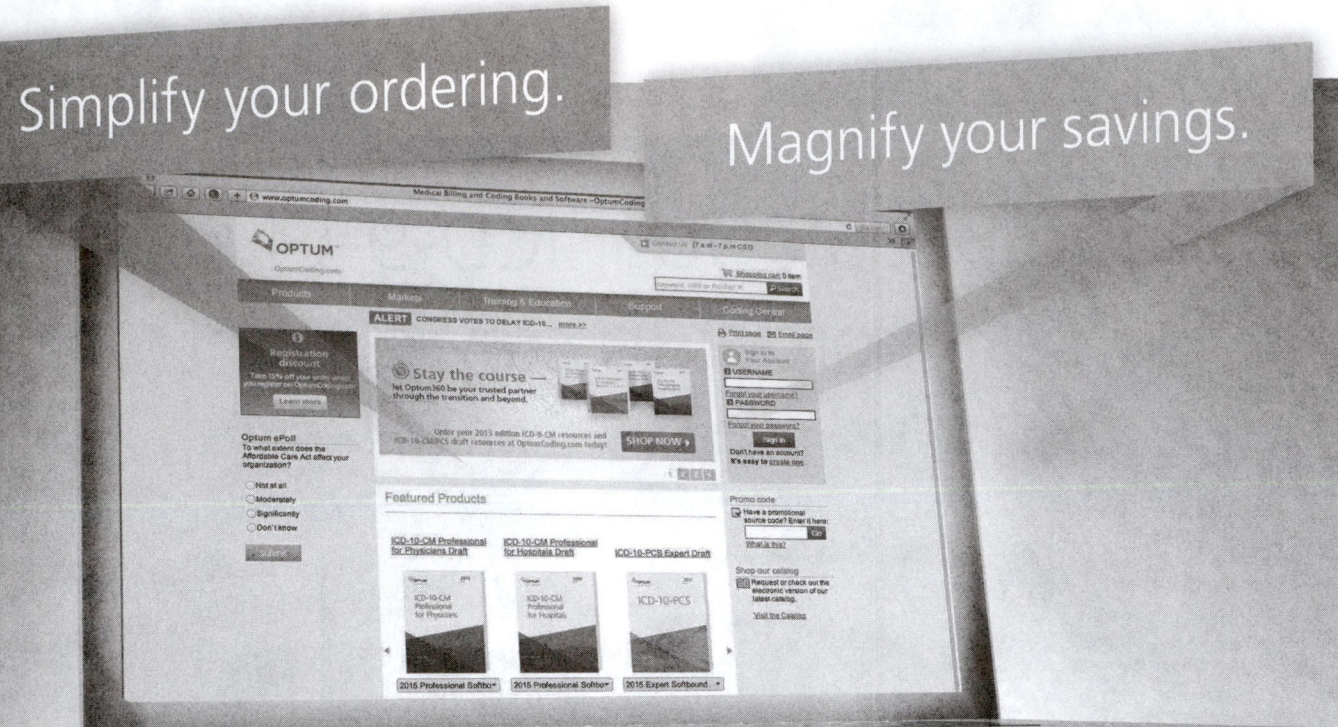

1 Click.

Visit optumcoding.com

- Find the products you need quickly and easily.
- View all available formats and edition years on the same page.
- Chat live with a customer service representative.
- Visit Coding Central for expert resources including articles, *Inside Track to ICD-10* and coding scenarios to test your knowledge.
- View our catalog online. Utilize our interactive online catalog features to view product information quickly and easily.

2 Register.

By registering, you'll be able to:

- Enjoy special promotions, discounts and automatic rewards.
- Get recommendations based on your order history.
- Check on shipment status and tracking.
- View order and payment history.
- Pay invoices.
- Manage your address book and ship orders to multiple locations.
- Renew your order with a single click.
- Compile a wish list of the products you want and purchase when you're ready.

3 Save.

Get 15% off your next order

Register for an account and receive a coupon via email for 15% off your next order.

Plus, save even more with our no-cost eRewards program.

Register for an account and you're automatically enrolled in our eRewards program, where you'll get a $50 coupon for every $500 you spend*. When logged in at optumcoding.com, the eRewards meter keeps track of purchases toward your next reward.

OPTUM360°™

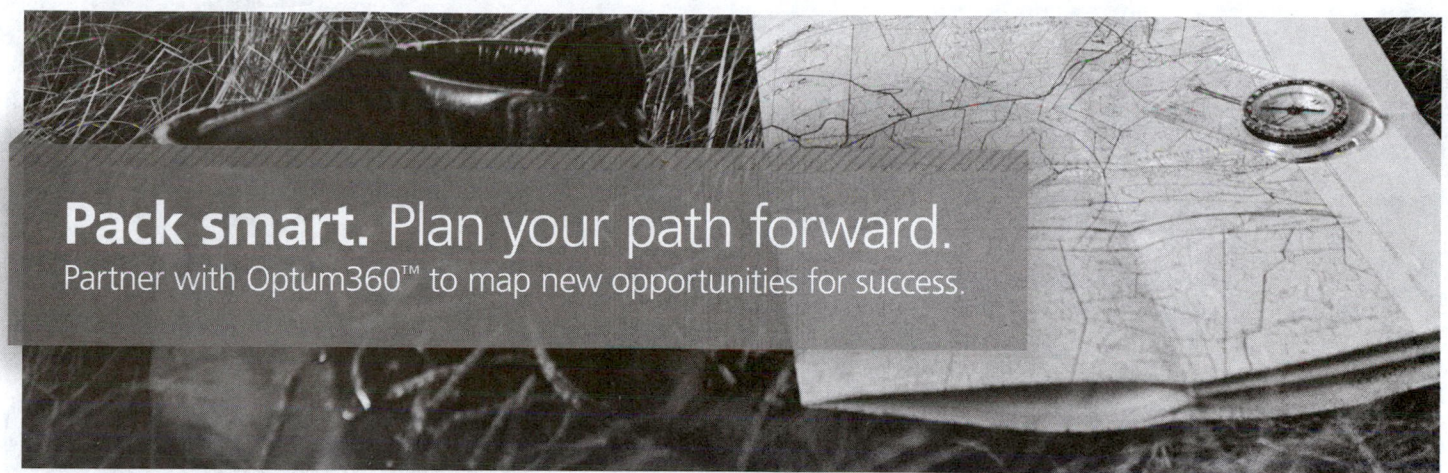

Pack smart. Plan your path forward.
Partner with Optum360™ to map new opportunities for success.

Stay the course - continue your training and preparation for the transition to ICD-10.

With Optum360 tools and resources at your fingertips, you can open a world of opportunities and help build the foundation for greater efficiencies, financial gains, and competitive advantages. For nearly 30 years, our print resources have remained trusted tools for coding professionals, and our 2015 editions offer the same quality and reliability you have come to expect from us.

Eliminate roadblocks with web-based coding solutions.
ICD-10 will have 668 percent more codes than ICD-9. Web-based coding solutions can help you experience a smooth, successful transition with fast access to ICD-10 codes, data and mapping tools, and can easily be used in conjunction with our ICD-10 training book. Learn more about EncoderPro.com and RevenueCyclePro.com today.

Explore. Plan. Conquer.
Save up to 25% on the ICD-10 resources you need.

Visit OptumCoding.com and enter
promo code **ICD10S25** to save 25%

Call 1.800.464.3649, option 1 and mention
promo code **ICD10S25** to save 20%

New ICD-10 training from Optum360™ offers eLearning, on-site and customized options.

Stay the course - continue your ICD-10 transition preparation and let Optum360 provide customized training for all members of your facility.

Optum360 ICD-10 education program levels:

Take online courses at your desk, invite a specialist to your office for on-the-job preparation, or ask our consulting professionals to assess your organization and suggest a tailor-made program.

Level 1: Overview training

High-level education, including the reasons for the ICD-10 mandate, its benefits, challenges, timelines and impacts. Available in an eLearning format.

Level 2: Knowledge-based skill transfer

Education and training that provide a deeper understanding of the ICD-10 code set. Designed for those who consistently use diagnosis data. Also available as eLearning or on-site training.

Level 3: On-the-job (OTJ) training

Transitions learners from a structured classroom or eLearning environment to an on-site environment. OTJ training solutions are customized to your organization's needs, whether that means building the training within current workflows or conducting it in a practice environment.

Optum360 gives you:

- **Actionable training:** Education you can apply to your day-to-day job functions.
- **Comprehensive approach:** Whether you're a coder, a physician or support staff, and you want eLearning, on-site training or consulting services, Optum360 has you covered.
- **Flexibility:** Load your eLearning courses into your own LMS or let us help. For more personalized training, choose our on-site or tailor-made options.

Choose the training that's right for you

We offer a range of price points, so it's easy to find the program that best suits your budget. Let us know what you need.

 Explore your options: optumcoding.com/ICD10Training

 Talk with an ICD-10 specialist: 1-800-464-3649, option 1

 **OPTUM**360°™

RENEW TODAY

SAVE UP TO 25%

when you renew your coding essentials.

Buy 1–2 items, save 15%

Buy 3–5 items, save 20%

Buy 6+ items, save 25%

ITEM #	TITLE INDICATE THE ITEMS YOU WISH TO PURCHASE	QUANTITY	PRICE PER PRODUCT	TOTAL

	Subtotal	
(AK, DE, HI, MT, NH & OR are exempt)	Sales Tax	
1 item $10.95 • 2–4 items $12.95 • 5+ CALL	Shipping & Handling	
	TOTAL AMOUNT ENCLOSED	

Save up to 25% when you renew.

 Visit **optumcoding.com** and enter your promo code.

 Call **1-800-464-3649, option 1,** and mention the promo code.

 Fax this order form with purchase order to **801-982-4033.** *Optum360 no longer accepts credit cards by fax.*

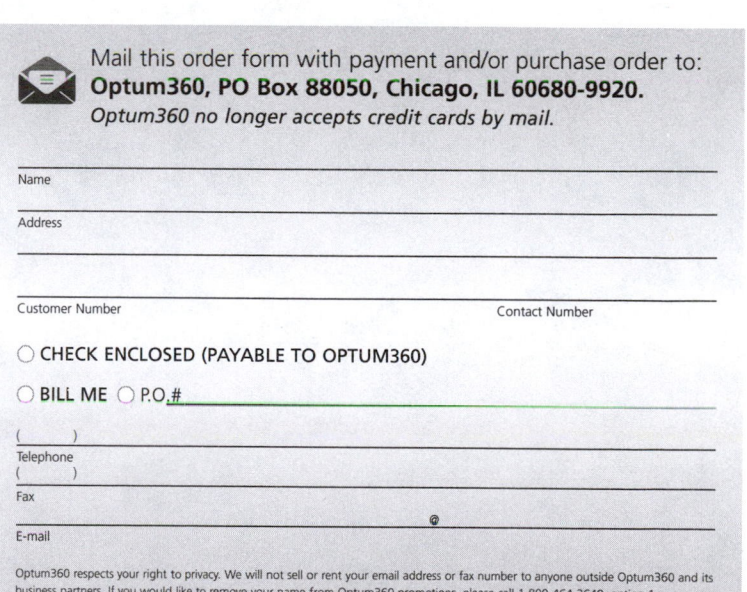

Mail this order form with payment and/or purchase order to:
Optum360, PO Box 88050, Chicago, IL 60680-9920.
Optum360 no longer accepts credit cards by mail.

Name

Address

Customer Number   Contact Number

○ CHECK ENCLOSED (PAYABLE TO OPTUM360)

○ BILL ME ○ P.O.#

( )
Telephone

( )
Fax

E-mail

Optum360 respects your right to privacy. We will not sell or rent your email address or fax number to anyone outside Optum360 and its business partners. If you would like to remove your name from Optum360 promotions, please call 1-800-464-3649, option 1.

PROMO CODE
FOBA15A

© 2014 Optum360, Inc. All rights reserved. OPTPRJ5486 SPRJ1697

ICD-9-CM

for Hospitals – Volumes 1, 2, & 3

2015 | Professional

International Classification of Diseases
9th Revision
Clinical Modification
Sixth Edition

Codes Valid October 1, 2014, through September 30, 2015

© 2014 OptumInsight, Inc.
All Rights Reserved

First Printing — August 2014
Made in the USA

IHP ISBN 978-1-62254-143-0

Publisher's Notice

All codes, indexes, and other material in the ICD-9-CM are compiled from official ICD-9-CM codes and instructions as well as the Medicare regulations and manuals issued or authorized by the Centers for Medicare and Medicaid Services. The code book is designed to provide accurate and authoritative information in regard to the subject covered, and every reasonable effort has been made to ensure the accuracy of the information within these pages. However, the ultimate responsibility for correct coding lies with the provider of services.

Optum, its employees, agents and staff make no representation, warranty or guarantee that this compilation of codes and narratives is error-free or that the use of this code book will prevent differences of opinion or disputes with Medicare or other third-party payers as to the codes that are accepted or the amounts that will be paid to providers for services, and will bear no responsibility or liability for the results or consequences of the use of this code book.

Our Commitment to Accuracy

Optum is committed to producing accurate and reliable materials. To report corrections, please visit www.optumcoding.com/accuracy or email accuracy@optum.com. You can also reach customer service by calling 1.800.464.3649, option 1.

Preface

Since the federal government implemented diagnosis-related groups (DRGs) on October 1, 1983, medical record professionals and others have had to refer to many sources for ICD-9-CM codes and coding and reimbursement principles.

ICD-9-CM for Hospitals, Volumes 1, 2 & 3, has been designed with the health information professional in mind. All three volumes of the most recent official government version of ICD-9-CM have been combined into one book.

Our technical experts have drawn upon their extensive hands-on experience to enhance the government's book with valuable features essential to correct coding and reimbursement. Without these enhancements, health information management departments would spend hours locating the information required to code each record accurately. Because of the thoroughness, accuracy, timeliness and ease of use of *ICD-9-CM for Hospitals*, health information departments nationwide have turned to them for their coding needs.

ICD-9-CM for Hospitals includes many of the enhancements described below in direct response to requests from our subscribers. As you review the content, you'll find the following:

- The complete ICD-9-CM official guidelines for coding and reporting, published by the U.S. Department of Health and Human Services and approved by the cooperating parties (American Hospital Association, American Health Information Management Association, Centers for Medicare and Medicaid Services and National Center for Health Statistics)
- All the official ICD-9-CM codes, indexes, notes, footnotes and symbols
- Color-highlighted illustrations and clearly worded definitions integrated in the tabular, provide important clinical information
- Exclusive color coding, symbols, and footnotes that alert coders to coding and reimbursement issues, including the majority of the Medicare code edits and identification of conditions that significantly affect DRG assignment.
- The complication and comorbidity (CC) exclusion list, integrated beneath the applicable codes makes it easier to determine complications and comorbidities excluded with a particular principal diagnosis
- The American Hospital Association (AHA's) *Coding Clinic for ICD-9-CM* references, integrated beneath the applicable codes to provide easy reference to official coding advice as designated by the four cooperating parties (AHA, AHIMA, CMS, and NCHS)
- Check fourth- and fifth-digit symbols identify codes that require the addition of a fourth or fifth digit for code specificity and validity
- Symbols identify new codes and text revisions and pages are dated to indicate when the changes were made
- Color coding and symbol legend at the bottom of each page
- Exclusive QuickFlip Color Tabs for quick, easy location of terms and codes in the index and Tabular List

Please review "How to Use *ICD-9-CM for Hospitals (Volumes 1, 2 & 3)*" in this section to learn about the features that will help you assign and report correct codes, ensuring appropriate reimbursement.

Use of Official Sources

The *ICD-9-CM for Hospitals* contains the official U.S. Department of Health and Human Services, Ninth Revision, Sixth Edition ICD-9-CM codes, effective for the current year.

The color-coding, footnotes and symbols, which identify coding and reimbursement issues, are derived from official federal government sources, including the Medicare Code Edits (MCE), Version 31.0.

The American Hospital Association's (AHA) *Coding Clinic for ICD-9-CM* references are used with permission of the AHA.

Technical Editors

Anita Schmidt, BS, RHIT, *Clinical Technical Editor*
Ms. Schmidt has expertise in Level I Adult and Pediatric Trauma hospital coding, specializing in ICD-9-CM, DRG, and CPT coding. Her experience includes analysis of medical record documentation and assignment of ICD-9-CM codes and DRGs, and CPT code assignments for same-day surgery cases. She has conducted coding training and auditing inclusive of DRG validation, conducted electronic health record training, and worked with clinical documentation specialists to identify documentation needs and potential areas for physician education. Ms. Schmidt is an active member of the American Health Information Management Association (AHIMA) and the Minnesota Health Information Management Association (MNHIMA).

Karen Schmidt, BSN, *Clinical Technical Director*
Ms. Schmidt has more than 25 years of health care experience beginning with a strong clinical background in critical care nursing and later functioning as director of case management, including the components of quality assurance, utilization management, concurrent coding, case-mix analysis, and discharge planning. Her areas of expertise include ICD-9-CM/DRG coding, outpatient observation, billing compliance, implementation of concurrent coding methodology, and physician documentation education. She is an active member of the American Health Information Management Association (AHIMA).

In addition to the editors, the following people have contributed to this book:

Stacy Perry, *Manager, Desktop Publishing*
Tracy Betzler, *Senior Desktop Publishing Specialist*
Hope M. Dunn, *Senior Desktop Publishing Specialist*
Katie Russell, *Desktop Publishing Specialist*
Kate Holden, *Editor*

What to Do If You Have Questions

If you have any questions call our customer service department toll-free at 800-464-3649, option 1.

If you have comments on the content of this book, please email them to accuracy@optum.com.

Additional Copies

Contact the customer service order department toll-free at 800-464-3649, option 1.

Introduction

History and Future of ICD-9-CM

The International Classification of Diseases, Ninth Revision, Clinical Modification (ICD-9-CM) is based on the official version of the World Health Organization's Ninth Revision, International Classification of Diseases (ICD-9). ICD-9 classifies morbidity and mortality information for statistical purposes, and for the indexing of hospital records by disease and operations, for data storage and retrieval.

This modification of ICD-9 supplants the Eighth Revision International Classification of Diseases, Adapted for Use in the United States (ICDA-8) and the Hospital Adaptation of ICDA (H-ICDA).

The concept of extending the International Classification of Diseases for use in hospital indexing was originally developed in response to a need for a more efficient basis for storage and retrieval of diagnostic data. In 1950, the U.S. Public Health Service and the Veterans Administration began independent tests of the International Classification of Diseases for hospital indexing purposes. The following year, the Columbia Presbyterian Medical Center in New York City adopted the International Classification of Diseases, Sixth Revision, with some modifications for use in its medical record department. A few years later, the Commission on Professional and Hospital Activities (CPHA) in Ann Arbor, Mich., adopted the International Classification of Diseases with similar modifications for use in hospitals participating in the Professional Activity Study.

The problem of adapting ICD for indexing hospital records was taken up by the U.S. National Committee on Vital and Health Statistics through its subcommittee on hospital statistics. The subcommittee reviewed the modifications made by the various users of ICD and proposed that uniform changes be made. This was done by a small working party.

In view of the growing interest in the use of the International Classification of Diseases for hospital indexing, a study was undertaken in 1956 by the American Hospital Association and the American Medical Record Association (then the American Association of Medical Record Librarians) of the relative efficiencies of coding systems for diagnostic indexing. This study indicated the International Classification of Diseases provided a suitable and efficient framework for indexing hospital records. The major users of the International Classification of Diseases for hospital indexing purposes then consolidated their experiences, and an adaptation was first published in December 1959. A revision was issued in 1962 and the first "Classification of Operations and Treatments" was included.

In 1966, the international conference for revising the International Classification of Diseases noted the eighth revision of ICD had been constructed with hospital indexing in mind and considered the revised classification suitable, in itself, for hospital use in some countries. However, it was recognized that the basic classification might provide inadequate detail for diagnostic indexing in other countries. A group of consultants was asked to study the eighth revision of ICD (ICD-8) for applicability to various users in the United States. This group recommended that further detail be provided for coding of hospital and morbidity data. The American Hospital Association was requested to develop the needed adaptation proposals. This was done by an advisory committee (the Advisory Committee to the Central Office on ICDA). In 1968 the United States Public Health Service published the product, Eighth Revision International Classification of Diseases, Adapted for Use in the United States. This became commonly known as ICDA-8, and beginning in 1968 it served as the basis for coding diagnostic data for both official morbidity and mortality statistics in the United States.

In 1968, the CPHA published the Hospital Adaptation of ICDA (H-ICDA) based on both the original ICD-8 and ICDA-8. In 1973, CPHA published a revision of H-ICDA, referred to as H-ICDA-2. Hospitals throughout the United States were divided in their use of these classifications until January 1979, when ICD-9-CM was made the single classification intended primarily for use in the United States, replacing these earlier related, but somewhat dissimilar, classifications.

Physicians have been required by law to submit diagnosis codes for Medicare reimbursement since the passage of the Medicare Catastrophic Coverage Act of 1988. This act requires physician offices to include the appropriate diagnosis codes when billing for services provided to Medicare beneficiaries on or after April 1, 1989. The Centers for Medicare and Medicaid Services (formerly known as Health Care Financing Administration) designated ICD-9-CM as the coding system physicians must use.

The ICD-10-CM classification system was developed by the National Center for Health Statistics (NCHS) as a clinical modification to the ICD-10 system developed by the World Health Organization (WHO), primarily as a unique system for use in the United States for morbidity and mortality reporting. Although ICD-10-CM has not yet been implemented for use in the United States, ICD-10 has been adopted for use in the coding and classification of mortality data from death certificates. ICD-10 replaced ICD-9 for this purpose as of January 1, 1999. The Department of Health and Human Services (HHS) published the final rule regarding the adoption of both ICD-10-CM and ICD-10-PCS in the January 16, 2009 *Federal Register* (45 CFR part 162[CMS—0013—F]). On April 2, 2014, Congress enacted the Protecting Access to Medicare Act of 2014, which contained a provision to delay the implementation of ICD-10-CM/PCS by at least one year. The act prohibits the Department of Health and Human Services (HHS) from adopting the ICD–10-CM/PCS code sets as the mandatory standard until at least October 1, 2015.

ICD-9-CM Background

In February 1977, a steering committee was convened by the National Center for Health Statistics to provide advice and counsel in developing a clinical modification of ICD-9. The organizations represented on the steering committee included the following:

- American Association of Health Data Systems
- American Hospital Association
- American Medical Record Association
- Association for Health Records
- Council on Clinical Classifications
- Centers for Medicare and Medicaid Services, Department of Health and Human Services
- WHO Center for Classification of Diseases for North America, sponsored by the National Center for Health Statistics, Department of Health and Human Services

The Council on Clinical Classifications was sponsored by the following:

- American Academy of Pediatrics
- American College of Obstetricians and Gynecologists
- American College of Physicians
- American College of Surgeons
- American Psychiatric Association
- Commission on Professional and Hospital Activities

The steering committee met periodically in 1977. Clinical guidance and technical input were provided by task forces on classification from the Council on Clinical Classification's sponsoring organizations.

ICD-9-CM is a clinical modification of the World Health Organization's ICD-9. The term "clinical" is used to emphasize the modification's intent: to serve as a useful tool to classify morbidity data for indexing medical records, medical care review, and ambulatory and other medical care programs, as well as for basic health statistics. To describe the clinical picture of the patient, the codes must be more precise than those needed only for statistical groupings and trend analysis.

Characteristics of ICD-9-CM

ICD-9-CM far exceeds its predecessors in the number of codes provided. The disease classification has been expanded to include health-related conditions and to provide greater specificity at the fifth-digit level of detail. These fifth digits are not optional; they are intended for use in recording the information substantiated in the clinical record.

Volume I (Tabular List) of ICD-9-CM contains four appendixes:

Appendix A:	Morphology of Neoplasms
Appendix B:	Deleted Effective October 1, 2004
Appendix C:	Classification of Drugs by American Hospital Formulary Service List Number and Their ICD-9-CM Equivalents
Appendix D:	Classification of Industrial Accidents According to Agency
Appendix E:	List of Three-Digit Categories

These appendixes are included as a reference to provide further information about the patient's clinical picture, to further define a diagnostic statement, to aid in classifying new drugs or to reference three-digit categories.

Volume 2 (Alphabetic Index) of ICD-9-CM contains many diagnostic terms that do not appear in Volume I since the index includes most diagnostic terms currently in use.

Volume 3 (Procedure Index and Procedure Tabular) of ICD-9-CM contains codes for operations and procedures. The format for the tabular is the same as Volume 1 disease tabular, except the codes consist of two digits with one or two digits following the decimal point. Conventions in the index follow Volume 2 conventions except some subterms appear immediately below the main term rather than following alphabetizing rules.

The Disease Classification

ICD-9-CM is totally compatible with its parent system, ICD-9, thus meeting the need for comparability of morbidity and mortality statistics at the international level. A few fourth-digit codes were created in existing three-digit rubrics only when the necessary detail could not be accommodated by the use of a fifth-digit subclassification. To ensure that each rubric of ICD-9-CM collapses back to its ICD-9 counterpart the following specifications governed the ICD-9-CM disease classification:

Specifications for the Tabular List:

1. Three-digit rubrics and their contents are unchanged from ICD-9.

2. The sequence of three-digit rubrics is unchanged from ICD-9.

3. Three-digit rubrics are not added to the main body of the classification.

4. Unsubdivided three-digit rubrics are subdivided where necessary to
   - add clinical detail
   - isolate terms for clinical accuracy.

5. The modification in ICD-9-CM is accomplished by adding a fifth digit to existing ICD-9 rubrics, except as noted under #7.

6. The optional dual classification in ICD-9 is modified.
   - Duplicate rubrics are deleted:
     - four-digit manifestation categories duplicating etiology entries
     - manifestation inclusion terms duplicating etiology entries
   - Manifestations of disease are identified, to the extent possible, by creating five-digit codes in the etiology rubrics.

- When the manifestation of a disease cannot be included in the etiology rubrics, provision for its identification is made by retaining the ICD-9 rubrics used for classifying manifestations of disease.

7. The format of ICD-9-CM is revised from that used in ICD-9.
   - American spelling of medical terms is used.
   - Inclusion terms are indented beneath the titles of codes.
   - Codes not to be used for primary tabulation of disease are printed in italics with the notation, "code first underlying disease."

Specifications for the Alphabetic Index:

1. The format of the Alphabetic Index follows that of ICD-9.

2. When two codes are required to indicate etiology and manifestation, the manifestation code appears in brackets (e.g., diabetic cataract 250.5 [366.41]).

The ICD-9-CM Coordination and Maintenance Committee

The ICD-9-CM Coordination and Maintenance Committee, a federal committee, was created as a forum for proposals to update International Classification of Diseases, Ninth Revision, Clinical Modification, Sixth Edition (ICD-9-CM). A representative from the National Center for Health Statistics (NCHS) and one from the Centers for Medicare and Medicaid Services (CMS) co-chair the ICD-9-CM Coordination and Maintenance Committee meetings. Responsibility for maintaining ICD-9-CM is divided between the two agencies, with NCHS classifying diagnoses (volumes 1 and 2) and CMS classifying procedures (volume 3).

Proposals for changes to the ICD-9-CM classification system are submitted and discussed in open forum meetings held in March and September of each year at the headquarters of CMS in Baltimore. Comments received during or after the meetings are then reviewed and evaluated. All final decisions are made by the director of NCHS and the administrator of CMS. The complete official document of changes to the classification system is released as the Addenda for the International Classification of Disease, Ninth Revision, Clinical Modification, Sixth Edition, Volume 1, 2 & 3.

The *ICD-9-CM for Hospitals, Volume 1, 2 & 3* is based on the official version of the International Classification of Diseases, Ninth Revision, Clinical Modification, Sixth Edition, issued by the U.S. Department of Health and Human Services. Annual code changes are implemented by the government and are effective October 1 and valid through September 30 of the following year. If a convincing case is made that requires a new code to capture new technology or an emerging disease, this new code may be implemented on April 1 of the following year.

Effective March 2014, the ICD-9-CM Coordination and Maintenance Committee was renamed the ICD-10 Coordination and Maintenance Committee.

How to Use the ICD-9-CM for Hospitals (Volumes 1, 2 & 3)

ICD-9-CM for Hospitals is based on the official version of the International Classification of Diseases, Ninth Revision, Clinical Modification, Sixth Edition, issued by the U.S. Department of Health and Human Services. Annual code changes are implemented by the government and are effective Oct. 1 and valid through Sept. 30 of the following year.

The code book is totally compatible with its parent system, ICD-9, thus meeting the need for comparability of morbidity and mortality statistics at the international level.

This book is consistent with the content of the government's version of ICD-9-CM. However, to accommodate the coder's approach to coding, the Alphabetic Index has been placed before the Tabular List in both the disease and procedure classifications. This allows the user to locate the correct codes in a logical, natural manner by locating the term in the index, then confirming the accuracy of the code in the Tabular List.

Steps to Correct Coding

1. Look up the main term in the Alphabetic Index and scan the subterm entries as appropriate. Follow any cross-references such as *"see"* and *"see also."* Do not code from the Alphabetic Index without verifying the accuracy of the code in the Tabular List.

2. Locate the code in the numerically arranged Tabular List.

3. Observe the punctuation, footnotes, cross-references, color-coded prompts and other conventions described in the 'Conventions' section.

4. To determine the appropriateness of the code selection, read all instructional material:

   - "includes" and *"excludes"* notes
   - *"see," "see also"* and *"see category"* cross-references
   - "use additional code" and *"code first underlying disease"* instructions
   - "code also" and *"omit code"* notes
   - fourth- and fifth-digit requirements
   - CC exclusions

5. Consult definitions, relevant illustrations, CC exclusions, color coding and reimbursement prompts, the check fourth- and fifth-digit, age and sex symbols. Refer to the color/symbol legend at the bottom of each page for symbols. Refer to the list of footnotes that is included in the "Additional Conventions" section of this book for a full explanation of a footnote associated with a code.

6. Consult the official ICD-9-CM guidelines for coding and reporting, and refer to the AHA's *Coding Clinic for ICD-9-CM* for coding guidelines governing the use of specific codes.

7. Confirm and transcribe the correct code.

Organization

Introduction
The introductory material in this book includes the history and future of ICD-9-CM as well as an overview of the classification system.

Official ICD-9-CM Conventions
This section provides a full explanation of all the official footnotes, symbols, instructional notes, and conventions found in the official government version.

Additional Conventions
Exclusive color-coding, symbols, and notations have been included in the *ICD-9-CM for Hospitals, Volumes 1, 2 & 3* to alert coders to important coding and reimbursement issues. This section provides a full explanation of the additional conventions used throughout this book.

ICD-10-CM Coding Proficiency and Documentation Self-Assessment
Use this self-assessment to identify the areas that may require additional coding training or documentation improvement before ICD-10-CM is implemented.

Coding Guidelines
Included in this book are the official ICD-9-CM coding guidelines as approved by the four cooperating parties of the ICD-9-CM Coordination and Maintenance Committee. Failure to comply with the official coding guidelines may result in denied or delayed claims.

Disease Classification: Alphabetic Index to Diseases
The Alphabetic Index to Diseases is separated by tabs labeled with the letters of the alphabet, contains diagnostic terms for illnesses, injuries and reasons for encounters with health care professionals. The Table of Drugs and Chemicals is easily located with the tab in this section.

The warning statement at the bottom of every page of the index, ▽ Subterms under main terms may continue to next column or page, is a reminder to always check for additional subterms before making final selection.

Disease Classification: Tabular List of Diseases
The Tabular List of Diseases arranges the ICD-9-CM codes and descriptors numerically. QuickFlip color tabs divide this section into chapters, identified by the code range on the tab.

The Tabular List includes two supplementary classifications:

- V Codes—Supplementary Classification of Factors Influencing Health Status and Contact with Health Services (V01–V91)
- E Codes—Supplementary Classification of External Causes of Injury and Poisoning (E000–E999)

ICD-9-CM includes four official appendixes.

- Appendix A   Morphology of Neoplasms
- Appendix B   Deleted Effective October 1, 2004
- Appendix C   Classification of Drugs by AHFS List
- Appendix D   Classification of Industrial Accidents According to Agency
- Appendix E   List of Three-digit Categories

These appendixes are included as a reference to provide further information about the patient's circumstances, help further define a diagnostic statement, maintain a tumor registry and aid in classifying new drugs.

Procedure Classification: Alphabetic Index to Procedures
The Alphabetic Index to Procedures lists common surgical and procedural terminology.

The warning statement at the bottom of every page of the index, ▽ Subterms under main terms may continue to next column or page, is a reminder to always check for additional subterms before making a final selection.

Procedure Classification: Tabular List of Procedures
The Tabular List of Procedures numerically arranges the procedure codes and their descriptors.

Resources

Listed below are the exclusive resources found **ONLY** in the *ICD-9-CM Expert for Hospitals, Volumes 1, 2 & 3* books.

Dx/MDC/DRG List

Provides the complete list of principal diagnosis codes and the MDC and medical MS-DRG to which they group, with the exception of a combination of principal and secondary diagnosis affecting DRG assignment.

MCC Condition List

A complete list of all codes considered MCC (Major Complications and Comorbidities) that will affect DRG assignment. This is an essential auditing tool for assigning the most appropriate DRG.

CC Condition List

A complete list of all codes considered CC (Complications and Comorbidities) that will affect DRG assignment. This an essential auditing tool for assigning the most appropriate DRG.

Pharmacological Listings

The most common generic and brand names of drugs are linked with the disease processes to assist in the identification of CC, thereby improving DRG assignment practices.

Valid Three-digit Code Table

ICD-9-CM is composed of codes with either 3, 4, or 5 digits. A code is invalid if it has not been coded to the full number of digits required for that code. There are a certain number codes that are valid for reporting as three digit codes. A list of the valid three-digit code is included as a convenient reference when auditing claims.

Present on Admission (POA) Indicator Tutorial

This resource presents an in-depth explanation of guidelines for assigning the present on admission (POA) indicators with case scenarios and exemptions. A table of official guidelines is included for quick reference regarding the use of information documented in the medical record.

10 Steps to Correct Coding

This is a valuable resource that takes the coder step by step through the coding process with detailed explanations accompanied by coding examples that demonstrate the practical application of ICD-9-CM conventions and coding guidelines in 10 steps.

ICD-9-CM Official Conventions

ICD-9-CM Footnotes, Symbols, Instructional Notes and Conventions

This *ICD-9-CM for Hospitals* preserves all the footnotes, symbols, instructional notes and conventions found in the government's official version. Accurate coding depends upon understanding the meaning of these elements.

The following appear in the disease Tabular List, unless otherwise noted.

Official Government Symbols

§   The section mark preceding a code denotes a footnote on the page. This symbol is used in the Tabular List of Diseases and in the Tabular List of Procedures.

ICD-9-CM Conventions Used in the Tabular List

In addition to the symbols and footnotes above, the ICD-9-CM disease tabular has certain abbreviations, punctuation, symbols and other conventions. Our *ICD-9-CM for Hospitals* preserves these conventions. Proper use of the conventions will lead to efficient and accurate coding.

Abbreviations

NEC   Not elsewhere classifiable
This abbreviation is used when the ICD-9-CM system does not provide a code specific for the patient's condition.

NOS   Not otherwise specified
This abbreviation is the equivalent of "unspecified" and is used only when the coder lacks the information necessary to code to a more specific four-digit subcategory.

[ ]   Brackets enclose synonyms, alternative terminology or explanatory phrases:

> **482.2   Pneumonia due to Hemophilus influenzae [H. influenzae]**

Brackets that appear beneath a code indicate the fifth digits that are considered valid fifth digits for the code. This convention is applied for those instances in ICD-9-CM where not all common fifth digits are considered valid for each subcategory within a category.

> **715.0   Osteoarthrosis, generalized**
> [0,4,9]

Generalized arthrosis can only be assigned in cases for which the degenerative joint disease involves multiple joints. Therefore, this code is considered for arthrosis in the sites described as unspecified, hand (which consists of multiple joints), or multiple sites. Therefore, only fifth digits 0, 4, and 9 are valid with subcategory 715.0.

[ ]   Slanted brackets that appear in the Alphabetic Indexes indicate mandatory multiple coding. Both codes must be assigned to fully describe the condition and are sequenced in the order listed.

> **Tachycardia**
> ventricular (paroxysmal)
> psychogenic 316 *[427.1]*

Psychogenic paroxysmal tachycardia is reported using both 316, Psychogenic factors associated with diseases classified elsewhere, and 427.1, Paroxysmal ventricular tachycardia.

> **Diversion**
> biliopancreatic (BPD) 43.7 *[45.51] [45.91]*

Code assignment of biliopancreatic diversion is reported using all three codes 43.7, Partial gastrectomy with anastomosis to jejunum, 45.51, Isolation of segment of small intestine, and 45.91, Small-to-small intestinal anastomosis.

( )   Parentheses enclose supplementary words, called nonessential modifiers, that may be present in the narrative description of a disease without affecting the code assignment:

> **198.4   Other parts of nervous system**
> Meninges (cerebral) (spinal)

:   Colons are used in the Tabular List after an incomplete term that needs one or more of the modifiers that follow in order to make it assignable to a given category:

> **021.1   Enteric tularemia**
> Tularemia:
>   cryptogenic
>   intestinal
>   typhoidal

}   Braces enclose a series of terms, each of which is modified by the statement appearing to the right of the brace:

> **560.2   Volvulus**
> Knotting
> Strangulation   }   of intestine, bowel, or
> Torsion   colon
> Twist

Other Conventions

Boldface   Boldface type is used for all codes and titles in the Tabular List.

Italicized   Italicized type is used for all exclusion notes and to identify codes that should not be used for describing the principal or first-listed diagnosis.

General Notes Used in the Tabular

These notes appear only in the Tabular List of Diseases:

Includes   An includes note further defines or clarifies the content of the chapter, subchapter, category, subcategory or subclassification. The includes note in the example below applies only to category 461.

Excludes   Terms following the word "Excludes" are not classified to the chapter, subchapter, category, subcategory or specific subclassification code under which it is found. The note also may provide the location of the excluded diagnosis. Excludes notes are italicized.

> **461   Acute sinusitis**
> [INCLUDES]   abscess
>   empyema   }   acute, of sinus
>   infection   (accessory)
>   inflammation   (nasal)
>   suppuration
> *EXCLUDES   chronic or unspecified sinusitis (473.0-473.9)*

Instructional Notes

The following official instructional notes are critical to correct coding practices. The instructional notes appear in red type in the Tabular List.

Use additional code:
This instruction signals the coder that an additional code should be used if the information is available to provide a more complete picture of that diagnosis.

For emphasis this instructional note appears in red type in the tabular section.

362.13 Changes in vascular appearance
Vascular sheathing of retina

Use additional code for any associated atherosclerosis (440.8)

There are coding circumstances outside of the etiology/ manifestation convention when multiple coding for a single condition is required. The "Use additional code" note will be found under the associated condition code in the tabular. In the index, the multiple coding requirement is indicated by the use of the slanted bracket. The two codes are to be sequenced as listed in the index. For example, retinal arteriosclerosis must be coded using two codes sequenced as listed in the index.

Arteriosclerosis, arteriosclerotic
retinal (vascular) 440.8 *[362.13]*

Code first underlying disease:

The "*Code first underlying disease*" instructional note found under certain codes is a sequencing rule. Most often this sequencing rule applies to the etiology/manifestation convention and is found under the manifestation code. The manifestation code may never be used alone or as a principal or first-listed diagnosis (i.e., sequenced first). The instructional note, the code and its descriptor appear in italics in the Tabular List.

590.81 *Pyelitis or pyelonephritis in diseases classified elsewhere*
Code first underlying disease as:
tuberculosis (016.0)

Not all codes with a "Code first underlying disease" instructional note are part of the etiology/manifestation convention. The "Code first" note will appear, but the title of the code and the instructional note are not in italics. These codes may be reported alone or as the secondary diagnosis. For example, disseminated chorioretinitis may be reported as a principal diagnosis. However, if the underlying condition that caused disseminated chorioretinitis is known, such as tuberculous disseminated chorioretinitis, two codes are required and sequenced as listed in the index.

363.13 Disseminated choroiditis and chorioretinitis, generalized
Code first underlying disease as:
tuberculosis (017.3)

For emphasis this instructional note appears in red type in the tabular section.

Code, if applicable, any causal condition first:

A code with this note indicates that this code may be assigned as a principal diagnosis when the causal condition is unknown or not applicable. If a causal condition is known, then the code for that condition should be sequenced as the principal or first-listed diagnosis.

590.0 Chronic pyelonephritis
Chronic pyelitis
Chronic pyonephrosis
Code, if applicable, any causal condition first

For emphasis this instructional note appears in red type in the tabular section.

Instructional Notes Used in the Index

Omit code:

"Omit code" is used to instruct the coder that no code is to be assigned. When this instruction is found in the Alphabetic Index to Diseases the medical term should not be coded as a diagnosis.

Metaplasia
cervix — *omit code*

When used in Volume 3, *omit code* is meant to indicate procedures that do not merit separate code assignments, such as minor procedures preformed in conjunction with more extensive procedures or procedures that represent an operative approach.

Arthrotomy 80.10
as operative approach — *omit code*

See Condition:

The "*see* condition" note found in the Alphabetic Index to Disease instructs the coder to refer to a main term for the condition. This note will follow index terms that are nouns for anatomical sites or adjectival forms of disease term. In the example below, the index terms "Cervix" and "Diffuse" are followed by the — *see* condition. Coders should search the index using a condition term such as atrophy or prolapse.

Cervix — *see* condition
Diffuse — *see* condition

Morphology Codes

For each neoplastic disease listed in the index, a morphology code is provided that identifies histological type and behavior.

Example:

Myelolipoma (M8870/0) — *see* Neoplasm, by site, benign

The histology is identified by the first four digits and the behavior is identified by the digit following the slash. Appendix A of Volume 1 contains a listing of morphology codes. This appendix is helpful when the pathology report identifies the neoplasm by using an M code. The coder may refer to Appendix A to determine the nomenclature of the neoplasm that will be the main term to search in the Index. The behavior classification is as follows:

0 Benign

1 Uncertain whether benign or malignant
Borderline malignancy

2 Carcinoma in situ
Intraepithelial
Noninfiltrating
Noninvasive

3 Malignant, primary site

6 Malignant, metastatic site
Secondary site

Additional Conventions

New and Revised Text Symbols

●   A bullet at a code or line of text indicates that that the entry is new.

▲   A triangle in the Tabular List indicates that the code title is revised. In the Alphabetic Index the triangle indicates that a code has changed.

►◄   These symbols appear at the beginning and at the end of a section of new or revised text.

Additional Digits Required

√3ʳᵈ   This symbol indicates that the code requires a third digit.

√4ᵗʰ   This symbol indicates that the code requires a fourth digit.

√5ᵗʰ   This symbol indicates that a code requires a fifth digit.

☑   This symbol found only in the Alphabetic Index sections and the Table of Drugs and Chemicals indicates that an additional digit is required. Referring to the tabular section is essential to locate the appropriate additional digit.

Definitions

DEF: This symbol indicates a definition of disease or procedure term. The definition will appear in blue type in the Disease and Procedure Tabular Lists.

AHA's *Coding Clinic for ICD-9-CM* References

The four cooperating parties have designated the AHA's *Coding Clinic for ICD-9-CM* as the official publication for coding guidelines. The references are identified by the notation **AHA:** followed by the issue, year and page number.

In the example below, AHA's *Coding Clinic for ICD-9-CM*, third quarter 1991, page 15, contains a discussion on code assignment for vitreous hemorrhage:

    379.23 Vitreous hemorrhage
        AHA: 3Q, '91, 15

The table below explains the abbreviations in the Coding Clinic references:

J-F	January/February
M-A	March/April
M-J	May/June
J-A	July/August
S-O	September/October
N-D	November/December
1Q	First quarter
2Q	Second quarter
3Q	Third quarter
4Q	Fourth quarter

AHA's *Coding Clinic for ICD-9-CM* references appear in blue type in the Tabular List.

Medicare Code Edits

Fiscal intermediaries use Medicare code edits (MCE) to check the coding accuracy on claims. The Medicare code edits are listed below:

- Invalid diagnosis or procedure code
- E-code as principal diagnosis
- Duplicate of principal diagnosis (PDx) (as applied to a secondary diagnosis)
- *Age conflict
- *Sex conflict
- *Manifestation code as principal diagnosis
- *Questionable admission

- *Unacceptable principal diagnosis
- *Noncovered procedure
- *Bilateral procedure
- Invalid age
- Invalid sex
- Invalid discharge status
- *Limited coverage procedure
- *Wrong surgery
- Length of stay less than four (4) days for mechanical ventilation

Starred edits are identified by colors, symbols or footnotes as described below.

Age and Sex Edit Symbols

The age edits below address MCE edit 4 and are used to detect inconsistencies between the patient's age and diagnosis. The following edit symbols appear in the Tabular List of Diseases to the right of the code description.

Newborn Age: 0   Ⓝ
These diagnoses are intended for newborns and neonates and the patient's age must be 0 years.

Pediatric Age: 0-17   Ⓟ
These diagnoses are intended for children and the patient's age must between 0 and 17 years.

Maternity Age: 12-55   Ⓜ
These diagnoses are intended for the patients between the age of 12 and 55 years.

Adult Age: 15-124   Ⓐ
These diagnoses are intended for the patients between the age of 15 and 124 years.

The sex symbols below are used to detect inconsistencies between the patient's sex and diagnosis or procedure. These symbols appear in the Tabular Lists to the right of the code description:

♂   **Male diagnosis or procedure only**
This symbol appears to the right of the code description. This reference appears in the disease and procedure Tabular List.

♀   **Female diagnosis or procedure only**
This symbol appears to the right of the code description. This reference appears in the disease and procedure Tabular List.

Color Coding

For a quick reference to the color codes and their meaning, refer to the color/symbol legend located at the bottom of each page.

To alert the coder to important reimbursement issues affected by the code assignment, color bars have been added. The colors represent Medicare code edits as well as other reimbursement issues.

Color coding appears in both Tabular Lists. Some codes carry more than one color. Please note that the same color may appear in the disease and procedure Tabular Lists, but with different meanings.

Disease Tabular List
Manifestation Code
These codes will appear in italic type as well as with a blue color bar over the code title. A manifestation code is not allowed to be reported as a principal or first-listed diagnosis because each describes a manifestation of some other underlying disease, not the disease process itself. In the Alphabetic Index these codes are listed as the secondary code in slanted brackets with the code for the underlying disease listed first.

Unacceptable PDx

These codes will appear with a gray color bar over the code title. These codes do not describe a current illness or injury, but a circumstance which influences a patient's health status. These are considered an unacceptable principal diagnosis for inpatient admission.

Questionable Admission

These codes will also appear with a gray color bar over the code title. These codes identify a condition that usually is insufficient justification for hospital admission. Since these codes are considered an unacceptable principal diagnoses for inpatient admission, they are color coded in the same manner as the "Unacceptable PDx" codes.

Nonspecific PDx

Effective October 1, 2007 the Medicare code edit for Non-Specific Diagnoses was deactivated. Therefore, these codes will no longer be identified by a yellow color bar over the code title.

Hospital Acquired Condition (HAC)

These codes will appear with a yellow color bar over the code title. These codes identify conditions that are high cost or high volume or both, a complication or comorbidity (CC) or major complication or comorbidity (MCC) that as a secondary diagnosis would result in assignment of a case to a higher-paying MS-DRG, and reasonably preventable through the application of evidence-based guidelines. If the condition is not present on admission, the case would not group to the higher-paying MS-DRG based solely upon the reporting of the HAC.

Procedure Tabular List
Nonspecific OR Procedure

Effective October 1, 2007 the Medicare code edit for Non-Specific OR was deactivated. Therefore, these codes will no longer be identified by a yellow color bar over the code title.

Valid OR

A procedure that triggers a change in DRG assignment and is designated by a gray color bar over the code title.

Non-OR Procedure

A non-operating room procedure that affects DRG assignment and is designated by a blue color bar over the code title.

Adjunct Codes

These codes are not to be reported alone and are indicated by the red color bar over the code title. Adjunct codes are assigned only in addition to a principal procedure. Their purpose is to provide supplemental information about the principal procedure performed. Adjunct codes are not procedure codes, but serve to provide additional detail about the principal procedure.

> *Example:*
>
> PTCA balloon inflation of two vessels, with insertion of one intravascular coronary stent.
>
> Code assignment:
>
> **00.66   Percutaneous transluminal coronary angioplasty [PTCA] or coronary atherectomy**
>
> **00.41   Procedure on two vessels**
>
> **00.45   Insertion of one vascular stent**
>
> In the above example, codes 00.41 and 00.45 are adjunct codes that provide specific detail about the PTCA procedure performed.

Footnotes

All footnotes are identified by a numerical superscript that appears to the upper left of the code:

> [1] **427.41 Ventricular fibrillation**   MCC

The footnote 1 indicates "MCC = Only if patient is discharged alive." This means that ventricular fibrillation is considered a major complication or comorbidity that may affect DRG assignment only if the patient is discharged alive. Otherwise ventricular fibrillation is assigned as a non CC condition.

The following list identifies the meaning of each footnote number and the classification in which the footnote appears:

Disease Tabular

1   Major complication or comorbidity (MCC) that may affect DRG assignment only if the patient is discharged alive.

2   These V codes may be used as principal diagnosis on Medicare patients.

3   This V code, with the fourth digit of 1 or 2, is unacceptable as a principal diagnosis.

4   These codes, with the fourth digit of 0, may be used as a principal diagnosis for Medicare patients.

5   Rehabilitation codes acceptable as a principal diagnosis when accompanied by a secondary diagnosis reflecting the condition treated.

6   These V codes are acceptable as principal diagnosis when accompanied by a diagnosis of personal history of malignancy. These codes group to MS-DRG 949-950.

7   Diagnosis code with fifth digit of 0 is considered a "Questionable Admission" diagnosis when used as a principal diagnosis.

8   These codes are considered CC/MCC conditions that affect DRG assignment, except when reported in combination with diagnosis code 996.64 and the condition is not present on admission.

9   This condition is designated as a hospital acquired condition (HAC) that when reported as not present upon admission and when in combination with a procedure code from 36.10-36.19 will not solely group the case to a higher-paying MS-DRG.

10   The codes within the category or subcategory qualify as hospital acquired conditions when not present upon admission and only for the valid CC and MCC codes within that range.

11   This condition is designated as a hospital acquired condition (HAC) when reported as a secondary condition with procedure codes 00.85–00.87, or 81.51, 81.52, or 81.54 and the condition is not present on admission.

12   This condition is designated as a hospital acquired condition (HAC) when reported as a secondary condition with procedure codes 81.01–81.08, 81.23–81.24, 81.31–81.38, 81.83, or 81.85 and the condition is not present on admission.

13   This condition is designated as a hospital acquired condition (HAC) when reported as a secondary condition with procedure codes 81.01–81.08, 81.23–81.24, 81.31–81.38, 81.83, 81.85, or procedure code 44.38, 44.39, or 44.95 with principal diagnosis code 278.01 and the condition is not present on admission.

14   This condition is designated as a hospital acquired condition (HAC) when reported with principal diagnosis 278.01 and with procedure code 44.38, 44.39, or 44.95 and the condition is not present on admission.

15   This condition is designated as a hospital acquired condition (HAC) when reported with procedure(s) 00.50-00.54, 37.74-37.77, 37.79, 37.80-37.89, 37.94, 37.96, or 37.98 and the condition is not present on admission.

16   This condition is designated as a hospital acquired condition (HAC) when reported with procedure 38.93 and the condition is not present on admission.

*   Wrong Surgery edit applies to the E code which when reported will trigger the Wrong Surgery edit and the claim will be denied and returned to the provider.

Procedure Tabular

1   Valid OR procedure code if accompanied by one of the following codes: 37.80, 37.81, 37.82, 37.85, 37.86, 37.87.

2   Valid OR procedure code if accompanied by one of the following codes: 37.80, 37.83.

3   Valid OR procedure code if accompanied by one of the following codes: 37.80, 37.85, 37.86, 37.87.

4   Valid OR procedure code if accompanied by any one of the following codes: 37.80, 37.81, 37.82, 37.83, 37.85, 37.86, 37.87.

5   Valid OR procedure code if accompanied by any one of the following codes: 37.70, 37.71, 37.73, 37.74.

6   Valid OR procedure code if accompanied by one of the following codes: 37.72, 37.74.

7   Non-covered except when reported with procedure code 00.65, Percutaneous insertion of intracranial vascular stent(s).

8   Non-covered procedure only when the following diagnoses are present as either a principal or secondary diagnosis: 204.00, 205.00, 205.10, 205.11, 206.00, 207.00, 208.00.

9   Non-covered procedure only when the following diagnoses are present as either a principal or secondary diagnosis: 203.00, 203.01.

10   Non-covered procedure unless reported with code 55.69 or a diagnosis code from 250.x1 or 250.x3 or 251.3.

11   Non-covered except when the patient is 60 years old or less.

12   Limited coverage for the procedure is provided only when reported in combination with diagnosis code V70.7. Medicare limits the coverage to a portion of the costs and only when certain criteria are met such as participation in a clinical study.

13   When the code representing mechanical ventilation for 96 or more consecutive hours (96.72) is assigned, the length of stay must be equal to or greater than four (4) days.

Other Notations

Alphabetic Indexes

▽ **Subterms under main terms may continue to next column or page.** This warning statement is a reminder to always check for additional subterms and information that may continue onto the next page or column before making a final selection.

Disease Tabular
TIPS:

This symbol precedes official coding advice found in the official coding guidelines and AHA's *Coding Clinic for ICD-9-CM*. Coding tips appear in blue type in the Tabular List.

I-10

In preparation for the transition to coding using the ICD-10-CM classification system, examples of ICD-10-CM codes have been provided for selected ICD-9-CM diagnosis codes. This symbol indicates that the code provided is an ICD-10-CM code to which the selected ICD-9-CM code is mapped.

Note: Coding professionals should keep in mind the following points when referring to the ICD-10-CM codes provided:

- ICD-10-CM codes are not currently valid for reporting purposes.

- The ICD-10-CM code may represent only one possible coding option. Since mappings between ICD-9-CM and ICD-10-CM are not always straightforward one-to-one correspondences due to the differences in terminology and clinical concepts, the mapping may result in a one-to-many code option. Not all code options for a particular ICD-9-CM code are provided. For cases in which many code alternatives are possible in ICD-10-CM, only one example is provided.

- The ICD-10-CM code examples are provided only for the most frequently reported ICD-9-CM codes in each chapter.

- The ICD-10-CM codes are examples only and are provided to ease the transition to the new classification system.

CC **CC Condition**

This symbol designates a complication or comorbidity diagnosis that may affect DRG assignment. A complication or comorbidity diagnosis, CC condition, is defined as a significant acute disease, a significant acute manifestation of a chronic disease, an advanced or end stage chronic disease, or a chronic disease associated with systemic physiological decompensation and debility that have consistently greater impact on hospital resources.

A CC listed with a digit or range of digits indicates that only the fifth-digit assignments stated for that code are to be considered CC conditions. For example, code 642.1 has a CC 3-4 which means that only codes 642.13 and 642.14 are considered CC conditions. Codes 642.11 and 642.12 are considered major complications or comorbidity (MCC) conditions. Code 642.10 is not designated as CC or MCC.

MCC **MCC Condition**

This symbol designates a complication or comorbidity diagnosis that meets the criteria established for the revised CC list and was an AP-DRG major CC and was an APR-DRG default severity level 3 (major) or level 4 (extensive) with the exception of the newborn, maternity, and congenital anomalies which are APR-DRG default severity level 3 (major) or level 4 (extensive) only.

An MCC listed with a digit or range of digits indicates that only the fifth-digit assignments stated for that code are to be considered MCC conditions. For example; code 642.1 has a CC 3-4 which means that only codes 642.13 and 642.14 are considered CC conditions. Codes 642.11 and 642.12 are considered major complications or comorbidity (MCC) conditions and code 642.1 also has an MCC 1-2 designation. Code 642.10 is not designated as CC or MCC.

CC Exclusion List

An exclusive feature of *ICD-9-CM for Hospitals* is the integration of the government's CC exclusion list with each affected code.

The CC exclusion list indicates secondary diagnosis codes that are excluded as CC or MCC conditions with certain principal diagnoses. This exclusion occurs because the cited conditions are inherent to the disease process of the principal diagnosis, conditions that could not coexist, nonspecific codes for the principal diagnosis, or conditions affecting proximal anatomical sites.

Listed below each code that is considered a complication or comorbidity (CC) or a major complication or comorbidity (MCC) are the codes or code ranges representing principal diagnoses for which the CC or MCC will not be recognized as such for DRG assignment.

In the example below, code 254.1 is considered a CC condition. However, the CC exclusion (CC Excl:) notation indicates that if a code from the listed code ranges is assigned as the principal diagnosis, the secondary diagnosis of 254.1 will not be recognized as a CC condition in DRG assignment.

> **254.1   Abscess of thymus**   **CC**
> **CC Excl:** 254.0-254.9, 259.50-259.9

Please note that the same notation, CC Exclusion (**CC Excl:**), is used for both the MCC and CC conditions. Both MCC and CC are considered complication and comorbidity conditions. And for both, the same criteria are applied in determining which principal diagnosis for which the designated CC or MCC will not affect DRG assignment.

HIV **HIV**

This symbol indicates that the condition is considered a major HIV related diagnosis. When the condition is coded in combination with a diagnosis of human immunodeficiency virus (HIV), code 042, the case will move from MS-DRG 977 to MS-DRGs 974–976.

Wrong Surgery Edit

The Wrong Surgery edit (MCE) was created to identify cases in which wrong surgeries occurred. Any claim submitted with a code from the E876.5-E876.7 code range, whether they are in the principal or secondary diagnosis position, will trigger the Wrong Surgery edit. The claim will be denied and returned to the provider. A surgical or other invasive procedure is considered to be a wrong procedure if:

- The procedure was performed on the wrong site

- The procedure was performed on the wrong patient, or

- The incorrect procedure was performed on a patient

V Code That May Be Principal or First-Listed Diagnosis

The instructions for V code use contained in the new official coding guidelines only identify those V codes that can only be used as a PDx. All

other V codes may either be SDx or PDx depending upon circumstances of the encounter, by meeting the definition of first-listed or principal diagnosis, and by following any specific V code guidelines in section I.C.18 a-e. With the elimination of the V Code Table, the responsibility of those assigning the V codes as PDx is to make sure the circumstances of the encounter meet the definition of first-listed or principal diagnosis, follow all coding instructions, and follow the V code specific guidelines.

Note: Please note that while the official guidelines [Section 1. C.18.e.] include the V codes that may be principal or first-listed diagnoses, the reporting designations indicated by this section are often in conflict with the Medicare code edits (MCE) for the inpatient prospective payment system (IPPS). Therefore, only the inpatient prospective payment system code edits are represented in this edition.

Procedure Tabular

NC Noncovered Procedure

A procedure not covered by Medicare. In some instances this procedure may also be identified as a valid operating room (OR) procedure that may trigger a DRG assignment. Even if a DRG assignment is made, Medicare may not reimburse for the noncovered procedure.

LC Limited Coverage Procedure

A procedure whose medical complexity and serious nature incur associated costs that are deemed extraordinary and Medicare limits coverage to a portion of the cost.

BI Bilateral Edit

Due to the lack of laterality in ICD-9-CM, there are certain lower extremity joint procedure codes that do not accurately reflect procedures that are performed in one admission on two different bilateral joints. To group to MS-DRG 461 or 462, Bilateral or Multiple Joint Procedures of Lower Extremity with or without MCC, a case must be coded with a combination of two or more different major lower extremity joint procedures. The bilateral procedure symbol identifies those procedure codes that when coded twice represent the same procedure performed on both of the same bilateral joints of the lower extremity. Otherwise, a code edit will instruct the fiscal intermediary to verify that the two different procedures were performed on two different bilateral joints.

ICD-10-CM Coding and Documentation Proficiency Self-Assessment

Introduction

This self-assessment covers ICD-10-CM coding guidance and the required level of detail for clinical documentation of heart disease, diabetes, and pneumonia. These high-volume diagnoses have numerous coding guidelines and documentation requirements. The assessment also covers ICD-10-CM conventions that are new or problematic. Use this self-assessment to identify the areas that may require additional coding training or documentation improvement before ICD-10-CM is implemented.

Instructions

Code assignments are based upon the 2015 ICD-10-CM diagnosis code set for all reportable diagnoses, including external causes of morbidity (V00–Y99), as appropriate, according to the instructions in ICD-10-CM conventions and the 2015 *ICD-10-CM Draft Official Guidelines for Coding and Reporting*. Answer each question based on the information provided. Note that for some questions, the codes in the answer are not based upon the information provided, requiring that the provider be queried for specific information because the documentation is insufficient to assign codes correctly.

The answers to the questions can be found on page xx immediately following the assessment.

Self-Assessment Questions

1. There are two classifications of pneumonia by anatomical site rather than cause. What are the anatomical classifications and which site of the lung does each affect?

   _____ pneumonia affecting _____ (sites) of lung

   _____ pneumonia affecting _____ (sites) of lung

2. The attending physician's final diagnosis on the progress note on the day of discharge: atypical pneumonia. Sputum results: normal flora. Chest x-ray: bilateral lower lobe consolidation.

   A Assign J18.9 Pneumonia, unspecified organism.

   B Documentation does not follow guidelines and/or the physician must be queried to determine the following:

   • Clinical significance of the sputum results

   • Clinical significance of the chest x-ray

3. What is the appropriate diagnosis code assignment(s) for ESRD due to type I diabetes on chronic dialysis via right arm AV shunt and hypertension as documented by the provider?

   Code assignment:_____

4. Attending admission note: Patient is a 42-year-old female who presents with diabetes with hypoglycemia.

   A Assign E11.649 Type II diabetes mellitus with hypoglycemia without coma.

   B Documentation does not follow guidelines and/or the physician must be queried to determine the following:

   • Type of diabetes mellitus

   • Cause of the hypoglycemia

5. Assign the appropriate code(s) for a diagnosis by the provider of ischemic heart disease and coronary artery disease without history of coronary bypass and current smoker.

   Code assignment:_____

6. Assign the appropriate code(s) for a patient diagnosed by the provider with community-acquired pneumonia who presented with hemoptysis, productive cough, fever, and an increased respiratory rate with sputum culture stain showing gram-negative bacilli.

   Code assignment:_____

7. Discharge summary: 1. VAP, with sputum stain identifying *Klebsiella pneumoniae*, sensitivity performed and Keflex administered. 2. Vent-dependent patient.

   A Assign J95.851 Ventilator associated pneumonia, B96.1 Klebsiella pneumoniae [K. pneumoniae] as the cause of diseases classified elsewhere, and Z99.11 Dependence on respirator [ventilator] status.

   B Documentation does not follow guidelines and/or the physician must be queried to determine the following:

   • Clinical significance of the sputum results

   • Pneumonia: present on admission or post admission

8. Assign the appropriate diagnosis code(s) for diabetes II with Charcôt joint, left hallux with ulcer, with dry gangrene and with chronic osteomyelitis. The patient is admitted for amputation due to osteomyelitis documented in the surgeon's admission note.

   Code assignment:_____

9. What is the appropriate code assignment for a diagnosis of ischemic cardiomyopathy and coronary artery disease, as documented by the provider?

   Code assignment:_____

10. Discharge summary: Patient was admitted from the ED for work-up of precordial chest pain, elevated troponin; history of CABG, congestive heart failure, hypertension. Final diagnosis: ASCAD with USA, s/p CABG, CHF. Most recent diagnostic left heart catheterization showed clean vein and mammary grafts with 90% atherosclerotic stenosis of the native LAD portion. Plans are for future coronary angioplasty as an outpatient. Continue Lasix, Norvasc, and Nitrolingual.

    A Assign I25.110 Atherosclerotic heart disease of native coronary artery with unstable angina, I11.9 Hypertensive heart disease without heart failure, I50.9 Heart failure, unspecified, Z95.1 Presence of aortocoronary bypass graft.

    B Documentation does not follow guidelines and/or the physician must be queried to determine the following:

    • Description of relationship between the hypertension and congestive heart failure

    • Type of congestive heart failure

11. What is the appropriate diagnosis code assignment for the postobstructive pneumonia, right middle lobe, due to hilar lung cancer right lobe when the treatment is directed only toward the pneumonia as documented in the admission note by the resident?

   Code assignment:_____

12. Discharge summary: RSV pneumonia with acute bronchiolitis in one-month-old, high-risk due to being ex-35-week preemie.

   A   Assign J12.1 Respiratory syncytial virus pneumonia, J21.0 Acute bronchiolitis due to RSV, P07.38 Preterm newborn, gestational age 35 completed weeks.

   B   Documentation does not follow guidelines and/or the physician must be queried to determine the following:

   - Clinical significance of the history of prematurity

   - Identification of the causal organism of the bronchiolitis

13. Assign the appropriate diagnosis code(s) for a subsequent encounter for a patient on prescribed steroids with steroid-induced diabetes mellitus, requiring insulin regimen, determined to be inadequately controlled due to dietary noncompliance as documented by the provider.

   Code assignment:_____

14. What is the appropriate code assignment for a diagnosis of unstable angina in a patient who is a nonsmoker with coronary artery disease due to second-hand smoke, as documented by the provider?

   Code assignment:_____

15. Order for outpatient pre-op labs via telephone by office manager of surgeon's office; registrar sends a fax-back form that confirms the order with physician signature. Both office and lab enter note into medical record of phone order. Reason for the surgery and history are furnished by the patient at registration: angioplasty of AV fistula, right arm due to stenosis, end-stage kidney disease, hypertension, on weekly dialysis.

   A   Assign Z01.812 Encounter for preprocedural laboratory examination, T82.858A Stenosis of vascular prosthetic devices, implants and grafts, initial encounter, I12.0 Hypertensive chronic kidney disease with stage 5 chronic kidney disease or end-stage renal disease, N18.6 End-stage renal disease, and Z99.2 Dependence on renal dialysis.

   B   Documentation does not follow guidelines and/or the physician must be queried to determine the following:

   - Etiology of the end-stage renal failure

   - Hypertension, further qualified

16. What is the appropriate code assignment for the diagnosis of mixed bacterial pneumonia due to *Streptococcus pneumoniae* and *Hemophilus influenzae* identified on sputum culture stain and confirmed by the attending physician in the discharge summary?

   Code assignment:_____

17. Discharge summary: Atypical pneumonia, based on presentation clinical indicators and chest CT showing bronchial wall thickening. Last progress note: Awaiting immunoassay results. Addendum to last progress note by PA: Change antibiotic to Azithromycin. At the time of coding, the immunoassay report is posted to the chart and indicates mycoplasma pneumonia. Upon review of the sensitivity test post discharge, the provider's PA ordered a different antibiotic after consulting the attending by phone.

   A   Assign J18.9 Pneumonia, unspecified organism.

   B   Documentation does not follow guidelines and/or the physician must be queried to determine the following:

   - Clinical significance of the immunoassay results and treatment re-evaluation

   - Provide an addendum if the type of pneumonia can be further specified

18. What is the appropriate diagnosis code assignment for physician documentation of a 15-year-old with diabetes on insulin regimen?

   Code assignment:_____

19. Discharge summary signed by attending: A diagnosis of borderline diabetes is listed and body of summary notes FPG test of 124 mg/dl and indicates a need for follow-up testing in three months with diabetic counseling on next office visit recommended.

   Code assignment:_____

20. What is the appropriate diagnosis code assignment for an admission documented by the resident as due to decompensated congestive heart failure with chronic diastolic heart failure, due to patient not refilling her prescription for Lanoxin because she cannot afford the medication this month?

   Code assignment:_____

21. Order for outpatient echocardiogram. Reason: O90.3, with stamped signature of treating physician. Patient presents to testing facility with order. States order is for monitoring since she is being treated for congestive heart failure and is two months post delivery.

   A   Assign O90.3 Peripartum cardiomyopathy, I50.9 Heart failure.

   B   Documentation does not follow guidelines and/or the physician must be queried to determine the following:

   - Provide signed/dated order

   - Provide a written diagnostic statement

22. Which code is appropriate for the diagnosis of gram-positive pneumonia: J15.8 Pneumonia due to other specified bacteria, or J15.9 Unspecified bacterial pneumonia?

   Code assignment:_____

23. What is the appropriate diagnosis code to reflect physician documentation of an office visit of a 14-year-old female G1P0 for evaluation of diet-controlled gestational diabetes, second trimester at 26 weeks?

   Code assignment:_____

24. **Progress note: Patient with chronic deep ulcer on right heel. Schedule surgery to debride and consult wound care. Monitor glucose levels for patient's diabetes 2.**

   A   Assign E11.621 Type 2 diabetes mellitus with foot ulcer, and L97.419 Non-pressure chronic ulcer of right heel and midfoot with unspecified severity.

   B   Documentation does not follow guidelines and/or the physician must be queried to determine the following:

   - Etiology of the ulcer

   - Stage or severity of the ulcer

25. **What is the appropriate diagnosis code when the PA documents a history of congestive heart failure and combined diastolic and systolic dysfunction under treatment?**

   Code assignment:_____

26. **Office note by provider: Patient presents today for prenatal visit. Patient is 36-year-old G1P2, at 32 weeks, with history of essential hypertension, currently treated and monitored for signs of pre-eclampsia, asymptomatic mitral valve prolapse, history of smoking that ceased prior to pregnancy.**

   A   Assign O09.523 Supervision of elderly multigravida, third trimester, O10.013 Pre-existing essential hypertension complicating pregnancy, third trimester, I34.1 Nonrheumatic mitral (valve) prolapse, Z3A.32 32 weeks gestation of pregnancy.

   B   Documentation does not follow guidelines and/or the physician must be queried to determine the following:

   - Type of hypertension

   - Significance of patient's age affecting the pregnancy

27. **Which of these two coding conventions means the information is insufficient to assign a more specific code; for example, for the diagnosis of bacterial pneumonia?**

   A   NOS

   B   NEC

28. **Discharge summary: CMV pneumonia right lung, s/p right lung transplant in 2010 for end-stage emphysema. History of smoking. Continue outpatient pulmonary rehab.**

   A   Assign T86.812 Lung transplant infection, B25.0 Cytomegaloviral pneumonitis, J43.9 Emphysema, unspecified.

   B   Documentation does not follow guidelines and/or the physician must be queried to determine the following:

   - Whether the CMV infection of the right lung transplant is a complication of the transplant or unrelated to the transplant

   - Whether the emphysema is a current diagnosis or by history only

   - History of smoking: former history of use or dependence

29. **What is the appropriate diagnosis code for an emergency department visit for an 89-year-old patient with bleeding of a left calf ulcer due to diabetes 2 with diabetic peripheral angiopathy, exacerbated by Coumadin use for chronic atrial fibrillation. The bleeding could not be controlled by pressure at nursing home as documented by the ED physician.**

   Code assignment:_____

30. **Physician office visit note by provider: Weekly obstetric visit. 27-year-old G4P2A1, now at 30 weeks with history of miscarriage, current gestational diabetes, being treated with insulin.**

   A   Assign O09.293 Supervision of pregnancy with other poor reproductive or obstetric history, third trimester, O24.414 Gestational diabetes mellitus in pregnancy, insulin controlled, Z3A.30 30 weeks gestation of pregnancy.

   B   Documentation does not follow guidelines and/or the physician must be queried to determine the following:

   - Insulin as a long-term medication

   - Clinical significance of previous miscarriage

31. **What is the appropriate code assignment for a diagnosis of hypertensive heart disease with congestive heart failure, as documented by the emergency department physician?**

   Code assignment:_____

32. **Observation record final diagnosis by nephrologist: Admitted to observation from emergency department due to fluid overload from missing weekly dialysis, acute renal failure, end-stage renal failure, hypertension, history of congestive heart failure on Lasix (compensated). Treated with dialysis.**

   A   Assign E87.70 Fluid overload unspecified, N17.9 Acute kidney failure, I50.9 heart failure, I12.0 Hypertensive chronic kidney disease with stage 5 chronic kidney disease or end-stage renal disease, N18.6 End-stage renal disease, Z91.15 Patient's noncompliance with renal dialysis.

   B   Documentation does not follow guidelines and/or the physician must be queried to determine the following:

   - End-stage renal failure relationship to hypertension

   - Etiology of the fluid overload

33. **Which of these two coding conventions means the information provides detail for which a specific code does not exist. An example of when the convention is used is for the diagnosis *Moraxella catarrhalis* pneumonia.**

   A   NOS

   B   NEC

34. **Admitting note LTCH: 1. Gram-negative pneumonia, resolving: Admit to continue antibiotics three days more to complete regimen ordered during acute inpatient admission, then repeat chest x-ray to evaluate for presence of previously seen consolidation.**

   A   Assign J15.9 Unspecified bacterial pneumonia.

   B   Documentation does not follow guidelines and/or the physician must be queried to determine the following:

   - Whether the diagnosis of pneumonia is current (acute phase) for this encounter or resolved on admission and sequela of illness is under treatment (specify residual)

   - Clinical significance of the repeat chest x-ray (results)

35. **What are the appropriate diagnosis codes for admission to the ASC, as documented by the procedure physician, for pancreatic transplant biopsy to evaluate ongoing rejection. The patient has diabetes type 1 with severe nonproliferative retinopathy and gastroparesis and is on the transplant list awaiting a second pancreas transplant. The patient has a functioning kidney allograft with CKD stage 1, due to diabetic renal disease.**

   Code assignment:_____

36. Wound care note by wound care nurse: 32-year-old male with diabetes 1 (poly)neuropathic ulcer, 2cmx1cm improvement from last week of 2cmx2xm, right lateral 5th toe, Grade 2 subcutaneous tissue involvement, presented with dry, clean dressing, no drainage present, no odor, granular tissue present, no signs of infection, will continue enzymatic debridement. Note: patient is status post kidney/pancreas transplants, which are functioning.

A   Assign E10.621 Type 1 diabetes mellitus with foot ulcer, E10.42 Type 1 diabetes mellitus with diabetic polyneuropathy, L97.512 Non-pressure chronic ulcer of other part of right foot with fat layer exposed, Z94.0 Kidney transplant status, Z94.83 Pancreas transplant status.

B   Documentation does not follow guidelines and/or the physician must be queried to determine the following:
   • Physician must co-sign wound care note
   • Diabetes current diagnosis

37. What is the appropriate diagnosis code for Hospital B for a transfer for therapeutic intervention due to an acute STEMI inferior wall myocardial infarction where the patient suffered an acute subendocardial myocardial infarction prior to discharge, as the physician documented in the discharge summary?

   Code assignment:_____

38. Script written by PCP for outpatient chest x-ray: Productive cough, increased respiratory rate, crackles on inspiration, fever, rule out pneumonia. Script written by PCP for outpatient urinalysis and culture: Fever, tachypnea, history of recurrent urinary tract infections. Radiologist final reading: Pneumonia, COPD. Lab results: Urinalysis was abnormal, culture showed *E. coli.* Sensitivity test results were also performed.

A   Radiology: Assign J18.9 Pneumonia, unspecified organism. Lab: Assign R50.9 Fever, unspecified, R06.82 Tachypnea, not elsewhere classified, Z87.440 Personal history of urinary (tract) infections.

B   Documentation does not follow guidelines and/or the physician must be queried to determine the following:
   • PCP: Etiology for the presenting symptoms identified
   • PCP: Clinical significance of the finding of COPD

39. What is the appropriate diagnosis code for a patient with diabetes 1, inadequately controlled, with an insulin pump who is admitted as an outpatient to evaluate insulin pump function. Insulin pump was found to be functioning. The insulin dosage and titration were changed, as documented by the procedure physician.

   Code assignment:_____

40. What is the appropriate diagnosis code for an encounter the emergency department physician documents as for cardiac arrest due to ventricular fibrillation with cardiogenic shock?

   Code assignment:_____

41. ED record, signed by ED attending: Cardiac arrest, history of coronary artery disease, s/p CABG in 2011, hypertension, history of myocardial infarction in 2011. Patient admitted in cardiac arrest, CPR and defibrillation in the ED, resuscitation was unsuccessful and patient expired. Labs: CK-MB: 12.6, troponin I: 5.0. EKG: ST segment elevation and ventricular fibrillation.

A   Assign I46.9 Cardiac arrest, cause unspecified, I25.10 Atherosclerotic heart disease of native coronary artery without angina pectoris, I10 Essential (primary) hypertension, Z95.1 Presence of aortocoronary bypass graft, I25.2 Old myocardial infarction.

B   Documentation does not follow guidelines and/or the physician must be queried to determine the following:
   • Etiology of cardiac arrest
   • Clinical significance of the lab results and EKG reading

42. What is the appropriate diagnosis code for the second episode in six months of *Pneumocystis jiroveci* pneumonia in a patient who is noted to be HIV positive, as documented by the provider?

   Code assignment:_____

43. Office visit note: Follow-up for recent pneumonia, course of antibiotics completed last week. Patient without complaint. Repeat chest x-ray is negative.

A   Assign Z09 Encounter for follow-up examination after completed treatment for conditions other than malignant neoplasm, Z87.01 Personal history of pneumonia (recurrent).

B   Documentation does not follow guidelines and/or the physician must be queried to determine the following:
   • Type of pneumonia be further specified
   • Pneumonia current or by history only

44. Emergency department record, signed by ED attending: Fractured nose, right black eye of eyelid/ocular area, due to battery assault by boyfriend during domestic abuse incident; apartment residence. Patient is 20-year-old female, G3P2 at 35 weeks with diabetes 1, on insulin, with poor control due to noncompliance and financial difficulties. Admit to labor and delivery observation.

A   Assign O9A.313 Physical abuse complicating pregnancy, third trimester, S02.2XXA Fracture of nasal bones, initial encounter for closed fracture, S00.11XA Contusion of right eyelid and periocular area, initial encounter, O24.013 Pre-existing diabetes mellitus, type 1, in pregnancy, third trimester, E10.65 Type 1 diabetes mellitus with hyperglycemia, T38.3X6A Underdosing of insulin and oral hypoglycemic [antidiabetic] drugs, initial encounter, Z3A.35 35 weeks gestation of pregnancy, Y04.0XXA Assault by unarmed brawl or fight, Y07.03 Male partner, perpetrator of maltreatment and neglect, Z91.14 Patient's other noncompliance with medication regimen, Z91.120 Patient's intentional underdosing of medication regimen due to financial hardship, Z79.4 Long-term (current) use of insulin, Y92.039 Unspecified place in apartment as the place of occurrence of the external cause.

B   Documentation does not follow guidelines and/or the physician must be queried to determine the following:
   • Medical significance of noncompliance
   • Effects of trauma on pregnancy

45. Progress note by critical care physician: Code blue called after patient arrived on floor after cardiac catheterization with stent placement for coronary artery disease stenosis, history of recent myocardial infarction, no intraop complications noted. Nurse found patient in cardiac arrest; responding team initiated CPR, defibrillation, endotrachial intubation, epinephrine administered. Patient was resuscitated successfully; admit to inpatient status.

   A   Assign I46.9 Cardiac arrest cause unspecified.

   B   Documentation does not follow guidelines and/or the physician must be queried to determine the following:

   • Cause of cardiac arrest

   • Whether the cardiac arrest was a complication of the procedure

46. What is the correct code if the resident documents the diagnosis of pneumonia due to mechanical ventilation and the lab record shows vent cultures growing yeast?

   Code assignment:_____

47. What is the appropriate diagnosis code when a surgeon documents that a newborn infant was delivered by cesarean on this encounter with macrosomia and the newborn has a diagnosis of syndrome of infant of a diabetic mother?

   Code assignment:_____

48. Visit to endocrinologist: Progress note, signed by provider: diabetes 2; 4 months postpartum who had developed gestational diabetes, now with peripartum diabetes 2, under treatment with metaformin.

   A   Assign E11.9 Type 2 diabetes mellitus without complications, Z86.32 Personal history of gestational diabetes, and O94 Sequela of complication of pregnancy, childbirth, and the puerperium.

   B   Documentation does not follow guidelines and/or the physician must be queried to determine the following:

   • Risk factors for diabetes

   • Diabetic complications

49. What is the appropriate diagnosis code assignment as documented by the emergency department physician for an encounter with a woman who had acute chest pain on inspiration while surveying the damage in the yard of her former home, with acute emotional stress reaction due to surviving a tornado and losing her home to it today?

   Code assignment:_____

50. Admit note by resident: PMH: h/o cardiac arrest due to acute myocardial infarction in 2010, treated by thrombolysis. Admit note: Found to have coronary artery disease, treated medically until now. Admitted today for CABG due to progressive angina. What past history would be appropriate to assign?

   A   Assign Z86.74 Personal history of sudden cardiac arrest, and I25.2 Old myocardial infarction.

   B   Documentation does not follow guidelines and/or the physician must be queried to determine the following:

   • Type of angina

   • Significance of history of myocardial infarction treatment

Coding and Documentation Review Answers

1. **Answer: Lobar pneumonia affects an area of a lobe of the lung; Bronch(o)(ial) pneumonia affects the walls of the bronchioles.**

   Rationale: Under the ICD-10-CM Alphabetic Index entry for pneumonia, the subterms that indicate anatomical areas, such as alveolar, apex, confluent, diffuse, etc., index to "see" references. The two "see" references are "see Pneumonia, lobar" or "see Pneumonia, broncho." These two terms are anatomical classifications of pneumonia that indicate the sites in the lung where clinical indicators of consolidation can be seen on radiologic displays. Since these types of pneumonia are identified by radiological findings rather than causal organism, they are classified as pneumonia caused by unspecified organism. Lobar affects an area of the lung lobe. Bronch(o)(ial)pneumonia or lobular pneumonia affects the walls of the bronchioles with multiple foci of isolated consolidation in one or more basal lobes of the lung.

2. **Answer: A Assign J18.9 Pneumonia, unspecified organism.**

   Rationale: The type of pneumonia is identified only as "atypical," and no specific organism is attributable; the Alphabetic Index entry for "Pneumonia, atypical" lists J18.9 Pneumonia, unspecified organism. Normal flora identified in a culture indicates a mixture of bacteria normally found at specific body sites and does not represent pathogens and is not clinically significant. The chest x-ray shows bilateral lower lobe consolidation, which can also be seen in congestive heart failure and empyema, among other causes. OCG.I.C.18.b states that signs or symptoms routinely associated with a disease process should not be identified with additional codes unless the physician instructs otherwise.

3. **Answer: E10.22 Type 1 diabetes mellitus with diabetic chronic kidney disease, I12.0 Hypertensive chronic kidney disease with stage 5 chronic kidney disease or end-stage renal disease, N18.6 End-stage renal disease, Z99.2 Dependence on renal dialysis**

   Rationale: The type of diabetes is stated as type I, and the chronic kidney disease is due to the diabetes; therefore, assign a code from category E10. ICD-10-CM assumes a cause-and-effect relationship when both hypertension and chronic kidney disease are present (*Official Coding Guidelines* [OCG], section I.C.9.a.2); consequently a code from category I12 is assigned. The tabular "code also" note indicates that the coder should assign an additional code to identify the stage of chronic kidney disease, in this case, end-stage renal disease, N18.6. An instructional note under code N18.6 instructs the coder to use an additional code to identify dialysis status, which is Z99.2 Dependence on renal dialysis.

4. **Answer: A E11.649 Type II diabetes mellitus with hypoglycemia without coma**

   Rationale: ICD-10-CM OCG section I.C.4.a.2 states that E11- Type 2 diabetes mellitus, is assigned as the default when the type is not specified. Guideline section I.A.15 indicates that the word "with" means "due to" in the Alphabetic Index; therefore, the documentation links the diabetes and hypoglycemia. Diabetes mellitus codes are combination codes, and the Alphabetic Index entry for diabetes with hypoglycemia, Type 2, refers to E11.649 Type II diabetes mellitus with hypoglycemia without coma.

5. **Answer: I25.10 Atherosclerotic heart disease of native coronary artery without angina pectoris, Z72.0 Tobacco use**

   Rationale: The ICD-10-CM Alphabetic Index main term "Disease, coronary (artery)" directs the coder to "see" Disease, heart, ischemic, atherosclerotic. Under "Disease/heart/ischemic/atherosclerotic," the code default is I25.10. Both stated conditions are classified to the single code I25.10 Atherosclerotic heart disease of native coronary artery without angina pectoris. When there is no history or documentation of a previous coronary artery bypass graft (CABG) or heart transplant, a code for atherosclerosis of native artery should be assigned. The Alphabetic Index lists code Z72.0 under "Tobacco, use."

6. **Answer: J18.9 Pneumonia, unspecified organism, R04.2 Hemoptysis**

   Rationale: The ICD-10-CM Alphabetic Index does not list the nonessential modifier "hemorrhagic" after the term "pneumonia." Therefore, unless documentation links this symptom to the pneumonia, the hemoptysis would be assigned as an additional code. The provider/documentation does not confirm that the sputum culture stain showing gram-negative bacilli is clinically significant. See OCG 1.C.18.b, "Use of a symptom code with a definitive diagnosis," and OCG III, "Reporting Additional Findings, B. Abnormal findings."

7. **Answer: A Assign J95.851 Ventilator associated pneumonia, B96.1 Klebsiella pneumoniae [K. pneumoniae] as the cause of diseases classified elsewhere, Z99.11 Dependence on respirator [ventilator] status.**

   Rationale: The ICD-10-CM OCG section I.C.10.d.1 states that the assignment of a complication code is based on the provider's documentation of the relationship between the pneumonia and the mechanical ventilation. In this case, the documentation describes the pneumonia as due to the ventilator. An additional code is assigned if an identified organism is attributed to the VAP, but not a pneumonia code from J12–J18.

8. **Answer: E11.610 Type 2 diabetes mellitus with diabetic neuropathic arthropathy, E11.621 Type 2 diabetes mellitus with foot ulcer, E11.52 Type 2 diabetes mellitus with diabetic peripheral angiopathy with gangrene, L97.524 Non-pressure chronic ulcer of other part of left foot with necrosis of bone**

   Rationale: ICD-10-CM OCG section I.A.15 states that the use of the term "with" is to be interpreted to mean "associated with" or "due to" when it appears in a code title, the Alphabetic Index, or an instructional note in the Tabular List. Therefore, the listed conditions are coded as diabetic complications. Guideline section I.C.4.a states that as many codes within a particular category should be assigned as describe all the complications, with sequencing based on the reason for a particular encounter. E11.610 Type 2 diabetes mellitus with diabetic neuropathic arthropathy is sequenced first since this describes the osteomyelitis.

9. **Answer: I25.5 Ischemic cardiomyopathy and I25.10 Atherosclerotic heart disease of native coronary artery without angina pectoris**

   Rationale: Ischemic cardiomyopathy is an extrinsic cardiomyopathy due to reduced blood flow to the heart muscle. The ICD-10-CM Alphabetic Index lists I25.5 Ischemic cardiomyopathy under the term "Cardiomyopathy, ischemic to." The "excludes2" note under I25.5 indicates that coronary atherosclerosis (I25.1-, I25.7-) is not included; therefore, these two conditions can be coded together when documented.

10. **Answer: B Documentation does not follow guidelines and/or the physician must be queried to determine the following: description of relationship between the hypertension and congestive heart failure, and specify type of the congestive heart failure.**

   Rationale: The relationship between hypertension and congestive heart failure is not assumed in ICD-10-CM and must be documented. Second, if the type of heart failure can be further specified as diastolic, systolic, or both, a more accurate code can be assigned from category I50 Heart failure. Heart disease without a stated causal relationship to hypertension is coded separately.

11. *Answer:* **J18.9 Pneumonia, unspecified organism, and C34.01 Malignant neoplasm of right main bronchus or lung**

    Rationale: There is no specific entry in the Alphabetic Index for postobstructive pneumonia; therefore, only the term "Pneumonia" is listed. When a specified type of pneumonia is not documented, J18.9 Pneumonia, unspecified organism, is the default code and should be assigned. The malignancy is sequenced as an additional code according to OCG section C.2.l.4.

12. *Answer:* <u>A</u> **Assign J12.1 Respiratory syncytial virus pneumonia, J21.0 Acute bronchiolitis due to RSV, P07.38 Preterm newborn, gestational age 35 completed weeks.**

    Rationale: The ICD-10-CM Alphabetic Index entry for "Pneumonia, respiratory syncytial virus" lists J12.1. Respiratory syncytial virus is a common community-acquired infection in children. OCG section I.C.16.a.5 states that if a newborn condition is community-acquired, a code from chapter 16, "Certain Conditions Originating in the Perinatal Period," is not assigned. RSV bronchiolitis is also documented and is also assigned. Both are acute conditions, and when the patient is admitted for both and both are equal in work-up, focus, and treatment, either can be sequenced as the principal diagnosis, following OCG section II.B. The additional information that the patient is a former preemie is coded as its clinical significance is documented and OCG section I.C.16.e states that prematurity is coded when it affects the patient's current health status.

13. *Answer:* **E09.65 Drug or chemical induced diabetes mellitus with hyperglycemia, T38.0X5D Adverse effect of glucocorticoids and synthetic analogues subsequent encounter, Z79.4 Long term (current) use of insulin, Z91.11 Patient's noncompliance with dietary regimen**

    Rationale: Since the steroid use is prescribed and there is no indication of incorrect usage, this is considered an adverse effect and not a poisoning. The diabetes is drug-induced, and according to OCG section I.C.4.a.6.b, sequencing is to "code first" E09 Drug or chemical induced diabetes mellitus, followed by an additional code for the adverse effect to identify the drug T36–T50 with a fifth/sixth character of 5. ICD-10-CM does not use the terms "uncontrolled," "inadequately controlled," or "out of control, poorly controlled." The index instructs the user to "code Diabetes, by type, with hyperglycemia." Therefore, the first-listed code is E09.65 Drug or chemical induced diabetes mellitus with hyperglycemia. This is followed by T38.0X5- Adverse effect of glucocorticoids and synthetic analogues, which is located in the Table of Drugs and Chemicals under the main term "Steroid" with the appropriate additional character requirement, which in this case is a character for a subsequent encounter (D). The patient is maintained on insulin, Z79.4, which OCG section I.C.4.a.6.a, indicates is coded when documented. The diabetes is inadequately controlled due to dietary noncompliance, Z91.11, which is located in the Alphabetic Index under "Noncompliance, with, dietary regimen."

14. *Answer:* **I25.110 Atherosclerotic heart disease of native coronary artery with unstable angina pectoris, Z77.22 Contact with and (suspected) exposure to environmental tobacco smoke (acute) (chronic)**

    Rationale: OCG section I.C.9.b states that ICD-10-CM provides combination codes that link coronary artery disease with angina since the relationship between them is to be assumed unless otherwise documented. No separate code is assigned from category I20 Angina pectoris. Code Z77.22 Contact with and (suspected) exposure to environmental tobacco smoke (acute) (chronic) is assigned as a secondary code when the provider documents that the second-hand smoke is the external cause of the patient's condition. Locate the code in the Alphabetic Index under the term "Exposure, second hand tobacco smoke (acute) (chronic)." When there is no history or documentation of a previous coronary artery bypass graft (CABG) or heart transplant, a code for atherosclerosis of native artery is assigned.

15. *Answer:* <u>A</u> **Assign Z01.812 Encounter for preprocedural laboratory examination, T82.858A Stenosis of vascular prosthetic devices, implants and grafts, initial encounter, I12.0 Hypertensive chronic kidney disease with stage 5 chronic kidney disease or end-stage renal disease, N18.6 End-stage renal disease, and Z99.2 Dependence on renal dialysis.**

    Rationale: A telephone call from the treating physician's office to the testing facility to order a diagnostic outpatient service is acceptable if, as required by the Centers for Medicare and Medicaid Services, payer, state, conditions of participation bylaws, Joint Commission and Office of Inspector General requirements, both the treating physician/office and the testing facility document the phone call in their copies of the patient's medical record. This information may be obtained from the patient or the medical record, but the coder should attempt to confirm this information with the physician, and it is recommended to have a "fax-back" policy in place for the registration sites. In the example, the reason for the order is to have pre-op lab testing performed; "Examination, pre-procedural (pre-operative), laboratory" in the Alphabetic Index lists Z01.812 Encounter for preprocedural laboratory examination. OCG section I.C.21.c.16 indicates that category Z01 is a "first-listed" diagnosis and therefore should be sequenced first followed by the reason for the surgery/procedure.

16. *Answer:* **J13 Pneumonia due to Streptococcus pneumoniae, and J14 Pneumonia due to Haemophilus influenzae**

    Rationale: Since the attending physician confirmed both identified infective organisms, both individual codes are assigned. If the organisms were not identified, then only pneumonia, bacterial (unspecified organism) would be assigned, not the "bacterial, specified" code, since the terms "mixed bacterial" do not identify specified organisms not elsewhere classified.

17. *Answer:* <u>B</u> **Documentation does not follow guidelines and/or the physician must be queried to determine the following: the clinical significance of the immunoassay results and treatment re-evaluation and provide an addendum if the type of pneumonia can be further specified.**

    Rationale: After the documentation is reviewed, a query is warranted to further specify the type of pneumonia. The physician assistant documented a change in treatment based upon the results of the immunoassay test. Although the test results are posted to the chart, the coder should ask about their clinical significance and the reason behind the change in medication. Additionally, the findings on chest x-ray further support a more specific pneumonia as due to the identified organism. Coders are responsible for querying when the clinical documentation as a whole suggests a higher level of specificity.

18. *Answer:* **E11.9 Type 2 diabetes mellitus without complications, and Z79.4 Long-term (current) use of insulin**

    Rationale: According to OCG section I.C.4.a.2.3, the type of diabetes mellitus cannot be determined by patient age or the use of insulin. The guideline further states that when the type of diabetes is not documented, the default is diabetes mellitus type 2 and that insulin documented as a maintenance drug is assigned as an additional code.

19. *Answer:* **Assign R73.09 Other abnormal glucose.**

    Rationale: Without further documentation of a diagnosis of diabetes, the attending's attestation to the discharge summary confirming the lab findings and the indication of clinical significance, only a code from subcategory "abnormal glucose" can be assigned. This can be found in the Alphabetic Index under the main term "Findings, abnormal, inconclusive, without findings, glucose" or by the documentation of borderline diabetes mellitus or diabetes, latent. Code R73.09 Other abnormal glucose, lists "prediabetes" and "latent diabetes" as inclusion terms.

20. *Answer:* I50.33 Acute on chronic diastolic (congestive) heart failure, T46.0X6A Underdosing of cardiac-stimulant glycosides and drugs of similar action initial encounter, and Z91.120 Patient's intentional underdosing of medication regimen due to financial hardship

Rationale: The code for "chronic on acute (i.e., acute on chronic)" is assigned because the acute exacerbation of a chronic condition is coded as acute on chronic, and when a combination code is available, only a single code is assigned. The exacerbation of the congestive heart failure was due to the lack of Lanoxin and is sequenced before the code for the underdosing, according to OCG section I.C.19.e.5.c. The seventh-character assignment of A, indicating the initial encounter, is required to complete code T46.0X6. An additional code to represent noncompliance and the reason and intent is assigned: Z91.120 Patient's intentional underdosing of medication regimen due to financial hardship. The ICD-10-CM Alphabetic Index and Tabular List now provide the nonessential modifier "congestive" in the descriptor of the diastolic and systolic types of heart failure. Therefore an additional code for "congestive heart failure" is not assigned.

21. *Answer:* **B** Documentation does not follow guidelines and/or the physician must be queried to determine the following: provide signed/dated order and provide a written diagnostic statement.

Rationale: A valid order must follow CMS, payer, state, conditions of participation, bylaws and Joint Commission and OIG requirements. Signatures are required for certain diagnostic tests, and CMS Transmittal 327 states that stamped signatures are not acceptable. The introduction to the OCG states that ICD-10-CM is a morbidity classification for classifying diagnoses and reason for health care visits. Codes are not diagnoses—they may not be used as a substitute for a written diagnostic statement within the medical record.

22. *Answer:* J15.9 Unspecified bacterial pneumonia

Rationale: Since the term "gram-positive" is nonspecific and does not identify a specific organism, assign J15.9 Unspecified bacterial pneumonia. When a specific bacterial organism is identified but has no specific entry in the Alphabetic Index or a corresponding ICD-10-CM diagnosis code, the default is J15.8 Pneumonia due to other specified bacteria. The same applies to viral pneumonia coding.

23. *Answer:* O09.612 Supervision of young primigravida, second trimester, O24.410 Gestational diabetes mellitus in pregnancy, diet controlled, Z3A.26, 26 weeks gestation of pregnancy

Rationale: OCG section I.C.15.i covers gestational diabetes. Since the patient is 14 years old and this is her first pregnancy (identified by "G1P0"), the coder would look in the index under "Pregnancy, supervision of, young mother, primigravida." The sixth character "2" specifies second trimester as defined by the note at the introduction to chapter 15. The Alphabetic Index lists the main term "Diabetes" with the subterm "gestational, diet controlled," which references code O24.410. Follow the instructional note for chapter 15 and use an additional code from category Z3A to describe the number of weeks of gestation.

24. *Answer:* **B** Documentation does not follow guidelines and/or the physician must be queried to determine the following: etiology of the ulcer and stage or severity of the ulcer.

Rationale: If the ulcer is of diabetic origin, the link to diabetes must be stated before the ulcer can be coded. The term "deep" does not indicate the tissues involved, and the tissues need to be documented to further classify the stage or level of necrosis for code severity specificity.

25. *Answer:* I50.42 Chronic combined systolic (congestive) and diastolic (congestive) heart failure

Rationale: The ICD-10-CM Alphabetic Index does not have entries for diastolic or systolic under the main term "Dysfunction." Diastolic dysfunction is the decline in performance of one or both ventricles of the heart during the time phase of diastole; left/systemic/body and right/pulmonary/lungs. Dysfunction has a subterm "ventricular/with congestive heart failure," which references I50.9 Heart failure unspecified. However, when there is diastolic or systolic dysfunction in the presence of heart failure, the relationship is assumed. In this example, the heart failure is specified as combined diastolic and systolic. Code I50.42 is the appropriate code. If diastolic or systolic dysfunction is documented without documentation of heart failure, assign I51.9 Heart disease, unspecified. In this case, however, because of the known history of heart failure, the case is coded as chronic.

26. *Answer:* **A** Assign O09.523 Supervision of elderly multigravida, third trimester, O10.013 Pre-existing essential hypertension complicating pregnancy third trimester, I34.1 Nonrheumatic mitral (valve) prolapse, Z3A.32 32 weeks gestation of pregnancy.

Rationale: For this scenario, OCG section I.C.15.b.2 states that the principal diagnosis should be a code from category O09 for supervision of a high-risk (elderly) pregnancy. The patient is 36 years old and has delivered once (G1P2). Assign code O09.523 as the first-listed diagnosis. The sixth character indicates the third trimester, as defined by the note in the introduction to chapter 15. Code Z3A.32 32 weeks gestation of pregnancy, is assigned according to the instructional note for chapter 15. Code O10.013 Pre-existing essential hypertension complicating pregnancy, third trimester, would be assigned as a secondary diagnosis code. Mitral valve prolapse, although asymptomatic, is coded because it is medically significant during pregnancy.

27. *Answer:* **A** NOS

Rationale: The coding convention NOS, or not otherwise specified, is the equivalent of "unspecified" and is assigned when the documentation does not provide more specific information about the condition. In the example, the term bacterial pneumonia means that the specified bacterial organism causing the pneumonia is unknown, or cannot be determined. What is known is that the causal organism is bacterial as opposed to viral. The Alphabetic Index lists the terms "Pneumonia, bacterial"; therefore, the default is J15.9 Unspecified bacterial pneumonia.

28. *Answer:* **A** Assign T86.812 Lung transplant infection, B25.0 Cytomegaloviral pneumonitis, J43.9 Emphysema, unspecified.

Rationale: According to OCG section I.C.19.g.3.a, the code for transplant complications is assigned only if the complication affects the function of the transplanted organ. The complication requires two codes, one from category T86 to identify the type of complication and a second to identify the manifestation. Cytomegaloviral pneumonitis, or CMV, is an opportunistic pneumonia. Since the pneumonitis is in the allograft, it is coded as a lung transplant complication, specifically as an infection. The transplant was performed only on the right, so the emphysema is not "cured" and is still present. Therefore, the emphysema is assigned as an additional diagnosis. Only history of tobacco dependence, not history of smoking or tobacco use, has an index entry. Therefore, the history of smoking is not coded.

29. *Answer:* **E11.622 Type 2 diabetes mellitus with other skin ulcer, T45.515A Adverse effect of anticoagulants, E11.51 Type 2 diabetes mellitus with diabetic peripheral angiopathy without gangrene, L97.229 Non-pressure chronic ulcer of left calf with unspecified severity, I48.2 Chronic atrial fibrillation**

    Rationale: As the bleeding from the ulcer is an adverse effect of the prescribed Coumadin, follow the guidelines in OCG section I.C.19.e.5.a and sequence the nature of the adverse effect first, which in this case is also a diabetic complication, E11.622 Type 2 diabetes mellitus with other skin ulcer. This is followed by the code identifying the drug and adverse effect, T45.515A Adverse effect of anticoagulants, found in the Table of Drugs and Chemicals. Code also all other diabetic complications, E11.51 Type 2 diabetes mellitus with diabetic peripheral angiopathy without gangrene. Also list code L97.229 Non-pressure chronic ulcer of left calf with unspecified severity to identify the site and severity of the ulcer per the "use additional code" instruction note under E11.622. Code I48.2 Chronic atrial fibrillation, indicates the condition for which the Coumadin is taken.

30. *Answer:* **A Assign O09.293 Supervision of pregnancy with other poor reproductive or obstetric history, third trimester, O24.414 Gestational diabetes mellitus in pregnancy, insulin controlled, Z3A.30, 30 weeks gestation of pregnancy.**

    Rationale: The provider's documentation indicates this is a routine prenatal visit for a high-risk pregnancy due to a history of miscarriage with current gestational diabetes. OCG section I.C.15.b.2 states that a code from category O09 Supervision of high-risk pregnancy, should be assigned as the first-listed diagnosis, followed by any other applicable chapter 15 codes to describe comorbid conditions affecting the pregnancy. The code for gestational diabetes does not indicate trimester, but the fourth character does represent "in pregnancy." From the instructional note "use additional code from category Z3A" for chapter 15, code Z3A.30 30 weeks gestation of pregnancy, is assigned. OCG section I.C.15.i notes that additional code Z79.4 Long-term (current) use of insulin, should not be assigned with codes from subcategory O24.4.

31. *Answer:* **I11.0 Hypertensive heart disease with heart failure, I50.9 Heart failure, unspecified**

    Rationale: According to OCG section I.C.9.1, when a causal relationship between hypertension and heart failure (I50.-) or heart disease (I51.4.-I51.9) is stated (due to) or implied (hypertensive), assign a code from category I11 Hypertensive heart disease. Also the OCG section I.A.15 states that in the Alphabetic Index, the subentry term "with" means "associated with" or "due to." Therefore, a diagnostic statement of "with" provides the link between two conditions. The tabular note instructs the coder to "use additional code to identify type of heart failure I50.-." In the example, the type is not documented; therefore an additional code for heart failure, unspecified is assigned.

32. *Answer:* **A Assign E87.70 Fluid overload unspecified, N17.9 Acute kidney failure, I50.9 Heart failure, I12.0 Hypertensive chronic kidney disease with stage 5 chronic kidney disease or end-stage renal disease, N18.6 End-stage renal disease, Z91.15 Patient's noncompliance with renal dialysis.**

    Rationale: The acute conditions necessitating admission were the fluid overload and the acute renal failure. Since the dialysis is treatment for both conditions, according to OCG section II.C either may be sequenced as the principal diagnosis unless one is considered the more significant problem. As long as the admission is clearly documented as to treat the fluid overload and as not related to the history of congestive heart failure, the fluid overload can be coded separately. The congestive heart failure is noted to be "compensated," meaning it is not in acute

exacerbation; note that unspecified heart failure I50.9 makes no distinction between acute or decompensated and compensated. If the record indicates that the type of heart failure can be specified further, the coder should query the physician for the type as well as a possible relationship between the heart failure and hypertension. Acute renal failure can be coded in the presence of end-stage kidney disease as there are no excludes or includes notes or instructional notes that indicate otherwise. The cause of the fluid overload was the noncompliance with dialysis, which is in the Alphabetic Index as "Noncompliance, with, dialysis," Z91.15. The dialysis status code is not assigned when the noncompliance is coded, Z91.15, as indicated by the "excludes1" note under Z99.2 Dependence on renal dialysis.

33. *Answer:* **B NEC**

    Rationale: The coding convention NEC, or not elsewhere classified, is the equivalent of "specified (other, other specified)" and applies when the documentation specifies a condition but there is no individual code for that condition. In the example, the type of bacteria causing the pneumonia is identified (specified), but the ICD-10-CM Alphabetic Index does not list an individual code for that particular organism. Therefore, the user would look in the index under "Pneumonia, specified, bacterium NEC," leading to J15.8 Pneumonia due to other specified bacteria.

34. *Answer:* **B Documentation does not follow guidelines and/or the physician must be queried to determine the following: diagnosis of pneumonia current (acute phase) for this encounter or resolved on admission and sequela of illness is under treatment (specify residual); and clinical significance of the repeat chest x-ray (results).**

    Rationale: Long-term care hospitals may assign codes for acute unresolved conditions, sequelae, or rehab. The selection of principal diagnosis follows the guidelines in OCG section II. When the patient is admitted for continuation of treatment of an acute condition, OCG section I.B.10 may apply if the acute phase has resolved and it is the sequela that is being treated. This provider must document that the residual condition is being treated and is the reason for admission. If the patient no longer has the clinical indicators of the acute disease, the coder should query the physician for clarification as to whether the acute condition is present or if a sequela is receiving the continuation of care and treatment. As long as an acute condition is the target of treatment, it is coded. For this example, the facility must decide how to address the issue of acute condition versus sequela for "resolving" conditions that may or may not have clinical indicators.

35. *Answer:* **T86.890 Other transplanted tissue rejection, E10.349 Type 1 diabetes mellitus with severe nonproliferative diabetic retinopathy without macular edema, E10.43 Type 1 diabetes mellitus with diabetic autonomic (poly)neuropathy (gastroparesis), E10.22 Type 1 diabetes mellitus with diabetic chronic kidney disease, N18.1 Chronic kidney disease, stage 1, Z94.0 Kidney transplant status, and Z76.82 Awaiting organ transplant status**

    Rationale: Rejection affects the transplanted pancreas and is a complication of the pancreas transplant. As the reason for the encounter, the transplant rejection is sequenced first. The patient has ongoing complications of retinopathy and gastroparesis due to diabetes 1, which must also be coded. The patient is also status post kidney transplant due to diabetic renal disease, and the transplanted kidney is functioning with mild CKD stage 1, which is not documented as a complication but is residual renal disease. OCG section I.C.14.a.2 indicates that the CKD stage with kidney transplant status should be assigned. Also indicate that the patient is awaiting transplant by looking in the index under "Transplant, awaiting organ," code Z76.82.

36. *Answer:* **A** Assign **E10.621 Type 1 diabetes mellitus with foot ulcer, E10.42 Type 1 diabetes mellitus with diabetic polyneuropathy, L97.512 Non-pressure chronic ulcer of other part of right foot with fat layer exposed, Z94.0 Kidney transplant status, Z94.83 Pancreas transplant status.**

Rationale: The term provider is used throughout the *Official Coding Guidelines* to indicate a physician or any qualified health care practitioner who is legally accountable for establishing the patient's diagnosis. State laws define the scope of practice and, for health care entities, regulatory laws establish who may provide documentation; wound care nursing documentation is recognized as valid. Although the patient has a functioning pancreas transplant, diabetes is coded since there are related complications. The diabetes 1 is linked to the ulcer by its description as diabetes 1 neuropathic ulcer. Because the Wagner non-pressure foot ulcer classification grade 2 is penetration through the subcutaneous tissue, the severity chosen is "with fat layer exposed." The ulcer is sequenced first before the neuropathy because it is the reason for the encounter.

37. *Answer:* **I21.19 ST elevation (STEMI) myocardial infarction involving other coronary artery of inferior wall, and I22.2 Subsequent non-ST elevation (NSTEMI) myocardial infarction**

Rationale: OCG section I.C.9.e.1 states that a code for the site is assigned for an acute STEMI myocardial infarction for encounters occurring when the MI is equal to or less than four weeks old, including transfers during this timeframe. New for ICD-10-CM, OCG section I.C.9.e.4 states that after an initial myocardial infarction, a subsequent or new acute myocardial infarction during the same four-week timeframe is coded to category I22 Subsequent ST elevation (STEMI) and non-ST elevation (NSTEMI) myocardial infarction. When there are both an initial and subsequent acute myocardial infarction, codes from both I21 and I22 are assigned, sequenced based on the circumstances of the encounter.

38. *Answer:* **A** Radiology: Assign **J18.9 Pneumonia, unspecified organism. Lab: Assign R50.9 Fever, unspecified, R06.82 Tachypnea, not elsewhere classified, Z87.440 Personal history of urinary (tract) infections.**

Rationale: In the outpatient setting, uncertain diagnoses cannot be assigned (OCG section IV.H). The referring provider should document signs, symptoms, and abnormal findings that prompt the outpatient encounter. If a physician has interpreted a diagnostic test and the results are available, the confirmed or definitive diagnosis is coded; the related or integral signs and symptoms are not coded, according to OCG section IV.K.. The second script lists signs and symptoms and history, but the test results are by lab only. Therefore, the signs and symptoms and history codes are assigned. When possible, the coder should ask the PCP to clarify the lab results. Until the PCP confirms the test results for the scripts, only the codes for the symptoms for which the tests were ordered are assigned.

39. *Answer:* **E10.65 Type 1 diabetes mellitus with hyperglycemia and Z46.81 Encounter for fitting and adjustment of insulin pump**

Rationale: The ICD-10-CM Alphabetic Index lists the terms inadequately controlled, out of control, and poorly controlled to represent diabetes mellitus uncontrolled, with the instruction to assign diabetes, by type, with hyperglycemia. Therefore, assign E10.65 Type 1 diabetes mellitus with hyperglycemia as the first diagnosis as the diabetes was symptomatic and the reason for the encounter, not just an evaluation of the insulin pump or for titration adjustment. Add Z46.81 Encounter for fitting and adjustment of insulin pump, since titration adjustment was performed. The status code Z96.41 Presence of insulin pump (external) (internal) is not assigned since the reason for encounter code indicates the type of status according to OCG section I.C.21.c.3.

40. *Answer:* **I49.01 Ventricular fibrillation, I46.2 Cardiac arrest due to underlying cardiac condition, and R57.0 Cardiogenic shock**

Rationale: The ICD-10-CM Alphabetic Index now provides separate codes for cardiac arrest due to underlying cardiac condition, due to (other) specified underlying condition (trauma, overdose, etc.) or unspecified cause. Codes for both the cardiac arrest and the underlying condition should be assigned, when the condition is known. In the example for the ED encounter, the ventricular fibrillation is known and should be sequenced first, followed by the code for the cardiac arrest as instructed by the tabular "code first" note under category I46 Cardiac arrest. If further work-up determines the cause of the ventricular fibrillation, such as cardiac ischemia or coronary artery disease, cardiomyopathy, acute myocardial infarction, trauma, overdose, etc., that condition is the principal diagnosis and the appropriate code from category I46 Cardiac arrest, is secondary, along with I49.01 Ventricular fibrillation. Since the cardiogenic shock is not integral to the ventricular fibrillation or the cardiac arrest, the code for shock is assigned even though it is not a chapter 18 code (OCG section I.C.18.b). Review and apply the guidelines in the OCG section II introduction for the UHDDS definition of principal diagnosis for inpatient, and in OCG section IV.G, IV.k and IV.l for the reason of the outpatient encounter. Keep in mind that, according to OCG section IV.A, the coding conventions and the general and disease-specific guidelines take precedence over the outpatient guidelines.

41. *Answer:* **A** Assign **I46.9 Cardiac arrest, cause unspecified, I25.10 Atherosclerotic heart disease of native coronary artery without angina pectoris, I10 Essential (primary) hypertension, Z95.1 Presence of aortocoronary bypass graft, I25.2 Old myocardial infarction.**

Rationale: When an emergency department patient dies before the cause of a cardiac arrest is known, the code for the cardiac arrest is the first-listed diagnosis. When the underlying condition is known, the code for the condition is sequenced first, with the code for cardiac arrest as an additional diagnosis. In ICD-10-CM, cardiac arrest now has three subcategories based on whether the underlying condition is known or not and whether it is cardiac or other specified condition. Since there is no documentation of recent cardiac catheterization, the coronary artery disease post CABG is assumed to be of native vessel without angina pectoris.

42. *Answer:* **B20 Human immunodeficiency virus [HIV] disease and B59 Pneumocystosis**

Rationale: ICD-10-CM OCG section I.C.1.a.1 instructs that confirmation of HIV status can be made by the provider's statement that the patient has an HIV-related illness. Also, section I.C.1.a.2.f states that cases involving patients with any known prior diagnosis of an HIV-related illness are assigned code B20 Human immunodeficiency virus [HIV] disease. The Centers for Disease Control (CDC) classifies *Pneumocystis jiroveci* pneumonia, an opportunistic pneumonia, as an AIDS-defining condition and one of the clinical criteria for HIV stage 3 or AIDS. Another clinical criterion is an HIV-positive patient having bacterial pneumonia twice within one year.

43. *Answer:* **A** Assign **Z09 Encounter for follow-up examination after completed treatment for conditions other than malignant neoplasm, Z87.01 Personal history of pneumonia (recurrent).**

Rationale: OCG section I.C.21.c.8 states that follow-up codes are assigned when the encounter is for surveillance following completed treatment and the condition no longer exists. Follow-up codes are not used for sequelae or ongoing care of a condition that is healing or resolving. A history code representing the healed/resolved condition is assigned as a secondary code to fully explain the reason for the encounter. The follow-up code is not assigned if the condition is found to have recurred on the follow-up encounter, and instead the code for the condition is listed first.

44. *Answer:* **A** Assign O9A.313 Physical abuse complicating pregnancy, third trimester, S02.2XXA Fracture of nasal bones, initial encounter for closed fracture, S00.11XA Contusion of right eyelid and periocular area, initial encounter, O24.013 Pre-existing diabetes mellitus, type 1, in pregnancy, third trimester, E10.65 Type 1 diabetes mellitus with hyperglycemia, T38.3X6A Underdosing of insulin and oral hypoglycemic [antidiabetic] drugs, initial encounter, Z3A.35 35 weeks gestation of pregnancy, Y04.0XXA Assault by unarmed brawl or fight, Y07.03 Male partner, perpetrator of maltreatment and neglect, Z91.120 Patient's intentional underdosing of medication regimen due to financial hardship, Z79.4 Long term (current) use of insulin, Y92.039 Unspecified place in apartment as the place of occurrence of the external cause

Rationale: The ED provider documentation that is attested by signature confirms the injuries are due to physical abuse. The *Official Coding Guidelines* section I.C.15.r states that abuse in a pregnant patient is sequenced first and coded to category O9A Physical abuse complicating pregnancy, childbirth, and the puerperium, when suspected or confirmed; associated injuries are coded as additional diagnoses. Pre-existing diabetes 1 with poor control is assigned to category O24 Diabetes mellitus in pregnancy, childbirth, and the puerperium, with an additional code from category E10 Type 1 diabetes mellitus, to further identify manifestation of hyperglycemia, indicated in the Alphabetic Index as poor control. Underdosing of medication is covered in OCG section I.C.19.e.5.c and is assigned from category T38 with the sixth character of 6. Sequencing of multiple codes from chapter 20, "External Causes of Morbidity," is explained in OCG section I.C.20.f.

45. *Answer:* **B** Documentation does not follow guidelines and/or the physician must be queried to determine the following: cause of cardiac arrest and whether the cardiac arrest a complication of the procedure.

Rationale: When a cardiac arrest occurs during an inpatient hospitalization and the patient is resuscitated, a code from category I46 Cardiac arrest, is assigned as an additional diagnosis. It would be appropriate to ask the physician the cause or contributing cause if it is not stated when there is clinical evidence to support the query. When a cardiac arrest is the reason for an inpatient death (the patient is not resuscitated) and the cause or contributing cause is known, the code for cardiac arrest is not assigned.

46. *Answer:* **J95.851 Ventilator associated pneumonia**

Rationale: ICD-10-CM OCG section I.C.10.d.1 states that the code for a complication is based on the provider's documentation of the relationship between the complication and the cause, in this case, the pneumonia and the mechanical ventilation. Therefore, code J95.851 Ventilator associated pneumonia, is assigned only when the link is expressly stated and not merely when a patient on a mechanical ventilator has pneumonia. An additional code is assigned if an identified organism is attributed to the VAP, but not a code from J12–J18. In the example, since the yeast cultures are identified only as a lab value and are not documented by the provider as related to the VAP, a code for the yeast organism is not assigned. The coder should ask the provider to state the clinical significance of the lab results; if the results are related to the VAP, B37.9 Candidiasis, unspecified, would be assigned.

47. *Answer:* **Z38.01 Single liveborn infant, delivered by cesarean, P70.1 Syndrome of infant of a diabetic mother**

Rationale: The code for a newborn delivered by cesarean on this admission is found by looking in the Alphabetic Index under "Newborn, born in hospital, by cesarean," code Z38.01. Macrosomia is not listed in the ICD-10-CM Alphabetic Index but is synonymous with "large for gestational age," or LGA, which the index entry for "Large, baby" indicates is coded with P08.1. This is not assigned, however, because subcategory E08.1 has an "excludes1" note indicating that LGA in "syndrome of diabetic mother" is to be included in P70.1.

48. *Answer:* **A** Assign E11.9 Type 2 diabetes mellitus without complications, Z86.32 Personal history of gestational diabetes, and O94 Sequela of complication of pregnancy, childbirth, and the puerperium.

Rationale: When diagnosed with gestational diabetes mellitus, patients have a high risk of developing diabetes 2 post delivery, which is why clinical guidelines recommend the patients return for postpartum glucose testing. When the postpartum impaired glucose regulation indicates diabetes, the case is coded as diabetes and no longer abnormal glucose finding. OCG section I.C.15.o.3 states that if the provider documents a condition as related to pregnancy, codes from chapter 15 may be assigned. OCG section I.C.15.p states that when an initial complication of a pregnancy develops a sequela requiring care or treatment, code O94 is assigned and sequenced after the code identifying the sequela condition. The documented personal history of gestational diabetes is also coded.

49. *Answer:* **R07.1 Chest pain on breathing, F43.0 Acute stress reaction, X37.1XXA Tornado, and Y92.017 Garden or yard in a single-family (private) house as the place of occurrence of the external cause**

Rationale: The ICD-10-CM Alphabetic Index no longer provides a separate code for other acute pain for use with a specified site of pain. Instead, only the pain of the site is coded when stated as acute of a specified site. The index entry for "Pain, acute" shows R52 Pain, unspecified, which has an "excludes1" note instructing the user to code to pain by site for localized pain of unspecified type. The chest pain is described as "on inspiration"; the Alphabetic Index lists "Pain, chest, on breathing or pleurodynia," R07.1. Always review the entire record for a description of the chest pain and assign a code of the highest level of specificity based on physician documentation; query when appropriate. Since the chest pain is not linked to the stress the patient is experiencing, code F43.9 Acute stress reaction is assigned. To describe the situation related to the diagnoses, assign X37.1XXA Tornado, and Y92.017 Garden or yard in a single-family (private) house, as the place of occurrence of the external cause, for this initial encounter, according to OCG section I.C.20.b.

50. *Answer:* **A** Assign Z86.74 Personal history of sudden cardiac arrest, and I25.2 Old myocardial infarction.

Rationale: The past medical history documents a past cardiac arrest and myocardial infarction. Since the patient presents for CABG due to progressive angina for which the history of cardiac arrest and myocardial infarction would be relevant, assign the personal history code for both. The Alphabetic Index lists "History, personal, cardiac arrest (death) successfully resuscitated," code Z86.74. The index entry for history of myocardial infarction is "History, personal, myocardial infarction (old)," code I25.2. History codes are appropriate for an encounter when facility policy requires them or when the history is significant to the encounter based on medical significance or in relationship to other diagnoses or conditions. OCG section III.A states that previous conditions may be coded as additional diagnoses when they affect current care or treatment.

Official ICD-9-CM Guidelines for Coding and Reporting

Effective October 1, 2011
Note: Since no official ICD-9-CM addendum to the guidelines has been released since 2011, the guidelines included in this book stand as the official guidelines effective October 1, 2014, through September 30, 2015.

The Centers for Medicare and Medicaid Services (CMS) and the National Center for Health Statistics (NCHS), two departments within the U.S. Federal Government's Department of Health and Human Services (DHHS) provide the following guidelines for coding and reporting using the International Classification of Diseases, 9th Revision, Clinical Modification (ICD-9-CM). These guidelines should be used as a companion document to the official version of the ICD-9-CM as published on CD-ROM by the U.S. Government Printing Office (GPO).

These guidelines have been approved by the four organizations that make up the Cooperating Parties for the ICD-9-CM: the American Hospital Association (AHA), the American Health Information Management Association (AHIMA), CMS, and NCHS. These guidelines are included on the official government version of the ICD-9-CM, and also appear in *"Coding Clinic for ICD-9-CM"* published by the AHA.

These guidelines are a set of rules that have been developed to accompany and complement the official conventions and instructions provided within the ICD-9-CM itself. The instructions and conventions of the classification take precedence over guidelines. These guidelines are based on the coding and sequencing instructions in Volumes I, II and III of ICD-9-CM, but provide additional instruction. Adherence to these guidelines when assigning ICD-9-CM diagnosis and procedure codes is required under the Health Insurance Portability and Accountability Act (HIPAA). The diagnosis codes (Volumes 1-2) have been adopted under HIPAA for all healthcare settings. Volume 3 procedure codes have been adopted for inpatient procedures reported by hospitals. A joint effort between the healthcare provider and the coder is essential to achieve complete and accurate documentation, code assignment, and reporting of diagnoses and procedures. These guidelines have been developed to assist both the healthcare provider and the coder in identifying those diagnoses and procedures that are to be reported. The importance of consistent, complete documentation in the medical record cannot be overemphasized. Without such documentation accurate coding cannot be achieved. The entire record should be reviewed to determine the specific reason for the encounter and the conditions treated.

The term encounter is used for all settings, including hospital admissions. In the context of these guidelines, the term provider is used throughout the guidelines to mean physician or any qualified health care practitioner who is legally accountable for establishing the patient's diagnosis. Only this set of guidelines, approved by the Cooperating Parties, is official.

The guidelines are organized into sections. Section I includes the structure and conventions of the classification and general guidelines that apply to the entire classification, and chapter-specific guidelines that correspond to the chapters as they are arranged in the classification. Section II includes guidelines for selection of principal diagnosis for non-outpatient settings. Section III includes guidelines for reporting additional diagnoses in non-outpatient settings. Section IV is for outpatient coding and reporting.

Section I. Conventions, general coding guidelines and chapter specific guidelines

A. Conventions for the ICD-9-CM
1. Format:
2. Abbreviations
    a. Index abbreviations
    b. Tabular abbreviations
3. Punctuation
4. Includes and Excludes Notes and Inclusion terms
5. Other and Unspecified codes
    a. "Other" codes
    b. "Unspecified" codes
6. Etiology/manifestation convention ("code first", "use additional code" and "in diseases classified elsewhere" notes)
7. "And"
8. "With"
9. "See" and "See Also"

B. General Coding Guidelines
1. Use of Both Alphabetic Index and Tabular List
2. Locate each term in the Alphabetic Index
3. Level of Detail in Coding
4. Code or codes from 001.0 through V91.99
5. Selection of codes 001.0 through 999.9
6. Signs and symptoms
7. Conditions that are an integral part of a disease process
8. Conditions that are not an integral part of a disease process
9. Multiple coding for a single condition
10. Acute and Chronic Conditions
11. Combination Code
12. Late Effects
13. Impending or Threatened Condition
14. Reporting Same Diagnosis Code More than Once
15. Admissions/Encounters for Rehabilitation
16. Documentation for BMI and Pressure Ulcer Stages
17. Syndromes
18. Documentation of Complications of Care

C. Chapter-Specific Coding Guidelines
1. Chapter 1: Infectious and Parasitic Diseases (001-139)
    a. Human Immunodeficiency Virus (HIV) Infections
    b. Septicemia, Systemic Inflammatory Response Syndrome (SIRS), Sepsis, Severe Sepsis and Septic Shock
    c. Methicillin Resistant *Staphylococcus aureus* (MRSA) Conditions
2. Chapter 2: Neoplasms (140-239)
    a. Treatment directed at the malignancy
    b. Treatment of secondary site
    c. Coding and sequencing of complications
    d. Primary malignancy previously excised
    e. Admissions/Encounters involving chemotherapy, immunotherapy and radiation therapy
    f. Admission/encounter to determine extent of malignancy
    g. Symptoms, signs, and ill-defined conditions listed in Chapter 16 associated with neoplasms
    h. Admission/encounter for pain control/management
    i. Malignant neoplasm associated with transplanted organ
3. Chapter 3: Endocrine, Nutritional, and Metabolic Diseases and Immunity Disorders (240-279)
    a. Diabetes mellitus
4. Chapter 4: Diseases of Blood and Blood Forming Organs (280-289)
    a. Anemia of chronic disease
5. Chapter 5: Mental Disorders (290-319)
    Reserved for future guideline expansion
6. Chapter 6: Diseases of Nervous System and Sense Organs (320-389)
    a. Pain - Category 338
    b. Glaucoma
7. Chapter 7: Diseases of Circulatory System (390-459)
    a. Hypertension
    b. Cerebral infarction/stroke/ from cerebrovascular accident (CVA)
    c. Postoperative cerebrovascular accident
    d. Late Effects of Cerebrovascular Disease
    e. Acute myocardial infarction (AMI)

Section II. Selection of Principal Diagnosis

Section III. Reporting Additional Diagnoses

Section IV. Diagnostic Coding and Reporting Guidelines for Outpatient Services

Appendix I: Present on Admission Reporting Guidelines

Section I. Conventions, general coding guidelines and chapter specific guidelines

The conventions, general guidelines and chapter-specific guidelines are applicable to all health care settings unless otherwise indicated. The conventions and instructions of the classification take precedence over guidelines.

A. Conventions for the ICD-9-CM

The conventions for the ICD-9-CM are the general rules for use of the classification independent of the guidelines. These conventions are incorporated within the index and tabular of the ICD-9-CM as instructional notes. The conventions are as follows:

1. **Format:**

   The ICD-9-CM uses an indented format for ease in reference

2. **Abbreviations**

   a. **Index abbreviations**

      NEC "Not elsewhere classifiable"

      This abbreviation in the index represents "other specified" when a specific code is not available for a condition the index directs the coder to the "other specified" code in the tabular.

   b. **Tabular abbreviations**

      NEC "Not elsewhere classifiable"

      This abbreviation in the tabular represents "other specified". When a specific code is not available for a condition the tabular includes an NEC entry under a code to identify the code as the "other specified" code.
      (See Section I.A.5.a. "Other" codes).

      NOS "Not otherwise specified"

      This abbreviation is the equivalent of unspecified.
      (See Section I.A.5.b., "Unspecified" codes)

3. **Punctuation**

   [ ] Brackets are used in the tabular list to enclose synonyms, alternative wording or explanatory phrases. Brackets are used in the index to identify manifestation codes.
   (See Section I.A.6. "Etiology/manifestations")

   ( ) Parentheses are used in both the index and tabular to enclose supplementary words that may be present or absent in the statement of a disease or procedure without affecting the code number to which it is assigned. The terms within the parentheses are referred to as nonessential modifiers.

   : Colons are used in the Tabular list after an incomplete term which needs one or more of the modifiers following the colon to make it assignable to a given category.

4. **Includes and Excludes Notes and Inclusion terms**

   Includes: This note appears immediately under a three-digit code title to further define, or give examples of, the content of the category.

   Excludes: An excludes note under a code indicates that the terms excluded from the code are to be coded elsewhere. In some cases the codes for the excluded terms should not be used in conjunction with the code from which it is excluded. An example of this is a congenital condition excluded from an acquired form of the same condition. The congenital and acquired codes should not be used together. In other cases, the excluded terms may be used together with an excluded code. An example of this is when fractures of different bones are coded to different codes. Both codes may be used together if both types of fractures are present.

   Inclusion terms: List of terms is included under certain four and five digit codes. These terms are the conditions for which that code number is to be used. The terms may be synonyms of the code title, or, in the case of "other specified" codes, the terms are a list of the various conditions assigned to that code. The inclusion terms are not necessarily exhaustive. Additional terms found only in the index may also be assigned to a code.

5. **Other and Unspecified codes**

   a. **"Other" codes**

      Codes titled "other" or "other specified" (usually a code with a 4th digit 8 or fifth-digit 9 for diagnosis codes) are for use when the information in the medical record provides detail for which a specific code does not exist. Index entries with NEC in the line designate "other" codes in the tabular. These index entries represent specific disease entities for which no specific code exists so the term is included within an "other" code.

   b. **"Unspecified" codes**

      Codes (usually a code with a 4th digit 9 or 5th digit 0 for diagnosis codes) titled "unspecified" are for use when the information in the medical record is insufficient to assign a more specific code.

6. **Etiology/manifestation convention ("code first", "use additional code" and "in diseases classified elsewhere" notes)**

   Certain conditions have both an underlying etiology and multiple body system manifestations due to the underlying etiology. For such conditions, the ICD-9-CM has a coding convention that requires the underlying condition be sequenced first followed by the manifestation. Wherever such a combination exists, there is a "use additional code" note at the etiology code, and a "code first" note at the manifestation code. These instructional notes indicate the proper sequencing order of the codes, etiology followed by manifestation.

   In most cases the manifestation codes will have in the code title, "in diseases classified elsewhere." Codes with this title are a component of the etiology/ manifestation convention. The code title indicates that it is a manifestation code. "In diseases classified elsewhere" codes are never permitted to be used as first listed or principal diagnosis codes. They must be used in conjunction with an underlying condition code and they must be listed following the underlying condition.

   There are manifestation codes that do not have "in diseases classified elsewhere" in the title. For such codes a "use additional code" note will still be present and the rules for sequencing apply.

   In addition to the notes in the tabular, these conditions also have a specific index entry structure. In the index both conditions are listed together with the etiology code first followed by the manifestation codes in brackets. The code in brackets is always to be sequenced second.

   The most commonly used etiology/manifestation combinations are the codes for Diabetes mellitus, category 250. For each code under category 250 there is a use additional code note for the manifestation that is specific for that particular diabetic manifestation. Should a patient have more than one manifestation of diabetes, more than one code from category 250 may be used with as many manifestation codes as are needed to fully describe the patient's complete diabetic condition. The category 250 diabetes codes should be sequenced first, followed by the manifestation codes.

   "Code first" and "Use additional code" notes are also used as sequencing rules in the classification for certain codes that are not part of an etiology/ manifestation combination.
   See - Section I.B.9. "Multiple coding for a single condition".

7. **"And"**

   The word "and" should be interpreted to mean either "and" or "or" when it appears in a title.

8. **"With"**

   The word "with" should be interpreted to mean "associated with" or "due to" when it appears in a code title, the Alphabetic Index, or an instructional note in the Tabular List.

   The word "with" in the alphabetic index is sequenced immediately following the main term, not in alphabetical order.

9. **"See" and "See Also"**

   The "see" instruction following a main term in the index indicates that another term should be referenced. It is necessary to go to the main term referenced with the "see" note to locate the correct code.

   A "see also" instruction following a main term in the index instructs that there is another main term that may also be referenced that may provide additional index entries that may be useful. It is not necessary

to follow the "see also" note when the original main term provides the necessary code.

B. General Coding Guidelines

1. Use of Both Alphabetic Index and Tabular List

Use both the Alphabetic Index and the Tabular List when locating and assigning a code. Reliance on only the Alphabetic Index or the Tabular List leads to errors in code assignments and less specificity in code selection.

2. Locate each term in the Alphabetic Index

Locate each term in the Alphabetic Index and verify the code selected in the Tabular List. Read and be guided by instructional notations that appear in both the Alphabetic Index and the Tabular List.

3. Level of Detail in Coding

Diagnosis and procedure codes are to be used at their highest number of digits available.

ICD-9-CM diagnosis codes are composed of codes with 3, 4, or 5 digits. Codes with three digits are included in ICD-9-CM as the heading of a category of codes that may be further subdivided by the use of fourth and/or fifth digits, which provide greater detail.

A three-digit code is to be used only if it is not further subdivided. Where fourth-digit subcategories and/or fifth-digit subclassifications are provided, they must be assigned. A code is invalid if it has not been coded to the full number of digits required for that code. For example, Acute myocardial infarction, code 410, has fourth digits that describe the location of the infarction (e.g., 410.2, Of inferolateral wall), and fifth digits that identify the episode of care. It would be incorrect to report a code in category 410 without a fourth and fifth digit.

ICD-9-CM Volume 3 procedure codes are composed of codes with either 3 or 4 digits. Codes with two digits are included in ICD-9-CM as the heading of a category of codes that may be further subdivided by the use of third and/or fourth digits, which provide greater detail.

4. Code or codes from 001.0 through V91.99

The appropriate code or codes from 001.0 through V91.99 must be used to identify diagnoses, symptoms, conditions, problems, complaints or other reason(s) for the encounter/visit.

5. Selection of codes 001.0 through 999.9

The selection of codes 001.0 through 999.9 will frequently be used to describe the reason for the admission/encounter. These codes are from the section of ICD-9-CM for the classification of diseases and injuries (e.g., infectious and parasitic diseases; neoplasms; symptoms, signs, and ill-defined conditions, etc.).

6. Signs and symptoms

Codes that describe symptoms and signs, as opposed to diagnoses, are acceptable for reporting purposes when a related definitive diagnosis has not been established (confirmed) by the provider. Chapter 16 of ICD-9-CM, Symptoms, Signs, and Ill-defined conditions (codes 780.0 - 799.9) contain many, but not all codes for symptoms.

7. Conditions that are an integral part of a disease process

Signs and symptoms that are associated routinely with a disease process should not be assigned as additional codes, unless otherwise instructed by the classification.

8. Conditions that are not an integral part of a disease process

Additional signs and symptoms that may not be associated routinely with a disease process should be coded when present.

9. Multiple coding for a single condition

In addition to the etiology/manifestation convention that requires two codes to fully describe a single condition that affects multiple body systems, there are other single conditions that also require more than one code. "Use additional code" notes are found in the tabular at codes that are not part of an etiology/manifestation pair where a secondary code is useful to fully describe a condition. The sequencing rule is the same as the etiology/manifestation pair - "use additional code" indicates that a secondary code should be added.

For example, for infections that are not included in chapter 1, a secondary code from category 041, Bacterial infection in conditions classified elsewhere and of unspecified site, may be required to

identify the bacterial organism causing the infection. A "use additional code" note will normally be found at the infectious disease code, indicating a need for the organism code to be added as a secondary code.

"Code first" notes are also under certain codes that are not specifically manifestation codes but may be due to an underlying cause. When a "code first" note is present and an underlying condition is present the underlying condition should be sequenced first.

"Code, if applicable, any causal condition first", notes indicate that this code may be assigned as a principal diagnosis when the causal condition is unknown or not applicable. If a causal condition is known, then the code for that condition should be sequenced as the principal or first-listed diagnosis.

Multiple codes may be needed for late effects, complication codes and obstetric codes to more fully describe a condition. See the specific guidelines for these conditions for further instruction.

10. Acute and Chronic Conditions

If the same condition is described as both acute (subacute) and chronic, and separate subentries exist in the Alphabetic Index at the same indentation level, code both and sequence the acute (subacute) code first.

11. Combination Code

A combination code is a single code used to classify:

- Two diagnoses, or
- A diagnosis with an associated secondary process (manifestation)
- A diagnosis with an associated complication

Combination codes are identified by referring to subterm entries in the Alphabetic Index and by reading the inclusion and exclusion notes in the Tabular List.

Assign only the combination code when that code fully identifies the diagnostic conditions involved or when the Alphabetic Index so directs. Multiple coding should not be used when the classification provides a combination code that clearly identifies all of the elements documented in the diagnosis. When the combination code lacks necessary specificity in describing the manifestation or complication, an additional code should be used as a secondary code.

12. Late Effects

A late effect is the residual effect (condition produced) after the acute phase of an illness or injury has terminated. There is no time limit on when a late effect code can be used. The residual may be apparent early, such as in cerebrovascular accident cases, or it may occur months or years later, such as that due to a previous injury. Coding of late effects generally requires two codes sequenced in the following order: The condition or nature of the late effect is sequenced first. The late effect code is sequenced second.

Exceptions to the above guidelines are those instances the late effect code has been expanded (at the fourth and fifth-digit levels) to include the manifestation(s) or the classification instructs otherwise. The code for the acute phase of an illness or injury that led to the late effect is never used with a code for the late effect.

13. Impending or Threatened Condition

Code any condition described at the time of discharge as "impending" or "threatened" as follows:

If it did occur, code as confirmed diagnosis.
If it did not occur, reference the Alphabetic Index to determine if the condition has a subentry term for "impending" or "threatened" and also reference main term entries for "Impending" and for "Threatened."
If the subterms are listed, assign the given code.
If the subterms are not listed, code the existing underlying condition(s) and not the condition described as impending or threatened.

14. Reporting Same Diagnosis Code More than Once

Each unique ICD-9-CM diagnosis code may be reported only once for an encounter. This applies to bilateral conditions or two different conditions classified to the same ICD-9-CM diagnosis code.

15. Admissions/Encounters for Rehabilitation

When the purpose for the admission/encounter is rehabilitation, sequence the appropriate V code from category V57, Care involving use of rehabilitation procedures, as the principal/first-listed diagnosis. The code for the condition for which the service is being performed should be reported as an additional diagnosis.

Only one code from category V57 is required. Code V57.89, Other specified rehabilitation procedures, should be assigned if more than one type of rehabilitation is performed during a single encounter. A procedure code should be reported to identify each type of rehabilitation therapy actually performed.

16. Documentation for BMI and Pressure Ulcer Stages

For the Body Mass Index (BMI) and pressure ulcer stage codes, code assignment may be based on medical record documentation from clinicians who are not the patient's provider (i.e., physician or other qualified healthcare practitioner legally accountable for establishing the patient's diagnosis), since this information is typically documented by other clinicians involved in the care of the patient (e.g., a dietitian often documents the BMI and nurses often documents the pressure ulcer stages). However, the associated diagnosis (such as overweight, obesity, or pressure ulcer) must be documented by the patient's provider. If there is conflicting medical record documentation, either from the same clinician or different clinicians, the patient's attending provider should be queried for clarification.

The BMI and pressure ulcer stage codes should only be reported as secondary diagnoses. As with all other secondary diagnosis codes, the BMI and pressure ulcer stage codes should only be assigned when they meet the definition of a reportable additional diagnosis (see Section III, Reporting Additional Diagnoses).

17. Syndromes

Follow the Alphabetic Index guidance when coding syndromes. In the absence of index guidance, assign codes for the documented manifestations of the syndrome.

18. Documentation of complications of care

Code assignment is based on the provider's documentation of the relationship between the condition and the care or procedure. The guideline extends to any complications of care, regardless of the chapter the code is located in. It is important to note that not all conditions that occur during or following medical care or surgery are classified as complications. There must be a cause-and-effect relationship between the care provided and the condition, and an indication in the documentation that it is a complication. Query the provider for clarification, if the complication is not clearly documented.

C. Chapter-Specific Coding Guidelines

In addition to general coding guidelines, there are guidelines for specific diagnoses and/or conditions in the classification. Unless otherwise indicated, these guidelines apply to all health care settings. Please refer to Section II for guidelines on the selection of principal diagnosis.

1. Chapter 1: Infectious and Parasitic Diseases (001-139)

a. Human Immunodeficiency Virus (HIV) Infections

1) Code only confirmed cases

Code only confirmed cases of HIV infection/illness. This is an exception to the hospital inpatient guideline Section II, H.

In this context, "confirmation" does not require documentation of positive serology or culture for HIV; the provider's diagnostic statement that the patient is HIV positive, or has an HIV-related illness is sufficient.

2) Selection and sequencing of HIV codes

(a) Patient admitted for HIV-related condition

If a patient is admitted for an HIV-related condition, the principal diagnosis should be 042, followed by additional diagnosis codes for all reported HIV-related conditions.

(b) Patient with HIV disease admitted for unrelated condition

If a patient with HIV disease is admitted for an unrelated condition (such as a traumatic injury), the code for the unrelated condition (e.g., the nature of injury code) should be the principal diagnosis. Other diagnoses would be 042 followed by additional diagnosis codes for all reported HIV-related conditions.

(c) Whether the patient is newly diagnosed

Whether the patient is newly diagnosed or has had previous admissions/encounters for HIV conditions is irrelevant to the sequencing decision.

(d) Asymptomatic human immunodeficiency virus

V08 Asymptomatic human immunodeficiency virus [HIV] infection, is to be applied when the patient without any documentation of symptoms is listed as being "HIV positive," "known HIV," "HIV test positive," or similar terminology. Do not use this code if the term "AIDS" is used or if the patient is treated for any HIV-related illness or is described as having any condition(s) resulting from his/her HIV positive status; use 042 in these cases.

(e) Patients with inconclusive HIV serology

Patients with inconclusive HIV serology, but no definitive diagnosis or manifestations of the illness, may be assigned code 795.71, Inconclusive serologic test for Human Immunodeficiency Virus [HIV].

(f) Previously diagnosed HIV-related illness

Patients with any known prior diagnosis of an HIV-related illness should be coded to 042. Once a patient has developed an HIV-related illness, the patient should always be assigned code 042 on every subsequent admission/encounter. Patients previously diagnosed with any HIV illness (042) should never be assigned to 795.71 or V08.

(g) HIV Infection in Pregnancy, Childbirth and the Puerperium

During pregnancy, childbirth or the puerperium, a patient admitted (or presenting for a health care encounter) because of an HIV-related illness should receive a principal diagnosis code of 647.6x, Other specified infectious and parasitic diseases in the mother classifiable elsewhere, but complicating the pregnancy, childbirth or the puerperium, followed by 042 and the code(s) for the HIV-related illness(es). Codes from Chapter 15 always take sequencing priority.

Patients with asymptomatic HIV infection status admitted (or presenting for a health care encounter) during pregnancy, childbirth, or the puerperium should receive codes of 647.6x and V08.

(h) Encounters for testing for HIV

If a patient is being seen to determine his/her HIV status, use code V73.89, Screening for other specified viral disease. Use code V69.8, Other problems related to lifestyle, as a secondary code if an asymptomatic patient is in a known high risk group for HIV. Should a patient with signs or symptoms or illness, or a confirmed HIV related diagnosis be tested for HIV, code the signs and symptoms or the diagnosis. An additional counseling code V65.44 may be used if counseling is provided during the encounter for the test.

When a patient returns to be informed of his/her HIV test results use code V65.44, HIV counseling, if the results of the test are negative.

If the results are positive but the patient is asymptomatic use code V08, Asymptomatic HIV infection. If the results are positive and the patient is symptomatic use code 042, HIV infection, with codes for the HIV related symptoms or diagnosis. The HIV

counseling code may also be used if counseling is provided for patients with positive test results.

b. Septicemia, Systemic Inflammatory Response Syndrome (SIRS), Sepsis, Severe Sepsis, and Septic Shock

1) SIRS, Septicemia, and Sepsis

(a) The terms *septicemia* and *sepsis* are often used interchangeably by providers, however they are not considered synonymous terms. The following descriptions are provided for reference but do not preclude querying the provider for clarification about terms used in the documentation:

(i) Septicemia generally refers to a systemic disease associated with the presence of pathological microorganisms or toxins in the blood, which can include bacteria, viruses, fungi or other organisms.

(ii) Systemic inflammatory response syndrome (SIRS) generally refers to the systemic response to infection, trauma/burns, or other insult (such as cancer) with symptoms including fever, tachycardia, tachypnea, and leukocytosis.

(iii) Sepsis generally refers to SIRS due to infection.

(iv) Severe sepsis generally refers to sepsis with associated acute organ dysfunction.

(b) The Coding of SIRS, sepsis and severe sepsis

The coding of SIRS, sepsis and severe sepsis requires a minimum of 2 codes: a code for the underlying cause (such as infection or trauma) and a code from subcategory 995.9 Systemic inflammatory response syndrome (SIRS).

(i) The code for the underlying cause (such as infection or trauma) must be sequenced before the code from subcategory 995.9 Systemic inflammatory response syndrome (SIRS).

(ii) Sepsis and severe sepsis require a code for the systemic infection (038.xx, 112.5, etc.) and either code 995.91, Sepsis, or 995.92, Severe sepsis. If the causal organism is not documented, assign code 038.9, Unspecified septicemia.

(iii) Severe sepsis requires additional code(s) for the associated acute organ dysfunction(s).

(iv) If a patient has sepsis with multiple organ dysfunctions, follow the instructions for coding severe sepsis.

(v) Either the term sepsis or SIRS must be documented to assign a code from subcategory 995.9.

(vi) *See Section I.C.17.g), Injury and poisoning, for information regarding systemic inflammatory response syndrome (SIRS) due to trauma/burns and other non-infectious processes.*

(c) Due to the complex nature of sepsis and severe sepsis, some cases may require querying the provider prior to assignment of the codes.

2) Sequencing sepsis and severe sepsis

(a) Sepsis and severe sepsis as principal diagnosis

If sepsis or severe sepsis is present on admission, and meets the definition of principal diagnosis, the systemic infection code (e.g., 038.xx, 112.5, etc) should be assigned as the principal diagnosis, followed by code 995.91, Sepsis, or 995.92, Severe sepsis, as required by the sequencing rules in the Tabular List. Codes from subcategory 995.9 can never be assigned as a principal diagnosis. A code should also be assigned for any localized infection, if present.

If the sepsis or severe sepsis is due to a postprocedural infection, see Section I.C.1.b.10 for guidelines related to sepsis due to postprocedural infection.

(b) Sepsis and severe sepsis as secondary diagnoses

When sepsis or severe sepsis develops during the encounter (it was not present on admission), the systemic infection code and code 995.91 or 995.92 should be assigned as secondary diagnoses.

(c) Documentation unclear as to whether sepsis or severe sepsis is present on admission

Sepsis or severe sepsis may be present on admission but the diagnosis may not be confirmed until sometime after admission. If the documentation is not clear whether the sepsis or severe sepsis was present on admission, the provider should be queried.

3) Sepsis/SIRS with Localized Infection

If the reason for admission is both sepsis, severe sepsis, or SIRS and a localized infection, such as pneumonia or cellulitis, a code for the systemic infection (038.xx, 112.5, etc) should be assigned first, then code 995.91 or 995.92, followed by the code for the localized infection. If the patient is admitted with a localized infection, such as pneumonia, and sepsis/SIRS doesn't develop until after admission, see guideline I.C.1.b.2.b).

If the localized infection is postprocedural, *see Section I.C.1.b.10 for guidelines related to sepsis due to postprocedural infection.*

Note: The term urosepsis is a nonspecific term. If that is the only term documented then only code 599.0 should be assigned based on the default for the term in the ICD-9-CM index, in addition to the code for the causal organism if known.

4) Bacterial Sepsis and Septicemia

In most cases, it will be a code from category 038, Septicemia, that will be used in conjunction with a code from subcategory 995.9 such as the following:

(a) Streptococcal sepsis

If the documentation in the record states streptococcal sepsis, codes 038.0, Streptococcal septicemia, and code 995.91 should be used, in that sequence.

(b) Streptococcal septicemia

If the documentation states streptococcal septicemia, only code 038.0 should be assigned, however, the provider should be queried whether the patient has sepsis, an infection with SIRS.

5) Acute organ dysfunction that is not clearly associated with the sepsis

If a patient has sepsis and an acute organ dysfunction, but the medical record documentation indicates that the acute organ dysfunction is related to a medical condition other than the sepsis, do not assign code 995.92, Severe sepsis. An acute organ dysfunction must be associated with the sepsis in order to assign the severe sepsis code. If the documentation is not clear as to whether an acute organ dysfunction is related to the sepsis or another medical condition, query the provider.

6) Septic shock

(a) Sequencing of septic shock

Septic shock generally refers to circulatory failure associated with severe sepsis, and, therefore, it represents a type of acute organ dysfunction.

For cases of septic shock, the code for the systemic infection should be sequenced first, followed by codes 995.92, Severe sepsis and 785.52, Septic shock or 998.02, Postoperative septic shock. Any additional codes for other acute organ dysfunctions should also be assigned. As noted in the sequencing instructions in the Tabular List, the code for septic shock cannot be assigned as a principal diagnosis.

(b) Septic Shock without documentation of severe sepsis

Since septic shock indicates the presence of severe sepsis, code 995.92, Severe sepsis, can be assigned with code 785.52, Septic shock, or code 998.02 Postoperative shock, septic, even if the term severe sepsis is not documented in the record.

7) Sepsis and septic shock complicating abortion and pregnancy

Sepsis and septic shock complicating abortion, ectopic pregnancy, and molar pregnancy are classified to category codes in Chapter 11 (630-639).

See section I.C.11.i.7. for information on the coding of puerperal sepsis.

8) Negative or inconclusive blood cultures

Negative or inconclusive blood cultures do not preclude a diagnosis of septicemia or sepsis in patients with clinical evidence of the condition, however, the provider should be queried.

9) Newborn sepsis

See Section I.C.15.j for information on the coding of newborn sepsis.

10) Sepsis due to a Postprocedural Infection

(a) Documentation of causal relationship

As with all postprocedural complications, code assignment is based on the provider's documentation of the relationship between the infection and the procedure.

(b) Sepsis due to postprocedural infection

In cases of postprocedural sepsis, the complication code, such as code 998.59, Other postoperative infection, or 674.3x, Other complications of obstetrical surgical wounds should be coded first followed by the appropriate sepsis codes (systemic infection code and either code 995.91or 995.92). An additional code(s) for any acute organ dysfunction should also be assigned for cases of severe sepsis.

See Section see Section I.C.1.b.6 if the sepsis or severe sepsis results in postprocedural septic shock.

(c) Postprocedural infection and postprocedural septic shock

In cases where a postprocedural infection has occurred and has resulted in severe sepsis and postprocedural septic shock, the code for the precipitating complication such as code 998.59, Other postoperative infection, or 674.3x, Other complications of obstetrical surgical wounds should be coded first followed by the appropriate sepsis codes (systemic infection code and code 995.92). Code 998.02, Postoperative septic shock, should be assigned as an additional code. In cases of severe sepsis, an additional code(s) for any acute organ dysfunction should also be assigned.

11) External cause of injury codes with SIRS

Refer to Section I.C.19.a.7 for instruction on the use of external cause of injury codes with codes for SIRS resulting from trauma.

12) Sepsis and Severe Sepsis Associated with Non-infectious Process

In some cases, a non-infectious process, such as trauma, may lead to an infection which can result in sepsis or severe sepsis. If sepsis or severe sepsis is documented as associated with a non-infectious condition, such as a burn or serious injury, and this condition meets the definition for principal diagnosis, the code for the non-infectious condition should be sequenced first, followed by the code for the systemic infection and either code 995.91, Sepsis, or 995.92, Severe sepsis. Additional codes for any associated acute organ dysfunction(s) should also be assigned for cases of severe sepsis. If the sepsis or severe sepsis meets the definition of

principal diagnosis, the systemic infection and sepsis codes should be sequenced before the non-infectious condition. When both the associated non-infectious condition and the sepsis or severe sepsis meet the definition of principal diagnosis, either may be assigned as principal diagnosis.

See Section I.C.1.b.2.a. for guidelines pertaining to sepsis or severe sepsis as the principal diagnosis.

Only one code from subcategory 995.9 should be assigned. Therefore, when a non-infectious condition leads to an infection resulting in sepsis or severe sepsis, assign either code 995.91 or 995.92. Do not additionally assign code 995.93, Systemic inflammatory response syndrome due to non-infectious process without acute organ dysfunction, or 995.94, Systemic inflammatory response syndrome with acute organ dysfunction.

See Section I.C.17.g for information on the coding of SIRS due to trauma/burns or other non-infectious disease processes.

c. Methicillin Resistant Staphylococcus aureus (MRSA) Conditions

1) Selection and sequencing of MRSA codes

(a) Combination codes for MRSA infection

When a patient is diagnosed with an infection that is due to methicillin resistant *Staphylococcus aureus* (MRSA), and that infection has a combination code that includes the causal organism (e.g., septicemia, pneumonia) assign the appropriate code for the condition (e.g., code 038.12, Methicillin resistant Staphylococcus aureus septicemia or code 482.42, Methicillin resistant pneumonia due to Staphylococcus aureus). Do not assign code 041.12, Methicillin resistant Staphylococcus aureus, as an additional code because the code includes the type of infection and the MRSA organism. Do not assign a code from subcategory V09.0, Infection with microorganisms resistant to penicillins, as an additional diagnosis.

See Section C.1.b.1 for instructions on coding and sequencing of septicemia.

(b) Other codes for MRSA infection

When there is documentation of a current infection (e.g., wound infection, stitch abscess, urinary tract infection) due to MRSA, and that infection does not have a combination code that includes the causal organism, select the appropriate code to identify the condition along with code 041.12, Methicillin resistant Staphylococcus aureus, for the MRSA infection. Do not assign a code from subcategory V09.0, Infection with microorganisms resistant to penicillins.

(c) Methicillin susceptible Staphylococcus aureus (MSSA) and MRSA colonization

The condition or state of being colonized or carrying MSSA or MRSA is called colonization or carriage, while an individual person is described as being colonized or being a carrier. Colonization means that MSSA or MSRA is present on or in the body without necessarily causing illness. A positive MRSA colonization test might be documented by the provider as "MRSA screen positive" or "MRSA nasal swab positive".

Assign code V02.54, Carrier or suspected carrier, Methicillin resistant Staphylococcus aureus, for patients documented as having MRSA colonization. Assign code V02.53, Carrier or suspected carrier, Methicillin susceptible Staphylococcus aureus, for patient documented as having MSSA colonization. Colonization is not necessarily indicative of a disease process or as the cause of a specific condition the patient may have unless documented as such by the provider.

Code V02.59, Other specified bacterial diseases, should be assigned for other types of staphylococcal colonization (e.g., S. *epidermidis*, S. *saprophyticus*). Code

V02.59 should not be assigned for colonization with any type of *Staphylococcus aureus* (MRSA, MSSA).

(d) MRSA colonization and infection

If a patient is documented as having both MRSA colonization and infection during a hospital admission, code V02.54, Carrier or suspected carrier, Methicillin resistant *Staphylococcus aureus*, and a code for the MRSA infection may both be assigned.

2. Chapter 2: Neoplasms (140-239)

General guidelines

Chapter 2 of the ICD-9-CM contains the codes for most benign and all malignant neoplasms. Certain benign neoplasms, such as prostatic adenomas, may be found in the specific body system chapters. To properly code a neoplasm it is necessary to determine from the record if the neoplasm is benign, in-situ, malignant, or of uncertain histologic behavior. If malignant, any secondary (metastatic) sites should also be determined.

The neoplasm table in the Alphabetic Index should be referenced first. However, if the histological term is documented, that term should be referenced first, rather than going immediately to the Neoplasm Table, in order to determine which column in the Neoplasm Table is appropriate. For example, if the documentation indicates "adenoma," refer to the term in the Alphabetic Index to review the entries under this term and the instructional note to "see also neoplasm, by site, benign." The table provides the proper code based on the type of neoplasm and the site. It is important to select the proper column in the table that corresponds to the type of neoplasm. The tabular should then be referenced to verify that the correct code has been selected from the table and that a more specific site code does not exist.

See Section I. C. 18.d.4. for information regarding V codes for genetic susceptibility to cancer.

a. Treatment directed at the malignancy

If the treatment is directed at the malignancy, designate the malignancy as the principal diagnosis.

The only exception to this guideline is if a patient admission/encounter is solely for the administration of chemotherapy, immunotherapy or radiation therapy, assign the appropriate V58.x code as the first-listed or principal diagnosis, and the diagnosis or problem for which the service is being performed as a secondary diagnosis.

b. Treatment of secondary site

When a patient is admitted because of a primary neoplasm with metastasis and treatment is directed toward the secondary site only, the secondary neoplasm is designated as the principal diagnosis even though the primary malignancy is still present.

c. Coding and sequencing of complications

Coding and sequencing of complications associated with the malignancies or with the therapy thereof are subject to the following guidelines:

1) Anemia associated with malignancy

When admission/encounter is for management of an anemia associated with the malignancy, and the treatment is only for anemia, the appropriate anemia code (such as code 285.22, Anemia in neoplastic disease) is designated as the principal diagnosis and is followed by the appropriate code(s) for the malignancy.

Code 285.22 may also be used as a secondary code if the patient suffers from anemia and is being treated for the malignancy.

If anemia in neoplastic disease and anemia due to antineoplastic chemotherapy are both documented, assign codes for both conditions.

2) Anemia associated with chemotherapy, immunotherapy and radiation therapy

When the admission/encounter is for management of an anemia associated with chemotherapy, immunotherapy or radiotherapy and the only treatment is for the anemia, the

anemia is sequenced first. The appropriate neoplasm code should be assigned as an additional code.

3) Management of dehydration due to the malignancy

When the admission/encounter is for management of dehydration due to the malignancy or the therapy, or a combination of both, and only the dehydration is being treated (intravenous rehydration), the dehydration is sequenced first, followed by the code(s) for the malignancy.

4) Treatment of a complication resulting from a surgical procedure

When the admission/encounter is for treatment of a complication resulting from a surgical procedure, designate the complication as the principal or first-listed diagnosis if treatment is directed at resolving the complication.

d. Primary malignancy previously excised

When a primary malignancy has been previously excised or eradicated from its site and there is no further treatment directed to that site and there is no evidence of any existing primary malignancy, a code from category V10, Personal history of malignant neoplasm, should be used to indicate the former site of the malignancy. Any mention of extension, invasion, or metastasis to another site is coded as a secondary malignant neoplasm to that site. The secondary site may be the principal or first-listed with the V10 code used as a secondary code.

e. Admissions/Encounters involving chemotherapy, immunotherapy and radiation therapy

1) Episode of care involves surgical removal of neoplasm

When an episode of care involves the surgical removal of a neoplasm, primary or secondary site, followed by adjunct chemotherapy or radiation treatment during the same episode of care, the neoplasm code should be assigned as principal or first-listed diagnosis, using codes in the 140-198 series or where appropriate in the 200-203 series.

2) Patient admission/encounter solely for administration of chemotherapy, immunotherapy and radiation therapy

If a patient admission/encounter is solely for the administration of chemotherapy, immunotherapy or radiation therapy assign code V58.0, Encounter for radiation therapy, or V58.11, Encounter for antineoplastic chemotherapy, or V58.12, Encounter for antineoplastic immunotherapy as the first-listed or principal diagnosis. If a patient receives more than one of these therapies during the same admission more than one of these codes may be assigned, in any sequence.

The malignancy for which the therapy is being administered should be assigned as a secondary diagnosis.

3) Patient admitted for radiotherapy/chemotherapy and immunotherapy and develops complications

When a patient is admitted for the purpose of radiotherapy, immunotherapy or chemotherapy and develops complications such as uncontrolled nausea and vomiting or dehydration, the principal or first-listed diagnosis is V58.0, Encounter for radiotherapy, or V58.11, Encounter for antineoplastic chemotherapy, or V58.12, Encounter for antineoplastic immunotherapy followed by any codes for the complications.

f. Admission/encounter to determine extent of malignancy

When the reason for admission/encounter is to determine the extent of the malignancy, or for a procedure such as paracentesis or thoracentesis, the primary malignancy or appropriate metastatic site is designated as the principal or first-listed diagnosis, even though chemotherapy or radiotherapy is administered.

g. Symptoms, signs, and ill-defined conditions listed in Chapter 16 associated with neoplasms

Symptoms, signs, and ill-defined conditions listed in Chapter 16 characteristic of, or associated with, an existing primary or

secondary site malignancy cannot be used to replace the malignancy as principal or first-listed diagnosis, regardless of the number of admissions or encounters for treatment and care of the neoplasm.

h. Admission/encounter for pain control/management

See Section I.C.6.a.5 for information on coding admission/encounter for pain control/management.

i. Malignant neoplasm associated with transplanted organ

A malignant neoplasm of a transplanted organ should be coded as a transplant complication. Assign first the appropriate code from subcategory 996.8, Complications of transplanted organ, followed by code 199.2, Malignant neoplasm associated with transplanted organ. Use an additional code for the specific malignancy.

3. Chapter 3: Endocrine, Nutritional, and Metabolic Diseases and Immunity Disorders (240-279)

a. Diabetes mellitus

Codes under category 250, Diabetes mellitus, identify complications/manifestations associated with diabetes mellitus. A fifth-digit is required for all category 250 codes to identify the type of diabetes mellitus and whether the diabetes is controlled or uncontrolled.

See I.C.3.a.7 for secondary diabetes

1) Fifth-digits for category 250:

The following are the fifth-digits for the codes under category 250:

0   type II or unspecified type, not stated as uncontrolled

1   type I, [juvenile type], not stated as uncontrolled

2   type II or unspecified type, uncontrolled

3   type I, [juvenile type], uncontrolled

The age of a patient is not the sole determining factor, though most type I diabetics develop the condition before reaching puberty. For this reason type I diabetes mellitus is also referred to as juvenile diabetes.

2) Type of diabetes mellitus not documented

If the type of diabetes mellitus is not documented in the medical record the default is type II.

3) Diabetes mellitus and the use of insulin

All type I diabetics must use insulin to replace what their bodies do not produce. However, the use of insulin does not mean that a patient is a type I diabetic. Some patients with type II diabetes mellitus are unable to control their blood sugar through diet and oral medication alone and do require insulin. If the documentation in a medical record does not indicate the type of diabetes but does indicate that the patient uses insulin, the appropriate fifth-digit for type II must be used. For type II patients who routinely use insulin, code V58.67, Long-term (current) use of insulin, should also be assigned to indicate that the patient uses insulin. Code V58.67 should not be assigned if insulin is given temporarily to bring a type II patient's blood sugar under control during an encounter.

4) Assigning and sequencing diabetes codes and associated conditions

When assigning codes for diabetes and its associated conditions, the code(s) from category 250 must be sequenced before the codes for the associated conditions. The diabetes codes and the secondary codes that correspond to them are paired codes that follow the etiology/manifestation convention of the classification *(See Section I.A.6., Etiology/manifestation convention)*. Assign as many codes from category 250 as needed to identify all of the associated conditions that the patient has. The corresponding secondary codes are listed under each of the diabetes codes.

(a) Diabetic retinopathy/diabetic macular edema

Diabetic macular edema, code 362.07, is only present with diabetic retinopathy. Another code from subcategory 362.0, Diabetic retinopathy, must be used with code 362.07. Codes under subcategory 362.0 are diabetes manifestation codes, so they must be used following the appropriate diabetes code.

5) Diabetes mellitus in pregnancy and gestational diabetes

(a) For diabetes mellitus complicating pregnancy, *see Section I.C.11.f., Diabetes mellitus in pregnancy.*

(b) For gestational diabetes, *see Section I.C.11, g., Gestational diabetes.*

6) Insulin pump malfunction

(a) Underdose of insulin due insulin pump failure

An underdose of insulin due to an insulin pump failure should be assigned 996.57, Mechanical complication due to insulin pump, as the principal or first listed code, followed by the appropriate diabetes mellitus code based on documentation.

(b) Overdose of insulin due to insulin pump failure

The principal or first listed code for an encounter due to an insulin pump malfunction resulting in an overdose of insulin, should also be 996.57, Mechanical complication due to insulin pump, followed by code 962.3, Poisoning by insulins and antidiabetic agents, and the appropriate diabetes mellitus code based on documentation.

7) Secondary Diabetes Mellitus

Codes under category 249, Secondary diabetes mellitus, identify complications/manifestations associated with secondary diabetes mellitus. Secondary diabetes is always caused by another condition or event (e.g., cystic fibrosis, malignant neoplasm of pancreas, pancreatectomy, adverse effect of drug, or poisoning).

(a) Fifth-digits for category 249:

A fifth-digit is required for all category 249 codes to identify whether the diabetes is controlled or uncontrolled.

(b) Secondary diabetes mellitus and the use of insulin

For patients who routinely use insulin, code V58.67, Long-term (current) use of insulin, should also be assigned. Code V58.67 should not be assigned if insulin is given temporarily to bring a patient's blood sugar under control during an encounter.

(c) Assigning and sequencing secondary diabetes codes and associated conditions

When assigning codes for secondary diabetes and its associated conditions (e.g. renal manifestations), the code(s) from category 249 must be sequenced before the codes for the associated conditions. The secondary diabetes codes and the diabetic manifestation codes that correspond to them are paired codes that follow the etiology/manifestation convention of the classification. Assign as many codes from category 249 as needed to identify all of the associated conditions that the patient has. The corresponding codes for the associated conditions are listed under each of the secondary diabetes codes. For example, secondary diabetes with diabetic nephrosis is assigned to code 249.40, followed by 581.81.

(d) Assigning and sequencing secondary diabetes codes and its causes

The sequencing of the secondary diabetes codes in relationship to codes for the cause of the diabetes is based on the reason for the encounter, applicable

ICD-9-CM sequencing conventions, and chapter-specific guidelines.

If a patient is seen for treatment of the secondary diabetes or one of its associated conditions, a code from category 249 is sequenced as the principal or first-listed diagnosis, with the cause of the secondary diabetes (e.g. cystic fibrosis) sequenced as an additional diagnosis.

If, however, the patient is seen for the treatment of the condition causing the secondary diabetes (e.g., malignant neoplasm of pancreas), the code for the cause of the secondary diabetes should be sequenced as the principal or first-listed diagnosis followed by a code from category 249.

(i) Secondary diabetes mellitus due to pancreatectomy

For postpancreatectomy diabetes mellitus (lack of insulin due to the surgical removal of all or part of the pancreas), assign code 251.3, Postsurgical hypoinsulinemia. Assign a code from subcategory 249, Secondary diabetes mellitus and a code from subcategory V88.1, Acquired absence of pancreas as additional codes. Code also any diabetic manifestations (e.g. diabetic nephrosis 581.81).

(ii) Secondary diabetes due to drugs

Secondary diabetes may be caused by an adverse effect of correctly administered medications, poisoning or late effect of poisoning.

See section I.C.17.e for coding of adverse effects and poisoning, and section I.C.19 for E code reporting.

4. Chapter 4: Diseases of Blood and Blood Forming Organs (280-289)

a. Anemia of chronic disease

Subcategory 285.2, Anemia in chronic illness, has codes for anemia in chronic kidney disease, code 285.21; anemia in neoplastic disease, code 285.22; and anemia in other chronic illness, code 285.29. These codes can be used as the principal/first listed code if the reason for the encounter is to treat the anemia. They may also be used as secondary codes if treatment of the anemia is a component of an encounter, but not the primary reason for the encounter. When using a code from subcategory 285 it is also necessary to use the code for the chronic condition causing the anemia.

1) Anemia in chronic kidney disease

When assigning code 285.21, Anemia in chronic kidney disease, it is also necessary to assign a code from category 585, Chronic kidney disease, to indicate the stage of chronic kidney disease.

See i.C.10.a. Chronic kidney disease (CKD).

2) Anemia in neoplastic disease

When assigning code 285.22, Anemia in neoplastic disease, it is also necessary to assign the neoplasm code that is responsible for the anemia. Code 285.22 is for use for anemia that is due to the malignancy, not for anemia due to antineoplastic chemotherapy drugs. Assign the appropriate code for anemia due to antineoplastic chemotherapy.

See I.C.2.c.1 Anemia associated with malignancy.

See I.C.2.c.2 Anemia associated with chemotherapy, immunotherapy and radiation therapy.

5. Chapter 5: Mental Disorders (290-319)

Reserved for future guideline expansion

6. Chapter 6: Diseases of Nervous System and Sense Organs (320-389)

a. Pain - Category 338

1) General coding information

Codes in category 338 may be used in conjunction with codes from other categories and chapters to provide more detail about acute or chronic pain and neoplasm-related pain, unless otherwise indicated below.

If the pain is not specified as acute or chronic, do not assign codes from category 338, except for post-thoracotomy pain, postoperative pain, neoplasm related pain, or central pain syndrome.

A code from subcategories 338.1 and 338.2 should not be assigned if the underlying (definitive) diagnosis is known, unless the reason for the encounter is pain control/management and not management of the underlying condition.

(a) Category 338 Codes as Principal or First-Listed Diagnosis

Category 338 codes are acceptable as principal diagnosis or the first-listed code:

- When pain control or pain management is the reason for the admission/encounter (e.g., a patient with displaced intervertebral disc, nerve impingement and severe back pain presents for injection of steroid into the spinal canal). The underlying cause of the pain should be reported as an additional diagnosis, if known.

- When an admission or encounter is for a procedure aimed at treating the underlying condition (e.g., spinal fusion, kyphoplasty), a code for the underlying condition (e.g., vertebral fracture, spinal stenosis) should be assigned as the principal diagnosis. No code from category 338 should be assigned.

- When a patient is admitted for the insertion of a neurostimulator for pain control, assign the appropriate pain code as the principal or first listed diagnosis. When an admission or encounter is for a procedure aimed at treating the underlying condition and a neurostimulator is inserted for pain control during the same admission/encounter, a code for the underlying condition should be assigned as the principal diagnosis and the appropriate pain code should be assigned as a secondary diagnosis.

(b) Use of Category 338 Codes in Conjunction with Site Specific Pain Codes

(i) Assigning Category 338 Codes and Site-Specific Pain Codes

Codes from category 338 may be used in conjunction with codes that identify the site of pain (including codes from chapter 16) if the category 338 code provides additional information. For example, if the code describes the site of the pain, but does not fully describe whether the pain is acute or chronic, then both codes should be assigned.

(ii) Sequencing of Category 338 Codes with Site-Specific Pain Codes

The sequencing of category 338 codes with site-specific pain codes (including chapter 16 codes), is dependent on the circumstances of the encounter/admission as follows:

- If the encounter is for pain control or pain management, assign the code from category 338 followed by the code identifying the specific site of pain (e.g., encounter for pain management for acute neck pain from trauma is assigned code 338.11, Acute pain due to trauma, followed by

code 723.1, Cervicalgia, to identify the site of pain).

- If the encounter is for any other reason except pain control or pain management, and a related definitive diagnosis has not been established (confirmed) by the provider, assign the code for the specific site of pain first, followed by the appropriate code from category 338.

2) Pain due to devices, implants and grafts

Pain associated with devices, implants or grafts left in a surgical site (for example painful hip prosthesis) is assigned to the appropriate code(s) found in Chapter 17, Injury and Poisoning. Use additional code(s) from category 338 to identify acute or chronic pain due to presence of the device, implant or graft (338.18-338.19 or 338.28-338.29).

3) Postoperative Pain

Post-thoracotomy pain and other postoperative pain are classified to subcategories 338.1 and 338.2, depending on whether the pain is acute or chronic. The default for post-thoracotomy and other postoperative pain not specified as acute or chronic is the code for the acute form.

Routine or expected postoperative pain immediately after surgery should not be coded.

(a) Postoperative pain not associated with specific postoperative complication

Postoperative pain not associated with a specific postoperative complication is assigned to the appropriate postoperative pain code in category 338.

(b) Postoperative pain associated with specific postoperative complication

Postoperative pain associated with a specific postoperative complication (such as painful wire sutures) is assigned to the appropriate code(s) found in Chapter 17, Injury and Poisoning. If appropriate, use additional code(s) from category 338 to identify acute or chronic pain (338.18 or 338.28). If pain control/management is the reason for the encounter, a code from category 338 should be assigned as the principal or first-listed diagnosis in accordance with *Section I.C.6.a.1.a above.*

(c) Postoperative pain as principal or first-listed diagnosis

Postoperative pain may be reported as the principal or first-listed diagnosis when the stated reason for the admission/encounter is documented as postoperative pain control/ management.

(d) Postoperative pain as secondary diagnosis

Postoperative pain may be reported as a secondary diagnosis code when a patient presents for outpatient surgery and develops an unusual or inordinate amount of postoperative pain.

The provider's documentation should be used to guide the coding of postoperative pain, as well as *Section III. Reporting Additional Diagnoses and Section IV. Diagnostic Coding and Reporting in the Outpatient Setting.*

See Section II.I.2 for information on sequencing of diagnoses for patients admitted to hospital inpatient care following post-operative observation.

See Section II.J for information on sequencing of diagnoses for patients admitted to hospital inpatient care from outpatient surgery.

See Section IV.A.2 for information on sequencing of diagnoses for patients admitted for observation.

4) Chronic pain

Chronic pain is classified to subcategory 338.2. There is no time frame defining when pain becomes chronic pain. The provider's documentation should be used to guide use of these codes.

5) Neoplasm Related Pain

Code 338.3 is assigned to pain documented as being related, associated or due to cancer, primary or secondary malignancy, or tumor. This code is assigned regardless of whether the pain is acute or chronic.

This code may be assigned as the principal or first-listed code when the stated reason for the admission/encounter is documented as pain control/pain management. The underlying neoplasm should be reported as an additional diagnosis.

When the reason for the admission/encounter is management of the neoplasm and the pain associated with the neoplasm is also documented, code 338.3 may be assigned as an additional diagnosis.

See Section I.C.2 for instructions on the sequencing of neoplasms for all other stated reasons for the admission/encounter (except for pain control/pain management).

6) Chronic pain syndrome

This condition is different than the term "chronic pain," and therefore this code should only be used when the provider has specifically documented this condition.

b. Glaucoma

1) Glaucoma

For types of glaucoma classified to subcategories 365.1-365.6, an additional code should be assigned from subcategory 365.7, Glaucoma stage, to identify the glaucoma stage. Codes from 365.7, Glaucoma stage, may not be assigned as a principal or first-listed diagnosis.

2) Bilateral glaucoma with same stage

When a patient has bilateral glaucoma and both are documented as being the same type and stage, report only the code for the type of glaucoma and one code for the stage.

3) Bilateral glaucoma stage with different stages

When a patient has bilateral glaucoma and each eye is documented as having a different stage, assign one code for the type of glaucoma and one code for the highest glaucoma stage.

4) Bilateral glaucoma with different types and different stages

When a patient has bilateral glaucoma and each eye is documented as having a different type and a different stage, assign one code for each type of glaucoma and one code for the highest glaucoma stage.

5) Patient admitted with glaucoma and stage evolves during the admission

If a patient is admitted with glaucoma and the stage progresses during the admission, assign the code for highest stage documented.

6) Indeterminate stage glaucoma

Assignment of code 365.74, Indeterminate stage glaucoma, should be based on the clinical documentation. Code 365.74 is used for glaucoma whose stage cannot be clinically determined. This code should not be confused with code 365.70, Glaucoma stage, unspecified. Code 365.70 should be assigned when there is no documentation regarding the stage of the glaucoma.

7. Chapter 7: Diseases of Circulatory System (390-459)

a. Hypertension

Hypertension Table

The Hypertension Table, found under the main term, "Hypertension", in the Alphabetic Index, contains a complete listing of all conditions due to or associated with hypertension and classifies them according to malignant, benign, and unspecified.

1) Hypertension, Essential, or NOS

Assign hypertension (arterial) (essential) (primary) (systemic) (NOS) to category code 401 with the appropriate fourth digit to indicate malignant (.0), benign (.1), or unspecified (.9). Do

not use either .0 malignant or .1 benign unless medical record documentation supports such a designation.

2) Hypertension with Heart Disease

Heart conditions (425.8, 429.0-429.3, 429.8, 429.9) are assigned to a code from category 402 when a causal relationship is stated (due to hypertension) or implied (hypertensive). Use an additional code from category 428 to identify the type of heart failure in those patients with heart failure. More than one code from category 428 may be assigned if the patient has systolic or diastolic failure and congestive heart failure.

The same heart conditions (425.8, 429.0-429.3, 429.8, 429.9) with hypertension, but without a stated causal relationship, are coded separately. Sequence according to the circumstances of the admission/encounter.

3) Hypertensive Chronic Kidney Disease

Assign codes from category 403, Hypertensive chronic kidney disease, when conditions classified to category 585 or code 587 are present with hypertension. Unlike hypertension with heart disease, ICD-9-CM presumes a cause-and-effect relationship and classifies chronic kidney disease (CKD) with hypertension as hypertensive chronic kidney disease.

Fifth digits for category 403 should be assigned as follows:

- 0 with CKD stage I through stage IV, or unspecified.
- 1 with CKD stage V or end stage renal disease.

The appropriate code from category 585, Chronic kidney disease, should be used as a secondary code with a code from category 403 to identify the stage of chronic kidney disease.

See Section I.C.10.a for information on the coding of chronic kidney disease.

4) Hypertensive Heart and Chronic Kidney Disease

Assign codes from combination category 404, Hypertensive heart and chronic kidney disease, when both hypertensive kidney disease and hypertensive heart disease are stated in the diagnosis. Assume a relationship between the hypertension and the chronic kidney disease, whether or not the condition is so designated. Assign an additional code from category 428, to identify the type of heart failure. More than one code from category 428 may be assigned if the patient has systolic or diastolic failure and congestive heart failure.

Fifth digits for category 404 should be assigned as follows:

- 0 without heart failure and with chronic kidney disease (CKD) stage I through stage IV, or unspecified
- 1 with heart failure and with CKD stage I through stage IV, or unspecified
- 2 without heart failure and with CKD stage V or end stage renal disease
- 3 with heart failure and with CKD stage V or end stage renal disease

The appropriate code from category 585, Chronic kidney disease, should be used as a secondary code with a code from category 404 to identify the stage of kidney disease.

See Section I.C.10.a for information on the coding of chronic kidney disease.

5) Hypertensive Cerebrovascular Disease

First assign codes from 430-438, Cerebrovascular disease, then the appropriate hypertension code from categories 401-405.

6) Hypertensive Retinopathy

Two codes are necessary to identify the condition. First assign the code from subcategory 362.11, Hypertensive retinopathy, then the appropriate code from categories 401-405 to indicate the type of hypertension.

7) Hypertension, Secondary

Two codes are required: one to identify the underlying etiology and one from category 405 to identify the hypertension. Sequencing of codes is determined by the reason for admission/encounter.

8) Hypertension, Transient

Assign code 796.2, Elevated blood pressure reading without diagnosis of hypertension, unless patient has an established diagnosis of hypertension. Assign code 642.3x for transient hypertension of pregnancy.

9) Hypertension, Controlled

Assign appropriate code from categories 401-405. This diagnostic statement usually refers to an existing state of hypertension under control by therapy.

10) Hypertension, Uncontrolled

Uncontrolled hypertension may refer to untreated hypertension or hypertension not responding to current therapeutic regimen. In either case, assign the appropriate code from categories 401-405 to designate the stage and type of hypertension. Code to the type of hypertension.

11) Elevated Blood Pressure

For a statement of elevated blood pressure without further specificity, assign code 796.2, Elevated blood pressure reading without diagnosis of hypertension, rather than a code from category 401.

b. Cerebral infarction/stroke/cerebrovascular accident (CVA)

The terms stroke and CVA are often used interchangeably to refer to a cerebral infarction. The terms stroke, CVA, and cerebral infarction NOS are all indexed to the default code 434.91, Cerebral artery occlusion, unspecified, with infarction.

Additional code(s) should be assigned for any neurologic deficits associated with the acute CVA, regardless of whether or not the neurologic deficit resolves prior to discharge.

See Section I.C.18.d.3 for information on coding status post administration of tPA in a different facility within the last 24 hours.

c. Postoperative cerebrovascular accident

A cerebrovascular hemorrhage or infarction that occurs as a result of medical intervention is coded to 997.02, Iatrogenic cerebrovascular infarction or hemorrhage. Medical record documentation should clearly specify the cause- and-effect relationship between the medical intervention and the cerebrovascular accident in order to assign this code. A secondary code from the code range 430-432 or from a code from subcategories 433 or 434 with a fifth digit of "1" should also be used to identify the type of hemorrhage or infarct.

This guideline conforms to the use additional code note instruction at category 997. Code 436, Acute, but ill-defined, cerebrovascular disease, should not be used as a secondary code with code 997.02.

d. Late Effects of Cerebrovascular Disease

1) Category 438, Late Effects of Cerebrovascular disease

Category 438 is used to indicate conditions classifiable to categories 430-437 as the causes of late effects (neurologic deficits), themselves classified elsewhere. These "late effects" include neurologic deficits that persist after initial onset of conditions classifiable to 430-437. The neurologic deficits caused by cerebrovascular disease may be present from the onset or may arise at any time after the onset of the condition classifiable to 430-437.

Codes in category 438 are only for use for late effects of cerebrovascular disease, not for neurologic deficits associated with an acute CVA.

2) Codes from category 438 with codes from 430-437

Codes from category 438 may be assigned on a health care record with codes from 430-437, if the patient has a current cerebrovascular accident (CVA) and deficits from an old CVA.

3) Code V12.54

Assign code V12.54, Transient ischemic attack (TIA), and cerebral infarction without residual deficits (and not a code from category 438) as an additional code for history of cerebrovascular disease when no neurologic deficits are present.

e. Acute myocardial infarction (AMI)

1) ST elevation myocardial infarction (STEMI) and non ST elevation myocardial infarction (NSTEMI)

The ICD-9-CM codes for acute myocardial infarction (AMI) identify the site, such as anterolateral wall or true posterior wall. Subcategories 410.0-410.6 and 410.8 are used for ST elevation myocardial infarction (STEMI). Subcategory 410.7, Subendocardial infarction, is used for non ST elevation myocardial infarction (NSTEMI) and nontransmural MIs.

2) Acute myocardial infarction, unspecified

Subcategory 410.9 is the default for the unspecified term acute myocardial infarction. If only STEMI or transmural MI without the site is documented, query the provider as to the site, or assign a code from subcategory 410.9.

3) AMI documented as nontransmural or subendocardial but site provided

If an AMI is documented as nontransmural or subendocardial, but the site is provided, it is still coded as a subendocardial AMI. If NSTEMI evolves to STEMI, assign the STEMI code. If STEMI converts to NSTEMI due to thrombolytic therapy, it is still coded as STEMI.

See Section I.C.18.d.3 for information on coding status post administration of tPA in a different facility within the last 24 hours.

8. Chapter 8: Diseases of Respiratory System (460-519)

See I.C.17.f. for ventilator-associated pneumonia.

a. Chronic Obstructive Pulmonary Disease [COPD] and Asthma

1) Conditions that comprise COPD and Asthma

The conditions that comprise COPD are obstructive chronic bronchitis, subcategory 491.2, and emphysema, category 492. All asthma codes are under category 493, Asthma. Code 496, Chronic airway obstruction, not elsewhere classified, is a nonspecific code that should only be used when the documentation in a medical record does not specify the type of COPD being treated.

2) Acute exacerbation of chronic obstructive bronchitis and asthma

The codes for chronic obstructive bronchitis and asthma distinguish between uncomplicated cases and those in acute exacerbation. An acute exacerbation is a worsening or a decompensation of a chronic condition. An acute exacerbation is not equivalent to an infection superimposed on a chronic condition, though an exacerbation may be triggered by an infection.

3) Overlapping nature of the conditions that comprise COPD and asthma

Due to the overlapping nature of the conditions that make up COPD and asthma, there are many variations in the way these conditions are documented. Code selection must be based on the terms as documented. When selecting the correct code for the documented type of COPD and asthma, it is essential to first review the index, and then verify the code in the tabular list. There are many instructional notes under the different COPD subcategories and codes. It is important that all such notes be reviewed to assure correct code assignment.

4) Acute exacerbation of asthma and status asthmaticus

An acute exacerbation of asthma is an increased severity of the asthma symptoms, such as wheezing and shortness of breath. Status asthmaticus refers to a patient's failure to respond to therapy administered during an asthmatic episode and is a life threatening complication that requires emergency care. If status asthmaticus is documented by the provider with any type of COPD or with acute bronchitis, the status asthmaticus should be sequenced first. It supersedes any type of COPD including that with acute exacerbation or acute bronchitis. It is inappropriate to assign an asthma code with 5th digit 2, with acute exacerbation, together with an asthma code with 5th digit 1, with status asthmatics. Only the 5th digit 1 should be assigned.

b. Chronic Obstructive Pulmonary Disease [COPD] and Bronchitis

1) Acute bronchitis with COPD

Acute bronchitis, code 466.0, is due to an infectious organism. When acute bronchitis is documented with COPD, code 491.22, Obstructive chronic bronchitis with acute bronchitis, should be assigned. It is not necessary to also assign code 466.0. If a medical record documents acute bronchitis with COPD with acute exacerbation, only code 491.22 should be assigned. The acute bronchitis included in code 491.22 supersedes the acute exacerbation. If a medical record documents COPD with acute exacerbation without mention of acute bronchitis, only code 491.21 should be assigned.

c. Acute Respiratory Failure

1) Acute respiratory failure as principal diagnosis

Code 518.81, Acute respiratory failure, may be assigned as a principal diagnosis when it is the condition established after study to be chiefly responsible for occasioning the admission to the hospital, and the selection is supported by the Alphabetic Index and Tabular List. However, chapter-specific coding guidelines (such as obstetrics, poisoning, HIV, newborn) that provide sequencing direction take precedence.

2) Acute respiratory failure as secondary diagnosis

Respiratory failure may be listed as a secondary diagnosis if it occurs after admission, or if it is present on admission, but does not meet the definition of principal diagnosis.

3) Sequencing of acute respiratory failure and another acute condition

When a patient is admitted with respiratory failure and another acute condition, (e.g., myocardial infarction, cerebrovascular accident, aspiration pneumonia), the principal diagnosis will not be the same in every situation. This applies whether the other acute condition is a respiratory or nonrespiratory condition. Selection of the principal diagnosis will be dependent on the circumstances of admission. If both the respiratory failure and the other acute condition are equally responsible for occasioning the admission to the hospital, and there are no chapter-specific sequencing rules, the guideline regarding two or more diagnoses that equally meet the definition for principal diagnosis *(Section II, C.)* may be applied in these situations.

If the documentation is not clear as to whether acute respiratory failure and another condition are equally responsible for occasioning the admission, query the provider for clarification.

d. Influenza due to certain identified viruses

Code only confirmed cases of avian influenza (codes 488.01-488.02, 488.09, Influenza due to identified avian influenza virus), 2009 H1N1 influenza virus (codes 488.11-488.12, 488.19), or novel influenza A (codes 488.81-488.82, 488.89, Influenza due to identified novel influenza A virus). This is an exception to the hospital inpatient guideline Section II, H. (Uncertain Diagnosis).

In this context, "confirmation" does not require documentation of positive laboratory testing specific for avian, 2009 H1N1 or novel influenza A virus. However, coding should be based on the provider's diagnostic statement that the patient has avian influenza, 2009 H1N1 influenza, or novel influenza A.

If the provider records "suspected" or "possible" or "probable" avian, 2009 H1N1, or novel influenza A, the appropriate influenza

code from category 487, Influenza should be assigned. A code from category 488, Influenza due to certain identified influenza viruses, should not be assigned.

9. **Chapter 9: Diseases of Digestive System (520-579)**

Reserved for future guideline expansion

10. **Chapter 10: Diseases of Genitourinary System (580-629)**

a. **Chronic kidney disease**

1) **Stages of chronic kidney disease (CKD)**

The ICD-9-CM classifies CKD based on severity. The severity of CKD is designated by stages I-V. Stage II, code 585.2, equates to mild CKD; stage III, code 585.3, equates to moderate CKD; and stage IV, code 585.4, equates to severe CKD. Code 585.6, End stage renal disease (ESRD), is assigned when the provider has documented end-stage-renal disease (ESRD).

If both a stage of CKD and ESRD are documented, assign code 585.6 only.

2) **Chronic kidney disease and kidney transplant status**

Patients who have undergone kidney transplant may still have some form of CKD, because the kidney transplant may not fully restore kidney function. Therefore, the presence of CKD alone does not constitute a transplant complication. Assign the appropriate 585 code for the patient's stage of CKD and code V42.0. If a transplant complication such as failure or rejection is documented, see section I.C.17.f.2.b for information on coding complications of a kidney transplant. If the documentation is unclear as to whether the patient has a complication of the transplant, query the provider.

3) **Chronic kidney disease with other conditions**

Patients with CKD may also suffer from other serious conditions, most commonly diabetes mellitus and hypertension. The sequencing of the CKD code in relationship to codes for other contributing conditions is based on the conventions in the tabular list.

See I.C.3.a.4 for sequencing instructions for diabetes.
See I.C.4.a.1 for anemia in CKD.
See I.C.7.a.3 for hypertensive chronic kidney disease.
See I.C.17.f.2.b, Kidney transplant complications, for instructions on coding of documented rejection or failure.

11. **Chapter 11: Complications of Pregnancy, Childbirth, and the Puerperium (630-679)**

a. **General Rules for Obstetric Cases**

1) **Codes from chapter 11 and sequencing priority**

Obstetric cases require codes from chapter 11, codes in the range 630-679, Complications of Pregnancy, Childbirth, and the Puerperium. Chapter 11 codes have sequencing priority over codes from other chapters. Additional codes from other chapters may be used in conjunction with chapter 11 codes to further specify conditions. Should the provider document that the pregnancy is incidental to the encounter, then code V22.2 should be used in place of any chapter 11 codes. It is the provider's responsibility to state that the condition being treated is not affecting the pregnancy.

2) **Chapter 11 codes used only on the maternal record**

Chapter 11 codes are to be used only on the maternal record, never on the record of the newborn.

3) **Chapter 11 fifth-digits**

Categories 640-648, 651-676 have required fifth-digits, which indicate whether the encounter is antepartum, postpartum and whether a delivery has also occurred.

4) **Fifth-digits, appropriate for each code**

The fifth-digits, which are appropriate for each code number, are listed in brackets under each code. The fifth-digits on each code should all be consistent with each other. That is, should a delivery occur all of the fifth-digits should indicate the delivery.

b. **Selection of OB Principal or First-listed Diagnosis**

1) **Routine outpatient prenatal visits**

For routine outpatient prenatal visits when no complications are present codes V22.0, Supervision of normal first pregnancy, and V22.1, Supervision of other normal pregnancy, should be used as the first-listed diagnoses. These codes should not be used in conjunction with chapter 11 codes.

2) **Prenatal outpatient visits for high-risk patients**

For routine prenatal outpatient visits for patients with high-risk pregnancies, a code from category V23, Supervision of high-risk pregnancy, should be used as the first-listed diagnosis. Secondary chapter 11 codes may be used in conjunction with these codes if appropriate.

3) **Episodes when no delivery occurs**

In episodes when no delivery occurs, the principal diagnosis should correspond to the principal complication of the pregnancy, which necessitated the encounter. Should more than one complication exist, all of which are treated or monitored, any of the complications codes may be sequenced first.

4) **When a delivery occurs**

When a delivery occurs, the principal diagnosis should correspond to the main circumstances or complication of the delivery. In cases of cesarean delivery, the selection of the principal diagnosis should be the condition established after study that was responsible for the patient's admission. If the patient was admitted with a condition that resulted in the performance of a cesarean procedure, that condition should be selected as the principal diagnosis. If the reason for the admission/encounter was unrelated to the condition resulting in the cesarean delivery, the condition related to the reason for the admission/encounter should be selected as the principal diagnosis, even if a cesarean was performed.

5) **Outcome of delivery**

An outcome of delivery code, V27.0-V27.9, should be included on every maternal record when a delivery has occurred. These codes are not to be used on subsequent records or on the newborn record.

c. **Fetal Conditions Affecting the Management of the Mother**

1) **Codes from categories 655 and 656**

Codes from categories 655, Known or suspected fetal abnormality affecting management of the mother, and 656, Other known or suspected fetal and placental problems affecting the management of the mother, are assigned only when the fetal condition is actually responsible for modifying the management of the mother, i.e., by requiring diagnostic studies, additional observation, special care, or termination of pregnancy. The fact that the fetal condition exists does not justify assigning a code from this series to the mother's record.

See I.C.18.d. for suspected maternal and fetal conditions not found

2) **In utero surgery**

In cases when surgery is performed on the fetus, a diagnosis code from category 655, Known or suspected fetal abnormalities affecting management of the mother, should be assigned identifying the fetal condition. Procedure code 75.36, Correction of fetal defect, should be assigned on the hospital inpatient record.

No code from Chapter 15, the perinatal codes, should be used on the mother's record to identify fetal conditions. Surgery performed in utero on a fetus is still to be coded as an obstetric encounter.

d. **HIV Infection in Pregnancy, Childbirth and the Puerperium**

During pregnancy, childbirth or the puerperium, a patient admitted because of an HIV-related illness should receive a principal diagnosis of 647.6x, Other specified infectious and

parasitic diseases in the mother classifiable elsewhere, but complicating the pregnancy, childbirth or the puerperium, followed by 042 and the code(s) for the HIV-related illness(es).

Patients with asymptomatic HIV infection status admitted during pregnancy, childbirth, or the puerperium should receive codes of 647.6x and V08.

e. Current Conditions Complicating Pregnancy

Assign a code from subcategory 648.x for patients that have current conditions when the condition affects the management of the pregnancy, childbirth, or the puerperium. Use additional secondary codes from other chapters to identify the conditions, as appropriate.

f. Diabetes mellitus in pregnancy

Diabetes mellitus is a significant complicating factor in pregnancy. Pregnant women who are diabetic should be assigned code 648.0x, Diabetes mellitus complicating pregnancy, and a secondary code from category 250, Diabetes mellitus, or category 249, Secondary diabetes to identify the type of diabetes.

Code V58.67, Long-term (current) use of insulin, should also be assigned if the diabetes mellitus is being treated with insulin.

g. Gestational diabetes

Gestational diabetes can occur during the second and third trimester of pregnancy in women who were not diabetic prior to pregnancy. Gestational diabetes can cause complications in the pregnancy similar to those of pre-existing diabetes mellitus. It also puts the woman at greater risk of developing diabetes after the pregnancy. Gestational diabetes is coded to 648.8x, Abnormal glucose tolerance. Codes 648.0x and 648.8x should never be used together on the same record.

Code V58.67, Long-term (current) use of insulin, should also be assigned if the gestational diabetes is being treated with insulin.

h. Normal Delivery, Code 650

1) Normal delivery

Code 650 is for use in cases when a woman is admitted for a full-term normal delivery and delivers a single, healthy infant without any complications antepartum, during the delivery, or postpartum during the delivery episode. Code 650 is always a principal diagnosis. It is not to be used if any other code from chapter 11 is needed to describe a current complication of the antenatal, delivery, or perinatal period. Additional codes from other chapters may be used with code 650 if they are not related to or are in any way complicating the pregnancy.

2) Normal delivery with resolved antepartum complication

Code 650 may be used if the patient had a complication at some point during her pregnancy, but the complication is not present at the time of the admission for delivery.

3) V27.0, Single liveborn, outcome of delivery

V27.0, Single liveborn, is the only outcome of delivery code appropriate for use with 650.

i. The Postpartum and Peripartum Periods

1) Postpartum and peripartum periods

The postpartum period begins immediately after delivery and continues for six weeks following delivery. The peripartum period is defined as the last month of pregnancy to five months postpartum.

2) Postpartum complication

A postpartum complication is any complication occurring within the six-week period.

3) Pregnancy-related complications after 6 week period

Chapter 11 codes may also be used to describe pregnancy-related complications after the six-week period should the provider document that a condition is pregnancy related.

4) Postpartum complications occurring during the same admission as delivery

Postpartum complications that occur during the same admission as the delivery are identified with a fifth digit of "2." Subsequent admissions/encounters for postpartum complications should be identified with a fifth digit of "4."

5) Admission for routine postpartum care following delivery outside hospital

When the mother delivers outside the hospital prior to admission and is admitted for routine postpartum care and no complications are noted, code V24.0, Postpartum care and examination immediately after delivery, should be assigned as the principal diagnosis.

6) Admission following delivery outside hospital with postpartum conditions

A delivery diagnosis code should not be used for a woman who has delivered prior to admission to the hospital. Any postpartum conditions and/or postpartum procedures should be coded.

7) Puerperal sepsis

Code 670.2x, Puerperal sepsis, should be assigned with a secondary code to identify the causal organism (e.g., for a bacterial infection, assign a code from category 041, Bacterial infections in conditions classified elsewhere and of unspecified site). A code from category 038, Septicemia, should not be used for puerperal sepsis. Do not assign code 995.91, Sepsis, as code 670.2x describes the sepsis. If applicable, use additional codes to identify severe sepsis (995.92) and any associated acute organ dysfunction.

j. Code 677, Late effect of complication of pregnancy

1) Code 677

Code 677, Late effect of complication of pregnancy, childbirth, and the puerperium is for use in those cases when an initial complication of a pregnancy develops a sequelae requiring care or treatment at a future date.

2) After the initial postpartum period

This code may be used at any time after the initial postpartum period.

3) Sequencing of Code 677

This code, like all late effect codes, is to be sequenced following the code describing the sequelae of the complication.

k. Abortions

1) Fifth-digits required for abortion categories

Fifth-digits are required for abortion categories 634-637. Fifth digit assignment is based on the status of the patient at the beginning (or start) of the encounter. Fifth-digit 1, incomplete, indicates that all of the products of conception have not been expelled from the uterus. Fifth-digit 2, complete, indicates that all products of conception have been expelled from the uterus.

2) Code from categories 640-648 and 651-659

A code from categories 640-648 and 651-659 may be used as additional codes with an abortion code to indicate the complication leading to the abortion.

Fifth digit 3 is assigned with codes from these categories when used with an abortion code because the other fifth digits will not apply. Codes from the 660-669 series are not to be used for complications of abortion.

3) Code 639 for complications

Code 639 is to be used for all complications following abortion. Code 639 cannot be assigned with codes from categories 634-638.

4) Abortion with Liveborn Fetus

When an attempted termination of pregnancy results in a liveborn fetus assign code 644.21, Early onset of delivery,

with an appropriate code from category V27, Outcome of Delivery. The procedure code for the attempted termination of pregnancy should also be assigned.

5) Retained Products of Conception following an abortion

Subsequent admissions for retained products of conception following a spontaneous or legally induced abortion are assigned the appropriate code from category 634, Spontaneous abortion, or 635 Legally induced abortion, with a fifth digit of "1" (incomplete). This advice is appropriate even when the patient was discharged previously with a discharge diagnosis of complete abortion.

12. Chapter 12: Diseases Skin and Subcutaneous Tissue (680-709)

a. Pressure ulcer stage codes

1) Pressure ulcer stages

Two codes are needed to completely describe a pressure ulcer: A code from subcategory 707.0, Pressure ulcer, to identify the site of the pressure ulcer and a code from subcategory 707.2, Pressure ulcer stages.

The codes in subcategory 707.2, Pressure ulcer stages, are to be used as an additional diagnosis with a code(s) from subcategory 707.0, Pressure Ulcer. Codes from 707.2, Pressure ulcer stages, may not be assigned as a principal or first-listed diagnosis. The pressure ulcer stage codes should only be used with pressure ulcers and not with other types of ulcers (e.g., stasis ulcer).

The ICD-9-CM classifies pressure ulcer stages based on severity, which is designated by stages I-IV and unstageable.

2) Unstageable pressure ulcers

Assignment of code 707.25, Pressure ulcer, unstageable, should be based on the clinical documentation. Code 707.25 is used for pressure ulcers whose stage cannot be clinically determined (e.g., the ulcer is covered by eschar or has been treated with a skin or muscle graft) and pressure ulcers that are documented as deep tissue injury but not documented as due to trauma. This code should not be confused with code 707.20, Pressure ulcer, stage unspecified. Code 707.20 should be assigned when there is no documentation regarding the stage of the pressure ulcer.

3) Documented pressure ulcer stage

Assignment of the pressure ulcer stage code should be guided by clinical documentation of the stage or documentation of the terms found in the index. For clinical terms describing the stage that are not found in the index, and there is no documentation of the stage, the provider should be queried.

4) Bilateral pressure ulcers with same stage

When a patient has bilateral pressure ulcers (e.g., both buttocks) and both pressure ulcers are documented as being the same stage, only the code for the site and one code for the stage should be reported.

5) Bilateral pressure ulcers with different stages

When a patient has bilateral pressure ulcers at the same site (e.g., both buttocks) and each pressure ulcer is documented as being at a different stage, assign one code for the site and the appropriate codes for the pressure ulcer stage.

6) Multiple pressure ulcers of different sites and stages

When a patient has multiple pressure ulcers at different sites (e.g., buttock, heel, shoulder) and each pressure ulcer is documented as being at different stages (e.g., stage 3 and stage 4), assign the appropriate codes for each different site and a code for each different pressure ulcer stage.

7) Patients admitted with pressure ulcers documented as healed

No code is assigned if the documentation states that the pressure ulcer is completely healed.

8) Patients admitted with pressure ulcers documented as healing

Pressure ulcers described as healing should be assigned the appropriate pressure ulcer stage code based on the documentation in the medical record. If the documentation does not provide information about the stage of the healing pressure ulcer, assign code 707.20, Pressure ulcer stage, unspecified.

If the documentation is unclear as to whether the patient has a current (new) pressure ulcer or if the patient is being treated for a healing pressure ulcer, query the provider.

9) Patient admitted with pressure ulcer evolving into another stage during the admission

If a patient is admitted with a pressure ulcer at one stage and it progresses to a higher stage, assign the code for highest stage reported for that site.

13. Chapter 13: Diseases of Musculoskeletal and Connective Tissue (710-739)

a. Coding of Pathologic Fractures

1) Acute Fractures vs. Aftercare

Pathologic fractures are reported using subcategory 733.1, when the fracture is newly diagnosed. Subcategory 733.1 may be used while the patient is receiving active treatment for the fracture. Examples of active treatment are: surgical treatment, emergency department encounter, evaluation and treatment by a new physician.

Fractures are coded using the aftercare codes (subcategories V54.0, V54.2, V54.8 or V54.9) for encounters after the patient has completed active treatment of the fracture and is receiving routine care for the fracture during the healing or recovery phase. Examples of fracture aftercare are: cast change or removal, removal of external or internal fixation device, medication adjustment, and follow up visits following fracture treatment.

Care for complications of surgical treatment for fracture repairs during the healing or recovery phase should be coded with the appropriate complication codes.

Care of complications of fractures, such as malunion and nonunion, should be reported with the appropriate codes.

See Section I. C. 17.b for information on the coding of traumatic fractures.

14. Chapter 14: Congenital Anomalies (740-759)

a. Codes in categories 740-759, Congenital Anomalies

Assign an appropriate code(s) from categories 740-759, Congenital Anomalies, when an anomaly is documented. A congenital anomaly may be the principal/first listed diagnosis on a record or a secondary diagnosis.

When a congenital anomaly does not have a unique code assignment, assign additional code(s) for any manifestations that may be present.

When the code assignment specifically identifies the congenital anomaly, manifestations that are an inherent component of the anomaly should not be coded separately. Additional codes should be assigned for manifestations that are not an inherent component.

Codes from Chapter 14 may be used throughout the life of the patient. If a congenital anomaly has been corrected, a personal history code should be used to identify the history of the anomaly. Although present at birth, a congenital anomaly may not be identified until later in life. Whenever the condition is diagnosed by the physician, it is appropriate to assign a code from codes 740-759.

For the birth admission, the appropriate code from category V30, Liveborn infants, according to type of birth should be sequenced as the principal diagnosis, followed by any congenital anomaly codes, 740-759.

15. Chapter 15: Newborn (Perinatal) Guidelines (760-779)

For coding and reporting purposes the perinatal period is defined as before birth through the 28th day following birth. The following guidelines are provided for reporting purposes. Hospitals may record other diagnoses as needed for internal data use.

a. General Perinatal Rules

1) Chapter 15 Codes

They are never for use on the maternal record. Codes from Chapter 11, the obstetric chapter, are never permitted on the newborn record. Chapter 15 code may be used throughout the life of the patient if the condition is still present.

2) Sequencing of perinatal codes

Generally, codes from Chapter 15 should be sequenced as the principal/first-listed diagnosis on the newborn record, with the exception of the appropriate V30 code for the birth episode, followed by codes from any other chapter that provide additional detail. The "use additional code" note at the beginning of the chapter supports this guideline. If the index does not provide a specific code for a perinatal condition, assign code 779.89, Other specified conditions originating in the perinatal period, followed by the code from another chapter that specifies the condition. Codes for signs and symptoms may be assigned when a definitive diagnosis has not been established.

3) Birth process or community acquired conditions

If a newborn has a condition that may be either due to the birth process or community acquired and the documentation does not indicate which it is, the default is due to the birth process and the code from Chapter 15 should be used. If the condition is community-acquired, a code from Chapter 15 should not be assigned.

4) Code all clinically significant conditions

All clinically significant conditions noted on routine newborn examination should be coded. A condition is clinically significant if it requires:

- clinical evaluation; or
- therapeutic treatment; or
- diagnostic procedures; or
- extended length of hospital stay; or
- increased nursing care and/or monitoring; or
- has implications for future health care needs

Note: The perinatal guidelines listed above are the same as the general coding guidelines for "additional diagnoses", except for the final point regarding implications for future health care needs. Codes should be assigned for conditions that have been specified by the provider as having implications for future health care needs. Codes from the perinatal chapter should not be assigned unless the provider has established a definitive diagnosis.

b. Use of codes V30-V39

When coding the birth of an infant, assign a code from categories V30-V39, according to the type of birth. A code from this series is assigned as a principal diagnosis, and assigned only once to a newborn at the time of birth.

c. Newborn transfers

If the newborn is transferred to another institution, the V30 series is not used at the receiving hospital.

d. Use of category V29

1) Assigning a code from category V29

Assign a code from category V29, Observation and evaluation of newborns and infants for suspected conditions not found, to identify those instances when a healthy newborn is evaluated for a suspected condition that is determined after study not to be present. Do not use a code from category V29 when the patient has identified signs or symptoms of a suspected problem; in such cases, code the sign or symptom.

A code from category V29 may also be assigned as a principal code for readmissions or encounters when the V30 code no longer applies. Codes from category V29 are for use only for healthy newborns and infants for which no condition after study is found to be present.

2) V29 code on a birth record

A V29 code is to be used as a secondary code after the V30, Outcome of delivery, code.

e. Use of other V codes on perinatal records

V codes other than V30 and V29 may be assigned on a perinatal or newborn record code. The codes may be used as a principal or first-listed diagnosis for specific types of encounters or for readmissions or encounters when the V30 code no longer applies.

See Section I.C.18 for information regarding the assignment of V codes.

f. Maternal Causes of Perinatal Morbidity

Codes from categories 760-763, Maternal causes of perinatal morbidity and mortality, are assigned only when the maternal condition has actually affected the fetus or newborn. The fact that the mother has an associated medical condition or experiences some complication of pregnancy, labor or delivery does not justify the routine assignment of codes from these categories to the newborn record.

g. Congenital Anomalies in Newborns

For the birth admission, the appropriate code from category V30, Liveborn infants according to type of birth, should be used, followed by any congenital anomaly codes, categories 740-759. Use additional secondary codes from other chapters to specify conditions associated with the anomaly, if applicable.

Also, see Section I.C.14 for information on the coding of congenital anomalies.

h. Coding Additional Perinatal Diagnoses

1) Assigning codes for conditions that require treatment

Assign codes for conditions that require treatment or further investigation, prolong the length of stay, or require resource utilization.

2) Codes for conditions specified as having implications for future health care needs

Assign codes for conditions that have been specified by the provider as having implications for future health care needs.

Note: This guideline should not be used for adult patients.

3) Codes for newborn conditions originating in the perinatal period

Assign a code for newborn conditions originating in the perinatal period (categories 760-779), as well as complications arising during the current episode of care classified in other chapters, only if the diagnoses have been documented by the responsible provider at the time of transfer or discharge as having affected the fetus or newborn.

i. Prematurity and Fetal Growth Retardation

Providers utilize different criteria in determining prematurity. A code for prematurity should not be assigned unless it is documented. The 5th digit assignment for codes from category 764 and subcategories 765.0 and 765.1 should be based on the recorded birth weight and estimated gestational age.

A code from subcategory 765.2, Weeks of gestation, should be assigned as an additional code with category 764 and codes from 765.0 and 765.1 to specify weeks of gestation as documented by the provider in the record.

j. Newborn sepsis

Code 771.81, Septicemia [sepsis] of newborn, should be assigned with a secondary code from category 041, Bacterial infections in

conditions classified elsewhere and of unspecified site, to identify the organism. A code from category 038, Septicemia, should not be used on a newborn record. Do not assign code 995.91, Sepsis, as code 771.81 describes the sepsis. If applicable, use additional codes to identify severe sepsis (995.92) and any associated acute organ dysfunction.

16. **Chapter 16: Signs, Symptoms and Ill-Defined Conditions (780-799)**

    Reserved for future guideline expansion

17. **Chapter 17: Injury and Poisoning (800-999)**

    a. **Coding of Injuries**

    When coding injuries, assign separate codes for each injury unless a combination code is provided, in which case the combination code is assigned. Multiple injury codes are provided in ICD-9-CM, but should not be assigned unless information for a more specific code is not available. These traumatic injury codes are not to be used for normal, healing surgical wounds or to identify complications of surgical wounds.

    The code for the most serious injury, as determined by the provider and the focus of treatment, is sequenced first.

    1) **Superficial injuries**

       Superficial injuries such as abrasions or contusions are not coded when associated with more severe injuries of the same site.

    2) **Primary injury with damage to nerves/blood vessels**

       When a primary injury results in minor damage to peripheral nerves or blood vessels, the primary injury is sequenced first with additional code(s) from categories 950-957, Injury to nerves and spinal cord, and/or 900-904, Injury to blood vessels. When the primary injury is to the blood vessels or nerves, that injury should be sequenced first.

    b. **Coding of Traumatic Fractures**

    The principles of multiple coding of injuries should be followed in coding fractures. Fractures of specified sites are coded individually by site in accordance with both the provisions within categories 800-829 and the level of detail furnished by medical record content. Combination categories for multiple fractures are provided for use when there is insufficient detail in the medical record (such as trauma cases transferred to another hospital), when the reporting form limits the number of codes that can be used in reporting pertinent clinical data, or when there is insufficient specificity at the fourth-digit or fifth-digit level. More specific guidelines are as follows:

    1) **Acute Fractures vs. Aftercare**

       Traumatic fractures are coded using the acute fracture codes (800-829) while the patient is receiving active treatment for the fracture. Examples of active treatment are: surgical treatment, emergency department encounter, and evaluation and treatment by a new physician.

       Fractures are coded using the aftercare codes (subcategories V54.0, V54.1, V54.8, or V54.9) for encounters after the patient has completed active treatment of the fracture and is receiving routine care for the fracture during the healing or recovery phase. Examples of fracture aftercare are: cast change or removal, removal of external or internal fixation device, medication adjustment, and follow up visits following fracture treatment.

       Care for complications of surgical treatment for fracture repairs during the healing or recovery phase should be coded with the appropriate complication codes.

       Care of complications of fractures, such as malunion and nonunion, should be reported with the appropriate codes.

       Pathologic fractures are not coded in the 800-829 range, but instead are assigned to subcategory 733.1. *See Section I.C.13.a for additional information.*

    2) **Multiple fractures of same limb**

       Multiple fractures of same limb classifiable to the same three-digit or four-digit category are coded to that category.

    3) **Multiple unilateral or bilateral fractures of same bone**

       Multiple unilateral or bilateral fractures of same bone(s) but classified to different fourth-digit subdivisions (bone part) within the same three-digit category are coded individually by site.

    4) **Multiple fracture categories 819 and 828**

       Multiple fracture categories 819 and 828 classify bilateral fractures of both upper limbs (819) and both lower limbs (828), but without any detail at the fourth-digit level other than open and closed type of fractures.

    5) **Multiple fractures sequencing**

       Multiple fractures are sequenced in accordance with the severity of the fracture. The provider should be asked to list the fracture diagnoses in the order of severity.

    c. **Coding of Burns**

    Current burns (940-948) are classified by depth, extent and by agent (E code). Burns are classified by depth as first degree (erythema), second degree (blistering), and third degree (full-thickness involvement).

    1) **Sequencing of burn and related condition codes**

       Sequence first the code that reflects the highest degree of burn when more than one burn is present.

       a. When the reason for the admission or encounter is for treatment of external multiple burns, sequence first the code that reflects the burn of the highest degree.

       b. When a patient has both internal and external burns, the circumstances of admission govern the selection of the principal diagnosis or first-listed diagnosis.

       c. When a patient is admitted for burn injuries and other related conditions such as smoke inhalation and/or respiratory failure, the circumstances of admission govern the selection of the principal or first-listed diagnosis.

    2) **Burns of the same local site**

       Classify burns of the same local site (three-digit category level, 940-947) but of different degrees to the subcategory identifying the highest degree recorded in the diagnosis.

    3) **Non-healing burns**

       Non-healing burns are coded as acute burns.

       Necrosis of burned skin should be coded as a non-healed burn.

    4) **Code 958.3, Posttraumatic wound infection**

       Assign code 958.3, Posttraumatic wound infection, not elsewhere classified, as an additional code for any documented infected burn site.

    5) **Assign separate codes for each burn site**

       When coding burns, assign separate codes for each burn site. Category 946 Burns of Multiple specified sites, should only be used if the location of the burns are not documented.

       Category 949, Burn, unspecified, is extremely vague and should rarely be used.

    6) **Assign codes from category 948, Burns**

       Burns classified according to extent of body surface involved, when the site of the burn is not specified or when there is a need for additional data. It is advisable to use category 948 as additional coding when needed to provide data for evaluating burn mortality, such as that needed by burn units. It is also advisable to use category 948 as an additional code for reporting purposes when there is mention of a third-degree burn involving 20 percent or more of the body surface.

       In assigning a code from category 948:

           Fourth-digit codes are used to identify the percentage of total body surface involved in a burn (all degree).

Fifth-digits are assigned to identify the percentage of body surface involved in third-degree burn.

Fifth-digit zero (0) is assigned when less than 10 percent or when no body surface is involved in a third-degree burn.

Category 948 is based on the classic "rule of nines" in estimating body surface involved: head and neck are assigned nine percent, each arm nine percent, each leg 18 percent, the anterior trunk 18 percent, posterior trunk 18 percent, and genitalia one percent. Providers may change these percentage assignments where necessary to accommodate infants and children who have proportionately larger heads than adults and patients who have large buttocks, thighs, or abdomen that involve burns.

7) **Encounters for treatment of late effects of burns**

Encounters for the treatment of the late effects of burns (i.e., scars or joint contractures) should be coded to the residual condition (sequelae) followed by the appropriate late effect code (906.5-906.9). A late effect E code may also be used, if desired.

8) **Sequelae with a late effect code and current burn**

When appropriate, both a sequelae with a late effect code, and a current burn code may be assigned on the same record (when both a current burn and sequelae of an old burn exist).

d. **Coding of Debridement of Wound, Infection, or Burn**

Excisional debridement involves surgical removal or cutting away, as opposed to a mechanical (brushing, scrubbing, washing) debridement.

For coding purposes, excisional debridement is assigned to code 86.22.

Nonexcisional debridement is assigned to code 86.28.

e. **Adverse Effects, Poisoning and Toxic Effects**

The properties of certain drugs, medicinal and biological substances or combinations of such substances, may cause toxic reactions. The occurrence of drug toxicity is classified in ICD-9-CM as follows:

1) **Adverse Effect**

When the drug was correctly prescribed and properly administered, code the reaction plus the appropriate code from the E930-E949 series. Codes from the E930-E949 series must be used to identify the causative substance for an adverse effect of drug, medicinal and biological substances, correctly prescribed and properly administered. The effect, such as tachycardia, delirium, gastrointestinal hemorrhaging, vomiting, hypokalemia, hepatitis, renal failure, or respiratory failure, is coded and followed by the appropriate code from the E930-E949 series.

Adverse effects of therapeutic substances correctly prescribed and properly administered (toxicity, synergistic reaction, side effect, and idiosyncratic reaction) may be due to (1) differences among patients, such as age, sex, disease, and genetic factors, and (2) drug-related factors, such as type of drug, route of administration, duration of therapy, dosage, and bioavailability.

2) **Poisoning**

(a) **Error was made in drug prescription**

Errors made in drug prescription or in the administration of the drug by provider, nurse, patient, or other person, use the appropriate poisoning code from the 960-979 series.

(b) **Overdose of a drug intentionally taken**

If an overdose of a drug was intentionally taken or administered and resulted in drug toxicity, it would be coded as a poisoning (960-979 series).

(c) **Nonprescribed drug taken with correctly prescribed and properly administered drug**

If a nonprescribed drug or medicinal agent was taken in combination with a correctly prescribed and properly administered drug, any drug toxicity or other reaction resulting from the interaction of the two drugs would be classified as a poisoning.

(d) **Interaction of drug(s) and alcohol**

When a reaction results from the interaction of a drug(s) and alcohol, this would be classified as poisoning.

(e) **Sequencing of poisoning**

When coding a poisoning or reaction to the improper use of a medication (e.g., wrong dose, wrong substance, wrong route of administration) the poisoning code is sequenced first, followed by a code for the manifestation. If there is also a diagnosis of drug abuse or dependence to the substance, the abuse or dependence is coded as an additional code.

See Section I.C.3.a.6.b. if poisoning is the result of insulin pump malfunctions and Section I.C.19 for general use of E-codes.

3) **Toxic Effects**

(a) **Toxic effect codes**

When a harmful substance is ingested or comes in contact with a person, this is classified as a toxic effect. The toxic effect codes are in categories 980-989.

(b) **Sequencing toxic effect codes**

A toxic effect code should be sequenced first, followed by the code(s) that identify the result of the toxic effect.

(c) **External cause codes for toxic effects**

An external cause code from categories E860-E869 for accidental exposure, codes E950.6 or E950.7 for intentional self-harm, category E962 for assault, or categories E980-E982, for undetermined, should also be assigned to indicate intent.

f. **Complications of care**

1) **Complications of care**

(a) **Documentation of complications of care**

See Section I.B.18. for information on documentation of complications of care.

(b) **Use additional code to identify nature of complication**

An additional code identifying the complication should be assigned with codes in categories 996-999, Complications of Surgical and Medical Care NEC, when the additional code provides greater specificity as to the nature of the condition. If the complication code fully describes the condition, no additional code is necessary.

2) **Transplant complications**

(a) **Transplant complications other than kidney**

Codes under subcategory 996.8, Complications of transplanted organ, are for use for both complications and rejection of transplanted organs. A transplant complication code is only assigned if the complication affects the function of the transplanted organ. Two codes are required to fully describe a transplant complication, the appropriate code from subcategory 996.8 and a secondary code that identifies the complication.

Pre-existing conditions or conditions that develop after the transplant are not coded as complications unless they affect the function of the transplanted organs.

See I.C.18.d.3 for transplant organ removal status

See I.C.2.i for malignant neoplasm associated with transplanted organ.

(b) Chronic kidney disease and kidney transplant complications

Patients who have undergone kidney transplant may still have some form of chronic kidney disease (CKD) because the kidney transplant may not fully restore kidney function. Code 996.81 should be assigned for documented complications of a kidney transplant, such as transplant failure or rejection or other transplant complication. Code 996.81 should not be assigned for post kidney transplant patients who have chronic kidney (CKD) unless a transplant complication such as transplant failure or rejection is documented. If the documentation is unclear as to whether the patient has a complication of the transplant, query the provider.

Conditions that affect the function of the transplanted kidney, other than CKD, should be assigned code 996.81, Complications of transplanted organ, Kidney, and a secondary code that identifies the complication.

For patients with CKD following a kidney transplant, but who do not have a complication such as failure or rejection, *see section I.C.10.a.2, Chronic kidney disease and kidney transplant status.*

3) Ventilator associated pneumonia

(a) Documentation of Ventilator associated Pneumonia

As with all procedural or postprocedural complications, code assignment is based on the provider's documentation of the relationship between the condition and the procedure.

Code 997.31, Ventilator associated pneumonia, should be assigned only when the provider has documented ventilator associated pneumonia (VAP). An additional code to identify the organism (e.g., Pseudomonas aeruginosa, code 041.7) should also be assigned. Do not assign an additional code from categories 480-484 to identify the type of pneumonia.

Code 997.31 should not be assigned for cases where the patient has pneumonia and is on a mechanical ventilator but the provider has not specifically stated that the pneumonia is ventilator-associated pneumonia.

If the documentation is unclear as to whether the patient has a pneumonia that is a complication attributable to the mechanical ventilator, query the provider.

(b) Patient admitted with pneumonia and develops VAP

A patient may be admitted with one type of pneumonia (e.g., code 481, Pneumococcal pneumonia) and subsequently develop VAP. In this instance, the principal diagnosis would be the appropriate code from categories 480-484 for the pneumonia diagnosed at the time of admission. Code 997.31, Ventilator associated pneumonia, would be assigned as an additional diagnosis when the provider has also documented the presence of ventilator associated pneumonia.

g. SIRS due to Non-infectious Process

The systemic inflammatory response syndrome (SIRS) can develop as a result of certain non-infectious disease processes, such as trauma, malignant neoplasm, or pancreatitis. When SIRS is documented with a noninfectious condition, and no subsequent infection is documented, the code for the underlying condition, such as an injury, should be assigned, followed by code 995.93, Systemic inflammatory response syndrome due to noninfectious process without acute organ dysfunction, or 995.94, Systemic inflammatory response syndrome due to non-infectious process with acute organ dysfunction. If an acute organ dysfunction is documented, the appropriate code(s) for the associated acute organ dysfunction(s) should be assigned in addition to code 995.94. If acute organ dysfunction is documented, but it cannot be determined if the acute organ

dysfunction is associated with SIRS or due to another condition (e.g., directly due to the trauma), the provider should be queried.

When the non-infectious condition has led to an infection that results in SIRS, *see Section I.C.1.b.12 for the guideline for sepsis and severe sepsis associated with a non-infectious process.*

18. Classification of Factors Influencing Health Status and Contact with Health Service (Supplemental V01-V91)

Note: The chapter specific guidelines provide additional information about the use of V codes for specified encounters.

a. Introduction

ICD-9-CM provides codes to deal with encounters for circumstances other than a disease or injury. The Supplementary Classification of Factors Influencing Health Status and Contact with Health Services (V01.0 - V91.99) is provided to deal with occasions when circumstances other than a disease or injury (codes 001-999) are recorded as a diagnosis or problem.

There are four primary circumstances for the use of V codes:

1) A person who is not currently sick encounters the health services for some specific reason, such as to act as an organ donor, to receive prophylactic care, such as inoculations or health screenings, or to receive counseling on health related issues.

2) A person with a resolving disease or injury, or a chronic, long-term condition requiring continuous care, encounters the health care system for specific aftercare of that disease or injury (e.g., dialysis for renal disease; chemotherapy for malignancy; cast change). A diagnosis/symptom code should be used whenever a current, acute, diagnosis is being treated or a sign or symptom is being studied.

3) Circumstances or problems influence a person's health status but are not in themselves a current illness or injury.

4) Newborns, to indicate birth status.

b. V codes use in any healthcare setting

V codes are for use in any healthcare setting. V codes may be used as either a first listed (principal diagnosis code in the inpatient setting) or secondary code, depending on the circumstances of the encounter. Certain V codes may only be used as first listed, others only as secondary codes.

See Section I.C.18.e, V Codes That May Only be Principal/First-Listed Diagnosis.

c. V Codes indicate a reason for an encounter

They are not procedure codes. A corresponding procedure code must accompany a V code to describe the procedure performed.

d. Categories of V Codes

1) Contact/Exposure

Category V01 indicates contact with or exposure to communicable diseases. These codes are for patients who do not show any sign or symptom of a disease but have been exposed to it by close personal contact with an infected individual or are in an area where a disease is epidemic. These codes may be used as a first listed code to explain an encounter for testing, or, more commonly, as a secondary code to identify a potential risk.

Codes V15.84 – V15.86 describe contact with or (suspected) exposure to asbestos, potentially hazardous body fluids, and lead.

Subcategories V87.0 – V87.3 describe contact with or (suspected) exposure to hazardous metals, aromatic compounds, other potentially hazardous chemicals, and other potentially hazardous substances.

2) Inoculations and vaccinations

Categories V03-V06 are for encounters for inoculations and vaccinations. They indicate that a patient is being seen to receive a prophylactic inoculation against a disease. The injection itself must be represented by the appropriate procedure code. A code from V03-V06 may be used as a

secondary code if the inoculation is given as a routine part of preventive health care, such as a well-baby visit.

3) Status

Status codes indicate that a patient is a carrier of a disease, has the sequelae or residual of a past disease or condition, or has another factor influencing a person's health status. This includes such things as the presence of prosthetic or mechanical devices resulting from past treatment. A status code is informative, because the status may affect the course of treatment and its outcome. A status code is distinct from a history code. The history code indicates that the patient no longer has the condition.

A status code should not be used with a diagnosis code from one of the body system chapters, if the diagnosis code includes the information provided by the status code. For example, code V42.1, Heart transplant status, should not be used with code 996.83, Complications of transplanted heart. The status code does not provide additional information. The complication code indicates that the patient is a heart transplant patient.

The status V codes/categories are:

V02   Carrier or suspected carrier of infectious diseases

Carrier status indicates that a person harbors the specific organisms of a disease without manifest symptoms and is capable of transmitting the infection.

V07.5x   Use of agents affecting estrogen receptors and estrogen level

This code indicates when a patient is receiving a drug that affects estrogen receptors and estrogen levels for prevention of cancer.

V08   Asymptomatic HIV infection status

This code indicates that a patient has tested positive for HIV but has manifested no signs or symptoms of the disease.

V09   Infection with drug-resistant microorganisms

This category indicates that a patient has an infection that is resistant to drug treatment. Sequence the infection code first.

V21   Constitutional states in development

V22.2   Pregnant state, incidental

This code is a secondary code only for use when the pregnancy is in no way complicating the reason for visit. Otherwise, a code from the obstetric chapter is required.

V26.5x   Sterilization status

V42   Organ or tissue replaced by transplant

V43   Organ or tissue replaced by other means

V44   Artificial opening status

V45   Other postsurgical states

Assign code V45.87, Transplant organ removal status, to indicate that a transplanted organ has been previously removed. This code should not be assigned for the encounter in which the transplanted organ is removed. The complication necessitating removal of the transplant organ should be assigned for that encounter.

See section I.C17.f.2. for information on the coding of organ transplant complications.

Assign code V45.88, Status post administration of tPA (rtPA) in a different facility within the last 24 hours prior to admission to the current facility, as a secondary diagnosis when a patient is received by transfer into a facility and documentation indicates they were administered tissue plasminogen activator (tPA) within the last 24 hours prior to admission to the current facility.

This guideline applies even if the patient is still receiving the tPA at the time they are received into the current facility.

The appropriate code for the condition for which the tPA was administered (such as cerebrovascular disease or myocardial infarction) should be assigned first.

Code V45.88 is only applicable to the receiving facility record and not to the transferring facility record.

V46   Other dependence on machines

V49.6   Upper limb amputation status

V49.7   Lower limb amputation status

Note: Categories V42-V46, and subcategories V49.6, V49.7 are for use only if there are no complications or malfunctions of the organ or tissue replaced, the amputation site or the equipment on which the patient is dependent.

V49.81   Asymptomatic postmenopausal status (age-related) (natural)

V49.82   Dental sealant status

V49.83   Awaiting organ transplant status

V49.86   Do not resuscitate status

This code may be used when it is documented by the provider that a patient is on do not resuscitate status at any time during the stay.

V49.87   Physical restraint status

This code may be used when it is documented by the provider that a patient has been put in restraints during the current encounter. Please note that this code should not be reported when it is documented by the provider that a patient is temporarily restrained during a procedure.

V58.6x   Long-term (current) drug use

Codes from this subcategory indicate a patient's continuous use of a prescribed drug (including such things as aspirin therapy) for the long-term treatment of a condition or for prophylactic use. It is not for use for patients who have addictions to drugs. This subcategory is not for use of medications for detoxification or maintenance programs to prevent withdrawal symptoms in patients with drug dependence (e.g., methadone maintenance for opiate dependence). Assign the appropriate code for the drug dependence instead.

Assign a code from subcategory V58.6, Long-term (current) drug use, if the patient is receiving a medication for an extended period as a prophylactic measure (such as for the prevention of deep vein thrombosis) or as treatment of a chronic condition (such as arthritis) or a disease requiring a lengthy course of treatment (such as cancer). Do not assign a code from subcategory V58.6 for medication being administered for a brief period of time to treat an acute illness or injury (such as a course of antibiotics to treat acute bronchitis).

V83   Genetic carrier status

Genetic carrier status indicates that a person carries a gene, associated with a particular disease, which may be passed to offspring who may develop that disease. The person does not have the disease and is not at risk of developing the disease.

V84   Genetic susceptibility status

Genetic susceptibility indicates that a person has a gene that increases the risk of that person developing the disease.

Codes from category V84, Genetic susceptibility to disease, should not be used as principal or first-listed codes. If the patient has the condition to which he/she is susceptible, and that condition is

the reason for the encounter, the code for the current condition should be sequenced first. If the patient is being seen for follow-up after completed treatment for this condition, and the condition no longer exists, a follow-up code should be sequenced first, followed by the appropriate personal history and genetic susceptibility codes. If the purpose of the encounter is genetic counseling associated with procreative management, a code from subcategory V26.3, Genetic counseling and testing, should be assigned as the first-listed code, followed by a code from category V84. Additional codes should be assigned for any applicable family or personal history.

See Section I.C. 18.d.14 for information on prophylactic organ removal due to a genetic susceptibility.

V85	Body Mass Index (BMI)
V86	Estrogen receptor status
V88	Acquired absence of other organs and tissue
V90	Retained foreign body

4) History (of)

There are two types of history V codes, personal and family. Personal history codes explain a patient's past medical condition that no longer exists and is not receiving any treatment, but that has the potential for recurrence, and therefore may require continued monitoring. The exceptions to this general rule are category V14, Personal history of allergy to medicinal agents, and subcategory V15.0, Allergy, other than to medicinal agents. A person who has had an allergic episode to a substance or food in the past should always be considered allergic to the substance.

Family history codes are for use when a patient has a family member(s) who has had a particular disease that causes the patient to be at higher risk of also contracting the disease.

Personal history codes may be used in conjunction with follow-up codes and family history codes may be used in conjunction with screening codes to explain the need for a test or procedure. History codes are also acceptable on any medical record regardless of the reason for visit. A history of an illness, even if no longer present, is important information that may alter the type of treatment ordered.

The history V code categories are:

V10	Personal history of malignant neoplasm
V12	Personal history of certain other diseases
V13	Personal history of other diseases

Except: V13.4, Personal history of arthritis, and subcategory V13.6, Personal history of congenital (corrected) malformations. These conditions are life-long so are not true history codes.

V14	Personal history of allergy to medicinal agents
V15	Other personal history presenting hazards to health

Except: Codes V15.7, Personal history of contraception; V15.84, Contact with and (suspected) exposure to asbestos; V15.85, Contact with and (suspected) exposure to potentially hazardous body fluids; V15.86, Contact with and (suspected) exposure to lead.

V16	Family history of malignant neoplasm
V17	Family history of certain chronic disabling diseases
V18	Family history of certain other specific diseases
V19	Family history of other conditions
V87	Other specified personal exposures and history presenting hazards to health

Except: Subcategories V87.0, Contact with and (suspected) exposure to hazardous metals; V87.1, Contact with and (suspected) exposure to hazardous aromatic compounds; V87.2, Contact with and (suspected) exposure to other potentially

hazardous chemicals; and V87.3, Contact with and (suspected) exposure to other potentially hazardous substances.

5) Screening

Screening is the testing for disease or disease precursors in seemingly well individuals so that early detection and treatment can be provided for those who test positive for the disease. Screenings that are recommended for many subgroups in a population include: routine mammograms for women over 40, a fecal occult blood test for everyone over 50, an amniocentesis to rule out a fetal anomaly for pregnant women over 35, because the incidence of breast cancer and colon cancer in these subgroups is higher than in the general population, as is the incidence of Down's syndrome in older mothers.

The testing of a person to rule out or confirm a suspected diagnosis because the patient has some sign or symptom is a diagnostic examination, not a screening. In these cases, the sign or symptom is used to explain the reason for the test.

A screening code may be a first listed code if the reason for the visit is specifically the screening exam. It may also be used as an additional code if the screening is done during an office visit for other health problems. A screening code is not necessary if the screening is inherent to a routine examination, such as a pap smear done during a routine pelvic examination.

Should a condition be discovered during the screening then the code for the condition may be assigned as an additional diagnosis.

The V code indicates that a screening exam is planned. A procedure code is required to confirm that the screening was performed.

The screening V code categories:

V28	Antenatal screening
V73-V82	Special screening examinations

6) Observation

There are three observation V code categories. They are for use in very limited circumstances when a person is being observed for a suspected condition that is ruled out. The observation codes are not for use if an injury or illness or any signs or symptoms related to the suspected condition are present. In such cases the diagnosis/symptom code is used with the corresponding E code to identify any external cause. The observation codes are to be used as principal diagnosis only. The only exception to this is when the principal diagnosis is required to be a code from the V30, Live born infant, category. Then the V29 observation code is sequenced after the V30 code. Additional codes may be used in addition to the observation code but only if they are unrelated to the suspected condition being observed.

Codes from subcategory V89.0, Suspected maternal and fetal conditions not found, may either be used as a first listed or as an additional code assignment depending on the case. They are for use in very limited circumstances on a maternal record when an encounter is for a suspected maternal or fetal condition that is ruled out during that encounter (for example, a maternal or fetal condition may be suspected due to an abnormal test result). These codes should not be used when the condition is confirmed. In those cases, the confirmed condition should be coded. In addition, these codes are not for use if an illness or any signs or symptoms related to the suspected condition or problem are present. In such cases the diagnosis/symptom code is used.

Additional codes may be used in addition to the code from subcategory V89.0, but only if they are unrelated to the suspected condition being evaluated.

Codes from subcategory V89.0 may not be used for encounters for antenatal screening of mother. *See Section I.C.18.d., Screening.*

For encounters for suspected fetal condition that are inconclusive following testing and evaluation, assign the appropriate code from category 655, 656, 657 or 658.

The observation V code categories:

V29   Observation and evaluation of newborns for suspected condition not found

For the birth encounter, a code from category V30 should be sequenced before the V29 code.

V71   Observation and evaluation for suspected condition not found

V89   Suspected maternal and fetal conditions not found

7)   Aftercare

Aftercare visit codes cover situations when the initial treatment of a disease or injury has been performed and the patient requires continued care during the healing or recovery phase, or for the long-term consequences of the disease. The aftercare V code should not be used if treatment is directed at a current, acute disease or injury. The diagnosis code is to be used in these cases. Exceptions to this rule are codes V58.0, Radiotherapy, and codes from subcategory V58.1, Encounter for chemotherapy and immunotherapy for neoplastic conditions. These codes are to be first listed, followed by the diagnosis code when a patient's encounter is solely to receive radiation therapy or chemotherapy for the treatment of a neoplasm. Should a patient receive both chemotherapy and radiation therapy during the same encounter code V58.0 and V58.1 may be used together on a record with either one being sequenced first.

The aftercare codes are generally first listed to explain the specific reason for the encounter. An aftercare code may be used as an additional code when some type of aftercare is provided in addition to the reason for admission and no diagnosis code is applicable. An example of this would be the closure of a colostomy during an encounter for treatment of another condition.

Aftercare codes should be used in conjunction with any other aftercare codes or other diagnosis codes to provide better detail on the specifics of an aftercare encounter visit, unless otherwise directed by the classification. The sequencing of multiple aftercare codes is discretionary.

Certain aftercare V code categories need a secondary diagnosis code to describe the resolving condition or sequelae, for others, the condition is inherent in the code title.

Additional V code aftercare category terms include fitting and adjustment, and attention to artificial openings.

Status V codes may be used with aftercare V codes to indicate the nature of the aftercare. For example code V45.81, Aortocoronary bypass status, may be used with code V58.73, Aftercare following surgery of the circulatory system, NEC, to indicate the surgery for which the aftercare is being performed. Also, a transplant status code may be used following code V58.44, Aftercare following organ transplant, to identify the organ transplanted. A status code should not be used when the aftercare code indicates the type of status, such as using V55.0, Attention to tracheostomy with V44.0, Tracheostomy status.

See Section I. B.16 Admissions/Encounter for Rehabilitation

The aftercare V category/codes:

V51.0   Encounter for breast reconstruction following mastectomy

V52   Fitting and adjustment of prosthetic device and implant

V53   Fitting and adjustment of other device

V54   Other orthopedic aftercare

V55   Attention to artificial openings

V56   Encounter for dialysis and dialysis catheter care

V57   Care involving the use of rehabilitation procedures

V58.0   Radiotherapy

V58.11   Encounter for antineoplastic chemotherapy

V58.12   Encounter for antineoplastic immunotherapy

V58.3x   Attention to dressings and sutures

V58.41   Encounter for planned post-operative wound closure

V58.42   Aftercare, surgery, neoplasm

V58.43   Aftercare, surgery, trauma

V58.44   Aftercare involving organ transplant

V58.49   Other specified aftercare following surgery

V58.7x   Aftercare following surgery

V58.81   Fitting and adjustment of vascular catheter

V58.82   Fitting and adjustment of non-vascular catheter

V58.83   Monitoring therapeutic drug

V58.89   Other specified aftercare

8)   Follow-up

The follow-up codes are used to explain continuing surveillance following completed treatment of a disease, condition, or injury. They imply that the condition has been fully treated and no longer exists. They should not be confused with aftercare codes that explain current treatment for a healing condition or its sequelae. Follow-up codes may be used in conjunction with history codes to provide the full picture of the healed condition and its treatment. The follow-up code is sequenced first, followed by the history code.

A follow-up code may be used to explain repeated visits. Should a condition be found to have recurred on the follow-up visit, then the diagnosis code should be used in place of the follow-up code.

The follow-up V code categories:

V24   Postpartum care and evaluation

V67   Follow-up examination

9)   Donor

Category V59 is the donor codes. They are used for living individuals who are donating blood or other body tissue. These codes are only for individuals donating for others, not for self donations. They are not for use to identify cadaveric donations.

10)   Counseling

Counseling V codes are used when a patient or family member receives assistance in the aftermath of an illness or injury, or when support is required in coping with family or social problems. They are not necessary for use in conjunction with a diagnosis code when the counseling component of care is considered integral to standard treatment.

The counseling V categories/codes:

V25.0   General counseling and advice for contraceptive management

V26.3   Genetic counseling

V26.4   General counseling and advice for procreative management

V61.x   Other family circumstances

V65.1   Person consulted on behalf of another person

V65.3   Dietary surveillance and counseling

V65.4   Other counseling, not elsewhere classified

11)   Obstetrics and related conditions

See Section I.C.11., the Obstetrics guidelines for further instruction on the use of these codes.

V codes for pregnancy are for use in those circumstances when none of the problems or complications included in the codes from the Obstetrics chapter exist (a routine prenatal visit or postpartum care). Codes V22.0, Supervision of normal first pregnancy, and V22.1, Supervision of other

normal pregnancy, are always first listed and are not to be used with any other code from the OB chapter.

The outcome of delivery, category V27, should be included on all maternal delivery records. It is always a secondary code.

V codes for family planning (contraceptive) or procreative management and counseling should be included on an obstetric record either during the pregnancy or the postpartum stage, if applicable.

Obstetrics and related conditions V code categories:

V22	Normal pregnancy
V23	Supervision of high-risk pregnancy
	Except: V23.2, Pregnancy with history of abortion. Code 646.3, Recurrent pregnancy loss, from the OB chapter is required to indicate a history of abortion during a pregnancy.
V24	Postpartum care and evaluation
V25	Encounter for contraceptive management
	Except V25.0x
	(See Section I.C.18.d.11, Counseling)
V26	Procreative management
	Except: V26.5x, Sterilization status, V26.3 and V26.4
	(See Section I.C.18.d.11., Counseling)
V27	Outcome of delivery
V28	Antenatal screening
	(See Section I.C.18.d.6., Screening)
V91	Multiple gestation placenta status

12) Newborn, infant and child

See Section I.C.15, the Newborn guidelines for further instruction on the use of these codes.

Newborn V code categories:

V20	Health supervision of infant or child
V29	Observation and evaluation of newborns for suspected condition not found
	(See Section I.C.18.d.7, Observation)
V30-V39	Liveborn infant according to type of birth

13) Routine and administrative examinations

The V codes allow for the description of encounters for routine examinations, such as, a general check-up, or examinations for administrative purposes, such as a pre-employment physical. The codes are not to be used if the examination is for diagnosis of a suspected condition or for treatment purposes. In such cases the diagnosis code is used. During a routine exam, should a diagnosis or condition be discovered, it should be coded as an additional code. Pre-existing and chronic conditions and history codes may also be included as additional codes as long as the examination is for administrative purposes and not focused on any particular condition.

Pre-operative examination and pre-procedural laboratory examination V codes are for use only in those situations when a patient is being cleared for a procedure or surgery and no treatment is given.

The V codes categories/code for routine and administrative examinations:

V20.2	Routine infant or child health check
	Any injections given should have a corresponding procedure code.
V70	General medical examination
V72	Special investigations and examinations
	Codes V72.5 and V72.62 may be used if the reason for the patient encounter is for routine laboratory/radiology testing in the absence of any signs, symptoms, or associated diagnosis. If routine testing is performed during the same encounter as

a test to evaluate a sign, symptom, or diagnosis, it is appropriate to assign both the V code and the code describing the reason for the non-routine test.

14) Miscellaneous V codes

The miscellaneous V codes capture a number of other health care encounters that do not fall into one of the other categories. Certain of these codes identify the reason for the encounter, others are for use as additional codes that provide useful information on circumstances that may affect a patient's care and treatment.

Prophylactic Organ Removal

For encounters specifically for prophylactic removal of breasts, ovaries, or another organ due to a genetic susceptibility to cancer or a family history of cancer, the principal or first listed code should be a code from subcategory V50.4, Prophylactic organ removal, followed by the appropriate genetic susceptibility code and the appropriate family history code.

If the patient has a malignancy of one site and is having prophylactic removal at another site to prevent either a new primary malignancy or metastatic disease, a code for the malignancy should also be assigned in addition to a code from subcategory V50.4. A V50.4 code should not be assigned if the patient is having organ removal for treatment of a malignancy, such as the removal of the testes for the treatment of prostate cancer.

Miscellaneous V code categories/codes:

V07	Need for isolation and other prophylactic or treatment measures
	Except V07.5X, Use of agents affecting estrogen receptors and estrogen levels
V40.31	Wandering in diseases classified elsewhere
V50	Elective surgery for purposes other than remedying health states
V58.5	Orthodontics
V60	Housing, household, and economic circumstances
V62	Other psychosocial circumstances
V63	Unavailability of other medical facilities for care
V64	Persons encountering health services for specific procedures, not carried out
V66	Convalescence and Palliative Care
V68	Encounters for administrative purposes
V69	Problems related to lifestyle

15) Nonspecific V codes

Certain V codes are so non-specific, or potentially redundant with other codes in the classification, that there can be little justification for their use in the inpatient setting. Their use in the outpatient setting should be limited to those instances when there is no further documentation to permit more precise coding. Otherwise, any sign or symptom or any other reason for visit that is captured in another code should be used.

Nonspecific V code categories/codes:

V11	Personal history of mental disorder
	A code from the mental disorders chapter, with an in remission fifth-digit, should be used.
V13.4	Personal history of arthritis
V13.6	Personal history of congenital malformations
V15.7	Personal history of contraception
V23.2	Pregnancy with history of abortion
V40	Mental and behavioral problems
	Exception: V40.31 Wandering in diseases classified elsewhere
V41	Problems with special senses and other special functions
V47	Other problems with internal organs

V48	Problems with head, neck, and trunk
V49	Problems with limbs and other problems
	Exceptions:
V49.6	Upper limb amputation status
V49.7	Lower limb amputation status
V49.81	Asymptomatic postmenopausal status (age-related) (natural)
V49.82	Dental sealant status
V49.83	Awaiting organ transplant status
V49.86	Do not resuscitate status
V49.87	Physical restraints status
V51.8	Other aftercare involving the use of plastic surgery
V58.2	Blood transfusion, without reported diagnosis
V58.9	Unspecified aftercare
	See Section IV.K. and Section IV.L. of the Outpatient guidelines.

e. V Codes That May Only be Principal/First-Listed Diagnosis

The list of V codes/categories below may only be reported as the principal/first-listed diagnosis, except when there are multiple encounters on the same day and the medical records for the encounters are combined or when there is more than one V code that meets the definition of principal diagnosis (e.g., a patient is admitted to home healthcare for both aftercare and rehabilitation and they equally meet the definition of principal diagnosis). These codes should not be reported if they do not meet the definition of principal or first-listed diagnosis.

See Section II and Section IV.A for information on selection of principal and first-listed diagnosis.

See Section II.C for information on two or more diagnoses that equally meet the definition for principal diagnosis.

V20.x	Health supervision of infant or child
V22.0	Supervision of normal first pregnancy
V22.1	Supervision of other normal pregnancy
V24.x	Postpartum care and examination
V26.81	Encounter for assisted reproductive fertility procedure cycle
V26.82	Encounter for fertility preservation procedure
V30.x	Single liveborn
V31.x	Twin, mate liveborn
V32.x	Twin, mate stillborn
V33.x	Twin, unspecified
V34.x	Other multiple, mates all liveborn
V35.x	Other multiple, mates all stillborn
V36.x	Other multiple, mates live- and stillborn
V37.x	Other multiple, unspecified
V39.x	Unspecified
V46.12	Encounter for respirator dependence during power failure
V46.13	Encounter for weaning from respirator [ventilator]
V51.0	Encounter for breast reconstruction following mastectomy
V56.0	Extracorporeal dialysis
V57.x	Care involving use of rehabilitation procedures
V58.0	Radiotherapy
V58.11	Encounter for antineoplastic chemotherapy
V58.12	Encounter for antineoplastic immunotherapy
V59.x	Donors
V66.0	Convalescence and palliative care following surgery
V66.1	Convalescence and palliative care following radiotherapy
V66.2	Convalescence and palliative care following chemotherapy
V66.3	Convalescence and palliative care following psychotherapy and other treatment for mental disorder

V66.4	Convalescence and palliative care following treatment of fracture
V66.5	Convalescence and palliative care following other treatment
V66.6	Convalescence and palliative care following combined treatment
V66.9	Unspecified convalescence
V68.x	Encounters for administrative purposes
V70.0	Routine general medical examination at a health care facility
V70.1	General psychiatric examination, requested by the authority
V70.2	General psychiatric examination, other and unspecified
V70.3	Other medical examination for administrative purposes
V70.4	Examination for medicolegal reasons
V70.5	Health examination of defined subpopulations
V70.6	Health examination in population surveys
V70.8	Other specified general medical examinations
V70.9	Unspecified general medical examination
V71.x	Observation and evaluation for suspected conditions not found

19. Supplemental Classification of External Causes of Injury and Poisoning (E-codes, E000-E999)

Introduction: These guidelines are provided for those who are currently collecting E codes in order that there will be standardization in the process. If your institution plans to begin collecting E codes, these guidelines are to be applied. The use of E codes is supplemental to the application of ICD-9-CM diagnosis codes.

External causes of injury and poisoning codes (categories E000 and E800-E999) are intended to provide data for injury research and evaluation of injury prevention strategies. Activity codes (categories E001-E030) are intended to be used to describe the activity of a person seeking care for injuries as well as other health conditions, when the injury or other health condition resulted from an activity or the activity contributed to a condition. E codes capture how the injury, poisoning, or adverse effect happened (cause), the intent (unintentional or accidental; or intentional, such as suicide or assault), the person's status (e.g. civilian, military), the associated activity and the place where the event occurred.

Some major categories of E codes include:

transport accidents

poisoning and adverse effects of drugs, medicinal substances and biologicals

accidental falls

accidents caused by fire and flames

accidents due to natural and environmental factors

late effects of accidents, assaults or self injury

assaults or purposely inflicted injury

suicide or self inflicted injury

These guidelines apply for the coding and collection of E codes from records in hospitals, outpatient clinics, emergency departments, other ambulatory care settings and provider offices, and nonacute care settings, except when other specific guidelines apply.

a. General E Code Coding Guidelines

1) Used with any code in the range of 001-V91

An E code from categories E800-E999 may be used with any code in the range of 001-V91, which indicates an injury, poisoning, or adverse effect due to an external cause.

An activity E code (categories E001-E030) may be used with any code in the range of 001-V91 that indicates an injury, or other health condition that resulted from an activity, or the activity contributed to a condition.

2) Assign the appropriate E code for all initial treatments

Assign the appropriate E code for the initial encounter of an injury, poisoning, or adverse effect of drugs, not for subsequent treatment.

External cause of injury codes (E-codes) may be assigned while the acute fracture codes are still applicable.

See Section I.C.17.b.1 for coding of acute fractures.

3) Use the full range of E codes

Use the full range of E codes (E800 – E999) to completely describe the cause, the intent and the place of occurrence, if applicable, for all injuries, poisonings, and adverse effects of drugs.

See a.1.), j.), and k.) in this section for information on the use of status and activity E codes.

4) Assign as many E codes as necessary

Assign as many E codes as necessary to fully explain each cause.

5) The selection of the appropriate E code

The selection of the appropriate E code is guided by the Index to External Causes, which is located after the alphabetical index to diseases and by Inclusion and Exclusion notes in the Tabular List.

6) E code can never be a principal diagnosis

An E code can never be a principal (first listed) diagnosis.

7) External cause code(s) with systemic inflammatory response syndrome (SIRS)

An external cause code is not appropriate with a code from subcategory 995.9, unless the patient also has another condition for which an E code would be appropriate (such as an injury, poisoning, or adverse effect of drugs).

8) Multiple Cause E Code Coding Guidelines

More than one E-code is required to fully describe the external cause of an illness, injury or poisoning. The assignment of E-codes should be sequenced in the following priority:

If two or more events cause separate injuries, an E code should be assigned for each cause. The first listed E code will be selected in the following order:

E codes for child and adult abuse take priority over all other E codes.

See Section I.C.19.e., Child and Adult abuse guidelines.

E codes for terrorism events take priority over all other E codes except child and adult abuse.

E codes for cataclysmic events take priority over all other E codes except child and adult abuse and terrorism.

E codes for transport accidents take priority over all other E codes except cataclysmic events, child and adult abuse and terrorism.

Activity and external cause status codes are assigned following all causal (intent) E codes.

The first-listed E code should correspond to the cause of the most serious diagnosis due to an assault, accident, or self-harm, following the order of hierarchy listed above.

9) If the reporting format limits the number of E codes

If the reporting format limits the number of E codes that can be used in reporting clinical data, report the code for the cause/intent most related to the principal diagnosis. If the format permits capture of additional E codes, the cause/intent, including medical misadventures, of the additional events should be reported rather than the codes for place, activity or external status.

b. Place of Occurrence Guideline

Use an additional code from category E849 to indicate the Place of Occurrence. The Place of Occurrence describes the place where

the event occurred and not the patient's activity at the time of the event.

Do not use E849.9 if the place of occurrence is not stated.

c. Adverse Effects of Drugs, Medicinal and Biological Substances Guidelines

1) Do not code directly from the Table of Drugs

Do not code directly from the Table of Drugs and Chemicals. Always refer back to the Tabular List.

2) Use as many codes as necessary to describe

Use as many codes as necessary to describe completely all drugs, medicinal or biological substances.

If the reporting format limits the number of E codes, and there are different fourth digit codes in the same three digit category, use the code for "Other specified" of that category of drugs, medicinal or biological substances. If there is no "Other specified" code in that category, use the appropriate "Unspecified" code in that category.

If the reporting format limits the number of E codes, and the codes are in different three digit categories, assign the appropriate E code for other multiple drugs and medicinal substances.

3) If the same E code would describe the causative agent

If the same E code would describe the causative agent for more than one adverse reaction, assign the code only once.

4) If two or more drugs, medicinal or biological substances

If two or more drugs, medicinal or biological substances are reported, code each individually unless the combination code is listed in the Table of Drugs and Chemicals. In that case, assign the E code for the combination.

5) When a reaction results from the interaction of a drug(s)

When a reaction results from the interaction of a drug(s) and alcohol, use poisoning codes and E codes for both.

6) Codes from the E930-E949 series

Codes from the E930-E949 series must be used to identify the causative substance for an adverse effect of drug, medicinal and biological substances, correctly prescribed and properly administered. The effect, such as tachycardia, delirium, gastrointestinal hemorrhaging, vomiting, hypokalemia, hepatitis, renal failure, or respiratory failure, is coded and followed by the appropriate code from the E930-E949 series.

d. Child and Adult Abuse Guideline

1) Intentional injury

When the cause of an injury or neglect is intentional child or adult abuse, the first listed E code should be assigned from categories E960-E968, Homicide and injury purposely inflicted by other persons, (except category E967). An E code from category E967, Child and adult battering and other maltreatment, should be added as an additional code to identify the perpetrator, if known.

2) Accidental intent

In cases of neglect when the intent is determined to be accidental E code E904.0, Abandonment or neglect of infant and helpless person, should be the first listed E code.

e. Unknown or Suspected Intent Guideline

1) If the intent (accident, self-harm, assault) of the cause of an injury or poisoning is unknown

If the intent (accident, self-harm, assault) of the cause of an injury or poisoning is unknown or unspecified, code the intent as undetermined E980-E989.

2) If the intent (accident, self-harm, assault) of the cause of an injury or poisoning is questionable

If the intent (accident, self-harm, assault) of the cause of an injury or poisoning is questionable, probable or suspected, code the intent as undetermined E980-E989.

f. **Undetermined Cause**

When the intent of an injury or poisoning is known, but the cause is unknown, use codes: E928.9, Unspecified accident, E958.9, Suicide and self-inflicted injury by unspecified means, and E968.9, Assault by unspecified means.

These E codes should rarely be used, as the documentation in the medical record, in both the inpatient outpatient and other settings, should normally provide sufficient detail to determine the cause of the injury.

g. **Late Effects of External Cause Guidelines**

1) **Late effect E codes**

Late effect E codes exist for injuries and poisonings but not for adverse effects of drugs, misadventures and surgical complications.

2) **Late effect E codes (E929, E959, E969, E977, E989, or E999.1)**

A late effect E code (E929, E959, E969, E977, E989, or E999.1) should be used with any report of a late effect or sequela resulting from a previous injury or poisoning (905-909).

3) **Late effect E code with a related current injury**

A late effect E code should never be used with a related current nature of injury code.

4) **Use of late effect E codes for subsequent visits**

Use a late effect E code for subsequent visits when a late effect of the initial injury or poisoning is being treated. There is no late effect E code for adverse effects of drugs.

Do not use a late effect E code for subsequent visits for follow-up care (e.g., to assess healing, to receive rehabilitative therapy) of the injury or poisoning when no late effect of the injury has been documented.

h. **Misadventures and Complications of Care Guidelines**

1) **Code range E870-E876**

Assign a code in the range of E870-E876 if misadventures are stated by the provider. When applying the E code guidelines pertaining to sequencing, these E codes are considered causal codes.

2) **Code range E878-E879**

Assign a code in the range of E878-E879 if the provider attributes an abnormal reaction or later complication to a surgical or medical procedure, but does not mention misadventure at the time of the procedure as the cause of the reaction.

i. **Terrorism Guidelines**

1) **Cause of injury identified by the Federal Government (FBI) as terrorism**

When the cause of an injury is identified by the Federal Government (FBI) as terrorism, the first-listed E-code should be a code from category E979, Terrorism. The definition of terrorism employed by the FBI is found at the inclusion note at E979. The terrorism E-code is the only E-code that should be assigned. Additional E codes from the assault categories should not be assigned.

2) **Cause of an injury is suspected to be the result of terrorism**

When the cause of an injury is suspected to be the result of terrorism a code from category E979 should not be assigned. Assign a code in the range of E codes based circumstances on the documentation of intent and mechanism.

3) **Code E979.9, Terrorism, secondary effects**

Assign code E979.9, Terrorism, secondary effects, for conditions occurring subsequent to the terrorist event. This code should not be assigned for conditions that are due to the initial terrorist act.

4) **Statistical tabulation of terrorism codes**

For statistical purposes these codes will be tabulated within the category for assault, expanding the current category from E960-E969 to include E979 and E999.1.

j. **Activity Code Guidelines**

Assign a code from category E001-E030 to describe the activity that caused or contributed to the injury or other health condition.

Unlike other E codes, activity E codes may be assigned to indicate a health condition (not just injuries) resulted from an activity, or the activity contributed to the condition.

The activity codes are not applicable to poisonings, adverse effects, misadventures or late effects.

Do not assign E030, Unspecified activity, if the activity is not stated.

k. **External cause status**

A code from category E000, External cause status, should be assigned whenever any other E code is assigned for an encounter, including an Activity E code, except for the events noted below. Assign a code from category E000, External cause status, to indicate the work status of the person at the time the event occurred. The status code indicates whether the event occurred during military activity, whether a non-military person was at work, whether an individual including a student or volunteer was involved in a non-work activity at the time of the causal event.

A code from E000, External cause status, should be assigned, when applicable, with other external cause codes, such as transport accidents and falls. The external cause status codes are not applicable to poisonings, adverse effects, misadventures or late effects.

Do not assign a code from category E000 if no other E codes (cause, activity) are applicable for the encounter.

Do not assign code E000.9, Unspecified external cause status, if the status is not stated.

Section II. Selection of Principal Diagnosis

The circumstances of inpatient admission always govern the selection of principal diagnosis. The principal diagnosis is defined in the Uniform Hospital Discharge Data Set (UHDDS) as "that condition established after study to be chiefly responsible for occasioning the admission of the patient to the hospital for care."

The UHDDS definitions are used by hospitals to report inpatient data elements in a standardized manner. These data elements and their definitions can be found in the July 31, 1985, Federal Register (Vol. 50, No, 147), pp. 31038-40.

Since that time the application of the UHDDS definitions has been expanded to include all non-outpatient settings (acute care, short term, long term care and psychiatric hospitals; home health agencies; rehab facilities; nursing homes, etc).

In determining principal diagnosis the coding conventions in the ICD-9-CM, Volumes I and II take precedence over these official coding guidelines.

(See Section I.A., Conventions for the ICD-9-CM)

The importance of consistent, complete documentation in the medical record cannot be overemphasized. Without such documentation the application of all coding guidelines is a difficult, if not impossible, task.

A. **Codes for symptoms, signs, and ill-defined conditions**

Codes for symptoms, signs, and ill-defined conditions from Chapter 16 are not to be used as principal diagnosis when a related definitive diagnosis has been established.

B. **Two or more interrelated conditions, each potentially meeting the definition for principal diagnosis.**

When there are two or more interrelated conditions (such as diseases in the same ICD-9-CM chapter or manifestations characteristically associated with a certain disease) potentially meeting the definition of principal diagnosis, either condition may be sequenced first, unless the circumstances of the admission, the therapy provided, the Tabular List, or the Alphabetic Index indicate otherwise.

C. Two or more diagnoses that equally meet the definition for principal diagnosis

In the unusual instance when two or more diagnoses equally meet the criteria for principal diagnosis as determined by the circumstances of admission, diagnostic workup and/or therapy provided, and the Alphabetic Index, Tabular List, or another coding guidelines does not provide sequencing direction, any one of the diagnoses may be sequenced first.

D. Two or more comparative or contrasting conditions.

In those rare instances when two or more contrasting or comparative diagnoses are documented as "either/or" (or similar terminology), they are coded as if the diagnoses were confirmed and the diagnoses are sequenced according to the circumstances of the admission. If no further determination can be made as to which diagnosis should be principal, either diagnosis may be sequenced first.

E. A symptom(s) followed by contrasting/comparative diagnoses

When a symptom(s) is followed by contrasting/comparative diagnoses, the symptom code is sequenced first. All the contrasting/comparative diagnoses should be coded as additional diagnoses.

F. Original treatment plan not carried out

Sequence as the principal diagnosis the condition, which after study occasioned the admission to the hospital, even though treatment may not have been carried out due to unforeseen circumstances.

G. Complications of surgery and other medical care

When the admission is for treatment of a complication resulting from surgery or other medical care, the complication code is sequenced as the principal diagnosis. If the complication is classified to the 996-999 series and the code lacks the necessary specificity in describing the complication, an additional code for the specific complication should be assigned.

H. Uncertain Diagnosis

If the diagnosis documented at the time of discharge is qualified as "probable", "suspected", "likely", "questionable", "possible", or "still to be ruled out", or other similar terms indicating uncertainty, code the condition as if it existed or was established. The bases for these guidelines are the diagnostic workup, arrangements for further workup or observation, and initial therapeutic approach that correspond most closely with the established diagnosis.

Note: This guideline is applicable only to inpatient admissions to short-term, acute, long-term care and psychiatric hospitals.

I. Admission from Observation Unit

1. Admission Following Medical Observation

When a patient is admitted to an observation unit for a medical condition, which either worsens or does not improve, and is subsequently admitted as an inpatient of the same hospital for this same medical condition, the principal diagnosis would be the medical condition which led to the hospital admission.

2. Admission Following Post-Operative Observation

When a patient is admitted to an observation unit to monitor a condition (or complication) that develops following outpatient surgery, and then is subsequently admitted as an inpatient of the same hospital, hospitals should apply the Uniform Hospital Discharge Data Set (UHDDS) definition of principal diagnosis as "that condition established after study to be chiefly responsible for occasioning the admission of the patient to the hospital for care."

J. Admission from Outpatient Surgery

When a patient receives surgery in the hospital's outpatient surgery department and is subsequently admitted for continuing inpatient care at the same hospital, the following guidelines should be followed in selecting the principal diagnosis for the inpatient admission:

- If the reason for the inpatient admission is a complication, assign the complication as the principal diagnosis.

- If no complication, or other condition, is documented as the reason for the inpatient admission, assign the reason for the outpatient surgery as the principal diagnosis.

- If the reason for the inpatient admission is another condition unrelated to the surgery, assign the unrelated condition as the principal diagnosis.

Section III. Reporting Additional Diagnoses
GENERAL RULES FOR OTHER (ADDITIONAL) DIAGNOSES

For reporting purposes the definition for "other diagnoses" is interpreted as additional conditions that affect patient care in terms of requiring:

clinical evaluation; or

therapeutic treatment; or

diagnostic procedures; or

extended length of hospital stay; or

increased nursing care and/or monitoring.

The UHDDS item #11-b defines Other Diagnoses as "all conditions that coexist at the time of admission, that develop subsequently, or that affect the treatment received and/or the length of stay. Diagnoses that relate to an earlier episode which have no bearing on the current hospital stay are to be excluded." UHDDS definitions apply to inpatients in acute care, short-term, long term care and psychiatric hospital setting. The UHDDS definitions are used by acute care short-term hospitals to report inpatient data elements in a standardized manner. These data elements and their definitions can be found in the July 31, 1985, Federal Register (Vol. 50, No, 147), pp. 31038-40.

Since that time the application of the UHDDS definitions has been expanded to include all non-outpatient settings (acute care, short term, long term care and psychiatric hospitals; home health agencies; rehab facilities; nursing homes, etc).

The following guidelines are to be applied in designating "other diagnoses" when neither the Alphabetic Index nor the Tabular List in ICD-9-CM provide direction. The listing of the diagnoses in the patient record is the responsibility of the attending provider.

A. Previous conditions

If the provider has included a diagnosis in the final diagnostic statement, such as the discharge summary or the face sheet, it should ordinarily be coded. Some providers include in the diagnostic statement resolved conditions or diagnoses and status-post procedures from previous admission that have no bearing on the current stay. Such conditions are not to be reported and are coded only if required by hospital policy.

However, history codes (V10-V19) may be used as secondary codes if the historical condition or family history has an impact on current care or influences treatment.

B. Abnormal findings

Abnormal findings (laboratory, x-ray, pathologic, and other diagnostic results) are not coded and reported unless the provider indicates their clinical significance. If the findings are outside the normal range and the attending provider has ordered other tests to evaluate the condition or prescribed treatment, it is appropriate to ask the provider whether the abnormal finding should be added.

Please note: This differs from the coding practices in the outpatient setting for coding encounters for diagnostic tests that have been interpreted by a provider.

C. Uncertain Diagnosis

If the diagnosis documented at the time of discharge is qualified as "probable", "suspected", "likely", "questionable", "possible", or "still to be ruled out" or other similar terms indicating uncertainty, code the condition as if it existed or was established. The bases for these guidelines are the diagnostic workup, arrangements for further workup or observation, and initial therapeutic approach that correspond most closely with the established diagnosis.

Note: This guideline is applicable only to inpatient admissions to short-term, acute, long-term care and psychiatric hospitals.

Section IV. Diagnostic Coding and Reporting Guidelines for Outpatient Services

These coding guidelines for outpatient diagnoses have been approved for use by hospitals/ providers in coding and reporting hospital-based outpatient services and provider-based office visits.

Information about the use of certain abbreviations, punctuation, symbols, and other conventions used in the ICD-9-CM Tabular List (code numbers and titles), can be found in Section IA of these guidelines, under "Conventions Used in the Tabular List." Information about the correct sequence to use in finding a code is also described in Section I.

The terms encounter and visit are often used interchangeably in describing outpatient service contacts and, therefore, appear together in these guidelines without distinguishing one from the other.

Though the conventions and general guidelines apply to all settings, coding guidelines for outpatient and provider reporting of diagnoses will vary in a number of instances from those for inpatient diagnoses, recognizing that:

The Uniform Hospital Discharge Data Set (UHDDS) definition of principal diagnosis applies only to inpatients in acute, short-term, long-term care and psychiatric hospitals.

Coding guidelines for inconclusive diagnoses (probable, suspected, rule out, etc.) were developed for inpatient reporting and do not apply to outpatients.

A. Selection of first-listed condition

In the outpatient setting, the term first-listed diagnosis is used in lieu of principal diagnosis.

In determining the first-listed diagnosis the coding conventions of ICD-9-CM, as well as the general and disease specific guidelines take precedence over the outpatient guidelines.

Diagnoses often are not established at the time of the initial encounter /visit. It may take two or more visits before the diagnosis is confirmed.

The most critical rule involves beginning the search for the correct code assignment through the Alphabetic Index. Never begin searching initially in the Tabular List as this will lead to coding errors.

1. Outpatient Surgery

When a patient presents for outpatient surgery, code the reason for the surgery as the first-listed diagnosis (reason for the encounter), even if the surgery is not performed due to a contraindication.

2. Observation Stay

When a patient is admitted for observation for a medical condition, assign a code for the medical condition as the first-listed diagnosis.

When a patient presents for outpatient surgery and develops complications requiring admission to observation, code the reason for the surgery as the first reported diagnosis (reason for the encounter), followed by codes for the complications as secondary diagnoses.

B. Codes from 001.0 through V91.99

The appropriate code or codes from 001.0 through V91.99 must be used to identify diagnoses, symptoms, conditions, problems, complaints, or other reason(s) for the encounter/visit.

C. Accurate reporting of ICD-9-CM diagnosis codes

For accurate reporting of ICD-9-CM diagnosis codes, the documentation should describe the patient's condition, using terminology which includes specific diagnoses as well as symptoms, problems, or reasons for the encounter. There are ICD-9-CM codes to describe all of these.

D. Selection of codes 001.0 through 999.9

The selection of codes 001.0 through 999.9 will frequently be used to describe the reason for the encounter. These codes are from the section of ICD-9-CM for the classification of diseases and injuries (e.g. Infectious and parasitic diseases; neoplasms; symptoms, signs, and ill-defined conditions, etc.).

E. Codes that describe symptoms and signs

Codes that describe symptoms and signs, as opposed to diagnoses, are acceptable for reporting purposes when a diagnosis has not been established (confirmed) by the provider. Chapter 16 of ICD-9-CM, Symptoms, Signs, and Ill-defined conditions (codes 780.0 - 799.9) contain many, but not all codes for symptoms.

F. Encounters for circumstances other than a disease or injury

ICD-9-CM provides codes to deal with encounters for circumstances other than a disease or injury. The Supplementary Classification of factors Influencing Health Status and Contact with Health Services (V01.0- V91.99) is provided to deal with occasions when circumstances other than a disease or injury are recorded as diagnosis or problems. *See Section I.C. 18 for information on V-codes.*

G. Level of Detail in Coding

1. ICD-9-CM codes with 3, 4, or 5 digits

ICD-9-CM is composed of codes with either 3, 4, or 5 digits. Codes with three digits are included in ICD-9-CM as the heading of a category of codes that may be further subdivided by the use of fourth and/or fifth digits, which provide greater specificity.

2. Use of full number of digits required for a code

A three-digit code is to be used only if it is not further subdivided. Where fourth-digit subcategories and/or fifth-digit subclassifications are provided, they must be assigned. A code is invalid if it has not been coded to the full number of digits required for that code.

See also discussion under Section I.b.3., General Coding Guidelines, Level of Detail in Coding.

H. ICD-9-CM code for the diagnosis, condition, problem, or other reason for encounter/visit

List first the ICD-9-CM code for the diagnosis, condition, problem, or other reason for encounter/visit shown in the medical record to be chiefly responsible for the services provided. List additional codes that describe any coexisting conditions. In some cases the first-listed diagnosis may be a symptom when a diagnosis has not been established (confirmed) by the physician.

I. Uncertain diagnosis

Do not code diagnoses documented as "probable", "suspected," "questionable," "rule out," or "working diagnosis" or other similar terms indicating uncertainty. Rather, code the condition(s) to the highest degree of certainty for that encounter/visit, such as symptoms, signs, abnormal test results, or other reason for the visit.

Please note: This differs from the coding practices used by short-term, acute care, long-term care and psychiatric hospitals.

J. Chronic diseases

Chronic diseases treated on an ongoing basis may be coded and reported as many times as the patient receives treatment and care for the condition(s)

K. Code all documented conditions that coexist

Code all documented conditions that coexist at the time of the encounter/visit, and require or affect patient care treatment or management. Do not code conditions that were previously treated and no longer exist. However, history codes (V10-V19) may be used as secondary codes if the historical condition or family history has an impact on current care or influences treatment.

L. Patients receiving diagnostic services only

For patients receiving diagnostic services only during an encounter/visit, sequence first the diagnosis, condition, problem, or other reason for encounter/visit shown in the medical record to be chiefly responsible for the outpatient services provided during the encounter/visit. Codes for other diagnoses (e.g., chronic conditions) may be sequenced as additional diagnoses.

For encounters for routine laboratory/radiology testing in the absence of any signs, symptoms, or associated diagnosis, assign V72.5 and/or a code from subcategory V72.6. If routine testing is performed during the same encounter as a test to evaluate a sign, symptom, or diagnosis, it is appropriate to assign both the V code and the code describing the reason for the non-routine test.

For outpatient encounters for diagnostic tests that have been interpreted by a physician, and the final report is available at the time of coding, code any confirmed or definitive diagnosis(es) documented in the interpretation. Do not code related signs and symptoms as additional diagnoses.

Please note: This differs from the coding practice in the hospital inpatient setting regarding abnormal findings on test results.

M. Patients receiving therapeutic services only

For patients receiving therapeutic services only during an encounter/visit, sequence first the diagnosis, condition, problem, or other reason for encounter/visit shown in the medical record to be chiefly responsible for the outpatient services provided during the encounter/visit. Codes for other diagnoses (e.g., chronic conditions) may be sequenced as additional diagnoses.

The only exception to this rule is that when the primary reason for the admission/encounter is chemotherapy, radiation therapy, or rehabilitation, the appropriate V code for the service is listed first, and the diagnosis or problem for which the service is being performed listed second.

N. Patients receiving preoperative evaluations only

For patients receiving preoperative evaluations only, sequence first a code from category V72.8, Other specified examinations, to describe the pre-op consultations. Assign a code for the condition to describe the reason for the surgery as an additional diagnosis. Code also any findings related to the pre-op evaluation.

O. Ambulatory surgery

For ambulatory surgery, code the diagnosis for which the surgery was performed. If the postoperative diagnosis is known to be different from the preoperative diagnosis at the time the diagnosis is confirmed, select the postoperative diagnosis for coding, since it is the most definitive.

P. Routine outpatient prenatal visits

For routine outpatient prenatal visits when no complications are present, codes V22.0, Supervision of normal first pregnancy, or V22.1, Supervision of other normal pregnancy, should be used as the principal diagnosis. These codes should not be used in conjunction with chapter 11 codes.

APPENDIX I. PRESENT ON ADMISSION REPORTING GUIDELINES

Introduction

These guidelines are to be used as a supplement to the *ICD-9-CM Official Guidelines for Coding and Reporting* to facilitate the assignment of the Present on Admission (POA) indicator for each diagnosis and external cause of injury code reported on claim forms (UB-04 and 837 Institutional).

These guidelines are not intended to replace any guidelines in the main body of the *ICD-9-CM Official Guidelines for Coding and Reporting*. The POA guidelines are not intended to provide guidance on when a condition should be coded, but rather, how to apply the POA indicator to the final set of diagnosis codes that have been assigned in accordance with Sections I, II, and III of the official coding guidelines. Subsequent to the assignment of the ICD-9-CM codes, the POA indicator should then be assigned to those conditions that have been coded.

As stated in the Introduction to the ICD-9-CM Official Guidelines for Coding and Reporting, a joint effort between the healthcare provider and the coder is essential to achieve complete and accurate documentation, code assignment, and reporting of diagnoses and procedures. The importance of consistent, complete documentation in the medical record cannot be overemphasized. Medical record documentation from any provider involved in the care and treatment of the patient may be used to support the determination of whether a condition was present on admission or not. In the context of the official coding guidelines, the term "provider" means a physician or any qualified healthcare practitioner who is legally accountable for establishing the patient's diagnosis.

These guidelines are not a substitute for the provider's clinical judgment as to the determination of whether a condition was/was not present on admission. The provider should be queried regarding issues related to the linking of signs/symptoms, timing of test results, and the timing of findings.

General Reporting Requirements

All claims involving inpatient admissions to general acute care hospitals or other facilities that are subject to a law or regulation mandating collection of present on admission information.

Present on admission is defined as present at the time the order for inpatient admission occurs -- conditions that develop during an outpatient encounter, including emergency department, observation, or outpatient surgery, are considered as present on admission.

POA indicator is assigned to principal and secondary diagnoses (as defined in Section II of the Official Guidelines for Coding and Reporting) and the external cause of injury codes.

Issues related to inconsistent, missing, conflicting or unclear documentation must still be resolved by the provider.

If a condition would not be coded and reported based on UHDDS definitions and current official coding guidelines, then the POA indicator would not be reported.

Reporting Options

Y - Yes

N - No

U - Unknown

W – Clinically undetermined

Unreported/Not used (or "1" for Medicare usage) – (Exempt from POA reporting)

Reporting Definitions

Y = present at the time of inpatient admission

N = not present at the time of inpatient admission

U = documentation is insufficient to determine if condition is present on admission

W = provider is unable to clinically determine whether condition was present on admission or not

Timeframe for POA Identification and Documentation

There is no required timeframe as to when a provider (per the definition of "provider" used in these guidelines) must identify or document a condition to be present on admission. In some clinical situations, it may not be possible for a provider to make a definitive diagnosis (or a condition may not be recognized or reported by the patient) for a period of time after admission. In some cases it may be several days before the provider arrives at a definitive diagnosis. This does not mean that the condition was not present on admission. Determination of whether the condition was present on admission or not will be based on the applicable POA guideline as identified in this document, or on the provider's best clinical judgment.

If at the time of code assignment the documentation is unclear as to whether a condition was present on admission or not, it is appropriate to query the provider for clarification.

ASSIGNING THE POA INDICATOR

Condition is on the "Exempt from Reporting" list

Leave the "present on admission" field blank if the condition is on the list of ICD-9-CM codes for which this field is not applicable. This is the only circumstance in which the field maybe left blank.

POA explicitly documented

Assign Y for any condition the provider explicitly documents as being present on admission.

Assign N for any condition the provider explicitly documents as not present at the time of admission.

Conditions diagnosed prior to inpatient admission

Assign "Y" for conditions that were diagnosed prior to admission (example: hypertension, diabetes mellitus, asthma)

Conditions diagnosed during the admission but clearly present before admission

Assign "Y" for conditions diagnosed during the admission that were clearly present but not diagnosed until after admission occurred.

Diagnoses subsequently confirmed after admission are considered present on admission if at the time of admission they are documented as suspected, possible, rule out, differential diagnosis, or constitute an underlying cause of a symptom that is present at the time of admission.

Condition develops during outpatient encounter prior to inpatient admission

Assign Y for any condition that develops during an outpatient encounter prior to a written order for inpatient admission.

Documentation does not indicate whether condition was present on admission

Assign "U" when the medical record documentation is unclear as to whether the condition was present on admission. "U" should not be routinely assigned and used only in very limited circumstances. Coders are encouraged to query the providers when the documentation is unclear.

Documentation states that it cannot be determined whether the condition was or was not present on admission

Assign "W" when the medical record documentation indicates that it cannot be clinically determined whether or not the condition was present on admission.

Chronic condition with acute exacerbation during the admission

If the code is a combination code that identifies both the chronic condition and the acute exacerbation, see POA guidelines pertaining to combination codes.

If the combination code only identifies the chronic condition and not the acute exacerbation (e.g., acute exacerbation of chronic leukemia), assign "Y."

Conditions documented as possible, probable, suspected, or rule out at the time of discharge

If the final diagnosis contains a possible, probable, suspected, or rule out diagnosis, and this diagnosis was based on signs, symptoms or clinical findings suspected at the time of inpatient admission, assign "Y."

If the final diagnosis contains a possible, probable, suspected, or rule out diagnosis, and this diagnosis was based on signs, symptoms or clinical findings that were not present on admission, assign "N".

Conditions documented as impending or threatened at the time of discharge

If the final diagnosis contains an impending or threatened diagnosis, and this diagnosis is based on symptoms or clinical findings that were present on admission, assign "Y".

If the final diagnosis contains an impending or threatened diagnosis, and this diagnosis is based on symptoms or clinical findings that were not present on admission, assign "N".

Acute and chronic conditions

Assign "Y" for acute conditions that are present at time of admission and N for acute conditions that are not present at time of admission.

Assign "Y" for chronic conditions, even though the condition may not be diagnosed until after admission.

If a single code identifies both an acute and chronic condition, see the POA guidelines for combination codes.

Combination codes

Assign "N" if any part of the combination code was not present on admission (e.g., obstructive chronic bronchitis with acute exacerbation and the exacerbation was not present on admission; gastric ulcer that does not start bleeding until after admission; asthma patient develops status asthmaticus after admission)

Assign "Y" if all parts of the combination code were present on admission (e.g., patient with diabetic nephropathy is admitted with uncontrolled diabetes).

If the final diagnosis includes comparative or contrasting diagnoses, and both were present, or suspected, at the time of admission, assign "Y".

For infection codes that include the causal organism, assign "Y" if the infection (or signs of the infection) was present on admission, even though the culture results may not be known until after admission (e.g., patient is admitted with pneumonia and the provider documents pseudomonas as the causal organism a few days later).

Same diagnosis code for two or more conditions

When the same ICD-9-CM diagnosis code applies to two or more conditions during the same encounter (e.g. bilateral condition, or two separate conditions classified to the same ICD-9-CM diagnosis code):

Assign "Y" if all conditions represented by the single ICD-9-CM code were present on admission (e.g. bilateral fracture of the same bone, same site, and both fractures were present on admission)

Assign "N" if any of the conditions represented by the single ICD-9-CM code was not present on admission (e.g. dehydration with hyponatremia is assigned to code 276.1, but only one of these conditions was present on admission).

Obstetrical conditions

Whether or not the patient delivers during the current hospitalization does not affect assignment of the POA indicator. The determining factor for POA assignment is whether the pregnancy complication or obstetrical condition described by the code was present at the time of admission or not.

If the pregnancy complication or obstetrical condition was present on admission (e.g., patient admitted in preterm labor), assign "Y".

If the pregnancy complication or obstetrical condition was not present on admission (e.g., 2nd degree laceration during delivery, postpartum hemorrhage that occurred during current hospitalization, fetal distress develops after admission), assign "N".

If the obstetrical code includes more than one diagnosis and any of the diagnoses identified by the code were not present on admission assign "N". (e.g., Code 642.7, Pre-eclampsia or eclampsia superimposed on pre-existing hypertension).

If the obstetrical code includes information that is not a diagnosis, do not consider that information in the POA determination. (e.g. Code 652.1x, Breech or other malpresentation successfully converted to cephalic presentation should be reported as present on admission if the fetus was breech on admission but was converted to cephalic presentation after admission (since the conversion to cephalic presentation does not represent a diagnosis, the fact that the conversion occurred after admission has no bearing on the POA determination).

Perinatal conditions

Newborns are not considered to be admitted until after birth. Therefore, any condition present at birth or that developed in utero is considered present at admission and should be assigned "Y". This includes conditions that occur during delivery (e.g., injury during delivery, meconium aspiration, exposure to streptococcus B in the vaginal canal).

Congenital conditions and anomalies

Assign "Y" for congenital conditions and anomalies, **except for categories 740-759, Congenital anomalies, which are on the exempt list.** Congenital conditions are always considered present on admission.

External cause of injury codes

Assign "Y" for any E code representing an external cause of injury or poisoning that occurred prior to inpatient admission (e.g., patient fell out of bed at home, patient fell out of bed in emergency room prior to admission)

Assign "N" for any E code representing an external cause of injury or poisoning that occurred during inpatient hospitalization (e.g., patient fell out of hospital bed during hospital stay, patient experienced an adverse reaction to a medication administered after inpatient admission)

CATEGORIES AND CODES EXEMPT FROM DIAGNOSIS PRESENT ON ADMISSION REQUIREMENT

Note: *"Diagnosis present on admission" for these code categories are exempt because they represent circumstances regarding the healthcare encounter or factors influencing health status that do not represent a current disease or injury or are always present on admission.*

Categories or subcategories listed are inclusive of all codes within those categories or subcategories, unless otherwise indicated. In order to streamline the POA exempt list and make it easier to read, where all of the codes in a code range are POA exempt, only the code range is shown, rather than listing each of the individual codes in the range.

137-139	Late effects of infectious and parasitic diseases
268.1	Rickets, late effect
326	Late effects of intracranial abscess or pyogenic infection
412	Old myocardial infarction
438	Late effects of cerebrovascular disease
650	Normal delivery
660.7	Failed forceps or vacuum extractor, unspecified
677	Late effect of complication of pregnancy, childbirth, and the puerperium
740-759	Congenital anomalies
905-909	Late effects of injuries, poisonings, toxic effects, and other external causes
V02	Carrier or suspected carrier of infectious diseases
V03	Need for prophylactic vaccination and inoculation against bacterial diseases
V04	Need for prophylactic vaccination and inoculation against certain viral diseases
V05	Need for other prophylactic vaccination and inoculation against single diseases
V06	Need for prophylactic vaccination and inoculation against combinations of diseases
V07	Need for isolation and other prophylactic or treatment measures

V10	Personal history of malignant neoplasm
V11	Personal history of mental disorder
V12	Personal history of certain other diseases
V13	Personal history of other diseases
V14	Personal history of allergy to medicinal agents
V15	Other personal history presenting hazards to health
V16	Family history of malignant neoplasm
V17	Family history of certain chronic disabling diseases
V18	Family history of certain other specific conditions
V19	Family history of other conditions
V20	Health supervision of infant or child
V21	Constitutional states in development
V22	Normal pregnancy
V23	Supervision of high-risk pregnancy
V24	Postpartum care and examination
V25	Encounter for contraceptive management
V26	Procreative management
V27	Outcome of delivery
V28	Antenatal screening
V29	Observation and evaluation of newborns for suspected condition not found
V30-V39	Liveborn infants according to type of birth
V42	Organ or tissue replaced by transplant
V43	Organ or tissue replaced by other means
V44	Artificial opening status
V45	Other postprocedural states
V46	Other dependence on machines and devices
V49.60-V49.77	Upper and lower limb amputation status
V49.81-V49.85	Other specified conditions influencing health status
V50	Elective surgery for purposes other than remedying health states
V51	Aftercare involving the use of plastic surgery
V52	Fitting and adjustment of prosthetic device and implant
V53	Fitting and adjustment of other device
V54	Other orthopedic aftercare
V55	Attention to artificial openings
V56	Encounter for dialysis and dialysis catheter care
V57	Care involving use of rehabilitation procedures
V58	Encounter for other and unspecified procedures and aftercare
V59	Donors
V60	Housing, household, and economic circumstances
V61	Other family circumstances
V62	Other psychosocial circumstances
V64	Persons encountering health services for specific procedures, not carried out
V65	Other persons seeking consultation
V66	Convalescence and palliative care
V67	Follow-up examination
V68	Encounters for administrative purposes
V69	Problems related to lifestyle
V70	General medical examination
V71	Observation and evaluation for suspected condition not found
V72	Special investigations and examinations
V73	Special screening examination for viral and chlamydial diseases
V74	Special screening examination for bacterial and spirochetal diseases
V75	Special screening examination for other infectious diseases
V76	Special screening for malignant neoplasms
V77	Special screening for endocrine, nutritional, metabolic, and immunity disorders
V78	Special screening for disorders of blood and blood-forming organs
V79	Special screening for mental disorders and developmental handicaps
V80	Special screening for neurological, eye, and ear diseases
V81	Special screening for cardiovascular, respiratory, and genitourinary diseases
V82	Special screening for other conditions
V83	Genetic carrier status
V84	Genetic susceptibility to disease
V85	Body Mass Index
V86	Estrogen receptor status
V87.32	Contact with and (suspected) exposure to algae bloom
V87.4	Personal history of drug therapy

V88	Acquired absence of other organs and tissue
V89	Suspected maternal and fetal conditions not found
V90	Retained foreign body
V91	Multiple gestation placenta status
E000	External cause status
E001-E030	Activity
E800-E807	Railway accidents
E810-E819	Motor vehicle traffic accidents
E820-E825	Motor vehicle nontraffic accidents
E826-E829	Other road vehicle accidents
E830-E838	Water transport accidents
E840-E845	Air and space transport accidents
E846-E848	Vehicle accidents not elsewhere classifiable
E849	Place of occurrence (Except E849.7)
E883.1	Accidental fall into well
E883.2	Accidental fall into storm drain or manhole
E884.0	Fall from playground equipment
E884.1	Fall from cliff
E885.0	Fall from (nonmotorized) scooter
E885.1	Fall from roller skates
E885.2	Fall from skateboard
E885.3	Fall from skis
E885.4	Fall from snowboard
E886.0	Fall on same level from collision, pushing, or shoving, by or with other person, In sports
E890.0-E890.9	Conflagration in private dwelling
E893.0	Accident caused by ignition of clothing, from controlled fire in private dwelling
E893.2	Accident caused by ignition of clothing, from controlled fire not in building or structure
E894	Ignition of highly inflammable material
E895	Accident caused by controlled fire in private dwelling
E897	Accident caused by controlled fire not in building or structure
E917.0	Striking against or struck accidentally by objects or persons, in sports without subsequent fall
E917.1	Striking against or struck accidentally by objects or persons, caused by a crowd, by collective fear or panic without subsequent fall
E917.2	Striking against or struck accidentally by objects or persons, in running water without subsequent fall
E917.5	Striking against or struck accidentally by objects or persons, object in sports with subsequent fall
E917.6	Striking against or struck accidentally by objects or persons, caused by a crowd, by collective fear or panic with subsequent fall
E919	Accident caused by machinery (Except E919.2)
E921	Accident caused by explosion of pressure vessel
E922	Accident caused by firearm and air gun missile
E926.2	Visible and ultraviolet light sources
E928.0-E928.8	Other and unspecified environmental and accidental causes
E929.0-E929.9	Late effects of accidental injury
E959	Late effects of self-inflicted injury
E970-E978	Legal intervention
E979	Terrorism
E981	Poisoning by gases in domestic use, undetermined whether accidentally or purposely inflicted
E982	Poisoning by other gases, undetermined whether accidentally or purposely inflicted
E985	Injury by firearms, air guns and explosives, undetermined whether accidentally or purposely inflicted
E987.0	Falling from high place, undetermined whether accidentally or purposely inflicted, residential premises
E987.2	Falling from high place, undetermined whether accidentally or purposely inflicted, natural sites
E989	Late effects of injury, undetermined whether accidentally or purposely inflicted
E990-E999	Injury resulting from operations of war

A

AAT (alpha-1 antitrypsin) deficiency 273.4
AAV (disease) (illness) (infection) — *see* Human immunodeficiency virus (disease) (illness) (infection)
Abactio — *see* Abortion, induced
Abactus venter — *see* Abortion, induced
Abarognosis 781.99
Abasia (-astasia) 307.9
  atactica 781.3
  choreic 781.3
  hysterical 300.11
  paroxysmal trepidant 781.3
  spastic 781.3
  trembling 781.3
  trepidans 781.3
Abderhalden-Kaufmann-Lignac syndrome (cystinosis) 270.0
Abdomen, abdominal — *see also* condition
  accordion 306.4
  acute 789.0 ☑
  angina 557.1
  burst 868.00
  convulsive equivalent (*see also* Epilepsy) 345.5 ☑
  heart 746.87
  muscle deficiency syndrome 756.79
  obstipum 756.79
Abdominalgia 789.0 ☑
  periodic 277.31
Abduction contracture, hip or other joint — *see* Contraction, joint
Abercrombie's syndrome (amyloid degeneration) 277.39
Aberrant (congenital) — *see also* Malposition, congenital
  adrenal gland 759.1
  blood vessel NEC 747.60
    arteriovenous NEC 747.60
    cerebrovascular 747.81
    gastrointestinal 747.61
    lower limb 747.64
    renal 747.62
    spinal 747.82
    upper limb 747.63
  breast 757.6
  endocrine gland NEC 759.2
  gastrointestinal vessel (peripheral) 747.61
  hepatic duct 751.69
  lower limb vessel (peripheral) 747.64
  pancreas 751.7
  parathyroid gland 759.2
  peripheral vascular vessel NEC 747.60
  pituitary gland (pharyngeal) 759.2
  renal blood vessel 747.62
  sebaceous glands, mucous membrane, mouth 750.26
  spinal vessel 747.82
  spleen 759.0
  testis (descent) 752.51
  thymus gland 759.2
  thyroid gland 759.2
  upper limb vessel (peripheral) 747.63
Aberratio
  lactis 757.6
  testis 752.51
Aberration — *see also* Anomaly
  chromosome — *see* Anomaly, chromosome(s)
  distantial 368.9
  mental (*see also* Disorder, mental, nonpsychotic) 300.9
Abetalipoproteinemia 272.5
Abionarce 780.79
Abiotrophy 799.89
Ablatio
  placentae — *see* Placenta, ablatio
  retinae (*see also* Detachment, retina) 361.9
Ablation
  pituitary (gland) (with hypofunction) 253.7
  placenta — *see* Placenta, ablatio
  uterus 621.8
Ablepharia, ablepharon, ablephary 743.62
Ablepsia — *see* Blindness
Ablepsy — *see* Blindness

Ablutomania 300.3
Abnormal, abnormality, abnormalities — *see also* Anomaly
  acid-base balance 276.4
    fetus or newborn — *see* Distress, fetal
  adaptation curve, dark 368.63
  alveolar ridge 525.9
  amnion 658.9 ☑
    affecting fetus or newborn 762.9
  anatomical relationship NEC 759.9
  apertures, congenital, diaphragm 756.6
  auditory perception NEC 388.40
  autosomes NEC 758.5
    13 758.1
    18 758.2
    21 or 22 758.0
    D_1 758.1
    E_3 758.2
    G 758.0
  ballistocardiogram 794.39
  basal metabolic rate (BMR) 794.7
  biosynthesis, testicular androgen 257.2
  blood level (of)
    cobalt 790.6
    copper 790.6
    iron 790.6
    lead 790.6
    lithium 790.6
    magnesium 790.6
    mineral 790.6
    zinc 790.6
  blood pressure
    elevated (without diagnosis of hypertension) 796.2
    low (*see also* Hypotension) 458.9
      reading (incidental) (isolated) (nonspecific) 796.3
  blood sugar 790.29
  bowel sounds 787.5
  breathing behavior — *see* Respiration
  caloric test 794.19
  cervix (acquired) NEC 622.9
    congenital 752.40
    in pregnancy or childbirth 654.6 ☑
      causing obstructed labor 660.2 ☑
        affecting fetus or newborn 763.1
  chemistry, blood NEC 790.6
  chest sounds 786.7
  chorion 658.9 ☑
    affecting fetus or newborn 762.9
  chromosomal NEC 758.89
    analysis, nonspecific result 795.2
    autosomes (*see also* Abnormal, autosomes NEC) 758.5
    fetal, (suspected) affecting management of pregnancy 655.1 ☑
    sex 758.81
  clinical findings NEC 796.4
  communication — *see* Fistula
  configuration of pupils 379.49
  coronary
    artery 746.85
    vein 746.9
  cortisol-binding globulin 255.8
  course, Eustachian tube 744.24
  creatinine clearance 794.4
  dentofacial NEC 524.9
    functional 524.50
    specified type NEC 524.89
  development, developmental NEC 759.9
    bone 756.9
    central nervous system 742.9
  direction, teeth 524.30
  Dynia (*see also* Defect, coagulation) 286.9
  Ebstein 746.2
  echocardiogram 793.2
  echoencephalogram 794.01
  echogram NEC — *see* Findings, abnormal, structure
  electrocardiogram (ECG) (EKG) 794.31
  electroencephalogram (EEG) 794.02
  electromyogram (EMG) 794.17
    ocular 794.14
  electro-oculogram (EOG) 794.12
  electroretinogram (ERG) 794.11
  erythrocytes 289.9

Abnormal, abnormality, abnormalities — *see also* Anomaly — *continued*
  erythrocytes — *continued*
    congenital, with perinatal jaundice 282.9 [774.0]
  Eustachian valve 746.9
  excitability under minor stress 301.9
  fat distribution 782.9
  feces 787.7
  fetal heart rate — *see* Distress, fetal
  fetus NEC
    affecting management of pregnancy — *see* Pregnancy, management affected by, fetal
    causing disproportion 653.7 ☑
      affecting fetus or newborn 763.1
      causing obstructed labor 660.1 ☑
        affecting fetus or newborn 763.1
  findings without manifest disease — *see* Findings, abnormal
  fluid
    amniotic 792.3
    cerebrospinal 792.0
    peritoneal 792.9
    pleural 792.9
    synovial 792.9
    vaginal 792.9
  forces of labor NEC 661.9 ☑
    affecting fetus or newborn 763.7
  form, teeth 520.2
  function studies
    auditory 794.15
    bladder 794.9
    brain 794.00
    cardiovascular 794.30
    endocrine NEC 794.6
    kidney 794.4
    liver 794.8
    nervous system
      central 794.00
      peripheral 794.19
    oculomotor 794.14
    pancreas 794.9
    placenta 794.9
    pulmonary 794.2
    retina 794.11
    special senses 794.19
    spleen 794.9
    thyroid 794.5
    vestibular 794.16
  gait 781.2
    hysterical 300.11
  gastrin secretion 251.5
  globulin
    cortisol-binding 255.8
    thyroid-binding 246.8
  glucagon secretion 251.4
  glucose 790.29
    in pregnancy, childbirth, or puerperium 648.8 ☑
      fetus or newborn 775.0
    non-fasting 790.29
  gravitational (G) forces or states 994.9
  hair NEC 704.2
  hard tissue formation in pulp 522.3
  head movement 781.0
  heart
    rate
      fetus, affecting liveborn infant
        before the onset of labor 763.81
        during labor 763.82
        unspecified as to time of onset 763.83
      intrauterine
        before the onset of labor 763.81
        during labor 763.82
        unspecified as to time of onset 763.83
      newborn
        before the onset of labor 763.81
        during labor 763.82
        unspecified as to time of onset 763.83
    shadow 793.2
    sounds NEC 785.3

Abnormal, abnormality, abnormalities — *see also* Anomaly — *continued*
  hemoglobin (*see also* Disease, hemoglobin) 282.7
    trait — *see* Trait, hemoglobin, abnormal
  hemorrhage, uterus — *see* Hemorrhage, uterus
  histology NEC 795.4
  increase
    in
      appetite 783.6
      development 783.9
  involuntary movement 781.0
  jaw closure 524.51
  karyotype 795.2
  knee jerk 796.1
  laboratory findings — *see* Findings, abnormal
  labor NEC 661.9 ☑
    affecting fetus or newborn 763.7
  length, organ or site, congenital — *see* Distortion
  liver function test 790.6
  loss of height 781.91
  loss of weight 783.21
  lung shadow 793.19
  mammogram 793.80
    calcification 793.89
    calculus 793.89
    microcalcification 793.81
  Mantoux test 795.51
  membranes (fetal)
    affecting fetus or newborn 762.9
    complicating pregnancy 658.8 ☑
  menstruation — *see* Menstruation
  metabolism (*see also* condition) 783.9
  movement 781.0
    disorder NEC 333.90
      sleep related, unspecified 780.58
      specified NEC 333.99
    head 781.0
    involuntary 781.0
    specified type NEC 333.99
  muscle contraction, localized 728.85
  myoglobin (Aberdeen) (Annapolis) 289.9
  narrowness, eyelid 743.62
  optokinetic response 379.57
  organs or tissues of pelvis NEC
    in pregnancy or childbirth 654.9 ☑
      affecting fetus or newborn 763.89
      causing obstructed labor 660.2 ☑
        affecting fetus or newborn 763.1
  origin — *see* Malposition, congenital
  palmar creases 757.2
  Papanicolaou (smear)
    anus 796.70
      with
        atypical squamous cells
          cannot exclude high grade squamous intraepithelial lesion (ASC-H) 796.72
          of undetermined significance (ASC-US) 796.71
        cytologic evidence of malignancy 796.76
        high grade squamous intraepithelial lesion (HGSIL) 796.74
        low grade squamous intraepithelial lesion (LGSIL) 796.73
        glandular 796.70
        specified finding NEC 796.79
    cervix 795.00
      with
        atypical squamous cells
          cannot exclude high grade squamous intraepithelial lesion (ASC-H) 795.02
          of undetermined significance (ASC-US) 795.01
        cytologic evidence of malignancy 795.06
        high grade squamous intraepithelial lesion (HGSIL) 795.04

Abnormal, abnormality, abnormalities —
see also Anomaly — continued
  Papanicolaou — continued
    cervix — continued
      with — continued
        low grade squamous intraepithe-
          lial lesion (LGSIL) 795.03
      nonspecific finding NEC 795.09
    other site 796.9
    vagina 795.10
      with
        atypical squamous cells
          cannot exclude high grade
            squamous intraepithe-
            lial lesion (ASC-H)
            795.12
          of undetermined significance
            (ASC-US) 795.11
        cytologic evidence of malignancy
          795.16
        high grade squamous intraepithe-
          lial lesion (HGSIL) 795.14
        low grade squamous intraepithe-
          lial lesion (LGSIL) 795.13
    glandular 795.10
    specified finding NEC 795.19
  parturition
    affecting fetus or newborn 763.9
    mother — see Delivery, complicated
  pelvis (bony) — see Deformity, pelvis
  percussion, chest 786.7
  periods (grossly) (see also Menstruation)
    626.9
  phonocardiogram 794.39
  placenta — see Placenta, abnormal
  plantar reflex 796.1
  plasma protein — see Deficiency, plasma,
    protein
  pleural folds 748.8
  position (see also Malposition)
    gravid uterus 654.4 ☑
      causing obstructed labor 660.2 ☑
        affecting fetus or newborn 763.1
  posture NEC 781.92
  presentation (fetus) — see Presentation,
    fetus, abnormal
  product of conception NEC 631.8
  puberty — see Puberty
  pulmonary
    artery 747.39
    function, newborn 770.89
    test results 794.2
    ventilation, newborn 770.89
      hyperventilation 786.01
  pulsations in neck 785.1
  pupil reflexes 379.40
  quality of milk 676.8 ☑
  radiological examination 793.99
    abdomen NEC 793.6
    biliary tract 793.3
    breast 793.89
      mammogram NOS 793.80
      mammographic
        calcification 793.89
        calculus 793.89
        microcalcification 793.81
    gastrointestinal tract 793.4
    genitourinary organs 793.5
    head 793.0
    image test inconclusive due to excess
      body fat 793.91
    intrathoracic organ NEC 793.2
    lung (field) 793.19
    musculoskeletal system 793.7
    retroperitoneum 793.6
    skin and subcutaneous tissue 793.99
    skull 793.0
  red blood cells 790.09
    morphology 790.09
    volume 790.09
  reflex NEC 796.1
  renal function test 794.4
  respiration signs — see Respiration
  response to nerve stimulation 794.10
  retinal correspondence 368.34
  rhythm, heart (see also Arrhythmia)

Abnormal, abnormality, abnormalities —
see also Anomaly — continued
  rhythm, heart (see also Arrhythmia) — con-
    tinued
    fetus — see Distress, fetal
  saliva 792.4
  scan
    brain 794.09
    kidney 794.4
    liver 794.8
    lung 794.2
    thyroid 794.5
  secretion
    gastrin 251.5
    glucagon 251.4
  semen 792.2
  serum level (of)
    acid phosphatase 790.5
    alkaline phosphatase 790.5
    amylase 790.5
    enzymes NEC 790.5
    lipase 790.5
  shape
    cornea 743.41
    gallbladder 751.69
    gravid uterus 654.4 ☑
      affecting fetus or newborn 763.89
      causing obstructed labor 660.2 ☑
        affecting fetus or newborn 763.1
    head (see also Anomaly, skull) 756.0
    organ or site, congenital NEC — see
      Distortion
  sinus venosus 747.40
  size
    fetus, complicating delivery 653.5 ☑
      causing obstructed labor 660.1 ☑
    gallbladder 751.69
    head (see also Anomaly, skull) 756.0
    organ or site, congenital NEC — see
      Distortion
    teeth 520.2
  skin and appendages, congenital NEC 757.9
  soft parts of pelvis — see Abnormal, organs
    or tissues of pelvis
  spermatozoa 792.2
  sputum (amount) (color) (excessive) (odor)
    (purulent) 786.4
  stool NEC 787.7
    bloody 578.1
      occult 792.1
    bulky 787.7
    color (dark) (light) 792.1
    content (fat) (mucus) (pus) 792.1
    occult blood 792.1
  synchondrosis 756.9
  test results without manifest disease — see
    Findings, abnormal
  thebesian valve 746.9
  thermography — see Findings, abnormal,
    structure
  threshold, cones or rods (eye) 368.63
  thyroid-binding globulin 246.8
  thyroid product 246.8
  toxicology (findings) NEC 796.0
  tracheal cartilage (congenital) 748.3
  transport protein 273.8
  ultrasound results — see Findings, abnor-
    mal, structure
  umbilical cord
    affecting fetus or newborn 762.6
    complicating delivery 663.9 ☑
    specified NEC 663.8 ☑
  union
    cricoid cartilage and thyroid cartilage
      748.3
    larynx and trachea 748.3
    thyroid cartilage and hyoid bone 748.3
  urination NEC 788.69
    psychogenic 306.53
    stream
      intermittent 788.61
      slowing 788.62
      splitting 788.61
      weak 788.62
    urgency 788.63
  urine (constituents) NEC 791.9

Abnormal, abnormality, abnormalities —
see also Anomaly — continued
  uterine hemorrhage (see also Hemorrhage,
    uterus) 626.9
    climacteric 627.0
    postmenopausal 627.1
  vagina (acquired) (congenital)
    in pregnancy or childbirth 654.7 ☑
      affecting fetus or newborn 763.89
      causing obstructed labor 660.2 ☑
        affecting fetus or newborn 763.1
  vascular sounds 785.9
  vectorcardiogram 794.39
  visually evoked potential (VEP) 794.13
  vulva (acquired) (congenital)
    in pregnancy or childbirth 654.8 ☑
      affecting fetus or newborn 763.89
      causing obstructed labor 660.2 ☑
        affecting fetus or newborn 763.1
  weight
    gain 783.1
      of pregnancy 646.1 ☑
        with hypertension — see Tox-
          emia, of pregnancy
    loss 783.21
  x-ray examination — see Abnormal, radio-
    logical examination
Abnormally formed uterus — see Anomaly,
  uterus
Abnormity (any organ or part) — see Anomaly
ABO
  hemolytic disease 773.1
  incompatibility (due to transfusion of blood
    or blood products)
    with hemolytic transfusion reaction
      (HTR) (not specified as acute or
      delayed) 999.61
      24 hours or more after transfusion
        999.63
      acute 999.62
      delayed 999.63
      less than 24 hours after transfusion
        999.62
      unspecified time after transfusion
        999.61
    reaction 999.60
      specified NEC 999.69
Abocclusion 524.20
Abolition, language 784.69
Aborter, habitual or recurrent NEC
  without current pregnancy 629.81
  current abortion (see also Abortion, sponta-
    neous) 634.9 ☑
    affecting fetus or newborn 761.8
  observation in current pregnancy 646.3 ☑
Abortion (complete) (incomplete) (inevitable)
  (with retained products of conception)
  637.9 ☑

> *Note* — Use the following fifth-digit
> subclassification with categories
> 634–637:
>
> 0   unspecified
>
> 1   incomplete
>
> 2   complete

  with
    complication(s) (any) following previous
      abortion — see category 639 ☑
    damage to pelvic organ (laceration)
      (rupture) (tear) 637.2 ☑
    embolism (air) (amniotic fluid) (blood
      clot) (pulmonary) (pyemic) (sep-
      tic) (soap) 637.6 ☑
    genital tract and pelvic infection
      637.0 ☑
    hemorrhage, delayed or excessive
      637.1 ☑
    metabolic disorder 637.4 ☑
    renal failure (acute) 637.3 ☑
    sepsis (genital tract) (pelvic organ)
      637.0 ☑
      urinary tract 637.7 ☑
    shock (postoperative) (septic) 637.5 ☑
    specified complication NEC 637.7 ☑

Abortion — continued
  with — continued
    toxemia 637.3 ☑
    unspecified complication(s) 637.8 ☑
    urinary tract infection 637.7 ☑
  accidental — see Abortion, spontaneous
  artificial — see Abortion, induced
  attempted (failed) — see Abortion, failed
  criminal — see Abortion, illegal
  early — see Abortion, spontaneous
  elective — see Abortion, legal
  failed (legal) 638.9
    with
      damage to pelvic organ (laceration)
        (rupture) (tear) 638.2
      embolism (air) (amniotic fluid) (blood
        clot) (pulmonary) (pyemic)
        (septic) (soap) 638.6
      genital tract and pelvic infection
        638.0
      hemorrhage, delayed or excessive
        638.1
      metabolic disorder 638.4
      renal failure (acute) 638.3
      sepsis (genital tract) (pelvic organ)
        638.0
        urinary tract 638.7
      shock (postoperative) (septic) 638.5
      specified complication NEC 638.7
      toxemia 638.3
      unspecified complication(s) 638.8
      urinary tract infection 638.7
  fetal indication — see Abortion, legal
  fetus 779.6
  following threatened abortion — see Abor-
    tion, by type
  habitual or recurrent (care during pregnan-
    cy) 646.3 ☑
    with current abortion (see also Abortion,
      spontaneous) 634.9 ☑
      affecting fetus or newborn 761.8
    without current pregnancy 629.81
  homicidal — see Abortion, illegal
  illegal 636.9 ☑
    with
      damage to pelvic organ (laceration)
        (rupture) (tear) 636.2 ☑
      embolism (air) (amniotic fluid) (blood
        clot) (pulmonary) (pyemic)
        (septic) (soap) 636.6 ☑
      genital tract and pelvic infection
        636.0 ☑
      hemorrhage, delayed or excessive
        636.1 ☑
      metabolic disorder 636.4 ☑
      renal failure 636.3 ☑
      sepsis (genital tract) (pelvic organ)
        636.0 ☑
        urinary tract 636.7 ☑
      shock (postoperative) (septic)
        636.5 ☑
      specified complication NEC 636.7 ☑
      toxemia 636.3 ☑
      unspecified complication(s) 636.8 ☑
      urinary tract infection 636.7 ☑
    fetus 779.6 ☑
  induced 637.9 ☑
    illegal — see Abortion, illegal
    legal indications — see Abortion, legal
    medical indications — see Abortion, le-
      gal
    therapeutic — see Abortion, legal
  late — see Abortion, spontaneous
  legal (legal indication) (medical indication)
    (under medical supervision) 635.9 ☑
    with
      damage to pelvic organ (laceration)
        (rupture) (tear) 635.2 ☑
      embolism (air) (amniotic fluid) (blood
        clot) (pulmonary) (pyemic)
        (septic) (soap) 635.6 ☑
      genital tract and pelvic infection
        635.0 ☑
      hemorrhage, delayed or excessive
        635.1 ☑

Abortion — continued
  legal — continued
    with — continued
      metabolic disorder 635.4 ☑
      renal failure (acute) 635.3 ☑
      sepsis (genital tract) (pelvic organ)
        635.0 ☑
        urinary tract 635.7 ☑
      shock (postoperative) (septic)
        635.5 ☑
      specified complication NEC 635.7 ☑
      toxemia 635.3 ☑
      unspecified complication(s) 635.8 ☑
      urinary tract infection 635.7 ☑
    fetus 779.6
  medical indication — see Abortion, legal
  mental hygiene problem — see Abortion,
    legal
  missed 632
  operative — see Abortion, legal
  psychiatric indication — see Abortion, legal
  recurrent — see Abortion, spontaneous
  self-induced — see Abortion, illegal
  septic — see Abortion, by type, with sepsis
  spontaneous 634.9 ☑
    with
      damage to pelvic organ (laceration)
        (rupture) (tear) 634.2 ☑
      embolism (air) (amniotic fluid) (blood
        clot) (pulmonary) (pyemic)
        (septic) (soap) 634.6 ☑
      genital tract and pelvic infection
        634.0 ☑
      hemorrhage, delayed or excessive
        634.1 ☑
      metabolic disorder 634.4 ☑
      renal failure 634.3 ☑
      sepsis (genital tract) (pelvic organ)
        634.0 ☑
        urinary tract 634.7 ☑
      shock (postoperative) (septic)
        634.5 ☑
      specified complication NEC 634.7 ☑
      toxemia 634.3 ☑
      unspecified complication(s) 634.8 ☑
      urinary tract infection 634.7 ☑
    fetus 761.8
    threatened 640.0 ☑
      affecting fetus or newborn 762.1
  surgical — see Abortion, legal
  therapeutic — see Abortion, legal
  threatened 640.0 ☑
    affecting fetus or newborn 762.1
  tubal — see Pregnancy, tubal
  voluntary — see Abortion, legal
Abortus fever 023.9
Aboulomania 301.6
Abrachia 755.20
Abrachiatism 755.20
Abrachiocephalia 759.89
Abrachiocephalus 759.89
Abrami's disease (acquired hemolytic jaundice) 283.9
Abramov-Fiedler myocarditis (acute isolated myocarditis) 422.91
Abrasion — see also Injury, superficial, by site
  cornea 918.1
  dental 521.20
    extending into
      dentine 521.22
      pulp 521.23
    generalized 521.25
    limited to enamel 521.21
    localized 521.24
  teeth, tooth (dentifrice) (habitual) (hard tissues) (occupational) (ritual) (traditional) (wedge defect) (see also Abrasion, dental) 521.20
Abrikossov's tumor (M9580/0) — see also Neoplasm, connective tissue, benign
  malignant (M9580/3) — see Neoplasm, connective tissue, malignant
Abrism 988.8
Abruption, placenta — see Placenta, abruptio
Abruptio placentae — see Placenta, abruptio

Abscess (acute) (chronic) (infectional) (lymphangitic) (metastatic) (multiple) (pyogenic) (septic) (with lymphangitis) — see also Cellulitis 682.9
  abdomen, abdominal
    cavity 567.22
    wall 682.2
  abdominopelvic 567.22
  accessory sinus (chronic) (see also Sinusitis) 473.9
  adrenal (capsule) (gland) 255.8
  alveolar 522.5
    with sinus 522.7
  ambic 006.3
    bladder 006.8
    brain (with liver or lung abscess) 006.5
    liver (without mention of brain or lung abscess) 006.3
      with
        brain abscess (and lung abscess) 006.5
        lung abscess 006.4
    lung (with liver abscess) 006.4
      with brain abscess 006.5
    seminal vesicle 006.8
    specified site NEC 006.8
    spleen 006.8
  anaerobic 040.0
  ankle 682.6
  anorectal 566
  antecubital space 682.3
  antrum (chronic) (Highmore) (see also Sinusitis, maxillary) 473.0
  anus 566
  apical (tooth) 522.5
    with sinus (alveolar) 522.7
  appendix 540.1
  areola (acute) (chronic) (nonpuerperal) 611.0
    puerperal, postpartum 675.1 ☑
  arm (any part, above wrist) 682.3
  artery (wall) 447.2
  atheromatous 447.2
  auditory canal (external) 380.10
  auricle (ear) (staphylococcal) (streptococcal) 380.10
  axilla, axillary (region) 682.3
    lymph gland or node 683
  back (any part) 682.2
  Bartholin's gland 616.3
    with
      abortion — see Abortion, by type, with sepsis
      ectopic pregnancy (see also categories 633.0–633.9) 639.0
      molar pregnancy (see also categories 630–632) 639.0
    complicating pregnancy or puerperium 646.6 ☑
    following
      abortion 639.0
      ectopic or molar pregnancy 639.0
  bartholinian 616.3
  Bezold's 383.01
  bile, biliary, duct or tract (see also Cholecystitis) 576.8
  bilharziasis 120.1
  bladder (wall) 595.89
    amebic 006.8
  bone (subperiosteal) (see also Osteomyelitis) 730.0
    accessory sinus (chronic) (see also Sinusitis) 473.9
    acute 730.0 ☑
    chronic or old 730.1 ☑
    jaw (lower) (upper) 526.4
    mastoid — see Mastoiditis, acute
    petrous 383.20
    spinal (tuberculous) (see also Tuberculosis) 015.0 ☑ [730.88]
      nontuberculous 730.08
  bowel 569.5
  brain (any part) 324.0
    amebic (with liver or lung abscess) 006.5
    cystic 324.0
    late effect — see category 326

Abscess — see also Cellulitis — continued
  brain — continued
    otogenic 324.0
    tuberculous (see also Tuberculosis) 013.3 ☑
  breast (acute) (chronic) (nonpuerperal) 611.0
    newborn 771.5
    puerperal, postpartum 675.1 ☑
    tuberculous (see also Tuberculosis) 017.9 ☑
  broad ligament (chronic) (see also Disease, pelvis, inflammatory) 614.4
    acute 614.3
  Brodie's (chronic) (localized) (see also Osteomyelitis) 730.1 ☑
  bronchus 519.19
  buccal cavity 528.3
  bulbourethral gland 597.0
  bursa 727.89
    pharyngeal 478.29
  buttock 682.5
  canaliculus, breast 611.0
  canthus 372.20
  cartilage 733.99
  cecum 569.5
    with appendicitis 540.1
  cerebellum, cerebellar 324.0
    late effect — see category 326
  cerebral (embolic) 324.0
    late effect — see category 326
  cervical (neck region) 682.1
    lymph gland or node 683
    stump (see also Cervicitis) 616.0
  cervix (stump) (uteri) (see also Cervicitis) 616.0
  cheek, external 682.0
    inner 528.3
  chest 510.9
    with fistula 510.0
    wall 682.2
  chin 682.0
  choroid 363.00
  ciliary body 364.3
  circumtonsillar 475
  cold (tuberculous) (see also Tuberculosis, abscess)
    articular — see Tuberculosis, joint
  colon (wall) 569.5
  colostomy or enterostomy 569.61
  conjunctiva 372.00
  connective tissue NEC 682.9
  cornea 370.55
    with ulcer 370.00
  corpus
    cavernosum 607.2
    luteum (see also Salpingo-oophoritis) 614.2
  Cowper's gland 597.0
  cranium 324.0
  cul-de-sac (Douglas') (posterior) (see also Disease, pelvis, inflammatory) 614.4
    acute 614.3
  dental 522.5
    with sinus (alveolar) 522.7
  dentoalveolar 522.5
    with sinus (alveolar) 522.7
  diaphragm, diaphragmatic 567.22
  digit NEC 681.9
  Douglas' cul-de-sac or pouch (see also Disease, pelvis, inflammatory) 614.4
    acute 614.3
  Dubois' 090.5
  ductless gland 259.8
  ear
    acute 382.00
    external 380.10
    inner 386.30
    middle — see Otitis media
  elbow 682.3
  endamebic — see Abscess, amebic
  entamebic — see Abscess, amebic
  enterostomy 569.61
  epididymis 604.0
  epidural 324.9
    brain 324.0

Abscess — see also Cellulitis — continued
  epidural — continued
    late effect — see category 326
    spinal cord 324.1
  epiglottis 478.79
  epiploon, epiploic 567.22
  erysipelatous (see also Erysipelas) 035
  esophagostomy 530.86
  esophagus 530.19
  ethmoid (bone) (chronic) (sinus) (see also Sinusitis, ethmoidal) 473.2
  external auditory canal 380.10
  extradural 324.9
    brain 324.0
    late effect — see category 326
    spinal cord 324.1
  extraperitoneal — see Abscess, peritoneum
  eye 360.00
  eyelid 373.13
  face (any part, except eye) 682.0
  fallopian tube (see also Salpingo-oophoritis) 614.2
  fascia 728.89
  fauces 478.29
  fecal 569.5
  femoral (region) 682.6
  filaria, filarial (see also Infestation, filarial) 125.9
  finger (any) (intrathecal) (periosteal) (subcutaneous) (subcuticular) 681.00
  fistulous NEC 682.9
  flank 682.2
  foot (except toe) 682.7
  forearm 682.3
  forehead 682.0
  frontal (sinus) (chronic) (see also Sinusitis, frontal) 473.1
  gallbladder (see also Cholecystitis, acute) 575.0
  gastric 535.0 ☑
  genital organ or tract NEC
    female 616.9
      with
        abortion — see Abortion, by type, with sepsis
        ectopic pregnancy (see also categories 633.0–633.9) 639.0
        molar pregnancy (see also categories 630–632) 639.0
      following
        abortion 639.0
        ectopic or molar pregnancy 639.0
      puerperal, postpartum, childbirth 670.8 ☑
    male 608.4
  genitourinary system, tuberculous (see also Tuberculosis) 016.9 ☑
  gingival 523.30
  gland, glandular (lymph) (acute) NEC 683
  glottis 478.79
  gluteal (region) 682.5
  gonorrheal NEC (see also Gonococcus) 098.0
  groin 682.2
  gum 523.30
  hand (except finger or thumb) 682.4
  head (except face) 682.8
  heart 429.89
  heel 682.7
  helminthic (see also Infestation, by specific parasite) 128.9
  hepatic 572.0
    amebic (see also Abscess, liver, amebic) 006.3
    duct 576.8
  hip 682.6
    tuberculous (active) (see also Tuberculosis) 015.1 ☑
  ileocecal 540.1
  ileostomy (bud) 569.61
  iliac (region) 682.2
    fossa 540.1
  iliopsoas 567.31
    nontuberculous 728.89
    tuberculous (see also Tuberculosis) 015.0 ☑ [730.88]
  infraclavicular (fossa) 682.3

☑ Additional Digit Required — Refer to the Tabular List for Digit Selection   ▽ Subterms under main terms may continue to next column or page

2015 ICD-9-CM   ▶◀ Revised Text   ● New Line   ▲ Revised Code   Volume 2 — 3

Abscess — see also Cellulitis — continued
  inguinal (region) 682.2
    lymph gland or node 683
  intersphincteric (anus) 566
  intestine, intestinal 569.5
    rectal 566
  intra-abdominal (see also Abscess, peritoneum) 567.22
    postoperative 998.59
  intracranial 324.0
    late effect — see category 326
  intramammary — see Abscess, breast
  intramastoid (see also Mastoiditis, acute) 383.00
  intraorbital 376.01
  intraperitoneal 567.22
  intraspinal 324.1
    late effect — see category 326
  intratonsillar 475
  iris 364.3
  ischiorectal 566
  jaw (bone) (lower) (upper) 526.4
    skin 682.0
  joint (see also Arthritis, pyogenic) 711.0 ☑
    vertebral (tuberculous) (see also Tuberculosis) 015.0 ☑ [730.88]
      nontuberculous 724.8
  kidney 590.2
    with
      abortion — see Abortion, by type, with urinary tract infection
      calculus 592.0
      ectopic pregnancy (see also categories 633.0–633.9) 639.8
      molar pregnancy (see also categories 630–632) 639.8
      complicating pregnancy or puerperium 646.6 ☑
        affecting fetus or newborn 760.1
      following
        abortion 639.8
        ectopic or molar pregnancy 639.8
  knee 682.6
    joint 711.06
    tuberculous (active) (see also Tuberculosis) 015.2 ☑
  labium (majus) (minus) 616.4
    complicating pregnancy, childbirth, or puerperium 646.6 ☑
  lacrimal (passages) (sac) (see also Dacryocystitis) 375.30
    caruncle 375.30
    gland (see also Dacryoadenitis) 375.00
  lacunar 597.0
  larynx 478.79
  lateral (alveolar) 522.5
    with sinus 522.7
  leg, except foot 682.6
  lens 360.00
  lid 373.13
  lingual 529.0
    tonsil 475
  lip 528.5
  Littre's gland 597.0
  liver 572.0
    amebic 006.3
      with
        brain abscess (and lung abscess) 006.5
        lung abscess 006.4
      due to Entamoeba histolytica 006.3
    dysenteric (see also Abscess, liver, amebic) 006.3
    pyogenic 572.0
    tropical (see also Abscess, liver, amebic) 006.3
  loin (region) 682.2
  lumbar (tuberculous) (see also Tuberculosis) 015.0 ☑ [730.88]
    nontuberculous 682.2
  lung (miliary) (putrid) 513.0
    amebic (with liver abscess) 006.4
      with brain abscess 006.5
  lymphangitic, acute — see Cellulitis
  lymph, lymphatic, gland or node (acute) 683
    any site, except mesenteric 683

Abscess — see also Cellulitis — continued
  lymph, lymphatic, gland or node — continued
    mesentery 289.2
  malar 526.4
  mammary gland — see Abscess, breast
  marginal (anus) 566
  mastoid (process) (see also Mastoiditis, acute) 383.00
    subperiosteal 383.01
  maxilla, maxillary 526.4
    molar (tooth) 522.5
      with sinus 522.7
    premolar 522.5
    sinus (chronic) (see also Sinusitis, maxillary) 473.0
  mediastinum 513.1
  meibomian gland 373.12
  meninges (see also Meningitis) 320.9
  mesentery, mesenteric 567.22
  mesosalpinx (see also Salpingo-oophoritis) 614.2
  milk 675.1 ☑
  Monro's (psoriasis) 696.1
  mons pubis 682.2
  mouth (floor) 528.3
  multiple sites NEC 682.9
  mural 682.2
  muscle 728.89
    psoas 567.31
  myocardium 422.92
  nabothian (follicle) (see also Cervicitis) 616.0
  nail (chronic) (with lymphangitis) 681.9
    finger 681.02
    toe 681.11
  nasal (fossa) (septum) 478.19
    sinus (chronic) (see also Sinusitis) 473.9
  nasopharyngeal 478.29
  nates 682.5
  navel 682.2
    newborn NEC 771.4
  neck (region) 682.1
    lymph gland or node 683
  nephritic (see also Abscess, kidney) 590.2
  nipple 611.0
    puerperal, postpartum 675.0 ☑
  nose (septum) 478.19
    external 682.0
  omentum 567.22
  operative wound 998.59
  orbit, orbital 376.01
  ossifluent — see Abscess, bone
  ovary, ovarian (corpus luteum) (see also Salpingo-oophoritis) 614.2
  oviduct (see also Salpingo-oophoritis) 614.2
  palate (soft) 528.3
    hard 526.4
  palmar (space) 682.4
  pancreas (duct) 577.0
  paradontal 523.30
  parafrenal 607.2
  parametric, parametrium (chronic) (see also Disease, pelvis, inflammatory) 614.4
    acute 614.3
  paranephric 590.2
  parapancreatic 577.0
  parapharyngeal 478.22
  pararectal 566
  parasinus (see also Sinusitis) 473.9
  parauterine (see also Disease, pelvis, inflammatory) 614.4
    acute 614.3
  paravaginal (see also Vaginitis) 616.10
  parietal region 682.8
  parodontal 523.30
  parotid (duct) (gland) 527.3
    region 528.3
  parumbilical 682.2
    newborn 771.4
  pectoral (region) 682.2
  pelvirectal 567.22
  pelvis, pelvic
    female (chronic) (see also Disease, pelvis, inflammatory) 614.4
      acute 614.3

Abscess — see also Cellulitis — continued
  pelvis, pelvic — continued
    male, peritoneal (cellular tissue) — see Abscess, peritoneum
    tuberculous (see also Tuberculosis) 016.9 ☑
  penis 607.2
    gonococcal (acute) 098.0
      chronic or duration of 2 months or over 098.2
  perianal 566
  periapical 522.5
    with sinus (alveolar) 522.7
  periappendiceal 540.1
  pericardial 420.99
  pericecal 540.1
  pericemental 523.30
  pericholecystic (see also Cholecystitis, acute) 575.0
  pericoronal 523.30
  peridental 523.30
  perigastric 535.0 ☑
  perimetric (see also Disease, pelvis, inflammatory) 614.4
    acute 614.3
  perinephric, perinephritic (see also Abscess, kidney) 590.2
  perineum, perineal (superficial) 682.2
    deep (with urethral involvement) 597.0
    urethra 597.0
  periodontal (parietal) 523.31
    apical 522.5
  periosteum, periosteal (see also Periostitis) 730.3 ☑
    with osteomyelitis (see also Osteomyelitis) 730.2 ☑
    acute or subacute 730.0 ☑
    chronic or old 730.1 ☑
  peripleuritic 510.9
    with fistula 510.0
  periproctic 566
  periprostatic 601.2
  perirectal (staphylococcal) 566
  perirenal (tissue) (see also Abscess, kidney) 590.2
  perisinuous (nose) (see also Sinusitis) 473.9
  peritoneum, peritoneal (perforated) (ruptured) 567.22
    with
      abortion — see Abortion, by type, with sepsis
      appendicitis 540.1
      ectopic pregnancy (see also categories 633.0–633.9) 639.0
      molar pregnancy (see also categories 630–632) 639.0
    following
      abortion 639.0
      ectopic or molar pregnancy 639.0
    pelvic, female (see also Disease, pelvis, inflammatory) 614.4
      acute 614.3
    postoperative 998.59
    puerperal, postpartum, childbirth 670.8 ☑
    tuberculous (see also Tuberculosis) 014.0 ☑
  peritonsillar 475
  perityphlic 540.1
  periureteral 593.89
  periurethral 597.0
    gonococcal (acute) 098.0
      chronic or duration of 2 months or over 098.2
  periuterine (see also Disease, pelvis, inflammatory) 614.4
    acute 614.3
  perivesical 595.89
  pernicious NEC 682.9
  petrous bone — see Petrositis
  phagedenic NEC 682.9
    chancroid 099.0
  pharynx, pharyngeal (lateral) 478.29
  phlegmonous NEC 682.9
  pilonidal 685.0
  pituitary (gland) 253.8

Abscess — see also Cellulitis — continued
  pleura 510.9
    with fistula 510.0
  popliteal 682.6
  postanal 566
  postcecal 540.1
  postlaryngeal 478.79
  postnasal 478.19
  postpharyngeal 478.24
  posttonsillar 475
  posttyphoid 002.0
  Pott's (see also Tuberculosis) 015.0 ☑ [730.88]
  pouch of Douglas (chronic) (see also Disease, pelvis, inflammatory) 614.4
  premammary — see Abscess, breast
  prepatellar 682.6
  prostate (see also Prostatitis) 601.2
    gonococcal (acute) 098.12
      chronic or duration of 2 months or over 098.32
  psoas 567.31
    nontuberculous 728.89
    tuberculous (see also Tuberculosis) 015.0 ☑ [730.88]
  pterygopalatine fossa 682.8
  pubis 682.2
  puerperal — see Puerperal, abscess, by site
  pulmonary — see Abscess, lung
  pulp, pulpal (dental) 522.0
    finger 681.01
    toe 681.10
  pyemic — see Septicemia
  pyloric valve 535.0 ☑
  rectovaginal septum 569.5
  rectovesical 595.89
  rectum 566
  regional NEC 682.9
  renal (see also Abscess, kidney) 590.2
  retina 363.00
  retrobulbar 376.01
  retrocecal 567.22
  retrolaryngeal 478.79
  retromammary — see Abscess, breast
  retroperineal 682.2
  retroperitoneal 567.38
    postprocedural 998.59
  retropharyngeal 478.24
    tuberculous (see also Tuberculosis) 012.8 ☑
  retrorectal 566
  retrouterine (see also Disease, pelvis, inflammatory) 614.4
    acute 614.3
  retrovesical 595.89
  root, tooth 522.5
    with sinus (alveolar) 522.7
  round ligament (see also Disease, pelvis, inflammatory) 614.4
    acute 614.3
  rupture (spontaneous) NEC 682.9
  sacrum (tuberculous) (see also Tuberculosis) 015.0 ☑ [730.88]
    nontuberculous 730.08
  salivary duct or gland 527.3
  scalp (any part) 682.8
  scapular 730.01
  sclera 379.09
  scrofulous (see also Tuberculosis) 017.2 ☑
  scrotum 608.4
  seminal vesicle 608.0
    amebic 006.8
  septal, dental 522.5
    with sinus (alveolar) 522.7
  septum (nasal) 478.19
  serous (see also Periostitis) 730.3 ☑
  shoulder 682.3
  side 682.2
  sigmoid 569.5
  sinus (accessory) (chronic) (nasal) (see also Sinusitis) 473.9
    intracranial venous (any) 324.0
    late effect — see category 326
  Skene's duct or gland 597.0
  skin NEC 682.9

☑ Additional Digit Required — Refer to the Tabular List for Digit Selection   Subterms under main terms may continue to next column or page

4 — Volume 2   ▶◀ Revised Text   ● New Line   ▲ Revised Code   2015 ICD-9-CM

Abscess — see also Cellulitis — continued
skin — continued
tuberculous (primary) (see also Tuberculosis) 017.0 ☑
sloughing NEC 682.9
specified site NEC 682.8
amebic 006.8
spermatic cord 608.4
sphenoidal (sinus) (see also Sinusitis, sphenoidal) 473.3
spinal
cord (any part) (staphylococcal) 324.1
tuberculous (see also Tuberculosis) 013.5 ☑
epidural 324.1
spine (column) (tuberculous) (see also Tuberculosis) 015.0 ☑ [730.88]
nontuberculous 730.08
spleen 289.59
amebic 006.8
staphylococcal NEC 682.9
stitch 998.59
stomach (wall) 535.0 ☑
strumous (tuberculous) (see also Tuberculosis) 017.2 ☑
subarachnoid 324.9
brain 324.0
cerebral 324.0
late effect — see category 326
spinal cord 324.1
subareolar (see also Abscess, breast)
puerperal, postpartum 675.1 ☑
subcecal 540.1
subcutaneous NEC 682.9
subdiaphragmatic 567.22
subdorsal 682.2
subdural 324.9
brain 324.0
late effect — see category 326
spinal cord 324.1
subgaleal 682.8
subhepatic 567.22
sublingual 528.3
gland 527.3
submammary — see Abscess, breast
submandibular (region) (space) (triangle) 682.0
gland 527.3
submaxillary (region) 682.0
gland 527.3
submental (pyogenic) 682.0
gland 527.3
subpectoral 682.2
subperiosteal — see Abscess, bone
subperitoneal 567.22
subphrenic (see also Abscess, peritoneum) 567.22
postoperative 998.59
subscapular 682.2
subungual 681.9
suburethral 597.0
sudoriparous 705.89
suppurative NEC 682.9
supraclavicular (fossa) 682.3
suprahepatic 567.22
suprapelvic (see also Disease, pelvis, inflammatory) 614.4
acute 614.3
suprapubic 682.2
suprarenal (capsule) (gland) 255.8
sweat gland 705.89
syphilitic 095.8
teeth, tooth (root) 522.5
with sinus (alveolar) 522.7
supporting structures NEC 523.30
temple 682.0
temporal region 682.0
temporosphenoidal 324.0
late effect — see category 326
tendon (sheath) 727.89
testicle — see Orchitis
thecal 728.89
thigh (acquired) 682.6
thorax 510.9
with fistula 510.0
throat 478.29

Abscess — see also Cellulitis — continued
thumb (intrathecal) (periosteal) (subcutaneous) (subcuticular) 681.00
thymus (gland) 254.1
thyroid (gland) 245.0
toe (any) (intrathecal) (periosteal) (subcutaneous) (subcuticular) 681.10
tongue (staphylococcal) 529.0
tonsil(s) (lingual) 475
tonsillopharyngeal 475
tooth, teeth (root) 522.5
with sinus (alveolar) 522.7
supporting structure NEC 523.30
trachea 478.9
trunk 682.2
tubal (see also Salpingo-oophoritis) 614.2
tuberculous — see Tuberculosis, abscess
tubo-ovarian (see also Salpingo-oophoritis) 614.2
tunica vaginalis 608.4
umbilicus NEC 682.2
newborn 771.4
upper arm 682.3
upper respiratory 478.9
urachus 682.2
urethra (gland) 597.0
urinary 597.0
uterus, uterine (wall) (see also Endometritis) 615.9
ligament (see also Disease, pelvis, inflammatory) 614.4
acute 614.3
neck (see also Cervicitis) 616.0
uvula 528.3
vagina (wall) (see also Vaginitis) 616.10
vaginorectal (see also Vaginitis) 616.10
vas deferens 608.4
vermiform appendix 540.1
vertebra (column) (tuberculous) (see also Tuberculosis) 015.0 ☑ [730.88]
nontuberculous 730.0 ☑
vesical 595.89
vesicouterine pouch (see also Disease, pelvis, inflammatory) 614.4
vitreous (humor) (pneumococcal) 360.04
vocal cord 478.5
von Bezold's 383.01
vulva 616.4
complicating pregnancy, childbirth, or puerperium 646.6 ☑
vulvovaginal gland (see also Vaginitis) 616.3
web-space 682.4
wrist 682.4
Absence (organ or part) (complete or partial)
acoustic nerve 742.8
adrenal (gland) (congenital) 759.1
acquired V45.79
albumin (blood) 273.8
alimentary tract (complete) (congenital) (partial) 751.8
lower 751.5
upper 750.8
alpha-fucosidase 271.8
alveolar process (acquired) 525.8
congenital 750.26
anus, anal (canal) (congenital) 751.2
aorta (congenital) 747.22
aortic valve (congenital) 746.89
appendix, congenital 751.2
arm (acquired) V49.60
above elbow V49.66
below elbow V49.65
congenital (see also Deformity, reduction, upper limb) 755.20
lower — see Absence, forearm, congenital
upper (complete) (partial) (with absence of distal elements, incomplete) 755.24
with
complete absence of distal elements 755.21
forearm (incomplete) 755.23
artery (congenital) (peripheral) NEC (see also Anomaly, peripheral vascular system) 747.60

Absence — continued
artery (see also Anomaly, peripheral vascular system) — continued
brain 747.81
cerebral 747.81
coronary 746.85
pulmonary 747.31
umbilical 747.5
atrial septum 745.69
auditory canal (congenital) (external) 744.01
auricle (ear) (with stenosis or atresia of auditory canal), congenital 744.01
bile, biliary duct (common) or passage (congenital) 751.61
bladder (acquired) V45.74
congenital 753.8
bone (congenital) NEC 756.9
marrow 284.9
acquired (secondary) 284.89
congenital 284.09
hereditary 284.09
idiopathic 284.9
skull 756.0
bowel sounds 787.5
brain 740.0
specified part 742.2
breast(s) (acquired) V45.71
congenital 757.6
broad ligament (congenital) 752.19
bronchus (congenital) 748.3
calvarium, calvaria (skull) 756.0
canaliculus lacrimalis, congenital 743.65
carpal(s) (congenital) (complete) (partial) (with absence of distal elements, incomplete) (see also Deformity, reduction, upper limb) 755.28
with complete absence of distal elements 755.21
cartilage 756.9
caudal spine 756.13
cecum (acquired) (postoperative) (posttraumatic) V45.72
congenital 751.2
cementum 520.4
cerebellum (congenital) (vermis) 742.2
cervix (acquired) (uteri) V88.01
with remaining uterus V88.03
and uterus V88.01
congenital 752.43
chin, congenital 744.89
cilia (congenital) 743.63
acquired 374.89
circulatory system, part NEC 747.89
clavicle 755.51
clitoris (congenital) 752.49
coccyx, congenital 756.13
cold sense (see also Disturbance, sensation) 782.0
colon (acquired) (postoperative) V45.72
congenital 751.2
congenital
lumen — see Atresia
organ or site NEC — see Agenesis
septum — see Imperfect, closure
corpus callosum (congenital) 742.2
cricoid cartilage 748.3
diaphragm (congenital) (with hernia) 756.6
with obstruction 756.6
digestive organ(s) or tract, congenital (complete) (partial) 751.8
acquired V45.79
lower 751.5
upper 750.8
ductus arteriosus 747.89
duodenum (acquired) (postoperative) V45.72
congenital 751.1
ear, congenital 744.09
acquired V45.79
auricle 744.01
external 744.01
inner 744.05
lobe, lobule 744.21
middle, except ossicles 744.03
ossicles 744.04
ossicles 744.04

Absence — continued
ejaculatory duct (congenital) 752.89
endocrine gland NEC (congenital) 759.2
epididymis (congenital) 752.89
acquired V45.77
epiglottis, congenital 748.3
epileptic (atonic) (typical) (see also Epilepsy) 345.0 ☑
erythrocyte 284.9
erythropoiesis 284.9
congenital 284.01
esophagus (congenital) 750.3
Eustachian tube (congenital) 744.24
extremity (acquired)
congenital (see also Deformity, reduction) 755.4
lower V49.70
upper V49.60
extrinsic muscle, eye 743.69
eye (acquired) V45.78
adnexa (congenital) 743.69
congenital 743.00
muscle (congenital) 743.69
eyelid (fold), congenital 743.62
acquired 374.89
face
bones NEC 756.0
specified part NEC 744.89
fallopian tube(s) (acquired) V45.77
congenital 752.19
femur, congenital (complete) (partial) (with absence of distal elements, incomplete) (see also Deformity, reduction, lower limb) 755.34
with
complete absence of distal elements 755.31
tibia and fibula (incomplete) 755.33
fibrin 790.92
fibrinogen (congenital) 286.3
acquired 286.6
fibula, congenital (complete) (partial) (with absence of distal elements, incomplete) (see also Deformity, reduction, lower limb) 755.37
with
complete absence of distal elements 755.31
tibia 755.35
with
complete absence of distal elements 755.31
femur (incomplete) 755.33
with complete absence of distal elements 755.31
finger (acquired) V49.62
congenital (complete) (partial) (see also Deformity, reduction, upper limb) 755.29
meaning all fingers (complete) (partial) 755.21
transverse 755.21
fissures of lungs (congenital) 748.5
foot (acquired) V49.73
congenital (complete) 755.31
forearm (acquired) V49.65
congenital (complete) (partial) (with absence of distal elements, incomplete) (see also Deformity, reduction, upper limb) 755.25
with
complete absence of distal elements (hand and fingers) 755.21
humerus (incomplete) 755.23
fovea centralis 743.55
fucosidase 271.8
gallbladder (acquired) V45.79
congenital 751.69
gamma globulin (blood) 279.00
genital organs
acquired V45.77
congenital
female 752.89
external 752.49

☑ Additional Digit Required — Refer to the Tabular List for Digit Selection
▽ Subterms under main terms may continue to next column or page
2015 ICD-9-CM
▶◀ Revised Text
● New Line
▲ Revised Code
Volume 2 — 5

Absence — continued
  genital organs — continued
    congenital — continued
      female — continued
        internal NEC 752.89
      male 752.89
        penis 752.69
  genitourinary organs, congenital NEC 752.89
  glottis 748.3
  gonadal, congenital NEC 758.6
  hair (congenital) 757.4
    acquired — see Alopecia
  hand (acquired) V49.63
    congenital (complete) (see also Deformity, reduction, upper limb) 755.21
  heart (congenital) 759.89
    acquired — see Status, organ replacement
  heat sense (see also Disturbance, sensation) 782.0
  humerus, congenital (complete) (partial) (with absence of distal elements, incomplete) (see also Deformity, reduction, upper limb) 755.24
    with
      complete absence of distal elements 755.21
      radius and ulna (incomplete) 755.23
  hymen (congenital) 752.49
  ileum (acquired) (postoperative) (posttraumatic) V45.72
    congenital 751.1
  immunoglobulin, isolated NEC 279.03
    IgA 279.01
    IgG 279.03
    IgM 279.02
  incus (acquired) 385.24
    congenital 744.04
  internal ear (congenital) 744.05
  intestine (acquired) (small) V45.72
    congenital 751.1
      large 751.2
    large V45.72
      congenital 751.2
  iris (congenital) 743.45
  jaw — see Absence, mandible
  jejunum (acquired) V45.72
    congenital 751.1
  joint (acquired) (following prior explantation of joint prosthesis) (with or without presence of antibiotic-impregnated cement spacer) NEC V88.29
    congenital NEC 755.8
    hip V88.21
    knee V88.22
  kidney(s) (acquired) V45.73
    congenital 753.0
  labium (congenital) (majus) (minus) 752.49
  labyrinth, membranous 744.05
  lacrimal apparatus (congenital) 743.65
  larynx (congenital) 748.3
  leg (acquired) V49.70
    above knee V49.76
    below knee V49.75
    congenital (partial) (unilateral) (see also Deformity, reduction, lower limb) 755.31
      lower (complete) (partial) (with absence of distal elements, incomplete) 755.35
        with
          complete absence of distal elements (foot and toes) 755.31
          thigh (incomplete) 755.33
            with complete absence of distal elements 755.31
      upper — see Absence, femur
  lens (congenital) 743.35
    acquired 379.31
  ligament, broad (congenital) 752.19
  limb (acquired)
    congenital (complete) (partial) (see also Deformity, reduction) 755.4
      lower 755.30

Absence — continued
  limb — continued
    congenital (see also Deformity, reduction) — continued
      lower — continued
        complete 755.31
        incomplete 755.32
        longitudinal — see Deficiency, lower limb, longitudinal
        transverse 755.31
      upper 755.20
        complete 755.21
        incomplete 755.22
        longitudinal — see Deficiency, upper limb, longitudinal
        transverse 755.21
      lower NEC V49.70
      upper NEC V49.60
  lip 750.26
  liver (congenital) (lobe) 751.69
  lumbar (congenital) (vertebra) 756.13
    isthmus 756.11
    pars articularis 756.11
  lumen — see Atresia
  lung (bilateral) (congenital) (fissure) (lobe) (unilateral) 748.5
    acquired (any part) V45.76
  mandible (congenital) 524.09
  maxilla (congenital) 524.09
  menstruation 626.0
  metacarpal(s), congenital (complete) (partial) (with absence of distal elements, incomplete) (see also Deformity, reduction, upper limb) 755.28
    with all fingers, complete 755.21
  metatarsal(s), congenital (complete) (partial) (with absence of distal elements, incomplete) (see also Deformity, reduction, lower limb) 755.38
    with complete absence of distal elements 755.31
  muscle (congenital) (pectoral) 756.81
    ocular 743.69
  musculoskeletal system (congenital) NEC 756.9
  nail(s) (congenital) 757.5
  neck, part 744.89
  nerve 742.8
  nervous system, part NEC 742.8
  neutrophil 288.00
  nipple (congenital) 757.6
    acquired V45.71
  nose (congenital) 748.1
    acquired 738.0
  nuclear 742.8
  ocular muscle (congenital) 743.69
  organ
    of Corti (congenital) 744.05
    or site
      acquired V45.79
      congenital NEC 759.89
  osseous meatus (ear) 744.03
  ovary (acquired) V45.77
    congenital 752.0
  oviduct (acquired) V45.77
    congenital 752.19
  pancreas (congenital) 751.7
    acquired (postoperative) (posttraumatic) V88.11
      partial V88.12
      total V88.11
  parathyroid gland (congenital) 759.2
  parotid gland(s) (congenital) 750.21
  patella, congenital 755.64
  pelvic girdle (congenital) 755.69
  penis (congenital) 752.69
    acquired V45.77
  pericardium (congenital) 746.89
  perineal body (congenital) 756.81
  phalange(s), congenital 755.4
    lower limb (complete) (intercalary) (partial) (terminal) (see also Deformity, reduction, lower limb) 755.39
      meaning all toes (complete) (partial) 755.31

Absence — continued
  phalange(s), congenital — continued
    lower limb (see also Deformity, reduction, lower limb) — continued
      transverse 755.31
    upper limb (complete) (intercalary) (partial) (terminal) (see also Deformity, reduction, upper limb) 755.29
      meaning all digits (complete) (partial) 755.21
      transverse 755.21
  pituitary gland (congenital) 759.2
  postoperative — see Absence, by site, acquired
  prostate (congenital) 752.89
    acquired V45.77
  pulmonary
    artery 747.31
    trunk 747.31
    valve (congenital) 746.01
    vein 747.49
  punctum lacrimale (congenital) 743.65
  radius, congenital (complete) (partial) (with absence of distal elements, incomplete) 755.26
    with
      complete absence of distal elements 755.21
      ulna 755.25
        with
          complete absence of distal elements 755.21
          humerus (incomplete) 755.23
  ray, congenital 755.4
    lower limb (complete) (partial) (see also Deformity, reduction, lower limb) 755.38
      meaning all rays 755.31
      transverse 755.31
    upper limb (complete) (partial) (see also Deformity, reduction, upper limb) 755.28
      meaning all rays 755.21
      transverse 755.21
  rectum (congenital) 751.2
    acquired V45.79
  red cell 284.9
    acquired (secondary) 284.81
    congenital 284.01
    hereditary 284.01
    idiopathic 284.9
  respiratory organ (congenital) NEC 748.9
  rib (acquired) 738.3
    congenital 756.3
  roof of orbit (congenital) 742.0
  round ligament (congenital) 752.89
  sacrum, congenital 756.13
  salivary gland(s) (congenital) 750.21
  scapula 755.59
  scrotum, congenital 752.89
  seminal tract or duct (congenital) 752.89
    acquired V45.77
  septum (congenital) (see also Imperfect, closure, septum)
    atrial 745.69
      and ventricular 745.7
    between aorta and pulmonary artery 745.0
    ventricular 745.3
      and atrial 745.7
  sex chromosomes 758.81
  shoulder girdle, congenital (complete) (partial) 755.59
  skin (congenital) 757.39
  skull bone 756.0
    with
      anencephalus 740.0
      encephalocele 742.0
      hydrocephalus 742.3
        with spina bifida (see also Spina bifida) 741.0 ☑
      microcephalus 742.1
  spermatic cord (congenital) 752.89
  spinal cord 742.59
  spine, congenital 756.13

Absence — continued
  spleen (congenital) 759.0
    acquired V45.79
  sternum, congenital 756.3
  stomach (acquired) (partial) (postoperative) V45.75
    with postgastric surgery syndrome 564.2
    congenital 750.7
  submaxillary gland(s) (congenital) 750.21
  superior vena cava (congenital) 747.49
  tarsal(s), congenital (complete) (partial) (with absence of distal elements, incomplete) (see also Deformity, reduction, lower limb) 755.38
  teeth, tooth (congenital) 520.0
    with abnormal spacing 524.30
    acquired 525.10
      with malocclusion 524.30
      due to
        caries 525.13
        extraction 525.10
        periodontal disease 525.12
        trauma 525.11
  tendon (congenital) 756.81
  testis (congenital) 752.89
    acquired V45.77
  thigh (acquired) 736.89
  thumb (acquired) V49.61
    congenital 755.29
  thymus gland (congenital) 759.2
  thyroid (gland) (surgical) 246.8
    with hypothyroidism 244.0
    cartilage, congenital 748.3
    congenital 243
  tibia, congenital (complete) (partial) (with absence of distal elements, incomplete) (see also Deformity, reduction, lower limb) 755.36
    with
      complete absence of distal elements 755.31
      fibula 755.35
        with
          complete absence of distal elements 755.31
          femur (incomplete) 755.33
            with complete absence of distal elements 755.31
  toe (acquired) V49.72
    congenital (complete) (partial) 755.39
      meaning all toes 755.31
      transverse 755.31
    great V49.71
  tongue (congenital) 750.11
  tooth, teeth (congenital) 520.0
    with abnormal spacing 524.30
    acquired 525.10
      with malocclusion 524.30
      due to
        caries 525.13
        extraction 525.10
        periodontal disease 525.12
        trauma 525.11
  trachea (cartilage) (congenital!) (rings) 748.3
  transverse aortic arch (congenital) 747.21
  tricuspid valve 746.1
  ulna, congenital (complete) (partial) (with absence of distal elements, incomplete) (see also Deformity, reduction, upper limb) 755.27
    with
      complete absence of distal elements 755.21
      radius 755.25
        with
          complete absence of distal elements 755.21
          humerus (incomplete) 755.23
  umbilical artery (congenital) 747.5
  ureter (congenital) 753.4
    acquired V45.74
  urethra, congenital 753.8
    acquired V45.74
  urinary system, part NEC, congenital 753.8
    acquired V45.74

☑ Additional Digit Required — Refer to the Tabular List for Digit Selection   ▽ Subterms under main terms may continue to next column or page

6 — Volume 2   ▶◀ Revised Text   ● New Line   ▲ Revised Code   2015 ICD-9-CM

Absence — *continued*
  uterus (acquired) V88.01
    with remaining cervical stump V88.02
      and cervix V88.01
    congenital 752.31
  uvula (congenital) 750.26
  vagina, congenital 752.45
    acquired V45.77
  vas deferens (congenital) 752.89
    acquired V45.77
  vein (congenital) (peripheral) NEC (*see also* Anomaly, peripheral vascular system) 747.60
    brain 747.81
    great 747.49
    portal 747.49
    pulmonary 747.49
  vena cava (congenital) (inferior) (superior) 747.49
  ventral horn cell 742.59
  ventricular septum 745.3
  vermis of cerebellum 742.2
  vertebra, congenital 756.13
  vulva, congenital 752.49
Absentia epileptica — *see also* Epilepsy 345.0 ☑
Absinthemia — *see also* Dependence 304.6 ☑
Absinthism — *see also* Dependence 304.6 ☑
Absorbent system disease 459.89
Absorption
  alcohol, through placenta or breast milk 760.71
  antibiotics, through placenta or breast milk 760.74
  anticonvulsants, through placenta or breast milk 760.77
  antifungals, through placenta or breast milk 760.74
  anti-infective, through placenta or breast milk 760.74
  antimetabolics, through placenta or breast milk 760.78
  chemical NEC 989.9
    specified chemical or substance — *see* Table of Drugs and Chemicals
    through placenta or breast milk (fetus or newborn) 760.70
      alcohol 760.71
      anticonvulsants 760.77
      antifungals 760.74
      anti-infective agents 760.74
      antimetabolics 760.78
      cocaine 760.75
      "crack" 760.75
      diethylstilbestrol [DES] 760.76
      hallucinogenic agents 760.73
      medicinal agents NEC 760.79
      narcotics 760.72
      obstetric anesthetic or analgesic drug 763.5
      specified agent NEC 760.79
      suspected, affecting management of pregnancy 655.5 ☑
  cocaine, through placenta or breast milk 760.75
  drug NEC (*see also* Reaction, drug)
    through placenta or breast milk (fetus or newborn) 760.70
      alcohol 760.71
      anticonvulsants 760.77
      antifungals 760.74
      anti-infective agents 760.74
      antimetabolics 760.78
      cocaine 760.75
      "crack" 760.75
      diethylstilbestrol [DES] 760.76
      hallucinogenic agents 760.73
      medicinal agents NEC 760.79
      narcotics 760.72
      obstetric anesthetic or analgesic drug 763.5
      specified agent NEC 760.79
      suspected, affecting management of pregnancy 655.5 ☑
  fat, disturbance 579.8

Absorption — *continued*
  hallucinogenic agents, through placenta or breast milk 760.73
  immune sera, through placenta or breast milk 760.79
  lactose defect 271.3
  medicinal agents NEC, through placenta or breast milk 760.79
  narcotics, through placenta or breast milk 760.72
  noxious substance — *see* Absorption, chemical
  protein, disturbance 579.8
  pus or septic, general — *see* Septicemia
  quinine, through placenta or breast milk 760.74
  toxic substance — *see* Absorption, chemical
  uremic — *see* Uremia
Abstinence symptoms or syndrome
  alcohol 291.81
  drug 292.0
  neonatal 779.5
Abt-Letterer-Siwe syndrome (acute histiocytosis X) (M9722/3) 202.5 ☑
Abulia 799.89
Abulomania 301.6
Abuse
  adult 995.80
    emotional 995.82
    multiple forms 995.85
    neglect (nutritional) 995.84
    physical 995.81
    psychological 995.82
    sexual 995.83
  alcohol — *see also* Alcoholism 305.0 ☑
    dependent 303.9 ☑
    non-dependent 305.0 ☑
  child 995.50
    counseling
      perpetrator
        non-parent V62.83
        parent V61.22
      victim V61.21
    emotional 995.51
    multiple forms 995.59
    neglect (nutritional) 995.52
    physical 995.54
      shaken infant syndrome 995.55
    psychological 995.51
    sexual 995.53
  drugs, nondependent 305.9 ☑

> *Note* — *Use the following fifth-digit subclassification with the following codes: 305.0, 305.2–305.9:*
>
> 0   *unspecified*
>
> 1   *continuous*
>
> 2   *episodic*
>
> 3   *in remission*

      amphetamine type 305.7 ☑
      antidepressants 305.8 ☑
      anxiolytic 305.4 ☑
      barbiturates 305.4 ☑
      caffeine 305.9 ☑
      cannabis 305.2 ☑
      cocaine type 305.6 ☑
      hallucinogens 305.3 ☑
      hashish 305.2 ☑
      hypnotic 305.4 ☑
      inhalant 305.9 ☑
      LSD 305.3 ☑
      marijuana 305.2 ☑
      mixed 305.9 ☑
      morphine type 305.5 ☑
      opioid type 305.5 ☑
      phencyclidine (PCP) 305.9 ☑
      sedative 305.4 ☑
      specified NEC 305.9 ☑
      tranquilizers 305.4 ☑
    spouse 995.80
    tobacco 305.1
Acalcerosis 275.40
Acalcicosis 275.40
Acalculia 784.69

Acalculia — *continued*
  developmental 315.1
Acanthocheilonemiasis 125.4
Acanthocytosis 272.5
Acanthokeratodermia 701.1
Acantholysis 701.8
  bullosa 757.39
Acanthoma (benign) (M8070/0) — *see also* Neoplasm, by site, benign
  malignant (M8070/3) — *see* Neoplasm, by site, malignant
Acanthosis (acquired) (nigricans) 701.2
  adult 701.2
  benign (congenital) 757.39
  congenital 757.39
  glycogenic
    esophagus 530.89
  juvenile 701.2
  tongue 529.8
Acanthrocytosis 272.5
Acapnia 276.3
Acarbia 276.2
Acardia 759.89
Acardiacus amorphus 759.89
Acardiotrophia 429.1
Acardius 759.89
Acariasis 133.9
  sarcoptic 133.0
Acaridiasis 133.9
Acarinosis 133.9
Acariosis 133.9
Acarodermatitis 133.9
  urticarioides 133.9
Acarophobia 300.29
Acatalasemia 277.89
Acatalasia 277.89
Acatamathesia 784.69
Acataphasia 784.59
Acathisia 781.0
  due to drugs 333.99
Acceleration, accelerated
  atrioventricular conduction 426.7
  idioventricular rhythm 427.89
Accessory (congenital)
  adrenal gland 759.1
  anus 751.5
  appendix 751.5
  atrioventricular conduction 426.7
  auditory ossicles 744.04
  auricle (ear) 744.1
  autosome(s) NEC 758.5
    21 or 22 758.0
  biliary duct or passage 751.69
  bladder 753.8
  blood vessels (peripheral) (congenital) NEC (*see also* Anomaly, peripheral vascular system) 747.60
    cerebral 747.81
    coronary 746.85
  bone NEC 756.9
    foot 755.67
  breast tissue, axilla 757.6
  carpal bones 755.56
  cecum 751.5
  cervix 752.44
  chromosome(s) NEC 758.5
    13-15 758.1
    16-18 758.2
    21 or 22 758.0
    autosome(s) NEC 758.5
    D_1 758.1
    E_3 758.2
    G 758.0
    sex 758.81
  coronary artery 746.85
  cusp(s), heart valve NEC 746.89
    pulmonary 746.09
  cystic duct 751.69
  digits 755.00
  ear (auricle) (lobe) 744.1
  endocrine gland NEC 759.2
  external os 752.44
  eyelid 743.62
  eye muscle 743.69
  face bone(s) 756.0
  fallopian tube (fimbria) (ostium) 752.19

Accessory — *continued*
  fingers 755.01
  foreskin 605
  frontonasal process 756.0
  gallbladder 751.69
  genital organ(s)
    female 752.89
      external 752.49
      internal NEC 752.89
    male NEC 752.89
      penis 752.69
  genitourinary organs NEC 752.89
  heart 746.89
    valve NEC 746.89
      pulmonary 746.09
  hepatic ducts 751.69
  hymen 752.49
  intestine (large) (small) 751.5
  kidney 753.3
  lacrimal canal 743.65
  leaflet, heart valve NEC 746.89
    pulmonary 746.09
  ligament, broad 752.19
  liver (duct) 751.69
  lobule (ear) 744.1
  lung (lobe) 748.69
  muscle 756.82
  navicular of carpus 755.56
  nervous system, part NEC 742.8
  nipple 757.6
  nose 748.1
  organ or site NEC — *see* Anomaly, specified type NEC
  ovary 752.0
  oviduct 752.19
  pancreas 751.7
  parathyroid gland 759.2
  parotid gland (and duct) 750.22
  pituitary gland 759.2
  placental lobe — *see* Placenta, abnormal
  preauricular appendage 744.1
  prepuce 605
  renal arteries (multiple) 747.62
  rib 756.3
    cervical 756.2
  roots (teeth) 520.2
  salivary gland 750.22
  sesamoids 755.8
  sinus — *see* condition
  skin tags 757.39
  spleen 759.0
  sternum 756.3
  submaxillary gland 750.22
  tarsal bones 755.67
  teeth, tooth 520.1
    causing crowding 524.31
  tendon 756.89
  thumb 755.01
  thymus gland 759.2
  thyroid gland 759.2
  toes 755.02
  tongue 750.13
  tragus 744.1
  ureter 753.4
  urethra 753.8
  urinary organ or tract NEC 753.8
  uterus 752.2
  vagina 752.49
  valve, heart NEC 746.89
    pulmonary 746.09
  vertebra 756.19
  vocal cords 748.3
  vulva 752.49
Accident, accidental — *see also* condition
  birth NEC 767.9
  cardiovascular (*see also* Disease, cardiovascular) 429.2
  cerebral (*see also* Disease, cerebrovascular, acute) 434.91
  cerebrovascular (current) (CVA) (*see also* Disease, cerebrovascular, acute) 434.91
    aborted 434.91
    embolic 434.11
    healed or old V12.54
    hemorrhagic — *see* Hemorrhage, brain

☑ Additional Digit Required — Refer to the Tabular List for Digit Selection   ▽ Subterms under main terms may continue to next column or page

Accident, accidental — see also condition — continued
  cerebrovascular (see also Disease, cerebrovascular, acute) — continued
    impending 435.9
    ischemic 434.91
    late effect — see Late effect(s) (of) cerebrovascular disease
    postoperative 997.02
    thrombotic 434.01
  coronary (see also Infarct, myocardium) 410.9 ☑
  craniovascular (see also Disease, cerebrovascular, acute) 436
  during pregnancy, to mother, affecting fetus or newborn 760.5
  heart, cardiac (see also Infarct, myocardium) 410.9 ☑
  intrauterine 779.89
  vascular — see Disease, cerebrovascular, acute
Accommodation
  disorder of 367.51
    drug-induced 367.89
    toxic 367.89
  insufficiency of 367.4
  paralysis of 367.51
    hysterical 300.11
  spasm of 367.53
Accouchement — see Delivery
Accreta placenta (without hemorrhage) 667.0 ☑
  with hemorrhage 666.0 ☑
Accretio cordis (nonrheumatic) 423.1
Accretions on teeth 523.6
Accumulation secretion, prostate 602.8
Acephalia, acephalism, acephaly 740.0
Acephalic 740.0
Acephalobrachia 759.89
Acephalocardia 759.89
Acephalocardius 759.89
Acephalochiria 759.89
Acephalochirus 759.89
Acephalogaster 759.89
Acephalostomus 759.89
Acephalothorax 759.89
Acephalus 740.0
Acetonemia 790.6
  diabetic 250.1 ☑
    due to secondary diabetes 249.1 ☑
Acetonglycosuria 982.8
Acetonuria 791.6
Achalasia 530.0
  cardia 530.0
  digestive organs congenital NEC 751.8
  esophagus 530.0
  pelvirectal 751.3
  psychogenic 306.4
  pylorus 750.5
  sphincteral NEC 564.89
Achard-Thiers syndrome (adrenogenital) 255.2
Ache(s) — see Pain
Acheilia 750.26
Acheiria 755.21
Achillobursitis 726.71
Achillodynia 726.71
Achlorhydria, achlorhydric 536.0
  anemia 280.9
  diarrhea 536.0
  neurogenic 536.0
  postvagotomy 564.2
  psychogenic 306.4
  secondary to vagotomy 564.2
Achloroblepsia 368.52
Achloropsia 368.52
Acholia 575.8
Acholuric jaundice (familial) (splenomegalic) — see also Spherocytosis 282.0
  acquired 283.9
Achondroplasia 756.4
Achrestic anemia 281.8
Achroacytosis, lacrimal gland 375.00
  tuberculous (see also Tuberculosis) 017.3 ☑
Achroma, cutis 709.00
Achromate (congenital) 368.54

Achromatopia 368.54
Achromatopsia (congenital) 368.54
Achromia
  congenital 270.2
  parasitica 111.0
  unguium 703.8
Achylia
  gastrica 536.8
    neurogenic 536.3
    psychogenic 306.4
  pancreatica 577.1
Achylosis 536.8
Acid
  burn (see also Burn, by site)
    from swallowing acid — see Burn, internal organs
  deficiency
    amide nicotinic 265.2
    amino 270.9
    ascorbic 267
    folic 266.2
    nicotinic (amide) 265.2
    pantothenic 266.2
  intoxication 276.2
  peptic disease 536.8
  stomach 536.8
    psychogenic 306.4
Acidemia 276.2
  arginosuccinic 270.6
  fetal
    affecting management of pregnancy 656.3 ☑
    before onset of labor, in liveborn infant 768.2
    during labor and delivery in liveborn infant 768.3
    intrauterine 656.3 ☑
    unspecified as to time of onset, in liveborn infant 768.4
  newborn 775.81
  pipecolic 270.7
Acidity, gastric (high) (low) 536.8
  psychogenic 306.4
Acidocytopenia 288.59
Acidocytosis 288.3
Acidopenia 288.59
Acidosis 276.2
  diabetic 250.1 ☑
    due to secondary diabetes 249.1 ☑
  fetal, affecting management of pregnancy 656.8 ☑
  fetal, affecting newborn 775.81
  kidney tubular 588.89
    newborn 775.81
  lactic 276.2
  metabolic NEC 276.2
    with respiratory acidosis 276.4
      of newborn 775.81
    late, of newborn 775.7
  newborn 775.81
  renal
    hyperchloremic 588.89
    tubular (distal) (proximal) 588.89
  respiratory 276.2
    complicated by
      metabolic acidosis 276.4
        of newborn 775.81
      metabolic alkalosis 276.4
Aciduria 791.9
  arginosuccinic 270.6
  beta-aminoisobutyric (BAIB) 277.2
  glutaric
    type I 270.7
    type II (type IIA, IIB, IIC) 277.85
    type III 277.86
  glycolic 271.8
  methylmalonic 270.3
    with glycinemia 270.7
  organic 270.9
  orotic (congenital) (hereditary) (pyrimidine deficiency) 281.4
Acladiosis 111.8
  skin 111.8
Aclasis
  diaphyseal 756.4
  tarsoepiphyseal 756.59

Acleistocardia 745.5
Aclusion 524.4
Acmesthesia 782.0
Acne (pustular) (vulgaris) 706.1
  agminata (see also Tuberculosis) 017.0 ☑
  artificialis 706.1
  atrophica 706.0
  cachecticorum (Hebra) 706.1
  conglobata 706.1
  conjunctiva 706.1
  cystic 706.1
  decalvans 704.09
  erythematosa 695.3
  eyelid 706.1
  frontalis 706.0
  indurata 706.1
  keloid 706.1
  lupoid 706.0
  necrotic, necrotica 706.0
    miliaris 704.8
  neonatal 706.1
  nodular 706.1
  occupational 706.1
  papulosa 706.1
  rodens 706.0
  rosacea 695.3
  scorbutica 267
  scrofulosorum (Bazin) (see also Tuberculosis) 017.0 ☑
  summer 692.72
  tropical 706.1
  varioliformis 706.0
Acneiform drug eruptions 692.3
Acnitis (primary) — see also Tuberculosis 017.0 ☑
Acomia 704.00
Acontractile bladder 344.61
Aconuresis — see also Incontinence 788.30
Acosta's disease 993.2
Acousma 780.1
Acoustic — see condition
Acousticophobia 300.29
Acquired — see condition
Acquired immune deficiency syndrome — see Human immunodeficiency virus (disease) (illness) (infection)
Acquired immunodeficiency syndrome — see Human immunodeficiency virus (disease) (illness) (infection)
Acragnosis 781.99
Acrania 740.0
Acroagnosis 781.99
Acroangiodermatitis 448.9
Acroasphyxia, chronic 443.89
Acrobrachycephaly 756.0
Acrobystiolith 608.89
Acrobystitis 607.2
Acrocephalopolysyndactyly 755.55
Acrocephalosyndactyly 755.55
Acrocephaly 756.0
Acrochondrohyperplasia 759.82
Acrocyanosis 443.89
  newborn 770.83
    meaning transient blue hands and feet — omit code
Acrodermatitis 686.8
  atrophicans (chronica) 701.8
  continua (Hallopeau) 696.1
  enteropathica 686.8
  Hallopeau's 696.1
  perstans 696.1
  pustulosa continua 696.1
  recalcitrant pustular 696.1
Acrodynia 985.0
Acrodysplasia 755.55
Acrohyperhidrosis — see also Hyperhidrosis 780.8
Acrokeratosis verruciformis 757.39
Acromastitis 611.0
Acromegaly, acromegalia (skin) 253.0
Acromelalgia 443.82
Acromicria, acromikria 756.59
Acronyx 703.0
Acropachyderma 757.39
Acropachy, thyroid — see also Thyrotoxicosis 242.9 ☑

Acroparesthesia 443.89
  simple (Schultz's type) 443.89
  vasomotor (Nothnagel's type) 443.89
Acropathy thyroid — see also Thyrotoxicosis 242.9 ☑
Acrophobia 300.29
Acroposthitis 607.2
Acroscleriasis — see also Scleroderma 710.1
Acroscleroderma — see also Scleroderma 710.1
Acrosclerosis — see also Scleroderma 710.1
Acrosphacelus 785.4
Acrosphenosyndactylia 755.55
Acrospiroma, eccrine (M8402/0) — see Neoplasm, skin, benign
Acrostealgia 732.9
Acrosyndactyly — see also Syndactylism 755.10
Acrotrophodynia 991.4
Actinic — see also condition
  cheilitis (due to sun) 692.72
    chronic NEC 692.74
    due to radiation, except from sun 692.82
  conjunctivitis 370.24
  dermatitis (due to sun) (see also Dermatitis, actinic) 692.70
  due to
    roentgen rays or radioactive substance 692.82
    ultraviolet radiation, except from sun 692.82
    sun NEC 692.70
  elastosis solare 692.74
  granuloma 692.73
  keratitis 370.24
  ophthalmia 370.24
  reticuloid 692.73
Actinobacillosis, general 027.8
Actinobacillus
  lignieresii 027.8
  mallei 024
  muris 026.1
Actinocutitis NEC — see also Dermatitis, actinic 692.70
Actinodermatitis NEC — see also Dermatitis, actinic 692.70
Actinomyces
  israelii (infection) — see Actinomycosis
  muris-ratti (infection) 026.1
Actinomycosis, actinomycotic 039.9
  with
    pneumonia 039.1
  abdominal 039.2
  cervicofacial 039.3
  cutaneous 039.0
  pulmonary 039.1
  specified site NEC 039.8
  thoracic 039.1
Actinoneuritis 357.89
Action, heart
  disorder 427.9
    postoperative 997.1
  irregular 427.9
    postoperative 997.1
    psychogenic 306.2
Active — see condition
Activity decrease, functional 780.99
Acute — see also condition
  abdomen NEC 789.0 ☑
  gallbladder (see also Cholecystitis, acute) 575.0
Acyanoblepsia 368.53
Acyanopsia 368.53
Acystia 753.8
Acystinervia — see Neurogenic, bladder
Acystineuria — see Neurogenic, bladder
Adactylia, adactyly (congenital) 755.4
  lower limb (complete) (intercalary) (partial) (terminal) (see also Deformity, reduction, lower limb) 755.39
    meaning all digits (complete) (partial) 755.31
    transverse (complete) (partial) 755.31
  upper limb (complete) (intercalary) (partial) (terminal) (see also Deformity, reduction, upper limb) 755.29

☑ Additional Digit Required — Refer to the Tabular List for Digit Selection   ⬇ Subterms under main terms may continue to next column or page

8 — Volume 2   ▶◀ Revised Text   ● New Line   ▲ Revised Code   2015 ICD-9-CM

Adactylia, adactyly — *continued*
  upper limb (*see also* Deformity, reduction, upper limb) — *continued*
      meaning all digits (complete) (partial) 755.21
      transverse (complete) (partial) 755.21
Adair-Dighton syndrome (brittle bones and blue sclera, deafness) 756.51
Adamantinoblastoma (M9310/0) — *see* Ameloblastoma
Adamantinoma (M9310/0) — *see* Ameloblastoma
Adamantoblastoma (M9310/0) — *see* Ameloblastoma
Adams-Stokes (-Morgagni) disease or syndrome (syncope with heart block) 426.9
Adaptation reaction — *see also* Reaction, adjustment 309.9
Addiction — *see also* Dependence
  absinthe 304.6 ☑
  alcoholic (ethyl) (methyl) (wood) 303.9 ☑
      complicating pregnancy, childbirth, or puerperium 648.4 ☑
          affecting fetus or newborn 760.71
          suspected damage to fetus affecting management of pregnancy 655.4 ☑
  drug (*see also* Dependence) 304.9 ☑
  ethyl alcohol 303.9 ☑
  heroin 304.0 ☑
  hospital 301.51
  methyl alcohol 303.9 ☑
  methylated spirit 303.9 ☑
  morphine (-like substances) 304.0 ☑
  nicotine 305.1
  opium 304.0 ☑
  tobacco 305.1
  wine 303.9 ☑
Addison's
  anemia (pernicious) 281.0
  disease (bronze) (primary adrenal insufficiency) 255.41
      tuberculous (*see also* Tuberculosis) 017.6 ☑
  keloid (morphea) 701.0
  melanoderma (adrenal cortical hypofunction) 255.41
Addison-Biermer anemia (pernicious) 281.0
Addison-Gull disease — *see* Xanthoma
Addisonian crisis or melanosis (acute adrenocortical insufficiency) 255.41
Additional — *see also* Accessory
  chromosome(s) 758.5
      13-15 758.1
      16-18 758.2
      21 758.0
      autosome(s) NEC 758.5
      sex 758.81
Adduction contracture, hip or other joint — *see* Contraction, joint
ADEM (acute disseminated encephalomyelitis) (postinfectious) 136.9 *[323.61]*
  infectious 136.9 *[323.61]*
  noninfectious 323.81
Adenasthenia gastrica 536.0
Aden fever 061
Adenitis — *see also* Lymphadenitis 289.3
  acute, unspecified site 683
      epidemic infectious 075
  axillary 289.3
      acute 683
      chronic or subacute 289.1
  Bartholin's gland 616.89
  bulbourethral gland (*see also* Urethritis) 597.89
  cervical 289.3
      acute 683
      chronic or subacute 289.1
  chancroid (Ducrey's bacillus) 099.0
  chronic (any lymph node, except mesenteric) 289.1
      mesenteric 289.2
  Cowper's gland (*see also* Urethritis) 597.89
  epidemic, acute 075
  gangrenous 683
  gonorrheal NEC 098.89

Adenitis — *see also* Lymphadenitis — *continued*
  groin 289.3
      acute 683
      chronic or subacute 289.1
  infectious 075
  inguinal (region) 289.3
      acute 683
      chronic or subacute 289.1
  lymph gland or node, except mesenteric 289.3
      acute 683
      chronic or subacute 289.1
  mesenteric (acute) (chronic) (nonspecific) (subacute) 289.2
  mesenteric (acute) (chronic) (nonspecific) (subacute) 289.2
      due to Pasteurella multocida (P. septica) 027.2
  parotid gland (suppurative) 527.2
  phlegmonous 683
  salivary duct or gland (any) (recurring) (suppurative) 527.2
  scrofulous (*see also* Tuberculosis) 017.2 ☑
  septic 289.3
  Skene's duct or gland (*see also* Urethritis) 597.89
  strumous, tuberculous (*see also* Tuberculosis) 017.2 ☑
  subacute, unspecified site 289.1
  sublingual gland (suppurative) 527.2
  submandibular gland (suppurative) 527.2
  submaxillary gland (suppurative) 527.2
  suppurative 683
  tuberculous — *see* Tuberculosis, lymph gland
  urethral gland (*see also* Urethritis) 597.89
  venereal NEC 099.8
  Wharton's duct (suppurative) 527.2
Adenoacanthoma (M8570/3) — *see* Neoplasm, by site, malignant
Adenoameloblastoma (M9300/0) 213.1
  upper jaw (bone) 213.0
Adenocarcinoma (M8140/3) — *see also* Neoplasm, by site, malignant

Note — The list of adjectival modifiers below is not exhaustive. A description of adenocarcinoma that does not appear in this list should be coded in the same manner as carcinoma with that description. Thus, "mixed acidophil-basophil adenocarcinoma," should be coded in the same manner as "mixed acidophil-basophil carcinoma," which appears in the list under "Carcinoma."

Except where otherwise indicated, the morphological varieties of adenocarcinoma in the list below should be coded by site as for "Neoplasm, malignant."

  with
      apocrine metaplasia (M8573/3)
      cartilaginous (and osseous) metaplasia (M8571/3)
      osseous (and cartilaginous) metaplasia (M8571/3)
      spindle cell metaplasia (M8572/3)
      squamous metaplasia (M8570/3)
  acidophil (M8280/3)
      specified site — *see* Neoplasm, by site, malignant
      unspecified site 194.3
  acinar (M8550/3)
  acinic cell (M8550/3)
  adrenal cortical (M8370/3) 194.0
  alveolar (M8251/3)
      and
          epidermoid carcinoma, mixed (M8560/3)
          squamous cell carcinoma, mixed (M8560/3)
  apocrine (M8401/3)
      breast — *see* Neoplasm, breast, malignant
      specified site NEC — *see* Neoplasm, skin, malignant

Adenocarcinoma — *see also* Neoplasm, by site, malignant — *continued*
  apocrine — *continued*
      unspecified site 173.99
  basophil (M8300/3)
      specified site — *see* Neoplasm, by site, malignant
      unspecified site 194.3
  bile duct type (M8160/3)
      liver 155.1
      specified site NEC — *see* Neoplasm, by site, malignant
      unspecified site 155.1
  bronchiolar (M8250/3) — *see* Neoplasm, lung, malignant
  ceruminous (M8420/3) 173.29
  chromophobe (M8270/3)
      specified site — *see* Neoplasm, by site, malignant
      unspecified site 194.3
  clear cell (mesonephroid type) (M8310/3)
  colloid (M8480/3)
  cylindroid type (M8200/3)
  diffuse type (M8145/3)
      specified site — *see* Neoplasm, by site, malignant
      unspecified site 151.9
  duct (infiltrating) (M8500/3)
      with Paget's disease (M8541/3) — *see* Neoplasm, breast, malignant
      specified site — *see* Neoplasm, by site, malignant
      unspecified site 174.9
  embryonal (M9070/3)
  endometrioid (M8380/3) — *see* Neoplasm, by site, malignant
  eosinophil (M8280/3)
      specified site — *see* Neoplasm, by site, malignant
      unspecified site 194.3
  follicular (M8330/3)
      and papillary (M8340/3) 193
      moderately differentiated type (M8332/3) 193
      pure follicle type (M8331/3) 193
      specified site — *see* Neoplasm, by site, malignant
      trabecular type (M8332/3) 193
      unspecified type 193
      well differentiated type (M8331/3) 193
  gelatinous (M8480/3)
  granular cell (M8320/3)
  Hürthle cell (M8290/3) 193
  in
      adenomatous
          polyp (M8210/3)
          polyposis coli (M8220/3) 153.9
      polypoid adenoma (M8210/3)
      tubular adenoma (M8210/3)
      villous adenoma (M8261/3)
  infiltrating duct (M8500/3)
      with Paget's disease (M8541/3) — *see* Neoplasm, breast, malignant
      specified site — *see* Neoplasm, by site, malignant
      unspecified site 174.9
  inflammatory (M8530/3)
      specified site — *see* Neoplasm, by site, malignant
      unspecified site 174.9
  in situ (M8140/2) — *see* Neoplasm, by site, in situ
  intestinal type (M8144/3)
      specified site — *see* Neoplasm, by site, malignant
      unspecified site 151.9
  intraductal (noninfiltrating) (M8500/2)
      papillary (M8503/2)
          specified site — *see* Neoplasm, by site, in situ
          unspecified site 233.0
      specified site — *see* Neoplasm, by site, in situ
      unspecified site 233.0

Adenocarcinoma — *see also* Neoplasm, by site, malignant — *continued*
  islet cell (M8150/3)
      and exocrine, mixed (M8154/3)
          specified site — *see* Neoplasm, by site, malignant
          unspecified site 157.9
      pancreas 157.4
      specified site NEC — *see* Neoplasm, by site, malignant
      unspecified site 157.4
  lobular (M8520/3)
      specified site — *see* Neoplasm, by site, malignant
      unspecified site 174.9
  medullary (M8510/3)
  mesonephric (M9110/3)
  mixed cell (M8323/3)
  mucinous (M8480/3)
  mucin-producing (M8481/3)
  mucoid (M8480/3) (*see also* Neoplasm, by site, malignant)
      cell (M8300/3)
          specified site — *see* Neoplasm, by site, malignant
          unspecified site 194.3
  nonencapsulated sclerosing (M8350/3) 193
  oncocytic (M8290/3)
  oxyphilic (M8290/3)
  papillary (M8260/3)
      and follicular (M8340/3) 193
      intraductal (noninfiltrating) (M8503/2)
          specified site — *see* Neoplasm, by site, in situ
          unspecified site 233.0
  serous (M8460/3)
      specified site — *see* Neoplasm, by site, malignant
      unspecified site 183.0
  papillocystic (M8450/3)
      specified site — *see* Neoplasm, by site, malignant
      unspecified site 183.0
  pseudomucinous (M8470/3)
      specified site — *see* Neoplasm, by site, malignant
      unspecified site 183.0
  renal cell (M8312/3) 189.0
  sebaceous (M8410/3)
  serous (M8441/3) (*see also* Neoplasm, by site, malignant)
      papillary
          specified site — *see* Neoplasm, by site, malignant
          unspecified site 183.0
  signet ring cell (M8490/3)
  superficial spreading (M8143/3)
  sweat gland (M8400/3) — *see* Neoplasm, skin, malignant
  trabecular (M8190/3)
  tubular (M8211/3)
  villous (M8262/3)
  water-clear cell (M8322/3) 194.1
Adenofibroma (M9013/0)
  clear cell (M8313/0) — *see* Neoplasm, by site, benign
  endometrioid (M8381/0) 220
      borderline malignancy (M8381/1) 236.2
      malignant (M8381/3) 183.0
  mucinous (M9015/0)
      specified site — *see* Neoplasm, by site, benign
      unspecified site 220
  prostate
      with
          other lower urinary tract symptoms (LUTS) 600.21
          urinary
              obstruction 600.21
              retention 600.21
  serous (M9014/0)
      specified site — *see* Neoplasm, by site, benign
      unspecified site 220
  specified site — *see* Neoplasm, by site, benign

Adenofibroma — *continued*
  unspecified site 220
Adenofibrosis
  breast 610.2
  endometrioid 617.0
Adenoiditis 474.01
  acute 463
  chronic 474.01
    with chronic tonsillitis 474.02
Adenoids (congenital) (of nasal fossa) 474.9
  hypertrophy 474.12
  vegetations 474.2
Adenolipomatosis (symmetrical) 272.8
Adenolymphoma (M8561/0)
  specified site — *see* Neoplasm, by site, benign
  unspecified 210.2
Adenomatosis (M8220/0)
  endocrine (multiple) (M8360/1)
    single specified site — *see* Neoplasm, by site, uncertain behavior
    two or more specified sites 237.4
    unspecified site 237.4
  erosive of nipple (M8506/0) 217
  pluriendocrine — *see* Adenomatosis, endocrine
  pulmonary (M8250/1) 235.7
    malignant (M8250/3) — *see* Neoplasm, lung, malignant
  specified site — *see* Neoplasm, by site, benign
  unspecified site 211.3
Adenomatous
  cyst, thyroid (gland) — *see* Goiter, nodular
  goiter (nontoxic) (*see also* Goiter, nodular) 241.9
    toxic or with hyperthyroidism 242.3 ☑
Adenoma (sessile) (M8140/0) — *see also* Neoplasm, by site, benign

Note — Except where otherwise indicated, the morphological varieties of adenoma in the list below should be coded by site as for "Neoplasm, benign."

acidophil (M8280/0)
  specified site — *see* Neoplasm, by site, benign
  unspecified site 227.3
acinar (cell) (M8550/0)
acinic cell (M8550/0)
adrenal (cortex) (cortical) (functioning) (M8370/0) 227.0
  clear cell type (M8373/0) 227.0
  compact cell type (M8371/0) 227.0
  glomerulosa cell type (M8374/0) 227.0
  heavily pigmented variant (M8372/0) 227.0
  mixed cell type (M8375/0) 227.0
alpha cell (M8152/0)
  pancreas 211.7
  specified site NEC — *see* Neoplasm, by site, benign
  unspecified site 211.7
alveolar (M8251/0)
apocrine (M8401/0)
  breast 217
  specified site NEC — *see* Neoplasm, skin, benign
  unspecified site 216.9
basal cell (M8147/0)
basophil (M8300/0)
  specified site — *see* Neoplasm, by site, benign
  unspecified site 227.3
beta cell (M8151/0)
  pancreas 211.7
  specified site NEC — *see* Neoplasm, by site, benign
  unspecified site 211.7
bile duct (M8160/0) 211.5
black (M8372/0) 227.0
bronchial (M8140/1) 235.7
  carcinoid type (M8240/3) — *see* Neoplasm, lung, malignant
  cylindroid type (M8200/3) — *see* Neoplasm, lung, malignant
ceruminous (M8420/0) 216.2

Adenoma — *see also* Neoplasm, by site, benign — *continued*
chief cell (M8321/0) 227.1
chromophobe (M8270/0)
  specified site — *see* Neoplasm, by site, benign
  unspecified site 227.3
clear cell (M8310/0)
colloid (M8334/0)
  specified site — *see* Neoplasm, by site, benign
  unspecified site 226
cylindroid type, bronchus (M8200/3) — *see* Neoplasm, lung, malignant
duct (M8503/0)
embryonal (M8191/0)
endocrine, multiple (M8360/1)
  single specified site — *see* Neoplasm, by site, uncertain behavior
  two or more specified sites 237.4
  unspecified site 237.4
endometrioid (M8380/0) (*see also* Neoplasm, by site, benign)
  borderline malignancy (M8380/1) — *see* Neoplasm, by site, uncertain behavior
eosinophil (M8280/0)
  specified site — *see* Neoplasm, by site, benign
  unspecified site 227.3
fetal (M8333/0)
  specified site — *see* Neoplasm, by site, benign
  unspecified site 226
follicular (M8330/0)
  specified site — *see* Neoplasm, by site, benign
  unspecified site 226
hepatocellular (M8170/0) 211.5
Hürthle cell (M8290/0) 226
intracystic papillary (M8504/0)
islet cell (functioning) (M8150/0)
  pancreas 211.7
  specified site NEC — *see* Neoplasm, by site, benign
  unspecified site 211.7
liver cell (M8170/0) 211.5
macrofollicular (M8334/0)
  specified site NEC — *see* Neoplasm, by site, benign
  unspecified site 226
malignant, malignum (M8140/3) — *see* Neoplasm, by site, malignant
mesonephric (M9110/0)
microfollicular (M8333/0)
  specified site — *see* Neoplasm, by site, benign
  unspecified site 226
mixed cell (M8323/0)
monomorphic (M8146/0)
mucinous (M8480/0)
mucoid cell (M8300/0)
  specified site — *see* Neoplasm, by site, benign
  unspecified site 227.3
multiple endocrine (M8360/1)
  single specified site — *see* Neoplasm, by site, uncertain behavior
  two or more specified sites 237.4
  unspecified site 237.4
nipple (M8506/0) 217
oncocytic (M8290/0)
oxyphilic (M8290/0)
papillary (M8260/0) (*see also* Neoplasm, by site, benign)
  intracystic (M8504/0)
papillotubular (M8263/0)
Pick's tubular (M8640/0)
  specified site — *see* Neoplasm, by site, benign
  unspecified site
    female 220
    male 222.0
pleomorphic (M8940/0)
polypoid (M8210/0)
prostate (benign) 600.20

Adenoma — *see also* Neoplasm, by site, benign — *continued*
prostate — *continued*
  with
    other lower urinary tract symptoms (LUTS) 600.21
    urinary
      obstruction 600.21
      retention 600.21
rete cell 222.0
sebaceous, sebaceum (gland) (senile) (M8410/0) (*see also* Neoplasm, skin, benign)
  disseminata 759.5
Sertoli cell (M8640/0)
  specified site — *see* Neoplasm, by site, benign
  unspecified site
    female 220
    male 222.0
skin appendage (M8390/0) — *see* Neoplasm, skin, benign
sudoriferous gland (M8400/0) — *see* Neoplasm, skin, benign
sweat gland or duct (M8400/0) — *see* Neoplasm, skin, benign
testicular (M8640/0)
  specified site — *see* Neoplasm, by site, benign
  unspecified site
    female 220
    male 222.0
thyroid 226
trabecular (M8190/0)
tubular (M8211/0) (*see also* Neoplasm, by site, benign)
  papillary (M8460/3)
  Pick's (M8640/0)
    specified site — *see* Neoplasm, by site, benign
    unspecified site
      female 220
      male 222.0
tubulovillous (M8263/0)
villoglandular (M8263/0)
villous (M8261/1) — *see* Neoplasm, by site, uncertain behavior
water-clear cell (M8322/0) 227.1
wolffian duct (M9110/0)
Adenomyoma (M8932/0) — *see also* Neoplasm, by site, benign
prostate 600.20
  with
    other lower urinary tract symptoms (LUTS) 600.21
    urinary
      obstruction 600.21
      retention 600.21
Adenomyometritis 617.0
Adenomyosis (uterus) (internal) 617.0
Adenopathy (lymph gland) 785.6
  inguinal 785.6
  mediastinal 785.6
  mesentery 785.6
  syphilitic (secondary) 091.4
  tracheobronchial 785.6
    tuberculous (*see also* Tuberculosis) 012.1 ☑
      primary, progressive 010.8 ☑
  tuberculous (*see also* Tuberculosis, lymph gland) 017.2 ☑
    tracheobronchial 012.1 ☑
      primary, progressive 010.8 ☑
Adenopharyngitis 462
Adenophlegmon 683
Adenosalpingitis 614.1
Adenosarcoma (M8960/3) 189.0
Adenosclerosis 289.3
Adenosis
  breast (sclerosing) 610.2
  vagina, congenital 752.49
Adentia (complete) (partial) — *see also* Absence, teeth 520.0
Adherent
  labium (minus) 624.4
  pericardium (nonrheumatic) 423.1

Adherent — *continued*
  pericardium — *continued*
    rheumatic 393
  placenta 667.0 ☑
    with hemorrhage 666.0 ☑
  prepuce 605
  scar (skin) NEC 709.2
  tendon in scar 709.2
Adhesion(s), adhesive (postinfectional) (postoperative)
  abdominal (wall) (*see also* Adhesions, peritoneum) 568.0
  amnion to fetus 658.8 ☑
    affecting fetus or newborn 762.8
  appendix 543.9
  arachnoiditis — *see* Meningitis
  auditory tube (Eustachian) 381.89
  bands (*see also* Adhesions, peritoneum)
    cervix 622.3
    uterus 621.5
  bile duct (any) 576.8
  bladder (sphincter) 596.89
  bowel (*see also* Adhesions, peritoneum) 568.0
  cardiac 423.1
    rheumatic 398.99
  cecum (*see also* Adhesions, peritoneum) 568.0
  cervicovaginal 622.3
    congenital 752.49
    postpartal 674.8 ☑
    old 622.3
  cervix 622.3
  clitoris 624.4
  colon (*see also* Adhesions, peritoneum) 568.0
  common duct 576.8
  congenital (*see also* Anomaly, specified type NEC)
    fingers (*see also* Syndactylism, fingers) 755.11
    labium (majus) (minus) 752.49
    omental, anomalous 751.4
    ovary 752.0
    peritoneal 751.4
    toes (*see also* Syndactylism, toes) 755.13
    tongue (to gum or roof of mouth) 750.12
  conjunctiva (acquired) (localized) 372.62
    congenital 743.63
    extensive 372.63
  cornea — *see* Opacity, cornea
  cystic duct 575.8
  diaphragm (*see also* Adhesions, peritoneum) 568.0
  due to foreign body — *see* Foreign body
  duodenum (*see also* Adhesions, peritoneum) 568.0
    with obstruction 537.3
  ear, middle — *see* Adhesions, middle ear
  epididymis 608.89
  epidural — *see* Adhesions, meninges
  epiglottis 478.79
  Eustachian tube 381.89
  eyelid 374.46
    postoperative 997.99
    surgically created V45.69
  gallbladder (*see also* Disease, gallbladder) 575.8
  globe 360.89
  heart 423.1
    rheumatic 398.99
  ileocecal (coil) (*see also* Adhesions, peritoneum) 568.0
  ileum (*see also* Adhesions, peritoneum) 568.0
  intestine (postoperative) (*see also* Adhesions, peritoneum) 568.0
    with obstruction 560.81
      with hernia (*see also* Hernia, by site, with obstruction)
        gangrenous — *see* Hernia, by site, with gangrene
  intra-abdominal (*see also* Adhesions, peritoneum) 568.0
  iris 364.70
    to corneal graft 996.79

Adhesion(s), adhesive — *continued*
joint (*see also* Ankylosis) 718.5 ☑
kidney 593.89
labium (majus) (minus), congenital 752.49
liver 572.8
lung 511.0
mediastinum 519.3
meninges 349.2
cerebral (any) 349.2
congenital 742.4
congenital 742.8
spinal (any) 349.2
congenital 742.59
tuberculous (cerebral) (spinal) (*see also*
Tuberculosis, meninges) 013.0 ☑
mesenteric (*see also* Adhesions, peritoneum)
568.0
middle ear (fibrous) 385.10
drum head 385.19
to
incus 385.11
promontorium 385.13
stapes 385.12
specified NEC 385.19
nasal (septum) (to turbinates) 478.19
nerve NEC 355.9
spinal 355.9
root 724.9
cervical NEC 723.4
lumbar NEC 724.4
lumbosacral 724.4
thoracic 724.4
ocular muscle 378.60
omentum (*see also* Adhesions, peritoneum)
568.0
organ or site, congenital NEC — *see*
Anomaly, specified type NEC
ovary 614.6
congenital (to cecum, kidney, or omentum) 752.0
parauterine 614.6
parovarian 614.6
pelvic (peritoneal)
female (postoperative) (postinfection)
614.6
male (postoperative) (postinfection) (*see
also* Adhesions, peritoneum)
568.0
postpartal (old) 614.6
tuberculous (*see also* Tuberculosis)
016.9 ☑
penis to scrotum (congenital) 752.69
periappendiceal (*see also* Adhesions, peritoneum) 568.0
pericardium (nonrheumatic) 423.1
rheumatic 393
tuberculous (*see also* Tuberculosis)
017.9 ☑ [420.0]
pericholecystic 575.8
perigastric (*see also* Adhesions, peritoneum)
568.0
periovarian 614.6
periprostatic 602.8
perirectal (*see also* Adhesions, peritoneum)
568.0
perirenal 593.89
peritoneum, peritoneal (fibrous) (postoperative) 568.0
with obstruction (intestinal) 560.81
with hernia (*see also* Hernia, by site,
with obstruction)
gangrenous — *see* Hernia, by site,
with gangrene
duodenum 537.3
congenital 751.4
female (postoperative) (postinfective)
614.6
pelvic, female 614.6
pelvic, male 568.0
postpartal, pelvic 614.6
to uterus 614.6
perituba l 614.6
periureteral 593.89
periuterine 621.5
perivesical 596.89
perivesicular (seminal vesicle) 608.89

Adhesion(s), adhesive — *continued*
pleura, pleuritic 511.0
tuberculous (*see also* Tuberculosis,
pleura) 012.0 ☑
pleuropericardial 511.0
postoperative (gastrointestinal tract) (*see
also* Adhesions, peritoneum) 568.0
eyelid 997.99
surgically created V45.69
pelvic female 614.9
pelvic male 568.0
urethra 598.2
postpartal, old 624.4
preputial, prepuce 605
pulmonary 511.0
pylorus (*see also* Adhesions, peritoneum)
568.0
Rosenmüller's fossa 478.29
sciatic nerve 355.0
seminal vesicle 608.89
shoulder (joint) 726.0
sigmoid flexure (*see also* Adhesions, peritoneum) 568.0
spermatic cord (acquired) 608.89
congenital 752.89
spinal canal 349.2
nerve 355.9
root 724.9
cervical NEC 723.4
lumbar NEC 724.4
lumbosacral 724.4
thoracic 724.4
stomach (*see also* Adhesions, peritoneum)
568.0
subscapular 726.2
tendonitis 726.90
shoulder 726.0
testicle 608.89
tongue (congenital) (to gum or roof of
mouth) 750.12
acquired 529.8
trachea 519.19
tubo-ovarian 614.6
tunica vaginalis 608.89
ureter 593.89
uterus 621.5
to abdominal wall 614.6
in pregnancy or childbirth 654.4 ☑
affecting fetus or newborn 763.89
vagina (chronic) (postoperative) (postradiation) 623.2
vaginitis (congenital) 752.49
vesical 596.89
vitreomacular adhesion 379.27
vitreous 379.29
Adie (-Holmes) syndrome (tonic pupillary reaction) 379.46
Adiponecrosis neonatorum 778.1
Adiposa dolorosa 272.8
Adiposalgia 272.8
Adiposis
cerebralis 253.8
dolorosa 272.8
tuberosa simplex 272.8
Adiposity 278.02
heart (*see also* Degeneration, myocardial)
429.1
localized 278.1
Adiposogenital dystrophy 253.8
Adjustment
prosthesis or other device — *see* Fitting of
reaction — *see* Reaction, adjustment
Administration, prophylactic
antibiotics, long-term V58.62
short-term use — *omit code*
antitoxin, any V07.2
antivenin V07.2
chemotherapeutic agent NEC V07.39
chemotherapy NEC V07.39
diphtheria antitoxin V07.2
fluoride V07.31
gamma globulin V07.2
immune sera (gamma globulin) V07.2
passive immunization agent V07.2
RhoGAM V07.2

Admission (encounter)
as organ donor — *see* Donor
by mistake V68.9
for
adequacy testing (for)
hemodialysis V56.31
peritoneal dialysis V56.32
adjustment (of)
artificial
arm (complete) (partial) V52.0
eye V52.2
leg (complete) (partial) V52.1
brain neuropacemaker V53.02
breast
implant V52.4
exchange (different material)
(different size) V52.4
prosthesis V52.4
cardiac device V53.39
defibrillator, automatic implantable (with syn-
chronous cardiac pacemak-
er) V53.32
pacemaker V53.31
carotid sinus V53.39
catheter
non-vascular V58.82
vascular V58.81
cerebral ventricle (communicating)
shunt V53.01
colostomy belt V55.3
contact lenses V53.1
cystostomy device V53.6
dental prosthesis V52.3
device, unspecified type V53.90
abdominal V53.59
cardiac V53.39
defibrillator, automatic implantable (with syn-
chronous cardiac pace-
maker V53.32
pacemaker V53.31
carotid sinus V53.39
cerebral ventricle (communicating) shunt V53.01
gastrointestinal NEC V53.59
insulin pump V53.91
intestinal V53.50
nervous system V53.09
orthodontic V53.4
other device V53.99
prosthetic V52.9
breast V52.4
dental V52.3
eye V52.2
specified type NEC V52.8
special senses V53.09
substitution
auditory V53.09
nervous system V53.09
visual V53.09
urinary V53.6
dialysis catheter
extracorporeal V56.1
peritoneal V56.2
diaphragm (contraceptive) V25.02
gastric lap band V53.51
gastrointestinal appliance and device
NEC V53.59
growth rod V54.02
hearing aid V53.2
ileostomy device V55.2
intestinal appliance and device
V53.50
neuropacemaker (brain) (peripheral
nerve) (spinal cord) V53.02
orthodontic device V53.4
orthopedic (device) V53.7
brace V53.7
cast V53.7
shoes V53.7
pacemaker
brain V53.02
cardiac V53.31
carotid sinus V53.39
peripheral nerve V53.02

Admission — *continued*
for — *continued*
adjustment — *continued*
pacemaker — *continued*
spinal cord V53.02
prosthesis V52.9
arm (complete) (partial) V52.0
breast V52.4
dental V52.3
eye V52.2
leg (complete) (partial) V52.1
specified type NEC V52.8
spectacles V53.1
wheelchair V53.8
adoption referral or proceedings V68.89
aftercare (*see also* Aftercare) V58.9
cardiac pacemaker V53.31
chemotherapy (oral) (intravenous)
V58.11
dialysis
extracorporeal (renal) V56.0
peritoneal V56.8
renal V56.0
fracture (*see also* Aftercare, fracture)
V54.9
medical NEC V58.89
organ transplant V58.44
orthopedic V54.9
following explanation of joint
prosthesis (for joint prosthesis insertion) (staged
procedure) V54.82
specified care NEC V54.89
pacemaker device
brain V53.02
cardiac V53.31
carotid sinus V53.39
nervous system V53.02
spinal cord V53.02
postoperative NEC V58.49
wound closure, planned V58.41
postpartum
immediately after delivery V24.0
routine follow-up V24.2
postradiation V58.0
radiation therapy V58.0
removal of
non-vascular catheter V58.82
vascular catheter V58.81
specified NEC V58.89
surgical NEC V58.49
wound closure, planned V58.41
antineoplastic
chemotherapy (oral) (intravenous)
V58.11
immunotherapy V58.12
artificial insemination V26.1
assisted reproductive fertility procedure
cycle V26.81
attention to artificial opening (of) V55.9
artificial vagina V55.7
colostomy V55.3
cystostomy V55.5
enterostomy V55.4
gastrostomy V55.1
ileostomy V55.2
jejunostomy V55.4
nephrostomy V55.6
specified site NEC V55.8
intestinal tract V55.4
urinary tract V55.6
tracheostomy V55.0
ureterostomy V55.6
urethrostomy V55.6
battery replacement
cardiac pacemaker V53.31
blood typing V72.86
Rh typing V72.86
boarding V65.0
breast
augmentation or reduction V50.1
implant exchange (different material)
(different size) V52.4
reconstruction following mastectomy
V51.0

Admission — continued
for — continued
  breast — continued
    removal
      prophylactic V50.41
      tissue expander without synchronous insertion of permanent implant V52.4
  change of
    cardiac pacemaker (battery) V53.31
    carotid sinus pacemaker V53.39
    catheter in artificial opening — see Attention to, artificial, opening
    drains V58.49
    dressing
      wound V58.30
        nonsurgical V58.30
        surgical V58.31
    fixation device
      external V54.89
      internal V54.01
    Kirschner wire V54.89
    neuropacemaker device (brain) (peripheral nerve) (spinal cord) V53.02
    nonsurgical wound dressing V58.30
    pacemaker device
      brain V53.02
      cardiac V53.31
      carotid sinus V53.39
      nervous system V53.02
    plaster cast V54.89
    splint, external V54.89
    Steinmann pin V54.89
    surgical wound dressing V58.31
    traction device V54.89
    wound packing V58.30
      nonsurgical V58.30
      surgical V58.31
  checkup only V70.0
  chemotherapy, (oral) (intravenous) antineoplastic V58.11
  circumcision, ritual or routine (in absence of medical indication) V50.2
  clinical research investigation (control) (normal comparison) (participant) V70.7
  closure of artificial opening — see Attention to, artificial, opening
  contraceptive
    counseling V25.09
      emergency V25.03
      postcoital V25.03
    management V25.9
      specified type NEC V25.8
  convalescence following V66.9
    chemotherapy V66.2
    psychotherapy V66.3
    radiotherapy V66.1
    surgery V66.0
    treatment (for) V66.5
      combined V66.6
      fracture V66.4
      mental disorder NEC V66.3
      specified condition NEC V66.5
  cosmetic surgery NEC V50.1
    breast reconstruction following mastectomy V51.0
    following healed injury or operation V51.8
  counseling (see also Counseling) V65.40
    without complaint or sickness V65.49
    contraceptive management V25.09
      emergency V25.03
      postcoital V25.03
    dietary V65.3
    exercise V65.41
    fertility preservation (prior to cancer therapy) (prior to surgical removal of gonads) V26.42
    for
      nonattending third party V65.19

Admission — continued
for — continued
  counseling (see also Counseling) — continued
    for — continued
      pediatric
        pre-adoption visit for adoptive parent(s) V65.11
        pre-birth visit for expectant parent(s) V65.11
      victim of abuse
        child V61.21
        partner or spouse V61.11
    genetic V26.33
    gonorrhea V65.45
    HIV V65.44
    human immunodeficiency virus V65.44
    injury prevention V65.43
    insulin pump training V65.46
    natural family planning
      procreative V26.41
      to avoid pregnancy V25.04
    procreative management V26.49
      using natural family planning V26.41
    sexually transmitted disease NEC V65.45
      HIV V65.44
    specified reason NEC V65.49
    substance use and abuse V65.42
    syphilis V65.45
    victim of abuse
      child V61.21
      partner or spouse V61.11
  desensitization to allergens V07.1
  dialysis V56.0
    catheter
      fitting and adjustment
        extracorporeal V56.1
        peritoneal V56.2
      removal or replacement
        extracorporeal V56.1
        peritoneal V56.2
    extracorporeal (renal) V56.0
    peritoneal V56.8
    renal V56.0
  dietary surveillance and counseling V65.3
  drug monitoring, therapeutic V58.83
  ear piercing V50.3
  elective surgery V50.9
    breast
      augmentation or reduction V50.1
      reconstruction following mastectomy V51.0
      removal, prophylactic V50.41
    circumcision, ritual or routine (in absence of medical indication) V50.2
    cosmetic NEC V50.1
      breast reconstruction following mastectomy V51.0
      following healed injury or operation V51.8
    ear piercing V50.3
    face-lift V50.1
    hair transplant V50.0
    plastic
      breast reconstruction following mastectomy V51.0
      cosmetic NEC V50.1
      following healed injury or operation V51.8
    prophylactic organ removal V50.49
      breast V50.41
      ovary V50.42
    repair of scarred tissue (following healed injury or operation) V51.8
    specified type NEC V50.8
  end-of-life care V66.7
  examination (see also Examination) V70.9
    administrative purpose NEC V70.3
    adoption V70.3

Admission — continued
for — continued
  examination (see also Examination) — continued
    allergy V72.7
    antibody response V72.61
    at health care facility V70.0
    athletic team V70.3
    camp V70.3
    cardiovascular, preoperative V72.81
    clinical research investigation (control) (participant) V70.7
    dental V72.2
    developmental testing (child) (infant) V20.2
    donor (potential) V70.8
    driver's license V70.3
    ear V72.19
    employment V70.5
    eye V72.0
    fertility preservation (prior to cancer therapy) (prior to surgical removal of gonads) V26.82
    follow-up (routine) — see Examination, follow-up
    for admission to
      old age home V70.3
      school V70.3
    general V70.9
      specified reason NEC V70.8
    gynecological V72.31
    health supervision
      child (over 28 days old) V20.2
      infant (over 28 days old) V20.2
      newborn
        8 to 28 days old V20.32
        under 8 days old V20.31
    hearing V72.19
      following failed hearing screening V72.11
    immigration V70.3
    infant
      8 to 28 days old V20.32
      over 28 days old, routine V20.2
      under 8 days old V20.31
    insurance certification V70.3
    laboratory V72.60
      ordered as part of a routine general medical examination V72.62
      pre-operative V72.63
      pre-procedural V72.63
      specified NEC V72.69
    marriage license V70.3
    medical (general) (see also Examination, medical) V70.9
    medicolegal reasons V70.4
    naturalization V70.3
    pelvic (annual) (periodic) V72.31
    postpartum checkup V24.2
    pregnancy (possible) (unconfirmed) V72.40
      negative result V72.41
      positive result V72.42
    preoperative V72.84
      cardiovascular V72.81
      respiratory V72.82
      specified NEC V72.83
    preprocedural V72.84
      cardiovascular V72.81
      general physical V72.83
      respiratory V72.82
      specified NEC V72.83
    prior to chemotherapy V72.83
    prison V70.3
    psychiatric (general) V70.2
      requested by authority V70.1
    radiological NEC V72.5
    respiratory, preoperative V72.82
    school V70.3
    screening — see Screening
    skin hypersensitivity V72.7
    specified type NEC V72.85
    sport competition V70.3
    vision V72.0
    well baby and child care V20.2

Admission — continued
for — continued
  exercise therapy V57.1
  face-lift, cosmetic reason V50.1
  fertility preservation (prior to cancer therapy) (prior to surgical removal of gonads) V26.82
  fitting (of)
    artificial
      arm (complete) (partial) V52.0
      eye V52.2
      leg (complete) (partial) V52.1
    biliary drainage tube V58.82
    brain neuropacemaker V53.02
    breast V52.4
      implant V52.4
      prosthesis V52.4
    cardiac pacemaker V53.31
    catheter
      non-vascular V58.82
      vascular V58.81
    cerebral ventricle (communicating) shunt V53.01
    chest tube V58.82
    colostomy belt V55.2
    contact lenses V53.1
    cystostomy device V53.6
    dental prosthesis V52.3
    device, unspecified type V53.90
      abdominal V53.59
      cerebral ventricle (communicating) shunt V53.01
      gastrointestinal NEC V53.59
      insulin pump V53.91
      intestinal V53.50
      intrauterine contraceptive
        insertion V25.11
        removal V25.12
          and reinsertion V25.13
        replacement V25.13
      nervous system V53.09
      orthodontic V53.4
      other device V53.99
      prosthetic V52.9
        breast V52.4
        dental V52.3
        eye V52.2
      special senses V53.09
      substitution
        auditory V53.09
        nervous system V53.09
        visual V53.09
    diaphragm (contraceptive) V25.02
    fistula (sinus tract) drainage tube V58.82
    gastric lap band V53.51
    gastrointestinal appliance and device NEC V53.59
    growth rod V54.02
    hearing aid V53.2
    ileostomy device V55.2
    intestinal appliance and device V53.50
    intrauterine contraceptive device
      insertion V25.11
      removal V25.12
        and reinsertion V25.13
      replacement V25.13
    neuropacemaker (brain) (peripheral nerve) (spinal cord) V53.02
    orthodontic device V53.4
    orthopedic (device) V53.7
      brace V53.7
      cast V53.7
      shoes V53.7
    pacemaker
      brain V53.02
      cardiac V53.31
      carotid sinus V53.39
      spinal cord V53.02
    pleural drainage tube V58.82
    portacath V58.81
    prosthesis V52.9
      arm (complete) (partial) V52.0
      breast V52.4
      dental V52.3

☑ **Additional Digit Required — Refer to the Tabular List for Digit Selection**
▽ **Subterms under main terms may continue to next column or page**

12 — Volume 2
▶◀ **Revised Text**
● **New Line**
▲ **Revised Code**
2015 ICD-9-CM

Admission — continued
for — continued
  fitting — continued
    prosthesis — continued
      eye V52.2
      leg (complete) (partial) V52.1
      specified type NEC V52.8
    spectacles V53.1
    wheelchair V53.8
  follow-up examination (routine) (following) V67.9
    cancer chemotherapy V67.2
    chemotherapy V67.2
    high-risk medication NEC V67.51
    injury NEC V67.59
    psychiatric V67.3
    psychotherapy V67.3
    radiotherapy V67.1
    specified surgery NEC V67.09
    surgery V67.00
      vaginal pap smear V67.01
    treatment (for) V67.9
      combined V67.6
      fracture V67.4
      involving high-risk medication NEC V67.51
      mental disorder V67.3
      specified NEC V67.59
  hair transplant, for cosmetic reason V50.0
  health advice, education, or instruction V65.4 ☑
  hearing conservation and treatment V72.12
  hormone replacement therapy (postmenopausal) V07.4
  hospice care V66.7
  immunizations (childhood) appropriate for age V20.2
  immunotherapy, antineoplastic V58.12
  insertion (of)
    intrauterine contraceptive device V25.11
    subdermal implantable contraceptive V25.5
  insulin pump titration V53.91
  insulin pump training V65.46
  intrauterine device
    insertion V25.11
    management V25.42
    removal V25.12
      and reinsertion V25.13
    replacement V25.13
  investigation to determine further disposition V63.8
  in vitro fertilization cycle V26.81
  isolation V07.0
  issue of
    disability examination certificate V68.01
    medical certificate NEC V68.09
    repeat prescription NEC V68.1
      contraceptive device NEC V25.49
  kidney dialysis V56.0
  lengthening of growth rod V54.02
  mental health evaluation V70.2
    requested by authority V70.1
  natural family planning counseling and advice
    procreative V26.41
    to avoid pregnancy V25.04
  nonmedical reason NEC V68.89
  nursing care evaluation V63.8
  observation (without need for further medical care) (see also Observation) V71.9
    accident V71.4
    alleged rape or seduction V71.5
    criminal assault V71.6
    following accident V71.4
      at work V71.3
    foreign body ingestion V71.89
    growth and development variations, childhood V21.0
    inflicted injury NEC V71.6

Admission — continued
for — continued
  observation (see also Observation) — continued
    ingestion of deleterious agent or foreign body V71.89
    injury V71.6
    malignant neoplasm V71.1
    mental disorder V71.09
    newborn — see Observation, suspected, condition, newborn
    rape V71.5
    specified NEC V71.89
    suspected
      abuse V71.81
      accident V71.4
        at work V71.3
      benign neoplasm V71.89
      cardiovascular V71.7
      disorder V71.9
      exposure
        anthrax V71.82
        biological agent NEC V71.83
        SARS V71.83
      heart V71.7
      inflicted injury NEC V71.6
      malignant neoplasm V71.1
      maternal and fetal problem not found
        amniotic cavity and membrane V89.01
        cervical shortening V89.05
        fetal anomaly V89.03
        fetal growth V89.04
        oligohydramnios V89.01
        other specified NEC V89.09
        placenta V89.02
        polyhydramnios V89.01
      mental NEC V71.09
      neglect V71.81
      specified condition NEC V71.89
      tuberculosis V71.2
    tuberculosis V71.2
  occupational therapy V57.21
  organ transplant, donor — see Donor
  ovary, ovarian removal, prophylactic V50.42
  palliative care V66.7
  Papanicolaou smear
    cervix V76.2
      for suspected malignant neoplasm V76.2
      no disease found V71.1
      routine, as part of gynecological examination V72.31
      to confirm findings of recent normal smear following initial abnormal smear V72.32
    vaginal V76.47
      following hysterectomy for malignant condition V67.01
  passage of sounds or bougie in artificial opening — see Attention to, artificial, opening
  paternity testing V70.4
  peritoneal dialysis V56.32
  physical therapy NEC V57.1
  plastic surgery
    breast reconstruction following mastectomy V51.0
    cosmetic NEC V50.1
    following healed injury or operation V51.8
  postmenopausal hormone replacement therapy V07.4
  postpartum observation
    immediately after delivery V24.0
    routine follow-up V24.2
  poststerilization (for restoration) V26.0
  procreative management V26.9
    assisted reproductive fertility procedure cycle V26.81
    in vitro fertilization cycle V26.81
    specified type NEC V26.89

Admission — continued
for — continued
  prophylactic
    administration of
      antibiotics, long-term V58.62
        short-term use — omit code
      antitoxin, any V07.2
      antivenin V07.2
      chemotherapeutic agent NEC V07.39
      chemotherapy NEC V07.39
      diphtheria antitoxin V07.2
      fluoride V07.31
      gamma globulin V07.2
      immune sera (gamma globulin) V07.2
      RhoGAM V07.2
      tetanus antitoxin V07.2
    breathing exercises V57.0
    chemotherapy NEC V07.39
      fluoride V07.31
    measure V07.9
      specified type NEC V07.8
    organ removal V50.49
      breast V50.41
      ovary V50.42
  psychiatric examination (general) V70.2
    requested by authority V70.1
  radiation management V58.0
  radiotherapy V58.0
  reconstruction following mastectomy V51.0
  reforming of artificial opening — see Attention to, artificial, opening
  rehabilitation V57.9
    multiple types V57.89
    occupational V57.21
    orthoptic V57.4
    orthotic V57.81
    physical NEC V57.1
    specified type NEC V57.89
    speech (-language) V57.3
    vocational V57.22
  removal of
    breast tissue expander without synchronous insertion of permanent implant V52.4
    cardiac pacemaker V53.31
    cast (plaster) V54.89
    catheter from artificial opening — see Attention to, artificial, opening
    cerebral ventricle (communicating) shunt V53.01
    cystostomy catheter V55.5
    device
      cerebral ventricle (communicating) shunt V53.01
      fixation
        external V54.89
        internal V54.01
      intrauterine contraceptive V25.12
      traction, external V54.89
    drains V58.49
    dressing
      wound V58.30
        nonsurgical V58.30
        surgical V58.31
    fixation device
      external V54.89
      internal V54.01
    intrauterine contraceptive device V25.12
    Kirschner wire V54.89
    neuropacemaker (brain) (peripheral nerve) (spinal cord) V53.02
    nonsurgical wound dressing V58.30
    orthopedic fixation device
      external V54.89
      internal V54.01
    pacemaker device
      brain V53.02
      cardiac V53.31
      carotid sinus V53.39
      nervous system V53.02
    plaster cast V54.89

Admission — continued
for — continued
  removal of — continued
    plate (fracture) V54.01
    rod V54.01
    screw (fracture) V54.01
    splint, traction V54.89
    staples V58.32
    Steinmann pin V54.89
    subdermal implantable contraceptive V25.43
    surgical wound dressing V58.31
    sutures V58.32
    traction device, external V54.89
    ureteral stent V53.6
    wound packing V58.30
      nonsurgical V58.30
      surgical V58.31
  repair of scarred tissue (following healed injury or operation) V51.8
  replacement of intrauterine contraceptive device V25.13
  reprogramming of cardiac pacemaker V53.31
  respirator [ventilator] dependence during
    mechanical failure V46.14
    power failure V46.12
    for weaning V46.13
  restoration of organ continuity (poststerilization) (tuboplasty) (vasoplasty) V26.0
  Rh typing V72.86
  routine infant and child vision and hearing testing V20.2
  sensitivity test (see also Test, skin)
    allergy NEC V72.7
    bacterial disease NEC V74.9
    Dick V74.8
    Kveim V82.89
    Mantoux V74.1
    mycotic infection NEC V75.4
    parasitic disease NEC V75.8
    Schick V74.3
    Schultz-Charlton V74.8
  social service (agency) referral or evaluation V63.8
  speech (-language) therapy V57.3
  sterilization V25.2
  suspected disorder (ruled out) (without need for further care) — see Observation
  terminal care V66.7
  tests only — see Test
  therapeutic drug monitoring V58.83
  therapy
    blood transfusion, without reported diagnosis V58.2
    breathing exercises V57.0
    chemotherapy, antineoplastic V58.11
      prophylactic NEC V07.39
      fluoride V07.31
    dialysis (intermittent) (treatment)
      extracorporeal V56.0
      peritoneal V56.8
      renal V56.0
      specified type NEC V56.8
    exercise (remedial) NEC V57.1
      breathing V57.0
    immunotherapy, antineoplastic V58.12
    long-term (current) (prophylactic) drug use NEC V58.69
      antibiotics V58.62
        short-term use — omit code
      anticoagulants V58.61
      anti-inflammatories, nonsteroidal (NSAID) V58.64
      antiplatelets V58.63
      antithrombotics V58.63
      aspirin V58.66
      bisphosphonates V58.68
      high-risk medications NEC V58.69
      insulin V58.67
      methadone for pain control V58.69

Admission — continued
for — continued
 therapy — continued
  long-term drug use — continued
   opiate analgesic V58.69
   steroids V58.65
  occupational V57.21
  orthoptic V57.4
  physical NEC V57.1
  radiation V58.0
  speech (-language) V57.3
  vocational V57.22
 toilet or cleaning
  of artificial opening — see Attention to, artificial, opening
  of non-vascular catheter V58.82
  of vascular catheter V58.81
 treatment
  measure V07.9
   specified type NEC V07.8
 tubal ligation V25.2
 tuboplasty for previous sterilization V26.0
 ultrasound, routine fetal V28.3
 vaccination, prophylactic (against)
  arthropod-borne virus, viral NEC V05.1
   disease NEC V05.1
   encephalitis V05.0
  Bacille Calmette Guérin (BCG) V03.2
  BCG V03.2
  chickenpox V05.4
  cholera alone V03.0
   with typhoid-paratyphoid (cholera + TAB) V06.0
  common cold V04.7
  dengue V05.1
  diphtheria alone V03.5
  diphtheria-tetanus-pertussis (DTP) (DTaP) V06.1
   with
    poliomyelitis (DTP + polio) V06.3
    typhoid-paratyphoid (DTP + TAB) V06.2
  diphtheria-tetanus [Td] [DT] without pertussis V06.5
  disease (single) NEC V05.9
   bacterial NEC V03.9
    specified type NEC V03.89
   combinations NEC V06.9
    specified type NEC V06.8
   specified type NEC V05.8
   viral NEC V04.89
  encephalitis, viral, arthropod-borne V05.0
  Hemophilus influenzae, type B [Hib] V03.81
  hepatitis, viral V05.3
  human papillomavirus (HPV) V04.89
  immune sera (gamma globulin) V07.2
  influenza V04.81
   with
    Streptococcus pneumoniae [pneumococcus] V06.6
  Leishmaniasis V05.2
  measles alone V04.2
  measles-mumps-rubella (MMR) V06.4
  mumps alone V04.6
   with measles and rubella (MMR) V06.4
  not done because of contraindication V64.09
  pertussis alone V03.6
  plague V03.3
  pneumonia V03.82
  poliomyelitis V04.0
   with diphtheria-tetanus-pertussis (DTP+ polio) V06.3
  rabies V04.5
  respiratory syncytial virus (RSV) V04.82
  rubella alone V04.3
   with measles and mumps (MMR) V06.4

Admission — continued
for — continued
 vaccination, prophylactic — continued
  smallpox V04.1
  specified type NEC V05.8
  Streptococcus pneumoniae [pneumococcus] V03.82
   with
    influenza V06.6
  tetanus toxoid alone V03.7
   with diphtheria [Td] [DT] V06.5
    and pertussis (DTP) (DTaP) V06.1
  tuberculosis (BCG) V03.2
  tularemia V03.4
  typhoid alone V03.1
   with diphtheria-tetanus-pertussis (TAB + DTP) V06.2
  typhoid-paratyphoid alone (TAB) V03.1
  typhus V05.8
  varicella (chicken pox) V05.4
  viral encephalitis, arthropod-borne V05.0
  viral hepatitis V05.3
  yellow fever V04.4
 vasectomy V25.2
 vasoplasty for previous sterilization V26.0
 vision examination V72.0
 vocational therapy V57.22
 waiting period for admission to other facility V63.2
  undergoing social agency investigation V63.8
 well baby and child care V20.2
 x-ray of chest
  for suspected tuberculosis V71.2
  routine V72.5
Adnexitis (suppurative) — see also Salpingo-oophoritis 614.2
Adolescence NEC V21.2
Adoption
 agency referral V68.89
 examination V70.3
 held for V68.89
Adrenal gland — see condition
Adrenalism 255.9
 tuberculous (see also Tuberculosis) 017.6 ☑
Adrenalitis, adrenitis 255.8
 meningococcal hemorrhagic 036.3
Adrenarche, precocious 259.1
Adrenocortical syndrome 255.2
Adrenogenital syndrome (acquired) (congenital) 255.2
 iatrogenic, fetus or newborn 760.79
Adrenoleukodystrophy 277.86
 neonatal 277.86
 x-linked 277.86
Adrenomyeloneuropathy 277.86
Adventitious bursa — see Bursitis
Adynamia (episodica) (hereditary) (periodic) 359.3
Adynamic
 ileus or intestine (see also Ileus) 560.1
 ureter 753.22
Aeration lung, imperfect, newborn 770.5
Aerobullosis 993.3
Aerocele — see Embolism, air
Aerodermectasia
 subcutaneous (traumatic) 958.7
  surgical 998.81
 surgical 998.81
Aerodontalgia 993.2
Aeroembolism 993.3
Aerogenes capsulatus infection — see also Gangrene, gas 040.0
Aero-otitis media 993.0
Aerophagy, aerophagia 306.4
 psychogenic 306.4
Aerosinusitis 993.1
Aerotitis 993.0
Affection, affections — see also Disease
 sacroiliac (joint), old 724.6
 shoulder region NEC 726.2

Afibrinogenemia 286.3
 acquired 286.6
 congenital 286.3
 postpartum 666.3 ☑
African
 sleeping sickness 086.5
 tick fever 087.1
 trypanosomiasis 086.5
  Gambian 086.3
  Rhodesian 086.4
Aftercare V58.9
 amputation stump V54.89
 artificial openings — see Attention to, artificial, opening
 blood transfusion without reported diagnosis V58.2
 breathing exercise V57.0
 cardiac device V53.39
  defibrillator, automatic implantable (with synchronous cardiac pacemaker) V53.32
  pacemaker V53.31
   carotid sinus V53.39
 carotid sinus pacemaker V53.39
 cerebral ventricle (communicating) shunt V53.01
 chemotherapy (oral) (intravenous) session (adjunctive) (maintenance) V58.11
 defibrillator, automatic implantable cardiac (with synchronous cardiac pacemaker) V53.32
 exercise (remedial) (therapeutic) V57.1
  breathing V57.0
 extracorporeal dialysis (intermittent) (treatment) V56.0
 following surgery NEC V58.49
  for
   injury V58.43
   neoplasm V58.42
   organ transplant V58.44
   trauma V58.43
  joint
   explantation of prosthesis (staged procedure) V54.82
   replacement V54.81
  of
   circulatory system V58.73
   digestive system V58.75
   genital organs V58.76
   genitourinary system V58.76
   musculoskeletal system V58.78
   nervous system V58.72
   oral cavity V58.75
   respiratory system V58.74
   sense organs V58.71
   skin V58.77
   subcutaneous tissue V58.77
   teeth V58.75
   urinary system V58.76
  spinal — see Aftercare, following surgery, of, specified body system
  wound closure, planned V58.41
 fracture V54.9
  healing V54.89
   pathologic
    ankle V54.29
    arm V54.20
     lower V54.22
     upper V54.21
    finger V54.29
    foot V54.29
    hand V54.29
    hip V54.23
    leg V54.24
     lower V54.26
     upper V54.25
    pelvis V54.29
    specified site NEC V54.29
    toe(s) V54.29
    vertebrae V54.27
    wrist V54.29
   traumatic
    ankle V54.19
    arm V54.10
     lower V54.12
     upper V54.11

Aftercare — continued
 fracture — continued
  healing — continued
   traumatic — continued
    finger V54.19
    foot V54.19
    hand V54.19
    hip V54.13
    leg V54.14
     lower V54.16
     upper V54.15
    pelvis V54.19
    specified site NEC V54.19
    toe(s) V54.19
    vertebrae V54.17
    wrist V54.19
  removal of
   external fixation device V54.89
   internal fixation device V54.01
  specified care NEC V54.89
 gait training V57.1
  for use of artificial limb(s) V57.81
 internal fixation device V54.09
 involving
  dialysis (intermittent) (treatment)
   extracorporeal V56.0
   peritoneal V56.8
   renal V56.0
  gait training V57.1
   for use of artificial limb(s) V57.81
  growth rod
   adjustment V54.02
   lengthening V54.02
  internal fixation device V54.09
  orthoptic training V57.4
  orthotic training V57.81
  radiotherapy session V58.0
  removal of
   drains V58.49
   dressings
    wound V58.30
     nonsurgical V58.30
     surgical V58.31
   fixation device
    external V54.89
    internal V54.01
   fracture plate V54.01
   nonsurgical wound dressing V58.30
   pins V54.01
   plaster cast V54.89
   rods V54.01
   screws V54.01
   staples V58.32
   surgical wound dressings V58.31
   sutures V58.32
   traction device, external V54.89
   wound packing V58.30
    nonsurgical V58.30
    surgical V58.31
  neuropacemaker (brain) (peripheral nerve) (spinal cord) V53.02
  occupational therapy V57.21
  orthodontic V58.5
  orthopedic V54.9
   change of external fixation or traction device V54.89
   following joint
    explantation of prosthesis (staged procedure) V54.82
    replacement V54.81
   internal fixation device V54.09
   removal of fixation device
    external V54.89
    internal V54.01
   specified care NEC V54.89
  orthoptic training V57.4
  orthotic training V57.81
  pacemaker
   brain V53.02
   cardiac V53.31
   carotid sinus V53.39
   peripheral nerve V53.02
   spinal cord V53.02
  peritoneal dialysis (intermittent) (treatment) V56.8
  physical therapy NEC V57.1

Aftercare — *continued*
  physical therapy — *continued*
    breathing exercises V57.0
  radiotherapy session V58.0
  rehabilitation procedure V57.9
    breathing exercises V57.0
    multiple types V57.89
    occupational V57.21
    orthoptic V57.4
    orthotic V57.81
    physical therapy NEC V57.1
    remedial exercises V57.1
    specified type NEC V57.89
    speech (-language) V57.3
    therapeutic exercises V57.1
    vocational V57.22
  renal dialysis (intermittent) (treatment) V56.0
  specified type NEC V58.89
    removal of non-vascular catheter V58.82
    removal of vascular catheter V58.81
  speech (-language) therapy V57.3
  stump, amputation V54.89
  vocational rehabilitation V57.22
After-cataract 366.50
  obscuring vision 366.53
  specified type, not obscuring vision 366.52
Agalactia 676.4 ☑
Agammaglobulinemia 279.00
  with lymphopenia 279.2
  acquired (primary) (secondary) 279.06
  Bruton's X-linked 279.04
  infantile sex-linked (Bruton's) (congenital) 279.04
  Swiss-type 279.2
Aganglionosis (bowel) (colon) 751.3
Age (old) — *see also* Senile 797
Agenesis — *see also* Absence, by site, congenital
  acoustic nerve 742.8
  adrenal (gland) 759.1
  alimentary tract (complete) (partial) NEC 751.8
    lower 751.2
    upper 750.8
  anus, anal (canal) 751.2
  aorta 747.22
  appendix 751.2
  arm (complete) (partial) (*see also* Deformity, reduction, upper limb) 755.20
  artery (peripheral) NEC (*see also* Anomaly, peripheral vascular system) 747.60
    brain 747.81
    coronary 746.85
    pulmonary 747.31
    umbilical 747.5
  auditory (canal) (external) 744.01
  auricle (ear) 744.01
  bile, biliary duct or passage 751.61
  bone NEC 756.9
  brain 740.0
    specified part 742.2
  breast 757.6
  bronchus 748.3
  canaliculus lacrimalis 743.65
  carpus NEC (*see also* Deformity, reduction, upper limb) 755.28
  cartilage 756.9
  cecum 751.2
  cerebellum 742.2
  cervix 752.43
  chin 744.89
  cilia 743.63
  circulatory system, part NEC 747.89
  clavicle 755.51
  clitoris 752.49
  coccyx 756.13
  colon 751.2
  corpus callosum 742.2
  cricoid cartilage 748.3
  diaphragm (with hernia) 756.6
  digestive organ(s) or tract (complete) (partial) NEC 751.8
    lower 751.2
    upper 750.8
  ductus arteriosus 747.89

Agenesis — *see also* Absence, by site, congenital — *continued*
  duodenum 751.1
  ear NEC 744.09
    auricle 744.01
    lobe 744.21
  ejaculatory duct 752.89
  endocrine (gland) NEC 759.2
  epiglottis 748.3
  esophagus 750.3
  Eustachian tube 744.24
  extrinsic muscle, eye 743.69
  eye 743.00
    adnexa 743.69
  eyelid (fold) 743.62
  face
    bones NEC 756.0
    specified part NEC 744.89
  fallopian tube 752.19
  femur NEC (*see also* Absence, femur, congenital) 755.34
  fibula NEC (*see also* Absence, fibula, congenital) 755.37
  finger NEC (*see also* Absence, finger, congenital) 755.29
  foot (complete) (*see also* Deformity, reduction, lower limb) 755.31
  gallbladder 751.69
  gastric 750.8
  genitalia, genital (organ)
    female 752.89
      external 752.49
      internal NEC 752.89
    male 752.89
      penis 752.69
  glottis 748.3
  gonadal 758.6
  hair 757.4
  hand (complete) (*see also* Deformity, reduction, upper limb) 755.21
  heart 746.89
    valve NEC 746.89
      aortic 746.89
      mitral 746.89
      pulmonary 746.01
  hepatic 751.69
  humerus NEC (*see also* Absence, humerus, congenital) 755.24
  hymen 752.49
  ileum 751.1
  incus 744.04
  intestine (small) 751.1
    large 751.2
  iris (dilator fibers) 743.45
  jaw 524.09
  jejunum 751.1
  kidney(s) (partial) (unilateral) 753.0
  labium (majus) (minus) 752.49
  labyrinth, membranous 744.05
  lacrimal apparatus (congenital) 743.65
  larynx 748.3
  leg NEC (*see also* Deformity, reduction, lower limb) 755.30
  lens 743.35
  limb (complete) (partial) (*see also* Deformity, reduction) 755.4
    lower NEC 755.30
    upper 755.20
  lip 750.26
  liver 751.69
  lung (bilateral) (fissures) (lobe) (unilateral) 748.5
  mandible 524.09
  maxilla 524.09
  metacarpus NEC 755.28
  metatarsus NEC 755.38
  muscle (any) 756.81
  musculoskeletal system NEC 756.9
  nail(s) 757.5
  neck, part 744.89
  nerve 742.8
  nervous system, part NEC 742.8
  nipple 757.6
  nose 748.1
  nuclear 742.8

Agenesis — *see also* Absence, by site, congenital — *continued*
  organ
    of Corti 744.05
    or site not listed — *see* Anomaly, specified type NEC
  osseous meatus (ear) 744.03
  ovary 752.0
  oviduct 752.19
  pancreas 751.7
  parathyroid (gland) 759.2
  patella 755.64
  pelvic girdle (complete) (partial) 755.69
  penis 752.69
  pericardium 746.89
  perineal body 756.81
  pituitary (gland) 759.2
  prostate 752.89
  pulmonary
    artery 747.31
    trunk 747.31
    vein 747.49
  punctum lacrimale 743.65
  radioulnar NEC (*see also* Absence, forearm, congenital) 755.25
  radius NEC (*see also* Absence, radius, congenital) 755.26
  rectum 751.2
  renal 753.0
  respiratory organ NEC 748.9
  rib 756.3
  roof of orbit 742.0
  round ligament 752.89
  sacrum 756.13
  salivary gland 750.21
  scapula 755.59
  scrotum 752.89
  seminal duct or tract 752.89
  septum
    atrial 745.69
    between aorta and pulmonary artery 745.0
    ventricular 745.3
  shoulder girdle (complete) (partial) 755.59
  skull (bone) 756.0
    with
      anencephalus 740.0
      encephalocele 742.0
      hydrocephalus 742.3
        with spina bifida (*see also* Spina bifida) 741.0 ☑
      microcephalus 742.1
  spermatic cord 752.89
  spinal cord 742.59
  spine 756.13
    lumbar 756.13
      isthmus 756.11
      pars articularis 756.11
  spleen 759.0
  sternum 756.3
  stomach 750.7
  tarsus NEC 755.38
  tendon 756.81
  testicular 752.89
  testis 752.89
  thymus (gland) 759.2
  thyroid (gland) 243
    cartilage 748.3
  tibia NEC (*see also* Absence, tibia, congenital) 755.36
  tibiofibular NEC 755.35
  toe (complete) (partial) (*see also* Absence, toe, congenital) 755.39
  tongue 750.11
  trachea (cartilage) 748.3
  ulna NEC (*see also* Absence, ulna, congenital) 755.27
  ureter 753.4
  urethra 753.8
  urinary tract NEC 753.8
  uterus 752.31
  uvula 750.26
  vagina (total) (partial) 752.45
  vas deferens 752.89
  vein(s) (peripheral) NEC (*see also* Anomaly, peripheral vascular system) 747.60

Agenesis — *see also* Absence, by site, congenital — *continued*
  vein(s) (*see also* Anomaly, peripheral vascular system) — *continued*
    brain 747.81
    great 747.49
    portal 747.49
    pulmonary 747.49
    vena cava (inferior) (superior) 747.49
  vermis of cerebellum 742.2
  vertebra 756.13
    lumbar 756.13
      isthmus 756.11
      pars articularis 756.11
  vulva 752.49
Ageusia — *see also* Disturbance, sensation 781.1
Aggressiveness 301.3
Aggressive outburst — *see also* Disturbance, conduct 312.0 ☑
  in children or adolescents 313.9
Aging skin 701.8
Agitated — *see* condition
Agitation 307.9
  catatonic (*see also* Schizophrenia) 295.2 ☑
Aglossia (congenital) 750.11
Aglycogenosis 271.0
Agnail (finger) (with lymphangitis) 681.02
Agnosia (body image) (tactile) 784.69
  verbal 784.69
    auditory 784.69
      secondary to organic lesion 784.69
    developmental 315.8
    secondary to organic lesion 784.69
  visual 368.16
    object 368.16
Agoraphobia 300.22
  with panic disorder 300.21
Agrammatism 784.69
Agranulocytopenia — *see also* Agranulocytosis 288.09
Agranulocytosis — *see also* Neutropenia 288.09
  chronic 288.09
  cyclical 288.02
  due to infection 288.04
  genetic 288.01
  infantile 288.01
  periodic 288.02
  pernicious 288.09
Agraphia (absolute) 784.69
  with alexia 784.61
  developmental 315.39
Agrypnia — *see also* Insomnia 780.52
Ague — *see also* Malaria 084.6
  brass-founders' 985.8
  dumb 084.6
  tertian 084.1
Agyria 742.2
AHTR (acute hemolytic transfusion reaction) — *see* Complications, transfusion
Ahumada-del Castillo syndrome (nonpuerperal galactorrhea and amenorrhea) 253.1
AIDS 042
AIDS-associated retrovirus (disease) (illness) 042
  infection — *see* Human immunodeficiency virus, infection
AIDS-associated virus (disease) (illness) 042
  infection — *see* Human immunodeficiency virus, infection
AIDS-like disease (illness) (syndrome) 042
AIDS-related complex 042
AIDS-related conditions 042
AIDS-related virus (disease) (illness) 042
  infection — *see* Human immunodeficiency virus, infection
AIDS virus (disease) (illness) 042
  infection — *see* Human immunodeficiency virus, infection
Ailment, heart — *see* Disease, heart
Ailurophobia 300.29
Ainhum (disease) 136.0
AIN I (anal intraepithelial neoplasia I) (histologically confirmed) 569.44

☑ Additional Digit Required — Refer to the Tabular List for Digit Selection   ▽ Subterms under main terms may continue to next column or page

2015 ICD-9-CM   ►◄ Revised Text   ● New Line   ▲ Revised Code   Volume 2 — 15

AIN II (anal intraepithelial neoplasia II) (histologically confirmed) 569.44
AIN III (anal intraepithelial neoplasia III) 230.6
anal canal 230.5
AIPHI (acute idiopathic pulmonary hemorrhage
in infants (over 28 days old)) 786.31
Air
anterior mediastinum 518.1
compressed, disease 993.3
embolism (any site) (artery) (cerebral) 958.0
with
abortion — see Abortion, by type,
with embolism
ectopic pregnancy (see also categories 633.0–633.9) 639.6
molar pregnancy (see also categories
630–632) 639.6
due to implanted device — see Complications, due to (presence of) any
device, implant, or graft classified
to 996.0–996.5 NEC
following
abortion 639.6
ectopic or molar pregnancy 639.6
infusion, perfusion, or transfusion
999.1
in pregnancy, childbirth, or puerperium
673.0 ☑
traumatic 958.0
hunger 786.09
psychogenic 306.1
leak (lung) (pulmonary) (thorax) 512.84
iatrogenic 512.1
persistent 512.84
postoperative 512.2
rarefied, effects of — see Effect, adverse,
high altitude
sickness 994.6
Airplane sickness 994.6
Akathisia, acathisia 781.0
due to drugs 333.99
neuroleptic-induced acute 333.99
Akinesia algeria 352.6
Akiyami 100.89
Akureyri disease (epidemic neuromyasthenia)
049.8
Alacrima (congenital) 743.65
Alactasia (hereditary) 271.3
Alagille syndrome 759.89
Alalia 784.3
developmental 315.31
receptive-expressive 315.32
secondary to organic lesion 784.3
Alaninemia 270.8
Alastrim 050.1
Albarrán's disease (colibacilluria) 791.9
Albers-Schönberg's disease (marble bones)
756.52
Albert's disease 726.71
Albinism, albino (choroid) (cutaneous) (eye)
(generalized) (isolated) (ocular) (oculocutaneous) (partial) 270.2
Albinismus 270.2
Albright (-Martin) (-Bantam) disease (pseudohypoparathyroidism) 275.49
Albright (-McCune) (-Sternberg) syndrome
(osteitis fibrosa disseminata) 756.59
Albuminous — see condition
Albuminuria, albuminuric (acute) (chronic)
(subacute) 791.0
Bence-Jones 791.0
cardiac 785.9
complicating pregnancy, childbirth, or
puerperium 646.2 ☑
with hypertension — see Toxemia, of
pregnancy
affecting fetus or newborn 760.1
cyclic 593.6
gestational 646.2 ☑
gravidarum 646.2 ☑
with hypertension — see Toxemia, of
pregnancy
affecting fetus or newborn 760.1
heart 785.9
idiopathic 593.6
orthostatic 593.6

Albuminuria, albuminuric — continued
postural 593.6
pre-eclamptic (mild) 642.4 ☑
affecting fetus or newborn 760.0
severe 642.5 ☑
affecting fetus or newborn 760.0
recurrent physiologic 593.6
scarlatinal 034.1
Albumosuria 791.0
Bence-Jones 791.0
myelopathic (M9730/3) 203.0 ☑
Alcaptonuria 270.2
Alcohol, alcoholic
abstinence 291.81
acute intoxication 305.0 ☑
with dependence 303.0 ☑
addiction (see also Alcoholism) 303.9 ☑
maternal
with suspected fetal damage affecting management of pregnan-
cy 655.4 ☑
affecting fetus or newborn 760.71
amnestic disorder, persisting 291.1
anxiety 291.89
brain syndrome, chronic 291.2
cardiopathy 425.5
chronic (see also Alcoholism) 303.9 ☑
cirrhosis (liver) 571.2
delirium 291.0
acute 291.0
chronic 291.1
tremens 291.0
withdrawal 291.0
dementia NEC 291.2
deterioration 291.2
drunkenness (simple) 305.0 ☑
hallucinosis (acute) 291.3
induced
circadian rhythm sleep disorder 291.82
hypersomnia 291.82
insomnia 291.82
mental disorder 291.9
anxiety 291.89
mood 291.89
sexual 291.89
sleep 291.82
specified type 291.89
parasomnia 291.82
persisting
amnestic disorder 291.1
dementia 291.2
psychotic disorder
with
delusions 291.5
hallucinations 291.3
sleep disorder 291.82
insanity 291.9
intoxication (acute) 305.0 ☑
with dependence 303.0 ☑
pathological 291.4
jealousy 291.5
Korsakoff's, Korsakov's, Korsakow's 291.1
liver NEC 571.3
acute 571.1
chronic 571.2
mania (acute) (chronic) 291.9
mood 291.89
paranoia 291.5
paranoid (type) psychosis 291.5
pellagra 265.2
poisoning, accidental (acute) NEC 980.9
specified type of alcohol — see Table of
Drugs and Chemicals
psychosis (see also Psychosis, alcoholic)
291.9
Korsakoff's, Korsakov's, Korsakow's 291.1
polyneuritic 291.1
with
delusions 291.5
hallucinations 291.3
related disorder 291.9
withdrawal symptoms, syndrome NEC
291.81
delirium 291.0
hallucinosis 291.3

Alcoholism 303.9 ☑

Note — Use the following fifth-digit
subclassification with category 303:

0   unspecified

1   continuous

2   episodic

3   in remission

with psychosis (see also Psychosis, alcoholic)
291.9
acute 303.0 ☑
chronic 303.9 ☑
with psychosis 291.9
complicating pregnancy, childbirth, or
puerperium 648.4 ☑
affecting fetus or newborn 760.71
history V11.3
Korsakoff's, Korsakov's, Korsakow's 291.1
suspected damage to fetus affecting management of pregnancy 655.4 ☑
Alder's anomaly or syndrome (leukocyte
granulation anomaly) 288.2
Alder-Reilly anomaly (leukocyte granulation)
288.2
Aldosteronism (primary) 255.10
congenital 255.10
familial type I 255.11
glucocorticoid-remediable 255.11
secondary 255.14
Aldosteronoma (M8370/1) 237.2
Aldrich (-Wiskott) syndrome (eczema-
thrombocytopenia) 279.12
Aleppo boil 085.1
Aleukemic — see condition
Aleukia
congenital 288.09
hemorrhagica 284.9
acquired (secondary) 284.89
congenital 284.09
idiopathic 284.9
splenica 289.4
Alexia (congenital) (developmental) 315.01
secondary to organic lesion 784.61
Algoneurodystrophy 733.7
Algophobia 300.29
Alibert-Bazin disease (M9700/3) 202.1 ☑
Alibert's disease (mycosis fungoides)
(M9700/3) 202.1 ☑
Alice in Wonderland syndrome 293.89
Alienation, mental — see also Psychosis 298.9
Alkalemia 276.3
Alkalosis 276.3
metabolic 276.3
with respiratory acidosis 276.4
respiratory 276.3
Alkaptonuria 270.2
Allen-Masters syndrome 620.6
Allergic bronchopulmonary aspergillosis
518.6
Allergy, allergic (reaction) 995.3
air-borne substance — see also Fever, hay
477.9
specified allergen NEC 477.8
alveolitis (extrinsic) 495.9
due to
Aspergillus clavatus 495.4
cryptostroma corticale 495.6
organisms (fungal, thermophilic
actinomycete, other) growing
in ventilation (air conditioning
systems) 495.7
specified type NEC 495.8
anaphylactic reaction or shock 995.0
due to food — see Anaphylactic reaction
or shock, due to, food
angioderma 995.1
angioneurotic edema 995.1
animal (cat) (dog) (epidermal) 477.8
dander 477.2
hair 477.2
arthritis (see also Arthritis, allergic) 716.2 ☑
asthma — see Asthma
bee sting (anaphylactic shock) 989.5
biological — see Allergy, drug

Allergy, allergic — continued
bronchial asthma — see Asthma
conjunctivitis (eczematous) 372.14
dander, animal (cat) (dog) 477.2
dandruff 477.8
dermatitis (venenata) — see Dermatitis
diathesis V15.09
drug, medicinal substance, and biological
(any) (correct medicinal substance
properly administered) (external)
(internal) 995.27
wrong substance given or taken NEC
977.9
specified drug or substance — see
Table of Drugs and Chemicals
dust (house) (stock) 477.8
eczema — see Eczema
endophthalmitis 360.19
epidermal (animal) 477.8
existing dental restorative material
feathers 477.8
food (any) (ingested) 693.1
atopic 691.8
in contact with skin 692.5
gastritis 535.4 ☑
gastroenteritis 558.3
gastrointestinal 558.3
grain 477.0
grass (pollen) 477.0
asthma (see also Asthma) 493.0 ☑
hay fever 477.0
hair, animal (cat) (dog) 477.2
hay fever (grass) (pollen) (ragweed) (tree)
(see also Fever, hay) 477.9
history (of) V15.09
to
arachnid bite V15.06
eggs V15.03
food additives V15.05
insect bite V15.06
latex V15.07
milk products V15.02
nuts V15.05
peanuts V15.01
radiographic dye V15.08
seafood V15.04
specified food NEC V15.05
spider bite V15.06
horse serum — see Allergy, serum
inhalant 477.9
dust 477.8
pollen 477.0
specified allergen other than pollen
477.8
kapok 477.8
medicine — see Allergy, drug
migraine 339.00
milk protein 558.3
pannus 370.62
pneumonia 518.3
pollen (any) (hay fever) 477.0
asthma (see also Asthma) 493.0 ☑
primrose 477.0
primula 477.0
purpura 287.0
ragweed (pollen) (Senecio jacobae) 477.0
asthma (see also Asthma) 493.0 ☑
hay fever 477.0
respiratory (see also Allergy, inhalant) 477.9
due to
drug — see Allergy, drug
food — see Allergy, food
rhinitis (see also Fever, hay) 477.9
due to food 477.1
rose 477.0
Senecio jacobae 477.0
serum (prophylactic) (therapeutic) 999.59
anaphylactic reaction or shock 999.49
shock (anaphylactic) (due to adverse effect
of correct medicinal substance
properly administered) 995.0
food — see Anaphylactic reaction or
shock, due to, food
from
administration of blood and blood
products 999.41

☑ **Additional Digit Required** — Refer to the Tabular List for Digit Selection   ▽ **Subterms under main terms may continue to next column or page**

16 — Volume 2   ▶◀ **Revised Text**   ● **New Line**   ▲ **Revised Code**   **2015 ICD-9-CM**

Allergy, allergic — *continued*
  shock — *continued*
    from — *continued*
      immunization 999.42
      serum NEC 999.49
  sinusitis (*see also* Fever, hay) 477.9
  skin reaction 692.9
    specified substance — *see* Dermatitis,
      due to
  tree (any) (hay fever) (pollen) 477.0
    asthma (*see also* Asthma) 493.0 ☑
  upper respiratory (*see also* Fever, hay) 477.9
  urethritis 597.89
  urticaria 708.0
  vaccine — *see* Allergy, serum
Allescheriosis 117.6
Alligator skin disease (ichthyosis congenita)
  757.1
  acquired 701.1
Allocheiria, allochiria — *see also* Disturbance,
  sensation 782.0
Almeida's disease (Brazilian blastomycosis)
  116.1
Alopecia (atrophicans) (pregnancy) (premature) (senile) 704.00
  adnata 757.4
  areata 704.01
  celsi 704.01
  cicatrisata 704.09
  circumscripta 704.01
  congenital, congenitalis 757.4
  disseminata 704.01
  effluvium (telogen) 704.02
  febrile 704.09
  generalisata 704.09
  hereditaria 704.09
  marginalis 704.01
  mucinosa 704.09
  postinfectional 704.09
  seborrheica 704.09
  specific 091.82
  syphilitic (secondary) 091.82
  telogen effluvium 704.02
  totalis 704.09
  toxica 704.09
  universalis 704.09
  x-ray 704.09
Alpers' disease 330.8
Alpha-lipoproteinemia 272.4
Alpha thalassemia 282.43
Alphos 696.1
Alpine sickness 993.2
Alport's syndrome (hereditary hematurianephropathy-deafness) 759.89
ALPS (autoimmune lymphoproliferative syndrome) 279.41
ALTE (apparent life threatening event) **in newborn and infant** 799.82
Alteration (of), altered
  awareness 780.09
    transient 780.02
  consciousness 780.09
    persistent vegetative state 780.03
    transient 780.02
  mental status 780.97
    amnesia (retrograde) 780.93
    memory loss 780.93
Alternaria (infection) 118
Alternating — *see* condition
Altitude, high (effects) — *see* Effect, adverse, high altitude
Aluminosis (of lung) 503
Alvarez syndrome (transient cerebral ischemia) 435.9
Alveolar capillary block syndrome 516.64
Alveolus, alveolar — *see* condition
Alymphocytosis (pure) 279.2
Alymphoplasia, thymic 279.2
Alzheimer's
  dementia (senile)
    with behavioral disturbance
      331.0 *[294.11]*
    without behavioral disturbance
      331.0 *[294.10]*
  disease or sclerosis 331.0

Alzheimer's — *continued*
  disease or sclerosis — *continued*
    with dementia — *see* Alzheimer's, dementia
Amastia — *see also* Absence, breast 611.89
Amaurosis (acquired) (congenital) — *see also*
  Blindness 369.00
  fugax 362.34
  hysterical 300.11
  Leber's (congenital) 362.76
  tobacco 377.34
  uremic — *see* Uremia
Amaurotic familial idiocy (infantile) (juvenile)
  (late) 330.1
Ambisexual 752.7
Amblyopia (acquired) (congenital) (partial)
  368.00
  color 368.59
    acquired 368.55
  deprivation 368.02
  ex anopsia 368.00
  hysterical 300.11
  nocturnal 368.60
    vitamin A deficiency 264.5
  refractive 368.03
  strabismic 368.01
  suppression 368.01
  tobacco 377.34
  toxic NEC 377.34
  uremic — *see* Uremia
Ameba, amebic (histolytica) — *see also* Amebiasis
  abscess 006.3
    bladder 006.8
    brain (with liver and lung abscess) 006.5
    liver 006.3
      with
        brain abscess (and lung abscess)
          006.5
        lung abscess 006.4
    lung (with liver abscess) 006.4
      with brain abscess 006.5
    seminal vesicle 006.8
    spleen 006.8
  carrier (suspected of) V02.2
  meningoencephalitis
    due to Naegleria (gruberi) 136.29
    primary 136.29
Amebiasis NEC 006.9
  with
    brain abscess (with liver or lung abscess)
      006.5
    liver abscess (without mention of brain
      or lung abscess) 006.3
    lung abscess (with liver abscess) 006.4
      with brain abscess 006.5
  acute 006.0
  bladder 006.8
  chronic 006.1
  cutaneous 006.6
  cutis 006.6
  due to organism other than Entamoeba
    histolytica 007.8
  hepatic (*see also* Abscess, liver, amebic)
    006.3
  nondysenteric 006.2
  seminal vesicle 006.8
  specified
    organism NEC 007.8
    site NEC 006.8
Ameboma 006.8
Amelia 755.4
  lower limb 755.31
  upper limb 755.21
Ameloblastoma (M9310/0) 213.1
  jaw (bone) (lower) 213.1
    upper 213.0
  long bones (M9261/3) — *see* Neoplasm, bone, malignant
  malignant (M9310/3) 170.1
    jaw (bone) (lower) 170.1
      upper 170.0
  mandible 213.1
  tibial (M9261/3) 170.7
Amelogenesis imperfecta 520.5
  nonhereditaria (segmentalis) 520.4

Amenorrhea (primary) (secondary) 626.0
  due to ovarian dysfunction 256.8
  hyperhormonal 256.8
Amentia — *see also* Disability, intellectual 319
  Meynert's (nonalcoholic) 294.0
    alcoholic 291.1
  nevoid 759.6
American
  leishmaniasis 085.5
  mountain tick fever 066.1
  trypanosomiasis — *see* Trypanosomiasis, American
Ametropia — *see also* Disorder, accommodation 367.9
Amianthosis 501
Amimia 784.69
Amino acid
  deficiency 270.9
    anemia 281.4
  metabolic disorder (*see also* Disorder, amino acid) 270.9
Aminoaciduria 270.9
  imidazole 270.5
Amnesia (retrograde) 780.93
  auditory 784.69
    developmental 315.31
    secondary to organic lesion 784.69
  dissociative 300.12
  hysterical or dissociative type 300.12
  psychogenic 300.12
  transient global 437.7
Amnestic (confabulatory) **syndrome** 294.0
  alcohol-induced persisting 291.1
  drug-induced persisting 292.83
  posttraumatic 294.0
Amniocentesis screening (for) V28.2
  alphafetoprotein level, raised V28.1
  chromosomal anomalies V28.0
Amnion, amniotic — *see also* condition
  nodosum 658.8 ☑
Amnionitis (complicating pregnancy) 658.4 ☑
  affecting fetus or newborn 762.7
Amoral trends 301.7
Amotio retinae — *see also* Detachment, retina
  361.9
Ampulla
  lower esophagus 530.89
  phrenic 530.89
Amputation
  any part of fetus, to facilitate delivery 763.89
  cervix (supravaginal) (uteri) 622.8
    in pregnancy or childbirth 654.6 ☑
      affecting fetus or newborn 763.89
  clitoris — *see* Wound, open, clitoris
  congenital
    lower limb 755.31
    upper limb 755.21
  neuroma (traumatic) (*see also* Injury, nerve, by site)
    surgical complication (late) 997.61
  penis — *see* Amputation, traumatic, penis
  status (without complication) — *see* Absence, by site, acquired
  stump (surgical) (posttraumatic)
    abnormal, painful, or with complication (late) 997.60
    healed or old NEC (*see also* Absence, by site, acquired)
      lower V49.70
      upper V49.60
  traumatic (complete) (partial)

> *Note* — "Complicated" includes traumatic amputation with delayed healing, delayed treatment, foreign body, or infection.

    arm 887.4
      at or above elbow 887.2
        complicated 887.3
      below elbow 887.0
        complicated 887.1
      both (bilateral) (any level(s)) 887.6
        complicated 887.7
      complicated 887.5
      finger(s) (one or both hands) 886.0
        with thumb(s) 885.0
        complicated 885.1

Amputation — *continued*
  traumatic — *continued*
    finger(s) — *continued*
      complicated 886.1
    foot (except toe(s) only) 896.0
      and other leg 897.6
        complicated 897.7
      both (bilateral) 896.2
        complicated 896.3
      complicated 896.1
      toe(s) only (one or both feet) 895.0
        complicated 895.1
    genital organ(s) (external) NEC 878.8
      complicated 878.9
    hand (except finger(s) only) 887.0
      and other arm 887.6
        complicated 887.7
      both (bilateral) 887.6
        complicated 887.7
      complicated 887.1
    finger(s) (one or both hands) 886.0
      with thumb(s) 885.0
        complicated 885.1
      complicated 886.1
      thumb(s) (with fingers of either hand) 885.0
        complicated 885.1
    head 874.9
    late effect — *see* Late, effects (of), amputation
    leg 897.4
      and other foot 897.6
        complicated 897.7
      at or above knee 897.2
        complicated 897.3
      below knee 897.0
        complicated 897.1
      both (bilateral) 897.6
        complicated 897.7
      complicated 897.5
    lower limb(s) except toe(s) — *see* Amputation, traumatic, leg
    nose — *see* Wound, open, nose
    penis 878.0
      complicated 878.1
    sites other than limbs — *see* Wound, open, by site
    thumb(s) (with finger(s) of either hand) 885.0
      complicated 885.1
    toe(s) (one or both feet) 895.0
      complicated 895.1
    upper limb(s) — *see* Amputation, traumatic, arm
Amputee (bilateral) (old) — *see also* Absence, by site, acquired V49.70
Amusia 784.69
  developmental 315.39
  secondary to organic lesion 784.69
Amyelencephalus 740.0
Amyelia 742.59
Amygdalitis — *see* Tonsillitis
Amygdalolith 474.8
Amyloid disease or degeneration 277.30
  heart 277.39 *[425.7]*
Amyloidosis (familial) (general) (generalized) (genetic) (primary) 277.30
  with lung involvement 277.39 *[517.8]*
  cardiac, hereditary 277.39
  heart 277.39 *[425.7]*
  nephropathic 277.39 *[583.81]*
  neuropathic (Portuguese) (Swiss) 277.39 *[357.4]*
  pulmonary 277.39 *[517.8]*
  secondary 277.39
  systemic, inherited 277.39
Amylopectinosis (brancher enzyme deficiency) 271.0
Amylophagia 307.52
Amyoplasia, congenita 756.89
Amyotonia 728.2
  congenita 358.8
Amyotrophia, amyotrophy, amyotrophic 728.2
  congenita 756.89
  diabetic 250.6 ☑ *[353.5]*

☑ Additional Digit Required — Refer to the Tabular List for Digit Selection   ▽ Subterms under main terms may continue to next column or page

2015 ICD-9-CM   ►◄ Revised Text   ● New Line   ▲ Revised Code   Volume 2 — 17

Allergy, allergic — Amyotrophia, amyotrophy, amyotrophic

Amyotrophia, amyotrophy, amyotrophic —
continued
  diabetic — continued
    due to secondary diabetes
      249.6 ☑ [353.5]
  lateral sclerosis (syndrome) 335.20
  neuralgic 353.5
  sclerosis (lateral) 335.20
  spinal progressive 335.21
Anacidity, gastric 536.0
  psychogenic 306.4
Anaerosis of newborn 770.88
Anaibuminemia 273.8
Analgesia — see also Anesthesia 782.0
Analphalipoproteinemia 272.5
Anaphylactic reaction or shock (correct
    substance properly administered) 995.0
  due to
    administration of blood and blood
      products 999.41
    chemical — see Table of Drugs and
      Chemicals
    correct medicinal substance properly
      administered 995.0
    drug or medicinal substance
      correct substance properly adminis-
        tered 995.0
      overdose or wrong substance given
        or taken 977.9
      specified drug — see Table of
        Drugs and Chemicals
    following sting(s) 989.5
    food 995.60
      additives 995.66
      crustaceans 995.62
      eggs 995.68
      fish 995.65
      fruits 995.63
      milk products 995.67
      nuts (tree) 995.64
      peanuts 995.61
      seeds 995.64
      specified NEC 995.69
      tree nuts 995.64
      vegetables 995.63
    immunization 999.42
    overdose or wrong substance given or
      taken 977.9
      specified drug — see Table of Drugs
        and Chemicals
    serum NEC 999.49
    following sting(s) 989.5
    purpura 287.0
    serum NEC 999.49
Anaphylactoid reaction or shock — see
    Anaphylactic reaction or shock
Anaphylaxis — see Anaphylactic reaction or
    shock
Anaplasia, cervix 622.10
Anaplasmosis, human 082.49
Anarthria 784.51
Anarthritic rheumatoid disease 446.5
Anasarca 782.3
  cardiac (see also Failure, heart) 428.0
  fetus or newborn 778.0
  lung 514
  nutritional 262
  pulmonary 514
  renal (see also Nephrosis) 581.9
Anaspadias 752.62
Anastomosis
  aneurysmal — see Aneurysm
  arteriovenous, congenital NEC (see also
    Anomaly, arteriovenous) 747.60
  ruptured, of brain (see also Hemorrhage,
    subarachnoid) 430
  intestinal 569.89
    complicated NEC 997.49
      involving urinary tract 997.5
  retinal and choroidal vessels 743.58
    acquired 362.17
Anatomical narrow angle (glaucoma) 365.02
Ancylostoma (infection) (infestation) 126.9
  americanus 126.1
  braziliense 126.2
  caninum 126.8

Ancylostoma — continued
  ceylanicum 126.3
  duodenale 126.0
  Necator americanus 126.1
Ancylostomiasis (intestinal) 126.9
  ancylostoma
    americanus 126.1
    caninum 126.8
    ceylanicum 126.3
    duodenale 126.0
    braziliense 126.2
    Necator americanus 126.1
Anders' disease or syndrome (adiposis
    tuberosa simplex) 272.8
Andersen's glycogen storage disease 271.0
Anderson's disease 272.7
Andes disease 993.2
Andrews' disease (bacterid) 686.8
Androblastoma (M8630/1)
  benign (M8630/0)
    specified site — see Neoplasm, by site,
      benign
    unspecified site
      female 220
      male 222.0
  malignant (M8630/3)
    specified site — see Neoplasm, by site,
      malignant
    unspecified site
      female 183.0
      male 186.9
  specified site — see Neoplasm, by site, un-
    certain behavior
  tubular (M8640/0)
    with lipid storage (M8641/0)
      specified site — see Neoplasm, by
        site, benign
      unspecified site
        female 220
        male 222.0
    specified site — see Neoplasm, by site,
      benign
    unspecified site
      female 220
      male 222.0
  unspecified site
    female 236.2
    male 236.4
Android pelvis 755.69
  with disproportion (fetopelvic) 653.3 ☑
    affecting fetus or newborn 763.1
    causing obstructed labor 660.1 ☑
      affecting fetus or newborn 763.1
Anectasis, pulmonary (newborn or fetus)
    770.5
Anemia 285.9
  with
    disorder of
      anaerobic glycolysis 282.3
      pentose phosphate pathway 282.2
    koilonychia 280.9
  6-phosphogluconic dehydrogenase deficien-
    cy 282.2
  achlorhydric 280.9
  achrestic 281.8
  Addison's (pernicious) 281.0
  Addison-Biermer (pernicious) 281.0
  agranulocytic 288.09
  amino acid deficiency 281.4
  antineoplastic chemotherapy induced 285.3
  aplastic 284.9
    acquired (secondary) 284.89
    congenital 284.01
    constitutional 284.01
    due to
      antineoplastic chemotherapy 284.89
      chronic systemic disease 284.89
      drugs 284.89
      infection 284.89
      radiation 284.89
    idiopathic 284.9
    myxedema 244.9
    of or complicating pregnancy 648.2 ☑
  red cell (acquired) (adult) (with thymo-
    ma) 284.81
    congenital 284.01

Anemia — continued
  aplastic — continued
    red cell — continued
      pure 284.01
      specified type NEC 284.89
      toxic (paralytic) 284.89
  aregenerative 284.9
    congenital 284.01
  asiderotic 280.9
  atypical (primary) 285.9
  autohemolysis of Selwyn and Dacie (type I)
    282.2
  autoimmune hemolytic 283.0
  Baghdad Spring 282.2
  Balantidium coli 007.0
  Biermer's (pernicious) 281.0
  blood loss (chronic) 280.0
    acute 285.1
  bothriocephalus 123.4
  brickmakers' (see also Ancylostomiasis)
    126.9
  cerebral 437.8
  childhood 282.9
  chlorotic 280.9
  chronic 285.9
    blood loss 280.0
    hemolytic 282.9
      idiopathic 283.9
    simple 281.9
  chronica congenita aregenerativa 284.01
  combined system disease NEC 281.0 [336.2]
    due to dietary deficiency 281.1 [336.2]
  complicating pregnancy or childbirth
    648.2 ☑
  congenital (following fetal blood loss) 776.5
    aplastic 284.01
    due to isoimmunization NEC 773.2
    Heinz-body 282.7
    hereditary hemolytic NEC 282.9
    nonspherocytic
      Type I 282.2
      Type II 282.3
    pernicious 281.0
    spherocytic (see also Spherocytosis)
      282.0
  Cooley's (erythroblastic) 282.44
  crescent — see Disease, sickle-cell
  cytogenic 281.0
  Dacie's (nonspherocytic)
    type I 282.2
    type II 282.3
  Davidson's (refractory) 284.9
  deficiency 281.9
    2, 3 diphosphoglycurate mutase 282.3
    2, 3 PG 282.3
    6-PGD 282.2
    6-phosphogluronic dehydrogenase
      282.2
    amino acid 281.4
    combined B₁₂ and folate 281.3
    enzyme, drug-induced (hemolytic) 282.2
    erythrocytic glutathione 282.2
    folate 281.2
      dietary 281.2
      drug-induced 281.2
    folic acid 281.2
      dietary 281.2
      drug-induced 281.2
    G-6-PD 282.2
    GGS-R 282.2
    glucose-6-phosphate dehydrogenase
      (G-6-PD) 282.2
    glucose-phosphate isomerase 282.3
    glutathione peroxidase 282.2
    glutathione reductase 282.2
    glyceraldehyde phosphate dehydroge-
      nase 282.3
    GPI 282.3
    G SH 282.2
    hexokinase 282.3
    iron (Fe) 280.9
      specified NEC 280.8
    nutritional 281.9
      with
        poor iron absorption 280.9
        specified deficiency NEC 281.8

Anemia — continued
  deficiency — continued
    nutritional — continued
      due to inadequate dietary iron intake
        280.1
      specified type NEC 281.8
    of or complicating pregnancy 648.2 ☑
    pentose phosphate pathway 282.2
    PFK 282.3
    phosphofructo-aldolase 282.3
    phosphofructokinase 282.3
    phosphoglycerate kinase 282.3
    PK 282.3
    protein 281.4
    pyruvate kinase (PK) 282.3
    TPI 282.3
    triosephosphate isomerase 282.3
    vitamin B₁₂ NEC 281.1
      dietary 281.1
      pernicious 281.0
  Diamond-Blackfan (congenital hypoplastic)
    284.01
  dibothriocephalus 123.4
  dimorphic 281.9
  diphasic 281.8
  diphtheritic 032.89
  Diphyllobothrium 123.4
  drepanocytic (see also Disease, sickle-cell)
    282.60
  due to
    antineoplastic chemotherapy 285.3
    blood loss (chronic) 280.0
      acute 285.1
    chemotherapy, antineoplastic 285.3
    defect of Embden-Meyerhof pathway
      glycolysis 282.3
    disorder of glutathione metabolism
      282.2
    drug — see Anemia, by type (see also
      Table of Drugs and Chemicals)
      chemotherapy, antineoplastic 285.3
    fetal blood loss 776.5
    fish tapeworm (D. latum) infestation
      123.4
    glutathione metabolism disorder 282.2
    hemorrhage (chronic) 280.0
      acute 285.1
    hexose monophosphate (HMP) shunt
      deficiency 282.2
    impaired absorption 280.9
    loss of blood (chronic) 280.0
      acute 285.1
    myxedema 244.9
    Necator americanus 126.1
    prematurity 776.6
    selective vitamin B₁₂ malabsorption with
      proteinuria 281.1
  Dyke-Young type (secondary)
    (symptomatic) 283.9
  dyserythropoietic (congenital) (types I, II,
    III) 285.8
  dyshemopoietic (congenital) 285.8
  Egypt (see also Ancylostomiasis) 126.9
  elliptocytosis (see also Elliptocytosis) 282.1
  enzyme deficiency, drug-induced 282.2
  epidemic (see also Ancylostomiasis) 126.9
  EPO resistant 285.21
  erythroblastic
    familial 282.44
    fetus or newborn (see also Disease,
      hemolytic) 773.2
    late 773.5
  erythrocytic glutathione deficiency 282.2
  erythropoietin-resistant (EPO resistant ane-
    mia) 285.21
  essential 285.9
  Faber's (achlorhydric anemia) 280.9
  factitious (self-induced blood letting) 280.0
  familial erythroblastic (microcytic) 282.44
  Fanconi's (congenital pancytopenia) 284.09
  favism 282.2
  fetal 678.0 ☑
    following blood loss, affecting newborn
      776.5

☑ Additional Digit Required — Refer to the Tabular List for Digit Selection   ▽ Subterms under main terms may continue to next column or page

18 — Volume 2   ▶◀ Revised Text   ● New Line   ▲ Revised Code   2015 ICD-9-CM

Anemia — *continued*
  fetus or newborn
    due to
      ABO
        antibodies 773.1
        incompatibility, maternal/fetal 773.1
        isoimmunization 773.1
      Rh
        antibodies 773.0
        incompatibility, maternal/fetal 773.0
        isoimmunization 773.0
    following fetal blood loss 776.5
  fish tapeworm (D. latum) infestation 123.4
  folate (folic acid) deficiency 281.2
    dietary 281.2
    drug-induced 281.2
  folate malabsorption, congenital 281.2
  folic acid deficiency 281.2
    dietary 281.2
    drug-induced 281.2
  G-6-PD 282.2
  general 285.9
  glucose-6-phosphate dehydrogenase deficiency 282.2
  glutathione-reductase deficiency 282.2
  goat's milk 281.2
  granulocytic 288.09
  Heinz-body, congenital 282.7
  hemoglobin deficiency 285.9
  hemolytic 283.9
    acquired 283.9
      with hemoglobinuria NEC 283.2
      autoimmune (cold type) (idiopathic) (primary) (secondary) (symptomatic) (warm type) 283.0
      due to
        cold reactive antibodies 283.0
        drug exposure 283.0
        warm reactive antibodies 283.0
      fragmentation 283.19
      idiopathic (chronic) 283.9
      infectious 283.19
        autoimmune 283.0
        non-autoimmune 283.10
      toxic 283.19
      traumatic cardiac 283.19
    acute 283.9
      due to enzyme deficiency NEC 282.3
      fetus or newborn (*see also* Disease, hemolytic) 773.2
        late 773.5
      Lederer's (acquired infectious hemolytic anemia) 283.19
    autoimmune (acquired) 283.0
    chronic 282.9
      idiopathic 283.9
    cold type (secondary) (symptomatic) 283.0
    congenital (spherocytic) (*see also* Spherocytosis) 282.0
      nonspherocytic — *see* Anemia, hemolytic, nonspherocytic, congenital
    drug-induced 283.0
      enzyme deficiency 282.2
    due to
      cardiac conditions 283.19
      drugs 283.0
      enzyme deficiency NEC 282.3
        drug-induced 282.2
      presence of shunt or other internal prosthetic device 283.19
      thrombotic thrombocytopenic purpura 446.6
    elliptocytotic (*see also* Elliptocytosis) 282.1
    familial 282.9
    hereditary 282.9
      due to enzyme deficiency NEC 282.3
        specified NEC 282.8
      idiopathic (chronic) 283.9
    infectious (acquired) 283.19
    mechanical 283.19
    microangiopathic 283.19

Anemia — *continued*
  hemolytic — *continued*
    non-autoimmune NEC 283.10
    nonspherocytic
      congenital or hereditary NEC 282.3
        glucose-6-phosphate dehydrogenase deficiency 282.2
        pyruvate kinase (PK) deficiency 282.3
        type I 282.2
        type II 282.3
      type I 282.2
      type II 282.3
      of or complicating pregnancy 648.2 ☑
      resulting from presence of shunt or other internal prosthetic device 283.19
    secondary 283.19
      autoimmune 283.0
    sickle-cell — *see* Disease, sickle-cell
    Stransky-Regala type (Hb-E) (*see also* Disease, hemoglobin) 282.7
    symptomatic 283.19
      autoimmune 283.0
    toxic (acquired) 283.19
    uremic (adult) (child) 283.11
    warm type (secondary) (symptomatic) 283.0
  hemorrhagic (chronic) 280.0
    acute 285.1
  HEMPAS 285.8
  hereditary erythroblast multinuclearity-positive acidified serum test 285.8
  Herrick's (hemoglobin S disease) 282.61
  hexokinase deficiency 282.3
  high A₂ 282.46
  hookworm (*see also* Ancylostomiasis) 126.9
  hypochromic (idiopathic) (microcytic) (normoblastic) 280.9
    with iron loading 285.0
    due to blood loss (chronic) 280.0
      acute 285.1
    familial sex linked 285.0
    pyridoxine-responsive 285.0
  hypoplasia, red blood cells 284.81
    congenital or familial 284.01
  hypoplastic (idiopathic) 284.9
    congenital 284.01
    familial 284.01
    of childhood 284.09
  idiopathic 285.9
    hemolytic, chronic 283.9
  in (due to) (with)
    chronic illness NEC 285.29
    chronic kidney disease 285.21
    end-stage renal disease 285.21
    neoplastic disease 285.22
  infantile 285.9
  infective, infectional 285.9
  intertropical (*see also* Ancylostomiasis) 126.9
  iron (Fe) deficiency 280.9
    due to blood loss (chronic) 280.0
      acute 285.1
    of or complicating pregnancy 648.2 ☑
    specified NEC 280.8
  Jaksch's (pseudoleukemia infantum) 285.8
  Joseph-Diamond-Blackfan (congenital hypoplastic) 284.01
  labyrinth 386.50
  Lederer's (acquired infectious hemolytic anemia) 283.19
  leptocytosis (hereditary) 282.40
  leukoerythroblastic 284.2
  macrocytic 281.9
    nutritional 281.2
    of or complicating pregnancy 648.2 ☑
    tropical 281.2
  malabsorption (familial), selective B₁₂ with proteinuria 281.1
  malarial (*see also* Malaria) 084.6
  malignant (progressive) 281.0
  malnutrition 281.9
  marsh (*see also* Malaria) 084.6
  Mediterranean 282.40
    with hemoglobinopathy 282.49
  megaloblastic 281.9

Anemia — *continued*
  megaloblastic — *continued*
    combined B₁₂ and folate deficiency 281.3
    nutritional (of infancy) 281.2
    of infancy 281.2
    of or complicating pregnancy 648.2 ☑
    refractory 281.3
    specified NEC 281.3
  megalocytic 281.9
  microangiopathic hemolytic 283.19
  microcytic (hypochromic) 280.9
    due to blood loss (chronic) 280.0
      acute 285.1
    familial 282.49
    hypochromic 280.9
  microdrepanocytosis 282.41
  miners' (*see also* Ancylostomiasis) 126.9
  myelopathic 285.8
  myelophthisic (normocytic) 284.2
  newborn (*see also* Disease, hemolytic) 773.2
    due to isoimmunization (*see also* Disease, hemolytic) 773.2
    late, due to isoimmunization 773.5
    posthemorrhagic 776.5
  nonregenerative 284.9
  nonspherocytic hemolytic — *see* Anemia, hemolytic, nonspherocytic
  normocytic (infectional) (not due to blood loss) 285.9
    due to blood loss (chronic) 280.0
      acute 285.1
    myelophthisic 284.2
  nutritional (deficiency) 281.9
    with
      poor iron absorption 280.9
      specified deficiency NEC 281.8
    due to inadequate dietary iron intake 280.1
    megaloblastic (of infancy) 281.2
  of childhood 282.9
  of chronic
    disease NEC 285.29
    illness NEC 285.29
  of or complicating pregnancy 648.2 ☑
    affecting fetus or newborn 760.8
  of prematurity 776.6
  orotic aciduric (congenital) (hereditary) 281.4
  osteosclerotic 289.89
  ovalocytosis (hereditary) (*see also* Elliptocytosis) 282.1
  paludal (*see also* Malaria) 084.6
  pentose phosphate pathway deficiency 282.2
  pernicious (combined system disease) (congenital) (dorsolateral spinal degeneration) (juvenile) (myelopathy) (neuropathy) (posterior sclerosis) (primary) (progressive) (spleen) 281.0
    of or complicating pregnancy 648.2 ☑
  pleochromic 285.9
    of sprue 281.8
  portal 285.8
  posthemorrhagic (chronic) 280.0
    acute 285.1
    newborn 776.5
  postoperative
    due to (acute) blood loss 285.1
      chronic blood loss 280.0
    other 285.9
  postpartum 648.2 ☑
  pressure 285.9
  primary 285.9
  profound 285.9
  progressive 285.9
    malignant 281.0
    pernicious 281.0
  protein-deficiency 281.4
  pseudoleukemica infantum 285.8
  puerperal 648.2 ☑
  pure red cell 284.81
    congenital 284.01
  pyridoxine-responsive (hypochromic) 285.0
  pyruvate kinase (PK) deficiency 282.3
  refractoria sideroblastica 238.72

Anemia — *continued*
  refractory (primary) 238.72
    with
      excess
        blasts-1 (RAEB-1) 238.72
        blasts-2 (RAEB-2) 238.73
        hemochromatosis 238.72
        ringed sideroblasts (RARS) 238.72
    due to
      drug 285.0
      myelodysplastic syndrome 238.72
      toxin 285.0
    hereditary 285.0
    idiopathic 238.72
    megaloblastic 281.3
    sideroblastic 238.72
      hereditary 285.0
    sideropenic 280.9
  Rietti-Greppi-Micheli (thalassemia minor) 282.46
  scorbutic 281.8
  secondary (to) 285.9
    blood loss (chronic) 280.0
      acute 285.1
    hemorrhage 280.0
      acute 285.1
    inadequate dietary iron intake 280.1
  semiplastic 284.9
  septic 285.9
  sickle-cell (*see also* Disease, sickle-cell) 282.60
  sideroachrestic 285.0
  sideroblastic (acquired) (any type) (congenital) (drug-induced) (due to disease) (hereditary) (primary) (secondary) (sex-linked hypochromic) (vitamin B₆ responsive) 285.0
    refractory 238.72
    congenital 285.0
    drug-induced 285.0
    hereditary 285.0
    sex-linked hypochromic 285.0
    vitamin B₆-responsive 285.0
  sideropenic (refractory) 280.9
    due to blood loss (chronic) 280.0
      acute 285.1
  simple chronic 281.9
  specified type NEC 285.8
  spherocytic (hereditary) (*see also* Spherocytosis) 282.0
  splenic 285.8
    familial (Gaucher's) 272.7
  splenomegalic 285.8
  stomatocytosis 282.8
  syphilitic 095.8
  target cell (oval) 285.8
    with thalassemia — *see* Thalassemia
  thalassemia 282.40
  thrombocytopenic (*see also* Thrombocytopenia) 287.5
  toxic 284.89
  triosephosphate isomerase deficiency 282.3
  tropical, macrocytic 281.2
  tuberculous (*see also* Tuberculosis) 017.9 ☑
  vegan's 281.1
  vitamin
    B₆-responsive 285.0
    B₁₂ deficiency (dietary) 281.1
      pernicious 281.0
  von Jaksch's (pseudoleukemia infantum) 285.8
  Witts' (achlorhydric anemia) 280.9
  Zuelzer (-Ogden) (nutritional megaloblastic anemia) 281.2
Anencephalus, anencephaly 740.0
  fetal, affecting management of pregnancy 655.0 ☑
Anergasia — *see also* Psychosis, organic 294.9
  senile 290.0
Anesthesia, anesthetic 782.0
  complication or reaction NEC 995.22
    due to
      correct substance properly administered 995.22

☑ **Additional Digit Required** — Refer to the Tabular List for Digit Selection   ▽ **Subterms under main terms may continue to next column or page**

Anesthesia, anesthetic — continued
  complication or reaction — continued
    due to — continued
      overdose or wrong substance given 968.4
      specified anesthetic — see Table of Drugs and Chemicals
  cornea 371.81
  death from
    correct substance properly administered 995.4
    during delivery 668.9 ☑
    overdose or wrong substance given 968.4
    specified anesthetic — see Table of Drugs and Chemicals
  eye 371.81
  functional 300.11
  hyperesthetic, thalamic 338.0
  hysterical 300.11
  local skin lesion 782.0
  olfactory 781.1
  sexual (psychogenic) 302.72
  shock
    due to
      correct substance properly administered 995.4
      overdose or wrong substance given 968.4
      specified anesthetic — see Table of Drugs and Chemicals
  skin 782.0
  tactile 782.0
  testicular 608.9
  thermal 782.0
Anetoderma (maculosum) 701.3
Aneuploidy NEC 758.5
Aneurin deficiency 265.1
Aneurysm (anastomotic) (artery) (cirsoid) (diffuse) (false) (fusiform) (multiple) (ruptured) (saccular) (varicose) 442.9
  abdominal (aorta) 441.4
    ruptured 441.3
    syphilitic 093.0
  aorta, aortic (nonsyphilitic) 441.9
    abdominal 441.4
      dissecting 441.02
      ruptured 441.3
      syphilitic 093.0
    arch 441.2
      ruptured 441.1
    arteriosclerotic NEC 441.9
      ruptured 441.5
    ascending 441.2
      ruptured 441.1
    congenital 747.29
    descending 441.9
      abdominal 441.4
        ruptured 441.3
      ruptured 441.5
      thoracic 441.2
        ruptured 441.1
    dissecting 441.00
      abdominal 441.02
      thoracic 441.01
      thoracoabdominal 441.03
    due to coarctation (aorta) 747.10
    ruptured 441.5
    sinus, right 747.29
    syphilitic 093.0
    thoracoabdominal 441.7
      ruptured 441.6
    thorax, thoracic (arch) (nonsyphilitic) 441.2
      dissecting 441.01
      ruptured 441.1
      syphilitic 093.0
    transverse 441.2
      ruptured 441.1
    valve (heart) (see also Endocarditis, aortic) 424.1
  arteriosclerotic NEC 442.9
    cerebral 437.3
      ruptured (see also Hemorrhage, subarachnoid) 430

Aneurysm — continued
  arteriovenous (congenital) (peripheral) NEC (see also Anomaly, arteriovenous) 747.60
    acquired NEC 447.0
      brain 437.3
        ruptured (see also Hemorrhage, subarachnoid) 430
      coronary 414.11
      pulmonary 417.0
    brain (cerebral) 747.81
      ruptured (see also Hemorrhage, subarachnoid) 430
    coronary 746.85
    pulmonary 747.32
    retina 743.58
    specified site NEC 747.89
      acquired 447.0
    traumatic (see also Injury, blood vessel, by site) 904.9
  basal — see Aneurysm, brain
  berry (congenital) (ruptured) (see also Hemorrhage, subarachnoid) 430
    nonruptured 437.3
  brain 437.3
    arteriosclerotic 437.3
      ruptured (see also Hemorrhage, subarachnoid) 430
    arteriovenous 747.81
      acquired 437.3
        ruptured (see also Hemorrhage, subarachnoid) 430
      ruptured (see also Hemorrhage, subarachnoid) 430
    berry (congenital) (ruptured) (see also Hemorrhage, subarachnoid) 430
      nonruptured 437.3
    congenital 747.81
      ruptured (see also Hemorrhage, subarachnoid) 430
    meninges 437.3
      ruptured (see also Hemorrhage, subarachnoid) 430
    miliary (congenital) (ruptured) (see also Hemorrhage, subarachnoid) 430
    mycotic 421.0
      ruptured (see also Hemorrhage, subarachnoid) 430
    nonruptured 437.3
    ruptured (see also Hemorrhage, subarachnoid) 430
    syphilitic 094.87
    traumatic — see Injury, intracranial
  cardiac (false) (see also Aneurysm, heart) 414.10
  carotid artery (common) (external) 442.81
    internal (intracranial portion) 437.3
      extracranial portion 442.81
      ruptured into brain (see also Hemorrhage, subarachnoid) 430
    syphilitic 093.89
      intracranial 094.87
  cavernous sinus (see also Aneurysm, brain) 437.3
    arteriovenous 747.81
      ruptured (see also Hemorrhage, subarachnoid) 430
    congenital 747.81
      ruptured (see also Hemorrhage, subarachnoid) 430
  celiac 442.84
  central nervous system, syphilitic 094.89
  cerebral — see Aneurysm, brain
  chest — see Aneurysm, thorax
  circle of Willis (see also Aneurysm, brain) 437.3
    congenital 747.81
      ruptured (see also Hemorrhage, subarachnoid) 430
    ruptured (see also Hemorrhage, subarachnoid) 430
  common iliac artery 442.2
  congenital (peripheral) NEC 747.60
    brain 747.81

Aneurysm — continued
  congenital — continued
    brain — continued
      ruptured (see also Hemorrhage, subarachnoid) 430
    cerebral — see Aneurysm, brain, congenital
    coronary 746.85
    gastrointestinal 747.61
    lower limb 747.64
    pulmonary 747.32
    renal 747.62
    retina 743.58
    specified site NEC 747.89
    spinal 747.82
    upper limb 747.63
  conjunctiva 372.74
  conus arteriosus (see also Aneurysm, heart) 414.10
  coronary (arteriosclerotic) (artery) (vein) (see also Aneurysm, heart) 414.11
    arteriovenous 746.85
    congenital 746.85
    syphilitic 093.89
  cylindrical 441.9
    ruptured 441.5
    syphilitic 093.9
  dissecting 442.9
    aorta 441.00
      abdominal 441.02
      thoracic 441.01
      thoracoabdominal 441.03
    syphilitic 093.9
  ductus arteriosus 747.0
  embolic — see Embolism, artery
  endocardial, infective (any valve) 421.0
  femoral 442.3
  gastroduodenal 442.84
  gastroepiploic 442.84
  heart (chronic or with a stated duration of over 8 weeks) (infectional) (wall) 414.10
    acute or with a stated duration of 8 weeks or less (see also Infarct, myocardium) 410.9 ☑
    congenital 746.89
    valve — see Endocarditis
  hepatic 442.84
  iliac (common) 442.2
  infective (any valve) 421.0
  innominate (nonsyphilitic) 442.89
    syphilitic 093.89
  interauricular septum (see also Aneurysm, heart) 414.10
  interventricular septum (see also Aneurysm, heart) 414.10
  intracranial — see Aneurysm, brain
  intrathoracic (nonsyphilitic) 441.2
    ruptured 441.1
    syphilitic 093.0
  jugular vein (acute) 453.89
    chronic 453.76
  lower extremity 442.3
  lung (pulmonary artery) 417.1
  malignant 093.9
  mediastinal (nonsyphilitic) 442.89
    syphilitic 093.89
  miliary (congenital) (ruptured) (see also Hemorrhage, subarachnoid) 430
  mitral (heart) (valve) 424.0
  mural (arteriovenous) (heart) (see also Aneurysm, heart) 414.10
  mycotic, any site 421.0
    without endocarditis — see Aneurysm by site
    ruptured, brain (see also Hemorrhage, subarachnoid) 430
  myocardium (see also Aneurysm, heart) 414.10
  neck 442.81
  pancreaticoduodenal 442.84
  patent ductus arteriosus 747.0
  peripheral NEC 442.89
    congenital NEC (see also Aneurysm, congenital) 747.60
  popliteal 442.3

Aneurysm — continued
  pulmonary 417.1
    arteriovenous 747.32
      acquired 417.0
    syphilitic 093.89
    valve (heart) (see also Endocarditis, pulmonary) 424.3
  racemose 442.9
    congenital (peripheral) NEC 747.60
  radial 442.0
  Rasmussen's (see also Tuberculosis) 011.2 ☑
  renal 442.1
  retinal (acquired) 362.17
    congenital 743.58
    diabetic 250.5 ☑ [362.01]
      due to secondary diabetes 249.5 ☑ [362.01]
  sinus, aortic (of Valsalva) 747.29
  specified site NEC 442.89
  spinal (cord) 442.89
    congenital 747.82
    syphilitic (hemorrhage) 094.89
  spleen, splenic 442.83
  subclavian 442.82
    syphilitic 093.89
  superior mesenteric 442.84
  syphilitic 093.9
    aorta 093.0
    central nervous system 094.89
    congenital 090.5
    spine, spinal 094.89
  thoracoabdominal 441.7
    ruptured 441.6
  thorax, thoracic (arch) (nonsyphilitic) 441.2
    dissecting 441.01
    ruptured 441.1
    syphilitic 093.0
  traumatic (complication) (early) — see Injury, blood vessel, by site
  tricuspid (heart) (valve) — see Endocarditis, tricuspid
  ulnar 442.0
  upper extremity 442.0
  valve, valvular — see Endocarditis
  venous 456.8
    congenital NEC (see also Aneurysm, congenital) 747.60
  ventricle (arteriovenous) (see also Aneurysm, heart) 414.10
  visceral artery NEC 442.84
Angiectasis 459.89
Angiectopia 459.9
Angiitis 447.6
  allergic granulomatous 446.4
  hypersensitivity 446.20
    Goodpasture's syndrome 446.21
    specified NEC 446.29
  necrotizing 446.0
  Wegener's (necrotizing respiratory granulomatosis) 446.4
Angina (attack) (cardiac) (chest) (effort) (heart) (pectoris) (syndrome) (vasomotor) 413.9
  abdominal 557.1
  accelerated 411.1
  agranulocytic 288.03
  aphthous 074.0
  catarrhal 462
  crescendo 411.1
  croupous 464.4
  cruris 443.9
    due to atherosclerosis NEC (see also Arteriosclerosis, extremities) 440.20
  decubitus 413.0
  diphtheritic (membranous) 032.0
  equivalent 413.9
  erysipelatous 034.0
  erythematous 462
  exudative, chronic 476.0
  faucium 478.29
  gangrenous 462
    diphtheritic 032.0
  infectious 462
  initial 411.1
  intestinal 557.1
  ludovici 528.3
  Ludwig's 528.3

☑ Additional Digit Required — Refer to the Tabular List for Digit Selection

▽ Subterms under main terms may continue to next column or page

Angina — *continued*
- malignant 462
  - diphtheritic 032.0
- membranous 464.4
  - diphtheritic 032.0
- mesenteric 557.1
- monocytic 075
- nocturnal 413.0
- phlegmonous 475
  - diphtheritic 032.0
- preinfarctional 411.1
- Prinzmetal's 413.1
- progressive 411.1
- pseudomembranous 101
- psychogenic 306.2
- pultaceous, diphtheritic 032.0
- scarlatinal 034.1
- septic 034.0
- simple 462
- stable NEC 413.9
- staphylococcal 462
- streptococcal 034.0
- stridulous, diphtheritic 032.3
- syphilitic 093.9
  - congenital 090.5
- tonsil 475
- trachealis 464.4
- unstable 411.1
- variant 413.1
- Vincent's 101

Angioblastoma (M9161/1) — *see* Neoplasm, connective tissue, uncertain behavior
Angiocholecystitis — *see also* Cholecystitis, acute 575.0
Angiocholitis — *see also* Cholecystitis, acute 576.1
Angiodysgensis spinalis 336.1
Angiodysplasia (intestinalis) (intestine) 569.84
- with hemorrhage 569.85
- duodenum 537.82
  - with hemorrhage 537.83
- stomach 537.82
  - with hemorrhage 537.83
Angioedema (allergic) (any site) (with urticaria) 995.1
- hereditary 277.6
Angioendothelioma (M9130/1) — *see also* Neoplasm, by site, uncertain behavior
- benign (M9130/0) (*see also* Hemangioma, by site) 228.00
- bone (M9260/3) — *see* Neoplasm, bone, malignant
- Ewing's (M9260/3) — *see* Neoplasm, bone, malignant
- nervous system (M9130/0) 228.09
Angiofibroma (M9160/0) — *see also* Neoplasm, by site, benign
- juvenile (M9160/0) 210.7
  - specified site — *see* Neoplasm, by site, benign
  - unspecified site 210.7
Angiohemophilia (A) (B) 286.4
Angioid streaks (choroid) (retina) 363.43
Angiokeratoma (M9141/0) — *see also* Neoplasm, skin, benign
- corporis diffusum 272.7
Angiokeratosis
- diffuse 272.7
Angioleiomyoma (M8894/0) — *see* Neoplasm, connective tissue, benign
Angioleucitis 683
Angiolipoma (M8861/0) — *see also* Lipoma, by site 214.9
- infiltrating (M8861/1) — *see* Neoplasm, connective tissue, uncertain behavior
Angioma (M9120/0) — *see also* Hemangioma, by site 228.00
- capillary 448.1
- hemorrhagicum hereditaria 448.0
- malignant (M9120/3) — *see* Neoplasm, connective tissue, malignant
- pigmentosum et atrophicum 757.33
- placenta — *see* Placenta, abnormal
- plexiform (M9131/0) — *see* Hemangioma, by site
- senile 448.1

Angioma — *see also* Hemangioma, by site — *continued*
- serpiginosum 709.1
- spider 448.1
- stellate 448.1
Angiomatosis 757.32
- bacillary 083.8
- corporis diffusum universale 272.7
- cutaneocerebral 759.6
- encephalocutaneous 759.6
- encephalofacial 759.6
- encephalotrigeminal 759.6
- hemorrhagic familial 448.0
- hereditary familial 448.0
- heredofamilial 448.0
- meningo-oculofacial 759.6
- multiple sites 228.09
- neuro-oculocutaneous 759.6
- retina (Hippel's disease) 759.6
- retinocerebellosa 759.6
- retinocerebral 759.6
- systemic 228.09
Angiomyolipoma (M8860/0)
- specified site — *see* Neoplasm, connective tissue, benign
- unspecified site 223.0
Angiomyoliposarcoma (M8860/3) — *see* Neoplasm, connective tissue, malignant
Angiomyoma (M8894/0) — *see* Neoplasm, connective tissue, benign
Angiomyosarcoma (M8894/3) — *see* Neoplasm, connective tissue, malignant
Angioneurosis 306.2
Angioneurotic edema (allergic) (any site) (with urticaria) 995.1
- hereditary 277.6
Angiopathia, angiopathy 459.9
- diabetic (peripheral) 250.7 ☑ *[443.81]*
  - due to secondary diabetes 249.7 ☑ *[443.81]*
- peripheral 443.9
  - diabetic 250.7 ☑ *[443.81]*
    - due to secondary diabetes 249.7 ☑ *[443.81]*
  - specified type NEC 443.89
- retinae syphilitica 093.89
- retinalis (juvenilis) 362.18
  - background 362.10
  - diabetic 250.5 ☑ *[362.01]*
    - due to secondary diabetes 249.5 ☑ *[362.01]*
  - proliferative 362.29
  - tuberculous (*see also* Tuberculosis) 017.3 ☑ *[362.18]*
Angiosarcoma (M9120/3) — *see* Neoplasm, connective tissue, malignant
Angiosclerosis — *see* Arteriosclerosis
Angioscotoma, enlarged 368.42
Angiospasm 443.9
- brachial plexus 353.0
- cerebral 435.9
- cervical plexus 353.2
- nerve
  - arm 354.9
    - axillary 353.0
    - median 354.1
    - ulnar 354.2
  - autonomic (*see also* Neuropathy, peripheral, autonomic) 337.9
  - axillary 353.0
  - leg 355.8
    - plantar 355.6
  - lower extremity — *see* Angiospasm, nerve, leg
  - median 354.1
  - peripheral NEC 355.9
  - spinal NEC 355.9
  - sympathetic (*see also* Neuropathy, peripheral, autonomic) 337.9
  - ulnar 354.2
  - upper extremity — *see* Angiospasm, nerve, arm
- peripheral NEC 443.9
- traumatic 443.9
  - foot 443.9
  - leg 443.9

Angiospasm — *continued*
- vessel 443.9
Angiospastic disease or edema 443.9
Angle's
- class I 524.21
- class II 524.22
- class III 524.23
Anguillulosis 127.2
Angulation
- cecum (*see also* Obstruction, intestine) 560.9
- coccyx (acquired) 738.6
  - congenital 756.19
- femur (acquired) 736.39
  - congenital 755.69
- intestine (large) (small) (*see also* Obstruction, intestine) 560.9
- sacrum (acquired) 738.5
  - congenital 756.19
- sigmoid (flexure) (*see also* Obstruction, intestine) 560.9
- spine (*see also* Curvature, spine) 737.9
- tibia (acquired) 736.89
  - congenital 755.69
- ureter 593.3
- wrist (acquired) 736.09
  - congenital 755.59
Angulus infectiosus 686.8
Anhedonia 780.99
Anhidrosis (lid) (neurogenic) (thermogenic) 705.0
Anhydration 276.51
- with
  - hypernatremia 276.0
  - hyponatremia 276.1
Anhydremia 276.52
- with
  - hypernatremia 276.0
  - hyponatremia 276.1
Anidrosis 705.0
Aniridia (congenital) 743.45
Anisakiasis (infection) (infestation) 127.1
Anisakis larva infestation 127.1
Aniseikonia 367.32
Anisocoria (pupil) 379.41
- congenital 743.46
Anisocytosis 790.09
Anisometropia (congenital) 367.31
Ankle — *see* condition
Ankyloblepharon (acquired) (eyelid) 374.46
- filiforme (adnatum) (congenital) 743.62
- total 743.62
Ankylodactly — *see also* Syndactylism 755.10
Ankyloglossia 750.0
Ankylosis (fibrous) (osseous) 718.50
- ankle 718.57
- any joint, produced by surgical fusion V45.4
- cricoarytenoid (cartilage) (joint) (larynx) 478.79
- dental 521.6
- ear ossicle NEC 385.22
  - malleus 385.21
- elbow 718.52
- finger 718.54
- hip 718.55
- incostapedial joint (infectional) 385.22
- joint, produced by surgical fusion NEC V45.4
- knee 718.56
- lumbosacral (joint) 724.6
- malleus 385.21
- multiple sites 718.59
- postoperative (status) V45.4
- sacroiliac (joint) 724.6
- shoulder 718.51
- specified site NEC 718.58
- spine NEC 724.9
- surgical V45.4
- teeth, tooth (hard tissues) 521.6
- temporomandibular joint 524.61
- wrist 718.53
Ankylostoma — *see* Ancylostoma
Ankylostomiasis (intestinal) — *see* Ancylostomiasis
Ankylurethria — *see also* Stricture, urethra 598.9
Annular — *see also* condition
- detachment, cervix 622.8

Annular — *see also* condition — *continued*
- organ or site, congenital NEC — *see* Distortion
- pancreas (congenital) 751.7
Anodontia (complete) (partial) (vera) 520.0
- with abnormal spacing 524.30
- acquired 525.10
  - causing malocclusion 524.30
  - due to
    - caries 525.13
    - extraction 525.10
    - periodontal disease 525.12
    - trauma 525.11
Anomaly, anomalous (congenital) (unspecified type) 759.9
- abdomen 759.9
- abdominal wall 756.70
- acoustic nerve 742.9
- adrenal (gland) 759.1
- Alder (-Reilly) (leukocyte granulation) 288.2
- alimentary tract 751.9
  - lower 751.5
    - specified type NEC 751.8
  - upper (any part, except tongue) 750.9
    - tongue 750.10
      - specified type NEC 750.19
- alveolar 524.70
  - ridge (process) 525.8
  - specified NEC 524.79
- ankle (joint) 755.69
- anus, anal (canal) 751.5
- aorta, aortic 747.20
  - arch 747.21
  - coarctation (postductal) (preductal) 747.10
  - cusp or valve NEC 746.9
  - septum 745.0
  - specified type NEC 747.29
- aorticopulmonary septum 745.0
- apertures, diaphragm 756.6
- appendix 751.5
- aqueduct of Sylvius 742.3
  - with spina bifida (*see also* Spina bifida) 741.0 ☑
- arm 755.50
  - reduction (*see also* Deformity, reduction, upper limb) 755.20
- arteriovenous (congenital) (peripheral) NEC 747.60
  - brain 747.81
  - cerebral 747.81
  - coronary 746.85
  - gastrointestinal 747.61
    - acquired — *see* Angiodysplasia
  - lower limb 747.64
  - renal 747.62
  - specified site NEC 747.69
  - spinal 747.82
  - upper limb 747.63
- artery (*see also* Anomaly, peripheral vascular system) NEC 747.60
  - brain 747.81
  - cerebral 747.81
  - coronary 746.85
  - eye 743.9
  - pulmonary 747.39
  - renal 747.62
  - retina 743.9
  - umbilical 747.5
- arytenoepiglottic folds 748.3
- atrial
  - bands 746.9
  - folds 746.9
  - septa 745.5
- atrioventricular
  - canal 745.69
  - common 745.69
  - conduction 426.7
  - excitation 426.7
  - septum 745.4
- atrium — *see* Anomaly, atrial
- auditory canal 744.3
  - specified type NEC 744.29
    - with hearing impairment 744.02
- auricle
  - ear 744.3

Angina — Anomaly, anomalous

Anomaly, anomalous — *continued*
  auricle — *continued*
    ear — *continued*
      causing impairment of hearing 744.02
      heart 746.9
        septum 745.5
  autosomes, autosomal NEC 758.5
  Axenfeld's 743.44
  back 759.9
  band
    atrial 746.9
    heart 746.9
    ventricular 746.9
  Bartholin's duct 750.9
  biliary duct or passage 751.60
    atresia 751.61
  bladder (neck) (sphincter) (trigone) 753.9
    specified type NEC 753.8
  blood vessel 747.9
    artery — *see* Anomaly, artery
    peripheral vascular — *see* Anomaly, peripheral vascular system
    vein — *see* Anomaly, vein
  bone NEC 756.9
    ankle 755.69
    arm 755.50
    chest 756.3
    cranium 756.0
    face 756.0
    finger 755.50
    foot 755.67
    forearm 755.50
    frontal 756.0
    head 756.0
    hip 755.63
    leg 755.60
    lumbosacral 756.10
    nose 748.1
    pelvic girdle 755.60
    rachitic 756.4
    rib 756.3
    shoulder girdle 755.50
    skull 756.0
      with
        anencephalus 740.0
        encephalocele 742.0
        hydrocephalus 742.3
          with spina bifida (*see also* Spina bifida) 741.0 ☑
        microcephalus 742.1
    toe 755.66
  brain 742.9
    multiple 742.4
    reduction 742.2
    specified type NEC 742.4
    vessel 747.81
  branchial cleft NEC 744.49
    cyst 744.42
    fistula 744.41
    persistent 744.41
    sinus (external) (internal) 744.41
  breast 757.6
  broad ligament 752.10
    specified type NEC 752.19
  bronchus 748.3
  bulbar septum 745.0
  bulbus cordis 745.9
    persistent (in left ventricle) 745.8
  bursa 756.9
  canal of Nuck 752.9
  canthus 743.9
  capillary NEC (*see also* Anomaly, peripheral vascular system) 747.60
  cardiac 746.9
    septal closure 745.9
      acquired 429.71
    valve NEC 746.9
      pulmonary 746.00
      specified type NEC 746.89
  cardiovascular system 746.9
    complicating pregnancy, childbirth, or puerperium 648.5 ☑
  carpus 755.50
  cartilage, trachea 748.3
  cartilaginous 756.9

Anomaly, anomalous — *continued*
  caruncle, lacrimal, lachrymal 743.9
  cascade stomach 750.7
  cauda equina 742.59
  cecum 751.5
  cerebral (*see also* Anomaly, brain vessels) 747.81
  cerebrovascular system 747.81
  cervix (uterus) 752.40
    with doubling of vagina and uterus 752.2
    in pregnancy or childbirth 654.6 ☑
      affecting fetus or newborn 763.89
      causing obstructed labor 660.2 ☑
        affecting fetus or newborn 763.1
  Chédiak-Higashi (-Steinbrinck) (congenital gigantism of peroxidase granules) 288.2
  cheek 744.9
  chest (wall) 756.3
  chin 744.9
    specified type NEC 744.89
  chordae tendineae 746.9
  choroid 743.9
    plexus 742.9
  chromosomes, chromosomal 758.9
    13 (13-15) 758.1
    18 (16-18) 758.2
    21 or 22 758.0
    autosomes NEC (*see also* Abnormal, autosomes) 758.5
      deletion 758.39
      Christchurch 758.39
      D_1 758.1
      E_3 758.2
      G 758.0
    mitochondrial 758.9
    mosaics 758.89
    sex 758.81
      complement, XO 758.6
      complement, XXX 758.81
      complement, XXY 758.7
      complement, XYY 758.81
      gonadal dysgenesis 758.6
      Klinefelter's 758.7
      Turner's 758.6
    trisomy 21 758.0
  cilia 743.9
  circulatory system 747.9
    specified type NEC 747.89
  clavicle 755.51
  clitoris 752.40
  coccyx 756.10
  colon 751.5
  common duct 751.60
  communication
    coronary artery 746.85
    left ventricle with right atrium 745.4
  concha (ear) 744.3
  connection
    renal vessels with kidney 747.62
    total pulmonary venous 747.41
  connective tissue 756.9
    specified type NEC 756.89
  cornea 743.9
    shape 743.41
    size 743.41
    specified type NEC 743.49
  coronary
    artery 746.85
    vein 746.89
  cranium — *see* Anomaly, skull
  cricoid cartilage 748.3
  cushion, endocardial 745.60
    specified type NEC 745.69
  cystic duct 751.60
  dental arch 524.20
    specified NEC 524.29
  dental arch relationship 524.20
    angle's class I 524.21
    angle's class II 524.22
    angle's class III 524.23
    articulation
      anterior 524.27
      posterior 524.27
      reverse 524.27

Anomaly, anomalous — *continued*
  dental arch relationship — *continued*
    disto-occlusion 524.22
      division I 524.22
      division II 524.22
    excessive horizontal overlap 524.26
    interarch distance (excessive) (inadequate) 524.28
    mesio-occlusion 524.23
    neutro-occlusion 524.21
    open
      anterior occlusal relationship 524.24
      posterior occlusal relationship 524.25
    specified NEC 524.29
  dentition 520.6
  dentofacial NEC 524.9
    functional 524.50
    specified type NEC 524.89
  dermatoglyphic 757.2
  Descemet's membrane 743.9
    specified type NEC 743.49
  development
    cervix 752.40
    vagina 752.40
    vulva 752.40
  diaphragm, diaphragmatic (apertures) NEC 756.6
  digestive organ(s) or system 751.9
    lower 751.5
      specified type NEC 751.8
    upper 750.9
  distribution, coronary artery 746.85
  ductus
    arteriosus 747.0
    Botalli 747.0
  duodenum 751.5
  dura 742.9
    brain 742.4
    spinal cord 742.59
  ear 744.3
    causing impairment of hearing 744.00
      specified type NEC 744.09
    external 744.3
      causing impairment of hearing 744.02
      specified type NEC 744.29
    inner (causing impairment of hearing) 744.05
    middle, except ossicles (causing impairment of hearing) 744.03
      ossicles 744.04
    ossicles 744.04
    prominent auricle 744.29
    specified type NEC 744.29
      with hearing impairment 744.09
  Ebstein's (heart) 746.2
    tricuspid valve 746.2
  ectodermal 757.9
  Eisenmenger's (ventricular septal defect) 745.4
  ejaculatory duct 752.9
    specified type NEC 752.89
  elbow (joint) 755.50
  endocardial cushion 745.60
    specified type NEC 745.69
  endocrine gland NEC 759.2
  epididymis 752.9
  epiglottis 748.3
  esophagus 750.9
    specified type NEC 750.4
  Eustachian tube 744.3
    specified type NEC 744.24
  eye (any part) 743.9
    adnexa 743.9
      specified type NEC 743.69
    anophthalmos 743.00
    anterior
      chamber and related structures 743.9
      angle 743.9
        specified type NEC 743.44
      specified type NEC 743.44
    segment 743.9
      combined 743.48
      multiple 743.48
      specified type NEC 743.49
    cataract (*see also* Cataract) 743.30

Anomaly, anomalous — *continued*
  eye — *continued*
    glaucoma (*see also* Buphthalmia) 743.20
    lid 743.9
      specified type NEC 743.63
    microphthalmos (*see also* Microphthalmos) 743.10
    posterior segment 743.9
      specified type NEC 743.59
      vascular 743.58
      vitreous 743.9
        specified type NEC 743.51
    ptosis (eyelid) 743.61
    retina 743.9
      specified type NEC 743.59
    sclera 743.9
      specified type NEC 743.47
    specified type NEC 743.8
  eyebrow 744.89
  eyelid 743.9
    specified type NEC 743.63
  face (any part) 744.9
    bone(s) 756.0
    specified type NEC 744.89
  fallopian tube 752.10
    specified type NEC 752.19
  fascia 756.9
    specified type NEC 756.89
  femur 755.60
  fibula 755.60
  finger 755.50
    supernumerary 755.01
    webbed (*see also* Syndactylism, fingers) 755.11
  fixation, intestine 751.4
  flexion (joint) 755.9
    hip or thigh (*see also* Dislocation, hip, congenital) 754.30
  folds, heart 746.9
  foot 755.67
  foramen
    Botalli 745.5
    ovale 745.5
  forearm 755.50
  forehead (*see also* Anomaly, skull) 756.0
  form, teeth 520.2
  fovea centralis 743.9
  frontal bone (*see also* Anomaly, skull) 756.0
  gallbladder 751.60
  Gartner's duct 752.41
  gastrointestinal tract 751.9
    specified type NEC 751.8
    vessel 747.61
  genitalia, genital organ(s) or system 752.9
    female 752.9
      external 752.40
        specified type NEC 752.49
      internal NEC 752.9
    male (external and internal) 752.9
      epispadias 752.62
      hidden penis 752.65
      hydrocele, congenital 778.6
      hypospadias 752.61
      micropenis 752.64
      testis, undescended 752.51
        retractile 752.52
    specified type NEC 752.89
  genitourinary NEC 752.9
  Gerbode 745.4
  globe (eye) 743.9
  glottis 748.3
  granulation or granulocyte, genetic 288.2
    constitutional 288.2
    leukocyte 288.2
  gum 750.9
  gyri 742.9
  hair 757.9
    specified type NEC 757.4
  hand 755.50
  hard tissue formation in pulp 522.3
  head (*see also* Anomaly, skull) 756.0
  heart 746.9
    auricle 746.9
    bands 746.9
    fibroelastosis cordis 425.3
    folds 746.9

☑ **Additional Digit Required — Refer to the Tabular List for Digit Selection**　　　　　　　　▽ **Subterms under main terms may continue to next column or page**

22 — Volume 2　　　　　▶◀ **Revised Text**　　　● **New Line**　　▲ **Revised Code**　　　　**2015 ICD-9-CM**

Anomaly, anomalous — *continued*
heart — *continued*
　malposition 746.87
　maternal, affecting fetus or newborn
　　760.3
　obstructive NEC 746.84
　patent ductus arteriosus (Botalli) 747.0
　septum 745.9
　　acquired 429.71
　　aortic 745.0
　　aorticopulmonary 745.0
　　atrial 745.5
　　auricular 745.5
　　between aorta and pulmonary artery
　　　745.0
　　endocardial cushion type 745.60
　　　specified type NEC 745.69
　　interatrial 745.5
　　interventricular 745.4
　　　with pulmonary stenosis or atre-
　　　　sia, dextraposition of aor-
　　　　ta, and hypertrophy of
　　　　right ventricle 745.2
　　　acquired 429.71
　　specified type NEC 745.8
　　ventricular 745.4
　　　with pulmonary stenosis or atre-
　　　　sia, dextraposition of aor-
　　　　ta, and hypertrophy of
　　　　right ventricle 745.2
　　　acquired 429.71
　specified type NEC 746.89
　tetralogy of Fallot 745.2
　valve NEC 746.9
　　aortic 746.9
　　　atresia 746.89
　　　bicuspid valve 746.4
　　　insufficiency 746.4
　　　specified type NEC 746.89
　　　stenosis 746.3
　　　　subaortic 746.81
　　　　supravalvular 747.22
　　mitral 746.9
　　　atresia 746.89
　　　insufficiency 746.6
　　　specified type NEC 746.89
　　　stenosis 746.5
　　pulmonary 746.00
　　　atresia 746.01
　　　insufficiency 746.09
　　　stenosis 746.02
　　　　infundibular 746.83
　　　　subvalvular 746.83
　　tricuspid 746.9
　　　atresia 746.1
　　　stenosis 746.1
　　ventricle 746.9
heel 755.67
Hegglin's 288.2
hemianencephaly 740.0
hemicephaly 740.0
hemicrania 740.0
hepatic duct 751.60
hip (joint) 755.63
hourglass
　bladder 753.8
　gallbladder 751.69
　stomach 750.7
humerus 755.50
hymen 752.40
hypersegmentation of neutrophils, heredi-
　tary 288.2
hypophyseal 759.2
ileocecal (coil) (valve) 751.5
ileum (intestine) 751.5
ilium 755.60
integument 757.9
　specified type NEC 757.8
interarch distance (excessive) (inadequate)
　524.28
intervertebral cartilage or disc 756.10
intestine (large) (small) 751.5
　fixational type 751.4
iris 743.9
　specified type NEC 743.46
ischium 755.60

Anomaly, anomalous — *continued*
jaw-cranial base relationship 524.10
　specified NEC 524.19
jaw NEC 524.9
　closure 524.51
　size (major) NEC 524.00
　specified type NEC 524.89
jejunum 751.5
joint 755.9
　hip
　　dislocation (*see also* Dislocation, hip,
　　　congenital) 754.30
　　predislocation (*see also* Subluxation,
　　　congenital, hip) 754.32
　　preluxation (*see also* Subluxation,
　　　congenital, hip) 754.32
　　subluxation (*see also* Subluxation,
　　　congenital, hip) 754.32
　lumbosacral 756.10
　　spondylolisthesis 756.12
　　spondylosis 756.11
　multiple arthrogryposis 754.89
　sacroiliac 755.69
Jordan's 288.2
kidney(s) (calyx) (pelvis) 753.9
　vessel 747.62
Klippel-Feil (brevicollis) 756.16
knee (joint) 755.64
labium (majus) (minus) 752.40
labyrinth, membranous (causing impair-
　ment of hearing) 744.05
lacrimal
　apparatus, duct or passage 743.9
　　specified type NEC 743.65
　gland 743.9
　　specified type NEC 743.64
Langdon Down (mongolism) 758.0
larynx, laryngeal (muscle) 748.3
　web, webbed 748.2
leg (lower) (upper) 755.60
　reduction NEC (*see also* Deformity, reduc-
　　tion, lower limb) 755.30
lens 743.9
　shape 743.36
　specified type NEC 743.39
leukocytes, genetic 288.2
　granulation (constitutional) 288.2
lid (fold) 743.9
ligament 756.9
　broad 752.10
　round 752.9
limb, except reduction deformity 755.9
　lower 755.60
　　reduction deformity (*see also* Defor-
　　　mity, reduction, lower limb)
　　　755.30
　　specified type NEC 755.69
　upper 755.50
　　reduction deformity (*see also* Defor-
　　　mity, reduction, upper limb)
　　　755.20
　　specified type NEC 755.59
lip 750.9
　harelip (*see also* Cleft, lip) 749.10
　specified type NEC 750.26
liver (duct) 751.60
　atresia 751.69
lower extremity 755.60
　vessel 747.64
lumbosacral (joint) (region) 756.10
lung (fissure) (lobe) NEC 748.60
　agenesis 748.5
　specified type NEC 748.69
lymphatic system 759.9
Madelung's (radius) 755.54
mandible 524.9
　size NEC 524.00
maxilla 524.9
　size NEC 524.00
May (-Hegglin) 288.2
meatus urinarius 753.9
　specified type NEC 753.8
meningeal bands or folds, constriction of
　742.8
meninges 742.9
　brain 742.4

Anomaly, anomalous — *continued*
meninges — *continued*
　spinal 742.59
meningocele (*see also* Spina bifida) 741.9 ☑
　acquired 349.2
mesentery 751.9
metacarpus 755.50
metatarsus 755.67
middle ear, except ossicles (causing impair-
　ment of hearing) 744.03
　ossicles 744.04
mitral (leaflets) (valve) 746.9
　atresia 746.89
　insufficiency 746.6
　specified type NEC 746.89
　stenosis 746.5
mouth 750.9
　specified type NEC 750.26
multiple NEC 759.7
　specified type NEC 759.89
muscle 756.9
　eye 743.9
　　specified type NEC 743.69
　specified type NEC 756.89
musculoskeletal system, except limbs 756.9
　specified type NEC 756.9
nail 757.9
　specified type NEC 757.5
narrowness, eyelid 743.62
nasal sinus or septum 748.1
neck (any part) 744.9
　specified type NEC 744.89
nerve 742.9
　acoustic 742.9
　　specified type NEC 742.8
　optic 742.9
　　specified type NEC 742.8
　specified type NEC 742.8
nervous system NEC 742.9
　brain 742.9
　　specified type NEC 742.4
　specified type NEC 742.8
neurological 742.9
nipple 757.6
nonteratogenic NEC 754.89
nose, nasal (bone) (cartilage) (septum) (si-
　nus) 748.1
ocular muscle 743.9
omphalomesenteric duct 751.0
opening, pulmonary veins 747.49
optic
　disc 743.9
　　specified type NEC 743.57
　nerve 742.9
opticociliary vessels 743.9
orbit (eye) 743.9
　specified type NEC 743.66
organ
　of Corti (causing impairment of hearing)
　　744.05
　or site 759.9
　　specified type NEC 759.89
origin
　both great arteries from same ventricle
　　745.11
　coronary artery 746.85
　innominate artery 747.69
　left coronary artery from pulmonary
　　artery 746.85
　pulmonary artery 747.39
　renal vessels 747.62
　subclavian artery (left) (right) 747.21
osseous meatus (ear) 744.03
ovary 752.0
oviduct 752.10
palate (hard) (soft) 750.9
　cleft (*see also* Cleft, palate) 749.00
pancreas (duct) 751.7
papillary muscles 746.9
parathyroid gland 759.2
paraurethral ducts 753.9
parotid (gland) 750.9
patella 755.64
Pelger-Huët (hereditary hyposegmentation)
　288.2
pelvic girdle 755.60

Anomaly, anomalous — *continued*
pelvic girdle — *continued*
　specified type NEC 755.69
pelvis (bony) 755.60
　complicating delivery 653.0 ☑
　rachitic 268.1
　　fetal 756.4
penis (glans) 752.69
pericardium 746.89
peripheral vascular system NEC 747.60
　gastrointestinal 747.61
　lower limb 747.64
　renal 747.62
　specified site NEC 747.69
　spinal 747.82
　upper limb 747.63
Peter's 743.44
pharynx 750.9
　branchial cleft 744.41
　specified type NEC 750.29
Pierre Robin 756.0
pigmentation 709.00
　congenital 757.33
　specified NEC 709.09
pituitary (gland) 759.2
pleural folds 748.8
portal vein 747.40
position tooth, teeth 524.30
　crowding 524.31
　displacement 524.30
　　horizontal 524.33
　　vertical 524.34
　distance
　　interocclusal
　　　excessive 524.37
　　　insufficient 524.36
　excessive spacing 524.32
　rotation 524.35
　specified NEC 524.39
preauricular sinus 744.46
prepuce 752.9
prostate 752.9
pulmonary 748.60
　artery 747.39
　circulation 747.39
　specified type NEC 748.69
　valve 746.00
　　atresia 746.01
　　insufficiency 746.09
　　specified type NEC 746.09
　　stenosis 746.02
　　　infundibular 746.83
　　　subvalvular 746.83
　vein 747.40
　venous
　　connection 747.49
　　　partial 747.42
　　　total 747.41
　　return 747.49
　　　partial 747.42
　　　total (TAPVR) (complete) (subdi-
　　　　aphragmatic) (supradi-
　　　　aphragmatic) 747.41
pupil 743.9
pylorus 750.9
　hypertrophy 750.5
　stenosis 750.5
rachitic, fetal 756.4
radius 755.50
rectovaginal (septum) 752.40
rectum 751.5
refraction 367.9
renal 753.9
　vessel 747.62
respiratory system 748.9
　specified type NEC 748.8
rib 756.3
　cervical 756.2
Rieger's 743.44
rings, trachea 748.3
rotation (*see also* Malrotation)
　hip or thigh (*see also* Subluxation, con-
　　genital, hip) 754.32
round ligament 752.9
sacroiliac (joint) 755.69
sacrum 756.10

☑ **Additional Digit Required** — Refer to the Tabular List for Digit Selection　　　　　　　　　　　　　　　ᵂ **Subterms under main terms may continue to next column or page**

2015 ICD-9-CM　　　　　▶◀ **Revised Text**　　　　● **New Line**　　　▲ **Revised Code**　　　　**Volume 2 — 23**

Anomaly, anomalous — *continued*
saddle
  back 754.2
  nose 754.0
    syphilitic 090.5
salivary gland or duct 750.9
  specified type NEC 750.26
scapula 755.50
sclera 743.9
  specified type NEC 743.47
scrotum 752.9
sebaceous gland 757.9
seminal duct or tract 752.9
sense organs 742.9
  specified type NEC 742.8
septum
  heart — *see* Anomaly, heart, septum
  nasal 748.1
sex chromosomes NEC (*see also* Anomaly, chromosomes) 758.81
shoulder (girdle) (joint) 755.50
  specified type NEC 755.59
sigmoid (flexure) 751.5
sinus of Valsalva 747.29
site NEC 759.9
skeleton generalized NEC 756.50
skin (appendage) 757.9
  specified type NEC 757.39
skull (bone) 756.0
  with
    anencephalus 740.0
    encephalocele 742.0
    hydrocephalus 742.3
      with spina bifida (*see also* Spina bifida) 741.0 ☑
    microcephalus 742.1
specified type NEC
  adrenal (gland) 759.1
  alimentary tract (complete) (partial) 751.8
    lower 751.5
    upper 750.8
  ankle 755.69
  anus, anal (canal) 751.5
  aorta, aortic 747.29
    arch 747.21
  appendix 751.5
  arm 755.59
  artery (peripheral) NEC (*see also* Anomaly, peripheral vascular system) 747.60
    brain 747.81
    coronary 746.85
    eye 743.58
    pulmonary 747.39
    retinal 743.58
    umbilical 747.5
  auditory canal 744.29
    causing impairment of hearing 744.02
  bile duct or passage 751.69
  bladder 753.8
    neck 753.8
  bone(s) 756.9
    arm 755.59
    face 756.0
    leg 755.69
    pelvic girdle 755.69
    shoulder girdle 755.59
    skull 756.0
      with
        anencephalus 740.0
        encephalocele 742.0
        hydrocephalus 742.3
          with spina bifida (*see also* Spina bifida) 741.0 ☑
        microcephalus 742.1
  brain 742.4
  breast 757.6
  broad ligament 752.19
  bronchus 748.3
  canal of Nuck 752.89
  cardiac septal closure 745.8
  carpus 755.59
  cartilaginous 756.9

Anomaly, anomalous — *continued*
specified type — *continued*
  cecum 751.5
  cervix 752.49
  chest (wall) 756.3
  chin 744.89
  ciliary body 743.46
  circulatory system 747.89
  clavicle 755.51
  clitoris 752.49
  coccyx 756.19
  colon 751.5
  common duct 751.69
  connective tissue 756.89
  cricoid cartilage 748.3
  cystic duct 751.69
  diaphragm 756.6
  digestive organ(s) or tract 751.8
    lower 751.5
    upper 750.8
  duodenum 751.5
  ear 744.29
    auricle 744.29
      causing impairment of hearing 744.02
    causing impairment of hearing 744.09
    inner (causing impairment of hearing) 744.05
    middle, except ossicles 744.03
      ossicles 744.04
  ejaculatory duct 752.89
  endocrine 759.2
  epiglottis 748.3
  esophagus 750.4
  Eustachian tube 744.24
  eye 743.8
    lid 743.63
    muscle 743.69
  face 744.89
    bone(s) 756.0
  fallopian tube 752.19
  fascia 756.89
  femur 755.69
  fibula 755.69
  finger 755.59
  foot 755.67
  fovea centralis 743.55
  gallbladder 751.69
  Gartner's duct 752.89
  gastrointestinal tract 751.8
  genitalia, genital organ(s)
    female 752.89
      external 752.49
      internal NEC 752.89
    male 752.89
      penis 752.69
      scrotal transposition 752.81
  genitourinary tract NEC 752.89
  glottis 748.3
  hair 757.4
  hand 755.59
  heart 746.89
    valve NEC 746.89
      pulmonary 746.09
  hepatic duct 751.69
  hydatid of Morgagni 752.89
  hymen 752.49
  integument 757.8
  intestine (large) (small) 751.5
    fixational type 751.4
  iris 743.46
  jejunum 751.5
  joint 755.8
  kidney 753.3
  knee 755.64
  labium (majus) (minus) 752.49
  labyrinth, membranous 744.05
  larynx 748.3
  leg 755.69
  limb, except reduction deformity 755.8
    lower 755.69
      reduction deformity (*see also* Deformity, reduction, lower limb) 755.30

Anomaly, anomalous — *continued*
specified type — *continued*
  limb, except reduction deformity — *continued*
    upper 755.59
      reduction deformity (*see also* Deformity, reduction, upper limb) 755.20
  lip 750.26
  liver 751.69
  lung (fissure) (lobe) 748.69
  meatus urinarius 753.8
  metacarpus 755.59
  mouth 750.26
  Müllerian
    cervix 752.49
    uterus 752.39
    vagina 752.49
  muscle 756.89
    eye 743.69
  musculoskeletal system, except limbs 756.9
  nail 757.5
  neck 744.89
  nerve 742.8
    acoustic 742.8
    optic 742.8
  nervous system 742.8
  nipple 757.6
  nose 748.1
  organ NEC 759.89
    of Corti 744.05
  osseous meatus (ear) 744.03
  ovary 752.0
  oviduct 752.19
  pancreas 751.7
  parathyroid 759.2
  patella 755.64
  pelvic girdle 755.69
  penis 752.69
  pericardium 746.89
  peripheral vascular system NEC (*see also* Anomaly, peripheral vascular system) 747.60
  pharynx 750.29
  pituitary 759.2
  prostate 752.89
  radius 755.59
  rectum 751.5
  respiratory system 748.8
  rib 756.3
  round ligament 752.89
  sacrum 756.19
  salivary duct or gland 750.26
  scapula 755.59
  sclera 743.47
  scrotum 752.89
    transposition 752.81
  seminal duct or tract 752.89
  shoulder girdle 755.59
  site NEC 759.89
  skin 757.39
  skull (bone(s)) 756.0
    with
      anencephalus 740.0
      encephalocele 742.0
      hydrocephalus 742.3
        with spina bifida (*see also* Spina bifida) 741.0 ☑
      microcephalus 742.1
  specified organ or site NEC 759.89
  spermatic cord 752.89
  spinal cord 742.59
  spine 756.19
  spleen 759.0
  sternum 756.3
  stomach 750.7
  tarsus 755.67
  tendon 756.89
  testis 752.89
  thorax (wall) 756.3
  thymus 759.2
  thyroid (gland) 759.2
    cartilage 748.3
  tibia 755.69
  toe 755.66

Anomaly, anomalous — *continued*
specified type — *continued*
  tongue 750.19
  trachea (cartilage) 748.3
  ulna 755.59
  urachus 753.7
  ureter 753.4
    obstructive 753.29
  urethra 753.8
    obstructive 753.6
  urinary tract 753.8
  uterus (Müllerian) 752.39
  uvula 750.26
  vagina 752.49
  vascular NEC (*see also* Anomaly, peripheral vascular system) 747.60
    brain 747.81
  vas deferens 752.89
  vein(s) (peripheral) NEC (*see also* Anomaly, peripheral vascular system) 747.60
    brain 747.81
    great 747.49
    portal 747.49
    pulmonary 747.49
  vena cava (inferior) (superior) 747.49
  vertebra 756.19
  vulva 752.49
spermatic cord 752.9
spine, spinal 756.10
  column 756.10
  cord 742.9
    meningocele (*see also* Spina bifida) 741.9 ☑
    specified type NEC 742.59
    spina bifida (*see also* Spina bifida) 741.9 ☑
    vessel 747.82
  meninges 742.59
  nerve root 742.9
spleen 759.0
Sprengel's 755.52
sternum 756.3
stomach 750.9
  specified type NEC 750.7
submaxillary gland 750.9
superior vena cava 747.40
talipes — *see* Talipes
tarsus 755.67
  with complete absence of distal elements 755.31
teeth, tooth NEC 520.9
  position 524.30
    crowding 524.31
    displacement 524.30
      horizontal 524.33
      vertical 524.34
    distance
      interocclusal
        excessive 524.37
        insufficient 524.36
    excessive spacing 524.32
    rotation 524.35
    specified NEC 524.39
  spacing 524.30
tendon 756.9
  specified type NEC 756.89
termination
  coronary artery 746.85
testis 752.9
thebesian valve 746.9
thigh 755.60
  flexion (*see also* Subluxation, congenital, hip) 754.32
thorax (wall) 756.3
throat 750.9
thumb 755.50
  supernumerary 755.01
thymus gland 759.2
thyroid (gland) 759.2
  cartilage 748.3
tibia 755.60
  saber 090.5
toe 755.66
  supernumerary 755.02

Anomaly, anomalous — *continued*
 toe — *continued*
  webbed (*see also* Syndactylism, toes) 755.13
 tongue 750.10
  specified type NEC 750.19
 trachea, tracheal 748.3
  cartilage 748.3
  rings 748.3
 tragus 744.3
 transverse aortic arch 747.21
 trichromata 368.59
 trichromatopsia 368.59
 tricuspid (leaflet) (valve) 746.9
  atresia 746.1
  Ebstein's 746.2
  specified type NEC 746.89
  stenosis 746.1
 trunk 759.9
 Uhl's (hypoplasia of myocardium, right ventricle) 746.84
 ulna 755.50
 umbilicus 759.9
  artery 747.5
 union, trachea with larynx 748.3
 unspecified site 759.9
 upper extremity 755.50
  vessel 747.63
 urachus 753.7
  specified type NEC 753.7
 ureter 753.9
  obstructive 753.20
  specified type NEC 753.4
   obstructive 753.29
 urethra (valve) 753.9
  obstructive 753.6
  specified type NEC 753.8
 urinary tract or system (any part, except urachus) 753.9
  specified type NEC 753.8
  urachus 753.7
 uterus 752.39
  with only one functioning horn 752.33
  in pregnancy or childbirth 654.0 ☑
   affecting fetus or newborn 763.89
   causing obstructed labor 660.2 ☑
    affecting fetus or newborn 763.1
 uvula 750.9
 vagina 752.40
 valleculae 748.3
 valve (heart) NEC 746.9
  formation, ureter 753.29
  pulmonary 746.00
  specified type NEC 746.89
 vascular NEC (*see also* Anomaly, peripheral vascular system) 747.60
  ring 747.21
 vas deferens 752.9
 vein(s) (peripheral) NEC (*see also* Anomaly, peripheral vascular system) 747.60
  brain 747.81
  cerebral 747.81
  coronary 746.89
  great 747.40
   specified type NEC 747.49
  portal 747.40
  pulmonary 747.40
  retina 743.9
 vena cava (inferior) (superior) 747.40
 venous — *see* Anomaly, vein
 venous return (pulmonary) 747.49
  partial 747.42
  total 747.41
 ventricle, ventricular (heart) 746.9
  bands 746.9
  folds 746.9
  septa 745.4
 vertebra 756.10
 vesicourethral orifice 753.9
 vessels NEC (*see also* Anomaly, peripheral vascular system) 747.60
  optic papilla 743.9
 vitelline duct 751.0
 vitreous humor 743.9
  specified type NEC 743.51
 vulva 752.40

Anomaly, anomalous — *continued*
 wrist (joint) 755.50
Anomia 784.69
Anonychia 757.5
 acquired 703.8
Anophthalmos, anophthalmus (clinical) (congenital) (globe) 743.00
 acquired V45.78
Anopsia (altitudinal) (quadrant) 368.46
Anorchia 752.89
Anorchism, anorchidism 752.89
Anorexia 783.0
 hysterical 300.11
 nervosa 307.1
Anosmia — *see also* Disturbance, sensation 781.1
 hysterical 300.11
 postinfectional 478.9
 psychogenic 306.7
 traumatic 951.8
Anosognosia 780.99
Anosphrasia 781.1
Anosteoplasia 756.50
Anotia 744.09
Anovulatory cycle 628.0
Anoxemia 799.02
 newborn 770.88
Anoxia 799.02
 altitude 993.2
 cerebral 348.1
  with
   abortion — *see* Abortion, by type, with specified complication NEC
   ectopic pregnancy (*see also* categories 633.0–633.9) 639.8
   molar pregnancy (*see also* categories 630–632) 639.8
  complicating
   delivery (cesarean) (instrumental) 669.4 ☑
   ectopic or molar pregnancy 639.8
   obstetric anesthesia or sedation 668.2 ☑
  during or resulting from a procedure 997.01
  following
   abortion 639.8
   ectopic or molar pregnancy 639.8
  newborn (*see also* Distress, fetal, liveborn infant) 770.88
 due to drowning 994.1
 fetal, affecting newborn 770.88
 heart — *see* Insufficiency, coronary
 high altitude 993.2
 intrauterine
  fetal death (before onset of labor) 768.0
   during labor 768.1
  liveborn infant — *see* Distress, fetal, liveborn infant
 myocardial — *see* Insufficiency, coronary
 newborn 768.9
  mild or moderate 768.6
  severe 768.5
 pathological 799.02
Anteflexion — *see* Anteversion
Antenatal
 care, normal pregnancy V22.1
  first V22.0
 sampling
  chorionic villus V28.89
 screening of mother (for) V28.9
  based on amniocentesis NEC V28.2
   chromosomal anomalies V28.0
   raised alphafetoprotein levels V28.1
  chromosomal anomalies V28.0
  fetal growth retardation using ulatrasonics V28.4
  genomic V28.89
  isoimmunization V28.5
  malformations using ulatrasonics V28.3
  proteomic V28.89
  raised alphafetoprotein levels in amniotic fluid V28.1
  risk
   pre-term labor V28.82

Antenatal — *continued*
 screening of mother — *continued*
  specified condition NEC V28.89
  Streptococcus B V28.6
 survey
  fetal anatomic V28.81
 testing
  nuchal translucency V28.89
Antepartum — *see* condition
Anterior — *see* condition
 spinal artery compression syndrome 721.1
Antero-occlusion 524.24
Anteversion
 cervix — *see* Anteversion, uterus
 femur (neck), congenital 755.63
 uterus, uterine (cervix) (postinfectional) (postpartal, old) 621.6
  congenital 752.39
  in pregnancy or childbirth 654.4 ☑
   affecting fetus or newborn 763.89
   causing obstructed labor 660.2 ☑
    affecting fetus or newborn 763.1
Anthracosilicosis (occupational) 500
Anthracosis (lung) (occupational) 500
 lingua 529.3
Anthrax 022.9
 with pneumonia 022.1 [484.5]
 colitis 022.2
 cutaneous 022.0
 gastrointestinal 022.2
 intestinal 022.2
 pulmonary 022.1
 respiratory 022.1
 septicemia 022.3
 specified manifestation NEC 022.8
Anthropoid pelvis 755.69
 with disproportion (fetopelvic) 653.2 ☑
  affecting fetus or newborn 763.1
  causing obstructed labor 660.1 ☑
   affecting fetus or newborn 763.1
Anthropophobia 300.29
Antibioma, breast 611.0
Antibodies
 maternal (blood group) (*see also* Incompatibility) 656.2 ☑
  anti-D, cord blood 656.1 ☑
   fetus or newborn 773.0
Antibody
 anticardiolipin 795.79
  with
   hemorrhagic disorder 286.53
   hypercoagulable state 289.81
 antiphosphatidylglycerol 795.79
  with
   hemorrhagic disorder 286.53
   hypercoagulable state 289.81
 antiphosphatidylinositol 795.79
  with
   hemorrhagic disorder 286.53
   hypercoagulable state 289.81
 antiphosphatidylserine 795.79
  with
   hemorrhagic disorder 286.53
   hypercoagulable state 289.81
 antiphospholipid 795.79
  with
   hemorrhagic disorder 286.53
   hypercoagulable state 289.81
 deficiency syndrome
  agammaglobulinemic 279.00
  congenital 279.04
  hypogammaglobulinemic 279.00
Anticoagulant
 intrinsic, circulating, causing hemorrhagic disorder (*see also* Circulating, anticoagulants) 286.59
 lupus (LAC) 795.79
  with
   hemorrhagic disorder 286.53
   hypercoagulable state 289.81
Antimongolism syndrome 758.39
Antimonial cholera 985.4
Antisocial personality 301.7
Antithrombinemia — *see also* Circulating anticoagulants 286.59

Antithromboplastinemia — *see also* Circulating anticoagulants 286.59
Antithromboplastinogenemia — *see also* Circulating anticoagulants 286.59
Antitoxin complication or reaction — *see* Complications, vaccination
Anton (-Babinski) syndrome (hemiasomatognosia) 307.9
Antritis (chronic) 473.0
 maxilla 473.0
  acute 461.0
 stomach 535.4 ☑
Antrum, antral — *see* condition
Anuria 788.5
 with
  abortion — *see* Abortion, by type, with renal failure
  ectopic pregnancy (*see also* categories 633.0–633.9) 639.3
  molar pregnancy (*see also* categories 630–632) 639.3
 calculus (impacted) (recurrent) 592.9
  kidney 592.0
  ureter 592.1
 congenital 753.3
 due to a procedure 997.5
 following
  abortion 639.3
  ectopic or molar pregnancy 639.3
 newborn 753.3
 postrenal 593.4
 puerperal, postpartum, childbirth 669.3 ☑
 specified as due to a procedure 997.5
 sulfonamide
  correct substance properly administered 788.5
  overdose or wrong substance given or taken 961.0
 traumatic (following crushing) 958.5
Anus, anal — *see also* condition
 high risk human papillomavirus (HPV) DNA test positive 796.75
 low risk human papillomavirus (HPV) DNA test positive 796.79
Anusitis 569.49
Anxiety (neurosis) (reaction) (state) 300.00
 alcohol-induced 291.89
 depression 300.4
 drug-induced 292.89
 due to or associated with physical condition 293.84
 generalized 300.02
 hysteria 300.20
 in
  acute stress reaction 308.0
  transient adjustment reaction 309.24
 panic type 300.01
 separation, abnormal 309.21
 syndrome (organic) (transient) 293.84
Aorta, aortic — *see* condition
Aortectasia — *see also* Ectasia, aortic 447.70
 with aneurysm 441.9
Aortitis (nonsyphilitic) 447.6
 arteriosclerotic 440.0
 calcific 447.6
 Döhle-Heller 093.1
 luetic 093.1
 rheumatic (*see also* Endocarditis, acute, rheumatic) 391.1
 rheumatoid — *see* Arthritis, rheumatoid
 specific 093.1
 syphilitic 093.1
  congenital 090.5
Apathetic 799.25
 thyroid storm (*see also* Thyrotoxicosis) 242.9 ☑
Apathy 799.25
Apepsia 536.8
 achlorhydric 536.0
 psychogenic 306.4
Aperistalsis, esophagus 530.0
Apert-Gallais syndrome (adrenogenital) 255.2
Apertognathia 524.20
Apert's syndrome (acrocephalosyndactyly) 755.55
Aphagia 787.20

☑ **Additional Digit Required** — Refer to the Tabular List for Digit Selection

▽ **Subterms under main terms may continue to next column or page**

Aphagia — continued
  psychogenic 307.1
Aphakia (acquired) (bilateral) (postoperative)
  (unilateral) 379.31
  congenital 743.35
Aphalangia (congenital) 755.4
  lower limb (complete) (intercalary) (partial)
    (terminal) 755.39
    meaning all digits (complete) (partial)
      755.31
    transverse 755.31
  upper limb (complete) (intercalary) (partial)
    (terminal) 755.29
    meaning all digits (complete) (partial)
      755.21
    transverse 755.21
Aphasia (amnestic) (ataxic) (auditory) (Broca's)
  (choreatic) (classic) (expressive) (global)
  (ideational) (ideokinetic) (ideomotor)
  (jargon) (motor) (nominal) (receptive)
  (semantic) (sensory) (syntactic) (verbal)
  (visual) (Wernicke's) 784.3
  developmental 315.31
  syphilis, tertiary 094.89
  uremic — see Uremia
Aphemia 784.3
  uremic — see Uremia
Aphonia 784.41
  clericorum 784.49
  hysterical 300.11
  organic 784.41
  psychogenic 306.1
Aphthae, aphthous — see also condition
  Bednar's 528.2
  cachectic 529.0
  epizootic 078.4
  fever 078.4
  oral 528.2
  stomatitis 528.2
  thrush 112.0
  ulcer (oral) (recurrent) 528.2
    genital organ(s) NEC
      female 616.50
      male 608.89
    larynx 478.79
Apical — see condition
Apical ballooning syndrome 429.83
Aplasia — see also Agenesis
  alveolar process (acquired) 525.8
    congenital 750.26
  aorta (congenital) 747.22
  aortic valve (congenital) 746.89
  axialis extracorticalis (congenital) 330.0
  bone marrow (myeloid) 284.9
    acquired (secondary) 284.89
    congenital 284.01
    idiopathic 284.9
  brain 740.0
    specified part 742.2
  breast 757.6
  bronchus 748.3
  cementum 520.4
  cerebellar 742.2
  congenital (pure) red cell 284.01
  corpus callosum 742.2
  erythrocyte 284.81
    congenital 284.01
  extracortical axial 330.0
  eye (congenital) 743.00
  fovea centralis (congenital) 743.55
  germinal (cell) 606.0
  iris 743.45
  labyrinth, membranous 744.05
  limb (congenital) 755.4
    lower NEC 755.30
    upper NEC 755.20
  lung (bilateral) (congenital) (unilateral)
    748.5
  nervous system NEC 742.8
  nuclear 742.8
  ovary 752.0
  Pelizaeus-Merzbacher 330.0
  prostate (congenital) 752.89
  red cell (with thymoma) 284.81
    acquired (secondary) 284.81
      due to drugs 284.81

Aplasia — see also Agenesis — continued
  red cell — continued
    adult 284.81
    congenital 284.01
    hereditary 284.01
    of infants 284.01
    primary 284.01
    pure 284.01
      due to drugs 284.81
  round ligament (congenital) 752.89
  salivary gland 750.21
  skin (congenital) 757.39
  spinal cord 742.59
  spleen 759.0
  testis (congenital) 752.89
  thymic, with immunodeficiency 279.2
  thyroid 243
  uterus 752.39
  ventral horn cell 742.59
Apleuria 756.3
Apnea, apneic (spells) 786.03
  newborn, neonatorum 770.81
    essential 770.81
    obstructive 770.82
    primary 770.81
    sleep 770.81
    specified NEC 770.82
  psychogenic 306.1
  sleep, unspecified 780.57
    with
      hypersomnia, unspecified 780.53
      hyposomnia, unspecified 780.51
      insomnia, unspecified 780.51
      sleep disturbance 780.57
    central, in conditions classified else-
      where 327.27
    obstructive (adult) (pediatric) 327.23
    organic 327.20
    other 327.29
    primary central 327.21
Apneumatosis newborn 770.4
Apodia 755.31
Aponeurosis 726.90
Apophysitis (bone) — see also Osteochondrosis 732.9
  calcaneus 732.5
  juvenile 732.6
Apoplectiform convulsions — see also Disease, cerebrovascular, acute 436
Apoplexia, apoplexy, apoplectic — see also
  Disease, cerebrovascular, acute 436
  abdominal 569.89
  adrenal 036.3
  attack 436
  basilar (see also Disease, cerebrovascular,
    acute) 436
  brain (see also Disease, cerebrovascular,
    acute) 436
  bulbar (see also Disease, cerebrovascular,
    acute) 436
  capillary (see also Disease, cerebrovascular,
    acute) 436
  cardiac (see also Infarct, myocardium)
    410.9 ☑
  cerebral (see also Disease, cerebrovascular,
    acute) 436
  chorea (see also Disease, cerebrovascular,
    acute) 436
  congestive (see also Disease, cerebrovascu-
    lar, acute) 436
    newborn 767.4
  embolic (see also Embolism, brain) 434.1 ☑
  fetus 767.0
  fit (see also Disease, cerebrovascular, acute)
    436
  healed or old V12.54
  heart (auricle) (ventricle) (see also Infarct,
    myocardium) 410.9 ☑
  heat 992.0
  hemiplegia (see also Disease, cerebrovascu-
    lar, acute) 436
  hemorrhagic (stroke) (see also Hemorrhage,
    brain) 432.9
  ingravescent (see also Disease, cerebrovas-
    cular, acute) 436

Apoplexia, apoplexy, apoplectic — see also
  Disease, cerebrovascular, acute —
  continued
  late effect — see Late effect(s) (of) cere-
    brovascular disease
  lung — see Embolism, pulmonary
  meninges, hemorrhagic (see also Hemor-
    rhage, subarachnoid) 430
  neonatorum 767.0
  newborn 767.0
  pancreatitis 577.0
  placenta 641.2 ☑
  progressive (see also Disease, cerebrovascu-
    lar, acute) 436
  pulmonary (artery) (vein) — see Embolism,
    pulmonary
  sanguineous (see also Disease, cerebrovas-
    cular, acute) 436
  seizure (see also Disease, cerebrovascular,
    acute) 436
  serous (see also Disease, cerebrovascular,
    acute) 436
  spleen 289.59
  stroke (see also Disease, cerebrovascular,
    acute) 436
  thrombotic (see also Thrombosis, brain)
    434.0 ☑
  uremic — see Uremia
  uteroplacental 641.2 ☑
Appendage
  fallopian tube (cyst of Morgagni) 752.11
  intestine (epiploic) 751.5
  preauricular 744.1
  testicular (organ of Morgagni) 752.89
Appendicitis 541
  with
    perforation, peritonitis (generalized), or
      rupture 540.0
      with peritoneal abscess 540.1
    peritoneal abscess 540.1
  acute (catarrhal) (fulminating) (gangrenous)
    (inflammatory) (obstructive) (retroce-
    cal) (suppurative) 540.9
    with
      perforation, peritonitis, or rupture
        540.0
        with peritoneal abscess 540.1
      peritoneal abscess 540.1
  amebic 006.8
  chronic (recurrent) 542
  exacerbation — see Appendicitis, acute
  fulminating — see Appendicitis, acute
  gangrenous — see Appendicitis, acute
  healed (obliterative) 542
  interval 542
  neurogenic 542
  obstructive 542
  pneumococcal 541
  recurrent 542
  relapsing 542
  retrocecal 541
  subacute (adhesive) 542
  subsiding 542
  suppurative — see Appendicitis, acute
  tuberculous (see also Tuberculosis) 014.8 ☑
Appendiclausis 543.9
Appendicolithiasis 543.9
Appendicopathia oxyurica 127.4
Appendix, appendicular — see also condition
  Morgagni (male) 752.89
    fallopian tube 752.11
Appetite
  depraved 307.52
  excessive 783.6
    psychogenic 307.51
  lack or loss (see also Anorexia) 783.0
    nonorganic origin 307.59
  perverted 307.52
    hysterical 300.11
Apprehension, apprehensiveness (abnormal)
  (state) 300.00
  specified type NEC 300.09
Approximal wear 521.10
Apraxia (classic) (ideational) (ideokinetic)
  (ideomotor) (motor) 784.69
  oculomotor, congenital 379.51

Apraxia — continued
  verbal 784.69
Aptyalism 527.7
Aqueous misdirection 365.83
Arabicum elephantiasis — see also Infesta-
  tion, filarial 125.9
Arachnidism 989.5
Arachnitis — see Meningitis
Arachnodactyly 759.82
Arachnoidism 989.5
Arachnoiditis (acute) (adhesive) (basic) (brain)
  (cerebrospinal) (chiasmal) (chronic)
  (spinal) — see also Meningitis 322.9
  meningococcal (chronic) 036.0
  syphilitic 094.2
  tuberculous (see also Tuberculosis,
    meninges) 013.0 ☑
Araneism 989.5
Arboencephalitis, Australian 062.4
Arborization block (heart) 426.6
Arbor virus, arbovirus (infection) NEC 066.9
ARC 042
Arches — see condition
Arcuate uterus 752.36
Arcuatus uterus 752.36
Arcus (cornea)
  juvenilis 743.43
    interfering with vision 743.42
  senilis 371.41
Arc-welders' lung 503
Arc-welders' syndrome (photokeratitis) 370.24
Areflexia 796.1
Areola — see condition
Argentaffinoma (M8241/1) — see also Neo-
  plasm, by site, uncertain behavior
  benign (M8241/0) — see Neoplasm, by site,
    benign
  malignant (M8241/3) — see Neoplasm, by
    site, malignant
  syndrome 259.2
Argentinian hemorrhagic fever 078.7
Arginosuccinicaciduria 270.6
Argonz-Del Castillo syndrome (nonpuerperal
  galactorrhea and amenorrhea) 253.1
**Argyll-Robertson phenomenon, pupil, or
  syndrome** (syphilitic) 094.89
  atypical 379.45
  nonluetic 379.45
  nonsyphilitic 379.45
  reversed 379.45
Argyria, argyriasis NEC 985.8
  conjunctiva 372.55
  cornea 371.16
  from drug or medicinal agent
    correct substance properly administered
      709.09
    overdose or wrong substance given or
      taken 961.2
Arhinencephaly 742.2
Arias-Stella phenomenon 621.30
Ariboflavinosis 266.0
Arizona enteritis 008.1
Arm — see condition
Armenian disease 277.31
Arnold-Chiari obstruction or syndrome —
  see also Spina bifida 741.0 ☑
  type I 348.4
  type II (see also Spina bifida) 741.0 ☑
  type III 742.0
  type IV 742.2
Arousals
  confusional 327.41
Arrest, arrested
  active phase of labor 661.1 ☑
    affecting fetus or newborn 763.7
  any plane in pelvis
    complicating delivery 660.1 ☑
      affecting fetus or newborn 763.1
  bone marrow (see also Anemia, aplastic)
    284.9
  cardiac 427.5
    with
      abortion — see Abortion, by type,
        with specified complication
        NEC

☑ Additional Digit Required — Refer to the Tabular List for Digit Selection   ▽ Subterms under main terms may continue to next column or page

Arrest, arrested — *continued*
cardiac — *continued*
with — *continued*
ectopic pregnancy (see also categories 633.0–633.9) 639.8
molar pregnancy (see also categories 630–632) 639.8
complicating
anesthesia
correct substance properly administered 427.5
obstetric 668.1 ☑
overdose or wrong substance given 968.4
specified anesthetic — see Table of Drugs and Chemicals
delivery (cesarean) (instrumental) 669.4 ☑
ectopic or molar pregnancy 639.8
surgery (nontherapeutic) (therapeutic) 997.1
fetus or newborn 779.85
following
abortion 639.8
ectopic or molar pregnancy 639.8
personal history, successfully resuscitated V12.53
postoperative (immediate) 997.1
long-term effect of cardiac surgery 429.4
cardiorespiratory (see also Arrest, cardiac) 427.5
deep transverse 660.3 ☑
affecting fetus or newborn 763.1
development or growth
bone 733.91
child 783.40
fetus 764.9 ☑
affecting management of pregnancy 656.5 ☑
tracheal rings 748.3
epiphyseal 733.91
granulopoiesis 288.09
heart — see Arrest, cardiac
respiratory 799.1
newborn 770.87
sinus 426.6
transverse (deep) 660.3 ☑
affecting fetus or newborn 763.1
Arrhenoblastoma (M8630/1)
benign (M8630/0)
specified site — see Neoplasm, by site, benign
unspecified site
female 220
male 222.0
malignant (M8630/3)
specified site — see Neoplasm, by site, malignant
unspecified site
female 183.0
male 186.9
specified site — see Neoplasm, by site, uncertain behavior
unspecified site
female 236.2
male 236.4
Arrhinencephaly 742.2
due to
trisomy 13 (13-15) 758.1
trisomy 18 (16-18) 758.2
Arrhythmia (auricle) (cardiac) (cordis) (gallop rhythm) (juvenile) (nodal) (reflex) (sinus) (supraventricular) (transitory) (ventricle) 427.9
bigeminal rhythm 427.89
block 426.9
bradycardia 427.89
contractions, premature 427.60
coronary sinus 427.89
ectopic 427.89
extrasystolic 427.60
postoperative 997.1
psychogenic 306.2
vagal 780.2

Arrillaga-Ayerza syndrome (pulmonary artery sclerosis with pulmonary hypertension) 416.0
Arsenical
dermatitis 692.4
keratosis 692.4
pigmentation 985.1
from drug or medicinal agent
correct substance properly administered 709.09
overdose or wrong substance given or taken 961.1
Arsenism 985.1
from drug or medicinal agent
correct substance properly administered 692.4
overdose or wrong substance given or taken 961.1
Arterial — see condition
Arteriectasis 447.8
Arteriofibrosis — see Arteriosclerosis
Arteriolar sclerosis — see Arteriosclerosis
Arteriolith — see Arteriosclerosis
Arteriolitis 447.6
necrotizing, kidney 447.5
renal — see Hypertension, kidney
Arteriolosclerosis — see Arteriosclerosis
Arterionephrosclerosis — see also Hypertension, kidney 403.90
Arteriopathy 447.9
Arteriosclerosis, arteriosclerotic (artery) (deformans) (diffuse) (disease) (endarteritis) (general) (obliterans) (obliterative) (occlusive) (senile) (with calcification) 440.9
with
gangrene 440.24
psychosis (see also Psychosis, arteriosclerotic) 290.40
ulceration 440.23
aorta 440.0
arteries of extremities — see Arteriosclerosis, extremities
basilar (artery) (see also Occlusion, artery, basilar) 433.0 ☑
brain 437.0
bypass graft
coronary artery 414.05
autologous artery (gastroepiploic) (internal mammary) 414.04
autologous vein 414.02
nonautologous biological 414.03
of transplanted heart 414.07
extremity 440.30
autologous vein 440.31
nonautologous biological 440.32
cardiac — see Arteriosclerosis, coronary
cardiopathy — see Arteriosclerosis, coronary
cardiorenal (see also Hypertension, cardiorenal) 404.90
cardiovascular (see also Disease, cardiovascular) 429.2
carotid (artery) (common) (internal) (see also Occlusion, artery, carotid) 433.1 ☑
central nervous system 437.0
cerebral 437.0
late effect — see Late effect(s) (of) cerebrovascular disease
cerebrospinal 437.0
cerebrovascular 437.0
coronary (artery) 414.00
due to
calcified coronary lesion (severely) 414.4
lipid rich plaque 414.3
graft — see Arteriosclerosis, bypass graft
native artery 414.01
of transplanted heart 414.06
extremities (native artery) NEC 440.20
bypass graft 440.30
autologous vein 440.31
nonautologous biological 440.32
claudication (intermittent) 440.21
and
gangrene 440.24
rest pain 440.22

Arteriosclerosis, arteriosclerotic — *continued*
extremities — *continued*
claudication — *continued*
and — *continued*
rest pain — *continued*
and
gangrene 440.24
ulceration 440.23
and gangrene 440.24
ulceration 440.23
and gangrene 440.24
gangrene 440.24
rest pain 440.22
and
gangrene 440.24
ulceration 440.23
and gangrene 440.24
specified site NEC 440.29
ulceration 440.23
and gangrene 440.24
heart (disease) (see also Arteriosclerosis, coronary)
valve 424.99
aortic 424.1
mitral 424.0
pulmonary 424.3
tricuspid 424.2
iliac 440.8
kidney (see also Hypertension, kidney) 403.90
labyrinth, labyrinthine 388.00
medial NEC (see also Arteriosclerosis, extremities) 440.20
mesentery (artery) 557.1
Mönckeberg's (see also Arteriosclerosis, extremities) 440.20
myocarditis 429.0
nephrosclerosis (see also Hypertension, kidney) 403.90
peripheral (of extremities) — see Arteriosclerosis, extremities
precerebral 433.9 ☑
specified artery NEC 433.8 ☑
pulmonary (idiopathic) 416.0
renal (see also Hypertension, kidney) 403.90
arterioles (see also Hypertension, kidney) 403.90
artery 440.1
retinal (vascular) 440.8 [362.13]
specified artery NEC 440.8
with gangrene 440.8 [785.4]
spinal (cord) 437.0
vertebral (artery) (see also Occlusion, artery, vertebral) 433.2 ☑
Arteriospasm 443.9
Arteriovenous — see condition
Arteritis 447.6
allergic (see also Angiitis, hypersensitivity) 446.20
aorta (nonsyphilitic) 447.6
syphilitic 093.1
aortic arch 446.7
brachiocephalica 446.7
brain 437.4
syphilitic 094.89
branchial 446.7
cerebral 437.4
late effect — see Late effect(s) (of) cerebrovascular disease
syphilitic 094.89
coronary (artery) (see also Arteriosclerosis, coronary)
rheumatic 391.9
chronic 398.99
syphilitic 093.89
cranial (left) (right) 446.5
deformans — see Arteriosclerosis
giant cell 446.5
necrosing or necrotizing 446.0
nodosa 446.0
obliterans (see also Arteriosclerosis)
subclaviocarotica 446.7
pulmonary 417.8
retina 362.18
rheumatic — see Fever, rheumatic

Arteritis — *continued*
senile — see Arteriosclerosis
suppurative 447.2
syphilitic (general) 093.89
brain 094.89
coronary 093.89
spinal 094.89
temporal 446.5
young female, syndrome 446.7
Artery, arterial — see condition
Arthralgia — see also Pain, joint 719.4 ☑
allergic (see also Pain, joint) 719.4 ☑
in caisson disease 993.3
psychogenic 307.89
rubella 056.71
Salmonella 003.23
temporomandibular joint 524.62
Arthritis, arthritic (acute) (chronic) (subacute) 716.9 ☑
meaning Osteoarthritis — see Osteoarthrosis

> *Note* — *Use the following fifth-digit subclassification with categories 711–712, 715–716:*
>
> 0 *site unspecified*
>
> 1 *shoulder region*
>
> 2 *upper arm*
>
> 3 *forearm*
>
> 4 *hand*
>
> 5 *pelvic region and thigh*
>
> 6 *lower leg*
>
> 7 *ankle and foot*
>
> 8 *other specified sites*
>
> 9 *multiple sites*

allergic 716.2 ☑
ankylosing (crippling) (spine) 720.0
sites other than spine 716.9 ☑
atrophic 714.0
spine 720.9
back (see also Arthritis, spine) 721.90
Bechterew's (ankylosing spondylitis) 720.0
blennorrhagic 098.50
cervical, cervicodorsal (see also Spondylosis, cervical) 721.0
Charcôt's 094.0 [713.5]
diabetic 250.6 ☑ [713.5]
due to secondary diabetes 249.6 ☑ [713.5]
syringomyelic 336.0 [713.5]
tabetic 094.0 [713.5]
chylous (see also Filariasis) 125.9 [711.7] ☑
climacteric NEC 716.3 ☑
coccyx 721.8
cricoarytenoid 478.79
crystal (-induced) — see Arthritis, due to crystals
deformans (see also Osteoarthrosis) 715.9 ☑
spine 721.90
with myelopathy 721.91
degenerative (see also Osteoarthrosis) 715.9 ☑
idiopathic 715.09
polyarticular 715.09
spine 721.90
with myelopathy 721.91
dermatoarthritis, lipoid 272.8 [713.0]
due to or associated with
acromegaly 253.0 [713.0]
actinomycosis 039.8 [711.4] ☑
amyloidosis 277.39 [713.7]
bacterial disease NEC 040.89 [711.4] ☑
Behçet's syndrome 136.1 [711.2] ☑
blastomycosis 116.0 [711.6] ☑
brucellosis (see also Brucellosis) 023.9 [711.4] ☑
caisson disease 993.3
coccidioidomycosis 114.3 [711.6] ☑
coliform (Escherichia coli) 711.0 ☑
colitis, ulcerative (see also Colitis, ulcerative) 556.9 [713.1]

☑ **Additional Digit Required — Refer to the Tabular List for Digit Selection**   ▽ **Subterms under main terms may continue to next column or page**

Arthritis, arthritic — continued
  due to or associated with — continued
    cowpox 051.01 [711.5] ☑
    crystals (see also Gout)
      dicalcium phosphate
        275.49 [712.1] ☑
      pyrophosphate 275.49 [712.2] ☑
      specified NEC 275.49 [712.8] ☑
    dermatoarthritis, lipoid 272.8 [713.0]
    dermatological disorder NEC
        709.9 [713.3]
    diabetes 250.6 ☑ [713.5]
      due to secondary diabetes
        249.6 ☑ [713.5]
    diphtheria 032.89 [711.4] ☑
    dracontiasis 125.7 [711.7] ☑
    dysentery 009.0 [711.3] ☑
    endocrine disorder NEC 259.9 [713.0]
    enteritis NEC 009.1 [711.3] ☑
      infectious (see also Enteritis, infec-
        tious) 009.0 [711.3] ☑
      specified organism NEC
        008.8 [711.3] ☑
      regional (see also Enteritis, regional)
        555.9 [713.1]
      specified organism NEC
        008.8 [711.3] ☑
    epiphyseal slip, nontraumatic (old)
        716.8 ☑
    erysipelas 035 [711.4] ☑
    erythema
      epidemic 026.1
      multiforme 695.10 [713.3]
      nodosum 695.2 [713.3]
    Escherichia coli 711.0 ☑
    filariasis NEC 125.9 [711.7] ☑
    gastrointestinal condition NEC
        569.9 [713.1]
    glanders 024 [711.4] ☑
    Gonococcus 098.50
    gout 274.00
    helminthiasis NEC 128.9 [711.7] ☑
    hematological disorder NEC 289.9 [713.2]
    hemochromatosis 275.03 [713.0]
    hemoglobinopathy NEC (see also Dis-
        ease, hemoglobin) 282.7 [713.2]
    hemophilia (see also Hemophilia)
        286.0 [713.2]
    Hemophilus influenzae (H. influenzae)
        711.0 ☑
    Henoch (-Schönlein) purpura
        287.0 [713.6]
    H. influenzae 711.0 ☑
    histoplasmosis NEC (see also Histoplas-
        mosis) 115.99 [711.6] ☑
    human parvovirus 079.83 [711.5] ☑
    hyperparathyroidism 252.00 [713.0]
    hypersensitivity reaction NEC
        995.3 [713.6]
    hypogammaglobulinemia (see also Hy-
        pogamma-globulinemia)
        279.00 [713.0]
    hypothyroidism NEC 244.9 [713.0]
    infection (see also Arthritis, infectious)
        711.9 ☑
    infectious disease NEC 136.9 [711.8] ☑
    leprosy (see also Leprosy)
        030.9 [711.4] ☑
    leukemia NEC (M9800/3) 208.9 [713.2]
    lipoid dermatoarthritis 272.8 [713.0]
    Lyme disease 088.81 [711.8] ☑
    Mediterranean fever, familial
        277.31 [713.7]
    meningococcal infection 036.82
    metabolic disorder NEC 277.9 [713.0]
    multiple myelomatosis (M9730/3) 203.0
        [713.2]
    mumps 072.79 [711.5] ☑
    mycobacteria 031.8 [711.4] ☑
    mycosis NEC 117.9 [711.6] ☑
    neurological disorder NEC 349.9 [713.5]
    ochronosis 270.2 [713.0]
    O'Nyong Nyong 066.3 [711.5] ☑
    parasitic disease NEC 136.9 [711.8] ☑

Arthritis, arthritic — continued
  due to or associated with — continued
    paratyphoid fever (see also Fever,
        paratyphoid) 002.9 [711.3] ☑
    parvovirus B19 079.83 [711.5] ☑
    Pneumococcus 711.0 ☑
    poliomyelitis (see also Poliomyelitis)
        045.9 ☑ [711.5] ☑
    Pseudomonas 711.0 ☑
    psoriasis 696.0
    pyogenic organism (E. coli) (H. influen-
        zae) (Pseudomonas) (Streptococ-
        cus) 711.0 ☑
    rat-bite fever 026.1 [711.4] ☑
    regional enteritis (see also Enteritis, re-
        gional) 555.9 [713.1]
    Reiter's disease 099.3 [711.1] ☑
    respiratory disorder NEC 519.9 [713.4]
    reticulosis, malignant (M9720/3) 202.3
        [713.2]
    rubella 056.71
    salmonellosis 003.23
    sarcoidosis 135 [713.7]
    serum sickness 999.59 [713.6]
    Staphylococcus 711.0 ☑
    Streptococcus 711.0 ☑
    syphilis (see also Syphilis)
        094.0 [711.4] ☑
    syringomyelia 336.0 [713.5]
    thalassemia (see also Thalassemia)
        282.40 [713.2]
    tuberculosis (see also Tuberculosis,
        arthritis) 015.9 ☑ [711.4] ☑
    typhoid fever 002.0 [711.3] ☑
    ulcerative colitis (see also Colitis, ulcera-
        tive) 556.9 [713.1]
    urethritis
      nongonococcal (see also Urethritis,
        nongonococcal)
        099.40 [711.1] ☑
      nonspecific (see also Urethritis, non-
        gonococcal) 099.40 [711.1] ☑
      Reiter's 099.3
    viral disease NEC 079.99 [711.5] ☑
  erythema epidemic 026.1
  gonococcal 098.50
  gouty 274.00
    acute 274.01
  hypertrophic (see also Osteoarthrosis)
        715.9 ☑
    spine 721.90
      with myelopathy 721.91
  idiopathic, blennorrheal 099.3
  in caisson disease 993.3 [713.8]
  infectious or infective (acute) (chronic)
        (subacute) NEC 711.9 ☑
    nonpyogenic 711.9 ☑
    spine 720.9
  inflammatory NEC 714.9
  juvenile rheumatoid (chronic) (polyarticular)
        714.30
    acute 714.31
    monoarticular 714.33
    pauciarticular 714.32
  lumbar (see also Spondylosis, lumbar) 721.3
  meningococcal 036.82
  menopausal NEC 716.3 ☑
  migratory — see Fever, rheumatic
  neuropathic (Charcôt's) 094.0 [713.5]
    diabetic 250.6 ☑ [713.5]
      due to secondary diabetes
        249.6 ☑ [713.5]
    nonsyphilitic NEC 349.9 [713.5]
    syringomyelic 336.0 [713.5]
    tabetic 094.0 [713.5]
  nodosa (see also Osteoarthrosis) 715.9 ☑
    spine 721.90
      with myelopathy 721.91
  nonpyogenic NEC 716.9 ☑
    spine 721.90
      with myelopathy 721.91
  ochronotic 270.2 [713.0]
  palindromic (see also Rheumatism, palin-
        dromic) 719.3 ☑
  pneumococcal 711.0 ☑

Arthritis, arthritic — continued
  postdysenteric 009.0 [711.3] ☑
  postrheumatic, chronic (Jaccoud's) 714.4
  primary progressive 714.0
    spine 720.9
  proliferative 714.0
    spine 720.0
  psoriatic 696.0
  purulent 711.0 ☑
  pyogenic or pyemic 711.0 ☑
  reactive 099.3
  rheumatic 714.0
    acute or subacute — see Fever,
        rheumatic
    chronic 714.0
    spine 720.9
  rheumatoid (nodular) 714.0
    with
      splenoadenomegaly and leukopenia
        714.1
      visceral or systemic involvement
        714.2
    aortitis 714.89
    carditis 714.2
    heart disease 714.2
    juvenile (chronic) (polyarticular) 714.30
      acute 714.31
      monoarticular 714.33
      pauciarticular 714.32
    spine 720.0
  rubella 056.71
  sacral, sacroiliac, sacrococcygeal (see also
        Spondylosis, sacral) 721.3
  scorbutic 267
  senile or senescent (see also Osteoarthrosis)
        715.9 ☑
    spine 721.90
      with myelopathy 721.91
  septic 711.0 ☑
  serum (nontherapeutic) (therapeutic)
        999.59 [713.6]
  specified form NEC 716.8 ☑
  spine 721.90
    with myelopathy 721.91
    atrophic 720.9
    degenerative 721.90
      with myelopathy 721.91
    hypertrophic (with deformity) 721.90
      with myelopathy 721.91
    infectious or infective NEC 720.9
    Marie-Strümpell 720.0
    nonpyogenic 721.90
      with myelopathy 721.91
    pyogenic 720.9
    rheumatoid 720.0
    traumatic (old) 721.7
    tuberculous (see also Tuberculosis)
        015.0 ☑ [720.81]
  staphylococcal 711.0 ☑
  streptococcal 711.0 ☑
  suppurative 711.0 ☑
  syphilitic 094.0 [713.5]
    congenital 090.49 [713.5]
  syphilitica deformans (Charcôt) 094.0 [713.5]
  temporomandibular joint 524.69
  thoracic (see also Spondylosis, thoracic)
        721.2
  toxic of menopause 716.3 ☑
  transient 716.4 ☑
  traumatic (chronic) (old) (post) 716.1 ☑
    current injury — see nature of injury
  tuberculous (see also Tuberculosis, arthritis)
        015.9 ☑ [711.4] ☑
  urethritica 099.3 [711.1] ☑
  urica, uratic 274.00
  venereal 099.3 [711.1] ☑
  vertebral (see also Arthritis, spine) 721.90
  villous 716.8 ☑
  von Bechterew's 720.0
Arthrocele — see also Effusion, joint 719.0 ☑
Arthrochondritis — see Arthritis
Arthrodesis status V45.4
Arthrodynia — see also Pain, joint 719.4 ☑
  psychogenic 307.89
Arthrodysplasia 755.9

Arthrofibrosis joint — see also Ankylosis
        718.5 ☑
Arthrogryposis 728.3
  multiplex, congenita 754.89
Arthrokatadysis 715.35
Arthrolithiasis 274.00
Arthro-onychodysplasia 756.89
Arthro-osteo-onychodysplasia 756.89
Arthropathy — see also Arthritis 716.9 ☑

> Note — Use the following fifth-digit
> subclassification with categories
> 711–712, 716:
>
> 0   site unspecified
> 1   shoulder region
> 2   upper arm
> 3   forearm
> 4   hand
> 5   pelvic region and thigh
> 6   lower leg
> 7   ankle and foot
> 8   other specified sites
> 9   multiple sites

  Behçet's 136.1 [711.2] ☑
  Charcôt's 094.0 [713.5]
    diabetic 250.6 ☑ [713.5]
      due to secondary diabetes
        249.6 ☑ [713.5]
    syringomyelic 336.0 [713.5]
    tabetic 094.0 [713.5]
  crystal (-induced) — see Arthritis, due to
        crystals
  gouty 274.00
    acute 274.01
    chronic (without mention of tophus
        (tophi)) 274.02
      with tophus (tophi) 274.03
  neurogenic, neuropathic (Charcôt's) (tabet-
        ic) 094.0 [713.5]
    diabetic 250.6 ☑ [713.5]
      due to secondary diabetes
        249.6 ☑ [713.5]
    nonsyphilitic NEC 349.9 [713.5]
    syringomyelic 336.0 [713.5]
  postdysenteric NEC 009.0 [711.3] ☑
  postrheumatic, chronic (Jaccoud's) 714.4
  psoriatic 696.0
  pulmonary 731.2
  specified NEC 716.8 ☑
  syringomyelia 336.0 [713.5]
  tabes dorsalis 094.0 [713.5]
  tabetic 094.0 [713.5]
  transient 716.4 ☑
  traumatic 716.1 ☑
  uric acid 274.00
Arthrophyte — see also Loose, body, joint
        718.1 ☑
Arthrophytis 719.80
  ankle 719.87
  elbow 719.82
  foot 719.87
  hand 719.84
  hip 719.85
  knee 719.86
  multiple sites 719.89
  pelvic region 719.85
  shoulder (region) 719.81
  specified site NEC 719.88
  wrist 719.83
Arthropyosis — see also Arthritis, pyogenic
        711.0 ☑
**Arthroscopic surgical procedure converted
  to open procedure** V64.43
Arthrosis (deformans) (degenerative) — see
        also Osteoarthrosis 715.9 ☑
  Charcôt's 094.0 [713.5]
  polyarticular 715.09
  spine (see also Spondylosis) 721.90
Arthus phenomenon 995.21

☑ Additional Digit Required — Refer to the Tabular List for Digit Selection   ⒱ Subterms under main terms may continue to next column or page

28 — Volume 2   ▶◀ Revised Text   ● New Line   ▲ Revised Code   2015 ICD-9-CM

Arthus phenomenon — continued
  due to
    correct substance properly administered 995.21
    overdose or wrong substance given or taken 977.9
      specified drug — see Table of Drugs and Chemicals
    serum 999.59
Articular — see also condition
  disc disorder (reducing or non-reducing) 524.63
  spondylolisthesis 756.12
Articulation
  anterior 524.27
  posterior 524.27
  reverse 524.27
Artificial
  device (prosthetic) — see Fitting, device
  insemination V26.1
  menopause (states) (symptoms) (syndrome) 627.4
  opening status (functioning) (without complication) V44.9
    anus (colostomy) V44.3
    colostomy V44.3
    cystostomy V44.50
      appendico-vesicostomy V44.52
      cutaneous-vesicostomy V44.51
      specified type NEC V44.59
    enterostomy V44.4
    gastrostomy V44.1
    ileostomy V44.2
    intestinal tract NEC V44.4
    jejunostomy V44.4
    nephrostomy V44.6
    specified site NEC V44.8
    tracheostomy V44.0
    ureterostomy V44.6
    urethrostomy V44.6
    urinary tract NEC V44.6
    vagina V44.7
    vagina status V44.7
ARV (disease) (illness) (infection) — see Human immunodeficiency virus (disease) (illness) (infection)
Arytenoid — see condition
Asbestosis (occupational) 501
Asboe-Hansen's disease (incontinentia pigmenti) 757.33
Ascariasis (intestinal) (lung) 127.0
Ascaridiasis 127.0
Ascaridosis 127.0
Ascaris 127.0
  lumbricoides (infestation) 127.0
  pneumonia 127.0
Ascending — see condition
ASC-H (atypical squamous cells cannot exclude high grade squamous intraepithelial lesion)
  anus 796.72
  cervix 795.02
  vagina 795.12
Aschoff's bodies — see also Myocarditis, rheumatic 398.0
Ascites 789.59
  abdominal NEC 789.59
  cancerous (M8000/6) 789.51
  cardiac 428.0
  chylous (nonfilarial) 457.8
    filarial (see also Infestation, filarial) 125.9
  congenital 778.0
  due to S. japonicum 120.2
  fetal, causing fetopelvic disproportion 653.7 ☑
  heart 428.0
  joint (see also Effusion, joint) 719.0 ☑
  malignant (M8000/6) 789.51
  pseudochylous 789.59
  syphilitic 095.2
  tuberculous (see also Tuberculosis) 014.0 ☑
Ascorbic acid (vitamin C) **deficiency** (scurvy) 267
ASC-US (atypical squamous cells of undetermined significance)
  anus 796.71

ASC-US — continued
  cervix 795.01
  vagina 795.11
ASCVD (arteriosclerotic cardiovascular disease) 429.2
Aseptic — see condition
Asherman's syndrome 621.5
Asialia 527.7
Asiatic cholera — see also Cholera 001.9
Asocial personality or trends 301.7
Asomatognosia 781.8
Aspergillosis 117.3
  with pneumonia 117.3 [484.6]
  allergic bronchopulmonary 518.6
  nonsyphilitic NEC 117.3
Aspergillus (flavus) (fumigatus) (infection) (terreus) 117.3
Aspermatogenesis 606.0
Aspermia (testis) 606.0
Asphyxia, asphyxiation (by) 799.01
  antenatal — see Distress, fetal
  bedclothes 994.7
  birth (see also Asphyxia, newborn) 768.9
  bunny bag 994.7
  carbon monoxide 986
  caul (see also Asphyxia, newborn) 768.9
  cave-in 994.7
    crushing — see Injury, internal, intrathoracic organs
  constriction 994.7
  crushing — see Injury, internal, intrathoracic organs
  drowning 994.1
  fetal, affecting newborn 768.9
  food or foreign body (in larynx) 933.1
    bronchioles 934.8
    bronchus (main) 934.1
    lung 934.8
    nasopharynx 933.0
    nose, nasal passages 932
    pharynx 933.0
    respiratory tract 934.9
      specified part NEC 934.8
    throat 933.0
    trachea 934.0
  gas, fumes, or vapor NEC 987.9
    specified — see Table of Drugs and Chemicals
  gravitational changes 994.7
  hanging 994.7
  inhalation — see Inhalation
  intrauterine
    fetal death (before onset of labor) 768.0
      during labor 768.1
    liveborn infant — see Distress, fetal, liveborn infant
  local 443.0
  mechanical 994.7
    during birth (see also Distress, fetal) 768.9
  mucus 933.1
    bronchus (main) 934.1
    larynx 933.1
    lung 934.8
    nasal passages 932
    newborn 770.18
    pharynx 933.0
    respiratory tract 934.9
      specified part NEC 934.8
    throat 933.0
    trachea 934.0
    vaginal (fetus or newborn) 770.18
  newborn 768.9
    with neurologic involvement 768.5
    blue 768.6
    livida 768.6
    mild or moderate 768.6
    pallida 768.5
    severe 768.5
    white 768.5
  pathological 799.01
  plastic bag 994.7
  postnatal (see also Asphyxia, newborn) 768.9
    mechanical 994.7
  pressure 994.7
  reticularis 782.61

Asphyxia, asphyxiation — continued
  strangulation 994.7
  submersion 994.1
  traumatic NEC — see Injury, internal, intrathoracic organs
  vomiting, vomitus — see Asphyxia, food or foreign body
Aspiration
  acid pulmonary (syndrome) 997.39
    obstetric 668.0 ☑
  amniotic fluid 770.13
    with respiratory symptoms 770.14
  bronchitis 507.0
  clear amniotic fluid 770.13
    with
      pneumonia 770.14
      pneumonitis 770.14
      respiratory symptoms 770.14
  contents of birth canal 770.17
    with respiratory symptoms 770.18
  fetal 770.10
    blood 770.15
      with
        pneumonia 770.16
        pneumonitis 770.16
    pneumonitis 770.18
  food, foreign body, or gasoline (with asphyxiation) — see Asphyxia, food or foreign body
  meconium 770.11
    with
      pneumonia 770.12
      pneumonitis 770.12
      respiratory symptoms 770.12
    below vocal cords 770.11
      with respiratory symptoms 770.12
  mucus 933.1
    into
      bronchus (main) 934.1
      lung 934.8
      respiratory tract 934.9
        specified part NEC 934.8
      trachea 934.0
    newborn 770.17
    vaginal (fetus or newborn) 770.17
  newborn 770.10
    with respiratory symptoms 770.18
    blood 770.15
      with
        pneumonia 770.16
        pneumonitis 770.16
        respiratory symptoms 770.16
    pneumonia 507.0
      fetus or newborn 770.18
        meconium 770.12
    pneumonitis 507.0
      fetus or newborn 770.18
        meconium 770.12
    obstetric 668.0 ☑
  postnatal stomach contents 770.85
    with
      pneumonia 770.86
      pneumonitis 770.86
      respiratory symptoms 770.86
  syndrome of newborn (massive) 770.18
    meconium 770.12
  vernix caseosa 770.12
Asplenia 759.0
  with mesocardia 746.87
Assam fever 085.0
Assimilation, pelvis
  with disproportion 653.2 ☑
    affecting fetus or newborn 763.1
    causing obstructed labor 660.1 ☑
      affecting fetus or newborn 763.1
Assmann's focus — see also Tuberculosis 011.0 ☑
Astasia (-abasia) 307.9
  hysterical 300.11
Asteatosis 706.8
  cutis 706.8
Astereognosis 780.99
Asterixis 781.3
  in liver disease 572.8
Asteroid hyalitis 379.22
Asthenia, asthenic 780.79

Asthenia, asthenic — continued
  cardiac (see also Failure, heart) 428.9
    psychogenic 306.2
  cardiovascular (see also Failure, heart) 428.9
    psychogenic 306.2
  heart (see also Failure, heart) 428.9
    psychogenic 306.2
  hysterical 300.11
  myocardial (see also Failure, heart) 428.9
    psychogenic 306.2
  nervous 300.5
  neurocirculatory 306.2
  neurotic 300.5
  psychogenic 300.5
  psychoneurotic 300.5
  reaction, psychoneurotic 300.5
  senile 797
  Stiller's 780.79
  tropical anhidrotic 705.1
Asthenopia 368.13
  accommodative 367.4
  hysterical (muscular) 300.11
  psychogenic 306.7
Asthenospermia 792.2
Asthma, asthmatic (bronchial) (catarrh) (spasmodic) 493.9 ☑

> *Note* — Use the following fifth-digit subclassification with codes 493.0–493.2, 493.9:
>
> 0   without mention of status asthmaticus or acute exacerbation or unspecified
>
> 1   with status asthmaticus
>
> 2   with acute exacerbation

  with
    chronic obstructive pulmonary disease (COPD) 493.2 ☑
    hay fever 493.0 ☑
    rhinitis, allergic 493.0 ☑
  allergic 493.9 ☑
    stated cause (external allergen) 493.0 ☑
  atopic 493.0 ☑
  cardiac (see also Failure, ventricular, left) 428.1
  cardiobronchial (see also Failure, ventricular, left) 428.1
  cardiorenal (see also Hypertension, cardiorenal) 404.90
  childhood 493.0 ☑
  Colliers' 500
  cough variant 493.82
  croup 493.9 ☑
  detergent 507.8
  due to
    detergent 507.8
    inhalation of fumes 506.3
    internal immunological process 493.0 ☑
  endogenous (intrinsic) 493.1 ☑
  eosinophilic 518.3
  exercise induced bronchospasm 493.81
  exogenous (cosmetics) (dander or dust) (drugs) (dust) (feathers) (food) (hay) (platinum) (pollen) 493.0 ☑
  extrinsic 493.0 ☑
  grinders' 502
  hay 493.0 ☑
  heart (see also Failure, ventricular, left) 428.1
  IgE 493.0 ☑
  infective 493.1 ☑
  intrinsic 493.1 ☑
  Kopp's 254.8
  late-onset 493.1 ☑
  meat-wrappers' 506.9
  Millar's (laryngismus stridulus) 478.75
  millstone makers' 502
  miners' 500
  Monday morning 504
  New Orleans (epidemic) 493.0 ☑
  platinum 493.0 ☑
  pneumoconiotic (occupational) NEC 505
  potters' 502
  psychogenic 316 [493.9] ☑

☑ Additional Digit Required — Refer to the Tabular List for Digit Selection   ▽ Subterms under main terms may continue to next column or page

Asthma, asthmatic — continued
pulmonary eosinophilic 518.3
red cedar 495.8
Rostan's (see also Failure, ventricular, left)
428.1
sandblasters' 502
sequoiosis 495.8
stonemasons' 502
thymic 254.8
tuberculous (see also Tuberculosis, pulmonary) 011.9 ☑
Wichmann's (laryngismus stridulus) 478.75
wood 495.8
Astigmatism (compound) (congenital) 367.20
irregular 367.22
regular 367.21
Astroblastoma (M9430/3)
nose 748.1
specified site — see Neoplasm, by site, malignant
unspecified site 191.9
Astrocytoma (cystic) (M9400/3)
anaplastic type (M9401/3)
specified site — see Neoplasm, by site, malignant
unspecified site 191.9
fibrillary (M9420/3)
specified site — see Neoplasm, by site, malignant
unspecified site 191.9
fibrous (M9420/3)
specified site — see Neoplasm, by site, malignant
unspecified site 191.9
gemistocytic (M9411/3)
specified site — see Neoplasm, by site, malignant
unspecified site 191.9
juvenile (M9421/3)
specified site — see Neoplasm, by site, malignant
unspecified site 191.9
nose 748.1
pilocytic (M9421/3)
specified site — see Neoplasm, by site, malignant
unspecified site 191.9
piloid (M9421/3)
specified site — see Neoplasm, by site, malignant
unspecified site 191.9
protoplasmic (M9410/3)
specified site — see Neoplasm, by site, malignant
unspecified site 191.9
specified site — see Neoplasm, by site, malignant
subependymal (M9383/1) 237.5
giant cell (M9384/1) 237.5
unspecified site 191.9
Astroglioma (M9400/3)
nose 748.1
specified site — see Neoplasm, by site, malignant
unspecified site 191.9
Asymbolia 784.60
Asymmetrical breathing 786.09
Asymmetry — see also Distortion
breast, between native and reconstructed
612.1
chest 786.9
face 754.0
jaw NEC 524.12
maxillary 524.11
pelvis with disproportion 653.0 ☑
affecting fetus or newborn 763.1
causing obstructed labor 660.1 ☑
affecting fetus or newborn 763.1
Asynergia 781.3
Asynergy 781.3
ventricular 429.89
Asystole (heart) — see also Arrest, cardiac
427.5
Ataxia, ataxy, ataxic 781.3
acute 781.3
brain 331.89

Ataxia, ataxy, ataxic — continued
cerebellar 334.3
hereditary (Marie's) 334.2
in
alcoholism 303.9 ☑ [334.4]
myxedema (see also Myxedema)
244.9 [334.4]
neoplastic disease NEC 239.9 [334.4]
cerebral 331.89
family, familial 334.2
cerebral (Marie's) 334.2
spinal (Friedreich's) 334.0
Friedreich's (heredofamilial) (spinal) 334.0
frontal lobe 781.3
gait 781.2
hysterical 300.11
general 781.3
hereditary NEC 334.2
cerebellar 334.2
spastic 334.1
spinal 334.0
heredofamilial (Marie's) 334.2
hysterical 300.11
locomotor (progressive) 094.0
diabetic 250.6 ☑ [337.1]
due to secondary diabetes
249.6 ☑ [337.1]
Marie's (cerebellar) (heredofamilial) 334.2
nonorganic origin 307.9
partial 094.0
postchickenpox 052.7
progressive locomotor 094.0
psychogenic 307.9
Sanger-Brown's 334.2
spastic 094.0
hereditary 334.1
syphilitic 094.0
spinal
hereditary 334.0
progressive locomotor 094.0
telangiectasia 334.8
Ataxia-telangiectasia 334.8
Atelectasis (absorption collapse) (complete)
(compression) (massive) (partial)
(postinfective) (pressure collapse) (pulmonary) (relaxation) 518.0
newborn (congenital) (partial) 770.5
primary 770.4
primary 770.4
tuberculous (see also Tuberculosis, pulmonary) 011.9 ☑
Ateleiosis, ateliosis 253.3
Atelia — see Distortion
Ateliosis 253.3
Atelocardia 746.9
Atelomyelia 742.59
Athelia 757.6
Atheroembolism
extremity
lower 445.02
upper 445.01
kidney 445.81
specified site NEC 445.89
Atheroma, atheromatous — see also Arteriosclerosis 440.9
aorta, aortic 440.0
valve (see also Endocarditis, aortic) 424.1
artery — see Arteriosclerosis
basilar (artery) (see also Occlusion, artery, basilar) 433.0 ☑
carotid (artery) (common) (internal) (see also Occlusion, artery, carotid) 433.1 ☑
cerebral (arteries) 437.0
coronary (artery) — see Arteriosclerosis, coronary
degeneration — see Arteriosclerosis
heart, cardiac — see Arteriosclerosis, coronary
mitral (valve) 424.0
myocardium, myocardial — see Arteriosclerosis, coronary
pulmonary valve (heart) (see also Endocarditis, pulmonary) 424.3
skin 706.2
tricuspid (heart) (valve) 424.2
valve, valvular — see Endocarditis

Atheroma, atheromatous — see also
Arteriosclerosis — continued
vertebral (artery) (see also Occlusion, artery, vertebral) 433.2 ☑
Atheromatosis — see also Arteriosclerosis
arterial, congenital 272.8
Atherosclerosis — see Arteriosclerosis
Athetosis (acquired) 781.0
bilateral 333.79
congenital (bilateral) 333.6
double 333.71
unilateral 781.0
Athlete's
foot 110.4
heart 429.3
Athletic team examination V70.3
Athrepsia 261
Athyrea (acquired) — see also Hypothyroidism
244.9
congenital 243
Athyreosis (congenital) 243
acquired — see Hypothyroidism
Athyroidism (acquired) — see also Hypothyroidism 244.9
congenital 243
Atmospheric pyrexia 992.0
Atonia, atony, atonic
abdominal wall 728.2
bladder (sphincter) 596.4
neurogenic NEC 596.54
with cauda equina syndrome 344.61
capillary 448.9
cecum 564.89
psychogenic 306.4
colon 564.89
psychogenic 306.4
congenital 779.89
dyspepsia 536.3
psychogenic 306.4
intestine 564.89
psychogenic 306.4
stomach 536.3
neurotic or psychogenic 306.4
psychogenic 306.4
uterus 661.2 ☑
with hemorrhage (postpartum) 666.1 ☑
without hemorrhage
intrapartum 661.2 ☑
postpartum 669.8 ☑
vesical 596.4
Atopy NEC V15.09
Atransferrinemia, congenital 273.8
Atresia, atretic (congenital) 759.89
alimentary organ or tract NEC 751.8
lower 751.2
upper 750.8
ani, anus, anal (canal) 751.2
aorta 747.22
with hypoplasia of ascending aorta and
defective development of left
ventricle (with mitral valve atresia) 746.7
arch 747.11
ring 747.21
aortic (orifice) (valve) 746.89
arch 747.11
aqueduct of Sylvius 742.3
with spina bifida (see also Spina bifida)
741.0 ☑
artery NEC (see also Atresia, blood vessel)
747.60
cerebral 747.81
coronary 746.85
eye 743.58
pulmonary 747.31
umbilical 747.5
auditory canal (external) 744.02
bile, biliary duct (common) or passage
751.61
acquired (see also Obstruction, biliary)
576.2
bladder (neck) 753.6
blood vessel (peripheral) NEC 747.60
cerebral 747.81
gastrointestinal 747.61
lower limb 747.64

Atresia, atretic — continued
blood vessel — continued
pulmonary artery 747.31
renal 747.62
spinal 747.82
upper limb 747.63
bronchus 748.3
canal, ear 744.02
cardiac
valve 746.89
aortic 746.89
mitral 746.89
pulmonary 746.01
tricuspid 746.1
cecum 751.2
cervix (acquired) 622.4
congenital 752.43
in pregnancy or childbirth 654.6 ☑
affecting fetus or newborn 763.89
causing obstructed labor 660.2 ☑
affecting fetus or newborn 763.1
choana 748.0
colon 751.2
cystic duct 751.61
acquired 575.8
with obstruction (see also Obstruction, gallbladder) 575.2
digestive organs NEC 751.8
duodenum 751.1
ear canal 744.02
ejaculatory duct 752.89
epiglottis 748.3
esophagus 750.3
Eustachian tube 744.24
fallopian tube (acquired) 628.2
congenital 752.19
follicular cyst 620.0
foramen of
Luschka 742.3
with spina bifida (see also Spina bifida) 741.0 ☑
Magendie 742.3
with spina bifida (see also Spina bifida) 741.0 ☑
gallbladder 751.69
genital organ
external
female 752.49
male NEC 752.89
penis 752.69
internal
female 752.89
male 752.89
glottis 748.3
gullet 750.3
heart
valve NEC 746.89
aortic 746.89
mitral 746.89
pulmonary 746.01
tricuspid 746.1
hymen 752.42
acquired 623.3
postinfective 623.3
ileum 751.1
intestine (small) 751.1
large 751.2
iris, filtration angle (see also Buphthalmia)
743.20
jejunum 751.1
kidney 753.3
lacrimal, apparatus 743.65
acquired — see Stenosis, lacrimal
larynx 748.3
ligament, broad 752.19
lung 748.5
meatus urinarius 753.6
mitral valve 746.89
with atresia or hypoplasia of aortic orifice or valve, with hypoplasia of
ascending aorta and defective
development of left ventricle
746.7
nares (anterior) (posterior) 748.0
nasolacrimal duct 743.65
nasopharynx 748.8

☑ Additional Digit Required — Refer to the Tabular List for Digit Selection   ▽ Subterms under main terms may continue to next column or page

30 — Volume 2   ►◄ Revised Text   ● New Line   ▲ Revised Code   2015 ICD-9-CM

Atresia, atretic — *continued*
- nose, nostril 748.0
  - acquired 738.0
- organ or site NEC — *see* Anomaly, specified type NEC
- osseous meatus (ear) 744.03
- oviduct (acquired) 628.2
  - congenital 752.19
- parotid duct 750.23
  - acquired 527.8
- pulmonary (artery) 747.31
  - valve 746.01
  - vein 747.49
- pulmonic 746.01
- pupil 743.46
- rectum 751.2
- salivary duct or gland 750.23
  - acquired 527.8
- sublingual duct 750.23
  - acquired 527.8
- submaxillary duct or gland 750.23
  - acquired 527.8
- trachea 748.3
- tricuspid valve 746.1
- ureter 753.29
- ureteropelvic junction 753.21
- ureterovesical orifice 753.22
- urethra (valvular) 753.6
- urinary tract NEC 753.29
- uterus 752.31
  - acquired 621.8
- vagina (acquired) 623.2
  - congenital (total) (partial) 752.45
  - postgonococcal (old) 098.2
  - postinfectional 623.2
  - senile 623.2
- vascular NEC (*see also* Atresia, blood vessel) 747.60
  - cerebral 747.81
- vas deferens 752.89
- vein NEC (*see also* Atresia, blood vessel) 747.60
  - cardiac 746.89
  - great 747.49
  - portal 747.49
  - pulmonary 747.49
- vena cava (inferior) (superior) 747.49
- vesicourethral orifice 753.6
- vulva 752.49
  - acquired 624.8

Atrichia, atrichosis 704.00
- congenital (universal) 757.4

Atrioventricularis commune 745.69

At risk for falling V15.88

Atrophia — *see also* Atrophy
- alba 709.09
- cutis 701.8
  - idiopathica progressiva 701.8
  - senilis 701.8
- dermatological, diffuse (idiopathic) 701.8
- flava hepatis (acuta) (subacuta) (*see also* Necrosis, liver) 570
- gyrata of choroid and retina (central) 363.54
  - generalized 363.57
- senilis 797
  - dermatological 701.8
- unguium 703.8
  - congenita 757.5

Atrophoderma, atrophodermia 701.9
- diffusum (idiopathic) 701.8
- maculatum 701.3
  - et striatum 701.3
    - due to syphilis 095.8
  - syphilitic 091.3
- neuriticum 701.8
- pigmentosum 757.33
- reticulatum symmetricum faciei 701.8
- senile 701.8
- symmetrical 701.8
- vermiculata 701.8

Atrophy, atrophic
- adrenal (autoimmune) (capsule) (cortex) (gland) 255.41
  - with hypofunction 255.41
- alveolar process or ridge (edentulous) 525.20

Atrophy, atrophic — *continued*
- alveolar process or ridge — *continued*
  - mandible 525.20
    - minimal 525.21
    - moderate 525.22
    - severe 525.23
  - maxilla 525.20
    - minimal 525.24
    - moderate 525.25
    - severe 525.26
- appendix 543.9
- Aran-Duchenne muscular 335.21
- arm 728.2
- arteriosclerotic — *see* Arteriosclerosis
- arthritis 714.0
  - spine 720.9
- bile duct (any) 576.8
- bladder 596.89
- blanche (of Milian) 701.3
- bone (senile) 733.99
  - due to
    - disuse 733.7
    - infection 733.99
    - tabes dorsalis (neurogenic) 094.0
  - posttraumatic 733.99
- brain (cortex) (progressive) 331.9
  - with dementia 290.10
    - Alzheimer's 331.0
      - with dementia — *see* Alzheimer's, dementia
  - circumscribed (Pick's) 331.11
    - with dementia
      - with behavioral disturbance 331.11 [294.11]
      - without behavioral disturbance 331.11 [294.10]
  - congenital 742.4
  - hereditary 331.9
  - senile 331.2
- breast 611.4
  - puerperal, postpartum 676.3 ☑
- buccal cavity 528.9
- cardiac (brown) (senile) (*see also* Degeneration, myocardial) 429.1
- cartilage (infectional) (joint) 733.99
- cast, plaster of Paris 728.2
- cerebellar — *see* Atrophy, brain
- cerebral — *see* Atrophy, brain
- cervix (endometrium) (mucosa) (myometrium) (senile) (uteri) 622.8
  - menopausal 627.8
- Charcôt-Marie-Tooth 356.1
- choroid 363.40
  - diffuse secondary 363.42
  - hereditary (*see also* Dystrophy, choroid) 363.50
    - gyrate
      - central 363.54
      - diffuse 363.57
      - generalized 363.57
  - senile 363.41
- ciliary body 364.57
- colloid, degenerative 701.3
- conjunctiva (senile) 372.89
- corpus cavernosum 607.89
- cortical (*see also* Atrophy, brain) 331.9
- Cruveilhier's 335.21
- cystic duct 576.8
- dacryosialadenopathy 710.2
- degenerative
  - colloid 701.3
  - senile 701.3
- Déjérine-Thomas 333.0
- diffuse idiopathic, dermatological 701.8
- disuse
  - bone 733.7
  - muscle 728.2
  - pelvic muscles and anal sphincter 618.83
- Duchenne-Aran 335.21
- ear 388.9
- edentulous alveolar ridge 525.20
  - mandible 525.20
    - minimal 525.21
    - moderate 525.22
    - severe 525.23
  - maxilla 525.20

Atrophy, atrophic — *continued*
- edentulous alveolar ridge — *continued*
  - maxilla — *continued*
    - minimal 525.24
    - moderate 525.25
    - severe 525.26
- emphysema, lung 492.8
- endometrium (senile) 621.8
  - cervix 622.8
- enteric 569.89
- epididymis 608.3
- eyeball, cause unknown 360.41
- eyelid (senile) 374.50
- facial (skin) 701.9
- facioscapulohumeral (Landouzy-Déjérine) 359.1
- fallopian tube (senile), acquired 620.3
- fatty, thymus (gland) 254.8
- gallbladder 575.8
- gastric 537.89
- gastritis (chronic) 535.1 ☑
- gastrointestinal 569.89
- genital organ, male 608.89
- glandular 289.3
- globe (phthisis bulbi) 360.41
- gum (*see also* Recession, gingival) 523.20
- hair 704.2
- heart (brown) (senile) (*see also* Degeneration, myocardial) 429.1
- hemifacial 754.0
  - Romberg 349.89
- hydronephrosis 591
- infantile 261
  - paralysis, acute (*see also* Poliomyelitis, with paralysis) 045.1 ☑
- intestine 569.89
- iris (generalized) (postinfectional) (sector shaped) 364.59
  - essential 364.51
  - progressive 364.51
  - sphincter 364.54
- kidney (senile) (*see also* Sclerosis, renal) 587
  - with hypertension (*see also* Hypertension, kidney) 403.90
  - congenital 753.0
  - hydronephrotic 591
  - infantile 753.0
- lacrimal apparatus (primary) 375.13
  - secondary 375.14
- Landouzy-Déjérine 359.1
- laryngitis, infection 476.0
- larynx 478.79
- Leber's optic 377.16
- lip 528.5
- liver (acute) (subacute) (*see also* Necrosis, liver) 570
  - chronic (yellow) 571.8
  - yellow (congenital) 570
    - with
      - abortion — *see* Abortion, by type, with specified complication NEC
      - ectopic pregnancy (*see also* categories 633.0–633.9) 639.8
      - molar pregnancy (*see also* categories 630–632) 639.8
    - chronic 571.8
    - complicating pregnancy 646.7 ☑
    - following
      - abortion 639.8
      - ectopic or molar pregnancy 639.8
    - from injection, inoculation or transfusion (onset within 8 months after administration) — *see* Hepatitis, viral
    - healed 571.5
    - obstetric 646.7 ☑
    - postabortal 639.8
    - postimmunization — *see* Hepatitis, viral
    - posttransfusion — *see* Hepatitis, viral
    - puerperal, postpartum 674.8 ☑
- lung (senile) 518.89
  - congenital 748.69
- macular (dermatological) 701.3
  - syphilitic, skin 091.3

Atrophy, atrophic — *continued*
- macular — *continued*
  - syphilitic, skin — *continued*
    - striated 095.8
- muscle, muscular 728.2
  - disuse 728.2
  - Duchenne-Aran 335.21
  - extremity (lower) (upper) 728.2
  - familial spinal 335.11
  - general 728.2
  - idiopathic 728.2
  - infantile spinal 335.0
  - myelopathic (progressive) 335.10
  - myotonic 359.21
  - neuritic 356.1
  - neuropathic (peroneal) (progressive) 356.1
  - peroneal 356.1
  - primary (idiopathic) 728.2
  - progressive (familial) (hereditary) (pure) 335.21
    - adult (spinal) 335.19
    - infantile (spinal) 335.0
    - juvenile (spinal) 335.11
    - spinal 335.10
      - adult 335.19
      - hereditary or familial 335.11
      - infantile 335.0
  - pseudohypertrophic 359.1
  - spinal (progressive) 335.10
    - adult 335.19
    - Aran-Duchenne 335.21
    - familial 335.11
    - hereditary 335.11
    - infantile 335.0
    - juvenile 335.11
  - syphilitic 095.6
- myocardium (*see also* Degeneration, myocardial) 429.1
- myometrium (senile) 621.8
  - cervix 622.8
- myotatic 728.2
- myotonia 359.21
- nail 703.8
  - congenital 757.5
- nasopharynx 472.2
- nerve (*see also* Disorder, nerve)
  - abducens 378.54
  - accessory 352.4
  - acoustic or auditory 388.5
  - cranial 352.9
    - first (olfactory) 352.0
    - second (optic) (*see also* Atrophy, optic nerve) 377.10
    - third (oculomotor) (partial) 378.51
      - total 378.52
    - fourth (trochlear) 378.53
    - fifth (trigeminal) 350.8
    - sixth (abducens) 378.54
    - seventh (facial) 351.8
    - eighth (auditory) 388.5
    - ninth (glossopharyngeal) 352.2
    - tenth (pneumogastric) (vagus) 352.3
    - eleventh (accessory) 352.4
    - twelfth (hypoglossal) 352.5
  - facial 351.8
  - glossopharyngeal 352.2
  - hypoglossal 352.5
  - oculomotor (partial) 378.51
    - total 378.52
  - olfactory 352.0
  - peripheral 355.9
  - pneumogastric 352.3
  - trigeminal 350.8
  - trochlear 378.53
  - vagus (pneumogastric) 352.3
- nervous system, congenital 742.8
- neuritic (*see also* Disorder, nerve) 355.9
- neurogenic NEC 355.9
  - bone
    - tabetic 094.0
- nutritional 261
- old age 797
- olivopontocerebellar 333.0

Atrophy, atrophic — continued
  optic nerve (ascending) (descending) (infectional) (nonfamilial) (papillomacular bundle) (postretinal) (secondary NEC) (simple) 377.10
    associated with retinal dystrophy 377.13
    dominant hereditary 377.16
    glaucomatous 377.14
    hereditary (dominant) (Leber's) 377.16
    Leber's (hereditary) 377.16
    partial 377.15
    postinflammatory 377.12
    primary 377.11
    syphilitic 094.84
      congenital 090.49
      tabes dorsalis 094.0
  orbit 376.45
  ovary (senile), acquired 620.3
  oviduct (senile), acquired 620.3
  palsy, diffuse 335.20
  pancreas (duct) (senile) 577.8
  papillary muscle 429.81
  paralysis 355.9
  parotid gland 527.0
  patches skin 701.3
    senile 701.8
  penis 607.89
  pharyngitis 472.1
  pharynx 478.29
  pluriglandular 258.8
  polyarthritis 714.0
  prostate 602.2
  pseudohypertrophic 359.1
  renal (see also Sclerosis, renal) 587
  reticulata 701.8
  retina (see also Degeneration, retina) 362.60
    hereditary (see also Dystrophy, retina) 362.70
  rhinitis 472.0
  salivary duct or gland 527.0
  scar NEC 709.2
  sclerosis, lobar (of brain) 331.0
    with dementia
      with behavioral disturbance 331.0 [294.11]
      without behavioral disturbance 331.0 [294.10]
  scrotum 608.89
  seminal vesicle 608.89
  senile 797
    degenerative, of skin 701.3
  skin (patches) (senile) 701.8
  spermatic cord 608.89
  spinal (cord) 336.8
    acute 336.8
    muscular (chronic) 335.10
      adult 335.19
      familial 335.11
      juvenile 335.10
    paralysis 335.10
      acute (see also Poliomyelitis, with paralysis) 045.1 ☑
  spine (column) 733.99
  spleen (senile) 289.59
  spots (skin) 701.3
    senile 701.8
  stomach 537.89
  striate and macular 701.3
    syphilitic 095.8
  subcutaneous 701.9
    due to injection 999.9
  sublingual gland 527.0
  submaxillary gland 527.0
  Sudeck's 733.7
  suprarenal (autoimmune) (capsule) (gland) 255.41
    with hypofunction 255.41
  tarso-orbital fascia, congenital 743.66
  testis 608.3
  thenar, partial 354.0
  throat 478.29
  thymus (fat) 254.8
  thyroid (gland) 246.8
    with
      cretinism 243
      myxedema 244.9

Atrophy, atrophic — continued
  thyroid — continued
    congenital 243
  tongue (senile) 529.8
    papillae 529.4
    smooth 529.4
  trachea 519.19
  tunica vaginalis 608.89
  turbinate 733.99
  tympanic membrane (nonflaccid) 384.82
    flaccid 384.81
  ulcer (see also Ulcer, skin) 707.9
  upper respiratory tract 478.9
  uterus, uterine (acquired) (senile) 621.8
    cervix 622.8
    due to radiation (intended effect) 621.8
  vagina (senile) 627.3
  vascular 459.89
  vas deferens 608.89
  vertebra (senile) 733.99
  vulva (primary) (senile) 624.1
  Werdnig-Hoffmann 335.0
  yellow (acute) (congenital) (liver) (subacute) (see also Necrosis, liver) 570
    chronic 571.8
    resulting from administration of blood, plasma, serum, or other biological substance (within 8 months of administration) — see Hepatitis, viral

Attack
  akinetic (see also Epilepsy) 345.0 ☑
  angina — see Angina
  apoplectic (see also Disease, cerebrovascular, acute) 436
  benign shuddering 333.93
  bilious — see Vomiting
  cataleptic 300.11
  cerebral (see also Disease, cerebrovascular, acute) 436
  coronary (see also Infarct, myocardium) 410.9 ☑
  cyanotic, newborn 770.83
  epileptic (see also Epilepsy) 345.9 ☑
  epileptiform 780.39
  heart (see also Infarct, myocardium) 410.9 ☑
  hemiplegia (see also Disease, cerebrovascular, acute) 436
  hysterical 300.11
  jacksonian (see also Epilepsy) 345.5 ☑
  myocardium, myocardial (see also Infarct, myocardium) 410.9 ☑
  myoclonic (see also Epilepsy) 345.1 ☑
  panic 300.01
  paralysis (see also Disease, cerebrovascular, acute) 436
  paroxysmal 780.39
  psychomotor (see also Epilepsy) 345.4 ☑
  salaam (see also Epilepsy) 345.6 ☑
  schizophreniform (see also Schizophrenia) 295.4 ☑
  sensory and motor 780.39
  syncope 780.2
  toxic, cerebral 780.39
  transient ischemic (TIA) 435.9
  unconsciousness 780.2
    hysterical 300.11
  vasomotor 780.2
  vasovagal (idiopathic) (paroxysmal) 780.2

Attention to
  artificial opening (of) V55.9
    digestive tract NEC V55.4
    specified site NEC V55.8
    urinary tract NEC V55.6
    vagina V55.7
  colostomy V55.3
  cystostomy V55.5
  dressing
    wound V58.30
      nonsurgical V58.30
      surgical V58.31
  gastrostomy V55.1
  ileostomy V55.2
  jejunostomy V55.4
  nephrostomy V55.6

Attention to — continued
  surgical dressings V58.31
  sutures V58.32
  tracheostomy V55.0
  ureterostomy V55.6
  urethrostomy V55.6

Attrition
  gum (see also Recession, gingival) 523.20
  teeth (hard tissues) 521.10
    excessive 521.10
      extending into
        dentine 521.12
        pulp 521.13
      generalized 521.15
      limited to enamel 521.11
      localized 521.14

Atypical — see also condition
  cells
    endocervical 795.00
    endometrial 795.00
    glandular
      anus 796.70
      cervical 795.00
      vaginal 795.10
  distribution, vessel (congenital) (peripheral) NEC 747.60
  endometrium 621.9
  kidney 593.89

Atypism, cervix 622.10

Audible tinnitus — see also Tinnitus 388.30

Auditory — see condition

Audry's syndrome (acropachyderma) 757.39

Aujeszky's disease 078.89

Aura
  jacksonian (see also Epilepsy) 345.5 ☑
  persistent migraine 346.5 ☑
    with cerebral infarction 346.6 ☑
    without cerebral infarction 346.5 ☑

Aurantiasis, cutis 278.3

Auricle, auricular — see condition

Auriculotemporal syndrome 350.8

Australian
  Q fever 083.0
  X disease 062.4

Autism, autistic (child) (infantile) 299.0 ☑

Autodigestion 799.89

Autoerythrocyte sensitization 287.2

Autographism 708.3

Autoimmune
  cold sensitivity 283.0
  disease NEC 279.49
  hemolytic anemia 283.0
  inhibitors to clotting factors 286.52
  lymphoproliferative syndrome (ALPS) 279.41
  thyroiditis 245.2

Autoinfection, septic — see Septicemia

Autointoxication 799.89

Automatism 348.89
  with temporal sclerosis 348.81
  epileptic (see also Epilepsy) 345.4 ☑
  paroxysmal, idiopathic (see also Epilepsy) 345.4 ☑

Autonomic, autonomous
  bladder 596.54
    neurogenic 596.54
      with cauda equina 344.61
  dysreflexia 337.3
  faciocephalalgia (see also Neuropathy, peripheral, autonomic) 337.9
  hysterical seizure 300.11
  imbalance (see also Neuropathy, peripheral, autonomic) 337.9

Autophony 388.40

Autosensitivity, erythrocyte 287.2

Autotopagnosia 780.99

Autotoxemia 799.89

Autumn — see condition

Avellis' syndrome 344.89

Aversion
  oral 783.3
    newborn 779.31
    nonorganic origin 307.59

Aviators
  disease or sickness (see also Effect, adverse, high altitude) 993.2

Aviators — continued
  ear 993.0
  effort syndrome 306.2

Avitaminosis (multiple NEC) — see also Deficiency, vitamin 269.2
  A 264.9
  B 266.9
    with
      beriberi 265.0
      pellagra 265.2
  B_1 265.1
  B_2 266.0
  B_6 266.1
  B_{12} 266.2
  C (with scurvy) 267
  D 268.9
    with
      osteomalacia 268.2
      rickets 268.0
  E 269.1
  G 266.0
  H 269.1
  K 269.0
  multiple 269.2
  nicotinic acid 265.2
  P 269.1

Avulsion (traumatic) 879.8
  blood vessel — see Injury, blood vessel, by site
  cartilage (see also Dislocation, by site)
    knee, current (see also Tear, meniscus) 836.2
    symphyseal (inner), complicating delivery 665.6 ☑
  complicated 879.9
  diaphragm — see Injury, internal, diaphragm
  ear — see Wound, open, ear
  epiphysis of bone — see Fracture, by site
  external site other than limb — see Wound, open, by site
  eye 871.3
  fingernail — see Wound, open, finger
  fracture — see Fracture, by site
  genital organs, external — see Wound, open, genital organs
  head (intracranial) NEC (see also Injury, intracranial, with open intracranial wound)
    complete 874.9
    external site NEC 873.8
      complicated 873.9
  internal organ or site — see Injury, internal, by site
  joint (see also Dislocation, by site)
    capsule — see Sprain, by site
  ligament — see Sprain, by site
  limb (see also Amputation, traumatic, by site)
    skin and subcutaneous tissue — see Wound, open, by site
  muscle — see Sprain, by site
  nerve (root) — see Injury, nerve, by site
  scalp — see Wound, open, scalp
  skin and subcutaneous tissue — see Wound, open, by site
  symphyseal cartilage (inner), complicating delivery 665.6 ☑
  tendon (see also Sprain, by site)
    with open wound — see Wound, open, by site
  toenail — see Wound, open, toe(s)
  tooth 873.63
    complicated 873.73

Awaiting organ transplant status V49.83

Awareness of heart beat 785.1

Axe grinders' disease 502

Axenfeld's anomaly or syndrome 743.44

Axilla, axillary — see also condition
  breast 757.6

Axonotmesis — see Injury, nerve, by site

Ayala's disease 756.89

Ayerza's disease or syndrome (pulmonary artery sclerosis with pulmonary hypertension) 416.0

☑ Additional Digit Required — Refer to the Tabular List for Digit Selection   ▽ Subterms under main terms may continue to next column or page

32 — Volume 2   ▶◀ Revised Text   ● New Line   ▲ Revised Code   2015 ICD-9-CM

Azoospermia 606.0
Azorean disease (of the nervous system) 334.8
Azotemia 790.6
    meaning uremia (see also Uremia) 586
Aztec ear 744.29
Azygos lobe, lung (fissure) 748.69

B

Baader's syndrome (erythema multiforme exudativum) 695.19
Baastrup's syndrome 721.5
Babesiasis 088.82
Babesiosis 088.82
Babington's disease (familial hemorrhagic telangiectasia) 448.0
Babinski-Fröhlich syndrome (adiposogenital dystrophy) 253.8
Babinski-Nageotte syndrome 344.89
Babinski's syndrome (cardiovascular syphilis) 093.89
Bacillary — see condition
Bacilluria 791.9
    asymptomatic, in pregnancy or puerperium 646.5 ☑
    tuberculous (see also Tuberculosis) 016.9 ☑
Bacillus — see also Infection, bacillus
    abortus infection 023.1
    anthracis infection 022.9
    coli
        infection 041.49
            generalized 038.42
            intestinal 008.00
        pyemia 038.42
        septicemia 038.42
    Flexner's 004.1
    fusiformis infestation 101
    mallei infection 024
    Shiga's 004.0
    suipestifer infection (see also Infection, Salmonella) 003.9
Back — see condition
Backache (postural) 724.5
    psychogenic 307.89
    sacroiliac 724.6
Backflow (pyelovenous) — see also Disease, renal 593.9
Backknee — see also Genu, recurvatum 736.5
Bacteremia 790.7
    newborn 771.83
Bacteria
    in blood (see also Bacteremia) 790.7
    in urine (see also Bacteriuria) 599.0
Bacterial — see condition
Bactericholia — see also Cholecystitis, acute 575.0
Bacterid, bacteride (Andrews' pustular) 686.8
Bacteriuria, bacteruria 791.9
    with
        urinary tract infection 599.0
    asymptomatic 791.9
        in pregnancy or puerperium 646.5 ☑
            affecting fetus or newborn 760.1
Bad
    breath 784.99
    heart — see Disease, heart
    trip (see also Abuse, drugs, nondependent) 305.3 ☑
Baehr-Schiffrin disease (thrombotic thrombocytopenic purpura) 446.6
Baelz's disease (cheilitis glandularis apostematosa) 528.5
Baerensprung's disease (eczema marginatum) 110.3
Bagassosis (occupational) 495.1
Baghdad boil 085.1
Bagratuni's syndrome (temporal arteritis) 446.5
Baker's
    cyst (knee) 727.51
        tuberculous (see also Tuberculosis) 015.2 ☑
    itch 692.89
Bakwin-Krida syndrome (craniometaphyseal dysplasia) 756.89
Balanitis (circinata) (gangraenosa) (infectious) (vulgaris) 607.1

Balanitis — continued
    amebic 006.8
    candidal 112.2
    chlamydial 099.53
    due to Ducrey's bacillus 099.0
    erosiva circinata et gangraenosa 607.1
    gangrenous 607.1
    gonococcal (acute) 098.0
        chronic or duration of 2 months or over 098.2
    nongonococcal 607.1
    phagedenic 607.1
    venereal NEC 099.8
    xerotica obliterans 607.81
Balanorrhagia — see Balanitis
Balanoposthitis 607.1
    chlamydial 099.53
    gonococcal (acute) 098.0
        chronic or duration of 2 months or over 098.2
    ulcerative NEC 099.8
Balantidiasis 007.0
Balantidiosis 007.0
Balbuties, balbutio — see also Disorder, fluency 315.35
Bald
    patches on scalp 704.00
    tongue 529.4
Baldness — see also Alopecia 704.00
Balfour's disease (chloroma) 205.3 ☑
Balint's syndrome (psychic paralysis of visual fixation) 368.16
Balkan grippe 083.0
Ball
    food 938
    hair 938
Ballantyne (-Runge) syndrome (postmaturity) 766.22
Balloon disease — see also Effect, adverse, high altitude 993.2
Ballooning posterior leaflet syndrome 424.0
Baló's disease or concentric sclerosis 341.1
Bamberger's disease (hypertrophic pulmonary osteoarthropathy) 731.2
Bamberger-Marie disease (hypertrophic pulmonary osteoarthropathy) 731.2
Bamboo spine 720.0
Bancroft's filariasis 125.0
Band(s)
    adhesive (see also Adhesions, peritoneum) 568.0
    amniotic 658.8 ☑
        affecting fetus or newborn 762.8
    anomalous or congenital (see also Anomaly, specified type NEC)
        atrial 746.9
        heart 746.9
        intestine 751.4
        omentum 751.4
        ventricular 746.9
    cervix 622.3
    gallbladder (congenital) 751.69
    intestinal (adhesive) (see also Adhesions, peritoneum) 568.0
        congenital 751.4
    obstructive (see also Obstruction, intestine) 560.81
    periappendiceal (congenital) 751.4
    peritoneal (adhesive) (see also Adhesions, peritoneum) 568.0
        with intestinal obstruction 560.81
        congenital 751.4
    uterus 621.5
    vagina 623.2
Bandemia (without diagnosis of specific infection) 288.66
Bandl's ring (contraction)
    complicating delivery 661.4 ☑
        affecting fetus or newborn 763.7
Bang's disease (Brucella abortus) 023.1
Bangkok hemorrhagic fever 065.4
Bannister's disease 995.1
Bantam-Albright-Martin disease (pseudohypoparathyroidism) 275.49

Banti's disease or syndrome (with cirrhosis) (with portal hypertension) — see Cirrhosis, liver
Bar
    calcaneocuboid 755.67
    calcaneonavicular 755.67
    cubonavicular 755.67
    prostate 600.90
        with
            other lower urinary tract symptoms (LUTS) 600.91
        urinary
            obstruction 600.91
            retention 600.91
    talocalcaneal 755.67
Baragnosis 780.99
Barasheh, barashek 266.2
Barcoo disease or rot — see also Ulcer, skin 707.9
Bard-Pic syndrome (carcinoma, head of pancreas) 157.0
Bärensprung's disease (eczema marginatum) 110.3
Baritosis 503
Barium lung disease 503
Barlow (-Möller) disease or syndrome (meaning infantile scurvy) 267
Barlow's syndrome (meaning mitral valve prolapse) 424.0
Barodontalgia 993.2
Baron Münchausen syndrome 301.51
Barosinusitis 993.1
Barotitis 993.0
Barotrauma 993.2
    odontalgia 993.2
    otitic 993.0
    sinus 993.1
Barraquer's disease or syndrome (progressive lipodystrophy) 272.6
Barré-Guillain syndrome 357.0
Barrel chest 738.3
Barré-Liéou syndrome (posterior cervical sympathetic) 723.2
Barrett's esophagus 530.85
Barrett's syndrome or ulcer (chronic peptic ulcer of esophagus) 530.85
Bársony-Polgár syndrome (corkscrew esophagus) 530.5
Bársony-Teschendorf syndrome (corkscrew esophagus) 530.5
Bartholin's
    adenitis (see also Bartholinitis) 616.89
    gland — see condition
Bartholinitis (suppurating) 616.89
    gonococcal (acute) 098.0
        chronic or duration of 2 months or over 098.2
Barth syndrome 759.89
Bartonellosis 088.0
Bartter's syndrome (secondary hyperaldosteronism with juxtaglomerular hyperplasia) 255.13
Basal — see condition
Basan's (hidrotic) ectodermal dysplasia 757.31
Baseball finger 842.13
Basedow's disease or syndrome (exophthalmic goiter) 242.0 ☑
Basic — see condition
Basilar — see condition
Bason's (hidrotic) ectodermal dysplasia 757.31
Basopenia 288.59
Basophilia 288.65
Basophilism (corticoadrenal) (Cushing's) (pituitary) (thymic) 255.0
Bassen-Kornzweig syndrome (abetalipoproteinemia) 272.5
Bat ear 744.29
Bateman's
    disease 078.0
    purpura (senile) 287.2
Bathing cramp 994.1
Bathophobia 300.23
Batten's disease, retina 330.1 [362.71]
Batten-Mayou disease 330.1 [362.71]

Batten-Steinert syndrome 359.21
Battered
    adult (syndrome) 995.81
    baby or child (syndrome) 995.54
    spouse (syndrome) 995.81
Battey mycobacterium infection 031.0
Battledore placenta — see Placenta, abnormal
Battle exhaustion — see also Reaction, stress, acute 308.9
Baumgarten-Cruveilhier (cirrhosis) disease, or syndrome 571.5
Bauxite
    fibrosis (of lung) 503
    workers' disease 503
Bayle's disease (dementia paralytica) 094.1
Bazin's disease (primary) — see also Tuberculosis 017.1 ☑
Beach ear 380.12
Beaded hair (congenital) 757.4
Beals syndrome 759.82
Beard's disease (neurasthenia) 300.5
Bearn-Kunkel (-Slater) syndrome (lupoid hepatitis) 571.49
Beat
    elbow 727.2
    hand 727.2
    knee 727.2
Beats
    ectopic 427.60
    escaped, heart 427.60
        postoperative 997.1
    premature (nodal) 427.60
        atrial 427.61
        auricular 427.61
        postoperative 997.1
        specified type NEC 427.69
        supraventricular 427.61
        ventricular 427.69
Beau's
    disease or syndrome (see also Degeneration, myocardial) 429.1
    lines (transverse furrows on fingernails) 703.8
Bechterew's disease (ankylosing spondylitis) 720.0
Bechterew-Strümpell-Marie syndrome (ankylosing spondylitis) 720.0
Becker's
    disease
        idiopathic mural endomyocardial disease 425.2
        myotonia congenita, recessive form 359.22
    dystrophy 359.22
Beck's syndrome (anterior spinal artery occlusion) 433.8 ☑
Beckwith (-Wiedemann) syndrome 759.89
Bedbugs bite(s) — see Injury, superficial, by site
Bedclothes, asphyxiation or suffocation by 994.7
Bed confinement status V49.84
Bednar's aphthae 528.2
Bedsore (see also Ulcer, pressure) 707.00
    with gangrene 707.00 [785.4]
Bedwetting — see also Enuresis 788.36
Beer-drinkers' heart (disease) 425.5
Bee sting (with allergic or anaphylactic shock) 989.5
Begbie's disease (exophthalmic goiter) 242.0 ☑
Behavior disorder, disturbance — see also Disturbance, conduct
    antisocial, without manifest psychiatric disorder
        adolescent V71.02
        adult V71.01
        child V71.02
    dyssocial, without manifest psychiatric disorder
        adolescent V71.02
        adult V71.01
        child V71.02
    high risk — see Problem
Behçet's syndrome 136.1
Behr's disease 362.50

☑ Additional Digit Required — Refer to the Tabular List for Digit Selection   ▽ Subterms under main terms may continue to next column or page

2015 ICD-9-CM   ►◄ Revised Text   ● New Line   ▲ Revised Code   Volume 2 — 33

Beigel's disease or morbus (white piedra) 111.2
Bejel 104.0
Bekhterev's disease (ankylosing spondylitis) 720.0
Bekhterev-Strümpell-Marie syndrome (ankylosing spondylitis) 720.0
Belching — *see also* Eructation 787.3
Bell's
　disease (*see also* Psychosis, affective) 296.0 ☑
　mania (*see also* Psychosis, affective) 296.0 ☑
　palsy, paralysis 351.0
　　infant 767.5
　　newborn 767.5
　　syphilitic 094.89
　spasm 351.0
Bence-Jones albuminuria, albuminosuria, or proteinuria 791.0
Bends 993.3
Benedikt's syndrome (paralysis) 344.89
Benign — *see also* condition
　cellular changes, cervix 795.09
　prostate
　　with
　　　other lower urinary tract symptoms (LUTS) 600.21
　　　urinary
　　　　obstruction 600.21
　　　　retention 600.21
　　hyperplasia 600.20
　　neoplasm 222.2
Bennett's
　disease (leukemia) 208.9 ☑
　fracture (closed) 815.01
　　open 815.11
Benson's disease 379.22
Bent
　back (hysterical) 300.11
　nose 738.0
　　congenital 754.0
Bereavement V62.82
　as adjustment reaction 309.0
Bergeron's disease (hysteroepilepsy) 300.11
Berger's paresthesia (lower limb) 782.0
Beriberi (acute) (atrophic) (chronic) (dry) (subacute) (wet) 265.0
　with polyneuropathy 265.0 [357.4]
　heart (disease) 265.0 [425.7]
　leprosy 030.1
　neuritis 265.0 [357.4]
Berlin's disease or edema (traumatic) 921.3
Berloque dermatitis 692.72
Bernard-Horner syndrome — *see also* Neuropathy, peripheral, autonomic 337.9
Bernard-Sergent syndrome (acute adrenocortical insufficiency) 255.41
Bernard-Soulier disease or thrombopathy 287.1
Bernhardt's disease or paresthesia 355.1
Bernhardt-Roth disease or syndrome (paresthesia) 355.1
Bernheim's syndrome — *see also* Failure, heart 428.0
Bertielliasis 123.8
Bertolotti's syndrome (sacralization of fifth lumbar vertebra) 756.15
Berylliosis (acute) (chronic) (lung) (occupational) 503
Besnier's
　lupus pernio 135
　prurigo (atopic dermatitis) (infantile eczema) 691.8
Besnier-Boeck disease or sarcoid 135
Besnier-Boeck-Schaumann disease (sarcoidosis) 135
Best's disease 362.76
Bestiality 302.1
Beta-adrenergic hyperdynamic circulatory state 429.82
Beta-aminoisobutyric aciduria 277.2
Beta-mercaptolactate-cysteine disulfiduria 270.0
Beta thalassemia (mixed) 282.44
　major 282.44
　minor 282.46

Beurmann's disease (sporotrichosis) 117.1
Bezoar 938
　intestine 936
　stomach 935.2
Bezold's abscess — *see also* Mastoiditis 383.01
Bianchi's syndrome (aphasia-apraxia-alexia) 784.69
Bicornuate or bicornis uterus (complete) (partial) 752.34
　in pregnancy or childbirth 654.0 ☑
　　with obstructed labor 660.2 ☑
　　　affecting fetus or newborn 763.1
　　affecting fetus or newborn 763.89
Bicuspid aortic valve 746.4
Biedl-Bardet syndrome 759.89
Bielschowsky's disease 330.1
Bielschowsky-Jansky
　amaurotic familial idiocy 330.1
　disease 330.1
Biemond's syndrome (obesity, polydactyly, and intellectual disabilities) 759.89
Biermer's anemia or disease (pernicious anemia) 281.0
Biett's disease 695.4
Bifid (congenital) — *see also* Imperfect, closure
　apex, heart 746.89
　clitoris 752.49
　epiglottis 748.3
　kidney 753.3
　nose 748.1
　patella 755.64
　scrotum 752.89
　toe 755.66
　tongue 750.13
　ureter 753.4
　uterus 752.34
　uvula 749.02
　　with cleft lip (*see also* Cleft, palate, with cleft lip) 749.20
Biforis uterus (suprasimplex) 752.34
Bifurcation (congenital) — *see also* Imperfect, closure
　gallbladder 751.69
　kidney pelvis 753.3
　renal pelvis 753.3
　rib 756.3
　tongue 750.13
　trachea 748.3
　ureter 753.4
　urethra 753.8
　uvula 749.02
　　with cleft lip (*see also* Cleft, palate, with cleft lip) 749.20
　vertebra 756.19
Bigeminal pulse 427.89
Bigeminy 427.89
Big spleen syndrome 289.4
Bilateral — *see* condition
Bile duct — *see* condition
Bile pigments in urine 791.4
Bilharziasis — *see also* Schistosomiasis 120.9
　chyluria 120.0
　cutaneous 120.3
　galacturia 120.0
　hematochyluria 120.0
　intestinal 120.1
　lipemia 120.9
　lipuria 120.0
　Oriental 120.2
　piarhemia 120.9
　pulmonary 120.2
　tropical hematuria 120.0
　vesical 120.0
Biliary — *see* condition
Bilious (attack) — *see also* Vomiting
　fever, hemoglobinuric 084.8
Bilirubinuria 791.4
Biliuria 791.4
Billroth's disease
　meningocele (*see also* Spina bifida) 741.9 ☑
Bilobate placenta — *see* Placenta, abnormal
Bilocular
　heart 745.7
　stomach 536.8
Bing-Horton syndrome (histamine cephalgia) 339.00

Binswanger's disease or dementia 290.12
Biörck (-Thorson) syndrome (malignant carcinoid) 259.2
Biparta, bipartite — *see also* Imperfect, closure
　carpal scaphoid 755.59
　patella 755.64
　placenta — *see* Placenta, abnormal
　vagina 752.49
Bird
　face 756.0
　fanciers' lung or disease 495.2
　flu — *see also* Influenza, avian 488.02
Bird's disease (oxaluria) 271.8
Birth
　abnormal fetus or newborn 763.9
　accident, fetus or newborn — *see* Birth, injury
　complications in mother — *see* Delivery, complicated
　compression during NEC 767.9
　defect — *see* Anomaly
　delayed, fetus 763.9
　difficult NEC, affecting fetus or newborn 763.9
　dry, affecting fetus or newborn 761.1
　forced, NEC, affecting fetus or newborn 763.89
　forceps, affecting fetus or newborn 763.2
　hematoma of sternomastoid 767.8
　immature 765.1 ☑
　　extremely 765.0 ☑
　inattention, after or at 995.52
　induced, affecting fetus or newborn 763.89
　infant — *see* Newborn
　injury NEC 767.9
　　adrenal gland 767.8
　　basal ganglia 767.0
　　brachial plexus (paralysis) 767.6
　　brain (compression) (pressure) 767.0
　　cerebellum 767.0
　　cerebral hemorrhage 767.0
　　conjunctiva 767.8
　　eye 767.8
　　fracture
　　　bone, any except clavicle or spine 767.3
　　　clavicle 767.2
　　　femur 767.3
　　　humerus 767.3
　　　long bone 767.3
　　　radius and ulna 767.3
　　　skeleton NEC 767.3
　　　skull 767.3
　　　spine 767.4
　　　tibia and fibula 767.3
　　hematoma 767.8
　　　liver (subcapsular) 767.8
　　　mastoid 767.8
　　　skull 767.19
　　　sternomastoid 767.8
　　　testes 767.8
　　　vulva 767.8
　　intracranial (edema) 767.0
　　laceration
　　　brain 767.0
　　　by scalpel 767.8
　　　peripheral nerve 767.7
　　liver 767.8
　　meninges
　　　brain 767.0
　　　spinal cord 767.4
　　nerves (cranial, peripheral) 767.7
　　　brachial plexus 767.6
　　　facial 767.5
　　paralysis 767.7
　　　brachial plexus 767.6
　　　Erb (-Duchenne) 767.6
　　　facial nerve 767.5
　　　Klumpke (-Déjérine) 767.6
　　　radial nerve 767.6
　　　spinal (cord) (hemorrhage) (laceration) (rupture) 767.4
　　rupture
　　　intracranial 767.0
　　　liver 767.8

Birth — *continued*
　injury — *continued*
　　rupture — *continued*
　　　spinal cord 767.4
　　　spleen 767.8
　　　viscera 767.8
　　scalp 767.19
　　scalpel wound 767.8
　　skeleton NEC 767.3
　　specified NEC 767.8
　　spinal cord 767.4
　　spleen 767.8
　　subdural hemorrhage 767.0
　　tentorial, tear 767.0
　　testes 767.8
　　vulva 767.8
　instrumental, NEC, affecting fetus or newborn 763.2
　lack of care, after or at 995.52
　multiple
　　affected by maternal complications of pregnancy 761.5
　　healthy liveborn — *see* Newborn, multiple
　neglect, after or at 995.52
　newborn — *see* Newborn
　palsy or paralysis NEC 767.7
　precipitate, fetus or newborn 763.6
　premature (infant) 765.1 ☑
　prolonged, affecting fetus or newborn 763.9
　retarded, fetus or newborn 763.9
　shock, newborn 779.89
　strangulation or suffocation
　　due to aspiration of clear amniotic fluid 770.13
　　　with respiratory symptoms 770.14
　　mechanical 767.8
　trauma NEC 767.9
　triplet
　　affected by maternal complications of pregnancy 761.5
　　healthy liveborn — *see* Newborn, multiple
　twin
　　affected by maternal complications of pregnancy 761.5
　　healthy liveborn — *see* Newborn, twin
　ventouse, affecting fetus or newborn 763.3
Birthmark 757.32
Birt-Hogg-Dube syndrome 759.89
Bisalbuminemia 273.8
Biskra button 085.1
Bite(s)
　with intact skin surface — *see* Contusion
　animal — *see* Wound, open, by site
　　intact skin surface — *see* Contusion
　bedbug — *see* Injury, superficial, by site
　centipede 989.5
　chigger 133.8
　fire ant 989.5
　flea — *see* Injury, superficial, by site
　human (open wound) (*see also* Wound, open, by site)
　　intact skin surface — *see* Contusion
　insect
　　nonvenomous — *see* Injury, superficial, by site
　　venomous 989.5
　mad dog (death from) 071
　open
　　anterior 524.24
　　posterior 524.25
　poisonous 989.5
　red bug 133.8
　reptile 989.5
　　nonvenomous — *see* Wound, open, by site
　snake 989.5
　　nonvenomous — *see* Wound, open, by site
　spider (venomous) 989.5
　　nonvenomous — *see* Injury, superficial, by site
　venomous 989.5
Biting
　cheek or lip 528.9

☑ Additional Digit Required — Refer to the Tabular List for Digit Selection　　　▽ Subterms under main terms may continue to next column or page

34 — Volume 2　　▶◀ Revised Text　　● New Line　　▲ Revised Code　　2015 ICD-9-CM

Biting — *continued*
nail 307.9
Black
death 020.9
eye NEC 921.0
hairy tongue 529.3
heel 924.20
lung disease 500
palm 923.20
Blackfan-Diamond anemia or syndrome
(congenital hypoplastic anemia) 284.01
Blackhead 706.1
Blackout 780.2
Blackwater fever 084.8
Bladder — *see* condition
Blast
blindness 921.3
concussion — *see* Blast, injury
injury 869.0
with open wound into cavity 869.1
abdomen or thorax — *see* Injury, internal, by site
brain (*see also* Concussion, brain) 850.9
with skull fracture — *see* Fracture, skull
ear (acoustic nerve trauma) 951.5
with perforation, tympanic membrane — *see* Wound, open, ear, drum
lung (*see also* Injury, internal, lung) 861.20
otitic (explosive) 388.11
Blastomycosis, blastomycotic (chronic) (cutaneous) (disseminated) (lung) (pulmonary) (systemic) 116.0
Brazilian 116.1
European 117.5
keloidal 116.2
North American 116.0
primary pulmonary 116.0
South American 116.1
Bleb(s) 709.8
emphysematous (bullous) (diffuse) (lung) (ruptured) (solitary) 492.0
filtering, eye (postglaucoma) (status) V45.69
with complication 997.99
postcataract extraction (complication) 997.99
lung (ruptured) 492.0
congenital 770.5
subpleural (emphysematous) 492.0
Bleeder (familial) (hereditary) — *see also* Defect, coagulation 286.9
nonfamilial 286.9
Bleeding — *see also* Hemorrhage 459.0
anal 569.3
anovulatory 628.0
atonic, following delivery 666.1 ☑
capillary 448.9
due to subinvolution 621.1
puerperal 666.2 ☑
ear 388.69
excessive, associated with menopausal onset 627.0
familial (*see also* Defect, coagulation) 286.9
following intercourse 626.7
gastrointestinal 578.9
gums 523.8
hemorrhoids — *see* Hemorrhoids, bleeding
intermenstrual
irregular 626.6
regular 626.5
intraoperative 998.11
irregular NEC 626.4
menopausal 627.0
mouth 528.9
nipple 611.79
nose 784.7
ovulation 626.5
postclimacteric 627.1
postcoital 626.7
postmenopausal 627.1
following induced menopause 627.4
postoperative 998.11
preclimacteric 627.0
puberty 626.3

Bleeding — *see also* Hemorrhage — *continued*
puberty — *continued*
excessive, with onset of menstrual periods 626.3
rectum, rectal 569.3
tendencies (*see also* Defect, coagulation) 286.9
throat 784.8
umbilical stump 772.3
umbilicus 789.9
unrelated to menstrual cycle 626.6
uterus, uterine 626.9
climacteric 627.0
dysfunctional 626.8
functional 626.8
unrelated to menstrual cycle 626.6
vagina, vaginal 623.8
functional 626.8
vicarious 625.8
Blennorrhagia, blennorrhagic — *see* Blennorrhea
Blennorrhea (acute) 098.0
adultorum 098.40
alveolaris 523.40
chronic or duration of 2 months or over 098.2
gonococcal (neonatorum) 098.40
inclusion (neonatal) (newborn) 771.6
neonatorum 098.40
Blepharelosis — *see also* Entropion 374.00
Blepharitis (eyelid) 373.00
angularis 373.01
ciliaris 373.00
with ulcer 373.01
marginal 373.00
with ulcer 373.01
scrofulous (*see also* Tuberculosis)
017.3 ☑ [373.00]
squamous 373.02
ulcerative 373.01
Blepharochalasis 374.34
congenital 743.62
Blepharoclonus 333.81
Blepharoconjunctivitis — *see also* Conjunctivitis 372.20
angular 372.21
contact 372.22
Blepharophimosis (eyelid) 374.46
congenital 743.62
Blepharoplegia 374.89
Blepharoptosis 374.30
congenital 743.61
Blepharopyorrhea 098.49
Blepharospasm 333.81
due to drugs 333.85
Blessig's cyst 362.62
Blighted ovum 631.8
Blind
bronchus (congenital) 748.3
eye (*see also* Blindness)
hypertensive 360.42
hypotensive 360.41
loop syndrome (postoperative) 579.2
sac, fallopian tube (congenital) 752.19
spot, enlarged 368.42
tract or tube (congenital) NEC — *see* Atresia
Blindness (acquired) (congenital) (both eyes) 369.00
with deafness V49.85
blast 921.3
with nerve injury — *see* Injury, nerve, optic
Bright's — *see* Uremia
color (congenital) 368.59
acquired 368.55
blue 368.53
green 368.52
red 368.51
total 368.54
concussion 950.9
cortical 377.75
day 368.10
acquired 368.10
congenital 368.10
hereditary 368.10

Blindness — *continued*
day — *continued*
specified type NEC 368.10
due to
injury NEC 950.9
refractive error — *see* Error, refractive
eclipse (total) 363.31
emotional 300.11
face 368.16
hysterical 300.11
legal (both eyes) (USA definition) 369.4
with impairment of better (less impaired) eye
near-total 369.02
with
lesser eye impairment 369.02
near-total 369.04
total 369.03
profound 369.05
with
lesser eye impairment 369.05
near-total 369.07
profound 369.08
total 369.06
severe 369.21
with
lesser eye impairment 369.21
blind 369.11
near-total 369.13
profound 369.14
severe 369.22
total 369.12
total
with lesser eye impairment
total 369.01
mind 784.69
moderate
both eyes 369.25
with impairment of lesser eye (specified as)
blind, not further specified 369.15
low vision, not further specified 369.23
near-total 369.17
profound 369.18
severe 369.24
total 369.16
one eye 369.74
with vision of other eye (specified as)
near-normal 369.75
normal 369.76
near-total
both eyes 369.04
with impairment of lesser eye (specified as)
blind, not further specified 369.02
total 369.03
one eye 369.64
with vision of other eye (specified as)
near-normal 369.65
normal 369.66
night 368.60
acquired 368.62
congenital (Japanese) 368.61
hereditary 368.61
specified type NEC 368.69
vitamin A deficiency 264.5
nocturnal — *see* Blindness, night
one eye 369.60
with low vision of other eye 369.10
profound
both eyes 369.08
with impairment of lesser eye (specified as)
blind, not further specified 369.05
near-total 369.07
total 369.06
one eye 369.67
with vision of other eye (specified as)
near-normal 369.68
normal 369.69
psychic 784.69
severe
both eyes 369.22

Blindness — *continued*
severe — *continued*
both eyes — *continued*
with impairment of lesser eye (specified as)
blind, not further specified 369.11
low vision, not further specified 369.21
near-total 369.13
profound 369.14
total 369.12
one eye 369.71
with vision of other eye (specified as)
near-normal 369.72
normal 369.73
snow 370.24
sun 363.31
temporary 368.12
total
both eyes 369.01
one eye 369.61
with vision of other eye (specified as)
near-normal 369.62
normal 369.63
transient 368.12
traumatic NEC 950.9
word (developmental) 315.01
acquired 784.61
secondary to organic lesion 784.61
Blister — *see also* Injury, superficial, by site
beetle dermatitis 692.89
due to burn — *see* Burn, by site, second degree
fever 054.9
fracture — *omit code*
multiple, skin, nontraumatic 709.8
Bloating 787.3
Bloch-Siemens syndrome (incontinentia pigmenti) 757.33
Bloch-Stauffer dyshormonal dermatosis 757.33
Bloch-Sulzberger disease or syndrome (incontinentia pigmenti) (melanoblastosis) 757.33
Block
alveolar capillary 516.8
arborization (heart) 426.6
arrhythmic 426.9
atrioventricular (AV) (incomplete) (partial) 426.10
with
2:1 atrioventricular response block 426.13
atrioventricular dissociation 426.0
first degree (incomplete) 426.11
second degree (Mobitz type I) 426.13
Mobitz (type) II 426.12
third degree 426.0
complete 426.0
congenital 746.86
congenital 746.86
Mobitz (incomplete)
type I (Wenckebach's) 426.13
type II 426.12
partial 426.13
auriculoventricular (*see also* Block, atrioventricular) 426.10
complete 426.0
congenital 746.86
congenital 746.86
bifascicular (cardiac) 426.53
bundle branch (complete) (false) (incomplete) 426.50
bilateral 426.53
left (complete) (main stem) 426.3
with right bundle branch block 426.53
anterior fascicular 426.2
with
posterior fascicular block 426.3
right bundle branch block 426.52
hemiblock 426.2
incomplete 426.2

☑ **Additional Digit Required** — Refer to the Tabular List for Digit Selection   ▽ **Subterms under main terms may continue to next column or page**

2015 ICD-9-CM   ▶◀ Revised Text   ● New Line   ▲ Revised Code   Volume 2 — 35

Block — *continued*
- bundle branch — *continued*
  - left — *continued*
    - incomplete — *continued*
      - with right bundle branch block 426.53
    - posterior fascicular 426.2
      - with
        - anterior fascicular block 426.3
        - right bundle branch block 426.51
    - right 426.4
      - with
        - left bundle branch block (incomplete) (main stem) 426.53
        - left fascicular block 426.53
          - anterior 426.52
          - posterior 426.51
    - Wilson's type 426.4
  - cardiac 426.9
  - conduction 426.9
    - complete 426.0
  - Eustachian tube (*see also* Obstruction, Eustachian tube) 381.60
  - fascicular (left anterior) (left posterior) 426.2
  - foramen Magendie (acquired) 331.3
    - congenital 742.3
      - with spina bifida (*see also* Spina bifida) 741.0 ☑
  - heart 426.9
    - first degree (atrioventricular) 426.11
    - second degree (atrioventricular) 426.13
    - third degree (atrioventricular) 426.0
    - bundle branch (complete) (false) (incomplete) 426.50
      - bilateral 426.53
      - left (*see also* Block, bundle branch, left) 426.3
      - right (*see also* Block, bundle branch, right) 426.4
    - complete (atrioventricular) 426.0
    - congenital 746.86
    - incomplete 426.13
    - intra-atrial 426.6
    - intraventricular NEC 426.6
    - sinoatrial 426.6
    - specified type NEC 426.6
  - hepatic vein 453.0
  - intraventricular (diffuse) (myofibrillar) 426.6
    - bundle branch (complete) (false) (incomplete) 426.50
      - bilateral 426.53
      - left (*see also* Block, bundle branch, left) 426.3
      - right (*see also* Block, bundle branch, right) 426.4
  - kidney (*see also* Disease, renal) 593.9
    - postcystoscopic 997.5
  - myocardial (*see also* Block, heart) 426.9
  - nodal 426.10
  - optic nerve 377.49
  - organ or site (congenital) NEC — *see* Atresia
  - parietal 426.6
  - peri-infarction 426.6
  - portal (vein) 452
  - sinoatrial 426.6
  - sinoauricular 426.6
  - spinal cord 336.9
  - trifascicular 426.54
  - tubal 628.2
  - vein NEC 453.9

Blocq's disease or syndrome (astasia-abasia) 307.9

Blood
- constituents, abnormal NEC 790.6
- disease 289.9
  - specified NEC 289.89
- donor V59.01
  - other blood components V59.09
  - stem cells V59.02
  - whole blood V59.01
- dyscrasia 289.9
  - with
    - abortion — *see* Abortion, by type, with hemorrhage, delayed or excessive

Blood — *continued*
- dyscrasia — *continued*
  - with — *continued*
    - ectopic pregnancy (*see also* categories 633.0–633.9) 639.1
    - molar pregnancy (*see also* categories 630–632) 639.1
  - following
    - abortion 639.1
    - ectopic or molar pregnancy 639.1
  - newborn NEC 776.9
  - puerperal, postpartum 666.3 ☑
- flukes NEC (*see also* Infestation, Schistosoma) 120.9
- in
  - feces (*see also* Melena) 578.1
    - occult 792.1
  - urine (*see also* Hematuria) 599.70
- mole 631.8
- occult 792.1
- poisoning (*see also* Septicemia) 038.9
- pressure
  - decreased, due to shock following injury 958.4
  - fluctuating 796.4
  - high (*see also* Hypertension) 401.9
    - borderline 796.2
      - incidental reading (isolated) (nonspecific), without diagnosis of hypertension 796.2
  - low (*see also* Hypotension) 458.9
    - incidental reading (isolated) (nonspecific), without diagnosis of hypotension 796.3
- spitting (*see also* Hemoptysis) 786.30
- staining cornea 371.12
- transfusion
  - without reported diagnosis V58.2
  - donor V59.01
    - stem cells V59.02
  - reaction or complication — *see* Complications, transfusion
- tumor — *see* Hematoma
- vessel rupture — *see* Hemorrhage
- vomiting (*see also* Hematemesis) 578.0

Blood-forming organ disease 289.9
Bloodgood's disease 610.1
Bloodshot eye 379.93
Bloom (-Machacek) (-Torre) syndrome 757.39
Blotch, palpebral 372.55
Blount-Barber syndrome (tibia vara) 732.4
Blount's disease (tibia vara) 732.4
Blue
- baby 746.9
- bloater 491.20
  - with
    - acute bronchitis 491.22
    - exacerbation (acute) 491.21
- diaper syndrome 270.0
- disease 746.9
- dome cyst 610.0
- drum syndrome 381.02
- sclera 743.47
  - with fragility of bone and deafness 756.51
- toe syndrome 445.02

Blueness — *see also* Cyanosis 782.5
Blurring, visual 368.8
Blushing (abnormal) (excessive) 782.62
BMI (body mass index)
- adult
  - 25.0-25.9 V85.21
  - 26.0-26.9 V85.22
  - 27.0-27.9 V85.23
  - 28.0-28.9 V85.24
  - 29.0-29.9 V85.25
  - 30.0-30.9 V85.30
  - 31.0-31.9 V85.31
  - 32.0-32.9 V85.32
  - 33.0-33.9 V85.33
  - 34.0-34.9 V85.34
  - 35.0-35.9 V85.35
  - 36.0-36.9 V85.36
  - 37.0-37.9 V85.37
  - 38.0-38.9 V85.38
  - 39.0-39.9 V85.39

BMI — *continued*
- adult — *continued*
  - 40.0-44.9 V85.41
  - 45.0-49.9 V85.42
  - 50.0-59.9 V85.43
  - 60.0-69.9 V85.44
  - 70 and over V85.45
  - between 19-24 V85.1
  - less than 19 V85.0
- pediatric
  - 5th percentile to less than 85th percentile for age V85.52
  - 85th percentile to less than 95th percentile for age V85.53
  - greater than or equal to 95th percentile for age V85.54
  - less than 5th percentile for age V85.51

Boarder, hospital V65.0
- infant V65.0

Bockhart's impetigo (superficial folliculitis) 704.8
Bodechtel-Guttmann disease (subacute sclerosing panencephalitis) 046.2
Boder-Sedgwick syndrome (ataxia-telangiectasia) 334.8
Body, bodies
- Aschoff (*see also* Myocarditis, rheumatic) 398.0
- asteroid, vitreous 379.22
- choroid, colloid (degenerative) 362.57
  - hereditary 362.77
- cytoid (retina) 362.82
- drusen (retina) (*see also* Drusen) 362.57
  - optic disc 377.21
- fibrin, pleura 511.0
- foreign — *see* Foreign body
- Hassall-Henle 371.41
- loose
  - joint (*see also* Loose, body, joint) 718.1 ☑
    - knee 717.6
  - knee 717.6
  - sheath, tendon 727.82
- Mallory's 034.1
- mass index (BMI)
  - adult
    - 25.0-25.9 V85.21
    - 26.0-26.9 V85.22
    - 27.0-27.9 V85.23
    - 28.0-28.9 V85.24
    - 29.0-29.9 V85.25
    - 30.0-30.9 V85.30
    - 31.0-31.9 V85.31
    - 32.0-32.9 V85.32
    - 33.0-33.9 V85.33
    - 34.0-34.9 V85.34
    - 35.0-35.9 V85.35
    - 36.0-36.9 V85.36
    - 37.0-37.9 V85.37
    - 38.0-38.9 V85.38
    - 39.0-39.9 V85.39
    - 40.0-44.9 V85.41
    - 45.0-49.9 V85.42
    - 50.0-59.9 V85.43
    - 60.0-69.9 V85.44
    - 70 and over V85.45
    - between 19-24 V85.1
    - less than 19 V85.0
  - pediatric
    - 5th percentile to less than 85th percentile for age V85.52
    - 85th percentile to less than 95th percentile for age V85.53
    - greater than or equal to 95th percentile for age V85.54
    - less than 5th percentile for age V85.51
- Mooser 081.0
- Negri 071
- rice (joint) (*see also* Loose, body, joint) 718.1 ☑
  - knee 717.6
- rocking 307.3

Boeck's
- disease (sarcoidosis) 135
- lupoid (miliary) 135

Boeck's — *continued*
- sarcoid 135

Boerhaave's syndrome (spontaneous esophageal rupture) 530.4
Boggy
- cervix 622.8
- uterus 621.8

Boil — *see also* Carbuncle 680.9
- abdominal wall 680.2
- Aleppo 085.1
- ankle 680.6
- anus 680.5
- arm (any part, above wrist) 680.3
- auditory canal, external 680.0
- axilla 680.3
- back (any part) 680.2
- Baghdad 085.1
- breast 680.2
- buttock 680.5
- chest wall 680.2
- corpus cavernosum 607.2
- Delhi 085.1
- ear (any part) 680.0
- eyelid 373.13
- face (any part, except eye) 680.0
- finger (any) 680.4
- flank 680.2
- foot (any part) 680.7
- forearm 680.3
- Gafsa 085.1
- genital organ, male 608.4
- gluteal (region) 680.5
- groin 680.2
- hand (any part) 680.4
- head (any part, except face) 680.8
- heel 680.7
- hip 680.6
- knee 680.6
- labia 616.4
- lacrimal (*see also* Dacryocystitis) 375.30
  - gland (*see also* Dacryoadenitis) 375.00
  - passages (duct) (sac) (*see also* Dacryocystitis) 375.30
- leg, any part, except foot 680.6
- multiple sites 680.9
- natal 085.1
- neck 680.1
- nose (external) (septum) 680.0
- orbit, orbital 376.01
- partes posteriores 680.5
- pectoral region 680.2
- penis 607.2
- perineum 680.2
- pinna 680.0
- scalp (any part) 680.8
- scrotum 608.4
- seminal vesicle 608.0
- shoulder 680.3
- skin NEC 680.9
- specified site NEC 680.8
- spermatic cord 608.4
- temple (region) 680.0
- testis 608.4
- thigh 680.6
- thumb 680.4
- toe (any) 680.7
- tropical 085.1
- trunk 680.2
- tunica vaginalis 608.4
- umbilicus 680.2
- upper arm 680.3
- vas deferens 608.4
- vulva 616.4
- wrist 680.4

Bold hives — *see also* Urticaria 708.9
Bolivian hemorrhagic fever 078.7
Bombé, iris 364.74
Bomford-Rhoads anemia (refractory) 238.72
Bone — *see* condition
Bonnevie-Ullrich syndrome 758.6
Bonnier's syndrome 386.19
Bonvale Dam fever 780.79
Bony block of joint 718.80
- ankle 718.87
- elbow 718.82
- foot 718.87

☑ **Additional Digit Required** — Refer to the Tabular List for Digit Selection   ▽ **Subterms under main terms may continue to next column or page**

Bony block of joint — *continued*
  hand 718.84
  hip 718.85
  knee 718.86
  multiple sites 718.89
  pelvic region 718.85
  shoulder (region) 718.81
  specified site NEC 718.88
  wrist 718.83
BOOP (bronchiolitis obliterans organized
    pneumonia) 516.8
Borderline
  diabetes mellitus 790.29
  hypertension 796.2
  intellectual functioning V62.89
  osteopenia 733.90
  pelvis 653.1 ☑
    with obstruction during labor 660.1 ☑
      affecting fetus or newborn 763.1
  psychosis (*see also* Schizophrenia) 295.5 ☑
    of childhood (*see also* Psychosis, child-
      hood) 299.8 ☑
  schizophrenia (*see also* Schizophrenia)
      295.5 ☑
Borna disease 062.9
Bornholm disease (epidemic pleurodynia)
    074.1
Borrelia vincentii (mouth) (pharynx) (tonsils)
    101
Bostock's catarrh — *see also* Fever, hay 477.9
Boston exanthem 048
Botalli, ductus (patent) (persistent) 747.0
Bothriocephalus latus infestation 123.4
Botulism 005.1
  food poisoning 005.1
  infant 040.41
  non-foodborne 040.42
  wound 040.42
Bouba — *see also* Yaws 102.9
Bouffée délirante 298.3
Bouillaud's disease or syndrome (rheumatic
    heart disease) 391.9
Bourneville's disease (tuberous sclerosis)
    759.5
Boutonneuse fever 082.1
Boutonniere
  deformity (finger) 736.21
  hand (intrinsic) 736.21
Bouveret (-Hoffmann) disease or syndrome
    (paroxysmal tachycardia) 427.2
Bovine heart — *see* Hypertrophy, cardiac
Bowel — *see* condition
Bowen's
  dermatosis (precancerous) (M8081/2) —
      see Neoplasm, skin, in situ
  disease (M8081/2) — *see* Neoplasm, skin,
      in situ
  epithelioma (M8081/2) — *see* Neoplasm,
      skin, in situ
  type
    epidermoid carcinoma in situ (M8081/2)
        — *see* Neoplasm, skin, in situ
    intraepidermal squamous cell carcinoma
        (M8081/2) — *see* Neoplasm, skin,
        in situ
Bowing
  femur 736.89
    congenital 754.42
  fibula 736.89
    congenital 754.43
  forearm 736.09
    away from midline (cubitus valgus)
        736.01
    toward midline (cubitus varus) 736.02
  leg(s), long bones, congenital 754.44
  radius 736.09
    away from midline (cubitus valgus)
        736.01
    toward midline (cubitus varus) 736.02
  tibia 736.89
    congenital 754.43
Bowleg(s) 736.42
  congenital 754.44
  rachitic 268.1
Boyd's dysentery 004.2
Brachial — *see* condition

Brachman-de Lange syndrome (Amsterdam
    dwarf, intellectual disabilities, and
    brachycephaly) 759.89
Brachycardia 427.89
Brachycephaly 756.0
Brachymorphism and ectopia lentis 759.89
Bradley's disease (epidemic vomiting) 078.82
Bradycardia 427.89
  chronic (sinus) 427.81
  newborn 779.81
  nodal 427.89
  postoperative 997.1
  reflex 337.09
  sinoatrial 427.89
    with paroxysmal tachyarrhythmia or
        tachycardia 427.81
    chronic 427.81
  sinus 427.89
    with paroxysmal tachyarrhythmia or
        tachycardia 427.81
    chronic 427.81
    persistent 427.81
    severe 427.81
  tachycardia syndrome 427.81
  vagal 427.89
Bradykinesia 781.0
Bradypnea 786.09
Brailsford's disease 732.3
  radial head 732.3
  tarsal scaphold 732.5
Brailsford-Morquio disease or syndrome
    (mucopolysaccharidosis IV) 277.5
Brain — *see also* condition
  death 348.82
  syndrome (acute) (chronic) (nonpsychotic)
      (organic) (with neurotic reaction)
      (with behavioral reaction) (*see also*
      Syndrome, brain) 310.9
    with
      presenile brain disease 290.10
      psychosis, psychotic reaction (*see al-
          so* Psychosis, organic) 294.9
    congenital (*see also* Disability, intellectu-
        al) 319
Branched-chain amino-acid disease 270.3
Branchial — *see* condition
Brandt's syndrome (acrodermatitis enteropath-
    ica) 686.8
Brash (water) 787.1
Brass-founders' ague 985.8
Bravais-Jacksonian epilepsy — *see also*
    Epilepsy 345.5 ☑
Braxton Hicks contractions 644.1 ☑
Braziers' disease 985.8
Brazilian
  blastomycosis 116.1
  leishmaniasis 085.5
BRBPR (bright red blood per rectum) 569.3
Break
  cardiorenal — *see* Hypertension, cardiorenal
  retina (*see also* Defect, retina) 361.30
Breakbone fever 061
Breakdown
  device, implant, or graft — *see* Complica-
      tions, mechanical
  nervous (*see also* Disorder, mental, nonpsy-
      chotic) 300.9
  perineum 674.2 ☑
Breast — *see also* condition
  buds 259.1
    in newborn 779.89
  dense 793.82
  nodule 793.89
Breast feeding difficulties 676.8 ☑
Breath
  foul 784.99
  holder, child 312.81
  holding spells 786.9
  shortness 786.05
Breathing
  asymmetrical 786.09
  bronchial 786.09
  exercises V57.0
  labored 786.09
  mouth 784.99
    causing malocclusion 524.59

Breathing — *continued*
  periodic 786.09
    high altitude 327.22
    tic 307.20
Breathlessness 786.09
Breda's disease — *see also* Yaws 102.9
Breech
  delivery, affecting fetus or newborn 763.0
  extraction, affecting fetus or newborn 763.0
  presentation (buttocks) (complete) (frank)
      652.2 ☑
    with successful version 652.1 ☑
      before labor, affecting fetus or newborn
          761.7
      during labor, affecting fetus or newborn
          763.0
Breisky's disease (kraurosis vulvae) 624.09
Brennemann's syndrome (acute mesenteric
    lymphadenitis) 289.2
Brenner's
  tumor (benign) (M9000/0) 220
    borderline malignancy (M9000/1) 236.2
    malignant (M9000/3) 183.0
    proliferating (M9000/1) 236.2
Bretonneau's disease (diphtheritic malignant
    angina) 032.0
Breus' mole 631.8
Brevicollis 756.16
Bricklayers' itch 692.89
Brickmakers' anemia 126.9
Bridge
  myocardial 746.85
Bright's
  blindness — *see* Uremia
  disease (*see also* Nephritis) 583.9
    arteriosclerotic (*see also* Hypertension,
        kidney) 403.90
Bright red blood per rectum (BRBPR) 569.3
Brill's disease (recrudescent typhus) 081.1
  flea-borne 081.0
  louse-borne 081.1
Brill-Symmers disease (follicular lymphoma)
    (M9690/3) 202.0 ☑
Brill-Zinsser disease (recrudescent typhus)
    081.1
Brinton's disease (linitis plastica) (M8142/3)
    151.9
Brion-Kayser disease — *see also* Fever,
    paratyphoid 002.9
Briquet's disorder or syndrome 300.81
Brissaud's
  infantilism (infantile myxedema) 244.9
  motor-verbal tic 307.23
Brissaud-Meige syndrome (infantile
    myxedema) 244.9
Brittle
  bones (congenital) 756.51
  nails 703.8
    congenital 757.5
Broad — *see also* condition
  beta disease 272.2
  ligament laceration syndrome 620.6
Brock's syndrome (atelectasis due to enlarged
    lymph nodes) 518.0
Brocq's disease 691.8
  atopic (diffuse) neurodermatitis 691.8
  lichen simplex chronicus 698.3
  parakeratosis psoriasiformis 696.2
  parapsoriasis 696.2
Brocq-Duhring disease (dermatitis herpeti-
    formis) 694.0
Brodie's
  abscess (localized) (chronic) (*see also* Os-
      teomyelitis) 730.1 ☑
  disease (joint) (*see also* Osteomyelitis)
      730.1 ☑
Broken
  arches 734
    congenital 755.67
  back — *see* Fracture, vertebra, by site
  bone — *see* Fracture, by site
  compensation — *see* Disease, heart
  heart syndrome 429.83
  implant or internal device — *see* listing un-
      der Complications, mechanical
  neck — *see* Fracture, vertebra, cervical

Broken — *continued*
  nose 802.0
    open 802.1
  tooth, teeth 873.63
    complicated 873.73
Bromhidrosis 705.89
Bromidism, bromism
  acute 967.3
    correct substance properly administered
        349.82
    overdose or wrong substance given or
        taken 967.3
  chronic (*see also* Dependence) 304.1 ☑
Bromidrosiphobia 300.23
Bromidrosis 705.89
Bronchi, bronchial — *see* condition
Bronchiectasis (cylindrical) (diffuse) (fusiform)
    (localized) (moniliform) (postinfectious)
    (recurrent) (saccular) 494.0
  with acute exacerbation 494.1
  congenital 748.61
  tuberculosis (*see also* Tuberculosis) 011.5 ☑
Bronchiolectasis — *see* Bronchiectasis
Bronchiolitis (acute) (infectious) (subacute)
    466.19
  with
    bronchospasm or obstruction 466.19
    influenza, flu, or grippe (*see also* Influen-
        za) 487.1
  catarrhal (acute) (subacute) 466.19
  chemical 506.0
    chronic 506.4
  chronic (obliterative) 491.8
  due to external agent — *see* Bronchitis,
      acute, due to
  fibrosa obliterans 491.8
  influenzal (*see also* Influenza) 487.1
  obliterans 491.8
    with organizing pneumonia (BOOP)
        516.8
    status post lung transplant 996.84
  obliterative (chronic) (diffuse) (subacute)
      491.8
    due to fumes or vapors 506.4
  respiratory syncytial virus 466.11
  vesicular — *see* Pneumonia, broncho-
Bronchitis (diffuse) (hypostatic) (infectious)
    (inflammatory) (simple) 490
  with
    emphysema — *see* Emphysema
    influenza, flu, or grippe (*see also* Influen-
        za) 487.1
    obstruction airway, chronic 491.20
      with
        acute bronchitis 491.22
        exacerbation (acute) 491.21
    tracheitis 490
      acute or subacute 466.0
        with bronchospasm or obstruc-
            tion 466.0
      chronic 491.8
  acute or subacute 466.0
    with
      bronchiectasis 494.1
      bronchospasm 466.0
      obstruction 466.0
      tracheitis 466.0
    chemical (due to fumes or vapors) 506.0
    due to
      fumes or vapors 506.0
      radiation 508.8
  allergic (acute) (*see also* Asthma) 493.9 ☑
  arachidic 934.1
  aspiration 507.0
    due to fumes or vapors 506.0
  asthmatic (acute) 493.90
    with
      acute exacerbation 493.92
      status asthmaticus 493.91
    chronic 493.2 ☑
  capillary 466.19
    with bronchospasm or obstruction
        466.19
    chronic 491.8
  caseous (*see also* Tuberculosis) 011.3 ☑
  Castellani's 104.8

☑ **Additional Digit Required** — Refer to the Tabular List for Digit Selection   ▽ **Subterms under main terms may continue to next column or page**

2015 ICD-9-CM   ▶◀ **Revised Text**   ● **New Line**   ▲ **Revised Code**   **Volume 2 — 37**

Bronchitis — *continued*
- catarrhal 490
  - acute — *see* Bronchitis, acute
  - chronic 491.0
- chemical (acute) (subacute) 506.0
  - chronic 506.4
  - due to fumes or vapors (acute) (subacute) 506.0
    - chronic 506.4
- chronic 491.9
  - with
    - tracheitis (chronic) 491.8
  - asthmatic 493.2 ☑
  - catarrhal 491.0
  - chemical (due to fumes and vapors) 506.4
  - due to
    - fumes or vapors (chemical) (inhalation) 506.4
    - radiation 508.8
    - tobacco smoking 491.0
  - mucopurulent 491.1
  - obstructive 491.20
    - with
      - acute bronchitis 491.22
      - exacerbation (acute) 491.21
  - purulent 491.1
  - simple 491.0
  - specified type NEC 491.8
- croupous 466.0
  - with bronchospasm or obstruction 466.0
  - due to fumes or vapors 506.0
- emphysematous 491.20
  - with
    - acute bronchitis 491.22
    - exacerbation (acute) 491.21
- exudative 466.0
- fetid (chronic) (recurrent) 491.1
- fibrinous, acute or subacute 466.0
  - with bronchospasm or obstruction 466.0
- grippal (*see also* Influenza) 487.1
- influenzal (*see also* Influenza) 487.1
- membranous, acute or subacute 466.0
  - with bronchospasm or obstruction 466.0
- moulders' 502
- mucopurulent (chronic) (recurrent) 491.1
  - acute or subacute 466.0
- obliterans 491.8
- obstructive (chronic) 491.20
  - with
    - acute bronchitis 491.22
    - exacerbation (acute) 491.21
- pituitous 491.1
- plastic (inflammatory) 466.0
- pneumococcal, acute or subacute 466.0
  - with bronchospasm or obstruction 466.0
- pseudomembranous 466.0
- purulent (chronic) (recurrent) 491.1
  - acute or subacute 466.0
    - with bronchospasm or obstruction 466.0
- putrid 491.1
- scrofulous (*see also* Tuberculosis) 011.3 ☑
- senile 491.9
- septic, acute or subacute 466.0
  - with bronchospasm or obstruction 466.0
- smokers' 491.0
- spirochetal 104.8
- suffocative, acute or subacute 466.0
- summer (*see also* Asthma) 493.9 ☑
- suppurative (chronic) 491.1
  - acute or subacute 466.0
- tuberculous (*see also* Tuberculosis) 011.3 ☑
- ulcerative 491.8
  - Vincent's 101
- Vincent's 101
- viral, acute or subacute 466.0
Bronchoalveolitis 485
Bronchoaspergillosis 117.3
Bronchocele
- meaning
  - dilatation of bronchus 519.19
  - goiter 240.9
Bronchogenic carcinoma 162.9
Bronchohemisporosis 117.9
Broncholithiasis 518.89

Broncholithiasis — *continued*
- tuberculous (*see also* Tuberculosis) 011.3 ☑
Bronchomalacia 748.3
Bronchomoniliasis 112.89
Bronchomycosis 112.89
Bronchonocardiosis 039.1
Bronchopleuropneumonia — *see* Pneumonia, broncho-
Bronchopneumonia — *see* Pneumonia, broncho-
Bronchopneumonitis — *see* Pneumonia, broncho-
Bronchopulmonary — *see* condition
Bronchopulmonitis — *see* Pneumonia, broncho-
Bronchorrhagia 786.30
- newborn 770.3
- tuberculous (*see also* Tuberculosis) 011.3 ☑
Bronchorrhea (chronic) (purulent) 491.0
- acute 466.0
Bronchospasm 519.11
- with
  - asthma — *see* Asthma
  - bronchiolitis, acute 466.19
    - due to respiratory syncytial virus 466.11
  - bronchitis — *see* Bronchitis
  - chronic obstructive pulmonary disease (COPD) 496
  - emphysema — *see* Emphysema
  - due to external agent — *see* Condition, respiratory, acute, due to
- acute 519.11
- exercise induced 493.81
Bronchospirochetosis 104.8
Bronchostenosis 519.19
Bronchus — *see* condition
Bronze, bronzed
- diabetes 275.01
- disease (Addison's) (skin) 255.41
  - tuberculous (*see also* Tuberculosis) 017.6 ☑
Brooke's disease or tumor (M8100/0) — *see* Neoplasm, skin, benign
Brown enamel of teeth (hereditary) 520.5
Brown-Séquard's paralysis (syndrome) 344.89
Brown's tendon sheath syndrome 378.61
Brow presentation complicating delivery 652.4 ☑
Brucella, brucellosis (infection) 023.9
- abortus 023.1
- canis 023.3
- dermatitis, skin 023.9
- melitensis 023.0
- mixed 023.8
- suis 023.2
Bruck-de Lange disease or syndrome (Amsterdam dwarf, intellectual disabilities, and brachycephaly) 759.89
Bruck's disease 733.99
Brugada syndrome 746.89
Brug's filariasis 125.1
Brugsch's syndrome (acropachyderma) 757.39
Bruhl's disease (splenic anemia with fever) 285.8
Bruise (skin surface intact) — *see also* Contusion
- with
  - fracture — *see* Fracture, by site
  - open wound — *see* Wound, open, by site
  - internal organ (abdomen, chest, or pelvis) — *see* Injury, internal, by site
- umbilical cord 663.6 ☑
  - affecting fetus or newborn 762.6
Bruit 785.9
- arterial (abdominal) (carotid) 785.9
- supraclavicular 785.9
Brushburn — *see* Injury, superficial, by site
Bruton's X-linked agammaglobulinemia 279.04
Bruxism 306.8
- sleep related 327.53
Bubbly lung syndrome 770.7
Bubo 289.3
- blennorrhagic 098.89

Bubo — *continued*
- chancroidal 099.0
- climatic 099.1
- due to Hemophilus ducreyi 099.0
- gonococcal 098.89
- indolent NEC 099.8
- inguinal NEC 099.8
  - chancroidal 099.0
  - climatic 099.1
  - due to H. ducreyi 099.0
- scrofulous (*see also* Tuberculosis) 017.2 ☑
- soft chancre 099.0
- suppurating 683
- syphilitic 091.0
  - congenital 090.0
- tropical 099.1
- venereal NEC 099.8
- virulent 099.0
Bubonic plague 020.0
Bubonocele — *see* Hernia, inguinal
Buccal — *see* condition
Buchanan's disease (juvenile osteochondrosis of iliac crest) 732.1
Buchem's syndrome (hyperostosis corticalis) 733.3
Buchman's disease (osteochondrosis, juvenile) 732.1
Bucket handle fracture (semilunar cartilage) — *see also* Tear, meniscus 836.2
Budd-Chiari syndrome (hepatic vein thrombosis) 453.0
Budgerigar-fanciers' disease or lung 495.2
Büdinger-Ludloff-Läwen disease 717.89
Buds
- breast 259.1
  - in newborn 779.89
Buerger's disease (thromboangiitis obliterans) 443.1
Bulbar — *see* condition
Bulbus cordis 745.9
- persistent (in left ventricle) 745.8
Bulging fontanels (congenital) 756.0
Bulimia 783.6
- nervosa 307.51
- nonorganic origin 307.51
Bulky uterus 621.2
Bulla(e) 709.8
- lung (emphysematous) (solitary) 492.0
Bullet wound — *see also* Wound, open, by site
- fracture — *see* Fracture, by site, open
- internal organ (abdomen, chest, or pelvis) — *see* Injury, internal, by site, with open wound
- intracranial — *see* Laceration, brain, with open wound
Bullis fever 082.8
Bullying — *see also* Disturbance, conduct 312.0 ☑
Bundle
- branch block (complete) (false) (incomplete) 426.50
  - bilateral 426.53
  - left (*see also* Block, bundle branch, left) 426.3
    - hemiblock 426.2
  - right (*see also* Block, bundle branch, right) 426.4
- of His — *see* condition
- of Kent syndrome (anomalous atrioventricular excitation) 426.7
Bungpagga 040.81
Bunion 727.1
Bunionette 727.1
Bunyamwera fever 066.3
Buphthalmia, buphthalmos (congenital) 743.20
- associated with
  - keratoglobus, congenital 743.22
  - megalocornea 743.22
  - ocular anomalies NEC 743.22
- isolated 743.21
- simple 743.21
Bürger-Grütz disease or syndrome (essential familial hyperlipemia) 272.3
Buried roots 525.3

Burke's syndrome 577.8
Burkitt's
- tumor (M9750/3) 200.2 ☑
- type malignant, lymphoma, lymphoblastic, or undifferentiated (M9750/3) 200.2 ☑
Burn (acid) (cathode ray) (caustic) (chemical) (electric heating appliance) (electricity) (fire) (flame) (hot liquid or object) (irradiation) (lime) (radiation) (steam) (thermal) (x-ray) 949.0

> *Note* — Use the following fifth-digit subclassification with category 948 to indicate the percent of body surface with third degree burn:
>
> 0   Less than 10% or unspecified
> 1   10–19%
> 2   20–29%
> 3   30–39%
> 4   40–49%
> 5   50–59%
> 6   60–69%
> 7   70–79%
> 8   80–89%
> 9   90% or more of body surface

- with
  - blisters — *see* Burn, by site, second degree
  - erythema — *see* Burn, by site, first degree
  - skin loss (epidermal) (*see also* Burn, by site, second degree)
    - full thickness (*see also* Burn, by site, third degree)
      - with necrosis of underlying tissues — *see* Burn, by site, third degree, deep
- first degree — *see* Burn, by site, first degree
- second degree — *see* Burn, by site, second degree
- third degree — *see* Burn, by site, third degree
  - deep — *see* Burn, by site, third degree, deep
- abdomen, abdominal (muscle) (wall) 942.03
  - with
    - trunk — *see* Burn, trunk, multiple sites
  - first degree 942.13
  - second degree 942.23
  - third degree 942.33
    - deep 942.43
      - with loss of body part 942.53
- ankle 945.03
  - with
    - lower limb(s) — *see* Burn, leg, multiple sites
  - first degree 945.13
  - second degree 945.23
  - third degree 945.33
    - deep 945.43
      - with loss of body part 945.53
- anus — *see* Burn, trunk, specified site NEC
- arm(s) 943.00
  - first degree 943.10
  - second degree 943.20
  - third degree 943.30
    - deep 943.40
      - with loss of body part 943.50
  - lower — *see* Burn, forearm(s)
  - multiple sites, except hand(s) or wrist(s) 943.09
    - first degree 943.19
    - second degree 943.29
    - third degree 943.39
      - deep 943.49
        - with loss of body part 943.59
  - upper 943.03
    - first degree 943.13
    - second degree 943.23
    - third degree 943.33

☑ **Additional Digit Required** — Refer to the Tabular List for Digit Selection   ▽ **Subterms under main terms may continue to next column or page**

38 — Volume 2   ▶◀ Revised Text   ● New Line   ▲ Revised Code   2015 ICD-9-CM

Burn — *continued*
  arm(s) — *continued*
    upper — *continued*
      third degree — *continued*
        deep 943.43
          with loss of body part 943.53
  auditory canal (external) — *see* Burn, ear
  auricle (ear) — *see* Burn, ear
  axilla 943.04
    with
      upper limb(s), except hand(s) or
        wrist(s) — *see* Burn, arm(s),
        multiple sites
    first degree 943.14
    second degree 943.24
    third degree 943.34
      deep 943.44
        with loss of body part 943.54
  back 942.04
    with
      trunk — *see* Burn, trunk, multiple
        sites
    first degree 942.14
    second degree 942.24
    third degree 942.34
      deep 942.44
        with loss of body part 942.54
  biceps
    brachii — *see* Burn, arm(s), upper
    femoris — *see* Burn, thigh
  breast(s) 942.01
    with
      trunk — *see* Burn, trunk, multiple
        sites
    first degree 942.11
    second degree 942.21
    third degree 942.31
      deep 942.41
        with loss of body part 942.51
  brow — *see* Burn, forehead
  buttock(s) — *see* Burn, back
  canthus (eye) 940.1
    chemical 940.0
  cervix (uteri) 947.4
  cheek (cutaneous) 941.07
    with
      face or head — *see* Burn, head, mul-
        tiple sites
    first degree 941.17
    second degree 941.27
    third degree 941.37
      deep 941.47
        with loss of body part 941.57
  chest wall (anterior) 942.02
    with
      trunk — *see* Burn, trunk, multiple
        sites
    first degree 942.12
    second degree 942.22
    third degree 942.32
      deep 942.42
        with loss of body part 942.52
  chin 941.04
    with
      face or head — *see* Burn, head, mul-
        tiple sites
    first degree 941.14
    second degree 941.24
    third degree 941.34
      deep 941.44
        with loss of body part 941.54
  clitoris — *see* Burn, genitourinary organs,
    external
  colon 947.3
  conjunctiva (and cornea) 940.4
    chemical
      acid 940.3
      alkaline 940.2
  cornea (and conjunctiva) 940.4
    chemical
      acid 940.3
      alkaline 940.2
  costal region — *see* Burn, chest wall
  due to ingested chemical agent — *see* Burn,
    internal organs
  ear (auricle) (canal) (drum) (external) 941.01

Burn — *continued*
  ear — *continued*
    with
      face or head — *see* Burn, head, mul-
        tiple sites
    first degree 941.11
    second degree 941.21
    third degree 941.31
      deep 941.41
        with loss of a body part 941.51
  elbow 943.02
    with
      hand(s) and wrist(s) — *see* Burn,
        multiple specified sites
      upper limb(s), except hand(s) or
        wrist(s) (*see also* Burn, arm(s),
        multiple sites)
    first degree 943.12
    second degree 943.22
    third degree 943.32
      deep 943.42
        with loss of body part 943.52
  electricity, electric current — *see* Burn, by
    site
  entire body — *see* Burn, multiple, specified
    sites
  epididymis — *see* Burn, genitourinary or-
    gans, external
  epigastric region — *see* Burn, abdomen
  epiglottis 947.1
  esophagus 947.2
  extent (percent of body surface)
    less than 10 percent 948.0 ☑
    10-19 percent 948.1 ☑
    20-29 percent 948.2 ☑
    30-39 percent 948.3 ☑
    40-49 percent 948.4 ☑
    50-59 percent 948.5 ☑
    60-69 percent 948.6 ☑
    70-79 percent 948.7 ☑
    80-89 percent 948.8 ☑
    90 percent or more 948.9 ☑
  extremity
    lower — *see* Burn, leg
    upper — *see* Burn, arm(s)
  eye(s) (and adnexa) (only) 940.9
    with
      face, head, or neck 941.02
        first degree 941.12
        second degree 941.22
        third degree 941.32
          deep 941.42
            with loss of body part
              941.52
      other sites (classifiable to more than
        one category in 940–945) —
        see Burn, multiple, specified
        sites
      resulting rupture and destruction of
        eyeball 940.5
    specified part — *see* Burn, by site
  eyeball (*see also* Burn, eye)
    with resulting rupture and destruction
      of eyeball 940.5
  eyelid(s) 940.1
    chemical 940.0
  face — *see* Burn, head
  finger (nail) (subungual) 944.01
    with
      hand(s) — *see* Burn, hand(s), multi-
        ple sites
      other sites — *see* Burn, multiple,
        specified sites
      thumb 944.04
        first degree 944.14
        second degree 944.24
        third degree 944.34
          deep 944.44
            with loss of body part
              944.54
    first degree 944.11
    second degree 944.21
    third degree 944.31
      deep 944.41
        with loss of body part 944.51
  multiple (digits) 944.03

Burn — *continued*
  finger — *continued*
    multiple — *continued*
      with thumb — *see* Burn, finger, with
        thumb
      first degree 944.13
      second degree 944.23
      third degree 944.33
        deep 944.43
          with loss of body part 944.53
  flank — *see* Burn, abdomen
  foot 945.02
    with
      lower limb(s) — *see* Burn, leg, multi-
        ple sites
    first degree 945.12
    second degree 945.22
    third degree 945.32
      deep 945.42
        with loss of body part 945.52
  forearm(s) 943.01
    with
      upper limb(s), except hand(s) or
        wrist(s) — *see* Burn, arm(s),
        multiple sites
    first degree 943.11
    second degree 943.21
    third degree 943.31
      deep 943.41
        with loss of body part 943.51
  forehead 941.07
    with
      face or head — *see* Burn, head, mul-
        tiple sites
    first degree 941.17
    second degree 941.27
    third degree 941.37
      deep 941.47
        with loss of body part 941.57
  fourth degree — *see* Burn, by site, third de-
    gree, deep
  friction — *see* Injury, superficial, by site
  from swallowing caustic or corrosive sub-
    stance NEC — *see* Burn, internal or-
    gans
  full thickness — *see* Burn, by site, third de-
    gree
  gastrointestinal tract 947.3
  genitourinary organs
    external 942.05
      with
        trunk — *see* Burn, trunk, multiple
          sites
      first degree 942.15
      second degree 942.25
      third degree 942.35
        deep 942.45
          with loss of body part 942.55
    internal 947.8
  globe (eye) — *see* Burn, eyeball
  groin — *see* Burn, abdomen
  gum 947.0
  hand(s) (phalanges) (and wrist) 944.00
    first degree 944.10
    second degree 944.20
    third degree 944.30
      deep 944.40
        with loss of body part 944.50
    back (dorsal surface) 944.06
      first degree 944.16
      second degree 944.26
      third degree 944.36
        deep 944.46
          with loss of body part 944.56
    multiple sites 944.08
      first degree 944.18
      second degree 944.28
      third degree 944.38
        deep 944.48
          with loss of body part 944.58
  head (and face) 941.00
    first degree 941.10
    second degree 941.20
    third degree 941.30
      deep 941.40
        with loss of body part 941.50

Burn — *continued*
  head — *continued*
    eye(s) only 940.9
      specified part — *see* Burn, by site
    multiple sites 941.09
      with eyes — *see* Burn, eyes, with
        face, head, or neck
      first degree 941.19
      second degree 941.29
      third degree 941.39
        deep 941.49
          with loss of body part 941.59
  heel — *see* Burn, foot
  hip — *see* Burn, leg, upper
  iliac region — *see* Burn, trunk, specified site
    NEC
  infected 958.3
  inhalation (*see also* Burn, internal organs)
    947.9
  internal organs 947.9
    from caustic or corrosive substance
      (swallowing) NEC 947.9
    specified NEC (*see also* Burn, by site)
      947.8
  interscapular region — *see* Burn, back
  intestine (large) (small) 947.3
  iris — *see* Burn, eyeball
  knee 945.05
    with
      lower limb(s) — *see* Burn, leg, multi-
        ple sites
    first degree 945.15
    second degree 945.25
    third degree 945.35
      deep 945.45
        with loss of body part 945.55
  labium (majus) (minus) — *see* Burn, geni-
    tourinary organs, external
  lacrimal apparatus, duct, gland, or sac 940.1
    chemical 940.0
  larynx 947.1
  late effect — *see* Late, effects (of), burn
  leg 945.00
    first degree 945.10
    second degree 945.20
    third degree 945.30
      deep 945.40
        with loss of body part 945.50
    lower 945.04
      with other part(s) of lower limb(s) —
        see Burn, leg, multiple sites
      first degree 945.14
      second degree 945.24
      third degree 945.34
        deep 945.44
          with loss of body part 945.54
    multiple sites 945.09
      first degree 945.19
      second degree 945.29
      third degree 945.39
        deep 945.49
          with loss of body part 945.59
    upper — *see* Burn, thigh
  lightning — *see* Burn, by site
  limb(s)
    lower (including foot or toe(s)) — *see*
      Burn, leg
    upper (except wrist and hand) — *see*
      Burn, arm(s)
  lip(s) 941.03
    with
      face or head — *see* Burn, head, mul-
        tiple sites
    first degree 941.13
    second degree 941.23
    third degree 941.33
      deep 941.43
        with loss of body part 941.53
  lumbar region — *see* Burn, back
  lung 947.1
  malar region — *see* Burn, cheek
  mastoid region — *see* Burn, scalp
  membrane, tympanic — *see* Burn, ear
  midthoracic region — *see* Burn, chest wall
  mouth 947.0
  multiple (*see also* Burn, unspecified) 949.0

☑ **Additional Digit Required — Refer to the Tabular List for Digit Selection**   ▽ **Subterms under main terms may continue to next column or page**

2015 ICD-9-CM   ▶◀ Revised Text   ● New Line   ▲ Revised Code   **Volume 2 — 39**

Burn — continued
　multiple (see also Burn, unspecified) — continued
　　specified sites classifiable to more than one category in 940-945 ☑, 946.0
　　　first degree 946.1
　　　second degree 946.2
　　　third degree 946.3
　　　deep 946.4
　　　　with loss of body part 946.5
　muscle, abdominal — see Burn, abdomen
　nasal (septum) — see Burn, nose
　neck 941.08
　　with
　　　face or head — see Burn, head, multiple sites
　　first degree 941.18
　　second degree 941.28
　　third degree 941.38
　　　deep 941.48
　　　　with loss of body part 941.58
　nose (septum) 941.05
　　with
　　　face or head — see Burn, head, multiple sites
　　first degree 941.15
　　second degree 941.25
　　third degree 941.35
　　　deep 941.45
　　　　with loss of body part 941.55
　occipital region — see Burn, scalp
　orbit region 940.1
　　chemical 940.0
　oronasopharynx 947.0
　palate 947.0
　palm(s) 944.05
　　with
　　　hand(s) and wrist(s) — see Burn, hand(s), multiple sites
　　first degree 944.15
　　second degree 944.25
　　third degree 944.35
　　　deep 944.45
　　　　with loss of a body part 944.55
　parietal region — see Burn, scalp
　penis — see Burn, genitourinary organs, external
　perineum — see Burn, genitourinary organs, external
　periocular area 940.1
　　chemical 940.0
　pharynx 947.0
　pleura 947.1
　popliteal space — see Burn, knee
　prepuce — see Burn, genitourinary organs, external
　pubic region — see Burn, genitourinary organs, external
　pudenda — see Burn, genitourinary organs, external
　rectum 947.3
　sac, lacrimal 940.1
　　chemical 940.0
　sacral region — see Burn, back
　salivary (ducts) (glands) 947.0
　scalp 941.06
　　with
　　　face or neck — see Burn, head, multiple sites
　　first degree 941.16
　　second degree 941.26
　　third degree 941.36
　　　deep 941.46
　　　　with loss of body part 941.56
　scapular region 943.06
　　with
　　　upper limb(s), except hand(s) or wrist(s) — see Burn, arm(s), multiple sites
　　first degree 943.16
　　second degree 943.26
　　third degree 943.36
　　　deep 943.46
　　　　with loss of body part 943.56
　sclera — see Burn, eyeball

Burn — continued
　scrotum — see Burn, genitourinary organs, external
　septum, nasal — see Burn, nose
　shoulder(s) 943.05
　　with
　　　hand(s) and wrist(s) — see Burn, multiple, specified sites
　　　upper limb(s), except hand(s) or wrist(s) — see Burn, arm(s), multiple sites
　　first degree 943.15
　　second degree 943.25
　　third degree 943.35
　　　deep 943.45
　　　　with loss of body part 943.55
　skin NEC (see also Burn, unspecified) 949.0
　skull — see Burn, head
　small intestine 947.3
　sternal region — see Burn, chest wall
　stomach 947.3
　subconjunctival — see Burn, conjunctiva
　subcutaneous — see Burn, by site, third degree
　submaxillary region — see Burn, head
　submental region — see Burn, chin
　sun — see Sunburn
　supraclavicular fossa — see Burn, neck
　supraorbital — see Burn, forehead
　temple — see Burn, scalp
　temporal region — see Burn, scalp
　testicle — see Burn, genitourinary organs, external
　testis — see Burn, genitourinary organs, external
　thigh 945.06
　　with
　　　lower limb(s) — see Burn, leg, multiple sites
　　first degree 945.16
　　second degree 945.26
　　third degree 945.36
　　　deep 945.46
　　　　with loss of body part 945.56
　thorax (external) — see Burn, chest wall
　throat 947.0
　thumb(s) (nail) (subungual) 944.02
　　with
　　　finger(s) — see Burn, finger, with other sites, thumb
　　　hand(s) and wrist(s) — see Burn, hand(s), multiple sites
　　first degree 944.12
　　second degree 944.22
　　third degree 944.32
　　　deep 944.42
　　　　with loss of body part 944.52
　toe (nail) (subungual) 945.01
　　with
　　　lower limb(s) — see Burn, leg, multiple sites
　　first degree 945.11
　　second degree 945.21
　　third degree 945.31
　　　deep 945.41
　　　　with loss of body part 945.51
　tongue 947.0
　tonsil 947.0
　trachea 947.1
　trunk 942.00
　　first degree 942.10
　　second degree 942.20
　　third degree 942.30
　　　deep 942.40
　　　　with loss of body part 942.50
　　multiple sites 942.09
　　　first degree 942.19
　　　second degree 942.29
　　　third degree 942.39
　　　　deep 942.49
　　　　　with loss of body part 942.59
　　specified site NEC 942.09
　　　first degree 942.19
　　　second degree 942.29
　　　third degree 942.39
　　　　deep 942.49

Burn — continued
　trunk — continued
　　specified site — continued
　　　third degree — continued
　　　　deep — continued
　　　　　with loss of body part 942.59
　tunica vaginalis — see Burn, genitourinary organs, external
　tympanic membrane — see Burn, ear
　tympanum — see Burn, ear
　ultraviolet 692.82
　unspecified site (multiple) 949.0
　　with extent of body surface involved specified
　　　less than 10 percent 948.0 ☑
　　　10-19 percent 948.1 ☑
　　　20-29 percent 948.2 ☑
　　　30-39 percent 948.3 ☑
　　　40-49 percent 948.4 ☑
　　　50-59 percent 948.5 ☑
　　　60-69 percent 948.6 ☑
　　　70-79 percent 948.7 ☑
　　　80-89 percent 948.8 ☑
　　　90 percent or more 948.9 ☑
　　first degree 949.1
　　second degree 949.2
　　third degree 949.3
　　　deep 949.4
　　　　with loss of body part 949.5
　uterus 947.4
　uvula 947.0
　vagina 947.4
　vulva — see Burn, genitourinary organs, external
　wrist(s) 944.07
　　with
　　　hand(s) — see Burn, hand(s), multiple sites
　　first degree 944.17
　　second degree 944.27
　　third degree 944.37
　　　deep 944.47
　　　　with loss of body part 944.57
Burnett's syndrome (milk-alkali) 275.42
Burnier's syndrome (hypophyseal dwarfism) 253.3
Burning
　feet syndrome 266.2
　sensation (see also Disturbance, sensation) 782.0
　tongue 529.6
Burns' disease (osteochondrosis, lower ulna) 732.3
Bursa — see also condition
　pharynx 478.29
Bursitis NEC 727.3
　Achilles tendon 726.71
　adhesive 726.90
　　shoulder 726.0
　ankle 726.79
　buttock 726.5
　calcaneal 726.79
　collateral ligament
　　fibular 726.63
　　tibial 726.62
　Duplay's 726.2
　elbow 726.33
　finger 726.8
　foot 726.79
　gonococcal 098.52
　hand 726.4
　hip 726.5
　infrapatellar 726.69
　ischiogluteal 726.5
　knee 726.60
　occupational NEC 727.2
　olecranon 726.33
　pes anserinus 726.61
　pharyngeal 478.29
　popliteal 727.51
　prepatellar 726.65
　radiohumeral 727.3
　scapulohumeral 726.19
　　adhesive 726.0
　shoulder 726.10
　　adhesive 726.0

Bursitis — continued
　subacromial 726.19
　　adhesive 726.0
　subcoracoid 726.19
　subdeltoid 726.19
　　adhesive 726.0
　subpatellar 726.69
　syphilitic 095.7
　Thornwaldt's, Tornwaldt's (pharyngeal) 478.29
　toe 726.79
　trochanteric area 726.5
　wrist 726.4
Burst stitches or sutures (complication of surgery) (external) (see also Dehiscence) 998.32
　internal 998.31
Buruli ulcer 031.1
Bury's disease (erythema elevatum diutinum) 695.89
Buschke's disease or scleredema (adultorum) 710.1
Busquet's disease (osteoperiostitis) — see also Osteomyelitis 730.1 ☑
Busse-Buschke disease (cryptococcosis) 117.5
Buttock — see condition
Button
　Biskra 085.1
　Delhi 085.1
　oriental 085.1
Buttonhole hand (intrinsic) 736.21
Bwamba fever (encephalitis) 066.3
Byssinosis (occupational) 504
Bywaters' syndrome 958.5

C

Cacergasia 300.9
Cachexia 799.4
　cancerous (see also Neoplasm, by site, malignant) 799.4
　cardiac — see Disease, heart
　dehydration 276.51
　　with
　　　hypernatremia 276.0
　　　hyponatremia 276.1
　due to malnutrition 799.4
　exophthalmic 242.0 ☑
　heart — see Disease, heart
　hypophyseal 253.2
　hypopituitary 253.2
　lead 984.9
　　specified type of lead — see Table of Drugs and Chemicals
　malaria 084.9
　malignant (see also Neoplasm, by site, malignant) 799.4
　marsh 084.9
　nervous 300.5
　old age 797
　pachydermic — see Hypothyroidism
　paludal 084.9
　pituitary (postpartum) 253.2
　renal (see also Disease, renal) 593.9
　saturnine 984.9
　　specified type of lead — see Table of Drugs and Chemicals
　senile 797
　Simmonds' (pituitary cachexia) 253.2
　splenica 289.59
　strumipriva (see also Hypothyroidism) 244.9
　tuberculous NEC (see also Tuberculosis) 011.9 ☑
Café au lait spots 709.09
Caffey's disease or syndrome (infantile cortical hyperostosis) 756.59
Caisson disease 993.3
Caked breast (puerperal, postpartum) 676.2 ☑
Cake kidney 753.3
Calabar swelling 125.2
Calcaneal spur 726.73
Calcaneoapophysitis 732.5
Calcaneonavicular bar 755.67
Calcareous — see condition
Calcicosis (occupational) 502
Calciferol (vitamin D) **deficiency** 268.9

☑ Additional Digit Required — Refer to the Tabular List for Digit Selection　　　　▽ Subterms under main terms may continue to next column or page

40 — Volume 2　　▶◀ Revised Text　　● New Line　　▲ Revised Code　　2015 ICD-9-CM

Calciferol (vitamin D) **deficiency** —
   continued
  with
    osteomalacia 268.2
    rickets (*see also* Rickets) 268.0
Calcification
  adrenal (capsule) (gland) 255.41
    tuberculous (*see also* Tuberculosis)
      017.6 ☑
  aorta 440.0
  artery (annular) — *see* Arteriosclerosis
  auricle (ear) 380.89
  bladder 596.89
    due to S. hematobium 120.0
  brain (cortex) — *see* Calcification, cerebral
  bronchus 519.19
  bursa 727.82
  cardiac (*see also* Degeneration, myocardial)
    429.1
  cartilage (postinfectional) 733.99
  cerebral (cortex) 348.89
    artery 437.0
  cervix (uteri) 622.8
  choroid plexus 349.2
  conjunctiva 372.54
  corpora cavernosa (penis) 607.89
  cortex (brain) — *see* Calcification, cerebral
  dental pulp (nodular) 522.2
  dentinal papilla 520.4
  disc, intervertebral 722.90
    cervical, cervicothoracic 722.91
    lumbar, lumbosacral 722.93
    thoracic, thoracolumbar 722.92
  fallopian tube 620.8
  falx cerebri — *see* Calcification, cerebral
  fascia 728.89
  gallbladder 575.8
  general 275.40
  heart (*see also* Degeneration, myocardial)
    429.1
    valve — *see* Endocarditis
  intervertebral cartilage or disc (postinfection-
    al) 722.90
    cervical, cervicothoracic 722.91
    lumbar, lumbosacral 722.93
    thoracic, thoracolumbar 722.92
  intracranial — *see* Calcification, cerebral
  intraspinal ligament 728.89
  joint 719.80
    ankle 719.87
    elbow 719.82
    foot 719.87
    hand 719.84
    hip 719.85
    knee 719.86
    multiple sites 719.89
    pelvic region 719.85
    shoulder (region) 719.81
    specified site NEC 719.88
    wrist 719.83
  kidney 593.89
    tuberculous (*see also* Tuberculosis)
      016.0 ☑
  larynx (senile) 478.79
  lens 366.8
  ligament 728.89
    intraspinal 728.89
    knee (medial collateral) 717.89
  lung 518.89
    active 518.89
    postinfectional 518.89
    tuberculous (*see also* Tuberculosis, pul-
      monary) 011.9 ☑
  lymph gland or node (postinfectional) 289.3
    tuberculous (*see also* Tuberculosis,
      lymph gland) 017.2 ☑
  mammographic 793.89
  massive (paraplegic) 728.10
  medial NEC (*see also* Arteriosclerosis, extrem-
    ities) 440.20
  meninges (cerebral) 349.2
  metastatic 275.40
  Mönckeberg's — *see* Arteriosclerosis
  muscle 728.10
    heterotopic, postoperative 728.13

Calcification — *continued*
  myocardium, myocardial (*see also* Degener-
    ation, myocardial) 429.1
  ovary 620.8
  pancreas 577.8
  penis 607.89
  periarticular 728.89
  pericardium (*see also* Pericarditis) 423.8
  pineal gland 259.8
  pleura 511.0
    postinfectional 518.89
    tuberculous (*see also* Tuberculosis,
      pleura) 012.0 ☑
  pulp (dental) (nodular) 522.2
  renal 593.89
  Rider's bone 733.99
  sclera 379.16
  semilunar cartilage 717.89
  spleen 289.59
  subcutaneous 709.3
  suprarenal (capsule) (gland) 255.41
  tendon (sheath) 727.82
    with bursitis, synovitis or tenosynovitis
      727.82
  trachea 519.19
  ureter 593.89
  uterus 621.8
  vitreous 379.29
Calcified — *see also* Calcification
  hematoma NEC 959.9
Calcinosis (generalized) (interstitial) (tumoral)
  (universalis) 275.49
  circumscripta 709.3
  cutis 709.3
  intervertebralis 275.49 [722.90]
  Raynaud's phenomenonsclerodactylytelang-
    iectasis (CRST) 710.1
Calciphylaxis — *see also* Calcification, by site
  275.49
Calcium
  blood
    high (*see also* Hypercalcemia) 275.42
    low (*see also* Hypocalcemia) 275.41
  deposits (*see also* Calcification, by site)
    in bursa 727.82
    in tendon (sheath) 727.82
      with bursitis, synovitis or tenosynovi-
        tis 727.82
  salts or soaps in vitreous 379.22
Calciuria 791.9
Calculi — *see* Calculus
Calculosis, intrahepatic — *see* Choledocholithiasis
Calculus, calculi, calculous 592.9
  ampulla of Vater — *see* Choledocholithiasis
  anuria (impacted) (recurrent) 592.0
  appendix 543.9
  bile duct (any) — *see* Choledocholithiasis
  biliary — *see* Cholelithiasis
  bilirubin, multiple — *see* Cholelithiasis
  bladder (encysted) (impacted) (urinary)
    594.1
    diverticulum 594.0
  bronchus 518.89
  calyx (kidney) (renal) 592.0
    congenital 753.3
  cholesterol (pure) (solitary) — *see*
    Cholelithiasis
  common duct (bile) — *see* Choledocholithi-
    asis
  conjunctiva 372.54
  cystic 594.1
    duct — *see* Cholelithiasis
  dental 523.6
    subgingival 523.6
    supragingival 523.6
  epididymis 608.89
  gallbladder (*see also* Cholelithiasis)
    congenital 751.69
  hepatic (duct) — *see* Choledocholithiasis
  intestine (impaction) (obstruction) 560.39
  kidney (impacted) (multiple) (pelvis) (recur-
    rent) (staghorn) 592.0
    congenital 753.3
  lacrimal (passages) 375.57
  liver (impacted) — *see* Choledocholithiasis

Calculus, calculi, calculous — *continued*
  lung 518.89
  mammographic 793.89
  nephritic (impacted) (recurrent) 592.0
  nose 478.19
  pancreas (duct) 577.8
  parotid gland 527.5
  pelvis, encysted 592.0
  prostate 602.0
  pulmonary 518.89
  renal (impacted) (recurrent) 592.0
    congenital 753.3
  salivary (duct) (gland) 527.5
  seminal vesicle 608.89
  staghorn 592.0
  Stensen's duct 527.5
  sublingual duct or gland 527.5
    congenital 750.26
  submaxillary duct, gland, or region 527.5
  suburethral 594.8
  tonsil 474.8
  tooth, teeth 523.6
  tunica vaginalis 608.89
  ureter (impacted) (recurrent) 592.1
  urethra (impacted) 594.2
  urinary (duct) (impacted) (passage) (tract)
    592.9
    lower tract NEC 594.9
      specified site 594.8
  vagina 623.8
  vesical (impacted) 594.1
  Wharton's duct 527.5
Caliectasis 593.89
California
  disease 114.0
  encephalitis 062.5
Caligo cornea 371.03
Callositas, callosity (infected) 700
Callus (infected) 700
  bone 726.91
  excessive, following fracture (*see also* Late,
    effect (of), fracture)
Calvé (-Perthes) disease (osteochondrosis,
  femoral capital) 732.1
Calvities — *see also* Alopecia 704.00
Cameroon fever — *see also* Malaria 084.6
Camptocormia 300.11
Camptodactyly (congenital) 755.59
Camurati-Engelmann disease (diaphyseal
  sclerosis) 756.59
Canal — *see* condition
Canaliculitis (lacrimal) (acute) 375.31
  Actinomyces 039.8
  chronic 375.41
Canavan's disease 330.0
Cancer (M8000/3) — *see also* Neoplasm, by
  site, malignant

> *Note* — *The term "cancer" when modi-*
> *fied by an adjective or adjectival phrase*
> *indicating a morphological type should*
> *be coded in the same manner as "carci-*
> *noma" with that adjective or phrase.*
> *Thus, "squamous-cell cancer" should be*
> *coded in the same manner as "squa-*
> *mous-cell carcinoma," which appears in*
> *the list under "Carcinoma."*

  bile duct type (M8160/3), liver 155.1
  hepatocellular (M8170/3) 155.0
Cancerous (M8000/3) — *see* Neoplasm, by site,
  malignant
Cancerphobia 300.29
Cancrum oris 528.1
Candidiasis, candidal 112.9
  with pneumonia 112.4
  balanitis 112.2
  congenital 771.7
  disseminated 112.5
  endocarditis 112.81
  esophagus 112.84
  intertrigo 112.3
  intestine 112.85
  lung 112.4
  meningitis 112.83
  mouth 112.0
  nails 112.3
  neonatal 771.7

Candidiasis, candidal — *continued*
  onychia 112.3
  otitis externa 112.82
  otomycosis 112.82
  paronychia 112.3
  perionyxis 112.3
  pneumonia 112.4
  pneumonitis 112.4
  skin 112.3
  specified site NEC 112.89
  systemic 112.5
  urogenital site NEC 112.2
  vagina 112.1
  vulva 112.1
  vulvovaginitis 112.1
Candidiosis — *see* Candidiasis
Candiru infection or infestation 136.8
Canities (premature) 704.3
  congenital 757.4
Canker (mouth) (sore) 528.2
  rash 034.1
Cannabinosis 504
Canton fever 081.9
Cap
  cradle 690.11
Capillariasis 127.5
Capillary — *see* condition
Caplan-Colinet syndrome 714.81
Caplan's syndrome 714.81
Capsule — *see* condition
Capsulitis (joint) 726.90
  adhesive (shoulder) 726.0
  hip 726.5
  knee 726.60
  labyrinthine 387.8
  thyroid 245.9
  wrist 726.4
Caput
  crepitus 756.0
  medusae 456.8
  succedaneum 767.19
Carapata disease 087.1
Carate — *see* Pinta
**Carbohydrate-deficient glycoprotein syn-
  drome** (CGDS) 271.8
Carboxyhemoglobinemia 986
Carbuncle 680.9
  abdominal wall 680.2
  ankle 680.6
  anus 680.5
  arm (any part, above wrist) 680.3
  auditory canal, external 680.0
  axilla 680.3
  back (any part) 680.2
  breast 680.2
  buttock 680.5
  chest wall 680.2
  corpus cavernosum 607.2
  ear (any part) (external) 680.0
  eyelid 373.13
  face (any part, except eye) 680.0
  finger (any) 680.4
  flank 680.2
  foot (any part) 680.7
  forearm 680.3
  genital organ (male) 608.4
  gluteal (region) 680.5
  groin 680.2
  hand (any part) 680.4
  head (any part, except face) 680.8
  heel 680.7
  hip 680.6
  kidney (*see also* Abscess, kidney) 590.2
  knee 680.6
  labia 616.4
  lacrimal
    gland (*see also* Dacryoadenitis) 375.00
    passages (duct) (sac) (*see also* Dacryocys-
      titis) 375.30
  leg, any part except foot 680.6
  lower extremity, any part except foot 680.6
  malignant 022.0
  multiple sites 680.9
  neck 680.1
  nose (external) (septum) 680.0
  orbit, orbital 376.01

☑ **Additional Digit Required** — **Refer to the Tabular List for Digit Selection**   **Subterms under main terms may continue to next column or page**

2015 ICD-9-CM   ▶◀ **Revised Text**   ● **New Line**   ▲ **Revised Code**   **Volume 2 — 41**

Carbuncle — *continued*
    partes posteriores 680.5
    pectoral region 680.2
    penis 607.2
    perineum 680.2
    pinna 680.0
    scalp (any part) 680.8
    scrotum 608.4
    seminal vesicle 608.0
    shoulder 680.3
    skin NEC 680.9
    specified site NEC 680.8
    spermatic cord 608.4
    temple (region) 680.0
    testis 608.4
    thigh 680.6
    thumb 680.4
    toe (any) 680.7
    trunk 680.2
    tunica vaginalis 608.4
    umbilicus 680.2
    upper arm 680.3
    urethra 597.0
    vas deferens 608.4
    vulva 616.4
    wrist 680.4
Carbunculus — *see also* Carbuncle 680.9
Carcinoid (tumor) (M8240/1) — *see* Tumor, carcinoid
Carcinoidosis 259.2
Carcinomaphobia 300.29
Carcinomatosis
    peritonei (M8010/6) 197.6
    specified site NEC (M8010/3) — *see* Neoplasm, by site, malignant
    unspecified site (M8010/6) 199.0
Carcinoma (M8010/3) — *see also* Neoplasm, by site, malignant

Note — Except where otherwise indicated, the morphological varieties of carcinoma in the list below should be coded by site as for "Neoplasm, malignant."

    with
        apocrine metaplasia (M8573/3)
        cartilaginous (and osseous) metaplasia (M8571/3)
        osseous (and cartilaginous) metaplasia (M8571/3)
        productive fibrosis (M8141/3)
        spindle cell metaplasia (M8572/3)
        squamous metaplasia (M8570/3)
    acidophil (M8280/3)
        specified site — *see* Neoplasm, by site, malignant
        unspecified site 194.3
    acidophil-basophil, mixed (M8281/3)
        specified site — *see* Neoplasm, by site, malignant
        unspecified site 194.3
    acinar (cell) (M8550/3)
    acinic cell (M8550/3)
    adenocystic (M8200/3)
    adenoid
        cystic (M8200/3)
        squamous cell (M8075/3)
    adenosquamous (M8560/3)
    adnexal (skin) (M8390/3) — *see* Neoplasm, skin, malignant
    adrenal cortical (M8370/3) 194.0
    alveolar (M8251/3)
        cell (M8250/3) — *see* Neoplasm, lung, malignant
    anaplastic type (M8021/3)
    apocrine (M8401/3)
        breast — *see* Neoplasm, breast, malignant
        specified site NEC — *see* Neoplasm, skin, malignant
        unspecified site 173.99
    basal cell (pigmented) (M8090/3) (*see also* Neoplasm, skin, malignant) 173.91
    fibro-epithelial type (M8093/3) — *see* Neoplasm, skin, malignant
    morphea type (M8092/3) — *see* Neoplasm, skin, malignant

Carcinoma — *see also* Neoplasm, by site, malignant — *continued*
    basal cell (*see also* Neoplasm, skin, malignant) — *continued*
        multicentric (M8091/3) — *see* Neoplasm, skin, malignant
    basaloid (M8123/3)
    basal-squamous cell, mixed (M8094/3) — *see* Neoplasm, skin, malignant
    basophil (M8300/3)
        specified site — *see* Neoplasm, by site, malignant
        unspecified site 194.3
    basophil-acidophil, mixed (M8281/3)
        specified site — *see* Neoplasm, by site, malignant
        unspecified site 194.3
    basosquamous (M8094/3) — *see* Neoplasm, skin, malignant
    bile duct type (M8160/3)
        and hepatocellular, mixed (M8180/3) 155.0
        liver 155.1
        specified site NEC — *see* Neoplasm, by site, malignant
        unspecified site 155.1
    branchial or branchiogenic 146.8
    bronchial or bronchogenic — *see* Neoplasm, lung, malignant
    bronchiolar (terminal) (M8250/3) — *see* Neoplasm, lung, malignant
    bronchiolo-alveolar (M8250/3) — *see* Neoplasm, lung, malignant
    bronchogenic (epidermoid) 162.9
    C cell (M8510/3)
        specified site — *see* Neoplasm, by site, malignant
        unspecified site 193
    ceruminous (M8420/3) 173.29
    chorionic (M9100/3)
        specified site — *see* Neoplasm, by site, malignant
        unspecified site
            female 181
            male 186.9
    chromophobe (M8270/3)
        specified site — *see* Neoplasm, by site, malignant
        unspecified site 194.3
    clear cell (mesonephroid type) (M8310/3)
    cloacogenic (M8124/3)
        specified site — *see* Neoplasm, by site, malignant
        unspecified site 154.8
    colloid (M8480/3)
    cribriform (M8201/3)
    cylindroid type (M8200/3)
    diffuse type (M8145/3)
        specified site — *see* Neoplasm, by site, malignant
        unspecified site 151.9
    duct (cell) (M8500/3)
        with Paget's disease (M8541/3) — *see* Neoplasm, breast, malignant
        infiltrating (M8500/3)
            specified site — *see* Neoplasm, by site, malignant
            unspecified site 174.9
    ductal (M8500/3)
    ductular, infiltrating (M8521/3)
    embryonal (M9070/3)
        and teratoma, mixed (M9081/3)
        combined with choriocarcinoma (M9101/3) — *see* Neoplasm, by site, malignant
        infantile type (M9071/3)
        liver 155.0
        polyembryonal type (M9072/3)
    endometrioid (M8380/3)
    eosinophil (M8280/3)
        specified site — *see* Neoplasm, by site, malignant
        unspecified site 194.3
    epidermoid (M8070/3) (*see also* Carcinoma, squamous cell)

Carcinoma — *see also* Neoplasm, by site, malignant — *continued*
    epidermoid (*see also* Carcinoma, squamous cell) — *continued*
        and adenocarcinoma, mixed (M8560/3)
        in situ, Bowen's type (M8081/2) — *see* Neoplasm, skin, in situ
        intradermal — *see* Neoplasm, skin, in situ
    fibroepithelial type basal cell (M8093/3) — *see* Neoplasm, skin, malignant
    follicular (M8330/3)
        and papillary (mixed) (M8340/3) 193
        moderately differentiated type (M8332/3) 193
        pure follicle type (M8331/3) 193
        specified site — *see* Neoplasm, by site, malignant
        trabecular type (M8332/3) 193
        unspecified site 193
        well differentiated type (M8331/3) 193
    gelatinous (M8480/3)
    giant cell (M8031/3)
        and spindle cell (M8030/3)
    granular cell (M8320/3)
    granulosa cell (M8620/3) 183.0
    hepatic (M8170/3) 155.0
    hepatocellular (M8170/3) 155.0
        and bile duct, mixed (M8180/3) 155.0
    hepatocholangiolitic (M8180/3) 155.0
    Hürthle cell (thyroid) 193
    hypernephroid (M8311/3)
    in
        adenomatous
            polyp (M8210/3)
            polyposis coli (M8220/3) 153.9
        pleomorphic adenoma (M8940/3)
        polypoid adenoma (M8210/3)
        situ (M8010/3) — *see* Carcinoma, in situ
        tubular adenoma (M8210/3)
        villous adenoma (M8261/3)
    infiltrating duct (M8500/3)
        with Paget's disease (M8541/3) — *see* Neoplasm, breast, malignant
        specified site — *see* Neoplasm, by site, malignant
        unspecified site 174.9
    inflammatory (M8530/3)
        specified site — *see* Neoplasm, by site, malignant
        unspecified site 174.9
    in situ (M8010/2) (*see also* Neoplasm, by site, in situ)
        epidermoid (M8070/2) (*see also* Neoplasm, by site, in situ)
            with questionable stromal invasion (M8076/2)
            specified site — *see* Neoplasm, by site, in situ
            unspecified site 233.1
        Bowen's type (M8081/2) — *see* Neoplasm, skin, in situ
    intraductal (M8500/2)
        specified site — *see* Neoplasm, by site, in situ
        unspecified site 233.0
    lobular (M8520/2)
        specified site — *see* Neoplasm, by site, in situ
        unspecified site 233.0
    papillary (M8050/2) — *see* Neoplasm, by site, in situ
    squamous cell (M8070/2) (*see also* Neoplasm, by site, in situ)
        with questionable stromal invasion (M8076/2)
        specified site — *see* Neoplasm, by site, in situ
        unspecified site 233.1
    transitional cell (M8120/2) — *see* Neoplasm, by site, in situ
    intestinal type (M8144/3)
        specified site — *see* Neoplasm, by site, malignant
        unspecified site 151.9

Carcinoma — *see also* Neoplasm, by site, malignant — *continued*
    intraductal (noninfiltrating) (M8500/2)
        papillary (M8503/2)
            specified site — *see* Neoplasm, by site, in situ
            unspecified site 233.0
        specified site — *see* Neoplasm, by site, in situ
        unspecified site 233.0
    intraepidermal (M8070/2) (*see also* Neoplasm, skin, in situ)
        squamous cell, Bowen's type (M8081/2) — *see* Neoplasm, skin, in situ
    intraepithelial (M8010/2) (*see also* Neoplasm, by site, in situ)
        squamous cell (M8072/2) — *see* Neoplasm, by site, in situ
    intraosseous (M9270/3) 170.1
        upper jaw (bone) 170.0
    islet cell (M8150/3)
        and exocrine, mixed (M8154/3)
            specified site — *see* Neoplasm, by site, malignant
            unspecified site 157.9
        pancreas 157.4
        specified site NEC — *see* Neoplasm, by site, malignant
        unspecified site 157.4
    juvenile, breast (M8502/3) — *see* Neoplasm, breast, malignant
    Kulchitsky's cell (carcinoid tumor of intestine) 259.2
    large cell (M8012/3)
        squamous cell, non-keratinizing type (M8072/3)
    Leydig cell (testis) (M8650/3)
        specified site — *see* Neoplasm, by site, malignant
        unspecified site 186.9
            female 183.0
            male 186.9
    liver cell (M8170/3) 155.0
    lobular (infiltrating) (M8520/3)
        non-infiltrating (M8520/3)
            specified site — *see* Neoplasm, by site, in situ
            unspecified site 233.0
        specified site — *see* Neoplasm, by site, malignant
        unspecified site 174.9
    lymphoepithelial (M8082/3)
    medullary (M8510/3)
        with
            amyloid stroma (M8511/3)
                specified site — *see* Neoplasm, by site, malignant
                unspecified site 193
            lymphoid stroma (M8512/3)
                specified site — *see* Neoplasm, by site, malignant
                unspecified site 174.9
    Merkel cell 209.36
        buttock 209.36
        ear 209.31
        eyelid, including canthus 209.31
        face 209.31
        genitals 209.36
        lip 209.31
        lower limb 209.34
        neck 209.32
        nodal presentation 209.75
        scalp 209.32
        secondary (any site) 209.75
        specified site NEC 209.36
        trunk 209.35
        unknown primary site 209.75
        upper limb 209.33
        visceral metastatic presentation 209.75
    mesometanephric (M9110/3)
    mesonephric (M9110/3)
    metastatic (M8010/6) — *see* Metastasis, cancer
    metatypical (M8095/3) — *see* Neoplasm, skin, malignant

Carcinoma — *see also* Neoplasm, by site, malignant — *continued*
  morphea type basal cell (M8092/3) — *see* Neoplasm, skin, malignant
  mucinous (M8480/3)
  mucin-producing (M8481/3)
  mucin-secreting (M8481/3)
  mucoepidermoid (M8430/3)
  mucoid (M8480/3)
    cell (M8300/3)
      specified site — *see* Neoplasm, by site, malignant
      unspecified site 194.3
  mucous (M8480/3)
  neuroendocrine
    high grade (M8240/3) 209.30
    malignant poorly differentiated (M8240/3) 209.30
  nonencapsulated sclerosing (M8350/3) 193
  noninfiltrating
    intracystic (M8504/2) — *see* Neoplasm, by site, in situ
    intraductal (M8500/2)
      papillary (M8503/2)
        specified site — *see* Neoplasm, by site, in situ
        unspecified site 233.0
      specified site — *see* Neoplasm, by site, in situ
      unspecified site 233.0
    lobular (M8520/2)
      specified site — *see* Neoplasm, by site, in situ
      unspecified site 233.0
  oat cell (M8042/3)
    specified site — *see* Neoplasm, by site, malignant
    unspecified site 162.9
  odontogenic (M9270/3) 170.1
    upper jaw (bone) 170.0
  onocytic (M8290/3)
  oxyphilic (M8290/3)
  papillary (M8050/3)
    and follicular (mixed) (M8340/3) 193
    epidermoid (M8052/3)
    intraductal (noninfiltrating) (M8503/2)
      specified site — *see* Neoplasm, by site, in situ
      unspecified site 233.0
    serous (M8460/3)
      specified site — *see* Neoplasm, by site, malignant
      surface (M8461/3)
        specified site — *see* Neoplasm, by site, malignant
        unspecified site 183.0
      unspecified site 183.0
    squamous cell (M8052/3)
    transitional cell (M8130/3)
  papillocystic (M8450/3)
    specified site — *see* Neoplasm, by site, malignant
    unspecified site 183.0
  parafollicular cell (M8510/3)
    specified site — *see* Neoplasm, by site, malignant
    unspecified site 193
  pleomorphic (M8022/3)
  polygonal cell (M8034/3)
  prickle cell (M8070/3)
  pseudoglandular, squamous cell (M8075/3)
  pseudomucinous (M8470/3)
    specified site — *see* Neoplasm, by site, malignant
    unspecified site 183.0
  pseudosarcomatous (M8033/3)
  regaud type (M8082/3) — *see* Neoplasm, nasopharynx, malignant
  renal cell (M8312/3) 189.0
  reserve cell (M8041/3)
  round cell (M8041/3)
  Schmincke (M8082/3) — *see* Neoplasm, nasopharynx, malignant
  Schneiderian (M8121/3)
    specified site — *see* Neoplasm, by site, malignant

Carcinoma — *see also* Neoplasm, by site, malignant — *continued*
  Schneiderian — *continued*
    unspecified site 160.0
  scirrhous (M8141/3)
  sebaceous (M8410/3) — *see* Neoplasm, skin, malignant
  secondary (M8010/6) — *see* Neoplasm, by site, malignant, secondary
  secretory, breast (M8502/3) — *see* Neoplasm, breast, malignant
  serous (M8441/3)
    papillary (M8460/3)
      specified site — *see* Neoplasm, by site, malignant
      unspecified site 183.0
    surface, papillary (M8461/3)
      specified site — *see* Neoplasm, by site, malignant
      unspecified site 183.0
  Sertoli cell (M8640/3)
    specified site — *see* Neoplasm, by site, malignant
    unspecified site 186.9
  signet ring cell (M8490/3)
    metastatic (M8490/6) — *see* Neoplasm, by site, secondary
  simplex (M8231/3)
  skin appendage (M8390/3) — *see* Neoplasm, skin, malignant
  small cell (M8041/3)
    fusiform cell type (M8043/3)
    squamous cell, non-keratinizing type (M8073/3)
  solid (M8230/3)
    with amyloid stroma (M8511/3)
      specified site — *see* Neoplasm, by site, malignant
      unspecified site 193
  spheroidal cell (M8035/3)
  spindle cell (M8032/3)
    and giant cell (M8030/3)
  spinous cell (M8070/3)
  squamous (cell) (M8070/3)
    adenoid type (M8075/3)
    and adenocarcinoma, mixed (M8560/3)
    intraepidermal, Bowen's type — *see* Neoplasm, skin, in situ
    keratinizing type (large cell) (M8071/3)
    large cell, non-keratinizing type (M8072/3)
    microinvasive (M8076/3)
      specified site — *see* Neoplasm, by site, malignant
      unspecified site 180.9
    non-keratinizing type (M8072/3)
    papillary (M8052/3)
    pseudoglandular (M8075/3)
    skin (*see also* Neoplasm, skin, malignant) 173.92
    small cell, non-keratinizing type (M8073/3)
    spindle cell type (M8074/3)
    verrucous (M8051/3)
  superficial spreading (M8143/3)
  sweat gland (M8400/3) — *see* Neoplasm, skin, malignant
  theca cell (M8600/3) 183.0
  thymic (M8580/3) 164.0
  trabecular (M8190/3)
  transitional (cell) (M8120/3)
    papillary (M8130/3)
    spindle cell type (M8122/3)
  tubular (M8211/3)
  undifferentiated type (M8020/3)
  urothelial (M8120/3)
  ventriculi 151.9
  verrucous (epidermoid) (squamous cell) (M8051/3)
  villous (M8262/3)
  water-clear cell (M8322/3) 194.1
  wolffian duct (M9110/3)
Carcinosarcoma (M8980/3) — *see also* Neoplasm, by site, malignant
  embryonal type (M8981/3) — *see* Neoplasm, by site, malignant

Cardiac — *see also* condition
  death — *see* Disease, heart
  device
    defibrillator, automatic implantable (with synchronous cardiac pacemaker) V45.02
    in situ NEC V45.00
    pacemaker
      cardiac
        fitting or adjustment V53.31
        in situ V45.01
      carotid sinus
        fitting or adjustment V53.39
        in situ V45.09
    pacemaker — *see* Cardiac, device, pacemaker
    tamponade 423.3
Cardia, cardial — *see* condition
Cardialgia — *see also* Pain, precordial 786.51
Cardiectasis — *see* Hypertrophy, cardiac
Cardiochalasia 530.81
Cardiomalacia — *see also* Degeneration, myocardial 429.1
Cardiomegalia glycogenica diffusa 271.0
Cardiomegaly — *see also* Hypertrophy, cardiac 429.3
  congenital 746.89
  glycogen 271.0
  hypertensive (*see also* Hypertension, heart) 402.90
  idiopathic 429.3
Cardiomyoliposis — *see also* Degeneration, myocardial 429.1
Cardiomyopathy (congestive) (constrictive) (familial) (infiltrative) (obstructive) (restrictive) (sporadic) 425.4
  alcoholic 425.5
  amyloid 277.39 [425.7]
  beriberi 265.0 [425.7]
  cobalt-beer 425.5
  congenital 425.3
  due to
    amyloidosis 277.39 [425.7]
    beriberi 265.0 [425.7]
    cardiac glycogenosis 271.0 [425.7]
    Chagas' disease 086.0
    Friedreich's ataxia 334.0 [425.8]
    hypertension — *see* Hypertension, with, heart involvement
    mucopolysaccharidosis 277.5 [425.7]
    myotonia atrophica 359.21 [425.8]
    progressive muscular dystrophy 359.1 [425.8]
    sarcoidosis 135 [425.8]
  glycogen storage 271.0 [425.7]
  hypertensive — *see* Hypertension, with, heart involvement
  hypertrophic 425.18
    nonobstructive 425.18
    obstructive 425.11
      congenital 746.84
  idiopathic (concentric) 425.4
  in
    Chagas' disease 086.0
    sarcoidosis 135 [425.8]
  ischemic 414.8
  metabolic NEC 277.9 [425.7]
    amyloid 277.39 [425.7]
    thyrotoxic (*see also* Thyrotoxicosis) 242.9 ☑ [425.7]
    thyrotoxicosis (*see also* Thyrotoxicosis) 242.9 ☑ [425.7]
  newborn 425.4
    congenital 425.3
  nutritional 269.9 [425.7]
    beriberi 265.0 [425.7]
  obscure of Africa 425.2
  peripartum 674.5 ☑
  postpartum 674.5 ☑
  primary 425.4
  secondary 425.9
  stress inuced 429.83
  takotsubo 429.83
  thyrotoxic (*see also* Thyrotoxicosis) 242.9 ☑ [425.7]
  toxic NEC 425.9

Cardiomyopathy — *continued*
  tuberculous (*see also* Tuberculosis) 017.9 ☑ [425.8]
Cardionephritis — *see* Hypertension, cardiorenal
Cardionephropathy — *see* Hypertension, cardiorenal
Cardionephrosis — *see* Hypertension, cardiorenal
Cardioneurosis 306.2
Cardiopathia nigra 416.0
Cardiopathy — *see also* Disease, heart 429.9
  hypertensive (*see also* Hypertension, heart) 402.90
  idiopathic 425.4
  mucopolysaccharidosis 277.5 [425.7]
Cardiopericarditis — *see also* Pericarditis 423.9
Cardiophobia 300.29
Cardioptosis 746.87
Cardiorenal — *see* condition
Cardiorrhexis — *see also* Infarct, myocardium 410.9 ☑
Cardiosclerosis — *see* Arteriosclerosis, coronary
Cardiosis — *see* Disease, heart
Cardiospasm (esophagus) (reflex) (stomach) 530.0
  congenital 750.7
Cardiostenosis — *see* Disease, heart
Cardiosymphysis 423.1
Cardiothyrotoxicosis — *see* Hyperthyroidism
Cardiovascular — *see* condition
Carditis (acute) (bacterial) (chronic) (subacute) 429.89
  Coxsackie 074.20
  hypertensive (*see also* Hypertension, heart) 402.90
  meningococcal 036.40
  rheumatic — *see* Disease, heart, rheumatic
  rheumatoid 714.2
Care (of)
  child (routine) V20.1
  convalescent following V66.9
    chemotherapy V66.2
    medical NEC V66.5
    psychotherapy V66.3
    radiotherapy V66.1
    surgery V66.0
    surgical NEC V66.0
    treatment (for) V66.5
      combined V66.6
      fracture V66.4
      mental disorder NEC V66.3
      specified type NEC V66.5
  end-of-life V66.7
  family member (handicapped) (sick)
    creating problem for family V61.49
    provided away from home for holiday relief V60.5
    unavailable, due to
      absence (person rendering care) (sufferer) V60.4
      inability (any reason) of person rendering care V60.4
  holiday relief V60.5
  hospice V66.7
  lack of (at or after birth) (infant) (child) 995.52
    adult 995.84
  lactation of mother V24.1
  palliative V66.7
  postpartum
    immediately after delivery V24.0
    routine follow-up V24.2
  prenatal V22.1
    first pregnancy V22.0
    high-risk pregnancy V23.9
      inconclusive fetal viability V23.87
      specified problem NEC V23.89
  terminal V66.7
  unavailable, due to
    absence of person rendering care V60.4
    inability (any reason) of person rendering care V60.4
  well baby V20.1

☑ Additional Digit Required — Refer to the Tabular List for Digit Selection   ▽ Subterms under main terms may continue to next column or page

Caries (bone) — *see also* Tuberculosis, bone
  015.9 ☑ *[730.8]* ☑
  arrested 521.04
  cementum 521.03
  cerebrospinal (tuberculous)
    015.0 ☑ *[730.88]*
  dental (acute) (chronic) (incipient) (infected)
    521.00
    with pulp exposure 521.03
    extending to
      dentine 521.02
      pulp 521.03
    other specified NEC 521.09
    pit and fissure 521.06
    primary
      pit and fissure origin 521.06
      root surface 521.08
      smooth surface origin 521.07
    root surface 521.08
    smooth surface 521.07
  dentin (acute) (chronic) 521.02
  enamel (acute) (chronic) (incipient) 521.01
  external meatus 380.89
  hip (*see also* Tuberculosis) 015.1 ☑ *[730.85]*
  initial 521.01
  knee 015.2 ☑ *[730.86]*
  labyrinth 386.8
  limb NEC 015.7 ☑ *[730.88]*
  mastoid (chronic) (process) 383.1
  middle ear 385.89
  nose 015.7 ☑ *[730.88]*
  orbit 015.7 ☑ *[730.88]*
  ossicle 385.24
  petrous bone 383.20
  sacrum (tuberculous) 015.0 ☑ *[730.88]*
  spine, spinal (column) (tuberculous)
    015.0 ☑ *[730.88]*
  syphilitic 095.5
    congenital 090.0 *[730.8]* ☑
  teeth (internal) 521.00
    initial 521.01
  vertebra (column) (tuberculous)
    015.0 ☑ *[730.88]*
Carini's syndrome (ichthyosis congenita) 757.1
Carious teeth 521.00
Carneous mole 631.8
Carnosinemia 270.5
Carotid body or sinus syndrome 337.01
Carotidynia 337.01
Carotinemia (dietary) 278.3
Carotinosis (cutis) (skin) 278.3
Carpal tunnel syndrome 354.0
Carpenter's syndrome 759.89
Carpopedal spasm — *see also* Tetany 781.7
Carpoptosis 736.05
Carrier (suspected) of
  amebiasis V02.2
  bacterial disease (meningococcal, staphylo-
    coccal) NEC V02.59
  cholera V02.0
  cystic fibrosis gene V83.81
  defective gene V83.89
  diphtheria V02.4
  dysentery (bacillary) V02.3
    amebic V02.2
  Endamoeba histolytica V02.2
  gastrointestinal pathogens NEC V02.3
  genetic defect V83.89
  gonorrhea V02.7
  group B streptococcus V02.51
  HAA (hepatitis Australian-antigen) V02.61
  hemophilia A (asymptomatic) V83.01
    symptomatic V83.02
  hepatitis V02.60
    Australian-antigen (HAA) V02.61
    B V02.61
    C V02.62
    serum V02.61
    specified type NEC V02.69
    viral V02.60
  infective organism NEC V02.9
  malaria V02.9
  paratyphoid V02.3
  Salmonella V02.3
    typhosa V02.1
  serum hepatitis V02.61

Carrier (suspected) of — *continued*
  Shigella V02.3
  Staphylococcus NEC V02.59
    methicillin
      resistant Staphylococcus aureus
        V02.54
      susceptible Staphylococcus aureus
        V02.53
  Streptococcus NEC V02.52
    group B V02.51
  typhoid V02.1
  venereal disease NEC V02.8
Carrión's disease (Bartonellosis) 088.0
Car sickness 994.6
Carter's
  relapsing fever (Asiatic) 087.0
Cartilage — *see* condition
Caruncle (inflamed)
  abscess, lacrimal (*see also* Dacryocystitis)
    375.30
  conjunctiva 372.00
    acute 372.00
  eyelid 373.00
  labium (majus) (minus) 616.89
  lacrimal 375.30
  urethra (benign) 599.3
  vagina (wall) 616.89
Cascade stomach 537.6
Caseation lymphatic gland — *see also* Tuberculosis 017.2 ☑
Caseous ☑
  bronchitis — *see* Tuberculosis, pulmonary
  meningitis 013.0 ☑
  pneumonia — *see* Tuberculosis, pulmonary
Cassidy (-Scholte) syndrome (malignant carcinoid) 259.2
Castellani's bronchitis 104.8
Castleman's tumor or lymphoma (mediastinal lymph node hyperplasia) 785.6
Castration, traumatic 878.2
  complicated 878.3
Casts in urine 791.7
Catalepsy 300.11
  catatonic (acute) (*see also* Schizophrenia)
    295.2 ☑
  hysterical 300.11
  schizophrenic (*see also* Schizophrenia)
    295.2 ☑
Cataphasia — *see also* Disorder, fluency 315.35
Cataplexy (idiopathic) — *see* Narcolepsy
Cataract (anterior cortical) (anterior polar)
  (black) (capsular) (central) (cortical) (hypermature) (immature) (incipient) (mature) 366.9
  anterior
    and posterior axial embryonal 743.33
    pyramidal 743.31
    subcapsular polar
      infantile, juvenile, or presenile 366.01
      senile 366.13
  associated with
    calcinosis 275.40 *[366.42]*
    craniofacial dysostosis 756.0 *[366.44]*
    galactosemia 271.1 *[366.44]*
    hypoparathyroidism 252.1 *[366.42]*
    myotonic disorders 359.21 *[366.43]*
    neovascularization 366.33
  blue dot 743.39
  cerulean 743.39
  complicated NEC 366.30
  congenital 743.30
    capsular or subcapsular 743.31
    cortical 743.32
    nuclear 743.33
    specified type NEC 743.39
    total or subtotal 743.34
    zonular 743.32
  coronary (congenital) 743.39
    acquired 366.12
  cupuliform 366.14
  diabetic 250.5 ☑ *[366.41]*
    due to secondary diabetes
      249.5 ☑ *[366.41]*
  drug-induced 366.45
  due to
    chalcosis 360.24 *[366.34]*

Cataract — *continued*
  due to — *continued*
    chronic choroiditis (*see also* Choroiditis)
      363.20 *[366.32]*
    degenerative myopia 360.21 *[366.34]*
    glaucoma (*see also* Glaucoma)
      365.9 *[366.31]*
    infection, intraocular NEC 366.32
    inflammatory ocular disorder NEC 366.32
    iridocyclitis, chronic 364.10 *[366.33]*
    pigmentary retinal dystrophy
      362.74 *[366.34]*
    radiation 366.46
  electric 366.46
  glassblowers' 366.46
  heat ray 366.46
  heterochromic 366.33
  in eye disease NEC 366.30
  infantile (*see also* Cataract, juvenile) 366.00
  intumescent 366.12
  irradiational 366.46
  juvenile 366.00
    anterior subcapsular polar 366.01
    combined forms 366.09
    cortical 366.03
    lamellar 366.03
    nuclear 366.04
    posterior subcapsular polar 366.02
    specified NEC 366.09
    zonular 366.03
  lamellar 743.32
    infantile, juvenile, or presenile 366.03
  morgagnian 366.18
  myotonic 359.21 *[366.43]*
  myxedema 244.9 *[366.44]*
  nuclear 366.16
  posterior, polar (capsular) 743.31
    infantile, juvenile, or presenile 366.02
    senile 366.14
  presenile (*see also* Cataract, juvenile) 366.00
  punctate
    acquired 366.12
    congenital 743.39
  secondary (membrane) 366.50
    obscuring vision 366.53
    specified type, not obscuring vision
      366.52
  senile 366.10
    anterior subcapsular polar 366.13
    combined forms 366.19
    cortical 366.15
    hypermature 366.18
    immature 366.12
    incipient 366.12
    mature 366.17
    nuclear 366.16
    posterior subcapsular polar 366.14
    specified NEC 366.19
    total or subtotal 366.17
  snowflake 250.5 ☑ *[366.41]*
    due to secondary diabetes
      249.5 ☑ *[366.41]*
  specified NEC 366.8
  subtotal (senile) 366.17
    congenital 743.34
  sunflower 360.24 *[366.34]*
  tetanic NEC 252.1 *[366.42]*
  total (mature) (senile) 366.17
    congenital 743.34
    localized 366.21
    traumatic 366.22
  toxic 366.45
  traumatic 366.20
    partially resolved 366.23
    total 366.22
  zonular (perinuclear) 743.32
    infantile, juvenile, or presenile 366.03
Cataracta 366.10
  brunescens 366.16
  cerulea 743.39
  complicata 366.30
  congenita 743.30
  coralliformis 743.39
  coronaria (congenital) 743.39
    acquired 366.12
  diabetic 250.5 ☑ *[366.41]*

Cataracta — *continued*
  diabetic — *continued*
    due to secondary diabetes
      249.5 ☑ *[366.41]*
  floriformis 360.24 *[366.34]*
  membranacea
    accreta 366.50
    congenita 743.39
  nigra 366.16
Catarrh, catarrhal (inflammation) — *see also*
  condition 460
  acute 460
  asthma, asthmatic (*see also* Asthma)
    493.9 ☑
  Bostock's (*see also* Fever, hay) 477.9
  bowel — *see* Enteritis
  bronchial 490
    acute 466.0
    chronic 491.0
    subacute 466.0
  cervix, cervical (canal) (uteri) — *see* Cervicitis
  chest (*see also* Bronchitis) 490
  chronic 472.0
  congestion 472.0
  conjunctivitis 372.03
  due to syphilis 095.9
    congenital 090.0
  enteric — *see* Enteritis
  epidemic (*see also* Influenza) 487.1
  Eustachian 381.50
  eye (acute) (vernal) 372.03
  fauces (*see also* Pharyngitis) 462
  febrile 460
  fibrinous acute 466.0
  gastroenteric — *see* Enteritis
  gastrointestinal — *see* Enteritis
  gingivitis 523.00
  hay (*see also* Fever, hay) 477.9
  infectious 460
  intestinal — *see* Enteritis
  larynx (*see also* Laryngitis, chronic) 476.0
  liver 070.1
    with hepatic coma 070.0
  lung (*see also* Bronchitis) 490
    acute 466.0
    chronic 491.0
  middle ear (chronic) — *see* Otitis media,
    chronic
  mouth 528.00
  nasal (chronic) (*see also* Rhinitis) 472.0
    acute 460
  nasobronchial 472.2
  nasopharyngeal (chronic) 472.2
    acute 460
  nose — *see* Catarrh, nasal
  ophthalmia 372.03
  pneumococcal, acute 466.0
  pulmonary (*see also* Bronchitis) 490
    acute 466.0
    chronic 491.0
  spring (eye) 372.13
  suffocating (*see also* Asthma) 493.9 ☑
  summer (hay) (*see also* Fever, hay) 477.9
  throat 472.1
  tracheitis 464.10
    with obstruction 464.11
  tubotympanal 381.4
    acute (*see also* Otitis media, acute, non-
      suppurative) 381.00
    chronic 381.10
  vasomotor (*see also* Fever, hay) 477.9
  vesical (bladder) — *see* Cystitis
Catarrhus aestivus — *see also* Fever, hay 477.9
Catastrophe, cerebral — *see also* Disease,
  cerebrovascular, acute 436
Catatonia, catatonic (acute) 781.99
  with
    affective psychosis — *see* Psychosis, af-
      fective
  agitation 295.2 ☑
  dementia (praecox) 295.2 ☑
  due to or associated with physical condition
    293.89
  excitation 295.2 ☑
  excited type 295.2 ☑
  in conditions classified elsewhere 293.89

☑ Additional Digit Required — Refer to the Tabular List for Digit Selection
▽ Subterms under main terms may continue to next column or page
44 — Volume 2   ▶◀ Revised Text   ● New Line   ▲ Revised Code   2015 ICD-9-CM

Catatonia, catatonic — *continued*
  schizophrenia 295.2 ☑
  stupor 295.2 ☑
Cat's ear 744.29
Cat-scratch — *see also* Injury, superficial
  disease or fever 078.3
Cauda equina — *see also* condition
  syndrome 344.60
Cauliflower ear 738.7
Caul over face 768.9
Causalgia 355.9
  lower limb 355.71
  upper limb 354.4
Cause
  external, general effects NEC 994.9
  not stated 799.9
  unknown 799.9
Caustic burn — *see also* Burn, by site
  from swallowing caustic or corrosive sub-
    stance — *see* Burn, internal organs
Cavare's disease (familial periodic paralysis)
  359.3
Cave-in, injury
  crushing (severe) (*see also* Crush, by site)
    869.1
  suffocation 994.7
Cavernitis (penis) 607.2
  lymph vessel — *see* Lymphangioma
Cavernositis 607.2
Cavernous — *see* condition
Cavitation of lung — *see also* Tuberculosis
  011.2 ☑
  nontuberculous 518.89
  primary, progressive 010.8 ☑
Cavity
  lung — *see* Cavitation of lung
  optic papilla 743.57
  pulmonary — *see* Cavitation of lung
  teeth 521.00
  vitreous (humor) 379.21
Cavovarus foot, congenital 754.59
Cavus foot (congenital) 754.71
  acquired 736.73
Cazenave's
  disease (pemphigus) NEC 694.4
  lupus (erythematosus) 695.4
CDGS (carbohydrate-deficient glycoprotein
  syndrome) 271.8
Cecitis — *see* Appendicitis
Cecocele — *see* Hernia
Cecum — *see* condition
Celiac
  artery compression syndrome 447.4
  disease 579.0
  infantilism 579.0
Cell, cellular — *see also* condition
  anterior chamber (eye) (positive aqueous
    ray) 364.04
Cellulitis (diffuse) (with lymphangitis) — *see
  also* Abscess 682.9
  abdominal wall 682.2
  anaerobic (*see also* Gas gangrene) 040.0
  ankle 682.6
  anus 566
  areola 611.0
  arm (any part, above wrist) 682.3
  auditory canal (external) 380.10
  axilla 682.3
  back (any part) 682.2
  breast 611.0
    postpartum 675.1 ☑
  broad ligament (*see also* Disease, pelvis, in-
    flammatory) 614.4
    acute 614.3
  buttock 682.5
  cervical (neck region) 682.1
  cervix (uteri) (*see also* Cervicitis) 616.0
  cheek, external 682.0
    internal 528.3
  chest wall 682.2
  chronic NEC 682.9
  colostomy 569.61
  corpus cavernosum 607.2
  digit 681.9

Cellulitis — *see also* Abscess — *continued*
  Douglas' cul-de-sac or pouch (chronic) (*see
    also* Disease, pelvis, inflammatory)
    614.4
    acute 614.3
  drainage site (following operation) 998.59
  ear, external 380.10
  enterostomy 569.61
  erysipelar (*see also* Erysipelas) 035
  esophagostomy 530.86
  eyelid 373.13
  face (any part, except eye) 682.0
  finger (intrathecal) (periosteal) (subcuta-
    neous) (subcuticular) 681.00
  flank 682.2
  foot (except toe) 682.7
  forearm 682.3
  gangrenous (*see also* Gangrene) 785.4
  genital organ NEC
    female — *see* Abscess, genital organ,
      female
    male 608.4
  glottis 478.71
  gluteal (region) 682.5
  gonococcal NEC 098.0
  groin 682.2
  hand (except finger or thumb) 682.4
  head (except face) NEC 682.8
  heel 682.7
  hip 682.6
  jaw (region) 682.0
  knee 682.6
  labium (majus) (minus) (*see also* Vulvitis)
    616.10
  larynx 478.71
  leg, except foot 682.6
  lip 528.5
  mammary gland 611.0
  mouth (floor) 528.3
  multiple sites NEC 682.9
  nasopharynx 478.21
  navel 682.2
    newborn NEC 771.4
  neck (region) 682.1
  nipple 611.0
  nose 478.19
    external 682.0
  orbit, orbital 376.01
  palate (soft) 528.3
  pectoral (region) 682.2
  pelvis, pelvic
    with
      abortion — *see* Abortion, by type,
        with sepsis
      ectopic pregnancy (*see also* cate-
        gories 633.0–633.9) 639.0
      molar pregnancy (*see also* categories
        630–632) 639.0
    female (*see also* Disease, pelvis, inflam-
      matory) 614.4
      acute 614.3
    following
      abortion 639.0
      ectopic or molar pregnancy 639.0
    male 567.21
    puerperal, postpartum, childbirth
      670.8 ☑
  penis 607.2
  perineal, perineum 682.2
  perirectal 566
  peritonsillar 475
  periurethral 597.0
  periuterine (*see also* Disease, pelvis, inflam-
    matory) 614.4
    acute 614.3
  pharynx 478.21
  phlegmonous NEC 682.9
  rectum 566
  retromammary 611.0
  retroperitoneal (*see also* Peritonitis)
    567.2 ☑, 567.38
  round ligament (*see also* Disease, pelvis, in-
    flammatory) 614.4
    acute 614.3
  scalp (any part) 682.8
    dissecting 704.8

Cellulitis — *see also* Abscess — *continued*
  scrotum 608.4
  seminal vesicle 608.0
  septic NEC 682.9
  shoulder 682.3
  specified sites NEC 682.8
  spermatic cord 608.4
  submandibular (region) (space) (triangle)
    682.0
    gland 527.3
  submaxillary 528.3
    gland 527.3
  submental (pyogenic) 682.0
    gland 527.3
  suppurative NEC 682.9
  testis 608.4
  thigh 682.6
  thumb (intrathecal) (periosteal) (subcuta-
    neous) (subcuticular) 681.00
  toe (intrathecal) (periosteal) (subcutaneous)
    (subcuticular) 681.10
  tonsil 475
  trunk 682.2
  tuberculous (primary) (*see also* Tuberculosis)
    017.0 ☑
  tunica vaginalis 608.4
  umbilical 682.2
    newborn NEC 771.4
  vaccinal 999.39
  vagina — *see* Vaginitis
  vas deferens 608.4
  vocal cords 478.5
  vulva (*see also* Vulvitis) 616.10
  wrist 682.4
Cementoblastoma, benign (M9273/0) 213.1
  upper jaw (bone) 213.0
Cementoma (M9273/0) 213.1
  gigantiform (M9275/0) 213.1
    upper jaw (bone) 213.0
  upper jaw (bone) 213.0
Cementoperiostitis 523.40
  acute 523.33
  apical 523.40
Cephalgia, cephalagia — *see also* Headache
  784.0
  histamine 339.00
  nonorganic origin 307.81
  other trigeminal autonomic (TACS) 339.09
  psychogenic 307.81
  tension 307.81
Cephalhematocele, cephalematocele
  due to birth injury 767.19
  fetus or newborn 767.19
  traumatic (*see also* Contusion, head) 920
Cephalhematoma, cephalematoma (calcified)
  due to birth injury 767.19
  fetus or newborn 767.19
  traumatic (*see also* Contusion, head) 920
Cephalic — *see* condition
Cephalitis — *see* Encephalitis
Cephalocele 742.0
Cephaloma — *see* Neoplasm, by site, malig-
  nant
Cephalomenia 625.8
Cephalopelvic — *see* condition
Cercomoniasis 007.3
Cerebellitis — *see* Encephalitis
Cerebellum (cerebellar) — *see* condition
Cerebral — *see* condition
Cerebritis — *see* Encephalitis
Cerebrohepatorenal syndrome 759.89
Cerebromacular degeneration 330.1
Cerebromalacia — *see also* Softening, brain
  348.89
  due to cerebrovascular accident 438.89
Cerebrosidosis 272.7
Cerebrospasticity — *see* Palsy, cerebral
Cerebrospinal — *see* condition
Cerebrum — *see* condition
Ceroid storage disease 272.7
Cerumen (accumulation) (impacted) 380.4
Cervical — *see also* condition
  auricle 744.43
  high risk human papillomavirus (HPV) DNA
    test positive 795.05

Cervical — *see also* condition — *continued*
  intraepithelial glandular neoplasia 233.1
  low risk human papillomavirus (HPV) DNA
    test positive 795.09
  rib 756.2
  shortening — *see* Short, cervical
Cervicalgia 723.1
Cervicitis (acute) (chronic) (nonvenereal)
  (subacute) (with erosion or ectropion)
  616.0
  with
    abortion — *see* Abortion, by type, with
      sepsis
    ectopic pregnancy (*see also* categories
      633.0–633.9) 639.0
    molar pregnancy (*see also* categories
      630–632) 639.0
    ulceration 616.0
  chlamydial 099.53
  complicating pregnancy or puerperium
    646.6 ☑
    affecting fetus or newborn 760.8
  following
    abortion 639.0
    ectopic or molar pregnancy 639.0
  gonococcal (acute) 098.15
    chronic or duration of 2 months or more
      098.35
  senile (atrophic) 616.0
  syphilitic 095.8
  trichomonal 131.09
  tuberculous (*see also* Tuberculosis) 016.7 ☑
Cervicoaural fistula 744.49
Cervicocolpitis (emphysematosa) — *see also*
  Cervicitis 616.0
Cervix — *see* condition
Cesarean delivery, operation or section NEC
  669.7 ☑
  affecting fetus or newborn 763.4
  (planned) occurring after 37 completed
    weeks of gestation but before 39
    completed weeks gestation due to
    (spontaneous) onset of labor
    649.8 ☑
  post mortem, affecting fetus or newborn
    761.6
  previous, affecting management of pregnan-
    cy 654.2 ☑
Céstan-Chenais paralysis 344.89
Céstan-Raymond syndrome 433.8 ☑
Céstan's syndrome 344.89
Cestode infestation NEC 123.9
  specified type NEC 123.8
Cestodiasis 123.9
CGF (congenital generalized fibromatosis)
  759.89
Chabert's disease 022.9
Chacaleh 266.2
Chafing 709.8
Chagas' disease — *see also* Trypanosomiasis,
  American 086.2
  with heart involvement 086.0
Chagres fever 084.0
Chalasia (cardiac sphincter) 530.81
Chalazion 373.2
Chalazoderma 757.39
Chalcosis 360.24
  cornea 371.15
  crystalline lens 360.24 [366.34]
  retina 360.24
Chalicosis (occupational) (pulmonum) 502
Chancre (any genital site) (hard) (indurated)
  (infecting) (primary) (recurrent) 091.0
  congenital 090.0
  conjunctiva 091.2
  Ducrey's 099.0
  extragenital 091.2
  eyelid 091.2
  Hunterian 091.0
  lip (syphilis) 091.2
  mixed 099.8
  nipple 091.2
  Nisbet's 099.0
  of
    carate 103.0
    pinta 103.0

☑ **Additional Digit Required** — Refer to the Tabular List for Digit Selection   ▽ **Subterms under main terms may continue to next column or page**

2015 ICD-9-CM   ►◄ Revised Text   ● New Line   ▲ Revised Code   Volume 2 — 45

Chancre — continued
of — continued
yaws 102.0
palate, soft 091.2
phagedenic 099.0
Ricord's 091.0
Rollet's (syphilitic) 091.0
seronegative 091.0
seropositive 091.0
simple 099.0
soft 099.0
bubo 099.0
urethra 091.0
yaws 102.0
Chancriform syndrome 114.1
Chancroid 099.0
anus 099.0
penis (Ducrey's bacillus) 099.0
perineum 099.0
rectum 099.0
scrotum 099.0
urethra 099.0
vulva 099.0
Chandipura fever 066.8
Chandler's disease (osteochondritis dissecans, hip) 732.7
Change(s) (of) — see also Removal of
arteriosclerotic — see Arteriosclerosis
battery
cardiac pacemaker V53.31
bone 733.90
diabetic 250.8 ☑ [731.8]
due to secondary diabetes
249.8 ☑ [731.8]
in disease, unknown cause 733.90
bowel habits 787.99
cardiorenal (vascular) (see also Hypertension, cardiorenal) 404.90
cardiovascular — see Disease, cardiovascular
circulatory 459.9
cognitive or personality change of other type, nonpsychotic 310.1
color, teeth, tooth
during formation 520.8
extrinsic 523.6
intrinsic posteruptive 521.7
contraceptive device V25.42
cornea, corneal
degenerative NEC 371.40
membrane NEC 371.30
senile 371.41
coronary (see also Ischemia, heart) 414.9
degenerative
chamber angle (anterior) (iris) 364.56
ciliary body 364.57
spine or vertebra (see also Spondylosis) 721.90
dental pulp, regressive 522.2
drains V58.49
dressing
wound V58.30
nonsurgical V58.30
surgical V58.31
fixation device V54.89
external V54.89
internal V54.01
heart (see also Disease, heart)
hip joint 718.95
hyperplastic larynx 478.79
hypertrophic
nasal sinus (see also Sinusitis) 473.9
turbinate, nasal 478.0
upper respiratory tract 478.9
inflammatory — see Inflammation
joint (see also Derangement, joint) 718.90
sacroiliac 724.6
Kirschner wire V54.89
knee 717.9
macular, congenital 743.55

Change(s) — see also Removal of — continued
malignant (M — — /3) (see also Neoplasm, by site, malignant)

> Note — for malignant change occurring in a neoplasm, use the appropriate M code with behavior digit /3 e.g., malignant change in uterine fibroid — M8890/3. For malignant change occurring in a nonneoplastic condition (e.g., gastric ulcer) use the M code M8000/3.

mental (status) NEC 780.97
due to or associated with physical condition — see Syndrome, brain
myocardium, myocardial — see Degeneration, myocardial
of life (see also Menopause) 627.2
pacemaker battery (cardiac) V53.31
peripheral nerve 355.9
personality (nonpsychotic) NEC 310.1
plaster cast V54.89
refractive, transient 367.81
regressive, dental pulp 522.2
retina 362.9
myopic (degenerative) (malignant) 360.21
vascular appearance 362.13
sacroiliac joint 724.6
scleral 379.19
degenerative 379.16
senile (see also Senility) 797
sensory (see also Disturbance, sensation) 782.0
skin texture 782.8
spinal cord 336.9
splint, external V54.89
subdermal implantable contraceptive V25.5
suture V58.32
traction device V54.89
trophic 355.9
arm NEC 354.9
leg NEC 355.8
lower extremity NEC 355.8
upper extremity NEC 354.9
vascular 459.9
vasomotor 443.9
voice 784.49
psychogenic 306.1
wound packing V58.30
nonsurgical V58.30
surgical V58.31
Changing sleep-work schedule, affecting sleep 327.36
Changuinola fever 066.0
Chapping skin 709.8
Character
depressive 301.12
Charcôt's
arthropathy 094.0 [713.5]
cirrhosis — see Cirrhosis, biliary
disease 094.0
spinal cord 094.0
fever (biliary) (hepatic) (intermittent) — see Choledocholithiasis
joint (disease) 094.0 [713.5]
diabetic 250.6 ☑ [713.5]
due to secondary diabetes 249.6 ☑ [713.5]
syringomyelic 336.0 [713.5]
syndrome (intermittent claudication) 443.9
due to atherosclerosis 440.21
Charcôt-Marie-Tooth disease, paralysis, or syndrome 356.1
CHARGE association (syndrome) 759.89
Charleyhorse (quadriceps) 843.8
muscle, except quadriceps — see Sprain, by site
Charlouis' disease — see also Yaws 102.9
Chauffeur's fracture — see Fracture, ulna, lower end
Cheadle (-Möller) (-Barlow) disease or syndrome (infantile scurvy) 267
Checking (of)
contraceptive device (intrauterine) V25.42
device
fixation V54.89

Checking — continued
device — continued
fixation — continued
external V54.89
internal V54.09
traction V54.89
Kirschner wire V54.89
plaster cast V54.89
splint, external V54.89
Checkup
following treatment — see Examination
health V70.0
infant (over 28 days old) (not sick) V20.2
newborn, routine
8 to 28 days old V20.32
over 28 days old, routine V20.2
under 8 days old V20.31
weight V20.32
pregnancy (normal) V22.1
first V22.0
high-risk pregnancy V23.9
inconclusive fetal viability V23.87
specified problem NEC V23.89
Chédiak-Higashi (-Steinbrinck) anomaly, disease, or syndrome (congenital gigantism of peroxidase granules) 288.2
Cheek — see also condition
biting 528.9
Cheese itch 133.8
Cheese washers' lung 495.8
Cheilitis 528.5
actinic (due to sun) 692.72
chronic NEC 692.74
due to radiation, except from sun 692.82
due to radiation, except from sun 692.82
acute 528.5
angular 528.5
catarrhal 528.5
chronic 528.5
exfoliative 528.5
gangrenous 528.5
glandularis apostematosa 528.5
granulomatosa 351.8
infectional 528.5
membranous 528.5
Miescher's 351.8
suppurative 528.5
ulcerative 528.5
vesicular 528.5
Cheilodynia 528.5
Cheilopalatoschisis — see also Cleft, palate, with cleft lip 749.20
Cheilophagia 528.9
Cheiloschisis — see also Cleft, lip 749.10
Cheilosis 528.5
with pellagra 265.2
angular 528.5
due to
dietary deficiency 266.0
vitamin deficiency 266.0
Cheiromegaly 729.89
Cheiropompholyx 705.81
Cheloid — see also Keloid 701.4
Chemical burn — see also Burn, by site
from swallowing chemical — see Burn, internal organs
Chemodectoma (M8693/1) — see Paraganglioma, nonchromaffin
Chemoprophylaxis NEC V07.39
Chemosis, conjunctiva 372.73
Chemotherapy
convalescence V66.2
encounter (for) (oral) (intravenous) V58.11
maintenance (oral) (intravenous) V58.11
prophylactic NEC V07.39
fluoride V07.31
Cherubism 526.89
Chest — see condition
Cheyne-Stokes respiration (periodic) 786.04
Chiari's
disease or syndrome (hepatic vein thrombosis) 453.0
malformation
type I 348.4
type II (see also Spina bifida) 741.0 ☑

Chiari's — continued
malformation — continued
type III 742.0
type IV 742.2
network 746.89
Chiari-Frommel syndrome 676.6 ☑
Chicago disease (North American blastomycosis) 116.0
Chickenpox — see also Varicella 052.9
exposure to V01.71
vaccination and inoculation (prophylactic) V05.4
Chiclero ulcer 085.4
Chiggers 133.8
Chignon 111.2
fetus or newborn (from vacuum extraction) 767.19
Chigoe disease 134.1
Chikungunya fever 066.3
Chilaiditi's syndrome (subphrenic displacement, colon) 751.4
Chilblains 991.5
lupus 991.5
Child
behavior causing concern V61.20
adopted child V61.24
biological child V61.23
foster child V61.25
Childbed fever 670.8 ☑
Childbirth — see also Delivery
puerperal complications — see Puerperal
Childhood, period of rapid growth V21.0
Chill(s) 780.64
with fever 780.60
without fever 780.64
congestive 780.99
in malarial regions 084.6
septic — see Septicemia
urethral 599.84
Chilomastigiasis 007.8
Chin — see condition
Chinese dysentery 004.9
Chiropractic dislocation — see also Lesion, nonallopathic, by site 739.9
Chitral fever 066.0
Chlamydia, chlamydial — see condition
Chloasma 709.09
cachecticorum 709.09
eyelid 374.52
congenital 757.33
hyperthyroid 242.0 ☑
gravidarum 646.8 ☑
idiopathic 709.09
skin 709.09
symptomatic 709.09
Chloroma (M9930/3) 205.3 ☑
Chlorosis 280.9
Egyptian (see also Ancylostomiasis) 126.9
miners' (see also Ancylostomiasis) 126.9
Chlorotic anemia 280.9
Chocolate cyst (ovary) 617.1
Choked
disk or disc — see Papilledema
on food, phlegm, or vomitus NEC (see also Asphyxia, food) 933.1
phlegm 933.1
while vomiting NEC (see also Asphyxia, food) 933.1
Chokes (resulting from bends) 993.3
Choking sensation 784.99
Cholangiectasis — see also Disease, gallbladder 575.8
Cholangiocarcinoma (M8160/3)
and hepatocellular carcinoma, combined (M8180/3) 155.0
liver 155.1
specified site NEC — see Neoplasm, by site, malignant
unspecified site 155.1
Cholangiohepatitis 575.8
due to fluke infestation 121.1
Cholangiohepatoma (M8180/3) 155.0
Cholangiolitis (acute) (chronic) (extrahepatic) (gangrenous) 576.1
intrahepatic 575.8

☑ Additional Digit Required — Refer to the Tabular List for Digit Selection
▽ Subterms under main terms may continue to next column or page
46 — Volume 2
▶◀ Revised Text ● New Line ▲ Revised Code
2015 ICD-9-CM

Cholangiolitis — *continued*
  paratyphoidal (*see also* Fever, paratyphoid)
    002.9
  typhoidal 002.0
Cholangioma (M8160/0) 211.5
  malignant — *see* Cholangiocarcinoma
Cholangitis (acute) (ascending) (catarrhal)
  (chronic) (infective) (malignant) (primary) (recurrent) (sclerosing) (secondary)
  (stenosing) (suppurative) 576.1
  chronic nonsuppurative destructive 571.6
  nonsuppurative destructive (chronic) 571.6
Cholecystdocholithiasis — *see* Choledocholithiasis
Cholecystitis 575.10
  with
    calculus, stones in
      bile duct (common) (hepatic) — *see*
        Choledocholithiasis
      gallbladder — *see* Cholelithiasis
  acute 575.0
  acute and chronic 575.12
  chronic 575.11
  emphysematous (acute) (*see also* Cholecys-
    titis, acute) 575.0
  gangrenous (*see also* Cholecystitis, acute)
    575.0
  paratyphoidal, current (*see also* Fever,
    paratyphoid) 002.9
  suppurative (*see also* Cholecystitis, acute)
    575.0
  typhoidal 002.0
Choledochitis (suppurative) 576.1
Choledocholith — *see* Choledocholithiasis
Choledocholithiasis 574.5 ☑

> Note — Use the following fifth-digit
> subclassification with category 574:
> 0   without mention of obstruction
> 1   with obstruction

  with
    cholecystitis 574.4 ☑
      acute 574.3 ☑
      chronic 574.4 ☑
    cholelithiasis 574.9 ☑
      with
        cholecystitis 574.7 ☑
          acute 574.6 ☑
            and chronic 574.8 ☑
          chronic 574.7 ☑
Cholelithiasis (impacted) (multiple) 574.2 ☑

> Note — Use the following fifth-digit
> subclassification with category 574:
> 0   without mention of obstruction
> 1   with obstruction

  with
    cholecystitis 574.1 ☑
      acute 574.0 ☑
      chronic 574.1 ☑
    choledocholithiasis 574.9 ☑
      with
        cholecystitis 574.7 ☑
          acute 574.6 ☑
            and chronic 574.8 ☑
          chronic cholecystitis 574.7 ☑
Cholemia — *see also* Jaundice 782.4
  familial 277.4
  Gilbert's (familial nonhemolytic) 277.4
Cholemic gallstone — *see* Cholelithiasis
Choleperitoneum, choleperitonitis — *see*
  also Disease, gallbladder 567.81
Cholera (algid) (Asiatic) (asphyctic) (epidemic)
  (gravis) (Indian) (malignant) (morbus)
  (pestilential) (spasmodic) 001.9
  antimonial 985.4
  carrier (suspected) of V02.0
  classical 001.0
  contact V01.0
  due to
    Vibrio
      cholerae (Inaba, Ogawa, Hikojima
        serotypes) 001.0
      El Tor 001.1

Cholera — *continued*
  El Tor 001.1
    exposure to V01.0
    vaccination, prophylactic (against) V03.0
Cholerine — *see also* Cholera 001.9
Cholestasis 576.8
  due to total parenteral nutrition (TPN) 573.8
Cholesteatoma (ear) 385.30
  attic (primary) 385.31
  diffuse 385.35
  external ear (canal) 380.21
  marginal (middle ear) 385.32
    with involvement of mastoid cavity
      385.33
    secondary (with middle ear involvement)
      385.33
  mastoid cavity 385.30
  middle ear (secondary) 385.32
    with involvement of mastoid cavity
      385.33
  postmastoidectomy cavity (recurrent)
    383.32
  primary 385.31
  recurrent, postmastoidectomy cavity 383.32
  secondary (middle ear) 385.32
    with involvement of mastoid cavity
      385.33
Cholesteatosis (middle ear) — *see also*
  Cholesteatoma 385.30
  diffuse 385.35
Cholesteremia 272.0
Cholesterin
  granuloma, middle ear 385.82
  in vitreous 379.22
Cholesterol
  deposit
    retina 362.82
    vitreous 379.22
  elevated (high) 272.0
    with elevated (high) triglycerides 272.2
  imbibition of gallbladder (*see also* Disease,
    gallbladder) 575.6
Cholesterolemia 272.0
  essential 272.0
  familial 272.0
  hereditary 272.0
Cholesterosis, cholesterolosis (gallbladder)
  575.6
  with
    cholecystitis — *see* Cholecystitis
    cholelithiasis — *see* Cholelithiasis
  middle ear (*see also* Cholesteatoma) 385.30
Cholocolic fistula — *see also* Fistula, gallbladder 575.5
Choluria 791.4
Chondritis (purulent) 733.99
  auricle 380.03
  costal 733.6
    Tietze's 733.6
  patella, posttraumatic 717.7
  pinna 380.03
  posttraumatica patellae 717.7
  tuberculous (active) (*see also* Tuberculosis)
    015.9 ☑
    intervertebral 015.0 ☑ [730.88]
Chondroangiopathia calcarea seu punctate
  756.59
Chondroblastoma (M9230/0) — *see also*
  Neoplasm, bone, benign
  malignant (M9230/3) — *see* Neoplasm,
    bone, malignant
Chondrocalcinosis (articular) (crystal deposition) (dihydrate) — *see also* Arthritis, due
  to, crystals 275.49 [712.3] ☑
  due to
    calcium pyrophosphate
      275.49 [712.2] ☑
    dicalcium phosphate crystals
      275.49 [712.1] ☑
    pyrophosphate crystals 275.49 [712.2] ☑
Chondrodermatitis nodularis helicis 380.00
Chondrodysplasia 756.4
  angiomatose 756.4
  calcificans congenita 756.59
  epiphysialis punctata 756.59
  hereditary deforming 756.4

Chondrodysplasia — *continued*
  rhizomelic punctata 277.86
Chondrodystrophia (fetalis) 756.4
  calcarea 756.4
  calcificans congenita 756.59
  fetalis hypoplastica 756.59
  hypoplastica calcinosa 756.59
  punctata 756.59
  tarda 277.5
Chondrodystrophy (familial) (hypoplastic)
  756.4
  myotonic (congenital) 359.23
Chondroectodermal dysplasia 756.55
Chondrolysis 733.99
Chondroma (M9220/0) — *see also* Neoplasm,
  cartilage, benign
  juxtacortical (M9221/0) — *see* Neoplasm,
    bone, benign
  periosteal (M9221/0) — *see* Neoplasm,
    bone, benign
Chondromalacia 733.92
  epiglottis (congenital) 748.3
  generalized 733.92
  knee 717.7
  larynx (congenital) 748.3
  localized, except patella 733.92
  patella, patellae 717.7
  systemic 733.92
  tibial plateau 733.92
  trachea (congenital) 748.3
Chondromatosis (M9220/1) — *see* Neoplasm,
  cartilage, uncertain behavior
Chondromyxosarcoma (M9220/3) — *see*
  Neoplasm, cartilage, malignant
Chondro-osteodysplasia (Morquio-Brailsford
  type) 277.5
Chondro-osteodystrophy 277.5
Chondro-osteoma (M9210/0) — *see* Neoplasm, bone, benign
Chondropathia tuberosa 733.6
Chondrosarcoma (M9220/3) — *see also* Neoplasm, cartilage, malignant
  juxtacortical (M9221/3) — *see* Neoplasm,
    bone, malignant
  mesenchymal (M9240/3) — *see* Neoplasm,
    connective tissue, malignant
Chordae tendineae rupture (chronic) 429.5
Chordee (nonvenereal) 607.89
  congenital 752.63
  gonococcal 098.2
Chorditis (fibrinous) (nodosa) (tuberosa) 478.5
Chordoma (M9370/3) — *see* Neoplasm, by site,
  malignant
Chorea (gravis) (minor) (spasmodic) 333.5
  with
    heart involvement — *see* Chorea with
      rheumatic heart disease
    rheumatic heart disease (chronic, inac-
      tive, or quiescent) (conditions
      classifiable to 393–398) (see
      rheumatic heart condition in-
      volved)
      active or acute (conditions classifi-
        able to 391) 392.0
  acute — *see* Chorea, Sydenham's
  apoplectic (*see also* Disease, cerebrovascu-
    lar, acute) 436
  chronic 333.4
  electric 049.8
  gravidarum — *see* Eclampsia, pregnancy
  habit 307.22
  hereditary 333.4
  Huntington's 333.4
  posthemiplegic 344.89
  pregnancy — *see* Eclampsia, pregnancy
  progressive 333.4
    chronic 333.4
    hereditary 333.4
  rheumatic (chronic) 392.9
    with heart disease or involvement — *see*
      Chorea, with rheumatic heart
      disease
  senile 333.5
  Sydenham's 392.9
    with heart involvement — *see* Chorea,
      with rheumatic heart disease

Chorea — *continued*
  Sydenham's — *continued*
    nonrheumatic 333.5
    variabilis 307.23
Choreoathetosis (paroxysmal) 333.5
Chorioadenoma (destruens) (M9100/1) 236.1
Chorioamnionitis 658.4 ☑
  affecting fetus or newborn 762.7
Chorioangioma (M9120/0) 219.8
Choriocarcinoma (M9100/3)
  combined with
    embryonal carcinoma (M9101/3) — *see*
      Neoplasm, by site, malignant
    teratoma (M9101/3) — *see* Neoplasm,
      by site, malignant
  specified site — *see* Neoplasm, by site, ma-
    lignant
  unspecified site
    female 181
    male 186.9
Chorioencephalitis, lymphocytic (acute)
  (serous) 049.0
Chorioepithelioma (M9100/3) — *see* Choriocarcinoma
Choriomeningitis (acute) (benign) (lymphocytic) (serous) 049.0
Chorionepithelioma (M9100/3) — *see* Choriocarcinoma
Chorionitis — *see also* Scleroderma 710.1
Chorioretinitis 363.20
  disseminated 363.10
    generalized 363.13
    in
      neurosyphilis 094.83
      secondary syphilis 091.51
    peripheral 363.12
    posterior pole 363.11
    tuberculous (*see also* Tuberculosis)
      017.3 ☑ [363.13]
  due to
    histoplasmosis (*see also* Histoplasmosis)
      115.92
    toxoplasmosis (acquired) 130.2
      congenital (active) 771.2
  focal 363.00
    juxtapapillary 363.01
    peripheral 363.04
    posterior pole NEC 363.03
  juxtapapillaris, juxtapapillary 363.01
  progressive myopia (degeneration) 360.21
  syphilitic (secondary) 091.51
    congenital (early) 090.0 [363.13]
    late 090.5 [363.13]
    late 095.8 [363.13]
  tuberculous (*see also* Tuberculosis)
    017.3 ☑ [363.13]
Choristoma — *see* Neoplasm, by site, benign
Choroid — *see* condition
Choroideremia, choroidermia (initial stage)
  (late stage) (partial or total atrophy)
  363.55
Choroiditis — *see also* Chorioretinitis 363.20
  leprous 030.9 [363.13]
  senile guttate 363.41
  sympathetic 360.11
  syphilitic (secondary) 091.51
    congenital (early) 090.0 [363.13]
    late 090.5 [363.13]
    late 095.8 [363.13]
  Tay's 363.41
  tuberculous (*see also* Tuberculosis)
    017.3 ☑ [363.13]
Choroidopathy NEC 363.9
  degenerative (*see also* Degeneration,
    choroid) 363.40
  hereditary (*see also* Dystrophy, choroid)
    363.50
  specified type NEC 363.8
Choroidoretinitis — *see* Chorioretinitis
Choroidosis, central serous 362.41
Choroidretinopathy, serous 362.41
Christian's syndrome (chronic histiocytosis X)
  277.89
Christian-Weber disease (nodular nonsuppu-
  rative panniculitis) 729.30
Christmas disease 286.1

☑ Additional Digit Required — Refer to the Tabular List for Digit Selection   ▼ Subterms under main terms may continue to next column or page

2015 ICD-9-CM   ▶◀ Revised Text   ● New Line   ▲ Revised Code   Volume 2 — 47

Cholangiolitis — Christmas disease

Chromaffinoma (M8700/0) — *see also* Neoplasm, by site, benign
   malignant (M8700/3) — *see* Neoplasm, by site, malignant
Chromatopsia 368.59
Chromhidrosis, chromidrosis 705.89
Chromoblastomycosis 117.2
Chromomycosis 117.2
Chromophytosis 111.0
Chromotrichomycosis 111.8
Chronic — *see* condition
Churg-Strauss syndrome 446.4
Chyle cyst, mesentery 457.8
Chylocele (nonfilarial) 457.8
   filarial (*see also* Infestation, filarial) 125.9
   tunica vaginalis (nonfilarial) 608.84
     filarial (*see also* Infestation, filarial) 125.9
Chylomicronemia (fasting) (with hyperprebetalipoproteinemia) 272.3
Chylopericardium (acute) 420.90
Chylothorax (nonfilarial) 457.8
   filarial (*see also* Infestation, filarial) 125.9
Chylous
   ascites 457.8
   cyst of peritoneum 457.8
   hydrocele 603.9
   hydrothorax (nonfilarial) 457.8
     filarial (*see also* Infestation, filarial) 125.9
Chyluria 791.1
   bilharziasis 120.0
   due to
     Brugia (malayi) 125.1
     Wuchereria (bancrofti) 125.0
       malayi 125.1
   filarial (*see also* Infestation, filarial) 125.9
   filariasis (*see also* Infestation, filarial) 125.9
   nonfilarial 791.1
Cicatricial (deformity) — *see* Cicatrix
Cicatrix (adherent) (contracted) (painful) (vicious) 709.2
   adenoid 474.8
   alveolar process 525.8
   anus 569.49
   auricle 380.89
   bile duct (*see also* Disease, biliary) 576.8
   bladder 596.89
   bone 733.99
   brain 348.89
   cervix (postoperative) (postpartal) 622.3
     in pregnancy or childbirth 654.6 ☑
       causing obstructed labor 660.2 ☑
   chorioretinal 363.30
     disseminated 363.35
     macular 363.32
     peripheral 363.34
     posterior pole NEC 363.33
   choroid — *see* Cicatrix, chorioretinal
   common duct (*see also* Disease, biliary) 576.8
   congenital 757.39
   conjunctiva 372.64
   cornea 371.00
     tuberculous (*see also* Tuberculosis) 017.3 ☑ [371.05]
   duodenum (bulb) 537.3
   esophagus 530.3
   eyelid 374.46
     with
       ectropion — *see* Ectropion
       entropion — *see* Entropion
   hypopharynx 478.29
   knee, semilunar cartilage 717.5
   lacrimal
     canaliculi 375.53
     duct
       acquired 375.56
       neonatal 375.55
     punctum 375.52
     sac 375.54
   larynx 478.79
   limbus (cystoid) 372.64
   lung 518.89
   macular 363.32
     disseminated 363.35
     peripheral 363.34
   middle ear 385.89

Cicatrix — *continued*
   mouth 528.9
   muscle 728.89
   nasolacrimal duct
     acquired 375.56
     neonatal 375.55
   nasopharynx 478.29
   palate (soft) 528.9
   penis 607.89
   prostate 602.8
   rectum 569.49
   retina 363.30
     disseminated 363.35
     macular 363.32
     peripheral 363.34
     posterior pole NEC 363.33
   semilunar cartilage — *see* Derangement, meniscus
   seminal vesicle 608.89
   skin 709.2
     infected 686.8
     postinfectional 709.2
     tuberculous (*see also* Tuberculosis) 017.0 ☑
   specified site NEC 709.2
   throat 478.29
   tongue 529.8
   tonsil (and adenoid) 474.8
   trachea 478.9
   tuberculous NEC (*see also* Tuberculosis) 011.9 ☑
   ureter 593.89
   urethra 599.84
   uterus 621.8
   vagina 623.4
     in pregnancy or childbirth 654.7 ☑
       causing obstructed labor 660.2 ☑
   vocal cord 478.5
   wrist, constricting (annular) 709.2
CIDP (chronic inflammatory demyelinating polyneuropathy) 357.81
CIN I (cervical intraepithelial neoplasia I) 622.11
CIN II (cervical intraepithelial neoplasia II) 622.12
CIN III (cervical intraepithelial neoplasia III) 233.1
Cinchonism
   correct substance properly administered 386.9
   overdose or wrong substance given or taken 961.4
Circine herpes 110.5
Circle of Willis — *see* condition
Circular — *see* condition
   hymen 752.49
Circulating anticoagulants, antibodies, or inhibitors — *see also* Anticoagulants 286.59
   extrinsic 287.8
   following childbirth 666.3 ☑
   intrinsic, causing hemorrhagic disorder 286.59
     with
       acquired hemophilia 286.52
       antiphospholipid antibody 286.53
   postpartum 666.3 ☑
Circulation
   collateral (venous), any site 459.89
   defective 459.9
     congenital 747.9
     lower extremity 459.89
   embryonic 747.9
   failure 799.89
     fetus or newborn 779.89
     peripheral 785.59
   fetal, persistent 747.83
   heart, incomplete 747.9
Circulatory system — *see* condition
Circulus senilis 371.41
Circumcision
   in absence of medical indication V50.2
   ritual V50.2
   routine V50.2
   status (post), female 629.20
Circumscribed — *see* condition

Circumvallata placenta — *see* Placenta, abnormal
Cirrhosis, cirrhotic 571.5
   with alcoholism 571.2
   alcoholic (liver) 571.2
   atrophic (of liver) — *see* Cirrhosis, portal
   Baumgarten-Cruveilhier 571.5
   biliary (cholangiolitic) (cholangitic) (cholestatic) (extrahepatic) (hypertrophic) (intrahepatic) (nonobstructive) (obstructive) (pericholangiolitic) (posthepatic) (primary) (secondary) (xanthomatous) 571.6
     due to
       clonorchiasis 121.1
       flukes 121.3
   brain 331.9
   capsular — *see* Cirrhosis, portal
   cardiac 571.5
     alcoholic 571.2
   central (liver) — *see* Cirrhosis, liver
   Charcôt's 571.6
   cholangiolitic — *see* Cirrhosis, biliary
   cholangitic — *see* Cirrhosis, biliary
   cholestatic — *see* Cirrhosis, biliary
   clitoris (hypertrophic) 624.2
   coarsely nodular 571.5
   congestive (liver) — *see* Cirrhosis, cardiac
   Cruveilhier-Baumgarten 571.5
   cryptogenic (of liver) 571.5
     alcoholic 571.2
   dietary (*see also* Cirrhosis, portal) 571.5
   due to
     bronzed diabetes 275.01
     congestive hepatomegaly — *see* Cirrhosis, cardiac
     cystic fibrosis 277.00
     hemochromatosis (*see also* Hemochromatosis) 275.03
     hepatolenticular degeneration 275.1
     passive congestion (chronic) — *see* Cirrhosis, cardiac
     Wilson's disease 275.1
     xanthomatosis 272.2
   extrahepatic (obstructive) — *see* Cirrhosis, biliary
   fatty 571.8
     alcoholic 571.0
   florid 571.2
   Glisson's — *see* Cirrhosis, portal
   Hanot's (hypertrophic) — *see* Cirrhosis, biliary
   hepatic — *see* Cirrhosis, liver
   hepatolienal — *see* Cirrhosis, liver
   hobnail — *see* Cirrhosis, portal
   hypertrophic (*see also* Cirrhosis, liver)
     biliary — *see* Cirrhosis, biliary
     Hanot's — *see* Cirrhosis, biliary
   infectious NEC — *see* Cirrhosis, portal
   insular — *see* Cirrhosis, portal
   intrahepatic (obstructive) (primary) (secondary) — *see* Cirrhosis, biliary
   juvenile (*see also* Cirrhosis, portal) 571.5
   kidney (*see also* Sclerosis, renal) 587
   Laennec's (of liver) 571.2
     nonalcoholic 571.5
   liver (chronic) (hepatolienal) (hypertrophic) (nodular) (splenomegalic) (unilobar) 571.5
     with alcoholism 571.2
     alcoholic 571.2
     congenital (due to failure of obliteration of umbilical vein) 777.8
     cryptogenic 571.5
       alcoholic 571.2
     fatty 571.8
       alcoholic 571.0
     macronodular 571.5
       alcoholic 571.2
     micronodular 571.5
       alcoholic 571.2
     nodular, diffuse 571.5
       alcoholic 571.2
     pigmentary 275.01
     portal 571.5
       alcoholic 571.2

Cirrhosis, cirrhotic — *continued*
   liver — *continued*
     postnecrotic 571.5
       alcoholic 571.2
       syphilitic 095.3
   lung (chronic) (*see also* Fibrosis, lung) 515
   macronodular (of liver) 571.5
     alcoholic 571.2
   malarial 084.9
   metabolic NEC 571.5
   micronodular (of liver) 571.5
     alcoholic 571.2
   monolobular — *see* Cirrhosis, portal
   multilobular — *see* Cirrhosis, portal
   nephritis (*see also* Sclerosis, renal) 587
   nodular — *see* Cirrhosis, liver
   nutritional (fatty) 571.5
   obstructive (biliary) (extrahepatic) (intrahepatic) — *see* Cirrhosis, biliary
   ovarian 620.8
   paludal 084.9
   pancreas (duct) 577.8
   pericholangiolitic — *see* Cirrhosis, biliary
   periportal — *see* Cirrhosis, portal
   pigment, pigmentary (of liver) 275.01
   portal (of liver) 571.5
     alcoholic 571.2
   posthepatitic (*see also* Cirrhosis, postnecrotic) 571.5
   postnecrotic (of liver) 571.5
     alcoholic 571.2
   primary (intrahepatic) — *see* Cirrhosis, biliary
   pulmonary (*see also* Fibrosis, lung) 515
   renal (*see also* Sclerosis, renal) 587
   septal (*see also* Cirrhosis, postnecrotic) 571.5
   spleen 289.51
   splenomegalic (of liver) — *see* Cirrhosis, liver
   stasis (liver) — *see* Cirrhosis, liver
   stomach 535.4 ☑
   Todd's (*see also* Cirrhosis, biliary) 571.6
   toxic (nodular) — *see* Cirrhosis, postnecrotic
   trabecular — *see* Cirrhosis, postnecrotic
   unilobar — *see* Cirrhosis, liver
   vascular (of liver) — *see* Cirrhosis, liver
   xanthomatous (biliary) (*see also* Cirrhosis, biliary) 571.6
     due to xanthomatosis (familial) (metabolic) (primary) 272.2
Cistern, subarachnoid 793.0
Citrullinemia 270.6
Citrullinuria 270.6
Ciuffini-Pancoast tumor (M8010/3) (carcinoma, pulmonary apex) 162.3
Civatte's disease or poikiloderma 709.09
CJD (Creutzfeldt-Jakob disease) 046.19
   variant (vCJD) 046.11
CLABSI (central line-associated bloodstream infection) 999.32
Clam diggers' itch 120.3
Clap — *see* Gonorrhea
Clarke-Hadfield syndrome (pancreatic infantilism) 577.8
Clark's paralysis 343.9
Clastothrix 704.2
Claude Bernard-Horner syndrome — *see also* Neuropathy, peripheral, autonomic 337.9
Claude's syndrome 352.6
Claudication, intermittent 443.9
   cerebral (artery) (*see also* Ischemia, cerebral, transient) 435.9
   due to atherosclerosis 440.21
   spinal cord (arteriosclerotic) 435.1
     syphilitic 094.89
   spinalis 435.1
   venous (axillary) 453.89
Claudicatio venosa intermittens 453.89
Claustrophobia 300.29
Clavus (infected) 700
Clawfoot (congenital) 754.71
   acquired 736.74
Clawhand (acquired) 736.06
   congenital 755.59
Clawtoe (congenital) 754.71

☑ **Additional Digit Required** — Refer to the Tabular List for Digit Selection   ▾ **Subterms under main terms may continue to next column or page**

48 — Volume 2   ▶◀ **Revised Text**   ● **New Line**   ▲ **Revised Code**   **2015 ICD-9-CM**

Clawtoe — *continued*
  acquired 735.5
Clay eating 307.52
Clay shovelers' fracture — *see* Fracture, vertebra, cervical
Cleansing of artificial opening — *see also* Attention to artificial opening V55.9
Cleft (congenital) — *see also* Imperfect, closure
  alveolar process 525.8
  branchial (persistent) 744.41
    cyst 744.42
  clitoris 752.49
  cricoid cartilage, posterior 748.3
  facial (*see also* Cleft, lip) 749.10
  lip 749.10
    with cleft palate 749.20
      bilateral (lip and palate) 749.24
        with unilateral lip or palate 749.25
        complete 749.23
        incomplete 749.24
      unilateral (lip and palate) 749.22
        with bilateral lip or palate 749.25
        complete 749.21
        incomplete 749.22
    bilateral 749.14
      with cleft palate, unilateral 749.25
      complete 749.13
      incomplete 749.14
    unilateral 749.12
      with cleft palate, bilateral 749.25
      complete 749.11
      incomplete 749.12
  nose 748.1
  palate 749.00
    with cleft lip 749.20
      bilateral (lip and palate) 749.24
        with unilateral lip or palate 749.25
        complete 749.23
        incomplete 749.24
      unilateral (lip and palate) 749.22
        with bilateral lip or palate 749.25
        complete 749.21
        incomplete 749.22
    bilateral 749.04
      with cleft lip, unilateral 749.25
      complete 749.03
      incomplete 749.04
    unilateral 749.02
      with cleft lip, bilateral 749.25
      complete 749.01
      incomplete 749.02
  penis 752.69
  posterior, cricoid cartilage 748.3
  scrotum 752.89
  sternum (congenital) 756.3
  thyroid cartilage (congenital) 748.3
  tongue 750.13
  uvula 749.02
    with cleft lip (*see also* Cleft, lip, with cleft palate) 749.20
  water 366.12
Cleft hand (congenital) 755.58
Cleidocranial dysostosis 755.59
Cleidotomy, fetal 763.89
Cleptomania 312.32
Clérambault's syndrome 297.8
  erotomania 302.89
Clergyman's sore throat 784.49
Click, clicking
  systolic syndrome 785.2
Clifford's syndrome (postmaturity) 766.22
Climacteric — *see also* Menopause 627.2
  arthritis NEC (*see also* Arthritis, climacteric) 716.3 ☑
  depression (*see also* Psychosis, affective) 296.2 ☑
  disease 627.2
    recurrent episode 296.3 ☑
    single episode 296.2 ☑
  female (symptoms) 627.2
  male (symptoms) (syndrome) 608.89
  melancholia (*see also* Psychosis, affective) 296.2 ☑
    recurrent episode 296.3 ☑

Climacteric — *see also* Menopause — *continued*
  melancholia (*see also* Psychosis, affective) — *continued*
    single episode 296.2 ☑
  paranoid state 297.2
  paraphrenia 297.2
  polyarthritis NEC 716.39
    male 608.89
  symptoms (female) 627.2
Clinical research investigation (control) (participant) V70.7
Clinodactyly 755.59
Clitoris — *see* condition
Cloaca, persistent 751.5
Clonorchiasis 121.1
Clonorchiosis 121.1
Clonorchis infection, liver 121.1
Clonus 781.0
Closed bite 524.20
Closed surgical procedure converted to open procedure
  arthroscopic V64.43
  laparoscopic V64.41
  thoracoscopic V64.42
Closure
  artificial opening (*see also* Attention to artificial opening) V55.9
  congenital, nose 748.0
  cranial sutures, premature 756.0
  defective or imperfect NEC — *see* Imperfect, closure
  fistula, delayed — *see* Fistula
  fontanelle, delayed 756.0
  foramen ovale, imperfect 745.5
  hymen 623.3
  interauricular septum, defective 745.5
  interventricular septum, defective 745.4
  lacrimal duct 375.56
    congenital 743.65
    neonatal 375.55
  nose (congenital) 748.0
    acquired 738.0
  primary angle without glaucoma damage 365.06
  vagina 623.2
  valve — *see* Endocarditis
  vulva 624.8
Clot (blood)
  artery (obstruction) (occlusion) (*see also* Embolism) 444.9
  atrial appendage 429.89
  bladder 596.7
  brain (extradural or intradural) (*see also* Thrombosis, brain) 434.0 ☑
    late effect — *see* Late effect(s) (of) cerebrovascular disease
  circulation 444.9
  heart (*see also* Infarct, myocardium) 410.9 ☑
    without myocardial infarction 429.89
  vein (*see also* Thrombosis) 453.9
Clotting defect NEC — *see also* Defect, coagulation 286.9
Clouded state 780.09
  epileptic (*see also* Epilepsy) 345.9 ☑
  paroxysmal (idiopathic) (*see also* Epilepsy) 345.9 ☑
Clouding
  corneal graft 996.51
Cloudy
  antrum, antra 473.0
  dialysis effluent 792.5
Clouston's (hidrotic) ectodermal dysplasia 757.31
Clubbing of fingers 781.5
Clubfinger 736.29
  acquired 736.29
  congenital 754.89
Clubfoot (congenital) 754.70
  acquired 736.71
  equinovarus 754.51
  paralytic 736.71
Club hand (congenital) 754.89
  acquired 736.07
Clubnail (acquired) 703.8

Clubnail — *continued*
  congenital 757.5
Clump kidney 753.3
Clumsiness 781.3
  syndrome 315.4
Cluttering — *see also* Disorder, fluency 315.35
Clutton's joints 090.5
Coagulation, intravascular (diffuse) (disseminated) — *see also* Fibrinolysis 286.6
  newborn 776.2
Coagulopathy — *see also* Defect, coagulation 286.9
  consumption 286.6
  intravascular (disseminated) NEC 286.6
    newborn 776.2
Coalition
  calcaneoscaphoid 755.67
  calcaneus 755.67
  tarsal 755.67
Coal miners'
  elbow 727.2
  lung 500
Coal workers' lung or pneumoconiosis 500
Coarctation
  aorta (postductal) (preductal) 747.10
  pulmonary artery 747.31
Coated tongue 529.3
Coats' disease 362.12
Cocainism — *see also* Dependence 304.2 ☑
Coccidioidal granuloma 114.3
Coccidioidomycosis 114.9
  with pneumonia 114.0
  cutaneous (primary) 114.1
  disseminated 114.3
  extrapulmonary (primary) 114.1
  lung 114.5
    acute 114.0
    chronic 114.4
    primary 114.0
  meninges 114.2
  primary (pulmonary) 114.0
    acute 114.0
  prostate 114.3
  pulmonary 114.5
    acute 114.0
    chronic 114.4
    primary 114.0
  specified site NEC 114.3
Coccidioidosis 114.9
  lung 114.5
    acute 114.0
    chronic 114.4
    primary 114.0
  meninges 114.2
Coccidiosis (colitis) (diarrhea) (dysentery) 007.2
Cocciuria 791.9
Coccus in urine 791.9
Coccydynia 724.79
Coccygodynia 724.79
Coccyx — *see* condition
Cochin-China
  diarrhea 579.1
    anguilluliasis 127.2
  ulcer 085.1
Cockayne's disease or syndrome (microcephaly and dwarfism) 759.89
Cockayne-Weber syndrome (epidermolysis bullosa) 757.39
Cocked-up toe 735.2
Cock's peculiar tumor 706.2
Codman's tumor (benign chondroblastoma) (M9230/0) — *see* Neoplasm, bone, benign
Coenurosis 123.8
Coffee workers' lung 495.8
Cogan's syndrome 370.52
  congenital oculomotor apraxia 379.51
  nonsyphilitic interstitial keratitis 370.52
Coiling, umbilical cord — *see* Complications, umbilical cord
Coitus, painful (female) 625.0
  male 608.89
  psychogenic 302.76
Cold 460
  with influenza, flu, or grippe (*see also* Influenza) 487.1

Cold — *continued*
  abscess (*see also* Tuberculosis, abscess)
    articular — *see* Tuberculosis, joint
  agglutinin
    disease (chronic) or syndrome 283.0
    hemoglobinuria 283.0
    paroxysmal (cold) (nocturnal) 283.2
  allergic (*see also* Fever, hay) 477.9
  bronchus or chest — *see* Bronchitis
    with grippe or influenza (*see also* Influenza) 487.1
  common (head) 460
    vaccination, prophylactic (against) V04.7
  deep 464.10
  effects of 991.9
    specified effect NEC 991.8
  excessive 991.9
    specified effect NEC 991.8
  exhaustion from 991.8
  exposure to 991.9
    specified effect NEC 991.8
  grippy (*see also* Influenza) 487.1
  head 460
  injury syndrome (newborn) 778.2
  intolerance 780.99
  on lung — *see* Bronchitis
  rose 477.0
  sensitivity, autoimmune 283.0
  virus 460
Coldsore — *see also* Herpes, simplex 054.9
Colibacillosis 041.49
  generalized 038.42
Colibacilluria 791.9
Colic (recurrent) 789.7
  abdomen 789.7
    psychogenic 307.89
  appendicular 543.9
  appendix 543.9
  bile duct — *see* Choledocholithiasis
  biliary — *see* Cholelithiasis
  bilious — *see* Cholelithiasis
  common duct — *see* Choledocholithiasis
  Devonshire NEC 984.9
    specified type of lead — *see* Table of Drugs and Chemicals
  flatulent 787.3
  gallbladder or gallstone — *see* Cholelithiasis
  gastric 536.8
  hepatic (duct) — *see* Choledocholithiasis
  hysterical 300.11
  in
    adult 789.0 ☑
    child over 12 months old 789.0 ☑
    infant 789.7
  infantile 789.7
  intestinal 789.7
  kidney 788.0
  lead NEC 984.9
    specified type of lead — *see* Table of Drugs and Chemicals
  liver (duct) — *see* Choledocholithiasis
  mucous 564.9
    psychogenic 316 [564.9]
  nephritic 788.0
  painter's NEC 984.9
  pancreas 577.8
  psychogenic 306.4
  renal 788.0
  saturnine NEC 984.9
    specified type of lead — *see* Table of Drugs and Chemicals
  spasmodic 789.7
  ureter 788.0
  urethral 599.84
    due to calculus 594.2
  uterus 625.8
    menstrual 625.3
  vermicular 543.9
  virus 460
  worm NEC 128.9
Colicystitis — *see also* Cystitis 595.9
Colitis (acute) (catarrhal) (croupous) (cystica superficialis) (exudative) (hemorrhagic) (noninfectious) (phlegmonous) (presumed noninfectious) 558.9
  adaptive 564.9

☑ Additional Digit Required — Refer to the Tabular List for Digit Selection   ⬇ Subterms under main terms may continue to next column or page

2015 ICD-9-CM   ▶◀ Revised Text   ● New Line   ▲ Revised Code   Volume 2 — 49

Colitis — continued

allergic 558.3

amebic (see also Amebiasis) 006.9

  nondysenteric 006.2

anthrax 022.2

bacillary (see also Infection, Shigella) 004.9

balantidial 007.0

chronic 558.9

  ulcerative (see also Colitis, ulcerative) 556.9

coccidial 007.2

dietetic 558.9

due to radiation 558.1

eosinophilic 558.42

functional 558.9

gangrenous 009.0

giardial 007.1

granulomatous 555.1

gravis (see also Colitis, ulcerative) 556.9

infectious (see also Enteritis, due to, specific organism) 009.0

  presumed 009.1

ischemic 557.9

  acute 557.0

  chronic 557.1

  due to mesenteric artery insufficiency 557.1

membranous 564.9

  psychogenic 316 [564.9]

mucous 564.9

  psychogenic 316 [564.9]

necrotic 009.0

polyposa (see also Colitis, ulcerative) 556.9

protozoal NEC 007.9

pseudomembranous 008.45

pseudomucinous 564.9

regional 555.1

segmental 555.1

septic (see also Enteritis, due to, specific organism) 009.0

spastic 564.9

  psychogenic 316 [564.9]

Staphylococcus 008.41

  food 005.0

thromboulcerative 557.0

toxic 558.2

transmural 555.1

trichomonal 007.3

tuberculous (ulcerative) 014.8 ☑

ulcerative (chronic) (idiopathic) (nonspecific) 556.9

  entero- 556.0

  fulminant 557.0

  ileo- 556.1

  left-sided 556.5

  procto- 556.2

  proctosigmoid 556.3

  psychogenic 316 [556] ☑

  specified NEC 556.8

  universal 556.6

Collagen disease NEC 710.9

nonvascular 710.9

vascular (allergic) (see also Angiitis, hypersensitivity) 446.20

Collagenosis — see also Collagen disease 710.9

cardiovascular 425.4

mediastinal 519.3

Collapse 780.2

adrenal 255.8

cardiorenal (see also Hypertension, cardiorenal) 404.90

cardiorespiratory 785.51

  fetus or newborn 779.85

cardiovascular (see also Disease, heart) 785.51

  fetus or newborn 779.85

circulatory (peripheral) 785.59

  with

    abortion — see Abortion, by type, with shock

    ectopic pregnancy (see also categories 633.0–633.9) 639.5

    molar pregnancy (see also categories 630–632) 639.5

  during or after labor and delivery 669.1 ☑

Collapse — continued

circulatory — continued

  fetus or newborn 779.85

  following

    abortion 639.5

    ectopic or molar pregnancy 639.5

  during or after labor and delivery 669.1 ☑

    fetus or newborn 779.89

during or resulting from a surgical procedure 998.00

external ear canal 380.50

  secondary to

    inflammation 380.53

    surgery 380.52

    trauma 380.51

general 780.2

heart — see Disease, heart

heat 992.1

hysterical 300.11

labyrinth, membranous (congenital) 744.05

lung (massive) (see also Atelectasis) 518.0

  pressure, during labor 668.0 ☑

myocardial — see Disease, heart

nervous (see also Disorder, mental, nonpsychotic) 300.9

neurocirculatory 306.2

nose 738.0

postoperative (cardiovascular) 998.09

pulmonary (see also Atelectasis) 518.0

  fetus or newborn 770.5

    partial 770.5

    primary 770.4

thorax 512.89

  iatrogenic 512.1

  postoperative 512.1

trachea 519.19

valvular — see Endocarditis

vascular (peripheral) 785.59

  with

    abortion — see Abortion, by type, with shock

    ectopic pregnancy (see also categories 633.0–633.9) 639.5

    molar pregnancy (see also categories 630–632) 639.5

  cerebral (see also Disease, cerebrovascular, acute) 436

  during or after labor and delivery 669.1 ☑

  fetus or newborn 779.89

  following

    abortion 639.5

    ectopic or molar pregnancy 639.5

vasomotor 785.59

vertebra 733.13

Collateral — see also condition

circulation (venous) 459.89

dilation, veins 459.89

Colles' fracture (closed) (reversed) (separation) 813.41

open 813.51

Collet-Sicard syndrome 352.6

Collet's syndrome 352.6

Colliculitis urethralis — see also Urethritis 597.89

Colliers'

asthma 500

lung 500

phthisis (see also Tuberculosis) 011.4 ☑

Collodion baby (ichthyosis congenita) 757.1

Colloid milium 709.3

Coloboma NEC 743.49

choroid 743.59

fundus 743.52

iris 743.46

lens 743.36

lids 743.62

optic disc (congenital) 743.57

  acquired 377.23

retina 743.56

sclera 743.47

Coloenteritis — see Enteritis

Colon — see condition

Colonization

MRSA (methicillin resistant Staphylococcus aureus) V02.54

Colonization — continued

MSSA (methicillin susceptible Staphylococcus aureus) V02.53

Coloptosis 569.89

Color

amblyopia NEC 368.59

  acquired 368.55

blindness NEC (congenital) 368.59

  acquired 368.55

Colostomy

attention to V55.3

fitting or adjustment V55.3

malfunctioning 569.62

status V44.3

Colpitis — see also Vaginitis 616.10

Colpocele 618.6

Colpocystitis — see also Vaginitis 616.10

Colporrhexis 665.4 ☑

Colpospasm 625.1

Column, spinal, vertebral — see condition

Coma 780.01

apoplectic (see also Disease, cerebrovascular, acute) 436

diabetic (with ketoacidosis) 250.3 ☑

  due to secondary diabetes 249.3 ☑

  hyperosmolar 250.2 ☑

    due to secondary diabetes 249.2 ☑

eclamptic (see also Eclampsia) 780.39

epileptic 345.3

hepatic 572.2

hyperglycemic 250.3 ☑

  due to secondary diabetes 249.3 ☑

hyperosmolar (diabetic) (nonketotic) 250.2 ☑

  due to secondary diabetes 249.2 ☑

hypoglycemic 251.0

  diabetic 250.3 ☑

    due to secondary diabetes 249.3 ☑

insulin 250.3 ☑

  due to secondary diabetes 249.3 ☑

  hyperosmolar 250.2 ☑

    due to secondary diabetes 249.2 ☑

  non-diabetic 251.0

  organic hyperinsulinism 251.0

Kussmaul's (diabetic) 250.3 ☑

  due to secondary diabetes 249.3 ☑

liver 572.2

newborn 779.2

prediabetic 250.2 ☑

  due to secondary diabetes 249.2 ☑

uremic — see Uremia

Combat fatigue — see also Reaction, stress, acute 308.9

Combined — see condition

Comedo 706.1

Comedocarcinoma (M8501/3) — see also Neoplasm, breast, malignant

noninfiltrating (M8501/2)

  specified site — see Neoplasm, by site, in situ

  unspecified site 233.0

Comedomastitis 610.4

Comedones 706.1

lanugo 757.4

Comma bacillus, carrier (suspected) of V02.3

Comminuted fracture — see Fracture, by site

Common

aortopulmonary trunk 745.0

atrioventricular canal (defect) 745.69

atrium 745.69

cold (head) 460

  vaccination, prophylactic (against) V04.7

truncus (arteriosus) 745.0

ventricle 745.3

Commotio (current)

cerebri (see also Concussion, brain) 850.9

  with skull fracture — see Fracture, skull, by site

retinae 921.3

spinalis — see Injury, spinal, by site

Commotion (current)

brain (without skull fracture) (see also Concussion, brain) 850.9

  with skull fracture — see Fracture, skull, by site

spinal cord — see Injury, spinal, by site

Communication

abnormal (see also Fistula)

  between

    base of aorta and pulmonary artery 745.0

    left ventricle and right atrium 745.4

    pericardial sac and pleural sac 748.8

    pulmonary artery and pulmonary vein 747.39

  congenital, between uterus and anterior abdominal wall 752.39

    bladder 752.39

    intestine 752.39

    rectum 752.39

  left ventricular — right atrial 745.4

  pulmonary artery-pulmonary vein 747.39

Compartment syndrome — see Syndrome, compartment

Compensation

broken — see Failure, heart

failure — see Failure, heart

neurosis, psychoneurosis 300.11

Complaint — see also Disease

bowel, functional 564.9

  psychogenic 306.4

intestine, functional 564.9

  psychogenic 306.4

kidney (see also Disease, renal) 593.9

liver 573.9

miners' 500

Complete — see condition

Complex

cardiorenal (see also Hypertension, cardiorenal) 404.90

castration 300.9

Costen's 524.60

ego-dystonic homosexuality 302.0

Eisenmenger's (ventricular septal defect) 745.4

homosexual, ego-dystonic 302.0

hypersexual 302.89

inferiority 301.9

jumped process

  spine — see Dislocation, vertebra

primary, tuberculosis (see also Tuberculosis) 010.0 ☑

regional pain syndrome 355.9

  type I 337.20

    lower limb 337.22

    specified site NEC 337.29

    upper limb 337.21

  type II

    lower limb 355.71

    upper limb 354.4

Taussig-Bing (transposition, aorta and overriding pulmonary artery) 745.11

Complications

abortion NEC — see categories 634-639 ☑

accidental puncture or laceration during a procedure 998.2

amniocentesis, fetal 679.1 ☑

amputation stump (late) (surgical) 997.60

  traumatic — see Amputation, traumatic

anastomosis (and bypass) (see also Complications, due to (presence of) any device, implant, or graft classified to 996.0–996.5 NEC)

  hemorrhage NEC 998.11

  intestinal (internal) NEC 997.49

    involving urinary tract 997.5

  mechanical — see Complications, mechanical, graft

  urinary tract (involving intestinal tract) 997.5

anesthesia, anesthetic NEC (see also Anesthesia, complication) 995.22

  in labor and delivery 668.9 ☑

    affecting fetus or newborn 763.5

    cardiac 668.1 ☑

    central nervous system 668.2 ☑

    pulmonary 668.0 ☑

    specified type NEC 668.8 ☑

aortocoronary (bypass) graft 996.03

  atherosclerosis — see Arteriosclerosis, coronary

  embolism 996.72

☑ **Additional Digit Required** — Refer to the Tabular List for Digit Selection ◢ Subterms under main terms may continue to next column or page

50 — Volume 2   ▶◀ Revised Text   ● New Line   ▲ Revised Code   2015 ICD-9-CM

Complications — continued
aortocoronary graft — continued
　occlusion NEC 996.72
　thrombus 996.72
arthroplasty (see also Complications, prosthetic joint) 996.49
artificial opening
　cecostomy 569.60
　colostomy 569.60
　cystostomy 596.83
　　infection 596.81
　　mechanical 596.82
　　specified complication NEC 596.83
　enterostomy 569.60
　esophagostomy 530.87
　　infection 530.86
　　mechanical 530.87
　gastrostomy 536.40
　ileostomy 569.60
　jejunostomy 569.60
　nephrostomy 997.5
　tracheostomy 519.00
　ureterostomy 997.5
　urethrostomy 997.5
bariatric surgery
　gastric band procedure 539.09
　　infection 539.01
　specified procedure NEC 539.89
　　infection 539.81
bile duct implant (prosthetic) NEC 996.79
　infection or inflammation 996.69
　mechanical 996.59
bleeding (intraoperative) (postoperative) 998.11
blood vessel graft 996.1
　aortocoronary 996.03
　　atherosclerosis — see Arteriosclerosis, coronary
　　embolism 996.72
　　occlusion NEC 996.72
　　thrombus 996.72
　atherosclerosis — see Arteriosclerosis, extremities
　embolism 996.74
　occlusion NEC 996.74
　thrombus 996.74
bone growth stimulator NEC 996.78
　infection or inflammation 996.67
bone marrow transplant 996.85
breast implant (prosthetic) NEC 996.79
　infection or inflammation 996.69
　mechanical 996.54
bypass (see also Complications, anastomosis)
　aortocoronary 996.03
　　atherosclerosis — see Arteriosclerosis, coronary
　　embolism 996.72
　　occlusion NEC 996.72
　　thrombus 996.72
　carotid artery 996.1
　　atherosclerosis — see Arteriosclerosis, extremities
　　embolism 996.74
　　occlusion NEC 996.74
　　thrombus 996.74
cardiac (see also Disease, heart) 429.9
　device, implant, or graft NEC 996.72
　　infection or inflammation 996.61
　　long-term effect 429.4
　　mechanical (see also Complications, mechanical, by type) 996.00
　　valve prosthesis 996.71
　　　infection or inflammation 996.61
　postoperative NEC 997.1
　long-term effect 429.4
cardiorenal (see also Hypertension, cardiorenal) 404.90
carotid artery bypass graft 996.1
　atherosclerosis — see Arteriosclerosis, extremities
　embolism 996.74
　occlusion NEC 996.74
　thrombus 996.74
cataract fragments in eye 998.82

Complications — continued
catheter device NEC (see also Complications, due to (presence of) any device, implant, or graft classified to 996.0–996.5 NEC)
　mechanical — see Complications, mechanical, catheter
cecostomy 569.60
cesarean section wound 674.3 ☑
chemotherapy (antineoplastic) 995.29
chin implant (prosthetic) NEC 996.79
　infection or inflammation 996.69
　mechanical 996.59
colostomy (enterostomy) 569.60
　specified type NEC 569.69
contraceptive device, intrauterine NEC 996.76
　infection 996.65
　inflammation 996.65
　mechanical 996.32
cord (umbilical) — see Complications, umbilical cord
cornea
　due to
　　contact lens 371.82
coronary (artery) bypass (graft) NEC 996.03
　atherosclerosis — see Arteriosclerosis, coronary
　embolism 996.72
　infection or inflammation 996.61
　mechanical 996.03
　occlusion NEC 996.72
　specified type NEC 996.72
　thrombus 996.72
cystostomy 596.83
　infection 596.81
　mechanical 596.82
　specified complication NEC 596.83
delivery 669.9 ☑
　procedure (instrumental) (manual) (surgical) 669.4 ☑
　specified type NEC 669.8 ☑
dialysis (hemodialysis) (peritoneal) (renal) NEC 999.9
　catheter NEC (see also Complications, due to (presence of) any device, implant, or graft classified to 996.0–996.5 NEC)
　　infection or inflammation 996.62
　　　peritoneal 996.68
　　mechanical 996.1
　　　peritoneal 996.56
drug NEC 995.29
due to (presence of) any device, implant, or graft classified to 996.0–996.5 NEC 996.70
　with infection or inflammation — see Complications, infection or inflammation, due to (presence of) any device, implant, or graft classified to 996.0–996.5 NEC
　arterial NEC 996.74
　　coronary NEC 996.03
　　　atherosclerosis — see Arteriosclerosis, coronary
　　　embolism 996.72
　　　occlusion NEC 996.72
　　　specified type NEC 996.72
　　　thrombus 996.72
　　renal dialysis 996.73
　arteriovenous fistula or shunt NEC 996.74
　bone growth stimulator 996.78
　breast NEC 996.79
　cardiac NEC 996.72
　　defibrillator 996.72
　　pacemaker 996.72
　　valve prosthesis 996.71
　catheter NEC 996.79
　　spinal 996.75
　　urinary, indwelling 996.76
　　vascular NEC 996.74
　　　renal dialysis 996.73
　　ventricular shunt 996.75
　coronary (artery) bypass (graft) NEC 996.03

Complications — continued
due to any device, implant, or graft classified to 996.0–996.5 — continued
　coronary bypass — continued
　　atherosclerosis — see Arteriosclerosis, coronary
　　embolism 996.72
　　occlusion NEC 996.72
　　thrombus 996.72
　electrodes
　　brain 996.75
　　heart 996.72
　esophagostomy 530.87
　gastrointestinal NEC 996.79
　genitourinary NEC 996.76
　heart valve prosthesis NEC 996.71
　infusion pump 996.74
　insulin pump 996.57
　internal
　　joint prosthesis 996.77
　　orthopedic NEC 996.78
　　specified type NEC 996.79
　intrauterine contraceptive device NEC 996.76
　joint prosthesis, internal NEC 996.77
　mechanical — see Complications, mechanical
　nervous system NEC 996.75
　ocular lens NEC 996.79
　orbital NEC 996.79
　orthopedic NEC 996.78
　　joint, internal 996.77
　renal dialysis 996.73
　specified type NEC 996.79
　urinary catheter, indwelling 996.76
　vascular NEC 996.74
　ventricular shunt 996.75
during dialysis NEC 999.9
ectopic or molar pregnancy NEC 639.9
electroshock therapy NEC 999.9
enterostomy 569.60
　specified type NEC 569.69
esophagostomy 530.87
　infection 530.86
　mechanical 530.87
external (fixation) device with internal component(s) NEC 996.78
　infection or inflammation 996.67
　mechanical 996.49
extracorporeal circulation NEC 999.9
eye implant (prosthetic) NEC 996.79
　infection or inflammation 996.69
　mechanical
　　ocular lens 996.53
　　orbital globe 996.59
fetal, from amniocentesis 679.1 ☑
gastrointestinal, postoperative NEC (see also Complications, surgical procedures) 997.49
gastrostomy 536.40
　specified type NEC 536.49
genitourinary device, implant or graft NEC 996.76
　erosion of implanted vaginal mesh 629.31
　exposure of implanted vaginal mesh 629.32
　infection or inflammation 996.65
　　urinary catheter, indwelling 996.64
　mechanical (see also Complications, mechanical, by type) 996.30
　　specified NEC 996.39
graft (bypass) (patch) (see also Complications, due to (presence of) any device, implant, or graft classified to 996.0–996.5 NEC)
　bone marrow 996.85
　corneal NEC 996.79
　　infection or inflammation 996.69
　　rejection or reaction 996.51
　　retroprosthetic membrane 996.51
　　mechanical — see Complications, mechanical, graft
　organ (immune or nonimmune cause) (partial) (total) 996.80
　　bone marrow 996.85

Complications — continued
graft (see also Complications, due to any device, implant, or graft classified to 996.0–996.5) — continued
　organ — continued
　　heart 996.83
　　intestines 996.87
　　kidney 996.81
　　liver 996.82
　　lung 996.84
　　pancreas 996.86
　　specified NEC 996.89
　skin NEC 996.79
　　infection or inflammation 996.69
　　rejection 996.52
　　　artificial 996.55
　　　decellularized allodermis 996.55
heart (see also Disease, heart transplant (immune or nonimmune cause)) 996.83
hematoma (intraoperative) (postoperative) 998.12
hemorrhage (intraoperative) (postoperative) 998.11
hyperalimentation therapy NEC 999.9
immunization (procedure) — see Complications, vaccination
implant (see also Complications, due to (presence of) any device, implant, or graft classified to 996.0–996.5 NEC)
　dental placement, hemorrhagic 525.71
　mechanical — see Complications, mechanical, implant
infection and inflammation
　due to (presence of) any device, implant or graft classified to 996.0–996.5 NEC 996.60
　　arterial NEC 996.62
　　　coronary 996.61
　　　renal dialysis 996.62
　　arteriovenous fistula or shunt 996.62
　　artificial heart 996.61
　　bone growth stimulator 996.67
　　breast 996.69
　　cardiac 996.61
　　catheter NEC 996.69
　　　central venous 999.31
　　　　bloodstream 999.32
　　　　localized 999.33
　　　Hickman 999.31
　　　　bloodstream 999.32
　　　　localized 999.33
　　　peripherally inserted central (PICC) 999.31
　　　　bloodstream 999.32
　　　　localized 999.33
　　　peritoneal 996.68
　　　portacath (port-a-cath) 999.31
　　　　bloodstream 999.32
　　　　localized 999.33
　　　spinal 996.63
　　　triple lumen 999.31
　　　　bloodstream 999.32
　　　　localized 999.33
　　　umbilical venous 999.31
　　　　bloodstream 999.32
　　　　localized 999.33
　　urinary, indwelling 996.64
　　vascular (arterial) (dialysis) (peripheral venous) NEC 996.62
　　ventricular shunt 996.63
　central venous catheter 999.31
　　bloodstream 999.32
　　localized 999.33
　coronary artery bypass 996.61
　electrodes
　　brain 996.63
　　heart 996.61
　gastrointestinal NEC 996.69
　genitourinary NEC 996.65
　　indwelling urinary catheter 996.64
　heart assist device 996.61
　heart valve 996.61
　Hickman catheter 999.31

Complications — *continued*
  infection and inflammation — *continued*
    due to any device, implant or graft classified to 996.0–996.5 — *continued*
      Hickman catheter — *continued*
        bloodstream 999.32
        localized 999.33
      infusion pump 996.62
      insulin pump 996.69
      intrauterine contraceptive device 996.65
      joint prosthesis, internal 996.66
      ocular lens 996.69
      orbital (implant) 996.69
      orthopedic NEC 996.67
        joint, internal 996.66
      peripherally inserted central catheter (PICC) 999.31
        bloodstream 999.32
        localized 999.33
      portacath (port-a-cath) 999.31
        bloodstream 999.32
        localized 999.33
      specified type NEC 996.69
      triple lumen catheter 999.31
        bloodstream 999.32
        localized 999.33
      umbilical venous catheter 999.31
        bloodstream 999.32
        localized 999.33
      urinary catheter, indwelling 996.64
      ventricular shunt 996.63
  infusion (procedure) 999.88
    blood — *see* Complications, transfusion
    infection NEC 999.39
    sepsis NEC 999.39
  inhalation therapy NEC 999.9
  injection (procedure) 999.9
    drug reaction (*see also* Reaction, drug) 995.27
    infection NEC 999.39
    sepsis NEC 999.39
    serum (prophylactic) (therapeutic) — *see* Complications, vaccination
    vaccine (any) — *see* Complications, vaccination
  inoculation (any) — *see* Complications, vaccination
  insulin pump 996.57
  internal device (catheter) (electronic) (fixation) (prosthetic) (*see also* Complications, due to (presence of) any device, implant, or graft classified to 996.0–996.5 NEC)
    mechanical — *see* Complications, mechanical
  intestinal pouch, specified NEC 569.79
  intestinal transplant (immune or nonimmune cause) 996.87
  intraoperative bleeding or hemorrhage 998.11
  intrauterine contraceptive device (*see also* Complications, contraceptive device) 996.76
    with fetal damage affecting management of pregnancy 655.8 ☑
    infection or inflammation 996.65
  in utero procedure
    fetal 679.1 ☑
    maternal 679.0 ☑
  jejunostomy 569.60
  kidney transplant (immune or nonimmune cause) 996.81
  labor 669.9 ☑
    specified condition NEC 669.8 ☑
  liver transplant (immune or nonimmune cause) 996.82
  lumbar puncture 349.0
  mechanical
    anastomosis — *see* Complications, mechanical, graft
    artificial heart 996.09
    bypass — *see* Complications, mechanical, graft

Complications — *continued*
  mechanical — *continued*
    catheter NEC 996.59
      cardiac 996.09
      cystostomy 596.82
      dialysis (hemodialysis) 996.1
        peritoneal 996.56
      during a procedure 998.2
      urethral, indwelling 996.31
    colostomy 569.62
    device NEC 996.59
      balloon (counterpulsation), intra-aortic 996.1
      cardiac 996.00
        automatic implantable defibrillator 996.04
        long-term effect 429.4
        specified NEC 996.09
      contraceptive, intrauterine 996.32
      counterpulsation, intra-aortic 996.1
      fixation, external, with internal components 996.49
      fixation, internal (nail, rod, plate) 996.40
      genitourinary 996.30
        specified NEC 996.39
      insulin pump 996.57
      nervous system 996.2
      orthopedic, internal 996.40
        prosthetic joint (*see also* Complications, mechanical, device, orthopedic, prosthetic, joint) 996.47
    prosthetic NEC 996.59
      joint 996.47
        articular bearing surface wear 996.46
        aseptic loosening 996.41
        breakage 996.43
        dislocation 996.42
        failure 996.47
        fracture 996.43
          around prosthetic 996.44
          peri-prosthetic 996.44
        instability 996.42
        loosening 996.41
        peri-prosthetic osteolysis 996.45
        subluxation 996.42
        wear 996.46
      umbrella, vena cava 996.1
      vascular 996.1
    dorsal column stimulator 996.2
    electrode NEC 996.59
      brain 996.2
      cardiac 996.01
      spinal column 996.2
    enterostomy 569.62
    esophagostomy 530.87
    fistula, arteriovenous, surgically created 996.1
    gastrostomy 536.42
    graft NEC 996.52
      aortic (bifurcation) 996.1
      aortocoronary bypass 996.03
      blood vessel NEC 996.1
      bone 996.49
      cardiac 996.00
      carotid artery bypass 996.1
      cartilage 996.49
      corneal 996.51
      coronary bypass 996.03
      decellularized allodermis 996.55
      genitourinary 996.30
        specified NEC 996.39
      muscle 996.49
      nervous system 996.2
      organ (immune or nonimmune cause) 996.80
        heart 996.83
        intestines 996.87
        kidney 996.81
        liver 996.82
        lung 996.84
        pancreas 996.86
        specified NEC 996.89

Complications — *continued*
  mechanical — *continued*
    graft — *continued*
      orthopedic, internal 996.49
      peripheral nerve 996.2
      prosthetic NEC 996.59
      skin 996.52
        artificial 996.55
        specified NEC 996.59
      tendon 996.49
      tissue NEC 996.52
      tooth 996.59
      ureter, without mention of resection 996.39
      vascular 996.1
    heart valve prosthesis 996.02
      long-term effect 429.4
    implant NEC 996.59
      cardiac 996.00
        automatic implantable defibrillator 996.04
        long-term effect 429.4
        specified NEC 996.09
      electrode NEC 996.59
        brain 996.2
        cardiac 996.01
        spinal column 996.2
      genitourinary 996.30
      nervous system 996.2
      orthopedic, internal 996.49
      prosthetic NEC 996.59
        in
          bile duct 996.59
          breast 996.54
          chin 996.59
          eye
            ocular lens 996.53
            orbital globe 996.59
      vascular 996.1
    insulin pump 996.57
    nonabsorbable surgical material 996.59
    pacemaker NEC 996.59
      brain 996.2
      cardiac 996.01
      nerve (phrenic) 996.2
    patch — *see* Complications, mechanical, graft
    prosthesis NEC 996.59
      bile duct 996.59
      breast 996.54
      chin 996.59
      ocular lens 996.53
      reconstruction, vas deferens 996.39
    reimplant NEC 996.59
      extremity (*see also* Complications, reattached, extremity) 996.90
      organ (*see also* Complications, transplant, organ, by site) 996.80
    repair — *see* Complications, mechanical, graft
    respirator [ventilator] V46.14
    shunt NEC 996.59
      arteriovenous, surgically created 996.1
      ventricular (communicating) 996.2
    stent NEC 996.59
    tracheostomy 519.02
    vas deferens reconstruction 996.39
    ventilator [respirator] V46.14
  medical care NEC 999.9
    cardiac NEC 997.1
    gastrointestinal NEC 997.49
    nervous system NEC 997.00
    peripheral vascular NEC 997.2
    respiratory NEC 997.39
    urinary NEC 997.5
    vascular
      mesenteric artery 997.71
      other vessels 997.79
      peripheral vessels 997.2
      renal artery 997.72
  nephrostomy 997.5
  nervous system
    device, implant, or graft NEC 349.1
      mechanical 996.2
    postoperative NEC 997.00

Complications — *continued*
  obstetric 669.9 ☑
    procedure (instrumental) (manual) (surgical) 669.4 ☑
    specified NEC 669.8 ☑
    surgical wound 674.3 ☑
  ocular lens implant NEC 996.79
    infection or inflammation 996.69
    mechanical 996.53
  organ transplant — *see* Complications, transplant, organ, by site
  orthopedic device, implant, or graft
    internal (fixation) (nail) (plate) (rod) NEC 996.78
      infection or inflammation 996.67
      joint prosthesis 996.77
        infection or inflammation 996.66
      mechanical 996.40
  pacemaker (cardiac) 996.72
    infection or inflammation 996.61
    mechanical 996.01
  pancreas transplant (immune or nonimmune cause) 996.86
  perfusion NEC 999.9
  perineal repair (obstetrical) 674.3 ☑
    disruption 674.2 ☑
  pessary (uterus) (vagina) — *see* Complications, contraceptive device
  phototherapy 990
  postcystoscopic 997.5
  postmastoidectomy NEC 383.30
  postoperative — *see* Complications, surgical procedures
  pregnancy NEC 646.9 ☑
    affecting fetus or newborn 761.9
  prosthetic device, internal (*see also* Complications, due to (presence of) any device, implant or graft classified to 996.0–996.5 NEC)
    mechanical NEC (*see also* Complications, mechanical) 996.59
  puerperium NEC (*see also* Puerperal) 674.9 ☑
  puncture, spinal 349.0
  pyelogram 997.5
  radiation 990
  radiotherapy 990
  reattached
    body part, except extremity 996.99
    extremity (infection) (rejection) 996.90
      arm(s) 996.94
        digit(s) (hand) 996.93
          foot 996.95
        finger(s) 996.93
        foot 996.95
        forearm 996.91
        hand 996.92
        leg 996.96
        lower NEC 996.96
        toe(s) 996.95
        upper NEC 996.94
  reimplant NEC (*see also* Complications, due to (presence of) any device, implant, or graft classified to 996.0–996.5 NEC)
    bone marrow 996.85
    extremity (*see also* Complications, reattached, extremity) 996.90
      due to infection 996.90
    mechanical — *see* Complications, mechanical, reimplant
    organ (immune or nonimmune cause) (partial) (total) (*see also* Complications, transplant, organ, by site) 996.80
  renal allograft 996.81
  renal dialysis — *see* Complications, dialysis
  respirator [ventilator], mechanical V46.14
  respiratory 519.9
    device, implant or graft NEC 996.79
      infection or inflammation 996.69
      mechanical 996.59
    distress syndrome, adult, following trauma and surgery 518.52
    insufficiency, acute, postoperative 518.52

☑ Additional Digit Required — Refer to the Tabular List for Digit Selection   ▽ Subterms under main terms may continue to next column or page

52 — Volume 2   ▶◀ Revised Text   ● New Line   ▲ Revised Code   2015 ICD-9-CM

Complications — *continued*
respiratory — *continued*
postoperative NEC 997.39
therapy NEC 999.9
sedation during labor and delivery 668.9 ☑
affecting fetus or newborn 763.5
cardiac 668.1 ☑
central nervous system 668.2 ☑
pulmonary 668.0 ☑
specified type NEC 668.8 ☑
seroma (intraoperative) (postoperative) (noninfected) 998.13
infected 998.51
shunt (*see also* Complications, due to (presence of) any device, implant, or graft classified to 996.0–996.5 NEC)
mechanical — *see* Complications, mechanical, shunt
specified body system NEC
device, implant, or graft — *see* Complications, due to (presence of) any device, implant, or graft classified to 996.0–996.5 NEC
postoperative NEC 997.99
spinal puncture or tap 349.0
stoma, external
gastrointestinal tract
colostomy 569.60
enterostomy 569.60
esophagostomy 530.87
infection 530.86
mechanical 530.87
gastrostomy 536.40
urinary tract 997.5
stomach banding 539.09
stomach stapling 539.89
surgical procedures 998.9
accidental puncture or laceration 998.2
amputation stump (late) 997.60
anastomosis — *see* Complications, anastomosis
burst stitches or sutures (external) (*also* Dehiscence) 998.32
internal 998.31
cardiac 997.1
long-term effect following cardiac surgery 429.4
cataract fragments in eye 998.82
catheter device — *see* Complications, catheter device
cecostomy malfunction 569.62
colostomy malfunction 569.62
cystostomy malfunction 596.82
infection 596.81
mechanical 596.82
specified complication NEC 596.83
dehiscence (of incision) (external) (*see also* Dehiscence) 998.32
internal 998.31
dialysis NEC (*see also* Complications, dialysis) 999.9
disruption (*see also* Dehiscence)
anastomosis (internal) — *see* Complications, mechanical, graft
internal suture (line) 998.31
wound (external) 998.32
internal 998.31
dumping syndrome (postgastrectomy) 564.2
elephantiasis or lymphedema 997.99
postmastectomy 457.0
emphysema (surgical) 998.81
enterostomy malfunction 569.62
esophagostomy malfunction 530.87
evisceration 998.32
fistula (persistent postoperative) 998.6
foreign body inadvertently left in wound (sponge) (suture) (swab) 998.4
from nonabsorbable surgical material (Dacron) (mesh) (permanent suture) (reinforcing) (Teflon) — *see* Complications, due to (presence of) any device, implant, or graft classified to 996.0–996.5 NEC
gastrointestinal NEC 997.49
gastrostomy malfunction 536.42

Complications — *continued*
surgical procedures — *continued*
hematoma 998.12
hemorrhage 998.11
ileostomy malfunction 569.62
internal prosthetic device NEC (*see also* Complications, internal device) 996.70
hemolytic anemia 283.19
infection or inflammation 996.60
malfunction — *see* Complications, mechanical
mechanical complication — *see* Complications, mechanical
thrombus 996.70
jejunostomy malfunction 569.62
nervous system NEC 997.00
obstruction, internal anastomosis — *see* Complications, mechanical, graft
other body system NEC 997.99
peripheral vascular NEC 997.2
postcardiotomy syndrome 429.4
postcholecystectomy syndrome 576.0
postcommissurotomy syndrome 429.4
postgastrectomy dumping syndrome 564.2
postmastectomy lymphedema syndrome 457.0
postmastoidectomy 383.30
cholesteatoma, recurrent 383.32
cyst, mucosal 383.31
granulation 383.33
inflammation, chronic 383.33
postvagotomy syndrome 564.2
postvalvulotomy syndrome 429.4
reattached extremity (infection) (rejection) (*see also* Complications, reattached, extremity) 996.90
respiratory NEC 997.39
seroma 998.13
shock (endotoxic) (septic) 998.02
hypovolemic 998.09
shunt, prosthetic (thrombus) (*see also* Complications, due to (presence of) any device, implant, or graft classified to 996.0–996.5 NEC)
hemolytic anemia 283.19
specified complication NEC 596.83
specified complication NEC 998.89
stitch abscess 998.59
transplant — *see* Complications, graft
ureterostomy malfunction 997.5
urethrostomy malfunction 997.5
urinary NEC 997.5
vascular
mesenteric artery 997.71
other vessels 997.79
peripheral vessels 997.2
renal artery 997.72
wound infection 998.59
therapeutic misadventure NEC 999.9
surgical treatment 998.9
tracheostomy 519.00
transfusion (blood) (lymphocytes) (plasma) 999.80
acute lung injury (TRALI) 518.7
atrophy, liver, yellow, subacute (within 8 months of administration) — *see* Hepatitis, viral
bone marrow 996.85
embolism
air 999.1
thrombus 999.2
febrile nonhemolytic reaction (FNHTR) 780.66
hemolysis NEC 999.89
bone marrow 996.85
hemolytic reaction, incompatibility unspecified 999.83
acute 999.84
delayed 999.85
hepatitis (serum) (type B) (within 8 months after administration) — *see* Hepatitis, viral
incompatibility reaction
ABO 999.60

Complications — *continued*
transfusion — *continued*
incompatibility reaction — *continued*
ABO — *continued*
with hemolytic transfusion reaction (HTR) (not specified as acute or delayed) 999.61
acute 999.62
delayed 999.63
specified type NEC 999.69
minor blood group 999.89
non-ABO (minor antigens) (Duffy) (Kell) (Kidd) (Lewis) (M) (N) (P) (S) 999.75
with hemolytic transfusion reaction (HTR) (not specified as acute or delayed) 999.76
acute 999.77
delayed 999.78
specified type NEC 999.79
Rh antigen (C) (c) (D) (E) (e) (factor) 999.70
with hemolytic transfusion reaction (HTR) (not specified as acute or delayed) 999.71
acute 999.72
delayed 999.73
specified type NEC 999.74
infection 999.39
acute 999.34
jaundice (serum) (within 8 months after administration) — *see* Hepatitis, viral
sepsis 999.39
shock or reaction NEC 999.89
bone marrow 996.85
specified reaction NEC 999.89
subacute yellow atrophy of liver (within 8 months after administration) — *see* Hepatitis, viral
thromboembolism 999.2
transplant NEC (*see also* Complications, due to (presence of) any device, implant, or graft classified to 996.0–996.5 NEC)
bone marrow 996.85
organ (immune or nonimmune cause) (partial) (total) 996.80
bone marrow 996.85
heart 996.83
intestines 996.87
kidney 996.81
liver 996.82
lung 996.84
pancreas 996.86
specified NEC 996.89
stem cell(s) 996.88
from
peripheral blood 996.88
umbilical cord 996.88
trauma NEC (early) 958.8
ultrasound therapy NEC 999.9
umbilical cord
affecting fetus or newborn 762.6
complicating delivery 663.9 ☑
affecting fetus or newborn 762.6
specified type NEC 663.8 ☑
urethral catheter NEC 996.76
infection or inflammation 996.64
mechanical 996.31
urinary, postoperative NEC 997.5
vaccination 999.9
anaphylaxis NEC 999.42
cellulitis 999.39
encephalitis or encephalomyelitis 323.51
hepatitis (serum) (type B) (within 8 months after administration) — *see* Hepatitis, viral
infection (general) (local) NEC 999.39
jaundice (serum) (within 8 months after administration) — *see* Hepatitis, viral
meningitis 997.09 [321.8]
myelitis 323.52
protein sickness 999.52

Complications — *continued*
vaccination — *continued*
reaction (allergic) 999.52
serum 999.52
sepsis 999.39
serum intoxication, sickness, rash, or other serum reaction NEC 999.52
shock (allergic) (anaphylactic) 999.49
subacute yellow atrophy of liver (within 8 months after administration) — *see* Hepatitis, viral
vaccinia (generalized) 999.0
localized 999.39
vascular
device, implant, or graft NEC 996.74
infection or inflammation 996.62
mechanical NEC 996.1
cardiac (*see also* Complications, mechanical, by type) 996.00
following infusion, perfusion, or transfusion 999.2
postoperative NEC 997.2
mesenteric artery 997.71
other vessels 997.79
peripheral vessels 997.2
renal artery 997.72
ventilation therapy NEC 999.9
ventilator [respirator], mechanical V46.14
Compound presentation, complicating delivery 652.8 ☑
causing obstructed labor 660.0 ☑
Compressed air disease 993.3
Compression
with injury — *see* specific injury
arm NEC 354.9
artery 447.1
celiac, syndrome 447.4
brachial plexus 353.0
brain (stem) 348.4
due to
contusion, brain — *see* Contusion, brain
injury NEC (*see also* Hemorrhage, brain, traumatic)
birth — *see* Birth, injury, brain
laceration, brain — *see* Laceration, brain
osteopathic 739.0
bronchus 519.19
by cicatrix — *see* Cicatrix
cardiac 423.9
cauda equina 344.60
with neurogenic bladder 344.61
celiac (artery) (axis) 447.4
cerebral — *see* Compression, brain
cervical plexus 353.2
cord (umbilical) — *see* Compression, umbilical cord
cranial nerve 352.9
second 377.49
third (partial) 378.51
total 378.52
fourth 378.53
fifth 350.8
sixth 378.54
seventh 351.8
divers' squeeze 993.3
duodenum (external) (*see also* Obstruction, duodenum) 537.3
during birth 767.9
esophagus 530.3
congenital, external 750.3
Eustachian tube 381.63
facies (congenital) 754.0
fracture — *see* Fracture, by site
heart — *see* Disease, heart
intestine (*see also* Obstruction, intestine) 560.9
with hernia — *see* Hernia, by site, with obstruction
laryngeal nerve, recurrent 478.79
leg NEC 355.8
lower extremity NEC 355.8
lumbosacral plexus 353.1
lung 518.89

☑ Additional Digit Required — Refer to the Tabular List for Digit Selection   ▽ Subterms under main terms may continue to next column or page

2015 ICD-9-CM   ▶◀ Revised Text   ● New Line   ▲ Revised Code   Volume 2 — 53

Compression — continued
- lymphatic vessel 457.1
- medulla — see Compression, brain
- nerve NEC (see also Disorder, nerve)
  - arm NEC 354.9
  - autonomic nervous system (see also Neuropathy, peripheral, autonomic) 337.9
  - axillary 353.0
  - cranial NEC 352.9
  - due to displacement of intervertebral disc 722.2
    - with myelopathy 722.70
    - cervical 722.0
      - with myelopathy 722.71
    - lumbar, lumbosacral 722.10
      - with myelopathy 722.73
    - thoracic, thoracolumbar 722.11
      - with myelopathy 722.72
  - iliohypogastric 355.79
  - ilioinguinal 355.79
  - leg NEC 355.8
  - lower extremity NEC 355.8
  - median (in carpal tunnel) 354.0
  - obturator 355.79
  - optic 377.49
  - plantar 355.6
  - posterior tibial (in tarsal tunnel) 355.5
  - root (by scar tissue) NEC 724.9
    - cervical NEC 723.4
    - lumbar NEC 724.4
    - lumbosacral 724.4
    - thoracic 724.4
  - saphenous 355.79
  - sciatic (acute) 355.0
  - sympathetic 337.9
  - traumatic — see Injury, nerve
  - ulnar 354.2
  - upper extremity NEC 354.9
- peripheral — see Compression, nerve
- spinal (cord) (old or nontraumatic) 336.9
  - by displacement of intervertebral disc — see Displacement, intervertebral disc
  - nerve
    - root NEC 724.9
      - postoperative 722.80
        - cervical region 722.81
        - lumbar region 722.83
        - thoracic region 722.82
      - traumatic — see Injury, nerve, spinal
    - traumatic — see Injury, nerve, spinal
  - spondylogenic 721.91
    - cervical 721.1
    - lumbar, lumbosacral 721.42
    - thoracic 721.41
  - traumatic (see also Injury, spinal, by site)
    - with fracture, vertebra — see Fracture, vertebra, by site, with spinal cord injury
  - spondylogenic — see Compression, spinal cord, spondylogenic
- subcostal nerve (syndrome) 354.8
- sympathetic nerve NEC 337.9
- syndrome 958.5
- thorax 512.89
  - iatrogenic 512.1
  - postoperative 512.1
- trachea 519.19
  - congenital 748.3
- ulnar nerve (by scar tissue) 354.2
- umbilical cord
  - affecting fetus or newborn 762.5
    - cord prolapsed 762.4
  - complicating delivery 663.2 ☑
    - cord around neck 663.1 ☑
    - cord prolapsed 663.0 ☑
- upper extremity NEC 354.9
- ureter 593.3
- urethra — see Stricture, urethra
- vein 459.2
- vena cava (inferior) (superior) 459.2
- vertebral NEC — see Compression, spinal (cord)

Compulsion, compulsive
- eating 307.51
- neurosis (obsessive) 300.3
- personality 301.4
- states (mixed) 300.3
- swearing 300.3
  - in Gilles de la Tourette's syndrome 307.23
- tics and spasms 307.22
- water drinking NEC (syndrome) 307.9

Concato's disease (pericardial polyserositis) 423.2
- peritoneal 568.82
- pleural — see Pleurisy

Concavity, chest wall 738.3

Concealed
- hemorrhage NEC 459.0
- penis 752.65

Concentric fading 368.12

Concern (normal) **about sick person in family** V61.49

Concrescence (teeth) 520.2

Concretio cordis 423.1
- rheumatic 393

Concretion — see also Calculus
- appendicular 543.9
- canaliculus 375.57
- clitoris 624.8
- conjunctiva 372.54
- eyelid 374.56
- intestine (impaction) (obstruction) 560.39
- lacrimal (passages) 375.57
- prepuce (male) 605
  - female (clitoris) 624.8
- salivary gland (any) 527.5
- seminal vesicle 608.89
- stomach 537.89
- tonsil 474.8

Concussion (current) 850.9
- with
  - loss of consciousness 850.5
    - brief (less than one hour)
      - 30 minutes or less 850.11
      - 31-59 minutes 850.12
    - moderate (1-24 hours) 850.2
    - prolonged (more than 24 hours)
      - (with complete recovery)
        - (with return to pre-existing conscious level) 850.3
      - without return to pre-existing conscious level 850.4
  - mental confusion or disorientation (without loss of consciousness) 850.0
    - with loss of consciousness — see Concussion, with, loss of consciousness
- without loss of consciousness 850.0
- blast (air) (hydraulic) (immersion) (underwater) 869.0
  - with open wound into cavity 869.1
  - abdomen or thorax — see Injury, internal, by site
  - brain — see Concussion, brain
  - ear (acoustic nerve trauma) 951.5
    - with perforation, tympanic membrane — see Wound, open, ear drum
  - thorax — see Injury, internal, intrathoracic organs NEC
- brain or cerebral (without skull fracture) 850.9
  - with
    - loss of consciousness 850.5
      - brief (less than one hour)
        - 30 minutes or less 850.11
        - 31-59 minutes 850.12
      - moderate (1-24 hours) 850.2
      - prolonged (more than 24 hours)
        - (with complete recovery)
          - (with return to pre-existing conscious level) 850.3
        - without return to pre-existing conscious level 850.4

Concussion — continued
- brain or cerebral — continued
  - with — continued
    - mental confusion or disorientation (without loss of consciousness) 850.0
      - with loss of consciousness — see Concussion, brain, with, loss of consciousness
    - skull fracture — see Fracture, skull, by site
  - without loss of consciousness 850.0
- cauda equina 952.4
- cerebral — see Concussion, brain
- conus medullaris (spine) 952.4
- hydraulic — see Concussion, blast
- internal organs — see Injury, internal, by site
- labyrinth — see Injury, intracranial
- ocular 921.3
- osseous labyrinth — see Injury, intracranial
- spinal (cord) (see also Injury, spinal, by site)
  - due to
    - broken
      - back — see Fracture, vertebra, by site, with spinal cord injury
      - neck — see Fracture, vertebra, cervical, with spinal cord injury
    - fracture, fracture dislocation, or compression fracture of spine or vertebra — see Fracture, vertebra, by site, with spinal cord injury
- syndrome 310.2
- underwater blast — see Concussion, blast

Condition — see also Disease
- fetal hematologic 678.0 ☑
- psychiatric 298.9
- respiratory NEC 519.9
  - acute or subacute NEC 519.9
    - due to
      - external agent 508.9
        - specified type NEC 508.8
      - fumes or vapors (chemical) (inhalation) 506.3
      - radiation 508.0
  - chronic NEC 519.9
    - due to
      - external agent 508.9
        - specified type NEC 508.8
      - fumes or vapors (chemical) (inhalation) 506.4
      - radiation 508.1
    - due to
      - external agent 508.9
        - specified type NEC 508.8
      - fumes or vapors (chemical) (inhalation) 506.9
      - smoke inhalation 508.2

Conduct disturbance — see also Disturbance, conduct 312.9
- adjustment reaction 309.3
- hyperkinetic 314.2

Condyloma NEC 078.11
- acuminatum 078.11
- gonorrheal 098.0
- latum 091.3
- syphilitic 091.3
  - congenital 090.0
- venereal, syphilitic 091.3

Confinement — see Delivery

Conflagration — see also Burn, by site
- asphyxia (by inhalation of gases, fumes, or vapors) 987.9
- specified agent — see Table of Drugs and Chemicals

Conflict
- family V61.9
  - specified circumstance NEC V61.8
- interpersonal NEC V62.81
- marital V61.10
  - involving
    - divorce V61.03
    - estrangement V61.09
  - parent (guardian)-child V61.20

Conflict — continued
- parent-child — continued
  - adopted child V61.24
  - biological child V61.23
  - foster child V61.25
- partner V61.10

Confluent — see condition

Confusional arousals 327.41

Confusion, confused (mental) (state) — see also State, confusional 298.9
- acute 293.0
- epileptic 293.0
- postoperative 293.9
- psychogenic 298.2
- reactive (from emotional stress, psychological trauma) 298.2
- subacute 293.1

Congelation 991.9

Congenital — see also condition
- aortic septum 747.29
- generalized fibromatosis (CGF) 759.89
- intrinsic factor deficiency 281.0
- malformation — see Anomaly

Congestion, congestive
- asphyxia, newborn 768.9
- bladder 596.89
- bowel 569.89
- brain (see also Disease, cerebrovascular NEC) 437.8
  - malarial 084.9
- breast 611.79
- bronchi 519.19
- bronchial tube 519.19
- catarrhal 472.0
- cerebral — see Congestion, brain
- cerebrospinal — see Congestion, brain
- chest 786.9
- chill 780.99
  - malarial (see also Malaria) 084.6
- circulatory NEC 459.9
- conjunctiva 372.71
- due to disturbance of circulation 459.9
- duodenum 537.3
- enteritis — see Enteritis
- eye 372.71
- fibrosis syndrome (pelvic) 625.5
- gastroenteritis — see Enteritis
- general 799.89
- glottis 476.0
- heart (see also Failure, heart) 428.0
- hepatic 573.0
- hypostatic (lung) 514
- intestine 569.89
- intracranial — see Congestion, brain
- kidney 593.89
- labyrinth 386.50
- larynx 476.0
- liver 573.0
- lung 786.9
  - active or acute (see also Pneumonia) 486
    - congenital 770.0
  - chronic 514
  - hypostatic 514
  - idiopathic, acute 518.52
  - passive 514
- malaria, malarial (brain) (fever) (see also Malaria) 084.6
- medulla — see Congestion, brain
- nasal 478.19
- nose 478.19
- orbit, orbital 376.33
  - inflammatory (chronic) 376.10
    - acute 376.00
- ovary 620.8
- pancreas 577.8
- pelvic, female 625.5
- pleural 511.0
- prostate (active) 602.1
- pulmonary — see Congestion, lung
- renal 593.89
- retina 362.89
- seminal vesicle 608.89
- spinal cord 336.1
- spleen 289.51
  - chronic 289.51
- stomach 537.89

Congestion, congestive — *continued*
trachea 464.11
urethra 599.84
uterus 625.5
with subinvolution 621.1
viscera 799.89
Congestive — *see* Congestion
Conical
cervix 622.6
cornea 371.60
teeth 520.2
Conjoined twins 759.4
causing disproportion (fetopelvic) 678.1 ☑
fetal 678.1 ☑
Conjugal maladjustment V61.10
involving
divorce V61.03
estrangement V61.09
Conjunctiva — *see* condition
Conjunctivitis (exposure) (infectious)
(nondiphtheritic) (pneumococcal) (pustular) (staphylococcal) (streptococcal)
NEC 372.30
actinic 370.24
acute 372.00
atopic 372.05
chemical 372.06
contagious 372.03
follicular 372.02
hemorrhagic (viral) 077.4
toxic 372.06
adenoviral (acute) 077.3
allergic (chronic) 372.14
with hay fever 372.05
anaphylactic 372.05
angular 372.03
Apollo (viral) 077.4
atopic 372.05
blennorrhagic (neonatorum) 098.40
catarrhal 372.03
chemical 372.06
allergic 372.05
meaning corrosion — *see* Burn, conjunctiva
chlamydial 077.98
due to
Chlamydia trachomatis — *see* Trachoma
paratrachoma 077.0
chronic 372.10
allergic 372.14
follicular 372.12
simple 372.11
specified type NEC 372.14
vernal 372.13
diphtheritic 032.81
due to
dust 372.05
enterovirus type 70 077.4
erythema multiforme 695.10 [372.33]
filariasis (*see also* Filariasis) 125.9 [372.15]
mucocutaneous
disease NEC 372.33
leishmaniasis 085.5 [372.15]
Reiter's disease 099.3 [372.33]
syphilis 095.8 [372.10]
toxoplasmosis (acquired) 130.1
congenital (active) 771.2
trachoma — *see* Trachoma
dust 372.05
eczematous 370.31
epidemic 077.1
hemorrhagic 077.4
follicular (acute) 372.02
adenoviral (acute) 077.3
chronic 372.12
glare 370.24
gonococcal (neonatorum) 098.40
granular (trachomatous) 076.1
late effect 139.1
hemorrhagic (acute) (epidemic) 077.4
herpetic (simplex) 054.43
zoster 053.21
inclusion 077.0
infantile 771.6
influenzal 372.03

Conjunctivitis — *continued*
Koch-Weeks 372.03
light 372.05
medicamentosa 372.05
membranous 372.04
meningococcic 036.89
Morax-Axenfeld 372.02
mucopurulent NEC 372.03
neonatal 771.6
gonococcal 098.40
Newcastle's 077.8
nodosa 360.14
of Beal 077.3
parasitic 372.15
filariasis (*see also* Filariasis) 125.9 [372.15]
mucocutaneous leishmaniasis
085.5 [372.15]
Parinaud's 372.02
petrificans 372.39
phlyctenular 370.31
pseudomembranous 372.04
diphtheritic 032.81
purulent 372.03
Reiter's 099.3 [372.33]
rosacea 695.3 [372.31]
serous 372.01
viral 077.99
simple chronic 372.11
specified NEC 372.39
sunlamp 372.04
swimming pool 077.0
toxic 372.06
trachomatous (follicular) 076.1
acute 076.0
late effect 139.1
traumatic NEC 372.39
tuberculous (*see also* Tuberculosis)
017.3 ☑ [370.31]
tularemic 021.3
tularensis 021.3
vernal 372.13
limbar 372.13 [370.32]
viral 077.99
acute hemorrhagic 077.4
specified NEC 077.8
Conjunctivochalasis 372.81
Conjunctoblepharitis — *see* Conjunctivitis
Connective tissue — *see* condition
Conn (-Louis) syndrome (primary aldosteronism) 255.12
Conradi (-Hünermann) syndrome or disease
(chondrodysplasia calcificans congenita)
756.59
Consanguinity V19.7
Consecutive — *see* condition
Consolidated lung (base) — *see* Pneumonia, lobar
Constipation 564.00
atonic 564.09
drug induced
correct substance properly administered
564.09
overdose or wrong substance given or
taken 977.9
specified drug — *see* Table of Drugs
and Chemicals
neurogenic 564.09
other specified NEC 564.09
outlet dysfunction 564.02
psychogenic 306.4
simple 564.00
slow transit 564.01
spastic 564.09
Constitutional — *see also* condition
arterial hypotension (*see also* Hypotension)
458.9
obesity 278.00
morbid 278.01
psychopathic state 301.9
short stature in childhood 783.43
state, developmental V21.9
specified development NEC V21.8
substandard 301.6
Constitutionally substandard 301.6
Constriction
anomalous, meningeal bands or folds 742.8

Constriction — *continued*
aortic arch (congenital) 747.10
asphyxiation or suffocation by 994.7
bronchus 519.19
canal, ear (*see also* Stricture, ear canal, acquired) 380.50
duodenum 537.3
gallbladder (*see also* Obstruction, gallbladder) 575.2
congenital 751.69
intestine (*see also* Obstruction, intestine)
560.9
larynx 478.74
congenital 748.3
meningeal bands or folds, anomalous 742.8
organ or site, congenital NEC — *see* Atresia
prepuce (congenital) 605
pylorus 537.0
adult hypertrophic 537.0
congenital or infantile 750.5
newborn 750.5
ring (uterus) 661.4 ☑
affecting fetus or newborn 763.7
spastic (*see also* Spasm)
ureter 593.3
urethra — *see* Stricture, urethra
stomach 537.89
ureter 593.3
urethra — *see* Stricture, urethra
visual field (functional) (peripheral) 368.45
Constrictive — *see* condition
Consultation
without complaint or sickness V65.9
feared complaint unfounded V65.5
specified reason NEC V65.8
medical (*see also* Counseling, medical)
specified reason NEC V65.8
Consumption — *see* Tuberculosis
Contact — *see also* Exposure (suspected)
with
AIDS virus V01.79
anthrax V01.81
asbestos V15.84
cholera V01.0
communicable disease V01.9
specified type NEC V01.89
viral NEC V01.79
Escherichia coli (E. coli) V01.83
German measles V01.4
gonorrhea V01.6
HIV V01.79
human immunodeficiency virus V01.79
lead V15.86
meningococcus V01.84
parasitic disease NEC V01.89
poliomyelitis V01.2
potentially hazardous body fluids V15.85
rabies V01.5
rubella V01.4
SARS-associated coronavirus V01.82
smallpox V01.3
syphilis V01.6
tuberculosis V01.1
varicella V01.71
venereal disease V01.6
viral disease NEC V01.79
dermatitis — *see* Dermatitis
Contamination, food — *see also* Poisoning,
food 005.9
Contraception, contraceptive
advice NEC V25.09
family planning V25.09
fitting of diaphragm V25.02
prescribing or use of
oral contraceptive agent V25.01
specified agent NEC V25.02
counseling NEC V25.09
emergency V25.03
family planning V25.09
fitting of diaphragm V25.02
prescribing or use of
oral contraceptive agent V25.01
emergency V25.03
postcoital V25.03
specified agent NEC V25.02
device (in situ) V45.59

Contraception, contraceptive — *continued*
device — *continued*
causing menorrhagia 996.76
checking V25.42
complications 996.32
insertion V25.11
intrauterine V45.51
reinsertion V25.13
removal V25.12
and reinsertion V25.13
replacement V25.13
subdermal V45.52
fitting of diaphragm V25.02
insertion
intrauterine contraceptive device V25.11
subdermal implantable V25.5
maintenance V25.40
examination V25.40
oral contraceptive V25.41
specified method NEC V25.49
subdermal implantable V25.43
intrauterine device V25.42
intrauterine device V25.42
oral contraceptive V25.41
specified method NEC V25.49
subdermal implantable V25.43
management NEC V25.49
prescription
oral contraceptive agent V25.01
emergency V25.03
postcoital V25.03
repeat V25.41
specified agent NEC V25.02
repeat V25.49
sterilization V25.2
surveillance V25.40
intrauterine device V25.42
oral contraceptive agent V25.41
subdermal implantable V25.43
specified method NEC V25.49
Contraction, contracture, contracted
Achilles tendon (*see also* Short, tendon,
Achilles) 727.81
anus 564.89
axilla 729.90
bile duct (*see also* Disease, biliary) 576.8
bladder 596.89
neck or sphincter 596.0
bowel (*see also* Obstruction, intestine) 560.9
Braxton Hicks 644.1 ☑
breast implant, capsular 611.83
bronchus 519.19
burn (old) — *see* Cicatrix
capsular, of breast implant 611.83
cecum (*see also* Obstruction, intestine) 560.9
cervix (*see also* Stricture, cervix) 622.4
congenital 752.49
cicatricial — *see* Cicatrix
colon (*see also* Obstruction, intestine) 560.9
conjunctiva trachomatous, active 076.1
late effect 139.1
Dupuytren's 728.6
eyelid 374.41
eye socket (after enucleation) 372.64
face 729.90
fascia (lata) (postural) 728.89
Dupuytren's 728.6
palmar 728.6
plantar 728.71
finger NEC 736.29
congenital 755.59
joint (*see also* Contraction, joint) 718.44
flaccid, paralytic
joint (*see also* Contraction, joint)
718.4 ☑
muscle 728.85
ocular 378.50
gallbladder (*see also* Obstruction, gallbladder) 575.2
hamstring 728.89
tendon 727.81
heart valve — *see* Endocarditis
Hicks' 644.1 ☑
hip (*see also* Contraction, joint) 718.4 ☑

☑ Additional Digit Required — Refer to the Tabular List for Digit Selection
⩗ Subterms under main terms may continue to next column or page

Contraction, contracture, contracted — *continued*
hourglass
  bladder 596.89
    congenital 753.8
  gallbladder (*see also* Obstruction, gall-
    bladder) 575.2
    congenital 751.69
  stomach 536.8
    congenital 750.7
    psychogenic 306.4
  uterus 661.4 ☑
    affecting fetus or newborn 763.7
hysterical 300.11
infantile (*see also* Epilepsy) 345.6 ☑
internal os (*see also* Stricture, cervix) 622.4
intestine (*see also* Obstruction, intestine)
  560.9
joint (abduction) (acquired) (adduction)
  (flexion) (rotation) 718.40
  ankle 718.47
  congenital NEC 755.8
    generalized or multiple 754.89
      lower limb joints 754.89
    hip (*see also* Subluxation, congenital,
      hip) 754.32
    lower limb (including pelvic girdle)
      not involving hip 754.89
    upper limb (including shoulder gir-
      dle) 755.59
  elbow 718.42
  foot 718.47
  hand 718.44
  hip 718.45
  hysterical 300.11
  knee 718.46
  multiple sites 718.49
  pelvic region 718.45
  shoulder (region) 718.41
  specified site NEC 718.48
  wrist 718.43
kidney (granular) (secondary) (*see also*
  Sclerosis, renal) 587
  congenital 753.3
  hydronephritic 591
  pyelonephritic (*see also* Pyelitis, chronic)
    590.00
  tuberculous (*see also* Tuberculosis)
    016.0 ☑
ligament 728.89
  congenital 756.89
liver — *see* Cirrhosis, liver
muscle (postinfectional) (postural) NEC
  728.85
  congenital 756.89
    sternocleidomastoid 754.1
  extraocular 378.60
  eye (extrinsic) (*see also* Strabismus) 378.9
    paralytic (*see also* Strabismus, paralyt-
      ic) 378.50
  flaccid 728.85
  hysterical 300.11
  ischemic (Volkmann's) 958.6
  paralytic 728.85
  posttraumatic 958.6
  psychogenic 306.0
    specified as conversion reaction
      300.11
  myotonic 728.85
neck (*see also* Torticollis) 723.5
  congenital 754.1
  psychogenic 306.0
ocular muscle (*see also* Strabismus) 378.9
  paralytic (*see also* Strabismus, paralytic)
    378.50
organ or site, congenital NEC — *see* Atresia
outlet (pelvis) — *see* Contraction, pelvis
palmar fascia 728.6
paralytic
  joint (*see also* Contraction, joint)
    718.4 ☑
  muscle 728.85
    ocular (*see also* Strabismus, paralytic)
      378.50
pelvis (acquired) (general) 738.6
  affecting fetus or newborn 763.1

Contraction, contracture, contracted —
continued
pelvis — *continued*
  complicating delivery 653.1 ☑
    causing obstructed labor 660.1 ☑ ☑
    generally contracted 653.1 ☑
      causing obstructed labor
        660.1 ☑
    inlet 653.2 ☑
      causing obstructed labor
        660.1 ☑
    midpelvic 653.8 ☑
      causing obstructed labor
        660.1 ☑
    midplane 653.8 ☑
      causing obstructed labor
        660.1 ☑
    outlet 653.3 ☑
      causing obstructed labor
        660.1 ☑
plantar fascia 728.71
premature
  atrial 427.61
  auricular 427.61
  auriculoventricular 427.61
  heart (junctional) (nodal) 427.60
  supraventricular 427.61
  ventricular 427.69
prostate 602.8
pylorus (*see also* Pylorospasm) 537.81
rectosigmoid (*see also* Obstruction, intestine) 560.9
rectum, rectal (sphincter) 564.89
  psychogenic 306.4
ring (Bandl's) 661.4 ☑
  affecting fetus or newborn 763.7
scar — *see* Cicatrix
sigmoid (*see also* Obstruction, intestine)
  560.9
socket, eye 372.64
spine (*see also* Curvature, spine) 737.9
stomach 536.8
  hourglass 536.8
    congenital 750.7
  psychogenic 306.4
tendon (sheath) (*see also* Short, tendon)
  727.81
toe 735.8
ureterovesical orifice (postinfectional) 593.3
urethra 599.84
uterus 621.8
  abnormal 661.9 ☑
    affecting fetus or newborn 763.7
  clonic, hourglass or tetanic 661.4 ☑
    affecting fetus or newborn 763.7
  dyscoordinate 661.4 ☑
    affecting fetus or newborn 763.7
  hourglass 661.4 ☑
    affecting fetus or newborn 763.7
  hypotonic NEC 661.2 ☑
    affecting fetus or newborn 763.7
  incoordinate 661.4 ☑
    affecting fetus or newborn 763.7
  inefficient or poor 661.2 ☑
    affecting fetus or newborn 763.7
  irregular 661.2 ☑
    affecting fetus or newborn 763.7
  tetanic 661.4 ☑
    affecting fetus or newborn 763.7
vagina (outlet) 623.2
vesical 596.89
  neck or urethral orifice 596.0
visual field, generalized 368.45
Volkmann's (ischemic) 958.6
Contusion (skin surface intact) 924.9
with
  crush injury — *see* Crush
  dislocation — *see* Dislocation, by site
  fracture — *see* Fracture, by site
  internal injury (*see also* Injury, internal,
    by site)
    heart — *see* Contusion, cardiac
    kidney — *see* Contusion, kidney
    liver — *see* Contusion, liver
    lung — *see* Contusion, lung
    spleen — *see* Contusion, spleen

Contusion — *continued*
with — *continued*
  intracranial injury — *see* Injury, intracra-
    nial
  nerve injury — *see* Injury, nerve
  open wound — *see* Wound, open, by
    site
abdomen, abdominal (muscle) (wall) 922.2
  organ(s) NEC 868.00
adnexa, eye NEC 921.9
ankle 924.21
  with other parts of foot 924.20
arm 923.9
  lower (with elbow) 923.10
  upper 923.03
    with shoulder or axillary region
      923.09
auditory canal (external) (meatus) (and
  other part(s) of neck, scalp, or face,
  except eye) 920
auricle, ear (and other part(s) of neck, scalp,
  or face except eye) 920
axilla 923.02
  with shoulder or upper arm 923.09
back 922.31
bone NEC 924.9
brain (cerebral) (membrane) (with hemorrhage) 851.8 ☑

> Note — Use the following fifth-digit
> subclassification with categories
> 851–854:
>
> 0   unspecified state of consciousness
>
> 1   with no loss of consciousness
>
> 2   with brief [less than one hour]
>   loss of consciousness
>
> 3   with moderate [1–24 hours] loss
>   of consciousness
>
> 4   with prolonged [more than 24
>   hours] loss of consciousness and
>   return to pre-existing conscious
>   level
>
> 5   with prolonged [more than 24
>   hours] loss of consciousness,
>   without return to pre-existing
>   conscious level
>
> Use fifth-digit 5 to designate when a
> patient is unconscious and dies before
> regaining consciousness, regardless of
> the duration of the loss of consciousness
>
> 6   with loss of consciousness of un-
>   specified duration
>
> 9   with concussion, unspecified

  with
    open intracranial wound 851.9 ☑
    skull fracture — *see* Fracture, skull,
      by site
  cerebellum 851.4 ☑
    with open intracranial wound
      851.5 ☑
  cortex 851.0 ☑
    with open intracranial wound
      851.1 ☑
  occipital lobe 851.4 ☑
    with open intracranial wound
      851.5 ☑
  stem 851.4 ☑
    with open intracranial wound
      851.5 ☑
breast 922.0
brow (and other part(s) of neck, scalp, or
  face, except eye) 920
buttock 922.32
canthus 921.1
cardiac 861.01
  with open wound into thorax 861.11
cauda equina (spine) 952.4
cerebellum — *see* Contusion, brain, cerebellum
cerebral — *see* Contusion, brain
cheek(s) (and other part(s) of neck, scalp, or
  face, except eye) 920

Contusion — *continued*
chest (wall) 922.1
chin (and other part(s) of neck, scalp, or face,
  except eye) 920
clitoris 922.4
conjunctiva 921.1
conus medullaris (spine) 952.4
cornea 921.3
corpus cavernosum 922.4
cortex (brain) (cerebral) — *see* Contusion,
  brain, cortex
costal region 922.1
ear (and other part(s) of neck, scalp, or face
  except eye) 920
elbow 923.11
  with forearm 923.10
epididymis 922.4
epigastric region 922.2
eyeball 921.3
eyelid(s) (and periocular area) 921.1
eye NEC 921.9
face (and neck, or scalp, any part, except
  eye) 920
femoral triangle 922.2
fetus or newborn 772.6
finger(s) (nail) (subungual) 923.3
flank 922.2
foot (with ankle) (excluding toe(s)) 924.20
forearm (and elbow) 923.10
forehead (and other part(s) of neck, scalp,
  or face, except eye) 920
genital organs, external 922.4
globe (eye) 921.3
groin 922.2
gum(s) (and other part(s) of neck, scalp, or
  face, except eye) 920
hand(s) (except fingers alone) 923.20
head (any part, except eye) (and face) (and
  neck) 920
heart — *see* Contusion, cardiac
heel 924.20
hip 924.01
  with thigh 924.00
iliac region 922.2
inguinal region 922.2
internal organs (abdomen, chest, or pelvis)
  NEC — *see* Injury, internal, by site
interscapular region 922.33
iris (eye) 921.3
kidney 866.01
  with open wound into cavity 866.11
knee 924.11
  with lower leg 924.10
labium (majus) (minus) 922.4
lacrimal apparatus, gland, or sac 921.1
larynx (and other part(s) of neck, scalp, or
  face, except eye) 920
late effect — *see* Late, effects (of), contusion
leg 924.5
  lower (with knee) 924.10
lens 921.3
lingual (and other part(s) of neck, scalp, or
  face, except eye) 920
lip(s) (and other part(s) of neck, scalp, or
  face, except eye) 920
liver 864.01
  with
    laceration — *see* Laceration, liver
    open wound into cavity 864.11
lower extremity 924.5
  multiple sites 924.4
lumbar region 922.31
lung 861.21
  with open wound into thorax 861.31
malar region (and other part(s) of neck,
  scalp, or face, except eye) 920
mandibular joint (and other part(s) of neck,
  scalp, or face, except eye) 920
mastoid region (and other part(s) of neck,
  scalp, or face, except eye) 920
membrane, brain — *see* Contusion, brain
midthoracic region 922.1
mouth (and other part(s) of neck, scalp, or
  face, except eye) 920
multiple sites (not classifiable to same three-
  digit category) 924.8

Contusion — *continued*
multiple sites — *continued*
lower limb 924.4
trunk 922.8
upper limb 923.8
muscle NEC 924.9
myocardium — *see* Contusion, cardiac
nasal (septum) (and other part(s) of neck, scalp, or face, except eye) 920
neck (and scalp or face, any part, except eye) 920
nerve — *see* Injury, nerve, by site
nose (and other part(s) of neck, scalp, or face, except eye) 920
occipital region (scalp) (and neck or face, except eye) 920
lobe — *see* Contusion, brain, occipital lobe
orbit (region) (tissues) 921.2
palate (soft) (and other part(s) of neck, scalp, or face, except eye) 920
parietal region (scalp) (and neck or face, except eye) 920
lobe — *see* Contusion, brain
penis 922.4
pericardium — *see* Contusion, cardiac
perineum 922.4
periocular area 921.1
pharynx (and other part(s) of neck, scalp, or face, except eye) 920
popliteal space (*see also* Contusion, knee) 924.11
prepuce 922.4
pubic region 922.4
pudenda 922.4
pulmonary — *see* Contusion, lung
quadriceps femoralis 924.00
rib cage 922.1
sacral region 922.32
salivary ducts or glands (and other part(s) of neck, scalp, or face, except eye) 920
scalp (and neck or face, except eye) 920
scapular region 923.01
with shoulder or upper arm 923.09
sclera (eye) 921.3
scrotum 922.4
shoulder 923.00
with upper arm or axillar regions 923.09
skin NEC 924.9
skull 920
spermatic cord 922.4
spinal cord (*see also* Injury, spinal, by site)
cauda equina 952.4
conus medullaris 952.4
spleen 865.01
with open wound into cavity 865.11
sternal region 922.1
stomach — *see* Injury, internal, stomach
subconjunctival 921.1
subcutaneous NEC 924.9
submaxillary region (and other part(s) of neck, scalp, or face, except eye) 920
submental region (and other part(s) of neck, scalp, or face, except eye) 920
subperiosteal NEC 924.9
supraclavicular fossa (and other part(s) of neck, scalp, or face, except eye) 920
supraorbital (and other part(s) of neck, scalp, or face, except eye) 920
temple (region) (and other part(s) of neck, scalp, or face, except eye) 920
testis 922.4
thigh (and hip) 924.00
thorax 922.1
organ — *see* Injury, internal, intrathoracic
throat (and other part(s) of neck, scalp, or face, except eye) 920
thumb(s) (nail) (subungual) 923.3
toe(s) (nail) (subungual) 924.3
tongue (and other part(s) of neck, scalp, or face, except eye) 920
trunk 922.9
multiple sites 922.8

Contusion — *continued*
trunk — *continued*
specified site — *see* Contusion, by site
tunica vaginalis 922.4
tympanum (membrane) (and other part(s) of neck, scalp, or face, except eye) 920
upper extremity 923.9
multiple sites 923.8
uvula (and other part(s) of neck, scalp, or face, except eye) 920
vagina 922.4
vocal cord(s) (and other part(s) of neck, scalp, or face, except eye) 920
vulva 922.4
wrist 923.21
with hand(s), except finger(s) alone 923.20
Conus (any type) (congenital) 743.57
acquired 371.60
medullaris syndrome 336.8
Convalescence (following) V66.9
chemotherapy V66.2
medical NEC V66.5
psychotherapy V66.3
radiotherapy V66.1
surgery NEC V66.0
treatment (for) NEC V66.5
combined V66.6
fracture V66.4
mental disorder NEC V66.3
specified disorder NEC V66.5
Conversion
closed surgical procedure to open procedure
arthroscopic V64.43
laparoscopic V64.41
thoracoscopic V64.42
hysteria, hysterical, any type 300.11
neurosis, any 300.11
reaction, any 300.11
Converter, tuberculosis (test reaction) 795.51
Convulsions (idiopathic) 780.39
apoplectiform (*see also* Disease, cerebrovascular, acute) 436
brain 780.39
cerebral 780.39
cerebrospinal 780.39
due to trauma NEC — *see* Injury, intracranial
eclamptic (*see also* Eclampsia) 780.39
epileptic (*see also* Epilepsy) 345.9 ☑
epileptiform (*see also* Seizure, epileptiform) 780.39
epileptoid (*see also* Seizure, epileptiform) 780.39
ether
anesthetic
correct substance properly administered 780.39
overdose or wrong substance given 968.2
other specified type — *see* Table of Drugs and Chemicals
febrile (simple) 780.31
complex 780.32
generalized 780.39
hysterical 300.11
infantile 780.39
epilepsy — *see* Epilepsy
internal 780.39
jacksonian (*see also* Epilepsy) 345.5 ☑
myoclonic 333.2
newborn 779.0
paretic 094.1
pregnancy (nephritic) (uremic) — *see* Eclampsia, pregnancy
psychomotor (*see also* Epilepsy) 345.4 ☑
puerperal, postpartum — *see* Eclampsia, pregnancy
recurrent 780.39
epileptic — *see* Epilepsy
reflex 781.0
repetitive 780.39
epileptic — *see* Epilepsy
salaam (*see also* Epilepsy) 345.6 ☑
scarlatinal 034.1

Convulsions — *continued*
spasmodic 780.39
tetanus, tetanic (*see also* Tetanus) 037
thymic 254.8
uncinate 780.39
uremic 586
Convulsive — *see also* Convulsions
disorder or state 780.39
epileptic — *see* Epilepsy
equivalent, abdominal (*see also* Epilepsy) 345.5 ☑
Cooke-Apert-Gallais syndrome (adrenogenital) 255.2
Cooley's anemia (erythroblastic) 282.44
Coolie itch 126.9
Cooper's
disease 610.1
hernia — *see* Hernia, Cooper's
Coordination disturbance 781.3
Copper wire arteries, retina 362.13
Copra itch 133.8
Coprolith 560.39
Coprophilia 302.89
Coproporphyria, hereditary 277.1
Coprostasis 560.32
with hernia (*see also* Hernia, by site, with obstruction)
gangrenous — *see* Hernia, by site, with gangrene
Cor
biloculare 745.7
bovinum — *see* Hypertrophy, cardiac
bovis (*see also* Hypertrophy, cardiac)
pulmonale (chronic) 416.9
acute 415.0
triatriatum, triatrium 746.82
triloculare 745.8
biatriatum 745.3
biventriculare 745.69
Corbus' disease 607.1
Cord — *see also* condition
around neck (tightly) (with compression)
affecting fetus or newborn 762.5
complicating delivery 663.1 ☑
without compression 663.3 ☑
affecting fetus or newborn 762.6
bladder NEC 344.61
tabetic 094.0
prolapse
affecting fetus or newborn 762.4
complicating delivery 663.0 ☑
Cord's angiopathy — *see also* Tuberculosis 017.3 ☑ [362.18]
Cordis ectopia 746.87
Corditis (spermatic) 608.4
Corectopia 743.46
Cori type glycogen storage disease — *see* Disease, glycogen storage
Cork-handlers' disease or lung 495.3
Corkscrew esophagus 530.5
Corlett's pyosis (impetigo) 684
Corn (infected) 700
Cornea — *see also* condition
donor V59.5
guttata (dystrophy) 371.57
plana 743.41
Cornelia de Lange's syndrome (Amsterdam dwarf, intellectual disabilities, and brachycephaly) 759.89
Cornual gestation or pregnancy — *see* Pregnancy, cornual
Cornu cutaneum 702.8
Coronary (artery) — *see also* condition
arising from aorta or pulmonary trunk 746.85
Corpora — *see also* condition
amylacea (prostate) 602.8
cavernosa — *see* condition
Corpulence — *see* Obesity
Corpus — *see* condition
Corrigan's disease — *see* Insufficiency, aortic
Corrosive burn — *see* Burn, by site
Corsican fever — *see also* Malaria 084.6
Cortical — *see also* condition
blindness 377.75
necrosis, kidney (bilateral) 583.6

Corticoadrenal — *see* condition
Corticosexual syndrome 255.2
Coryza (acute) 460
with grippe or influenza (*see also* Influenza) 487.1
syphilitic 095.8
congenital (chronic) 090.0
Costen's syndrome or complex 524.60
Costiveness — *see also* Constipation 564.00
Costochondritis 733.6
Cotard's syndrome (paranoia) 297.1
Cot death 798.0
Cotia virus 059.8
Cotungo's disease 724.3
Cough 786.2
with hemorrhage (*see also* Hemoptysis) 786.39
affected 786.2
bronchial 786.2
with grippe or influenza (*see also* Influenza) 487.1
chronic 786.2
epidemic 786.2
functional 306.1
hemorrhagic 786.39
hysterical 300.11
laryngeal, spasmodic 786.2
nervous 786.2
psychogenic 306.1
smokers' 491.0
tea tasters' 112.89
Counseling NEC V65.40
without complaint or sickness V65.49
abuse victim NEC V62.89
child V61.21
partner V61.11
spouse V61.11
child abuse, maltreatment, or neglect V61.21
contraceptive NEC V25.09
device (intrauterine) V25.02
maintenance V25.40
intrauterine contraceptive device V25.42
oral contraceptive (pill) V25.41
specified type NEC V25.49
subdermal implantable V25.43
management NEC V25.9
oral contraceptive (pill) V25.01
emergency V25.03
postcoital V25.03
prescription NEC V25.02
oral contraceptive (pill) V25.01
emergency V25.03
postcoital V25.03
repeat prescription V25.41
repeat prescription V25.40
subdermal implantable V25.43
surveillance NEC V25.40
dietary V65.3
exercise V65.41
expectant parent(s)
pediatric pre-adoption visit V65.11
pediatric pre-birth visit V65.11
explanation of
investigation finding NEC V65.49
medication NEC V65.49
family planning V25.09
natural
procreative V26.41
to avoid pregnancy V25.04
for nonattending third party V65.19
genetic V26.33
gonorrhea V65.45
health (advice) (education) (instruction) NEC V65.49
HIV V65.44
human immunodeficiency virus V65.44
injury prevention V65.43
insulin pump training V65.46
marital V61.10
medical (for) V65.9
boarding school resident V60.6
condition not demonstrated V65.5
feared complaint and no disease found V65.5

☑ Additional Digit Required — Refer to the Tabular List for Digit Selection
▽ Subterms under main terms may continue to next column or page
2015 ICD-9-CM
▶◀ Revised Text ● New Line ▲ Revised Code
Volume 2 — 57

Counseling — *continued*
  medical — *continued*
    institutional resident V60.6
    on behalf of another V65.19
    person living alone V60.3
  natural family planning
    procreative V26.41
    to avoid pregnancy V25.04
  parent (guardian)-child conflict V61.20
    adopted child V61.24
    biological child V61.23
    foster child V61.25
    specified problem NEC V61.29
  partner abuse
    perpetrator V61.12
    victim V61.11
  pediatric
    pre-adoption visit for adoptive parent(s)
      V65.11
    pre-birth visit for expectant parents
      V65.11
  perpetrator of
    child abuse V62.83
      parental V61.22
    partner abuse V61.12
    spouse abuse V61.12
  procreative V65.49
  sex NEC V65.49
    transmitted disease NEC V65.45
      HIV V65.44
  specified reason NEC V65.49
  spousal abuse
    perpetrator V61.12
    victim V61.11
  substance use and abuse V65.42
  syphilis V65.45
  victim (of)
    abuse NEC V62.89
    child abuse V61.21
    partner abuse V61.11
    spousal abuse V61.11
Coupled rhythm 427.89
Couvelaire uterus (complicating delivery) —
  see Placenta, separation
Cowper's gland — *see* condition
Cowperitis — *see also* Urethritis 597.89
  gonorrheal (acute) 098.0
    chronic or duration of 2 months or over
      098.2
Cowpox (abortive) 051.01
  due to vaccination 999.0
  eyelid 051.01 *[373.5]*
    postvaccination 999.0 *[373.5]*
Coxa
  plana 732.1
  valga (acquired) 736.31
    congenital 755.61
    late effect of rickets 268.1
  vara (acquired) 736.32
    congenital 755.62
    late effect of rickets 268.1
Coxae malum senilis 715.25
Coxalgia (nontuberculous) 719.45
  tuberculous (*see also* Tuberculosis)
    015.1 ☑ *[730.85]*
Coxalgic pelvis 736.30
Coxitis 716.65
Coxsackie (infection) (virus) 079.2
  central nervous system NEC 048
  endocarditis 074.22
  enteritis 008.67
  meningitis (aseptic) 047.0
  myocarditis 074.23
  pericarditis 074.21
  pharyngitis 074.0
  pleurodynia 074.1
  specific disease NEC 074.8
Crabs, meaning pubic lice 132.2
Crack baby 760.75
Cracked
  nipple 611.2
    puerperal, postpartum 676.1 ☑
  tooth 521.81
Cradle cap 690.11
Craft neurosis 300.89
Craigiasis 007.8

Cramp(s) 729.82
  abdominal 789.0 ☑
  bathing 994.1
  colic 789.7
    infantile 789.7
    psychogenic 306.4
  due to immersion 994.1
  extremity (lower) (upper) NEC 729.82
  fireman 992.2
  heat 992.2
  hysterical 300.11
  immersion 994.1
  intestinal 789.0 ☑
    psychogenic 306.4
  linotypist's 300.89
    organic 333.84
  muscle (extremity) (general) 729.82
    due to immersion 994.1
    hysterical 300.11
  occupational (hand) 300.89
    organic 333.84
  psychogenic 307.89
  salt depletion 276.1
  sleep related leg 327.52
  stoker 992.2
  stomach 789.0 ☑
  telegraphers' 300.89
    organic 333.84
  typists' 300.89
    organic 333.84
  uterus 625.8
    menstrual 625.3
  writers' 333.84
    organic 333.84
    psychogenic 300.89
Cranial — *see* condition
Cranioclasis, fetal 763.89
Craniocleidodysostosis 755.59
Craniofenestria (skull) 756.0
Craniolacunia (skull) 756.0
Craniopagus 759.4
Craniopathy, metabolic 733.3
Craniopharyngeal — *see* condition
Craniopharyngioma (M9350/1) 237.0
Craniorachischisis (totalis) 740.1
Cranioschisis 756.0
Craniostenosis 756.0
Craniosynostosis 756.0
Craniotabes (cause unknown) 733.3
  rachitic 268.1
  syphilitic 090.5
Craniotomy, fetal 763.89
Cranium — *see* condition
Craw-craw 125.3
CRBSI (catheter-related bloodstream infection)
  999.31
Creaking joint 719.60
  ankle 719.67
  elbow 719.62
  foot 719.67
  hand 719.64
  hip 719.65
  knee 719.66
  multiple sites 719.69
  pelvic region 719.65
  shoulder (region) 719.61
  specified site NEC 719.68
  wrist 719.63
Creeping
  eruption 126.9
  palsy 335.21
  paralysis 335.21
Crenated tongue 529.8
Creotoxism 005.9
Crepitus
  caput 756.0
  joint 719.60
    ankle 719.67
    elbow 719.62
    foot 719.67
    hand 719.64
    hip 719.65
    knee 719.66
    multiple sites 719.69
    pelvic region 719.65
    shoulder (region) 719.61

Crepitus — *continued*
  joint — *continued*
    specified site NEC 719.68
    wrist 719.63
Crescent or conus choroid, congenital 743.57
Cretin, cretinism (athyrotic) (congenital) (endemic) (metabolic) (nongoitrous) (sporadic) 243
  goitrous (sporadic) 246.1
  pelvis (dwarf type) (male type) 243
    with disproportion (fetopelvic) 653.1 ☑
      affecting fetus or newborn 763.1
      causing obstructed labor 660.1 ☑
        affecting fetus or newborn 763.1
  pituitary 253.3
Cretinoid degeneration 243
Creutzfeldt-Jakob disease (CJD) (syndrome)
  046.19
  with dementia
    with behavioral disturbance
      046.19 *[294.11]*
    without behavioral disturbance
      046.19 *[294.10]*
  familial 046.19
  iatrogenic 046.19
  specified NEC 046.19
  sporadic 046.19
  variant (vCJD) 046.11
    with dementia
      with behavioral disturbance
        046.11 *[294.11]*
      without behavioral disturbance
        046.11 *[294.10]*
Crib death 798.0
Cribriform hymen 752.49
Cri-du-chat syndrome 758.31
Crigler-Najjar disease or syndrome (congenital hyperbilirubinemia) 277.4
Crimean hemorrhagic fever 065.0
Criminalism 301.7
Crisis
  abdomen 789.0 ☑
  addisonian (acute adrenocortical insufficien-
    cy) 255.41
  adrenal (cortical) 255.41
  asthmatic — *see* Asthma
  brain, cerebral (*see also* Disease, cerebrovas-
    cular, acute) 436
  celiac 579.0
  Dietl's 593.4
  emotional NEC 309.29
    acute reaction to stress 308.0
    adjustment reaction 309.9
    specific to childhood or adolescence
      313.9
  gastric (tabetic) 094.0
  glaucomatocyclitic 364.22
  heart (*see also* Failure, heart) 428.9
  hypertensive — *see* Hypertension
  nitritoid
    correct substance properly administered
      458.29
    overdose or wrong substance given or
      taken 961.1
  oculogyric 378.87
    psychogenic 306.7
  Pel's 094.0
  psychosexual identity 302.6
  rectum 094.0
  renal 593.81
  sickle cell 282.62
  stomach (tabetic) 094.0
  tabetic 094.0
  thyroid (*see also* Thyrotoxicosis) 242.9 ☑
  thyrotoxic (*see also* Thyrotoxicosis) 242.9 ☑
  vascular — *see* Disease, cerebrovascular,
    acute
Crocq's disease (acrocyanosis) 443.89
Crohn's disease — *see also* Enteritis, regional
  555.9
Cronkhite-Canada syndrome 211.3
Crooked septum, nasal 470
Cross
  birth (of fetus) complicating delivery
    652.3 ☑
    with successful version 652.1 ☑

Cross — *continued*
  birth complicating delivery — *continued*
    causing obstructed labor 660.0 ☑
  bite, anterior or posterior 524.27
  eye (*see also* Esotropia) 378.00
Crossed ectopia of kidney 753.3
Crossfoot 754.50
Croup, croupous (acute) (angina) (catarrhal)
  (infective) (inflammatory) (laryngeal)
  (membranous) (nondiphtheritic) (pseudomembranous) 464.4
  asthmatic (*see also* Asthma) 493.9 ☑
  bronchial 466.0
  diphtheritic (membranous) 032.3
  false 478.75
  spasmodic 478.75
    diphtheritic 032.3
  stridulous 478.75
    diphtheritic 032.3
Crouzon's disease (craniofacial dysostosis)
  756.0
Crowding, teeth 524.31
CRST syndrome (cutaneous systemic sclerosis)
  710.1
Cruchet's disease (encephalitis lethargica)
  049.8
Cruelty in children — *see also* Disturbance,
  conduct 312.9
Crural ulcer — *see also* Ulcer, lower extremity
  707.10
Crush, crushed, crushing (injury) 929.9
  abdomen 926.19
    internal — *see* Injury, internal, abdomen
  ankle 928.21
    with other parts of foot 928.20
  arm 927.9
    lower (and elbow) 927.10
    upper 927.03
      with shoulder or axillary region
        927.09
  axilla 927.02
    with shoulder or upper arm 927.09
  back 926.11
  breast 926.19
  buttock 926.12
  cheek 925.1
  chest — *see* Injury, internal, chest
  ear 925.1
  elbow 927.11
    with forearm 927.10
  face 925.1
  finger(s) 927.3
    with hand(s) 927.20
      and wrist(s) 927.21
  flank 926.19
  foot, excluding toe(s) alone (with ankle)
    928.20
  forearm (and elbow) 927.10
  genitalia, external (female) (male) 926.0
    internal — *see* Injury, internal, genital
      organ NEC
  hand, except finger(s) alone (and wrist)
    927.20
  head — *see* Fracture, skull, by site
  heel 928.20
  hip 928.01
    with thigh 928.00
  internal organ (abdomen, chest, or pelvis)
    — *see* Injury, internal, by site
  knee 928.11
    with leg, lower 928.10
  labium (majus) (minus) 926.0
  larynx 925.2
  late effect — *see* Late, effects (of), crushing
  leg 928.9
    lower 928.10
      and knee 928.11
    upper 928.00
  limb
    lower 928.9
      multiple sites 928.8
    upper 927.9
      multiple sites 927.8
  multiple sites NEC 929.0
  neck 925.2
  nerve — *see* Injury, nerve, by site

☑ **Additional Digit Required** — Refer to the Tabular List for Digit Selection   ▽ Subterms under main terms may continue to next column or page

58 — Volume 2   ►◄ Revised Text   ● New Line   ▲ Revised Code   2015 ICD-9-CM

Crush, crushed, crushing — *continued*
  nose 802.0
    open 802.1
  penis 926.0
  pharynx 925.2
  scalp 925.1
  scapular region 927.01
    with shoulder or upper arm 927.09
  scrotum 926.0
  shoulder 927.00
    with upper arm or axillary region 927.09
  skull or cranium — *see* Fracture, skull, by site
  spinal cord — *see* Injury, spinal, by site
  syndrome (complication of trauma) 958.5
  testis 926.0
  thigh (with hip) 928.00
  throat 925.2
  thumb(s) (and fingers) 927.3
  toe(s) 928.3
    with foot 928.20
      and ankle 928.21
  tonsil 925.2
  trunk 926.9
    chest — *see* Injury, internal, intrathoracic organs NEC
    internal organ — *see* Injury, internal, by site
    multiple sites 926.8
    specified site NEC 926.19
  vulva 926.0
  wrist 927.21
    with hand(s), except fingers alone 927.20
Crusta lactea 690.11
Crusts 782.8
Crutch paralysis 953.4
Cruveilhier-Baumgarten cirrhosis, disease, or syndrome 571.5
Cruveilhier's disease 335.21
Cruz-Chagas disease — *see also* Trypanosomiasis 086.2
Crying
  constant, continuous
    adolescent 780.95
    adult 780.95
    baby 780.92
    child 780.95
    infant 780.92
    newborn 780.92
  excessive
    adolescent 780.95
    adult 780.95
    baby 780.92
    child 780.95
    infant 780.92
    newborn 780.92
Cryofibrinogenemia 273.2
Cryoglobulinemia (mixed) 273.2
Crypt (anal) (rectal) 569.49
Cryptitis (anal) (rectal) 569.49
Cryptococcosis (European) (pulmonary) (systemic) 117.5
Cryptococcus 117.5
  epidermicus 117.5
  neoformans, infection by 117.5
Cryptopapillitis (anus) 569.49
Cryptophthalmos (eyelid) 743.06
Cryptorchid, cryptorchism, cryptorchidism 752.51
Cryptosporidiosis 007.4
  hepatobiliary 136.8
  respiratory 136.8
Cryptotia 744.29
Crystallopathy
  calcium pyrophosphate (*see also* Arthritis) 275.49 *[712.2]* ☑
  dicalcium phosphate (*see also* Arthritis) 275.49 *[712.1]* ☑
  gouty 274.00
  pyrophosphate NEC (*see also* Arthritis) 275.49 *[712.2]* ☑
  uric acid 274.00
Crystalluria 791.9
Csillag's disease (lichen sclerosis et atrophicus) 701.0
Cuban itch 050.1

Cubitus
  valgus (acquired) 736.01
    congenital 755.59
    late effect of rickets 268.1
  varus (acquired) 736.02
    congenital 755.59
    late effect of rickets 268.1
Cultural deprivation V62.4
Cupping of optic disc 377.14
Curling esophagus 530.5
Curling's ulcer — *see* Ulcer, duodenum
Curschmann (-Batten) (-Steinert) disease or syndrome 359.21
Curvature
  organ or site, congenital NEC — *see* Distortion
  penis (lateral) 752.69
  Pott's (spinal) (*see also* Tuberculosis) 015.0 ☑ *[737.43]*
  radius, idiopathic, progressive (congenital) 755.54
  spine (acquired) (angular) (idiopathic) (incorrect) (postural) 737.9
    congenital 754.2
    due to or associated with
      Charcôt-Marie-Tooth disease 356.1 *[737.40]*
      mucopolysaccharidosis 277.5 *[737.40]*
      neurofibromatosis 237.71 *[737.40]*
      osteitis
        deformans 731.0 *[737.40]*
        fibrosa cystica 252.01 *[737.40]*
      osteoporosis (*see also* Osteoporosis) 733.00 *[737.40]*
      poliomyelitis (*see also* Poliomyelitis) 138 *[737.40]*
      tuberculosis (Pott's curvature) (*see also* Tuberculosis) 015.0 ☑ *[737.43]*
    kyphoscoliotic (*see also* Kyphoscoliosis) 737.30
    kyphotic (*see also* Kyphosis) 737.10
    late effect of rickets 268.1 *[737.40]*
    Pott's 015.0 ☑ *[737.40]*
    scoliotic (*see also* Scoliosis) 737.30
    specified NEC 737.8
    tuberculous 015.0 ☑ *[737.40]*
Cushing's
  basophilism, disease, or syndrome (iatrogenic) (idiopathic) (pituitary basophilism) (pituitary dependent) 255.0
  ulcer — *see* Ulcer, peptic
Cushingoid due to steroid therapy
  correct substance properly administered 255.0
  overdose or wrong substance given or taken 962.0
Cut (external) — *see* Wound, open, by site
Cutaneous — *see also* condition
  hemorrhage 782.7
  horn (cheek) (eyelid) (mouth) 702.8
  larva migrans 126.9
Cutis — *see also* condition
  hyperelastic 756.83
    acquired 701.8
  laxa 756.83
    senilis 701.8
  marmorata 782.61
  osteosis 709.3
  pendula 756.83
    acquired 701.8
  rhomboidalis nuchae 701.8
  verticis gyrata 757.39
    acquired 701.8
Cyanopathy, newborn 770.83
Cyanosis 782.5
  autotoxic 289.7
  common atrioventricular canal 745.69
  congenital 770.83
  conjunctiva 372.71
  due to
    endocardial cushion defect 745.60
    nonclosure, foramen botalli 745.5
    patent foramen botalli 745.5

Cyanosis — *continued*
  due to — *continued*
    persistent foramen ovale 745.5
  enterogenous 289.7
  fetus or newborn 770.83
  ostium primum defect 745.61
  paroxysmal digital 443.0
  retina, retinal 362.10
Cycle
  anovulatory 628.0
  menstrual, irregular 626.4
Cyclencephaly 759.89
Cyclical vomiting 536.2
  associated with migraine 346.2 ☑
  psychogenic 306.4
Cyclitic membrane 364.74
Cyclitis — *see also* Iridocyclitis 364.3
  acute 364.00
    primary 364.01
    recurrent 364.02
  chronic 364.10
    in
      sarcoidosis 135 *[364.11]*
      tuberculosis (*see also* Tuberculosis) 017.3 ☑ *[364.11]*
  Fuchs' heterochromic 364.21
  granulomatous 364.10
  lens induced 364.23
  nongranulomatous 364.00
  posterior 363.21
  primary 364.01
  recurrent 364.02
  secondary (noninfectious) 364.04
    infectious 364.03
  subacute 364.00
    primary 364.01
    recurrent 364.02
Cyclokeratitis — *see* Keratitis
Cyclophoria 378.44
Cyclopia, cyclops 759.89
Cycloplegia 367.51
Cyclospasm 367.53
Cyclosporiasis 007.5
Cyclothymia 301.13
Cyclothymic personality 301.13
Cyclotropia 378.33
Cyesis — *see* Pregnancy
Cylindroma (M8200/3) — *see also* Neoplasm, by site, malignant
  eccrine dermal (M8200/0) — *see* Neoplasm, skin, benign
  skin (M8200/0) — *see* Neoplasm, skin, benign
Cylindruria 791.7
Cyllosoma 759.89
Cynanche
  diphtheritic 032.3
  tonsillaris 475
Cynorexia 783.6
Cyphosis — *see* Kyphosis
Cyprus fever — *see also* Brucellosis 023.9
Cyriax's syndrome (slipping rib) 733.99
Cyst (mucus) (retention) (serous) (simple)

> *Note* — In general, cysts are not neoplastic and are classified to the appropriate category for disease of the specified anatomical site. This generalization does not apply to certain types of cysts which are neoplastic in nature, for example, dermoid, nor does it apply to cysts of certain structures, for example, branchial cleft, which are classified as developmental anomalies.
>
> The following listing includes some of the most frequently reported sites of cysts as well as qualifiers which indicate the type of cyst. The latter qualifiers usually are not repeated under the anatomical sites. Since the code assignment for a given site may vary depending upon the type of cyst, the coder should refer to the listings under the specified type of cyst before consideration is given to the site.

  accessory, fallopian tube 752.11

Cyst — *continued*
  adenoid (infected) 474.8
  adrenal gland 255.8
    congenital 759.1
  air, lung 518.89
  allantoic 753.7
  alveolar process (jaw bone) 526.2
  amnion, amniotic 658.8 ☑
  anterior chamber (eye) 364.60
    exudative 364.62
    implantation (surgical) (traumatic) 364.61
    parasitic 360.13
  anterior nasopalatine 526.1
  antrum 478.19
  anus 569.49
  apical (periodontal) (tooth) 522.8
  appendix 543.9
  arachnoid, brain 348.0
  arytenoid 478.79
  auricle 706.2
  Baker's (knee) 727.51
    tuberculous (*see also* Tuberculosis) 015.2 ☑
  Bartholin's gland or duct 616.2
  bile duct (*see also* Disease, biliary) 576.8
  bladder (multiple) (trigone) 596.89
  Blessig's 362.62
  blood, endocardial (*see also* Endocarditis) 424.90
  blue dome 610.0
  bone (local) 733.20
    aneurysmal 733.22
    jaw 526.2
      developmental (odontogenic) 526.0
      fissural 526.1
      latent 526.89
    solitary 733.21
    unicameral 733.21
  brain 348.0
    congenital 742.4
    hydatid (*see also* Echinococcus) 122.9
    third ventricle (colloid) 742.4
  branchial (cleft) 744.42
  branchiogenic 744.42
  breast (benign) (blue dome) (pedunculated) (solitary) (traumatic) 610.0
    involution 610.4
    sebaceous 610.8
  broad ligament (benign) 620.8
    embryonic 752.11
  bronchogenic (mediastinal) (sequestration) 518.89
    congenital 748.4
  buccal 528.4
  bulbourethral gland (Cowper's) 599.89
  bursa, bursal 727.49
    pharyngeal 478.26
  calcifying odontogenic (M9301/0) 213.1
    upper jaw (bone) 213.0
  canal of Nuck (acquired) (serous) 629.1
    congenital 752.41
  canthus 372.75
  carcinomatous (M8010/3) — *see* Neoplasm, by site, malignant
  cartilage (joint) — *see* Derangement, joint
  cauda equina 336.8
  cavum septi pellucidi NEC 348.0
  celomic (pericardium) 746.89
  cerebellopontine (angle) — *see* Cyst, brain
  cerebellum — *see* Cyst, brain
  cerebral — *see* Cyst, brain
  cervical lateral 744.42
  cervix 622.8
    embryonal 752.41
    nabothian (gland) 616.0
  chamber, anterior (eye) 364.60
    exudative 364.62
    implantation (surgical) (traumatic) 364.61
    parasitic 360.13
  chiasmal, optic NEC (*see also* Lesion, chiasmal) 377.54
  chocolate (ovary) 617.1
  choledochal (congenital) 751.69
    acquired 576.8

☑ Additional Digit Required — Refer to the Tabular List for Digit Selection

▽ Subterms under main terms may continue to next column or page

Cyst — *continued*

choledochus 751.69
chorion 658.8 ☑
choroid plexus 348.0
chyle, mesentery 457.8
ciliary body 364.60
   exudative 364.64
   implantation 364.61
   primary 364.63
clitoris 624.8
coccyx (*see also* Cyst, bone) 733.20
colloid
   third ventricle (brain) 742.4
   thyroid gland — *see* Goiter
colon 569.89
common (bile) duct (*see also* Disease, biliary) 576.8
congenital NEC 759.89
   adrenal glands 759.1
   epiglottis 748.3
   esophagus 750.4
   fallopian tube 752.11
   kidney 753.10
      multiple 753.19
      single 753.11
   larynx 748.3
   liver 751.62
   lung 748.4
   mediastinum 748.8
   ovary 752.0
   oviduct 752.11
   pancreas 751.7
   periurethral (tissue) 753.8
   prepuce NEC 752.69
      penis 752.69
   sublingual 750.26
   submaxillary gland 750.26
   thymus (gland) 759.2
   tongue 750.19
   ureterovesical orifice 753.4
   vulva 752.41
conjunctiva 372.75
cornea 371.23
corpora quadrigemina 348.0
corpus
   albicans (ovary) 620.2
   luteum (ruptured) 620.1
Cowper's gland (benign) (infected) 599.89
cranial meninges 348.0
craniobuccal pouch 253.8
craniopharyngeal pouch 253.8
cystic duct (*see also* Disease, gallbladder) 575.8
Cysticercus (any site) 123.1
Dandy-Walker 742.3
   with spina bifida (*see also* Spina bifida) 741.0 ☑
dental 522.8
   developmental 526.0
   eruption 526.0
   lateral periodontal 526.0
   primordial (keratocyst) 526.0
   root 522.8
dentigerous 526.0
   mandible 526.0
   maxilla 526.0
dermoid (M9084/0) (*see also* Neoplasm, by site, benign)
   with malignant transformation (M9084/3) 183.0
   implantation
      external area or site (skin) NEC 709.8
      iris 364.61
      skin 709.8
      vagina 623.8
      vulva 624.8
   mouth 528.4
   oral soft tissue 528.4
   sacrococcygeal 685.1
      with abscess 685.0
developmental of ovary, ovarian 752.0
dura (cerebral) 348.0
   spinal 349.2
ear (external) 706.2
echinococcal (*see also* Echinococcus) 122.9

Cyst — *continued*

embryonal
   cervix uteri 752.41
   genitalia, female external 752.41
   uterus 752.39
   vagina 752.41
endometrial 621.8
   ectopic 617.9
endometrium (uterus) 621.8
   ectopic — *see* Endometriosis
enteric 751.5
enterogenous 751.5
epidermal (inclusion) (*see also* Cyst, skin) 706.2
epidermoid (inclusion) (*see also* Cyst, skin) 706.2
   mouth 528.4
   not of skin — *see* Cyst, by site
   oral soft tissue 528.4
epididymis 608.89
epiglottis 478.79
epiphysis cerebri 259.8
epithelial (inclusion) (*see also* Cyst, skin) 706.2
epoophoron 752.11
eruption 526.0
esophagus 530.89
ethmoid sinus 478.19
eye (retention) 379.8
   congenital 743.03
   posterior segment, congenital 743.54
eyebrow 706.2
eyelid (sebaceous) 374.84
   infected 373.13
   sweat glands or ducts 374.84
falciform ligament (inflammatory) 573.8
fallopian tube 620.8
   congenital 752.11
female genital organs NEC 629.89
fimbrial (congenital) 752.11
fissural (oral region) 526.1
follicle (atretic) (graafian) (ovarian) 620.0
   nabothian (gland) 616.0
follicular (atretic) (ovarian) 620.0
   dentigerous 526.0
frontal sinus 478.19
gallbladder or duct 575.8
ganglion 727.43
Gartner's duct 752.41
gas, of mesentery 568.89
gingiva 523.8
gland of moll 374.84
globulomaxillary 526.1
graafian follicle 620.0
granulosal lutein 620.2
hemangiomatous (M9121/0) (*see also* Hemangioma) 228.00
hydatid (*see also* Echinococcus) 122.9
   fallopian tube (Morgagni) 752.11
   liver NEC 122.8
   lung NEC 122.9
   Morgagni 752.89
      fallopian tube 752.11
   specified site NEC 122.9
hymen 623.8
   embryonal 752.41
hypopharynx 478.26
hypophysis, hypophyseal (duct) (recurrent) 253.8
   cerebri 253.8
implantation (dermoid)
   anterior chamber (eye) 364.61
   external area or site (skin) NEC 709.8
   iris 364.61
   vagina 623.8
   vulva 624.8
incisor, incisive canal 526.1
inclusion (epidermal) (epithelial) (epidermoid) (mucous) (squamous) (*see also* Cyst, skin) 706.2
   not of skin — *see* Neoplasm, by site, benign
intestine (large) (small) 569.89
intracranial — *see* Cyst, brain
intraligamentous 728.89
   knee 717.89

Cyst — *continued*

intrasellar 253.8
iris (idiopathic) 364.60
   exudative 364.62
   implantation (surgical) (traumatic) 364.61
   miotic pupillary 364.55
   parasitic 360.13
Iwanoff's 362.62
jaw (bone) (aneurysmal) (extravasation) (hemorrhagic) (traumatic) 526.2
   developmental (odontogenic) 526.0
   fissural 526.1
keratin 706.2
kidney (congenital) 753.10
   acquired 593.2
   calyceal (*see also* Hydronephrosis) 591
   multiple 753.19
   pyelogenic (*see also* Hydronephrosis) 591
   simple 593.2
   single 753.11
   solitary (not congenital) 593.2
labium (majus) (minus) 624.8
   sebaceous 624.8
lacrimal
   apparatus 375.43
   gland or sac 375.12
larynx 478.79
lens 379.39
   congenital 743.39
lip (gland) 528.5
liver 573.8
   congenital 751.62
   hydatid (*see also* Echinococcus) 122.8
      granulosis 122.0
      multilocularis 122.5
lung 518.89
   congenital 748.4
   giant bullous 492.0
lutein 620.1
lymphangiomatous (M9173/0) 228.1
lymphoepithelial
   mouth 528.4
   oral soft tissue 528.4
macula 362.54
malignant (M8000/3) — *see* Neoplasm, by site, malignant
mammary gland (sweat gland) (*see also* Cyst, breast) 610.0
mandible 526.2
   dentigerous 526.0
   radicular 522.8
maxilla 526.2
   dentigerous 526.0
   radicular 522.8
median
   anterior maxillary 526.1
   palatal 526.1
mediastinum (congenital) 748.8
meibomian (gland) (retention) 373.2
   infected 373.12
membrane, brain 348.0
meninges (cerebral) 348.0
   spinal 349.2
meniscus knee 717.5
mesentery, mesenteric (gas) 568.89
   chyle 457.8
   gas 568.89
mesonephric duct 752.89
mesothelial
   peritoneum 568.89
   pleura (peritoneal) 568.89
milk 611.5
miotic pupillary (iris) 364.55
Morgagni (hydatid) 752.89
   fallopian tube 752.11
mouth 528.4
Müllerian duct 752.89
   appendix testis 608.89
   cervix (embryonal) 752.41
   fallopian tube 752.11
   prostatic utricle 599.89
   vagina (embryonal) 752.41
multilocular (ovary) (M8000/1) 239.5
myometrium 621.8

Cyst — *continued*

nabothian (follicle) (ruptured) 616.0
nasal sinus 478.19
nasoalveolar 528.4
nasolabial 528.4
nasopalatine (duct) 526.1
   anterior 526.1
nasopharynx 478.26
neoplastic (M8000/1) (*see also* Neoplasm, by site, unspecified nature)
   benign (M8000/0) — *see* Neoplasm, by site, benign
   uterus 621.8
nervous system — *see* Cyst, brain
neuroenteric 742.59
neuroepithelial ventricle 348.0
nipple 610.0
nose 478.19
   skin of 706.2
odontogenic, developmental 526.0
omentum (lesser) 568.89
   congenital 751.8
oral soft tissue (dermoid) (epidermoid) (lymphoepithelial) 528.4
ora serrata 361.19
orbit 376.81
ovary, ovarian (twisted) 620.2
   adherent 620.2
   chocolate 617.1
   corpus
      albicans 620.2
      luteum 620.1
   dermoid (M9084/0) 220
   developmental 752.0
   due to failure of involution NEC 620.2
   endometrial 617.1
   follicular (atretic) (graafian) (hemorrhagic) 620.0
   hemorrhagic 620.2
   in pregnancy or childbirth 654.4 ☑
      affecting fetus or newborn 763.89
      causing obstructed labor 660.2 ☑
         affecting fetus or newborn 763.1
   multilocular (M8000/1) 239.5
   pseudomucinous (M8470/0) 220
   retention 620.2
   serous 620.2
   theca lutein 620.2
   tuberculous (*see also* Tuberculosis) 016.6 ☑
   unspecified 620.2
oviduct 620.8
palatal papilla (jaw) 526.1
palate 526.1
   fissural 526.1
   median (fissural) 526.1
palatine, of papilla 526.1
pancreas, pancreatic 577.2
   congenital 751.7
   false 577.2
   hemorrhagic 577.2
   true 577.2
paralabral
   hip 718.85
   shoulder 840.7
paramesonephric duct — *see* Cyst, Müllerian duct
paranephric 593.2
para ovarian 752.11
paraphysis, cerebri 742.4
parasitic NEC 136.9
parathyroid (gland) 252.8
paratubal (fallopian) 620.8
paraurethral duct 599.89
paroophoron 752.11
parotid gland 527.6
   mucous extravasation or retention 527.6
parovarian 752.11
pars planus 364.60
   exudative 364.64
   primary 364.63
pelvis, female
   in pregnancy or childbirth 654.4 ☑
      affecting fetus or newborn 763.89
      causing obstructed labor 660.2 ☑
         affecting fetus or newborn 763.1

☑ **Additional Digit Required** — Refer to the Tabular List for Digit Selection   ▽ **Subterms under main terms may continue to next column or page**

60 — Volume 2   ▶◀ **Revised Text**   ● **New Line**   ▲ **Revised Code**   **2015 ICD-9-CM**

Cyst — continued
  penis (sebaceous) 607.89
  periapical 522.8
  pericardial (congenital) 746.89
    acquired (secondary) 423.8
  pericoronal 526.0
  perineural (Tarlov's) 355.9
  periodontal 522.8
    lateral 526.0
  peripancreatic 577.2
  peripelvic (lymphatic) 593.2
  peritoneum 568.89
    chylous 457.8
  pharynx (wall) 478.26
  pilar 704.41
  pilonidal (infected) (rectum) 685.1
    with abscess 685.0
    malignant (M9084/3) 173.59
  pituitary (duct) (gland) 253.8
  placenta (amniotic) — see Placenta, abnormal
  pleura 519.8
  popliteal 727.51
  porencephalic 742.4
    acquired 348.0
  postanal (infected) 685.1
    with abscess 685.0
  posterior segment of eye, congenital 743.54
  postmastoidectomy cavity 383.31
  preauricular 744.47
  prepuce 607.89
    congenital 752.69
  primordial (jaw) 526.0
  prostate 600.3
  pseudomucinous (ovary) (M8470/0) 220
  pudenda (sweat glands) 624.8
  pupillary, miotic 364.55
    sebaceous 624.8
  radicular (residual) 522.8
  radiculodental 522.8
  ranular 527.6
  Rathke's pouch 253.8
  rectum (epithelium) (mucous) 569.49
  renal — see Cyst, kidney
  residual (radicular) 522.8
  retention (ovary) 620.2
  retina 361.19
    macular 362.54
    parasitic 360.13
    primary 361.13
    secondary 361.14
  retroperitoneal 568.89
  sacrococcygeal (dermoid) 685.1
    with abscess 685.0
  salivary gland or duct 527.6
    mucous extravasation or retention 527.6
  Sampson's 617.1
  sclera 379.19
  scrotum (sebaceous) 706.2
    sweat glands 706.2
  sebaceous (duct) (gland) 706.2
    breast 610.8
    eyelid 374.84
    genital organ NEC
      female 629.89
      male 608.89
    scrotum 706.2
  semilunar cartilage (knee) (multiple) 717.5
  seminal vesicle 608.89
  serous (ovary) 620.2
  sinus (antral) (ethmoidal) (frontal) (maxillary) (nasal) (sphenoidal) 478.19
  Skene's gland 599.89
  skin (epidermal) (epidermoid, inclusion) (epithelial) (inclusion) (retention) (sebaceous) 706.2
    breast 610.8
    eyelid 374.84
    genital organ NEC
      female 629.89
      male 608.89
    neoplastic 216.3
    scrotum 706.2
    sweat gland or duct 705.89
  solitary
    bone 733.21

Cyst — continued
  solitary — continued
    kidney 593.2
  spermatic cord 608.89
  sphenoid sinus 478.19
  spinal meninges 349.2
  spine (see also Cyst, bone) 733.20
  spleen NEC 289.59
    congenital 759.0
    hydatid (see also Echinococcus) 122.9
  spring water (pericardium) 746.89
  subarachnoid 348.0
    intrasellar 793.0
  subdural (cerebral) 348.0
    spinal cord 349.2
  sublingual gland 527.6
    mucous extravasation or retention 527.6
  submaxillary gland 527.6
    mucous extravasation or retention 527.6
  suburethral 599.89
  suprarenal gland 255.8
  suprasellar — see Cyst, brain
  sweat gland or duct 705.89
  sympathetic nervous system 337.9
  synovial 727.40
    popliteal space 727.51
  Tarlov's 355.9
  tarsal 373.2
  tendon (sheath) 727.42
  testis 608.89
  theca-lutein (ovary) 620.2
  Thornwaldt's, Tornwaldt's 478.26
  thymus (gland) 254.8
  thyroglossal (duct) (infected) (persistent) 759.2
  thyroid (gland) 246.2
    adenomatous — see Goiter, nodular
    colloid (see also Goiter) 240.9
  thyrolingual duct (infected) (persistent) 759.2
  tongue (mucous) 529.8
  tonsil 474.8
  tooth (dental root) 522.8
  trichilemmal (proliferating) 704.42
  tubo-ovarian 620.8
    inflammatory 614.1
  tunica vaginalis 608.89
  turbinate (nose) (see also Cyst, bone) 733.20
  Tyson's gland (benign) (infected) 607.89
  umbilicus 759.89
  urachus 753.7
  ureter 593.89
  ureterovesical orifice 593.89
    congenital 753.4
  urethra 599.84
  urethral gland (Cowper's) 599.89
  uterine
    ligament 620.8
      embryonic 752.11
    tube 620.8
  uterus (body) (corpus) (recurrent) 621.8
    embryonal 752.39
  utricle (ear) 386.8
    prostatic 599.89
  utriculus masculinus 599.89
  vagina, vaginal (squamous cell) (wall) 623.8
    embryonal 752.41
    implantation 623.8
    inclusion 623.8
  vallecula, vallecular 478.79
  ventricle, neuroepithelial 348.0
  verumontanum 599.89
  vesical (orifice) 596.89
  vitreous humor 379.29
  vulva (sweat glands) 624.8
    congenital 752.41
    implantation 624.8
    inclusion 624.8
    sebaceous gland 624.8
  vulvovaginal gland 624.8
  wolffian 752.89
Cystadenocarcinoma (M8440/3) — see also Neoplasm, by site, malignant
  bile duct type (M8161/3) 155.1
  endometrioid (M8380/3) — see Neoplasm, by site, malignant

Cystadenocarcinoma — see also Neoplasm, by site, malignant — continued
  mucinous (M8470/3)
    papillary (M8471/3)
      specified site — see Neoplasm, by site, malignant
      unspecified site 183.0
    specified site — see Neoplasm, by site, malignant
    unspecified site 183.0
  papillary (M8450/3)
    mucinous (M8471/3)
      specified site — see Neoplasm, by site, malignant
      unspecified site 183.0
    pseudomucinous (M8471/3)
      specified site — see Neoplasm, by site, malignant
      unspecified site 183.0
    serous (M8460/3)
      specified site — see Neoplasm, by site, malignant
      unspecified site 183.0
    specified site — see Neoplasm, by site, malignant
    unspecified 183.0
  pseudomucinous (M8470/3)
    papillary (M8471/3)
      specified site — see Neoplasm, by site, malignant
      unspecified site 183.0
    specified site — see Neoplasm, by site, malignant
    unspecified site 183.0
  serous (M8441/3)
    papillary (M8460/3)
      specified site — see Neoplasm, by site, malignant
      unspecified site 183.0
    specified site — see Neoplasm, by site, malignant
    unspecified site 183.0
Cystadenofibroma (M9013/0)
  clear cell (M8313/0) — see Neoplasm, by site, benign
  endometrioid (M8381/0) 220
    borderline malignancy (M8381/1) 236.2
    malignant (M8381/3) 183.0
  mucinous (M9015/0)
    specified site — see Neoplasm, by site, benign
    unspecified site 220
  serous (M9014/0)
    specified site — see Neoplasm, by site, benign
    unspecified site 220
  specified site — see Neoplasm, by site, benign
  unspecified site 220
Cystadenoma (M8440/0) — see also Neoplasm, by site, benign
  bile duct (M8161/0) 211.5
  endometrioid (M8380/0) (see also Neoplasm, by site, benign)
    borderline malignancy (M8380/1) — see Neoplasm, by site, uncertain behavior
  malignant (M8440/3) — see Neoplasm, by site, malignant
  mucinous (M8470/0)
    borderline malignancy (M8470/1)
      specified site — see Neoplasm, uncertain behavior
      unspecified site 236.2
    papillary (M8471/0)
      borderline malignancy (M8471/1)
        specified site — see Neoplasm, by site, uncertain behavior
        unspecified site 236.2
      specified site — see Neoplasm, by site, benign
      unspecified site 220
    specified site — see Neoplasm, by site, benign
    unspecified site 220

Cystadenoma — see also Neoplasm, by site, benign — continued
  papillary (M8450/0)
    borderline malignancy (M8450/1)
      specified site — see Neoplasm, by site, uncertain behavior
      unspecified site 236.2
    lymphomatosum (M8561/0) 210.2
    mucinous (M8471/0)
      borderline malignancy (M8471/1)
        specified site — see Neoplasm, by site, uncertain behavior
        unspecified site 236.2
      specified site — see Neoplasm, by site, benign
      unspecified site 220
    pseudomucinous (M8471/0)
      borderline malignancy (M8471/1)
        specified site — see Neoplasm, by site, uncertain behavior
        unspecified site 236.2
      specified site — see Neoplasm, by site, benign
      unspecified site 220
    serous (M8460/0)
      borderline malignancy (M8460/1)
        specified site — see Neoplasm, by site, uncertain behavior
        unspecified site 236.2
      specified site — see Neoplasm, by site, benign
      unspecified site 220
    specified site — see Neoplasm, by site, benign
    unspecified site 220
  pseudomucinous (M8470/0)
    borderline malignancy (M8470/1)
      specified site — see Neoplasm, by site, uncertain behavior
      unspecified site 236.2
    papillary (M8471/0)
      borderline malignancy (M8471/1)
        specified site — see Neoplasm, by site, uncertain behavior
        unspecified site 236.2
      specified site — see Neoplasm, by site, benign
      unspecified site 220
    specified site — see Neoplasm, by site, benign
    unspecified site 220
  serous (M8441/0)
    borderline malignancy (M8441/1)
      specified site — see Neoplasm, by site, uncertain behavior
      unspecified site 236.2
    papillary (M8460/0)
      borderline malignancy (M8460/1)
        specified site — see Neoplasm, by site, uncertain behavior
        unspecified site 236.2
      specified site — see Neoplasm, by site, benign
      unspecified site 220
    specified site — see Neoplasm, by site, benign
    unspecified site 220
  thyroid 226
Cystathioninemia 270.4
Cystathioninuria 270.4
Cystic — see also condition
  breast, chronic 610.1
  corpora lutea 620.1
  degeneration, congenital
    brain 742.4
    kidney (see also Cystic, disease, kidney) 753.10
  disease
    breast, chronic 610.1
    kidney, congenital 753.10
      medullary 753.16
      multiple 753.19
      polycystic — see Polycystic, kidney
      single 753.11
      specified NEC 753.19
    liver, congenital 751.62

☑ **Additional Digit Required** — Refer to the Tabular List for Digit Selection   ▽ **Subterms under main terms may continue to next column or page**

2015 ICD-9-CM   ▶◀ **Revised Text**   ● **New Line**   ▲ **Revised Code**   **Volume 2 — 61**

Cystic — see also condition — continued
  disease — continued
    lung 518.89
      congenital 748.4
    pancreas, congenital 751.7
    semilunar cartilage 717.5
  duct — see condition
  eyeball, congenital 743.03
  fibrosis (pancreas) 277.00
    with
      manifestations
        gastrointestinal 277.03
        pulmonary 277.02
        specified NEC 277.09
      meconium ileus 277.01
      pulmonary exacerbation 277.02
  hygroma (M9173/0) 228.1
  kidney, congenital 753.10
    medullary 753.16
    multiple 753.19
    polycystic — see Polycystic, kidney
    single 753.11
    specified NEC 753.19
  liver, congenital 751.62
  lung 518.89
    congenital 748.4
  mass — see Cyst
  mastitis, chronic 610.1
  ovary 620.2
  pancreas, congenital 751.7

Cysticerciasis 123.1
Cysticercosis (mammary) (subretinal) 123.1
Cysticercus 123.1
  cellulosae infestation 123.1
Cystinosis (malignant) 270.0
Cystinuria 270.0
Cystitis (bacillary) (colli) (diffuse) (exudative)
  (hemorrhagic) (purulent) (recurrent)
  (septic) (suppurative) (ulcerative) 595.9
  with
    abortion — see Abortion, by type, with
      urinary tract infection
    ectopic pregnancy (see also categories
      633.0–633.9) 639.8

Cystitis — continued
  with — continued
    fibrosis 595.1
    leukoplakia 595.1
    malakoplakia 595.1
    metaplasia 595.1
    molar pregnancy (see also categories
      630–632) 639.8
  actinomycotic 039.8 [595.4]
  acute 595.0
    of trigone 595.3
  allergic 595.89
  amebic 006.8 [595.4]
  bilharzial 120.9 [595.4]
  blennorrhagic (acute) 098.11
    chronic or duration of 2 months or more
      098.31
  bullous 595.89
  calculous 594.1
  chlamydial 099.53
  chronic 595.2
    interstitial 595.1
    of trigone 595.3
  complicating pregnancy, childbirth, or
    puerperium 646.6 ☑
    affecting fetus or newborn 760.1
  cystic(a) 595.81
  diphtheritic 032.84
  echinococcal
    granulosus 122.3 [595.4]
    multilocularis 122.6 [595.4]
  emphysematous 595.89
  encysted 595.81
  follicular 595.3
  following
    abortion 639.8
    ectopic or molar pregnancy 639.8
  gangrenous 595.89
  glandularis 595.89
  gonococcal (acute) 098.11
    chronic or duration of 2 months or more
      098.31
  incrusted 595.89
  interstitial 595.1

Cystitis — continued
  irradiation 595.82
  irritation 595.89
  malignant 595.89
  monilial 112.2
  of trigone 595.3
  panmural 595.1
  polyposa 595.89
  prostatic 601.3
  radiation 595.82
  Reiter's (abacterial) 099.3
  specified NEC 595.89
  subacute 595.2
  submucous 595.1
  syphilitic 095.8
  trichomoniasis 131.09
  tuberculous (see also Tuberculosis) 016.1 ☑
  ulcerative 595.1
Cystocele
  female (without uterine prolapse) 618.01
    with uterine prolapse 618.4
      complete 618.3
      incomplete 618.2
    lateral 618.02
    midline 618.01
    paravaginal 618.02
  in pregnancy or childbirth 654.4 ☑
    affecting fetus or newborn 763.89
    causing obstructed labor 660.2 ☑
      affecting fetus or newborn 763.1
  male 596.89
Cystoid
  cicatrix limbus 372.64
  degeneration macula 362.53
Cystolithiasis 594.1
Cystoma (M8440/0) — see also Neoplasm, by
  site, benign
  endometrial, ovary 617.1
  mucinous (M8470/0)
    specified site — see Neoplasm, by site,
      benign
    unspecified site 220

Cystoma — see also Neoplasm, by site, benign
  — continued
  serous (M8441/0)
    specified site — see Neoplasm, by site,
      benign
    unspecified site 220
  simple (ovary) 620.2
Cystoplegia 596.53
Cystoptosis 596.89
Cystopyelitis — see also Pyelitis 590.80
Cystorrhagia 596.89
Cystosarcoma phyllodes (M9020/1) 238.3
  benign (M9020/0) 217
  malignant (M9020/3) — see Neoplasm,
    breast, malignant
Cystostomy status V44.50
  with complication 596.83
    infection 596.81
    mechanical 596.82
    specified complication NEC 596.83
  appendico-vesicostomy V44.52
  cutaneous-vesicostomy V44.51
  specified type NEC V44.59
Cystourethritis — see also Urethritis 597.89
Cystourethrocele — see also Cystocele
  female (without uterine prolapse) 618.09
    with uterine prolapse 618.4
      complete 618.3
      incomplete 618.2
  male 596.89
Cytomegalic inclusion disease 078.5
  congenital 771.1
Cytomycosis, reticuloendothelial — see also
  Histoplasmosis, American 115.00
Cytopenia 289.9
  refractory
    with
      multilineage dysplasia (RCMD)
        238.72
      and ringed sideroblasts (RCMD-
        RS) 238.72

D

Daae (-Finsen) disease (epidemic pleurodynia) 074.1
Dabney's grip 074.1
Da Costa's syndrome (neurocirculatory asthenia) 306.2
Dacryoadenitis, dacryadenitis 375.00
  acute 375.01
  chronic 375.02
Dacryocystitis 375.30
  acute 375.32
  chronic 375.42
  neonatal 771.6
  phlegmonous 375.33
  syphilitic 095.8
    congenital 090.0
  trachomatous, active 076.1
    late effect 139.1
  tuberculous (see also Tuberculosis) 017.3 ☑
Dacryocystoblenorrhea 375.42
Dacryocystocele 375.43
Dacryolith, dacryolithiasis 375.57
Dacryoma 375.43
Dacryopericystitis (acute) (subacute) 375.32
  chronic 375.42
Dacryops 375.11
Dacryosialadenopathy, atrophic 710.2
Dacryostenosis 375.56
  congenital 743.65
Dactylitis
  bone (see also Osteomyelitis) 730.2 ☑
  sickle-cell 282.62
    Hb-C 282.64
    Hb-SS 282.62
    specified NEC 282.69
  syphilitic 095.5
  tuberculous (see also Tuberculosis) 015.5 ☑
Dactylolysis spontanea 136.0
Dactylosymphysis — see also Syndactylism 755.10
Damage
  arteriosclerotic — see Arteriosclerosis
  brain 348.9
    anoxic, hypoxic 348.1
      during or resulting from a procedure 997.01
      ischemic, in newborn 768.70
        mild 768.71
        moderate 768.72
        severe 768.73
    child NEC 343.9
    due to birth injury 767.0
    minimal (child) (see also Hyperkinesia) 314.9
    newborn 767.0
  cardiac (see also Disease, heart)
  cardiorenal (vascular) (see also Hypertension, cardiorenal) 404.90
  central nervous system — see Damage, brain
  cerebral NEC — see Damage, brain
  coccyx, complicating delivery 665.6 ☑
  coronary (see also Ischemia, heart) 414.9
  eye, birth injury 767.8
  heart (see also Disease, heart)
    valve — see Endocarditis
  hypothalamus NEC 348.9
  liver 571.9
    alcoholic 571.3
  medication 995.20
  myocardium (see also Degeneration, myocardial) 429.1
  pelvic
    joint or ligament, during delivery 665.6 ☑
    organ NEC
      with
        abortion — see Abortion, by type, with damage to pelvic organs
        ectopic pregnancy (see also categories 633.0–633.9) 639.2
        molar pregnancy (see also categories 630–632) 639.2
      during delivery 665.5 ☑

Damage — continued
  pelvic — continued
    organ — continued
      following
        abortion 639.2
        ectopic or molar pregnancy 639.2
  renal (see also Disease, renal) 593.9
  skin, solar 692.79
    acute 692.72
    chronic 692.74
  subendocardium, subendocardial (see also Degeneration, myocardial) 429.1
  vascular 459.9
Dameshek's syndrome (erythroblastic anemia) 282.49
Dana-Putnam syndrome (subacute combined sclerosis with pernicious anemia) 281.0 [336.2]
Danbolt (-Closs) syndrome (acrodermatitis enteropathica) 686.8
Dandruff 690.18
Dandy fever 061
Dandy-Walker deformity or syndrome (atresia, foramen of Magendie) 742.3
  with spina bifida (see also Spina bifida) 741.0 ☑
Dangle foot 736.79
Danielssen's disease (anesthetic leprosy) 030.1
Danlos' syndrome 756.83
Darier's disease (congenital) (keratosis follicularis) 757.39
  due to vitamin A deficiency 264.8
  meaning erythema annulare centrifugum 695.0
Darier-Roussy sarcoid 135
Dark area on retina 239.81
Darling's
  disease (see also Histoplasmosis, American) 115.00
  histoplasmosis (see also Histoplasmosis, American) 115.00
Dartre 054.9
Darwin's tubercle 744.29
Davidson's anemia (refractory) 284.9
Davies-Colley syndrome (slipping rib) 733.99
Davies' disease 425.0
Dawson's encephalitis 046.2
Day blindness — see also Blindness, day 368.60
Dead
  fetus
    retained (in utero) 656.4 ☑
      early pregnancy (death before 22 completed weeks gestation) 632
      late (death after 22 completed weeks gestation) 656.4 ☑
    syndrome 641.3 ☑
  labyrinth 386.50
  ovum, retained 631.8
Deaf and dumb NEC 389.7
Deaf mutism (acquired) (congenital) NEC 389.7
  endemic 243
  hysterical 300.11
  syphilitic, congenital 090.0
Deafness (acquired) (complete) (congenital) (hereditary) (middle ear) (partial) 389.9
  with
    blindness V49.85
    blue sclera and fragility of bone 756.51
  auditory fatigue 389.9
  aviation 993.0
    nerve injury 951.5
  boilermakers' 951.5
  central 389.14
    with conductive hearing loss 389.20
      bilateral 389.22
      unilateral 389.21
  conductive (air) 389.00
    with sensorineural hearing loss 389.20
      bilateral 389.22
      unilateral 389.21
    bilateral 389.06
    combined types 389.08
    external ear 389.01

Deafness — continued
  conductive — continued
    inner ear 389.04
    middle ear 389.03
    multiple types 389.08
    tympanic membrane 389.02
    unilateral 389.05
  emotional (complete) 300.11
  functional (complete) 300.11
  high frequency 389.8
  hysterical (complete) 300.11
  injury 951.5
  low frequency 389.8
  mental 784.69
  mixed conductive and sensorineural 389.20
    bilateral 389.22
    unilateral 389.21
  nerve
    with conductive hearing loss 389.20
      bilateral 389.22
      unilateral 389.21
    bilateral 389.12
    unilateral 389.13
  neural
    with conductive hearing loss 389.20
      bilateral 389.22
      unilateral 389.21
    bilateral 389.12
    unilateral 389.13
  noise-induced 388.12
    nerve injury 951.5
  nonspeaking 389.7
  perceptive 389.10
    with conductive hearing loss 389.20
      bilateral 389.22
      unilateral 389.21
    central 389.14
    neural
      bilateral 389.12
      unilateral 389.13
    sensorineural 389.10
      asymmetrical 389.16
      bilateral 389.18
      unilateral 389.15
    sensory
      bilateral 389.11
      unilateral 389.17
  psychogenic (complete) 306.7
  sensorineural (see also Deafness, perceptive) 389.10
    asymmetrical 389.16
    bilateral 389.18
    unilateral 389.15
  sensory
    with conductive hearing loss 389.20
      bilateral 389.22
      unilateral 389.21
    bilateral 389.11
    unilateral 389.17
  specified type NEC 389.8
  sudden NEC 388.2
  syphilitic 094.89
  transient ischemic 388.02
  transmission — see Deafness, conductive
  traumatic 951.5
  word (secondary to organic lesion) 784.69
    developmental 315.31
Death
  after delivery (cause not stated) (sudden) 674.9 ☑
  anesthetic
    due to
      correct substance properly administered 995.4
      overdose or wrong substance given 968.4
      specified anesthetic — see Table of Drugs and Chemicals
    during delivery 668.9 ☑
  brain 348.82
  cardiac (sudden) (SCD) — code to underlying condition
    family history of V17.41
    personal history of, successfully resuscitated V12.53
  cause unknown 798.2

Death — continued
  cot (infant) 798.0
  crib (infant) 798.0
  fetus, fetal (cause not stated) (intrauterine) 779.9
    early, with retention (before 22 completed weeks gestation) 632
    from asphyxia or anoxia (before labor) 768.0
      during labor 768.1
    late, affecting management of pregnancy (after 22 completed weeks gestation) 656.4 ☑
  from pregnancy NEC 646.9 ☑
  instantaneous 798.1
  intrauterine (see also Death, fetus) 779.9
    complicating pregnancy 656.4 ☑
  maternal, affecting fetus or newborn 761.6
  neonatal NEC 779.9
  sudden (cause unknown) 798.1
    cardiac (SCD)
      family history of V17.41
      personal history of, successfully resuscitated V12.53
    during delivery 669.9 ☑
      under anesthesia NEC 668.9 ☑
    infant, syndrome (SIDS) 798.0
    puerperal, during puerperium 674.9 ☑
  unattended (cause unknown) 798.9
  under anesthesia NEC
    due to
      correct substance properly administered 995.4
      overdose or wrong substance given 968.4
      specified anesthetic — see Table of Drugs and Chemicals
    during delivery 668.9 ☑
  violent 798.1
de Beurmann-Gougerot disease (sporotrichosis) 117.1
Debility (general) (infantile) (postinfectional) 799.3
  with nutritional difficulty 269.9
  congenital or neonatal NEC 779.9
  nervous 300.5
  old age 797
  senile 797
Débove's disease (splenomegaly) 789.2
Decalcification
  bone (see also Osteoporosis) 733.00
  teeth 521.89
Decapitation 874.9
  fetal (to facilitate delivery) 763.89
Decapsulation, kidney 593.89
Decay
  dental 521.00
  senile 797
  tooth, teeth 521.00
Decensus, uterus — see Prolapse, uterus
Deciduitis (acute)
  with
    abortion — see Abortion, by type, with sepsis
    ectopic pregnancy (see also categories 633.0–633.9) 639.0
    molar pregnancy (see also categories 630–632) 639.0
  affecting fetus or newborn 760.8
  following
    abortion 639.0
    ectopic or molar pregnancy 639.0
  in pregnancy 646.6 ☑
  puerperal, postpartum 670.1 ☑
Deciduoma malignum (M9100/3) 181
Deciduous tooth (retained) 520.6
Decline (general) — see also Debility 799.3
Decompensation
  cardiac (acute) (chronic) (see also Disease, heart) 429.9
    failure — see Failure, heart
  cardiorenal (see also Hypertension, cardiorenal) 404.90
  cardiovascular (see also Disease, cardiovascular) 429.2
  heart (see also Disease, heart) 429.9

☑ Additional Digit Required — Refer to the Tabular List for Digit Selection   ▽ Subterms under main terms may continue to next column or page

2015 ICD-9-CM   ►◄ Revised Text   ● New Line   ▲ Revised Code   Volume 2 — 63

Decompensation — *continued*
heart (*see also* Disease, heart) — *continued*
  failure — *see* Failure, heart
  hepatic 572.2
  myocardial (acute) (chronic) (*see also* Disease, heart) 429.9
    failure — *see* Failure, heart
  respiratory 519.9
Decompression sickness 993.3
Decrease, decreased
  blood
    platelets (*see also* Thrombocytopenia) 287.5
    pressure 796.3
      due to shock following
        injury 958.4
        operation 998.00
    white cell count 288.50
      specified NEC 288.59
  cardiac reserve — *see* Disease, heart
  estrogen 256.39
    postablative 256.2
  fetal movements 655.7 ☑
  fragility of erythrocytes 289.89
  function
    adrenal (cortex) 255.41
      medulla 255.5
    ovary in hypopituitarism 253.4
    parenchyma of pancreas 577.8
    pituitary (gland) (lobe) (anterior) 253.2
      posterior (lobe) 253.8
  functional activity 780.99
  glucose 790.29
  haptoglobin (serum) NEC 273.8
  leukocytes 288.50
  libido 799.81
  lymphocytes 288.51
  platelets (*see also* Thrombocytopenia) 287.5
  pulse pressure 785.9
  respiration due to shock following injury 958.4
  sexual desire 799.81
  tear secretion NEC 375.15
  tolerance
    fat 579.8
    salt and water 276.9
  vision NEC 369.9
  white blood cell count 288.50
Decubital gangrene — *see also* Ulcer, pressure 707.00 [785.4]
Decubiti — *see also* Ulcer, pressure 707.00
Decubitus (ulcer) — *see also* Ulcer, pressure 707.00
  with gangrene 707.00 [785.4]
  ankle 707.06
  back
    lower 707.03
    upper 707.02
  buttock 707.05
  coccyx 707.03
  elbow 707.01
  head 707.09
  heel 707.07
  hip 707.04
  other site 707.09
  sacrum 707.03
  shoulder blades 707.02
Deepening acetabulum 718.85
Defect, defective 759.9
  3-beta-hydroxysteroid dehydrogenase 255.2
  11-hydroxylase 255.2
  21-hydroxylase 255.2
  abdominal wall, congenital 756.70
  aorticopulmonary septum 745.0
  aortic septal 745.0
  atrial septal (ostium secundum type) 745.5
    acquired 429.71
    ostium primum type 745.61
    sinus venosus 745.8
  atrioventricular
    canal 745.69
    septum 745.4
      acquired 429.71
  atrium secundum 745.5
    acquired 429.71

Defect, defective — *continued*
  auricular septal 745.5
    acquired 429.71
  bilirubin excretion 277.4
  biosynthesis, testicular androgen 257.2
  bridge 525.60
  bulbar septum 745.0
  butanol-insoluble iodide 246.1
  chromosome — *see* Anomaly, chromosome
  circulation (acquired) 459.9
    congenital 747.9
    newborn 747.9
  clotting NEC (*see also* Defect, coagulation) 286.9
  coagulation (factor) (*see also* Deficiency, coagulation factor) 286.9
    with
      abortion — *see* Abortion, by type, with hemorrhage
      ectopic pregnancy (*see also* categories 634–638) 639.1
      molar pregnancy (*see also* categories 630–632) 639.1
    acquired (any) 286.7
    antepartum or intrapartum 641.3 ☑
      affecting fetus or newborn 762.1
    causing hemorrhage of pregnancy or delivery 641.3 ☑
    complicating pregnancy, childbirth, or puerperium 649.3 ☑
    due to
      liver disease 286.7
      vitamin K deficiency 286.7
    newborn, transient 776.3
    postpartum 666.3 ☑
    specified type NEC 286.9
  conduction (heart) 426.9
    bone (*see also* Deafness, conductive) 389.00
  congenital, organ or site NEC (*see also* Anomaly)
    circulation 747.9
    Descemet's membrane 743.9
      specified type NEC 743.49
    diaphragm 756.6
    ectodermal 757.9
    esophagus 750.9
    pulmonic cusps — *see* Anomaly, heart valve
    respiratory system 748.9
      specified type NEC 748.8
  crown 525.60
  cushion endocardial 745.60
  dental restoration 525.60
  dentin (hereditary) 520.5
  Descemet's membrane (congenital) 743.9
    acquired 371.30
    specific type NEC 743.49
  deutan 368.52
  developmental (*see also* Anomaly, by site)
    cauda equina 742.59
    left ventricle 746.9
      with atresia or hypoplasia of aortic orifice or valve, with hypoplasia of ascending aorta 746.7
      in hypoplastic left heart syndrome 746.7
    testis 752.9
    vessel 747.9
  diaphragm
    with elevation, eventration, or hernia — *see* Hernia, diaphragm
    congenital 756.6
      with elevation, eventration, or hernia 756.6
      gross (with elevation, eventration, or hernia) 756.6
  ectodermal, congenital 757.9
  Eisenmenger's (ventricular septal defect) 745.4
  endocardial cushion 745.60
    specified type NEC 745.69
  esophagus, congenital 750.9
  extensor retinaculum 728.9
  fibrin polymerization (*see also* Defect, coagulation) 286.3

Defect, defective — *continued*
  filling
    biliary tract 793.3
    bladder 793.5
    dental 525.60
    gallbladder 793.3
    kidney 793.5
    stomach 793.4
    ureter 793.5
  fossa ovalis 745.5
  gene, carrier (suspected) of V83.89
  Gerbode 745.4
  glaucomatous, without elevated tension 365.89
  Hageman (factor) (*see also* Defect, coagulation) 286.3
  hearing (*see also* Deafness) 389.9
  high grade 317
  homogentisic acid 270.2
  interatrial septal 745.5
    acquired 429.71
  interauricular septal 745.5
    acquired 429.71
  interventricular septal 745.4
    with pulmonary stenosis or atresia, dextraposition of aorta, and hypertrophy of right ventricle 745.2
    acquired 429.71
    in tetralogy of Fallot 745.2
  iodide trapping 246.1
  iodotyrosine dehalogenase 246.1
  kynureninase 270.2
  learning, specific 315.2
  major osseous 731.3
  mental (*see also* Disability, intellectual) 319
  osseous, major 731.3
  osteochondral NEC 738.8
  ostium
    primum 745.61
    secundum 745.5
  pericardium 746.89
  peroxidase-binding 246.1
  placental blood supply — *see* Placenta, insufficiency
  platelet (qualitative) 287.1
    constitutional 286.4
  postural, spine 737.9
  protan 368.51
  pulmonic cusps, congenital 746.00
  renal pelvis 753.9
    obstructive 753.29
    specified type NEC 753.3
  respiratory system, congenital 748.9
    specified type NEC 748.8
  retina, retinal 361.30
    with detachment (*see also* Detachment, retina, with retinal defect) 361.00
    multiple 361.33
      with detachment 361.02
    nerve fiber bundle 362.85
    single 361.30
      with detachment 361.01
  septal (closure) (heart) NEC 745.9
    acquired 429.71
    atrial 745.5
    specified type NEC 745.8
  speech NEC 784.59
    developmental 315.39
    late effect of cerebrovascular disease — *see* Late effect(s) (of) cerebrovascular disease, speech and language deficit
    secondary to organic lesion 784.59
  Taussig-Bing (transposition, aorta and overriding pulmonary artery) 745.11
  teeth, wedge 521.20
  thyroid hormone synthesis 246.1
  tritan 368.53
  ureter 753.9
    obstructive 753.29
  vascular (acquired) (local) 459.9
    congenital (peripheral) NEC 747.60
      gastrointestinal 747.61
      lower limb 747.64
      renal 747.62
      specified NEC 747.69

Defect, defective — *continued*
  vascular — *continued*
    congenital — *continued*
      spinal 747.82
      upper limb 747.63
  ventricular septal 745.4
    with pulmonary stenosis or atresia, dextraposition of aorta, and hypertrophy of right ventricle 745.2
    acquired 429.71
    atrioventricular canal type 745.69
    between infundibulum and anterior portion 745.4
    in tetralogy of Fallot 745.2
    isolated anterior 745.4
  vision NEC 369.9
  visual field 368.40
    arcuate 368.43
    heteronymous, bilateral 368.47
    homonymous, bilateral 368.46
    localized NEC 368.44
    nasal step 368.44
    peripheral 368.44
    sector 368.43
  voice and resonance 784.40
  wedge, teeth (abrasion) 521.20
Defeminization syndrome 255.2
Deferentitis 608.4
  gonorrheal (acute) 098.14
    chronic or duration of 2 months or over 098.34
Defibrination syndrome — *see also* Fibrinolysis 286.6
Deficiency, deficient
  3-beta-hydroxysteroid dehydrogenase 255.2
  6-phosphogluconic dehydrogenase (anemia) 282.2
  11-beta-hydroxylase 255.2
  17-alpha-hydroxylase 255.2
  18-hydroxysteroid dehydrogenase 255.2
  20-alpha-hydroxylase 255.2
  21-hydroxylase 255.2
  AAT (alpha-1 antitrypsin) 273.4
  abdominal muscle syndrome 756.79
  accelerator globulin (Ac G) (blood) (*see also* Defect, coagulation) 286.3
  AC globulin (congenital) (*see also* Defect, coagulation) 286.3
    acquired 286.7
  activating factor (blood) (*see also* Defect, coagulation) 286.3
  adenohypophyseal 253.2
  adenosine deaminase 277.2
  aldolase (hereditary) 271.2
  alpha-1-antitrypsin 273.4
  alpha-1-trypsin inhibitor 273.4
  alpha-fucosidase 271.8
  alpha-lipoprotein 272.5
  alpha-mannosidase 271.8
  amino acid 270.9
  anemia — *see* Anemia, deficiency
  aneurin 265.1
    with beriberi 265.0
  antibody NEC 279.00
  antidiuretic hormone 253.5
  antihemophilic
    factor (A) 286.0
      B 286.1
      C 286.2
    globulin (AHG) NEC 286.0
  antithrombin III 289.81
  antitrypsin 273.4
  argininosuccinate synthetase or lyase 270.6
  ascorbic acid (with scurvy) 267
  autoprothrombin
    I (*see also* Defect, coagulation) 286.3
    II 286.1
    C (*see also* Defect, coagulation) 286.3
  bile salt 579.8
  biotin 266.2
  biotinidase 277.6
  bradykinase-1 277.6
  brancher enzyme (amylopectinosis) 271.0
  calciferol 268.9
    with
      osteomalacia 268.2

☑ **Additional Digit Required** — Refer to the Tabular List for Digit Selection   ▽ Subterms under main terms may continue to next column or page

64 — Volume 2   ▶◀ Revised Text   ● New Line   ▲ Revised Code   **2015 ICD-9-CM**

Deficiency, deficient — continued
  calciferol — continued
    with — continued
      rickets (see also Rickets) 268.0
  calcium 275.40
    dietary 269.3
  calorie, severe 261
  carbamyl phosphate synthetase 270.6
  cardiac (see also Insufficiency, myocardial) 428.0
  carnitine 277.81
    due to
      hemodialysis 277.83
      inborn errors of metabolism 277.82
      valproic acid therapy 277.83
    iatrogenic 277.83
    palmitoyltransferase (CPT1, CPT2) 277.85
    palmityl transferase (CPT1, CPT2) 277.85
    primary 277.81
    secondary 277.84
  carotene 264.9
  Carr factor (see also Defect, coagulation) 286.9
  central nervous system 349.9
  ceruloplasmin 275.1
  cevitamic acid (with scurvy) 267
  choline 266.2
  Christmas factor 286.1
  chromium 269.3
  citrin 269.1
  clotting (blood) (see also Defect, coagulation) 286.9
  coagulation factor NEC 286.9
    with
      abortion — see Abortion, by type, with hemorrhage
      ectopic pregnancy (see also categories 634–638) 639.1
      molar pregnancy (see also categories 630–632) 639.1
    acquired (any) 286.7
    antepartum or intrapartum 641.3 ☑
      affecting fetus or newborn 762.1
    complicating pregnancy, childbirth, or puerperium 649.3 ☑
    due to
      liver disease 286.7
      vitamin K deficiency 286.7
    newborn, transient 776.3
    postpartum 666.3 ☑
    specified type NEC 286.3
  color vision (congenital) 368.59
    acquired 368.55
  combined glucocorticoid and mineralocorticoid 255.41
  combined, two or more coagulation factors (see also Defect, coagulation) 286.9
  complement factor NEC 279.8
  contact factor (see also Defect, coagulation) 286.3
  copper NEC 275.1
  corticoadrenal 255.41
  craniofacial axis 756.0
  cyanocobalamin (vitamin B₁₂) 266.2
  debrancher enzyme (limit dextrinosis) 271.0
  desmolase 255.2
  diet 269.9
  dihydrofolate reductase 281.2
  dihydropteridine reductase 270.1
  dihydropyrimidine dehydrogenase (DPD) 277.6
  disaccharidase (intestinal) 271.3
  disease NEC 269.9
  ear(s) V48.8
  edema 262
  endocrine 259.9
  enzymes, circulating NEC (see also Deficiency, by specific enzyme) 277.6
  ergosterol 268.9
    with
      osteomalacia 268.2
      rickets (see also Rickets) 268.0
  erythrocytic glutathione (anemia) 282.2
  eyelid(s) V48.8
  factor (see also Defect, coagulation) 286.9
    I (congenital) (fibrinogen) 286.3

Deficiency, deficient — continued
  factor (see also Defect, coagulation) — continued
    I — continued
      antepartum or intrapartum 641.3 ☑
        affecting fetus or newborn 762.1
      newborn, transient 776.3
      postpartum 666.3 ☑
    II (congenital) (prothrombin) 286.3
    V (congenital) (labile) 286.3
    VII (congenital) (stable) 286.3
    VIII (congenital) (functional) 286.0
      with
        functional defect 286.0
        vascular defect 286.4
    IX (Christmas) (congenital) (functional) 286.1
    X (congenital) (Stuart-Prower) 286.3
    XI (congenital) (plasma thromboplastin antecedent) 286.2
    XII (congenital) (Hageman) 286.3
    XIII (congenital) (fibrin stabilizing) 286.3
    Hageman 286.3
    multiple (congenital) 286.9
      acquired 286.7
  fibrinase (see also Defect, coagulation) 286.3
  fibrinogen (congenital) (see also Defect, coagulation) 286.3
    acquired 286.6
  fibrin-stabilizing factor (congenital) (see also Defect, coagulation) 286.3
  finger — see Absence, finger
  fletcher factor (see also Defect, coagulation) 286.9
  fluorine 269.3
  folate, anemia 281.2
  folic acid (vitamin B₆) 266.2
    anemia 281.2
  follicle-stimulating hormone (FSH) 253.4
  fructokinase 271.2
  fructose-1, 6-diphosphate 271.2
  fructose-1-phosphate aldolase 271.2
  FSH (follicle-stimulating hormone) 253.4
  fucosidase 271.8
  galactokinase 271.1
  galactose-1-phosphate uridyl transferase 271.1
  gamma globulin in blood 279.00
  glass factor (see also Defect, coagulation) 286.3
  glucocorticoid 255.41
  glucose-6-phosphatase 271.0
  glucose-6-phosphate dehydrogenase anemia 282.2
  glucuronyl transferase 277.4
  glutathione-reductase (anemia) 282.2
  glycogen synthetase 271.0
  growth hormone 253.3
  Hageman factor (congenital) (see also Defect, coagulation) 286.3
  head V48.0
  hemoglobin (see also Anemia) 285.9
  hepatophosphorylase 271.0
  hexose monophosphate (HMP) shunt 282.2
  HGH (human growth hormone) 253.3
  HG-PRT 277.2
  homogentisic acid oxidase 270.2
  hormone (see also Deficiency, by specific hormone)
    anterior pituitary (isolated) (partial) NEC 253.4
      growth (human) 253.3
      follicle-stimulating 253.4
      growth (human) (isolated) 253.3
      human growth 253.3
      interstitial cell-stimulating 253.4
      luteinizing 253.4
      melanocyte-stimulating 253.4
      testicular 257.2
  human growth hormone 253.3
  humoral 279.00
    with
      hyper-IgM 279.05
        autosomal recessive 279.05
        X-linked 279.05
      increased IgM 279.05

Deficiency, deficient — continued
  humoral — continued
    congenital hypogammaglobulinemia 279.04
    non-sex-linked 279.06
    selective immunoglobulin NEC 279.03
      IgA 279.01
      IgG 279.03
      IgM 279.02
        increased 279.05
    specified NEC 279.09
  hydroxylase 255.2
  hypoxanthine-guanine phosphoribosyltransferase (HG-PRT) 277.2
  ICSH (interstitial cell-stimulating hormone) 253.4
  immunity NEC 279.3
    cell-mediated 279.10
      with
        hyperimmunoglobulinemia 279.2
        thrombocytopenia and eczema 279.12
      specified NEC 279.19
    combined (severe) 279.2
      syndrome 279.2
    common variable 279.06
    humoral NEC 279.00
    IgA (secretory) 279.01
    IgG 279.03
    IgM 279.02
  immunoglobulin, selective NEC 279.03
    IgA 279.01
    IgG 279.03
    IgM 279.02
  inositol (B complex) 266.2
  interferon 279.49
  internal organ V47.0
  interstitial cell-stimulating hormone (ICSH) 253.4
  intrinsic factor (Castle's) (congenital) 281.0
  intrinsic (urethral) sphincter (ISD) 599.82
  invertase 271.3
  iodine 269.3
  iron, anemia 280.9
  labile factor (congenital) (see also Defect, coagulation) 286.3
    acquired 286.7
  lacrimal fluid (acquired) 375.15
    congenital 743.64
  lactase 271.3
  Laki-Lorand factor (see also Defect, coagulation) 286.3
  lecithin-cholesterol acyltranferase 272.5
  LH (luteinizing hormone) 253.4
  limb V49.0
    lower V49.0
      congenital (see also Deficiency, lower limb, congenital) 755.30
    upper V49.0
      congenital (see also Deficiency, upper limb, congenital) 755.20
  lipocaic 577.8
  lipoid (high-density) 272.5
  lipoprotein (familial) (high density) 272.5
  liver phosphorylase 271.0
  long chain 3-hydroxyacyl CoA dehydrogenase (LCHAD) 277.85
  long chain/very long chain acyl CoA dehydrogenase (LCAD, VLCAD) 277.85
  lower limb V49.0
    congenital 755.30
      with complete absence of distal elements 755.31
      longitudinal (complete) (partial) (with distal deficiencies, incomplete) 755.32
        with complete absence of distal elements 755.31
        combined femoral, tibial, fibular (incomplete) 755.33
        femoral 755.34
        fibular 755.37
        metatarsal(s) 755.38
        phalange(s) 755.39
          meaning all digits 755.31
        tarsal(s) 755.38

Deficiency, deficient — continued
  lower limb — continued
    congenital — continued
      longitudinal — continued
        tibia 755.36
        tibiofibular 755.35
        transverse 755.31
  luteinizing hormone (LH) 253.4
  lysosomal alpha-1, 4 glucosidase 271.0
  magnesium 275.2
  mannosidase 271.8
  medium chain acyl CoA dehydrogenase (MCAD) 277.85
  melanocyte-stimulating hormone (MSH) 253.4
  menadione (vitamin K) 269.0
    newborn 776.0
  mental (familial) (hereditary) (see also Disability, intellectual) 319
  methylenetetrahydrofolate reductase (MTHFR) 270.4
  mineralocorticoid 255.42
  mineral NEC 269.3
  molybdenum 269.3
  moral 301.7
  multiple, syndrome 260
  myocardial (see also Insufficiency, myocardial) 428.0
  myophosphorylase 271.0
  NADH-diaphorase or reductase (congenital) 289.7
  NADH (DPNH)-methemoglobin-reductase (congenital) 289.7
  neck V48.1
  niacin (amide) (-tryptophan) 265.2
  nicotinamide 265.2
  nicotinic acid (amide) 265.2
  nose V48.8
  number of teeth (see also Anodontia) 520.0
  nutrition, nutritional 269.9
    specified NEC 269.8
  ornithine transcarbamylase 270.6
  ovarian 256.39
  oxygen (see also Anoxia) 799.02
  pantothenic acid 266.2
  parathyroid (gland) 252.1
  phenylalanine hydroxylase 270.1
  phosphoenolpyruvate carboxykinase 271.8
  phosphofructokinase 271.2
  phosphoglucomutase 271.0
  phosphohexosisomerase 271.0
  phosphomannomutase 271.8
  phosphomannose isomerase 271.8
  phosphomannosyl mutase 271.8
  phosphorylase kinase, liver 271.0
  pituitary (anterior) 253.2
    posterior 253.5
  placenta — see Placenta, insufficiency
  plasma
    cell 279.00
    protein (paraproteinemia) (pyroglobulinemia) 273.8
      gamma globulin 279.00
    thromboplastin
      antecedent (PTA) 286.2
      component (PTC) 286.1
  platelet NEC 287.1
    constitutional 286.4
  polyglandular 258.9
  potassium (K) 276.8
  proaccelerin (congenital) (see also Defect, congenital) 286.3
    acquired 286.7
  proconvertin factor (congenital) (see also Defect, coagulation) 286.3
    acquired 286.7
  prolactin 253.4
  protein 260
    anemia 281.4
    C 289.81
    plasma — see Deficiency, plasma, protein
    S 289.81
  prothrombin (congenital) (see also Defect, coagulation) 286.3
    acquired 286.7

☑ Additional Digit Required — Refer to the Tabular List for Digit Selection   ▽ Subterms under main terms may continue to next column or page

2015 ICD-9-CM   ▶◀ Revised Text   ● New Line   ▲ Revised Code   Volume 2 — 65

Deficiency, deficient — *continued*

Prower factor (*see also* Defect, coagulation) 286.3
PRT 277.2
pseudocholinesterase 289.89
psychobiological 301.6
PTA 286.2
PTC 286.1
purine nucleoside phosphorylase 277.2
pyracin (alpha) (beta) 266.1
pyridoxal 266.1
pyridoxamine 266.1
pyridoxine (derivatives) 266.1
pyruvate carboxylase 271.8
pyruvate dehydrogenase 271.8
pyruvate kinase (PK) 282.3
riboflavin (vitamin B_2) 266.0
saccadic eye movements 379.57
salivation 527.7
salt 276.1
secretion
  ovary 256.39
  salivary gland (any) 527.7
  urine 788.5
selenium 269.3
serum
  antitrypsin, familial 273.4
  protein (congenital) 273.8
short chain acyl CoA dehydrogenase (SCAD) 277.85
short stature homeobox gene (SHOX)
  with
    dyschondrosteosis 756.89
    short stature (idiopathic) 783.43
    Turner's syndrome 758.6
smooth pursuit movements (eye) 379.58
sodium (Na) 276.1
SPCA (*see also* Defect, coagulation) 286.3
specified NEC 269.8
stable factor (congenital) (*see also* Defect, coagulation) 286.3
  acquired 286.7
Stuart (-Prower) factor (*see also* Defect, co-agulation) 286.3
sucrase 271.3
sucrase-isomaltase 271.3
sulfite oxidase 270.0
syndrome, multiple 260
thiamine, thiaminic (chloride) 265.1
thrombokinase (*see also* Defect, coagulation) 286.3
  newborn 776.0
thrombopoieten 287.39
thymolymphatic 279.2
thyroid (gland) 244.9
tocopherol 269.1
toe — *see* Absence, toe
tooth bud (*see also* Anodontia) 520.0
trunk V48.1
UDPG-glycogen transferase 271.0
upper limb V49.0
  congenital 755.20
    with complete absence of distal elements 755.21
    longitudinal (complete) (partial) (with distal deficiencies, incomplete) 755.22
      carpal(s) 755.28
      combined humeral, radial, ulnar (incomplete) 755.23
      humeral 755.24
      metacarpal(s) 755.28
      phalange(s) 755.29
        meaning all digits 755.21
      radial 755.26
      radioulnar 755.25
      ulnar 755.27
    transverse (complete) (partial) 755.21
vascular 459.9
vasopressin 253.5
viosterol (*see also* Deficiency, calciferol) 268.9
vitamin (multiple) NEC 269.2
  A 264.9
    with
      Bitôt's spot 264.1

Deficiency, deficient — *continued*
vitamin — *continued*
  A — *continued*
    with — *continued*
      Bitôt's spot — *continued*
        corneal 264.2
          with corneal ulceration 264.3
      keratomalacia 264.4
      keratosis, follicular 264.8
      night blindness 264.5
      scar of cornea, xerophthalmic 264.6
      specified manifestation NEC 264.8
        ocular 264.7
      xeroderma 264.8
      xerophthalmia 264.7
      xerosis
        conjunctival 264.0
          with Bitôt's spot 264.1
        corneal 264.2
          with corneal ulceration 264.3
  B_1 NEC 265.1
    beriberi 265.0
  B_2 266.0
  B_6 266.1
  B_{12} 266.2
  B_c (folic acid) 266.2
  B (complex) NEC 266.9
    with
      beriberi 265.0
      pellagra 265.2
    specified type NEC 266.2
  C (ascorbic acid) (with scurvy) 267
  D (calciferol) (ergosterol) 268.9
    with
      osteomalacia 268.2
      rickets (*see also* Rickets) 268.0
  E 269.1
  folic acid 266.2
  G 266.0
  H 266.2
  K 269.0
    of newborn 776.0
  nicotinic acid 265.2
  P 269.1
  PP 265.2
  specified NEC 269.1
  zinc 269.3
Deficient — *see also* Deficiency
blink reflex 374.45
craniofacial axis 756.0
number of teeth (*see also* Anodontia) 520.0
secretion of urine 788.5
Deficit
attention 799.51
cognitive communication 799.52
concentration 799.51
executive function 799.55
frontal lobe 799.55
neurologic NEC 781.99
  due to
    cerebrovascular lesion (*see also* Disease, cerebrovascular, acute) 436
    late effect — *see* Late effect(s) (of) cerebrovascular disease
    transient ischemic attack 435.9
  ischemic
    reversible (RIND) 434.91
      history of (personal) V12.54
      prolonged (PRIND) 434.91
        history of (personal) V12.54
oxygen 799.02
psychomotor 799.54
visuospatial 799.53
Deflection
radius 736.09
septum (acquired) (nasal) (nose) 470
spine — *see* Curvature, spine
turbinate (nose) 470
Defluvium
capillorum (*see also* Alopecia) 704.00
cil|orum 374.55

Defluvium — *continued*
unguium 703.8
Deformity 738.9
abdomen, congenital 759.9
abdominal wall
  acquired 738.8
  congenital 756.70
  muscle deficiency syndrome 756.79
acquired (unspecified site) 738.9
  specified site NEC 738.8
adrenal gland (congenital) 759.1
alimentary tract, congenital 751.9
  lower 751.5
  specified type NEC 751.8
  upper (any part, except tongue) 750.9
    specified type NEC 750.8
    tongue 750.10
      specified type NEC 750.19
ankle (joint) (acquired) 736.70
  abduction 718.47
  congenital 755.69
  contraction 718.47
  specified NEC 736.79
anus (congenital) 751.5
  acquired 569.49
aorta (congenital) 747.20
  acquired 447.8
  arch 747.21
    acquired 447.8
  coarctation 747.10
aortic
  arch 747.21
    acquired 447.8
  cusp or valve (congenital) 746.9
    acquired (*see also* Endocarditis, aortic) 424.1
  ring 747.21
appendix 751.5
arm (acquired) 736.89
  congenital 755.50
arteriovenous (congenital) (peripheral) NEC 747.60
  gastrointestinal 747.61
  lower limb 747.64
  renal 747.62
  specified NEC 747.69
  spinal 747.82
  upper limb 747.63
artery (congenital) (peripheral) NEC (*see also* Deformity, vascular) 747.60
  acquired 447.8
  cerebral 747.81
  coronary (congenital) 746.85
    acquired (*see also* Ischemia, heart) 414.9
  retinal 743.9
  umbilical 747.5
atrial septal (congenital) (heart) 745.5
auditory canal (congenital) (external) (*see also* Deformity, ear) 744.3
  acquired 380.50
auricle
  ear (congenital) (*see also* Deformity, ear) 744.3
    acquired 380.32
  heart (congenital) 746.9
back (acquired) — *see* Deformity, spine
Bartholin's duct (congenital) 750.9
bile duct (congenital) 751.60
  acquired 576.8
    with calculus, choledocholithiasis, or stones — *see* Choledocholithiasis
biliary duct or passage (congenital) 751.60
  acquired 576.8
    with calculus, choledocholithiasis, or stones — *see* Choledocholithiasis
bladder (neck) (sphincter) (trigone) (acquired) 596.89
  congenital 753.9
bone (acquired) NEC 738.9
  congenital 756.9
  turbinate 738.0
boutonniere (finger) 736.21
brain (congenital) 742.9

Deformity — *continued*
brain — *continued*
  acquired 348.89
  multiple 742.4
  reduction 742.2
  vessel (congenital) 747.81
breast (acquired) 611.89
  congenital 757.6
  reconstructed 612.0
bronchus (congenital) 748.3
  acquired 519.19
bursa, congenital 756.9
canal of Nuck 752.9
canthus (congenital) 743.9
  acquired 374.89
capillary (acquired) 448.9
  congenital NEC (*see also* Deformity, vascular) 747.60
cardiac — *see* Deformity, heart
cardiovascular system (congenital) 746.9
caruncle, lacrimal (congenital) 743.9
  acquired 375.69
cascade, stomach 537.6
cecum (congenital) 751.5
  acquired 569.89
cerebral (congenital) 742.9
  acquired 348.89
cervix (acquired) (uterus) 622.8
  congenital 752.40
cheek (acquired) 738.19
  congenital 744.9
chest (wall) (acquired) 738.3
  congenital 754.89
  late effect of rickets 268.1
chin (acquired) 738.19
  congenital 744.9
choroid (congenital) 743.9
  acquired 363.8
  plexus (congenital) 742.9
    acquired 349.2
cicatricial — *see* Cicatrix
cilia (congenital) 743.9
  acquired 374.89
circulatory system (congenital) 747.9
clavicle (acquired) 738.8
  congenital 755.51
clitoris (congenital) 752.40
  acquired 624.8
clubfoot — *see* Clubfoot
coccyx (acquired) 738.6
  congenital 756.10
colon (congenital) 751.5
  acquired 569.89
concha (ear) (congenital) (*see also* Deformity, ear) 744.3
  acquired 380.32
congenital, organ or site not listed (*see also* Anomaly) 759.9
cornea (congenital) 743.9
  acquired 371.70
coronary artery (congenital) 746.85
  acquired (*see also* Ischemia, heart) 414.9
cranium (acquired) 738.19
  congenital (*see also* Deformity, skull, congenital) 756.0
cricoid cartilage (congenital) 748.3
  acquired 478.79
cystic duct (congenital) 751.60
  acquired 575.8
Dandy-Walker 742.3
  with spina bifida (*see also* Spina bifida) 741.0 ☑
diaphragm (congenital) 756.6
  acquired 738.8
digestive organ(s) or system (congenital) NEC 751.9
  specified type NEC 751.8
ductus arteriosus 747.0
duodenal bulb 537.89
duodenum (congenital) 751.5
  acquired 537.89
dura (congenital) 742.9
  brain 742.4
    acquired 349.2
  spinal 742.59
    acquired 349.2

Deformity — *continued*
  ear (congenital) 744.3
    acquired 380.32
    auricle 744.3
      causing impairment of hearing
        744.02
      causing impairment of hearing 744.00
    external 744.3
      causing impairment of hearing
        744.02
    internal 744.05
    lobule 744.3
    middle 744.03
      ossicles 744.04
    ossicles 744.04
  ectodermal (congenital) NEC 757.9
    specified type NEC 757.8
  ejaculatory duct (congenital) 752.9
    acquired 608.89
  elbow (joint) (acquired) 736.00
    congenital 755.50
    contraction 718.42
  endocrine gland NEC 759.2
  epididymis (congenital) 752.9
    acquired 608.89
    torsion 608.24
  epiglottis (congenital) 748.3
    acquired 478.79
  esophagus (congenital) 750.9
    acquired 530.89
  Eustachian tube (congenital) NEC 744.3
    specified type NEC 744.24
  extremity (acquired) 736.9
    congenital, except reduction deformity
      755.9
      lower 755.60
      upper 755.50
    reduction — *see* Deformity, reduction
  eye (congenital) 743.9
    acquired 379.8
    muscle 743.9
  eyebrow (congenital) 744.89
  eyelid (congenital) 743.9
    acquired 374.89
    specified type NEC 743.62
  face (acquired) 738.19
    congenital (any part) 744.9
      due to intrauterine malposition and
        pressure 754.0
  fallopian tube (congenital) 752.10
    acquired 620.8
  femur (acquired) 736.89
    congenital 755.60
  fetal
    with fetopelvic disproportion 653.7 ☑
      affecting fetus or newborn 763.1
    causing obstructed labor 660.1 ☑
      affecting fetus or newborn 763.1
    known or suspected, affecting manage-
      ment of pregnancy 655.9 ☑
  finger (acquired) 736.20
    boutonniere type 736.21
    congenital 755.50
    flexion contracture 718.44
    swan neck 736.22
  flexion (joint) (acquired) 736.9
    congenital NEC 755.9
    hip or thigh (acquired) 736.39
      congenital (*see also* Subluxation,
        congenital, hip) 754.32
  foot (acquired) 736.70
    cavovarus 736.75
      congenital 754.59
    congenital NEC 754.70
      specified type NEC 754.79
    valgus (acquired) 736.79
      congenital 754.60
        specified type NEC 754.69
    varus (acquired) 736.79
      congenital 754.50
        specified type NEC 754.59
  forearm (acquired) 736.00
    congenital 755.50
  forehead (acquired) 738.19
    congenital (*see also* Deformity, skull,
      congenital) 756.0

Deformity — *continued*
  frontal bone (acquired) 738.19
    congenital (*see also* Deformity, skull,
      congenital) 756.0
  gallbladder (congenital) 751.60
    acquired 575.8
  gastrointestinal tract (congenital) NEC 751.9
    acquired 569.89
    specified type NEC 751.8
  genitalia, genital organ(s) or system NEC
    congenital 752.9
    female (congenital) 752.9
      acquired 629.89
      external 752.40
      internal 752.9
    male (congenital) 752.9
      acquired 608.89
  globe (eye) (congenital) 743.9
    acquired 360.89
  gum (congenital) 750.9
    acquired 523.9
  gunstock 736.02
  hand (acquired) 736.00
    claw 736.06
    congenital 755.50
    minus (and plus) (intrinsic) 736.09
    pill roller (intrinsic) 736.09
    plus (and minus) (intrinsic) 736.09
    swan neck (intrinsic) 736.09
  head (acquired) 738.10
    congenital (*see also* Deformity, skull
      congenital) 756.0
    specified NEC 738.19
  heart (congenital) 746.9
    auricle (congenital) 746.9
    septum 745.9
      auricular 745.5
      specified type NEC 745.8
      ventricular 745.4
    valve (congenital) NEC 746.9
      acquired — *see* Endocarditis
      pulmonary (congenital) 746.00
      specified type NEC 746.89
    ventricle (congenital) 746.9
  heel (acquired) 736.76
    congenital 755.67
  hepatic duct (congenital) 751.60
    acquired 576.8
      with calculus, choledocholithiasis, or
        stones — *see* Choledocholithi-
        asis
  hip (joint) (acquired) 736.30
    congenital NEC 755.63
    flexion 718.45
      congenital (*see also* Subluxation,
        congenital, hip) 754.32
  hourglass — *see* Contraction, hourglass
  humerus (acquired) 736.89
    congenital 755.50
  hymen (congenital) 752.40
  hypophyseal (congenital) 759.2
  ileocecal (coil) (valve) (congenital) 751.5
    acquired 569.89
  ileum (intestine) (congenital) 751.5
    acquired 569.89
  ilium (acquired) 738.6
    congenital 755.60
  integument (congenital) 757.9
  intervertebral cartilage or disc (acquired)
    (*see also* Displacement, intervertebral
    disc)
    congenital 756.10
  intestine (large) (small) (congenital) 751.5
    acquired 569.89
  iris (acquired) 364.75
    congenital 743.9
    prolapse 364.89
  ischium (acquired) 738.6
    congenital 755.60
  jaw (acquired) (congenital) NEC 524.9
    due to intrauterine malposition and
      pressure 754.0
  joint (acquired) NEC 738.8
    congenital 755.9

Deformity — *continued*
  joint — *continued*
    contraction (abduction) (adduction)
      (extension) (flexion) — *see* Con-
      traction, joint
  kidney(s) (calyx) (pelvis) (congenital) 753.9
    acquired 593.89
    vessel 747.62
      acquired 459.9
  Klippel-Feil (brevicollis) 756.16
  knee (acquired) NEC 736.6
    congenital 755.64
  labium (majus) (minus) (congenital) 752.40
    acquired 624.8
  lacrimal apparatus or duct (congenital)
    743.9
    acquired 375.69
  larynx (muscle) (congenital) 748.3
    acquired 478.79
    web (glottic) (subglottic) 748.2
  leg (lower) (upper) (acquired) NEC 736.89
    congenital 755.60
      reduction — *see* Deformity, reduc-
        tion, lower limb
  lens (congenital) 743.9
    acquired 379.39
  lid (fold) (congenital) 743.9
    acquired 374.89
  ligament (acquired) 728.9
    congenital 756.9
  limb (acquired) 736.9
    congenital, except reduction deformity
      755.9
      lower 755.60
        reduction (*see also* Deformity,
          reduction, lower limb)
          755.30
      upper 755.50
        reduction (*see also* Deformity, re-
          duction, upper limb)
          755.20
    specified NEC 736.89
  lip (congenital) NEC 750.9
    acquired 528.5
    specified type NEC 750.26
  liver (congenital) 751.60
    acquired 573.8
    duct (congenital) 751.60
      acquired 576.8
        with calculus, choledocholithiasis,
          or stones — *see* Choledo-
          cholithi-asis
  lower extremity — *see* Deformity, leg
  lumbosacral (joint) (region) (congenital)
    756.10
    acquired 738.5
  lung (congenital) 748.60
    acquired 518.89
    specified type NEC 748.69
  lymphatic system, congenital 759.9
  Madelung's (radius) 755.54
  maxilla (acquired) (congenital) 524.9
  meninges or membrane (congenital) 742.9
    brain 742.4
      acquired 349.2
    spinal (cord) 742.59
      acquired 349.2
  mesentery (congenital) 751.9
    acquired 568.89
  metacarpus (acquired) 736.00
    congenital 755.50
  metatarsus (acquired) 736.70
    congenital 754.70
  middle ear, except ossicles (congenital)
    744.03
    ossicles 744.04
  mitral (leaflets) (valve) (congenital) 746.9
    acquired — *see* Endocarditis, mitral
    Ebstein's 746.89
    parachute 746.5
    specified type NEC 746.89
    stenosis, congenital 746.5
  mouth (acquired) 528.9
    congenital NEC 750.9
      specified type NEC 750.26
  multiple, congenital NEC 759.7

Deformity — *continued*
  multiple, congenital — *continued*
    specified type NEC 759.89
  muscle (acquired) 728.9
    congenital 756.9
      specified type NEC 756.89
      sternocleidomastoid (due to intrauter-
        ine malposition and pressure)
        754.1
  musculoskeletal system, congenital NEC
    756.9
    specified type NEC 756.9
  nail (acquired) 703.9
    congenital 757.9
  nasal — *see* Deformity, nose
  neck (acquired) NEC 738.2
    congenital (any part) 744.9
      sternocleidomastoid 754.1
  nervous system (congenital) 742.9
  nipple (congenital) 757.6
    acquired 611.89
  nose, nasal (cartilage) (acquired) 738.0
    bone (turbinate) 738.0
    congenital 748.1
      bent 754.0
      squashed 754.0
    saddle 738.0
      syphilitic 090.5
    septum 470
      congenital 748.1
    sinus (wall) (congenital) 748.1
      acquired 738.0
    syphilitic (congenital) 090.5
      late 095.8
  ocular muscle (congenital) 743.9
    acquired 378.60
  opticociliary vessels (congenital) 743.9
  orbit (congenital) (eye) 743.9
    acquired NEC 376.40
      associated with craniofacial deformi-
        ties 376.44
      due to
        bone disease 376.43
        surgery 376.47
        trauma 376.47
  organ of Corti (congenital) 744.05
  ovary (congenital) 752.0
    acquired 620.8
  oviduct (congenital) 752.10
    acquired 620.8
  palate (congenital) 750.9
    acquired 526.89
    cleft (congenital) (*see also* Cleft, palate)
      749.00
    hard, acquired 526.89
    soft, acquired 528.9
  pancreas (congenital) 751.7
    acquired 577.8
  parachute, mitral valve 746.5
  parathyroid (gland) 759.2
  parotid (gland) (congenital) 750.9
    acquired 527.8
  patella (acquired) 736.6
    congenital 755.64
  pelvis, pelvic (acquired) (bony) 738.6
    with disproportion (fetopelvic) 653.0 ☑
      affecting fetus or newborn 763.1
      causing obstructed labor 660.1 ☑
        affecting fetus or newborn 763.1
    congenital 755.60
    rachitic (late effect) 268.1
  penis (glans) (congenital) 752.9
    acquired 607.89
  pericardium (congenital) 746.9
    acquired — *see* Pericarditis
  pharynx (congenital) 750.9
    acquired 478.29
  Pierre Robin (congenital) 756.0
  pinna (acquired) 380.32
    congenital 744.3
  pituitary (congenital) 759.2
  pleural folds (congenital) 748.8
  portal vein (congenital) 747.40
  posture — *see* Curvature, spine
  prepuce (congenital) 752.9
    acquired 607.89

☑ Additional Digit Required — Refer to the Tabular List for Digit Selection
▽ Subterms under main terms may continue to next column or page

2015 ICD-9-CM   ▶◀ Revised Text   ● New Line   ▲ Revised Code   Volume 2 — 67

Deformity — Deformity

Deformity — *continued*
  prostate (congenital) 752.9
    acquired 602.8
  pulmonary valve — *see* Endocarditis, pulmonary
  pupil (congenital) 743.9
    acquired 364.75
  pylorus (congenital) 750.9
    acquired 537.89
  rachitic (acquired), healed or old 268.1
  radius (acquired) 736.00
    congenital 755.50
      reduction — *see* Deformity, reduction, upper limb
  rectovaginal septum (congenital) 752.40
    acquired 623.8
  rectum 751.5
    acquired 569.49
  reduction (extremity) (limb) 755.4
    brain 742.2
    lower limb 755.30
      with complete absence of distal elements 755.31
      longitudinal (complete) (partial) (with distal deficiencies, incomplete) 755.32
        with complete absence of distal elements 755.31
        combined femoral, tibial, fibular (incomplete) 755.33
        femoral 755.34
        fibular 755.37
        metatarsal(s) 755.38
        phalange(s) 755.39
          meaning all digits 755.31
        tarsal(s) 755.38
        tibia 755.36
        tibiofibular 755.35
      transverse 755.31
    upper limb 755.20
      with complete absence of distal elements 755.21
      longitudinal (complete) (partial) (with distal deficiencies, incomplete) 755.22
        with complete absence of distal elements 755.21
        carpal(s) 755.28
        combined humeral, radial, ulnar (incomplete) 755.23
        humeral 755.24
        metacarpal(s) 755.28
        phalange(s) 755.29
          meaning all digits 755.21
        radial 755.26
        radioulnar 755.25
        ulnar 755.27
      transverse (complete) (partial) 755.21
  renal — *see* Deformity, kidney
  respiratory system (congenital) 748.9
    specified type NEC 748.8
  rib (acquired) 738.3
    congenital 756.3
      cervical 756.2
  rotation (joint) (acquired) 736.9
    congenital 755.9
    hip or thigh 736.39
      congenital (*see also* Subluxation, congenital, hip) 754.32
  sacroiliac joint (congenital) 755.69
    acquired 738.5
  sacrum (acquired) 738.5
    congenital 756.10
  saddle
    back 737.8
    nose 738.0
      syphilitic 090.5
  salivary gland or duct (congenital) 750.9
    acquired 527.8
  scapula (acquired) 736.89
    congenital 755.50
  scrotum (congenital) 752.9
    acquired 608.89
  sebaceous gland, acquired 706.8
  seminal tract or duct (congenital) 752.9
    acquired 608.89

Deformity — *continued*
  septum (nasal) (acquired) 470
    congenital 748.1
  shoulder (joint) (acquired) 736.89
    congenital 755.50
      specified type NEC 755.59
    contraction 718.41
  sigmoid (flexure) (congenital) 751.5
    acquired 569.89
  sinus of Valsalva 747.29
  skin (congenital) 757.9
    acquired NEC 709.8
  skull (acquired) 738.19
    congenital 756.0
      with
        anencephalus 740.0
        encephalocele 742.0
        hydrocephalus 742.3
          with spina bifida (*see also* Spina bifida) 741.0 ☑
        microcephalus 742.1
      due to intrauterine malposition and pressure 754.0
  soft parts, organs or tissues (of pelvis)
    in pregnancy or childbirth NEC 654.9 ☑
      affecting fetus or newborn 763.89
      causing obstructed labor 660.2 ☑
        affecting fetus or newborn 763.1
  spermatic cord (congenital) 752.9
    acquired 608.89
      torsion 608.22
        extravaginal 608.21
        intravaginal 608.22
  spinal
    column — *see* Deformity, spine
    cord (congenital) 742.9
      acquired 336.8
      vessel (congenital) 747.82
    nerve root (congenital) 742.9
      acquired 724.9
  spine (acquired) NEC 738.5
    congenital 756.10
      due to intrauterine malposition and pressure 754.2
    kyphoscoliotic (*see also* Kyphoscoliosis) 737.30
    kyphotic (*see also* Kyphosis) 737.10
    lordotic (*see also* Lordosis) 737.20
    rachitic 268.1
    scoliotic (*see also* Scoliosis) 737.30
  spleen
    acquired 289.59
    congenital 759.0
  Sprengel's (congenital) 755.52
  sternum (acquired) 738.3
    congenital 756.3
  stomach (congenital) 750.9
    acquired 537.89
  submaxillary gland (congenital) 750.9
    acquired 527.8
  swan neck (acquired)
    finger 736.22
    hand 736.09
  talipes — *see* Talipes
  teeth, tooth NEC 520.9
  testis (congenital) 752.9
    acquired 608.89
      torsion 608.20
  thigh (acquired) 736.89
    congenital 755.60
  thorax (acquired) (wall) 738.3
    congenital 754.89
    late effect of rickets 268.1
  thumb (acquired) 736.20
    congenital 755.50
  thymus (tissue) (congenital) 759.2
  thyroid (gland) (congenital) 759.2
    cartilage 748.3
      acquired 478.79
  tibia (acquired) 736.89
    congenital 755.60
    saber 090.5
  toe (acquired) 735.9
    congenital 755.66
    specified NEC 735.8
  tongue (congenital) 750.10

Deformity — *continued*
  tongue — *continued*
    acquired 529.8
  tooth, teeth NEC 520.9
  trachea (rings) (congenital) 748.3
    acquired 519.19
  transverse aortic arch (congenital) 747.21
  tricuspid (leaflets) (valve) (congenital) 746.9
    acquired — *see* Endocarditis, tricuspid
    atresia or stenosis 746.1
    specified type NEC 746.89
  trunk (acquired) 738.3
    congenital 759.9
  ulna (acquired) 736.00
    congenital 755.50
  upper extremity — *see* Deformity, arm
  urachus (congenital) 753.7
  ureter (opening) (congenital) 753.9
    acquired 593.89
  urethra (valve) (congenital) 753.9
    acquired 599.84
  urinary tract or system (congenital) 753.9
    urachus 753.7
  uterus (congenital) 752.39
    acquired 621.8
  uvula (congenital) 750.9
    acquired 528.9
  vagina (congenital) 752.40
    acquired 623.8
  valve, valvular (heart) (congenital) 746.9
    acquired — *see* Endocarditis
    pulmonary 746.00
    specified type NEC 746.89
  vascular (congenital) (peripheral) NEC 747.60
    acquired 459.9
    gastrointestinal 747.61
    lower limb 747.64
    renal 747.62
    specified site NEC 747.69
    spinal 747.82
    upper limb 747.63
  vas deferens (congenital) 752.9
    acquired 608.89
  vein (congenital) NEC (*see also* Deformity, vascular) 747.60
    brain 747.81
    coronary 746.9
    great 747.40
  vena cava (inferior) (superior) (congenital) 747.40
  vertebra — *see* Deformity, spine
  vesicourethral orifice (acquired) 596.89
    congenital NEC 753.9
      specified type NEC 753.8
  vessels of optic papilla (congenital) 743.9
  visual field (contraction) 368.45
  vitreous humor (congenital) 743.9
    acquired 379.29
  vulva (congenital) 752.40
    acquired 624.8
  wrist (joint) (acquired) 736.00
    congenital 755.50
    contraction 718.43
    valgus 736.03
      congenital 755.59
    varus 736.04
      congenital 755.59

Degeneration, degenerative
  adrenal (capsule) (gland) 255.8
    with hypofunction 255.41
    fatty 255.8
    hyaline 255.8
    infectional 255.8
    lardaceous 277.39
  amyloid (any site) (general) 277.39
  anterior cornua, spinal cord 336.8
  anterior labral 840.8
  aorta, aortic 440.0
    fatty 447.8
    valve (heart) (*see also* Endocarditis, aortic) 424.1
  arteriovascular — *see* Arteriosclerosis
  artery, arterial (atheromatous) (calcareous) (*see also* Arteriosclerosis)
    amyloid 277.39

Degeneration, degenerative — *continued*
  artery, arterial (*see also* Arteriosclerosis) — *continued*
    lardaceous 277.39
    medial NEC (*see also* Arteriosclerosis, extremities) 440.20
  articular cartilage NEC (*see also* Disorder, cartilage, articular) 718.0 ☑
    elbow 718.02
    knee 717.5
    patella 717.7
    shoulder 718.01
    spine (*see also* Spondylosis) 721.90
  atheromatous — *see* Arteriosclerosis
  bacony (any site) 277.39
  basal nuclei or ganglia NEC 333.0
  bone 733.90
  brachial plexus 353.0
  brain (cortical) (progressive) 331.9
    arteriosclerotic 437.0
    childhood 330.9
      specified type NEC 330.8
    congenital 742.4
    cystic 348.0
      congenital 742.4
    familial NEC 331.89
    grey matter 330.8
    heredofamilial NEC 331.89
    in
      alcoholism 303.9 ☑ *[331.7]*
      beriberi 265.0 *[331.7]*
      cerebrovascular disease 437.9 *[331.7]*
      congenital hydrocephalus 742.3 *[331.7]*
        with spina bifida (*see also* Spina bifida) 741.0 ☑ *[331.7]*
      Fabry's disease 272.7 *[330.2]*
      Gaucher's disease 272.7 *[330.2]*
      Hunter's disease or syndrome 277.5 *[330.3]*
      lipidosis
        cerebral 330.1
        generalized 272.7 *[330.2]*
      mucopolysaccharidosis 277.5 *[330.3]*
      myxedema (*see also* Myxedema) 244.9 *[331.7]*
      neoplastic disease NEC (M8000/1) 239.9 *[331.7]*
      Niemann-Pick disease 272.7 *[330.2]*
      sphingolipidosis 272.7 *[330.2]*
      vitamin B_{12} deficiency 266.2 *[331.7]*
    motor centers 331.89
    senile 331.2
    specified type NEC 331.89
  breast — *see* Disease, breast
  Bruch's membrane 363.40
  bundle of His 426.50
    left 426.3
    right 426.4
  calcareous NEC 275.49
  capillaries 448.9
    amyloid 277.39
    fatty 448.9
    lardaceous 277.39
  cardiac (brown) (calcareous) (fatty) (fibrous) (hyaline) (mural) (muscular) (pigmentary) (senile) (with arteriosclerosis) (*see also* Degeneration, myocardial) 429.1
    valve, valvular — *see* Endocarditis
  cardiorenal (*see also* Hypertension, cardiorenal) 404.90
  cardiovascular (*see also* Disease, cardiovascular) 429.2
    renal (*see also* Hypertension, cardiorenal) 404.90
  cartilage (joint) — *see* Derangement, joint
  cerebellar NEC 334.9
    primary (hereditary) (sporadic) 334.2
  cerebral — *see* Degeneration, brain
  cerebromacular 330.1
  cerebrovascular 437.1
    due to hypertension 437.2
    late effect — *see* Late effect(s) (of) cerebrovascular disease
  cervical plexus 353.2

☑ **Additional Digit Required** — Refer to the Tabular List for Digit Selection   ▽ **Subterms under main terms may continue to next column or page**

68 — Volume 2   ▶◀ Revised Text   ● New Line   ▲ Revised Code   2015 ICD-9-CM

Degeneration, degenerative — *continued*

cervix 622.8
  due to radiation (intended effect) 622.8
    adverse effect or misadventure 622.8
changes, spine or vertebra (*see also*
  Spondylosis) 721.90
chitinous 277.39
chorioretinal 363.40
  congenital 743.53
  hereditary 363.50
choroid (colloid) (drusen) 363.40
  hereditary 363.50
  senile 363.41
    diffuse secondary 363.42
cochlear 386.8
collateral ligament (knee) (medial) 717.82
  lateral 717.81
combined (spinal cord) (subacute)
  266.2 *[336.2]*
  with anemia (pernicious) 281.0 *[336.2]*
    due to dietary deficiency
      281.1 *[336.2]*
    due to vitamin B$_{12}$ deficiency anemia
      (dietary) 281.1 *[336.2]*
conjunctiva 372.50
  amyloid 277.39 *[372.50]*
cornea 371.40
  calcerous 371.44
  familial (hereditary) (*see also* Dystrophy,
    cornea) 371.50
    macular 371.55
    reticular 371.54
  hyaline (of old scars) 371.41
  marginal (Terrien's) 371.48
  mosaic (shagreen) 371.41
  nodular 371.46
  peripheral 371.48
  senile 371.41
cortical (cerebellar) (parenchymatous) 334.2
  alcoholic 303.9 ☑ *[334.4]*
  diffuse, due to arteriopathy 437.0
corticobasal 331.6
corticostriatal-spinal 334.8
cretinoid 243
cruciate ligament (knee) (posterior) 717.84
  anterior 717.83
cutis 709.3
  amyloid 277.39
dental pulp 522.2
disc disease — *see* Degeneration, intervertebral disc
dorsolateral (spinal cord) — *see* Degeneration, combined
endocardial 424.90
extrapyramidal NEC 333.90
eye NEC 360.40
  macular (*see also* Degeneration, macula)
    362.50
    congenital 362.75
    hereditary 362.76
fatty (diffuse) (general) 272.8
  liver 571.8
    alcoholic 571.0
  localized site — *see* Degeneration, by
    site, fatty
  placenta — *see* Placenta, abnormal
globe (eye) NEC 360.40
  macular — *see* Degeneration, macula
grey matter 330.8
heart (brown) (calcareous) (fatty) (fibrous)
  (hyaline) (mural) (muscular) (pigmentary) (senile) (with arteriosclerosis)
  (*see also* Degeneration, myocardial)
  429.1
  amyloid 277.39 *[425.7]*
  atheromatous — *see* Arteriosclerosis,
    coronary
  gouty 274.82
  hypertensive (*see also* Hypertension,
    heart) 402.90
  ischemic 414.9
  valve, valvular — *see* Endocarditis
hepatolenticular (Wilson's) 275.1
hepatorenal 572.4
heredofamilial
  brain NEC 331.89

Degeneration, degenerative — *continued*

heredofamilial — *continued*
  spinal cord NEC 336.8
hyaline (diffuse) (generalized) 728.9
  localized (*see also* Degeneration, by site)
    cornea 371.41
    keratitis 371.41
hypertensive vascular — *see* Hypertension
infrapatellar fat pad 729.31
internal semilunar cartilage 717.3
intervertebral disc 722.6
  with myelopathy 722.70
  cervical, cervicothoracic 722.4
    with myelopathy 722.71
  lumbar, lumbosacral 722.52
    with myelopathy 722.73
  thoracic, thoracolumbar 722.51
    with myelopathy 722.72
intestine 569.89
  amyloid 277.39
  lardaceous 277.39
iris (generalized) (*see also* Atrophy, iris)
  364.59
  pigmentary 364.53
  pupillary margin 364.54
ischemic — *see* Ischemia
joint disease (*see also* Osteoarthrosis)
  715.9 ☑
  multiple sites 715.09
  spine (*see also* Spondylosis) 721.90
kidney (*see also* Sclerosis, renal) 587
  amyloid 277.39 *[583.81]*
  cyst, cystic (multiple) (solitary) 593.2
    congenital (*see also* Cystic, disease,
      kidney) 753.10
  fatty 593.89
  fibrocystic (congenital) 753.19
  lardaceous 277.39 *[583.81]*
  polycystic (congenital) 753.12
    adult type (APKD) 753.13
    autosomal dominant 753.13
    autosomal recessive 753.14
    childhood type (CPKD) 753.14
    infantile type 753.14
  waxy 277.39 *[583.81]*
Kuhnt-Junius (retina) 362.52
labyrinth, osseous 386.8
lacrimal passages, cystic 375.12
lardaceous (any site) 277.39
lateral column (posterior), spinal cord (*see
  also* Degeneration, combined)
  266.2 *[336.2]*
lattice 362.63
lens 366.9
  infantile, juvenile, or presenile 366.00
  senile 366.10
lenticular (familial) (progressive) (Wilson's)
  (with cirrhosis of liver) 275.1
  striate artery 437.0
lethal ball, prosthetic heart valve 996.02
ligament
  collateral (knee) (medial) 717.82
    lateral 717.81
  cruciate (knee) (posterior) 717.84
    anterior 717.83
liver (diffuse) 572.8
  amyloid 277.39
  congenital (cystic) 751.62
  cystic 572.8
    congenital 751.62
  fatty 571.8
    alcoholic 571.0
  hypertrophic 572.8
  lardaceous 277.39
  parenchymatous, acute or subacute (*see
    also* Necrosis, liver) 570
  pigmentary 572.8
  toxic (acute) 573.8
  waxy 277.39
lung 518.89
lymph gland 289.3
  hyaline 289.3
  lardaceous 277.39
macula (acquired) (senile) 362.50
  atrophic 362.51
  Best's 362.76

Degeneration, degenerative — *continued*

macula — *continued*
  congenital 362.75
  cystic 362.54
  cystoid 362.53
  disciform 362.52
  dry 362.51
  exudative 362.52
  familial pseudoinflammatory 362.77
  hereditary 362.76
  hole 362.54
  juvenile (Stargardt's) 362.75
  nonexudative 362.51
  pseudohole 362.54
  wet 362.52
medullary — *see* Degeneration, brain
membranous labyrinth, congenital (causing
  impairment of hearing) 744.05
meniscus — *see* Derangement, joint
microcystoid 362.62
mitral — *see* Insufficiency, mitral
Mönckeberg's (*see also* Arteriosclerosis, extremities) 440.20
moral 301.7
motor centers, senile 331.2
mural (*see also* Degeneration, myocardial)
  429.1
  heart, cardiac (*see also* Degeneration,
    myocardial) 429.1
  myocardium, myocardial (*see also* Degen-
    eration, myocardial) 429.1
muscle 728.9
  fatty 728.9
  fibrous 728.9
  heart (*see also* Degeneration, myocar-
    dial) 429.1
  hyaline 728.9
muscular progressive 728.2
myelin, central nervous system NEC 341.9
myocardium, myocardial (brown) (calcareous) (fatty) (fibrous) (hyaline) (mural)
  (muscular) (pigmentary) (senile)
  (with arteriosclerosis) 429.1
  with rheumatic fever (conditions classifi-
    able to 390) 398.0
    active, acute, or subacute 391.2
      with chorea 392.0
    inactive or quiescent (with chorea)
      398.0
  amyloid 277.39 *[425.7]*
  congenital 746.89
  fetus or newborn 779.89
  gouty 274.82
  hypertensive (*see also* Hypertension,
    heart) 402.90
  ischemic 414.8
  rheumatic (*see also* Degeneration, my-
    ocardium, with rheumatic fever)
    398.0
  syphilitic 093.82
nasal sinus (mucosa) (*see also* Sinusitis)
  473.9
  frontal 473.1
  maxillary 473.0
nerve — *see* Disorder, nerve
nervous system 349.89
  amyloid 277.39 *[357.4]*
  autonomic (*see also* Neuropathy, periph-
    eral, autonomic) 337.9
  fatty 349.89
  peripheral autonomic NEC (*see also*
    Neuropathy, peripheral, autonom-
    ic) 337.9
nipple 611.9
nose 478.19
oculoacousticocerebral, congenital (progressive) 743.8
olivopontocerebellar (familial) (hereditary)
  333.0
osseous labyrinth 386.8
ovary 620.8
  cystic 620.2
  microcystic 620.2
pallidal, pigmentary (progressive) 333.0
pancreas 577.8

Degeneration, degenerative — *continued*

pancreas — *continued*
  tuberculous (*see also* Tuberculosis)
    017.9 ☑
papillary muscle 429.81
paving stone 362.61
penis 607.89
peritoneum 568.89
pigmentary (diffuse) (general)
  localized — *see* Degeneration, by site
  pallidal (progressive) 333.0
  secondary 362.65
pineal gland 259.8
pituitary (gland) 253.8
placenta (fatty) (fibrinoid) (fibroid) — *see*
  Placenta, abnormal
popliteal fat pad 729.31
posterolateral (spinal cord) (*see also* Degeneration, combined) 266.2 *[336.2]*
pulmonary valve (heart) (*see also* Endocarditis, pulmonary) 424.3
pulp (tooth) 522.2
pupillary margin 364.54
renal (*see also* Sclerosis, renal) 587
  fibrocystic 753.19
  polycystic 753.12
    adult type (APKD) 753.13
    autosomal dominant 753.13
    autosomal recessive 753.14
    childhood type (CPKD) 753.14
    infantile type 753.14
reticuloendothelial system 289.89
retina (peripheral) 362.60
  with retinal defect (*see also* Detachment,
    retina, with retinal defect) 361.00
  cystic (senile) 362.50
  cystoid 362.53
  hereditary (*see also* Dystrophy, retina)
    362.70
    cerebroretinal 362.71
    congenital 362.75
    juvenile (Stargardt's) 362.75
    macula 362.76
  Kuhnt-Junius 362.52
  lattice 362.63
  macular (*see also* Degeneration, macula)
    362.50
  microcystoid 362.62
  palisade 362.63
  paving stone 362.61
  pigmentary (primary) 362.74
    secondary 362.65
  posterior pole (*see also* Degeneration,
    macula) 362.50
  secondary 362.66
  senile 362.60
    cystic 362.53
    reticular 362.64
saccule, congenital (causing impairment of
  hearing) 744.05
sacculocochlear 386.8
senile 797
  brain 331.2
  cardiac, heart, or myocardium (*see also*
    Degeneration, myocardial) 429.1
  motor centers 331.2
  reticule 362.64
  retina, cystic 362.50
  vascular — *see* Arteriosclerosis
silicone rubber poppet (prosthetic valve)
  996.02
sinus (cystic) (*see also* Sinusitis) 473.9
  polypoid 471.1
skin 709.3
  amyloid 277.39
  colloid 709.3
spinal (cord) 336.8
  amyloid 277.39
  column 733.90
  combined (subacute) (*see also* Degener-
    ation, combined) 266.2 *[336.2]*
    with anemia (pernicious)
      281.0 *[336.2]*
  dorsolateral (*see also* Degeneration,
    combined) 266.2 *[336.2]*
  familial NEC 336.8

☑ Additional Digit Required — Refer to the Tabular List for Digit Selection   ▽ Subterms under main terms may continue to next column or page

2015 ICD-9-CM   ▶◀ Revised Text   ● New Line   ▲ Revised Code   Volume 2 — 69

Degeneration, degenerative — continued
spinal — continued
  fatty 336.8
  funicular (see also Degeneration, combined) 266.2 [336.2]
  heredofamilial NEC 336.8
  posterolateral (see also Degeneration, combined) 266.2 [336.2]
  subacute combined — see Degeneration, combined
  tuberculous (see also Tuberculosis) 013.8 ☑
spine 733.90
spleen 289.59
  amyloid 277.39
  lardaceous 277.39
stomach 537.89
  lardaceous 277.39
strionigral 333.0
sudoriparous (cystic) 705.89
suprarenal (capsule) (gland) 255.8
  with hypofunction 255.41
sweat gland 705.89
synovial membrane (pulpy) 727.9
tapetoretinal 362.74
  adult or presenile form 362.50
testis (postinfectional) 608.89
thymus (gland) 254.8
  fatty 254.8
  lardaceous 277.39
thyroid (gland) 246.8
tricuspid (heart) (valve) — see Endocarditis, tricuspid
tuberculous NEC (see also Tuberculosis) 011.9 ☑
turbinate 733.90
uterus 621.8
  cystic 621.8
vascular (senile) (see also Arteriosclerosis)
  hypertensive — see Hypertension
vitreoretinal (primary) 362.73
  secondary 362.66
vitreous humor (with infiltration) 379.21
wallerian NEC — see Disorder, nerve
waxy (any site) 277.39
Wilson's hepatolenticular 275.1

Deglutition
paralysis 784.99
  hysterical 300.11
pneumonia 507.0

Degos' disease or syndrome 447.8

Degradation disorder, branched-chain amino acid 270.3

Dehiscence
anastomosis — see Complications, anastomosis
cesarean wound 674.1 ☑
closure of
  cornea 998.32
  fascia, superficial or muscular 998.31
  internal organ 998.31
  mucosa 998.32
  muscle or muscle flap 998.31
  ribs or rib cage 998.31
  skin 998.32
  skull or craniotomy 998.31
  sternum or sternotomy 998.31
  subcutaneous tissue 998.32
  tendon or ligament 998.31
  traumatic laceration (external) (internal) 998.33
episiotomy 674.2 ☑
operation wound 998.32
  deep 998.31
  external 998.32
  internal 998.31
  superficial 998.32
perineal wound (postpartum) 674.2 ☑
postoperative 998.32
  abdomen 998.32
    internal 998.31
  internal 998.31
traumatic injury wound repair 998.33
uterine wound 674.1 ☑

Dehydration (cachexia) 276.51

Dehydration — continued
with
  hypernatremia 276.0
  hyponatremia 276.1
newborn 775.5

Deiters' nucleus syndrome 386.19
Déjérine's disease 356.0
Déjérine-Klumpke paralysis 767.6
Déjérine-Roussy syndrome 338.0
Déjérine-Sottas disease or neuropathy (hypertrophic) 356.0
Déjérine-Thomas atrophy or syndrome 333.0
de Lange's syndrome (Amsterdam dwarf, intellectual disabilities, and brachycephaly) 759.89

Delay, delayed
adaptation, cones or rods 368.63
any plane in pelvis
  affecting fetus or newborn 763.1
  complicating delivery 660.1 ☑
birth or delivery NEC 662.1 ☑
  affecting fetus or newborn 763.89
  second twin, triplet, or multiple mate 662.3 ☑
closure (see also Fistula)
  cranial suture 756.0
  fontanel 756.0
coagulation NEC 790.92
conduction (cardiac) (ventricular) 426.9
delivery NEC 662.1 ☑
  second twin, triplet, etc. 662.3 ☑
    affecting fetus or newborn 763.89
development
  in childhood 783.40
    physiological 783.40
  intellectual NEC 315.9
  learning NEC 315.2
  reading 315.00
  sexual 259.0
  speech 315.39
    and language due to hearing loss 315.34
    associated with hyperkinesis 314.1
  spelling 315.09
gastric emptying 536.8
menarche 256.39
  due to pituitary hypofunction 253.4
menstruation (cause unknown) 626.8
milestone in childhood 783.42
motility — see Hypomotility
passage of meconium (newborn) 777.1
primary respiration 768.9
puberty 259.0
separation of umbilical cord 779.83
sexual maturation, female 259.0
vaccination V64.00

Del Castillo's syndrome (germinal aplasia) 606.0
Déleage's disease 359.89

Deletion syndrome
5p 758.31
22q11.2 758.32
autosomal NEC 758.39
constitutional 5q deletion 758.39

Delhi (boil) (button) (sore) 085.1

Delinquency (juvenile) 312.9
group (see also Disturbance, conduct) 312.2 ☑
neurotic 312.4

Delirium, delirious 780.09
acute 780.09
  due to conditions classified elsewhere 293.0
alcoholic 291.0
  acute 291.0
  chronic 291.1
alcoholicum 291.0
chronic (see also Psychosis) 293.89
  due to or associated with physical condition — see Psychosis, organic
drug-induced 292.81
due to conditions classified elsewhere 293.0
eclamptic (see also Eclampsia) 780.39
exhaustion (see also Reaction, stress, acute) 308.9
hysterical 300.11

Delirium, delirious — continued
in
  presenile dementia 290.11
  senile dementia 290.3
induced by drug 292.81
manic, maniacal (acute) (see also Psychosis, affective) 296.0 ☑
  recurrent episode 296.1 ☑
  single episode 296.0 ☑
puerperal 293.9
senile 290.3
subacute (psychotic) 293.1
thyroid (see also Thyrotoxicosis) 242.9 ☑
traumatic (see also Injury, intracranial)
  with
    lesion, spinal cord — see Injury, spinal, by site
    shock, spinal — see Injury, spinal, by site
tremens (impending) 291.0
uremic — see Uremia
withdrawal
  alcoholic (acute) 291.0
    chronic 291.1
  drug 292.0

Delivery

Note — Use the following fifth-digit subclassification with categories 640–649, 651–676:

0   unspecified as to episode of care

1   delivered, with or without mention of antepartum condition

2   delivered, with mention of postpartum complication

3   antepartum condition or complication

4   postpartum condition or complication

breech (assisted) (buttocks) (complete) (frank) (spontaneous) 652.2 ☑
  affecting fetus or newborn 763.0
  extraction NEC 669.6 ☑
cesarean (for) 669.7 ☑
  abnormal
    cervix 654.6 ☑
    pelvic organs or tissues 654.9 ☑
    pelvis (bony) (major) NEC 653.0 ☑
    presentation or position 652.9 ☑
      in multiple gestation 652.6 ☑
    size, fetus 653.5 ☑
    soft parts (of pelvis) 654.9 ☑
    uterus, congenital 654.0 ☑
    vagina 654.7 ☑
    vulva 654.8 ☑
  abruptio placentae 641.2 ☑
  acromion presentation 652.8 ☑
  affecting fetus or newborn 763.4
  anteversion, cervix or uterus 654.4 ☑
  atony, uterus 661.2 ☑
    with hemorrhage 666.1 ☑
  bicornis or bicornuate uterus 654.0 ☑
  breech presentation (buttocks) (complete) (frank) 652.2 ☑
  brow presentation 652.4 ☑
  cephalopelvic disproportion (normally formed fetus) 653.4 ☑
  chin presentation 652.4 ☑
  cicatrix of cervix 654.6 ☑
  contracted pelvis (general) 653.1 ☑
    inlet 653.2 ☑
    outlet 653.3 ☑
  cord presentation or prolapse 663.0 ☑
  cystocele 654.4 ☑
  deformity (acquired) (congenital)
    pelvic organs or tissues NEC 654.9 ☑
    pelvis (bony) NEC 653.0 ☑
  displacement, uterus NEC 654.4 ☑
  disproportion NEC 653.9 ☑
  distress
    fetal 656.8 ☑
    maternal 669.0 ☑
  eclampsia 642.6 ☑

Delivery — continued
cesarean — continued
  face presentation 652.4 ☑
  failed
    forceps 660.7 ☑
    trial of labor NEC 660.6 ☑
    vacuum extraction 660.7 ☑
    ventouse 660.7 ☑
  fetal deformity 653.7 ☑
  fetal-maternal hemorrhage 656.0 ☑
  fetus, fetal
    distress 656.8 ☑
    prematurity 656.8 ☑
  fibroid (tumor) (uterus) 654.1 ☑
  footling 652.8 ☑
    with successful version 652.1 ☑
  hemorrhage (antepartum) (intrapartum) NEC 641.9 ☑
  hydrocephalic fetus 653.6 ☑
  incarceration of uterus 654.3 ☑
  incoordinate uterine action 661.4 ☑
  inertia, uterus 661.2 ☑
    primary 661.0 ☑
    secondary 661.1 ☑
  lateroversion, uterus or cervix 654.4 ☑
  mal lie 652.9 ☑
  malposition
    fetus 652.9 ☑
      in multiple gestation 652.6 ☑
    pelvic organs or tissues NEC 654.9 ☑
    uterus NEC or cervix 654.4 ☑
  malpresentation NEC 652.9 ☑
    in multiple gestation 652.6 ☑
  maternal
    diabetes mellitus (conditions classifiable to 249 and 250) 648.0 ☑
    heart disease NEC 648.6 ☑
  meconium in liquor 656.8 ☑
    staining only 792.3
  oblique presentation 652.3 ☑
  oversize fetus 653.5 ☑
  pelvic tumor NEC 654.9 ☑
  placental insufficiency 656.5 ☑
  placenta previa 641.0 ☑
    with hemorrhage 641.1 ☑
  (planned) occurring after 37 completed weeks of gestation but before 39 completed weeks gestation due to (spontaneous) onset of labor 649.8 ☑
  poor dilation, cervix 661.0 ☑
  pre-eclampsia 642.4 ☑
    severe 642.5 ☑
  previous
    cesarean delivery, section 654.2 ☑
    surgery (to)
      cervix 654.6 ☑
      gynecological NEC 654.9 ☑
      rectum 654.8 ☑
      uterus NEC 654.9 ☑
        previous cesarean delivery, section 654.2 ☑
      vagina 654.7 ☑
  prolapse
    arm or hand 652.7 ☑
    uterus 654.4 ☑
  prolonged labor 662.1 ☑
  rectocele 654.4 ☑
  retroversion, uterus or cervix 654.3 ☑
  rigid
    cervix 654.6 ☑
    pelvic floor 654.4 ☑
    perineum 654.8 ☑
    vagina 654.7 ☑
    vulva 654.8 ☑
  sacculation, pregnant uterus 654.4 ☑
  scar(s)
    cervix 654.6 ☑
    cesarean delivery, section 654.2 ☑
    uterus NEC 654.9 ☑
      due to previous cesarean delivery, section 654.2 ☑
  Shirodkar suture in situ 654.5 ☑
  shoulder presentation 652.8 ☑

☑ Additional Digit Required — Refer to the Tabular List for Digit Selection ▽ Subterms under main terms may continue to next column or page

70 — Volume 2   ►◄ Revised Text   ● New Line   ▲ Revised Code   2015 ICD-9-CM

Delivery — *continued*
  cesarean — *continued*
    stenosis or stricture, cervix 654.6 ☑
    transverse presentation or lie 652.3 ☑
    tumor, pelvic organs or tissues NEC 654.4 ☑
    umbilical cord presentation or prolapse 663.0 ☑
  completely normal case — *see* category 650
  complicated (by) NEC 669.9 ☑
    abdominal tumor, fetal 653.7 ☑
      causing obstructed labor 660.1 ☑
    abnormal, abnormality of
      cervix 654.6 ☑
        causing obstructed labor 660.2 ☑
      forces of labor 661.9 ☑
      formation of uterus 654.0 ☑
      pelvic organs or tissues 654.9 ☑
        causing obstructed labor 660.2 ☑
      pelvis (bony) (major) NEC 653.0 ☑
        causing obstructed labor 660.1 ☑
      presentation or position NEC 652.9 ☑
        causing obstructed labor 660.0 ☑
      size, fetus 653.5 ☑
        causing obstructed labor 660.1 ☑
      soft parts (of pelvis) 654.9 ☑
        causing obstructed labor 660.2 ☑
      uterine contractions NEC 661.9 ☑
      uterus (formation) 654.0 ☑
        causing obstructed labor 660.2 ☑
      vagina 654.7 ☑
        causing obstructed labor 660.2 ☑
    abnormally formed uterus (any type) (congenital) 654.0 ☑
      causing obstructed labor 660.2 ☑
    acromion presentation 652.8 ☑
      causing obstructed labor 660.0 ☑
    adherent placenta 667.0 ☑
      with hemorrhage 666.0 ☑
    adhesions, uterus (to abdominal wall) 654.4 ☑
    advanced maternal age NEC 659.6 ☑
      multigravida 659.6 ☑
      primigravida 659.5 ☑
    air embolism 673.0 ☑
    amnionitis 658.4 ☑
    amniotic fluid embolism 673.1 ☑
    anesthetic death 668.9 ☑
    annular detachment, cervix 665.3 ☑
    antepartum hemorrhage — *see* Delivery, complicated, hemorrhage
    anteversion, cervix or uterus 654.4 ☑
      causing obstructed labor 660.2 ☑
    apoplexy 674.0 ☑
      placenta 641.2 ☑
    arrested active phase 661.1 ☑
    asymmetrical pelvis bone 653.0 ☑
      causing obstructed labor 660.1 ☑
    atony, uterus with hemorrhage (hypotonic) (inertia) 666.1 ☑
      hypertonic 661.4 ☑
    Bandl's ring 661.4 ☑
    battledore placenta — *see* Placenta, abnormal
    bicornis or bicornuate uterus 654.0 ☑
      causing obstructed labor 660.2 ☑
    birth injury to mother NEC 665.9 ☑
    bleeding (*see also* Delivery, complicated, hemorrhage) 641.9 ☑
    breech presentation (assisted) (buttocks) (complete) (frank) (spontaneous) 652.2 ☑
      with successful version 652.1 ☑
    brow presentation 652.4 ☑

Delivery — *continued*
  complicated — *continued*
    cephalopelvic disproportion (normally formed fetus) 653.4 ☑
      causing obstructed labor 660.1 ☑
    cerebral hemorrhage 674.0 ☑
    cervical dystocia 661.2 ☑
    chin presentation 652.4 ☑
      causing obstructed labor 660.0 ☑
    cicatrix
      cervix 654.6 ☑
        causing obstructed labor 660.2 ☑
      vagina 654.7 ☑
        causing obstructed labor 660.2 ☑
    coagulation defect 649.3 ☑
    colporrhexis 665.4 ☑
      with perineal laceration 664.0 ☑
    compound presentation 652.8 ☑
      causing obstructed labor 660.0 ☑
    compression of cord (umbilical) 663.2 ☑
      around neck 663.1 ☑
      cord prolapsed 663.0 ☑
    contraction, contracted pelvis 653.1 ☑
      causing obstructed labor 660.1 ☑
      general 653.1 ☑
        causing obstructed labor 660.1 ☑
      inlet 653.2 ☑
        causing obstructed labor 660.1 ☑
      midpelvic 653.8 ☑
        causing obstructed labor 660.1 ☑
      midplane 653.8 ☑
        causing obstructed labor 660.1 ☑
      outlet 653.3 ☑
        causing obstructed labor 660.1 ☑
    contraction ring 661.4 ☑
    cord (umbilical) 663.9 ☑
      around neck, tightly or with compression 663.1 ☑
        without compression 663.3 ☑
      bruising 663.6 ☑
      complication NEC 663.9 ☑
        specified type NEC 663.8 ☑
      compression NEC 663.2 ☑
      entanglement NEC 663.3 ☑
        with compression 663.2 ☑
      forelying 663.0 ☑
      hematoma 663.6 ☑
      marginal attachment 663.8 ☑
      presentation 663.0 ☑
      prolapse (complete) (occult) (partial) 663.0 ☑
      short 663.4 ☑
      specified complication NEC 663.8 ☑
      thrombosis (vessels) 663.6 ☑
      vascular lesion 663.6 ☑
      velamentous insertion 663.8 ☑
    Couvelaire uterus 641.2 ☑
    cretin pelvis (dwarf type) (male type) 653.1 ☑
      causing obstructed labor 660.1 ☑
    crossbirth 652.3 ☑
      with successful version 652.1 ☑
      causing obstructed labor 660.0 ☑
    cyst (Gartner's duct) 654.7 ☑
    cystocele 654.4 ☑
      causing obstructed labor 660.2 ☑
    death of fetus (near term) 656.4 ☑
      early (before 22 completed weeks gestation) 632
    deformity (acquired) (congenital)
      fetus 653.7 ☑
        causing obstructed labor 660.1 ☑
      pelvic organs or tissues NEC 654.9 ☑
        causing obstructed labor 660.2 ☑
      pelvis (bony) NEC 653.0 ☑

Delivery — *continued*
  complicated — *continued*
    deformity — *continued*
      pelvis — *continued*
        causing obstructed labor 660.1 ☑
    delay, delayed
      delivery in multiple pregnancy 662.3 ☑
      due to locked mates 660.5 ☑
      following rupture of membranes (spontaneous) 658.2 ☑
        artificial 658.3 ☑
    depressed fetal heart tones 659.7 ☑
    diastasis recti 665.8 ☑
    dilatation
      bladder 654.4 ☑
        causing obstructed labor 660.2 ☑
      cervix, incomplete, poor or slow 661.0 ☑
    diseased placenta 656.7 ☑
    displacement uterus NEC 654.4 ☑
      causing obstructed labor 660.2 ☑
    disproportion NEC 653.9 ☑
      causing obstructed labor 660.1 ☑
    disruptio uteri — *see* Delivery, complicated, rupture, uterus
    distress
      fetal 656.8 ☑
      maternal 669.0 ☑
    double uterus (congenital) 654.0 ☑
      causing obstructed labor 660.2 ☑
    dropsy amnion 657.0 ☑
    dysfunction, uterus 661.9 ☑
      hypertonic 661.4 ☑
      hypotonic 661.2 ☑
        primary 661.0 ☑
        secondary 661.1 ☑
      incoordinate 661.4 ☑
    dystocia
      cervical 661.2 ☑
      fetal — *see* Delivery, complicated, abnormal, presentation
      maternal — *see* Delivery, complicated, prolonged labor
      pelvic — *see* Delivery, complicated, contraction pelvis
      positional 652.8 ☑
      shoulder girdle 660.4 ☑
    eclampsia 642.6 ☑
    ectopic kidney 654.4 ☑
      causing obstructed labor 660.2 ☑
    edema, cervix 654.6 ☑
      causing obstructed labor 660.2 ☑
    effusion, amniotic fluid 658.1 ☑
    elderly multigravida 659.6 ☑
    elderly primigravida 659.5 ☑
    embolism (pulmonary) 673.2 ☑
      air 673.0 ☑
      amniotic fluid 673.1 ☑
      blood clot 673.2 ☑
      cerebral 674.0 ☑
      fat 673.8 ☑
      pyemic 673.3 ☑
      septic 673.3 ☑
    entanglement, umbilical cord 663.3 ☑
      with compression 663.2 ☑
      around neck (with compression) 663.1 ☑
    eversion, cervix or uterus 665.2 ☑
    excessive
      fetal growth 653.5 ☑
        causing obstructed labor 660.1 ☑
      size of fetus 653.5 ☑
        causing obstructed labor 660.1 ☑
    face presentation 652.4 ☑
      causing obstructed labor 660.0 ☑
      to pubes 660.3 ☑
    failure, fetal head to enter pelvic brim 652.5 ☑
      causing obstructed labor 660.0 ☑

Delivery — *continued*
  complicated — *continued*
    female genital mutilation 660.8 ☑
    fetal
      acid-base balance 656.8 ☑
      death (near term) NEC 656.4 ☑
        early (before 22 completed weeks gestation) 632
      deformity 653.7 ☑
        causing obstructed labor 660.1 ☑
      distress 656.8 ☑
      heart rate or rhythm 659.7 ☑
      reduction of multiple fetuses reduced to single fetus 651.7 ☑
    fetopelvic disproportion 653.4 ☑
      causing obstructed labor 660.1 ☑
    fever during labor 659.2 ☑
    fibroid (tumor) (uterus) 654.1 ☑
      causing obstructed labor 660.2 ☑
    fibromyomata 654.1 ☑
      causing obstructed labor 660.2 ☑
    forelying umbilical cord 663.0 ☑
    fracture of coccyx 665.6 ☑
    hematoma 664.5 ☑
      broad ligament 665.7 ☑
      ischial spine 665.7 ☑
      pelvic 665.7 ☑
      perineum 664.5 ☑
      soft tissues 665.7 ☑
      subdural 674.0 ☑
      umbilical cord 663.6 ☑
      vagina 665.7 ☑
      vulva or perineum 664.5 ☑
    hemorrhage (uterine) (antepartum) (intrapartum) (pregnancy) 641.9 ☑
      accidental 641.2 ☑
      associated with
        afibrinogenemia 641.3 ☑
        coagulation defect 641.3 ☑
          hyperfibrinolysis 641.3 ☑
          hypofibrinogenemia 641.3 ☑
      cerebral 674.0 ☑
      due to
        low-lying placenta 641.1 ☑
        placenta previa 641.1 ☑
        premature separation of placenta (normally implanted) 641.2 ☑
        retained placenta 666.0 ☑
        trauma 641.8 ☑
        uterine leiomyoma 641.8 ☑
      marginal sinus rupture 641.2 ☑
      placenta NEC 641.9 ☑
      postpartum (atonic) (immediate) (within 24 hours) 666.1 ☑
        with retained or trapped placenta 666.0 ☑
        delayed 666.2 ☑
        secondary 666.2 ☑
        third stage 666.0 ☑
    hourglass contraction, uterus 661.4 ☑
    hydramnios 657.0 ☑
    hydrocephalic fetus 653.6 ☑
      causing obstructed labor 660.1 ☑
    hydrops fetalis 653.7 ☑
      causing obstructed labor 660.1 ☑
    hypertension — *see* Hypertension, complicating pregnancy
    hypertonic uterine dysfunction 661.4 ☑
    hypotonic uterine dysfunction 661.2 ☑
    impacted shoulders 660.4 ☑
    incarceration, uterus 654.3 ☑
      causing obstructed labor 660.2 ☑
    incomplete dilation (cervix) 661.0 ☑
    incoordinate uterus 661.4 ☑
    indication NEC 659.9 ☑
      specified type NEC 659.8 ☑
    inertia, uterus 661.2 ☑
      hypertonic 661.4 ☑
      hypotonic 661.2 ☑
        primary 661.0 ☑
        secondary 661.1 ☑

☑ Additional Digit Required — Refer to the Tabular List for Digit Selection   ▽ Subterms under main terms may continue to next column or page

Delivery — *continued*
  complicated — *continued*
    infantile
      genitalia 654.4 ☑
        causing obstructed labor
          660.2 ☑
      uterus (os) 654.4 ☑
        causing obstructed labor
          660.2 ☑
    injury (to mother) NEC 665.9 ☑
    intrauterine fetal death (near term) NEC
      656.4 ☑
      early (before 22 completed weeks
        gestation) 632
    inversion, uterus 665.2 ☑
    kidney, ectopic 654.4 ☑
      causing obstructed labor 660.2 ☑
    knot (true), umbilical cord 663.2 ☑
    labor
      onset (spontaneous) after 37 complet-
        ed weeks of gestation but be-
        fore 39 completed weeks
        gestation with delivery by
        (planned) cesarean section
        649.8 ☑
      premature (before 37 completed
        weeks gestation) 644.2 ☑
    laceration 664.9 ☑
      anus (sphincter) (healed) (old)
        654.8 ☑
        with mucosa 664.3 ☑
        not associated with third-degree
          perineal laceration
          664.6 ☑
      bladder (urinary) 665.5 ☑
      bowel 665.5 ☑
      central 664.4 ☑
      cervix (uteri) 665.3 ☑
      fourchette 664.0 ☑
      hymen 664.0 ☑
      labia (majora) (minora) 664.0 ☑
      pelvic
        floor 664.1 ☑
        organ NEC 665.5 ☑
      perineum, perineal 664.4 ☑
        first degree 664.0 ☑
        second degree 664.1 ☑
        third degree 664.2 ☑
        fourth degree 664.3 ☑
        central 664.4 ☑
        extensive NEC 664.4 ☑
        muscles 664.1 ☑
        skin 664.0 ☑
        slight 664.0 ☑
      peritoneum (pelvic) 665.5 ☑
      periurethral tissue 664.8 ☑
      rectovaginal (septum) (without per-
        ineal laceration) 665.4 ☑
        with perineum 664.2 ☑
          with anal or rectal mucosa
            664.3 ☑
      skin (perineum) 664.0 ☑
      specified site or type NEC 664.8 ☑
      sphincter ani (healed) (old) 654.8 ☑
        with mucosa 664.3 ☑
        not associated with third-degree
          perineal laceration
          664.6 ☑
      urethra 665.5 ☑
      uterus 665.1 ☑
        before labor 665.0 ☑
      vagina, vaginal (deep) (high) (sulcus)
        (wall) (without perineal lacer-
        ation) 665.4 ☑
        with perineum 664.0 ☑
        muscles, with perineum 664.1 ☑
      vulva 664.0 ☑
    lateroversion, uterus or cervix 654.4 ☑
      causing obstructed labor 660.2 ☑
    locked mates 660.5 ☑
    low implantation of placenta — *see* De-
      livery, complicated, placenta,
      previa
    mal lie 652.9 ☑

Delivery — *continued*
  complicated — *continued*
    malposition
      fetus NEC 652.9 ☑
        causing obstructed labor
          660.0 ☑
      pelvic organs or tissues NEC 654.9 ☑
        causing obstructed labor
          660.2 ☑
      placenta 641.1 ☑
        without hemorrhage 641.0 ☑
      uterus NEC or cervix 654.4 ☑
        causing obstructed labor
          660.2 ☑
    malpresentation 652.9 ☑
      causing obstructed labor 660.0 ☑
    marginal sinus (bleeding) (rupture)
      641.2 ☑
    maternal hypotension syndrome
      669.2 ☑
    meconium in liquor 656.8 ☑
    membranes, retained — *see* Delivery,
      complicated, placenta, retained
    mentum presentation 652.4 ☑
      causing obstructed labor 660.0 ☑
    metrorrhagia (myopathia) — *see* Deliv-
      ery, complicated, hemorrhage
    metrorrhexis — *see* Delivery, complicat-
      ed, rupture, uterus
    multiparity (grand) 659.4 ☑
    myelomeningocele, fetus 653.7 ☑
      causing obstructed labor 660.1 ☑
    Nägele's pelvis 653.0 ☑
      causing obstructed labor 660.1 ☑
    nonengagement, fetal head 652.5 ☑
      causing obstructed labor 660.0 ☑
    oblique presentation 652.3 ☑
      causing obstructed labor 660.0 ☑
    obstetric
      shock 669.1 ☑
      trauma NEC 665.9 ☑
    obstructed labor 660.9 ☑
      due to
        abnormality of pelvic organs or
          tissues (conditions classifi-
          able to 654.0–654.9)
          660.2 ☑
        deep transverse arrest 660.3 ☑
        impacted shoulders 660.4 ☑
        locked twins 660.5 ☑
        malposition and malpresentation
          of fetus (conditions classi-
          fiable to 652.0–652.9)
          660.0 ☑
        persistent occipitoposterior
          660.3 ☑
        shoulder dystocia 660.4 ☑
    occult prolapse of umbilical cord
      663.0 ☑
    oversize fetus 653.5 ☑
      causing obstructed labor 660.1 ☑
    pathological retraction ring, uterus
      661.4 ☑
    pelvic
      arrest (deep) (high) (of fetal head)
        (transverse) 660.3 ☑
      deformity (bone) (*see also* Deformity,
        pelvis, with disproportion)
        soft tissue 654.9 ☑
          causing obstructed labor
            660.2 ☑
      tumor NEC 654.9 ☑
        causing obstructed labor
          660.2 ☑
    penetration, pregnant uterus by instru-
      ment 665.1 ☑
    perforation — *see* Delivery, complicated,
      laceration
    persistent
      hymen 654.8 ☑
        causing obstructed labor
          660.2 ☑
      occipitoposterior 660.3 ☑

Delivery — *continued*
  complicated — *continued*
    placenta, placental
      ablatio 641.2 ☑
      abnormality 656.7 ☑
        with hemorrhage 641.2 ☑
      abruptio 641.2 ☑
      accreta 667.0 ☑
        with hemorrhage 666.0 ☑
      adherent (without hemorrhage)
        667.0 ☑
        with hemorrhage 666.0 ☑
      apoplexy 641.2 ☑
      battledore placenta — *see* Placenta,
        abnormal
      detachment (premature) 641.2 ☑
      disease 656.7 ☑
      hemorrhage NEC 641.9 ☑
      increta (without hemorrhage)
        667.0 ☑
        with hemorrhage 666.0 ☑
      low (implantation) 641.1 ☑
        without hemorrhage 641.0 ☑
      malformation 656.7 ☑
        with hemorrhage 641.2 ☑
      malposition 641.1 ☑
        without hemorrhage 641.0 ☑
      marginal sinus rupture 641.2 ☑
      percreta 667.0 ☑
        with hemorrhage 666.0 ☑
      premature separation 641.2 ☑
      previa (central) (lateral) (marginal)
        (partial) 641.1 ☑
        without hemorrhage 641.0 ☑
      retained (with hemorrhage) 666.0 ☑
        without hemorrhage 667.0 ☑
      rupture of marginal sinus 641.2 ☑
      separation (premature) 641.2 ☑
      trapped 666.0 ☑
        without hemorrhage 667.0 ☑
      vicious insertion 641.1 ☑
    polyhydramnios 657.0 ☑
    polyp, cervix 654.6 ☑
      causing obstructed labor 660.2 ☑
    precipitate labor 661.3 ☑
    premature
      labor (before 37 completed weeks
        gestation) 644.2 ☑
      rupture, membranes 658.1 ☑
        delayed delivery following
          658.2 ☑
    presenting umbilical cord 663.0 ☑
    previous
      cesarean delivery, section 654.2 ☑
      surgery
        cervix 654.6 ☑
          causing obstructed labor
            660.2 ☑
        gynecological NEC 654.9 ☑
          causing obstructed labor
            660.2 ☑
        perineum 654.8 ☑
        rectum 654.8 ☑
        uterus NEC 654.9 ☑
          due to previous cesarean de-
            livery, section 654.2 ☑
        vagina 654.7 ☑
          causing obstructed labor
            660.2 ☑
        vulva 654.8 ☑
    primary uterine inertia 661.0 ☑
    primipara, elderly or old 659.5 ☑
    prolapse
      arm or hand 652.7 ☑
        causing obstructed labor
          660.0 ☑
      cord (umbilical) 663.0 ☑
      fetal extremity 652.8 ☑
      foot or leg 652.8 ☑
        causing obstructed labor
          660.0 ☑
      umbilical cord (complete) (occult)
        (partial) 663.0 ☑
      uterus 654.4 ☑

Delivery — *continued*
  complicated — *continued*
    prolapse — *continued*
      uterus — *continued*
        causing obstructed labor
          660.2 ☑
    prolonged labor 662.1 ☑
      first stage 662.0 ☑
      second stage 662.2 ☑
      active phase 661.2 ☑
      due to
        cervical dystocia 661.2 ☑
        contraction ring 661.4 ☑
        tetanic uterus 661.4 ☑
        uterine inertia 661.2 ☑
          primary 661.0 ☑
          secondary 661.1 ☑
      latent phase 661.0 ☑
    pyrexia during labor 659.2 ☑
    rachitic pelvis 653.2 ☑
      causing obstructed labor 660.1 ☑
    rectocele 654.4 ☑
      causing obstructed labor 660.2 ☑
    retained membranes or portions of pla-
      centa 666.2 ☑
      without hemorrhage 667.1 ☑
    retarded (prolonged) birth 662.1 ☑
    retention secundines (with hemorrhage)
      666.2 ☑
      without hemorrhage 667.1 ☑
    retroversion, uterus or cervix 654.3 ☑
      causing obstructed labor 660.2 ☑
    rigid
      cervix 654.6 ☑
        causing obstructed labor
          660.2 ☑
      pelvic floor 654.4 ☑
        causing obstructed labor
          660.2 ☑
      perineum or vulva 654.8 ☑
        causing obstructed labor
          660.2 ☑
      vagina 654.7 ☑
        causing obstructed labor
          660.2 ☑
    Robert's pelvis 653.0 ☑
      causing obstructed labor 660.1 ☑
    rupture (*see also* Delivery, complicated,
      laceration)
      bladder (urinary) 665.5 ☑
      cervix 665.3 ☑
      marginal sinus 641.2 ☑
      membranes, premature 658.1 ☑
      pelvic organ NEC 665.5 ☑
      perineum (without mention of other
        laceration) — *see* Delivery,
        complicated, laceration, per-
        ineum
      peritoneum (pelvic) 665.5 ☑
      urethra 665.5 ☑
      uterus (during labor) 665.1 ☑
        before labor 665.0 ☑
    sacculation, pregnant uterus 654.4 ☑
    sacral teratomas, fetal 653.7 ☑
      causing obstructed labor 660.1 ☑
    scar(s)
      cervix 654.6 ☑
        causing obstructed labor
          660.2 ☑
      cesarean delivery, section 654.2 ☑
        causing obstructed labor
          660.2 ☑
      perineum 654.8 ☑
        causing obstructed labor
          660.2 ☑
      uterus NEC 654.9 ☑
        causing obstructed labor
          660.2 ☑
        due to previous cesarean delivery,
          section 654.2 ☑
      vagina 654.7 ☑
        causing obstructed labor
          660.2 ☑
      vulva 654.8 ☑

☑ **Additional Digit Required** — Refer to the Tabular List for Digit Selection   ▽ **Subterms under main terms may continue to next column or page**

Delivery — continued
  complicated — continued
    scar(s) — continued
      vulva — continued
        causing obstructed labor
          660.2 ☑
    scoliotic pelvis 653.0 ☑
      causing obstructed labor 660.1 ☑
    secondary uterine inertia 661.1 ☑
    secundines, retained — see Delivery,
      complicated, placenta, retained
    separation
      placenta (premature) 641.2 ☑
      pubic bone 665.6 ☑
      symphysis pubis 665.6 ☑
    septate vagina 654.7 ☑
      causing obstructed labor 660.2 ☑
    shock (birth) (obstetric) (puerperal)
      669.1 ☑
    short cord syndrome 663.4 ☑
    shoulder
      girdle dystocia 660.4 ☑
      presentation 652.8 ☑
        causing obstructed labor
          660.0 ☑
    Siamese twins 678.1 ☑
    slow slope active phase 661.2 ☑
    spasm
      cervix 661.4 ☑
      uterus 661.4 ☑
    spondylolisthesis, pelvis 653.3 ☑
      causing obstructed labor 660.1 ☑
    spondylolysis (lumbosacral) 653.3 ☑
      causing obstructed labor 660.1 ☑
    spondylosis 653.0 ☑
      causing obstructed labor 660.1 ☑
    stenosis or stricture
      cervix 654.6 ☑
        causing obstructed labor
          660.2 ☑
      vagina 654.7 ☑
        causing obstructed labor
          660.2 ☑
    sudden death, unknown cause 669.9 ☑
    tear (pelvic organ) (see also Delivery,
      complicated, laceration) 664.9 ☑
      anal sphincter (healed) (old) 654.8 ☑
        not associated with third-degree
          perineal laceration
          664.6 ☑
    teratomas, sacral, fetal 653.7 ☑
      causing obstructed labor 660.1 ☑
    tetanic uterus 661.4 ☑
    tipping pelvis 653.0 ☑
      causing obstructed labor 660.1 ☑
    transverse
      arrest (deep) 660.3 ☑
      presentation or lie 652.3 ☑
        with successful version 652.1 ☑
        causing obstructed labor
          660.0 ☑
    trauma (obstetrical) NEC 665.9 ☑
      periurethral 664.8 ☑
    tumor
      abdominal, fetal 653.7 ☑
        causing obstructed labor
          660.1 ☑
      pelvic organs or tissues NEC 654.9 ☑
        causing obstructed labor
          660.2 ☑
    umbilical cord (see also Delivery, compli-
      cated, cord) 663.9 ☑
      around neck tightly, or with compres-
        sion 663.1 ☑
      entanglement NEC 663.3 ☑
        with compression 663.2 ☑
      prolapse (complete) (occult) (partial)
        663.0 ☑
    unstable lie 652.0 ☑
      causing obstructed labor 660.0 ☑
    uterine
      inertia (see also Delivery, complicat-
        ed, inertia, uterus) 661.2 ☑
      spasm 661.4 ☑

Delivery — continued
  complicated — continued
    vasa previa 663.5 ☑
    velamentous insertion of cord 663.8 ☑
    young maternal age 659.8 ☑
  delayed NEC 662.1 ☑
    following rupture of membranes (spon-
      taneous) 658.2 ☑
      artificial 658.3 ☑
    second twin, triplet, etc. 662.3 ☑
  difficult NEC 669.9 ☑
    previous, affecting management of
      pregnancy or childbirth V23.49
    specified type NEC 669.8 ☑
  early onset (spontaneous) 644.2 ☑
  footling 652.8 ☑
    with successful version 652.1 ☑
  forceps NEC 669.5 ☑
    affecting fetus or newborn 763.2
  missed (at or near term) 656.4 ☑
  multiple gestation NEC 651.9 ☑
    with fetal loss and retention of one or
      more fetus(es) 651.6 ☑
    following (elective) fetal reduction
      651.7 ☑
    specified type NEC 651.8 ☑
      with fetal loss and retention of one
        or more fetus(es) 651.6 ☑
      following (elective) fetal reduction
        651.7 ☑
  nonviable infant 656.4 ☑
  normal — see category 650
  precipitate 661.3 ☑
    affecting fetus or newborn 763.6
  premature NEC (before 37 completed weeks
    gestation) 644.2 ☑
    previous, affecting management of
      pregnancy V23.41
  quadruplet NEC 651.2 ☑
    with fetal loss and retention of one or
      more fetus(es) 651.5 ☑
    following (elective) fetal reduction
      651.7 ☑
  quintuplet NEC 651.8 ☑
    with fetal loss and retention of one or
      more fetus(es) 651.6 ☑
    following (elective) fetal reduction
      651.7 ☑
  sextuplet NEC 651.8 ☑
    with fetal loss and retention of one or
      more fetus(es) 651.6 ☑
    following (elective) fetal reduction
      651.7 ☑
  specified complication NEC 669.8 ☑
  stillbirth (near term) NEC 656.4 ☑
    early (before 22 completed weeks gesta-
      tion) 632
  term pregnancy (live birth) NEC — see cate-
    gory 650
    stillbirth NEC 656.4 ☑
  threatened premature 644.2 ☑
  triplets NEC 651.1 ☑
    with fetal loss and retention of one or
      more fetus(es) 651.4 ☑
    delayed delivery (one or more mates)
      662.3 ☑
    following (elective) fetal reduction
      651.7 ☑
    locked mates 660.5 ☑
  twins NEC 651.0 ☑
    with fetal loss and retention of one fetus
      651.3 ☑
    delayed delivery (one or more mates)
      662.3 ☑
    following (elective) fetal reduction
      651.7 ☑
    locked mates 660.5 ☑
  uncomplicated — see category 650
  vacuum extractor NEC 669.5 ☑
    affecting fetus or newborn 763.3
  ventouse NEC 669.5 ☑
    affecting fetus or newborn 763.3
Dellen, cornea 371.41
Delusions (paranoid) 297.9

Delusions — continued
  grandiose 297.1
  parasitosis 300.29
  systematized 297.1
Dementia 294.20
  with behavioral disturbance (aggressive)
    (combative) (violent) 294.21
  alcohol-induced persisting (see also Psy-
    chosis, alcoholic) 291.2
  Alzheimer's — see Alzheimer's, dementia
  arteriosclerotic (simple type) (uncomplicat-
    ed) 290.40
    with
      acute confusional state 290.41
      delirium 290.41
      delusions 290.42
      depressed mood 290.43
    depressed type 290.43
    paranoid type 290.42
  Binswanger's 290.12
  catatonic (acute) (see also Schizophrenia)
    295.2 ☑
  congenital (see also Disability, intellectual)
    319
  degenerative 290.9
    presenile-onset — see Dementia, prese-
      nile
    senile-onset — see Dementia, senile
  developmental (see also Schizophrenia)
    295.9 ☑
  dialysis 294.8
    transient 293.9
  drug-induced persisting (see also Psychosis,
    drug) 292.82
  due to or associated with condition(s) clas-
    sified elsewhere
    Alzheimer's
      with behavioral disturbance
        331.0 [294.11]
      without behavioral disturbance
        331.0 [294.10]
    cerebral lipidoses
      with behavioral disturbance
        330.1 [294.11]
      without behavioral disturbance
        330.1 [294.10]
    epilepsy
      with behavioral disturbance
        345.9 ☑ [294.11]
      without behavioral disturbance
        345.9 ☑ [294.10]
    hepatolenticular degeneration
      with behavioral disturbance
        275.1 [294.11]
      without behavioral disturbance
        275.1 [294.10]
    HIV
      with behavioral disturbance
        042 [294.11]
      without behavioral disturbance
        042 [294.10]
    Huntington's chorea
      with behavioral disturbance
        333.4 [294.11]
      without behavioral disturbance
        333.4 [294.10]
    Jakob-Creutzfeldt disease (CJD)
      with behavioral disturbance
        046.19 [294.11]
      without behavioral disturbance
        046.19 [294.10]
      variant (vCJD) 046.11
        with dementia
          with behavioral disturbance
            046.11 [294.11]
          without behavioral disbur-
            bance 046.11 [294.10]
    Lewy bodies
      with behavioral disturbance
        331.82 [294.11]
      without behavioral disturbance
        331.82 [294.10]
    multiple sclerosis
      with behavioral disturbance
        340 [294.11]

Dementia — continued
  due to or associated with condition(s) classi-
    fied elsewhere — continued
    multiple sclerosis — continued
      without behavioral disturbance
        340 [294.10]
    neurosyphilis
      with behavioral disturbance
        094.9 [294.11]
      without behavioral disturbance
        094.9 [294.10]
    Parkinsonism
      with behavioral disturbance
        331.82 [294.11]
      without behavioral disturbance
        331.82 [294.10]
    Parkinson's disease
      with behavioral disturbance
        332.0 [294.11]
      without behavioral disturbance
        332.0 [294.10]
    Pelizaeus-Merzbacher disease
      with behavioral disturbance
        333.0 [294.11]
      without behavioral disturbance
        333.0 [294.10]
    Pick's disease
      with behavioral disturbance
        331.11 [294.11]
      without behavioral disturbance
        331.11 [294.10]
    polyarteritis nodosa
      with behavioral disturbance
        446.0 [294.11]
      without behavioral disturbance
        446.0 [294.10]
    syphilis
      with behavioral disturbance
        094.1 [294.11]
      without behavioral disturbance
        094.1 [294.10]
    Wilson's disease
      with behavioral disturbance
        275.1 [294.11]
      without behavioral disturbance
        275.1 [294.10]
  frontal 331.19
    with behavioral disturbance
      331.19 [294.11]
    without behavioral disturbance
      331.19 [294.10]
  frontotemporal 331.19
    with behavioral disturbance
      331.19 [294.11]
    without behavioral disturbance
      331.19 [294.10]
  hebephrenic (acute) 295.1 ☑
  Heller's (infantile psychosis) (see also Psy-
    chosis, childhood) 299.1 ☑
  idiopathic 290.9
    presenile-onset — see Dementia, prese-
      nile
    senile-onset — see Dementia, senile
  in
    arteriosclerotic brain disease 290.40
    senility 290.0
  induced by drug 292.82
  infantile, infantilia (see also Psychosis,
    childhood) 299.0 ☑
  Lewy body 331.82
    with behavioral disturbance
      331.82 [294.11]
    without behavioral disturbance
      331.82 [294.10]
  multi-infarct (cerebrovascular) (see also De-
    mentia, arterlosclerotic) 290.40
  old age 290.0
  paralytica, paralytic 094.1
    juvenilis 090.40
    syphilitic 094.1
      congenital 090.40
    tabetic form 094.1
  paranoid (see also Schizophrenia) 295.3 ☑
  paraphrenic (see also Schizophrenia)
    295.3 ☑
  paretic 094.1

☑ Additional Digit Required — Refer to the Tabular List for Digit Selection   ▽ Subterms under main terms may continue to next column or page

2015 ICD-9-CM   ▶◀ Revised Text   ● New Line   ▲ Revised Code   Volume 2 — 73

Dementia — continued
  praecox (see also Schizophrenia) 295.9 ☑
  presenile 290.10
    with
      acute confusional state 290.11
      delirium 290.11
      delusional features 290.12
      depressive features 290.13
    depressed type 290.13
    paranoid type 290.12
    simple type 290.10
    uncomplicated 290.10
  primary (acute) (see also Schizophrenia)
    295.0 ☑
  progressive, syphilitic 094.1
  puerperal — see Psychosis, puerperal
  schizophrenic (see also Schizophrenia)
    295.9 ☑
  senile 290.0
    with
      acute confusional state 290.3
      delirium 290.3
      delusional features 290.20
      depressive features 290.21
    depressed type 290.21
    exhaustion 290.0
    paranoid type 290.20
  simple type (acute) (see also Schizophrenia)
    295.0 ☑
  simplex (acute) (see also Schizophrenia)
    295.0 ☑
  syphilitic 094.1
  uremic — see Uremia
  vascular 290.40
    with
      delirium 290.41
      delusions 290.42
      depressed mood 290.43
Demerol dependence — see also Dependence
  304.0 ☑
Demineralization, ankle — see also Osteoporosis 733.00
Demodex folliculorum (infestation) 133.8
Demoralization 799.25
de Morgan's spots (senile angiomas) 448.1
Demyelinating
  polyneuritis, chronic inflammatory 357.81
Demyelination, demyelinization
  central nervous system 341.9
    specified NEC 341.8
  corpus callosum (central) 341.8
  global 340
Dengue (fever) 061
  sandfly 061
  vaccination, prophylactic (against) V05.1
  virus hemorrhagic fever 065.4
Dens
  evaginatus 520.2
  in dente 520.2
  invaginatus 520.2
Dense
  breast(s) 793.82
Density
  increased, bone (disseminated) (general-
    ized) (spotted) 733.99
  lung (nodular) 518.89
Dental — see also condition
  examination only V72.2
Dentia praecox 520.6
Denticles (in pulp) 522.2
Dentigerous cyst 526.0
Dentin
  irregular (in pulp) 522.3
  opalescent 520.5
  secondary (in pulp) 522.3
  sensitive 521.89
Dentinogenesis imperfecta 520.5
Dentinoma (M9271/0) 213.1
  upper jaw (bone) 213.0
Dentition 520.7
  abnormal 520.6
  anomaly 520.6
  delayed 520.6
  difficult 520.7
  disorder of 520.6
  precocious 520.6

Dentition — continued
  retarded 520.6
Denture sore (mouth) 528.9
Dependence

Note — Use the following fifth-digit
subclassification with category 304:

  0 unspecified
  1 continuous
  2 episodic
  3 in remission

  with
    withdrawal symptoms
      alcohol 291.81
      drug 292.0
  14-hydroxy-dihydromorphinone 304.0 ☑
  absinthe 304.6 ☑
  acemorphan 304.0 ☑
  acetanilid(e) 304.6 ☑
  acetophenetidin 304.6 ☑
  acetorphine 304.0 ☑
  acetyldihydrocodeine 304.0 ☑
  acetyldihydrocodeinone 304.0 ☑
  Adalin 304.1 ☑
  Afghanistan black 304.3 ☑
  agrypnal 304.1 ☑
  alcohol, alcoholic (ethyl) (methyl) (wood)
    303.9 ☑
    maternal, with suspected fetal damage
      affecting management of preg-
      nancy 655.4 ☑
  allobarbitone 304.1 ☑
  allonal 304.1 ☑
  allylisopropylacetylurea 304.1 ☑
  alphaprodine (hydrochloride) 304.0 ☑
  Alurate 304.1 ☑
  Alvodine 304.0 ☑
  amethocaine 304.6 ☑
  amidone 304.0 ☑
  amidopyrine 304.6 ☑
  aminopyrine 304.6 ☑
  amobarbital 304.1 ☑
  amphetamine(s) (type) (drugs classifiable
    to 969.7) 304.4 ☑
  amylene hydrate 304.6 ☑
  amylobarbitone 304.1 ☑
  amylocaine 304.6 ☑
  Amytal (sodium) 304.1 ☑
  analgesic (drug) NEC 304.6 ☑
    synthetic with morphine-like effect
      304.0 ☑
  anesthetic (agent) (drug) (gas) (general)
    (local) NEC 304.6 ☑
  Angel dust 304.6 ☑
  anileridine 304.0 ☑
  antipyrine 304.6 ☑
  anxiolytic 304.1 ☑
  aprobarbital 304.1 ☑
  aprobarbitone 304.1 ☑
  atropine 304.6 ☑
  Avertin (bromide) 304.6 ☑
  barbenyl 304.1 ☑
  barbital(s) 304.1 ☑
  barbitone 304.1 ☑
  barbiturate(s) (compounds) (drugs classifi-
    able to 967.0) 304.1 ☑
  barbituric acid (and compounds) 304.1 ☑
  benzedrine 304.4 ☑
  benzylmorphine 304.0 ☑
  Beta-chlor 304.1 ☑
  bhang 304.3 ☑
  blue velvet 304.0 ☑
  Brevital 304.1 ☑
  bromal (hydrate) 304.1 ☑
  bromide(s) NEC 304.1 ☑
  bromine compounds NEC 304.1 ☑
  bromisovalum 304.1 ☑
  bromoform 304.1 ☑
  Bromo-seltzer 304.1 ☑
  bromural 304.1 ☑
  butabarbital (sodium) 304.1 ☑
  butabarpal 304.1 ☑

Dependence — continued
  butallylonal 304.1 ☑
  butethal 304.1 ☑
  buthalitone (sodium) 304.1 ☑
  Butisol 304.1 ☑
  butobarbitone 304.1 ☑
  butyl chloral (hydrate) 304.1 ☑
  caffeine 304.4 ☑
  cannabis (indica) (sativa) (resin) (derivatives)
    (type) 304.3 ☑
  carbamazepine 304.6 ☑
  Carbrital 304.1 ☑
  carbromal 304.1 ☑
  carisoprodol 304.6 ☑
  Catha (edulis) 304.4 ☑
  chloral (betaine) (hydrate) 304.1 ☑
  chloralamide 304.1 ☑
  chloralformamide 304.1 ☑
  chloralose 304.1 ☑
  chlordiazepoxide 304.1 ☑
  Chloretone 304.1 ☑
  chlorobutanol 304.1 ☑
  chlorodyne 304.1 ☑
  chloroform 304.6 ☑
  Cliradon 304.0 ☑
  coca (leaf) and derivatives 304.2 ☑
  cocaine 304.2 ☑
    hydrochloride 304.2 ☑
    salt (any) 304.2 ☑
  codeine 304.0 ☑
  combination of drugs (excluding morphine
    or opioid type drug) NEC 304.8 ☑
    morphine or opioid type drug with any
      other drug 304.7 ☑
  croton-chloral 304.1 ☑
  cyclobarbital 304.1 ☑
  cyclobarbitone 304.1 ☑
  dagga 304.3 ☑
  Delvinal 304.1 ☑
  Demerol 304.0 ☑
  desocodeine 304.0 ☑
  desomorphine 304.0 ☑
  desoxyephedrine 304.4 ☑
  DET 304.5 ☑
  dexamphetamine 304.4 ☑
  dexedrine 304.4 ☑
  dextromethorphan 304.0 ☑
  dextromoramide 304.0 ☑
  dextronorpseudoephedrine 304.4 ☑
  dextrorphan 304.0 ☑
  diacetylmorphine 304.0 ☑
  Dial 304.1 ☑
  diallylbarbituric acid 304.1 ☑
  diamorphine 304.0 ☑
  diazepam 304.1 ☑
  dibucaine 304.6 ☑
  dichloroethane 304.6 ☑
  diethyl barbituric acid 304.1 ☑
  diethylsulfone-diethylmethane 304.1 ☑
  difencloxazine 304.0 ☑
  dihydrocodeine 304.0 ☑
  dihydrocodeinone 304.0 ☑
  dihydrohydroxycodeinone 304.0 ☑
  dihydroisocodeine 304.0 ☑
  dihydromorphine 304.0 ☑
  dihydromorphinone 304.0 ☑
  dihydroxcodeinone 304.0 ☑
  Dilaudid 304.0 ☑
  dimenhydrinate 304.6 ☑
  dimethylmeperidine 304.0 ☑
  dimethyltriptamine 304.5 ☑
  Dionin 304.0 ☑
  diphenoxylate 304.6 ☑
  dipipanone 304.0 ☑
  d-lysergic acid diethylamide 304.5 ☑
  DMT 304.5 ☑
  Dolophine 304.0 ☑
  DOM 304.2 ☑
  Doriden 304.1 ☑
  dormiral 304.1 ☑
  Dormison 304.1 ☑
  Dromoran 304.0 ☑
  drug NEC 304.9 ☑

Dependence — continued
  drug — continued
    analgesic NEC 304.6 ☑
    combination (excluding morphine or
      opioid type drug) NEC 304.8 ☑
      morphine or opioid type drug with
        any other drug 304.7 ☑
    complicating pregnancy, childbirth, or
      puerperium 648.3 ☑
      affecting fetus or newborn 779.5
    hallucinogenic 304.5 ☑
    hypnotic NEC 304.1 ☑
    narcotic NEC 304.9 ☑
    psychostimulant NEC 304.4 ☑
    sedative 304.1 ☑
    soporific NEC 304.1 ☑
    specified type NEC 304.6 ☑
    suspected damage to fetus affecting
      management of pregnancy
      655.5 ☑
    synthetic, with morphine-like effect
      304.0 ☑
    tranquilizing 304.1 ☑
  duboisine 304.6 ☑
  ectylurea 304.1 ☑
  Endocaine 304.6 ☑
  Equanil 304.1 ☑
  Eskabarb 304.1 ☑
  ethchlorvynol 304.1 ☑
  ether (ethyl) (liquid) (vapor) (vinyl) 304.6 ☑
  ethidene 304.6 ☑
  ethinamate 304.1 ☑
  ethoheptazine 304.6 ☑
  ethyl
    alcohol 303.9 ☑
    bromide 304.6 ☑
    carbamate 304.6 ☑
    chloride 304.6 ☑
    morphine 304.0 ☑
  ethylene (gas) 304.6 ☑
    dichloride 304.6 ☑
  ethylidene chloride 304.6 ☑
  etilfen 304.1 ☑
  etorphine 304.0 ☑
  etoval 304.1 ☑
  eucodal 304.0 ☑
  euneryl 304.1 ☑
  Evipal 304.1 ☑
  Evipan 304.1 ☑
  fentanyl 304.0 ☑
  ganja 304.3 ☑
  gardenal 304.1 ☑
  gardenpanyl 304.1 ☑
  gelsemine 304.6 ☑
  Gelsemium 304.6 ☑
  Gemonil 304.1 ☑
  glucochloral 304.1 ☑
  glue (airplane) (sniffing) 304.6 ☑
  glutethimide 304.1 ☑
  hallucinogenics 304.5 ☑
  hashish 304.3 ☑
  headache powder NEC 304.6 ☑
  Heavenly Blue 304.5 ☑
  hedonal 304.1 ☑
  hemp 304.3 ☑
  heptabarbital 304.1 ☑
  Heptalgin 304.0 ☑
  heptobarbitone 304.1 ☑
  heroin 304.0 ☑
    salt (any) 304.0 ☑
  hexethal (sodium) 304.1 ☑
  hexobarbital 304.1 ☑
  Hycodan 304.0 ☑
  hydrocodone 304.0 ☑
  hydromorphinol 304.0 ☑
  hydromorphinone 304.0 ☑
  hydromorphone 304.0 ☑
  hydroxycodeine 304.0 ☑
  hypnotic NEC 304.1 ☑
  Indian hemp 304.3 ☑
  inhalant 304.6 ☑
  intranarcon 304.1 ☑
  Kemithal 304.1 ☑

☑ Additional Digit Required — Refer to the Tabular List for Digit Selection

⑆ Subterms under main terms may continue to next column or page

Dependence — *continued*
- ketobemidone 304.0 ☑
- khat 304.4 ☑
- kif 304.3 ☑
- Lactuca (virosa) extract 304.1 ☑
- lactucarium 304.1 ☑
- laudanum 304.0 ☑
- Lebanese red 304.3 ☑
- Leritine 304.0 ☑
- lettuce opium 304.1 ☑
- Levanil 304.1 ☑
- Levo-Dromoran 304.0 ☑
- levo-iso-methadone 304.0 ☑
- levorphanol 304.0 ☑
- Librium 304.1 ☑
- Lomotil 304.6 ☑
- Lotusate 304.1 ☑
- LSD (-25) (and derivatives) 304.5 ☑
- Luminal 304.1 ☑
- lysergic acid 304.5 ☑
  - amide 304.5 ☑
- maconha 304.3 ☑
- magic mushroom 304.5 ☑
- marihuana 304.3 ☑
- MDA (methylene dioxyamphetamine) 304.4 ☑
- Mebaral 304.1 ☑
- Medinal 304.1 ☑
- Medomin 304.1 ☑
- megahallucinogenics 304.5 ☑
- meperidine 304.0 ☑
- mephobarbital 304.1 ☑
- meprobamate 304.1 ☑
- mescaline 304.5 ☑
- methadone 304.0 ☑
- methamphetamine(s) 304.4 ☑
- methaqualone 304.1 ☑
- metharbital 304.1 ☑
- methitural 304.1 ☑
- methobarbitone 304.1 ☑
- methohexital 304.1 ☑
- methopholine 304.6 ☑
- methyl
  - alcohol 303.9 ☑
  - bromide 304.6 ☑
  - morphine 304.0 ☑
  - sulfonal 304.1 ☑
- methylaparafynol 304.1 ☑
- methylated spirit 303.9 ☑
- methylbutinol 304.6 ☑
- methyldihydromorphinone 304.0 ☑
- methylene
  - chloride 304.6 ☑
  - dichloride 304.6 ☑
  - dioxyamphetamine (MDA) 304.4 ☑
- methylphenidate 304.4 ☑
- methyprylone 304.1 ☑
- metopon 304.0 ☑
- Miltown 304.1 ☑
- morning glory seeds 304.5 ☑
- morphinan(s) 304.0 ☑
- morphine (sulfate) (sulfite) (type) (drugs classifiable to 965.00–965.09) 304.0 ☑
- morphine or opioid type drug (drugs classifiable to 965.00–965.09) with any other drug 304.7 ☑
- morphinol(s) 304.0 ☑
- morphinon 304.0 ☑
- morpholinylethylmorphine 304.0 ☑
- mylomide 304.1 ☑
- myristicin 304.5 ☑
- narcotic (drug) NEC 304.9 ☑
- nealbarbital 304.1 ☑
- nealbarbitone 304.1 ☑
- Nembutal 304.1 ☑
- Neonal 304.1 ☑
- Neraval 304.1 ☑
- Neravan 304.1 ☑
- neurobarb 304.1 ☑
- nicotine 305.1
- Nisentil 304.0 ☑
- nitrous oxide 304.6 ☑

Dependence — *continued*
- Noctec 304.1 ☑
- Noludar 304.1 ☑
- nonbarbiturate sedatives and tranquilizers with similar effect 304.1 ☑
- noptil 304.1 ☑
- normorphine 304.0 ☑
- noscapine 304.0 ☑
- Novocaine 304.6 ☑
- Numorphan 304.0 ☑
- nunol 304.1 ☑
- Nupercaine 304.6 ☑
- Oblivon 304.1 ☑
- on
  - aspirator V46.0
  - hemodialysis V45.11
  - hyperbaric chamber V46.8
  - iron lung V46.11
  - machine (enabling) V46.9
    - specified type NEC V46.8
  - peritoneal dialysis V45.11
  - Possum (Patient-Operated-Selector-Mechanism) V46.8
  - renal dialysis machine V45.11
  - respirator [ventilator] V46.11
    - encounter
      - during
        - mechanical failure V46.14
        - power failure V46.12
      - for weaning V46.13
  - supplemental oxygen V46.2
  - wheelchair V46.3
- opiate 304.0 ☑
- opioids 304.0 ☑
- opioid type drug 304.0 ☑
  - with any other drug 304.7 ☑
- opium (alkaloids) (derivatives) (tincture) 304.0 ☑
- ortal 304.1 ☑
- Oxazepam 304.1 ☑
- oxycodone 304.0 ☑
- oxymorphone 304.0 ☑
- Palfium 304.0 ☑
- Panadol 304.6 ☑
- pantopium 304.0 ☑
- pantopon 304.0 ☑
- papaverine 304.0 ☑
- paracetamol 304.6 ☑
- paracodin 304.0 ☑
- paraldehyde 304.1 ☑
- paregoric 304.0 ☑
- Parzone 304.0 ☑
- PCP (phencyclidine) 304.6 ☑
- Pearly Gates 304.5 ☑
- pentazocine 304.0 ☑
- pentobarbital 304.1 ☑
- pentobarbitone (sodium) 304.1 ☑
- Pentothal 304.1 ☑
- Percaine 304.6 ☑
- Percodan 304.0 ☑
- Perichlor 304.1 ☑
- Pernocton 304.1 ☑
- Pernoston 304.1 ☑
- peronine 304.0 ☑
- pethidine (hydrochloride) 304.0 ☑
- petrichloral 304.1 ☑
- peyote 304.5 ☑
- Phanodron 304.1 ☑
- phenacetin 304.6 ☑
- phenadoxone 304.0 ☑
- phenaglycodol 304.1 ☑
- phenazocine 304.0 ☑
- phencyclidine 304.6 ☑
- phenmetrazine 304.4 ☑
- phenobal 304.1 ☑
- phenobarbital 304.1 ☑
- phenobarbitone 304.1 ☑
- phenomorphan 304.0 ☑
- phenonyl 304.1 ☑
- phenoperidine 304.0 ☑
- pholcodine 304.0 ☑
- piminodine 304.0 ☑
- Pipadone 304.0 ☑
- Pitkin's solution 304.6 ☑

Dependence — *continued*
- Placidyl 304.1 ☑
- polysubstance 304.8 ☑
- Pontocaine 304.6 ☑
- pot 304.3 ☑
- potassium bromide 304.1 ☑
- Preludin 304.4 ☑
- Prinadol 304.0 ☑
- probarbital 304.1 ☑
- procaine 304.6 ☑
- propanal 304.1 ☑
- propoxyphene 304.6 ☑
- psilocibin 304.5 ☑
- psilocin 304.5 ☑
- psilocybin 304.5 ☑
- psilocyline 304.5 ☑
- psilocyn 304.5 ☑
- psychedelic agents 304.5 ☑
- psychostimulant NEC 304.4 ☑
- psychotomimetic agents 304.5 ☑
- pyrahexyl 304.3 ☑
- Pyramidon 304.6 ☑
- quinalbarbitone 304.1 ☑
- racemoramide 304.0 ☑
- racemorphan 304.0 ☑
- Rela 304.6 ☑
- scopolamine 304.6 ☑
- secobarbital 304.1 ☑
- Seconal 304.1 ☑
- sedative NEC 304.1 ☑
  - nonbarbiturate with barbiturate effect 304.1 ☑
- Sedormid 304.1 ☑
- sernyl 304.1 ☑
- sodium bromide 304.1 ☑
- Soma 304.6 ☑
- Somnal 304.1 ☑
- Somnos 304.1 ☑
- Soneryl 304.1 ☑
- soporific (drug) NEC 304.1 ☑
  - specified drug NEC 304.6 ☑
- speed 304.4 ☑
- spinocaine 304.6 ☑
- Stovaine 304.6 ☑
- STP 304.5 ☑
- stramonium 304.6 ☑
- Sulfonal 304.1 ☑
- sulfonethylmethane 304.1 ☑
- sulfonmethane 304.1 ☑
- Surital 304.1 ☑
- synthetic drug with morphine-like effect 304.0 ☑
- talbutal 304.1 ☑
- tetracaine 304.6 ☑
- tetrahydrocannabinol 304.3 ☑
- tetronal 304.1 ☑
- THC 304.3 ☑
- thebacon 304.0 ☑
- thebaine 304.0 ☑
- thiamil 304.1 ☑
- thiamylal 304.1 ☑
- thiopental 304.1 ☑
- tobacco 305.1
- toluene, toluol 304.6 ☑
- tranquilizer NEC 304.1 ☑
  - nonbarbiturate with barbiturate effect 304.1 ☑
- tribromacetaldehyde 304.6 ☑
- tribromethanol 304.6 ☑
- tribromomethane 304.6 ☑
- trichloroethanol 304.6 ☑
- trichoroethyl phosphate 304.1 ☑
- triclofos 304.1 ☑
- Trional 304.1 ☑
- Tuinal 304.1 ☑
- Turkish Green 304.3 ☑
- urethan(e) 304.6 ☑
- Valium 304.1 ☑
- Valmid 304.1 ☑
- veganin 304.0 ☑
- veramon 304.1 ☑
- Veronal 304.1 ☑
- versidyne 304.6 ☑

Dependence — *continued*
- vinbarbital 304.1 ☑
- vinbarbitone 304.1 ☑
- vinyl bitone 304.1 ☑
- vitamin B$_6$ 266.1
- wine 303.9 ☑
- Zactane 304.6 ☑

Dependency
- passive 301.6
- reactions 301.6

Depersonalization (episode, in neurotic state) (neurotic) (syndrome) 300.6

Depletion
- carbohydrates 271.9
- complement factor 279.8
- extracellular fluid 276.52
- plasma 276.52
- potassium 276.8
  - nephropathy 588.89
- salt or sodium 276.1
  - causing heat exhaustion or prostration 992.4
  - nephropathy 593.9
- volume 276.50
  - extracellular fluid 276.52
  - plasma 276.52

Deployment (military)
- personal history of V62.22
- returned from V62.22
- status V62.21

Deposit
- argentous, cornea 371.16
- bone, in Boeck's sarcoid 135
- calcareous, calcium — *see* Calcification
- cholesterol
  - retina 362.82
  - skin 709.3
  - vitreous (humor) 379.22
- conjunctival 372.56
- cornea, corneal NEC 371.10
  - argentous 371.16
  - in
    - cystinosis 270.0 [371.15]
    - mucopolysaccharidosis 277.5 [371.15]
- crystalline, vitreous (humor) 379.22
- hemosiderin, in old scars of cornea 371.11
- metallic, in lens 366.45
- skin 709.3
- teeth, tooth (betel) (black) (green) (materia alba) (orange) (soft) (tobacco) 523.6
- urate, in kidney (*see also* Disease, renal) 593.9

Depraved appetite 307.52

Depression 311
- acute (*see also* Psychosis, affective) 296.2 ☑
  - recurrent episode 296.3 ☑
  - single episode 296.2 ☑
- agitated (*see also* Psychosis, affective) 296.2 ☑
  - recurrent episode 296.3 ☑
  - single episode 296.2 ☑
- anaclitic 309.21
- anxiety 300.4
- arches 734
  - congenital 754.61
- autogenous (*see also* Psychosis, affective) 296.2 ☑
  - recurrent episode 296.3 ☑
  - single episode 296.2 ☑
- basal metabolic rate (BMR) 794.7
- bone marrow 289.9
- central nervous system 799.1
  - newborn 779.2
- cerebral 331.9
  - newborn 779.2
- cerebrovascular 437.8
  - newborn 779.2
- chest wall 738.3
- endogenous (*see also* Psychosis, affective) 296.2 ☑
  - recurrent episode 296.3 ☑
  - single episode 296.2 ☑
- functional activity 780.99
- hysterical 300.11

☑ Additional Digit Required — Refer to the Tabular List for Digit Selection   ▽ Subterms under main terms may continue to next column or page

2015 ICD-9-CM   ►◄ Revised Text   ● New Line   ▲ Revised Code   Volume 2 — 75

Depression — continued

involutional, climacteric, or menopausal (see also Psychosis, affective) 296.2 ☑
  recurrent episode 296.3 ☑
  single episode 296.2 ☑
major 296.2 ☑
  recurrent episode 296.3 ☑
  single episode 296.2 ☑
manic (see also Psychosis, affective) 296.80
medullary 348.89
  newborn 779.2
mental 300.4
metatarsal heads — see Depression, arches
metatarsus — see Depression, arches
monopolar (see also Psychosis, affective) 296.2 ☑
  recurrent episode 296.3 ☑
  single episode 296.2 ☑
nervous 300.4
neurotic 300.4
nose 738.0
postpartum 648.4 ☑
psychogenic 300.4
  reactive 298.0
psychoneurotic 300.4
psychotic (see also Psychosis, affective) 296.2 ☑
  reactive 298.0
  recurrent episode 296.3 ☑
  single episode 296.2 ☑
reactive 300.4
  neurotic 300.4
  psychogenic 298.0
  psychoneurotic 300.4
  psychotic 298.0
recurrent 296.3 ☑
respiratory center 348.89
  newborn 770.89
scapula 736.89
senile 290.21
situational (acute) (brief) 309.0
  prolonged 309.1
skull 754.0
sternum 738.3
visual field 368.40

Depressive reaction — see also Reaction, depressive

acute (transient) 309.0
  with anxiety 309.28
prolonged 309.1
situational (acute) 309.0
  prolonged 309.1

Deprivation

cultural V62.4
emotional V62.89
  affecting
    adult 995.82
    infant or child 995.51
food 994.2
  specific substance NEC 269.8
protein (familial) (kwashiorkor) 260
sleep V69.4
social V62.4
  affecting
    adult 995.82
    infant or child 995.51
symptoms, syndrome
  alcohol 291.81
  drug 292.0
vitamins (see also Deficiency, vitamin) 269.2
water 994.3

de Quervain's

disease (tendon sheath) 727.04
syndrome 259.51
thyroiditis (subacute granulomatous thyroiditis) 245.1

Derangement

ankle (internal) 718.97
  current injury (see also Dislocation, ankle) 837.0
  recurrent 718.37
cartilage (articular) NEC (see also Disorder, cartilage, articular) 718.0 ☑
  knee 717.9
    recurrent 718.36
  recurrent 718.3 ☑

Derangement — continued

collateral ligament (knee) (medial) (tibial) 717.82
  current injury 844.1
    lateral (fibular) 844.0
  lateral (fibular) 717.81
    current injury 844.0
cruciate ligament (knee) (posterior) 717.84
  anterior 717.83
    current injury 844.2
  current injury 844.2
elbow (internal) 718.92
  current injury (see also Dislocation, elbow) 832.00
  recurrent 718.32
gastrointestinal 536.9
heart — see Disease, heart
hip (joint) (internal) (old) 718.95
  current injury (see also Dislocation, hip) 835.00
  recurrent 718.35
intervertebral disc — see Displacement, intervertebral disc
joint (internal) 718.90
  ankle 718.97
  current injury (see also Dislocation, by site)
    knee, meniscus or cartilage (see also Tear, meniscus) 836.2
  elbow 718.92
  foot 718.97
  hand 718.94
  hip 718.95
  knee 717.9
  multiple sites 718.99
  pelvic region 718.95
  recurrent 718.30
    ankle 718.37
    elbow 718.32
    foot 718.37
    hand 718.34
    hip 718.35
    knee 718.36
    multiple sites 718.39
    pelvic region 718.35
    shoulder (region) 718.31
    specified site NEC 718.38
    temporomandibular (old) 524.69
    wrist 718.33
  shoulder (region) 718.91
  specified site NEC 718.98
  spine NEC 724.9
  temporomandibular 524.69
  wrist 718.93
knee (cartilage) (internal) 717.9
  current injury (see also Tear, meniscus) 836.2
  ligament 717.89
    capsular 717.85
    collateral — see Derangement, collateral ligament
    cruciate — see Derangement, cruciate ligament
    specified NEC 717.85
    recurrent 718.36
  low back NEC 724.9
  meniscus NEC (knee) 717.5
    current injury (see also Tear, meniscus) 836.2
    lateral 717.40
      anterior horn 717.42
      posterior horn 717.43
      specified NEC 717.49
    medial 717.3
      anterior horn 717.1
      posterior horn 717.2
    recurrent 718.3 ☑
    site other than knee — see Disorder, cartilage, articular
  mental (see also Psychosis) 298.9
  rotator cuff (recurrent) (tear) 726.10
    current 840.4
  sacroiliac (old) 724.6
    current — see Dislocation, sacroiliac
  semilunar cartilage (knee) 717.5
    current injury 836.2

Derangement — continued

semilunar cartilage — continued
  current injury — continued
    lateral 836.1
    medial 836.0
  recurrent 718.3 ☑
shoulder (internal) 718.91
  current injury (see also Dislocation, shoulder) 831.00
  recurrent 718.31
spine (recurrent) NEC 724.9
  current — see Dislocation, spine
temporomandibular (internal) (joint) (old) 524.69
  current — see Dislocation, jaw

Dercum's disease or syndrome (adiposis dolorosa) 272.8

Derealization (neurotic) 300.6

Dermal — see condition

Dermaphytid — see Dermatophytosis

Dermatergosis — see Dermatitis

Dermatitis (allergic) (contact) (occupational) (venenata) 692.9
ab igne 692.82
acneiform 692.9
actinic (due to sun) 692.70
  acute 692.72
  chronic NEC 692.74
  other than from sun NEC 692.82
ambustionis
  due to
    burn or scald — see Burn, by site
    sunburn (see also Sunburn) 692.71
amebic 006.6
ammonia 691.0
anaphylactoid NEC 692.9
arsenical 692.4
artefacta 698.4
  psychogenic 316 [698.4]
asthmatic 691.8
atopic (allergic) (intrinsic) 691.8
  psychogenic 316 [691.8]
atrophicans 701.8
  diffusa 701.8
  maculosa 701.3
autoimmune progesterone 279.49
berlock, berloque 692.72
blastomycetic 116.0
blister beetle 692.89
Brucella NEC 023.9
bullosa 694.9
  striata pratensis 692.6
bullous 694.9
  mucosynechial, atrophic 694.60
    with ocular involvement 694.61
  seasonal 694.8
calorica
  due to
    burn or scald — see Burn, by site
    cold 692.89
    sunburn (see also Sunburn) 692.71
caterpillar 692.89
cercarial 120.3
combustionis
  due to
    burn or scald — see Burn, by site
    sunburn (see also Sunburn) 692.71
congelationis 991.5
contusiformis 695.2
diabetic 250.8 ☑
diaper 691.0
diphtheritica 032.85
due to
  acetone 692.2
  acids 692.4
  adhesive plaster 692.4
  alcohol (skin contact) (substances classifiable to 980.0–980.9) 692.4
    taken internally 693.8
  alkalis 692.4
  allergy NEC 692.9
  ammonia (household) (liquid) 692.4
  animal
    dander (cat) (dog) 692.84
    hair (cat) (dog) 692.84
  arnica 692.3

Dermatitis — continued

due to — continued
  arsenic 692.4
    taken internally 693.8
  blister beetle 692.89
  cantharides 692.3
  carbon disulphide 692.2
  caterpillar 692.89
  caustics 692.4
  cereal (ingested) 693.1
    contact with skin 692.5
  chemical(s) NEC 692.4
    internal 693.8
    irritant NEC 692.4
    taken internally 693.8
  chlorocompounds 692.2
  coffee (ingested) 693.1
    contact with skin 692.5
  cold weather 692.89
  cosmetics 692.81
  cyclohexanes 692.2
  dander, animal (cat) (dog) 692.84
  deodorant 692.81
  detergents 692.0
  dichromate 692.4
  drugs and medicinals (correct substance properly administered) (internal use) 693.0
    external (in contact with skin) 692.3
    wrong substance given or taken 976.6
      specified substance — see Table of Drugs and Chemicals
    wrong substance given or taken 977.9
      specified substance — see Table of Drugs and Chemicals
  dyes 692.89
    hair 692.89
  epidermophytosis — see Dermatophytosis
  esters 692.2
  external irritant NEC 692.9
    specified agent NEC 692.89
  eye shadow 692.81
  fish (ingested) 693.1
    contact with skin 692.5
  flour (ingested) 693.1
    contact with skin 692.5
  food (ingested) 693.1
    in contact with skin 692.5
  fruit (ingested) 693.1
    contact with skin 692.5
  fungicides 692.3
  furs 692.84
  glycols 692.2
  greases NEC 692.1
  hair, animal (cat) (dog) 692.84
  hair dyes 692.89
  hot
    objects and materials — see Burn, by site
    weather or places 692.89
  hydrocarbons 692.2
  infrared rays, except from sun 692.82
    solar NEC (see also Dermatitis, due to, sun) 692.70
  ingested substance 693.9
    drugs and medicinals (see also Dermatitis, due to, drugs and medicinals) 693.0
    food 693.1
    specified substance NEC 693.8
  ingestion or injection of chemical 693.8
    drug (correct substance properly administered) 693.0
    wrong substance given or taken 977.9
      specified substance — see Table of Drugs and Chemicals
  insecticides 692.4
  internal agent 693.9
    drugs and medicinals (see also Dermatitis, due to, drugs and medicinals) 693.0

☑ Additional Digit Required — Refer to the Tabular List for Digit Selection
▽ Subterms under main terms may continue to next column or page

76 — Volume 2
▶◀ Revised Text   ● New Line   ▲ Revised Code
2015 ICD-9-CM

Dermatitis — continued
due to — continued
  internal agent — continued
    food (ingested) 693.1
      in contact with skin 692.5
      specified agent NEC 693.8
  iodine 692.3
  iodoform 692.3
  irradiation 692.82
  jewelry 692.83
  keratolytics 692.3
  ketones 692.2
  lacquer tree (Rhus verniciflua) 692.6
  light (sun) NEC (see also Dermatitis, due to, sun) 692.70
    other 692.82
  low temperature 692.89
  mascara 692.81
  meat (ingested) 693.1
    contact with skin 692.5
  mercury, mercurials 692.3
  metals 692.83
  milk (ingested) 693.1
    contact with skin 692.5
  Neomycin 692.3
  nylon 692.4
  oils NEC 692.1
  paint solvent 692.2
  pediculocides 692.3
  petroleum products (substances classifiable to 981) 692.4
  phenol 692.3
  photosensitiveness, photosensitivity (sun) 692.72
    other light 692.82
  plants NEC 692.6
  plasters, medicated (any) 692.3
  plastic 692.4
  poison
    ivy (Rhus toxicodendron) 692.6
    oak (Rhus diversiloba) 692.6
    plant or vine 692.6
    sumac (Rhus venenata) 692.6
    vine (Rhus radicans) 692.6
  preservatives 692.89
  primrose (primula) 692.6
  primula 692.6
  radiation 692.82
    sun NEC (see also Dermatitis, due to, sun) 692.70
    tanning bed 692.82
  radioactive substance 692.82
  radium 692.82
  ragweed (Senecio jacobae) 692.6
  Rhus (diversiloba) (radicans) (toxicodendron) (venenata) (verniciflua) 692.6
  rubber 692.4
  scabicides 692.3
  Senecio jacobae 692.6
  solar radiation — see Dermatitis, due to, sun
  solvents (any) (substances classifiable to 982.0–982.8) 692.2
    chlorocompound group 692.2
    cyclohexane group 692.2
    ester group 692.2
    glycol group 692.2
    hydrocarbon group 692.2
    ketone group 692.2
    paint 692.2
  specified agent NEC 692.89
  sun 692.70
    acute 692.72
    chronic NEC 692.74
    specified NEC 692.79
  sunburn (see also Sunburn) 692.71
  sunshine NEC (see also Dermatitis, due to, sun) 692.70
  tanning bed 692.82
  tetrachlorethylene 692.2
  toluene 692.2
  topical medications 692.3
  turpentine 692.2
  ultraviolet rays, except from sun 692.82

Dermatitis — continued
due to — continued
  ultraviolet rays, except from sun — continued
    sun NEC (see also Dermatitis, due to, sun) 692.70
  vaccine or vaccination (correct substance properly administered) 693.0
    wrong substance given or taken
      bacterial vaccine 978.8
        specified — see Table of Drugs and Chemicals
      other vaccines NEC 979.9
        specified — see Table of Drugs and Chemicals
  varicose veins (see also Varicose, vein, inflamed or infected) 454.1
  x-rays 692.82
dyshydrotic 705.81
dysmenorrheica 625.8
eczematoid NEC 692.9
  infectious 690.8
eczematous NEC 692.9
epidemica 695.89
erysipelatosa 695.81
escharotica — see Burn, by site
exfoliativa, exfoliative 695.89
  generalized 695.89
  infantum 695.81
  neonatorum 695.81
eyelid 373.31
  allergic 373.32
  contact 373.32
  eczematous 373.31
  herpes (zoster) 053.20
    simplex 054.41
  infective 373.5
    due to
      actinomycosis 039.3 [373.5]
      herpes
        simplex 054.41
        zoster 053.20
      impetigo 684 [373.5]
      leprosy (see also Leprosy) 030.0 [373.4]
      lupus vulgaris (tuberculous) (see also Tuberculosis) 017.0 ☑ [373.4]
      mycotic dermatitis (see also Dermatomycosis) 111.9 [373.5]
      vaccinia 051.02 [373.5]
        postvaccination 999.0 [373.5]
      yaws (see also Yaws) 102.9 [373.4]
facta, factitia 698.4
  psychogenic 316 [698.4]
ficta 698.4
  psychogenic 316 [698.4]
flexural 691.8
follicularis 704.8
friction 709.8
fungus 111.9
  specified type NEC 111.8
gangrenosa, gangrenous (infantum) (see also Gangrene) 785.4
gestationis 646.8 ☑
gonococcal 098.89
gouty 274.89
harvest mite 133.8
heat 692.89
herpetiformis (bullous) (erythematous) (pustular) (vesicular) 694.0
  juvenile 694.2
  senile 694.5
hiemalis 692.89
hypostatic, hypostatica 454.1
  with ulcer 454.2
impetiginous 684
infantile (acute) (chronic) (intertriginous) (intrinsic) (seborrheic) 690.12
infectiosa eczematoides 690.8
infectious (staphylococcal) (streptococcal) 686.9
  eczematoid 690.8
infective eczematoid 690.8
Jacquet's (diaper dermatitis) 691.0

Dermatitis — continued
leptus 133.8
lichenified NEC 692.9
lichenoid, chronic 701.0
lichenoides purpurica pigmentosa 709.1
meadow 692.6
medicamentosa (correct substance properly administered) (internal use) (see also Dermatitis, due to, drugs or medicinals) 693.0
  due to contact with skin 692.3
mite 133.8
multiformis 694.0
  juvenile 694.2
  senile 694.5
napkin 691.0
neuro 698.3
neurotica 694.0
nummular NEC 692.9
osteatosis, osteatotic 706.8
papillaris capillitii 706.1
pellagrous 265.2
perioral 695.3
perstans 696.1
photosensitivity (sun) 692.72
  other light 692.82
pigmented purpuric lichenoid 709.1
polymorpha dolorosa 694.0
primary irritant 692.9
pruriginosa 694.0
pruritic NEC 692.9
psoriasiform nodularis 696.2
psychogenic 316
purulent 686.00
pustular contagious 051.2
pyococcal 686.00
pyocyaneus 686.09
pyogenica 686.00
radiation 692.82
repens 696.1
Ritter's (exfoliativa) 695.81
Schamberg's (progressive pigmentary dermatosis) 709.09
schistosome 120.3
seasonal bullous 694.8
seborrheic 690.10
  infantile 690.12
sensitization NEC 692.9
septic (see also Septicemia) 686.00
  gonococcal 098.89
solar, solare NEC (see also Dermatitis, due to, sun) 692.70
stasis 454.1
  due to
    postphlebitic syndrome 459.12
      with ulcer 459.13
    varicose veins — see Varicose
  ulcerated or with ulcer (varicose) 454.2
sunburn (see also Sunburn) 692.71
suppurative 686.00
traumatic NEC 709.8
trophoneurotica 694.0
ultraviolet, except from sun 692.82
  due to sun NEC (see also Dermatitis, due to, sun) 692.82
varicose 454.1
  with ulcer 454.2
vegetans 686.8
verrucosa 117.2
xerotic 706.8
Dermatoarthritis, lipoid 272.8 [713.0]
Dermatochalasia, dermatochalasis 374.87
Dermatofibroma (lenticulare) (M8832/0) — see also Neoplasm, skin, benign
  protuberans (M8832/1) — see Neoplasm, skin, uncertain behavior
Dermatofibrosarcoma (protuberans) (M8832/3) — see Neoplasm, skin, malignant
Dermatographia 708.3
Dermatolysis (congenital) (exfoliativa) 757.39
  acquired 701.8
  eyelids 374.34
  palpebrarum 374.34
  senile 701.8
Dermatomegaly NEC 701.8

Dermatomucomyositis 710.3
Dermatomycosis 111.9
  furfuracea 111.0
  specified type NEC 111.8
Dermatomyositis (acute) (chronic) 710.3
Dermatoneuritis of children 985.0
Dermatophiliasis 134.1
Dermatophytide — see Dermatophytosis
Dermatophytosis (Epidermophyton) (infection) (microsporum) (tinea) (Trichophyton) 110.9
  beard 110.0
  body 110.5
  deep seated 110.6
  fingernails 110.1
  foot 110.4
  groin 110.3
  hand 110.2
  nail 110.1
  perianal (area) 110.3
  scalp 110.0
  scrotal 110.8
  specified site NEC 110.8
  toenails 110.1
  vulva 110.8
Dermatopolyneuritis 985.0
Dermatorrhexis 756.83
  acquired 701.8
Dermatosclerosis — see also Scleroderma 710.1
  localized 701.0
Dermatosis 709.9
  Andrews' 686.8
  atopic 691.8
  Bowen's (M8081/2) — see Neoplasm, skin, in situ
  bullous 694.9
    specified type NEC 694.8
  erythematosquamous 690.8
  exfoliativa 695.89
  factitial 698.4
  gonococcal 098.89
  herpetiformis 694.0
    juvenile 694.2
    senile 694.5
  hysterical 300.11
  linear IgA 694.8
  menstrual NEC 709.8
  neutrophilic, acute febrile 695.89
  occupational (see also Dermatitis) 692.9
  papulosa nigra 709.8
  pigmentary NEC 709.00
    progressive 709.09
    Schamberg's 709.09
    Siemens-Bloch 757.33
  progressive pigmentary 709.09
  psychogenic 316
  pustular subcorneal 694.1
  Schamberg's (progressive pigmentary) 709.09
  senile NEC 709.3
  specified NEC 702.8
  Unna's (seborrheic dermatitis) 690.10
Dermographia 708.3
Dermographism 708.3
Dermoid (cyst) (M9084/0) — see also Neoplasm, by site, benign
  with malignant transformation (M9084/3) 183.0
Dermopathy
  infiltrative, with thyrotoxicosis 242.0 ☑
  nephrogenic fibrosing 701.8
  senile NEC 709.3
Dermophytosis — see Dermatophytosis
Descemet's membrane — see condition
Descemetocele 371.72
Descending — see condition
Descensus uteri (complete) (incomplete) (partial) (without vaginal wall prolapse) 618.1
  with mention of vaginal wall prolapse — see Prolapse, uterovaginal
Desensitization to allergens V07.1
Desert
  rheumatism 114.0
  sore (see also Ulcer, skin) 707.9

☑ Additional Digit Required — Refer to the Tabular List for Digit Selection   ▽ Subterms under main terms may continue to next column or page

2015 ICD-9-CM   ▶◀ Revised Text   ● New Line   ▲ Revised Code   Volume 2 — 77

Desertion (child) (newborn) 995.52
  adult 995.84
Desmoid (extra-abdominal) (tumor) (M8821/1)
    — *see also* Neoplasm, connective tissue,
    uncertain behavior
  abdominal (M8822/1) — *see* Neoplasm,
    connective tissue, uncertain behavior
Despondency 300.4
Desquamative dermatitis NEC 695.89
Destruction
  articular facet (*see also* Derangement, joint)
    718.9 ☑
    vertebra 724.9
  bone 733.90
    syphilitic 095.5
  joint (*see also* Derangement, joint) 718.9 ☑
    sacroiliac 724.6
  kidney 593.89
  live fetus to facilitate birth NEC 763.89
  ossicles (ear) 385.24
  rectal sphincter 569.49
  septum (nasal) 478.19
  tuberculous NEC (*see also* Tuberculosis)
    011.9 ☑
  tympanic membrane 384.82
  tympanum 385.89
  vertebral disc — *see* Degeneration, interver-
    tebral disc
Destructiveness — *see also* Disturbance, con-
    duct 312.9
  adjustment reaction 309.3
Detachment
  cartilage (*see also* Sprain, by site)
    knee — *see* Tear, meniscus
  cervix, annular 622.8
    complicating delivery 665.3 ☑
  choroid (old) (postinfectional) (simple)
    (spontaneous) 363.70
    hemorrhagic 363.72
    serous 363.71
  knee, medial meniscus (old) 717.3
    current injury 836.0
  ligament — *see* Sprain, by site
  placenta (premature) — *see* Placenta, sepa-
    ration
  retina (recent) 361.9
    with retinal defect (rhegmatogenous)
      361.00
      giant tear 361.03
      multiple 361.02
      partial
        with
          giant tear 361.03
          multiple defects 361.02
          retinal dialysis (juvenile)
            361.04
          single defect 361.01
        retinal dialysis (juvenile) 361.04
        single 361.01
        subtotal 361.05
        total 361.05
    delimited (old) (partial) 361.06
    old
      delimited 361.06
      partial 361.06
      total or subtotal 361.07
    pigment epithelium (RPE) (serous)
      362.42
      exudative 362.42
      hemorrhagic 362.43
    rhegmatogenous (*see also* Detachment,
      retina, with retinal defect) 361.00
    serous (without retinal defect) 361.2
    specified type NEC 361.89
    traction (with vitreoretinal organization)
      361.81
  vitreous humor 379.21
Detergent asthma 507.8
Deterioration
  epileptic
    with behavioral disturbance
      345.9 ☑ [294.11]
    without behavioral disturbance
      345.9 ☑ [294.10]
  heart, cardiac (*see also* Degeneration, my-
    ocardial) 429.1

Deterioration — *continued*
  mental (*see also* Psychosis) 298.9
  myocardium, myocardial (*see also* Degener-
    ation, myocardial) 429.1
  senile (simple) 797
  transplanted organ — *see* Complications,
    transplant, organ, by site
de Toni-Fanconi syndrome (cystinosis) 270.0
Deuteranomaly 368.52
Deuteranopia (anomalous trichromat) (com-
    plete) (incomplete) 368.52
Deutschländer's disease — *see* Fracture, foot
Development
  abnormal, bone 756.9
  arrested 783.40
    bone 733.91
    child 783.40
    due to malnutrition (protein-calorie)
      263.2
    fetus or newborn 764.9 ☑
    tracheal rings (congenital) 748.3
  defective, congenital (*see also* Anomaly)
    cauda equina 742.59
    left ventricle 746.9
      with atresia or hypoplasia of aortic
        orifice or valve with hypopla-
        sia of ascending aorta 746.7
      in hypoplastic left heart syndrome
        746.7
  delayed (*see also* Delay, development)
    783.40
    arithmetical skills 315.1
    language (skills) 315.31
      and speech due to hearing loss
        315.34
      expressive 315.31
      mixed receptive-expressive 315.32
    learning skill, specified NEC 315.2
    mixed skills 315.5
    motor coordination 315.4
    reading 315.00
    specified
      learning skill NEC 315.2
      type NEC, except learning 315.8
    speech 315.39
      and language due to hearing loss
        315.34
      associated with hyperkinesia 314.1
      phonological 315.39
    spelling 315.09
    written expression 315.2
  imperfect, congenital (*see also* Anomaly)
    heart 746.9
    lungs 748.60
  improper (fetus or newborn) 764.9 ☑
  incomplete (fetus or newborn) 764.9 ☑
    affecting management of pregnancy
      656.5 ☑
    bronchial tree 748.3
    organ or site not listed — *see* Hypoplasia
    respiratory system 748.9
  sexual, precocious NEC 259.1
  tardy, mental (*see also* Disability, intellectu-
    al) 319
Developmental — *see* condition
Devergie's disease (pityriasis rubra pilaris)
    696.4
Deviation
  conjugate (eye) 378.87
    palsy 378.81
    spasm, spastic 378.82
  esophagus 530.89
  eye, skew 378.87
  mandible, opening and closing 524.53
  midline (jaw) (teeth) 524.29
    specified site NEC — *see* Malposition
  occlusal plane 524.76
  organ or site, congenital NEC — *see* Malpo-
    sition, congenital
  septum (acquired) (nasal) 470
    congenital 754.0
  sexual 302.9
    bestiality 302.1
    coprophilia 302.89
    ego-dystonic
      homosexuality 302.0

Deviation — *continued*
  sexual — *continued*
    ego-dystonic — *continued*
      lesbianism 302.0
      erotomania 302.89
        Clérambault's 297.8
      exhibitionism (sexual) 302.4
      fetishism 302.81
        transvestic 302.3
      frotteurism 302.89
      homosexuality, ego-dystonic 302.0
        pedophilic 302.2
      lesbianism, ego-dystonic 302.0
      masochism 302.83
      narcissism 302.89
      necrophilia 302.89
      nymphomania 302.89
      pederosis 302.2
      pedophilia 302.2
      sadism 302.84
      sadomasochism 302.84
      satyriasis 302.89
      specified type NEC 302.89
      transvestic fetishism 302.3
      transvestism 302.3
      voyeurism 302.82
      zoophilia (erotica) 302.1
    teeth, midline 524.29
    trachea 519.19
    ureter (congenital) 753.4
Devic's disease 341.0
Device
  cerebral ventricle (communicating) in situ
    V45.2
  contraceptive — *see* Contraceptive, device
  drainage, cerebrospinal fluid V45.2
Devil's
  grip 074.1
  pinches (purpura simplex) 287.2
Devitalized tooth 522.9
Devonshire colic 984.9
  specified type of lead — *see* Table of Drugs
    and Chemicals
Dextraposition, aorta 747.21
  with ventricular septal defect, pulmonary
    stenosis or atresia, and hypertrophy
    of right ventricle 745.2
  in tetralogy of Fallot 745.2
Dextratransposition, aorta 745.11
Dextrinosis, limit (debrancher enzyme defi-
    ciency) 271.0
Dextrocardia (corrected) (false) (isolated)
    (secondary) (true) 746.87
  with
    complete transposition of viscera 759.3
    situs inversus 759.3
Dextroversion, kidney (left) 753.3
Dhobie itch 110.3
DHTR (delayed hemolytic transfusion reaction)
    — *see* Complications, transfusion
Diabetes, diabetic (brittle) (congenital) (famil-
    ial) (mellitus) (severe) (slight) (without
    complication) 250.0 ☑

  Note — Use the following fifth-digit
  subclassification with category 250:

  0   type II or unspecified type, not
        stated as uncontrolled

  Fifth-digit 0 is for use for type II pa-
  tients, even if the patient requires insulin

  1   type I [juvenile type], not stated
        as uncontrolled

  2   type II or unspecified type, uncon-
        trolled

  Fifth-digit 2 is for use for type II pa-
  tients, even if the patient requires insulin

  3   type I [juvenile type], uncontrolled

  with
    coma (with ketoacidosis) 250.3 ☑
      due to secondary diabetes 249.3 ☑
      hyperosmolar (nonketotic) 250.2 ☑
        due to secondary diabetes
          249.2 ☑

Diabetes, diabetic — *continued*
  with — *continued*
    complication NEC 250.9 ☑
      due to secondary diabetes 249.9 ☑
      specified NEC 250.8 ☑
        due to secondary diabetes
          249.8 ☑
    gangrene 250.7 ☑ [785.4]
      due to secondary diabetes
        249.7 ☑ [785.4]
    hyperglycemia — code to Diabetes, by
      type, with 5th digit for not stated
      as uncontrolled
    hyperosmolarity 250.2 ☑
      due to secondary diabetes 249.2 ☑
    ketosis, ketoacidosis 250.1 ☑
      due to secondary diabetes 249.1 ☑
    loss of protective sensation (LOPS) —
      see Diabetes, neuropathy
    osteomyelitis 250.8 ☑ [731.8]
      due to secondary diabetes
        249.8 ☑ [731.8]
    specified manisfestations NEC 250.8 ☑
      due to secondary diabetes 249.8 ☑
  acetonemia 250.1 ☑
    due to secondary diabetes 249.1 ☑
  acidosis 250.1 ☑
    due to secondary diabetes 249.1 ☑
  amyotrophy 250.6 ☑ [353.5]
    due to secondary diabetes
      249.6 ☑ [353.5]
  angiopathy, peripheral 250.7 ☑ [443.81]
    due to secondary diabetes
      249.7 ☑ [443.81]
  asymptomatic 790.29
  autonomic neuropathy (peripheral)
    250.6 ☑ [337.1]
    due to secondary diabetes
      249.6 ☑ [337.1]
  bone change 250.8 ☑ [731.8]
    due to secondary diabetes
      249.8 ☑ [731.8]
  borderline 790.29
  bronze, bronzed 275.01
  cataract 250.5 ☑ [366.41]
    due to secondary diabetes
      249.5 ☑ [366.41]
  chemical induced — *see* Diabetes, sec-
    ondary
  complicating pregnancy, childbirth, or
    puerperium 648.0 ☑
  coma (with ketoacidosis) 250.3 ☑
    due to secondary diabetes 249.3 ☑
    hyperglycemic 250.3 ☑
      due to secondary diabetes 249.3 ☑
    hyperosmolar (nonketotic) 250.2 ☑
      due to secondary diabetes 249.2 ☑
    hypoglycemic 250.3 ☑
      due to secondary diabetes 249.3 ☑
    insulin 250.3 ☑
      due to secondary diabetes 249.3 ☑
  complicating pregnancy, childbirth, or
    puerperium (maternal) (conditions
    classifiable to 249 and 250) 648.0 ☑
    affecting fetus or newborn 775.0
  complication NEC 250.9 ☑
    due to secondary diabetes 249.9 ☑
    specified NEC 250.8 ☑
      due to secondary diabetes 249.8 ☑
  dorsal sclerosis 250.6 ☑ [340]
    due to secondary diabetes
      249.6 ☑ [340]
  drug-induced — *see also* Diabetes, sec-
    ondary
    overdose or wrong substance given or
      taken — *see* Table of Drugs and
      Chemicals
  due to
    cystic fibrosis — *see* Diabetes, secondary
    infection — *see* Diabetes, secondary
  dwarfism-obesity syndrome 258.1
  gangrene 250.7 ☑ [785.4]
    due to secondary diabetes
      249.7 ☑ [785.4]

Diabetes, diabetic — *continued*
  gastroparesis 250.6 ☑ *[536.3]*
    due to secondary diabetes
      249.6 ☑ *[536.3]*
  gestational 648.8 ☑
    complicating pregnancy, childbirth, or
      puerperium 648.8 ☑
  glaucoma 250.5 ☑ *[365.44]*
    due to secondary diabetes
      249.5 ☑ *[365.44]*
  glomerulosclerosis (intercapillary)
      250.4 ☑ *[581.81]*
    due to secondary diabetes
      249.4 ☑ *[581.81]*
  glycogenosis, secondary 250.8 ☑ *[259.8]*
    due to secondary diabetes
      249.8 ☑ *[259.8]*
  hemochromatosis (*see also* Hemochromato-
      sis) 275.03
  hyperosmolar coma 250.2 ☑
    due to secondary diabetes 249.2 ☑
  hyperosmolarity 250.2 ☑
    due to secondary diabetes 249.2 ☑
  hypertension-nephrosis syndrome
      250.4 ☑ *[581.81]*
    due to secondary diabetes
      249.4 ☑ *[581.81]*
  hypoglycemia 250.8 ☑
    due to secondary diabetes 249.8 ☑
  hypoglycemic shock 250.8 ☑
    due to secondary diabetes 249.8 ☑
  inadequately controlled — code to Dia-
    betes, by type, with 5th digit for not
    stated as uncontrolled
  insipidus 253.5
    nephrogenic 588.1
    pituitary 253.5
    vasopressin-resistant 588.1
  intercapillary glomerulosclerosis
      250.4 ☑ *[581.81]*
    due to secondary diabetes
      249.4 ☑ *[581.81]*
  iritis 250.5 *[364.42]*
    due to secondary diabetes
      249.5 ☑ *[364.42]*
  ketosis, ketoacidosis 250.1 ☑
    due to secondary diabetes 249.1 ☑
  Kimmelstiel (-Wilson) disease or syndrome
    (intercapillary glomerulosclerosis)
      250.4 ☑ *[581.81]*
    due to secondary diabetes
      249.4 ☑ *[581.81]*
  Lancereaux's (diabetes mellitus with marked
    emaciation) 250.8 ☑ *[261]*
    due to secondary diabetes
      249.8 ☑ *[261]*
  latent (chemical) — *see* Diabetes, secondary
    complicating pregnancy, childbirth, or
      puerperium 648.0 ☑
  lipoidosis 250.8 ☑ *[272.7]*
    due to secondary diabetes
      249.8 ☑ *[272.7]*
  macular edema 250.5 ☑ *[362.07]*
    due to secondary diabetes
      249.5 ☑ *[362.07]*
  maternal
    with manifest disease in the infant 775.1
    affecting fetus or newborn 775.0
  microaneurysms, retinal 250.5 ☑ *[362.01]*
    due to secondary diabetes
      249.5 ☑ *[362.01]*
  mononeuropathy 250.6 ☑ *[355.9]*
    due to secondary diabetes
      249.6 ☑ *[355.9]*
  neonatal, transient 775.1
  nephropathy 250.4 ☑ *[583.81]*
    due to secondary diabetes
      249.4 ☑ *[583.81]*
  nephrosis (syndrome) 250.4 ☑ *[581.81]*
    due to secondary diabetes
      249.4 ☑ *[581.81]*
  neuralgia 250.6 ☑ *[357.2]*
    due to secondary diabetes
      249.6 ☑ *[357.2]*

Diabetes, diabetic — *continued*
  neuritis 250.6 ☑ *[357.2]*
    due to secondary diabetes
      249.6 ☑ *[357.2]*
  neurogenic arthropathy 250.6 ☑ *[713.5]*
    due to secondary diabetes
      249.6 ☑ *[713.5]*
  neuropathy 250.6 ☑ *[357.2]*
    autonomic (peripheral) 250.6 ☑ *[337.1]*
      due to secondary diabetes
        249.6 ☑ *[337.1]*
    due to secondary diabetes
      249.6 ☑ *[357.2]*
  nonclinical 790.29
  osteomyelitis 250.8 ☑ *[731.8]*
    due to secondary diabetes
      249.8 ☑ *[731.8]*
  out of control — code to Diabetes, by type,
    with 5th digit for uncontrolled
  peripheral autonomic neuropathy
      250.6 ☑ *[337.1]*
    due to secondary diabetes
      249.6 ☑ *[337.1]*
  phosphate 275.3
  polyneuropathy 250.6 ☑ *[357.2]*
    due to secondary diabetes
      249.6 ☑ *[357.2]*
  poorly controlled — code to Diabetes, by
    type, with 5th digit for not stated as
    uncontrolled
  renal (true) 271.4
  retinal
    edema 250.5 *[362.07]*
      due to secondary diabetes
        249.5 ☑ *[362.07]*
    hemorrhage 250.5 *[362.01]*
      due to secondary diabetes
        249.5 ☑ *[362.01]*
    microaneurysms 250.5 *[362.01]*
      due to secondary diabetes
        249.5 ☑ *[362.01]*
    retinitis 250.5 ☑ *[362.01]*
      due to secondary diabetes
        249.5 ☑ *[362.01]*
    retinopathy 250.5 ☑ *[362.01]*
      background 250.5 ☑ *[362.01]*
        due to secondary diabetes
          249.5 ☑ *[362.01]*
      due to secondary diabetes
        249.5 ☑ *[362.01]*
      nonproliferative 250.5 ☑ *[362.03]*
        due to secondary diabetes
          249.5 ☑ *[362.03]*
        mild 250.5 ☑ *[362.04]*
          due to secondary diabetes
            249.5 ☑ *[362.04]*
        moderate 250.5 ☑ *[362.05]*
          due to secondary diabetes
            249.5 ☑ *[362.05]*
        severe 250.5 ☑ *[362.06]*
          due to secondary diabetes
            249.5 ☑ *[362.06]*
      proliferative 250.5 ☑ *[362.02]*
        due to secondary diabetes
          249.5 ☑ *[362.02]*
  secondary (chemical-induced) (due to
    chronic condition) (due to infection)
    (drug-induced) 249.0 ☑
    with
      coma (with ketoacidosis) 249.3 ☑
        hyperosmolar (nonketotic)
          249.2 ☑
      complication NEC 249.9 ☑
        specified NEC 249.8 ☑
      gangrene 249.7 ☑ *[785.4]*
      hyperosmolarity 249.2 ☑
      ketosis, ketoacidosis 249.1 ☑
      osteomyelitis 249.8 ☑ *[731.8]*
      specified manifestations NEC
        249.8 ☑
    acetonemia 249.1 ☑
    acidosis 249.1 ☑
    amyotrophy 249.6 ☑ *[353.5]*
    angiopathy, peripheral 249.7 ☑ *[443.81]*

Diabetes, diabetic — *continued*
  secondary — *continued*
    autonomic neuropathy (peripheral)
      249.6 ☑ *[337.1]*
    bone change 249.8 ☑ *[731.8]*
    cataract 249.5 ☑ *[366.41]*
    coma (with ketoacidosis) 249.3 ☑
      hyperglycemic 249.3 ☑
      hyperosmolar (nonketotic) 249.2 ☑
      hypoglycemic 249.3 ☑
      insulin 249.3 ☑
    complicating pregnancy, childbirth, or
      puerperium (maternal) 648.0 ☑
      affecting fetus or newborn 775.0
    complication NEC 249.9 ☑
      specified NEC 249.8 ☑
    dorsal sclerosis 249.6 ☑ *[340]*
    due to overdose or wrong substance
      given or taken — *see* Table of
      Drugs and Chemicals
    gangrene 249.7 ☑ *[785.4]*
    gastroparesis 249.6 ☑ *[536.3]*
    glaucoma 249.5 ☑ *[365.44]*
    glomerulosclerosis (intercapillary)
      249.4 ☑ *[581.81]*
    glycogenosis, secondary 249.8 ☑ *[259.8]*
    hyperosmolar coma 249.2 ☑
    hyperosmolarity 249.2 ☑
    hypertension-nephrosis syndrome
      249.4 ☑ *[581.81]*
    hypoglycemia 249.8 ☑
    hypoglycemic shock 249.8 ☑
    intercapillary glomerulosclerosis
      249.4 ☑ *[581.81]*
    iritis 249.5 ☑ *[364.42]*
    ketosis, ketoacidosis 249.1 ☑
    Kimmelstiel (-Wilson) disease or syn-
      drome (intercapillary glomeru-
      losclerosis) 249.4 ☑ *[581.81]*
    Lancereaux's (diabetes mellitus with
      marked emaciation)
      249.8 ☑ *[261]*
    lipoidosis 249.8 ☑ *[272.7]*
    macular edema 249.5 ☑ *[362.07]*
    maternal
      with manifest disease in the infant
        775.1
      affecting fetus or newborn 775.0
    microaneurysms, retinal
      249.5 ☑ *[362.01]*
    mononeuropathy 249.6 ☑ *[355.9]*
    nephropathy 249.4 ☑ *[583.81]*
    nephrosis (syndrome) 249.4 ☑ *[581.81]*
    neuralgia 249.6 ☑ *[357.2]*
    neuritis 249.6 ☑ *[357.2]*
    neurogenic arthropathy 249.6 ☑ *[713.5]*
    neuropathy 249.6 ☑ *[357.2]*
      autonomic (peripheral)
        249.6 ☑ *[337.1]*
    osteomyelitis 249.8 ☑ *[731.8]*
    peripheral autonomic neuropathy
      249.6 ☑ *[337.1]*
    polyneuropathy 249.6 ☑ *[357.2]*
    retinal
      edema 249.5 ☑ *[362.07]*
      hemorrhage 249.5 ☑ *[362.01]*
      microaneurysms 249.5 ☑ *[362.01]*
    retinitis 249.5 ☑ *[362.01]*
    retinopathy 249.5 ☑ *[362.01]*
      background 249.5 ☑ *[362.01]*
      nonproliferative 249.5 ☑ *[362.03]*
        mild 249.5 ☑ *[362.04]*
        moderate 249.5 ☑ *[362.05]*
        severe 249.5 ☑ *[362.06]*
      proliferative 249.5 ☑ *[362.02]*
    ulcer (skin) 249.8 ☑ *[707.9]*
      lower extremity 249.8 ☑ *[707.10]*
        ankle 249.8 ☑ *[707.13]*
        calf 249.8 ☑ *[707.12]*
        foot 249.8 ☑ *[707.15]*
        heel 249.8 ☑ *[707.14]*
        knee 249.8 ☑ *[707.19]*
        specified site NEC
          249.8 ☑ *[707.19]*

Diabetes, diabetic — *continued*
  secondary — *continued*
    ulcer — *continued*
      lower extremity — *continued*
        thigh 249.8 ☑ *[707.11]*
        toes 249.8 ☑ *[707.15]*
      specified site NEC 249.8 ☑ *[707.8]*
      xanthoma 249.8 ☑ *[272.2]*
    steroid induced — *see also* Diabetes, sec-
      ondary
    overdose or wrong substance given or
      taken 962.0
  stress 790.29
  subclinical 790.29
  subliminal 790.29
  sugar 250.0 ☑
  ulcer (skin) 250.8 ☑ *[707.9]*
    due to secondary diabetes
      249.8 ☑ *[707.9]*
    lower extremity 250.8 ☑ *[707.10]*
      ankle 250.8 ☑ *[707.13]*
        due to secondary diabetes
          249.8 ☑ *[707.13]*
      calf 250.8 ☑ *[707.12]*
        due to secondary diabetes
          249.8 ☑ *[707.12]*
      due to secondary diabetes
        249.8 ☑ *[707.10]*
      foot 250.8 ☑ *[707.15]*
        due to secondary diabetes
          249.8 ☑ *[707.15]*
      heel 250.8 ☑ *[707.14]*
        due to secondary diabetes
          249.8 ☑ *[707.14]*
      knee 250.8 ☑ *[707.19]*
        due to secondary diabetes
          249.8 ☑ *[707.19]*
      specified site NEC 250.8 ☑ *[707.19]*
        due to secondary diabetes
          249.8 ☑ *[707.19]*
      thigh 250.8 ☑ *[707.11]*
        due to secondary diabetes
          249.8 ☑ *[707.11]*
      toes 250.8 ☑ *[707.15]*
        due to secondary diabetes
          249.8 ☑ *[707.15]*
    specified site NEC 250.8 ☑ *[707.8]*
      due to secondary diabetes
        249.8 ☑ *[707.8]*
    xanthoma 250.8 ☑ *[272.2]*
      due to secondary diabetes
        249.8 ☑ *[272.2]*
Diacyclothrombopathia 287.1
Diagnosis deferred 799.9
Dialysis (intermittent) (treatment)
  anterior retinal (juvenile) (with detachment)
    361.04
  extracorporeal V56.0
  hemodialysis V56.0
    status only V45.11
  peritoneal V56.8
    status only V45.11
  renal V56.0
    status only V45.11
  specified type NEC V56.8
Diamond-Blackfan anemia or syndrome
  (congenital hypoplastic anemia) 284.01
Diamond-Gardener syndrome (autoerythrocyte sensitization) 287.2
Diaper rash 691.0
Diaphoresis (excessive) NEC — *see also* Hyperhidrosis) 780.8
Diaphragm — *see* condition
Diaphragmalgia 786.52
Diaphragmitis 519.4
Diaphyseal aclasis 756.4
Diaphysitis 733.99
Diarrhea, diarrheal (acute) (autumn) (bilious)
  (bloody) (catarrhal) (choleraic) (chronic)
  (gravis) (green) (infantile) (lienteric)
  (noninfectious) (presumed noninfectious) (putrefactive) (secondary) (sporadic) (summer) (symptomatic) (thermic)
  787.91
  achlorhydric 536.0

☑ **Additional Digit Required — Refer to the Tabular List for Digit Selection**

☷ **Subterms under main terms may continue to next column or page**

2015 ICD-9-CM

▶◀ **Revised Text**

● **New Line**

▲ **Revised Code**

Volume 2 — 79

Diarrhea, diarrheal — *continued*
allergic 558.3
amebic (*see also* Amebiasis) 006.9
    with abscess — *see* Abscess, amebic
    acute 006.0
    chronic 006.1
    nondysenteric 006.2
bacillary — *see* Dysentery, bacillary
bacterial NEC 008.5
balantidial 007.0
bile salt-induced 579.8
cachectic NEC 787.91
chilomastix 007.8
choleriformis 001.1
coccidial 007.2
Cochin-China 579.1
    anguilluliasis 127.2
    psilosis 579.1
Dientamoeba 007.8
dietetic 787.91
due to
    achylia gastrica 536.8
    Aerobacter aerogenes 008.2
    Bacillus coli — *see* Enteritis, E. coli
    bacteria NEC 008.5
    bile salts 579.8
    Capillaria
        hepatica 128.8
        philippinensis 127.5
    Clostridium perfringens (C) (F) 008.46
    Enterobacter aerogenes 008.2
    enterococci 008.49
    Escherichia coli — *see* Enteritis, E. coli
    Giardia lamblia 007.1
    Heterophyes heterophyes 121.6
    irritating foods 787.91
    Metagonimus yokogawai 121.5
    Necator americanus 126.1
    Paracolobactrum arizonae 008.1
    Paracolon bacillus NEC 008.47
        Arizona 008.1
    Proteus (bacillus) (mirabilis) (Morganii) 008.3
    Pseudomonas aeruginosa 008.42
    S. japonicum 120.2
    specified organism NEC 008.8
        bacterial 008.49
        viral NEC 008.69
    Staphylococcus 008.41
    Streptococcus 008.49
        anaerobic 008.46
    Strongyloides stercoralis 127.2
    Trichuris trichiuria 127.3
    virus NEC (*see also* Enteritis, viral) 008.69
dysenteric 009.2
    due to specified organism NEC 008.8
dyspeptic 787.91
endemic 009.3
    due to specified organism NEC 008.8
epidemic 009.2
    due to specified organism NEC 008.8
fermentative 787.91
flagellate 007.9
Flexner's (ulcerative) 004.1
functional 564.5
    following gastrointestinal surgery 564.4
    psychogenic 306.4
giardial 007.1
Giardia lamblia 007.1
hill 579.1
hyperperistalsis (nervous) 306.4
infectious 009.2
    due to specified organism NEC 008.8
    presumed 009.3
inflammatory 787.91
    due to specified organism NEC 008.8
malarial (*see also* Malaria) 084.6
mite 133.8
mycotic 117.9
nervous 306.4
neurogenic 564.5
parenteral NEC 009.2
postgastrectomy 564.4
postvagotomy 564.4
prostaglandin induced 579.8
protozoal NEC 007.9

Diarrhea, diarrheal — *continued*
psychogenic 306.4
septic 009.2
    due to specified organism NEC 008.8
specified organism NEC 008.8
    bacterial 008.49
    viral NEC 008.69
Staphylococcus 008.41
Streptococcus 008.49
    anaerobic 008.46
toxic 558.2
travelers' 009.2
    due to specified organism NEC 008.8
trichomonal 007.3
tropical 579.1
tuberculous 014.8 ☑
ulcerative (chronic) (*see also* Colitis, ulcerative) 556.9
viral (*see also* Enteritis, viral) 008.8
zymotic NEC 009.2
Diastasis
cranial bones 733.99
    congenital 756.0
joint (traumatic) — *see* Dislocation, by site
muscle 728.84
    congenital 756.89
recti (abdomen) 728.84
    complicating delivery 665.8 ☑
    congenital 756.79
Diastema, teeth, tooth 524.30
Diastematomyelia 742.51
Diataxia, cerebral, infantile 343.0
Diathesis
allergic V15.09
bleeding (familial) 287.9
cystine (familial) 270.0
gouty 274.9
hemorrhagic (familial) 287.9
    newborn NEC 776.0
oxalic 271.8
scrofulous (*see also* Tuberculosis) 017.2 ☑
spasmophilic (*see also* Tetany) 781.7
ulcer 536.9
uric acid 274.9
Diaz's disease or osteochondrosis 732.5
Dibothriocephaliasis 123.4
    larval 123.5
Dibothriocephalus (infection) (infestation) (latus) 123.4
    larval 123.5
Dicephalus 759.4
Dichotomy, teeth 520.2
Dichromat, dichromata (congenital) 368.59
Dichromatopsia (congenital) 368.59
Dichuchwa 104.0
Dicroceliasis 121.8
Didelphys, didelphic — *see also* Double uterus 752.2
Didymitis — *see also* Epididymitis 604.90
Died — *see also* Death
    without
        medical attention (cause unknown) 798.9
        sign of disease 798.2
Dientamoeba diarrhea 007.8
Dietary
inadequacy or deficiency 269.9
surveillance and counseling V65.3
Dietl's crisis 593.4
Dieulafoy lesion (hemorrhagic)
    of
        duodenum 537.84
        esophagus 530.82
        intestine 569.86
        stomach 537.84
Difficult
birth, affecting fetus or newborn 763.9
delivery NEC 669.9 ☑
Difficulty
feeding 783.3
    adult 783.3
    breast 676.8 ☑
    child 783.3
    elderly 783.3
    infant 783.3
    newborn 779.31

Difficulty — *continued*
feeding — *continued*
    nonorganic (infant) NEC 307.59
mechanical, gastroduodenal stoma 537.89
reading 315.00
    specific, spelling 315.09
swallowing (*see also* Dysphagia) 787.20
walking 719.7
Diffuse — *see* condition
Diffused ganglion 727.42
Di George's syndrome (thymic hypoplasia) 279.11
Digestive — *see* condition
Di Guglielmo's disease or syndrome (M9841/3) 207.0 ☑
Dihydropyrimidine dehydrogenase disease (DPD) 277.6
Diktyoma (M9051/3) — *see* Neoplasm, by site, malignant
Dilaceration, tooth 520.4
Dilatation
anus 564.89
    venule — *see* Hemorrhoids
aorta (focal) (general) (*see also* Ectasia, aortic) 447.70
    with aneurysm 441.9
    congenital 747.29
    infectional 093.0
    ruptured 441.5
    syphilitic 093.0
appendix (cystic) 543.9
artery 447.8
bile duct (common) (congenital) 751.69
    acquired 576.8
bladder (sphincter) 596.89
    congenital 753.8
    in pregnancy or childbirth 654.4 ☑
        causing obstructed labor 660.2 ☑
            affecting fetus or newborn 763.1
blood vessel 459.89
bronchus, bronchi 494.0
    with acute exacerbation 494.1
calyx (due to obstruction) 593.89
capillaries 448.9
cardiac (acute) (chronic) (*see also* Hypertrophy, cardiac) 429.3
    congenital 746.89
        valve NEC 746.89
            pulmonary 746.09
    hypertensive (*see also* Hypertension, heart) 402.90
cavum septi pellucidi 742.4
cecum 564.89
    psychogenic 306.4
cervix (uteri) (*see also* Incompetency, cervix)
    incomplete, poor, slow
        affecting fetus or newborn 763.7
        complicating delivery 661.0 ☑
            affecting fetus or newborn 763.7
colon 564.7
    congenital 751.3
    due to mechanical obstruction 560.89
    psychogenic 306.4
common bile duct (congenital) 751.69
    acquired 576.8
        with calculus, choledocholithiasis, or stones — *see* Choledocholithiasis
cystic duct 751.69
    acquired (any bile duct) 575.8
duct, mammary 610.4
duodenum 564.89
esophagus 530.89
    congenital 750.4
    due to
        achalasia 530.0
        cardiospasm 530.0
Eustachian tube, congenital 744.24
fontanel 756.0
gallbladder 575.8
    congenital 751.69
gastric 536.8
    acute 536.1
    psychogenic 306.4
heart (acute) (chronic) (*see also* Hypertrophy, cardiac) 429.3

Dilatation — *continued*
heart (*see also* Hypertrophy, cardiac) — *continued*
    congenital 746.89
    hypertensive (*see also* Hypertension, heart) 402.90
    valve (*see also* Endocarditis)
        congenital 746.89
ileum 564.89
    psychogenic 306.4
inguinal rings — *see* Hernia, inguinal
jejunum 564.89
    psychogenic 306.4
kidney (calyx) (collecting structures) (cystic) (parenchyma) (pelvis) 593.89
lacrimal passages 375.69
lymphatic vessel 457.1
mammary duct 610.4
Meckel's diverticulum (congenital) 751.0
meningeal vessels, congenital 742.8
myocardium (acute) (chronic) (*see also* Hypertrophy, cardiac) 429.3
organ or site, congenital NEC — *see* Distortion
pancreatic duct 577.8
pelvis, kidney 593.89
pericardium — *see* Pericarditis
pharynx 478.29
prostate 602.8
pulmonary
    artery (idiopathic) 417.8
        congenital 747.39
    valve, congenital 746.09
pupil 379.43
rectum 564.89
renal 593.89
saccule vestibularis, congenital 744.05
salivary gland (duct) 527.8
sphincter ani 564.89
stomach 536.8
    acute 536.1
    psychogenic 306.4
submaxillary duct 527.8
trachea, congenital 748.3
ureter (idiopathic) 593.89
    congenital 753.20
    due to obstruction 593.5
urethra (acquired) 599.84
vasomotor 443.9
vein 459.89
ventricular, ventricle (acute) (chronic) (*see also* Hypertrophy, cardiac) 429.3
    cerebral, congenital 742.4
    hypertensive (*see also* Hypertension, heart) 402.90
venule 459.89
    anus — *see* Hemorrhoids
vesical orifice 596.89
Dilated, dilation — *see* Dilatation
Diminished
hearing (acuity) (*see also* Deafness) 389.9
pulse pressure 785.9
vision NEC 369.9
vital capacity 794.2
Diminuta taenia 123.6
Diminution, sense or sensation (cold) (heat) (tactile) (vibratory) — *see also* Disturbance, sensation 782.0
Dimitri-Sturge-Weber disease (encephalocutaneous angiomatosis) 759.6
Dimple
parasacral 685.1
    with abscess 685.0
pilonidal 685.1
    with abscess 685.0
postanal 685.1
    with abscess 685.0
Dioctophyma renale (infection) (infestation) 128.8
Dipetalonemiasis 125.4
Diphallus 752.69
Diphtheria, diphtheritic (gangrenous) (hemorrhagic) 032.9
carrier (suspected) of V02.4
cutaneous 032.85
cystitis 032.84

☑ Additional Digit Required — Refer to the Tabular List for Digit Selection   ▽ Subterms under main terms may continue to next column or page

80 — Volume 2   ►◄ Revised Text   ● New Line   ▲ Revised Code   2015 ICD-9-CM

Disease, diseased — *see also* Syndrome — *continued*

bone — *continued*
  Paget's (osteitis deformans) 731.0
  specified type NEC 733.99
  von Recklinghausen's (osteitis fibrosa cystica) 252.01
Bonfils' — *see* Disease, Hodgkin's
Borna 062.9
Bornholm (epidemic pleurodynia) 074.1
Bostock's (*see also* Fever, hay) 477.9
Bouchard's (myopathic dilatation of the stomach) 536.1
Bouillaud's (rheumatic heart disease) 391.9
Bourneville (-Brissaud) (tuberous sclerosis) 759.5
Bouveret (-Hoffmann) (paroxysmal tachycardia) 427.2
bowel 569.9
  functional 564.9
    psychogenic 306.4
Bowen's (M8081/2) — *see* Neoplasm, skin, in situ
Bozzolo's (multiple myeloma) (M9730/3) 203.0 ☑
Bradley's (epidemic vomiting) 078.82
Brailsford's 732.3
  radius, head 732.3
  tarsal, scaphoid 732.5
Brailsford-Morquio (mucopolysaccharidosis IV) 277.5
brain 348.9
  Alzheimer's 331.0
    with dementia — *see* Alzheimer's, dementia
  arterial, artery 437.9
  arteriosclerotic 437.0
  congenital 742.9
  degenerative — *see* Degeneration, brain
  inflammatory (*see also* Encephalitis)
    late effect — *see* category 326
  organic 348.9
    arteriosclerotic 437.0
  parasitic NEC 123.9
  Pick's 331.11
    with dementia
      with behavioral disturbance 331.11 [294.11]
      without behavioral disturbance 331.11 [294.10]
  senile 331.2
braziers' 985.8
breast 611.9
  cystic (chronic) 610.1
  fibrocystic 610.1
  inflammatory 611.0
  Paget's (M8540/3) 174.0
  puerperal, postpartum NEC 676.3 ☑
  specified NEC 611.89
Breda's (*see also* Yaws) 102.9
Breisky's (kraurosis vulvae) 624.09
Bretonneau's (diphtheritic malignant angina) 032.0
Bright's (*see also* Nephritis) 583.9
  arteriosclerotic (*see also* Hypertension, kidney) 403.90
Brill's (recrudescent typhus) 081.1
  flea-borne 081.0
  louse-borne 081.1
Brill-Symmers (follicular lymphoma) (M9690/3) 202.0 ☑
Brill-Zinsser (recrudescent typhus) 081.1
Brinton's (leather bottle stomach) (M8142/3) 151.9
Brion-Kayser (*see also* Fever, paratyphoid) 002.9
broad
  beta 272.2
  ligament, noninflammatory 620.9
    specified NEC 620.8
Brocq's 691.8
  meaning
    atopic (diffuse) neurodermatitis 691.8
    dermatitis herpetiformis 694.0
    lichen simplex chronicus 698.3

Disease, diseased — *see also* Syndrome — *continued*

Brocq's — *continued*
  meaning — *continued*
    parapsoriasis 696.2
    prurigo 698.2
Brocq-Duhring (dermatitis herpetiformis) 694.0
Brodie's (joint) (*see also* Osteomyelitis) 730.1 ☑
bronchi 519.19
bronchopulmonary 519.19
bronze (Addison's) 255.41
  tuberculous (*see also* Tuberculosis) 017.6 ☑
Brown-Séquard 344.89
Bruck's 733.99
Bruck-de Lange (Amsterdam dwarf, intellectual disabilities, and brachycephaly) 759.89
Bruhl's (splenic anemia with fever) 285.8
Bruton's (X-linked agammaglobulinemia) 279.04
buccal cavity 528.9
Buchanan's (juvenile osteochondrosis, iliac crest) 732.1
Buchman's (osteochondrosis juvenile) 732.1
Budgerigar-Fanciers' 495.2
Büdinger-Ludloff-Läwen 717.89
Buerger's (thromboangiitis obliterans) 443.1
Bürger-Grütz (essential familial hyperlipemia) 272.3
Burns' (lower ulna) 732.3
bursa 727.9
Bury's (erythema elevatum diutinum) 695.89
Buschke's 710.1
Busquet's (*see also* Osteomyelitis) 730.1 ☑
Busse-Buschke (cryptococcosis) 117.5
C₂ (*see also* Alcoholism) 303.9 ☑
Caffey's (infantile cortical hyperostosis) 756.59
caisson 993.3
calculous 592.9
California 114.0
Calvé (-Perthes) (osteochondrosis, femoral capital) 732.1
Camurati-Engelmann (diaphyseal sclerosis) 756.59
Canavan's 330.0
capillaries 448.9
Carapata 087.1
cardiac — *see* Disease, heart
cardiopulmonary, chronic 416.9
cardiorenal (arteriosclerotic) (hepatic) (hypertensive) (vascular) (*see also* Hypertension, cardiorenal) 404.90
cardiovascular (arteriosclerotic) 429.2
  congenital 746.9
  hypertensive (*see also* Hypertension, heart) 402.90
    benign 402.10
    malignant 402.00
  renal (*see also* Hypertension, cardiorenal) 404.90
  syphilitic (asymptomatic) 093.9
carotid gland 259.8
Carrión's (Bartonellosis) 088.0
cartilage NEC 733.90
  specified NEC 733.99
Castellani's 104.8
cat-scratch 078.3
Cavare's (familial periodic paralysis) 359.3
Cazenave's (pemphigus) 694.4
cecum 569.9
celiac (adult) 579.0
  infantile 579.0
cellular tissue NEC 709.9
central core 359.0
cerebellar, cerebellum — *see* Disease, brain
cerebral (*see also* Disease, brain) 348.9
  arterial, artery 437.9
  degenerative — *see* Degeneration, brain
cerebrospinal 349.9
cerebrovascular NEC 437.9
  acute 436
    embolic — *see* Embolism, brain

Disease, diseased — *see also* Syndrome — *continued*

cerebrovascular — *continued*
  acute — *continued*
    late effect — *see* Late effect(s) (of) cerebrovascular disease
    puerperal, postpartum, childbirth 674.0 ☑
    thrombotic — *see* Thrombosis, brain
  arteriosclerotic 437.0
  embolic — *see* Embolism, brain
  ischemic, generalized NEC 437.1
  late effect — *see* Late effect(s) (of) cerebrovascular disease
  occlusive 437.1
  puerperal, postpartum, childbirth 674.0 ☑
  specified type NEC 437.8
  thrombotic — *see* Thrombosis, brain
ceroid storage 272.7
cervix (uteri)
  inflammatory 616.0
  noninflammatory 622.9
    specified NEC 622.8
Chabert's 022.9
Chagas' (*see also* Trypanosomiasis, American) 086.2
Chandler's (osteochondritis dissecans, hip) 732.7
Charcôt-Marie-Tooth 356.1
Charcôt's (joint) 094.0 [713.5]
  spinal cord 094.0
Charlouis' (*see also* Yaws) 102.9
Cheadle (-Möller) (-Barlow) (infantile scurvy) 267
cheek, inner 528.9
chest 519.9
Chiari's (hepatic vein thrombosis) 453.0
Chicago (North American blastomycosis) 116.0
chignon (white piedra) 111.2
chigoe, chigo (jigger) 134.1
childhood granulomatous 288.1
Chinese liver fluke 121.1
chlamydial NEC 078.88
cholecystic (*see also* Disease, gallbladder) 575.9
choroid 363.9
  degenerative (*see also* Degeneration, choroid) 363.40
  hereditary (*see also* Dystrophy, choroid) 363.50
  specified type NEC 363.8
Christian's (chronic histiocytosis X) 277.89
Christian-Weber (nodular nonsuppurative panniculitis) 729.30
Christmas 286.1
ciliary body 364.9
  specified NEC 364.89
circulatory (system) NEC 459.9
  chronic, maternal, affecting fetus or newborn 760.3
  specified NEC 459.89
  syphilitic 093.9
    congenital 090.5
Civatte's (poikiloderma) 709.09
climacteric 627.2
  male 608.89
coagulation factor deficiency (congenital) (*see also* Defect, coagulation) 286.9
Coats' 362.12
coccidioidal pulmonary 114.5
  acute 114.0
  chronic 114.4
  primary 114.0
  residual 114.4
Cockayne's (microcephaly and dwarfism) 759.89
Cogan's 370.52
cold
  agglutinin 283.0
    or hemoglobinuria 283.0

Disease, diseased — *see also* Syndrome — *continued*

cold — *continued*
  agglutinin — *continued*
    or hemoglobinuria — *continued*
      paroxysmal (cold) (nocturnal) 283.2
  hemagglutinin (chronic) 283.0
collagen NEC 710.9
  nonvascular 710.9
  specified NEC 710.8
  vascular (allergic) (*see also* Angiitis, hypersensitivity) 446.20
colon 569.9
  functional 564.9
    congenital 751.3
  ischemic 557.0
combined system (of spinal cord) 266.2 [336.2]
  with anemia (pernicious) 281.0 [336.2]
compressed air 993.3
Concato's (pericardial polyserositis) 423.2
  peritoneal 568.82
  pleural — *see* Pleurisy
congenital NEC 799.89
conjunctiva 372.9
  chlamydial 077.98
    specified NEC 077.8
  specified type NEC 372.89
  viral 077.99
    specified NEC 077.8
connective tissue, diffuse (*see also* Disease, collagen) 710.9
Conor and Bruch's (boutonneuse fever) 082.1
Conradi (-Hünermann) 756.59
Cooley's (erythroblastic anemia) 282.44
Cooper's 610.1
Corbus' 607.1
cork-handlers' 495.3
cornea (*see also* Keratopathy) 371.9
coronary (*see also* Ischemia, heart) 414.9
  congenital 746.85
  ostial, syphilitic 093.20
    aortic 093.22
    mitral 093.21
    pulmonary 093.24
    tricuspid 093.23
Corrigan's — *see* Insufficiency, aortic
Cotugno's 724.3
Coxsackie (virus) NEC 074.8
cranial nerve NEC 352.9
Creutzfeldt-Jakob (CJD) 046.19
  with dementia
    with behavioral disturbance 046.19 [294.11]
    without behavioral disturbance 046.19 [294.10]
  familial 046.19
  iatrogenic 046.19
  specified NEC 046.19
  sporadic 046.19
  variant (vCJD) 046.11
    with dementia
      with behavioral disturbance 046.11 [294.11]
      without behavioral disturbance 046.11 [294.10]
Crigler-Najjar (congenital hyperbilirubinemia) 277.4
Crocq's (acrocyanosis) 443.89
Crohn's (intestine) (*see also* Enteritis, regional) 555.9
Crouzon's (craniofacial dysostosis) 756.0
Cruchet's (encephalitis lethargica) 049.8
Cruveilhier's 335.21
Cruz-Chagas (*see also* Trypanosomiasis, American) 086.2
crystal deposition (*see also* Arthritis, due to, crystals) 712.9 ☑
Csillag's (lichen sclerosus et atrophicus) 701.0
Curschmann's 359.21
Cushing's (pituitary basophilism) 255.0
cystic
  breast (chronic) 610.1

☑ **Additional Digit Required — Refer to the Tabular List for Digit Selection**   ▽ **Subterms under main terms may continue to next column or page**

82 — Volume 2   ▶◀ Revised Text   ● New Line   ▲ Revised Code   2015 ICD-9-CM

Disease, diseased — *see also* Syndrome — *continued*

cystic — *continued*

kidney, congenital (*see also* Cystic, disease, kidney) 753.10

liver, congenital 751.62

lung 518.89

congenital 748.4

pancreas 577.2

congenital 751.7

renal, congenital (*see also* Cystic, disease, kidney) 753.10

semilunar cartilage 717.5

cysticercus 123.1

cystine storage (with renal sclerosis) 270.0

cytomegalic inclusion (generalized) 078.5

with

pneumonia 078.5 [484.1]

congenital 771.1

Daae (-Finsen) (epidemic pleurodynia) 074.1

dancing 297.8

Danielssen's (anesthetic leprosy) 030.1

Darier's (congenital) (keratosis follicularis) 757.39

erythema annulare centrifugum 695.0

vitamin A deficiency 264.8

Darling's (histoplasmosis) (*see also* Histoplasmosis, American) 115.00

Davies' 425.0

de Beurmann-Gougerot (sporotrichosis) 117.1

Débove's (splenomegaly) 789.2

deer fly (*see also* Tularemia) 021.9

deficiency 269.9

degenerative (*see also* Degeneration)

disc — *see* Degeneration, intervertebral disc

Degos' 447.8

Déjérine (-Sottas) 356.0

Déléage's 359.89

demyelinating, demyelinizating (brain stem) (central nervous system) 341.9

multiple sclerosis 340

specified NEC 341.8

de Quervain's (tendon sheath) 727.04

thyroid (subacute granulomatous thyroiditis) 245.1

Dercum's (adiposis dolorosa) 272.8

Deutschländer's — *see* Fracture, foot

Devergie's (pityriasis rubra pilaris) 696.4

Devic's 341.0

diaphorase deficiency 289.7

diaphragm 519.4

diarrheal, infectious 009.2

diatomaceous earth 502

Diaz's (osteochondrosis astragalus) 732.5

digestive system 569.9

Di Guglielmo's (erythemic myelosis) (M9841/3) 207.0

Dimitri-Sturge-Weber (encephalocutaneous angiomatosis) 759.6

disc, degenerative — *see* Degeneration, intervertebral disc

discogenic (*see also* Disease, intervertebral disc) 722.90

diverticular — *see* Diverticula

Down's (mongolism) 758.0

Dubini's (electric chorea) 049.8

Dubois' (thymus gland) 090.5

Duchenne's 094.0

locomotor ataxia 094.0

muscular dystrophy 359.1

paralysis 335.22

pseudohypertrophy, muscles 359.1

Duchenne-Griesinger 359.1

ductless glands 259.9

Duhring's (dermatitis herpetiformis) 694.0

Dukes (-Filatov) 057.8

duodenum NEC 537.9

specified NEC 537.89

Duplay's 726.2

Dupré's (meningism) 781.6

Dupuytren's (muscle contracture) 728.6

Durand-Nicolas-Favre (climatic bubo) 099.1

Duroziez's (congenital mitral stenosis) 746.5

Dutton's (trypanosomiasis) 086.9

Disease, diseased — *see also* Syndrome — *continued*

Eales' 362.18

ear (chronic) (inner) NEC 388.9

middle 385.9

adhesive (*see also* Adhesions, middle ear) 385.10

specified NEC 385.89

Eberth's (typhoid fever) 002.0

Ebstein's

heart 746.2

meaning diabetes 250.4 ☑ [581.81]

due to secondary diabetes 249.4 ☑ [581.81]

Echinococcus (*see also* Echinococcus) 122.9

ECHO virus NEC 078.89

Economo's (encephalitis lethargica) 049.8

Eddowes' (brittle bones and blue sclera) 756.51

Edsall's 992.2

Eichstedt's (pityriasis versicolor) 111.0

Ellis-van Creveld (chondroectodermal dysplasia) 756.55

endocardium — *see* Endocarditis

endocrine glands or system NEC 259.9

specified NEC 259.8

endomyocardial, idiopathic mural 425.2

Engelmann's (diaphyseal sclerosis) 756.59

Engel-von Recklinghausen (osteitis fibrosa cystica) 252.01

English (rickets) 268.0

Engman's (infectious eczematoid dermatitis) 690.8

enteroviral, enterovirus NEC 078.89

central nervous system NEC 048

epidemic NEC 136.9

epididymis 608.9

epigastric, functional 536.9

psychogenic 306.4

Erb (-Landouzy) 359.1

Erb-Goldflam 358.00

Erdheim-Chester (ECD) 277.89

Erichsen's (railway spine) 300.16

esophagus 530.9

functional 530.5

psychogenic 306.4

Eulenburg's (congenital paramyotonia) 359.29

Eustachian tube 381.9

Evans' (thrombocytopenic purpura) 287.32

external auditory canal 380.9

extrapyramidal NEC 333.90

eye 379.90

anterior chamber 364.9

inflammatory NEC 364.3

muscle 378.9

eyeball 360.9

eyelid 374.9

eyeworm of Africa 125.2

Fabry's (angiokeratoma corporis diffusum) 272.7

facial nerve (seventh) 351.9

newborn 767.5

Fahr-Volhard (malignant nephrosclerosis) 403.00

fallopian tube, noninflammatory 620.9

specified NEC 620.8

familial periodic 277.31

paralysis 359.3

Fanconi's (congenital pancytopenia) 284.09

Farber's (disseminated lipogranulomatosis) 272.8

fascia 728.9

inflammatory 728.9

Fauchard's (periodontitis) 523.40

Favre-Durand-Nicolas (climatic bubo) 099.1

Favre-Racouchot (elastoidosis cutanea nodularis) 701.8

Fede's 529.0

Feer's 985.0

Felix's (juvenile osteochondrosis, hip) 732.1

Fenwick's (gastric atrophy) 537.89

Fernels' (aortic aneurysm) 441.9

fibrocaseous, of lung (*see also* Tuberculosis, pulmonary) 011.9 ☑

fibrocystic (*see also* Fibrocystic, disease)

Disease, diseased — *see also* Syndrome — *continued*

fibrocystic (*see also* Fibrocystic, disease) — *continued*

newborn 277.01

Fiedler's (leptospiral jaundice) 100.0

fifth 057.0

Filatoff's (infectious mononucleosis) 075

Filatov's (infectious mononucleosis) 075

file-cutters' 984.9

specified type of lead — *see* Table of Drugs and Chemicals

filterable virus NEC 078.89

fish skin 757.1

acquired 701.1

Flajani (-Basedow) (exophthalmic goiter) 242.0 ☑

Flatau-Schilder 341.1

flax-dressers' 504

Fleischner's 732.3

flint 502

fluke — *see* Infestation, fluke

Følling's (phenylketonuria) 270.1

foot and mouth 078.4

foot process 581.3

Forbes' (glycogenosis III) 271.0

Fordyce's (ectopic sebaceous glands) (mouth) 750.26

Fordyce-Fox (apocrine miliaria) 705.82

Fothergill's

meaning scarlatina anginosa 034.1

neuralgia (*see also* Neuralgia, trigeminal) 350.1

Fournier's 608.83

female 616.89

fourth 057.8

Fox (-Fordyce) (apocrine miliaria) 705.82

Francis' (*see also* Tularemia) 021.9

Franklin's (heavy chain) 273.2

Frei's (climatic bubo) 099.1

Freiberg's (flattening metatarsal) 732.5

Friedländer's (endarteritis obliterans) — *see* Arteriosclerosis

Friedreich's

combined systemic or ataxia 334.0

facial hemihypertrophy 756.0

myoclonia 333.2

Fröhlich's (adiposogenital dystrophy) 253.8

Frommel's 676.6 ☑

frontal sinus (chronic) 473.1

acute 461.1

Fuller's earth 502

fungus, fungous NEC 117.9

Gaisböck's (polycythemia hypertonica) 289.0

gallbladder 575.9

congenital 751.60

Gamna's (siderotic splenomegaly) 289.51

Gamstorp's (adynamia episodica hereditaria) 359.3

Gandy-Nanta (siderotic splenomegaly) 289.51

Gannister (occupational) 502

Garré's (*see also* Osteomyelitis) 730.1 ☑

gastric (*see also* Disease, stomach) 537.9

gastroesophageal reflux (GERD) 530.81

gastrointestinal (tract) 569.9

amyloid 277.39

functional 536.9

psychogenic 306.4

Gaucher's (adult) (cerebroside lipidosis) (infantile) 272.7

Gayet's (superior hemorrhagic polioencephalitis) 265.1

Gee (-Herter) (-Heubner) (-Thaysen) (nontropical sprue) 579.0

generalized neoplastic (M8000/6) 199.0

genital organs NEC

female 629.9

specified NEC 629.89

male 608.9

Gerhardt's (erythromelalgia) 443.82

Gerlier's (epidemic vertigo) 078.81

Gibert's (pityriasis rosea) 696.3

Gibney's (perispondylitis) 720.9

Gierke's (glycogenosis I) 271.0

Disease, diseased — *see also* Syndrome — *continued*

Gilbert's (familial nonhemolytic jaundice) 277.4

Gilchrist's (North American blastomycosis) 116.0

Gilford (-Hutchinson) (progeria) 259.8

Gilles de la Tourette's (motor-verbal tic) 307.23

Giovannini's 117.9

gland (lymph) 289.9

Glanzmann's (hereditary hemorrhagic thrombasthenia) 287.1

glassblowers' 527.1

Glénard's (enteroptosis) 569.89

Glisson's (*see also* Rickets) 268.0

glomerular

membranous, idiopathic 581.1

minimal change 581.3

glycogen storage (Andersen's) (Cori types 1-7) (Forbes') (McArdle-Schmid-Pearson) (Pompe's) (types I-VII) 271.0

cardiac 271.0 [425.7]

generalized 271.0

glucose–6–phosphatase deficiency 271.0

heart 271.0 [425.7]

hepatorenal 271.0

liver and kidneys 271.0

myocardium 271.0 [425.7]

von Gierke's (glycogenosis I) 271.0

Goldflam-Erb 358.00

Goldscheider's (epidermolysis bullosa) 757.39

Goldstein's (familial hemorrhagic telangiectasia) 448.0

gonococcal NEC 098.0

Goodall's (epidemic vomiting) 078.82

Gordon's (exudative enteropathy) 579.8

Gougerot's (trisymptomatic) 709.1

Gougerot-Carteaud (confluent reticulate papillomatosis) 701.8

Gougerot-Hailey-Hailey (benign familial chronic pemphigus) 757.39

graft-versus-host 279.50

acute 279.51

on chronic 279.53

chronic 279.52

grain-handlers' 495.8

Grancher's (splenopneumonia) — *see* Pneumonia

granulomatous (childhood) (chronic) 288.1

graphite lung 503

Graves' (exophthalmic goiter) 242.0 ☑

Greenfield's 330.0

green monkey 078.89

Griesinger's (*see also* Ancylostomiasis) 126.9

grinders' 502

Grisel's 723.5

Gruby's (tinea tonsurans) 110.0

Guertin's (electric chorea) 049.8

Guillain-Barré 357.0

Guinon's (motor-verbal tic) 307.23

Gull's (thyroid atrophy with myxedema) 244.8

Gull and Sutton's — *see* Hypertension, kidney

gum NEC 523.9

Günther's (congenital erythropoietic porphyria) 277.1

gynecological 629.9

specified NEC 629.89

H 270.0

Haas' 732.3

Habermann's (acute parapsoriasis varioliformis) 696.2

Haff 985.1

Hageman (congenital factor XII deficiency) (*see also* Defect, congenital) 286.3

Haglund's (osteochondrosis os tibiale externum) 732.5

Hagner's (hypertrophic pulmonary osteoarthropathy) 731.2

Hailey-Hailey (benign familial chronic pemphigus) 757.39

hair (follicles) NEC 704.9

☑ Additional Digit Required — Refer to the Tabular List for Digit Selection ⍦ Subterms under main terms may continue to next column or page

2015 ICD-9-CM ►◄ Revised Text ● New Line ▲ Revised Code Volume 2 — 83

Disease, diseased — Disease, diseased

Disease, diseased — *see also* Syndrome — *continued*

hair — *continued*
 specified type NEC 704.8
Hallervorden-Spatz 333.0
Hallopeau's (lichen sclerosus et atrophicus) 701.0
Hamman's (spontaneous mediastinal emphysema) 518.1
hand, foot, and mouth 074.3
Hand-Schüller-Christian (chronic histiocytosis X) 277.89
Hanot's — *see* Cirrhosis, biliary
Hansen's (leprosy) 030.9
 benign form 030.1
 malignant form 030.0
Harada's 363.22
Harley's (intermittent hemoglobinuria) 283.2
Hartnup (pellagra-cerebellar ataxia-renal aminoaciduria) 270.0
Hart's (pellagra-cerebellar ataxia-renal aminoaciduria) 270.0
Hashimoto's (struma lymphomatosa) 245.2
Hb — *see* Disease, hemoglobin
heart (organic) 429.9
 with
  acute pulmonary edema (*see also* Failure, ventricular, left) 428.1
  hypertensive 402.91
   with renal failure 404.93
   benign 402.11
    with renal failure 404.13
   malignant 402.01
    with renal failure 404.03
  kidney disease — *see* Hypertension, cardiorenal
  rheumatic fever (conditions classifiable to 390)
   active 391.9
    with chorea 392.0
   inactive or quiescent (with chorea) 398.90
 amyloid 277.39 *[425.7]*
 aortic (valve) (*see also* Endocarditis, aortic) 424.1
 arteriosclerotic or sclerotic (minimal) (senile) — *see* Arteriosclerosis, coronary
 artery, arterial — *see* Arteriosclerosis, coronary
 atherosclerotic — *see* Arteriosclerosis, coronary
 beer drinkers' 425.5
 beriberi 265.0 *[425.7]*
 black 416.0
 congenital NEC 746.9
  cyanotic 746.9
  maternal, affecting fetus or newborn 760.3
  specified type NEC 746.89
 congestive (*see also* Failure, heart) 428.0
 coronary 414.9
 cryptogenic 429.9
 due to
  amyloidosis 277.39 *[425.7]*
  beriberi 265.0 *[425.7]*
  cardiac glycogenosis 271.0 *[425.7]*
  Friedreich's ataxia 334.0 *[425.7]*
  gout 274.82
  mucopolysaccharidosis 277.5 *[425.7]*
  myotonia atrophica 359.21 *[425.8]*
  progressive muscular dystrophy 359.1 *[425.8]*
  sarcoidosis 135 *[425.8]*
 fetal 746.9
  inflammatory 746.89
 fibroid (*see also* Myocarditis) 429.0
 functional 427.9
  postoperative 997.1
  psychogenic 306.2
 glycogen storage 271.0 *[425.7]*
 gonococcal NEC 098.85
 gouty 274.82
 hypertensive (*see also* Hypertension, heart) 402.90

Disease, diseased — *see also* Syndrome — *continued*

heart — *continued*
 hypertensive (*see also* Hypertension, heart) — *continued*
  benign 402.10
  malignant 402.00
 hyperthyroid (*see also* Hyperthyroidism) 242.9 ☑ *[425.7]*
 incompletely diagnosed — *see* Disease, heart
 ischemic (chronic) (*see also* Ischemia, heart) 414.9
  acute (*see also* Infarct, myocardium) 410.9 ☑
   without myocardial infarction 411.89
    with coronary (artery) occlusion 411.81
  asymptomatic 412
  diagnosed on ECG or other special investigation but currently presenting no symptoms 412
 kyphoscoliotic 416.1
 mitral (*see also* Endocarditis, mitral) 394.9
 muscular (*see also* Degeneration, myocardial) 429.1
 postpartum 674.8 ☑
 psychogenic (functional) 306.2
 pulmonary (chronic) 416.9
  acute 415.0
  specified NEC 416.8
 rheumatic (chronic) (inactive) (old) (quiescent) (with chorea) 398.90
  active or acute 391.9
   with chorea (active) (rheumatic) (Sydenham's) 392.0
  specified type NEC 391.8
 maternal, affecting fetus or newborn 760.3
 rheumatoid — *see* Arthritis, rheumatoid
 sclerotic — *see* Arteriosclerosis, coronary
 senile (*see also* Myocarditis) 429.0
 specified type NEC 429.89
 syphilitic 093.89
  aortic 093.1
   aneurysm 093.0
  asymptomatic 093.89
  congenital 090.5
 thyroid (gland) (*see also* Hyper-thyroidism) 242.9 ☑ *[425.7]*
 thyrotoxic (*see also* Thyrotoxicosis) 242.9 ☑ *[425.7]*
 tuberculous (*see also* Tuberculosis) 017.9 ☑ *[425.8]*
 valve, valvular (obstructive) (regurgitant) (*see also* Endocarditis)
  congenital NEC (*see also* Anomaly, heart, valve) 746.9
  pulmonary 746.00
  specified type NEC 746.89
 vascular — *see* Disease, cardiovascular
heavy-chain (gamma G) 273.2
Heberden's 715.04
Hebra's
 dermatitis exfoliativa 695.89
 erythema multiforme exudativum 695.19
 pityriasis
  maculata et circinata 696.3
  rubra 695.89
  pilaris 696.4
 prurigo 698.2
Heerfordt's (uveoparotitis) 135
Heidenhain's 290.10
 with dementia 290.10
Heilmeyer-Schöner (M9842/3) 207.1 ☑
Heine-Medin (*see also* Poliomyelitis) 045.9 ☑
Heller's (*see also* Psychosis, childhood) 299.1 ☑
Heller-Döhle (syphilitic aortitis) 093.1
hematopoietic organs 289.9
hemoglobin (Hb) 282.7
 with thalassemia 282.49

Disease, diseased — *see also* Syndrome — *continued*

hemoglobin — *continued*
 abnormal (mixed) NEC 282.7
  with thalassemia 282.49
 AS genotype 282.5
 Bart's 282.43
 C (Hb-C) 282.7
  with other abnormal hemoglobin NEC 282.7
  elliptocytosis 282.7
  Hb-S (without crisis) 282.63
   with
    crisis 282.64
    vaso-occlusive pain 282.64
  sickle-cell (without crisis) 282.63
   with
    crisis 282.64
    vaso-occlusive pain 282.64
  thalassemia 282.49
 constant spring 282.7
 D (Hb-D) 282.7
  with other abnormal hemoglobin NEC 282.7
  Hb-S (without crisis) 282.68
   with crisis 282.69
  sickle-cell (without crisis) 282.68
   with crisis 282.69
  thalassemia 282.49
 E (Hb-E) 282.7
  with other abnormal hemoglobin NEC 282.7
  Hb-S (without crisis) 282.68
   with crisis 282.69
  sickle-cell (without crisis) 282.68
   with crisis 282.69
  thalassemia 282.47
 elliptocytosis 282.7
 F (Hb-F) 282.7
 G (Hb-G) 282.7
 H (Hb-H) 282.43
 hereditary persistence, fetal (HPFH) ("Swiss variety") 282.7
 high fetal gene 282.7
 I thalassemia 282.49
 M 289.7
 S (*see also* Disease, sickle-cell, Hb-S)
  thalassemia (without crisis) 282.41
   with
    crisis 282.42
    vaso-occlusive pain 282.42
 spherocytosis 282.7
 unstable, hemolytic 282.7
 Zurich (Hb-Zurich) 282.7
hemolytic (fetus) (newborn) 773.2
 autoimmune (cold type) (warm type) 283.0
 due to or with
  incompatibility
   ABO (blood group) 773.1
   blood (group) (Duffy) (Kell) (Kidd) (Lewis) (M) (S) NEC 773.2
   Rh (blood group) (factor) 773.0
  Rh negative mother 773.0
 unstable hemoglobin 282.7
hemorrhagic 287.9
 newborn 776.0
Henoch (-Schönlein) (purpura nervosa) 287.0
hepatic — *see* Disease, liver
hepatolenticular 275.1
heredodegenerative NEC
 brain 331.89
 spinal cord 336.8
Hers' (glycogenosis VI) 271.0
Herter (-Gee) (-Heubner) (nontropical sprue) 579.0
Herxheimer's (diffuse idiopathic cutaneous atrophy) 701.8
Heubner's 094.89
Heubner-Herter (nontropical sprue) 579.0
high fetal gene or hemoglobin thalassemia (*see also* Thalassemia) 282.40
Hildenbrand's (typhus) 081.9
Hippel's (retinocerebral angiomatosis) 759.6
hip (joint) NEC 719.95

Disease, diseased — *see also* Syndrome — *continued*

hip — *continued*
 congenital 755.63
 suppurative 711.05
 tuberculous (*see also* Tuberculosis) 015.1 ☑ *[730.85]*
Hirschfeld's (acute diabetes mellitus) (*see also* Diabetes) 250.0 ☑
 due to secondary diabetes 249.0 ☑
Hirschsprung's (congenital megacolon) 751.3
His (-Werner) (trench fever) 083.1
HIV 042
Hodgkin's (M9650/3) 201.9 ☑

> *Note* — *Use the following fifth-digit subclassification with category 201:*
>
> 0 *unspecified site*
>
> 1 *lymph nodes of head, face, and neck*
>
> 2 *intrathoracic lymph nodes*
>
> 3 *intra-abdominal lymph nodes*
>
> 4 *lymph nodes of axilla and upper limb*
>
> 5 *lymph nodes of inguinal region and lower limb*
>
> 6 *intrapelvic lymph nodes*
>
> 7 *spleen*
>
> 8 *lymph nodes of multiple sites*

 lymphocytic
  depletion (M9653/3) 201.7 ☑
  diffuse fibrosis (M9654/3) 201.7 ☑
  reticular type (M9655/3) 201.7 ☑
  predominance (M9651/3) 201.4 ☑
 lymphocytic-histiocytic predominance (M9651/3) 201.4 ☑
 mixed cellularity (M9652/3) 201.6 ☑
 nodular sclerosis (M9656/3) 201.5 ☑
  cellular phase (M9657/3) 201.5 ☑
Hodgson's 441.9
 ruptured 441.5
Hoffa (-Kastert) (liposynovitis prepatellaris) 272.8
Holla (*see also* Spherocytosis) 282.0
homozygous-Hb-S 282.61
hoof and mouth 078.4
hookworm (*see also* Ancylostomiasis) 126.9
Horton's (temporal arteritis) 446.5
host-versus-graft (immune or nonimmune cause) 279.50
HPFH (hereditary persistence of fetal hemoglobin) ("Swiss variety") 282.7
Huchard's disease (continued arterial hypertension) 401.9
Huguier's (uterine fibroma) 218.9
human immunodeficiency (virus) 042
hunger 251.1
Hunt's
 dyssynergia cerebellaris myoclonica 334.2
 herpetic geniculate ganglionitis 053.11
Huntington's 333.4
Huppert's (multiple myeloma) (M9730/3) 203.0 ☑
Hurler's (mucopolysaccharidosis I) 277.5
Hutchinson-Boeck (sarcoidosis) 135
Hutchinson-Gilford (progeria) 259.8
Hutchinson's, meaning
 angioma serpiginosum 709.1
 cheiropompholyx 705.81
 prurigo estivalis 692.72
hyaline (diffuse) (generalized) 728.9
 membrane (lung) (newborn) 769
hydatid (*see also* Echinococcus) 122.9
Hyde's (prurigo nodularis) 698.3
hyperkinetic (*see also* Hyperkinesia) 314.9
 heart 429.82
hypertensive (*see also* Hypertension) 401.9
hypophysis 253.9
 hyperfunction 253.1

Disease, diseased — *see also* Syndrome — *continued*

hypophysis — *continued*
  hypofunction 253.2
Iceland (epidemic neuromyasthenia) 049.8
I cell 272.7
ill-defined 799.89
immunologic NEC 279.9 ☑
immunoproliferative 203.8 ☑
inclusion 078.5
  salivary gland 078.5
infancy, early NEC 779.9
infective NEC 136.9
inguinal gland 289.9
internal semilunar cartilage, cystic 717.5
intervertebral disc 722.90
  with myelopathy 722.70
  cervical, cervicothoracic 722.91
    with myelopathy 722.71
  lumbar, lumbosacral 722.93
    with myelopathy 722.73
  thoracic, thoracolumbar 722.92
    with myelopathy 722.72
intestine 569.9
  functional 564.9
    congenital 751.3
    psychogenic 306.4
  lardaceous 277.39
  organic 569.9
  protozoal NEC 007.9
iris 364.9
  specified NEC 364.89
iron
  metabolism (*see also* Hemochromatosis) 275.09
  storage (*see also* Hemochromatosis) 275.03
Isambert's (*see also* Tuberculosis, larynx) 012.3 ☑
Iselin's (osteochondrosis, fifth metatarsal) 732.5
island (scrub typhus) 081.2
itai-itai 985.5
Jadassohn's (maculopapular erythroderma) 696.2
Jadassohn-Pellizari's (anetoderma) 701.3
Jakob-Creutzfeldt (CJD) 046.19
  with dementia
    with behavioral disturbance 046.19 [294.11]
    without behavioral disturbance 046.19 [294.10]
  familial 046.19
  iatrogenic 046.19
  specified NEC 046.19
  sporadic 046.19
  variant (vCJD) 046.11
    with dementia
      with behavioral disturbance 046.11 [294.11]
      without behavioral disturbance 046.11 [294.10]
Jaksch (-Luzet) (pseudoleukemia infantum) 285.8
Janet's 300.89
Jansky-Bielschowsky 330.1
jaw NEC 526.9
  fibrocystic 526.2
Jensen's 363.05
Jeune's (asphyxiating thoracic dystrophy) 756.4
jigger 134.1
Johnson-Stevens (erythema multiforme exudativum) 695.13
joint NEC 719.9 ☑
  ankle 719.97
  Charcôt 094.0 [713.5]
  degenerative (*see also* Osteoarthrosis) 715.9 ☑
    multiple 715.09
    spine (*see also* Spondylosis) 721.90
  elbow 719.92
  foot 719.97
  hand 719.94
  hip 719.95

Disease, diseased — *see also* Syndrome — *continued*

joint — *continued*
  hypertrophic (chronic) (degenerative) (*see also* Osteoarthrosis) 715.9 ☑
    spine (*see also* Spondylosis) 721.90
  knee 719.96
  Luschka 721.90
  multiple sites 719.99
  pelvic region 719.95
  sacroiliac 724.6
  shoulder (region) 719.91
  specified site NEC 719.98
  spine NEC 724.9
    pseudarthrosis following fusion 733.82
    sacroiliac 724.6
  wrist 719.93
Jourdain's (acute gingivitis) 523.00
Jüngling's (sarcoidosis) 135
Kahler (-Bozzolo) (multiple myeloma) (M9730/3) 203.0 ☑
Kalischer's 759.6
Kaposi's 757.33
  lichen ruber 697.8
    acuminatus 696.4
    moniliformis 697.8
  xeroderma pigmentosum 757.33
Kaschin-Beck (endemic polyarthritis) 716.00
  ankle 716.07
  arm 716.02
    lower (and wrist) 716.03
    upper (and elbow) 716.02
  foot (and ankle) 716.07
  forearm (and wrist) 716.03
  hand 716.04
  leg 716.06
    lower 716.06
    upper 716.05
  multiple sites 716.09
  pelvic region (hip) (thigh) 716.05
  shoulder region 716.01
  specified site NEC 716.08
Katayama 120.2
Kawasaki 446.1
Kedani (scrub typhus) 081.2
kidney (functional) (pelvis) (*see also* Disease, renal) 593.9
  chronic 585.9
    requiring chronic dialysis 585.6
    stage
      I 585.1
      II (mild) 585.2
      III (moderate) 585.3
      IV (severe) 585.4
      V 585.5
  cystic (congenital) 753.10
    multiple 753.19
    single 753.11
    specified NEC 753.19
  fibrocystic (congenital) 753.19
  in gout 274.10
  polycystic (congenital) 753.12
    adult type (APKD) 753.13
    autosomal dominant 753.13
    autosomal recessive 753.14
    childhood type (CPKD) 753.14
    infantile type 753.14
Kienböck's (carpal lunate) (wrist) 732.3
Kimmelstiel (-Wilson) (intercapillary glomerulosclerosis) 250.4 ☑ [581.81]
  due to secondary diabetes 249.4 ☑ [581.81]
Kinnier Wilson's (hepatolenticular degeneration) 275.1
kissing 075
Kleb's (*see also* Nephritis) 583.9
Klinger's 446.4
Klippel's 723.8
Klippel-Feil (brevicollis) 756.16
knight's 911.1
Köbner's (epidermolysis bullosa) 757.39
Koenig-Wichmann (pemphigus) 694.4
Köhler's
  first (osteoarthrosis juvenilis) 732.5

Disease, diseased — *see also* Syndrome — *continued*

Köhler's — *continued*
  second (Freiberg's infraction, metatarsal head) 732.5
  patellar 732.4
  tarsal navicular (bone) (osteoarthrosis juvenilis) 732.5
Köhler-Freiberg (infraction, metatarsal head) 732.5
Köhler-Mouchet (osteoarthrosis juvenilis) 732.5
Köhler-Pellegrini-Stieda (calcification, knee joint) 726.62
Kok 759.89
König's (osteochondritis dissecans) 732.7
Korsakoff's (nonalcoholic) 294.0
  alcoholic 291.1
Kostmann's (infantile genetic agranulocytosis) 288.01
Krabbe's 330.0
Kraepelin-Morel (*see also* Schizophrenia) 295.9 ☑
Kraft-Weber-Dimitri 759.6
Kufs' 330.1
Kugelberg-Welander 335.11
Kuhnt-Junius 362.52
Kümmell's (-Verneuil) (spondylitis) 721.7
Kundrat's (lymphosarcoma) 200.1 ☑
kuru 046.0
Kussmaul (-Meier) (polyarteritis nodosa) 446.0
Kyasanur Forest 065.2
Kyrle's (hyperkeratosis follicularis in cutem penetrans) 701.1
labia
  inflammatory 616.10
  noninflammatory 624.9
    specified NEC 624.8
labyrinth, ear 386.8
lacrimal system (apparatus) (passages) 375.9
  gland 375.00
  specified NEC 375.89
Lafora's 333.2
Lagleyze-von Hippel (retinocerebral angiomatosis) 759.6
Lancereaux-Mathieu (leptospiral jaundice) 100.0
Landry's 357.0
Lane's 569.89
lardaceous (any site) 277.39
Larrey-Weil (leptospiral jaundice) 100.0
Larsen (-Johansson) (juvenile osteopathia patellae) 732.4
larynx 478.70
Lasègue's (persecution mania) 297.9
Leber's 377.16
Lederer's (acquired infectious hemolytic anemia) 283.19
Legg's (capital femoral osteochondrosis) 732.1
Legg-Calvé-Perthes (capital femoral osteochondrosis) 732.1
Legg-Calvé-Waldenström (femoral capital osteochondrosis) 732.1
Legg-Perthes (femoral capital osteochondrosis) 732.1
Legionnaires' 482.84
Leigh's 330.8
Leiner's (exfoliative dermatitis) 695.89
Leloir's (lupus erythematosus) 695.4
Lenegre's 426.0
lens (eye) 379.39
Leriche's (osteoporosis, posttraumatic) 733.7
Letterer-Siwe (acute histiocytosis X) (M9722/3) 202.5 ☑
Lev's (acquired complete heart block) 426.0
Lewandowski's (*see also* Tuberculosis) 017.0 ☑
Lewandowski-Lutz (epidermodysplasia verruciformis) 078.19
Lewy body 331.82
  with dementia
    with behavioral disturbance 331.82 [294.11]

Disease, diseased — *see also* Syndrome — *continued*

Lewy body — *continued*
  with dementia — *continued*
    without behavioral disturbance 331.82 [294.10]
Leyden's (periodic vomiting) 536.2
Libman-Sacks (verrucous endocarditis) 710.0 [424.91]
Lichtheim's (subacute combined sclerosis with pernicious anemia) 281.0 [336.2]
ligament 728.9
light chain 203.0 ☑
Lightwood's (renal tubular acidosis) 588.89
Lignac's (cystinosis) 270.0
Lindau's (retinocerebral angiomatosis) 759.6
Lindau-von Hippel (angiomatosis retinocerebellosa) 759.6
lipidosis 272.7
lipoid storage NEC 272.7
Lipschütz's 616.50
lip NEC 528.5
Little's — *see* Palsy, cerebral
liver 573.9
  alcoholic 571.3
    acute 571.1
    chronic 571.3
  chronic 571.9
    alcoholic 571.3
  cystic, congenital 751.62
  drug-induced 573.3
  due to
    chemicals 573.3
    fluorinated agents 573.3
    hypersensitivity drugs 573.3
    isoniazids 573.3
  end stage NEC 572.8
    due to hepatitis — *see* Hepatitis
  fibrocystic (congenital) 751.62
  glycogen storage 271.0
  organic 573.9
  polycystic (congenital) 751.62
Lobo's (keloid blastomycosis) 116.2
Lobstein's (brittle bones and blue sclera) 756.51
locomotor system 334.9
Lorain's (pituitary dwarfism) 253.3
Lou Gehrig's 335.20
Lucas-Championnière (fibrinous bronchitis) 466.0
Ludwig's (submaxillary cellulitis) 528.3
luetic — *see* Syphilis
lumbosacral region 724.6
lung NEC 518.89
  black 500
  congenital 748.60
  cystic 518.89
    congenital 748.4
  fibroid (chronic) (*see also* Fibrosis, lung) 515
  fluke 121.2
    oriental 121.2
  in
    amyloidosis 277.39 [517.8]
    polymyositis 710.4 [517.8]
    sarcoidosis 135 [517.8]
    Sjögren's syndrome 710.2 [517.8]
    syphilis 095.1
    systemic lupus erythematosus 710.0 [517.8]
    systemic sclerosis 710.1 [517.2]
  interstitial (chronic) 515
    acute 136.3
    respiratory bronchiolitis 516.34
  nonspecific, chronic 496
  obstructive (chronic) (COPD) 496
    with
      acute
        bronchitis 491.22
        exacerbation NEC 491.21
      alveolitis, allergic (*see also* Alveolitis, allergic) 495.9
      asthma (chronic) (obstructive) 493.2 ☑
      bronchiectasis 494.0
        with acute exacerbation 494.1

Disease, diseased — *see also* Syndrome — *continued*

lung — *continued*
   obstructive — *continued*
      with — *continued*
         bronchitis (chronic) 491.20
            with
               acute bronchitis 491.22
               exacerbation (acute) 491.21
            decompensated 491.21
               with exacerbation 491.21
            emphysema NEC 492.8
      diffuse (with fibrosis) 496
      of childhood, specific NEC 516.69
      polycystic 518.89
         asthma (chronic) (obstructive) 493.2 ☑
         congenital 748.4
      purulent (cavitary) 513.0
      restrictive 518.89
      rheumatoid 714.81
         diffuse interstitial 714.81
      specified NEC 518.89
Lutembacher's (atrial septal defect with mitral stenosis) 745.5
Lutz-Miescher (elastosis perforans serpiginosa) 701.1
Lutz-Splendore-de Almeida (Brazilian blastomycosis) 116.1
Lyell's (toxic epidermal necrolysis) 695.15
   due to drug
      correct substance properly administered 695.15
      overdose or wrong substance given or taken 977.9
         specific drug — *see* Table of Drugs and Chemicals
Lyme 088.81
lymphatic (gland) (system) 289.9
   channel (noninfective) 457.9
   vessel (noninfective) 457.9
      specified NEC 457.8
lymphoproliferative (chronic) (M9970/1) 238.79
   X linked 759.89
Machado-Joseph 334.8
Madelung's (lipomatosis) 272.8
Madura (actinomycotic) 039.9
   mycotic 117.4
Magitot's 526.4
Majocchi's (purpura annularis telangiectodes) 709.1
malarial (*see also* Malaria) 084.6
Malassez's (cystic) 608.89
Malibu 919.8
   infected 919.9
malignant (M8000/3) (*see also* Neoplasm, by site, malignant)
   previous, affecting management of pregnancy V23.89
Manson's 120.1
maple bark 495.6
maple syrup (urine) 270.3
Marburg (virus) 078.89
Marchiafava (-Bignami) 341.8
Marfan's 090.49
   congenital syphilis 090.49
   meaning Marfan's syndrome 759.82
Marie-Bamberger (hypertrophic pulmonary osteoarthropathy) (secondary) 731.2
   primary or idiopathic (acropachyderma) 757.39
   pulmonary (hypertrophic osteoarthropathy) 731.2
Marie-Strümpell (ankylosing spondylitis) 720.0
Marion's (bladder neck obstruction) 596.0
Marsh's (exophthalmic goiter) 242.0 ☑
Martin's 715.27
mast cell 757.33
   systemic (M9741/3) 202.6 ☑
mastoid (*see also* Mastoiditis) 383.9
   process 385.9
maternal, unrelated to pregnancy NEC, affecting fetus or newborn 760.9

Disease, diseased — *see also* Syndrome — *continued*

Mathieu's (leptospiral jaundice) 100.0
Mauclaire's 732.3
Mauriac's (erythema nodosum syphiliticum) 091.3
Maxcy's 081.0
McArdle (-Schmid-Pearson) (glycogenosis V) 271.0
mediastinum NEC 519.3
Medin's (*see also* Poliomyelitis) 045.9 ☑
Mediterranean 282.40
   with hemoglobinopathy 282.49
medullary center (idiopathic) (respiratory) 348.89
Meige's (chronic hereditary edema) 757.0
Meleda 757.39
Ménétrier's (hypertrophic gastritis) 535.2 ☑
Ménière's (active) 386.00
   cochlear 386.02
   cochleovestibular 386.01
   inactive 386.04
   in remission 386.04
   vestibular 386.03
meningeal — *see* Meningitis
mental (*see also* Psychosis) 298.9
Merzbacher-Pelizaeus 330.0
mesenchymal 710.9
mesenteric embolic 557.0
metabolic NEC 277.9
metal polishers' 502
metastatic — *see* Metastasis
Mibelli's 757.39
microdrepanocytic 282.41
microvascular — code to condition
microvillus
   atrophy 751.5
   inclusion (MVD) 751.5
Miescher's 709.3
Mikulicz's (dryness of mouth, absent or decreased lacrimation) 527.1
Milkman (-Looser) (osteomalacia with pseudofractures) 268.2
Miller's (osteomalacia) 268.2
Mills' 335.29
Milroy's (chronic hereditary edema) 757.0
Minamata 985.0
Minor's 336.1
Minot's (hemorrhagic disease, newborn) 776.0
Minot-von Willebrand-Jürgens (angiohemophilia) 286.4
Mitchell's (erythromelalgia) 443.82
mitral — *see* Endocarditis, mitral
Mljet (mal de Meleda) 757.39
Möbius', Moebius' 346.2 ☑
Moeller's 267
Möller (-Barlow) (infantile scurvy) 267
Mönckeberg's (*see also* Arteriosclerosis, extremities) 440.20
Mondor's (thrombophlebitis of breast) 451.89
Monge's 993.2
Morel-Kraepelin (*see also* Schizophrenia) 295.9 ☑
Morgagni's (syndrome) (hyperostosis frontalis interna) 733.3
Morgagni-Adams-Stokes (syncope with heart block) 426.9
Morquio (-Brailsford) (-Ullrich) (mucopolysaccharidosis IV) 277.5
Morton's (with metatarsalgia) 355.6
Morvan's 336.0
motor neuron (bulbar) (mixed type) 335.20
Mouchet's (juvenile osteochondrosis, foot) 732.5
mouth 528.9
Moyamoya 437.5
Mucha (acute parapsoriasis varioliformis) 696.2
mu-chain 273.2
mucolipidosis (I) (II) (III) 272.7
Münchmeyer's (exostosis luxurians) 728.11
Murri's (intermittent hemoglobinuria) 283.2
muscle 359.9
   inflammatory 728.9

Disease, diseased — *see also* Syndrome — *continued*

muscle — *continued*
   ocular 378.9
   musculoskeletal system 729.90
mushroom workers' 495.5
mycotic 117.9
myeloproliferative (chronic) (M9960/1) 238.79
myocardium, myocardial (*see also* Degeneration, myocardial) 429.1
   hypertensive (*see also* Hypertension, heart 402.90
   primary (idiopathic) 425.4
myoneural 358.9
Naegeli's 287.1
nail 703.9
   specified type NEC 703.8
Nairobi sheep 066.1
nasal 478.19
   cavity NEC 478.19
   sinus (chronic) — *see* Sinusitis
navel (newborn) NEC 779.89
   delayed separation of umbilical cord 779.83
nemaline body 359.0
neoplastic, generalized (M8000/6) 199.0
nerve — *see* Disorder, nerve
nervous system (central) 349.9
   autonomic, peripheral (*see also* Neuropathy, peripheral, autonomic) 337.9
   congenital 742.9
   inflammatory — *see* Encephalitis
   parasympathetic (*see also* Neuropathy, peripheral, autonomic) 337.9
   peripheral NEC 355.9
   prion NEC 046.79
   specified NEC 349.89
   sympathetic (*see also* Neuropathy, peripheral, autonomic) 337.9
   vegetative (*see also* Neuropathy, peripheral, autonomic) 337.9
Nettleship's (urticaria pigmentosa) 757.33
Neumann's (pemphigus vegetans) 694.4
neurologic (central) NEC (*see also* Disease, nervous system) 349.9
   peripheral NEC 355.9
neuromuscular system NEC 358.9
Newcastle 077.8
Nicolas (-Durand) — Favre (climatic bubo) 099.1
Niemann-Pick (lipid histiocytosis) 272.7
nipple 611.9
   Paget's (M8540/3) 174.0
Nishimoto (-Takeuchi) 437.5
nonarthropod-borne NEC 078.89
   central nervous system NEC 049.9
   enterovirus NEC 078.89
nonautoimmune hemolytic NEC 283.10
Nonne-Milroy-Meige (chronic hereditary edema) 757.0
Norrie's (congenital progressive oculoacousticocerebral degeneration) 743.8
nose 478.19
nucleus pulposus — *see* Disease, intervertebral disc
nutritional 269.9
   maternal, affecting fetus or newborn 760.4
oasthouse, urine 270.2
obliterative vascular 447.1
Odelberg's (juvenile osteochondrosis) 732.1
Oguchi's (retina) 368.61
Ohara's (*see also* Tularemia) 021.9
Ollier's (chondrodysplasia) 756.4
Opitz's (congestive splenomegaly) 289.51
Oppenheim's 358.8
Oppenheim-Urbach (necrobiosis lipoidica diabeticorum) 250.8 ☑ [709.3]
   due to secondary diabetes 249.8 ☑ [709.3]
optic nerve NEC 377.49
orbit 376.9
   specified NEC 376.89
Oriental liver fluke 121.1

Disease, diseased — *see also* Syndrome — *continued*

Oriental lung fluke 121.2
Ormond's 593.4
Osgood-Schlatter 732.4
Osgood's tibia (tubercle) 732.4
Osler (-Vaquez) (polycythemia vera) (M9950/1) 238.4
Osler-Rendu (familial hemorrhagic telangiectasia) 448.0
osteofibrocystic 252.01
Otto's 715.35
outer ear 380.9
ovary (noninflammatory) NEC 620.9
   cystic 620.2
   polycystic 256.4
   specified NEC 620.8
Owren's (congenital) (*see also* Defect, coagulation) 286.3
Paas' 756.59
Paget's (osteitis deformans) 731.0
   with infiltrating duct carcinoma of the breast (M8541/3) — *see* Neoplasm, breast, malignant
   bone 731.0
      osteosarcoma in (M9184/3) — *see* Neoplasm, bone, malignant
   breast (M8540/3) 174.0
      extramammary (M8542/3) (*see also* Neoplasm, skin, malignant)
         anus 154.3
         skin 173.59
      malignant (M8540/3)
         breast 174.0
         specified site NEC (M8542/3) — *see* Neoplasm, skin, malignant
         unspecified site 174.0
      mammary (M8540/3) 174.0
      nipple (M8540/3) 174.0
palate (soft) 528.9
Paltauf-Sternberg 201.9 ☑
pancreas 577.9
   cystic 577.2
      congenital 751.7
   fibrocystic 277.00
Panner's 732.3
   capitellum humeri 732.3
   head of humerus 732.3
   tarsal navicular (bone) (osteochondrosis) 732.5
panvalvular — *see* Endocarditis, mitral
parametrium 629.9
parasitic NEC 136.9
   cerebral NEC 123.9
   intestinal NEC 129
   mouth 112.0
   skin NEC 134.9
   specified type — *see* Infestation
   tongue 112.0
parathyroid (gland) 252.9
   specified NEC 252.8
Parkinson's 332.0
parodontal 523.9
Parrot's (syphilitic osteochondritis) 090.0
Parry's (exophthalmic goiter) 242.0 ☑
Parson's (exophthalmic goiter) 242.0 ☑
Pavy's 593.6
Paxton's (white piedra) 111.2
Payr's (splenic flexure syndrome) 569.89
pearl-workers' (chronic osteomyelitis) (*see also* Osteomyelitis) 730.1 ☑
Pel-Ebstein — *see* Disease, Hodgkin's
Pelizaeus-Merzbacher 330.0
   with dementia
      with behavioral disturbance 330.0 [294.11]
      without behavioral disturbance 330.0 [294.10]
Pellegrini-Stieda (calcification, knee joint) 726.62
pelvis, pelvic
   female NEC 629.9
      specified NEC 629.89
   gonococcal (acute) 098.19
      chronic or duration of 2 months or over 098.39

☑ **Additional Digit Required — Refer to the Tabular List for Digit Selection**   ▽ **Subterms under main terms may continue to next column or page**

Disease, diseased — *see also* Syndrome — *continued*

pelvis, pelvic — *continued*

infection (*see also* Disease, pelvis, inflammatory) 614.9

inflammatory (female) (PID) 614.9

with

abortion — *see* Abortion, by type, with sepsis

ectopic pregnancy (*see also* categories 633.0–633.9) 639.0

molar pregnancy (*see also* categories 630–632) 639.0

acute 614.3

chronic 614.4

complicating pregnancy 646.6 ☑

affecting fetus or newborn 760.8

following

abortion 639.0

ectopic or molar pregnancy 639.0

peritonitis (acute) 614.5

chronic NEC 614.7

puerperal, postpartum, childbirth 670.8 ☑

specified NEC 614.8

organ, female NEC 629.9

specified NEC 629.89

peritoneum, female NEC 629.9

specified NEC 629.89

penis 607.9

inflammatory 607.2

peptic NEC 536.9

acid 536.8

periapical tissues NEC 522.9

pericardium 423.9

specified type NEC 423.8

perineum

female

inflammatory 616.9

specified NEC 616.89

noninflammatory 624.9

specified NEC 624.8

male (inflammatory) 682.2

periodic (familial) (Reimann's) NEC 277.31

paralysis 359.3

periodontal NEC 523.9

specified NEC 523.8

periosteum 733.90

peripheral

arterial 443.9

autonomic nervous system (*see also* Neuropathy, autonomic) 337.9

nerve NEC (*see also* Neuropathy) 356.9

multiple — *see* Polyneuropathy

vascular 443.9

specified type NEC 443.89

peritoneum 568.9

pelvic, female 629.9

specified NEC 629.89

Perrin-Ferraton (snapping hip) 719.65

persistent mucosal (middle ear) (with posterior or superior marginal perforation of ear drum) 382.2

Perthes' (capital femoral osteochondrosis) 732.1

Petit's (*see also* Hernia, lumbar) 553.8

Peutz-Jeghers 759.6

Peyronie's 607.85

Pfeiffer's (infectious mononucleosis) 075

pharynx 478.20

Phocas' 610.1

photochromogenic (acid-fast bacilli) (pulmonary) 031.0

nonpulmonary 031.9

Pick's

brain 331.11

with dementia

with behavioral disturbance 331.11 [294.11]

without behavioral disturbance 331.11 [294.10]

cerebral atrophy 331.11

with dementia

with behavioral disturbance 331.11 [294.11]

Disease, diseased — *see also* Syndrome — *continued*

Pick's — *continued*

cerebral atrophy — *continued*

with dementia — *continued*

without behavioral disturbance 331.11 [294.10]

lipid histiocytosis 272.7

liver (pericardial pseudocirrhosis of liver) 423.2

pericardium (pericardial pseudocirrhosis of liver) 423.2

polyserositis (pericardial pseudocirrhosis of liver) 423.2

Pierson's (osteochondrosis) 732.1

pigeon fanciers' or breeders' 495.2

pineal gland 259.8

pink 985.0

Pinkus' (lichen nitidus) 697.1

pinworm 127.4

pituitary (gland) 253.9

hyperfunction 253.1

hypofunction 253.2

pituitary snuff-takers' 495.8

placenta

affecting fetus or newborn 762.2

complicating pregnancy or childbirth 656.7 ☑

pleura (cavity) (*see also* Pleurisy) 511.0

Plummer's (toxic nodular goiter) 242.3 ☑

pneumatic

drill 994.9

hammer 994.9

policeman's 729.2

Pollitzer's (hidradenitis suppurativa) 705.83

polycystic (congenital) 759.89

congenital 748.4

kidney or renal 753.12

adult type (APKD) 753.13

autosomal dominant 753.13

autosomal recessive 753.14

childhood type (CPKD) 753.14

infantile type 753.14

liver or hepatic 751.62

lung or pulmonary 518.89

ovary, ovaries 256.4

spleen 759.0

polyethylene 996.45

Pompe's (glycogenosis II) 271.0

Poncet's (tuberculous rheumatism) (*see also* Tuberculosis) 015.9 ☑

Posada-Wernicke 114.9

Potain's (pulmonary edema) 514

Pott's (*see also* Tuberculosis) 015.0 ☑ [730.88]

osteomyelitis 015.0 ☑ [730.88]

paraplegia 015.0 ☑ [730.88]

spinal curvature 015.0 ☑ [737.43]

spondylitis 015.0 ☑ [720.81]

Potter's 753.0

Poulet's 714.2

pregnancy NEC (*see also* Pregnancy) 646.9 ☑

Preiser's (osteoporosis) 733.09

Pringle's (tuberous sclerosis) 759.5

Profichet's 729.90

prostate 602.9

specified type NEC 602.8

protozoal NEC 136.8

intestine, intestinal NEC 007.9

pseudo-Hurler's (mucolipidosis III) 272.7

psychiatric (*see also* Psychosis) 298.9

psychotic (*see also* Psychosis) 298.9

Puente's (simple glandular cheilitis) 528.5

puerperal NEC (*see also* Puerperal) 674.9 ☑

pulmonary (*see also* Disease, lung)

amyloid 277.39 [517.8]

artery 417.9

circulation, circulatory 417.9

specified NEC 417.8

diffuse obstructive (chronic) 496

with

acute bronchitis 491.22

asthma (chronic) (obstructive) 493.2 ☑

exacerbation NEC (acute) 491.21

Disease, diseased — *see also* Syndrome — *continued*

pulmonary (*see also* Disease, lung) — *continued*

heart (chronic) 416.9

specified NEC 416.8

hypertensive (vascular) 416.0

cardiovascular 416.0

obstructive diffuse (chronic) 496

with

acute bronchitis 491.22

asthma (chronic) (obstructive) 493.2 ☑

bronchitis (chronic) 491.20

with

exacerbation (acute) 491.21

acute 491.22

exacerbation NEC (acute) 491.21

decompensated 491.21

with exacerbation 491.21

valve (*see also* Endocarditis, pulmonary) 424.3

pulp (dental) NEC 522.9

pulseless 446.7

Putnam's (subacute combined sclerosis with pernicious anemia) 281.0 [336.2]

Pyle (-Cohn) (craniometaphyseal dysplasia) 756.89

pyramidal tract 333.90

Quervain's

tendon sheath 727.04

thyroid (subacute granulomatous thyroiditis) 245.1

Quincke's — *see* Edema, angioneurotic

Quinquaud (acne decalvans) 704.09

rag sorters' 022.1

Raynaud's (paroxysmal digital cyanosis) 443.0

reactive airway — *see* Asthma

Recklinghausen's (M9540/1) 237.71

bone (osteitis fibrosa cystica) 252.01

Recklinghausen-Applebaum (hemochromatosis) (*see also* Hemochromatosis) 275.03

Reclus' (cystic) 610.1

rectum NEC 569.49

Refsum's (heredopathia atactica polyneuritiformis) 356.3

Reichmann's (gastrosuccorrhea) 536.8

Reimann's (periodic) 277.31

Reiter's 099.3

renal (functional) (pelvis) (*see also* Disease, kidney) 593.9

with

edema (*see also* Nephrosis) 581.9

exudative nephritis 583.89

lesion of interstitial nephritis 583.89

stated generalized cause — *see* Nephritis

acute 593.9

basement membrane NEC 583.89

with

pulmonary hemorrhage (Goodpasture's syndrome) 446.21 [583.81]

chronic (*see also* Disease, kidney, chronic) 585.9

complicating pregnancy or puerperium NEC 646.2 ☑

with hypertension — *see* Toxemia, of pregnancy

affecting fetus or newborn 760.1

cystic, congenital (*see also* Cystic, disease, kidney) 753.10

diabetic 250.4 ☑ [583.81]

due to secondary diabetes 249.4 ☑ [581.81]

due to

amyloidosis 277.39 [583.81]

diabetes mellitus 250.4 ☑ [583.81]

due to secondary diabetes 249.4 ☑ [581.81]

systemic lupus erythematosis 710.0 [583.81]

Disease, diseased — *see also* Syndrome — *continued*

renal (*see also* Disease, kidney) — *continued*

end-stage 585.6

exudative 583.89

fibrocystic (congenital) 753.19

gonococcal 098.19 [583.81]

gouty 274.10

hypertensive (*see also* Hypertension, kidney) 403.90

immune complex NEC 583.89

interstitial (diffuse) (focal) 583.89

lupus 710.0 [583.81]

maternal, affecting fetus or newborn 760.1

hypertensive 760.0

phosphate-losing (tubular) 588.0

polycystic (congenital) 753.12

adult type (APKD) 753.13

autosomal dominant 753.13

autosomal recessive 753.14

childhood type (CPKD) 753.14

infantile type 753.14

specified lesion or cause NEC (*see also* Glomerulonephritis) 583.89

subacute 581.9

syphilitic 095.4

tuberculous (*see also* Tuberculosis) 016.0 ☑ [583.81]

tubular (*see also* Nephrosis, tubular) 584.5

Rendu-Osler-Weber (familial hemorrhagic telangiectasia) 448.0

renovascular (arteriosclerotic) (*see also* Hypertension, kidney) 403.90

respiratory (tract) 519.9

acute or subacute (upper) NEC 465.9

due to fumes or vapors 506.3

multiple sites NEC 465.8

noninfectious 478.9

streptococcal 034.0

chronic 519.9

arising in the perinatal period 770.7

due to fumes or vapors 506.4

due to

aspiration of liquids or solids 508.9

external agents NEC 508.9

specified NEC 508.8

fumes or vapors 506.9

acute or subacute NEC 506.3

chronic 506.4

fetus or newborn NEC 770.9

obstructive 496

smoke inhalation 508.2

specified type NEC 519.8

upper (acute) (infectious) NEC 465.9

multiple sites NEC 465.8

noninfectious NEC 478.9

streptococcal 034.0

retina, retinal NEC 362.9

Batten's or Batten-Mayou 330.1 [362.71]

degeneration 362.89

vascular lesion 362.17

rheumatic (*see also* Arthritis) 716.8 ☑

heart — *see* Disease, heart, rheumatic

rheumatoid (heart) — *see* Arthritis, rheumatoid

rickettsial NEC 083.9

specified type NEC 083.8

Riedel's (ligneous thyroiditis) 245.3

Riga (-Fede) (cachectic aphthae) 529.0

Riggs' (compound periodontitis) 523.40

Ritter's 695.81

Rivalta's (cervicofacial actinomycosis) 039.3

Robles' (onchocerciasis) 125.3 [360.13]

Roger's (congenital interventricular septal defect) 745.4

Rokitansky's (*see also* Necrosis, liver) 570

Romberg's 349.89

Rosenthal's (factor XI deficiency) 286.2

Rossbach's (hyperchlorhydria) 536.8

psychogenic 306.4

Roth (-Bernhardt) 355.1

Runeberg's (progressive pernicious anemia) 281.0

Disease, diseased — *see also* Syndrome — *continued*

Rust's (tuberculous spondylitis) (*see also* Tuberculosis) 015.0 ☑ [720.81]
Rustitskii's (multiple myeloma) (M9730/3) 203.0 ☑
Ruysch's (Hirschsprung's disease) 751.3
Sachs (-Tay) 330.1
sacroiliac NEC 724.6
salivary gland or duct NEC 527.9
   inclusion 078.5
     streptococcal 034.0
   virus 078.5
Sander's (paranoia) 297.1
Sandhoff's 330.1
sandworm 126.9
Savill's (epidemic exfoliative dermatitis) 695.89
Schamberg's (progressive pigmentary dermatosis) 709.09
Schaumann's (sarcoidosis) 135
Schenck's (sporotrichosis) 117.1
Scheuermann's (osteochondrosis) 732.0
Schilder (-Flatau) 341.1
Schimmelbusch's 610.1
Schlatter-Osgood 732.4
Schlatter's tibia (tubercle) 732.4
Schmorl's 722.30
   cervical 722.39
   lumbar, lumbosacral 722.32
   specified region NEC 722.39
   thoracic, thoracolumbar 722.31
Scholz's 330.0
Schönlein (-Henoch) (purpura rheumatica) 287.0
Schottmüller's (*see also* Fever, paratyphoid) 002.9
Schüller-Christian (chronic histiocytosis X) 277.89
Schultz's (agranulocytosis) 288.09
Schwalbe-Ziehen-Oppenheimer 333.6
Schwartz-Jampel 359.23
Schweninger-Buzzi (macular atrophy) 701.3
sclera 379.19
scrofulous (*see also* Tuberculosis) 017.2 ☑
scrotum 608.9
sebaceous glands NEC 706.9
Secretan's (posttraumatic edema) 782.3
semilunar cartilage, cystic 717.5
seminal vesicle 608.9
Senear-Usher (pemphigus erythematosus) 694.4
serum NEC 999.59
Sever's (osteochondrosis calcaneum) 732.5
sexually transmitted — *see* Disease, venereal
Sézary's (reticulosis) (M9701/3) 202.2 ☑
Shaver's (bauxite pneumoconiosis) 503
Sheehan's (postpartum pituitary necrosis) 253.2
shimamushi (scrub typhus) 081.2
shipyard 077.1
sickle cell 282.60
   with
     crisis 282.62
     Hb-S disease 282.61
     other abnormal hemoglobin (Hb-D) (Hb-E) (Hb-G) (Hb-J) (Hb-K) (Hb-O) (Hb-P) (high fetal gene) (without crisis) 282.68
       with crisis 282.69
   elliptocytosis 282.60
   Hb-C (without crisis) 282.63
     with
       crisis 282.64
       vaso-occlusive pain 282.64
   Hb-S 282.61
     with
       crisis 282.62
       Hb-C (without crisis) 282.63
         with
           crisis 282.64
           vaso-occlusive pain 282.64

Disease, diseased — *see also* Syndrome — *continued*

sickle cell — *continued*
   Hb-S — *continued*
     with — *continued*
       other abnormal hemoglobin (Hb-D) (Hb-E) (Hb-G) (Hb-J) (Hb-K) (Hb-O) (Hb-P) (high fetal gene) (without crisis) 282.68
       with crisis 282.69
   spherocytosis 282.60
   thalassemia (without crisis) 282.41
     with
       crisis 282.42
       vaso-occlusive pain 282.42
Siegal-Cattan-Mamou (periodic) 277.31
silo fillers' 506.9
Simian B 054.3
Simmonds' (pituitary cachexia) 253.2
Simons' (progressive lipodystrophy) 272.6
Sinding-Larsen (juvenile osteopathia patellae) 732.4
sinus (*see also* Sinusitis)
   brain 437.9
   specified NEC 478.19
Sirkari's 085.0
sixth (*see also* Exanthem subitum) 058.10
Sjögren (-Gougerot) 710.2
   with lung involvement 710.2 [517.8]
Skevas-Zerfus 989.5
skin NEC 709.9
   due to metabolic disorder 277.9
   specified type NEC 709.8
sleeping (*see also* Narcolepsy) 347.00
   meaning sleeping sickness (*see also* Trypanosomiasis) 086.5
small vessel 443.9
Smith-Strang (oasthouse urine) 270.2
Sneddon-Wilkinson (subcorneal pustular dermatosis) 694.1
South African creeping 133.8
Spencer's (epidemic vomiting) 078.82
Spielmeyer-Stock 330.1
Spielmeyer-Vogt 330.1
spine, spinal 733.90
   combined system (*see also* Degeneration, combined) 266.2 [336.2]
     with pernicious anemia 281.0 [336.2]
   cord NEC 336.9
     congenital 742.9
   demyelinating NEC 341.8
   joint (*see also* Disease, joint, spine) 724.9
     tuberculous 015.0 ☑ [730.8] ☑
spinocerebellar 334.9
   specified NEC 334.8
spleen (organic) (postinfectional) 289.50
   amyloid 277.39
   lardaceous 277.39
   polycystic 759.0
   specified NEC 289.59
sponge divers' 989.5
Stanton's (melioidosis) 025
Stargardt's 362.75
Startle 759.89
Steinert's 359.21
Sternberg's — *see* Disease, Hodgkin's
Stevens-Johnson (erythema multiforme exudativum) 695.13
Sticker's (erythema infectiosum) 057.0
Stieda's (calcification, knee joint) 726.62
Still's (juvenile rheumatoid arthritis) 714.30
   adult onset 714.2
Stiller's (asthenia) 780.79
Stokes' (exophthalmic goiter) 242.0 ☑
Stokes-Adams (syncope with heart block) 426.9
Stokvis (-Talma) (enterogenous cyanosis) 289.7
stomach NEC (organic) 537.9
   functional 536.9
     psychogenic 306.4
   lardaceous 277.39
stonemasons' 502

Disease, diseased — *see also* Syndrome — *continued*

storage
   glycogen (*see also* Disease, glycogen storage) 271.0
   lipid 272.7
   mucopolysaccharide 277.5
striatopallidal system 333.90
   specified NEC 333.89
Strümpell-Marie (ankylosing spondylitis) 720.0
Stuart's (congenital factor X deficiency) (*see also* Defect, coagulation) 286.3
Stuart-Prower (congenital factor X deficiency) (*see also* Defect, coagulation) 286.3
Sturge (-Weber) (-Dimitri) (encephalocutaneous angiomatosis) 759.6
Stuttgart 100.89
Sudeck's 733.7
supporting structures of teeth NEC 525.9
suprarenal (gland) (capsule) 255.9
   hyperfunction 255.3
   hypofunction 255.41
Sutton's 709.09
Sutton and Gull's — *see* Hypertension, kidney
sweat glands NEC 705.9
   specified type NEC 705.89
sweating 078.2
Sweeley-Klionsky 272.7
Swift (-Feer) 985.0
swimming pool (bacillus) 031.1
swineherd's 100.89
Sylvest's (epidemic pleurodynia) 074.1
Symmers (follicular lymphoma) (M9690/3) 202.0 ☑
sympathetic nervous system (*see also* Neuropathy, peripheral, autonomic) 337.9
synovium 727.9
syphilitic — *see* Syphilis
systemic tissue mast cell (M9741/3) 202.6 ☑
Taenzer's 757.4
Takayasu's (pulseless) 446.7
Talma's 728.85
Tangier (familial high-density lipoprotein deficiency) 272.5
Tarral-Besnier (pityriasis rubra pilaris) 696.4
Taylor's 701.8
Tay-Sachs 330.1
tear duct 375.69
teeth, tooth 525.9
   hard tissues 521.9
     specified NEC 521.89
   pulp NEC 522.9
tendon 727.9
   inflammatory NEC 727.9
terminal vessel 443.9
testis 608.9
Thaysen-Gee (nontropical sprue) 579.0
Thomsen's 359.22
Thomson's (congenital poikiloderma) 757.33
Thornwaldt's, Tornwaldt's (pharyngeal bursitis) 478.29
throat 478.20
   septic 034.0
thromboembolic (*see also* Embolism) 444.9
thymus (gland) 254.9
   specified NEC 254.8
thyroid (gland) NEC 246.9
   heart (*see also* Hyperthyroidism) 242.9 ☑ [425.7]
   lardaceous 277.39
   specified NEC 246.8
Tietze's 733.6
Tommaselli's
   correct substance properly administered 599.70
   overdose or wrong substance given or taken 961.4
tongue 529.9
tonsils, tonsillar (and adenoids) (chronic) 474.9
   specified NEC 474.8
tooth, teeth 525.9

Disease, diseased — *see also* Syndrome — *continued*

tooth, teeth — *continued*
   hard tissues 521.9
     specified NEC 521.89
   pulp NEC 522.9
Tornwaldt's (pharyngeal bursitis) 478.29
Tourette's 307.23
trachea 519.19
tricuspid — *see* Endocarditis, tricuspid
triglyceride-storage, type I, II, III 272.7
triple vessel (coronary arteries) — *see* Arteriosclerosis, coronary
trisymptomatic, Gougerot's 709.1
trophoblastic (*see also* Hydatidiform mole) 630
   previous, affecting management of pregnancy V23.1
tsutsugamushi (scrub typhus) 081.2
tube (fallopian), noninflammatory 620.9
   specified NEC 620.8
tuberculous NEC (*see also* Tuberculosis) 011.9 ☑
tubo-ovarian
   inflammatory (*see also* Salpingo-oophoritis) 614.2
   noninflammatory 620.9
     specified NEC 620.8
tubotympanic, chronic (with anterior perforation of ear drum) 382.1
tympanum 385.9
Uhl's 746.84
umbilicus (newborn) NEC 779.89
   delayed separation 779.83
Underwood's (sclerema neonatorum) 778.1
undiagnosed 799.9
Unna's (seborrheic dermatitis) 690.18
unstable hemoglobin hemolytic 282.7
Unverricht (-Lundborg) 345.1 ☑
Urbach-Oppenheim (necrobiosis lipoidica diabeticorum) 250.8 ☑ [709.3]
   due to secondary diabetes 249.8 ☑ [709.3]
Urbach-Wiethe (lipoid proteinosis) 272.8
ureter 593.9
urethra 599.9
   specified type NEC 599.84
urinary (tract) 599.9
   bladder 596.9
     specified NEC 596.89
   maternal, affecting fetus or newborn 760.1
Usher-Senear (pemphigus erythematosus) 694.4
uterus (organic) 621.9
   infective (*see also* Endometritis) 615.9
   inflammatory (*see also* Endometritis) 615.9
   noninflammatory 621.9
     specified type NEC 621.8
uveal tract
   anterior 364.9
   posterior 363.9
vagabonds' 132.1
vagina, vaginal
   inflammatory 616.10
   noninflammatory 623.9
     specified NEC 623.8
Valsuani's (progressive pernicious anemia, puerperal) 648.2 ☑
   complicating pregnancy or puerperium 648.2 ☑
valve, valvular — *see also* Endocarditis
   congenital NEC (*see also* Anomaly, heart, valve) 746.9
   pulmonary 746.00
     specified type NEC 746.89
van Bogaert-Nijssen (-Peiffer) 330.0
van Creveld-von Gierke (glycogenosis I) 271.0
van den Bergh's (enterogenous cyanosis) 289.7
van Neck's (juvenile osteochondrosis) 732.1
Vaquez (-Osler) (polycythemia vera) (M9950/1) 238.4
vascular 459.9

☑ **Additional Digit Required** — Refer to the Tabular List for Digit Selection   ▽ **Subterms under main terms may continue to next column or page**

88 — Volume 2   ▶◀ Revised Text   ● New Line   ▲ Revised Code   2015 ICD-9-CM

Disease, diseased — see also Syndrome — continued
vascular — continued
  arteriosclerotic — see Arteriosclerosis
  hypertensive — see Hypertension
  obliterative 447.1
    peripheral 443.9
  occlusive 459.9
  peripheral (occlusive) 443.9
    in (due to) (with) diabetes mellitus
      250.7 ☑ [443.81]
    in (due to) (with) secondary dia-
      betes 249.7 ☑ [443.81]
    specified type NEC 443.89
  vas deferens 608.9
  vasomotor 443.9
  vasospastic 443.9
  vein 459.9
  venereal 099.9
    chlamydial NEC 099.50
      anus 099.52
      bladder 099.53
      cervix 099.53
      epididymis 099.54
      genitourinary NEC 099.55
        lower 099.53
        specified NEC 099.54
      pelvic inflammatory disease 099.54
      perihepatic 099.56
      peritoneum 099.56
      pharynx 099.51
      rectum 099.52
      specified site NEC 099.59
      testis 099.54
      vagina 099.53
      vulva 099.53
    complicating pregnancy, childbirth, or
      puerperium 647.2 ☑
    fifth 099.1
    sixth 099.1
    specified nature or type NEC 099.8
      chlamydial — see Disease, venereal,
        chlamydial
Verneuil's (syphilitic bursitis) 095.7
Verse's (calcinosis intervertebralis)
    275.49 [722.90]
vertebra, vertebral NEC 733.90
  disc — see Disease, Intervertebral disc
vibration NEC 994.9
Vidal's (lichen simplex chronicus) 698.3
Vincent's (trench mouth) 101
Virchow's 733.99
virus (filterable) NEC 078.89
  arbovirus NEC 066.9
  arthropod-borne NEC 066.9
  central nervous system NEC 049.9
    specified type NEC 049.8
  complicating pregnancy, childbirth, or
    puerperium 647.6 ☑
  contact (with) V01.79
    varicella V01.71
  exposure to V01.79
    varicella V01.71
  Marburg 078.89
  maternal
    with fetal damage affecting manage-
      ment of pregnancy 655.3 ☑
  nonarthropod-borne NEC 078.89
    central nervous system NEC 049.9
    specified type NEC 049.8
  vaccination, prophylactic (against)
    V04.89
vitreous 379.29
vocal cords NEC 478.5
Vogt's (Cecile) 333.71
Vogt-Spielmeyer 330.1
Volhard-Fahr (malignant nephrosclerosis)
    403.00
Volkmann's
  acquired 958.6
von Bechterew's (ankylosing spondylitis)
    720.0
von Economo's (encephalitis lethargica)
    049.8
von Eulenburg's (congenital paramyotonia)
    359.29

Disease, diseased — see also Syndrome — continued
von Gierke's (glycogenosis I) 271.0
von Graefe's 378.72
von Hippel's (retinocerebral angiomatosis)
    759.6
von Hippel-Lindau (angiomatosis
    retinocerebellosa) 759.6
von Jaksch's (pseudoleukemia infantum)
    285.8
von Recklinghausen's (M9540/1) 237.71
  bone (osteitis fibrosa cystica) 252.01
von Recklinghausen-Applebaum
    (hemochromatosis) (see also
    Hemochromatosis) 275.03
von Willebrand (-Jürgens) (angiohemophil-
    ia) 286.4
von Zambusch's (lichen sclerosus et atroph-
    icus) 701.0
Voorhoeve's (dyschondroplasia) 756.4
Vrolik's (osteogenesis imperfecta) 756.51
vulva
  inflammatory 616.10
  noninflammatory 624.9
    specified NEC 624.8
Wagner's (colloid milium) 709.3
Waldenström's (osteochondrosis capital
    femoral) 732.1
Wallgren's (obstruction of splenic vein with
    collateral circulation) 459.89
Wardrop's (with lymphangitis) 681.9
  finger 681.02
  toe 681.11
Wassilieff's (leptospiral jaundice) 100.0
wasting NEC 799.4
  due to malnutrition 261
  paralysis 335.21
Waterhouse-Friderichsen 036.3
waxy (any site) 277.39
Weber-Christian (nodular nonsuppurative
    panniculitis) 729.30
Wegner's (syphilitic osteochondritis) 090.0
Weil's (leptospiral jaundice) 100.0
  of lung 100.0
Weir Mitchell's (erythromelalgia) 443.82
Werdnig-Hoffmann 335.0
Werlhof's (see also Purpura, thrombocy-
    topenic) 287.39
Wermer's 258.01
Werner's (progeria adultorum) 259.8
Werner-His (trench fever) 083.1
Werner-Schultz (agranulocytosis) 288.09
Wernicke's (superior hemorrhagic polioen-
    cephalitis) 265.1
Wernicke-Posadas 114.9
Whipple's (intestinal lipodystrophy) 040.2
whipworm 127.3
white
White's (congenital) (keratosis follicularis)
    757.39
  blood cell 288.9
    specified NEC 288.8
  spot 701.0
Whitmore's (melioidosis) 025
Widal-Abrami (acquired hemolytic jaundice)
    283.9
Wilkie's 557.1
Wilkinson-Sneddon (subcorneal pustular
    dermatosis) 694.1
Willis' (diabetes mellitus) (see also Diabetes)
    250.0 ☑
  due to secondary diabetes 249.0 ☑
Wilson's (hepatolenticular degeneration)
    275.1
Wilson-Brocq (dermatitis exfoliativa) 695.89
winter vomiting 078.82
Wise's 696.2
Wohlfart-Kugelberg-Welander 335.11
Woillez's (acute idiopathic pulmonary con-
    gestion) 518.52
Wolman's (primary familial xanthomatosis)
    272.7
wool-sorters' 022.1
Zagari's (xerostomia) 527.7
Zahorsky's (exanthem subitum) 058.10
Ziehen-Oppenheim 333.6

Disease, diseased — see also Syndrome — continued
  zoonotic, bacterial NEC 027.9
    specified type NEC 027.8
Disfigurement (due to scar) 709.2
  head V48.6
  limb V49.4
  neck V48.7
  trunk V48.7
Disgerminoma — see Dysgerminoma
Disinsertion, retina 361.04
Disintegration, complete, of the body 799.89
  traumatic 869.1
Disk kidney 753.3
Dislocatable hip, congenital — see also Dislocation, hip, congenital 754.30
Dislocation (articulation) (closed) (displacement) (simple) (subluxation) 839.8

> Note — "Closed" includes simple, com-
> plete, partial, uncomplicated, and unspec-
> ified dislocation.
>
> "Open" includes dislocation specified as
> infected or compound and dislocation
> with foreign body.
>
> "Chronic," "habitual," "old," or "recur-
> rent" dislocations should be coded as
> indicated under the entry "Dislocation,
> recurrent," and "pathological" as indicat-
> ed under the entry "Dislocation, patho-
> logical."
>
> For late effect of dislocation see Late,
> effect, dislocation.

  with fracture — see Fracture, by site
  acromioclavicular (joint) (closed) 831.04
    open 831.14
  anatomical site (closed)
    specified NEC 839.69
      open 839.79
    unspecified or ill-defined 839.8
      open 839.9
  ankle (scaphoid bone) (closed) 837.0
    open 837.1
  arm (closed) 839.8
    open 839.9
  astragalus (closed) 837.0
    open 837.1
  atlanto-axial (closed) 839.01
    open 839.11
  atlas (closed) 839.01
    open 839.11
  axis (closed) 839.02
    open 839.12
  back (closed) 839.8
    open 839.9
  Bell-Daly 723.8
  breast bone (closed) 839.61
    open 839.71
  capsule, joint — see Dislocation, by site
  carpal (bone) — see Dislocation, wrist
  carpometacarpal (joint) (closed) 833.04
    open 833.14
  cartilage (joint) (see also Dislocation, by site)
    knee — see Tear, meniscus
  cervical, cervicodorsal, or cervicothoracic
    (spine) (vertebra) — see Dislocation,
    vertebra, cervical
  chiropractic (see also Lesion, nonallopathic)
    739.9
  chondrocostal — see Dislocation, costochon-
    dral
  chronic — see Dislocation, recurrent
  clavicle (closed) 831.04
    open 831.14
  coccyx (closed) 839.41
    open 839.51
  collar bone (closed) 831.04
    open 831.14
  compound (open) NEC 839.9
  congenital NEC 755.8
    hip (see also Dislocation, hip, congenital)
      754.30
    lens 743.37
    rib 756.3
    sacroiliac 755.69

Dislocation — continued
  congenital — continued
    spine NEC 756.19
    vertebra 756.19
  coracoid (closed) 831.09
    open 831.19
  costal cartilage (closed) 839.69
    open 839.79
  costochondral (closed) 839.69
    open 839.79
  cricoarytenoid articulation (closed) 839.69
    open 839.79
  cricothyroid (cartilage) articulation (closed)
    839.69
    open 839.79
  dorsal vertebrae (closed) 839.21
    open 839.31
  ear ossicle 385.23
  elbow (closed) 832.00
    anterior (closed) 832.01
      open 832.11
    congenital 754.89
    divergent (closed) 832.09
      open 832.19
    lateral (closed) 832.04
      open 832.14
    medial (closed) 832.03
      open 832.13
    open 832.10
    posterior (closed) 832.02
      open 832.12
    recurrent 718.32
    specified type NEC 832.09
      open 832.19
  eye 360.81
    lateral 376.36
  eyeball 360.81
    lateral 376.36
  femur
    distal end (closed) 836.50
      anterior 836.52
        open 836.62
      lateral 836.54
        open 836.64
      medial 836.53
        open 836.63
      open 836.60
      posterior 836.51
        open 836.61
    proximal end (closed) 835.00
      anterior (pubic) 835.03
        open 835.13
      obturator 835.02
        open 835.12
      open 835.10
      posterior 835.01
        open 835.11
  fibula
    distal end (closed) 837.0
      open 837.1
    proximal end (closed) 836.59
      open 836.69
  finger(s) (phalanx) (thumb) (closed) 834.00
    interphalangeal (joint) 834.02
      open 834.12
    metacarpal (bone), distal end 834.01
      open 834.11
    metacarpophalangeal (joint) 834.01
      open 834.11
    open 834.10
    recurrent 718.34
  foot (closed) 838.00
    open 838.10
    recurrent 718.37
  forearm (closed) 839.8
    open 839.9
  fracture — see Fracture, by site
  glenoid (closed) 831.09
    open 831.19
  habitual — see Dislocation, recurrent
  hand (closed) 839.8
    open 839.9
  hip (closed) 835.00
    anterior 835.03
      obturator 835.02
        open 835.12

☑ Additional Digit Required — Refer to the Tabular List for Digit Selection   ▽ Subterms under main terms may continue to next column or page

2015 ICD-9-CM   ▶◀ Revised Text   ● New Line   ▲ Revised Code   Volume 2 — 89

Dislocation — *continued*
hip — *continued*
  anterior — *continued*
    open 835.13
  congenital (unilateral) 754.30
    with subluxation of other hip 754.35
    bilateral 754.31
  developmental 718.75
  open 835.10
  posterior 835.01
    open 835.11
  recurrent 718.35
humerus (closed) 831.00
  distal end (*see also* Dislocation, elbow) 832.00
    open 831.10
  proximal end (closed) 831.00
    anterior (subclavicular) (subcoracoid) (subglenoid) (closed) 831.01
      open 831.11
    inferior (closed) 831.03
      open 831.13
    open 831.10
    posterior (closed) 831.02
      open 831.12
implant — *see* Complications, mechanical
incus 385.23
infracoracoid (closed) 831.01
  open 831.11
innominate (pubic junction) (sacral junction) (closed) 839.69
  acetabulum (*see also* Dislocation, hip) 835.00
  open 839.79
interphalangeal (joint)
  finger or hand (closed) 834.02
    open 834.12
  foot or toe (closed) 838.06
    open 838.16
jaw (cartilage) (meniscus) (closed) 830.0
  open 830.1
  recurrent 524.69
joint NEC (closed) 839.8
  developmental 718.7 ☑
  open 839.9
  pathological — *see* Dislocation, pathological
  recurrent — *see* Dislocation, recurrent
knee (closed) 836.50
  anterior 836.51
    open 836.61
  congenital (with genu recurvatum) 754.41
  habitual 718.36
  lateral 836.54
    open 836.64
  medial 836.53
    open 836.63
  old 718.36
  open 836.60
  posterior 836.52
    open 836.62
  recurrent 718.36
  rotatory 836.59
    open 836.69
lacrimal gland 375.16
leg (closed) 839.8
  open 839.9
lens (crystalline) (complete) (partial) 379.32
  anterior 379.33
  congenital 743.37
  ocular implant 996.53
  posterior 379.34
  traumatic 921.3
ligament — *see* Dislocation, by site
lumbar (vertebrae) (closed) 839.20
  open 839.30
lumbosacral (vertebrae) (closed) 839.20
  congenital 756.19
  open 839.30
mandible (closed) 830.0
  open 830.1
maxilla (inferior) (closed) 830.0
  open 830.1
meniscus (knee) (*see also* Tear, meniscus)
  other sites — *see* Dislocation, by site

Dislocation — *continued*
metacarpal (bone)
  distal end (closed) 834.01
    open 834.11
  proximal end (closed) 833.05
    open 833.15
metacarpophalangeal (joint) (closed) 834.01
  open 834.11
metatarsal (bone) (closed) 838.04
  open 838.14
metatarsophalangeal (joint) (closed) 838.05
  open 838.15
midcarpal (joint) (closed) 833.03
  open 833.13
midtarsal (joint) (closed) 838.02
  open 838.12
Monteggia's — *see* Dislocation, hip
multiple locations (except fingers only or toes only) (closed) 839.8
  open 839.9
navicular (bone) foot (closed) 837.0
  open 837.1
neck (*see also* Dislocation, vertebra, cervical) 839.00
Nélaton's — *see* Dislocation, ankle
nontraumatic (joint) — *see* Dislocation, pathological
nose (closed) 839.69
  open 839.79
not recurrent, not current injury — *see* Dislocation, pathological
occiput from atlas (closed) 839.01
  open 839.11
old — *see* Dislocation, recurrent
open (compound) NEC 839.9
ossicle, ear 385.23
paralytic (flaccid) (spastic) — *see* Dislocation, pathological
patella (closed) 836.3
  congenital 755.64
  open 836.4
pathological NEC 718.20
  ankle 718.27
  elbow 718.22
  foot 718.27
  hand 718.24
  hip 718.25
  knee 718.26
  lumbosacral joint 724.6
  multiple sites 718.29
  pelvic region 718.25
  sacroiliac 724.6
  shoulder (region) 718.21
  specified site NEC 718.28
  spine 724.8
    sacroiliac 724.6
  wrist 718.23
pelvis (closed) 839.69
  acetabulum (*see also* Dislocation, hip) 835.00
  open 839.79
phalanx
  foot or toe (closed) 838.09
    open 838.19
  hand or finger (*see also* Dislocation, finger) 834.00
postpoliomyelitic — *see* Dislocation, pathological
prosthesis, internal — *see* Complications, mechanical
radiocarpal (joint) (closed) 833.02
  open 833.12
radioulnar (joint)
  distal end (closed) 833.01
    open 833.11
  proximal end (*see also* Dislocation, elbow) 832.00
radius
  distal end (closed) 833.00
    open 833.10
  proximal end (closed) 832.01
    open 832.11
recurrent (*see also* Derangement, joint, recurrent) 718.3 ☑
  elbow 718.32
  hip 718.35

Dislocation — *continued*
recurrent (*see also* Derangement, joint, recurrent) — *continued*
  joint NEC 718.38
  knee 718.36
  lumbosacral (joint) 724.6
  patella 718.36
  sacroiliac 724.6
  shoulder 718.31
  temporomandibular 524.69
rib (cartilage) (closed) 839.69
  congenital 756.3
  open 839.79
sacrococcygeal (closed) 839.42
  open 839.52
sacroiliac (joint) (ligament) (closed) 839.42
  congenital 755.69
  open 839.52
  recurrent 724.6
sacrum (closed) 839.42
  open 839.52
scaphoid (bone)
  ankle or foot (closed) 837.0
    open 837.1
  wrist (closed) (*see also* Dislocation, wrist) 833.00
    open 833.10
scapula (closed) 831.09
  open 831.19
semilunar cartilage, knee — *see* Tear, meniscus
septal cartilage (nose) (closed) 839.69
  open 839.79
septum (nasal) (old) 470
sesamoid bone — *see* Dislocation, by site
shoulder (blade) (ligament) (closed) 831.00
  anterior (subclavicular) (subcoracoid) (subglenoid) (closed) 831.01
    open 831.11
  chronic 718.31
  inferior 831.03
    open 831.13
  open 831.10
  posterior (closed) 831.02
    open 831.12
  recurrent 718.31
skull — *see* Injury, intracranial
Smith's — *see* Dislocation, foot
spine (articular process) (*see also* Dislocation, vertebra) (closed) 839.40
  atlanto-axial (closed) 839.01
    open 839.11
    recurrent 723.8
  cervical, cervicodorsal, cervicothoracic (closed) (*see also* Dislocation, vertebrae, cervical) 839.00
    open 839.10
    recurrent 723.8
  coccyx 839.41
    open 839.51
  congenital 756.19
  due to birth trauma 767.4
  open 839.50
  recurrent 724.9
  sacroiliac 839.42
    recurrent 724.6
  sacrum (sacrococcygeal) (sacroiliac) 839.42
    open 839.52
  spontaneous — *see* Dislocation, pathological
sternoclavicular (joint) (closed) 839.61
  open 839.71
sternum (closed) 839.61
  open 839.71
subastragalar — *see* Dislocation, foot
subglenoid (closed) 831.01
  open 831.11
symphysis
  jaw (closed) 830.0
    open 830.1
  mandibular (closed) 830.0
    open 830.1
  pubis (closed) 839.69
    open 839.79
tarsal (bone) (joint) 838.01

Dislocation — *continued*
tarsal — *continued*
  open 838.11
tarsometatarsal (joint) 838.03
  open 838.13
temporomandibular (joint) (closed) 830.0
  open 830.1
  recurrent 524.69
thigh
  distal end (*see also* Dislocation, femur, distal end) 836.50
  proximal end (*see also* Dislocation, hip) 835.00
thoracic (vertebrae) (closed) 839.21
  open 839.31
thumb(s) (*see also* Dislocation, finger) 834.00
thyroid cartilage (closed) 839.69
  open 839.79
tibia
  distal end (closed) 837.0
    open 837.1
  proximal end (closed) 836.50
    anterior 836.51
      open 836.61
    lateral 836.54
      open 836.64
    medial 836.53
      open 836.63
    open 836.60
    posterior 836.52
      open 836.62
    rotatory 836.59
      open 836.69
tibiofibular
  distal (closed) 837.0
    open 837.1
  superior (closed) 836.59
    open 836.69
toe(s) (closed) 838.09
  open 838.19
trachea (closed) 839.69
  open 839.79
ulna
  distal end (closed) 833.09
    open 833.19
  proximal end — *see* Dislocation, elbow
vertebra (articular process) (body) (closed) (traumatic) 839.40
  cervical, cervicodorsal or cervicothoracic (closed) 839.00
    first (atlas) 839.01
      open 839.11
    second (axis) 839.02
      open 839.12
    third 839.03
      open 839.13
    fourth 839.04
      open 839.14
    fifth 839.05
      open 839.15
    sixth 839.06
      open 839.16
    seventh 839.07
      open 839.17
    congenital 756.19
    multiple sites 839.08
      open 839.18
    open 839.10
  congenital 756.19
  dorsal 839.21
    open 839.31
    recurrent 724.9
  lumbar, lumbosacral 839.20
    open 839.30
  non-traumatic — *see* Displacement, intervertebral disc
  open NEC 839.50
  recurrent 724.9
  specified region NEC 839.49
    open 839.59
  thoracic 839.21
    open 839.31
wrist (carpal bone) (scaphoid) (semilunar) (closed) 833.00
  carpometacarpal (joint) 833.04
    open 833.14

☑ **Additional Digit Required** — Refer to the Tabular List for Digit Selection   ▽ Subterms under main terms may continue to next column or page

90 — Volume 2   ▶◀ Revised Text   ● New Line   ▲ Revised Code   2015 ICD-9-CM

Dislocation — continued
  wrist — continued
    metacarpal bone, proximal end 833.05
      open 833.15
    midcarpal (joint) 833.03
      open 833.13
    open 833.10
    radiocarpal (joint) 833.02
      open 833.12
    radioulnar (joint) 833.01
      open 833.11
    recurrent 718.33
    specified site NEC 833.09
      open 833.19
  xiphoid cartilage (closed) 839.61
    open 839.71

Dislodgement
  artificial skin graft 996.55
  decellularized allodermis graft 996.55

Disobedience, hostile (covert) (overt) — see
  also Disturbance, conduct 312.0 ☑

Disorder — see also Disease
  academic underachievement, childhood
    and adolescence 313.83
  accommodation 367.51
    drug-induced 367.89
    toxic 367.89
  adjustment (see also Reaction, adjustment)
    309.9
    with
      anxiety 309.24
      anxiety and depressed mood 309.28
      depressed mood 309.0
      disturbance of conduct 309.3
      disturbance of emotions and conduct
        309.4
  adrenal (capsule) (cortex) (gland) 255.9
    specified type NEC 255.8
  adrenogenital 255.2
  affective (see also Psychosis, affective)
    296.90
    atypical 296.81
  aggressive, unsocialized (see also Distur-
    bance, conduct) 312.0 ☑
  alcohol, alcoholic (see also Alcohol) 291.9
    induced mood 291.89
  allergic — see Allergy
  amino acid (metabolic) (see also Distur-
    bance, metabolism, amino acid)
    270.9
    albinism 270.2
    alkaptonuria 270.2
    argininosuccinicaciduria 270.6
    beta-amino-isobutyricaciduria 277.2
    cystathioninuria 270.4
    cystinosis 270.0
    cystinuria 270.0
    glycinuria 270.0
    homocystinuria 270.4
    imidazole 270.5
    maple syrup (urine) disease 270.3
    neonatal, transitory 775.89
    oasthouse urine disease 270.2
    ochronosis 270.2
    phenylketonuria 270.1
    phenylpyruvic oligophrenia 270.1
    purine NEC 277.2
    pyrimidine NEC 277.2
    renal transport NEC 270.0
    specified type NEC 270.8
    transport NEC 270.0
      renal 270.0
    xanthinuria 277.2
  amnestic (see also Amnestic syndrome)
    294.8
    alcohol-induced persisting 291.1
    drug-induced persisting 292.83
    in conditions classified elsewhere 294.0
  anaerobic glycolysis with anemia 282.3
  anxiety (see also Anxiety) 300.00
    due to or associated with physical condi-
      tion 293.84
  arteriole 447.9
    specified type NEC 447.8
  artery 447.9
    specified type NEC 447.8

Disorder — see also Disease — continued
  articulation — see Disorder, joint
  Asperger's 299.8 ☑
  attachment of infancy or early childhood
    313.89
  attention deficit 314.00
    with hyperactivity 314.01
    predominantly
      combined hyperactive/inattentive
        314.01
      hyperactive/impulsive 314.01
      inattentive 314.00
    residual type 314.8
  auditory processing disorder 388.45
    acquired 388.45
    developmental 315.32
  autistic 299.0 ☑
  autoimmune NEC 279.49
    hemolytic (cold type) (warm type) 283.0
    parathyroid 252.1
    thyroid 245.2
  avoidant, childhood or adolescence 313.21
  balance
    acid-base 276.9
      mixed (with hypercapnia) 276.4
    electrolyte 276.9
    fluid 276.9
  behavior NEC (see also Disturbance, con-
    duct) 312.9
    disruptive 312.9
  bilirubin excretion 277.4
  bipolar (affective) (alternating) 296.80

> Note — Use the following fifth-digit
> subclassification with categories
> 296.0–296.6:
>
> 0   unspecified
>
> 1   mild
>
> 2   moderate
>
> 3   severe, without mention of psy-
>   chotic behavior
>
> 4   severe, specified as with psychotic
>   behavior
>
> 5   in partial or unspecified remission
>
> 6   in full remission

    atypical 296.7
    currently
      depressed 296.5 ☑
      hypomanic 296.4 ☑
      manic 296.4 ☑
    mixed 296.6 ☑
    specified type NEC 296.89
    type I 296.7
      most recent episode (or current)
        depressed 296.5 ☑
        hypomanic 296.4 ☑
        manic 296.4 ☑
        mixed 296.6 ☑
        unspecified 296.7
      single manic episode 296.0 ☑
    type II (recurrent major depressive
      episodes with hypomania) 296.89
  bladder 596.9
    functional NEC 596.59
    specified NEC 596.89
  bleeding 286.9
  bone NEC 733.90
    specified NEC 733.99
  brachial plexus 353.0
  branched-chain amino-acid degradation
    270.3
  breast 611.9
    puerperal, postpartum 676.3 ☑
    specified NEC 611.89
  Briquet's 300.81
  bursa 727.9
    shoulder region 726.10
  carbohydrate metabolism, congenital 271.9
  cardiac, functional 427.9
    postoperative 997.1
    psychogenic 306.2
  cardiovascular, psychogenic 306.2
  cartilage NEC 733.90

Disorder — see also Disease — continued
  cartilage — continued
    articular 718.00
      ankle 718.07
      elbow 718.02
      foot 718.07
      hand 718.04
      hip 718.05
      knee 717.9
      multiple sites 718.09
      pelvic region 718.05
      shoulder region 718.01
      specified
        site NEC 718.08
        type NEC 733.99
      wrist 718.03
  catatonic — see Catatonia
  central auditory processing 315.32
    acquired 388.45
    developmental 315.32
  cervical region NEC 723.9
  cervical root (nerve) NEC 353.2
  character NEC (see also Disorder, personali-
    ty) 301.9
  ciliary body 364.9
    specified NEC 364.89
  coagulation (factor) (see also Defect, coagu-
    lation) 286.9
    factor VIII (congenital) (functional) 286.0
    factor IX (congenital) (functional) 286.1
    neonatal, transitory 776.3
  coccyx 724.70
    specified NEC 724.79
  cognitive 294.9
  colon 569.9
    functional 564.9
      congenital 751.3
  communication 307.9
  conduct (see also Disturbance, conduct)
    312.9
    adjustment reaction 309.3
    adolescent onset type 312.82
    childhood onset type 312.81
    compulsive 312.30
      specified type NEC 312.39
    hyperkinetic 314.2
    onset unspecified 312.89
    socialized (type) 312.20
      aggressive 312.23
      unaggressive 312.21
    specified NEC 312.89
  conduction, heart 426.9
    specified NEC 426.89
  conflict
    sexual orientation 302.0
  congenital
    glycosylation (CDG) 271.8
  convulsive (secondary) (see also Convul-
    sions) 780.39
    due to injury at birth 767.0
    idiopathic 780.39
  coordination 781.3
  cornea NEC 371.89
    due to contact lens 371.82
  corticosteroid metabolism NEC 255.2
  cranial nerve — see Disorder, nerve, cranial
  cyclothymic 301.13
  degradation, branched-chain amino acid
    270.3
  delusional 297.1
  dentition 520.6
  depersonalization 300.6
  depressive NEC 311
    atypical 296.82
    major (see also Psychosis, affective)
      296.2 ☑
      recurrent episode 296.3 ☑
      single episode 296.2 ☑
  development, specific 315.9
    associated with hyperkinesia 314.1
    coordination 315.4
    language 315.31
      and speech due to hearing loss
        315.34
    learning 315.2
      arithmetical 315.1

Disorder — see also Disease — continued
  development, specific — continued
    learning — continued
      reading 315.00
    mixed 315.5
    motor coordination 315.4
    specified type NEC 315.8
    speech 315.39
      and language due to hearing loss
        315.34
  diaphragm 519.4
  digestive 536.9
    fetus or newborn 777.9
      specified NEC 777.8
    psychogenic 306.4
  disintegrative, childhood 299.1 ☑
  dissociative 300.15
    identity 300.14
    nocturnal 307.47
  drug-related 292.9
  dysmorphic body 300.7
  dysthymic 300.4
  ear 388.9
    degenerative NEC 388.00
    external 380.9
      specified 380.89
    pinna 380.30
    specified type NEC 388.8
    vascular NEC 388.00
  eating NEC 307.50
  electrolyte NEC 276.9
    with
      abortion — see Abortion, by type,
        with metabolic disorder
      ectopic pregnancy (see also cate-
        gories 633.0–633.9) 639.4
      molar pregnancy (see also categories
        630–632) 639.4
    acidosis 276.2
      metabolic 276.2
      respiratory 276.2
    alkalosis 276.3
      metabolic 276.3
      respiratory 276.3
    following
      abortion 639.4
      ectopic or molar pregnancy 639.4
    neonatal, transitory NEC 775.5
  emancipation as adjustment reaction 309.22
  emotional (see also Disorder, mental,
    nonpsychotic) V40.9
  endocrine 259.9
    specified type NEC 259.8
  esophagus 530.9
    functional 530.5
    psychogenic 306.4
  explosive
    intermittent 312.34
    isolated 312.35
  expressive language 315.31
  eye 379.90
    globe — see Disorder, globe
    ill-defined NEC 379.99
    limited duction NEC 378.63
    specified NEC 379.8
  eyelid 374.9
    degenerative 374.50
    sensory 374.44
    specified type NEC 374.89
    vascular 374.85
  factitious (with combined psychological and
    physical signs and symptoms) (with
    predominantly physical signs and
    symptoms) 300.19
    with predominantly psychological signs
      and symptoms 300.16
  factor, coagulation (see also Defect, coagu-
    lation) 286.9
    IX (congenital) (functional) 286.1
    VIII (congenital) (functional) 286.0
  fascia 728.9
  fatty acid oxidation 277.85
  feeding — see Feeding
  female sexual arousal 302.72
  fluency 315.35
    adult onset 307.0

Disorder — *see also* Disease — *continued*
fluency — *continued*
    childhood onset 315.35
    due to late effect of cerebrovascular accident 438.14
    in conditions classified elsewhere 784.52
fluid NEC 276.9
gastric (functional) 536.9
  motility 536.8
  psychogenic 306.4
  secretion 536.8
gastrointestinal (functional) NEC 536.9
  newborn (neonatal) 777.9
    specified NEC 777.8
  psychogenic 306.4
gender (child) 302.6
  adult 302.85
gender identity (childhood) 302.6
  adolescents 302.85
  adults (-life) 302.85
genitourinary system, psychogenic 306.50
globe 360.9
  degenerative 360.20
    specified NEC 360.29
  specified type NEC 360.89
hearing (*see also* Deafness)
  conductive type (air) (*see also* Deafness, conductive) 389.00
  mixed conductive and sensorineural 389.20
    bilateral 389.22
    unilateral 389.21
  nerve
    bilateral 389.12
    unilateral 389.13
  perceptive (*see also* Deafness, perceptive) 389.10
  sensorineural type NEC (*see also* Deafness, sensorineural 389.10
heart action 427.9
  postoperative 997.1
hematological, transient neonatal 776.9
  specified type NEC 776.8
hematopoietic organs 289.9
hemorrhagic NEC 287.9
  due to intrinsic circulating anticoagulants, antibodies, or inhibitors 286.59
    with
      acquired hemophilia 286.52
      antiphospholipid antibody 286.53
  specified type NEC 287.8
hemostasis (*see also* Defect, coagulation) 286.9
homosexual conflict 302.0
hypomanic (chronic) 301.11
identity
  childhood and adolescence 313.82
    gender 302.6
immune mechanism (immunity) 279.9
  single complement (C1-C9) 279.8
  specified type NEC 279.8
impulse control (*see also* Disturbance, conduct, compulsive) 312.30
infant sialic acid storage 271.8
integument, fetus or newborn 778.9
  specified type NEC 778.8
interactional psychotic (childhood) (*see also* Psychosis, childhood) 299.1 ☑
intermittent explosive 312.34
intervertebral disc 722.90
  cervical, cervicothoracic 722.91
  lumbar, lumbosacral 722.93
  thoracic, thoracolumbar 722.92
intestinal 569.9
  functional NEC 564.9
    congenital 751.3
    postoperative 564.4
  psychogenic 306.4
introverted, of childhood and adolescence 313.22
involuntary emotional expression (IEED) 310.81
iris 364.9
  specified NEC 364.89
iron, metabolism 275.09

Disorder — *see also* Disease — *continued*
iron, metabolism — *continued*
  specified type NEC 275.09
isolated explosive 312.35
joint NEC 719.90
  ankle 719.97
  elbow 719.92
  foot 719.97
  hand 719.94
  hip 719.95
  knee 719.96
  multiple sites 719.99
  pelvic region 719.95
  psychogenic 306.0
  shoulder (region) 719.91
  specified site NEC 719.98
  temporomandibular 524.60
    sounds on opening or closing 524.64
    specified NEC 524.69
  wrist 719.93
kidney 593.9
  functional 588.9
    specified NEC 588.89
labyrinth, labyrinthine 386.9
  specified type NEC 386.8
lactation 676.9 ☑
language (developmental) (expressive) 315.31
  mixed receptive-expressive 315.32
learning 315.9
ligament 728.9
ligamentous attachments, peripheral (*see also* Enthesopathy)
  spine 720.1
limb NEC 729.90
  psychogenic 306.0
lipid
  metabolism, congenital 272.9
  storage 272.7
lipoprotein deficiency (familial) 272.5
low back NEC 724.9
  psychogenic 306.0
lumbosacral
  plexus 353.1
  root (nerve) NEC 353.4
lymphoproliferative (chronic) NEC (M9970/1) 238.79
  post-transplant (PTLD) 238.77
major depressive (*see also* Psychosis, affective) 296.2 ☑
  recurrent episode 296.3 ☑
  single episode 296.2 ☑
male erectile 607.84
  nonorganic origin 302.72
manic (*see also* Psychosis, affective) 296.0 ☑
  atypical 296.81
mathematics 315.1
meniscus NEC (*see also* Disorder, cartilage, articular) 718.0 ☑
menopausal 627.9
  specified NEC 627.8
menstrual 626.9
  psychogenic 306.52
  specified NEC 626.8
mental (nonpsychotic) 300.9
  affecting management of pregnancy, childbirth, or puerperium 648.4 ☑
  drug-induced 292.9
    hallucinogen persisting perception 292.89
    specified type NEC 292.89
  due to or associated with
    alcoholism 291.9
    drug consumption NEC 292.9
      specified type NEC 292.89
    physical condition NEC 293.9
  induced by drug 292.9
    specified type NEC 292.89
  neurotic (*see also* Neurosis) 300.9
  of infancy, childhood or adolescence 313.9
  persistent
    other
      due to conditions classified elsewhere 294.8

Disorder — *see also* Disease — *continued*
mental — *continued*
  persistent — *continued*
    unspecified
      due to conditions classified elsewhere 294.9
  presenile 310.1
    psychotic NEC 290.10
  previous, affecting management of pregnancy V23.89
  psychoneurotic (*see also* Neurosis) 300.9
  psychotic (*see also* Psychosis) 298.9
    brief 298.8
    senile 290.20
  specific, following organic brain damage 310.9
    cognitive or personality change of other type 310.1
    frontal lobe syndrome 310.0
    postconcussional syndrome 310.2
    specified type NEC 310.89
  transient
    in conditions classified elsewhere 293.9
metabolism NEC 277.9
  with
    abortion — *see* Abortion, by type, with metabolic disorder
    ectopic pregnancy (*see also* categories 633.0–633.9) 639.4
    molar pregnancy (*see also* categories 630–632) 639.4
  alkaptonuria 270.2
  amino acid (*see also* Disorder, amino acid) 270.9
    specified type NEC 270.8
  ammonia 270.6
  arginine 270.6
  argininosuccinic acid 270.6
  basal 794.7
  bilirubin 277.4
  calcium 275.40
  carbohydrate 271.9
    specified type NEC 271.8
  cholesterol 272.9
  citrulline 270.6
  copper 275.1
  corticosteroid 255.2
  cystine storage 270.0
  cystinuria 270.0
  fat 272.9
  fatty acid oxidation 277.85
  following
    abortion 639.4
    ectopic or molar pregnancy 639.4
  fructosemia 271.2
  fructosuria 271.2
  fucosidosis 271.8
  galactose-1-phosphate uridyl transferase 271.1
  glutamine 270.7
  glycine 270.7
  glycogen storage NEC 271.0
    hepatorenal 271.0
  hemochromatosis (*see also* Hemochromatosis) 275.03
  in labor and delivery 669.0 ☑
  iron 275.09
  lactose 271.3
  lipid 272.9
    specified type NEC 272.8
    storage 272.7
  lipoprotein (*see also* Hyperlipemia deficiency (familial)) 272.5
  lysine 270.7
  magnesium 275.2
  mannosidosis 271.8
  mineral 275.9
    specified type NEC 275.8
  mitochondrial 277.87
  mucopolysaccharide 277.5
  nitrogen 270.9
  ornithine 270.6
  oxalosis 271.8
  pentosuria 271.8
  phenylketonuria 270.1

Disorder — *see also* Disease — *continued*
metabolism — *continued*
  phosphate 275.3
  phosphorous 275.3
  plasma protein 273.9
    specified type NEC 273.8
  porphyrin 277.1
  purine 277.2
  pyrimidine 277.2
  serine 270.7
  sodium 276.9
  specified type NEC 277.89
  steroid 255.2
  threonine 270.7
  urea cycle 270.6
  xylose 271.8
micturition NEC 788.69
  psychogenic 306.53
misery and unhappiness, of childhood and adolescence 313.1
mitochondrial metabolism 277.87
mitral valve 424.0
mood (*see also* Disorder, bipolar) 296.90
  alcohol-induced 291.89
  episodic 296.90
    specified NEC 296.99
  in conditions classified elsewhere 293.83
motor tic 307.20
  chronic 307.22
  transient (childhood) 307.21
movement NEC 333.90
  hysterical 300.11
  medication-induced 333.90
  periodic limb 327.51
  sleep related, unspecified 780.58
    other organic 327.59
  specified type NEC 333.99
  stereotypic 307.3
mucopolysaccharide 277.5
muscle 728.9
  psychogenic 306.0
  specified type NEC 728.3
muscular attachments, peripheral (*see also* Enthesopathy)
  spine 720.1
musculoskeletal system NEC 729.90
  psychogenic 306.0
myeloproliferative (chronic) NEC (M9960/1) 238.79
myoneural 358.9
  due to lead 358.2
  specified type NEC 358.8
  toxic 358.2
myotonic 359.29
neck region NEC 723.9
nerve 349.9
  abducens NEC 378.54
  accessory 352.4
  acoustic 388.5
  auditory 388.5
  auriculotemporal 350.8
  axillary 353.0
  cerebral — *see* Disorder, nerve, cranial
  cranial 352.9
    first 352.0
    second 377.49
    third
      partial 378.51
      total 378.52
    fourth 378.53
    fifth 350.9
    sixth 378.54
    seventh NEC 351.9
    eighth 388.5
    ninth 352.2
    tenth 352.3
    eleventh 352.4
    twelfth 352.5
    multiple 352.6
  entrapment — *see* Neuropathy, entrapment
  facial 351.9
    specified NEC 351.8
  femoral 355.2
  glossopharyngeal NEC 352.2
  hypoglossal 352.5

Disorder — see also Disease — continued

nerve — continued
iliohypogastric 355.79
ilioinguinal 355.79
intercostal 353.8
lateral
cutaneous of thigh 355.1
popliteal 355.3
lower limb NEC 355.8
medial, popliteal 355.4
median NEC 354.1
obturator 355.79
oculomotor
partial 378.51
total 378.52
olfactory 352.0
optic 377.49
hypoplasia 377.43
ischemic 377.41
nutritional 377.33
toxic 377.34
peroneal 355.3
phrenic 354.8
plantar 355.6
pneumogastric 352.3
posterior tibial 355.5
radial 354.3
recurrent laryngeal 352.3
root 353.9
specified NEC 353.8
saphenous 355.79
sciatic NEC 355.0
specified NEC 355.9
lower limb 355.79
upper limb 354.8
spinal 355.9
sympathetic NEC 337.9
trigeminal 350.9
specified NEC 350.8
trochlear 378.53
ulnar 354.2
upper limb NEC 354.9
vagus 352.3
nervous system NEC 349.9
autonomic (peripheral) (see also Neuropathy, peripheral, autonomic) 337.9
cranial 352.9
parasympathetic (see also Neuropathy, peripheral, autonomic) 337.9
specified type NEC 349.89
sympathetic (see also Neuropathy, peripheral, autonomic) 337.9
vegetative (see also Neuropathy, peripheral, autonomic) 337.9
neurohypophysis NEC 253.6
neurological NEC 781.99
peripheral NEC 355.9
neuromuscular NEC 358.9
hereditary NEC 359.1
specified NEC 358.8
toxic 358.2
neurotic 300.9
specified type NEC 300.89
neutrophil, polymorphonuclear (functional) 288.1
nightmare 307.47
night terror 307.46
obsessive-compulsive 300.3
oppositional defiant, childhood and adolescence 313.81
optic
chiasm 377.54
associated with
inflammatory disorders 377.54
neoplasm NEC 377.52
pituitary 377.51
pituitary disorders 377.51
vascular disorders 377.53
nerve 377.49
radiations 377.63
tracts 377.63
orbit 376.9
specified NEC 376.89
orgasmic
female 302.73
male 302.74

Disorder — see also Disease — continued

overanxious, of childhood and adolescence 313.0
oxidation, fatty acid 277.85
pancreas, internal secretion (other than diabetes mellitus) 251.9
specified type NEC 251.8
panic 300.01
with agoraphobia 300.21
papillary muscle NEC 429.81
paranoid 297.9
induced 297.3
shared 297.3
parathyroid 252.9
specified type NEC 252.8
paroxysmal, mixed 780.39
pentose phosphate pathway with anemia 282.2
periodic limb movement 327.51
peroxisomal 277.86
personality 301.9
affective 301.10
aggressive 301.3
amoral 301.7
anancastic, anankastic 301.4
antisocial 301.7
asocial 301.7
asthenic 301.6
avoidant 301.82
borderline 301.83
compulsive 301.4
cyclothymic 301.13
dependent-passive 301.6
dyssocial 301.7
emotional instability 301.59
epileptoid 301.3
explosive 301.3
following organic brain damage 310.1
histrionic 301.50
hyperthymic 301.11
hypomanic (chronic) 301.11
hypothymic 301.12
hysterical 301.50
immature 301.89
inadequate 301.6
introverted 301.21
labile 301.59
moral deficiency 301.7
narcissistic 301.81
obsessional 301.4
obsessive-compulsive 301.4
overconscientious 301.4
paranoid 301.0
passive (-dependent) 301.6
passive-aggressive 301.84
pathological NEC 301.9
pseudosocial 301.7
psychopathic 301.9
schizoid 301.20
introverted 301.21
schizotypal 301.22
schizotypal 301.22
seductive 301.59
type A 301.4
unstable 301.59
pervasive developmental 299.9 ☑
childhood-onset 299.8 ☑
specified NEC 299.8 ☑
phonological 315.39
pigmentation, choroid (congenital) 743.53
pinna 380.30
specified type NEC 380.39
pituitary, thalamic 253.9
anterior NEC 253.4
iatrogenic 253.7
postablative 253.7
specified NEC 253.8
pityriasis-like NEC 696.8
platelets (blood) 287.1
polymorphonuclear neutrophils (functional) 288.1
porphyrin metabolism 277.1
postmenopausal 627.9
specified type NEC 627.8
post-transplant lymphoproliferative (PTLD) 238.77

Disorder — see also Disease — continued

post-traumatic stress (PTSD) 309.81
posttraumatic stress 309.81
acute 309.81
brief 309.81
chronic 309.81
premenstrual dysphoric (PMDD) 625.4
psoriatic-like NEC 696.8
psychic, with diseases classified elsewhere 316
psychogenic NEC (see also condition) 300.9
allergic NEC
respiratory 306.1
anxiety 300.00
atypical 300.00
generalized 300.02
appetite 307.59
articulation, joint 306.0
asthenic 300.5
blood 306.8
cardiovascular (system) 306.2
compulsive 300.3
cutaneous 306.3
depressive 300.4
digestive (system) 306.4
dysmenorrheic 306.52
dyspneic 306.1
eczematous 306.3
endocrine (system) 306.6
eye 306.7
feeding 307.59
functional NEC 306.9
gastric 306.4
gastrointestinal (system) 306.4
genitourinary (system) 306.50
heart (function) (rhythm) 306.2
hemic 306.8
hyperventilatory 306.1
hypochondriacal 300.7
hysterical 300.10
intestinal 306.4
joint 306.0
learning 315.2
limb 306.0
lymphatic (system) 306.8
menstrual 306.52
micturition 306.53
monoplegic NEC 306.0
motor 307.9
muscle 306.0
musculoskeletal 306.0
neurocirculatory 306.2
obsessive 300.3
occupational 300.89
organ or part of body NEC 306.9
organs of special sense 306.7
paralytic NEC 306.0
phobic 300.20
physical NEC 306.9
pruritic 306.3
rectal 306.4
respiratory (system) 306.1
rheumatic 306.0
sexual (function) 302.70
specified type NEC 302.79
sexual orientation conflict 302.0
skin (allergic) (eczematous) (pruritic) 306.3
sleep 307.40
initiation or maintenance 307.41
persistent 307.42
transient 307.41
movement 780.58
sleep terror 307.46
specified type NEC 307.49
specified part of body NEC 306.8
stomach 306.4
psychomotor NEC 307.9
hysterical 300.11
psychoneurotic (see also Neurosis) 300.9
mixed 300.89
psychophysiologic (see also Disorder, psychosomatic) 306.9
psychosexual identity (childhood) 302.6
adult-life 302.85
psychosomatic NEC 306.9

Disorder — see also Disease — continued

psychosomatic — continued
allergic NEC
respiratory 306.1
articulation, joint 306.0
cardiovascular (system) 306.2
cutaneous 306.3
digestive (system) 306.4
dysmenorrheic 306.52
dyspneic 306.1
endocrine (system) 306.6
eye 306.7
gastric 306.4
gastrointestinal (system) 306.4
genitourinary (system) 306.50
heart (functional) (rhythm) 306.2
hyperventilatory 306.1
intestinal 306.4
joint 306.0
limb 306.0
lymphatic (system) 306.8
menstrual 306.52
micturition 306.53
monoplegic NEC 306.0
muscle 306.0
musculoskeletal 306.0
neurocirculatory 306.2
organs of special sense 306.7
paralytic NEC 306.0
pruritic 306.3
rectal 306.4
respiratory (system) 306.1
rheumatic 306.0
sexual (function) 302.70
skin 306.3
specified part of body NEC 306.8
specified type NEC 302.79
stomach 306.4
psychotic (see also Psychosis) 298.9
brief 298.8
purine metabolism NEC 277.2
pyrimidine metabolism NEC 277.2
reactive attachment of infancy or early childhood 313.89
reading, developmental 315.00
reflex 796.1
REM sleep behavior 327.42
renal function, impaired 588.9
specified type NEC 588.89
renal transport NEC 588.89
respiration, respiratory NEC 519.9
due to
aspiration of liquids or solids 508.9
inhalation of fumes or vapors 506.9
smoke inhalation 508.2
psychogenic 306.1
retina 362.9
specified type NEC 362.89
rumination 307.53
sacroiliac joint NEC 724.6
sacrum 724.6
schizo-affective (see also Schizophrenia) 295.7 ☑
schizoid, childhood or adolescence 313.22
schizophreniform 295.4 ☑
schizotypal personality 301.22
secretion, thyrocalcitonin 246.0
seizure 345.9 ☑
recurrent 345.9 ☑
epileptic — see Epilepsy
semantic pragmatic 315.39
with autism 299.0 ☑
sense of smell 781.1
psychogenic 306.7
separation anxiety 309.21
sexual (see also Deviation, sexual) 302.9
aversion 302.79
desire, hypoactive 302.71
function, psychogenic 302.70
shyness, of childhood and adolescence 313.21
single complement (C1-C9) 279.8
skin NEC 709.9
fetus or newborn 778.9
specified type 778.8

☑ Additional Digit Required — Refer to the Tabular List for Digit Selection

▽ Subterms under main terms may continue to next column or page

2015 ICD-9-CM

►◄ Revised Text   ● New Line   ▲ Revised Code

Volume 2 — 93

Disorder — Disorder

Disorder — *see also* Disease — *continued*
  skin — *continued*
    psychogenic (allergic) (eczematous)
      (pruritic) 306.3
    specified type NEC 709.8
    vascular 709.1
  sleep 780.50
    with apnea — *see* Apnea, sleep
    alcohol induced 291.82
    arousal 307.46
      confusional 327.41
    circadian rhythm 327.30
      advanced sleep phase type 327.32
      alcohol induced 291.82
      delayed sleep phase type 327.31
      drug induced 292.85
      free running type 327.34
      in conditions classified elsewhere
        327.37
      irregular sleep-wake type 327.33
      jet lag type 327.35
      other 327.39
      shift work type 327.36
    drug induced 292.85
    initiation or maintenance (*see also* Insom-
      nia) 780.52
      nonorganic origin (transient) 307.41
        persistent 307.42
    nonorganic origin 307.40
      specified type NEC 307.49
    organic specified type NEC 327.8
    periodic limb movement 327.51
    specified NEC 780.59
    wake
      cycle — *see* Disorder, sleep, circadian
        rhythm
      schedule — *see* Disorer, sleep, circa-
        dian rhythm
  social, of childhood and adolescence 313.22
  soft tissue 729.90
    specified type NEC 729.99
  somatization 300.81
  somatoform (atypical) (undifferentiated)
    300.82
    severe 300.81
    specified type NEC 300.89
  speech NEC 784.59
    nonorganic origin 307.9
  spine NEC 724.9
    ligamentous or muscular attachments,
      peripheral 720.1
  steroid metabolism NEC 255.2
  stomach (functional) (*see also* Disorder,
    gastric) 536.9
    psychogenic 306.4
  storage, iron 275.09
  stress (*see also* Reaction, stress, acute) 308.3
    posttraumatic
      acute 309.81
      brief 309.81
      chronic 309.81
  substitution 300.11
  suspected — *see* Observation
  synovium 727.9
  temperature regulation, fetus or newborn
    778.4
  temporomandibular joint NEC 524.60
    sounds on opening or closing 524.64
    specified NEC 524.69
  tendon 727.9
    shoulder region 726.10
  thoracic root (nerve) NEC 353.3
  thyrocalcitonin secretion 246.0
  thyroid (gland) NEC 246.9
    specified type NEC 246.8
  tic 307.20
    chronic (motor or vocal) 307.22
    motor-verbal 307.23
    organic origin 333.1
    transient (of childhood) 307.21
  tooth NEC 525.9
    development NEC 520.9
      specified type NEC 520.8
    eruption 520.6
    specified type NEC 525.8
  Tourette's 307.23

Disorder — *see also* Disease — *continued*
  transport, carbohydrate 271.9
    specified type NEC 271.8
  tubular, phosphate-losing 588.0
  tympanic membrane 384.9
  unaggressive, unsocialized (*see also* Distur-
    bance, conduct) 312.1
  undersocialized, unsocialized (*see also* Dis-
    turbance, conduct)
    aggressive (type) 312.0
    unaggressive (type) 312.1
  vision, visual NEC 368.9
    binocular NEC 368.30
    cortex 377.73
      associated with
        inflammatory disorders 377.73
        neoplasms 377.71
        vascular disorders 377.72
    pathway NEC 377.63
      associated with
        inflammatory disorders 377.63
        neoplasms 377.61
        vascular disorders 377.62
  vocal tic
    chronic 307.22
  wakefulness (*see also* Hypersomnia) 780.54
    nonorganic origin (transient) 307.43
      persistent 307.44
  written expression 315.2
Disorganized globe 360.29
Displacement, displaced

> Note — For acquired displacement of
> bones, cartilage, joints, tendons, due to
> injury, see also Dislocation.
>
> Displacements at ages under one year
> should be considered congenital, provid-
> ed there is no indication the condition
> was acquired after birth.

  acquired traumatic of bone, cartilage, joint,
    tendon NEC (without fracture) (*see
    also* Dislocation) 839.8
    with fracture — *see* Fracture, by site
  adrenal gland (congenital) 759.1
  alveolus and teeth, vertical 524.75
  appendix, retrocecal (congenital) 751.5
  auricle (congenital) 744.29
  bladder (acquired) 596.89
    congenital 753.8
  brachial plexus (congenital) 742.8
  brain stem, caudal 742.4
  canaliculus lacrimalis 743.65
  cardia, through esophageal hiatus 750.6
  cerebellum, caudal 742.4
  cervix — *see* Displacement, uterus
  colon (congenital) 751.4
  device, implant, or graft — *see* Complica-
    tions, mechanical
  epithelium
    columnar of cervix 622.10
    cuboidal, beyond limits of external os
      (uterus) 752.49
  esophageal mucosa into cardia of stomach,
    congenital 750.4
  esophagus (acquired) 530.89
    congenital 750.4
  eyeball (acquired) (old) 376.36
    congenital 743.8
    current injury 871.3
    lateral 376.36
  fallopian tube (acquired) 620.4
    congenital 752.19
    opening (congenital) 752.19
  gallbladder (congenital) 751.69
  gastric mucosa 750.7
    into
      duodenum 750.7
      esophagus 750.7
      Meckel's diverticulum, congenital
        750.7
  globe (acquired) (lateral) (old) 376.36
    current injury 871.3
  graft
    artificial skin graft 996.55
    decellularized allodermis graft 996.55
  heart (congenital) 746.87

Displacement, displaced — *continued*
  heart — *continued*
    acquired 429.89
  hymen (congenital) (upward) 752.49
  internal prosthesis NEC — *see* Complica-
    tions, mechanical
  intervertebral disc (with neuritis, radiculitis,
    sciatica, or other pain) 722.2
    with myelopathy 722.70
    cervical, cervicodorsal, cervicothoracic
      722.0
      with myelopathy 722.71
      due to major trauma — *see* Disloca-
        tion, vertebra, cervical
    due to trauma — *see* Dislocation, verte-
      bra
    lumbar, lumbosacral 722.10
      with myelopathy 722.73
      due to major trauma — *see* Disloca-
        tion, vertebra, lumbar
    thoracic, thoracolumbar 722.11
      with myelopathy 722.72
      due to major trauma — *see* Disloca-
        tion, vertebra, thoracic
  intrauterine device 996.32
  kidney (acquired) 593.0
    congenital 753.3
  lacrimal apparatus or duct (congenital)
    743.65
  macula (congenital) 743.55
  Meckel's diverticulum (congenital) 751.0
  nail (congenital) 757.5
    acquired 703.8
  opening of Wharton's duct in mouth 750.26
  organ or site, congenital NEC — *see* Malpo-
    sition, congenital
  ovary (acquired) 620.4
    congenital 752.0
    free in peritoneal cavity (congenital)
      752.0
    into hernial sac 620.4
  oviduct (acquired) 620.4
    congenital 752.19
  parathyroid (gland) 252.8
  parotid gland (congenital) 750.26
  punctum lacrimale (congenital) 743.65
  sacroiliac (congenital) (joint) 755.69
    current injury — *see* Dislocation,
      sacroiliac
    old 724.6
  spine (congenital) 756.19
  spleen, congenital 759.0
  stomach (congenital) 750.7
    acquired 537.89
  subglenoid (closed) 831.01
  sublingual duct (congenital) 750.26
  teeth, tooth 524.30
    horizontal 524.33
    vertical 524.34
  tongue (congenital) (downward) 750.19
  trachea (congenital) 748.3
  ureter or ureteric opening or orifice (congen-
    ital) 753.4
  uterine opening of oviducts or fallopian
    tubes 752.19
  uterus, uterine (*see also* Malposition, uterus)
    621.6
    congenital 752.39
  ventricular septum 746.89
    with rudimentary ventricle 746.89
  xyphoid bone (process) 738.3
Disproportion 653.9 ☑
  affecting fetus or newborn 763.1
  breast, reconstructed 612.1
    between native and reconstructed 612.1
  caused by
    conjoined twins 678.1 ☑
    contraction, pelvis (general) 653.1 ☑
      inlet 653.2 ☑
      midpelvic 653.8 ☑
      midplane 653.8 ☑
      outlet 653.3 ☑
    fetal
      ascites 653.7 ☑
      hydrocephalus 653.6 ☑
      hydrops 653.7 ☑

Disproportion — *continued*
  caused by — *continued*
    fetal – – *continued*
      meningomyelocele 653.7 ☑
      sacral teratoma 653.7 ☑
      tumor 653.7 ☑
    hydrocephalic fetus 653.6 ☑
    pelvis, pelvic, abnormality (bony) NEC
      653.0 ☑
    unusually large fetus 653.5 ☑
  causing obstructed labor 660.1 ☑
  cephalopelvic, normally formed fetus
    653.4 ☑
    causing obstructed labor 660.1 ☑
  fetal NEC 653.5 ☑
    causing obstructed labor 660.1 ☑
  fetopelvic, normally formed fetus 653.4 ☑
    causing obstructed labor 660.1 ☑
  mixed maternal and fetal origin, normally
    formed fetus 653.4 ☑
  pelvis, pelvic (bony) NEC 653.1 ☑
    causing obstructed labor 660.1 ☑
  specified type NEC 653.8 ☑
Disruption
  cesarean wound 674.1 ☑
  family V61.09
    due to
      child in
        care of non-parental family
          member V61.06
        foster care V61.06
        welfare custody V61.05
      death of family member V61.07
      divorce V61.03
      estrangement V61.09
        parent-child V61.04
      extended absence of family member
        NEC V61.08
      family member
        on military deployment V61.01
        return from military deployment
          V61.02
      legal separation V61.03
  gastrointestinal anastomosis 997.49
  ligament(s) (*see also* Sprain)
    knee
      current injury — *see* Dislocation,
        knee
      old 717.89
        capsular 717.85
        collateral (medial) 717.82
          lateral 717.81
        cruciate (posterior) 717.84
          anterior 717.83
        specified site NEC 717.85
  marital V61.10
    involving
      divorce V61.03
      estrangement V61.09
  operation wound (external) (*see also* Dehis-
    cence) 998.32
    internal 998.31
  organ transplant, anastomosis site — *see*
    Complications, transplant, organ, by
    site
  ossicles, ossicular chain 385.23
    traumatic — *see* Fracture, skull, base
  parenchyma
    liver (hepatic) — *see* Laceration, liver,
      major
    spleen — *see* Laceration, spleen,
      parenchyma, massive
  phase-shift, of 24-hour sleep-wake cycle,
    unspecified 780.55
    nonorganic origin 307.45
  sleep-wake cycle (24-hour), unspecified
    780.55
    circadian rhythm 327.33
    nonorganic origin 307.45
  suture line (external) (*see also* Dehiscence)
    998.32
    internal 998.31
  wound 998.30
    cesarean operation 674.1 ☑
    episiotomy 674.2 ☑
    operation (surgical) 998.32

☑ **Additional Digit Required** — Refer to the Tabular List for Digit Selection   ▽ **Subterms under main terms may continue to next column or page**

94 — Volume 2   ▶◀ Revised Text   ● New Line   ▲ Revised Code   2015 ICD-9-CM

Disruption — *continued*
  wound — *continued*
    operation — *continued*
      cesarean 674.1 ☑
      internal 998.31
      perineal (obstetric) 674.2 ☑
      uterine 674.1 ☑
Disruptio uteri — *see also* Rupture, uterus
  complicating delivery — *see* Delivery, complicated, rupture, uterus
Dissatisfaction with
  employment V62.29
  school environment V62.3
Dissecting — *see* condition
Dissection
  aorta 441.00
    abdominal 441.02
    thoracic 441.01
    thoracoabdominal 441.03
  artery, arterial
    carotid 443.21
    coronary 414.12
    iliac 443.22
    renal 443.23
    specified NEC 443.29
    vertebral 443.24
  vascular 459.9
  wound — *see* Wound, open, by site
Disseminated — *see* condition
Dissociated personality NEC 300.15
Dissociation
  auriculoventricular or atrioventricular (any degree) (AV) 426.89
    with heart block 426.0
  interference 426.89
  isorhythmic 426.89
  rhythm
    atrioventricular (AV) 426.89
    interference 426.89
Dissociative
  identity disorder 300.14
  reaction NEC 300.15
Dissolution, vertebra — *see also* Osteoporosis 733.00
Distention
  abdomen (gaseous) 787.3
  bladder 596.89
  cecum 569.89
  colon 569.89
  gallbladder 575.8
  gaseous (abdomen) 787.3
  intestine 569.89
  kidney 593.89
  liver 573.9
  seminal vesicle 608.89
  stomach 536.8
    acute 536.1
    psychogenic 306.4
  ureter 593.5
  uterus 621.8
Distichia, distichiasis (eyelid) 743.63
Distoma hepaticum infestation 121.3
Distomiasis 121.9
  bile passages 121.3
    due to Clonorchis sinensis 121.1
  hemic 120.9
  hepatic (liver) 121.3
    due to Clonorchis sinensis (clonorchiasis) 121.1
  intestinal 121.4
  liver 121.3
    due to Clonorchis sinensis 121.1
  lung 121.2
  pulmonary 121.2
Distomolar (fourth molar) 520.1
  causing crowding 524.31
Disto-occlusion (division I) (division II) 524.22
Distortion (congenital)
  adrenal (gland) 759.1
  ankle (joint) 755.69
  anus 751.5
  aorta 747.29
  appendix 751.5
  arm 755.59
  artery (peripheral) NEC (*see also* Distortion, peripheral vascular system) 747.60

Distortion — *continued*
  artery (*see also* Distortion, peripheral vascular system) — *continued*
    cerebral 747.81
    coronary 746.85
    pulmonary 747.39
    retinal 743.58
    umbilical 747.5
  auditory canal 744.29
    causing impairment of hearing 744.02
  bile duct or passage 751.69
  bladder 753.8
  brain 742.4
  bronchus 748.3
  cecum 751.5
  cervix (uteri) 752.49
  chest (wall) 756.3
  clavicle 755.51
  clitoris 752.49
  coccyx 756.19
  colon 751.5
  common duct 751.69
  cornea 743.41
  cricoid cartilage 748.3
  cystic duct 751.69
  duodenum 751.5
  ear 744.29
    auricle 744.29
      causing impairment of hearing 744.02
    causing impairment of hearing 744.09
    external 744.29
      causing impairment of hearing 744.02
    inner 744.05
    middle, except ossicles 744.03
      ossicles 744.04
    ossicles 744.04
  endocrine (gland) NEC 759.2
  epiglottis 748.3
  Eustachian tube 744.24
  eye 743.8
    adnexa 743.69
  face bone(s) 756.0
  fallopian tube 752.19
  femur 755.69
  fibula 755.69
  finger(s) 755.59
  foot 755.67
  gallbladder 751.69
  genitalia, genital organ(s)
    female 752.89
      external 752.49
      internal NEC 752.89
    male 752.89
      penis 752.69
  glottis 748.3
  gyri 742.4
  hand bone(s) 755.59
  heart (auricle) (ventricle) 746.89
    valve (cusp) 746.89
  hepatic duct 751.69
  humerus 755.59
  hymen 752.49
  ileum 751.5
  intestine (large) (small) 751.5
    with anomalous adhesions, fixation or malrotation 751.4
  jaw NEC 524.89
  jejunum 751.5
  kidney 753.3
  knee (joint) 755.64
  labium (majus) (minus) 752.49
  larynx 748.3
  leg 755.69
  lens 743.36
  liver 751.69
  lumbar spine 756.19
    with disproportion (fetopelvic) 653.0 ☑
      affecting fetus or newborn 763.1
      causing obstructed labor 660.1 ☑
  lumbosacral (joint) (region) 756.19
  lung (fissures) (lobe) 748.69
  nerve 742.8
  nose 748.1

Distortion — *continued*
  organ
    of Corti 744.05
    of site not listed — *see* Anomaly, specified type NEC
  ossicles, ear 744.04
  ovary 752.0
  oviduct 752.19
  pancreas 751.7
  parathyroid (gland) 759.2
  patella 755.64
  peripheral vascular system NEC 747.60
    gastrointestinal 747.61
    lower limb 747.64
    renal 747.62
    spinal 747.82
    upper limb 747.63
  pituitary (gland) 759.2
  radius 755.59
  rectum 751.5
  rib 756.3
  sacroiliac joint 755.69
  sacrum 756.19
  scapula 755.59
  shoulder girdle 755.59
  site not listed — *see* Anomaly, specified type NEC
  skull bone(s) 756.0
    with
      anencephalus 740.0
      encephalocele 742.0
      hydrocephalus 742.3
        with spina bifida (*see also* Spina bifida) 741.0 ☑
      microcephalus 742.1
  spinal cord 742.59
  spine 756.19
  spleen 759.0
  sternum 756.3
  thorax (wall) 756.3
  thymus (gland) 759.2
  thyroid (gland) 759.2
    cartilage 748.3
  tibia 755.59
  toe(s) 755.66
  tongue 750.19
  trachea (cartilage) 748.3
  ulna 755.59
  ureter 753.4
    causing obstruction 753.20
  urethra 753.8
    causing obstruction 753.6
  uterus 752.39
  vagina 752.49
  vein (peripheral) NEC (*see also* Distortion, peripheral vascular system) 747.60
    great 747.49
    portal 747.49
    pulmonary 747.49
  vena cava (inferior) (superior) 747.49
  vertebra 756.19
  visual NEC 368.15
    shape or size 368.14
  vulva 752.49
  wrist (bones) (joint) 755.59
Distress
  abdomen 789.0 ☑
  colon 564.9
  emotional V40.9
  epigastric 789.0 ☑
  fetal (syndrome) 768.4
    affecting management of pregnancy or childbirth 656.8 ☑
    liveborn infant 768.4
    first noted
      before onset of labor 768.2
      during labor and delivery 768.3
    stillborn infant (death before onset of labor) 768.0
      death during labor 768.1
  gastrointestinal (functional) 536.9
    psychogenic 306.4
  intestinal (functional) NEC 564.9
    psychogenic 306.4
  intrauterine — *see* Distress, fetal
  leg 729.5

Distress — *continued*
  maternal 669.0 ☑
  mental V40.9
  respiratory 786.09
    acute (adult) 518.82
    adult syndrome (following trauma and surgery) 518.52
      specified NEC 518.82
    fetus or newborn 770.89
    syndrome (idiopathic) (newborn) 769
  stomach 536.9
    psychogenic 306.4
Distribution vessel, atypical NEC 747.60
  coronary artery 746.85
  spinal 747.82
Districhiasis 704.2
Disturbance — *see also* Disease
  absorption NEC 579.9
    calcium 269.3
    carbohydrate 579.8
    fat 579.8
    protein 579.8
    specified type NEC 579.8
    vitamin (*see also* Deficiency, vitamin) 269.2
  acid-base equilibrium 276.9
  activity and attention, simple, with hyperkinesis 314.01
  amino acid (metabolic) (*see also* Disorder, amino acid) 270.9
    imidazole 270.5
    maple syrup (urine) disease 270.3
    transport 270.0
  assimilation, food 579.9
  attention, simple 314.00
    with hyperactivity 314.01
  auditory, nerve, except deafness 388.5
  behavior (*see also* Disturbance, conduct) 312.9
  blood clotting (hypoproteinemia) (mechanism) (*see also* Defect, coagulation) 286.9
  central nervous system NEC 349.9
  cerebral nerve NEC 352.9
  circulatory 459.9
  conduct 312.9

> *Note — Use the following fifth-digit subclassification with categories 312.0–312.2:*
>
> 0   *unspecified*
>
> 1   *mild*
>
> 2   *moderate*
>
> 3   *severe*

    adjustment reaction 309.3
    adolescent onset type 312.82
    childhood onset type 312.81
    compulsive 312.30
      intermittent explosive disorder 312.34
      isolated explosive disorder 312.35
      kleptomania 312.32
      pathological gambling 312.31
      pyromania 312.33
    hyperkinetic 314.2
    intermittent explosive 312.34
    isolated explosive 312.35
    mixed with emotions 312.4
    socialized (type) 312.20
      aggressive 312.23
      unaggressive 312.21
    specified type NEC 312.89
    undersocialized, unsocialized
      aggressive (type) 312.0 ☑
      unaggressive (type) 312.1 ☑
  coordination 781.3
  cranial nerve NEC 352.9
  deep sensibility — *see* Disturbance, sensation
  digestive 536.9
    psychogenic 306.4
  electrolyte — *see* Imbalance, electrolyte
  emotions specific to childhood or adolescence 313.9

☑ **Additional Digit Required** — Refer to the Tabular List for Digit Selection   ▽ **Subterms under main terms may continue to next column or page**

2015 ICD-9-CM   ▶◀ Revised Text   ● New Line   ▲ Revised Code   **Volume 2 — 95**

Diverticula, diverticulosis, diverticulum — *continued*
vesical (urinary) 596.3
congenital 753.8
Zenker's (esophagus) 530.6
Diverticulitis (acute) — *see also* Diverticula 562.11
with hemorrhage 562.13
bladder (urinary) 596.3
cecum (perforated) 562.11
with hemorrhage 562.13
colon (perforated) 562.11
with hemorrhage 562.13
duodenum 562.01
with hemorrhage 562.03
esophagus 530.6
ileum (perforated) 562.01
with hemorrhage 562.03
intestine (large) (perforated) 562.11
with hemorrhage 562.13
small 562.01
with hemorrhage 562.03
jejunum (perforated) 562.01
with hemorrhage 562.03
Meckel's (perforated) 751.0
pharyngoesophageal 530.6
rectosigmoid (perforated) 562.11
with hemorrhage 562.13
rectum 562.11
with hemorrhage 562.13
sigmoid (old) (perforated) 562.11
with hemorrhage 562.13
small intestine (perforated) 562.01
with hemorrhage 562.03
vesical (urinary) 596.3
Diverticulosis — *see* Diverticula
Division
cervix uteri 622.8
external os into two openings by frenum 752.44
external (cervical) into two openings by frenum 752.44
glans penis 752.69
hymen 752.49
labia minora (congenital) 752.49
ligament (partial or complete) (current) (*see also* Sprain, by site)
with open wound — *see* Wound, open, by site
muscle (partial or complete) (current) (*see also* Sprain, by site)
with open wound — *see* Wound, open, by site
nerve — *see* Injury, nerve, by site
penis glans 752.69
spinal cord — *see* Injury, spinal, by site
vein 459.9
traumatic — *see* Injury, vascular, by site
Divorce V61.03
Dix-Hallpike neurolabyrinthitis 386.12
Dizziness 780.4
hysterical 300.11
psychogenic 306.9
Doan-Wiseman syndrome (primary splenic neutropenia) 289.53
Dog bite — *see* Wound, open, by site
Döhle body-panmyelopathic syndrome 288.2
Döhle-Heller aortitis 093.1
Dolichocephaly, dolichocephalus 754.0
Dolichocolon 751.5
Dolichostenomelia 759.82
Donohue's syndrome (leprechaunism) 259.8
Donor
blood V59.01
other blood components V59.09
stem cells V59.02
whole blood V59.01
bone V59.2
marrow V59.3
cornea V59.5
egg (oocyte) (ovum) V59.70
over age 35 V59.73
anonymous recipient V59.73
designated recipient V59.74
under age 35 V59.71

Donor — *continued*
egg — *continued*
under age 35 — *continued*
anonymous recipient V59.71
designated recipient V59.72
heart V59.8
kidney V59.4
liver V59.6
lung V59.8
lymphocyte V59.8
organ V59.9
specified NEC V59.8
potential, examination of V70.8
skin V59.1
specified organ or tissue NEC V59.8
sperm V59.8
stem cells V59.02
tissue V59.9
specified type NEC V59.8
Donovanosis (granuloma venereum) 099.2
DOPS (diffuse obstructive pulmonary syndrome) 496
Double
alburnin 273.8
aortic arch 747.21
auditory canal 744.29
auricle (heart) 746.82
bladder 753.8
external (cervical) os 752.44
kidney with double pelvis (renal) 753.3
larynx 748.3
meatus urinarius 753.8
organ or site NEC — *see* Accessory orifice
heart valve NEC 746.89
pulmonary 746.09
outlet, right ventricle 745.11
pelvis (renal) with double ureter 753.4
penis 752.69
tongue 750.13
ureter (one or both sides) 753.4
with double pelvis (renal) 753.4
urethra 753.8
urinary meatus 753.8
uterus (any degree) 752.2
with doubling of cervix and vagina 752.2
in pregnancy or childbirth 654.0 ☑
affecting fetus or newborn 763.89
vagina 752.47
with doubling of cervix and uterus 752.2
vision 368.2
vocal cords 748.3
vulva 752.49
whammy (syndrome) 360.81
Douglas' pouch, cul-de-sac — *see* condition
Down's disease or syndrome (mongolism) 758.0
Down-growth, epithelial (anterior chamber) 364.61
DPD (dihydropyrimidine dehydrogenase deficiency) 277.6
Dracontiasis 125.7
Dracunculiasis 125.7
Dracunculosis 125.7
Drainage
abscess (spontaneous) — *see* Abscess
anomalous pulmonary veins to hepatic veins or right atrium 747.41
stump (amputation) (surgical) 997.62
suprapubic, bladder 596.89
Dream state, hysterical 300.13
Drepanocytic anemia — *see also* Disease, sickle cell 282.60
Dresbach's syndrome (elliptocytosis) 282.1
Dreschlera (infection) 118
hawaiiensis 117.8
Dressler's syndrome (postmyocardial infarction) 411.0
Dribbling (post-void) 788.35
Drift, ulnar 736.09
Drinking (alcohol) — *see also* Alcoholism
excessive, to excess NEC (*see also* Abuse, drugs, nondependent) 305.0 ☑
bouts, periodic 305.0 ☑
continual 303.9 ☑
episodic 305.0 ☑

Drinking (alcohol) — *see also* Alcoholism — *continued*
excessive, to excess (*see also* Abuse, drugs, nondependent) — *continued*
habitual 303.9 ☑
periodic 305.0 ☑
Drip, postnasal (chronic) 784.91
due to
allergic rhinitis — *see* Rhinitis, allergic
common cold 460
gastroesophageal reflux — *see* Reflux, gastroesophageal
nasopharyngitis — *see* Nasopharyngitis
other known condition — code to condition
sinusitis — *see* Sinusitis
Drivers' license examination V70.3
Droop
Cooper's 611.81
facial 781.94
Drop
finger 736.29
foot 736.79
hematocrit (precipitous) 790.01
hemoglobin 790.01
toe 735.8
wrist 736.05
Dropped
dead 798.1
heart beats 426.6
Dropsy, dropsical — *see also* Edema 782.3
abdomen 789.59
amnion (*see also* Hydramnios) 657.0 ☑
brain — *see* Hydrocephalus
cardiac (*see also* Failure, heart) 428.0
cardiorenal (*see also* Hypertension, cardiorenal) 404.90
chest 511.9
fetus or newborn 778.0
due to isoimmunization 773.3
gangrenous (*see also* Gangrene) 785.4
heart (*see also* Failure, heart) 428.0
hepatic — *see* Cirrhosis, liver
infantile — *see* Hydrops, fetalis
kidney (*see also* Nephrosis) 581.9
liver — *see* Cirrhosis, liver
lung 514
malarial (*see also* Malaria) 084.9
neonatorum — *see* Hydrops, fetalis
nephritic 581.9
newborn — *see* Hydrops, fetalis
nutritional 269.9
ovary 620.8
pericardium (*see also* Pericarditis) 423.9
renal (*see also* Nephrosis) 581.9
uremic — *see* Uremia
Drowned, drowning (near) 994.1
lung 518.52
Drowsiness 780.09
Drug — *see also* condition
addiction (*see also* listing under Dependence) 304.9 ☑
adverse effect, correct substance properly administered 995.20
allergy 995.27
dependence (*see also* listing under Dependence) 304.9 ☑
habit (*see also* listing under Dependence) 304.9 ☑
hypersensitivity 995.27
induced
circadian rhythm sleep disorder 292.85
hypersomnia 292.85
insomnia 292.85
mental disorder 292.9
anxiety 292.89
mood 292.84
sexual 292.89
sleep 292.85
specified type 292.89
parasomnia 292.85
persisting
amnestic disorder 292.83
dementia 292.82

Drug — *see also* condition — *continued*
induced — *continued*
psychotic disorder
with
delusions 292.11
hallucinations 292.12
sleep disorder 292.85
intoxication 292.89
overdose — *see* Table of Drugs and Chemicals
poisoning — *see* Table of Drugs and Chemicals
therapy (maintenance) status NEC
chemotherapy, antineoplastic V58.11
immunotherapy, antineoplastic V58.12
long-term (current) (prophylactic) use V58.69
antibiotics V58.62
anticoagulants V58.61
anti-inflammatories, non-steroidal (NSAID) V58.64
antiplatelets V58.63
antithrombotics V58.63
aspirin V58.66
bisphosphonates V58.68
high-risk medications NEC V58.69
insulin V58.67
methadone for pain control V58.69
opiate analgesic V58.69
steroids V58.65
methadone 304.00
wrong substance given or taken in error — *see* Table of Drugs and Chemicals
Drunkenness — *see also* Abuse, drugs, nondependent 305.0 ☑
acute in alcoholism (*see also* Alcoholism) 303.0 ☑
chronic (*see also* Alcoholism) 303.9 ☑
pathologic 291.4
simple (acute) 305.0 ☑
in alcoholism 303.0 ☑
sleep 307.47
Drusen
optic disc or papilla 377.21
retina (colloid) (hyaloid degeneration) 362.57
hereditary 362.77
Drusenfieber 075
Dry, dryness — *see also* condition
eye 375.15
syndrome 375.15
larynx 478.79
mouth 527.7
nose 478.19
skin syndrome 701.1
socket (teeth) 526.5
throat 478.29
DSAP (disseminated superficial actinic porokeratosis) 692.75
DSTR (delayed serologic transfusion reaction)
due to or resulting from
incompatibility
ABO 999.69
non-ABO antigen (minor) (Duffy) (Kell) (Kidd) (Lewis) (M) (N) (P) (S) 999.79
Rh antigen (C) (c) (D) (E) (e) 999.74
Duane's retraction syndrome 378.71
Duane-Stilling-Türk syndrome (ocular retraction syndrome) 378.71
Dubini's disease (electric chorea) 049.8
Dubin-Johnson disease or syndrome 277.4
Dubois' abscess or disease 090.5
Duchenne's
disease 094.0
locomotor ataxia 094.0
muscular dystrophy 359.1
pseudohypertrophy, muscles 359.1
paralysis 335.22
syndrome 335.22
Duchenne-Aran myelopathic, muscular atrophy (nonprogressive) (progressive) 335.21
Duchenne-Griesinger disease 359.1
Ducrey's
bacillus 099.0

Ducrey's — *continued*
 chancre 099.0
 disease (chancroid) 099.0
Duct, ductus — *see* condition
Duengero 061
Duhring's disease (dermatitis herpetiformis)
  694.0
Dukes (-Filatov) disease 057.8
Dullness
 cardiac (decreased) (increased) 785.3
Dumb ague — *see also* Malaria 084.6
Dumbness — *see also* Aphasia 784.3
Dumdum fever 085.0
Dumping syndrome (postgastrectomy) 564.2
 nonsurgical 536.8
Duodenitis (nonspecific) (peptic) 535.60
 with hemorrhage 535.61
 due to
  Strongyloides stercoralis 127.2
Duodenocholangitis 575.8
Duodenum, duodenal — *see* condition
Duplay's disease, periarthritis, or syndrome
  726.2
Duplex — *see also* Accessory
 kidney 753.3
 placenta — *see* Placenta, abnormal
 uterus 752.2
Duplication — *see also* Accessory
 anus 751.5
 aortic arch 747.21
 appendix 751.5
 biliary duct (any) 751.69
 bladder 753.8
 cecum 751.5
  and appendix 751.5
 cervical, cervix 752.44
 clitoris 752.49
 cystic duct 751.69
 digestive organs 751.8
 duodenum 751.5
 esophagus 750.4
 fallopian tube 752.19
 frontonasal process 756.0
 gallbladder 751.69
 ileum 751.5
 intestine (large) (small) 751.5
 jejunum 751.5
 kidney 753.3
 liver 751.69
 nose 748.1
 pancreas 751.7
 penis 752.69
 respiratory organs NEC 748.9
 salivary duct 750.22
 spinal cord (incomplete) 742.51
 stomach 750.7
 ureter 753.4
 vagina 752.47
 vas deferens 752.89
 vocal cords 748.3
Dupré's disease or syndrome (meningism)
  781.6
Dupuytren's
 contraction 728.6
 disease (muscle contracture) 728.6
 fracture (closed) 824.4
  ankle (closed) 824.4
   open 824.5
  fibula (closed) 824.4
   open 824.5
  radius (closed) 813.42
   open 813.52
 muscle contracture 728.6
Durand-Nicolas-Favre disease (climatic bubo)
  099.1
Durotomy, incidental (inadvertent) — *see also*
  Tear, dural 349.31
Duroziez's disease (congenital mitral stenosis)
  746.5
Dust
 conjunctivitis 372.05
 reticulation (occupational) 504
Dutton's
 disease (trypanosomiasis) 086.9
 relapsing fever (West African) 087.1

Dwarf, dwarfism 259.4
 with infantilism (hypophyseal) 253.3
 achondroplastic 756.4
 Amsterdam 759.89
 bird-headed 759.89
 congenital 259.4
 constitutional 259.4
 hypophyseal 253.3
 infantile 259.4
 Levi type 253.3
 Lorain-Levi (pituitary) 253.3
 Lorain type (pituitary) 253.3
 metatropic 756.4
 nephrotic-glycosuric, with hypophosphatemic rickets 270.0
 nutritional 263.2
 ovarian 758.6
 pancreatic 577.8
 pituitary 253.3
 polydystrophic 277.5
 primordial 253.3
 psychosocial 259.4
 renal 588.0
  with hypertension — *see* Hypertension,
    kidney
 Russell's (uterine dwarfism and craniofacial
   dysostosis) 759.89
Dyke-Young anemia or syndrome (acquired
  macrocytic hemolytic anemia) (secondary) (symptomatic) 283.9
Dynia abnormality — *see also* Defect, coagulation 286.9
Dysacousis 388.40
Dysadrenocortism 255.9
 hyperfunction 255.3
 hypofunction 255.41
Dysarthria 784.51
 due to late effect of cerebrovascular disease
   (*see also* Late effect(s) (of) cerebrovascular disease) 438.13
Dysautonomia — *see also* Neuropathy, peripheral, autonomic 337.9
 familial 742.8
Dysbarism 993.3
Dysbasia 719.7
 angiosclerotica intermittens 443.9
  due to atherosclerosis 440.21
 hysterical 300.11
 lordotica (progressiva) 333.6
 nonorganic origin 307.9
 psychogenic 307.9
Dysbetalipoproteinemia (familial) 272.2
Dyscalculia 315.1
Dyschezia — *see also* Constipation 564.00
Dyschondroplasia (with hemangiomata) 756.4
 Voorhoeve's 756.4
Dyschondrosteosis 756.59
Dyschromia 709.00
Dyscollagenosis 710.9
Dyscoria 743.41
Dyscraniopyophalangy 759.89
Dyscrasia
 blood 289.9
  with antepartum hemorrhage 641.3 ☑
   hemorrhage, subungual 287.8
  puerperal, postpartum 666.3 ☑
 ovary 256.8
 plasma cell 273.9
 pluriglandular 258.9
 polyglandular 258.9
Dysdiadochokinesia 781.3
Dysectasia, vesical neck 596.89
Dysendocrinism 259.9
Dysentery, dysenteric (bilious) (catarrhal)
  (diarrhea) (epidemic) (gangrenous)
  (hemorrhagic) (infectious) (sporadic)
  (tropical) (ulcerative) 009.0
 abscess, liver (*see also* Abscess, amebic)
   006.3
 amebic (*see also* Amebiasis) 006.9
  with abscess — *see* Abscess, amebic
  acute 006.0
  carrier (suspected) of V02.2
  chronic 006.1
  arthritis (*see also* Arthritis, due to, dysentery)
   009.0 *[711.3]* ☑

Dysentery, dysenteric — *continued*
 arthritis (*see also* Arthritis, due to, dysentery)
   — *continued*
  bacillary 004.9 *[711.3]* ☑
 asylum 004.9
 bacillary 004.9
  arthritis 004.9 *[711.3]* ☑
  Boyd 004.2
  Flexner 004.1
  Schmitz (-Stutzer) 004.0
  Shiga 004.0
  Shigella 004.9
   group A 004.0
   group B 004.1
   group C 004.2
   group D 004.3
   specified type NEC 004.8
  Sonne 004.3
  specified type NEC 004.8
 bacterium 004.9
 balantidial 007.0
 Balantidium coli 007.0
 Boyd's 004.2
 Chilomastix 007.8
 Chinese 004.9
 choleriform 001.1
 coccidial 007.2
 Dientamoeba fragilis 007.8
 due to specified organism NEC — *see* Enteritis, due to, by organism
 Embadomonas 007.8
 Endolimax nana — *see* Dysentery, amebic
 Entamoba, entambic — *see* Dysentery,
   amebic
 Flexner's 004.1
 Flexner-Boyd 004.2
 giardial 007.1
 Giardia lamblia 007.1
 Hiss-Russell 004.1
 lamblia 007.1
 leishmanial 085.0
 malarial (*see also* Malaria) 084.6
 metazoal 127.9
 Monilia 112.89
 protozoal NEC 007.9
 Russell's 004.8
 salmonella 003.0
 schistosomal 120.1
 Schmitz (-Stutzer) 004.0
 Shiga 004.0
 Shigella NEC (*see also* Dysentery, bacillary)
   004.9
  boydii 004.2
  dysenteriae 004.0
   Schmitz 004.0
   Shiga 004.0
  flexneri 004.1
  group A 004.0
  group B 004.1
  group C 004.2
  group D 004.3
  Schmitz 004.0
  Shiga 004.0
  Sonnei 004.3
 Sonne 004.3
 strongyloidiasis 127.2
 trichomonal 007.3
 tuberculous (*see also* Tuberculosis) 014.8 ☑
 viral (*see also* Enteritis, viral) 008.8
Dysequilibrium 780.4
Dysesthesia 782.0
 hysterical 300.11
Dysfibrinogenemia (congenital) — *see also*
  Defect, coagulation 286.3
Dysfunction
 adrenal (cortical) 255.9
  hyperfunction 255.3
  hypofunction 255.41
 associated with sleep stages or arousal from
   sleep 780.56
  nonorganic origin 307.47
 bladder NEC 596.59
 bleeding, uterus 626.8
 brain, minimal (*see also* Hyperkinesia) 314.9
 cerebral 348.30
 colon 564.9

Dysfunction — *continued*
 colon — *continued*
  psychogenic 306.4
 colostomy or enterostomy 569.62
 cystic duct 575.8
 diastolic 429.9
  with heart failure — *see* Failure, heart
  due to
   cardiomyopathy — *see* Cardiomyopa-
     thy
   hypertension — *see* Hypertension,
     heart
 endocrine NEC 259.9
 endometrium 621.8
 enteric stoma 569.62
 enterostomy 569.62
 erectile 607.84
  nonorganic origin 302.72
 esophagostomy 530.87
 Eustachian tube 381.81
 gallbladder 575.8
 gastrointestinal 536.9
 gland, glandular NEC 259.9
 heart 427.9
  postoperative (immediate) 997.1
   long-term effect of cardiac surgery
     429.4
 hemoglobin 289.89
 hepatic 573.9
 hepatocellular NEC 573.9
 hypophysis 253.9
  hyperfunction 253.1
  hypofunction 253.2
  posterior lobe 253.6
   hypofunction 253.5
 kidney (*see also* Disease, renal) 593.9
 labyrinthine 386.50
  specified NEC 386.58
 liver 573.9
  constitutional 277.4
 minimal brain (child) (*see also* Hyperkinesia)
   314.9
 ovary, ovarian 256.9
  hyperfunction 256.1
   estrogen 256.0
  hypofunction 256.39
   postablative 256.2
  postablative 256.2
  specified NEC 256.8
 papillary muscle 429.81
  with myocardial infarction 410.8 ☑
 parathyroid 252.8
  hyperfunction 252.00
  hypofunction 252.1
 pineal gland 259.8
 pituitary (gland) 253.9
  hyperfunction 253.1
  hypofunction 253.2
  posterior 253.6
   hypofunction 253.5
 placental — *see* Placenta, insufficiency
 platelets (blood) 287.1
 polyglandular 258.9
  specified NEC 258.8
 psychosexual 302.70
  with
   dyspareunia (functional) (psy-
     chogenic) 302.76
   frigidity 302.72
   impotence 302.72
   inhibition
    orgasm
     female 302.73
     male 302.74
    sexual
     desire 302.71
     excitement 302.72
   premature ejaculation 302.75
   sexual aversion 302.79
   specified disorder NEC 302.79
   vaginismus 306.51
 pylorus 537.9
 rectum 564.9
  psychogenic 306.4
 segmental (*see also* Dysfunction, somatic)
   739.9

☑ **Additional Digit Required** — **Refer to the Tabular List for Digit Selection**   ▽ **Subterms under main terms may continue to next column or page**

Dysfunction — continued
  senile 797
  sexual 302.70
  sinoatrial node 427.81
  somatic 739.9
    abdomen 739.9
    acromioclavicular 739.7
    cervical 739.1
    cervicothoracic 739.1
    costochondral 739.8
    costovertebral 739.8
    extremities
      lower 739.6
      upper 739.7
    head 739.0
    hip 739.5
    lumbar, lumbosacral 739.3
    occipitocervical 739.0
    pelvic 739.5
    pubic 739.5
    rib cage 739.8
    sacral 739.4
    sacrococcygeal 739.4
    sacroiliac 739.4
    specified site NEC 739.9
    sternochondral 739.8
    sternoclavicular 739.7
    temporomandibular 739.0
    thoracic, thoracolumbar 739.2
  stomach 536.9
    psychogenic 306.4
  suprarenal 255.9
    hyperfunction 255.3
    hypofunction 255.41
  symbolic NEC 784.60
    specified type NEC 784.69
  systolic 429.9
    with heart failure — see Failure, heart
  temporomandibular (joint) (joint-pain-syndrome) NEC 524.60
    sounds on opening or closing 524.64
    specified NEC 524.69
  testicular 257.9
    hyperfunction 257.0
    hypofunction 257.2
    specified type NEC 257.8
  thymus 254.9
  thyroid 246.9
    complicating pregnancy, childbirth, or puerperium 648.1 ☑
    hyperfunction — see Hyperthyroidism
    hypofunction — see Hypothyroidism
  uterus, complicating delivery 661.9 ☑
    affecting fetus or newborn 763.7
    hypertonic 661.4 ☑
    hypotonic 661.2 ☑
      primary 661.0 ☑
      secondary 661.1 ☑
  velopharyngeal (acquired) 528.9
    congenital 750.29
  ventricular 429.9
    with congestive heart failure (see also Failure, heart) 428.0
    due to
      cardiomyopathy — see Cardiomyopathy
      hypertension — see Hypertension, heart
    left, reversible following sudden emotional stress 429.83
  vesicourethral NEC 596.59
  vestibular 386.50
    specified type NEC 386.58
Dysgammaglobulinemia 279.06
Dysgenesis
  gonadal (due to chromosomal anomaly) 758.6
    pure 752.7
  kidney(s) 753.0
  ovarian 758.6
  renal 753.0
  reticular 279.2
  seminiferous tubules 758.6
  tidal platelet 287.31

Dysgerminoma (M9060/3)
  specified site — see Neoplasm, by site, malignant
  unspecified site
    female 183.0
    male 186.9
Dysgeusia 781.1
Dysgraphia 781.3
Dyshidrosis 705.81
Dysidrosis 705.81
Dysinsulinism 251.8
Dyskaryotic cervical smear 795.09
Dyskeratosis — see also Keratosis 701.1
  bullosa hereditaria 757.39
  cervix 622.10
  congenital 757.39
  follicularis 757.39
    vitamin A deficiency 264.8
  gingiva 523.8
  oral soft tissue NEC 528.79
  tongue 528.79
  uterus NEC 621.8
Dyskinesia 781.3
  biliary 575.8
  esophagus 530.5
  hysterical 300.11
  intestinal 564.89
  neuroleptic-induced tardive 333.85
  nonorganic origin 307.9
  orofacial 333.82
    due to drugs 333.85
  psychogenic 307.9
  subacute, due to drugs 333.85
  tardive (oral) 333.85
Dyslalia 784.59
  developmental 315.39
Dyslexia 784.61
  developmental 315.02
  secondary to organic lesion 784.61
Dyslipidemia 272.4
Dysmaturity — see also Immaturity 765.1 ☑
  lung 770.4
  pulmonary 770.4
Dysmenorrhea (essential) (exfoliative) (functional) (intrinsic) (membranous) (primary) (secondary) 625.3
  psychogenic 306.52
Dysmetabolic syndrome X 277.7
Dysmetria 781.3
Dysmorodystrophia mesodermalis congenita 759.82
Dysnomia 784.3
Dysorexia 783.0
  hysterical 300.11
Dysostosis
  cleidocranial, cleidocranialis 755.59
  craniofacial 756.0
  Fairbank's (idiopathic familial generalized osteophytosis) 756.50
  mandibularis 756.0
  mandibulofacial, incomplete 756.0
  multiplex 277.5
  orodigitofacial 759.89
Dyspareunia (female) 625.0
  male 608.89
  psychogenic 302.76
Dyspepsia (allergic) (congenital) (fermentative) (flatulent) (functional) (gastric) (gastrointestinal) (neurogenic) (occupational) (reflex) 536.8
  acid 536.8
  atonic 536.3
    psychogenic 306.4
  diarrhea 787.91
    psychogenic 306.4
  intestinal 564.89
    psychogenic 306.4
  nervous 306.4
  neurotic 306.4
  psychogenic 306.4
Dysphagia 787.20
  cervical 787.29
  functional 300.11
  hysterical 300.11
  nervous 300.11
  neurogenic 787.29

Dysphagia — continued
  oral phase 787.21
  oropharyngeal phase 787.22
  pharyngeal phase 787.23
  pharyngoesophageal phase 787.24
  psychogenic 306.4
  sideropenic 280.8
  spastica 530.5
  specified NEC 787.29
Dysphagocytosis, congenital 288.1
Dysphasia 784.59
Dysphonia 784.42
  clericorum 784.49
  functional 300.11
  hysterical 300.11
  psychogenic 306.1
  spastica 478.79
Dyspigmentation — see also Pigmentation
  eyelid (acquired) 374.52
Dyspituitarism 253.9
  hyperfunction 253.1
  hypofunction 253.2
  posterior lobe 253.6
Dysplasia — see also Anomaly
  alveolar capillary, with vein misalignment 516.64
  anus 569.44
    intraepithelial neoplasia I (AIN I) (histologically confirmed) 569.44
    intraepithelial neoplasia II (AIN II) (histologically confirmed) 569.44
    intraepithelial neoplasia III (AIN III) 230.6
      anal canal 230.5
    mild (histologically confirmed) 569.44
    moderate (histologically confirmed) 569.44
    severe 230.6
      anal canal 230.5
  artery
    fibromuscular NEC 447.8
      carotid 447.8
      renal 447.3
  bladder 596.89
  bone (fibrous) NEC 733.29
    diaphyseal, progressive 756.59
    jaw 526.89
    monostotic 733.29
    polyostotic 756.54
    solitary 733.29
  brain 742.9
  bronchopulmonary, fetus or newborn 770.7
  cervix (uteri) 622.10
    cervical intraepithelial neoplasia I (CIN I) 622.11
    cervical intraepithelial neoplasia II (CIN II) 622.12
    cervical intraepithelial neoplasia III (CIN III) 233.1
    CIN I 622.11
    CIN II 622.12
    CIN III 233.1
    mild 622.11
    moderate 622.12
    severe 233.1
  chondroectodermal 756.55
  chondromatose 756.4
  colon 211.3
  craniocarpotarsal 759.89
  craniometaphyseal 756.89
  dentinal 520.5
  diaphyseal, progressive 756.59
  ectodermal (anhidrotic) (Bason) (Clouston's) (congenital) (Feinmesser) (hereditary) (hidrotic) (Marshall) (Robinson's) 757.31
  epiphysealis 756.9
    multiplex 756.56
    punctata 756.59
  epiphysis 756.9
    multiple 756.56
  epithelial
    epiglottis 478.79
    uterine cervix 622.10
  erythroid NEC 289.89
  eye (see also Microphthalmos) 743.10
  familial metaphyseal 756.89

Dysplasia — see also Anomaly — continued
  fibromuscular, artery NEC 447.8
    carotid 447.8
    renal 447.3
  fibrous
    bone NEC 733.29
    diaphyseal, progressive 756.59
    jaw 526.89
    monostotic 733.29
    polyostotic 756.54
    solitary 733.29
  high-grade, focal — see Neoplasm, by site, benign
  hip (congenital) 755.63
    with dislocation (see also Dislocation, hip, congenital) 754.30
  hypohidrotic ectodermal 757.31
  joint 755.8
  kidney 753.15
  leg 755.69
  linguofacialis 759.89
  lung 748.5
  macular 743.55
  mammary (benign) (gland) 610.9
    cystic 610.1
    specified type NEC 610.8
  metaphyseal 756.9
    familial 756.89
  monostotic fibrous 733.29
  muscle 756.89
  myeloid NEC 289.89
  nervous system (general) 742.9
  neuroectodermal 759.6
  oculoauriculovertebral 756.0
  oculodentodigital 759.89
  olfactogenital 253.4
  osteo-onycho-arthro (hereditary) 756.89
  periosteum 733.99
  polyostotic fibrous 756.54
  progressive diaphyseal 756.59
  prostate 602.3
    intraepithelial neoplasia I [PIN I] 602.3
    intraepithelial neoplasia II [PIN II] 602.3
    intraepithelial neoplasia III [PIN III] 233.4
  renal 753.15
  renofacialis 753.0
  retinal NEC 743.56
  retrolental (see also Retinopathy of prematurity) 362.21
  skin 709.8
  spinal cord 742.9
  thymic, with immunodeficiency 279.2
  vagina 623.0
    mild 623.0
    moderate 623.0
    severe 233.31
  vocal cord 478.5
  vulva 624.8
    intraepithelial neoplasia I (VIN I) 624.01
    intraepithelial neoplasia II (VIN II) 624.02
    intraepithelial neoplasia III (VIN III) 233.32
    mild 624.01
    moderate 624.02
    severe 233.32
    VIN I 624.01
    VIN II 624.02
    VIN III 233.32
Dyspnea (nocturnal) (paroxysmal) 786.09
  asthmatic (bronchial) (see also Asthma) 493.9 ☑
    with bronchitis (see also Asthma) 493.9 ☑
      chronic 493.2 ☑
    cardiac (see also Failure, ventricular, left) 428.1
  cardiac (see also Failure, ventricular, left) 428.1
  functional 300.11
  hyperventilation 786.01
  hysterical 300.11
  Monday morning 504
  newborn 770.89
  psychogenic 306.1
  uremic — see Uremia

☑ **Additional Digit Required** — Refer to the Tabular List for Digit Selection   ▽ **Subterms under main terms may continue to next column or page**

2015 ICD-9-CM   ▶◀ Revised Text   ● New Line   ▲ Revised Code   Volume 2 — 99

Dyspraxia 781.3
  syndrome 315.4
Dysproteinemia 273.8
  transient with copper deficiency 281.4
Dysprothrombinemia (constitutional) — see
  also Defect, coagulation 286.3
Dysreflexia, autonomic 337.3
Dysrhythmia
  cardiac 427.9
    postoperative (immediate) 997.1
      long-term effect of cardiac surgery
        429.4
    specified type NEC 427.89
  cerebral or cortical 348.30
Dyssecretosis, mucoserous 710.2
**Dyssocial reaction, without manifest psychi-
  atric disorder**
  adolescent V71.02
  adult V71.01
  child V71.02
Dyssomnia NEC 780.56
  nonorganic origin 307.47
Dyssplenism 289.4
Dyssynergia
  biliary (see also Disease, biliary) 576.8
  cerebellaris myoclonica 334.2
  detrusor sphincter (bladder) 596.55
  ventricular 429.89
Dystasia, hereditary areflexic 334.3
Dysthymia 300.4
Dysthymic disorder 300.4
Dysthyroidism 246.9
Dystocia 660.9 ☑
  affecting fetus or newborn 763.1
  cervical 661.2 ☑
    affecting fetus or newborn 763.7
  contraction ring 661.4 ☑
    affecting fetus or newborn 763.7
  fetal 660.9 ☑
    abnormal size 653.5 ☑
    affecting fetus or newborn 763.1
    deformity 653.7 ☑
  maternal 660.9 ☑
    affecting fetus or newborn 763.1
  positional 660.0 ☑
    affecting fetus or newborn 763.1
  shoulder (girdle) 660.4 ☑
    affecting fetus or newborn 763.1
  uterine NEC 661.4 ☑
    affecting fetus or newborn 763.7
Dystonia
  acute
    due to drugs 333.72
      neuroleptic-induced acute 333.72
  deformans progressiva 333.6
  lenticularis 333.6
  musculorum deformans 333.6
  torsion (idiopathic) 333.6
    acquired 333.79
    fragments (of) 333.89
    genetic 333.6
    symptomatic 333.79
Dystonic
  movements 781.0
Dystopia kidney 753.3
Dystrophia myotonica 359.2 ☑
Dystrophy, dystrophia 783.9
  adiposogenital 253.8
  asphyxiating thoracic 756.4
  Becker's type 359.22
  brevicollis 756.16
  Bruch's membrane 362.77
  cervical (sympathetic) NEC 337.09
  chondro-osseus with punctate epiphyseal
    dysplasia 756.59
  choroid (hereditary) 363.50
    central (areolar) (partial) 363.53
      total (gyrate) 363.54
    circinate 363.53
    circumpapillary (partial) 363.51
      total 363.52
    diffuse
      partial 363.56
      total 363.57
    generalized
      partial 363.56

Dystrophy, dystrophia — continued
  choroid — continued
    generalized — continued
      total 363.57
    gyrate
      central 363.54
      generalized 363.57
    helicoid 363.52
    peripapillary — see Dystrophy, choroid,
      circumpapillary
    serpiginous 363.54
  cornea (hereditary) 371.50
    anterior NEC 371.52
    Cogan's 371.52
    combined 371.57
    crystalline 371.56
    endothelial (Fuchs') 371.57
    epithelial 371.50
      juvenile 371.51
      microscopic cystic 371.52
    granular 371.53
    lattice 371.54
    macular 371.55
    marginal (Terrien's) 371.48
    Meesman's 371.51
    microscopic cystic (epithelial) 371.52
    nodular, Salzmann's 371.46
    polymorphous 371.58
    posterior NEC 371.58
    ring-like 371.52
    Salzmann's nodular 371.46
    stromal NEC 371.56
  dermatochondrocorneal 371.50
  Duchenne's 359.1
  due to malnutrition 263.9
  Erb's 359.1
  familial
    hyperplastic periosteal 756.59
    osseous 277.5
  foveal 362.77
  Fuchs', cornea 371.57
  Gowers' muscular 359.1
  hair 704.2
  hereditary, progressive muscular 359.1
  hypogenital, with diabetic tendency 759.81
  Landouzy-Déjérine 359.1
  Leyden-Möbius 359.1
  mesodermalis congenita 759.82
  muscular 359.1
    congenital (hereditary) 359.0
      myotonic 359.22
    distal 359.1
    Duchenne's 359.1
    Erb's 359.1
    fascioscapulohumeral 359.1
    Gowers' 359.1
    hereditary (progressive) 359.1
    Landouzy-Déjérine 359.1
    limb-girdle 359.1
    myotonic 359.21
    progressive (hereditary) 359.1
      Charcôt-Marie-Tooth 356.1
    pseudohypertrophic (infantile) 359.1
  myocardium, myocardial (see also Degener-
    ation, myocardial) 429.1
  myotonic 359.21
  myotonica 359.21
  nail 703.8
    congenital 757.5
  neurovascular (traumatic) (see also Neuropa-
    thy, peripheral, autonomic) 337.9
  nutritional 263.9
  ocular 359.1
  oculocerebrorenal 270.8
  oculopharyngeal 359.1
  ovarian 620.8
  papillary (and pigmentary) 701.1
  pelvicrural atrophic 359.1
  pigmentary (see also Acanthosis) 701.2
  pituitary (gland) 253.8
  polyglandular 258.8
  posttraumatic sympathetic — see Dystro-
    phy, sympathetic
  progressive ophthalmoplegic 359.1
  reflex neuromuscular — see Dystrophy,
    sympathetic

Dystrophy, dystrophia — continued
  retina, retinal (hereditary) 362.70
    albipunctate 362.74
    Bruch's membrane 362.77
    cone, progressive 362.75
    hyaline 362.77
    in
      Bassen-Kornzweig syndrome
        272.5 [362.72]
      cerebroretinal lipidosis 330.1 [362.71]
      Refsum's disease 356.3 [362.72]
      systemic lipidosis 272.7 [362.71]
    juvenile (Stargardt's) 362.75
    pigmentary 362.74
    pigment epithelium 362.76
    progressive cone (-rod) 362.75
    pseudoinflammatory foveal 362.77
    rod, progressive 362.75
    sensory 362.75
    vitelliform 362.76
  Salzmann's nodular 371.46
  scapuloperoneal 359.1
  skin NEC 709.9
  sympathetic (posttraumatic) (reflex) 337.20
    lower limb 337.22
    specified site NEC 337.29
    upper limb 337.21
  tapetoretinal NEC 362.74
  thoracic asphyxiating 756.4
  unguium 703.8
    congenital 757.5
  vitreoretinal (primary) 362.73
    secondary 362.66
  vulva 624.09
Dysuria 788.1
  psychogenic 306.53

E

Eagle-Barrett syndrome 756.71
Eales' disease (syndrome) 362.18
Ear — see also condition
  ache 388.70
    otogenic 388.71
    referred 388.72
  lop 744.29
  piercing V50.3
  swimmers' acute 380.12
  tank 380.12
  tropical 111.8 [380.15]
  wax 380.4
Earache 388.70
  otogenic 388.71
  referred 388.72
Early satiety 780.94
Eaton-Lambert syndrome — see also Syndrome, Lambert-Eaton 358.30
Eberth's disease (typhoid fever) 002.0
Ebstein's
  anomaly or syndrome (downward displace-
    ment, tricuspid valve into right ven-
    tricle) 746.2
  disease (diabetes) 250.4 ☑ [581.81]
    due to secondary diabetes
      249.4 ☑ [581.81]
Eccentro-osteochondrodysplasia 277.5
Ecchondroma (M9210/0) — see Neoplasm,
  bone, benign
Ecchondrosis (M9210/1) 238.0
Ecchordosis physaliphora 756.0
Ecchymosis (multiple) 459.89
  conjunctiva 372.72
  eye (traumatic) 921.0
  eyelids (traumatic) 921.1
  newborn 772.6
  spontaneous 782.7
  traumatic — see Contusion
ECD (Erdheim-Chester disease) 277.89
Echinococciasis — see Echinococcus
Echinococcosis — see Echinococcus
Echinococcus (infection) 122.9
  granulosus 122.4
    liver 122.0
    lung 122.1
    orbit 122.3 [376.13]
    specified site NEC 122.3
    thyroid 122.2

Echinococcus — continued
  liver NEC 122.8
    granulosus 122.0
    multilocularis 122.5
  lung NEC 122.9
    granulosus 122.1
    multilocularis 122.6
  multilocularis 122.7
    liver 122.5
    specified site NEC 122.6
  orbit 122.9 [376.13]
    granulosus 122.3 [376.13]
    multilocularis 122.6 [376.13]
  specified site NEC 122.9
    granulosus 122.3
    multilocularis 122.6 [376.13]
  thyroid NEC 122.9
    granulosus 122.2
    multilocularis 122.6
Echinorhynchiasis 127.7
Echinostomiasis 121.8
Echolalia 784.69
ECHO virus infection NEC 079.1
Eclampsia, eclamptic (coma) (convulsions)
  (delirium) 780.39
  female, child-bearing age NEC — see
    Eclampsia, pregnancy
  gravidarum — see Eclampsia, pregnancy
  male 780.39
  not associated with pregnancy or childbirth
    780.39
  pregnancy, childbirth, or puerperium
    642.6 ☑
    with pre-existing hypertension 642.7 ☑
      affecting fetus or newborn 760.0
  uremic 586
Eclipse blindness (total) 363.31
Economic circumstance affecting care V60.9
  specified type NEC V60.89
Economo's disease (encephalitis lethargica)
  049.8
Ectasia, ectasis
  annuloaortic 424.1
  aorta (see also Ectasia, aortic) 447.70
    with aneurysm 441.9
      ruptured 441.5
  aortic 447.70
    with aneurysm 441.9
    abdominal 447.72
    thoracic 447.71
    thoracoabdominal 447.73
  breast 610.4
  capillary 448.9
  cornea (marginal) (postinfectional) 371.71
  duct (mammary) 610.4
  gastric antral vascular (GAVE) 537.82
    with hemorrhage 537.83
    without hemorrhage 537.82
  kidney 593.89
  mammary duct (gland) 610.4
  papillary 448.9
  renal 593.89
  salivary gland (duct) 527.8
  scar, cornea 371.71
  sclera 379.11
Ecthyma 686.8
  contagiosum 051.2
  gangrenosum 686.09
  infectiosum 051.2
Ectocardia 746.87
Ectodermal dysplasia, congenital 757.31
Ectodermosis erosiva pluriorificialis 695.19
Ectopic, ectopia (congenital) 759.89
  abdominal viscera 751.8
    due to defect in anterior abdominal wall
      756.79
  ACTH syndrome 255.0
  adrenal gland 759.1
  anus 751.5
  auricular beats 427.61
  beats 427.60
  bladder 753.5
  bone and cartilage in lung 748.69
  brain 742.4
  breast tissue 757.6
  cardiac 746.87

☑ **Additional Digit Required** — Refer to the Tabular List for Digit Selection   ▽ **Subterms under main terms may continue to next column or page**

100 — Volume 2   ▶◀ **Revised Text**   ● **New Line**   ▲ **Revised Code**   **2015 ICD-9-CM**

Ectopic, ectopia — *continued*
  cerebral 742.4
  cordis 746.87
  endometrium 617.9
  gallbladder 751.69
  gastric mucosa 750.7
  gestation — *see* Pregnancy, ectopic
  heart 746.87
  hormone secretion NEC 259.3
  hyperparathyroidism 259.3
  kidney (crossed) (intrathoracic) (pelvis)
      753.3
      in pregnancy or childbirth 654.4 ☑
          causing obstructed labor 660.2 ☑
  lens 743.37
  lentis 743.37
  mole — *see* Pregnancy, ectopic
  organ or site NEC — *see* Malposition, con-
      genital
  ovary 752.0
  pancreas, pancreatic tissue 751.7
  pregnancy — *see* Pregnancy, ectopic
  pupil 364.75
  renal 753.3
  sebaceous glands of mouth 750.26
  secretion
      ACTH 255.0
      adrenal hormone 259.3
      adrenalin 259.3
      adrenocorticotropin 255.0
      antidiuretic hormone (ADH) 259.3
      epinephrine 259.3
      hormone NEC 259.3
      norepinephrine 259.3
      pituitary (posterior) 259.3
  spleen 759.0
  testis 752.51
  thyroid 759.2
  ureter 753.4
  ventricular beats 427.69
  vesicae 753.5
Ectrodactyly 755.4
  finger (*see also* Absence, finger, congenital)
      755.29
  toe (*see also* Absence, toe, congenital)
      755.39
Ectromelia 755.4
  lower limb 755.30
  upper limb 755.20
Ectropion 374.10
  anus 569.49
  cervix 622.0
      with mention of cervicitis 616.0
  cicatricial 374.14
  congenital 743.62
  eyelid 374.10
      cicatricial 374.14
      congenital 743.62
      mechanical 374.12
      paralytic 374.12
      senile 374.11
      spastic 374.13
  iris (pigment epithelium) 364.54
  lip (congenital) 750.26
      acquired 528.5
  mechanical 374.12
  paralytic 374.12
  rectum 569.49
  senile 374.11
  spastic 374.13
  urethra 599.84
  uvea 364.54
Eczema (acute) (allergic) (chronic) (erythema-
    tous) (fissum) (occupational) (rubrum)
    (squamous) 692.9
  asteatotic 706.8
  atopic 691.8
  contact NEC 692.9
  dermatitis NEC 692.9
  due to specified cause — *see* Dermatitis,
      due to
  dyshidrotic 705.81
  external ear 380.22
  flexural 691.8
  gouty 274.89
  herpeticum 054.0

Eczema — *continued*
  hypertrophicum 701.8
  hypostatic — *see* Varicose, vein
  impetiginous 684
  infantile (acute) (chronic) (due to any sub-
      stance) (intertriginous) (seborrheic)
      690.12
  intertriginous NEC 692.9
      infantile 690.12
  intrinsic 691.8
  lichenified NEC 692.9
  marginatum 110.3
  nummular 692.9
  pustular 686.8
  seborrheic 690.18
      infantile 690.12
  solare 692.72
  stasis (lower extremity) 454.1
      ulcerated 454.2
  vaccination, vaccinatum 999.0
  varicose (lower extremity) — *see* Varicose,
      vein
  verrucosum callosum 698.3
Eczematoid, exudative 691.8
Eddowes' syndrome (brittle bones and blue
    sclera) 756.51
Edema, edematous 782.3
  with nephritis (*see also* Nephrosis) 581.9
  allergic 995.1
  angioneurotic (allergic) (any site) (with ur-
      ticaria) 995.1
      hereditary 277.6
  angiospastic 443.9
  Berlin's (traumatic) 921.3
  brain (cytotoxic) (vasogenic) 348.5
      due to birth injury 767.8
      fetus or newborn 767.8
  cardiac (*see also* Failure, heart) 428.0
  cardiovascular (*see also* Failure, heart) 428.0
  cerebral — *see* Edema, brain
  cerebrospinal vessel — *see* Edema, brain
  cervix (acute) (uteri) 622.8
      puerperal, postpartum 674.8 ☑
  chronic hereditary 757.0
  circumscribed, acute 995.1
      hereditary 277.6
  complicating pregnancy (gestational)
      646.1 ☑
      with hypertension — *see* Toxemia, of
          pregnancy
  conjunctiva 372.73
  connective tissue 782.3
  cornea 371.20
      due to contact lenses 371.24
      idiopathic 371.21
      secondary 371.22
  cystoid macular 362.53
  due to
      lymphatic obstruction — *see* Edema,
          lymphatic
      salt retention 276.0
  epiglottis — *see* Edema, glottis
  essential, acute 995.1
      hereditary 277.6
  extremities, lower — *see* Edema, legs
  eyelid NEC 374.82
  familial, hereditary (legs) 757.0
  famine 262
  fetus or newborn 778.5
  genital organs
      female 629.89
      male 608.86
  gestational 646.1 ☑
      with hypertension — *see* Toxemia, of
          pregnancy
  glottis, glottic, glottides (obstructive) (pas-
      sive) 478.6
      allergic 995.1
          hereditary 277.6
      due to external agent — *see* Condition,
          respiratory, acute, due to speci-
          fied agent
  heart (*see also* Failure, heart) 428.0
      newborn 779.89
  heat 992.7
  hereditary (legs) 757.0

Edema, edematous — *continued*
  inanition 262
  infectious 782.3
  intracranial 348.5
      due to injury at birth 767.8
  iris 364.89
  joint (*see also* Effusion, joint) 719.0 ☑
  larynx (*see also* Edema, glottis) 478.6
  legs 782.3
      due to venous obstruction 459.2
      hereditary 757.0
  localized 782.3
      due to venous obstruction 459.2
          lower extremity 459.2
  lower extremities — *see* Edema, legs
  lung 514
      acute 518.4
          with heart disease or failure (*see also*
              Failure, ventricular, left) 428.1
              congestive 428.0
          chemical (due to fumes or vapors)
              506.1
          due to
              external agent(s) NEC 508.9
                  specified NEC 508.8
              fumes and vapors (chemical) (in-
                  halation) 506.1
              radiation 508.0
      chemical (acute) 506.1
          chronic 506.4
      chronic 514
          chemical (due to fumes or vapors)
              506.4
          due to
              external agent(s) NEC 508.9
                  specified NEC 508.8
              fumes or vapors (chemical) (in-
                  halation) 506.4
              radiation 508.1
      due to
          external agent 508.9
              specified NEC 508.8
          high altitude 993.2
          near drowning 994.1
      postoperative 518.4
      terminal 514
  lymphatic 457.1
      due to mastectomy operation 457.0
  macula 362.83
      cystoid 362.53
      diabetic 250.5 ☑ [362.07]
          due to secondary diabetes
              249.5 ☑ [362.07]
  malignant (*see also* Gangrene, gas) 040.0
  Milroy's 757.0
  nasopharynx 478.25
  neonatorum 778.5
  nutritional (newborn) 262
      with dyspigmentation, skin and hair 260
  optic disc or nerve — *see* Papilledema
  orbit 376.33
      circulatory 459.89
  palate (soft) (hard) 528.9
  pancreas 577.8
  penis 607.83
  periodic 995.1
      hereditary 277.6
  pharynx 478.25
  pitting 782.3
  pulmonary — *see* Edema, lung
  Quincke's 995.1
      hereditary 277.6
  renal (*see also* Nephrosis) 581.9
  retina (localized) (macular) (peripheral)
      362.83
      cystoid 362.53
      diabetic 250.5 ☑ [362.07]
          due to secondary diabetes
              249.5 ☑ [362.07]
  salt 276.0
  scrotum 608.86
  seminal vesicle 608.86
  spermatic cord 608.86
  spinal cord 336.1
  starvation 262
  stasis (*see also* Hypertension, venous) 459.30

Edema, edematous — *continued*
  subconjunctival 372.73
  subglottic (*see also* Edema, glottis) 478.6
  supraglottic (*see also* Edema, glottis) 478.6
  testis 608.86
  toxic NEC 782.3
  traumatic NEC 782.3
  tunica vaginalis 608.86
  vas deferens 608.86
  vocal cord — *see* Edema, glottis
  vulva (acute) 624.8
Edentia (complete) (partial) — *see also* Ab-
    sence, tooth 520.0
  acquired (*see also* Edentulism) 525.40
      due to
          caries 525.13
          extraction 525.10
          periodontal disease 525.12
          specified NEC 525.19
          trauma 525.11
      causing malocclusion 524.30
  congenital (deficiency of tooth buds) 520.0
Edentulism 525.40
  complete 525.40
      class I 525.41
      class II 525.42
      class III 525.43
      class IV 525.44
  partial 525.50
      class I 525.51
      class II 525.52
      class III 525.53
      class IV 525.54
Edsall's disease 992.2
Educational handicap V62.3
Edwards' syndrome 758.2
Effect, adverse NEC
  abnormal gravitational (G) forces or states
      994.9
  air pressure — *see* Effect, adverse, atmo-
      spheric pressure
  altitude (high) — *see* Effect, adverse, high
      altitude
  anesthetic
      in labor and delivery NEC 668.9 ☑
          affecting fetus or newborn 763.5
  antitoxin — *see* Complications, vaccination
  atmospheric pressure 993.9
      due to explosion 993.4
      high 993.3
      low — *see* Effect, adverse, high altitude
      specified effect NEC 993.8
  biological, correct substance properly admin-
      istered (*see also* Effect, adverse, drug)
      995.20
  blood (derivatives) (serum) (transfusion) —
      see Complications, transfusion
  chemical substance NEC 989.9
      specified — *see* Table of Drugs and
          Chemicals
  cobalt, radioactive (*see also* Effect, adverse,
      radioactive substance) 990
  cold (temperature) (weather) 991.9
      chilblains 991.5
      frostbite — *see* Frostbite
      specified effect NEC 991.8
  drugs and medicinals 995.20
      correct substance properly administered
          995.20
      overdose or wrong substance given or
          taken 977.9
          specified drug — *see* Table of Drugs
              and Chemicals
  electric current (shock) 994.8
      burn — *see* Burn, by site
  electricity (electrocution) (shock) 994.8
      burn — *see* Burn, by site
  exertion (excessive) 994.5
  exposure 994.9
      exhaustion 994.4
  external cause NEC 994.9
  fallout (radioactive) NEC 990
  fluoroscopy NEC 990

☑ **Additional Digit Required — Refer to the Tabular List for Digit Selection**

▽ **Subterms under main terms may continue to next column or page**

Effect, adverse — continued
foodstuffs
anaphylactic reaction or shock due to food NEC — see Anaphylactic reaction or shock, due to food
noxious 988.9
specified type NEC (see also Poisoning, by name of noxious foodstuff) 988.8
gases, fumes, or vapors — see Table of Drugs and Chemicals
glue (airplane) sniffing 304.6 ☑
heat — see Heat
high altitude NEC 993.2
anoxia 993.2
on
ears 993.0
sinuses 993.1
polycythemia 289.0
hot weather — see Heat
hunger 994.2
immersion, foot 991.4
immunization — see Complications, vaccination
immunological agents — see Complications, vaccination
implantation (removable) of isotope or radium NEC 990
infrared (radiation) (rays) NEC 990
burn — see Burn, by site
dermatitis or eczema 692.82
infusion — see Complications, infusion
ingestion or injection of isotope (therapeutic) NEC 990
irradiation NEC (see also Effect, adverse, radiation) 990
isotope (radioactive) NEC 990
lack of care (child) (infant) (newborn) 995.52
adult 995.84
lightning 994.0
burn — see Burn, by site
Lirugin — see Complications, vaccination
medicinal substance, correct, properly administered (see also Effect, adverse, drugs) 995.20
mesothorium NEC 990
motion 994.6
noise, inner ear 388.10
other drug, medicinal and biological substance 995.29
overheated places — see Heat
polonium NEC 990
psychosocial, of work environment V62.1
radiation (diagnostic) (fallout) (infrared) (natural source) (therapeutic) (tracer) (ultraviolet) (x-ray) NEC 990
with pulmonary manifestations
acute 508.0
chronic 508.1
dermatitis or eczema 692.82
due to sun NEC (see also Dermatitis, due to, sun) 692.70
fibrosis of lungs 508.1
maternal with suspected damage to fetus affecting management of pregnancy 655.6 ☑
pneumonitis 508.0
radioactive substance NEC 990
dermatitis or eczema 692.82
radioactivity NEC 990
radiotherapy NEC 990
dermatitis or eczema 692.82
radium NEC 990
reduced temperature 991.9
frostbite — see Frostbite
immersion, foot (hand) 991.4
specified effect NEC 991.8
roentgenography NEC 990
roentgenoscopy NEC 990
roentgen rays NEC 990
serum (prophylactic) (therapeutic) NEC 999.59
specified NEC 995.89
external cause NEC 994.9
strangulation 994.7
submersion 994.1

Effect, adverse — continued
teletherapy NEC 990
thirst 994.3
transfusion — see Complications, transfusion
ultraviolet (radiation) (rays) NEC 990
burn (see also Burn, by site)
from sun (see also Sunburn) 692.71
dermatitis or eczema 692.82
due to sun NEC (see also Dermatitis, due to, sun) 692.70
uranium NEC 990
vaccine (any) — see Complications, vaccination
weightlessness 994.9
whole blood (see also Complications, transfusion)
overdose or wrong substance given (see also Table of Drugs and Chemicals) 964.7
working environment V62.1
x-rays NEC 990
dermatitis or eczema 692.82

Effect, remote
of cancer — see condition

Effects, late — see Late, effect (of)

Effluvium, telogen 704.02

Effort
intolerance 306.2
syndrome (aviators) (psychogenic) 306.2

Effusion
amniotic fluid (see also Rupture, membranes, premature) 658.1 ☑
brain (serous) 348.5
bronchial (see also Bronchitis) 490
cerebral 348.5
cerebrospinal (see also Meningitis) 322.9
vessel 348.5
chest — see Effusion, pleura
intracranial 348.5
joint 719.00
ankle 719.07
elbow 719.02
foot 719.07
hand 719.04
hip 719.05
knee 719.06
multiple sites 719.09
pelvic region 719.05
shoulder (region) 719.01
specified site NEC 719.08
wrist 719.03
meninges (see also Meningitis) 322.9
pericardium, pericardial (see also Pericarditis) 423.9
acute 420.90
peritoneal (chronic) 568.82
pleura, pleurisy, pleuritic, pleuropericardial 511.9
bacterial, nontuberculous 511.1
fetus or newborn 511.9
malignant 511.81
nontuberculous 511.9
bacterial 511.1
pneumococcal 511.1
staphylococcal 511.1
streptococcal 511.1
traumatic 862.29
with open wound 862.39
tuberculous (see also Tuberculosis, pleura) 012.0 ☑
primary progressive 010.1 ☑
pulmonary — see Effusion, pleura
spinal (see also Meningitis) 322.9
thorax, thoracic — see Effusion, pleura

Egg (oocyte) (ovum)
donor V59.70
over age 35 V59.73
anonymous recipient V59.73
designated recipient V59.74
under age 35 V59.71
anonymous recipient V59.71
designated recipient V59.72

Eggshell nails 703.8
congenital 757.5

Ego-dystonic
homosexuality 302.0
lesbianism 302.0
sexual orientation 302.0

Egyptian splenomegaly 120.1

Ehlers-Danlos syndrome 756.83

Ehrlichiosis 082.40
chaffeensis 082.41
specified type NEC 082.49

Eichstedt's disease (pityriasis versicolor) 111.0

EIN (endometrial intraepithelial neoplasia) 621.35

Eisenmenger's complex or syndrome (ventricular septal defect) 745.4

Ejaculation, semen
painful 608.89
psychogenic 306.59
premature 302.75
retrograde 608.87

Ekbom syndrome (restless legs) 333.94

Ekman's syndrome (brittle bones and blue sclera) 756.51

Elastic skin 756.83
acquired 701.8

Elastofibroma (M8820/0) — see Neoplasm, connective tissue, benign

Elastoidosis
cutanea nodularis 701.8
cutis cystica et comedonica 701.8

Elastoma 757.39
juvenile 757.39
Miescher's (elastosis perforans serpiginosa) 701.1

Elastomyofibrosis 425.3

Elastosis 701.8
atrophicans 701.8
perforans serpiginosa 701.1
reactive perforating 701.1
senilis 701.8
solar (actinic) 692.74

Elbow — see condition

Electric
current, electricity, effects (concussion) (fatal) (nonfatal) (shock) 994.8
burn — see Burn, by site
feet (foot) syndrome 266.2
shock from electroshock gun (taser) 994.8

Electrocution 994.8

Electrolyte imbalance 276.9
with
abortion — see Abortion, by type, with metabolic disorder
ectopic pregnancy (see also categories 633.0–633.9) 639.4
hyperemesis gravidarum (before 22 completed weeks gestation) 643.1 ☑
molar pregnancy (see also categories 630–632) 639.4
following
abortion 639.4
ectopic or molar pregnancy 639.4

Elephantiasis (nonfilarial) 457.1
arabicum (see also Infestation, filarial) 125.9
congenita hereditaria 757.0
congenital (any site) 757.0
due to
Brugia (malayi) 125.1
mastectomy operation 457.0
Wuchereria (bancrofti) 125.0
malayi 125.1
eyelid 374.83
filarial (see also Infestation, filarial) 125.9
filariensis (see also Infestation, filarial) 125.9
gingival 523.8
glandular 457.1
graecorum 030.9
lymphangiectatic 457.1
lymphatic vessel 457.1
due to mastectomy operation 457.0
neuromatosa 237.71
postmastectomy 457.0
scrotum 457.1
streptococcal 457.1
surgical 997.99
postmastectomy 457.0

Elephantiasis — continued
telangiectodes 457.1
vulva (nonfilarial) 624.8

Elephant man syndrome 237.71

Elevated — see Elevation
findings on laboratory examination — see Findings, abnormal, without diagnosis (examination) (laboratory test)
GFR (glomerular filtration rate) — see Findings, abnormal, without diagnosis (examination) (laboratory test)

Elevation
17-ketosteroids 791.9
acid phosphatase 790.5
alkaline phosphatase 790.5
amylase 790.5
antibody titers 795.79
basal metabolic rate (BMR) 794.7
blood pressure (see also Hypertension) 401.9
reading (incidental) (isolated) (nonspecific), no diagnosis of hypertension 796.2
blood sugar 790.29
body temperature (of unknown origin) (see also Pyrexia) 780.60
cancer antigen 125 [CA 125] 795.82
carcinoembryonic antigen [CEA] 795.81
cholesterol 272.0
with high triglycerides 272.2
conjugate, eye 378.81
C-reactive protein (CRP) 790.95
CRP (C-reactive protein) 790.95
diaphragm, congenital 756.6
GFR (glomerular filtration rate) — see Findings, abnormal, without diagnosis (examination) (laboratory test)
glucose
fasting 790.21
tolerance test 790.22
immunoglobulin level 795.79
indolacetic acid 791.9
lactic acid dehydrogenase (LDH) level 790.4
leukocytes 288.60
lipase 790.5
lipoprotein a level 272.8
liver function test (LFT) 790.6
alkaline phosphatase 790.5
aminotransferase 790.4
bilirubin 782.4
hepatic enzyme NEC 790.5
lactate dehydrogenase 790.4
lymphocytes 288.61
prostate specific antigen (PSA) 790.93
renin 790.99
in hypertension (see also Hypertension, renovascular) 405.91
Rh titer (see also Complications, transfusion) 999.70
scapula, congenital 755.52
sedimentation rate 790.1
SGOT 790.4
SGPT 790.4
transaminase 790.4
triglycerides 272.1
with high cholesterol 272.2
vanillylmandelic acid 791.9
venous pressure 459.89
VMA 791.9
white blood cell count 288.60
specified NEC 288.69

Elliptocytosis (congenital) (hereditary) 282.1
Hb-C (disease) 282.7
hemoglobin disease 282.7
sickle-cell (disease) 282.60
trait 282.5

Ellison-Zollinger syndrome (gastric hypersecretion with pancreatic islet cell tumor) 251.5

Ellis-van Creveld disease or syndrome (chondroectodermal dysplasia) 756.55

Elongation, elongated (congenital) — see also Distortion
bone 756.9
cervix (uteri) 752.49
acquired 622.6
hypertrophic 622.6

Elongation, elongated — see also Distortion — continued
  colon 751.5
  common bile duct 751.69
  cystic duct 751.69
  frenulum, penis 752.69
  labia minora, acquired 624.8
  ligamentum patellae 756.89
  petiolus (epiglottidis) 748.3
  styloid bone (process) 733.99
  tooth, teeth 520.2
  uvula 750.26
    acquired 528.9
Elschnig bodies or pearls 366.51
El Tor cholera 001.1
Emaciation (due to malnutrition) 261
Emancipation disorder 309.22
Embadomoniasis 007.8
Embarrassment heart, cardiac — see Disease, heart
Embedded
  fragment (status) — see Foreign body, retained
  splinter (status) — see Foreign body, retained
  tooth, teeth 520.6
    root only 525.3
Embolic — see condition
Embolism 444.9
  with
    abortion — see Abortion, by type, with embolism
    ectopic pregnancy (see also categories 633.0–633.9) 639.6
    molar pregnancy (see also categories 630–632) 639.6
  air (any site) 958.0
    with
      abortion — see Abortion, by type, with embolism
      ectopic pregnancy (see also categories 633.0–633.9) 639.6
      molar pregnancy (see also categories 630–632) 639.6
    due to implanted device — see Complications, due to (presence of) any device, implant, or graft classified to 996.0–996.5 NEC
    following
      abortion 639.6
      ectopic or molar pregnancy 639.6
      infusion, perfusion, or transfusion 999.1
    in pregnancy, childbirth, or puerperium 673.0 ✔
    traumatic 958.0
  amniotic fluid (pulmonary) 673.1 ✔
    with
      abortion — see Abortion, by type, with embolism
      ectopic pregnancy (see also categories 633.0–633.9) 639.6
      molar pregnancy (see also categories 630–632) 639.6
    following
      abortion 639.6
      ectopic or molar pregnancy 639.6
  aorta, aortic 444.1
    abdominal 444.09
      saddle 444.01
    bifurcation 444.09
    saddle 444.01
    thoracic 444.1
  artery 444.9
    auditory, internal 433.8 ✔
    basilar (see also Occlusion, artery, basilar) 433.0 ✔
    bladder 444.89
    carotid (common) (internal) (see also Occlusion, artery, carotid) 433.1 ✔
    cerebellar (anterior inferior) (posterior inferior) (superior) 433.8 ✔
    cerebral (see also Embolism, brain) 434.1 ✔
    choroidal (anterior) 433.8 ✔

Embolism — continued
  artery — continued
    communicating posterior 433.8 ✔
    coronary (see also Infarct, myocardium) 410.9 ✔
      without myocardial infarction 411.81
    extremity 444.22
      lower 444.22
      upper 444.21
    hypophyseal 433.8 ✔
    mesenteric (with gangrene) 557.0
    ophthalmic (see also Occlusion, retina) 362.30
    peripheral 444.22
    pontine 433.8 ✔
    precerebral NEC — see Occlusion, artery, precerebral
    pulmonary — see Embolism, pulmonary
    pyemic 449
      pulmonary 415.12
    renal 593.81
    retinal (see also Occlusion, retina) 362.30
    septic 449
      pulmonary 415.12
    specified site NEC 444.89
    vertebral (see also Occlusion, artery, vertebral) 433.2 ✔
  auditory, internal 433.8 ✔
  basilar (artery) (see also Occlusion, artery, basilar) 433.0 ✔
  birth, mother — see Embolism, obstetrical
  blood-clot
    with
      abortion — see Abortion, by type, with embolism
      ectopic pregnancy (see also categories 633.0–633.9) 639.6
      molar pregnancy (see also categories 630–632) 639.6
    following
      abortion 639.6
      ectopic or molar pregnancy 639.6
    in pregnancy, childbirth, or puerperium 673.2 ✔
  brain 434.1 ✔
    with
      abortion — see Abortion, by type, with embolism
      ectopic pregnancy (see also categories 633.0–633.9) 639.6
      molar pregnancy (see also categories 630–632) 639.6
    following
      abortion 639.6
      ectopic or molar pregnancy 639.6
    late effect — see Late effect(s) (of) cerebrovascular disease
    puerperal, postpartum, childbirth 674.0 ✔
  capillary 448.9
  cardiac (see also Infarct, myocardium) 410.9 ✔
  carotid (artery) (common) (internal) (see also Occlusion, artery, carotid) 433.1 ✔
  cavernous sinus (venous) — see Embolism, intracranial venous sinus
  cerebral (see also Embolism, brain) 434.1 ✔
  cholesterol — see Atheroembolism
  choroidal (anterior) (artery) 433.8 ✔
  coronary (artery or vein) (systemic) (see also Infarct, myocardium) 410.9 ✔
    without myocardial infarction 411.81
  due to (presence of) any device, implant, or graft classifiable to 996.0–996.5 — see Complications, due to (presence of) any device, implant, or graft classified to 996.0–996.5 NEC
  encephalomalacia (see also Embolism, brain) 434.1 ✔
  extremities 444.22
    lower 444.22
    upper 444.21
  eye 362.30
  fat (cerebral) (pulmonary) (systemic) 958.1

Embolism — continued
  fat — continued
    with
      abortion — see Abortion, by type, with embolism
      ectopic pregnancy (see also categories 633.0–633.9) 639.6
      molar pregnancy (see also categories 630–632) 639.6
    complicating delivery or puerperium 673.8 ✔
    following
      abortion 639.6
      ectopic or molar pregnancy 639.6
    in pregnancy, childbirth, or the puerperium 673.8 ✔
  femoral (artery) 444.22
    vein 453.6
      deep 453.41
  following
    abortion 639.6
    ectopic or molar pregnancy 639.6
    infusion, perfusion, or transfusion
      air 999.1
      thrombus 999.2
  heart (fatty) (see also Infarct, myocardium) 410.9 ✔
  hepatic (vein) 453.0
  iliac (artery) 444.81
  iliofemoral 444.81
  in pregnancy, childbirth, or puerperium (pulmonary) — see Embolism, obstetrical
  intestine (artery) (vein) (with gangrene) 557.0
  intracranial (see also Embolism, brain) 434.1 ✔
    venous sinus (any) 325
      late effect — see category 326
      nonpyogenic 437.6
        in pregnancy or puerperium 671.5 ✔
  kidney (artery) 593.81
  lateral sinus (venous) — see Embolism, intracranial venous sinus
  longitudinal sinus (venous) — see Embolism, intracranial venous sinus
  lower extremity 444.22
  lung (massive) — see Embolism, pulmonary
  meninges (see also Embolism, brain) 434.1 ✔
  mesenteric (artery) (with gangrene) 557.0
  multiple NEC 444.9
  obstetrical (pulmonary) 673.2 ✔
    air 673.0 ✔
    amniotic fluid (pulmonary) 673.1 ✔
    blood-clot 673.2 ✔
    cardiac 674.8 ✔
    fat 673.8 ✔
    heart 674.8 ✔
    pyemic 673.3 ✔
    septic 673.3 ✔
    specified NEC 674.8 ✔
  ophthalmic (see also Occlusion, retina) 362.30
  paradoxical NEC 444.9
  penis 607.82
  peripheral arteries NEC 444.22
    lower 444.22
    upper 444.21
  pituitary 253.8
  popliteal (artery) 444.22
  portal (vein) 452
  postoperative NEC 997.2
    cerebral 997.02
    mesenteric artery 997.71
    other vessels 997.79
    peripheral vascular 997.2
    pulmonary 415.11
      septic 415.11
    renal artery 997.72
  precerebral artery (see also Occlusion, artery, precerebral) 433.9 ✔
  puerperal — see Embolism, obstetrical
  pulmonary (acute) (artery) (vein) 415.19

Embolism — continued
  pulmonary — continued
    with
      abortion — see Abortion, by type, with embolism
      ectopic pregnancy (see also categories 633.0–633.9) 639.6
      molar pregnancy (see also categories 630–632) 639.6
    chronic 416.2
    following
      abortion 639.6
      ectopic or molar pregnancy 639.6
    healed or old V12.55
    iatrogenic 415.11
    in pregnancy, childbirth, or puerperium — see Embolism, obstetrical
    personal history of V12.55
    postoperative 415.11
    septic 415.12
  pyemic (multiple) (see also Septicemia) 415.12
    with
      abortion — see Abortion, by type, with embolism
      ectopic pregnancy (see also categories 633.0–633.9) 639.6
      molar pregnancy (see also categories 630–632) 639.6
    Aerobacter aerogenes 415.12
    enteric gram-negative bacilli 415.12
    Enterobacter aerogenes 415.12
    Escherichia coli 415.12
    following
      abortion 639.6
      ectopic or molar pregnancy 639.6
    Hemophilus influenzae 415.12
    pneumococcal 415.12
    Proteus vulgaris 415.12
    Pseudomonas (aeruginosa) 415.12
    puerperal, postpartum, childbirth (any organism) 673.3 ✔
    Serratia 415.12
    specified organism NEC 415.12
    staphylococcal 415.12
      aureus 415.12
      specified organism NEC 415.12
    streptococcal 415.12
  renal (artery) 593.81
    vein 453.3
  retina, retinal (see also Occlusion, retina) 362.30
  saddle
    abdominal aorta 444.01
    pulmonary artery 415.13
  septic 415.12
    arterial 449
  septicemic — see Embolism, pyemic
  sinus — see Embolism, intracranial venous sinus
  soap
    with
      abortion — see Abortion, by type, with embolism
      ectopic pregnancy (see also categories 633.0–633.9) 639.6
      molar pregnancy (see also categories 630–632) 639.6
    following
      abortion 639.6
      ectopic or molar pregnancy 639.6
  spinal cord (nonpyogenic) 336.1
    in pregnancy or puerperium 671.5 ✔
    pyogenic origin 324.1
    late effect — see category 326
  spleen, splenic (artery) 444.89
  thrombus (thromboembolism) following infusion, perfusion, or transfusion 999.2
  upper extremity 444.21
  vein 453.9
    with inflammation or phlebitis — see Thrombophlebitis
    antecubital (acute) 453.81
      chronic 453.71
    axillary (acute) 453.84

✔ **Additional Digit Required** — Refer to the Tabular List for Digit Selection

▽ Subterms under main terms may continue to next column or page

Embolism — continued
vein — continued
axillary — continued
chronic 453.74
basilic (acute) 453.81
chronic 453.71
brachial (acute) 453.82
chronic 453.72
brachiocephalic (acute) (innominate)
453.87
chronic 453.77
cephalic (acute) 453.81
chronic 453.71
cerebral (see also Embolism, brain)
434.1 ☑
coronary (see also Infarct, myocardium)
410.9 ☑
without myocardial infarction 411.81
hepatic 453.0
internal jugular (acute) 453.86
chronic 453.76
lower extremity (superficial) 453.6
deep 453.40
acute 453.40
calf 453.42
distal (lower leg) 453.42
femoral 453.41
iliac 453.41
lower leg 453.42
peroneal 453.42
popliteal 453.41
proximal (upper leg) 453.41
thigh 453.41
tibial 453.42
chronic 453.50
calf 453.52
disal (lower leg) 453.52
femoral 453.51
iliac 453.51
lower leg 453.52
peroneal 453.52
popliteal 453.51
proximal (upper leg) 453.51
thigh 453.51
tibial 453.52
saphenous (greater) (lesser) 453.6
superficial 453.6
mesenteric (with gangrene) 557.0
portal 452
pulmonary — see Embolism, pulmonary
radial (acute) 453.82
chronic 453.72
renal 453.3
saphenous (greater) (lesser) 453.6
specified NEC (acute) 453.89
with inflammation or phlebitis — see
Thrombophlebitis
chronic 453.79
subclavian (acute) 453.85
chronic 453.75
superior vena cava (acute) 453.87
chronic 453.77
thoracic (acute) 453.87
chronic 453.77
ulnar (acute) 453.82
chronic 453.72
upper extremity (acute) 453.83
chronic 453.73
deep 453.72
superficial 453.71
deep 453.82
superficial 453.81
vena cava
inferior 453.2
superior (acute) 453.87
chronic 453.77
vessels of brain (see also Embolism, brain)
434.1 ☑
Embolization — see Embolism
Embolus — see Embolism
Embryoma (M9080/1) — see also Neoplasm,
by site, uncertain behavior
benign (M9080/0) — see Neoplasm, by site,
benign
kidney (M8960/3) 189.0
liver (M8970/3) 155.0

Embryoma (M9080/1) — see also Neoplasm,
by site, uncertain behavior —
continued
malignant (M9080/3) (see also Neoplasm,
by site, malignant)
kidney (M8960/3) 189.0
liver (M8970/3) 155.0
testis (M9070/3) 186.9
undescended 186.0
testis (M9070/3) 186.9
undescended 186.0
Embryonic
circulation 747.9
heart 747.9
vas deferens 752.89
Embryopathia NEC 759.9
Embryotomy, fetal 763.89
Embryotoxon 743.43
interfering with vision 743.42
Emesis — see also Vomiting
bilious 787.04
gravidarum — see Hyperemesis, gravidarum
Emissions, nocturnal (semen) 608.89
Emotional
crisis — see Crisis, emotional
disorder (see also Disorder, mental) 300.9
instability (excessive) 301.3
lability 799.24
overlay — see Reaction, adjustment
upset 300.9
Emotionality, pathological 301.3
Emotogenic disease — see also Disorder,
psychogenic 306.9
Emphysema (atrophic) (centriacinar) (centrilob-
ular) (chronic) (diffuse) (essential) (hypertrophic) (interlobular) (lung) (obstructive) (panlobular) (paracicatricial)
(paracinar) (postural) (pulmonary) (senile) (subpleural) (traction) (unilateral)
(unilobular) (vesicular) 492.8
with bronchitis
chronic 491.20
with
acute bronchitis 491.22
exacerbation (acute) 491.21
bullous (giant) 492.0
cellular tissue 958.7
surgical 998.81
compensatory 518.2
congenital 770.2
conjunctiva 372.89
connective tissue 958.7
surgical 998.81
due to fumes or vapors 506.4
eye 376.89
eyelid 374.85
surgical 998.81
traumatic 958.7
fetus or newborn (interstitial) (mediastinal)
(unilobular) 770.2
heart 416.9
interstitial 518.1
congenital 770.2
fetus or newborn 770.2
laminated tissue 958.7
surgical 998.81
mediastinal 518.1
fetus or newborn 770.2
newborn (interstitial) (mediastinal) (unilobular) 770.2
obstructive diffuse with fibrosis 492.8
orbit 376.89
subcutaneous 958.7
due to trauma 958.7
nontraumatic 518.1
surgical 998.81
surgical 998.81
thymus (gland) (congenital) 254.8
traumatic 958.7
tuberculous (see also Tuberculosis, pulmonary) 011.9 ☑
Employment examination (certification) V70.5
Empty sella (turcica) syndrome 253.8

Empyema (chest) (diaphragmatic) (double)
(encapsulated) (general) (interlobar)
(lung) (medial) (necessitatis) (perforating
chest wall) (pleura) (pneumococcal)
(residual) (sacculated) (streptococcal)
(supradiaphragmatic) 510.9
with fistula 510.0
accessory sinus (chronic) (see also Sinusitis)
473.9
acute 510.9
with fistula 510.0
antrum (chronic) (see also Sinusitis, maxillary) 473.0
brain (any part) (see also Abscess, brain)
324.0
ethmoidal (sinus) (chronic) (see also Sinusitis, ethmoidal) 473.2
extradural (see also Abscess, extradural)
324.9
frontal (sinus) (chronic) (see also Sinusitis,
frontal) 473.1
gallbladder (see also Cholecystitis, acute)
575.0
mastoid (process) (acute) (see also Mastoiditis, acute) 383.00
maxilla, maxillary 526.4
sinus (chronic) (see also Sinusitis, maxillary) 473.0
nasal sinus (chronic) (see also Sinusitis) 473.9
sinus (accessory) (nasal) (see also Sinusitis)
473.9
sphenoidal (chronic) (sinus) (see also Sinusitis, sphenoidal) 473.3
subarachnoid (see also Abscess, extradural)
324.9
subdural (see also Abscess, extradural) 324.9
tuberculous (see also Tuberculosis, pleura)
012.0 ☑
ureter (see also Ureteritis) 593.89
ventricular (see also Abscess, brain) 324.0
Enameloma 520.2
Encephalitis (bacterial) (chronic) (hemorrhagic)
(idiopathic) (nonepidemic) (spurious)
(subacute) 323.9
acute (see also Encephalitis, viral)
disseminated (postinfectious) NEC
136.9 [323.61]
postimmunization or postvaccination
323.51
inclusional 049.8
inclusion body 049.8
necrotizing 049.8
arboviral, arbovirus NEC 064
arthropod-borne (see also Encephalitis, viral,
arthropod-borne) 064
Australian X 062.4
Bwamba fever 066.3
California (virus) 062.5
Central European 063.2
Czechoslovakian 063.2
Dawson's (inclusion body) 046.2
diffuse sclerosing 046.2
due to
actinomycosis 039.8 [323.41]
cat-scratch disease 078.3 [323.01]
human herpesvirus 6 058.21
human herpesvirus 7 058.29
human herpesvirus NEC 058.29
human immunodeficiency virus (HIV)
disease 042 [323.01]
infectious mononucleosis 075 [323.01]
malaria (see also Malaria) 084.6 [323.2]
Negishi virus 064
ornithosis 073.7 [323.01]
other infection classified elsewhere
136.9 [323.41]
prophylactic inoculation against smallpox 323.51
rickettsiosis (see also Rickettsiosis)
083.9 [323.1]
rubella 056.01
toxoplasmosis (acquired) 130.0
congenital (active) 771.2 [323.41]
typhus (fever) (see also Typhus)
081.9 [323.1]
vaccination (smallpox) 323.51

Encephalitis — continued
Eastern equine 062.2
endemic 049.8
epidemic 049.8
equine (acute) (infectious) (viral) 062.9
Eastern 062.2
Venezuelan 066.2
Western 062.1
Far Eastern 063.0
following vaccination or other immunization
procedure 323.51
herpes 054.3
human herpesvirus 6 058.21
human herpesvirus 7 058.29
human herpesvirus NEC 058.29
Ilheus (virus) 062.8
inclusion body 046.2
infectious (acute) (virus) NEC 049.8
influenzal (see also Influenza) 487.8 [323.41]
lethargic 049.8
Japanese (B type) 062.0
La Crosse 062.5
Langat 063.8
late effect — see Late, effect, encephalitis
lead 984.9 [323.71]
lethargic (acute) (infectious) (influenzal)
049.8
lethargica 049.8
louping ill 063.1
lupus 710.0 [323.81]
lymphatica 049.0
Mengo 049.8
meningococcal 036.1
mumps 072.2
Murray Valley 062.4
myoclonic 049.8
Negishi virus 064
otitic NEC 382.4 [323.41]
parasitic NEC 123.9 [323.41]
periaxialis (concentrica) (diffusa) 341.1
postchickenpox 052.0
postexanthematous NEC 057.9 [323.62]
postimmunization 323.51
postinfectious NEC 136.9 [323.62]
postmeasles 055.0
posttraumatic 323.81
postvaccinal (smallpox) 323.51
postvaricella 052.0
postviral NEC 079.99 [323.62]
postexanthematous 057.9 [323.62]
specified NEC 057.8 [323.62]
Powassan 063.8
progressive subcortical (Binswanger's)
290.12
Rasmussen 323.81
Rio Bravo 049.8
rubella 056.01
Russian
autumnal 062.0
spring-summer type (taiga) 063.0
saturnine 984.9 [323.71]
Semliki Forest 062.8
serous 048
slow-acting virus NEC 046.8
specified cause NEC 323.81
St. Louis type 062.3
subacute sclerosing 046.2
subcorticalis chronica 290.12
summer 062.0
suppurative 324.0
syphilitic 094.81
congenital 090.41
tick-borne 063.9
torula, torular 117.5 [323.41]
toxic NEC 989.9 [323.71]
toxoplasmic (acquired) 130.0
congenital (active) 771.2 [323.41]
trichinosis 124 [323.41]
Trypanosomiasis (see also Trypanosomiasis)
086.9 [323.2]
tuberculous (see also Tuberculosis) 013.6 ☑
type B (Japanese) 062.0
type C 062.3
van Bogaert's 046.2
Venezuelan 066.2
Vienna type 049.8

Encephalitis — continued
viral, virus 049.9
  arthropod-borne NEC 064
    mosquito-borne 062.9
      Australian X disease 062.4
      California virus 062.5
      Eastern equine 062.2
      Ilheus virus 062.8
      Japanese (B type) 062.0
      Murray Valley 062.4
      specified type NEC 062.8
      St. Louis 062.3
      type B 062.0
      type C 062.3
      Western equine 062.1
    tick-borne 063.9
      biundulant 063.2
      Central European 063.2
      Czechoslovakian 063.2
      diphasic meningoencephalitis 063.2
      Far Eastern 063.0
      Langat 063.8
      louping ill 063.1
      Powassan 063.8
      Russian spring-summer (taiga) 063.0
      specified type NEC 063.8
      vector unknown 064
      Western equine 062.1
    slow acting NEC 046.8
    specified type NEC 049.8
    vaccination, prophylactic (against) V05.0
    von Economo's 049.8
    Western equine 062.1
    West Nile type 066.41
Encephalocele 742.0
  orbit 376.81
Encephalocystocele 742.0
Encephaloduroarteriomyosynangiosis (EDAMS) 437.5
Encephalomalacia (brain) (cerebellar) (cerebral) (cerebrospinal) — see also Softening, brain 348.89
  due to
    hemorrhage (see also Hemorrhage, brain) 431
    recurrent spasm of artery 435.9
  embolic (cerebral) (see also Embolism, brain) 434.1 ☑
  subcorticalis chronicus arteriosclerotica 290.12
  thrombotic (see also Thrombosis, brain) 434.0 ☑
Encephalomeningitis — see Meningoencephalitis
Encephalomeningocele 742.0
Encephalomeningomyelitis — see Meningoencephalitis
Encephalomeningopathy — see also Meningoencephalitis 349.9
Encephalomyelitis (chronic) (granulomatous) (myalgic, benign) — see also Encephalitis 323.9
  abortive disseminated 049.8
  acute disseminated (ADEM) (postinfectious) 136.9 [323.61]
    infectious 136.9 [323.61]
    noninfectious 323.81
    postimmunization 323.51
  due to
    cat-scratch disease 078.3 [323.01]
    infectious mononucleosis 075 [323.01]
    ornithosis 073.7 [323.01]
    vaccination (any) 323.51
  equine (acute) (infectious) 062.9
    Eastern 062.2
    Venezuelan 066.2
    Western 062.1
  funicularis infectiosa 049.8
  late effect — see Late, effect, encephalitis
  Munch-Peterson's 049.8
  postchickenpox 052.0
  postimmunization 323.51
  postmeasles 055.0
  postvaccinal (smallpox) 323.51

Encephalomyelitis — see also Encephalitis — continued
  rubella 056.01
  specified cause NEC 323.81
  syphilitic 094.81
  West Nile 066.41
Encephalomyelocele 742.0
Encephalomyelomeningitis — see Meningoencephalitis
Encephalomyeloneuropathy 349.9
Encephalomyelopathy 349.9
  subacute necrotizing (infantile) 330.8
Encephalomyeloradiculitis (acute) 357.0
Encephalomyeloradiculoneuritis (acute) 357.0
Encephalomyeloradiculopathy 349.9
Encephalomyocarditis 074.23
Encephalopathia hyperbilirubinemica, newborn 774.7
  due to isoimmunization (conditions classifiable to 773.0–773.2) 773.4
Encephalopathy (acute) 348.30
  alcoholic 291.2
  anoxic — see Damage, brain, anoxic
  arteriosclerotic 437.0
    late effect — see Late effect(s) (of) cerebrovascular disease
  bilirubin, newborn 774.7
    due to isoimmunization 773.4
  congenital 742.9
  demyelinating (callosal) 341.8
  due to
    birth injury (intracranial) 767.8
    dialysis 294.8
      transient 293.9
    drugs — (see also Table of Drugs and Chemicals) 349.82
    hyperinsulinism — see Hyperinsulinism
    influenza (virus) (see also Influenza) 487.8
      identified
        avian 488.09
        (novel) 2009 H1N1 488.19
    lack of vitamin (see also Deficiency, vitamin) 269.2
    nicotinic acid deficiency 291.2
    serum (nontherapeutic) (therapeutic) 999.59
    syphilis 094.81
    trauma (postconcussional) 310.2
      current (see also Concussion, brain) 850.9
        with skull fracture — see Fracture, skull, by site, with intracranial injury
    vaccination 323.51
  hepatic 572.2
  hyperbilirubinemic, newborn 774.7
    due to isoimmunization (conditions classifiable to 773.0–773.2) 773.4
  hypertensive 437.2
  hypoglycemic 251.2
  hypoxic (see also Damage, brain, anoxic)
    ischemic (HIE) 768.70
      mild 768.71
      moderate 768.72
      severe 768.73
  infantile cystic necrotizing (congenital) 341.8
  lead 984.9 [323.71]
  leukopolio 330.0
  metabolic (see also Delirium) 348.31
    drug induced 349.82
    toxic 349.82
  necrotizing
    hemorrhagic (acute) 323.61
    subacute 330.8
  other specified type NEC 348.39
  pellagrous 265.2
  portal-systemic 572.2
  postcontusional 310.2
  posttraumatic 310.2
  saturnine 984.9 [323.71]
  septic 348.31
  spongioform, subacute (viral) 046.19

Encephalopathy — continued
  subacute
    necrotizing 330.8
    spongiform 046.19
    viral, spongioform 046.19
  subcortical progressive (Schilder) 341.1
    chronic (Binswanger's) 290.12
  toxic 349.82
    metabolic 349.82
  traumatic (postconcussional) 310.2
    current (see also Concussion, brain) 850.9
      with skull fracture — see Fracture, skull, by site, with intracranial injury
  vitamin B deficiency NEC 266.9
  Wernicke's (superior hemorrhagic polioencephalitis) 265.1
Encephalorrhagia — see also Hemorrhage, brain 432.9
  healed or old V12.54
  late effect — see Late effect(s) (of) cerebrovascular disease
Encephalosis, posttraumatic 310.2
Enchondroma (M9220/0) — see also Neoplasm, bone, benign
  multiple, congenital 756.4
Enchondromatosis (cartilaginous) (congenital) (multiple) 756.4
Enchondroses, multiple (cartilaginous) (congenital) 756.4
Encopresis — see also Incontinence, feces 787.60
  nonorganic origin 307.7
Encounter for — see also Admission for
  administrative purpose only V68.9
    referral of patient without examination or treatment V68.81
    specified purpose NEC V68.89
  chemotherapy, (oral) (intravenous), antineoplastic V58.11
  determination of fetal viability of pregnancy V23.87
  dialysis
    extracorporeal (renal) V56.0
    peritoneal V56.8
  disability examination V68.01
  end-of-life care V66.7
  hospice care V66.7
  immunizations (childhood) appropriate for age V20.2
  immunotherapy, antineoplastic V58.12
  joint prosthesis insertion following prior explantation of joint prosthesis V54.82
  palliative care V66.7
  paternity testing V70.4
  radiotherapy V58.0
  respirator [ventilator] dependence
    during
      mechanical failure V46.14
      power failure V46.12
    for weaning V46.13
  routine infant and child vision and hearing testing V20.2
  school examination V70.3
    following surgery V67.09
  screening mammogram NEC V76.12
    for high-risk patient V76.11
  terminal care V66.7
  weaning from respirator [ventilator] V46.13
Encystment — see Cyst
Endamebiasis — see Amebiasis
Endamoeba — see Amebiasis
Endarteritis (bacterial, subacute) (infective) (septic) 447.6
  brain, cerebral or cerebrospinal 437.4
    late effect — see Late effect(s) (of) cerebrovascular disease
  coronary (artery) — see Arteriosclerosis, coronary
  deformans — see Arteriosclerosis
  embolic (see also Embolism) 444.9
  obliterans (see also Arteriosclerosis)
    pulmonary 417.8
  pulmonary 417.8
  retina 362.18

Endarteritis — continued
  senile — see Arteriosclerosis
  syphilitic 093.89
    brain or cerebral 094.89
    congenital 090.5
    spinal 094.89
  tuberculous (see also Tuberculosis) 017.9 ☑
Endemic — see condition
Endocarditis (chronic) (indeterminate) (interstitial) (marantic) (nonbacterial thrombotic) (residual) (sclerotic) (sclerous) (senile) (valvular) 424.90
  with
    rheumatic fever (conditions classifiable to 390)
      active — see Endocarditis, acute, rheumatic
      inactive or quiescent (with chorea) 397.9
  acute or subacute 421.9
    rheumatic (aortic) (mitral) (pulmonary) (tricuspid) 391.1
      with chorea (acute) (rheumatic) (Sydenham's) 392.0
  aortic (heart) (nonrheumatic) (valve) 424.1
    with
      mitral (valve) disease 396.9
        active or acute 391.1
          with chorea (acute) (rheumatic) (Sydenham's) 392.0
      bacterial 421.0
      rheumatic fever (conditions classifiable to 390)
        active — see Endocarditis, acute, rheumatic
        inactive or quiescent (with chorea) 395.9
          with mitral disease 396.9
    acute or subacute 421.9
    arteriosclerotic 424.1
    congenital 746.89
    hypertensive 424.1
    rheumatic (chronic) (inactive) 395.9
      with mitral (valve) disease 396.9
        active or acute 391.1
          with chorea (acute) (rheumatic) (Sydenham's) 392.0
        active or acute 391.1
          with chorea (acute) (rheumatic) (Sydenham's) 392.0
    specified cause, except rheumatic 424.1
    syphilitic 093.22
  arteriosclerotic or due to arteriosclerosis 424.99
  atypical verrucous (Libman-Sacks) 710.0 [424.91]
  bacterial (acute) (any valve) (chronic) (subacute) 421.0
  blastomycotic 116.0 [421.1]
  candidal 112.81
  congenital 425.3
  constrictive 421.0
  Coxsackie 074.22
  due to
    blastomycosis 116.0 [421.1]
    candidiasis 112.81
    Coxsackie (virus) 074.22
    disseminated lupus erythematosus 710.0 [424.91]
    histoplasmosis (see also Histoplasmosis) 115.94
    hypertension (benign) 424.99
    moniliasis 112.81
    prosthetic cardiac valve 996.61
    Q fever 083.0 [421.1]
    serratia marcescens 421.0
    typhoid (fever) 002.0 [421.1]
  fetal 425.3
  gonococcal 098.84
  hypertensive 424.99
  infectious or infective (acute) (any valve) (chronic) (subacute) 421.0
  lenta (acute) (any valve) (chronic) (subacute) 421.0

Enteritis — *continued*
  chronic — *continued*
    ulcerative (*see also* Colitis, ulcerative)
      556.9
  cicatrizing (chronic) 555.0
  Clostridium
    botulinum 005.1
    difficile 008.45
    haemolyticum 008.46
    novyi 008.46
    perfringens (C) (F) 008.46
    specified type NEC 008.46
  coccidial 007.2
  dietetic 558.9
  due to
    achylia gastrica 536.8
    adenovirus 008.62
    Aerobacter aerogenes 008.2
    anaerobes (*see also* Enteritis, anaerobic)
      008.46
    Arizona (bacillus) 008.1
    astrovirus 008.66
    Bacillus coli — *see* Enteritis, E. coli
    bacteria NEC 008.5
      specified NEC 008.49
    Bacteroides (*see also* Enteritis, Bac-
      teroides) 008.46
    Butyrivibrio (fibrisolvens) 008.46
    calicivirus 008.65
    Camplyobacter 008.43
    Clostridium — *see* Enteritis, Clostridium
    Cockle agent 008.64
    Coxsackie (virus) 008.67
    Ditchling agent 008.64
    ECHO virus 008.67
    Enterobacter aerogenes 008.2
    enterococci 008.49
    enterovirus NEC 008.67
    Escherichia coli — *see* Enteritis, E. coli
    Eubacterium 008.46
    Fusobacterium (nucleatum) 008.46
    gram-negative bacteria NEC 008.47
      anaerobic NEC 008.46
    Hawaii agent 008.63
    irritating foods 558.9
    Klebsiella aerogenes 008.47
    Marin County agent 008.66
    Montgomery County agent 008.63
    norovirus 008.63
    Norwalk-like agent 008.63
    Norwalk virus 008.63
    Otofuke agent 008.63
    Paracolobactrum arizonae 008.1
    paracolon bacillus NEC 008.47
      Arizona 008.1
    Paramatta agent 008.64
    Peptococcus 008.46
    Peptostreptococcus 008.46
    Proprionibacterium 008.46
    Proteus (bacillus) (mirabilis) (morganii)
      008.3
    Pseudomonas aeruginosa 008.42
    Rotavirus 008.61
    Sapporo agent 008.63
    small round virus (SRV) NEC 008.64
      featureless NEC 008.63
      structured NEC 008.63
    Snow Mountain (SM) agent 008.63
    specified
      bacteria NEC 008.49
      organism, nonbacterial NEC 008.8
      virus NEC 008.69
    Staphylococcus 008.41
    Streptococcus 008.49
      anaerobic 008.46
    Taunton agent 008.63
    Torovirus 008.69
    Treponema 008.46
    Veillonella 008.46
    virus 008.8
      specified type NEC 008.69
    Wollan (W) agent 008.64
    Yersinia enterocolitica 008.44
  dysentery — *see* Dysentery
  E. coli 008.00
    enterohemorrhagic 008.04

Enteritis — *continued*
  E. coli — *continued*
    enteroinvasive 008.03
    enteropathogenic 008.01
    enterotoxigenic 008.02
    specified type NEC 008.09
  el tor 001.1
  embadomonial 007.8
  eosinophilic 558.41
  epidemic 009.0
  Eubacterium 008.46
  fermentative 558.9
  fulminant 557.0
  Fusobacterium (nucleatum) 008.46
  gangrenous (*see also* Enteritis, due to, by
    organism) 009.0
  giardial 007.1
  gram-negative bacteria NEC 008.47
    anaerobic NEC 008.46
  infectious NEC (*see also* Enteritis, due to, by
    organism) 009.0
    presumed 009.1
  influenzal (*see also* Influenza) 487.8
  ischemic 557.9
    acute 557.0
    chronic 557.1
    due to mesenteric artery insufficiency
      557.1
  membranous 564.9
  mucous 564.9
  myxomembranous 564.9
  necrotic (*see also* Enteritis, due to, by organ-
    ism) 009.0
  necroticans 005.2
  necrotizing of fetus or newborn (*see also*
    Enterocolitis, necrotizing, newborn)
    777.50
  neurogenic 564.9
  newborn 777.8
    necrotizing (*see also* Enterocolitis,
      necrotizing, newborn) 777.50
  parasitic NEC 129
  paratyphoid (fever) (*see also* Fever, paraty-
    phoid) 002.9
  Peptococcus 008.46
  Peptostreptococcus 008.46
  Proprionibacterium 008.46
  protozoal NEC 007.9
  radiation 558.1
  regional (of) 555.9
    intestine
      large (bowel, colon, or rectum) 555.1
        with small intestine 555.2
      small (duodenum, ileum, or jejunum)
        555.0
        with large intestine 555.2
  Salmonella infection 003.0
  salmonellosis 003.0
  segmental (*see also* Enteritis, regional) 555.9
  septic (*see also* Enteritis, due to, by organ-
    ism) 009.0
  Shigella 004.9
  simple 558.9
  spasmodic 564.9
  spastic 564.9
  staphylococcal 008.41
    due to food 005.0
  streptococcal 008.49
    anaerobic 008.46
  toxic 558.2
  Treponema (denticola) (macrodentium)
    008.46
  trichomonal 007.3
  tuberculous (*see also* Tuberculosis) 014.8 ☑
  typhosa 002.0
  ulcerative (chronic) (*see also* Colitis, ulcera-
    tive) 556.9
  Veillonella 008.46
  viral 008.8
    adenovirus 008.62
    enterovirus 008.67
    specified virus NEC 008.69
  Yersinia enterocolitica 008.44
  zymotic 009.0
Enteroarticular syndrome 099.3
Enterobiasis 127.4

Enterobius vermicularis 127.4
Enterocele — *see also* Hernia 553.9
  pelvis, pelvic (acquired) (congenital) 618.6
  vagina, vaginal (acquired) (congenital) 618.6
Enterocolitis — *see also* Enteritis
  fetus or newborn (*see also* Enterocolitis,
    necrotizing, newborn) 777.8
    necrotizing 777.50
  fulminant 557.0
  granulomatous 555.2
  hemorrhagic (acute) 557.0
    chronic 557.1
  necrotizing (acute) (membranous) 557.0
    newborn 777.50
      with
        perforation 777.53
        pneumatosis and perforation
          777.53
        pneumatosis without perforation
          777.52
        without pneumatosis, without perfo-
          ration 777.51
      stage I 777.51
      stage II 777.52
      stage III 777.53
    primary necrotizing (*see also* Enterocolitis,
      necrotizing, newborn) 777.50
  pseudomembranous 008.45
    newborn 008.45
  radiation 558.1
    newborn (*see also* Enterocolitis, necrotiz-
      ing, newborn) 777.50
  ulcerative 556.0
Enterocystoma 751.5
Enterogastritis — *see* Enteritis
Enterogenous cyanosis 289.7
Enterolith, enterolithiasis (impaction) 560.39
  with hernia (*see also* Hernia, by site, with
    obstruction)
    gangrenous — *see* Hernia, by site, with
      gangrene
Enteropathy 569.9
  exudative (of Gordon) 579.8
  gluten 579.0
  hemorrhagic, terminal 557.0
  protein-losing 579.8
Enteroperitonitis — *see also* Peritonitis 567.9
Enteroptosis 569.89
Enterorrhagia 578.9
Enterospasm 564.9
  psychogenic 306.4
Enterostenosis — *see also* Obstruction, intestine 560.9
Enterostomy status V44.4
  with complication 569.60
Enthesopathy 726.90
  ankle and tarsus 726.70
  elbow region 726.30
    specified NEC 726.39
  hip 726.5
  knee 726.60
  peripheral NEC 726.8
  shoulder region 726.10
    adhesive 726.0
  spinal 720.1
  wrist and carpus 726.4
Entrance, air into vein — *see* Embolism, air
Entrapment, nerve — *see* Neuropathy, entrapment
Entropion (eyelid) 374.00
  cicatricial 374.04
  congenital 743.62
  late effect of trachoma (healed) 139.1
  mechanical 374.02
  paralytic 374.02
  senile 374.01
  spastic 374.03
Enucleation of eye (current) (traumatic) 871.3
Enuresis 788.30
  habit disturbance 307.6
  nocturnal 788.36
    psychogenic 307.6
  nonorganic origin 307.6
  psychogenic 307.6
Enzymopathy 277.9
Eosinopenia 288.59

Eosinophilia 288.3
  with
    angiolymphoid hyperplasia (ALHE)
      228.01
  allergic 288.3
  hereditary 288.3
  idiopathic 288.3
  infiltrative 518.3
  Loeffler's 518.3
  myalgia syndrome 710.5
  pulmonary (tropical) 518.3
  secondary 288.3
  tropical 518.3
Eosinophilic — *see also* condition
  fasciitis 728.89
  granuloma (bone) 277.89
  infiltration lung 518.3
Ependymitis (acute) (cerebral) (chronic)
  (granular) — *see also* Meningitis 322.9
Ependymoblastoma (M9392/3)
  specified site — *see* Neoplasm, by site, ma-
    lignant
  unspecified site 191.9
Ependymoma (epithelial) (malignant)
  (M9391/3)
  anaplastic type (M9392/3)
    specified site — *see* Neoplasm, by site,
      malignant
    unspecified site 191.9
  benign (M9391/0)
    specified site — *see* Neoplasm, by site,
      benign
    unspecified site 225.0
  myxopapillary (M9394/1) 237.5
  papillary (M9393/1) 237.5
  specified site — *see* Neoplasm, by site, ma-
    lignant
  unspecified site 191.9
Ependymopathy 349.2
  spinal cord 349.2
Ephelides, ephelis 709.09
Ephemeral fever — *see also* Pyrexia 780.60
Epiblepharon (congenital) 743.62
Epicanthus, epicanthic fold (congenital)
  (eyelid) 743.63
Epicondylitis (elbow) (lateral) 726.32
  medial 726.31
Epicystitis — *see also* Cystitis 595.9
Epidemic — *see* condition
Epidermidalization, cervix — *see* condition
Epidermidization, cervix — *see* condition
Epidermis, epidermal — *see* condition
Epidermization, cervix — *see* condition
Epidermodysplasia verruciformis 078.19
Epidermoid
  cholesteatoma — *see* Cholesteatoma
  inclusion (*see also* Cyst, skin) 706.2
Epidermolysis
  acuta (combustiformis) (toxica) 695.15
  bullosa 757.39
  necroticans combustiformis 695.15
    due to drug
      correct substance properly adminis-
        tered 695.15
      overdose or wrong substance given
        or taken 977.9
      specified drug — *see* Table of
        Drugs and Chemicals
Epidermophytid — *see* Dermatophytosis
Epidermophytosis (infected) — *see* Dermatophytosis
Epidermosis, ear (middle) — *see also*
  Cholesteatoma 385.30
Epididymis — *see* condition
Epididymitis (nonvenereal) 604.90
  with abscess 604.0
  acute 604.99
  blennorrhagic (acute) 098.0
    chronic or duration of 2 months or over
      098.2
  caseous (*see also* Tuberculosis) 016.4 ☑
  chlamydial 099.54
  diphtheritic 032.89 *[604.91]*
  filarial 125.9 *[604.91]*
  gonococcal (acute) 098.0

☑ **Additional Digit Required** — Refer to the Tabular List for Digit Selection   ▽ **Subterms under main terms may continue to next column or page**

2015 ICD-9-CM   ▶◀ Revised Text   ● New Line   ▲ Revised Code   **Volume 2 — 107**

Epididymitis — *continued*
gonococcal — *continued*
chronic or duration of 2 months or over 098.2
recurrent 604.99
residual 604.99
syphilitic 095.8 [604.91]
tuberculous (*see also* Tuberculosis) 016.4 ☑
Epididymo-orchitis — *see also* Epididymitis 604.90
with abscess 604.0
chlamydial 099.54
gonococcal (acute) 098.13
chronic or duration of 2 months or over 098.33
Epidural — *see* condition
Epigastritis — *see also* Gastritis 535.5 ☑
Epigastrium, epigastric — *see* condition
Epigastrocele — *see also* Hernia, epigastric 553.29
Epiglottiditis (acute) 464.30
with obstruction 464.31
chronic 476.1
viral 464.30
with obstruction 464.31
Epiglottis — *see* condition
Epiglottitis (acute) 464.30
with obstruction 464.31
chronic 476.1
viral 464.30
with obstruction 464.31
Epignathus 759.4
Epilepsia
partialis continua (*see also* Epilepsy) 345.7 ☑
procursiva (*see also* Epilepsy) 345.8 ☑
Epilepsy, epileptic (idiopathic) 345.9 ☑

Note — use the following fifth-digit subclassification with categories 345.0, 345.1, 345.4–345.9:

0 *without mention of intractable epilepsy*

1 *with intractable epilepsy*

pharmacoresistant (pharmacologically resistant)

poorly controlled

refractory (medically)

treatment resistant

abdominal 345.5 ☑
absence (attack) 345.0 ☑
akinetic 345.0 ☑
psychomotor 345.4 ☑
automatism 345.4 ☑
autonomic diencephalic 345.5 ☑
brain 345.9 ☑
Bravais-Jacksonian 345.5 ☑
cerebral 345.9 ☑
climacteric 345.9 ☑
clonic 345.1 ☑
clouded state 345.9 ☑
coma 345.3
communicating 345.4 ☑
complicating pregnancy, childbirth, or the puerperium 649.4 ☑
congenital 345.9 ☑
convulsions 345.9 ☑
cortical (focal) (motor) 345.5 ☑
cursive (running) 345.8 ☑
cysticercosis 123.1
deterioration
with behavioral disturbance 345.9 [294.11]
without behavioral disturbance 345.9 [294.10]
due to syphilis 094.89
equivalent 345.5 ☑
fit 345.9 ☑
focal (motor) 345.5 ☑
gelastic 345.8 ☑
generalized 345.9 ☑
convulsive 345.1 ☑

Epilepsy, epileptic — *continued*
generalized — *continued*
flexion 345.1 ☑
nonconvulsive 345.0 ☑
grand mal (idiopathic) 345.1 ☑
Jacksonian (motor) (sensory) 345.5 ☑
Kojevnikoff's, Kojevnikov's, Kojewnikoff's 345.7 ☑
laryngeal 786.2
limbic system 345.4 ☑
localization related (focal) (partial) and epileptic syndromes
with
complex partial seizures 345.4 ☑
simple partial seizures 345.5 ☑
major (motor) 345.1 ☑
minor 345.0 ☑
mixed (type) 345.9 ☑
motor partial 345.5 ☑
musicogenic 345.1 ☑
myoclonus, myoclonic 345.1 ☑
progressive (familial) 345.1 ☑
nonconvulsive, generalized 345.0 ☑
parasitic NEC 123.9
partial (focalized) 345.5 ☑
with
impairment of consciousness 345.4 ☑
memory and ideational disturbances 345.4 ☑
without impairment of consciousness 345.5 ☑
abdominal type 345.5 ☑
motor type 345.5 ☑
psychomotor type 345.4 ☑
psychosensory type 345.4 ☑
secondarily generalized 345.4 ☑
sensory type 345.5 ☑
somatomotor type 345.5 ☑
somatosensory type 345.5 ☑
temporal lobe type 345.4 ☑
visceral type 345.5 ☑
visual type 345.5 ☑
peripheral 345.9 ☑
petit mal 345.0 ☑
photokinetic 345.8 ☑
progressive myoclonic (familial) 345.1 ☑
psychic equivalent 345.5 ☑
psychomotor 345.4 ☑
psychosensory 345.4 ☑
reflex 345.1 ☑
seizure 345.9 ☑
senile 345.9 ☑
sensory-induced 345.5 ☑
sleep (*see also* Narcolepsy) 347.00
somatomotor type 345.5 ☑
somatosensory 345.5 ☑
specified type NEC 345.8 ☑
status (grand mal) 345.3
focal motor 345.7 ☑
petit mal 345.2
psychomotor 345.7 ☑
temporal lobe 345.7 ☑
symptomatic 345.9 ☑
temporal lobe 345.4 ☑
tonic (-clonic) 345.1 ☑
traumatic (injury unspecified) 907.0
injury specified — *see* Late, effect (of) specified injury
twilight 293.0
uncinate (gyrus) 345.4 ☑
Unverricht (-Lundborg) (familial myoclonic) 345.1 ☑
visceral 345.5 ☑
visual 345.5 ☑
Epileptiform
convulsions 780.39
seizure 780.39
Epiloia 759.5
Epimenorrhea 626.2
Epipharyngitis — *see also* Nasopharyngitis 460
Epiphora 375.20

Epiphora — *continued*
due to
excess lacrimation 375.21
insufficient drainage 375.22
Epiphyseal arrest 733.91
femoral head 732.2
Epiphyseolysis, epiphysiolysis — *see also* Osteochondrosis 732.9
Epiphysitis — *see also* Osteochondrosis 732.9
juvenile 732.6
marginal (Scheuermann's) 732.0
os calcis 732.5
syphilitic (congenital) 090.0
vertebral (Scheuermann's) 732.0
Epiplocele — *see also* Hernia 553.9
Epiploitis — *see also* Peritonitis 567.9
Epiplosarcomphalocele — *see also* Hernia, umbilicus 553.1
Episcleritis 379.00
gouty 274.89 [379.09]
nodular 379.02
periodica fugax 379.01
angioneurotic — *see* Edema, angioneurotic
specified NEC 379.09
staphylococcal 379.00
suppurative 379.00
syphilitic 095.0
tuberculous (*see also* Tuberculosis) 017.3 [379.09]
Episode
brain (*see also* Disease, cerebrovascular, acute) 436
cerebral (*see also* Disease, cerebrovascular, acute) 436
depersonalization (in neurotic state) 300.6
hyporesponsive 780.09
psychotic (*see also* Psychosis) 298.9
organic, transient 293.9
schizophrenic (acute) NEC (*see also* Schizophrenia) 295.4 ☑
Epispadias
female 753.8
male 752.62
Episplenitis 289.59
Epistaxis (multiple) 784.7
hereditary 448.0
vicarious menstruation 625.8
Epithelioma (malignant) (M8011/3) — *see also* Neoplasm, by site, malignant
adenoides cysticum (M8100/0) — *see* Neoplasm, skin, benign
basal cell (M8090/3) — *see* Neoplasm, skin, malignant
benign (M8011/0) — *see* Neoplasm, by site, benign
Bowen's (M8081/2) — *see* Neoplasm, skin, in situ
calcifying (benign) (Malherbe's) (M8110/0) — *see* Neoplasm, skin, benign
external site — *see* Neoplasm, skin, malignant
intraepidermal, Jadassohn (M8096/0) — *see* Neoplasm, skin, benign
squamous cell (M8070/3) — *see* Neoplasm, by site, malignant
Epitheliopathy
pigment, retina 363.15
posterior multifocal placoid (acute) 363.15
Epithelium, epithelial — *see* condition
Epituberculosis (allergic) (with atelectasis) — *see also* Tuberculosis 010.8 ☑
Eponychia 757.5
Epstein's
nephrosis or syndrome (*see also* Nephrosis) 581.9
pearl (mouth) 528.4
Epstein-Barr infection (viral) 075
chronic 780.79 [139.8]
Epulis (giant cell) (gingiva) 523.8
Equinia 024
Equinovarus (congenital) 754.51
acquired 736.71
Equivalent
angina 413.9

Equivalent — *continued*
convulsive (abdominal) (*see also* Epilepsy) 345.5 ☑
epileptic (psychic) (*see also* Epilepsy) 345.5 ☑
Erb's
disease 359.1
palsy, paralysis (birth) (brachial) (newborn) 767.6
spinal (spastic) syphilitic 094.89
pseudohypertrophic muscular dystrophy 359.1
Erb-Goldflam disease or syndrome 358.00
Erb (-Duchenne) paralysis (birth injury) (newborn) 767.6
Erdheim-Chester disease (ECD) 277.89
Erdheim's syndrome (acromegalic macrospondylitis) 253.0
Erection, painful (persistent) 607.3
Ergosterol deficiency (vitamin D) 268.9
with
osteomalacia 268.2
rickets (*see also* Rickets) 268.0
Ergotism (ergotized grain) 988.2
from ergot used as drug (migraine therapy)
correct substance properly administered 349.82
overdose or wrong substance given or taken 975.0
Erichsen's disease (railway spine) 300.16
Erlacher-Blount syndrome (tibia vara) 732.4
Erosio interdigitalis blastomycetica 112.3
Erosion
arteriosclerotic plaque — *see* Arteriosclerosis, by site
artery NEC 447.2
without rupture 447.8
bone 733.99
bronchus 519.19
cartilage (joint) 733.99
cervix (uteri) (acquired) (chronic) (congenital) 622.0
with mention of cervicitis 616.0
cornea (recurrent) (*see also* Keratitis) 371.42
traumatic 918.1
dental (idiopathic) (occupational) 521.30
extending into
dentine 521.32
pulp 521.33
generalized 521.35
limited to enamel 521.31
localized 521.34
duodenum, postpyloric — *see* Ulcer, duodenum
esophagus 530.89
gastric 535.4 ☑
implanted vaginal mesh
in, into
pelvic floor muscles 629.31
surrounding organ(s) or tissue 629.31
intestine 569.89
lymphatic vessel 457.8
pylorus, pyloric (ulcer) 535.4 ☑
sclera 379.16
spine, aneurysmal 094.89
spleen 289.59
stomach 535.4 ☑
teeth (idiopathic) (occupational) (*see also* Erosion, dental) 521.30
due to
medicine 521.30
persistent vomiting 521.30
urethra 599.84
uterus 621.8
vaginal prosthetic materials NEC
in, into
pelvic floor muscles 629.31
surrounding organ(s) or tissue 629.31
vertebra 733.99
Erotomania 302.89
Clérambault's 297.8
Error
in diet 269.9
refractive 367.9
astigmatism (*see also* Astigmatism) 367.20

☑ **Additional Digit Required — Refer to the Tabular List for Digit Selection**

▽ Subterms under main terms may continue to next column or page

108 — Volume 2

▶◀ **Revised Text**

● **New Line**

▲ **Revised Code**

2015 ICD-9-CM

Error — *continued*
  refractive — *continued*
    drug-induced 367.89
    hypermetropia 367.0
    hyperopia 367.0
    myopia 367.1
    presbyopia 367.4
    toxic 367.89
Eructation 787.3
  nervous 306.4
  psychogenic 306.4
Eruption
  creeping 126.9
  drug — *see* Dermatitis, due to, drug
  Hutchinson, summer 692.72
  Kaposi's varicelliform 054.0
  napkin (psoriasiform) 691.0
  polymorphous
    light (sun) 692.72
      other source 692.82
  psoriasiform, napkin 691.0
  recalcitrant pustular 694.8
  ringed 695.89
  skin (*see also* Dermatitis) 782.1
    creeping (meaning hookworm) 126.9
    due to
      chemical(s) NEC 692.4
        internal use 693.8
      drug — *see* Dermatitis, due to, drug
      prophylactic inoculation or vaccina-
        tion against disease — *see*
        Dermatitis, due to, vaccine
      smallpox vaccination NEC — *see*
        Dermatitis, due to, vaccine
    erysipeloid 027.1
    feigned 698.4
    Hutchinson, summer 692.72
    Kaposi's, varicelliform 054.0
      vaccinia 999.0
    lichenoid, axilla 698.3
    polymorphous, due to light 692.72
    toxic NEC 695.0
    vesicular 709.8
  teeth, tooth
    accelerated 520.6
    delayed 520.6
    difficult 520.6
    disturbance of 520.6
    in abnormal sequence 520.6
    incomplete 520.6
    late 520.6
    natal 520.6
    neonatal 520.6
    obstructed 520.6
    partial 520.6
    persistent primary 520.6
    premature 520.6
    prenatal 520.6
  vesicular 709.8
Erysipelas (gangrenous) (infantile) (newborn)
  (phlegmonous) (suppurative) 035
  external ear 035 *[380.13]*
  puerperal, postpartum, childbirth 670.8 ☑
Erysipelatoid (Rosenbach's) 027.1
Erysipeloid (Rosenbach's) 027.1
Erythema, erythematous (generalized) 695.9
  ab igne — *see* Burn, by site, first degree
  annulare (centrifugum) (rheumaticum)
    695.0
  arthriticum epidemicum 026.1
  brucellum (*see also* Brucellosis) 023.9
  bullosum 695.19
  caloricum — *see* Burn, by site, first degree
  chronicum migrans 088.81
  circinatum 695.19
  diaper 691.0
  due to
    chemical (contact) NEC 692.4
      internal 693.8
    drug (internal use) 693.0
      contact 692.3
  elevatum diutinum 695.89
  endemic 265.2
  epidemic, arthritic 026.1
  figuratum perstans 695.0
  gluteal 691.0

Erythema, erythematous — *continued*
  gyratum (perstans) (repens) 695.19
  heat — *see* Burn, by site, first degree
  ichthyosiforme congenitum 757.1
  induratum (primary) (scrofulosorum) (*see*
    also Tuberculosis) 017.1 ☑
    nontuberculous 695.2
  infantum febrile 057.8
  infectional NEC 695.9
  infectiosum 057.0
  inflammation NEC 695.9
  intertrigo 695.89
  iris 695.10
  lupus (discoid) (localized) (*see also* Lupus,
    erythematosus) 695.4
  marginatum 695.0
    rheumaticum — *see* Fever, rheumatic
  medicamentosum — *see* Dermatitis, due
    to, drug
  migrans 529.1
    chronicum 088.81
  multiforme 695.10
    bullosum 695.19
    conjunctiva 695.19
    exudativum (Hebra) 695.19
    major 695.12
    minor 695.11
    pemphigoides 694.5
  napkin 691.0
  neonatorum 778.8
  nodosum 695.2
    tuberculous (*see also* Tuberculosis)
      017.1 ☑
  nummular, nummulare 695.19
  palmar 695.0
  palmaris hereditarium 695.0
  pernio 991.5
  perstans solare 692.72
  rash, newborn 778.8
  scarlatiniform (exfoliative) (recurrent) 695.0
  simplex marginatum 057.8
  solare (*see also* Sunburn) 692.71
  streptogenes 696.5
  toxic, toxicum NEC 695.0
    newborn 778.8
  tuberculous (primary) (*see also* Tuberculosis)
    017.0 ☑
  venenatum 695.0
Erythematosus — *see* condition
Erythematous — *see* condition
Erythermalgia (primary) 443.82
Erythralgia 443.82
Erythrasma 039.0
Erythredema 985.0
  polyneuritica 985.0
  polyneuropathy 985.0
Erythremia (acute) (M9841/3) 207.0 ☑
  chronic (M9842/3) 207.1 ☑
  secondary 289.0
Erythroblastopenia (acquired) 284.89
  congenital 284.01
Erythroblastophthisis 284.01
Erythroblastosis (fetalis) (newborn) 773.2
  due to
    ABO
      antibodies 773.1
      incompatibility, maternal/fetal 773.1
      isoimmunization 773.1
    Rh
      antibodies 773.0
      incompatibility, maternal/fetal 773.0
      isoimmunization 773.0
Erythrocyanosis (crurum) 443.89
Erythrocythemia — *see* Erythremia
Erythrocytopenia 285.9
Erythrocytosis (megalosplenic)
  familial 289.6
  oval, hereditary (*see also* Elliptocytosis)
    282.1
  secondary 289.0
  stress 289.0
Erythroderma — *see also* Erythema 695.9
  desquamativa (in infants) 695.89
  exfoliative 695.89
  ichthyosiform, congenital 757.1
  infantum 695.89

Erythroderma — *see also* Erythema —
  continued
  maculopapular 696.2
  neonatorum 778.8
  psoriaticum 696.1
  secondary 695.9
Erythrodysesthesia, palmar plantar (PPE)
  693.0
Erythrogenesis imperfecta 284.09
Erythroleukemia (M9840/3) 207.0 ☑
Erythromelalgia 443.82
Erythromelia 701.8
Erythropenia 285.9
Erythrophagocytosis 289.9
Erythrophobia 300.23
Erythroplakia
  oral mucosa 528.79
  tongue 528.79
Erythroplasia (Queyrat) (M8080/2)
  specified site — *see* Neoplasm, skin, in situ
  unspecified site 233.5
Erythropoiesis, idiopathic ineffective 285.0
Escaped beats, heart 427.60
  postoperative 997.1
Escherichia coli (E. coli) — *see* Infection, Es-
  cherichia coli
Esoenteritis — *see* Enteritis
Esophagalgia 530.89
Esophagectasis 530.89
  due to cardiospasm 530.0
Esophagismus 530.5
Esophagitis (alkaline) (chemical) (chronic) (in-
  fectional) (necrotic) (peptic) (postopera-
  tive) (regurgitant) 530.10
  acute 530.12
  candidal 112.84
  eosinophilic 530.13
  reflux 530.11
  specified NEC 530.19
  tuberculous (*see also* Tuberculosis) 017.8 ☑
  ulcerative 530.19
Esophagocele 530.6
Esophagodynia 530.89
Esophagomalacia 530.89
Esophagoptosis 530.89
Esophagospasm 530.5
Esophagostenosis 530.3
Esophagostomiasis 127.7
Esophagostomy
  complication 530.87
    infection 530.86
    malfunctioning 530.87
    mechanical 530.87
Esophagotracheal — *see* condition
Esophagus — *see* condition
Esophoria 378.41
  convergence, excess 378.84
  divergence, insufficiency 378.85
Esotropia (nonaccommodative) 378.00
  accommodative 378.35
  alternating 378.05
    with
      A pattern 378.06
      specified noncomitancy NEC 378.08
      V pattern 378.07
      X pattern 378.08
      Y pattern 378.08
    intermittent 378.22
  intermittent 378.20
    alternating 378.22
    monocular 378.21
  monocular 378.01
    with
      A pattern 378.02
      specified noncomitancy NEC 378.04
      V pattern 378.03
      X pattern 378.04
      Y pattern 378.04
    intermittent 378.21
Espundia 085.5
Essential — *see* condition
Esterapenia 289.89
Esthesioneuroblastoma (M9522/3) 160.0
Esthesioneurocytoma (M9521/3) 160.0
Esthesioneuroepithelioma (M9523/3) 160.0
Esthiomene 099.1

Estivo-autumnal
  fever 084.0
  malaria 084.0
Estrangement V61.09
Estriasis 134.0
Ethanolaminuria 270.8
Ethanolism — *see also* Alcoholism 303.9 ☑
Ether dependence, dependency — *see also*
  Dependence 304.6 ☑
Etherism — *see also* Dependence 304.6 ☑
Ethmoid, ethmoidal — *see* condition
Ethmoiditis (chronic) (nonpurulent) (purulent)
  — *see also* Sinusitis, ethmoidal 473.2
  influenzal (*see also* Influenza) 487.1
  Woakes' 471.1
Ethylism — *see also* Alcoholism 303.9 ☑
Eulenburg's disease (congenital paramyoto-
  nia) 359.3
Eunuchism 257.2
Eunuchoidism 257.2
  hypogonadotropic 257.2
European blastomycosis 117.5
Eustachian — *see* condition
Euthyroidism 244.9
Euthyroid sick syndrome 790.94
Evaluation
  fetal lung maturity 659.8 ☑
  for suspected condition (*see also* Observa-
    tion) V71.9
    abuse V71.81
    exposure
      anthrax V71.82
      biologic agent NEC V71.83
      SARS V71.83
    neglect V71.81
    newborn — *see* Observation, suspected,
      condition, newborn
    specified condition NEC V71.89
  mental health V70.2
    requested by authority V70.1
  nursing care V63.8
  social service V63.8
Evans' syndrome (thrombocytopenic purpura)
  287.32
Event, apparent life threatening in newborn
  and infant (ALTE) 799.82
Eventration
  colon into chest — *see* Hernia, diaphragm
  diaphragm (congenital) 756.6
Eversion
  bladder 596.89
  cervix (uteri) 622.0
    with mention of cervicitis 616.0
  foot NEC 736.79
    congenital 755.67
  lacrimal punctum 375.51
  punctum lacrimale (postinfectional) (senile)
    375.51
  ureter (meatus) 593.89
  urethra (meatus) 599.84
  uterus 618.1
    complicating delivery 665.2 ☑
      affecting fetus or newborn 763.89
    puerperal, postpartum 674.8 ☑
Evidence
  of malignancy
    cytologic
      without histologic confirmation
        anus 796.76
        cervix 795.06
        vagina 795.16
Evisceration
  birth injury 767.8
  bowel (congenital) — *see* Hernia, ventral
  congenital (*see also* Hernia, ventral) 553.29
  operative wound 998.32
  traumatic NEC 869.1
    eye 871.3
Evulsion — *see* Avulsion
Ewing's
  angioendothelioma (M9260/3) — *see* Neo-
    plasm, bone, malignant
  sarcoma (M9260/3) — *see* Neoplasm, bone,
    malignant
  tumor (M9260/3) — *see* Neoplasm, bone,
    malignant

☑ **Additional Digit Required** — Refer to the Tabular List for Digit Selection   ▽ **Subterms under main terms may continue to next column or page**

2015 ICD-9-CM   ▶◀ **Revised Text**   ● **New Line**   ▲ **Revised Code**   **Volume 2 — 109**

Exaggerated lumbosacral angle (with imping-
ing spine) 756.12
Examination (general) (routine) (of) (for) V70.9
  allergy V72.7
  annual V70.0
  cardiovascular preoperative V72.81
  cervical Papanicolaou smear V76.2
    as a part of routine gynecological exam-
      ination V72.31
    to confirm findings of recent normal
      smear following initial abnormal
      smear V72.32
  child care (routine) V20.2
  clinical research investigation (normal con-
    trol patient) (participant) V70.7
  dental V72.2
  developmental testing (child) (infant) V20.2
  donor (potential) V70.8
  ear V72.19
  eye V72.0
  following
    accident (motor vehicle) V71.4
    alleged rape or seduction (victim or cul-
      prit) V71.5
    inflicted injury (victim or culprit) NEC
      V71.6
    rape or seduction, alleged (victim or
      culprit) V71.5
    treatment (for) V67.9
      combined V67.6
      fracture V67.4
      involving high-risk medication NEC
        V67.51
      mental disorder V67.3
      specified condition NEC V67.59
  follow-up (routine) (following) V67.9
    cancer chemotherapy V67.2
    chemotherapy V67.2
    disease NEC V67.59
    high-risk medication NEC V67.51
    injury NEC V67.59
    population survey V70.6
    postpartum V24.2
    psychiatric V67.3
    psychotherapy V67.3
    radiotherapy V67.1
    specified surgery NEC V67.09
    surgery V67.00
      vaginal pap smear V67.01
  gynecological V72.31
    for contraceptive maintenance V25.40
      intrauterine device V25.42
      pill V25.41
      specified method NEC V25.49
  health (of)
    armed forces personnel V70.5
    checkup V70.0
    child, routine V20.2
    defined subpopulation NEC V70.5
    inhabitants of institutions V70.5
    occupational V70.5
    pre-employment screening V70.5
    preschool children V70.5
      for admission to school V70.3
    prisoners V70.5
      for entrance into prison V70.3
    prostitutes V70.5
    refugees V70.5
    school children V70.5
    students V70.5
  hearing V72.19
    following failed hearing screening
      V72.11
  infant
    8 to 28 days old V20.32
    over 28 days old, routine V20.2
    under 8 days old V20.31
  laboratory V72.60
    ordered as part of a routine general
      medical examination V72.62
    pre-operative V72.63
    pre-procedural V72.63
    specified NEC V72.69
  lactating mother V24.1
  medical (for) (of) V70.9
    administrative purpose NEC V70.3

Examination — *continued*
  medical — *continued*
    admission to
      old age home V70.3
      prison V70.3
      school V70.3
    adoption V70.3
    armed forces personnel V70.5
    at health care facility V70.0
    camp V70.3
    child, routine V20.2
    clinical research (control) (normal com-
      parison) (participant) V70.7
    defined subpopulation NEC V70.5
    donor (potential) V70.8
    driving license V70.3
    general V70.9
      routine V70.0
      specified reason NEC V70.8
    immigration V70.3
    inhabitants of institutions V70.5
    insurance certification V70.3
    marriage V70.3
    medicolegal reasons V70.4
    naturalization V70.3
    occupational V70.5
    population survey V70.6
    pre-employment V70.5
    preschool children V70.5
      for admission to school V70.3
    prison V70.3
    prisoners V70.5
      for entrance into prison V70.3
    prostitutes V70.5
    refugees V70.5
    school children V70.5
    specified reason NEC V70.8
    sport competition V70.3
    students V70.5
  medicolegal reason V70.4
  pelvic (annual) (periodic) V72.31
  periodic (annual) (routine) V70.0
  postpartum
    immediately after delivery V24.0
    routine follow-up V24.2
  pregnancy (unconfirmed) (possible) V72.40
    negative result V72.41
    positive result V72.42
  prenatal V22.1
    first pregnancy V22.0
    high-risk pregnancy V23.9
      specified problem NEC V23.89
      to determine fetal viability V23.87
  preoperative V72.84
    cardiovascular V72.81
    respiratory V72.82
    specified NEC V72.83
  preprocedural V72.84
    cardiovascular V72.81
    general physical V72.83
    respiratory V72.82
    specified NEC V72.83
  prior to chemotherapy V72.83
  psychiatric V70.2
    follow-up not needing further care V67.3
    requested by authority V70.1
  radiological NEC V72.5
  respiratory preoperative V72.82
  screening — *see* Screening
  sensitization V72.7
  skin V72.7
    hypersensitivity V72.7
  special V72.9
  specified type or reason NEC V72.85
    preoperative V72.83
    specified NEC V72.83
  teeth V72.2
  vaginal Papanicolaou smear V76.47
    following hysterectomy for malignant
      condition V67.01
  victim or culprit following
    alleged rape or seduction V71.5
    inflicted injury NEC V71.6
  vision V72.0
  well baby V20.2
Exanthem, exanthema — *see also* Rash 782.1

Exanthem, exanthema — *see also* Rash —
  continued
  Boston 048
  epidemic, with meningitis 048
  lichenoid psoriasiform 696.2
  subitum 058.10
    due to
      human herpesvirus 6 058.11
      human herpesvirus 7 058.12
  viral, virus NEC 057.9
    specified type NEC 057.8
Excess, excessive, excessively
  alcohol level in blood 790.3
  carbohydrate tissue, localized 278.1
  carotene (dietary) 278.3
  cold 991.9
    specified effect NEC 991.8
  convergence 378.84
  crying 780.95
    of
      adolescent 780.95
      adult 780.95
      baby 780.92
      child 780.95
      infant (baby) 780.92
      newborn 780.92
  development, breast 611.1
  diaphoresis (*see also* Hyperhidrosis) 780.8
  distance, interarch 524.28
  divergence 378.85
  drinking (alcohol) NEC (*see also* Abuse,
    drugs, nondependent) 305.0 ☑
    continual (*see also* Alcoholism) 303.9 ☑
    habitual (*see also* Alcoholism) 303.9 ☑
  eating 783.6
  eyelid fold (congenital) 743.62
  fat 278.02
    in heart (*see also* Degeneration, myocar-
      dial) 429.1
    tissue, localized 278.1
  foreskin 605
  gas 787.3
  gastrin 251.5
  glucagon 251.4
  heat (*see also* Heat) 992.9
  horizontal
    overjet 524.26
    overlap 524.26
  interarch distance 524.28
  intermaxillary vertical dimension 524.37
  interocclusal distance of teeth 524.37
  large
    colon 564.7
      congenital 751.3
    fetus or infant 766.0
      with obstructed labor 660.1 ☑
      affecting management of pregnancy
        656.6 ☑
      causing disproportion 653.5 ☑
    newborn (weight of 4500 grams or
      more) 766.0
    organ or site, congenital NEC — *see*
      Anomaly, specified type NEC
  lid fold (congenital) 743.62
  long
    colon 751.5
    organ or site, congenital NEC — *see*
      Anomaly, specified type NEC
    umbilical cord (entangled)
      affecting fetus or newborn 762.5
      in pregnancy or childbirth 663.3 ☑
      with compression 663.2 ☑
  menstruation 626.2
  number of teeth 520.1
    causing crowding 524.31
  nutrients (dietary) NEC 783.6
  potassium (K) 276.7
  salivation (*see also* Ptyalism) 527.7
  secretion (*see also* Hypersecretion)
    milk 676.6 ☑
    sputum 786.4
    sweat (*see also* Hyperhidrosis) 780.8
  short
    organ or site, congenital NEC — *see*
      Anomaly, specified type NEC

Excess, excessive, excessively —
  continued
  short — *continued*
    umbilical cord
      affecting fetus or newborn 762.6
      in pregnancy or childbirth 663.4 ☑
  skin NEC 701.9
    eyelid 743.62
      acquired 374.30
  sodium (Na) 276.0
  spacing of teeth 524.32
  sputum 786.4
  sweating (*see also* Hyperhidrosis) 780.8
  tearing (ducts) (eye) (*see also* Epiphora)
    375.20
  thirst 783.5
    due to deprivation of water 994.3
  tissue in reconstructed breast 612.0
  tuberosity 524.07
  vitamin
    A (dietary) 278.2
      administered as drug (chronic) (pro-
        longed excessive intake) 278.2
      reaction to sudden overdose
        963.5
    D (dietary) 278.4
      administered as drug (chronic) (pro-
        longed excessive intake) 278.4
      reaction to sudden overdose
        963.5
  weight 278.02
    gain 783.1
      of pregnancy 646.1 ☑
    loss 783.21
Excitability, abnormal, under minor stress
  309.29
Excitation
  catatonic (*see also* Schizophrenia) 295.2 ☑
  psychogenic 298.1
  reactive (from emotional stress, psycholog-
    ical trauma) 298.1
Excitement
  manic (*see also* Psychosis, affective) 296.0 ☑
    recurrent episode 296.1 ☑
    single episode 296.0 ☑
  mental, reactive (from emotional stress,
    psychological trauma) 298.1
  state, reactive (from emotional stress, psy-
    chological trauma) 298.1
Excluded pupils 364.76
Excoriation (traumatic) — *see also* Injury, superficial, by site 919.8
  neurotic 698.4
Excyclophoria 378.44
Excyclotropia 378.33
Exencephalus, exencephaly 742.0
Exercise
  breathing V57.0
  remedial NEC V57.1
  therapeutic NEC V57.1
Exfoliation
  skin
    due to erythematous condition 695.50
      involving (percent of body surface)
        less than 10 percent 695.50
        10-19 percent 695.51
        20-29 percent 695.52
        30-39 percent 695.53
        40-49 percent 695.54
        50-59 percent 695.55
        60-69 percent 695.56
        70-79 percent 695.57
        80-89 percent 695.58
        90 percent or more 695.59
  teeth
    due to systemic causes 525.0
Exfoliative — *see also* condition
  dermatitis 695.89
Exhaustion, exhaustive (physical NEC) 780.79
  battle (*see also* Reaction, stress, acute) 308.9
  cardiac (*see also* Failure, heart) 428.9
  delirium (*see also* Reaction, stress, acute)
    308.9
  due to
    cold 991.8
    excessive exertion 994.5

☑ **Additional Digit Required** — Refer to the Tabular List for Digit Selection   ▽ **Subterms under main terms may continue to next column or page**

110 — Volume 2   ▶◀ Revised Text   ● New Line   ▲ Revised Code   2015 ICD-9-CM

Exhaustion, exhaustive — *continued*
  due to — *continued*
    exposure 994.4
      overexertion 994.5
    fetus or newborn 779.89
    heart (*see also* Failure, heart) 428.9
    heat 992.5
      due to
        salt depletion 992.4
        water depletion 992.3
  manic (*see also* Psychosis, affective) 296.0 ☑
    recurrent episode 296.1 ☑
    single episode 296.0 ☑
  maternal, complicating delivery 669.8 ☑
    affecting fetus or newborn 763.89
  mental 300.5
  myocardium, myocardial (*see also* Failure, heart) 428.9
  nervous 300.5
  old age 797
  postinfectional NEC 780.79
  psychogenic 300.5
  psychosis (*see also* Reaction, stress, acute) 308.9
  senile 797
    dementia 290.0
Exhibitionism (sexual) 302.4
Exomphalos 756.72
Exophoria 378.42
  convergence, insufficiency 378.83
  divergence, excess 378.85
Exophthalmic
  cachexia 242.0 ☑
  goiter 242.0 ☑
  ophthalmoplegia 242.0 ☑ [376.22]
Exophthalmos 376.30
  congenital 743.66
  constant 376.31
  endocrine NEC 259.9 [376.22]
  hyperthyroidism 242.0 ☑ [376.21]
  intermittent NEC 376.34
  malignant 242.0 ☑ [376.21]
  pulsating 376.35
    endocrine NEC 259.9 [376.22]
  thyrotoxic 242.0 ☑ [376.21]
Exostosis 726.91
  cartilaginous (M9210/0) — *see* Neoplasm, bone, benign
  congenital 756.4
  ear canal, external 380.81
  gonococcal 098.89
  hip 726.5
  intracranial 733.3
  jaw (bone) 526.81
  luxurians 728.11
  multiple (cancellous) (congenital) (hereditary) 756.4
  nasal bones 726.91
  orbit, orbital 376.42
  osteocartilaginous (M9210/0) — *see* Neoplasm, bone, benign
  spine 721.8
    with spondylosis — *see* Spondylosis
  syphilitic 095.5
  wrist 726.4
Exotropia 378.10
  alternating 378.15
    with
      A pattern 378.16
      specified noncomitancy NEC 378.18
      V pattern 378.17
      X pattern 378.18
      Y pattern 378.18
    intermittent 378.24
  intermittent 378.20
    alternating 378.24
    monocular 378.23
  monocular 378.11
    with
      A pattern 378.12
      specified noncomitancy NEC 378.14
      V pattern 378.13
      X pattern 378.14
      Y pattern 378.14
    intermittent 378.23

Explanation of
  investigation finding V65.4 ☑
  medication V65.4 ☑
Exposure (suspected) 994.9
  algae bloom V87.32
  cold 991.9
    specified effect NEC 991.8
  effects of 994.9
  exhaustion due to 994.4
  implanted vaginal mesh
    into vagina 629.32
    through vaginal wall 629.32
  to
    AIDS virus V01.79
    anthrax V01.81
    aromatic
      amines V87.11
      dyes V87.19
    arsenic V87.01
    asbestos V15.84
    benzene V87.12
    body fluids (hazardous) V15.85
    cholera V01.0
    chromium compounds V87.09
    communicable disease V01.9
      specified type NEC V01.89
    dyes V87.2
      aromatic V87.19
    Escherichia coli (E. coli) V01.83
    German measles V01.4
    gonorrhea V01.6
    hazardous
      aromatic compounds NEC V87.19
      body fluids V15.85
      chemicals NEC V87.2
      metals V87.09
      substances V87.39
    HIV V01.79
    human immunodeficiency virus V01.79
    lead V15.86
    meningococcus V01.84
    mold V87.31
    nickel dust V87.09
    parasitic disease V01.89
    poliomyelitis V01.2
    polycyclic aromatic hydrocarbons V87.19
    potentially hazardous body fluids V15.85
    rabies V01.5
    rubella V01.4
    SARS-associated coronavirus V01.82
    smallpox V01.3
    syphilis V01.6
    tuberculosis V01.1
    uranium V87.02
    varicella V01.71
    venereal disease V01.6
    viral disease NEC V01.79
      varicella V01.71
  vaginal prosthetic materials NEC
    into vagina 629.32
    through vaginal wall 629.32
Exsanguination, fetal 772.0
Exstrophy
  abdominal content 751.8
  bladder (urinary) 753.5
Extensive — *see* condition
Extra — *see also* Accessory
  rib 756.3
    cervical 756.2
Extraction
  with hook 763.89
  breech NEC 669.6 ☑
    affecting fetus or newborn 763.0
  cataract postsurgical V45.61
  manual NEC 669.8 ☑
    affecting fetus or newborn 763.89
Extrasystole 427.60
  atrial 427.61
  postoperative 997.1
  ventricular 427.69
Extrauterine gestation or pregnancy — *see* Pregnancy, ectopic
Extravasation
  blood 459.0
    lower extremity 459.0
  chemotherapy, vesicant 999.81

Extravasation — *continued*
  chyle into mesentery 457.8
  pelvicalyceal 593.4
  pyelosinus 593.4
  urine 788.8
    from ureter 788.8
  vesicant
    agent NEC 999.82
    chemotherapy 999.81
Extremity — *see* condition
Extrophy — *see* Exstrophy
Extroversion
  bladder 753.5
  uterus 618.1
    complicating delivery 665.2 ☑
      affecting fetus or newborn 763.89
    postpartal (old) 618.1
Extruded tooth 524.34
Extrusion
  alveolus and teeth 524.75
  breast implant (prosthetic) 996.54
  device, implant, or graft — *see* Complications, mechanical
  eye implant (ball) (globe) 996.59
  intervertebral disc — *see* Displacement, intervertebral disc
  lacrimal gland 375.43
  mesh (reinforcing) 996.59
  ocular lens implant 996.53
  prosthetic device NEC — *see* Complications, mechanical
  vitreous 379.26
Exudate, pleura — *see* Effusion, pleura
Exudates, retina 362.82
Exudative — *see* condition
Eye, eyeball, eyelid — *see* condition
Eyestrain 368.13
Eyeworm disease of Africa 125.2

F

Faber's anemia or syndrome (achlorhydric anemia) 280.9
Fabry's disease (angiokeratoma corporis diffusum) 272.7
Face, facial — *see* condition
Facet of cornea 371.44
Faciocephalalgia, autonomic — *see also* Neuropathy, peripheral, autonomic 337.9
Facioscapulohumeral myopathy 359.1
Factitious disorder, illness — *see* Illness, factitious
Factor
  deficiency — *see* Deficiency, factor
  psychic, associated with diseases classified elsewhere 316
  risk — *see* Problem
  V Leiden mutation 289.81
Fahr-Volhard disease (malignant nephrosclerosis) 403.00
Failure, failed
  adenohypophyseal 253.2
  attempted abortion (legal) (*see also* Abortion, failed) 638.9
  bone marrow (anemia) 284.9
    acquired (secondary) 284.89
    congenital 284.09
    idiopathic 284.9
  cardiac (*see also* Failure, heart) 428.9
    newborn 779.89
  cardiorenal (chronic) 428.9
    hypertensive (*see also* Hypertension, cardiorenal) 404.93
  cardiorespiratory 799.1
    specified during or due to a procedure 997.1
      long-term effect of cardiac surgery 429.4
  cardiovascular (chronic) 428.9
  cerebrovascular 437.8
  cervical dilatation in labor 661.0 ☑
    affecting fetus or newborn 763.7
  circulation, circulatory 799.89
    fetus or newborn 779.89
    peripheral 785.50
      postoperative 998.00

Failure, failed — *continued*
  compensation — *see* Disease, heart
  congestive (*see also* Failure, heart) 428.0
  conscious sedation, during procedure 995.24
  coronary (*see also* Insufficiency, coronary) 411.89
  dental implant 525.79
    due to
      infection 525.71
      lack of attached gingiva 525.72
      occlusal trauma (caused by poor prosthetic design) 525.72
      parafunctional habits 525.72
      periodontal infection (peri-implantitis) 525.72
      poor oral hygiene 525.72
      unintentional loading 525.71
    endosseous NEC 525.79
    mechanical 525.73
    osseointegration 525.71
      due to
        complications of systemic disease 525.71
        poor bone quality 525.71
        premature loading 525.71
      iatrogenic 525.71
      prior to intentional prosthetic loading 525.71
    post-osseointegration
      biological 525.72
        iatrogenic 525.72
      due to complications of systemic disease 525.72
      mechanical 525.73
    pre-integration 525.71
    pre-osseointegration 525.71
  dental prosthesis causing loss of dental implant 525.73
  dental restoration
    marginal integrity 525.61
    periodontal anatomical integrity 525.65
  descent of head (at term) 652.5 ☑
    affecting fetus or newborn 763.1
    in labor 660.0 ☑
      affecting fetus or newborn 763.1
  device, implant, or graft — *see* Complications, mechanical
  engagement of head NEC 652.5 ☑
    in labor 660.0 ☑
  extrarenal 788.99
  fetal head to enter pelvic brim 652.5 ☑
    affecting fetus or newborn 763.1
    in labor 660.0 ☑
      affecting fetus or newborn 763.1
  forceps NEC 660.7 ☑
    affecting fetus or newborn 763.1
  fusion (joint) (spinal) 996.49
  growth in childhood 783.43
  heart (acute) (sudden) 428.9
    with
      abortion — *see* Abortion, by type, with specified complication NEC
      acute pulmonary edema (*see also* Failure, ventricular, left) 428.1
        with congestion (*see also* Failure, heart) 428.0
      decompensation (*see also* Failure, heart) 428.0
      dilation — *see* Disease, heart
      ectopic pregnancy (*see also* categories 633.0–633.9) 639.8
      molar pregnancy (*see also* categories 630–632) 639.8
    arteriosclerotic 440.9
    combined left-right sided 428.0
    combined systolic and diastolic 428.40
      acute 428.41
      acute on chronic 428.43
      chronic 428.42
    compensated (*see also* Failure, heart) 428.0

Failure, failed — *continued*
  heart — *continued*
    complicating
      abortion — *see* Abortion, by type, with specified complication NEC
      delivery (cesarean) (instrumental) 669.4 ☑
      ectopic pregnancy (*see also* categories 633.0–633.9) 639.8
      molar pregnancy (*see also* categories 630–632) 639.8
      obstetric anesthesia or sedation 668.1 ☑
      surgery 997.1
    congestive (compensated) (decompensated) (*see also* Failure, heart) 428.0
      with rheumatic fever (conditions classifiable to 390)
        active 391.8
        inactive or quiescent (with chorea) 398.91
      fetus or newborn 779.89
      hypertensive (*see also* Hypertension, heart) 402.91
        with renal disease (*see also* Hypertension, cardiorenal) 404.91
          with renal failure 404.93
        benign 402.11
        malignant 402.01
      rheumatic (chronic) (inactive) (with chorea) 398.91
        active or acute 391.8
          with chorea (Sydenham's) 392.0
    decompensated (*see also* Failure, heart) 428.0
    degenerative (*see also* Degeneration, myocardial) 429.1
    diastolic 428.30
      acute 428.31
      acute on chronic 428.33
      chronic 428.32
    due to presence of (cardiac) prosthesis 429.4
    fetus or newborn 779.89
    following
      abortion 639.8
      cardiac surgery 429.4
      ectopic or molar pregnancy 639.8
    high output NEC 428.9
    hypertensive (*see also* Hypertension, heart) 402.91
      with renal disease (*see also* Hypertension, cardiorenal) 404.91
        with renal failure 404.93
      benign 402.11
      malignant 402.01
    left (ventricular) (*see also* Failure, ventricular, left) 428.1
      with right-sided failure (see also Failure, heart) 428.0
    low output (syndrome) NEC 428.9
    organic — *see* Disease, heart
    postoperative (immediate) 997.1
      long term effect of cardiac surgery 429.4
    rheumatic (chronic) (congestive) (inactive) 398.91
    right (secondary to left heart failure, conditions classifiable to 428.1) (ventricular) (*see also* Failure, heart) 428.0
    senile 797
    specified during or due to a procedure 997.1
      long-term effect of cardiac surgery 429.4
    systolic 428.20
      acute 428.21
      acute on chronic 428.23
      chronic 428.22
    thyrotoxic (*see also* Thyrotoxicosis) 242.9 ☑ [425.7]

Failure, failed — *continued*
  heart — *continued*
    valvular — *see* Endocarditis
  hepatic 572.8
    acute 570
    due to a procedure 997.49
  hepatorenal 572.4
  hypertensive heart (*see also* Hypertension, heart) 402.91
    benign 402.11
    malignant 402.01
  induction (of labor) 659.1 ☑
    abortion (legal) (*see also* Abortion, failed) 638.9
    affecting fetus or newborn 763.89
    by oxytocic drugs 659.1 ☑
    instrumental 659.0 ☑
    mechanical 659.0 ☑
    medical 659.1 ☑
    surgical 659.0 ☑
  initial alveolar expansion, newborn 770.4
  involution, thymus (gland) 254.8
  kidney — *see* Failure, renal
  lactation 676.4 ☑
  Leydig's cell, adult 257.2
  liver 572.8
    acute 570
  medullary 799.89
  mitral — *see* Endocarditis, mitral
  moderate sedation, during procedure 995.24
  myocardium, myocardial (*see also* Failure, heart) 428.9
    chronic (*see also* Failure, heart) 428.0
    congestive (*see also* Failure, heart) 428.0
  ovarian (primary) 256.39
    iatrogenic 256.2
    postablative 256.2
    postirradiation 256.2
    postsurgical 256.2
  ovulation 628.0
  prerenal 788.99
  renal (kidney) 586
    with
      abortion — *see* Abortion, by type, with renal failure
      ectopic pregnancy (*see also* categories 633.0–633.9) 639.3
      edema (*see also* Nephrosis) 581.9
      hypertension (*see also* Hypertension, kidney) 403.91
      hypertensive heart disease (conditions classifiable to 402) 404.92
        with heart failure 404.93
        benign 404.12
          with heart failure 404.13
        malignant 404.02
          with heart failure 404.03
      molar pregnancy (*see also* categories 630–632) 639.3
      tubular necrosis (acute) 584.5
    acute 584.9
      with lesion of
        necrosis
          cortical (renal) 584.6
          medullary (renal) (papillary) 584.7
          tubular 584.5
        specified pathology NEC 584.8
    chronic 585.9
      hypertensive or with hypertension (*see also* Hypertension, kidney) 403.91
    due to a procedure 997.5
    following
      abortion 639.3
      crushing 958.5
      ectopic or molar pregnancy 639.3
      labor and delivery (acute) 669.3 ☑
    hypertensive (*see also* Hypertension, kidney) 403.91
    puerperal, postpartum 669.3 ☑
  respiration, respiratory 518.81
    acute 518.81
      following trauma and surgery 518.51

Failure, failed — *continued*
  respiration, respiratory — *continued*
    acute and chronic 518.84
      following trauma and surgery 518.53
    center 348.89
      newborn 770.84
    chronic 518.83
      following trauma and surgery or shock 518.51
      newborn 770.84
  rotation
    cecum 751.4
    colon 751.4
    intestine 751.4
    kidney 753.3
  sedation, during procedure
    conscious 995.24
    moderate 995.24
  segmentation (*see also* Fusion)
    fingers (*see also* Syndactylism, fingers) 755.11
    toes (*see also* Syndactylism, toes) 755.13
  seminiferous tubule, adult 257.2
  senile (general) 797
    with psychosis 290.20
  testis, primary (seminal) 257.2
  to progress 661.2 ☑
  to thrive
    adult 783.7
    child 783.41
    newborn 779.34
  transplant 996.80
    bone marrow 996.85
    organ (immune or nonimmune cause) 996.80
      bone marrow 996.85
      heart 996.83
      intestines 996.87
      kidney 996.81
      liver 996.82
      lung 996.84
      pancreas 996.86
      specified NEC 996.89
    skin 996.52
      artificial 996.55
      decellularized allodermis 996.55
      temporary allograft or pigskin graft — omit code
    stem cell(s) 996.88
      from
        peripheral blood 996.88
        umbilical cord 996.88
  trial of labor NEC 660.6 ☑
    affecting fetus or newborn 763.1
  tubal ligation 998.89
  urinary 586
  vacuum extraction
    abortion — *see* Abortion, failed
    delivery NEC 660.7 ☑
      affecting fetus or newborn 763.1
  vasectomy 998.89
  ventouse NEC 660.7 ☑
    affecting fetus or newborn 763.1
  ventricular (*see also* Failure, heart) 428.9
    left 428.1
      with rheumatic fever (conditions classifiable to 390)
        active 391.8
          with chorea 392.0
        inactive or quiescent (with chorea) 398.91
      hypertensive (*see also* Hypertension, heart) 402.91
        benign 402.11
        malignant 402.01
      rheumatic (chronic) (inactive) (with chorea) 398.91
        active or acute 391.8
          with chorea 392.0
    right (*see also* Failure, heart) 428.0
  vital centers, fetus or newborn 779.89
  weight gain in childhood 783.41
Fainting (fit) (spell) 780.2
Falciform hymen 752.49
Fallen arches 734
Falling, any organ or part — *see* Prolapse

Fall, maternal, affecting fetus or newborn 760.5
Fallopian
  insufflation
    fertility testing V26.21
    following sterilization reversal V26.22
  tube — *see* condition
Fallot's
  pentalogy 745.2
  tetrad or tetralogy 745.2
  triad or trilogy 746.09
Fallout, radioactive (adverse effect) NEC 990
False — *see also* condition
  bundle branch block 426.50
  bursa 727.89
  croup 478.75
  joint 733.82
  labor (pains) 644.1 ☑
  opening, urinary, male 752.69
  passage, urethra (prostatic) 599.4
  positive
    serological test for syphilis 795.6
    Wassermann reaction 795.6
  pregnancy 300.11
Family, familial — *see also* condition
  affected by
    family member
      currently on deployment (military) V61.01
      returned from deployment (military) (current or past conflict) V61.02
  disruption (*see also* Disruption, family) V61.09
  estrangement V61.09
  hemophagocytic
    lymphohistiocytosis 288.4
    reticulosis 288.4
  Li-Fraumeni (syndrome) V84.01
  planning advice V25.09
    natural
      procreative V26.41
      to avoid pregnancy V25.04
  problem V61.9
    specified circumstance NEC V61.8
  retinoblastoma (syndrome) 190.5
Famine 994.2
  edema 262
Fanconi's anemia (congenital pancytopenia) 284.09
Fanconi (-de Toni) (-Debré) syndrome (cystinosis) 270.0
Farber (-Uzman) syndrome or disease (disseminated lipogranulomatosis) 272.8
Farcin 024
Farcy 024
Farmers'
  lung 495.0
  skin 692.74
Farsightedness 367.0
Fascia — *see* condition
Fasciculation 781.0
Fasciculitis optica 377.32
Fasciitis 729.4
  eosinophilic 728.89
  necrotizing 728.86
  nodular 728.79
  perirenal 593.4
  plantar 728.71
  pseudosarcomatous 728.79
  traumatic (old) NEC 728.79
    current — *see* Sprain, by site
Fasciola hepatica infestation 121.3
Fascioliasis 121.3
Fasciolopsiasis (small intestine) 121.4
Fasciolopsis (small intestine) 121.4
Fast pulse 785.0
Fat
  embolism (cerebral) (pulmonary) (systemic) 958.1
    with
      abortion — *see* Abortion, by type, with embolism
      ectopic pregnancy (*see also* categories 633.0–633.9) 639.6

☑ Additional Digit Required — Refer to the Tabular List for Digit Selection   ▽ Subterms under main terms may continue to next column or page

112 — Volume 2   ▶◀ Revised Text   ● New Line   ▲ Revised Code   2015 ICD-9-CM

Fat — *continued*
  embolism — *continued*
    with — *continued*
      molar pregnancy (*see also* categories
        630–632) 639.6
      complicating delivery or puerperium
        673.8 ☑
      following
        abortion 639.6
        ectopic or molar pregnancy 639.6
      in pregnancy, childbirth, or the puerperi-
        um 673.8 ☑
    excessive 278.02
      in heart (*see also* Degeneration, myocar-
        dial) 429.1
  general 278.02
  hernia, herniation 729.30
    eyelid 374.34
    knee 729.31
    orbit 374.34
    retro-orbital 374.34
    retropatellar 729.31
    specified site NEC 729.39
  indigestion 579.8
  in stool 792.1
  localized (pad) 278.1
    heart (*see also* Degeneration, myocar-
      dial) 429.1
    knee 729.31
    retropatellar 729.31
  necrosis (*see also* Fatty, degeneration)
    breast (aseptic) (segmental) 611.3
    mesentery 567.82
    omentum 567.82
    peritoneum 567.82
  pad 278.1
Fatal familial insomnia (FFI) 046.72
Fatal syncope 798.1
Fatigue 780.79
  auditory deafness (*see also* Deafness) 389.9
  chronic, syndrome 780.71
  combat (*see also* Reaction, stress, acute)
    308.9
  during pregnancy 646.8 ☑
  general 780.79
    psychogenic 300.5
  heat (transient) 992.6
  muscle 729.89
  myocardium (*see also* Failure, heart) 428.9
  nervous 300.5
  neurosis 300.5
  operational 300.89
  postural 729.89
  posture 729.89
  psychogenic (general) 300.5
  senile 797
  syndrome NEC 300.5
    chronic 780.71
  undue 780.79
  voice 784.49
Fatness 278.02
Fatty — *see also* condition
  apron 278.1
  degeneration (diffuse) (general) NEC 272.8
    localized — *see* Degeneration, by site,
      fatty
    placenta — *see* Placenta, abnormal
  heart (enlarged) (*see also* Degeneration,
    myocardial) 429.1
  infiltration (diffuse) (general) (*see also* De-
    generation, by site, fatty) 272.8
    heart (enlarged) (*see also* Degeneration,
      myocardial) 429.1
  liver 571.8
    alcoholic 571.0
  necrosis — *see* Degeneration, fatty
  phanerosis 272.8
Fauces — *see* condition
Fauchard's disease (periodontitis) 523.40
Faucitis 478.29
Faulty — *see also* condition
  position of teeth 524.30
Favism (anemia) 282.2
Favre-Racouchot disease (elastoidosis cu-
  tanea nodularis) 701.8
Favus 110.9

Favus — *continued*
  beard 110.0
  capitis 110.0
  corporis 110.5
  eyelid 110.8
  foot 110.4
  hand 110.2
  scalp 110.0
  specified site NEC 110.8
Feared complaint unfounded V65.5
Fear, fearfulness (complex) (reaction) 300.20
  child 313.0
  of
    animals 300.29
    closed spaces 300.29
    crowds 300.29
    eating in public 300.23
    heights 300.29
    open spaces 300.22
      with panic attacks 300.21
    public speaking 300.23
    streets 300.22
      with panic attacks 300.21
    travel 300.22
      with panic attacks 300.21
    washing in public 300.23
  transient 308.0
Febricula (continued) (simple) — *see also*
  Pyrexia 780.60
Febrile — *see also* Pyrexia 780.60
  convulsion (simple) 780.31
    complex 780.32
    nonhemolytic transfusion reaction (FNHTR)
      780.66
  seizure (simple) 780.31
    atypical 780.32
    complex 780.32
    complicated 780.32
Febris — *see also* Fever 780.60
  aestiva (*see also* Fever, hay) 477.9
  flava (*see also* Fever, yellow) 060.9
  melitensis 023.0
  pestis (*see also* Plague) 020.9
  puerperalis 672.0 ☑
  recurrens (*see also* Fever, relapsing) 087.9
    pediculo vestimenti 087.0
  rubra 034.1
  typhoidea 002.0
  typhosa 002.0
Fecal — *see* condition
Fecalith (impaction) 560.32
  with hernia (*see also* Hernia, by site, with
    obstruction)
    gangrenous — *see* Hernia, by site, with
      gangrene
  appendix 543.9
  congenital 777.1
Fede's disease 529.0
Feeble-minded 317
**Feeble rapid pulse due to shock following
  injury** 958.4
Feeding
  faulty (elderly) (infant) 783.3
    newborn 779.31
  formula check V20.2
  improper (elderly) (infant) 783.3
    newborn 779.31
  problem (elderly) (infant) 783.3
    newborn 779.31
    nonorganic origin 307.59
Feeling of foreign body in throat 784.99
Feer's disease 985.0
Feet — *see* condition
Feigned illness V65.2
Feil-Klippel syndrome (brevicollis) 756.16
Feinmesser's (hidrotic) **ectodermal dysplasia**
  757.31
Felix's disease (juvenile osteochondrosis, hip)
  732.1
Felon (any digit) (with lymphangitis) 681.01
  herpetic 054.6
Felty's syndrome (rheumatoid arthritis with
  splenomegaly and leukopenia) 714.1
Feminism in boys 302.6
Feminization, testicular 259.51
  with pseudohermaphroditism, male 259.51

Femoral hernia — *see* Hernia, femoral
Femora vara 736.32
Femur, femoral — *see* condition
Fenestrata placenta — *see* Placenta, abnormal
Fenestration, fenestrated — *see also* Imperfect, closure
  aorta-pulmonary 745.0
  aorticopulmonary 745.0
  aortopulmonary 745.0
  cusps, heart valve NEC 746.89
    pulmonary 746.09
  hymen 752.49
  pulmonic cusps 746.09
Fenwick's disease 537.89
Fermentation (gastric) (gastrointestinal)
  (stomach) 536.8
  intestine 564.89
    psychogenic 306.4
  psychogenic 306.4
Fernell's disease (aortic aneurysm) 441.9
Fertile eunuch syndrome 257.2
Fertility, meaning multiparity — *see* Multiparity
Fetal
  alcohol syndrome 760.71
  anemia 678.0 ☑
  thrombocytopenia 678.0 ☑
  twin to twin transfusion 678.0 ☑
Fetalis uterus 752.39
Fetid
  breath 784.99
  sweat 705.89
Fetishism 302.81
  transvestic 302.3
Fetomaternal hemorrhage
  affecting management of pregnancy
    656.0 ☑
  fetus or newborn 772.0
Fetus, fetal — *see also* condition
  papyraceous 779.89
  type lung tissue 770.4
Fever 780.60
  with chills 780.60
    in malarial regions (*see also* Malaria)
      084.6
  abortus NEC 023.9
  aden 061
  African tick-borne 087.1
  American
    mountain tick 066.1
    spotted 082.0
  and ague (*see also* Malaria) 084.6
  aphthous 078.4
  arbovirus hemorrhagic 065.9
  Assam 085.0
  Australian A or Q 083.0
  Bangkok hemorrhagic 065.4
  biliary, Charcôt's intermittent — *see* Chole-
    docholithiasis
  bilious, hemoglobinuric 084.8
  blackwater 084.8
  blister 054.9
  Bonvale Dam 780.79
  boutonneuse 082.1
  brain 323.9
    late effect — *see* category 326
  breakbone 061
  Bullis 082.8
  Bunyamwera 066.3
  Burdwan 085.0
  Bwamba (encephalitis) 066.3
  Cameroon (*see also* Malaria) 084.6
  Canton 081.9
  catarrhal (acute) 460
    chronic 472.0
  cat-scratch 078.3
  cerebral 323.9
    late effect — *see* category 326
  cerebrospinal (meningococcal) (*see also*
    Meningitis, cerebrospinal) 036.0
  Chagres 084.0
  Chandipura 066.8
  changuinola 066.0
  Charcôt's (biliary) (hepatic) (intermittent)
    — *see* Choledocholithiasis
  Chikungunya (viral) 066.3

Fever — *continued*
  Chikungunya — *continued*
    hemorrhagic 065.4
  childbed 670.8 ☑
  Chitral 066.0
  Colombo (*see also* Fever, paratyphoid) 002.9
  Colorado tick (virus) 066.1
  congestive
    malarial (*see also* Malaria) 084.6
    remittent (*see also* Malaria) 084.6
  Congo virus 065.0
  continued 780.60
    malarial 084.0
  Corsican (*see also* Malaria) 084.6
  Crimean hemorrhagic 065.0
  Cyprus (*see also* Brucellosis) 023.9
  dandy 061
  deer fly (*see also* Tularemia) 021.9
  dehydration, newborn 778.4
  dengue (virus) 061
    hemorrhagic 065.4
  desert 114.0
  due to heat 992.0
  Dumdum 085.0
  enteric 002.0
  ephemeral (of unknown origin) (*see also*
    Pyrexia) 780.60
  epidemic, hemorrhagic of the Far East 065.0
  erysipelatous (*see also* Erysipelas) 035
  estivo-autumnal (malarial) 084.0
  etiocholanolone 277.31
  famine (*see also* Fever, relapsing)
    meaning typhus — *see* Typhus
  Far Eastern hemorrhagic 065.0
  five day 083.1
  Fort Bragg 100.89
  gastroenteric 002.0
  gastromalarial (*see also* Malaria) 084.6
  Gibraltar (*see also* Brucellosis) 023.9
  glandular 075
  Guama (viral) 066.3
  Haverhill 026.1
  hay (allergic) (with rhinitis) 477.9
    with
      asthma (bronchial) (*see also* Asthma)
        493.0 ☑
    due to
      dander, animal (cat) (dog) 477.2
      dust 477.8
      fowl 477.8
      hair, animal (cat) (dog) 477.2
      pollen, any plant or tree 477.0
      specified allergen other than pollen
        477.8
  heat (effects) 992.0
  hematuric, bilious 084.8
  hemoglobinuric (malarial) 084.8
    bilious 084.8
  hemorrhagic (arthropod-borne) NEC 065.9
    with renal syndrome 078.6
    arenaviral 078.7
    Argentine 078.7
    Bangkok 065.4
    Bolivian 078.7
    Central Asian 065.0
    chikungunya 065.4
    Crimean 065.0
    dengue (virus) 065.4
    Ebola 065.8
    epidemic 078.6
      of Far East 065.0
    Far Eastern 065.0
    Junin virus 078.7
    Korean 078.6
    Kyasanur forest 065.2
    Machupo virus 078.7
    mite-borne NEC 065.8
    mosquito-borne 065.4
    Omsk 065.1
    Philippine 065.4
    Russian (Yaroslav) 078.6
    Singapore 065.4
    Southeast Asia 065.4
    Thailand 065.4
    tick-borne NEC 065.3
  hepatic (*see also* Cholecystitis) 575.8

☑ Additional Digit Required — Refer to the Tabular List for Digit Selection
▽ Subterms under main terms may continue to next column or page
2015 ICD-9-CM
▶◀ Revised Text
● New Line
▲ Revised Code
Volume 2 — 113

Fat — Fever

Fever — *continued*
  hepatic (*see also* Cholecystitis) — *continued*
    intermittent (Charcôt's) — *see* Choledo-cholithiasis
  herpetic (*see also* Herpes) 054.9
  Hyalomma tick 065.0
  icterohemorrhagic 100.0
  inanition 780.60
    newborn 778.4
  in conditions classified elsewhere 780.61
  infective NEC 136.9
  intermittent (bilious) (*see also* Malaria) 084.6
    hepatic (Charcôt) — *see* Choledocholithi-asis
    of unknown origin (*see also* Pyrexia) 780.60
    pernicious 084.0
  iodide
    correct substance properly administered 780.60
    overdose or wrong substance given or taken 975.5
  Japanese river 081.2
  jungle yellow 060.0
  Junin virus, hemorrhagic 078.7
  Katayama 120.2
  Kedani 081.2
  Kenya 082.1
  Korean hemorrhagic 078.6
  Lassa 078.89
  Lone Star 082.8
  lung — *see* Pneumonia
  Machupo virus, hemorrhagic 078.7
  malaria, malarial (*see also* Malaria) 084.6
  Malta (*see also* Brucellosis) 023.9
  Marseilles 082.1
  marsh (*see also* Malaria) 084.6
  Mayaro (viral) 066.3
  Mediterranean (*see also* Brucellosis) 023.9
    familial 277.31
    tick 082.1
  meningeal — *see* Meningitis
  metal fumes NEC 985.8
  Meuse 083.1
  Mexican — *see* Typhus, Mexican
  Mianeh 087.1
  miasmatic (*see also* Malaria) 084.6
  miliary 078.2
  milk, female 672.0 ☑
  mill 504
  mite-borne hemorrhagic 065.8
  Monday 504
  mosquito-borne NEC 066.3
    hemorrhagic NEC 065.4
  mountain 066.1
    meaning
      Rocky Mountain spotted 082.0
      undulant fever (*see also* Brucellosis) 023.9
    tick (American) 066.1
  Mucambo (viral) 066.3
  mud 100.89
  Neapolitan (*see also* Brucellosis) 023.9
  neutropenic 288.00
  newborn (environmentally-induced) 778.4
  nine-mile 083.0
  nonexanthematous tick 066.1
  North Asian tick-borne typhus 082.2
  Omsk hemorrhagic 065.1
  O'nyong-nyong (viral) 066.3
  Oropouche (viral) 066.3
  Oroya 088.0
  paludal (*see also* Malaria) 084.6
  Panama 084.0
  pappataci 066.0
  paratyphoid 002.9
    A 002.1
    B (Schottmüller's) 002.2
    C (Hirschfeld) 002.3
  parrot 073.9
  periodic 277.31
  pernicious, acute 084.0
  persistent (of unknown origin) (*see also* Pyrexia) 780.60
  petechial 036.0

Fever — *continued*
  pharyngoconjunctival 077.2
    adenoviral type 3 077.2
  Philippine hemorrhagic 065.4
  phlebotomus 066.0
  Piry 066.8
  Pixuna (viral) 066.3
  Plasmodium ovale 084.3
  pleural (*see also* Pleurisy) 511.0
  pneumonic — *see* Pneumonia
  polymer fume 987.8
  postimmunization 780.63
  postoperative 780.62
    due to infection 998.59
  posttransfusion 780.66
  postvaccination 780.63
  pretibial 100.89
  puerperal, postpartum 672.0 ☑
  putrid — *see* Septicemia
  pyemic — *see* Septicemia
  Q 083.0
    with pneumonia 083.0 [484.8]
  quadrilateral 083.0
  quartan (malaria) 084.2
  Queensland (coastal) 083.0
    seven-day 100.89
  Quintan (A) 083.1
  quotidian 084.0
  rabbit (*see also* Tularemia) 021.9
  rat-bite 026.9
    due to
      Spirillum minor or minus 026.0
      Spirochaeta morsus muris 026.0
      Streptobacillus moniliformis 026.1
  recurrent — *see* Fever, relapsing
  relapsing 087.9
    Carter's (Asiatic) 087.0
    Dutton's (West African) 087.1
    Koch's 087.9
    louse-borne (epidemic) 087.0
    Novy's (American) 087.1
    Obermeyer's (European) 087.0
    spirillum NEC 087.9
    tick-borne (endemic) 087.1
  remittent (bilious) (congestive) (gastric) (*see also* Malaria) 084.6
  rheumatic (active) (acute) (chronic) (suba-cute) 390
    with heart involvement 391.9
      carditis 391.9
      endocarditis (aortic) (mitral) (pulmonary) (tricuspid) 391.1
      multiple sites 391.8
      myocarditis 391.2
      pancarditis, acute 391.8
      pericarditis 391.0
      specified type NEC 391.8
      valvulitis 391.1
    cardiac hypertrophy 398.99
    inactive or quiescent
      with cardiac hypertrophy 398.99
      carditis 398.90
      endocarditis 397.9
        aortic (valve) 395.9
          with mitral (valve) disease 396.9
        mitral (valve) 394.9
          with aortic (valve) disease 396.9
        pulmonary (valve) 397.1
        tricuspid (valve) 397.0
      heart conditions (classifiable to 429.3, 429.6, 429.9) 398.99
        failure (congestive) (conditions classifiable to 428.0, 428.9) 398.91
      left ventricular failure (conditions classifiable to 428.1) 398.91
      myocardial degeneration (conditions classifiable to 429.1) 398.0
      myocarditis (conditions classifiable to 429.0) 398.0
      pancarditis 398.99
      pericarditis 393
  Rift Valley (viral) 066.3
  Rocky Mountain spotted 082.0

Fever — *continued*
  rose 477.0
  Ross river (viral) 066.3
  Russian hemorrhagic 078.6
  sandfly 066.0
  San Joaquin (valley) 114.0
  São Paulo 082.0
  scarlet 034.1
  septic — *see* Septicemia
  seven-day 061
    Japan 100.89
    Queensland 100.89
  shin bone 083.1
  Singapore hemorrhagic 065.4
  solar 061
  sore 054.9
  South African tick-bite 087.1
  Southeast Asia hemorrhagic 065.4
  spinal — *see* Meningitis
  spirillary 026.0
  splenic (*see also* Anthrax) 022.9
  spotted (Rocky Mountain) 082.0
    American 082.0
    Brazilian 082.0
    Colombian 082.0
    meaning
      cerebrospinal meningitis 036.0
      typhus 082.9
  spring 309.23
  steroid
    correct substance properly administered 780.60
    overdose or wrong substance given or taken 962.0
  streptobacillary 026.1
  subtertian 084.0
  Sumatran mite 081.2
  sun 061
  swamp 100.89
  sweating 078.2
  swine 003.8
  sylvatic yellow 060.0
  Tahyna 062.5
  tertian — *see* Malaria, tertian
  Thailand hemorrhagic 065.4
  thermic 992.0
  three day 066.0
    with Coxsackie exanthem 074.8
  tick
    American mountain 066.1
    Colorado 066.1
    Kemerovo 066.1
    Mediterranean 082.1
    mountain 066.1
    nonexanthematous 066.1
    Quaranfil 066.1
  tick-bite NEC 066.1
  tick-borne NEC 066.1
    hemorrhagic NEC 065.3
  transitory of newborn 778.4
  trench 083.1
  tsutsugamushi 081.2
  typhogastric 002.0
  typhoid (abortive) (ambulant) (any site) (hemorrhagic) (infection) (intermittent) (malignant) (rheumatic) 002.0
  typhomalarial (*see also* Malaria) 084.6
  typhus — *see* Typhus
  undulant (*see also* Brucellosis) 023.9
  unknown origin (*see also* Pyrexia) 780.60
  uremic — *see* Uremia
  uveoparotid 135
  valley (Coccidioidomycosis) 114.0
  Venezuelan equine 066.2
  Volhynian 083.1
  Wesselsbron (viral) 066.3
  West
    African 084.8
    Nile (viral) 066.40
      with
        cranial nerve disorders 066.42
        encephalitis 066.41
        optic neuritis 066.42
        other complications 066.49
        other neurologic manifestations 066.42

Fever — *continued*
  West — *continued*
    Nile — *continued*
      with — *continued*
        polyradiculitis 066.42
  Whitmore's 025
  Wolhynian 083.1
  worm 128.9
  Yaroslav hemorrhagic 078.6
  yellow 060.9
    jungle 060.0
    sylvatic 060.0
    urban 060.1
    vaccination, prophylactic (against) V04.4
  Zika (viral) 066.3

Fibrillation
  atrial (established) (paroxysmal) 427.31
  auricular (atrial) (established) 427.31
  cardiac (ventricular) 427.41
  coronary (*see also* Infarct, myocardium) 410.9 ☑
  heart (ventricular) 427.41
  muscular 728.9
  postoperative 997.1
  ventricular 427.41

Fibrin
  ball or bodies, pleural (sac) 511.0
  chamber, anterior (eye) (gelatinous exudate) 364.04

Fibrinogenolysis (hemorrhagic) — *see* Fibrinolysis

Fibrinogenopenia (congenital) (hereditary) — *see also* Defect, coagulation 286.3
  acquired 286.6

Fibrinolysis (acquired) (hemorrhagic) (pathologic) 286.6
  with
    abortion — *see* Abortion, by type, with hemorrhage, delayed or excessive
    ectopic pregnancy (*see also* categories 633.0–633.9) 639.1
    molar pregnancy (*see also* categories 630–632) 639.1
  antepartum or intrapartum 641.3 ☑
    affecting fetus or newborn 762.1
  following
    abortion 639.1
    ectopic or molar pregnancy 639.1
  newborn, transient 776.2
  postpartum 666.3 ☑

Fibrinopenia (hereditary) — *see also* Defect, coagulation 286.3
  acquired 286.6

Fibrinopurulent — *see* condition

Fibrinous — *see* condition

Fibroadenoma (M9010/0)
  cellular intracanalicular (M9020/0) 217
  giant (intracanalicular) (M9020/0) 217
  intracanalicular (M9011/0)
    cellular (M9020/0) 217
    giant (M9020/0) 217
    specified site — *see* Neoplasm, by site, benign
    unspecified site 217
  juvenile (M9030/0) 217
  pericanicular (M9012/0)
    specified site — *see* Neoplasm, by site, benign
    unspecified site 217
  phyllodes (M9020/0) 217
  prostate 600.20
    with
      other lower urinary tract symptoms (LUTS) 600.21
      urinary
        obstruction 600.21
        retention 600.21
  specified site — *see* Neoplasm, by site, benign
  unspecified site 217

Fibroadenosis, breast (chronic) (cystic) (diffuse) (periodic) (segmental) 610.2

Fibroangioma (M9160/0) — *see also* Neoplasm, by site, benign

Fibroangioma — *see also* Neoplasm, by site,
   benign — *continued*
    juvenile (M9160/0)
      specified site — *see* Neoplasm, by site,
        benign
      unspecified site 210.7
Fibrocellulitis progressiva ossificans 728.11
Fibrochondrosarcoma (M9220/3) — *see*
   Neoplasm, cartilage, malignant
Fibrocystic
   disease 277.00
    bone NEC 733.29
    breast 610.1
    jaw 526.2
    kidney (congenital) 753.19
    liver 751.62
    lung 518.89
      congenital 748.4
    pancreas 277.00
   kidney (congenital) 753.19
Fibrodysplasia ossificans multiplex (progressiva) 728.11
Fibroelastosis (cordis) (endocardial) (endomyocardial) 425.3
Fibroid (tumor) (M8890/0) — *see also* Neoplasm, connective tissue, benign
   disease, lung (chronic) (*see also* Fibrosis,
    lung) 515
   heart (disease) (*see also* Myocarditis) 429.0
   induration, lung (chronic) (*see also* Fibrosis,
    lung) 515
   in pregnancy or childbirth 654.1 ☑
    affecting fetus or newborn 763.89
    causing obstructed labor 660.2 ☑
      affecting fetus or newborn 763.1
   liver — *see* Cirrhosis, liver
   lung (*see also* Fibrosis, lung) 515
   pneumonia (chronic) (*see also* Fibrosis, lung)
    515
   uterus (M8890/0) (*see also* Leiomyoma,
    uterus) 218.9
Fibrolipoma (M8851/0) — *see also* Lipoma, by
   site 214.9
Fibroliposarcoma (M8850/3) — *see* Neoplasm,
   connective tissue, malignant
Fibroma (M8810/0) — *see also* Neoplasm,
   connective tissue, benign
   ameloblastic (M9330/0) 213.1
    upper jaw (bone) 213.0
   bone (nonossifying) 733.99
    ossifying (M9262/0) — *see* Neoplasm,
     bone, benign
   cementifying (M9274/0) — *see* Neoplasm,
    bone, benign
   chondromyxoid (M9241/0) — *see* Neo-
    plasm, bone, benign
   desmoplastic (M8823/1) — *see* Neoplasm,
    connective tissue, uncertain behavior
   facial (M8813/0) — *see* Neoplasm, connec-
    tive tissue, benign
   invasive (M8821/1) — *see* Neoplasm, con-
    nective tissue, uncertain behavior
   molle (M8851/0) (*see also* Lipoma, by site)
    214.9
   myxoid (M8811/0) — *see* Neoplasm, connec-
    tive tissue, benign
   nasopharynx, nasopharyngeal (juvenile)
    (M9160/0) 210.7
   nonosteogenic (nonossifying) — *see* Dyspla-
    sia, fibrous
   odontogenic (M9321/0) 213.1
    upper jaw (bone) 213.0
   ossifying (M9262/0) — *see* Neoplasm, bone,
    benign
   periosteal (M8812/0) — *see* Neoplasm,
    bone, benign
   prostate 600.20
    with
      other lower urinary tract symptoms
        (LUTS) 600.21
      urinary
        obstruction 600.21
        retention 600.21
   soft (M8851/0) (*see also* Lipoma, by site)
    214.9
Fibromatosis 728.79

Fibromatosis — *continued*
   abdominal (M8822/1) — *see* Neoplasm,
    connective tissue, uncertain behavior
   aggressive (M8821/1) — *see* Neoplasm,
    connective tissue, uncertain behavior
   congenital generalized (CGF) 759.89
   Dupuytren's 728.6
   gingival 523.8
   plantar fascia 728.71
   proliferative 728.79
   pseudosarcomatous (proliferative) (subcu-
    taneous) 728.79
   subcutaneous pseudosarcomatous (prolifer-
    ative) 728.79
Fibromyalgia 729.1
Fibromyoma (M8890/0) — *see also* Neoplasm,
   connective tissue, benign
   uterus (corpus) (*see also* Leiomyoma, uterus)
    218.9
    in pregnancy or childbirth 654.1 ☑
      affecting fetus or newborn 763.89
      causing obstructed labor 660.2 ☑
        affecting fetus or newborn 763.1
Fibromyositis — *see also* Myositis 729.1
   scapulohumeral 726.2
Fibromyxolipoma (M8852/0) — *see also*
   Lipoma, by site 214.9
Fibromyxoma (M8811/0) — *see* Neoplasm,
   connective tissue, benign
Fibromyxosarcoma (M8811/3) — *see* Neoplasm, connective tissue, malignant
Fibro-odontoma, ameloblastic (M9290/0)
   213.1
   upper jaw (bone) 213.0
Fibro-osteoma (M9262/0) — *see* Neoplasm,
   bone, benign
Fibroplasia, retrolental (*see also* Retinopathy
   of prematurity) 362.21
Fibropurulent — *see* condition
Fibrosarcoma (M8810/3) — *see also* Neoplasm,
   connective tissue, malignant
   ameloblastic (M9330/3) 170.1
    upper jaw (bone) 170.0
   congenital (M8814/3) — *see* Neoplasm,
    connective tissue, malignant
   fascial (M8813/3) — *see* Neoplasm, connec-
    tive tissue, malignant
   infantile (M8814/3) — *see* Neoplasm, con-
    nective tissue, malignant
   odontogenic (M9330/3) 170.1
    upper jaw (bone) 170.0
   periosteal (M8812/3) — *see* Neoplasm,
    bone, malignant
Fibrosclerosis
   breast 610.3
   corpora cavernosa (penis) 607.89
   familial multifocal NEC 710.8
   multifocal (idiopathic) NEC 710.8
   penis (corpora cavernosa) 607.89
Fibrosis, fibrotic
   adrenal (gland) 255.8
   alveolar (diffuse) 516.31
   amnion 658.8 ☑
   anal papillae 569.49
   anus 569.49
   appendix, appendiceal, noninflammatory
    543.9
   arteriocapillary — *see* Arteriosclerosis
   bauxite (of lung) 503
   biliary 576.8
    due to Clonorchis sinensis 121.1
   bladder 596.89
    interstitial 595.1
    localized submucosal 595.1
    panmural 595.1
   bone, diffuse 756.59
   breast 610.3
   capillary (*see also* Arteriosclerosis)
    lung (chronic) (*see also* Fibrosis, lung)
     515
   cardiac (*see also* Myocarditis) 429.0
   cervix 622.8
   chorion 658.8 ☑
   corpus cavernosum 607.89
   cystic (of pancreas) 277.00

Fibrosis, fibrotic — *continued*
   cystic — *continued*
    with
      manifestations
        gastrointestinal 277.03
        pulmonary 277.02
        specified NEC 277.09
      meconium ileus 277.01
      pulmonary exacerbation 277.02
   due to (presence of) any device, implant, or
    graft — *see* Complications, due to
    (presence of) any device, implant, or
    graft classified to 996.0–996.5 NEC
   ejaculatory duct 608.89
   endocardium (*see also* Endocarditis) 424.90
   endomyocardial (African) 425.0
   epididymis 608.89
   eye muscle 378.62
   graphite (of lung) 503
   heart (*see also* Myocarditis) 429.0
   hepatic (*see also* Cirrhosis, liver)
    due to Clonorchis sinensis 121.1
   hepatolienal — *see* Cirrhosis, liver
   hepatosplenic — *see* Cirrhosis, liver
   infrapatellar fat pad 729.31
   interstitial pulmonary, newborn 770.7
   intrascrotal 608.89
   kidney (*see also* Sclerosis, renal) 587
   liver — *see* Cirrhosis, liver
   lung (atrophic) (capillary) (chronic) (conflu-
    ent) (massive) (perialveolar) (peri-
    bronchial) 515
    with
      anthracosilicosis (occupational) 500
      anthracosis (occupational) 500
      asbestosis (occupational) 501
      bagassosis (occupational) 495.1
      bauxite 503
      berylliosis (occupational) 503
      byssinosis (occupational) 504
      calcicosis (occupational) 502
      chalicosis (occupational) 502
      dust reticulation (occupational) 504
      farmers' lung 495.0
      gannister disease (occupational) 502
      graphite 503
      pneumoconiosis (occupational)
       505
      pneumosiderosis (occupational) 503
      siderosis (occupational) 503
      silicosis (occupational) 502
      tuberculosis (*see also* Tuberculosis)
       011.4 ☑
    diffuse (idiopathic) (interstitial) 516.31
    due to
      bauxite 503
      fumes or vapors (chemical) (inhala-
       tion) 506.4
      graphite 503
    following radiation 508.1
    postinflammatory 515
    silicotic (massive) (occupational) 502
    tuberculous (*see also* Tuberculosis)
      011.4 ☑
   lymphatic gland 289.3
   median bar 600.90
    with
      other lower urinary tract symptoms
        (LUTS) 600.91
      urinary
        obstruction 600.91
        retention 600.91
   mediastinum (idiopathic) 519.3
   meninges 349.2
   muscle NEC 728.2
    iatrogenic (from injection) 999.9
   myocardium, myocardial (*see also* Myocardi-
    tis) 429.0
   oral submucous 528.8
   ovary 620.8
   oviduct 620.8
   pancreas 577.8
    cystic 277.00
      with
        manifestations
          gastrointestinal 277.03

Fibrosis, fibrotic — *continued*
   pancreas — *continued*
    cystic — *continued*
      with — *continued*
        manifestations — *continued*
          pulmonary 277.02
          specified NEC 277.09
        meconium ileus 277.01
        pulmonary exacerbation 277.02
   penis 607.89
   periappendiceal 543.9
   periarticular (*see also* Ankylosis) 718.5 ☑
   pericardium 423.1
   perineum, in pregnancy or childbirth
    654.8 ☑
    affecting fetus or newborn 763.89
    causing obstructed labor 660.2 ☑
      affecting fetus or newborn 763.1
   perineural NEC 355.9
    foot 355.6
   periureteral 593.89
   placenta — *see* Placenta, abnormal
   pleura 511.0
   popliteal fat pad 729.31
   preretinal 362.56
   prostate (chronic) 600.90
    with
      other lower urinary tract symptoms
        (LUTS) 600.91
      urinary
        obstruction 600.91
        retention 600.91
   pulmonary (chronic) (*see also* Fibrosis, lung)
    515
    alveolar capillary block 516.8
    idiopathic 516.31
    interstitial
      diffuse (idiopathic) 516.31
      newborn 770.7
   radiation — *see* Effect, adverse, radiation
   rectal sphincter 569.49
   retroperitoneal, idiopathic 593.4
   sclerosing mesenteric (idiopathic) 567.82
   scrotum 608.89
   seminal vesicle 608.89
   senile 797
   skin NEC 709.2
   spermatic cord 608.89
   spleen 289.59
    bilharzial (*see also* Schistosomiasis) 120.9
   subepidermal nodular (M8832/0) — *see*
    Neoplasm, skin, benign
   submucous NEC 709.2
    oral 528.8
    tongue 528.8
   syncytium — *see* Placenta, abnormal
   testis 608.89
    chronic, due to syphilis 095.8
   thymus (gland) 254.8
   tunica vaginalis 608.89
   ureter 593.89
   urethra 599.84
   uterus (nonneoplastic) 621.8
    bilharzial (*see also* Schistosomiasis) 120.9
    neoplastic (*see also* Leiomyoma, uterus)
     218.9
   vagina 623.8
   valve, heart (*see also* Endocarditis) 424.90
   vas deferens 608.89
   vein 459.89
    lower extremities 459.89
   vesical 595.1
Fibrositis (periarticular) (rheumatoid) 729.0
   humeroscapular region 726.2
   nodular, chronic
    Jaccoud's 714.4
    rheumatoid 714.4
   ossificans 728.11
   scapulohumeral 726.2
Fibrothorax 511.0
Fibrotic — *see* Fibrosis
Fibrous — *see* condition
Fibroxanthoma (M8831/0) — *see also* Neoplasm, connective tissue, benign
   atypical (M8831/1) — *see* Neoplasm, con-
    nective tissue, uncertain behavior

☑ **Additional Digit Required** — Refer to the Tabular List for Digit Selection   ▽ **Subterms under main terms may continue to next column or page**

Fibroxanthoma — *see also* Neoplasm, connective tissue, benign — *continued*
  malignant (M8831/3) — *see* Neoplasm, connective tissue, malignant
Fibroxanthosarcoma (M8831/3) — *see* Neoplasm, connective tissue, malignant
Fiedler's
  disease (leptospiral jaundice) 100.0
  myocarditis or syndrome (acute isolated myocarditis) 422.91
Fiessinger-Leroy (-Reiter) syndrome 099.3
Fiessinger-Rendu syndrome (erythema muliforme exudativum) 695.19
Fifth disease (eruptive) 057.0
  venereal 099.1
Filaria, filarial — *see* Infestation, filarial
Filariasis — *see also* Infestation, filarial 125.9
  bancroftian 125.0
  Brug's 125.1
  due to
    bancrofti 125.0
    Brugia (Wuchereria) (malayi) 125.1
    Loa loa 125.2
    malayi 125.1
    organism NEC 125.6
    Wuchereria (bancrofti) 125.0
      malayi 125.1
  Malayan 125.1
  ozzardi 125.5
  specified type NEC 125.6
Filatoff's, Filatov's, Filatow's disease (infectious mononucleosis) 075
File-cutters' disease 984.9
  specified type of lead — *see* Table of Drugs and Chemicals
Filling defect
  biliary tract 793.3
  bladder 793.5
  duodenum 793.4
  gallbladder 793.3
  gastrointestinal tract 793.4
  intestine 793.4
  kidney 793.5
  stomach 793.4
  ureter 793.5
Filtering bleb, eye (postglaucoma) (status) V45.69
  with complication or rupture 997.99
  postcataract extraction (complication) 997.99
Fimbrial cyst (congenital) 752.11
Fimbriated hymen 752.49
Financial problem affecting care V60.2
Findings, (abnormal), without diagnosis (examination) (laboratory test) 796.4
  17-ketosteroids, elevated 791.9
  acetonuria 791.6
  acid phosphatase 790.5
  albumin-globulin ratio 790.99
  albuminuria 791.0
  alcohol in blood 790.3
  alkaline phosphatase 790.5
  amniotic fluid 792.3
  amylase 790.5
  anisocytosis 790.09
  antenatal screening 796.5
  anthrax, positive 795.31
  antibody titers, elevated 795.79
  anticardiolipin antibody 795.79
  antigen-antibody reaction 795.79
  antiphosphatidylglycerol antibody 795.79
  antiphosphatidylinositol antibody 795.79
  antiphosphatidylserine antibody 795.79
  antiphospholipid antibody 795.79
  bacteriuria 791.9
  ballistocardiogram 794.39
  bicarbonate 276.9
  bile in urine 791.4
  bilirubin 277.4
  bleeding time (prolonged) 790.92
  blood culture, positive 790.7
  blood gas level (arterial) 790.91
  blood sugar level 790.29
    high 790.29
      fasting glucose 790.21

Findings, (abnormal), without diagnosis — *continued*
  blood sugar level — *continued*
    high — *continued*
      glucose tolerance test 790.22
    low 251.2
  calcium 275.40
  cancer antigen 125 [CA 125] 795.82
  carbonate 276.9
  carcinoembryonic antigen [CEA] 795.81
  casts, urine 791.7
  catecholamines 791.9
  cells, urine 791.7
  cerebrospinal fluid (color) (content) (pressure) 792.0
  cervical
    high risk human papillomavirus (HPV) DNA test positive 795.05
    low risk human papillomavirus (HPV) DNA test positive 795.09
    non-atypical endometrial cells 795.09
  chloride 276.9
  cholesterol 272.9
    high 272.0
      with high triglycerides 272.2
  chromosome analysis 795.2
  chyluria 791.1
  circulation time 794.39
  cloudy dialysis effluent 792.5
  cloudy urine 791.9
  coagulation study 790.92
  cobalt, blood 790.6
  color of urine (unusual) NEC 791.9
  copper, blood 790.6
  C-reactive protein (CRP) 790.95
  creatinine clearance 794.4
  crystals, urine 791.9
  culture, positive NEC 795.39
    blood 790.7
    HIV V08
    human immunodeficiency virus V08
    nose 795.39
      Staphylococcus — *see* Carrier (suspected) of, Staphylococcus
    skin lesion NEC 795.39
    spinal fluid 792.0
    sputum 795.39
    stool 792.1
    throat 795.39
    urine 791.9
    viral
      human immunodeficiency V08
    wound 795.39
  cytology specified site NEC 796.9
  echocardiogram 793.2
  echoencephalogram 794.01
  echogram NEC — *see* Findings, abnormal, structure
  electrocardiogram (ECG) (EKG) 794.31
  electroencephalogram (EEG) 794.02
  electrolyte level, urinary 791.9
  electromyogram (EMG) 794.17
    ocular 794.14
  electro-oculogram (EOG) 794.12
  electroretinogram (ERG) 794.11
  enzymes, serum NEC 790.5
  fibrinogen titer coagulation study 790.92
  filling defect — *see* Filling defect
  function study NEC 794.9
    auditory 794.15
    bladder 794.9
    brain 794.00
    cardiac 794.30
    endocrine NEC 794.6
      thyroid 794.5
    kidney 794.4
    liver 794.8
    nervous system
      central 794.00
      peripheral 794.19
    oculomotor 794.14
    pancreas 794.9
    placenta 794.9
    pulmonary 794.2
    retina 794.11
    special senses 794.19

Findings, (abnormal), without diagnosis — *continued*
  function study — *continued*
    spleen 794.9
    vestibular 794.16
  gallbladder, nonvisualization 793.3
  glucose 790.29
    elevated
      fasting 790.21
      tolerance test 790.22
  glycosuria 791.5
  heart
    shadow 793.2
    sounds 785.3
  hematinuria 791.2
  hematocrit
    drop (precipitous) 790.01
    elevated 282.7
    low 285.9
  hematologic NEC 790.99
  hematuria 599.70
  hemoglobin
    drop 790.01
    elevated 282.7
    low 285.9
  hemoglobinuria 791.2
  histological NEC 795.4
  hormones 259.9
  immunoglobulins, elevated 795.79
  indolacetic acid, elevated 791.9
  iron 790.6
  karyotype 795.2
  ketonuria 791.6
  lactic acid dehydrogenase (LDH) 790.4
  lead 790.6
  lipase 790.5
  lipids NEC 272.9
  lithium, blood 790.6
  liver function test 790.6
  lung field (shadow) 793.19
    coin lesion 793.11
  magnesium, blood 790.6
  mammogram 793.80
    calcification 793.89
    calculus 793.89
    dense breasts 793.82
    inconclusive 793.82
      due to dense breasts 793.82
    microcalcification 793.81
  mediastinal shift 793.2
  melanin, urine 791.9
  microbiologic NEC 795.39
  mineral, blood NEC 790.6
  myoglobinuria 791.3
  nasal swab, anthrax 795.31
  neonatal screening 796.6
  nitrogen derivatives, blood 790.6
  nonvisualization of gallbladder 793.3
  nose culture, positive 795.39
  odor of urine (unusual) NEC 791.9
  oxygen saturation 790.91
  Papanicolaou (smear) 796.9
    anus 796.70
      with
        atypical squamous cells
          cannot exclude high grade squamous intraepithelial lesion (ASC-H) 796.72
          of undetermined significance (ASC-US) 796.71
        cytologic evidence of malignancy 796.76
        high grade squamous intraepithelial lesion (HGSIL) 796.74
        low grade squamous intraepithelial lesion (LGSIL) 796.73
      glandular 796.70
      specified finding NEC 796.79
    cervix 795.00
      with
        atypical squamous cells
          cannot exclude high grade squamous intraepithelial lesion (ASC-H) 795.02

Findings, (abnormal), without diagnosis — *continued*
  Papanicolaou — *continued*
    cervix — *continued*
      with — *continued*
        atypical squamous cells — *continued*
          of undetermined significance (ASC-US) 795.01
        cytologic evidence of malignancy 795.06
        high grade squamous intraepithelial lesion (HGSIL) 795.04
        low grade squamous intraepithelial lesion (LGSIL) 795.03
        non-atypical endometrial cells 795.09
      dyskaryotic 795.09
      non-atypical endometrial cells 795.09
      nonspecific finding NEC 795.09
    other site 796.9
    vagina 795.10
      with
        atypical squamous cells
          cannot exclude high grade squamous intraepithelial lesion (ASC-H) 795.12
          of undetermined significance (ASC-US) 795.11
        cytologic evidence of malignancy 795.16
        high grade squamous intraepithelial lesion (HGSIL) 795.14
        low grade squamous intraepithelial lesion (LGSIL) 795.13
      glandular 795.10
      specified NEC 795.19
  peritoneal fluid 792.9
  phonocardiogram 794.39
  phosphorus 275.3
  pleural fluid 792.9
  pneumoencephalogram 793.0
  PO$_2$-oxygen ratio 790.91
  poikilocytosis 790.09
  potassium
    deficiency 276.8
    excess 276.7
  PPD 795.51
  prostate specific antigen (PSA) 790.93
  protein, serum NEC 790.99
  proteinuria 791.0
  prothrombin time (partial) (prolonged) (PT) (PTT) 790.92
  pyuria 791.9
  radiologic (x-ray) 793.99
    abdomen 793.6
    biliary tract 793.3
    breast 793.89
      abnormal mammogram NOS 793.80
      mammographic
        calcification 793.89
        calculus 793.89
        microcalcification 793.81
    gastrointestinal tract 793.4
    genitourinary organs 793.5
    head 793.0
    image test inconclusive due to excess body fat 793.91
    intrathoracic organs NEC 793.2
    lung 793.19
    musculoskeletal 793.7
    placenta 793.99
    retroperitoneum 793.6
    skin 793.99
    skull 793.0
    subcutaneous tissue 793.99
  red blood cell 790.09
    count 790.09
    morphology 790.09
    sickling 790.09
    volume 790.09
  saliva 792.4
  scan NEC 794.9
    bladder 794.9
    bone 794.9

☑ **Additional Digit Required** — Refer to the Tabular List for Digit Selection   ▽ **Subterms under main terms may continue to next column or page**

116 — Volume 2   ▶◀ **Revised Text**   ● **New Line**   ▲ **Revised Code**   **2015 ICD-9-CM**

Findings, (abnormal), without diagnosis — *continued*
  scan — *continued*
    brain 794.09
    kidney 794.4
    liver 794.8
    lung 794.2
    pancreas 794.9
    placental 794.9
    spleen 794.9
    thyroid 794.5
  sedimentation rate, elevated 790.1
  semen 792.2
  serological (for)
    human immunodeficiency virus (HIV)
      inconclusive 795.71
      positive V08
    syphilis — *see* Findings, serology for syphilis
  serology for syphilis
    false positive 795.6
    positive 097.1
      false 795.6
      follow-up of latent syphilis — *see* Syphilis, latent
      only finding — *see* Syphilis, latent
  serum 790.99
    blood NEC 790.99
    enzymes NEC 790.5
    proteins 790.99
  SGOT 790.4
  SGPT 790.4
  sickling of red blood cells 790.09
  skin test, positive 795.79
    tuberculin (without active tuberculosis) 795.51
  sodium 790.6
    deficiency 276.1
    excess 276.0
  specified NEC 796.9
  spermatozoa 792.2
  spinal fluid 792.0
    culture, positive 792.0
  sputum culture, positive 795.39
    for acid-fast bacilli 795.39
  stool NEC 792.1
    bloody 578.1
      occult 792.1
    color 792.1
    culture, positive 792.1
    occult blood 792.1
  stress test 794.39
  structure, body (echogram) (thermogram) (ultrasound) (x-ray) NEC 793.99
    abdomen 793.6
    breast 793.89
      abnormal mammogram 793.80
      mammographic
        calcification 793.89
        calculus 793.89
        microcalcification 793.81
    gastrointestinal tract 793.4
    genitourinary organs 793.5
    head 793.0
      echogram (ultrasound) 794.01
    intrathoracic organs NEC 793.2
    lung 793.19
    musculoskeletal 793.7
    placenta 793.99
    retroperitoneum 793.6
    skin 793.99
    subcutaneous tissue NEC 793.99
  synovial fluid 792.9
  thermogram — *see* Findings, abnormal, structure
  throat culture, positive 795.39
  thyroid (function) 794.5
    metabolism (rate) 794.5
    scan 794.5
    uptake 794.5
  total proteins 790.99
  toxicology (drugs) (heavy metals) 796.0
  transaminase (level) 790.4
  triglycerides 272.9
    high 272.1
      with high cholesterol 272.2

Findings, (abnormal), without diagnosis — *continued*
  tuberculin skin test (without active tuberculosis) 795.51
  tumor markers NEC 795.89
  ultrasound (*see also* Findings, abnormal, structure)
    cardiogram 793.2
  uric acid, blood 790.6
  urine, urinary constituents 791.9
    acetone 791.6
    albumin 791.0
    bacteria 791.9
    bile 791.4
    blood 599.70
    casts or cells 791.7
    chyle 791.1
    culture, positive 791.9
    glucose 791.5
    hemoglobin 791.2
    ketone 791.6
    protein 791.0
    pus 791.9
    sugar 791.5
  vaginal
    fluid 792.9
    high risk human papillomavirus (HPV) DNA test positive 795.15
    low risk human papillomavirus (HPV) DNA test positive 795.19
  vanillylmandelic acid, elevated 791.9
  vectorcardiogram (VCG) 794.39
  ventriculogram (cerebral) 793.0
  VMA, elevated 791.9
  Wassermann reaction
    false positive 795.6
    positive 097.1
      follow-up of latent syphilis — *see* Syphilis, latent
      only finding — *see* Syphilis, latent
  white blood cell 288.9
    count 288.9
      elevated 288.60
      low 288.50
    differential 288.9
    morphology 288.9
  wound culture 795.39
  xerography 793.89
  zinc, blood 790.6
Finger — *see* condition
Finnish type nephrosis (congenital) 759.89
Fire, St. Anthony's — *see also* Erysipelas 035
Fish
  hook stomach 537.89
  meal workers' lung 495.8
Fisher's syndrome 357.0
Fissure, fissured
  abdominal wall (congenital) 756.79
  anus, anal 565.0
    congenital 751.5
  buccal cavity 528.9
  clitoris (congenital) 752.49
  ear, lobule (congenital) 744.29
  epiglottis (congenital) 748.3
  larynx 478.79
    congenital 748.3
  lip 528.5
    congenital (*see also* Cleft, lip) 749.10
  nipple 611.2
    puerperal, postpartum 676.1 ☑
  palate (congenital) (*see also* Cleft, palate) 749.00
  postanal 565.0
  rectum 565.0
  skin 709.8
    streptococcal 686.9
  spine (congenital) (*see also* Spina bifida) 741.9 ☑
  sternum (congenital) 756.3
  tongue (acquired) 529.5
    congenital 750.13
Fistula (sinus) 686.9
  abdomen (wall) 569.81
    bladder 596.2
    intestine 569.81
    ureter 593.82

Fistula — *continued*
  abdomen — *continued*
    uterus 619.2
  abdominorectal 569.81
  abdominosigmoidal 569.81
  abdominothoracic 510.0
  abdominouterine 619.2
    congenital 752.39
  abdominovesical 596.2
  accessory sinuses (*see also* Sinusitis) 473.9
  actinomycotic — *see* Actinomycosis
  alveolar
    antrum (*see also* Sinusitis, maxillary) 473.0
    process 522.7
  anorectal 565.1
  antrobuccal (*see also* Sinusitis, maxillary) 473.0
  antrum (*see also* Sinusitis, maxillary) 473.0
  anus, anal (infectional) (recurrent) 565.1
    congenital 751.5
    tuberculous (*see also* Tuberculosis) 014.8 ☑
  aortic sinus 747.29
  aortoduodenal 447.2
  appendix, appendicular 543.9
  arteriovenous (acquired) 447.0
    brain 437.3
      congenital 747.81
        ruptured (*see also* Hemorrhage, subarachnoid) 430
      ruptured (*see also* Hemorrhage, subarachnoid) 430
    cerebral 437.3
      congenital 747.81
    congenital (peripheral) 747.60
      brain — *see* Fistula, arteriovenous, brain, congenital
      coronary 746.85
      gastrointestinal 747.61
      lower limb 747.64
      pulmonary 747.39
      renal 747.62
      specified site NEC 747.69
      upper limb 747.63
    coronary 414.19
      congenital 746.85
    heart 414.19
    pulmonary (vessels) 417.0
      congenital 747.39
    surgically created (for dialysis) V45.11
      complication NEC 996.73
        atherosclerosis — *see* Arteriosclerosis, extremities
        embolism 996.74
        infection or inflammation 996.62
        mechanical 996.1
        occlusion NEC 996.74
        thrombus 996.74
    traumatic — *see* Injury, blood vessel, by site
  artery 447.2
  aural 383.81
    congenital 744.49
  auricle 383.81
    congenital 744.49
  Bartholin's gland 619.8
  bile duct (*see also* Fistula, biliary) 576.4
  biliary (duct) (tract) 576.4
    congenital 751.69
  bladder (neck) (sphincter) 596.2
    into seminal vesicle 596.2
  bone 733.99
  brain 348.89
    arteriovenous — *see* Fistula, arteriovenous, brain
  branchial (cleft) 744.41
  branchiogenous 744.41
  breast 611.0
    puerperal, postpartum 675.1 ☑
  bronchial 510.0
  bronchocutaneous, bronchomediastinal, bronchopleural, bronchopleuromediastinal (infective) 510.0
    tuberculous (*see also* Tuberculosis) 011.3 ☑

Fistula — *continued*
  bronchoesophageal 530.89
    congenital 750.3
  buccal cavity (infective) 528.3
  canal, ear 380.89
  carotid-cavernous
    congenital 747.81
      with hemorrhage 430
    traumatic 900.82
      with hemorrhage (*see also* Hemorrhage, brain, traumatic) 853.0 ☑
        late effect 908.3
  cecosigmoidal 569.81
  cecum 569.81
  cerebrospinal (fluid) 349.81
  cervical, lateral (congenital) 744.41
  cervicoaural (congenital) 744.49
  cervicosigmoidal 619.1
  cervicovesical 619.0
  cervix 619.8
  chest (wall) 510.0
  cholecystocolic (*see also* Fistula, gallbladder) 575.5
  cholecystocolonic (*see also* Fistula, gallbladder) 575.5
  cholecystoduodenal (*see also* Fistula, gallbladder) 575.5
  cholecystoenteric (*see also* Fistula, gallbladder) 575.5
  cholecystogastric (*see also* Fistula, gallbladder) 575.5
  cholecystointestinal (*see also* Fistula, gallbladder) 575.5
  choledochoduodenal 576.4
  cholocolic (*see also* Fistula, gallbladder) 575.5
  coccyx 685.1
    with abscess 685.0
  colon 569.81
  colostomy 569.69
  colovaginal (acquired) 619.1
  common duct (bile duct) 576.4
  congenital, NEC — *see* Anomaly, specified type NEC
  cornea, causing hypotony 360.32
  coronary, arteriovenous 414.19
    congenital 746.85
  costal region 510.0
  cul-de-sac, Douglas' 619.8
  cutaneous 686.9
  cystic duct (*see also* Fistula, gallbladder) 575.5
    congenital 751.69
  cystostomy 596.83
  dental 522.7
  diaphragm 510.0
    bronchovisceral 510.0
    pleuroperitoneal 510.0
    pulmonoperitoneal 510.0
  duodenum 537.4
  ear (canal) (external) 380.89
  enterocolic 569.81
  enterocutaneous 569.81
  enteroenteric 569.81
  entero-uterine 619.1
    congenital 752.39
  enterovaginal 619.1
    congenital 752.49
  enterovesical 596.1
  epididymis 608.89
    tuberculous (*see also* Tuberculosis) 016.4 ☑
  esophagobronchial 530.89
    congenital 750.3
  esophagocutaneous 530.89
  esophagopleurocutaneous 530.89
  esophagotracheal 530.84
    congenital 750.3
  esophagus 530.89
    congenital 750.4
  ethmoid (*see also* Sinusitis, ethmoidal) 473.2
  eyeball (cornea) (sclera) 360.32
  eyelid 373.11
  fallopian tube (external) 619.2
  fecal 569.81

☑ **Additional Digit Required** — Refer to the Tabular List for Digit Selection   ▽ **Subterms under main terms may continue to next column or page**

2015 ICD-9-CM   ▶◀ Revised Text   ● New Line   ▲ Revised Code   Volume 2 — 117

☑ Additional Digit Required — Refer to the Tabular List for Digit Selection   ▽ Subterms under main terms may continue to next column or page

118 — Volume 2   ►◄ Revised Text   ● New Line   ▲ Revised Code   2015 ICD-9-CM

Fitting — *continued*
  device, unspecified type — *continued*
    prosthetic — *continued*
      specified type NEC V52.8
      special senses V53.09
      substitution
        auditory V53.09
        nervous system V53.09
        visual V53.09
      urinary V53.6
  diaphragm (contraceptive) V25.02
  gastric lap band V53.51
  gastrointestinal appliance and device NEC V53.59
  glasses (reading) V53.1
  growth rod V54.02
  hearing aid V53.2
  ileostomy device V53.5 ☑
  intestinal appliance and device V53.50
  intestinal appliance or device NEC V53.5 ☑
  intrauterine contraceptive device
    insertion V25.11
    removal V25.12
      and reinsertion V25.13
    replacement V25.13
  neuropacemaker (brain) (peripheral nerve) (spinal cord) V53.02
  orthodontic device V53.4
  orthopedic (device) V53.7
    brace V53.7
    cast V53.7
    corset V53.7
    shoes V53.7
  pacemaker (cardiac) V53.31
    brain V53.02
    carotid sinus V53.39
    peripheral nerve V53.02
    spinal cord V53.02
  prosthesis V52.9
    arm (complete) (partial) V52.0
    breast V52.4
      implant exchange (different material) (different size) V52.4
    dental V52.3
    eye V52.2
    leg (complete) (partial) V52.1
    specified type NEC V52.8
  spectacles V53.1
  wheelchair V53.8
Fitz-Hugh and Curtis syndrome 098.86
  due to
    Chlamydia trachomatis 099.56
    Neisseria gonorrhoeae (gonococcal peritonitis) 098.86
Fitz's syndrome (acute hemorrhagic pancreatitis) 577.0
Fixation
  joint — *see* Ankylosis
  larynx 478.79
  pupil 364.76
  stapes 385.22
    deafness (*see also* Deafness, conductive) 389.04
  uterus (acquired) — *see* Malposition, uterus
  vocal cord 478.5
Flaccid — *see also* condition
  foot 736.79
  forearm 736.09
  palate, congenital 750.26
Flail
  chest 807.4
    newborn 767.3
  joint (paralytic) 718.80
    ankle 718.87
    elbow 718.82
    foot 718.87
    hand 718.84
    hip 718.85
    knee 718.86
    multiple sites 718.89
    pelvic region 718.85
    shoulder (region) 718.81
    specified site NEC 718.88
    wrist 718.83
Flajani (-Basedow) syndrome or disease (exophthalmic goiter) 242.0 ☑

Flap, liver 572.8
Flare, anterior chamber (aqueous) (eye) 364.04
Flashback phenomena (drug) (hallucinogenic) 292.89
Flat
  chamber (anterior) (eye) 360.34
  chest, congenital 754.89
  electroencephalogram (EEG) 348.89
  foot (acquired) (fixed type) (painful) (postural) (spastic) 734
    congenital 754.61
      rocker bottom 754.61
      vertical talus 754.61
    rachitic 268.1
    rocker bottom (congenital) 754.61
    vertical talus, congenital 754.61
  organ or site, congenital NEC — *see* Anomaly, specified type NEC
  pelvis 738.6
    with disproportion (fetopelvic) 653.2 ☑
      affecting fetus or newborn 763.1
      causing obstructed labor 660.1 ☑
        affecting fetus or newborn 763.1
    congenital 755.69
Flatau-Schilder disease 341.1
Flattening
  head, femur 736.39
  hip 736.39
  lip (congenital) 744.89
  nose (congenital) 754.0
    acquired 738.0
Flatulence 787.3
Flatus 787.3
  vaginalis 629.89
Flax dressers' disease 504
Flea bite — *see* Injury, superficial, by site
Fleischer (-Kayser) ring (corneal pigmentation) 275.1 *[371.14]*
Fleischner's disease 732.3
Fleshy mole 631.8
Flexibilitas cerea — *see also* Catalepsy 300.11
Flexion
  cervix — *see* Flexion, uterus
  contracture, joint (*see also* Contraction, joint) 718.4 ☑
  deformity, joint (*see also* Contraction, joint) 736.9
    hip, congenital (*see also* Subluxation, congenital, hip) 754.32
  uterus (*see also* Malposition, uterus) 621.6
Flexner's
  bacillus 004.1
  diarrhea (ulcerative) 004.1
  dysentery 004.1
Flexner-Boyd dysentery 004.2
Flexure — *see* condition
Floater, vitreous 379.24
Floating
  cartilage (joint) (*see also* Disorder, cartilage, articular) 718.0 ☑
    knee 717.6
  gallbladder (congenital) 751.69
  kidney 593.0
    congenital 753.3
  liver (congenital) 751.69
  rib 756.3
  spleen 289.59
Flooding 626.2
Floor — *see* condition
Floppy
  infant NEC 781.99
  iris syndrome 364.81
  valve syndrome (mitral) 424.0
Flu — *see also* Influenza
  bird (*see also* Influenza, avian) 488.02
  gastric NEC 008.8
  swine — *see* Influenza (novel) 2009 H1N1
Fluctuating blood pressure 796.4
Fluid
  abdomen 789.59
  chest (*see also* Pleurisy, with effusion) 511.9
  heart (*see also* Failure, heart) 428.0
  joint (*see also* Effusion, joint) 719.0 ☑
  loss (acute) 276.50

Fluid — *continued*
  loss — *continued*
    with
      hypernatremia 276.0
      hyponatremia 276.1
  lung (*see also* Edema, lung)
    encysted 511.89
  peritoneal cavity 789.59
    malignant 789.51
  pleural cavity (*see also* Pleurisy, with effusion) 511.9
  retention 276.69
Flukes NEC — *see also* Infestation, fluke 121.9
  blood NEC (*see also* Infestation, Schistosoma) 120.9
  liver 121.3
Fluor (albus) (vaginalis) 623.5
  trichomonal (Trichomonas vaginalis) 131.00
Fluorosis (dental) (chronic) 520.3
Flushing 782.62
  menopausal 627.2
Flush syndrome 259.2
Flutter
  atrial or auricular 427.32
  heart (ventricular) 427.42
    atrial 427.32
  impure 427.32
  postoperative 997.1
  ventricular 427.42
Flux (bloody) (serosanguineous) 009.0
FNHTR (febrile nonhemolytic transfusion reaction) 780.66
Focal — *see* condition
Fochier's abscess — *see* Abscess, by site
Focus, Assmann's — *see also* Tuberculosis 011.0 ☑
Fogo selvagem 694.4
Foix-Alajouanine syndrome 336.1
Folds, anomalous — *see also* Anomaly, specified type NEC
  Bowman's membrane 371.31
  Descemet's membrane 371.32
  epicanthic 743.63
  heart 746.89
  posterior segment of eye, congenital 743.54
Folie à deux 297.3
Follicle
  cervix (nabothian) (ruptured) 616.0
  graafian, ruptured, with hemorrhage 620.0
  nabothian 616.0
Folliclis (primary) — *see also* Tuberculosis 017.0 ☑
Follicular — *see also* condition
  cyst (atretic) 620.0
Folliculitis 704.8
  abscedens et suffodiens 704.8
  decalvans 704.09
  gonorrheal (acute) 098.0
    chronic or duration of 2 months or more 098.2
  keloid, keloidalis 706.1
  pustular 704.8
  ulerythematosa reticulata 701.8
Folliculosis, conjunctival 372.02
Følling's disease (phenylketonuria) 270.1
Follow-up (examination) (routine) (following) V67.9
  cancer chemotherapy V67.2
  chemotherapy V67.2
  fracture V67.4
  high-risk medication V67.51
  injury NEC V67.59
  postpartum
    immediately after delivery V24.0
    routine V24.2
  psychiatric V67.3
  psychotherapy V67.3
  radiotherapy V67.1
  specified condition NEC V67.59
  specified surgery NEC V67.09
  surgery V67.00
    vaginal pap smear V67.01
  treatment V67.9
    combined NEC V67.6
    fracture V67.4

Follow-up — *continued*
  treatment — *continued*
    involving high-risk medication NEC V67.51
    mental disorder V67.3
    specified NEC V67.59
Fong's syndrome (hereditary osteoonychodysplasia) 756.89
Food
  allergy 693.1
  anaphylactic reaction or shock due to food 995.60
  asphyxia (from aspiration or inhalation) (*see also* Asphyxia, food) 933.1
  choked on (*see also* Asphyxia, food) 933.1
  deprivation 994.2
    specified kind of food NEC 269.8
  intoxication (*see also* Poisoning, food) 005.9
  lack of 994.2
  poisoning (*see also* Poisoning, food) 005.9
  refusal or rejection NEC 307.59
  strangulation or suffocation (*see also* Asphyxia, food) 933.1
  toxemia (*see also* Poisoning, food) 005.9
Foot — *see also* condition
  and mouth disease 078.4
  process disease 581.3
Foramen ovale (nonclosure) (patent) (persistent) 745.5
Forbes-Albright syndrome (nonpuerperal amenorrhea and lactation associated with pituitary tumor) 253.1
Forbes' (glycogen storage) disease 271.0
Forced birth or delivery NEC 669.8 ☑
  affecting fetus or newborn NEC 763.89
Forceps
  delivery NEC 669.5 ☑
    affecting fetus or newborn 763.2
Fordyce's disease (ectopic sebaceous glands) (mouth) 750.26
Fordyce-Fox disease (apocrine miliaria) 705.82
Forearm — *see* condition
Foreign body

> *Note* — For foreign body with open wound, or other injury, see Wound, open, or the type of injury specified.

  accidentally left during a procedure 998.4
  anterior chamber (eye) 871.6
    magnetic 871.5
      retained or old 360.51
    retained or old 360.61
  ciliary body (eye) 871.6
    magnetic 871.5
      retained or old 360.52
    retained or old 360.62
  entering through orifice (current) (old)
    accessory sinus 932
    air passage (upper) 933.0
      lower 934.8
    alimentary canal 938
    alveolar process 935.0
    antrum (Highmore) 932
    anus 937
    appendix 936
    asphyxia due to (*see also* Asphyxia, food) 933.1
    auditory canal 931
    auricle 931
    bladder 939.0
    bronchioles 934.8
    bronchus (main) 934.1
    buccal cavity 935.0
    canthus (inner) 930.1
    cecum 936
    cervix (canal) uterine 939.1
    coil, ileocecal 936
    colon 936
    conjunctiva 930.1
    conjunctival sac 930.1
    cornea 930.0
    digestive organ or tract NEC 938
    duodenum 936
    ear (external) 931
    esophagus 935.1
    eye (external) 930.9
      combined sites 930.8

☑ **Additional Digit Required** — Refer to the Tabular List for Digit Selection   ▽ **Subterms under main terms may continue to next column or page**

2015 ICD-9-CM   ▶◀ Revised Text   ● New Line   ▲ Revised Code   **Volume 2 — 119**

Foreign body — *continued*
  entering through orifice — *continued*
    eye — *continued*
      intraocular — *see* Foreign body, by
        site
      specified site NEC 930.8
    eyeball 930.8
      intraocular — *see* Foreign body, in-
        traocular
    eyelid 930.1
      retained or old 374.86
    frontal sinus 932
    gastrointestinal tract 938
    genitourinary tract 939.9
    globe 930.8
      penetrating 871.6
        magnetic 871.5
          retained or old 360.50
        retained or old 360.60
    gum 935.0
    Highmore's antrum 932
    hypopharynx 933.0
    ileocecal coil 936
    ileum 936
    inspiration (of) 933.1
    intestine (large) (small) 936
    lacrimal apparatus, duct, gland, or sac
      930.2
    larynx 933.1
    lung 934.8
    maxillary sinus 932
    mouth 935.0
    nasal sinus 932
    nasopharynx 933.0
    nose (passage) 932
    nostril 932
    oral cavity 935.0
    palate 935.0
    penis 939.3
    pharynx 933.0
    pyriform sinus 933.0
    rectosigmoid 937
      junction 937
    rectum 937
    respiratory tract 934.9
      specified part NEC 934.8
    sclera 930.1
    sinus 932
      accessory 932
      frontal 932
      maxillary 932
      nasal 932
      pyriform 933.0
    small intestine 936
    stomach (hairball) 935.2
    suffocation by (*see also* Asphyxia, food)
      933.1
    swallowed 938
      tongue 933.0
    tear ducts or glands 930.2
    throat 933.0
    tongue 935.0
      swallowed 933.0
    tonsil, tonsillar 933.0
      fossa 933.0
    trachea 934.0
    ureter 939.0
    urethra 939.0
    uterus (any part) 939.1
    vagina 939.2
    vulva 939.2
    wind pipe 934.0
  feeling of, in throat 784.99
  granuloma (old) 728.82
    bone 733.99
    in operative wound (inadvertently left)
      998.4
      due to surgical material intentionally
        left — *see* Complications, due
        to (presence of) any device,
        implant, or graft classified to
        996.0–996.5 NEC
    muscle 728.82
    skin 709.4
    soft tissue 709.4
    subcutaneous tissue 709.4

Foreign body — *continued*
  in
    bone (residual) 733.99
    open wound — *see* Wound, open, by
      site
    soft tissue (residual) 729.6
    site complicated
  inadvertently left in operation wound
    (causing adhesions, obstruction, or
    perforation) 998.4
  ingestion, ingested NEC 938
  inhalation or inspiration (*see also* Asphyxia,
    food) 933.1
  internal organ, not entering through an
    orifice — *see* Injury, internal, by site,
    with open wound
  intraocular (nonmagnetic) 871.6
    combined sites 871.6
      magnetic 871.5
        retained or old 360.59
      retained or old 360.69
    magnetic 871.5
      retained or old 360.50
    retained or old 360.60
    specified site NEC 871.6
      magnetic 871.5
        retained or old 360.59
      retained or old 360.69
    iris (nonmagnetic) 871.6
      magnetic 871.5
        retained or old 360.52
      retained or old 360.62
    lens (nonmagnetic) 871.6
      magnetic 871.5
        retained or old 360.53
      retained or old 360.63
    lid, eye 930.1
    ocular muscle 870.4
      retained or old 376.6
    old or residual
      bone 733.99
      eyelid 374.86
      middle ear 385.83
      muscle 729.6
        ocular 376.6
      retrobulbar 376.6
      skin 729.6
        with granuloma 709.4
      soft tissue 729.6
        with granuloma 709.4
      subcutaneous tissue 729.6
        with granuloma 709.4
    operation wound, left accidentally 998.4
    orbit 870.4
      retained or old 376.6
    posterior wall, eye 871.6
      magnetic 871.5
        retained or old 360.55
      retained or old 360.65
    respiratory tree 934.9
      specified site NEC 934.8
    retained (old) (nonmagnetic) (in) V90.9
      anterior chamber (eye) 360.61
        magnetic 360.51
      ciliary body 360.62
        magnetic 360.52
      eyelid 374.86
      fragment(s)
        acrylics V90.2
        animal quills V90.31
        animal spines V90.31
        cement V90.83
        concrete V90.83
        crystalline V90.83
        depleted
          isotope V90.09
          uranium V90.01
        diethylhexylphthalates V90.2
        glass V90.81
        isocyanate V90.2
        metal V90.10
          magnetic V90.11
          nonmagnetic V90.12
        organic NEC V90.39
        plastic V90.2
        radioactive
          nontherapeutic V90.09

Foreign body — *continued*
  retained — *continued*
    fragment(s) — *continued*
      radioactive — *continued*
        specified NEC V90.09
      stone V90.83
      tooth V90.32
      wood V90.33
    globe 360.60
      magnetic 360.50
    intraocular 360.60
      magnetic 360.50
      specified site NEC 360.69
        magnetic 360.59
    iris 360.62
      magnetic 360.52
    lens 360.63
      magnetic 360.53
    muscle 729.6
    orbit 376.6
    posterior wall of globe 360.65
      magnetic 360.55
    retina 360.65
      magnetic 360.55
    retrobulbar 376.6
    skin 729.6
      with granuloma 709.4
    soft tissue 729.6
      with granuloma 709.4
    specified NEC V90.89
    subcutaneous tissue 729.6
      with granuloma 709.4
    vitreous 360.64
      magnetic 360.54
  retina 871.6
    magnetic 871.5
      retained or old 360.55
    retained or old 360.65
  superficial, without major open wound (*see*
    also Injury, superficial, by site) 919.6
  swallowed NEC 938
  throat, feeling of 784.99
  vitreous (humor) 871.6
    magnetic 871.5
      retained or old 360.54
    retained or old 360.64

Forking, aqueduct of Sylvius 742.3
  with spina bifida (*see also* Spina bifida)
    741.0 ☑
Formation
  bone in scar tissue (skin) 709.3
  connective tissue in vitreous 379.25
  Elschnig pearls (postcataract extraction)
    366.51
  hyaline in cornea 371.49
  sequestrum in bone (due to infection) (*see*
    also Osteomyelitis) 730.1 ☑
  valve
    colon, congenital 751.5
    ureter (congenital) 753.29
Formication 782.0
Fort Bragg fever 100.89
Fossa — *see also* condition
  pyriform — *see* condition
Foster care (status) V60.81
Foster-Kennedy syndrome 377.04
Fothergill's
  disease, meaning scarlatina anginosa 034.1
  neuralgia (*see also* Neuralgia, trigeminal)
    350.1
Foul breath 784.99
Found dead (cause unknown) 798.9
Foundling V20.0
Fournier's disease (idiopathic gangrene)
  608.83
  female 616.89
Fourth
  cranial nerve — *see* condition
  disease 057.8
  molar 520.1
Foville's syndrome 344.89
Fox's
  disease (apocrine miliaria) 705.82
  impetigo (contagiosa) 684
Fox-Fordyce disease (apocrine miliaria) 705.82

Fracture (abduction) (adduction) (avulsion)
  (compression) (crush) (dislocation)
  (oblique) (separation) (closed) 829.0

> *Note* — For fracture of any of the fol-
> lowing sites with fracture of other bones
> — *see* Fracture, multiple.
>
> "Closed" includes the following descrip-
> tions of fractures, with or without de-
> layed healing, unless they are specified
> as open or compound:
>
> | | |
> |---|---|
> | comminuted | linear |
> | depressed | simple |
> | elevated | slipped epiphysis |
> | fissured | spiral |
> | greenstick | unspecified |
> | impacted | |
>
> "Open" includes the following descrip-
> tions of fractures, with or without de-
> layed healing:
>
> | | |
> |---|---|
> | compound | puncture |
> | infected | with foreign body |
> | missile | |
>
> For late effect of fracture, see Late, ef-
> fect, fracture, by site.

  with
    internal injuries in same region (condi-
      tions classifiable to 860–869) (*see*
      also Injury, internal, by site)
    pelvic region — *see* Fracture, pelvis
  acetabulum (with visceral injury) (closed)
    808.0
    open 808.1
  acromion (process) (closed) 811.01
    open 811.11
  alveolus (closed) 802.8
    open 802.9
  ankle (malleolus) (closed) 824.8
    bimalleolar (Dupuytren's) (Pott's) 824.4
      open 824.5
    bone 825.21
      open 825.31
    lateral malleolus only (fibular) 824.2
      open 824.3
    medial malleolus only (tibial) 824.0
      open 824.1
    open 824.9
    pathologic 733.16
    talus 825.21
      open 825.31
    trimalleolar 824.6
      open 824.7
  antrum — *see* Fracture, skull, base
  arm (closed) 818.0
    and leg(s) (any bones) 828.0
      open 828.1
    both (any bones) (with rib(s)) (with ster-
      num) 819.0
      open 819.1
    lower 813.80
      open 813.90
    open 818.1
    upper — *see* Fracture, humerus
  astragalus (closed) 825.21
    open 825.31
  atlas — *see* Fracture, vertebra, cervical, first
  axis — *see* Fracture, vertebra, cervical, sec-
    ond
  back — *see* Fracture, vertebra, by site
  Barton's — *see* Fracture, radius, lower end
  basal (skull) — *see* Fracture, skull, base
  Bennett's (closed) 815.01
    open 815.11
  bimalleolar (closed) 824.4
    open 824.5
  bone (closed) NEC 829.0
    birth injury NEC 767.3
    open 829.1
    pathologic NEC (*see also* Fracture,
      pathologic) 733.10

☑ **Additional Digit Required** — Refer to the Tabular List for Digit Selection   ▽ **Subterms under main terms may continue to next column or page**

120 — Volume 2   ►◄ **Revised Text**   ● **New Line**   ▲ **Revised Code**   2015 ICD-9-CM

Fracture — *continued*
- bone — *continued*
  - stress NEC (*see also* Fracture, stress) 733.95
  - boot top — *see* Fracture, fibula
  - boxers' — *see* Fracture, metacarpal bone(s)
  - breast bone — *see* Fracture, sternum
  - bucket handle (semilunar cartilage) — *see* Tear, meniscus
  - buckle — *see* Fracture, torus
  - burst — *see* Fracture, traumatic, by site
  - bursting — *see* Fracture, phalanx, hand, distal
- calcaneus (closed) 825.0
  - open 825.1
- capitate (bone) (closed) 814.07
  - open 814.17
- capitellum (humerus) (closed) 812.49
  - open 812.59
- carpal bone(s) (wrist NEC) (closed) 814.00
  - open 814.10
  - specified site NEC 814.09
    - open 814.19
- cartilage, knee (semilunar) — *see* Tear, meniscus
- cervical — *see* Fracture, vertebra, cervical
- chauffeur's — *see* Fracture, ulna, lower end
- chisel — *see* Fracture, radius, upper end
- chronic — *see* Fracture, pathologic
- clavicle (interligamentous part) (closed) 810.00
  - acromial end 810.03
    - open 810.13
  - due to birth trauma 767.2
  - open 810.10
  - shaft (middle third) 810.02
    - open 810.12
  - sternal end 810.01
    - open 810.11
- clayshovelers' — *see* Fracture, vertebra, cervical
- coccyx (*see also* Fracture, vertebra, coccyx)
  - complicating delivery 665.6 ☑
- collar bone — *see* Fracture, clavicle
- Colles' (reversed) (closed) 813.41
  - open 813.51
- comminuted — *see* Fracture, by site
- compression (*see also* Fracture, by site)
  - nontraumatic — *see* Fracture, pathologic
- congenital 756.9
- coracoid process (closed) 811.02
  - open 811.12
- coronoid process (ulna) (closed) 813.02
  - mandible (closed) 802.23
    - open 802.33
  - open 813.12
- corpus cavernosum penis 959.13
- costochondral junction — *see* Fracture, rib
- costosternal junction — *see* Fracture, rib
- cranium — *see* Fracture, skull, by site
- cricoid cartilage (closed) 807.5
  - open 807.6
- cuboid (ankle) (closed) 825.23
  - open 825.33
- cuneiform
  - foot (closed) 825.24
    - open 825.34
  - wrist (closed) 814.03
    - open 814.13
- dental implant 525.73
- dental restorative material
  - with loss of material 525.64
  - without loss of material 525.63
- due to
  - birth injury — *see* Birth injury, fracture
  - gunshot — *see* Fracture, by site, open
  - neoplasm — *see* Fracture, pathologic
  - osteoporosis — *see* Fracture, pathologic
- Dupuytren's (ankle) (fibula) (closed) 824.4
  - open 824.5
  - radius 813.42
    - open 813.52
- Duverney's — *see* Fracture, ilium
- elbow (*see also* Fracture, humerus, lower end)
  - olecranon (process) (closed) 813.01

Fracture — *continued*
- elbow (*see also* Fracture, humerus, lower end) — *continued*
  - olecranon — *continued*
    - open 813.11
  - supracondylar (closed) 812.41
    - open 812.51
- ethmoid (bone) (sinus) — *see* Fracture, skull, base
- face bone(s) (closed) NEC 802.8
  - with
    - other bone(s) — *see* Fracture, multiple, skull
    - skull (*see also* Fracture, skull)
      - involving other bones — *see* Fracture, multiple, skull
  - open 802.9
- fatigue — *see* Fracture, march
- femur, femoral (closed) 821.00
  - cervicotrochanteric 820.03
    - open 820.13
  - condyles, epicondyles 821.21
    - open 821.31
  - distal end — *see* Fracture, femur, lower end
  - epiphysis (separation)
    - capital 820.01
      - open 820.11
    - head 820.01
      - open 820.11
    - lower 821.22
      - open 821.32
    - trochanteric 820.01
      - open 820.11
    - upper 820.01
      - open 820.11
  - head 820.09
    - open 820.19
  - lower end or extremity (distal end) (closed) 821.20
    - condyles, epicondyles 821.21
      - open 821.31
    - epiphysis (separation) 821.22
      - open 821.32
    - multiple sites 821.29
      - open 821.39
    - open 821.30
    - specified site NEC 821.29
      - open 821.39
    - supracondylar 821.23
      - open 821.33
    - T-shaped 821.21
      - open 821.31
  - neck (closed) 820.8
    - base (cervicotrochanteric) 820.03
      - open 820.13
    - extracapsular 820.20
      - open 820.30
    - intertrochanteric (section) 820.21
      - open 820.31
    - intracapsular 820.00
      - open 820.10
    - intratrochanteric 820.21
      - open 820.31
    - midcervical 820.02
      - open 820.12
    - open 820.9
    - pathologic 733.14
      - specified part NEC 733.15
    - specified site NEC 820.09
      - open 820.19
    - stress 733.96
    - transcervical 820.02
      - open 820.12
    - transtrochanteric 820.20
      - open 820.30
  - open 821.10
  - pathologic 733.14
    - specified part NEC 733.15
  - peritrochanteric (section) 820.20
    - open 820.30
  - shaft (lower third) (middle third) (upper third) 821.01
    - open 821.11
    - stress 733.97
  - subcapital 820.09

Fracture — *continued*
- femur, femoral — *continued*
  - subcapital — *continued*
    - open 820.19
    - subtrochanteric (region) (section) 820.22
      - open 820.32
    - supracondylar 821.23
      - open 821.33
    - transepiphyseal 820.01
      - open 820.11
    - trochanter (greater) (lesser) (*see also* Fracture, femur, neck, by site) 820.20
      - open 820.30
    - T-shaped, into knee joint 821.21
      - open 821.31
    - upper end 820.8
      - open 820.9
- fibula (closed) 823.81
  - with tibia 823.82
    - open 823.92
  - distal end 824.8
    - open 824.9
  - epiphysis
    - lower 824.8
      - open 824.9
    - upper — *see* Fracture, fibula, upper end
  - head — *see* Fracture, fibula, upper end
  - involving ankle 824.2
    - open 824.3
  - lower end or extremity 824.8
    - open 824.9
  - malleolus (external) (lateral) 824.2
    - open 824.3
  - open NEC 823.91
  - pathologic 733.16
  - proximal end — *see* Fracture, fibula, upper end
  - shaft 823.21
    - with tibia 823.22
      - open 823.32
    - open 823.31
  - stress 733.93
  - torus 823.41
    - with tibia 823.42
  - upper end or extremity (epiphysis) (head) (proximal end) (styloid) 823.01
    - with tibia 823.02
      - open 823.12
    - open 823.11
- finger(s), of one hand (closed) (*see also* Fracture, phalanx, hand) 816.00
  - with
    - metacarpal bone(s), of same hand 817.0
      - open 817.1
    - thumb of same hand 816.03
      - open 816.13
  - open 816.10
- foot, except toe(s) alone (closed) 825.20
  - open 825.30
- forearm (closed) NEC 813.80
  - lower end (distal end) (lower epiphysis) 813.40
    - open 813.50
  - open 813.90
  - shaft 813.20
    - open 813.30
  - upper end (proximal end) (upper epiphysis) 813.00
    - open 813.10
- fossa, anterior, middle, or posterior — *see* Fracture, skull, base
- Fracture (abduction) (adduction) (avulsion) (compression) (crush) (dislocation) (oblique) (separation) (closed) 829.0
- frontal (bone) (*see also* Fracture, skull, vault)
  - sinus — *see* Fracture, skull, base
- Galeazzi's — *see* Fracture, radius, lower end
- glenoid (cavity) (fossa) (scapula) (closed) 811.03
  - open 811.13
- Gosselin's — *see* Fracture, ankle
- greenstick — *see* Fracture, by site

Fracture — *continued*
- grenade-throwers' — *see* Fracture, humerus, shaft
- gutter — *see* Fracture, skull, vault
- hamate (closed) 814.08
  - open 814.18
- hand, one (closed) 815.00
  - carpals 814.00
    - open 814.10
    - specified site NEC 814.09
      - open 814.19
  - metacarpals 815.00
    - open 815.10
  - multiple, bones of one hand 817.0
    - open 817.1
  - open 815.10
  - phalanges (*see also* Fracture, phalanx, hand) 816.00
    - open 816.10
- healing
  - aftercare (*see also* Aftercare, fracture) V54.89
  - change of cast V54.89
  - complications — *see* condition
  - convalescence V66.4
  - removal of
    - cast V54.89
    - fixation device
      - external V54.89
      - internal V54.01
- heel bone (closed) 825.0
  - open 825.1
- Hill-Sachs 812.09
- hip (closed) (*see also* Fracture, femur, neck) 820.8
  - open 820.9
  - pathologic 733.14
- humerus (closed) 812.20
  - anatomical neck 812.02
    - open 812.12
  - articular process (*see also* Fracture humerus, condyle(s)) 812.44
    - open 812.54
  - capitellum 812.49
    - open 812.59
  - condyle(s) 812.44
    - lateral (external) 812.42
      - open 812.52
    - medial (internal epicondyle) 812.43
      - open 812.53
    - open 812.54
  - distal end — *see* Fracture, humerus, lower end
  - epiphysis
    - lower (*see also* Fracture, humerus, condyle(s)) 812.44
      - open 812.54
    - upper 812.09
      - open 812.19
  - external condyle 812.42
    - open 812.52
  - great tuberosity 812.03
    - open 812.13
  - head 812.09
    - open 812.19
  - internal epicondyle 812.43
    - open 812.53
  - lesser tuberosity 812.09
    - open 812.19
  - lower end or extremity (distal end) (*see also* Fracture, humerus, by site) 812.40
    - multiple sites NEC 812.49
      - open 812.59
    - open 812.50
    - specified site NEC 812.49
      - open 812.59
  - neck 812.01
    - open 812.11
  - open 812.30
  - pathologic 733.11
  - proximal end — *see* Fracture, humerus, upper end
  - shaft 812.21
    - open 812.31
  - supracondylar 812.41

☑ **Additional Digit Required** — Refer to the Tabular List for Digit Selection   ▽ **Subterms under main terms may continue to next column or page**

Fracture — *continued*

humerus — *continued*

supracondylar — *continued*

open 812.51

surgical neck 812.01

open 812.11

trochlea 812.49

open 812.59

T-shaped 812.44

open 812.54

tuberosity — *see* Fracture, humerus, upper end

upper end or extremity (proximal end) (*see also* Fracture, humerus, by site) 812.00

open 812.10

specified site NEC 812.09

open 812.19

hyoid bone (closed) 807.5

open 807.6

hyperextension — *see* Fracture, radius, lower end

ilium (with visceral injury) (closed) 808.41

open 808.51

impaction, impacted — *see* Fracture, by site

incus — *see* Fracture, skull, base

innominate bone (with visceral injury) (closed) 808.49

open 808.59

instep, of one foot (closed) 825.20

with toe(s) of same foot 827.0

open 827.1

open 825.30

insufficiency — *see* Fracture, pathologic, by site

internal

ear — *see* Fracture, skull, base

semilunar cartilage, knee — *see* Tear, meniscus, medial

intertrochanteric — *see* Fracture, femur, neck, intertrochanteric

ischium (with visceral injury) (closed) 808.42

open 808.52

jaw (bone) (lower) (closed) (*see also* Fracture, mandible) 802.20

angle 802.25

open 802.35

open 802.30

upper — *see* Fracture, maxilla

knee

cap (closed) 822.0

open 822.1

cartilage (semilunar) — *see* Tear, meniscus

labyrinth (osseous) — *see* Fracture, skull, base

larynx (closed) 807.5

open 807.6

late effect — *see* Late, effects (of), fracture

Le Fort's — *see* Fracture, maxilla

leg (closed) 827.0

with rib(s) or sternum 828.0

open 828.1

both (any bones) 828.0

open 828.1

lower — *see* Fracture, tibia

open 827.1

upper — *see* Fracture, femur

limb

lower (multiple) (closed) NEC 827.0

open 827.1

upper (multiple) (closed) NEC 818.0

open 818.1

long bones, due to birth trauma — *see* Birth injury, fracture

lower end or extremity (anterior lip) (posterior) 824.8

open 824.9

lumbar — *see* Fracture, vertebra, lumbar

lunate bone (closed) 814.02

open 814.12

malar bone (closed) 802.4

open 802.5

Malgaigne's (closed) 808.43

open 808.53

malleolus (closed) 824.8

Fracture — *continued*

malleolus — *continued*

bimalleolar 824.4

open 824.5

lateral 824.2

and medial (*see also* Fracture, malleolus, bimalleolar)

with lip of tibia — *see* Fracture, malleolus, trimalleolar

open 824.3

medial (closed) 824.0

and lateral (*see also* Fracture, malleolus, bimalleolar)

with lip of tibia — *see* Fracture, malleolus, trimalleolar

open 824.1

open 824.9

trimalleolar (closed) 824.6

open 824.7

malleus — *see* Fracture, skull, base

malunion 733.81

mandible (closed) 802.20

angle 802.25

open 802.35

body 802.28

alveolar border 802.27

open 802.37

open 802.38

symphysis 802.26

open 802.36

condylar process 802.21

open 802.31

coronoid process 802.23

open 802.33

multiple sites 802.29

open 802.39

open 802.30

ramus NEC 802.24

open 802.34

subcondylar 802.22

open 802.32

manubrium — *see* Fracture, sternum

march 733.95

femoral neck 733.96

fibula 733.93

metatarsals 733.94

pelvis 733.98

shaft of femur 733.97

tibia 733.93

maxilla, maxillary (superior) (upper jaw) (closed) 802.4

inferior — *see* Fracture, mandible

open 802.5

meniscus, knee — *see* Tear, meniscus

metacarpus, metacarpal (bone(s)), of one hand (closed) 815.00

with phalanx, phalanges, hand (finger(s)) (thumb) of same hand 817.0

open 817.1

base 815.02

first metacarpal 815.01

open 815.11

open 815.12

thumb 815.01

open 815.11

multiple sites 815.09

open 815.19

neck 815.04

open 815.14

open 815.10

shaft 815.03

open 815.13

metatarsus, metatarsal (bone(s)), of one foot (closed) 825.25

with tarsal bone(s) 825.29

open 825.39

open 825.35

Monteggia's (closed) 813.03

open 813.13

Moore's — *see* Fracture, radius, lower end

multangular bone (closed)

larger 814.05

open 814.15

smaller 814.06

open 814.16

Fracture — *continued*

multiple (closed) 829.0

Note — Multiple fractures of sites classifiable to the same three- or four-digit category are coded to that category, except for sites classifiable to 810–818 or 820–827 in different limbs.

Multiple fractures of sites classifiable to different fourth-digit subdivisions within the same three-digit category should be dealt with according to coding rules.

Multiple fractures of sites classifiable to different three-digit categories (identifiable from the listing under "Fracture"), and of sites classifiable to 810–818 or 820–827 in different limbs should be coded according to the following list, which should be referred to in the following priority order: skull or face bones, pelvis or vertebral column, legs, arms.

arm (multiple bones in same arm except in hand alone) (sites classifiable to 810–817 with sites classifiable to a different three-digit category in 810–817 in same arm) (closed) 818.0

open 818.1

arms, both or arm(s) with rib(s) or sternum (sites classifiable to 810–818 with sites classifiable to same range of categories in other limb or to 807) (closed) 819.0

open 819.1

bones of trunk NEC (closed) 809.0

open 809.1

hand, metacarpal bone(s) with phalanx or phalanges of same hand (sites classifiable to 815 with sites classifiable to 816 in same hand) (closed) 817.0

open 817.1

leg (multiple bones in same leg) (sites classifiable to 820–826 with sites classifiable to a different three-digit category in that range in same leg) (closed) 827.0

open 827.1

legs, both or leg(s) with arm(s), rib(s), or sternum (sites classifiable to 820–827 with sites classifiable to same range of categories in other leg or to 807 or 810–819) (closed) 828.0

open 828.1

open 829.1

pelvis with other bones except skull or face bones (sites classifiable to 808 with sites classifiable to 805–807 or 810–829) (closed) 809.0

open 809.1

Fracture — *continued*

multiple — *continued*

skull, specified or unspecified bones, or face bone(s) with any other bone(s) (sites classifiable to 800–803 with sites classifiable to 805–829) (closed) 804.0 ☑

Note — Use the following fifth-digit subclassification with categories 800, 801, 803, and 804:

0 *unspecified state of consciousness*

1 *with no loss of consciousness*

2 *with brief [less than one hour] loss of consciousness*

3 *with moderate [1–24 hours] loss of consciousness*

4 *with prolonged [more than 24 hours] loss of consciousness and return to pre-existing conscious level*

5 *with prolonged [more than 24 hours] loss of consciousness, without return to pre-existing conscious level*

Use fifth-digit 5 to designate when a patient is unconscious and dies before regaining consciousness, regardless of the duration of the loss of consciousness

6 *with loss of consciousness of unspecified duration*

9 *with concussion, unspecified*

with

contusion, cerebral 804.1 ☑

epidural hemorrhage 804.2 ☑

extradural hemorrhage 804.2 ☑

hemorrhage (intracranial) NEC 804.3 ☑

intracranial injury NEC 804.4 ☑

laceration, cerebral 804.1 ☑

subarachnoid hemorrhage 804.2 ☑

subdural hemorrhage 804.2 ☑

open 804.5 ☑

with

contusion, cerebral 804.6 ☑

epidural hemorrhage 804.7 ☑

extradural hemorrhage 804.7 ☑

hemorrhage (intracranial) NEC 804.8 ☑

intracranial injury NEC 804.9 ☑

laceration, cerebral 804.6 ☑

subarachnoid hemorrhage 804.7 ☑

subdural hemorrhage 804.7 ☑

vertebral column with other bones, except skull or face bones (sites classifiable to 805 or 806 with sites classifiable to 807–808 or 810–829) (closed) 809.0

open 809.1

nasal (bone(s)) (closed) 802.0

open 802.1

sinus — *see* Fracture, skull, base

navicular

carpal (wrist) (closed) 814.01

open 814.11

tarsal (ankle) (closed) 825.22

open 825.32

neck — *see* Fracture, vertebra, cervical

neural arch — *see* Fracture, vertebra, by site

nonunion 733.82

nose, nasal, (bone) (septum) (closed) 802.0

open 802.1

occiput — *see* Fracture, skull, base

odontoid process — *see* Fracture, vertebra, cervical

olecranon (process) (ulna) (closed) 813.01

☑ **Additional Digit Required** — Refer to the Tabular List for Digit Selection

▽ **Subterms under main terms may continue to next column or page**

▶◀ Revised Text   ● New Line   ▲ Revised Code

Fracture — *continued*
olecranon — *continued*
    open 813.11
  open 829.1
orbit, orbital (bone) (region) (closed) 802.8
  floor (blow-out) 802.6
    open 802.7
  open 802.9
  roof — *see* Fracture, skull, base
  specified part NEC 802.8
    open 802.9
os
  calcis (closed) 825.0
    open 825.1
  magnum (closed) 814.07
    open 814.17
  pubis (with visceral injury) (closed) 808.2
    open 808.3
  triquetrum (closed) 814.03
    open 814.13
osseous
  auditory meatus — *see* Fracture, skull, base
  labyrinth — *see* Fracture, skull, base
  ossicles, auditory (incus) (malleus) (stapes) — *see* Fracture, skull, base
osteoporotic — *see* Fracture, pathologic
palate (closed) 802.8
  open 802.9
paratrooper — *see* Fracture, tibia, lower end
parietal bone — *see* Fracture, skull, vault
parry — *see* Fracture, Monteggia's
patella (closed) 822.0
  open 822.1
pathologic (cause unknown) 733.10
  ankle 733.16
  femur (neck) 733.14
    specified NEC 733.15
  fibula 733.16
  hip 733.14
  humerus 733.11
  radius (distal) 733.12
  specified site NEC 733.19
  tibia 733.16
  ulna 733.12
  vertebrae (collapse) 733.13
  wrist 733.12
pedicle (of vertebral arch) — *see* Fracture, vertebra, by site
pelvis, pelvic (bone(s)) (with visceral injury) (closed) 808.8
  multiple
    with
      disruption of pelvic circle 808.43
        open 808.53
      disruption of pelvic ring 808.43
        open 808.53
    without
      disruption of pelvic circle 808.44
        open 808.54
      disruption of pelvic ring 808.44
        open 808.54
  open 808.9
  rim (closed) 808.49
    open 808.59
  stress 733.98
peritrochanteric (closed) 820.20
  open 820.30
phalanx, phalanges, of one
  foot (closed) 826.0
    with bone(s) of same lower limb 827.0
      open 827.1
    open 826.1
  hand (closed) 816.00
    with metacarpal bone(s) of same hand 817.0
      open 817.1
    distal 816.02
      open 816.12
    middle 816.01
      open 816.11
    multiple sites NEC 816.03
      open 816.13
    open 816.10
    proximal 816.01

Fracture — *continued*
phalanx, phalanges, of one — *continued*
  hand — *continued*
    proximal — *continued*
      open 816.11
pisiform (closed) 814.04
  open 814.14
pond — *see* Fracture, skull, vault
Pott's (closed) 824.4
  open 824.5
prosthetic device, internal — *see* Complications, mechanical
pubis (with visceral injury) (closed) 808.2
  open 808.3
Quervain's (closed) 814.01
  open 814.11
radius (alone) (closed) 813.81
  with ulna NEC 813.83
    open 813.93
  distal end — *see* Fracture, radius, lower end
  epiphysis
    lower — *see* Fracture, radius, lower end
    upper — *see* Fracture, radius, upper end
  head — *see* Fracture, radius, upper end
  lower end or extremity (distal end) (lower epiphysis) 813.42
    with ulna (lower end) 813.44
      open 813.54
    open 813.52
    torus 813.45
      with ulna 813.47
  neck — *see* Fracture, radius, upper end
  open NEC 813.91
  pathologic 733.12
  proximal end — *see* Fracture, radius, upper end
  shaft (closed) 813.21
    with ulna (shaft) 813.23
      open 813.33
    open 813.31
  upper end 813.07
    with ulna (upper end) 813.08
      open 813.18
    epiphysis 813.05
      open 813.15
    head 813.05
      open 813.15
    multiple sites 813.07
      open 813.17
    neck 813.06
      open 813.16
    open 813.17
    specified site NEC 813.07
      open 813.17
ramus
  inferior or superior (with visceral injury) (closed) 808.2
    open 808.3
  ischium — *see* Fracture, ischium
  mandible 802.24
    open 802.34
rib(s) (closed) 807.0 ☑

> *Note* — Use the following fifth-digit subclassification with categories 807.0–807.1:
>
> 0 rib(s), unspecified
> 1 one rib
> 2 two ribs
> 3 three ribs
> 4 four ribs
> 5 five ribs
> 6 six ribs
> 7 seven ribs
> 8 eight or more ribs
> 9 multiple ribs, unspecified

  with flail chest (open) 807.4
  open 807.1 ☑
root, tooth 873.63

Fracture — *continued*
root, tooth — *continued*
  complicated 873.73
sacrum — *see* Fracture, vertebra, sacrum
scaphoid
  ankle (closed) 825.22
    open 825.32
  wrist (closed) 814.01
    open 814.11
scapula (closed) 811.00
  acromial, acromion (process) 811.01
    open 811.11
  body 811.09
    open 811.19
  coracoid process 811.02
    open 811.12
  glenoid (cavity) (fossa) 811.03
    open 811.13
  neck 811.03
    open 811.13
  open 811.10
semilunar
  bone, wrist (closed) 814.02
    open 814.12
  cartilage (interior) (knee) — *see* Tear, meniscus
sesamoid bone — *see* Fracture, by site
Shepherd's (closed) 825.21
  open 825.31
shoulder (*see also* Fracture, humerus, upper end)
  blade — *see* Fracture, scapula
silverfork — *see* Fracture, radius, lower end
sinus (ethmoid) (frontal) (maxillary) (nasal) (sphenoidal) — *see* Fracture, skull, base
Skillern's — *see* Fracture, radius, shaft
skull (multiple NEC) (with face bones) (closed) 803.0 ☑

> *Note* — Use the following fifth-digit subclassification with categories 800, 801, 803, and 804:
>
> 0 unspecified state of consciousness
> 1 with no loss of consciousness
> 2 with brief [less than one hour] loss of consciousness
> 3 with moderate [1-24 hours] loss of consciousness
> 4 with prolonged [more than 24 hours] loss of consciousness and return to pre-existing conscious level
> 5 with prolonged [more than 24 hours] loss of consciousness, without return to pre-existing conscious level
>
> Use fifth-digit 5 to designate when a patient is unconscious and dies before regaining consciousness, regardless of the duration of the loss of consciousness
>
> 6 with loss of consciousness of unspecified duration
> 9 with concussion, unspecified

  with
    contusion, cerebral 803.1 ☑
    epidural hemorrhage 803.2 ☑
    extradural hemorrhage 803.2 ☑
    hemorrhage (intracranial) NEC 803.3 ☑
    intracranial injury NEC 803.4 ☑
    laceration, cerebral 803.1 ☑
    other bones — *see* Fracture, multiple, skull
    subarachnoid hemorrhage 803.2 ☑
    subdural hemorrhage 803.2 ☑
  base (antrum) (ethmoid bone) (fossa) (internal ear) (nasal sinus) (occiput) (sphenoid) (temporal bone) (closed) 801.0 ☑

Fracture — *continued*
skull — *continued*
  base — *continued*
    with
      contusion, cerebral 801.1 ☑
      epidural hemorrhage 801.2 ☑
      extradural hemorrhage 801.2 ☑
      hemorrhage (intracranial) NEC 801.3 ☑
      intracranial injury NEC 801.4 ☑
      laceration, cerebral 801.1 ☑
      subarachnoid hemorrhage 801.2 ☑
      subdural hemorrhage 801.2 ☑
    open 801.5 ☑
      with
        contusion, cerebral 801.6 ☑
        epidural hemorrhage 801.7 ☑
        extradural hemorrhage 801.7 ☑
        hemorrhage (intracranial) NEC 801.8 ☑
        intracranial injury NEC 801.9 ☑
        laceration, cerebral 801.6 ☑
        subarachnoid hemorrhage 801.7 ☑
        subdural hemorrhage 801.7 ☑
  birth injury 767.3
  face bones — *see* Fracture, face bones
  open 803.5 ☑
    with
      contusion, cerebral 803.6 ☑
      epidural hemorrhage 803.7 ☑
      extradural hemorrhage 803.7 ☑
      hemorrhage (intracranial) NEC 803.8 ☑
      intracranial injury NEC 803.9 ☑
      laceration, cerebral 803.6 ☑
      subarachnoid hemorrhage 803.7 ☑
      subdural hemorrhage 803.7 ☑
  vault (frontal bone) (parietal bone) (vertex) (closed) 800.0 ☑
    with
      contusion, cerebral 800.1 ☑
      epidural hemorrhage 800.2 ☑
      extradural hemorrhage 800.2 ☑
      hemorrhage (intracranial) NEC 800.3 ☑
      intracranial injury NEC 800.4 ☑
      laceration, cerebral 800.1 ☑
      subarachnoid hemorrhage 800.2 ☑
      subdural hemorrhage 800.2 ☑
    open 800.5 ☑
      with
        contusion, cerebral 800.6 ☑
        epidural hemorrhage 800.7 ☑
        extradural hemorrhage 800.7 ☑
        hemorrhage (intracranial) NEC 800.8 ☑
        intracranial injury NEC 800.9 ☑
        laceration, cerebral 800.6 ☑
        subarachnoid hemorrhage 800.7 ☑
        subdural hemorrhage 800.7 ☑
Smith's 813.41
  open 813.51
sphenoid (bone) (sinus) — *see* Fracture, skull, base
spine (*see also* Fracture, vertebra, by site due to birth trauma) 767.4
spinous process — *see* Fracture, vertebra, by site
spontaneous — *see* Fracture, pathologic
sprinters' — *see* Fracture, ilium
stapes — *see* Fracture, skull, base

Fracture — continued

stave (see also Fracture, metacarpus, metacarpal bone(s))
  spine — see Fracture, tibia, upper end
sternum (closed) 807.2
  with flail chest (open) 807.4
  open 807.3
Stieda's — see Fracture, femur, lower end
stress 733.95
  femoral neck 733.96
  fibula 733.93
  metatarsals 733.94
  pelvis 733.98
  shaft of femur 733.97
  specified site NEC 733.95
  tibia 733.93
styloid process
  metacarpal (closed) 815.02
    open 815.12
  radius — see Fracture, radius, lower end
  temporal bone — see Fracture, skull, base
  ulna — see Fracture, ulna, lower end
supracondylar, elbow 812.41
  open 812.51
symphysis pubis (with visceral injury) (closed) 808.2
  open 808.3
talus (ankle bone) (closed) 825.21
  open 825.31
tarsus, tarsal bone(s) (with metatarsus) of one foot (closed) NEC 825.29
  open 825.39
temporal bone (styloid) — see Fracture, skull, base
tendon — see Sprain, by site
thigh — see Fracture, femur, shaft
thumb (and finger(s)) of one hand (closed) (see also Fracture, phalanx, hand) 816.00
  with metacarpal bone(s) of same hand 817.0
    open 817.1
  metacarpal(s) — see Fracture, metacarpus
  open 816.10
thyroid cartilage (closed) 807.5
  open 807.6
tibia (closed) 823.80
  with fibula 823.82
    open 823.92
  condyles — see Fracture, tibia, upper end
  distal end 824.8
    open 824.9
  epiphysis
    lower 824.8
      open 824.9
    upper — see Fracture, tibia, upper end
  head (involving knee joint) — see Fracture, tibia, upper end
  intercondyloid eminence — see Fracture, tibia, upper end
  involving ankle 824.0
    open 824.9
  lower end or extremity (anterior lip) (posterior lip) 824.8
    open 824.9
  malleolus (internal) (medial) 824.0
    open 824.1
  open NEC 823.90
  pathologic 733.16
  proximal end — see Fracture, tibia, upper end
  shaft 823.20
    with fibula 823.22
      open 823.32
    open 823.30
  spine — see Fracture, tibia, upper end
  stress 733.93
  torus 823.40
    with fibula 823.42
  tuberosity — see Fracture, tibia, upper end

Fracture — continued

tibia — continued
  upper end or extremity (condyle) (epiphysis) (head) (spine) (proximal end) (tuberosity) 823.00
    with fibula 823.02
      open 823.12
    open 823.10
toe(s), of one foot (closed) 826.0
  with bone(s) of same lower limb 827.0
    open 827.1
  open 826.1
tooth (root) 873.63
  complicated 873.73
torus
  fibula 823.41
    with tibia 823.42
  humerus 812.49
  radius (alone) 813.45
    with ulna 813.47
  tibia 823.40
    with fibula 823.42
  ulna (alone) 813.46
    with radius 813.47
trachea (closed) 807.5
  open 807.6
transverse process — see Fracture, vertebra, by site
trapezium (closed) 814.05
  open 814.15
trapezoid bone (closed) 814.06
  open 814.16
trimalleolar (closed) 824.6
  open 824.7
triquetral (bone) (closed) 814.03
  open 814.13
trochanter (greater) (lesser) (closed) (see also Fracture, femur, neck, by site) 820.20
  open 820.30
trunk (bones) (closed) 809.0
  open 809.1
tuberosity (external) — see Fracture, by site
ulna (alone) (closed) 813.82
  with radius NEC 813.83
    open 813.93
  coronoid process (closed) 813.02
    open 813.12
  distal end — see Fracture, ulna, lower end
  epiphysis
    lower — see Fracture, ulna, lower end
    upper — see Fracture, ulna, upper end
  head — see Fracture, ulna, lower end
  lower end (distal end) (head) (lower epiphysis) (styloid process) 813.43
    with radius (lower end) 813.44
      open 813.54
    open 813.53
  olecranon process (closed) 813.01
    open 813.11
  open NEC 813.92
  pathologic 733.12
  proximal end — see Fracture, ulna, upper end
  shaft 813.22
    with radius (shaft) 813.23
      open 813.33
    open 813.32
  styloid process — see Fracture, ulna, lower end
  torus 813.46
    with radius 813.47
  transverse — see Fracture, ulna, by site
  upper end (epiphysis) 813.04
    with radius (upper end) 813.08
      open 813.18
    multiple sites 813.04
      open 813.14
    specified site NEC 813.04
      open 813.14
unciform (closed) 814.08
  open 814.18

Fracture — continued

vertebra, vertebral (back) (body) (column) (neural arch) (pedicle) (spine) (spinous process) (transverse process) (closed) 805.8
  with
    hematomyelia — see Fracture, vertebra, by site, with spinal cord injury
    injury to
      cauda equina — see Fracture, vertebra, sacrum, with spinal cord injury
      nerve — see Fracture, vertebra, by site, with spinal cord injury
    paralysis — see Fracture, vertebra, by site, with spinal cord injury
    paraplegia — see Fracture, vertebra, by site, with spinal cord injury
    quadriplegia — see Fracture, vertebra, by site, with spinal cord injury
    spinal concussion — see Fracture, vertebra, by site, with spinal cord injury
    spinal cord injury (closed) NEC 806.8

> *Note* — Use the following fifth-digit subclassification with categories 806.0–806.3:
>
> C_1–C_4 or unspecified level and D_1–D_6 (T_1–T_6) or unspecified level with
>
> 0   unspecified spinal cord injury
> 1   complete lesion of cord
> 2   anterior cord syndrome
> 3   central cord syndrome
> 4   specified injury NEC
>
> C_5–C_7 level and D_7–D_{12} level with:
>
> 5   unspecified spinal cord injury
> 6   complete lesion of cord
> 7   anterior cord syndrome
> 8   central cord syndrome
> 9   specified injury NEC

      cervical 806.0 ☑
        open 806.1 ☑
      dorsal, dorsolumbar 806.2 ☑
        open 806.3 ☑
        open 806.9
      thoracic, thoracolumbar 806.2 ☑
        open 806.3 ☑
  atlanto-axial — see Fracture, vertebra, cervical
  cervical (hangman) (teardrop) (closed) 805.00
    with spinal cord injury — see Fracture, vertebra, with spinal cord injury, cervical
    first (atlas) 805.01
      open 805.11
    second (axis) 805.02
      open 805.12
    third 805.03
      open 805.13
    fourth 805.04
      open 805.14
    fifth 805.05
      open 805.15
    sixth 805.06
      open 805.16
    seventh 805.07
      open 805.17
    multiple sites 805.08
      open 805.18
    open 805.10
  chronic 733.13
  coccyx (closed) 805.6
    with spinal cord injury (closed) 806.60
      cauda equina injury 806.62

Fracture — continued

vertebra, vertebral — continued
  coccyx — continued
    with spinal cord injury — continued
      cauda equina injury — continued
        complete lesion 806.61
          open 806.71
        open 806.72
      open 806.70
      specified type NEC 806.69
        open 806.79
    open 805.7
  collapsed 733.13
  compression, not due to trauma 733.13
  dorsal (closed) 805.2
    with spinal cord injury — see Fracture, vertebra, with spinal cord injury, dorsal
    open 805.3
  dorsolumbar (closed) 805.2
    with spinal cord injury — see Fracture, vertebra, with spinal cord injury, dorsal
    open 805.3
  due to osteoporosis 733.13
  fetus or newborn 767.4
  lumbar (closed) 805.4
    with spinal cord injury (closed) 806.4
      open 806.5
    open 805.5
  nontraumatic 733.13
  open NEC 805.9
  pathologic (any site) 733.13
  sacrum (closed) 805.6
    with spinal cord injury 806.60
      cauda equina injury 806.62
        complete lesion 806.61
          open 806.71
        open 806.72
      open 806.70
      specified type NEC 806.69
        open 806.79
    open 805.7
  site unspecified (closed) 805.8
    with spinal cord injury (closed) 806.8
      open 806.9
    open 805.9
  stress (any site) 733.95
  thoracic (closed) 805.2
    with spinal cord injury — see Fracture, vertebra, with spinal cord injury, thoracic
    open 805.3
  vertex — see Fracture, skull, vault
  vomer (bone) 802.0
    open 802.1
  Wagstaffe's — see Fracture, ankle
  wrist (closed) 814.00
    open 814.10
    pathologic 733.12
  xiphoid (process) — see Fracture, sternum
  zygoma (zygomatic arch) (closed) 802.4
    open 802.5

Fragile X syndrome 759.83
Fragilitas
  crinium 704.2
  hair 704.2
  ossium 756.51
    with blue sclera 756.51
  unguium 703.8
    congenital 757.5
Fragility
  bone 756.51
    with deafness and blue sclera 756.51
  capillary (hereditary) 287.8
  hair 704.2
  nails 703.8
Fragmentation — see Fracture, by site
Frailty 797
Frambesia, frambesial (tropica) — see also Yaws 102.9
  initial lesion or ulcer 102.0
  primary 102.0

☑ **Additional Digit Required** — Refer to the Tabular List for Digit Selection   ▽ **Subterms under main terms may continue to next column or page**

124 — Volume 2   ▶◀ Revised Text   ● New Line   ▲ Revised Code   2015 ICD-9-CM

Frambeside
  gummatous 102.4
  of early yaws 102.2
Frambesioma 102.1
Franceschetti's syndrome (mandibulofacial dysostosis) 756.0
Francis' disease — *see also* Tularemia 021.9
Franklin's disease (heavy chain) 273.2
Frank's essential thrombocytopenia — *see also* Purpura, thrombocytopenic 287.39
Fraser's syndrome 759.89
Freckle 709.09
  malignant melanoma in (M8742/3) — *see* Melanoma
  melanotic (of Hutchinson) (M8742/2) — *see* Neoplasm, skin, in situ
  retinal 239.81
Freeman-Sheldon syndrome 759.89
Freezing 991.9
  specified effect NEC 991.8
Freiberg's
  disease (osteochondrosis, second metatarsal) 732.5
  infraction of metatarsal head 732.5
  osteochondrosis 732.5
Frei's disease (climatic bubo) 099.1
Fremitus, friction, cardiac 785.3
Frenulum linguae 750.0
Frenum
  external os 752.44
  tongue 750.0
Frequency (urinary) NEC 788.41
  micturition 788.41
  nocturnal 788.43
  polyuria 788.42
  psychogenic 306.53
Frey's syndrome (auriculotemporal syndrome) 705.22
Friction
  burn (*see also* Injury, superficial, by site) 919.0
  fremitus, cardiac 785.3
  precordial 785.3
  sounds, chest 786.7
Friderichsen-Waterhouse syndrome or disease 036.3
Friedländer's
  B (bacillus) NEC (*see also* condition) 041.3
    sepsis or septicemia 038.49
  disease (endarteritis obliterans) — *see* Arteriosclerosis
Friedreich's
  ataxia 334.0
  combined systemic disease 334.0
  disease 333.2
    combined systemic 334.0
  myoclonia 333.2
  sclerosis (spinal cord) 334.0
Friedrich-Erb-Arnold syndrome (acropachyderma) 757.39
Frigidity 302.72
  psychic or psychogenic 302.72
Fröhlich's disease or syndrome (adiposogenital dystrophy) 253.8
Froin's syndrome 336.8
Frommel-Chiari syndrome 676.6 ☑
Frommel's disease 676.6 ☑
Frontal — *see also* condition
  lobe syndrome 310.0

Frostbite 991.3
  face 991.0
  foot 991.2
  hand 991.1
  specified site NEC 991.3
Frotteurism 302.89
Frozen 991.9
  pelvis 620.8
  shoulder 726.0
Fructosemia 271.2
Fructosuria (benign) (essential) 271.2
Fuchs'
  black spot (myopic) 360.21
  corneal dystrophy (endothelial) 371.57
  heterochromic cyclitis 364.21
Fucosidosis 271.8
Fugue 780.99
  dissociative 300.13
  hysterical (dissociative) 300.13
  reaction to exceptional stress (transient) 308.1
Fukuhara syndrome 277.87
Fuller Albright's syndrome (osteitis fibrosa disseminata) 756.59
Fuller's earth disease 502
Fulminant, fulminating — *see* condition
Functional — *see* condition
Functioning
  borderline intellectual V62.89
Fundus — *see also* condition
  flavimaculatus 362.76
Fungemia 117.9
Fungus, fungous
  cerebral 348.89
  disease NEC 117.9
  infection — *see* Infection, fungus
  testis (*see also* Tuberculosis) 016.5 ☑ [608.81]
Funiculitis (acute) 608.4
  chronic 608.4
  endemic 608.4
  gonococcal (acute) 098.14
    chronic or duration of 2 months or over 098.34
  tuberculous (*see also* Tuberculosis) 016.5 ☑
Funnel
  breast (acquired) 738.3
    congenital 754.81
    late effect of rickets 268.1
  chest (acquired) 738.3
    congenital 754.81
    late effect of rickets 268.1
  pelvis (acquired) 738.6
    with disproportion (fetopelvic) 653.3 ☑
      affecting fetus or newborn 763.1
      causing obstructed labor 660.1 ☑
        affecting fetus or newborn 763.1
    congenital 755.69
    tuberculous (*see also* Tuberculosis) 016.9 ☑
FUO — *see also* Pyrexia 780.60
Furfur 690.18
  microsporon 111.0
Furor, paroxysmal (idiopathic) — *see also* Epilepsy 345.8 ☑
Furriers' lung 495.8
Furrowed tongue 529.5
  congenital 750.13
Furrowing nail(s) (transverse) 703.8

Furrowing nail(s) — *continued*
  congenital 757.5
Furuncle 680.9
  abdominal wall 680.2
  ankle 680.6
  anus 680.5
  arm (any part, above wrist) 680.3
  auditory canal, external 680.0
  axilla 680.3
  back (any part) 680.2
  breast 680.2
  buttock 680.5
  chest wall 680.2
  corpus cavernosum 607.2
  ear (any part) 680.0
  eyelid 373.13
  face (any part, except eye) 680.0
  finger (any) 680.4
  flank 680.2
  foot (any part) 680.7
  forearm 680.3
  gluteal (region) 680.5
  groin 680.2
  hand (any part) 680.4
  head (any part, except face) 680.8
  heel 680.7
  hip 680.6
  kidney (*see also* Abscess, kidney) 590.2
  knee 680.6
  labium (majus) (minus) 616.4
  lacrimal
    gland (*see also* Dacryoadenitis) 375.00
    passages (duct) (sac) (*see also* Dacryocystitis) 375.30
  leg, any part except foot 680.6
  malignant 022.0
  multiple sites 680.9
  neck 680.1
  nose (external) (septum) 680.0
  orbit 376.01
  partes posteriores 680.5
  pectoral region 680.2
  penis 607.2
  perineum 680.2
  pinna 680.0
  scalp (any part) 680.8
  scrotum 608.4
  seminal vesicle 608.0
  shoulder 680.3
  skin NEC 680.9
  specified site NEC 680.8
  spermatic cord 608.4
  temple (region) 680.0
  testis 604.90
  thigh 680.6
  thumb 680.4
  toe (any) 680.7
  trunk 680.2
  tunica vaginalis 608.4
  umbilicus 680.2
  upper arm 680.3
  vas deferens 608.4
  vulva 616.4
  wrist 680.4
Furunculosis — *see also* Furuncle 680.9
  external auditory meatus 680.0 [380.13]
Fusarium (infection) 118
Fusion, fused (congenital)
  anal (with urogenital canal) 751.5

Fusion, fused — *continued*
  aorta and pulmonary artery 745.0
  astragaloscaphoid 755.67
  atria 745.5
  atrium and ventricle 745.69
  auditory canal 744.02
  auricles, heart 745.5
  binocular, with defective stereopsis 368.33
  bone 756.9
  cervical spine — *see* Fusion, spine
  choanal 748.0
  commissure, mitral valve 746.5
  cranial sutures, premature 756.0
  cusps, heart valve NEC 746.89
    mitral 746.5
    tricuspid 746.89
  ear ossicles 744.04
  fingers (*see also* Syndactylism, fingers) 755.11
  hymen 752.42
  hymeno-urethral 599.89
    causing obstructed labor 660.1 ☑
      affecting fetus or newborn 763.1
  joint (acquired) (*see also* Ankylosis)
    congenital 755.8
  kidneys (incomplete) 753.3
  labium (majus) (minus) 752.49
  larynx and trachea 748.3
  limb 755.8
    lower 755.69
    upper 755.59
  lobe, lung 748.5
  lumbosacral (acquired) 724.6
    congenital 756.15
    surgical V45.4
  nares (anterior) (posterior) 748.0
  nose, nasal 748.0
  nostril(s) 748.0
  organ or site NEC — *see* Anomaly, specified type NEC
  ossicles 756.9
    auditory 744.04
  pulmonary valve segment 746.02
  pulmonic cusps 746.02
  ribs 756.3
  sacroiliac (acquired) (joint) 724.6
    congenital 755.69
    surgical V45.4
  skull, imperfect 756.0
  spine (acquired) 724.9
    arthrodesis status V45.4
    congenital (vertebra) 756.15
    postoperative status V45.4
  sublingual duct with submaxillary duct at opening in mouth 750.26
  talonavicular (bar) 755.67
  teeth, tooth 520.2
  testes 752.89
  toes (*see also* Syndactylism, toes) 755.13
  trachea and esophagus 750.3
  twins 759.4
  urethral-hymenal 599.89
  vagina 752.49
  valve cusps — *see* Fusion, cusps, heart valve
  ventricles, heart 745.4
  vertebra (arch) — *see* Fusion, spine
  vulva 752.49
Fusospirillosis (mouth) (tongue) (tonsil) 101
Fussy infant (baby) 780.91

☑ Additional Digit Required — Refer to the Tabular List for Digit Selection   ▽ Subterms under main terms may continue to next column or page

G

Gafsa boil 085.1
Gain, weight (abnormal) (excessive) — *see also*
    Weight, gain 783.1
Gaisböck's disease or syndrome (poly-
    cythemia hypertonica) 289.0
Gait
    abnormality 781.2
        hysterical 300.11
    ataxic 781.2
        hysterical 300.11
    disturbance 781.2
        hysterical 300.11
    paralytic 781.2
    scissor 781.2
    spastic 781.2
    staggering 781.2
        hysterical 300.11
Galactocele (breast) (infected) 611.5
    puerperal, postpartum 676.8 ☑
Galactophoritis 611.0
    puerperal, postpartum 675.2 ☑
Galactorrhea 676.6 ☑
    not associated with childbirth 611.6
Galactosemia (classic) (congenital) 271.1
Galactosuria 271.1
Galacturia 791.1
    bilharziasis 120.0
Galen's vein — *see* condition
Gallbladder — *see also* condition
    acute (*see also* Disease, gallbladder) 575.0
Gall duct — *see* condition
Gallop rhythm 427.89
Gallstone (cholemic) (colic) (impacted) — *see*
    also Cholelithiasis
    causing intestinal obstruction 560.31
Gambling, pathological 312.31
Gammaloidosis 277.39
Gammopathy 273.9
    macroglobulinemia 273.3
    monoclonal (benign) (essential) (idiopathic)
        (with lymphoplasmacytic dyscrasia)
        273.1
Gamna's disease (siderotic splenomegaly)
    289.51
Gampsodactylia (congenital) 754.71
Gamstorp's disease (adynamia episodica
    hereditaria) 359.3
Gandy-Nanta disease (siderotic splenomegaly)
    289.51
Gang activity, without manifest psychiatric
    disorder V71.09
    adolescent V71.02
    adult V71.01
    child V71.02
Gangliocytoma (M9490/0) — *see* Neoplasm,
    connective tissue, benign
Ganglioglioma (M9505/1) — *see* Neoplasm,
    by site, uncertain behavior
Ganglion 727.43
    joint 727.41
    of yaws (early) (late) 102.6
    periosteal (*see also* Periostitis) 730.3 ☑
    tendon sheath (compound) (diffuse) 727.42
    tuberculous (*see also* Tuberculosis) 015.9 ☑
Ganglioneuroblastoma (M9490/3) — *see*
    Neoplasm, connective tissue, malignant
Ganglioneuroma (M9490/0) — *see also* Neo-
    plasm, connective tissue, benign
    malignant (M9490/3) — *see* Neoplasm,
        connective tissue, malignant
Ganglioneuromatosis (M9491/0) — *see* Neo-
    plasm, connective tissue, benign
Ganglionitis
    fifth nerve (*see also* Neuralgia, trigeminal)
        350.1
    gasserian 350.1
    geniculate 351.1
        herpetic 053.11
        newborn 767.5
    herpes zoster 053.11
    herpetic geniculate (Hunt's syndrome)
        053.11
Gangliosidosis 330.1
Gangosa 102.5

Gangrene, gangrenous (anemia) (artery)
    (cellulitis) (dermatitis) (dry) (infective)
    (moist) (pemphigus) (septic) (skin) (sta-
    sis) (ulcer) 785.4
    with
        arteriosclerosis (native artery) 440.24
            bypass graft 440.30
                autologous vein 440.31
                nonautologous biological 440.32
        diabetes (mellitus) 250.7 ☑ *[785.4]*
            due to secondary diabetes
                249.7 ☑ *[785.4]*
    abdomen (wall) 785.4
    adenitis 683
    alveolar 526.5
    angina 462
        diphtheritic 032.0
    anus 569.49
    appendices epiploicae — *see* Gangrene,
        mesentery
    appendix — *see* Appendicitis, acute
    arteriosclerotic — *see* Arteriosclerosis, with,
        gangrene
    auricle 785.4
    Bacillus welchii (*see also* Gangrene, gas)
        040.0
    bile duct (*see also* Cholangitis) 576.8
    bladder 595.89
    bowel — *see* Gangrene, intestine
    cecum — *see* Gangrene, intestine
    Clostridium perfringens or welchii (*see also*
        Gangrene, gas) 040.0
    colon — *see* Gangrene, intestine
    connective tissue 785.4
    cornea 371.40
    corpora cavernosa (infective) 607.2
        noninfective 607.89
    cutaneous, spreading 785.4
    decubital (*see also* Ulcer, pressure)
        707.00 *[785.4]*
    diabetic (any site) 250.7 ☑ *[785.4]*
        due to secondary diabetes
            249.7 ☑ *[785.4]*
    dropsical 785.4
    emphysematous (*see also* Gangrene, gas)
        040.0
    epidemic (ergotized grain) 988.2
    epididymis (infectional) (*see also* Epididymi-
        tis) 604.99
    erysipelas (*see also* Erysipelas) 035
    extremity (lower) (upper) 785.4
    gallbladder or duct (*see also* Cholecystitis,
        acute) 575.0
    gas (bacillus) 040.0
        with
            abortion — *see* Abortion, by type,
                with sepsis
            ectopic pregnancy (*see also* cate-
                gories 633.0–633.9) 639.0
            molar pregnancy (*see also* categories
                630–632) 639.0
        following
            abortion 639.0
            ectopic or molar pregnancy 639.0
        puerperal, postpartum, childbirth
            670.8 ☑
    glossitis 529.0
    gum 523.8
    hernia — *see* Hernia, by site, with gangrene
    hospital noma 528.1
    intestine, intestinal (acute) (hemorrhagic)
        (massive) 557.0
        with
            hernia — *see* Hernia, by site, with
                gangrene
            mesenteric embolism or infarction
                557.0
            obstruction (*see also* Obstruction, in-
                testine) 560.9
    laryngitis 464.00
        with obstruction 464.01
    liver 573.8
    lung 513.0
        spirochetal 104.8
    lymphangitis 457.2
    Meleney's (cutaneous) 686.09

Gangrene, gangrenous — *continued*
    mesentery 557.0
        with
            embolism or infarction 557.0
            intestinal obstruction (*see also* Ob-
                struction, intestine) 560.9
    mouth 528.1
    noma 528.1
    orchitis 604.90
    ovary (*see also* Salpingo-oophoritis) 614.2
    pancreas 577.0
    penis (infectional) 607.2
        noninfective 607.89
    perineum 785.4
    pharynx 462
    pneumonia 513.0
    Pott's 440.24
    presenile 443.1
    pulmonary 513.0
    pulp, tooth 522.1
    quinsy 475
    Raynaud's (symmetric gangrene)
        443.0 *[785.4]*
    rectum 569.49
    retropharyngeal 478.24
    rupture — *see* Hernia, by site, with gan-
        grene
    scrotum 608.4
        noninfective 608.83
    senile 440.24
    septic 034.0
    septic 034.0
    sore throat 462
    spermatic cord 608.4
        noninfective 608.89
    spine 785.4
    spirochetal NEC 104.8
    spreading cutaneous 785.4
    stomach 537.89
    stomatitis 528.1
    symmetrical 443.0 *[785.4]*
    testis (infectional) (*see also* Orchitis) 604.99
        noninfective 608.89
    throat 462
        diphtheritic 032.0
    thyroid (gland) 246.8
    tonsillitis (acute) 463
    tooth (pulp) 522.1
    tuberculous NEC (*see also* Tuberculosis)
        011.9 ☑
    tunica vaginalis 608.4
        noninfective 608.89
    umbilicus 785.4
    uterus (*see also* Endometritis) 615.9
    uvulitis 528.3
    vas deferens 608.4
        noninfective 608.89
    vulva (*see also* Vulvitis) 616.10
Gannister disease (occupational) 502
    with tuberculosis — *see* Tuberculosis, pul-
        monary
Ganser's syndrome, hysterical 300.16
Gardner-Diamond syndrome (autoerythro-
    cyte sensitization) 287.2
Gargoylism 277.5
Garré's
    disease (*see also* Osteomyelitis) 730.1 ☑
    osteitis (sclerosing) (*see also* Osteomyelitis)
        730.1 ☑
    osteomyelitis (*see also* Osteomyelitis)
        730.1 ☑
Garrod's pads, knuckle 728.79
Gartner's duct
    cyst 752.41
    persistent 752.41
Gas 787.3
    asphyxia, asphyxiation, inhalation, poison-
        ing, suffocation NEC 987.9
        specified gas — *see* Table of Drugs and
            Chemicals
    bacillus gangrene or infection — *see* Gas,
        gangrene
    cyst, mesentery 568.89
    excessive 787.3
    gangrene 040.0

Gas — *continued*
    gangrene — *continued*
        with
            abortion — *see* Abortion, by type,
                with sepsis
            ectopic pregnancy (*see also* cate-
                gories 633.0–633.9) 639.0
            molar pregnancy (*see also* categories
                630–632) 639.0
        following
            abortion 639.0
            ectopic or molar pregnancy 639.0
        puerperal, postpartum, childbirth
            670.8 ☑
    on stomach 787.3
    pains 787.3
Gastradenitis 535.0 ☑
Gastralgia 536.8
    psychogenic 307.89
Gastrectasis, gastrectasia 536.1
    psychogenic 306.4
Gastric — *see* condition
Gastrinoma (M8153/1)
    malignant (M8153/3)
        pancreas 157.4
        specified site NEC — *see* Neoplasm, by
            site, malignant
        unspecified site 157.4
    specified site — *see* Neoplasm, by site, un-
        certain behavior
    unspecified site 235.5
Gastritis 535.5 ☑

> *Note* — *Use the following fifth-digit*
> *subclassification for category 535:*
>
> *0*   *without mention of hemorrhage*
>
> *1*   *with hemorrhage*

    acute 535.0 ☑
    alcoholic 535.3 ☑
    allergic 535.4 ☑
    antral 535.4 ☑
    atrophic 535.1 ☑
    atrophic-hyperplastic 535.1 ☑
    bile-induced 535.4 ☑
    catarrhal 535.0 ☑
    chronic (atrophic) 535.1 ☑
    cirrhotic 535.4 ☑
    corrosive (acute) 535.4 ☑
    dietetic 535.4 ☑
    due to diet deficiency 269.9 *[535.4]* ☑
    eosinophilic 535.7 ☑
    erosive 535.4 ☑
    follicular 535.4 ☑
        chronic 535.1 ☑
    giant hypertrophic 535.2 ☑
    glandular 535.4 ☑
        chronic 535.1 ☑
    hypertrophic (mucosa) 535.2 ☑
        chronic giant 211.1
    irritant 535.4 ☑
    nervous 306.4
    phlegmonous 535.0 ☑
    psychogenic 306.4
    sclerotic 535.4 ☑
    spastic 536.8
    subacute 535.0 ☑
    superficial 535.4 ☑
    suppurative 535.0 ☑
    toxic 535.4 ☑
    tuberculous (*see also* Tuberculosis) 017.9 ☑
Gastrocarcinoma (M8010/3) 151.9
Gastrocolic — *see* condition
Gastrocolitis — *see* Enteritis
Gastrodisciasis 121.8
Gastroduodenitis — *see also* Gastritis 535.5 ☑
    catarrhal 535.0 ☑
    infectional 535.0 ☑
    virus, viral 008.8
        specified type NEC 008.69
Gastrodynia 536.8
Gastroenteritis (acute) (catarrhal) (congestive)
    (hemorrhagic) (noninfectious) — *see also*
    Enteritis 558.9
    aertrycke infection 003.0

☑ **Additional Digit Required** — Refer to the Tabular List for Digit Selection   ▽ **Subterms under main terms may continue to next column or page**

2015 ICD-9-CM   ▶◀ **Revised Text**   ● **New Line**   ▲ **Revised Code**   **Volume 2 — 127**

Gastroenteritis — *see also* Enteritis — *continued*
  allergic 558.3
  chronic 558.9
    ulcerative (*see also* Colitis, ulcerative) 556.9
  dietetic 558.9
  due to
    antineoplastic chemotherapy 558.9
    food poisoning (*see also* Poisoning, food) 005.9
    radiation 558.1
  eosinophilic 558.41
  epidemic 009.0
  functional 558.9
  infectious (*see also* Enteritis, due to, by organism) 009.0
    presumed 009.1
  salmonella 003.0
  septic (*see also* Enteritis, due to, by organism) 009.0
  toxic 558.2
  tuberculous (*see also* Tuberculosis) 014.8 ☑
  ulcerative (*see also* Colitis, ulcerative) 556.9
  viral NEC 008.8
    specified type NEC 008.69
  zymotic 009.0
Gastroenterocolitis — *see* Enteritis
Gastroenteropathy, protein-losing 579.8
Gastroenteroptosis 569.89
Gastroesophageal laceration-hemorrhage syndrome 530.7
Gastroesophagitis 530.19
Gastrohepatitis — *see also* Gastritis 535.5 ☑
Gastrointestinal — *see* condition
Gastrojejunal — *see* condition
Gastrojejunitis — *see also* Gastritis 535.5 ☑
Gastrojejunocolic — *see* condition
Gastroliths 537.89
Gastromalacia 537.89
Gastroparalysis 536.3
  diabetic 250.6 ☑ [536.3]
    due to secondary diabetes 249.6 ☑ [536.3]
Gastroparesis 536.3
  diabetic 250.6 ☑ [536.3]
    due to secondary diabetes 249.6 ☑ [536.3]
Gastropathy 537.9
  congestive portal 537.89
  erythematous 535.5 ☑
  exudative 579.8
  portal hypertensive 537.89
Gastroptosis 537.5
Gastrorrhagia 578.0
Gastrorrhea 536.8
  psychogenic 306.4
Gastroschisis (congenital) 756.73
  acquired 569.89
Gastrospasm (neurogenic) (reflex) 536.8
  neurotic 306.4
  psychogenic 306.4
Gastrostaxis 578.0
Gastrostenosis 537.89
Gastrostomy
  attention to V55.1
  complication 536.40
    specified type 536.49
  infection 536.41
  malfunctioning 536.42
  status V44.1
Gastrosuccorrhea (continuous) (intermittent) 536.8
  neurotic 306.4
  psychogenic 306.4
Gaucher's
  disease (adult) (cerebroside lipidosis) (infantile) 272.7
  hepatomegaly 272.7
  splenomegaly (cerebroside lipidosis) 272.7
GAVE (gastric antral vascular ectasia) 537.82
  with hemorrhage 537.83
  without hemorrhage 537.82
Gayet's disease (superior hemorrhagic polioencephalitis) 265.1

Gayet-Wernicke's syndrome (superior hemorrhagic polioencephalitis) 265.1
Gee (-Herter) (-Heubner) (-Thaysen) disease or syndrome (nontropical sprue) 579.0
Gélineau's syndrome — *see also* Narcolepsy 347.00
Gemination, teeth 520.2
Gemistocytoma (M9411/3)
  specified site — *see* Neoplasm, by site, malignant
  unspecified site 191.9
General, generalized — *see* condtion
Genetic
  susceptibility to
    MEN (multiple endocrine neoplasia) V84.81
    neoplasia
      multiple endocrine (MEN) V84.81
    neoplasm
      malignant, of
        breast V84.01
        endometrium V84.04
        other V84.09
        ovary V84.02
        prostate V84.03
    specified disease NEC V84.89
Genital — *see* condition
  warts 078.11
Genito-anorectal syndrome 099.1
Genitourinary system — *see* condition
Genu
  congenital 755.64
  extrorsum (acquired) 736.42
    congenital 755.64
    late effects of rickets 268.1
  introrsum (acquired) 736.41
    congenital 755.64
    late effects of rickets 268.1
  rachitic (old) 268.1
  recurvatum (acquired) 736.5
    congenital 754.40
      with dislocation of knee 754.41
    late effects of rickets 268.1
  valgum (acquired) (knock-knee) 736.41
    congenital 755.64
    late effects of rickets 268.1
  varum (acquired) (bowleg) 736.42
    congenital 755.64
    late effect of rickets 268.1
Geographic tongue 529.1
Geophagia 307.52
Geotrichosis 117.9
  intestine 117.9
  lung 117.9
  mouth 117.9
Gephyrophobia 300.29
Gerbode defect 745.4
GERD (gastroesophageal reflux disease) 530.81
Gerhardt's
  disease (erythromelalgia) 443.82
  syndrome (vocal cord paralysis) 478.30
Gerlier's disease (epidemic vertigo) 078.81
German measles 056.9
  exposure to V01.4
Germinoblastoma (diffuse) (M9614/3) 202.8 ☑
  follicular (M9692/3) 202.0 ☑
Germinoma (M9064/3) — *see* Neoplasm, by site, malignant
Gerontoxon 371.41
Gerstmann-Sträussler-Scheinker syndrome (GSS) 046.71
Gerstmann's syndrome (finger agnosia) 784.69
Gestation (period) — *see also* Pregnancy
  ectopic NEC (*see also* Pregnancy, ectopic) 633.90
    with intrauterine pregnancy 633.91
  multiple
    placenta status
      quadruplet
        two or more monoamniotic fetuses V91.22
        two or more monochorionic fetuses V91.21

Gestation — *see also* Pregnancy — *continued*
  multiple — *continued*
    placenta status — *continued*
      quadruplet — *continued*
        unable to determine number of placenta and number of amniotic sacs V91.29
        unspecified number of placenta and unspecified number of amniotic sacs V91.20
      specified (greater than quadruplets) NEC
        two or more monoamniotic fetuses V91.92
        two or more monochorionic fetuses V91.91
        unable to determine number of placenta and number of amniotic sacs V91.99
        unspecified number of placenta and unspecified number of amniotic sacs V91.90
      triplet
        two or more monoamniotic fetuses V91.12
        two or more monochorionic fetuses V91.11
        unable to determine number of placenta and number of amniotic sacs V91.19
        unspecified number of placenta, unspecified number of amniotic sacs V91.10
      twin
        dichorionic/diamniotic (two placentae, two amniotic sacs) V91.03
        monochorionic/diamniotic (one placenta, two amniotic sacs) V91.02
        monochorionic/monoamniotic (one placenta, one amniotic sac) V91.01
        unable to determine number of placenta and number of amniotic sacs V91.09
        unspecified number of placenta, unspecified number of amniotic sacs V91.00
Gestational proteinuria 646.2 ☑
  with hypertension — *see* Toxemia, of pregnancy
Ghon tubercle primary infection — *see also* Tuberculosis 010.0 ☑
Ghost
  teeth 520.4
  vessels, cornea 370.64
Ghoul hand 102.3
Gianotti Crosti syndrome 057.8
  due to known virus — *see* Infection, virus
  due to unknown virus 057.8
Giant
  cell
    epulis 523.8
    peripheral (gingiva) 523.8
    tumor, tendon sheath 727.02
  colon (congenital) 751.3
  esophagus (congenital) 750.4
  kidney 753.3
  urticaria 995.1
    hereditary 277.6
Giardia lamblia infestation 007.1
Giardiasis 007.1
Gibert's disease (pityriasis rosea) 696.3
Gibraltar fever — *see* Brucellosis
Giddiness 780.4
  hysterical 300.11
  psychogenic 306.9
Gierke's disease (glycogenosis I) 271.0
Gigantism (cerebral) (hypophyseal) (pituitary) 253.0
Gilbert's disease or cholemia (familial nonhemolytic jaundice) 277.4
Gilchrist's disease (North American blastomycosis) 116.0

Gilford (-Hutchinson) disease or syndrome (progeria) 259.8
Gilles de la Tourette's disease (motor-verbal tic) 307.23
Gillespie's syndrome (dysplasia oculodentodigitalis) 759.89
Gingivitis 523.10
  acute 523.00
    necrotizing 101
    non-plaque induced 523.01
    plaque induced 523.00
  catarrhal 523.00
  chronic 523.10
    non-plaque induced 523.11
  desquamative 523.10
  expulsiva 523.40
  hyperplastic 523.10
  marginal, simple 523.10
  necrotizing, acute 101
  non-plaque induced 523.11
  pellagrous 265.2
  plaque induced 523.10
  ulcerative 523.10
    acute necrotizing 101
  Vincent's 101
Gingivoglossitis 529.0
Gingivopericementitis 523.40
Gingivosis 523.10
Gingivostomatitis 523.10
  herpetic 054.2
Giovannini's disease 117.9
GISA (glycopeptide intermediate staphylococcus aureus) V09.8 ☑
Glanders 024
Gland, glandular — *see* condition
Glanzmann (-Naegeli) disease or thrombasthenia 287.1
Glassblowers' disease 527.1
Glaucoma (capsular) (inflammatory) (noninflammatory) (primary) 365.9
  with increased episcleral venous pressure 365.82
  absolute 360.42
  acute 365.22
    narrow angle 365.22
    secondary 365.60
  angle closure 365.20
    acute 365.22
    attack 365.22
    chronic 365.23
    crisis 365.22
    intermittent 365.21
    interval 365.21
    primary 365.20
      chronic 365.23
    residual stage 365.24
    subacute 365.21
  angle recession 365.65
  borderline 365.00
  chronic 365.11
    noncongestive 365.11
    open angle 365.11
    simple 365.11
  closed angle — *see* Glaucoma, angle closure
  congenital 743.20
    associated with other eye anomalies 743.22
    simple 743.21
  congestive — *see* Glaucoma, narrow angle
  corticosteroid-induced (glaucomatous stage) 365.31
    residual stage 365.32
  exfoliation 365.52
  hemorrhagic 365.60
  hypersecretion 365.81
  infantile 365.14
    congenital 743.20
      associated with other eye anomalies 743.22
      simple 743.21
  inflammatory 365.62
  in or with
    aniridia 365.42
    Axenfeld's anomaly 365.41
    congenital syndromes NEC 759.89 [365.44]

Glaucoma — *continued*
  in or with — *continued*
    disorder of lens NEC 365.59
    inflammation, ocular 365.62
    iris
      anomalies NEC 365.42
      atrophy, essential 365.42
      bombé 365.61
    microcornea 365.43
    neurofibromatosis 237.71 [365.44]
    ocular
      cysts NEC 365.64
      disorders NEC 365.60
      trauma 365.65
      tumors NEC 365.64
    pupillary block or seclusion 365.61
    Rieger's anomaly or syndrome 365.41
    seclusion of pupil 365.61
    Sturge-Weber (-Dimitri) syndrome
      759.6 [365.44]
    systemic syndrome NEC 365.44
    tumor of globe 365.64
    vascular disorders NEC 365.63
  juvenile 365.14
  low tension 365.12
  malignant 365.83
  narrow angle (primary) 365.20
    acute 365.22
    chronic 365.23
    intermittent 365.21
    interval 365.21
    residual stage 365.24
    subacute 365.21
  neovascular 365.63
  newborn 743.20
    associated with other eye anomalies
      743.22
    simple 743.21
  noncongestive (chronic) 365.11
  nonobstructive (chronic) 365.11
  normal tension 365.12
  obstructive 365.60
    due to lens changes 365.59
  open angle 365.10
    with
      abnormal optic disc appearance or
        asymmetry 365.01
      borderline findings
        high risk 365.05
        intraocular pressure 365.01
        low risk 365.01
      cupping of optic discs 365.01
      thin central corneal thickness
        (pachymetry) 365.01
    high risk 365.05
    low risk 365.01
    primary 365.11
    residual stage 365.15
  phacoanaphylactic 365.59
  phacolytic 365.51
  phacomorphic
    acute 365.22
    borderline 365.06
  pigmentary 365.13
  pigment dispersion 365.13
  postinfectious 365.60
  pseudoexfoliation 365.52
  secondary NEC 365.60
    due to
      steroids 365.31
      surgery 365.60
  simple (chronic) 365.11
  simplex 365.11
  stage
    advanced 365.73
    early 365.71
    end-stage 365.73
    indeterminate 365.74
    mild 365.71
    moderate 365.72
    severe 365.73
    unspecified 365.70
  steroid
    induced 365.31
    responders 365.03
  suspect 365.00

Glaucoma — *continued*
  suspect — *continued*
    primary angle closure 365.02
  syphilitic 095.8
  traumatic NEC 365.65
    newborn 767.8
  uveitic 365.62
  wide angle (*see also* Glaucoma, open angle) 365.10
Glaucomatous flecks (subcapsular) 366.31
Glazed tongue 529.4
Gleet 098.2
Glénard's disease or syndrome (enteroptosis) 569.89
Glinski-Simmonds syndrome (pituitary cachexia) 253.2
Glioblastoma (multiforme) (M9440/3)
  with sarcomatous component (M9442/3)
    specified site — *see* Neoplasm, by site, malignant
    unspecified site 191.9
  giant cell (M9441/3)
    specified site — *see* Neoplasm, by site, malignant
    unspecified site 191.9
  specified site — *see* Neoplasm, by site, malignant
  unspecified site 191.9
Glioma (malignant) (M9380/3)
  astrocytic (M9400/3)
    specified site — *see* Neoplasm, by site, malignant
    unspecified site 191.9
  mixed (M9382/3)
    specified site — *see* Neoplasm, by site, malignant
    unspecified site 191.9
  nose 748.1
  specified site NEC — *see* Neoplasm, by site, malignant
  subependymal (M9383/1) 237.5
  unspecified site 191.9
Gliomatosis cerebri (M9381/3) 191.0
Glioneuroma (M9505/1) — *see* Neoplasm, by site, uncertain behavior
Gliosarcoma (M9380/3)
  specified site — *see* Neoplasm, by site, malignant
  unspecified site 191.9
Gliosis (cerebral) 349.89
  spinal 336.0
Glisson's
  cirrhosis — *see* Cirrhosis, portal
  disease (*see also* Rickets) 268.0
Glissonitis 573.3
Globinuria 791.2
Globus 306.4
  hystericus 300.11
Glomangioma (M8712/0) — *see also* Hemangioma 228.00
Glomangiosarcoma (M8710/3) — *see* Neoplasm, connective tissue, malignant
Glomerular nephritis — *see also* Nephritis 583.9
Glomerulitis — *see also* Nephritis 583.9
Glomerulonephritis — *see also* Nephritis 583.9
  with
    edema (*see also* Nephrosis) 581.9
    lesion of
      exudative nephritis 583.89
      interstitial nephritis (diffuse) (focal) 583.89
      necrotizing glomerulitis 583.4
        acute 580.4
        chronic 582.4
      renal necrosis 583.9
        cortical 583.6
        medullary 583.7
      specified pathology NEC 583.89
        acute 580.89
        chronic 582.89
    necrosis, renal 583.9
      cortical 583.6
      medullary (papillary) 583.7
    specified pathology or lesion NEC 583.89
  acute 580.9

Glomerulonephritis — *see also* Nephritis — *continued*
  acute — *continued*
    with
      exudative nephritis 580.89
      interstitial nephritis (diffuse) (focal) 580.89
      necrotizing glomerulitis 580.4
    extracapillary with epithelial crescents 580.4
    poststreptococcal 580.0
    proliferative (diffuse) 580.0
    rapidly progressive 580.4
    specified pathology NEC 580.89
  arteriolar (*see also* Hypertension, kidney) 403.90
  arteriosclerotic (*see also* Hypertension, kidney) 403.90
  ascending (*see also* Pyelitis) 590.80
  basement membrane NEC 583.89
    with
      pulmonary hemorrhage (Goodpasture's syndrome) 446.21 [583.81]
  chronic 582.9
    with
      exudative nephritis 582.89
      interstitial nephritis (diffuse) (focal) 582.89
      necrotizing glomerulitis 582.4
      specified pathology or lesion NEC 582.89
    endothelial 582.2
    extracapillary with epithelial crescents 582.4
    hypocomplementemic persistent 582.2
    lobular 582.2
    membranoproliferative 582.2
    membranous 582.1
      and proliferative (mixed) 582.2
      sclerosing 582.1
    mesangiocapillary 582.2
    mixed membranous and proliferative 582.2
    proliferative (diffuse) 582.0
    rapidly progressive 582.4
    sclerosing 582.1
  cirrhotic — *see* Sclerosis, renal
  desquamative — *see* Nephrosis
  due to or associated with
    amyloidosis 277.39 [583.81]
      with nephrotic syndrome 277.39 [581.81]
      chronic 277.39 [582.81]
    diabetes mellitus 250.4 ☑ [583.81]
      with nephrotic syndrome 250.4 ☑ [581.81]
        due to secondary diabetes 249.4 ☑ [581.81]
      due to secondary diabetes 249.4 ☑ [581.81]
    diphtheria 032.89 [580.81]
    gonococcal infection (acute) 098.19 [583.81]
      chronic or duration of 2 months or over 098.39 [583.81]
    infectious hepatitis 070.9 [580.81]
    malaria (with nephrotic syndrome) 084.9 [581.81]
    mumps 072.79 [580.81]
    polyarteritis (nodosa) (with nephrotic syndrome) 446.0 [581.81]
    specified pathology NEC 583.89
      acute 580.89
      chronic 582.89
    streptotrichosis 039.8 [583.81]
    subacute bacterial endocarditis 421.0 [580.81]
    syphilis (late) 095.4
      congenital 090.5 [583.81]
      early 091.69 [583.81]
    systemic lupus erythematosus 710.0 [583.81]
      with nephrotic syndrome 710.0 [581.81]
      chronic 710.0 [582.81]

Glomerulonephritis — *see also* Nephritis — *continued*
  due to or associated with — *continued*
    tuberculosis (*see also* Tuberculosis) 016.0 ☑ [583.81]
    typhoid fever 002.0 [580.81]
  extracapillary with epithelial crescents 583.4
    acute 580.4
    chronic 582.4
  exudative 583.89
    acute 580.89
    chronic 582.89
  focal (*see also* Nephritis) 583.9
    embolic 580.4
  granular 582.89
  granulomatous 582.89
  hydremic (*see also* Nephrosis) 581.9
  hypocomplementemic persistent 583.2
    with nephrotic syndrome 581.2
    chronic 582.2
  immune complex NEC 583.89
  infective (*see also* Pyelitis) 590.80
  interstitial (diffuse) (focal) 583.89
    with nephrotic syndrome 581.89
    acute 580.89
    chronic 582.89
  latent or quiescent 582.9
  lobular 583.2
    with nephrotic syndrome 581.2
    chronic 582.2
  membranoproliferative 583.2
    with nephrotic syndrome 581.2
    chronic 582.2
  membranous 583.1
    with nephrotic syndrome 581.1
    and proliferative (mixed) 583.2
      with nephrotic syndrome 581.2
      chronic 582.2
    chronic 582.1
    sclerosing 582.1
      with nephrotic syndrome 581.1
  mesangiocapillary 583.2
    with nephrotic syndrome 581.2
    chronic 582.2
  minimal change 581.3
  mixed membranous and proliferative 583.2
    with nephrotic syndrome 581.2
    chronic 582.2
  necrotizing 583.4
    acute 580.4
    chronic 582.4
  nephrotic (*see also* Nephrosis) 581.9
  old — *see* Glomerulonephritis, chronic
  parenchymatous 581.89
  poststreptococcal 580.0
  proliferative (diffuse) 583.0
    with nephrotic syndrome 581.0
    acute 580.0
    chronic 582.0
  purulent (*see also* Pyelitis) 590.80
  quiescent — *see* Nephritis, chronic
  rapidly progressive 583.4
    acute 580.4
    chronic 582.4
  sclerosing membranous (chronic) 582.1
    with nephrotic syndrome 581.1
  septic (*see also* Pyelitis) 590.80
  specified pathology or lesion NEC 583.89
    with nephrotic syndrome 581.89
    acute 580.89
    chronic 582.89
  suppurative (acute) (disseminated) (*see also* Pyelitis) 590.80
  toxic — *see* Nephritis, acute
  tubal, tubular — *see* Nephrosis, tubular
  type II (Ellis) — *see* Nephrosis
  vascular — *see* Hypertension, kidney
Glomerulosclerosis — *see also* Sclerosis, renal 587
  focal 582.1
    with nephrotic syndrome 581.1
  intercapillary (nodular) (with diabetes) 250.4 ☑ [581.81]
    due to secondary diabetes 249.4 ☑ [581.81]
Glossagra 529.6

Glossalgia 529.6
Glossitis 529.0
  areata exfoliativa 529.1
  atrophic 529.4
  benign migratory 529.1
  gangrenous 529.0
  Hunter's 529.4
  median rhomboid 529.2
  Moeller's 529.4
  pellagrous 265.2
Glossocele 529.8
Glossodynia 529.6
  exfoliativa 529.4
Glossoncus 529.8
Glossophytia 529.3
Glossoplegia 529.8
Glossoptosis 529.8
Glossopyrosis 529.6
Glossotrichia 529.3
Glossy skin 701.9
Glottis — see condition
Glottitis — see Glossitis
Glucagonoma (M8152/0)
  malignant (M8152/3)
    pancreas 157.4
    specified site NEC — see Neoplasm, by
      site, malignant
    unspecified site 157.4
  pancreas 211.7
  specified site NEC — see Neoplasm, by site,
    benign
  unspecified site 211.7
Glucoglycinuria 270.7
Glue ear syndrome 381.20
Glue sniffing (airplane glue) — see also Depen-
  dence 304.6 ☑
Glycinemia (with methylmalonic acidemia)
  270.7
Glycinuria (renal) (with ketosis) 270.0
Glycogen
  infiltration (see also Disease, glycogen stor-
    age) 271.0
  storage disease (see also Disease, glycogen
    storage) 271.0
Glycogenosis — see also Disease, glycogen
  storage 271.0
  cardiac 271.0 [425.7]
  Cori, types I-VII 271.0
  diabetic, secondary 250.8 ☑ [259.8]
    due to secondary diabetes
      249.8 ☑ [259.8]
  diffuse (with hepatic cirrhosis) 271.0
  generalized 271.0
  glucose-6-phosphatase deficiency 271.0
  hepatophosphorylase deficiency 271.0
  hepatorenal 271.0
  myophosphorylase deficiency 271.0
  pulmonary interstitial 516.62
Glycopenia 251.2
Glycopeptide
  intermediate staphylococcus aureus (GISA)
    V09.8 ☑
  resistant
    enterococcus V09.8 ☑
    staphylococcus aureus (GRSA) V09.8 ☑
Glycoprolinuria 270.8
Glycosuria 791.5
  renal 271.4
Gnathostoma (spinigerum) (infection) (infestation) 128.1
  wandering swellings from 128.1
Gnathostomiasis 128.1
Goiter (adolescent) (colloid) (diffuse) (dipping)
  (due to iodine deficiency) (endemic)
  (euthyroid) (heart) (hyperplastic) (internal) (intrathoracic) (juvenile) (mixed
  type) (nonendemic) (parenchymatous)
  (plunging) (sporadic) (subclavicular)
  (substernal) 240.9
  with
    hyperthyroidism (recurrent) (see also
      Goiter, toxic) 242.0 ☑
    thyrotoxicosis (see also Goiter, toxic)
      242.0 ☑
  adenomatous (see also Goiter, nodular)
    241.9

Goiter — continued
  cancerous (M8000/3) 193
  complicating pregnancy, childbirth, or
    puerperium 648.1 ☑
  congenital 246.1
  cystic (see also Goiter, nodular) 241.9
  due to enzyme defect in synthesis of thyroid
    hormone (butane-insoluble iodine)
    (coupling) (deiodinase) (iodide trap-
    ping or organification) (iodotyrosine
    dehalogenase) (peroxidase) 246.1
  dyshormonogenic 246.1
  exophthalmic (see also Goiter, toxic)
    242.0 ☑
  familial (with deaf-mutism) 243
  fibrous 245.3
  lingual 759.2
  lymphadenoid 245.2
  malignant (M8000/3) 193
  multinodular (nontoxic) 241.1
    toxic or with hyperthyroidism (see also
      Goiter, toxic) 242.2 ☑
  nodular (nontoxic) 241.9
    with
      hyperthyroidism (see also Goiter,
        toxic) 242.3 ☑
      thyrotoxicosis (see also Goiter, toxic)
        242.3 ☑
    endemic 241.9
    exophthalmic (diffuse) (see also Goiter,
      toxic) 242.0 ☑
    multinodular (nontoxic) 241.1
    sporadic 241.9
    toxic (see also Goiter, toxic) 242.3 ☑
    uninodular (nontoxic) 241.0
  nontoxic (nodular) 241.9
    multinodular 241.1
    uninodular 241.0
  pulsating (see also Goiter, toxic) 242.0 ☑
  simple 240.0
  toxic 242.0 ☑

> Note — Use the following fifth-digit
> subclassification with category 242:
>
> 0 without mention of thyrotoxic
>   crisis or storm
>
> 1 with mention of thyrotoxic crisis
>   or storm

    adenomatous 242.3 ☑
      multinodular 242.2 ☑
      uninodular 242.1 ☑
    multinodular 242.2 ☑
    nodular 242.3 ☑
      multinodular 242.2 ☑
      uninodular 242.1 ☑
    uninodular 242.1 ☑
  uninodular (nontoxic) 241.0
    toxic or with hyperthyroidism (see also
      Goiter, toxic) 242.1 ☑
Goldberg (-Maxwell) (-Morris) syndrome
  (testicular feminization) 259.51
Goldblatt's
  hypertension 440.1
  kidney 440.1
Goldenhar's syndrome (oculoauriculovertebral dysplasia) 756.0
Goldflam-Erb disease or syndrome 358.00
Goldscheider's disease (epidermolysis bullosa)
  757.39
Goldstein's disease (familial hemorrhagic
  telangiectasia) 448.0
Golfer's elbow 726.32
Goltz-Gorlin syndrome (dermal hypoplasia)
  757.39
Gonadoblastoma (M9073/1)
  specified site — see Neoplasm, by site un-
    certain behavior
  unspecified site
    female 236.2
    male 236.4
Gonecystitis — see also Vesiculitis 608.0
Gongylonemiasis 125.6
  mouth 125.6
Goniosynechiae 364.73
Gonococcemia 098.89

Gonococcus, gonococcal (disease) (infection)
  — see also condition 098.0
  anus 098.7
  bursa 098.52
  chronic NEC 098.2
  complicating pregnancy, childbirth, or
    puerperium 647.1 ☑
    affecting fetus or newborn 760.2
  conjunctiva, conjunctivitis (neonatorum)
    098.40
  dermatosis 098.89
  endocardium 098.84
  epididymo-orchitis 098.13
    chronic or duration of 2 months or over
      098.33
  eye (newborn) 098.40
  fallopian tube (chronic) 098.37
    acute 098.17
  genitourinary (acute) (organ) (system) (tract)
    (see also Gonorrhea) 098.0
    lower 098.0
      chronic 098.2
    upper 098.10
      chronic 098.30
  heart NEC 098.85
  joint 098.50
  keratoderma 098.81
  keratosis (blennorrhagica) 098.81
  lymphatic (gland) (node) 098.89
  meninges 098.82
  orchitis (acute) 098.13
    chronic or duration of 2 months or over
      098.33
  pelvis (acute) 098.19
    chronic or duration of 2 months or over
      098.39
  pericarditis 098.83
  peritonitis 098.86
  pharyngitis 098.6
  pharynx 098.6
  proctitis 098.7
  pyosalpinx (chronic) 098.37
    acute 098.17
  rectum 098.7
  septicemia 098.89
  skin 098.89
  specified site NEC 098.89
  synovitis 098.51
  tendon sheath 098.51
  throat 098.6
  urethra (acute) 098.0
    chronic or duration of 2 months or over
      098.2
  vulva (acute) 098.0
    chronic or duration of 2 months or over
      098.2
Gonocytoma (M9073/1)
  specified site — see Neoplasm, by site, un-
    certain behavior
  unspecified site
    female 236.2
    male 236.4
Gonorrhea 098.0
  acute 098.0
  Bartholin's gland (acute) 098.0
    chronic or duration of 2 months or over
      098.2
  bladder (acute) 098.11
    chronic or duration of 2 months or over
      098.31
  carrier (suspected of) V02.7
  cervix (acute) 098.15
    chronic or duration of 2 months or over
      098.35
  chronic 098.2
  complicating pregnancy, childbirth, or
    puerperium 647.1 ☑
    affecting fetus or newborn 760.2
  conjunctiva, conjunctivitis (neonatorum)
    098.40
  contact V01.6
  Cowper's gland (acute) 098.0
    chronic or duration of 2 months or over
      098.2
  duration of two months or over 098.2
  exposure to V01.6

Gonorrhea — continued
  fallopian tube (chronic) 098.37
    acute 098.17
  genitourinary (acute) (organ) (system) (tract)
    098.0
    chronic 098.2
    duration of two months or over 098.2
  kidney (acute) 098.19
    chronic or duration of 2 months or over
      098.39
  ovary (acute) 098.19
    chronic or duration of 2 months or over
      098.39
  pelvis (acute) 098.19
    chronic or duration of 2 months or over
      098.39
  penis (acute) 098.0
    chronic or duration of 2 months or over
      098.2
  prostate (acute) 098.12
    chronic or duration of 2 months or over
      098.32
  seminal vesicle (acute) 098.14
    chronic or duration of 2 months or over
      098.34
  specified site NEC — see Gonococcus
  spermatic cord (acute) 098.14
    chronic or duration of 2 months or over
      098.34
  urethra (acute) 098.0
    chronic or duration of 2 months or over
      098.2
  vagina (acute) 098.0
    chronic or duration of 2 months or over
      098.2
  vas deferens (acute) 098.14
    chronic or duration of 2 months or over
      098.34
  vulva (acute) 098.0
    chronic or duration of 2 months or over
      098.2
Goodpasture's syndrome (pneumorenal)
  446.21
Good's syndrome 279.06
Gopalan's syndrome (burning feet) 266.2
Gordon's disease (exudative enteropathy)
  579.8
Gorlin-Chaudhry-Moss syndrome 759.89
Gougerot-Blum syndrome (pigmented pur-
  puric lichenoid dermatitis) 709.1
Gougerot-Carteaud disease or syndrome
  (confluent reticulate papillomatosis)
  701.8
Gougerot-Hailey-Hailey disease (benign fa-
  milial chronic pemphigus) 757.39
Gougerot (-Houwer) -Sjögren syndrome
  (keratoconjunctivitis sicca) 710.2
Gougerot's syndrome (trisymptomatic) 709.1
Gouley's syndrome (constrictive pericarditis)
  423.2
Goundou 102.6
Gout, gouty 274.9
  with
    specified manifestations NEC 274.89
    tophi (tophus) 274.03
  acute 274.01
  arthritis 274.00
    acute 274.01
  arthropathy 274.00
    acute 274.01
    chronic (without mention of tophus
      (tophi)) 274.02
      with tophus (tophi) 274.03
  attack 274.01
  chronic 274.02
    tophaceous 274.03
  degeneration, heart 274.82
  diathesis 274.9
  eczema 274.89
  episcleritis 274.89 [379.09]
  external ear (tophus) 274.81
  flare 274.01
  glomerulonephritis 274.10
  iritis 274.89 [364.11]
  joint 274.00
  kidney 274.10

☑ **Additional Digit Required — Refer to the Tabular List for Digit Selection**
▽ **Subterms under main terms may continue to next column or page**

130 — Volume 2
▶️ Revised Text
● New Line
▲ Revised Code
2015 ICD-9-CM

Gout, gouty — *continued*
  lead 984.9
    specified type of lead — *see* Table of
      Drugs and Chemicals
  nephritis 274.10
  neuritis 274.89 [357.4]
  phlebitis 274.89 [451.9]
  rheumatic 714.0
  saturnine 984.9
    specified type of lead — *see* Table of
      Drugs and Chemicals
  spondylitis 274.00
  synovitis 274.00
  syphilitic 095.8
  tophi 274.03
    ear 274.81
    heart 274.82
    specified site NEC 274.82
Gowers'
  muscular dystrophy 359.1
  syndrome (vasovagal attack) 780.2
Gowers-Paton-Kennedy syndrome 377.04
Gradenigo's syndrome 383.02
Graft-versus-host disease 279.50
  due to organ transplant NEC — *see* Compli-
    cations, transplant, organ
Graham Steell's murmur (pulmonic regurgi-
    tation) — *see also* Endocarditis, pul-
    monary 424.3
Grain-handlers' disease or lung 495.8
Grain mite (itch) 133.8
Grand
  mal (idiopathic) (*see also* Epilepsy) 345.1 ☑
    hysteria of Charcôt 300.11
    nonrecurrent or isolated 780.39
  multipara
    affecting management of labor and de-
      livery 659.4 ☑
    status only (not pregnant) V61.5
Granite workers' lung 502
Granular — *see also* condition
  inflammation, pharynx 472.1
  kidney (contracting) (*see also* Sclerosis, re-
    nal) 587
  liver — *see* Cirrhosis, liver
  nephritis — *see* Nephritis
Granulation tissue, abnormal — *see also*
    Granuloma
  abnormal or excessive 701.5
  postmastoidectomy cavity 383.33
  postoperative 701.5
  skin 701.5
Granulocytopenia, granulocytopenic (prima-
    ry) 288.00
  malignant 288.09
Granulomatosis NEC 686.1
  disciformis chronica et progressiva 709.3
  infantiseptica 771.2
  lipoid 277.89
  lipophagic, intestinal 040.2
  miliary 027.0
  necrotizing, respiratory 446.4
  progressive, septic 288.1
  Wegener's (necrotizing respiratory) 446.4
Granuiomatous tissue — *see* Granuloma
Granuloma NEC 686.1
  abdomen (wall) 568.89
    skin (pyogenicum) 686.1
      from residual foreign body 709.4
  annulare 695.89
  anus 569.49
  apical 522.6
  appendix 543.9
  aural 380.23
  beryllium (skin) 709.4
    lung 503
  bone (*see also* Osteomyelitis) 730.1 ☑
    eosinophilic 277.89
    from residual foreign body 733.99
  canaliculus lacrimalis 375.81
  cerebral 348.89
  cholesterin, middle ear 385.82
  coccidioidal (progressive) 114.3
    lung 114.4
    meninges 114.2
    primary (lung) 114.0

Granuloma — *continued*
  colon 569.89
  conjunctiva 372.61
  dental 522.6
  ear, middle (cholesterin) 385.82
    with otitis media — *see* Otitis media
  eosinophilic 277.89
    bone 277.89
    lung 277.89
    oral mucosa 528.9
  exuberant 701.5
  eyelid 374.89
  facial
    lethal midline 446.3
    malignant 446.3
  faciale 701.8
  fissuratum (gum) 523.8
  foot NEC 686.1
  foreign body (in soft tissue) NEC 728.82
    bone 733.99
    in operative wound 998.4
    muscle 728.82
    skin 709.4
    subcutaneous tissue 709.4
  fungoides 202.1 ☑
  gangraenescens 446.3
  giant cell (central) (jaw) (reparative) 526.3
    gingiva 523.8
    peripheral (gingiva) 523.8
  gland (lymph) 289.3
  Hodgkin's (M9661/3) 201.1 ☑
  ileum 569.89
  infectious NEC 136.9
  inguinale (Donovan) 099.2
    venereal 099.2
  intestine 569.89
  iridocyclitis 364.10
  jaw (bone) 526.3
    reparative giant cell 526.3
  kidney (*see also* Infection, kidney) 590.9
  lacrimal sac 375.81
  larynx 478.79
  lethal midline 446.3
  lipid 277.89
  lipoid 277.89
  liver 572.8
  lung (infectious) (*see also* Fibrosis, lung) 515
    coccidioidal 114.4
    eosinophilic 277.89
  lymph gland 289.3
  Majocchi's 110.6
  malignant, face 446.3
  mandible 526.3
  mediastinum 519.3
  midline 446.3
  monilial 112.3
  muscle 728.82
    from residual foreign body 728.82
  nasal sinus (*see also* Sinusitis) 473.9
  operation wound 998.59
    foreign body 998.4
    stitch (external) 998.89
      internal wound 998.89
    talc 998.7
  oral mucosa, eosinophilic or pyogenic 528.9
  orbit, orbital 376.11
  paracoccidioidal 116.1
  penis, venereal 099.2
  periapical 522.6
  peritoneum 568.89
    due to ova of helminths NEC (*see also*
      Helminthiasis) 128.9
  postmastoidectomy cavity 383.33
  postoperative — *see* Granuloma, operation
    wound
  prostate 601.8
  pudendi (ulcerating) 099.2
  pudendorum (ulcerative) 099.2
  pulp, internal (tooth) 521.49
  pyogenic, pyogenicum (skin) 686.1
    maxillary alveolar ridge 522.6
    oral mucosa 528.9
  rectum 569.49
  reticulohistiocytic 277.89
  rubrum nasi 705.89
  sarcoid 135

Granuloma — *continued*
  Schistosoma 120.9
  septic (skin) 686.1
  silica (skin) 709.4
  sinus (accessory) (infectional) (nasal) (*see
    also* Sinusitis) 473.9
  skin (pyogenicum) 686.1
    from foreign body or material 709.4
  sperm 608.89
  spine
    syphilitic (epidural) 094.89
    tuberculous (*see also* Tuberculosis)
      015.0 ☑ [730.88]
  stitch (postoperative) 998.89
    internal wound 998.89
  suppurative (skin) 686.1
  suture (postoperative) 998.89
    internal wound 998.89
  swimming pool 031.1
  talc 728.82
    in operation wound 998.7
  telangiectaticum (skin) 686.1
  tracheostomy 519.09
  trichophyticum 110.6
  tropicum 102.4
  umbilicus 686.1
    newborn 771.4
  urethra 599.84
  uveitis 364.10
  vagina 099.2
  venereum 099.2
  vocal cords 478.5
  Wegener's (necrotizing respiratory granulo-
    matosis) 446.4
Granulosis rubra nasi 705.89
Graphite fibrosis (of lung) 503
Graphospasm 300.89
  organic 333.84
Grating scapula 733.99
Gravel (urinary) — *see also* Calculus 592.9
Graves' disease (exophthalmic goiter) — *see
    also* Goiter, toxic 242.0 ☑
Gravis — *see* condition
Grawitz's tumor (hypernephroma) (M8312/3)
    189.0
Grayness, hair (premature) 704.3
  congenital 757.4
Gray or grey syndrome (chloramphenicol)
    (newborn) 779.4
Greenfield's disease 330.0
Green sickness 280.9
Greenstick fracture — *see* Fracture, by site
Greig's syndrome (hypertelorism) 756.0
Grief 309.0
Griesinger's disease — *see also* Ancylostomi-
    asis 126.9
Grinders'
  asthma 502
  lung 502
  phthisis (*see also* Tuberculosis) 011.4 ☑
Grinding, teeth 306.8
Grip
  Dabney's 074.1
  devil's 074.1
Grippe, grippal — *see also* Influenza
  Balkan 083.0
  intestinal (*see also* Influenza) 487.8
  summer 074.8
Grippy cold — *see also* Influenza 487.1
Grisel's disease 723.5
Groin — *see* condition
Grooved
  nails (transverse) 703.8
  tongue 529.5
    congenital 750.13
Ground itch 126.9
Growing pains, children 781.99
Growth (fungoid) (neoplastic) (new) (M8000/1)
    — *see also* Neoplasm, by site, unspeci-
    fied nature
  adenoid (vegetative) 474.12
  benign (M8000/0) — *see* Neoplasm, by site,
    benign
  fetal, poor 764.9 ☑
    affecting management of pregnancy
      656.5 ☑

Growth — *see also* Neoplasm, by site,
    unspecified nature — *continued*
  malignant (M8000/3) — *see* Neoplasm, by
    site, malignant
  rapid, childhood V21.0
  secondary (M8000/6) — *see* Neoplasm, by
    site, malignant, secondary
GRSA (glycopeptide resistant staphylococcus
    aureus) V09.8 ☑
Gruber's hernia — *see* Hernia, Gruber's
Gruby's disease (tinea tonsurans) 110.0
GSS (Gerstmann-Sträussler-Scheinker syn-
    drome) 046.71
G-trisomy 758.0
Guama fever 066.3
Gubler (-Millard) paralysis or syndrome
    344.89
Guérin-Stern syndrome (arthrogryposis mul-
    tiplex congenita) 754.89
Guertin's disease (electric chorea) 049.8
Guillain-Barré disease or syndrome 357.0
Guinea worms (infection) (infestation) 125.7
Guinon's disease (motor-verbal tic) 307.23
Gull and Sutton's disease — *see* Hyperten-
    sion, kidney
Gull's disease (thyroid atrophy with myxede-
    ma) 244.8
Gum — *see* condition
Gumboil 522.7
Gumma (syphilitic) 095.9
  artery 093.89
    cerebral or spinal 094.89
  bone 095.5
    of yaws (late) 102.6
  brain 094.89
  cauda equina 094.89
  central nervous system NEC 094.9
  ciliary body 095.8 [364.11]
  congenital 090.5
    testis 090.5
  eyelid 095.8 [373.5]
  heart 093.89
  intracranial 094.89
  iris 095.8 [364.11]
  kidney 095.4
  larynx 095.8
  leptomeninges 094.2
  liver 095.3
  meninges 094.2
  myocardium 093.82
  nasopharynx 095.8
  neurosyphilitic 094.9
  nose 095.8
  orbit 095.8
  palate (soft) 095.8
  penis 095.8
  pericardium 093.81
  pharynx 095.8
  pituitary 095.8
  scrofulous (*see also* Tuberculosis) 017.0 ☑
  skin 095.8
  specified site NEC 095.8
  spinal cord 094.89
  tongue 095.8
  tonsil 095.8
  trachea 095.8
  tuberculous (*see also* Tuberculosis) 017.0 ☑
  ulcerative due to yaws 102.4
  ureter 095.8
  yaws 102.4
    bone 102.6
Gunn's syndrome (jaw-winking syndrome)
    742.8
Gunshot wound — *see also* Wound, open, by
    site
  fracture — *see* Fracture, by site, open
  internal organs (abdomen, chest, or pelvis)
    — *see* Injury, internal, by site, with
    open wound
  intracranial — *see* Laceration, brain, with
    open intracranial wound
Günther's disease or syndrome (congenital
    erythropoietic porphyria) 277.1
Gustatory hallucination 780.1
Gynandrism 752.7

☑ **Additional Digit Required** — Refer to the Tabular List for Digit Selection   ▽ **Subterms under main terms may continue to next column or page**

2015 ICD-9-CM   ◀▶ **Revised Text**   ● **New Line**   ▲ **Revised Code**   Volume 2 — **131**

Gynandroblastoma (M8632/1)
  specified site — *see* Neoplasm, by site, uncertain behavior
  unspecified site
    female 236.2
    male 236.4
Gynandromorphism 752.7
Gynatresia (congenital) 752.49
Gynecoid pelvis, male 738.6
Gynecological examination V72.31
  for contraceptive maintenance V25.40
Gynecomastia 611.1
Gynephobia 300.29
Gyrate scalp 757.39

H

Haas' disease (osteochondrosis head of humerus) 732.3
Habermann's disease (acute parapsoriasis varioliformis) 696.2
Habit, habituation
  chorea 307.22
  disturbance, child 307.9
  drug (*see also* Dependence) 304.9 ☑
  laxative (*see also* Abuse, drugs, nondependent) 305.9 ☑
  spasm 307.20
    chronic 307.22
    transient (of childhood) 307.21
  tic 307.20
    chronic 307.22
    transient (of childhood) 307.21
  use of
    nonprescribed drugs (*see also* Abuse, drugs, nondependent) 305.9 ☑
    patent medicines (*see also* Abuse, drugs, nondependent) 305.9 ☑
  vomiting 536.2
Hadfield-Clarke syndrome (pancreatic infantilism) 577.8
Haff disease 985.1
Hageman factor defect, deficiency, or disease — *see also* Defect, coagulation 286.3
Haglund's disease (osteochondrosis os tibiale externum) 732.5
Haglund-Läwen-Fründ syndrome 717.89
Hagner's disease (hypertrophic pulmonary osteoarthropathy) 731.2
Hag teeth, tooth 524.39
Hailey-Hailey disease (benign familial chronic pemphigus) 757.39
Hair — *see also* condition
  plucking 307.9
Hairball in stomach 935.2
Hairy black tongue 529.3
Half vertebra 756.14
Halitosis 784.99
Hallermann-Streiff syndrome 756.0
Hallervorden-Spatz disease or syndrome 333.0
Hallopeau's
  acrodermatitis (continua) 696.1
  disease (lichen sclerosis et atrophicus) 701.0
Hallucination (auditory) (gustatory) (olfactory) (tactile) 780.1
  alcohol-induced 291.3
  drug-induced 292.12
  visual 368.16
Hallucinosis 298.9
  alcohol-induced (acute) 291.3
  drug-induced 292.12
Hallus — *see* Hallux
Hallux 735.9
  limitus 735.8
  malleus (acquired) 735.3
  rigidus (acquired) 735.2
    congenital 755.66
    late effects of rickets 268.1
  valgus (acquired) 735.0
    congenital 755.66
  varus (acquired) 735.1
    congenital 755.66
Halo, visual 368.15
Hamartoblastoma 759.6
Hamartoma 759.6

Hamartoma — *continued*
  epithelial (gingival), odontogenic, central, or peripheral (M9321/0) 213.1
    upper jaw (bone) 213.0
  vascular 757.32
Hamartosis, hamartoses NEC 759.6
Hamman's disease or syndrome (spontaneous mediastinal emphysema) 518.1
Hamman-Rich syndrome (diffuse interstitial pulmonary fibrosis) 516.33
Hammer toe (acquired) 735.4
  congenital 755.66
  late effects of rickets 268.1
Hand — *see* condition
Hand-foot syndrome 693.0
Hand-Schüller-Christian disease or syndrome (chronic histiocytosis x) 277.89
Hanging (asphyxia) (strangulation) (suffocation) 994.7
Hangnail (finger) (with lymphangitis) 681.02
Hangover (alcohol) — *see also* Abuse, drugs, nondependent 305.0 ☑
Hanot-Chauffard (-Troisier) syndrome (bronze diabetes) 275.01
Hanot's cirrhosis or disease — *see* Cirrhosis, biliary
Hansen's disease (leprosy) 030.9
  benign form 030.1
  malignant form 030.0
Harada's disease or syndrome 363.22
Hard chancre 091.0
Hardening
  artery — *see* Arteriosclerosis
  brain 348.89
  liver 571.8
Hard firm prostate 600.10
  with
    urinary
      obstruction 600.11
      retention 600.11
Harelip — *see also* Cleft, lip 749.10
Hare's syndrome (M8010/3) (carcinoma, pulmonary apex) 162.3
Harkavy's syndrome 446.0
Harlequin (fetus) 757.1
  color change syndrome 779.89
Harley's disease (intermittent hemoglobinuria) 283.2
Harris'
  lines 733.91
  syndrome (organic hyperinsulinism) 251.1
Hart's disease or syndrome (pellagra-cerebellar ataxia-renal aminoaciduria) 270.0
Hartmann's pouch (abnormal sacculation of gallbladder neck) 575.8
  of intestine V44.3
    attention to V55.3
Hartnup disease (pellagra-cerebellar ataxia-renal aminoaciduria) 270.0
Harvester lung 495.0
Hashimoto's disease or struma (struma lymphomatosa) 245.2
Hassall-Henle bodies (corneal warts) 371.41
Haut mal — *see also* Epilepsy 345.1 ☑
Haverhill fever 026.1
Hawaiian wood rose dependence 304.5 ☑
Hawkins' keloid 701.4
Hay
  asthma (*see also* Asthma) 493.0 ☑
  fever (allergic) (with rhinitis) 477.9
    with asthma (bronchial) (*see also* Asthma) 493.0 ☑
    allergic, due to grass, pollen, ragweed, or tree 477.0
    conjunctivitis 372.05
    due to
      dander, animal (cat) (dog) 477.2
      dust 477.8
      fowl 477.8
      hair, animal (cat) (dog) 477.2
      pollen 477.0
      specified allergen other than pollen 477.8
Hayem-Faber syndrome (achlorhydric anemia) 280.9

Hayem-Widal syndrome (acquired hemolytic jaundice) 283.9
Haygarth's nodosities 715.04
Hazard-Crile tumor (M8350/3) 193
Hb (abnormal)
  disease — *see* Disease, hemoglobin
  trait — *see* Trait
H disease 270.0
Head — *see also* condition
  banging 307.3
Headache 784.0
  allergic 339.00
  associated with sexual activity 339.82
  cluster 339.00
    chronic 339.02
    episodic 339.01
  daily
    chronic 784.0
    new persistent (NPDH) 339.42
  drug induced 339.3
  due to
    loss, spinal fluid 349.0
    lumbar puncture 349.0
    saddle block 349.0
  emotional 307.81
  histamine 339.00
  hypnic 339.81
  lumbar puncture 349.0
  medication overuse 339.3
  menopausal 627.2
  menstrual 346.4 ☑
  migraine 346.9 ☑
  nasal septum 784.0
  nonorganic origin 307.81
  orgasmic 339.82
  postspinal 349.0
  post-traumatic 339.20
    acute 339.21
    chronic 339.22
  premenstrual 346.4 ☑
  preorgasmic 339.82
  primary
    cough 339.83
    exertional 339.84
    stabbing 339.85
    thunderclap 339.43
  psychogenic 307.81
  psychophysiologic 307.81
  rebound 339.3
  short lasting unilateral neuralgiform with conjunctival injection and tearing (SUNCT) 339.05
  sick 346.9 ☑
  spinal 349.0
    complicating labor and delivery 668.8 ☑
    postpartum 668.8 ☑
  spinal fluid loss 349.0
  syndrome
    cluster 339.00
    complicated NEC 339.44
    periodic in child or adolescent 346.2 ☑
    specified NEC 339.89
  tension 307.81
    type 339.10
      chronic 339.12
      episodic 339.11
  vascular 784.0
    migraine type 346.9 ☑
  vasomotor 346.9 ☑
Health
  advice V65.4 ☑
  audit V70.0
  checkup V70.0
  education V65.4 ☑
  hazard (*see also* History of) V15.9
    falling V15.88
    specified cause NEC V15.89
  instruction V65.4 ☑
  services provided because (of)
    boarding school residence V60.6
    holiday relief for person providing home care V60.5
    inadequate
      housing V60.1
      resources V60.2
    lack of housing V60.0

Health — *continued*
  services provided because — *continued*
    no care available in home V60.4
    person living alone V60.3
    poverty V60.3
    residence in institution V60.6
    specified cause NEC V60.89
    vacation relief for person providing home care V60.5
Healthy
  donor (*see also* Donor) V59.9
  infant or child
    accompanying sick mother V65.0
    receiving care V20.1
  person
    accompanying sick relative V65.0
    admitted for sterilization V25.2
    receiving prophylactic inoculation or vaccination (*see also* Vaccination, prophylactic) V05.9
Hearing
  conservation and treatment V72.12
  examination V72.19
    following failed hearing screening V72.11
Heart — *see* condition
Heartburn 787.1
  psychogenic 306.4
Heat (effects) 992.9
  apoplexy 992.0
  burn (*see also* Burn, by site)
    from sun (*see also* Sunburn) 692.71
  collapse 992.1
  cramps 992.2
  dermatitis or eczema 692.89
  edema 992.7
  erythema — *see* Burn, by site
  excessive 992.9
    specified effect NEC 992.8
  exhaustion 992.5
    anhydrotic 992.3
    due to
      salt (and water) depletion 992.4
      water depletion 992.3
  fatigue (transient) 992.6
  fever 992.0
  hyperpyrexia 992.0
  prickly 705.1
  prostration — *see* Heat, exhaustion
  pyrexia 992.0
  rash 705.1
  specified effect NEC 992.8
  stroke 992.0
  sunburn (*see also* Sunburn) 692.71
  syncope 992.1
Heavy-chain disease 273.2
Heavy-for-dates (fetus or infant) 766.1
  4500 grams or more 766.0
  exceptionally 766.0
Hebephrenia, hebephrenic (acute) — *see also* Schizophrenia 295.1 ☑
  dementia (praecox) (*see also* Schizophrenia) 295.1 ☑
  schizophrenia (*see also* Schizophrenia) 295.1 ☑
Heberden's
  disease or nodes 715.04
  syndrome (angina pectoris) 413.9
Hebra's disease
  dermatitis exfoliativa 695.89
  erythema multiforme exudativum 695.19
  pityriasis 695.89
    maculata et circinata 696.3
    rubra 695.89
      pilaris 696.4
  prurigo 698.2
Hebra, nose 040.1
Hedinger's syndrome (malignant carcinoid) 259.2
Heel — *see* condition
Heerfordt's disease or syndrome (uveoparotitis) 135
Hegglin's anomaly or syndrome 288.2
Heidenhain's disease 290.10
  with dementia 290.10

☑ Additional Digit Required — Refer to the Tabular List for Digit Selection   Subterms under main terms may continue to next column or page

132 — Volume 2   ▶◀ Revised Text   ● New Line   ▲ Revised Code   2015 ICD-9-CM

Heilmeyer-Schöner disease (M9842/3) 207.1 ☑
Heine-Medin disease — see also Poliomyelitis 045.9 ☑
Heinz-body anemia, congenital 282.7
Heller's disease or syndrome (infantile psychosis) — see also Psychosis, childhood 299.1 ☑
H.E.L.L.P 642.5 ☑
Helminthiasis — see also Infestation, by specific parasite 128.9
  Ancylostoma (see also Ancylostoma) 126.9
  intestinal 127.9
    mixed types (types classifiable to more than one of the categories 120.0–127.7) 127.8
    specified type 127.7
  mixed types (intestinal) (types classifiable to more than one of the categories 120.0–127.7) 127.8
  Necator americanus 126.1
  specified type NEC 128.8
  Trichinella 124
Heloma 700
Hemangioblastoma (M9161/1) — see also Neoplasm, connective tissue, uncertain behavior
  malignant (M9161/3) — see Neoplasm, connective tissue, malignant
Hemangioblastomatosis, cerebelloretinal 759.6
Hemangioendothelioma (M9130/1) — see also Neoplasm, by site, uncertain behavior
  benign (M9130/0) 228.00
  bone (diffuse) (M9130/3) — see Neoplasm, bone, malignant
  malignant (M9130/3) — see Neoplasm, connective tissue, malignant
  nervous system (M9130/0) 228.09
Hemangioendotheliosarcoma (M9130/3) — see Neoplasm, connective tissue, malignant
Hemangiofibroma (M9160/0) — see Neoplasm, by site, benign
Hemangiolipoma (M8861/0) — see Lipoma
Hemangioma (M9120/0) 228.00
  arteriovenous (M9123/0) — see Hemangioma, by site
  brain 228.02
  capillary (M9131/0) — see Hemangioma, by site
  cavernous (M9121/0) — see Hemangioma, by site
  central nervous system NEC 228.09
  choroid 228.09
  heart 228.09
  infantile (M9131/0) — see Hemangioma, by site
  intra-abdominal structures 228.04
  intracranial structures 228.02
  intramuscular (M9132/0) — see Hemangioma, by site
  iris 228.09
  juvenile (M9131/0) — see Hemangioma, by site
  malignant (M9120/3) — see Neoplasm, connective tissue, malignant
  meninges 228.09
    brain 228.02
    spinal cord 228.09
  peritoneum 228.04
  placenta — see Placenta, abnormal
  plexiform (M9131/0) — see Hemangioma, by site
  racemose (M9123/0) — see Hemangioma, by site
  retina 228.03
  retroperitoneal tissue 228.04
  sclerosing (M8832/0) — see Neoplasm, skin, benign
  simplex (M9131/0) — see Hemangioma, by site
  skin and subcutaneous tissue 228.01
  specified site NEC 228.09
  spinal cord 228.09

Hemangioma — continued
  venous (M9122/0) — see Hemangioma, by site
  verrucous keratotic (M9142/0) — see Hemangioma, by site
Hemangiomatosis (systemic) 757.32
  involving single site — see Hemangioma
Hemangiopericytoma (M9150/1) — see also Neoplasm, connective tissue, uncertain behavior
  benign (M9150/0) — see Neoplasm, connective tissue, benign
  malignant (M9150/3) — see Neoplasm, connective tissue, malignant
Hemangiosarcoma (M9120/3) — see Neoplasm, connective tissue, malignant
Hemarthrosis (nontraumatic) 719.10
  ankle 719.17
  elbow 719.12
  foot 719.17
  hand 719.14
  hip 719.15
  knee 719.16
  multiple sites 719.19
  pelvic region 719.15
  shoulder (region) 719.11
  specified site NEC 719.18
  traumatic — see Sprain, by site
  wrist 719.13
Hematemesis 578.0
  with ulcer — see Ulcer, by site, with hemorrhage
  due to S. japonicum 120.2
  Goldstein's (familial hemorrhagic telangiectasia) 448.0
  newborn 772.4
    due to swallowed maternal blood 777.3
Hematidrosis 705.89
Hematinuria — see also Hemoglobinuria 791.2
  malarial 084.8
  paroxysmal 283.2
Hematite miners' lung 503
Hematobilia 576.8
Hematocele (congenital) (diffuse) (idiopathic) 608.83
  broad ligament 620.7
  canal of Nuck 629.0
  cord, male 608.83
  fallopian tube 620.8
  female NEC 629.0
  ischiorectal 569.89
  male NEC 608.83
  ovary 629.0
  pelvis, pelvic
    female 629.0
      with ectopic pregnancy (see also Pregnancy, ectopic) 633.90
      with intrauterine pregnancy 633.91
    male 608.83
  periuterine 629.0
  retrouterine 629.0
  scrotum 608.83
  spermatic cord (diffuse) 608.83
  testis 608.84
  traumatic — see Injury, internal, pelvis
  tunica vaginalis 608.83
  uterine ligament 629.0
  uterus 621.4
  vagina 623.6
  vulva 624.5
Hematocephalus 742.4
Hematochezia — see also Melena 578.1
Hematochyluria — see also Infestation, filarial 125.9
Hematocolpos 626.8
Hematocornea 371.12
Hematogenous — see condition

Hematoma (skin surface intact) (traumatic) — see also Contusion

> *Note — Hematomas are coded according to origin and the nature and site of the hematoma or the accompanying injury. Hematomas of unspecified origin are coded as injuries of the sites involved, except:*
>
> *(a) hematomas of genital organs which are coded as diseases of the organ involved unless they complicate pregnancy or delivery*
>
> *(b) hematomas of the eye which are coded as diseases of the eye.*
>
> *For late effect of hematoma classifiable to 920–924 see Late, effect, contusion*

  with
    crush injury — see Crush
    fracture — see Fracture, by site
    injury of internal organs (see also Injury, internal, by site)
      kidney — see Hematoma, kidney traumatic
      liver — see Hematoma, liver, traumatic
      spleen — see Hematoma, spleen
    nerve injury — see Injury, nerve
    open wound — see Wound, open, by site
    skin surface intact — see Contusion
  abdomen (wall) — see Contusion, abdomen
  amnion 658.8 ☑
  aorta, dissecting 441.00
    abdominal 441.02
    thoracic 441.01
    thoracoabdominal 441.03
  aortic intramural — see Dissection, aorta
  arterial (complicating trauma) 904.9
    specified site — see Injury, blood vessel, by site
  auricle (ear) 380.31
  birth injury 767.8
    skull 767.19
  brain (traumatic) 853.0 ☑

> *Note — Use the following fifth-digit subclassification with categories 851–854:*
>
> *0   unspecified state of consciousness*
>
> *1   with no loss of consciousness*
>
> *2   with brief [less than one hour] loss of consciousness*
>
> *3   with moderate [1–24 hours] loss of consciousness*
>
> *4   with prolonged [more than 24 hours] loss of consciousness and return to pre-existing conscious level*
>
> *5   with prolonged [more than 24 hours] loss of consciousness, without return to pre-existing conscious level*
>
> *Use fifth-digit 5 to designate when a patient is unconscious and dies before regaining consciousness, regardless of the duration of the loss of consciousness*
>
> *6   with loss of consciousness of unspecified duration*
>
> *9   with concussion, unspecified*

    with
      cerebral
        contusion — see Contusion, brain
        laceration — see Laceration, brain
      open intracranial wound 853.1 ☑
      skull fracture — see Fracture, skull, by site
    extradural or epidural 852.4 ☑
      with open intracranial wound 852.5 ☑
      fetus or newborn 767.0

Hematoma — see also Contusion — continued
  brain — continued
    extradural or epidural — continued
      nontraumatic 432.0
    fetus or newborn NEC 767.0
    nontraumatic (see also Hemorrhage, brain) 431
      epidural or extradural 432.0
      newborn NEC 772.8
      subarachnoid, arachnoid, or meningeal (see also Hemorrhage, subarachnoid) 430
      subdural (see also Hemorrhage, subdural) 432.1
    subarachnoid, arachnoid, or meningeal 852.0 ☑
      with open intracranial wound 852.1 ☑
      fetus or newborn 772.2
      nontraumatic (see also Hemorrhage, subarachnoid) 430
    subdural 852.2 ☑
      with open intracranial wound 852.3 ☑
      fetus or newborn (localized) 767.0
      nontraumatic (see also Hemorrhage, subdural) 432.1
  breast (nontraumatic) 611.89
  broad ligament (nontraumatic) 620.7
    complicating delivery 665.7 ☑
    traumatic — see Injury, internal, broad ligament
  calcified NEC 959.9
  capitis 920
    due to birth injury 767.19
    newborn 767.19
  cerebral — see Hematoma, brain
  cesarean section wound 674.3 ☑
  chorion — see Placenta, abnormal
  complicating delivery (perineum) (vulva) 664.5 ☑
    pelvic 665.7 ☑
    vagina 665.7 ☑
  corpus
    cavernosum (nontraumatic) 607.82
    luteum (nontraumatic) (ruptured) 620.1
  dura (mater) — see Hematoma, brain, subdural
  epididymis (nontraumatic) 608.83
  epidural (traumatic) (see also Hematoma, brain, extradural)
    spinal — see Injury, spinal, by site
  episiotomy 674.3 ☑
  external ear 380.31
  extradural (see also Hematoma, brain, extradural)
    fetus or newborn 767.0
    nontraumatic 432.0
    fetus or newborn 767.0
  fallopian tube 620.8
  genital organ (nontraumatic)
    female NEC 629.89
    male NEC 608.83
    traumatic (external site) 922.4
      internal — see Injury, internal, genital organ
  graafian follicle (ruptured) 620.0
  internal organs (abdomen, chest, or pelvis) (see also Injury, internal, by site)
    kidney — see Hematoma, kidney, traumatic
    liver — see Hematoma, liver, traumatic
    spleen — see Hematoma, spleen
  intracranial — see Hematoma, brain
  kidney, cystic 593.81
    traumatic 866.01
      with open wound into cavity 866.11
  labia (nontraumatic) 624.5
  lingual (and other parts of neck, scalp, or face, except eye) 920
  liver (subcapsular) 573.8
    birth injury 767.8
    fetus or newborn 767.8
    traumatic NEC 864.01

Hematoma — *see also* Contusion — *continued*
  liver — *continued*
    traumatic — *continued*
      with
        laceration — *see* Laceration, liver
        open wound into cavity 864.11
  mediastinum — *see* Injury, internal, mediastinum
  meninges, meningeal (brain) (*see also* Hematoma, brain, subarachnoid)
    spinal — *see* Injury, spinal, by site
  mesosalpinx (nontraumatic) 620.8
    traumatic — *see* Injury, internal, pelvis
  muscle (traumatic) — *see* Contusion, by site
    nontraumatic 729.92
  nasal (septum) (and other part(s) of neck, scalp, or face, except eye) 920
  obstetrical surgical wound 674.3 ☑
  orbit, orbital (nontraumatic) 376.32
    traumatic 921.2
  ovary (corpus luteum) (nontraumatic) 620.1
    traumatic — *see* Injury, internal, ovary
  pelvis (female) (nontraumatic) 629.89
    complicating delivery 665.7 ☑
    male 608.83
    traumatic (*see also* Injury, internal, pelvis)
      specified organ NEC (*see also* Injury, internal, pelvis) 867.6
  penis (nontraumatic) 607.82
  pericranial (and neck, or face any part, except eye) 920
    due to injury at birth 767.19
  perineal wound (obstetrical) 674.3 ☑
    complicating delivery 664.5 ☑
  perirenal, cystic 593.81
  pinna 380.31
  placenta — *see* Placenta, abnormal
  postoperative 998.12
  retroperitoneal (nontraumatic) 568.81
    traumatic — *see* Injury, internal, retroperitoneum
  retropubic, male 568.81
  scalp (and neck, or face any part, except eye) 920
    fetus or newborn 767.19
  scrotum (nontraumatic) 608.83
    traumatic 922.4
  seminal vesicle (nontraumatic) 608.83
    traumatic — *see* Injury, internal, seminal, vesicle
  soft tissue 729.92
  spermatic cord (*see also* Injury, internal, spermatic cord)
    nontraumatic 608.83
  spinal (cord) (meninges) (*see also* Injury, spinal, by site)
    fetus or newborn 767.4
    nontraumatic 336.1
  spleen 865.01
    with
      laceration — *see* Laceration, spleen
      open wound into cavity 865.11
  sternocleidomastoid, birth injury 767.8
  sternomastoid, birth injury 767.8
  subarachnoid (*see also* Hematoma, brain, subarachnoid)
    fetus or newborn 772.2
    nontraumatic (*see also* Hemorrhage, subarachnoid) 430
    newborn 772.2
  subdural (*see also* Hematoma, brain, subdural)
    fetus or newborn (localized) 767.0
    nontraumatic (*see also* Hemorrhage, subdural) 432.1
  subperiosteal (syndrome) 267
    traumatic — *see* Hematoma, by site
  superficial, fetus or newborn 772.6
  syncytium — *see* Placenta, abnormal
  testis (nontraumatic) 608.83
    birth injury 767.8
    traumatic 922.4
  tunica vaginalis (nontraumatic) 608.83
  umbilical cord 663.6 ☑
    affecting fetus or newborn 762.6

Hematoma — *see also* Contusion — *continued*
  uterine ligament (nontraumatic) 620.7
    traumatic — *see* Injury, internal, pelvis
  uterus 621.4
    traumatic — *see* Injury, internal, pelvis
  vagina (nontraumatic) (ruptured) 623.6
    complicating delivery 665.7 ☑
    traumatic 922.4
  vas deferens (nontraumatic) 608.83
    traumatic — *see* Injury, internal, vas deferens
  vitreous 379.23
  vocal cord 920
  vulva (nontraumatic) 624.5
    complicating delivery 664.5 ☑
    fetus or newborn 767.8
    traumatic 922.4
Hematometra 621.4
Hematomyelia 336.1
  with fracture of vertebra (*see also* Fracture, vertebra, by site, with spinal cord injury) 806.8
  fetus or newborn 767.4
Hematomyelitis 323.9
  late effect — *see* category 326
Hematoperitoneum — *see also* Hemoperitoneum 568.81
Hematopneumothorax — *see also* Hemothorax 511.89
Hematopoiesis, cyclic 288.02
Hematoporphyria (acquired) (congenital) 277.1
Hematoporphyrinuria (acquired) (congenital) 277.1
Hematorachis, hematorrhachis 336.1
  fetus or newborn 767.4
Hematosalpinx 620.8
  with
    ectopic pregnancy (*see also* categories 633.0–633.9) 639.2
    infectional (*see also* Salpingo-oophoritis) 614.2
    molar pregnancy (*see also* categories 630–632) 639.2
Hematospermia 608.82
Hematothorax — *see also* Hemothorax 511.89
Hematotympanum 381.03
Hematuria (benign) (essential) (idiopathic) 599.70
  due to S. hematobium 120.0
  endemic 120.0
  gross 599.71
  intermittent 599.70
  malarial 084.8
  microscopic 599.72
  paroxysmal 599.70
  sulfonamide
    correct substance properly administered 599.70
    overdose or wrong substance given or taken 961.0
  tropical (bilharziasis) 120.0
  tuberculous (*see also* Tuberculosis) 016.9 ☑
Hematuric bilious fever 084.8
Hemeralopia 368.10
Hemiabiotrophy 799.89
Hemi-akinesia 781.8
Hemianalgesia — *see also* Disturbance, sensation 782.0
Hemianencephaly 740.0
Hemianesthesia — *see also* Disturbance, sensation 782.0
Hemianopia, hemianopsia (altitudinal) (homonymous) 368.46
  binasal 368.47
  bitemporal 368.47
  heteronymous 368.47
  syphilitic 095.8
Hemiasomatognosia 307.9
Hemiathetosis 781.0
Hemiatrophy 799.89
  cerebellar 334.8
  face 349.89
    progressive 349.89
  fascia 728.9

Hemiatrophy — *continued*
  leg 728.2
  tongue 529.8
Hemiballism (us) 333.5
Hemiblock (cardiac) (heart) (left) 426.2
Hemicardia 746.89
Hemicephalus, hemicephaly 740.0
Hemichorea 333.5
Hemicrania 346.9 ☑
  congenital malformation 740.0
  continua 339.41
  paroxysmal 339.03
    chronic 339.04
    episodic 339.03
Hemidystrophy — *see* Hemiatrophy
Hemiectromelia 755.4
Hemihypalgesia — *see also* Disturbance, sensation 782.0
Hemihypertrophy (congenital) 759.89
  cranial 756.0
Hemihypesthesia — *see also* Disturbance, sensation 782.0
Hemi-inattention 781.8
Hemimelia 755.4
  lower limb 755.30
    paraxial (complete) (incomplete) (intercalary) (terminal) 755.32
      fibula 755.37
      tibia 755.36
    transverse (complete) (partial) 755.31
  upper limb 755.20
    paraxial (complete) (incomplete) (intercalary) (terminal) 755.22
      radial 755.26
      ulnar 755.27
    transverse (complete) (partial) 755.21
Hemiparalysis — *see also* Hemiplegia 342.9 ☑
Hemiparesis — *see also* Hemiplegia 342.9 ☑
Hemiparesthesia — *see also* Disturbance, sensation 782.0
Hemiplegia 342.9 ☑
  acute (*see also* Disease, cerebrovascular, acute) 436
  alternans facialis 344.89
  apoplectic (*see also* Disease, cerebrovascular, acute) 436
    late effect or residual
      affecting
        dominant side 438.21
        nondominant side 438.22
        unspecified side 438.20
  arteriosclerotic 437.0
    late effect or residual
      affecting
        dominant side 438.21
        nondominant side 438.22
        unspecified side 438.20
  ascending (spinal) NEC 344.89
  attack (*see also* Disease, cerebrovascular, acute) 436
  brain, cerebral (current episode) 437.8
    congenital 343.1
  cerebral — *see* Hemiplegia, brain
  congenital (cerebral) (spastic) (spinal) 343.1
  conversion neurosis (hysterical) 300.11
  cortical — *see* Hemiplegia, brain
  due to
    arteriosclerosis 437.0
      late effect or residual
        affecting
          dominant side 438.21
          nondominant side 438.22
          unspecified side 438.20
    cerebrovascular lesion (*see also* Disease, cerebrovascular, acute) 436
      late effect
        affecting
          dominant side 438.21
          nondominant side 438.22
          unspecified side 438.20
  embolic (current) (*see also* Embolism, brain) 434.1 ☑
    late effect
      affecting
        dominant side 438.21
        nondominant side 438.22

Hemiplegia — *continued*
  embolic (*see also* Embolism, brain) — *continued*
    late effect — *continued*
      affecting — *continued*
        unspecified side 438.20
  flaccid 342.0 ☑
  hypertensive (current episode) 437.8
  infantile (postnatal) 343.4
  late effect
    birth injury, intracranial or spinal 343.4
    cerebrovascular lesion —– *see* Late effect(s) (of) cerebrovascular disease
    viral encephalitis 139.0
  middle alternating NEC 344.89
  newborn NEC 767.0
  seizure (current episode) (*see also* Disease, cerebrovascular, acute) 436
  spastic 342.1 ☑
    congenital or infantile 343.1
  specified NEC 342.8 ☑
  thrombotic (current) (*see also* Thrombosis, brain) 434.0 ☑
    late effect —- *see* Late effect(s) (of) cerebrovascular disease
Hemisection, spinal cord — *see* Fracture, vertebra, by site, with spinal cord injury
Hemispasm 781.0
  facial 781.0
Hemispatial neglect 781.8
Hemisporosis 117.9
Hemitremor 781.0
Hemivertebra 756.14
Hemobilia 576.8
Hemocholecyst 575.8
Hemochromatosis (acquired) (liver) (myocardium) (secondary) 275.03
  with refractory anemia 238.72
  diabetic 275.03
  due to repeated red blood cell transfusions 275.02
  hereditary 275.01
  primary idiopathic 275.01
  specified NEC 275.03
  transfusion associated (red blood cell) 275.02
Hemodialysis V56.0
Hemoglobin — *see also* condition
  abnormal (disease) — *see* Disease, hemoglobin
  AS genotype 282.5
  fetal, hereditary persistence 282.7
  H Constant Spring 282.43
  H disease 282.43
  high-oxygen-affinity 289.0
  low NEC 285.9
  S (Hb-S), heterozygous 282.5
Hemoglobinemia 283.2
  due to blood transfusion NEC 999.89
    bone marrow 996.85
  paroxysmal 283.2
Hemoglobinopathy (mixed) — *see also* Disease, hemoglobin 282.7
  with thalassemia 282.49
  sickle-cell 282.60
    with thalassemia (without crisis) 282.41
      with
        crisis 282.42
        vaso-occlusive pain 282.42
Hemoglobinuria, hemoglobinuric 791.2
  with anemia, hemolytic, acquired (chronic) NEC 283.2
  cold (agglutinin) (paroxysmal) (with Raynaud's syndrome) 283.2
  due to
    exertion 283.2
    hemolysis (from external causes) NEC 283.2
  exercise 283.2
  fever (malaria) 084.8
  infantile 791.2
  intermittent 283.2
  malarial 084.8
  march 283.2
  nocturnal (paroxysmal) 283.2

☑ Additional Digit Required — Refer to the Tabular List for Digit Selection

▽ Subterms under main terms may continue to next column or page

Hemoglobinuria, hemoglobinuric —
continued
 paroxysmal (cold) (nocturnal) 283.2
Hemolymphangioma (M9175/0) 228.1
Hemolysis
 fetal — *see* Jaundice, fetus or newborn
 intravascular (disseminated) NEC 286.6
 with
  abortion — *see* Abortion, by type,
   with hemorrhage, delayed or
   excessive
  ectopic pregnancy (*see also* categories 633.0–633.9) 639.1
  hemorrhage of pregnancy 641.3 ☑
   affecting fetus or newborn 762.1
  molar pregnancy (*see also* categories
   630–632) 639.1
 acute 283.2
 following
  abortion 639.1
  ectopic or molar pregnancy 639.1
 neonatal — *see* Jaundice, fetus or newborn
 transfusion NEC 999.89
  bone marrow 996.85
Hemolytic — *see also* condition
 anemia — *see* Anemia, hemolytic
 uremic syndrome 283.11
Hemometra 621.4
Hemopericardium (with effusion) 423.0
 newborn 772.8
 traumatic (*see also* Hemothorax, traumatic)
  860.2
  with open wound into thorax 860.3
Hemoperitoneum 568.81
 infectional (*see also* Peritonitis) 567.29
 traumatic — *see* Injury, internal, peritoneum
Hemophagocytic syndrome 288.4
 infection-associated 288.4
Hemophilia (familial) (hereditary) 286.0
 A 286.0
  carrier (asymptomatic) V83.01
   symptomatic V83.02
 acquired 286.52
 autoimmune 286.52
 B (Leyden) 286.1
 C 286.2
 calcipriva (*see also* Fibrinolysis) 286.7
 classical 286.0
 nonfamilial 286.7
 secondary 286.52
 vascular 286.4
Hemophilus influenzae NEC 041.5
 arachnoiditis (basic) (brain) (spinal) 320.0
  late effect — *see* category 326
 bronchopneumonia 482.2
 cerebral ventriculitis 320.0
  late effect — *see* category 326
 cerebrospinal inflammation 320.0
  late effect — *see* category 326
 infection NEC 041.5
 leptomeningitis 320.0
  late effect — *see* category 326
 meningitis (cerebral) (cerebrospinal) (spinal)
  320.0
  late effect — *see* category 326
 meningomyelitis 320.0
  late effect — *see* category 326
 pachymeningitis (adhesive) (fibrous) (hemorrhagic) (hypertrophic) (spinal)
  320.0
  late effect — *see* category 326
 pneumonia (broncho-) 482.2
Hemophthalmos 360.43
Hemopneumothorax — *see also* Hemothorax
 511.89
 traumatic 860.4
  with open wound into thorax 860.5
Hemoptysis 786.30
 due to Paragonimus (westermani) 121.2
 newborn 770.3
 specified NEC 786.39
 tuberculous (*see also* Tuberculosis, pulmonary) 011.9 ☑
Hemorrhage, hemorrhagic (nontraumatic)
 459.0
 abdomen 459.0

Hemorrhage, hemorrhagic — *continued*
 accidental (antepartum) 641.2 ☑
  affecting fetus or newborn 762.1
 adenoid 474.8
 adrenal (capsule) (gland) (medulla) 255.41
  newborn 772.5
 after labor — *see* Hemorrhage, postpartum
 alveolar
  lung, newborn 770.3
  process 525.8
 alveolus 525.8
 amputation stump (surgical) 998.11
  secondary, delayed 997.69
 anemia (chronic) 280.0
  acute 285.1
 antepartum — *see* Hemorrhage, pregnancy
 anus (sphincter) 569.3
 apoplexy (stroke) 432.9
 arachnoid — *see* Hemorrhage, subarachnoid
 artery NEC 459.0
  brain (*see also* Hemorrhage, brain) 431
   middle meningeal — *see* Hemorrhage,
    subarachnoid
 basilar (ganglion) (*see also* Hemorrhage,
  brain) 431
 bladder 596.89
 blood dyscrasia 289.9
 bowel 578.9
  newborn 772.4
 brain (miliary) (nontraumatic) 431
  with
   birth injury 767.0
   arachnoid — *see* Hemorrhage, subarach-
    noid
  due to
   birth injury 767.0
   rupture of aneurysm (congenital) (*see
    also* Hemorrhage, subarach-
    noid) 430
   mycotic 431
   syphilis 094.89
  epidural or extradural — *see* Hemorrhage, extradural
  fetus or newborn (anoxic) (hypoxic) (due
   to birth trauma) (nontraumatic)
   767.0
   intraventricular 772.10
    grade I 772.11
    grade II 772.12
    grade III 772.13
    grade IV 772.14
  iatrogenic 997.02
  postoperative 997.02
  puerperal, postpartum, childbirth
   674.0 ☑
  stem 431
  subarachnoid, arachnoid, or meningeal
   — *see* Hemorrhage, subarachnoid
  subdural — *see* Hemorrhage, subdural

Hemorrhage, hemorrhagic — *continued*
 brain — *continued*
  traumatic NEC 853.0 ☑

> *Note* — *Use the following fifth-digit
> subclassification with categories
> 851–854:*
>
> *0   unspecified state of consciousness*
>
> *1   with no loss of consciousness*
>
> *2   with brief [less than one hour]
>   loss of consciousness*
>
> *3   with moderate [1–24 hours] loss
>   of consciousness*
>
> *4   with prolonged [more than 24
>   hours] loss of consciousness and
>   return to pre–existing conscious
>   level*
>
> *5   with prolonged [more than 24
>   hours] loss of consciousness,
>   without return to pre–existing
>   conscious level*
>
> *Use fifth-digit 5 to designate when a
> patient is unconscious and dies before
> regaining consciousness, regardless of
> the duration of the loss of consciousness*
>
> *6   with loss of consciousness of un-
>   specified duration*
>
> *9   with concussion, unspecified*

   with
    cerebral
     contusion — *see* Contusion,
      brain
     laceration — *see* Laceration,
      brain
    open intracranial wound 853.1 ☑
    skull fracture — *see* Fracture,
     skull, by site
   extradural or epidural 852.4 ☑
    with open intracranial wound
     852.5 ☑
   subarachnoid 852.0 ☑
    with open intracranial wound
     852.1 ☑
   subdural 852.2 ☑
    with open intracranial wound
     852.3 ☑
 breast 611.79
 bronchial tube — *see* Hemorrhage, lung
 bronchopulmonary — *see* Hemorrhage,
  lung
 bronchus (cause unknown) (*see also* Hemorrhage, lung) 786.30
 bulbar (*see also* Hemorrhage, brain) 431
 bursa 727.89
 capillary 448.9
  primary 287.8
 capsular — *see* Hemorrhage, brain
 cardiovascular 429.89
 cecum 578.9
 cephalic (*see also* Hemorrhage, brain) 431
 cerebellar (*see also* Hemorrhage, brain) 431
 cerebellum (*see also* Hemorrhage, brain) 431
 cerebral (*see also* Hemorrhage, brain) 431
  fetus or newborn (anoxic) (traumatic)
   767.0
 cerebromeningeal (*see also* Hemorrhage,
  brain) 431
 cerebrospinal (*see also* Hemorrhage, brain)
  431
 cerebrovascular accident — *see* Hemorrhage, brain
 cerebrum (*see also* Hemorrhage, brain) 431
 cervix (stump) (uteri) 622.8
 cesarean section wound 674.3 ☑
 chamber, anterior (eye) 364.41
 childbirth — *see* Hemorrhage, complicating,
  delivery
 choroid 363.61
  expulsive 363.62
 ciliary body 364.41
 cochlea 386.8
 colon — *see* Hemorrhage, intestine

Hemorrhage, hemorrhagic — *continued*
 complicating
  delivery 641.9 ☑
   affecting fetus or newborn 762.1
   associated with
    afibrinogenemia 641.3 ☑
     affecting fetus or newborn
      763.89
    coagulation defect 641.3 ☑
     affecting fetus or newborn
      763.89
    hyperfibrinolysis 641.3 ☑
     affecting fetus or newborn
      763.89
    hypofibrinogenemia 641.3 ☑
     affecting fetus or newborn
      763.89
   due to
    low-lying placenta 641.1 ☑
     affecting fetus or newborn
      762.0
    placenta previa 641.1 ☑
     affecting fetus or newborn
      762.0
    premature separation of placenta
     641.2 ☑
     affecting fetus or newborn
      762.1
   retained
    placenta 666.0 ☑
    secundines 666.2 ☑
   trauma 641.8 ☑
    affecting fetus or newborn
     763.89
   uterine leiomyoma 641.8 ☑
    affecting fetus or newborn
     763.89
  surgical procedure 998.11
 complication(s)
  of dental implant placement 525.71
 concealed NEC 459.0
 congenital 772.9
 conjunctiva 372.72
  newborn 772.8
 cord, newborn 772.0
  slipped ligature 772.3
  stump 772.3
 corpus luteum (ruptured) 620.1
 cortical (*see also* Hemorrhage, brain) 431
 cranial 432.9
 cutaneous 782.7
  newborn 772.6
 cystitis — *see* Cystitis
 cyst, pancreas 577.2
 delayed
  with
   abortion — *see* Abortion, by type,
    with hemorrhage, delayed or
    excessive
   ectopic pregnancy (*see also* cate-
    gories 633.0–633.9) 639.1
   molar pregnancy (*see also* categories
    630–632) 639.1
  following
   abortion 639.1
   ectopic or molar pregnancy 639.1
  postpartum 666.2 ☑
 diathesis (familial) 287.9
  newborn 776.0
 disease 287.9
  newborn 776.0
  specified type NEC 287.8
 disorder 287.9
  due to intrinsic circulating anticoagulants, antibodies, or inhibitors
   286.59
   with
    acquired hemophilia 286.52
    antiphospholipid antibody 286.53
  specified type NEC 287.8
 due to
  any device, implant or graft (presence
   of) classifiable to 996.0–996.5 —
   see Complications, due to (presence of) any device, implant, or
   graft classified to 996.0–996.5 NEC

☑ **Additional Digit Required — Refer to the Tabular List for Digit Selection**   ₜₑₓₜ **Subterms under main terms may continue to next column or page**

2015 ICD-9-CM   ▶◀ **Revised Text**   ● **New Line**   ▲ **Revised Code**   **Volume 2 — 135**

Hemorrhage, hemorrhagic — *continued*
- due to — *continued*
  - intrinsic circulating anticoagulant, antibodies, or inhibitors 286.59
    - with
      - acquired hemophilia 286.52
      - antiphospholipid antibody 286.53
- duodenum, duodenal 537.89
  - ulcer — *see* Ulcer, duodenum, with hemorrhage
- dura mater — *see* Hemorrhage, subdural
- endotracheal — *see* Hemorrhage, lung
- epicranial subaponeurotic (massive) 767.11
- epidural — *see* Hemorrhage, extradural
- episiotomy 674.3 ☑
- esophagus 530.82
  - varix (*see also* Varix, esophagus, bleeding) 456.0
- excessive
  - with
    - abortion — *see* Abortion, by type, with hemorrhage, delayed or excessive
    - ectopic pregnancy (*see also* categories 633.0–633.9) 639.1
    - molar pregnancy (*see also* categories 630–632) 639.1
  - following
    - abortion 639.1
    - ectopic or molar pregnancy 639.1
- external 459.0
- extradural (traumatic) (*see also* Hemorrhage, brain, traumatic, extradural)
  - birth injury 767.0
  - fetus or newborn (anoxic) (traumatic) 767.0
  - nontraumatic 432.0
- eye 360.43
  - chamber (anterior) (aqueous) 364.41
  - fundus 362.81
- eyelid 374.81
- fallopian tube 620.8
- fetomaternal 772.0
  - affecting management of pregnancy or puerperium 656.0 ☑
- fetus, fetal, affecting newborn 772.0
  - from
    - cut end of co-twin's cord 772.0
    - placenta 772.0
    - ruptured cord 772.0
    - vasa previa 772.0
  - into
    - co-twin 772.0
    - mother's circulation 772.0
      - affecting management of pregnancy or puerperium 656.0 ☑
- fever (*see also* Fever, hemorrhagic) 065.9
  - with renal syndrome 078.6
  - arthropod-borne NEC 065.9
  - Bangkok 065.4
  - Crimean 065.0
  - dengue virus 065.4
  - epidemic 078.6
  - Junin virus 078.7
  - Korean 078.6
  - Machupo virus 078.7
  - mite-borne 065.8
  - mosquito-borne 065.4
  - Philippine 065.4
  - Russian (Yaroslav) 078.6
  - Singapore 065.4
  - southeast Asia 065.4
  - Thailand 065.4
  - tick-borne NEC 065.3
- fibrinogenolysis (*see also* Fibrinolysis) 286.6
- fibrinolytic (acquired) (*see also* Fibrinolysis) 286.6
- fontanel 767.19
- from tracheostomy stoma 519.09
- fundus, eye 362.81
- funis
  - affecting fetus or newborn 772.0
  - complicating delivery 663.8 ☑
- gastric (*see also* Hemorrhage, stomach) 578.9

Hemorrhage, hemorrhagic — *continued*
- gastroenteric 578.9
  - newborn 772.4
- gastrointestinal (tract) 578.9
  - newborn 772.4
- genitourinary (tract) NEC 599.89
- gingiva 523.8
- globe 360.43
- gravidarum — *see* Hemorrhage, pregnancy
- gum 523.8
- heart 429.89
- hypopharyngeal (throat) 784.8
- intermenstrual 626.6
  - irregular 626.6
  - regular 626.5
- internal (organs) 459.0
  - capsule (*see also* Hemorrhage, brain) 431
  - ear 386.8
  - newborn 772.8
- intestine 578.9
  - congenital 772.4
  - newborn 772.4
- into
  - bladder wall 596.7
  - bursa 727.89
  - corpus luysii (*see also* Hemorrhage, brain) 431
- intra-abdominal 459.0
  - during or following surgery 998.11
- intra-alveolar, newborn (lung) 770.3
- intracerebral (*see also* Hemorrhage, brain) 431
- intracranial NEC 432.9
  - puerperal, postpartum, childbirth 674.0 ☑
  - traumatic — *see* Hemorrhage, brain, traumatic
- intramedullary NEC 336.1
- intraocular 360.43
- intraoperative 998.11
- intrapartum — *see* Hemorrhage, complicating, delivery
- intrapelvic
  - female 629.89
  - male 459.0
- intraperitoneal 459.0
- intrapontine (*see also* Hemorrhage, brain) 431
- intrauterine 621.4
  - complicating delivery — *see* Hemorrhage, complicating, delivery
  - in pregnancy or childbirth — *see* Hemorrhage, pregnancy
  - postpartum (*see also* Hemorrhage, postpartum) 666.1 ☑
- intraventricular (*see also* Hemorrhage, brain) 431
  - fetus or newborn (anoxic) (traumatic) 772.10
    - grade I 772.11
    - grade II 772.12
    - grade III 772.13
    - grade IV 772.14
- intravesical 596.7
- iris (postinfectional) (postinflammatory) (toxic) 364.41
- joint (nontraumatic) 719.10
  - ankle 719.17
  - elbow 719.12
  - foot 719.17
  - forearm 719.13
  - hand 719.14
  - hip 719.15
  - knee 719.16
  - lower leg 719.16
  - multiple sites 719.19
  - pelvic region 719.15
  - shoulder (region) 719.11
  - specified site NEC 719.18
  - thigh 719.15
  - upper arm 719.12
  - wrist 719.13
- kidney 593.81
- knee (joint) 719.16
- labyrinth 386.8
- leg NEC 459.0

Hemorrhage, hemorrhagic — *continued*
- lenticular striate artery (*see also* Hemorrhage, brain) 431
- ligature, vessel 998.11
- liver 573.8
- lower extremity NEC 459.0
- lung 786.30
  - newborn 770.3
  - tuberculous (*see also* Tuberculosis, pulmonary) 011.9 ☑
- malaria 084.8
- marginal sinus 641.2 ☑
- massive subaponeurotic, birth injury 767.11
- maternal, affecting fetus or newborn 762.1
- mediastinum 786.30
- medulla (*see also* Hemorrhage, brain) 431
- membrane (brain) (*see also* Hemorrhage, subarachnoid) 430
  - spinal cord — *see* Hemorrhage, spinal cord
- meninges, meningeal (brain) (middle) (*see also* Hemorrhage, subarachnoid) 430
  - spinal cord — *see* Hemorrhage, spinal cord
- mesentery 568.81
- metritis 626.8
- midbrain (*see also* Hemorrhage, brain) 431
- mole 631.8
- mouth 528.9
- mucous membrane NEC 459.0
  - newborn 772.8
- muscle 728.89
- nail (subungual) 703.8
- nasal turbinate 784.7
  - newborn 772.8
- nasopharynx 478.29
- navel, newborn 772.3
- newborn 772.9
  - adrenal 772.5
  - alveolar (lung) 770.3
  - brain (anoxic) (hypoxic) (due to birth trauma) 767.0
  - cerebral (anoxic) (hypoxic) (due to birth trauma) 767.0
  - conjunctiva 772.8
  - cutaneous 772.6
  - diathesis 776.0
  - due to vitamin K deficiency 776.0
  - epicranial subaponeurotic (massive) 767.11
  - gastrointestinal 772.4
  - internal (organs) 772.8
  - intestines 772.4
  - intra-alveolar (lung) 770.3
  - intracranial (from any perinatal cause) 767.0
  - intraventricular (from any perinatal cause) 772.10
    - grade I 772.11
    - grade II 772.12
    - grade III 772.13
    - grade IV 772.14
  - lung 770.3
  - pulmonary (massive) 770.3
  - spinal cord, traumatic 767.4
  - stomach 772.4
  - subaponeurotic (massive) 767.11
  - subarachnoid (from any perinatal cause) 772.2
  - subconjunctival 772.8
  - subgaleal 767.11
  - umbilicus 772.0
    - slipped ligature 772.3
    - vasa previa 772.0
- nipple 611.79
- nose 784.7
  - newborn 772.8
- obstetrical surgical wound 674.3 ☑
- omentum 568.89
  - newborn 772.4
- optic nerve (sheath) 377.42
- orbit 376.32
- ovary 620.1
- oviduct 620.8
- pancreas 577.8
- parathyroid (gland) (spontaneous) 252.8

Hemorrhage, hemorrhagic — *continued*
- parturition — *see* Hemorrhage, complicating, delivery
- penis 607.82
- pericardium, pericarditis 423.0
- perineal wound (obstetrical) 674.3 ☑
- peritoneum, peritoneal 459.0
- peritonsillar tissue 474.8
  - after operation on tonsils 998.11
  - due to infection 475
- petechial 782.7
- pituitary (gland) 253.8
- placenta NEC 641.9 ☑
  - affecting fetus or newborn 762.1
  - from surgical or instrumental damage 641.8 ☑
    - affecting fetus or newborn 762.1
  - previa 641.1 ☑
    - affecting fetus or newborn 762.0
- pleura — *see* Hemorrhage, lung
- polioencephalitis, superior 265.1
- polymyositis — *see* Polymyositis
- pons (*see also* Hemorrhage, brain) 431
- pontine (*see also* Hemorrhage, brain) 431
- popliteal 459.0
- postcoital 626.7
- postextraction (dental) 998.11
- postmenopausal 627.1
- postnasal 784.7
- postoperative 998.11
- postpartum (atonic) (following delivery of placenta) 666.1 ☑
  - delayed or secondary (after 24 hours) 666.2 ☑
  - retained placenta 666.0 ☑
  - third stage 666.0 ☑
- pregnancy (concealed) 641.9 ☑
  - accidental 641.2 ☑
    - affecting fetus or newborn 762.1
  - affecting fetus or newborn 762.1
  - before 22 completed weeks gestation 640.9 ☑
    - affecting fetus or newborn 762.1
  - due to
    - abruptio placenta 641.2 ☑
      - affecting fetus or newborn 762.1
    - afibrinogenemia or other coagulation defect (conditions classifiable to 286.0–286.9) 641.3 ☑
      - affecting fetus or newborn 762.1
    - coagulation defect 641.3 ☑
      - affecting fetus or newborn 762.1
    - hyperfibrinolysis 641.3 ☑
      - affecting fetus or newborn 762.1
    - hypofibrinogenemia 641.3 ☑
      - affecting fetus or newborn 762.1
    - leiomyoma, uterus 641.8 ☑
      - affecting fetus or newborn 762.1
    - low-lying placenta 641.1 ☑
      - affecting fetus or newborn 762.1
    - marginal sinus (rupture) 641.2 ☑
      - affecting fetus or newborn 762.1
    - placenta previa 641.1 ☑
      - affecting fetus or newborn 762.0
    - premature separation of placenta (normally implanted) 641.2 ☑
      - affecting fetus or newborn 762.1
    - threatened abortion 640.0 ☑
      - affecting fetus or newborn 762.1
    - trauma 641.8 ☑
      - affecting fetus or newborn 762.1
  - early (before 22 completed weeks gestation) 640.9 ☑
    - affecting fetus or newborn 762.1
  - previous, affecting management of pregnancy or childbirth V23.49
  - unavoidable — *see* Hemorrhage, pregnancy, due to placenta previa
- prepartum (mother) — *see* Hemorrhage, pregnancy
- preretinal, cause unspecified 362.81
- prostate 602.1
- puerperal (*see also* Hemorrhage, postpartum) 666.1 ☑

☑ **Additional Digit Required — Refer to the Tabular List for Digit Selection**   ▽ **Subterms under main terms may continue to next column or page**

Hemorrhage, hemorrhagic — *continued*
pulmonary (*see also* Hemorrhage, lung) 786.30
　acute idiopathic in infants (AIPHI) (over 28 days old) 786.31
　newborn (massive) 770.3
　renal syndrome 446.21
purpura (primary) (*see also* Purpura, thrombocytopenic) 287.39
rectum (sphincter) 569.3
recurring, following initial hemorrhage at time of injury 958.2
renal 593.81
　pulmonary syndrome 446.21
respiratory tract (*see also* Hemorrhage, lung) 786.30
retina, retinal (deep) (superficial) (vessels) 362.81
　diabetic 250.5 ☑ *[362.01]*
　　due to secondary diabetes 249.5 ☑ *[362.01]*
　due to birth injury 772.8
retrobulbar 376.89
retroperitoneal 459.0
retroplacental (*see also* Placenta, separation) 641.2 ☑
scalp 459.0
　due to injury at birth 767.19
scrotum 608.83
secondary (nontraumatic) 459.0
　following initial hemorrhage at time of injury 958.2
seminal vesicle 608.83
skin 782.7
　newborn 772.6
spermatic cord 608.83
spinal (cord) 336.1
　aneurysm (ruptured) 336.1
　　syphilitic 094.89
　due to birth injury 767.4
　fetus or newborn 767.4
spleen 289.59
spontaneous NEC 459.0
　petechial 782.7
stomach 578.9
　newborn 772.4
　ulcer — *see* Ulcer, stomach, with hemorrhage
subaponeurotic, newborn 767.11
　massive (birth injury) 767.11
subarachnoid (nontraumatic) 430
　fetus or newborn (anoxic) (traumatic) 772.2
　puerperal, postpartum, childbirth 674.0 ☑
　traumatic — *see* Hemorrhage, brain, traumatic, subarachnoid
subconjunctival 372.72
　due to birth injury 772.8
　newborn 772.8
subcortical (*see also* Hemorrhage, brain) 431
subcutaneous 782.7
subdiaphragmatic 459.0
subdural (nontraumatic) 432.1
　due to birth injury 767.0
　fetus or newborn (anoxic) (hypoxic) (due to birth trauma) 767.0
　puerperal, postpartum, childbirth 674.0 ☑
　spinal 336.1
　traumatic — *see* Hemorrhage, brain, traumatic, subdural
subgaleal 767.11
subhyaloid 362.81
subperiosteal 733.99
subretinal 362.81
subtentorial (*see also* Hemorrhage, subdural) 432.1
subungual 703.8
　due to blood dyscrasia 287.8
suprarenal (capsule) (gland) 255.41
　fetus or newborn 772.5
tentorium (traumatic) (*see also* Hemorrhage, brain, traumatic)
　fetus or newborn 767.0

Hemorrhage, hemorrhagic — *continued*
tentorium (*see also* Hemorrhage, brain, traumatic) — *continued*
　nontraumatic — *see* Hemorrhage, subdural
testis 608.83
thigh 459.0
third stage 666.0 ☑
thorax — *see* Hemorrhage, lung
throat 784.8
thrombocythemia 238.71
thymus (gland) 254.8
thyroid (gland) 246.3
　cyst 246.3
tongue 529.8
tonsil 474.8
　postoperative 998.11
tooth socket (postextraction) 998.11
trachea — *see* Hemorrhage, lung
traumatic (*see also* nature of injury)
　brain — *see* Hemorrhage, brain, traumatic
　recurring or secondary (following initial hemorrhage at time of injury) 958.2
tuberculous NEC (*see also* Tuberculosis, pulmonary) 011.9 ☑
tunica vaginalis 608.83
ulcer — *see* Ulcer, by site, with hemorrhage
umbilicus, umbilical cord 772.0
　after birth, newborn 772.3
　complicating delivery 663.8 ☑
　　affecting fetus or newborn 772.0
　slipped ligature 772.3
　stump 772.3
unavoidable (due to placenta previa) 641.1 ☑
　affecting fetus or newborn 762.0
upper extremity 459.0
urethra (idiopathic) 599.84
uterus, uterine (abnormal) 626.9
　climacteric 627.0
　complicating delivery — *see* Hemorrhage, complicating, delivery
　due to
　　intrauterine contraceptive device 996.76
　　perforating uterus 996.32
　functional or dysfunctional 626.8
　in pregnancy — *see* Hemorrhage, pregnancy
　intermenstrual 626.6
　　irregular 626.6
　　regular 626.5
　postmenopausal 627.1
　postpartum (*see also* Hemorrhage, postpartum) 666.1 ☑
　prepubertal 626.8
　pubertal 626.3
　puerperal (immediate) 666.1 ☑
vagina 623.8
vasa previa 663.5 ☑
　affecting fetus or newborn 772.0
vas deferens 608.83
ventricular (*see also* Hemorrhage, brain) 431
vesical 596.89
viscera 459.0
　newborn 772.8
vitreous (humor) (intraocular) 379.23
vocal cord 478.5
vulva 624.8
Hemorrhoids (anus) (rectum) (without complication) 455.6
bleeding, prolapsed, strangulated, or ulcerated NEC 455.8
　external 455.5
　internal 455.2
complicated NEC 455.8
complicating pregnancy and puerperium 671.8 ☑
external 455.3
　with complication NEC 455.5
　bleeding, prolapsed, strangulated, or ulcerated 455.5
　thrombosed 455.4
internal 455.0

Hemorrhoids — *continued*
internal — *continued*
　with complication NEC 455.2
　　bleeding, prolapsed, strangulated, or ulcerated 455.2
　thrombosed 455.1
residual skin tag 455.9
sentinel pile 455.9
thrombosed NEC 455.7
　external 455.4
　internal 455.1
Hemosalpinx 620.8
Hemosiderosis 275.09
dietary 275.09
pulmonary (idiopathic) 275.09 *[516.1]*
transfusion NEC 275.02
　bone marrow 996.85
Hemospermia 608.82
Hemothorax 511.89
bacterial, nontuberculous 511.1
newborn 772.8
nontuberculous 511.89
　bacterial 511.1
pneumococcal 511.1
postoperative 998.11
staphylococcal 511.1
streptococcal 511.1
traumatic 860.2
　with
　　open wound Into thorax 860.3
　　pneumothorax 860.4
　　　with open wound into thorax 860.5
tuberculous (*see also* Tuberculosis, pleura) 012.0 ☑
Hemotympanum 385.89
Hench-Rosenberg syndrome (palindromic arthritis) — *see also* Rheumatism, palindromic 719.3 ☑
Henle's warts 371.41
Henoch (-Schönlein)
　disease or syndrome (allergic purpura) 287.0
　purpura (allergic) 287.0
Henpue, henpuye 102.6
Heparin-induced thrombocytopenia (HIT) 289.84
Heparitinuria 277.5
Hepar lobatum 095.3
Hepatalgia 573.8
Hepatic — *see also* condition
　flexure syndrome 569.89
Hepatitis 573.3
acute (*see also* Necrosis, liver) 570
　alcoholic 571.1
　infective 070.1
　　with hepatic coma 070.0
alcoholic 571.1
ambic — *see* Abscess, liver, amebic
anicteric (acute) — *see* Hepatitis, viral
antigen-associated (HAA) — *see* Hepatitis, viral, type B
Australian antigen (positive) — *see* Hepatitis, viral, type B
autoimmune 571.42
catarrhal (acute) 070.1
　with hepatic coma 070.0
　chronic 571.40
　newborn 070.1
　　with hepatic coma 070.0
chemical 573.3
cholangiolitic 573.8
cholestatic 573.8
chronic 571.40
　active 571.49
　　viral — *see* Hepatitis, viral
　aggressive 571.49
　persistent 571.41
　viral — *see* Hepatitis, viral
cytomegalic inclusion virus 078.5 *[573.1]*
diffuse 573.3
"dirty needle" — *see* Hepatitis, viral
drug-induced 573.3
due to
　Coxsackie 074.8 *[573.1]*
　cytomegalic inclusion virus 078.5 *[573.1]*
　infectious mononucleosis 075 *[573.1]*

Hepatitis — *continued*
due to — *continued*
　malaria 084.9 *[573.2]*
　mumps 072.71
　secondary syphilis 091.62
　toxoplasmosis (acquired) 130.5
　　congenital (active) 771.2
epidemic — *see* Hepatitis, viral, type A
fetus or newborn 774.4
fibrous (chronic) 571.49
　acute 570
from injection, inoculation, or transfusion (blood) (other substance) (plasma) (serum) (onset within 8 months after administration) — *see* Hepatitis, viral
fulminant (viral) (*see also* Hepatitis, viral) 070.9
　with hepatic coma 070.6
　type A 070.1
　　with hepatic coma 070.0
　type B — *see* Hepatitis, viral, type B
giant cell (neonatal) 774.4
hemorrhagic 573.8
history of
　B V12.09
　C V12.09
homologous serum — *see* Hepatitis, viral
hypertrophic (chronic) 571.49
　acute 570
infectious, infective (acute) (chronic) (subacute) 070.1
　with hepatic coma 070.0
inoculation — *see* Hepatitis, viral
interstitial (chronic) 571.49
　acute 570
lupoid 571.49
malarial 084.9 *[573.2]*
malignant (*see also* Necrosis, liver) 570
neonatal (toxic) 774.4
newborn 774.4
parenchymatous (acute) (*see also* Necrosis, liver) 570
peliosis 573.3
persistent, chronic 571.41
plasma cell 571.49
postimmunization — *see* Hepatitis, viral
postnecrotic 571.49
posttransfusion — *see* Hepatitis, viral
recurrent 571.49
septic 573.3
serum — *see* Hepatitis, viral
　carrier (suspected of) V02.61
subacute (*see also* Necrosis, liver) 570
suppurative (diffuse) 572.0
syphilitic (late) 095.3
　congenital (early) 090.0 *[573.2]*
　　late 090.5 *[573.2]*
　secondary 091.62
toxic (noninfectious) 573.3
　fetus or newborn 774.4
tuberculous (*see also* Tuberculosis) 017.9 ☑
viral (acute) (anicteric) (cholangiolitic) (cholestatic) (chronic) (subacute) 070.9
　with hepatic coma 070.6
　AU-SH type virus — *see* Hepatitis, viral, type B
　Australian antigen — *see* Hepatitis, viral, type B
　B-antigen — *see* Hepatitis, viral, type B
　Coxsackie 074.8 *[573.1]*
　cytomegalic inclusion 078.5 *[573.1]*
　IH (virus) — *see* Hepatitis, viral, type A
　infectious hepatitis virus — *see* Hepatitis, viral, type A
　serum hepatitis virus — *see* Hepatitis, viral, type B
　SH — *see* Hepatitis, viral, type B
　specified type NEC 070.59
　　with hepatic coma 070.49
　type A 070.1
　　with hepatic coma 070.0
　type B (acute) 070.30
　　with
　　　hepatic coma 070.20
　　　　with hepatitis delta 070.21

☑ Additional Digit Required — Refer to the Tabular List for Digit Selection
🔽 Subterms under main terms may continue to next column or page
2015 ICD-9-CM
▶◀ Revised Text　● New Line　▲ Revised Code
Volume 2 — 137

Hepatitis — continued
viral — continued
type B — continued
with — continued
hepatitis delta 070.31
with hepatic coma 070.21
carrier status V02.61
chronic 070.32
with
hepatic coma 070.22
with hepatitis delta 070.23
hepatitis delta 070.33
with hepatic coma 070.23
type C
acute 070.51
with hepatic coma 070.41
carrier status V02.62
chronic 070.54
with hepatic coma 070.44
in remission 070.54
unspecified 070.70
with hepatic coma 070.71
type delta (with hepatitis B carrier state) 070.52
with
active hepatitis B disease — see Hepatitis, viral, type B
hepatic coma 070.42
type E 070.53
with hepatic coma 070.43
vaccination and inoculation (prophylactic) V05.3
Waldenström's (lupoid hepatitis) 571.49
Hepatization, lung (acute) — see also Pneumonia, lobar
chronic (see also Fibrosis, lung) 515
Hepatoblastoma (M8970/3) 155.0
Hepatocarcinoma (M8170/3) 155.0
Hepatocholangiocarcinoma (M8180/3) 155.0
Hepatocholangioma, benign (M8180/0) 211.5
Hepatocholangitis 573.8
Hepatocystitis — see also Cholecystitis 575.10
Hepatodystrophy 570
Hepatolenticular degeneration 275.1
Hepatolithiasis — see Choledocholithiasis
Hepatoma (malignant) (M8170/3) 155.0
benign (M8170/0) 211.5
congenital (M8970/3) 155.0
embryonal (M8970/3) 155.0
Hepatomegalia glycogenica diffusa 271.0
Hepatomegaly — see also Hypertrophy, liver 789.1
congenital 751.69
syphilitic 090.0
due to Clonorchis sinensis 121.1
Gaucher's 272.7
syphilitic (congenital) 090.0
Hepatoptosis 573.8
Hepatorrhexis 573.8
Hepatosis, toxic 573.8
Hepatosplenomegaly 571.8
due to S. japonicum 120.2
hyperlipemic (Bürger-Grutz type) 272.3
Herald patch 696.3
Hereditary — see condition
Heredodegeneration 330.9
macular 362.70
Heredopathia atactica polyneuritiformis 356.3
Heredosyphilis — see also Syphilis, congenital 090.9
Hermaphroditism (true) 752.7
with specified chromosomal anomaly — see Anomaly, chromosomes, sex
Hernia, hernial (acquired) (recurrent) 553.9
with
gangrene (obstructed) NEC 551.9
obstruction NEC 552.9
and gangrene 551.9
abdomen (wall) — see Hernia, ventral
abdominal, specified site NEC 553.8
with
gangrene (obstructed) 551.8
obstruction 552.8
and gangrene 551.8
appendix 553.8

Hernia, hernial — continued
appendix — continued
with
gangrene (obstructed) 551.8
obstruction 552.8
and gangrene 551.8
bilateral (inguinal) — see Hernia, inguinal
bladder (sphincter)
congenital (female) (male) 756.71
female (see also Cystocele, female) 618.01
male 596.89
brain 348.4
congenital 742.0
broad ligament 553.8
cartilage, vertebral — see Displacement, intervertebral disc
cerebral 348.4
congenital 742.0
endaural 742.0
ciliary body 364.89
traumatic 871.1
colic 553.9
with
gangrene (obstructed) 551.9
obstruction 552.9
and gangrene 551.9
colon 553.9
with
gangrene (obstructed) 551.9
obstruction 552.9
and gangrene 551.9
colostomy (stoma) 569.69
Cooper's (retroperitoneal) 553.8
with
gangrene (obstructed) 551.8
obstruction 552.8
and gangrene 551.8
crural — see Hernia, femoral
cystostomy 596.83
diaphragm, diaphragmatic 553.3
with
gangrene (obstructed) 551.3
obstruction 552.3
and gangrene 551.3
congenital 756.6
due to gross defect of diaphragm 756.6
traumatic 862.0
with open wound into cavity 862.1
direct (inguinal) — see Hernia, inguinal
disc, intervertebral — see Displacement, intervertebral disc
diverticulum, intestine 553.9
with
gangrene (obstructed) 551.9
obstruction 552.9
and gangrene 551.9
double (inguinal) — see Hernia, inguinal
due to adhesion with obstruction 552.9
duodenojejunal 553.8
with
gangrene (obstructed) 551.8
obstruction 552.8
and gangrene 551.8
en glissade — see Hernia, inguinal
enterostomy (stoma) 569.69
epigastric 553.29
with
gangrene (obstruction) 551.29
obstruction 552.29
and gangrene 551.29
recurrent 553.21
with
gangrene (obstructed) 551.21
obstruction 552.21
and gangrene 551.21
esophageal hiatus (sliding) 553.3
with
gangrene (obstructed) 551.3
obstruction 552.3
and gangrene 551.3
congenital 750.6
external (inguinal) — see Hernia, inguinal
fallopian tube 620.4
fascia 728.89
fat 729.30

Hernia, hernial — continued
fat — continued
eyelid 374.34
orbital 374.34
pad 729.30
eye, eyelid 374.34
knee 729.31
orbit 374.34
popliteal (space) 729.31
specified site NEC 729.39
femoral (unilateral) 553.00
with
gangrene (obstructed) 551.00
obstruction 552.00
with gangrene 551.00
bilateral 553.02
gangrenous (obstructed) 551.02
obstructed 552.02
with gangrene 551.02
recurrent 553.03
gangrenous (obstructed) 551.03
obstructed 552.03
with gangrene 551.03
recurrent (unilateral) 553.01
bilateral 553.03
gangrenous (obstructed) 551.03
obstructed 552.03
with gangrene 551.01
gangrenous (obstructed) 551.01
obstructed 552.01
with gangrene 551.01
foramen
Bochdalek 553.3
with
gangrene (obstructed) 551.3
obstruction 552.3
and gangrene 551.3
congenital 756.6
magnum 348.4
Morgagni, Morgagnian 553.3
with
gangrene 551.3
obstruction 552.3
and gangrene 551.3
congenital 756.6
funicular (umbilical) 553.1
with
gangrene (obstructed) 551.1
obstruction 552.1
and gangrene 551.1
spermatic cord — see Hernia, inguinal
gangrenous — see Hernia, by site, with gangrene
gastrointestinal tract 553.9
with
gangrene (obstructed) 551.9
obstruction 552.9
and gangrene 551.9
gluteal — see Hernia, femoral
Gruber's (internal mesogastric) 553.8
with
gangrene (obstructed) 551.8
obstruction 552.8
and gangrene 551.8
Hesselbach's 553.8
with
gangrene (obstructed) 551.8
obstruction 552.8
and gangrene 551.8
hiatal (esophageal) (sliding) 553.3
with
gangrene (obstructed) 551.3
obstruction 552.3
and gangrene 551.3
congenital 750.6
incarcerated (see also Hernia, by site, with obstruction) 552.9
gangrenous (see also Hernia, by site, with gangrene) 551.9
incisional 553.21
with
gangrene (obstructed) 551.21
obstruction 552.21
and gangrene 551.21
lumbar — see Hernia, lumbar
recurrent 553.21

Hernia, hernial — continued
incisional — continued
recurrent — continued
with
gangrene (obstructed) 551.21
obstruction 552.21
and gangrene 551.21
indirect (inguinal) — see Hernia, inguinal
infantile — see Hernia, inguinal
infrapatellar fat pad 729.31
inguinal (direct) (double) (encysted) (external) (funicular) (indirect) (infantile) (internal) (interstitial) (oblique) (scrotal) (sliding) 550.9 ☑

Note — Use the following fifth-digit subclassification with category 550:

0   unilateral or unspecified (not specified as recurrent)

1   unilateral or unspecified, recurrent

2   bilateral (not specified as recurrent)

3   bilateral, recurrent

with
gangrene (obstructed) 550.0 ☑
obstruction 550.1 ☑
and gangrene 550.0 ☑
internal 553.8
with
gangrene (obstructed) 551.8
obstruction 552.8
and gangrene 551.8
inguinal — see Hernia, inguinal
interstitial 553.9
with
gangrene (obstructed) 551.9
obstruction 552.9
and gangrene 551.9
inguinal — see Hernia, inguinal
intervertebral cartilage or disc — see Displacement, intervertebral disc
intestine, intestinal 553.9
with
gangrene (obstructed) 551.9
obstruction 552.9
and gangrene 551.9
intra-abdominal 553.9
with
gangrene (obstructed) 551.9
obstruction 552.9
and gangrene 551.9
intraparietal 553.9
with
gangrene (obstructed) 551.9
obstruction 552.9
and gangrene 551.9
iris 364.89
traumatic 871.1
irreducible (see also Hernia, by site, with obstruction) 552.9
gangrenous (with obstruction) (see also Hernia, by site, with gangrene) 551.9
ischiatic 553.8
with
gangrene (obstructed) 551.8
obstruction 552.8
and gangrene 551.8
ischiorectal 553.8
with
gangrene (obstructed) 551.8
obstruction 552.8
and gangrene 551.8
lens 379.32
traumatic 871.1
linea
alba — see Hernia, epigastric
semilunaris — see Hernia, spigelian
Littre's (diverticular) 553.9
with
gangrene (obstructed) 551.9
obstruction 552.9
and gangrene 551.9
lumbar 553.8

☑ **Additional Digit Required** — Refer to the Tabular List for Digit Selection   ▿ᵇⁱ **Subterms under main terms may continue to next column or page**

Hernia, hernial — *continued*
  lumbar — *continued*
    with
      gangrene (obstructed) 551.8
      obstruction 552.8
        and gangrene 551.8
    intervertebral disc 722.10
  lung (subcutaneous) 518.89
    congenital 748.69
  mediastinum 519.3
  mesenteric (internal) 553.8
    with
      gangrene (obstructed) 551.8
      obstruction 552.8
        and gangrene 551.8
  mesocolon 553.8
    with
      gangrene (obstructed) 551.8
      obstruction 552.8
        and gangrene 551.8
  muscle (sheath) 728.89
  nucleus pulposus — *see* Displacement, intervertebral disc
  oblique (inguinal) — *see* Hernia, inguinal
  obstructive (*see also* Hernia, by site, with obstruction) 552.9
    gangrenous (with obstruction) (*see also* Hernia, by site, with gangrene) 551.9
  obturator 553.8
    with
      gangrene (obstructed) 551.8
      obstruction 552.8
        and gangrene 551.8
  omental 553.8
    with
      gangrene (obstructed) 551.8
      obstruction 552.8
        and gangrene 551.8
  orbital fat (pad) 374.34
  ovary 620.4
  oviduct 620.4
  paracolostomy (stoma) 569.69
  paraduodenal 553.8
    with
      gangrene (obstructed) 551.8
      obstruction 552.8
        and gangrene 551.8
  paraesophageal 553.3
    with
      gangrene (obstructed) 551.3
      obstruction 552.3
        and gangrene 551.3
    congenital 750.6
  parahiatal 553.3
    with
      gangrene (obstructed) 551.3
      obstruction 552.3
        and gangrene 551.3
  paraumbilical 553.1
    with
      gangrene (obstructed) 551.1
      obstruction 552.1
        and gangrene 551.1
  parietal 553.9
    with
      gangrene (obstructed) 551.9
      obstruction 552.9
        and gangrene 551.9
  perineal 553.8
    with
      gangrene (obstructed) 551.8
      obstruction 552.8
        and gangrene 551.8
  peritoneal sac, lesser 553.8
    with
      gangrene (obstructed) 551.8
      obstruction 552.8
        and gangrene 551.8
  popliteal fat pad 729.31
  postoperative 553.21
    with
      gangrene (obstructed) 551.21
      obstruction 552.21
        and gangrene 551.21
  pregnant uterus 654.4 ☑

Hernia, hernial — *continued*
  prevesical 596.89
  properitoneal 553.8
    with
      gangrene (obstructed) 551.8
      obstruction 552.8
        and gangrene 551.8
  pudendal 553.8
    with
      gangrene (obstructed) 551.8
      obstruction 552.8
        and gangrene 551.8
  rectovaginal 618.6
  retroperitoneal 553.8
    with
      gangrene (obstructed) 551.8
      obstruction 552.8
        and gangrene 551.8
  Richter's (parietal) 553.9
    with
      gangrene (obstructed) 551.9
      obstruction 552.9
        and gangrene 551.9
  Rieux's, Riex's (retrocecal) 553.8
    with
      gangrene (obstructed) 551.8
      obstruction 552.8
        and gangrene 551.8
  sciatic 553.8
    with
      gangrene (obstructed) 551.8
      obstruction 552.8
        and gangrene 551.8
  scrotum, scrotal — *see* Hernia, inguinal
  sliding (inguinal) (*see also* Hernia, inguinal)
    hiatus — *see* Hernia, hiatal
  spigelian 553.29
    with
      gangrene (obstructed) 551.29
      obstruction 552.29
        and gangrene 551.29
  spinal (*see also* Spina bifida) 741.9 ☑
    with hydrocephalus 741.0 ☑
  strangulated (*see also* Hernia, by site, with obstruction) 552.9
    gangrenous (with obstruction) (*see also* Hernia, by site, with gangrene) 551.9
  supraumbilicus (linea alba) — *see* Hernia, epigastric
  tendon 727.9
  testis (nontraumatic) 550.9 ☑
    meaning
      scrotal hernia 550.9 ☑
      symptomatic late syphilis 095.8
  Treitz's (fossa) 553.8
    with
      gangrene (obstructed) 551.8
      obstruction 552.8
        and gangrene 551.8
  tunica
    albuginea 608.89
    vaginalis 752.89
  umbilicus, umbilical 553.1
    with
      gangrene (obstructed) 551.1
      obstruction 552.1
        and gangrene 551.1
  ureter 593.89
    with obstruction 593.4
  uterus 621.8
    pregnant 654.4 ☑
  vaginal (posterior) 618.6
  Velpeau's (femoral) (*see also* Hernia, femoral) 553.00
  ventral 553.20
    with
      gangrene (obstructed) 551.20
      obstruction 552.20
        and gangrene 551.20
    incisional 553.21
    recurrent 553.21
      with
        gangrene (obstructed) 551.21
        obstruction 552.21
          and gangrene 551.21

Hernia, hernial — *continued*
  vesical
    congenital (female) (male) 756.71
    female (*see also* Cystocele, female) 618.01
    male 596.89
  vitreous (into anterior chamber) 379.21
    traumatic 871.1
Herniation — *see also* Hernia
  brain (stem) 348.4
  cerebral 348.4
  gastric mucosa (into duodenal bulb) 537.89
  mediastinum 519.3
  nucleus pulposus — *see* Displacement, intervertebral disc
Herpangina 074.0
Herpes, herpetic 054.9
  auricularis (zoster) 053.71
    simplex 054.73
  blepharitis (zoster) 053.20
    simplex 054.41
  circinate 110.5
  circinatus 110.5
    bullous 694.5
  conjunctiva (simplex) 054.43
    zoster 053.21
  cornea (simplex) 054.43
    disciform (simplex) 054.43
    zoster 053.21
  encephalitis 054.3
  eye (zoster) 053.29
    simplex 054.40
  eyelid (zoster) 053.20
    simplex 054.41
  febrilis 054.9
  fever 054.9
  geniculate ganglionitis 053.11
  genital, genitalis 054.10
    specified site NEC 054.19
  gestationis 646.8 ☑
  gingivostomatitis 054.2
  iridocyclitis (simplex) 054.44
    zoster 053.22
  iris (any site) 695.10
  iritis (simplex) 054.44
  keratitis (simplex) 054.43
    dendritic 054.42
    disciform 054.43
    interstitial 054.43
    zoster 053.21
  keratoconjunctivitis (simplex) 054.43
    zoster 053.21
  labialis 054.9
    meningococcal 036.89
  lip 054.9
  meningitis (simplex) 054.72
    zoster 053.0
  ophthalmicus (zoster) 053.20
    simplex 054.40
  otitis externa (zoster) 053.71
    simplex 054.73
  penis 054.13
  perianal 054.10
  pharyngitis 054.79
  progenitalis 054.10
  scrotum 054.19
  septicemia 054.5
  simplex 054.9
    complicated 054.8
      ophthalmic 054.40
        specified NEC 054.49
      specified NEC 054.79
    congenital 771.2
    external ear 054.73
    keratitis 054.43
      dendritic 054.42
    meningitis 054.72
    myelitis 054.74
    neuritis 054.79
    specified complication NEC 054.79
      ophthalmic 054.49
    visceral 054.71
  stomatitis 054.2
  tonsurans 110.0
    maculosus (of Hebra) 696.3
  visceral 054.71

Herpes, herpetic — *continued*
  vulva 054.12
  vulvovaginitis 054.11
  whitlow 054.6
  zoster 053.9
    auricularis 053.71
    complicated 053.8
      specified NEC 053.79
    conjunctiva 053.21
    cornea 053.21
    ear 053.71
    eye 053.29
    geniculate 053.11
    keratitis 053.21
      interstitial 053.21
    myelitis 053.14
    neuritis 053.10
    ophthalmicus(a) 053.20
    oticus 053.71
    otitis externa 053.71
    specified complication NEC 053.79
    specified site NEC 053.9
    zosteriform, intermediate type 053.9
Herrick's
  anemia (hemoglobin S disease) 282.61
  syndrome (hemoglobin S disease) 282.61
Hers' disease (glycogenosis VI) 271.0
Herter (-Gee) disease or syndrome (nontropical sprue) 579.0
Herter's infantilism (nontropical sprue) 579.0
Herxheimer's disease (diffuse idiopathic cutaneous atrophy) 701.8
Herxheimer's reaction 995.91
Hesitancy, urinary 788.64
Hesselbach's hernia — *see* Hernia, Hesselbach's
Heterochromia (congenital) 743.46
  acquired 364.53
  cataract 366.33
  cyclitis 364.21
  hair 704.3
  iritis 364.21
  retained metallic foreign body 360.62
    magnetic 360.52
  uveitis 364.21
Heterophoria 378.40
  alternating 378.45
  vertical 378.43
Heterophyes, small intestine 121.6
Heterophyiasis 121.6
Heteropsia 368.8
Heterotopia, heterotopic — *see also* Malposition, congenital
  cerebralis 742.4
  pancreas, pancreatic 751.7
  spinalis 742.59
Heterotropia 378.30
  intermittent 378.20
    vertical 378.31
  vertical (constant) (intermittent) 378.31
Heubner's disease 094.89
Heubner-Herter disease or syndrome (nontropical sprue) 579.0
Hexadactylism 755.0 ☑
Heyd's syndrome (hepatorenal) 572.4
HGSIL (high grade squamous intraepithelial lesion) (cytologic finding) (Pap smear finding)
  anus 796.74
  cervix 795.04
    biopsy finding — code to CIN II or CIN III
  vagina 795.14
Hibernoma (M8880/0) — *see* Lipoma
Hiccough 786.8
  epidemic 078.89
  psychogenic 306.1
Hiccup — *see also* Hiccough 786.8
Hicks (-Braxton) contractures 644.1 ☑
Hidden penis 752.65
Hidradenitis (axillaris) (suppurative) 705.83
Hidradenoma (nodular) (M8400/0) — *see also* Neoplasm, skin, benign
  clear cell (M8402/0) — *see* Neoplasm, skin, benign

☑ Additional Digit Required — Refer to the Tabular List for Digit Selection   ▼ Subterms under main terms may continue to next column or page

2015 ICD-9-CM   ▶◀ Revised Text   ● New Line   ▲ Revised Code   Volume 2 — 139

Hidradenoma — *see also* Neoplasm, skin, benign — *continued*
  papillary (M8405/0) — *see* Neoplasm, skin, benign
Hidrocystoma (M8404/0) — *see* Neoplasm, skin, benign
HIE (hypoxic-ischemic encephalopathy) 768.70
  mild 768.71
  moderate 768.72
  severe 768.73
High
  A₂ anemia 282.46
  altitude effects 993.2
    anoxia 993.2
    on
      ears 993.0
      sinuses 993.1
    polycythemia 289.0
  arch
    foot 755.67
    palate 750.26
  artery (arterial) tension (*see also* Hypertension) 401.9
    without diagnosis of hypertension 796.2
  basal metabolic rate (BMR) 794.7
  blood pressure (*see also* Hypertension) 401.9
    borderline 796.2
    incidental reading (isolated) (nonspecific), no diagnosis of hypertension 796.2
  cholesterol 272.0
    with high triglycerides 272.2
  compliance bladder 596.4
  diaphragm (congenital) 756.6
  frequency deafness (congenital) (regional) 389.8
  head at term 652.5 ☑
    affecting fetus or newborn 763.1
  output failure (cardiac) (*see also* Failure, heart) 428.9
  oxygen-affinity hemoglobin 289.0
  palate 750.26
  risk
    behavior — *see* Problem
    family situation V61.9
      specified circumstance NEC V61.8
    human papillomavirus (HPV) DNA test positive
      anal 796.75
      cervical 795.05
      vaginal 795.15
    individual NEC V62.89
    infant NEC V20.1
    patient taking drugs (prescribed) V67.51
      nonprescribed (*see also* Abuse, drugs, nondependent) 305.9 ☑
    pregnancy V23.9
      inadequate prenatal care V23.7
      inconclusive fetal viability V23.87
      specified problem NEC V23.89
  temperature (of unknown origin) (*see also* Pyrexia) 780.60
  thoracic rib 756.3
  triglycerides 272.1
    with high cholesterol 272.2
Hildenbrand's disease (typhus) 081.9
Hilger's syndrome 337.09
Hill diarrhea 579.1
Hilliard's lupus — *see also* Tuberculosis 017.0 ☑
Hilum — *see* condition
Hip — *see* condition
Hippel's disease (retinocerebral angiomatosis) 759.6
Hippus 379.49
Hirschfeld's disease (acute diabetes mellitus) — *see also* Diabetes 250.0 ☑
  due to secondary diabetes 249.0 ☑
Hirschsprung's disease or megacolon (congenital) 751.3
Hirsuties — *see also* Hypertrichosis 704.1
Hirsutism — *see also* Hypertrichosis 704.1
Hirudiniasis (external) (internal) 134.2
Hiss-Russell dysentery 004.1
Histamine cephalgia 339.00
Histidinemia 270.5

Histidinuria 270.5
Histiocytic syndromes 288.4
Histiocytoma (M8832/0) — *see also* Neoplasm, skin, benign
  fibrous (M8830/0) (*see also* Neoplasm, skin, benign)
    atypical (M8830/1) — *see* Neoplasm, connective tissue, uncertain behavior
    malignant (M8830/3) — *see* Neoplasm, connective tissue, malignant
Histiocytosis (acute) (chronic) (subacute) 277.89
  acute differentiated progressive (M9722/3) 202.5 ☑
  adult pulmonary Langerhans cell (PLCH) 516.5
  cholesterol 277.89
  essential 277.89
  lipid, lipoid (essential) 272.7
  lipochrome (familial) 288.1
  malignant (M9720/3) 202.3 ☑
  non-Langerhans cell 277.89
  polyostotic sclerosing 277.89
  X (chronic) 277.89
    acute (progressive) (M9722/3) 202.5 ☑
Histoplasmosis 115.90
  with
    endocarditis 115.94
    meningitis 115.91
    pericarditis 115.93
    pneumonia 115.95
    retinitis 115.92
    specified manifestation NEC 115.99
  African (due to Histoplasma duboisii) 115.10
    with
      endocarditis 115.14
      meningitis 115.11
      pericarditis 115.13
      pneumonia 115.15
      retinitis 115.12
      specified manifestation NEC 115.19
  American (due to Histoplasma capsulatum) 115.00
    with
      endocarditis 115.04
      meningitis 115.01
      pericarditis 115.03
      pneumonia 115.05
      retinitis 115.02
      specified manifestation NEC 115.09
  Darling's — *see* Histoplasmosis, American
  large form (*see also* Histoplasmosis, African) 115.10
  lung 115.05
  small form (*see also* Histoplasmosis, American) 115.00
History (personal) of
  abuse
    emotional V15.42
    neglect V15.42
    physical V15.41
    sexual V15.41
  affective psychosis V11.1
  alcoholism V11.3
    specified as drinking problem (*see also* Abuse, drugs, nondependent) 305.0 ☑
  allergy to V15.09
    analgesic agent NEC V14.6
    anesthetic NEC V14.4
    antibiotic agent NEC V14.1
      penicillin V14.0
    anti-infective agent NEC V14.3
    arachnid bite V15.06
    diathesis V15.09
    drug V14.9
      specified type NEC V14.8
    eggs V15.03
    food additives V15.05
    insect bite V15.06
    latex V15.07
    medicinal agents V14.9
      specified type NEC V14.8
    milk products V15.02
    narcotic agent NEC V14.5

History of — *continued*
  allergy to — *continued*
    nuts V15.05
      peanuts V15.01
    penicillin V14.0
    radiographic dye V15.08
    seafood V15.04
    serum V14.7
    specified food NEC V15.05
    specified nonmedicinal agents NEC V15.09
    spider bite V15.06
    sulfa V14.2
    sulfonamides V14.2
    therapeutic agent NEC V15.09
    vaccine V14.7
  anaphylactic reaction or shock V13.81
  anaphylaxis V13.81
  anemia V12.3
  arrest, sudden cardiac V12.53
  arthritis V13.4
  attack, transient ischemic (TIA) V12.54
  benign neoplasm of brain V12.41
  blood disease V12.3
  calculi, urinary V13.01
  cardiovascular disease V12.50
    myocardial infarction 412
  chemotherapy, antineoplastic V87.41
  child abuse V15.41
  cigarette smoking V15.82
  circulatory system disease V12.50
    myocardial infarction 412
  cleft lip and palate, corrected V13.64
  combat and operational stress reaction V11.4
  congenital malformation (corrected)
    circulatory system V13.65
    digestive system V13.67
    ear V13.64
    eye V13.64
    face V13.64
    genitourinary system V13.62
    heart V13.65
    integument V13.68
    limbs V13.68
    musculoskeletal V13.68
    neck V13.64
    nervous system V13.63
    respiratory system V13.66
    specified type NEC V13.69
  contraception V15.7
  death, sudden, successfully resuscitated V12.53
  deficit
    prolonged reversible ischemic neurologic (PRIND) V12.54
    reversible ischemic neurologic (RIND) V12.54
  diathesis, allergic V15.09
  digestive system disease V12.70
    peptic ulcer V12.71
    polyps, colonic V12.72
    specified NEC V12.79
  disease (of) V13.9
    blood V12.3
    blood-forming organs V12.3
    cardiovascular system V12.50
    circulatory system V12.50
      specified NEC V12.59
    digestive system V12.70
      peptic ulcer V12.71
      polyps, colonic V12.72
      specified NEC V12.79
    infectious V12.00
      malaria V12.03
      methicillin resistant Staphylococcus aureus (MRSA) V12.04
      MRSA (methicillin resistant Staphylococcus aureus) V12.04
      poliomyelitis V12.02
      specified NEC V12.09
      tuberculosis V12.01
    parasitic V12.00
      specified NEC V12.09
    respiratory system V12.60
      pneumonia V12.61

History of — *continued*
  disease — *continued*
    respiratory system — *continued*
      specified NEC V12.69
    skin V13.3
    specified site NEC V13.89
    subcutaneous tissue V13.3
    trophoblastic V13.1
      affecting management of pregnancy V23.1
  disorder (of) V13.9
    endocrine V12.29
      gestational diabetes V12.21
    genital system V13.29
    hematological V12.3
    immunity V12.29
    mental V11.9
      affective type V11.1
      manic-depressive V11.1
      neurosis V11.2
      schizophrenia V11.0
      specified type NEC V11.8
    metabolic V12.29
    musculoskeletal NEC V13.59
    nervous system V12.40
      specified type NEC V12.49
    obstetric V13.29
      affecting management of current pregnancy V23.49
      ectopic pregnancy V23.42
      pre-term labor V23.41
    pre-term labor V13.21
    sense organs V12.40
      specified type NEC V12.49
    specified site NEC V13.89
    urinary system V13.00
      calculi V13.01
      infection V13.02
      nephrotic syndrome V13.03
      specified NEC V13.09
  drug use
    nonprescribed (*see also* Abuse, drugs, nondependent) 305.9 ☑
    patent (*see also* Abuse, drugs, non-dependent) 305.9 ☑
  dysplasia
    cervical (conditions classifiable to 622.10-622.12) V13.22
    vaginal (conditions classifiable to 623.0) V13.23
    vulvar (conditions classifiable to 624.01-624.02) V13.24
  effect NEC of external cause V15.89
  embolism V12.51
    pulmonary V12.55
  emotional abuse V15.42
  encephalitis V12.42
  endocrine disorder V12.29
    gestational diabetes V12.21
  estrogen therapy V87.43
  extracorporeal membrane oxygenation (ECMO) V15.87
  failed
    conscious sedation V15.80
    moderate sedation V15.80
  falling V15.88
  family
    allergy V19.6
    anemia V18.2
    arteriosclerosis V17.49
    arthritis V17.7
    asthma V17.5
    blindness V19.0
    blood disorder NEC V18.3
    cardiovascular disease V17.49
    carrier, genetic disease V18.9
    cerebrovascular disease V17.1
    chronic respiratory condition NEC V17.6
    colonic polyps V18.51
    congenital anomalies V19.5
    consanguinity V19.7
    coronary artery disease V17.3
    cystic fibrosis V18.19
    deafness V19.2
    diabetes mellitus V18.0
    digestive disorders V18.59

History of — *continued*
  family — *continued*
    disabilities, intellectual V18.4
    disease or disorder (of)
      allergic V19.6
      blood NEC V18.3
      cardiovascular NEC V17.49
      cerebrovascular V17.1
      colonic polyps V18.51
      coronary artery V17.3
      death, sudden cardiac (SCD) V17.41
      digestive V18.59
      ear NEC V19.3
      endocrine V18.19
        multiple neoplasia (MEN) syndrome V18.11
      eye NEC V19.19
        glaucoma V19.11
      genitourinary NEC V18.7
      glaucoma V19.11
      hypertensive V17.49
      infectious V18.8
      ischemic heart V17.3
      kidney V18.69
        polycystic V18.61
      mental V17.0
      metabolic V18.19
      musculoskeletal NEC V17.89
        osteoporosis V17.81
      neurological NEC V17.2
      parasitic V18.8
      psychiatric condition V17.0
      skin condition V19.4
    ear disorder NEC V19.3
    endocrine disease V18.19
      multiple neoplasia (MEN) syndrome V18.11
    epilepsy V17.2
    eye disorder NEC V19.19
      glaucoma V19.11
    genetic disease carrier V18.9
    genitourinary disease NEC V18.7
    glaucoma V19.11
    glomerulonephritis V18.69
    gout V18.19
    hay fever V17.6
    hearing loss V19.2
    hematopoietic neoplasia V16.7
    Hodgkin's disease V16.7
    Huntington's chorea V17.2
    hydrocephalus V19.5
    hypertension V17.49
    infarction, myocardial V17.3
    infectious disease V18.8
    intellectual disabilities V18.4
    ischemic heart disease V17.3
    kidney disease V18.69
      polycystic V18.61
    leukemia V16.6
    lymphatic malignant neoplasia NEC V16.7
    malignant neoplasm (of) NEC V16.9
      anorectal V16.0
      anus V16.0
      appendix V16.0
      bladder V16.52
      bone V16.8
      brain V16.8
      breast V16.3
        male V16.8
      bronchus V16.1
      cecum V16.0
      cervix V16.49
      colon V16.0
      duodenum V16.0
      esophagus V16.0
      eye V16.8
      gallbladder V16.0
      gastrointestinal tract V16.0
      genital organs V16.40
      hemopoietic NEC V16.7
      ileum V16.0
      ilium V16.8
      intestine V16.0
      intrathoracic organs NEC V16.2
      kidney V16.51

History of — *continued*
  family — *continued*
    malignant neoplasm — *continued*
      larynx V16.2
      liver V16.0
      lung V16.1
      lymphatic NEC V16.7
      ovary V16.41
      oviduct V16.41
      pancreas V16.0
      penis V16.49
      prostate V16.42
      rectum V16.0
      respiratory organs NEC V16.2
      skin V16.8
      specified site NEC V16.8
      stomach V16.0
      testis V16.43
      trachea V16.1
      ureter V16.59
      urethra V16.59
      urinary organs V16.59
      uterus V16.49
      vagina V16.49
      vulva V16.49
    MEN (multiple endocrine neoplasia syndrome) V18.11
    mental retardation — *see* History, family, intellectual disabilities
    metabolic disease NEC V18.19
    mongolism V19.5
    multiple
      endocrine neoplasia (MEN) syndrome V18.11
      myeloma V16.7
    musculoskeletal disease NEC V17.89
      osteoporosis V17.81
    myocardial infarction V17.3
    nephritis V18.69
    nephrosis V18.69
    osteoporosis V17.81
    parasitic disease V18.8
    polycystic kidney disease V18.61
    psychiatric disorder V17.0
    psychosis V17.0
    retinitis pigmentosa V19.19
    schizophrenia V17.0
    skin conditions V19.4
    specified condition NEC V19.8
    stroke (cerebrovascular) V17.1
    sudden cardiac death (SCD) V17.41
    visual loss V19.0
  foreign body fully removed V15.53
  fracture, healed
    pathologic V13.51
    stress V13.52
    traumatic V15.51
  genital system disorder V13.29
    pre-term labor V13.21
  gestational diabetes V12.21
  health hazard V15.9
    falling V15.88
    specified cause NEC V15.89
  hepatitis
    B V12.09
    C V12.09
  Hodgkin's disease V10.72
  hypospadias (corrected) V13.61
  immunity disorder V12.29
  immunosuppression therapy V87.46
  infarction, cerebral, without residual deficits V12.54
  infection
    central nervous system V12.42
    urinary (tract) V13.02
  infectious disease V12.00
    malaria V12.03
    methicillin resistant Staphylococcus aureus (MRSA) V12.04
    MRSA (methicillin resistant Staphylococcus aureus) V12.04
    poliomyelitis V12.02
    specified NEC V12.09
    tuberculosis V12.01
  injury NEC V15.59
    traumatic brain V15.52

History of — *continued*
  insufficient prenatal care V23.7
  in utero procedure
    during pregnancy V15.21
    while a fetus V15.22
  irradiation V15.3
  leukemia V10.60
    lymphoid V10.61
    monocytic V10.63
    myeloid V10.62
    specified type NEC V10.69
  little or no prenatal care V23.7
  low birth weight (*see also* Status, low birth weight) V21.30
  lymphosarcoma V10.71
  malaria V12.03
  malignant carcinoid tumor V10.91
  malignant neoplasm (of) V10.90
    accessory sinus V10.22
    adrenal V10.88
    anus V10.06
    bile duct V10.09
    bladder V10.51
    bone V10.81
    brain V10.85
    breast V10.3
    bronchus V10.11
    cervix uteri V10.41
    colon V10.05
    connective tissue NEC V10.89
    corpus uteri V10.42
    digestive system V10.00
      specified part NEC V10.09
    duodenum V10.09
    endocrine gland NEC V10.88
    epididymis V10.48
    esophagus V10.03
    eye V10.84
    fallopian tube V10.44
    female genital organ V10.40
      specified site NEC V10.44
    gallbladder V10.09
    gastrointestinal tract V10.00
    gum V10.02
    hematopoietic NEC V10.79
    hypopharynx V10.02
    ileum V10.09
    intrathoracic organs NEC V10.20
    jejunum V10.09
    kidney V10.52
    large intestine V10.05
    larynx V10.21
    lip V10.02
    liver V10.07
    lung V10.11
    lymphatic NEC V10.79
    lymph glands or nodes NEC V10.79
    male genital organ V10.45
      specified site NEC V10.49
    mediastinum V10.29
    melanoma (of skin) V10.82
    middle ear V10.22
    mouth V10.02
      specified part NEC V10.02
    nasal cavities V10.22
    nasopharynx V10.02
    nervous system NEC V10.86
    nose V10.22
    oropharynx V10.02
    ovary V10.43
    pancreas V10.09
    parathyroid V10.88
    penis V10.49
    pharynx V10.02
    pineal V10.88
    pituitary V10.88
    placenta V10.44
    pleura V10.29
    prostate V10.46
    rectosigmoid junction V10.06
    rectum V10.06
    renal pelvis V10.53
    respiratory organs NEC V10.20
    salivary gland V10.02
    skin V10.83
      melanoma V10.82

History of — *continued*
  malignant neoplasm — *continued*
    small intestine NEC V10.09
    soft tissue NEC V10.89
    specified site NEC V10.89
    stomach V10.04
    testis V10.47
    thymus V10.29
    thyroid V10.87
    tongue V10.01
    trachea V10.12
    ureter V10.59
    urethra V10.59
    urinary organ V10.50
    uterine adnexa V10.44
    uterus V10.42
    vagina V10.44
    vulva V10.44
  malignant neuroendocrine tumor V10.91
  manic-depressive psychosis V11.1
  meningitis V12.42
  mental disorder V11.9
    affective type V11.1
    manic-depressive V11.1
    neurosis V11.2
    schizophrenia V11.0
    specified type NEC V11.8
  Merkel cell carcinoma V10.91
  metabolic disorder V12.29
  methicillin resistant Staphylococcus aureus (MRSA) V12.04
  MRSA (methicillin resistant Staphylococcus aureus) V12.04
  musculoskeletal disorder NEC V13.59
  myocardial infarction 412
  neglect (emotional) V15.42
  nephrotic syndrome V13.03
  nervous system disorder V12.40
    specified type NEC V12.49
  neurosis V11.2
  noncompliance with medical treatment V15.81
  nutritional deficiency V12.1
  obstetric disorder V13.29
    affecting management of current pregnancy V23.49
      ectopic pregnancy V23.42
      pre-term labor V23.41
    pre-term labor V13.21
  parasitic disease V12.00
    specified NEC V12.09
  perinatal problems V13.7
    low birth weight (*see also* Status, low birth weight) V21.30
  physical abuse V15.41
  poisoning V15.6
  poliomyelitis V12.02
  polyps, colonic V12.72
  poor obstetric V13.29
    affecting management of current pregnancy V23.49
      ectopic pregnancy V23.42
      pre-term labor V23.41
    pre-term labor V13.21
  prolonged reversible ischemic neurologic deficit (PRIND) V12.54
  psychiatric disorder V11.9
    affective type V11.1
    manic-depressive V11.1
    neurosis V11.2
    schizophrenia V11.0
    specified type NEC V11.8
  psychological trauma V15.49
    emotional abuse V15.42
    neglect V15.42
    physical abuse V15.41
    rape V15.41
  psychoneurosis V11.2
  radiation therapy V15.3
  rape V15.41
  respiratory system disease V12.60
    pneumonia V12.61
    specified NEC V12.69
  reticulosarcoma V10.71
  return from military deployment V62.22

☑ Additional Digit Required — Refer to the Tabular List for Digit Selection   ▽ Subterms under main terms may continue to next column or page

2015 ICD-9-CM   ►◄ Revised Text   ● New Line   ▲ Revised Code   Volume 2 — 141

History of — *continued*
reversible ischemic neurologic deficit (RIND) V12.54
schizophrenia V11.0
skin disease V13.3
smoking (tobacco) V15.82
steroid therapy V87.45
inhaled V87.44
systemic V87.45
stroke without residual deficits V12.54
subcutaneous tissue disease V13.3
sudden
cardiac
arrest V12.53
death (successfully resuscitated) V12.53
surgery to
great vessels V15.1
heart V15.1
in utero
during pregnancy V15.21
while a fetus V15.22
organs NEC V15.29
syndrome, nephrotic V13.03
therapy
antineoplastic drug V87.41
drug NEC V87.49
estrogen V87.43
immunosuppression V87.46
monoclonal drug V87.42
steroid V87.45
inhaled V87.44
systemic V87.45
thrombophlebitis V12.52
thrombosis V12.51
pulmonary V12.55
tobacco use V15.82
trophoblastic disease V13.1
affecting management of pregnancy V23.1
tuberculosis V12.01
ulcer, peptic V12.71
urinary system disorder V13.00
calculi V13.01
infection V13.02
nephrotic syndrome V13.03
specified NEC V13.09
His-Werner disease (trench fever) 083.1
HIT (heparin-induced thrombocytopenia) 289.84
Hives (bold) — *see also* Urticaria 708.9
HIV infection (disease) (illness) — *see* Human immunodeficiency virus (disease) (illness) (infection)
Hoarseness 784.42
Hobnail liver — *see* Cirrhosis, portal
Hobo, hoboism V60.0
Hodgkin's
disease (M9650/3) 201.9 ☑
lymphocytic
depletion (M9653/3) 201.7 ☑
diffuse fibrosis (M9654/3) 201.7 ☑
reticular type (M9655/3) 201.7 ☑
predominance (M9651/3) 201.4 ☑
lymphocytic-histiocytic predominance (M9651/3) 201.4 ☑
mixed cellularity (M9652/3) 201.6 ☑
nodular sclerosis (M9656/3) 201.5 ☑
cellular phase (M9657/3) 201.5 ☑
granuloma (M9661/3) 201.1 ☑
lymphogranulomatosis (M9650/3) 201.9 ☑
lymphoma (M9650/3) 201.9 ☑
lymphosarcoma (M9650/3) 201.9 ☑
paragranuloma (M9660/3) 201.0 ☑
sarcoma (M9662/3) 201.2 ☑
Hodgson's disease (aneurysmal dilatation of aorta) 441.9
ruptured 441.5
Hodi-potsy 111.0
Hoffa (-Kastert) disease or syndrome (liposynovitis prepatellaris) 272.8
Hoffmann-Bouveret syndrome (paroxysmal tachycardia) 427.2
Hoffman's syndrome 244.9 [359.5]

Hole
macula 362.54
optic disc, crater-like 377.22
retina (macula) 362.54
round 361.31
with detachment 361.01
Holla disease — *see also* Spherocytosis 282.0
Holländer-Simons syndrome (progressive lipodystrophy) 272.6
Hollow foot (congenital) 754.71
acquired 736.73
Holmes' syndrome (visual disorientation) 368.16
Holoprosencephaly 742.2
due to
trisomy 13 758.1
trisomy 18 758.2
Holthouse's hernia — *see* Hernia, inguinal
Homesickness 309.89
Homicidal ideation V62.85
Homocystinemia 270.4
Homocystinuria 270.4
Homologous serum jaundice (prophylactic) (therapeutic) — *see* Hepatitis, viral
Homosexuality — omit code
ego-dystonic 302.0
pedophilic 302.2
problems with 302.0
Homozygous Hb-S disease 282.61
Honeycomb lung 518.89
congenital 748.4
Hong Kong ear 117.3
HOOD (hereditary osteo-onychodysplasia) 756.89
Hooded
clitoris 752.49
penis 752.69
Hookworm (anemia) (disease) (infestation) — *see* Ancylostomiasis
Hoppe-Goldflam syndrome 358.00
Hordeolum (external) (eyelid) 373.11
internal 373.12
Horn
cutaneous 702.8
cheek 702.8
eyelid 702.8
penis 702.8
iliac 756.89
nail 703.8
congenital 757.5
papillary 700
Horner's
syndrome (*see also* Neuropathy, peripheral, autonomic) 337.9
traumatic 954.0
teeth 520.4
Horseshoe kidney (congenital) 753.3
Horton's
disease (temporal arteritis) 446.5
headache or neuralgia 339.00
Hospice care V66.7
Hospitalism (in children) NEC 309.83
Hourglass contraction, contracture
bladder 596.89
gallbladder 575.2
congenital 751.69
stomach 536.8
congenital 750.7
psychogenic 306.4
uterus 661.4 ☑
affecting fetus or newborn 763.7
Household circumstance affecting care V60.9
specified type NEC V60.89
Housemaid's knee 727.2
Housing circumstance affecting care V60.9
specified type NEC V60.89
HTLV-I infection 079.51
HTLV-II infection 079.52
HTLV-III/LAV (disease) (illness) (infection) — *see* Human immunodeficiency virus (disease) (illness) (infection)
HTLV-III (disease) (illness) (infection) — *see* Human immunodeficiency virus (disease) (illness) (infection)

HTR (hemolytic transfusion reaction)
due to or resulting from
incompatibility
ABO 999.61
acute 999.62
delayed 999.63
non-ABO antigen (minor) (Duffy) (Kell) (Kidd) (Lewis) (M) (N) (P) (S) 999.76
acute 999.77
delayed 999.78
Rh antigen (C) (c) (D) (E) (e) 999.71
acute 999.72
delayed 999.73
Huchard's disease (continued arterial hypertension) 401.9
Hudson-Ståhli lines 371.11
Huguier's disease (uterine fibroma) 218.9
Human bite (open wound) — *see also* Wound, open, by site
intact skin surface — *see* Contusion
Human immunodeficiency virus (disease) (illness) 042
infection V08
with symptoms, symptomatic 042
Human immunodeficiency virus-2 infection 079.53
Human immunovirus (disease) (illness) (infection) — *see* Human immunodeficiency virus (disease) (illness) (infection)
Human papillomavirus 079.4
high risk, DNA test positive
anal 796.75
cervical 795.05
vaginal 795.15
low risk, DNA test positive
anal 796.79
cervical 795.09
vaginal 795.19
Human parvovirus 079.83
Human T-cell lymphotrophic virus-I infection 079.51
Human T-cell lymphotrophic virus-II infection 079.52
Human T-cell lymphotrophic virus-III (disease) (illness) (infection) — *see* Human immunodeficiency virus (disease) (illness) (infection)
Humpback (acquired) 737.9
congenital 756.19
Hum, venous — omit code
Hunchback (acquired) 737.9
congenital 756.19
Hunger 994.2
air, psychogenic 306.1
disease 251.1
Hungry bone syndrome 275.5
Hunner's ulcer — *see also* Cystitis 595.1
Hunt's
neuralgia 053.11
syndrome (herpetic geniculate ganglionitis) 053.11
dyssynergia cerebellaris myoclonica 334.2
Hunter's glossitis 529.4
Hunterian chancre 091.0
Hunter (-Hurler) syndrome (mucopolysaccharidosis II) 277.5
Huntington's
chorea 333.4
disease 333.4
Huppert's disease (multiple myeloma) (M9730/3) 203.0 ☑
Hurler (-Hunter) disease or syndrome (mucopolysaccharidosis II) 277.5
Hürthle cell
adenocarcinoma (M8290/3) 193
adenoma (M8290/0) 226
carcinoma (M8290/3) 193
tumor (M8290/0) 226
Hutchinson's
disease meaning
angioma serpiginosum 709.1
cheiropompholyx 705.81
prurigo estivalis 692.72

Hutchinson's — *continued*
disease meaning — *continued*
summer eruption, or summer prurigo 692.72
incisors 090.5
melanotic freckle (M8742/2) (*see also* Neoplasm, skin, in situ)
malignant melanoma in (M8742/3) — *see* Melanoma
teeth or incisors (congenital syphilis) 090.5
Hutchinson-Boeck disease or syndrome (sarcoidosis) 135
Hutchinson-Gilford disease or syndrome (progeria) 259.8
Hyaline
degeneration (diffuse) (generalized) 728.9
localized — *see* Degeneration, by site
membrane (disease) (lung) (newborn) 769
Hyalinosis cutis et mucosae 272.8
Hyalin plaque, sclera, senile 379.16
Hyalitis (asteroid) 379.22
syphilitic 095.8
Hydatid
cyst or tumor (*see also* Echinococcus)
fallopian tube 752.11
mole — *see* Hydatidiform mole
Morgagni (congenital) 752.89
fallopian tube 752.11
Hydatidiform mole (benign) (complicating pregnancy) (delivered) (undelivered) 630
invasive (M9100/1) 236.1
malignant (M9100/1) 236.1
previous, affecting management of pregnancy V23.1
Hydatidosis — *see* Echinococcus
Hyde's disease (prurigo nodularis) 698.3
Hydradenitis 705.83
Hydradenoma (M8400/0) — *see* Hidradenoma
Hydralazine lupus or syndrome
correct substance properly administered 695.4
overdose or wrong substance given or taken 972.6
Hydramnios 657.0 ☑
affecting fetus or newborn 761.3
Hydrancephaly 742.3
with spina bifida (*see also* Spina bifida) 741.0 ☑
Hydranencephaly 742.3
with spina bifida (*see also* Spina bifida) 741.0 ☑
Hydrargyrism NEC 985.0
Hydrarthrosis — *see also* Effusion, joint 719.0 ☑
gonococcal 098.50
intermittent (*see also* Rheumatism, palindromic) 719.3 ☑
of yaws (early) (late) 102.6
syphilitic 095.8
congenital 090.5
Hydremia 285.9
Hydrencephalocele (congenital) 742.0
Hydrencephalomeningocele (congenital) 742.0
Hydroa 694.0
aestivale 692.72
gestationis 646.8 ☑
herpetiformis 694.0
pruriginosa 694.0
vacciniforme 692.72
Hydroadenitis 705.83
Hydrocalycosis — *see also* Hydronephrosis 591
congenital 753.29
Hydrocalyx — *see also* Hydronephrosis 591
Hydrocele (calcified) (chylous) (idiopathic) (infantile) (inguinal canal) (recurrent) (senile) (spermatic cord) (testis) (tunica vaginalis) 603.9
canal of Nuck (female) 629.1
male 603.9
congenital 778.6
encysted 603.0
congenital 778.6
female NEC 629.89
infected 603.1
round ligament 629.89

☑ **Additional Digit Required** — Refer to the Tabular List for Digit Selection   ▼ **Subterms under main terms may continue to next column or page**

142 — Volume 2   ▶◀ **Revised Text**   ● **New Line**   ▲ **Revised Code**   2015 ICD-9-CM

Hydrocele — *continued*
  specified type NEC 603.8
    congenital 778.6
  spinalis (*see also* Spina bifida) 741.9 ☑
  vulva 624.8
Hydrocephalic fetus
  affecting management or pregnancy 655.0 ☑
  causing disproportion 653.6 ☑
    with obstructed labor 660.1 ☑
      affecting fetus or newborn 763.1
Hydrocephalus (acquired) (external) (internal) (malignant) (noncommunicating) (obstructive) (recurrent) 331.4
  aqueduct of Sylvius stricture 742.3
    with spina bifida (*see also* Spina bifida) 741.0 ☑
  chronic 742.3
    with spina bifida (*see also* Spina bifida) 741.0 ☑
  communicating 331.3
  congenital (external) (internal) 742.3
    with spina bifida (*see also* Spina bifida) 741.0 ☑
  due to
    stricture of aqueduct of Sylvius 742.3
      with spina bifida (*see also* Spina bifida) 741.0 ☑
    toxoplasmosis (congenital) 771.2
  fetal affecting management of pregnancy 655.0 ☑
  foramen Magendie block (acquired) 331.3
    congenital 742.3
      with spina bifida (*see also* Spina bifida) 741.0 ☑
  newborn 742.3
    with spina bifida (*see also* Spina bifida) 741.0 ☑
  normal pressure 331.5
    idiopathic (INPH) 331.5
    secondary 331.3
  otitic 348.2
  syphilitic, congenital 090.49
  tuberculous (*see also* Tuberculosis) 013.8 ☑
Hydrocolpos (congenital) 623.8
Hydrocystoma (M8404/0) — *see* Neoplasm, skin, benign
Hydroencephalocele (congenital) 742.0
Hydroencephalomeningocele (congenital) 742.0
Hydrohematopneumothorax — *see also* Hemothorax 511.89
Hydromeningitis — *see* Meningitis
Hydromeningocele (spinal) — *see also* Spina bifida 741.9 ☑
  cranial 742.0
Hydrometra 621.8
Hydrometrocolpos 623.8
Hydromicrocephaly 742.1
Hydromphalus (congenital) (since birth) 757.39
Hydromyelia 742.53
Hydromyelocele — *see also* Spina bifida 741.9 ☑
Hydronephrosis 591
  atrophic 591
  congenital 753.29
  due to S. hematobium 120.0
  early 591
  functionless (infected) 591
  infected 591
  intermittent 591
  primary 591
  secondary 591
  tuberculous (*see also* Tuberculosis) 016.0 ☑
Hydropericarditis — *see also* Pericarditis 423.9
Hydropericardium — *see also* Pericarditis 423.9
Hydroperitoneum 789.59
Hydrophobia 071
Hydrophthalmos — *see also* Buphthalmia 743.20
Hydropneumohemothorax — *see also* Hemothorax 511.89
Hydropneumopericarditis — *see also* Pericarditis 423.9

Hydropneumopericardium — *see also* Pericarditis 423.9
Hydropneumothorax 511.89
  nontuberculous 511.89
    bacterial 511.1
  pneumococcal 511.1
  staphylococcal 511.1
  streptococcal 511.1
  traumatic 860.0
    with open wound into thorax 860.1
  tuberculous (*see also* Tuberculosis, pleura) 012.0 ☑
Hydrops 782.3
  abdominis 789.59
  amnii (complicating pregnancy) (*see also* Hydramnios) 657.0 ☑
  articulorum intermittens (*see also* Rheumatism, palindromic) 719.3 ☑
  cardiac (*see also* Failure, heart) 428.0
  congenital — *see* Hydrops, fetalis
  endolymphatic (*see also* Disease, Ménière's) 386.00
  fetal, fetalis or newborn 778.0
    due to
      alpha thalassemia 282.43
      isoimmunization 773.3
    not due to isoimmunization 778.0
  gallbladder 575.3
  idiopathic (fetus or newborn) 778.0
  joint (see also Effusion, joint) 719.0 ☑
  labyrinth (*see also* Disease, Ménière's) 386.00
  meningeal NEC 331.4
  nutritional 262
  pericardium — *see* Pericarditis
  pleura (*see also* Hydrothorax) 511.89
  renal (*see also* Nephrosis) 581.9
  spermatic cord (*see also* Hydrocele) 603.9
Hydropyonephrosis — *see also* Pyelitis 590.80
  chronic 590.00
Hydrorachis 742.53
Hydrorrhea (nasal) 478.19
  gravidarum 658.1 ☑
  pregnancy 658.1 ☑
Hydrosadenitis 705.83
Hydrosalpinx (fallopian tube) (follicularis) 614.1
Hydrothorax (double) (pleural) 511.89
  chylous (nonfilarial) 457.8
    filaria (*see also* Infestation, filarial) 125.9
  nontuberculous 511.89
    bacterial 511.1
  pneumococcal 511.1
  staphylococcal 511.1
  streptococcal 511.1
  traumatic 862.29
    with open wound into thorax 862.39
  tuberculous (*see also* Tuberculosis, pleura) 012.0 ☑
Hydroureter 593.5
  congenital 753.22
Hydroureteronephrosis — *see also* Hydronephrosis 591
Hydrourethra 599.84
Hydroxykynureninuria 270.2
Hydroxyprolinemia 270.8
Hydroxyprolinuria 270.8
Hygroma (congenital) (cystic) (M9173/0) 228.1
  prepatellar 727.3
  subdural — *see* Hematoma, subdural
Hymen — *see* condition
Hymenolepiasis (diminuta) (infection) (infestation) (nana) 123.6
Hymenolepsis (diminuta) (infection) (infestation) (nana) 123.6
Hypalgesia — *see also* Disturbance, sensation 782.0
Hyperabduction syndrome 447.8
Hyperacidity, gastric 536.8
  psychogenic 306.4
Hyperactive, hyperactivity 314.01
  basal cell, uterine cervix 622.10
  bladder 596.51
  bowel (syndrome) 564.9
    sounds 787.5
  cervix epithelial (basal) 622.10
  child 314.01

Hyperactive, hyperactivity — *continued*
  colon 564.9
  gastrointestinal 536.8
    psychogenic 306.4
  intestine 564.9
  labyrinth (unilateral) 386.51
    with loss of labyrinthine reactivity 386.58
    bilateral 386.52
  nasal mucous membrane 478.19
  stomach 536.8
  thyroid (gland) (*see also* Thyrotoxicosis) 242.9 ☑
Hyperacusis 388.42
Hyperadrenalism (cortical) 255.3
  medullary 255.6
Hyperadrenocorticism 255.3
  congenital 255.2
  iatrogenic
    correct substance properly administered 255.3
    overdose or wrong substance given or taken 962.0
Hyperaffectivity 301.11
Hyperaldosteronism (atypical) (hyperplastic) (normoaldosteronal) (normotensive) (primary) 255.10
  secondary 255.14
Hyperalgesia — *see also* Disturbance, sensation 782.0
Hyperalimentation 783.6
  carotene 278.3
  specified NEC 278.8
  vitamin A 278.2
  vitamin D 278.4
Hyperaminoaciduria 270.9
  arginine 270.6
  citrulline 270.6
  cystine 270.0
  glycine 270.0
  lysine 270.7
  ornithine 270.6
  renal (types I, II, III) 270.0
Hyperammonemia (congenital) 270.6
Hyperamnesia 780.99
Hyperamylasemia 790.5
Hyperaphia 782.0
Hyperazotemia 791.9
Hyperbetalipoproteinemia (acquired) (essential) (familial) (hereditary) (primary) (secondary) 272.0
  with prebetalipoproteinemia 272.2
Hyperbilirubinemia 782.4
  congenital 277.4
  constitutional 277.4
  neonatal (transient) (*see also* Jaundice, fetus or newborn) 774.6
    of prematurity 774.2
Hyperbilirubinemica encephalopathia, newborn 774.7
  due to isoimmunization 773.4
Hypercalcemia, hypercalcemic (idiopathic) 275.42
  nephropathy 588.89
Hypercalcinuria 275.40
Hypercapnia 786.09
  with mixed acid-based disorder 276.4
  fetal, affecting newborn 770.89
Hypercarotinemia 278.3
Hypercementosis 521.5
Hyperchloremia 276.9
Hyperchlorhydria 536.8
  neurotic 306.4
  psychogenic 306.4
Hypercholesterinemia — *see* Hypercholesterolemia
Hypercholesterolemia 272.0
  with hyperglyceridemia, endogenous 272.2
  essential 272.0
  familial 272.0
  hereditary 272.0
  primary 272.0
  pure 272.0
Hypercholesterolosis 272.0
Hyperchylia gastrica 536.8
  psychogenic 306.4

Hyperchylomicronemia (familial) (with hyper-betalipoproteinemia) 272.3
Hypercoagulation syndrome (primary) 289.81
  secondary 289.82
Hypercorticosteronism
  correct substance properly administered 255.3
  overdose or wrong substance given or taken 962.0
Hypercortisonism
  correct substance properly administered 255.3
  overdose or wrong substance given or taken 962.0
Hyperdynamic beta-adrenergic state or syndrome (circulatory) 429.82
Hyperekplexia 759.89
Hyperelectrolytemia 276.9
Hyperemesis 536.2
  arising during pregnancy — *see* Hyperemesis, gravidarum
  gravidarum (mild) (before 22 completed weeks gestation) 643.0 ☑
    with
      carbohydrate depletion 643.1 ☑
      dehydration 643.1 ☑
      electrolyte imbalance 643.1 ☑
      metabolic disturbance 643.1 ☑
    affecting fetus or newborn 761.8
    severe (with metabolic disturbance) 643.1 ☑
  psychogenic 306.4
Hyperemia (acute) 780.99
  anal mucosa 569.49
  bladder 596.7
  cerebral 437.8
  conjunctiva 372.71
  ear, internal, acute 386.30
  enteric 564.89
  eye 372.71
  eyelid (active) (passive) 374.82
  intestine 564.89
  iris 364.41
  kidney 593.81
  labyrinth 386.30
  liver (active) (passive) 573.8
  lung 514
  ovary 620.8
  passive 780.99
  pulmonary 514
  renal 593.81
  retina 362.89
  spleen 289.59
  stomach 537.89
Hyperesthesia (body surface) — *see also* Disturbance, sensation 782.0
  larynx (reflex) 478.79
    hysterical 300.11
  pharynx (reflex) 478.29
Hyperestrinism 256.0
Hyperestrogenism 256.0
Hyperestrogenosis 256.0
Hyperexplexia 759.89
Hyperextension, joint 718.80
  ankle 718.87
  elbow 718.82
  foot 718.87
  hand 718.84
  hip 718.85
  knee 718.86
  multiple sites 718.89
  pelvic region 718.85
  shoulder (region) 718.81
  specified site NEC 718.88
  wrist 718.83
Hyperfibrinolysis — *see* Fibrinolysis
Hyperfolliculinism 256.0
Hyperfructosemia 271.2
Hyperfunction
  adrenal (cortex) 255.3
    androgenic, acquired benign 255.3
    medulla 255.6
    virilism 255.2
  corticoadrenal NEC 255.3
  labyrinth — *see* Hyperactive, labyrinth
  medulloadrenal 255.6

Hyperfunction — continued
ovary 256.1
estrogen 256.0
pancreas 577.8
parathyroid (gland) 252.00
pituitary (anterior) (gland) (lobe) 253.1
testicular 257.0
Hypergammaglobulinemia 289.89
monoclonal, benign (BMH) 273.1
polyclonal 273.0
Waldenström's 273.0
Hyperglobulinemia 273.8
Hyperglycemia 790.29
maternal
affecting fetus or newborn 775.0
manifest diabetes in infant 775.1
postpancreatectomy (complete) (partial)
251.3
Hyperglyceridemia 272.1
endogenous 272.1
essential 272.1
familial 272.1
hereditary 272.1
mixed 272.3
pure 272.1
Hyperglycinemia 270.7
Hypergonadism
ovarian 256.1
testicular (infantile) (primary) 257.0
Hyperheparinemia — see also Circulating, intrinsic anticoagulants 287.5
Hyperhidrosis, hyperidrosis 705.21
axilla 705.21
face 705.21
focal (localized) 705.21
primary 705.21
axilla 705.21
face 705.21
palms 705.21
soles 705.21
secondary 705.22
axilla 705.22
face 705.22
palms 705.22
soles 705.22
generalized 780.8
palms 705.21
psychogenic 306.3
secondary 780.8
soles 705.21
Hyperhistidinemia 270.5
Hyperinsulinism (ectopic) (functional) (organic) NEC 251.1
iatrogenic 251.0
reactive 251.2
spontaneous 251.2
therapeutic misadventure (from administration of insulin) 962.3
Hyperiodemia 276.9
Hyperirritability (cerebral), in newborn 779.1
Hyperkalemia 276.7
Hyperkeratosis — see also Keratosis 701.1
cervix 622.2
congenital 757.39
cornea 371.89
due to yaws (early) (late) (palmar or plantar)
102.3
eccentrica 757.39
figurata centrifuga atrophica 757.39
follicularis 757.39
in cutem penetrans 701.1
limbic (cornea) 371.89
palmoplantaris climacterica 701.1
pinta (carate) 103.1
senile (with pruritus) 702.0
tongue 528.79
universalis congenita 757.1
vagina 623.1
vocal cord 478.5
vulva 624.09
Hyperkinesia, hyperkinetic (disease) (reaction) (syndrome) 314.9
with
attention deficit — see Disorder, attention deficit
conduct disorder 314.2

Hyperkinesia, hyperkinetic — continued
with — continued
developmental delay 314.1
simple disturbance of activity and attention 314.01
specified manifestation NEC 314.8
heart (disease) 429.82
of childhood or adolescence NEC 314.9
Hyperlacrimation — see also Epiphora 375.20
Hyperlipemia — see also Hyperlipidemia 272.4
Hyperlipidemia 272.4
carbohydrate-induced 272.1
combined 272.2
endogenous 272.1
exogenous 272.3
fat-induced 272.3
group
A 272.0
B 272.1
C 272.2
D 272.3
mixed 272.2
specified type NEC 272.4
Hyperlipidosis 272.7
hereditary 272.7
Hyperlipoproteinemia (acquired) (essential)
(familial) (hereditary) (primary) (secondary) 272.4
Fredrickson type
I 272.3
IIa 272.0
IIb 272.2
III 272.2
IV 272.1
V 272.3
low-density-lipoid-type (LDL) 272.0
very-low-density-lipoid-type (VLDL) 272.1
Hyperlucent lung, unilateral 492.8
Hyperluteinization 256.1
Hyperlysinemia 270.7
Hypermagnesemia 275.2
neonatal 775.5
Hypermaturity (fetus or newborn)
post-term infant 766.21
prolonged gestation infant 766.22
Hypermenorrhea 626.2
Hypermetabolism 794.7
Hypermethioninemia 270.4
Hypermetropia (congenital) 367.0
Hypermobility
cecum 564.9
coccyx 724.71
colon 564.9
psychogenic 306.4
ileum 564.89
joint (acquired) 718.80
ankle 718.87
elbow 718.82
foot 718.87
hand 718.84
hip 718.85
knee 718.86
multiple sites 718.89
pelvic region 718.85
shoulder (region) 718.81
specified site NEC 718.88
wrist 718.83
kidney, congenital 753.3
meniscus (knee) 717.5
scapula 718.81
stomach 536.8
psychogenic 306.4
syndrome 728.5
testis, congenital 752.52
urethral 599.81
Hypermotility
gastrointestinal 536.8
intestine 564.9
psychogenic 306.4
stomach 536.8
Hypernasality 784.43
Hypernatremia 276.0
with water depletion 276.0
Hypernephroma (M8312/3) 189.0
Hyperopia 367.0
Hyperorexia 783.6

Hyperornithinemia 270.6
Hyperosmia — see also Disturbance, sensation
781.1
Hyperosmolality 276.0
Hyperosteogenesis 733.99
Hyperostosis 733.99
calvarial 733.3
cortical 733.3
infantile 756.59
frontal, internal of skull 733.3
interna frontalis 733.3
monomelic 733.99
skull 733.3
congenital 756.0
vertebral 721.8
with spondylosis — see Spondylosis
ankylosing 721.6
Hyperovarianism 256.1
Hyperovarism, hyperovaria 256.1
Hyperoxaluria (primary) 271.8
Hyperoxia 987.8
Hyperparathyroidism 252.00
ectopic 259.3
other 252.08
primary 252.01
secondary (of renal origin) 588.81
non-renal 252.02
tertiary 252.08
Hyperpathia — see also Disturbance, sensation
782.0
psychogenic 307.80
Hyperperistalsis 787.4
psychogenic 306.4
Hyperpermeability, capillary 448.9
Hyperphagia 783.6
Hyperphenylalaninemia 270.1
Hyperphoria 378.40
alternating 378.45
Hyperphosphatemia 275.3
Hyperpiesia — see also Hypertension 401.9
Hyperpiesis — see also Hypertension 401.9
Hyperpigmentation — see Pigmentation
Hyperpinealism 259.8
Hyperpipecolatemia 270.7
Hyperpituitarism 253.1
Hyperplasia, hyperplastic
adenoids (lymphoid tissue) 474.12
and tonsils 474.10
adrenal (capsule) (cortex) (gland) 255.8
with
sexual precocity (male) 255.2
virilism, adrenal 255.2
virilization (female) 255.2
congenital 255.2
due to excess ACTH (ectopic) (pituitary)
255.0
medulla 255.8
alpha cells (pancreatic)
with
gastrin excess 251.5
glucagon excess 251.4
angiolymphoid, with eosinophilia (ALHE)
228.01
appendix (lymphoid) 543.0
artery, fibromuscular NEC 447.8
carotid 447.8
renal 447.3
bone 733.99
marrow 289.9
breast (see also Hypertrophy, breast) 611.1
ductal 610.8
atypical 610.8
carotid artery 447.8
cementation, cementum (teeth) (tooth)
521.5
cervical gland 785.6
cervix (uteri) 622.10
basal cell 622.10
congenital 752.49
endometrium 622.10
polypoid 622.10
chin 524.05
clitoris, congenital 752.49
dentin 521.5
endocervicitis 616.0

Hyperplasia, hyperplastic — continued
endometrium, endometrial (adenomatous)
(atypical) (cystic) (glandular) (polypoid) (uterus) 621.30
with atypia 621.33
without atypia
complex 621.32
simple 621.31
benign 621.34
cervix 622.10
epithelial 709.8
focal, oral, including tongue 528.79
mouth (focal) 528.79
nipple 611.89
skin 709.8
tongue (focal) 528.79
vaginal wall 623.0
erythroid 289.9
fascialis ossificans (progressiva) 728.11
fibromuscular, artery NEC 447.8
carotid 447.8
renal 447.3
genital
female 629.89
male 608.89
gingiva 523.8
glandularis
cystica uteri 621.30
endometrium (uterus) 621.30
interstitialis uteri 621.30
granulocytic 288.69
gum 523.8
hymen, congenital 752.49
islands of Langerhans 251.1
islet cell (pancreatic) 251.9
alpha cells
with excess
gastrin 251.5
glucagon 251.4
beta cells 251.1
juxtaglomerular (complex) (kidney) 593.89
kidney (congenital) 753.3
liver (congenital) 751.69
lymph node (gland) 785.6
lymphoid (diffuse) (nodular) 785.6
appendix 543.0
intestine 569.89
mandibular 524.02
alveolar 524.72
unilateral condylar 526.89
Marchand multiple nodular (liver) — see
Cirrhosis, postnecrotic
maxillary 524.01
alveolar 524.71
medulla, adrenal 255.8
myometrium, myometrial 621.2
neuroendocrine cell, of infancy 516.61
nose (lymphoid) (polypoid) 478.19
oral soft tissue (inflammatory) (irritative)
(mucosa) NEC 528.9
gingiva 523.8
tongue 529.8
organ or site, congenital NEC — see
Anomaly, specified type NEC
ovary 620.8
palate, papillary 528.9
pancreatic islet cells 251.9
alpha
with excess
gastrin 251.5
glucagon 251.4
beta 251.1
parathyroid (gland) 252.01
persistent, vitreous (primary) 743.51
pharynx (lymphoid) 478.29
prostate 600.90
with
other lower urinary tract symptoms
(LUTS) 600.91
urinary
obstruction 600.91
retention 600.91
adenofibromatous 600.20
with
other lower urinary tract symptoms (LUTS) 600.21

Hyperplasia, hyperplastic — *continued*
  prostate — *continued*
    adenofibromatous — *continued*
      with — *continued*
        urinary
          obstruction 600.21
          retention 600.21
    nodular 600.10
      with
        urinary
          obstruction 600.11
          retention 600.11
  renal artery (fibromuscular) 447.3
  reticuloendothelial (cell) 289.9
  salivary gland (any) 527.1
  Schimmelbusch's 610.1
  suprarenal (capsule) (gland) 255.8
  thymus (gland) (persistent) 254.0
  thyroid (*see also* Goiter) 240.9
    primary 242.0 ☑
    secondary 242.2 ☑
  tonsil (lymphoid tissue) 474.11
    and adenoids 474.10
  urethrovaginal 599.89
  uterus, uterine (myometrium) 621.2
    endometrium (*see also* Hyperplasia, en-
      dometrium) 621.30
  vitreous (humor), primary persistent 743.51
  vulva 624.3
  zygoma 738.11
Hyperpnea — *see also* Hyperventilation 786.01
Hyperpotassemia 276.7
Hyperprebetalipoproteinemia 272.1
  with chylomicronemia 272.3
  familial 272.1

Hyperprolactinemia 253.1
Hyperprolinemia 270.8
Hyperproteinemia 273.8
Hyperprothrombinemia 289.89
Hyperpselaphesia 782.0
Hyperpyrexia 780.60
  heat (effects of) 992.0
  malarial (*see also* Malaria) 084.6
  malignant, due to anesthetic 995.86
  rheumatic — *see* Fever, rheumatic
  unknown origin (*see also* Pyrexia) 780.60
Hyperreactor, vascular 780.2
Hyperreflexia 796.1
  bladder, autonomic 596.54
    with cauda equina 344.61
  detrusor 344.61
Hypersalivation — *see also* Ptyalism 527.7
Hypersarcosinemia 270.8
Hypersecretion
  ACTH 255.3
  androgens (ovarian) 256.1
  calcitonin 246.0
  corticoadrenal 255.3
  cortisol 255.0
  estrogen 256.0
  gastric 536.8
    psychogenic 306.4
  gastrin 251.5
  glucagon 251.4
  hormone
    ACTH 255.3
    anterior pituitary 253.1
    growth NEC 253.0
    ovarian androgen 256.1
    testicular 257.0

Hypersecretion — *continued*
  hormone — *continued*
    thyroid stimulating 242.8 ☑
  insulin — *see* Hyperinsulinism
  lacrimal glands (*see also* Epiphora) 375.20
  medulloadrenal 255.6
  milk 676.6 ☑
  ovarian androgens 256.1
  pituitary (anterior) 253.1
  salivary gland (any) 527.7
  testicular hormones 257.0
  thyrocalcitonin 246.0
  upper respiratory 478.9
Hypersegmentation, hereditary 288.2
  eosinophils 288.2
  neutrophil nuclei 288.2
Hypersensitive, hypersensitiveness, hyper-
  sensitivity — *see also* Allergy
  angiitis 446.20
    specified NEC 446.29
  carotid sinus 337.01
  colon 564.9
    psychogenic 306.4
  DNA (deoxyribonucleic acid) NEC 287.2
  drug (*see also* Allergy, drug) 995.27
  due to correct medical substance properly
    administered 995.27
  esophagus 530.89
  insect bites — *see* Injury, superficial, by site
  labyrinth 386.58
  pain (*see also* Disturbance, sensation) 782.0
  pneumonitis NEC 495.9
  reaction (*see also* Allergy) 995.3
    upper respiratory tract NEC 478.8
  stomach (allergic) (nonallergic) 536.8

Hypersensitive, hypersensitiveness,
  hypersensitivity — *see also* Allergy —
    continued
  stomach — *continued*
    psychogenic 306.4
Hypersomatotropism (classic) 253.0
Hypersomnia, unspecified 780.54
  with sleep apnea, unspecified 780.53
  alcohol induced 291.82
  drug induced 292.85
  due to
    medical condition classified elsewhere
      327.14
    mental disorder 327.15
  idiopathic
    with long sleep time 327.11
    without long sleep time 327.12
  menstrual related 327.13
  nonorganic origin 307.43
    persistent (primary) 307.44
    transient 307.43
  organic 327.10
    other 327.19
  primary 307.44
  recurrent 327.13
Hypersplenia 289.4
Hypersplenism 289.4
Hypersteatosis 706.3
Hyperstimulation, ovarian 256.1
Hypersuprarenalism 255.3
Hypersusceptibility — *see* Allergy
Hyper-TBG-nemia 246.8
Hypertelorism 756.0
  orbit, orbital 376.41

☑ **Additional Digit Required — Refer to the Tabular List for Digit Selection**

▽ **Subterms under main terms may continue to next column or page**

2015 ICD-9-CM

▶◀ **Revised Text**

● **New Line**

▲ **Revised Code**

Volume 2 — 145

	Malignant	Benign	Unspecified
Hypertension, hypertensive (arterial) (arteriolar) (crisis) (degeneration) (disease) (essential) (fluctuating) (idiopathic) (intermittent) (labile) (low renin) (orthostatic) (paroxysmal) (primary) (systemic) (uncontrolled) (vascular)	401.0	401.1	401.9
with			
chronic kidney disease			
stage I through stage IV, or unspecified	403.00	403.10	403.90
stage V or end stage renal disese	403.01	403.11	403.91
heart involvement (conditions classifiable to 429.0–429.3, 429.8, 429.9 due to hypertension) (see also Hypertension, heart)	402.00	402.10	402.90
with kidney involvement — see Hypertension, cardiorenal			
renal (kidney) involvement (only conditions classifiable to 585, 587) (excludes conditions classifiable to 584) (see also Hypertension, kidney)	403.00	403.10	403.90
with heart involvement — see Hypertension, cardiorenal			
failure (and sclerosis) (see also Hypertension, kidney)	403.01	403.11	403.91
sclerosis without failure (see also Hypertension, kidney)	403.00	403.10	403.90
accelerated (see also Hypertension, by type, malignant))	401.0	—	—
antepartum — see Hypertension, complicating pregnancy, childbirth, or the puerperium			
borderline	—	—	796.2
cardiorenal (disease)	404.00	404.10	404.90
with			
chronic kidney disease			
stage I through stage IV, or unspecified	404.00	404.10	404.90
and heart failure	404.01	404.11	404.91
stage V or end stage renal disease	404.02	404.12	404.92
and heart failure	404.03	404.13	404.93
heart failure	404.01	404.11	404.91
and chronic kidney disease	404.01	404.11	404.91
stage I through stage IV or unspecified	404.01	404.11	404.91
stave V or end stage renal disease	404.03	404.13	404.93
cardiovascular disease (arteriosclerotic) (sclerotic)	402.00	402.10	402.90
with			
heart failure	402.01	402.11	402.91
renal involvement (conditions classifiable to 403) (see also Hypertension, cardiorenal)	404.00	404.10	404.90
cardiovascular renal (disease) (sclerosis) (see also Hypertension, cardiorenal)	404.00	404.10	404.90
cerebrovascular disease NEC	437.2	—	—
complicating pregnancy, childbirth, or the puerperium	642.2	642.0	642.9
with			
albuminuria (and edema) (mild)	—	—	642.4
severe	—	—	642.5
chronic kidney disesae	642.2	—	—
and heart disease	642.2	—	—
edema (mild)	—	—	642.4
severe	—	—	642.5
heart disease	642.2	—	—
and chronic kidney disease	642.2	—	—
renal disease	642.2	—	—
and heart disease	642.2	—	—
chronic	642.2	642.0	—
with pre-eclampsia or eclampsia	642.7	—	—
fetus or newborn	760.0	—	—
essential	—	642.0	—
with pre-eclampsia or eclampsia	—	642.7	—
fetus or newborn	760.0	—	—
fetus or newborn	760.0	—	—
gestational	—	—	642.3
pre-existing	642.2	642.0	—
with pre-eclampsia or eclampsia	642.7	—	—
fetus or newborn	760.0	—	—
secondary to renal disease	642.1	—	—
with pre-eclampsia or eclampsia	642.7	—	—
fetus or newborn	760.0	—	—
transient	—	—	642.3
due to			
aldosteronism, primary	405.09	405.19	405.99
brain tumor	405.09	405.19	405.99
bulbar poliomyelitis	405.09	405.19	405.99
calculus			
kidney	405.09	405.19	405.99

	Malignant	Benign	Unspecified
Hypertension, hypertensive — *continued*			
due to — *continued*			
calculus — *continued*			
ureter	405.09	405.19	405.99
coarctation, aorta	405.09	405.19	405.99
Cushing's disease	405.09	405.19	405.99
glomerulosclerosis (see also Hypertension, kidney)	403.00	403.10	403.90
periarteritis nodosa	405.09	405.19	405.99
pheochromocytoma	405.09	405.19	405.99
polycystic kidney(s)	405.09	405.19	405.99
polycythemia	405.09	405.19	405.99
porphyria	405.09	405.19	405.99
pyelonephritis	405.09	405.19	405.99
renal (artery)			
aneurysm	405.01	405.11	405.91
anomaly	405.01	405.11	405.91
embolism	405.01	405.11	405.91
fibromuscular hyperplasia	405.01	405.11	405.91
occlusion	405.01	405.11	405.91
stenosis	405.01	405.11	405.91
thrombosis	405.01	405.11	405.91
encephalopathy	437.2	—	—
gestational (transient) NEC	—	—	642.3
Goldblatt's	440.1	—	—
heart (disease) (conditions classifiable to 429.0–429.3, 429.8, 429.9 due to hypertension)	402.00	402.10	402.90
with heart failure	402.01	402.11	402.91
hypertensive kidney disease (conditions classifiable to 403) (see also Hypertension, cardiorenal)	404.00	404.10	404.90
renal sclerosis (see also Hypertension, cardiorenal)	404.00	404.10	404.90
intracranial, benign	—	348.2	—
intraocular	—	—	365.04
kidney	403.00	403.10	403.90
with			
chronic kidney disease			
stage I through stage IV, or unspecified	403.00	403.10	403.90
stage V or end stage renal disese	403.01	403.11	403.91
heart involvement (conditions classifiable to 429.0–429.3, 429.8, 429.9 due to hypertension) (see also Hypertension, cardiorenal)	404.00	404.10	404.90
hypertensive heart (disease) (conditions classifiable to 402) (see also Hypertension, cardiorenal)	404.00	404.10	404.90
lesser circulation	—	—	416.0
necrotizing	401.0	—	—
ocular	—	—	365.04
pancreatic duct — code to underlying condition			
with			
chronic pancreatitis	—	—	577.1
portal (due to chronic liver disease)	—	—	572.3
postoperative	—	—	997.91
psychogenic	—	—	306.2
puerperal, postpartum — see Hypertension, complicating pregnancy, childbirth, or the puerperium			
pulmonary (artery) (secondary)	—	—	416.8
with			
cor pulmonale (chronic)	—	—	416.8
acute	—	—	415.0
right heart ventricular strain/failure	—	—	416.8
acute	—	—	415.0
idiopathic	—	—	416.0
primary	—	—	416.0
of newborn	—	—	747.83
secondary	—	—	416.8
renal (disease) (see also Hypertension, kidney)	403.00	403.10	403.90
renovascular NEC	405.01	405.11	405.91
secondary NEC	405.09	405.19	405.99
due to			
aldosteronism, primary	405.09	405.19	405.99
brain tumor	405.09	405.19	405.99
bulbar poliomyelitis	405.09	405.19	405.99
calculus			
kidney	405.09	405.19	405.99
ureter	405.09	405.19	405.99
coarctation, aorta	405.09	405.19	405.99
Cushing's disease	405.09	405.19	405.99
glomerulosclerosis (see also Hypertension, kidney)	403.00	403.10	403.90

☑ **Additional Digit Required** — Refer to the Tabular List for Digit Selection ▽ Subterms under main terms may continue to next column or page

	Malignant	Benign	Unspecified
Hypertension, hypertensive — *continued*			
secondary — *continued*			
due to — *continued*			
periarteritis nodosa	405.09	405.19	405.99
pheochromocytoma	405.09	405.19	405.99
polycystic kidney(s)	405.09	405.19	405.99
polycythemia	405.09	405.19	405.99
porphyria	405.09	405.19	405.99
pyelonephritis	405.09	405.19	405.99
renal (artery)			
aneurysm	405.01	405.11	405.91
anomaly	405.01	405.11	405.91
embolism	405.01	405.11	405.91
fibromuscular hyperplasia	405.01	405.11	405.91
occlusion	405.01	405.11	405.91
stenosis	405.01	405.11	405.91
thrombosis	405.01	405.11	405.91
transient	—	—	796.2
of pregnancy	—	—	642.3
vascular degeneration	401.0	401.1	401.9
venous, chronic (asymptomatic) (idiopathic)	—	—	459.30
with			
complication, NEC	—	—	459.39
inflammation	—	—	459.32
with ulcer	—	—	459.33
ulcer	—	—	459.31
with inflammation	—	—	459.33
due to			
deep vein thrombosis (*see also* Syndrome, postphlebetic)	—	—	459.10

☑ **Additional Digit Required** — Refer to the Tabular List for Digit Selection   ▽ **Subterms under main terms may continue to next column or page**

2015 ICD-9-CM   ►◄ Revised Text   ● New Line   ▲ Revised Code   **Volume 2 — 147**

Index

Hypertensive urgency — Hypertrophy, hypertrophic

Hypertensive urgency — *see* Hypertension
Hyperthecosis, ovary 256.8
Hyperthermia (of unknown origin) — *see also*
  Pyrexia 780.60
  malignant (due to anesthesia) 995.86
  newborn 778.4
Hyperthymergasia — *see also* Psychosis, affective 296.0 ☑
  reactive (from emotional stress, psychological trauma) 298.1
  recurrent episode 296.1 ☑
  single episode 296.0 ☑
Hyperthymism 254.8
Hyperthyroid (recurrent) — *see* Hyperthyroidism
Hyperthyroidism (latent) (preadult) (recurrent) (without goiter) 242.9 ☑

  Note — Use the following fifth-digit subclassification with category 242:
  0   without mention of thyrotoxic crisis or storm
  1   with mention of thyrotoxic crisis or storm

  with
    goiter (diffuse) 242.0 ☑
      adenomatous 242.3 ☑
        multinodular 242.2 ☑
        uninodular 242.1 ☑
      nodular 242.3 ☑
        multinodular 242.2 ☑
        uninodular 242.1 ☑
      thyroid nodule 242.1 ☑
    complicating pregnancy, childbirth, or puerperium 648.1 ☑
  neonatal (transient) 775.3
Hypertonia — *see* Hypertonicity
Hypertonicity
  bladder 596.51
  fetus or newborn 779.89
  gastrointestinal (tract) 536.8
  infancy 779.89
    due to electrolyte imbalance 779.89
  muscle 728.85
  stomach 536.8
    psychogenic 306.4
  uterus, uterine (contractions) 661.4 ☑
    affecting fetus or newborn 763.7
Hypertony — *see* Hypertonicity
Hypertransaminemia 790.4
Hypertrichosis 704.1
  congenital 757.4
  eyelid 374.54
  lanuginosa 757.4
    acquired 704.1
Hypertriglyceridemia, essential 272.1
Hypertrophy, hypertrophic
  adenoids (infectional) 474.12
    and tonsils (faucial) (infective) (lingual) (lymphoid) 474.10
  adrenal 255.8
  alveolar process or ridge 525.8
  anal papillae 569.49
  apocrine gland 705.82
  artery NEC 447.8
    carotid 447.8
    congenital (peripheral) NEC 747.60
      gastrointestinal 747.61
      lower limb 747.64
      renal 747.62
      specified NEC 747.69
      spinal 747.82
      upper limb 747.63
    renal 447.3
  arthritis (chronic) (*see also* Osteoarthrosis) 715.9 ☑
    spine (*see also* Spondylosis) 721.90
  arytenoid 478.79
  asymmetrical (heart) 429.9
  auricular — *see* Hypertrophy, cardiac
  Bartholin's gland 624.8
  bile duct 576.8
  bladder (sphincter) (trigone) 596.89
  blind spot, visual field 368.42
  bone 733.99

Hypertrophy, hypertrophic — *continued*
  brain 348.89
  breast 611.1
    cystic 610.1
    fetus or newborn 778.7
    fibrocystic 610.1
    massive pubertal 611.1
    puerperal, postpartum 676.3 ☑
    senile (parenchymatous) 611.1
  cardiac (chronic) (idiopathic) 429.3
    with
      rheumatic fever (conditions classifiable to 390)
        active 391.8
          with chorea 392.0
        inactive or quiescent (with chorea) 398.99
      congenital NEC 746.89
      fatty (*see also* Degeneration, myocardial) 429.1
      hypertensive (*see also* Hypertension, heart) 402.90
      rheumatic (with chorea) 398.99
        active or acute 391.8
          with chorea 392.0
      valve (*see also* Endocarditis) 424.90
        congenital NEC 746.89
  cartilage 733.99
  cecum 569.89
  cervix (uteri) 622.6
    congenital 752.49
    elongation 622.6
  clitoris (cirrhotic) 624.2
    congenital 752.49
  colon 569.89
    congenital 751.3
  conjunctiva, lymphoid 372.73
  cornea 371.89
  corpora cavernosa 607.89
  duodenum 537.89
  endometrium (uterus) (*see also* Hyperplasia, endometrium) 621.30
    cervix 622.6
  epididymis 608.89
  esophageal hiatus (congenital) 756.6
    with hernia — *see* Hernia, diaphragm
  eyelid 374.30
  falx, skull 733.99
  fat pad 729.30
    infrapatellar 729.31
    knee 729.31
    orbital 374.34
    popliteal 729.31
    prepatellar 729.31
    retropatellar 729.31
    specified site NEC 729.39
  foot (congenital) 755.67
  frenum, frenulum (tongue) 529.8
    linguae 529.8
    lip 528.5
  gallbladder or cystic duct 575.8
  gastric mucosa 535.2 ☑
  gingiva 523.8
  gland, glandular (general) NEC 785.6
  gum (mucous membrane) 523.8
  heart (idiopathic) (*see also* Hypertrophy, cardiac)
    valve (*see also* Endocarditis)
      congenital NEC 746.89
  hemifacial 754.0
  hepatic — *see* Hypertrophy, liver
  hiatus (esophageal) 756.6
  hilus gland 785.6
  hymen, congenital 752.49
  ileum 569.89
  infrapatellar fat pad 729.31
  intestine 569.89
  jejunum 569.89
  kidney (compensatory) 593.1
    congenital 753.3
  labial frenulum 528.5
  labium (majus) (minus) 624.3
  lacrimal gland, chronic 375.03
  ligament 728.9
    spinal 724.8
  linguae frenulum 529.8

Hypertrophy, hypertrophic — *continued*
  lingual tonsil (infectional) 474.11
  lip (frenum) 528.5
    congenital 744.81
  liver 789.1
    acute 573.8
    cirrhotic — *see* Cirrhosis, liver
    congenital 751.69
    fatty — *see* Fatty, liver
  lymph gland 785.6
    tuberculous — *see* Tuberculosis, lymph gland
  mammary gland — *see* Hypertrophy, breast
  maxillary frenulum 528.5
  Meckel's diverticulum (congenital) 751.0
  medial meniscus, acquired 717.3
  median bar 600.90
    with
      other lower urinary tract symptoms (LUTS) 600.91
      urinary
        obstruction 600.91
        retention 600.91
  mediastinum 519.3
  meibomian gland 373.2
  meniscus, knee, congenital 755.64
  metatarsal head 733.99
  metatarsus 733.99
  mouth 528.9
  mucous membrane
    alveolar process 523.8
    nose 478.19
    turbinate (nasal) 478.0
  muscle 728.9
  muscular coat, artery NEC 447.8
    carotid 447.8
    renal 447.3
  myocardium (*see also* Hypertrophy, cardiac) 429.3
    idiopathic 425.18
  myometrium 621.2
  nail 703.8
    congenital 757.5
  nasal 478.19
    alae 478.19
    bone 738.0
    cartilage 478.19
    mucous membrane (septum) 478.19
    sinus (*see also* Sinusitis) 473.9
    turbinate 478.0
  nasopharynx, lymphoid (infectional) (tissue) (wall) 478.29
  neck, uterus 622.6
  nipple 611.1
  normal aperture diaphragm (congenital) 756.6
  nose (*see also* Hypertrophy, nasal) 478.19
  orbit 376.46
  organ or site, congenital NEC — *see* Anomaly, specified type NEC
  osteoarthropathy (pulmonary) 731.2
  ovary 620.8
  palate (hard) 526.89
    soft 528.9
  pancreas (congenital) 751.7
  papillae
    anal 569.49
    tongue 529.3
  parathyroid (gland) 252.01
  parotid gland 527.1
  penis 607.89
  phallus 607.89
    female (clitoris) 624.2
  pharyngeal tonsil 474.12
  pharyngitis 472.1
  pharynx 478.29
    lymphoid (infectional) (tissue) (wall) 478.29
  pituitary (fossa) (gland) 253.8
  popliteal fat pad 729.31
  preauricular (lymph) gland (Hampstead) 785.6
  prepuce (congenital) 605
    female 624.2
  prostate (asymptomatic) (early) (recurrent) 600.90

Hypertrophy, hypertrophic — *continued*
  prostate — *continued*
    with
      other lower urinary tract symptoms (LUTS) 600.91
      urinary
        obstruction 600.91
        retention 600.91
    adenofibromatous 600.20
      with
        other lower urinary tract symptoms (LUTS) 600.21
        urinary
          obstruction 600.21
          retention 600.21
    benign 600.00
      with
        other lower urinary tract symptoms (LUTS) 600.01
        urinary
          obstruction 600.01
          retention 600.01
    congenital 752.89
  pseudoedematous hypodermal 757.0
  pseudomuscular 359.1
  pylorus (muscle) (sphincter) 537.0
    congenital 750.5
    infantile 750.5
  rectal sphincter 569.49
  rectum 569.49
  renal 593.1
  rhinitis (turbinate) 472.0
  salivary duct or gland 527.1
    congenital 750.26
  scaphoid (tarsal) 733.99
  scar 701.4
  scrotum 608.89
  sella turcica 253.8
  seminal vesicle 608.89
  sigmoid 569.89
  skin condition NEC 701.9
  spermatic cord 608.89
  spinal ligament 724.8
  spleen — *see* Splenomegaly
  spondylitis (spine) (*see also* Spondylosis) 721.90
  stomach 537.89
  subaortic stenosis (idiopathic) 425.11
  sublingual gland 527.1
    congenital 750.26
  submaxillary gland 527.1
  suprarenal (gland) 255.8
  tendon 727.9
  testis 608.89
    congenital 752.89
  thymic, thymus (congenital) (gland) 254.0
  thyroid (gland) (*see also* Goiter) 240.9
    primary 242.0 ☑
    secondary 242.2 ☑
  toe (congenital) 755.65
    acquired 735.8
  tongue 529.8
    congenital 750.15
    frenum 529.8
    papillae (foliate) 529.3
  tonsil (faucial) (infective) (lingual) (lymphoid) 474.11
    with
      adenoiditis 474.01
      tonsillitis 474.00
        and adenoiditis 474.02
      and adenoids 474.10
  tunica vaginalis 608.89
  turbinate (mucous membrane) 478.0
  ureter 593.89
  urethra 599.84
  uterus 621.2
    puerperal, postpartum 674.8 ☑
  uvula 528.9
  vagina 623.8
  vas deferens 608.89
  vein 459.89
  ventricle, ventricular (heart) (left) (right) (*see also* Hypertrophy, cardiac)
    congenital 746.89

☑ **Additional Digit Required — Refer to the Tabular List for Digit Selection**   ▽ Subterms under main terms may continue to next column or page

Hypertrophy, hypertrophic — continued
  ventricle, ventricular (see also Hypertrophy, cardiac) — continued
    due to hypertension (left) (right) (see also Hypertension, heart) 402.90
      benign 402.10
      malignant 402.00
    right with ventricular septal defect, pulmonary stenosis or atresia, and dextraposition of aorta 745.2
  verumontanum 599.89
  vesical 596.89
  vocal cord 478.5
  vulva 624.3
    stasis (nonfilarial) 624.3
Hypertropia (intermittent) (periodic) 378.31
Hypertyrosinemia 270.2
Hyperuricemia 790.6
Hypervalinemia 270.3
Hyperventilation (tetany) 786.01
  hysterical 300.11
  psychogenic 306.1
  syndrome 306.1
Hyperviscidosis 277.00
Hyperviscosity (of serum) (syndrome) NEC 273.3
  polycythemic 289.0
  sclerocythemic 282.8
Hypervitaminosis (dietary) NEC 278.8
  A (dietary) 278.2
  D (dietary) 278.4
  from excessive administration or use of vitamin preparations (chronic) 278.8
    reaction to sudden overdose 963.5
  vitamin A 278.2
    reaction to sudden overdose 963.5
  vitamin D 278.4
    reaction to sudden overdose 963.5
  vitamin K
    correct substance properly administered 278.8
    overdose or wrong substance given or taken 964.3
Hypervolemia 276.69
Hypesthesia — see also Disturbance, sensation 782.0
  cornea 371.81
Hyphema (anterior chamber) (ciliary body) (iris) 364.41
  traumatic 921.3
Hyphemia — see Hyphema
Hypoacidity, gastric 536.8
  psychogenic 306.4
Hypoactive labyrinth (function) — see Hypofunction, labyrinth
Hypoadrenalism 255.41
  tuberculous (see also Tuberculosis) 017.6 ☑
Hypoadrenocorticism 255.41
  pituitary 253.4
Hypoalbuminemia 273.8
Hypoaldosteronism 255.42
Hypoalphalipoproteinemia 272.5
Hypobarism 993.2
Hypobaropathy 993.2
Hypobetalipoproteinemia (familial) 272.5
Hypocalcemia 275.41
  cow's milk 775.4
  dietary 269.3
  neonatal 775.4
  phosphate-loading 775.4
Hypocalcification, teeth 520.4
Hypochloremia 276.9
Hypochlorhydria 536.8
  neurotic 306.4
  psychogenic 306.4
Hypocholesteremia 272.5
Hypochondria (reaction) 300.7
Hypochondriac 300.7
Hypochondriasis 300.7
Hypochromasia blood cells 280.9
Hypochromic anemia 280.9
  due to blood loss (chronic) 280.0
    acute 285.1
  microcytic 280.9
Hypocoagulability — see also Defect, coagulation 286.9

Hypocomplementemia 279.8
Hypocythemia (progressive) 284.9
Hypodontia — see also Anodontia 520.0
Hypoeosinophilia 288.59
Hypoesthesia — see also Disturbance, sensation 782.0
  cornea 371.81
  tactile 782.0
Hypoestrinism 256.39
Hypoestrogenism 256.39
Hypoferremia 280.9
  due to blood loss (chronic) 280.0
Hypofertility
  female 628.9
  male 606.1
Hypofibrinogenemia 286.3
  acquired 286.6
  congenital 286.3
Hypofunction
  adrenal (gland) 255.41
    cortex 255.41
    medulla 255.5
    specified NEC 255.5
  cerebral 331.9
  corticoadrenal NEC 255.41
  intestinal 564.89
  labyrinth (unilateral) 386.53
    with loss of labyrinthine reactivity 386.55
    bilateral 386.54
      with loss of labyrinthine reactivity 386.56
  Leydig cell 257.2
  ovary 256.39
    postablative 256.2
  pituitary (anterior) (gland) (lobe) 253.2
    posterior 253.5
  testicular 257.2
    iatrogenic 257.1
    postablative 257.1
    postirradiation 257.1
    postsurgical 257.1
Hypogammaglobulinemia 279.00
  acquired primary 279.06
  non-sex-linked, congenital 279.06
  sporadic 279.06
  transient of infancy 279.09
Hypogenitalism (congenital) (female) (male) 752.89
  penis 752.69
Hypoglycemia (spontaneous) 251.2
  coma 251.0
    diabetic 250.3 ☑
      due to secondary diabetes 249.3 ☑
  diabetic 250.8 ☑
    due to secondary diabetes 249.8 ☑
  due to insulin 251.0
    therapeutic misadventure 962.3
  familial (idiopathic) 251.2
  following gastrointestinal surgery 579.3
  infantile (idiopathic) 251.2
  in infant of diabetic mother 775.0
  leucine-induced 270.3
  neonatal 775.6
  reactive 251.2
  specified NEC 251.1
Hypoglycemic shock 251.0
  diabetic 250.8 ☑
    due to secondary diabetes 249.8 ☑
  due to insulin 251.0
  functional (syndrome) 251.1
Hypogonadism
  female 256.39
  gonadotrophic (isolated) 253.4
  hypogonadotropic (isolated) (with anosmia) 253.4
  isolated 253.4
  male 257.2
    hereditary familial (Reifenstein's syndrome) 259.52
  ovarian (primary) 256.39
  pituitary (secondary) 253.4
  testicular (primary) (secondary) 257.2
Hypohidrosis 705.0
Hypohidrotic ectodermal dysplasia 757.31
Hypoidrosis 705.0
Hypoinsulinemia, postsurgical 251.3

Hypoinsulinemia, postsurgical — continued
  postpancreatectomy (complete) (partial) 251.3
Hypokalemia 276.8
Hypokinesia 780.99
Hypoleukia splenica 289.4
Hypoleukocytosis 288.50
Hypolipidemia 272.5
Hypolipoproteinemia 272.5
Hypomagnesemia 275.2
  neonatal 775.4
Hypomania, hypomanic reaction — see also Psychosis, affective 296.0 ☑
  recurrent episode 296.1 ☑
  single episode 296.0 ☑
Hypomastia (congenital) 611.82
Hypomenorrhea 626.1
Hypometabolism 783.9
Hypomotility
  gastrointestinal tract 536.8
    psychogenic 306.4
  intestine 564.89
    psychogenic 306.4
  stomach 536.8
    psychogenic 306.4
Hyponasality 784.44
Hyponatremia 276.1
Hypo-ovarianism 256.39
Hypo-ovarism 256.39
Hypoparathyroidism (idiopathic) (surgically induced) 252.1
  neonatal 775.4
Hypoperfusion (in)
  newborn 779.89
Hypopharyngitis 462
Hypophoria 378.40
Hypophosphatasia 275.3
Hypophosphatemia (acquired) (congenital) (familial) 275.3
  renal 275.3
Hypophyseal, hypophysis — see also condition
  dwarfism 253.3
  gigantism 253.0
  syndrome 253.8
Hypophyseothalamic syndrome 253.8
Hypopiesis — see Hypotension
Hypopigmentation 709.00
  eyelid 374.53
Hypopinealism 259.8
Hypopituitarism (juvenile) (syndrome) 253.2
  due to
    hormone therapy 253.7
    hypophysectomy 253.7
    radiotherapy 253.7
  postablative 253.7
  postpartum hemorrhage 253.2
Hypoplasia, hypoplasis 759.89
  adrenal (gland) 759.1
  alimentary tract 751.8
    lower 751.2
    upper 750.8
  angiolymphoid, with eosinophilia (ALHE) 228.01
  anus, anal (canal) 751.2
  aorta 747.22
  aortic
    arch (tubular) 747.10
    orifice or valve with hypoplasia of ascending aorta and defective development of left ventricle (with mitral valve atresia) 746.7
  appendix 751.2
  areola 757.6
  arm (see also Absence, arm, congenital) 755.20
  artery (congenital) (peripheral) 747.60
    brain 747.81
    cerebral 747.81
    coronary 746.85
    gastrointestinal 747.61
    lower limb 747.64
    pulmonary 747.31
    renal 747.62
    retinal 743.58

Hypoplasia, hypoplasis — continued
  artery — continued
    specified NEC 747.69
    spinal 747.82
    umbilical 747.5
    upper limb 747.63
  auditory canal 744.29
    causing impairment of hearing 744.02
  biliary duct (common) or passage 751.61
  bladder 753.8
  bone NEC 756.9
    face 756.0
    malar 756.0
    mandible 524.04
      alveolar 524.74
    marrow 284.9
      acquired (secondary) 284.89
      congenital 284.09
      idiopathic 284.9
    maxilla 524.03
      alveolar 524.73
    skull (see also Hypoplasia, skull) 756.0
  brain 742.1
    gyri 742.2
    specified part 742.2
  breast (areola) 611.82
  bronchus (tree) 748.3
  cardiac 746.89
    valve — see Hypoplasia, heart, valve
    vein 746.89
  carpus (see also Absence, carpal, congenital) 755.28
  cartilaginous 756.9
  cecum 751.2
  cementum 520.4
    hereditary 520.5
  cephalic 742.1
  cerebellum 742.2
  cervix (uteri) 752.43
  chin 524.06
  clavicle 755.51
  coccyx 756.19
  colon 751.2
  corpus callosum 742.2
  cricoid cartilage 748.3
  dermal, focal (Goltz) 757.39
  digestive organ(s) or tract NEC 751.8
    lower 751.2
    upper 750.8
  ear 744.29
    auricle 744.23
    lobe 744.29
    middle, except ossicles 744.03
      ossicles 744.04
    ossicles 744.04
  enamel of teeth (neonatal) (postnatal) (prenatal) 520.4
    hereditary 520.5
  endocrine (gland) NEC 759.2
  endometrium 621.8
  epididymis 752.89
  epiglottis 748.3
  erythroid, congenital 284.01
  erythropoietic, chronic acquired 284.81
  esophagus 750.3
  Eustachian tube 744.24
  eye (see also Microphthalmos) 743.10
    lid 743.62
  face 744.89
    bone(s) 756.0
  fallopian tube 752.19
  femur (see also Absence, femur, congenital) 755.34
  fibula (see also Absence, fibula, congenital) 755.37
  finger (see also Absence, finger, congenital) 755.29
  focal dermal 757.39
  foot 755.31
  gallbladder 751.69
  genitalia, genital organ(s)
    female 752.89
      external 752.49
      internal NEC 752.89
    in adiposogenital dystrophy 253.8
    male 752.89

☑ Additional Digit Required — Refer to the Tabular List for Digit Selection ▽ Subterms under main terms may continue to next column or page

2015 ICD-9-CM   ▶◀ Revised Text   ● New Line   ▲ Revised Code   **Volume 2 — 149**

Hypoplasia, hypoplasis — continued

genitalia, genital organ(s) — continued
- male — continued
  - penis 752.69
- glottis 748.3
- hair 757.4
- hand 755.21
- heart 746.89
  - left (complex) (syndrome) 746.7
  - valve NEC 746.89
  - pulmonary 746.01
- humerus (see also Absence, humerus, congenital) 755.24
- hymen 752.49
- intestine (small) 751.1
  - large 751.2
- iris 743.46
- jaw 524.09
- kidney(s) 753.0
- labium (majus) (minus) 752.49
- labyrinth, membranous 744.05
- lacrimal duct (apparatus) 743.65
- larynx 748.3
- leg (see also Absence, limb, congenital, lower) 755.30
- limb 755.4
  - lower (see also Absence, limb, congenital, lower) 755.30
  - upper (see also Absence, limb, congenital, upper) 755.20
- liver 751.69
- lung (lobe) 748.5
- mammary (areolar) 611.82
- mandibular 524.04
  - alveolar 524.74
  - unilateral condylar 526.89
- maxillary 524.03
  - alveolar 524.73
- medullary 284.9
- megakaryocytic 287.30
- metacarpus (see also Absence, metacarpal, congenital) 755.28
- metatarsus (see also Absence, metatarsal, congenital) 755.38
- muscle 756.89
  - eye 743.69
- myocardium (congenital) (Uhl's anomaly) 746.84
- nail(s) 757.5
- nasolacrimal duct 743.65
- nervous system NEC 742.8
- neural 742.8
- nose, nasal 748.1
- ophthalmic (see also Microphthalmos) 743.10
- optic nerve 377.43
- organ
  - of Corti 744.05
  - or site NEC — see Anomaly, by site
- osseous meatus (ear) 744.03
- ovary 752.0
- oviduct 752.19
- pancreas 751.7
- parathyroid (gland) 759.2
- parotid gland 750.26
- patella 755.64
- pelvis, pelvic girdle 755.69
- penis 752.69
- peripheral vascular system (congenital) NEC 747.60
  - gastrointestinal 747.61
  - lower limb 747.64
  - renal 747.62
  - specified NEC 747.69
  - spinal 747.82
  - upper limb 747.63
- pituitary (gland) 759.2
- pulmonary 748.5

Hypoplasia, hypoplasis — continued

pulmonary — continued
- arteriovenous 747.32
- artery 747.31
- valve 746.01
- punctum lacrimale 743.65
- radioulnar (see also Absence, radius, congenital, with ulna) 755.25
- radius (see also Absence, radius, congenital) 755.26
- rectum 751.2
- respiratory system NEC 748.9
- rib 756.3
- sacrum 756.19
- scapula 755.59
- shoulder girdle 755.59
- skin 757.39
- skull (bone) 756.0
  - with
    - anencephalus 740.0
    - encephalocele 742.0
    - hydrocephalus 742.3
      - with spina bifida (see also Spina bifida) 741.0 ☑
    - microcephalus 742.1
- spinal (cord) (ventral horn cell) 742.59
  - vessel 747.82
- spine 756.19
- spleen 759.0
- sternum 756.3
- tarsus (see also Absence, tarsal, congenital) 755.38
- testis, testicle 752.89
- thymus (gland) 279.11
- thyroid (gland) 243
  - cartilage 748.3
- tibiofibular (see also Absence, tibia, congenital, with fibula) 755.35
- toe (see also Absence, toe, congenital) 755.39
- tongue 750.16
- trachea (cartilage) (rings) 748.3
- Turner's (tooth) 520.4
- ulna (see also Absence, ulna, congenital) 755.27
- umbilical artery 747.5
- ureter 753.29
- uterus 752.32
- vagina 752.45
- vascular (peripheral) NEC (see also Hypoplasia, peripheral vascular system) 747.60
  - brain 747.81
- vein(s) (peripheral) NEC (see also Hypoplasia, peripheral vascular system) 747.60
  - brain 747.81
  - cardiac 746.89
  - great 747.49
  - portal 747.49
  - pulmonary 747.49
- vena cava (inferior) (superior) 747.49
- vertebra 756.19
- vulva 752.49
- zonule (ciliary) 743.39
- zygoma 738.12

Hypopotassemia 276.8

Hypoproaccelerinemia — see also Defect, coagulation 286.3

Hypoproconvertinemia (congenital) — see also Defect, coagulation 286.3

Hypoproteinemia (essential) (hypermetabolic) (idiopathic) 273.8

Hypoproteinosis 260

Hypoprothrombinemia (congenital) (hereditary) (idiopathic) — see also Defect, coagulation 286.3
- acquired 286.7
- newborn 776.3

Hypopselaphesia 782.0

Hypopyon (anterior chamber) (eye) 364.05
- iritis 364.05
- ulcer (cornea) 370.04

Hypopyrexia 780.99

Hyporeflex 796.1

Hyporeninemia, extreme 790.99
- in primary aldosteronism 255.10

Hyporesponsive episode 780.09

Hyposecretion
- ACTH 253.4
- ovary 256.39
  - postablative 256.2
- salivary gland (any) 527.7

Hyposegmentation of neutrophils, hereditary 288.2

Hyposiderinemia 280.9

Hyposmolality 276.1
- syndrome 276.1

Hyposomatotropism 253.3

Hyposomnia, unspecified — see also Insomnia 780.52
- with sleep apnea, unspecified 780.51

Hypospadias (male) 752.61
- female 753.8

Hypospermatogenesis 606.1

Hyposphagma 372.72

Hyposplenism 289.59

Hypostasis, pulmonary 514

Hypostatic — see condition

Hyposthenuria 593.89

Hyposuprarenalism 255.41

Hypo-TBG-nemia 246.8

Hypotension (arterial) (constitutional) 458.9
- chronic 458.1
- iatrogenic 458.29
- maternal, syndrome (following labor and delivery) 669.2 ☑
- of hemodialysis 458.21
- orthostatic (chronic) 458.0
  - dysautonomic-dyskinetic syndrome 333.0
- permanent idiopathic 458.1
- postoperative 458.29
- postural 458.0
- specified type NEC 458.8
- transient 796.3

Hypothermia (accidental) 991.6
- anesthetic 995.89
- associated with low environmental temperature 991.6
- newborn NEC 778.3
- not associated with low environmental temperature 780.65

Hypothymergasia — see also Psychosis, affective 296.2 ☑
- recurrent episode 296.3 ☑
- single episode 296.2 ☑

Hypothyroidism (acquired) 244.9
- complicating pregnancy, childbirth, or puerperium 648.1 ☑
- congenital 243
- due to
  - ablation 244.1
    - radioactive iodine 244.1
    - surgical 244.0
  - iodine (administration) (ingestion) 244.2
    - radioactive 244.1
  - irradiation therapy 244.1
  - p-aminosalicylic acid (PAS) 244.3
  - phenylbutazone 244.3
  - resorcinol 244.3
  - specified cause NEC 244.8
  - surgery 244.0
- goitrous (sporadic) 246.1
- iatrogenic NEC 244.3
- iodine 244.2

Hypothyroidism — continued

- pituitary 244.8
- postablative NEC 244.1
- postsurgical 244.0
- primary 244.9
- secondary NEC 244.8
- specified cause NEC 244.8
- sporadic goitrous 246.1

Hypotonia, hypotonicity, hypotony 781.3
- benign congenital 358.8
- bladder 596.4
- congenital 779.89
  - benign 358.8
- eye 360.30
  - due to
    - fistula 360.32
    - ocular disorder NEC 360.33
  - following loss of aqueous or vitreous 360.33
  - primary 360.31
- infantile muscular (benign) 359.0
- muscle 728.9
- uterus, uterine (contractions) — see Inertia, uterus

Hypotrichosis 704.09
- congenital 757.4
- lid (congenital) 757.4
  - acquired 374.55
- postinfectional NEC 704.09

Hypotropia 378.32

Hypoventilation 786.09
- congenital central alveolar syndrome 327.25
- idiopathic sleep related nonobstructive alveolar 327.24
- obesity 278.03
- sleep related, in conditions classifiable elsewhere 327.26

Hypovitaminosis — see also Deficiency, vitamin 269.2

Hypovolemia 276.52
- surgical shock 998.09
- traumatic (shock) 958.4

Hypoxemia — see also Anoxia 799.02
- sleep related, in conditions classifiable elsewhere 327.26

Hypoxia — see also Anoxia 799.02
- cerebral 348.1
  - during or resulting from a procedure 997.01
  - newborn 770.88
    - mild or moderate 768.6
    - severe 768.5
- fetal, affecting newborn 770.88
- intrauterine — see Distress, fetal
- myocardial (see also Insufficiency, coronary) 411.89
  - arteriosclerotic — see Arteriosclerosis, coronary
- newborn 770.88
- sleep related 327.24

Hypoxic-ischemic encephalopathy (HIE) 768.70
- mild 768.71
- moderate 768.72
- severe 768.73

Hypsarrhythmia — see also Epilepsy 345.6 ☑

Hysteralgia, pregnant uterus 646.8 ☑

Hysteria, hysterical 300.10
- anxiety 300.20
- Charcôt's gland 300.11
- conversion (any manifestation) 300.11
- dissociative type NEC 300.15
- psychosis, acute 298.1

Hysteroepilepsy 300.11

Hysterotomy, affecting fetus or newborn 763.89

☑ Additional Digit Required — Refer to the Tabular List for Digit Selection ▽ Subterms under main terms may continue to next column or page

150 — Volume 2 ▶◀ Revised Text ● New Line ▲ Revised Code 2015 ICD-9-CM

I

Iatrogenic syndrome of excess cortisol 255.0
IBM (inclusion body myositis) 359.71
Iceland disease (epidemic neuromyasthenia) 049.8
Ichthyosis (congenita) 757.1
  acquired 701.1
  fetalis gravior 757.1
  follicularis 757.1
  hystrix 757.39
  lamellar 757.1
  lingual 528.6
  palmaris and plantaris 757.39
  simplex 757.1
  vera 757.1
  vulgaris 757.1
Ichthyotoxism 988.0
  bacterial (*see also* Poisoning, food) 005.9
Icteroanemia, hemolytic (acquired) 283.9
  congenital (*see also* Spherocytosis) 282.0
Icterus — *see also* Jaundice 782.4
  catarrhal — *see* Icterus, infectious
  conjunctiva 782.4
    newborn 774.6
  epidemic — *see* Icterus, infectious
  febrilis — *see* Icterus, infectious
  fetus or newborn — *see* Jaundice, fetus or newborn
  gravis (*see also* Necrosis, liver) 570
    complicating pregnancy 646.7 ☑
      affecting fetus or newborn 760.8
    fetus or newborn NEC 773.0
    obstetrical 646.7 ☑
      affecting fetus or newborn 760.8
  hematogenous (acquired) 283.9
  hemolytic (acquired) 283.9
    congenital (*see also* Spherocytosis) 282.0
  hemorrhagic (acute) 100.0
    leptospiral 100.0
    newborn 776.0
    spirochetal 100.0
  infectious 070.1
    with hepatic coma 070.0
    leptospiral 100.0
    spirochetal 100.0
  intermittens juvenilis 277.4
  malignant (*see also* Necrosis, liver) 570
  neonatorum (*see also* Jaundice, fetus or newborn) 774.6
  pernicious (*see also* Necrosis, liver) 570
  spirochetal 100.0
Ictus solaris, solis 992.0
Ideation
  homicidal V62.85
  suicidal V62.84
Identity disorder 313.82
  dissociative 300.14
  gender role (child) 302.6
    adult 302.85
  psychosexual (child) 302.6
    adult 302.85
Idioglossia 307.9
Idiopathic — *see* condition
Idiosyncrasy — *see also* Allergy 995.3
  drug, medicinal substance, and biological — *see* Allergy, drug
Idiot, idiocy (congenital) 318.2
  amaurotic (Bielschowsky) (-Jansky) (family) (infantile) (late) (juvenile) (late) (Vogt-Spielmeyer) 330.1
  microcephalic 742.1
  Mongolian 758.0
  oxycephalic 756.0
Id reaction (due to bacteria) 692.89
IEED (involuntary emotional expression disorder) 310.81
IFIS (intraoperative floppy iris syndrome) 364.81
IgE asthma 493.0 ☑
Ileitis (chronic) — *see also* Enteritis 558.9
  infectious 009.0
  noninfectious 558.9
  regional (ulcerative) 555.0
    with large intestine 555.2
  segmental 555.0

Ileitis — *see also* Enteritis — *continued*
  segmental — *continued*
    with large intestine 555.2
  terminal (ulcerative) 555.0
    with large intestine 555.2
Ileocolitis — *see also* Enteritis 558.9
  infectious 009.0
  regional 555.2
  ulcerative 556.1
Ileostomy status V44.2
  with complication 569.60
Ileotyphus 002.0
Ileum — *see* condition
Ileus (adynamic) (bowel) (colon) (inhibitory) (intestine) (neurogenic) (paralytic) 560.1
  arteriomesenteric duodenal 537.2
  due to gallstone (in intestine) 560.31
  duodenal, chronic 537.2
  following gastrointestinal surgery 997.49
  gallstone 560.31
  mechanical (*see also* Obstruction, intestine) 560.9
  meconium 777.1
    due to cystic fibrosis 277.01
  myxedema 564.89
  postoperative 997.49
  transitory, newborn 777.4
Iliac — *see* condition
Iliotibial band friction syndrome 728.89
Illegitimacy V61.6
Ill, louping 063.1
Illness — *see also* Disease
  factitious 300.19
    with
      combined psychological and physical signs and symptoms 300.19
      predominantly
        physical signs and symptoms 300.19
        psychological symptoms 300.16
    chronic (with physical symptoms) 301.51
  heart — *see* Disease, heart
  manic-depressive (*see also* Psychosis, affective) 296.80
  mental (*see also* Disorder, mental) 300.9
Imbalance 781.2
  autonomic (*see also* Neuropathy, peripheral, autonomic) 337.9
  electrolyte 276.9
    with
      abortion — *see* Abortion, by type, with metabolic disorder
      ectopic pregnancy (*see also* categories 633.0–633.9) 639.4
      hyperemesis gravidarum (before 22 completed weeks gestation) 643.1 ☑
      molar pregnancy (*see also* categories 630–632) 639.4
    following
      abortion 639.4
      ectopic or molar pregnancy 639.4
    neonatal, transitory NEC 775.5
  endocrine 259.9
  eye muscle NEC 378.9
    heterophoria — *see* Heterophoria
  glomerulotubular NEC 593.89
  hormone 259.9
  hysterical (*see also* Hysteria) 300.10
  labyrinth NEC 386.50
  posture 729.90
  sympathetic (*see also* Neuropathy, peripheral, autonomic) 337.9
Imbecile, imbecility 318.0
  moral 301.7
  old age 290.9
  senile 290.9
  specified IQ — *see* IQ
  unspecified IQ 318.0
Imbedding, intrauterine device 996.32
Imbibition, cholesterol (gallbladder) 575.6
Imerslund (-Gräsbeck) syndrome (anemia due to familial selective vitamin B$_{12}$ malabsorption) 281.1
Iminoacidopathy 270.8
Iminoglycinuria, familial 270.8

Immature — *see also* Immaturity
  personality 301.89
Immaturity 765.1 ☑
  extreme 765.0 ☑
  fetus or infant light-for-dates — *see* Light-for-dates
  lung, fetus or newborn 770.4
  organ or site NEC — *see* Hypoplasia
  pulmonary, fetus or newborn 770.4
  reaction 301.89
  sexual (female) (male) 259.0
Immersion 994.1
  foot 991.4
  hand 991.4
Immobile, immobility
  complete
    due to severe physical disability or frailty 780.72
  intestine 564.89
  joint — *see* Ankylosis
  syndrome (paraplegic) 728.3
Immunization
  ABO
    affecting management of pregnancy 656.2 ☑
      fetus or newborn 773.1
  complication — *see* Complications, vaccination
  Rh factor
    affecting management of pregnancy 656.1 ☑
      fetus or newborn 773.0
      from transfusion (*see also* Complications, transfusion) 999.70
Immunodeficiency 279.3
  with
    adenosine-deaminase deficiency 279.2
    defect, predominant
      B-cell 279.00
      T-cell 279.10
    hyperimmunoglobulinemia 279.2
    lymphopenia, hereditary 279.2
    thrombocytopenia and eczema 279.12
    thymic
      aplasia 279.2
      dysplasia 279.2
  autosomal recessive, Swiss-type 279.2
  common variable 279.06
  severe combined (SCID) 279.2
  to Rh factor
    affecting management of pregnancy 656.1 ☑
      fetus or newborn 773.0
  X-linked, with increased IgM 279.05
Immunotherapy, prophylactic V07.2
  antineoplastic V58.12
Impaction, impacted
  bowel, colon, rectum 560.30
    with hernia (*see also* Hernia, by site, with obstruction)
      gangrenous — *see* Hernia, by site, with gangrene
    by
      calculus 560.32
      gallstone 560.31
      fecal 560.32
      specified type NEC 560.32
  calculus — *see* Calculus
  cerumen (ear) (external) 380.4
  cuspid 520.6
  dental 520.6
  fecal, feces 560.32
    with hernia (*see also* Hernia, by site, with obstruction)
      gangrenous — *see* Hernia, by site, with gangrene
  fracture — *see* Fracture, by site
  gallbladder — *see* Cholelithiasis
  gallstone(s) — *see* Cholelithiasis
    in intestine (any part) 560.31
  intestine(s) 560.30
    with hernia (*see also* Hernia, by site, with obstruction)
      gangrenous — *see* Hernia, by site, with gangrene

Impaction, impacted — *continued*
  intestine(s) — *continued*
    by
      calculus 560.32
      gallstone 560.31
      fecal 560.32
      specified type NEC 560.32
  intrauterine device (IUD) 996.32
  molar 520.6
  shoulder 660.4 ☑
    affecting fetus or newborn 763.1
  tooth, teeth 520.6
  turbinate 733.99
Impaired, impairment (function)
  arm V49.1
    movement, involving
      musculoskeletal system V49.1
      nervous system V49.2
  auditory discrimination 388.43
  back V48.3
  body (entire) V49.89
  cognitive, mild, so stated 331.83
  combined visual hearing V49.85
  dual sensory V49.85
  glucose
    fasting 790.21
    tolerance test (oral) 790.22
  hearing (*see also* Deafness) 389.9
    combined with visual impairment V49.85
  heart — *see* Disease, heart
  kidney (*see also* Disease, renal) 593.9
    disorder resulting from 588.9
      specified NEC 588.89
  leg V49.1
    movement, involving
      musculoskeletal system V49.1
      nervous system V49.2
  limb V49.1
    movement, involving
      musculoskeletal system V49.1
      nervous system V49.2
  liver 573.8
  mastication 524.9
  mild cognitive, so stated 331.83
  mobility
    ear ossicles NEC 385.22
    incostapedial joint 385.22
    malleus 385.21
  myocardium, myocardial (*see also* Insufficiency, myocardial) 428.0
  neuromusculoskeletal NEC V49.89
    back V48.3
    head V48.2
    limb V49.2
    neck V48.3
    spine V48.3
    trunk V48.3
  rectal sphincter 787.99
  renal (*see also* Disease, renal) 593.9
    disorder resulting from 588.9
      specified NEC 588.89
  spine V48.3
  vision NEC 369.9
    both eyes NEC 369.3
    combined with hearing impairment V49.85
    moderate 369.74
      both eyes 369.25
        with impairment of lesser eye (specified as)
          blind, not further specified 369.15
          low vision, not further specified 369.23
          near-total 369.17
          profound 369.18
          severe 369.24
          total 369.16
      one eye 369.74
        with vision of other eye (specified as)
          near-normal 369.75
          normal 369.76
    near-total 369.64
      both eyes 369.04

☑ **Additional Digit Required** — Refer to the Tabular List for Digit Selection   ▽ **Subterms under main terms may continue to next column or page**

2015 ICD-9-CM   ▶◀ **Revised Text**   ● **New Line**   ▲ **Revised Code**   **Volume 2 — 151**

Impaired, impairment — continued
  vision — continued
    near-total — continued
      both eyes — continued
        with impairment of lesser eye
          (specified as)
          blind, not further specified
            369.02
          total 369.03
      one eye 369.64
        with vision of other eye (specified
          as)
          near normal 369.65
          normal 369.66
    one eye 369.60
      with low vision of other eye 369.10
    profound 369.67
      both eyes 369.08
        with impairment of lesser eye
          (specified as)
          blind, not further specified
            369.05
          near-total 369.07
          total 369.06
      one eye 369.67
        with vision of other eye (specified
          as)
          near-normal 369.68
          normal 369.69
    severe 369.71
      both eyes 369.22
        with impairment of lesser eye
          (specified as)
          blind, not further specified
            369.11
          low vision, not further speci-
            fied 369.21
          near-total 369.13
          profound 369.14
          total 369.12
      one eye 369.71
        with vision of other eye (specified
          as)
          near-normal 369.72
          normal 369.73
    total
      both eyes 369.01
      one eye 369.61
        with vision of other eye (specified
          as)
          near-normal 369.62
          normal 369.63

Impaludism — see Malaria
Impediment, speech NEC 784.59
  psychogenic 307.9
  secondary to organic lesion 784.59
Impending
  cerebrovascular accident or attack 435.9
  coronary syndrome 411.1
  delirium tremens 291.0
  myocardial infarction 411.1
Imperception, auditory (acquired) (congenital) 389.9
Imperfect
  aeration, lung (newborn) 770.5
  closure (congenital)
    alimentary tract NEC 751.8
      lower 751.5
      upper 750.8
    atrioventricular ostium 745.69
    atrium (secundum) 745.5
      primum 745.61
    branchial cleft or sinus 744.41
    choroid 743.59
    cricoid cartilage 748.3
    cusps, heart valve NEC 746.89
      pulmonary 746.09
    ductus
      arteriosus 747.0
      Botalli 747.0
    ear drum 744.29
      causing impairment of hearing
        744.03
    endocardial cushion 745.60
    epiglottis 748.3

Imperfect — continued
  closure — continued
    esophagus with communication to
      bronchus or trachea 750.3
    Eustachian valve 746.89
    eyelid 743.62
    face, facial (see also Cleft, lip) 749.10
    foramen
      Botalli 745.5
      ovale 745.5
    genitalia, genital organ(s) or system
      female 752.89
        external 752.49
        internal NEC 752.89
        uterus 752.39
      male 752.89
        penis 752.69
    glottis 748.3
    heart valve (cusps) NEC 746.89
    interatrial ostium or septum 745.5
    interauricular ostium or septum 745.5
    interventricular ostium or septum 745.4
    iris 743.46
    kidney 753.3
    larynx 748.3
    lens 743.36
    lip (see also Cleft, lip) 749.10
    nasal septum or sinus 748.1
    nose 748.1
    omphalomesenteric duct 751.0
    optic nerve entry 743.57
    organ or site NEC — see Anomaly, spec-
      ified type, by site
    ostium
      interatrial 745.5
      interauricular 745.5
      interventricular 745.4
    palate (see also Cleft, palate) 749.00
    preauricular sinus 744.46
    retina 743.56
    roof of orbit 742.0
    sclera 743.47
    septum
      aortic 745.0
      aorticopulmonary 745.0
      atrial (secundum) 745.5
        primum 745.61
      between aorta and pulmonary artery
        745.0
      heart 745.9
      interatrial (secundum) 745.5
        primum 745.61
      interauricular (secundum) 745.5
        primum 745.61
      interventricular 745.4
        with pulmonary stenosis or atre-
          sia, dextraposition of aor-
          ta, and hypertrophy of
          right ventricle 745.2
        in tetralogy of Fallot 745.2
      nasal 748.1
      ventricular 745.4
        with pulmonary stenosis or atre-
          sia, dextraposition of aor-
          ta, and hypertrophy of
          right ventricle 745.2
        in tetralogy of Fallot 745.2
    skull 756.0
      with
        anencephalus 740.0
        encephalocele 742.0
        hydrocephalus 742.3
          with spina bifida (see also
            Spina bifida) 741.0 ☑
        microcephalus 742.1
    spine (with meningocele) (see also Spina
      bifida) 741.90
    thyroid cartilage 748.3
    trachea 748.3
    tympanic membrane 744.29
      causing impairment of hearing
        744.03
    uterus (with communication to bladder,
      intestine, or rectum) 752.39
    uvula 749.02

Imperfect — continued
  closure — continued
    uvula — continued
      with cleft lip (see also Cleft, palate,
        with cleft lip) 749.20
      vitelline duct 751.0
  development — see Anomaly, by site
  erection 607.84
  fusion — see Imperfect, closure
  inflation lung (newborn) 770.5
  intestinal canal 751.5
  poise 729.90
  rotation — see Malrotation
  septum, ventricular 745.4
Imperfectly descended testis 752.51
Imperforate (congenital) — see also Atresia
  anus 751.2
  bile duct 751.61
  cervix (uteri) 752.49
  esophagus 750.3
  hymen 752.42
  intestine (small) 751.1
    large 751.2
  jejunum 751.1
  pharynx 750.29
  rectum 751.2
  salivary duct 750.23
  urethra 753.6
  urinary meatus 753.6
  vagina 752.49
Impervious (congenital) — see also Atresia
  anus 751.2
  bile duct 751.61
  esophagus 750.3
  intestine (small) 751.1
    large 751.5
  rectum 751.2
  urethra 753.6
Impetiginization of other dermatoses 684
Impetigo (any organism) (any site) (bullous)
  (circinate) (contagiosa) (neonatorum)
  (simplex) 684
  Bockhart's (superficial folliculitis) 704.8
  external ear 684 [380.13]
  eyelid 684 [373.5]
  Fox's (contagiosa) 684
  furfuracea 696.5
  herpetiformis 694.3
    nonobstetrical 694.3
  staphylococcal infection 684
  ulcerative 686.8
  vulgaris 684
Impingement, soft tissue between teeth
  524.89
  anterior 524.81
  posterior 524.82
Implantation
  anomalous (see also Anomaly, specified
    type, by site)
    ureter 753.4
  cyst
    external area or site (skin) NEC 709.8
    iris 364.61
    vagina 623.8
    vulva 624.8
  dermoid (cyst)
    external area or site (skin) NEC 709.8
    iris 364.61
    vagina 623.8
    vulva 624.8
  placenta, low or marginal — see Placenta
    previa
Implant, endometrial 617.9
Impotence (sexual) 607.84
  organic origin NEC 607.84
  psychogenic 302.72
Impoverished blood 285.9
Impression, basilar 756.0
Imprisonment V62.5
Improper
  development, infant 764.9 ☑
Improperly tied umbilical cord (causing
  hemorrhage) 772.3
Impulses, obsessional 300.3
Impulsive 799.23
  neurosis 300.3

Impulsiveness 799.23
Inaction, kidney — see also Disease, renal
  593.9
Inactive — see condition
Inadequate, inadequacy
  aesthetics of dental restoration 525.67
  biologic 301.6
  cardiac and renal — see Hypertension, car-
    diorenal
  constitutional 301.6
  development
    child 783.40
    fetus 764.9 ☑
      affecting management of pregnancy
        656.5 ☑
    genitalia
      after puberty NEC 259.0
      congenital — see Hypoplasia, geni-
        talia
    lungs 748.5
    organ or site NEC — see Hypoplasia, by
      site
  dietary 269.9
  distance, interarch 524.28
  education V62.3
  environment
    economic problem V60.2
    household condition NEC V60.1
    poverty V60.2
    unemployment V62.0
  functional 301.6
  household care, due to
    family member
      handicapped or ill V60.4
      temporarily away from home V60.4
        on vacation V60.5
    technical defects in home V60.1
    temporary absence from home of person
      rendering care V60.4
  housing (heating) (space) V60.1
  interarch distance 524.28
  material resources V60.2
  mental (see also Disability, intellectual) 319
  nervous system 799.29
  personality 301.6
  prenatal care in current pregnancy V23.7
  pulmonary
    function 786.09
      newborn 770.89
    ventilation, newborn 770.89
  respiration 786.09
    newborn 770.89
  sample
    cytology
      anal 796.78
      cervical 795.08
      vaginal 795.18
  social 301.6
Inanition 263.9
  with edema 262
  due to
    deprivation of food 994.2
    malnutrition 263.9
  fever 780.60
Inappropriate
  change in quantitative human chorionic
    gonadotropin (hCG) in early pregnan-
    cy 631.0
  level of quantitative human chorionic go-
    nadotropin (hCG) for gestational age
    in early pregnancy 631.0
  secretion
    ACTH 255.0
    antidiuretic hormone (ADH) (excessive)
      253.6
      deficiency 253.5
    ectopic hormone NEC 259.3
    pituitary (posterior) 253.6
Inattention after or at birth 995.52
Inborn errors of metabolism — see Disorder,
  metabolism
Incarceration, incarcerated
  bubonocele (see also Hernia, inguinal, with
    obstruction)
    gangrenous — see Hernia, inguinal, with
      gangrene

☑ **Additional Digit Required** — Refer to the Tabular List for Digit Selection   ▽ **Subterms under main terms may continue to next column or page**

152 — Volume 2   ▶◀ **Revised Text**   ● **New Line**   ▲ **Revised Code**   2015 ICD-9-CM

Incarceration, incarcerated — *continued*
  colon (by hernia) (*see also* Hernia, by site with obstruction)
    gangrenous — *see* Hernia, by site, with gangrene
  enterocele 552.9
    gangrenous 551.9
  epigastrocele 552.29
    gangrenous 551.29
  epiplocele 552.9
    gangrenous 551.9
  exomphalos 552.1
    gangrenous 551.1
  fallopian tube 620.8
  hernia (*see also* Hernia, by site, with obstruction)
    gangrenous — *see* Hernia, by site, with gangrene
  iris, in wound 871.1
  lens, in wound 871.1
  merocele (*see also* Hernia, femoral, with obstruction) 552.00
  omentum (by hernia) (*see also* Hernia, by site, with obstruction)
    gangrenous — *see* Hernia, by site, with gangrene
  omphalocele 756.72
  rupture (meaning hernia) (*see also* Hernia, by site, with obstruction) 552.9
    gangrenous (*see also* Hernia, by site, with gangrene) 551.9
  sarcoepiplocele 552.9
    gangrenous 551.9
  sarcoepiplomphalocele 552.1
    with gangrene 551.1
  uterus 621.8
    gravid 654.3 ☑
      causing obstructed labor 660.2 ☑
        affecting fetus or newborn 763.1
Incident, cerebrovascular — *see also* Disease, cerebrovascular, acute 436
Incineration (entire body) (from fire, conflagration, electricity, or lightning) — *see* Burn, multiple, specified sites
Incised wound
  external — *see* Wound, open, by site
  internal organs (abdomen, chest, or pelvis) — *see* Injury, internal, by site, with open wound
Incision, incisional
  hernia — *see* Hernia, incisional
  surgical, complication — *see* Complications, surgical procedures
  traumatic
    external — *see* Wound, open, by site
    internal organs (abdomen, chest, or pelvis) — *see* Injury, internal, by site, with open wound
Inclusion
  azurophilic leukocytic 288.2
  blennorrhea (neonatal) (newborn) 771.6
  cyst — *see* Cyst, skin
  gallbladder in liver (congenital) 751.69
Incompatibility
  ABO
    affecting management of pregnancy 656.2 ☑
    fetus or newborn 773.1
    infusion or transfusion reaction (*see also* Complications, transfusion) 999.60
  blood (group) (Duffy) (E) (K(ell)) (Kidd) (Lewis) (M) (N) (P) (S) NEC
    affecting management of pregnancy 656.2 ☑
    fetus or newborn 773.2
    infusion or transfusion reaction (*see also* Complications, transfusion) 999.75
  contour of existing restoration of tooth with oral health 525.65
  marital V61.10
    involving
      divorce V61.03
      estrangement V61.09

Incompatibility — *continued*
  non-ABO (*see also* Complications, transfusion) 999.75
  Rh (antigen) (C) (c) (D) (E) (e) (blood group) (factor)
    affecting management of pregnancy 656.1 ☑
    fetus or newborn 773.0
    infusion or transfusion reaction (*see also* Complications, transfusion) 999.70
  Rhesus — *see* Incompatibility, Rh
Incompetency, incompetence, incompetent
  annular
    aortic (valve) (*see also* Insufficiency, aortic) 424.1
    mitral (valve) (*see also* Insufficiency, mitral) 424.0
    pulmonary valve (heart) (*see also* Endocarditis, pulmonary) 424.3
  aortic (valve) (*see also* Insufficiency, aortic) 424.1
    syphilitic 093.22
  cardiac (orifice) 530.0
    valve — *see* Endocarditis
  cervix, cervical (os) 622.5
    in pregnancy 654.5 ☑
      affecting fetus or newborn 761.0
  chronotropic 426.89
    with
      autonomic dysfunction 337.9
      ischemic heart disease 414.9
      left ventricular dysfunction 429.89
      sinus node dysfunction 427.81
  esophagogastric (junction) (sphincter) 530.0
  heart valve, congenital 746.89
  mitral (valve) — *see* Insufficiency, mitral
  papillary muscle (heart) 429.81
  pelvic fundus
    pubocervical tissue 618.81
    rectovaginal tissue 618.82
  pulmonary valve (heart) (*see also* Endocarditis, pulmonary) 424.3
    congenital 746.09
  tricuspid (annular) (rheumatic) (valve) (*see also* Endocarditis, tricuspid) 397.0
  valvular — *see* Endocarditis
  vein, venous (saphenous) (varicose) (*see also* Varicose, vein) 454.9
  velopharyngeal (closure)
    acquired 528.9
    congenital 750.29
Incomplete — *see also* condition
  bladder emptying 788.21
  defecation 787.61
  expansion lungs (newborn) 770.5
  gestation (liveborn) — *see* Immaturity
  rotation — *see* Malrotation
Inconclusive
  image test due to excess body fat 793.91
  mammogram, mammography 793.82
    due to dense breasts 793.82
Incontinence 788.30
  without sensory awareness 788.34
  anal sphincter 787.60
  continuous leakage 788.37
  feces, fecal 787.60
    due to hysteria 300.11
    nonorganic origin 307.7
  hysterical 300.11
  mixed (male) (female) (urge and stress) 788.33
  overflow 788.38
  paradoxical 788.39
  rectal 787.60
  specified NEC 788.39
  stress (female) 625.6
    male NEC 788.32
  urethral sphincter 599.84
  urge 788.31
    and stress (male) (female) 788.33
  urine 788.30
    active 788.30
    due to
      cognitive impairment 788.91
      immobility 788.91

Incontinence — *continued*
  urine — *continued*
    due to — *continued*
      severe physical disability 788.91
    functional 788.91
    male 788.30
      stress 788.32
        and urge 788.33
    neurogenic 788.39
    nonorganic origin 307.6
    stress (female) 625.6
      male NEC 788.32
    urge 788.31
      and stress 788.33
Incontinentia pigmenti 757.33
Incoordinate
  uterus (action) (contractions) 661.4 ☑
    affecting fetus or newborn 763.7
Incoordination
  esophageal-pharyngeal (newborn) 787.24
  muscular 781.3
  papillary muscle 429.81
Increase, increased
  abnormal, in development 783.9
  androgens (ovarian) 256.1
  anticoagulants (antithrombin) (anti-II) (anti-VIIIa) (anti-IXa) (anti-XIa) (prothrombin) (*see also* Anticoagulants 286.59
    anti-IIa 287.8
    anti-Xa 287.8
    extrinsic 287.8
    postpartum 666.3 ☑
  cold sense (*see also* Disturbance, sensation) 782.0
  estrogen 256.0
  function
    adrenal (cortex) 255.3
      medulla 255.6
    pituitary (anterior) (gland) (lobe) 253.1
      posterior 253.6
  heat sense (*see also* Disturbance, sensation) 782.0
  intracranial pressure 781.99
    injury at birth 767.8
  light reflex of retina 362.13
  permeability, capillary 448.9
  pressure
    intracranial 781.99
      injury at birth 767.8
    intraocular 365.00
  pulsations 785.9
  pulse pressure 785.9
  sphericity, lens 743.36
  splenic activity 289.4
  venous pressure 459.89
    portal 572.3
Incrustation, cornea, lead or zinc 930.0
Incyclophoria 378.44
Incyclotropia 378.33
Indeterminate sex 752.7
India rubber skin 756.83
Indicanuria 270.2
Indigestion (bilious) (functional) 536.8
  acid 536.8
  catarrhal 536.8
  due to decomposed food NEC 005.9
  fat 579.8
  nervous 306.4
  psychogenic 306.4
Indirect — *see* condition
Indolent bubo NEC 099.8
Induced
  abortion — *see* Abortion, induced
  birth, affecting fetus or newborn 763.89
  delivery — *see* Delivery
  labor — *see* Delivery
Induration, indurated
  brain 348.89
  breast (fibrous) 611.79
    puerperal, postpartum 676.3 ☑
  broad ligament 620.8
  chancre 091.0
    anus 091.1
    congenital 090.0
    extragenital NEC 091.2
  corpora cavernosa (penis) (plastic) 607.89

Induration, indurated — *continued*
  liver (chronic) 573.8
    acute 573.8
  lung (black) (brown) (chronic) (fibroid) (*see also* Fibrosis, lung) 515
    essential brown 275.09 *[516.1]*
  penile 607.89
  phlebitic — *see* Phlebitis
  skin 782.8
  stomach 537.89
Induratio penis plastica 607.89
Industrial — *see* condition
Inebriety — *see also* Abuse, drugs, nondependent 305.0 ☑
Inefficiency
  kidney (*see also* Disease, renal) 593.9
  thyroid (acquired) (gland) 244.9
Inelasticity, skin 782.8
Inequality, leg (acquired) (length) 736.81
  congenital 755.30
Inertia
  bladder 596.4
    neurogenic 596.54
      with cauda equina syndrome 344.61
  stomach 536.8
    psychogenic 306.4
  uterus, uterine 661.2 ☑
    affecting fetus or newborn 763.7
    primary 661.0 ☑
    secondary 661.1 ☑
  vesical 596.4
    neurogenic 596.54
      with cauda equina 344.61
Infant — *see also* condition
  excessive crying of 780.92
  fussy (baby) 780.91
  held for adoption V68.89
  newborn — *see* Newborn
  post-term (gestation period over 40 completed weeks to 42 completed weeks) 766.21
  prolonged gestation of (period over 42 completed weeks) 766.22
  syndrome of diabetic mother 775.0
"Infant Hercules" syndrome 255.2
Infantile — *see also* condition
  genitalia, genitals 259.0
    in pregnancy or childbirth NEC 654.4 ☑
      affecting fetus or newborn 763.89
      causing obstructed labor 660.2 ☑
        affecting fetus or newborn 763.1
  heart 746.9
  kidney 753.3
  lack of care 995.52
  macula degeneration 362.75
  melanodontia 521.05
  os, uterus (*see also* Infantile, genitalia) 259.0
  pelvis 738.6
    with disproportion (fetopelvic) 653.1 ☑
      affecting fetus or newborn 763.1
      causing obstructed labor 660.1 ☑
        affecting fetus or newborn 763.1
  penis 259.0
  testis 257.2
  uterus (*see also* Infantile, genitalia) 259.0
  vulva 752.49
Infantilism 259.9
  with dwarfism (hypophyseal) 253.3
  Brissaud's (infantile myxedema) 244.9
  celiac 579.0
  Herter's (nontropical sprue) 579.0
  hypophyseal 253.3
  hypothalamic (with obesity) 253.8
  idiopathic 259.9
  intestinal 579.0
  pancreatic 577.8
  pituitary 253.3
  renal 588.0
  sexual (with obesity) 259.0
Infants, healthy liveborn — *see* Newborn
Infarct, infarction
  adrenal (capsule) (gland) 255.41
  amnion 658.8 ☑
  anterior (with contiguous portion of intraventricular septum) NEC (*see also* Infarct, myocardium) 410.1 ☑

☑ **Additional Digit Required** — Refer to the Tabular List for Digit Selection
▽ **Subterms under main terms may continue to next column or page**

2015 ICD-9-CM
▶◀ Revised Text   ● New Line   ▲ Revised Code
Volume 2 — 153

Infarct, infarction — *continued*
appendices epiploicae 557.0
bowel 557.0
brain (stem) 434.91
  embolic (*see also* Embolism, brain)
    434.11
  healed or old without residuals V12.54
  iatrogenic 997.02
  lacunar 434.91
  late effect — *see* Late effect(s) (of) cere-
    brovascular disease
  postoperative 997.02
  puerperal, postpartum, childbirth
    674.0 ☑
  thrombotic (*see also* Thrombosis, brain)
    434.01
breast 611.89
Brewer's (kidney) 593.81
cardiac (*see also* Infarct, myocardium)
  410.9 ☑
cerebellar (*see also* Infarct, brain) 434.91
  embolic (*see also* Embolism, brain)
    434.11
cerebral (*see also* Infarct, brain) 434.91
  aborted 434.91
  embolic (*see also* Embolism, brain)
    434.11
  thrombotic (*see also* Infarct, brain)
    434.01
chorion 658.8 ☑
colon (acute) (agnogenic) (embolic) (hemor-
    rhagic) (nonocclusive) (nonthrombot-
    ic) (occlusive) (segmental) (thrombot-
    ic) (with gangrene) 557.0
coronary artery (*see also* Infarct, myocardi-
    um) 410.9 ☑
cortical 434.91
embolic (*see also* Embolism) 444.9
fallopian tube 620.8
gallbladder 575.8
heart (*see also* Infarct, myocardium)
    410.9 ☑
hepatic 573.4
hypophysis (anterior lobe) 253.8
impending (myocardium) 411.1
intestine (acute) (agnogenic) (embolic)
    (hemorrhagic) (nonocclusive) (non-
    thrombotic) (occlusive) (thrombotic)
    (with gangrene) 557.0
kidney 593.81
lacunar 434.91
liver 573.4
lung (embolic) (thrombotic) 415.19
  with
    abortion — *see* Abortion, by type,
      with, embolism
    ectopic pregnancy (*see also* cate-
      gories 633.0–633.9) 639.6
    molar pregnancy (*see also* categories
      630–632) 639.6
  following
    abortion 639.6
    ectopic or molar pregnancy 639.6
  iatrogenic 415.11
  in pregnancy, childbirth, or puerperium
    — *see* Embolism, obstetrical
  postoperative 415.11
  septic 415.12
lymph node or vessel 457.8
medullary (brain) — *see* Infarct, brain
meibomian gland (eyelid) 374.85
mesentery, mesenteric (embolic) (thrombot-
    ic) (with gangrene) 557.0
midbrain — *see* Infarct, brain
myocardium, myocardial (acute or with a
    stated duration of 8 weeks or less)
    (with hypertension) 410.9 ☑

Note — *Use the following fifth-digit
subclassification with category 410:*

0   *episode unspecified*

1   *initial episode*

2   *subsequent episode without recur-
    rence*

Infarct, infarction — *continued*
myocardium, myocardial — *continued*
  with symptoms after 8 weeks from date
    of infarction 414.8
  anterior (wall) (with contiguous portion
    of intraventricular septum) NEC
    410.1 ☑
  anteroapical (with contiguous portion
    of intraventricular septum)
    410.1 ☑
  anterolateral (wall) 410.0 ☑
  anteroseptal (with contiguous portion
    of intraventricular septum)
    410.1 ☑
  apical-lateral 410.5 ☑
  atrial 410.8 ☑
  basal-lateral 410.5 ☑
  chronic (with symptoms after 8 weeks
    from date of infarction) 414.8
  diagnosed on ECG, but presenting no
    symptoms 412
  diaphragmatic wall (with contiguous
    portion of intraventricular sep-
    tum) 410.4 ☑
  healed or old, currently presenting no
    symptoms 412
  high lateral 410.5 ☑
  impending 411.1
  inferior (wall) (with contiguous portion
    of intraventricular septum)
    410.4 ☑
  inferolateral (wall) 410.2 ☑
  inferoposterior wall 410.3 ☑
  intraoperative 997.1
  lateral wall 410.5 ☑
  non-Q wave 410.7 ☑
  non-ST elevation (NSTEMI)
  nontransmural 410.7 ☑
  papillary muscle 410.8 ☑
  past (diagnosed on ECG or other special
    investigation, but currently pre-
    senting no symptoms) 412
    with symptoms NEC 414.8
  posterior (strictly) (true) (wall) 410.6 ☑
  posterobasal 410.6 ☑
  posteroinferior 410.3 ☑
  posterolateral 410.5 ☑
  postprocedural 997.1
  previous, currently presenting no symp-
    toms 412
  Q wave (*see also* Infarct, myo-cardium,
    by site) 410.9 ☑
  septal 410.8 ☑
  specified site NEC 410.8 ☑
  ST elevation (STEMI) 410.9 ☑
    anterior (wall) 410.1 ☑
    anterolateral (wall) 410.0 ☑
    inferior (wall) 410.4 ☑
    inferolateral (wall) 410.2 ☑
    inferoposterior wall 410.3 ☑
    lateral wall 410.5 ☑
    posterior (strictly) (true) (wall)
      410.6 ☑
    specified site NEC 410.8 ☑
  subendocardial 410.7 ☑
  syphilitic 093.82
  non-ST elevation myocardial infarction
    (NSTEMI) 410.7 ☑
  nontransmural 410.7 ☑
omentum 557.0
ovary 620.8
pancreas 577.8
papillary muscle (*see also* Infarct, myocardi-
    um) 410.8 ☑
parathyroid gland 252.8
pituitary (gland) 253.8
placenta (complicating pregnancy) 656.7 ☑
  affecting fetus or newborn 762.2
pontine — *see* Infarct, brain
posterior NEC (*see also* Infarct, myocardium)
    410.6 ☑
prostate 602.8
pulmonary (artery) (hemorrhagic) (vein)
    415.19

Infarct, infarction — *continued*
pulmonary — *continued*
  with
    abortion — *see* Abortion, by type,
      with embolism
    ectopic pregnancy (*see also* cate-
      gories 633.0–633.9) 639.6
    molar pregnancy (*see also* categories
      630–632) 639.6
  following
    abortion 639.6
    ectopic or molar pregnancy 639.6
  iatrogenic 415.11
  in pregnancy, childbirth, or puerperium
    — *see* Embolism, obstetrical
  postoperative 415.11
  septic 415.12
renal 593.81
  embolic or thrombotic 593.81
retina, retinal 362.84
  with occlusion — *see* Occlusion, retina
spinal (acute) (cord) (embolic) (nonembolic)
    336.1
spleen 289.59
  embolic or thrombotic 444.89
subchorionic — *see* Infarct, placenta
subendocardial (*see also* Infarct, myocardi-
    um) 410.7 ☑
suprarenal (capsule) (gland) 255.41
syncytium — *see* Infarct, placenta
testis 608.83
thrombotic (*see also* Thrombosis) 453.9
  artery, arterial — *see* Embolism
thyroid (gland) 246.3
ventricle (heart) (*see also* Infarct, myocardi-
    um) 410.9 ☑
Infecting — *see* condition
Infection, infected, infective (opportunistic)
    136.9
  with
    influenza viruses occurring in pigs or
      other animals — *see* Influenza,
      due to identified, novel influenza
      A virus
    lymphangitis — *see* Lymphangitis
  abortion — *see* Abortion, by type, with,
    sepsis
  abscess (skin) — *see* Abscess, by site
  Absidia 117.7
  acanthamoeba 136.21
  Acanthocheilonema (perstans) 125.4
    streptocerca 125.6
  accessory sinus (chronic) (*see also* Sinusitis)
    473.9
  Achorion — *see* Dermatophytosis
  Acremonium falciforme 117.4
  acromioclavicular (joint) 711.91
  actinobacillus
    lignieresii 027.8
    mallei 024
    muris 026.1
  actinomadura — *see* Actinomycosis
  Actinomyces (israelii) (*see also* Actinomyco-
    sis)
    muris-ratti 026.1
  Actinomycetales (actinomadura) (Actino-
    myces) (Nocardia) (Streptomyces) —
    see Actinomycosis
  actinomycotic NEC (*see also* Actinomycosis)
    039.9
  adenoid (chronic) 474.01
    acute 463
    and tonsil (chronic) 474.02
      acute or subacute 463
  adenovirus NEC 079.0
    in diseases classified elsewhere — *see*
      category 079 ☑
    unspecified nature or site 079.0
  Aerobacter aerogenes NEC 041.85
    enteritis 008.2
  aerogenes capsulatus (*see also* Gangrene,
    gas) 040.0
  aertrycke (*see also* Infection, Salmonella)
    003.9
  ajellomyces dermatitidis 116.0

Infection, infected, infective — *continued*
alimentary canal NEC (*see also* Enteritis, due
    to, by organism) 009.0
Allescheria boydii 117.6
Alternaria 118
alveolus, alveolar (process) (pulpal origin)
    522.4
ameba, amebic (histolytica) (*see also* Amebi-
    asis) 006.9
  acute 006.0
  chronic 006.1
  free-living 136.29
  hartmanni 007.8
  specified
    site NEC 006.8
    type NEC 007.8
amniotic fluid or cavity 658.4 ☑
  affecting fetus or newborn 762.7
anaerobes (cocci) (gram-negative) (gram-
    positive) (mixed) NEC 041.84
anal canal 569.49
Ancylostoma braziliense 126.2
Angiostrongylus cantonensis 128.8
anisakiasis 127.1
Anisakis larva 127.1
anthrax (*see also* Anthrax) 022.9
antrum (chronic) (*see also* Sinusitis, maxil-
    lary) 473.0
anus (papillae) (sphincter) 569.49
arbor virus NEC 066.9
arbovirus NEC 066.9
argentophil-rod 027.0
Ascaris lumbricoides 127.0
ascomycetes 117.4
Aspergillus (flavus) (fumigatus) (terreus)
    117.3
atypical
  acid-fast (bacilli) (*see also* Mycobacteri-
    um, atypical) 031.9
  mycobacteria (*see also* Mycobacterium,
    atypical) 031.9
auditory meatus (circumscribed) (diffuse)
    (external) (*see also* Otitis, externa)
    380.10
auricle (ear) (*see also* Otitis, externa) 380.10
axillary gland 683
Babesiasis 088.82
Babesiosis 088.82
Bacillus NEC 041.89
  abortus 023.1
  anthracis (*see also* Anthrax) 022.9
  cereus (food poisoning) 005.89
  coli — *see* Infection, Escherichia coli
  coliform NEC 041.85
  Ducrey's (any location) 099.0
  Flexner's 004.1
  Friedländer's NEC 041.3
  fusiformis 101
  gas (gangrene) (*see also* Gangrene, gas)
    040.0
  mallei 024
  melitensis 023.0
  paratyphoid, paratyphosus 002.9
    A 002.1
    B 002.2
    C 002.3
  Schmorl's 040.3
  Shiga 004.0
  suipestifer (*see also* Infection, Salmonel-
    la) 003.9
  swimming pool 031.1
  typhosa 002.0
  welchii (*see also* Gangrene, gas) 040.0
  Whitmore's 025
bacterial NEC 041.9
  specified NEC 041.89
    anaerobic NEC 041.84
    gram-negative NEC 041.85
      anaerobic NEC 041.84
Bacterium
  paratyphosum 002.9
    A 002.1
    B 002.2
    C 002.3
  typhosum 002.0

Infection, infected, infective — *continued*
- Bacteroides (fragilis) (melaninogenicus) (oralis) NEC 041.82
- balantidium coli 007.0
- Bartholin's gland 616.89
- Basidiobolus 117.7
- Bedsonia 079.98
  - specified NEC 079.88
- bile duct 576.1
- bladder (see also Cystitis) 595.9
- Blastomyces, blastomycotic 116.0
  - brasiliensis 116.1
  - dermatitidis 116.0
  - European 117.5
  - loboi 116.2
  - North American 116.0
  - South American 116.1
- bleb
  - postprocedural 379.60
    - stage 1 379.61
    - stage 2 379.62
    - stage 3 379.63
- blood stream (see also Septicemia)
  - catheter-related (CRBSI) 999.31
  - central line-associated (CLABSI) 999.32
  - due to central venous catheter 999.32
- bone 730.9 ☑
  - specified — see Osteomyelitis
- Bordetella 033.9
  - bronchiseptica 033.8
  - parapertussis 033.1
  - pertussis 033.0
- Borrelia
  - bergdorfi 088.81
  - vincentii (mouth) (pharynx) (tonsil) 101
- bovine stomatitis 059.11
- brain (see also Encephalitis) 323.9
  - late effect — see category 326
  - membranes (see also Meningitis) 322.9
  - septic 324.0
    - late effect — see category 326
    - meninges (see also Meningitis) 320.9
- branchial cyst 744.42
- breast 611.0
  - puerperal, postpartum 675.2 ☑
    - with nipple 675.9 ☑
      - specified type NEC 675.8 ☑
    - nonpurulent 675.2 ☑
    - purulent 675.1 ☑
- bronchus (see also Bronchitis) 490
  - fungus NEC 117.9
- Brucella 023.9
  - abortus 023.1
  - canis 023.3
  - melitensis 023.0
  - mixed 023.8
  - suis 023.2
- Brugia (Wuchereria) malayi 125.1
- bursa — see Bursitis
- buttocks (skin) 686.9
- Candida (albicans) (tropicalis) (see also Candidiasis) 112.9
  - congenital 771.7
- Candiru 136.8
- Capillaria
  - hepatica 128.8
  - philippinensis 127.5
- cartilage 733.99
- catheter-related bloodstream (CRBSI) 999.31
- cat liver fluke 121.0
- cellulitis — see Cellulitis, by site
- central line-associated 999.31
  - bloodstream 999.32
- Cephalosporum falciforme 117.4
- Cercomonas hominis (intestinal) 007.3
- cerebrospinal (see also Meningitis) 322.9
  - late effect — see category 326
- cervical gland 683
- cervix (see also Cervicitis) 616.0
- cesarean section wound 674.3 ☑
- Chilomastix (intestinal) 007.8
- Chlamydia 079.98
  - specified NEC 079.88
- cholera (see also Cholera) 001.9
- chorionic plate 658.8 ☑

Infection, infected, infective — *continued*
- Cladosporium
  - bantianum 117.8
  - carrionii 117.2
  - mansoni 111.1
  - trichoides 117.8
  - wernecki 111.1
- Clonorchis (sinensis) (liver) 121.1
- Clostridium (haemolyticum) (novyi) NEC 041.84
  - botulinum 005.1
  - histolyticum (see also Gangrene, gas) 040.0
  - oedematiens (see also Gangrene, gas) 040.0
  - perfringens 041.83
    - due to food 005.2
  - septicum (see also Gangrene, gas) 040.0
  - sordellii (see also Gangrene, gas) 040.0
  - welchii (see also Gangrene, gas) 040.0
    - due to food 005.2
- Coccidioides (immitis) (see also Coccidioidomycosis) 114.9
- coccus NEC 041.89
- colon (see also Enteritis, due to, by organism) 009.0
  - bacillus — see Infection, Escherichia coli
- colostomy or enterostomy 569.61
- common duct 576.1
- complicating pregnancy, childbirth, or puerperium NEC 647.9 ☑
  - affecting fetus or newborn 760.2
- Condiobolus 117.7
- congenital NEC 771.89
  - Candida albicans 771.7
  - chronic 771.2
  - cytomegalovirus 771.1
  - hepatitis, viral 771.2
  - herpes simplex 771.2
  - listeriosis 771.2
  - malaria 771.2
  - poliomyelitis 771.2
  - rubella 771.0
  - toxoplasmosis 771.2
  - tuberculosis 771.2
  - urinary (tract) 771.82
  - vaccinia 771.2
- coronavirus 079.89
  - SARS-associated 079.82
- corpus luteum (see also Salpingo-oophoritis) 614.2
- Corynebacterium diphtheriae — see Diphtheria
- cotia virus 059.8
- Coxsackie (see also Coxsackie) 079.2
  - endocardium 074.22
  - heart NEC 074.20
  - in diseases classified elsewhere — see category 079 ☑
  - meninges 047.0
  - myocardium 074.23
  - pericardium 074.21
  - pharynx 074.0
  - specified disease NEC 074.8
  - unspecified nature or site 079.2
- Cryptococcus neoformans 117.5
- Cryptosporidia 007.4
- Cunninghamella 117.7
- cyst — see Cyst
- Cysticercus cellulosae 123.1
- cystostomy 596.83
- cytomegalovirus 078.5
  - congenital 771.1
- dental (pulpal origin) 522.4
- deuteromycetes 117.4
- Dicrocoelium dendriticum 121.8
- Dipetalonema (perstans) 125.4
  - streptocerca 125.6
- diphtherial — see Diphtheria
- Diphyllobothrium (adult) (latum) (pacificum) 123.4
  - larval 123.5
- Diplogonoporus (grandis) 123.8
- Dipylidium (caninum) 123.8
- Dirofilaria 125.6
- dog tapeworm 123.8

Infection, infected, infective — *continued*
- Dracunculus medinensis 125.7
- Dreschlera 118
  - hawaiiensis 117.8
- Ducrey's bacillus (any site) 099.0
- due to or resulting from
  - central venous catheter (see also Complications, due to, catheter, central venous) 999.31
    - bloodstream 999.32
    - localized 999.33
  - device, implant, or graft (any) (presence of) — see Complications, Infection and inflammation, due to (presence of) any device, implant, or graft classified to 996.0–996.5 NEC
  - injection, inoculation, infusion, transfusion, or vaccination (prophylactic) (therapeutic) 999.39
    - blood and blood products
      - acute 999.34
  - injury NEC — see Wound, open, by site, complicated
  - surgery 998.59
- duodenum 535.6 ☑
- ear (see also Otitis)
  - external (see also Otitis, externa) 380.10
  - inner (see also Labyrinthitis) 386.30
  - middle — see Otitis, media
- Eaton's agent NEC 041.81
- Eberthella typhosa 002.0
- Ebola 078.89
- echinococcosis 122.9
- Echinococcus (see also Echinococcus) 122.9
- Echinostoma 121.8
- ECHO virus 079.1
  - in diseases classified elsewhere — see category 079 ☑
  - unspecified nature or site 079.1
- Ehrlichiosis 082.40
  - chaffeensis 082.41
  - specified type NEC 082.49
- Endamoeba — see Infection, ameba
- endocardium (see also Endocarditis) 421.0
- endocervix (see also Cervicitis) 616.0
- Entamoeba — see Infection, ameba
- enteric (see also Enteritis, due to, by organism) 009.0
- Enterobacter aerogenes NEC 041.85
- Enterobacter sakazakii 041.85
- Enterobius vermicularis 127.4
- enterococcus NEC 041.04
- enterovirus NEC 079.89
  - central nervous system NEC 048
  - enteritis 008.67
  - meningitis 047.9
- Entomophthora 117.7
- Epidermophyton — see Dermatophytosis
- epidermophytosis — see Dermatophytosis
- episiotomy 674.3 ☑
- Epstein-Barr virus 075
  - chronic 780.79 [139.8]
- erysipeloid 027.1
- Erysipelothrix (insidiosa) (rhusiopathiae) 027.1
- erythema infectiosum 057.0
- Escherichia coli (E. coli) 041.49
  - enteritis — see Enteritis, E. coli
  - generalized 038.42
  - intestinal — see Enteritis, E. coli
  - non-Shiga toxin-producing 041.49
  - Shiga toxin-producing (STEC) 041.43
    - with
      - unspecified O group 041.43
      - non-O157 (with known O group) 041.43
      - O157 (with confirmation of Shiga toxin when H antigen is unknown, or is not H7) 041.41
      - O157:H7 with or without confirmation of Shiga toxin-production 041.41
      - O157H:- (nonmotile) with confirmation of Shiga toxin 041.41
    - specified NEC 041.42

Infection, infected, infective — *continued*
- esophagostomy 530.86
- ethmoidal (chronic) (sinus) (see also Sinusitis, ethmoidal) 473.2
- Eubacterium 041.84
- Eustachian tube (ear) 381.50
  - acute 381.51
  - chronic 381.52
- exanthema subitum (see also Exanthem subitum) 058.10
- exit site 999.33
- external auditory canal (meatus) (see also Otitis, externa) 380.10
- eyelid 373.9
  - specified NEC 373.8
- eye NEC 360.00
- fallopian tube (see also Salpingo-oophoritis) 614.2
- fascia 728.89
- Fasciola
  - gigantica 121.3
  - hepatica 121.3
- Fasciolopsis (buski) 121.4
- fetus (intra-amniotic) — see Infection, congenital
- filarial — see Infestation, filarial
- finger (skin) 686.9
  - abscess (with lymphangitis) 681.00
    - pulp 681.01
  - cellulitis (with lymphangitis) 681.00
  - distal closed space (with lymphangitis) 681.00
  - nail 681.02
    - fungus 110.1
- fish tapeworm 123.4
  - larval 123.5
- flagellate, intestinal 007.9
- fluke — see Infestation, fluke
- focal
  - teeth (pulpal origin) 522.4
  - tonsils 474.00
    - and adenoids 474.02
- Fonsecaea
  - compactum 117.2
  - pedrosoi 117.2
- food (see also Poisoning, food) 005.9
- foot (skin) 686.9
  - fungus 110.4
- Francisella tularensis (see also Tularemia) 021.9
- frontal sinus (chronic) (see also Sinusitis, frontal) 473.1
- fungus NEC 117.9
  - beard 110.0
  - body 110.5
  - dermatiacious NEC 117.8
  - foot 110.4
  - groin 110.3
  - hand 110.2
  - nail 110.1
  - pathogenic to compromised host only 118
  - perianal (area) 110.3
  - scalp 110.0
  - scrotum 110.8
  - skin 111.9
    - foot 110.4
    - hand 110.2
  - toenails 110.1
  - trachea 117.9
- Fusarium 118
- Fusobacterium 041.84
- gallbladder (see also Cholecystitis, acute) 575.0
- Gardnerella vaginalis 041.89
- gas bacillus (see also Gas, gangrene) 040.0
- gastric (see also Gastritis) 535.5 ☑
- Gastrodiscoides hominis 121.8
- gastroenteric (see also Enteritis, due to, by organism) 009.0
- gastrointestinal (see also Enteritis, due to, by organism) 009.0
- gastrostomy 536.41
- generalized NEC (see also Septicemia) 038.9
- genital organ or tract NEC
  - female 614.9

Infection, infected, infective — *continued*
  genital organ or tract — *continued*
    female — *continued*
      with
        abortion — *see* Abortion, by type, with sepsis
        ectopic pregnancy (*see also* categories 633.0–633.9) 639.0
        molar pregnancy (*see also* categories 630–632) 639.0
      complicating pregnancy 646.6 ☑
        affecting fetus or newborn 760.8
      following
        abortion 639.0
        ectopic or molar pregnancy 639.0
      puerperal, postpartum, childbirth 670.8 ☑
        minor or localized 646.6 ☑
          affecting fetus or newborn 760.8
    male 608.4
  genitourinary tract NEC 599.0
  Ghon tubercle, primary (*see also* Tuberculosis) 010.0 ☑
  Giardia lamblia 007.1
  gingival (chronic) 523.10
    acute 523.00
    Vincent's 101
  glanders 024
  Glenosporopsis amazonica 116.2
  Gnathostoma spinigerum 128.1
  Gongylonema 125.6
  gonococcal NEC (*see also* Gonococcus) 098.0
  gram-negative bacilli NEC 041.85
    anaerobic 041.84
  guinea worm 125.7
  gum (*see also* Infection, gingival) 523.10
  Hantavirus 079.81
  heart 429.89
  Helicobacter pylori [H. pylori] 041.86
  helminths NEC 128.9
    intestinal 127.9
      mixed (types classifiable to more than one category in 120.0–127.7) 127.8
      specified type NEC 127.7
    specified type NEC 128.8
  Hemophilus influenzae NEC 041.5
    generalized 038.41
  herpes (simplex) (*see also* Herpes, simplex) 054.9
    congenital 771.2
    zoster (*see also* Herpes, zoster) 053.9
    eye NEC 053.29
  Heterophyes heterophyes 121.6
  Histoplasma (*see also* Histoplasmosis) 115.90
    capsulatum (*see also* Histoplasmosis, American) 115.00
    duboisii (*see also* Histoplasmosis, African) 115.10
  HIV V08
    with symptoms, symptomatic 042
  hookworm (*see also* Ancylostomiasis) 126.9
  human herpesvirus 6 058.81
  human herpesvirus 7 058.82
  human herpesvirus 8 058.89
  human herpesvirus NEC 058.89
  human immunodeficiency virus V08
    with symptoms, symptomatic 042
  human papillomavirus 079.4
  hydrocele 603.1
  hydronephrosis 591
  Hymenolepis 123.6
  hypopharynx 478.29
  inguinal glands 683
    due to soft chancre 099.0
  insertion site 999.33
  intestine, intestinal (*see also* Enteritis, due to, by organism) 009.0
  intrauterine (*see also* Endometritis) 615.9
    complicating delivery 646.6 ☑
  isospora belli or hominis 007.2
  Japanese B encephalitis 062.0
  jaw (bone) (acute) (chronic) (lower) (subacute) (upper) 526.4
  joint — *see* Arthritis, infectious or infective

Infection, infected, infective — *continued*
  Kaposi's sarcoma-associated herpesvirus 058.89
  kidney (cortex) (hematogenous) 590.9
    with
      abortion — *see* Abortion, by type, with urinary tract infection
    calculus 592.0
    ectopic pregnancy (*see also* categories 633.0–633.9) 639.8
    molar pregnancy (*see also* categories 630–632) 639.8
  complicating pregnancy or puerperium 646.6 ☑
    affecting fetus or newborn 760.1
  following
    abortion 639.8
    ectopic or molar pregnancy 639.8
  pelvis and ureter 590.3
  Klebsiella pneumoniae NEC 041.3
  knee (skin) NEC 686.9
    joint — *see* Arthritis, infectious
  Koch's (*see also* Tuberculosis, pulmonary) 011.9 ☑
  labia (majora) (minora) (*see also* Vulvitis) 616.10
  lacrimal
    gland (*see also* Dacryoadenitis) 375.00
    passages (duct) (sac) (*see also* Dacryocystitis) 375.30
  larynx NEC 478.79
  leg (skin) NEC 686.9
  Leishmania (*see also* Leishmaniasis) 085.9
    braziliensis 085.5
    donovani 085.0
    ethiopica 085.3
    furunculosa 085.1
    infantum 085.0
    mexicana 085.4
    tropica (minor) 085.1
      major 085.2
  Leptosphaeria senegalensis 117.4
  leptospira (*see also* Leptospirosis) 100.9
    Australis 100.89
    Bataviae 100.89
    pyrogenes 100.89
    specified type NEC 100.89
  leptospirochetal NEC (*see also* Leptospirosis) 100.9
  Leptothrix — *see* Actinomycosis
  Listeria monocytogenes (listeriosis) 027.0
    congenital 771.2
  liver fluke — *see* Infestation, fluke, liver
  Loa loa 125.2
    eyelid 125.2 [373.6]
  Loboa loboi 116.2
  local, skin (staphylococcal) (streptococcal) NEC 686.9
    abscess — *see* Abscess, by site
    cellulitis — *see* Cellulitis, by site
    ulcer (*see also* Ulcer, skin) 707.9
  Loefflerella
    mallei 024
    whitmori 025
  lung 518.89
    atypical Mycobacterium 031.0
      tuberculous (*see also* Tuberculosis, pulmonary) 011.9 ☑
    basilar 518.89
    chronic 518.89
    fungus NEC 117.9
    spirochetal 104.8
    virus — *see* Pneumonia, virus
  lymph gland (axillary) (cervical) (inguinal) 683
    mesenteric 289.2
  lymphoid tissue, base of tongue or posterior pharynx, NEC 474.00
  maduralla
    grisea 117.4
    mycetomii 117.4
  major
    with
      abortion — *see* Abortion, by type, with sepsis

Infection, infected, infective — *continued*
  major — *continued*
    with — *continued*
      ectopic pregnancy (*see also* categories 633.0–633.9) 639.0
      molar pregnancy (*see also* categories 630–632) 639.0
    following
      abortion 639.0
      ectopic or molar pregnancy 639.0
    puerperal, postpartum, childbirth 670.0 ☑
  Malassezia furfur 111.0
  Malleomyces
    mallei 024
    pseudomallei 025
  mammary gland 611.0
    puerperal, postpartum 675.2 ☑
  Mansonella (ozzardi) 125.5
  mastoid (suppurative) — *see* Mastoiditis
  maxilla, maxillary 526.4
    sinus (chronic) (*see also* Sinusitis, maxillary) 473.0
  mediastinum 519.2
  medina 125.7
  meibomian
    cyst 373.12
    gland 373.12
  melioidosis 025
  meninges (*see also* Meningitis) 320.9
  meningococcal (*see also* condition) 036.9
    brain 036.1
    cerebrospinal 036.0
    endocardium 036.42
    generalized 036.2
    meninges 036.0
    meningococcemia 036.2
    specified site NEC 036.89
  mesenteric lymph nodes or glands NEC 289.2
  Metagonimus 121.5
  metatarsophalangeal 711.97
  methicillin
    resistant Staphylococcus aureus (MRSA) 041.12
    susceptible Staphylococcus aureus (MSSA) 041.11
  microorganism resistant to drugs — *see* Resistance (to), drugs by microorganisms
  Microsporidia 136.8
  microsporum, microsporic — *see* Dermatophytosis
  Mima polymorpha NEC 041.85
  mixed flora NEC 041.89
  Monilia (*see also* Candidiasis) 112.9
    neonatal 771.7
  monkeypox 059.01
  Monosporium apiospermum 117.6
  mouth (focus) NEC 528.9
    parasitic 136.9
  MRSA (methicillin resistant Staphylococcus aureus) 041.12
  MSSA (methicillin susceptible Staphylococcus aureus) 041.11
  Mucor 117.7
  muscle NEC 728.89
  mycelium NEC 117.9
  mycetoma
    actinomycotic NEC (*see also* Actinomycosis) 039.9
    mycotic NEC 117.4
  Mycobacterium, mycobacterial (*see also* Mycobacterium) 031.9
  Mycoplasma NEC 041.81
  mycotic NEC 117.9
    pathogenic to compromised host only 118
    skin NEC 111.9
    systemic 117.9
  myocardium NEC 422.90
  nail (chronic) (with lymphangitis) 681.9
    finger 681.02
      fungus 110.1
    ingrowing 703.0
    toe 681.11

Infection, infected, infective — *continued*
  nail — *continued*
    toe — *continued*
      fungus 110.1
  nasal sinus (chronic) (*see also* Sinusitis) 473.9
  nasopharynx (chronic) 478.29
    acute 460
  navel 686.9
    newborn 771.4
  Neisserian — *see* Gonococcus
  Neotestudina rosatii 117.4
  newborn, generalized 771.89
  nipple 611.0
    puerperal, postpartum 675.0 ☑
      with breast 675.9 ☑
        specified type NEC 675.8 ☑
  Nocardia — *see* Actinomycosis
  nose 478.19
  nostril 478.19
  obstetrical surgical wound 674.3 ☑
  Oesophagostomum (apiostomum) 127.7
  Oestrus ovis 134.0
  Oidium albicans (*see also* Candidiasis) 112.9
  Onchocerca (volvulus) 125.3
    eye 125.3 [360.13]
    eyelid 125.3 [373.6]
  operation wound 998.59
  Opisthorchis (felineus) (tenuicollis) (viverrini) 121.0
  orbit 376.00
    chronic 376.10
  orthopoxvirus 059.00
    specified NEC 059.09
  ovary (*see also* Salpingo-oophoritis) 614.2
  Oxyuris vermicularis 127.4
  pancreas 577.0
  Paracoccidioides brasiliensis 116.1
  Paragonimus (westermani) 121.2
  parainfluenza virus 079.89
  parameningococcus NEC 036.9
    with meningitis 036.0
  parapoxvirus 059.10
    specified NEC 059.19
  parasitic NEC 136.9
  paratyphoid 002.9
    type A 002.1
    type B 002.2
    type C 002.3
  paraurethral ducts 597.89
  parotid gland 527.2
  Pasteurella NEC 027.2
    multocida (cat-bite) (dog-bite) 027.2
    pestis (*see also* Plague) 020.9
    pseudotuberculosis 027.2
    septica (cat-bite) (dog-bite) 027.2
    tularensis (*see also* Tularemia) 021.9
  pelvic, female (*see also* Disease, pelvis, inflammatory) 614.9
  penis (glans) (retention) NEC 607.2
    herpetic 054.13
  Peptococcus 041.84
  Peptostreptococcus 041.84
  periapical (pulpal origin) 522.4
  peridental 523.30
  perineal wound (obstetrical) 674.3 ☑
  periodontal 523.31
  periorbital 376.00
    chronic 376.10
  perirectal 569.49
  perirenal (*see also* Infection, kidney) 590.9
  peritoneal (*see also* Peritonitis) 567.9
  periureteral 593.89
  periurethral 597.89
  Petriellidium boydii 117.6
  pharynx 478.29
    Coxsackie virus 074.0
    phlegmonous 462
    posterior, lymphoid 474.00
  Phialophora
    gougerotii 117.8
    jeanselmei 117.8
    verrucosa 117.2
  Piedraia hortai 111.3
  pinna, acute 380.11
  pinta 103.9
    intermediate 103.1

☑ **Additional Digit Required** — Refer to the Tabular List for Digit Selection

ᴺᴱᶜ **Subterms under main terms may continue to next column or page**

Infection, infected, infective — *continued*
  pinta — *continued*
    late 103.2
    mixed 103.3
    primary 103.0
  pinworm 127.4
  pityrosporum furfur 111.0
  pleuropneumonia-like organisms NEC (PP-LO) 041.81
  pneumococcal NEC 041.2
    generalized (purulent) 038.2
  Pneumococcus NEC 041.2
  port 999.33
  postoperative wound 998.59
  posttraumatic NEC 958.3
  postvaccinal 999.39
  poxvirus 059.9
    specified NEC 059.8
  prepuce NEC 607.1
  Proprionibacterium 041.84
  prostate (capsule) (*see also* Prostatitis) 601.9
  Proteus (mirabilis) (morganii) (vulgaris) NEC 041.6
    enteritis 008.3
  protozoal NEC 136.8
    intestinal NEC 007.9
  Pseudomonas NEC 041.7
    mallei 024
    pneumonia 482.1
    pseudomallei 025
  psittacosis 073.9
  puerperal, postpartum (major) 670.0 ☑
    minor 646.6 ☑
  pulmonary — *see* Infection, lung
  purulent — *see* Abscess
  putrid, generalized — *see* Septicemia
  pyemic — *see* Septicemia
  Pyrenochaeta romeroi 117.4
  Q fever 083.0
  rabies 071
  rectum (sphincter) 569.49
  renal (*see also* Infection, kidney) 590.9
    pelvis and ureter 590.3
  reservoir 999.33
  resistant to drugs — *see* Resistance (to), drugs by microorganisms
  respiratory 519.8
    chronic 519.8
    influenzal (acute) (upper) (*see also* Influenza) 487.1
    lung 518.89
    rhinovirus 460
    syncytial virus 079.6
    upper (acute) (infectious) NEC 465.9
      with flu, grippe, or influenza (*see also* Influenza) 487.1
      influenzal (*see also* Influenza) 487.1
      multiple sites NEC 465.8
      streptococcal 034.0
      viral NEC 465.9
  respiratory syncytial virus (RSV) 079.6
  resulting from presence of shunt or other internal prosthetic device — *see* Complications, infection and inflammation, due to (presence of) any device, implant, or graft classified to 996.0–996.5 NEC
  retroperitoneal 567.39
  retrovirus 079.50
    human immunodeficiency virus type 2 (HIV2) 079.53
    human T-cell lymphotrophic virus type I (HTLV-I) 079.51
    human T-cell lymphotrophic virus type II (HTLV-II) 079.52
    specified NEC 079.59
  Rhinocladium 117.1
  Rhinosporidium — *see* beri 117.0
  rhinovirus
    in diseases classified elsewhere — *see* category 079 ☑
    unspecified nature or site 079.3
  Rhizopus 117.7
  rickettsial 083.9
  rickettsialpox 083.2
  rubella (*see also* Rubella) 056.9

Infection, infected, infective — *continued*
  rubella (*see also* Rubella) — *continued*
    congenital 771.0
  Saccharomyces (*see also* Candidiasis) 112.9
  Saksenaea 117.7
  salivary duct or gland (any) 527.2
  Salmonella (aertrycke) (callinarum) (choleraesuis) (enteritidis) (suipestifer) (typhimurium) 003.9
    with
      arthritis 003.23
      gastroenteritis 003.0
      localized infection 003.20
        specified type NEC 003.29
      meningitis 003.21
      osteomyelitis 003.24
      pneumonia 003.22
      septicemia 003.1
      specified manifestation NEC 003.8
    due to food (poisoning) (any serotype) (*see also* Poisoning, food, due to, Salmonella)
    hirschfeldii 002.3
    localized 003.20
      specified type NEC 003.29
    paratyphi 002.9
      A 002.1
      B 002.2
      C 002.3
    schottmuelleri 002.2
    specified type NEC 003.8
    typhi 002.0
    typhosa 002.0
  saprophytic 136.8
  Sarcocystis, lindemanni 136.5
  SARS-associated coronavirus 079.82
  scabies 133.0
  Schistosoma — *see* Infestation, Schistosoma
  Schmorl's bacillus 040.3
  scratch or other superficial injury — *see* Injury, superficial, by site
  scrotum (acute) NEC 608.4
  sealpox 059.12
  secondary, burn or open wound (dislocation) (fracture) 958.3
  seminal vesicle (*see also* Vesiculitis) 608.0
  septic
    generalized — *see* Septicemia
    localized, skin (*see also* Abscess) 682.9
  septicemic — *see* Septicemia
  seroma 998.51
  Serratia (marcescens) 041.85
    generalized 038.44
  sheep liver fluke 121.3
  Shigella 004.9
    boydii 004.2
    dysenteriae 004.0
    flexneri 004.1
    group
      A 004.0
      B 004.1
      C 004.2
      D 004.3
    Schmitz (-Stutzer) 004.0
    schmitzii 004.0
    Shiga 004.0
    sonnei 004.3
    specified type NEC 004.8
  Sin Nombre virus 079.81
  sinus (*see also* Sinusitis) 473.9
    pilonidal 685.1
      with abscess 685.0
    skin NEC 686.9
  Skene's duct or gland (*see also* Urethritis) 597.89
  skin (local) (staphylococcal) (streptococcal) NEC 686.9
    abscess — *see* Abscess, by site
    cellulitis — *see* Cellulitis, by site
    due to fungus 111.9
      specified type NEC 111.8
    mycotic 111.9
      specified type NEC 111.8
    ulcer (*see also* Ulcer, skin) 707.9
  slow virus 046.9
    specified condition NEC 046.8

Infection, infected, infective — *continued*
  Sparganum (mansoni) (proliferum) 123.5
  spermatic cord NEC 608.4
  sphenoidal (chronic) (sinus) (*see also* Sinusitis, sphenoidal) 473.3
  Spherophorus necrophorus 040.3
  spinal cord NEC (*see also* Encephalitis) 323.9
    abscess 324.1
      late effect — *see* category 326
    late effect — *see* category 326
    meninges — *see* Meningitis
    streptococcal 320.2
  Spirillum
    minus or minor 026.0
    morsus muris 026.0
    obermeieri 087.0
  spirochetal NEC 104.9
    lung 104.8
    specified nature or site NEC 104.8
  spleen 289.59
  Sporothrix schenckii 117.1
  Sporotrichum (schenckii) 117.1
  Sporozoa 136.8
  staphylococcal NEC 041.10
    aureus 041.11
      methicillin
        resistant (MRSA) 041.12
        susceptible (MSSA) 041.11
    food poisoning 005.0
    generalized (purulent) 038.10
      aureus 038.11
        methicillin
          resistant 038.12
          susceptible 038.11
      specified organism NEC 038.19
    pneumonia 482.40
      aureus 482.41
        methicillin
          resistant (MRSA) 482.42
          susceptible (MSSA) 482.41
      MRSA (methicillin resistant Staphylococcus aureus) 482.42
      MSSA (methicillin susceptible Staphylococcus aureus) 482.41
      specified type NEC 482.49
    septicemia 038.10
      aureus 038.11
        methicillin
          resistant (MRSA) 038.12
          susceptible (MSSA) 038.11
      MRSA (methicillin resistant Staphylococcus aureus) 038.12
      MSSA (methicillin susceptible Staphylococcus aureus) 038.11
      specified organism NEC 038.19
    specified NEC 041.19
  steatoma 706.2
  Stellantchasmus falcatus 121.6
  Streptobacillus moniliformis 026.1
  streptococcal NEC 041.00
    generalized (purulent) 038.0
    Group
      A 041.01
      B 041.02
      C 041.03
      D [enterococcus] 041.04
      G 041.05
    pneumonia — *see* Pneumonia, streptococcal
    septicemia 038.0
    sore throat 034.0
    specified NEC 041.09
  Streptomyces — *see* Actinomycosis
  streptotrichosis — *see* Actinomycosis
  Strongyloides (stercoralis) 127.2
  stump (amputation) (posttraumatic) (surgical) 997.62
    traumatic — *see* Amputation, traumatic, by site, complicated
  subcutaneous tissue, local NEC 686.9
  submaxillary region 528.9
  suipestifer (*see also* Infection, Salmonella) 003.9
  swimming pool bacillus 031.1

Infection, infected, infective — *continued*
  syphilitic — *see* Syphilis
  systemic — *see* Septicemia
  Taenia — *see* Infestation, Taenia
  Taeniarhynchus saginatus 123.2
  tanapox 059.21
  tapeworm — *see* Infestation, tapeworm
  tendon (sheath) 727.89
  Ternidens diminutus 127.7
  testis (*see also* Orchitis) 604.90
  thigh (skin) 686.9
  threadworm 127.4
  throat 478.29
    pneumococcal 462
    staphylococcal 462
    streptococcal 034.0
    viral NEC (*see also* Pharyngitis) 462
  thumb (skin) 686.9
    abscess (with lymphangitis) 681.00
      pulp 681.01
    cellulitis (with lymphangitis) 681.00
    nail 681.02
  thyroglossal duct 529.8
  toe (skin) 686.9
    abscess (with lymphangitis) 681.10
    cellulitis (with lymphangitis) 681.10
    nail 681.11
      fungus 110.1
  tongue NEC 529.0
    parasitic 112.0
  tonsil (faucial) (lingual) (pharyngeal) 474.00
    acute or subacute 463
    and adenoid 474.02
    tag 474.00
  tooth, teeth 522.4
    periapical (pulpal origin) 522.4
    peridental 523.30
    periodontal 523.31
    pulp 522.0
    socket 526.5
  TORCH — *see* Infection, congenital NEC
    without active infection 760.2
  Torula histolytica 117.5
  Toxocara (cani) (cati) (felis) 128.0
  Toxoplasma gondii (*see also* Toxoplasmosis) 130.9
  trachea, chronic 491.8
    fungus 117.9
  traumatic NEC 958.3
  trematode NEC 121.9
  trench fever 083.1
  Treponema
    denticola 041.84
    macrodenticum 041.84
    pallidum (*see also* Syphilis) 097.9
  Trichinella (spiralis) 124
  Trichomonas 131.9
    bladder 131.09
    cervix 131.09
    hominis 007.3
    intestine 007.3
    prostate 131.03
    specified site NEC 131.8
    urethra 131.02
    urogenitalis 131.00
    vagina 131.01
    vulva 131.01
  Trichophyton, trichophytid — *see* Dermatophytosis
  Trichosporon (beigelii) cutaneum 111.2
  Trichostrongylus 127.6
  Trichuris (trichiuria) 127.3
  Trombicula (irritans) 133.8
  Trypanosoma (*see also* Trypanosomiasis) 086.9
    cruzi 086.2
  tubal (*see also* Salpingo-oophoritis) 614.2
  tuberculous NEC (*see also* Tuberculosis) 011.9 ☑
  tubo-ovarian (*see also* Salpingo-oophoritis) 614.2
  tunica vaginalis 608.4
  tunnel 999.33
  tympanic membrane — *see* Myringitis
  typhoid (abortive) (ambulant) (bacillus) 002.0

☑ **Additional Digit Required** — Refer to the Tabular List for Digit Selection
▽ **Subterms under main terms may continue to next column or page**

Infection, infected, infective — *continued*
- typhus 081.9
  - flea-borne (endemic) 081.0
  - louse-borne (epidemic) 080
  - mite-borne 081.2
  - recrudescent 081.1
  - tick-borne 082.9
    - African 082.1
    - North Asian 082.2
- umbilicus (septic) 686.9
  - newborn NEC 771.4
- ureter 593.89
- urethra (*see also* Urethritis) 597.80
- urinary (tract) NEC 599.0
  - with
    - abortion — *see* Abortion, by type, with urinary tract infection
    - ectopic pregnancy (*see also* categories 633.0–633.9) 639.8
    - molar pregnancy (*see also* categories 630–632) 639.8
  - candidal 112.2
  - complicating pregnancy, childbirth, or puerperium 646.6 ☑
    - affecting fetus or newborn 760.1
    - asymptomatic 646.5 ☑
      - affecting fetus or newborn 760.1
  - diplococcal (acute) 098.0
    - chronic 098.2
  - due to Trichomonas (vaginalis) 131.00
  - following
    - abortion 639.8
    - ectopic or molar pregnancy 639.8
  - gonococcal (acute) 098.0
    - chronic or duration of 2 months or over 098.2
  - newborn 771.82
  - trichomonal 131.00
  - tuberculous (*see also* Tuberculosis) 016.3 ☑
- uterus, uterine (*see also* Endometritis) 615.9
- utriculus masculinus NEC 597.89
- vaccination 999.39
- vagina (granulation tissue) (wall) (*see also* Vaginitis) 616.10
- varicella 052.9
- varicose veins — *see* Varicose, veins
- variola 050.9
  - major 050.0
  - minor 050.1
- vas deferens NEC 608.4
- Veillonella 041.84
- verumontanum 597.89
- vesical (*see also* Cystitis) 595.9
- Vibrio
  - cholerae 001.0
    - El Tor 001.1
  - parahaemolyticus (food poisoning) 005.4
  - vulnificus 041.85
- Vincent's (gums) (mouth) (tonsil) 101
- vaccination 999.39
- virus, viral 079.99
  - adenovirus
    - in diseases classified elsewhere — *see* category 079 ☑
    - unspecified nature or site 079.0
  - central nervous system NEC 049.9
    - enterovirus 048
      - meningitis 047.9
        - specified type NEC 047.8
    - slow virus 046.9
    - specified condition NEC 046.8
  - chest 519.8
  - conjunctivitis 077.99
    - specified type NEC 077.8
  - coronavirus 079.89
    - SARS-associated 079.82
  - Coxsackie (*see also* Infection, Coxsackie) 079.2
  - Ebola 065.8
  - ECHO
    - in diseases classified elsewhere — *see* category 079 ☑
    - unspecified nature or site 079.1

Infection, infected, infective — *continued*
- virus, viral — *continued*
  - encephalitis 049.9
    - arthropod-borne NEC 064
    - tick-borne 063.9
      - specified type NEC 063.8
  - enteritis NEC (*see also* Enteritis, viral) 008.8
  - exanthem NEC 057.9
  - Hantavirus 079.81
  - human papilloma 079.4
  - in diseases classified elsewhere — *see* category 079 ☑
  - intestine (*see also* Enteritis, viral) 008.8
  - lung — *see* Pneumonia, viral
  - respiratory syncytial (RSV) 079.6
  - retrovirus 079.50
  - rhinovirus
    - in diseases classified elsewhere — *see* category 079 ☑
    - unspecified nature or site 079.3
  - salivary gland disease 078.5
  - slow 046.9
    - specified condition NEC 046.8
  - specified type NEC 079.89
    - in diseases classified elsewhere — *see* category 079 ☑
  - unspecified nature or site 079.99
  - warts 078.10
    - specified NEC 078.19
  - yaba monkey tumor 059.22
- vulva (*see also* Vulvitis) 616.10
- whipworm 127.3
- Whitmore's bacillus 025
- wound (local) (posttraumatic) NEC 958.3
  - with
    - dislocation — *see* Dislocation, by site, open
    - fracture — *see* Fracture, by site, open
    - open wound — *see* Wound, open, by site, complicated
  - postoperative 998.59
  - surgical 998.59
- Wuchereria 125.0
  - bancrofti 125.0
  - malayi 125.1
- yaba monkey tumor virus 059.22
- yatapoxvirus 059.20
- yaws — *see* Yaws
- yeast (*see also* Candidiasis) 112.9
- yellow fever (*see also* Fever, yellow) 060.9
- Yersinia pestis (*see also* Plague) 020.9
- Zeis' gland 373.12
- zoonotic bacterial NEC 027.9
- Zopfia senegalensis 117.4

Infective, infectious — *see* condition

Inferiority complex 301.9
- constitutional psychopathic 301.7

Infertility
- female 628.9
  - age related 628.8
  - associated with
    - adhesions, peritubal 614.6 [628.2]
    - anomaly
      - cervical mucus 628.4
      - congenital
        - cervix 628.4
        - fallopian tube 628.2
        - uterus 628.3
        - vagina 628.4
    - anovulation 628.0
    - dysmucorrhea 628.4
    - endometritis, tuberculous (*see also* Tuberculosis) 016.7 ☑ [628.3]
    - Stein-Leventhal syndrome 256.4 [628.0]
  - due to
    - adiposogenital dystrophy 253.8 [628.1]
    - anterior pituitary disorder NEC 253.4 [628.1]
      - hyperfunction 253.1 [628.1]
    - cervical anomaly 628.4
    - fallopian tube anomaly 628.2
    - ovarian failure 256.39 [628.0]

Infertility — *continued*
- female — *continued*
  - due to — *continued*
    - Stein-Leventhal syndrome 256.4 [628.0]
    - uterine anomaly 628.3
    - vaginal anomaly 628.4
  - nonimplantation 628.3
  - origin
    - cervical 628.4
    - pituitary-hypothalamus NEC 253.8 [628.1]
      - anterior pituitary NEC 253.4 [628.1]
        - hyperfunction NEC 253.1 [628.1]
        - dwarfism 253.3 [628.1]
        - panhypopituitarism 253.2 [628.1]
  - specified NEC 628.8
  - tubal (block) (occlusion) (stenosis) 628.2
    - adhesions 614.6 [628.2]
  - uterine 628.3
  - vaginal 628.4
  - previous, requiring supervision of pregnancy V23.0
- male 606.9
  - absolute 606.0
  - due to
    - azoospermia 606.0
    - drug therapy 606.8
    - extratesticular cause NEC 606.8
    - germinal cell
      - aplasia 606.0
      - desquamation 606.1
    - hypospermatogenesis 606.1
    - infection 606.8
    - obstruction, afferent ducts 606.8
    - oligospermia 606.1
    - radiation 606.8
    - spermatogenic arrest (complete) 606.0
      - incomplete 606.1
    - systemic disease 606.8

Infestation 134.9
- Acanthocheilonema (perstans) 125.4
  - streptocerca 125.6
- Acariasis 133.9
  - demodex folliculorum 133.8
  - Sarcoptes scabiei 133.0
  - trombiculae 133.8
- Agamofilaria streptocerca 125.6
- Ancylostoma, Ankylostoma 126.9
  - americanum 126.1
  - braziliense 126.2
  - canium 126.8
  - ceylanicum 126.3
  - duodenale 126.0
  - new world 126.1
  - old world 126.0
- Angiostrongylus cantonensis 128.8
- anisakiasis 127.1
- Anisakis larva 127.1
- arthropod NEC 134.1
- Ascaris lumbricoides 127.0
- Bacillus fusiformis 101
- Balantidium coli 007.0
- beef tapeworm 123.2
- Bothriocephalus (latus) 123.4
  - larval 123.5
- broad tapeworm 123.4
  - larval 123.5
- Brugia malayi 125.1
- Candiru 136.8
- Capillaria
  - hepatica 128.8
  - philippinensis 127.5
- cat liver fluke 121.0
- Cercomonas hominis (intestinal) 007.3
- cestodes 123.9
  - specified type NEC 123.8
- chigger 133.8
- chigoe 134.1
- Chilomastix 007.8
- Clonorchis (sinensis) (liver) 121.1
- coccidia 007.2

Infestation — *continued*
- complicating pregnancy, childbirth, or puerperium 647.9 ☑
  - affecting fetus or newborn 760.8
- Cysticercus cellulosae 123.1
- Demodex folliculorum 133.8
- Dermatobia (hominis) 134.0
- Dibothriocephalus (latus) 123.4
  - larval 123.5
- Dicrocoelium dendriticum 121.8
- Diphyllobothrium (adult) (intestinal) (latum) (pacificum) 123.4
  - larval 123.5
- Diplogonoporus (grandis) 123.8
- Dipylidium (caninum) 123.8
- Distoma hepaticum 121.3
- dog tapeworm 123.8
- Dracunculus medinensis 125.7
- dragon worm 125.7
- dwarf tapeworm 123.6
- Echinococcus (*see also* Echinococcus) 122.9
- Echinostoma ilocanum 121.8
- Embadomonas 007.8
- Endamoeba (histolytica) — *see* Infection, ameba
- Entamoeba (histolytica) — *see* Infection, ameba
- Enterobius vermicularis 127.4
- Epidermophyton — *see* Dermatophytosis
- eyeworm 125.2
- Fasciola
  - gigantica 121.3
  - hepatica 121.3
- Fasciolopsis (buski) (small intestine) 121.4
  - blood NEC (*see also* Schistosomiasis) 120.9
  - cat liver 121.0
- filarial 125.9
  - due to
    - Acanthocheilonema (perstans) 125.4
      - streptocerca 125.6
    - Brugia (Wuchereria) malayi 125.1
    - Dracunculus medinensis 125.7
    - guinea worms 125.7
    - Mansonella (ozzardi) 125.5
    - Onchocerca volvulus 125.3
      - eye 125.3 [360.13]
      - eyelid 125.3 [373.6]
    - Wuchereria (bancrofti) 125.0
      - malayi 125.1
  - specified type NEC 125.6
- fish tapeworm 123.4
  - larval 123.5
- fluke 121.9
  - intestinal (giant) 121.4
  - liver (sheep) 121.3
    - cat 121.0
    - Chinese 121.1
    - clonorchiasis 121.1
    - fascioliasis 121.3
    - Oriental 121.1
  - lung (oriental) 121.2
  - sheep liver 121.3
- fly larva 134.0
- Gasterophilus (intestinalis) 134.0
- Gastrodiscoides hominis 121.8
- Giardia lamblia 007.1
- Gnathostoma (spinigerum) 128.1
- Gongylonema 125.6
- guinea worm 125.7
- helminth NEC 128.9
  - intestinal 127.9
    - mixed (types classifiable to more than one category in 120.0–127.7) 127.8
    - specified type NEC 127.7
  - specified type NEC 128.8
- Heterophyes heterophyes (small intestine) 121.6
- hookworm (*see also* Infestation, ancylostoma) 126.9
- Hymenolepis (diminuta) (nana) 123.6
- intestinal NEC 129
- leeches (aquatic) (land) 134.2
- Leishmania — *see* Leishmaniasis

Infestation — *continued*
lice (*see also* Infestation, pediculus) 132.9
Linguatulidae, linguatula (pentastoma)
(serrata) 134.1
Loa loa 125.2
eyelid 125.2 [373.6]
louse (*see also* Infestation, pediculus) 132.9
body 132.1
head 132.0
pubic 132.2
maggots 134.0
Mansonella (ozzardi) 125.5
medina 125.7
Metagonimus yokogawai (small intestine)
121.5
Microfilaria streptocerca 125.3
eye 125.3 [360.13]
eyelid 125.3 [373.6]
Microsporon furfur 111.0
microsporum — *see* Dermatophytosis
mites 133.9
scabic 133.0
specified type NEC 133.8
monilia (albicans) (*see also* Candidiasis)
112.9
vagina 112.1
vulva 112.1
mouth 112.0
Necator americanus 126.1
nematode (intestinal) 127.9
Ancylostoma (*see also* Ancylostoma)
126.9
Ascaris lumbricoides 127.0
conjunctiva NEC 128.9
Dioctophyma 128.8
Enterobius vermicularis 127.4
Gnathostoma spinigerum 128.1
Oesophagostomum (apiostomum) 127.7
Physaloptera 127.4
specified type NEC 127.7
Strongyloides stercoralis 127.2
Ternidens diminutus 127.7
Trichinella spiralis 124
Trichostrongylus 127.6
Trichuris (trichiuria) 127.3
Oesophagostomum (apiostomum) 127.7
Oestrus ovis 134.0
Onchocerca (volvulus) 125.3
eye 125.3 [360.13]
eyelid 125.3 [373.6]
Opisthorchis (felineus) (tenuicollis) (viverrini) 121.0
Oxyuris vermicularis 127.4
Paragonimus (westermani) 121.2
parasite, parasitic NEC 136.9
eyelid 134.9 [373.6]
intestinal 129
mouth 112.0
orbit 376.13
skin 134.9
tongue 112.0
pediculus 132.9
capitis (humanus) (any site) 132.0
corporis (humanus) (any site) 132.1
eyelid 132.0 [373.6]
mixed (classifiable to more than one
category in 132.0–132.2) 132.3
pubis (any site) 132.2
phthirus (pubis) (any site) 132.2
with any infestation classifiable to 132.0,
132.1 and 132.3
pinworm 127.4
pork tapeworm (adult) 123.0
protozoal NEC 136.8
pubic louse 132.2
rat tapeworm 123.6
red bug 133.8
roundworm (large) NEC 127.0
sand flea 134.1
saprophytic NEC 136.8
Sarcoptes scabiei 133.0
scabies 133.0
Schistosoma 120.9
bovis 120.8
cercariae 120.3
hematobium 120.0

Infestation — *continued*
Schistosoma — *continued*
intercalatum 120.8
japonicum 120.2
mansoni 120.1
mattheii 120.8
specified
site — *see* Schistosomiasis
type NEC 120.8
spindale 120.8
screw worms 134.0
skin NEC 134.9
Sparganum (mansoni) (proliferum) 123.5
larval 123.5
specified type NEC 134.8
Spirometra larvae 123.5
Sporozoa NEC 136.8
Stellantchasmus falcatus 121.6
Strongyloides 127.2
Strongylus (gibsoni) 127.7
Taenia 123.3
diminuta 123.6
Echinococcus (*see also* Echinococcus)
122.9
mediocanellata 123.2
nana 123.6
saginata (mediocanellata) 123.2
solium (intestinal form) 123.0
larval form 123.1
Taeniarhynchus saginatus 123.2
tapeworm 123.9
beef 123.2
broad 123.4
larval 123.5
dog 123.8
dwarf 123.6
fish 123.4
larval 123.5
pork 123.0
rat 123.6
Ternidens diminutus 127.7
Tetranychus molestissimus 133.8
threadworm 127.4
tongue 112.0
Toxocara (cani) (cati) (felis) 128.0
trematode(s) NEC 121.9
Trichina spiralis 124
Trichinella spiralis 124
Trichocephalus 127.3
Trichomonas 131.9
bladder 131.09
cervix 131.09
intestine 007.3
prostate 131.03
specified site NEC 131.8
urethra (female) (male) 131.02
urogenital 131.00
vagina 131.01
vulva 131.01
Trichophyton — *see* Dermatophytosis
Trichostrongylus instabilis 127.6
Trichuris (trichiuria) 127.3
Trombicula (irritans) 133.8
Trypanosoma — *see* Trypanosomiasis
Tunga penetrans 134.1
Uncinaria americana 126.1
whipworm 127.3
worms NEC 128.9
intestinal 127.9
Wuchereria 125.0
bancrofti 125.0
malayi 125.1

Infiltrate, infiltration
with an iron compound 275.09
amyloid (any site) (generalized) 277.39
calcareous (muscle) NEC 275.49
localized — *see* Degeneration, by site
calcium salt (muscle) 275.49
chemotherapy, vesicant 999.81
corneal (*see also* Edema, cornea) 371.20
eyelid 373.9
fatty (diffuse) (generalized) 272.8
localized — *see* Degeneration, by site,
fatty
glycogen, glycogenic (*see also* Disease,
glycogen storage) 271.0

Infiltrate, infiltration — *continued*
heart, cardiac
fatty (*see also* Degeneration, myocardial)
429.1
glycogenic 271.0 [425.7]
inflammatory in vitreous 379.29
kidney (*see also* Disease, renal) 593.9
leukemic (M9800/3) — *see* Leukemia
liver 573.8
fatty — *see* Fatty, liver
glycogen (*see also* Disease, glycogen
storage) 271.0
lung (*see also* Infiltrate, pulmonary) 793.19
eosinophilic 518.3
x-ray finding only 793.19
lymphatic (*see also* Leukemia, lymphatic)
204.9 ☑
gland, pigmentary 289.3
muscle, fatty 728.9
myelogenous (*see also* Leukemia, myeloid)
205.9 ☑
myocardium, myocardial
fatty (*see also* Degeneration, myocardial)
429.1
glycogenic 271.0 [425.7]
pulmonary 793.19
with
eosinophilia 518.3
pneumonia — *see* Pneumonia, by
type
x-ray finding only 793.19
Ranke's primary (*see also* Tuberculosis)
010.0 ☑
skin, lymphocytic (benign) 709.8
thymus (gland) (fatty) 254.8
urine 788.8
vesicant
agent NEC 999.82
chemotherapy 999.81
vitreous humor 379.29
Infirmity 799.89
senile 797

Inflammation, inflamed, inflammatory (with
exudation)
abducens (nerve) 378.54
accessory sinus (chronic) (*see also* Sinusitis)
473.9
adrenal (gland) 255.8
alimentary canal — *see* Enteritis
alveoli (teeth) 526.5
scorbutic 267
amnion — *see* Amnionitis
anal canal 569.49
antrum (chronic) (*see also* Sinusitis, maxillary) 473.0
anus 569.49
appendix (*see also* Appendicitis) 541
arachnoid — *see* Meningitis
areola 611.0
puerperal, postpartum 675.0 ☑
areolar tissue NEC 686.9
artery — *see* Arteritis
auditory meatus (external) (*see also* Otitis,
externa) 380.10
Bartholin's gland 616.89
bile duct or passage 576.1
bladder (*see also* Cystitis) 595.9
bleb
postprocedural 379.60
stage 1 379.61
stage 2 379.62
stage 3 379.63
bone — *see* Osteomyelitis
bowel (*see also* Enteritis) 558.9
brain (*see also* Encephalitis) 323.9
late effect — *see* category 326
membrane — *see* Meningitis
breast 611.0
puerperal, postpartum 675.2 ☑
broad ligament (*see also* Disease, pelvis, inflammatory) 614.4
acute 614.3
bronchus — *see* Bronchitis
bursa — *see* Bursitis
capsule
liver 573.3

Inflammation, inflamed, inflammatory —
continued
capsule — *continued*
spleen 289.59
catarrhal (*see also* Catarrh) 460
vagina 616.10
cecum (*see also* Appendicitis) 541
cerebral (*see also* Encephalitis) 323.9
late effect — *see* category 326
membrane — *see* Meningitis
cerebrospinal (*see also* Meningitis) 322.9
late effect — *see* category 326
meningococcal 036.0
tuberculous (*see also* Tuberculosis)
013.6 ☑
cervix (uteri) (*see also* Cervicitis) 616.0
chest 519.9
choroid NEC (*see also* Choroiditis) 363.20
cicatrix (tissue) — *see* Cicatrix
colon (*see also* Enteritis) 558.9
granulomatous 555.1
newborn 558.9
connective tissue (diffuse) NEC 728.9
cornea (*see also* Keratitis) 370.9
with ulcer (*see also* Ulcer, cornea) 370.00
corpora cavernosa (penis) 607.2
cranial nerve — *see* Disorder, nerve, cranial
diarrhea — *see* Diarrhea
disc (intervertebral) (space) 722.90
cervical, cervicothoracic 722.91
lumbar, lumbosacral 722.93
thoracic, thoracolumbar 722.92
Douglas' cul-de-sac or pouch (chronic) (*see
also* Disease, pelvis, inflammatory)
614.4
acute 614.3
due to (presence of) any device, implant, or
graft classifiable to 996.0–996.5 —
see Complications, infection and inflammation, due to (presence of) any
device, implant, or graft classified to
996.0–996.5 NEC
duodenum 535.6 ☑
dura mater — *see* Meningitis
ear (*see also* Otitis)
external (*see also* Otitis, externa) 380.10
inner (*see also* Labyrinthitis) 386.30
middle — *see* Otitis media
esophagus 530.10
ethmoidal (chronic) (sinus) (*see also* Sinusitis, ethmoidal) 473.2
Eustachian tube (catarrhal) 381.50
acute 381.51
chronic 381.52
extrarectal 569.49
eye 379.99
eyelid 373.9
specified NEC 373.8
fallopian tube (*see also* Salpingo-oophoritis)
614.2
fascia 728.9
fetal membranes (acute) 658.4 ☑
affecting fetus or newborn 762.7
follicular, pharynx 472.1
frontal (chronic) (sinus) (*see also* Sinusitis,
frontal) 473.1
gallbladder (*see also* Cholecystitis, acute)
575.0
gall duct (*see also* Cholecystitis) 575.10
gastrointestinal (*see also* Enteritis) 558.9
genital organ (diffuse) (internal)
female 614.9
with
abortion — *see* Abortion, by type,
with sepsis
ectopic pregnancy (*see also* categories 633.0–633.9) 639.0
molar pregnancy (*see also* categories 630–632) 639.0
complicating pregnancy, childbirth,
or puerperium 646.6 ☑
affecting fetus or newborn 760.8
following
abortion 639.0
ectopic or molar pregnancy 639.0
male 608.4

☑ **Additional Digit Required** — Refer to the Tabular List for Digit Selection
2015 ICD-9-CM   ▶◀ Revised Text   ● New Line   ▲ Revised Code
▽ **Subterms under main terms may continue to next column or page**
Volume 2 — 159

Inflammation, inflamed, inflammatory — continued

gland (lymph) (see also Lymphadenitis) 289.3
glottis (see also Laryngitis) 464.00
  with obstruction 464.01
granular, pharynx 472.1
gum 523.10
heart (see also Carditis) 429.89
hepatic duct 576.8
hernial sac — see Hernia, by site
ileum (see also Enteritis) 558.9
  terminal or regional 555.0
    with large intestine 555.2
intervertebral disc 722.90
  cervical, cervicothoracic 722.91
  lumbar, lumbosacral 722.93
  thoracic, thoracolumbar 722.92
intestine (see also Enteritis) 558.9
jaw (acute) (bone) (chronic) (lower) (suppurative) (upper) 526.4
jejunum — see Enteritis
joint NEC (see also Arthritis) 716.9 ☑
  sacroiliac 720.2
kidney (see also Nephritis) 583.9
knee (joint) 716.66
  tuberculous (active) (see also Tuberculosis) 015.2 ☑
labium (majus) (minus) (see also Vulvitis) 616.10
lacrimal
  gland (see also Dacryoadenitis) 375.00
  passages (duct) (sac) (see also Dacryocystitis) 375.30
larynx (see also Laryngitis) 464.00
  with obstruction 464.01
  diphtheritic 032.3
leg NEC 686.9
lip 528.5
liver (capsule) (see also Hepatitis) 573.3
  acute 570
  chronic 571.40
  suppurative 572.0
lung (acute) (see also Pneumonia) 486
  chronic (interstitial) 518.89
lymphatic vessel (see also Lymphangitis) 457.2
lymph node or gland (see also Lymphadenitis) 289.3
mammary gland 611.0
  puerperal, postpartum 675.2 ☑
maxilla, maxillary 526.4
  sinus (chronic) (see also Sinusitis, maxillary) 473.0
membranes of brain or spinal cord — see Meningitis
meninges — see Meningitis
mouth 528.00
muscle 728.9
myocardium (see also Myocarditis) 429.0
nasal sinus (chronic) (see also Sinusitis) 473.9
nasopharynx — see Nasopharyngitis
navel 686.9
  newborn NEC 771.4
nerve NEC 729.2
nipple 611.0
  puerperal, postpartum 675.0 ☑
nose 478.19
  suppurative 472.0
oculomotor nerve 378.51
optic nerve 377.30
orbit (chronic) 376.10
  acute 376.00
  chronic 376.10
ovary (see also Salpingo-oophoritis) 614.2
oviduct (see also Salpingo-oophoritis) 614.2
pancreas — see Pancreatitis
parametrium (chronic) (see also Disease, pelvis, inflammatory) 614.4
  acute 614.3
parotid region 686.9
  gland 527.2
pelvis, female (see also Disease, pelvis, inflammatory) 614.9
penis (corpora cavernosa) 607.2
perianal 569.49

Inflammation, inflamed, inflammatory — continued

pericardium (see also Pericarditis) 423.9
perineum (female) (male) 686.9
perirectal 569.49
peritoneum (see also Peritonitis) 567.9
periuterine (see also Disease, pelvis, inflammatory) 614.9
perivesical (see also Cystitis) 595.9
petrous bone (see also Petrositis) 383.20
pharynx (see also Pharyngitis) 462
  follicular 472.1
  granular 472.1
pia mater — see Meningitis
pleura — see Pleurisy
postmastoidectomy cavity 383.30
  chronic 383.33
pouch, internal ileoanal 569.71
prostate (see also Prostatitis) 601.9
rectosigmoid — see Rectosigmoiditis
rectum (see also Proctitis) 569.49
respiratory, upper (see also Infection, respiratory, upper) 465.9
  chronic, due to external agent — see Condition, respiratory, chronic, due to, external agent
  due to
    fumes or vapors (chemical) (inhalation) 506.2
    radiation 508.1
retina (see also Retinitis) 363.20
retrocecal (see also Appendicitis) 541
retroperitoneal (see also Peritonitis) 567.9
salivary duct or gland (any) (suppurative) 527.2
scorbutic, alveoli, teeth 267
scrotum 608.4
sigmoid — see Enteritis
sinus (see also Sinusitis) 473.9
Skene's duct or gland (see also Urethritis) 597.89
skin 686.9
spermatic cord 608.4
sphenoidal (sinus) (see also Sinusitis, sphenoidal) 473.3
spinal
  cord (see also Encephalitis) 323.9
    late effect — see category 326
  membrane — see Meningitis
  nerve — see Disorder, nerve
spine (see also Spondylitis) 720.9
spleen (capsule) 289.59
stomach — see Gastritis
stricture, rectum 569.49
subcutaneous tissue NEC 686.9
suprarenal (gland) 255.8
synovial (fringe) (membrane) — see Bursitis
tendon (sheath) NEC 726.90
testis (see also Orchitis) 604.90
thigh 686.9
throat (see also Sore throat) 462
thymus (gland) 254.8
thyroid (gland) (see also Thyroiditis) 245.9
tongue 529.0
tonsil — see Tonsillitis
trachea — see Tracheitis
trochlear nerve 378.53
tubal (see also Salpingo-oophoritis) 614.2
tuberculous NEC (see also Tuberculosis) 011.9 ☑
tubo-ovarian (see also Salpingo-oophoritis) 614.2
tunica vaginalis 608.4
tympanic membrane — see Myringitis
umbilicus, umbilical 686.9
  newborn NEC 771.4
uterine ligament (see also Disease, pelvis, inflammatory) 614.4
  acute 614.3
uterus (catarrhal) (see also Endometritis) 615.9
uveal tract (anterior) (see also Iridocyclitis) 364.3
  posterior — see Chorioretinitis
  sympathetic 360.11
vagina (see also Vaginitis) 616.10

Inflammation, inflamed, inflammatory — continued

vas deferens 608.4
vein (see also Phlebitis) 451.9
  thrombotic 451.9
    cerebral (see also Thrombosis, brain) 434.0 ☑
    leg 451.2
      deep (vessels) NEC 451.19
      superficial (vessels) 451.0
    lower extremity 451.2
      deep (vessels) NEC 451.19
      superficial (vessels) 451.0
vocal cord 478.5
vulva (see also Vulvitis) 616.10

Inflation, lung imperfect (newborn) 770.5

Influenza, influenzal 487.1
  with
    bronchitis 487.1
    bronchopneumonia 487.0
    cold (any type) 487.1
    digestive manifestations 487.8
    hemoptysis 487.1
    involvement of
      gastrointestinal tract 487.8
      nervous system 487.8
    laryngitis 487.1
    manifestations NEC 487.8
      respiratory 487.1
        pneumonia 487.0
    pharyngitis 487.1
    pneumonia (any form classifiable to 480–483, 485–486) 487.0
    respiratory manifestations NEC 487.1
    sinusitis 487.1
    sore throat 487.1
    tonsillitis 487.1
    tracheitis 487.1
    upper respiratory infection (acute) 487.1
  abdominal 487.8
  A/H5N1 (see also Influenza, avian) 488.02
  Asian 487.1
  avian 488.02
    with involvement of gastrointestinal tract 488.09
    bronchopneumonia 488.01
    laryngitis 488.02
    manifestations NEC 488.09
      respiratory 488.02
    pharyngitis 488.02
    pneumonia (any form classifiable to 480–483, 485–486) 488.01
    respiratory infection (acute) (upper) 488.02
  bronchial 487.1
  bronchopneumonia 487.0
  catarrhal 487.1
  due to identified
    animal origin influenza virus — see Influenza, due to identified, novel influenza A virus
    avian influenza virus 488.02
      with
        manifestations NEC 488.09
          respiratory 488.02
        pneumonia (any form classifiable to 480–483, 485–486) 488.01
    (novel 2009) H1N1 influenza virus 488.12
      with
        manifestations NEC 488.19
          respiratory 488.12
        pneumonia 488.11
    novel influenza A virus 488.82
      with
        encephalopathy 488.89
        involvement of gastrointestinal tract 488.89
        laryngitis 488.82
        manifestations NEC 488.89
          respiratory (acute) (upper) 488.82
        pharyngitis 488.82
        pneumonia 488.81
  epidemic 487.1
  gastric 487.8

Influenza, influenzal — continued

intestinal 487.8
laryngitis 487.1
maternal affecting fetus or newborn 760.2
  manifest influenza in infant 771.2
(novel) 2009 H1N1 488.12
  with involvement of gastrointestinal tract 488.19
  bronchopneumonia 488.11
  laryngitis 488.12
  manifestations NEC 488.19
    respiratory 488.12
  pharyngitis 488.12
  pneumonia (any form classifiable to 480–483, 485–486) 488.11
  respiratory infection (acute) (upper) 488.12
novel A/H1N1 (see also Influenza, (novel) 2009 H1N1) 488.12
novel influenza A viruses not previously found in humans — see Influenza, due to identified, novel influenza A virus
pharyngitis 487.1
pneumonia (any form) 487.0
respiratory (upper) 487.1
specified NEC 487.1
stomach 487.8
vaccination, prophylactic (against) V04.81

Influenza-like disease — see also Influenza 487.1

Infraction, Freiberg's (metatarsal head) 732.5

Infraeruption, teeth 524.34

Infusion complication, misadventure, or reaction — see Complication, infusion

Ingestion
chemical — see Table of Drugs and Chemicals
drug or medicinal substance
  overdose or wrong substance given or taken 977.9
    specified drug — see Table of Drugs and Chemicals
foreign body NEC (see also Foreign body) 938

Ingrowing
hair 704.8
nail (finger) (toe) (infected) 703.0

inguinal — see also condition
testis 752.51

Inhalation
carbon monoxide 986
flame
  lung 947.1
  mouth 947.0
food or foreign body (see also Asphyxia, food or foreign body) 933.1
gas, fumes, or vapor (noxious) 987.9
  specified agent — see Table of Drugs and Chemicals
liquid or vomitus (see also Asphyxia, food or foreign body) 933.1
  lower respiratory tract NEC 934.9
meconium (fetus or newborn) 770.11
  with respiratory symptoms 770.12
mucus (see also Asphyxia, mucus) 933.1
oil (causing suffocation) (see also Asphyxia, food or foreign body) 933.1
pneumonia — see Pneumonia, aspiration
smoke 508.2
steam 987.9
stomach contents or secretions (see also Asphyxia, food or foreign body) 933.1
  in labor and delivery 668.0 ☑

Inhibition, inhibited
academic as adjustment reaction 309.23
orgasm
  female 302.73
  male 302.74
sexual
  desire 302.71
  excitement 302.72
work as adjustment reaction 309.23

Inhibitor
autoimmune, to clotting factors 286.52

☑ Additional Digit Required — Refer to the Tabular List for Digit Selection   ▽ Subterms under main terms may continue to next column or page

160 — Volume 2   ▶◀ Revised Text   ● New Line   ▲ Revised Code   2015 ICD-9-CM

Inhibitor — *continued*
    systemic lupus erythematosus (presence of) 795.79
        with
            hemorrhagic disorder 286.53
            hypercoagulable state 289.81
Iniencephalus, iniencephaly 740.2
Injected eye 372.74
Injury 959.9

> *Note* — For abrasion, insect bite (non-venomous), blister, or scratch, see Injury, superficial.
>
> For laceration, traumatic rupture, tear, or penetrating wound of internal organs, such as heart, lung, liver, kidney, pelvic organs, whether or not accompanied by open wound in the same region, see Injury, internal.
>
> For nerve injury, see Injury, nerve.
>
> For late effect of injuries classifiable to 850–854, 860–869, 900–919, 950–959, see Late, effect, injury, by type.

    abdomen, abdominal (viscera) (*see also* Injury, internal, abdomen)
        muscle or wall 959.12
    acoustic, resulting in deafness 951.5
    adenoid 959.09
    adrenal (gland) — *see* Injury, internal, adrenal
    alveolar (process) 959.09
    ankle (and foot) (and knee) (and leg, except thigh) 959.7
    anterior chamber, eye 921.3
    anus 959.19
    aorta (thoracic) 901.0
        abdominal 902.0
    appendix — *see* Injury, internal, appendix
    arm, upper (and shoulder) 959.2
    artery (complicating trauma) (*see also* Injury, blood vessel, by site) 904.9
        cerebral or meningeal (*see also* Hemorrhage, brain, traumatic, subarachnoid) 852.0 ☑
    auditory canal (external) (meatus) 959.09
    auricle, auris, ear 959.09
    axilla 959.2
    back 959.19
    bile duct — *see* Injury, internal, bile duct
    birth (*see also* Birth, injury)
        canal NEC, complicating delivery 665.9 ☑
    bladder (sphincter) — *see* Injury, internal, bladder
    blast (air) (hydraulic) (immersion) (underwater) NEC 869.0
        with open wound into cavity NEC 869.1
        abdomen or thorax — *see* Injury, internal, by site
        brain — *see* Concussion, brain
        ear (acoustic nerve trauma) 951.5
            with perforation of tympanic membrane — *see* Wound, open, ear, drum
    blood vessel NEC 904.9
        abdomen 902.9
            multiple 902.87
            specified NEC 902.89
        aorta (thoracic) 901.0
            abdominal 902.0
        arm NEC 903.9
        axillary 903.00
            artery 903.01
            vein 903.02
        azygos vein 901.89
        basilic vein 903.1
        brachial (artery) (vein) 903.1
        bronchial 901.89
        carotid artery 900.00
            common 900.01
            external 900.02
            internal 900.03
        celiac artery 902.20
            specified branch NEC 902.24
        cephalic vein (arm) 903.1

Injury — *continued*
    blood vessel — *continued*
        colica dextra 902.26
        cystic
            artery 902.24
            vein 902.39
        deep plantar 904.6
        digital (artery) (vein) 903.5
        due to accidental puncture or laceration during procedure 998.2
        extremity
            lower 904.8
                multiple 904.7
                specified NEC 904.7
            upper 903.9
                multiple 903.8
                specified NEC 903.8
        femoral
            artery (superficial) 904.1
                above profunda origin 904.0
                common 904.0
            vein 904.2
        gastric
            artery 902.21
            vein 902.39
        head 900.9
            intracranial — *see* Injury, intracranial
            multiple 900.82
            specified NEC 900.89
        hemiazygos vein 901.89
        hepatic
            artery 902.22
            vein 902.11
        hypogastric 902.59
            artery 902.51
            vein 902.52
        ileocolic
            artery 902.26
            vein 902.31
        iliac 902.50
            artery 902.53
            specified branch NEC 902.59
            vein 902.54
        innominate
            artery 901.1
            vein 901.3
        intercostal (artery) (vein) 901.81
        jugular vein (external) 900.81
            internal 900.1
        leg NEC 904.8
        mammary (artery) (vein) 901.82
        mesenteric
            artery 902.20
                inferior 902.27
                specified branch NEC 902.29
                superior (trunk) 902.25
                  branches, primary 902.26
            vein 902.39
                inferior 902.32
                superior (and primary subdivisions) 902.31
        neck 900.9
            multiple 900.82
            specified NEC 900.89
        ovarian 902.89
            artery 902.81
            vein 902.82
        palmar artery 903.4
        pelvis 902.9
            multiple 902.87
            specified NEC 902.89
        plantar (deep) (artery) (vein) 904.6
        popliteal 904.40
            artery 904.41
            vein 904.42
        portal 902.33
        pulmonary 901.40
            artery 901.41
            vein 901.42
        radial (artery) (vein) 903.2
        renal 902.40
            artery 902.41
            specified NEC 902.49
            vein 902.42
        saphenous
            artery 904.7

Injury — *continued*
    blood vessel — *continued*
        saphenous — *continued*
            vein (greater) (lesser) 904.3
        splenic
            artery 902.23
            vein 902.34
        subclavian
            artery 901.1
            vein 901.3
        suprarenal 902.49
        thoracic 901.9
            multiple 901.83
            specified NEC 901.89
        tibial 904.50
            artery 904.50
                anterior 904.51
                posterior 904.53
            vein 904.50
                anterior 904.52
                posterior 904.54
        ulnar (artery) (vein) 903.3
        uterine 902.59
            artery 902.55
            vein 902.56
        vena cava
            inferior 902.10
                specified branches NEC 902.19
            superior 901.2
    brachial plexus 953.4
        newborn 767.6
    brain (traumatic) NEC (*see also* Injury, intracranial) 854.0 ☑
        due to fracture of skull — *see* Fracture, skull, by site
    breast 959.19
    broad ligament — *see* Injury, internal, broad ligament
    bronchus, bronchi — *see* Injury, internal, bronchus
    brow 959.09
    buttock 959.19
    canthus, eye 921.1
    cathode ray 990
    cauda equina 952.4
        with fracture, vertebra — *see* Fracture, vertebra, sacrum
    cavernous sinus (*see also* Injury, intracranial) 854.0 ☑
    cecum — *see* Injury, internal, cecum
    celiac ganglion or plexus 954.1
    cerebellum (*see also* Injury, intracranial) 854.0 ☑
    cervix (uteri) — *see* Injury, internal, cervix
    cheek 959.09
    chest (*see also* Injury, internal, chest)
        wall 959.11
    childbirth (*see also* Birth, injury)
        maternal NEC 665.9 ☑
    chin 959.09
    choroid (eye) 921.3
    clitoris 959.14
    coccyx 959.19
        complicating delivery 665.6 ☑
    colon — *see* Injury, internal, colon
    common duct — *see* Injury, internal, common duct
    conjunctiva 921.1
        superficial 918.2
    cord
        spermatic — *see* Injury, internal, spermatic cord
        spinal — *see* Injury, spinal, by site
    cornea 921.3
        abrasion 918.1
            due to contact lens 371.82
        penetrating — *see* Injury, eyeball, penetrating
        superficial 918.1
            due to contact lens 371.82
    cortex (cerebral) (*see also* Injury, intracranial) 854.0 ☑
        visual 950.3
    costal region 959.11
    costochondral 959.11

Injury — *continued*
    cranial
        bones — *see* Fracture, skull, by site
        cavity (*see also* Injury, intracranial) 854.0 ☑
        nerve — *see* Injury, nerve, cranial
    crushing — *see* Crush
    cutaneous sensory nerve
        lower limb 956.4
        upper limb 955.5
    deep tissue — *see* Contusion, by site
        meaning pressure ulcer 707.25
    delivery (*see also* Birth, injury)
        maternal NEC 665.9 ☑
    Descemet's membrane — *see* Injury, eyeball, penetrating
    diaphragm — *see* Injury, internal, diaphragm
    diffuse axonal — *see* Injury, intracranial
    duodenum — *see* Injury, internal, duodenum
    ear (auricle) (canal) (drum) (external) 959.09
    elbow (and forearm) (and wrist) 959.3
    epididymis 959.14
    epigastric region 959.12
    epiglottis 959.09
    epiphyseal, current — *see* Fracture, by site
    esophagus — *see* Injury, internal, esophagus
    Eustachian tube 959.09
    extremity (lower) (upper) NEC 959.8
    eye 921.9
        penetrating eyeball — *see* Injury, eyeball, penetrating
        superficial 918.9
    eyeball 921.3
        penetrating 871.7
            with
                partial loss (of intraocular tissue) 871.2
                prolapse or exposure (of intraocular tissue) 871.1
            without prolapse 871.0
            foreign body (nonmagnetic) 871.6
                magnetic 871.5
        superficial 918.9
    eyebrow 959.09
    eyelid(s) 921.1
        laceration — *see* Laceration, eyelid
        superficial 918.0
    face (and neck) 959.09
    fallopian tube — *see* Injury, internal, fallopian tube
    finger(s) (nail) 959.5
    flank 959.19
    foot (and ankle) (and knee) (and leg, except thigh) 959.7
    forceps NEC 767.9
        scalp 767.19
    forearm (and elbow) (and wrist) 959.3
    forehead 959.09
    gallbladder — *see* Injury, internal, gallbladder
    gasserian ganglion 951.2
    gastrointestinal tract — *see* Injury, internal, gastrointestinal tract
    genital organ(s)
        with
            abortion — *see* Abortion, by type, with, damage to pelvic organs
            ectopic pregnancy (*see also* categories 633.0–633.9) 639.2
            molar pregnancy (*see also* categories 630–632) 639.2
        external 959.14
            fracture of corpus cavernosum penis 959.13
        following
            abortion 639.2
            ectopic or molar pregnancy 639.2
        internal — *see* Injury, internal, genital organs
        obstetrical trauma NEC 665.9 ☑
            affecting fetus or newborn 763.89
    gland
        lacrimal 921.1

Injury — *continued*
  gland — *continued*
    lacrimal — *continued*
      laceration 870.8
    parathyroid 959.09
    salivary 959.09
    thyroid 959.09
  globe (eye) (*see also* Injury, eyeball) 921.3
  grease gun — *see* Wound, open, by site, complicated
  groin 959.19
  gum 959.09
  hand(s) (except fingers) 959.4
  head NEC 959.01
    with
      loss of consciousness 850.5
      skull fracture — *see* Fracture, skull, by site
  heart — *see* Injury, internal, heart
  heel 959.7
  hip (and thigh) 959.6
  hymen 959.14
  hyperextension (cervical) (vertebra) 847.0
  ileum — *see* Injury, internal, ileum
  iliac region 959.19
  infrared rays NEC 990
  instrumental (during surgery) 998.2
    birth injury — *see* Birth, injury
    nonsurgical (*see also* Injury, by site) 959.9
    obstetrical 665.9 ☑
      affecting fetus or newborn 763.89
      bladder 665.5 ☑
      cervix 665.3 ☑
      high vaginal 665.4 ☑
      perineal NEC 664.9 ☑
      urethra 665.5 ☑
      uterus 665.5 ☑
  internal 869.0

> *Note* — For injury of internal organ(s) by foreign body entering through a natural orifice (e.g., inhaled, ingested, or swallowed) — *see* Foreign body, entering through orifice.
>
> For internal injury of any of the following sites with internal injury of any other of the sites — *see* Injury, internal, multiple.

    with
      fracture
        pelvis — *see* Fracture, pelvis
        specified site, except pelvis — *see* Injury, internal, by site
    open wound into cavity 869.1
  abdomen, abdominal (viscera) NEC 868.00
    with
      fracture, pelvis — *see* Fracture, pelvis
      open wound into cavity 868.10
    specified site NEC 868.09
      with open wound into cavity 868.19
  adrenal (gland) 868.01
    with open wound into cavity 868.11
  aorta (thoracic) 901.0
    abdominal 902.0
  appendix 863.85
    with open wound into cavity 863.95
  bile duct 868.02
    with open wound into cavity 868.12
  bladder (sphincter) 867.0
    with
      abortion — *see* Abortion, by type, with damage to pelvic organs
      ectopic pregnancy (*see also* categories 633.0–633.9) 639.2
      molar pregnancy (*see also* categories 630–632) 639.2
      open wound into cavity 867.1
    following
      abortion 639.2
      ectopic or molar pregnancy 639.2
    obstetrical trauma 665.5 ☑

Injury — *continued*
  internal — *continued*
    bladder — *continued*
      obstetrical trauma — *continued*
        affecting fetus or newborn 763.89
    blood vessel — *see* Injury, blood vessel, by site
    broad ligament 867.6
      with open wound into cavity 867.7
    bronchus, bronchi 862.21
      with open wound into cavity 862.31
    cecum 863.89
      with open wound into cavity 863.99
    cervix (uteri) 867.4
      with
        abortion — *see* Abortion, by type, with damage to pelvic organs
        ectopic pregnancy (*see also* categories 633.0–633.9) 639.2
        molar pregnancy (*see also* categories 630–632) 639.2
        open wound into cavity 867.5
      following
        abortion 639.2
        ectopic or molar pregnancy 639.2
      obstetrical trauma 665.3 ☑
      affecting fetus or newborn 763.89
    chest (*see also* Injury, internal, intrathoracic organs) 862.8
      with open wound into cavity 862.9
    colon 863.40
      with
        open wound into cavity 863.50
        rectum 863.46
          with open wound into cavity 863.56
      ascending (right) 863.41
        with open wound into cavity 863.51
      descending (left) 863.43
        with open wound into cavity 863.53
      multiple sites 863.46
        with open wound into cavity 863.56
      sigmoid 863.44
        with open wound into cavity 863.54
      specified site NEC 863.49
        with open wound into cavity 863.59
      transverse 863.42
        with open wound into cavity 863.52
    common duct 868.02
      with open wound into cavity 868.12
    complicating delivery 665.9 ☑
      affecting fetus or newborn 763.89
    diaphragm 862.0
      with open wound into cavity 862.1
    duodenum 863.21
      with open wound into cavity 863.31
    esophagus (intrathoracic) 862.22
      with open wound into cavity 862.32
      cervical region 874.4
        complicated 874.5
    fallopian tube 867.6
      with open wound into cavity 867.7
    gallbladder 868.02
      with open wound into cavity 868.12
    gastrointestinal tract NEC 863.80
      with open wound into cavity 863.90
    genital organ NEC 867.6
      with open wound into cavity 867.7
    heart 861.00
      with open wound into thorax 861.10
    ileum 863.29
      with open wound into cavity 863.39
    intestine NEC 863.89
      with open wound into cavity 863.99
      large NEC 863.40
        with open wound into cavity 863.50
      small NEC 863.20

Injury — *continued*
  internal — *continued*
    intestine — *continued*
      small — *continued*
        with open wound into cavity 863.30
    intra-abdominal (organ) 868.00
      with open wound into cavity 868.10
      multiple sites 868.09
        with open wound into cavity 868.19
      specified site NEC 868.09
        with open wound into cavity 868.19
    intrathoracic organs (multiple) 862.8
      with open wound into cavity 862.9
      diaphragm (only) — *see* Injury, internal, diaphragm
      heart (only) — *see* Injury, internal, heart
      lung (only) — *see* Injury, internal, lung
      specified site NEC 862.29
        with open wound into cavity 862.39
    intrauterine (*see also* Injury, internal, uterus) 867.4
      with open wound into cavity 867.5
    jejunum 863.29
      with open wound into cavity 863.39
    kidney (subcapsular) 866.00
      with
        disruption of parenchyma (complete) 866.03
          with open wound into cavity 866.13
        hematoma (without rupture of capsule) 866.01
          with open wound into cavity 866.11
        laceration 866.02
          with open wound into cavity 866.12
        open wound into cavity 866.10
    liver 864.00
      with
        contusion 864.01
          with open wound into cavity 864.11
        hematoma 864.01
          with open wound into cavity 864.11
        laceration 864.05
          with open wound into cavity 864.15
        major (disruption of hepatic parenchyma) 864.04
          with open wound into cavity 864.14
        minor (capsule only) 864.02
          with open wound into cavity 864.12
        moderate (involving parenchyma) 864.03
          with open wound into cavity 864.13
        multiple 864.04
        stellate 864.04
          with open wound into cavity 864.14
        open wound into cavity 864.10
    lung 861.20
      with open wound into thorax 861.30
      aspiration 507.0
      hemopneumothorax — *see* Hemopneumothorax, traumatic
      hemothorax — *see* Hemothorax, traumatic
      pneumohemothorax — *see* Pneumohemothorax, traumatic
      pneumothorax — *see* Pneumothorax, traumatic
      transfusion related, acute (TRALI) 518.7
    mediastinum 862.29
      with open wound into cavity 862.39

Injury — *continued*
  internal — *continued*
    mesentery 863.89
      with open wound into cavity 863.99
    mesosalpinx 867.6
      with open wound into cavity 867.7
    multiple 869.0

> *Note* — Multiple internal injuries of sites classifiable to the same three- or four-digit category should be classified to that category.
>
> Multiple injuries classifiable to different fourth-digit subdivisions of 861 (heart and lung injuries) should be dealt with according to coding rules.

    internal
      with open wound into cavity 869.1
    intra–abdominal organ (sites classifiable to 863–868)
      with
        intrathoracic organ(s) (sites classifiable to 861–862) 869.0
          with open wound into cavity 869.1
        other intra–abdominal organ(s) (sites classifiable to 863–868, except where classifiable to the same three–digit category) 868.09
          with open wound into cavity 868.19
    intrathoracic organ (sites classifiable to 861–862)
      with
        intra–abdominal organ(s) (sites classifiable to 863–868) 869.0
          with open wound into cavity 869.1
        other intrathoracic organ(s) (sites classifiable to 861–862, except where classifiable to the same three–digit category) 862.8
          with open wound into cavity 862.9
    myocardium — *see* Injury, internal, heart
    ovary 867.6
      with open wound into cavity 867.7
    pancreas (multiple sites) 863.84
      with open wound into cavity 863.94
      body 863.82
        with open wound into cavity 863.92
      head 863.81
        with open wound into cavity 863.91
      tail 863.83
        with open wound into cavity 863.93
    pelvis, pelvic (organs) (viscera) 867.8
      with
        fracture, pelvis — *see* Fracture, pelvis
        open wound into cavity 867.9
      specified site NEC 867.6
        with open wound into cavity 867.7
    peritoneum 868.03
      with open wound into cavity 868.13
    pleura 862.29
      with open wound into cavity 862.39
    prostate 867.6
      with open wound into cavity 867.7
    rectum 863.45
      with
        colon 863.46
          with open wound into cavity 863.56
      open wound into cavity 863.55
    retroperitoneum 868.04

☑ **Additional Digit Required** — Refer to the Tabular List for Digit Selection

▽ **Subterms under main terms may continue to next column or page**

Injury — *continued*
  internal — *continued*
    retroperitoneum — *continued*
      with open wound into cavity 868.14
    round ligament 867.6
      with open wound into cavity 867.7
    seminal vesicle 867.6
      with open wound into cavity 867.7
    spermatic cord 867.6
      with open wound into cavity 867.7
      scrotal — *see* Wound, open, spermatic cord
    spleen 865.00
      with
        disruption of parenchyma (massive) 865.04
          with open wound into cavity 865.14
        hematoma (without rupture of capsule) 865.01
          with open wound into cavity 865.11
        open wound into cavity 865.10
        tear, capsular 865.02
          with open wound into cavity 865.12
        extending into parenchyma 865.03
          with open wound into cavity 865.13
    stomach 863.0
      with open wound into cavity 863.1
    suprarenal gland (multiple) 868.01
      with open wound into cavity 868.11
    thorax, thoracic (cavity) (organs) (multiple) (*see also* Injury, internal, intrathoracic organs) 862.8
      with open wound into cavity 862.9
    thymus (gland) 862.29
      with open wound into cavity 862.39
    trachea (intrathoracic) 862.29
      with open wound into cavity 862.39
      cervical region (*see also* Wound, open, trachea) 874.02
    ureter 867.2
      with open wound into cavity 867.3
    urethra (sphincter) 867.0
      with
        abortion — *see* Abortion, by type, with damage to pelvic organs
        ectopic pregnancy (*see also* categories 633.0–633.9) 639.2
        molar pregnancy (*see also* categories 630–632) 639.2
        open wound into cavity 867.1
      following
        abortion 639.2
        ectopic or molar pregnancy 639.2
      obstetrical trauma 665.5
        affecting fetus or newborn 763.89
    uterus 867.4
      with
        abortion — *see* Abortion, by type, with damage to pelvic organs
        ectopic pregnancy (*see also* categories 633.0–633.9) 639.2
        molar pregnancy (*see also* categories 630–632) 639.2
        open wound into cavity 867.5
      following
        abortion 639.2
        ectopic or molar pregnancy 639.2
      obstetrical trauma NEC 665.5
        affecting fetus or newborn 763.89
    vas deferens 867.6
      with open wound into cavity 867.7
    vesical (sphincter) 867.0
      with open wound into cavity 867.1
    viscera (abdominal) (*see also* Injury, internal, multiple) 868.00
      with
        fracture, pelvis — *see* Fracture, pelvis
        open wound into cavity 868.10

Injury — *continued*
  internal — *continued*
    viscera (*see also* Injury, internal, multiple) — *continued*
      thoracic NEC (*see also* Injury, internal, intrathoracic organs) 862.8
        with open wound into cavity 862.9
    interscapular region 959.19
    intervertebral disc 959.19
    intestine — *see* Injury, internal, intestine
    intra-abdominal (organs) NEC — *see* Injury, internal, intra-abdominal
    intracranial (traumatic) 854.0 ☑

> **Note** — *Use the following fifth-digit subclassification with categories 851–854:*
>
> 0   *unspecified state of consciousness*
>
> 1   *with no loss of consciousness*
>
> 2   *with brief [less than one hour] loss of consciousness*
>
> 3   *with moderate [1–24 hours] loss of consciousness*
>
> 4   *with prolonged [more than 24 hours] loss of consciousness and return to pre–existing conscious level*
>
> 5   *with prolonged [more than 24 hours] loss of consciousness, without return to pre–existing conscious level*
>
> *Use fifth-digit 5 to designate when a patient is unconscious and dies before regaining consciousness, regardless of the duration of the loss of consciousness*
>
> 6   *with loss of consciousness of unspecified duration*
>
> 9   *with concussion, unspecified*

      with
        open intracranial wound 854.1 ☑
        skull fracture — *see* Fracture, skull, by site
      contusion 851.8 ☑
        with open intracranial wound 851.9 ☑
        brain stem 851.4 ☑
          with open intracranial wound 851.5 ☑
        cerebellum 851.4 ☑
          with open intracranial wound 851.5 ☑
        cortex (cerebral) 851.0 ☑
          with open intracranial wound 851.2 ☑
      hematoma — *see* Injury, intracranial, hemorrhage
      hemorrhage 853.0 ☑
        with
          laceration — *see* Injury, intracranial, laceration
          open intracranial wound 853.1 ☑
        extradural 852.4 ☑
          with open intracranial wound 852.5 ☑
        subarachnoid 852.0 ☑
          with open intracranial wound 852.1 ☑
        subdural 852.2 ☑
          with open intracranial wound 852.3 ☑
      laceration 851.8 ☑
        with open intracranial wound 851.9 ☑
        brain stem 851.6 ☑
          with open intracranial wound 851.7 ☑
        cerebellum 851.6 ☑
          with open intracranial wound 851.7 ☑
        cortex (cerebral) 851.2 ☑

Injury — *continued*
  intracranial — *continued*
    laceration — *continued*
      cortex — *continued*
        with open intracranial wound 851.3 ☑
    intraocular — *see* Injury, eyeball, penetrating
    intrathoracic organs (multiple) — *see* Injury, internal, intrathoracic organs
    intrauterine — *see* Injury, internal, intrauterine
    iris 921.3
      penetrating — *see* Injury, eyeball, penetrating
    jaw 959.09
    jejunum — *see* Injury, internal, jejunum
    joint NEC 959.9
      old or residual 718.80
        ankle 718.87
        elbow 718.82
        foot 718.87
        hand 718.84
        hip 718.85
        knee 718.86
        multiple sites 718.89
        pelvic region 718.85
        shoulder (region) 718.81
        specified site NEC 718.88
        wrist 718.83
    kidney — *see* Injury, internal, kidney
      acute (nontraumatic) 584.9
    knee (and ankle) (and foot) (and leg, except thigh) 959.7
    labium (majus) (minus) 959.14
    labyrinth, ear 959.09
    lacrimal apparatus, gland, or sac 921.1
      laceration 870.8
    larynx 959.09
    late effect — *see* Late, effects (of), injury
    leg, except thigh (and ankle) (and foot) (and knee) 959.7
      upper or thigh 959.6
    lens, eye 921.3
      penetrating — *see* Injury, eyeball, penetrating
    lid, eye — *see* Injury, eyelid
    lip 959.09
    liver — *see* Injury, internal, liver
    lobe, parietal — *see* Injury, intracranial
    lumbar (region) 959.19
      plexus 953.5
    lumbosacral (region) 959.19
      plexus 953.5
    lung — *see* Injury, internal, lung
    malar region 959.09
    mastoid region 959.09
    maternal, during pregnancy, affecting fetus or newborn 760.5
    maxilla 959.09
    mediastinum — *see* Injury, internal, mediastinum
    membrane
      brain (*see also* Injury, intracranial) 854.0 ☑
      tympanic 959.09
    meningeal artery — *see* Hemorrhage, brain, traumatic, subarachnoid
    meninges (cerebral) — *see* Injury, intracranial
    mesenteric
      artery — *see* Injury, blood vessel, mesenteric, artery
      plexus, inferior 954.1
      vein — *see* Injury, blood vessel, mesenteric, vein
    mesentery — *see* Injury, internal, mesentery
    mesosalpinx — *see* Injury, internal, mesosalpinx
    middle ear 959.09
    midthoracic region 959.11
    mouth 959.09
    multiple (sites not classifiable to the same four–digit category in 959.0–959.7) 959.8
      internal 869.0

Injury — *continued*
  multiple — *continued*
    internal — *continued*
      with open wound into cavity 869.1
  musculocutaneous nerve 955.4
  nail
    finger 959.5
    toe 959.7
  nasal (septum) (sinus) 959.09
  nasopharynx 959.09
  neck (and face) 959.09
  nerve 957.9
    abducens 951.3
    abducent 951.3
    accessory 951.6
    acoustic 951.5
    ankle and foot 956.9
    anterior crural, femoral 956.1
    arm (*see also* Injury, nerve, upper limb) 955.9
    auditory 951.5
    axillary 955.0
    brachial plexus 953.4
    cervical sympathetic 954.0
    cranial 951.9
      first or olfactory 951.8
      second or optic 950.0
      third or oculomotor 951.0
      fourth or trochlear 951.1
      fifth or trigeminal 951.2
      sixth or abducens 951.3
      seventh or facial 951.4
      eighth, acoustic, or auditory 951.5
      ninth or glossopharyngeal 951.8
      tenth, pneumogastric, or vagus 951.8
      eleventh or accessory 951.6
      twelfth or hypoglossal 951.7
      newborn 767.7
    cutaneous sensory
      lower limb 956.4
      upper limb 955.5
    digital (finger) 955.6
      toe 956.5
    facial 951.4
      newborn 767.5
    femoral 956.1
    finger 955.9
    foot and ankle 956.9
    forearm 955.9
    glossopharyngeal 951.8
    hand and wrist 955.9
    head and neck, superficial 957.0
    hypoglossal 951.7
    involving several parts of body 957.8
    leg (*see also* Injury, nerve, lower limb) 956.9
    lower limb 956.9
      multiple 956.8
      specified site NEC 956.5
    lumbar plexus 953.5
    lumbosacral plexus 953.5
    median 955.1
      forearm 955.1
      wrist and hand 955.1
    multiple (in several parts of body) (sites not classifiable to the same three-digit category) 957.8
    musculocutaneous 955.4
    musculospiral 955.3
      upper arm 955.3
    oculomotor 951.0
    olfactory 951.8
    optic 950.0
    pelvic girdle 956.9
      multiple sites 956.8
      specified site NEC 956.5
    peripheral 957.9
      multiple (in several regions) (sites not classifiable to the same three-digit category) 957.8
      specified site NEC 957.1
    peroneal 956.3
      ankle and foot 956.3
      lower leg 956.3
    plantar 956.5
    plexus 957.9

☑ **Additional Digit Required** — Refer to the Tabular List for Digit Selection   ⁿᵉʷ **Subterms under main terms may continue to next column or page**

2015 ICD-9-CM   ▶◀ **Revised Text**   ● **New Line**   ▲ **Revised Code**   **Volume 2 — 163**

Injury — Injury

Injury — continued
  nerve — continued
    plexus — continued
      celiac 954.1
      mesenteric, inferior 954.1
      spinal 953.9
        brachial 953.4
        lumbosacral 953.5
        multiple sites 953.8
      sympathetic NEC 954.1
    pneumogastric 951.8
    radial 955.3
      wrist and hand 955.3
    sacral plexus 953.5
    sciatic 956.0
      thigh 956.0
    shoulder girdle 955.9
      multiple 955.8
      specified site NEC 955.7
    specified site NEC 957.1
    spinal 953.9
      plexus — see Injury, nerve, plexus, spinal
      root 953.9
        cervical 953.0
        dorsal 953.1
        lumbar 953.2
        multiple sites 953.8
        sacral 953.3
    splanchnic 954.1
    sympathetic NEC 954.1
      cervical 954.0
    thigh 956.9
    tibial 956.5
      ankle and foot 956.2
      lower leg 956.5
      posterior 956.2
    toe 956.9
    trigeminal 951.2
    trochlear 951.1
    trunk, excluding shoulder and pelvic girdles 954.9
      specified site NEC 954.8
      sympathetic NEC 954.1
    ulnar 955.2
      forearm 955.2
      wrist (and hand) 955.2
    upper limb 955.9
      multiple 955.8
      specified site NEC 955.7
    vagus 951.8
    wrist and hand 955.9
  nervous system, diffuse 957.8
  nose (septum) 959.09
  obstetrical NEC 665.9 ☑
    affecting fetus or newborn 763.89
  occipital (region) (scalp) 959.09
    lobe (see also Injury, intracranial) 854.0 ☑
  optic 950.9
    chiasm 950.1
    cortex 950.3
    nerve 950.0
    pathways 950.2
  orbit, orbital (region) 921.2
    penetrating 870.3
      with foreign body 870.4
  ovary — see Injury, internal, ovary
  paint-gun — see Wound, open, by site, complicated
  palate (soft) 959.09
  pancreas — see Injury, internal, pancreas
  parathyroid (gland) 959.09
  parietal (region) (scalp) 959.09
    lobe — see Injury, intracranial
  pelvic
    floor 959.19
      complicating delivery 664.1 ☑
        affecting fetus or newborn 763.89
    joint or ligament, complicating delivery 665.6 ☑
      affecting fetus or newborn 763.89
    organs (see also Injury, internal, pelvis)

Injury — continued
  pelvic — continued
    organs (see also Injury, internal, pelvis) — continued
      with
        abortion — see Abortion, by type, with damage to pelvic organs
        ectopic pregnancy (see also categories 633.0–633.9) 639.2
        molar pregnancy (see also categories 633.0–633.9) 639.2
      following
        abortion 639.2
        ectopic or molar pregnancy 639.2
      obstetrical trauma 665.5 ☑
        affecting fetus or newborn 763.89
  pelvis 959.19
  penis 959.14
    fracture of corpus cavernosum 959.13
  perineum 959.14
  peritoneum — see Injury, internal, peritoneum
  periurethral tissue
    with
      abortion — see Abortion, by type, with damage to pelvic organs
      ectopic pregnancy (see also categories 633.0–633.9) 639.2
      molar pregnancy (see also categories 630–632) 639.2
    complicating delivery 664.8 ☑
      affecting fetus or newborn 763.89
    following
      abortion 639.2
      ectopic or molar pregnancy 639.2
  phalanges
    foot 959.7
    hand 959.5
  pharynx 959.09
  pleura — see Injury, internal, pleura
  popliteal space 959.7
  post-cardiac surgery (syndrome) 429.4
  prepuce 959.14
  prostate — see Injury, internal, prostate
  pubic region 959.19
  pudenda 959.14
  radiation NEC 990
  radioactive substance or radium NEC 990
  rectovaginal septum 959.14
  rectum — see Injury, internal, rectum
  retina 921.3
    penetrating — see Injury, eyeball, penetrating
  retroperitoneal — see Injury, internal, retroperitoneum
  roentgen rays NEC 990
  round ligament — see Injury, internal, round ligament
  sacral (region) 959.19
    plexus 953.5
  sacroiliac ligament NEC 959.19
  sacrum 959.19
  salivary ducts or glands 959.09
  scalp 959.09
    due to birth trauma 767.19
    fetus or newborn 767.19
  scapular region 959.2
  sclera 921.3
    penetrating — see Injury, eyeball, penetrating
    superficial 918.2
  scrotum 959.14
  seminal vesicle — see Injury, internal, seminal vesicle
  shoulder (and upper arm) 959.2
  sinus
    cavernous (see also Injury, intracranial) 854.0 ☑
    nasal 959.09
  skeleton NEC, birth injury 767.3
  skin NEC 959.9
  skull — see Fracture, skull, by site
  soft tissue (of external sites) (severe) — see Wound, open, by site
  specified site NEC 959.8

Injury — continued
  spermatic cord — see Injury, internal, spermatic cord
  spinal (cord) 952.9
    with fracture, vertebra — see Fracture, vertebra, by site, with spinal cord injury
    cervical (C_1-C_4) 952.00
      with
        anterior cord syndrome 952.02
        central cord syndrome 952.03
        complete lesion of cord 952.01
        incomplete lesion NEC 952.04
        posterior cord syndrome 952.04
    C_5-C_7 level 952.05
      with
        anterior cord syndrome 952.07
        central cord syndrome 952.08
        complete lesion of cord 952.06
        incomplete lesion NEC 952.09
        posterior cord syndrome 952.09
      specified type NEC 952.09
    specified type NEC 952.04
    dorsal (D_1-D_6) (T_1-T_6) (thoracic) 952.10
      with
        anterior cord syndrome 952.12
        central cord syndrome 952.13
        complete lesion of cord 952.11
        incomplete lesion NEC 952.14
        posterior cord syndrome 952.14
    D_7-D_{12} level (T_7-T_{12}) 952.15
      with
        anterior cord syndrome 952.17
        central cord syndrome 952.18
        complete lesion of cord 952.16
        incomplete lesion NEC 952.19
        posterior cord syndrome 952.19
      specified type NEC 952.19
    specified type NEC 952.14
    lumbar 952.2
    multiple sites 952.8
    nerve (root) NEC — see Injury, nerve, spinal, root
    plexus 953.9
      brachial 953.4
      lumbosacral 953.5
      multiple sites 953.8
    sacral 953.3
    thoracic (see also Injury, spinal, dorsal) 952.10
  spleen — see Injury, internal, spleen
  stellate ganglion 954.1
  sternal region 959.11
  stomach — see Injury, internal, stomach
  subconjunctival 921.1
  subcutaneous 959.9
  subdural — see Injury, intracranial
  submaxillary region 959.09
  submental region 959.09
  subungual
    fingers 959.5
    toes 959.7

Injury — continued
  superficial 919 ☑

> Note — Use the following fourth-digit subdivisions with categories 910–919:
>
> 0 Abrasion or friction burn without mention of infection
>
> 1 Abrasion or friction burn, infected
>
> 2 Blister without mention of infection
>
> 3 Blister, infected
>
> 4 Insect bite, nonvenomous, without mention of infection
>
> 5 Insect bite, nonvenomous, infected
>
> 6 Superficial foreign body (splinter) without major open wound and without mention of infection
>
> 7 Superficial foreign body (splinter) without major open wound, infected
>
> 8 Other and unspecified superficial injury without mention of infection
>
> 9 Other and unspecified superficial injury, infected
>
> For late effects of superficial injury, see category 906.2.

    abdomen, abdominal (muscle) (wall) (and other part(s) of trunk) 911 ☑
    ankle (and hip, knee, leg, or thigh) 916 ☑
    anus (and other part(s) of trunk) 911 ☑
    arm 913 ☑
      upper (and shoulder) 912 ☑
    auditory canal (external) (meatus) (and other part(s) of face, neck, or scalp, except eye) 910 ☑
    axilla (and upper arm) 912 ☑
    back (and other part(s) of trunk) 911 ☑
    breast (and other part(s) of trunk) 911 ☑
    brow (and other part(s) of face, neck, or scalp, except eye) 910 ☑
    buttock (and other part(s) of trunk) 911 ☑
    canthus, eye 918.0
    cheek(s) (and other part(s) of face, neck, or scalp, except eye) 910 ☑
    chest wall (and other part(s) of trunk) 911 ☑
    chin (and other part(s) of face, neck, or scalp, except eye) 910 ☑
    clitoris (and other part(s) of trunk) 911 ☑
    conjunctiva 918.2
    cornea 918.1
      due to contact lens 371.82
    costal region (and other part(s) of trunk) 911 ☑
    ear(s) (auricle) (canal) (drum) (external) (and other part(s) of face, neck, or scalp, except eye) 910 ☑
    elbow (and forearm) (and wrist) 913 ☑
    epididymis (and other part(s) of trunk) 911 ☑
    epigastric region (and other part(s) of trunk) 911 ☑
    epiglottis (and other part(s) of face, neck, or scalp, except eye) 910 ☑
    eyelid(s) (and periocular area) 918.0
    eye(s) (and adnexa) NEC 918.9
    face (any part(s), except eye) (and neck or scalp) 910 ☑
    finger(s) (nail) (any) 915 ☑
    flank (and other part(s) of trunk) 911 ☑
    foot (phalanges) (and toe(s)) 917 ☑
    forearm (and elbow) (and wrist) 913 ☑
    forehead (and other part(s) of face, neck, or scalp, except eye) 910 ☑
    globe (eye) 918.9

☑ **Additional Digit Required** — Refer to the Tabular List for Digit Selection   ☞ **Subterms under main terms may continue to next column or page**

164 — Volume 2   ►◄ Revised Text   ● New Line   ▲ Revised Code   2015 ICD-9-CM

Injury — continued

superficial — continued

groin (and other part(s) of trunk) 911 ☑

gum(s) (and other part(s) of face, neck, or scalp, except eye) 910 ☑

hand(s) (except fingers alone) 914 ☑

head (and other part(s) of face, neck, or scalp, except eye) 910 ☑

heel (and foot or toe) 917 ☑

hip (and ankle, knee, leg, or thigh) 916 ☑

iliac region (and other part(s) of trunk) 911 ☑

interscapular region (and other part(s) of trunk) 911 ☑

iris 918.9

knee (and ankle, hip, leg, or thigh) 916 ☑

labium (majus) (minus) (and other part(s) of trunk) 911 ☑

lacrimal (apparatus) (gland) (sac) 918.0

leg (lower) (upper) (and ankle, hip, knee, or thigh) 916 ☑

lip(s) (and other part(s) of face, neck, or scalp, except eye) 910 ☑

lower extremity (except foot) 916 ☑

lumbar region (and other part(s) of trunk) 911 ☑

malar region (and other part(s) of face, neck, or scalp, except eye) 910 ☑

mastoid region (and other part(s) of face, neck, or scalp, except eye) 910 ☑

midthoracic region (and other part(s) of trunk) 911 ☑

mouth (and other part(s) of face, neck, or scalp, except eye) 910 ☑

multiple sites (not classifiable to the same three-digit category) 919 ☑

nasal (septum) (and other part(s) of face, neck, or scalp, except eye) 910 ☑

neck (and face or scalp, any part(s), except eye) 910 ☑

nose (septum) (and other part(s) of face, neck, or scalp, except eye) 910 ☑

occipital region (and other part(s) of face, neck, or scalp, except eye) 910 ☑

orbital region 918.0

palate (soft) (and other part(s) of face, neck, or scalp, except eye) 910 ☑

parietal region (and other part(s) of face, neck, or scalp, except eye) 910 ☑

penis (and other part(s) of trunk) 911 ☑

perineum (and other part(s) of trunk) 911 ☑

periocular area 918.0

pharynx (and other part(s) of face, neck, or scalp, except eye) 910 ☑

popliteal space (and ankle, hip, leg, or thigh) 916 ☑

prepuce (and other part(s) of trunk) 911 ☑

pubic region (and other part(s) of trunk) 911 ☑

pudenda (and other part(s) of trunk) 911 ☑

sacral region (and other part(s) of trunk) 911 ☑

salivary (ducts) (glands) (and other part(s) of face, neck, or scalp, except eye) 910 ☑

scalp (and other part(s) of face or neck, except eye) 910 ☑

scapular region (and upper arm) 912 ☑

sclera 918.2

scrotum (and other part(s) of trunk) 911 ☑

shoulder (and upper arm) 912 ☑

skin NEC 919 ☑

specified site(s) NEC 919 ☑

sternal region (and other part(s) of trunk) 911 ☑

subconjunctival 918.2

subcutaneous NEC 919 ☑

Injury — continued

superficial — continued

submaxillary region (and other part(s) of face, neck, or scalp, except eye) 910 ☑

submental region (and other part(s) of face, neck, or scalp, except eye) 910 ☑

supraclavicular fossa (and other part(s) of face, neck, or scalp, except eye) 910 ☑

supraorbital 918.0

temple (and other part(s) of face, neck, or scalp, except eye) 910 ☑

temporal region (and other part(s) of face, neck, or scalp, except eye) 910 ☑

testis (and other part(s) of trunk) 911 ☑

thigh (and ankle, hip, knee, or leg) 916 ☑

thorax, thoracic (external) (and other part(s) of trunk) 911 ☑

throat (and other part(s) of face, neck, or scalp, except eye) 910 ☑

thumb(s) (nail) 915 ☑

toe(s) (nail) (subungual) (and foot) 917 ☑

tongue (and other part(s) of face, neck, or scalp, except eye) 910 ☑

tooth, teeth (see also Abrasion, dental) 521.20

trunk (any part(s)) 911 ☑

tunica vaginalis 959.14

tympanum, tympanic membrane (and other part(s) of face, neck, or scalp, except eye) 910 ☑

upper extremity NEC 913 ☑

uvula (and other part(s) of face, neck, or scalp, except eye) 910 ☑

vagina (and other part(s) of trunk) 911 ☑

vulva (and other part(s) of trunk) 911 ☑

wrist (and elbow) (and forearm) 913 ☑

supraclavicular fossa 959.19

supraorbital 959.09

surgical complication (external or internal site) 998.2

symphysis pubis 959.19

complicating delivery 665.6 ☑

affecting fetus or newborn 763.89

temple 959.09

temporal region 959.09

testis 959.14

thigh (and hip) 959.6

thorax, thoracic (external) 959.11

cavity — see Injury, internal, thorax

internal — see Injury, internal, intrathoracic organs

throat 959.09

thumb(s) (nail) 959.5

thymus — see Injury, internal, thymus

thyroid (gland) 959.09

toe (nail) (any) 959.7

tongue 959.09

tonsil 959.09

tooth NEC 873.63

complicated 873.73

trachea — see Injury, internal, trachea

trunk 959.19

tunica vaginalis 959.14

tympanum, tympanic membrane 959.09

ultraviolet rays NEC 990

ureter — see Injury, internal, ureter

urethra (sphincter) — see Injury, internal, urethra

uterus — see Injury, internal, uterus

uvula 959.09

vagina 959.14

vascular — see Injury, blood vessel

vas deferens — see Injury, internal, vas deferens

vein (see also Injury, blood vessel, by site) 904.9

vena cava

inferior 902.10

superior 901.2

Injury — continued

vesical (sphincter) — see Injury, internal, vesical

viscera (abdominal) — see Injury, internal, viscera

with fracture, pelvis — see Fracture, pelvis

visual 950.9

cortex 950.3

vitreous (humor) 871.2

vulva 959.14

whiplash (cervical spine) 847.0

wringer — see Crush, by site

wrist (and elbow) (and forearm) 959.3

x-ray NEC 990

Inoculation — see also Vaccination

complication or reaction — see Complication, vaccination

INPH (idiopathic normal pressure hydrocephalus) 331.5

Insanity, insane — see also Psychosis 298.9

adolescent (see also Schizophrenia) 295.9 ☑

alternating (see also Psychosis, affective, circular) 296.7

confusional 298.9

acute 293.0

subacute 293.1

delusional 298.9

paralysis, general 094.1

progressive 094.1

paresis, general 094.1

senile 290.20

Insect

bite — see Injury, superficial, by site

venomous, poisoning by 989.5

Insemination, artificial V26.1

Insensitivity

adrenocorticotropin hormone (ACTH) 255.41

androgen 259.50

complete 259.51

partial 259.52

Insertion

cord (umbilical) lateral or velamentous 663.8 ☑

affecting fetus or newborn 762.6

intrauterine contraceptive device V25.11

placenta, vicious — see Placenta, previa

subdermal implantable contraceptive V25.5

velamentous, umbilical cord 663.8 ☑

affecting fetus or newborn 762.6

Insolation 992.0

meaning sunstroke 992.0

Insomnia, unspecified 780.52

with sleep apnea, unspecified 780.51

adjustment 307.41

alcohol induced 291.82

behavioral, of childhood V69.5

drug induced 292.85

due to

medical condition classified elsewhere 327.01

mental disorder 327.02

fatal familial (FFI) 046.72

idiopathic 307.42

nonorganic origin 307.41

persistent (primary) 307.42

transient 307.41

organic 327.00

other 327.09

paradoxical 307.42

primary 307.42

psychophysiological 307.42

subjective complaint 307.49

Inspiration

food or foreign body (see also Asphyxia, food or foreign body) 933.1

mucus (see also Asphyxia, mucus) 933.1

Inspissated bile syndrome, newborn 774.4

Instability

detrusor 596.59

emotional (excessive) 301.3

joint (posttraumatic) 718.80

ankle 718.87

elbow 718.82

foot 718.87

Instability — continued

joint — continued

hand 718.84

hip 718.85

knee 718.86

lumbosacral 724.6

multiple sites 718.89

pelvic region 718.85

sacroiliac 724.6

shoulder (region) 718.81

specified site NEC 718.88

wrist 718.83

lumbosacral 724.6

nervous 301.89

personality (emotional) 301.59

thyroid, paroxysmal 242.9 ☑

urethral 599.83

vasomotor 780.2

Insufficiency, insufficient

accommodation 367.4

adrenal (gland) (acute) (chronic) 255.41

medulla 255.5

primary 255.41

specified site NEC 255.5

adrenocortical 255.41

anterior (occlusal) guidance 524.54

anus 569.49

aortic (valve) 424.1

with

mitral (valve) disease 396.1

insufficiency, incompetence, or regurgitation 396.3

stenosis or obstruction 396.1

stenosis or obstruction 424.1

with mitral (valve) disease 396.8

congenital 746.4

rheumatic 395.1

with

mitral (valve) disease 396.1

insufficiency, incompetence, or regurgitation 396.3

stenosis or obstruction 396.1

stenosis or obstruction 395.2

with mitral (valve) disease 396.8

specified cause NEC 424.1

syphilitic 093.22

arterial 447.1

basilar artery 435.0

carotid artery 435.8

cerebral 437.1

coronary (acute or subacute) 411.89

mesenteric 557.1

peripheral 443.9

precerebral 435.9

vertebral artery 435.1

vertebrobasilar 435.3

arteriovenous 459.9

basilar artery 435.0

biliary 575.8

cardiac (see also Insufficiency, myocardial) 428.0

complicating surgery 997.1

due to presence of (cardiac) prosthesis 429.4

postoperative 997.1

long-term effect of cardiac surgery 429.4

specified during or due to a procedure 997.1

long-term effect of cardiac surgery 429.4

cardiorenal (see also Hypertension, cardiorenal) 404.90

cardiovascular (see also Disease, cardiovascular) 429.2

renal (see also Hypertension, cardiorenal) 404.90

carotid artery 435.8

cerebral (vascular) 437.9

cerebrovascular 437.9

with transient focal neurological signs and symptoms 435.9

acute 437.1

with transient focal neurological signs and symptoms 435.9

☑ **Additional Digit Required — Refer to the Tabular List for Digit Selection**   ⧖ **Subterms under main terms may continue to next column or page**

2015 ICD-9-CM   ▶◀ Revised Text   ● New Line   ▲ Revised Code   Volume 2 — 165

Insufficiency, insufficient — *continued*
circulatory NEC 459.9
  fetus or newborn 779.89
convergence 378.83
coronary (acute or subacute) 411.89
  chronic or with a stated duration of over
    8 weeks 414.8
corticoadrenal 255.41
dietary 269.9
divergence 378.85
food 994.2
gastroesophageal 530.89
gonadal
  ovary 256.39
  testis 257.2
gonadotropic hormone secretion 253.4
heart (*see also* Insufficiency, myocardial)
  fetus or newborn 779.89
  valve (*see also* Endocarditis) 424.90
    congenital NEC 746.89
hepatic 573.8
idiopathic autonomic 333.0
interocclusal distance of teeth (ridge) 524.36
kidney
  acute 593.9
  chronic 585.9
labyrinth, labyrinthine (function) 386.53
  bilateral 386.54
  unilateral 386.53
lacrimal 375.15
liver 573.8
lung (acute) (*see also* Insufficiency, pul-
    monary) 518.82
  following trauma and surgery 518.52
  newborn 770.89
mental (congenital) (*see also* Disability, intel-
    lectual) 319
mesenteric 557.1
mitral (valve) 424.0
  with
    aortic (valve) disease 396.3
      insufficiency, incompetence, or
        regurgitation 396.3
      stenosis or obstruction 396.2
    obstruction or stenosis 394.2
      with aortic valve disease 396.8
  congenital 746.6
  rheumatic 394.1
    with
      aortic (valve) disease 396.3
        insufficiency, incompetence,
          or regurgitation 396.3
        stenosis or obstruction 396.2
      obstruction or stenosis 394.2
        with aortic valve disease 396.8
    active or acute 391.1
      with chorea, rheumatic (Syden-
        ham's) 392.0
  specified cause, except rheumatic 424.0
muscle
  heart — *see* Insufficiency, myocardial
  ocular (*see also* Strabismus) 378.9
myocardial, myocardium (with arterioscle-
    rosis) 428.0
  with rheumatic fever (conditions classifi-
    able to 390)
    active, acute, or subacute 391.2
      with chorea 392.0
    inactive or quiescent (with chorea)
      398.0
  congenital 746.89
  due to presence of (cardiac) prosthesis
    429.4
  fetus or newborn 779.89
  following cardiac surgery 429.4
  hypertensive (*see also* Hypertension,
    heart) 402.91
    benign 402.11
    malignant 402.01
  postoperative 997.1
    long-term effect of cardiac surgery
      429.4
  rheumatic 398.0
    active, acute, or subacute 391.2
      with chorea (Sydenham's) 392.0
  syphilitic 093.82

Insufficiency, insufficient — *continued*
nourishment 994.2
organic 799.89
ovary 256.39
  postablative 256.2
pancreatic 577.8
parathyroid (gland) 252.1
peripheral vascular (arterial) 443.9
pituitary (anterior) 253.2
  posterior 253.5
placental — *see* Placenta, insufficiency
platelets 287.5
prenatal care in current pregnancy V23.7
progressive pluriglandular 258.9
pseudocholinesterase 289.89
pulmonary (acute) 518.82
  following
    shock 518.52
    surgery 518.52
    trauma 518.52
  newborn 770.89
  valve (*see also* Endocarditis, pulmonary)
    424.3
    congenital 746.09
pyloric 537.0
renal 593.9
  acute 593.9
  chronic 585.9
  due to a procedure 997.5
respiratory 786.09
  acute 518.82
    following trauma and surgery 518.52
  newborn 770.89
rotation — *see* Malrotation
suprarenal 255.41
  medulla 255.5
tarso-orbital fascia, congenital 743.66
tear film 375.15
testis 257.2
thyroid (gland) (acquired) (*see also* Hypothy-
    roidism)
    congenital 243
tricuspid (*see also* Endocarditis, tricuspid)
    397.0
    congenital 746.89
    syphilitic 093.23
urethral sphincter 599.84
valve, valvular (heart) (*see also* Endocarditis)
    424.90
vascular 459.9
    intestine NEC 557.9
    mesenteric 557.1
    peripheral 443.9
    renal (*see also* Hypertension, kidney)
      403.90
velopharyngeal
  acquired 528.9
  congenital 750.29
venous (peripheral) 459.81
ventricular — *see* Insufficiency, myocardial
vertebral artery 435.1
vertebrobasilar artery 435.3
weight gain during pregnancy 646.8 ☑
zinc 269.3

Insufflation
fallopian
  fertility testing V26.21
  following sterilization reversal V26.22
meconium 770.11
  with respiratory symptoms 770.12

Insular — *see* condition

Insulinoma (M8151/0)
malignant (M8151/3)
  pancreas 157.4
  specified site — *see* Neoplasm, by site,
    malignant
  unspecified site 157.4
pancreas 211.7
specified site — *see* Neoplasm, by site, be-
    nign
unspecified site 211.7

Insuloma — *see* Insulinoma

Insult
brain 437.9
  acute 436
cerebral 437.9

Insult — *continued*
cerebral — *continued*
  acute 436
cerebrovascular 437.9
  acute 436
vascular NEC 437.9
  acute 436

Insurance examination (certification) V70.3

Intemperance — *see also* Alcoholism 303.9

Interception of pregnancy (menstrual extrac-
    tion) V25.3

Interference
balancing side 524.56
non-working side 524.56

Intermenstrual
bleeding 626.6
  irregular 626.6
  regular 626.5
hemorrhage 626.6
  irregular 626.6
  regular 626.5
pain(s) 625.2

Intermittent — *see* condition

Internal — *see* condition

Interproximal wear 521.10

Interrogation
cardiac defibrillator (automatic) (im-
    plantable) V53.32
cardiac pacemaker V53.31
cardiac (event) (loop) recorder V53.39
infusion pump (implanted) (intrathecal)
    V53.09
neurostimulator V53.02

Interruption
aortic arch 747.11
bundle of His 426.50
fallopian tube (for sterilization) V25.2
phase-shift, sleep cycle 307.45
repeated REM-sleep 307.48
sleep
  due to perceived environmental distur-
    bances 307.48
  phase-shift, of 24-hour sleep-wake cycle
    307.45
  repeated REM-sleep type 307.48
vas deferens (for sterilization) V25.2

Intersexuality 752.7

Interstitial — *see* condition

Intertrigo 695.89
labialis 528.5

Intervertebral disc — *see* condition

Intestine, intestinal — *see also* condition
flu 487.8

Intolerance
carbohydrate NEC 579.8
cardiovascular exercise, with pain (at rest)
    (with less than ordinary activity)
    (with ordinary activity) V47.2
cold 780.99
dissacharide (hereditary) 271.3
drug
  correct substance properly administered
    995.27
  wrong substance given or taken in error
    977.9
  specified drug — *see* Table of Drugs
    and Chemicals
effort 306.2
fat NEC 579.8
foods NEC 579.8
fructose (hereditary) 271.2
glucose (-galactose) (congenital) 271.3
gluten 579.0
lactose (hereditary) (infantile) 271.3
lysine (congenital) 270.7
milk NEC 579.8
protein (familial) 270.7
starch NEC 579.8
sucrose (-isomaltose) (congenital) 271.3

Intoxicated NEC — *see also* Alcoholism
    305.0 ☑

Intoxication
acid 276.2
acute
  alcoholic 305.0 ☑
    with alcoholism 303.0 ☑

Intoxication — *continued*
acute — *continued*
  alcoholic — *continued*
    hangover effects 305.0 ☑
    caffeine 305.9 ☑
    hallucinogenic (*see also* Abuse, drugs,
      nondependent) 305.3 ☑
  alcohol (acute) 305.0 ☑
    with alcoholism 303.0 ☑
    hangover effects 305.0 ☑
    idiosyncratic 291.4
    pathological 291.4
  alimentary canal 558.2
  ammonia (hepatic) 572.2
  caffeine 305.9 ☑
  chemical (*see also* Table of Drugs and
      Chemicals)
    via placenta or breast milk 760.70
      alcohol 760.71
      anticonvulsants
      antifungals
      anti-infective agents 760.74
      antimetabolics
      cocaine 760.75
      "crack" 760.75
      hallucinogenic agents NEC 760.73
      medicinal agents NEC 760.79
      narcotics 760.72
      obstetric anesthetic or analgesic drug
        763.5
      specified agent NEC 760.79
      suspected, affecting management of
        pregnancy 655.5 ☑
  cocaine, through placenta or breast milk
    760.75
  delirium
    alcohol 291.0
    drug 292.81
  drug 292.89
    with delirium 292.81
    correct substance properly administered
      (*see also* Allergy, drug) 995.27
    newborn 779.4
    obstetric anesthetic or sedation 668.9 ☑
      affecting fetus or newborn 763.5
    overdose or wrong substance given or
      taken — *see* Table of Drugs and
      Chemicals
    pathologic 292.2
    specific to newborn 779.4
    via placenta or breast milk 760.70
      alcohol 760.71
      anticonvulsants 760.77
      antifungals 760.74
      anti-infective agents 760.74
      antimetabolics 760.78
      cocaine 760.75
      "crack" 760.75
      hallucinogenic agents 760.73
      medicinal agents NEC 760.79
      narcotics 760.72
      obstetric anesthetic or analgesic drug
        763.5
      specified agent NEC 760.79
      suspected, affecting management of
        pregnancy 655.5 ☑
  enteric — *see* Intoxication, intestinal
  fetus or newborn, via placenta or breast milk
    760.70
    alcohol 760.71
    anticonvulsants 760.77
    antifungals 760.74
    anti-infective agents 760.74
    antimetabolics 760.78
    cocaine 760.75
    "crack" 760.75
    hallucinogenic agents 760.73
    medicinal agents NEC 760.79
    narcotics 760.72
    obstetric anesthetic or analgesic drug
      763.5
    specified agent NEC 760.79
    suspected, affecting management of
      pregnancy 655.5 ☑
  food — *see* Poisoning, food
  gastrointestinal 558.2

☑ **Additional Digit Required — Refer to the Tabular List for Digit Selection**
▽ **Subterms under main terms may continue to next column or page**

166 — Volume 2   ▶◀ Revised Text   ● New Line   ▲ Revised Code   2015 ICD-9-CM

Intoxication — *continued*
  hallucinogenic (acute) 305.3 ☑
  hepatocerebral 572.2
  idiosyncratic alcohol 291.4
  intestinal 569.89
    due to putrefaction of food 005.9
  methyl alcohol (*see also* Alcoholism)
    305.0 ☑
    with alcoholism 303.0 ☑
  non-foodborne due to toxins of Clostridium
    botulinum [C. botulinum] — *see* Bo-
    tulism
  pathologic 291.4
    drug 292.2
  potassium (K) 276.7
  septic
    with
      abortion — *see* Abortion, by type,
        with sepsis
      ectopic pregnancy (*see also* cate-
        gories 633.0–633.9) 639.0
      molar pregnancy (*see also* categories
        630–632) 639.0
    during labor 659.3 ☑
    following
      abortion 639.0
      ectopic or molar pregnancy 639.0
    generalized — *see* Septicemia
    puerperal, postpartum, childbirth
      670.2 ☑
  serum (prophylactic) (therapeutic) 999.59
  uremic — *see* Uremia
  water 276.69
Intracranial — *see* condition
Intrahepatic gallbladder 751.69
Intraligamentous — *see also* condition
  pregnancy — *see* Pregnancy, cornual
Intraocular — *see also* condition
  sepsis 360.00
Intrathoracic — *see also* condition
  kidney 753.3
  stomach — *see* Hernia, diaphragm
Intrauterine contraceptive device
  checking V25.42
  insertion V25.11
  in situ V45.51
  management V25.42
  prescription V25.02
    repeat V25.42
  reinsertion V25.13
  removal V25.12
    and reinsertion V25.13
  replacement V25.13
Intraventricular — *see* condition
Intrinsic deformity — *see* Deformity
Intruded tooth 524.34
Intrusion, repetitive, of sleep (due to environmental disturbances) (with atypical
  polysomnographic features) 307.48
Intumescent, lens (eye) NEC 366.9
  senile 366.12
Intussusception (colon) (enteric) (intestine)
  (rectum) 560.0
  appendix 543.9
  congenital 751.5
  fallopian tube 620.8
  ileocecal 560.0
  ileocolic 560.0
  ureter (with obstruction) 593.4
Invagination
  basilar 756.0
  colon or intestine 560.0
Invalid (since birth) 799.89
Invalidism (chronic) 799.89
Inversion
  albumin-globulin (A-G) ratio 273.8
  bladder 596.89
  cecum (*see also* Intussusception) 560.0
  cervix 622.8
  nipple 611.79
    congenital 757.6
    puerperal, postpartum 676.3 ☑
  optic papilla 743.57
  organ or site, congenital NEC — *see*
    Anomaly, specified type NEC
  sleep rhythm 327.39

Inversion — *continued*
  sleep rhythm — *continued*
    nonorganic origin 307.45
  testis (congenital) 752.51
  uterus (postinfectional) (postpartal, old)
    621.7
    chronic 621.7
    complicating delivery 665.2 ☑
      affecting fetus or newborn 763.89
  vagina — *see* Prolapse, vagina
Investigation
  allergens V72.7
  clinical research (control) (normal compari-
    son) (participant) V70.7
Inviability — *see* Immaturity
Involuntary movement, abnormal 781.0
Involution, involutional — *see also* condition
  breast, cystic or fibrocystic 610.1
  depression (*see also* Psychosis, affective)
    296.2 ☑
    recurrent episode 296.3 ☑
    single episode 296.2 ☑
  melancholia (*see also* Psychosis, affective)
    296.2 ☑
    recurrent episode 296.3 ☑
    single episode 296.2 ☑
  ovary, senile 620.3
  paranoid state (reaction) 297.2
  paraphrenia (climacteric) (menopause)
    297.2
  psychosis 298.8
  thymus failure 254.8
IQ
  under 20 318.2
  20-34 318.1
  35-49 318.0
  50-70 317
IRDS 769
Irideremia 743.45
Iridis rubeosis 364.42
  diabetic 250.5 ☑ [364.42]
    due to secondary diabetes
      249.5 ☑ [364.42]
Iridochoroiditis (panuveitis) 360.12
Iridocyclitis NEC 364.3
  acute 364.00
    primary 364.01
    recurrent 364.02
  chronic 364.10
    in
      lepromatous leprosy 030.0 [364.11]
      sarcoidosis 135 [364.11]
      tuberculosis (*see also* Tuberculosis)
        017.3 ☑ [364.11]
  due to allergy 364.04
  endogenous 364.01
  gonococcal 098.41
  granulomatous 364.10
  herpetic (simplex) 054.44
    zoster 053.22
  hypopyon 364.05
  lens induced 364.23
  nongranulomatous 364.00
  primary 364.01
  recurrent 364.02
  rheumatic 364.10
  secondary 364.04
    infectious 364.03
    noninfectious 364.04
  subacute 364.00
    primary 364.01
    recurrent 364.02
  sympathetic 360.11
  syphilitic (secondary) 091.52
  tuberculous (chronic) (*see also* Tuberculosis)
    017.3 ☑ [364.11]
Iridocyclochoroiditis (panuveitis) 360.12
Iridodialysis 364.76
Iridodonesis 364.89
Iridoplegia (complete) (partial) (reflex) 379.49
Iridoschisis 364.52
IRIS (Immune Reconstitution Inflammatory
  Syndrome) 995.90
Iris — *see* condition
Iritis 364.3
  acute 364.00

Iritis — *continued*
  acute — *continued*
    primary 364.01
    recurrent 364.02
  chronic 364.10
    in
      sarcoidosis 135 [364.11]
      tuberculosis (*see also* Tuberculosis)
        017.3 ☑ [364.11]
  diabetic 250.5 ☑ [364.42]
    due to secondary diabetes
      249.5 ☑ [364.42]
  due to
    allergy 364.04
    herpes simplex 054.44
    leprosy 030.0 [364.11]
  endogenous 364.01
  gonococcal 098.41
  gouty 274.89 [364.11]
  granulomatous 364.10
  hypopyon 364.05
  lens induced 364.23
  nongranulomatous 364.00
  papulosa 095.8 [364.11]
  primary 364.01
  recurrent 364.02
  rheumatic 364.10
  secondary 364.04
    infectious 364.03
    noninfectious 364.04
  subacute 364.00
    primary 364.01
    recurrent 364.02
  sympathetic 360.11
  syphilitic (secondary) 091.52
    congenital 090.0 [364.11]
    late 095.8 [364.11]
  tuberculous (*see also* Tuberculosis)
    017.3 ☑ [364.11]
  uratic 274.89 [364.11]
Iron
  deficiency anemia 280.9
  metabolism disease 275.09
  storage disease 275.09
Iron-miners' lung 503
Irradiated enamel (tooth, teeth) 521.89
Irradiation
  burn — *see* Burn, by site
  effects, adverse 990
Irreducible, irreducibility — *see* condition
Irregular, irregularity
  action, heart 427.9
  alveolar process 525.8
  bleeding NEC 626.4
  breathing 786.09
  colon 569.89
  contour
    acquired 371.70
    of cornea 743.41
      acquired 371.70
    reconstructed breast 612.0
  dentin in pulp 522.3
  eye movements NEC 379.59
  menstruation (cause unknown) 626.4
  periods 626.4
  prostate 602.9
  pupil 364.75
  respiratory 786.09
  septum (nasal) 470
  shape, organ or site, congenital NEC — *see*
    Distortion
  sleep-wake rhythm (non-24-hour) 327.39
    nonorganic origin 307.45
  vertebra 733.99
Irritability 799.22
  bladder 596.89
    neurogenic 596.54
      with cauda equina syndrome 344.61
  bowel (syndrome) 564.1
  bronchial (*see also* Bronchitis) 490
  cerebral, newborn 779.1
  colon 564.1
    psychogenic 306.4
  duodenum 564.89
  heart (psychogenic) 306.2
  ileum 564.89

Irritability — *continued*
  jejunum 564.89
  myocardium 306.2
  nervousness 799.21
  rectum 564.89
  stomach 536.9
    psychogenic 306.4
  sympathetic (nervous system) (*see also*
    Neuropathy, peripheral, autonomic)
    337.9
  urethra 599.84
  ventricular (heart) (psychogenic) 306.2
Irritable — *see also* Irritability 799.22
Irritation
  anus 569.49
  axillary nerve 353.0
  bladder 596.89
  brachial plexus 353.0
  brain (traumatic) (*see also* Injury, intracra-
    nial) 854.0 ☑
    nontraumatic — *see* Encephalitis
  bronchial (*see also* Bronchitis) 490
  cerebral (traumatic) (*see also* Injury, intracra-
    nial) 854.0 ☑
    nontraumatic — *see* Encephalitis
  cervical plexus 353.2
  cervix (*see also* Cervicitis) 616.0
  choroid, sympathetic 360.11
  cranial nerve — *see* Disorder, nerve, cranial
  digestive tract 536.9
    psychogenic 306.4
  gastric 536.9
    psychogenic 306.4
  gastrointestinal (tract) 536.9
    functional 536.9
    psychogenic 306.4
  globe, sympathetic 360.11
  intestinal (bowel) 564.9
  labyrinth 386.50
  lumbosacral plexus 353.1
  meninges (traumatic) (*see also* Injury, in-
    tracranial) 854.0 ☑
    nontraumatic — *see* Meningitis
  myocardium 306.2
  nerve — *see* Disorder, nerve
  nervous 799.21
  nose 478.19
  penis 607.89
  perineum 709.9
  peripheral
    autonomic nervous system (*see also*
      Neuropathy, peripheral, autonom-
      ic) 337.9
    nerve — *see* Disorder, nerve
  peritoneum (*see also* Peritonitis) 567.9
  pharynx 478.29
  plantar nerve 355.6
  spinal (cord) (traumatic) (*see also* Injury,
    spinal, by site)
    nerve (*see also* Disorder, nerve)
      root NEC 724.9
      traumatic — *see* Injury, nerve, spinal
    nontraumatic — *see* Myelitis
  stomach 536.9
    psychogenic 306.4
  sympathetic nerve NEC (*see also* Neuropa-
    thy, peripheral, autonomic) 337.9
  ulnar nerve 354.2
  vagina 623.9
Isambert's disease 012.3 ☑
Ischemia, ischemic 459.9
  basilar artery (with transient neurologic
    deficit) 435.0
  bone NEC 733.40
  bowel (transient) 557.9
    acute 557.0
    chronic 557.1
    due to mesenteric artery insufficiency
      557.1
  brain (*see also* Ischemia, cerebral)
    recurrent focal 435.9
  cardiac (*see also* Ischemia, heart) 414.9
  cardiomyopathy 414.8
  carotid artery (with transient neurologic
    deficit) 435.8
  cerebral (chronic) (generalized) 437.1

☑ **Additional Digit Required** — Refer to the Tabular List for Digit Selection   ▽ **Subterms under main terms may continue to next column or page**

2015 ICD-9-CM   ▶◀ **Revised Text**   ● **New Line**   ▲ **Revised Code**   **Volume 2 — 167**

Ischemia, ischemic — *continued*
 cerebral — *continued*
  arteriosclerotic 437.0
  intermittent (with transient neurologic
   deficit) 435.9
  newborn 779.2
  puerperal, postpartum, childbirth
   674.0 ☑
  recurrent focal (with transient neurologic
   deficit) 435.9
  transient (with transient neurologic
   deficit) 435.9
 colon 557.9
  acute 557.0
  chronic 557.1
  due to mesenteric artery insufficiency
   557.1
 coronary (chronic) (*see also* Ischemia, heart)
  414.9
 demand 411.89
 heart (chronic or with a stated duration of
  over 8 weeks) 414.9
  acute or with a stated duration of 8
   weeks or less (*see also* Infarct,
   myocardium) 410.9 ☑
   without myocardial infarction 411.89
    with coronary (artery) occlusion
     411.81
  subacute 411.89
 intestine (transient) 557.9
  acute 557.0
  chronic 557.1
  due to mesenteric artery insufficiency
   557.1
 kidney 593.81
 labyrinth 386.50

Ischemia, ischemic — *continued*
 muscles, leg 728.89
 myocardium, myocardial (chronic or with a
  stated duration of over 8 weeks)
  414.8
  acute (*see also* Infarct, myocardium)
   410.9 ☑
   without myocardial infarction 411.89
    with coronary (artery) occlusion
     411.81
 renal 593.81
 retina, retinal 362.84
 small bowel 557.9
  acute 557.0
  chronic 557.1
  due to mesenteric artery insufficiency
   557.1
 spinal cord 336.1
 subendocardial (*see also* Insufficiency,
  coronary) 411.89
 supply (*see also* Angina) 414.9
 vertebral artery (with transient neurologic
  deficit) 435.1
Ischialgia — *see also* Sciatica 724.3
Ischiopagus 759.4
Ischium, ischial — *see* condition
Ischomenia 626.8
Ischuria 788.5
Iselin's disease or osteochondrosis 732.5
Islands of
 parotid tissue in
  lymph nodes 750.26
  neck structures 750.26
 submaxillary glands in
  fascia 750.26
  lymph nodes 750.26

Islands of — *continued*
 submaxillary glands in — *continued*
  neck muscles 750.26
Islet cell tumor, pancreas (M8150/0) 211.7
Isoimmunization NEC — *see also* Incompatibility 656.2 ☑
 anti-E 656.2 ☑
 fetus or newborn 773.2
  ABO blood groups 773.1
  Rhesus (Rh) factor 773.0
Isolation V07.0
 social V62.4
Isosporosis 007.2
Issue
 medical certificate NEC V68.09
  cause of death V68.09
  disability examination V68.01
  fitness V68.09
  incapacity V68.09
 repeat prescription NEC V68.1
  appliance V68.1
  contraceptive V25.40
   device NEC V25.49
    intrauterine V25.42
    specified type NEC V25.49
   pill V25.41
  glasses V68.1
  medicinal substance V68.1
Itch — *see also* Pruritus 698.9
 bakers' 692.89
 barbers' 110.0
 bricklayers' 692.89
 cheese 133.8
 clam diggers' 120.3
 coolie 126.9
 copra 133.8

Itch — *see also* Pruritus — *continued*
 Cuban 050.1
 dew 126.9
 dhobie 110.3
 eye 379.99
 filarial (*see also* Infestation, filarial) 125.9
 grain 133.8
 grocers' 133.8
 ground 126.9
 harvest 133.8
 jock 110.3
 Malabar 110.9
  beard 110.0
  foot 110.4
  scalp 110.0
 meaning scabies 133.0
 Norwegian 133.0
 perianal 698.0
 poultrymen's 133.8
 sarcoptic 133.0
 scrub 134.1
 seven year V61.10
  meaning scabies 133.0
 straw 133.8
 swimmers' 120.3
 washerwoman's 692.4
 water 120.3
 winter 698.8
Itsenko-Cushing syndrome (pituitary basophilism) 255.0
Ivemark's syndrome (asplenia with congenital
 heart disease) 759.0
Ivory bones 756.52
Ixodes 134.8
Ixodiasis 134.8

☑ **Additional Digit Required** — Refer to the Tabular List for Digit Selection   ▽ **Subterms under main terms may continue to next column or page**

168 — Volume 2   ►◄ **Revised Text**   ● **New Line** ▲ **Revised Code**   **2015 ICD-9-CM**

J

Jaccoud's nodular fibrositis, chronic (Jaccoud's syndrome) 714.4
Jackson's
  membrane 751.4
  paralysis or syndrome 344.89
  veil 751.4
Jacksonian
  epilepsy (see also Epilepsy) 345.5 ☑
  seizures (focal) (see also Epilepsy) 345.5 ☑
Jacob's ulcer (M8090/3) — see Neoplasm, skin, malignant, by site
Jacquet's dermatitis (diaper dermatitis) 691.0
Jadassohn's
  blue nevus (M8780/0) — see Neoplasm, skin, benign
  disease (maculopapular erythroderma) 696.2
  intraepidermal epithelioma (M8096/0) — see Neoplasm, skin, benign
Jadassohn-Lewandowski syndrome (pachyonychia congenita) 757.5
Jadassohn-Pellizari's disease (anetoderma) 701.3
Jadassohn-Tièche nevus (M8780/0) — see Neoplasm, skin, benign
Jaffe-Lichtenstein (-Uehlinger) syndrome 252.01
Jahnke's syndrome (encephalocutaneous angiomatosis) 759.6
Jakob-Creutzfeldt disease (CJD) (syndrome) 046.19
  with dementia
    with behavioral disturbance 046.19 [294.11]
    without behavioral disturbance 046.19 [294.10]
  familial 046.19
  iatrogenic 046.19
  specified NEC 046.19
  sporadic 046.19
  variant (vCJD) 046.11
    with dementia
      with behavioral disturbance 046.11 [294.11]
      without behavioral disturbance 046.11 [294.10]
Jaksch (-Luzet) disease or syndrome (pseudoleukemia infantum) 285.8
Jamaican
  neuropathy 349.82
  paraplegic tropical ataxic-spastic syndrome 349.82
Janet's disease (psychasthenia) 300.89
Janiceps 759.4
Jansky-Bielschowsky amaurotic familial idiocy 330.1
Japanese
  B type encephalitis 062.0
  river fever 081.2
  seven-day fever 100.89
Jaundice (yellow) 782.4
  acholuric (familial) (splenomegalic) (see also Spherocytosis) 282.0
    acquired 283.9
  breast milk 774.39
  catarrhal (acute) 070.1
    with hepatic coma 070.0
    chronic 571.9
    epidemic — see Jaundice, epidemic
  cholestatic (benign) 782.4
  chronic idiopathic 277.4
  epidemic (catarrhal) 070.1
    with hepatic coma 070.0
    leptospiral 100.0
    spirochetal 100.0
  febrile (acute) 070.1
    with hepatic coma 070.0
    leptospiral 100.0
    spirochetal 100.0
  fetus or newborn 774.6
    due to or associated with
      ABO
        absence or deficiency of enzyme system for bilirubin conjugation (congenital) 774.39

Jaundice — continued
  fetus or newborn — continued
    due to or associated with — continued
      antibodies 773.1
      blood group incompatibility NEC 773.2
      breast milk inhibitors to conjugation 774.39
        associated with preterm delivery 774.2
      bruising 774.1
      Crigler-Najjar syndrome 277.4 [774.31]
      delayed conjugation 774.30
        associated with preterm delivery 774.2
        development 774.39
      drugs or toxins transmitted from mother 774.1
      G-6-PD deficiency 282.2 [774.0]
      galactosemia 271.1 [774.5]
      Gilbert's syndrome 277.4 [774.31]
      hepatocellular damage 774.4
      hereditary hemolytic anemia (see also Anemia, hemolytic) 282.9 [774.0]
      hypothyroidism, congenital 243 [774.31]
      incompatibility, maternal/fetal 773.1
      incompatibility, maternal/fetal NEC 773.2
      infection 774.1
      inspissated bile syndrome 774.4
      isoimmunization 773.1
      isoimmunization NEC 773.2
      mucoviscidosis 277.01 [774.5]
      obliteration of bile duct, congenital 751.61 [774.5]
      polycythemia 774.1
      preterm delivery 774.2
      red cell defect 282.9 [774.0]
      Rh
        antibodies 773.0
        incompatibility, maternal/fetal 773.0
        isoimmunization 773.0
      spherocytosis (congenital) 282.0 [774.0]
      swallowed maternal blood 774.1
    physiological NEC 774.6
  from injection, inoculation, infusion, or transfusion (blood) (plasma) (serum) (other substance) (onset within 8 months after administration) — see Hepatitis, viral
  Gilbert's (familial nonhemolytic) 277.4
  hematogenous 283.9
  hemolytic (acquired) 283.9
    congenital (see also Spherocytosis) 282.0
  hemorrhagic (acute) 100.0
    leptospiral 100.0
    newborn 776.0
    spirochetal 100.0
  hepatocellular 573.8
  homologous (serum) — see Hepatitis, viral
  idiopathic, chronic 277.4
  infectious (acute) (subacute) 070.1
    with hepatic coma 070.0
    leptospiral 100.0
    spirochetal 100.0
  leptospiral 100.0
  malignant (see also Necrosis, liver) 570
  newborn (physiological) (see also Jaundice, fetus or newborn) 774.6
  nonhemolytic, congenital familial (Gilbert's) 277.4
  nuclear, newborn (see also Kernicterus of newborn) 774.7
  obstructive NEC (see also Obstruction, biliary) 576.8
  postimmunization — see Hepatitis, viral
  posttransfusion — see Hepatitis, viral
  regurgitation (see also Obstruction, biliary) 576.8

Jaundice — continued
  serum (homologous) (prophylactic) (therapeutic) — see Hepatitis, viral
  spirochetal (hemorrhagic) 100.0
  symptomatic 782.4
    newborn 774.6
Jaw — see condition
Jaw-blinking 374.43
  congenital 742.8
Jaw-winking phenomenon or syndrome 742.8
Jealousy
  alcoholic 291.5
  childhood 313.3
  sibling 313.3
Jejunitis — see also Enteritis 558.9
Jejunostomy status V44.4
Jejunum, jejunal — see condition
Jensen's disease 363.05
Jericho boil 085.1
Jerks, myoclonic 333.2
Jervell-Lange-Nielsen syndrome 426.82
Jeune's disease or syndrome (asphyxiating thoracic dystrophy) 756.4
Jigger disease 134.1
Job's syndrome (chronic granulomatous disease) 288.1
Jod-Basedow phenomenon 242.8 ☑
Johnson-Stevens disease (erythema multiforme exudativum) 695.13
Joint — see also condition
  Charcôt's 094.0 [713.5]
  false 733.82
  flail — see Flail, joint
  mice — see Loose, body, joint, by site
  sinus to bone 730.9 ☑
  von Gies' 095.8
Jordan's anomaly or syndrome 288.2
Josephs-Diamond-Blackfan anemia (congenital hypoplastic) 284.01
Joubert syndrome 759.89
Jumpers' knee 727.2
Jungle yellow fever 060.0
Jüngling's disease (sarcoidosis) 135
Junin virus hemorrhagic fever 078.7
Juvenile — see also condition
  delinquent 312.9
    group (see also Disturbance, conduct) 312.2 ☑
    neurotic 312.4

K

Kabuki syndrome 759.89
Kahler (-Bozzolo) disease (multiple myeloma) (M9730/3) 203.0 ☑
Kakergasia 300.9
Kakke 265.0
Kala-azar (Indian) (infantile) (Mediterranean) (Sudanese) 085.0
Kalischer's syndrome (encephalocutaneous angiomatosis) 759.6
Kallmann's syndrome (hypogonadotropic hypogonadism with anosmia) 253.4
Kanner's syndrome (autism) — see also Psychosis, childhood 299.0 ☑
Kaolinosis 502
Kaposi's
  disease 757.33
    lichen ruber 696.4
      acuminatus 696.4
      moniliformis 697.8
    xeroderma pigmentosum 757.33
  sarcoma (M9140/3) 176.9
    adipose tissue 176.1
    aponeurosis 176.1
    artery 176.1
    associated herpesvirus infection 058.89
    blood vessel 176.1
    bursa 176.1
    connective tissue 176.1
    external genitalia 176.8
    fascia 176.1
    fatty tissue 176.1
    fibrous tissue 176.1
    gastrointestinal tract NEC 176.3
    ligament 176.1

Kaposi's — continued
  sarcoma — continued
    lung 176.4
    lymph
      gland(s) 176.5
      node(s) 176.5
    lymphatic(s) NEC 176.1
    muscle (skeletal) 176.1
    oral cavity NEC 176.8
    palate 176.2
    scrotum 176.8
    skin 176.0
    soft tissue 176.1
    specified site NEC 176.8
    subcutaneous tissue 176.1
    synovia 176.1
    tendon (sheath) 176.1
    vein 176.1
    vessel 176.1
    viscera NEC 176.9
    vulva 176.8
  varicelliform eruption 054.0
  vaccinia 999.0
Kartagener's syndrome or triad (sinusitis, bronchiectasis, situs inversus) 759.3
Kasabach-Merritt syndrome (capillary hemangioma associated with thrombocytopenic purpura) 287.39
Kaschin-Beck disease (endemic polyarthritis) — see Disease, Kaschin-Beck
Kast's syndrome (dyschondroplasia with hemangiomas) 756.4
Katatonia — see Catatonia
Katayama disease or fever 120.2
Kathisophobia 781.0
Kawasaki disease 446.1
Kayser-Fleischer ring (cornea) (pseudosclerosis) 275.1 [371.14]
Kaznelson's syndrome (congenital hypoplastic anemia) 284.01
Kearns-Sayre syndrome 277.87
Kedani fever 081.2
Kelis 701.4
Kelly (-Patterson) syndrome (sideropenic dysphagia) 280.8
Keloid, cheloid 701.4
  Addison's (morphea) 701.0
  cornea 371.00
  Hawkins' 701.4
  scar 701.4
Keloma 701.4
Kenya fever 082.1
Keratectasia 371.71
  congenital 743.41
Keratinization NEC
  alveolar ridge mucosa
    excessive 528.72
    minimal 528.71
Keratitis (nodular) (nonulcerative) (simple) (zonular) NEC 370.9
  with ulceration (see also Ulcer, cornea) 370.00
  actinic 370.24
  arborescens 054.42
  areolar 370.22
  bullosa 370.8
  deep — see Keratitis, interstitial
  dendritic(a) 054.42
  desiccation 370.34
  diffuse interstitial 370.52
  disciform(is) 054.43
    varicella 052.7 [370.44]
  epithelialis vernalis 372.13 [370.32]
  exposure 370.34
  filamentary 370.23
  gonococcal (congenital) (prenatal) 098.43
  herpes, herpetic (simplex) NEC 054.43
    zoster 053.21
  hypopyon 370.04
  in
    chickenpox 052.7 [370.44]
    exanthema (see also Exanthem) 057.9 [370.44]
    paravaccinia (see also Paravaccinia) 051.9 [370.44]

☑ **Additional Digit Required** — Refer to the Tabular List for Digit Selection   ▽ **Subterms under main terms may continue to next column or page**

Keratitis — *continued*
  in — *continued*
    smallpox (*see also* Smallpox)
      050.9 [*370.44*]
    vernal conjunctivitis 372.13 [*370.32*]
  interstitial (nonsyphilitic) 370.50
    with ulcer (*see also* Ulcer, cornea) 370.00
    diffuse 370.52
    herpes, herpetic (simplex) 054.43
      zoster 053.21
    syphilitic (congenital) (hereditary) 090.3
    tuberculous (*see also* Tuberculosis)
      017.3 ☑ [*370.59*]
  lagophthalmic 370.34
  macular 370.22
  neuroparalytic 370.35
  neurotrophic 370.35
  nummular 370.22
  oyster-shuckers' 370.8
  parenchymatous — *see* Keratitis, interstitial
  petrificans 370.8
  phlyctenular 370.31
  postmeasles 055.71
  punctata, punctate 370.21
    leprosa 030.0 [*370.21*]
    profunda 090.3
    superficial (Thygeson's) 370.21
  purulent 370.8
  pustuliformis profunda 090.3
  rosacea 695.3 [*370.49*]
  sclerosing 370.54
  specified type NEC 370.8
  stellate 370.22
  striate 370.22
  superficial 370.20
    with conjunctivitis (*see also* Keratocon-
      junctivitis) 370.40
    punctate (Thygeson's) 370.21
  suppurative 370.8
  syphilitic (congenital) (prenatal) 090.3
  trachomatous 076.1
    late effect 139.1
  tuberculous (phlyctenular) (see also Tuber-
    culosis) 017.3 ☑ [*370.31*]
  ulcerated (*see also* Ulcer, cornea) 370.00
  vesicular 370.8
  welders' 370.24
  xerotic (*see also* Keratomalacia) 371.45
    vitamin A deficiency 264.4
Keratoacanthoma 238.2
Keratocele 371.72
Keratoconjunctivitis — *see also* Keratitis
    370.40
  adenovirus type 8 077.1
  epidemic 077.1
  exposure 370.34
  gonococcal 098.43
  herpetic (simplex) 054.43
    zoster 053.21
  in
    chickenpox 052.7 [*370.44*]
    exanthema (*see also* Exanthem)
      057.9 [*370.44*]
    paravaccinia (*see also* Paravaccinia)
      051.9 [*370.44*]
    smallpox (*see also* Smallpox)
      050.9 [*370.44*]
  infectious 077.1
  neurotrophic 370.35
  phlyctenular 370.31
  postmeasles 055.71
  shipyard 077.1
  sicca (Sjögren's syndrome) 710.2
    not in Sjögren's syndrome 370.33
  specified type NEC 370.49
  tuberculous (phlyctenular) (see also Tuber-
    culosis) 017.3 ☑ [*370.31*]
Keratoconus 371.60
  acute hydrops 371.62
  congenital 743.41
  stable 371.61
Keratocyst (dental) 526.0
Keratoderma, keratodermia (congenital)
    (palmaris et plantaris) (symmetrical)
    757.39
  acquired 701.1

Keratoderma, keratodermia — *continued*
  blennorrhagica 701.1
    gonococcal 098.81
  climacterium 701.1
  eccentrica 757.39
  gonorrheal 098.81
  punctata 701.1
  tylodes, progressive 701.1
Keratodermatocele 371.72
Keratoglobus 371.70
  congenital 743.41
    associated with buphthalmos 743.22
Keratohemia 371.12
Keratoiritis — *see also* Iridocyclitis 364.3
  syphilitic 090.3
  tuberculous (*see also* Tuberculosis)
    017.3 ☑ [*364.11*]
Keratolysis exfoliativa (congenital) 757.39
  acquired 695.89
  neonatorum 757.39
Keratoma 701.1
  congenital 757.39
  malignum congenitale 757.1
  palmaris et plantaris hereditarium 757.39
  senile 702.0
Keratomalacia 371.45
  vitamin A deficiency 264.4
Keratomegaly 743.41
Keratomycosis 111.1
  nigricans (palmaris) 111.1
Keratopathy 371.40
  band (*see also* Keratitis) 371.43
  bullous (*see also* Keratitis) 371.23
  degenerative (*see also* Degeneration,
    cornea) 371.40
    hereditary (*see also* Dystrophy, cornea)
      371.50
  discrete colliquative 371.49
Keratoscleritis, tuberculous — *see also* Tuber-
    culosis 017.3 ☑ [*370.31*]
Keratosis 701.1
  actinic 702.0
  arsenical 692.4
  blennorrhagica 701.1
    gonococcal 098.81
  congenital (any type) 757.39
  ear (middle) (*see also* Cholesteatoma) 385.30
  female genital (external) 629.89
  follicularis 757.39
    acquired 701.1
    congenital (acneiformis) (Siemens')
      757.39
    spinulosa (decalvans) 757.39
    vitamin A deficiency 264.8
  follicular, vitamin A deficiency 264.8
    gonococcal 098.81
  larynx, laryngeal 478.79
  male genital (external) 608.89
  middle ear (*see also* Cholesteatoma) 385.30
  nigricans 701.2
    congenital 757.39
  obturans 380.21
  oral epithelium
    residual ridge mucosa
      excessive 528.72
      minimal 528.71
  palmaris et plantaris (symmetrical) 757.39
  penile 607.89
  pharyngeus 478.29
  pilaris 757.39
    acquired 701.1
  punctata (palmaris et plantaris) 701.1
  scrotal 608.89
  seborrheic 702.19
    inflamed 702.11
  senilis 702.0
  solar 702.0
  suprafollicularis 757.39
  tonsillaris 478.29
  vagina 623.1
  vegetans 757.39
  vitamin A deficiency 264.8
Kerato-uveitis — *see also* Iridocyclitis 364.3
Keraunoparalysis 994.0
Kerion (celsi) 110.0

Kernicterus of newborn (not due to isoimmu-
    nization) 774.7
  due to isoimmunization (conditions classifi-
    able to 773.0–773.2) 773.4
Ketoacidosis 276.2
  diabetic 250.1 ☑
    due to secondary diabetes 249.1 ☑
Ketonuria 791.6
  branched-chain, intermittent 270.3
Ketosis 276.2
  diabetic 250.1 ☑
    due to secondary diabetes 249.1 ☑
Kidney — *see* condition
Kienböck's
  disease 732.3
    adult 732.8
  osteochondrosis 732.3
Kimmelstiel (-Wilson) disease or syndrome
    (intercapillary glomerulosclerosis)
    250.4 ☑ [*581.81*]
  due to secondary diabetes 249.4 ☑ [*581.81*]
Kink, kinking
  appendix 543.9
  artery 447.1
  cystic duct, congenital 751.61
  hair (acquired) 704.2
  ileum or intestine (*see also* Obstruction, in-
    testine) 560.9
  Lane's (*see also* Obstruction, intestine) 560.9
  organ or site, congenital NEC — *see*
    Anomaly, specified type NEC, by site
  ureter (pelvic junction) 593.3
    congenital 753.20
  vein(s) 459.2
    caval 459.2
    peripheral 459.2
Kinnier Wilson's disease (hepatolenticular
    degeneration) 275.1
Kissing
  osteophytes 721.5
  spine 721.5
  vertebra 721.5
Klauder's syndrome (erythema multiforme,
    exudativum) 695.19
Klebs' disease — *see also* Nephritis 583.9
Kleine-Levin syndrome 327.13
Klein-Waardenburg syndrome (ptosisepican-
    thus) 270.2
Kleptomania 312.32
Klinefelter's syndrome 758.7
Klinger's disease 446.4
Klippel's disease 723.8
Klippel-Feil disease or syndrome (brevicollis)
    756.16
Klippel-Trenaunay syndrome 759.89
Klumpke (-Déjérine) palsy, paralysis (birth)
    (newborn) 767.6
Klüver-Bucy (-Terzian) syndrome 310.0
Knee — *see* condition
Knifegrinders' rot — *see also* Tuberculosis
    011.4 ☑
Knock-knee (acquired) 736.41
  congenital 755.64
Knot
  intestinal, syndrome (volvulus) 560.2
  umbilical cord (true) 663.2 ☑
    affecting fetus or newborn 762.5
Knots, surfer 919.8
  infected 919.9
Knotting (of)
  hair 704.2
  intestine 560.2
Knuckle pads (Garrod's) 728.79
Köbner's disease (epidermolysis bullosa)
    757.39
Koch's
  infection (*see also* Tuberculosis, pulmonary)
    011.9 ☑
  relapsing fever 087.9
Koch-Weeks conjunctivitis 372.03
Koenig-Wichman disease (pemphigus) 694.4
Köhler's disease (osteochondrosis) 732.5
  first (osteochondrosis juvenilis) 732.5
  second (Freiburg's infarction, metatarsal
    head) 732.5
  patellar 732.4

Köhler's disease — *continued*
  tarsal navicular (bone) (osteoarthrosis juve-
    nilis) 732.5
Köhler-Mouchet disease (osteoarthrosis juve-
    nilis) 732.5
**Köhler-Pellegrini-Stieda disease or syn-
    drome** (calcification, knee joint) 726.62
Koilonychia 703.8
  congenital 757.5
Kojevnikov's, Kojewnikoff's epilepsy — *see
    also* Epilepsy 345.7 ☑
König's
  disease (osteochondritis dissecans) 732.7
  syndrome 564.89
Koniophthisis — *see also* Tuberculosis
    011.4 ☑
Koplik's spots 055.9
Kopp's asthma 254.8
Korean hemorrhagic fever 078.6
**Korsakoff (-Wernicke) disease, psychosis,
    or syndrome** (nonalcoholic) 294.0
  alcoholic 291.1
Korsakov's disease — *see* Korsakoff's disease
Korsakow's disease — *see* Korsakoff's disease
Kostmann's disease or syndrome (infantile
    genetic agranulocytosis) 288.01
Krabbe's
  disease (leukodystrophy) 330.0
  syndrome
    congenital muscle hypoplasia 756.89
    cutaneocerebral angioma 759.6
Kraepelin-Morel disease — *see also*
    Schizophrenia 295.9 ☑
Kraft-Weber-Dimitri disease 759.6
Kraurosis
  ani 569.49
  penis 607.0
  vagina 623.8
  vulva 624.09
Kreotoxism 005.9
Krukenberg's
  spindle 371.13
  tumor (M8490/6) 198.6
Kufs' disease 330.1
Kugelberg-Welander disease 335.11
Kuhnt-Junius degeneration or disease
    362.52
Kulchitsky's cell carcinoma (carcinoid tumor
    of intestine) 259.2
Kümmell's disease or spondylitis 721.7
Kundrat's disease (lymphosarcoma) 200.1 ☑
Kunekune — *see* Dermatophytosis
Kunkel syndrome (lupoid hepatitis) 571.49
Kupffer cell sarcoma (M9124/3) 155.0
Kuru 046.0
Kussmaul's
  coma (diabetic) 250.3 ☑
    due to secondary diabetes 249.3 ☑
  disease (polyarteritis nodosa) 446.0
  respiration (air hunger) 786.09
Kwashiorkor (marasmus type) 260
Kyasanur Forest disease 065.2
Kyphoscoliosis, kyphoscoliotic (acquired) —
    see also Scoliosis 737.30
  congenital 756.19
  due to radiation 737.33
  heart (disease) 416.1
  idiopathic 737.30
    infantile
      progressive 737.32
      resolving 737.31
  late effect of rickets 268.1 [*737.43*]
  specified NEC 737.39
  thoracogenic 737.34
  tuberculous (*see also* Tuberculosis)
    015.0 ☑ [*737.43*]
Kyphosis, kyphotic (acquired) (postural)
    737.10
  adolescent postural 737.0
  congenital 756.19
  dorsalis juvenilis 732.0
  due to or associated with
    Charcôt-Marie-Tooth disease
      356.1 [*737.41*]
    mucopolysaccharidosis 277.5 [*737.41*]
    neurofibromatosis 237.71 [*737.41*]

☑ Additional Digit Required — Refer to the Tabular List for Digit Selection   ▽ Subterms under main terms may continue to next column or page

170 — Volume 2   ▶◀ Revised Text   ● New Line   ▲ Revised Code   2015 ICD-9-CM

Kyphosis, kyphotic — *continued*
  due to or associated with — *continued*
    osteitis
      deformans 731.0 *[737.41]*
      fibrosa cystica 252.01 *[737.41]*
    osteoporosis (*see also* Osteoporosis)
      733.0 ☑ *[737.41]*
    poliomyelitis (*see also* Poliomyelitis)
      138 *[737.41]*
    radiation 737.11
    tuberculosis (*see also* Tuberculosis)
      015.0 ☑ *[737.41]*
  Kümmell's 721.7
  late effect of rickets 268.1 *[737.41]*
  Morquio-Brailsford type (spinal)
    277.5 *[737.41]*
  pelvis 738.6
  postlaminectomy 737.12
  specified cause NEC 737.19
  syphilitic, congenital 090.5 *[737.41]*
  tuberculous (*see also* Tuberculosis)
    015.0 ☑ *[737.41]*
Kyrle's disease (hyperkeratosis follicularis in cutem penetrans) 701.1

L

Labia, labium — *see* condition
Labiated hymen 752.49
Labile
  blood pressure 796.2
  emotions, emotionality 301.3
  vasomotor system 443.9
Lability, emotional 799.24
Labioglossal paralysis 335.22
Labium leporinum — *see also* Cleft, lip 749.10
Labor — *see also* Delivery
  with complications — *see* Delivery, complicated
  abnormal NEC 661.9 ☑
    affecting fetus or newborn 763.7
  arrested active phase 661.1 ☑
    affecting fetus or newborn 763.7
  desultory 661.2 ☑
    affecting fetus or newborn 763.7
  dyscoordinate 661.4 ☑
    affecting fetus or newborn 763.7
  early onset (22-36 weeks gestation)
    644.2 ☑
  failed
    induction 659.1 ☑
      mechanical 659.0 ☑
      medical 659.1 ☑
      surgical 659.0 ☑
    trial (vaginal delivery) 660.6 ☑
  false 644.1 ☑
  forced or induced, affecting fetus or newborn 763.89
  hypertonic 661.4 ☑
    affecting fetus or newborn 763.7
  hypotonic 661.2 ☑
    affecting fetus or newborn 763.7
    primary 661.0 ☑
      affecting fetus or newborn 763.7
    secondary 661.1 ☑
      affecting fetus or newborn 763.7
  incoordinate 661.4 ☑
    affecting fetus or newborn 763.7
  irregular 661.2 ☑
    affecting fetus or newborn 763.7
  long — *see* Labor, prolonged
  missed (at or near term) 656.4 ☑
  obstructed NEC 660.9 ☑
    affecting fetus or newborn 763.1
    due to female genital mutilation
      660.8 ☑
    specified cause NEC 660.8 ☑
      affecting fetus or newborn 763.1
  pains, spurious 644.1 ☑
  precipitate 661.3 ☑
    affecting fetus or newborn 763.6
  premature 644.2 ☑
    threatened 644.0 ☑
  prolonged or protracted 662.1 ☑
    first stage 662.0 ☑
      affecting fetus or newborn 763.89

Labor — *see also* Delivery — *continued*
  prolonged or protracted — *continued*
    second stage 662.2 ☑
      affecting fetus or newborn 763.89
    affecting fetus or newborn 763.89
  threatened NEC 644.1 ☑
  undelivered 644.1 ☑
Labored breathing — *see also* Hyperventilation 786.09
Labyrinthitis (inner ear) (destructive) (latent)
  386.30
  circumscribed 386.32
  diffuse 386.31
  focal 386.32
  purulent 386.33
  serous 386.31
  suppurative 386.33
  syphilitic 095.8
  toxic 386.34
  viral 386.35
Laceration — *see also* Wound, open, by site
  accidental, complicating surgery 998.2
  Achilles tendon 845.09
    with open wound 892.2
  anus (sphincter) 879.6
    with
      abortion — *see* Abortion, by type,
        with damage to pelvic organs
      ectopic pregnancy (*see also* categories 633.0–633.9) 639.2
      molar pregnancy (*see also* categories 630–632) 639.2
    complicated 879.7
    complicating delivery (healed) (old)
      654.8 ☑
    with laceration of anal or rectal mucosa 664.3 ☑
    not associated with third-degree
      perineal laceration 664.6 ☑
    following
      abortion 639.2
      ectopic or molar pregnancy 639.2
    nontraumatic, nonpuerperal (healed)
      (old) 569.43
  bladder (urinary)
    with
      abortion — *see* Abortion, by type,
        with damage to pelvic organs
      ectopic pregnancy (*see also* categories 633.0–633.9) 639.2
      molar pregnancy (*see also* categories 630–632) 639.2
    following
      abortion 639.2
      ectopic or molar pregnancy 639.2
    obstetrical trauma 665.5 ☑
  blood vessel — *see* Injury, blood vessel, by site
  bowel
    with
      abortion — *see* Abortion, by type,
        with damage to pelvic organs
      ectopic pregnancy (*see also* categories 633.0–633.9) 639.2
      molar pregnancy (*see also* categories 630–632) 639.2
    following
      abortion 639.2
      ectopic or molar pregnancy 639.2
    obstetrical trauma 665.5 ☑

Laceration — *see also* Wound, open, by site — *continued*
  brain (cerebral) (membrane) (with hemorrhage) 851.8 ☑

> *Note* — Use the following fifth-digit subclassification with categories *851–854:*
>
> 0   *unspecified state of consciousness*
>
> 1   *with no loss of consciousness*
>
> 2   *with brief [less than one hour] loss of consciousness*
>
> 3   *with moderate [1–24 hours] loss of consciousness*
>
> 4   *with prolonged [more than 24 hours] loss of consciousness and return to pre–existing conscious level*
>
> 5   *with prolonged [more than 24 hours] loss of consciousness, without return to pre–existing conscious level*
>
> *Use fifth-digit 5 to designate when a patient is unconscious and dies before regaining consciousness, regardless of the duration of the loss of consciousness*
>
> 6   *with loss of consciousness of unspecified duration*
>
> 9   *with concussion, unspecified*

      with
        open intracranial wound 851.9 ☑
        skull fracture — *see* Fracture, skull, by site
      cerebellum 851.6 ☑
        with open intracranial wound
          851.7 ☑
      cortex 851.2 ☑
        with open intracranial wound
          851.3 ☑
      during birth 767.0
      stem 851.6 ☑
        with open intracranial wound
          851.7 ☑
    broad ligament
      with
        abortion — *see* Abortion, by type,
          with damage to pelvic organs
        ectopic pregnancy (*see also* categories 633.0–633.9) 639.2
        molar pregnancy (*see also* categories 630–632) 639.2
      following
        abortion 639.2
        ectopic or molar pregnancy 639.2
      nontraumatic 620.6
      obstetrical trauma 665.6 ☑
      syndrome (nontraumatic) 620.6
    capsule, joint — *see* Sprain, by site
    cardiac — *see* Laceration, heart
    causing eversion of cervix uteri (old) 622.0
    central, complicating delivery 664.4 ☑
    cerebellum — *see* Laceration, brain, cerebellum
    cerebral (*see also* Laceration, brain)
      during birth 767.0
    cervix (uteri)
      with
        abortion — *see* Abortion, by type,
          with damage to pelvic organs
        ectopic pregnancy (*see also* categories 633.0–633.9) 639.2
        molar pregnancy (*see also* categories 630–632) 639.2
      following
        abortion 639.2
        ectopic or molar pregnancy 639.2
      nonpuerperal, nontraumatic 622.3
      obstetrical trauma (current) 665.3 ☑
      old (postpartal) 622.3
      traumatic — *see* Injury, internal, cervix
    chordae heart 429.5
    complicated 879.9

Laceration — *see also* Wound, open, by site — *continued*
  cornea — *see* Laceration, eyeball
    superficial 918.1
  cortex (cerebral) — *see* Laceration, brain, cortex
  esophagus 530.89
  eye(s) — *see* Laceration, ocular
  eyeball NEC 871.4
    with prolapse or exposure of intraocular tissue 871.1
    penetrating — *see* Penetrating wound, eyeball
    specified as without prolapse of intraocular tissue 871.0
  eyelid NEC 870.8
    full thickness 870.1
      involving lacrimal passages 870.2
    skin (and periocular area) 870.0
      penetrating — *see* Penetrating wound, orbit
  fourchette
    with
      abortion — *see* Abortion, by type,
        with damage to pelvic organs
      ectopic pregnancy (*see also* categories 633.0–633.9) 639.2
      molar pregnancy (*see also* categories 630–632) 639.2
    complicating delivery 664.0 ☑
    following
      abortion 639.2
      ectopic or molar pregnancy 639.2
  heart (without penetration of heart chambers) 861.02
    with
      open wound into thorax 861.12
      penetration of heart chambers
        861.03
        with open wound into thorax
          861.13
  hernial sac — *see* Hernia, by site
  internal organ (abdomen) (chest) (pelvis)
    NEC — *see* Injury, internal, by site
    NEC — *see* Injury, internal, by site
  kidney (parenchyma) 866.02
    with
      complete disruption of parenchyma
        (rupture) 866.03
        with open wound into cavity
          866.13
      open wound into cavity 866.12
  labia
    complicating delivery 664.0 ☑
  ligament (*see also* Sprain, by site)
    with open wound — *see* Wound, open, by site
  liver 864.05
    with open wound into cavity 864.15
    major (disruption of hepatic parenchyma) 864.04
      with open wound into cavity 864.14
    minor (capsule only) 864.02
      with open wound into cavity 864.12
    moderate (involving parenchyma without major disruption) 864.03
      with open wound into cavity 864.13
    multiple 864.04
      with open wound into cavity
        864.14
    stellate 864.04
      with open wound into cavity 864.14
  lung 861.22
    with open wound into thorax 861.32
  meninges — *see* Laceration, brain
  meniscus (knee) (*see also* Tear, meniscus)
    836.2
    old 717.5
    site other than knee (*see also* Sprain, by site)
      old NEC (*see also* Disorder, cartilage, articular) 718.0 ☑
  muscle (*see also* Sprain, by site)
    with open wound — *see* Wound, open, by site
  myocardium — *see* Laceration, heart

Laceration — *see also* Wound, open, by site
— *continued*
nerve — *see* Injury, nerve, by site
ocular NEC (*see also* Laceration, eyeball)
871.4
adnexa NEC 870.8
penetrating 870.3
with foreign body 870.4
orbit (eye) 870.8
penetrating 870.3
with foreign body 870.4
pelvic
floor (muscles)
with
abortion — *see* Abortion, by type,
with damage to pelvic or-
gans
ectopic pregnancy (*see also* categories 633.0–633.9) 639.2
molar pregnancy (*see also* categories 630–632) 639.2
complicating delivery 664.1 ☑
following
abortion 639.2
ectopic or molar pregnancy 639.2
nonpuerperal 618.7
old (postpartal) 618.7
organ NEC
with
abortion — *see* Abortion, by type,
with damage to pelvic or-
gans
ectopic pregnancy (*see also* categories 633.0–633.9) 639.2
molar pregnancy (*see also* categories 630–632) 639.2
complicating delivery 665.5 ☑
affecting fetus or newborn 763.89
following
abortion 639.2
ectopic or molar pregnancy 639.2
obstetrical trauma 665.5 ☑
perineum, perineal (old) (postpartal) 618.7
with
abortion — *see* Abortion, by type,
with damage to pelvic floor
ectopic pregnancy (*see also* categories 633.0–633.9) 639.2
molar pregnancy (*see also* categories
630–632) 639.2
complicating delivery 664.4 ☑
first degree 664.0 ☑
second degree 664.1 ☑
third degree 664.2 ☑
fourth degree 664.3 ☑
anal sphincter (healed) (old) 654.8 ☑
not associated with third-degree
perineal laceration
664.6 ☑
sphincter (anal) (healed) (old)
654.8 ☑
not associated with third-degree perineal lacera-
tion 664.6 ☑
central 664.4 ☑
involving
anal sphincter 664.2 ☑
fourchette 664.0 ☑
hymen 664.0 ☑
labia 664.0 ☑
pelvic floor 664.1 ☑
perineal muscles 664.1 ☑
rectovaginal septum 664.2 ☑
with anal mucosa 664.3 ☑
skin 664.0 ☑
sphincter (anal) 664.2 ☑
with anal mucosa 664.3 ☑
vagina 664.0 ☑
vaginal muscles 664.1 ☑
vulva 664.0 ☑
secondary 674.2 ☑
following
abortion 639.2
ectopic or molar pregnancy 639.2
male 879.6

Laceration — *see also* Wound, open, by site
— *continued*
perineum, perineal — *continued*
male — *continued*
complicated 879.7
muscles, complicating delivery 664.1 ☑
nonpuerperal, current injury 879.6
complicated 879.7
secondary (postpartal) 674.2 ☑
peritoneum
with
abortion — *see* Abortion, by type,
with damage to pelvic organs
ectopic pregnancy (*see also* categories 633.0–633.9) 639.2
molar pregnancy (*see also* categories
630–632) 639.2
following
abortion 639.2
ectopic or molar pregnancy 639.2
obstetrical trauma 665.5 ☑
periurethral tissue
with
abortion — *see* Abortion, by type,
with damage to pelvic organs
ectopic pregnancy (*see also* categories 633.0–633.9) 639.2
molar pregnancy (*see also* categories
630–632) 639.2
following
abortion 639.2
ectopic or molar pregnancy 639.2
obstetrical trauma 664.8 ☑
rectovaginal (septum)
with
abortion — *see* Abortion, by type,
with damage to pelvic organs
ectopic pregnancy (*see also* categories 633.0–633.9) 639.2
molar pregnancy (*see also* categories
630–632) 639.2
complicating delivery 665.4 ☑
with perineum 664.2 ☑
involving anal or rectal mucosa
664.3 ☑
following
abortion 639.2
ectopic or molar pregnancy 639.2
nonpuerperal 623.4
old (postpartal) 623.4
spinal cord (meninges) (*see also* Injury,
spinal, by site)
due to injury at birth 767.4
fetus or newborn 767.4
spleen 865.09
with
disruption of parenchyma (massive)
865.04
with open wound into cavity
865.14
open wound into cavity 865.19
capsule (without disruption of
parenchyma) 865.02
with open wound into cavity 865.12
parenchyma 865.03
with open wound into cavity 865.13
massive disruption (rupture) 865.04
with open wound into cavity
865.14
tendon 848.9
with open wound — *see* Wound, open,
by site
Achilles 845.09
with open wound 892.2
lower limb NEC 844.9
with open wound NEC 894.2
upper limb NEC 840.9
with open wound NEC 884.2
tentorium cerebelli — *see* Laceration, brain,
cerebellum
tongue 873.64
complicated 873.74
urethra
with
abortion — *see* Abortion, by type,
with damage to pelvic organs

Laceration — *see also* Wound, open, by site
— *continued*
urethra — *continued*
with — *continued*
ectopic pregnancy (*see also* categories 633.0–633.9) 639.2
molar pregnancy (*see also* categories
630–632) 639.2
following
abortion 639.2
ectopic or molar pregnancy 639.2
nonpuerperal, nontraumatic 599.84
obstetrical trauma 665.5 ☑
uterus
with
abortion — *see* Abortion, by type,
with damage to pelvic organs
ectopic pregnancy (*see also* categories 633.0–633.9) 639.2
molar pregnancy (*see also* categories
630–632) 639.2
following
abortion 639.2
ectopic or molar pregnancy 639.2
nonpuerperal, nontraumatic 621.8
obstetrical trauma NEC 665.5 ☑
old (postpartal) 621.8
vagina
with
abortion — *see* Abortion, by type,
with damage to pelvic organs
ectopic pregnancy (*see also* categories 633.0–633.9) 639.2
molar pregnancy (*see also* categories
630–632) 639.2
perineal involvement, complicating
delivery 664.0 ☑
complicating delivery 665.4 ☑
first degree 664.0 ☑
second degree 664.1 ☑
third degree 664.2 ☑
fourth degree 664.3 ☑
high 665.4 ☑
muscles 664.1 ☑
sulcus 665.4 ☑
wall 665.4 ☑
following
abortion 639.2
ectopic or molar pregnancy 639.2
nonpuerperal, nontraumatic 623.4
old (postpartal) 623.4
valve, heart — *see* Endocarditis
vulva
with
abortion — *see* Abortion, by type,
with damage to pelvic organs
ectopic pregnancy (*see also* categories 633.0–633.9) 639.2
molar pregnancy (*see also* categories
630–632) 639.2
complicating delivery 664.0 ☑
following
abortion 639.2
ectopic or molar pregnancy 639.2
nonpuerperal, nontraumatic 624.4
old (postpartal) 624.4
Lachrymal — *see* condition
Lachrymonasal duct — *see* condition
Lack of
adequate intermaxillary vertical dimension
524.36
appetite (*see also* Anorexia) 783.0
care
in home V60.4
of adult 995.84
of infant (at or after birth) 995.52
coordination 781.3
development (*see also* Hypoplasia)
physiological in childhood 783.40
education V62.3
energy 780.79
financial resources V60.2
food 994.2
in environment V60.89
growth in childhood 783.43
heating V60.1

Lack of — *continued*
housing (permanent) (temporary) V60.0
adequate V60.1
material resources V60.2
medical attention 799.89
memory (*see also* Amnesia) 780.93
mild, following organic brain damage
310.89
ovulation 628.0
person able to render necessary care V60.4
physical exercise V69.0
physiologic development in childhood
783.40
posterior occlusal support 524.57
prenatal care in current pregnancy V23.7
shelter V60.0
sleep V69.4
water 994.3
Lacrimal — *see* condition
Lacrimation, abnormal — *see also* Epiphora
375.20
Lacrimonasal duct — *see* condition
Lactation, lactating (breast) (puerperal)
(postpartum)
defective 676.4 ☑
disorder 676.9 ☑
specified type NEC 676.8 ☑
excessive 676.6 ☑
failed 676.4 ☑
mastitis NEC 675.2 ☑
mother (care and/or examination) V24.1
nonpuerperal 611.6
suppressed 676.5 ☑
Lacticemia 271.3
excessive 276.2
Lactosuria 271.3
Lacunar skull 756.0
Laennec's cirrhosis (alcoholic) 571.2
nonalcoholic 571.5
Lafora's disease 333.2
Lagleyze-von Hippel disease (retinocerebral
angiomatosis) 759.6
Lag, lid (nervous) 374.41
Lagophthalmos (eyelid) (nervous) 374.20
cicatricial 374.23
keratitis (*see also* Keratitis) 370.34
mechanical 374.22
paralytic 374.21
La grippe — *see* Influenza
Lahore sore 085.1
Lakes, venous (cerebral) 437.8
Laki-Lorand factor deficiency — *see also* De-
fect, coagulation 286.3
Lalling 307.9
Lambliasis 007.1
Lame back 724.5
Lancereaux's diabetes (diabetes mellitus with
marked emaciation) 250.8 ☑ [261]
due to secondary diabetes 249.8 ☑ [261]
Landau-Kleffner syndrome 345.8 ☑
Landouzy-Déjérine dystrophy (fascioscapu-
lohumeral atrophy) 359.1
Landry's disease or paralysis 357.0
Landry-Guillain-Barré syndrome 357.0
Lane's
band 751.4
disease 569.89
kink (*see also* Obstruction, intestine) 560.9
Langdon Down's syndrome (mongolism)
758.0
Language abolition 784.69
Lanugo (persistent) 757.4
**Laparoscopic surgical procedure converted
to open procedure** V64.41
Lardaceous
degeneration (any site) 277.39
disease 277.39
kidney 277.39 [583.81]
liver 277.39
Large
baby (regardless of gestational age) 766.1
exceptionally (weight of 4500 grams or
more) 766.0
of diabetic mother 775.0
ear 744.22
fetus (*see also* Oversize, fetus)

☑ **Additional Digit Required — Refer to the Tabular List for Digit Selection**   ▽ **Subterms under main terms may continue to next column or page**

172 — Volume 2   ▶◀ Revised Text   ● New Line   ▲ Revised Code   **2015 ICD-9-CM**

Large — *continued*
  fetus (*see also* Oversize, fetus) — *contin-ued*
    causing disproportion 653.5 ☑
      with obstructed labor 660.1 ☑
    for dates
      fetus or newborn (regardless of gesta-tional age) 766.1
        affecting management of pregnancy 656.6 ☑
      exceptionally (weight of 4500 grams or more) 766.0
  physiological cup 743.57
  stature 783.9
  waxy liver 277.39
  white kidney — *see* Nephrosis
Larsen-Johansson disease (juvenile os-teopathia patellae) 732.4
Larsen's syndrome (flattened facies and mul-tiple congenital dislocations) 755.8
Larva migrans
  cutaneous NEC 126.9
    ancylostoma 126.9
  of Diptera in vitreous 128.0
  visceral NEC 128.0
Laryngeal — *see also* condition 786.2
  syncope 786.2
Laryngismus (acute) (infectious) (stridulous) 478.75
  congenital 748.3
  diphtheritic 032.3
Laryngitis (acute) (edematous) (fibrinous) (gangrenous) (infective) (infiltrative) (malignant) (membranous) (phleg-monous) (pneumococcal) (pseudomem-branous) (septic) (subglottic) (suppura-tive) (ulcerative) (viral) 464.00
  with
    influenza, flu, or grippe (*see also* Influen-za) 487.1
    obstruction 464.01
    tracheitis (*see also* Laryngotracheitis) 464.20
      with obstruction 464.21
      acute 464.20
        with obstruction 464.21
      chronic 476.1
  atrophic 476.0
  Borrelia vincentii 101
  catarrhal 476.0
  chronic 476.0
    with tracheitis (chronic) 476.1
    due to external agent — *see* Condition, respiratory, chronic, due to
  diphtheritic (membranous) 032.3
  due to external agent — *see* Inflammation, respiratory, upper, due to
  Hemophilus influenzae 464.00
    with obstruction 464.01
  H. influenzae 464.00
    with obstruction 464.01
  hypertrophic 476.0
  influenzal (*see also* Influenza) 487.1
  pachydermic 478.79
  sicca 476.0
  spasmodic 478.75
    acute 464.00
      with obstruction 464.01
  streptococcal 034.0
  stridulous 478.75
  syphilitic 095.8
    congenital 090.5
  tuberculous (*see also* Tuberculosis, larynx) 012.3 ☑
  Vincent's 101
Laryngocele (congenital) (ventricular) 748.3
Laryngofissure 478.79
  congenital 748.3
Laryngomalacia (congenital) 748.3
Laryngopharyngitis (acute) 465.0
  chronic 478.9
    due to external agent — *see* Condition, respiratory, chronic, due to
  due to external agent — *see* Inflammation, respiratory, upper, due to
  septic 034.0

Laryngoplegia — *see also* Paralysis, vocal cord 478.30
Laryngoptosis 478.79
Laryngospasm 478.75
  due to external agent — *see* Condition, respiratory, acute, due to
Laryngostenosis 478.74
  congenital 748.3
Laryngotracheitis (acute) (infectional) (viral) — *see also* Laryngitis 464.20
  with obstruction 464.21
  atrophic 476.1
  Borrelia vincenti 101
  catarrhal 476.1
  chronic 476.1
    due to external agent — *see* Condition, respiratory, chronic, due to
  diphtheritic (membranous) 032.3
  due to external agent — *see* Inflammation, respiratory, upper, due to
  H. influenzae 464.20
    with obstruction 464.21
  hypertrophic 476.1
  influenzal (*see also* Influenza) 487.1
  pachydermic 478.75
  sicca 476.1
  spasmodic 478.75
    acute 464.20
      with obstruction 464.21
  streptococcal 034.0
  stridulous 478.75
  syphilitic 095.8
    congenital 090.5
  tuberculous (*see also* Tuberculosis, larynx) 012.3 ☑
  Vincent's 101
Laryngotracheobronchitis — *see also* Bron-chitis 490
  acute 466.0
  chronic 491.8
  viral 466.0
Laryngotracheobronchopneumonitis — *see* Pneumonia, broncho-
Larynx, laryngeal — *see* condition
Lasègue's disease (persecution mania) 297.9
Lassa fever 078.89
Lassitude — *see also* Weakness 780.79
Late — *see also* condition
  effect(s) (of) (*see also* condition)
    abscess
      intracranial or intraspinal (conditions classifiable to 324) — *see* cat-egory 326
    adverse effect of drug, medicinal or bio-logical substance 909.5
    allergic reaction 909.9
    amputation
      postoperative (late) 997.60
      traumatic (injury classifiable to 885–887 and 895–897) 905.9
    burn (injury classifiable to 948–949) 906.9
      extremities NEC (injury classifiable to 943 or 945) 906.7
      hand or wrist (injury classifiable to 944) 906.6
      eye (injury classifiable to 940) 906.5
      face, head, and neck (injury classifi-able to 941) 906.5
      specified site NEC (injury classifiable to 942 and 946–947) 906.8
    cerebrovascular disease (conditions classifiable to 430–437) 438.9
      with
        alterations of sensations 438.6
        aphasia 438.11
        apraxia 438.81
        ataxia 438.84
        cognitive deficits 438.0
        disturbances of vision 438.7
        dysarthria 438.13
        dysphagia 438.82
        dysphasia 438.12
        facial droop 438.83
        facial weakness 438.83
        fluency disorder 438.14

Late — *see also* condition — *continued*
  effect(s) (*see also* condition) — *contin-ued*
    cerebrovascular disease — *contin-ued*
      with — *continued*
        hemiplegia/hemiparesis
          affecting
            dominant side 438.21
            nondominant side 438.22
            unspecified side 438.20
        monoplegia of lower limb
          affecting
            dominant side 438.41
            nondominant side 438.42
            unspecified side 438.40
        monoplegia of upper limb
          affecting
            dominant side 438.31
            nondominant side 438.32
            unspecified side 438.30
        paralytic syndrome NEC
          affecting
            bilateral 438.53
            dominant side 438.51
            nondominant side 438.52
            unspecified side 438.50
        speech and language deficit 438.10
          specified type NEC 438.19
        stuttering 438.14
        vertigo 438.85
      specified type NEC 438.89
    childbirth complication(s) 677
    complication(s) of
      childbirth 677
      delivery 677
      pregnancy 677
      puerperium 677
      surgical and medical care (conditions classifiable to 996–999) 909.3
      trauma (conditions classifiable to 958) 908.6
    contusion (injury classifiable to 920–924) 906.3
    crushing (injury classifiable to 925–929) 906.4
    delivery complication(s) 677
    dislocation (injury classifiable to 830–839) 905.6
    encephalitis or encephalomyelitis (con-ditions classifiable to 323) — *see* category 326
      in infectious diseases 139.8
      viral (conditions classifiable to 049.8, 049.9, 062–064) 139.0
    external cause NEC (conditions classifi-able to 995) 909.9
      certain conditions classifiable to cat-egories 991-994 909.4
    foreign body in orifice (injury classifiable to 930–939) 908.5
    fracture (multiple) (injury classifiable to 828–829) 905.5
      extremity
        lower (injury classifiable to 821–827) 905.4
          neck of femur (injury classifi-able to 820) 905.3
        upper (injury classifiable to 810–819) 905.2
      face and skull (injury classifiable to 800–804) 905.0
      skull and face (injury classifiable to 800–804) 905.0
      spine and trunk (injury classifiable to 805 and 807–809) 905.1
        with spinal cord lesion (injury classifiable to 806) 907.2
    infection
      pyogenic, intracranial — *see* catego-ry 326
    infectious diseases (conditions classifi-able to 001–136) NEC 139.8
    injury (injury classifiable to 959) 908.9

Late — *see also* condition — *continued*
  effect(s) (*see also* condition) — *contin-ued*
    injury — *continued*
      blood vessel 908.3
        abdomen and pelvis (injury classi-fiable to 902) 908.4
        extremity (injury classifiable to 903–904) 908.3
        head and neck (injury classifiable to 900) 908.3
        intracranial (injury classifiable to 850–854) 907.0
          with skull fracture 905.0
        thorax (injury classifiable to 901) 908.4
      internal organ NEC (injury classifiable to 867 and 869) 908.2
        abdomen (injury classifiable to 863–866 and 868) 908.1
        thorax (injury classifiable to 860–862) 908.0
      intracranial (injury classifiable to 850–854) 907.0
        with skull fracture (injury classifi-able to 800–801 and 803–804) 905.0
      nerve NEC (injury classifiable to 957) 907.9
        cranial (injury classifiable to 950–951) 907.1
        peripheral NEC (injury classifiable to 957) 907.9
          lower limb and pelvic girdle (injury classifiable to 956) 907.5
          upper limb and shoulder gir-dle (injury classifiable to 955) 907.4
        roots and plexus(es), spinal (in-jury classifiable to 953) 907.3
        trunk (injury classifiable to 954) 907.3
      spinal
        cord (injury classifiable to 806 and 952) 907.2
        nerve root(s) and plexus(es) (in-jury classifiable to 953) 907.3
      superficial (injury classifiable to 910–919) 906.2
      tendon (tendon injury classifiable to 840–848, 880–884 with .2, and 890–894 with .2) 905.8
    meningitis
      bacterial (conditions classifiable to 320) — *see* category 326
      unspecified cause (conditions classi-fiable to 322) — *see* category 326
    myelitis (*see also* Late, effect(s) (of), en-cephalitis) — *see* category 326
    parasitic diseases (conditions classifiable to 001–136 NEC) 139.8
    phlebitis or thrombophlebitis of intracra-nial venous sinuses (conditions classifiable to 325) — *see* catego-ry 326
    poisoning due to drug, medicinal or bio-logical substance (conditions classifiable to 960–979) 909.0
    poliomyelitis, acute (conditions classifi-able to 045) 138
    pregnancy complication(s) 677
    puerperal complication(s) 677
    radiation (conditions classifiable to 990) 909.2
    rickets 268.1
    sprain and strain without mention of tendon injury (injury classifiable to 840–848, except tendon injury) 905.7
      tendon involvement 905.8

☑ **Additional Digit Required** — Refer to the Tabular List for Digit Selection   ▽ **Subterms under main terms may continue to next column or page**

2015 ICD-9-CM   ▶◀ **Revised Text**   ● **New Line**   ▲ **Revised Code**   **Volume 2 — 173**

Large — Late

Late — see also condition — continued
  effect(s) (see also condition) — continued
    toxic effect of
      drug, medicinal or biological substance (conditions classifiable to 960–979) 909.0
      nonmedical substance (conditions classifiable to 980–989) 909.1
    trachoma (conditions classifiable to 076) 139.1
    tuberculosis 137.0
      bones and joints (conditions classifiable to 015) 137.3
      central nervous system (conditions classifiable to 013) 137.1
      genitourinary (conditions classifiable to 016) 137.2
      pulmonary (conditions classifiable to 010–012) 137.0
      specified organs NEC (conditions classifiable to 014, 017–018) 137.4
    viral encephalitis (conditions classifiable to 049.8, 049.9, 062–064) 139.0
    wound, open
      extremity (injury classifiable to 880–884 and 890–894, except .2) 906.1
      tendon (injury classifiable to 880–884 with .2 and 890–894 with .2) 905.8
      head, neck, and trunk (injury classifiable to 870–879) 906.0
  infant
    post-term (gestation period over 40 completed weeks to 42 completed weeks) 766.21
    prolonged gestation (period over 42 completed weeks) 766.22
Latent — see condition
Lateral — see condition
Laterocession — see Lateroversion
Lateroflexion — see Lateroversion
Lateroversion
  cervix — see Lateroversion, uterus
  uterus, uterine (cervix) (postinfectional) (postpartal, old) 621.6
    congenital 752.39
    in pregnancy or childbirth 654.4 ☑
      affecting fetus or newborn 763.89
Lathyrism 988.2
Launois-Bensaude's lipomatosis 272.8
Launois-Cléret syndrome (adiposogenital dystrophy) 253.8
Launois' syndrome (pituitary gigantism) 253.0
Laurence-Moon-Biedl syndrome (obesity, polydactyly, and intellectual disabilities) 759.89
LAV (disease) (illness) (infection) — see Human immunodeficiency virus (disease) (illness) (infection)
LAV/HTLV-III (disease) (illness) (infection) — see Human immunodeficiency virus (disease) (illness) (infection)
Lawford's syndrome (encephalocutaneous angiomatosis) 759.6
Laxative habit — see also Abuse, drugs, nondependent 305.9 ☑
Lax, laxity — see also Relaxation
  ligament 728.4
  skin (acquired) 701.8
    congenital 756.83
Lazy leukocyte syndrome 288.09
LCAD (long chain/very long chain acyl CoA dehydrogenase deficiency, VLCAD) 277.85
LCHAD (long chain 3-hydroxyacyl CoA dehydrogenase deficiency) 277.85
Lead — see also condition
  exposure (suspected) to V15.86
  incrustation of cornea 371.15
  poisoning 984.9
    specified type of lead — see Table of Drugs and Chemicals
Lead miners' lung 503

Leakage
  amniotic fluid 658.1 ☑
    with delayed delivery 658.2 ☑
    affecting fetus or newborn 761.1
  bile from drainage tube (T tube) 997.49
  blood (microscopic), fetal, into maternal circulation 656.0 ☑
    affecting management of pregnancy or puerperium 656.0 ☑
  device, implant, or graft — see Complications, mechanical
  spinal fluid at lumbar puncture site 997.09
  urine, continuous 788.37
Leaky heart — see Endocarditis
Learning defect, specific NEC (strephosymbolia) 315.2
Leather bottle stomach (M8142/3) 151.9
Leber's
  congenital amaurosis 362.76
  optic atrophy (hereditary) 377.16
Lederer's anemia or disease (acquired infectious hemolytic anemia) 283.19
Lederer-Brill syndrome (acquired infectious hemolytic anemia) 283.19
Leeches (aquatic) (land) 134.2
Leiofibromyoma (M8890/0) — see also Leiomyoma
  uterus (cervix) (corpus) (see also Leiomyoma, uterus) 218.9
Leiomyoblastoma (M8891/1) — see Neoplasm, connective tissue, uncertain behavior
Leiomyofibroma (M8890/0) — see also Neoplasm, connective tissue, benign
  uterus (cervix) (corpus) (see also Leiomyoma, uterus) 218.9
Leiomyoma (M8890/0) — see also Neoplasm, connective tissue, benign
  bizarre (M8893/0) — see Neoplasm, connective tissue, benign
  cellular (M8892/1) — see Neoplasm, connective tissue, uncertain behavior
  epithelioid (M8891/1) — see Neoplasm, connective tissue, uncertain behavior
  prostate (polypoid) 600.20
    with
      other lower urinary tract symptoms (LUTS) 600.21
      urinary
        obstruction 600.21
        retention 600.21
  uterus (cervix) (corpus) 218.9
    interstitial 218.1
    intramural 218.1
    submucous 218.0
    subperitoneal 218.2
    subserous 218.2
  vascular (M8894/0) — see Neoplasm, connective tissue, benign
Leiomyomatosis (intravascular) (M8890/1) — see Neoplasm, connective tissue, uncertain behavior
Leiomyosarcoma (M8890/3) — see also Neoplasm, connective tissue, malignant
  epithelioid (M8891/3) — see Neoplasm, connective tissue, malignant
Leishmaniasis 085.9
  American 085.5
    cutaneous 085.4
    mucocutaneous 085.5
  Asian desert 085.2
  Brazilian 085.5
  cutaneous 085.9
    acute necrotizing 085.2
    American 085.4
    Asian desert 085.2
    diffuse 085.3
    dry form 085.1

Leishmaniasis — continued
  cutaneous — continued
    Ethiopian 085.3
    eyelid 085.5 [373.6]
    late 085.1
    lepromatous 085.3
    recurrent 085.1
    rural 085.2
    ulcerating 085.1
    urban 085.1
    wet form 085.2
    zoonotic form 085.2
  dermal (see also Leishmaniasis, cutaneous)
    post kala-azar 085.0
  eyelid 085.5 [373.6]
  infantile 085.0
  Mediterranean 085.0
  mucocutaneous (American) 085.5
  naso-oral 085.5
  nasopharyngeal 085.5
  Old World 085.1
  tegumentaria diffusa 085.4
  vaccination, prophylactic (against) V05.2
  visceral (Indian) 085.0
Leishmanoid, dermal — see also Leishmaniasis, cutaneous
  post kala-azar 085.0
Leloir's disease 695.4
Lemiere syndrome 451.89
Lenegre's disease 426.0
Lengthening, leg 736.81
Lennox-Gastaut syndrome 345.0 ☑
  with tonic seizures 345.1 ☑
Lennox's syndrome — see also Epilepsy 345.0 ☑
Lens — see condition
Lenticonus (anterior) (posterior) (congenital) 743.36
Lenticular degeneration, progressive 275.1
Lentiglobus (posterior) (congenital) 743.36
Lentigo (congenital) 709.09
  juvenile 709.09
  Maligna (M8742/2) (see also Neoplasm, skin, in situ)
    melanoma (M8742/3) — see Melanoma
  senile 709.09
Leonine leprosy 030.0
Leontiasis
  ossium 733.3
  syphilitic 095.8
    congenital 090.5
Léopold-Lévi's syndrome (paroxysmal thyroid instability) 242.9 ☑
Lepore hemoglobin syndrome 282.45
Lepothrix 039.0
Lepra 030.9
  Willan's 696.1
Leprechaunism 259.8
Lepromatous leprosy 030.0
Leprosy 030.9
  anesthetic 030.1
  beriberi 030.1
  borderline (group B) (infiltrated) (neuritic) 030.3
  cornea (see also Leprosy, by type) 030.9 [371.89]
  dimorphous (group B) (infiltrated) (lepromatous) (neuritic) (tuberculoid) 030.3
  eyelid 085.5 [373.4]
  indeterminate (group I) (macular) (neuritic) (uncharacteristic) 030.2
  leonine 030.0
  lepromatous (diffuse) (infiltrated) (macular) (neuritic) (nodular) (type L) 030.0
  macular (early) (neuritic) (simple) 030.2
  maculoanesthetic 030.1
  mixed 030.1
  neuro 030.1
  nodular 030.0
  primary neuritic 030.3
  specified type or group NEC 030.8
  tubercular 030.1
  tuberculoid (macular) (maculoanesthetic) (major) (minor) (neuritic) (type T) 030.1
Leptocytosis, hereditary 282.40

Leptomeningitis (chronic) (circumscribed) (hemorrhagic) (nonsuppurative) — see also Meningitis 322.9
  aseptic 047.9
    adenovirus 049.1
    Coxsackie virus 047.0
    ECHO virus 047.1
    enterovirus 047.9
    lymphocytic choriomeningitis 049.0
  epidemic 036.0
  late effect — see category 326
  meningococcal 036.0
  pneumococcal 320.1
  syphilitic 094.2
  tuberculous (see also Tuberculosis, meninges) 013.0 ☑
Leptomeningopathy — see also Meningitis 322.9
Leptospiral — see condition
Leptospirochetal — see condition
Leptospirosis 100.9
  autumnalis 100.89
  canicula 100.89
  grippotyphosa 100.89
  hebdomidis 100.89
  icterohemorrhagica 100.0
  nanukayami 100.89
  pomona 100.89
  Weil's disease 100.0
Leptothricosis — see Actinomycosis
Leptothrix infestation — see Actinomycosis
Leptotricosis — see Actinomycosis
Leptus dermatitis 133.8
Leriche's syndrome (aortic bifurcation occlusion) 444.09
Léris pleonosteosis 756.89
Léri-Weill syndrome 756.59
Lermoyez's syndrome — see also Disease, Ménière's 386.00
Lesbianism — omit code
  ego-dystonic 302.0
  problems with 302.0
Lesch-Nyhan syndrome (hypoxanthineguanine-phosphoribosyltransferase deficiency) 277.2
Lesion(s)
  abducens nerve 378.54
  alveolar process 525.8
  anorectal 569.49
  aortic (valve) — see Endocarditis, aortic
  auditory nerve 388.5
  basal ganglion 333.90
  bile duct (see also Disease, biliary) 576.8
  bladder 596.9
  bone 733.90
  brachial plexus 353.0
  brain 348.89
    congenital 742.9
    vascular (see also Lesion, cerebrovascular) 437.9
      degenerative 437.1
      healed or old without residuals V12.54
      hypertensive 437.2
      late effect — see Late effect(s) (of) cerebrovascular disease
  buccal 528.9
  calcified — see Calcification
  canthus 373.9
  carate — see Pinta, lesions
  cardia 537.89
  cardiac — see also Disease, heart
    congenital 746.9
    valvular — see Endocarditis
  cauda equina 344.60
    with neurogenic bladder 344.61
  cecum 569.89
  cerebral — see Lesion, brain
  cerebrovascular (see also Disease, cerebrovascular NEC) 437.9
    degenerative 437.1
    healed or old without residuals V12.54
    hypertensive 437.2
    specified type NEC 437.8
  cervical root (nerve) NEC 353.2

☑ **Additional Digit Required** — Refer to the Tabular List for Digit Selection   ▽ **Subterms under main terms may continue to next column or page**

Lesion(s) — *continued*
- chiasmal 377.54
  - associated with
    - inflammatory disorders 377.54
    - neoplasm NEC 377.52
      - pituitary 377.51
    - pituitary disorders 377.51
    - vascular disorders 377.53
- chorda tympani 351.8
- coin, lung 793.11
- colon 569.89
- congenital — *see* Anomaly
- conjunctiva 372.9
- coronary artery (*see also* Ischemia, heart) 414.9
- cranial nerve 352.9
  - first 352.0
  - second 377.49
  - third
    - partial 378.51
    - total 378.52
  - fourth 378.53
  - fifth 350.9
  - sixth 378.54
  - seventh 351.9
  - eighth 388.5
  - ninth 352.2
  - tenth 352.3
  - eleventh 352.4
  - twelfth 352.5
- cystic — *see* Cyst
- degenerative — *see* Degeneration
- dermal (skin) 709.9
- Dieulafoy (hemorrhagic)
  - of
    - duodenum 537.84
    - intestine 569.86
    - stomach 537.84
- duodenum 537.89
  - with obstruction 537.3
- eyelid 373.9
- gasserian ganglion 350.8
- gastric 537.89
- gastroduodenal 537.89
- gastrointestinal 569.89
- glossopharyngeal nerve 352.2
- heart (organic) (*see also* Disease, heart)
  - vascular — *see* Disease, cardiovascular
- helix (ear) 709.9
- high grade myelodysplastic syndrome 238.73
- hyperchromic, due to pinta (carate) 103.1
- hyperkeratotic (*see also* Hyperkeratosis) 701.1
- hypoglossal nerve 352.5
- hypopharynx 478.29
- hypothalamic 253.9
- ileocecal coil 569.89
- ileum 569.89
- iliohypogastric nerve 355.79
- ilioinguinal nerve 355.79
- in continuity — *see* Injury, nerve, by site
- Inflammatory — *see* Inflammation
- intestine 569.89
- intracerebral — *see* Lesion, brain
- intrachiasmal (optic) (*see also* Lesion, chiasmal) 377.54
- intracranial, space-occupying NEC 784.2
- joint 719.90
  - ankle 719.97
  - elbow 719.92
  - foot 719.97
  - hand 719.94
  - hip 719.95
  - knee 719.96
  - multiple sites 719.99
  - pelvic region 719.95
  - sacroiliac (old) 724.6
  - shoulder (region) 719.91
  - specified site NEC 719.98
  - wrist 719.93
- keratotic (*see also* Keratosis) 701.1
- kidney (*see also* Disease, renal) 593.9
- laryngeal nerve (recurrent) 352.3
- leonine 030.0
- lip 528.5

Lesion(s) — *continued*
- liver 573.8
- low grade myelodysplastic syndrome 238.72
- lumbosacral
  - plexus 353.1
  - root (nerve) NEC 353.4
- lung 518.89
  - coin 793.11
- maxillary sinus 473.0
- mitral — *see* Endocarditis, mitral
- Morel Lavallée — *see* Hematoma, by site
- motor cortex 348.89
- nerve (*see also* Disorder, nerve) 355.9
- nervous system 349.9
  - congenital 742.9
- nonallopathic NEC 739.9
  - in region (of)
    - abdomen 739.9
    - acromioclavicular 739.7
    - cervical, cervicothoracic 739.1
    - costochondral 739.8
    - costovertebral 739.8
    - extremity
      - lower 739.6
      - upper 739.7
    - head 739.0
    - hip 739.5
    - lower extremity 739.6
    - lumbar, lumbosacral 739.3
    - occipitocervical 739.0
    - pelvic 739.5
    - pubic 739.5
    - rib cage 739.8
    - sacral, sacrococcygeal, sacroiliac 739.4
    - sternochondral 739.8
    - sternoclavicular 739.7
    - thoracic, thoracolumbar 739.2
    - upper extremity 739.7
- nose (internal) 478.19
- obstructive — *see* Obstruction
- obturator nerve 355.79
- occlusive
  - artery — *see* Embolism, artery
- organ or site NEC — *see* Disease, by site
- osteolytic 733.90
- paramacular, of retina 363.32
- peptic 537.89
- periodontal, due to traumatic occlusion 523.8
- perirectal 569.49
- peritoneum (granulomatous) 568.89
- pigmented (skin) 709.00
- pinta — *see* Pinta, lesions
- polypoid — *see* Polyp
- prechiasmal (optic) (*see also* Lesion, chiasmal) 377.54
- primary (*see also* Syphilis, primary)
  - carate 103.0
  - pinta 103.0
  - yaws 102.0
- pulmonary 518.89
  - valve (*see also* Endocarditis, pulmonary) 424.3
- pylorus 537.89
- radiation NEC 990
- radium NEC 990
- rectosigmoid 569.89
- retina, retinal (*see also* Retinopathy)
  - vascular 362.17
- retroperitoneal 568.89
- romanus 720.1
- sacroiliac (joint) 724.6
- salivary gland 527.8
  - benign lymphoepithelial 527.8
- saphenous nerve 355.79
- secondary — *see* Syphilis, secondary
- sigmoid 569.89
- sinus (accessory) (nasal) (*see also* Sinusitis) 473.9
- skin 709.9
  - suppurative 686.00
- SLAP (superior glenoid labrum) 840.7
- space-occupying, intracranial NEC 784.2
- spinal cord 336.9
  - congenital 742.9

Lesion(s) — *continued*
- spinal cord — *continued*
  - traumatic (complete) (incomplete) (transverse) (*see also* Injury, spinal, by site)
    - with
      - broken
        - back — *see* Fracture, vertebra, by site, with spinal cord injury
        - neck — *see* Fracture, vertebra, cervical, with spinal cord injury
      - fracture, vertebra — *see* Fracture, vertebra, by site, with spinal cord injury
- spleen 289.50
- stomach 537.89
- superior glenoid labrum (SLAP) 840.7
- syphilitic — *see* Syphilis
- tertiary — *see* Syphilis, tertiary
- thoracic root (nerve) 353.3
- tonsillar fossa 474.9
- tooth, teeth 525.8
  - white spot 521.01
- traumatic NEC (*see also* nature and site of injury) 959.9
- tricuspid (valve) — *see* Endocarditis, tricuspid
- trigeminal nerve 350.9
- ulcerated or ulcerative — *see* Ulcer
- uterus NEC 621.9
- vagina 623.8
- vagus nerve 352.3
- valvular — *see* Endocarditis
- vascular 459.9
  - affecting central nervous system (*see also* Lesion, cerebrovascular) 437.9
  - following trauma (*see also* Injury, blood vessel, by site) 904.9
  - retina 362.17
  - traumatic — *see* Injury, blood vessel, by site
  - umbilical cord 663.6 ☑
    - affecting fetus or newborn 762.6
- visual
  - cortex NEC (*see also* Disorder, visual, cortex) 377.73
  - pathway NEC (*see also* Disorder, visual, pathway) 377.63
- warty — *see* Verruca
- white spot, on teeth 521.01
- x-ray NEC 990

Lethargic — *see* condition

Lethargy 780.79

Letterer-Siwe disease (acute histiocytosis X) (M9722/3) 202.5 ☑

Leucinosis 270.3

Leucocoria 360.44

Leucosarcoma (M9850/3) 207.8 ☑

Leukasmus 270.2

Leukemia, leukemic (congenital) (M9800/3) 208.9 ☑

> *Note* – Use the following fifth-digit subclassification for categories 203–208:
>
> 0　without mention of having achieved remission
>
> 　　　failed remission
>
> 1　with remission
>
> 2　in relapse

- acute NEC (M9801/3) 208.0 ☑
- aleukemic NEC (M9804/3) 208.0 ☑
  - granulocytic (M9864/3) 205.8 ☑
- basophilic (M9870/3) 205.1 ☑
- blast (cell) (M9801/3) 208.0 ☑
- blastic (M9801/3) 208.0 ☑
  - granulocytic (M9861/3) 205.0 ☑
- chronic NEC (M9803/3) 208.1 ☑
- compound (M9810/3) 207.8 ☑
- eosinophilic (M9880/3) 205.1 ☑
- giant cell (M9910/3) 207.2 ☑
- granulocytic (M9860/3) 205.9 ☑
  - acute (M9861/3) 205.0 ☑

Leukemia, leukemic — *continued*
- granulocytic — *continued*
  - aleukemic (M9864/3) 205.8 ☑
  - blastic (M9861/3) 205.0 ☑
  - chronic (M9863/3) 205.1 ☑
  - subacute (M9862/3) 205.2 ☑
  - subleukemic (M9864/3) 205.8 ☑
- hairy cell (M9940/3) 202.4 ☑
- hemoblastic (M9801/3) 208.0 ☑
- histiocytic (M9890/3) 206.9 ☑
- lymphatic (M9820/3) 204.9 ☑
  - acute (M9821/3) 204.0 ☑
  - aleukemic (M9824/3) 204.8 ☑
  - chronic (M9823/3) 204.1 ☑
  - subacute (M9822/3) 204.2 ☑
  - subleukemic (M9824/3) 204.8 ☑
- lymphoblastic (M9821/3) 204.0 ☑
- lymphocytic (M9820/3) 204.9 ☑
  - acute (M9821/3) 204.0 ☑
  - aleukemic (M9824/3) 204.8 ☑
  - chronic (M9823/3) 204.1 ☑
  - granular
    - large T-cell 204.8 ☑
  - subacute (M9822/3) 204.2 ☑
  - subleukemic (M9824/3) 204.8 ☑
- lymphogenous (M9820/3) — *see* Leukemia, lymphoid
- lymphoid (M9820/3) 204.9 ☑
  - acute (M9821/3) 204.0 ☑
  - aleukemic (M9824/3) 204.8 ☑
  - blastic (M9821/3) 204.0 ☑
  - chronic (M9823/3) 204.1 ☑
  - subacute (M9822/3) 204.2 ☑
  - subleukemic (M9824/3) 204.8 ☑
- lymphosarcoma cell (M9850/3) 207.8 ☑
- mast cell (M9900/3) 207.8 ☑
- megakaryocytic (M9910/3) 207.2 ☑
- megakaryocytoid (M9910/3) 207.2 ☑
- mixed (cell) (M9810/3) 207.8 ☑
- monoblastic (M9891/3) 206.0 ☑
- monocytic (Schilling-type) (M9890/3) 206.9 ☑
  - acute (M9891/3) 206.0 ☑
  - aleukemic (M9894/3) 206.8 ☑
  - chronic (M9893/3) 206.1 ☑
  - Naegeli-type (M9863/3) 205.1 ☑
  - subacute (M9892/3) 206.2 ☑
  - subleukemic (M9894/3) 206.8 ☑
- monocytoid (M9890/3) 206.9 ☑
  - acute (M9891/3) 206.0 ☑
  - aleukemic (M9894/3) 206.8 ☑
  - chronic (M9893/3) 206.1 ☑
  - myelogenous (M9863/3) 205.1 ☑
  - subacute (M9892/3) 206.2 ☑
  - subleukemic (M9894/3) 206.8 ☑
- monomyelocytic (M9860/3) — *see* Leukemia, myelomonocytic
- myeloblastic (M9861/3) 205.0 ☑
- myelocytic (M9863/3) 205.1 ☑
  - acute (M9861/3) 205.0 ☑
- myelogenous (M9860/3) 205.9 ☑
  - acute (M9861/3) 205.0 ☑
  - aleukemic (M9864/3) 205.8 ☑
  - chronic (M9863/3) 205.1 ☑
  - monocytoid (M9863/3) 205.1 ☑
  - subacute (M9862/3) 205.2 ☑
  - subleukemic (M9864) 205.8 ☑
- myeloid (M9860/3) 205.9 ☑
  - acute (M9861/3) 205.0 ☑
  - aleukemic (M9864/3) 205.8 ☑
  - chronic (M9863/3) 205.1 ☑
  - subacute (M9862/3) 205.2 ☑
  - subleukemic (M9864/3) 205.8 ☑
- myelomonocytic (M9860/3) 205.9 ☑
  - acute (M9861/3) 205.0 ☑
  - chronic (M9863/3) 205.1 ☑
- Naegeli-type monocytic (M9863/3) 205.1 ☑
- neutrophilic (M9865/3) 205.1 ☑
- plasma cell (M9830/3) 203.1 ☑
- plasmacytic (M9830/3) 203.1 ☑
- prolymphocytic (M9825/3) — *see* Leukemia, lymphoid
- promyelocytic, acute (M9866/3) 205.0 ☑

☑ **Additional Digit Required — Refer to the Tabular List for Digit Selection**　　　　　▽ **Subterms under main terms may continue to next column or page**

Leukemia, leukemic — *continued*
  Schilling-type monocytic (M9890/3) — *see* Leukemia, monocytic
  stem cell (M9801/3) 208.0 ☑
  subacute NEC (M9802/3) 208.2 ☑
  subleukemic NEC (M9804/3) 208.8 ☑
  thrombocytic (M9910/3) 207.2 ☑
  undifferentiated (M9801/3) 208.0 ☑
Leukemoid reaction (basophilic) (lymphocytic) (monocytic) (myelocytic) (neutrophilic) 288.62
Leukoaraiosis (hypertensive) 437.1
Leukoariosis — *see* Leukoaraiosis
Leukoclastic vasculitis 446.29
Leukocoria 360.44
Leukocythemia — *see* Leukemia
Leukocytopenia 288.50
Leukocytosis 288.60
  basophilic 288.8
  eosinophilic 288.3
  lymphocytic 288.8
  monocytic 288.8
  neutrophilic 288.8
Leukoderma 709.09
  syphilitic 091.3
    late 095.8
Leukodermia — *see also* Leukoderma 709.09
Leukodystrophy (cerebral) (globoid cell) (metachromatic) (progressive) (sudanophilic) 330.0
Leukoedema, mouth or tongue 528.79
Leukoencephalitis
  acute hemorrhagic (postinfectious) NEC 136.9 [323.61]
    postimmunization or postvaccinal 323.51
  subacute sclerosing 046.2
    van Bogaert's 046.2
  van Bogaert's (sclerosing) 046.2
Leukoencephalopathy — *see also* Encephalitis 323.9
  acute necrotizing hemorrhagic (postinfectious) 136.9 [323.61]
    postimmunization or postvaccinal 323.51
  arteriosclerotic 437.0
  Binswanger's 290.12
  metachromatic 330.0
  multifocal (progressive) 046.3
  progressive multifocal 046.3
  reversible, posterior 348.5
Leukoerythroblastosis 289.9
Leukoerythrosis 289.0
Leukokeratosis — *see also* Leukoplakia 702.8
  mouth 528.6
  nicotina palati 528.79
  tongue 528.6
Leukokoria 360.44
Leukokraurosis vulva, vulvae 624.09
Leukolymphosarcoma (M9850/3) 207.8 ☑
Leukoma (cornea) (interfering with central vision) 371.03
  adherent 371.04
Leukomalacia, periventricular 779.7
Leukomelanopathy, hereditary 288.2
Leukonychia (punctata) (striata) 703.8
  congenital 757.5
Leukopathia
  unguium 703.8
    congenital 757.5
Leukopenia 288.50
  basophilic 288.59
  cyclic 288.02
  eosinophilic 288.59
  familial 288.59
  malignant (*see also* Agranulocytosis) 288.09
  periodic 288.02
  transitory neonatal 776.7
Leukopenic — *see* condition
Leukoplakia 702.8
  anus 569.49
  bladder (postinfectional) 596.89
  buccal 528.6
  cervix (uteri) 622.2
  esophagus 530.83
  gingiva 528.6

Leukoplakia — *continued*
  kidney (pelvis) 593.89
  larynx 478.79
  lip 528.6
  mouth 528.6
  oral soft tissue (including tongue) (mucosa) 528.6
  palate 528.6
  pelvis (kidney) 593.89
  penis (infectional) 607.0
  rectum 569.49
  syphilitic 095.8
  tongue 528.6
  tonsil 478.29
  ureter (postinfectional) 593.89
  urethra (postinfectional) 599.84
  uterus 621.8
  vagina 623.1
  vesical 596.89
  vocal cords 478.5
  vulva 624.09
Leukopolioencephalopathy 330.0
Leukorrhea (vagina) 623.5
  due to trichomonas (vaginalis) 131.00
  trichomonal (Trichomonas vaginalis) 131.00
Leukosarcoma (M9850/3) 207.8 ☑
Leukosis (M9800/3) — *see* Leukemia
Lev's disease or syndrome (acquired complete heart block) 426.0
Levi's syndrome (pituitary dwarfism) 253.3
Levocardia (isolated) 746.87
  with situs inversus 759.3
Levulosuria 271.2
Lewandowski's disease (primary) — *see also* Tuberculosis 017.0 ☑
Lewandowski-Lutz disease (epidermodysplasia verruciformis) 078.19
Lewy body dementia 331.82
Lewy body disease 331.82
Leyden's disease (periodic vomiting) 536.2
Leyden-Möbius dystrophy 359.1
Leydig cell
  carcinoma (M8650/3)
    specified site — *see* Neoplasm, by site, malignant
    unspecified site
      female 183.0
      male 186.9
  tumor (M8650/1)
    benign (M8650/0)
      specified site — *see* Neoplasm, by site, benign
      unspecified site
        female 220
        male 222.0
    malignant (M8650/3)
      specified site — *see* Neoplasm, by site, malignant
      unspecified site
        female 183.0
        male 186.9
    specified site — *see* Neoplasm, by site, uncertain behavior
    unspecified site
      female 236.2
      male 236.4
Leydig-Sertoli cell tumor (M8631/0)
  specified site — *see* Neoplasm, by site, benign
  unspecified site
    female 220
    male 222.0
LGSIL (low grade squamous intraepithelial lesion)
  anus 796.73
  cervix 795.03
  vagina 795.13
Liar, pathologic 301.7
Libman-Sacks disease or syndrome 710.0 [424.91]
Lice (infestation) 132.9
  body (pediculus corporis) 132.1
  crab 132.2
  head (pediculus capitis) 132.0
  mixed (classifiable to more than one of the categories 132.0–132.2) 132.3

Lice — *continued*
  pubic (pediculus pubis) 132.2
Lichen 697.9
  albus 701.0
  annularis 695.89
  atrophicus 701.0
  corneus obtusus 698.3
  myxedematous 701.8
  nitidus 697.1
  pilaris 757.39
    acquired 701.1
  planopilaris 697.0
  planus (acute) (chronicus) (hypertrophic) (verrucous) 697.0
    morphoeicus 701.0
    sclerosus (et atrophicus) 701.0
  ruber 696.4
    acuminatus 696.4
    moniliformis 697.8
    obtusus corneus 698.3
    of Wilson 697.0
    planus 697.0
  sclerosus (et atrophicus) 701.0
  scrofulosus (primary) (*see also* Tuberculosis) 017.0 ☑
  simplex (Vidal's) 698.3
    chronicus 698.3
    circumscriptus 698.3
  spinulosus 757.39
    mycotic 117.9
  striata 697.8
  urticatus 698.2
Lichenification 698.3
  nodular 698.3
Lichenoides tuberculosis (primary) — *see also* Tuberculosis 017.0 ☑
Lichtheim's disease or syndrome (subacute combined sclerosis with pernicious anemia) 281.0 [336.2]
Lien migrans 289.59
Lientery — *see also* Diarrhea 787.91
  infectious 009.2
Life circumstance problem NEC V62.89
Li-Fraumeni cancer syndrome V84.01
Ligament — *see* condition
Light-for-dates (infant) 764.0 ☑
  with signs of fetal malnutrition 764.1 ☑
  affecting management of pregnancy 656.5 ☑
Light-headedness 780.4
Lightning (effects) (shock) (stroke) (struck by) 994.0
  burn — *see* Burn, by site
  foot 266.2
Lightwood's disease or syndrome (renal tubular acidosis) 588.89
Lignac's disease (cystinosis) 270.0
Lignac (-de Toni) (-Fanconi) (-Debré) syndrome (cystinosis) 270.0
Lignac (-Fanconi) syndrome (cystinosis) 270.0
Ligneous thyroiditis 245.3
Likoff's syndrome (angina in menopausal women) 413.9
Limb — *see* condition
Limitation of joint motion — *see also* Stiffness, joint 719.5 ☑
  sacroiliac 724.6
Limit dextrinosis 271.0
Limited
  cardiac reserve — *see* Disease, heart
  duction, eye NEC 378.63
  mandibular range of motion 524.52
Lindau's disease (retinocerebral angiomatosis) 759.6
Lindau (-von Hippel) disease (angiomatosis retinocerebellosa) 759.6
Linea corneae senilis 371.41
Lines
  Beau's (transverse furrows on fingernails) 703.8
  Harris' 733.91
  Hudson-Ståhli 371.11
  Ståhli's 371.11
Lingua
  geographical 529.1
  nigra (villosa) 529.3

Lingua — *continued*
  plicata 529.5
    congenital 750.13
  tylosis 528.6
Lingual (tongue) — *see also* condition
  thyroid 759.2
Linitis (gastric) 535.4 ☑
  plastica (M8142/3) 151.9
Lioderma essentialis (cum melanosis et telangiectasia) 757.33
Lip — *see also* condition
  biting 528.9
Lipalgia 272.8
Lipedema — *see* Edema
Lipemia — *see also* Hyperlipidemia 272.4
  retina, retinalis 272.3
Lipidosis 272.7
  cephalin 272.7
  cerebral (infantile) (juvenile) (late) 330.1
  cerebroretinal 330.1 [362.71]
  cerebroside 272.7
  cerebrospinal 272.7
  chemically-induced 272.7
  cholesterol 272.7
  diabetic 250.8 ☑ [272.7]
    due to secondary diabetes 249.8 ☑ [272.7]
  dystopic (hereditary) 272.7
  glycolipid 272.7
  hepatosplenomegalic 272.3
  hereditary, dystopic 272.7
  sulfatide 330.0
Lipoadenoma (M8324/0) — *see* Neoplasm, by site, benign
Lipoblastoma (M8881/0) — *see* Lipoma, by site
Lipoblastomatosis (M8881/0) — *see* Lipoma, by site
Lipochondrodystrophy 277.5
Lipochrome histiocytosis (familial) 288.1
Lipodermatosclerosis 729.39
Lipodystrophia progressiva 272.6
Lipodystrophy (progressive) 272.6
  insulin 272.6
  intestinal 040.2
  mesenteric 567.82
Lipofibroma (M8851/0) — *see* Lipoma, by site
Lipoglycoproteinosis 272.8
Lipogranuloma, sclerosing 709.8
Lipogranulomatosis (disseminated) 272.8
  kidney 272.8
Lipoid — *see also* condition
  histiocytosis 272.7
    essential 272.7
  nephrosis (*see also* Nephrosis) 581.3
  proteinosis of Urbach 272.8
Lipoidemia — *see also* Hyperlipidemia 272.4
Lipoidosis — *see also* Lipidosis 272.7
Lipoma (M8850/0) 214.9
  breast (skin) 214.1
  face 214.0
  fetal (M8881/0) (*see also* Lipoma, by site)
    fat cell (M8880/0) — *see* Lipoma, by site
  infiltrating (M8856/0) — *see* Lipoma, by site
  intra-abdominal 214.3
  intramuscular (M8856/0) — *see* Lipoma, by site
  intrathoracic 214.2
  kidney 214.3
  mediastinum 214.2
  muscle 214.8
  peritoneum 214.3
  retroperitoneum 214.3
  skin 214.1
    face 214.0
  spermatic cord 214.4
  spindle cell (M8857/0) — *see* Lipoma, by site
  stomach 214.3
  subcutaneous tissue 214.1
    face 214.0
  thymus 214.2
  thyroid gland 214.2
Lipomatosis (dolorosa) 272.8
  epidural 214.8
  fetal (M8881/0) — *see* Lipoma, by site

☑ **Additional Digit Required** — Refer to the Tabular List for Digit Selection   ▽ **Subterms under main terms may continue to next column or page**

176 — Volume 2   ▶◀ **Revised Text**   ● **New Line**   ▲ **Revised Code**   **2015 ICD-9-CM**

Lipomatosis — continued
    Launois-Bensaude's 272.8
Lipomyohemangioma (M8860/0)
    specified site — see Neoplasm, connective
        tissue, benign
    unspecified site 223.0
Lipomyoma (M8860/0)
    specified site — see Neoplasm, connective
        tissue, benign
    unspecified site 223.0
Lipomyxoma (M8852/0) — see Lipoma, by site
Lipomyxosarcoma (M8852/3) — see Neo-
    plasm, connective tissue, malignant
Lipophagocytosis 289.89
Lipoproteinemia (alpha) 272.4
    broad-beta 272.2
    floating-beta 272.2
    hyper-pre-beta 272.1
Lipoproteinosis (Rössle-Urbach-Wiethe) 272.8
Liposarcoma (M8850/3) — see also Neoplasm,
    connective tissue, malignant
    differentiated type (M8851/3) — see Neo-
        plasm, connective tissue, malignant
    embryonal (M8852/3) — see Neoplasm,
        connective tissue, malignant
    mixed type (M8855/3) — see Neoplasm,
        connective tissue, malignant
    myxoid (M8852/3) — see Neoplasm, connec-
        tive tissue, malignant
    pleomorphic (M8854/3) — see Neoplasm,
        connective tissue, malignant
    round cell (M8853/3) — see Neoplasm,
        connective tissue, malignant
    well differentiated type (M8851/3) — see
        Neoplasm, connective tissue, malig-
        nant
Liposynovitis prepatellaris 272.8
Lipping
    cervix 622.0
    spine (see also Spondylosis) 721.90
    vertebra (see also Spondylosis) 721.90
Lip pits (mucus), congenital 750.25
Lipschütz disease or ulcer 616.50
Lipuria 791.1
    bilharziasis 120.0
Lisping 307.9
Lissauer's paralysis 094.1
Lissencephalia, lissencephaly 742.2
Listerellose 027.0
Listeriose 027.0
Listeriosis 027.0
    congenital 771.2
    fetal 771.2
    suspected fetal damage affecting manage-
        ment of pregnancy 655.4 ☑
Listlessness 780.79
Lithemia 790.6
Lithiasis — see also Calculus
    hepatic (duct) — see Choledocholithiasis
    urinary 592.9
Lithopedion 779.9
    affecting management of pregnancy
        656.8 ☑
Lithosis (occupational) 502
    with tuberculosis — see Tuberculosis, pul-
        monary
Lithuria 791.9
Litigation V62.5
Little
    league elbow 718.82
    stroke syndrome 435.9
Little's disease — see Palsy, cerebral
Littre's
    gland — see condition
    hernia — see Hernia, Littre's
Littritis — see also Urethritis 597.89
Livedo 782.61
    annularis 782.61
    racemose 782.61
    reticularis 782.61
Live flesh 781.0
Liver — see also condition
    donor V59.6
Livida, asphyxia
    newborn 768.6

Living
    alone V60.3
        with handicapped person V60.4
Lloyd's syndrome 258.1
Loa loa 125.2
Loasis 125.2
Lobe, lobar — see condition
Lobo's disease or blastomycosis 116.2
Lobomycosis 116.2
Lobotomy syndrome 310.0
Lobstein's disease (brittle bones and blue
    sclera) 756.51
Lobster-claw hand 755.58
Lobulation (congenital) — see also Anomaly,
    specified type NEC, by site
    kidney, fetal 753.3
    liver, abnormal 751.69
    spleen 759.0
Lobule, lobular — see condition
Local, localized — see condition
Locked bowel or intestine — see also Obstruc-
    tion, intestine 560.9
Locked-in state 344.81
Locked twins 660.5 ☑
    affecting fetus or newborn 763.1
Locking
    joint (see also Derangement, joint) 718.90
    knee 717.9
Lockjaw — see also Tetanus 037
Locomotor ataxia (progressive) 094.0
Löffler's
    endocarditis 421.0
    eosinophilia or syndrome 518.3
    pneumonia 518.3
    syndrome (eosinophilic pneumonitis) 518.3
Löfgren's syndrome (sarcoidosis) 135
Loiasis 125.2
    eyelid 125.2 [373.6]
Loneliness V62.89
Lone star fever 082.8
Longitudinal stripes or grooves, nails 703.8
    congenital 757.5
Long labor 662.1 ☑
    affecting fetus or newborn 763.89
    first stage 662.0 ☑
    second stage 662.2 ☑
Long-term (current) (prophylactic) **drug use**
        V58.69
    antibiotics V58.62
    anticoagulants V58.61
    anti-inflammatories, non-steroidal (NSAID)
        V58.64
    antiplatelets/antithrombotics V58.63
    aspirin V58.66
    bisphosphonates V58.68
    high-risk medications NEC V58.69
    insulin V58.67
    methadone for pain control V58.69
    opiate analgesic V58.69
    pain killers V58.69
        anti-inflammatories, non-steroidal
            (NSAID) V58.64
        aspirin V58.66
    steroids V58.65
    tamoxifen V07.51
Loop
    intestine (see also Volvulus) 560.2
    intrascleral nerve 379.29
    vascular on papilla (optic) 743.57
Loose — see also condition
    body
        in tendon sheath 727.82
        joint 718.10
            ankle 718.17
            elbow 718.12
            foot 718.17
            hand 718.14
            hip 718.15
            knee 717.6
            multiple sites 718.19
            pelvic region 718.15
            prosthetic implant — see Complica-
                tions, mechanical
            shoulder (region) 718.11
            specified site NEC 718.18
            wrist 718.13

Loose — see also condition — continued
    cartilage (joint) (see also Loose, body, joint)
        718.1 ☑
        knee 717.6
    facet (vertebral) 724.9
    prosthetic implant — see Complications,
        mechanical
    sesamoid, joint (see also Loose, body, joint)
        718.1 ☑
    tooth, teeth 525.8
Loosening epiphysis 732.9
Looser (-Debray) -Milkman syndrome (osteo-
    malacia with pseudofractures) 268.2
Lop ear (deformity) 744.29
Lorain's disease or syndrome (pituitary
    dwarfism) 253.3
Lorain-Levi syndrome (pituitary dwarfism)
    253.3
Lordosis (acquired) (postural) 737.20
    congenital 754.2
    due to or associated with
        Charcôt-Marie-Tooth disease
            356.1 [737.42]
        mucopolysaccharidosis 277.5 [737.42]
        neurofibromatosis 237.71 [737.42]
        osteitis
            deformans 731.0 [737.42]
            fibrosa cystica 252.01 [737.42]
        osteoporosis (see also Osteoporosis)
            733.00 [737.42]
        poliomyelitis (see also Poliomyelitis)
            138 [737.42]
        tuberculosis (see also Tuberculosis)
            015.0 ☑ [737.42]
    late effect of rickets 268.1 [737.42]
    postlaminectomy 737.21
    postsurgical NEC 737.22
    rachitic 268.1 [737.42]
    specified NEC 737.29
    tuberculous (see also Tuberculosis)
        015.0 ☑ [737.42]
Loss
    appetite 783.0
        hysterical 300.11
        nonorganic origin 307.59
        psychogenic 307.59
    blood — see Hemorrhage
    central vision 368.41
    consciousness 780.09
        transient 780.2
    control, sphincter, rectum 787.60
        nonorganic origin 307.7
    ear ossicle, partial 385.24
    elasticity, skin 782.8
    extremity or member, traumatic, current —
        see Amputation, traumatic
    fluid (acute) 276.50
        with
            hypernatremia 276.0
            hyponatremia 276.1
        fetus or newborn 775.5
    hair 704.00
    hearing (see also Deafness)
        central 389.14
        conductive (air) 389.00
            with sensorineural hearing loss
                389.20
            bilateral 389.22
            unilateral 389.21
            bilateral 389.06
            combined types 389.08
            external ear 389.01
            inner ear 389.04
            middle ear 389.03
            multiple types 389.08
            tympanic membrane 389.02
            unilateral 389.05
        mixed conductive and sensorineural
            389.20
            bilateral 389.22
            unilateral 389.21
        mixed type 389.20
            bilateral 389.22
            unilateral 389.21
        nerve
            bilateral 389.12

Loss — continued
    hearing (see also Deafness) — continued
        nerve — continued
            unilateral 389.13
        neural
            bilateral 389.12
            unilateral 389.13
        noise-induced 388.12
        perceptive NEC (see also Loss, hearing,
            sensorineural) 389.10
        sensorineural 389.10
            with conductive hearing loss 389.20
                bilateral 389.22
                unilateral 389.21
            asymmetrical 389.16
            bilateral 389.18
            central 389.14
            neural 389.12
                bilateral 389.12
                unilateral 389.13
            sensory
                bilateral 389.11
                unilateral 389.17
            unilateral 389.15
        sensory
            bilateral 389.11
            unilateral 389.17
        specified type NEC 389.8
        sudden NEC 388.2
    height 781.91
    labyrinthine reactivity (unilateral) 386.55
        bilateral 386.56
    memory (see also Amnesia) 780.93
        mild, following organic brain damage
            310.89
    mind (see also Psychosis) 298.9
    occlusal vertical dimension 524.37
    organ or part — see Absence, by site, ac-
        quired
    recurrent pregnancy — see Pregnancy,
        management affected by, abortion,
        habitual
    sensation 782.0
    sense of
        smell (see also Disturbance, sensation)
            781.1
        taste (see also Disturbance, sensation)
            781.1
        touch (see also Disturbance, sensation)
            781.1
    sight (acquired) (complete) (congenital) —
        see Blindness
    spinal fluid
        headache 349.0
    substance of
        bone (see also Osteoporosis) 733.00
        cartilage 733.99
        ear 380.32
        vitreous (humor) 379.26
    tooth, teeth
        acquired 525.10
            due to
                caries 525.13
                extraction 525.10
                periodontal disease 525.12
                specified NEC 525.19
                trauma 525.11
    vision, visual (see also Blindness) 369.9
        both eyes (see also Blindness, both eyes)
            369.3
        complete (see also Blindness, both eyes)
            369.00
        one eye 369.8
        sudden 368.11
        transient 368.12
    vitreous 379.26
    voice (see also Aphonia) 784.41
    weight (cause unknown) 783.21
Lou Gehrig's disease 335.20
Louis-Bar syndrome (ataxia-telangiectasia)
    334.8
Louping ill 063.1
Lousiness — see Lice
Low
    back syndrome 724.2
    basal metabolic rate (BMR) 794.7

☑ **Additional Digit Required** — Refer to the Tabular List for Digit Selection   ▽ **Subterms under main terms may continue to next column or page**

2015 ICD-9-CM   ▶◀ Revised Text   ● New Line   ▲ Revised Code   Volume 2 — 177

Low — *continued*
 birthweight 765.1 ☑
  extreme (less than 1000 grams) 765.0 ☑
  for gestational age 764.0 ☑
  status (*see also* Status, low birth weight) V21.30
 bladder compliance 596.52
 blood pressure (*see also* Hypotension) 458.9
  reading (incidental) (isolated) (nonspecific) 796.3
 cardiac reserve — *see* Disease, heart
 compliance bladder 596.52
 frequency deafness — *see* Disorder, hearing
 function (*see also* Hypofunction)
  kidney (*see also* Disease, renal) 593.9
  liver 573.9
 hemoglobin 285.9
 implantation, placenta — *see* Placenta, previa
 insertion, placenta — *see* Placenta, previa
 lying
  kidney 593.0
  organ or site, congenital — *see* Malposition, congenital
  placenta — *see* Placenta, previa
 output syndrome (cardiac) (*see also* Failure, heart) 428.9
 platelets (blood) (*see also* Thrombocytopenia) 287.5
 reserve, kidney (*see also* Disease, renal) 593.9
 risk
  human papillomavirus (HPA) DNA test positive
   anal 796.79
   cervical 795.09
   vaginal 795.19
 salt syndrome 593.9
 tension glaucoma 365.12
 vision 369.9
  both eyes 369.20
  one eye 369.70
Lower extremity — *see* condition
Lowe (-Terrey-MacLachlan) syndrome (oculocerebrorenal dystrophy) 270.8
Lown (-Ganong) -Levine syndrome (short P-R interval, normal QRS complex, and paroxysmal supraventricular tachycardia) 426.81
LSD reaction — *see also* Abuse, drugs, nondependent 305.3 ☑
L-shaped kidney 753.3
Lucas-Championnière disease (fibrinous bronchitis) 466.0
Lucey-Driscoll syndrome (jaundice due to delayed conjugation) 774.30
Ludwig's
 angina 528.3
 disease (submaxillary cellulitis) 528.3
Lues (venerea), **luetic** — *see* Syphilis
Luetscher's syndrome (dehydration) 276.51
Lumbago 724.2
 due to displacement, intervertebral disc 722.10
Lumbalgia 724.2
 due to displacement, intervertebral disc 722.10
Lumbar — *see* condition
Lumbarization, vertebra 756.15
Lumbermen's itch 133.8
Lump — *see also* Mass
 abdominal 789.3 ☑
 breast 611.72
 chest 786.6
 epigastric 789.3 ☑
 head 784.2
 kidney 753.3
 liver 789.1
 lung 786.6
 mediastinal 786.6
 neck 784.2
 nose or sinus 784.2
 pelvic 789.3 ☑
 skin 782.2
 substernal 786.6
 throat 784.2

Lump — *see also* Mass — *continued*
 umbilicus 789.3 ☑
Lunacy — *see also* Psychosis 298.9
Lunatomalacia 732.3
Lung — *see also* condition
 donor V59.8
 drug addict's 417.8
 mainliners' 417.8
 vanishing 492.0
Lupoid (miliary) **of Boeck** 135
Lupus 710.0
 anticoagulant 795.79
  with
   hemorrhagic disorder 286.53
   hypercoagulable state 289.81
 Cazenave's (erythematosus) 695.4
 discoid (local) 695.4
 disseminated 710.0
 erythematodes (discoid) (local) 695.4
 erythematosus (discoid) (local) 695.4
  disseminated 710.0
  eyelid 373.34
  systemic 710.0
   with
    encephalitis 710.0 *[323.81]*
    lung involvement 710.0 *[517.8]*
   inhibitor (presence of) 795.79
    with hypercoagulable state 289.81
 exedens 017.0 ☑
 eyelid (*see also* Tuberculosis) 017.0 ☑ *[373.4]*
 Hilliard's 017.0 ☑
 hydralazine
  correct substance properly administered 695.4
  overdose or wrong substance given or taken 972.6
 miliaris disseminatus faciei 017.0 ☑
 nephritis 710.0 *[583.81]*
  acute 710.0 *[580.81]*
  chronic 710.0 *[582.81]*
 nontuberculous, not disseminated 695.4
 pernio (Besnier) 135
 tuberculous (*see also* Tuberculosis) 017.0 ☑
  eyelid (*see also* Tuberculosis) 017.0 ☑ *[373.4]*
 vulgaris 017.0 ☑
Luschka's joint disease 721.90
Luteinoma (M8610/0) 220
Lutembacher's disease or syndrome (atrial septal defect with mitral stenosis) 745.5
Luteoma (M8610/0) 220
Lutz-Miescher disease (elastosis perforans serpiginosa) 701.1
Lutz-Splendore-de Almeida disease (Brazilian blastomycosis) 116.1
Luxatio
 bulbi due to birth injury 767.8
 coxae congenita (*see also* Dislocation, hip, congenital) 754.30
 erecta — *see* Dislocation, shoulder
 imperfecta — *see* Sprain, by site
 perinealis — *see* Dislocation, hip
Luxation — *see also* Dislocation, by site
 eyeball 360.81
  due to birth injury 767.8
  lateral 376.36
 genital organs (external) NEC — *see* Wound, open, genital organs
 globe (eye) 360.81
  lateral 376.36
 lacrimal gland (postinfectional) 375.16
 lens (old) (partial) 379.32
  congenital 743.37
   syphilitic 090.49 *[379.32]*
  Marfan's disease 090.49
  spontaneous 379.32
 penis — *see* Wound, open, penis
 scrotum — *see* Wound, open, scrotum
 testis — *see* Wound, open, testis
L-xyloketosuria 271.8
Lycanthropy — *see also* Psychosis 298.9
Lyell's disease or syndrome (toxic epidermal necrolysis) 695.15

Lyell's disease or syndrome — *continued*
 due to drug
  correct substance properly administered 695.15
  overdose or wrong substance given or taken 977.9
  specified drug — *see* Table of Drugs and Chemicals
Lyme disease 088.81
Lymph
 gland or node — *see* condition
 scrotum (*see also* Infestation, filarial) 125.9
Lymphadenitis 289.3
 with
  abortion — *see* Abortion, by type, with sepsis
  ectopic pregnancy (*see also* categories 633.0–633.9) 639.0
  molar pregnancy (*see also* categories 630–632) 639.0
 acute 683
  mesenteric 289.2
 any site, except mesenteric 289.3
  acute 683
  chronic 289.1
  mesenteric (acute) (chronic) (nonspecific) (subacute) 289.2
  subacute 289.1
   mesenteric 289.2
 breast, puerperal, postpartum 675.2 ☑
 chancroidal (congenital) 099.0
 chronic 289.1
  mesenteric 289.2
 dermatopathic 695.89
 due to
  anthracosis (occupational) 500
  Brugia (Wuchereria) malayi 125.1
  diphtheria (toxin) 032.89
  lymphogranuloma venereum 099.1
  Wuchereria bancrofti 125.0
 following
  abortion 639.0
  ectopic or molar pregnancy 639.0
 generalized 289.3
 gonorrheal 098.89
 granulomatous 289.1
 infectional 683
 mesenteric (acute) (chronic) (nonspecific) (subacute) 289.2
  due to Bacillus typhi 002.0
  tuberculous (*see also* Tuberculosis) 014.8 ☑
 mycobacterial 031.8
 purulent 683
 pyogenic 683
 regional 078.3
 septic 683
 streptococcal 683
 subacute, unspecified site 289.1
 suppurative 683
 syphilitic (early) (secondary) 091.4
  late 095.8
 tuberculous — *see* Tuberculosis, lymph gland
 venereal 099.1
Lymphadenoid goiter 245.2
Lymphadenopathy (general) 785.6
 due to toxoplasmosis (acquired) 130.7
  congenital (active) 771.2
Lymphadenopathy-associated virus (disease) (illness) (infection) — *see* Human immunodeficiency virus (disease) (illness) (infection)
Lymphadenosis 785.6
 acute 075
Lymphangiectasis 457.1
 conjunctiva 372.89
 postinfectional 457.1
 scrotum 457.1
Lymphangiectatic elephantiasis, nonfilarial 457.1
Lymphangioendothelioma (M9170/0) 228.1
 malignant (M9170/3) — *see* Neoplasm, connective tissue, malignant
Lymphangioleiomyomatosis 516.4
Lymphangioma (M9170/0) 228.1

Lymphangioma — *continued*
 capillary (M9171/0) 228.1
 cavernous (M9172/0) 228.1
 cystic (M9173/0) 228.1
 malignant (M9170/3) — *see* Neoplasm, connective tissue, malignant
Lymphangiomyoma (M9174/0) 228.1
Lymphangiomyomatosis 516.4
Lymphangiosarcoma (M9170/3) — *see* Neoplasm, connective tissue, malignant
Lymphangitis 457.2
 with
  abortion — *see* Abortion, by type, with sepsis
  abscess — *see* Abscess, by site
  cellulitis — *see* Abscess, by site
  ectopic pregnancy (*see also* categories 633.0–633.9) 639.0
  molar pregnancy (*see also* categories 630–632) 639.0
 acute (with abscess or cellulitis) 682.9
  specified site — *see* Abscess, by site
 breast, puerperal, postpartum 675.2 ☑
 chancroidal 099.0
 chronic (any site) 457.2
 due to
  Brugia (Wuchereria) malayi 125.1
  Wuchereria bancrofti 125.0
 following
  abortion 639.0
  ectopic or molar pregnancy 639.0
 gangrenous 457.2
 penis
  acute 607.2
  gonococcal (acute) 098.0
   chronic or duration of 2 months or more 098.2
 puerperal, postpartum, childbirth 670.8 ☑
 strumous, tuberculous (*see also* Tuberculosis) 017.2 ☑
 subacute (any site) 457.2
 tuberculous — *see* Tuberculosis, lymph gland
Lymphatic (vessel) — *see* condition
Lymphatism 254.8
 scrofulous (*see also* Tuberculosis) 017.2 ☑
Lymphectasia 457.1
Lymphedema — *see also* Elephantiasis 457.1
 acquired (chronic) 457.1
 chronic hereditary 757.0
 congenital 757.0
 idiopathic hereditary 757.0
 praecox 457.1
 secondary 457.1
 surgical NEC 997.99
  postmastectomy (syndrome) 457.0
Lymph-hemangioma (M9120/0) — *see* Hemangioma, by site
Lymphoblastic — *see* condition
Lymphoblastoma (diffuse) (M9630/3) 200.1 ☑
 giant follicular (M9690/3) 202.0 ☑
 macrofollicular (M9690/3) 202.0 ☑
Lymphoblastosis, acute benign 075
Lymphocele 457.8
Lymphocythemia 288.51
Lymphocytic — *see also* condition
 chorioencephalitis (acute) (serous) 049.0
 choriomeningitis (acute) (serous) 049.0
Lymphocytoma (diffuse) (malignant) (M9620/3) 200.1 ☑
Lymphocytomatosis (M9620/3) 200.1 ☑
Lymphocytopenia 288.51
Lymphocytosis (symptomatic) 288.61
 infectious (acute) 078.89
Lymphoepithelioma (M8082/3) — *see* Neoplasm, by site, malignant
Lymphogranuloma (malignant) (M9650/3) 201.9 ☑
 inguinale 099.1
 venereal (any site) 099.1
  with stricture of rectum 099.1
 venereum 099.1
Lymphogranulomatosis (malignant) (M9650/3) 201.9 ☑
 benign (Boeck's sarcoid) (Schaumann's) 135
 Hodgkin's (M9650/3) 201.9 ☑

☑ **Additional Digit Required — Refer to the Tabular List for Digit Selection**

ⓦ **Subterms under main terms may continue to next column or page**

Lymphohistiocytosis, familial hemophagocytic 288.4
Lymphoid — see condition
Lympholeukoblastoma (M9850/3) 207.8 ☑
Lympholeukosarcoma (M9850/3) 207.8 ☑
Lymphoma (malignant) (M9590/3) 200.8 ☑

Note — Use the following fifth-digit subclassification with categories 200–202:

0   unspecified site, extranodal and solid organ sites
1   lymph nodes of head, face, and neck
2   intrathoracic lymph nodes
3   intra–abdominal lymph nodes
4   lymph nodes of axilla and upper limb
5   lymph nodes of inguinal region and lower limb
6   intrapelvic lymph nodes
7   spleen
8   lymph nodes of multiple sites

  benign (M9590/0) — see Neoplasm, by site, benign
  Burkitt's type (lymphoblastic) (undifferentiated) (M9750/3) 200.2 ☑
  Castleman's (mediastinal lymph node hyperplasia) 785.6
  centroblastic-centrocytic
    diffuse (M9614/3) 202.8 ☑
    follicular (M9692/3) 202.0 ☑
  centroblastic type (diffuse) (M9632/3) 202.8 ☑
    follicular (M9697/3) 202.0 ☑
  centrocytic (M9622/3) 202.8 ☑
  compound (M9613/3) 200.8 ☑
  convoluted cell type (lymphoblastic) (M9602/3) 202.8 ☑
  diffuse NEC (M9590/3) 202.8 ☑
    large B cell 202.8 ☑
  follicular (giant) (M9690/3) 202.0 ☑
    center cell (diffuse) (M9615/3) 202.8 ☑
    cleaved (diffuse) (M9623/3) 202.8 ☑
      follicular (M9695/3) 202.0 ☑
    non-cleaved (diffuse) (M9633/3) 202.8 ☑
      follicular (M9698/3) 202.0 ☑
    centroblastic-centrocytic (M9692/3) 202.0 ☑
    centroblastic type (M9697/3) 202.0 ☑
    large cell 202.0 ☑
    lymphocytic
      intermediate differentiation (M9694/3) 202.0 ☑
      poorly differentiated (M9696/3) 202.0 ☑
    mixed (cell type) (lymphocytic-histiocytic) (small cell and large cell) (M9691/3) 202.0 ☑
  germinocytic (M9622/3) 202.8 ☑
  giant, follicular or follicle (M9690/3) 202.0 ☑
  histiocytic (diffuse) (M9640/3) 200.0 ☑
    nodular (M9642/3) 200.0 ☑
    pleomorphic cell type (M9641/3) 200.0 ☑
  Hodgkin's (M9650/3) (see also Disease, Hodgkin's) 201.9 ☑
  immunoblastic (type) (M9612/3) 200.8 ☑
  large cell (M9640/3) 200.7 ☑
    anaplastic 200.6 ☑
    nodular (M9642/3) 202.0 ☑
    pleomorphic cell type (M9641/3) 200.0 ☑
  lymphoblastic (diffuse) (M9630/3) 200.1 ☑
    Burkitt's type (M9750/3) 200.2 ☑
    convoluted cell type (M9602/3) 202.8 ☑
  lymphocytic (cell type) (diffuse) (M9620/3) 200.1 ☑

Lymphoma — continued
  lymphocytic — continued
    with plasmacytoid differentiation, diffuse (M9611/3) 200.8 ☑
    intermediate differentiation (diffuse) (M9621/3) 200.1 ☑
      follicular (M9694/3) 202.0 ☑
      nodular (M9694/3) 202.0 ☑
    nodular (M9690/3) 202.0 ☑
    poorly differentiated (diffuse) (M9630/3) 200.1 ☑
      follicular (M9696/3) 202.0 ☑
      nodular (M9696/3) 202.0 ☑
    well differentiated (diffuse) (M9620/3) 200.1 ☑
      follicular (M9693/3) 202.0 ☑
      nodular (M9693/3) 202.0 ☑
  lymphocytic-histiocytic, mixed (diffuse) (M9613/3) 200.8 ☑
    follicular (M9691/3) 202.0 ☑
    nodular (M9691/3) 202.0 ☑
  lymphoplasmacytoid type (M9611/3) 200.8 ☑
  lymphosarcoma type (M9610/3) 200.1 ☑
  macrofollicular (M9690/3) 202.0 ☑
  mantle cell 200.4 ☑
  marginal zone 200.3 ☑
    extranodal B-cell 200.3 ☑
    nodal B-cell 200.3 ☑
    splenic B-cell 200.3 ☑
  mixed cell type (diffuse) (M9613/3) 200.8 ☑
    follicular (M9691/3) 202.0 ☑
    nodular (M9691/3) 202.0 ☑
  nodular (M9690/3) 202.0 ☑
    histiocytic (M9642/3) 200.0 ☑
    lymphocytic (M9690/3) 202.0 ☑
      intermediate differentiation (M9694/3) 202.0 ☑
      poorly differentiated (M9696/3) 202.0 ☑
    mixed (cell type) (lymphocytic-histiocytic) (small cell and large cell) (M9691/3) 202.0 ☑
  non-Hodgkin's type NEC (M9591/3) 202.8 ☑
  peripheral T-cell 202.7 ☑
  primary central nervous system 200.5 ☑
  reticulum cell (type) (M9640/3) 200.0 ☑
  small cell and large cell, mixed (diffuse) (M9613/3) 200.8 ☑
    follicular (M9691/3) 202.0 ☑
    nodular (M9691/3) 202.0 ☑
  stem cell (type) (M9601/3) 202.8 ☑
  T-cell 202.1 ☑
    peripheral 202.7 ☑
  undifferentiated (cell type) (non-Burkitt's) (M9600/3) 202.8 ☑
    Burkitt's type (M9750/3) 200.2 ☑
Lymphomatosis (M9590/3) — see also Lymphoma
  granulomatous 099.1
Lymphopathia
  venereum 099.1
  veneris 099.1
Lymphopenia 288.51
  familial 279.2
Lymphoreticulosis, benign (of inoculation) 078.3
Lymphorrhea 457.8
Lymphosarcoma (M9610/3) 200.1 ☑
  diffuse (M9610/3) 200.1 ☑
    with plasmacytoid differentiation (M9611/3) 200.8 ☑
    lymphoplasmacytic (M9611/3) 200.8 ☑
  follicular (giant) (M9690/3) 202.0 ☑
    lymphoblastic (M9696/3) 202.0 ☑
    lymphocytic, intermediate differentiation (M9694/3) 202.0 ☑
    mixed cell type (M9691/3) 202.0 ☑
  giant follicular (M9690/3) 202.0 ☑
  Hodgkin's (M9650/3) 201.9 ☑
  immunoblastic (M9612/3) 200.8 ☑
  lymphoblastic (diffuse) (M9630/3) 200.1 ☑
    follicular (M9696/3) 202.0 ☑
    nodular (M9696/3) 202.0 ☑

Lymphosarcoma — continued
  lymphocytic (diffuse) (M9620/3) 200.1 ☑
    intermediate differentiation (diffuse) (M9621/3) 200.1 ☑
      follicular (M9694/3) 202.0 ☑
      nodular (M9694/3) 202.0 ☑
  mixed cell type (diffuse) (M9613/3) 200.8 ☑
    follicular (M9691/3) 202.0 ☑
    nodular (M9691/3) 202.0 ☑
  nodular (M9690/3) 202.0 ☑
    lymphoblastic (M9696/3) 202.0 ☑
    lymphocytic, intermediate differentiation (M9694/3) 202.0 ☑
    mixed cell type (M9691/3) 202.0 ☑
  prolymphocytic (M9631/3) 200.1 ☑
  reticulum cell (M9640/3) 200.0 ☑
Lymphostasis 457.8
Lypemania — see also Melancholia 296.2 ☑
Lyssa 071

M

Macacus ear 744.29
Maceration
  fetus (cause not stated) 779.9
  wet feet, tropical (syndrome) 991.4
Machado-Joseph disease 334.8
Machupo virus hemorrhagic fever 078.7
Macleod's syndrome (abnormal transradiancy, one lung) 492.8
Macrocephalia, macrocephaly 756.0
Macrocheilia (congenital) 744.81
Macrochilia (congenital) 744.81
Macrocolon (congenital) 751.3
Macrocornea 743.41
  associated with buphthalmos 743.22
Macrocytic — see condition
Macrocytosis 289.89
Macrodactylia, macrodactylism (fingers) (thumbs) 755.57
  toes 755.65
Macrodontia 520.2
Macroencephaly 742.4
Macrogenia 524.05
Macrogenitosomia (female) (male) (praecox) 255.2
Macrogingivae 523.8
Macroglobulinemia (essential) (idiopathic) (monoclonal) (primary) (syndrome) (Waldenström's) 273.3
Macroglossia (congenital) 750.15
  acquired 529.8
Macrognathia, macrognathism (congenital) 524.00
  mandibular 524.02
    alveolar 524.72
  maxillary 524.01
    alveolar 524.71
Macrogyria (congenital) 742.4
Macrohydrocephalus — see also Hydrocephalus 331.4
Macromastia — see also Hypertrophy, breast 611.1
Macrophage activation syndrome 288.4
Macropsia 368.14
Macrosigmoid 564.7
  congenital 751.3
Macrospondylitis, acromegalic 253.0
Macrostomia (congenital) 744.83
Macrotia (external ear) (congenital) 744.22
Macula
  cornea, corneal
    congenital 743.43
      interfering with vision 743.42
    interfering with central vision 371.03
    not interfering with central vision 371.02
  degeneration (see also Degeneration, macula) 362.50
    hereditary (see also Dystrophy, retina) 362.70
  edema, cystoid 362.53
Maculae ceruleae 132.1
Macules and papules 709.8
Maculopathy, toxic 362.55
Madarosis 374.55

Madelung's
  deformity (radius) 755.54
  disease (lipomatosis) 272.8
  lipomatosis 272.8
Madness — see also Psychosis 298.9
  myxedema (acute) 293.0
    subacute 293.1
Madura
  disease (actinomycotic) 039.9
    mycotic 117.4
  foot (actinomycotic) 039.4
    mycotic 117.4
Maduromycosis (actinomycotic) 039.9
  mycotic 117.4
Maffucci's syndrome (dyschondroplasia with hemangiomas) 756.4
Magenblase syndrome 306.4
Main en griffe (acquired) 736.06
  congenital 755.59
Maintenance
  chemotherapy regimen or treatment V58.11
  dialysis regimen or treatment
    extracorporeal (renal) V56.0
    peritoneal V56.8
    renal V56.0
  drug therapy or regimen
    chemotherapy, antineoplastic V58.11
    immunotherapy, antineoplastic V58.12
  external fixation NEC V54.89
  methadone 304.00
  radiotherapy V58.0
  traction NEC V54.89
Majocchi's
  disease (purpura annularis telangiectodes) 709.1
  granuloma 110.6
Major — see condition
Mal
  cerebral (idiopathic) (see also Epilepsy) 345.9 ☑
  comital (see also Epilepsy) 345.9 ☑
  de los pintos (see also Pinta) 103.9
  de Meleda 757.39
  de mer 994.6
  lie — see Presentation, fetal
  perforant (see also Ulcer, lower extremity) 707.15
Malabar itch 110.9
  beard 110.0
  foot 110.4
  scalp 110.0
Malabsorption 579.9
  calcium 579.8
  carbohydrate 579.8
  disaccharide 271.3
  drug-induced 579.8
  due to bacterial overgrowth 579.8
  fat 579.8
  folate, congenital 281.2
  galactose 271.1
  glucose-galactose (congenital) 271.3
  intestinal 579.9
  isomaltose 271.3
  lactose (hereditary) 271.3
  methionine 270.4
  monosaccharide 271.8
  postgastrectomy 579.3
  postsurgical 579.3
  protein 579.8
  sucrose (-isomaltose) (congenital) 271.3
  syndrome 579.9
    postgastrectomy 579.3
    postsurgical 579.3
Malacia, bone 268.2
  juvenile (see also Rickets) 268.0
  Kienböck's (juvenile) (lunate) (wrist) 732.3
    adult 732.8
Malacoplakia
  bladder 596.89
  colon 569.89
  pelvis (kidney) 593.89
  ureter 593.89
  urethra 599.84
Malacosteon 268.2
  juvenile (see also Rickets) 268.0
Maladaptation — see Maladjustment

☑ Additional Digit Required — Refer to the Tabular List for Digit Selection   ▽ Subterms under main terms may continue to next column or page

2015 ICD-9-CM   ▶◀ Revised Text   ● New Line   ▲ Revised Code   Volume 2 — 179

Maladie de Roger 745.4
Maladjustment
  conjugal V61.10
    involving
      divorce V61.03
      estrangement V61.09
  educational V62.3
  family V61.9
    specified circumstance NEC V61.8
  marital V61.10
    involving
      divorce V61.03
      estrangement V61.09
  occupational V62.29
    current military deployment status V62.21
  simple, adult (see also Reaction, adjustment) 309.9
  situational acute (see also Reaction, adjustment) 309.9
  social V62.4
Malaise 780.79
Malakoplakia — see Malacoplakia
Malaria, malarial (fever) 084.6
  algid 084.9
  any type, with
    algid malaria 084.9
    blackwater fever 084.8
    fever
      blackwater 084.8
      hemoglobinuric (bilious) 084.8
    hemoglobinuria, malarial 084.8
    hepatitis 084.9 [573.2]
    nephrosis 084.9 [581.81]
    pernicious complication NEC 084.9
      cardiac 084.9
      cerebral 084.9
  cardiac 084.9
  carrier (suspected) of V02.9
  cerebral 084.9
  complicating pregnancy, childbirth, or puerperium 647.4 ☑
  congenital 771.2
  congestion, congestive 084.6
    brain 084.9
  continued 084.0
  estivo-autumnal 084.0
  falciparum (malignant tertian) 084.0
  hematinuria 084.8
  hematuria 084.8
  hemoglobinuria 084.8
  hemorrhagic 084.6
  induced (therapeutically) 084.7
    accidental — see Malaria, by type
  liver 084.9 [573.2]
  malariae (quartan) 084.2
  malignant (tertian) 084.0
  mixed infections 084.5
  monkey 084.4
  ovale 084.3
  pernicious, acute 084.0
  Plasmodium, P.
    falciparum 084.0
    malariae 084.2
    ovale 084.3
    vivax 084.1
  quartan 084.2
  quotidian 084.0
  recurrent 084.6
    induced (therapeutically) 084.7
      accidental — see Malaria, by type
  remittent 084.6
  specified types NEC 084.4
  spleen 084.6
  subtertian 084.0
  tertian (benign) 084.1
    malignant 084.0
  tropical 084.0
  typhoid 084.6
  vivax (benign tertian) 084.1
Malassez's disease (testicular cyst) 608.89
Malassimilation 579.9
Maldescent, testis 752.51
Maldevelopment — see also Anomaly, by site
  brain 742.9
  colon 751.5

Maldevelopment — see also Anomaly, by site — continued
  hip (joint) 755.63
    congenital dislocation (see also Dislocation, hip, congenital) 754.30
  mastoid process 756.0
  middle ear, except ossicles 744.03
    ossicles 744.04
  newborn (not malformation) 764.9 ☑
  ossicles, ear 744.04
  spine 756.10
  toe 755.66
Male type pelvis 755.69
  with disproportion (fetopelvic) 653.2 ☑
    affecting fetus or newborn 763.1
    causing obstructed labor 660.1 ☑
      affecting fetus or newborn 763.1
Malformation (congenital) — see also
  Anomaly
  arteriovenous
    pulmonary 747.32
  bone 756.9
  bursa 756.9
  Chiari
    type I 348.4
    type II (see also Spina bifida) 741.0 ☑
    type III 742.0
    type IV 742.2
  circulatory system NEC 747.9
    specified type NEC 747.89
  cochlea 744.05
  digestive system NEC 751.9
    lower 751.5
    specified type NEC 751.8
    upper 750.9
  eye 743.9
  gum 750.9
  heart NEC 746.9
    specified type NEC 746.89
    valve 746.9
  internal ear 744.05
  joint NEC 755.9
    specified type NEC 755.8
  Mondini's (congenital) (malformation, cochlea) 744.05
  muscle 756.9
  nervous system (central) 742.9
  pelvic organs or tissues
    in pregnancy or childbirth 654.9 ☑
      affecting fetus or newborn 763.89
      causing obstructed labor 660.2 ☑
        affecting fetus or newborn 763.1
  placenta (see also Placenta, abnormal) 656.7 ☑
  respiratory organs 748.9
    specified type NEC 748.8
  Rieger's 743.44
  sense organs NEC 742.9
    specified type NEC 742.8
  skin 757.9
    specified type NEC 757.8
  spinal cord 742.9
  teeth, tooth NEC 520.9
  tendon 756.9
  throat 750.9
  umbilical cord (complicating delivery) 663.9 ☑
    affecting fetus or newborn 762.6
  umbilicus 759.9
  urinary system NEC 753.9
    specified type NEC 753.8
  venous — see Anomaly, vein
Malfunction — see also Dysfunction
  arterial graft 996.1
  cardiac pacemaker 996.01
  catheter device — see Complications, mechanical, catheter
  colostomy 569.62
    valve 569.62
  cystostomy 596.82
    infection 596.81
    mechanical 596.82
    specified complication NEC 596.83
  device, implant, or graft NEC — see Complications, mechanical
  enteric stoma 569.62

Malfunction — see also Dysfunction — continued
  enterostomy 569.62
  esophagostomy 530.87
  gastroenteric 536.8
  gastrostomy 536.42
  ileostomy
    valve 569.62
  nephrostomy 997.5
  pacemaker — see Complications, mechanical, pacemaker
  prosthetic device, internal — see Complications, mechanical
  tracheostomy 519.02
  valve
    colostomy 569.62
    ileostomy 569.62
  vascular graft or shunt 996.1
Malgaigne's fracture (closed) 808.43
  open 808.53
Malherbe's
  calcifying epithelioma (M8110/0) — see Neoplasm, skin, benign
  tumor (M8110/0) — see Neoplasm, skin, benign
Malibu disease 919.8
  infected 919.9
Malignancy (M8000/3) — See Neoplasm, by site, malignant
Malignant — see condition
Malingerer, malingering V65.2
Mallet, finger (acquired) 736.1
  congenital 755.59
  late effect of rickets 268.1
Malleus 024
Mallory's bodies 034.1
Mallory-Weiss syndrome 530.7
Malnutrition (calorie) 263.9
  complicating pregnancy 648.9 ☑
  degree
    first 263.1
    second 263.0
    third 262
    mild (protein) 263.1
    moderate (protein) 263.0
    severe 261
      protein-calorie 262
  fetus 764.2 ☑
    "light-for-dates" 764.1 ☑
  following gastrointestinal surgery 579.3
  intrauterine or fetal 764.2 ☑
    fetus or infant "light-for-dates" 764.1 ☑
  lack of care, or neglect (child) (infant) 995.52
    adult 995.84
  malignant 260
  mild (protein) 263.1
  moderate (protein) 263.0
  protein 260
  protein-calorie 263.9
    mild 263.1
    moderate 263.0
    severe 262
    specified type NEC 263.8
  severe 261
    protein-calorie NEC 262
Malocclusion (teeth) 524.4
  angle's class I 524.21
  angle's class II 524.22
  angle's class III 524.23
  due to
    abnormal swallowing 524.59
    accessory teeth (causing crowding) 524.31
    dentofacial abnormality NEC 524.89
    impacted teeth (causing crowding) 520.6
    missing teeth 524.30
    mouth breathing 524.59
    sleep postures 524.59
    supernumerary teeth (causing crowding) 524.31
    thumb sucking 524.59
    tongue, lip, or finger habits 524.59
  temporomandibular (joint) 524.69
Malposition
  cardiac apex (congenital) 746.87
  cervix — see Malposition, uterus

Malposition — continued
  congenital
    adrenal (gland) 759.1
    alimentary tract 751.8
      lower 751.5
      upper 750.8
    aorta 747.21
    appendix 751.5
    arterial trunk 747.29
    artery (peripheral) NEC (see also Malposition, congenital, peripheral vascular system) 747.60
      coronary 746.85
      pulmonary 747.39
    auditory canal 744.29
      causing impairment of hearing 744.02
    auricle (ear) 744.29
      causing impairment of hearing 744.02
    cervical 744.43
    biliary duct or passage 751.69
    bladder (mucosa) 753.8
      exteriorized or extroverted 753.5
    brachial plexus 742.8
    brain tissue 742.4
    breast 757.6
    bronchus 748.3
    cardiac apex 746.87
    cecum 751.5
    clavicle 755.51
    colon 751.5
    digestive organ or tract NEC 751.8
      lower 751.5
      upper 750.8
    ear (auricle) (external) 744.29
      ossicles 744.04
    endocrine (gland) NEC 759.2
    epiglottis 748.3
    Eustachian tube 744.24
    eye 743.8
    facial features 744.89
    fallopian tube 752.19
    finger(s) 755.59
      supernumerary 755.01
    foot 755.67
    gallbladder 751.69
    gastrointestinal tract 751.8
    genitalia, genital organ(s) or tract
      female 752.89
        external 752.49
        internal NEC 752.89
      male 752.89
        penis 752.69
        scrotal transposition 752.81
    glottis 748.3
    hand 755.59
    heart 746.87
      dextrocardia 746.87
        with complete transposition of viscera 759.3
    hepatic duct 751.69
    hip (joint) (see also Dislocation, hip, congenital) 754.30
    intestine (large) (small) 751.5
      with anomalous adhesions, fixation, or malrotation 751.4
    joint NEC 755.8
    kidney 753.3
    larynx 748.3
    limb 755.8
      lower 755.69
      upper 755.59
    liver 751.69
    lung (lobe) 748.69
    nail(s) 757.5
    nerve 742.8
    nervous system NEC 742.8
    nose, nasal (septum) 748.1
    organ or site NEC — see Anomaly, specified type NEC, by site
    ovary 752.0
    pancreas 751.7
    parathyroid (gland) 759.2
    patella 755.64
    peripheral vascular system 747.60

☑ Additional Digit Required — Refer to the Tabular List for Digit Selection   ▽ Subterms under main terms may continue to next column or page

180 — Volume 2   ▶◀ Revised Text   ● New Line   ▲ Revised Code   2015 ICD-9-CM

Malposition — *continued*
  congenital — *continued*
    peripheral vascular system — *continued*
      gastrointestinal 747.61
      lower limb 747.64
      renal 747.62
      specified NEC 747.69
      spinal 747.82
      upper limb 747.63
    pituitary (gland) 759.2
    respiratory organ or system NEC 748.9
    rib (cage) 756.3
      supernumerary in cervical region 756.2
    scapula 755.59
    shoulder 755.59
    spinal cord 742.59
    spine 756.19
    spleen 759.0
    sternum 756.3
    stomach 750.7
    symphysis pubis 755.69
    testis (undescended) 752.51
    thymus (gland) 759.2
    thyroid (gland) (tissue) 759.2
      cartilage 748.3
    toe(s) 755.66
      supernumerary 755.02
    tongue 750.19
    trachea 748.3
    uterus 752.39
    vein(s) (peripheral) NEC (*see also* Malposition, congenital, peripheral vascular system) 747.60
      great 747.49
      portal 747.49
      pulmonary 747.49
      vena cava (inferior) (superior) 747.49
  device, implant, or graft — *see* Complications, mechanical
  fetus NEC (*see also* Presentation, fetal) 652.9 ☑
    with successful version 652.1 ☑
    affecting fetus or newborn 763.1
    before labor, affecting fetus or newborn 761.7
    causing obstructed labor 660.0 ☑
    in multiple gestation (one fetus or more) 652.6 ☑
      with locking 660.5 ☑
      causing obstructed labor 660.0 ☑
  gallbladder (*see also* Disease, gallbladder) 575.8
  gastrointestinal tract 569.89
    congenital 751.8
  heart (*see also* Malposition, congenital, heart) 746.87
  intestine 569.89
    congenital 751.5
  pelvic organs or tissues
    in pregnancy or childbirth 654.4 ☑
      affecting fetus or newborn 763.89
      causing obstructed labor 660.2 ☑
        affecting fetus or newborn 763.1
  placenta — *see* Placenta, previa
  stomach 537.89
    congenital 750.7
  tooth, teeth 524.30
    with impaction 520.6
  uterus (acquired) (acute) (adherent) (any degree) (asymptomatic) (postinfectional) (postpartal, old) 621.6
    anteflexion or anteversion (*see also* Anteversion, uterus) 621.6
    congenital 752.39
    flexion 621.6
      lateral (*see also* Lateroversion, uterus) 621.6
    in pregnancy or childbirth 654.4 ☑
      affecting fetus or newborn 763.89
      causing obstructed labor 660.2 ☑
        affecting fetus or newborn 763.1
    inversion 621.6
    lateral (flexion) (version) (*see also* Lateroversion, uterus) 621.6

Malposition — *continued*
  uterus — *continued*
    lateroflexion (*see also* Lateroversion, uterus) 621.6
    lateroversion (*see also* Lateroversion, uterus) 621.6
    retroflexion or retroversion (*see also* Retroversion, uterus) 621.6
Malposture 729.90
Malpresentation, fetus — *see also* Presentation, fetal 652.9 ☑
Malrotation
  cecum 751.4
  colon 751.4
  intestine 751.4
  kidney 753.3
MALT (mucosa associated lymphoid tissue) 200.3 ☑
Malta fever — *see also* Brucellosis 023.9
Maltosuria 271.3
Maltreatment (of)
  adult 995.80
    emotional 995.82
    multiple forms 995.85
    neglect (nutritional) 995.84
    physical 995.81
    psychological 995.82
    sexual 995.83
  child 995.50
    emotional 995.51
    multiple forms 995.59
    neglect (nutritional) 995.52
    physical 995.54
      shaken infant syndrome 995.55
    psychological 995.51
    sexual 995.53
  spouse (*see also* Maltreatment, adult) 995.80
Malt workers' lung 495.4
Malum coxae senilis 715.25
Malunion, fracture 733.81
Mammillitis — *see also* Mastitis 611.0
  puerperal, postpartum 675.2 ☑
Mammitis — *see also* Mastitis 611.0
  puerperal, postpartum 675.2 ☑
Mammographic
  calcification 793.89
  calculus 793.89
  microcalcification 793.81
Mammoplasia 611.1
Management
  contraceptive V25.9
    specified type NEC V25.8
  procreative V26.9
    specified type NEC V26.89
Mangled NEC — *see also* nature and site of injury 959.9
Mania (monopolar) — *see also* Psychosis, affective 296.0 ☑
  alcoholic (acute) (chronic) 291.9
  Bell's — *see* Mania, chronic
  chronic 296.0 ☑
    recurrent episode 296.1 ☑
    single episode 296.0 ☑
  compulsive 300.3
  delirious (acute) 296.0 ☑
    recurrent episode 296.1 ☑
    single episode 296.0 ☑
  epileptic (*see also* Epilepsy) 345.4 ☑
  hysterical 300.10
  inhibited 296.89
  puerperal (after delivery) 296.0 ☑
    recurrent episode 296.1 ☑
    single episode 296.0 ☑
  recurrent episode 296.1 ☑
  senile 290.8
  single episode 296.0 ☑
  stupor 296.89
  stuporous 296.89
  unproductive 296.89
Manic-depressive insanity, psychosis, reaction, or syndrome — *see also* Psychosis, affective 296.80
  circular (alternating) 296.7
    currently
      depressed 296.5 ☑
      episode unspecified 296.7

Manic-depressive insanity, psychosis, reaction, or syndrome — *see also* Psychosis, affective — *continued*
  circular — *continued*
    currently — *continued*
      hypomanic, previously depressed 296.4 ☑
      manic 296.4 ☑
      mixed 296.6 ☑
  depressed (type), depressive 296.2 ☑
    atypical 296.82
    recurrent episode 296.3 ☑
    single episode 296.2 ☑
  hypomanic 296.0 ☑
    recurrent episode 296.1 ☑
    single episode 296.0 ☑
  manic 296.0 ☑
    atypical 296.81
    recurrent episode 296.1 ☑
    single episode 296.0 ☑
  mixed NEC 296.89
  perplexed 296.89
  stuporous 296.89
Manifestations, rheumatoid
  lungs 714.81
  pannus — *see* Arthritis, rheumatoid
  subcutaneous nodules — *see* Arthritis, rheumatoid
Mankowsky's syndrome (familial dysplastic osteopathy) 731.2
Mannoheptulosuria 271.8
Mannosidosis 271.8
Manson's
  disease (schistosomiasis) 120.1
  pyosis (pemphigus contagiosus) 684
  schistosomiasis 120.1
Mansonellosis 125.5
Manual — *see* condition
Maple bark disease 495.6
Maple bark-strippers' lung 495.6
Maple syrup (urine) disease or syndrome 270.3
Marable's syndrome (celiac artery compression) 447.4
Marasmus 261
  brain 331.9
  due to malnutrition 261
  intestinal 569.89
  nutritional 261
  senile 797
  tuberculous NEC (*see also* Tuberculosis) 011.9 ☑
Marble
  bones 756.52
  skin 782.61
Marburg disease (virus) 078.89
March
  foot 733.94
  hemoglobinuria 283.2
Marchand multiple nodular hyperplasia (liver) 571.5
Marchesani (-Weill) syndrome (brachymorphism and ectopia lentis) 759.89
Marchiafava (-Bignami) disease or syndrome 341.8
Marchiafava-Micheli syndrome (paroxysmal nocturnal hemoglobinuria) 283.2
Marcus Gunn's syndrome (jaw-winking syndrome) 742.8
Marfan's
  congenital syphilis 090.49
  disease 090.49
  syndrome (arachnodactyly) 759.82
    meaning congenital syphilis 090.49
    with luxation of lens 090.49 [379.32]
Marginal
  implantation, placenta — *see* Placenta, previa
  placenta — *see* Placenta, previa
  sinus (hemorrhage) (rupture) 641.2 ☑
    affecting fetus or newborn 762.1
Marie's
  cerebellar ataxia 334.2
  syndrome (acromegaly) 253.0

Marie-Bamberger disease or syndrome (hypertrophic) (pulmonary) (secondary) 731.2
  idiopathic (acropachyderma) 757.39
  primary (acropachyderma) 757.39
Marie-Charcôt-Tooth neuropathic atrophy, muscle 356.1
Marie-Strümpell arthritis or disease (ankylosing spondylitis) 720.0
Marihuana, marijuana
  abuse (*see also* Abuse, drugs, nondependent) 305.2 ☑
  dependence (*see also* Dependence) 304.3 ☑
Marion's disease (bladder neck obstruction) 596.0
Marital conflict V61.10
Mark
  port wine 757.32
  raspberry 757.32
  strawberry 757.32
  stretch 701.3
  tattoo 709.09
Maroteaux-Lamy syndrome (mucopolysaccharidosis VI) 277.5
Marriage license examination V70.3
Marrow (bone)
  arrest 284.9
  megakaryocytic 287.30
  poor function 289.9
Marseilles fever 082.1
Marshall's (hidrotic) **ectodermal dysplasia** 757.31
Marsh's disease (exophthalmic goiter) 242.0 ☑
Marsh fever — *see also* Malaria 084.6
Martin-Albright syndrome (pseudohypoparathyroidism) 275.49
Martin's disease 715.27
Martorell-Fabre syndrome (pulseless disease) 446.7
Masculinization, female, with adrenal hyperplasia 255.2
Masculinovoblastoma (M8670/0) 220
Masochism 302.83
Masons' lung 502
Mass
  abdominal 789.3 ☑
  anus 787.99
  bone 733.90
  breast 611.72
  cheek 784.2
  chest 786.6
  cystic — *see* Cyst
  ear 388.8
  epigastric 789.3 ☑
  eye 379.92
  female genital organ 625.8
  gum 784.2
  head 784.2
  intracranial 784.2
  joint 719.60
    ankle 719.67
    elbow 719.62
    foot 719.67
    hand 719.64
    hip 719.65
    knee 719.66
    multiple sites 719.69
    pelvic region 719.65
    shoulder (region) 719.61
    specified site NEC 719.68
    wrist 719.63
  kidney (*see also* Disease, kidney) 593.9
  lung 786.6
  lymph node 785.6
  malignant (M8000/3) — *see* Neoplasm, by site, malignant
  mediastinal 786.6
  mouth 784.2
  muscle (limb) 729.89
  neck 784.2
  nose or sinus 784.2
  palate 784.2
  pelvis, pelvic 789.3 ☑
  penis 607.89
  perineum 625.8

☑ Additional Digit Required — Refer to the Tabular List for Digit Selection   ▽ Subterms under main terms may continue to next column or page

182 — Volume 2   ▶◀ Revised Text   ● New Line   ▲ Revised Code   2015 ICD-9-CM

Megaduodenum 537.3
Megaesophagus (functional) 530.0
  congenital 750.4
Megakaryocytic — *see* condition
Megalencephaly 742.4
Megalerythema (epidermicum) (infectiosum) 057.0
Megalia, cutis et ossium 757.39
Megaloappendix 751.5
Megalocephalus, megalocephaly NEC 756.0
Megalocornea 743.41
  associated with buphthalmos 743.22
Megalocytic anemia 281.9
Megalodactylia (fingers) (thumbs) 755.57
  toes 755.65
Megaloduodenum 751.5
Megaloesophagus (functional) 530.0
  congenital 750.4
Megalogastria (congenital) 750.7
Megalomania 307.9
Megalophthalmos 743.8
Megalopsia 368.14
Megalosplenia — *see also* Splenomegaly 789.2
Megaloureter 593.89
  congenital 753.22
Megarectum 569.49
Megasigmoid 564.7
  congenital 751.3
Megaureter 593.89
  congenital 753.22
Megrim 346.9 ☑
Meibomian
  cyst 373.2
    infected 373.12
  gland — *see* condition
  infarct (eyelid) 374.85
  stye 373.11
Meibomitis 373.12
Meige
  -Milroy disease (chronic hereditary edema) 757.0
  syndrome (blepharospasm-oromandibular dystonia) 333.82
Melalgia, nutritional 266.2
Melancholia — *see also* Psychosis, affective 296.90
  climacteric 296.2 ☑
    recurrent episode 296.3 ☑
    single episode 296.2 ☑
  hypochondriac 300.7
  intermittent 296.2 ☑
    recurrent episode 296.3 ☑
    single episode 296.2 ☑
  involutional 296.2 ☑
    recurrent episode 296.3 ☑
    single episode 296.2 ☑
  menopausal 296.2 ☑
    recurrent episode 296.3 ☑
    single episode 296.2 ☑
  puerperal 296.2 ☑
  reactive (from emotional stress, psychological trauma) 298.0
  recurrent 296.3 ☑
  senile 290.21
  stuporous 296.2 ☑
    recurrent episode 296.3 ☑
    single episode 296.2 ☑
Melanemia 275.09
Melanoameloblastoma (M9363/0) — *see* Neoplasm, bone, benign
Melanoblastoma (M8720/3) — *see* Melanoma
Melanoblastosis
  Block-Sulzberger 757.33
  cutis linearis sive systematisata 757.33
Melanocarcinoma (M8720/3) — *see* Melanoma
Melanocytoma, eyeball (M8726/0) 224.0
Melanocytosis, neurocutaneous 757.33
Melanoderma, melanodermia 709.09
  Addison's (primary adrenal insufficiency) 255.41
Melanodontia, infantile 521.05
Melanodontoclasia 521.05
Melanoepithelioma (M8720/3) — *see* Melanoma

Melanoma (malignant) (M8720/3) 172.9

> *Note* — *Except where otherwise indicated, the morphological varieties of melanoma in the list below should be coded by site as for "Melanoma (malignant)". Internal sites should be coded to malignant neoplasm of those sites.*

  abdominal wall 172.5
  ala nasi 172.3
  amelanotic (M8730/3) — *see* Melanoma, by site
  ankle 172.7
  anus, anal 154.3
    canal 154.2
  arm 172.6
  auditory canal (external) 172.2
  auricle (ear) 172.2
  auricular canal (external) 172.2
  axilla 172.5
  axillary fold 172.5
  back 172.5
  balloon cell (M8722/3) — *see* Melanoma, by site
  benign (M8720/0) — *see* Neoplasm, skin, benign
  breast (female) (male) 172.5
  brow 172.3
  buttock 172.5
  canthus (eye) 172.1
  cheek (external) 172.3
  chest wall 172.5
  chin 172.3
  choroid 190.6
  conjunctiva 190.3
  ear (external) 172.2
  epithelioid cell (M8771/3) (*see also* Melanoma, by site)
    and spindle cell, mixed (M8775/3) — *see* Melanoma, by site
  external meatus (ear) 172.2
  eye 190.9
  eyebrow 172.3
  eyelid (lower) (upper) 172.1
  face NEC 172.3
  female genital organ (external) NEC 184.4
  finger 172.6
  flank 172.5
  foot 172.7
  forearm 172.6
  forehead 172.3
  foreskin 187.1
  gluteal region 172.5
  groin 172.5
  hand 172.6
  heel 172.7
  helix 172.2
  hip 172.7
  in
    giant pigmented nevus (M8761/3) — *see* Melanoma, by site
    Hutchinson's melanotic freckle (M8742/3) — *see* Melanoma, by site
    junctional nevus (M8740/3) — *see* Melanoma, by site
    precancerous melanosis (M8741/3) — *see* Melanoma, by site
  in situ — *see* Melanoma, by site
    skin 172.9
  interscapular region 172.5
  iris 190.0
  jaw 172.3
  juvenile (M8770/0) — *see* Neoplasm, skin, benign
  knee 172.7
  labium
    majus 184.1
    minus 184.2
  lacrimal gland 190.2
  leg 172.7
  lip (lower) (upper) 172.0
  liver 197.7
  lower limb NEC 172.7
  male genital organ (external) NEC 187.9
  meatus, acoustic (external) 172.2
  meibomian gland 172.1

Melanoma — *continued*
  metastatic
    of or from specified site — *see* Melanoma, by site
    site not of skin — *see* Neoplasm, by site, malignant, secondary
    to specified site — *see* Neoplasm, by site, malignant, secondary
    unspecified site 172.9
  nail 172.9
    finger 172.6
    toe 172.7
  neck 172.4
  nodular (M8721/3) — *see* Melanoma, by site
  nose, external 172.3
  orbit 190.1
  penis 187.4
  perianal skin 172.5
  perineum 172.5
  pinna 172.2
  popliteal (fossa) (space) 172.7
  prepuce 187.1
  pubes 172.5
  pudendum 184.4
  retina 190.5
  scalp 172.4
  scrotum 187.7
  septum nasal (skin) 172.3
  shoulder 172.6
  skin NEC 172.8
    in situ 172.9
  spindle cell (M8772/3) (*see also* Melanoma, by site)
    type A (M8773/3) 190.0
    type B (M8774/3) 190.0
  submammary fold 172.5
  superficial spreading (M8743/3) — *see* Melanoma, by site
  temple 172.3
  thigh 172.7
  toe 172.7
  trunk NEC 172.5
  umbilicus 172.5
  upper limb NEC 172.6
  vagina vault 184.0
  vulva 184.4
Melanoplakia 528.9
Melanosarcoma (M8720/3) — *see also* Melanoma
  epithelioid cell (M8771/3) — *see* Melanoma
Melanosis 709.09
  addisonian (primary adrenal insufficiency) 255.41
    tuberculous (*see also* Tuberculosis) 017.6 ☑
  adrenal 255.41
  colon 569.89
  conjunctiva 372.55
    congenital 743.49
  corii degenerativa 757.33
  cornea (presenile) (senile) 371.12
    congenital 743.43
      interfering with vision 743.42
  eye 372.55
    congenital 743.49
  jute spinners' 709.09
  lenticularis progressiva 757.33
  liver 573.8
  precancerous (M8741/2) (*see also* Neoplasm, skin, in situ)
    malignant melanoma in (M8741/3) — *see* Melanoma
  prenatal 743.43
    interfering with vision 743.42
  Riehl's 709.09
  sclera 379.19
    congenital 743.47
  suprarenal 255.41
  tar 709.09
  toxic 709.09
Melanuria 791.9
Melasma 709.09
  adrenal (gland) 255.41
  suprarenal (gland) 255.41

MELAS syndrome (mitochondrial encephalopathy, lactic acidosis and stroke-like episodes) 277.87
Melena 578.1
  due to
    swallowed maternal blood 777.3
    ulcer — *see* Ulcer, by site, with hemorrhage
  newborn 772.4
    due to swallowed maternal blood 777.3
Meleney's
  gangrene (cutaneous) 686.09
  ulcer (chronic undermining) 686.09
Melioidosis 025
Melitensis, febris 023.0
Melitococcosis 023.0
Melkersson (-Rosenthal) syndrome 351.8
Mellitus, diabetes — *see* Diabetes
Melorheostosis (bone) (leri) 733.99
Meloschisis 744.83
Melotia 744.29
Membrana
  capsularis lentis posterior 743.39
  epipapillaris 743.57
Membranacea placenta — *see* Placenta, abnormal
Membranaceous uterus 621.8
Membrane, membranous — *see also* condition
  folds, congenital — *see* Web
  Jackson's 751.4
  over face (causing asphyxia), fetus or newborn 768.9
  premature rupture — *see* Rupture, membranes, premature
  pupillary 364.74
    persistent 743.46
  retained (complicating delivery) (with hemorrhage) 666.2 ☑
    without hemorrhage 667.1 ☑
  secondary (eye) 366.50
  unruptured (causing asphyxia) 768.9
  vitreous humor 379.25
Membranitis, fetal 658.4 ☑
  affecting fetus or newborn 762.7
Memory disturbance, loss or lack — *see also* Amnesia 780.93
  mild, following organic brain damage 310.89
MEN (multiple endocrine neoplasia) (syndromes)
  type I 258.01
  type IIA 258.02
  type IIB 258.03
Menadione (vitamin K) **deficiency** 269.0
Menarche, precocious 259.1
Mendacity, pathologic 301.7
Mendelson's syndrome (resulting from a procedure) 997.32
  obstetric 668.0 ☑
Mende's syndrome (ptosis-epicanthus) 270.2
Ménétrier's disease or syndrome (hypertrophic gastritis) 535.2 ☑
Ménière's disease, syndrome, or vertigo 386.00
  cochlear 386.02
  cochleovestibular 386.01
  inactive 386.04
  in remission 386.04
  vestibular 386.03
Meninges, meningeal — *see* condition
Meningioma (M9530/0) — *see also* Neoplasm, meninges, benign
  angioblastic (M9535/0) — *see* Neoplasm, meninges, benign
  angiomatous (M9534/0) — *see* Neoplasm, meninges, benign
  endotheliomatous (M9531/0) — *see* Neoplasm, meninges, benign
  fibroblastic (M9532/0) — *see* Neoplasm, meninges, benign
  fibrous (M9532/0) — *see* Neoplasm, meninges, benign
  hemangioblastic (M9535/0) — *see* Neoplasm, meninges, benign

☑ Additional Digit Required — Refer to the Tabular List for Digit Selection   ▽ Subterms under main terms may continue to next column or page

2015 ICD-9-CM   ▶◀ Revised Text   ● New Line   ▲ Revised Code   Volume 2 — 183

Meningioma — see also Neoplasm, meninges, benign — continued
  hemangiopericytic (M9536/0) — see Neoplasm, meninges, benign
  malignant (M9530/3) — see Neoplasm, meninges, malignant
  meningiothelial (M9531/0) — see Neoplasm, meninges, benign
  meningotheliomatous (M9531/0) — see Neoplasm, meninges, benign
  mixed (M9537/0) — see Neoplasm, meninges, benign
  multiple (M9530/1) 237.6
  papillary (M9538/1) 237.6
  psammomatous (M9533/0) — see Neoplasm, meninges, benign
  syncytial (M9531/0) — see Neoplasm, meninges, benign
  transitional (M9537/0) — see Neoplasm, meninges, benign
Meningiomatosis (diffuse) (M9530/1) 237.6
Meningism — see also Meningismus 781.6
Meningismus (infectional) (pneumococcal) 781.6
  due to serum or vaccine 997.09 [321.8]
  influenzal NEC (see also Influenza) 487.8
Meningitis (basal) (basic) (basilar) (brain) (cerebral) (cervical) (congestive) (diffuse) (hemorrhagic) (infantile) (membranous) (metastatic) (nonspecific) (pontine) (progressive) (simple) (spinal) (subacute) (sympathetica) (toxic) 322.9
  abacterial NEC (see also Meningitis, aseptic) 047.9
  actinomycotic 039.8 [320.7]
  adenoviral 049.1
  Aerobacter aerogenes 320.82
  anaerobes (cocci) (gram-negative) (gram-positive) (mixed) (NEC) 320.81
  arbovirus NEC 066.9 [321.2]
    specified type NEC 066.8 [321.2]
  aseptic (acute) NEC 047.9
    adenovirus 049.1
    Coxsackie virus 047.0
    due to
      adenovirus 049.1
      Coxsackie virus 047.0
      ECHO virus 047.1
      enterovirus 047.9
      mumps 072.1
      poliovirus (see also Poliomyelitis) 045.2 ☑ [321.2]
    ECHO virus 047.1
    herpes (simplex) virus 054.72
      zoster 053.0
    leptospiral 100.81
    lymphocytic choriomeningitis 049.0
    noninfective 322.0
  Bacillus pyocyaneus 320.89
  bacterial NEC 320.9
    anaerobic 320.81
    gram-negative 320.82
      anaerobic 320.81
  Bacteroides (fragilis) (oralis) (melaninogenicus) 320.81
  cancerous (M8000/6) 198.4
  candidal 112.83
  carcinomatous (M8010/6) 198.4
  caseous (see also Tuberculosis, meninges) 013.0 ☑
  cerebrospinal (acute) (chronic) (diplococcal) (endemic) (epidemic) (fulminant) (infectious) (malignant) (meningococcal) (sporadic) 036.0
    carrier (suspected) of V02.59
  chronic NEC 322.2
  clear cerebrospinal fluid NEC 322.0
  Clostridium (haemolyticum) (novyi) NEC 320.81
  coccidioidomycosis 114.2
  Coxsackie virus 047.0
  cryptococcal 117.5 [321.0]
  diplococcal 036.0
    gram-negative 036.0
    gram-positive 320.1

Meningitis — continued
  Diplococcus pneumoniae 320.1
  due to
    actinomycosis 039.8 [320.7]
    adenovirus 049.1
    coccidiomycosis 114.2
    enterovirus 047.9
      specified NEC 047.8
    histoplasmosis (see also Histoplasmosis) 115.91
    Listerosis 027.0 [320.7]
    Lyme disease 088.81 [320.7]
    moniliasis 112.83
    mumps 072.1
    neurosyphilis 094.2
    nonbacterial organisms NEC 321.8
    oidiomycosis 112.83
    poliovirus (see also Poliomyelitis) 045.2 ☑ [321.2]
    preventive immunization, inoculation, or vaccination 997.09 [321.8]
    sarcoidosis 135 [321.4]
    sporotrichosis 117.1 [321.1]
    syphilis 094.2
      acute 091.81
      congenital 090.42
      secondary 091.81
    trypanosomiasis (see also Trypanosomiasis) 086.9 [321.3]
    whooping cough 033.9 [320.7]
  ECHO virus 047.1
  E. coli 320.82
  endothelial-leukocytic, benign, recurrent 047.9
  Enterobacter aerogenes 320.82
  enteroviral 047.9
    specified type NEC 047.8
  enterovirus 047.9
    specified NEC 047.8
  eosinophilic 322.1
  epidemic NEC 036.0
  Escherichia coli (E. coli) 320.82
  Eubacterium 320.81
  fibrinopurulent NEC 320.9
    specified type NEC 320.89
  Friedländer (bacillus) 320.82
  fungal NEC 117.9 [321.1]
  Fusobacterium 320.81
  gonococcal 098.82
  gram-negative bacteria NEC 320.82
    anaerobic 320.81
    cocci 036.0
      specified NEC 320.82
  gram-negative cocci NEC 036.0
    specified NEC 320.82
  gram-positive cocci NEC 320.9
  herpes (simplex) virus 054.72
    zoster 053.0
  H. influenzae 320.0
  infectious NEC 320.9
  influenzal 320.0
  Klebsiella pneumoniae 320.82
  late effect — see Late, effect, meningitis
  leptospiral (aseptic) 100.81
  Listerella (monocytogenes) 027.0 [320.7]
  Listeria monocytogenes 027.0 [320.7]
  lymphocytic (acute) (benign) (serous) 049.0
    choriomeningitis virus 049.0
  meningococcal (chronic) 036.0
  Mima polymorpha 320.82
  Mollaret's 047.9
  monilial 112.83
  mumps (virus) 072.1
  mycotic NEC 117.9 [321.1]
  Neisseria 036.0
  neurosyphilis 094.2
  nonbacterial NEC (see also Meningitis, aseptic) 047.9
  nonpyogenic NEC 322.0
  oidiomycosis 112.83
  ossificans 349.2
  Peptococcus 320.81
  Peptostreptococcus 320.81
  pneumococcal 320.1
  poliovirus (see also Poliomyelitis) 045.2 ☑ [321.2]

Meningitis — continued
  Proprionibacterium 320.81
  Proteus morganii 320.82
  Pseudomonas (aeruginosa) (pyocyaneus) 320.82
  purulent NEC 320.9
    specified organism NEC 320.89
  pyogenic NEC 320.9
    specified organism NEC 320.89
  Salmonella 003.21
  septic NEC 320.9
    specified organism NEC 320.89
  serosa circumscripta NEC 322.0
  serous NEC (see also Meningitis, aseptic) 047.9
    lymphocytic 049.0
    syndrome 348.2
  Serratia (marcescens) 320.82
  specified organism NEC 320.89
  sporadic cerebrospinal 036.0
  sporotrichosis 117.1 [321.1]
  staphylococcal 320.3
  sterile 997.09
  streptococcal (acute) 320.2
  suppurative 320.9
    specified organism NEC 320.89
  syphilitic 094.2
    acute 091.81
    congenital 090.42
    secondary 091.81
  torula 117.5 [321.0]
  traumatic (complication of injury) 958.8
  Treponema (denticola) (macrodenticum) 320.81
  trypanosomiasis 086.1 [321.3]
  tuberculous (see also Tuberculosis, meninges) 013.0 ☑
  typhoid 002.0 [320.7]
  Veillonella 320.81
  Vibrio vulnificus 320.82
  viral, virus NEC (see also Meningitis, aseptic) 047.9
  Wallgren's (see also Meningitis, aseptic) 047.9
Meningocele (congenital) (spinal) — see also Spina bifida 741.9 ☑
  acquired (traumatic) 349.2
  cerebral 742.0
  cranial 742.0
Meningocerebritis — see Meningoencephalitis
Meningococcemia (acute) (chronic) 036.2
Meningococcus, meningococcal — see also condition 036.9
  adrenalitis, hemorrhagic 036.3
  carditis 036.40
  carrier (suspected) of V02.59
  cerebrospinal fever 036.0
  encephalitis 036.1
  endocarditis 036.42
  exposure to V01.84
  infection NEC 036.9
  meningitis (cerebrospinal) 036.0
  myocarditis 036.43
  optic neuritis 036.81
  pericarditis 036.41
  septicemia (chronic) 036.2
Meningoencephalitis — see also Encephalitis 323.9
  acute NEC 048
  bacterial, purulent, pyogenic, or septic — see Meningitis
  chronic NEC 094.1
  diffuse NEC 094.1
  diphasic 063.2
  due to
    actinomycosis 039.8 [320.7]
    blastomycosis NEC (see also Blastomycosis) 116.0 [323.41]
    free-living amebae 136.29
    Listeria monocytogenes 027.0 [320.7]
    Lyme disease 088.81 [320.7]
    mumps 072.2
    Naegleria (amebae) (gruberi) (organisms) 136.29
    rubella 056.01

Meningoencephalitis — see also Encephalitis — continued
  due to — continued
    sporotrichosis 117.1 [321.1]
    toxoplasmosis (acquired) 130.0
      congenital (active) 771.2 [323.41]
    Trypanosoma 086.1 [323.2]
  epidemic 036.0
  herpes 054.3
  herpetic 054.3
  H. influenzae 320.0
  infectious (acute) 048
  influenzal 320.0
  late effect — see category 326
  Listeria monocytogenes 027.0 [320.7]
  lymphocytic (serous) 049.0
  mumps 072.2
  parasitic NEC 123.9 [323.41]
  pneumococcal 320.1
  primary amebic 136.29
  rubella 056.01
  serous 048
    lymphocytic 049.0
  specific 094.2
  staphylococcal 320.3
  streptococcal 320.2
  syphilitic 094.2
  toxic NEC 989.9 [323.71]
    due to
      carbon tetrachloride (vapor) 987.8 [323.71]
      hydroxyquinoline derivatives poisoning 961.3 [323.71]
      lead 984.9 [323.71]
      mercury 985.0 [323.71]
      thallium 985.8 [323.71]
  toxoplasmosis (acquired) 130.0
  trypanosomic 086.1 [323.2]
  tuberculous (see also Tuberculosis, meninges) 013.0 ☑
  virus NEC 048
Meningoencephalocele 742.0
  syphilitic 094.89
  congenital 090.49
Meningoencephalomyelitis — see also Meningoencephalitis 323.9
  acute NEC 048
    disseminated (postinfectious) 136.9 [323.61]
      postimmunization or postvaccination 323.51
  due to
    actinomycosis 039.8 [320.7]
    torula 117.5 [323.41]
    toxoplasma or toxoplasmosis (acquired) 130.0
      congenital (active) 771.2 [323.41]
  late effect — see category 326
Meningoencephalomyelopathy — see also Meningoencephalomyelitis 349.9
Meningoencephalopathy — see also Meningoencephalitis 348.39
Meningoencephalopoliomyelitis — see also Poliomyelitis, bulbar 045.0 ☑
  late effect 138
Meningomyelitis — see also Meningoencephalitis 323.9
  blastomycotic NEC (see also Blastomycosis) 116.0 [323.41]
  due to
    actinomycosis 039.8 [320.7]
    blastomycosis (see also Blastomycosis) 116.0 [323.41]
    Meningococcus 036.0
    sporotrichosis 117.1 [323.41]
    torula 117.5 [323.41]
  late effect — see category 326
  lethargic 049.8
  meningococcal 036.0
  syphilitic 094.2
  tuberculous (see also Tuberculosis, meninges) 013.0 ☑
Meningomyelocele — see also Spina bifida 741.9 ☑
  syphilitic 094.89

☑ Additional Digit Required — Refer to the Tabular List for Digit Selection   ▽ Subterms under main terms may continue to next column or page

184 — Volume 2   ▶◀ Revised Text   ● New Line   ▲ Revised Code   2015 ICD-9-CM

Meningomyeloneuritis — *see* Meningoencephalitis
Meningoradiculitis — *see* Meningitis
Meningovascular — *see* condition
Meniscocytosis 282.60
Menkes' syndrome — *see* Syndrome, Menkes'
Menolipsis 626.0
Menometrorrhagia 626.2
Menopause, menopausal (symptoms) (syndrome) 627.2
  arthritis (any site) NEC 716.3 ☑
  artificial 627.4
  bleeding 627.0
  crisis 627.2
  depression (*see also* Psychosis, affective)
    296.2 ☑
    agitated 296.2 ☑
      recurrent episode 296.3 ☑
      single episode 296.2 ☑
    psychotic 296.2 ☑
      recurrent episode 296.3 ☑
      single episode 296.2 ☑
    recurrent episode 296.3 ☑
    single episode 296.2 ☑
  melancholia (*see also* Psychosis, affective)
    296.2 ☑
    recurrent episode 296.3 ☑
    single episode 296.2 ☑
  paranoid state 297.2
  paraphrenia 297.2
  postsurgical 627.4
  premature 256.31
    postirradiation 256.2
    postsurgical 256.2
  psychoneurosis 627.2
  psychosis NEC 298.8
  surgical 627.4
  toxic polyarthritis NEC 716.39
Menorrhagia (primary) 626.2
  climacteric 627.0
  menopausal 627.0
  postclimacteric 627.1
  postmenopausal 627.1
  preclimacteric 627.0
  premenopausal 627.0
  puberty (menses retained) 626.3
Menorrhalgia 625.3
Menoschesis 626.8
Menostaxis 626.2
Menses, retention 626.8
Menstrual — *see also* Menstruation
  cycle, irregular 626.4
  disorders NEC 626.9
  extraction V25.3
  fluid, retained 626.8
  molimen 625.4
  period, normal V65.5
  regulation V25.3
Menstruation
  absent 626.0
  anovulatory 628.0
  delayed 626.8
  difficult 625.3
  disorder 626.9
    psychogenic 306.52
    specified NEC 626.8
  during pregnancy 640.8 ☑
  excessive 626.2
  frequent 626.2
  infrequent 626.1
  irregular 626.4
  latent 626.8
  membranous 626.8
  painful (primary) (secondary) 625.3
    psychogenic 306.52
  passage of clots 626.2
  precocious 259.1
  protracted 626.8
  retained 626.8
  retrograde 626.8
  scanty 626.1
  suppression 626.8
  vicarious (nasal) 625.8
Mentagra — *see also* Sycosis 704.8
Mental — *see also* condition

Mental — *see also* condition — *continued*
  deficiency (*see also* Disability, intellectual)
    319
  deterioration (*see also* Psychosis) 298.9
  disorder (*see also* Disorder, mental) 300.9
  exhaustion 300.5
  insufficiency (congenital) (*see also* Disability,
    intellectual) 319
  observation without need for further medi-
    cal care NEC V71.09
  retardation —*see* Disability, intellectual
  subnormality (*see also* Disability, intellectu-
    al) 319
    mild 317
    moderate 318.0
    profound 318.2
    severe 318.1
  upset (*see also* Disorder, mental) 300.9
Meralgia paresthetica 355.1
Mercurial — *see* condition
Mercurialism NEC 985.0
Merergasia 300.9
Merkel cell tumor — *see* Carcinoma, Merkel
  cell
Merocele — *see also* Hernia, femoral 553.00
Meromelia 755.4
  lower limb 755.30
    intercalary 755.32
      femur 755.34
        tibiofibular (complete) (incom-
          plete) 755.33
      fibula 755.37
      metatarsal(s) 755.38
      tarsal(s) 755.38
      tibia 755.36
      tibiofibular 755.35
    terminal (complete) (partial) (transverse)
      755.31
    longitudinal 755.32
      metatarsal(s) 755.38
      phalange(s) 755.39
      tarsal(s) 755.38
    transverse 755.31
  upper limb 755.20
    intercalary 755.22
      carpal(s) 755.28
      humeral 755.24
        radioulnar (complete) (incom-
          plete) 755.23
      metacarpal(s) 755.28
      phalange(s) 755.29
      radial 755.26
      radioulnar 755.25
      ulnar 755.27
    terminal (complete) (partial) (transverse)
      755.21
    longitudinal 755.22
      carpal(s) 755.28
      metacarpal(s) 755.28
      phalange(s) 755.29
    transverse 755.21
Merosmia 781.1
MERRF syndrome (myoclonus with epilepsy
  and with ragged red fibers) 277.87
Merycism — *see also* Vomiting
  psychogenic 307.53
Merzbacher-Pelizaeus disease 330.0
Mesaortitis — *see* Aortitis
Mesarteritis — *see* Arteritis
Mesencephalitis — *see also* Encephalitis 323.9
  late effect — *see* category 326
Mesenchymoma (M8990/1) — *see also* Neo-
  plasm, connective tissue, uncertain be-
  havior
  benign (M8990/0) — *see* Neoplasm, connec-
    tive tissue, benign
  malignant (M8990/3) — *see* Neoplasm,
    connective tissue, malignant
Mesenteritis
  retractile 567.82
  sclerosing 567.82
Mesentery, mesenteric — *see* condition
Mesiodens, mesiodentes 520.1
  causing crowding 524.31
Mesio-occlusion 524.23
Mesocardia (with asplenia) 746.87

Mesocolon — *see* condition
Mesonephroma (malignant) (M9110/3) — *see*
  also Neoplasm, by site, malignant
  benign (M9110/0) — *see* Neoplasm, by site,
    benign
Mesophlebitis — *see* Phlebitis
Mesostromal dysgenesis 743.51
Mesothelioma (malignant) (M9050/3) — *see*
  also Neoplasm, by site, malignant
  benign (M9050/0) — *see* Neoplasm, by site,
    benign
  biphasic type (M9053/3) (*see also* Neoplasm,
    by site, malignant)
    benign (M9053/0) — *see* Neoplasm, by
      site, benign
  epithelioid (M9052/3) (*see also* Neoplasm,
    by site, malignant)
    benign (M9052/0) — *see* Neoplasm, by
      site, benign
  fibrous (M9051/3) (*see also* Neoplasm, by
    site, malignant)
    benign (M9051/0) — *see* Neoplasm, by
      site, benign
Metabolic syndrome 277.7
Metabolism disorder 277.9
  specified type NEC 277.89
Metagonimiasis 121.5
Metagonimus infestation (small intestine)
  121.5
Metal
  pigmentation (skin) 709.00
  polishers' disease 502
Metalliferous miners' lung 503
Metamorphopsia 368.14
Metaplasia
  bone, in skin 709.3
  breast 611.89
  cervix — *omit code*
  endometrium (squamous) 621.8
  esophagus 530.85
  intestinal, of gastric mucosa 537.89
  kidney (pelvis) (squamous) (*see also* Disease,
    renal) 593.89
  myelogenous 289.89
  myeloid 289.89
    agnogenic 238.76
    megakaryocytic 238.76
  spleen 289.59
  squamous cell
    amnion 658.8 ☑
    bladder 596.89
    cervix — *see* condition
    trachea 519.19
    tracheobronchial tree 519.19
    uterus 621.8
    cervix — *see* condition
Metastasis, metastatic
  abscess — *see* Abscess
  calcification 275.40
  cancer, neoplasm, or disease
    from specified site (M8000/3) — *see*
      Neoplasm, by site, malignant
    to specified site (M8000/6) — *see* Neo-
      plasm, by site, secondary
  deposits (in) (M8000/6) — *see* Neoplasm,
    by site, secondary
  mesentery, of neuroendocrine tumor 209.74
  pneumonia 038.8 *[484.8]*
  spread (to) (M8000/6) — *see* Neoplasm, by
    site, secondary
Metatarsalgia 726.70
  anterior 355.6
  due to Freiberg's disease 732.5
  Morton's 355.6
Metatarsus, metatarsal — *see also* condition
  abductus valgus (congenital) 754.60
  adductus varus (congenital) 754.53
  primus varus 754.52
  valgus (adductus) (congenital) 754.60
  varus (abductus) (congenital) 754.53
    primus 754.52
Methadone use 304.00
Methemoglobinemia 289.7
  acquired (with sulfhemoglobinemia) 289.7
  congenital 289.7
  enzymatic 289.7

Methemoglobinemia — *continued*
  Hb-M disease 289.7
  hereditary 289.7
  toxic 289.7
Methemoglobinuria — *see also*
  Hemoglobinuria 791.2
Methicillin
  resistant staphyloccocus aureus (MRSA)
    041.12
    colonization V02.54
    personal history of V12.04
  susceptible staphylococcus aureus (MSSA)
    041.11
    colonization V02.53
Methioninemia 270.4
Metritis (catarrhal) (septic) (suppurative) —
  see also Endometritis 615.9
  blennorrhagic 098.16
    chronic or duration of 2 months or over
      098.36
  cervical (*see also* Cervicitis) 616.0
  gonococcal 098.16
    chronic or duration of 2 months or over
      098.36
  hemorrhagic 626.8
  puerperal, postpartum, childbirth 670.1 ☑
    septic 670.2 ☑
  tuberculous (*see also* Tuberculosis) 016.7 ☑
Metropathia hemorrhagica 626.8
Metroperitonitis — *see also* Peritonitis, pelvic,
  female 614.5
Metrorrhagia 626.6
  arising during pregnancy — *see* Hemor-
    rhage, pregnancy
  postpartum NEC 666.2 ☑
  primary 626.6
  psychogenic 306.59
  puerperal 666.2 ☑
Metrorrhexis — *see* Rupture, uterus
Metrosalpingitis — *see also* Salpingo-
  oophoritis 614.2
Metrostaxis 626.6
Metrovaginitis — *see also* Endometritis 615.9
  gonococcal (acute) 098.16
    chronic or duration of 2 months or over
      098.36
Mexican fever — *see* Typhus, Mexican
Meyenburg-Altherr-Uehlinger syndrome
  733.99
Meyer-Schwickerath and Weyers syndrome
  (dysplasia oculodentodigitalis) 759.89
Meynert's amentia (nonalcoholic) 294.0
  alcoholic 291.1
Mibelli's disease 757.39
Mice, joint — *see also* Loose, body, joint
  718.1 ☑
  knee 717.6
Micheli-Rietti syndrome (thalassemia minor)
  282.46
Michotte's syndrome 721.5
Micrencephalon, micrencephaly 742.1
Microalbuminuria 791.0
Microaneurysm, retina 362.14
  diabetic 250.5 ☑ *[362.01]*
    due to secondary diabetes
      249.5 ☑ *[362.01]*
Microangiopathy 443.9
  diabetic (peripheral) 250.7 ☑ *[443.81]*
    due to secondary diabetes
      249.7 ☑ *[443.81]*
    retinal 250.5 ☑ *[362.01]*
      due to secondary diabetes
        249.5 ☑ *[362.01]*
  peripheral 443.9
    diabetic 250.7 ☑ *[443.81]*
      due to secondary diabetes
        249.7 ☑ *[443.81]*
  retinal 362.18
    diabetic 250.5 ☑ *[362.01]*
      due to secondary diabetes
        249.5 ☑ *[362.01]*
  thrombotic 446.6
    Moschcowitz's (thrombotic thrombocy-
      topenic purpura) 446.6
Microcalcification, mammographic 793.81

☑ Additional Digit Required — Refer to the Tabular List for Digit Selection   ▽ Subterms under main terms may continue to next column or page

Microcephalus, microcephalic, microcephaly 742.1
  due to toxoplasmosis (congenital) 771.2
Microcheilia 744.82
Microcolon (congenital) 751.5
Microcornea (congenital) 743.41
Microcytic — see condition
Microdeletions NEC 758.33
Microdontia 520.2
Microdrepanocytosis (thalassemia-Hb-S disease) 282.41
  with sickle cell crisis 282.42
Microembolism
  atherothrombotic — see Atheroembolism
  retina 362.33
Microencephalon 742.1
Microfilaria streptocerca infestation 125.3
Microgastria (congenital) 750.7
Microgenia 524.06
Microgenitalia (congenital) 752.89
  penis 752.64
Microglioma (M9710/3)
  specified site — see Neoplasm, by site, malignant
  unspecified site 191.9
Microglossia (congenital) 750.16
Micrognathia, micrognathism (congenital) 524.00
  mandibular 524.04
    alveolar 524.74
  maxillary 524.03
    alveolar 524.73
Microgyria (congenital) 742.2
Microinfarct, heart — see also Insufficiency, coronary 411.89
Microlithiasis, alveolar, pulmonary 516.2
Micromastia 611.82
Micromyelia (congenital) 742.59
Micropenis 752.64
Microphakia (congenital) 743.36
Microphthalmia (congenital) — see also Microphthalmos 743.10
Microphthalmos (congenital) 743.10
  associated with eye and adnexal anomalies NEC 743.12
  due to toxoplasmosis (congenital) 771.2
  isolated 743.11
  simple 743.11
  syndrome 759.89
Micropsia 368.14
Microsporidiosis 136.8
Microsporon furfur infestation 111.0
Microsporosis — see also Dermatophytosis 110.9
  nigra 111.1
Microstomia (congenital) 744.84
Microthelia 757.6
Microthromboembolism — see Embolism
Microtia (congenital) (external ear) 744.23
Microtropia 378.34
Microvillus inclusion disease (MVD) 751.5
Micturition
  disorder NEC 788.69
    psychogenic 306.53
  frequency 788.41
    psychogenic 306.53
  nocturnal 788.43
  painful 788.1
    psychogenic 306.53
Middle
  ear — see condition
  lobe (right) syndrome 518.0
Midplane — see condition
Miescher's disease 709.3
  cheilitis 351.8
  granulomatosis disciformis 709.3
Miescher-Leder syndrome or granulomatosis 709.3
Mieten's syndrome 759.89

Migraine (idiopathic) 346.9 ☑

Note — The following fifth digit subclassification is for use with category 346:

0 *without mention of intractable migraine without mention of status migrainosus*

  without mention of refractory migraine without mention of status migrainosus

1 *with intractable migraine, so stated, without mention of status migrainosus*

  with refractory migraine, so stated, without mention of status migrainosus

2 *without mention of intractable migraine with status migrainosus*

  without mention of refractory migraine with status migrainosus

3 *with intractable migraine, so stated, with status migrainosus*

  with refractory migraine, so stated, with status migrainosus

  with aura (acute-onset) (without headache) (prolonged) (typical) 346.0 ☑
  without aura 346.1 ☑
    chronic 346.7 ☑
      transformed 346.7 ☑
  abdominal (syndrome) 346.2 ☑
  allergic (histamine) 346.2 ☑
  atypical 346.8 ☑
  basilar 346.0 ☑
  chronic without aura 346.7 ☑
  classic(al) 346.0 ☑
  common 346.1 ☑
  complicated 346.0 ☑
  hemiplegic 346.3 ☑
    familial 346.3 ☑
    sporadic 346.3 ☑
  lower-half 339.00
  menstrual 346.4 ☑
  menstrually related 346.4 ☑
  ophthalmic 346.8 ☑
  ophthalmoplegic 346.2 ☑
  premenstrual 346.4 ☑
  pure menstrual 346.4 ☑
  retinal 346.0 ☑
  specified form NEC 346.8 ☑
  transformed without aura 346.7 ☑
  variant 346.2 ☑
Migrant, social V60.0
Migratory, migrating — see also condition
  person V60.0
  testis, congenital 752.52
Mikulicz's disease or syndrome (dryness of mouth, absent or decreased lacrimation) 527.1
Milian atrophia blanche 701.3
Miliaria (crystallina) (rubra) (tropicalis) 705.1
  apocrine 705.82
Miliary — see condition
Milium — see also Cyst, sebaceous 706.2
  colloid 709.3
  eyelid 374.84
Milk
  crust 690.11
  excess secretion 676.6 ☑
  fever, female 672.0 ☑
  poisoning 988.8
  retention 676.2 ☑
  sickness 988.8
  spots 423.1
Milkers' nodes 051.1
Milk-leg (deep vessels) 671.4 ☑
  complicating pregnancy 671.3 ☑
  nonpuerperal 451.19
  puerperal, postpartum, childbirth 671.4 ☑
Milkman (-Looser) disease or syndrome (osteomalacia with pseudofractures) 268.2

Milky urine — see also Chyluria 791.1
Millar's asthma (laryngismus stridulus) 478.75
Millard-Gubler-Foville paralysis 344.89
Millard-Gubler paralysis or syndrome 344.89
Miller-Dieker syndrome 758.33
Miller's disease (osteomalacia) 268.2
Miller Fisher's syndrome 357.0
Milles' syndrome (encephalocutaneous angiomatosis) 759.6
Mills' disease 335.29
Millstone makers' asthma or lung 502
Milroy's disease (chronic hereditary edema) 757.0
Miners' — see also condition
  asthma 500
  elbow 727.2
  knee 727.2
  lung 500
  nystagmus 300.89
  phthisis (see also Tuberculosis) 011.4 ☑
  tuberculosis (see also Tuberculosis) 011.4 ☑
Minkowski-Chauffard syndrome — see also Spherocytosis 282.0
Minor — see condition
Minor's disease 336.1
Minot's disease (hemorrhagic disease, newborn) 776.0
Minot-von Willebrand (-Jürgens) disease or syndrome (angiohemophilia) 286.4
Minus (and plus) hand (intrinsic) 736.09
Miosis (persistent) (pupil) 379.42
Mirizzi's syndrome (hepatic duct stenosis) — see also Obstruction, biliary 576.2
  with calculus, cholelithiasis, or stones — see Choledocholithiasis
Mirror writing 315.09
  secondary to organic lesion 784.69
Misadventure (prophylactic) (therapeutic) — see also Complications 999.9
  administration of insulin 962.3
  infusion — see Complications, infusion
  local applications (of fomentations, plasters, etc.) 999.9
    burn or scald — see Burn, by site
  medical care (early) (late) NEC 999.9
    adverse effect of drugs or chemicals — see Table of Drugs and Chemicals
    burn or scald — see Burn, by site
  radiation NEC 990
  radiotherapy NEC 990
  surgical procedure (early) (late) — see Complications, surgical procedure
  transfusion — see Complications, transfusion
  vaccination or other immunological procedure — see Complications, vaccination
Misanthropy 301.7
Miscarriage — see Abortion, spontaneous
Mischief, malicious, child — see also Disturbance, conduct 312.0 ☑
Misdirection
  aqueous 365.83
Mismanagement, feeding 783.3
Misplaced, misplacement
  kidney (see also Disease, renal) 593.0
    congenital 753.3
  organ or site, congenital NEC — see Malposition, congenital
Missed
  abortion 632
  delivery (at or near term) 656.4 ☑
  labor (at or near term) 656.4 ☑
Misshapen reconstructed breast 612.0
Missing — see also Absence
  teeth (acquired) 525.10
    congenital (see also Anodontia) 520.0
    due to
      caries 525.13
      extraction 525.10
      periodontal disease 525.12
      specified NEC 525.19
      trauma 525.11
  vertebrae (congenital) 756.13
Misuse of drugs NEC — see also Abuse, drug, nondependent 305.9 ☑

Mitchell's disease (erythromelalgia) 443.82
Mite(s)
  diarrhea 133.8
  grain (itch) 133.8
  hair follicle (itch) 133.8
  in sputum 133.8
Mitochondrial encephalopathy, lactic acidosis and stroke-like episodes (MELAS syndrome) 277.87
Mitochondrial neurogastrointestinal encephalopathy syndrome (MNGIE) 277.87
Mitral — see condition
Mittelschmerz 625.2
Mixed — see condition
Mljet disease (mal de Meleda) 757.39
Mobile, mobility
  cecum 751.4
  coccyx 733.99
  excessive — see Hypermobility
  gallbladder 751.69
  kidney 593.0
    congenital 753.3
  organ or site, congenital NEC — see Malposition, congenital
  spleen 289.59
Mobitz heart block (atrioventricular) 426.10
  type I (Wenckebach's) 426.13
  type II 426.12
Möbius'
  disease 346.2 ☑
  syndrome
    congenital oculofacial paralysis 352.6
    ophthalmoplegic migraine 346.2 ☑
Moeller(-Barlow) disease (infantile scurvy) 267
  glossitis 529.4
Mohr's syndrome (types I and II) 759.89
Mola destruens (M9100/1) 236.1
Molarization, premolars 520.2
Molar pregnancy 631.8
  hydatidiform (delivered) (undelivered) 630
Molding, head (during birth) — omit code
Mold(s) in vitreous 117.9
Mole (pigmented) (M8720/0) — see also Neoplasm, skin, benign
  blood 631.8
  Breus' 631.8
  cancerous (M8720/3) — see Melanoma
  carneous 631.8
  destructive (M9100/1) 236.1
  ectopic — see Pregnancy, ectopic
  fleshy 631.8
  hemorrhagic 631.8
  hydatid, hydatidiform (benign) (complicating pregnancy) (delivered) (undelivered) (see also Hydatidiform mole) 630
    invasive (M9100/1) 236.1
    malignant (M9100/1) 236.1
    previous, affecting management of pregnancy V23.1
  invasive (hydatidiform) (M9100/1) 236.1
  malignant
    meaning
      malignant hydatidiform mole (M9100/1) 236.1
      melanoma (M8720/3) — see Melanoma
  nonpigmented (M8730/0) — see Neoplasm, skin, benign
  pregnancy NEC 631.8
  skin (M8720/0) — see Neoplasm, skin, benign
  stone 631.8
  tubal — see Pregnancy, tubal
  vesicular (see also Hydatidiform mole) 630
Molimen, molimina (menstrual) 625.4
Mollaret's meningitis 047.9
Mollities (cerebellar) (cerebral) 437.8
  ossium 268.2
Molluscum
  contagiosum 078.0
  epitheliale 078.0
  fibrosum (M8851/0) — see Lipoma, by site
  pendulum (M8851/0) — see Lipoma, by site

Mönckeberg's arteriosclerosis, degeneration, disease, or sclerosis — see also Arteriosclerosis, extremities 440.20
Monday fever 504
Monday morning dyspnea or asthma 504
Mondini's malformation (cochlea) 744.05
Mondor's disease (thrombophlebitis of breast) 451.89
Mongolian, mongolianism, mongolism, mongoloid 758.0
  spot 757.33
Monilethrix (congenital) 757.4
Monilia infestation — see Candidiasis
Moniliasis — see also Candidiasis
  neonatal 771.7
  vulvovaginitis 112.1
Monkeypox 059.01
Monoarthritis 716.60
  ankle 716.67
  arm 716.62
    lower (and wrist) 716.63
    upper (and elbow) 716.62
  foot (and ankle) 716.67
  forearm (and wrist) 716.63
  hand 716.64
  leg 716.66
    lower 716.66
    upper 716.65
  pelvic region (hip) (thigh) 716.65
  shoulder (region) 716.61
  specified site NEC 716.68
Monoblastic — see condition
Monochromatism (cone) (rod) 368.54
Monocytic — see condition
Monocytopenia 288.59
Monocytosis (symptomatic) 288.63
Monofixation syndrome 378.34
Monomania — see also Psychosis 298.9
Mononeuritis 355.9
  cranial nerve — see Disorder, nerve, cranial
  femoral nerve 355.2
  lateral
    cutaneous nerve of thigh 355.1
    popliteal nerve 355.3
  lower limb 355.8
    specified nerve NEC 355.79
  medial popliteal nerve 355.4
  median nerve 354.1
  multiplex 354.5
  plantar nerve 355.6
  posterior tibial nerve 355.5
  radial nerve 354.3
  sciatic nerve 355.0
  ulnar nerve 354.2
  upper limb 354.9
    specified nerve NEC 354.8
  vestibular 388.5
Mononeuropathy — see also Mononeuritis 355.9
  diabetic NEC 250.6 ☑ [355.9]
    due to secondary diabetes 249.6 ☑ [355.9]
    lower limb 250.6 ☑ [355.8]
      due to secondary diabetes 249.6 ☑ [355.8]
    upper limb 250.6 ☑ [354.9]
      due to secondary diabetes 249.6 ☑ [354.9]
  iliohypogastric nerve 355.79
  ilioinguinal nerve 355.79
  obturator nerve 355.79
  saphenous nerve 355.79
Mononucleosis, infectious 075
  with hepatitis 075 [573.1]
Monoplegia 344.5
  brain (current episode) (see also Paralysis, brain) 437.8
    fetus or newborn 767.8
  cerebral (current episode) (see also Paralysis, brain) 437.8
  congenital or infantile (cerebral) (spastic) (spinal) 343.3
  embolic (current) (see also Embolism, brain) 434.1 ☑
    late effect — see Late effect(s) (of) cerebrovascular disease

Monoplegia — continued
  infantile (cerebral) (spastic) (spinal) 343.3
  lower limb 344.30
    affecting
      dominant side 344.31
      nondominant side 344.32
    due to late effect of cerebrovascular accident — see Late effect(s) (of) cerebrovascular accident
    newborn 767.8
    psychogenic 306.0
      specified as conversion reaction 300.11
    thrombotic (current) (see also Thrombosis, brain) 434.0 ☑
      late effect — see Late effect(s) (of) cerebrovascular disease
  transient 781.4
  upper limb 344.40
    affecting
      dominant side 344.41
      nondominant side 344.42
    due to late effect of cerebrovascular accident — see Late effect(s) (of) cerebrovascular accident
Monorchism, monorchidism 752.89
Monteggia's fracture (closed) 813.03
  open 813.13
Mood swings
  brief compensatory 296.99
  rebound 296.99
Mooren's ulcer (cornea) 370.07
Moore's syndrome — see also Epilepsy 345.5 ☑
Mooser bodies 081.0
Mooser-Neill reaction 081.0
Moral
  deficiency 301.7
  imbecility 301.7
Morax-Axenfeld conjunctivitis 372.03
Morbilli — see also Measles 055.9
Morbus
  anglicus, anglorum 268.0
  Beigel 111.2
  caducus (see also Epilepsy) 345.9 ☑
  caeruleus 746.89
  celiacus 579.0
  comitialis (see also Epilepsy) 345.9 ☑
  cordis (see also Disease, heart)
    valvulorum — see Endocarditis
  coxae 719.95
    tuberculous (see also Tuberculosis) 015.1 ☑
  hemorrhagicus neonatorum 776.0
  maculosus neonatorum 772.6
  renum 593.0
  senilis (see also Osteoarthrosis) 715.9 ☑
Morel-Kraepelin disease — see also Schizophrenia 295.9 ☑
Morel-Moore syndrome (hyperostosis frontalis interna) 733.3
Morel-Morgagni syndrome (hyperostosis frontalis interna) 733.3
Morgagni
  cyst, organ, hydatid, or appendage 752.89
    fallopian tube 752.11
  disease or syndrome (hyperostosis frontalis interna) 733.3
Morgagni-Adams-Stokes syndrome (syncope with heart block) 426.9
Morgagni-Stewart-Morel syndrome (hyperostosis frontalis interna) 733.3
Moria — see also Psychosis 298.9
Morning sickness 643.0 ☑
Moron 317
Morphea (guttate) (linear) 701.0
Morphine dependence — see also Dependence 304.0 ☑
Morphinism — see also Dependence 304.0 ☑
Morphinomania — see also Dependence 304.0 ☑
Morphoea 701.0
Morquio (-Brailsford) (-Ullrich) disease or syndrome (mucopolysaccharidosis IV) 277.5
  kyphosis 277.5

Morris syndrome (testicular feminization) 259.51
Morsus humanus (open wound) — see also Wound, open, by site
  skin surface intact — see Contusion
Mortification (dry) (moist) — see also Gangrene 785.4
Morton's
  disease 355.6
  foot 355.6
  metatarsalgia (syndrome) 355.6
  neuralgia 355.6
  neuroma 355.6
  syndrome (metatarsalgia) (neuralgia) 355.6
  toe 355.6
Morvan's disease 336.0
Mosaicism, mosaic (chromosomal) 758.9
  autosomal 758.5
  sex 758.81
Moschcowitz's syndrome (thrombotic thrombocytopenic purpura) 446.6
Mother yaw 102.0
Motion sickness (from travel, any vehicle) (from roundabouts or swings) 994.6
Mottled teeth (enamel) (endemic) (nonendemic) 520.3
Mottling enamel (endemic) (nonendemic) (teeth) 520.3
Mouchet's disease 732.5
Mould(s) (in vitreous) 117.9
Moulders'
  bronchitis 502
  tuberculosis (see also Tuberculosis) 011.4 ☑
Mounier-Kuhn syndrome 748.3
  with
    acute exacerbation 494.1
    bronchiectasis 494.0
      with (acute) exacerbation 494.1
  acquired 519.19
    with bronchiectasis 494.0
      with (acute) exacerbation 494.1
Mountain
  fever — see Fever, mountain
  sickness 993.2
    with polycythemia, acquired 289.0
      acute 289.0
  tick fever 066.1
Mouse, joint — see also Loose, body, joint 718.1 ☑
  knee 717.6
Mouth — see condition
Movable
  coccyx 724.71
  kidney (see also Disease, renal) 593.0
    congenital 753.3
  organ or site, congenital NEC — see Malposition, congenital
  spleen 289.59
Movement
  abnormal (dystonic) (involuntary) 781.0
  decreased fetal 655.7 ☑
  paradoxical facial 374.43
Moya Moya disease 437.5
Mozart's ear 744.29
MRSA (methicillin-resistant staphylococcus aureus) 041.12
  colonization V02.54
  personal history of V12.04
MSSA (methicillin susceptible staphylococcus aureus) 041.11
  colonization V02.53
Mucha's disease (acute parapsoriasis varioliformis) 696.2
Mucha-Haberman syndrome (acute parapsoriasis varioliformis) 696.2
Mu-chain disease 273.2
Mucinosis (cutaneous) (papular) 701.8
Mucocele
  appendix 543.9
  buccal cavity 528.9
  gallbladder (see also Disease, gallbladder) 575.3
  lacrimal sac 375.43
  orbit (eye) 376.81
  salivary gland (any) 527.6
  sinus (accessory) (nasal) 478.19

Mucocele — continued
  turbinate (bone) (middle) (nasal) 478.19
  uterus 621.8
Mucocutaneous lymph node syndrome (acute) (febrile) (infantile) 446.1
Mucoenteritis 564.9
Mucolipidosis I, II, III 272.7
Mucopolysaccharidosis (types 1-6) 277.5
  cardiopathy 277.5 [425.7]
Mucormycosis (lung) 117.7
Mucosa associated lymphoid tissue (MALT) 200.3 ☑
Mucositis — see also Inflammation, by site 528.00
  cervix (ulcerative) 616.81
  due to
    antineoplastic therapy (ulcerative) 528.01
    other drugs (ulcerative) 528.02
    specified NEC 528.09
  gastrointestinal (ulcerative) 538
  nasal (ulcerative) 478.11
  necroticans agranulocytica (see also Agranulocytosis) 288.09
  ulcerative 528.00
  vagina (ulcerative) 616.81
  vulva (ulcerative) 616.81
Mucous — see also condition
  patches (syphilitic) 091.3
    congenital 090.0
Mucoviscidosis 277.00
  with meconium obstruction 277.01
Mucus
  asphyxia or suffocation (see also Asphyxia, mucus) 933.1
    newborn 770.18
  in stool 792.1
  plug (see also Asphyxia, mucus) 933.1
    aspiration, of newborn 770.17
    tracheobronchial 519.19
      newborn 770.18
Muguet 112.0
Mulberry molars 090.5
Müllerian mixed tumor (M8950/3) — see Neoplasm, by site, malignant
Multicystic kidney 753.19
Multilobed placenta — see Placenta, abnormal
Multinodular prostate 600.10
  with
    urinary
      obstruction 600.11
      retention 600.11
Multiparity V61.5
  affecting
    fetus or newborn 763.89
  management of
    labor and delivery 659.4 ☑
    pregnancy V23.3
  requiring contraceptive management (see also Contraception) V25.9
Multipartita placenta — see Placenta, abnormal
Multiple, multiplex — see also condition
  birth
    affecting fetus or newborn 761.5
    healthy liveborn — see Newborn, multiple
  digits (congenital) 755.00
    fingers 755.01
    toes 755.02
  organ or site NEC — see Accessory
  personality 300.14
  renal arteries 747.62
Mumps 072.9
  with complication 072.8
    specified type NEC 072.79
  encephalitis 072.2
  hepatitis 072.71
  meningitis (aseptic) 072.1
  meningoencephalitis 072.2
  oophoritis 072.79
  orchitis 072.0
  pancreatitis 072.3
  polyneuropathy 072.72
  vaccination, prophylactic (against) V04.6

☑ **Additional Digit Required** — Refer to the Tabular List for Digit Selection
▽ **Subterms under main terms may continue to next column or page**
2015 ICD-9-CM
►◄ Revised Text
● New Line
▲ Revised Code
Volume 2 — 187

Mumu — *see also* Infestation, filarial 125.9
Münchausen syndrome 301.51
Münchmeyer's disease or syndrome (exostosis luxurians) 728.11
Mural — *see* condition
Murmur (cardiac) (heart) (nonorganic) (organic) 785.2
  abdominal 787.5
  aortic (valve) (*see also* Endocarditis, aortic) 424.1
  benign — *omit code*
  cardiorespiratory 785.2
  diastolic — *see* condition
  Flint (*see also* Endocarditis, aortic) 424.1
  functional — *omit code*
  Graham Steell (pulmonic regurgitation) (*see also* Endocarditis, pulmonary) 424.3
  innocent — *omit code*
  insignificant — *omit code*
  midsystolic 785.2
  mitral (valve) — *see* Stenosis, mitral
  physiologic — *see* condition
  presystolic, mitral — *see* Insufficiency, mitral
  pulmonic (valve) (*see also* Endocarditis, pulmonary) 424.3
  Still's (vibratory) — *omit code*
  systolic (valvular) — *see* condition
  tricuspid (valve) — *see* Endocarditis, tricuspid
  undiagnosed 785.2
  valvular — *see* condition
  vibratory — *omit code*
Murri's disease (intermittent hemoglobinuria) 283.2
Muscae volitantes 379.24
Muscle, muscular — *see* condition
Musculoneuralgia 729.1
Mushrooming hip 718.95
Mushroom workers' (pickers') lung 495.5
Mutation(s)
  factor V Leiden 289.81
  prothrombin gene 289.81
  surfactant, of lung 516.63
Mutism — *see also* Aphasia 784.3
  akinetic 784.3
  deaf (acquired) (congenital) 389.7
  hysterical 300.11
  selective (elective) 313.23
    adjustment reaction 309.83
MVD (microvillus inclusion disease) 751.5
MVID (microvillus inclusion disease) 751.5
Myà's disease (congenital dilation, colon) 751.3
Myalgia (intercostal) 729.1
  eosinophilia syndrome 710.5
  epidemic 074.1
    cervical 078.89
  psychogenic 307.89
  traumatic NEC 959.9
Myasthenia 358.00
  cordis — *see* Failure, heart
  gravis 358.00
    with exacerbation (acute) 358.01
    in crisis 358.01
    neonatal 775.2
    pseudoparalytica 358.00
  stomach 536.8
    psychogenic 306.4
  syndrome
    in
      botulism 005.1 *[358.1]*
      diabetes mellitus 250.6 ☑ *[358.1]*
        due to secondary diabetes 249.6 ☑ *[358.1]*
      hypothyroidism (*see also* Hypothyroidism) 244.9 *[358.1]*
      malignant neoplasm NEC 199.1 *[358.1]*
      pernicious anemia 281.0 *[358.1]*
      thyrotoxicosis (*see also* Thyrotoxicosis) 242.9 ☑ *[358.1]*
Myasthenic 728.87
Mycelium infection NEC 117.9
Mycetismus 988.1
Mycetoma (actinomycotic) 039.9
  bone 039.8

Mycetoma — *continued*
  bone — *continued*
    mycotic 117.4
  foot 039.4
    mycotic 117.4
  madurae 039.9
    mycotic 117.4
  maduromycotic 039.9
    mycotic 117.4
  mycotic 117.4
  nocardial 039.9
Mycobacteriosis — *see* Mycobacterium
Mycobacterium, mycobacterial (infection) 031.9
  acid-fast (bacilli) 031.9
  anonymous (*see also* Mycobacterium, atypical) 031.9
  atypical (acid-fast bacilli) 031.9
    cutaneous 031.1
    pulmonary 031.0
      tuberculous (*see also* Tuberculosis, pulmonary) 011.9 ☑
    specified site NEC 031.8
  avium 031.0
    intracellulare complex bacteremia (MAC) 031.2
  balnei 031.1
  Battey 031.0
  cutaneous 031.1
  disseminated 031.2
    avium-intracellulare complex (DMAC) 031.2
  fortuitum 031.0
  intracellulare (battey bacillus) 031.0
  kakerifu 031.8
  kansasii 031.0
  kasongo 031.8
  leprae — *see* Leprosy
  luciflavum 031.0
  marinum 031.1
  pulmonary 031.0
    tuberculous (*see also* Tuberculosis, pulmonary) 011.9 ☑
  scrofulaceum 031.1
  tuberculosis (human, bovine) (*see also* Tuberculosis)
    avian type 031.0
  ulcerans 031.1
  xenopi 031.0
Mycosis, mycotic 117.9
  cutaneous NEC 111.9
  ear 111.8 *[380.15]*
  fungoides (M9700/3) 202.1 ☑
  mouth 112.0
  pharynx 117.9
  skin NEC 111.9
  stomatitis 112.0
  systemic NEC 117.9
  tonsil 117.9
  vagina, vaginitis 112.1
Mydriasis (persistent) (pupil) 379.43
Myelatelia 742.59
Myelinoclasis, perivascular, acute (postinfectious) NEC 136.9 *[323.61]*
  postimmunization or postvaccinal 323.51
Myelinosis, central pontine 341.8
Myelitis (ascending) (cerebellar) (childhood) (chronic) (descending) (diffuse) (disseminated) (pressure) (progressive) (spinal cord) (subacute) — *see also* Encephalitis 323.9
  acute (transverse) 341.20
    idiopathic 341.22
    in conditions classified elsewhere 341.21
  due to
    other infection classified elsewhere 136.9 *[323.42]*
    specified cause NEC 323.82
    vaccination (any) 323.52
    viral diseases classified elsewhere 323.02
  herpes simplex 054.74
  herpes zoster 053.14
  late effect — *see* category 326
  optic neuritis in 341.0
  postchickenpox 052.2
  postimmunization 323.52

Myelitis — *see also* Encephalitis — *continued*
  postinfectious 136.9 *[323.63]*
  postvaccinal 323.52
  postvaricella 052.2
  syphilitic (transverse) 094.89
  toxic 989.9 *[323.72]*
  transverse 323.82
    acute 341.20
      idiopathic 341.22
      in conditions classified elsewhere 341.21
    idiopathic 341.22
  tuberculous (*see also* Tuberculosis) 013.6 ☑
  virus 049.9
Myeloblastic — *see* condition
Myelocele — *see also* Spina bifida 741.9 ☑
  with hydrocephalus 741.0 ☑
Myelocystocele — *see also* Spina bifida 741.9 ☑
Myelocytic — *see* condition
Myelocytoma 205.1 ☑
Myelodysplasia (spinal cord) 742.59
  meaning myelodysplastic syndrome — *see* Syndrome, myelodysplastic
Myeloencephalitis — *see* Encephalitis
Myelofibrosis 289.83
  with myeloid metaplasia 238.76
  idiopathic (chronic) 238.76
  megakaryocytic 238.79
  primary 238.76
  secondary 289.83
Myelogenous — *see* condition
Myeloid — *see* condition
Myelokathexis 288.09
Myeloleukodystrophy 330.0
Myelolipoma (M8870/0) — *see* Neoplasm, by site, benign
Myeloma (multiple) (plasma cell) (plasmacytic) (M9730/3) 203.0 ☑
  monostotic (M9731/1) 238.6
  solitary (M9731/1) 238.6
Myelomalacia 336.8
Myelomata, multiple (M9730/3) 203.0 ☑
Myelomatosis (M9730/3) 203.0 ☑
Myelomeningitis — *see* Meningoencephalitis
Myelomeningocele (spinal cord) — *see also* Spina bifida 741.9 ☑
  fetal, causing fetopelvic disproportion 653.7 ☑
Myelo-osteo-musculodysplasia hereditaria 756.89
Myelopathic — *see* condition
Myelopathy (spinal cord) 336.9
  cervical 721.1
  diabetic 250.6 ☑ *[336.3]*
    due to secondary diabetes 249.6 ☑ *[336.3]*
  drug-induced 336.8
  due to or with
    carbon tetrachloride 987.8 *[323.72]*
    degeneration or displacement, intervertebral disc 722.70
      cervical, cervicothoracic 722.71
      lumbar, lumbosacral 722.73
      thoracic, thoracolumbar 722.72
    hydroxyquinoline derivatives 961.3 *[323.72]*
    infection — *see* Encephalitis
    intervertebral disc disorder 722.70
      cervical, cervicothoracic 722.71
      lumbar, lumbosacral 722.73
      thoracic, thoracolumbar 722.72
    lead 984.9 *[323.72]*
    mercury 985.0 *[323.72]*
    neoplastic disease (*see also* Neoplasm, by site) 239.9 *[336.3]*
    pernicious anemia 281.0 *[336.3]*
    spondylosis 721.91
      cervical 721.1
      lumbar, lumbosacral 721.42
      thoracic 721.41
    thallium 985.8 *[323.72]*
  lumbar, lumbosacral 721.42
  necrotic (subacute) 336.1
  radiation-induced 336.8

Myelopathy — *continued*
  spondylogenic NEC 721.91
    cervical 721.1
    lumbar, lumbosacral 721.42
    thoracic 721.41
  thoracic 721.41
  toxic NEC 989.9 *[323.72]*
  transverse (*see also* Myelitis) 323.82
  vascular 336.1
Myelophthisis 284.2
Myeloproliferative disease (M9960/1) 238.79
Myeloradiculitis — *see also* Polyneuropathy 357.0
Myeloradiculodysplasia (spinal) 742.59
Myelosarcoma (M9930/3) 205.3 ☑
Myelosclerosis 289.89
  with myeloid metaplasia (M9961/1) 238.76
  disseminated, of nervous system 340
  megakaryocytic (M9961/1) 238.79
Myelosis (M9860/3) — *see also* Leukemia, myeloid 205.9 ☑
  acute (M9861/3) 205.0 ☑
  aleukemic (M9864/3) 205.8 ☑
  chronic (M9863/3) 205.1 ☑
  erythremic (M9840/3) 207.0 ☑
    acute (M9841/3) 207.0 ☑
  megakaryocytic (M9920/3) 207.2 ☑
  nonleukemic (chronic) 288.8
  subacute (M9862/3) 205.2 ☑
Myesthenia — *see* Myasthenia
Myiasis (cavernous) 134.0
  orbit 134.0 *[376.13]*
Myoadenoma, prostate 600.20
  with
    other lower urinary tract symptoms (LUTS) 600.21
    urinary
      obstruction 600.21
      retention 600.21
Myoblastoma
  granular cell (M9580/0) (*see also* Neoplasm, connective tissue, benign)
    malignant (M9580/3) — *see* Neoplasm, connective tissue, malignant
  tongue (M9580/0) 210.1
Myocardial — *see* condition
Myocardiopathy (congestive) (constrictive) (familial) (idiopathic) (infiltrative) (obstructive) (primary) (restrictive) (sporadic) 425.4
  alcoholic 425.5
  amyloid 277.39 *[425.7]*
  beriberi 265.0 *[425.7]*
  cobalt-beer 425.5
  due to
    amyloidosis 277.39 *[425.7]*
    beriberi 265.0 *[425.7]*
    cardiac glycogenosis 271.0 *[425.7]*
    Chagas' disease 086.0
    Friedreich's ataxia 334.0 *[425.8]*
    influenza (*see also* Influenza) 487.8 *[425.8]*
    mucopolysaccharidosis 277.5 *[425.7]*
    myotonia atrophica 359.21 *[425.8]*
    progressive muscular dystrophy 359.1 *[425.8]*
    sarcoidosis 135 *[425.8]*
  glycogen storage 271.0 *[425.7]*
  hypertrophic 425.18
    nonobstructive 425.18
    obstructive 425.11
  metabolic NEC 277.9 *[425.7]*
  nutritional 269.9 *[425.7]*
  obscure (African) 425.2
  peripartum 674.5 ☑
  postpartum 674.5 ☑
  secondary 425.9
  thyrotoxic (*see also* Thyrotoxicosis) 242.9 ☑ *[425.7]*
  toxic NEC 425.9
Myocarditis (fibroid) (interstitial) (old) (progressive) (senile) (with arteriosclerosis) 429.0
  with
    rheumatic fever (conditions classifiable to 390) 398.0

☑ **Additional Digit Required** — Refer to the Tabular List for Digit Selection   ▽ **Subterms under main terms may continue to next column or page**

188 — Volume 2   ▶◀ Revised Text   ● New Line   ▲ Revised Code   2015 ICD-9-CM

Myocarditis — *continued*
  with — *continued*
    rheumatic fever — *continued*
      active (*see also* Myocarditis, acute,
        rheumatic) 391.2
      inactive or quiescent (with chorea)
        398.0
    active (nonrheumatic) 422.90
      rheumatic 391.2
        with chorea (acute) (rheumatic)
          (Sydenham's) 392.0
    acute or subacute (interstitial) 422.90
      due to Streptococcus (beta-hemolytic)
        391.2
      idiopathic 422.91
      rheumatic 391.2
        with chorea (acute) (rheumatic)
          (Sydenham's) 392.0
      specified type NEC 422.99
  aseptic of newborn 074.23
  bacterial (acute) 422.92
  chagasic 086.0
  chronic (interstitial) 429.0
  congenital 746.89
  constrictive 425.4
  Coxsackie (virus) 074.23
  diphtheritic 032.82
  due to or in
    Coxsackie (virus) 074.23
    diphtheria 032.82
    epidemic louse-borne typhus 080 *[422.0]*
    influenza (*see also* Influenza)
      487.8 *[422.0]*
    Lyme disease 088.81 *[422.0]*
    scarlet fever 034.1 *[422.0]*
    toxoplasmosis (acquired) 130.3
    tuberculosis (*see also* Tuberculosis)
      017.9 ☑ *[422.0]*
    typhoid 002.0 *[422.0]*
    typhus NEC 081.9 *[422.0]*
  eosinophilic 422.91
  epidemic of newborn 074.23
  Fiedler's (acute) (isolated) (subacute) 422.91
  giant cell (acute) (subacute) 422.91
  gonococcal 098.85
  granulomatous (idiopathic) (isolated) (non-
    specific) 422.91
  hypertensive (*see also* Hypertension, heart)
    402.90
  idiopathic 422.91
    granulomatous 422.91
  infective 422.92
  influenzal (*see also* Influenza) 487.8 *[422.0]*
  isolated (diffuse) (granulomatous) 422.91
  malignant 422.99
  meningococcal 036.43
  nonrheumatic, active 422.90
  parenchymatous 422.90
  pneumococcal (acute) (subacute) 422.92
  rheumatic (chronic) (inactive) (with chorea)
    398.0
    active or acute 391.2
      with chorea (acute) (rheumatic)
        (Sydenham's) 392.0
  septic 422.92
  specific (giant cell) (productive) 422.91
  staphylococcal (acute) (subacute) 422.92
  suppurative 422.92
  syphilitic (chronic) 093.82
  toxic 422.93
    rheumatic (*see also* Myocarditis, acute
      rheumatic) 391.2
  tuberculous (*see also* Tuberculosis)
    017.9 ☑ *[422.0]*
  typhoid 002.0 *[422.0]*
  valvular — *see* Endocarditis
  viral, except Coxsackie 422.91
    Coxsackie 074.23
    of newborn (Coxsackie) 074.23
Myocardium, myocardial — *see* condition
Myocardosis — *see also* Cardiomyopathy 425.4
Myoclonia (essential) 333.2
  epileptica 345.1 ☑
  Friedrich's 333.2
  massive 333.2

Myoclonic
  epilepsy, familial (progressive) 345.1 ☑
  jerks 333.2
Myoclonus (familial essential) (multifocal)
  (simplex) 333.2
  with epilepsy and with ragged red fibers
    (MERRF syndrome) 277.87
  facial 351.8
  massive (infantile) 333.2
  palatal 333.2
  pharyngeal 333.2
Myocytolysis 429.1
Myodiastasis 728.84
Myoendocarditis — *see also* Endocarditis
  acute or subacute 421.9
Myoepithelioma (M8982/0) — *see* Neoplasm,
  by site, benign
Myofascitis (acute) 729.1
  low back 724.2
Myofibroma (M8890/0) — *see also* Neoplasm,
  connective tissue, benign
  uterus (cervix) (corpus) (*see also* Leiomy-
    oma) 218.9
Myofibromatosis
  infantile 759.89
Myofibrosis 728.2
  heart (*see also* Myocarditis) 429.0
  humeroscapular region 726.2
  scapulohumeral 726.2
Myofibrositis — *see also* Myositis 729.1
  scapulohumeral 726.2
Myogelosis (occupational) 728.89
Myoglobinuria 791.3
Myoglobulinuria, primary 791.3
Myokymia — *see also* Myoclonus
  facial 351.8
Myolipoma (M8860/0)
  specified site — *see* Neoplasm, connective
    tissue, benign
  unspecified site 223.0
Myoma (M8895/0) — *see also* Neoplasm, connective tissue, benign
  cervix (stump) (uterus) (*see also* Leiomyoma)
    218.9
  malignant (M8895/3) — *see* Neoplasm,
    connective tissue, malignant
  prostate 600.20
    with
      other lower urinary tract symptoms
        (LUTS) 600.21
      urinary
        obstruction 600.21
        retention 600.21
  uterus (cervix) (corpus) (*see also* Leiomy-
    oma) 218.9
  in pregnancy or childbirth 654.1 ☑
    affecting fetus or newborn 763.89
    causing obstructed labor 660.2 ☑
      affecting fetus or newborn 763.1
Myomalacia 728.9
  cordis, heart (*see also* Degeneration, myocar-
    dial) 429.1
Myometritis — *see also* Endometritis 615.9
Myometrium — *see* condition
Myonecrosis, clostridial 040.0
Myopathy 359.9
  alcoholic 359.4
  amyloid 277.39 *[359.6]*
  benign, congenital 359.0
  central core 359.0
  centronuclear 359.0
  congenital (benign) 359.0
  critical illness 359.81
  distal 359.1
  due to drugs 359.4
  endocrine 259.9 *[359.5]*
    specified type NEC 259.8 *[359.5]*
  extraocular muscles 376.82
  facioscapulohumeral 359.1
  in
    Addison's disease 255.41 *[359.5]*
    amyloidosis 277.39 *[359.6]*
    cretinism 243 *[359.5]*
    Cushing's syndrome 255.0 *[359.5]*
    disseminated lupus erythematosus
      710.0 *[359.6]*

Myopathy — *continued*
  in — *continued*
    giant cell arteritis 446.5 *[359.6]*
    hyperadrenocorticism NEC 255.3 *[359.5]*
    hyperparathyroidism 252.01 *[359.5]*
    hypopituitarism 253.2 *[359.5]*
    hypothyroidism (*see also* Hypothy-
      roidism) 244.9 *[359.5]*
    malignant neoplasm NEC (M8000/3)
      199.1 *[359.6]*
    myxedema (*see also* Myxedema)
      244.9 *[359.5]*
    polyarteritis nodosa 446.0 *[359.6]*
    rheumatoid arthritis 714.0 *[359.6]*
    sarcoidosis 135 *[359.6]*
    scleroderma 710.1 *[359.6]*
    Sjögren's disease 710.2 *[359.6]*
    thyrotoxicosis (*see also* Thyrotoxicosis)
      242.9 ☑ *[359.5]*
  inflammatory 359.79
    immune NEC 359.79
    specified NEC 359.79
  intensive care (ICU) 359.81
  limb-girdle 359.1
  myotubular 359.0
  necrotizing, acute 359.81
  nemaline 359.0
  ocular 359.1
  oculopharyngeal 359.1
  of critical illness 359.81
  primary 359.89
  progressive NEC 359.89
  proximal myotonic (PROMM) 359.21
  quadriplegic, acute 359.81
  rod body 359.0
  scapulohumeral 359.1
  specified type NEC 359.89
  toxic 359.4
Myopericarditis — *see also* Pericarditis 423.9
Myopia (axial) (congenital) (increased curvature
  or refraction, nucleus of lens) 367.1
  degenerative, malignant 360.21
  malignant 360.21
  progressive high (degenerative) 360.21
Myosarcoma (M8895/3) — *see* Neoplasm,
  connective tissue, malignant
Myosis (persistent) 379.42
  stromal (endolymphatic) (M8931/1) 236.0
Myositis 729.1
  clostridial 040.0
  due to posture 729.1
  epidemic 074.1
  fibrosa or fibrous (chronic) 728.2
    Volkmann's (complicating trauma) 958.6
  inclusion body (IBM) 359.71
  infective 728.0
  interstitial 728.81
  multiple — *see* Polymyositis
  occupational 729.1
  orbital, chronic 376.12
  ossificans 728.12
    circumscribed 728.12
    progressive 728.11
    traumatic 728.12
  progressive fibrosing 728.11
  purulent 728.0
  rheumatic 729.1
  rheumatoid 729.1
  suppurative 728.0
  syphilitic 095.6
  traumatic (old) 729.1
Myospasia impulsiva 307.23
Myotonia (acquisita) (intermittens) 728.85
  atrophica 359.21
  congenita 359.22
    acetazolamide responsive 359.22
    dominant form 359.22
    recessive form 359.22
  drug-induced 359.24
  dystrophica 359.21
  fluctuans 359.29
  levior 359.22
  permanens 359.29
Myotonic pupil 379.46
Myriapodiasis 134.1

Myringitis
  with otitis media — *see* Otitis media
  acute 384.00
    specified type NEC 384.09
  bullosa hemorrhagica 384.01
  bullous 384.01
  chronic 384.1
Mysophobia 300.29
Mytilotoxism 988.0
Myxadenitis labialis 528.5
Myxedema (adult) (idiocy) (infantile) (juvenile)
  (thyroid gland) — *see also* Hypothyroidism 244.9
  circumscribed 242.9 ☑
  congenital 243
  cutis 701.8
  localized (pretibial) 242.9 ☑
  madness (acute) 293.0
    subacute 293.1
  papular 701.8
  pituitary 244.8
  postpartum 674.8 ☑
  pretibial 242.9 ☑
  primary 244.9
Myxochondrosarcoma (M9220/3) — *see*
  Neoplasm, cartilage, malignant
Myxofibroma (M8811/0) — *see also* Neoplasm,
  connective tissue, benign
  odontogenic (M9320/0) 213.1
    upper jaw (bone) 213.0
Myxofibrosarcoma (M8811/3) — *see* Neoplasm, connective tissue, malignant
Myxolipoma (M8852/0) — *see* Lipoma, by
  site 214.9
Myxoliposarcoma (M8852/3) — *see* Neoplasm,
  connective tissue, malignant
Myxoma (M8840/0) — *see also* Neoplasm,
  connective tissue, benign
  odontogenic (M9320/0) 213.1
    upper jaw (bone) 213.0
Myxosarcoma (M8840/3) — *see* Neoplasm,
  connective tissue, malignant

N

Naegeli's
  disease (hereditary hemorrhagic thrombas-
    thenia) 287.1
  leukemia, monocytic (M9863/3) 205.1 ☑
  syndrome (incontinentia pigmenti) 757.33
Naffziger's syndrome 353.0
Naga sore — *see also* Ulcer, skin 707.9
Nägele's pelvis 738.6
  with disproportion (fetopelvic) 653.0 ☑
    affecting fetus or newborn 763.1
    causing obstructed labor 660.1 ☑
      affecting fetus or newborn 763.1
Nager-de Reynier syndrome (dysostosis
  mandibularis) 756.0
Nail — *see also* condition
  biting 307.9
  patella syndrome (hereditary osteoony-
    chodysplasia) 756.89
Nanism, nanosomia — *see also* Dwarfism
  259.4
  hypophyseal 253.3
  pituitary 253.3
  renis, renalis 588.0
Nanukayami 100.89
Napkin rash 691.0
Narcissism 301.81
Narcolepsy 347.00
  with cataplexy 347.01
  in conditions classified elsewhere 347.10
    with cataplexy 347.11
Narcosis
  carbon dioxide (respiratory) 786.09
  due to drug
    correct substance properly administered
      780.09
    overdose or wrong substance given or
      taken 977.9
    specified drug — *see* Table of Drugs
      and Chemicals
Narcotism (chronic) — *see also* Dependence
  304.9 ☑

☑ **Additional Digit Required** — Refer to the Tabular List for Digit Selection   ▽ **Subterms under main terms may continue to next column or page**

2015 ICD-9-CM   ▶◀ Revised Text   ● New Line   ▲ Revised Code   Volume 2 — 189

Narcotism (chronic) — *see also* Dependence
— *continued*
  acute
    correct substance properly administered 349.82
    overdose or wrong substance given or taken 967.8
      specified drug — *see* Table of Drugs and Chemicals
NARP (ataxia and retinitis pigmentosa) 277.87
Narrow
  anterior chamber angle 365.02
  pelvis (inlet) (outlet) — *see* Contraction, pelvis
Narrowing
  artery NEC 447.1
    auditory, internal 433.8 ☑
    basilar 433.0 ☑
      with other precerebral artery 433.3 ☑
        bilateral 433.3 ☑
    carotid 433.1 ☑
      with other precerebral artery 433.3 ☑
        bilateral 433.3 ☑
    cerebellar 433.8 ☑
    choroidal 433.8 ☑
    communicating posterior 433.8 ☑
    coronary (*see also* Arteriosclerosis, coronary)
      congenital 746.85
        due to syphilis 090.5
    hypophyseal 433.8 ☑
    pontine 433.8 ☑
    precerebral NEC 433.9 ☑
      multiple or bilateral 433.3 ☑
      specified NEC 433.8 ☑
    vertebral 433.2 ☑
      with other precerebral artery 433.3 ☑
        bilateral 433.3 ☑
  auditory canal (external) (*see also* Stricture, ear canal, acquired) 380.50
  cerebral arteries 437.0
  cicatricial — *see* Cicatrix
  congenital — *see* Anomaly, congenital
  coronary artery — *see* Narrowing, artery, coronary
  ear, middle 385.22
  Eustachian tube (*see also* Obstruction, Eustachian tube) 381.60
  eyelid 374.46
    congenital 743.62
  intervertebral disc or space NEC — *see* Degeneration, intervertebral disc
  joint space, hip 719.85
  larynx 478.74
  lids 374.46
    congenital 743.62
  mesenteric artery (with gangrene) 557.0
  palate 524.89
  palpebral fissure 374.46
  retinal artery 362.13
  ureter 593.3
  urethra (*see also* Stricture, urethra) 598.9
Narrowness, abnormal, eyelid 743.62
Nasal — *see* condition
Nasolacrimal — *see* condition
Nasopharyngeal — *see also* condition
  bursa 478.29
  pituitary gland 759.2
  torticollis 723.5
Nasopharyngitis (acute) (infective) (subacute) 460
  chronic 472.2
    due to external agent — *see* Condition, respiratory, chronic, due to
  due to external agent — *see* Condition, respiratory, due to
  septic 034.0
  streptococcal 034.0
  suppurative (chronic) 472.2
  ulcerative (chronic) 472.2
Nasopharynx, nasopharyngeal — *see* condition
Natal tooth, teeth 520.6

Nausea — *see also* Vomiting 787.02
  with vomiting 787.01
  epidemic 078.82
  gravidarum — *see* Hyperemesis, gravidarum
  marina 994.6
Navel — *see* condition
Neapolitan fever — *see also* Brucellosis 023.9
Near drowning 994.1
Nearsightedness 367.1
Near-syncope 780.2
Nebécourt's syndrome 253.3
Nebula, cornea (eye) 371.01
  congenital 743.43
    interfering with vision 743.42
Necator americanus infestation 126.1
Necatoriasis 126.1
Neck — *see* condition
Necrencephalus — *see also* Softening, brain 437.8
Necrobacillosis 040.3
Necrobiosis 799.89
  brain or cerebral (*see also* Softening, brain) 437.8
  lipoidica 709.3
    diabeticorum 250.8 ☑ [709.3]
      due to secondary diabetes 249.8 ☑ [709.3]
Necrodermolysis 695.15
Necrolysis, toxic epidermal 695.15
  due to drug
    correct substance properly administered 695.15
    overdose or wrong substance given or taken 977.9
      specified drug — *see* Table of Drugs and Chemicals
  Stevens-Johnson syndrome overlap (SJS-TEN overlap syndrome) 695.14
Necrophilia 302.89
Necrosis, necrotic
  adrenal (capsule) (gland) 255.8
  antrum, nasal sinus 478.19
  aorta (hyaline) (*see also* Aneurysm, aorta) 441.9
    cystic medial 441.00
      abdominal 441.02
      thoracic 441.01
      thoracoabdominal 441.03
    ruptured 441.5
  arteritis 446.0
  artery 447.5
  aseptic, bone 733.40
    femur (head) (neck) 733.42
      medial condyle 733.43
    humoral head 733.41
    jaw 733.45
    medial femoral condyle 733.43
    specific site NEC 733.49
    talus 733.44
  avascular, bone NEC (*see also* Necrosis, aseptic, bone) 733.40
  bladder (aseptic) (sphincter) 596.89
  bone (*see also* Osteomyelitis) 730.1 ☑
    acute 730.0 ☑
    aseptic or avascular 733.40
      femur (head) (neck) 733.42
        medial condyle 733.43
      humoral head 733.41
      jaw 733.45
      medial femoral condyle 733.43
      specified site NEC 733.49
      talus 733.44
    ethmoid 478.19
    ischemic 733.40
    jaw 526.4
      aseptic 733.45
    marrow 289.89
    Paget's (osteitis deformans) 731.0
    tuberculous — *see* Tuberculosis, bone
  brain (softening) (*see also* Softening, brain) 437.8
  breast (aseptic) (fat) (segmental) 611.3
  bronchus, bronchi 519.19
  central nervous system NEC (*see also* Softening, brain) 437.8
  cerebellar (*see also* Softening, brain) 437.8

Necrosis, necrotic — *continued*
  cerebral (softening) (*see also* Softening, brain) 437.8
  cerebrospinal (softening) (*see also* Softening, brain) 437.8
  colon 557.0
  cornea (*see also* Keratitis) 371.40
  cortical, kidney 583.6
  cystic medial (aorta) 441.00
    abdominal 441.02
    thoracic 441.01
    thoracoabdominal 441.03
  dental 521.09
    pulp 522.1
  due to swallowing corrosive substance — *see* Burn, by site
  ear (ossicle) 385.24
  esophagus 530.89
  ethmoid (bone) 478.19
  eyelid 374.50
  fat, fatty (generalized) (*see also* Degeneration, fatty) 272.8
    abdominal wall 567.82
    breast (aseptic) (segmental) 611.3
    intestine 569.89
    localized — *see* Degeneration, by site, fatty
    mesentery 567.82
    omentum 567.82
    pancreas 577.8
    peritoneum 567.82
    skin (subcutaneous) 709.3
      newborn 778.1
  femur (aseptic) (avascular) 733.42
    head 733.42
    medial condyle 733.43
    neck 733.42
  gallbladder (*see also* Cholecystitis, acute) 575.0
  gangrenous 785.4
  gastric 537.89
  glottis 478.79
  heart (myocardium) — *see* Infarct, myocardium
  hepatic (*see also* Necrosis, liver) 570
  hip (aseptic) (avascular) 733.42
  intestine (acute) (hemorrhagic) (massive) 557.0
  ischemic 785.4
  jaw 526.4
    aseptic 733.45
  kidney (bilateral) 583.9
    acute 584.9
    cortical 583.6
      acute 584.6
        with
          abortion — *see* Abortion, by type, with renal failure
          ectopic pregnancy (*see also* categories 633.0–633.9) 639.3
          molar pregnancy (*see also* categories 630–632) 639.3
        complicating pregnancy 646.2 ☑
          affecting fetus or newborn 760.1
        following labor and delivery 669.3 ☑
    medullary (papillary) (*see also* Pyelitis) 590.80
      in
        acute renal failure 584.7
        nephritis, nephropathy 583.7
    papillary (*see also* Pyelitis) 590.80
      in
        acute renal failure 584.7
        nephritis, nephropathy 583.7
    tubular 584.5
      with
        abortion — *see* Abortion, by type, with renal failure
        ectopic pregnancy (*see also* categories 633.0–633.9) 639.3
        molar pregnancy (*see also* categories 630–632) 639.3

Necrosis, necrotic — *continued*
  kidney — *continued*
    tubular — *continued*
      complicating
        abortion 639.3
        ectopic or molar pregnancy 639.3
        pregnancy 646.2 ☑
          affecting fetus or newborn 760.1
      following labor and delivery 669.3 ☑
      traumatic 958.5
  larynx 478.79
  liver (acute) (congenital) (diffuse) (massive) (subacute) 570
    with
      abortion — *see* Abortion, by type, with specified complication NEC
      ectopic pregnancy (*see also* categories 633.0–633.9) 639.8
      molar pregnancy (*see also* categories 630–632) 639.8
    complicating pregnancy 646.7 ☑
      affecting fetus or newborn 760.8
    following
      abortion 639.8
      ectopic or molar pregnancy 639.8
    obstetrical 646.7 ☑
    postabortal 639.8
    puerperal, postpartum 674.8 ☑
    toxic 573.3
  lung 513.0
  lymphatic gland 683
  mammary gland 611.3
  mastoid (chronic) 383.1
  mesentery 557.0
    fat 567.82
  mitral valve — *see* Insufficiency, mitral
  myocardium, myocardial — *see* Infarct, myocardium
  nose (septum) 478.19
  omentum 557.0
    with mesenteric infarction 557.0
    fat 567.82
  orbit, orbital 376.10
  ossicles, ear (aseptic) 385.24
  ovary (*see also* Salpingo-oophoritis) 614.2
  pancreas (aseptic) (duct) (fat) 577.8
    acute 577.0
    infective 577.0
  papillary, kidney (*see also* Pyelitis) 590.80
  perineum 624.8
  peritoneum 557.0
    with mesenteric infarction 557.0
    fat 567.82
  pharynx 462
    in granulocytopenia 288.09
  phosphorus 983.9
  pituitary (gland) (postpartum) (Sheehan) 253.2
  placenta (*see also* Placenta, abnormal) 656.7 ☑
  pneumonia 513.0
  pulmonary 513.0
  pulp (dental) 522.1
  pylorus 537.89
  radiation — *see* Necrosis, by site
  radium — *see* Necrosis, by site
  renal — *see* Necrosis, kidney
  sclera 379.19
  scrotum 608.89
  skin or subcutaneous tissue 709.8
    due to burn — *see* Burn, by site
    gangrenous 785.4
  spine, spinal (column) 730.18
    acute 730.18
    cord 336.1
  spleen 289.59
  stomach 537.89
  stomatitis 528.1
  subcutaneous fat 709.3
    fetus or newborn 778.1
  subendocardial — *see* Infarct, myocardium
  suprarenal (capsule) (gland) 255.8
  teeth, tooth 521.09
  testis 608.89

☑ **Additional Digit Required** — Refer to the Tabular List for Digit Selection   ▽ Subterms under main terms may continue to next column or page

Necrosis, necrotic — *continued*
 thymus (gland) 254.8
 tonsil 474.8
 trachea 519.19
 tuberculous NEC — *see* Tuberculosis
 tubular (acute) (anoxic) (toxic) 584.5
  due to a procedure 997.5
 umbilical cord, affecting fetus or newborn
   762.6
 vagina 623.8
 vertebra (lumbar) 730.18
  acute 730.18
  tuberculous (*see also* Tuberculosis)
    015.0 ☑ [730.8] ☑
 vesical (aseptic) (bladder) 596.89
 vulva 624.8

Necrosis, necrotic — *continued*
 x-ray — *see* Necrosis, by site
Necrospermia 606.0
Necrotizing angiitis 446.0
Negativism 301.7
Neglect (child) (newborn) NEC 995.52
 adult 995.84
 after or at birth 995.52
 hemispatial 781.8
 left-sided 781.8
 sensory 781.8
 visuospatial 781.8
Negri bodies 071
Neill-Dingwall syndrome (microcephaly and
  dwarfism) 759.89
Neisserian infection NEC — *see* Gonococcus

Nematodiasis NEC — *see also* Infestation, Nematode 127.9
 ancylostoma (*see also* Ancylostomiasis)
  126.9
Neoformans cryptococcus infection 117.5
Neonatal — *see also* condition
 abstinence syndrome 779.5
 adrenoleukodystrophy 277.86
 teeth, tooth 520.6
Neonatorum — *see* condition
Neoplasia
 anal intraepithelial I (AIN I) (histologically
  confirmed) 569.44
 anal intraepithelial II (AIN II) (histologically
  confirmed) 569.44
 anal intraepithelial III (AIN III) 230.6

Neoplasia — *continued*
 anal intraepithelial III — *continued*
  anal canal 230.5
 endometrial intraepithelial (EIN) 621.35
 multiple endocrine (MEN)
  type I 258.01
  type IIA 258.02
  type IIB 258.03
 vaginal intraepithelial I (VAIN I) 623.0
 vaginal intraepithelial II (VAIN II) 623.0
 vaginal intraepithelial III (VAIN III) 233.31
 vulvular intraepithelial I (VIN I) 624.01
 vulvular intraepithelial II (VIN II) 624.02
 vulvular intraepithelial III (VIN III) 233.32

☑ **Additional Digit Required** — Refer to the Tabular List for Digit Selection   ▽ **Subterms under main terms may continue to next column or page**

2015 ICD-9-CM   ▶◀ **Revised Text**   ● **New Line**   ▲ **Revised Code**   **Volume 2 — 191**

	Malignant			Benign	Uncertain Behavior	Unspecified
	Primary	Secondary	Ca in situ			
Neoplasm, neoplastic	199.1	—	234.9	229.9	238.9	239.9

Notes — 1. The list below gives the code numbers for neoplasms by anatomical site. For each site there are six possible code numbers according to whether the neoplasm in question is malignant, benign, in situ, of uncertain behavior, or of unspecified nature. The description of the neoplasm will often indicate which of the six columns is appropriate; e.g., malignant melanoma of skin, benign fibroadenoma of breast, carcinoma in situ of cervix uteri.

Where such descriptors are not present, the remainder of the Index should be consulted where guidance is given to the appropriate column for each morphological (histological) variety listed; e.g., Mesonephroma — see Neoplasm, malignant; Embryoma — see also Neoplasm, uncertain behavior; Disease, Bowen's — see Neoplasm, skin, in situ. However, the guidance in the Index can be overridden if one of the descriptors mentioned above is present; e.g., malignant adenoma of colon is coded to 153.9 and not to 211.3 as the adjective "malignant" overrides the Index entry "Adenoma — see also Neoplasm, benign."

2. Sites marked with the sign * (e.g., face NEC*) should be classified to malignant neoplasm of skin of these sites if the variety of neoplasm is a squamous cell carcinoma or an epidermoid carcinoma, and to benign neoplasm of skin of these sites if the variety of neoplasm is a papilloma (any type).

	Malignant			Benign	Uncertain Behavior	Unspecified
	Primary	Secondary	Ca in situ			
abdomen, abdominal	195.2	198.89	234.8	229.8	238.8	239.89
cavity	195.2	198.89	234.8	229.8	238.8	239.89
organ	195.2	198.89	234.8	229.8	238.8	239.89
viscera	195.2	198.89	234.8	229.8	238.8	239.89
wall	173.50	198.2	232.5	216.5	238.2	239.2
basal cell carcinoma	173.51	—	—	—	—	—
connective tissue	171.5	198.89	—	215.5	238.1	239.2
specified type NEC	173.59	—	—	—	—	—
squamous cell carcinoma	173.52	—	—	—	—	—
abdominopelvic	195.8	198.89	234.8	229.8	238.8	239.89
accessory sinus — see Neoplasm, sinus						
acoustic nerve	192.0	198.4	—	225.1	237.9	239.7
acromion (process)	170.4	198.5	—	213.4	238.0	239.2
adenoid (pharynx) (tissue)	147.1	198.89	230.0	210.7	235.1	239.0
adipose tissue (see also Neoplasm, connective tissue)	171.9	198.89	—	215.9	238.1	239.2
adnexa (uterine)	183.9	198.82	233.39	221.8	236.3	239.5
adrenal (cortex) (gland) (medulla)	194.0	198.7	234.8	227.0	237.2	239.7
ala nasi (external)	173.30	198.2	232.3	216.3	238.2	239.2
alimentary canal or tract NEC	159.9	197.8	230.9	211.9	235.5	239.0
alveolar	143.9	198.89	230.0	210.4	235.1	239.0
mucosa	143.9	198.89	230.0	210.4	235.1	239.0
lower	143.1	198.89	230.0	210.4	235.1	239.0
upper	143.0	198.89	230.0	210.4	235.1	239.0
ridge or process	170.1	198.5	—	213.1	238.0	239.2
carcinoma	143.9	—	—	—	—	—
lower	143.1	—	—	—	—	—
upper	143.0	—	—	—	—	—
lower	170.1	198.5	—	213.1	238.0	239.2
mucosa	143.9	198.89	230.0	210.4	235.1	239.0
lower	143.1	198.89	230.0	210.4	235.1	239.0
upper	143.0	198.89	230.0	210.4	235.1	239.0
upper	170.0	198.5	—	213.0	238.0	239.2
sulcus	145.1	198.89	230.0	210.4	235.1	239.0
alveolus	143.9	198.89	230.0	210.4	235.1	239.0
lower	143.1	198.89	230.0	210.4	235.1	239.0
upper	143.0	198.89	230.0	210.4	235.1	239.0
ampulla of Vater	156.2	197.8	230.8	211.5	235.3	239.0
ankle NEC*	195.5	198.89	232.7	229.8	238.8	239.89
anorectum, anorectal (junction)	154.8	197.5	230.7	211.4	235.2	239.0
antecubital fossa or space*	195.4	198.89	232.6	229.8	238.8	239.89

	Malignant			Benign	Uncertain Behavior	Unspecified
	Primary	Secondary	Ca in situ			
Neoplasm, neoplastic — continued						
antrum (Highmore) (maxillary)	160.2	197.3	231.8	212.0	235.9	239.1
pyloric	151.2	197.8	230.2	211.1	235.2	239.0
tympanicum	160.1	197.3	231.8	212.0	235.9	239.1
anus, anal	154.3	197.5	230.6	211.4	235.5	239.0
canal	154.2	197.5	230.5	211.4	235.5	239.0
contiguous sites with rectosigmoid junction or rectum	154.8	—	—			
margin (see also Neoplasm, anus, skin)	173.50	198.2	232.5	216.6	238.2	239.2
skin	173.50	198.2	232.5	216.5	238.2	239.2
basal cell carcinoma	173.51	—	—			
specified type NEC	173.59	—	—	—	—	—
squamous cell carcinoma	173.52	—	—	—	—	—
sphincter	154.2	197.5	230.5	211.4	235.5	239.0
aorta (thoracic)	171.4	198.89	—	215.4	238.1	239.2
abdominal	171.5	198.89	—	215.5	238.1	239.2
aortic body	194.6	198.89	—	227.6	237.3	239.7
aponeurosis	171.9	198.89	—	215.9	238.1	239.2
palmar	171.2	198.89	—	215.2	238.1	239.2
plantar	171.3	198.89	—	215.3	238.1	239.2
appendix	153.5	197.5	230.3	211.3	235.2	239.0
arachnoid (cerebral)	192.1	198.4	—	225.2	237.6	239.7
spinal	192.3	198.4	—	225.4	237.6	239.7
areola (female)	174.0	198.81	233.0	217	238.3	239.3
male	175.0	198.81	233.0	217	238.3	239.3
arm NEC*	195.4	198.89	232.6	229.8	238.8	239.89
artery — see Neoplasm, connective tissue						
aryepiglottic fold	148.2	198.89	230.0	210.8	235.1	239.0
hypopharyngeal aspect	148.2	198.89	230.0	210.8	235.1	239.0
laryngeal aspect	161.1	197.3	231.0	212.1	235.6	239.1
marginal zone	148.2	198.89	230.0	210.8	235.1	239.0
arytenoid (cartilage)	161.3	197.3	231.0	212.1	235.6	239.1
fold — see Neoplasm, aryepiglottic						
associated with transplanted organ	199.2	—		—	—	—
atlas	170.2	198.5		213.2	238.0	239.2
atrium, cardiac	164.1	198.89	—	212.7	238.8	239.89
auditory canal (external) (skin) (see also Neoplasm, skin, ear)	173.20	198.2	232.2	216.2	238.2	239.2
internal	160.1	197.3	231.8	212.0	235.9	239.1
nerve	192.0	198.4	—	225.1	237.9	239.7
tube	160.1	197.3	231.8	212.0	235.9	239.1
Eustachian	160.1	197.3	231.8	212.0	235.9	239.1
opening	147.2	198.89	230.0	210.7	235.1	239.0
auricle, ear see also Neoplasm, skin, ear)	173.20	198.2	232.2	216.2	238.2	239.2
cartilage	171.0	198.89	—	215.0	238.1	239.2
auricular canal (external) (see also Neoplasm, skin, ear)	173.20	198.2	232.2	216.2	238.2	239.2
internal	160.1	197.3	231.8	212.0	235.9	239.1
autonomic nerve or nervous system NEC	171.9	198.89	—	215.9	238.1	239.2
axilla, axillary	195.1	198.89	234.8	229.8	238.8	239.89
fold (see also Neoplasm, skin, trunk)	173.50	198.2	232.5	216.5	238.2	239.2

☑ Additional Digit Required — Refer to the Tabular List for Digit Selection   ▽ Subterms under main terms may continue to next column or page

2015 ICD-9-CM   ▶◀ Revised Text   ● New Line   ▲ Revised Code   Volume 2 — 193

	Malignant					
	Primary	Secondary	Ca in situ	Benign	Uncertain Behavior	Unspecified
Neoplasm, neoplastic — *continued*						
back NEC*	195.8	198.89	232.5	229.8	238.8	239.89
Bartholin's gland	184.1	198.82	233.32	221.2	236.3	239.5
basal ganglia	191.0	198.3	—	225.0	237.5	239.6
basis pedunculi	191.7	198.3	—	225.0	237.5	239.6
bile or biliary						
(tract)	156.9	197.8	230.8	211.5	235.3	239.0
canaliculi (biliferi) (intrahepatic)	155.1	197.8	230.8	211.5	235.3	239.0
canals, interlobular	155.1	197.8	230.8	211.5	235.3	239.0
contiguous sites	156.8	—		—	—	—
duct or passage (common) (cystic) (extrahepatic)	156.1	197.8	230.8	211.5	235.3	239.0
contiguous sites with gallbladder	156.8	—		—	—	—
interlobular	155.1	197.8	230.8	211.5	235.3	239.0
intrahepatic	155.1	197.8	230.8	211.5	235.3	239.0
and extrahepatic	156.9	197.8	230.8	211.5	235.3	239.0
bladder (urinary)	188.9	198.1	233.7	223.3	236.7	239.4
contiguous sites	188.8	—	—	—	—	—
dome	188.1	198.1	233.7	223.3	236.7	239.4
neck	188.5	198.1	233.7	223.3	236.7	239.4
orifice	188.9	198.1	233.7	223.3	236.7	239.4
ureteric	188.6	198.1	233.7	223.3	236.7	239.4
urethral	188.5	198.1	233.7	223.3	236.7	239.4
sphincter	188.8	198.1	233.7	223.3	236.7	239.4
trigone	188.0	198.1	233.7	223.3	236.7	239.4
urachus	188.7	—	233.7	223.3	236.7	239.4
wall	188.9	198.1	233.7	223.3	236.7	239.4
anterior	188.3	198.1	233.7	223.3	236.7	239.4
lateral	188.2	198.1	233.7	223.3	236.7	239.4
posterior	188.4	198.1	233.7	223.3	236.7	239.4
blood vessel — *see* Neoplasm, connective tissue						
bone (periosteum)	170.9	198.5	—	213.9	238.0	239.2

Note — Carcinomas and adenocarcinomas, of any type other than intraosseous or odontogenic, of the sites listed under "Neoplasm, bone" should be considered as constituting metastatic spread from an unspecified primary site and coded to 198.5 for morbidity coding.

	Primary	Secondary	Ca in situ	Benign	Uncertain Behavior	Unspecified
acetabulum	170.6	198.5	—	213.6	238.0	239.2
acromion (process)	170.4	198.5	—	213.4	238.0	239.2
ankle	170.8	198.5	—	213.8	238.0	239.2
arm NEC	170.4	198.5	—	213.4	238.0	239.2
astragalus	170.8	198.5	—	213.8	238.0	239.2
atlas	170.2	198.5	—	213.2	238.0	239.2
axis	170.2	198.5	—	213.2	238.0	239.2
back NEC	170.2	198.5	—	213.2	238.0	239.2
calcaneus	170.8	198.5	—	213.8	238.0	239.2
calvarium	170.0	198.5	—	213.0	238.0	239.2
carpus (any)	170.5	198.5	—	213.5	238.0	239.2
cartilage NEC	170.9	198.5	—	213.9	238.0	239.2
clavicle	170.3	198.5	—	213.3	238.0	239.2
clivus	170.0	198.5	—	213.0	238.0	239.2
coccygeal vertebra	170.6	198.5	—	213.6	238.0	239.2
coccyx	170.6	198.5	—	213.6	238.0	239.2
costal cartilage	170.3	198.5	—	213.3	238.0	239.2
costovertebral joint	170.3	198.5	—	213.3	238.0	239.2
cranial	170.0	198.5	—	213.0	238.0	239.2
cuboid	170.8	198.5	—	213.8	238.0	239.2
cuneiform	170.9	198.5	—	213.9	238.0	239.2
ankle	170.8	198.5	—	213.8	238.0	239.2
wrist	170.5	198.5	—	213.5	238.0	239.2
digital	170.9	198.5	—	213.9	238.0	239.2
finger	170.5	198.5	—	213.5	238.0	239.2
toe	170.8	198.5	—	213.8	238.0	239.2

	Malignant					
	Primary	Secondary	Ca in situ	Benign	Uncertain Behavior	Unspecified
Neoplasm, neoplastic — *continued*						
bone — *continued*						
elbow	170.4	198.5	—	213.4	238.0	239.2
ethmoid (labyrinth)	170.0	198.5	—	213.0	238.0	239.2
face	170.0	198.5	—	213.0	238.0	239.2
lower jaw	170.1	198.5	—	213.1	238.0	239.2
femur (any part)	170.7	198.5	—	213.7	238.0	239.2
fibula (any part)	170.7	198.5	—	213.7	238.0	239.2
finger (any)	170.5	198.5	—	213.5	238.0	239.2
foot	170.8	198.5	—	213.8	238.0	239.2
forearm	170.4	198.5	—	213.4	238.0	239.2
frontal	170.0	198.5	—	213.0	238.0	239.2
hand	170.5	198.5	—	213.5	238.0	239.2
heel	170.8	198.5	—	213.8	238.0	239.2
hip	170.6	198.5	—	213.6	238.0	239.2
humerus (any part)	170.4	198.5	—	213.4	238.0	239.2
hyoid	170.0	198.5	—	213.0	238.0	239.2
ilium	170.6	198.5	—	213.6	238.0	239.2
innominate	170.6	198.5	—	213.6	238.0	239.2
intervertebral cartilage or disc	170.2	198.5	—	213.2	238.0	239.2
ischium	170.6	198.5	—	213.6	238.0	239.2
jaw (lower)	170.1	198.5	—	213.1	238.0	239.2
upper	170.0	198.5	—	213.0	238.0	239.2
knee	170.7	198.5	—	213.7	238.0	239.2
leg NEC	170.7	198.5	—	213.7	238.0	239.2
limb NEC	170.9	198.5	—	213.9	238.0	239.2
lower (long bones)	170.7	198.5	—	213.7	238.0	239.2
short bones	170.8	198.5	—	213.8	238.0	239.2
upper (long bones)	170.4	198.5	—	213.4	238.0	239.2
short bones	170.5	198.5	—	213.5	238.0	239.2
long	170.9	198.5	—	213.9	238.0	239.2
lower limbs NEC	170.7	198.5	—	213.7	238.0	239.2
upper limbs NEC	170.4	198.5	—	213.4	238.0	239.2
malar	170.0	198.5	—	213.0	238.0	239.2
mandible	170.1	198.5	—	213.1	238.0	239.2
marrow NEC	202.9	198.5	—	—	—	238.79
mastoid	170.0	198.5	—	213.0	238.0	239.2
maxilla, maxillary (superior)	170.0	198.5	—	213.0	238.0	239.2
inferior	170.1	198.5	—	213.1	238.0	239.2
metacarpus (any)	170.5	198.5	—	213.5	238.0	239.2
metatarsus (any)	170.8	198.5	—	213.8	238.0	239.2
navicular (ankle)	170.8	198.5	—	213.8	238.0	239.2
hand	170.5	198.5	—	213.5	238.0	239.2
nose, nasal	170.0	198.5	—	213.0	238.0	239.2
occipital	170.0	198.5	—	213.0	238.0	239.2
orbit	170.0	198.5	—	213.0	238.0	239.2
parietal	170.0	198.5	—	213.0	238.0	239.2
patella	170.8	198.5	—	213.8	238.0	239.2
pelvic	170.6	198.5	—	213.6	238.0	239.2
phalanges	170.9	198.5	—	213.9	238.0	239.2
foot	170.8	198.5	—	213.8	238.0	239.2
hand	170.5	198.5	—	213.5	238.0	239.2
pubic	170.6	198.5	—	213.6	238.0	239.2
radius (any part)	170.4	198.5	—	213.4	238.0	239.2
rib	170.3	198.5	—	213.3	238.0	239.2
sacral vertebra	170.6	198.5	—	213.6	238.0	239.2
sacrum	170.6	198.5	—	213.6	238.0	239.2
scaphoid (of hand)	170.5	198.5	—	213.5	238.0	239.2
of ankle	170.8	198.5	—	213.8	238.0	239.2
scapula (any part)	170.4	198.5	—	213.4	238.0	239.2
sella turcica	170.0	198.5	—	213.0	238.0	239.2
short	170.9	198.5	—	213.9	238.0	239.2
lower limb	170.8	198.5	—	213.8	238.0	239.2

	Malignant					
	Primary	Secondary	Ca in situ	Benign	Uncertain Behavior	Unspecified
Neoplasm, neoplastic — *continued*						
bone — *continued*						
short — *continued*						
upper limb	170.5	198.5	—	213.5	238.0	239.2
shoulder	170.4	198.5	—	213.4	238.0	239.2
skeleton, skeletal NEC	170.9	198.5	—	213.9	238.0	239.2
skull	170.0	198.5	—	213.0	238.0	239.2
sphenoid	170.0	198.5	—	213.0	238.0	239.2
spine, spinal (column)	170.2	198.5	—	213.2	238.0	239.2
coccyx	170.6	198.5	—	213.6	238.0	239.2
sacrum	170.6	198.5	—	213.6	238.0	239.2
sternum	170.3	198.5	—	213.3	238.0	239.2
tarsus (any)	170.8	198.5	—	213.8	238.0	239.2
temporal	170.0	198.5	—	213.0	238.0	239.2
thumb	170.5	198.5	—	213.5	238.0	239.2
tibia (any part)	170.7	198.5	—	213.7	238.0	239.2
toe (any)	170.8	198.5	—	213.8	238.0	239.2
trapezium	170.5	198.5	—	213.5	238.0	239.2
trapezoid	170.5	198.5	—	213.5	238.0	239.2
turbinate	170.0	198.5	—	213.0	238.0	239.2
ulna (any part)	170.4	198.5	—	213.4	238.0	239.2
unciform	170.5	198.5	—	213.5	238.0	239.2
vertebra (column)	170.2	198.5	—	213.2	238.0	239.2
coccyx	170.6	198.5	—	213.6	238.0	239.2
sacrum	170.6	198.5	—	213.6	238.0	239.2
vomer	170.0	198.5	—	213.0	238.0	239.2
wrist	170.5	198.5	—	213.5	238.0	239.2
xiphoid process	170.3	198.5	—	213.3	238.0	239.2
zygomatic	170.0	198.5	—	213.0	238.0	239.2
book-leaf (mouth)	145.8	198.89	230.0	210.4	235.1	239.0
bowel — *see* Neoplasm, intestine						
brachial plexus	171.2	198.89	—	215.2	238.1	239.2
brain NEC	191.9	198.3	—	225.0	237.5	239.6
basal ganglia	191.0	198.3	—	225.0	237.5	239.6
cerebellopontine angle	191.6	198.3	—	225.0	237.5	239.6
cerebellum NOS	191.6	198.3	—	225.0	237.5	239.6
cerebrum	191.0	198.3	—	225.0	237.5	239.6
choroid plexus	191.5	198.3	—	225.0	237.5	239.6
contiguous sites	191.8	—	—	—	—	—
corpus callosum	191.8	198.3	—	225.0	237.5	239.6
corpus striatum	191.0	198.3	—	225.0	237.5	239.6
cortex (cerebral)	191.0	198.3	—	225.0	237.5	239.6
frontal lobe	191.1	198.3	—	225.0	237.5	239.6
globus pallidus	191.0	198.3	—	225.0	237.5	239.6
hippocampus	191.2	198.3	—	225.0	237.5	239.6
hypothalamus	191.0	198.3	—	225.0	237.5	239.6
internal capsule	191.0	198.3	—	225.0	237.5	239.6
medulla oblongata	191.7	198.3	—	225.0	237.5	239.6
meninges	192.1	198.4	—	225.2	237.6	239.7
midbrain	191.7	198.3	—	225.0	237.5	239.6
occipital lobe	191.4	198.3	—	225.0	237.5	239.6
parietal lobe	191.3	198.3	—	225.0	237.5	239.6
peduncle	191.7	198.3	—	225.0	237.5	239.6
pons	191.7	198.3	—	225.0	237.5	239.6
stem	191.7	198.3	—	225.0	237.5	239.6
tapetum	191.8	198.3	—	225.0	237.5	239.6
temporal lobe	191.2	198.3	—	225.0	237.5	239.6
thalamus	191.0	198.3	—	225.0	237.5	239.6
uncus	191.2	198.3	—	225.0	237.5	239.6
ventricle (floor)	191.5	198.3	—	225.0	237.5	239.6
branchial (cleft) (vestiges)	146.8	198.89	230.0	210.6	235.1	239.0
breast (connective tissue) (female) (glandular tissue) (soft parts)	174.9	198.81	233.0	217	238.3	239.3
areola	174.0	198.81	233.0	217	238.3	239.3
male	175.0	198.81	233.0	217	238.3	239.3
axillary tail	174.6	198.81	233.0	217	238.3	239.3

	Malignant					
	Primary	Secondary	Ca in situ	Benign	Uncertain Behavior	Unspecified
Neoplasm, neoplastic — *continued*						
breast — *continued*						
central portion	174.1	198.81	233.0	217	238.3	239.3
contiguous sites	174.8	—	—	—	—	—
ectopic sites	174.8	198.81	233.0	217	238.3	239.3
inner	174.8	198.81	233.0	217	238.3	239.3
lower	174.8	198.81	233.0	217	238.3	239.3
lower-inner quadrant	174.3	198.81	233.0	217	238.3	239.3
lower-outer quadrant	174.5	198.81	233.0	217	238.3	239.3
male	175.9	198.81	233.0	217	238.3	239.3
areola	175.0	198.81	233.0	217	238.3	239.3
ectopic tissue	175.9	198.81	233.0	217	238.3	239.3
nipple	175.0	198.81	233.0	217	238.3	239.3
mastectomy site (skin) (*see also* Neoplasm, mastectomy site)	173.50	198.2	—	—	—	—
specified as breast tissue	174.8	198.81	—	—	—	—
midline	174.8	198.81	233.0	217	238.3	239.3
nipple	174.0	198.81	233.0	217	238.3	239.3
male	175.0	198.81	233.0	217	238.3	239.3
outer	174.8	198.81	233.0	217	238.3	239.3
skin (*see also* Neoplasm, mastectomy site)	173.50	198.2	232.5	216.5	238.2	239.2
tail (axillary)	174.6	198.81	233.0	217	238.3	239.3
upper	174.8	198.81	233.0	217	238.3	239.3
upper-inner quadrant	174.2	198.81	233.0	217	238.3	239.3
upper-outer quadrant	174.4	198.81	233.0	217	238.3	239.3
broad ligament	183.3	198.82	233.39	221.0	236.3	239.5
bronchiogenic, bronchogenic (lung)	162.9	197.0	231.2	212.3	235.7	239.1
bronchiole	162.9	197.0	231.2	212.3	235.7	239.1
bronchus	162.9	197.0	231.2	212.3	235.7	239.1
carina	162.2	197.0	231.2	212.3	235.7	239.1
contiguous sites with lung or trachea	162.8	—	—	—	—	—
lower lobe of lung	162.5	197.0	231.2	212.3	235.7	239.1
main	162.2	197.0	231.2	212.3	235.7	239.1
middle lobe of lung	162.4	197.0	231.2	212.3	235.7	239.1
upper lobe of lung	162.3	197.0	231.2	212.3	235.7	239.1
brow	173.30	198.2	232.3	216.3	238.2	239.2
basal cell carcinoma	173.31	—	—	—	—	—
specified type NEC	173.39	—	—	—	—	—
squamous cell carcinoma	173.32	—	—	—	—	—
buccal (cavity)	145.9	198.89	230.0	210.4	235.1	239.0
commissure	145.0	198.89	230.0	210.4	235.1	239.0
groove (lower) (upper)	145.1	198.89	230.0	210.4	235.1	239.0
mucosa	145.0	198.89	230.0	210.4	235.1	239.0
sulcus (lower) (upper)	145.1	198.89	230.0	210.4	235.1	239.0
bulbourethral gland	189.3	198.1	233.9	223.81	236.99	239.5
bursa — *see* Neoplasm, connective tissue						
buttock NEC*	195.3	198.89	232.5	229.8	238.8	239.89
calf*	195.5	198.89	232.7	229.8	238.8	239.89
calvarium	170.0	198.5	—	213.0	238.0	239.2
calyx, renal	189.1	198.0	233.9	223.1	236.91	239.5
canal						
anal	154.2	197.5	230.5	211.4	235.5	239.0

☑ **Additional Digit Required** — Refer to the Tabular List for Digit Selection

Subterms under main terms may continue to next column or page

	Malignant			Benign	Uncertain Behavior	Unspecified
	Primary	Secondary	Ca in situ			
Neoplasm, neoplastic — *continued*						
canal — *continued*						
auditory (external) (*see also* Neoplasm, skin, ear)	173.20	198.2	232.2	216.2	238.2	239.2
auricular (external) (*see also* Neoplasm, skin, ear)	173.20	198.2	232.2	216.2	238.2	239.2
canaliculi, biliary (biliferi) (intrahepatic)	155.1	197.8	230.8	211.5	235.3	239.0
canthus (eye) (inner) (outer)	173.10	198.2	232.1	216.1	238.2	239.2
basal cell carcinoma	173.11	—	—	—	—	—
specified type NEC	173.19	—	—	—	—	—
squamous cell carcinoma	173.12	—	—	—	—	—
capillary — *see* Neoplasm, connective tissue						
caput coli	153.4	197.5	230.3	211.3	235.2	239.0
cardia (gastric)	151.0	197.8	230.2	211.1	235.2	239.0
cardiac orifice (stomach)	151.0	197.8	230.2	211.1	235.2	239.0
cardio-esophageal junction	151.0	197.8	230.2	211.1	235.2	239.0
cardio-esophagus	151.0	197.8	230.2	211.1	235.2	239.0
carina (bronchus)	162.2	197.0	231.2	212.3	235.7	239.1
carotid (artery)	171.0	198.89	—	215.0	238.1	239.2
body	194.5	198.89	—	227.5	237.3	239.7
carpus (any bone)	170.5	198.5	—	213.5	238.0	239.2
cartilage (articular) (joint) NEC (*see also* Neoplasm, bone)	170.9	198.5	—	213.9	238.0	239.2
arytenoid	161.3	197.3	231.0	212.1	235.6	239.1
auricular	171.0	198.89	—	215.0	238.1	239.2
bronchi	162.2	197.3	—	212.3	235.7	239.1
connective tissue — *see* Neoplasm, connective tissue						
costal	170.3	198.5	—	213.3	238.0	239.2
cricoid	161.3	197.3	231.0	212.1	235.6	239.1
cuneiform	161.3	197.3	231.0	212.1	235.6	239.1
ear (external)	171.0	198.89	—	215.0	238.1	239.2
ensiform	170.3	198.5	—	213.3	238.0	239.2
epiglottis	161.1	197.3	231.0	212.1	235.6	239.1
anterior surface	146.4	198.89	230.0	210.6	235.1	239.0
eyelid	171.0	198.89	—	215.0	238.1	239.2
intervertebral	170.2	198.5	—	213.2	238.0	239.2
larynx, laryngeal	161.3	197.3	231.0	212.1	235.6	239.1
nose, nasal	160.0	197.3	231.8	212.0	235.9	239.1
pinna	171.0	198.89	—	215.0	238.1	239.2
rib	170.3	198.5	—	213.3	238.0	239.2
semilunar (knee)	170.7	198.5	—	213.7	238.0	239.2
thyroid	161.3	197.3	231.0	212.1	235.6	239.1
trachea	162.0	197.3	231.1	212.2	235.7	239.1
cauda equina	192.2	198.3	—	225.3	237.5	239.7
cavity						
buccal	145.9	198.89	230.0	210.4	235.1	239.0
nasal	160.0	197.3	231.8	212.0	235.9	239.1
oral	145.9	198.89	230.0	210.4	235.1	239.0
peritoneal	158.9	197.6	—	211.8	235.4	239.0
tympanic	160.1	197.3	231.8	212.0	235.9	239.1
cecum	153.4	197.5	230.3	211.3	235.2	239.0
central nervous system — *see* Neoplasm, nervous system						
white matter	191.0	198.3	—	225.0	237.5	239.6
Neoplasm, neoplastic — *continued*						
cerebellopontine (angle)	191.6	198.3	—	225.0	237.5	239.6
cerebellum, cerebellar	191.6	198.3	—	225.0	237.5	239.6
cerebrum, cerebral (cortex) (hemisphere) (white matter)	191.0	198.3	—	225.0	237.5	239.6
meninges	192.1	198.4	—	225.2	237.6	239.7
peduncle	191.7	198.3	—	225.0	237.5	239.6
ventricle (any)	191.5	198.3	—	225.0	237.5	239.6
cervical region	195.0	198.89	234.8	229.8	238.8	239.89
cervix (cervical) (uteri) (uterus)	180.9	198.82	233.1	219.0	236.0	239.5
canal	180.0	198.82	233.1	219.0	236.0	239.5
contiguous sites	180.8	—	—	—	—	—
endocervix (canal) (gland)	180.0	198.82	233.1	219.0	236.0	239.5
exocervix	180.1	198.82	233.1	219.0	236.0	239.5
external os	180.1	198.82	233.1	219.0	236.0	239.5
internal os	180.0	198.82	233.1	219.0	236.0	239.5
nabothian gland	180.0	198.82	233.1	219.0	236.0	239.5
squamocolumnar junction	180.8	198.82	233.1	219.0	236.0	239.5
stump	180.8	198.82	233.1	219.0	236.0	239.5
cheek	195.0	198.89	234.8	229.8	238.8	239.89
external	173.30	198.2	232.3	216.3	238.2	239.2
basal cell carcinoma	173.31	—	—	—	—	—
specified type NEC	173.39	—	—	—	—	—
squamous cell carcinoma	173.32	—	—	—	—	—
inner aspect	145.0	198.89	230.0	210.4	235.1	239.0
internal	145.0	198.89	230.0	210.4	235.1	239.0
mucosa	145.0	198.89	230.0	210.4	235.1	239.0
chest (wall) NEC	195.1	198.89	234.8	229.8	238.8	239.89
chiasma opticum	192.0	198.4	—	225.1	237.9	239.7
chin	173.30	198.2	232.3	216.3	238.2	239.2
basal cell carcinoma	173.31	—	—	—	—	—
specified type NEC	173.39	—	—	—	—	—
squamous cell carcinoma	173.32	—	—	—	—	—
choana	147.3	198.89	230.0	210.7	235.1	239.0
cholangiole	155.1	197.8	230.8	211.5	235.3	239.0
choledochal duct	156.1	197.8	230.8	211.5	235.3	239.0
choroid	190.6	198.4	234.0	224.6	238.8	239.81
plexus	191.5	198.3	—	225.0	237.5	239.6
ciliary body	190.0	198.4	234.0	224.0	238.8	239.89
clavicle	170.3	198.5	—	213.3	238.0	239.2
clitoris	184.3	198.82	233.32	221.2	236.3	239.5
clivus	170.0	198.5	—	213.0	238.0	239.2
cloacogenic zone	154.8	197.5	230.7	211.4	235.5	239.0
coccygeal body or glomus	194.6	198.89	—	227.6	237.3	239.7
vertebra	170.6	198.5	—	213.6	238.0	239.2
coccyx	170.6	198.5	—	213.6	238.0	239.2
colon — *see also* Neoplasm, intestine, large	153.9	197.5	230.3	211.3	235.2	239.0
with rectum	154.0	197.5	230.4	211.4	235.2	239.0
columnella (*see also* Neoplasm, skin, face)	173.30	198.2	232.3	216.3	238.2	239.2
column, spinal — *see* Neoplasm, spine						
commissure labial, lip	140.6	198.89	230.0	210.4	235.1	239.0
laryngeal	161.0	197.3	231.0	212.1	235.6	239.1
common (bile) duct	156.1	197.8	230.8	211.5	235.3	239.0

☑ Additional Digit Required — Refer to the Tabular List for Digit Selection   ▽ Subterms under main terms may continue to next column or page

Neoplasm, neoplastic— continued

	Malignant					
	Primary	Secondary	Ca in situ	Benign	Uncertain Behavior	Unspecified
concha (see also Neoplasm, skin, ear)	173.20	198.2	232.2	216.2	238.2	239.2
nose	160.0	197.3	231.8	212.0	235.9	239.1
conjunctiva	190.3	198.4	234.0	224.3	238.8	239.89
connective tissue NEC	171.9	198.89	—	215.9	238.1	239.2

Note — For neoplasms of connective tissue (blood vessel, bursa, fascia, ligament, muscle, peripheral nerves, sympathetic and parasympathetic nerves and ganglia, synovia, tendon, etc.) or of morphological types that indicate connective tissue, code according to the list under "Neoplasm, connective tissue"; for sites that do not appear in this list, code to neoplasm of that site; e.g.,

liposarcoma, shoulder 171.2

leiomyosarcoma, stomach 151.9

neurofibroma, chest wall 215.4

Morphological types that indicate connective tissue appear in the proper place in the alphabetic index with the instruction "see Neoplasm, connective tissue…"

	Primary	Secondary	Ca in situ	Benign	Uncertain Behavior	Unspecified
abdomen	171.5	198.89	—	215.5	238.1	239.2
abdominal wall	171.5	198.89	—	215.5	238.1	239.2
ankle	171.3	198.89	—	215.3	238.1	239.2
antecubital fossa or space	171.2	198.89	—	215.2	238.1	239.2
arm	171.2	198.89	—	215.2	238.1	239.2
auricle (ear)	171.0	198.89	—	215.0	238.1	239.2
axilla	171.4	198.89	—	215.4	238.1	239.2
back	171.7	198.89	—	215.7	238.1	239.2
breast (female) (see also Neoplasm, breast)	174.9	198.81	233.0	217	238.3	239.3
male	175.9	198.81	233.0	217	238.3	239.3
buttock	171.6	198.89	—	215.6	238.1	239.2
calf	171.3	198.89	—	215.3	238.1	239.2
cervical region	171.0	198.89	—	215.0	238.1	239.2
cheek	171.0	198.89	—	215.0	238.1	239.2
chest (wall)	171.4	198.89	—	215.4	238.1	239.2
chin	171.0	198.89	—	215.0	238.1	239.2
contiguous sites	171.8	—	—	—	—	—
diaphragm	171.4	198.89	—	215.4	238.1	239.2
ear (external)	171.0	198.89	—	215.0	238.1	239.2
elbow	171.2	198.89	—	215.2	238.1	239.2
extrarectal	171.6	198.89	—	215.6	238.1	239.2
extremity	171.8	198.89	—	215.8	238.1	239.2
lower	171.3	198.89	—	215.3	238.1	239.2
upper	171.2	198.89	—	215.2	238.1	239.2
eyelid	171.0	198.89	—	215.0	238.1	239.2
face	171.0	198.89	—	215.0	238.1	239.2
finger	171.2	198.89	—	215.2	238.1	239.2
flank	171.7	198.89	—	215.7	238.1	239.2
foot	171.3	198.89	—	215.3	238.1	239.2
forearm	171.2	198.89	—	215.2	238.1	239.2
forehead	171.0	198.89	—	215.0	238.1	239.2
gastric	171.5	198.89	—	215.5	238.1	—
gastrointestinal	171.5	198.89	—	215.5	238.1	—
gluteal region	171.6	198.89	—	215.6	238.1	239.2
great vessels NEC	171.4	198.89	—	215.4	238.1	239.2
groin	171.6	198.89	—	215.6	238.1	239.2
hand	171.2	198.89	—	215.2	238.1	239.2
head	171.0	198.89	—	215.0	238.1	239.2
heel	171.3	198.89	—	215.3	238.1	239.2
hip	171.3	198.89	—	215.3	238.1	239.2
hypochondrium	171.5	198.89	—	215.5	238.1	239.2
iliopsoas muscle	171.6	198.89	—	215.6	238.1	239.2
infraclavicular region	171.4	198.89	—	215.4	238.1	239.2
inguinal (canal) (region)	171.6	198.89	—	215.6	238.1	239.2
intestine	171.5	198.89	—	215.5	238.1	—
intrathoracic	171.4	198.89	—	215.4	238.1	239.2
ischorectal fossa	171.6	198.89	—	215.6	238.1	239.2
jaw	143.9	198.89	230.0	210.4	235.1	239.0

Neoplasm, neoplastic— continued

connective tissue — continued

	Primary	Secondary	Ca in situ	Benign	Uncertain Behavior	Unspecified
knee	171.3	198.89	—	215.3	238.1	239.2
leg	171.3	198.89	—	215.3	238.1	239.2
limb NEC	171.9	198.89	—	215.8	238.1	239.2
lower	171.3	198.89	—	215.3	238.1	239.2
upper	171.2	198.89	—	215.2	238.1	239.2
nates	171.6	198.89	—	215.6	238.1	239.2
neck	171.0	198.89	—	215.0	238.1	239.2
orbit	190.1	198.4	234.0	224.1	238.8	239.89
pararectal	171.6	198.89	—	215.6	238.1	239.2
para-urethral	171.6	198.89	—	215.6	238.1	239.2
paravaginal	171.6	198.89	—	215.6	238.1	239.2
pelvis (floor)	171.6	198.89	—	215.6	238.1	239.2
pelvo-abdominal	171.8	198.89	—	215.8	238.1	239.2
perineum	171.6	198.89	—	215.6	238.1	239.2
perirectal (tissue)	171.6	198.89	—	215.6	238.1	239.2
periurethral (tissue)	171.6	198.89	—	215.6	238.1	239.2
popliteal fossa or space	171.3	198.89	—	215.3	238.1	239.2
presacral	171.6	198.89	—	215.6	238.1	239.2
psoas muscle	171.5	198.89	—	215.5	238.1	239.2
pterygoid fossa	171.0	198.89	—	215.0	238.1	239.2
rectovaginal septum or wall	171.6	198.89	—	215.6	238.1	239.2
rectovesical	171.6	198.89	—	215.6	238.1	239.2
retroperitoneum	158.0	197.6	—	211.8	235.4	239.0
sacrococcygeal region	171.6	198.89	—	215.6	238.1	239.2
scalp	171.0	198.89	—	215.0	238.1	239.2
scapular region	171.4	198.89	—	215.4	238.1	239.2
shoulder	171.2	198.89	—	215.2	238.1	239.2
skin (dermis) NEC	173.90	198.2	232.9	216.9	238.2	239.2
stomach	171.5	198.89	—	215.5	238.1	—
submental	171.0	198.89	—	215.0	238.1	239.2
supraclavicular region	171.0	198.89	—	215.0	238.1	239.2
temple	171.0	198.89	—	215.0	238.1	239.2
temporal region	171.0	198.89	—	215.0	238.1	239.2
thigh	171.3	198.89	—	215.3	238.1	239.2
thoracic (duct) (wall)	171.4	198.89	—	215.4	238.1	239.2
thorax	171.4	198.89	—	215.4	238.1	239.2
thumb	171.2	198.89	—	215.2	238.1	239.2
toe	171.3	198.89	—	215.3	238.1	239.2
trunk	171.7	198.89	—	215.7	238.1	239.2
umbilicus	171.5	198.89	—	215.5	238.1	239.2
vesicorectal	171.6	198.89	—	215.6	238.1	239.2
wrist	171.2	198.89	—	215.2	238.1	239.2
conus medullaris	192.2	198.3	—	225.3	237.5	239.7
cord (true) (vocal)	161.0	197.3	231.0	212.1	235.6	239.1
false	161.1	197.3	231.0	212.1	235.6	239.1
spermatic	187.6	198.82	233.6	222.8	236.6	239.5
spinal (cervical) (lumbar) (thoracic)	192.2	198.3	—	225.3	237.5	239.7
cornea (limbus)	190.4	198.4	234.0	224.4	238.8	239.89
corpus						
albicans	183.0	198.6	233.39	220	236.2	239.5
callosum, brain	191.8	198.3	—	225.0	237.5	239.6
cavernosum	187.3	198.82	233.5	222.1	236.6	239.5
gastric	151.4	197.8	230.2	211.1	235.2	239.0
penis	187.3	198.82	233.5	222.1	236.6	239.5
striatum, cerebrum	191.0	198.3	—	225.0	237.5	239.6
uteri	182.0	198.82	233.2	219.1	236.0	239.5
isthmus	182.1	198.82	233.2	219.1	236.0	239.5
cortex						
adrenal	194.0	198.7	234.8	227.0	237.2	239.7
cerebral	191.0	198.3	—	225.0	237.5	239.6
costal cartilage	170.3	198.5	—	213.3	238.0	239.2

☑ Additional Digit Required — Refer to the Tabular List for Digit Selection

🄬 Subterms under main terms may continue to next column or page

Neoplasm, costovertebral joint — Neoplasm, eye

Neoplasm, neoplastic — continued	Malignant Primary	Malignant Secondary	Malignant Ca in situ	Benign	Uncertain Behavior	Unspecified
costovertebral joint	170.3	198.5	—	213.3	238.0	239.2
Cowper's gland	189.3	198.1	233.9	223.81	236.99	239.5
cranial (fossa, any)	191.9	198.3	—	225.0	237.5	239.6
meninges	192.1	198.4	—	225.2	237.6	239.7
nerve (any)	192.0	198.4	—	225.1	237.9	239.7
craniobuccal pouch	194.3	198.89	234.8	227.3	237.0	239.7
craniopharyngeal (duct) (pouch)	194.3	198.89	234.8	227.3	237.0	239.7
cricoid	148.0	198.89	230.0	210.8	235.1	239.0
cartilage	161.3	197.3	231.0	212.1	235.6	239.1
cricopharynx	148.0	198.89	230.0	210.8	235.1	239.0
crypt of Morgagni	154.8	197.5	230.7	211.4	235.2	239.0
crystalline lens	190.0	198.4	234.0	224.0	238.8	239.89
cul-de-sac (Douglas')	158.8	197.6	—	211.8	235.4	239.0
cuneiform cartilage	161.3	197.3	231.0	212.1	235.6	239.1
cutaneous — see Neoplasm, skin						
cutis — see Neoplasm, skin						
cystic (bile) duct (common)	156.1	197.8	230.8	211.5	235.3	239.0
dermis — see Neoplasm, skin						
diaphragm	171.4	198.89	—	215.4	238.1	239.2
digestive organs, system, tube, or tract NEC	159.9	197.8	230.9	211.9	235.5	239.0
contiguous sites with peritoneum	159.8	—	—	—	—	—
disc, intervertebral	170.2	198.5	—	213.2	238.0	239.2
disease, generalized	199.0	—	234.9	229.9	238.9	—
disseminated	199.0	—	234.9	229.9	238.9	—
Douglas' cul-de-sac or pouch	158.8	197.6	—	211.8	235.4	239.0
duodenojejunal junction	152.8	197.4	230.7	211.2	235.2	239.0
duodenum	152.0	197.4	230.7	211.2	235.2	239.0
dura (cranial) (mater)	192.1	198.4	—	225.2	237.6	239.7
cerebral	192.1	198.4	—	225.2	237.6	239.7
spinal	192.3	198.4	—	225.4	237.6	239.7
ear (external) (see also Neoplasm, ear, skin)	173.20	198.2	232.2	216.2	238.2	239.2
auricle or auris (see also Neoplasm, ear, skin)	173.20	198.2	232.2	216.2	238.2	239.2
canal, external (see also Neoplasm, ear, skin)	173.20	198.2	232.2	216.2	238.2	239.2
cartilage	171.0	198.89	—	215.0	238.1	239.2
external meatus (see also Neoplasm, ear, skin)	173.20	198.2	232.2	216.2	238.2	239.2
inner	160.1	197.3	231.8	212.0	235.9	239.89
lobule (see also Neoplasm, ear, skin)	173.20	198.2	232.2	216.2	238.2	239.2
middle	160.1	197.3	231.8	212.0	235.9	239.89
contiguous sites with accessory sinuses or nasal cavities	160.8	—	—	—	—	—
skin	173.20	198.2	232.2	216.2	238.2	239.2
basal cell carcinoma	173.21	—	—	—	—	—
specified type NEC	173.29	—	—	—	—	—
squamous cell carcinoma	173.22	—	—	—	—	—
earlobe	173.20	198.2	232.2	216.2	238.2	239.2

Neoplasm, neoplastic — continued	Malignant Primary	Malignant Secondary	Malignant Ca in situ	Benign	Uncertain Behavior	Unspecified
earlobe — continued						
basal cell carcinoma	173.21	—	—	—	—	—
specified type NEC	173.29	—	—	—	—	—
squamous cell carcinoma	173.22	—	—	—	—	—
ejaculatory duct	187.8	198.82	233.6	222.8	236.6	239.5
elbow NEC*	195.4	198.89	232.6	229.8	238.8	239.89
endocardium	164.1	198.89	—	212.7	238.8	239.89
endocervix (canal) (gland)	180.0	198.82	233.1	219.0	236.0	239.5
endocrine gland NEC	194.9	198.89	—	227.9	237.4	239.7
pluriglandular NEC	194.8	198.89	234.8	227.8	237.4	239.7
endometrium (gland) (stroma)	182.0	198.82	233.2	219.1	236.0	239.5
ensiform cartilage	170.3	198.5	—	213.3	238.0	239.2
enteric — see Neoplasm, intestine						
ependyma (brain)	191.5	198.3	—	225.0	237.5	239.6
epicardium	164.1	198.89	—	212.7	238.8	239.89
epididymis	187.5	198.82	233.6	222.3	236.6	239.5
epidural	192.9	198.4	—	225.9	237.9	239.7
epiglottis	161.1	197.3	231.0	212.1	235.6	239.1
anterior aspect or surface	146.4	198.89	230.0	210.6	235.1	239.0
cartilage	161.3	197.3	231.0	212.1	235.6	239.1
free border (margin)	146.4	198.89	230.0	210.6	235.1	239.0
junctional region	146.5	198.89	230.0	210.6	235.1	239.0
posterior (laryngeal) surface	161.1	197.3	231.0	212.1	235.6	239.1
suprahyoid portion	161.1	197.3	231.0	212.1	235.6	239.1
esophagogastric junction	151.0	197.8	230.2	211.1	235.2	239.0
esophagus	150.9	197.8	230.1	211.0	235.5	239.0
abdominal	150.2	197.8	230.1	211.0	235.5	239.0
cervical	150.0	197.8	230.1	211.0	235.5	239.0
contiguous sites	150.8	—	—	—	—	—
distal (third)	150.5	197.8	230.1	211.0	235.5	239.0
lower (third)	150.5	197.8	230.1	211.0	235.5	239.0
middle (third)	150.4	197.8	230.1	211.0	235.5	239.0
proximal (third)	150.3	197.8	230.1	211.0	235.5	239.0
specified part NEC	150.8	197.8	230.1	211.0	235.5	239.0
thoracic	150.1	197.8	230.1	211.0	235.5	239.0
upper (third)	150.3	197.8	230.1	211.0	235.5	239.0
ethmoid (sinus)	160.3	197.3	231.8	212.0	235.9	239.1
bone or labyrinth	170.0	198.5	—	213.0	238.0	239.2
Eustachian tube	160.1	197.3	231.8	212.0	235.9	239.1
exocervix	180.1	198.82	233.1	219.0	236.0	239.5
external meatus (ear) (see also Neoplasm, skin, ear)	173.20	198.2	232.2	216.2	238.2	239.2
os, cervix uteri	180.1	198.82	233.1	219.0	236.0	239.5
extradural	192.9	198.4	—	225.9	237.9	239.7
extrahepatic (bile) duct	156.1	197.8	230.8	211.5	235.3	239.0
contiguous sites with gallbladder	156.8	—	—	—	—	—
extraocular muscle	190.1	198.4	234.0	224.1	238.8	239.89
extrarectal	195.3	198.89	234.8	229.8	238.8	239.89
extremity*	195.8	198.89	232.8	229.8	238.8	239.89
lower*	195.5	198.89	232.7	229.8	238.8	239.89
upper*	195.4	198.89	232.6	229.8	238.8	239.89
eye NEC	190.9	198.4	234.0	224.9	238.8	239.89
contiguous sites	190.8	—	—	—	—	—

☑ Additional Digit Required — Refer to the Tabular List for Digit Selection

▽ Subterms under main terms may continue to next column or page

Neoplasm, neoplastic — continued	Malignant			Benign	Uncertain Behavior	Unspecified
	Primary	Secondary	Ca in situ			
eye — *continued*						
specified sites						
NEC	190.8	198.4	234.0	224.8	238.8	239.89
eyeball	190.0	198.4	234.0	224.0	238.8	239.89
eyebrow	173.30	198.2	232.3	216.3	238.2	239.2
basal cell carcinoma	173.31	—	—	—	—	—
specified type NEC	173.39	—	—	—	—	—
squamous cell carcinoma	173.32	—	—	—	—	—
eyelid (lower) (skin) (upper)	173.10	198.2	232.1	216.1	238.2	239.2
basal cell carcinoma	173.11	—	—	—	—	—
cartilage	171.0	198.89	—	215.0	238.1	239.2
specified type NEC	173.19	—	—	—	—	—
squamous cell carcinoma	173.12	—	—	—	—	—
face NEC*	195.0	198.89	232.3	229.8	238.8	239.89
fallopian tube (accessory)	183.2	198.82	233.39	221.0	236.3	239.5
falx (cerebelli) (cerebri)	192.1	198.4	—	225.2	237.6	239.7
fascia (*see also* Neoplasm, connective tissue)						
palmar	171.2	198.89	—	215.2	238.1	239.2
plantar	171.3	198.89	—	215.3	238.1	239.2
fatty tissue — *see* Neoplasm, connective tissue						
fauces, faucial NEC	146.9	198.89	230.0	210.6	235.1	239.0
pillars	146.2	198.89	230.0	210.6	235.1	239.0
tonsil	146.0	198.89	230.0	210.5	235.1	239.0
femur (any part)	170.7	198.5	—	213.7	238.0	239.2
fetal membrane	181	198.82	233.2	219.8	236.1	239.5
fibrous tissue — *see* Neoplasm, connective tissue						
fibula (any part)	170.7	198.5	—	213.7	238.0	239.2
filum terminale	192.2	198.3	—	225.3	237.5	239.7
finger NEC*	195.4	198.89	232.6	229.8	238.8	239.89
flank NEC*	195.8	198.89	232.5	229.8	238.8	239.89
follicle, nabothian	180.0	198.82	233.1	219.0	236.0	239.5
foot NEC*	195.5	198.89	232.7	229.8	238.8	239.89
forearm NEC*	195.4	198.89	232.6	229.8	238.8	239.89
forehead (skin)	173.30	198.2	232.3	216.3	238.2	239.2
basal cell carcinoma	173.31	—	—	—	—	—
specified type NEC	173.39	—	—	—	—	—
squamous cell carcinoma	173.32	—	—	—	—	—
foreskin	187.1	198.82	233.5	222.1	236.6	239.5
fornix						
pharyngeal	147.3	198.89	230.0	210.7	235.1	239.0
vagina	184.0	198.82	233.31	221.1	236.3	239.5
fossa (of)						
anterior (cranial)	191.9	198.3	—	225.0	237.5	239.6
cranial	191.9	198.3	—	225.0	237.5	239.6
ischiorectal	195.3	198.89	234.8	229.8	238.8	239.89
middle (cranial)	191.9	198.3	—	225.0	237.5	239.6
pituitary	194.3	198.89	234.8	227.3	237.0	239.7
posterior (cranial)	191.9	198.3	—	225.0	237.5	239.6
pterygoid	171.0	198.89	—	215.0	238.1	239.2
pyriform	148.1	198.89	230.0	210.8	235.1	239.0
Rosenmüller	147.2	198.89	230.0	210.7	235.1	239.0
tonsillar	146.1	198.89	230.0	210.6	235.1	239.0
fourchette	184.4	198.82	233.32	221.2	236.3	239.5
frenulum						
labii — *see* Neoplasm, lip, internal						

Neoplasm, neoplastic — continued	Malignant			Benign	Uncertain Behavior	Unspecified
	Primary	Secondary	Ca in situ			
frenulum — *continued*						
linguae	141.3	198.89	230.0	210.1	235.1	239.0
frontal						
bone	170.0	198.5	—	213.0	238.0	239.2
lobe, brain	191.1	198.3	—	225.0	237.5	239.6
meninges	192.1	198.4	—	225.2	237.6	239.7
pole	191.1	198.3	—	225.0	237.5	239.6
sinus	160.4	197.3	231.8	212.0	235.9	239.1
fundus						
stomach	151.3	197.8	230.2	211.1	235.2	239.0
uterus	182.0	198.82	233.2	219.1	236.0	239.5
gallbladder	156.0	197.8	230.8	211.5	235.3	239.0
contiguous sites with extrahepatic bile ducts	156.8	—	—	—	—	—
gall duct (extrahepatic)	156.1	197.8	230.8	211.5	235.3	239.0
intrahepatic	155.1	197.8	230.8	211.5	235.3	239.0
ganglia (*see also* Neoplasm, connective tissue)	171.9	198.89	—	215.9	238.1	239.2
basal	191.0	198.3	—	225.0	237.5	239.6
ganglion (*see also* Neoplasm, connective tissue)	171.9	198.89	—	215.9	238.1	239.2
cranial nerve	192.0	198.4	—	225.1	237.9	239.7
Gartner's duct	184.0	198.82	233.31	221.1	236.3	239.5
gastric — *see* Neoplasm, stomach						
gastrocolic	159.8	197.8	230.9	211.9	235.5	239.0
gastroesophageal junction	151.0	197.8	230.2	211.1	235.2	239.0
gastrointestinal (tract) NEC	159.9	197.8	230.9	211.9	235.5	239.0
generalized	199.0	—	234.9	229.9	238.9	—
genital organ or tract						
female NEC	184.9	198.82	233.39	221.9	236.3	239.5
contiguous sites	184.8	—	—	—	—	—
specified site NEC	184.8	198.82	233.39	221.8	236.3	239.5
male NEC	187.9	198.82	233.6	222.9	236.6	239.5
contiguous sites	187.8	—	—	—	—	—
specified site NEC	187.8	198.82	233.6	222.8	236.6	239.5
genitourinary tract						
female	184.9	198.82	233.39	221.9	236.3	239.5
male	187.9	198.82	233.6	222.9	236.6	239.5
gingiva (alveolar) (marginal)	143.9	198.89	230.0	210.4	235.1	239.0
lower	143.1	198.89	230.0	210.4	235.1	239.0
mandibular	143.1	198.89	230.0	210.4	235.1	239.0
maxillary	143.0	198.89	230.0	210.4	235.1	239.0
upper	143.0	198.89	230.0	210.4	235.1	239.0
gland, glandular (lymphatic) (system) (*see also* Neoplasm, lymph gland)						
endocrine NEC	194.9	198.89	—	227.9	237.4	239.7
salivary — *see* Neoplasm, salivary, gland						
glans penis	187.2	198.82	233.5	222.1	236.6	239.5
globus pallidus	191.0	198.3	—	225.0	237.5	239.6
glomus						
coccygeal	194.6	198.89		227.6	237.3	239.7
jugularis	194.6	198.89		227.6	237.3	239.7
glosso-epiglottic fold(s)	146.4	198.89	230.0	210.6	235.1	239.0
glossopalatine fold	146.2	198.89	230.0	210.6	235.1	239.0
glossopharyngeal sulcus	146.1	198.89	230.0	210.6	235.1	239.0

☑ Additional Digit Required — Refer to the Tabular List for Digit Selection

▽ Subterms under main terms may continue to next column or page

	Malignant			Benign	Uncertain Behavior	Unspecified
	Primary	Secondary	Ca in situ			

Neoplasm, neoplastic — continued

	Primary	Secondary	Ca in situ	Benign	Uncertain Behavior	Unspecified
glottis	161.0	197.3	231.0	212.1	235.6	239.1
gluteal region*	195.3	198.89	232.5	229.8	238.8	239.89
great vessels NEC	171.4	198.89	—	215.4	238.1	239.2
groin NEC	195.3	198.89	232.5	229.8	238.8	239.89
gum	143.9	198.89	230.0	210.4	235.1	239.0
contiguous sites	143.8	—	—	—	—	—
lower	143.1	198.89	230.0	210.4	235.1	239.0
upper	143.0	198.89	230.0	210.4	235.1	239.0
hand NEC*	195.4	198.89	232.6	229.8	238.8	239.89
head NEC*	195.0	198.89	232.4	229.8	238.8	239.89
heart	164.1	198.89	—	212.7	238.8	239.89
contiguous sites with mediastinum or thymus	164.8	—	—	—	—	—
heel NEC*	195.5	198.89	232.7	229.8	238.8	239.89
helix (see also Neoplasm, skin, ear)	173.20	198.2	232.2	216.2	238.2	239.2
hematopoietic, hemopoietic tissue NEC	202.8	198.89	—	—	—	238.79
hemisphere, cerebral	191.0	198.3	—	225.0	237.5	239.6
hemorrhoidal zone	154.2	197.5	230.5	211.4	235.5	239.0
hepatic	155.2	197.7	230.8	211.5	235.3	239.0
duct (bile)	156.1	197.8	230.8	211.5	235.3	239.0
flexure (colon)	153.0	197.5	230.3	211.3	235.2	239.0
primary	155.0	—	—	—	—	—
hilus of lung	162.2	197.0	231.2	212.3	235.7	239.1
hip NEC*	195.5	198.89	232.7	229.8	238.8	239.89
hippocampus, brain	191.2	198.3	—	225.0	237.5	239.6
humerus (any part)	170.4	198.5	—	213.4	238.0	239.2
hymen	184.0	198.82	233.31	221.1	236.3	239.5
hypopharynx, hypopharyngeal NEC	148.9	198.89	230.0	210.8	235.1	239.0
contiguous sites	148.8	—	—	—	—	—
postcricoid region	148.0	198.89	230.0	210.8	235.1	239.0
posterior wall	148.3	198.89	230.0	210.8	235.1	239.0
pyriform fossa (sinus)	148.1	198.89	230.0	210.8	235.1	239.0
specified site NEC	148.8	198.89	230.0	210.8	235.1	239.0
wall	148.9	198.89	230.0	210.8	235.1	239.0
posterior	148.3	198.89	230.0	210.8	235.1	239.0
hypophysis	194.3	198.89	234.8	227.3	237.0	239.7
hypothalamus	191.0	198.3	—	225.0	237.5	239.6
ileocecum, ileocecal (coil) (junction) (valve)	153.4	197.5	230.3	211.3	235.2	239.0
ileum	152.2	197.4	230.7	211.2	235.2	239.0
ilium	170.6	198.5	—	213.6	238.0	239.2
immunoproliferative NEC	203.8	—	—	—	—	—
infraclavicular (region)*	195.1	198.89	232.5	229.8	238.8	239.89
inguinal (region)*	195.3	198.89	232.5	229.8	238.8	239.89
insula	191.0	198.3	—	225.0	237.5	239.6
insular tissue (pancreas)	157.4	197.8	230.9	211.7	235.5	239.0
brain	191.0	198.3	—	225.0	237.5	239.6
interarytenoid fold	148.2	198.89	230.0	210.8	235.1	239.0
hypopharyngeal aspect	148.2	198.89	230.0	210.8	235.1	239.0
laryngeal aspect	161.1	197.3	231.0	212.1	235.6	239.1
marginal zone	148.2	198.89	230.0	210.8	235.1	239.0
interdental papillae	143.9	198.89	230.0	210.4	235.1	239.0
lower	143.1	198.89	230.0	210.4	235.1	239.0
upper	143.0	198.89	230.0	210.4	235.1	239.0
internal capsule	191.0	198.3	—	225.0	237.5	239.6
os (cervix)	180.0	198.82	233.1	219.0	236.0	239.5

Neoplasm, neoplastic — continued

	Primary	Secondary	Ca in situ	Benign	Uncertain Behavior	Unspecified
intervertebral cartilage or disc	170.2	198.5	—	213.2	238.0	239.2
intestine, intestinal	159.0	197.8	230.7	211.9	235.2	239.0
large	153.9	197.5	230.3	211.3	235.2	239.0
appendix	153.5	197.5	230.3	211.3	235.2	239.0
caput coli	153.4	197.5	230.3	211.3	235.2	239.0
cecum	153.4	197.5	230.3	211.3	235.2	239.0
colon	153.9	197.5	230.3	211.3	235.2	239.0
and rectum	154.0	197.5	230.4	211.4	235.2	239.0
ascending	153.6	197.5	230.3	211.3	235.2	239.0
caput	153.4	197.5	230.3	211.3	235.2	239.0
contiguous sites	153.8	—	230.3	—	—	—
descending	153.2	197.5	230.3	211.3	235.2	239.0
distal	153.2	197.5	230.3	211.3	235.2	239.0
left	153.2	197.5	230.3	211.3	235.2	239.0
pelvic	153.3	197.5	230.3	211.3	235.2	239.0
right	153.6	197.5	230.3	211.3	235.2	239.0
sigmoid (flexure)	153.3	197.5	230.3	211.3	235.2	239.0
transverse	153.1	197.5	230.3	211.3	235.2	239.0
contiguous sites	153.8	—	—	—	—	—
hepatic flexure	153.0	197.5	230.3	211.3	235.2	239.0
ileocecum, ileocecal (coil) (valve)	153.4	197.5	230.3	211.3	235.2	239.0
sigmoid flexure (lower) (upper)	153.3	197.5	230.3	211.3	235.2	239.0
splenic flexure	153.7	197.5	230.3	211.3	235.2	239.0
small	152.9	197.4	230.7	211.2	235.2	239.0
contiguous sites	152.8	—	—	—	—	—
duodenum	152.0	197.4	230.7	211.2	235.2	239.0
ileum	152.2	197.4	230.7	211.2	235.2	239.0
jejunum	152.1	197.4	230.7	211.2	235.2	239.0
tract NEC	159.0	197.8	230.7	211.9	235.2	239.0
intra-abdominal	195.2	198.89	234.8	229.8	238.8	239.89
intracranial NEC	191.9	198.3	—	225.0	237.5	239.6
intrahepatic (bile) duct	155.1	197.8	230.8	211.5	235.3	239.0
intraocular	190.0	198.4	234.0	224.0	238.8	239.89
intraorbital	190.1	198.4	234.0	224.1	238.8	239.89
intrasellar	194.3	198.89	234.8	227.3	237.0	239.7
intrathoracic (cavity) (organs NEC)	195.1	198.89	234.8	229.8	238.8	239.89
contiguous sites with respiratory organs	165.8	—	—	—	—	—
iris	190.0	198.4	234.0	224.0	238.8	239.89
ischiorectal (fossa)	195.3	198.89	234.8	229.8	238.8	239.89
ischium	170.6	198.5	—	213.6	238.0	239.2
island of Reil	191.0	198.3	—	225.0	237.5	239.6
islands or islets of Langerhans	157.4	197.8	230.9	211.7	235.5	239.0
isthmus uteri	182.1	198.82	233.2	219.1	236.0	239.5
jaw	195.0	198.89	234.8	229.8	238.8	239.89
bone	170.1	198.5	—	213.1	238.0	239.2
carcinoma	143.9	—	—	—	—	—
lower	143.1	—	—	—	—	—
upper	143.0	—	—	—	—	—
lower	170.1	198.5	—	213.1	238.0	239.2
upper	170.0	198.5	—	213.0	238.0	239.2
carcinoma (any type) (lower) (upper)	195.0	—	—	—	—	—
skin (see also Neoplasm, skin, face)	173.30	198.2	232.3	216.3	238.2	239.2
soft tissues	143.9	198.89	230.0	210.4	235.1	239.0
lower	143.1	198.89	230.0	210.4	235.1	239.0
upper	143.0	198.89	230.0	210.4	235.1	239.0
jejunum	152.1	197.4	230.7	211.2	235.2	239.0

Neoplasm, neoplastic— continued	Malignant			Benign	Uncertain Behavior	Unspecified
	Primary	Secondary	Ca in situ			
joint NEC (see also Neoplasm, bone)	170.9	198.5	—	213.9	238.0	239.2
acromioclavicular	170.4	198.5	—	213.4	238.0	239.2
bursa or synovial membrane — see Neoplasm, connective tissue						
costovertebral	170.3	198.5	—	213.3	238.0	239.2
sternocostal	170.3	198.5	—	213.3	238.0	239.2
temporomandibular	170.1	198.5	—	213.1	238.0	239.2
junction						
anorectal	154.8	197.5	230.7	211.4	235.5	239.0
cardioesophageal	151.0	197.8	230.2	211.1	235.2	239.0
esophagogastric	151.0	197.8	230.2	211.1	235.2	239.0
gastroesophageal	151.0	197.8	230.2	211.1	235.2	239.0
hard and soft palate	145.5	198.89	230.0	210.4	235.1	239.0
ileocecal	153.4	197.5	230.3	211.3	235.2	239.0
pelvirectal	154.0	197.5	230.4	211.4	235.2	239.0
pelviureteric	189.1	198.0	233.9	223.1	236.91	239.5
rectosigmoid	154.0	197.5	230.4	211.4	235.2	239.0
squamocolumnar, of cervix	180.8	198.82	233.1	219.0	236.0	239.5
kidney						
(parenchyma)	189.0	198.0	233.9	223.0	236.91	239.5
calyx	189.1	198.0	233.9	223.1	236.91	239.5
hilus	189.1	198.0	233.9	223.1	236.91	239.5
pelvis	189.1	198.0	233.9	223.1	236.91	239.5
knee NEC*	195.5	198.89	232.7	229.8	238.8	239.89
labia (skin)	184.4	198.82	233.32	221.2	236.3	239.5
majora	184.1	198.82	233.32	221.2	236.3	239.5
minora	184.2	198.82	233.32	221.2	236.3	239.5
labial (see also Neoplasm, lip) sulcus (lower) (upper)	145.1	198.89	230.0	210.4	235.1	239.0
labium (skin)	184.4	198.82	233.32	221.2	236.3	239.5
majus	184.1	198.82	233.32	221.2	236.3	239.5
minus	184.2	198.82	233.32	221.2	236.3	239.5
lacrimal						
canaliculi	190.7	198.4	234.0	224.7	238.8	239.89
duct (nasal)	190.7	198.4	234.0	224.7	238.8	239.89
gland	190.2	198.4	234.0	224.2	238.8	239.89
punctum	190.7	198.4	234.0	224.7	238.8	239.89
sac	190.7	198.4	234.0	224.7	238.8	239.89
Langerhans, islands or islets	157.4	197.8	230.9	211.7	235.5	239.0
laryngopharynx	148.9	198.89	230.0	210.8	235.1	239.0
larynx, laryngeal NEC	161.9	197.3	231.0	212.1	235.6	239.1
aryepiglottic fold	161.1	197.3	231.0	212.1	235.6	239.1
cartilage (arytenoid) (cricoid) (cuneiform) (thyroid)	161.3	197.3	231.0	212.1	235.6	239.1
commissure (anterior) (posterior)	161.0	197.3	231.0	212.1	235.6	239.1
contiguous sites	161.8	—	—	—	—	—
extrinsic NEC	161.1	197.3	231.0	212.1	235.6	239.1
meaning hypopharynx	148.9	198.89	230.0	210.8	235.1	239.0
interarytenoid fold	161.1	197.3	231.0	212.1	235.6	239.1
Intrinsic	161.0	197.3	231.0	212.1	235.6	239.1
ventricular band	161.1	197.3	231.0	212.1	235.6	239.1
leg NEC*	195.5	198.89	232.7	229.8	238.8	239.89
lens, crystalline	190.0	198.4	234.0	224.0	238.8	239.89
lid (lower) (upper)	173.10	198.2	232.1	216.1	238.2	239.2
basal cell carcinoma	173.11	—	—	—	—	—
specified type NEC	173.19	—	—	—	—	—
squamous cell carcinoma	173.12					

Neoplasm, neoplastic— continued	Malignant			Benign	Uncertain Behavior	Unspecified
	Primary	Secondary	Ca in situ			
ligament (see also Neoplasm, connective tissue)						
broad	183.3	198.82	233.39	221.0	236.3	239.5
Mackenrodt's	183.8	198.82	233.39	221.8	236.3	239.5
non-uterine — see Neoplasm, connective tissue						
round	183.5	198.82	—	221.0	236.3	239.5
sacro-uterine	183.4	198.82	—	221.0	236.3	239.5
uterine	183.4	198.82	—	221.0	236.3	239.5
utero-ovarian	183.8	198.82	233.39	221.8	236.3	239.5
uterosacral	183.4	198.82	—	221.0	236.3	239.5
limb*	195.8	198.89	232.8	229.8	238.8	239.89
lower*	195.5	198.89	232.7	229.8	238.8	239.89
upper*	195.4	198.89	232.6	229.8	238.8	239.89
limbus of cornea	190.4	198.4	234.0	224.4	238.8	239.89
lingual NEC (see also Neoplasm, tongue)	141.9	198.89	230.0	210.1	235.1	239.0
lingula, lung	162.3	197.0	231.2	212.3	235.7	239.1
lip (external) (lipstick area) (vermillion border)	140.9	198.89	230.0	210.0	235.1	239.0
buccal aspect — see Neoplasm, lip, internal						
commissure	140.6	198.89	230.0	210.4	235.1	239.0
contiguous sites	140.8	—	—	—	—	—
with oral cavity or pharynx	149.8	—	—	—	—	—
frenulum — see Neoplasm, lip, internal						
inner aspect — see Neoplasm, lip, internal						
internal (buccal) (frenulum) (mucosa) (oral)	140.5	198.89	230.0	210.0	235.1	239.0
lower	140.4	198.89	230.0	210.0	235.1	239.0
upper	140.3	198.89	230.0	210.0	235.1	239.0
lower	140.1	198.89	230.0	210.0	235.1	239.0
internal (buccal) (frenulum) (mucosa) (oral)	140.4	198.89	230.0	210.0	235.1	239.0
mucosa — see Neoplasm, lip, internal						
oral aspect — see Neoplasm, lip, internal						
skin (commissure) (lower) (upper)	173.00	198.2	232.0	216.0	238.2	239.2
basal cell carcinoma	173.01	—	—	—	—	—
specified type NEC	173.09	—	—	—	—	—
squamous cell carcinoma	173.02	—	—	—	—	—
upper	140.0	198.89	230.0	210.0	235.1	239.0
internal (buccal) (frenulum) (mucosa) (oral)	140.3	198.89	230.0	210.0	235.1	239.0
liver	155.2	197.7	230.8	211.5	235.3	239.0
primary	155.0	—	—	—	—	—
lobe						
azygos	162.3	197.0	231.2	212.3	235.7	239.1
frontal	191.1	198.3	—	225.0	237.5	239.6
lower	162.5	197.0	231.2	212.3	235.7	239.1
middle	162.4	197.0	231.2	212.3	235.7	239.1
occipital	191.4	198.3	—	225.0	237.5	239.6

Neoplasm, lobe — Neoplasm, mandible *(Index sidebar)*

	Malignant			Benign	Uncertain Behavior	Unspecified
	Primary	Secondary	Ca in situ			

Neoplasm, neoplastic — *continued*
lobe — *continued*

	Primary	Secondary	Ca in situ	Benign	Uncertain Behavior	Unspecified
parietal	191.3	198.3	—	225.0	237.5	239.6
temporal	191.2	198.3	—	225.0	237.5	239.6
upper	162.3	197.0	231.2	212.3	235.7	239.1
lumbosacral plexus	171.6	198.4	—	215.6	238.1	239.2
lung	162.9	197.0	231.2	212.3	235.7	239.1
azygos lobe	162.3	197.0	231.2	212.3	235.7	239.1
carina	162.2	197.0	231.2	212.3	235.7	239.1
contiguous sites with bronchus or trachea	162.8	—	—	—	—	—
hilus	162.2	197.0	231.2	212.3	235.7	239.1
lingula	162.3	197.0	231.2	212.3	235.7	239.1
lobe NEC	162.9	197.0	231.2	212.3	235.7	239.1
lower lobe	162.5	197.0	231.2	212.3	235.7	239.1
main bronchus	162.2	197.0	231.2	212.3	235.7	239.1
middle lobe	162.4	197.0	231.2	212.3	235.7	239.1
upper lobe	162.3	197.0	231.2	212.3	235.7	239.1
lymph, lymphatic channel NEC *(see also* Neoplasm, connective tissue)*	171.9	198.89	—	215.9	238.1	239.2
gland (secondary)	—	196.9	—	229.0	238.8	239.89
abdominal	—	196.2	—	229.0	238.8	239.89
aortic	—	196.2	—	229.0	238.8	239.89
arm	—	196.3	—	229.0	238.8	239.89
auricular (anterior) (posterior)	—	196.0	—	229.0	238.8	239.89
axilla, axillary	—	196.3	—	229.0	238.8	239.89
brachial	—	196.3	—	229.0	238.8	239.89
bronchial	—	196.1	—	229.0	238.8	239.89
bronchopulmonary	—	196.1	—	229.0	238.8	239.89
celiac	—	196.2	—	229.0	238.8	239.89
cervical	—	196.0	—	229.0	238.8	239.89
cervicofacial	—	196.0	—	229.0	238.8	239.89
Cloquet	—	196.5	—	229.0	238.8	239.89
colic	—	196.2	—	229.0	238.8	239.89
common duct	—	196.2	—	229.0	238.8	239.89
cubital	—	196.3	—	229.0	238.8	239.89
diaphragmatic	—	196.1	—	229.0	238.8	239.89
epigastric, inferior	—	196.6	—	229.0	238.8	239.89
epitrochlear	—	196.3	—	229.0	238.8	239.89
esophageal	—	196.1	—	229.0	238.8	239.89
face	—	196.0	—	229.0	238.8	239.89
femoral	—	196.5	—	229.0	238.8	239.89
gastric	—	196.2	—	229.0	238.8	239.89
groin	—	196.5	—	229.0	238.8	239.89
head	—	196.0	—	229.0	238.8	239.89
hepatic	—	196.2	—	229.0	238.8	239.89
hilar (pulmonary)	—	196.1	—	229.0	238.8	239.89
splenic	—	196.2	—	229.0	238.8	239.89
hypogastric	—	196.6	—	229.0	238.8	239.89
ileocolic	—	196.2	—	229.0	238.8	239.89
iliac	—	196.6	—	229.0	238.8	239.89
infraclavicular	—	196.3	—	229.0	238.8	239.89
inguina, inguinal	—	196.5	—	229.0	238.8	239.89
innominate	—	196.1	—	229.0	238.8	239.89
intercostal	—	196.1	—	229.0	238.8	239.89
intestinal	—	196.2	—	229.0	238.8	239.89
intra-abdominal	—	196.2	—	229.0	238.8	239.89
intrapelvic	—	196.6	—	229.0	238.8	239.89
intrathoracic	—	196.1	—	229.0	238.8	239.9
jugular	—	196.0	—	229.0	238.8	239.89
leg	—	196.5	—	229.0	238.8	239.89
limb lower	—	196.5	—	229.0	238.8	239.9
upper	—	196.3	—	229.0	238.8	239.89
lower limb	—	196.5	—	229.0	238.8	239.9
lumbar	—	196.2	—	229.0	238.8	239.89

Neoplasm, neoplastic — *continued*
lymph, lymphatic — *continued*
gland — *continued*

	Primary	Secondary	Ca in situ	Benign	Uncertain Behavior	Unspecified
mandibular	—	196.0	—	229.0	238.8	239.89
mediastinal	—	196.1	—	229.0	238.8	239.89
mesenteric (inferior) (superior)	—	196.2	—	229.0	238.8	239.89
midcolic	—	196.2	—	229.0	238.8	239.89
multiple sites in categories 196.0–196.6	—	196.8	—	229.0	238.8	239.89
neck	—	196.0	—	229.0	238.8	239.89
obturator	—	196.6	—	229.0	238.8	239.89
occipital	—	196.0	—	229.0	238.8	239.89
pancreatic	—	196.2	—	229.0	238.8	239.89
para-aortic	—	196.2	—	229.0	238.8	239.89
paracervical	—	196.6	—	229.0	238.8	239.89
parametrial	—	196.6	—	229.0	238.8	239.89
parasternal	—	196.1	—	229.0	238.8	239.89
parotid	—	196.0	—	229.0	238.8	239.89
pectoral	—	196.3	—	229.0	238.8	239.89
pelvic	—	196.6	—	229.0	238.8	239.89
peri-aortic	—	196.2	—	229.0	238.8	239.89
peripancreatic	—	196.2	—	229.0	238.8	239.89
popliteal	—	196.5	—	229.0	238.8	239.89
porta hepatis	—	196.2	—	229.0	238.8	239.89
portal	—	196.2	—	229.0	238.8	239.89
preauricular	—	196.0	—	229.0	238.8	239.89
prelaryngeal	—	196.0	—	229.0	238.8	239.89
presymphysial	—	196.6	—	229.0	238.8	239.89
pretracheal	—	196.0	—	229.0	238.8	239.89
primary (any site) NEC	202.9	—	—	—	—	—
pulmonary (hiler)	—	196.1	—	229.0	238.8	239.89
pyloric	—	196.2	—	229.0	238.8	239.89
retroperitoneal	—	196.2	—	229.0	238.8	239.89
retropharyngeal	—	196.0	—	229.0	238.8	239.89
Rosenmüller's	—	196.5	—	229.0	238.8	239.89
sacral	—	196.6	—	229.0	238.8	239.89
scalene	—	196.0	—	229.0	238.8	239.89
site NEC	—	196.9	—	229.0	238.8	239.89
splenic (hilar)	—	196.2	—	229.0	238.8	239.89
subclavicular	—	196.3	—	229.0	238.8	239.89
subinguinal	—	196.5	—	229.0	238.8	239.89
sublingual	—	196.0	—	229.0	238.8	239.89
submandibular	—	196.0	—	229.0	238.8	239.89
submaxillary	—	196.0	—	229.0	238.8	239.89
submental	—	196.0	—	229.0	238.8	239.89
subscapular	—	196.3	—	229.0	238.8	239.89
supraclavicular	—	196.0	—	229.0	238.8	239.89
thoracic	—	196.1	—	229.0	238.8	239.89
tibial	—	196.5	—	229.0	238.8	239.89
tracheal	—	196.1	—	229.0	238.8	239.89
tracheobronchial	—	196.1	—	229.0	238.8	239.89
upper limb	—	196.3	—	229.0	238.8	239.89
Virchow's	—	196.0	—	229.0	238.8	239.89
node *(see also* Neoplasm, lymph gland)* primary NEC	202.9	—	—	—	—	—
vessel *(see also* Neoplasm, connective tissue)*	171.9	198.89	—	215.9	238.1	239.2
Mackenrodt's ligament	183.8	198.82	233.39	221.8	236.3	239.5
malar	170.0	198.5	—	213.0	238.0	239.2
region — *see* Neoplasm, cheek						
mammary gland — *see* Neoplasm, breast						
mandible	170.1	198.5	—	213.1	238.0	239.2
alveolar						

☑ **Additional Digit Required — Refer to the Tabular List for Digit Selection**

▽ Subterms under main terms may continue to next column or page

	Malignant					
	Primary	Secondary	Ca in situ	Benign	Uncertain Behavior	Unspecified
Neoplasm, neoplastic — *continued*						
mandible — *continued*						
alveolar — *continued*						
mucosa	143.1	198.89	230.0	210.4	235.1	239.0
mucose	143.1	198.89	230.0	210.4	235.1	239.0
ridge or process	170.1	198.5	—	213.1	238.0	239.2
carcinoma	143.1	—	—	—	—	—
carcinoma	143.1	—	—	—	—	—
marrow (bone) NEC	202.9	198.5	—	—	—	238.79
mastectomy site (skin)	173.50	198.2	—	—	—	—
basal cell carcinoma	173.51	—	—	—	—	—
specified as breast tissue	174.8	198.81	—	—	—	—
specified type NEC	173.59	—	—	—	—	—
squamous cell carcinoma	173.52	—	—	—	—	—
mastoid (air cells) (antrum) (cavity)	160.1	197.3	231.8	212.0	235.9	239.1
bone or process	170.0	198.5	—	213.0	238.0	239.2
maxilla, maxillary (superior)	170.0	198.5	—	213.0	238.0	239.2
alveolar						
mucosa	143.0	198.89	230.0	210.4	235.1	239.0
ridge or process	170.0	198.5	—	213.0	238.0	239.2
carcinoma	143.0	—	—	—	—	—
antrum	160.2	197.3	231.8	212.0	235.9	239.1
carcinoma	143.0	—	—	—	—	—
inferior — *see* Neoplasm, mandible						
sinus	160.2	197.3	231.8	212.0	235.9	239.1
meatus						
external (ear) (*see also* Neoplasm, skin, ear)	173.20	198.2	232.2	216.2	238.2	239.2
Meckel's diverticulum	152.3	197.4	230.7	211.2	235.2	239.0
mediastinum, mediastinal	164.9	197.1	—	212.5	235.8	239.89
anterior	164.2	197.1	—	212.5	235.8	239.89
contiguous sites with heart and thymus	164.8	—	—	—	—	—
posterior	164.3	197.1	—	212.5	235.8	239.89
medulla						
adrenal	194.0	198.7	234.8	227.0	237.2	239.7
oblongata	191.7	198.3	—	225.0	237.5	239.6
meibomian gland	173.10	198.2	232.1	216.1	238.2	239.2
basal cell carcinoma	173.11	—	—	—	—	—
specified type NEC	173.19	—	—	—	—	—
squamous cell carcinoma	173.12	—	—	—	—	—
meninges (brain) (cerebral) (cranial) (intracranial)	192.1	198.4	—	225.2	237.6	239.7
spinal (cord)	192.3	198.4	—	225.4	237.6	239.7
meniscus, knee joint (lateral) (medial)	170.7	198.5	—	213.7	238.0	239.2
mesentery, mesenteric	158.8	197.6	—	211.8	235.4	239.0
mesoappendix	158.8	197.6	—	211.8	235.4	239.0
mesocolon	158.8	197.6	—	211.8	235.4	239.0
mesopharynx — *see* Neoplasm, oropharynx						
mesosalpinx	183.3	198.82	233.39	221.0	236.3	239.5
mesovarium	183.3	198.82	233.39	221.0	236.3	239.5

	Malignant					
	Primary	Secondary	Ca in situ	Benign	Uncertain Behavior	Unspecified
Neoplasm, neoplastic — *continued*						
metacarpus (any bone)	170.5	198.5	—	213.5	238.0	239.2
metastatic NEC (*see also* Neoplasm, by site, secondary)	—	199.1	—	—	—	—
metatarsus (any bone)	170.8	198.5	—	213.8	238.0	239.2
midbrain	191.7	198.3	—	225.0	237.5	239.6
milk duct — *see* Neoplasm, breast						
mons						
pubis	184.4	198.82	233.32	221.2	236.3	239.5
veneris	184.4	198.82	233.32	221.2	236.3	239.5
motor tract	192.9	198.4	—	225.9	237.9	239.7
brain	191.9	198.3	—	225.0	237.5	239.6
spinal	192.2	198.3	—	225.3	237.5	239.7
mouth	145.9	198.89	230.0	210.4	235.1	239.0
contiguous sites	145.8	—	—	—	—	—
floor	144.9	198.89	230.0	210.3	235.1	239.0
anterior portion	144.0	198.89	230.0	210.3	235.1	239.0
contiguous sites	144.8	—	—	—	—	—
lateral portion	144.1	198.89	230.0	210.3	235.1	239.0
roof	145.5	198.89	230.0	210.4	235.1	239.0
specified part NEC	145.8	198.89	230.0	210.4	235.1	239.0
vestibule	145.1	198.89	230.0	210.4	235.1	239.0
mucosa						
alveolar (ridge or process)	143.9	198.89	230.0	210.4	235.1	239.0
lower	143.1	198.89	230.0	210.4	235.1	239.0
upper	143.0	198.89	230.0	210.4	235.1	239.0
buccal	145.0	198.89	230.0	210.4	235.1	239.0
cheek	145.0	198.89	230.0	210.4	235.1	239.0
lip — *see* Neoplasm, lip, internal						
nasal	160.0	197.3	231.8	212.0	235.9	239.1
oral	145.0	198.89	230.0	210.4	235.1	239.0
Müllerian duct						
female	184.8	198.82	233.39	221.8	236.3	239.5
male	187.8	198.82	233.6	222.8	236.6	239.5
multiple sites NEC	199.0	—	234.9	229.9	238.9	—
muscle (*see also* Neoplasm, connective tissue)						
extraocular	190.1	198.4	234.0	224.1	238.8	239.89
myocardium	164.1	198.89	—	212.7	238.8	239.89
myometrium	182.0	198.82	233.2	219.1	236.0	239.5
myopericardium	164.1	198.89	—	212.7	238.8	239.89
nabothian gland (follicle)	180.0	198.82	233.1	219.0	236.0	239.5
nail	173.90	198.2	232.9	216.9	238.2	239.2
finger (*see also* Neoplasm, skin, limb, upper)	173.60	198.2	232.6	216.6	238.2	239.2
toe (*see also* Neoplasm, skin, limb, lower)	173.70	198.2	232.7	216.7	238.2	239.2
nares, naris (anterior) (posterior)	160.0	197.3	231.8	212.0	235.9	239.1
nasal — *see* Neoplasm, nose						
nasolabial groove (*see also* Neoplasm, skin, face)	173.30	198.2	232.3	216.3	238.2	239.2
nasolacrimal duct	190.7	198.4	234.0	224.7	238.8	239.89
nasopharynx, nasopharyngeal	147.9	198.89	230.0	210.7	235.1	239.0
contiguous sites	147.8	—	—	—	—	—
floor	147.3	198.89	230.0	210.7	235.1	239.0
roof	147.0	198.89	230.0	210.7	235.1	239.0
specified site NEC	147.8	198.89	230.0	210.7	235.1	239.0
wall	147.9	198.89	230.0	210.7	235.1	239.0

☑ Additional Digit Required — Refer to the Tabular List for Digit Selection

Ⓝᴱ Subterms under main terms may continue to next column or page

| | Malignant | | | | | |
---	Primary	Secondary	Ca in situ	Benign	Uncertain Behavior	Unspecified
Neoplasm, neoplastic — *continued*						
nasopharynx, nasopharyngeal — *continued*						
wall — *continued*						
anterior	147.3	198.89	230.0	210.7	235.1	239.0
lateral	147.2	198.89	230.0	210.7	235.1	239.0
posterior	147.1	198.89	230.0	210.7	235.1	239.0
superior	147.0	198.89	230.0	210.7	235.1	239.0
nates (see also Neoplasm, skin, trunk)	173.50	198.2	232.5	216.5	238.2	239.2
neck NEC*	195.0	198.89	234.8	229.8	238.8	239.89
skin	173.40	198.2	232.4	216.4	238.2	239.2
basal cell carcinoma	173.41	—	—	—	—	—
specified type NEC	173.49	—	—	—	—	—
squamous cell carcinoma	173.42	—	—	—	—	—
nerve (autonomic) (ganglion) (parasympathetic) (peripheral) (sympathetic) (see also Neoplasm, connective tissue)						
abducens	192.0	198.4	—	225.1	237.9	239.7
accessory (spinal)	192.0	198.4	—	225.1	237.9	239.7
acoustic	192.0	198.4	—	225.1	237.9	239.7
auditory	192.0	198.4	—	225.1	237.9	239.7
brachial	171.2	198.89	—	215.2	238.1	239.2
cranial (any)	192.0	198.4	—	225.1	237.9	239.7
facial	192.0	198.4	—	225.1	237.9	239.7
femoral	171.3	198.89	—	215.3	238.1	239.2
glossopharyngeal	192.0	198.4	—	225.1	237.9	239.7
hypoglossal	192.0	198.4	—	225.1	237.9	239.7
intercostal	171.4	198.89	—	215.4	238.1	239.2
lumbar	171.7	198.89	—	215.7	238.1	239.2
median	171.2	198.89	—	215.2	238.1	239.2
obturator	171.3	198.89	—	215.3	238.1	239.2
oculomotor	192.0	198.4	—	225.1	237.9	239.7
olfactory	192.0	198.4	—	225.1	237.9	239.7
optic	192.0	198.4	—	225.1	237.9	239.7
peripheral NEC	171.9	198.89	—	215.9	238.1	239.2
radial	171.2	198.89	—	215.2	238.1	239.2
sacral	171.6	198.89	—	215.6	238.1	239.2
sciatic	171.3	198.89	—	215.3	238.1	239.2
spinal NEC	171.9	198.89	—	215.9	238.1	239.2
trigeminal	192.0	198.4	—	225.1	237.9	239.7
trochlear	192.0	198.4	—	225.1	237.9	239.7
ulnar	171.2	198.89	—	215.2	238.1	239.2
vagus	192.0	198.4	—	225.1	237.9	239.7
nervous system (central) NEC	192.9	198.4	—	225.9	237.9	239.7
autonomic NEC	171.9	198.89	—	215.9	238.1	239.2
brain (see also Neoplasm, brain)						
membrane or meninges	192.1	198.4	—	225.2	237.6	239.7
contiguous sites	192.8	—	—	—	—	—
parasympathetic NEC	171.9	198.89	—	215.9	238.1	239.2
sympathetic NEC	171.9	198.89	—	215.9	238.1	239.2
nipple (female)	174.0	198.81	233.0	217	238.3	239.3
male	175.0	198.81	233.0	217	238.3	239.3
nose, nasal	195.0	198.89	234.8	229.8	238.8	239.89
ala (external) (see also Neoplasm, nose, skin)	173.30	198.2	232.3	216.3	238.2	239.2
bone	170.0	198.5	—	213.0	238.0	239.2
cartilage	160.0	197.3	231.8	212.0	235.9	239.1

| | Malignant | | | | | |
---	Primary	Secondary	Ca in situ	Benign	Uncertain Behavior	Unspecified
Neoplasm, neoplastic — *continued*						
nose, nasal — *continued*						
cavity	160.0	197.3	231.8	212.0	235.9	239.1
contiguous sites with accessory sinuses or middle ear	160.8	—	—	—	—	—
choana	147.3	198.89	230.0	210.7	235.1	239.0
external (skin) (see also Neoplasm, nose, skin)	173.30	198.2	232.3	216.3	238.2	239.2
fossa	160.0	197.3	231.8	212.0	235.9	239.1
internal	160.0	197.3	231.8	212.0	235.9	239.1
mucosa	160.0	197.3	231.8	212.0	235.9	239.1
septum	160.0	197.3	231.8	212.0	235.9	239.1
posterior margin	147.3	198.89	230.0	210.7	235.1	239.0
sinus — see Neoplasm, sinus						
skin	173.30	198.2	232.3	216.3	238.2	239.2
basal cell carcinoma	173.31	—	—	—	—	—
specified type NEC	173.39	—	—	—	—	—
squamous cell carcinoma	173.32	—	—	—	—	—
turbinate (mucosa)	160.0	197.3	231.8	212.0	235.9	239.1
bone	170.0	198.5	—	213.0	238.0	239.2
vestibule	160.0	197.3	231.8	212.0	235.9	239.1
nostril	160.0	197.3	231.8	212.0	235.9	239.1
nucleus pulposus	170.2	198.5	—	213.2	238.0	239.2
occipital bone	170.0	198.5	—	213.0	238.0	239.2
lobe or pole, brain	191.4	198.3	—	225.0	237.5	239.6
odontogenic — see Neoplasm, jaw bone						
oesophagus — see Neoplasm, esophagus						
olfactory nerve or bulb	192.0	198.4	—	225.1	237.9	239.7
olive (brain)	191.7	198.3	—	225.0	237.5	239.6
omentum	158.8	197.6	—	211.8	235.4	239.0
operculum (brain)	191.0	198.3	—	225.0	237.5	239.6
optic nerve, chiasm, or tract	192.0	198.4	—	225.1	237.9	239.7
oral (cavity)	145.9	198.89	230.0	210.4	235.1	239.0
contiguous sites with lip or pharynx	149.8	—	—	—	—	—
ill-defined	149.9	198.89	230.0	210.4	235.1	239.0
mucosa	145.9	198.89	230.0	210.4	235.1	239.0
orbit	190.1	198.4	234.0	224.1	238.8	239.89
bone	170.0	198.5	—	213.0	238.0	239.2
eye	190.1	198.4	234.0	224.1	238.8	239.89
soft parts	190.1	198.4	234.0	224.1	238.8	239.89
organ of Zuckerkandl	194.6	198.89	—	227.6	237.3	239.7
oropharynx	146.9	198.89	230.0	210.6	235.1	239.0
branchial cleft (vestige)	146.8	198.89	230.0	210.6	235.1	239.0
contiguous sites	146.8	—	—	—	—	—
junctional region	146.5	198.89	230.0	210.6	235.1	239.0
lateral wall	146.6	198.89	230.0	210.6	235.1	239.0
pillars of fauces	146.2	198.89	230.0	210.6	235.1	239.0
posterior wall	146.7	198.89	230.0	210.6	235.1	239.0
specified part NEC	146.8	198.89	230.0	210.6	235.1	239.0
vallecula	146.3	198.89	230.0	210.6	235.1	239.0
os						
external	180.1	198.82	233.1	219.0	236.0	239.5

Neoplasm, neoplastic—	Primary	Secondary	Ca in situ	Benign	Uncertain Behavior	Unspecified
continued						
os — *continued*						
internal	180.0	198.82	233.1	219.0	236.0	239.5
ovary	183.0	198.6	233.39	220	236.2	239.5
oviduct	183.2	198.82	233.39	221.0	236.3	239.5
palate	145.5	198.89	230.0	210.4	235.1	239.0
hard	145.2	198.89	230.0	210.4	235.1	239.0
junction of hard and soft palate	145.5	198.89	230.0	210.4	235.1	239.0
soft	145.3	198.89	230.0	210.4	235.1	239.0
nasopharyngeal surface	147.3	198.89	230.0	210.7	235.1	239.0
posterior surface	147.3	198.89	230.0	210.7	235.1	239.0
superior surface	147.3	198.89	230.0	210.7	235.1	239.0
palatoglossal arch	146.2	198.89	230.0	210.6	235.1	239.0
palatopharyngeal arch	146.2	198.89	230.0	210.6	235.1	239.0
pallium	191.0	198.3	—	225.0	237.5	239.6
palpebra	173.10	198.2	232.1	216.1	238.2	239.2
basal cell carcinoma	173.11	—	—	—	—	—
specified type NEC	173.19					
squamous cell carcinoma	173.12	—	—	—	—	—
pancreas	157.9	197.8	230.9	211.6	235.5	239.0
body	157.1	197.8	230.9	211.6	235.5	239.0
contiguous sites	157.8	—	—			
duct (of Santorini) (of Wirsung)	157.3	197.8	230.9	211.6	235.5	239.0
ectopic tissue	157.8	197.8	230.9	211.6	235.5	239.0
head	157.0	197.8	230.9	211.6	235.5	239.0
islet cells	157.4	197.8	230.9	211.7	235.5	239.0
neck	157.8	197.8	230.9	211.6	235.5	239.0
tail	157.2	197.8	230.9	211.6	235.5	239.0
para-aortic body	194.6	198.89	—	227.6	237.3	239.7
paraganglion NEC	194.6	198.89	—	227.6	237.3	239.7
parametrium	183.4	198.82	—	221.0	236.3	239.5
paranephric	158.0	197.6	—	211.8	235.4	239.0
pararectal	195.3	198.89	—	229.8	238.8	239.89
parasagittal (region)	195.0	198.89	234.8	229.8	238.8	239.89
parasellar	192.9	198.4	—	225.9	237.9	239.7
parathyroid (gland)	194.1	198.89	234.8	227.1	237.4	239.7
paraurethral	195.3	198.89	—	229.8	238.8	239.89
gland	189.4	198.1	233.9	223.89	236.99	239.5
paravaginal	195.3	198.89	—	229.8	238.8	239.89
parenchyma, kidney	189.0	198.0	233.9	223.0	236.91	239.5
parietal bone	170.0	198.5	—	213.0	238.0	239.2
lobe, brain	191.3	198.3	—	225.0	237.5	239.6
paroophoron	183.3	198.82	233.39	221.0	236.3	239.5
parotid (duct) (gland)	142.0	198.89	230.0	210.2	235.0	239.0
parovarium	183.3	198.82	233.39	221.0	236.3	239.5
patella	170.8	198.5	—	213.8	238.0	239.2
peduncle, cerebral	191.7	198.3	—	225.0	237.5	239.6
pelvirectal junction	154.0	197.5	230.4	211.4	235.2	239.0
pelvis, pelvic	195.3	198.89	234.8	229.8	238.8	239.89
bone	170.6	198.5	—	213.6	238.0	239.2
floor	195.3	198.89	234.8	229.8	238.8	239.89
renal	189.1	198.0	233.9	223.1	236.91	239.5
viscera	195.3	198.89	234.8	229.8	238.8	239.89
wall	195.3	198.89	234.8	229.8	238.8	239.89
pelvo-abdominal	195.8	198.89	234.8	229.8	238.8	239.89
penis	187.4	198.82	233.5	222.1	236.6	239.5
body	187.3	198.82	233.5	222.1	236.6	239.5
corpus (cavernosum)	187.3	198.82	233.5	222.1	236.6	239.5
glans	187.2	198.82	233.5	222.1	236.6	239.5
skin NEC	187.4	198.82	233.5	222.1	236.6	239.5
periadrenal (tissue)	158.0	197.6	—	211.8	235.4	239.0

Neoplasm, neoplastic—	Primary	Secondary	Ca in situ	Benign	Uncertain Behavior	Unspecified
continued						
perianal (skin) (*see also* Neoplasm, skin, anus)	173.50	198.2	232.5	216.5	238.2	239.2
pericardium	164.1	198.89	—	212.7	238.8	239.89
perinephric	158.0	197.6	—	211.8	235.4	239.0
perineum	195.3	198.89	234.8	229.8	238.8	239.89
periodontal tissue NEC	143.9	198.89	230.0	210.4	235.1	239.0
periosteum — *see* Neoplasm, bone						
peripancreatic	158.0	197.6	—	211.8	235.4	239.0
peripheral nerve NEC	171.9	198.89	—	215.9	238.1	239.2
perirectal (tissue)	195.3	198.89	—	229.8	238.8	239.89
perirenal (tissue)	158.0	197.6	—	211.8	235.4	239.0
peritoneum, peritoneal (cavity)	158.9	197.6	—	211.8	235.4	239.0
contiguous sites	158.8	—	—	—	—	—
with digestive organs	159.8	—	—	—	—	—
parietal	158.8	197.6	—	211.8	235.4	239.0
pelvic	158.8	197.6	—	211.8	235.4	239.0
specified part NEC	158.8	197.6	—	211.8	235.4	239.0
peritonsillar (tissue)	195.0	198.89	234.8	229.8	238.8	239.89
periurethral tissue	195.3	198.89	—	229.8	238.8	239.89
phalanges	170.9	198.5	—	213.9	238.0	239.2
foot	170.8	198.5	—	213.8	238.0	239.2
hand	170.5	198.5	—	213.5	238.0	239.2
pharynx, pharyngeal	149.0	198.89	230.0	210.9	235.1	239.0
bursa	147.1	198.89	230.0	210.7	235.1	239.0
fornix	147.3	198.89	230.0	210.7	235.1	239.0
recess	147.2	198.89	230.0	210.7	235.1	239.0
region	149.0	198.89	230.0	210.9	235.1	239.0
tonsil	147.1	198.89	230.0	210.7	235.1	239.0
wall (lateral) (posterior)	149.0	198.89	230.0	210.9	235.1	239.0
pia mater (cerebral) (cranial)	192.1	198.4	—	225.2	237.6	239.7
spinal	192.3	198.4	—	225.4	237.6	239.7
pillars of fauces	146.2	198.89	230.0	210.6	235.1	239.0
pineal (body) (gland)	194.4	198.89	234.8	227.4	237.1	239.7
pinna (ear) NEC (*see also* Neoplasm, skin, ear)	173.20	198.2	232.2	216.2	238.2	239.2
cartilage	171.0	198.89	—	215.0	238.1	239.2
piriform fossa or sinus	148.1	198.89	230.0	210.8	235.1	239.0
pituitary (body) (fossa) (gland) (lobe)	194.3	198.89	234.8	227.3	237.0	239.7
placenta	181	198.82	233.2	219.8	236.1	239.5
pleura, pleural (cavity)	163.9	197.2	—	212.4	235.8	239.1
contiguous sites	163.8	—	—	—	—	—
parietal	163.0	197.2	—	212.4	235.8	239.1
visceral	163.1	197.2	—	212.4	235.8	239.1
plexus brachial	171.2	198.89	—	215.2	238.1	239.2
cervical	171.0	198.89	—	215.0	238.1	239.2
choroid	191.5	198.3	—	225.0	237.5	239.6
lumbosacral	171.6	198.89	—	215.6	238.1	239.2
sacral	171.6	198.89	—	215.6	238.1	239.2
pluri-endocrine	194.8	198.89	234.8	227.8	237.4	239.7
pole frontal	191.1	198.3	—	225.0	237.5	239.6
occipital	191.4	198.3	—	225.0	237.5	239.6
pons (varolii)	191.7	198.3	—	225.0	237.5	239.6
popliteal fossa or space*	195.5	198.89	234.8	229.8	238.8	239.89
postcricoid (region)	148.0	198.89	230.0	210.8	235.1	239.0

☑ Additional Digit Required — Refer to the Tabular List for Digit Selection

▽ Subterms under main terms may continue to next column or page

Neoplasm, posterior fossa — Neoplasm, skin NOS

	Malignant					
	Primary	Secondary	Ca in situ	Benign	Uncertain Behavior	Unspecified
Neoplasm, neoplastic— *continued*						
posterior fossa (cranial)	191.9	198.3	—	225.0	237.5	239.6
postnasal space	147.9	198.89	230.0	210.7	235.1	239.0
prepuce	187.1	198.82	233.5	222.1	236.6	239.5
prepylorus	151.1	197.8	230.2	211.1	235.2	239.0
presacral (region)	195.3	198.89	—	229.8	238.8	239.89
prostate (gland)	185	198.82	233.4	222.2	236.5	239.5
utricle	189.3	198.1	233.9	223.81	236.99	239.5
pterygoid fossa	171.0	198.89	—	215.0	238.1	239.2
pubic bone	170.6	198.5	—	213.6	238.0	239.2
pudenda, pudendum (female)	184.4	198.82	233.32	221.2	236.3	239.5
pulmonary	162.9	197.0	231.2	212.3	235.7	239.1
putamen	191.0	198.3	—	225.0	237.5	239.6
pyloric						
antrum	151.2	197.8	230.2	211.1	235.2	239.0
canal	151.1	197.8	230.2	211.1	235.2	239.0
pylorus	151.1	197.8	230.2	211.1	235.2	239.0
pyramid (brain)	191.7	198.3	—	225.0	237.5	239.6
pyriform fossa or sinus	148.1	198.89	230.0	210.8	235.1	239.0
radius (any part)	170.4	198.5	—	213.4	238.0	239.2
Rathke's pouch	194.3	198.89	234.8	227.3	237.0	239.7
rectosigmoid (colon) (junction)	154.0	197.5	230.4	211.4	235.2	239.0
contiguous sites with anus or rectum	154.8	—	—	—	—	—
rectouterine pouch	158.8	197.6	—	211.8	235.4	239.0
rectovaginal septum or wall	195.3	198.89	234.8	229.8	238.8	239.89
rectovesical septum	195.3	198.89	234.8	229.8	238.8	239.89
rectum (ampulla)	154.1	197.5	230.4	211.4	235.2	239.0
and colon	154.0	197.5	230.4	211.4	235.2	239.0
contiguous sites with anus or rectosigmoid junction	154.8	—	—	—	—	—
renal	189.0	198.0	233.9	223.0	236.91	239.5
calyx	189.1	198.0	233.9	223.1	236.91	239.5
hilus	189.1	198.0	233.9	223.1	236.91	239.5
parenchyma	189.0	198.0	233.9	223.0	236.91	239.5
pelvis	189.1	198.0	233.9	223.1	236.91	239.5
respiratory organs or system NEC	165.9	197.3	231.9	212.9	235.9	239.1
contiguous sites with intrathoracic organs	165.8	—	—	—	—	—
specified sites NEC	165.8	197.3	231.8	212.8	235.9	239.1
tract NEC	165.9	197.3	231.9	212.9	235.9	239.1
upper	165.0	197.3	231.9	212.9	235.9	239.1
retina	190.5	198.4	234.0	224.5	238.8	239.81
retrobulbar	190.1	198.4	—	224.1	238.8	239.89
retrocecal	158.0	197.6	—	211.8	235.4	239.0
retromolar (area) (triangle) (trigone)	145.6	198.89	230.0	210.4	235.1	239.0
retro-orbital	195.0	198.89	234.8	229.8	238.8	239.89
retroperitoneal (space) (tissue)	158.0	197.6	—	211.8	235.4	239.0
contiguous sites	158.8	—	—	—	—	—
retroperitoneum	158.0	197.6	—	211.8	235.4	239.0
contiguous sites	158.8	—	—	—	—	—
retropharyngeal	149.0	198.89	230.0	210.9	235.1	239.0
retrovesical (septum)	195.3	198.89	234.8	229.8	238.8	239.89
rhinencephalon	191.0	198.3	—	225.0	237.5	239.6
rib	170.3	198.5	—	213.3	238.0	239.2
Rosenmüller's fossa	147.2	198.89	230.0	210.7	235.1	239.0
round ligament	183.5	198.82	—	221.0	236.3	239.5
Neoplasm, neoplastic— *continued*						
sacrococcyx, sacrococcygeal	170.6	198.5	—	213.6	238.0	239.2
region	195.3	198.89	234.8	229.8	238.8	239.89
sacrouterine ligament	183.4	198.82		221.0	236.3	239.5
sacrum, sacral (vertebra)	170.6	198.5	—	213.6	238.0	239.2
salivary gland or duct (major)	142.9	198.89	230.0	210.2	235.0	239.0
contiguous sites	142.8	—	—	—	—	—
minor NEC	145.9	198.89	230.0	210.4	235.1	239.0
parotid	142.0	198.89	230.0	210.2	235.0	239.0
pluriglandular	142.8	198.89	—	210.2	235.0	239.0
sublingual	142.2	198.89	230.0	210.2	235.0	239.0
submandibular	142.1	198.89	230.0	210.2	235.0	239.0
submaxillary	142.1	198.89	230.0	210.2	235.0	239.0
salpinx (uterine)	183.2	198.82	233.39	221.0	236.3	239.5
Santorini's duct	157.3	197.8	230.9	211.6	235.5	239.0
scalp	173.40	198.2	232.4	216.4	238.2	239.2
basal cell carcinoma	173.41	—	—	—	—	—
specified type NEC	173.49	—	—	—	—	—
squamous cell carcinoma	173.42	—	—	—	—	—
scapula (any part)	170.4	198.5	—	213.4	238.0	239.2
scapular region	195.1	198.89	234.8	229.8	238.8	239.89
scar NEC (*see also* Neoplasm, skin)	173.90	198.2	232.9	216.9	238.2	239.2
sciatic nerve	171.3	198.89	—	215.3	238.1	239.2
sclera	190.0	198.4	234.0	224.0	238.8	239.89
scrotum (skin)	187.7	198.82	—	222.4	236.6	239.5
sebaceous gland — *see* Neoplasm, skin						
sella turcica	194.3	198.89	234.8	227.3	237.0	239.7
bone	170.0	198.5	—	213.0	238.0	239.2
semilunar cartilage (knee)	170.7	198.5	—	213.7	238.0	239.2
seminal vesicle	187.8	198.82	233.6	222.8	236.6	239.5
septum nasal	160.0	197.3	231.8	212.0	235.9	239.1
posterior margin	147.3	198.89	230.0	210.7	235.1	239.0
rectovaginal	195.3	198.89	234.8	229.8	238.8	239.89
rectovesical	195.3	198.89	234.8	229.8	238.8	239.89
urethrovaginal	184.9	198.82	233.39	221.9	236.3	239.5
vesicovaginal	184.9	198.82	233.39	221.9	236.3	239.5
shoulder NEC*	195.4	198.89	232.6	229.8	238.8	239.89
sigmoid flexure (lower) (upper)	153.3	197.5	230.3	211.3	235.2	239.0
sinus (accessory)	160.9	197.3	231.8	212.0	235.9	239.1
bone (any)	170.0	198.5	—	213.0	238.0	239.2
contiguous sites with middle ear or nasal cavities	160.8	—	—	—	—	—
ethmoidal	160.3	197.3	231.8	212.0	235.9	239.1
frontal	160.4	197.3	231.8	212.0	235.9	239.1
maxillary	160.2	197.3	231.8	212.0	235.9	239.1
nasal, paranasal NEC	160.9	197.3	231.8	212.0	235.9	239.1
pyriform	148.1	198.89	230.0	210.8	235.1	239.0
sphenoidal	160.5	197.3	231.8	212.0	235.9	239.1
skeleton, skeletal NEC	170.9	198.5	—	213.9	238.0	239.2
Skene's gland	189.4	198.1	233.9	223.89	236.99	239.5
skin NOS	173.90	198.2	232.9	216.9	238.2	239.2
abdominal wall	173.50	198.2	232.5	216.5	238.2	239.2
basal cell carcinoma	173.51	—	—	—	—	—
specified type NEC	173.59	—	—	—	—	—
squamous cell carcinoma	173.52	—	—	—	—	—

☑ **Additional Digit Required** — Refer to the Tabular List for Digit Selection

▽ Subterms under main terms may continue to next column or page

Neoplasm, neoplastic— continued	Malignant			Benign	Uncertain Behavior	Unspecified
	Primary	Secondary	Ca in situ			
skin — continued						
ala nasi (see also Neoplasm, skin, face)	173.30	198.2	232.3	216.3	238.2	239.2
ankle (see also Neoplasm, skin, limb, lower)	173.70	198.2	232.7	216.7	238.2	239.2
antecubital space (see also Neoplasm, skin, limb, upper)	173.60	198.2	232.6	216.6	238.2	239.2
anus	173.50	198.2	232.5	216.5	238.2	239.2
basal cell carcinoma	173.51	—	—	—	—	—
specified type NEC	173.59	—	—	—	—	—
squamous cell carcinoma	173.52	—	—	—	—	—
arm (see also Neoplasm, skin, limb, upper)	173.60	198.2	232.6	216.6	238.2	239.2
auditory canal (external) (see also Neoplasm, skin, ear)	173.20	198.2	232.2	216.2	238.2	239.2
auricle (ear) (see also Neoplasm, skin, ear)	173.20	198.2	232.2	216.2	238.2	239.2
auricular canal (external) (see also Neoplasm, skin, ear)	173.20	198.2	232.2	216.2	238.2	239.2
axilla, axillary fold (see also Neoplasm, skin, trunk)	173.50	198.2	232.5	216.5	238.2	239.2
back	173.50	198.2	232.5	216.5	238.2	239.2
basal cell carcinoma	173.51	—	—	—	—	—
specified type NEC	173.59	—	—	—	—	—
squamous cell carcinoma	173.52	—	—	—	—	—
basal cell carcinoma, unspecified site	173.91	—	—	—	—	—
breast (see also Neoplasm, skin, trunk)	173.50	198.2	232.5	216.5	238.2	239.2
brow (see also Neoplasm, skin, face)	173.30	198.2	232.3	216.3	238.2	239.2
buttock (see also Neoplasm, skin, trunk)	173.50	198.2	232.5	216.5	238.2	239.2
calf (see also Neoplasm, skin, limb, lower)	173.70	198.2	232.7	216.7	238.2	239.2
canthus (eye) (inner) (outer)	173.10	198.2	232.1	216.1	238.2	239.2
basal cell carcinoma	173.11	—	—	—	—	—
specified type NEC	173.19	—	—	—	—	—
squamous cell carcinoma	173.12	—	—	—	—	—
cervical region (see also Neoplasm, skin, neck)	173.40	198.2	232.4	216.4	238.2	239.2
cheek (external) (see also Neoplasm, skin, face)	173.30	198.2	232.3	216.3	238.2	239.2
chest (wall) (see also Neoplasm, skin, trunk)	173.50	198.2	232.5	216.5	238.2	239.2
chin (see also Neoplasm, skin, face)	173.30	198.2	232.3	216.3	238.2	239.2

Neoplasm, neoplastic— continued	Malignant			Benign	Uncertain Behavior	Unspecified
	Primary	Secondary	Ca in situ			
skin — continued						
clavicular area (see also Neoplasm, skin, trunk)	173.50	198.2	232.5	216.5	238.2	239.2
clitoris	—	198.82	233.32	221.2	236.3	239.5
columnella (see also Neoplasm, skin, face)	173.30	198.2	232.3	216.3	238.2	239.2
concha (see also Neoplasm, skin, ear)	173.20	198.2	232.2	216.2	238.2	239.2
contiguous sites	173.80	—	—	—	—	—
basal cell carcinoma	173.81	—	—	—	—	—
specified type NEC	173.89	—	—	—	—	—
squamous cell carcinoma	173.82	—	—	—	—	—
ear (external)	173.20	198.2	232.2	216.2	238.2	239.2
basal cell carcinoma	173.21	—	—	—	—	—
specified type NEC	173.29	—	—	—	—	—
squamous cell carcinoma	173.22	—	—	—	—	—
elbow (see also Neoplasm, skin, limb, upper)	173.60	198.2	232.6	216.6	238.2	239.2
eyebrow (see also Neoplasm, skin, face)	173.30	198.2	232.3	216.3	238.2	239.2
eyelid	173.10	198.2	232.1	—	238.2	239.2
basal cell carcinoma	173.11	—	—	—	—	—
specified type NEC	173.19	—	—	—	—	—
squamous cell carcinoma	173.12	—	—	—	—	—
face NEC	173.30	198.2	232.3	216.3	238.2	239.2
basal cell carcinoma	173.31	—	—	—	—	—
specified type NEC	173.39	—	—	—	—	—
squamous cell carcinoma	173.32	—	—	—	—	—
female genital organs (external)	184.4	198.82	233.30	221.2	236.3	239.5
clitoris	184.3	198.82	233.32	221.2	236.3	239.5
labium NEC	184.4	198.82	233.32	221.2	236.3	239.5
majus	184.1	198.82	233.32	221.2	236.3	239.5
minus	184.2	198.82	233.32	221.2	236.3	239.5
pudendum	184.4	198.82	233.32	221.2	236.3	239.5
vulva	184.4	198.82	233.32	221.2	236.3	239.5
finger (see also Neoplasm, skin, limb, upper)	173.60	198.2	232.6	216.6	238.2	239.2
flank (see also Neoplasm, skin, trunk)	173.50	198.2	232.5	216.5	238.2	239.2
foot (see also Neoplasm, skin, limb, lower)	173.70	198.2	232.7	216.7	238.2	239.2
forearm (see also Neoplasm, skin, limb, upper)	173.60	198.2	232.6	216.6	238.2	239.2
forehead (see also Neoplasm, skin, face)	173.30	198.2	232.3	216.3	238.2	239.2
glabella (see also Neoplasm, skin, face)	173.30	198.2	232.3	216.3	238.2	239.2
gluteal region (see also Neoplasm, skin, trunk)	173.50	198.2	232.5	216.5	238.2	239.2
groin (see also Neoplasm, skin, trunk)	173.50	198.2	232.5	216.5	238.2	239.2

☑ **Additional Digit Required** — Refer to the Tabular List for Digit Selection   ▽ Subterms under main terms may continue to next column or page

Neoplasm, neoplastic — continued
skin — continued

	Malignant			Benign	Uncertain Behavior	Unspecified
	Primary	Secondary	Ca in situ			
hand (see also Neoplasm, skin, limb, upper)	173.60	198.2	232.6	216.6	238.2	239.2
head NEC (see also Neoplasm, skin, scalp)	173.40	198.2	232.4	216.4	238.2	239.2
heel (see also Neoplasm, skin, limb, lower)	173.70	198.2	232.7	216.7	238.2	239.2
helix (see also Neoplasm, skin, ear)	173.20	198.2	—	216.2	238.2	239.2
hip	173.70	198.2	232.7	216.7	238.2	239.2
basal cell carcinoma	173.71	—	—	—	—	—
specified type NEC	173.79	—	—	—	—	—
squamous cell carcinoma	173.72	—	—	—	—	—
infraclavicular region (see also Neoplasm, skin, trunk)	173.50	198.2	232.5	216.5	238.2	239.2
inguinal region (see also Neoplasm, skin, trunk)	173.50	198.2	232.5	216.5	238.2	239.2
jaw (see also Neoplasm, skin, face)	173.30	198.2	232.3	216.3	238.2	239.2
knee (see also Neoplasm, skin, limb, lower)	173.70	198.2	232.7	216.7	238.2	239.2
labia						
majora	184.1	198.82	233.32	221.2	236.3	239.5
minora	184.2	198.82	233.32	221.2	236.3	239.5
leg (see also Neoplasm, skin, limb, lower)	173.70	198.2	232.7	216.7	238.2	239.2
lid (lower) (upper)	173.10	198.2	232.1	216.1	238.2	239.2
basal cell carcinoma	173.11	—	—	—	—	—
specified type NEC	173.19	—	—	—	—	—
squamous cell carcinoma	173.12	—	—	—	—	—
limb NEC	173.90	198.2	232.9	216.9	238.2	239.5
lower	173.70	198.2	232.7	216.7	238.2	239.2
basal cell carcinoma	173.71	—	—	—	—	—
specified type NEC	173.79	—	—	—	—	—
squamous cell carcinoma	173.72	—	—	—	—	—
upper	173.60	198.2	232.6	216.6	238.2	239.2
basal cell carcinoma	173.61	—	—	—	—	—
specified type NEC	173.69	—	—	—	—	—
squamous cell carcinoma	173.62	—	—	—	—	—
lip (lower) (upper)	173.00	198.2	232.0	216.0	238.2	239.2
basal cell carcinoma	173.01	—	—	—	—	—
specified type NEC	173.09	—	—	—	—	—
squamous cell carcinoma	173.02	—	—	—	—	—
male genital organs	187.9	198.82	233.6	222.9	236.6	239.5
penis	187.4	198.82	233.5	222.1	236.6	239.5
prepuce	187.1	198.82	233.5	222.1	236.6	239.5
scrotum	187.7	198.82	233.6	222.4	236.6	239.5
mastectomy site (see also Neoplasm, skin, trunk)	173.50	198.2	—	—	—	—
specified as breast tissue	174.8	198.81	—	—	—	—
meatus, acoustic (external) (see also Neoplasm, skin, ear)	173.20	198.2	232.2	216.2	238.2	239.2
nates (see also Neoplasm, skin, trunk)	173.50	198.2	232.5	216.5	238.2	239.0
neck	173.40	198.2	232.4	216.4	238.2	239.2
basal cell carcinoma	173.41	—	—	—	—	—
specified type NEC	173.49	—	—	—	—	—
squamous cell carcinoma	173.42	—	—	—	—	—
nose (external) (see also Neoplasm, skin, face)	173.30	198.2	232.3	216.3	238.2	239.2
palm (see also Neoplasm, skin, limb, upper)	173.60	198.2	232.6	216.6	238.2	239.2
palpebra	173.10	198.2	232.1	216.1	238.2	239.2
basal cell carcinoma	173.11	—	—	—	—	—
specified type NEC	173.19	—	—	—	—	—
squamous cell carcinoma	173.12	—	—	—	—	—
penis NEC	187.4	198.82	233.5	222.1	236.6	239.5
perianal (see also Neoplasm, skin, anus)	173.50	198.2	232.5	216.5	238.2	239.2
perineum (see also Neoplasm, skin, anus)	173.50	198.2	232.5	216.5	238.2	239.2
pinna (see also Neoplasm, skin, ear)	173.20	198.2	232.2	216.2	238.2	239.2
plantar (see also Neoplasm, skin, limb, lower)	173.70	198.2	232.7	216.7	238.2	239.2
popliteal fossa or space (see also Neoplasm, skin, limb, lower)	173.70	198.2	232.7	216.7	238.2	239.2
prepuce	187.1	198.82	233.5	222.1	236.6	239.5
pubes (see also Neoplasm, skin, trunk)	173.50	198.2	232.5	216.5	238.2	239.2
sacrococcygeal region (see also Neoplasm, skin, trunk)	173.50	198.2	232.5	216.5	238.2	239.2
scalp	173.40	198.2	232.4	216.4	238.2	239.2
basal cell carcinoma	173.41	—	—	—	—	—
specified type NEC	173.49	—	—	—	—	—
squamous cell carcinoma	173.42	—	—	—	—	—
scapular region (see also Neoplasm, skin, trunk)	173.50	198.2	232.5	216.5	238.2	239.2
scrotum	187.7	198.82	233.6	222.4	236.6	239.5
shoulder	173.60	198.2	232.6	216.6	238.2	239.2
basal cell carcinoma	173.61	—	—	—	—	—
specified type NEC	173.69	—	—	—	—	—
squamous cell carcinoma	173.62	—	—	—	—	—

☑ Additional Digit Required — Refer to the Tabular List for Digit Selection

▽ Subterms under main terms may continue to next column or page

Neoplasm, neoplastic — continued

	Malignant			Benign	Uncertain Behavior	Unspecified
	Primary	Secondary	Ca in situ			
skin — *continued*						
sole (foot) (*see also* Neoplasm, skin, limb, lower)	173.70	198.2	232.7	216.7	238.2	239.2
specified sites NEC	173.80	198.2	232.8	216.8	—	239.2
basal cell carcinoma	173.81	—	—	—	—	—
specified type NEC	173.89	—	—	—	—	—
squamous cell carcinoma	173.82	—	—	—	—	—
specified type NEC, unspecified site	173.99	—	—	—	—	—
squamous cell carcinoma, unspecified site	173.92	—	—	—	—	—
submammary fold (*see also* Neoplasm, skin, trunk)	173.50	198.2	232.5	216.5	238.2	239.2
supraclavicular region (*see also* Neoplasm, skin, neck)	173.40	198.2	232.4	216.4	238.2	239.2
temple (*see also* Neoplasm, skin, face)	173.30	198.2	232.3	216.3	238.2	239.2
thigh (*see also* Neoplasm, skin, limb, lower)	173.70	198.2	232.7	216.7	238.2	239.2
thoracic wall (*see also* Neoplasm, skin, trunk)	173.50	198.2	232.5	216.5	238.2	239.2
thumb (*see also* Neoplasm, skin, limb, upper)	173.60	198.2	232.6	216.6	238.2	239.2
toe (*see also* Neoplasm, skin, limb, lower)	173.70	198.2	232.7	216.7	238.2	239.2
tragus (*see also* Neoplasm, skin, ear)	173.20	198.2	232.2	216.2	238.2	239.2
trunk	173.50	198.2	232.5	216.5	238.2	239.2
basal cell carcinoma	173.51	—	—	—	—	—
specified type NEC	173.59	—	—	—	—	—
squamous cell carcinoma	173.52	—	—	—	—	—
umbilicus (*see also* Neoplasm, skin, trunk)	173.50	198.2	232.5	216.5	238.2	239.2
vulva	184.4	198.82	233.32	221.2	236.3	239.5
wrist (*see also* Neoplasm, skin, limb, upper)	173.60	198.2	232.6	216.6	238.2	239.2
skull	170.0	198.5	—	213.0	238.0	239.2
soft parts or tissues — *see* Neoplasm, connective tissue						
specified site NEC	195.8	198.89	234.8	229.8	238.8	239.89
specified site — *see* Neoplasm, skin						
spermatic cord	187.6	198.82	233.6	222.8	236.6	239.5
sphenoid	160.5	197.3	231.8	212.0	235.9	239.1
bone	170.0	198.5	—	213.0	238.0	239.2
sinus	160.5	197.3	231.8	212.0	235.9	239.1
sphincter						
anal	154.2	197.5	230.5	211.4	235.5	239.0
of Oddi	156.1	197.8	230.8	211.5	235.3	239.0
spine, spinal (column)	170.2	198.5	—	213.2	238.0	239.2
bulb	191.7	198.3	—	225.0	237.5	239.6
coccyx	170.6	198.5	—	213.6	238.0	239.2

Neoplasm, neoplastic — continued

	Malignant			Benign	Uncertain Behavior	Unspecified
	Primary	Secondary	Ca in situ			
spine, spinal — *continued*						
cord (cervical) (lumbar) (sacral) (thoracic)	192.2	198.3	—	225.3	237.5	239.7
dura mater	192.3	198.4	—	225.4	237.6	239.7
lumbosacral	170.2	198.5	—	213.2	238.0	239.2
membrane	192.3	198.4	—	225.4	237.6	239.7
meninges	192.3	198.4	—	225.4	237.6	239.7
nerve (root)	171.9	198.89	—	215.9	238.1	239.2
pia mater	192.3	198.4	—	225.4	237.6	239.7
root	171.9	198.89	—	215.9	238.1	239.2
sacrum	170.6	198.5	—	213.6	238.0	239.2
spleen, splenic NEC	159.1	197.8	230.9	211.9	235.5	239.0
flexure (colon)	153.7	197.5	230.3	211.3	235.2	239.0
stem, brain	191.7	198.3	—	225.0	237.5	239.6
Stensen's duct	142.0	198.89	230.0	210.2	235.0	239.0
sternum	170.3	198.5	—	213.3	238.0	239.2
stomach	151.9	197.8	230.2	211.1	235.2	239.0
antrum (pyloric)	151.2	197.8	230.2	211.1	235.2	239.0
body	151.4	197.8	230.2	211.1	235.2	239.0
cardia	151.0	197.8	230.2	211.1	235.2	239.0
cardiac orifice	151.0	197.8	230.2	211.1	235.2	239.0
contiguous sites	151.8	—	—	—	—	—
corpus	151.4	197.8	230.2	211.1	235.2	239.0
fundus	151.3	197.8	230.2	211.1	235.2	239.0
greater curvature NEC	151.6	197.8	230.2	211.1	235.2	239.0
lesser curvature NEC	151.5	197.8	230.2	211.1	235.2	239.0
prepylorus	151.1	197.8	230.2	211.1	235.2	239.0
pylorus	151.1	197.8	230.2	211.1	235.2	239.0
wall NEC	151.9	197.8	230.2	211.1	235.2	239.0
anterior NEC	151.8	197.8	230.2	211.1	235.2	239.0
posterior NEC	151.8	197.8	230.2	211.1	235.2	239.0
stroma, endometrial	182.0	198.82	233.2	219.1	236.0	239.5
stump, cervical	180.8	198.82	233.1	219.0	236.0	239.5
subcutaneous (nodule) (tissue) NEC — *see* Neoplasm, connective tissue						
subdural	192.1	198.4	—	225.2	237.6	239.7
subglottis, subglottic	161.2	197.3	231.0	212.1	235.6	239.1
sublingual	144.9	198.89	230.0	210.3	235.1	239.0
gland or duct	142.2	198.89	230.0	210.2	235.0	239.0
submandibular gland	142.1	198.89	230.0	210.2	235.0	239.0
submaxillary gland or duct	142.1	198.89	230.0	210.2	235.0	239.0
submental	195.0	198.89	234.8	229.8	238.8	239.89
subpleural	162.9	197.0	—	212.3	235.7	239.1
substernal	164.2	197.1	—	212.5	235.8	239.89
sudoriferous, sudoriparous gland, site unspecified	173.90	198.2	232.9	216.9	238.2	239.2
specified site — *see* Neoplasm, skin						
supraclavicular region	195.0	198.89	234.8	229.8	238.8	239.89
supraglottis	161.1	197.3	231.0	212.1	235.6	239.1
suprarenal (capsule) (cortex) (gland) (medulla)	194.0	198.7	234.8	227.0	237.2	239.7
suprasellar (region)	191.9	198.3	—	225.0	237.5	239.6
sweat gland (apocrine) (eccrine), site unspecified	173.90	198.2	232.9	216.9	238.2	239.2
sympathetic nerve or nervous system NEC	171.9	198.89	—	215.9	238.1	239.2

Neoplasm, neoplastic—	Primary	Secondary	Ca in situ	Benign	Uncertain Behavior	Unspecified
continued						
symphysis pubis	170.6	198.5	—	213.6	238.0	239.2
synovial membrane — *see* Neoplasm, connective tissue						
tapetum, brain	191.8	198.3	—	225.0	237.5	239.6
tarsus (any bone)	170.8	198.5	—	213.8	238.0	239.2
temple (skin) (*see also* Neoplasm, skin, face)	173.30	198.2	232.3	216.3	238.2	239.2
temporal						
bone	170.0	198.5	—	213.0	238.0	239.2
lobe or pole	191.2	198.3	—	225.0	237.5	239.6
region	195.0	198.89	234.8	229.8	238.8	239.89
skin (*see also* Neoplasm, skin, face)	173.30	198.2	232.3	216.3	238.2	239.2
tendon (sheath) — *see* Neoplasm, connective tissue						
tentorium (cerebelli)	192.1	198.4	—	225.2	237.6	239.7
testis, testes (descended) (scrotal)	186.9	198.82	233.6	222.0	236.4	239.5
ectopic	186.0	198.82	233.6	222.0	236.4	239.5
retained	186.0	198.82	233.6	222.0	236.4	239.5
undescended	186.0	198.82	233.6	222.0	236.4	239.5
thalamus	191.0	198.3	—	225.0	237.5	239.6
thigh NEC*	195.5	198.89	234.8	229.8	238.8	239.89
thorax, thoracic (cavity) (organs NEC)	195.1	198.89	234.8	229.8	238.8	239.89
duct	171.4	198.89	—	215.4	238.1	239.2
wall NEC	195.1	198.89	234.8	229.8	238.8	239.89
throat	149.0	198.89	230.0	210.9	235.1	239.0
thumb NEC*	195.4	198.89	232.6	229.8	238.8	239.89
thymus (gland)	164.0	198.89	—	212.6	235.8	239.89
contiguous sites with heart and mediastinum	164.8	—	—	—	—	—
thyroglossal duct	193	198.89	234.8	226	237.4	239.7
thyroid (gland)	193	198.89	234.8	226	237.4	239.7
cartilage	161.3	197.3	231.0	212.1	235.6	239.1
tibia (any part)	170.7	198.5	—	213.7	238.0	239.2
toe NEC*	195.5	198.89	232.7	229.8	238.8	239.89
tongue	141.9	198.89	230.0	210.1	235.1	239.0
anterior (two-thirds) NEC	141.4	198.89	230.0	210.1	235.1	239.0
dorsal surface	141.1	198.89	230.0	210.1	235.1	239.0
ventral surface	141.3	198.89	230.0	210.1	235.1	239.0
base (dorsal surface)	141.0	198.89	230.0	210.1	235.1	239.0
border (lateral)	141.2	198.89	230.0	210.1	235.1	239.0
contiguous sites	141.8	—	—	—	—	—
dorsal surface NEC	141.1	198.89	230.0	210.1	235.1	239.0
fixed part NEC	141.0	198.89	230.0	210.1	235.1	239.0
foreamen cecum	141.1	198.89	230.0	210.1	235.1	239.0
frenulum linguae	141.3	198.89	230.0	210.1	235.1	239.0
junctional zone	141.5	198.89	230.0	210.1	235.1	239.0
margin (lateral)	141.2	198.89	230.0	210.1	235.1	239.0
midline NEC	141.1	198.89	230.0	210.1	235.1	239.0
mobile part NEC	141.4	198.89	230.0	210.1	235.1	239.0
posterior (third)	141.0	198.89	230.0	210.1	235.1	239.0
root	141.0	198.89	230.0	210.1	235.1	239.0
surface (dorsal)	141.1	198.89	230.0	210.1	235.1	239.0
base	141.0	198.89	230.0	210.1	235.1	239.0
ventral	141.3	198.89	230.0	210.1	235.1	239.0
tip	141.2	198.89	230.0	210.1	235.1	239.0
tonsil	141.6	198.89	230.0	210.1	235.1	239.0
tonsil	146.0	198.89	230.0	210.5	235.1	239.0
fauces, faucial	146.0	198.89	230.0	210.5	235.1	239.0
lingual	141.6	198.89	230.0	210.1	235.1	239.0
palatine	146.0	198.89	230.0	210.5	235.1	239.0
pharyngeal	147.1	198.89	230.0	210.7	235.1	239.0

Neoplasm, neoplastic—	Primary	Secondary	Ca in situ	Benign	Uncertain Behavior	Unspecified
continued						
tonsil — *continued*						
pillar (anterior) (posterior)	146.2	198.89	230.0	210.6	235.1	239.0
tonsillar fossa	146.1	198.89	230.0	210.6	235.1	239.0
tooth socket NEC	143.9	198.89	230.0	210.4	235.1	239.0
trachea (cartilage) (mucosa)	162.0	197.3	231.1	212.2	235.7	239.1
contiguous sites with bronchus or lung	162.8	—	—	—	—	—
tracheobronchial	162.8	197.3	231.1	212.2	235.7	239.1
contiguous sites with lung	162.8	—	—	—	—	—
tragus (*see also* Neoplasm, skin, ear)	173.20	198.2	232.2	216.2	238.2	239.2
trunk NEC*	195.8	198.89	232.5	229.8	238.8	239.89
tubo-ovarian	183.8	198.82	233.39	221.8	236.3	239.5
tunica vaginalis	187.8	198.82	233.6	222.8	236.6	239.5
turbinate (bone)	170.0	198.5	—	213.0	238.0	239.2
nasal	160.0	197.3	231.8	212.0	235.9	239.1
tympanic cavity	160.1	197.3	231.8	212.0	235.9	239.1
ulna (any part)	170.4	198.5	—	213.4	238.0	239.2
umbilicus, umbilical (*see also* Neoplasm, skin, trunk)	173.50	198.2	232.5	216.5	238.2	239.2
uncus, brain	191.2	198.3	—	225.0	237.5	239.6
unknown site or unspecified	199.1	199.1	234.9	229.9	238.9	239.9
urachus	188.7	198.1	233.7	223.3	236.7	239.4
ureter-bladder junction	188.6	198.1	233.7	223.3	236.7	239.4
ureter, ureteral	189.2	198.1	233.9	223.2	236.91	239.5
orifice (bladder)	188.6	198.1	233.7	223.3	236.7	239.4
urethra, urethral (gland)	189.3	198.1	233.9	223.81	236.99	239.5
orifice, internal	188.5	198.1	233.7	223.3	236.7	239.4
urethrovaginal (septum)	184.9	198.82	233.39	221.9	236.3	239.5
urinary organ or system NEC	189.9	198.1	233.9	223.9	236.99	239.5
bladder — *see* Neoplasm, bladder						
contiguous sites	189.8	—	—	—	—	—
specified sites NEC	189.8	198.1	233.9	223.89	236.99	239.5
utero-ovarian	183.8	198.82	233.39	221.8	236.3	239.5
ligament	183.3	198.82		221.0	236.3	239.5
uterosacral ligament	183.4	198.82		221.0	236.3	239.5
uterus, uteri, uterine	179	198.82	233.2	219.9	236.0	239.5
adnexa NEC	183.9	198.82	233.39	221.8	236.3	239.5
contiguous sites	183.8	—	—	—	—	—
body	182.0	198.82	233.2	219.1	236.0	239.5
contiguous sites	182.8	—	—	—	—	—
cervix	180.9	198.82	233.1	219.0	236.0	239.5
cornu	182.0	198.82	233.2	219.1	236.0	239.5
corpus	182.0	198.82	233.2	219.1	236.0	239.5
endocervix (canal) (gland)	180.0	198.82	233.1	219.0	236.0	239.5
endometrium	182.0	198.82	233.2	219.1	236.0	239.5
exocervix	180.1	198.82	233.1	219.0	236.0	239.5
external os	180.1	198.82	233.1	219.0	236.0	239.5
fundus	182.0	198.82	233.2	219.1	236.0	239.5
internal os	180.0	198.82	233.1	219.0	236.0	239.5
isthmus	182.1	198.82	233.2	219.1	236.0	239.5
ligament	183.4	198.82	—	221.0	236.3	239.5
broad	183.3	198.82	233.39	221.0	236.3	239.5
round	183.5	198.82		221.0	236.3	239.5
lower segment	182.1	198.82	233.2	219.1	236.0	239.5
myometrium	182.0	198.82	233.2	219.1	236.0	239.5

☑ Additional Digit Required — Refer to the Tabular List for Digit Selection   ▽ Subterms under main terms may continue to next column or page

210— Volume 2   ►◄ Revised Text   ● New Line   ▲ Revised Code   2015 ICD-9-CM

	Malignant					
	Primary	Secondary	Ca in situ	Benign	Uncertain Behavior	Unspecified
Neoplasm, neoplastic — *continued*						
uterus, uteri, uterine — *continued*						
squamocolumnar junction	180.8	198.82	233.1	219.0	236.0	239.5
tube	183.2	198.82	233.39	221.0	236.3	239.5
utricle, prostatic	189.3	198.1	233.9	223.81	236.99	239.5
uveal tract	190.0	198.4	234.0	224.0	238.8	239.89
uvula	145.4	198.89	230.0	210.4	235.1	239.0
vagina, vaginal (fornix) (vault) (wall)	184.0	198.82	233.31	221.1	236.3	239.5
vaginovesical	184.9	198.82	233.39	221.9	236.3	239.5
septum	184.9	198.82	233.39	221.9	236.3	239.5
vallecula (epiglottis)	146.3	198.89	230.0	210.6	235.1	239.0
vascular — *see* Neoplasm, connective tissue						
vas deferens	187.6	198.82	233.6	222.8	236.6	239.5
Vater's ampulla	156.2	197.8	230.8	211.5	235.3	239.0
vein, venous — *see* Neoplasm, connective tissue						
vena cava (abdominal) (inferior)	171.5	198.89	—	215.5	238.1	239.2
superior	171.4	198.89	—	215.4	238.1	239.2
ventricle (cerebral) (floor) (fourth) (lateral) (third)	191.5	198.3	—	225.0	237.5	239.6
cardiac (left) (right)	164.1	198.89	—	212.7	238.8	239.89
ventricular band of larynx	161.1	197.3	231.0	212.1	235.6	239.1
ventriculus — see Neoplasm, stomach						
vermillion border — *see* Neoplasm, lip						
vermis, cerebellum	191.6	198.3	—	225.0	237.5	239.6
vertebra (column)	170.2	198.5	—	213.2	238.0	239.2
coccyx	170.6	198.5	—	213.6	238.0	239.2
sacrum	170.6	198.5	—	213.6	238.0	239.2
vesical — *see* Neoplasm, bladder						
vesicle, seminal	187.8	198.82	233.6	222.8	236.6	239.5
vesicocervical tissue	184.9	198.82	233.39	221.9	236.3	239.5
vesicorectal	195.3	198.89	234.8	229.8	238.8	239.89
vesicovaginal	184.9	198.82	233.39	221.9	236.3	239.5
septum	184.9	198.82	233.39	221.9	236.3	239.5
vessel (blood) — *see* Neoplasm, connective tissue						
vestibular gland, greater	184.1	198.82	233.32	221.2	236.3	239.5
vestibule						
mouth	145.1	198.89	230.0	210.4	235.1	239.0
nose	160.0	197.3	231.8	212.0	235.9	239.1
Virchow's gland	—	196.0	—	229.0	238.8	239.89
viscera NEC	195.8	198.89	234.8	229.8	238.8	239.89
vocal cords (true)	161.0	197.3	231.0	212.1	235.6	239.1
false	161.1	197.3	231.0	212.1	235.6	239.1
vomer	170.0	198.5	—	213.0	238.0	239.2
vulva	184.4	198.82	233.32	221.2	236.3	239.5
vulvovaginal gland	184.4	198.82	233.32	221.2	236.3	239.5
Waldeyer's ring	149.1	198.89	230.0	210.9	235.1	239.0
Wharton's duct	142.1	198.89	230.0	210.2	235.0	239.0
white matter (central) (cerebral)	191.0	198.3	—	225.0	237.5	239.6
windpipe	162.0	197.3	231.1	212.2	235.7	239.1
Wirsung's duct	157.3	197.8	230.9	211.6	235.5	239.0
wolffian (body) (duct) female	184.8	198.82	233.39	221.8	236.3	239.5
male	187.8	198.82	233.6	222.8	236.6	239.5
womb — *see* Neoplasm, uterus						
Neoplasm, neoplastic — *continued*						
wrist NEC*	195.4	198.89	232.6	229.8	238.8	239.89
xiphoid process	170.3	198.5	—	213.3	238.0	239.2
Zuckerkandl's organ	194.6	198.89	—	227.6	237.3	239.7

Neovascularization
  choroid 362.16
  ciliary body 364.42
  cornea 370.60
    deep 370.63
    localized 370.61
  iris 364.42
  retina 362.16
  subretinal 362.16
Nephralgia 788.0
Nephritis, nephritic (albuminuric) (azotemic)
  (congenital) (degenerative) (diffuse)
  (disseminated) (epithelial) (familial) (focal) (granulomatous) (hemorrhagic) (infantile) (nonsuppurative, excretory)
  (uremic) 583.9
  with
    edema — see Nephrosis
    lesion of
      glomerulonephritis
        hypocomplementemic persistent
          583.2
          with nephrotic syndrome
            581.2
          chronic 582.2
        lobular 583.2
          with nephrotic syndrome
            581.2
          chronic 582.2
        membranoproliferative 583.2
          with nephrotic syndrome
            581.2
          chronic 582.2
        membranous 583.1
          with nephrotic syndrome
            581.1
          chronic 582.1
        mesangiocapillary 583.2
          with nephrotic syndrome
            581.2
          chronic 582.2
        mixed membranous and prolifer-
          ative 583.2
          with nephrotic syndrome
            581.2
          chronic 582.2
        proliferative (diffuse) 583.0
          with nephrotic syndrome
            581.0
          acute 580.0
          chronic 582.0
        rapidly progressive 583.4
          acute 580.4
          chronic 582.4
        interstitial nephritis (diffuse) (focal)
          583.89
          with nephrotic syndrome 581.89
          acute 580.89
          chronic 582.89
        necrotizing glomerulitis 583.4
          acute 580.4
          chronic 582.4
        renal necrosis 583.9
          cortical 583.6
          medullary 583.7
        specified pathology NEC 583.89
          with nephrotic syndrome 581.89
          acute 580.89
          chronic 582.89
    necrosis, renal 583.9
      cortical 583.6
      medullary (papillary) 583.7
    nephrotic syndrome (see also Nephrosis)
      581.9
    papillary necrosis 583.7
    specified pathology NEC 583.89
  acute 580.9
    extracapillary with epithelial crescents
      580.4
    hypertensive (see also Hypertension,
      kidney) 403.90
    necrotizing 580.4
    poststreptococcal 580.0
    proliferative (diffuse) 580.0
    rapidly progressive 580.4
    specified pathology NEC 580.89

Nephritis, nephritic — continued
  amyloid 277.39 [583.81]
    chronic 277.39 [582.81]
  arteriolar (see also Hypertension, kidney)
    403.90
  arteriosclerotic (see also Hypertension, kid-
    ney) 403.90
  ascending (see also Pyelitis) 590.80
  atrophic 582.9
  basement membrane NEC 583.89
    with
      pulmonary hemorrhage (Goodpas-
        ture's syndrome)
        446.21 [583.81]
  calculous, calculus 592.0
  cardiac (see also Hypertension, kidney)
    403.90
  cardiovascular (see also Hypertension, kid-
    ney) 403.90
  chronic 582.9
    arteriosclerotic (see also Hypertension,
      kidney) 403.90
    hypertensive (see also Hypertension,
      kidney) 403.90
  cirrhotic (see also Sclerosis, renal) 587
  complicating pregnancy, childbirth, or
    puerperium 646.2 ☑
    with hypertension 642.1 ☑
      affecting fetus or newborn 760.0
    affecting fetus or newborn 760.1
  croupous 580.9
  desquamative — see Nephrosis
  due to
    amyloidosis 277.39 [583.81]
      chronic 277.39 [582.81]
    arteriosclerosis (see also Hypertension,
      kidney) 403.90
    diabetes mellitus 250.4 ☑ [583.81]
      with nephrotic syndrome
        250.4 ☑ [581.81]
      due to secondary diabetes
        249.4 ☑ [583.81]
      due to secondary diabetes
        249.4 ☑ [583.81]
    diphtheria 032.89 [580.81]
    gonococcal infection (acute)
      098.19 [583.81]
      chronic or duration of 2 months or
        over 098.39 [583.81]
    gout 274.10
    infectious hepatitis 070.9 [580.81]
    mumps 072.79 [580.81]
    specified kidney pathology NEC 583.89
      acute 580.89
      chronic 582.89
    streptotrichosis 039.8 [583.81]
    subacute bacterial endocarditis
      421.0 [580.81]
    systemic lupus erythematosus
      710.0 [583.81]
      chronic 710.0 [582.81]
    typhoid fever 002.0 [580.81]
  endothelial 582.2
  end stage (chronic) (terminal) NEC 585.6
  epimembranous 581.1
  exudative 583.89
    with nephrotic syndrome 581.89
    acute 580.89
    chronic 582.89
  gonococcal (acute) 098.19 [583.81]
    chronic or duration of 2 months or over
      098.39 [583.81]
  gouty 274.10
  hereditary (Alport's syndrome) 759.89
  hydremic — see Nephrosis
  hypertensive (see also Hypertension, kidney)
    403.90
  hypocomplementemic persistent 583.2
    with nephrotic syndrome 581.2
    chronic 582.2
  immune complex NEC 583.89
  infective (see also Pyelitis) 590.80
  interstitial (diffuse) (focal) 583.89
    with nephrotic syndrome 581.89
    acute 580.89
    chronic 582.89

Nephritis, nephritic — continued
  latent or quiescent — see Nephritis, chronic
  lead 984.9
    specified type of lead — see Table of
      Drugs and Chemicals
  lobular 583.2
    with nephrotic syndrome 581.2
    chronic 582.2
  lupus 710.0 [583.81]
    acute 710.0 [580.81]
    chronic 710.0 [582.81]
  membranoproliferative 583.2
    with nephrotic syndrome 581.2
    chronic 582.2
  membranous 583.1
    with nephrotic syndrome 581.1
    chronic 582.1
  mesangiocapillary 583.2
    with nephrotic syndrome 581.2
    chronic 582.2
  minimal change 581.3
  mixed membranous and proliferative 583.2
    with nephrotic syndrome 581.2
    chronic 582.2
  necrotic, necrotizing 583.4
    acute 580.4
    chronic 582.4
  nephrotic — see Nephrosis
  old — see Nephritis, chronic
  parenchymatous 581.89
  polycystic 753.12
    adult type (APKD) 753.13
    autosomal dominant 753.13
    autosomal recessive 753.14
    childhood type (CPKD) 753.14
    infantile type 753.14
  poststreptococcal 580.0
  pregnancy — see Nephritis, complicating
    pregnancy
  proliferative 583.0
    with nephrotic syndrome 581.0
    acute 580.0
    chronic 582.0
  purulent (see also Pyelitis) 590.80
  rapidly progressive 583.4
    acute 580.4
    chronic 582.4
  salt-losing or salt-wasting (see also Disease,
    renal) 593.9
  saturnine 584.9
    specified type of lead — see Table of
      Drugs and Chemicals
  septic (see also Pyelitis) 590.80
  specified pathology NEC 583.89
    acute 580.89
    chronic 582.89
  staphylococcal (see also Pyelitis) 590.80
  streptotrichosis 039.8 [583.81]
  subacute (see also Nephrosis) 581.9
  suppurative (see also Pyelitis) 590.80
  syphilitic (late) 095.4
    congenital 090.5 [583.81]
    early 091.69 [583.81]
  terminal (chronic) (end-stage) NEC 585.6
  toxic — see Nephritis, acute
  tubal, tubular — see Nephrosis, tubular
  tuberculous (see also Tuberculosis)
    016.0 ☑ [583.81]
  type II (Ellis) — see Nephrosis
  vascular — see Hypertension, kidney
  war 580.9
Nephroblastoma (M8960/3) 189.0
  epithelial (M8961/3) 189.0
  mesenchymal (M8962/3) 189.0
Nephrocalcinosis 275.49
Nephrocystitis, pustular — see also Pyelitis
  590.80
Nephrolithiasis (congenital) (pelvis) (recurrent)
  592.0
  uric acid 274.11
Nephroma (M8960/3) 189.0
  mesoblastic (M8960/1) 236.9 ☑
Nephronephritis — see also Nephrosis 581.9
Nephronopthisis 753.16
Nephropathy — see also Nephritis 583.9

Nephropathy — see also Nephritis —
  continued
  with
    exudative nephritis 583.89
    interstitial nephritis (diffuse) (focal)
      583.89
    medullary necrosis 583.7
    necrosis 583.9
      cortical 583.6
      medullary or papillary 583.7
    papillary necrosis 583.7
    specified lesion or cause NEC 583.89
  analgesic 583.89
    with medullary necrosis, acute 584.7
  arteriolar (see also Hypertension, kidney)
    403.90
  arteriosclerotic (see also Hypertension, kid-
    ney) 403.90
  complicating pregnancy 646.2 ☑
  diabetic 250.4 ☑ [583.81]
    due to secondary diabetes
      249.4 ☑ [583.81]
  gouty 274.10
    specified type NEC 274.19
  hereditary amyloid 277.31
  hypercalcemic 588.89
  hypertensive (see also Hypertension, kidney)
    403.90
  hypokalemic (vacuolar) 588.89
  IgA 583.9
  obstructive 593.89
    congenital 753.20
  phenacetin 584.7
  phosphate-losing 588.0
  potassium depletion 588.89
  proliferative (see also Nephritis, proliferative)
    583.0
  protein-losing 588.89
  salt-losing or salt-wasting (see also Disease,
    renal) 593.9
  sickle-cell (see also Disease, sickle-cell)
    282.60 [583.81]
  toxic 584.5
  vasomotor 584.5
  water-losing 588.89
Nephroptosis — see also Disease, renal 593.0
  congenital (displaced) 753.3
Nephropyosis — see also Abscess, kidney
  590.2
Nephrorrhagia 593.81
Nephrosclerosis (arteriolar) (arteriosclerotic)
  (chronic) (hyaline) — see also Hypertension, kidney 403.90
  gouty 274.10
  hyperplastic (arteriolar) (see also Hyperten-
    sion, kidney) 403.90
  senile (see also Sclerosis, renal) 587
Nephrosis, nephrotic (Epstein's) (syndrome)
  581.9
  with
    lesion of
      focal glomerulosclerosis 581.1
      glomerulonephritis
        endothelial 581.2
        hypocomplementemic persistent
          581.2
        lobular 581.2
        membranoproliferative 581.2
        membranous 581.1
        mesangiocapillary 581.2
        minimal change 581.3
        mixed membranous and prolifer-
          ative 581.2
        proliferative 581.0
      segmental hyalinosis 581.1
      specified pathology NEC 581.89
  acute — see Nephrosis, tubular
  anoxic — see Nephrosis, tubular
  arteriosclerotic (see also Hypertension, kid-
    ney) 403.90
  chemical — see Nephrosis, tubular
  cholemic 572.4
  complicating pregnancy, childbirth, or
    puerperium — see Nephritis, compli-
    cating pregnancy
  diabetic 250.4 ☑ [581.81]

☑ **Additional Digit Required** — Refer to the Tabular List for Digit Selection   ⚕ **Subterms under main terms may continue to next column or page**

212 — Volume 2   ▶◀ Revised Text   ● New Line   ▲ Revised Code   2015 ICD-9-CM

Nephrosis, nephrotic — *continued*
  diabetic — *continued*
    due to secondary diabetes
      249.4 ☑ *[581.81]*
    Finnish type (congenital) 759.89
    hemoglobinuric — *see* Nephrosis, tubular
      in
        amyloidosis 277.39 *[581.81]*
        diabetes mellitus 250.4 ☑ *[581.81]*
          due to secondary diabetes
            249.4 ☑ *[581.81]*
        epidemic hemorrhagic fever 078.6
        malaria 084.9 *[581.81]*
        polyarteritis 446.0 *[581.81]*
        systemic lupus erythematosus
          710.0 *[581.81]*
    ischemic — *see* Nephrosis, tubular
    lipoid 581.3
    lower nephron — *see* Nephrosis, tubular
    lupoid 710.0 *[581.81]*
    lupus 710.0 *[581.81]*
    malarial 084.9 *[581.81]*
    minimal change 581.3
    necrotizing — *see* Nephrosis, tubular
    osmotic (sucrose) 588.89
    polyarteritic 446.0 *[581.81]*
    radiation 581.9
    specified lesion or cause NEC 581.89
    syphilitic 095.4
    toxic — *see* Nephrosis, tubular
    tubular (acute) 584.5
      due to a procedure 997.5
      radiation 581.9
Nephrosonephritis hemorrhagic (endemic)
  078.6
Nephrostomy status V44.6
  with complication 997.5
Nerve — *see* condition
Nerves 799.21
Nervous — *see also* condition 799.21
  breakdown 300.9
  heart 306.2
  stomach 306.4
  tension 799.21
Nervousness 799.21
Nesidioblastoma (M8150/0)
  pancreas 211.7
  specified site NEC — *see* Neoplasm, by site,
    benign
  unspecified site 211.7
Netherton's syndrome (ichthyosiform erythroderma) 757.1
Nettle rash 708.8
Nettleship's disease (urticaria pigmentosa)
  757.33
Neumann's disease (pemphigus vegetans)
  694.4
Neuralgia, neuralgic (acute) — *see also* Neuritis 729.2
  accessory (nerve) 352.4
  acoustic (nerve) 388.5
  ankle 355.8
  anterior crural 355.8
  anus 787.99
  arm 723.4
  auditory (nerve) 388.5
  axilla 353.0
  bladder 788.1
  brachial 723.4
  brain — *see* Disorder, nerve, cranial
  broad ligament 625.9
  cerebral — *see* Disorder, nerve, cranial
  ciliary 339.00
  cranial nerve (*see also* Disorder, nerve, cra-
    nial)
    fifth or trigeminal (*see also* Neuralgia,
      trigeminal) 350.1
  ear 388.71
    middle 352.1
  facial 351.8
  finger 354.9
  flank 355.8
  foot 355.8
  forearm 354.9
  Fothergill's (*see also* Neuralgia, trigeminal)
    350.1

Neuralgia, neuralgic — *see also* Neuritis —
  continued
  Fothergill's (*see also* Neuralgia, trigeminal)
    — *continued*
    postherpetic 053.12
  glossopharyngeal (nerve) 352.1
  groin 355.8
  hand 354.9
  heel 355.8
  Horton's 339.00
  Hunt's 053.11
  hypoglossal (nerve) 352.5
  iliac region 355.8
  infraorbital (*see also* Neuralgia, trigeminal)
    350.1
  inguinal 355.8
  intercostal (nerve) 353.8
    postherpetic 053.19
  jaw 352.1
  kidney 788.0
  knee 355.8
  loin 355.8
  malarial (*see also* Malaria) 084.6
  mastoid 385.89
  maxilla 352.1
  median thenar 354.1
  metatarsal 355.6
  middle ear 352.1
  migrainous 339.00
  Morton's 355.6
  nerve, cranial — *see* Disorder, nerve, cranial
  nose 352.0
  occipital 723.8
  olfactory (nerve) 352.0
  ophthalmic 377.30
    postherpetic 053.19
  optic (nerve) 377.30
  penis 607.9
  perineum 355.8
  pleura 511.0
  postherpetic NEC 053.19
    geniculate ganglion 053.11
    ophthalmic 053.19
    trifacial 053.12
    trigeminal 053.12
  pubic region 355.8
  radial (nerve) 723.4
  rectum 787.99
  sacroiliac joint 724.3
  sciatic (nerve) 724.3
  scrotum 608.9
  seminal vesicle 608.9
  shoulder 354.9
  Sluder's 337.09
  specified nerve NEC — *see* Disorder, nerve
  spermatic cord 608.9
  sphenopalatine (ganglion) 337.09
  subscapular (nerve) 723.4
  suprascapular (nerve) 723.4
  testis 608.89
  thenar (median) 354.1
  thigh 355.8
  tongue 352.5
  trifacial (nerve) (*see also* Neuralgia, trigemi-
    nal) 350.1
  trigeminal (nerve) 350.1
    postherpetic 053.12
  tympanic plexus 388.71
  ulnar (nerve) 723.4
  vagus (nerve) 352.3
  wrist 354.9
  writers' 300.89
    organic 333.84
Neurapraxia — *see* Injury, nerve, by site
Neurasthenia 300.5
  cardiac 306.2
  gastric 306.4
  heart 306.2
  postfebrile 780.79
  postviral 780.79
Neurilemmoma (M9560/0) — *see also* Neoplasm, connective tissue, benign
  acoustic (nerve) 225.1
  malignant (M9560/3) (*see also* Neoplasm,
    connective tissue, malignant)
    acoustic (nerve) 192.0

Neurilemmosarcoma (M9560/3) — *see* Neoplasm, connective tissue, malignant
Neurilemoma — *see* Neurilemmoma
Neurinoma (M9560/0) — *see* Neurilemmoma
Neurinomatosis (M9560/1) — *see also* Neoplasm, connective tissue, uncertain behavior
  centralis 759.5
Neuritis — *see also* Neuralgia 729.2
  abducens (nerve) 378.54
  accessory (nerve) 352.4
  acoustic (nerve) 388.5
    syphilitic 094.86
  alcoholic 357.5
    with psychosis 291.1
  amyloid, any site 277.39 *[357.4]*
  anterior crural 355.8
  arising during pregnancy 646.4 ☑
  arm 723.4
  ascending 355.2
  auditory (nerve) 388.5
  brachial (nerve) NEC 723.4
    due to displacement, intervertebral disc
      722.0
  cervical 723.4
  chest (wall) 353.8
  costal region 353.8
  cranial nerve (*see also* Disorder, nerve, cra-
    nial)
    first or olfactory 352.0
    second or optic 377.30
    third or oculomotor 378.52
    fourth or trochlear 378.53
    fifth or trigeminal (*see also* Neuralgia,
      trigeminal) 350.1
    sixth or abducens 378.54
    seventh or facial 351.8
      newborn 767.5
    eighth or acoustic 388.5
    ninth or glossopharyngeal 352.1
    tenth or vagus 352.3
    eleventh or accessory 352.4
    twelfth or hypoglossal 352.5
  Déjérine-Sottas 356.0
  diabetic 250.6 ☑ *[357.2]*
    due to secondary diabetes
      249.6 ☑ *[357.2]*
  diphtheritic 032.89 *[357.4]*
  due to
    beriberi 265.0 *[357.4]*
    displacement, prolapse, protrusion, or
      rupture of intervertebral disc
      722.2
      cervical 722.0
      lumbar, lumbosacral 722.10
      thoracic, thoracolumbar 722.11
    herniation, nucleus pulposus 722.2
      cervical 722.0
      lumbar, lumbosacral 722.10
      thoracic, thoracolumbar 722.11
  endemic 265.0 *[357.4]*
  facial (nerve) 351.8
    newborn 767.5
  general — *see* Polyneuropathy
  geniculate ganglion 351.1
    due to herpes 053.11
  glossopharyngeal (nerve) 352.1
  gouty 274.89 *[357.4]*
  hypoglossal (nerve) 352.5
  ilioinguinal (nerve) 355.8
  in diseases classified elsewhere — *see*
    Polyneuropathy, in
  infectious (multiple) 357.0
  intercostal (nerve) 353.8
  interstitial hypertrophic progressive NEC
    356.9
  leg 355.8
  lumbosacral NEC 724.4
  median (nerve) 354.1
    thenar 354.1
  multiple (acute) (infective) 356.9
    endemic 265.0 *[357.4]*
  multiplex endemica 265.0 *[357.4]*
  nerve root (*see also* Radiculitis) 729.2
  oculomotor (nerve) 378.52
  olfactory (nerve) 352.0

Neuritis — *see also* Neuralgia — *continued*
  optic (nerve) 377.30
    in myelitis 341.0
    meningococcal 036.81
  pelvic 355.8
  peripheral (nerve) (*see also* Neuropathy,
    peripheral)
    complicating pregnancy or puerperium
      646.4 ☑
    specified nerve NEC — *see* Mononeuritis
  pneumogastric (nerve) 352.3
  postchickenpox 052.7
  postherpetic 053.19
  progressive hypertrophic interstitial NEC
    356.9
  puerperal, postpartum 646.4 ☑
  radial (nerve) 723.4
  retrobulbar 377.32
    syphilitic 094.85
  rheumatic (chronic) 729.2
  sacral region 355.8
  sciatic (nerve) 724.3
    due to displacement of intervertebral
      disc 722.10
  serum 999.59
  specified nerve NEC — *see* Disorder, nerve
  spinal (nerve) 355.9
    root (*see also* Radiculitis) 729.2
  subscapular (nerve) 723.4
  suprascapular (nerve) 723.4
  syphilitic 095.8
  thenar (median) 354.1
  thoracic NEC 724.4
  toxic NEC 357.7
  trochlear (nerve) 378.53
  ulnar (nerve) 723.4
  vagus (nerve) 352.3
Neuroangiomatosis, encephalofacial 759.6
Neuroastrocytoma (M9505/1) — *see* Neoplasm, by site, uncertain behavior
Neuro-avitaminosis 269.2
Neuroblastoma (M9500/3)
  olfactory (M9522/3) 160.0
  specified site — *see* Neoplasm, by site, ma-
    lignant
  unspecified site 194.0
Neurochorioretinitis — *see also* Chorioretinitis
  363.20
Neurocirculatory asthenia 306.2
Neurocytoma (M9506/0) — *see* Neoplasm, by
  site, benign
Neurodermatitis (circumscribed) (circumscripta) (local) 698.3
  atopic 691.8
  diffuse (Brocq) 691.8
  disseminated 691.8
  nodulosa 698.3
Neuroencephalomyelopathy, optic 341.0
Neuroendocrine tumor — *see* Tumor, neuroendocrine
Neuroepithelioma (M9503/3) — *see also*
  Neoplasm, by site, malignant
  olfactory (M9521/3) 160.0
Neurofibroma (M9540/0) — *see also* Neoplasm, connective tissue, benign
  melanotic (M9541/0) — *see* Neoplasm,
    connective tissue, benign
  multiple (M9540/1) 237.70
    type 1 237.71
    type 2 237.72
  plexiform (M9550/0) — *see* Neoplasm,
    connective tissue, benign
Neurofibromatosis (multiple) (M9540/1)
  237.70
  acoustic 237.72
  malignant (M9540/3) — *see* Neoplasm,
    connective tissue, malignant
  Schwannomatosis 237.73
  specified type NEC 237.79
  type 1 237.71
  type 2 237.72
  von Recklinghausen's 237.71
Neurofibrosarcoma (M9540/3) — *see* Neoplasm, connective tissue, malignant
Neurogenic — *see also* condition

☑ Additional Digit Required — Refer to the Tabular List for Digit Selection   ▽ Subterms under main terms may continue to next column or page

2015 ICD-9-CM   ▶◀ Revised Text   ● New Line   ▲ Revised Code   Volume 2 — 213

Neurogenic — see also condition — continued
  bladder (atonic) (automatic) (autonomic) (flaccid) (hypertonic) (hypotonic) (inertia) (infranuclear) (irritable) (motor) (nonreflex) (nuclear) (paralysis) (reflex) (sensory) (spastic) (supranuclear) (uninhibited) 596.54
    with cauda equina syndrome 344.61
  bowel 564.81
  heart 306.2
Neuroglioma (M9505/1) — see Neoplasm, by site, uncertain behavior
Neurolabyrinthitis (of Dix and Hallpike) 386.12
Neurolathyrism 988.2
Neuroleprosy 030.1
Neuroleptic malignant syndrome 333.92
Neurolipomatosis 272.8
Neuroma (M9570/0) — see also Neoplasm, connective tissue, benign
  acoustic (nerve) (M9560/0) 225.1
  amputation (traumatic) (see also Injury, nerve, by site)
    surgical complication (late) 997.61
  appendix 211.3
  auditory nerve 225.1
  digital 355.6
    toe 355.6
  interdigital (toe) 355.6
  intermetatarsal 355.6
  Morton's 355.6
  multiple 237.70
    type 1 237.71
    type 2 237.72
  nonneoplastic 355.9
    arm NEC 354.9
    leg NEC 355.8
    lower extremity NEC 355.8
    specified site NEC — see Mononeuritis, by site
    upper extremity NEC 354.9
  optic (nerve) 225.1
  plantar 355.6
  plexiform (M9550/0) — see Neoplasm, connective tissue, benign
  surgical (nonneoplastic) 355.9
    arm NEC 354.9
    leg NEC 355.8
    lower extremity NEC 355.8
    upper extremity NEC 354.9
  traumatic (see also Injury, nerve, by site)
    old — see Neuroma, nonneoplastic
Neuromyalgia 729.1
Neuromyasthenia (epidemic) 049.8
Neuromyelitis 341.8
  ascending 357.0
  optica 341.0
Neuromyopathy NEC 358.9
Neuromyositis 729.1
Neuronevus (M8725/0) — see Neoplasm, skin, benign
Neuronitis 357.0
  ascending (acute) 355.2
  vestibular 386.12
Neuroparalytic — see condition
Neuropathy, neuropathic — see also Disorder, nerve 355.9
  acute motor 357.82
  alcoholic 357.5
    with psychosis 291.1
  arm NEC 354.9
  ataxia and retinitis pigmentosa (NARP syndrome) 277.87
  autonomic (peripheral) — see Neuropathy, peripheral, autonomic
  axillary nerve 353.0
  brachial plexus 353.0
  cervical plexus 353.2
  chronic
    progressive segmentally demyelinating 357.89
    relapsing demyelinating 357.89
  congenital sensory 356.2
  Déjérine-Sottas 356.0
  diabetic 250.6 ☑ [357.2]
    autonomic (peripheral) 250.6 ☑ [337.1]

Neuropathy, neuropathic — see also Disorder, nerve — continued
  diabetic — continued
    due to secondary diabetes 249.6 ☑ [357.2]
      autonomic (peripheral) 249.6 ☑ [337.1]
  entrapment 355.9
    iliohypogastric nerve 355.79
    ilioinguinal nerve 355.79
    lateral cutaneous nerve of thigh 355.1
    median nerve 354.0
    obturator nerve 355.79
    peroneal nerve 355.3
    posterior tibial nerve 355.5
    saphenous nerve 355.79
    ulnar nerve 354.2
  facial nerve 351.9
  hereditary 356.9
    peripheral 356.0
    sensory (radicular) 356.2
  hypertrophic
    Charcôt-Marie-Tooth 356.1
    Déjérine-Sottas 356.0
    interstitial 356.9
    Refsum 356.3
  intercostal nerve 354.8
  ischemic — see Disorder, nerve
  Jamaican (ginger) 357.7
  leg NEC 355.8
  lower extremity NEC 355.8
  lumbar plexus 353.1
  median nerve 354.1
  motor
    acute 357.82
  multiple (acute) (chronic) (see also Polyneuropathy) 356.9
  optic 377.39
    ischemic 377.41
    nutritional 377.33
    toxic 377.34
  peripheral (nerve) (see also Polyneuropathy) 356.9
    arm NEC 354.9
    autonomic 337.9
      amyloid 277.39 [337.1]
      idiopathic 337.00
      in
        amyloidosis 277.39 [337.1]
        diabetes (mellitus) 250.6 ☑ [337.1]
          due to secondary diabetes 249.6 ☑ [337.1]
        diseases classified elsewhere 337.1
        gout 274.89 [337.1]
        hyperthyroidism 242.9 ☑ [337.1]
    due to
      antitetanus serum 357.6
      arsenic 357.7
      drugs 357.6
      lead 357.7
      organophosphate compounds 357.7
      toxic agent NEC 357.7
    hereditary 356.0
    idiopathic 356.9
      progressive 356.4
      specified type NEC 356.8
    in diseases classified elsewhere — see Polyneuropathy, in
    leg NEC 355.8
    lower extremity NEC 355.8
    upper extremity NEC 354.9
  plantar nerves 355.6
  progressive
    hypertrophic interstitial 356.9
    inflammatory 357.89
  radicular NEC 729.2
    brachial 723.4
    cervical NEC 723.4
    hereditary sensory 356.2
    lumbar 724.4
    lumbosacral 724.4
    thoracic NEC 724.4
  sacral plexus 353.1
  sciatic 355.0

Neuropathy, neuropathic — see also Disorder, nerve — continued
  spinal nerve NEC 355.9
    root (see also Radiculitis) 729.2
  toxic 357.7
  trigeminal sensory 350.8
  ulnar nerve 354.2
  upper extremity NEC 354.9
  uremic 585.9 [357.4]
  vitamin B₁₂ 266.2 [357.4]
    with anemia (pernicious) 281.0 [357.4]
      due to dietary deficiency 281.1 [357.4]
Neurophthisis — see also Disorder, nerve
  diabetic 250.6 ☑ [357.2]
    due to secondary diabetes 249.6 ☑ [357.2]
  peripheral 356.9
Neuropraxia — see Injury, nerve
Neuroretinitis 363.05
  syphilitic 094.85
Neurosarcoma (M9540/3) — see Neoplasm, connective tissue, malignant
Neurosclerosis — see Disorder, nerve
Neurosis, neurotic 300.9
  accident 300.16
  anancastic, anankastic 300.3
  anxiety (state) 300.00
    generalized 300.02
    panic type 300.01
  asthenic 300.5
  bladder 306.53
  cardiac (reflex) 306.2
  cardiovascular 306.2
  climacteric, unspecified type 627.2
  colon 306.4
  compensation 300.16
  compulsive, compulsion 300.3
  conversion 300.11
  craft 300.89
  cutaneous 306.3
  depersonalization 300.6
  depressive (reaction) (type) 300.4
  endocrine 306.6
  environmental 300.89
  fatigue 300.5
  functional (see also Disorder, psychosomatic) 306.9
  gastric 306.4
  gastrointestinal 306.4
  genitourinary 306.50
  heart 306.2
  hypochondriacal 300.7
  hysterical 300.10
    conversion type 300.11
    dissociative type 300.15
  impulsive 300.3
  incoordination 306.0
    larynx 306.1
    vocal cord 306.1
  intestine 306.4
  larynx 306.1
    hysterical 300.11
    sensory 306.1
  menopause, unspecified type 627.2
  mixed NEC 300.89
  musculoskeletal 306.0
  obsessional 300.3
    phobia 300.3
  obsessive-compulsive 300.3
  occupational 300.89
  ocular 306.7
  oral (see also Disorder, fluency) 315.35
  organ (see also Disorder, psychosomatic) 306.9
  pharynx 306.1
  phobic 300.20
  posttraumatic (acute) (situational) 309.81
    chronic 309.81
  psychasthenic (type) 300.89
  railroad 300.16
  rectum 306.4
  respiratory 306.1
  rumination 306.4
  senile 300.89
  sexual 302.70

Neurosis, neurotic — continued
  situational 300.89
  specified type NEC 300.89
  state 300.9
    with depersonalization episode 300.6
  stomach 306.4
  vasomotor 306.2
  visceral 306.4
  war 300.16
Neurospongioblastosis diffusa 759.5
Neurosyphilis (arrested) (early) (inactive) (late) (latent) (recurrent) 094.9
  with ataxia (cerebellar) (locomotor) (spastic) (spinal) 094.0
  acute meningitis 094.2
  aneurysm 094.89
  arachnoid (adhesive) 094.2
  arteritis (any artery) 094.89
  asymptomatic 094.3
  congenital 090.40
  dura (mater) 094.89
  general paresis 094.1
  gumma 094.9
  hemorrhagic 094.9
  juvenile (asymptomatic) (meningeal) 090.40
  leptomeninges (aseptic) 094.2
  meningeal 094.2
  meninges (adhesive) 094.2
  meningovascular (diffuse) 094.2
  optic atrophy 094.84
  parenchymatous (degenerative) 094.1
  paresis (see also Paresis, general) 094.1
  paretic (see also Paresis, general) 094.1
  relapse 094.9
  remission in (sustained) 094.9
  serological 094.3
  specified nature or site NEC 094.89
  tabes (dorsalis) 094.0
    juvenile 090.40
  tabetic 094.0
    juvenile 090.40
  taboparesis 094.1
    juvenile 090.40
  thrombosis 094.89
  vascular 094.89
Neurotic — see also Neurosis 300.9
  excoriation 698.4
    psychogenic 306.3
Neurotmesis — see Injury, nerve, by site
Neurotoxemia — see Toxemia
Neutro-occlusion 524.21
Neutropenia, neutropenic (idiopathic) (pernicious) (primary) 288.00
  chronic 288.09
    hypoplastic 288.09
  congenital (nontransient) 288.01
  cyclic 288.02
  drug induced 288.03
  due to infection 288.04
  fever 288.00
  genetic 288.01
  immune 288.09
  infantile 288.01
  malignant 288.09
  neonatal, transitory (isoimmune) (maternal transfer) 776.7
  periodic 288.02
  splenic 289.53
  splenomegaly 289.53
  toxic 288.09
Neutrophilia, hereditary giant 288.2
Nevocarcinoma (M8720/3) — see Melanoma
Nevus (M8720/0) — see also Neoplasm, skin, benign

Note — Except where otherwise indicated, varieties of nevus in the list below that are followed by a morphology code number (M----/0) should be coded by site as for "Neoplasm, skin, benign."

  acanthotic 702.8
  achromic (M8730/0)
  amelanotic (M8730/0)
  anemic, anemicus 709.09
  angiomatous (M9120/0) (see also Hemangioma) 228.00
  araneus 448.1

☑ Additional Digit Required — Refer to the Tabular List for Digit Selection   ▽ Subterms under main terms may continue to next column or page

214 — Volume 2   ►◄ Revised Text   ● New Line   ▲ Revised Code   2015 ICD-9-CM

Nevus — *see also* Neoplasm, skin, benign —
  continued
  avasculosus 709.09
  balloon cell (M8722/0)
  bathing trunk (M8761/1) 238.2
  blue (M8780/0)
    cellular (M8790/0)
    giant (M8790/0)
    Jadassohn's (M8780/0)
    malignant (M8780/3) — *see* Melanoma
  capillary (M9131/0) (*see also* Hemangioma)
    228.00
  cavernous (M9121/0) (*see also* Heman-
    gioma) 228.00
  cellular (M8720/0)
    blue (M8790/0)
  comedonicus 757.33
  compound (M8760/0)
  conjunctiva (M8720/0) 224.3
  dermal (M8750/0)
    and epidermal (M8760/0)
  epithelioid cell (and spindle cell) (M8770/0)
  flammeus 757.32
    osteohypertrophic 759.89
  hairy (M8720/0)
  halo (M8723/0)
  hemangiomatous (M9120/0) (*see also* He-
    mangioma) 228.00
  intradermal (M8750/0)
  intraepidermal (M8740/0)
  involuting (M8724/0)
  Jadassohn's (blue) (M8780/0)
  junction, junctional (M8740/0)
    malignant melanoma in (M8740/3) —
      see Melanoma
  juvenile (M8770/0)
  lymphatic (M9170/0) 228.1
  magnocellular (M8726/0)
    specified site — *see* Neoplasm, by site,
      benign
    unspecified site 224.0
  malignant (M8720/3) — *see* Melanoma
  meaning hemangioma (M9120/0) (*see also*
    Hemangioma) 228.00
  melanotic (pigmented) (M8720/0)
  multiplex 759.5
  nonneoplastic 448.1
  nonpigmented (M8730/0)
  nonvascular (M8720/0)
  oral mucosa, white sponge 750.26
  osteohypertrophic, flammeus 759.89
  papillaris (M8720/0)
  papillomatosus (M8720/0)
  pigmented (M8720/0)
    giant (M8761/1) (*see also* Neoplasm, skin,
      uncertain behavior)
      malignant melanoma in (M8761/3)
        — *see* Melanoma
    systematicus 757.33
  pilosus (M8720/0)
  port wine 757.32
  sanguineous 757.32
  sebaceous (senile) 702.8
  senile 448.1
  spider 448.1
  spindle cell (and epithelioid cell) (M8770/0)
  stellar 448.1
  strawberry 757.32
  syringocystadenomatous papilliferous
    (M8406/0)
  unius lateris 757.33
  Unna's 757.32
  vascular 757.32
  verrucous 757.33
  white sponge (oral mucosa) 750.26
Newborn (infant) (liveborn)
  abstinence syndrome 779.5
  affected by
    amniocentesis 760.61
    maternal abuse of drugs (gestational)
      (via placenta) (via breast milk)
      (*see also* Noxious, substances
      transmitted through placenta or
      breast milk (affecting fetus or
      newborn)) 760.70
      methamphetamine(s) 760.72

Newborn — *continued*
  affected by — *continued*
    procedure
      amniocentesis 760.61
      in utero NEC 760.62
    surgical on mother
      during pregnancy NEC 760.63
      previous not associated with
        pregnancy 760.64
  apnea 770.81
    obstructive 770.82
    specified NEC 770.82
  breast buds 779.89
  cardiomyopathy 425.4
    congenital 425.3
  convulsion 779.0
  electrolyte imbalance NEC (transitory) 775.5
  fever (environmentally-induced) 778.4
  gestation
    24 completed weeks 765.22
    25-26 completed weeks 765.23
    27-28 completed weeks 765.24
    29-30 completed weeks 765.25
    31-32 completed weeks 765.26
    33-34 completed weeks 765.27
    35-36 completed weeks 765.28
    37 or more completed weeks 765.29
    less than 24 completed weeks 765.21
    unspecified completed weeks 765.20
  infection 771.89
    candida 771.7
    mastitis 771.5
    specified NEC 771.89
    urinary tract 771.82
  mastitis 771.5
  multiple NEC
    born in hospital (without mention of
      cesarean delivery or section)
      V37.00
      with cesarean delivery or section
        V37.01
    born outside hospital
      hospitalized V37.1
      not hospitalized V37.2
    mates all liveborn
      born in hospital (without mention of
        cesarean delivery or section)
        V34.00
        with cesarean delivery or section
          V34.01
      born outside hospital
        hospitalized V34.1
        not hospitalized V34.2
    mates all stillborn
      born in hospital (without mention of
        cesarean delivery or section)
        V35.00
        with cesarean delivery or section
          V35.01
      born outside hospital
        hospitalized V35.1
        not hospitalized V35.2
    mates liveborn and stillborn
      born in hospital (without mention of
        cesarean delivery or section)
        V36.00
        with cesarean delivery or section
          V36.01
      born outside hospital
        hospitalized V36.1
        not hospitalized V36.2
  omphalitis 771.4
  seizure 779.0
  sepsis 771.81
  single
    born in hospital (without mention of
      cesarean delivery or section)
      V30.00
      with cesarean delivery or section
        V30.01
    born outside hospital
      hospitalized V30.1
      not hospitalized V30.2
  specified condition NEC 779.89

Newborn — *continued*
  twin NEC
    born in hospital (without mention of
      cesarean delivery or section)
      V33.00
      with cesarean delivery or section
        V33.01
    born outside hospital
      hospitalized V33.1
      not hospitalized V33.2
    mate liveborn
      born in hospital V31.0 ☑
      born outside hospital
        hospitalized V31.1
        not hospitalized V31.2
    mate stillborn
      born in hospital V32.0 ☑
      born outside hospital
        hospitalized V32.1
        not hospitalized V32.2
    unspecified as to single or multiple birth
      born in hospital (without mention of
        cesarean delivery or section)
        V39.00
        with cesarean delivery or section
          V39.01
      born outside hospital
        hospitalized V39.1
        not hospitalized V39.2
  weight check V20.32
Newcastle's conjunctivitis or disease 077.8
Nezelof's syndrome (pure alymphocytosis)
  279.13
Niacin (amide) **deficiency** 265.2
Nicolas-Durand-Favre disease (climatic bubo)
  099.1
Nicolas-Favre disease (climatic bubo) 099.1
Nicotinic acid (amide) **deficiency** 265.2
Niemann-Pick disease (lipid histiocytosis)
  (splenomegaly) 272.7
Night
  blindness (*see also* Blindness, night) 368.60
    congenital 368.61
    vitamin A deficiency 264.5
  cramps 729.82
  sweats 780.8
  terrors, child 307.46
Nightmare 307.47
  REM-sleep type 307.47
Nipple — *see* condition
Nisbet's chancre 099.0
Nishimoto (-Takeuchi) disease 437.5
Nitritoid crisis or reaction — *see* Crisis, nitritoid
Nitrogen retention, extrarenal 788.99
Nitrosohemoglobinemia 289.89
Njovera 104.0
No
  diagnosis 799.9
  disease (found) V71.9
  room at the inn V65.0
Nocardiasis — *see* Nocardiosis
Nocardiosis 039.9
  with pneumonia 039.1
  lung 039.1
  specified type NEC 039.8
Nocturia 788.43
  psychogenic 306.53
Nocturnal — *see also* condition
  dyspnea (paroxysmal) 786.09
  emissions 608.89
  enuresis 788.36
    psychogenic 307.6
  frequency (micturition) 788.43
    psychogenic 306.53
Nodal rhythm disorder 427.89
Nodding of head 781.0
Node(s) — *see also* Nodule(s)
  Heberden's 715.04
  larynx 478.79
  lymph — *see* condition
  milkers' 051.1
  Osler's 421.0
  rheumatic 729.89
  Schmorl's 722.30
    lumbar, lumbosacral 722.32

Node(s) — *see also* Nodule(s) — *continued*
  Schmorl's — *continued*
    specified region NEC 722.39
    thoracic, thoracolumbar 722.31
  singers' 478.5
  skin NEC 782.2
  tuberculous — *see* Tuberculosis, lymph
    gland
  vocal cords 478.5
Nodosities, Haygarth's 715.04
Nodule(s), nodular
  actinomycotic (*see also* Actinomycosis) 039.9
  arthritic — *see* Arthritis, nodosa
  breast 793.89
  cutaneous 782.2
  Haygarth's 715.04
  inflammatory — *see* Inflammation
  juxta-articular 102.7
    syphilitic 095.7
    yaws 102.7
  larynx 478.79
  lung
    emphysematous 492.8
    solitary 793.11
  milkers' 051.1
  prostate 600.10
    with
      urinary
        obstruction 600.11
        retention 600.11
  pulmonary, solitary (subsegmental branch
    of the bronchial tree) 793.11
    multiple 793.19
  retrocardiac 785.9
  rheumatic 729.89
  rheumatoid — *see* Arthritis, rheumatoid
  scrotum (inflammatory) 608.4
  singers' 478.5
  skin NEC 782.2
  solitary, lung 793.11
    emphysematous 492.8
  subcutaneous 782.2
  thyroid (gland) (nontoxic) (uninodular)
    241.0
    with
      hyperthyroidism 242.1 ☑
      thyrotoxicosis 242.1 ☑
    toxic or with hyperthyroidism 242.1 ☑
  vocal cords 478.5
Noma (gangrenous) (hospital) (infective) 528.1
  auricle (*see also* Gangrene) 785.4
  mouth 528.1
  pudendi (*see also* Vulvitis) 616.10
  vulvae (*see also* Vulvitis) 616.10
Nomadism V60.0
Non-adherence
  artificial skin graft 996.55
  decellularized allodermis graft 996.55
Non-autoimmune hemolytic anemia NEC
  283.10
Nonclosure — *see also* Imperfect, closure
  ductus
    arteriosus 747.0
    Botalli 747.0
  Eustachian valve 746.89
  foramen
    Botalli 745.5
    ovale 745.5
Noncompliance with medical treatment
  V15.81
  renal dialysis V45.12
Nondescent (congenital) — *see also* Malposition, congenital
  cecum 751.4
  colon 751.4
  testis 752.51
Nondevelopment
  brain 742.1
    specified part 742.2
  heart 746.89
  organ or site, congenital NEC — *see* Hypopla-
    sia
Nonengagement
  head NEC 652.5 ☑
    in labor 660.1 ☑
      affecting fetus or newborn 763.1

☑ Additional Digit Required — Refer to the Tabular List for Digit Selection   ▽ Subterms under main terms may continue to next column or page

Nonexanthematous tick fever 066.1
Nonexpansion, lung (newborn) NEC 770.4
Nonfunctioning
   cystic duct (*see also* Disease, gallbladder)
    575.8
   gallbladder (*see also* Disease, gallbladder)
    575.8
   kidney (*see also* Disease, renal) 593.9
   labyrinth 386.58
Nonhealing
   stump (surgical) 997.69
   wound, surgical 998.83
Nonimplantation of ovum, causing infertility 628.3
Noninsufflation, fallopian tube 628.2
Nonne-Milroy-Meige syndrome (chronic hereditary edema) 757.0
Nonovulation 628.0
Nonpatent fallopian tube 628.2
Nonpneumatization, lung NEC 770.4
Nonreflex bladder 596.54
   with cauda equina 344.61
Nonretention of food — *see* Vomiting
Nonrotation — *see* Malrotation
Nonsecretion, urine — *see also* Anuria 788.5
   newborn 753.3
Nonunion
   fracture 733.82
   organ or site, congenital NEC — *see* Imperfect, closure
   symphysis pubis, congenital 755.69
   top sacrum, congenital 756.19
Nonviability 765.0 ☑
Nonvisualization, gallbladder 793.3
Nonvitalized tooth 522.9
Non-working side interference 524.56
Normal
   delivery — *see* category 650
   menses V65.5
   state (feared complaint unfounded) V65.5
Normoblastosis 289.89

Normocytic anemia (infectional) 285.9
   due to blood loss (chronic) 280.0
    acute 285.1
Norrie's disease (congenital) (progressive oculoacousticocerebral degeneration) 743.8
North American blastomycosis 116.0
Norwegian itch 133.0
Nosebleed 784.7
Nose, nasal — *see* condition
Nosomania 298.9
Nosophobia 300.29
Nostalgia 309.89
Notched lip, congenital — *see also* Cleft, lip 749.10
Notching nose, congenital (tip) 748.1
Notch of iris 743.46
Nothnagel's
   syndrome 378.52
   vasomotor acroparesthesia 443.89
Novy's relapsing fever (American) 087.1
Noxious
   foodstuffs, poisoning by
    fish 988.0
    fungi 988.1
    mushrooms 988.1
    plants (food) 988.2
    shellfish 988.0
    specified type NEC 988.8
    toadstool 988.1
   substances transmitted through placenta or breast milk (affecting fetus or newborn) 760.70
    acetretin 760.78
    alcohol 760.71
    aminopterin 760.78
    antiandrogens 760.79
    anticonvulsant 760.77
    antifungal 760.74
    anti-infective agents 760.74
    antimetabolic 760.78

Noxious — *continued*
   substances transmitted through placenta or breast milk — *continued*
    atorvastatin 760.78
    carbamazepine 760.77
    cocaine 760.75
    "crack" 760.75
    diethylstilbestrol (DES) 760.76
    divalproex sodium 760.77
    endocrine disrupting chemicals 760.79
    estrogens 760.79
    etretinate 760.78
    fluconazole 760.74
    fluvastatin 760.78
    hallucinogenic agents NEC 760.73
    hormones 760.79
    lithium 760.79
    lovastatin 760.78
    medicinal agents NEC 760.79
    methotrexate 760.78
    misoprostil 760.79
    narcotics 760.72
    obstetric anesthetic or analgesic 763.5
    phenobarbital 760.77
    phenytoin 760.77
    pravastatin 760.78
    progestins 760.79
    retinoic acid 760.78
    simvastatin 760.78
    solvents 760.79
    specified agent NEC 760.79
    statins 760.78
    suspected, affecting management of pregnancy 655.5 ☑
    tetracycline 760.74
    thalidomide 760.79
    trimethadione 760.77
    valproate 760.77
    valproic acid 760.77
    vitamin A 760.78
NPDH (new persistent daily headache) 339.42

Nuchal hitch (arm) 652.8 ☑
Nucleus pulposus — *see* condition
Numbness 782.0
Nuns' knee 727.2
Nursemaid's
   elbow 832.2
   shoulder 831.0 ☑
Nutmeg liver 573.8
Nutrition, deficient or insufficient (particular kind of food) 269.9
   due to
    insufficient food 994.2
    lack of
     care (child) (infant) 995.52
      adult 995.84
     food 994.2
Nyctalopia — *see also* Blindness, night 368.60
   vitamin A deficiency 264.5
Nycturia 788.43
   psychogenic 306.53
Nymphomania 302.89
Nystagmus 379.50
   associated with vestibular system disorders 379.54
   benign paroxysmal positional 386.11
   central positional 386.2
   congenital 379.51
   deprivation 379.53
   dissociated 379.55
   latent 379.52
   miners' 300.89
   positional
    benign paroxysmal 386.11
    central 386.2
   specified NEC 379.56
   vestibular 379.54
   visual deprivation 379.53

☑ **Additional Digit Required — Refer to the Tabular List for Digit Selection**   ⩗ **Subterms under main terms may continue to next column or page**

216 — Volume 2   ▶◀ **Revised Text**   ● **New Line**   ▲ **Revised Code**   **2015 ICD-9-CM**

O

Oasthouse urine disease 270.2
Obermeyer's relapsing fever (European) 087.0
Obesity (constitutional) (exogenous) (familial) (nutritional) (simple) 278.00
  adrenal 255.8
  complicating pregnancy, childbirth, or puerperium 649.1 ☑
  due to hyperalimentation 278.00
  endocrine NEC 259.9
  endogenous 259.9
  Fröhlich's (adiposogenital dystrophy) 253.8
  glandular NEC 259.9
  hypothyroid (see also Hypothyroidism) 244.9
  hypoventilation syndrome 278.03
  morbid 278.01
  of pregnancy 649.1 ☑
  pituitary 253.8
  severe 278.01
  thyroid (see also Hypothyroidism) 244.9
Oblique — see also condition
  lie before labor, affecting fetus or newborn 761.7
Obliquity, pelvis 738.6
Obliteration
  abdominal aorta 446.7
  appendix (lumen) 543.9
  artery 447.1
  ascending aorta 446.7
  bile ducts 576.8
    with calculus, choledocholithiasis, or stones — see Choledocholithiasis
    congenital 751.61
      jaundice from 751.61 [774.5]
  common duct 576.8
    with calculus, choledocholithiasis, or stones — see Choledocholithiasis
    congenital 751.61
  cystic duct 575.8
    with calculus, choledocholithiasis, or stones — see Choledocholithiasis
  disease, arteriolar 447.1
  endometrium 621.8
  eye, anterior chamber 360.34
  fallopian tube 628.2
  lymphatic vessel 457.1
    postmastectomy 457.0
  organ or site, congenital NEC — see Atresia
  placental blood vessels — see Placenta, abnormal
  supra-aortic branches 446.7
  ureter 593.89
  urethra 599.84
  vein 459.9
  vestibule (oral) 525.8
Observation (for) V71.9
  without need for further medical care V71.9
  accident NEC V71.4
    at work V71.3
  criminal assault V71.6
  deleterious agent ingestion V71.89
  disease V71.9
    cardiovascular V71.7
    heart V71.7
    mental V71.09
    specified condition NEC V71.89
  foreign body ingestion V71.89
  growth and development variations V21.8
  injuries (accidental) V71.4
    inflicted NEC V71.6
      during alleged rape or seduction V71.5
  malignant neoplasm, suspected V71.1
  postpartum
    immediately after delivery V24.0
    routine follow-up V24.2
  pregnancy
    high-risk V23.9
      inconclusive fetal viability V23.87
      specified problem NEC V23.89
    normal (without complication) V22.1
      with nonobstetric complication V22.2
      first V22.0
  rape or seduction, alleged V71.5
    injury during V71.5

Observation — continued
  suicide attempt, alleged V71.89
  suspected (undiagnosed) (unproven)
    abuse V71.81
    cardiovascular disease V71.7
    child or wife battering victim V71.6
    concussion (cerebral) V71.6
    condition NEC V71.89
      infant — see Observation, suspected, condition, newborn
    maternal and fetal
      amniotic cavity and membrane problem V89.01
      cervical shortening V89.05
      fetal anomaly V89.03
      fetal growth problem V89.04
      oligohydramnios V89.01
      other specified problem NEC V89.09
      placental problem V89.02
      polyhydramnios V89.01
    newborn V29.9
      cardiovascular disease V29.8
      congenital anomaly V29.8
      genetic V29.3
      infectious V29.0
      ingestion foreign object V29.8
      injury V29.8
      metabolic V29.3
      neoplasm V29.8
      neurological V29.1
      poison, poisoning V29.8
      respiratory V29.2
      specified NEC V29.8
    exposure
      anthrax V71.82
      biologic agent NEC V71.83
      SARS V71.83
    infectious disease not requiring isolation V71.89
    malignant neoplasm V71.1
    mental disorder V71.09
    neglect V71.81
    neoplasm
      benign V71.89
      malignant V71.1
    specified condition NEC V71.89
    tuberculosis V71.2
  tuberculosis, suspected V71.2
Obsession, obsessional 300.3
  ideas and mental images 300.3
  impulses 300.3
  neurosis 300.3
  phobia 300.3
  psychasthenia 300.3
  ruminations 300.3
  state 300.3
  syndrome 300.3
Obsessive-compulsive 300.3
  neurosis 300.3
  personality 301.4
  reaction 300.3
Obstetrical trauma NEC (complicating delivery) 665.9 ☑
  with
    abortion — see Abortion, by type, with damage to pelvic organs
    ectopic pregnancy (see also categories 633.0–633.9) 639.2
    molar pregnancy (see also categories 630–632) 639.2
  affecting fetus or newborn 763.89
  following
    abortion 639.2
    ectopic or molar pregnancy 639.2
Obstipation — see also Constipation 564.00
  psychogenic 306.4
Obstruction, obstructed, obstructive
  airway NEC 519.8
    with
      allergic alveolitis NEC 495.9
      asthma NEC (see also Asthma) 493.9 ☑
      bronchiectasis 494.0
        with acute exacerbation 494.1

Obstruction, obstructed, obstructive — continued
  airway — continued
    with — continued
      bronchitis (chronic) (see also Bronchitis, with, obstruction) 491.20
      emphysema NEC 492.8
    chronic 496
      with
        allergic alveolitis NEC 495.5
        asthma NEC (see also Asthma) 493.2 ☑
        bronchiectasis 494.0
          with acute exacerbation 494.1
        bronchitis (chronic) (see also Bronchitis, with, obstruction) 491.20
        emphysema NEC 492.8
    due to
      bronchospasm 519.11
      foreign body 934.9
      inhalation of fumes or vapors 506.9
      laryngospasm 478.75
  alimentary canal (see also Obstruction, intestine) 560.9
  ampulla of Vater 576.2
    with calculus, cholelithiasis, or stones — see Choledocholithiasis
  aortic (heart) (valve) (see also Stenosis, aortic) 424.1
    rheumatic (see also Stenosis, aortic, rheumatic) 395.0
  aortoiliac 444.09
  aqueduct of Sylvius 331.4
    congenital 742.3
      with spina bifida (see also Spina bifida) 741.0 ☑
  Arnold-Chiari (see also Spina bifida) 741.0 ☑
  artery (see also Embolism, artery) 444.9
    basilar (complete) (partial) (see also Occlusion, artery, basilar) 433.0 ☑
    carotid (complete) (partial) (see also Occlusion, artery, carotid) 433.1 ☑
    precerebral — see Occlusion, artery, precerebral NEC
    retinal (central) (see also Occlusion, retina) 362.30
    vertebral (complete) (partial) (see also Occlusion, artery, vertebral) 433.2 ☑
  asthma (chronic) (with obstructive pulmonary disease) 493.2 ☑
  band (intestinal) 560.81
  bile duct or passage (see also Obstruction, biliary) 576.2
    congenital 751.61
      jaundice from 751.61 [774.5]
  biliary (duct) (tract) 576.2
    with calculus 574.51
      with cholecystitis (chronic) 574.41
        acute 574.31
    congenital 751.61
      jaundice from 751.61 [774.5]
    gallbladder 575.2
      with calculus 574.21
        with cholecystitis (chronic) 574.11
          acute 574.01
  bladder neck (acquired) 596.0
    congenital 753.6
  bowel (see also Obstruction, intestine) 560.9
  bronchus 519.19
  canal, ear (see also Stricture, ear canal, acquired) 380.50
  cardia 537.89
  caval veins (inferior) (superior) 459.2
  cecum (see also Obstruction, intestine) 560.9
  circulatory 459.9
  colon (see also Obstruction, intestine) 560.9
    sympathicotonic 560.89
  common duct (see also Obstruction, biliary) 576.2
    congenital 751.61
  coronary (artery) (heart) (see also Arteriosclerosis, coronary)
    acute (see also Infarct, myocardium) 410.9 ☑

Obstruction, obstructed, obstructive — continued
  coronary (see also Arteriosclerosis, coronary) — continued
    acute (see also Infarct, myocardium) — continued
      without myocardial infarction 411.81
  cystic duct (see also Obstruction, gallbladder) 575.2
    congenital 751.61
  device, implant, or graft — see Complications, due to (presence of) any device, implant, or graft classified to 996.0–996.5 NEC
  due to foreign body accidentally left in operation wound 998.4
  duodenum 537.3
    congenital 751.1
    due to
      compression NEC 537.3
      cyst 537.3
      intrinsic lesion or disease NEC 537.3
      scarring 537.3
      torsion 537.3
      ulcer 532.91
      volvulus 537.3
  ejaculatory duct 608.89
  endocardium 424.90
    arteriosclerotic 424.99
    specified cause, except rheumatic 424.99
  esophagus 530.3
  eustachian tube (complete) (partial) 381.60
    cartilaginous
      extrinsic 381.63
      intrinsic 381.62
    due to
      cholesteatoma 381.61
      osseous lesion NEC 381.61
      polyp 381.61
    osseous 381.61
  fallopian tube (bilateral) 628.2
  fecal 560.32
    with hernia (see also Hernia, by site, with obstruction)
      gangrenous — see Hernia, by site, with gangrene
  foramen of Monro (congenital) 742.3
    with spina bifida (see also Spina bifida) 741.0 ☑
  foreign body — see Foreign body
  gallbladder 575.2
    with calculus, cholelithiasis, or stones 574.21
      with cholecystitis (chronic) 574.11
        acute 574.01
    congenital 751.69
      jaundice from 751.69 [774.5]
  gastric outlet 537.0
  gastrointestinal (see also Obstruction, intestine) 560.9
  glottis 478.79
  hepatic 573.8
    duct (see also Obstruction, biliary) 576.2
    congenital 751.61
  icterus (see also Obstruction, biliary) 576.8
    congenital 751.61
  ileocecal coil (see also Obstruction, intestine) 560.9
  ileum (see also Obstruction, intestine) 560.9
  iliofemoral (artery) 444.81
  internal anastomosis — see Complications, mechanical, graft
  intestine (mechanical) (neurogenic) (paroxysmal) (postinfectional) (reflex) 560.9
    with
      adhesions (intestinal) (peritoneal) 560.81
      hernia (see also Hernia, by site, with obstruction)
        gangrenous — see Hernia, by site, with gangrene
    adynamic (see also Ileus) 560.1
    by gallstone 560.31
    congenital or infantile (small) 751.1
      large 751.2

☑ Additional Digit Required — Refer to the Tabular List for Digit Selection   ⓦ Subterms under main terms may continue to next column or page

2015 ICD-9-CM   ▶◀ Revised Text   ● New Line   ▲ Revised Code   Volume 2 — 217

Obstruction, obstructed, obstructive — *continued*
intestine — *continued*
  due to
    Ascaris lumbricoides 127.0
    mural thickening 560.89
    procedure 997.49
      involving urinary tract 997.5
  impaction 560.32
  infantile — *see* Obstruction, intestine, congenital
  newborn
    due to
      fecaliths 777.1
      inspissated milk 777.2
      meconium (plug) 777.1
        in mucoviscidosis 277.01
    transitory 777.4
  specified cause NEC 560.89
  transitory, newborn 777.4
  volvulus 560.2
intracardiac ball valve prosthesis 996.02
jaundice (*see also* Obstruction, biliary) 576.8
  congenital 751.61
jejunum (*see also* Obstruction, intestine) 560.9
kidney 593.89
labor 660.9 ☑
  affecting fetus or newborn 763.1
  by
    bony pelvis (conditions classifiable to 653.0–653.9) 660.1 ☑
    deep transverse arrest 660.3 ☑
    impacted shoulder 660.4 ☑
    locked twins 660.5 ☑
    malposition (fetus) (conditions classifiable to 652.0–652.9) 660.0 ☑
      head during labor 660.3 ☑
    persistent occipitoposterior position 660.3 ☑
    soft tissue, pelvic (conditions classifiable to 654.0–654.9) 660.2 ☑
lacrimal
  canaliculi 375.53
  congenital 743.65
  punctum 375.52
  sac 375.54
lacrimonasal duct 375.56
  congenital 743.65
  neonatal 375.55
lacteal, with steatorrhea 579.2
laryngitis (*see also* Laryngitis) 464.01
larynx 478.79
  congenital 748.3
liver 573.8
  cirrhotic (*see also* Cirrhosis, liver) 571.5
lung 518.89
  with
    asthma — *see* Asthma
    bronchitis (chronic) 491.20
    emphysema NEC 492.8
  airway, chronic 496
  chronic NEC 496
    with
      asthma (chronic) (obstructive) 493.2 ☑
  disease, chronic 496
    with
      asthma (chronic) (obstructive) 493.2 ☑
  emphysematous 492.8
lymphatic 457.1
meconium
  fetus or newborn 777.1
    in mucoviscidosis 277.01
  newborn due to fecaliths 777.1
mediastinum 519.3
mitral (rheumatic) — *see* Stenosis, mitral
nasal 478.19
  duct 375.56
    neonatal 375.55
  sinus — *see* Sinusitis
nasolacrimal duct 375.56
  congenital 743.65
  neonatal 375.55

Obstruction, obstructed, obstructive — *continued*
nasopharynx 478.29
nose 478.19
organ or site, congenital NEC — *see* Atresia
pancreatic duct 577.8
parotid gland 527.8
pelviureteral junction (*see also* Obstruction, ureter) 593.4
pharynx 478.29
portal (circulation) (vein) 452
prostate 600.90
  with
    other lower urinary tract symptoms (LUTS) 600.91
    urinary
      obstruction 600.91
      retention 600.91
  valve (urinary) 596.0
pulmonary
  valve (heart) (*see also* Endocarditis, pulmonary) 424.3
  vein, isolated 747.49
pyemic — *see* Septicemia
pylorus (acquired) 537.0
  congenital 750.5
  infantile 750.5
rectosigmoid (*see also* Obstruction, intestine) 560.9
rectum 569.49
renal 593.89
respiratory 519.8
  chronic 496
retinal (artery) (vein) (central) (*see also* Occlusion, retina) 362.30
salivary duct (any) 527.8
  with calculus 527.5
sigmoid (*see also* Obstruction, intestine) 560.9
sinus (accessory) (nasal) (*see also* Sinusitis) 473.9
Stensen's duct 527.8
stomach 537.89
  acute 536.1
  congenital 750.7
submaxillary gland 527.8
  with calculus 527.5
thoracic duct 457.1
thrombotic — *see* Thrombosis
tooth eruption 520.6
trachea 519.19
tracheostomy airway 519.09
tricuspid — *see* Endocarditis, tricuspid
upper respiratory, congenital 748.8
ureter (functional) 593.4
  congenital 753.20
  due to calculus 592.1
ureteropelvic junction, congenital 753.21
ureterovesical junction, congenital 753.22
urethra 599.60
  congenital 753.6
urinary (moderate) 599.60
  organ or tract (lower) 599.60
    due to
      benign prostatic hypertrophy (BPH) - see category 600
    specified NEC 599.69
      due to
        benign prostatic hypertrophy (BPH) — see category 600
  prostatic valve 596.0
uropathy 599.60
uterus 621.8
vagina 623.2
valvular — *see* Endocarditis
vascular graft or shunt 996.1
  atherosclerosis — *see* Arteriosclerosis, coronary
  embolism 996.74
  occlusion NEC 996.74
  thrombus 996.74
  vein, venous 459.2
    caval (inferior) (superior) 459.2
    thrombotic — *see* Thrombosis
  vena cava (inferior) (superior) 459.2

Obstruction, obstructed, obstructive — *continued*
ventricular shunt 996.2
vesical 596.0
vesicourethral orifice 596.0
vessel NEC 459.9
Obturator — *see* condition
Occlusal
plane deviation 524.76
wear, teeth 521.10
Occlusion
anus 569.49
  congenital 751.2
  infantile 751.2
aortoiliac (chronic) 444.09
aqueduct of Sylvius 331.4
  congenital 742.3
    with spina bifida (*see also* Spina bifida) 741.0 ☑
arteries of extremities, lower 444.22
  without thrombus or embolus (*see also* Arteriosclerosis, extremities) 440.20
  due to stricture or stenosis 447.1
  upper 444.21
    without thrombus or embolus (*see also* Arteriosclerosis, extremities) 440.20
    due to stricture or stenosis 447.1
artery NEC (*see also* Embolism, artery) 444.9
  auditory, internal 433.8 ☑
  basilar 433.0 ☑
    with other precerebral artery 433.3 ☑
    bilateral 433.3 ☑
  brain or cerebral (*see also* Infarct, brain) 434.9 ☑
  carotid 433.1 ☑
    with other precerebral artery 433.3 ☑
    bilateral 433.3 ☑
  cerebellar (anterior inferior) (posterior inferior) (superior) 433.8 ☑
  cerebral (*see also* Infarct, brain) 434.9 ☑
  choroidal (anterior) 433.8 ☑
  chronic total
    coronary 414.2
    extremity(ies) 440.4
  communicating posterior 433.8 ☑
  complete
    coronary 414.2
    extremity(ies) 440.4
  coronary (thrombotic) (*see also* Infarct, myocardium) 410.9 ☑
    acute 410.9 ☑
      without myocardial infarction 411.81
    chronic total 414.2
    complete 414.2
    healed or old 412
    total 414.2
  extremity(ies)
    chronic total 440.4
    complete 440.4
    total 440.4
  hypophyseal 433.8 ☑
  iliac (artery) 444.81
  mesenteric (embolic) (thrombotic) (with gangrene) 557.0
  pontine 433.8 ☑
  precerebral NEC 433.9 ☑
    late effect — *see* Late effect(s) (of) cerebrovascular disease
    multiple or bilateral 433.3 ☑
    puerperal, postpartum, childbirth 674.0 ☑
    specified NEC 433.8 ☑
  renal 593.81
  retinal — *see* Occlusion, retina, artery
  spinal 433.8 ☑
  vertebral 433.2 ☑
    with other precerebral artery 433.3 ☑
    bilateral 433.3 ☑

Occlusion — *continued*
basilar (artery) — *see* Occlusion, artery, basilar
bile duct (any) (*see also* Obstruction, biliary) 576.2
bowel (*see also* Obstruction, intestine) 560.9
brain (artery) (vascular) (*see also* Infarct, brain) 434.9 ☑
breast (duct) 611.89
carotid (artery) (common) (internal) — *see* Occlusion, artery, carotid
cerebellar (anterior inferior) (artery) (posterior inferior) (superior) 433.8 ☑
cerebral (artery) (*see also* Infarct, brain) 434.9 ☑
cerebrovascular (*see also* Infarct, brain) 434.9 ☑
  diffuse 437.0
cervical canal (*see also* Stricture, cervix) 622.4
  by falciparum malaria 084.0
cervix (uteri) (*see also* Stricture, cervix) 622.4
choanal 748.0
choroidal (artery) 433.8 ☑
colon (*see also* Obstruction, intestine) 560.9
communicating posterior artery 433.8 ☑
coronary (artery) (thrombotic) (*see also* Infarct, myocardium) 410.9 ☑
  without myocardial infarction 411.81
  acute 410.9 ☑
    without myocardial infarction 411.81
  healed or old 412
cystic duct (*see also* Obstruction, gallbladder) 575.2
  congenital 751.69
disto
  division I 524.22
  division II 524.22
embolic — *see* Embolism
fallopian tube 628.2
  congenital 752.19
gallbladder (*see also* Obstruction, gallbladder) 575.2
  congenital 751.69
    jaundice from 751.69 [774.5]
gingiva, traumatic 523.8
hymen 623.3
  congenital 752.42
hypophyseal (artery) 433.8 ☑
iliac artery 444.81
intestine (*see also* Obstruction, intestine) 560.9
kidney 593.89
lacrimal apparatus — *see* Stenosis, lacrimal
lung 518.89
lymph or lymphatic channel 457.1
mammary duct 611.89
mesenteric artery (embolic) (thrombotic) (with gangrene) 557.0
nose 478.1 ☑
  congenital 748.0
organ or site, congenital NEC — *see* Atresia
oviduct 628.2
  congenital 752.19
periodontal, traumatic 523.8
peripheral arteries (lower extremity) 444.22
  without thrombus or embolus (*see also* Arteriosclerosis, extremities) 440.20
  due to stricture or stenosis 447.1
  upper extremity 444.21
    without thrombus or embolus (*see also* Arteriosclerosis, extremities) 440.20
    due to stricture or stenosis 447.1
pontine (artery) 433.8 ☑
posterior lingual, of mandibular teeth 524.29
precerebral artery — *see* Occlusion, artery, precerebral NEC
puncta lacrimalia 375.52
pupil 364.74
pylorus (*see also* Stricture, pylorus) 537.0
renal artery 593.81
retina, retinal (vascular) 362.30
  artery, arterial 362.30

Occlusion — continued
retina, retinal — continued
artery, arterial — continued
branch 362.32
central (total) 362.31
partial 362.33
transient 362.34
tributary 362.32
vein 362.30
branch 362.36
central (total) 362.35
incipient 362.37
partial 362.37
tributary 362.36
spinal artery 433.8 ☑
stent
coronary 996.72
teeth (mandibular) (posterior lingual) 524.29
thoracic duct 457.1
tubal 628.2
ureter (complete) (partial) 593.4
congenital 753.29
urethra (see also Stricture, urethra) 598.9
congenital 753.6
uterus 621.8
vagina 623.2
vascular NEC 459.9
vein — see Thrombosis
vena cava
inferior 453.2
superior (acute) 453.87
chronic 453.77
ventricle (brain) NEC 331.4
vertebral (artery) — see Occlusion, artery, vertebral
vessel (blood) NEC 459.9
vulva 624.8
Occlusio pupillae 364.74
Occupational
problems NEC V62.29
therapy V57.21
Ochlophobia 300.29
Ochronosis (alkaptonuric) (congenital) (endogenous) 270.2
with chloasma of eyelid 270.2
Ocular muscle — see also condition
myopathy 359.1
torticollis 781.93
Oculoauriculovertebral dysplasia 756.0
Oculogyric
crisis or disturbance 378.87
psychogenic 306.7
Oculomotor syndrome 378.81
Oddi's sphincter spasm 576.5
Odelberg's disease (juvenile osteochondrosis) 732.1
Odontalgia 525.9
Odontoameloblastoma (M9311/0) 213.1
upper jaw (bone) 213.0
Odontoclasia 521.05
Odontoclasis 873.63
complicated 873.73
Odontodysplasia, regional 520.4
Odontogenesis imperfecta 520.5
Odontoma (M9280/0) 213.1
ameloblastic (M9311/0) 213.1
upper jaw (bone) 213.0
calcified (M9280/0) 213.1
upper jaw (bone) 213.0
complex (M9282/0) 213.1
upper jaw (bone) 213.0
compound (M9281/0) 213.1
upper jaw (bone) 213.0
fibroameloblastic (M9290/0) 213.1
upper jaw (bone) 213.0
follicular 526.0
upper jaw (bone) 213.0
Odontomyelitis (closed) (open) 522.0
Odontonecrosis 521.09
Odontorrhagia 525.8
Odontosarcoma, ameloblastic (M9290/3) 170.1
upper jaw (bone) 170.0
Odynophagia 787.20
Oesophagostomiasis 127.7
Oesophagostomum infestation 127.7

Oestriasis 134.0
Ogilvie's syndrome (sympathicotonic colon obstruction) 560.89
Oguchi's disease (retina) 368.61
Ohara's disease — see also Tularemia 021.9
Oidiomycosis — see also Candidiasis 112.9
Oidiomycotic meningitis 112.83
Oidium albicans infection — see also Candidiasis 112.9
Old age 797
dementia (of) 290.0
Olfactory — see condition
Oligemia 285.9
Oligergasia — see also Disability, intellectual 319
Oligoamnios 658.0 ☑
affecting fetus or newborn 761.2
Oligoastrocytoma, mixed (M9382/3)
specified site — see Neoplasm, by site, malignant
unspecified site 191.9
Oligocythemia 285.9
Oligodendroblastoma (M9460/3)
specified site — see Neoplasm, by site, malignant
unspecified site 191.9
Oligodendroglioma (M9450/3)
anaplastic type (M9451/3)
specified site — see Neoplasm, by site, malignant
unspecified site 191.9
specified site — see Neoplasm, by site, malignant
unspecified site 191.9
Oligodendroma — see Oligodendroglioma
Oligodontia — see also Anodontia 520.0
Oligoencephalon 742.1
Oligohydramnios 658.0 ☑
affecting fetus or newborn 761.2
due to premature rupture of membranes 658.1 ☑
affecting fetus or newborn 761.2
Oligohydrosis 705.0
Oligomenorrhea 626.1
Oligophrenia — see also Disability, intellectual 319
phenylpyruvic 270.1
Oligospermia 606.1
Oligotrichia 704.09
congenita 757.4
Oliguria 788.5
with
abortion — see Abortion, by type, with renal failure
ectopic pregnancy (see also categories 633.0–633.9) 639.3
molar pregnancy (see also categories 630–632) 639.3
complicating
abortion 639.3
ectopic or molar pregnancy 639.3
pregnancy 646.2 ☑
with hypertension — see Toxemia, of pregnancy
due to a procedure 997.5
following labor and delivery 669.3 ☑
heart or cardiac — see Failure, heart
puerperal, postpartum 669.3 ☑
specified due to a procedure 997.5
Ollier's disease (chondrodysplasia) 756.4
Omentitis — see also Peritonitis 567.9
Omentocele — see also Hernia, omental 553.8
Omentum, omental — see condition
Omphalitis (congenital) (newborn) 771.4
not of newborn 686.9
tetanus 771.3
Omphalocele 756.72
Omphalomesenteric duct, persistent 751.0
Omphalorrhagia, newborn 772.3
Omsk hemorrhagic fever 065.1
Onanism 307.9
Onchocerciasis 125.3
eye 125.3 [360.13]
Onchocercosis 125.3
Oncocytoma (M8290/0) — see Neoplasm, by site, benign

Ondine's curse 348.89
Oneirophrenia — see also Schizophrenia 295.4 ☑
Onychauxis 703.8
congenital 757.5
Onychia (with lymphangitis) 681.9
dermatophytic 110.1
finger 681.02
toe 681.11
Onychitis (with lymphangitis) 681.9
finger 681.02
toe 681.11
Onychocryptosis 703.0
Onychodystrophy 703.8
congenital 757.5
Onychogryphosis 703.8
Onychogryposis 703.8
Onycholysis 703.8
Onychomadesis 703.8
Onychomalacia 703.8
Onychomycosis 110.1
finger 110.1
toe 110.1
Onycho-osteodysplasia 756.89
Onychophagy 307.9
Onychoptosis 703.8
Onychorrhexis 703.8
congenital 757.5
Onychoschizia 703.8
Onychotrophia — see also Atrophy, nail 703.8
O'nyong-nyong fever 066.3
Onyxis (finger) (toe) 703.0
Onyxitis (with lymphangitis) 681.9
finger 681.02
toe 681.11
Oocyte (egg) (ovum)
donor V59.70
over age 35 V59.73
anonymous recipient V59.73
designated recipient V59.74
under age 35 V59.71
anonymous recipient V59.71
designated recipient V59.72
Oophoritis (cystic) (infectional) (interstitial) — see also Salpingo-oophoritis 614.2
complicating pregnancy 646.6 ☑
fetal (acute) 752.0
gonococcal (acute) 098.19
chronic or duration of 2 months or over 098.39
tuberculous (see also Tuberculosis) 016.6 ☑
Opacity, opacities
cornea 371.00
central 371.03
congenital 743.43
interfering with vision 743.42
degenerative (see also Degeneration, cornea) 371.40
hereditary (see also Dystrophy, cornea) 371.50
inflammatory (see also Keratitis) 370.9
late effect of trachoma (healed) 139.1
minor 371.01
peripheral 371.02
enamel (fluoride) (nonfluoride) (teeth) 520.3
lens (see also Cataract) 366.9
snowball 379.22
vitreous (humor) 379.24
congenital 743.51
Opalescent dentin (hereditary) 520.5
Open, opening
abnormal, organ or site, congenital — see Imperfect, closure
angle
with
borderline findings
high risk 365.05
intraocular pressure 365.01
low risk 365.01
cupping of discs 365.01
high risk 365.05
low risk 365.01
bite
anterior 524.24
posterior 524.25
false — see Imperfect, closure

Open, opening — continued
margin on tooth restoration 525.61
restoration margins 525.61
wound — see Wound, open, by site
Operation
causing mutilation of fetus 763.89
destructive, on live fetus, to facilitate birth 763.89
for delivery, fetus or newborn 763.89
maternal, unrelated to current delivery, affecting fetus or newborn (see also Newborn, affected by) 760.64
Operational fatigue 300.89
Operative — see condition
Operculitis (chronic) 523.40
acute 523.30
Operculum, retina 361.32
with detachment 361.01
Ophiasis 704.01
Ophthalmia — see also Conjunctivitis 372.30
actinic rays 370.24
allergic (acute) 372.05
chronic 372.14
blennorrhagic (neonatorum) 098.40
catarrhal 372.03
diphtheritic 032.81
Egyptian 076.1
electric, electrica 370.24
gonococcal (neonatorum) 098.40
metastatic 360.11
migraine 346.8 ☑
neonatorum, newborn 771.6
gonococcal 098.40
nodosa 360.14
phlyctenular 370.31
with ulcer (see also Ulcer, cornea) 370.00
sympathetic 360.11
Ophthalmitis — see Ophthalmia
Ophthalmocele (congenital) 743.66
Ophthalmoneuromyelitis 341.0
Ophthalmopathy, infiltrative with thyrotoxicosis 242.0 ☑
Ophthalmoplegia — see also Strabismus 378.9
anterior internuclear 378.86
ataxia-areflexia syndrome 357.0
bilateral 378.9
diabetic 250.5 ☑ [378.86]
due to secondary diabetes 249.5 ☑ [378.86]
exophthalmic 242.0 ☑ [376.22]
external 378.55
progressive 378.72
total 378.56
internal (complete) (total) 367.52
internuclear 378.86
migraine 346.2 ☑
painful 378.55
Parinaud's 378.81
progressive external 378.72
supranuclear, progressive 333.0
total (external) 378.56
internal 367.52
unilateral 378.9
Opisthognathism 524.00
Opisthorchiasis (felineus) (tenuicollis) (viverrini) 121.0
Opisthotonos, opisthotonus 781.0
Opitz's disease (congestive splenomegaly) 289.51
Opiumism — see also Dependence 304.0 ☑
Oppenheim's disease 358.8
Oppenheim-Urbach disease or syndrome (necrobiosis lipoidica diabeticorum) 250.8 ☑ [709.3]
due to secondary diabetes 249.8 ☑ [709.3]
Opsoclonia 379.59
Optic nerve — see condition
Orbit — see condition
Orchioblastoma (M9071/3) 186.9
Orchitis (nonspecific) (septic) 604.90
with abscess 604.0
blennorrhagic (acute) 098.13
chronic or duration of 2 months or over 098.33
diphtheritic 032.89 [604.91]
filarial 125.9 [604.91]

Orchitis — *continued*
  gangrenous 604.99
  gonococcal (acute) 098.13
    chronic or duration of 2 months or over 098.33
  mumps 072.0
  parotidea 072.0
  suppurative 604.99
  syphilitic 095.8 *[604.91]*
  tuberculous (*see also* Tuberculosis) 016.5 ☑ *[608.81]*
Orf 051.2
Organic — *see also* condition
  heart — *see* Disease, heart
  insufficiency 799.89
Oriental
  bilharziasis 120.2
  schistosomiasis 120.2
  sore 085.1
Orientation
  ego-dystonic sexual 302.0
Orifice — *see* condition
Origin, both great vessels from right ventricle 745.11
Ormond's disease or syndrome 593.4
Ornithosis 073.9
  with
    complication 073.8
      specified NEC 073.7
    pneumonia 073.0
    pneumonitis (lobular) 073.0
Orodigitofacial dysostosis 759.89
Oropouche fever 066.3
Orotaciduria, oroticaciduria (congenital) (hereditary) (pyrimidine deficiency) 281.4
Oroya fever 088.0
Orthodontics V58.5
  adjustment V53.4
  aftercare V58.5
  fitting V53.4
Orthopnea 786.02
Orthoptic training V57.4
Osgood-Schlatter
  disease 732.4
  osteochondrosis 732.4
Osler's
  disease (M9950/1) (polycythemia vera) 238.4
  nodes 421.0
Osler-Rendu disease (familial hemorrhagic telangiectasia) 448.0
Osler-Vaquez disease (M9950/1) (polycythemia vera) 238.4
Osler-Weber-Rendu syndrome (familial hemorrhagic telangiectasia) 448.0
Osmidrosis 705.89
Osseous — *see* condition
Ossification
  artery — *see* Arteriosclerosis
  auricle (ear) 380.39
  bronchus 519.19
  cardiac (*see also* Degeneration, myocardial) 429.1
  cartilage (senile) 733.99
  coronary (artery) — *see* Arteriosclerosis, coronary
  diaphragm 728.10
  ear 380.39
    middle (*see also* Otosclerosis) 387.9
  falx cerebri 349.2
  fascia 728.10
  fontanel
    defective or delayed 756.0
    premature 756.0
  heart (*see also* Degeneration, myocardial) 429.1
    valve — *see* Endocarditis
  larynx 478.79
  ligament
    posterior longitudinal 724.8
      cervical 723.7
  meninges (cerebral) 349.2
    spinal 336.8
  multiple, eccentric centers 733.99
  muscle 728.10

Ossification — *continued*
  muscle — *continued*
    heterotopic, postoperative 728.13
  myocardium, myocardial (*see also* Degeneration, myocardial) 429.1
  penis 607.81
  periarticular 728.89
  sclera 379.16
  tendon 727.82
  trachea 519.19
  tympanic membrane (*see also* Tympanosclerosis) 385.00
  vitreous (humor) 360.44
Osteitis — *see also* Osteomyelitis 730.2 ☑
  acute 730.0 ☑
  alveolar 526.5
  chronic 730.1 ☑
  condensans (ilii) 733.5
  deformans (Paget's) 731.0
    due to or associated with malignant neoplasm (*see also* Neoplasm, bone, malignant) 170.9 *[731.1]*
  due to yaws 102.6
  fibrosa NEC 733.29
    cystica (generalisata) 252.01
    disseminata 756.59
    osteoplastica 252.01
  fragilitans 756.51
  Garré's (sclerosing) 730.1 ☑
  infectious (acute) (subacute) 730.0 ☑
    chronic or old 730.1 ☑
  jaw (acute) (chronic) (lower) (neonatal) (suppurative) (upper) 526.4
  parathyroid 252.01
  petrous bone (*see also* Petrositis) 383.20
  pubis 733.5
  sclerotic, nonsuppurative 730.1 ☑
  syphilitic 095.5
  tuberculosa
    cystica (of Jüngling) 135
    multiplex cystoides 135
Osteoarthritica spondylitis (spine) — *see also* Spondylosis 721.90
Osteoarthritis — *see also* Osteoarthrosis 715.9 ☑
  distal interphalangeal 715.9 ☑
  hyperplastic 731.2
  interspinalis (*see also* Spondylosis) 721.90
  spine, spinal NEC (*see also* Spondylosis) 721.90
Osteoarthropathy — *see also* Osteoarthrosis 715.9 ☑
  chronic idiopathic hypertrophic 757.39
  familial idiopathic 757.39
  hypertrophic pulmonary 731.2
    secondary 731.2
  idiopathic hypertrophic 757.39
  primary hypertrophic 731.2
  pulmonary hypertrophic 731.2
  secondary hypertrophic 731.2
Osteoarthrosis (degenerative) (hypertrophic) (rheumatoid) 715.9 ☑

Note — Use the following fifth-digit subclassification with category 715:

0 site unspecified

1 shoulder region

2 upper arm

3 forearm

4 hand

5 pelvic region and thigh

6 lower leg

7 ankle and foot

8 other specified sites except spine

9 multiple sites

  Deformans alkaptonurica 270.2
  generalized 715.09
  juvenilis (Köhler's) 732.5
  localized 715.3 ☑
    idiopathic 715.1 ☑
    primary 715.1 ☑

Osteoarthrosis — *continued*
  localized — *continued*
    secondary 715.2 ☑
  multiple sites, not specified as generalized 715.89
  polyarticular 715.09
  spine (*see also* Spondylosis) 721.90
  temporomandibular joint 524.69
Osteoblastoma (M9200/0) — *see* Neoplasm, bone, benign
Osteochondritis — *see also* Osteochondrosis 732.9
  dissecans 732.7
  hip 732.7
  ischiopubica 732.1
  multiple 756.59
  syphilitic (congenital) 090.0
Osteochondrodermodysplasia 756.59
Osteochondrodystrophy 277.5
  deformans 277.5
  familial 277.5
  fetalis 756.4
Osteochondrolysis 732.7
Osteochondroma (M9210/0) — *see also* Neoplasm, bone, benign
  multiple, congenital 756.4
Osteochondromatosis (M9210/1) 238.0
  synovial 727.82
Osteochondromyxosarcoma (M9180/3) — *see* Neoplasm, bone, malignant
Osteochondropathy NEC 732.9
Osteochondrosarcoma (M9180/3) — *see* Neoplasm, bone, malignant
Osteochondrosis 732.9
  acetabulum 732.1
  adult spine 732.8
  astragalus 732.5
  Blount's 732.4
  Buchanan's (juvenile osteochondrosis of iliac crest) 732.1
  Buchman's (juvenile osteochondrosis) 732.1
  Burns' 732.3
  calcaneus 732.5
  capitular epiphysis (femur) 732.1
  carpal
    lunate (wrist) 732.3
    scaphoid 732.3
  coxae juvenilis 732.1
  deformans juvenilis (coxae) (hip) 732.1
    Scheuermann's 732.0
    spine 732.0
    tibia 732.4
    vertebra 732.0
  Diaz's (astragalus) 732.5
  dissecans (knee) (shoulder) 732.7
  femoral capital epiphysis 732.1
  femur (head) (juvenile) 732.1
  foot (juvenile) 732.5
  Freiberg's (disease) (second metatarsal) 732.5
  Haas' 732.3
  Haglund's (os tibiale externum) 732.5
  hand (juvenile) 732.3
  head of
    femur 732.1
    humerus (juvenile) 732.3
  hip (juvenile) 732.1
  humerus (juvenile) 732.3
  iliac crest (juvenile) 732.1
  ilium (juvenile) 732.1
  ischiopubic synchondrosis 732.1
  Iselin's (osteochondrosis fifth metatarsal) 732.5
  juvenile, juvenilis 732.6
    arm 732.3
    capital femoral epiphysis 732.1
    capitellum humeri 732.3
    capitular epiphysis 732.1
    carpal scaphoid 732.3
    clavicle, sternal epiphysis 732.6
    coxae 732.1
    deformans 732.1
    foot 732.5
    hand 732.3
    hip and pelvis 732.1
    lower extremity, except foot 732.4

Osteochondrosis — *continued*
  juvenile, juvenilis — *continued*
    lunate, wrist 732.3
    medial cuneiform bone 732.5
    metatarsal (head) 732.5
    metatarsophalangeal 732.5
    navicular, ankle 732.5
    patella 732.4
    primary patellar center (of Köhler) 732.4
    specified site NEC 732.6
    spine 732.0
    tarsal scaphoid 732.5
    tibia (epiphysis) (tuberosity) 732.4
    upper extremity 732.3
    vertebra (body) (Calvé) 732.0
      epiphyseal plates (of Scheuermann) 732.0
  Kienböck's (disease) 732.3
  Köhler's (disease) (navicular, ankle) 732.5
    patellar 732.4
    tarsal navicular 732.5
  Legg-Calvé-Perthes (disease) 732.1
  lower extremity (juvenile) 732.4
  lunate bone 732.3
  Mauclaire's 732.3
  metacarpal heads (of Mauclaire) 732.3
  metatarsal (fifth) (head) (second) 732.5
  navicular, ankle 732.5
  os calcis 732.5
  Osgood-Schlatter 732.4
  os tibiale externum 732.5
  Panner's 732.3
  patella (juvenile) 732.4
  patellar center
    primary (of Köhler) 732.4
    secondary (of Sinding-Larsen) 732.4
  pelvis (juvenile) 732.1
  Pierson's 732.1
  radial head (juvenile) 732.3
  Scheuermann's 732.0
  Sever's (calcaneum) 732.5
  Sinding-Larsen (secondary patellar center) 732.4
  spine (juvenile) 732.0
    adult 732.8
  symphysis pubis (of Pierson) (juvenile) 732.1
  syphilitic (congenital) 090.0
  tarsal (navicular) (scaphoid) 732.5
  tibia (proximal) (tubercle) 732.4
  tuberculous — *see* Tuberculosis, bone
  ulna 732.3
  upper extremity (juvenile) 732.3
  van Neck's (juvenile osteochondrosis) 732.1
  vertebral (juvenile) 732.0
    adult 732.8
Osteoclastoma (M9250/1) 238.0
  malignant (M9250/3) — *see* Neoplasm, bone, malignant
Osteocopic pain 733.90
Osteodynia 733.90
Osteodystrophy
  azotemic 588.0
  chronica deformans hypertrophica 731.0
  congenital 756.50
    specified type NEC 756.59
  deformans 731.0
  fibrosa localisata 731.0
  parathyroid 252.01
  renal 588.0
Osteofibroma (M9262/0) — *see* Neoplasm, bone, benign
Osteofibrosarcoma (M9182/3) — *see* Neoplasm, bone, malignant
Osteogenesis imperfecta 756.51
Osteogenic — *see* condition
Osteoma (M9180/0) — *see also* Neoplasm, bone, benign
  osteoid (M9191/0) (*see also* Neoplasm, bone, benign)
    giant (M9200/0) — *see* Neoplasm, bone, benign
Osteomalacia 268.2
  chronica deformans hypertrophica 731.0
  due to vitamin D deficiency 268.2
  infantile (*see also* Rickets) 268.0
  juvenile (*see also* Rickets) 268.0

☑ Additional Digit Required — Refer to the Tabular List for Digit Selection   ᴵᴺᴰ Subterms under main terms may continue to next column or page

☑ **Additional Digit Required** — Refer to the Tabular List for Digit Selection ▽ **Subterms under main terms may continue to next column or page**

2015 ICD-9-CM ►◄ Revised Text ● New Line ▲ Revised Code Volume 2 — 221

Outcome of delivery — *continued*
  single — *continued*
    stillborn V27.1
    twins V27.9
      both liveborn V27.2
      both stillborn V27.4
      one liveborn, one stillborn V27.3
Outlet — *see also* condition
  syndrome (thoracic) 353.0
Outstanding ears (bilateral) 744.29
Ovalocytosis (congenital) (hereditary) — *see also* Elliptocytosis 282.1
Ovarian — *see also* condition
  pregnancy — *see* Pregnancy, ovarian
  remnant syndrome 620.8
  vein syndrome 593.4
Ovaritis (cystic) — *see also* Salpingo-oophoritis 614.2
Ovary, ovarian — *see* condition
Overactive — *see also* Hyperfunction
  bladder 596.51
  eye muscle (*see also* Strabismus) 378.9
  hypothalamus 253.8
  thyroid (*see also* Thyrotoxicosis) 242.9 ☑
Overactivity, child 314.01
Overbite (deep) (excessive) (horizontal) (vertical) 524.29
Overbreathing — *see also* Hyperventilation 786.01
Overconscientious personality 301.4
Overdevelopment — *see also* Hypertrophy
  breast (female) (male) 611.1
  nasal bones 738.0
  prostate, congenital 752.89
Overdistention — *see* Distention
Overdose overdosage (drug) 977.9
  specified drug or substance — *see* Table of Drugs and Chemicals
Overeating 783.6
  nonorganic origin 307.51
Overexertion (effects) (exhaustion) 994.5
Overexposure (effects) 994.9
  exhaustion 994.4
Overfeeding — *see also* Overeating 783.6
Overfill, endodontic 526.62
Overgrowth, bone NEC 733.99
Overhanging
  tooth restoration 525.62
  unrepairable, dental restorative materials 525.62
Overheated (effects) (places) — *see* Heat
Overinhibited child 313.0
Overjet 524.29
  excessive horizontal 524.26
Overlaid, overlying (suffocation) 994.7
Overlap
  excessive horizontal 524.26
Overlapping toe (acquired) 735.8
  congenital (fifth toe) 755.66
Overload
  fluid 276.69
    due to transfusion (blood) (blood components) 276.61
  iron, due to repeated red blood cell transfusions 275.02
  potassium (K) 276.7
  sodium (Na) 276.0
  transfusion associated circulatory (TACO) 276.61
Overnutrition — *see also* Hyperalimentation 783.6
Overproduction — *see also* Hypersecretion
  ACTH 255.3
  cortisol 255.0
  growth hormone 253.0
  thyroid-stimulating hormone (TSH) 242.8 ☑
Overriding
  aorta 747.21
  finger (acquired) 736.29
    congenital 755.59
  toe (acquired) 735.8
    congenital 755.66
Oversize
  fetus (weight of 4500 grams or more) 766.0
    affecting management of pregnancy 656.6 ☑

Oversize — *continued*
  fetus — *continued*
    causing disproportion 653.5 ☑
      with obstructed labor 660.1 ☑
    affecting fetus or newborn 763.1
Overstimulation, ovarian 256.1
Overstrained 780.79
  heart — *see* Hypertrophy, cardiac
Overweight — *see also* Obesity 278.02
Overwork 780.79
Oviduct — *see* condition
Ovotestis 752.7
Ovulation (cycle)
  failure or lack of 628.0
  pain 625.2
Ovum
  blighted 631.8
  donor V59.70
    over age 35 V59.73
      anonymous recipient V59.73
      designated recipient V59.74
    under age 35 V59.71
      anonymous recipient V59.71
      designated recipient V59.72
  dropsical 631.8
  pathologic 631.8
Owren's disease or syndrome (parahemophilia) — *see also* Defect, coagulation 286.3
Oxalosis 271.8
Oxaluria 271.8
Ox heart — *see* Hypertrophy, cardiac
OX syndrome 758.6
Oxycephaly, oxycephalic 756.0
  syphilitic, congenital 090.0
Oxyuriasis 127.4
Oxyuris vermicularis (infestation) 127.4
Ozena 472.0

P

Pacemaker syndrome 429.4
Pachyderma, pachydermia 701.8
  laryngis 478.5
  laryngitis 478.79
  larynx (verrucosa) 478.79
Pachydermatitis 701.8
Pachydermatocele (congenital) 757.39
  acquired 701.8
Pachydermatosis 701.8
Pachydermoperiostitis
  secondary 731.2
Pachydermoperiostosis
  primary idiopathic 757.39
  secondary 731.2
Pachymeningitis (adhesive) (basal) (brain) (cerebral) (cervical) (chronic) (circumscribed) (external) (fibrous) (hemorrhagic) (hypertrophic) (internal) (purulent) (spinal) (suppurative) — *see also* Meningitis 322.9
  gonococcal 098.82
Pachyonychia (congenital) 757.5
  acquired 703.8
Pachyperiosteodermia
  primary or idiopathic 757.39
  secondary 731.2
Pachyperiostosis
  primary or idiopathic 757.39
  secondary 731.2
Pacinian tumor (M9507/0) — *see* Neoplasm, skin, benign
Pads, knuckle or Garrod's 728.79
Paget's disease (osteitis deformans) 731.0
  with infiltrating duct carcinoma of the breast (M8541/3) — *see* Neoplasm, breast, malignant
  bone 731.0
    osteosarcoma in (M9184/3) — *see* Neoplasm, bone, malignant
  breast (M8540/3) 174.0
  extramammary (M8542/3) (*see also* Neoplasm, skin, malignant)
    anus 154.3
    skin 173.59
  malignant (M8540/3)
    breast 174.0

Paget's disease — *continued*
  malignant — *continued*
    specified site NEC (M8542/3) — *see* Neoplasm, skin, malignant
    unspecified site 174.0
  mammary (M8540/3) 174.0
  necrosis of bone 731.0
  nipple (M8540/3) 174.0
  osteitis deformans 731.0
Paget-Schroetter syndrome (intermittent venous claudication) 453.89
Pain(s) — *see also* Painful 780.96
  abdominal 789.0 ☑
  acute 338.19
    due to trauma 338.11
    postoperative 338.18
      post-thoracotomy 338.12
  adnexa (uteri) 625.9
  alimentary, due to vascular insufficiency 557.9
  anginoid (*see also* Pain, precordial) 786.51
  anus 569.42
  arch 729.5
  arm 729.5
  axillary 729.5
  back (postural) 724.5
    low 724.2
    psychogenic 307.89
  bile duct 576.9
  bladder 788.99
  bone 733.90
  breast 611.71
    psychogenic 307.89
  broad ligament 625.9
  cancer associated 338.3
  cartilage NEC 733.90
  cecum 789.0 ☑
  cervicobrachial 723.3
  chest (central) 786.50
    atypical 786.59
    midsternal 786.51
    musculoskeletal 786.59
    noncardiac 786.59
    substernal 786.51
    wall (anterior) 786.52
  chronic 338.29
    associated with significant psychosocial dysfunction 338.4
    due to trauma 338.21
    postoperative 338.28
      post-thoracotomy 338.22
    syndrome 338.4
  coccyx 724.79
  colon 789.0 ☑
  common duct 576.9
  coronary — *see* Angina
  costochondral 786.52
  diaphragm 786.52
  due to (presence of) any device, implant, or graft classifiable to 996.0–996.5 — *see* Complications, due to (presence of) any device, implant, or graft classified to 996.0–996.5 NEC
    malignancy (primary) (secondary) 338.3
  ear (*see also* Otalgia) 388.70
  epigastric, epigastrium 789.06
  extremity (lower) (upper) 729.5
  eye 379.91
  face, facial 784.0
    atypical 350.2
    nerve 351.8
  false (labor) 644.1 ☑
  female genital organ NEC 625.9
    psychogenic 307.89
  finger 729.5
  flank 789.0 ☑
  foot 729.5
  gallbladder 575.9
  gas (intestinal) 787.3
  gastric 536.8
  generalized 780.96
  genital organ
    female 625.9
    male 608.9
    psychogenic 307.89
  groin 789.0 ☑

Pain(s) — *see also* Painful — *continued*
  growing 781.99
  hand 729.5
  head (*see also* Headache) 784.0
  heart (see also Pain, precordial) 786.51
  infraorbital (*see also* Neuralgia, trigeminal) 350.1
  intermenstrual 625.2
  jaw 784.92
  joint 719.40
    ankle 719.47
    elbow 719.42
    foot 719.47
    hand 719.44
    hip 719.45
    knee 719.46
    multiple sites 719.49
    pelvic region 719.45
    psychogenic 307.89
    shoulder (region) 719.41
    specified site NEC 719.48
    wrist 719.43
  kidney 788.0
  labor, false or spurious 644.1 ☑
  laryngeal 784.1
  leg 729.5
  limb 729.5
  low back 724.2
  lumbar region 724.2
  mandible, mandibular 784.92
  mastoid (*see also* Otalgia) 388.70
  maxilla 784.92
  menstrual 625.3
  metacarpophalangeal (joint) 719.44
  metatarsophalangeal (joint) 719.47
  mouth 528.9
  muscle 729.1
    intercostal 786.59
  musculoskeletal (see also Pain, by site) 729.1
  nasal 478.19
  nasopharynx 478.29
  neck NEC 723.1
    psychogenic 307.89
  neoplasm related (acute) (chronic) 338.3
  nerve NEC 729.2
  neuromuscular 729.1
  nose 478.19
  ocular 379.91
  ophthalmic 379.91
  orbital region 379.91
  osteocopic 733.90
  ovary 625.9
    psychogenic 307.89
  over heart (*see also* Pain, precordial) 786.51
  ovulation 625.2
  pelvic (female) 625.9
    male NEC 789.0 ☑
      psychogenic 307.89
    psychogenic 307.89
  penis 607.9
    psychogenic 307.89
  pericardial (*see also* Pain, precordial) 786.51
  perineum
    female 625.9
    male 608.9
  pharynx 478.29
  pleura, pleural, pleuritic 786.52
  postoperative 338.18
    acute 338.18
    chronic 338.28
  post-thoracotomy 338.12
    acute 338.12
    chronic 338.22
  preauricular 388.70
  precordial (region) 786.51
    psychogenic 307.89
  premenstrual 625.4
  psychogenic 307.80
    cardiovascular system 307.89
    gastrointestinal system 307.89
    genitourinary system 307.89
    heart 307.89
    musculoskeletal system 307.89
    respiratory system 307.89
    skin 306.3
  radicular (spinal) (*see also* Radiculitis) 729.2

☑ Additional Digit Required — Refer to the Tabular List for Digit Selection   ▼ Subterms under main terms may continue to next column or page

222 — Volume 2   ▶◀ Revised Text   ● New Line   ▲ Revised Code   2015 ICD-9-CM

Pain(s) — *see also* Painful — *continued*
  rectum 569.42
  respiration 786.52
  retrosternal 786.51
  rheumatic NEC 729.0
    muscular 729.1
  rib 786.50
  root (spinal) (*see also* Radiculitis) 729.2
  round ligament (stretch) 625.9
  sacroiliac 724.6
  sciatic 724.3
  scrotum 608.9
    psychogenic 307.89
  seminal vesicle 608.9
  sinus 478.19
  skin 782.0
  spermatic cord 608.9
  spinal root (*see also* Radiculitis) 729.2
  stomach 536.8
    psychogenic 307.89
  substernal 786.51
  testis 608.9
    psychogenic 307.89
  thoracic spine 724.1
    with radicular and visceral pain 724.4
  throat 784.1
  tibia 733.90
  toe 729.5
  tongue 529.6
  tooth 525.9
  total hip replacement 996.77
  total knee replacement 996.77
  trigeminal (*see also* Neuralgia, trigeminal) 350.1
  tumor associated 338.3
  umbilicus 789.05
  ureter 788.0
  urinary (organ) (system) 788.0
  uterus 625.9
    psychogenic 307.89
  vagina 625.9
  vertebrogenic (syndrome) 724.5
  vesical 788.99
  vulva 625.9
  xiphoid 733.90
Painful — *see also* Pain
  arc syndrome 726.19
  coitus
    female 625.0
    male 608.89
      psychogenic 302.76
  ejaculation (semen) 608.89
    psychogenic 302.79
  erection 607.3
  feet syndrome 266.2
  menstruation 625.3
    psychogenic 306.52
  micturition 788.1
  ophthalmoplegia 378.55
  respiration 786.52
  scar NEC 709.2
  urination 788.1
  wire sutures 998.89
Painters' colic 984.9
  specified type of lead — *see* Table of Drugs and Chemicals
Palate — *see* condition
Palatoplegia 528.9
Palatoschisis — *see also* Cleft, palate 749.00
Palilalia 784.69
Palindromic arthritis — *see also* Rheumatism, palindromic 719.3 ☑
Palliative care V66.7
Pallor 782.61
  temporal, optic disc 377.15
Palmar — *see also* condition
  fascia — *see* condition
Palpable
  cecum 569.89
  kidney 593.89
  liver 573.9
  lymph nodes 785.6
  ovary 620.8
  prostate 602.9
  spleen (*see also* Splenomegaly) 789.2
  uterus 625.8

Palpitation (heart) 785.1
  psychogenic 306.2
Palsy — *see also* Paralysis 344.9
  atrophic diffuse 335.20
  Bell's 351.0
    newborn 767.5
  birth 767.7
  brachial plexus 353.0
    fetus or newborn 767.6
  brain (*see also* Palsy, cerebral)
    noncongenital or noninfantile 344.89
      late effect — *see* Late effect(s) (of) cerebrovascular disease
    syphilitic 094.89
      congenital 090.49
  bulbar (chronic) (progressive) 335.22
    pseudo NEC 335.23
    supranuclear NEC 344.8 ☑
  cerebral (congenital) (infantile) (spastic) 343.9
    athetoid 333.71
    diplegic 343.0
      late effect — *see* Late effect(s) (of) cerebrovascular disease
    hemiplegic 343.1
    monoplegic 343.3
    noncongenital or noninfantile 437.8
      late effect — *see* Late effect(s) (of) cerebrovascular disease
    paraplegic 343.0
    quadriplegic 343.2
    spastic, not congenital or infantile 344.89
    syphilitic 094.89
      congenital 090.49
    tetraplegic 343.2
  cranial nerve (*see also* Disorder, nerve, cranial)
    multiple 352.6
  creeping 335.21
  divers' 993.3
  Erb's (birth injury) 767.6
  facial 351.0
    newborn 767.5
  glossopharyngeal 352.2
  Klumpke (-Déjérine) 767.6
  lead 984.9
    specified type of lead — *see* Table of Drugs and Chemicals
  median nerve (tardy) 354.0
  peroneal nerve (acute) (tardy) 355.3
  progressive supranuclear 333.0
  pseudobulbar NEC 335.23
  radial nerve (acute) 354.3
  seventh nerve 351.0
    newborn 767.5
  shaking (*see also* Parkinsonism) 332.0
  spastic (cerebral) (spinal) 343.9
    hemiplegic 343.1
  specified nerve NEC — *see* Disorder, nerve
  supranuclear NEC 356.8
    progressive 333.0
  ulnar nerve (tardy) 354.2
  wasting 335.21
Paltauf-Sternberg disease 201.9 ☑
Paludism — *see* Malaria
Panama fever 084.0
Panaris (with lymphangitis) 681.9
  finger 681.02
  toe 681.11
Panaritium (with lymphangitis) 681.9
  finger 681.02
  toe 681.11
Panarteritis (nodosa) 446.0
  brain or cerebral 437.4
Pancake heart 793.2
  with cor pulmonale (chronic) 416.9
Pancarditis (acute) (chronic) 429.89
  with
    rheumatic
      fever (active) (acute) (chronic) (subacute) 391.8
        inactive or quiescent 398.99
  rheumatic, acute 391.8
    chronic or inactive 398.99

Pancoast's syndrome or tumor (carcinoma, pulmonary apex) (M8010/3) 162.3
Pancoast-Tobias syndrome (M8010/3) (carcinoma, pulmonary apex) 162.3
Pancolitis 556.6
Pancreas, pancreatic — *see* condition
Pancreatitis 577.0
  acute (edematous) (hemorrhagic) (recurrent) 577.0
  annular 577.0
  apoplectic 577.0
  calcerceous 577.0
  chronic (infectious) 577.1
    recurrent 577.1
  cystic 577.2
  fibrous 577.8
  gangrenous 577.0
  hemorrhagic (acute) 577.0
  interstitial (chronic) 577.1
    acute 577.0
  malignant 577.0
  mumps 072.3
  painless 577.1
  recurrent 577.1
  relapsing 577.1
  subacute 577.0
  suppurative 577.0
  syphilitic 095.8
Pancreatolithiasis 577.8
Pancytolysis 289.9
Pancytopenia (acquired) 284.19
  with
    malformations 284.09
    myelodysplastic syndrome — *see* Syndrome, myelodysplastic
  congenital 284.09
  due to
    antineoplastic chemotherapy 284.11
    drug, specified NEC 284.12
  specified NEC 284.19
Panencephalitis — *see also* Encephalitis
  subacute, sclerosing 046.2
Panhematopenia 284.81
  congenital 284.09
  constitutional 284.09
  splenic, primary 289.4
Panhemocytopenia 284.81
  congenital 284.09
  constitutional 284.09
Panhypogonadism 257.2
Panhypopituitarism 253.2
  prepubertal 253.3
Panic (attack) (state) 300.01
  reaction to exceptional stress (transient) 308.0
Panmyelopathy, familial constitutional 284.09
Panmyelophthisis 284.2
  acquired (secondary) 284.81
  congenital 284.2
  idiopathic 284.9
Panmyelosis (acute) (M9951/1) 238.79
Panner's disease 732.3
  capitellum humeri 732.3
  head of humerus 732.3
  tarsal navicular (bone) (osteochondrosis) 732.5
Panneuritis endemica 265.0 [357.4]
Panniculitis 729.30
  back 724.8
  knee 729.31
  mesenteric 567.82
  neck 723.6
  nodular, nonsuppurative 729.30
  sacral 724.8
  specified site NEC 729.39
Panniculus adiposus (abdominal) 278.1
Pannus (corneal) 370.62
  abdominal (symptomatic) 278.1
  allergic eczematous 370.62
  degenerativus 370.62
  keratic 370.62
  rheumatoid — *see* Arthritis, rheumatoid
  trachomatosus, trachomatous (active) 076.1 [370.62]
    late effect 139.1

Panophthalmitis 360.02
Panotitis — *see* Otitis media
Pansinusitis (chronic) (hyperplastic) (nonpurulent) (purulent) 473.8
  acute 461.8
  due to fungus NEC 117.9
  tuberculous (*see also* Tuberculosis) 012.8 ☑
Panuveitis 360.12
  sympathetic 360.11
Panvalvular disease — *see* Endocarditis, mitral
Papageienkrankheit 073.9
Papanicolaou smear
  anus 796.70
    with
      atypical squamous cells
        cannot exclude high grade squamous intraepithelial lesion (ASC-H) 796.72
        of undetermined significance (ASC-US) 796.71
      cytologic evidence of malignancy 796.76
      high grade squamous intraepithelial lesion (HGSIL) 796.74
      low grade squamous intraepithelial lesion (LGSIL) 796.73
    glandular 796.70
    specified finding NEC 796.79
    unsatisfactory cytology 796.78
  cervix (screening test) V76.2
    as part of gynecological examination V72.31
    for suspected malignant neoplasm V76.2
      no disease found V71.1
    inadequate cytology sample 795.08
    nonspecific abnormal finding 795.00
      with
        atypical squamous cells
          cannot exclude high grade squamous intraepithelial lesion (ASC-H) 795.02
          of undetermined significance (ASC-US) 795.01
        cytologic evidence of malignancy 795.06
        high grade squamous intraepithelial lesion (HGSIL) 795.04
        low grade squamous intraepithelial lesion (LGSIL) 795.03
    nonspecific finding NEC 795.09
    to confirm findings of recent normal smear following initial abnormal smear V72.32
    satisfactory smear but lacking transformation zone 795.07
    unsatisfactory cervical cytology 795.08
  other specified site (*see also* Screening, malignant neoplasm)
    for suspected malignant neoplasm (*see also* Screening, malignant neoplasm)
      no disease found V71.1
    nonspecific abnormal finding 796.9
  vagina V76.47
    with
      atypical squamous cells
        cannot exclude high grade squamous intraepithelial lesion (ASC-H) 795.12
        of undetermined significance (ASC-US) 795.11
      cytologic evidence of malignancy 795.16
      high grade squamous intraepithelial lesion (HGSIL) 795.14
      low grade squamous intraepithelial lesion (LGSIL) 795.13
    abnormal NEC 795.19
    following hysterectomy for malignant condition V67.01
    inadequate cytology sample 795.18
    unsatisfactory cytology 795.18
Papilledema 377.00
  associated with
    decreased ocular pressure 377.02

☑ Additional Digit Required — Refer to the Tabular List for Digit Selection

▽ Subterms under main terms may continue to next column or page

Papilledema — *continued*
 associated with — *continued*
  increased intracranial pressure 377.01
  retinal disorder 377.03
 choked disc 377.00
 infectional 377.00
Papillitis 377.31
 anus 569.49
 chronic lingual 529.4
 necrotizing, kidney 584.7
 optic 377.31
 rectum 569.49
 renal, necrotizing 584.7
 tongue 529.0
Papilloma (M8050/0) — *see also* Neoplasm, by site, benign

> Note — Except where otherwise indicated, the morphological varieties of papilloma in the list below should be coded by site as for "Neoplasm, benign."

 acuminatum (female) (male) 078.11
 bladder (urinary) (transitional cell) (M8120/1) 236.7
  benign (M8120/0) 223.3
 choroid plexus (M9390/0) 225.0
  anaplastic type (M9390/3) 191.5
  malignant (M9390/3) 191.5
 ductal (M8503/0)
 dyskeratotic (M8052/0)
 epidermoid (M8052/0)
 hyperkeratotic (M8052/0)
 intracystic (M8504/0)
 intraductal (M8503/0)
 inverted (M8053/0)
 keratotic (M8052/0)
 parakeratotic (M8052/0)
 pinta (primary) 103.0
 renal pelvis (transitional cell) (M8120/1) 236.99
  benign (M8120/0) 223.1
 Schneiderian (M8121/0)
  specified site — *see* Neoplasm, by site, benign
  unspecified site 212.0
 serous surface (M8461/0)
  borderline malignancy (M8461/1)
   specified site — *see* Neoplasm, by site, uncertain behavior
   unspecified site 236.2
  specified site — *see* Neoplasm, by site, benign
  unspecified site 220
 squamous (cell) (M8052/0)
 transitional (cell) (M8120/0)
  bladder (urinary) (M8120/1) 236.7
  inverted type (M8121/1) — *see* Neoplasm, by site, uncertain behavior
  renal pelvis (M8120/1) 236.91
  ureter (M8120/1) 236.91
 ureter (transitional cell) (M8120/1) 236.91
  benign (M8120/0) 223.2
 urothelial (M8120/1) — *see* Neoplasm, by site, uncertain behavior
 verrucous (M8051/0)
 villous (M8261/1) — *see* Neoplasm, by site, uncertain behavior
 yaws, plantar or palmar 102.1
Papillomata, multiple, of yaws 102.1
Papillomatosis (M8060/0) — *see also* Neoplasm, by site, benign
 confluent and reticulate 701.8
 cutaneous 701.8
 ductal, breast 610.1
 Gougerot-Carteaud (confluent reticulate) 701.8
 intraductal (diffuse) (M8505/0) — *see* Neoplasm, by site, benign
 subareolar duct (M8506/0) 217
Papillon-Léage and Psaume syndrome (orodigitofacial dysostosis) 759.89
Papule 709.8
 carate (primary) 103.0
 fibrous, of nose (M8724/0) 216.3
 pinta (primary) 103.0
Papulosis
 lymphomatoid 709.8

Papulosis — *continued*
 malignant 447.8
Papyraceous fetus 779.89
 complicating pregnancy 646.0 ☑
Paracephalus 759.7
Parachute mitral valve 746.5
Paracoccidioidomycosis 116.1
 mucocutaneous-lymphangitic 116.1
 pulmonary 116.1
 visceral 116.1
Paracoccidiomycosis — *see* Paracoccidioidomycosis
Paracusis 388.40
Paradentosis 523.5
Paradoxical facial movements 374.43
Paraffinoma 999.9
Paraganglioma (M8680/1)
 adrenal (M8700/0) 227.0
  malignant (M8700/3) 194.0
 aortic body (M8691/1) 237.3
  malignant (M8691/3) 194.6
 carotid body (M8692/1) 237.3
  malignant (M8692/3) 194.5
 chromaffin (M8700/0) (*see also* Neoplasm, by site, benign)
  malignant (M8700/3) — *see* Neoplasm, by site, malignant
 extra-adrenal (M8693/1)
  malignant (M8693/3)
   specified site — *see* Neoplasm, by site, malignant
   unspecified site 194.6
  specified site — *see* Neoplasm, by site, uncertain behavior
  unspecified site 237.3
 glomus jugulare (M8690/1) 237.3
  malignant (M8690/3) 194.6
 jugular (M8690/1) 237.3
  malignant (M8680/3)
   specified site — *see* Neoplasm, by site, malignant
   unspecified site 194.6
 nonchromaffin (M8693/1)
  malignant (M8693/3)
   specified site — *see* Neoplasm, by site, malignant
   unspecified site 194.6
  specified site — *see* Neoplasm, by site, uncertain behavior
  unspecified site 237.3
 parasympathetic (M8682/1)
  specified site — *see* Neoplasm, by site, uncertain behavior
  unspecified site 237.3
 specified site — *see* Neoplasm, by site, uncertain behavior
 sympathetic (M8681/1)
  specified site — *see* Neoplasm, by site, uncertain behavior
  unspecified site 237.3
 unspecified site 237.3
Parageusia 781.1
 psychogenic 306.7
Paragonimiasis 121.2
Paragranuloma, Hodgkin's (M9660/3) 201.0 ☑
Parahemophilia — *see also* Defect, coagulation 286.3
Parakeratosis 690.8
 psoriasiformis 696.2
 variegata 696.2
Paralysis, paralytic (complete) (incomplete) 344.9
 with
  broken
   back — *see* Fracture, vertebra, by site, with spinal cord injury
   neck — *see* Fracture, vertebra, cervical, with spinal cord injury
  fracture, vertebra — *see* Fracture, vertebra, by site, with spinal cord injury
 syphilis 094.89
 abdomen and back muscles 355.9
 abdominal muscles 355.9
 abducens (nerve) 378.54

Paralysis, paralytic — *continued*
 abductor 355.9
  lower extremity 355.8
  upper extremity 354.9
 accessory nerve 352.4
 accommodation 367.51
  hysterical 300.11
 acoustic nerve 388.5
 agitans 332.0
  arteriosclerotic 332.0
 alternating 344.89
  oculomotor 344.89
 amyotrophic 335.20
 ankle 355.8
 anterior serratus 355.9
 anus (sphincter) 569.49
 apoplectic (current episode) (*see also* Disease, cerebrovascular, acute) 436
  late effect — *see* Late effect(s) (of) cerebrovascular disease
 arm 344.40
  affecting
   dominant side 344.41
   nondominant side 344.42
  both 344.2
  hysterical 300.11
  late effect — *see* Late effect(s) (of) cerebrovascular disease
  psychogenic 306.0
   transient 781.4
  traumatic NEC (*see also* Injury, nerve, upper limb) 955.9
 arteriosclerotic (current episode) 437.0
  late effect — *see* Late effect(s) (of) cerebrovascular disease
 ascending (spinal), acute 357.0
 associated, nuclear 344.89
 asthenic bulbar 358.00
 ataxic NEC 334.9
  general 094.1
 athetoid 333.71
 atrophic 356.9
  infantile, acute (*see also* Poliomyelitis, with paralysis) 045.1 ☑
  muscle NEC 355.9
  progressive 335.21
  spinal (acute) (*see also* Poliomyelitis, with paralysis) 045.1 ☑
 attack (*see also* Disease, cerebrovascular, acute) 436
 axillary 353.0
 Babinski-Nageotte's 344.89
 Bell's 351.0
  newborn 767.5
 Benedikt's 344.89
 birth (injury) 767.7
  brain 767.0
  intracranial 767.0
  spinal cord 767.4
 bladder (sphincter) 596.53
  neurogenic 596.54
   with cauda equina syndrome 344.61
  puerperal, postpartum, childbirth 665.5 ☑
  sensory 596.54
   with cauda equina 344.61
  spastic 596.54
   with cauda equina 344.61
 bowel, colon, or intestine (*see also* Ileus) 560.1
 brachial plexus 353.0
  due to birth injury 767.6
  newborn 767.6
 brain
  congenital — *see* Palsy, cerebral
  current episode 437.8
  diplegia 344.2
  hemiplegia 342.9 ☑
   late effect — *see* Late effect(s) (of) cerebrovascular disease
  infantile — *see* Palsy, cerebral
  late effect — *see* Late effect(s) (of) cerebrovascular disease
  monoplegia (*see also* Monoplegia)
   late effect — *see* Late effect(s) (of) cerebrovascular disease

Paralysis, paralytic — *continued*
 brain — *continued*
  paraplegia 344.1
  quadriplegia — *see* Quadriplegia
  syphilitic, congenital 090.49
  triplegia 344.89
 bronchi 519.19
 Brown-Séquard's 344.89
 bulbar (chronic) (progressive) 335.22
  infantile (*see also* Poliomyelitis, bulbar) 045.0 ☑
  poliomyelitic (*see also* Poliomyelitis, bulbar) 045.0 ☑
  pseudo 335.23
  supranuclear 344.89
 bulbospinal 358.00
 cardiac (*see also* Failure, heart) 428.9
 cerebral
  current episode 437.8
  spastic, infantile — *see* Palsy, cerebral
 cerebrocerebellar 437.8
  diplegic infantile 343.0
 cervical
  plexus 353.2
  sympathetic NEC 337.09
 Céstan-Chenais 344.89
 Charcôt-Marie-Tooth type 356.1
 childhood — *see* Palsy, cerebral
 Clark's 343.9
 colon (*see also* Ileus) 560.1
 compressed air 993.3
 compression
  arm NEC 354.9
  cerebral — *see* Paralysis, brain
  leg NEC 355.8
  lower extremity NEC 355.8
  upper extremity NEC 354.9
 congenital (cerebral) (spastic) (spinal) — *see* Palsy, cerebral
 conjugate movement (of eye) 378.81
  cortical (nuclear) (supranuclear) 378.81
 convergence 378.83
 cordis (*see also* Failure, heart) 428.9
 cortical (*see also* Paralysis, brain) 437.8
 cranial or cerebral nerve (*see also* Disorder, nerve, cranial) 352.9
 creeping 335.21
 crossed leg 344.89
 crutch 953.4
 deglutition 784.99
  hysterical 300.11
 dementia 094.1
 descending (spinal) NEC 335.9
 diaphragm (flaccid) 519.4
  due to accidental section of phrenic nerve during procedure 998.2
 digestive organs NEC 564.89
 diplegic — *see* Diplegia
 divergence (nuclear) 378.85
 divers' 993.3
 Duchenne's 335.22
 due to intracranial or spinal birth injury — *see* Palsy, cerebral
 embolic (current episode) (*see also* Embolism, brain) 434.1 ☑
  late effect — *see* Late effect(s) (of) cerebrovascular disease
 enteric (*see also* Ileus) 560.1
  with hernia — *see* Hernia, by site, with obstruction
 Erb (-Duchenne) (birth) (newborn) 767.6
 Erb's syphilitic spastic spinal 094.89
 esophagus 530.89
 essential, infancy (*see also* Poliomyelitis) 045.9 ☑
 extremity
  lower — *see* Paralysis, leg
  spastic (hereditary) 343.3
   noncongenital or noninfantile 344.1
   transient (cause unknown) 781.4
  upper — *see* Paralysis, arm
 eye muscle (extrinsic) 378.55
  intrinsic 367.51
 facial (nerve) 351.0
  birth injury 767.5
  congenital 767.5

Paralysis, paralytic — *continued*
  facial — *continued*
    following operation NEC 998.2
      newborn 767.5
    familial 359.3
      periodic 359.3
      spastic 334.1
    fauces 478.29
    finger NEC 354.9
    foot NEC 355.8
    gait 781.2
    gastric nerve 352.3
    gaze 378.81
    general 094.1
      ataxic 094.1
      insane 094.1
      juvenile 090.40
      progressive 094.1
      tabetic 094.1
    glossopharyngeal (nerve) 352.2
    glottis (*see also* Paralysis, vocal cord) 478.30
    gluteal 353.4
    Gubler (-Millard) 344.89
    hand 354.9
      hysterical 300.11
      psychogenic 306.0
    heart (*see also* Failure, heart) 428.9
    hemifacial, progressive 349.89
    hemiplegic — *see* Hemiplegia
    hyperkalemic periodic (familial) 359.3
    hypertensive (current episode) 437.8
    hypoglossal (nerve) 352.5
    hypokalemic periodic 359.3
    Hyrtl's sphincter (rectum) 569.49
    hysterical 300.11
    ileus (*see also* Ileus) 560.1
    infantile (*see also* Poliomyelitis) 045.9 ☑
      atrophic acute 045.1 ☑
      bulbar 045.0 ☑
      cerebral — *see* Palsy, cerebral
      paralytic 045.1 ☑
      progressive acute 045.9 ☑
      spastic — *see* Palsy, cerebral
      spinal 045.9 ☑
    infective (*see also* Poliomyelitis) 045.9 ☑
    inferior nuclear 344.9
    insane, general or progressive 094.1
    internuclear 378.86
    interosseous 355.9
    intestine (*see also* Ileus) 560.1
    intracranial (current episode) (*see also* Paralysis, brain) 437.8
      due to birth injury 767.0
    iris 379.49
      due to diphtheria (toxin) 032.81 [379.49]
    ischemic, Volkmann's (complicating trauma) 958.6
    isolated sleep, recurrent
    Jackson's 344.89
    jake 357.7
    Jamaica ginger (jake) 357.7
    juvenile general 090.40
    Klumpke (-Déjérine) (birth) (newborn) 767.6
    labioglossal (laryngeal) (pharyngeal) 335.22
    Landry's 357.0
    laryngeal nerve (recurrent) (superior) (*see also* Paralysis, vocal cord) 478.30
    larynx (*see also* Paralysis, vocal cord) 478.30
      due to diphtheria (toxin) 032.3
    late effect
      due to
        birth injury, brain or spinal (cord) — *see* Palsy, cerebral
        edema, brain or cerebral — *see* Paralysis, brain
        lesion
          late effect — *see* Late effect(s) (of) cerebrovascular disease
          spinal (cord) — *see* Paralysis, spinal
    lateral 335.24
    lead 984.9
      specified type of lead — *see* Table of Drugs and Chemicals
    left side — *see* Hemiplegia
    leg 344.30

Paralysis, paralytic — *continued*
  leg — *continued*
    affecting
      dominant side 344.31
      nondominant side 344.32
    both (*see also* Paraplegia) 344.1
    crossed 344.89
    hysterical 300.11
    psychogenic 306.0
    transient or transitory 781.4
      traumatic NEC (*see also* Injury, nerve, lower limb) 956.9
    levator palpebrae superioris 374.31
    limb NEC 344.5
      all four — *see* Quadriplegia
      quadriplegia — *see* Quadriplegia
    lip 528.5
    Lissauer's 094.1
    local 355.9
    lower limb (*see also* Paralysis, leg)
      both (*see also* Paraplegia) 344.1
    lung 518.89
      newborn 770.89
    median nerve 354.1
    medullary (tegmental) 344.89
    mesencephalic NEC 344.89
      tegmental 344.89
    middle alternating 344.89
    Millard-Gubler-Foville 344.89
    monoplegic — *see* Monoplegia
    motor NEC 344.9
      cerebral — *see* Paralysis, brain
      spinal — *see* Paralysis, spinal
    multiple
      cerebral — *see* Paralysis, brain
      spinal — *see* Paralysis, spinal
    muscle (flaccid) 359.9
      due to nerve lesion NEC 355.9
      eye (extrinsic) 378.55
        intrinsic 367.51
        oblique 378.51
      iris sphincter 364.89
      ischemic (complicating trauma) (Volkmann's) 958.6
      pseudohypertrophic 359.1
    muscular (atrophic) 359.9
      progressive 335.21
    musculocutaneous nerve 354.9
    musculospiral 354.9
    nerve (*see also* Disorder, nerve)
      third or oculomotor (partial) 378.51
        total 378.52
      fourth or trochlear 378.53
      sixth or abducens 378.54
      seventh or facial 351.0
        birth injury 767.5
        due to
          injection NEC 999.9
          operation NEC 997.09
        newborn 767.5
      accessory 352.4
      auditory 388.5
      birth injury 767.7
      cranial or cerebral (*see also* Disorder, nerve, cranial) 352.9
      facial 351.0
        birth injury 767.5
        newborn 767.5
      laryngeal (*see also* Paralysis, vocal cord) 478.30
      newborn 767.7
      phrenic 354.8
        newborn 767.7
      radial 354.3
        birth injury 767.6
        newborn 767.6
      syphilitic 094.89
      traumatic NEC (*see also* Injury, nerve, by site) 957.9
      trigeminal 350.9
      ulnar 354.2
    newborn NEC 767.0
    normokalemic periodic 359.3
    obstetrical, newborn 767.7
    ocular 378.9
    oculofacial, congenital 352.6

Paralysis, paralytic — *continued*
  oculomotor (nerve) (partial) 378.51
    alternating 344.89
    external bilateral 378.55
    total 378.52
  olfactory nerve 352.0
  palate 528.9
  palatopharyngolaryngeal 352.6
  paratrigeminal 350.9
  periodic (familial) (hyperkalemic) (hypokalemic) (normokalemic) (potassium sensitive) (secondary) 359.3
  peripheral
    autonomic nervous system — *see* Neuropathy, peripheral, autonomic
    nerve NEC 355.9
  peroneal (nerve) 355.3
  pharynx 478.29
  phrenic nerve 354.8
  plantar nerves 355.6
  pneumogastric nerve 352.3
  poliomyelitis (current) (*see also* Poliomyelitis, with paralysis) 045.1 ☑
    bulbar 045.0 ☑
  popliteal nerve 355.3
  pressure (*see also* Neuropathy, entrapment) 355.9
  progressive 335.21
    atrophic 335.21
    bulbar 335.22
    general 094.1
    hemifacial 349.89
    infantile, acute (*see also* Poliomyelitis) 045.9 ☑
    multiple 335.20
  pseudobulbar 335.23
  pseudohypertrophic 359.1
    muscle 359.1
  psychogenic 306.0
  pupil, pupillary 379.49
  quadriceps 355.8
  quadriplegic (*see also* Quadriplegia) 344.0 ☑
  radial nerve 354.3
    birth injury 767.6
  rectum (sphincter) 569.49
  rectus muscle (eye) 378.55
  recurrent
    isolated sleep 327.43
    laryngeal nerve (*see also* Paralysis, vocal cord) 478.30
  respiratory (muscle) (system) (tract) 786.09
    center NEC 344.89
      fetus or newborn 770.87
    congenital 768.9
    newborn 768.9
  right side — *see* Hemiplegia
  Saturday night 354.3
  saturnine 984.9
    specified type of lead — *see* Table of Drugs and Chemicals
  sciatic nerve 355.0
  secondary — *see* Paralysis, late effect
  seizure (cerebral) (current episode) (*see also* Disease, cerebrovascular, acute) 436
    late effect — *see* Late effect(s) (of) cerebrovascular disease
  senile NEC 344.9
  serratus magnus 355.9
  shaking (*see also* Parkinsonism) 332.0
  shock (*see also* Disease, cerebrovascular, acute) 436
    late effect — *see* Late effect(s) (of) cerebrovascular disease
  shoulder 354.9
  soft palate 528.9
  spasmodic — *see* Paralysis, spastic
  spastic 344.9
    cerebral infantile — *see* Palsy, cerebral
    congenital (cerebral) — *see* Palsy, cerebral
    familial 334.1
    hereditary 334.1
    infantile 343.9
    noncongenital or noninfantile, cerebral 344.9

Paralysis, paralytic — *continued*
  spastic — *continued*
    syphilitic 094.0
      spinal 094.89
  sphincter, bladder (*see also* Paralysis, bladder) 596.53
  spinal (cord) NEC 344.1
    accessory nerve 352.4
    acute (*see also* Poliomyelitis) 045.9 ☑
    ascending acute 357.0
    atrophic (acute) (*see also* Poliomyelitis, with paralysis) 045.1 ☑
      spastic, syphilitic 094.89
    congenital NEC 343.9
    hemiplegic — *see* Hemiplegia
    hereditary 336.8
    infantile (*see also* Poliomyelitis) 045.9 ☑
    late effect NEC 344.89
    monoplegic — *see* Monoplegia
    nerve 355.9
    progressive 335.10
    quadriplegic — *see* Quadriplegia
    spastic NEC 343.9
    traumatic — *see* Injury, spinal, by site
  sternomastoid 352.4
  stomach 536.3
    diabetic 250.6 ☑ [536.3]
      due to secondary diabetes 249.6 ☑ [536.3]
    nerve (nondiabetic) 352.3
  stroke (current episode) — *see* Infarct, brain
    late effect — *see* Late effect(s) (of) cerebrovascular disease
  subscapularis 354.8
  superior nuclear NEC 334.9
  supranuclear 356.8
  sympathetic
    cervical NEC 337.09
    nerve NEC (*see also* Neuropathy, peripheral, autonomic) 337.9
    nervous system — *see* Neuropathy, peripheral, autonomic
  syndrome 344.9
    specified NEC 344.89
  syphilitic spastic spinal (Erb's) 094.89
  tabetic general 094.1
  thigh 355.8
  throat 478.29
    diphtheritic 032.0
    muscle 478.29
  thrombotic (current episode) (*see also* Thrombosis, brain) 434.0 ☑
    late effect — *see* Late effect(s) (of) cerebrovascular disease
  thumb NEC 354.9
  tick (-bite) 989.5
  Todd's (postepileptic transitory paralysis) 344.89
  toe 355.6
  tongue 529.8
  transient
    arm or leg NEC 781.4
    traumatic NEC (*see also* Injury, nerve, by site) 957.9
  trapezius 352.4
  traumatic, transient NEC (*see also* Injury, nerve, by site) 957.9
  trembling (*see also* Parkinsonism) 332.0
  triceps brachii 354.9
  trigeminal nerve 350.9
  trochlear nerve 378.53
  ulnar nerve 354.2
  upper limb (*see also* Paralysis, arm)
    both (*see also* Diplegia) 344.2
  uremic — *see* Uremia
  uveoparotitic 135
  uvula 528.9
    hysterical 300.11
    postdiphtheritic 032.0
  vagus nerve 352.3
  vasomotor NEC 337.9
  velum palati 528.9
  vesical (*see also* Paralysis, bladder) 596.53
  vestibular nerve 388.5
  visual field, psychic 368.16
  vocal cord 478.30

☑ Additional Digit Required — Refer to the Tabular List for Digit Selection   Subterms under main terms may continue to next column or page

2015 ICD-9-CM   ►◄ Revised Text   ● New Line   ▲ Revised Code   Volume 2 — 225

Paralysis, paralytic — continued
  vocal cord — continued
    bilateral (partial) 478.33
      complete 478.34
    complete (bilateral) 478.34
    unilateral (partial) 478.31
      complete 478.32
  Volkmann's (complicating trauma) 958.6
  wasting 335.21
  Weber's 344.89
  wrist NEC 354.9
Paramedial orifice, urethrovesical 753.8
Paramenia 626.9
Parametritis (chronic) — see also Disease,
    pelvis, inflammatory 614.4
  acute 614.3
  puerperal, postpartum, childbirth 670.8 ☑
Parametrium, parametric — see condition
Paramnesia — see also Amnesia 780.93
Paramolar 520.1
  causing crowding 524.31
Paramyloidosis 277.30
Paramyoclonus multiplex 333.2
Paramyotonia 359.29
  congenita (of von Eulenburg) 359.29
Paraneoplastic syndrome — see condition
Parangi — see Yaws 102.9
Paranoia 297.1
  alcoholic 291.5
  querulans 297.8
  senile 290.20
Paranoid
  dementia (see also Schizophrenia) 295.3 ☑
    praecox (acute) 295.3 ☑
    senile 290.20
  personality 301.0
  psychosis 297.9
    alcoholic 291.5
    climacteric 297.2
    drug-induced 292.11
    involutional 297.2
    menopausal 297.2
    protracted reactive 298.4
    psychogenic 298.4
      acute 298.3
    senile 290.20
  reaction (chronic) 297.9
    acute 298.3
  schizophrenia (acute) (see also Schizophre-
    nia) 295.3 ☑
  state 297.9
    alcohol-induced 291.5
    climacteric 297.2
    drug-induced 292.11
    due to or associated with
      arteriosclerosis (cerebrovascular)
        290.42
      presenile brain disease 290.12
      senile brain disease 290.20
    involutional 297.2
    menopausal 297.2
    senile 290.20
    simple 297.0
    specified type NEC 297.8
  tendencies 301.0
  traits 301.0
  trends 301.0
  type, psychopathic personality 301.0
Paraparesis — see also Paraplegia 344.1
Paraphasia 784.3
Paraphilia — see also Deviation, sexual 302.9
Paraphimosis (congenital) 605
  chancroidal 099.0
Paraphrenia, paraphrenic (late) 297.2
  climacteric 297.2
  dementia (see also Schizophrenia) 295.3 ☑
  involutional 297.2
  menopausal 297.2
  schizophrenia (acute) (see also Schizophre-
    nia) 295.3 ☑
Paraplegia 344.1
  with
    broken back — see Fracture, vertebra,
      by site, with spinal cord injury

Paraplegia — continued
  with — continued
    fracture, vertebra — see Fracture, verte-
      bra, by site, with spinal cord in-
      jury
    ataxic — see Degeneration, combined,
      spinal cord
    brain (current episode) (see also Paralysis,
      brain) 437.8
    cerebral (current episode) (see also Paralysis,
      brain) 437.8
    congenital or infantile (cerebral) (spastic)
      (spinal) 343.0
    cortical — see Paralysis, brain
    familial spastic 334.1
    functional (hysterical) 300.11
    hysterical 300.11
    infantile 343.0
    late effect 344.1
    Pott's (see also Tuberculosis)
      015.0 ☑ [730.88]
    psychogenic 306.0
    spastic
      Erb's spinal 094.89
      hereditary 334.1
      not infantile or congenital 344.1
    spinal (cord)
      traumatic NEC — see Injury, spinal, by
        site
    syphilitic (spastic) 094.89
    traumatic NEC — see Injury, spinal, by site
Paraproteinemia 273.2
  benign (familial) 273.1
  monoclonal 273.1
  secondary to malignant or inflammatory
    disease 273.1
Parapsoriasis 696.2
  en plaques 696.2
  guttata 696.2
  lichenoides chronica 696.2
  retiformis 696.2
  varioliformis (acuta) 696.2
Parascarlatina 057.8
Parasitic — see also condition
  disease NEC (see also Infestation, parasitic)
    136.9
    contact V01.89
    exposure to V01.89
    intestinal NEC 129
    skin NEC 134.9
  stomatitis 112.0
  sycosis 110.0
    beard 110.0
    scalp 110.0
  twin 759.4
Parasitism NEC 136.9
  intestinal NEC 129
  skin NEC 134.9
  specified — see Infestation
Parasitophobia 300.29
Parasomnia 307.47
  alcohol induced 291.82
  drug induced 292.85
  nonorganic origin 307.47
  organic 327.40
    in conditions classified elsewhere 327.44
  other 327.49
Paraspadias 752.69
Paraspasm facialis 351.8
Parathyroid gland — see condition
Parathyroiditis (autoimmune) 252.1
Parathyroprival tetany 252.1
Paratrachoma 077.0
Paratyphilitis — see also Appendicitis 541
Paratyphoid (fever) — see Fever, paratyphoid
Paratyphus — see Fever, paratyphoid
Paraurethral duct 753.8
Para-urethritis 597.89
  gonococcal (acute) 098.0
    chronic or duration of 2 months or over
      098.2
Paravaccinia NEC 051.9
  milkers' node 051.1
Paravaginitis — see also Vaginitis 616.10
Parencephalitis — see also Encephalitis 323.9
  late effect — see category 326

Parergasia 298.9
Paresis — see also Paralysis 344.9
  accommodation 367.51
  bladder (spastic) (sphincter) (see also Paral-
    ysis, bladder) 596.53
    tabetic 094.0
  bowel, colon, or intestine (see also Ileus)
    560.1
  brain or cerebral — see Paralysis, brain
  extrinsic muscle, eye 378.55
  general 094.1
    arrested 094.1
    brain 094.1
    cerebral 094.1
    insane 094.1
    juvenile 090.40
      remission 090.49
    progressive 094.1
    remission (sustained) 094.1
    tabetic 094.1
  heart (see also Failure, heart) 428.9
  infantile (see also Poliomyelitis) 045.9 ☑
  insane 094.1
  juvenile 090.40
  late effect — see Paralysis, late effect
  luetic (general) 094.1
  peripheral progressive 356.9
  pseudohypertrophic 359.1
  senile NEC 344.9
  stomach 536.3
    diabetic 250.6 ☑ [536.3]
      due to secondary diabetes
        249.6 ☑ [536.3]
  syphilitic (general) 094.1
    congenital 090.40
  transient, limb 781.4
  vesical (sphincter) NEC 596.53
Paresthesia — see also Disturbance, sensation
    782.0
  Berger's (paresthesia of lower limb) 782.0
  Bernhardt 355.1
  Magnan's 782.0
Paretic — see condition
Parinaud's
  conjunctivitis 372.02
  oculoglandular syndrome 372.02
  ophthalmoplegia 378.81
  syndrome (paralysis of conjugate upward
    gaze) 378.81
Parkes Weber and Dimitri syndrome (en-
    cephalocutaneous angiomatosis) 759.6
Parkinson's disease, syndrome, or tremor
    — see Parkinsonism
Parkinsonism (arteriosclerotic) (idiopathic)
    (primary) 332.0
  associated with orthostatic hypotension
    (idiopathic) (symptomatic) 333.0
  due to drugs 332.1
  neuroleptic-induced 332.1
  secondary 332.1
  syphilitic 094.82
Parodontitis 523.40
Parodontosis 523.5
Paronychia (with lymphangitis) 681.9
  candidal (chronic) 112.3
  chronic 681.9
    candidal 112.3
    finger 681.02
    toe 681.11
  finger 681.02
  toe 681.11
  tuberculous (primary) (see also Tuberculosis)
    017.0 ☑
Parorexia NEC 307.52
  hysterical 300.11
Parosmia 781.1
  psychogenic 306.7
Parotid gland — see condition
Parotiditis — see also Parotitis 527.2
  epidemic 072.9
  infectious 072.9
Parotitis 527.2
  allergic 527.2
  chronic 527.2
  epidemic (see also Mumps) 072.9
  infectious (see also Mumps) 072.9

Parotitis — continued
  noninfectious 527.2
  nonspecific toxic 527.2
  not mumps 527.2
  postoperative 527.2
  purulent 527.2
  septic 527.2
  suppurative (acute) 527.2
  surgical 527.2
  toxic 527.2
Paroxysmal — see also condition
  dyspnea (nocturnal) 786.09
Parrot's disease (syphilitic osteochondritis)
    090.0
Parrot fever 073.9
Parry's disease or syndrome (exophthalmic
    goiter) 242.0 ☑
Parry-Romberg syndrome 349.89
Parsonage-Aldren-Turner syndrome 353.5
Parsonage-Turner syndrome 353.5
Parson's disease (exophthalmic goiter)
    242.0 ☑
Pars planitis 363.21
Particolored infant 757.39
Parturition — see Delivery
Parvovirus 079.83
  B19 079.83
  human 079.83
Passage
  false, urethra 599.4
  meconium noted during delivery 763.84
  of sounds or bougies (see also Attention to
    artificial opening) V55.9
Passive — see condition
Pasteurella septica 027.2
Pasteurellosis — see also Infection, Pasteurella
    027.2
PAT (paroxysmal atrial tachycardia) 427.0
Patau's syndrome (trisomy D1) 758.1
Patch
  herald 696.3
Patches
  mucous (syphilitic) 091.3
    congenital 090.0
  smokers' (mouth) 528.6
Patellar — see condition
Patellofemoral syndrome 719.46
Patent — see also Imperfect closure
  atrioventricular ostium 745.69
  canal of Nuck 752.41
  cervix 622.5
    complicating pregnancy 654.5 ☑
      affecting fetus or newborn 761.0
  ductus arteriosus or Botalli 747.0
  Eustachian
    tube 381.7
    valve 746.89
  foramen
    Botalli 745.5
    ovale 745.5
  interauricular septum 745.5
  interventricular septum 745.4
  omphalomesenteric duct 751.0
  os (uteri) — see Patent, cervix
  ostium secundum 745.5
  urachus 753.7
  vitelline duct 751.0
Paternity testing V70.4
Paterson-Kelly syndrome or web (sideropenic
    dysphagia) 280.8
Paterson (-Brown) (-Kelly) syndrome
    (sideropenic dysphagia) 280.8
Paterson's syndrome (sideropenic dysphagia)
    280.8
Pathologic, pathological — see also condition
  asphyxia 799.01
  drunkenness 291.4
  emotionality 301.3
  fracture — see Fracture, pathologic
  liar 301.7
  personality 301.9
  resorption, tooth 521.40
    external 521.42
    internal 521.41
    specified NEC 521.49
  sexuality (see also Deviation, sexual) 302.9

☑ Additional Digit Required — Refer to the Tabular List for Digit Selection   ▽ Subterms under main terms may continue to next column or page

226 — Volume 2   ►◄ Revised Text   ● New Line   ▲ Revised Code   2015 ICD-9-CM

Pathology (of) — *see also* Disease
   periradicular, associated with previous endodontic treatment 526.69
Patterned motor discharge, idiopathic — *see also* Epilepsy 345.5 ☑
Patulous — *see also* Patent
   anus 569.49
   Eustachian tube 381.7
Pause, sinoatrial 427.81
Pavor nocturnus 307.46
Pavy's disease 593.6
Paxton's disease (white piedra) 111.2
Payr's disease or syndrome (splenic flexure syndrome) 569.89
PBA (pseudobulbar affect) 310.81
Pearls
   Elschnig 366.51
   enamel 520.2
Pearl-workers' disease (chronic osteomyelitis) — *see also* Osteomyelitis 730.1 ☑
Pectenitis 569.49
Pectenosis 569.49
Pectoral — *see* condition
Pectus
   carinatum (congenital) 754.82
     acquired 738.3
     rachitic (*see also* Rickets) 268.0
   excavatum (congenital) 754.81
     acquired 738.3
     rachitic (*see also* Rickets) 268.0
   recurvatum (congenital) 754.81
     acquired 738.3
Pedatrophia 261
Pederosis 302.2
Pediculosis (infestation) 132.9
   capitis (head louse) (any site) 132.0
   corporis (body louse) (any site) 132.1
   eyelid 132.0 [373.6]
   mixed (classifiable to more than one category in 132.0–132.2) 132.3
   pubis (pubic louse) (any site) 132.2
   vestimenti 132.1
   vulvae 132.2
Pediculus (infestation) — *see* Pediculosis
Pedophilia 302.2
Peg-shaped teeth 520.2
Peiade 704.01
Pel's crisis 094.0
Pel-Ebstein disease — *see* Disease, Hodgkin's
Pelger-Huët anomaly or syndrome (hereditary hyposegmentation) 288.2
Peliosis (rheumatica) 287.0
Pelizaeus-Merzbacher
   disease 330.0
   sclerosis, diffuse cerebral 330.0
Pellagra (alcoholic or with alcoholism) 265.2
   with polyneuropathy 265.2 [357.4]
Pellagra-cerebellar-ataxia-renal aminoaciduria syndrome 270.0
Pellegrini's disease (calcification, knee joint) 726.62
Pellegrini (-Stieda) disease or syndrome (calcification, knee joint) 726.62
Pellizzi's syndrome (pineal) 259.8
Pelvic — *see also* condition
   congestion-fibrosis syndrome 625.5
   kidney 753.3
Pelvioectasis 591
Pelviolithiasis 592.0
Pelviperitonitis
   female (*see also* Peritonitis, pelvic, female) 614.5
   male (*see also* Peritonitis) 567.21
Pelvis, pelvic — *see also* condition or type
   infantile 738.6
   Nägele's 738.6
   obliquity 738.6
   Robert's 755.69
Pemphigoid 694.5
   benign, mucous membrane 694.60
     with ocular involvement 694.61
   bullous 694.5
   cicatricial 694.60
     with ocular involvement 694.61
   juvenile 694.2
Pemphigus 694.4

Pemphigus — *continued*
   benign 694.5
     chronic familial 757.39
   Brazilian 694.4
   circinatus 694.0
   congenital, traumatic 757.39
   conjunctiva 694.61
   contagiosus 684
   erythematodes 694.4
   erythematosus 694.4
   foliaceus 694.4
   frambesiodes 694.4
   gangrenous (*see also* Gangrene) 785.4
   malignant 694.4
   neonatorum, newborn 684
   ocular 694.61
   papillaris 694.4
   seborrheic 694.4
   South American 694.4
   syphilitic (congenital) 090.0
   vegetans 694.4
   vulgaris 694.4
   wildfire 694.4
Pendred's syndrome (familial goiter with deaf-mutism) 243
Pendulous
   abdomen 701.9
     in pregnancy or childbirth 654.4 ☑
       affecting fetus or newborn 763.89
   breast 611.89
Penetrating wound — *see also* Wound, open, by site
   with internal injury — *see* Injury, internal, by site, with open wound
   eyeball 871.7
     with foreign body (nonmagnetic) 871.6
       magnetic 871.5
   ocular (*see also* Penetrating wound, eyeball) 871.7
   adnexa 870.3
     with foreign body 870.4
   orbit 870.3
     with foreign body 870.4
Penetration, pregnant uterus by instrument
   with
     abortion — *see* Abortion, by type, with damage to pelvic organs
     ectopic pregnancy (*see also* categories 633.0–633.9) 639.2
     molar pregnancy (*see also* categories 630–632) 639.2
   complication of delivery 665.1 ☑
     affecting fetus or newborn 763.89
   following
     abortion 639.2
     ectopic or molar pregnancy 639.2
Penfield's syndrome — *see also* Epilepsy 345.5 ☑
Penicilliosis of lung 117.3
Penis — *see* condition
Penitis 607.2
Pentalogy (of Fallot) 745.2
Penta X syndrome 758.81
Pentosuria (benign) (essential) 271.8
Peptic acid disease 536.8
Peregrinating patient V65.2
Perforated — *see* Perforation
Perforation, perforative (nontraumatic)
   antrum (*see also* Sinusitis, maxillary) 473.0
   appendix 540.0
     with peritoneal abscess 540.1
   atrial septum, multiple 745.5
   attic, ear 384.22
     healed 384.81
   bile duct, except cystic (*see also* Disease, biliary) 576.3
     cystic 575.4
   bladder (urinary) 596.6
     with
       abortion — *see* Abortion, by type, with damage to pelvic organs
       ectopic pregnancy (*see also* categories 633.0–633.9) 639.2
       molar pregnancy (*see also* categories 630–632) 639.2

Perforation, perforative — *continued*
   bladder — *continued*
     following
       abortion 639.2
       ectopic or molar pregnancy 639.2
     obstetrical trauma 665.5 ☑
   bowel 569.83
     with
       abortion — *see* Abortion, by type, with damage to pelvic organs
       ectopic pregnancy (*see also* categories 633.0–633.9) 639.2
       molar pregnancy (*see also* categories 630–632) 639.2
     fetus or newborn 777.6
     following
       abortion 639.2
       ectopic or molar pregnancy 639.2
     obstetrical trauma 665.5 ☑
   broad ligament
     with
       abortion — *see* Abortion, by type, with damage to pelvic organs
       ectopic pregnancy (*see also* categories 633.0–633.9) 639.2
       molar pregnancy (*see also* categories 630–632) 639.2
     following
       abortion 639.2
       ectopic or molar pregnancy 639.2
     obstetrical trauma 665.6 ☑
   by
     device, implant, or graft — *see* Complications, mechanical
     foreign body left accidentally in operation wound 998.4
     instrument (any) during a procedure, accidental 998.2
   cecum 540.0
     with peritoneal abscess 540.1
   cervix (uteri) (*see also* Injury, internal, cervix)
     with
       abortion — *see* Abortion, by type, with damage to pelvic organs
       ectopic pregnancy (*see also* categories 633.0–633.9) 639.2
       molar pregnancy (*see also* categories 630–632) 639.2
     following
       abortion 639.2
       ectopic or molar pregnancy 639.2
     obstetrical trauma 665.3 ☑
   colon 569.83
   common duct (bile) 576.3
   cornea (*see also* Ulcer, cornea) 370.00
     due to ulceration 370.06
   cystic duct 575.4
   diverticulum (*see also* Diverticula) 562.10
     small intestine 562.00
   duodenum, duodenal (ulcer) — *see* Ulcer, duodenum, with perforation
   ear drum — *see* Perforation, tympanum
   enteritis — *see* Enteritis
   esophagus 530.4
   ethmoidal sinus (*see also* Sinusitis, ethmoidal) 473.2
   foreign body (external site) (*see also* Wound, open, by site, complicated)
     internal site, by ingested object — *see* Foreign body
   frontal sinus (*see also* Sinusitis, frontal) 473.1
   gallbladder or duct (*see also* Disease, gallbladder) 575.4
   gastric (ulcer) — *see* Ulcer, stomach, with perforation
   heart valve — *see* Endocarditis
   ileum (*see also* Perforation, intestine) 569.83
   instrumental
     external — *see* Wound, open, by site
     pregnant uterus, complicating delivery 665.9 ☑
     surgical (accidental) (blood vessel) (nerve) (organ) 998.2
   intestine 569.83

Perforation, perforative — *continued*
   intestine — *continued*
     with
       abortion — *see* Abortion, by type, with damage to pelvic organs
       ectopic pregnancy (*see also* categories 633.0–633.9) 639.2
       molar pregnancy (*see also* categories 630–632) 639.2
     fetus or newborn 777.6
     obstetrical trauma 665.5 ☑
     ulcerative NEC 569.83
   jejunum, jejunal 569.83
     ulcer — *see* Ulcer, gastrojejunal, with perforation
   mastoid (antrum) (cell) 383.89
   maxillary sinus (*see also* Sinusitis, maxillary) 473.0
   membrana tympani — *see* Perforation, tympanum
   nasal
     septum 478.19
       congenital 748.1
       syphilitic 095.8
     sinus (*see also* Sinusitis) 473.9
       congenital 748.1
   palate (hard) 526.89
     soft 528.9
       syphilitic 095.8
     syphilitic 095.8
   palatine vault 526.89
     syphilitic 095.8
       congenital 090.5
   pelvic
     floor
       with
         abortion — *see* Abortion, by type, with damage to pelvic organs
         ectopic pregnancy (*see also* categories 633.0–633.9) 639.2
         molar pregnancy (*see also* categories 630–632) 639.2
       obstetrical trauma 664.1 ☑
     organ
       with
         abortion — *see* Abortion, by type, with damage to pelvic organs
         ectopic pregnancy (*see also* categories 633.0–633.9) 639.2
         molar pregnancy (*see also* categories 630–632) 639.2
       following
         abortion 639.2
         ectopic or molar pregnancy 639.2
       obstetrical trauma 665.5 ☑
   perineum — *see* Laceration, perineum
   periurethral tissue
     with
       abortion — *see* Abortion, by type, with damage to pelvic organs
       ectopic pregnancy (*see also* categories 633.0–633.9) 639.2
       molar pregnancy (*see also* categories 630–632) 639.2
   pharynx 478.29
   pylorus, pyloric (ulcer) — *see* Ulcer, stomach, with perforation
   rectum 569.49
   root canal space 526.61
   sigmoid 569.83
   sinus (accessory) (chronic) (nasal) (*see also* Sinusitis) 473.9
   sphenoidal sinus (*see also* Sinusitis, sphenoidal) 473.3
   stomach (due to ulcer) — *see* Ulcer, stomach, with perforation
   surgical (accidental) (by instrument) (blood vessel) (nerve) (organ) 998.2
   traumatic
     external — *see* Wound, open, by site
     eye (*see also* Penetrating wound, ocular) 871.7
     internal organ — *see* Injury, internal, by site

☑ **Additional Digit Required** — Refer to the Tabular List for Digit Selection   ▽ **Subterms under main terms may continue to next column or page**

2015 ICD-9-CM   ►◄ Revised Text   ● New Line   ▲ Revised Code   **Volume 2 — 227**

Perforation, perforative — *continued*
tympanum (membrane) (persistent posttraumatic) (postinflammatory) 384.20
with
otitis media — *see* Otitis media
attic 384.22
central 384.21
healed 384.81
marginal NEC 384.23
multiple 384.24
pars flaccida 384.22
total 384.25
traumatic — *see* Wound, open, ear,
drum
typhoid, gastrointestinal 002.0
ulcer — *see* Ulcer, by site, with perforation
ureter 593.89
urethra
with
abortion — *see* Abortion, by type,
with damage to pelvic organs
ectopic pregnancy (*see also* categories 633.0–633.9) 639.2
molar pregnancy (*see also* categories
630–632) 639.2
following
abortion 639.2
ectopic or molar pregnancy 639.2
obstetrical trauma 665.5 ☑
uterus (*see also* Injury, internal, uterus)
with
abortion — *see* Abortion, by type,
with damage to pelvic organs
ectopic pregnancy (*see also* categories 633.0–633.9) 639.2
molar pregnancy (*see also* categories
630–632) 639.2
by intrauterine contraceptive device
996.32
following
abortion 639.2
ectopic or molar pregnancy 639.2
obstetrical trauma — *see* Injury, internal,
uterus, obstetrical trauma
uvula 528.9
syphilitic 095.8
vagina — *see* Laceration, vagina
viscus NEC 799.89
traumatic 868.00
with open wound into cavity 868.10
Periadenitis mucosa necrotica recurrens
528.2
Periangiitis 446.0
Periantritis 535.4 ☑
Periappendicitis (acute) — *see also* Appendicitis 541
Periarteritis (disseminated) (infectious)
(necrotizing) (nodosa) 446.0
Periarthritis (joint) 726.90
Duplay's 726.2
gonococcal 098.50
humeroscapularis 726.2
scapulohumeral 726.2
shoulder 726.2
wrist 726.4
Periarthrosis (angioneural) — *see* Periarthritis
Peribronchitis 491.9
tuberculous (*see also* Tuberculosis) 011.3 ☑
Pericapsulitis, adhesive (shoulder) 726.0
Pericarditis (granular) (with decompensation)
(with effusion) 423.9
with
rheumatic fever (conditions classifiable
to 390)
active (*see also* Pericarditis,
rheumatic) 391.0
inactive or quiescent 393
actinomycotic 039.8 *[420.0]*
acute (nonrheumatic) 420.90
with chorea (acute) (rheumatic) (Sydenham's) 392.0
bacterial 420.99
benign 420.91
hemorrhagic 420.90
idiopathic 420.91
infective 420.90

Pericarditis — *continued*
acute — *continued*
nonspecific 420.91
rheumatic 391.0
with chorea (acute) (rheumatic)
(Sydenham's) 392.0
sicca 420.90
viral 420.91
adhesive or adherent (external) (internal)
423.1
acute — *see* Pericarditis, acute
rheumatic (external) (internal) 393
amebic 006.8 *[420.0]*
bacterial (acute) (subacute) (with serous or
seropurulent effusion) 420.99
calcareous 423.2
cholesterol (chronic) 423.8
acute 420.90
chronic (nonrheumatic) 423.8
rheumatic 393
constrictive 423.2
Coxsackie 074.21
due to
actinomycosis 039.8 *[420.0]*
amebiasis 006.8 *[420.0]*
Coxsackie (virus) 074.21
histoplasmosis (*see also* Histoplasmosis)
115.93
nocardiosis 039.8 *[420.0]*
tuberculosis (*see also* Tuberculosis)
017.9 ☑ *[420.0]*
fibrinocaseous (*see also* Tuberculosis)
017.9 ☑ *[420.0]*
fibrinopurulent 420.99
fibrinous — *see* Pericarditis, rheumatic
fibropurulent 420.99
fibrous 423.1
gonococcal 098.83
hemorrhagic 423.0
idiopathic (acute) 420.91
infective (acute) 420.90
meningococcal 036.41
neoplastic (chronic) 423.8
acute 420.90
nonspecific 420.91
obliterans, obliterating 423.1
plastic 423.1
pneumococcal (acute) 420.99
postinfarction 411.0
purulent (acute) 420.99
rheumatic (active) (acute) (with effusion)
(with pneumonia) 391.0
with chorea (acute) (rheumatic) (Sydenham's) 392.0
chronic or inactive (with chorea) 393
septic (acute) 420.99
serofibrinous — *see* Pericarditis, rheumatic
staphylococcal (acute) 420.99
streptococcal (acute) 420.99
suppurative (acute) 420.99
syphilitic 093.81
tuberculous (acute) (chronic) (*see also* Tuberculosis) 017.9 ☑ *[420.0]*
uremic 585.9 *[420.0]*
viral (acute) 420.91
Pericardium, pericardial — *see* condition
Pericellulitis — *see also* Cellulitis 682.9
Pericementitis 523.40
acute 523.30
chronic (suppurative) 523.40
Pericholecystitis — *see also* Cholecystitis
575.10
Perichondritis
auricle 380.00
acute 380.01
chronic 380.02
bronchus 491.9
ear (external) 380.00
acute 380.01
chronic 380.02
larynx 478.71
syphilitic 095.8
typhoid 002.0 *[478.71]*
nose 478.19
pinna 380.00
acute 380.01

Perichondritis — *continued*
pinna — *continued*
chronic 380.02
trachea 478.9
Periclasia 523.5
Pericolitis 569.89
Pericoronitis (chronic) 523.40
acute 523.33
Pericystitis — *see also* Cystitis 595.9
Pericytoma (M9150/1) — *see also* Neoplasm,
connective tissue, uncertain behavior
benign (M9150/0) — *see* Neoplasm, connective tissue, benign
malignant (M9150/3) — *see* Neoplasm,
connective tissue, malignant
Peridacryocystitis, acute 375.32
Peridiverticulitis — *see also* Diverticulitis
562.11
Periduodenitis 535.6 ☑
Periendocarditis — *see also* Endocarditis
424.90
acute or subacute 421.9
Periepididymitis — *see also* Epididymitis
604.90
Perifolliculitis (abscedens) 704.8
capitis, abscedens et suffodiens 704.8
dissecting, scalp 704.8
scalp 704.8
superficial pustular 704.8
Perigastritis (acute) 535.0 ☑
Perigastrojejunitis (acute) 535.0 ☑
Perihepatitis (acute) 573.3
chlamydial 099.56
gonococcal 098.86
Peri-ileitis (subacute) 569.89
Perilabyrinthitis (acute) — *see* Labyrinthitis
Perimeningitis — *see* Meningitis
Perimetritis — *see also* Endometritis 615.9
Perimetrosalpingitis — *see also* Salpingo-
oophoritis 614.2
Perineocele 618.05
Perinephric — *see* condition
Perinephritic — *see* condition
Perinephritis — *see also* Infection, kidney
590.9
purulent (*see also* Abscess, kidney) 590.2
Perineum, perineal — *see* condition
Perineuritis NEC 729.2
Periodic — *see also* condition
disease (familial) 277.31
edema 995.1
hereditary 277.6
fever 277.31
headache syndromes in child or adolescent
346.2 ☑
limb movement disorder 327.51
paralysis (familial) 359.3
peritonitis 277.31
polyserositis 277.31
somnolence (*see also* Narcolepsy) 347.00
Periodontal
cyst 522.8
pocket 523.8
Periodontitis (chronic) (complex) (compound)
(simplex) 523.40
acute 523.33
aggressive 523.30
generalized 523.32
localized 523.31
apical 522.6
acute (pulpal origin) 522.4
generalized 523.42
localized 523.41
Periodontoclasia 523.5
Periodontosis 523.5
Periods — *see also* Menstruation
heavy 626.2
irregular 626.4
Perionychia (with lymphangitis) 681.9
finger 681.02
toe 681.11
Perioophoritis — *see also* Salpingo-oophoritis
614.2
Periorchitis — *see also* Orchitis 604.90
Periosteum, periosteal — *see* condition

Periostitis (circumscribed) (diffuse) (infective)
730.3 ☑

> *Note* — Use the following fifth-digit
> subclassification with category 730:
>
> 0   site unspecified
> 1   shoulder region
> 2   upper arm
> 3   forearm
> 4   hand
> 5   pelvic region and thigh
> 6   lower leg
> 7   ankle and foot
> 8   other specified sites
> 9   multiple sites

with osteomyelitis (*see also* Osteomyelitis)
730.2 ☑
acute or subacute 730.0 ☑
chronic or old 730.1 ☑
albuminosa, albuminosus 730.3 ☑
alveolar 526.5
alveolodental 526.5
dental 526.5
gonorrheal 098.89
hyperplastica, generalized 731.2
jaw (lower) (upper) 526.4
monomelic 733.99
orbital 376.02
syphilitic 095.5
congenital 090.0 *[730.8]* ☑
secondary 091.61
tuberculous (*see also* Tuberculosis, bone)
015.9 ☑ *[730.8]* ☑
yaws (early) (hypertrophic) (late) 102.6
Periostosis — *see also* Periostitis 730.3 ☑
with osteomyelitis (*see also* Osteomyelitis)
730.2 ☑
acute or subacute 730.0 ☑
chronic or old 730.1 ☑
hyperplastic 756.59
Peripartum cardiomyopathy 674.5 ☑
Periphlebitis — *see also* Phlebitis 451.9
lower extremity 451.2
deep (vessels) 451.19
superficial (vessels) 451.0
portal 572.1
retina 362.18
superficial (vessels) 451.0
tuberculous (*see also* Tuberculosis) 017.9 ☑
retina 017.3 ☑ *[362.18]*
Peripneumonia — *see* Pneumonia
Periproctitis 569.49
Periprostatitis — *see also* Prostatitis 601.9
Perirectal — *see* condition
Perirenal — *see* condition
Perisalpingitis — *see also* Salpingo-oophoritis
614.2
Perisigmoiditis 569.89
Perisplenitis (infectional) 289.59
Perispondylitis — *see* Spondylitis
Peristalsis reversed or visible 787.4
Peritendinitis — *see also* Tenosynovitis 726.90
adhesive (shoulder) 726.0
Perithelioma (M9150/1) — *see* Pericytoma
Peritoneum, peritoneal — *see also* condition
equilibration test V56.32
Peritonitis (acute) (adhesive) (fibrinous)
(hemorrhagic) (idiopathic) (localized)
(perforative) (primary) (with adhesions)
(with effusion) 567.9
with or following
abortion — *see* Abortion, by type, with
sepsis
abscess 567.21
appendicitis 540.0
with peritoneal abscess 540.1
ectopic pregnancy (*see also* categories
633.0–633.9) 639.0
molar pregnancy (*see also* categories
630–632) 639.0
aseptic 998.7

Peritonitis — *continued*
bacterial 567.29
  spontaneous 567.23
bile, biliary 567.81
chemical 998.7
chlamydial 099.56
chronic proliferative 567.89
congenital NEC 777.6
diaphragmatic 567.22
diffuse NEC 567.29
diphtheritic 032.83
disseminated NEC 567.29
due to
  bile 567.81
  foreign
    body or object accidentally left during a procedure (instrument) (sponge) (swab) 998.4
    substance accidentally left during a procedure (chemical) (powder) (talc) 998.7
  talc 998.7
  urine 567.89
fibrinopurulent 567.29
fibrinous 567.29
fibrocaseous (*see also* Tuberculosis) 014.0 ☑
fibropurulent 567.29
general, generalized (acute) 567.21
gonococcal 098.86
in infective disease NEC 136.9 [567.0]
meconium (newborn) 777.6
pancreatic 577.8
paroxysmal, benign 277.31
pelvic
  female (acute) 614.5
    chronic NEC 614.7
      with adhesions 614.6
    puerperal, postpartum, childbirth 670.8 ☑
  male (acute) 567.21
periodic (familial) 277.31
phlegmonous 567.29
pneumococcal 567.1
postabortal 639.0
proliferative, chronic 567.89
puerperal, postpartum, childbirth 670.8 ☑
purulent 567.29
septic 567.29
spontaneous bacterial 567.23
staphylococcal 567.29
streptococcal 567.29
subdiaphragmatic 567.29
subphrenic 567.29
suppurative 567.29
syphilitic 095.2
  congenital 090.0 [567.0]
talc 998.7
tuberculous (*see also* Tuberculosis) 014.0 ☑
urine 567.89
Peritonsillar — *see* condition
Peritonsillitis 475
Perityphlitis — *see also* Appendicitis 541
Periureteritis 593.89
Periurethral — *see* condition
Periurethritis (gangrenous) 597.89
Periuterine — *see* condition
Perivaginitis — *see also* Vaginitis 616.10
Perivasculitis, retinal 362.18
Perivasitis (chronic) 608.4
Periventricular leukomalacia 779.7
Perivesiculitis (seminal) — *see also* Vesiculitis 608.0
Perlèche 686.8
due to
  moniliasis 112.0
  riboflavin deficiency 266.0
Pernicious — *see* condition
Pernio, perniosis 991.5
Persecution
delusion 297.9
social V62.4
Perseveration (tonic) 784.69
Persistence, persistent (congenital) 759.89
anal membrane 751.2
arteria stapedia 744.04
atrioventricular canal 745.69

Persistence, persistent — *continued*
bloody ejaculate 792.2
branchial cleft 744.41
bulbus cordis in left ventricle 745.8
canal of Cloquet 743.51
capsule (opaque) 743.51
cilioretinal artery or vein 743.51
cloaca 751.5
communication — *see* Fistula, congenital
convolutions
  aortic arch 747.21
  fallopian tube 752.19
  oviduct 752.19
  uterine tube 752.19
double aortic arch 747.21
ductus
  arteriosus 747.0
  Botalli 747.0
fetal
  circulation 747.83
  form of cervix (uteri) 752.49
  hemoglobin (hereditary) ("Swiss variety") 282.7
  pulmonary hypertension 747.83
foramen
  Botalli 745.5
  ovale 745.5
Gartner's duct 752.41
hemoglobin, fetal (hereditary) (HPFH) 282.7
hyaloid
  artery (generally incomplete) 743.51
  system 743.51
hymen (tag)
  in pregnancy or childbirth 654.8 ☑
    causing obstructed labor 660.2 ☑
lanugo 757.4
left
  posterior cardinal vein 747.49
  root with right arch of aorta 747.21
  superior vena cava 747.49
Meckel's diverticulum 751.0
mesonephric duct 752.89
  fallopian tube 752.11
mucosal disease (middle ear) (with posterior or superior marginal perforation of ear drum) 382.2
nail(s), anomalous 757.5
occiput, anterior or posterior 660.3 ☑
  fetus or newborn 763.1
omphalomesenteric duct 751.0
organ or site NEC — *see* Anomaly, specified type NEC
ostium
  atrioventriculare commune 745.69
  primum 745.61
  secundum 745.5
ovarian rests in fallopian tube 752.19
pancreatic tissue in intestinal tract 751.5
primary (deciduous)
  teeth 520.6
  vitreous hyperplasia 743.51
pulmonary hypertension 747.83
pupillary membrane 743.46
  iris 743.46
Rhesus (Rh) titer (*see also* Complications, transfusion) 999.70
right aortic arch 747.21
sinus
  urogenitalis 752.89
  venosus with imperfect incorporation in right auricle 747.49
thymus (gland) 254.8
  hyperplasia 254.0
thyroglossal duct 759.2
thyrolingual duct 759.2
truncus arteriosus or communis 745.0
tunica vasculosa lentis 743.39
umbilical sinus 753.7
urachus 753.7
vegetative state 780.03
vitelline duct 751.0
wolffian duct 752.89
Person (with)
admitted for clinical research, as participant or control subject V70.7

Person — *continued*
affected by
  family member
    currently on deployment (military) V61.01
    returned from deployment (military) (current or past conflict) V61.02
awaiting admission to adequate facility elsewhere V63.2
undergoing social agency investigation V63.8
concern (normal) about sick person in family V61.49
consulting on behalf of another V65.19
  pediatric
    pre-adoption visit for adoptive parents V65.11
    pre-birth visit for expectant parents V65.11
currently deployed in theater or in support of military war, peacekeeping and humanitarian operations V62.21
feared
  complaint in whom no diagnosis was made V65.5
  condition not demonstrated V65.5
feigning illness V65.2
healthy, accompanying sick person V65.0
history of military war, peacekeeping and humanitarian deployment (current or past conflict) V62.22
living (in)
  without
    adequate
      financial resources V60.2
      housing (heating) (space) V60.1
    housing (permanent) (temporary) V60.0
    material resources V60.2
    person able to render necessary care V60.4
    shelter V60.0
  alone V60.3
  boarding school V60.6
  residence remote from hospital or medical care facility V63.0
  residential institution V60.6
medical services in home not available V63.1
on waiting list V63.2
  undergoing social agency investigation V63.8
sick or handicapped in family V61.49
"worried well" V65.5
Personality
affective 301.10
aggressive 301.3
amoral 301.7
anancastic, anankastic 301.4
antisocial 301.7
asocial 301.7
asthenic 301.6
avoidant 301.82
borderline 301.83
change 310.1
compulsive 301.4
cycloid 301.13
cyclothymic 301.13
dependent 301.6
depressive (chronic) 301.12
disorder, disturbance NEC 301.9
  with
    antisocial disturbance 301.7
    pattern disturbance NEC 301.9
    sociopathic disturbance 301.7
    trait disturbance 301.9
dual 300.14
dyssocial 301.7
eccentric 301.89
  "haltlose" type 301.89
emotionally unstable 301.59
epileptoid 301.3
explosive 301.3
fanatic 301.0
histrionic 301.50
hyperthymic 301.11

Personality — *continued*
hypomanic 301.11
hypothymic 301.12
hysterical 301.50
immature 301.89
inadequate 301.6
labile 301.59
masochistic 301.89
morally defective 301.7
multiple 300.14
narcissistic 301.81
obsessional 301.4
obsessive-compulsive 301.4
overconscientious 301.4
paranoid 301.0
passive (-dependent) 301.6
passive-aggressive 301.84
pathologic NEC 301.9
pattern defect or disturbance 301.9
pseudosocial 301.7
psychoinfantile 301.59
psychoneurotic NEC 301.89
psychopathic 301.9
  with
    amoral trend 301.7
    antisocial trend 301.7
    asocial trend 301.7
    pathologic sexuality (*see also* Deviation, sexual) 302.9
  mixed types 301.9
schizoid 301.20
type A 301.4
unstable (emotional) 301.59
Perthes' disease (capital femoral osteochondrosis) 732.1
Pertussis — *see also* Whooping cough 033.9
vaccination, prophylactic (against) V03.6
Peruvian wart 088.0
Perversion, perverted
appetite 307.52
  hysterical 300.11
function
  pineal gland 259.8
  pituitary gland 253.9
    anterior lobe
      deficient 253.2
      excessive 253.1
    posterior lobe 253.6
  placenta — *see* Placenta, abnormal
sense of smell or taste 781.1
  psychogenic 306.7
sexual (*see also* Deviation, sexual) 302.9
Pervious, congenital — *see also* Imperfect, closure
ductus arteriosus 747.0
Pes (congenital) — *see also* Talipes 754.70
abductus (congenital) 754.60
  acquired 736.79
acquired NEC 736.79
  planus 734
adductus (congenital) 754.79
  acquired 736.79
cavus 754.71
  acquired 736.73
planovalgus (congenital) 754.69
  acquired 736.79
planus (acquired) (any degree) 734
  congenital 754.61
  rachitic 268.1
valgus (congenital) 754.61
  acquired 736.79
varus (congenital) 754.50
  acquired 736.79
Pest — *see also* Plague 020.9
Pestis — *see also* Plague 020.9
bubonica 020.0
fulminans 020.0
minor 020.8
pneumonica — *see* Plague, pneumonic
Petechial
fever 036.0
typhus 081.9
Petechia, petechiae 782.7
fetus or newborn 772.6
Petges-Cléjat or Petges-Clégat syndrome (poikilodermatomyositis) 710.3

☑ **Additional Digit Required** — Refer to the Tabular List for Digit Selection   ▽ **Subterms under main terms may continue to next column or page**

2015 ICD-9-CM   ▶◀ **Revised Text**   ● **New Line**   ▲ **Revised Code**   **Volume 2 — 229**

Peritonitis — Petges-Cléjat or Petges-Clégat syndrome

☑ Additional Digit Required — Refer to the Tabular List for Digit Selection   ▽ Subterms under main terms may continue to next column or page

230 — Volume 2   ▶◀ Revised Text   ● New Line   ▲ Revised Code   2015 ICD-9-CM

Pick's — *continued*
  cerebral atrophy — *continued*
    with dementia
      with behavioral disturbance
        331.11 *[294.11]*
      without behavioral disturbance
        331.11 *[294.10]*
  disease
    brain 331.11
      dementia in
        with behavioral disturbance
          331.11 *[294.11]*
        without behavioral disturbance
          331.11 *[294.10]*
    lipid histiocytosis 272.7
    liver (pericardial pseudocirrhosis of liver) 423.2
    pericardium (pericardial pseudocirrhosis of liver) 423.2
    polyserositis (pericardial pseudocirrhosis of liver) 423.2
  syndrome
    heart (pericardial pseudocirrhosis of liver) 423.2
    liver (pericardial pseudocirrhosis of liver) 423.2
  tubular adenoma (M8640/0)
    specified site — *see* Neoplasm, by site, benign
    unspecified site
      female 220
      male 222.0
Pick-Herxheimer syndrome (diffuse idiopathic cutaneous atrophy) 701.8
Pick-Niemann disease (lipid histiocytosis) 272.7
Pickwickian syndrome (cardiopulmonary obesity) 278.03
Piebaldism, classic 709.09
Piedra 111.2
  beard 111.2
    black 111.3
    white 111.2
  black 111.3
  scalp 111.3
    black 111.3
    white 111.2
  white 111.2
Pierre Marie-Bamberger syndrome (hypertrophic pulmonary osteoarthropathy) 731.2
Pierre Marie's syndrome (pulmonary hypertrophic osteoarthropathy) 731.2
Pierre Mauriac's syndrome (diabetes-dwarfism-obesity) 258.1
Pierre Robin deformity or syndrome (congenital) 756.0
Pierson's disease or osteochondrosis 732.1
Pigeon
  breast or chest (acquired) 738.3
    congenital 754.82
    rachitic (*see also* Rickets) 268.0
  breeders' disease or lung 495.2
  fanciers' disease or lung 495.2
  toe 735.8
Pigmentation (abnormal) 709.00
  anomaly 709.00
    congenital 757.33
    specified NEC 709.09
  conjunctiva 372.55
  cornea 371.10
    anterior 371.11
    posterior 371.13
    stromal 371.12
  lids (congenital) 757.33
    acquired 374.52
  limbus corneae 371.10
  metals 709.00
  optic papilla, congenital 743.57
  retina (congenital) (grouped) (nevoid) 743.53
    acquired 362.74
  scrotum, congenital 757.33
Piles — *see* Hemorrhoids
Pili
  annulati or torti (congenital) 757.4

Pili — *continued*
  incarnati 704.8
Pill roller hand (intrinsic) 736.09
Pilomatrixoma (M8110/0) — *see* Neoplasm, skin, benign
Pilonidal — *see* condition
Pimple 709.8
PIN I (prostatic intraepithelial neoplasia I) 602.3
PIN II (prostatic intraepithelial neoplasia II) 602.3
PIN III (prostatic intraepithelial neoplasia III) 233.4
Pinched nerve — *see* Neuropathy, entrapment
Pineal body or gland — *see* condition
Pinealoblastoma (M9362/3) 194.4
Pinealoma (M9360/1) 237.1
  malignant (M9360/3) 194.4
Pineoblastoma (M9362/3) 194.4
Pineocytoma (M9361/1) 237.1
Pinguecula 372.51
Pingueculitis 372.34
Pinhole meatus — *see also* Stricture, urethra 598.9
Pink
  disease 985.0
  eye 372.03
  puffer 492.8
Pinkus' disease (lichen nitidus) 697.1
Pinpoint
  meatus (*see also* Stricture, urethra) 598.9
  os uteri (*see also* Stricture, cervix) 622.4
Pinselhaare (congenital) 757.4
Pinta 103.9
  cardiovascular lesions 103.2
  chancre (primary) 103.0
  erythematous plaques 103.1
  hyperchromic lesions 103.1
  hyperkeratosis 103.1
  lesions 103.9
    cardiovascular 103.2
    hyperchromic 103.1
    intermediate 103.1
    late 103.2
    mixed 103.3
    primary 103.0
    skin (achromic) (cicatricial) (dyschromic) 103.2
      hyperchromic 103.1
      mixed (achromic and hyperchromic) 103.3
  papule (primary) 103.0
  skin lesions (achromic) (cicatricial) (dyschromic) 103.2
    hyperchromic 103.1
    mixed (achromic and hyperchromic) 103.3
  vitiligo 103.2
Pintid 103.0
Pinworms (disease) (infection) (infestation) 127.4
Piry fever 066.8
Pistol wound — *see* Gunshot wound
Pitchers' elbow 718.82
Pithecoid pelvis 755.69
  with disproportion (fetopelvic) 653.2 ☑
    affecting fetus or newborn 763.1
    causing obstructed labor 660.1 ☑
Pithiatism 300.11
Pit, lip (mucus), **congenital** 750.25
Pitted — *see also* Pitting
  teeth 520.4
Pitting (edema) — *see also* Edema 782.3
  lip 782.3
  nail 703.8
    congenital 757.5
Pituitary gland — *see* condition
Pituitary snuff-takers' disease 495.8
Pityriasis 696.5
  alba 696.5
  capitis 690.11
  circinata (et maculata) 696.3
  Hebra's (exfoliative dermatitis) 695.89
  lichenoides et varioliformis 696.2
  maculata (et circinata) 696.3
  nigra 111.1
  pilaris 757.39

Pityriasis — *continued*
  pilaris — *continued*
    acquired 701.1
    Hebra's 696.4
  rosea 696.3
  rotunda 696.3
  rubra (Hebra) 695.89
    pilaris 696.4
  sicca 690.18
  simplex 690.18
  specified type NEC 696.5
  streptogenes 696.5
  versicolor 111.0
  scrotal 111.0
Placenta, placental
  ablatio 641.2 ☑
    affecting fetus or newborn 762.1
  abnormal, abnormality 656.7 ☑
    with hemorrhage 641.8 ☑
      affecting fetus or newborn 762.1
    affecting fetus or newborn 762.2
  abruptio 641.2 ☑
    affecting fetus or newborn 762.1
  accessory lobe — *see* Placenta, abnormal
  accreta (without hemorrhage) 667.0 ☑
    with hemorrhage 666.0 ☑
  adherent (without hemorrhage) 667.0 ☑
    with hemorrhage 666.0 ☑
  apoplexy — *see* Placenta, separation
  battledore — *see* Placenta, abnormal
  bilobate — *see* Placenta, abnormal
  bipartita — *see* Placenta, abnormal
  carneous mole 631.8
  centralis — *see* Placenta, previa
  circumvallata — *see* Placenta, abnormal
  cyst (amniotic) — *see* Placenta, abnormal
  deficiency — *see* Placenta, insufficiency
  degeneration — *see* Placenta, insufficiency
  detachment (partial) (premature) (with hemorrhage) 641.2 ☑
    affecting fetus or newborn 762.1
  dimidiata — *see* Placenta, abnormal
  disease 656.7 ☑
    affecting fetus or newborn 762.2
  duplex — *see* Placenta, abnormal
  dysfunction — *see* Placenta, insufficiency
  fenestrata — *see* Placenta, abnormal
  fibrosis — *see* Placenta, abnormal
  fleshy mole 631.8
  hematoma — *see* Placenta, abnormal
  hemorrhage NEC — *see* Placenta, separation
  hormone disturbance or malfunction — *see* Placenta, abnormal
  hyperplasia — *see* Placenta, abnormal
  increta (without hemorrhage) 667.0 ☑
    with hemorrhage 666.0 ☑
  infarction 656.7 ☑
    affecting fetus or newborn 762.2
  insertion, vicious — *see* Placenta, previa
  insufficiency
    affecting
      fetus or newborn 762.2
      management of pregnancy 656.5 ☑
  lateral — *see* Placenta, previa
  low implantation or insertion — *see* Placenta, previa
  low-lying — *see* Placenta, previa
  malformation — *see* Placenta, abnormal
  malposition — *see* Placenta, previa
  marginalis, marginata — *see* Placenta, previa
  marginal sinus (hemorrhage) (rupture) 641.2 ☑
    affecting fetus or newborn 762.1
  membranacea — *see* Placenta, abnormal
  multilobed — *see* Placenta, abnormal
  multipartita — *see* Placenta, abnormal
  necrosis — *see* Placenta, abnormal
  percreta (without hemorrhage) 667.0 ☑
    with hemorrhage 666.0 ☑
  polyp 674.4 ☑
  previa (central) (centralis) (complete) (lateral) (marginal) (marginalis) (partial) (partialis) (total) (with hemorrhage) 641.1 ☑

Placenta, placental — *continued*
  previa — *continued*
    without hemorrhage (before labor and delivery) (during pregnancy) 641.0 ☑
      affecting fetus or newborn 762.0
    noted
      before labor, without hemorrhage (with cesarean delivery) 641.0 ☑
      during pregnancy (without hemorrhage) 641.0 ☑
  retention (with hemorrhage) 666.0 ☑
    without hemorrhage 667.0 ☑
    fragments, complicating puerperium (delayed hemorrhage) 666.2 ☑
      without hemorrhage 667.1 ☑
    postpartum, puerperal 666.2 ☑
  separation (normally implanted) (partial) (premature) (with hemorrhage) 641.2 ☑
    affecting fetus or newborn 762.1
  septuplex — *see* Placenta, abnormal
  small — *see* Placenta, insufficiency
  softening (premature) — *see* Placenta, abnormal
  spuria — *see* Placenta, abnormal
  succenturiata — *see* Placenta, abnormal
  syphilitic 095.8
  transfusion syndromes 762.3
  transmission of chemical substance — *see* Absorption, chemical, through placenta
  trapped (with hemorrhage) 666.0 ☑
    without hemorrhage 667.0 ☑
  trilobate — *see* Placenta, abnormal
  tripartita — *see* Placenta, abnormal
  triplex — *see* Placenta, abnormal
  varicose vessel — *see* Placenta, abnormal
  vicious insertion — *see* Placenta, previa
Placentitis
  affecting fetus or newborn 762.7
  complicating pregnancy 658.4 ☑
Plagiocephaly (skull) 754.0
Plague 020.9
  abortive 020.8
  ambulatory 020.8
  bubonic 020.0
  cellulocutaneous 020.1
  lymphatic gland 020.0
  pneumonic 020.5
    primary 020.3
    secondary 020.4
  pulmonary — *see* Plague, pneumonic
  pulmonic — *see* Plague, pneumonic
  septicemic 020.2
  tonsillar 020.9
    septicemic 020.2
  vaccination, prophylactic (against) V03.3
Planning, family V25.09
  contraception V25.9
  natural
    procreative V26.41
    to avoid pregnancy V25.04
  procreation V26.49
    natural V26.41
Plaque
  artery, arterial — *see* Arteriosclerosis
  calcareous — *see* Calcification
  Hollenhorst's (retinal) 362.33
  tongue 528.6
Plasma cell myeloma 203.0 ☑
Plasmacytoma, plasmocytoma (solitary) (M9731/1) 238.6
  benign (M9731/0) — *see* Neoplasm, by site, benign
  malignant (M9731/3) 203.8 ☑
Plasmacytopenia 288.59
Plasmacytosis 288.64
Plaster ulcer — *see also* Ulcer, pressure 707.00
Plateau iris syndrome (without glaucoma) 364.82
  with glaucoma 365.23
Platybasia 756.0
Platyonychia (congenital) 757.5
  acquired 703.8

☑ Additional Digit Required — Refer to the Tabular List for Digit Selection   ▼ Subterms under main terms may continue to next column or page

2015 ICD-9-CM   ▶◀ Revised Text   ● New Line   ▲ Revised Code   Volume 2 — 231

Index

Pick's — Platyonychia

Platypelloid pelvis 738.6
  with disproportion (fetopelvic) 653.2 ☑
    affecting fetus or newborn 763.1
    causing obstructed labor 660.1 ☑
      affecting fetus or newborn 763.1
  congenital 755.69
Platyspondylia 756.19
Plethora 782.62
  newborn 776.4
Pleuralgia 786.52
Pleura, pleural — *see* condition
Pleurisy (acute) (adhesive) (chronic) (costal)
    (diaphragmatic) (double) (dry) (fetid)
    (fibrinous) (fibrous) (interlobar) (latent)
    (lung) (old) (plastic) (primary) (residual)
    (sicca) (sterile) (subacute) (unresolved)
    (with adherent pleura) 511.0
  with
    effusion (without mention of cause)
        511.9
      bacterial, nontuberculous 511.1
      nontuberculous NEC 511.9
        bacterial 511.1
      pneumococcal 511.1
      specified type NEC 511.89
      staphylococcal 511.1
      streptococcal 511.1
      tuberculous (*see also* Tuberculosis,
          pleura) 012.0 ☑
        primary, progressive 010.1 ☑
    influenza, flu, or grippe (*see also* Influen-
        za) 487.1
    tuberculosis — *see* Pleurisy, tuberculous
  encysted 511.89
  exudative (*see also* Pleurisy, with effusion)
      511.9
    bacterial, nontuberculous 511.1
  fibrinopurulent 510.9
    with fistula 510.0
  fibropurulent 510.9
    with fistula 510.0
  hemorrhagic 511.89
  influenzal (*see also* Influenza) 487.1
  pneumococcal 511.0
    with effusion 511.1
  purulent 510.9
    with fistula 510.0
  septic 510.9
    with fistula 510.0
  serofibrinous (*see also* Pleurisy, with effu-
      sion) 511.9
    bacterial, nontuberculous 511.1
  seropurulent 510.9
    with fistula 510.0
  serous (*see also* Pleurisy, with effusion) 511.9
    bacterial, nontuberculous 511.1
  staphylococcal 511.0
    with effusion 511.1
  streptococcal 511.0
    with effusion 511.1
  suppurative 510.9
    with fistula 510.0
  traumatic (post) (current) 862.29
    with open wound into cavity 862.39
  tuberculous (with effusion) (*see also* Tuber-
      culosis, pleura) 012.0 ☑
    primary, progressive 010.1 ☑
Pleuritis sicca — *see* Pleurisy
Pleurobronchopneumonia — *see also* Pneu-
    monia, broncho- 485
Pleurodynia 786.52
  epidemic 074.1
  viral 074.1
Pleurohepatitis 573.8
Pleuropericarditis — *see also* Pericarditis 423.9
  acute 420.90
Pleuropneumonia (acute) (bilateral) (double)
    (septic) — *see also* Pneumonia 486
  chronic (*see also* Fibrosis, lung) 515
Pleurorrhea — *see also* Hydrothorax 511.89
Plexitis, brachial 353.0
Plica
  knee 727.83
  polonica 132.0
  syndrome 727.83
  tonsil 474.8

Plicae dysphonia ventricularis 784.49
Plicated tongue 529.5
  congenital 750.13
Plug
  bronchus NEC 519.19
  meconium (newborn) NEC 777.1
  mucus — *see* Mucus, plug
Plumbism 984.9
  specified type of lead — *see* Table of Drugs
      and Chemicals
Plummer's disease (toxic nodular goiter)
    242.3 ☑
Plummer-Vinson syndrome (sideropenic
    dysphagia) 280.8
Pluricarential syndrome of infancy 260
Plurideficiency syndrome of infancy 260
Plus (and minus) hand (intrinsic) 736.09
PMDD (premenstrual dysphoric disorder) 625.4
PMS 625.4
Pneumathemia — *see* Air, embolism, by type
Pneumatic drill or hammer disease 994.9
Pneumatocele (lung) 518.89
  intracranial 348.89
  tension 492.0
Pneumatosis
  cystoides intestinalis 569.89
  peritonei 568.89
  pulmonum 492.8
Pneumaturia 599.84
Pneumoblastoma (M8981/3) — *see* Neoplasm,
    lung, malignant
Pneumocephalus 348.89
Pneumococcemia 038.2
Pneumococcus, pneumococcal — *see* condi-
    tion
Pneumoconiosis (due to) (inhalation of) 505
  aluminum 503
  asbestos 501
  bagasse 495.1
  bauxite 503
  beryllium 503
  carbon electrode makers' 503
  coal
    miners' (simple) 500
    workers' (simple) 500
  cotton dust 504
  diatomite fibrosis 502
  dust NEC 504
    inorganic 503
    lime 502
    marble 502
    organic NEC 504
  fumes or vapors (from silo) 506.9
  graphite 503
  hard metal 503
  mica 502
  moldy hay 495.0
  rheumatoid 714.81
  silicate NEC 502
  silica NEC 502
    and carbon 500
  talc 502
Pneumocystis carinii pneumonia 136.3
Pneumocystis jiroveci pneumonia 136.3
Pneumocystosis 136.3
  with pneumonia 136.3
Pneumoenteritis 025
Pneumohemopericardium — *see also* Peri-
    carditis 423.9
Pneumohemothorax — *see also* Hemothorax
    511.89
  traumatic 860.4
    with open wound into thorax 860.5
Pneumohydropericardium — *see also* Peri-
    carditis 423.9
Pneumohydrothorax — *see also* Hydrothorax
    511.89
Pneumomediastinum 518.1
  congenital 770.2
  fetus or newborn 770.2
Pneumomycosis 117.9

Pneumonia (acute) (Alpenstich) (benign) (bi-
    lateral) (brain) (cerebral) (circumscribed)
    (congestive) (creeping) (delayed resolu-
    tion) (double) (epidemic) (fever) (flash)
    (fulminant) (fungoid) (granulomatous)
    (hemorrhagic) (incipient) (infantile) (in-
    fectious) (infiltration) (insular) (intermit-
    tent) (latent) (lobe) (migratory) (new-
    born) (organized) (overwhelming) (pri-
    mary) (progressive) (pseudolobar) (puru-
    lent) (resolved) (secondary) (senile)
    (septic) (suppurative) (terminal) (true)
    (unresolved) (vesicular) 486
  with influenza, flu, or grippe 487.0
    due to
      identified (virus)
        avian 488.01
        (novel) 2009 H1N1 488.11
        novel influenza A 488.81
  adenoviral 480.0
  adynamic 514
  alba 090.0
  allergic 518.3
  alveolar — *see* Pneumonia, lobar
  anaerobes 482.81
  anthrax 022.1 *[484.5]*
  apex, apical — *see* Pneumonia, lobar
  ascaris 127.0 *[484.8]*
  aspiration 507.0
    due to
      aspiration of microorganisms
        bacterial 482.9
          specified type NEC 482.89
        specified organism NEC 483.8
          bacterial NEC 482.89
        viral 480.9
          specified type NEC 480.8
      food (regurgitated) 507.0
      gastric secretions 507.0
      milk 507.0
      oils, essences 507.1
      solids, liquids NEC 507.8
      vomitus 507.0
    fetal 770.18
      due to
        blood 770.16
        clear amniotic fluid 770.14
        meconium 770.12
        postnatal stomach contents
            770.86
    newborn 770.18
      due to
        blood 770.16
        clear amniotic fluid 770.14
        meconium 770.12
        postnatal stomach contents
            770.86
  asthenic 514
  atypical (disseminated) (focal) (primary) 486
    with influenza (*see also* Influenza) 487.0
  bacillus 482.9
    specified type NEC 482.89
  bacterial 482.9
    specified type NEC 482.89
  Bacteroides (fragilis) (oralis) (melaninogeni-
      cus) 482.81
  basal, basic, basilar — *see* Pneumonia, by
      type
  bronchiolitis obliterans organized (BOOP)
      516.8
  broncho-, bronchial (confluent) (croupous)
      (diffuse) (disseminated) (hemorrhag-
      ic) (involving lobes) (lobar) (terminal)
      485
    with influenza 487.0
      due to
        identified (virus)
          avian 488.01
          (novel) 2009 H1N1 488.11
          novel influenza A 488.81
    allergic 518.3
    aspiration (*see also* Pneumonia, aspira-
        tion) 507.0
    bacterial 482.9
      specified type NEC 482.89
    capillary 466.19

Pneumonia — *continued*
  broncho-, bronchial — *continued*
    capillary — *continued*
      with bronchospasm or obstruction
          466.19
    chronic (*see also* Fibrosis, lung) 515
    congenital (infective) 770.0
    diplococcal 481
    Eaton's agent 483.0
    Escherichia coli (E. coli) 482.82
    Friedländer's bacillus 482.0
    Hemophilus influenzae 482.2
    hiberno-vernal 083.0 *[484.8]*
    hypostatic 514
    influenzal (*see also* Influenza) 487.0
    inhalation (*see also* Pneumonia, aspira-
        tion) 507.0
      due to fumes or vapors (chemical)
          506.0
    Klebsiella 482.0
    lipid 507.1
      endogenous 516.8
    Mycoplasma (pneumoniae) 483.0
    ornithosis 073.0
    pleuropneumonia-like organisms (PPLO)
        483.0
    pneumococcal 481
    Proteus 482.83
    Pseudomonas 482.1
    specified organism NEC 483.8
      bacterial NEC 482.89
    staphylococcal 482.40
      aureus 482.41
      methicillin
        resistant (MRSA) 482.42
        susceptible (MSSA) 482.41
      specified type NEC 482.49
    streptococcal — *see* Pneumonia, strep-
        tococcal
    typhoid 002.0 *[484.8]*
    viral, virus (*see also* Pneumonia, viral)
        480.9
  Butyrivibrio (fibriosolvens) 482.81
  Candida 112.4
  capillary 466.19
    with bronchospasm or obstruction
        466.19
  caseous (*see also* Tuberculosis) 011.6 ☑
  catarrhal — *see* Pneumonia, broncho-
  central — *see* Pneumonia, lobar
  Chlamydia, chlamydial 483.1
    pneumoniae 483.1
    psittaci 073.0
    specified type NEC 483.1
    trachomatis 483.1
  cholesterol 516.8
  chronic (*see also* Fibrosis, lung) 515
  cirrhotic (chronic) (*see also* Fibrosis, lung)
      515
  Clostridium (haemolyticum) (novyi) NEC
      482.81
  confluent — *see* Pneumonia, broncho-
  congenital (infective) 770.0
    aspiration 770.18
  croupous — *see* Pneumonia, lobar
  cryptogenic organizing 516.36
  cytomegalic inclusion 078.5 *[484.1]*
  deglutition (*see also* Pneumonia, aspiration)
      507.0
  desquamative interstitial 516.37
  diffuse — *see* Pneumonia, broncho-
  diplococcal, diplococcus (broncho-) (lobar)
      481
  disseminated (focal) — *see* Pneumonia,
      broncho-
  due to
    adenovirus 480.0
    anaerobes 482.81
    Bacterium anitratum 482.83
    Chlamydia, chlamydial 483.1
      pneumoniae 483.1
      psittaci 073.0
      specified type NEC 483.1
      trachomatis 483.1
    coccidioidomycosis 114.0
    Diplococcus (pneumoniae) 481

☑ **Additional Digit Required** — Refer to the Tabular List for Digit Selection   ▽ **Subterms under main terms may continue to next column or page**

232 — Volume 2   ▶◀ Revised Text   ● New Line   ▲ Revised Code   2015 ICD-9-CM

Pneumonia — continued
  due to — continued
    Eaton's agent 483.0
    Escherichia coli (E. coli) 482.82
    Friedländer's bacillus 482.0
    fumes or vapors (chemical) (inhalation) 506.0
    fungus NEC 117.9 [484.7]
      coccidioidomycosis 114.0
    Hemophilus influenzae (H. influenzae) 482.2
    Herellea 482.83
    influenza (see also Influenza) 487.0
    Klebsiella pneumoniae 482.0
    Mycoplasma (pneumoniae) 483.0
    parainfluenza virus 480.2
    pleuropneumonia-like organism (PPLO) 483.0
    Pneumococcus 481
    Pneumocystis carinii 136.3
    Pneumocystis jiroveci 136.3
    Proteus 482.83
    Pseudomonas 482.1
    respiratory syncytial virus 480.1
    rickettsia 083.9 [484.8]
    SARS-associated coronavirus 480.3
    specified
      bacteria NEC 482.89
      organism NEC 483.8
      virus NEC 480.8
    Staphylococcus 482.40
      aureus 482.41
        methicillin
          resistant (MRSA) 482.42
          susceptible (MSSA) 482.41
        specified type NEC 482.49
    Streptococcus (see also Pneumonia, streptococcal)
      pneumoniae 481
    virus (see also Pneumonia, viral) 480.9
      SARS-associated coronavirus 480.3
  Eaton's agent 483.0
  embolic, embolism — (see Embolism, pulmonary)
  eosinophilic 518.3
  Escherichia coli (E. coli) 482.82
  Eubacterium 482.81
  fibrinous — see Pneumonia, lobar
  fibroid (chronic) (see also Fibrosis, lung) 515
  fibrous (see also Fibrosis, lung) 515
  Friedländer's bacillus 482.0
  Fusobacterium (nucleatum) 482.81
  gangrenous 513.0
  giant cell (see also Pneumonia, viral) 480.9
  gram-negative bacteria NEC 482.83
    anaerobic 482.81
  grippal (see also Influenza) 487.0
  Hemophilus influenzae (bronchial) (lobar) 482.2
  hypostatic (broncho-) (lobar) 514
  in
    actinomycosis 039.1
    anthrax 022.1 [484.5]
    aspergillosis 117.3 [484.6]
    candidiasis 112.4
    coccidioidomycosis 114.0
    cytomegalic inclusion disease 078.5 [484.1]
    histoplasmosis (see also Histoplasmosis) 115.95
    infectious disease NEC 136.9 [484.8]
    measles 055.1
    mycosis, systemic NEC 117.9 [484.7]
    nocardiasis, nocardiosis 039.1
    ornithosis 073.0
    pneumocystosis 136.3
    psittacosis 073.0
    Q fever 083.0 [484.8]
    salmonellosis 003.22
    toxoplasmosis 130.4
    tularemia 021.2
    typhoid (fever) 002.0 [484.8]
    varicella 052.1
    whooping cough (see also Whooping cough) 033.9 [484.3]
  infective, acquired prenatally 770.0

Pneumonia — continued
  influenzal (broncho) (lobar) (virus) (see also Influenza) 487.0
  inhalation (see also Pneumonia, aspiration) 507.0
    fumes or vapors (chemical) 506.0
  interstitial 516.8
    with influenzal (see also Influenza) 487.0
    acute
      due to Pneumocystis (carinii) (jiroveci) 136.3
      meaning:
        acute interstitial pneumonitis 516.33
        atypical pneumonia — see Pneumonia, atypical
        bacterial pneumonia — see Pneumonia, bacterial
    chronic (see also Fibrosis, lung) 515
    desquamative 516.37
    hypostatic 514
    idiopathic 516.30
      lymphoid 516.35
    lipoid 507.1
    lymphoid (due to known underlying cause) 516.8
    non-specific (due to known underlying cause) 516.8
    organizing (due to known underlying cause) 516.8
    plasma cell 136.3
    Pseudomonas 482.1
  intrauterine (infective) 770.0
    aspiration 770.18
      blood 770.16
      clear amniotic fluid 770.14
      meconium 770.12
      postnatal stomach contents 770.86
  Klebsiella pneumoniae 482.0
  Legionnaires' 482.84
  lipid, lipoid (exogenous) (interstitial) 507.1
    endogenous 516.8
  lobar (diplococcal) (disseminated) (double) (interstitial) (pneumococcal, any type) 481
    with influenza (see also Influenza) 487.0
    bacterial 482.9
      specified type NEC 482.89
    chronic (see also Fibrosis, lung) 515
    Escherichia coli (E. coli) 482.82
    Friedländer's bacillus 482.0
    Hemophilus influenzae (H. influenzae) 482.2
    hypostatic 514
    influenzal (see also Influenza) 487.0
    Klebsiella 482.0
    ornithosis 073.0
    Proteus 482.83
    Pseudomonas 482.1
    psittacosis 073.0
    specified organism NEC 483.8
      bacterial NEC 482.89
    staphylococcal 482.40
      aureus 482.41
        methicillin
          resistant (MRSA) 482.42
          susceptible (MSSA) 482.41
        specified type NEC 482.49
    streptococcal — see Pneumonia, streptococcal
    viral, virus (see also Pneumonia, viral) 480.9
  lobular (confluent) — see Pneumonia, broncho-
  Löffler's 518.3
  massive — see Pneumonia, lobar
  meconium aspiration 770.12
  metastatic NEC 038.8 [484.8]
  methicillin resistant Staphylococcus aureus (MRSA) 482.42
  methicillin susceptible Staphylococcus aureus (MSSA) 482.41
  MRSA (methicillin resistant Staphylococcus aureus) 482.42
  MSSA (methicillin susceptible Staphylococcus aureus) 482.41

Pneumonia — continued
  multilobar — see Pneumonia, by type
  Mycoplasma (pneumoniae) 483.0
  necrotic 513.0
  nitrogen dioxide 506.9
  orthostatic 514
  parainfluenza virus 480.2
  parenchymatous (see also Fibrosis, lung) 515
  passive 514
  patchy — see Pneumonia, broncho-
  Peptococcus 482.81
  Peptostreptococcus 482.81
  plasma cell 136.3
  pleurolobar — see Pneumonia, lobar
  pleuropneumonia-like organism (PPLO) 483.0
  pneumococcal (broncho) (lobar) 481
  Pneumocystis (carinii) (jiroveci) 136.3
  postinfectional NEC 136.9 [484.8]
  postmeasles 055.1
  postoperative 997.39
    aspiration 997.32
  primary atypical 486
  Proprionibacterium 482.81
  Proteus 482.83
  Pseudomonas 482.1
  psittacosis 073.0
  radiation 508.0
  respiratory syncytial virus 480.1
  resulting from a procedure 997.39
    aspiration 997.32
  rheumatic 390 [517.1]
  Salmonella 003.22
  SARS-associated coronavirus 480.3
  segmented, segmental — see Pneumonia, broncho-
  Serratia (marcescens) 482.83
  specified
    bacteria NEC 482.89
    organism NEC 483.8
    virus NEC 480.8
  spirochetal 104.8 [484.8]
  staphylococcal (broncho) (lobar) 482.40
    aureus 482.41
      methicillin
        resistant 482.42
        susceptible (MSSA) 482.41
      specified type NEC 482.49
  static, stasis 514
  streptococcal (broncho) (lobar) NEC 482.30
    Group
      A 482.31
      B 482.32
      specified NEC 482.39
    pneumoniae 481
    specified type NEC 482.39
  Streptococcus pneumoniae 481
  traumatic (complication) (early) (secondary) 958.8
  tuberculous (any) (see also Tuberculosis) 011.6 ☑
  tularemic 021.2
  TWAR agent 483.1
  varicella 052.1
  Veillonella 482.81
  ventilator associated 997.31
  viral, virus (broncho) (interstitial) (lobar) 480.9
    with influenza, flu, or grippe (see also Influenza) 487.0
    adenoviral 480.0
    parainfluenza 480.2
    respiratory syncytial 480.1
    SARS-associated coronavirus 480.3
    specified type NEC 480.8
  white (congenital) 090.0
Pneumonic — see condition
Pneumonitis (acute) (primary) — see also Pneumonia 486
  allergic 495.9
    specified type NEC 495.8
  aspiration 507.0
    due to fumes or gases 506.0
    fetal 770.18
      due to
        blood 770.16

Pneumonitis — see also Pneumonia — continued
  aspiration — continued
    fetal — continued
      due to — continued
        clear amniotic fluid 770.14
        meconium 770.12
        postnatal stomach contents 770.86
      newborn 770.18
        due to
          blood 770.16
          clear amniotic fluid 770.14
          meconium 770.12
          postnatal stomach contents 770.86
      obstetric 668.0 ☑
  chemical 506.0
    due to fumes or gases 506.0
    resulting from a procedure 997.32
  cholesterol 516.8
  chronic (see also Fibrosis, lung) 515
  congenital rubella 771.0
  crack 506.0
  due to
    crack (cocaine) 506.0
    fumes or vapors 506.0
    inhalation
      food (regurgitated), milk, vomitus 507.0
      oils, essences 507.1
      saliva 507.0
      solids, liquids NEC 507.8
    toxoplasmosis (acquired) 130.4
      congenital (active) 771.2 [484.8]
  eosinophilic 518.3
  fetal aspiration 770.18
    due to
      blood 770.16
      clear amniotic fluid 770.14
      meconium 770.12
      postnatal stomach contents 770.86
  hypersensitivity 495.9
  interstitial (chronic) (see also Fibrosis, lung) 515
    acute 516.33
    idiopathic
      lymphocytic 516.35
      non-specific 516.32
    lymphoid 516.8
  lymphoid, interstitial 516.8
  meconium aspiration 770.12
  postanesthetic
    correct substance properly administered 507.0
    obstetric 668.0 ☑
    overdose or wrong substance given 968.4
    specified anesthetic — see Table of Drugs and Chemicals
  postoperative 997.3 ☑
    aspiration 997.32
    obstetric 668.0 ☑
  radiation 508.0
  rubella, congenital 771.0
  "ventilation" 495.7
  ventilator associated 997.31
  wood-dust 495.8
Pneumonoconiosis — see Pneumoconiosis
Pneumoparotid 527.8
Pneumopathy NEC 518.89
  alveolar 516.9
    specified NEC 516.8
  due to dust NEC 504
  parietoalveolar 516.9
    specified condition NEC 516.8
Pneumopericarditis — see also Pericarditis 423.9
  acute 420.90
Pneumopericardium — see also Pericarditis
  congenital 770.2
  fetus or newborn 770.2
  traumatic (post) (see also Pneumothorax, traumatic) 860.0
    with open wound into thorax 860.1
Pneumoperitoneum 568.89

Pneumoperitoneum — *continued*
  fetus or newborn 770.2
Pneumophagia (psychogenic) 306.4
Pneumopleurisy, pneumopleuritis — *see also* Pneumonia 486
Pneumopyopericardium 420.99
Pneumopyothorax — *see also* Pyopneumothorax 510.9
  with fistula 510.0
Pneumorrhagia 786.30
  newborn 770.3
  tuberculous (*see also* Tuberculosis, pulmonary) 011.9 ☑
Pneumosiderosis (occupational) 503
Pneumothorax 512.89
  acute 512.89
  chronic 512.83
  congenital 770.2
  due to operative injury of chest wall or lung 512.1
    accidental puncture or laceration 512.1
  fetus or newborn 770.2
  iatrogenic 512.1
  postoperative 512.1
  specified type NEC 512.89
  spontaneous 512.89
    fetus or newborn 770.2
    primary 512.81
    secondary 512.82
    tension 512.0
  sucking 512.89
    iatrogenic 512.1
    postoperative 512.1
  tense valvular, infectional 512.0
  tension 512.0
    iatrogenic 512.1
    postoperative 512.1
    spontaneous 512.0
  traumatic 860.0
    with
      hemothorax 860.4
        with open wound into thorax 860.5
      open wound into thorax 860.1
  tuberculous (*see also* Tuberculosis) 011.7 ☑
Pocket(s)
  endocardial (*see also* Endocarditis) 424.90
  periodontal 523.8
Podagra 274.01
Podencephalus 759.89
Poikilocytosis 790.09
Poikiloderma 709.09
  Civatte's 709.09
  congenital 757.33
  vasculare atrophicans 696.2
Poikilodermatomyositis 710.3
Pointed ear 744.29
Poise imperfect 729.90
Poisoned — *see* Poisoning
Poisoning (acute) — *see also* Table of Drugs and Chemicals
  Bacillus, B.
    aertrycke (*see also* Infection, Salmonella) 003.9
    botulinus 005.1
    cholerae (suis) (*see also* Infection, Salmonella) 003.9
    paratyphosus (*see also* Infection, Salmonella) 003.9
    suipestifer (*see also* Infection, Salmonella) 003.9
  bacterial toxins NEC 005.9
  berries, noxious 988.2
  blood (general) — *see* Septicemia
  botulism 005.1
  bread, moldy, mouldy — *see* Poisoning, food
  Ciguatera 988.0
  damaged meat — *see* Poisoning, food
  death-cap (Amanita phalloides) (Amanita verna) 988.1
  decomposed food — *see* Poisoning, food
  diseased food — *see* Poisoning, food
  drug — *see* Table of Drugs and Chemicals
  epidemic, fish, meat, or other food — *see* Poisoning, food

Poisoning — *see also* Table of Drugs and Chemicals — *continued*
  fava bean 282.2
  fish (bacterial) (*see also* Poisoning, food)
    noxious 988.0
  food (acute) (bacterial) (diseased) (infected) NEC 005.9
    due to
      bacillus
        aertrycke (*see also* Poisoning, food, due to Salmonella) 003.9
        botulinus 005.1
        cereus 005.89
        choleraesuis (*see also* Poisoning, food, due to Salmonella) 003.9
        paratyphosus (*see also* Poisoning, food, due to Salmonella) 003.9
        suipestifer (*see also* Poisoning, food, due to Salmonella) 003.9
      Clostridium 005.3
        botulinum 005.1
        perfringens 005.2
        welchii 005.2
      Salmonella (aertrycke) (callinarum) (choleraesuis) (enteritidis) (paratyphi) (suipestifer) 003.9
        with
          gastroenteritis 003.0
          localized infection(s) (*see also* Infection, Salmonella) 003.20
          septicemia 003.1
          specified manifestation NEC 003.8
      specified bacterium NEC 005.89
      Staphylococcus 005.0
      Streptococcus 005.89
      Vibrio parahaemolyticus 005.4
      Vibrio vulnificus 005.81
    noxious or naturally toxic 988.0
      berries 988.2
      fish 988.0
      mushroom 988.1
      plants NEC 988.2
  ice cream — *see* Poisoning, food
  ichthyotoxism (bacterial) 005.9
  kreotoxism, food 005.9
  malarial — *see* Malaria
  meat — *see* Poisoning, food
  mushroom (noxious) 988.1
  mussel (*see also* Poisoning, food)
    noxious 988.0
  noxious foodstuffs (*see also* Poisoning, food, noxious) 988.9
    specified type NEC 988.8
  plants, noxious 988.2
  pork (*see also* Poisoning, food)
    specified NEC 988.8
    Trichinosis 124
  ptomaine — *see* Poisoning, food
  putrefaction, food — *see* Poisoning, food
  radiation 508.0
  Salmonella (*see also* Infection, Salmonella) 003.9
  sausage (*see also* Poisoning, food)
    Trichinosis 124
  saxitoxin 988.0
  shellfish (*see also* Poisoning, food)
    noxious (amnesic) (azaspiracid) (diarrheic) (neurotoxic) (paralytic) 988.0
  Staphylococcus, food 005.0
  toxic, from disease NEC 799.89
  truffles — *see* Poisoning, food
  uremic — *see* Uremia
  uric acid 274.9
  water 276.69
Poison ivy, oak, sumac or other plant dermatitis 692.6
Poker spine 720.0
Policeman's disease 729.2
Polioencephalitis (acute) (bulbar) — *see also* Poliomyelitis, bulbar 045.0 ☑

Polioencephalitis — *see also* Poliomyelitis, bulbar — *continued*
  inferior 335.22
  influenzal (*see also* Influenza) 487.8
  superior hemorrhagic (acute) (Wernicke's) 265.1
  Wernicke's (superior hemorrhagic) 265.1
Polioencephalomyelitis (acute) (anterior) (bulbar) — *see also* Polioencephalitis 045.0 ☑
Polioencephalopathy, superior hemorrhagic 265.1
  with
    beriberi 265.0
    pellagra 265.2
Poliomeningoencephalitis — *see* Meningoencephalitis
Poliomyelitis (acute) (anterior) (epidemic) 045.9 ☑

Note — *Use the following fifth-digit subclassification with category 045:*

0   *poliovirus, unspecified type*
1   *poliovirus, type I*
2   *poliovirus, type II*
3   *poliovirus, type III*

  with
    paralysis 045.1 ☑
      bulbar 045.0 ☑
  abortive 045.2 ☑
  ascending 045.9 ☑
    progressive 045.9 ☑
  bulbar 045.0 ☑
  cerebral 045.0 ☑
  chronic 335.21
  congenital 771.2
  contact V01.2
  deformities 138
  exposure to V01.2
  late effect 138
  nonepidemic 045.9 ☑
  nonparalytic 045.2 ☑
  old with deformity 138
  posterior, acute 053.19
  residual 138
  sequelae 138
  spinal, acute 045.9 ☑
  syphilitic (chronic) 094.89
  vaccination, prophylactic (against) V04.0
Poliosis (eyebrow) (eyelashes) 704.3
  circumscripta (congenital) 757.4
    acquired 704.3
  congenital 757.4
Pollakiuria 788.41
  psychogenic 306.53
Pollinosis 477.0
Pollitzer's disease (hidradenitis suppurativa) 705.83
Polyadenitis — *see also* Adenitis 289.3
  malignant 020.0
Polyalgia 729.99
Polyangiitis (essential) 446.0
Polyarteritis (nodosa) (renal) 446.0
Polyarthralgia 719.49
  psychogenic 306.0
Polyarthritis, polyarthropathy NEC 716.59
  due to or associated with other specified conditions — *see* Arthritis, due to or associated with
  endemic (*see also* Disease, Kaschin-Beck) 716.0 ☑
  inflammatory 714.9
    specified type NEC 714.89
  juvenile (chronic) 714.30
    acute 714.31
  migratory — *see* Fever, rheumatic
  rheumatic 714.0
    fever (acute) — *see* Fever, rheumatic
Polycarential syndrome of infancy 260
Polychondritis (atrophic) (chronic) (relapsing) 733.99
Polycoria 743.46
Polycystic (congenital) (disease) 759.89

Polycystic — *continued*
  degeneration, kidney — *see* Polycystic, kidney
  kidney (congenital) 753.12
    adult type (APKD) 753.13
    autosomal dominant 753.13
    autosomal recessive 753.14
    childhood type (CPKD) 753.14
    infantile type 753.14
  liver 751.62
  lung 518.89
    congenital 748.4
  ovary, ovaries 256.4
  spleen 759.0
Polycythemia (primary) (rubra) (vera) (M9950/1) 238.4
  acquired 289.0
  benign 289.0
    familial 289.6
  due to
    donor twin 776.4
    fall in plasma volume 289.0
    high altitude 289.0
    maternal-fetal transfusion 776.4
    stress 289.0
  emotional 289.0
  erythropoietin 289.0
  familial (benign) 289.6
  Gaisböck's (hypertonica) 289.0
  high altitude 289.0
  hypertonica 289.0
  hypoxemic 289.0
  neonatorum 776.4
  nephrogenous 289.0
  relative 289.0
  secondary 289.0
  spurious 289.0
  stress 289.0
Polycytosis cryptogenica 289.0
Polydactylism, polydactyly 755.00
  fingers 755.01
  toes 755.02
Polydipsia 783.5
Polydystrophic oligophrenia 277.5
Polyembryoma (M9072/3) — *see* Neoplasm, by site, malignant
Polygalactia 676.6 ☑
Polyglandular
  deficiency 258.9
  dyscrasia 258.9
  dysfunction 258.9
  syndrome 258.8
Polyhydramnios — *see also* Hydramnios 657.0 ☑
Polymastia 757.6
Polymenorrhea 626.2
Polymicrogyria 742.2
Polymyalgia 725
  arteritica 446.5
  rheumatica 725
Polymyositis (acute) (chronic) (hemorrhagic) 710.4
  with involvement of
    lung 710.4 [517.8]
    skin 710.3
  ossificans (generalisata) (progressiva) 728.19
  Wagner's (dermatomyositis) 710.3
Polyneuritis, polyneuritic — *see also* Polyneuropathy 356.9
  alcoholic 357.5
    with psychosis 291.1
  cranialis 352.6
  demyelinating, chronic inflammatory (CIDP) 357.81
  diabetic 250.6 ☑ [357.2]
    due to secondary diabetes 249.6 ☑ [357.2]
  due to lack of vitamin NEC 269.2 [357.4]
  endemic 265.0 [357.4]
  erythredema 985.0
  febrile 357.0
  hereditary ataxic 356.3
  idiopathic, acute 357.0
  infective (acute) 357.0
  nutritional 269.9 [357.4]
  postinfectious 357.0

☑ **Additional Digit Required** — Refer to the Tabular List for Digit Selection   ▽ Subterms under main terms may continue to next column or page

Polyneuropathy (peripheral) 356.9
  alcoholic 357.5
  amyloid 277.39 [357.4]
  arsenical 357.7
  critical illness 357.82
  demyelinating, chronic inflammatory (CIDP) 357.81
  diabetic 250.6 ☑ [357.2]
    due to secondary diabetes 249.6 ☑ [357.2]
  due to
    antitetanus serum 357.6
    arsenic 357.7
    drug or medicinal substance 357.6
      correct substance properly administered 357.6
      overdose or wrong substance given or taken 977.9
      specified drug — see Table of Drugs and Chemicals
    lack of vitamin NEC 269.2 [357.4]
    lead 357.7
    organophosphate compounds 357.7
    pellagra 265.2 [357.4]
    porphyria 277.1 [357.4]
    serum 357.6
    toxic agent NEC 357.7
  hereditary 356.0
  idiopathic 356.9
    progressive 356.4
  in
    amyloidosis 277.39 [357.4]
    avitaminosis 269.2 [357.4]
      specified NEC 269.1 [357.4]
    beriberi 265.0 [357.4]
    collagen vascular disease NEC 710.9 [357.1]
    deficiency
      B-complex NEC 266.2 [357.4]
      vitamin B 266.1 [357.4]
      vitamin B6 266.9 [357.4]
    diabetes 250.6 ☑ [357.2]
      due to secondary diabetes 249.6 ☑ [357.2]
    diphtheria (see also Diphtheria) 032.89 [357.4]
    disseminated lupus erythematosus 710.0 [357.1]
    herpes zoster 053.13
    hypoglycemia 251.2 [357.4]
    malignant neoplasm (M8000/3) NEC 199.1 [357.3]
    mumps 072.72
    pellagra 265.2 [357.4]
    polyarteritis nodosa 446.0 [357.1]
    porphyria 277.1 [357.4]
    rheumatoid arthritis 714.0 [357.1]
    sarcoidosis 135 [357.4]
    uremia 585.9 [357.4]
  lead 357.7
  nutritional 269.9 [357.4]
    specified NEC 269.8 [357.4]
  postherpetic 053.13
  progressive 356.4
  sensory (hereditary) 356.2
  specified NEC 356.8
Polyonychia 757.5
Polyopia 368.2
  refractive 368.15
Polyorchism, polyorchidism (three testes) 752.89
Polyorrhymenitis (peritoneal) — see also Polyserositis 568.82
  pericardial 423.2
Polyostotic fibrous dysplasia 756.54
Polyotia 744.1
Polyphagia 783.6
Polypoid — see condition
Polyposis — see also Polyp
  coli (adenomatous) (M8220/0) 211.3
    adenocarcinoma in (M8220/3) 153.9
    carcinoma in (M8220/3) 153.9
  familial (M8220/0) 211.3
  intestinal (adenomatous) (M8220/0) 211.3
  multiple (M8221/0) — see Neoplasm, by site, benign

Polyp, polypus

Note — Polyps of organs or sites that do not appear in the list below should be coded to the residual category for diseases of the organ or site concerned.

  accessory sinus 471.8
  adenoid tissue 471.0
  adenomatous (M8210/0) (see also Neoplasm, by site, benign)
    adenocarcinoma in (M8210/3) — see Neoplasm, by site, malignant
    carcinoma in (M8210/3) — see Neoplasm, by site, malignant
    multiple (M8221/0) — see Neoplasm, by site, benign
  antrum 471.8
  anus, anal (canal) (nonadenomatous) 569.0
    adenomatous 211.4
  Bartholin's gland 624.6
  bladder (M8120/1) 236.7
  broad ligament 620.8
  cervix (uteri) 622.7
    adenomatous 219.0
    in pregnancy or childbirth 654.6 ☑
      affecting fetus or newborn 763.89
      causing obstructed labor 660.2 ☑
    mucous 622.7
    nonneoplastic 622.7
  choanal 471.0
  cholesterol 575.6
  clitoris 624.6
  colon (M8210/0) (see also Polyp, adenomatous) 211.3
  corpus uteri 621.0
  dental 522.0
  ear (middle) 385.30
  endometrium 621.0
  ethmoidal (sinus) 471.8
  fallopian tube 620.8
  female genital organs NEC 624.8
  frontal (sinus) 471.8
  gallbladder 575.6
  gingiva 523.8
  gum 523.8
  labia 624.6
  larynx (mucous) 478.4
  malignant (M8000/3) — see Neoplasm, by site, malignant
  maxillary (sinus) 471.8
  middle ear 385.30
  myometrium 621.0
  nares
    anterior 471.9
    posterior 471.0
  nasal (mucous) 471.9
    cavity 471.0
    septum 471.9
  nasopharyngeal 471.0
  neoplastic (M8210/0) — see Neoplasm, by site, benign
  nose (mucous) 471.9
  oviduct 620.8
  paratubal 620.8
  pharynx 478.29
    congenital 750.29
  placenta, placental 674.4 ☑
  prostate 600.20
    with
      other lower urinary tract symptoms (LUTS) 600.21
      urinary
        obstruction 600.21
        retention 600.21
  pudenda 624.6
  pulp (dental) 522.0
  rectosigmoid 211.4
  rectum (nonadenomatous) 569.0
    adenomatous 211.4
  septum (nasal) 471.9
  sinus (accessory) (ethmoidal) (frontal) (maxillary) (sphenoidal) 471.8
  sphenoidal (sinus) 471.8
  stomach (M8210/0) 211.1
  tube, fallopian 620.8
  turbinate, mucous membrane 471.8
  ureter 593.89

Polyp, polypus — continued
  urethra 599.3
  uterine
    ligament 620.8
    tube 620.8
  uterus (body) (corpus) (mucous) 621.0
    in pregnancy or childbirth 654.1 ☑
      affecting fetus or newborn 763.89
      causing obstructed labor 660.2 ☑
  vagina 623.7
  vocal cord (mucous) 478.4
  vulva 624.6
Polyradiculitis (acute) 357.0
Polyradiculoneuropathy (acute) (segmentally demyelinating) 357.0
Polysarcia 278.00
Polyserositis (peritoneal) 568.82
  due to pericarditis 423.2
  paroxysmal (familial) 277.31
  pericardial 423.2
  periodic (familial) 277.31
  pleural — see Pleurisy
  recurrent 277.31
  tuberculous (see also Tuberculosis, polyserositis) 018.9 ☑
Polysialia 527.7
Polysplenia syndrome 759.0
Polythelia 757.6
Polytrichia — see also Hypertrichosis 704.1
Polyunguia (congenital) 757.5
  acquired 703.8
Polyuria 788.42
Pompe's disease (glycogenosis II) 271.0
Pompholyx 705.81
Poncet's disease (tuberculous rheumatism) — see also Tuberculosis 015.9 ☑
Pond fracture — see Fracture, skull, vault
Ponos 085.0
Pons, pontine — see condition
Poor
  aesthetics of existing restoration of tooth 525.67
  contractions, labor 661.2 ☑
    affecting fetus or newborn 763.7
  fetal growth NEC 764.9 ☑
    affecting management of pregnancy 656.5 ☑
  incorporation
    artificial skin graft 996.55
    decellularized allodermis graft 996.55
  obstetrical history V13.29
    affecting management of current pregnancy V23.49
    ectopic pregnancy V23.42
    pre-term labor V23.41
    pre-term labor V13.21
  sucking reflex (newborn) 796.1
  vision NEC 369.9
Poradenitis, nostras 099.1
Porencephaly (congenital) (developmental) (true) 742.4
  acquired 348.0
  nondevelopmental 348.0
  traumatic (post) 310.2
Porocephaliasis 134.1
Porokeratosis 757.39
  disseminated superficial actinic (DSAP) 692.75
Poroma, eccrine (M8402/0) — see Neoplasm, skin, benign
Porphyria (acute) (congenital) (constitutional) (erythropoietic) (familial) (hepatica) (idiopathic) (idiosyncratic) (intermittent) (latent) (mixed hepatic) (photosensitive) (South African genetic) (Swedish) 277.1
  acquired 277.1
  cuteanatarda
    hereditaria 277.1
    symptomatica 277.1
  due to drugs
    correct substance properly administered 277.1
    overdose or wrong substance given or taken 977.9
    specified drug — see Table of Drugs and Chemicals

Porphyria — continued
  secondary 277.1
  toxic NEC 277.1
  variegata 277.1
Porphyrinuria (acquired) (congenital) (secondary) 277.1
Porphyruria (acquired) (congenital) 277.1
Portal — see condition
Port wine nevus or mark 757.32
Posadas-Wernicke disease 114.9
Position
  fetus, abnormal (see also Presentation, fetal) 652.9 ☑
  teeth, faulty (see also Anomaly, position tooth) 524.30
Positive
  culture (nonspecific) 795.39
    AIDS virus V08
    blood 790.7
    HIV V08
    human immunodeficiency virus V08
    nose 795.39
      Staphylococcus — see Carrier (suspected) of, Staphylococcus
    skin lesion NEC 795.39
    spinal fluid 792.0
    sputum 795.39
    stool 792.1
    throat 795.39
    urine 791.9
    wound 795.39
  findings, anthrax 795.31
  HIV V08
  human immunodeficiency virus (HIV) V08
  PPD 795.51
  serology
    AIDS virus V08
      inconclusive 795.71
    HIV V08
      inconclusive 795.71
    human immunodeficiency virus (HIV) V08
      inconclusive 795.71
    syphilis 097.1
      with signs or symptoms — see Syphilis, by site and stage
      false 795.6
  skin test 795.7 ☑
    tuberculin (without active tuberculosis) 795.51
  VDRL 097.1
    with signs or symptoms — see Syphilis, by site and stage
    false 795.6
  Wassermann reaction 097.1
    false 795.6
Postcardiotomy syndrome 429.4
Postcaval ureter 753.4
Postcholecystectomy syndrome 576.0
Postclimacteric bleeding 627.1
Postcommissurotomy syndrome 429.4
Postconcussional syndrome 310.2
Postcontusional syndrome 310.2
Postcricoid region — see condition
Post-dates (pregnancy) — see Pregnancy
Postencephalitic — see also condition
  syndrome 310.89
Posterior — see condition
Posterolateral sclerosis (spinal cord) — see Degeneration, combined
Postexanthematous — see condition
Postfebrile — see condition
Postgastrectomy dumping syndrome 564.2
Posthemiplegic chorea 344.89
Posthemorrhagic anemia (chronic) 280.0
  acute 285.1
  newborn 776.5
Posthepatitis syndrome 780.79
Postherpetic neuralgia (intercostal) (syndrome) (zoster) 053.19
  geniculate ganglion 053.11
  ophthalmica 053.19
  trigeminal 053.12
Posthitis 607.1
Postimmunization complication or reaction — see Complications, vaccination

Postinfectious — see condition
Postinfluenzal syndrome 780.79
Postlaminectomy syndrome 722.80
  cervical, cervicothoracic 722.81
  kyphosis 737.12
  lumbar, lumbosacral 722.83
  thoracic, thoracolumbar 722.82
Postleukotomy syndrome 310.0
Postlobectomy syndrome 310.0
Postmastectomy lymphedema (syndrome) 457.0
Postmaturity, postmature (fetus or newborn) (gestation period over 42 completed weeks) 766.22
  affecting management of pregnancy
    post-term pregnancy 645.1 ☑
    prolonged pregnancy 645.2 ☑
  syndrome 766.22
Postmeasles — see also condition
  complication 055.8
    specified NEC 055.79
Postmenopausal
  endometrium (atrophic) 627.8
    suppurative (see also Endometritis) 615.9
  hormone replacement therapy V07.4
  status (age related) (natural) V49.81
Postnasal drip 784.91
Postnatal — see condition
Postoperative — see also condition
  confusion state 293.9
  psychosis 293.9
  status NEC (see also Status (post)) V45.89
Postpancreatectomy hyperglycemia 251.3
Postpartum — see also condition
  anemia 648.2 ☑
  cardiomyopathy 674.5 ☑
  observation
    immediately after delivery V24.0
    routine follow-up V24.2
Postperfusion syndrome NEC 999.89
  bone marrow 996.85
Postpoliomyelitic — see condition
Postsurgery status NEC — see also Status (post V45.89
Post-term (pregnancy) 645.1 ☑
  infant (gestation period over 40 completed weeks to 42 completed weeks) 766.21
Post-transplant lymphoproliferative disorder (PTLD) 238.77
Posttraumatic — see condition
Posttraumatic brain syndrome, nonpsychotic 310.2
Post-traumatic stress disorder (PTSD) 309.81
Post-typhoid abscess 002.0
Postures, hysterical 300.11
Postvaccinal reaction or complication — see Complications, vaccination
Postvagotomy syndrome 564.2
Postvalvulotomy syndrome 429.4
Postvasectomy sperm count V25.8
Potain's disease (pulmonary edema) 514
Potain's syndrome (gastrectasis with dyspepsia) 536.1
Pott's
  curvature (spinal) (see also Tuberculosis) 015.0 ☑ [737.43]
  disease or paraplegia (see also Tuberculosis) 015.0 ☑ [730.88]
  fracture (closed) 824.4
    open 824.5
  gangrene 440.24
  osteomyelitis (see also Tuberculosis) 015.0 ☑ [730.88]
  spinal curvature (see also Tuberculosis) 015.0 ☑ [737.43]
  tumor, puffy (see also Osteomyelitis) 730.2 ☑
Potter's
  asthma 502
  disease 753.0
  facies 754.0
  lung 502
  syndrome (with renal agenesis) 753.0

Pouch
  bronchus 748.3
  Douglas' — see condition
  esophagus, esophageal (congenital) 750.4
    acquired 530.6
  gastric 537.1
  Hartmann's (abnormal sacculation of gall-bladder neck) 575.8
    of intestine V44.3
      attention to V55.3
  pharynx, pharyngeal (congenital) 750.27
Pouchitis 569.71
Poulet's disease 714.2
Poultrymen's itch 133.8
Poverty V60.2
PPE (palmar plantar erythrodysesthesia) 693.0
Prader-Labhart-Willi-Fanconi syndrome (hypogenital dystrophy with diabetic tendency) 759.81
Prader-Willi syndrome (hypogenital dystrophy with diabetic tendency) 759.81
Preachers' voice 784.49
Pre-AIDS — see Human immunodeficiency virus (disease) (illness) (infection)
Preauricular appendage 744.1
Prebetalipoproteinemia (acquired) (essential) (familial) (hereditary) (primary) (secondary) 272.1
  with chylomicronemia 272.3
Precipitate labor 661.3 ☑
  affecting fetus or newborn 763.6
Preclimacteric bleeding 627.0
  menorrhagia 627.0
Precocious
  adrenarche 259.1
  menarche 259.1
  menstruation 259.1
  pubarche 259.1
  puberty NEC 259.1
  sexual development NEC 259.1
  thelarche 259.1
Precocity, sexual (constitutional) (cryptogenic) (female) (idiopathic) (male) NEC 259.1
  with adrenal hyperplasia 255.2
Precordial pain 786.51
  psychogenic 307.89
Predeciduous teeth 520.2
Prediabetes, prediabetic 790.29
  complicating pregnancy, childbirth, or puerperium 648.8 ☑
  fetus or newborn 775.89
Predislocation status of hip, at birth — see also Subluxation, congenital, hip 754.32
Preeclampsia (mild) 642.4 ☑
  with pre-existing hypertension 642.7 ☑
  affecting fetus or newborn 760.0
  severe 642.5 ☑
  superimposed on pre-existing hypertensive disease 642.7 ☑
Preeruptive color change, teeth, tooth 520.8
Preexcitation 426.7
  atrioventricular conduction 426.7
  ventricular 426.7
Preglaucoma 365.00
Pregnancy (single) (uterine) (without sickness) V22.2

> Note — Use the following fifth-digit subclassification with categories 640–649, 651–679:
>
> 0   unspecified as to episode of care
>
> 1   delivered, with or without mention of antepartum condition
>
> 2   delivered, with mention of postpartum complication
>
> 3   antepartum condition or complication
>
> 4   postpartum condition or complication

  abdominal (ectopic) 633.00
    with intrauterine pregnancy 633.01
    affecting fetus or newborn 761.4
  abnormal NEC 646.9 ☑
  ampullar — see Pregnancy, tubal

Pregnancy — continued
  biochemical 631.0
  broad ligament — see Pregnancy, cornual
  cervical — see Pregnancy, cornual
  chemical 631.0
  combined (extrauterine and intrauterine) — see Pregnancy, cornual
  complicated (by) 646.9 ☑
    abnormal, abnormality NEC 646.9 ☑
      cervix 654.6 ☑
      cord (umbilical) 663.9 ☑
      glucose tolerance (conditions classifiable to 790.21–790.29) 648.8 ☑
      pelvic organs or tissues NEC 654.9 ☑
      pelvis (bony) 653.0 ☑
      perineum or vulva 654.8 ☑
      placenta, placental (vessel) 656.7 ☑
      position
        cervix 654.4 ☑
        placenta 641.1 ☑
          without hemorrhage 641.0 ☑
        uterus 654.4 ☑
      size, fetus 653.5 ☑
      uterus (congenital) 654.0 ☑
    abscess or cellulitis
      bladder 646.6 ☑
      genitourinary tract (conditions classifiable to 590, 595, 597, 599.0, 614.0–614.5, 614.7–614.9, 615) 646.6 ☑
      kidney 646.6 ☑
      urinary tract NEC 646.6 ☑
    adhesion, pelvic peritoneal 648.9 ☑
    air embolism 673.0 ☑
    albuminuria 646.2 ☑
      with hypertension — see Toxemia, of pregnancy
    amnionitis 658.4 ☑
    amniotic fluid embolism 673.1 ☑
    anemia (conditions classifiable to 280–285) 648.2 ☑
    appendicitis 648.9 ☑
    atrophy, yellow (acute) (liver) (subacute) 646.7 ☑
    bacilluria, asymptomatic 646.5 ☑
    bacteriuria, asymptomatic 646.5 ☑
    bariatric surgery status 649.2 ☑
    bicornis or bicornuate uterus 654.0 ☑
    biliary problems 646.8 ☑
    bone and joint disorders (conditions classifiable to 720–724 or conditions affecting lower limbs classifiable to 711–719, 725–738) 648.7 ☑
    breech presentation (buttocks) (complete) (frank) 652.2 ☑
      with successful version 652.1 ☑
    cardiovascular disease (conditions classifiable to 390–398, 410–429) 648.6 ☑
      congenital (conditions classifiable to 745–747) 648.5 ☑
    cerebrovascular disorders (conditions classifiable to 430–434, 436–437) 674.0 ☑
    cervicitis (conditions classifiable to 616.0) 646.6 ☑
    chloasma (gravidarum) 646.8 ☑
    cholelithiasis 646.8 ☑
    cholestasis 646.7 ☑
    chorea (gravidarum) — see Eclampsia, pregnancy
    coagulation defect 649.3 ☑
    conjoined twins 678.1 ☑
    contraction, pelvis (general) 653.1 ☑
      inlet 653.2 ☑
      outlet 653.3 ☑
    convulsions (eclamptic) (uremic) 642.6 ☑
      with pre-existing hypertension 642.7 ☑

Pregnancy — continued
  complicated — continued
    current disease or condition (nonobstetric)
      abnormal glucose tolerance 648.8 ☑
      anemia 648.2 ☑
      biliary tract 646.7 ☑
      bone and joint (lower limb) 648.7 ☑
      cardiovascular 648.6 ☑
        congenital 648.5 ☑
      cerebrovascular 674.0 ☑
      diabetes (conditions classifiable to 249 and 250) 648.0 ☑
      drug dependence 648.3 ☑
      female genital mutilation 648.9 ☑
      genital organ or tract 646.6 ☑
      gonorrheal 647.1 ☑
      hypertension 642.2 ☑
        chronic kidney 642.2 ☑
        renal 642.1 ☑
      infectious 647.9 ☑
        specified type NEC 647.8 ☑
      liver 646.7 ☑
      malarial 647.4 ☑
      nutritional deficiency 648.9 ☑
      parasitic NEC 647.8 ☑
      periodontal disease 648.9 ☑
      renal 646.2 ☑
        hypertensive 642.1 ☑
      rubella 647.5 ☑
      specified condition NEC 648.9 ☑
      syphilitic 647.0 ☑
      thyroid 648.1 ☑
      tuberculous 647.3 ☑
      urinary 646.6 ☑
      venereal 647.2 ☑
      viral NEC 647.6 ☑
    cystitis 646.6 ☑
    cystocele 654.4 ☑
    death of fetus (near term) 656.4 ☑
      early pregnancy (before 22 completed weeks gestation) 632
    deciduitis 646.6 ☑
    decreased fetal movements 655.7 ☑
    diabetes (mellitus) (conditions classifiable to 249 and 250) 648.0 ☑
    disorders of liver and biliary tract 646.7 ☑
    displacement, uterus NEC 654.4 ☑
    disproportion — see Disproportion
    double uterus 654.0 ☑
    drug dependence (conditions classifiable to 304) 648.3 ☑
    dysplasia, cervix 654.6 ☑
    early onset of delivery (spontaneous) 644.2 ☑
    eclampsia, eclamptic (coma) (convulsions) (delirium) (nephritis) (uremia) 642.6 ☑
      with pre-existing hypertension 642.7 ☑
    edema 646.1 ☑
      with hypertension — see Toxemia, of pregnancy
    effusion, amniotic fluid 658.1 ☑
      delayed delivery following 658.2 ☑
    embolism
      air 673.0 ☑
      amniotic fluid 673.1 ☑
      blood-clot 673.2 ☑
      cerebral 674.0 ☑
      pulmonary NEC 673.2 ☑
      pyemic 673.3 ☑
      septic 673.3 ☑
    emesis (gravidarum) — see Pregnancy, complicated, vomiting
    endometritis (conditions classifiable to 615.0–615.9) 670.1 ☑
      decidual 646.6 ☑
    epilepsy 649.4 ☑
    excessive weight gain NEC 646.1 ☑
    face presentation 652.4 ☑
    failure, fetal head to enter pelvic brim 652.5 ☑

☑ **Additional Digit Required** — Refer to the Tabular List for Digit Selection   ▽ **Subterms under main terms may continue to next column or page**

Pregnancy — *continued*
  complicated — *continued*
    false labor (pains) 644.1 ☑
    fatigue 646.8 ☑
    fatty metamorphosis of liver 646.7 ☑
    female genital mutilation 648.9 ☑
    fetal
      anemia 678.0 ☑
      complications from in utero proce-
        dure 679.1 ☑
      conjoined twins 678.1 ☑
      death (near term) 656.4 ☑
        early (before 22 completed weeks
          gestation) 632
      deformity 653.7 ☑
      distress 656.8 ☑
      hematologic conditions 678.0 ☑
      reduction of multiple fetuses reduced
        to single fetus 651.7 ☑
      thrombocytopenia 678.0 ☑
      twin to twin transfusion 678.0 ☑
    fibroid (tumor) (uterus) 654.1 ☑
    footling presentation 652.8 ☑
      with successful version 652.1 ☑
    gallbladder disease 646.8 ☑
    gastric banding status 649.2 ☑
    gastric bypass status for obesity
    genital herpes (asymptomatic) (history
      of) (inactive) 647.6 ☑
    goiter 648.1 ☑
    gonococcal infection (conditions classifi-
      able to 098) 647.1 ☑
    gonorrhea (conditions classifiable to
      098) 647.1 ☑
    hemorrhage 641.9 ☑
      accidental 641.2 ☑
      before 22 completed weeks gesta-
        tion NEC 640.9 ☑
      cerebrovascular 674.0 ☑
      due to
        afibrinogenemia or other coagu-
          lation defect (conditions
          classifiable to 286.0–286.9)
          641.3 ☑
        leiomyoma, uterine 641.8 ☑
        marginal sinus (rupture) 641.2 ☑
        premature separation, placenta
          641.2 ☑
        trauma 641.8 ☑
      early (before 22 completed weeks
        gestation) 640.9 ☑
      threatened abortion 640.0 ☑
      unavoidable 641.1 ☑
    hepatitis (acute) (malignant) (subacute)
      646.7 ☑
      viral 647.6 ☑
    herniation of uterus 654.4 ☑
    high head at term 652.5 ☑
    hydatidiform mole (delivered) (undeliv-
      ered) 630
    hydramnios 657.0 ☑
    hydrocephalic fetus 653.6 ☑
    hydrops amnii 657.0 ☑
    hydrorrhea 658.1 ☑
    hyperemesis (gravidarum) — *see* Hyper-
      emesis, gravidarum
    hypertension — *see* Hypertension,
      complicating pregnancy
    hypertensive
      chronic kidney disease 642.2 ☑
      heart and chronic kidney disease
        642.2 ☑
      heart and renal disease 642.2 ☑
      heart disease 642.2 ☑
      renal disease 642.2 ☑
    hypertensive heart and chronic kidney
      disease 642.2 ☑
    hyperthyroidism 648.1 ☑
    hypothyroidism 648.1 ☑
    hysteralgia 646.8 ☑
    icterus gravis 646.7 ☑
    incarceration, uterus 654.3 ☑
    incompetent cervix (os) 654.5 ☑
    infection 647.9 ☑

Pregnancy — *continued*
  complicated — *continued*
    infection — *continued*
      amniotic fluid 658.4 ☑
      bladder 646.6 ☑
      genital organ (conditions classifiable
        to 614.0–614.5, 614.7–614.9,
        615) 646.6 ☑
      kidney (conditions classifiable to
        590.0–590.9) 646.6 ☑
      urinary (tract) 646.6 ☑
        asymptomatic 646.5 ☑
    infective and parasitic diseases NEC
      647.8 ☑
    inflammation
      bladder 646.6 ☑
      genital organ (conditions classifiable
        to 614.0–614.5, 614.7–614.9,
        615) 646.6 ☑
      urinary tract NEC 646.6 ☑
    insufficient weight gain 646.8 ☑
    insulin resistance 648.8 ☑
    intrauterine fetal death (near term) NEC
      656.4 ☑
      early (before 22 completed weeks'
        gestation) 632
    malaria (conditions classifiable to 084)
      647.4 ☑
    malformation, uterus (congenital)
      654.0 ☑
    malnutrition (conditions classifiable to
      260–269) 648.9 ☑
    malposition
      fetus — *see* Pregnancy, complicated,
        malpresentation
      uterus or cervix 654.4 ☑
    malpresentation 652.9 ☑
      with successful version 652.1 ☑
      in multiple gestation 652.6 ☑
      specified type NEC 652.8 ☑
    marginal sinus hemorrhage or rupture
      641.2 ☑
    maternal complications from in utero
      procedure 679.0 ☑
    maternal drug abuse 648.4 ☑
    maternal obesity syndrome 646.1 ☑
    menstruation 640.8 ☑
    mental disorders (conditions classifiable
      to 290–303, 305.0, 305.2-305.9,
      306–316, 317–319) 648.4 ☑
    mentum presentation 652.4 ☑
    missed
      abortion 632
      delivery (at or near term) 656.4 ☑
      labor (at or near term) 656.4 ☑
    necrosis
      genital organ or tract (conditions
        classifiable to 614.0–614.5,
        614.7–614.9, 615) 646.6 ☑
      liver (conditions classifiable to 570)
        646.7 ☑
      renal, cortical 646.2 ☑
    nephritis or nephrosis (conditions classi-
      fiable to 580–589) 646.2 ☑
      with hypertension 642.1 ☑
    nephropathy NEC 646.2 ☑
    neuritis (peripheral) 646.4 ☑
    nutritional deficiency (conditions classi-
      fiable to 260–269) 648.9 ☑
    obesity 649.1 ☑
      surgery status 649.2 ☑
    oblique lie or presentation 652.3 ☑
      with successful version 652.1 ☑
    obstetrical trauma NEC 665.9 ☑
    oligohydramnios NEC 658.0 ☑
    onset of contractions before 37 weeks
      644.0 ☑
    oversize fetus 653.5 ☑
    papyraceous fetus 646.0 ☑
    patent cervix 654.5 ☑
    pelvic inflammatory disease (conditions
      classifiable to 614.0–614.5,
      614.7–614.9, 615) 646.6 ☑
    pelvic peritoneal adhesion 648.9 ☑

Pregnancy — *continued*
  complicated — *continued*
    placenta, placental
      abnormality 656.7 ☑
      abruptio or ablatio 641.2 ☑
      detachment 641.2 ☑
      disease 656.7 ☑
      infarct 656.7 ☑
      low implantation 641.1 ☑
        without hemorrhage 641.0 ☑
      malformation 656.7 ☑
      malposition 641.1 ☑
        without hemorrhage 641.0 ☑
      marginal sinus hemorrhage 641.2 ☑
      previa 641.1 ☑
        without hemorrhage 641.0 ☑
      separation (premature) (undelivered)
        641.2 ☑
    placentitis 658.4 ☑
    pneumonia 648.9 ☑
    polyhydramnios 657.0 ☑
    postmaturity
      post-term 645.1 ☑
      prolonged 645.2 ☑
    prediabetes 648.8 ☑
    pre-eclampsia (mild) 642.4 ☑
      severe 642.5 ☑
      superimposed on pre-existing hyper-
        tensive disease 642.7 ☑
    premature rupture of membranes
      658.1 ☑
      with delayed delivery 658.2 ☑
    previous
      ectopic pregnancy V23.42
      infertility V23.0
      in utero procedure during previous
        pregnancy V23.86
      nonobstetric condition V23.89
      poor obstetric history V23.49
      premature delivery V23.41
      trophoblastic disease (conditions
        classifiable to 630) V23.1
    prolapse, uterus 654.4 ☑
    proteinuria (gestational) 646.2 ☑
      with hypertension — *see* Toxemia,
        of pregnancy
    pruritus (neurogenic) 646.8 ☑
    psychosis or psychoneurosis 648.4 ☑
    ptyalism 646.8 ☑
    pyelitis (conditions classifiable to
      590.0–590.9) 646.6 ☑
    renal disease or failure NEC 646.2 ☑
      with secondary hypertension
        642.1 ☑
      hypertensive 642.2 ☑
    retention, retained dead ovum 631.8
    retroversion, uterus 654.3 ☑
    Rh immunization, incompatibility, or
      sensitization 656.1 ☑
    rubella (conditions classifiable to 056)
      647.5 ☑
    rupture
      amnion (premature) 658.1 ☑
        with delayed delivery 658.2 ☑
      marginal sinus (hemorrhage)
        641.2 ☑
      membranes (premature) 658.1 ☑
        with delayed delivery 658.2 ☑
      uterus (before onset of labor)
        665.0 ☑
    salivation (excessive) 646.8 ☑
    salpingo–oophoritis (conditions classifi-
      able to 614.0–614.2) 646.6 ☑
    septicemia (conditions classifiable to
      038.0–038.9) 647.8 ☑
      postpartum 670.2 ☑
      puerperal 670.2 ☑
    smoking 649.0 ☑
    spasms, uterus (abnormal) 646.8 ☑
    specified condition NEC 646.8 ☑
    spotting 649.5 ☑
    spurious labor pains 644.1 ☑
    status post
      bariatric surgery 649.2 ☑

Pregnancy — *continued*
  complicated — *continued*
    status post — *continued*
      gastric banding 649.2 ☑
      gastric bypass for obesity 649.2 ☑
      obesity surgery 649.2 ☑
    superfecundation 651.9 ☑
    superfetation 651.9 ☑
    syphilis (conditions classifiable to
      090–097) 647.0 ☑
    threatened
      abortion 640.0 ☑
      premature delivery 644.2 ☑
      premature labor 644.0 ☑
    thrombophlebitis (superficial) 671.2 ☑
      deep 671.3 ☑
      septic 670.3 ☑
    thrombosis 671.2 ☑
      venous (superficial) 671.2 ☑
        deep 671.3 ☑
    thyroid dysfunction (conditions classifi-
      able to 240–246) 648.1 ☑
    thyroiditis 648.1 ☑
    thyrotoxicosis 648.1 ☑
    tobacco use disorder 649.0 ☑
    torsion of uterus 654.4 ☑
    toxemia — *see* Toxemia, of pregnancy
    transverse lie or presentation 652.3 ☑
      with successful version 652.1 ☑
    trauma 648.9 ☑
      obstetrical 665.9 ☑
    tuberculosis (conditions classifiable to
      010–018) 647.3 ☑
    tumor
      cervix 654.6 ☑
      ovary 654.4 ☑
      pelvic organs or tissue NEC 654.4 ☑
      uterus (body) 654.1 ☑
        cervix 654.6 ☑
      vagina 654.7 ☑
      vulva 654.8 ☑
    unstable lie 652.0 ☑
    uremia — *see* Pregnancy, complicated,
      renal disease
    urethritis 646.6 ☑
    vaginitis or vulvitis (conditions classifi-
      able to 616.1) 646.6 ☑
    varicose
      placental vessels 656.7 ☑
      veins (legs) 671.0 ☑
        perineum 671.1 ☑
        vulva 671.1 ☑
    varicosity, labia or vulva 671.1 ☑
    venereal disease NEC (conditions classi-
      fiable to 099) 647.2 ☑
    venous complication 671.9 ☑
    viral disease NEC (conditions classifiable
      to 042, 050–055, 057–079,
      795.05, 795.15, 796.75) 647.6 ☑
    vomiting (incoercible) (pernicious) (per-
      sistent) (uncontrollable) (vicious)
      643.9 ☑
      due to organic disease or other cause
        643.8 ☑
      early — *see* Hyperemesis, gravi-
        darum
      late (after 22 completed weeks gesta-
        tion) 643.2 ☑
    young maternal age 659.8 ☑
  complications NEC 646.9 ☑
  cornual 633.80
    with intrauterine pregnancy 633.81
    affecting fetus or newborn 761.4
  death, maternal NEC 646.9 ☑
  delivered — *see* Delivery
  ectopic (ruptured) NEC 633.90
    with intrauterine pregnancy 633.91
    abdominal — *see* Pregnancy, abdominal
    affecting fetus or newborn 761.4
    combined (extrauterine and intrauter-
      ine) — *see* Pregnancy, cornual
    ovarian — *see* Pregnancy, ovarian
    specified type NEC 633.80
      with intrauterine pregnancy 633.81

☑ **Additional Digit Required** — Refer to the Tabular List for Digit Selection

▽ **Subterms under main terms may continue to next column or page**

☑ Additional Digit Required — Refer to the Tabular List for Digit Selection   ▽ Subterms under main terms may continue to next column or page

238 — Volume 2   ►◄ Revised Text   ● New Line   ▲ Revised Code   2015 ICD-9-CM

Premyeloma 273.1
Prenatal
care, normal pregnancy V22.1
first V22.0
death, cause unknown — see Death, fetus
screening — see Antenatal, screening
teeth 520.6
Prepartum — see condition
Preponderance, left or right ventricular
429.3
Prepuce — see condition
PRES (posterior reversible encephalopathy
syndrome) 348.39
Presbycardia 797
hypertensive (see also Hypertension, heart)
402.90
Presbycusis 388.01
Presbyesophagus 530.89
Presbyophrenia 310.1
Presbyopia 367.4
Prescription of contraceptives NEC V25.02
diaphragm V25.02
oral (pill) V25.01
emergency V25.03
postcoital V25.03
repeat V25.41
repeat V25.40
oral (pill) V25.41
Presenile — see also condition
aging 259.8
dementia (see also Dementia, presenile)
290.10
Presenility 259.8
Presentation, fetal
abnormal 652.9 ☑
with successful version 652.1 ☑
before labor, affecting fetus or newborn
761.7
causing obstructed labor 660.0 ☑
affecting fetus or newborn, any, except breech 763.1
in multiple gestation (one or more)
652.6 ☑
specified NEC 652.8 ☑
arm 652.7 ☑
causing obstructed labor 660.0 ☑
breech (buttocks) (complete) (frank)
652.2 ☑
with successful version 652.1 ☑
before labor, affecting fetus or newborn 761.7
before labor, affecting fetus or newborn
761.7
brow 652.4 ☑
causing obstructed labor 660.0 ☑
buttocks 652.2 ☑
chin 652.4 ☑
complete 652.2 ☑
compound 652.8 ☑
cord 663.0 ☑
extended head 652.4 ☑
face 652.4 ☑
to pubes 652.8 ☑
footling 652.8 ☑
frank 652.2 ☑
hand, leg, or foot NEC 652.8 ☑
incomplete 652.8 ☑
mentum 652.4 ☑
multiple gestation (one fetus or more)
652.6 ☑
oblique 652.3 ☑
with successful version 652.1 ☑
shoulder 652.8 ☑
affecting fetus or newborn 763.1
transverse 652.3 ☑
with successful version 652.1 ☑
umbilical cord 663.0 ☑
unstable 652.0 ☑
Prespondylolisthesis (congenital) (lumbosacral) 756.11
Pressure
area, skin ulcer (see also Ulcer, pressure)
707.00
atrophy, spine 733.99
birth, fetus or newborn NEC 767.9

Pressure — continued
brachial plexus 353.0
brain 348.4
injury at birth 767.0
cerebral — see Pressure, brain
chest 786.59
cone, tentorial 348.4
injury at birth 767.0
funis — see Compression, umbilical cord
hyposystolic (see also Hypotension) 458.9
increased
intracranial 781.99
due to
benign intracranial hypertension
348.2
hydrocephalus — see hydrocephalus
injury at birth 767.8
intraocular 365.00
lumbosacral plexus 353.1
mediastinum 519.3
necrosis (chronic) (skin) (see also Decubitus)
707.00
nerve — see Compression, nerve
paralysis (see also Neuropathy, entrapment)
355.9
pre-ulcer skin changes limited to persistent
focal erythema (see also Ulcer, pressure) 707.21
sore (chronic) (see also Ulcer, pressure)
707.00
spinal cord 336.9
ulcer (chronic) (see also Ulcer, pressure)
707.00
umbilical cord — see Compression, umbilical cord
venous, increased 459.89
Pre-syncope 780.2
Preterm infant NEC 765.1 ☑
extreme 765.0 ☑
Priapism (penis) 607.3
Prickling sensation — see also Disturbance,
sensation 782.0
Prickly heat 705.1
Primary — see also condition
angle closure suspect 365.02
Primigravida, elderly
affecting
fetus or newborn 763.89
management of pregnancy, labor, and
delivery 659.5 ☑
Primipara, old
affecting
fetus or newborn 763.89
management of pregnancy, labor, and
delivery 659.5 ☑
Primula dermatitis 692.6
Primus varus (bilateral) (metatarsus) 754.52
PRIND (prolonged reversible ischemic neurologic deficit) 434.91
history of (personal) V12.54
Pringle's disease (tuberous sclerosis) 759.5
Prinzmetal's angina 413.1
Prinzmetal-Massumi syndrome (anterior
chest wall) 786.52
Prizefighter ear 738.7
Problem (with) V49.9
academic V62.3
acculturation V62.4
adopted child V61.24
aged
in-law V61.3
parent V61.3
person NEC V61.8
alcoholism in family V61.41
anger reaction (see also Disturbance, conduct) 312.0 ☑
behavioral V40.9
specified NEC V40.39
behavior, child 312.9
betting V69.3
biological child V61.23
cardiorespiratory NEC V47.2
career choice V62.29
care of sick or handicapped person in family
or household V61.49

Problem — continued
communication V40.1
conscience regarding medical care V62.6
delinquency (juvenile) 312.9
diet, inappropriate V69.1
digestive NEC V47.3
ear NEC V41.3
eating habits, inappropriate V69.1
economic V60.2
affecting care V60.9
specified type NEC V60.89
educational V62.3
enuresis, child 307.6
exercise, lack of V69.0
eye NEC V41.1
family V61.9
specified circumstance NEC V61.8
fear reaction, child 313.0
feeding (elderly) (infant) 783.3
newborn 779.31
nonorganic 307.59
fetal, affecting management of pregnancy
656.9 ☑
specified type NEC 656.8 ☑
financial V60.2
foster child V61.25
functional V41.9
specified type NEC V41.8
gambling V69.3
genital NEC V47.5
head V48.9
deficiency V48.0
disfigurement V48.6
mechanical V48.2
motor V48.2
movement of V48.2
sensory V48.4
specified condition NEC V48.8
hearing V41.2
high-risk sexual behavior V69.2
identity 313.82
influencing health status NEC V49.89
internal organ NEC V47.9
deficiency V47.0
mechanical or motor V47.1
interpersonal NEC V62.81
jealousy, child 313.3
learning V40.0
legal V62.5
life circumstance NEC V62.89
lifestyle V69.9
specified NEC V69.8
limb V49.9
deficiency V49.0
disfigurement V49.4
mechanical V49.1
motor V49.2
movement, involving
musculoskeletal system V49.1
nervous system V49.2
sensory V49.3
specified condition NEC V49.5
litigation V62.5
living alone V60.3
loneliness NEC V62.89
marital V61.10
involving
divorce V61.03
estrangement V61.09
psychosexual disorder 302.9
sexual function V41.7
relationship V61.10
mastication V41.6
medical care, within family V61.49
mental V40.9
specified NEC V40.2
mental hygiene, adult V40.9
multiparity V61.5
nail biting, child 307.9
neck V48.9
deficiency V48.1
disfigurement V48.7
mechanical V48.3
motor V48.3
movement V48.3
sensory V48.5

Problem — continued
neck — continued
specified condition NEC V48.8
neurological NEC 781.99
none (feared complaint unfounded) V65.5
occupational V62.29
parent-child V61.20
adopted child V61.24
biological child V61.23
foster child V61.25
relationship V61.20
partner V61.10
relationship V61.10
personality (see also Disorder, personality)
301.9
personal NEC V62.89
interpersonal conflict NEC V62.81
phase of life V62.89
placenta, affecting management of pregnancy 656.9 ☑
specified type NEC 656.8 ☑
poverty V60.2
presence of sick or handicapped person in
family or household V61.49
psychiatric 300.9
psychosocial V62.9
specified type NEC V62.89
relational NEC V62.81
relationship, childhood 313.3
religious or spiritual belief
other than medical care V62.89
regarding medical care V62.6
self-damaging behavior V69.8
sexual
behavior, high-risk V69.2
function NEC V41.7
sibling
relational V61.8
relationship V61.8
sight V41.0
sleep disorder, child 307.40
sleep, lack of V69.4
smell V41.5
speech V40.1
spite reaction, child (see also Disturbance,
conduct) 312.0 ☑
spoiled child reaction (see also Disturbance,
conduct) 312.1 ☑
substance abuse in family V61.42
swallowing V41.6
tantrum, child (see also Disturbance, conduct) 312.1 ☑
taste V41.5
thumb sucking, child 307.9
tic (child) 307.21
trunk V48.9
deficiency V48.1
disfigurement V48.7
mechanical V48.3
motor V48.3
movement V48.3
sensory V48.5
specified condition NEC V48.8
unemployment V62.0
urinary NEC V47.4
voice production V41.4
Procedure (surgical) **not done** NEC V64.3
because of
contraindication V64.1
patient's decision V64.2
for reasons of conscience or religion
V62.6
specified reason NEC V64.3
Procidentia
anus (sphincter) 569.1
rectum (sphincter) 569.1
stomach 537.89
uteri 618.1
Proctalgia 569.42
fugax 564.6
spasmodic 564.6
psychogenic 307.89
Proctitis 569.49
amebic 006.8
chlamydial 099.52
gonococcal 098.7

☑ **Additional Digit Required** — Refer to the Tabular List for Digit Selection   ▽ **Subterms under main terms may continue to next column or page**

2015 ICD-9-CM   ▶◀ **Revised Text**   ● **New Line**   ▲ **Revised Code**   **Volume 2 — 239**

Proctitis — *continued*
  granulomatous 555.1
  idiopathic 556.2
    with ulcerative sigmoiditis 556.3
  tuberculous (*see also* Tuberculosis) 014.8 ☑
  ulcerative (chronic) (nonspecific) 556.2
    with ulcerative sigmoiditis 556.3
Proctocele
  female (without uterine prolapse) 618.04
    with uterine prolapse 618.4
      complete 618.3
      incomplete 618.2
  male 569.49
Proctocolitis, idiopathic 556.2
  with ulcerative sigmoiditis 556.3
Proctoptosis 569.1
Proctosigmoiditis 569.89
  ulcerative (chronic) 556.3
Proctospasm 564.6
  psychogenic 306.4
Prodromal-AIDS — *see* Human immunodeficiency virus (disease) (illness) (infection)
Profichet's disease or syndrome 729.90
Progeria (adultorum) (syndrome) 259.8
Prognathism (mandibular) (maxillary) 524.10
Progonoma (melanotic) (M9363/0) — *see* Neoplasm, by site, benign
Progressive — *see* condition
Prolapse, prolapsed
  anus, anal (canal) (sphincter) 569.1
  arm or hand, complicating delivery 652.7 ☑
    causing obstructed labor 660.0 ☑
      affecting fetus or newborn 763.1
    fetus or newborn 763.1
  bladder (acquired) (mucosa) (sphincter)
    congenital (female) (male) 756.71
    female (*see also* Cystocele, female) 618.01
    male 596.89
  breast implant (prosthetic) 996.54
  cecostomy 569.69
  cecum 569.89
  cervix, cervical (hypertrophied) 618.1
    anterior lip, obstructing labor 660.2 ☑
      affecting fetus or newborn 763.1
    congenital 752.49
    postpartal (old) 618.1
    stump 618.84
  ciliary body 871.1
  colon (pedunculated) 569.89
  colostomy 569.69
  conjunctiva 372.73
  cord — *see* Prolapse, umbilical cord
  cystostomy 596.83
  disc (intervertebral) — *see* Displacement, intervertebral disc
  duodenum 537.89
  eye implant (orbital) 996.59
    lens (ocular) 996.53
  fallopian tube 620.4
  fetal extremity, complicating delivery 652.8 ☑
    causing obstructed labor 660.0 ☑
    fetus or newborn 763.1
  funis — *see* Prolapse, umbilical cord
  gastric (mucosa) 537.89
  genital, female 618.9
    specified NEC 618.89
  globe 360.81
  ileostomy bud 569.69
  intervertebral disc — *see* Displacement, intervertebral disc
  intestine (small) 569.89
  iris 364.89
    traumatic 871.1
  kidney (*see also* Disease, renal) 593.0
    congenital 753.3
  laryngeal muscles or ventricle 478.79
  leg, complicating delivery 652.8 ☑
    causing obstructed labor 660.0 ☑
    fetus or newborn 763.1
  liver 573.8
  meatus urinarius 599.5
  mitral valve 424.0
  ocular lens implant 996.53

Prolapse, prolapsed — *continued*
  organ or site, congenital NEC — *see* Malposition, congenital
  ovary 620.4
  pelvic (floor), female 618.89
  perineum, female 618.89
  pregnant uterus 654.4 ☑
  rectum (mucosa) (sphincter) 569.1
    due to Trichuris trichiuria 127.3
  spleen 289.59
  stomach 537.89
  umbilical cord
    affecting fetus or newborn 762.4
    complicating delivery 663.0 ☑
  ureter 593.89
    with obstruction 593.4
  ureterovesical orifice 593.89
  urethra (acquired) (infected) (mucosa) 599.5
    congenital 753.8
  uterovaginal 618.4
    complete 618.3
    incomplete 618.2
    specified NEC 618.89
  uterus (first degree) (second degree) (third degree) (complete) (without vaginal wall prolapse) 618.1
    with mention of vaginal wall prolapse — *see* Prolapse, uterovaginal
    congenital 752.39
    in pregnancy or childbirth 654.4 ☑
      affecting fetus or newborn 763.1
      causing obstructed labor 660.2 ☑
        affecting fetus or newborn 763.1
    postpartal (old) 618.1
  uveal 871.1
  vagina (anterior) (posterior) (vault) (wall) (without uterine prolapse) 618.00
    with uterine prolapse 618.4
      complete 618.3
      incomplete 618.2
    paravaginal 618.02
    posthysterectomy 618.5
    specified NEC 618.09
  vitreous (humor) 379.26
    traumatic 871.1
  womb — *see* Prolapse, uterus
Prolapsus, female 618.9
Proliferative — *see* condition
Prolinemia 270.8
Prolinuria 270.8
Prolonged, prolongation
  bleeding time (*see also* Defect, coagulation) 790.92
    "idiopathic" (in von Willebrand's disease) 286.4
  coagulation time (*see also* Defect, coagulation) 790.92
  gestation syndrome 766.22
  labor 662.1 ☑
    affecting fetus or newborn 763.89
    first stage 662.0 ☑
    second stage 662.2 ☑
  pregnancy 645.2 ☑
  PR interval 426.11
  prothrombin time (*see also* Defect, coagulation) 790.92
  QT interval 794.31
    syndrome 426.82
  rupture of membranes (24 hours or more prior to onset of labor) 658.2 ☑
  uterine contractions in labor 661.4 ☑
    affecting fetus or newborn 763.7
Prominauris 744.29
Prominence
  auricle (ear) (congenital) 744.29
    acquired 380.32
  ischial spine or sacral promontory
    with disproportion (fetopelvic) 653.3 ☑
      affecting fetus or newborn 763.1
      causing obstructed labor 660.1 ☑
        affecting fetus or newborn 763.1
  nose (congenital) 748.1
    acquired 738.0
PROMM (proximal myotonic myotonia) 359.21
Pronation
  ankle 736.79

Pronation — *continued*
  foot 736.79
    congenital 755.67
Prophylactic
  administration of
    antibiotics, long-term V58.62
      short-term — *omit code*
    antitoxin, any V07.2
    antivenin V07.2
    chemotherapeutic agent NEC V07.39
      fluoride V07.31
    diphtheria antitoxin V07.2
    drug V07.39
    exemestar (Aromasin) V07.52
    gamma globulin V07.2
    immune sera (gamma globulin) V07.2
    RhoGAM V07.2
    tetanus antitoxin V07.2
  chemotherapy NEC V07.39
    fluoride V07.31
  hormone replacement (postmenopausal) V07.4
  immunotherapy V07.2
  measure V07.9
    specified type NEC V07.8
  medication V07.39
  postmenopausal hormone replacement V07.4
  sterilization V25.2
Proptosis (ocular) — *see also* Exophthalmos 376.30
  thyroid 242.0 ☑
Propulsion
  eyeball 360.81
Prosecution, anxiety concerning V62.5
Prosopagnosia 368.16
Prostate, prostatic — *see* condition
Prostatism 600.90
  with
    other lower urinary tract symptoms (LUTS) 600.91
    urinary
      obstruction 600.91
      retention 600.91
Prostatitis (congestive) (suppurative) 601.9
  acute 601.0
  cavitary 601.8
  chlamydial 099.54
  chronic 601.1
  diverticular 601.8
  due to Trichomonas (vaginalis) 131.03
  fibrous 600.90
    with
      other lower urinary tract symptoms (LUTS) 600.91
      urinary
        obstruction 600.91
        retention 600.91
  gonococcal (acute) 098.12
    chronic or duration of 2 months or over 098.32
  granulomatous 601.8
  hypertrophic 600.00
    with
      other lower urinary tract symptoms (LUTS) 600.01
      urinary
        obstruction 600.01
        retention 600.01
  specified type NEC 601.8
  subacute 601.1
  trichomonal 131.03
  tuberculous (*see also* Tuberculosis) 016.5 ☑ [601.4]
Prostatocystitis 601.3
Prostatorrhea 602.8
Prostatoseminovesiculitis, trichomonal 131.03
Prostration 780.79
  heat 992.5
    anhydrotic 992.3
    due to
      salt (and water) depletion 992.4
      water depletion 992.3
  nervous 300.5
  newborn 779.89

Prostration — *continued*
  senile 797
Protanomaly 368.51
Protanopia (anomalous trichromat) (complete) (incomplete) 368.51
Protection (against) (from) — *see* Prophylactic
Protein
  deficiency 260
  malnutrition 260
  sickness (prophylactic) (therapeutic) 999.59
Proteinemia 790.99
Proteinosis
  alveolar, lung or pulmonary 516.0
  lipid 272.8
  lipoid (of Urbach) 272.8
Proteinuria — *see also* Albuminuria 791.0
  Bence-Jones NEC 791.0
  gestational 646.2 ☑
    with hypertension — *see* Toxemia, of pregnancy
  orthostatic 593.6
  postural 593.6
Proteolysis, pathologic 286.6
Protocoproporphyria 277.1
Protoporphyria (erythrohepatic) (erythropoietic) 277.1
Protrusio acetabuli 718.65
Protrusion
  acetabulum (into pelvis) 718.65
  device, implant, or graft — *see* Complications, mechanical
  ear, congenital 744.29
  intervertebral disc — *see* Displacement, intervertebral disc
  nucleus pulposus — *see* Displacement, intervertebral disc
Proud flesh 701.5
Prune belly (syndrome) 756.71
Prurigo (ferox) (gravis) (Hebra's) (hebrae) (mitis) (simplex) 698.2
  agria 698.3
  asthma syndrome 691.8
  Besnier's (atopic dermatitis) (infantile eczema) 691.8
  eczematodes allergicum 691.8
  estivalis (Hutchinson's) 692.72
  Hutchinson's 692.72
  nodularis 698.3
  psychogenic 306.3
Pruritus, pruritic 698.9
  ani 698.0
    psychogenic 306.3
  conditions NEC 698.9
    psychogenic 306.3
  due to Onchocerca volvulus 125.3
  ear 698.9
  essential 698.9
  genital organ(s) 698.1
    psychogenic 306.3
  gravidarum 646.8 ☑
  hiemalis 698.8
  neurogenic (any site) 306.3
  perianal 698.0
  psychogenic (any site) 306.3
  scrotum 698.1
    psychogenic 306.3
  senile, senilis 698.8
  Trichomonas 131.9
  vulva, vulvae 698.1
    psychogenic 306.3
Psammocarcinoma (M8140/3) — *see* Neoplasm, by site, malignant
Pseudarthrosis, pseudoarthrosis (bone) 733.82
  joint following fusion V45.4
Pseudoacanthosis
  nigricans 701.8
Pseudoaneurysm — *see* Aneurysm
Pseudoangina (pectoris) — *see* Angina
Pseudoangioma 452
Pseudo-Argyll-Robertson pupil 379.45
Pseudoarteriosus 747.89
Pseudoarthrosis — *see* Pseudarthrosis
Pseudoataxia 799.89
Pseudobulbar affect (PBA) 310.81
Pseudobursa 727.89

☑ Additional Digit Required — Refer to the Tabular List for Digit Selection
▽ Subterms under main terms may continue to next column or page

240 — Volume 2
▶◀ Revised Text   ● New Line   ▲ Revised Code
2015 ICD-9-CM

Pseudocholera 025

Pseudochromidrosis 705.89

Pseudocirrhosis, liver, pericardial 423.2

Pseudocoarctation 747.21

Pseudocowpox 051.1

Pseudocoxalgia 732.1

Pseudocroup 478.75

Pseudocyesis 300.11

Pseudocyst
  lung 518.89
  pancreas 577.2
  retina 361.19

Pseudodementia 300.16

Pseudoelephantiasis neuroarthritica 757.0

Pseudoemphysema 518.89

Pseudoencephalitis
  superior (acute) hemorrhagic 265.1

Pseudoerosion cervix, congenital 752.49

Pseudoexfoliation, lens capsule 366.11

Pseudofracture (idiopathic) (multiple) (spontaneous) (symmetrical) 268.2

Pseudoglanders 025

Pseudoglioma 360.44

Pseudogout — see Chondrocalcinosis

Pseudohallucination 780.1

Pseudohemianesthesia 782.0

Pseudohemophilia (Bernuth's) (hereditary) (typeB) 286.4
  type A 287.8
  vascular 287.8

Pseudohermaphroditism 752.7
  with chromosomal anomaly — see Anomaly, chromosomal
  adrenal 255.2
  female (without adrenocortical disorder) 752.7
    with adrenocortical disorder 255.2
    adrenal 255.2
  male (without gonadal disorder) 752.7
    with
      adrenocortical disorder 255.2
      cleft scrotum 752.7
      feminizing testis 259.51
      gonadal disorder 257.9
    adrenal 255.2

Pseudohole, macula 362.54

Pseudo-Hurler's disease (mucolipidosis III) 272.7

Pseudohydrocephalus 348.2

Pseudohypertrophic muscular dystrophy (Erb's) 359.1

Pseudohypertrophy, muscle 359.1

Pseudohypoparathyroidism 275.49

Pseudoinfluenza — see also Influenza 487.1

Pseudoinsomnia 307.49

Pseudoleukemia 288.8
  infantile 285.8

Pseudomembranous — see condition

Pseudomeningocele (cerebral) (infective) 349.2
  postprocedural 997.01
  spinal 349.2

Pseudomenstruation 626.8

Pseudomucinous
  cyst (ovary) (M8470/0) 220
  peritoneum 568.89

Pseudomyeloma 273.1

Pseudomyxoma peritonei (M8480/6) 197.6

Pseudoneuritis optic (nerve) 377.24
  papilla 377.24
  congenital 743.57

Pseudoneuroma — see Injury, nerve, by site

Pseudo-obstruction
  intestine (chronic) (idiopathic) (intermittent secondary) (primary) 564.89
  acute 560.89

Pseudopapilledema 377.24

Pseudoparalysis
  arm or leg 781.4
  atonic, congenital 358.8

Pseudopelade 704.09

Pseudophakia V43.1

Pseudopolycythemia 289.0

Pseudopolyposis, colon 556.4

Pseudoporencephaly 348.0

Pseudopseudohypoparathyroidism 275.49

Pseudopsychosis 300.16

Pseudopterygium 372.52

Pseudoptosis (eyelid) 374.34

Pseudorabies 078.89

Pseudoretinitis, pigmentosa 362.65

Pseudorickets 588.0
  senile (Pozzi's) 731.0

Pseudorubella 057.8

Pseudoscarlatina 057.8

Pseudosclerema 778.1

Pseudosclerosis (brain)
  Jakob's 046.19
  of Westphal (-Strümpell) (hepatolenticular degeneration) 275.1
  spastic 046.19
    with dementia
      with behavioral disturbance 046.19 [294.11]
      without behavioral disturbance 046.19 [294.10]

Pseudoseizure 780.39
  non-psychiatric 780.39
  psychiatric 300.11

Pseudotabes 799.89
  diabetic 250.6 ☑ [337.1]
    due to secondary diabetes 249.6 ☑ [337.1]

Pseudotetanus — see also Convulsions 780.39

Pseudotetany 781.7
  hysterical 300.11

Pseudothalassemia 285.0

Pseudotrichinosis 710.3

Pseudotruncus arteriosus 747.29

Pseudotuberculosis, pasteurella (infection) 027.2

Pseudotumor
  cerebri 348.2
  orbit (inflammatory) 376.11

Pseudo-Turner's syndrome 759.89

Pseudoxanthoma elasticum 757.39

Psilosis (sprue) (tropical) 579.1
  Monilia 112.89
  nontropical 579.0
  not sprue 704.00

Psittacosis 073.9

Psoitis 728.5

Psora NEC 696.1

Psoriasis 696.1
  any type, except arthropathic 696.1
  arthritic, arthropathic 696.0
  buccal 528.6
  flexural 696.1
  follicularis 696.1
  guttate 696.1
  inverse 696.1
  mouth 528.6
  nummularis 696.1
  psychogenic 316 [696.1]
  punctata 696.1
  pustular 696.1
  rupioides 696.1
  vulgaris 696.1

Psorospermiasis 136.4

Psorospermosis 136.4
  follicularis (vegetans) 757.39

Psychalgia 307.80

Psychasthenia 300.89
  compulsive 300.3
  mixed compulsive states 300.3
  obsession 300.3

Psychiatric disorder or problem NEC 300.9

Psychogenic — see also condition
  factors associated with physical conditions 316

Psychoneurosis, psychoneurotic — see also Neurosis 300.9
  anxiety (state) 300.00
  climacteric 627.2
  compensation 300.16
  compulsion 300.3
  conversion hysteria 300.11
  depersonalization 300.6
  depressive type 300.4
  dissociative hysteria 300.15
  hypochondriacal 300.7
  hysteria 300.10

Psychoneurosis, psychoneurotic — see also Neurosis — continued
  hysteria — continued
    conversion type 300.11
    dissociative type 300.15
  mixed NEC 300.89
  neurasthenic 300.5
  obsessional 300.3
  obsessive-compulsive 300.3
  occupational 300.89
  personality NEC 301.89
  phobia 300.20
  senile NEC 300.89

Psychopathic — see also condition
  constitution, posttraumatic 310.2
    with psychosis 293.9
  personality 301.9
    amoral trends 301.7
    antisocial trends 301.7
    asocial trends 301.7
    mixed types 301.7
  state 301.9

Psychopathy, sexual — see also Deviation, sexual 302.9

Psychophysiologic, psychophysiological condition — see Reaction, psychophysiologic

Psychose passionelle 297.8

Psychosexual identity disorder 302.6
  adult-life 302.85
  childhood 302.6

Psychosis 298.9
  acute hysterical 298.1
  affecting management of pregnancy, childbirth, or puerperium 648.4 ☑
  affective (see also Disorder, mood) 296.90

Note — Use the following fifth-digit subclassification with categories 296.0–296.6:

0   unspecified

1   mild

2   moderate

3   severe, without mention of psychotic behavior

4   severe, specified as with psychotic behavior

5   in partial or unspecified remission

6   in full remission

  drug-induced 292.84
  due to or associated with physical condition 293.83
  involutional 293.83
    recurrent episode 296.3 ☑
    single episode 296.2 ☑
  manic-depressive 296.80
    circular (alternating) 296.7
      currently depressed 296.5 ☑
      currently manic 296.4 ☑
    depressed type 296.2 ☑
      atypical 296.82
      recurrent episode 296.3 ☑
      single episode 296.2 ☑
    manic 296.0 ☑
      atypical 296.81
      recurrent episode 296.1 ☑
      single episode 296.0 ☑
    mixed type NEC 296.89
    specified type NEC 296.89
  senile 290.21
  specified type NEC 296.99
  alcoholic 291.9
    with
      anxiety 291.89
      delirium tremens 291.0
      delusions 291.5
      dementia 291.2
      hallucinosis 291.3
      jealousy 291.5
      mood disturbance 291.89
      paranoia 291.5
      persisting amnesia 291.1
      sexual dysfunction 291.89

Psychosis — continued
  alcoholic — continued
    with — continued
      sleep disturbance 291.89
    amnestic confabulatory 291.1
    delirium tremens 291.0
    hallucinosis 291.3
    Korsakoff's, Korsakov's, Korsakow's 291.1
    paranoid type 291.5
    pathological intoxication 291.4
    polyneuritic 291.1
    specified type NEC 291.89
  alternating (see also Psychosis, manic-depressive, circular) 296.7
  anergastic (see also Psychosis, organic) 294.9
  arteriosclerotic 290.40
    with
      acute confusional state 290.41
      delirium 290.41
      delusions 290.42
      depressed mood 290.43
    depressed type 290.43
    paranoid type 290.42
    simple type 290.40
    uncomplicated 290.40
  atypical 298.9
    depressive 296.82
    manic 296.81
  borderline (schizophrenia) (see also Schizophrenia) 295.5 ☑
    of childhood (see also Psychosis, childhood) 299.8 ☑
    prepubertal 299.8 ☑
  brief reactive 298.8
  childhood, with origin specific to 299.9 ☑

Note — Use the following fifth-digit subclassification with category 299:

0   current or active state

1   residual state

    atypical 299.8 ☑
    specified type NEC 299.8 ☑
  circular (see also Psychosis, manic-depressive, circular) 296.7
  climacteric (see also Psychosis, involutional) 298.8
  confusional 298.9
    acute 293.0
    reactive 298.2
    subacute 293.1
  depressive (see also Psychosis, affective) 296.2 ☑
    atypical 296.82
    involutional 296.2 ☑
      with hypomania (bipolar II) 296.89
      recurrent episode 296.3 ☑
      single episode 296.2 ☑
    psychogenic 298.0
    reactive (emotional stress) (psychological trauma) 298.0
    recurrent episode 296.3 ☑
      with hypomania (bipolar II) 296.89
    single episode 296.2 ☑
  disintegrative, childhood (see also Psychosis, childhood) 299.1 ☑
  drug 292.9
    with
      affective syndrome 292.84
      amnestic syndrome 292.83
      anxiety 292.89
      delirium 292.81
        withdrawal 292.0
      delusions 292.11
      dementia 292.82
      depressive state 292.84
      hallucinations 292.12
      hallucinosis 292.12
      mood disorder 292.84
      mood disturbance 292.84
      organic personality syndrome NEC 292.89
      sexual dysfunction 292.89
      sleep disturbance 292.89
      withdrawal syndrome (and delirium) 292.0

Index

Pseudocholera — Psychosis

☑ Additional Digit Required — Refer to the Tabular List for Digit Selection   ▼ Subterms under main terms may continue to next column or page

2015 ICD-9-CM   ▶◀ Revised Text   ● New Line   ▲ Revised Code   Volume 2 — 241

Psychosis — *continued*
  drug — *continued*
    affective syndrome 292.84
    delusions 292.11
    hallucinatory state 292.12
    hallucinosis 292.12
    paranoid state 292.11
    specified type NEC 292.89
    withdrawal syndrome (and delirium) 292.0
  due to or associated with physical condition (*see also* Psychosis, organic) 293.9
  epileptic NEC 293.9
  excitation (psychogenic) (reactive) 298.1
  exhaustive (*see also* Reaction, stress, acute) 308.9
  hypomanic (*see also* Psychosis, affective) 296.0 ☑
    recurrent episode 296.1 ☑
    single episode 296.0 ☑
  hysterical 298.8
    acute 298.1
  in
    conditions classified elsewhere
      with
        delusions 293.81
        hallucinations 293.82
    pregnancy, childbirth, or puerperium 648.4 ☑
  incipient 298.8
    schizophrenic (*see also* Schizophrenia) 295.5 ☑
  induced 297.3
  infantile (*see also* Psychosis, childhood) 299.0 ☑
  infective 293.9
    acute 293.0
    subacute 293.1
  interactional (childhood) (*see also* Psychosis, childhood) 299.1 ☑
  involutional 298.8
    depressive (*see also* Psychosis, affective) 296.2 ☑
      recurrent episode 296.3 ☑
      single episode 296.2 ☑
    melancholic 296.2 ☑
      recurrent episode 296.3 ☑
      single episode 296.2 ☑
    paranoid state 297.2
    paraphrenia 297.2
  Korsakoff's, Korakov's, Korsakow's (nonalcoholic) 294.0
    alcoholic 291.1
  mania (phase) (*see also* Psychosis, affective) 296.0 ☑
    recurrent episode 296.1 ☑
    single episode 296.0 ☑
  manic (*see also* Psychosis, affective) 296.0 ☑
    atypical 296.81
    recurrent episode 296.1 ☑
    single episode 296.0 ☑
  manic-depressive 296.80
    circular 296.7
      currently
        depressed 296.5 ☑
        manic 296.4 ☑
        mixed 296.6 ☑
    depressive 296.2 ☑
      recurrent episode 296.3 ☑
        with hypomania (bipolar II) 296.89
      single episode 296.2 ☑
    hypomanic 296.0 ☑
      recurrent episode 296.1 ☑
      single episode 296.0 ☑
    manic 296.0 ☑
      atypical 296.81
      recurrent episode 296.1 ☑
      single episode 296.0 ☑
    mixed NEC 296.89
    perplexed 296.89
    stuporous 296.89
  menopausal (*see also* Psychosis, involutional) 298.8

Psychosis — *continued*
  mixed schizophrenic and affective (*see also* Schizophrenia) 295.7 ☑
  multi-infarct (cerebrovascular) (*see also* Psychosis, arteriosclerotic) 290.40
  organic NEC 294.9
    due to or associated with
      addiction
        alcohol (*see also* Psychosis, alcoholic) 291.9
        drug (*see also* Psychosis, drug) 292.9
      alcohol intoxication, acute (*see also* Psychosis, alcoholic) 291.9
      alcoholism (*see also* Psychosis, alcoholic) 291.9
      arteriosclerosis (cerebral) (*see also* Psychosis, arteriosclerotic) 290.40
      cerebrovascular disease
        acute (psychosis) 293.0
        arteriosclerotic (*see also* Psychosis, arteriosclerotic) 290.40
      childbirth — *see* Psychosis, puerperal
      dependence
        alcohol (*see also* Psychosis, alcoholic) 291.9
        drug 292.9
      disease
        alcoholic liver (*see also* Psychosis, alcoholic) 291.9
        brain
          arteriosclerotic (*see also* Psychosis, arteriosclerotic) 290.40
          cerebrovascular
            acute (psychosis) 293.0
            arteriosclerotic (*see also* Psychosis, arteriosclerotic) 290.40
          endocrine or metabolic 293.9
            acute (psychosis) 293.0
            subacute (psychosis) 293.1
          Jakob-Creutzfeldt 046.19
            with behavioral disturbance 046.19 *[294.11]*
            without behavioral disturbance 046.19 *[294.10]*
            familial 046.19
            iatrogenic 046.19
            specified NEC 046.19
            sporadic 046.19
            variant 046.11
              with dementia
                with behavioral disturbance 046.11 *[294.11]*
                without behavioral disturbance 046.11 *[294.10]*
          liver, alcoholic (*see also* Psychosis, alcoholic) 291.9
      disorder
        cerebrovascular
          acute (psychosis) 293.0
        endocrine or metabolic 293.9
          acute (psychosis) 293.0
          subacute (psychosis) 293.1
      epilepsy
        with behavioral disturbance 345.9 ☑ *[294.11]*
        without behavioral disturbance 345.9 ☑ *[294.10]*
        transient (acute) 293.0
      Huntington's chorea
        with behavioral disturbance 333.4 *[294.11]*
        without behavioral disturbance 333.4 *[294.10]*
      infection
        brain 293.9
          acute (psychosis) 293.0
          chronic 294.8
          subacute (psychosis) 293.1
        intracranial NEC 293.9

Psychosis — *continued*
  organic — *continued*
    due to or associated with — *continued*
      infection — *continued*
        intracranial — *continued*
          acute (psychosis) 293.0
          chronic 294.8
          subacute (psychosis) 293.1
      intoxication
        alcoholic (acute) (*see also* Psychosis, alcoholic) 291.9
          pathological 291.4
        drug (*see also* Psychosis, drug) 292.9
      ischemia
        cerebrovascular (generalized) (*see also* Psychosis, arteriosclerotic) 290.40
      Jakob-Creutzfeldt disease (syndrome) 046.19
        with behavioral disturbance 046.19 *[294.11]*
        without behavioral disturbance 046.19 *[294.10]*
        variant 046.11
          with dementia
            with behavioral disturbance 046.11 *[294.11]*
            without behavioral disturbance 046.11 *[294.10]*
      multiple sclerosis
        with behavioral disturbance 340 *[294.11]*
        without behavioral disturbance 340 *[294.10]*
      physical condition NEC 293.9
        with
          delusions 293.81
          hallucinations 293.82
      presenility 290.10
      puerperium — *see* Psychosis, puerperal
      sclerosis, multiple
        with behavioral disturbance 340 *[294.11]*
        without behavioral disturbance 340 *[294.10]*
      senility 290.20
      status epilepticus
        with behavioral disturbance 345.3 *[294.11]*
        without behavioral disturbance 345.3 *[294.10]*
      trauma
        brain (birth) (from electrical current) (surgical) 293.9
          acute (psychosis) 293.0
          chronic 294.8
          subacute (psychosis) 293.1
        unspecified physical condition 293.9
          with
            delusion 293.81
            hallucinations 293.82
    infective 293.9
      acute (psychosis) 293.0
      subacute 293.1
    posttraumatic 293.9
      acute 293.0
      subacute 293.1
    specified type NEC 294.8
    transient 293.9
      with
        anxiety 293.84
        delusions 293.81
        depression 293.83
        hallucinations 293.82
      depressive type 293.83
      hallucinatory type 293.82
      paranoid type 293.81
      specified type NEC 293.89
  paranoic 297.1
  paranoid (chronic) 297.9

Psychosis — *continued*
  paranoid — *continued*
    alcoholic 291.5
    chronic 297.1
    climacteric 297.2
    involutional 297.2
    menopausal 297.2
    protracted reactive 298.4
    psychogenic 298.4
      acute 298.3
    schizophrenic (*see also* Schizophrenia) 295.3 ☑
    senile 290.20
  paroxysmal 298.9
    senile 290.20
  polyneuritic, alcoholic 291.1
  postoperative 293.9
  postpartum — *see* Psychosis, puerperal
  prepsychotic (*see also* Schizophrenia) 295.5 ☑
  presbyophrenic (type) 290.8
  presenile (*see also* Dementia, presenile) 290.10
  prison 300.16
  psychogenic 298.8
    depressive 298.0
    paranoid 298.4
      acute 298.3
  puerperal
    specified type — *see* categories 295-298 ☑
    unspecified type 293.89
      acute 293.0
      chronic 293.89
      subacute 293.1
  reactive (emotional stress) (psychological trauma) 298.8
    brief 298.8
    confusion 298.2
    depressive 298.0
    excitation 298.1
  schizo-affective (depressed) (excited) (*see also* Schizophrenia) 295.7 ☑
  schizophrenia, schizophrenic (*see also* Schizophrenia) 295.9 ☑
    borderline type 295.5 ☑
      of childhood (*see also* Psychosis, childhood) 299.8 ☑
    catatonic (excited) (withdrawn) 295.2 ☑
    childhood type (*see also* Psychosis, childhood) 299.9 ☑
    hebephrenic 295.1 ☑
    incipient 295.5 ☑
    latent 295.5 ☑
    paranoid 295.3 ☑
    prepsychotic 295.5 ☑
    prodromal 295.5 ☑
    pseudoneurotic 295.5 ☑
    pseudopsychopathic 295.5 ☑
    schizophreniform 295.4 ☑
    simple 295.0 ☑
    undifferentiated type 295.9 ☑
  schizophreniform 295.4 ☑
  senile NEC 290.20
    with
      delusional features 290.20
      depressive features 290.21
    depressed type 290.21
    paranoid type 290.20
    simple deterioration 290.20
    specified type — *see* categories 295-298 ☑
  shared 297.3
  situational (reactive) 298.8
  symbiotic (childhood) (*see also* Psychosis, childhood) 299.1 ☑
  toxic (acute) 293.9
Psychotic — *see also* condition 298.9
  episode 298.9
    due to or associated with physical conditions (*see also* Psychosis, organic) 293.9
Pterygium (eye) 372.40
  central 372.43
  colli 744.5

☑ **Additional Digit Required** — Refer to the Tabular List for Digit Selection   ▼ Subterms under main terms may continue to next column or page

242 — Volume 2   ▶◀ **Revised Text**   ● **New Line**   ▲ **Revised Code**   2015 ICD-9-CM

Pterygium — continued
  double 372.44
  peripheral (stationary) 372.41
    progressive 372.42
    recurrent 372.45
Ptilosis 374.55
PTLD (post-transplant lymphoproliferative disorder) 238.77
Ptomaine (poisoning) — see also Poisoning, food 005.9
Ptosis (adiposa) 374.30
  breast 611.81
  cecum 569.89
  colon 569.89
  congenital (eyelid) 743.61
    specified site NEC — see Anomaly, specified type NEC
  epicanthus syndrome 270.2
  eyelid 374.30
    congenital 743.61
    mechanical 374.33
    myogenic 374.32
    paralytic 374.31
  gastric 537.5
  intestine 569.89
  kidney (see also Disease, renal) 593.0
    congenital 753.3
  liver 573.8
  renal (see also Disease, renal) 593.0
    congenital 753.3
  splanchnic 569.89
  spleen 289.59
  stomach 537.5
  viscera 569.89
PTP (posttransfusion purpura) 287.41
PTSD (Post-traumatic stress disorder) 309.81
Ptyalism 527.7
  hysterical 300.11
  periodic 527.2
  pregnancy 646.8 ☑
  psychogenic 306.4
Ptyalolithiasis 527.5
Pubalgia 848.8
Pubarche, precocious 259.1
Pubertas praecox 259.1
Puberty V21.1
  abnormal 259.9
  bleeding 626.3
  delayed 259.0
  precocious (constitutional) (cryptogenic) (idiopathic) NEC 259.1
    due to
      adrenal
        cortical hyperfunction 255.2
        hyperplasia 255.2
      cortical hyperfunction 255.2
      ovarian hyperfunction 256.1
        estrogen 256.0
      pineal tumor 259.8
      testicular hyperfunction 257.0
    premature 259.1
      due to
        adrenal cortical hyperfunction 255.2
        pineal tumor 259.8
        pituitary (anterior) hyperfunction 253.1
Puckering, macula 362.56
Pudenda, pudendum — see condition
Puente's disease (simple glandular cheilitis) 528.5
Puerperal
  abscess
    areola 675.1 ☑
    Bartholin's gland 646.6 ☑
    breast 675.1 ☑
    cervix (uteri) 670.8 ☑
    fallopian tube 670.8 ☑
    genital organ 670.8 ☑
    kidney 646.6 ☑
    mammary 675.1 ☑
    mesosalpinx 670.8 ☑
    nabothian 646.6 ☑
    nipple 675.0 ☑
    ovary, ovarian 670.8 ☑
    oviduct 670.8 ☑
    parametric 670.8 ☑

Puerperal — continued
  abscess — continued
    para-uterine 670.8 ☑
    pelvic 670.8 ☑
    perimetric 670.8 ☑
    periuterine 670.8 ☑
    retro-uterine 670.8 ☑
    subareolar 675.1 ☑
    suprapelvic 670.8 ☑
    tubal (ruptured) 670.8 ☑
    tubo-ovarian 670.8 ☑
    urinary tract NEC 646.6 ☑
    uterine, uterus 670.8 ☑
    vagina (wall) 646.6 ☑
    vaginorectal 646.6 ☑
    vulvovaginal gland 646.6 ☑
  accident 674.9 ☑
  adnexitis 670.8 ☑
  afibrinogenemia, or other coagulation defect 666.3 ☑
  albuminuria (acute) (subacute) 646.2 ☑
    pre-eclamptic 642.4 ☑
  anemia (conditions classifiable to 280–285) 648.2 ☑
  anuria 669.3 ☑
  apoplexy 674.0 ☑
  asymptomatic bacteriuria 646.5 ☑
  atrophy, breast 676.3 ☑
  blood dyscrasia 666.3 ☑
  caked breast 676.2 ☑
  cardiomyopathy 674.5 ☑
  cellulitis — see Puerperal, abscess
  cerebrovascular disorder (conditions classifiable to 430–434, 436–437) 674.0 ☑
  cervicitis (conditions classifiable to 616.0) 646.6 ☑
  coagulopathy (any) 666.3 ☑
  complications 674.9 ☑
    specified type NEC 674.8 ☑
  convulsions (eclamptic) (uremic) 642.6 ☑
    with pre-existing hypertension 642.7 ☑
  cracked nipple 676.1 ☑
  cystitis 646.6 ☑
  cystopyelitis 646.6 ☑
  deciduitis (acute) 670.8 ☑
  delirium NEC 293.9
  diabetes (mellitus) (conditions classifiable to 249 and 250) 648.0 ☑
  disease 674.9 ☑
    breast NEC 676.3 ☑
    cerebrovascular (acute) 674.0 ☑
    nonobstetric NEC (see also Pregnancy, complicated, current disease or condition) 648.9 ☑
    pelvis inflammatory 670.8 ☑
    renal NEC 646.2 ☑
    tubo-ovarian 670.8 ☑
    Valsuani's (progressive pernicious anemia) 648.2 ☑
  disorder
    lactation 676.9 ☑
      specified type NEC 676.8 ☑
    nonobstetric NEC (see also Pregnancy, complicated, current disease or condition) 648.9 ☑
  disruption
    cesarean wound 674.1 ☑
    episiotomy wound 674.2 ☑
    perineal laceration wound 674.2 ☑
  drug dependence (conditions classifiable to 304) 648.3 ☑
  eclampsia 642.6 ☑
    with pre-existing hypertension 642.7 ☑
  embolism (pulmonary) 673.2 ☑
    air 673.0 ☑
    amniotic fluid 673.1 ☑
    blood-clot 673.2 ☑
    brain or cerebral 674.0 ☑
    cardiac 674.8 ☑
    fat 673.8 ☑
    intracranial sinus (venous) 671.5 ☑
    pyemic 673.3 ☑
    septic 673.3 ☑
    spinal cord 671.5 ☑

Puerperal — continued
  endometritis (conditions classifiable to 615.0–615.9) 670.1 ☑
  endophlebitis — see Puerperal, phlebitis
  endotrachelitis 646.6 ☑
  engorgement, breasts 676.2 ☑
  erysipelas 670.8 ☑
  failure
    lactation 676.4 ☑
    renal, acute 669.3 ☑
  fever 672 ☑
    meaning pyrexia (of unknown origin) 672.0 ☑
    meaning sepsis 670.2 ☑
  fissure, nipple 676.1 ☑
  fistula
    breast 675.1 ☑
    mammary gland 675.1 ☑
    nipple 675.0 ☑
  galactophoritis 675.2 ☑
  galactorrhea 676.6 ☑
  gangrene
    gas 670.8 ☑
      with sepsis 670.2 ☑
    uterus 670.8 ☑
  gonorrhea (conditions classifiable to 098) 647.1 ☑
  hematoma, subdural 674.0 ☑
  hematosalpinx, infectional 670.8 ☑
  hemiplegia, cerebral 674.0 ☑
  hemorrhage 666.1 ☑
    brain 674.0 ☑
    bulbar 674.0 ☑
    cerebellar 674.0 ☑
    cerebral 674.0 ☑
    cortical 674.0 ☑
    delayed (after 24 hours) (uterine) 666.2 ☑
    extradural 674.0 ☑
    internal capsule 674.0 ☑
    intracranial 674.0 ☑
    intrapontine 674.0 ☑
    meningeal 674.0 ☑
    pontine 674.0 ☑
    subarachnoid 674.0 ☑
    subcortical 674.0 ☑
    subdural 674.0 ☑
    uterine, delayed 666.2 ☑
    ventricular 674.0 ☑
  hemorrhoids 671.8 ☑
  hepatorenal syndrome 674.8 ☑
  hypertrophy
    breast 676.3 ☑
    mammary gland 676.3 ☑
  induration breast (fibrous) 676.3 ☑
  infarction
    lung — see Puerperal, embolism
    pulmonary — see Puerperal, embolism
  infection
    Bartholin's gland 646.6 ☑
    breast 675.2 ☑
      with nipple 675.9 ☑
        specified type NEC 675.8 ☑
    cervix 646.6 ☑
    endocervix 646.6 ☑
    fallopian tube 670.8 ☑
    generalized 670.0 ☑
    genital tract (major) 670.0 ☑
      minor or localized 646.6 ☑
    kidney (bacillus coli) 646.6 ☑
    mammary gland 675.2 ☑
      with nipple 675.9 ☑
        specified type NEC 675.8 ☑
    nipple 675.0 ☑
      with breast 675.9 ☑
        specified type NEC 675.8 ☑
    ovary 670.8 ☑
    pelvic 670.8 ☑
    peritoneum 670.8 ☑
    renal 646.6 ☑
    tubo-ovarian 670.8 ☑
    urinary (tract) NEC 646.6 ☑
      asymptomatic 646.5 ☑

Puerperal — continued
  infection — continued
    uterus, uterine 670.8 ☑
    vagina 646.6 ☑
  inflammation (see also Puerperal, infection)
    areola 675.1 ☑
    Bartholin's gland 646.6 ☑
    breast 675.2 ☑
    broad ligament 670.8 ☑
    cervix (uteri) 646.6 ☑
    fallopian tube 670.8 ☑
    genital organs 670.8 ☑
      localized 646.6 ☑
    mammary gland 675.2 ☑
    nipple 675.0 ☑
    ovary 670.8 ☑
    oviduct 670.8 ☑
    pelvis 670.8 ☑
    periuterine 670.8 ☑
    tubal 670.8 ☑
    vagina 646.6 ☑
    vein — see Puerperal, phlebitis
  inversion, nipple 676.3 ☑
  ischemia, cerebral 674.0 ☑
  lymphangitis 670.8 ☑
    breast 675.2 ☑
  malaria (conditions classifiable to 084) 647.4 ☑
  malnutrition 648.9 ☑
  mammillitis 675.0 ☑
  mammitis 675.2 ☑
  mania 296.0 ☑
    recurrent episode 296.1 ☑
    single episode 296.0 ☑
  mastitis 675.2 ☑
    purulent 675.1 ☑
    retromammary 675.1 ☑
    submammary 675.1 ☑
  melancholia 296.2 ☑
    recurrent episode 296.3 ☑
    single episode 296.2 ☑
  mental disorder (conditions classifiable to 290–303, 305.0, 305.2–305.9, 306–316, 317–319) 648.4 ☑
  metritis (suppurative) 670.1 ☑
    septic 670.2 ☑
  metroperitonitis 670.8 ☑
  metrorrhagia 666.2 ☑
  metrosalpingitis 670.8 ☑
  metrovaginitis 670.8 ☑
  milk leg 671.4 ☑
  monoplegia, cerebral 674.0 ☑
  necrosis
    kidney, tubular 669.3 ☑
    liver (acute) (subacute) (conditions classifiable to 570) 674.8 ☑
    ovary 670.8 ☑
    renal cortex 669.3 ☑
  nephritis or nephrosis (conditions classifiable to 580–589) 646.2 ☑
    with hypertension 642.1 ☑
  nutritional deficiency (conditions classifiable to 260–269) 648.9 ☑
  occlusion, precerebral artery 674.0 ☑
  oliguria 669.3 ☑
  oophoritis 670.8 ☑
  ovaritis 670.8 ☑
  paralysis
    bladder (sphincter) 665.5 ☑
    cerebral 674.0 ☑
  paralytic stroke 674.0 ☑
  parametritis 670.8 ☑
  paravaginitis 646.6 ☑
  pelviperitonitis 670.8 ☑
  perimetritis 670.8 ☑
  perimetrosalpingitis 670.8 ☑
  perinephritis 646.6 ☑
  perioophoritis 670.8 ☑
  periphlebitis — see Puerperal, phlebitis
  perisalpingitis 670.8 ☑
  peritoneal infection 670.8 ☑
  peritonitis (pelvic) 670.8 ☑
  perivaginitis 646.6 ☑

☑ Additional Digit Required — Refer to the Tabular List for Digit Selection   ▽ Subterms under main terms may continue to next column or page

Puerperal — *continued*
  phlebitis 671.2 ☑
    deep 671.4 ☑
    intracranial sinus (venous) 671.5 ☑
    pelvic 671.4 ☑
    specified site NEC 671.5 ☑
    superficial 671.2 ☑
  phlegmasia alba dolens 671.4 ☑
  placental polyp 674.4 ☑
  pneumonia, embolic — *see* Puerperal, embolism
  prediabetes 648.8 ☑
  pre-eclampsia (mild) 642.4 ☑
    with pre-existing hypertension 642.7 ☑
    severe 642.5 ☑
  psychosis, unspecified (*see also* Psychosis, puerperal) 293.89
  pyelitis 646.6 ☑
  pyelocystitis 646.6 ☑
  pyelohydronephrosis 646.6 ☑
  pyelonephritis 646.6 ☑
  pyelonephrosis 646.6 ☑
  pyemia 670.2 ☑
  pyocystitis 646.6 ☑
  pyohemia 670.2 ☑
  pyometra 670.8 ☑
  pyonephritis 646.6 ☑
  pyonephrosis 646.6 ☑
  pyo-oophoritis 670.8 ☑
  pyosalpingitis 670.8 ☑
  pyosalpinx 670.8 ☑
  pyrexia (of unknown origin) 672.0 ☑
  renal
    disease NEC 646.2 ☑
    failure, acute 669.3 ☑
  retention
    decidua (fragments) (with delayed hemorrhage) 666.2 ☑
      without hemorrhage 667.1 ☑
    placenta (fragments) (with delayed hemorrhage) 666.2 ☑
      without hemorrhage 667.1 ☑
    secundines (fragments) (with delayed hemorrhage) 666.2 ☑
      without hemorrhage 667.1 ☑
  retracted nipple 676.0 ☑
  rubella (conditions classifiable to 056) 647.5 ☑
  salpingitis 670.8 ☑
  salpingo-oophoritis 670.8 ☑
  salpingo-ovaritis 670.8 ☑
  salpingoperitonitis 670.8 ☑
  sapremia 670.2 ☑
  secondary perineal tear 674.2 ☑
  sepsis (pelvic) 670.2 ☑
  septicemia 670.2 ☑
  subinvolution (uterus) 674.8 ☑
  sudden death (cause unknown) 674.9 ☑
  suppuration — *see* Puerperal, abscess
  syphilis (conditions classifiable to 090–097) 647.0 ☑
  tetanus 670.8 ☑
  thelitis 675.0 ☑
  thrombocytopenia 666.3 ☑
  thrombophlebitis (superficial) 671.2 ☑
    deep 671.4 ☑
    pelvic 671.4 ☑
    septic 670.3 ☑
    specified site NEC 671.5 ☑
  thrombosis (venous) — *see* Thrombosis, puerperal
  thyroid dysfunction (conditions classifiable to 240–246) 648.1 ☑
  toxemia (*see also* Toxemia, of pregnancy) 642.4 ☑
    eclamptic 642.6 ☑
      with pre-existing hypertension 642.7 ☑
    pre-eclamptic (mild) 642.4 ☑
      with
        convulsions 642.6 ☑
        pre-existing hypertension 642.7 ☑
        severe 642.5 ☑

Puerperal — *continued*
  tuberculosis (conditions classifiable to 010–018) 647.3 ☑
  uremia 669.3 ☑
  vaginitis (conditions classifiable to 616.1) 646.6 ☑
  varicose veins (legs) 671.0 ☑
    vulva or perineum 671.1 ☑
  venous complication 671.9 ☑
  vulvitis (conditions classifiable to 616.1) 646.6 ☑
  vulvovaginitis (conditions classifiable to 616.1) 646.6 ☑
  white leg 671.4 ☑
Pulled muscle — *see* Sprain, by site
Pulmolithiasis 518.89
Pulmonary — *see* condition
Pulmonitis (unknown etiology) 486
Pulpitis (acute) (anachoretic) (chronic) (hyperplastic) (putrescent) (suppurative) (ulcerative) 522.0
Pulpless tooth 522.9
Pulse
  alternating 427.89
    psychogenic 306.2
  bigeminal 427.89
  fast 785.0
  feeble, rapid, due to shock following injury 958.4
  rapid 785.0
  slow 427.89
  strong 785.9
  trigeminal 427.89
  water-hammer (*see also* Insufficiency, aortic) 424.1
  weak 785.9
Pulseless disease 446.7
Pulsus
  alternans or trigeminy 427.89
    psychogenic 306.2
Punch drunk 310.2
Puncta lacrimalia occlusion 375.52
Punctiform hymen 752.49
Puncture (traumatic) — *see also* Wound, open, by site
  accidental, complicating surgery 998.2
  bladder, nontraumatic 596.6
  by
    device, implant, or graft — *see* Complications, mechanical
    foreign body
      internal organs (*see also* Injury, internal, by site)
        by ingested object — *see* Foreign body
      left accidentally in operation wound 998.4
    instrument (any) during a procedure, accidental 998.2
  internal organs, abdomen, chest, or pelvis — *see* Injury, internal, by site
  kidney, nontraumatic 593.89
Pupil — *see* condition
Pupillary membrane 364.74
  persistent 743.46
Pupillotonia 379.46
  pseudotabetic 379.46
Purpura 287.2
  abdominal 287.0
  allergic 287.0
  anaphylactoid 287.0
  annularis telangiectodes 709.1
  arthritic 287.0
  autoerythrocyte sensitization 287.2
  autoimmune 287.0
  bacterial 287.0
  Bateman's (senile) 287.2
  capillary fragility (hereditary) (idiopathic) 287.8
  cryoglobulinemic 273.2
  devil's pinches 287.2
  fibrinolytic (*see also* Fibrinolysis) 286.6
  fulminans, fulminous 286.6
  gangrenous 287.0
  hemorrhagic (*see also* Purpura, thrombocytopenic) 287.39

Purpura — *continued*
  hemorrhagic (*see also* Purpura, thrombocytopenic) — *continued*
    nodular 272.7
    nonthrombocytopenic 287.0
    thrombocytopenic 287.39
  Henoch's (purpura nervosa) 287.0
  Henoch-Schönlein (allergic) 287.0
  hypergammaglobulinemic (benign primary) (Waldenström's) 273.0
  idiopathic 287.31
    nonthrombocytopenic 287.0
    thrombocytopenic 287.31
  immune thrombocytopenic 287.31
  infectious 287.0
  malignant 287.0
  neonatorum 772.6
  nervosa 287.0
  newborn NEC 772.6
  nonthrombocytopenic 287.2
    hemorrhagic 287.0
    idiopathic 287.0
  nonthrombopenic 287.2
  peliosis rheumatica 287.0
  pigmentosa, progressiva 709.09
  posttransfusion (PTP) 287.41
    from whole blood (fresh) or blood products 287.41
  primary 287.0
  primitive 287.0
  red cell membrane sensitivity 287.2
  rheumatica 287.0
  Schönlein (-Henoch) (allergic) 287.0
  scorbutic 267
  senile 287.2
  simplex 287.2
  symptomatica 287.0
  telangiectasia annularis 709.1
  thrombocytopenic (*see also* Thrombocytopenia) 287.30
    congenital 287.33
    essential 287.30
    hereditary 287.31
    idiopathic 287.31
    immune 287.31
    neonatal, transitory (*see also* Thrombocytopenia, neonatal transitory) 776.1
    primary 287.30
    puerperal, postpartum 666.3 ☑
    thrombotic 446.6
  thrombohemolytic (*see also* Fibrinolysis) 286.6
  thrombopenic (*see also* Thrombocytopenia) 287.30
    congenital 287.33
    essential 287.30
    thrombotic 446.6
      thrombocytic 446.6
      thrombocytopenic 446.6
  toxic 287.0
  variolosa 050.0
  vascular 287.0
  visceral symptoms 287.0
  Werlhof's (*see also* Purpura, thrombocytopenic) 287.39
Purpuric spots 782.7
Purulent — *see* condition
Pus
  absorption, general — *see* Septicemia
  in
    stool 792.1
    urine 791.9
  tube (rupture) (*see also* Salpingo-oophoritis) 614.2
Pustular rash 782.1
Pustule 686.9
  malignant 022.0
  nonmalignant 686.9
Putnam-Dana syndrome (subacute combined sclerosis with pernicious anemia) 281.0 *[336.2]*
Putnam's disease (subacute combined sclerosis with pernicious anemia) 281.0 *[336.2]*
Putrefaction, intestinal 569.89
Putrescent pulp (dental) 522.1

Purpura — *continued*
Pyarthritis — *see* Pyarthrosis
Pyarthrosis — *see also* Arthritis, pyogenic 711.0 ☑
  tuberculous — *see* Tuberculosis, joint
Pycnoepilepsy, pycnolepsy (idiopathic) — *see also* Epilepsy 345.0 ☑
Pyelectasia 593.89
Pyelectasis 593.89
Pyelitis (congenital) (uremic) 590.80
  with
    abortion — *see* Abortion, by type, with specified complication NEC
    contracted kidney 590.00
    ectopic pregnancy (*see also* categories 633.0–633.9) 639.8
    molar pregnancy (*see also* categories 630–632) 639.8
  acute 590.10
    with renal medullary necrosis 590.11
  chronic 590.00
    with
      renal medullary necrosis 590.01
  complicating pregnancy, childbirth, or puerperium 646.6 ☑
    affecting fetus or newborn 760.1
  cystica 590.3
  following
    abortion 639.8
    ectopic or molar pregnancy 639.8
  gonococcal 098.19
    chronic or duration of 2 months or over 098.39
  tuberculous (*see also* Tuberculosis) 016.0 ☑ *[590.81]*
Pyelocaliectasis 593.89
Pyelocystitis — *see also* Pyelitis 590.80
Pyelohydronephrosis 591
Pyelonephritis — *see also* Pyelitis 590.80
  acute 590.10
    with renal medullary necrosis 590.11
  chronic 590.00
  syphilitic (late) 095.4
  tuberculous (*see also* Tuberculosis) 016.0 ☑ *[590.81]*
Pyelonephrosis — *see also* Pyelitis 590.80
  chronic 590.00
Pyelophlebitis 451.89
Pyelo-ureteritis cystica 590.3
Pyemia, pyemic (purulent) — *see also* Septicemia 038.9
  abscess — *see* Abscess
  arthritis (*see also* Arthritis, pyogenic) 711.0 ☑
  Bacillus coli 038.42
  embolism (*see also* Septicemia) 415.12
  fever 038.9
  infection 038.9
  joint (*see also* Arthritis, pyogenic) 711.0 ☑
  liver 572.1
  meningococcal 036.2
  newborn 771.81
  phlebitis — *see* Phlebitis
  pneumococcal 038.2
  portal 572.1
  postvaccinal 999.39
  puerperal 670.2 ☑
  specified organism NEC 038.8
  staphylococcal 038.10
    aureus 038.11
      methicillin
        resistant 038.12
        susceptible 038.11
    specified organism NEC 038.19
  streptococcal 038.0
  tuberculous — *see* Tuberculosis, miliary
Pygopagus 759.4
Pykno-epilepsy, pyknolepsy (idiopathic) — *see also* Epilepsy 345.0 ☑
Pyle (-Cohn) disease (craniometaphyseal dysplasia) 756.89
Pylephlebitis (suppurative) 572.1
Pylethrombophlebitis 572.1
Pylethrombosis 572.1
Pyloritis — *see also* Gastritis 535.5 ☑
Pylorospasm (reflex) 537.81
  congenital or infantile 750.5

☑ **Additional Digit Required** — Refer to the Tabular List for Digit Selection   ▽ **Subterms under main terms may continue to next column or page**

244 — Volume 2   ▶◀ Revised Text   ● New Line   ▲ Revised Code   2015 ICD-9-CM

Pylorospasm –– *continued*
- neurotic 306.4
- newborn 750.5
- psychogenic 306.4

Pylorus, pyloric — *see* condition
Pyoarthrosis — *see* Pyarthrosis
Pyocele
- mastoid 383.00
- sinus (accessory) (nasal) (*see also* Sinusitis) 473.9
- turbinate (bone) 473.9
- urethra (*see also* Urethritis) 597.0

Pyococcal dermatitis 686.00
Pyococcide, skin 686.00
Pyocolpos — *see also* Vaginitis 616.10
Pyocyaneus dermatitis 686.09
Pyocystitis — *see also* Cystitis 595.9
Pyoderma, pyodermia 686.00
- gangrenosum 686.01
- specified type NEC 686.09
- vegetans 686.8

Pyodermatitis 686.00
- vegetans 686.8

Pyogenic — *see* condition
Pyohemia — *see* Septicemia
Pyohydronephrosis — *see also* Pyelitis 590.80
Pyometra 615.9
Pyometritis — *see also* Endometritis 615.9
Pyometrium — *see also* Endometritis 615.9
Pyomyositis 728.0
- ossificans 728.19
- tropical (bungpagga) 040.81

Pyonephritis — *see also* Pyelitis 590.80
- chronic 590.00

Pyonephrosis (congenital) — *see also* Pyelitis 590.80
- acute 590.10

Pyo-oophoritis — *see also* Salpingo-oophoritis 614.2
Pyo-ovarium — *see also* Salpingo-oophoritis 614.2
Pyopericarditis 420.99
Pyopericardium 420.99
Pyophlebitis — *see* Phlebitis
Pyopneumopericardium 420.99
Pyopneumothorax (infectional) 510.9
- with fistula 510.0
- subdiaphragmatic (*see also* Peritonitis) 567.29
- subphrenic (*see also* Peritonitis) 567.29
- tuberculous (*see also* Tuberculosis, pleura) 012.0 ☑

Pyorrhea (alveolar) (alveolaris) 523.40
- degenerative 523.5

Pyosalpingitis — *see also* Salpingo-oophoritis 614.2
Pyosalpinx — *see also* Salpingo-oophoritis 614.2
Pyosepticemia — *see* Septicemia
Pyosis
- Corlett's (impetigo) 684
- Manson's (pemphigus contagiosus) 684

Pyothorax 510.9
- with fistula 510.0
- tuberculous (*see also* Tuberculosis, pleura) 012.0 ☑

Pyoureter 593.89
- tuberculous (*see also* Tuberculosis) 016.2 ☑

Pyramidopallidonigral syndrome 332.0
Pyrexia (of unknown origin) (P.U.O.) 780.60
- atmospheric 992.0
- during labor 659.2 ☑
- environmentally-induced newborn 778.4
- heat 992.0
- newborn, environmentally-induced 778.4
- puerperal 672.0 ☑

Pyroglobulinemia 273.8
Pyromania 312.33
Pyrosis 787.1
Pyrroloporphyria 277.1
Pyuria (bacterial) 791.9

Q

Q fever 083.0
- with pneumonia 083.0 [484.8]

Quadricuspid aortic valve 746.89

Quadrilateral fever 083.0
Quadriparesis — *see* Quadriplegia
- meaning muscle weakness 728.87

Quadriplegia 344.00
- with fracture, vertebra (process) — *see* Fracture, vertebra, cervical, with spinal cord injury
- brain (current episode) 437.8
- C1–C4
  - complete 344.01
  - incomplete 344.02
- C5–C7
  - complete 344.03
  - incomplete 344.04
- cerebral (current episode) 437.8
- congenital or infantile (cerebral) (spastic) (spinal) 343.2
- cortical 437.8
- embolic (current episode) (*see also* Embolism, brain) 434.1 ☑
- functional 780.72
- infantile (cerebral) (spastic) (spinal) 343.2
- newborn NEC 767.0
- specified NEC 344.09
- thrombotic (current episode) (*see also* Thrombosis, brain) 434.0 ☑
- traumatic — *see* Injury, spinal, cervical

Quadruplet
- affected by maternal complications of pregnancy 761.5
- healthy liveborn — *see* Newborn, multiple
- pregnancy (complicating delivery) NEC 651.8 ☑
  - with fetal loss and retention of one or more fetus(es) 651.5 ☑
  - following (elective) fetal reduction 651.7 ☑

Quarrelsomeness 301.3
Quartan
- fever 084.2
- malaria (fever) 084.2

Queensland fever 083.0
- coastal 083.0
- seven-day 100.89

Quervain's disease 727.04
- thyroid (subacute granulomatous thyroiditis) 245.1

Queyrat's erythroplasia (M8080/2)
- specified site — *see* Neoplasm, skin, in situ
- unspecified site 233.5

Quincke's disease or edema — *see* Edema, angioneurotic
Quinquaud's disease (acne decalvans) 704.09
Quinsy (gangrenous) 475
Quintan fever 083.1
Quintuplet
- affected by maternal complications of pregnancy 761.5
- healthy liveborn — *see* Newborn, multiple
- pregnancy (complicating delivery) NEC 651.2 ☑
  - with fetal loss and retention of one or more fetus(es) 651.6 ☑
  - following (elective) fetal reduction 651.7 ☑

Quotidian
- fever 084.0
- malaria (fever) 084.0

R

Rabbia 071
Rabbit fever — *see also* Tularemia 021.9
Rabies 071
- contact V01.5
- exposure to V01.5
- inoculation V04.5
  - reaction — *see* Complications, vaccination
- vaccination, prophylactic (against) V04.5

Rachischisis — *see also* Spina bifida 741.9 ☑
Rachitic — *see also* condition
- deformities of spine 268.1
- pelvis 268.1
  - with disproportion (fetopelvic) 653.2 ☑
  - affecting fetus or newborn 763.1

Rachitic — *see also* condition — *continued*
- pelvis — *continued*
  - with disproportion — *continued*
    - causing obstructed labor 660.1 ☑
    - affecting fetus or newborn 763.1

Rachitis, rachitism — *see also* Rickets
- acute 268.0
- fetalis 756.4
- renalis 588.0
- tarda 268.0

Racket nail 757.5
Radial nerve — *see* condition
Radiation effects or sickness — *see also* Effect, adverse, radiation
- cataract 366.46
- dermatitis 692.82
  - sunburn (*see also* Sunburn) 692.71

Radiculitis (pressure) (vertebrogenic) 729.2
- accessory nerve 723.4
- anterior crural 724.4
- arm 723.4
- brachial 723.4
- cervical NEC 723.4
- due to displacement of intervertebral disc — *see* Neuritis, due to, displacement intervertebral disc
- leg 724.4
- lumbar NEC 724.4
- lumbosacral 724.4
- rheumatic 729.2
- syphilitic 094.89
- thoracic (with visceral pain) 724.4

Radiculomyelitis 357.0
- toxic, due to
  - Clostridium tetani 037
  - Corynebacterium diphtheriae 032.89

Radiculopathy — *see also* Radiculitis 729.2
Radioactive substances, adverse effect — *see* Effect, adverse, radioactive substance
Radiodermal burns (acute) (chronic) (occupational) — *see* Burn, by site
Radiodermatitis 692.82
Radionecrosis — *see* Effect, adverse, radiation
Radiotherapy session V58.0
Radium, adverse effect — *see* Effect, adverse, radioactive substance
Raeder-Harbitz syndrome (pulseless disease) 446.7
Rage — *see also* Disturbance, conduct 312.0 ☑
- meaning rabies 071

Rag sorters' disease 022.1
Raillietiniasis 123.8
Railroad neurosis 300.16
Railway spine 300.16
Raised — *see* Elevation
Raiva 071
Rake teeth, tooth 524.39
Rales 786.7
Ramifying renal pelvis 753.3
Ramsay Hunt syndrome (herpetic geniculate ganglionitis) 053.11
- meaning dyssynergia cerebellaris myoclonica 334.2

Ranke's primary infiltration — *see also* Tuberculosis 010.0 ☑
Ranula 527.6
- congenital 750.26

Rape
- adult 995.83
- alleged, observation or examination V71.5
- child 995.53

Rapid
- feeble pulse, due to shock, following injury 958.4
- heart (beat) 785.0
  - psychogenic 306.2
- respiration 786.06
  - psychogenic 306.1
- second stage (delivery) 661.3 ☑
  - affecting fetus or newborn 763.6
- time-zone change syndrome 327.35

Rarefaction, bone 733.99
Rash 782.1
- canker 034.1
- diaper 691.0
- drug (internal use) 693.0

Rash — *continued*
- drug — *continued*
  - contact 692.3
- ECHO 9 virus 078.89
- enema 692.89
- food (*see also* Allergy, food) 693.1
- heat 705.1
- napkin 691.0
- nettle 708.8
- pustular 782.1
- rose 782.1
  - epidemic 056.9
  - of infants 057.8
- scarlet 034.1
- serum (prophylactic) (therapeutic) 999.59
- toxic 782.1
- wandering tongue 529.1

Rasmussen's aneurysm — *see also* Tuberculosis 011.2 ☑
Rat-bite fever 026.9
- due to Streptobacillus moniliformis 026.1
- spirochetal (morsus muris) 026.0

Rathke's pouch tumor (M9350/1) 237.0
Raymond (-Céstan) syndrome 433.8 ☑
Raynaud's
- disease or syndrome (paroxysmal digital cyanosis) 443.0
- gangrene (symmetric) 443.0 [785.4]
- phenomenon (paroxysmal digital cyanosis) (secondary) 443.0

RDS 769
Reaction
- acute situational maladjustment (*see also* Reaction, adjustment) 309.9
- adaptation (*see also* Reaction, adjustment) 309.9
- adjustment 309.9
  - with
    - anxious mood 309.24
      - with depressed mood 309.28
    - conduct disturbance 309.3
      - combined with disturbance of emotions 309.4
    - depressed mood 309.0
      - brief 309.0
        - with anxious mood 309.28
      - prolonged 309.1
    - elective mutism 309.83
    - mixed emotions and conduct 309.4
    - mutism, elective 309.83
    - physical symptoms 309.82
    - predominant disturbance (of)
      - conduct 309.3
      - emotions NEC 309.29
        - mixed 309.28
      - mixed, emotions and conduct 309.4
    - specified type NEC 309.89
  - specific academic or work inhibition 309.23
  - withdrawal 309.83
- depressive 309.0
  - with conduct disturbance 309.4
  - brief 309.0
  - prolonged 309.1
  - specified type NEC 309.89
- adverse food NEC 995.7
- affective (*see also* Psychosis, affective) 296.90
  - specified type NEC 296.99
- aggressive 301.3
  - unsocialized (*see also* Disturbance, conduct) 312.0 ☑
- allergic (*see also* Allergy) 995.3
  - drug, medicinal substance, and biological — *see* Allergy, drug
  - due to correct medical substance properly administered 995.27
  - food — *see* Allergy, food
  - serum 999.59
- anaphylactic — *see* Anaphylactic reaction
- anesthesia — *see* Anesthesia, complication
- anger 312.0 ☑
- antisocial 301.7
- antitoxin (prophylactic) (therapeutic) — *see* Complications, vaccination

☑ Additional Digit Required — Refer to the Tabular List for Digit Selection

Subterms under main terms may continue to next column or page

2015 ICD-9-CM

▶◀ Revised Text   ● New Line   ▲ Revised Code

Volume 2 — 245

Pylorospasm — Reaction

Reaction — *continued*
anxiety 300.00
Arthus 995.21
asthenic 300.5
compulsive 300.3
conversion (anesthetic) (autonomic) (hyperkinetic) (mixed paralytic) (paresthetic) 300.11
deoxyribonuclease (DNA) (DNase) hypersensitivity NEC 287.2
depressive 300.4
    acute 309.0
    affective (*see also* Psychosis, affective) 296.2 ☑
        recurrent episode 296.3 ☑
        single episode 296.2 ☑
    brief 309.0
    manic (*see also* Psychosis, affective) 296.80
    neurotic 300.4
    psychoneurotic 300.4
    psychotic 298.0
dissociative 300.15
drug NEC (*see also* Table of Drugs and Chemicals) 995.20
    allergic (*see also* Allergy, drug) 995.27
    correct substance properly administered 995.20
    obstetric anesthetic or analgesic NEC 668.9 ☑
        affecting fetus or newborn 763.5
        specified drug — *see* Table of Drugs and Chemicals
    overdose or poisoning 977.9
        specified drug — *see* Table of Drugs and Chemicals
    specific to newborn 779.4
    transmitted via placenta or breast milk — *see* Absorption, drug, through placenta
    withdrawal NEC 292.0
        infant of dependent mother 779.5
    wrong substance given or taken in error 977.9
        specified drug — *see* Table of Drugs and Chemicals
dyssocial 301.7
dystonic, acute, due to drugs 333.72
erysipeloid 027.1
fear 300.20
    child 313.0
fluid loss, cerebrospinal 349.0
food (*see also* Allergy, food)
    adverse NEC 995.7
    anaphylactic shock — *see* Anaphylactic reaction or shock, due to, food
foreign
    body NEC 728.82
        in operative wound (inadvertently left) 998.4
        due to surgical material intentionally left — *see* Complications, due to (presence of) any device, implant, or graft classified to 996.0–996.5 NEC
    substance accidentally left during a procedure (chemical) (powder) (talc) 998.7
    body or object (instrument) (sponge) (swab) 998.4
graft-versus-host (GVH) 279.50
grief (acute) (brief) 309.0
    prolonged 309.1
gross stress (*see also* Reaction, stress, acute) 308.9
group delinquent (*see also* Disturbance, conduct) 312.2 ☑
Herxheimer's 995.91
hyperkinetic (*see also* Hyperkinesia) 314.9
hypochondriacal 300.7
hypoglycemic, due to insulin 251.0
    therapeutic misadventure 962.3
hypomanic (*see also* Psychosis, affective) 296.0 ☑
    recurrent episode 296.1 ☑

Reaction — *continued*
hypomanic (*see also* Psychosis, affective) — *continued*
    single episode 296.0 ☑
hysterical 300.10
    conversion type 300.11
    dissociative 300.15
id (bacterial cause) 692.89
immaturity NEC 301.89
    aggressive 301.3
    emotional instability 301.59
immunization — *see* Complications, vaccination
incompatibility
    blood group (*see also* Complications, transfusion) 999.80
        ABO (due to transfusion of blood or blood products) (*see also* Complications, transfusion) 999.60
        minor blood group 999.89
        non-ABO — *see also* Complications, transfusion 999.75
        Rh antigen (C) (c) (D) (E) (e) (factor) (infusion) (transfusion) (*see also* Complications, transfusion) 999.70
inflammatory — *see* Infection
infusion — *see* Complications, infusion
inoculation (immune serum) — *see* Complications, vaccination
insulin 995.23
involutional
    paranoid 297.2
    psychotic (*see also* Psychosis, affective, depressive) 296.2 ☑
leukemoid (basophilic) (lymphocytic) (monocytic) (myelocytic) (neutrophilic) 288.62
LSD (*see also* Abuse, drugs, nondependent) 305.3 ☑
lumbar puncture 349.0
manic-depressive (*see also* Psychosis, affective) 296.80
    depressed 296.2 ☑
        recurrent episode 296.3 ☑
        single episode 296.2 ☑
    hypomanic 296.0 ☑
neurasthenic 300.5
neurogenic (*see also* Neurosis) 300.9
neurotic-depressive 300.4
neurotic NEC 300.9
nitritoid — *see* Crisis, nitritoid
nonspecific
    to
        cell mediated immunity measurement of gamma interferon antigen response without active tuberculosis 795.52
        QuantiFERON-TB test (QFT) without active tuberculosis 795.52
        tuberculin test (*see also* Reaction, tuberculin skin test) 795.51
obsessive compulsive 300.3
organic 293.9
    acute 293.0
    subacute 293.1
overanxious, child or adolescent 313.0
paranoid (chronic) 297.9
    acute 298.3
    climacteric 297.2
    involutional 297.2
    menopausal 297.2
    senile 290.20
    simple 297.0
passive
    aggressive 301.84
    dependency 301.6
personality (*see also* Disorder, personality) 301.9
phobic 300.20
postradiation — *see* Effect, adverse, radiation
psychogenic NEC 300.9
psychoneurotic (*see also* Neurosis) 300.9
    anxiety 300.00
    compulsive 300.3

Reaction — *continued*
psychoneurotic (*see also* Neurosis) — *continued*
    conversion 300.11
    depersonalization 300.6
    depressive 300.4
    dissociative 300.15
    hypochondriacal 300.7
    hysterical 300.10
        conversion type 300.11
        dissociative type 300.15
    neurasthenic 300.5
    obsessive 300.3
    obsessive-compulsive 300.3
    phobic 300.20
    tension state 300.9
psychophysiologic NEC (*see also* Disorder, psychosomatic) 306.9
    cardiovascular 306.2
    digestive 306.4
    endocrine 306.6
    gastrointestinal 306.4
    genitourinary 306.50
    heart 306.2
    hemic 306.8
    intestinal (large) (small) 306.4
    laryngeal 306.1
    lymphatic 306.8
    musculoskeletal 306.0
    pharyngeal 306.1
    respiratory 306.1
    skin 306.3
    special sense organs 306.7
psychosomatic (*see also* Disorder, psychosomatic) 306.9
psychotic (*see also* Psychosis) 298.9
    depressive 298.0
    due to or associated with physical condition (*see also* Psychosis, organic) 293.9
    involutional (*see also* Psychosis, affective) 296.2 ☑
        recurrent episode 296.3 ☑
        single episode 296.2 ☑
pupillary (myotonic) (tonic) 379.46
radiation — *see* Effect, adverse, radiation
runaway (*see also* Disturbance, conduct)
    socialized 312.2 ☑
    undersocialized, unsocialized 312.1 ☑
scarlet fever toxin — *see* Complications, vaccination
schizophrenic (*see also* Schizophrenia) 295.9 ☑
    latent 295.5 ☑
serological for syphilis — *see* Serology for syphilis
serum (prophylactic) (therapeutic) 999.59
    anaphylactic 999.49
    due to
        administration of blood and blood products 999.51
            anaphylactic 999.41
        vaccination 999.52
            anaphylactic 999.41
    immediate 999.49
situational (*see also* Reaction, adjustment) 309.9
    acute, to stress 308.3
    adjustment (*see also* Reaction, adjustment) 309.9
somatization (*see also* Disorder, psychosomatic) 306.9
spinal puncture 349.0
spite, child (*see also* Disturbance, conduct) 312.0 ☑
stress, acute 308.9
    with predominant disturbance (of)
        consciousness 308.1
        emotions 308.0
        mixed 308.4
        psychomotor 308.2
        specified type NEC 308.3
    bone or cartilage — *see* Fracture, stress
surgical procedure — *see* Complications, surgical procedure

Reaction — *continued*
tetanus antitoxin — *see* Complications, vaccination
toxin-antitoxin — *see* Complications, vaccination
transfusion (blood) (bone marrow) (lymphocytes) (allergic) (*see also* Complications, transfusion) 999.80
tuberculin skin test, nonspecific (without active tuberculosis) 795.51
    positive (without active tuberculosis) 795.51
ultraviolet — *see* Effect, adverse, ultraviolet
undersocialized, unsocialized (*see also* Disturbance, conduct)
    aggressive (type) 312.0 ☑
    unaggressive (type) 312.1 ☑
vaccination (any) — *see* Complications, vaccination
white graft (skin) 996.52
withdrawing, child or adolescent 313.22
x-ray — *see* Effect, adverse, x-rays
Reactive depression — *see also* Reaction, depressive 300.4
    neurotic 300.4
    psychoneurotic 300.4
    psychotic 298.0
Rebound tenderness 789.6 ☑
Recalcitrant patient V15.81
Recanalization, thrombus — *see* Thrombosis
Recession, receding
    chamber angle (eye) 364.77
    chin 524.06
    gingival (postinfective) (postoperative) 523.20
        generalized 523.25
        localized 523.24
        minimal 523.21
        moderate 523.22
        severe 523.23
Recklinghausen-Applebaum disease (hemochromatosis) 275.03
Recklinghausen's disease (M9540/1) 237.71
    bones (osteitis fibrosa cystica) 252.01
Reclus' disease (cystic) 610.1
Recrudescent typhus (fever) 081.1
Recruitment, auditory 388.44
Rectalgia 569.42
Rectitis 569.49
Rectocele
    female (without uterine prolapse) 618.04
        with uterine prolapse 618.4
            complete 618.3
            incomplete 618.2
    in pregnancy or childbirth 654.4 ☑
        causing obstructed labor 660.2 ☑
            affecting fetus or newborn 763.1
    male 569.49
    vagina, vaginal (outlet) 618.04
Rectosigmoiditis 569.89
    ulcerative (chronic) 556.3
Rectosigmoid junction — *see* condition
Rectourethral — *see* condition
Rectovaginal — *see* condition
Rectovesical — *see* condition
Rectum, rectal — *see* condition
Recurrent — *see* condition
    pregnancy loss — *see* Pregnancy, management affected by, abortion, habitual
Red bugs 133.8
Red cedar asthma 495.8
Redness
    conjunctiva 379.93
    eye 379.93
    nose 478.19
Reduced ventilatory or vital capacity 794.2
Reduction
    function
        kidney (*see also* Disease, renal) 593.9
        liver 573.8
    ventilatory capacity 794.2
    vital capacity 794.2
Redundant, redundancy
    abdomen 701.9
    anus 751.5
    cardia 537.89

☑ **Additional Digit Required** — **Refer to the Tabular List for Digit Selection**

▽ **Subterms under main terms may continue to next column or page**

Redundant, redundancy — *continued*
clitoris 624.2
colon (congenital) 751.5
foreskin (congenital) 605
intestine 751.5
labia 624.3
organ or site, congenital NEC — *see* Accessory
panniculus (abdominal) 278.1
prepuce (congenital) 605
pylorus 537.89
rectum 751.5
scrotum 608.89
sigmoid 751.5
skin (of face) 701.9
eyelids 374.30
stomach 537.89
uvula 528.9
vagina 623.8
Reduplication — *see* Duplication
Referral
adoption (agency) V68.89
nursing care V63.8
patient without examination or treatment V68.81
social services V63.8
Reflex — *see also* condition
blink, deficient 374.45
hyperactive gag 478.29
neurogenic bladder NEC 596.54
atonic 596.54
with cauda equina syndrome 344.61
vasoconstriction 443.9
vasovagal 780.2
Reflux 530.81
acid 530.81
esophageal 530.81
with esophagitis 530.11
esophagitis 530.11
gastroesophageal 530.81
mitral — *see* Insufficiency, mitral
ureteral — *see* Reflux, vesicoureteral
vesicoureteral 593.70
with
reflux nephropathy 593.73
bilateral 593.72
unilateral 593.71
Reformed gallbladder 576.0
Reforming, artificial openings — *see also*
Attention to, artificial, opening V55.9
Refractive error — *see also* Error, refractive 367.9
Refsum's disease or syndrome (heredopathia atactica polyneuritiformis) 356.3
Refusal of
food 307.59
hysterical 300.11
treatment because of, due to
patient's decision NEC V64.2
reason of conscience or religion V62.6
Regaud
tumor (M8082/3) — *see* Neoplasm, nasopharynx, malignant
type carcinoma (M8082/3) — *see* Neoplasm, nasopharynx, malignant
Regional — *see* condition
Regulation feeding (elderly) (infant) 783.3
newborn 779.31
Regurgitated
food, choked on 933.1
stomach contents, choked on 933.1
Regurgitation 787.03
aortic (valve) (*see also* Insufficiency, aortic) 424.1
congenital 746.4
syphilitic 093.22
food (*see also* Vomiting)
with reswallowing — *see* Rumination
newborn 779.33
gastric contents — *see* Vomiting
heart — *see* Endocarditis
mitral (valve) (*see also* Insufficiency, mitral) 424.0
congenital 746.6
myocardial — *see* Endocarditis
pulmonary (heart) (valve) (*see also* Endocarditis, pulmonary) 424.3

Regurgitation — *continued*
stomach — *see* Vomiting
tricuspid — *see* Endocarditis, tricuspid
valve, valvular — *see* Endocarditis
vesicoureteral — *see* Reflux, vesicoureteral
Rehabilitation V57.9
multiple types V57.89
occupational V57.21
specified type NEC V57.89
speech (-language) V57.3
vocational V57.22
Reichmann's disease or syndrome (gastrosuccorrhea) 536.8
Reifenstein's syndrome (hereditary familial hypogonadism, male) 259.52
Reilly's syndrome or phenomenon — *see also* Neuropathy, peripheral, autonomic 337.9
Reimann's periodic disease 277.31
Reinsertion, contraceptive device V25.42
intrauterine V25.13
Reiter's disease, syndrome, or urethritis 099.3 *[711.1]* ☑
Rejection
food, hysterical 300.11
transplant 996.80
bone marrow 996.85
corneal 996.51
organ (immune or nonimmune cause) 996.80
bone marrow 996.85
heart 996.83
intestines 996.87
kidney 996.81
liver 996.82
lung 996.84
pancreas 996.86
specified NEC 996.89
skin 996.52
artificial 996.55
decellularized allodermis 996.55
stem cells(s) 996.88
from
peripheral blood 996.88
umbilical cord 996.88
Relapsing fever 087.9
Carter's (Asiatic) 087.0
Dutton's (West African) 087.1
Koch's 087.9
louse-borne (epidemic) 087.0
Novy's (American) 087.1
Obermeyer's (European) 087.0
Spirillum 087.9
tick-borne (endemic) 087.1
Relaxation
anus (sphincter) 569.49
due to hysteria 300.11
arch (foot) 734
congenital 754.61
back ligaments 728.4
bladder (sphincter) 596.59
cardio-esophageal 530.89
cervix (*see also* Incompetency, cervix) 622.5
diaphragm 519.4
inguinal rings — *see* Hernia, inguinal
joint (capsule) (ligament) (paralytic) (*see also* Derangement, joint) 718.90
congenital 755.8
lumbosacral joint 724.6
pelvic floor 618.89
pelvis 618.89
perineum 618.89
posture 729.90
rectum (sphincter) 569.49
sacroiliac (joint) 724.6
scrotum 608.89
urethra (sphincter) 599.84
uterus (outlet) 618.89
vagina (outlet) 618.89
vesical 596.59
Remains
canal of Cloquet 743.51
capsule (opaque) 743.51
Remittent fever (malarial) 084.6
Remnant
canal of Cloquet 743.51

Remnant — *continued*
capsule (opaque) 743.51
cervix, cervical stump (acquired) (postoperative) 622.8
cystic duct, postcholecystectomy 576.0
fingernail 703.8
congenital 757.5
meniscus, knee 717.5
thyroglossal duct 759.2
tonsil 474.8
infected 474.00
urachus 753.7
Remote effect of cancer — *see* condition
Removal (of)
catheter (urinary) (indwelling) V53.6
from artificial opening — *see* Attention to, artificial, opening
non-vascular V58.82
vascular V58.81
cerebral ventricle (communicating) shunt V53.01
device (*see also* Fitting (of))
contraceptive V25.12
with reinsertion V25.13
fixation
external V54.89
internal V54.01
traction V54.89
drains V58.49
dressing
wound V58.30
nonsurgical V58.30
surgical V58.31
ileostomy V55.2
Kirschner wire V54.89
nonvascular catheter V58.82
pin V54.01
plaster cast V54.89
plate (fracture) V54.01
rod V54.01
screw V54.01
splint, external V54.89
staples V58.32
subdermal implantable contraceptive V25.43
sutures V58.32
traction device, external V54.89
vascular catheter V58.81
wound packing V58.30
nonsurgical V58.30
surgical V58.31
Ren
arcuatus 753.3
mobile, mobilis (*see also* Disease, renal) 593.0
congenital 753.3
unguliformis 753.3
Renal — *see also* condition
glomerulohyalinosis-diabetic syndrome 250.4 ☑ *[581.81]*
due to secondary diabetes 249.4 ☑ *[581.81]*
Rendu-Osler-Weber disease or syndrome (familial hemorrhagic telangiectasia) 448.0
Reninoma (M8361/1) 236.91
Rénon-Delille syndrome 253.8
Repair
pelvic floor, previous, in pregnancy or childbirth 654.4 ☑
affecting fetus or newborn 763.89
scarred tissue V51.8
Replacement by artificial or mechanical device or prosthesis of — *see also* Fitting (of)
artificial skin V43.83
bladder V43.5
blood vessel V43.4
breast V43.82
eye globe V43.0
heart
with
assist device V43.21
fully implantable artificial heart V43.22
valve V43.3

Replacement by artificial or mechanical device or prosthesis of — *see also* Fitting (of) — *continued*
intestine V43.89
joint V43.60
ankle V43.66
elbow V43.62
finger V43.69
hip (partial) (total) V43.64
knee V43.65
shoulder V43.61
specified NEC V43.69
wrist V43.63
kidney V43.89
larynx V43.81
lens V43.1
limb(s) V43.7
liver V43.89
lung V43.89
organ NEC V43.89
pancreas V43.89
skin (artificial) V43.83
tissue NEC V43.89
Reprogramming
cardiac pacemaker V53.31
Request for expert evidence V68.2
Reserve, decreased or low
cardiac — *see* Disease, heart
kidney (*see also* Disease, renal) 593.9
Residual — *see also* condition
bladder 596.89
foreign body — *see* Retention, foreign body
state, schizophrenic (*see also* Schizophrenia) 295.6 ☑
urine 788.69
Resistance, resistant (to)
activated protein C 289.81

Note — use the following subclassification for categories V09.5, V09.7, V09.8, V09.9:

0   *without mention of resistance to multiple drugs*

1   *with resistance to multiple drugs*

V09.5 *quinolones and fluoroquinolones*

V09.7 *antimycobacterial agents*

V09.8 *specified drugs NEC*

V09.9 *unspecified drugs*

drugs by microorganisms V09.9 ☑
Amikacin V09.4
aminoglycosides V09.4
Amodiaquine V09.5 ☑
Amoxicillin V09.0
Ampicillin V09.0
antimycobacterial agents V09.7 ☑
Azithromycin V09.2
Azlocillin V09.0
Aztreonam V09.1
Bacampicillin V09.0
Bacitracin V09.8 ☑
Benznidazole V09.8 ☑
B-lactam antibiotics V09.1
Capreomycin V09.7 ☑
Carbenicillin V09.0
Cefaclor V09.1
Cefadroxil V09.1
Cefamandole V09.1
Cefatetan V09.1
Cefazolin V09.1
Cefixime V09.1
Cefonicid V09.1
Cefoperazone V09.1
Ceforanide V09.1
Cefotaxime V09.1
Cefoxitin V09.1
Ceftazidime V09.1
Ceftizoxime V09.1
Ceftriaxone V09.1
Cefuroxime V09.1
Cephalexin V09.1
Cephaloglycin V09.1
Cephaloridine V09.1

☑ **Additional Digit Required** — Refer to the Tabular List for Digit Selection

▽ **Subterms under main terms may continue to next column or page**

Resistance, resistant — *continued*
  drugs by microorganisms — *continued*
    Cephalosporins V09.1
    Cephalothin V09.1
    Cephapirin V09.1
    Cephradine V09.1
    Chloramphenicol V09.8 ☑
    Chloroquine V09.5 ☑
    Chlorguanide V09.8 ☑
    Chlorproguanil V09.8 ☑
    Chlortetracycline V09.3
    Cinoxacin V09.5 ☑
    Ciprofloxacin V09.5 ☑
    Clarithromycin V09.2
    Clindamycin V09.8 ☑
    Clioquinol V09.5 ☑
    Clofazimine V09.7 ☑
    Cloxacillin V09.0
    Cyclacillin V09.0
    Cycloserine V09.7 ☑
    Dapsone [DZ] V09.7 ☑
    Demeclocycline V09.3
    Dicloxacillin V09.0
    Doxycycline V09.3
    Enoxacin V09.5 ☑
    Erythromycin V09.2
    Ethambutol [EMB] V09.7 ☑
    Ethionamide [ETA] V09.7 ☑
    fluoroquinolones V09.5 ☑
    Gentamicin V09.4
    Halofantrine V09.8 ☑
    Imipenem V09.1
    Iodoquinol V09.5 ☑
    Isoniazid [INH] V09.7 ☑
    Kanamycin V09.4
    macrolides V09.2
    Mafenide V09.6
    MDRO (multiple drug resistant organisms) NOS V09.91
    Mefloquine V09.8 ☑
    Melasoprol V09.8 ☑
    Methacycline V09.3
    Methenamine V09.8 ☑
    Methicillin — *see* Infection, Methicillin V09.0
    Metronidazole V09.8 ☑
    Mezlocillin V09.0
    Minocycline V09.3
    multiple drug resistant organisms NOS V09.91
    Nafcillin V09.0
    Nalidixic acid V09.5 ☑
    Natamycin V09.2
    Neomycin V09.4
    Netilmicin V09.4
    Nimorazole V09.8 ☑
    Nitrofurantoin V09.8 ☑
    Nitrofurtimox V09.8 ☑
    Norfloxacin V09.5 ☑
    Nystatin V09.2
    Ofloxacin V09.5 ☑
    Oleandomycin V09.2
    Oxacillin V09.0
    Oxytetracycline V09.3
    Para-amino salicylic acid [PAS] V09.7 ☑
    Paromomycin V09.4
    Penicillin (G) (V) (VK) V09.0
    penicillins V09.0
    Pentamidine V09.8 ☑
    Piperacillin V09.0
    Primaquine V09.5 ☑
    Proguanil V09.8 ☑
    Pyrazinamide [PZA] V09.7 ☑
    Pyrimethamine/Sulfalene V09.8 ☑
    Pyrimethamine/Sulfodoxine V09.8 ☑
    Quinacrine V09.5 ☑
    Quinidine V09.8 ☑
    Quinine V09.8 ☑
    quinolones V09.5 ☑
    Rifabutin V09.7 ☑
    Rifampin [RIF] V09.7 ☑
    Rifamycin V09.7 ☑
    Rolitetracycline V09.3
    specified drugs NEC V09.8 ☑
    Spectinomycin V09.8 ☑

Resistance, resistant — *continued*
  drugs by microorganisms — *continued*
    Spiramycin V09.2
    Streptomycin [SM] V09.4
    Sulfacetamide V09.6
    Sulfacytine V09.6
    Sulfadiazine V09.6
    Sulfadoxine V09.6
    Sulfamethoxazole V09.6
    Sulfapyridine V09.6
    Sulfasalizine V09.6
    Sulfasoxazole V09.6
    sulfonamides V09.6
    Sulfoxone V09.7 ☑
    tetracycline V09.3
    tetracyclines V09.3
    Thiamphenicol V09.8 ☑
    Ticarcillin V09.0
    Tinidazole V09.8 ☑
    Tobramycin V09.4
    Triamphenicol V09.8 ☑
    Trimethoprim V09.8 ☑
    Vancomycin V09.8 ☑
  insulin 277.7
    complicating pregnancy 648.8 ☑
  thyroid hormone 246.8
Resorption
  biliary 576.8
    purulent or putrid (*see also* Cholecystitis) 576.8
  dental (roots) 521.40
    alveoli 525.8
    pathological
      external 521.42
      internal 521.41
      specified NEC 521.49
  septic — *see* Septicemia
  teeth (roots) 521.40
    pathological
      external 521.42
      internal 521.41
      specified NEC 521.49
Respiration
  asymmetrical 786.09
  bronchial 786.09
  Cheyne-Stokes (periodic respiration) 786.04
  decreased, due to shock following injury 958.4
  disorder of 786.00
    psychogenic 306.1
    specified NEC 786.09
  failure 518.81
    acute 518.81
      following trauma and surgery 518.51
    acute and chronic 518.84
      following trauma and surgery 518.53
    chronic 518.83
    following trauma and surgery 518.51
    newborn 770.84
  insufficiency 786.09
    acute 518.82
    newborn NEC 770.89
  Kussmaul (air hunger) 786.09
  painful 786.52
  periodic 786.09
    high altitude 327.22
  poor 786.09
    newborn NEC 770.89
  sighing 786.7
    psychogenic 306.1
  wheezing 786.07
Respiratory — *see also* condition
  distress 786.09
    acute 518.82
    fetus or newborn NEC 770.89
    syndrome (newborn) 769
      adult (following trauma and surgery) 518.52
      specified NEC 518.82
  failure 518.81
    acute 518.81
      following trauma and surgery 518.51
    acute and chronic 518.84
      following trauma and surgery 518.53
    chronic 518.83
    following trauma and surgery 518.51

Respiratory syncytial virus (RSV) 079.6
  bronchiolitis 466.11
  pneumonia 480.1
  vaccination, prophylactic (against) V04.82
Response
  photoallergic 692.72
  phototoxic 692.72
Restless legs syndrome (RLS) 333.94
Restlessness 799.29
Restoration of organ continuity from previous sterilization (tuboplasty) (vasoplasty) V26.0
Rest, rests
  mesonephric duct 752.89
    fallopian tube 752.11
  ovarian, in fallopian tubes 752.19
  wolffian duct 752.89
Restriction of housing space V60.1
Restzustand, schizophrenic — *see also*
  Schizophrenia 295.6 ☑
Retained — *see* Retention
Retardation
  development, developmental, specific (*see also* Disorder, development, specific) 315.9
    learning, specific 315.2
      arithmetical 315.1
      language (skills) 315.31
        expressive 315.31
        mixed receptive-expressive 315.32
      mathematics 315.1
      reading 315.00
        phonological 315.39
        written expression 315.2
      motor 315.4
  endochondral bone growth 733.91
  growth (physical) in childhood 783.43
    due to malnutrition 263.2
    fetal (intrauterine) 764.9 ☑
      affecting management of pregnancy 656.5 ☑
  intrauterine growth 764.9 ☑
    affecting management of pregnancy 656.5 ☑
  mental — *see* Disability, intellectual
  motor, specific 315.4
  physical 783.43
    child 783.43
      due to malnutrition 263.2
    fetus (intrauterine) 764.9 ☑
      affecting management of pregnancy 656.5 ☑
  psychomotor NEC 307.9
  reading 315.00
Retching — *see* Vomiting
Retention, retained
  bladder (*see also* Retention, urine) 788.20
    psychogenic 306.53
  carbon dioxide 276.2
  cholelithiasis, following cholecystectomy 997.41
  cyst — *see* Cyst
  dead
    fetus (after 22 completed weeks gestation) 656.4 ☑
      early fetal death (before 22 completed weeks gestation) 632
    ovum 631.8
  decidua (following delivery) (fragments) (with hemorrhage) 666.2 ☑
    without hemorrhage 667.1 ☑
  deciduous tooth 520.6
  dental root 525.3
  fecal (*see also* Constipation) 564.00
  fluid 276.69
  foreign body (*see also* Foreign body, retained)
    bone 733.99
    current trauma — *see* Foreign body, by site or type
    middle ear 385.83
    muscle 729.6
    soft tissue NEC 729.6
  gallstones, following cholecystectomy 997.41

Retention, retained — *continued*
  gastric 536.8
  membranes (following delivery) (with hemorrhage) 666.2 ☑
    with abortion — *see* Abortion, by type
    without hemorrhage 667.1 ☑
  menses 626.8
  milk (puerperal) 676.2 ☑
  nitrogen, extrarenal 788.99
  placenta (total) (with hemorrhage) 666.0 ☑
    with abortion — *see* Abortion, by type
    without hemorrhage 667.0 ☑
    portions or fragments 666.2 ☑
      without hemorrhage 667.1 ☑
  products of conception
    early pregnancy (fetal death before 22 completed weeks gestation) 632
    following
      abortion — *see* Abortion, by type
      delivery 666.2 ☑
        with hemorrhage 666.2 ☑
        without hemorrhage 667.1 ☑
    secundines (following delivery) (with hemorrhage) 666.2 ☑
      with abortion — *see* Abortion, by type
      without hemorrhage 667.1 ☑
    complicating puerperium (delayed hemorrhage) 666.2 ☑
  smegma, clitoris 624.8
  urine NEC 788.20
    bladder, incomplete emptying 788.21
    due to
      benign prostatic hypertrophy (BPH) — see category 600
    due to
      benign prostatic hypertrophy (BPH) — see category 600
    psychogenic 306.53
    specified NEC 788.29
  water (in tissue) (*see also* Edema) 782.3
Reticulation, dust (occupational) 504
Reticulocytosis NEC 790.99
Reticuloendotheliosis
  acute infantile (M9722/3) 202.5 ☑
  leukemic (M9940/3) 202.4 ☑
  malignant (M9720/3) 202.3 ☑
  nonlipid (M9722/3) 202.5 ☑
Reticulohistiocytoma (giant cell) 277.89
Reticulohistiocytosis, multicentric 272.8
Reticulolymphosarcoma (diffuse) (M9613/3) 200.8 ☑
  follicular (M9691/3) 202.0 ☑
  nodular (M9691/3) 202.0 ☑
Reticulosarcoma (M9640/3) 200.0 ☑
  nodular (M9642/3) 200.0 ☑
  pleomorphic cell type (M9641/3) 200.0 ☑
Reticulosis (skin)
  acute of infancy (M9722/3) 202.5 ☑
  familial hemophagocytic 288.4
  histiocytic medullary (M9721/3) 202.3 ☑
  lipomelanotic 695.89
  malignant (M9720/3) 202.3 ☑
  Sézary's (M9701/3) 202.2 ☑
Retina, retinal — *see* condition
Retinitis — *see also* Chorioretinitis 363.20
  albuminurica 585.9 [363.10]
  arteriosclerotic 440.8 [362.13]
  central angiospastic 362.41
  Coat's 362.12
  diabetic 250.5 ☑ [362.01]
    due to secondary diabetes 249.5 ☑ [362.01]
  disciformis 362.52
  disseminated 363.10
    metastatic 363.14
    neurosyphilitic 094.83
    pigment epitheliopathy 363.15
  exudative 362.12
  focal 363.00
    in histoplasmosis 115.92
      capsulatum 115.02
      duboisii 115.12
    juxtapapillary 363.05
    macular 363.06
    paramacular 363.06

Retinitis — *see also* Chorioretinitis —
continued
  focal — *continued*
    peripheral 363.08
    posterior pole NEC 363.07
  gravidarum 646.8 ☑
  hemorrhagica externa 362.12
  juxtapapillary (Jensen's) 363.05
  luetic — *see* Retinitis, syphilitic
  metastatic 363.14
  pigmentosa 362.74
  proliferans 362.29
  proliferating 362.29
  punctata albescens 362.76
  renal 585.9 *[363.13]*
  syphilitic (secondary) 091.51
    congenital 090.0 *[363.13]*
    early 091.51
    late 095.8 *[363.13]*
  syphilitica, central, recurrent 095.8 *[363.13]*
  tuberculous (*see also* Tuberculous)
    017.3 ☑ *[363.13]*
Retinoblastoma (M9510/3) 190.5
  differentiated type (M9511/3) 190.5
  undifferentiated type (M9512/3) 190.5
Retinochoroiditis — *see also* Chorioretinitis
  363.20
  central angiospastic 362.41
  disseminated 363.10
    metastatic 363.14
    neurosyphilitic 094.83
    pigment epitheliopathy 363.15
    syphilitic 094.83
  due to toxoplasmosis (acquired) (focal)
    130.2
  focal 363.00
    in histoplasmosis 115.92
      capsulatum 115.02
      duboisii 115.12
    juxtapapillary (Jensen's) 363.05
    macular 363.06
    paramacular 363.06
    peripheral 363.08
    posterior pole NEC 363.07
  juxtapapillaris 363.05
  syphilitic (disseminated) 094.83
Retinopathy (background) 362.10
  arteriosclerotic 440.8 *[362.13]*
  atherosclerotic 440.8 *[362.13]*
  central serous 362.41
  circinate 362.10
  Coat's 362.12
  diabetic 250.5 ☑ *[362.01]*
    due to secondary diabetes
      249.5 ☑ *[362.01]*
    nonproliferative 250.5 ☑ *[362.03]*
      due to secondary diabetes
        249.5 ☑ *[362.03]*
      mild 250.5 ☑ *[362.04]*
        due to secondary diabetes
          249.5 ☑ *[362.04]*
      moderate 250.5 ☑ *[362.05]*
        due to secondary diabetes
          249.5 ☑ *[362.05]*
      severe 250.5 ☑ *[362.06]*
        due to secondary diabetes
          249.5 ☑ *[362.06]*
    proliferative 250.5 ☑ *[362.02]*
      due to secondary diabetes
        249.5 ☑ *[362.02]*
  exudative 362.12
  hypertensive 362.11
  nonproliferative
    diabetic 250.5 ☑ *[362.03]*
      due to secondary diabetes
        249.5 ☑ *[362.03]*
      mild 250.5 ☑ *[362.04]*
        due to secondary diabetes
          249.5 ☑ *[362.04]*
      moderate 250.5 ☑ *[362.05]*
        due to secondary diabetes
          249.5 ☑ *[362.05]*
      severe 250.5 ☑ *[362.06]*
        due to secondary diabetes
          249.5 ☑ *[362.06]*
  of prematurity 362.20

Retinopathy — *continued*
  of prematurity — *continued*
    cicatricial 362.21
    stage
      0 362.22
      1 362.23
      2 362.24
      3 362.25
      4 362.26
      5 362.27
  pigmentary, congenital 362.74
  proliferative 362.29
    diabetic 250.5 ☑ *[362.02]*
      due to secondary diabetes
        249.5 ☑ *[362.02]*
  sickle-cell 282.60 *[362.29]*
  solar 363.31
Retinoschisis 361.10
  bullous 361.12
  congenital 743.56
  flat 361.11
  juvenile 362.73
Retractile testis 752.52
Retraction
  cervix — *see* Retraction, uterus
  drum (membrane) 384.82
  eyelid 374.41
  finger 736.29
  head 781.0
  lid 374.41
  lung 518.89
  mediastinum 519.3
  nipple 611.79
    congenital 757.6
    puerperal, postpartum 676.0 ☑
  palmar fascia 728.6
  pleura (*see also* Pleurisy) 511.0
  ring, uterus (Bandl's) (pathological) 661.4 ☑
    affecting fetus or newborn 763.7
  sternum (congenital) 756.3
    acquired 738.3
    during respiration 786.9
  substernal 738.3
  supraclavicular 738.8
  syndrome (Duane's) 378.71
  uterus 621.6
  valve (heart) — *see* Endocarditis
Retrobulbar — *see* condition
Retrocaval ureter 753.4
Retrocecal — *see also* condition
  appendix (congenital) 751.5
Retrocession — *see* Retroversion
Retrodisplacement — *see* Retroversion
Retroflection, retroflexion — *see* Retroversion
Retrognathia, retrognathism (mandibular)
  (maxillary) 524.10
Retrograde
  ejaculation 608.87
  menstruation 626.8
Retroiliac ureter 753.4
Retroperineal — *see* condition
Retroperitoneal — *see* condition
Retroperitonitis 567.39
Retropharyngeal — *see* condition
Retroplacental — *see* condition
Retroposition — *see* Retroversion
Retroprosthetic membrane 996.51
Retrosternal thyroid (congenital) 759.2
Retroversion, retroverted
  cervix — *see* Retroversion, uterus
  female NEC (*see also* Retroversion, uterus)
    621.6
  iris 364.70
  testis (congenital) 752.51
  uterus, uterine (acquired) (acute) (adherent)
    (any degree) (asymptomatic) (cervix)
    (postinfectional) (postpartal, old)
    621.6
    congenital 752.39
    in pregnancy or childbirth 654.3 ☑
      affecting fetus or newborn 763.89
      causing obstructed labor 660.2 ☑
        affecting fetus or newborn 763.1
Retrusion, premaxilla (developmental) 524.04
Rett's syndrome 330.8

Reverse, reversed
  peristalsis 787.4
Reye-Sheehan syndrome (postpartum pituitary necrosis) 253.2
Reye's syndrome 331.81
Rhabdomyolysis (idiopathic) 728.88
Rhabdomyoma (M8900/0) — *see also* Neoplasm, connective tissue, benign
  adult (M8904/0) — *see* Neoplasm, connective tissue, benign
  fetal (M8903/0) — *see* Neoplasm, connective tissue, benign
  glycogenic (M8904/0) — *see* Neoplasm, connective tissue, benign
Rhabdomyosarcoma (M8900/3) — *see also* Neoplasm, connective tissue, malignant
  alveolar (M8920/3) — *see* Neoplasm, connective tissue, malignant
  embryonal (M8910/3) — *see* Neoplasm, connective tissue, malignant
  mixed type (M8902/3) — *see* Neoplasm, connective tissue, malignant
  pleomorphic (M8901/3) — *see* Neoplasm, connective tissue, malignant
Rhabdosarcoma (M8900/3) — *see* Rhabdomyosarcoma
Rh antigen (C) (c) (D) (E) (e) (factor)
  hemolytic disease 773.0
  incompatibility, immunization, or sensitization
    affecting management of pregnancy
      656.1 ☑
    fetus or newborn 773.0
    transfusion reaction (*see also* Complications, transfusion) 999.70
  negative mother, affecting fetus or newborn
    773.0
  titer elevated (*see also* Complications, transfusion) 999.70
  transfusion reaction (*see also* Complications, transfusion) 999.70
Rhesus (factor) (Rh) incompatibility — *see* Rh, incompatibility
Rheumaticosis — *see* Rheumatism
Rheumatism, rheumatic (acute NEC) 729.0
  adherent pericardium 393
  arthritis
    acute or subacute — *see* Fever, rheumatic
    chronic 714.0
      spine 720.0
    articular (chronic) NEC (*see also* Arthritis)
      716.9 ☑
      acute or subacute — *see* Fever, rheumatic
  back 724.9
  blennorrhagic 098.59
  carditis — *see* Disease, heart, rheumatic
  cerebral — *see* Fever, rheumatic
  chorea (acute) — *see* Chorea, rheumatic
  chronic NEC 729.0
  coronary arteritis 391.9
    chronic 398.99
  degeneration, myocardium (*see also* Degeneration, myocardium, with rheumatic fever) 398.0
  desert 114.0
  febrile — *see* Fever, rheumatic
  fever — *see* Fever, rheumatic
  gonococcal 098.59
  gout 714.0
  heart
    disease (*see also* Disease, heart, rheumatic) 398.90
    failure (chronic) (congestive) (inactive) 398.91
  hemopericardium — *see* Rheumatic, pericarditis
  hydropericardium — *see* Rheumatic, pericarditis
  inflammatory (acute) (chronic) (subacute) — *see* Fever, rheumatic
  intercostal 729.0
    meaning Tietze's disease 733.6
  joint (chronic) NEC (*see also* Arthritis)
    716.9 ☑

Rheumatism, rheumatic — *continued*
  joint (*see also* Arthritis) — *continued*
    acute — *see* Fever, rheumatic
    mediastinopericarditis — *see* Rheumatic, pericarditis
  muscular 729.0
  myocardial degeneration (*see also* Degeneration, myocardium, with rheumatic fever) 398.0
  myocarditis (chronic) (inactive) (with chorea) 398.0
    active or acute 391.2
      with chorea (acute) (rheumatic) (Sydenham's) 392.0
  myositis 729.1
  neck 724.9
  neuralgic 729.0
  neuritis (acute) (chronic) 729.2
  neuromuscular 729.0
  nodose — *see* Arthritis, nodosa
  nonarticular 729.0
  palindromic 719.30
    ankle 719.37
    elbow 719.32
    foot 719.37
    hand 719.34
    hip 719.35
    knee 719.36
    multiple sites 719.39
    pelvic region 719.35
    shoulder (region) 719.31
    specified site NEC 719.38
    wrist 719.33
  pancarditis, acute 391.8
    with chorea (acute) (rheumatic) (Sydenham's) 392.0
    chronic or inactive 398.99
  pericarditis (active) (acute) (with effusion) (with pneumonia) 391.0
    with chorea (acute) (rheumatic) (Sydenham's) 392.0
    chronic or inactive 393
  pericardium — *see* Rheumatic, pericarditis
  pleuropericarditis — *see* Rheumatic, pericarditis
  pneumonia 390 *[517.1]*
  pneumonitis 390 *[517.1]*
  pneumopericarditis — *see* Rheumatic, pericarditis
  polyarthritis
    acute or subacute — *see* Fever, rheumatic
    chronic 714.0
  polyarticular NEC (*see also* Arthritis) 716.9 ☑
  psychogenic 306.0
  radiculitis 729.2
  sciatic 724.3
  septic — *see* Fever, rheumatic
  spine 724.9
  subacute NEC 729.0
  torticollis 723.5
  tuberculous NEC (*see also* Tuberculosis)
    015.9 ☑
  typhoid fever 002.0
Rheumatoid — *see also* condition
  lungs 714.81
Rhinitis (atrophic) (catarrhal) (chronic)
  (croupous) (fibrinous) (hyperplastic)
  (hypertrophic) (membranous) (purulent)
  (suppurative) (ulcerative) 472.0
  with
    hay fever (*see also* Fever, hay) 477.9
      with asthma (bronchial) 493.0 ☑
    sore throat — *see* Nasopharyngitis
  acute 460
  allergic (nonseasonal) (seasonal) (*see also* Fever, hay) 477.9
    with asthma (*see also* Asthma) 493.0 ☑
    due to food 477.1
  granulomatous 472.0
  infective 460
  obstructive 472.0
  pneumococcal 460
  syphilitic 095.8
    congenital 090.0
  tuberculous (*see also* Tuberculosis) 012.8 ☑

☑ **Additional Digit Required** — Refer to the Tabular List for Digit Selection   ▽ **Subterms under main terms may continue to next column or page**

2015 ICD-9-CM   ▶◀ **Revised Text**   ● **New Line**   ▲ **Revised Code**   **Volume 2 — 249**

Rhinitis — *continued*
vasomotor (*see also* Fever, hay) 477.9
Rhinoantritis (chronic) 473.0
acute 461.0
Rhinodacryolith 375.57
Rhinolalia (aperta) (clausa) (open) 784.43
Rhinolith 478.19
nasal sinus (*see also* Sinusitis) 473.9
Rhinomegaly 478.19
Rhinopharyngitis (acute) (subacute) — *see also* Nasopharyngitis 460
chronic 472.2
destructive ulcerating 102.5
mutilans 102.5
Rhinophyma 695.3
Rhinorrhea 478.19
cerebrospinal (fluid) 349.81
paroxysmal (*see also* Fever, hay) 477.9
spasmodic (*see also* Fever, hay) 477.9
Rhinosalpingitis 381.50
acute 381.51
chronic 381.52
Rhinoscleroma 040.1
Rhinosporidiosis 117.0
Rhinovirus infection 079.3
Rhizomelic chrondrodysplasia punctata 277.86
Rhizomelique, pseudopolyarthritic 446.5
Rhoads and Bomford anemia (refractory) 238.72
Rhus
diversiloba dermatitis 692.6
radicans dermatitis 692.6
toxicodendron dermatitis 692.6
venenata dermatitis 692.6
verniciflua dermatitis 692.6
Rhythm
atrioventricular nodal 427.89
disorder 427.9
coronary sinus 427.89
ectopic 427.89
nodal 427.89
escape 427.89
heart, abnormal 427.9
fetus or newborn — *see* Abnormal, heart rate
idioventricular 426.89
accelerated 427.89
nodal 427.89
sleep, inversion 327.39
nonorganic origin 307.45
Rhytidosis facialis 701.8
Rib — *see also* condition
cervical 756.2
Riboflavin deficiency 266.0
Rice bodies — *see also* Loose, body, joint 718.1 ☑
knee 717.6
Richter's hernia — *see* Hernia, Richter's
Ricinism 988.2
Rickets (active) (acute) (adolescent) (adult) (chest wall) (congenital) (current) (infantile) (intestinal) 268.0
celiac 579.0
fetal 756.4
hemorrhagic 267
hypophosphatemic with nephrotic-glycosuric dwarfism 270.0
kidney 588.0
late effect 268.1
renal 588.0
scurvy 267
vitamin D-resistant 275.3
Rickettsial disease 083.9
specified type NEC 083.8
Rickettsialpox 083.2
Rickettsiosis NEC 083.9
specified type NEC 083.8
tick-borne 082.9
specified type NEC 082.8
vesicular 083.2
Ricord's chancre 091.0
Riddoch's syndrome (visual disorientation) 368.16
Rider's
bone 733.99

Rider's — *continued*
chancre 091.0
Ridge, alveolus — *see also* condition
edentulous
atrophy 525.20
mandible 525.20
minimal 525.21
moderate 525.22
severe 525.23
maxilla 525.20
minimal 525.24
moderate 525.25
severe 525.26
flabby 525.20
Ridged ear 744.29
Riedel's
disease (ligneous thyroiditis) 245.3
lobe, liver 751.69
struma (ligneous thyroiditis) 245.3
thyroiditis (ligneous) 245.3
Rieger's anomaly or syndrome (mesodermal dysgenesis, anterior ocular segment) 743.44
Riehl's melanosis 709.09
Rietti-Greppi-Micheli anemia or syndrome 282.46
Rieux's hernia — *see* Hernia, Rieux's
Rift Valley fever 066.3
Riga's disease (cachectic aphthae) 529.0
Riga-Fede disease (cachectic aphthae) 529.0
Riggs' disease (compound periodontitis) 523.40
Right middle lobe syndrome 518.0
Rigid, rigidity — *see also* condition
abdominal 789.4 ☑
articular, multiple congenital 754.89
back 724.8
cervix uteri
in pregnancy or childbirth 654.6 ☑
affecting fetus or newborn 763.89
causing obstructed labor 660.2 ☑
affecting fetus or newborn 763.1
hymen (acquired) (congenital) 623.3
nuchal 781.6
pelvic floor
in pregnancy or childbirth 654.4 ☑
affecting fetus or newborn 763.89
causing obstructed labor 660.2 ☑
affecting fetus or newborn 763.1
perineum or vulva
in pregnancy or childbirth 654.8 ☑
affecting fetus or newborn 763.89
causing obstructed labor 660.2 ☑
affecting fetus or newborn 763.1
spine 724.8
vagina
in pregnancy or childbirth 654.7 ☑
affecting fetus or newborn 763.89
causing obstructed labor 660.2 ☑
affecting fetus or newborn 763.1
Rigors 780.99
Riley-Day syndrome (familial dysautonomia) 742.8
RIND (reversible ischemic neurological deficit) 434.91
history of (personal) V12.54
Ring(s)
aorta 747.21
Bandl's, complicating delivery 661.4 ☑
affecting fetus or newborn 763.7
contraction, complicating delivery 661.4 ☑
affecting fetus or newborn 763.7
esophageal (congenital) 750.3
Fleischer (-Kayser) (cornea) 275.1 [371.14]
hymenal, tight (acquired) (congenital) 623.3
Kayser-Fleischer (cornea) 275.1 [371.14]
retraction, uterus, pathological 661.4 ☑
affecting fetus or newborn 763.7
Schatzki's (esophagus) (congenital) (lower) 750.3
acquired 530.3
Soemmering's 366.51
trachea, abnormal 748.3
vascular (congenital) 747.21
Vossius' 921.3
late effect 366.21

Ringed hair (congenital) 757.4
Ringing in the ear — *see also* Tinnitus 388.30
Ringworm 110.9
beard 110.0
body 110.5
Burmese 110.9
corporeal 110.5
foot 110.4
groin 110.3
hand 110.2
honeycomb 110.0
nails 110.1
perianal (area) 110.3
scalp 110.0
specified site NEC 110.8
Tokelau 110.5
Rise, venous pressure 459.89
Risk
factor — *see* Problem
falling V15.88
suicidal 300.9
Ritter's disease (dermatitis exfoliativa neonatorum) 695.81
Rivalry, sibling 313.3
Rivalta's disease (cervicofacial actinomycosis) 039.3
River blindness 125.3 [360.13]
Robert's pelvis 755.69
with disproportion (fetopelvic) 653.0 ☑
affecting fetus or newborn 763.1
causing obstructed labor 660.1 ☑
affecting fetus or newborn 763.1
Robinson's (hidrotic) **ectodermal dysplasia** 757.31
Robin's syndrome 756.0
Robles' disease (onchocerciasis) 125.3 [360.13]
Rochalimea — *see* Rickettsial disease
Rocky Mountain fever (spotted) 082.0
Rodent ulcer (M8090/3) — *see also* Neoplasm, skin, malignant
cornea 370.07
Roentgen ray, adverse effect — *see* Effect, adverse, x-ray
Roetheln 056.9
Roger's disease (congenital interventricular septal defect) 745.4
Rokitansky's
disease (*see also* Necrosis, liver) 570
tumor 620.2
Rokitansky-Aschoff sinuses (mucosal outpouching of gallbladder) — *see also* Disease, gallbladder 575.8
Rokitansky-Kuster-Hauser syndrome (congenital absence vagina) 752.45
Rollet's chancre (syphilitic) 091.0
Rolling of head 781.0
Romano-Ward syndrome (prolonged QT interval syndrome) 426.82
Romanus lesion 720.1
Romberg's disease or syndrome 349.89
Roof, mouth — *see* condition
Rosacea 695.3
acne 695.3
keratitis 695.3 [370.49]
Rosary, rachitic 268.0
Rose
cold 477.0
fever 477.0
rash 782.1
epidemic 056.9
of infants 057.8
Rosenbach's erysipelatoid or erysipeloid 027.1
Rosen-Castleman-Liebow syndrome (pulmonary proteinosis) 516.0
Rosenthal's disease (factor XI deficiency) 286.2
Roseola 057.8
infantum, infantilis (*see also* Exanthem subitum) 058.10
Rossbach's disease (hyperchlorhydria) 536.8
psychogenic 306.4
Rössle-Urbach-Wiethe lipoproteinosis 272.8
Ross river fever 066.3
Rostan's asthma (cardiac) — *see also* Failure, ventricular, left 428.1

Rot
Barcoo (*see also* Ulcer, skin) 707.9
knife-grinders' (*see also* Tuberculosis) 011.4 ☑
Rotation
anomalous, incomplete or insufficient — *see* Malrotation
cecum (congenital) 751.4
colon (congenital) 751.4
manual, affecting fetus or newborn 763.89
spine, incomplete or insufficient 737.8
tooth, teeth 524.35
vertebra, incomplete or insufficient 737.8
Rot-Bernhardt disease 355.1
Röteln 056.9
Roth-Bernhardt disease or syndrome 355.1
Roth's disease or meralgia 355.1
Rothmund (-Thomson) syndrome 757.33
Rotor's disease or syndrome (idiopathic hyperbilirubinemia) 277.4
Rotundum ulcus — *see* Ulcer, stomach
Round
back (with wedging of vertebrae) 737.10
late effect of rickets 268.1
hole, retina 361.31
with detachment 361.01
ulcer (stomach) — *see* Ulcer, stomach
worms (infestation) (large) NEC 127.0
Roussy-Lévy syndrome 334.3
Routine postpartum follow-up V24.2
Roy (-Jutras) syndrome (acropachyderma) 757.39
Rubella (German measles) 056.9
complicating pregnancy, childbirth, or puerperium 647.5 ☑
complication 056.8
neurological 056.00
encephalomyelitis 056.01
specified type NEC 056.09
specified type NEC 056.79
congenital 771.0
contact V01.4
exposure to V01.4
maternal
with suspected fetal damage affecting management of pregnancy 655.3 ☑
affecting fetus or newborn 760.2
manifest rubella in infant 771.0
specified complications NEC 056.79
vaccination, prophylactic (against) V04.3
Rubeola (measles) — *see also* Measles 055.9
complicated 055.8
meaning rubella (*see also* Rubella) 056.9
scarlatinosis 057.8
Rubeosis iridis 364.42
diabetica 250.5 ☑ [364.42]
due to secondary diabetes 249.5 ☑ [364.42]
Rubinstein-Taybi's syndrome (brachydactylia, short stature and intellectual disabilities) 759.89
Rudimentary (congenital) — *see also* Agenesis
arm 755.22
bone 756.9
cervix uteri 752.43
eye (*see also* Microphthalmos) 743.10
fallopian tube 752.19
leg 755.32
lobule of ear 744.21
patella 755.64
respiratory organs in thoracopagus 759.4
tracheal bronchus 748.3
uterine horn 752.39
uterus 752.39
in male 752.7
solid or with cavity 752.39
vagina 752.45
Rud's syndrome (mental deficiency, epilepsy, and infantilism) 759.89
Ruiter-Pompen (-Wyers) syndrome (angiokeratoma corporis diffusum) 272.7
Ruled out condition — *see also* Observation, suspected V71.9
Rumination — *see also* Vomiting
disorder 307.53

☑ **Additional Digit Required** — Refer to the Tabular List for Digit Selection   ▼ Subterms under main terms may continue to next column or page

250 — Volume 2   ▶◀ Revised Text   ● New Line   ▲ Revised Code   2015 ICD-9-CM

Rumination — *see also* Vomiting — *continued*
   neurotic 300.3
   obsessional 300.3
   psychogenic 307.53
Runaway reaction — *see also* Disturbance, conduct
   socialized 312.2 ☑
   undersocialized, unsocialized 312.1 ☑
Runeberg's disease (progressive pernicious anemia) 281.0
Runge's syndrome (postmaturity) 766.22
Runny nose 784.99
Rupia 091.3
   congenital 090.0
   tertiary 095.9
Rupture, ruptured 553.9
   abdominal viscera NEC 799.89
      obstetrical trauma 665.5 ☑
   abscess (spontaneous) — *see* Abscess, by site
   amnion — *see* Rupture, membranes
   aneurysm — *see* Aneurysm
   anus (sphincter) — *see* Laceration, anus
   aorta, aortic 441.5
      abdominal 441.3
      arch 441.1
      ascending 441.1
      descending 441.5
         abdominal 441.3
         thoracic 441.1
      syphilitic 093.0
      thoracoabdominal 441.6
      thorax, thoracic 441.1
      transverse 441.1
      traumatic (thoracic) 901.0
         abdominal 902.0
      valve or cusp (*see also* Endocarditis, aortic) 424.1
   appendix (with peritonitis) 540.0
      with peritoneal abscess 540.1
      traumatic — *see* Injury, internal, gastrointestinal tract
   arteriovenous fistula, brain (congenital) 430
   artery 447.2
      brain (*see also* Hemorrhage, brain) 431
      coronary (*see also* Infarct, myocardium) 410.9 ☑
      heart (*see also* Infarct, myocardium) 410.9 ☑
      pulmonary 417.8
      traumatic (complication) (*see also* Injury, blood vessel, by site) 904.9
   bile duct, except cystic (*see also* Disease, biliary) 576.3
      cystic 575.4
      traumatic — *see* Injury, internal, intra-abdominal
   bladder (sphincter) 596.6
      with
         abortion — *see* Abortion, by type, with damage to pelvic organs
         ectopic pregnancy (*see also* categories 633.0–633.9) 639.2
         molar pregnancy (*see also* categories 630–632) 639.2
      following
         abortion 639.2
         ectopic or molar pregnancy 639.2
      nontraumatic 596.6
      obstetrical trauma 665.5 ☑
      spontaneous 596.6
      traumatic — *see* Injury, internal, bladder
   blood vessel (*see also* Hemorrhage) 459.0
      brain (*see also* Hemorrhage, brain) 431
      heart (*see also* Infarct, myocardium) 410.9 ☑
      traumatic (complication) (*see also* Injury, blood vessel, by site) 904.9
   bone — *see* Fracture, by site
   bowel 569.89
      traumatic — *see* Injury, internal, intestine
   Bowman's membrane 371.31

Rupture, ruptured — *continued*
   brain
      aneurysm (congenital) (*see also* Hemorrhage, subarachnoid) 430
         late effect — *see* Late effect(s) (of) cerebrovascular disease
         syphilitic 094.87
      hemorrhagic (*see also* Hemorrhage, brain) 431
      injury at birth 767.0
      syphilitic 094.89
   capillaries 448.9
   cardiac (*see also* Infarct, myocardium) 410.9 ☑
   cartilage (articular) (current) (*see also* Sprain, by site)
      knee — *see* Tear, meniscus
      semilunar — *see* Tear, meniscus
   cecum (with peritonitis) 540.0
      with peritoneal abscess 540.1
      traumatic 863.89
         with open wound into cavity 863.99
   cerebral aneurysm (congenital) (*see also* Hemorrhage, subarachnoid) 430
      late effect — *see* Late effect(s) (of) cerebrovascular disease
   cervix (uteri)
      with
         abortion — *see* Abortion, by type, with damage to pelvic organs
         ectopic pregnancy (*see also* categories 633.0–633.9) 639.2
         molar pregnancy (*see also* categories 630–632) 639.2
      following
         abortion 639.2
         ectopic or molar pregnancy 639.2
      obstetrical trauma 665.3 ☑
      traumatic — *see* Injury, internal, cervix
   chordae tendineae 429.5
   choroid (direct) (indirect) (traumatic) 363.63
   circle of Willis (*see also* Hemorrhage, subarachnoid) 430
      late effect — *see* Late effect(s) (of) cerebrovascular disease
   colon 569.89
      traumatic — *see* Injury, internal, colon
   cornea (traumatic) (*see also* Rupture, eye)
      due to ulcer 370.00
   coronary (artery) (thrombotic) (*see also* Infarct, myocardium) 410.9 ☑
   corpus luteum (infected) (ovary) 620.1
   cyst — *see* Cyst
   cystic duct (*see also* Disease, gallbladder) 575.4
   Descemet's membrane 371.33
      traumatic — *see* Rupture, eye
   diaphragm (*see also* Hernia, diaphragm)
      traumatic — *see* Injury, internal, diaphragm
   diverticulum
      bladder 596.3
      intestine (large) (*see also* Diverticula) 562.10
         small 562.00
   duodenal stump 537.89
   duodenum (ulcer) — *see* Ulcer, duodenum, with perforation
   ear drum (*see also* Perforation, tympanum) 384.20
      with otitis media — *see* Otitis media
      traumatic — *see* Wound, open, ear
   esophagus 530.4
      traumatic 862.22
         with open wound into cavity 862.32
         cervical region — *see* Wound, open, esophagus
   eye (without prolapse of intraocular tissue) 871.0
      with
         exposure of intraocular tissue 871.1
         partial loss of intraocular tissue 871.2
         prolapse of intraocular tissue 871.1
      due to burn 940.5
   fallopian tube 620.8

Rupture, ruptured — *continued*
   fallopian tube — *continued*
      due to pregnancy — *see* Pregnancy, tubal
      traumatic — *see* Injury, internal, fallopian tube
   fontanel 767.3
   free wall (ventricle) (*see also* Infarct, myocardium) 410.9 ☑
   gallbladder or duct (*see also* Disease, gallbladder) 575.4
      traumatic — *see* Injury, internal, gallbladder
   gastric (*see also* Rupture, stomach) 537.89
      vessel 459.0
   globe (eye) (traumatic) — *see* Rupture, eye
   graafian follicle (hematoma) 620.0
   heart (auricle) (ventricle) (*see also* Infarct, myocardium) 410.9 ☑
      infectional 422.90
      traumatic — *see* Rupture, myocardium, traumatic
   hymen 623.8
   internal
      organ, traumatic (*see also* Injury, internal, by site)
         heart — *see* Rupture, myocardium, traumatic
         kidney — *see* Rupture, kidney
         liver — *see* Rupture, liver
         spleen — *see* Rupture, spleen, traumatic
      semilunar cartilage — *see* Tear, meniscus
   intervertebral disc — *see* Displacement, intervertebral disc
      traumatic (current) — *see* Dislocation, vertebra
   intestine 569.89
      traumatic — *see* Injury, internal, intestine
   intracranial, birth injury 767.0
   iris 364.76
      traumatic — *see* Rupture, eye
   joint capsule — *see* Sprain, by site
   kidney (traumatic) 866.03
      with open wound into cavity 866.13
      due to birth injury 767.8
      nontraumatic 593.89
   lacrimal apparatus (traumatic) 870.2
   lens (traumatic) 366.20
   ligament (*see also* Sprain, by site)
      with open wound — *see* Wound, open, by site
      old (*see also* Disorder, cartilage, articular) 718.0 ☑
   liver (traumatic) 864.04
      with open wound into cavity 864.14
      due to birth injury 767.8
      nontraumatic 573.8
   lymphatic (node) (vessel) 457.8
   marginal sinus (placental) (with hemorrhage) 641.2 ☑
      affecting fetus or newborn 762.1
   meaning hernia — *see* Hernia
   membrana tympani (*see also* Perforation, tympanum) 384.20
      with otitis media — *see* Otitis media
      traumatic — *see* Wound, open, ear
   membranes (spontaneous)
      artificial
         delayed delivery following 658.3 ☑
            affecting fetus or newborn 761.1
         fetus or newborn 761.1
      delayed delivery following 658.2 ☑
         affecting fetus or newborn 761.1
      premature (less than 24 hours prior to onset of labor) 658.1 ☑
         affecting fetus or newborn 761.1
      delayed delivery following 658.2 ☑
         affecting fetus or newborn 761.1
   meningeal artery (*see also* Hemorrhage, subarachnoid) 430
      late effect — *see* Late effect(s) (of) cerebrovascular disease
   meniscus (knee) (*see also* Tear, meniscus)

Rupture, ruptured — *continued*
   meniscus (*see also* Tear, meniscus) — *continued*
      old (*see also* Derangement, meniscus) 717.5
      site other than knee — *see* Disorder, cartilage, articular
      site other than knee — *see* Sprain, by site
   mesentery 568.89
      traumatic — *see* Injury, internal, mesentery
   mitral — *see* Insufficiency, mitral
   muscle (traumatic) NEC (*see also* Sprain, by site)
      with open wound — *see* Wound, open, by site
      nontraumatic 728.83
   musculotendinous cuff (nontraumatic) (shoulder) 840.4
   mycotic aneurysm, causing cerebral hemorrhage (*see also* Hemorrhage, subarachnoid) 430
      late effect — *see* Late effect(s) (of) cerebrovascular disease
   myocardium, myocardial (*see also* Infarct, myocardium) 410.9 ☑
      traumatic 861.03
         with open wound into thorax 861.13
   nontraumatic (meaning hernia) (*see also* Hernia, by site) 553.9
   obstructed (*see also* Hernia, by site, with obstruction) 552.9
      gangrenous (*see also* Hernia, by site, with gangrene) 551.9
   operation wound (*see also* Dehiscence) 998.32
      internal 998.31
   ovary, ovarian 620.8
      corpus luteum 620.1
      follicle (graafian) 620.0
   oviduct 620.8
      due to pregnancy — *see* Pregnancy, tubal
   pancreas 577.8
      traumatic — *see* Injury, internal, pancreas
   papillary muscle (ventricular) 429.6
   pelvic
      floor, complicating delivery 664.1 ☑
      organ NEC — *see* Injury, pelvic, organs
   penis (traumatic) — *see* Wound, open, penis
   perineum 624.8
      during delivery (*see also* Laceration, perineum, complicating delivery) 664.4 ☑
   pharynx (nontraumatic) (spontaneous) 478.29
   pregnant uterus (before onset of labor) 665.0 ☑
   prostate (traumatic) — *see* Injury, internal, prostate
   pulmonary
      artery 417.8
      valve (heart) (*see also* Endocarditis, pulmonary) 424.3
      vein 417.8
      vessel 417.8
   pupil, sphincter 364.75
   pus tube (*see also* Salpingo-oophoritis) 614.2
   pyosalpinx (*see also* Salpingo-oophoritis) 614.2
   rectum 569.49
      traumatic — *see* Injury, internal, rectum
   retina, retinal (traumatic) (without detachment) 361.30
      with detachment (*see also* Detachment, retina, with retinal defect) 361.00
   rotator cuff (capsule) (traumatic) 840.4
      nontraumatic (complete) 727.61
         partial 726.13
   sclera 871.0
   semilunar cartilage, knee (*see also* Tear, meniscus) 836.2

☑ **Additional Digit Required** — Refer to the Tabular List for Digit Selection
▽ **Subterms under main terms may continue to next column or page**

2015 ICD-9-CM   ▶◀ Revised Text   ● New Line   ▲ Revised Code   Volume 2 — 251

Rupture, ruptured — *continued*
  semilunar cartilage, knee (*see also* Tear, meniscus) — *continued*
    old (*see also* Derangement, meniscus) 717.5
  septum (cardiac) 410.8 ☑
  sigmoid 569.89
    traumatic — *see* Injury, internal, colon, sigmoid
  sinus of Valsalva 747.29
  spinal cord (*see also* Injury, spinal, by site)
    due to injury at birth 767.4
    fetus or newborn 767.4
    syphilitic 094.89
    traumatic (*see also* Injury, spinal, by site)
      with fracture — *see* Fracture, vertebra, by site, with spinal cord injury
  spleen 289.59
    congenital 767.8
    due to injury at birth 767.8
    malarial 084.9
    nontraumatic 289.59
    spontaneous 289.59
    traumatic 865.04
      with open wound into cavity 865.14
  splenic vein 459.0
  stomach 537.89
    due to injury at birth 767.8
    traumatic — *see* Injury, internal, stomach
    ulcer — *see* Ulcer, stomach, with perforation
  synovium 727.50
    specified site NEC 727.59
  tendon (traumatic) (*see also* Sprain, by site)
    with open wound — *see* Wound, open, by site
    Achilles 845.09
      nontraumatic 727.67
    ankle 845.09
      nontraumatic 727.68
    biceps (long bead) 840.8
      nontraumatic 727.62
    foot 845.10
      interphalangeal (joint) 845.13

Rupture, ruptured — *continued*
  tendon (*see also* Sprain, by site) — *continued*
    foot — *continued*
      metatarsophalangeal (joint) 845.12
      nontraumatic 727.68
      specified site NEC 845.19
      tarsometatarsal (joint) 845.11
    hand 842.10
      carpometacarpal (joint) 842.11
      interphalangeal (joint) 842.13
      metacarpophalangeal (joint) 842.12
      nontraumatic 727.63
        extensors 727.63
        flexors 727.64
      specified site NEC 842.19
    nontraumatic 727.60
      specified site NEC 727.69
    patellar 844.8
      nontraumatic 727.66
    quadriceps 844.8
      nontraumatic 727.65
    rotator cuff (capsule) 840.4
      nontraumatic (complete) 727.61
        partial 726.13
    wrist 842.00
      carpal (joint) 842.01
      nontraumatic 727.63
        extensors 727.63
        flexors 727.64
      radiocarpal (joint) (ligament) 842.02
      radioulnar (joint), distal 842.09
      specified site NEC 842.09
  testis (traumatic) 878.2
    complicated 878.3
    due to syphilis 095.8
  thoracic duct 457.8
  tonsil 474.8
  traumatic
    with open wound — *see* Wound, open, by site
    aorta — *see* Rupture, aorta, traumatic
    ear drum — *see* Wound, open, ear, drum
    external site — *see* Wound, open, by site
    eye 871.2
    globe (eye) — *see* Wound, open, eyeball

Rupture, ruptured — *continued*
  traumatic — *continued*
    internal organ (abdomen, chest, or pelvis) (*see also* Injury, internal, by site)
      heart — *see* Rupture, myocardium, traumatic
      kidney — *see* Rupture, kidney
      liver — *see* Rupture, liver
      spleen — *see* Rupture, spleen, traumatic
    ligament, muscle, or tendon (*see also* Sprain, by site)
      with open wound — *see* Wound, open, by site
    meaning hernia — *see* Hernia
  tricuspid (heart) (valve) — *see* Endocarditis, tricuspid
  tube, tubal 620.8
    abscess (*see also* Salpingo-oophoritis) 614.2
    due to pregnancy — *see* Pregnancy, tubal
  tympanum, tympanic (membrane) (*see also* Perforation, tympanum) 384.20
    with otitis media — *see* Otitis media
    traumatic — *see* Wound, open, ear, drum
  umbilical cord 663.8 ☑
    fetus or newborn 772.0
  ureter (traumatic) (*see also* Injury, internal, ureter) 867.2
    nontraumatic 593.89
  urethra 599.84
    with
      abortion — *see* Abortion, by type, with damage to pelvic organs
      ectopic pregnancy (*see also* categories 633.0–633.9) 639.2
      molar pregnancy (*see also* categories 630–632) 639.2
    following
      abortion 639.2
      ectopic or molar pregnancy 639.2
    obstetrical trauma 665.5 ☑
    traumatic — *see* Injury, internal urethra

Rupture, ruptured — *continued*
  uterosacral ligament 620.8
  uterus (traumatic) (*see also* Injury, internal uterus)
    affecting fetus or newborn 763.89
    during labor 665.1 ☑
    nonpuerperal, nontraumatic 621.8
    nontraumatic 621.8
    pregnant (during labor) 665.1 ☑
      before labor 665.0 ☑
  vagina 878.6
    complicated 878.7
    complicating delivery — *see* Laceration, vagina, complicating delivery
  valve, valvular (heart) — *see* Endocarditis
  varicose vein — *see* Varicose, vein
  varix — *see* Varix
  vena cava 459.0
  ventricle (free wall) (left) (*see also* Infarct, myocardium) 410.9 ☑
  vesical (urinary) 596.6
    traumatic — *see* Injury, internal, bladder
  vessel (blood) 459.0
    pulmonary 417.8
  viscus 799.89
  vulva 878.4
    complicated 878.5
    complicating delivery 664.0 ☑
Russell's dwarf (uterine dwarfism and craniofacial dysostosis) 759.89
Russell's dysentery 004.8
Russell (-Silver) syndrome (congenital hemihypertrophy and short stature) 759.89
Russian spring-summer type encephalitis 063.0
Rust's disease (tuberculous spondylitis) 015.0 ☑ *[720.81]*
Rustitskii's disease (multiple myeloma) (M9730/3) 203.0 ☑
Ruysch's disease (Hirschsprung's disease) 751.3
Rytand-Lipsitch syndrome (complete atrioventricular block) 426.0

☑ **Additional Digit Required** — *see* **Refer to the Tabular List for Digit Selection**
⬗ **Subterms under main terms may continue to next column or page**

Scapulalgia

S

Saber
shin 090.5
tibia 090.5
Saccharomyces infection — *see also* Candidiasis 112.9
Saccharopinuria 270.7
Saccular — *see* condition
Sacculation
aorta (nonsyphilitic) (*see also* Aneurysm, aorta) 441.9
ruptured 441.5
syphilitic 093.0
bladder 596.3
colon 569.89
intralaryngeal (congenital) (ventricular) 748.3
larynx (congenital) (ventricular) 748.3
organ or site, congenital — *see* Distortion
pregnant uterus, complicating delivery 654.4 ☑
affecting fetus or newborn 763.1
causing obstructed labor 660.2 ☑
affecting fetus or newborn 763.1
rectosigmoid 569.89
sigmoid 569.89
ureter 593.89
urethra 599.2
vesical 596.3
Sachs (-Tay) disease (amaurotic familial idiocy) 330.1
Sacks-Libman disease 710.0 [424.91]
Sac, lacrimal — *see* condition
Sacralgia 724.6
Sacralization
fifth lumbar vertebra 756.15
incomplete (vertebra) 756.15
Sacrodynia 724.6
Sacroiliac joint — *see* condition
Sacroiliitis NEC 720.2
Sacrum — *see* condition
Saddle
back 737.8
embolus
abdominal aorta 444.01
pulmonary artery 415.13
injury — code to condition
nose 738.0
congenital 754.0
due to syphilis 090.5
Sadism (sexual) 302.84
Saemisch's ulcer 370.04
Saenger's syndrome 379.46
Sago spleen 277.39
Sailors' skin 692.74
Saint
Anthony's fire (*see also* Erysipelas) 035
Guy's dance — *see* Chorea
Louis-type encephalitis 062.3
triad (*see also* Hernia, diaphragm) 553.3
Vitus' dance — *see* Chorea
Salicylism
correct substance properly administered 535.4 ☑
overdose or wrong substance given or taken 965.1
Salivary duct or gland — *see also* condition
virus disease 078.5
Salivation (excessive) — *see also* Ptyalism 527.7
Salmonella (aertrycke) (choleraesuis) (enteritidis) (gallinarum) (suipestifer) (typhimurium) — *see also* Infection, Salmonella 003.9
arthritis 003.23
carrier (suspected) of V02.3
meningitis 003.21
osteomyelitis 003.24
pneumonia 003.22
septicemia 003.1
typhosa 002.0
carrier (suspected) of V02.1
Salmonellosis 003.0
with pneumonia 003.22

Salpingitis (catarrhal) (fallopian tube) (nodular) (pseudofollicular) (purulent) (septic) — *see also* Salpingo-oophoritis 614.2
ear 381.50
acute 381.51
chronic 381.52
Eustachian (tube) 381.50
acute 381.51
chronic 381.52
follicularis 614.1
gonococcal (chronic) 098.37
acute 098.17
interstitial, chronic 614.1
isthmica nodosa 614.1
old — *see* Salpingo-oophoritis, chronic
puerperal, postpartum, childbirth 670.8 ☑
specific (chronic) 098.37
acute 098.17
tuberculous (acute) (chronic) (*see also* Tuberculosis) 016.6 ☑
venereal (chronic) 098.37
acute 098.17
Salpingocele 620.4
Salpingo-oophoritis (catarrhal) (purulent) (ruptured) (septic) (suppurative) 614.2
acute 614.0
with
abortion — *see* Abortion, by type, with sepsis
ectopic pregnancy (*see also* categories 633.0–633.9) 639.0
molar pregnancy (*see also* categories 630–632) 639.0
following
abortion 639.0
ectopic or molar pregnancy 639.0
gonococcal 098.17
puerperal, postpartum, childbirth 670.8 ☑
tuberculous (*see also* Tuberculosis) 016.6 ☑
chronic 614.1
gonococcal 098.37
tuberculous (*see also* Tuberculosis) 016.6 ☑
complicating pregnancy 646.6 ☑
affecting fetus or newborn 760.8
gonococcal (chronic) 098.37
acute 098.17
old — *see* Salpingo-oophoritis, chronic
puerperal 670.8 ☑
specific — *see* Salpingo-oophoritis, gonococcal
subacute (*see also* Salpingo-oophoritis, acute) 614.0
tuberculous (acute) (chronic) (*see also* Tuberculosis) 016.6 ☑
venereal — *see* Salpingo-oophoritis, gonococcal
Salpingo-ovaritis — *see also* Salpingo-oophoritis 614.2
Salpingoperitonitis — *see also* Salpingo-oophoritis 614.2
Salt-losing
nephritis (*see also* Disease, renal) 593.9
syndrome (*see also* Disease, renal) 593.9
Salt-rheum — *see also* Eczema 692.9
Salzmann's nodular dystrophy 371.46
Sampling
chorionic villus V28.89
Sampson's cyst or tumor 617.1
Sandblasters'
asthma 502
lung 502
Sander's disease (paranoia) 297.1
Sandfly fever 066.0
Sandhoff's disease 330.1
Sanfilippo's syndrome (mucopolysaccharidosis III) 277.5
Sanger-Brown's ataxia 334.2
San Joaquin Valley fever 114.0
Sao Paulo fever or typhus 082.0
Saponification, mesenteric 567.89
Sapremia — *see* Septicemia
Sarcocele (benign)
syphilitic 095.8

Sarcocele — *continued*
syphilitic — *continued*
congenital 090.5
Sarcoepiplocele — *see also* Hernia 553.9
Sarcoepiplomphalocele — *see also* Hernia, umbilicus 553.1
Sarcoid (any site) 135
with lung involvement 135 [517.8]
Boeck's 135
Darier-Roussy 135
Spiegler-Fendt 686.8
Sarcoidosis 135
cardiac 135 [425.8]
lung 135 [517.8]
Sarcoma (M8800/3) — *see also* Neoplasm, connective tissue, malignant
alveolar soft part (M9581/3) — *see* Neoplasm, connective tissue, malignant
ameloblastic (M9330/3) 170.1
upper jaw (bone) 170.0
botryoid (M8910/3) — *see* Neoplasm, connective tissue, malignant
botryoides (M8910/3) — *see* Neoplasm, connective tissue, malignant
cerebellar (M9480/3) 191.6
circumscribed (arachnoidal) (M9471/3) 191.6
circumscribed (arachnoidal) cerebellar (M9471/3) 191.6
clear cell, of tendons and aponeuroses (M9044/3) — *see* Neoplasm, connective tissue, malignant
embryonal (M8991/3) — *see* Neoplasm, connective tissue, malignant
endometrial (stromal) (M8930/3) 182.0
isthmus 182.1
endothelial (M9130/3) (*see also* Neoplasm, connective tissue, malignant)
bone (M9260/3) — *see* Neoplasm, bone, malignant
epithelioid cell (M8804/3) — *see* Neoplasm, connective tissue, malignant
Ewing's (M9260/3) — *see* Neoplasm, bone, malignant
follicular dendritic cell 202.9 ☑
germinoblastic (diffuse) (M9632/3) 202.8 ☑
follicular (M9697/3) 202.0 ☑
giant cell (M8802/3) (*see also* Neoplasm, connective tissue, malignant)
bone (M9250/3) — *see* Neoplasm, bone, malignant
glomoid (M8710/3) — *see* Neoplasm, connective tissue, malignant
granulocytic (M9930/3) 205.3 ☑
hemangioendothelial (M9130/3) — *see* Neoplasm, connective tissue, malignant
hemorrhagic, multiple (M9140/3) — *see* Kaposi's, sarcoma
Hodgkin's (M9662/3) 201.2 ☑
immunoblastic (M9612/3) 200.8 ☑
interdigitating dendritic cell 202.9 ☑
Kaposi's (M9140/3) — *see* Kaposi's, sarcoma
Kupffer cell (M9124/3) 155.0
Langerhans cell 202.9 ☑
leptomeningeal (M9530/3) — *see* Neoplasm, meninges, malignant
lymphangioendothelial (M9170/3) — *see* Neoplasm, connective tissue, malignant
lymphoblastic (M9630/3) 200.1 ☑
lymphocytic (M9620/3) 200.1 ☑
mast cell (M9740/3) 202.6 ☑
melanotic (M8720/3) — *see* Melanoma
meningeal (M9530/3) — *see* Neoplasm, meninges, malignant
meningothelial (M9530/3) — *see* Neoplasm, meninges, malignant
mesenchymal (M8800/3) (*see also* Neoplasm, connective tissue, malignant)
mixed (M8990/3) — *see* Neoplasm, connective tissue, malignant
mesothelial (M9050/3) — *see* Neoplasm, by site, malignant

Sarcoma — *see also* Neoplasm, connective tissue, malignant — *continued*
monstrocellular (M9481/3)
specified site — *see* Neoplasm, by site, malignant
unspecified site 191.9
myeloid (M9930/3) 205.3 ☑
neurogenic (M9540/3) — *see* Neoplasm, connective tissue, malignant
odontogenic (M9270/3) 170.1
upper jaw (bone) 170.0
osteoblastic (M9180/3) — *see* Neoplasm, bone, malignant
osteogenic (M9180/3) (*see also* Neoplasm, bone, malignant)
juxtacortical (M9190/3) — *see* Neoplasm, bone, malignant
periosteal (M9190/3) — *see* Neoplasm, bone, malignant
periosteal (M8812/3) (*see also* Neoplasm, bone, malignant)
osteogenic (M9190/3) — *see* Neoplasm, bone, malignant
plasma cell (M9731/3) 203.8 ☑
pleomorphic cell (M8802/3) — *see* Neoplasm, connective tissue, malignant
reticuloendothelial (M9720/3) 202.3 ☑
reticulum cell (M9640/3) 200.0 ☑
nodular (M9642/3) 200.0 ☑
pleomorphic cell type (M9641/3) 200.0 ☑
round cell (M8803/3) — *see* Neoplasm, connective tissue, malignant
small cell (M8803/3) — *see* Neoplasm, connective tissue, malignant
spindle cell (M8801/3) — *see* Neoplasm, connective tissue, malignant
stromal (endometrial) (M8930/3) 182.0
isthmus 182.1
synovial (M9040/3) (*see also* Neoplasm, connective tissue, malignant)
biphasic type (M9043/3) — *see* Neoplasm, connective tissue, malignant
epithelioid cell type (M9042/3) — *see* Neoplasm, connective tissue, malignant
spindle cell type (M9041/3) — *see* Neoplasm, connective tissue, malignant
Sarcomatosis
meningeal (M9539/3) — *see* Neoplasm, meninges, malignant
specified site NEC (M8800/3) — *see* Neoplasm, connective tissue, malignant
unspecified site (M8800/6) 171.9
Sarcosinemia 270.8
Sarcosporidiosis 136.5
Satiety, early 780.94
Satisfactory smear but lacking transformation zone
anal 796.77
cervical 795.07
Saturnine — *see* condition
Saturnism 984.9
specified type of lead — *see* Table of Drugs and Chemicals
Satyriasis 302.89
Sauriasis — *see* Ichthyosis
Sauriderma 757.39
Sauriosis — *see* Ichthyosis
Savill's disease (epidemic exfoliative dermatitis) 695.89
SBE (subacute bacterial endocarditis) 421.0
Scabies (any site) 133.0
Scabs 782.8
Scaglietti-Dagnini syndrome (acromegalic macrospondylitis) 253.0
Scald, scalded — *see also* Burn, by site
skin syndrome 695.81
Scalenus anticus (anterior) syndrome 353.0
Scales 782.8
Scalp — *see* condition
Scaphocephaly 756.0
Scaphoiditis, tarsal 732.5
Scapulalgia 733.90

Scapulohumeral myopathy 359.1
Scarabiasis 134.1
Scarlatina 034.1
   anginosa 034.1
   maligna 034.1
   myocarditis, acute 034.1 *[422.0]*
     old (*see also* Myocarditis) 429.0
   otitis media 034.1 *[382.02]*
   ulcerosa 034.1
Scarlatinella 057.8
Scarlet fever (albuminuria) (angina) (convulsions) (lesions of lid) (rash) 034.1
Scar, scarring — *see also* Cicatrix 709.2
   adherent 709.2
   atrophic 709.2
   cervix
     in pregnancy or childbirth 654.6 ☑
       affecting fetus or newborn 763.89
       causing obstructed labor 660.2 ☑
         affecting fetus or newborn 763.1
   cheloid 701.4
   chorioretinal 363.30
     disseminated 363.35
     macular 363.32
     peripheral 363.34
     posterior pole NEC 363.33
   choroid (*see also* Scar, chorioretinal) 363.30
   compression, pericardial 423.9
   congenital 757.39
   conjunctiva 372.64
   cornea 371.00
     xerophthalmic 264.6
   due to previous cesarean delivery, complicating pregnancy or childbirth 654.2 ☑
     affecting fetus or newborn 763.89
   duodenal (bulb) (cap) 537.3
   hypertrophic 701.4
   keloid 701.4
   labia 624.4
   lung (base) 518.89
   macula 363.32
     disseminated 363.35
     peripheral 363.34
   muscle 728.89
   myocardium, myocardial 412
   painful 709.2
   papillary muscle 429.81
   posterior pole NEC 363.33
     macular — *see* Scar, macula
   postnecrotic (hepatic) (liver) 571.9
   psychic V15.49
   retina (*see also* Scar, chorioretinal) 363.30
   trachea 478.9
   uterus 621.8
     in pregnancy or childbirth NEC 654.9 ☑
       affecting fetus or newborn 763.89
       due to previous cesarean delivery 654.2 ☑
   vulva 624.4
Schamberg's disease, dermatitis, or dermatosis (progressive pigmentary dermatosis) 709.09
Schatzki's ring (esophagus) (lower) (congenital) 750.3
   acquired 530.3
Schaufenster krankheit 413.9
Schaumann's
   benign lymphogranulomatosis 135
   disease (sarcoidosis) 135
   syndrome (sarcoidosis) 135
Scheie's syndrome (mucopolysaccharidosis IS) 277.5
Schenck's disease (sporotrichosis) 117.1
Scheuermann's disease or osteochondrosis 732.0
Scheuthauer-Marie-Sainton syndrome (cleidocranialis dysostosis) 755.59
Schilder (-Flatau) disease 341.1
Schilling-type monocytic leukemia (M9890/3) 206.9 ☑
Schimmelbusch's disease, cystic mastitis, or hyperplasia 610.1
Schirmer's syndrome (encephalocutaneous angiomatosis) 759.6
Schistocelia 756.79

Schistoglossia 750.13
Schistosoma infestation — *see* Infestation, Schistosoma
Schistosomiasis 120.9
   Asiatic 120.2
   bladder 120.0
   chestermani 120.8
   colon 120.1
   cutaneous 120.3
   due to
     S. hematobium 120.0
     S. japonicum 120.2
     S. mansoni 120.1
     S. mattheii 120.8
   eastern 120.2
   genitourinary tract 120.0
   intestinal 120.1
   lung 120.2
   Manson's (intestinal) 120.1
   Oriental 120.2
   pulmonary 120.2
   specified type NEC 120.8
   vesical 120.0
Schizencephaly 742.4
Schizo-affective psychosis — *see also* Schizophrenia 295.7 ☑
Schizodontia 520.2
Schizoid personality 301.20
   introverted 301.21
   schizotypal 301.22
Schizophrenia, schizophrenic (reaction) 295.9 ☑

> *Note* — Use the following fifth-digit subclassification with category 295:
>
> 0   *unspecified*
>
> 1   *subchronic*
>
> 2   *chronic*
>
> 3   *subchronic with acute exacerbation*
>
> 4   *chronic with acute exacerbation*
>
> 5   *in remission*

   acute (attack) NEC 295.8 ☑
     episode 295.4 ☑
   atypical form 295.8 ☑
   borderline 295.5 ☑
   catalepsy 295.2 ☑
   catatonic (type) (acute) (excited) (withdrawn) 295.2 ☑
   childhood (type) (*see also* Psychosis, childhood) 299.9 ☑
   chronic NEC 295.6 ☑
   coenesthesiopathic 295.8 ☑
   cyclic (type) 295.7 ☑
   disorganized (type) 295.1 ☑
   flexibilitas cerea 295.2 ☑
   hebephrenic (type) (acute) 295.1 ☑
   incipient 295.5 ☑
   latent 295.5 ☑
   paranoid (type) (acute) 295.3 ☑
   paraphrenic (acute) 295.3 ☑
   prepsychotic 295.5 ☑
   primary (acute) 295.0 ☑
   prodromal 295.5 ☑
   pseudoneurotic 295.5 ☑
   pseudopsychopathic 295.5 ☑
   reaction 295.9 ☑
   residual type (state) 295.6 ☑
   restzustand 295.6 ☑
   schizo-affective (type) (depressed) (excited) 295.7 ☑
   schizophreniform type 295.4 ☑
   simple (type) (acute) 295.0 ☑
   simplex (acute) 295.0 ☑
   specified type NEC 295.8 ☑
   syndrome of childhood NEC (*see also* Psychosis, childhood) 299.9 ☑
   undifferentiated type 295.9 ☑
     acute 295.8 ☑
     chronic 295.6 ☑
Schizothymia 301.20
   introverted 301.21

Schizothymia — *continued*
   schizotypal 301.22
Schlafkrankheit 086.5
Schlatter-Osgood disease (osteochondrosis, tibial tubercle) 732.4
Schlatter's tibia (osteochondrosis) 732.4
Schloffer's tumor — *see also* Peritonitis 567.29
Schmidt's syndrome
   sphallo-pharyngo-laryngeal hemiplegia 352.6
   thyroid-adrenocortical insufficiency 258.1
   vagoaccessory 352.6
Schmincke
   carcinoma (M8082/3) — *see* Neoplasm, nasopharynx, malignant
   tumor (M8082/3) — *see* Neoplasm, nasopharynx, malignant
Schmitz (-Stutzer) dysentery 004.0
Schmorl's disease or nodes 722.30
   lumbar, lumbosacral 722.32
   specified region NEC 722.39
   thoracic, thoracolumbar 722.31
Schneiderian
   carcinoma (M8121/3)
     specified site — *see* Neoplasm, by site, malignant
     unspecified site 160.0
   papilloma (M8121/0)
     specified site — *see* Neoplasm, by site, benign
     unspecified site 212.0
Schneider's syndrome 047.9
Schnitzler syndrome 273.1
Schoffer's tumor — *see also* Peritonitis 567.29
Scholte's syndrome (malignant carcinoid) 259.2
Scholz's disease 330.0
Scholz (-Bielschowsky-Henneberg) syndrome 330.0
Schönlein (-Henoch) disease (primary) (purpura) (rheumatic) 287.0
School examination V70.3
   following surgery V67.09
Schottmüller's disease — *see also* Fever, paratyphoid 002.9
Schroeder's syndrome (endocrine-hypertensive) 255.3
Schüller-Christian disease or syndrome (chronic histiocytosis X) 277.89
Schultz's disease or syndrome (agranulocytosis) 288.09
Schultze's acroparesthesia, simple 443.89
Schwalbe-Ziehen-Oppenheimer disease 333.6
Schwannoma (M9560/0) — *see also* Neoplasm, connective tissue, benign
   malignant (M9560/3) — *see* Neoplasm, connective tissue, malignant
Schwannomatosis 237.73
Schwartz-Bartter syndrome (inappropriate secretion of antidiuretic hormone) 253.6
Schwartz (-Jampel) syndrome 359.23
Schweninger-Buzzi disease (macular atrophy) 701.3
Sciatic — *see* condition
Sciatica (infectional) 724.3
   due to
     displacement of intervertebral disc 722.10
     herniation, nucleus pulposus 722.10
   wallet 724.3
Scimitar syndrome (anomalous venous drainage, right lung to inferior vena cava) 747.49
Sclera — *see* condition
Sclerectasia 379.11
Scleredema
   adultorum 710.1
   Buschke's 710.1
   newborn 778.1
Sclerema
   adiposum (newborn) 778.1
   adultorum 710.1
   edematosum (newborn) 778.1
   neonatorum 778.1
   newborn 778.1

Scleriasis — *see* Scleroderma
Scleritis 379.00
   with corneal involvement 379.05
   anterior (annular) (localized) 379.03
   brawny 379.06
   granulomatous 379.09
   posterior 379.07
   specified NEC 379.09
   suppurative 379.09
   syphilitic 095.0
   tuberculous (nodular) (*see also* Tuberculosis) 017.3 ☑ *[379.09]*
Sclerochoroiditis — *see also* Scleritis 379.00
Scleroconjunctivitis — *see also* Scleritis 379.00
Sclerocystic ovary (syndrome) 256.4
Sclerodactylia 701.0
Scleroderma, sclerodermia (acrosclerotic) (diffuse) (generalized) (progressive) (pulmonary) 710.1
   circumscribed 701.0
   linear 701.0
   localized (linear) 701.0
   newborn 778.1
Sclerokeratitis 379.05
   meaning sclerosing keratitis 370.54
   tuberculous (*see also* Tuberculosis) 017.3 ☑ *[379.09]*
Scleromalacia
   multiple 731.0
   perforans 379.04
Scleroma, trachea 040.1
Scleromyxedema 701.8
Scleroperikeratitis 379.05
Sclerose en plaques 340
Sclerosis, sclerotic
   adrenal (gland) 255.8
   Alzheimer's 331.0
     with dementia — *see* Alzheimer's, dementia
   amyotrophic (lateral) 335.20
   annularis fibrosi
     aortic 424.1
     mitral 424.0
   aorta, aortic 440.0
     valve (*see also* Endocarditis, aortic) 424.1
   artery, arterial, arteriolar, arteriovascular — *see* Arteriosclerosis
   ascending multiple 340
   Baló's (concentric) 341.1
   basilar — *see* Sclerosis, brain
   bone (localized) NEC 733.99
   brain (general) (lobular) 348.89
     Alzheimer's — *see* Alzheimer's, dementia
     artery, arterial 437.0
     atrophic lobar 331.0
       with dementia
         with behavioral disturbance 331.0 *[294.11]*
         without behavioral disturbance 331.0 *[294.10]*
     diffuse 341.1
       familial (chronic) (infantile) 330.0
       infantile (chronic) (familial) 330.0
       Pelizaeus-Merzbacher type 330.0
     disseminated 340
     hereditary 334.2
     hippocampal 348.81
     infantile (degenerative) (diffuse) 330.0
     insular 340
     Krabbe's 330.0
     mesial temporal 348.81
     miliary 340
     multiple 340
     Pelizaeus-Merzbacher 330.0
     progressive familial 330.0
     senile 437.0
     temporal 348.81
       mesial 348.81
     tuberous 759.5
   bulbar, progressive 340
   bundle of His 426.50
     left 426.3
     right 426.4
   cardiac — *see* Arteriosclerosis, coronary

☑ **Additional Digit Required** — Refer to the Tabular List for Digit Selection   ⬲ **Subterms under main terms may continue to next column or page**

254 — Volume 2   ▶◀ **Revised Text**   ● **New Line**   ▲ **Revised Code**   **2015 ICD-9-CM**

Sclerosis, sclerotic — *continued*
cardiorenal (*see also* Hypertension, cardiorenal) 404.90
cardiovascular (*see also* Disease, cardiovascular) 429.2
renal (*see also* Hypertension, cardiorenal) 404.90
centrolobar, familial 330.0
cerebellar — *see* Sclerosis, brain
cerebral — *see* Sclerosis, brain
cerebrospinal 340
disseminated 340
multiple 340
cerebrovascular 437.0
choroid 363.40
diffuse 363.56
combined (spinal cord) (*see also* Degeneration, combined)
multiple 340
concentric, Baló's 341.1
cornea 370.54
coronary (artery) — *see* Arteriosclerosis, coronary
corpus cavernosum
female 624.8
male 607.89
Dewitzky's
aortic 424.1
mitral 424.0
diffuse NEC 341.1
disease, heart — *see* Arteriosclerosis, coronary
disseminated 340
dorsal 340
dorsolateral (spinal cord) — *see* Degeneration, combined
endometrium 621.8
extrapyramidal 333.90
eye, nuclear (senile) 366.16
Friedreich's (spinal cord) 334.0
funicular (spermatic cord) 608.89
gastritis 535.4 ☑
general (vascular) — *see* Arteriosclerosis
gland (lymphatic) 457.8
hepatic 571.9
hereditary
cerebellar 334.2
spinal 334.0
hippocampal 348.81
idiopathic cortical (Garré's) (*see also* Osteomyelitis) 730.1 ☑
ilium, piriform 733.5
insular 340
pancreas 251.8
Islands of Langerhans 251.8
kidney — *see* Sclerosis, renal
larynx 478.79
lateral 335.24
amyotrophic 335.20
descending 335.24
primary 335.24
spinal 335.24
liver 571.9
lobar, atrophic (of brain) 331.0
with dementia
with behavioral disturbance 331.0 [294.11]
without behavioral disturbance 331.0 [294.10]
lung (*see also* Fibrosis, lung) 515
mastoid 383.1
mesial temporal 348.81
mitral — *see* Endocarditis, mitral
Mönckeberg's (medial) (*see also* Arteriosclerosis, extremities) 440.20
multiple (brain stem) (cerebral) (generalized) 340
myocardium, myocardial — *see* Arteriosclerosis, coronary
nuclear (senile), eye 366.16
ovary 620.8
pancreas 577.8
penis 607.89
peripheral arteries (*see also* Arteriosclerosis, extremities) 440.20
plaques 340

Sclerosis, sclerotic — *continued*
pluriglandular 258.8
polyglandular 258.8
posterior (spinal cord) (syphilitic) 094.0
posterolateral (spinal cord) — *see* Degeneration, combined
prepuce 607.89
primary lateral 335.24
progressive systemic 710.1
pulmonary (*see also* Fibrosis, lung) 515
artery 416.0
valve (heart) (*see also* Endocarditis, pulmonary) 424.3
renal 587
with
cystine storage disease 270.0
hypertension (*see also* Hypertension, kidney) 403.90
hypertensive heart disease (conditions classifiable to 402) (*see also* Hypertension, cardiorenal) 404.90
arteriolar (hyaline) (*see also* Hypertension, kidney) 403.90
hyperplastic (*see also* Hypertension, kidney) 403.90
retina (senile) (vascular) 362.17
rheumatic
aortic valve 395.9
mitral valve 394.9
Schilder's 341.1
senile — *see* Arteriosclerosis
spinal (cord) (general) (progressive) (transverse) 336.8
ascending 357.0
combined (*see also* Degeneration, combined)
multiple 340
syphilitic 094.89
disseminated 340
dorsolateral — *see* Degeneration, combined
hereditary (Friedreich's) (mixed form) 334.0
lateral (amyotrophic) 335.24
multiple 340
posterior (syphilitic) 094.0
stomach 537.89
subendocardial, congenital 425.3
systemic (progressive) 710.1
with lung involvement 710.1 [517.2]
temporal 348.81
mesial 348.81
tricuspid (heart) (valve) — *see* Endocarditis, tricuspid
tuberous (brain) 759.5
tympanic membrane (*see also* Tympanosclerosis) 385.00
valve, valvular (heart) — *see* Endocarditis
vascular — *see* Arteriosclerosis
vein 459.89
Sclerotenonitis 379.07
Sclerotitis — *see also* Scleritis 379.00
syphilitic 095.0
tuberculous (*see also* Tuberculosis) 017.3 ☑ [379.09]
Scoliosis (acquired) (postural) 737.30
congenital 754.2
due to or associated with
Charcôt-Marie-Tooth disease 356.1 [737.43]
mucopolysaccharidosis 277.5 [737.43]
neurofibromatosis 237.71 [737.43]
osteitis
deformans 731.0 [737.43]
fibrosa cystica 252.01 [737.43]
osteoporosis (*see also* Osteoporosis) 733.00 [737.43]
poliomyelitis 138 [737.43]
radiation 737.33
tuberculosis (*see also* Tuberculosis) 015.0 ☑ [737.43]
idiopathic 737.30
infantile
progressive 737.32
resolving 737.31

Scoliosis — *continued*
paralytic 737.39
rachitic 268.1
sciatic 724.3
specified NEC 737.39
thoracogenic 737.34
tuberculous (*see also* Tuberculosis) 015.0 ☑ [737.43]
Scoliotic pelvis 738.6
with disproportion (fetopelvic) 653.0 ☑
affecting fetus or newborn 763.1
causing obstructed labor 660.1 ☑
affecting fetus or newborn 763.1
Scorbutus, scorbutic 267
anemia 281.8
Scotoma (ring) 368.44
arcuate 368.43
Bjerrum 368.43
blind spot area 368.42
central 368.41
centrocecal 368.41
paracecal 368.42
paracentral 368.41
scintillating 368.12
Seidel 368.43
Scratch — *see* Injury, superficial, by site
Scratchy throat 784.99
Screening (for) V82.9
alcoholism V79.1
anemia, deficiency NEC V78.1
iron V78.0
anomaly, congenital V82.89
antenatal, of mother V28.9
alphafetoprotein levels, raised V28.1
based on amniocentesis V28.2
chromosomal anomalies V28.0
raised alphafetoprotein levels V28.1
fetal growth retardation using ultrasonics V28.4
ultrasonics V28.4
genomic V28.89
isoimmunization V28.5
malformations using ultrasonics V28.3
proteomic V28.89
raised alphafetoprotein levels V28.1
risk
pre-term labor V28.82
specified condition NEC V28.89
Streptococcus B V28.6
arterial hypertension V81.1
arthropod-borne viral disease NEC V73.5
asymptomatic bacteriuria V81.5
bacterial
and spirochetal sexually transmitted diseases V74.5
conjunctivitis V74.4
disease V74.9
sexually transmitted V74.5
specified condition NEC V74.8
bacteriuria, asymptomatic V81.5
blood disorder NEC V78.9
specified type NEC V78.8
bronchitis, chronic V81.3
brucellosis V74.8
cancer — *see* Screening, malignant neoplasm
cardiovascular disease NEC V81.2
cataract V80.2
Chagas' disease V75.3
chemical poisoning V82.5
cholera V74.0
cholesterol level V77.91
chromosomal
anomalies
by amniocentesis, antenatal V28.0
maternal postnatal V82.4
athletes V70.3
colonoscopy V76.51
condition
cardiovascular NEC V81.2
eye NEC V80.2
genitourinary NEC V81.6
neurological NEC V80.09
respiratory NEC V81.4
skin V82.0
specified NEC V82.89

Screening — *continued*
congenital
anomaly V82.89
eye V80.2
dislocation of hip V82.3
eye condition or disease V80.2
conjunctivitis, bacterial V74.4
contamination NEC (*see also* Poisoning) V82.5
coronary artery disease V81.0
cystic fibrosis V77.6
deficiency anemia NEC V78.1
iron V78.0
dengue fever V73.5
depression V79.0
developmental handicap V79.9
in early childhood V79.3
specified type NEC V79.8
diabetes mellitus V77.1
diphtheria V74.3
disease or disorder V82.9
bacterial V74.9
specified NEC V74.8
blood V78.9
specified type NEC V78.8
blood-forming organ V78.9
specified type NEC V78.8
cardiovascular NEC V81.2
hypertensive V81.1
ischemic V81.0
Chagas' V75.3
chlamydial V73.98
specified NEC V73.88
ear NEC V80.3
endocrine NEC V77.99
eye NEC V80.2
genitourinary NEC V81.6
heart NEC V81.2
hypertensive V81.1
ischemic V81.0
HPV (human papillomavirus) V73.81
human papillomavirus V73.81
immunity V77.99
infectious NEC V75.9
lipoid NEC V77.91
mental V79.9
specified type NEC V79.8
metabolic NEC V77.99
inborn NEC V77.7
neurological NEC V80.09
nutritional NEC V77.99
rheumatic NEC V82.2
rickettsial V75.0
sexually transmitted V74.5
bacterial V74.5
spirochetal V74.5
sickle-cell V78.2
trait V78.2
specified type NEC V82.89
thyroid V77.0
vascular NEC V81.2
ischemic V81.0
venereal V74.5
viral V73.99
arthropod-borne NEC V73.5
specified type NEC V73.89
dislocation of hip, congenital V82.3
drugs in athletes V70.3
elevated titer V82.9
emphysema (chronic) V81.3
encephalitis, viral (mosquito or tick borne) V73.5
endocrine disorder NEC V77.99
eye disorder NEC V80.2
congenital V80.2
fever
dengue V73.5
hemorrhagic V73.5
yellow V73.4
filariasis V75.6
galactosemia V77.4
genetic V82.79
disease carrier status V82.71
genitourinary condition NEC V81.6
glaucoma V80.1
gonorrhea V74.5

Separation — *continued*	**Septic** — *see also* condition — *continued*	**Septicemia, septicemic** — *continued*	**Sertoli cell** — *continued*

Separation — *continued*
  anxiety, abnormal 309.21
  apophysis, traumatic — *see* Fracture, by site
  choroid 363.70
    hemorrhagic 363.72
    serous 363.71
  costochondral (simple) (traumatic) — *see* Dislocation, costochondral
  delayed
    umbilical cord 779.83
  epiphysis, epiphyseal
    nontraumatic 732.9
      upper femoral 732.2
    traumatic — *see* Fracture, by site
  fracture — *see* Fracture, by site
  infundibulum cardiac from right ventricle by a partition 746.83
  joint (current) (traumatic) — *see* Dislocation, by site
  placenta (normally implanted) — *see* Placenta, separation
  pubic bone, obstetrical trauma 665.6 ☑
  retina, retinal (*see also* Detachment, retina) 361.9
    layers 362.40
      sensory (*see also* Retinoschisis) 361.10
    pigment epithelium (exudative) 362.42
      hemorrhagic 362.43
  sternoclavicular (traumatic) — *see* Dislocation, sternoclavicular
  symphysis pubis, obstetrical trauma 665.6 ☑
  tracheal ring, incomplete (congenital) 748.3
Sepsis (generalized) 995.91
  with
    abortion — *see* Abortion, by type, with sepsis
    acute organ dysfunction 995.92
    ectopic pregnancy (*see also* categories 633.0–633.9) 639.0
    molar pregnancy (*see also* categories 630–632) 639.0
    multiple organ dysfunction (MOD) 995.92
  buccal 528.3
  complicating labor 659.3 ☑
  dental (pulpal origin) 522.4
  female genital organ NEC 614.9
  fetus (intrauterine) 771.81
  following
    abortion 639.0
    ectopic or molar pregnancy 639.0
    infusion, perfusion, or transfusion 999.39
  Friedländer's 038.49
  intra-abdominal 567.22
  intraocular 360.00
  localized — code to specific localized infection
    in operation wound 998.59
    skin (*see also* Abscess) 682.9
  malleus 024
  nadir 038.9
  newborn (organism unspecified) NEC 771.81
  oral 528.3
  puerperal, postpartum, childbirth (pelvic) 670.2 ☑
  resulting from infusion, injection, transfusion, or vaccination 999.39
  severe 995.92
  skin, localized (*see also* Abscess) 682.9
  umbilical (newborn) (organism unspecified) 771.89
    tetanus 771.3
  urinary 599.0
    meaning sepsis 995.91
    meaning urinary tract infection 599.0
Septate — *see also* Septum
Septic — *see also* condition
  adenoids 474.01
    and tonsils 474.02
  arm (with lymphangitis) 682.3
  embolus — *see* Embolism
  finger (with lymphangitis) 681.00
  foot (with lymphangitis) 682.7
  gallbladder (*see also* Cholecystitis) 575.8

Septic — *see also* condition — *continued*
  hand (with lymphangitis) 682.4
  joint (*see also* Arthritis, septic) 711.0 ☑
  kidney (*see also* Infection, kidney) 590.9
  leg (with lymphangitis) 682.6
  mouth 528.3
  nail 681.9
    finger 681.02
    toe 681.11
  shock (endotoxic) 785.52
    postoperative 998.02
  sore (*see also* Abscess) 682.9
    throat 034.0
      milk-borne 034.0
      streptococcal 034.0
  spleen (acute) 289.59
  teeth (pulpal origin) 522.4
  throat 034.0
  thrombus — *see* Thrombosis
  toe (with lymphangitis) 681.10
  tonsils 474.00
    and adenoids 474.02
  umbilical cord (newborn) (organism unspecified) 771.89
  uterus (*see also* Endometritis) 615.9
Septicemia, septicemic (generalized) (suppurative) 038.9
  with
    abortion — *see* Abortion, by type, with sepsis
    ectopic pregnancy (*see also* categories 633.0–633.9) 639.0
    molar pregnancy (*see also* categories 630–632) 639.0
  Aerobacter aerogenes 038.49
  anaerobic 038.3
  anthrax 022.3
  Bacillus coli 038.42
  Bacteroides 038.3
  Clostridium 038.3
  complicating labor 659.3 ☑
  cryptogenic 038.9
  enteric gram-negative bacilli 038.40
  Enterobacter aerogenes 038.49
  Erysipelothrix (insidiosa) (rhusiopathiae) 027.1
  Escherichia coli 038.42
  following
    abortion 639.0
    ectopic or molar pregnancy 639.0
    infusion, injection, transfusion, or vaccination 999.39
  Friedländer's (bacillus) 038.49
  gangrenous 038.9
  gonococcal 098.89
  gram-negative (organism) 038.40
    anaerobic 038.3
  Hemophilus influenzae 038.41
  herpes (simplex) 054.5
  herpetic 054.5
  Listeria monocytogenes 027.0
  meningeal — *see* Meningitis
  meningococcal (chronic) (fulminating) 036.2
  methicillin
    resistant Staphylococcus aureus (MRSA) 038.12
    susceptible Staphylococcus aureus (MSSA) 038.11
  MRSA (methicillin resistant Staphylococcus aureus) 038.12
  MSSA (methicillin susceptible Staphylococcus aureus) 038.11
  navel, newborn (organism unspecified) 771.89
  newborn (organism unspecified) 771.81
  plague 020.2
  pneumococcal 038.2
  postabortal 639.0
  postoperative 998.59
  Proteus vulgaris 038.49
  Pseudomonas (aeruginosa) 038.43
  puerperal, postpartum 670.2 ☑
  Salmonella (aertrycke) (callinarum) (choleraesuis) (enteritidis) (suipestifer) 003.1
  Serratia 038.44
  Shigella (*see also* Dysentery, bacillary) 004.9

Septicemia, septicemic — *continued*
  specified organism NEC 038.8
  staphylococcal 038.10
    aureus 038.11
      methicillin
        resistant (MRSA) 038.12
        susceptible (MSSA) 038.11
    specified organism NEC 038.19
  streptococcal (anaerobic) 038.0
  Streptococcus pneumoniae 038.2
  suipestifer 003.1
  umbilicus, newborn (organism unspecified) 771.89
  viral 079.99
  Yersinia enterocolitica 038.49
Septum, septate (congenital) — *see also* Anomaly, specified type NEC
  anal 751.2
  aqueduct of Sylvius 742.3
    with spina bifida (*see also* Spina bifida) 741.0 ☑
  hymen 752.49
  uterus (complete) (partial) 752.35
  vagina
    in pregnancy or childbirth 654.7 ☑
      affecting fetus or newborn 763.89
      causing obstructed labor 660.2 ☑
        affecting fetus or newborn 763.1
    longitudinal (with or without obstruction) 752.47
    transverse 752.46
Sequestration
  lung (congenital) (extralobar) (intralobar) 748.5
  orbit 376.10
  pulmonary artery (congenital) 747.39
  splenic 289.52
Sequestrum
  bone (*see also* Osteomyelitis) 730.1 ☑
    jaw 526.4
  dental 525.8
  jaw bone 526.4
  sinus (accessory) (nasal) (*see also* Sinusitis) 473.9
    maxillary 473.0
Sequoiosis asthma 495.8
Serology for syphilis
  doubtful
    with signs or symptoms — *see* Syphilis, by site and stage
    follow-up of latent syphilis — *see* Syphilis, latent
  false positive 795.6
  negative, with signs or symptoms — *see* Syphilis, by site and stage
  positive 097.1
    with signs or symptoms — *see* Syphilis, by site and stage
    false 795.6
    follow-up of latent syphilis — *see* Syphilis, latent
    only finding — *see* Syphilis, latent
  reactivated 097.1
Seroma (postoperative) (non-infected) 998.13
  infected 998.51
  post-traumatic 729.91
Seropurulent — *see* condition
Serositis, multiple 569.89
  pericardial 423.2
  peritoneal 568.82
  pleural — *see* Pleurisy
Serotonin syndrome 333.99
Serous — *see* condition
Sertoli cell
  adenoma (M8640/0)
    specified site — *see* Neoplasm, by site, benign
    unspecified site
      female 220
      male 222.0
  carcinoma (M8640/3)
    specified site — *see* Neoplasm, by site, malignant
    unspecified site 186.9
  syndrome (germinal aplasia) 606.0

Sertoli cell — *continued*
  tumor (M8640/0)
    with lipid storage (M8641/0)
      specified site — *see* Neoplasm, by site, benign
      unspecified site
        female 220
        male 222.0
    specified site — *see* Neoplasm, by site, benign
    unspecified site
      female 220
      male 222.0
Sertoli-Leydig cell tumor (M8631/0)
  specified site — *see* Neoplasm, by site, benign
  unspecified site
    female 220
    male 222.0
Serum
  allergy, allergic reaction 999.59
    shock 999.49
  arthritis 999.59 [713.6]
  complication or reaction NEC 999.59
  disease NEC 999.59
  hepatitis 070.3
  intoxication 999.59
  jaundice (homologous) — *see* Hepatitis, viral, type B
  neuritis 999.59
  poisoning NEC 999.59
  rash NEC 999.59
  reaction NEC 999.59
  sickness NEC 999.59
Sesamoiditis 733.99
Seven-day fever 061
  of
    Japan 100.89
    Queensland 100.89
Sever's disease or osteochondrosis (calcaneum) 732.5
Sex chromosome mosaics 758.81
Sex reassignment surgery status (*see also* Trans-sexualism) 302.50
Sextuplet
  affected by maternal complications of pregnancy 761.5
  healthy liveborn — *see* Newborn, multiple
  pregnancy (complicating delivery) NEC 651.8 ☑
    with fetal loss and retention of one or more fetus(es) 651.6 ☑
    following (elective) fetal reduction 651.7 ☑
Sexual
  anesthesia 302.72
  deviation (*see also* Deviation, sexual) 302.9
  disorder (*see also* Deviation, sexual) 302.9
  frigidity (female) 302.72
  function, disorder of (psychogenic) 302.70
    specified type NEC 302.79
  immaturity (female) (male) 259.0
  impotence 607.84
    organic origin NEC 607.84
    psychogenic 302.72
  precocity (constitutional) (cryptogenic) (female) (idiopathic) (male) NEC 259.1
    with adrenal hyperplasia 255.2
  sadism 302.84
Sexuality, pathological — *see also* Deviation, sexual 302.9
Sézary's disease, reticulosis, or syndrome (M9701/3) 202.2 ☑
Shadow, lung 793.19
Shaken infant syndrome 995.55
Shaking
  head (tremor) 781.0
  palsy or paralysis (*see also* Parkinsonism) 332.0
Shallowness, acetabulum 736.39
Shaver's disease or syndrome (bauxite pneumoconiosis) 503
Shearing
  artificial skin graft 996.55
  decellularized allodermis graft 996.55
Sheath (tendon) — *see* condition

☑ Additional Digit Required — Refer to the Tabular List for Digit Selection   ▽ Subterms under main terms may continue to next column or page

2015 ICD-9-CM   ▶◀ Revised Text   ● New Line   ▲ Revised Code   Volume 2 — 257

Shedding
nail 703.8
teeth, premature, primary (deciduous) 520.6
Sheehan's disease or syndrome (postpartum pituitary necrosis) 253.2
Shelf, rectal 569.49
Shell
shock (current) (see also Reaction, stress, acute) 308.9
lasting state 300.16
teeth 520.5
Shield kidney 753.3
Shifting
pacemaker 427.89
sleep-work schedule (affecting sleep) 327.36
Shift, mediastinal 793.2
Shiga's
bacillus 004.0
dysentery 004.0
Shigella (dysentery) — see also Dysentery, bacillary 004.9
carrier (suspected) of V02.3
Shigellosis — see also Dysentery, bacillary 004.9
Shingles — see also Herpes, zoster 053.9
eye NEC 053.29
Shin splints 844.9
Shipyard eye or disease 077.1
Shirodkar suture, in pregnancy 654.5 ☑
Shock 785.50
with
abortion — see Abortion, by type, with shock
ectopic pregnancy (see also categories 633.0–633.9) 639.5
molar pregnancy (see also categories 630–632) 639.5
allergic — see Anaphylactic reaction or shock
anaclitic 309.21
anaphylactic — see also Anaphylactic reaction or shock
due to administration of blood and blood products 999.41
anaphylactoid — see Anaphylactic reaction or shock
anesthetic
correct substance properly administered 995.4
overdose or wrong substance given 968.4
specified anesthetic — see Table of Drugs and Chemicals
birth, fetus or newborn NEC 779.89
cardiogenic 785.51
chemical substance — see Table of Drugs and Chemicals
circulatory 785.59
complicating
abortion — see Abortion, by type, with shock
ectopic pregnancy (see also categories 633.0–633.9) 639.5
labor and delivery 669.1 ☑
molar pregnancy (see also categories 630–632) 639.5
culture 309.29
due to
drug 995.0
correct substance properly administered 995.0
overdose or wrong substance given or taken 977.9
specified drug — see Table of Drugs and Chemicals
food — see Anaphylactic shock, due to, food
during labor and delivery 669.1 ☑
electric 994.8
from electroshock gun (taser) 994.8
endotoxic 785.52
due to surgical procedure 998.02
postoperative 998.02
following
abortion 639.5
ectopic or molar pregnancy 639.5

Shock — continued
following — continued
injury (immediate) (delayed) 958.4
labor and delivery 669.1 ☑
gram-negative 785.52
postoperative 998.02
hematogenic 785.59
hemorrhagic
due to
disease 785.59
surgery (intraoperative) (postoperative) 998.09
trauma 958.4
hypovolemic NEC 785.59
surgical 998.09
traumatic 958.4
insulin 251.0
therapeutic misadventure 962.3
kidney 584.5
traumatic (following crushing) 958.5
lightning 994.0
lung 518.82
related to trauma and surgery 518.52
nervous (see also Reaction, stress, acute) 308.9
obstetric 669.1 ☑
with
abortion — see Abortion, by type, with shock
ectopic pregnancy (see also categories 633.0–633.9) 639.5
molar pregnancy (see also categories 630–632) 639.5
following
abortion 639.5
ectopic or molar pregnancy 639.5
paralysis, paralytic (see also Disease, cerebrovascular, acute) 436
late effect — see Late effect(s) (of) cerebrovascular disease
pleural (surgical) 998.09
due to trauma 958.4
postoperative 998.00
with
abortion — see Abortion, by type, with shock
ectopic pregnancy (see also categories 633.0–633.9) 639.5
molar pregnancy (see also categories 630–632) 639.5
cardiogenic 998.01
following
abortion 639.5
ectopic or molar pregnancy 639.5
hypovolemic 998.09
septic (endotoxic) (gram-negative) 998.02
specified NEC 998.09
psychic (see also Reaction, stress, acute) 308.9
past history (of) V15.49
psychogenic (see also Reaction, stress, acute) 308.9
septic 785.52
with
abortion — see Abortion, by type, with shock
ectopic pregnancy (see also categories 633.0–633.9) 639.5
molar pregnancy (see also categories 630–632) 639.5
due to
surgical procedure 998.02
transfusion NEC 999.89
bone marrow 996.85
following
abortion 639.5
ectopic or molar pregnancy 639.5
surgical procedure 998.02
transfusion NEC 999.89
bone marrow 996.85
postoperative 998.02
spinal (see also Injury, spinal, by site)
with spinal bone injury — see Fracture, vertebra, by site, with spinal cord injury

Shock — continued
surgical 998.00
therapeutic misadventure NEC (see also Complications) 998.89
thyroxin 962.7
toxic 040.82
transfusion — see Complications, transfusion
traumatic (immediate) (delayed) 958.4
Shoemakers' chest 738.3
Short, shortening, shortness
Achilles tendon (acquired) 727.81
arm 736.89
congenital 755.20
back 737.9
bowel syndrome 579.3
breath 786.05
cervical, cervix 649.7 ☑
gravid uterus 649.7 ☑
non-gravid uterus 622.5
acquired 622.5
congenital 752.49
chain acyl CoA dehydrogenase deficiency (SCAD) 277.85
common bile duct, congenital 751.69
cord (umbilical) 663.4 ☑
affecting fetus or newborn 762.6
cystic duct, congenital 751.69
esophagus (congenital) 750.4
femur (acquired) 736.81
congenital 755.34
frenulum linguae 750.0
frenum, lingual 750.0
hamstrings 727.81
hip (acquired) 736.39
congenital 755.63
leg (acquired) 736.81
congenital 755.30
metatarsus (congenital) 754.79
acquired 736.79
organ or site, congenital NEC — see Distortion
palate (congenital) 750.26
P-R interval syndrome 426.81
radius (acquired) 736.09
congenital 755.26
round ligament 629.89
sleeper 307.49
stature, constitutional (hereditary) (idiopathic) 783.43
tendon 727.81
Achilles (acquired) 727.81
congenital 754.79
congenital 756.89
thigh (acquired) 736.81
congenital 755.34
tibialis anticus 727.81
umbilical cord 663.4 ☑
affecting fetus or newborn 762.6
urethra 599.84
uvula (congenital) 750.26
vagina 623.8
Shortsightedness 367.1
Shoshin (acute fulminating beriberi) 265.0
Shoulder — see condition
Shovel-shaped incisors 520.2
Shower, thromboembolic — see Embolism
Shunt (status)
aortocoronary bypass V45.81
arterial-venous (dialysis) V45.11
arteriovenous, pulmonary (acquired) 417.0
congenital 747.39
traumatic (complication) 901.40
cerebral ventricle (communicating) in situ V45.2
coronary artery bypass V45.81
surgical, prosthetic, with complications — see Complications, shunt
vascular NEC V45.89
Shutdown
renal 586
with
abortion — see Abortion, by type, with renal failure
ectopic pregnancy (see also categories 633.0–633.9) 639.3

Shutdown — continued
renal — continued
with — continued
molar pregnancy (see also categories 630–632) 639.3
complicating
abortion 639.3
ectopic or molar pregnancy 639.3
following labor and delivery 669.3 ☑
Shwachman's syndrome 288.02
Shy-Drager syndrome (orthostatic hypotension with multisystem degeneration) 333.0
Sialadenitis (any gland) (chronic) (suppurative) 527.2
epidemic — see Mumps
Sialadenosis, periodic 527.2
Sialaporia 527.7
Sialectasia 527.8
Sialitis 527.2
Sialoadenitis — see also Sialadenitis 527.2
Sialoangitis 527.2
Sialodochitis (fibrinosa) 527.2
Sialodocholithiasis 527.5
Sialolithiasis 527.5
Sialorrhea — see also Ptyalism 527.7
periodic 527.2
Sialosis 527.8
rheumatic 710.2
Siamese twin 759.4
complicating pregnancy 678.1 ☑
Sicard's syndrome 352.6
Sicca syndrome (keratoconjunctivitis) 710.2
Sick 799.9
cilia syndrome 759.89
or handicapped person in family V61.49
Sickle-cell
anemia (see also Disease, sickle-cell) 282.60
disease (see also Disease, sickle-cell) 282.60
hemoglobin
C disease (without crisis) 282.63
with
crisis 282.64
vaso-occlusive pain 282.64
D disease (without crisis) 282.68
with crisis 282.69
E disease (without crisis) 282.68
with crisis 282.69
thalassemia (without crisis) 282.41
with
crisis 282.42
vaso-occlusive pain 282.42
trait 282.5
Sicklemia — see also Disease, sickle-cell 282.60
trait 282.5
Sickness
air (travel) 994.6
airplane 994.6
alpine 993.2
altitude 993.2
Andes 993.2
aviators' 993.2
balloon 993.2
car 994.6
compressed air 993.3
decompression 993.3
green 280.9
harvest 100.89
milk 988.8
morning 643.0 ☑
motion 994.6
mountain 993.2
acute 289.0
protein (see also Complications, vaccination) 999.59
radiation NEC 990
roundabout (motion) 994.6
sea 994.6
serum NEC 999.59
sleeping (African) 086.5
by Trypanosoma 086.5
gambiense 086.3
rhodesiense 086.4
Gambian 086.3
late effect 139.8
Rhodesian 086.4

☑ **Additional Digit Required** — Refer to the Tabular List for Digit Selection   ▽ **Subterms under main terms may continue to next column or page**

258 — Volume 2   ▶◀ Revised Text   ● New Line   ▲ Revised Code   2015 ICD-9-CM

Sickness — *continued*
  sweating 078.2
  swing (motion) 994.6
  train (railway) (travel) 994.6
  travel (any vehicle) 994.6
Sick sinus syndrome 427.81
Sideropenia — *see also* Anemia, iron deficiency 280.9
Siderosis (lung) (occupational) 503
  central nervous system (CNS) 437.8
  cornea 371.15
  eye (bulbi) (vitreous) 360.23
  lens 360.23
Siegal-Cattan-Mamou disease (periodic) 277.31
Siemens' syndrome
  ectodermal dysplasia 757.31
  keratosis follicularis spinulosa (decalvans) 757.39
Sighing respiration 786.7
Sigmoid
  flexure — *see* condition
  kidney 753.3
Sigmoiditis — *see* Enteritis
Silfverskiöld's syndrome 756.50
Silicosis, silicotic (complicated) (occupational) (simple) 502
  fibrosis, lung (confluent) (massive) (occupational) 502
  non-nodular 503
  pulmonum 502
Silicotuberculosis — *see also* Tuberculosis 011.4 ☑
Silo fillers' disease 506.9
Silver's syndrome (congenital hemihypertrophy and short stature) 759.89
Silver wire arteries, retina 362.13
Silvestroni-Bianco syndrome (thalassemia minima) 282.49
Simian crease 757.2
Simmonds' cachexia or disease (pituitary cachexia) 253.2
Simons' disease or syndrome (progressive lipodystrophy) 272.6
Simple, simplex — *see* condition
Sinding-Larsen disease (juvenile osteopathia patellae) 732.4
Singapore hemorrhagic fever 065.4
Singers' node or nodule 478.5
Single
  atrium 745.69
  coronary artery 746.85
  umbilical artery 747.5
  ventricle 745.3
Singultus 786.8
  epidemicus 078.89
Sinus — *see also* Fistula
  abdominal 569.81
  arrest 426.6
  arrhythmia 427.89
  bradycardia 427.89
    chronic 427.81
  branchial cleft (external) (internal) 744.41
  coccygeal (infected) 685.1
    with abscess 685.0
  dental 522.7
  dermal (congenital) 685.1
    with abscess 685.0
  draining — *see* Fistula
  infected, skin NEC 686.9
  marginal, ruptured or bleeding 641.2 ☑
    affecting fetus or newborn 762.1
  pause 426.6
  pericranii 742.0
  pilonidal (infected) (rectum) 685.1
    with abscess 685.0
  preauricular 744.46
  rectovaginal 619.1
  sacrococcygeal (dermoid) (infected) 685.1
    with abscess 685.0
  skin
    infected NEC 686.9
    noninfected — *see* Ulcer, skin
  tachycardia 427.89
  tarsi syndrome 726.79
  testis 608.89

Sinus — *see also* Fistula — *continued*
  tract (postinfectional) — *see* Fistula
  urachus 753.7
Sinuses, Rokitansky-Aschoff — *see also* Disease, gallbladder 575.8
Sinusitis (accessory) (nasal) (hyperplastic) (nonpurulent) (purulent) (chronic) 473.9
  with influenza, flu, or grippe (*see also* Influenza) 487.1
  acute 461.9
    ethmoidal 461.2
    frontal 461.1
    maxillary 461.0
    specified type NEC 461.8
    sphenoidal 461.3
  allergic (*see also* Fever, hay) 477.9
  antrum — *see* Sinusitis, maxillary
  due to
    fungus, any sinus 117.9
    high altitude 993.1
  ethmoidal 473.2
    acute 461.2
  frontal 473.1
    acute 461.1
  influenzal (*see also* Influenza) 487.1
  maxillary 473.0
    acute 461.0
  specified site NEC 473.8
  sphenoidal 473.3
    acute 461.3
  syphilitic, any sinus 095.8
  tuberculous, any sinus (*see also* Tuberculosis) 012.8 ☑
Sinusitis-bronchiectasis-situs inversus (syndrome) (triad) 759.3
Sioloangitis 527.2
Sipple's syndrome (medullary thyroid carcinoma-pheochromocytoma) 258.02
Sirenomelia 759.89
Siriasis 992.0
Sirkari's disease 085.0
SIRS (systemic inflammatory response syndrome) 995.90
  due to
    infectious process 995.91
      with acute organ dysfunction 995.92
    non-infectious process 995.93
      with acute organ dysfunction 995.94
Siti 104.0
Sitophobia 300.29
Situational
  disturbance (transient) (*see also* Reaction, adjustment) 309.9
    acute 308.3
  maladjustment, acute (*see also* Reaction, adjustment) 309.9
  reaction (*see also* Reaction, adjustment) 309.9
    acute 308.3
Situation, psychiatric 300.9
Situs inversus or transversus 759.3
  abdominalis 759.3
  thoracis 759.3
Sixth disease
  due to
    human herpesvirus 6 058.11
    human herpesvirus 7 058.12
Sjögren-Larsson syndrome (ichthyosis congenita) 757.1
Sjögren (-Gougerot) syndrome or disease (keratoconjunctivitis sicca) 710.2
  with lung involvement 710.2 [517.8]
SJS-TEN (Stevens-Johnson syndrome - toxic epidermal necrolysis overlap syndrome) 695.14
Skeletal — *see* condition
Skene's gland — *see* condition
Skenitis — *see also* Urethritis 597.89
  gonorrheal (acute) 098.0
    chronic or duration of 2 months or over 098.2
Skerljevo 104.0
Skevas-Zerfus disease 989.5
Skin — *see also* condition
  donor V59.1
  hidebound 710.9

SLAP lesion (superior glenoid labrum) 840.7
Slate-dressers' lung 502
Slate-miners' lung 502
Sleep
  deprivation V69.4
  disorder 780.50
    with apnea — *see* Apnea, sleep
      child 307.40
    movement, unspecified 780.58
    nonorganic origin 307.40
      specified type NEC 307.49
  disturbance 780.50
    with apnea — *see* Apnea, sleep
    nonorganic origin 307.40
      specified type NEC 307.49
  drunkenness 307.47
  movement disorder, unspecified 780.58
  paroxysmal (*see also* Narcolepsy) 347.00
  related movement disorder, unspecified 780.58
  rhythm inversion 327.39
    nonorganic origin 307.45
  walking 307.46
    hysterical 300.13
Sleeping sickness 086.5
  late effect 139.8
Sleeplessness — *see also* Insomnia 780.52
  menopausal 627.2
  nonorganic origin 307.41
Slipped, slipping
  epiphysis (postinfectional) 732.9
    traumatic (old) 732.9
      current — *see* Fracture, by site
    upper femoral (nontraumatic) 732.2
  intervertebral disc — *see* Displacement, intervertebral disc
  ligature, umbilical 772.3
  patella 717.89
  rib 733.99
  sacroiliac joint 724.6
  tendon 727.9
  ulnar nerve, nontraumatic 354.2
  vertebra NEC (*see also* Spondylolisthesis) 756.12
Slocumb's syndrome 255.3
Sloughing (multiple) (skin) 686.9
  abscess — *see* Abscess, by site
  appendix 543.9
  bladder 596.89
  fascia 728.9
  graft — *see* Complications, graft
  phagedena (*see also* Gangrene) 785.4
  reattached extremity (*see also* Complications, reattached extremity) 996.90
  rectum 569.49
  scrotum 608.89
  tendon 727.9
  transplanted organ (*see also* Rejection, transplant, organ, by site) 996.80
  ulcer (*see also* Ulcer, skin) 707.9
Slow
  feeding newborn 779.31
  fetal, growth NEC 764.9 ☑
    affecting management of pregnancy 656.5 ☑
Slowing
  heart 427.89
  urinary stream 788.62
Sluder's neuralgia or syndrome 337.09
Slurred, slurring, speech 784.59
Small-for-dates — *see also* Light-for-dates 764.0 ☑
  affecting management of pregnancy 656.5 ☑
Smallpox 050.9
  contact V01.3
  exposure to V01.3
  hemorrhagic (pustular) 050.0
  malignant 050.0
  modified 050.2
  vaccination
    complications — *see* Complications, vaccination
    prophylactic (against) V04.1
Small, smallness
  cardiac reserve — *see* Disease, heart

Small, smallness — *continued*
  for dates
    fetus or newborn 764.0 ☑
      with malnutrition 764.1 ☑
      affecting management of pregnancy 656.5 ☑
    infant, term 764.0 ☑
      with malnutrition 764.1 ☑
      affecting management of pregnancy 656.5 ☑
  introitus, vagina 623.3
  kidney, unknown cause 589.9
    bilateral 589.1
    unilateral 589.0
  ovary 620.8
  pelvis
    with disproportion (fetopelvic) 653.1 ☑
      affecting fetus or newborn 763.1
    causing obstructed labor 660.1 ☑
      affecting fetus or newborn 763.1
  placenta — *see* Placenta, insufficiency
  uterus 621.8
  white kidney 582.9
Smearing, fecal 787.62
Smith's fracture (separation) (closed) 813.41
  open 813.51
Smith-Lemli Opitz syndrome (cerebrohepatorenal syndrome) 759.89
Smith-Magenis syndrome 758.33
Smith-Strang disease (oasthouse urine) 270.2
Smokers'
  bronchitis 491.0
  cough 491.0
  syndrome (*see also* Abuse, drugs, nondependent) 305.1
  throat 472.1
  tongue 528.6
Smoking complicating pregnancy, childbirth, or the puerperium 649.0 ☑
Smothering spells 786.09
Snaggle teeth, tooth 524.39
Snapping
  finger 727.05
  hip 719.65
  jaw 524.69
    temporomandibular joint sounds on opening or closing 524.64
  knee 717.9
  thumb 727.05
Sneddon-Wilkinson disease or syndrome (subcorneal pustular dermatosis) 694.1
Sneezing 784.99
  intractable 478.19
Sniffing
  cocaine (*see also* Dependence) 304.2 ☑
  ether (*see also* Dependence) 304.6 ☑
  glue (airplane) (*see also* Dependence) 304.6 ☑
Snoring 786.09
Snow blindness 370.24
Snuffles (nonsyphilitic) 460
  syphilitic (infant) 090.0
Social migrant V60.0
Sodoku 026.0
Soemmering's ring 366.51
Soft — *see also* condition
  enlarged prostate 600.00
    with
      other lower urinary tract symptoms (LUTS) 600.01
      urinary
        obstruction 600.01
        retention 600.01
  nails 703.8
Softening
  bone 268.2
  brain (necrotic) (progressive) 348.89
    arteriosclerotic 437.0
    congenital 742.4
    due to cerebrovascular accident 438.89
    embolic (*see also* Embolism, brain) 434.1 ☑
    hemorrhagic (*see also* Hemorrhage, brain) 431
    occlusive 434.9 ☑

☑ **Additional Digit Required** — Refer to the Tabular List for Digit Selection   ☜ **Subterms under main terms may continue to next column or page**

2015 ICD-9-CM   ▶◀ **Revised Text**   ● **New Line**   ▲ **Revised Code**   **Volume 2 — 259**

Softening — *continued*
  brain — *continued*
    thrombotic (*see also* Thrombosis, brain)
      434.0 ☑
    cartilage 733.92
    cerebellar — *see* Softening, brain
    cerebral — *see* Softening, brain
    cerebrospinal — *see* Softening, brain
    myocardial, heart (*see also* Degeneration, myocardial) 429.1
    nails 703.8
    spinal cord 336.8
    stomach 537.89
Soiling, fecal 787.62
Solar fever 061
Soldier's
  heart 306.2
  patches 423.1
Solitary
  cyst
    bone 733.21
    kidney 593.2
  kidney (congenital) 753.0
  tubercle, brain (*see also* Tuberculosis, brain) 013.2 ☑
  ulcer, bladder 596.89
Somatization reaction, somatic reaction — *see also* Disorder, psychosomatic 306.9
  disorder 300.81
Somatoform disorder 300.82
  atypical 300.82
  severe 300.81
  undifferentiated 300.82
Somnambulism 307.46
  hysterical 300.13
Somnolence 780.09
  nonorganic origin 307.43
  periodic 349.89
Sonne dysentery 004.3
Soor 112.0
Sore
  Delhi 085.1
  desert (*see also* Ulcer, skin) 707.9
  eye 379.99
  Lahore 085.1
  mouth 528.9
    canker 528.2
    due to dentures 528.9
  muscle 729.1
  Naga (*see also* Ulcer, skin) 707.9
  oriental 085.1
  pressure (*see also* Ulcer, pressure) 707.00
    with gangrene (*see also* Ulcer, pressure) 707.00 [785.4]
  skin NEC 709.9
  soft 099.0
  throat 462
    with influenza, flu, or grippe (*see also* Influenza) 487.1
    acute 462
    chronic 472.1
    clergyman's 784.49
    coxsackie (virus) 074.0
    diphtheritic 032.0
    epidemic 034.0
    gangrenous 462
    herpetic 054.79
    influenzal (*see also* Influenza) 487.1
    malignant 462
    purulent 462
    putrid 462
    septic 034.0
    streptococcal (ulcerative) 034.0
    ulcerated 462
    viral NEC 462
      Coxsackie 074.0
  tropical (*see also* Ulcer, skin) 707.9
  veldt (*see also* Ulcer, skin) 707.9
Sotos' syndrome (cerebral gigantism) 253.0
Sounds
  friction, pleural 786.7
  succussion, chest 786.7
  temporomandibular joint
    on opening or closing 524.64
South African cardiomyopathy syndrome 425.2

South American
  blastomycosis 116.1
  trypanosomiasis — *see* Trypanosomiasis
Southeast Asian hemorrhagic fever 065.4
Spacing, teeth, abnormal 524.30
  excessive 524.32
Spade-like hand (congenital) 754.89
Spading nail 703.8
  congenital 757.5
Spanemia 285.9
Spanish collar 605
Sparganosis 123.5
Spasmodic — *see* condition
Spasmophilia — *see also* Tetany 781.7
Spasm, spastic, spasticity — *see also* condition 781.0
  accommodation 367.53
  ampulla of Vater (*see also* Disease, gallbladder) 576.8
  anus, ani (sphincter) (reflex) 564.6
    psychogenic 306.4
  artery NEC 443.9
    basilar 435.0
    carotid 435.8
    cerebral 435.9
      specified artery NEC 435.8
    retinal (*see also* Occlusion, retinal, artery) 362.30
    vertebral 435.1
    vertebrobasilar 435.3
  Bell's 351.0
  bladder (sphincter, external or internal) 596.89
  bowel 564.9
    psychogenic 306.4
  bronchus, bronchiole 519.11
  cardia 530.0
  cardiac — *see* Angina
  carpopedal (*see also* Tetany) 781.7
  cecum 564.9
    psychogenic 306.4
  cerebral (arteries) (vascular) 435.9
    specified artery NEC 435.8
  cerebrovascular 435.9
  cervix, complicating delivery 661.4 ☑
    affecting fetus or newborn 763.7
  ciliary body (of accommodation) 367.53
  colon 564.1
    psychogenic 306.4
  common duct (*see also* Disease, biliary) 576.8
  compulsive 307.22
  conjugate 378.82
  convergence 378.84
  coronary (artery) — *see* Angina
  diaphragm (reflex) 786.8
    psychogenic 306.1
  duodenum, duodenal (bulb) 564.89
  esophagus (diffuse) 530.5
    psychogenic 306.4
  facial 351.8
  fallopian tube 620.8
  gait 781.2
  gastrointestinal (tract) 536.8
    psychogenic 306.4
  glottis 478.75
    hysterical 300.11
    psychogenic 306.1
      specified as conversion reaction 300.11
    reflex through recurrent laryngeal nerve 478.75
  habit 307.20
    chronic 307.22
    transient (of childhood) 307.21
  heart — *see* Angina
  hourglass — *see* Contraction, hourglass
  hysterical 300.11
  infantile (*see also* Epilepsy) 345.6 ☑
  internal oblique, eye 378.51
  intestinal 564.9
    psychogenic 306.4
  larynx, laryngeal 478.75
    hysterical 300.11
    psychogenic 306.1

Spasm, spastic, spasticity — *see also* condition — *continued*
  larynx, laryngeal — *continued*
    psychogenic — *continued*
      specified as conversion reaction 300.11
    levator palpebrae superioris 333.81
  lightning (*see also* Epilepsy) 345.6 ☑
  mobile 781.0
  muscle 728.85
    back 724.8
    psychogenic 306.0
  nerve, trigeminal 350.1
  nervous 306.0
  nodding 307.3
    infantile (*see also* Epilepsy) 345.6 ☑
  occupational 300.89
  oculogyric 378.87
  ophthalmic artery 362.30
  orbicularis 781.0
  perineal 625.8
  peroneo-extensor (*see also* Flat, foot) 734
  pharynx (reflex) 478.29
    hysterical 300.11
    psychogenic 306.1
      specified as conversion reaction 300.11
  pregnant uterus, complicating delivery 661.4 ☑
  psychogenic 306.0
  pylorus 537.81
    adult hypertrophic 537.0
    congenital or infantile 750.5
    psychogenic 306.4
  rectum (sphincter) 564.6
    psychogenic 306.4
  retinal artery NEC (*see also* Occlusion, retina, artery) 362.30
  sacroiliac 724.6
  salaam (infantile) (*see also* Epilepsy) 345.6 ☑
  saltatory 781.0
  sigmoid 564.9
    psychogenic 306.4
  sphincter of Oddi (*see also* Disease, gallbladder) 576.5
  stomach 536.8
    neurotic 306.4
  throat 478.29
    hysterical 300.11
    psychogenic 306.1
      specified as conversion reaction 300.11
  tic 307.20
    chronic 307.22
    transient (of childhood) 307.21
  tongue 529.8
  torsion 333.6
  trigeminal nerve 350.1
    postherpetic 053.12
  ureter 593.89
  urethra (sphincter) 599.84
  uterus 625.8
    complicating labor 661.4 ☑
      affecting fetus or newborn 763.7
  vagina 625.1
    psychogenic 306.51
  vascular NEC 443.9
  vasomotor NEC 443.9
  vein NEC 459.89
  vesical (sphincter, external or internal) 596.89
  viscera 625.8 ☑
Spasmus nutans 307.3
Spastic — *see also* Spasm
  child 343.9
Spasticity — *see also* Spasm
  cerebral, child 343.9
Speakers' throat 784.49
Specific, specified — *see* condition
Speech
  defect, disorder, disturbance, impediment NEC 784.59
    psychogenic 307.9
  (language) therapy V57.3
Spells 780.39

Spells — *continued*
  breath-holding 786.9
Spencer's disease (epidemic vomiting) 078.82
Spens' syndrome (syncope with heart block) 426.9
Spermatic cord — *see* condition
Spermatocele 608.1
  congenital 752.89
Spermatocystitis 608.4
Spermatocytoma (M9063/3)
  specified site — *see* Neoplasm, by site, malignant
  unspecified site 186.9
Spermatorrhea 608.89
Sperm counts
  fertility testing V26.21
  following sterilization reversal V26.22
  postvasectomy V25.8
Sphacelus — *see also* Gangrene 785.4
Sphenoidal — *see* condition
Sphenoiditis (chronic) — *see also* Sinusitis, sphenoidal 473.3
Sphenopalatine ganglion neuralgia 337.09
Sphericity, increased, lens 743.36
Spherocytosis (congenital) (familial) (hereditary) 282.0
  hemoglobin disease 282.7
  sickle-cell (disease) 282.60
Spherophakia 743.36
Sphincter — *see* condition
Sphincteritis, sphincter of Oddi — *see also* Cholecystitis 576.8
Sphingolipidosis 272.7
Sphingolipodystrophy 272.7
Sphingomyelinosis 272.7
Spicule tooth 520.2
Spider
  finger 755.59
  nevus 448.1
  vascular 448.1
Spiegler-Fendt sarcoid 686.8
Spielmeyer-Stock disease 330.1
Spielmeyer-Vogt disease 330.1
Spina bifida (aperta) 741.9 ☑

> *Note* — Use the following fifth-digit subclassification with category 741:
>
> 0   unspecified region
>
> 1   cervical region
>
> 2   dorsal [thoracic] region
>
> 3   lumbar region

  with hydrocephalus 741.0 ☑
    fetal (suspected), affecting management of pregnancy 655.0 ☑
  occulta 756.17
Spindle, Krukenberg's 371.13
Spine, spinal — *see* condition
Spiradenoma (eccrine) (M8403/0) — *see* Neoplasm, skin, benign
Spirillosis NEC — *see also* Fever, relapsing 087.9
Spirillum minus 026.0
Spirillum obermeieri infection 087.0
Spirochetal — *see* condition
Spirochetosis 104.9
  arthritic, arthritica 104.9 [711.8] ☑
  bronchopulmonary 104.8
  icterohemorrhagica 100.0
  lung 104.8
Spitting blood — *see also* Hemoptysis 786.30
Splanchnomegaly 569.89
Splanchnoptosis 569.89
Spleen, splenic — *see also* condition
  agenesis 759.0
  flexure syndrome 569.89
  neutropenia syndrome 289.53
  sequestration syndrome 289.52
Splenectasis — *see also* Splenomegaly 789.2
Splenitis (interstitial) (malignant) (nonspecific) 289.59
  malarial (*see also* Malaria) 084.6
  tuberculous (*see also* Tuberculosis) 017.7 ☑
Splenocele 289.59
Splenomegalia — *see* Splenomegaly
Splenomegalic — *see* condition

☑ Additional Digit Required — Refer to the Tabular List for Digit Selection   ▽ Subterms under main terms may continue to next column or page

Splenomegaly 789.2
  Bengal 789.2
  cirrhotic 289.51
  congenital 759.0
  congestive, chronic 289.51
  cryptogenic 789.2
  Egyptian 120.1
  Gaucher's (cerebroside lipidosis) 272.7
  idiopathic 789.2
  malarial (see also Malaria) 084.6
  neutropenic 289.53
  Niemann-Pick (lipid histiocytosis) 272.7
  siderotic 289.51
  syphilitic 095.8
    congenital 090.0
  tropical (Bengal) (idiopathic) 789.2
Splenopathy 289.50
Splenopneumonia — see Pneumonia
Splenoptosis 289.59
Splinter — see Injury, superficial, by site
Split, splitting
  heart sounds 427.89
  lip, congenital (see also Cleft, lip) 749.10
  nails 703.8
  urinary stream 788.61
Spoiled child reaction — see also Disturbance,
  conduct 312.1 ☑
Spondylarthritis — see also Spondylosis
  721.90
Spondylarthrosis — see also Spondylosis
  721.90
Spondylitis 720.9
  ankylopoietica 720.0
  ankylosing (chronic) 720.0
  atrophic 720.9
    ligamentous 720.9
  chronic (traumatic) (see also Spondylosis)
    721.90
  deformans (chronic) (see also Spondylosis)
    721.90
  gonococcal 098.53
  gouty 274.00
  hypertrophic (see also Spondylosis) 721.90
  infectious NEC 720.9
  juvenile (adolescent) 720.0
  Kümmell's 721.7
  Marie-Strümpell (ankylosing) 720.0
  muscularis 720.9
  ossificans ligamentosa 721.6
  osteoarthritica (see also Spondylosis) 721.90
  posttraumatic 721.7
  proliferative 720.0
  rheumatoid 720.0
  rhizomelica 720.0
  sacroiliac NEC 720.2
  senescent (see also Spondylosis) 721.90
  senile (see also Spondylosis) 721.90
  static (see also Spondylosis) 721.90
  traumatic (chronic) (see also Spondylosis)
    721.90
  tuberculous (see also Tuberculosis)
    015.0 ☑ [720.81]
  typhosa 002.0 [720.81]
Spondyloarthrosis — see also Spondylosis
  721.90
Spondylolisthesis (congenital) (lumbosacral)
  756.12
  with disproportion (fetopelvic) 653.3 ☑
    affecting fetus or newborn 763.1
    causing obstructed labor 660.1 ☑
      affecting fetus or newborn 763.1
  acquired 738.4
  degenerative 738.4
  traumatic 738.4
    acute (lumbar) — see Fracture, vertebra,
      lumbar
    site other than lumbosacral — see
      Fracture, vertebra, by site
Spondylolysis (congenital) 756.11
  acquired 738.4
  cervical 756.19
  lumbosacral region 756.11
    with disproportion (fetopelvic) 653.3 ☑
      affecting fetus or newborn 763.1
      causing obstructed labor 660.1 ☑
        affecting fetus or newborn 763.1

Spondylopathy
  inflammatory 720.9
    specified type NEC 720.89
  traumatic 721.7
Spondylose rhizomelique 720.0
Spondylosis 721.90
  with
    disproportion 653.3 ☑
      affecting fetus or newborn 763.1
      causing obstructed labor 660.1 ☑
        affecting fetus or newborn 763.1
    myelopathy NEC 721.91
  cervical, cervicodorsal 721.0
    with myelopathy 721.1
  inflammatory 720.9
  lumbar, lumbosacral 721.3
    with myelopathy 721.42
  sacral 721.3
    with myelopathy 721.42
  thoracic 721.2
    with myelopathy 721.41
  traumatic 721.7
Sponge
  divers' disease 989.5
  inadvertently left in operation wound 998.4
  kidney (medullary) 753.17
Spongioblastoma (M9422/3)
  multiforme (M9440/3)
    specified site — see Neoplasm, by site,
      malignant
    unspecified site 191.9
  polare (M9423/3)
    specified site — see Neoplasm, by site,
      malignant
    unspecified site 191.9
  primitive polar (M9443/3)
    specified site — see Neoplasm, by site,
      malignant
    unspecified site 191.9
  specified site — see Neoplasm, by site, ma-
    lignant
  unspecified site 191.9
Spongiocytoma (M9400/3)
  specified site — see Neoplasm, by site, ma-
    lignant
  unspecified site 191.9
Spongioneuroblastoma (M9504/3) — see
  Neoplasm, by site, malignant
Spontaneous — see also condition
  fracture — see Fracture, pathologic
Spoon nail 703.8
  congenital 757.5
Sporadic — see condition
Sporotrichosis (bones) (cutaneous) (disseminated) (epidermal) (lymphatic) (lymphocutaneous) (mucous membranes) (pulmonary) (skeletal) (visceral) 117.1
Sporotrichum schenckii infection 117.1
Spots, spotting
  atrophic (skin) 701.3
  Bitôt's (in the young child) 264.1
  café au lait 709.09
  cayenne pepper 448.1
  complicating pregnancy 649.5 ☑
  cotton wool (retina) 362.83
  de Morgan's (senile angiomas) 448.1
  Fúchs' black (myopic) 360.21
  intermenstrual
    irregular 626.6
    regular 626.5
  interpalpebral 372.53
  Koplik's 055.9
  liver 709.09
  Mongolian (pigmented) 757.33
  of pregnancy 649.5 ☑
  purpuric 782.7
  ruby 448.1
Spotted fever — see Fever, spotted
Sprain, strain (joint) (ligament) (muscle) (tendon) 848.9
  abdominal wall (muscle) 848.8
  Achilles tendon 845.09
  acromioclavicular 840.0
  ankle 845.00
    and foot 845.00
  anterior longitudinal, cervical 847.0

Sprain, strain — continued
  arm 840.9
    upper 840.9
      and shoulder 840.9
  astragalus 845.00
  atlanto-axial 847.0
  atlanto-occipital 847.0
  atlas 847.0
  axis 847.0
  back (see also Sprain, spine) 847.9
  breast bone 848.40
  broad ligament — see Injury, internal, broad
    ligament
  calcaneofibular 845.02
  carpal 842.01
  carpometacarpal 842.11
  cartilage
    costal, without mention of injury to
      sternum 848.3
      involving sternum 848.42
    ear 848.8
    knee 844.9
      with current tear (see also Tear,
        meniscus) 836.2
    semilunar (knee) 844.8
      with current tear (see also Tear,
        meniscus) 836.2
    septal, nose 848.0
    thyroid region 848.2
    xiphoid 848.49
  cervical, cervicodorsal, cervicothoracic 847.0
  chondrocostal, without mention of injury
    to sternum 848.3
    involving sternum 848.42
  chondrosternal 848.42
  chronic (joint) — see Derangement, joint
  clavicle 840.9
  coccyx 847.4
  collar bone 840.9
  collateral, knee (medial) (tibial) 844.1
    lateral (fibular) 844.0
    recurrent or old 717.89
      lateral 717.81
      medial 717.82
  coracoacromial 840.8
  coracoclavicular 840.1
  coracohumeral 840.2
  coracoid (process) 840.9
  coronary, knee 844.8
  costal cartilage, without mention of injury
    to sternum 848.3
    involving sternum 848.42
  cricoarytenoid articulation 848.2
  cricothyroid articulation 848.2
  cruciate
    knee 844.2
    old 717.89
      anterior 717.83
      posterior 717.84
  deltoid
    ankle 845.01
    shoulder 840.8
  dorsal (spine) 847.1
  ear cartilage 848.8
  elbow 841.9
    and forearm 841.9
    specified site NEC 841.8
  femur (proximal end) 843.9
    distal end 844.9
  fibula (proximal end) 844.9
    distal end 845.00
  fibulocalcaneal 845.02
  finger(s) 842.10
  foot 845.10
    and ankle 845.00
  forearm 841.9
    and elbow 841.9
    specified site NEC 841.8
  glenoid (shoulder) (see also SLAP lesion)
    840.8
  hand 842.10
  hip 843.9
    and thigh 843.9
  humerus (proximal end) 840.9
    distal end 841.9
  iliofemoral 843.0

Sprain, strain — continued
  infraspinatus 840.3
  innominate
    acetabulum 843.9
    pubic junction 848.5
    sacral junction 846.1
  internal
    collateral, ankle 845.01
    semilunar cartilage 844.8
      with current tear (see also Tear,
        meniscus) 836.2
      old 717.5
  interphalangeal
    finger 842.13
    toe 845.13
  ischiocapsular 843.1
  jaw (cartilage) (meniscus) 848.1
    old 524.69
  knee 844.9
    and leg 844.9
    old 717.5
      collateral
        lateral 717.81
        medial 717.82
      cruciate
        anterior 717.83
        posterior 717.84
  late effect — see Late, effects (of), sprain
  lateral collateral, knee 844.0
    old 717.81
  leg 844.9
    and knee 844.9
  ligamentum teres femoris 843.8
  low back 846.9
  lumbar (spine) 847.2
  lumbosacral 846.0
    chronic or old 724.6
  mandible 848.1
    old 524.69
  maxilla 848.1
  medial collateral, knee 844.1
    old 717.82
  meniscus
    jaw 848.1
      old 524.69
    knee 844.8
      with current tear (see also Tear,
        meniscus) 836.2
      old 717.5
    mandible 848.1
      old 524.69
    specified site NEC 848.8
  metacarpal 842.10
    distal 842.12
    proximal 842.11
  metacarpophalangeal 842.12
  metatarsal 845.10
  metatarsophalangeal 845.12
  midcarpal 842.19
  midtarsal 845.19
  multiple sites, except fingers alone or toes
    alone 848.8
  neck 847.0
  nose (septal cartilage) 848.0
  occiput from atlas 847.0
  old — see Derangement, joint
  orbicular, hip 843.8
  patella(r) 844.8
    old 717.89
  pelvis 848.5
  phalanx
    finger 842.10
    toe 845.10
  radiocarpal 842.02
  radiohumeral 841.2
  radioulnar 841.9
    distal 842.09
  radius, radial (proximal end) 841.9
    and ulna 841.9
      distal 842.09
    collateral 841.0
    distal end 842.00
  recurrent — see Sprain, by site
  rib (cage), without mention of injury to
    sternum 848.3
    involving sternum 848.42

☑ Additional Digit Required — Refer to the Tabular List for Digit Selection   ▽ Subterms under main terms may continue to next column or page

2015 ICD-9-CM   ►◄ Revised Text   ● New Line   ▲ Revised Code   Volume 2 — 261

Sprain, strain — *continued*
  rotator cuff (capsule) 840.4
  round ligament (*see also* Injury, internal,
      round ligament)
    femur 843.8
  sacral (spine) 847.3
  sacrococcygeal 847.3
  sacroiliac (region) 846.9
    chronic or old 724.6
    ligament 846.1
    specified site NEC 846.8
  sacrospinatus 846.2
  sacrospinous 846.2
  sacrotuberous 846.3
  scaphoid bone, ankle 845.00
  scapula(r) 840.9
  semilunar cartilage (knee) 844.8
    with current tear (*see also* Tear, menis-
        cus) 836.2
    old 717.5
  septal cartilage (nose) 848.0
  shoulder 840.9
    and arm, upper 840.9
    blade 840.9
  specified site NEC 848.8
  spine 847.9
    cervical 847.0
    coccyx 847.4
    dorsal 847.1
    lumbar 847.2
    lumbosacral 846.0
      chronic or old 724.6
    sacral 847.3
    sacroiliac (*see also* Sprain, sacroiliac)
        846.9
      chronic or old 724.6
    thoracic 847.1
  sternoclavicular 848.41
  sternum 848.40
  subglenoid (*see also* SLAP lesion) 840.8
  subscapularis 840.5
  supraspinatus 840.6
  symphysis
    jaw 848.1
      old 524.69
    mandibular 848.1
      old 524.69
    pubis 848.5
  talofibular 845.09
  tarsal 845.10
  tarsometatarsal 845.11
  temporomandibular 848.1
    old 524.69
  teres
    ligamentum femoris 843.8
    major or minor 840.8
  thigh (proximal end) 843.9
    and hip 843.9
    distal end 844.9
  thoracic (spine) 847.1
  thorax 848.8
  thumb 842.10
  thyroid cartilage or region 848.2
  tibia (proximal end) 844.9
    distal end 845.00
  tibiofibular
    distal 845.03
    superior 844.3
  toe(s) 845.10
  trachea 848.8
  trapezoid 840.8
  ulna, ulnar (proximal end) 841.9
    collateral 841.1
    distal end 842.00
  ulnohumeral 841.3
  vertebrae (*see also* Sprain, spine) 847.9
    cervical, cervicodorsal, cervicothoracic
        847.0
  wrist (cuneiform) (scaphoid) (semilunar)
      842.00
  xiphoid cartilage 848.49
Sprengel's deformity (congenital) 755.52
Spring fever 309.23
Sprue 579.1
  celiac 579.0
  idiopathic 579.0

Sprue — *continued*
  meaning thrush 112.0
  nontropical 579.0
  tropical 579.1
Spur — *see also* Exostosis
  bone 726.91
    calcaneal 726.73
  calcaneal 726.73
  iliac crest 726.5
  nose (septum) 478.19
    bone 726.91
  septal 478.19
Spuria placenta — *see* Placenta, abnormal
Spurway's syndrome (brittle bones and blue
    sclera) 756.51
Sputum, abnormal (amount) (color) (exces-
    sive) (odor) (purulent) 786.4
  bloody 786.30
Squamous — *see also* condition
  cell metaplasia
    bladder 596.89
    cervix — *see* condition
  epithelium in
    cervical canal (congenital) 752.49
    uterine mucosa (congenital) 752.39
  metaplasia
    bladder 596.89
    cervix — *see* condition
Squashed nose 738.0
  congenital 754.0
Squeeze, divers' 993.3
Squint — *see also* Strabismus 378.9
  accommodative (*see also* Esotropia) 378.00
  concomitant (*see also* Heterotropia) 378.30
Stab — *see also* Wound, open, by site
  internal organs — *see* Injury, internal, by
      site, with open wound
Staggering gait 781.2
  hysterical 300.11
Staghorn calculus 592.0
Stain, staining
  meconium 779.84
  port wine 757.32
  tooth, teeth (hard tissues) 521.7
    due to
      accretions 523.6
      deposits (betel) (black) (green) (ma-
          teria alba) (orange) (tobacco)
          523.6
      metals (copper) (silver) 521.7
      nicotine 523.6
      pulpal bleeding 521.7
      tobacco 523.6
Stälh's
  ear 744.29
  pigment line (cornea) 371.11
Stälhi's pigment lines (cornea) 371.11
Stammering — *see* Disorder, fluency
    315.35
Standstill
  atrial 426.6
  auricular 426.6
  cardiac (*see also* Arrest, cardiac) 427.5
  sinoatrial 426.6
  sinus 426.6
  ventricular (*see also* Arrest, cardiac) 427.5
Stannosis 503
Stanton's disease (melioidosis) 025
Staphylitis (acute) (catarrhal) (chronic) (gan-
    grenous) (membranous) (suppurative)
    (ulcerative) 528.3
Staphylococcemia 038.10
  aureus 038.11
  specified organism NEC 038.19
Staphylococcus, staphylococcal — *see* condi-
    tion
Staphyloderma (skin) 686.00
Staphyloma 379.11
  anterior, localized 379.14
  ciliary 379.11
  cornea 371.73
  equatorial 379.13
  posterior 379.12
  posticum 379.12
  ring 379.15
  sclera NEC 379.11

Starch eating 307.52
Stargardt's disease 362.75
Starvation (inanition) (due to lack of food)
    994.2
  edema 262
  voluntary NEC 307.1
Stasis
  bile (duct) (*see also* Disease, biliary) 576.8
  bronchus (*see also* Bronchitis) 490
  cardiac (*see also* Failure, heart) 428.0
  cecum 564.89
  colon 564.89
  dermatitis (*see also* Varix, with stasis dermati-
      tis) 454.1
  duodenal 536.8
  eczema (*see also* Varix, with stasis dermati-
      tis) 454.1
  edema (*see also* Hypertension, venous)
      459.30
  foot 991.4
  gastric 536.3
  ileocecal coil 564.89
  ileum 564.89
  intestinal 564.89
  jejunum 564.89
  kidney 586
  liver 571.9
    cirrhotic — *see* Cirrhosis, liver
  lymphatic 457.8
  pneumonia 514
  portal 571.9
  pulmonary 514
  rectal 564.89
  renal 586
    tubular 584.5
  stomach 536.3
  ulcer
    with varicose veins 454.0
    without varicose veins 459.81
  urine NEC (*see also* Retention, urine) 788.20
  venous 459.81
State
  affective and paranoid, mixed, organic psy-
      chotic 294.8
  agitated 307.9
    acute reaction to stress 308.2
  anxiety (neurotic) (*see also* Anxiety) 300.00
    specified type NEC 300.09
  apprehension (*see also* Anxiety) 300.00
    specified type NEC 300.09
  climacteric, female 627.2
    following induced menopause 627.4
  clouded
    epileptic (*see also* Epilepsy) 345.9 ☑
    paroxysmal (idiopathic) (*see also* Epilep-
        sy) 345.9 ☑
  compulsive (mixed) (with obsession) 300.3
  confusional 298.9
    acute 293.0
      with
        arteriosclerotic dementia 290.41
        presenile brain disease 290.11
        senility 290.3
      alcoholic 291.0
      drug-induced 292.81
    epileptic 293.0
    postoperative 293.9
    reactive (emotional stress) (psychologi-
        cal trauma) 298.2
    subacute 293.1
  constitutional psychopathic 301.9
  convulsive (*see also* Convulsions) 780.39
  depressive NEC 311
    induced by drug 292.84
    neurotic 300.4
  dissociative 300.15
  hallucinatory 780.1
    induced by drug 292.12
  hypercoagulable (primary) 289.81
    secondary 289.82
  hyperdynamic beta-adrenergic circulatory
      429.82
  locked-in 344.81
  menopausal 627.2
    artificial 627.4
    following induced menopause 627.4

State — *continued*
  neurotic NEC 300.9
    with depersonalization episode 300.6
  obsessional 300.3
  oneiroid (*see also* Schizophrenia) 295.4 ☑
  panic 300.01
  paranoid 297.9
    alcohol-induced 291.5
    arteriosclerotic 290.42
    climacteric 297.2
    drug-induced 292.11
    in
      presenile brain disease 290.12
      senile brain disease 290.20
    involutional 297.2
    menopausal 297.2
    senile 290.20
    simple 297.0
  postleukotomy 310.0
  pregnant (*see also* Pregnancy) V22.2
  psychogenic, twilight 298.2
  psychotic, organic (*see also* Psychosis, organ-
      ic) 294.9
    mixed paranoid and affective 294.8
    senile or presenile NEC 290.9
    transient NEC 293.9
      with
        anxiety 293.84
        delusions 293.81
        depression 293.83
        hallucinations 293.82
  residual schizophrenic (*see also*
      Schizophrenia) 295.6 ☑
  tension (*see also* Anxiety) 300.9
  transient organic psychotic 293.9
    anxiety type 293.84
    depressive type 293.83
    hallucinatory type 293.83
    paranoid type 293.81
    specified type NEC 293.89
  twilight
    epileptic 293.0
    psychogenic 298.2
  vegetative (persistent) 780.03
Status (post)
  absence
    epileptic (*see also* Epilepsy) 345.2
    of organ, acquired (postsurgical) — *see*
        Absence, by site, acquired
  administration of tPA(rtPA) in a different
      institution within the last 24 hours
      prior to admission to facility V45.88
  anastomosis of intestine (for bypass) V45.3
  anginosus 413.9
  angioplasty, percutaneous transluminal
      coronary V45.82
  ankle prosthesis V43.66
  aortocoronary bypass or shunt V45.81
  arthrodesis V45.4
  artificially induced condition NEC V45.89
  artificial opening (of) V44.9
    gastrointestinal tract NEC V44.4
    specified site NEC V44.8
    urinary tract NEC V44.6
    vagina V44.7
  aspirator V46.0
  asthmaticus (*see also* Asthma) 493.9 ☑
  awaiting organ transplant V49.83
  bariatric surgery V45.86
    complicating pregnancy, childbirth, or
        the puerperium 649.2 ☑
  bed confinement V49.84
  breast
    correction V43.82
    implant removal V45.83
    reconstruction V43.82
  cardiac
    device (in situ) V45.00
      carotid sinus V45.09
        fitting or adjustment V53.39
      defibrillator, automatic implantable
          (with synchronous cardiac
          pacemaker) V45.02
      pacemaker V45.01
        fitting or adjustment V53.31
  carotid sinus stimulator V45.09

☑ **Additional Digit Required** — Refer to the Tabular List for Digit Selection   � **Subterms under main terms may continue to next column or page**

262 — Volume 2   ▶◀ Revised Text   ● New Line   ▲ Revised Code   2015 ICD-9-CM

Status — *continued*
- cataract extraction V45.61
- chemotherapy V66.2
  - current V58.69
- circumcision, female 629.20
- clitorectomy (female genital mutilation type I) 629.21
  - with excision of labia minora (female genital mutilation type II) 629.22
- colonization — *see* Carrier (suspected) of
- colostomy V44.3
- contraceptive device V45.59
  - intrauterine V45.51
  - subdermal V45.52
- convulsivus idiopathicus (*see also* Epilepsy) 345.3
- coronary artery bypass or shunt V45.81
- cutting
  - female genital 629.20
    - specified NEC 629.29
    - type I 629.21
    - type II 629.22
    - type III 629.23
    - type IV 629.29
- cystostomy V44.50
  - appendico-vesicostomy V44.52
  - cutaneous-vesicostomy V44.51
  - specified type NEC V44.59
- defibrillator, automatic implantable cardiac (with synchronous cardiac pacemaker) V45.02
- delinquent immunization V15.83
- dental crowns V45.84
- dental fillings V45.84
- dental restoration V45.84
- dental sealant V49.82
- dialysis (hemo) (peritoneal) V45.11
- donor V59.9
- do not resuscitate V49.86
- drug therapy or regimen V67.59
  - high-risk medication NEC V67.51
- elbow prosthesis V43.62
- embedded
  - fragment — *see* Foreign body, retained
  - splinter — *see* Foreign body, retained
- enterostomy V44.4
- epileptic, epilepticus (absence) (grand mal) (*see also* Epilepsy) 345.3
  - focal motor 345.7 ☑
  - partial 345.7 ☑
  - petit mal 345.2
  - psychomotor 345.7 ☑
  - temporal lobe 345.7 ☑
- estrogen receptor
  - negative [ER-] V86.1
  - positive [ER+] V86.0
- explantation of joint prosthesis NEC V88.29
  - hip V88.21
  - knee V88.22
- eye (adnexa) surgery V45.69
- female genital
  - cutting 629.20
    - specified NEC 629.29
    - type I 629.21
    - type II 629.22
    - type III 629.23
    - type IV 629.29
  - mutilation 629.20
    - type I 629.21
    - type II 629.22
    - type III 629.23
    - type IV 629.29
- filtering bleb (eye) (postglaucoma) V45.69
  - with rupture or complication 997.99
  - postcataract extraction (complication) 997.99
- finger joint prosthesis V43.69
- foster care V60.81
- gastric
  - banding V45.86
    - complicating pregnancy, childbirth, or the puerperium 649.2 ☑
  - bypass for obesity V45.86
    - complicating pregnancy, childbirth, or the puerperium 649.2 ☑
- gastrostomy V44.1

Status — *continued*
- grand mal 345.3
- heart valve prosthesis V43.3
- hemodialysis V45.11
- hip prosthesis (joint) (partial) (total) V43.64
  - explantation V88.21
- hysterectomy V88.01
  - partial with remaining cervical stump V88.02
  - total V88.01
- ileostomy V44.2
- infibulation (female genital mutilation type III) 629.23
- insulin pump V45.85
- intestinal bypass V45.3
- intrauterine contraceptive device V45.51
- jejunostomy V44.4
- joint prosthesis NEC V43.69
  - explantation V88.29
- knee joint prosthesis V43.65
  - explantation V88.22
- lacunaris 437.8
- lacunosis 437.8
- lapsed immunization schedule V15.83
- low birth weight V21.30
  - less than 500 grams V21.31
  - 1000–1499 grams V21.33
  - 1500–1999 grams V21.34
  - 2000–2500 grams V21.35
  - 500–999 grams V21.32
- lymphaticus 254.8
- malignant neoplasm, ablated or excised — *see* History, malignant neoplasm
- marmoratus 333.79
- military deployment V62.22
- mutilation, female 629.20
  - type I 629.21
  - type II 629.22
  - type III 629.23
  - type IV 629.29
- nephrostomy V44.6
- neuropacemaker NEC V45.89
  - brain V45.89
  - carotid sinus V45.09
  - neurologic NEC V45.89
- obesity surgery V45.86
  - complicating pregnancy, childbirth, or the puerperium 649.2 ☑
- organ replacement
  - by artificial or mechanical device or prosthesis of
    - artery V43.4
    - artificial skin V43.83
    - bladder V43.5
    - blood vessel V43.4
    - breast V43.82
    - eye globe V43.0
    - heart
      - assist device V43.21
      - fully implantable artificial heart V43.22
      - valve V43.3
    - intestine V43.89
    - joint V43.60
      - ankle V43.66
      - elbow V43.62
      - finger V43.69
      - hip (partial) (total) V43.64
      - knee V43.65
      - shoulder V43.61
      - specified NEC V43.69
      - wrist V43.63
    - kidney V43.89
    - larynx V43.81
    - lens V43.1
    - limb(s) V43.7
    - liver V43.89
    - lung V43.89
    - organ NEC V43.89
    - pancreas V43.89
    - skin (artificial) V43.83
    - tissue NEC V43.89
    - vein V43.4
  - by organ transplant (heterologous) (homologous) — *see* Status, transplant

Status — *continued*
- pacemaker
  - brain V45.89
  - cardiac V45.01
  - carotid sinus V45.09
  - neurologic NEC V45.89
  - specified site NEC V45.89
- percutaneous transluminal coronary angioplasty V45.82
- peritoneal dialysis V45.11
- petit mal 345.2
- physical restraints V49.87
- postcommotio cerebri 310.2
- postmenopausal (age related) (natural) V49.81
- postoperative NEC V45.89
- postpartum NEC V24.2
  - care immediately following delivery V24.0
  - routine follow-up V24.2
- postsurgical NEC V45.89
- renal dialysis V45.11
  - noncompliance V45.12
- respirator [ventilator] V46.11
  - encounter
    - during
      - mechanical failure V46.14
      - power failure V46.12
    - for weaning V46.13
- retained foreign body — *see* Foreign body, retained
- reversed jejunal transposition (for bypass) V45.3
- sex reassignment surgery (*see also* Transsexualism) 302.50
- shoulder prosthesis V43.61
- shunt
  - aortocoronary bypass V45.81
  - arteriovenous (for dialysis) V45.11
  - cerebrospinal fluid V45.2
  - vascular NEC V45.89
    - aortocoronary (bypass) V45.81
  - ventricular (communicating) (for drainage) V45.2
- sterilization
  - tubal ligation V26.51
  - vasectomy V26.52
- subdermal contraceptive device V45.52
- thymicolymphaticus 254.8
- thymicus 254.8
- thymolymphaticus 254.8
- tooth extraction 525.10
- tracheostomy V44.0
- transplant
  - blood vessel V42.89
  - bone V42.4
    - marrow V42.81
  - cornea V42.5
  - heart V42.1
    - valve V42.2
  - intestine V42.84
  - kidney V42.0
  - liver V42.7
  - lung V42.6
  - organ V42.9
    - removal (due to complication, failure, rejection or infection) V45.87
    - specified site NEC V42.89
  - pancreas V42.83
  - peripheral stem cells V42.82
  - skin V42.3
  - stem cells, peripheral V42.82
  - tissue V42.9
    - specified type NEC V42.89
  - vessel, blood V42.89
- tubal ligation V26.51
- underimmunization V15.83
- ureterostomy V44.6
- urethrostomy V44.6
- vagina, artificial V44.7
- vascular shunt NEC V45.89
  - aortocoronary (bypass) V45.81
- vasectomy V26.52
- ventilator [respirator] V46.11

Status — *continued*
- ventilator [respirator] — *continued*
  - encounter
    - during
      - mechanical failure V46.14
      - power failure V46.12
    - for weaning V46.13
  - wheelchair confinement V46.3
  - wrist prosthesis V43.63
- **Stave fracture** — *see* Fracture, metacarpus, metacarpal bone(s)
- **Steal**
  - subclavian artery 435.2
  - vertebral artery 435.1
- **Stealing, solitary, child problem** — *see also* Disturbance, conduct 312.1 ☑
- **Steam burn** — *see* Burn, by site
- **Steatocystoma multiplex** 706.2
- **Steatoma** (infected) 706.2
  - eyelid (cystic) 374.84
  - infected 373.13
- **Steatorrhea** (chronic) 579.8
  - with lacteal obstruction 579.2
  - idiopathic 579.0
    - adult 579.0
    - infantile 579.0
  - pancreatic 579.4
  - primary 579.0
  - secondary 579.8
  - specified cause NEC 579.8
  - tropical 579.1
- **Steatosis** 272.8
  - heart (*see also* Degeneration, myocardial) 429.1
  - kidney 593.89
  - liver 571.8
- **Steele-Richardson (-Olszewski) Syndrome** 333.0
- **Steinbrocker's syndrome** — *see also* Neuropathy, peripheral, autonomic 337.9
- **Steinert's disease** 359.21
- **Stein-Leventhal syndrome** (polycystic ovary) 256.4
- **Stein's syndrome** (polycystic ovary) 256.4
- **STEMI** (ST elevation myocardial infarction — *see also* — Infarct, myocardium, ST elevation 410.9 ☑
- **Stenocardia** — *see also* Angina 413.9
- **Stenocephaly** 756.0
- **Stenosis** (cicatricial) — *see also* Stricture
  - ampulla of Vater 576.2
    - with calculus, cholelithiasis, or stones — *see* Choledocholithiasis
  - anus, anal (canal) (sphincter) 569.2
    - congenital 751.2
  - aorta (ascending) 747.22
    - arch 747.10
    - arteriosclerotic 440.0
    - calcified 440.0
  - aortic (valve) 424.1
    - with
      - mitral (valve)
        - insufficiency or incompetence 396.2
        - stenosis or obstruction 396.0
    - atypical 396.0
    - congenital 746.3
    - rheumatic 395.0
      - with
        - insufficiency, incompetency or regurgitation 395.2
          - with mitral (valve) disease 396.8
        - mitral (valve)
          - disease (stenosis) 396.0
          - insufficiency or incompetence 396.2
          - stenosis or obstruction 396.0
    - specified cause, except rheumatic 424.1
    - syphilitic 093.22
  - aqueduct of Sylvius (congenital) 742.3
    - with spina bifida (*see also* Spina bifida) 741.0 ☑
    - acquired 331.4
  - artery NEC (*see also* Arteriosclerosis) 447.1
    - basilar — *see* Narrowing, artery, basilar

Stenosis — see also Stricture — continued
artery (see also Arteriosclerosis) — continued
  carotid (common) (internal) — see Narrowing, artery, carotid
  celiac 447.4
  cerebral 437.0
    due to
      embolism (see also Embolism, brain) 434.1 ☑
      thrombus (see also Thrombosis, brain) 434.0 ☑
  extremities 440.20
  precerebral — see Narrowing, artery, precerebral
  pulmonary (congenital) 747.31
    acquired 417.8
  renal 440.1
  vertebral — see Narrowing, artery, vertebral
bile duct or biliary passage (see also Obstruction, biliary) 576.2
  congenital 751.61
bladder neck (acquired) 596.0
  congenital 753.6
brain 348.89
bronchus 519.19
  syphilitic 095.8
cardia (stomach) 537.89
  congenital 750.7
cardiovascular (see also Disease, cardiovascular) 429.2
carotid artery — see Narrowing, artery, carotid
cervix, cervical (canal) 622.4
  congenital 752.49
  in pregnancy or childbirth 654.6 ☑
    affecting fetus or newborn 763.89
    causing obstructed labor 660.2 ☑
      affecting fetus or newborn 763.1
colon (see also Obstruction, intestine) 560.9
  congenital 751.2
colostomy 569.62
common bile duct (see also Obstruction, biliary) 576.2
  congenital 751.61
coronary (artery) — see Arteriosclerosis, coronary
cystic duct (see also Obstruction, gallbladder) 575.2
  congenital 751.61
due to (presence of) any device, implant, or graft classifiable to 996.0–996.5 — see Complications, due to (presence of) any device, implant, or graft classified to 996.0–996.5 NEC
duodenum 537.3
  congenital 751.1
ejaculatory duct NEC 608.89
endocervical os — see Stenosis, cervix
enterostomy 569.62
esophagostomy 530.87
esophagus 530.3
  congenital 750.3
  syphilitic 095.8
    congenital 090.5
external ear canal 380.50
  secondary to
    inflammation 380.53
    surgery 380.52
    trauma 380.51
gallbladder (see also Obstruction, gallbladder) 575.2
glottis 478.74
heart valve (acquired) (see also Endocarditis)
  congenital NEC 746.89
    aortic 746.3
    mitral 746.5
    pulmonary 746.02
    tricuspid 746.1
hepatic duct (see also Obstruction, biliary) 576.2
hymen 623.3
hypertrophic subaortic (idiopathic) 425.11
infundibulum cardiac 746.83

Stenosis — see also Stricture — continued
intestine (see also Obstruction, intestine) 560.9
  congenital (small) 751.1
    large 751.2
lacrimal
  canaliculi 375.53
  duct 375.56
    congenital 743.65
  punctum 375.52
    congenital 743.65
  sac 375.54
    congenital 743.65
lacrimonasal duct 375.56
  congenital 743.65
  neonatal 375.55
larynx 478.74
  congenital 748.3
  syphilitic 095.8
    congenital 090.5
mitral (valve) (chronic) (inactive) 394.0
  with
    aortic (valve)
      disease (insufficiency) 396.1
      insufficiency or incompetence 396.1
      stenosis or obstruction 396.0
    incompetency, insufficiency or regurgitation 394.2
      with aortic valve disease 396.8
  active or acute 391.1
    with chorea (acute) (rheumatic) (Sydenham's) 392.0
  congenital 746.5
  specified cause, except rheumatic 424.0
  syphilitic 093.21
myocardium, myocardial (see also Degeneration, myocardial) 429.1
  hypertrophic subaortic (idiopathic) 425.11
nares (anterior) (posterior) 478.19
  congenital 748.0
nasal duct 375.56
  congenital 743.65
nasolacrimal duct 375.56
  congenital 743.65
  neonatal 375.55
organ or site, congenital NEC — see Atresia
papilla of Vater 576.2
  with calculus, cholelithiasis, or stones — see Choledocholithiasis
pulmonary (artery) (congenital) 747.31
  with ventricular septal defect, dextraposition of aorta and hypertrophy of right ventricle 745.2
  acquired 417.8
  infundibular 746.83
  in tetralogy of Fallot 745.2
  subvalvular 746.83
  valve (see also Endocarditis, pulmonary) 424.3
    congenital 746.02
  vein 747.49
    acquired 417.8
  vessel NEC 417.8
pulmonic (congenital) 746.02
  infundibular 746.83
  subvalvular 746.83
pylorus (hypertrophic) 537.0
  adult 537.0
  congenital 750.5
  infantile 750.5
rectum (sphincter) (see also Stricture, rectum) 569.2
renal artery 440.1
salivary duct (any) 527.8
sphincter of Oddi (see also Obstruction, biliary) 576.2
spinal 724.00
  cervical 723.0
  lumbar, lumbosacral (without neurogenic claudication) 724.02
    with neurogenic claudication 724.03
  nerve (root) NEC 724.9
  specified region NEC 724.09
  thoracic, thoracolumbar 724.01

Stenosis — see also Stricture — continued
stomach, hourglass 537.6
subaortic 746.81
  hypertrophic (idiopathic) 425.11
supra (valvular)-aortic 747.22
trachea 519.19
  congenital 748.3
  syphilitic 095.8
  tuberculous (see also Tuberculosis) 012.8 ☑
tracheostomy 519.02
tricuspid (valve) (see also Endocarditis, tricuspid) 397.0
  congenital 746.1
  nonrheumatic 424.2
tubal 628.2
ureter (see also Stricture, ureter) 593.3
  congenital 753.29
urethra (see also Stricture, urethra) 598.9
vagina 623.2
  congenital 752.49
  in pregnancy or childbirth 654.7 ☑
    affecting fetus or newborn 763.89
    causing obstructed labor 660.2 ☑
      affecting fetus or newborn 763.1
valve (cardiac) (heart) (see also Endocarditis) 424.90
  congenital NEC 746.89
    aortic 746.3
    mitral 746.5
    pulmonary 746.02
    tricuspid 746.1
    urethra 753.6
valvular (see also Endocarditis) 424.90
  congenital NEC 746.89
    urethra 753.6
vascular graft or shunt 996.1
  atherosclerosis — see Arteriosclerosis, extremities
  embolism 996.74
  occlusion NEC 996.74
  thrombus 996.74
vena cava (inferior) (superior) 459.2
  congenital 747.49
ventricular shunt 996.2
vulva 624.8
Stent jail 996.72
Stercolith — see also Fecalith 560.32
  appendix 543.9
Stercoraceous, stercoral ulcer 569.82
  anus or rectum 569.41
Stereopsis, defective
  with fusion 368.33
  without fusion 368.32
Stereotypes NEC 307.3
Sterility
  female — see Infertility, female
  male (see also Infertility, male) 606.9
Sterilization, admission for V25.2
  status
    tubal ligation V26.51
    vasectomy V26.52
Sternalgia — see also Angina 413.9
Sternopagus 759.4
Sternum bifidum 756.3
Sternutation 784.99
Steroid
  effects (adverse) (iatrogenic)
    cushingoid
      correct substance properly administered 255.0
      overdose or wrong substance given or taken 962.0
    diabetes — see Diabetes, secondary
      correct substance properly administered 251.8
      overdose or wrong substance given or taken 962.0
    due to
      correct substance properly administered 255.8
      overdose or wrong substance given or taken 962.0
    fever
      correct substance properly administered 780.60

Steroid — continued
  effects — continued
    fever — continued
      overdose or wrong substance given or taken 962.0
    withdrawal
      correct substance properly administered 255.41
      overdose or wrong substance given or taken 962.0
  responder 365.03
Stevens-Johnson disease or syndrome (erythema multiforme exudativum) 695.13
  toxic epidermal necrolysis overlap (SJS-TEN overlap syndrome) 695.14
Stewart-Morel syndrome (hyperostosis frontalis interna) 733.3
Sticker's disease (erythema infectiosum) 057.0
Stickler syndrome 759.89
Sticky eye 372.03
Stieda's disease (calcification, knee joint) 726.62
Stiff
  back 724.8
  neck (see also Torticollis) 723.5
Stiff-baby 759.89
Stiff-man syndrome 333.91
Stiffness, joint NEC 719.50
  ankle 719.57
  back 724.8
  elbow 719.52
  finger 719.54
  hip 719.55
  knee 719.56
  multiple sites 719.59
  sacroiliac 724.6
  shoulder 719.51
  specified site NEC 719.58
  spine 724.9
  surgical fusion V45.4
  wrist 719.53
Stigmata, congenital syphilis 090.5
Stillbirth, stillborn NEC 779.9
Still's disease or syndrome 714.30
  adult onset 714.2
Stiller's disease (asthenia) 780.79
Still-Felty syndrome (rheumatoid arthritis with splenomegaly and leukopenia) 714.1
Stilling-Türk-Duane syndrome (ocular retraction syndrome) 378.71
Stimulation, ovary 256.1
Sting (animal) (bee) (fish) (insect) (jellyfish) (Portuguese man-o-war) (wasp) (venomous) 989.5
  anaphylactic shock or reaction 989.5
  plant 692.6
Stippled epiphyses 756.59
Stitch
  abscess 998.59
  burst (in external operation wound) (see also Dehiscence) 998.32
    internal 998.31
  in back 724.5
Stojano's (subcostal) **syndrome** 098.86
Stokes-Adams syndrome (syncope with heart block) 426.9
Stokes' disease (exophthalmic goiter) 242.0 ☑
Stokvis' (-Talma) disease (enterogenous cyanosis) 289.7
Stomach — see condition
Stoma malfunction
  colostomy 569.62
  cystostomy 596.82
    infection 596.81
    mechanical 596.82
    specified complication NEC 596.83
  enterostomy 569.62
  esophagostomy 530.87
  gastrostomy 536.42
  ileostomy 569.62
  nephrostomy 997.5
  tracheostomy 519.02
  ureterostomy 997.5
Stomatitis 528.00
  angular 528.5

☑ Additional Digit Required — Refer to the Tabular List for Digit Selection   ▽ Subterms under main terms may continue to next column or page

264 — Volume 2   ▶◀ Revised Text   ● New Line   ▲ Revised Code   2015 ICD-9-CM

Stomatitis — *continued*
    angular — *continued*
        due to dietary or vitamin deficiency 266.0
    aphthous 528.2
    bovine 059.11
    candidal 112.0
    catarrhal 528.00
    denture 528.9
    diphtheritic (membranous) 032.0
    due to
        dietary deficiency 266.0
        thrush 112.0
        vitamin deficiency 266.0
    epidemic 078.4
    epizootic 078.4
    follicular 528.00
    gangrenous 528.1
    herpetic 054.2
    herpetiformis 528.2
    malignant 528.00
    membranous acute 528.00
    monilial 112.0
    mycotic 112.0
    necrotic 528.1
        ulcerative 101
    necrotizing ulcerative 101
    parasitic 112.0
    septic 528.00
    specified NEC 528.09
    spirochetal 101
    suppurative (acute) 528.00
    ulcerative 528.00
        necrotizing 101
    ulceromembranous 101
    vesicular 528.00
        with exanthem 074.3
    Vincent's 101
Stomatocytosis 282.8
Stomatomycosis 112.0
Stomatorrhagia 528.9
Stone(s) — *see also* Calculus
    bladder 594.1
        diverticulum 594.0
    cystine 270.0
    heart syndrome (*see also* Failure, ventricular, left) 428.1
    kidney 592.0
    prostate 602.0
    pulp (dental) 522.2
    renal 592.0
    salivary duct or gland (any) 527.5
    ureter 592.1
    urethra (impacted) 594.2
    urinary (duct) (impacted) (passage) 592.9
        bladder 594.1
            diverticulum 594.0
        lower tract NEC 594.9
        specified site 594.8
    xanthine 277.2
Stonecutters' lung 502
    tuberculous (*see also* Tuberculosis) 011.4 ☑
Stonemasons'
    asthma, disease, or lung 502
        tuberculous (*see also* Tuberculosis) 011.4 ☑
    phthisis (*see also* Tuberculosis) 011.4 ☑
Stoppage
    bowel (*see also* Obstruction, intestine) 560.9
    heart (*see also* Arrest, cardiac) 427.5
    intestine (*see also* Obstruction, intestine) 560.9
    urine NEC (*see also* Retention, urine) 788.20
Storm, thyroid (apathetic) — *see also* Thyrotoxicosis 242.9 ☑
Strabismus (alternating) (congenital) (nonparalytic) 378.9
    concomitant (*see also* Heterotropia) 378.30
        convergent (*see also* Esotropia) 378.00
        divergent (*see also* Exotropia) 378.10
    convergent (*see also* Esotropia) 378.00
    divergent (*see also* Exotropia) 378.10
    due to adhesions, scars — *see* Strabismus, mechanical
    in neuromuscular disorder NEC 378.73
        intermittent 378.20

Strabismus — *continued*
    in neuromuscular disorder — *continued*
        intermittent — *continued*
            vertical 378.31
    latent 378.40
        convergent (esophoria) 378.41
        divergent (exophoria) 378.42
        vertical 378.43
    mechanical 378.60
        due to
            Brown's tendon sheath syndrome 378.61
            specified musculofascial disorder NEC 378.62
    paralytic 378.50
        third or oculomotor nerve (partial) 378.51
            total 378.52
        fourth or trochlear nerve 378.53
        sixth or abducens nerve 378.54
    specified type NEC 378.73
    vertical (hypertropia) 378.31
Strain — *see also* Sprain, by site
    eye NEC 368.13
    heart — *see* Disease, heart
    meaning gonorrhea — *see* Gonorrhea
    on urination 788.65
    physical NEC V62.89
    postural 729.90
    psychological NEC V62.89
Strands
    conjunctiva 372.62
    vitreous humor 379.25
Strangulation, strangulated 994.7
    appendix 543.9
    asphyxiation or suffocation by 994.7
    bladder neck 596.0
    bowel — *see* Strangulation, intestine
    colon — *see* Strangulation, intestine
    cord (umbilical) — *see* Compression, umbilical cord
    due to birth injury 767.8
    food or foreign body (*see also* Asphyxia, food) 933.1
    hemorrhoids 455.8
        external 455.5
        internal 455.2
    hernia (*see also* Hernia, by site, with obstruction)
        gangrenous — *see* Hernia, by site, with gangrene
    intestine (large) (small) 560.2
        with hernia (*see also* Hernia, by site, with obstruction)
            gangrenous — *see* Hernia, by site, with gangrene
        congenital (small) 751.1
            large 751.2
    mesentery 560.2
    mucus (*see also* Asphyxia, mucus) 933.1
        newborn 770.18
    omentum 560.2
    organ or site, congenital NEC — *see* Atresia
    ovary 620.8
        due to hernia 620.4
    penis 607.89
        foreign body 939.3
    rupture (*see also* Hernia, by site, with obstruction) 552.9
        gangrenous (*see also* Hernia, by site, with gangrene) 551.9
    stomach, due to hernia (*see also* Hernia, by site, with obstruction) 552.9
        with gangrene (*see also* Hernia, by site, with gangrene) 551.9
    umbilical cord — *see* Compression, umbilical cord
    vesicourethral orifice 596.0
Strangury 788.1
Strawberry
    gallbladder (*see also* Disease, gallbladder) 575.6
    mark 757.32
    tongue (red) (white) 529.3
Straw itch 133.8
Streak, ovarian 752.0

Strephosymbolia 315.01
    secondary to organic lesion 784.69
Streptobacillary fever 026.1
Streptobacillus moniliformis 026.1
Streptococcemia 038.0
Streptococcicosis — *see* Infection, streptococcal
Streptococcus, streptococcal — *see* condition
Streptoderma 686.00
Streptomycosis — *see* Actinomycosis
Streptothricosis — *see* Actinomycosis
Streptothrix — *see* Actinomycosis
Streptotrichosis — *see* Actinomycosis
Stress 308.9
    fracture — *see* Fracture, stress
    polycythemia 289.0
    reaction (gross) (*see also* Reaction, stress, acute) 308.9
Stretching, nerve — *see* Injury, nerve, by site
Striae (albicantes) (atrophicae) (cutis distensae) (distensae) 701.3
Striations of nails 703.8
Stricture — *see also* Stenosis 799.89
    ampulla of Vater 576.2
        with calculus, cholelithiasis, or stones — *see* Choledocholithiasis
    anus (sphincter) 569.2
        congenital 751.2
        infantile 751.2
    aorta (ascending) 747.22
        arch 747.10
        arteriosclerotic 440.0
        calcified 440.0
    aortic (valve) (*see also* Stenosis, aortic) 424.1
        congenital 746.3
    aqueduct of Sylvius (congenital) 742.3
        with spina bifida (*see also* Spina bifida) 741.0 ☑
        acquired 331.4
    artery 447.1
        basilar — *see* Narrowing, artery, basilar
        carotid (common) (internal) — *see* Narrowing, artery, carotid
        celiac 447.4
        cerebral 437.0
            congenital 747.81
            due to
                embolism (*see also* Embolism, brain) 434.1 ☑
                thrombus (*see also* Thrombosis, brain) 434.0 ☑
        congenital (peripheral) 747.60
            cerebral 747.81
            coronary 746.85
            gastrointestinal 747.61
            lower limb 747.64
            renal 747.62
            retinal 743.58
            specified NEC 747.69
            spinal 747.82
            umbilical 747.5
            upper limb 747.63
        coronary — *see* Arteriosclerosis, coronary
            congenital 746.85
        precerebral — *see* Narrowing, artery, precerebral NEC
        pulmonary (congenital) 747.31
            acquired 417.8
        renal 440.1
        vertebral — *see* Narrowing, artery, vertebral
    auditory canal (congenital) (external) 744.02
        acquired (*see also* Stricture, ear canal, acquired) 380.50
    bile duct or passage (any) (postoperative) (*see also* Obstruction, biliary) 576.2
        congenital 751.61
    bladder 596.89
        congenital 753.6
        neck 596.0
            congenital 753.6
    bowel (*see also* Obstruction, intestine) 560.9
    brain 348.89
    bronchus 519.19
        syphilitic 095.8

Stricture — *see also* Stenosis — *continued*
    cardia (stomach) 537.89
        congenital 750.7
    cardiac (*see also* Disease, heart)
        orifice (stomach) 537.89
    cardiovascular (*see also* Disease, cardiovascular) 429.2
    carotid artery — *see* Narrowing, artery, carotid
    cecum (*see also* Obstruction, intestine) 560.9
    cervix, cervical (canal) 622.4
        congenital 752.49
        in pregnancy or childbirth 654.6 ☑
            affecting fetus or newborn 763.89
            causing obstructed labor 660.2 ☑
                affecting fetus or newborn 763.1
    colon (*see also* Obstruction, intestine) 560.9
        congenital 751.2
    colostomy 569.62
    common bile duct (*see also* Obstruction, biliary) 576.2
        congenital 751.61
    coronary (artery) — *see* Arteriosclerosis, coronary
        congenital 746.85
    cystic duct (*see also* Obstruction, gallbladder) 575.2
        congenital 751.61
    cystostomy 596.83
    digestive organs NEC, congenital 751.8
    duodenum 537.3
        congenital 751.1
    ear canal (external) (congenital) 744.02
        acquired 380.50
            secondary to
                inflammation 380.53
                surgery 380.52
                trauma 380.51
    ejaculatory duct 608.85
    enterostomy 569.62
    esophagostomy 530.87
    esophagus (corrosive) (peptic) 530.3
        congenital 750.3
        syphilitic 095.8
            congenital 090.5
    eustachian tube (*see also* Obstruction, Eustachian tube) 381.60
        congenital 744.24
    fallopian tube 628.2
        gonococcal (chronic) 098.37
            acute 098.17
        tuberculous (*see also* Tuberculosis) 016.6 ☑
    gallbladder (*see also* Obstruction, gallbladder) 575.2
        congenital 751.69
    glottis 478.74
    heart (*see also* Disease, heart)
        congenital NEC 746.89
        valve (*see also* Endocarditis)
            congenital NEC 746.89
                aortic 746.3
                mitral 746.5
                pulmonary 746.02
                tricuspid 746.1
    hepatic duct (*see also* Obstruction, biliary) 576.2
    hourglass, of stomach 537.6
    hymen 623.3
    hypopharynx 478.29
    intestine (*see also* Obstruction, intestine) 560.9
        congenital (small) 751.1
            large 751.2
        ischemic 557.1
    lacrimal
        canaliculi 375.53
            congenital 743.65
        punctum 375.52
            congenital 743.65
        sac 375.54
            congenital 743.65
    lacrimonasal duct 375.56
        congenital 743.65
        neonatal 375.55
    larynx 478.79

☑ **Additional Digit Required** — Refer to the Tabular List for Digit Selection   ▽ **Subterms under main terms may continue to next column or page**

2015 ICD-9-CM   ▶◀ Revised Text   ● New Line   ▲ Revised Code   Volume 2 — 265

Stricture — *see also* Stenosis — *continued*
larynx — *continued*
   congenital 748.3
   syphilitic 095.8
      congenital 090.5
lung 518.89
meatus
   ear (congenital) 744.02
      acquired (*see also* Stricture, ear canal, acquired) 380.50
   osseous (congenital) (ear) 744.03
      acquired (*see also* Stricture, ear canal, acquired) 380.50
   urinarius (*see also* Stricture, urethra) 598.9
      congenital 753.6
mitral (valve) (*see also* Stenosis, mitral) 394.0
   congenital 746.5
   specified cause, except rheumatic 424.0
myocardium, myocardial (*see also* Degeneration, myocardial) 429.1
   hypertrophic subaortic (idiopathic) 425.11
nares (anterior) (posterior) 478.19
   congenital 748.0
nasal duct 375.56
   congenital 743.65
   neonatal 375.55
nasolacrimal duct 375.56
   congenital 743.65
   neonatal 375.55
nasopharynx 478.29
   syphilitic 095.8
nephrostomy 997.5
nose 478.19
   congenital 748.0
nostril (anterior) (posterior) 478.19
   congenital 748.0
organ or site, congenital NEC — *see* Atresia
osseous meatus (congenital) (ear) 744.03
   acquired (*see also* Stricture, ear canal, acquired) 380.50
os uteri (*see also* Stricture, cervix) 622.4
oviduct — *see* Stricture, fallopian tube
pelviureteric junction 593.3
pharynx (dilation) 478.29
prostate 602.8
pulmonary, pulmonic
   artery (congenital) 747.31
      acquired 417.8
      noncongenital 417.8
   infundibulum (congenital) 746.83
   valve (*see also* Endocarditis, pulmonary) 424.3
      congenital 746.02
   vein (congenital) 747.49
      acquired 417.8
   vessel NEC 417.8
punctum lacrimale 375.52
   congenital 743.65
pylorus (hypertrophic) 537.0
   adult 537.0
   congenital 750.5
   infantile 750.5
rectosigmoid 569.89
rectum (sphincter) 569.2
   congenital 751.2
   due to
      chemical burn 947.3
      irradiation 569.2
      lymphogranuloma venereum 099.1
   gonococcal 098.7
   inflammatory 099.1
   syphilitic 095.8
   tuberculous (*see also* Tuberculosis) 014.8 ☑
renal artery 440.1
salivary duct or gland (any) 527.8
sigmoid (flexure) (*see also* Obstruction, intestine) 560.9
spermatic cord 608.85
stoma (following) (of)
   colostomy 569.62
   cystostomy 596.83
   enterostomy 569.62
   esophagostomy 530.87

Stricture — *see also* Stenosis — *continued*
stoma — *continued*
   gastrostomy 536.42
   ileostomy 569.62
   nephrostomy 997.5
   tracheostomy 519.02
   ureterostomy 997.5
stomach 537.89
   congenital 750.7
   hourglass 537.6
subaortic 746.81
   hypertrophic (acquired) (idiopathic) 425.11
subglottic 478.74
syphilitic NEC 095.8
tendon (sheath) 727.81
trachea 519.19
   congenital 748.3
   syphilitic 095.8
   tuberculous (*see also* Tuberculosis) 012.8 ☑
tracheostomy 519.02
tricuspid (valve) (*see also* Endocarditis, tricuspid) 397.0
   congenital 746.1
   nonrheumatic 424.2
tunica vaginalis 608.85
ureter (postoperative) 593.3
   congenital 753.29
   tuberculous (*see also* Tuberculosis) 016.2 ☑
ureteropelvic junction 593.3
   congenital 753.21
ureterovesical orifice 593.3
   congenital 753.22
urethra (anterior) (meatal) (organic) (posterior) (spasmodic) 598.9
   associated with schistosomiasis (*see also* Schistosomiasis) 120.9 [598.01]
   congenital (valvular) 753.6
   due to
      infection 598.00
         syphilis 095.8 [598.01]
      trauma 598.1
   gonococcal 098.2 [598.01]
   gonorrheal 098.2 [598.01]
   infective 598.00
   late effect of injury 598.1
   postcatheterization 598.2
   postobstetric 598.1
   postoperative 598.2
   specified cause NEC 598.8
   syphilitic 095.8 [598.01]
   traumatic 598.1
   valvular, congenital 753.6
urinary meatus (*see also* Stricture, urethra) 598.9
   congenital 753.6
uterus, uterine 621.5
   os (external) (internal) — *see* Stricture, cervix
vagina (outlet) 623.2
   congenital 752.49
valve (cardiac) (heart) (*see also* Endocarditis) 424.90
   congenital (cardiac) (heart) NEC 746.89
      aortic 746.3
      mitral 746.5
      pulmonary 746.02
      tricuspid 746.1
      urethra 753.6
valvular (*see also* Endocarditis) 424.90
vascular graft or shunt 996.1
   atherosclerosis — *see* Arteriosclerosis, extremities
   embolism 996.74
   occlusion NEC 996.74
   thrombus 996.74
vas deferens 608.85
   congenital 752.89
vein 459.2
vena cava (inferior) (superior) NEC 459.2
   congenital 747.49
ventricular shunt 996.2
vesicourethral orifice 596.0
   congenital 753.6

Stricture — *see also* Stenosis — *continued*
vulva (acquired) 624.8
Stridor 786.1
   congenital (larynx) 748.3
Stridulous — *see* condition
Strippling of nails 703.8
Stroke 434.91
   apoplectic (*see also* Disease, cerebrovascular, acute) 436
   brain — *see* Infarct, brain
   embolic 434.11
   epileptic — *see* Epilepsy
   healed or old V12.54
   heart — *see* Disease, heart
   heat 992.0
   hemorrhagic — *see* Hemorrhage, brain
   iatrogenic 997.02
   in evolution 434.91
   ischemic 434.91
   late effect — *see* Late effect(s) (of) cerebrovascular disease
   lightning 994.0
   paralytic — *see* Infarct, brain
   postoperative 997.02
   progressive 435.9
   thrombotic 434.01
Stromatosis, endometrial (M8931/1) 236.0
Strong pulse 785.9
Strongyloides stercoralis infestation 127.2
Strongyloidiasis 127.2
Strongyloidosis 127.2
Strongylus (gibsoni) infestation 127.7
Strophulus (newborn) 779.89
   pruriginosus 698.2
Struck by lightning 994.0
Struma — *see also* Goiter 240.9
   fibrosa 245.3
   Hashimoto (struma lymphomatosa) 245.2
   lymphomatosa 245.2
   nodosa (simplex) 241.9
      endemic 241.9
      multinodular 241.1
      sporadic 241.9
      toxic or with hyperthyroidism 242.3 ☑
         multinodular 242.2 ☑
         uninodular 242.1 ☑
      toxicosa 242.3 ☑
         multinodular 242.2 ☑
         uninodular 242.1 ☑
      uninodular 241.0
   ovarii (M9090/0) 220
      and carcinoid (M9091/1) 236.2
      malignant (M9090/3) 183.0
   Riedel's (ligneous thyroiditis) 245.3
   scrofulous (*see also* Tuberculosis) 017.2 ☑
   tuberculous (*see also* Tuberculosis) 017.2 ☑
      abscess 017.2 ☑
      adenitis 017.2 ☑
      lymphangitis 017.2 ☑
      ulcer 017.2 ☑
Strumipriva cachexia — *see also* Hypothyroidism 244.9
Strümpell-Marie disease or spine (ankylosing spondylitis) 720.0
Strümpell-Westphal pseudosclerosis (hepatolenticular degeneration) 275.1
Stuart's disease (congenital factor X deficiency) — *see also* Defect, coagulation 286.3
Stuart-Prower factor deficiency (congenital factor X deficiency) — *see also* Defect, coagulation 286.3
Students' elbow 727.2
Stuffy nose 478.19
Stump — *see also* Amputation
   cervix, cervical (healed) 622.8
Stupor 780.09
   catatonic (*see also* Schizophrenia) 295.2 ☑
   circular (*see also* Psychosis, manic-depressive, circular) 296.7
   manic 296.89
   manic-depressive (*see also* Psychosis, affective) 296.89
   mental (anergic) (delusional) 298.9
   psychogenic 298.8
   reaction to exceptional stress (transient) 308.2

Stupor — *continued*
   traumatic NEC (*see also* Injury, intracranial)
      with spinal (cord)
         lesion — *see* Injury, spinal, by site
         shock — *see* Injury, spinal, by site
Sturge (-Weber) (-Dimitri) disease or syndrome (encephalocutaneous angiomatosis) 759.6
Sturge-Kalischer-Weber syndrome (encephalocutaneous angiomatosis) 759.6
Stuttering 315.35
   adult onset 307.0
   childhood onset 315.35
   due to late effect of cerebrovascular disease (*see also* Late effect(s) (of) cerebrovascular disease) 438.14
   in conditions classified elsewhere 784.52
Sty, stye 373.11
   external 373.11
   internal 373.12
   meibomian 373.12
Subacidity, gastric 536.8
   psychogenic 306.4
Subacute — *see* condition
Subarachnoid — *see* condition
Subclavian steal syndrome 435.2
Subcortical — *see* condition
Subcostal syndrome 098.86
   nerve compression 354.8
Subcutaneous, subcuticular — *see* condition
Subdelirium 293.1
Subdural — *see* condition
Subendocardium — *see* condition
Subependymoma (M9383/1) 237.5
Suberosis 495.3
Subglossitis — *see* Glossitis
Subhemophilia 286.0
Subinvolution (uterus) 621.1
   breast (postlactational) (postpartum) 611.89
   chronic 621.1
   puerperal, postpartum 674.8 ☑
Sublingual — *see* condition
Sublinguitis 527.2
Subluxation — *see also* Dislocation, by site
   congenital NEC (*see also* Malposition, congenital)
      hip (unilateral) 754.32
         with dislocation of other hip 754.35
         bilateral 754.33
      joint
         lower limb 755.69
         shoulder 755.59
         upper limb 755.59
      lower limb (joint) 755.69
      shoulder (joint) 755.59
      upper limb (joint) 755.59
   lens 379.32
      anterior 379.33
      posterior 379.34
   radial head 832.2
   rotary, cervical region of spine — *see* Fracture, vertebra, cervical
Submaxillary — *see* condition
Submersion (fatal) (nonfatal) 994.1
Submissiveness (undue), in child 313.0
Submucous — *see* condition
Subnormal, subnormality
   accommodation (*see also* Disorder, accommodation) 367.9
   mental (*see also* Disability, intellectual) 319
      mild 317
      moderate 318.0
      profound 318.2
      severe 318.1
   temperature (accidental) 991.6
      not associated with low environmental temperature 780.99
Subphrenic — *see* condition
Subscapular nerve — *see* condition
Subseptus uterus 752.35
Subsiding appendicitis 542
Substance abuse in family V61.42
Substernal thyroid — *see* Goiter 240.9
   congenital 759.2
Substitution disorder 300.11
Subtentorial — *see* condition

☑ Additional Digit Required — Refer to the Tabular List for Digit Selection   ▽ Subterms under main terms may continue to next column or page

266 — Volume 2   ▶◀ Revised Text   ● New Line   ▲ Revised Code   2015 ICD-9-CM

Subtertian
- fever 084.0
- malaria (fever) 084.0

Subthyroidism (acquired) — see also Hypothyroidism 244.9
- congenital 243

Succenturiata placenta — see Placenta, abnormal

Succussion sounds, chest 786.7

Sucking thumb, child 307.9

Sudamen 705.1

Sudamina 705.1

Sudanese kala-azar 085.0

Sudden
- death, cause unknown (less than 24 hours) 798.1
  - cardiac (SCD)
    - family history of V17.41
    - personal history of, successfully resuscitated V12.53
  - during childbirth 669.9 ☑
  - infant 798.0
  - puerperal, postpartum 674.9 ☑
- hearing loss NEC 388.2
- heart failure (see also Failure, heart) 428.9
- infant death syndrome 798.0

Sudeck's atrophy, disease, or syndrome 733.7

SUDS (sudden unexplained death) 798.2

Suffocation — see also Asphyxia 799.01
- by
  - bed clothes 994.7
  - bunny bag 994.7
  - cave-in 994.7
  - constriction 994.7
  - drowning 994.1
  - inhalation
    - food or foreign body (see also Asphyxia, food or foreign body) 933.1
    - oil or gasoline (see also Asphyxia, food or foreign body) 933.1
  - overlying 994.7
  - plastic bag 994.7
  - pressure 994.7
  - strangulation 994.7
- during birth 768.1
- mechanical 994.7

Sugar
- blood
  - high 790.29
  - low 251.2
- in urine 791.5

Suicide, suicidal (attempted)
- by poisoning — see Table of Drugs and Chemicals
- ideation V62.84
- risk 300.9
- tendencies 300.9
- trauma NEC (see also nature and site of injury) 959.9

Suipestifer infection — see also Infection, Salmonella 003.9

Sulfatidosis 330.0

Sulfhemoglobinemia, sulphemoglobinemia (acquired) (congenital) 289.7

Sumatran mite fever 081.2

Summer — see condition

Sunburn 692.71
- first degree 692.71
- second degree 692.76
- third degree 692.77
- dermatitis 692.71
- due to
  - other ultraviolet radiation 692.82
  - tanning bed 692.82

SUNCT (short lasting unilateral neuralgiform headache with conjunctival injection and tearing) 339.05

Sunken
- acetabulum 718.85
- fontanels 756.0

Sunstroke 992.0

Superfecundation 651.9 ☑
- with fetal loss and retention of one or more fetus(es) 651.6 ☑
- following (elective) fetal reduction 651.7 ☑

Superfetation 651.9 ☑
- with fetal loss and retention of one or more fetus(es) 651.6 ☑
- following (elective) fetal reduction 651.7 ☑

Superinvolution uterus 621.8

Supernumerary (congenital)
- aortic cusps 746.89
- auditory ossicles 744.04
- bone 756.9
- breast 757.6
- carpal bones 755.56
- cusps, heart valve NEC 746.89
  - mitral 746.5
  - pulmonary 746.09
- digit(s) 755.00
  - finger 755.01
  - toe 755.02
- ear (lobule) 744.1
- fallopian tube 752.19
- finger 755.01
- hymen 752.49
- kidney 753.3
- lacrimal glands 743.64
- lacrimonasal duct 743.65
- lobule (ear) 744.1
- mitral cusps 746.5
- muscle 756.82
- nipples 757.6
- organ or site NEC — see Accessory
- ossicles, auditory 744.04
- ovary 752.0
- oviduct 752.19
- pulmonic cusps 746.09
- rib 756.3
  - cervical or first 756.2
    - syndrome 756.2
- roots (of teeth) 520.2
- spinal vertebra 756.19
- spleen 759.0
- tarsal bones 755.67
- teeth 520.1
  - causing crowding 524.31
- testis 752.89
- thumb 755.01
- toe 755.02
- uterus 752.2
- vagina 752.49
- vertebra 756.19

Supervision (of)
- contraceptive method previously prescribed V25.40
  - intrauterine device V25.42
  - oral contraceptive (pill) V25.41
  - specified type NEC V25.49
  - subdermal implantable contraceptive V25.43
- dietary (for) V65.3
  - allergy (food) V65.3
  - colitis V65.3
  - diabetes mellitus V65.3
  - food allergy intolerance V65.3
  - gastritis V65.3
  - hypercholesterolemia V65.3
  - hypoglycemia V65.3
  - intolerance (food) V65.3
  - obesity V65.3
  - specified NEC V65.3
- lactation V24.1
- newborn health
  - 8 to 28 days old V20.32
  - under 8 days old V20.31
- pregnancy — see Pregnancy, supervision of

Supplemental teeth 520.1
- causing crowding 524.31

Suppression
- binocular vision 368.31
- lactation 676.5 ☑
- menstruation 626.8
- ovarian secretion 256.39
- renal 586
- urinary secretion 788.5
- urine 788.5

Suppuration, suppurative — see also condition

Suppuration, suppurative — see also condition — continued
- accessory sinus (chronic) (see also Sinusitis) 473.9
- adrenal gland 255.8
- antrum (chronic) (see also Sinusitis, maxillary) 473.0
- bladder (see also Cystitis) 595.89
- bowel 569.89
- brain 324.0
  - late effect 326
- breast 611.0
  - puerperal, postpartum 675.1 ☑
- dental periosteum 526.5
- diffuse (skin) 686.00
- ear (middle) (see also Otitis media) 382.4
  - external (see also Otitis, externa) 380.10
  - internal 386.33
- ethmoidal (sinus) (chronic) (see also Sinusitis, ethmoidal) 473.2
- fallopian tube (see also Salpingo-oophoritis) 614.2
- frontal (sinus) (chronic) (see also Sinusitis, frontal) 473.1
- gallbladder (see also Cholecystitis, acute) 575.0
- gum 523.30
- hernial sac — see Hernia, by site
- intestine 569.89
- joint (see also Arthritis, suppurative) 711.0 ☑
- labyrinthine 386.33
- lung 513.0
- mammary gland 611.0
  - puerperal, postpartum 675.1 ☑
- maxilla, maxillary 526.4
  - sinus (chronic) (see also Sinusitis, maxillary) 473.0
- muscle 728.0
- nasal sinus (chronic) (see also Sinusitis) 473.9
- pancreas 577.0
- parotid gland 527.2
- pelvis, pelvic
  - female (see also Disease, pelvis, inflammatory) 614.4
    - acute 614.3
  - male (see also Peritonitis) 567.21
- pericranial (see also Osteomyelitis) 730.2 ☑
- salivary duct or gland (any) 527.2
- sinus (nasal) (see also Sinusitis) 473.9
- sphenoidal (sinus) (chronic) (see also Sinusitis, sphenoidal) 473.3
- thymus (gland) 254.1
- thyroid (gland) 245.0
- tonsil 474.8
- uterus (see also Endometritis) 615.9
- vagina 616.10
- wound (see also Wound, open, by site, complicated)
  - dislocation — see Dislocation, by site, compound
  - fracture — see Fracture, by site, open
  - scratch or other superficial injury — see Injury, superficial, by site

Supraeruption, teeth 524.34

Supraglottitis 464.50
- with obstruction 464.51

Suprapubic drainage 596.89

Suprarenal (gland) — see condition

Suprascapular nerve — see condition

Suprasellar — see condition

Supraspinatus syndrome 726.10

Surfer knots 919.8
- infected 919.9

Surgery
- cosmetic NEC V50.1
  - breast reconstruction following mastectomy V51.0
  - following healed injury or operation V51.8
  - hair transplant V50.0
- elective V50.9
  - breast
    - augmentation or reduction V50.1
    - reconstruction following mastectomy V51.0

Surgery — continued
- elective — continued
  - circumcision, ritual or routine (in absence of medical indication) V50.2
  - cosmetic NEC V50.1
  - ear piercing V50.3
  - face-lift V50.1
  - following healed injury or operation V51.8
  - hair transplant V50.0
- not done because of
  - contraindication V64.1
  - patient's decision V64.2
  - specified reason NEC V64.3
- plastic
  - breast
    - augmentation or reduction V50.1
    - reconstruction following mastectomy V51.0
  - cosmetic V50.1
  - face-lift V50.1
  - following healed injury or operation V51.8
  - repair of scarred tissue (following healed injury or operation) V51.8
  - specified type NEC V50.8
- previous, in pregnancy or childbirth
  - cervix 654.6 ☑
    - affecting fetus or newborn (see also Newborn, affected by) 760.63
    - causing obstructed labor 660.2 ☑
      - affecting fetus or newborn 763.1
  - pelvic soft tissues NEC 654.9 ☑
    - affecting fetus or newborn (see also Newborn, affected by) 760.63
    - causing obstructed labor 660.2 ☑
      - affecting fetus or newborn 763.1
  - perineum or vulva 654.8 ☑
  - uterus NEC 654.9 ☑
    - affecting fetus or newborn (see also Newborn, affected by) 760.63
    - causing obstructed labor 660.2 ☑
      - affecting fetus or newborn 763.1
    - due to previous cesarean delivery 654.2 ☑
  - vagina 654.7 ☑

Surgical
- abortion — see Abortion, legal
- emphysema 998.81
- kidney (see also Pyelitis) 590.80
- operation NEC 799.9
- procedures, complication or misadventure — see Complications, surgical procedure
- shock 998.00

Survey
- fetal anatomic V28.81

Susceptibility
- genetic
  - to
    - MEN (multiple endocrine neoplasia) V84.81
    - neoplasia
      - multiple endocrine (MEN) V84.81
    - neoplasm
      - malignant, of
        - breast V84.01
        - endometrium V84.04
        - other V84.09
        - ovary V84.02
        - prostate V84.03
      - specified disease V84.89

Suspected condition, ruled out — see also Observation, suspected V71.9
- specified condition NEC V71.89

Suspended uterus, in pregnancy or childbirth 654.4 ☑
- affecting fetus or newborn 763.89
- causing obstructed labor 660.2 ☑
  - affecting fetus or newborn 763.1

Sutton and Gull's disease (arteriolar nephrosclerosis) — see also Hypertension, kidney 403.90

Sutton's disease 709.09

☑ Additional Digit Required — Refer to the Tabular List for Digit Selection   ▽ Subterms under main terms may continue to next column or page

2015 ICD-9-CM   ▶◀ Revised Text   ● New Line   ▲ Revised Code   Volume 2 — 267

Suture

burst (in external operation wound) (see also Dehiscence) 998.32
  internal 998.31
inadvertently left in operation wound 998.4
removal V58.32
Shirodkar, in pregnancy (with or without cervical incompetence) 654.5 ☑

Swab inadvertently left in operation wound 998.4

Swallowed, swallowing
difficulty (see also Dysphagia) 787.20
foreign body NEC (see also Foreign body) 938

Swamp fever 100.89

Swan neck hand (intrinsic) 736.09

Sweat(s), sweating
disease or sickness 078.2
excessive (see also Hyperhidrosis) 780.8
fetid 705.89
fever 078.2
gland disease 705.9
  specified type NEC 705.89
miliary 078.2
night 780.8

Sweeley-Klionsky disease (angiokeratoma corporis diffusum) 272.7

Sweet's syndrome (acute febrile neutrophilic dermatosis) 695.89

Swelling 782.3
abdominal (not referable to specific organ) 789.3 ☑
adrenal gland, cloudy 255.8
ankle 719.07
anus 787.99
arm 729.81
breast 611.72
Calabar 125.2
cervical gland 785.6
cheek 784.2
chest 786.6
ear 388.8
epigastric 789.3 ☑
extremity (lower) (upper) 729.81
eye 379.92
female genital organ 625.8
finger 729.81
foot 729.81
glands 785.6
gum 784.2
hand 729.81
head 784.2
inflammatory — see Inflammation
joint (see also Effusion, joint) 719.0 ☑
  tuberculous — see Tuberculosis, joint
kidney, cloudy 593.89
leg 729.81
limb 729.81
liver 573.8
lung 786.6
lymph nodes 785.6
mediastinal 786.6
mouth 784.2
muscle (limb) 729.81
neck 784.2
nose or sinus 784.2
palate 784.2
pelvis 789.3 ☑
penis 607.83
perineum 625.8
rectum 787.99
scrotum 608.86
skin 782.2
splenic (see also Splenomegaly) 789.2
substernal 786.6
superficial, localized (skin) 782.2
testicle 608.86
throat 784.2
toe 729.81
tongue 784.2
tubular (see also Disease, renal) 593.9
umbilicus 789.3 ☑
uterus 625.8
vagina 625.8
vulva 625.8

Swelling — continued
wandering, due to Gnathostoma (spinigerum) 128.1
white — see Tuberculosis, arthritis

Swift's disease 985.0

Swimmers'
ear (acute) 380.12
itch 120.3

Swimming in the head 780.4

Swollen — see also Swelling
glands 785.6

Swyer-James syndrome (unilateral hyperlucent lung) 492.8

Swyer's syndrome (XY pure gonadal dysgenesis) 752.7

Sycosis 704.8
barbae (not parasitic) 704.8
contagiosa 110.0
lupoid 704.8
mycotic 110.0
parasitic 110.0
vulgaris 704.8

Sydenham's chorea — see Chorea, Sydenham's

Sylvatic yellow fever 060.0

Sylvest's disease (epidemic pleurodynia) 074.1

Symblepharon 372.63
congenital 743.62

Symonds' syndrome 348.2

Sympathetic — see condition

Sympatheticotonia — see also Neuropathy, peripheral, autonomic 337.9

Sympathicoblastoma (M9500/3)
specified site — see Neoplasm, by site, malignant
unspecified site 194.0

Sympathicogonioma (M9500/3) — see Sympathicoblastoma

Sympathoblastoma (M9500/3) — see Sympathicoblastoma

Sympathogonioma (M9500/3) — see Sympathicoblastoma

Symphalangy — see also Syndactylism 755.10

Symptoms, specified (general) NEC 780.99
abdomen NEC 789.9
bone NEC 733.90
breast NEC 611.79
cardiac NEC 785.9
cardiovascular NEC 785.9
chest NEC 786.9
cognition 799.59
development NEC 783.9
digestive system NEC 787.99
emotional state NEC 799.29
eye NEC 379.99
gastrointestinal tract NEC 787.99
genital organs NEC
  female 625.9
  male 608.9
head and neck NEC 784.99
heart NEC 785.9
jaw 784.92
joint NEC 719.60
  ankle 719.67
  elbow 719.62
  foot 719.67
  hand 719.64
  hip 719.65
  knee 719.66
  multiple sites 719.69
  pelvic region 719.65
  shoulder (region) 719.61
  specified site NEC 719.68
  temporomandibular 524.69
  wrist 719.63
larynx NEC 784.99
limbs NEC 729.89
lymphatic system NEC 785.9
maxilla 784.92
menopausal 627.2
metabolism NEC 783.9
mouth NEC 528.9
muscle NEC 728.9
musculoskeletal NEC 781.99
  limbs NEC 729.89
nervous system NEC 781.99

Symptoms, specified — continued
neurotic NEC 300.9
nutrition, metabolism, and development NEC 783.9
pelvis NEC 789.9
  female 625.9
peritoneum NEC 789.9
respiratory system NEC 786.9
skin and integument NEC 782.9
subcutaneous tissue NEC 782.9
throat NEC 784.99
tonsil NEC 784.99
urinary system NEC 788.99
vascular NEC 785.9

Sympus 759.89

Synarthrosis 719.80
ankle 719.87
elbow 719.82
foot 719.87
hand 719.84
hip 719.85
knee 719.86
multiple sites 719.89
pelvic region 719.85
shoulder (region) 719.81
specified site NEC 719.88
wrist 719.83

Syncephalus 759.4

Synchondrosis 756.9
abnormal (congenital) 756.9
ischiopubic (van Neck's) 732.1

Synchysis (senile) (vitreous humor) 379.21
scintillans 379.22

Syncope (near) (pre-) 780.2
anginosa 413.9
bradycardia 427.89
cardiac 780.2
carotid sinus 337.01
complicating delivery 669.2 ☑
due to lumbar puncture 349.0
fatal 798.1
heart 780.2
heat 992.1
laryngeal 786.2
tussive 786.2
vasoconstriction 780.2
vasodepressor 780.2
vasomotor 780.2
vasovagal 780.2

Syncytial infarct — see Placenta, abnormal

Syndactylism, syndactyly (multiple sites) 755.10
fingers (without fusion of bone) 755.11
  with fusion of bone 755.12
toes (without fusion of bone) 755.13
  with fusion of bone 755.14

Syndrome — see also Disease
with 5q deletion 238.74
5q minus 238.74
abdominal
  acute 789.0 ☑
  migraine 346.2 ☑
  muscle deficiency 756.79
Abercrombie's (amyloid degeneration) 277.39
abnormal innervation 374.43
abstinence
  alcohol 291.81
  drug 292.0
  neonatal 779.5
Abt-Letterer-Siwe (acute histiocytosis X) (M9722/3) 202.5 ☑
Achard-Thiers (adrenogenital) 255.2
acid pulmonary aspiration 997.39
  obstetric (Mendelson's) 668.0 ☑
acquired immune deficiency 042
acquired immunodeficiency 042
acrocephalosyndactylism 755.55
acute abdominal 789.0 ☑
acute chest 517.3
acute coronary 411.1
Adair-Dighton (brittle bones and blue sclera, deafness) 756.51
Adams-Stokes (-Morgagni) (syncope with heart block) 426.9
Addisonian 255.41

Syndrome — see also Disease — continued
Adie (-Holmes) (pupil) 379.46
adiposogenital 253.8
adrenal
  hemorrhage 036.3
  meningococcic 036.3
adrenocortical 255.3
adrenogenital (acquired) (congenital) 255.2
  feminizing 255.2
  iatrogenic 760.79
  virilism (acquired) (congenital) 255.2
affective organic NEC 293.89
  drug-induced 292.84
afferent loop NEC 537.89
African macroglobulinemia 273.3
Ahumada-Del Castillo (nonpuerperal galactorrhea and amenorrhea) 253.1
air blast concussion — see Injury, internal, by site
Alagille 759.89
Albright (-Martin) (pseudohypoparathyroidism) 275.49
Albright-McCune-Sternberg (osteitis fibrosa disseminata) 756.59
alcohol withdrawal 291.81
Alder's (leukocyte granulation anomaly) 288.2
Aldrich (-Wiskott) (eczema-thrombocytopenia) 279.12
Alibert-Bazin (mycosis fungoides) (M9700/3) 202.1 ☑
Alice in Wonderland 293.89
alien hand 781.8
Allen-Masters 620.6
Alligator baby (ichthyosis congenita) 757.1
Alport's (hereditary hematuria-nephropathy-deafness) 759.89
Alvarez (transient cerebral ischemia) 435.9
alveolar capillary block 516.8
Alzheimer's 331.0
  with dementia — see Alzheimer's, dementia
amnestic (confabulatory) 294.0
  alcohol-induced persisting 291.1
  drug-induced 292.83
  posttraumatic 294.0
amotivational 292.89
amyostatic 275.1
amyotrophic lateral sclerosis 335.20
androgen insensitivity 259.51
  partial 259.52
Angelman 759.89
angina (see also Angina) 413.9
ankyloglossia superior 750.0
anterior
  chest wall 786.52
  compartment (tibial) 958.8
  spinal artery 433.8 ☑
    compression 721.1
  tibial (compartment) 958.8
antibody deficiency 279.00
  agammaglobulinemic 279.00
  congenital 279.04
  hypogammaglobulinemic 279.00
anticardiolipin antibody 289.81
antimongolism 758.39
antiphospholipid antibody 289.81
Anton (-Babinski) (hemiasomatognosia) 307.9
anxiety (see also Anxiety) 300.00
  organic 293.84
aortic
  arch 446.7
  bifurcation (occlusion) 444.09
  ring 747.21
Apert's (acrocephalosyndactyly) 755.55
Apert-Gallais (adrenogenital) 255.2
aphasia-apraxia-alexia 784.69
apical ballooning 429.83
"approximate answers" 300.16
arcuate ligament (-celiac axis) 447.4
arcus aortae 446.7
arc welders' 370.24
argentaffin, argintaffinoma 259.2
Argonz-Del Castillo (nonpuerperal galactorrhea and amenorrhea) 253.1

☑ Additional Digit Required — Refer to the Tabular List for Digit Selection
  Subterms under main terms may continue to next column or page

268 — Volume 2
▶◀ Revised Text
● New Line
▲ Revised Code
2015 ICD-9-CM

Syndrome — *see also* Disease — *continued*

Argyll Robertson's (syphilitic) 094.89
  nonsyphilitic 379.45
Armenian 277.31
arm-shoulder (*see also* Neuropathy, peripheral, autonomic) 337.9
Arnold-Chiari (*see also* Spina bifida) 741.0 ☑
  type I 348.4
  type II 741.0 ☑
  type III 742.0
  type IV 742.2
Arrillaga-Ayerza (pulmonary artery sclerosis with pulmonary hypertension) 416.0
arteriomesenteric duodenum occlusion 537.89
arteriovenous steal 996.73
arteritis, young female (obliterative brachiocephalic) 446.7
aseptic meningitis — *see* Meningitis, aseptic
Asherman's 621.5
Asperger's 299.8 ☑
asphyctic (*see also* Anxiety) 300.00
aspiration, of newborn (massive) 770.18
  meconium 770.12
ataxia-telangiectasia 334.8
Audry's (acropachyderma) 757.39
auriculotemporal 350.8
autoimmune lymphoproliferative (ALPS) 279.41
autosomal (*see also* Abnormal, autosomes NEC)
  deletion 758.39
    5p 758.31
    22q11.2 758.32
Avellis' 344.89
Axenfeld's 743.44
Ayerza (-Arrillaga) (pulmonary artery sclerosis with pulmonary hypertension) 416.0
Baader's (erythema multiforme exudativum) 695.19
Baastrup's 721.5
Babinski (-Vaquez) (cardiovascular syphilis) 093.89
Babinski-Fröhlich (adiposogenital dystrophy) 253.8
Babinski-Nageotte 344.89
Bagratuni's (temporal arteritis) 446.5
Bakwin-Krida (craniometaphyseal dysplasia) 756.89
Balint's (psychic paralysis of visual disorientation) 368.16
Ballantyne (-Runge) (postmaturity) 766.22
ballooning posterior leaflet 424.0
Banti's — *see* Cirrhosis, liver
Bardet-Biedl (obesity, polydactyly, and intellectual disabiilties) 759.89
Bard-Pic's (carcinoma, head of pancreas) 157.0
Barlow's (mitral valve prolapse) 424.0
Barlow (-Möller) (infantile scurvy) 267
Baron Munchausen's 301.51
Barré-Guillain 357.0
Barré-Liéou (posterior cervical sympathetic) 723.2
Barrett's (chronic peptic ulcer of esophagus) 530.85
Bársony-Polgár (corkscrew esophagus) 530.5
Bársony-Teschendorf (corkscrew esophagus) 530.5
Barth 759.89
Bartter's (secondary hyperaldosteronism with juxtaglomerular hyperplasia) 255.13
basal cell nevus 759.89
Basedow's (exophthalmic goiter) 242.0 ☑
basilar artery 435.0
basofrontal 377.04
Bassen-Kornzweig (abetalipoproteinemia) 272.5
Batten-Steinert 359.21
battered
  adult 995.81
  baby or child 995.54
  spouse 995.81

Syndrome — *see also* Disease — *continued*

Baumgarten-Cruveilhier (cirrhosis of liver) 571.5
Beals 759.82
Bearn-Kunkel (-Slater) (lupoid hepatitis) 571.49
Beau's (*see also* Degeneration, myocardial) 429.1
Bechterew-Strümpell-Marie (ankylosing spondylitis) 720.0
Beck's (anterior spinal artery occlusion) 433.8 ☑
Beckwith (-Wiedemann) 759.89
Behçet's 136.1
Bekhterev-Strümpell-Marie (ankylosing spondylitis) 720.0
Benedikt's 344.89
Béquez César (-Steinbrinck-Chédiak-Higashi) (congenital gigantism of peroxidase granules) 288.2
Bernard-Horner (*see also* Neuropathy, peripheral, autonomic) 337.9
Bernard-Sergent (acute adrenocortical insufficiency) 255.41
Bernhardt-Roth 355.1
Bernheim's (*see also* Failure, heart) 428.0
Bertolotti's (sacralization of fifth lumbar vertebra) 756.15
Besnier-Boeck-Schaumann (sarcoidosis) 135
Bianchi's (aphasia-apraxia-alexia syndrome) 784.69
Biedl-Bardet (obesity, polydactyly, and intellectual disabilities) 759.89
Biemond's (obesity, polydactyly, and intellectual disabilities) 759.89
big spleen 289.4
bilateral polycystic ovarian 256.4
Bing-Horton's 339.00
Biörck (-Thorson) (malignant carcinoid) 259.2
Birt-Hogg-Dube 759.89
Blackfan-Diamond (congenital hypoplastic anemia) 284.01
black lung 500
black widow spider bite 989.5
bladder neck (*see also* Incontinence, urine) 788.30
blast (concussion) — *see* Blast, injury
blind loop (postoperative) 579.2
Bloch-Siemens (incontinentia pigmenti) 757.33
Bloch-Sulzberger (incontinentia pigmenti) 757.33
Bloom (-Machacek) (-Torre) 757.39
Blount-Barber (tibia vara) 732.4
blue
  bloater 491.20
    with
      acute bronchitis 491.22
        exacerbation (acute) 491.21
  diaper 270.0
  drum 381.02
  sclera 756.51
  toe 445.02
Boder-Sedgwick (ataxia-telangiectasia) 334.8
Boerhaave's (spontaneous esophageal rupture) 530.4
Bonnevie-Ullrich 758.6
Bonnier's 386.19
Borjeson-Forssman-Lehmann 759.89
Bouillaud's (rheumatic heart disease) 391.9
Bourneville (-Pringle) (tuberous sclerosis) 759.5
Bouveret (-Hoffmann) (paroxysmal tachycardia) 427.2
brachial plexus 353.0
Brachman-de Lange (Amsterdam dwarf, intellectual disabilities, and brachycephaly) 759.89
bradycardia-tachycardia 427.81
Brailsford-Morquio (dystrophy) (mucopolysaccharidosis IV) 277.5
brain (acute) (chronic) (nonpsychotic) (organic) (with behavioral reaction) (with neurotic reaction) 310.9

Syndrome — *see also* Disease — *continued*

brain — *continued*
  with
    presenile brain disease (*see also* Dementia, presenile) 290.10
    psychosis, psychotic reaction (*see also* Psychosis, organic) 294.9
  chronic alcoholic 291.2
  congenital (*see also* Disability, intellectual) 319
  postcontusional 310.2
  posttraumatic
    nonpsychotic 310.2
    psychotic 293.9
      acute 293.0
      chronic (*see also* Psychosis, organic) 294.8
      subacute 293.1
  psycho-organic (*see also* Syndrome, psycho-organic) 310.9
  psychotic (*see also* Psychosis, organic) 294.9
  senile (*see also* Dementia, senile) 290.0
branchial arch 744.41
Brandt's (acrodermatitis enteropathica) 686.8
Brennemann's 289.2
Briquet's 300.81
Brissaud-Meige (infantile myxedema) 244.9
broad ligament laceration 620.6
Brock's (atelectasis due to enlarged lymph nodes) 518.0
broken heart 429.83
Brown-Séquard 344.89
brown spot 756.59
Brown's tendon sheath 378.61
Brugada 746.89
Brugsch's (acropachyderma) 757.39
bubbly lung 770.7
Buchem's (hyperostosis corticalis) 733.3
Budd-Chiari (hepatic vein thrombosis) 453.0
Büdinger-Ludloff-Läwen 717.89
bulbar 335.22
  lateral (*see also* Disease, cerebrovascular, acute) 436
Bullis fever 082.8
bundle of Kent (anomalous atrioventricular excitation) 426.7
Bürger-Grütz (essential familial hyperlipemia) 272.3
Burke's (pancreatic insufficiency and chronic neutropenia) 577.8
Burnett's (milk-alkali) 275.42
Burnier's (hypophyseal dwarfism) 253.3
burning feet 266.2
Bywaters' 958.5
Caffey's (infantile cortical hyperostosis) 756.59
Calvé-Legg-Perthes (osteochondrosis, femoral capital) 732.1
Caplan (-Colinet) syndrome 714.81
capsular thrombosis (*see also* Thrombosis, brain) 434.0 ☑
carbohydrate-deficient glycoprotein (CDGS) 271.8
carcinogenic thrombophlebitis 453.1
carcinoid 259.2
cardiac asthma (*see also* Failure, ventricular, left) 428.1
cardiacos negros 416.0
cardiofaciocutaneous 759.89
cardiopulmonary obesity 278.03
cardiorenal (*see also* Hypertension, cardiorenal) 404.90
cardiorespiratory distress (idiopathic), newborn 769
cardiovascular renal (*see also* Hypertension, cardiorenal) 404.90
cardiovasorenal 272.7
Carini's (ichthyosis congenita) 757.1
carotid
  artery (internal) 435.8
  body or sinus 337.01
carpal tunnel 354.0
Carpenter's 759.89

Syndrome — *see also* Disease — *continued*

Cassidy (-Scholte) (malignant carcinoid) 259.2
cat-cry 758.31
cauda equina 344.60
causalgia 355.9
  lower limb 355.71
  upper limb 354.4
cavernous sinus 437.6
celiac 579.0
  artery compression 447.4
  axis 447.4
central pain 338.0
cerebellomedullary malformation (*see also* Spina bifida) 741.0 ☑
cerebral gigantism 253.0
cerebrohepatorenal 759.89
cervical (root) (spine) NEC 723.8
  disc 722.71
  posterior, sympathetic 723.2
  rib 353.0
  sympathetic paralysis 337.09
  traumatic (acute) NEC 847.0
cervicobrachial (diffuse) 723.3
cervicocranial 723.2
cervicodorsal outlet 353.2
Céstan's 344.89
Céstan (-Raymond) 433.8 ☑
Céstan-Chenais 344.89
chancriform 114.1
Charcôt's (intermittent claudication) 443.9
  angina cruris 443.9
  due to atherosclerosis 440.21
Charcôt-Marie-Tooth 356.1
Charcôt-Weiss-Baker 337.01
CHARGE association 759.89
Cheadle (-Möller) (-Barlow) (infantile scurvy) 267
Chédiak-Higashi (-Steinbrinck) (congenital gigantism of peroxidase granules) 288.2
chest wall 786.52
Chiari's (hepatic vein thrombosis) 453.0
Chiari-Frommel 676.6 ☑
chiasmatic 368.41
Chilaiditi's (subphrenic displacement, colon) 751.4
chondroectodermal dysplasia 756.55
chorea-athetosis-agitans 275.1
Christian's (chronic histiocytosis X) 277.89
chromosome 4 short arm deletion 758.39
chronic pain 338.4
Churg-Strauss 446.4
Clarke-Hadfield (pancreatic infantilism) 577.8
Claude's 352.6
Claude Bernard-Horner (*see also* Neuropathy, peripheral, autonomic) 337.9
Clérambault's
  automatism 348.89
  erotomania 297.8
Clifford's (postmaturity) 766.22
climacteric 627.2
Clouston's (hidrotic ectodermal dysplasia) 757.31
clumsiness 315.4
Cockayne's (microencephaly and dwarfism) 759.89
Cockayne-Weber (epidermolysis bullosa) 757.39
Coffin-Lowry 759.89
Cogan's (nonsyphilitic interstitial keratitis) 370.52
cold injury (newborn) 778.2
Collet (-Sicard) 352.6
combined immunity deficiency 279.2
compartment(al) (anterior) (deep) (posterior) 958.8
  nontraumatic
    abdomen 729.73
    arm 729.71
    buttock 729.72
    fingers 729.71
    foot 729.72
    forearm 729.71
    hand 729.71

☑ **Additional Digit Required — Refer to the Tabular List for Digit Selection**   ▽ **Subterms under main terms may continue to next column or page**

Syndrome — *see also* Disease — *continued*
  compartment — *continued*
    nontraumatic — *continued*
      hip 729.72
      leg 729.72
      lower extremity 729.72
      shoulder 729.71
      specified site NEC 729.79
      thigh 729.72
      toes 729.72
      upper extremity 729.71
      wrist 729.71
    post-surgical (*see also* Syndrome, compartment, non-traumatic) 998.89
    traumatic 958.90
      adomen 958.93
      arm 958.91
      buttock 958.92
      fingers 958.91
      foot 958.92
      forearm 958.91
      hand 958.91
      hip 958.92
      leg 958.92
      lower extremity 958.92
      shoulder 958.91
      specified site NEC 958.99
      thigh 958.92
      tibial 958.92
      toes 958.92
      upper extremity 958.91
      wrist 958.91
  complex regional pain — *see also* Dystrophy, sympathetic
    type I — *see* Dystrophy, sympathetic (posttraumatic) (reflex)
    type II — *see* Causalgia
  compression 958.5
    cauda equina 344.60
      with neurogenic bladder 344.61
  concussion 310.2
  congenital
    affecting more than one system 759.7
      specified type NEC 759.89
    congenital central alveolar hypoventilation 327.25
    facial diplegia 352.6
    muscular hypertrophy-cerebral 759.89
  congestion-fibrosis (pelvic) 625.5
  conjunctivourethrosynovial 099.3
  Conn (-Louis) (primary aldosteronism) 255.12
  Conradi (-Hünermann) (chondrodysplasia calcificans congenita) 756.59
  conus medullaris 336.8
  Cooke-Apert-Gallais (adrenogenital) 255.2
  Cornelia de Lange's (Amsterdam dwarf, intellectual disabilities, and brachycephaly) 759.8 ☑
  coronary insufficiency or intermediate 411.1
  cor pulmonale 416.9
  corticosexual 255.2
  Costen's (complex) 524.60
  costochondral junction 733.6
  costoclavicular 353.0
  costovertebral 253.0
  Cotard's (paranoia) 297.1
  Cowden 759.6
  craniovertebral 723.2
  Creutzfeldt-Jakob 046.19
    with dementia
      with behavioral disturbance 046.19 [294.11]
      without behavioral disturbance 046.19 [294.10]
    variant 046.11
      with dementia
        with behavioral disturbance 046.11 [294.11]
        without behavioral disturbance 046.11 [294.10]
  crib death 798.0
  cricopharyngeal 787.20
  cri-du-chat 758.31
  Crigler-Najjar (congenital hyperbilirubinemia) 277.4

Syndrome — *see also* Disease — *continued*
  crocodile tears 351.8
  Cronkhite-Canada 211.3
  croup 464.4
  CRST (cutaneous systemic sclerosis) 710.1
  crush 958.5
  crushed lung (*see also* Injury, internal, lung) 861.20
  Cruveilhier-Baumgarten (cirrhosis of liver) 571.5
  cubital tunnel 354.2
  Cuiffini-Pancoast (M8010/3) (carcinoma, pulmonary apex) 162.3
  Curschmann (-Batten) (-Steinert) 359.21
  Cushing's (iatrogenic) (idiopathic) (pituitary basophilism) (pituitary-dependent) 255.0
    overdose or wrong substance given or taken 962.0
  Cyriax's (slipping rib) 733.99
  cystic duct stump 576.0
  Da Costa's (neurocirculatory asthenia) 306.2
  Dameshek's (erythroblastic anemia) 282.49
  Dana-Putnam (subacute combined sclerosis with pernicious anemia) 281.0 [336.2]
  Danbolt (-Closs) (acrodermatitis enteropathica) 686.8
  Dandy-Walker (atresia, foramen of Magendie) 742.3
    with spina bifida (*see also* Spina bifida) 741.0 ☑
  Danlos' 756.83
  Davies-Colley (slipping rib) 733.99
  dead fetus 641.3 ☑
  defeminization 255.2
  defibrination (*see also* Fibrinolysis) 286.6
  Degos' 447.8
  Deiters' nucleus 386.19
  Déjérine-Roussy 338.0
  Déjérine-Thomas 333.0
  de Lange's (Amsterdam dwarf, intellectual disabilities, and brachycephaly) (Cornelia) 759.89
  Del Castillo's (germinal aplasia) 606.0
  deletion chromosomes 758.39
  delusional
    induced by drug 292.11
  dementia-aphonia, of childhood (*see also* Psychosis, childhood) 299.1 ☑
  demyelinating NEC 341.9
  denial visual hallucination 307.9
  depersonalization 300.6
  de Quervain's 259.51
  Dercum's (adiposis dolorosa) 272.8
  de Toni-Fanconi (-Debré) (cystinosis) 270.0
  diabetes-dwarfism-obesity (juvenile) 258.1
  diabetes mellitus-hypertension-nephrosis 250.4 ☑ [581.81]
    due to secondary diabetes 249.4 ☑ [581.81]
  diabetes mellitus in newborn infant 775.1
  diabetes-nephrosis 250.4 ☑ [581.81]
    due to secondary diabetes 249.4 ☑ [581.81]
  diabetic amyotrophy 250.6 ☑ [353.5]
    due to secondary diabetes 249.6 ☑ [353.5]
  Diamond-Blackfan (congenital hypoplastic anemia) 284.01
  Diamond-Gardener (autoerythrocyte sensitization) 287.2
  DIC (diffuse or disseminated intravascular coagulopathy) (*see also* Fibrinolysis) 286.6
  diencephalohypophyseal NEC 253.8
  diffuse cervicobrachial 723.3
  diffuse obstructive pulmonary 496
  DiGeorge's (thymic hypoplasia) 279.11
  Dighton's 756.51
  Di Guglielmo's (erythremic myelosis) (M9841/3) 207.0 ☑
  disequilibrium 276.9
  disseminated platelet thrombosis 446.6
  Ditthomska 307.81
  Doan-Wisemann (primary splenic neutropenia) 289.53

Syndrome — *see also* Disease — *continued*
  Döhle body-panmyelopathic 288.2
  Donohue's (leprechaunism) 259.8
  dorsolateral medullary (*see also* Disease, cerebrovascular, acute) 436
  double athetosis 333.71
  double whammy 360.81
  Down's (mongolism) 758.0
  Dresbach's (elliptocytosis) 282.1
  Dressler's (postmyocardial infarction) 411.0
    hemoglobinuria 283.2
    postcardiotomy 429.4
  drug withdrawal, infant, of dependent mother 779.5
  dry skin 701.1
    eye 375.15
  DSAP (disseminated superficial actinic porokeratosis) 692.75
  Duane's (retraction) 378.71
  Duane-Stilling-Türk (ocular retraction syndrome) 378.71
  Dubin-Johnson (constitutional hyperbilirubinemia) 277.4
  Dubin-Sprinz (constitutional hyperbilirubinemia) 277.4
  Duchenne's 335.22
  due to abnormality
    autosomal NEC (*see also* Abnormal, autosomes NEC) 758.5
      13 758.1
      18 758.2
      21 or 22 758.0
      D1 758.1
      E3 758.2
      G 758.0
    chromosomal 758.89
      sex 758.81
  dumping 564.2
    nonsurgical 536.8
  Duplay's 726.2
  Dupré's (meningism) 781.6
  Dyke-Young (acquired macrocytic hemolytic anemia) 283.9
  dyspraxia 315.4
  dystocia, dystrophia 654.9 ☑
  Eagle-Barret 756.71
  Eales' 362.18
  Eaton-Lambert (*see also* Syndrome, Lambert-Eaton) 358.30
  Ebstein's (downward displacement, tricuspid valve into right ventricle) 746.2
  ectopic ACTH secretion 255.0
  eczema-thrombocytopenia 279.12
  Eddowes' (brittle bones and blue sclera) 756.51
  Edwards' 758.2
  efferent loop 537.89
  effort (aviators') (psychogenic) 306.2
  Ehlers-Danlos 756.83
  Eisenmenger's (ventricular septal defect) 745.4
  Ekbom's (restless legs) 333.94
  Ekman's (brittle bones and blue sclera) 756.51
  electric feet 266.2
  Elephant man 237.71
  Ellison-Zollinger (gastric hypersecretion with pancreatic islet cell tumor) 251.5
  Ellis-van Creveld (chondroectodermal dysplasia) 756.55
  embryonic fixation 270.2
  empty sella (turcica) 253.8
  endocrine-hypertensive 255.3
  Engel-von Recklinghausen (osteitis fibrosa cystica) 252.01
  enteroarticular 099.3
  entrapment — *see* Neuropathy, entrapment
  eosinophilia myalgia 710.5
  epidemic vomiting 078.82
  Epstein's — *see* Nephrosis
  Erb (-Oppenheim)-Goldflam 358.00
  Erdheim's (acromegalic macrospondylitis) 253.0
  Erdheim-Chester 277.89
  Erlacher-Blount (tibia vara) 732.4
  erythrocyte fragmentation 283.19

Syndrome — *see also* Disease — *continued*
  euthyroid sick 790.94
  Evans' (thrombocytopenic purpura) 287.32
  excess cortisol, iatrogenic 255.0
  exhaustion 300.5
  extrapyramidal 333.90
  eyelid-malar-mandible 756.0
  eye retraction 378.71
  Faber's (achlorhydric anemia) 280.9
  Fabry (-Anderson) (angiokeratoma corporis diffusum) 272.7
  facet 724.8
  Fallot's 745.2
  falx (*see also* Hemorrhage, brain) 431
  familial eczema-thrombocytopenia 279.12
  Fanconi's (anemia) (congenital pancytopenia) 284.09
  Fanconi (-de Toni) (-Debré) (cystinosis) 270.0
  Farber (-Uzman) (disseminated lipogranulomatosis) 272.8
  fatigue NEC 300.5
    chronic 780.71
  faulty bowel habit (idiopathic megacolon) 564.7
  FDH (focal dermal hypoplasia) 757.39
  fecal reservoir 560.39
  Feil-Klippel (brevicollis) 756.16
  Felty's (rheumatoid arthritis with splenomegaly and leukopenia) 714.1
  fertile eunuch 257.2
  fetal alcohol 760.71
    late effect 760.71
  fibrillation-flutter 427.32
  fibrositis (periarticular) 729.0
  Fiedler's (acute isolated myocarditis) 422.91
  Fiessinger-Leroy (-Reiter) 099.3
  Fiessinger-Rendu (erythema multiforme exudativum) 695.19
  first arch 756.0
  Fisher's 357.0
  fish odor 270.8
  Fitz's (acute hemorrhagic pancreatitis) 577.0
  Fitz-Hugh and Curtis 098.86
    due to
      Chlamydia trachomatis 099.56
      Neisseria gonorrhoeae (gonococcal peritonitis) 098.86
  Flajani (-Basedow) (exophthalmic goiter) 242.0 ☑
  flat back
    acquired 737.29
    postprocedural 738.5
  floppy
    infant 781.99
    iris 364.81
    valve (mitral) 424.0
  flush 259.2
  Foix-Alajouanine 336.1
  Fong's (hereditary osteo-onychodysplasia) 756.89
  foramen magnum 348.4
  Forbes-Albright (nonpuerperal amenorrhea and lactation associated with pituitary tumor) 253.1
  Foster-Kennedy 377.04
  Foville's (peduncular) 344.89
  fragile X 759.83
  Franceschetti's (mandibulofacial dysostosis) 756.0
  Fraser's 759.89
  Freeman-Sheldon 759.89
  Frey's (auriculotemporal) 705.22
  Friderichsen-Waterhouse 036.3
  Friedrich-Erb-Arnold (acropachyderma) 757.39
  Fröhlich's (adiposogenital dystrophy) 253.8
  Froin's 336.8
  Frommel-Chiari 676.6 ☑
  frontal lobe 310.0
  Fukuhara 277.87
  Fuller Albright's (osteitis fibrosa disseminata) 756.59
  functional
    bowel 564.9
    prepubertal castrate 752.89

☑ **Additional Digit Required** — Refer to the Tabular List for Digit Selection

ᴺᴱᶜ **Subterms under main terms may continue to next column or page**

Syndrome — *see also* Disease — *continued*

Gaisböck's (polycythemia hypertonica) 289.0
ganglion (basal, brain) 333.90
geniculi 351.1
Ganser's, hysterical 300.16
Gardner-Diamond (autoerythrocyte sensitization) 287.2
gastroesophageal junction 530.0
gastroesophageal laceration-hemorrhage 530.7
gastrojejunal loop obstruction 537.89
Gayet-Wernicke's (superior hemorrhagic polioencephalitis) 265.1
Gee-Herter-Heubner (nontropical sprue) 579.0
Gélineau's (*see also* Narcolepsy) 347.00
genito-anorectal 099.1
Gerhardt's (vocal cord paralysis) 478.30
Gerstmann's (finger agnosia) 784.69
Gerstmann-Sträussler-Scheinker (GSS) 046.71
Gianotti Crosti 057.8
due to known virus — *see* Infection, virus
due to unknown virus 057.8
Gilbert's 277.4
Gilford (-Hutchinson) (progeria) 259.8
Gilles de la Tourette's 307.23
Gillespie's (dysplasia oculodentodigitalis) 759.89
Glénard's (enteroptosis) 569.89
Glinski-Simmonds (pituitary cachexia) 253.2
glucuronyl transferase 277.4
glue ear 381.20
Goldberg (-Maxwell) (-Morris) (testicular feminization) 259.51
Goldenhar's (oculoauriculovertebral dysplasia) 756.0
Goldflam-Erb 358.00
Goltz-Gorlin (dermal hypoplasia) 757.39
Good's 279.06
Goodpasture's (pneumorenal) 446.21
Gopalan's (burning feet) 266.2
Gorlin's 759.89
Gorlin-Chaudhry-Moss 759.89
Gougerot-Blum (pigmented purpuric lichenoid dermatitis) 709.1
Gougerot-Carteaud (confluent reticulate papillomatosis) 701.8
Gougerot (-Houwer)-Sjögren (keratoconjunctivitis sicca) 710.2
Gouley's (constrictive pericarditis) 423.2
Gowers' (vasovagal attack) 780.2
Gowers-Paton-Kennedy 377.04
Gradenigo's 383.02
gray or grey (chloramphenicol) (newborn) 779.4
Greig's (hypertelorism) 756.0
GSS (Gerstmann-Sträussler-Scheinker) 046.71
Gubler-Millard 344.89
Guérin-Stern (arthrogryposis multiplex congenita) 754.89
Guillain-Barré (-Strohl) 357.0
Gunn's (jaw-winking syndrome) 742.8
Günther's (congenital erythropoietic porphyria) 277.1
gustatory sweating 350.8
H₃O 759.81
Hadfield-Clarke (pancreatic infantilism) 577.8
Haglund-Läwen-Fründ 717.89
hairless women 257.8
hair tourniquet (*see also* Injury, superficial, by site)
finger 915.8
infected 915.9
penis 911.8
infected 911.9
toe 917.8
infected 917.9
Hallermann-Streiff 756.0
Hallervorden-Spatz 333.0
Hamman's (spontaneous mediastinal emphysema) 518.1

Syndrome — *see also* Disease — *continued*

Hamman-Rich (diffuse interstitial pulmonary fibrosis) 516.33
hand-foot 693.0
Hand-Schüller-Christian (chronic histiocytosis X) 277.89
Hanot-Chauffard (-Troisier) (bronze diabetes) 275.01
Harada's 363.22
Hare's (M8010/3) (carcinoma, pulmonary apex) 162.3
Harkavy's 446.0
harlequin color change 779.89
Harris' (organic hyperinsulinism) 251.1
Hart's (pellagra-cerebellar ataxia-renal aminoaciduria) 270.0
Hayem-Faber (achlorhydric anemia) 280.9
Hayem-Widal (acquired hemolytic jaundice) 283.9
headache — *see* Headache, syndrome
Heberden's (angina pectoris) 413.9
Hedinger's (malignant carcinoid) 259.2
Hegglin's 288.2
Heller's (infantile psychosis) (*see also* Psychosis, childhood) 299.1 ☑
H.E.L.L.P 642.5 ☑
hemolytic-uremic (adult) (child) 283.11
hemophagocytic 288.4
infection-associated 288.4
Hench-Rosenberg (palindromic arthritis) (*see also* Rheumatism, palindromic) 719.3 ☑
Henoch-Schönlein (allergic purpura) 287.0
hepatic flexure 569.89
hepatopulmonary 573.5
hepatorenal 572.4
due to a procedure 997.49
following delivery 674.8 ☑
hepatourologic 572.4
Herrick's (hemoglobin S disease) 282.61
Herter (-Gee) (nontropical sprue) 579.0
Heubner-Herter (nontropical sprue) 579.0
Heyd's (hepatorenal) 572.4
HHHO 759.81
high grade myelodysplastic 238.73
with 5q deletion 238.73
Hilger's 337.09
histiocytic 288.4
Hoffa (-Kastert) (liposynovitis prepatellaris) 272.8
Hoffmann's 244.9 [359.5]
Hoffmann-Bouveret (paroxysmal tachycardia) 427.2
Hoffmann-Werdnig 335.0
Holländer-Simons (progressive lipodystrophy) 272.6
Holmes' (visual disorientation) 368.16
Holmes-Adie 379.46
Hoppe-Goldflam 358.00
Horner's (*see also* Neuropathy, peripheral, autonomic) 337.9
traumatic — *see* Injury, nerve, cervical sympathetic
hospital addiction 301.51
hungry bone 275.5
Hunt's (herpetic geniculate ganglionitis) 053.11
dyssynergia cerebellaris myoclonica 334.2
Hunter (-Hurler) (mucopolysaccharidosis II) 277.5
hunterian glossitis 529.4
Hurler (-Hunter) (mucopolysaccharidosis II) 277.5
Hutchinson-Boeck (sarcoidosis) 135
Hutchinson-Gilford (progeria) 259.8
Hutchinson's incisors or teeth 090.5
hydralazine
correct substance properly administered 695.4
overdose or wrong substance given or taken 972.6
hydraulic concussion (abdomen) (*see also* Injury, internal, abdomen) 868.00
hyperabduction 447.8
hyperactive bowel 564.9

Syndrome — *see also* Disease — *continued*

hyperaldosteronism with hypokalemic alkalosis (Bartter's) 255.13
hypercalcemic 275.42
hypercoagulation NEC 289.89
hypereosinophilic (idiopathic) 288.3
hyperkalemic 276.7
hyperkinetic (*see also* Hyperkinesia)
heart 429.82
hyperlipemia-hemolytic anemia-icterus 571.1
hypermobility 728.5
hypernatremia 276.0
hyperosmolarity 276.0
hyperperfusion 997.01
hypersomnia-bulimia 349.89
hypersplenic 289.4
hypersympathetic (*see also* Neuropathy, peripheral, autonomic) 337.9
hypertransfusion, newborn 776.4
hyperventilation, psychogenic 306.1
hyperviscosity (of serum) NEC 273.3
polycythemic 289.0
sclerothymic 282.8
hypoglycemic (familial) (neonatal) 251.2
functional 251.1
hypokalemic 276.8
hypophyseal 253.8
hypophyseothalamic 253.8
hypopituitarism 253.2
hypoplastic left heart 746.7
hypopotassemia 276.8
hyposmolality 276.1
hypotension, maternal 669.2 ☑
hypothenar hammer 443.89
hypotonia-hypomentia-hypogonadism-obesity 759.81
ICF (intravascular coagulation-fibrinolysis) (*see also* Fibrinolysis) 286.6
idiopathic cardiorespiratory distress, newborn 769
idiopathic nephrotic (infantile) 581.9
iliotibial band 728.89
Imerslund (-Gräsbeck) (anemia due to familial selective vitamin B₁₂ malabsorption) 281.1
immobility (paraplegic) 728.3
immune reconstitution inflammatory (IRIS) 995.90
immunity deficiency, combined 279.2
impending coronary 411.1
impingement
shoulder 726.2
vertebral bodies 724.4
inappropriate secretion of antidiuretic hormone (ADH) 253.6
incomplete
mandibulofacial 756.0
infant
death, sudden (SIDS) 798.0
Hercules 255.2
of diabetic mother 775.0
shaken 995.55
infantilism 253.3
inferior vena cava 459.2
influenza-like (*see also* Influenza) 487.1
inspissated bile, newborn 774.4
insufficient sleep 307.44
intermediate coronary (artery) 411.1
internal carotid artery (*see also* Occlusion, artery, carotid) 433.1 ☑
interspinous ligament 724.8
intestinal
carcinoid 259.2
gas 787.3
knot 560.2
intraoperative floppy iris (IFIS) 364.81
intravascular
coagulation-fibrinolysis (ICF) (*see also* Fibrinolysis) 286.6
coagulopathy (*see also* Fibrinolysis) 286.6
inverted Marfan's 759.89
IRDS (idiopathic respiratory distress, newborn) 769
irritable
bowel 564.1

irritable — *continued*
heart 306.2
weakness 300.5
ischemic bowel (transient) 557.9
chronic 557.1
due to mesenteric artery insufficiency 557.1
Itsenko-Cushing (pituitary basophilism) 255.0
IVC (intravascular coagulopathy) (*see also* Fibrinolysis) 286.6
Ivemark's (asplenia with congenital heart disease) 759.0
Jaccoud's 714.4
Jackson's 344.89
Jadassohn-Lewandowski (pachyonchia congenita) 757.5
Jaffe-Lichtenstein (-Uehlinger) 252.01
Jahnke's (encephalocutaneous angiomatosis) 759.6
Jakob-Creutzfeldt 046.19
with dementia
with behavioral disturbance 046.19 [294.11]
without behavioral disturbance 046.19 [294.10]
variant 046.11
with dementia
with behavioral disturbance 046.11 [294.11]
without behavioral disturbance 046.11 [294.10]
Jaksch's (pseudoleukemia infantum) 285.8
Jaksch-Hayem (-Luzet) (pseudoleukemia infantum) 285.8
jaw-winking 742.8
jejunal 564.2
Jervell-Lange-Nielsen 426.82
jet lag 327.35
Jeune's (asphyxiating thoracic dystrophy of newborn) 756.4
Job's (chronic granulomatous disease) 288.1
Jordan's 288.2
Joseph-Diamond-Blackfan (congenital hypoplastic anemia) 284.01
Joubert 759.89
jugular foramen 352.6
Kabuki 759.89
Kahler's (multiple myeloma) (M9730/3) 203.0 ☑
Kalischer's (encephalocutaneous angiomatosis) 759.6
Kallmann's (hypogonadotropic hypogonadism with anosmia) 253.4
Kanner's (autism) (*see also* Psychosis, childhood) 299.0 ☑
Kartagener's (sinusitis, bronchiectasis, situs inversus) 759.3
Kasabach-Merritt (capillary hemangioma associated with thrombocytopenic purpura) 287.39
Kast's (dyschondroplasia with hemangiomas) 756.4
Kaznelson's (congenital hypoplastic anemia) 284.01
Kearns-Sayre 277.87
Kelly's (sideropenic dysphagia) 280.8
Kimmelstiel-Wilson (intercapillary glomerulosclerosis) 250.4 ☑ [581.81]
due to secondary diabetes 249.4 ☑ [581.81]
Klauder's (erythema multiforme exudativum) 695.19
Kleine-Levin 327.13
Klein-Waardenburg (ptosis-epicanthus) 270.2
Klinefelter's 758.7
Klippel-Feil (brevicollis) 756.16
Klippel-Trenaunay 759.89
Klumpke (-Déjérine) (injury to brachial plexus at birth) 767.6
Klüver-Bucy (-Terzian) 310.0
Köhler-Pellegrini-Stieda (calcification, knee joint) 726.62
König's 564.89

☑ **Additional Digit Required** — Refer to the Tabular List for Digit Selection   ▽ **Subterms under main terms may continue to next column or page**

2015 ICD-9-CM   ▶◀ **Revised Text**   ● **New Line**   ▲ **Revised Code**   **Volume 2 — 271**

Syndrome — Syndrome

Syndrome — *see also* Disease — *continued*

Korsakoff's (nonalcoholic) 294.0
Korsakoff (-Wernicke) (nonalcoholic) 294.0
  alcoholic 291.1
  alcoholic 291.1
Kostmann's (infantile genetic agranulocytosis) 288.01
Krabbe's
  congenital muscle hypoplasia 756.89
  cutaneocerebral angioma 759.6
Kunkel (lupoid hepatitis) 571.49
labyrinthine 386.50
laceration, broad ligament 620.6
Lambert-Eaton 358.30
  in
    diseases classified elsewhere 358.39
    neoplastic disease 358.31
Landau-Kieffner 345.8 ☑
Langdon Down (mongolism) 758.0
Larsen's (flattened facies and multiple congenital dislocations) 755.8
lateral
  cutaneous nerve of thigh 355.1
  medullary (*see also* Disease, cerebrovascular acute) 436
Launois' (pituitary gigantism) 253.0
Launois-Cléret (adiposogenital dystrophy) 253.8
Laurence-Moon (-Bardet)-Biedl (obesity, polydactyly, and intellectual disabilities) 759.89
Lawford's (encephalocutaneous angiomatosis) 759.6
lazy
  leukocyte 288.09
  posture 728.3
Lederer-Brill (acquired infectious hemolytic anemia) 283.19
Legg-Calvé-Perthes (osteochondrosis capital femoral) 732.1
Lemiere 451.89
Lennox's (*see also* Epilepsy) 345.0 ☑
Lennox-Gastaut syndrome 345.0 ☑
  with tonic seizures 345.1 ☑
lenticular 275.1
Léopold-Lévi's (paroxysmal thyroid instability) 242.9 ☑
Lepore hemoglobin 282.45
Leriche's (aortic bifurcation occlusion) 444.09
Léri-Weill 756.59
Lermoyez's (*see also* Disease, Ménière's) 386.00
Lesch-Nyhan (hypoxanthine-guanine-phosphoribosyltransferase deficiency) 277.2
leukoencephalopathy, reversible, posterior 348.5
Lev's (acquired complete heart block) 426.0
Levi's (pituitary dwarfism) 253.3
Lévy-Roussy 334.3
Lichtheim's (subacute combined sclerosis with pernicious anemia) 281.0 [336.2]
Li-Fraumeni V84.01
Lightwood's (renal tubular acidosis) 588.89
Lignac (-de Toni) (-Fanconi) (-Debré) (cystinosis) 270.0
Likoff's (angina in menopausal women) 413.9
liver-kidney 572.4
Lloyd's 258.1
lobotomy 310.0
Löffler's (eosinophilic pneumonitis) 518.3
Löfgren's (sarcoidosis) 135
long arm 18 or 21 deletion 758.39
Looser (-Debray)-Milkman (osteomalacia with pseudofractures) 268.2
Lorain-Levi (pituitary dwarfism) 253.3
Louis-Bar (ataxia-telangiectasia) 334.8
low
  atmospheric pressure 993.2
  back 724.2
    psychogenic 306.0
  output (cardiac) (*see also* Failure, heart) 428.9
Lowe's (oculocerebrorenal dystrophy) 270.8

Syndrome — *see also* Disease — *continued*

lower radicular, newborn 767.4
Lowe-Terrey-MacLachlan (oculocerebrorenal dystrophy) 270.8
Lown (-Ganong)-Levine (short P-R interval, normal QRS complex, and supraventricular tachycardia) 426.81
Lucey-Driscoll (jaundice due to delayed conjugation) 774.30
Luetscher's (dehydration) 276.51
lumbar vertebral 724.4
Lutembacher's (atrial septal defect with mitral stenosis) 745.5
Lyell's (toxic epidermal necrolysis) 695.15
  due to drug
    correct substance properly administered 695.15
    overdose or wrong substance given or taken 977.9
      specified drug — *see* Table of Drugs and Chemicals
MacLeod's 492.8
macrogenitosomia praecox 259.8
macroglobulinemia 273.3
macrophage activation 288.4
Maffucci's (dyschondroplasia with hemangiomas) 756.4
Magenblase 306.4
magnesium-deficiency 781.7
malabsorption 579.9
  postsurgical 579.3
  spinal fluid 331.3
Mal de Debarquement 780.4
malignant carcinoid 259.2
Mallory-Weiss 530.7
mandibulofacial dysostosis 756.0
manic-depressive (*see also* Psychosis, affective) 296.80
Mankowsky's (familial dysplastic osteopathy) 731.2
maple syrup (urine) 270.3
Marable's (celiac artery compression) 447.4
Marchesani (-Weill) (brachymorphism and ectopia lentis) 759.89
Marchiafava-Bignami 341.8
Marchiafava-Micheli (paroxysmal nocturnal hemoglobinuria) 283.2
Marcus Gunn's (jaw-winking syndrome) 742.8
Marfan's (arachnodactyly) 759.82
  meaning congenital syphilis 090.49
    with luxation of lens 090.49 [379.32]
Marie's (acromegaly) 253.0
  primary or idiopathic (acropachyderma) 757.39
  secondary (hypertrophic pulmonary osteoarthropathy) 731.2
Markus-Adie 379.46
Maroteaux-Lamy (mucopolysaccharidosis VI) 277.5
Martin's 715.27
Martin-Albright (pseudohypoparathyroidism) 275.49
Martorell-Fabré (pulseless disease) 446.7
massive aspiration of newborn 770.18
Masters-Allen 620.6
mastocytosis 757.33
maternal hypotension 669.2 ☑
maternal obesity 646.1 ☑
May (-Hegglin) 288.2
McArdle (-Schmid) (-Pearson) (glycogenosis V) 271.0
McCune-Albright (osteitis fibrosa disseminata) 756.59
McQuarrie's (idiopathic familial hypoglycemia) 251.2
meconium
  aspiration 770.12
  plug (newborn) NEC 777.1
median arcuate ligament 447.4
mediastinal fibrosis 519.3
Meekeren-Ehlers-Danlos 756.83
Meige (blepharospasm-oromandibular dystonia) 333.82
  -Milroy (chronic hereditary edema) 757.0

Syndrome — *see also* Disease — *continued*

MELAS (mitochondrial encephalopathy, lactic acidosis and stroke-like episodes) 277.87
Melkersson (-Rosenthal) 351.8
MEN (multiple endocrine neoplasia)
  type I 258.01
  type IIA 258.02
  type IIB 258.03
Mende's (ptosis-epicanthus) 270.2
Mendelson's (resulting from a procedure) 997.32
  during labor 668.0 ☑
  obstetric 668.0 ☑
Ménétrier's (hypertrophic gastritis) 535.2 ☑
Ménière's (*see also* Disease, Ménière's) 386.00
meningo-eruptive 047.1
Menkes' 759.89
  glutamic acid 759.89
  maple syrup (urine) disease 270.3
menopause 627.2
  postartificial 627.4
menstruation 625.4
MERRF (myoclonus with epilepsy and with ragged red fibers) 277.87
mesenteric
  artery, superior 557.1
  vascular insufficiency (with gangrene) 557.1
metabolic 277.7
metastatic carcinoid 259.2
Meyenburg-Altherr-Uehlinger 733.99
Meyer-Schwickerath and Weyers (dysplasia oculodentodigitalis) 759.89
Micheli-Rietti (thalassemia minor) 282.46
Michotte's 721.5
micrognathia-glossoptosis 756.0
microphthalmos (congenital) 759.89
midbrain 348.89
middle
  lobe (lung) (right) 518.0
  radicular 353.0
Miescher's
  familial acanthosis nigricans 701.2
  granulomatosis disciformis 709.3
Mieten's 759.89
migraine 346.0 ☑
Mikity-Wilson (pulmonary dysmaturity) 770.7
Mikulicz's (dryness of mouth, absent or decreased lacrimation) 527.1
milk alkali (milk drinkers') 275.42
Milkman (-Looser) (osteomalacia with pseudofractures) 268.2
Millard-Gubler 344.89
Miller-Dieker 758.33
Miller Fisher's 357.0
Milles' (encephalocutaneous angiomatosis) 759.6
Minkowicz-Chauffard (*see also* Spherocytosis) 282.0
Mirizzi's (hepatic duct stenosis) 576.2
  with calculus, cholelithiasis, or stones — *see* Choledocholithiasis
mitochondrial neurogastrointestinal encephalopathy (MNGIE) 277.87
mitral
  click (-murmur) 785.2
  valve prolapse 424.0
MNGIE (mitochondrial neurogastrointestinal encephalopathy) 277.87
Möbius'
  congenital oculofacial paralysis 352.6
  ophthalmoplegic migraine 346.2 ☑
Mohr's (types I and II) 759.89
monofixation 378.34
Moore's (*see also* Epilepsy) 345.5 ☑
Morel-Moore (hyperostosis frontalis interna) 733.3
Morel-Morgagni (hyperostosis frontalis interna) 733.3
Morgagni (-Stewart-Morel) (hyperostosis frontalis interna) 733.3
Morgagni-Adams-Stokes (syncope with heart block) 426.9

Syndrome — *see also* Disease — *continued*

Morquio (-Brailsford) (-Ullrich) (mucopolysaccharidosis IV) 277.5
Morris (testicular feminization) 259.51
Morton's (foot) (metatarsalgia) (metatarsal neuralgia) (neuralgia) (neuroma) (toe) 355.6
Moschcowitz (-Singer-Symmers) (thrombotic thrombocytopenic purpura) 446.6
Mounier-Kuhn 748.3
  with
    acute exacerbation 494.1
    bronchiectasis 494.0
      with (acute) exacerbation 494.1
  acquired 519.19
    with bronchiectasis 494.0
      with (acute) exacerbation 494.1
Mucha-Haberman (acute parapsoriasis varioliformis) 696.2
mucocutaneous lymph node (acute) (febrile) (infantile) (MCLS) 446.1
multiple
  deficiency 260
  endocrine neoplasia (MEN)
    type I 258.01
    type IIA 258.02
    type IIB 258.03
  operations 301.51
Munchausen's 301.51
Münchmeyer's (exostosis luxurians) 728.11
Murchison-Sanderson — *see* Disease, Hodgkin's
myasthenic — *see* Myasthenia, syndrome
myelodysplastic 238.75
  with 5q deletion 238.74
  high grade with 5q deletion 238.73
  lesions, low grade 238.72
  therapy-related 289.83
myeloproliferative (chronic) (M9960/1) 238.79
myofascial pain NEC 729.1
Naffziger's 353.0
Nager-de Reynier (dysostosis mandibularis) 756.0
nail-patella (hereditary osteo-onychodysplasia) 756.89
NARP (neuropathy, ataxia and retinitis pigmentosa) 277.87
Nebécourt's 253.3
Neill-Dingwall (microencephaly and dwarfism) 759.89
nephrotic (*see also* Nephrosis) 581.9
  diabetic 250.4 ☑ [581.81]
    due to secondary diabetes 249.4 ☑ [581.81]
Netherton's (ichthyosiform erythroderma) 757.1
neurocutaneous 759.6
neuroleptic malignant 333.92
Nezelof's (pure alymphocytosis) 279.13
Niemann-Pick (lipid histiocytosis) 272.7
Nonne-Milroy-Meige (chronic hereditary edema) 757.0
nonsense 300.16
Noonan's 759.89
Nothnagel's
  ophthalmoplegia-cerebellar ataxia 378.52
  vasomotor acroparesthesia 443.89
nucleus ambiguous-hypoglossal 352.6
OAV (oculoauriculovertebral dysplasia) 756.0
obesity hypoventilation 278.03
obsessional 300.3
oculocutaneous 364.24
oculomotor 378.81
oculourethroarticular 099.3
Ogilvie's (sympathicotonic colon obstruction) 560.89
ophthalmoplegia-cerebellar ataxia 378.52
Oppenheim-Urbach (necrobiosis lipoidica diabeticorum) 250.8 ☑ [709.3]
  due to secondary diabetes 249.8 ☑ [709.3]
oral-facial-digital 759.89

☑ **Additional Digit Required** — Refer to the Tabular List for Digit Selection

▽ **Subterms under main terms may continue to next column or page**

Syndrome — see also Disease — continued
organic
affective NEC 293.83
drug-induced 292.84
anxiety 293.84
delusional 293.81
alcohol-induced 291.5
drug-induced 292.11
due to or associated with
arteriosclerosis 290.42
presenile brain disease 290.12
senility 290.20
depressive 293.83
drug-induced 292.84
due to or associated with
arteriosclerosis 290.43
presenile brain disease 290.13
senile brain disease 290.21
hallucinosis 293.82
drug-induced 292.84
organic affective 293.83
induced by drug 292.84
organic personality 310.1
induced by drug 292.89
Ormond's 593.4
orodigitofacial 759.89
orthostatic hypotensive-dysautonomic
dyskinetic 333.0
Osler-Weber-Rendu (familial hemorrhagic
telangiectasia) 448.0
osteodermopathic hyperostosis 757.39
osteoporosis-osteomalacia 268.2
Österreicher-Turner (hereditary osteo-onychodysplasia) 756.89
os trigonum 755.69
Ostrum-Furst 756.59
otolith 386.19
otopalatodigital 759.89
outlet (thoracic) 353.0
ovarian remnant 620.8
Owren's (see also Defect, coagulation) 286.3
OX 758.6
pacemaker 429.4
Paget-Schroetter (intermittent venous
claudication) 453.89
pain (see also Pain)
central 338.0
chronic 338.4
complex regional 355.9
type I 337.20
lower limb 337.22
specified site NEC 337.29
upper limb 337.21
type II
lower limb 355.71
upper limb 354.4
myelopathic 338.0
thalamic (hyperesthetic) 338.0
painful
apicocostal vertebral (M8010/3) 162.3
arc 726.19
bruising 287.2
feet 266.2
Pancoast's (carcinoma, pulmonary apex)
(M8010/3) 162.3
panhypopituitary (postpartum) 253.2
papillary muscle 429.81
with myocardial infarction 410.8 ☑
Papillon-Léage and Psaume (orodigitofacial
dysostosis) 759.89
parabiotic (transfusion)
donor (twin) 772.0
recipient (twin) 776.4
paralysis agitans 332.0
paralytic 344.9
specified type NEC 344.89
paraneoplastic — see condition
Parinaud's (paralysis of conjugate upward
gaze) 378.81
oculoglandular 372.02
Parkes Weber and Dimitri (encephalocutaneous angiomatosis) 759.6
Parkinson's (see also Parkinsonism) 332.0
parkinsonian (see also Parkinsonism) 332.0
Parry's (exophthalmic goiter) 242.0 ☑
Parry-Romberg 349.89

Syndrome — see also Disease — continued
Parsonage-Aldren-Turner 353.5
Parsonage-Turner 353.5
Patau's (trisomy D1) 758.1
patella clunk 719.66
patellofemoral 719.46
Paterson (-Brown) (-Kelly) (sideropenic dysphagia) 280.8
Payr's (splenic flexure syndrome) 569.89
pectoral girdle 447.8
pectoralis minor 447.8
Pelger-Huët (hereditary hyposegmentation)
288.2
pellagra-cerebellar ataxia-renal
aminoaciduria 270.0
pellagroid 265.2
Pellegrini-Stieda 726.62
Pellizzi's (pineal) 259.8
pelvic congestion (-fibrosis) 625.5
Pendred's (familial goiter with deaf-mutism)
243
Penfield's (see also Epilepsy) 345.5 ☑
Penta X 758.81
peptic ulcer — see Ulcer, peptic 533.9 ☑
perabduction 447.8
periodic 277.31
periurethral fibrosis 593.4
persistent fetal circulation 747.83
Petges-Cléjat (poikilodermatomyositis)
710.3
Peutz-Jeghers 759.6
Pfeiffer (acrocephalosyndactyly) 755.55
phantom limb 353.6
pharyngeal pouch 279.11
Pick's (pericardial pseudocirrhosis of liver)
423.2
heart 423.2
liver 423.2
Pick-Herxheimer (diffuse idiopathic cutaneous atrophy) 701.8
Pickwickian (cardiopulmonary obesity)
278.03
PIE (pulmonary infiltration with eosinophilia) 518.3
Pierre Marie-Bamberger (hypertrophic pulmonary osteoarthropathy) 731.2
Pierre Mauriac's (diabetes-dwarfism-obesity)
258.1
Pierre Robin 756.0
pigment dispersion, iris 364.53
pineal 259.8
pink puffer 492.8
pituitary 253.0
placental
dysfunction 762.2
insufficiency 762.2
transfusion 762.3
plantar fascia 728.71
plateau iris (without glaucoma) 364.82
with glaucoma 365.23
plica knee 727.83
Plummer-Vinson (sideropenic dysphagia)
280.8
pluricarential of infancy 260
plurideficiency of infancy 260
pluriglandular (compensatory) 258.8
Poland 756.81
polycarential of infancy 260
polyglandular 258.8
polysplenia 759.0
pontine 433.8 ☑
popliteal
artery entrapment 447.8
web 756.89
postartificial menopause 627.4
postcardiac injury
postcardiotomy 429.4
postmyocardial infarction 411.0
postcardiotomy 429.4
post chemoembolization — code to associated conditions
postcholecystectomy 576.0
postcommissurotomy 429.4
postconcussional 310.2
postcontusional 310.2
postencephalitic 310.89

Syndrome — see also Disease — continued
posterior
cervical sympathetic 723.2
fossa compression 348.4
inferior cerebellar artery (see also Disease, cerebrovascular, acute) 436
reversible encephalopathy (PRES) 348.39
postgastrectomy (dumping) 564.2
post-gastric surgery 564.2
posthepatitis 780.79
postherpetic (neuralgia) (zoster) 053.19
geniculate ganglion 053.11
ophthalmica 053.19
postimmunization — see Complications,
vaccination
postinfarction 411.0
postinfluenza (asthenia) 780.79
postirradiation 990
postlaminectomy 722.80
cervical, cervicothoracic 722.81
lumbar, lumbosacral 722.83
thoracic, thoracolumbar 722.82
postleukotomy 310.0
postlobotomy 310.0
postmastectomy lymphedema 457.0
postmature (of newborn) 766.22
postmyocardial infarction 411.0
postoperative NEC 998.9
blind loop 579.2
postpartum panhypopituitary 253.2
postperfusion NEC 999.89
bone marrow 996.85
postpericardiotomy 429.4
postphlebitic (asymptomatic) 459.10
with
complications NEC 459.19
inflammation 459.12
and ulcer 459.13
stasis dermatitis 459.12
with ulcer 459.13
ulcer 459.11
with inflammation 459.13
postpolio (myelitis) 138
postvagotomy 564.2
postvalvulotomy 429.4
postviral (asthenia) NEC 780.79
Potain's (gastrectasis with dyspepsia) 536.1
potassium intoxication 276.7
Potter's 753.0
Prader (-Labhart) -Willi (-Fanconi) 759.81
preinfarction 411.1
preleukemic 238.75
premature senility 259.8
premenstrual 625.4
premenstrual tension 625.4
pre ulcer 536.9
Prinzmetal-Massumi (anterior chest wall
syndrome) 786.52
Profichet's 729.90
progeria 259.8
progressive pallidal degeneration 333.0
prolonged gestation 766.22
Proteus (dermal hypoplasia) 757.39
prune belly 756.71
prurigo-asthma 691.8
pseudocarpal tunnel (sublimis) 354.0
pseudohermaphroditism-virilism-hirsutism
255.2
pseudoparalytica 358.00
pseudo-Turner's 759.89
psycho-organic 293.9
acute 293.0
anxiety type 293.84
depressive type 293.83
hallucinatory type 293.82
nonpsychotic severity 310.1
specified focal (partial) NEC 310.89
paranoid type 293.81
specified type NEC 293.89
subacute 293.1
pterygolymphangiectasia 758.6
ptosis-epicanthus 270.2
pulmonary
arteriosclerosis 416.0
hypoperfusion (idiopathic) 769
renal (hemorrhagic) 446.21

Syndrome — see also Disease — continued
pulseless 446.7
Putnam-Dana (subacute combined sclerosis
with pernicious anemia) 281.0 [336.2]
pyloroduodenal 537.89
pyramidopallidonigral 332.0
pyriformis 355.0
QT interval prolongation 426.82
radicular NEC 729.2
lower limbs 724.4
upper limbs 723.4
newborn 767.4
Raeder-Harbitz (pulseless disease) 446.7
Ramsay Hunt's
dyssynergia cerebellaris myoclonica
334.2
herpetic geniculate ganglionitis 053.11
rapid time-zone change 327.35
Raymond (-Céstan) 433.8 ☑
Raynaud's (paroxysmal digital cyanosis)
443.0
RDS (respiratory distress syndrome, newborn) 769
Refsum's (heredopathia atactica polyneuritiformis) 356.3
Reichmann's (gastrosuccorrhea) 536.8
Reifenstein's (hereditary familial hypogonadism, male) 259.52
Reilly's (see also Neuropathy, peripheral,
autonomic) 337.9
Reiter's 099.3
renal glomerulohyalinosis-diabetic
250.4 ☑ [581.81]
due to secondary diabetes
249.4 ☑ [581.81]
Rendu-Osler-Weber (familial hemorrhagic
telangiectasia) 448.0
renofacial (congenital biliary fibroan-
giomatosis) 753.0
Rénon-Delille 253.8
respiratory distress (idiopathic) (newborn)
769
adult (following trauma and surgery)
518.52
specified NEC 518.82
type II 770.6
restless legs (RLS) 333.94
retinoblastoma (familial) 190.5
retraction (Duane's) 378.71
retroperitoneal fibrosis 593.4
retroviral seroconversion (acute) V08
Rett's 330.8
Reye's 331.81
Reye-Sheehan (postpartum pituitary
necrosis) 253.2
Riddoch's (visual disorientation) 368.16
Ridley's (see also Failure, ventricular, left)
428.1
Rieger's (mesodermal dysgenesis, anterior
ocular segment) 743.44
Rietti-Greppi-Micheli (thalassemia minor)
282.46
right ventricular obstruction — see Failure,
heart
Riley-Day (familial dysautonomia) 742.8
Robin's 756.0
Rokitansky-Kuster-Hauser (congenital ab-
sence, vagina) 752.45
Romano-Ward (prolonged QT interval syn-
drome) 426.82
Romberg's 349.89
Rosen-Castleman-Liebow (pulmonary pro-
teinosis) 516.0
rotator cuff, shoulder 726.10
Roth's 355.1
Rothmund's (congenital poikiloderma)
757.33
Rotor's (idiopathic hyperbilirubinemia)
277.4
Roussy-Lévy 334.3
Roy (-Jutras) (acropachyderma) 757.39
rubella (congenital) 771.0
Rubinstein-Taybi's (brachydactylia, short
stature, and intellectual disabilities)
759.89

☑ Additional Digit Required — Refer to the Tabular List for Digit Selection   ▽ Subterms under main terms may continue to next column or page

2015 ICD-9-CM   ▶◀ Revised Text   ● New Line   ▲ Revised Code   Volume 2 — 273

Syndrome — *see also* Disease — *continued*

vagohypoglossal 352.6

vagovagal 780.2

van Buchem's (hyperostosis corticalis) 733.3

van der Hoeve's (brittle bones and blue sclera, deafness) 756.51

van der Hoeve-Halbertsma-Waardenburg (ptosis-epicanthus) 270.2

van der Hoeve-Waardenburg-Gualdi (ptosis-epicanthus) 270.2

vanishing twin 651.33

van Neck-Odelberg (juvenile osteochondrosis) 732.1

vascular splanchnic 557.0

vasomotor 443.9

vasovagal 780.2

VATER 759.89

Velo-cardio-facial 758.32

vena cava (inferior) (superior) (obstruction) 459.2

Verbiest's (claudicatio intermittens spinalis) 435.1

Vernet's 352.6

vertebral

artery 435.1

compression 721.1

lumbar 724.4

steal 435.1

vertebrogenic (pain) 724.5

vertiginous NEC 386.9

video display tube 723.8

Villaret's 352.6

Vinson-Plummer (sideropenic dysphagia) 280.8

virilizing adrenocortical hyperplasia, congenital 255.2

virus, viral 079.99

visceral larval migrans 128.0

visual disorientation 368.16

vitamin B_6 deficiency 266.1

vitreous touch 997.99

Vogt's (corpus striatum) 333.71

Vogt-Koyanagi 364.24

Volkmann's 958.6

von Bechterew-Strümpell (ankylosing spondylitis) 720.0

von Graefe's 378.72

von Hippel-Lindau (angiomatosis retinocerebellosa) 759.6

von Schroetter's (intermittent venous claudication) 453.89

von Willebrand (-Jürgens) (angiohemophilia) 286.4

Waardenburg-Klein (ptosis epicanthus) 270.2

Wagner (-Unverricht) (dermatomyositis) 710.3

Waldenström's (macroglobulinemia) 273.3

Waldenström-Kjellberg (sideropenic dysphagia) 280.8

Wallenberg's (posterior inferior cerebellar artery) (*see also* Disease, cerebrovascular, acute) 436

Waterhouse (-Friderichsen) 036.3

water retention 276.69

Weber's 344.89

Weber-Christian (nodular nonsuppurative panniculitis) 729.30

Weber-Cockayne (epidermolysis bullosa) 757.39

Weber-Dimitri (encephalocutaneous angiomatosis) 759.6

Weber-Gubler 344.89

Weber-Leyden 344.89

Weber-Osler (familial hemorrhagic telangiectasia) 448.0

Wegener's (necrotizing respiratory granulomatosis) 446.4

Weill-Marchesani (brachymorphism and ectopia lentis) 759.89

Weingarten's (tropical eosinophilia) 518.3

Weiss-Baker (carotid sinus syncope) 337.01

Weissenbach-Thibierge (cutaneous systemic sclerosis) 710.1

Werdnig-Hoffmann 335.0

Syndrome — *see also* Disease — *continued*

Werlhof-Wichmann (*see also* Purpura, thrombocytopenic) 287.39

Wermer's (polyendocrine adenomatosis) 258.01

Werner's (progeria adultorum) 259.8

Wernicke's (nonalcoholic) (superior hemorrhagic polioencephalitis) 265.1

Wernicke-Korsakoff (nonalcoholic) 294.0

alcoholic 291.1

Westphal-Strümpell (hepatolenticular degeneration) 275.1

wet

brain (alcoholic) 303.9 ☑

feet (maceration) (tropical) 991.4

lung

adult 518.52

newborn 770.6

whiplash 847.0

Whipple's (intestinal lipodystrophy) 040.2

"whistling face" (craniocarpotarsal dystrophy) 759.89

Widal (-Abrami) (acquired hemolytic jaundice) 283.9

Wilkie's 557.1

Wilkinson-Sneddon (subcorneal pustular dermatosis) 694.1

Willan-Plumbe (psoriasis) 696.1

Willebrand (-Jürgens) (angiohemophilia) 286.4

Willi-Prader (hypogenital dystrophy with diabetic tendency) 759.81

Wilson's (hepatolenticular degeneration) 275.1

Wilson-Mikity 770.7

Wiskott-Aldrich (eczema-thrombocytopenia) 279.12

withdrawal

alcohol 291.81

drug 292.0

infant of dependent mother 779.5

Woakes' (ethmoiditis) 471.1

Wolff-Parkinson-White (anomalous atrioventricular excitation) 426.7

Wright's (hyperabduction) 447.8

X

cardiac 413.9

dysmetabolic 277.7

xiphoidalgia 733.99

XO 758.6

XXX 758.81

XXXXY 758.81

XXY 758.7

yellow vernix (placental dysfunction) 762.2

Zahorsky's 074.0

Zellweger 277.86

Zieve's (jaundice, hyperlipemia and hemolytic anemia) 571.1

Zollinger-Ellison (gastric hypersecretion with pancreatic islet cell tumor) 251.5

Zuelzer-Ogden (nutritional megaloblastic anemia) 281.2

Synechia (iris) (pupil) 364.70

anterior 364.72

peripheral 364.73

intrauterine (traumatic) 621.5

posterior 364.71

vulvae, congenital 752.49

Synesthesia — *see also* Disturbance, sensation 782.0

Synodontia 520.2

Synophthalmus 759.89

Synorchidism 752.89

Synorchism 752.89

Synostosis (congenital) 756.59

astragaloscaphoid 755.67

radioulnar 755.53

talonavicular (bar) 755.67

tarsal 755.67

Synovial — *see* condition

Synovioma (M9040/3) — *see also* Neoplasm, connective tissue, malignant

benign (M9040/0) — *see* Neoplasm, connective tissue, benign

Synoviosarcoma (M9040/3) — *see* Neoplasm, connective tissue, malignant

Synovitis — *see also* Tenosynovitis 727.00

chronic crepitant, wrist 727.2

due to crystals — *see* Arthritis, due to crystals

gonococcal 098.51

gouty 274.00

specified NEC 727.09

syphilitic 095.7

congenital 090.0

traumatic, current — *see* Sprain, by site

tuberculous — *see* Tuberculosis, synovitis

villonodular 719.20

ankle 719.27

elbow 719.22

foot 719.27

hand 719.24

hip 719.25

knee 719.26

multiple sites 719.29

pelvic region 719.25

shoulder (region) 719.21

specified site NEC 719.28

wrist 719.23

Syphilide 091.3

congenital 090.0

newborn 090.0

tubercular 095.8

congenital 090.0

Syphilis, syphilitic (acquired) 097.9

with lung involvement 095.1

abdomen (late) 095.2

acoustic nerve 094.86

adenopathy (secondary) 091.4

adrenal (gland) 095.8

with cortical hypofunction 095.8

age under 2 years NEC (*see also* Syphilis, congenital) 090.9

acquired 097.9

alopecia (secondary) 091.82

anemia 095.8

aneurysm (artery) (ruptured) 093.89

aorta 093.0

central nervous system 094.89

congenital 090.5

anus 095.8

primary 091.1

secondary 091.3

aorta, aortic (arch) (abdominal) (insufficiency) (pulmonary) (regurgitation) (stenosis) (thoracic) 093.89

aneurysm 093.0

arachnoid (adhesive) 094.2

artery 093.89

cerebral 094.89

spinal 094.89

arthropathy (neurogenic) (tabetic) 094.0 [713.5]

asymptomatic — *see* Syphilis, latent

ataxia, locomotor (progressive) 094.0

atrophoderma maculatum 091.3

auricular fibrillation 093.89

Bell's palsy 094.89

bladder 095.8

bone 095.5

secondary 091.61

brain 094.89

breast 095.8

bronchus 095.8

bubo 091.0

bulbar palsy 094.89

bursa (late) 095.7

cardiac decompensation 093.89

cardiovascular (early) (late) (primary) (secondary) (tertiary) 093.9

specified type and site NEC 093.89

causing death under 2 years of age (*see also* Syphilis, congenital) 090.9

stated to be acquired NEC 097.9

central nervous system (any site) (early) (late) (latent) (primary) (recurrent) (relapse) (secondary) (tertiary) 094.9

with

ataxia 094.0

paralysis, general 094.1

juvenile 090.40

paresis (general) 094.1

Syphilis, syphilitic — *continued*

central nervous system — *continued*

with — *continued*

paresis — *continued*

juvenile 090.40

tabes (dorsalis) 094.0

juvenile 090.40

taboparesis 094.1

juvenile 090.40

aneurysm (ruptured) 094.87

congenital 090.40

juvenile 090.40

remission in (sustained) 094.9

serology doubtful, negative, or positive 094.9

specified nature or site NEC 094.89

vascular 094.89

cerebral 094.89

meningovascular 094.2

nerves 094.89

sclerosis 094.89

thrombosis 094.89

cerebrospinal 094.89

tabetic 094.0

cerebrovascular 094.89

cervix 095.8

chancre (multiple) 091.0

extragenital 091.2

Rollet's 091.2

Charcôt's joint 094.0 [713.5]

choked disc 094.89 [377.00]

chorioretinitis 091.51

congenital 090.0 [363.13]

late 094.83

choroiditis 091.51

congenital 090.0 [363.13]

late 094.83

prenatal 090.0 [363.13]

choroidoretinitis (secondary) 091.51

congenital 090.0 [363.13]

late 094.83

ciliary body (secondary) 091.52

late 095.8 [364.11]

colon (late) 095.8

combined sclerosis 094.89

complicating pregnancy, childbirth or puerperium 647.0 ☑

affecting fetus or newborn 760.2

condyloma (latum) 091.3

congenital 090.9

with

encephalitis 090.41

paresis (general) 090.40

tabes (dorsalis) 090.40

taboparesis 090.40

chorioretinitis, choroiditis 090.0 [363.13]

early or less than 2 years after birth NEC 090.2

with manifestations 090.0

latent (without manifestations) 090.1

negative spinal fluid test 090.1

serology, positive 090.1

symptomatic 090.0

interstitial keratitis 090.3

juvenile neurosyphilis 090.40

late or 2 years or more after birth NEC 090.7

chorioretinitis, choroiditis 090.5 [363.13]

interstitial keratitis 090.3

juvenile neurosyphilis NEC 090.40

latent (without manifestations) 090.6

negative spinal fluid test 090.6

serology, positive 090.6

symptomatic or with manifestations NEC 090.5

interstitial keratitis 090.3

conjugal 097.9

tabes 094.0

conjunctiva 095.8 [372.10]

contact V01.6

cord, bladder 094.0

cornea, late 095.8 [370.59]

coronary (artery) 093.89

sclerosis 093.89

coryza 095.8

☑ **Additional Digit Required** — Refer to the Tabular List for Digit Selection

▼ **Subterms under main terms** may continue to next column or page

Syphilis, syphilitic — *continued*
coryza — *continued*
 congenital 090.0
cranial nerve 094.89
cutaneous — *see* Syphilis, skin
dacryocystitis 095.8
degeneration, spinal cord 094.89
d'emblée 095.8
dementia 094.1
 paralytica 094.1
  juvenilis 090.40
destruction of bone 095.5
dilatation, aorta 093.0
due to blood transfusion 097.9
dura mater 094.89
ear 095.8
 inner 095.8
  nerve (eighth) 094.86
  neurorecurrence 094.86
early NEC 091.0
 cardiovascular 093.9
 central nervous system 094.9
  paresis 094.1
  tabes 094.0
 latent (without manifestations) (less
  than 2 years after infection) 092.9
 negative spinal fluid test 092.9
 serological relapse following treatment 092.0
 serology positive 092.9
 paresis 094.1
 relapse (treated, untreated) 091.7
 skin 091.3
 symptomatic NEC 091.89
  extragenital chancre 091.2
  primary, except extragenital chancre
   091.0
  secondary (*see also* Syphilis, secondary) 091.3
   relapse (treated, untreated) 091.7
 tabes 094.0
 ulcer 091.3
eighth nerve 094.86
endemic, nonvenereal 104.0
endocarditis 093.20
 aortic 093.22
 mitral 093.21
 pulmonary 093.24
 tricuspid 093.23
epididymis (late) 095.8
epiglottis 095.8
epiphysitis (congenital) 090.0
esophagus 095.8
Eustachian tube 095.8
exposure to V01.6
eye 095.8 [363.13]
 neuromuscular mechanism 094.85
eyelid 095.8 [373.5]
 with gumma 095.8 [373.5]
 ptosis 094.89
fallopian tube 095.8
fracture 095.5
gallbladder (late) 095.8
gastric 095.8
 crisis 094.0
 polyposis 095.8
general 097.9
 paralysis 094.1
  juvenile 090.40
genital (primary) 091.0
glaucoma 095.8
gumma (late) NEC 095.9
 cardiovascular system 093.9
 central nervous system 094.9
 congenital 090.5
 heart or artery 093.89
heart 093.89
 block 093.89
 decompensation 093.89
 disease 093.89
 failure 093.89
 valve (*see also* Syphilis, endocarditis)
  093.20
hemianesthesia 094.89
hemianopsia 095.8
hemiparesis 094.89

Syphilis, syphilitic — *continued*
hemiplegia 094.89
hepatic artery 093.89
hepatitis 095.3
hepatomegaly 095.3
 congenital 090.0
hereditaria tarda (*see also* Syphilis, congenital, late) 090.7
hereditary (*see also* Syphilis, congenital)
 090.9
 interstitial keratitis 090.3
Hutchinson's teeth 090.5
hyalitis 095.8
inactive — *see* Syphilis, latent
infantum NEC (*see also* Syphilis, congenital)
 090.9
inherited — *see* Syphilis, congenital
internal ear 095.8
intestine (late) 095.8
iris, iritis (secondary) 091.52
 late 095.8 [364.11]
joint (late) 095.8
keratitis (congenital) (early) (interstitial)
 (late) (parenchymatous) (punctata
 profunda) 090.3
kidney 095.4
lacrimal apparatus 095.8
laryngeal paralysis 095.8
larynx 095.8
late 097.0
 cardiovascular 093.9
 central nervous system 094.9
 latent or 2 years or more after infection
  (without manifestations) 096
  negative spinal fluid test 096
  serology positive 096
 paresis 094.1
 specified site NEC 095.8
 symptomatic or with symptoms 095.9
 tabes 094.0
latent 097.1
 central nervous system 094.9
 date of infection unspecified 097.1
 early or less than 2 years after infection
  092.9
 late or 2 years or more after infection 096
 serology
  doubtful
   follow-up of latent syphilis 097.1
    central nervous system 094.9
    date of infection unspecified
     097.1
    early or less than 2 years after
     infection 092.9
    late or 2 years or more after
     infection 096
  positive, only finding 097.1
   date of infection unspecified
    097.1
   early or less than 2 years after in-
    fection 097.1
   late or 2 years or more after infec-
    tion 097.1
lens 095.8
leukoderma 091.3
 late 095.8
lienis 095.8
lip 091.3
 chancre 091.2
 late 095.8
 primary 091.2
Lissauer's paralysis 094.1
liver 095.3
 secondary 091.62
locomotor ataxia 094.0
lung 095.1
lymphadenitis (secondary) 091.4
lymph gland (early) (secondary) 091.4
 late 095.8
macular atrophy of skin 091.3
 striated 095.8
maternal, affecting fetus or newborn 760.2
 manifest syphilis in newborn — *see*
  Syphilis, congenital
mediastinum (late) 095.8

Syphilis, syphilitic — *continued*
meninges (adhesive) (basilar) (brain) (spinal
 cord) 094.2
meningitis 094.2
 acute 091.81
 congenital 090.42
meningoencephalitis 094.2
meningovascular 094.2
 congenital 090.49
mesarteritis 093.89
 brain 094.89
 spine 094.89
middle ear 095.8
mitral stenosis 093.21
monoplegia 094.89
mouth (secondary) 091.3
 late 095.8
mucocutaneous 091.3
 late 095.8
mucous
 membrane 091.3
  late 095.8
 patches 091.3
  congenital 090.0
mulberry molars 090.5
muscle 095.6
myocardium 093.82
myositis 095.6
nasal sinus 095.8
neonatorum NEC (*see also* Syphilis, congenital) 090.9
nerve palsy (any cranial nerve) 094.89
nervous system, central 094.9
neuritis 095.8
 acoustic nerve 094.86
neurorecidive of retina 094.83
neuroretinitis 094.85
newborn (*see also* Syphilis, congenital) 090.9
nodular superficial 095.8
nonvenereal, endemic 104.0
nose 095.8
 saddle back deformity 090.5
 septum 095.8
  perforated 095.8
occlusive arterial disease 093.89
ophthalmic 095.8 [363.13]
ophthalmoplegia 094.89
optic nerve (atrophy) (neuritis) (papilla)
 094.84
orbit (late) 095.8
orchitis 095.8
organic 097.9
osseous (late) 095.5
osteochondritis (congenital) 090.0
osteoporosis 095.5
ovary 095.8
oviduct 095.8
palate 095.8
 gumma 095.8
 perforated 090.5
pancreas (late) 095.8
pancreatitis 095.8
paralysis 094.89
 general 094.1
 juvenile 090.40
paraplegia 094.89
paresis (general) 094.1
 juvenile 090.40
paresthesia 094.89
Parkinson's disease or syndrome 094.82
paroxysmal tachycardia 093.89
pemphigus (congenital) 090.0
penis 091.0
 chancre 091.0
 late 095.8
pericardium 093.81
perichondritis, larynx 095.8
periosteum 095.5
 congenital 090.0
 early 091.61
 secondary 091.61
peripheral nerve 095.8
petrous bone (late) 095.5
pharynx 095.8
 secondary 091.3
pituitary (gland) 095.8

Syphilis, syphilitic — *continued*
placenta 095.8
pleura (late) 095.8
pneumonia, white 090.0
pontine (lesion) 094.89
portal vein 093.89
primary NEC 091.2
 anal 091.1
 and secondary (*see also* Syphilis, secondary) 091.9
 cardiovascular 093.9
 central nervous system 094.9
 extragenital chancre NEC 091.2
 fingers 091.2
 genital 091.0
 lip 091.2
 specified site NEC 091.2
 tonsils 091.2
prostate 095.8
psychosis (intracranial gumma) 094.89
ptosis (eyelid) 094.89
pulmonary (late) 095.1
 artery 093.89
pulmonum 095.1
pyelonephritis 095.4
recently acquired, symptomatic NEC 091.89
rectum 095.8
respiratory tract 095.8
retina
 late 094.83
 neurorecidive 094.83
retrobulbar neuritis 094.85
salpingitis 095.8
sclera (late) 095.0
sclerosis
 cerebral 094.89
 coronary 093.89
 multiple 094.89
 subacute 094.89
scotoma (central) 095.8
scrotum 095.8
secondary (and primary) 091.9
 adenopathy 091.4
 anus 091.3
 bone 091.61
 cardiovascular 093.9
 central nervous system 094.9
 chorioretinitis, choroiditis 091.51
 hepatitis 091.62
 liver 091.62
 lymphadenitis 091.4
 meningitis, acute 091.81
 mouth 091.3
 mucous membranes 091.3
 periosteum 091.61
 periostitis 091.61
 pharynx 091.3
 relapse (treated) (untreated) 091.7
 skin 091.3
 specified form NEC 091.89
 tonsil 091.3
 ulcer 091.3
 viscera 091.69
 vulva 091.3
seminal vesicle (late) 095.8
seronegative
 with signs or symptoms — *see* Syphilis,
  by site or stage
seropositive
 with signs or symptoms — *see* Syphilis,
  by site and stage
 follow-up of latent syphilis — *see*
  Syphilis, latent
 only finding — *see* Syphilis, latent
seventh nerve (paralysis) 094.89
sinus 095.8
sinusitis 095.8
skeletal system 095.5
skin (early) (secondary) (with ulceration)
 091.3
 late or tertiary 095.8
small intestine 095.8
spastic spinal paralysis 094.0
spermatic cord (late) 095.8
spinal (cord) 094.89

☑ Additional Digit Required — Refer to the Tabular List for Digit Selection   ▽ Subterms under main terms may continue to next column or page

276 — Volume 2   ▶◀ Revised Text   ● New Line   ▲ Revised Code   2015 ICD-9-CM

Syphilis, syphilitic — *continued*
spinal — *continued*
with
paresis 094.1
tabes 094.0
spleen 095.8
splenomegaly 095.8
spondylitis 095.5
staphyloma 095.8
stigmata (congenital) 090.5
stomach 095.8
synovium (late) 095.7
tabes dorsalis (early) (late) 094.0
juvenile 090.40
tabetic type 094.0
juvenile 090.40
taboparesis 094.1
juvenile 090.40
tachycardia 093.89
tendon (late) 095.7
tertiary 097.0
with symptoms 095.8
cardiovascular 093.9
central nervous system 094.9
multiple NEC 095.8
specified site NEC 095.8
testis 095.8
thorax 095.8
throat 095.8
thymus (gland) 095.8
thyroid (late) 095.8
tongue 095.8
tonsil (lingual) 095.8
primary 091.2
secondary 091.3
trachea 095.8
tricuspid valve 093.23
tumor, brain 094.89
tunica vaginalis (late) 095.8
ulcer (any site) (early) (secondary) 091.3
late 095.9
perforating 095.9
foot 094.0
urethra (stricture) 095.8
urogenital 095.8
uterus 095.8
uveal tract (secondary) 091.50
late 095.8 [363.13]
uveitis (secondary) 091.50
late 095.8 [363.13]
uvula (late) 095.8
perforated 095.8
vagina 091.0
late 095.8
valvulitis NEC 093.20
vascular 093.89
brain or cerebral 094.89
vein 093.89
cerebral 094.89
ventriculi 095.8
vesicae urinariae 095.8
viscera (abdominal) 095.2
secondary 091.69
vitreous (hemorrhage) (opacities) 095.8
vulva 091.0
late 095.8
secondary 091.3
Syphiloma 095.9
cardiovascular system 093.9
central nervous system 094.9
circulatory system 093.9
congenital 090.5
Syphilophobia 300.29
Syringadenoma (M8400/0) — *see also* Neoplasm, skin, benign
papillary (M8406/0) — *see* Neoplasm, skin, benign
Syringobulbia 336.0
Syringocarcinoma (M8400/3) — *see* Neoplasm, skin, malignant
Syringocystadenoma (M8400/0) — *see also* Neoplasm, skin, benign
papillary (M8406/0) — *see* Neoplasm, skin, benign
Syringocystoma (M8407/0) — *see* Neoplasm, skin, benign

Syringoma (M8407/0) — *see also* Neoplasm, skin, benign
chondroid (M8940/0) — *see* Neoplasm, by site, benign
Syringomyelia 336.0
Syringomyelitis 323.9
late effect — *see* category 326
Syringomyelocele — *see also* Spina bifida 741.9 ☑
Syringopontia 336.0
System, systemic — *see also* condition
disease, combined — *see* Degeneration, combined
fibrosclerosing syndrome 710.8
inflammatory response syndrome (SIRS) 995.90
due to
infectious process 995.91
with acute organ dysfunction 995.92
non-infectious process 995.93
with acute organ dysfunction 995.94
lupus erythematosus 710.0
inhibitor 795.79

T

Tab — *see* Tag
Tabacism 989.84
Tabacosis 989.84
Tabardillo 080
flea-borne 081.0
louse-borne 080
Tabes, tabetic
with
central nervous system syphilis 094.0
Charcôt's joint 094.0 [713.5]
cord bladder 094.0
crisis, viscera (any) 094.0
paralysis, general 094.1
paresis (general) 094.1
perforating ulcer 094.0
arthropathy 094.0 [713.5]
bladder 094.0
bone 094.0
cerebrospinal 094.0
congenital 090.40
conjugal 094.0
dorsalis 094.0
neurosyphilis 094.0
early 094.0
juvenile 090.40
latent 094.0
mesenterica (*see also* Tuberculosis) 014.8 ☑
paralysis insane, general 094.1
peripheral (nonsyphilitic) 799.89
spasmodic 094.0
not dorsal or dorsalis 343.9
syphilis (cerebrospinal) 094.0
Taboparalysis 094.1
Taboparesis (remission) 094.1
with
Charcôt's joint 094.1 [713.5]
cord bladder 094.1
perforating ulcer 094.1
juvenile 090.40
Tache noir 923.20
Tachyalimentation 579.3
Tachyarrhythmia, tachyrhythmia — *see also* Tachycardia
paroxysmal with sinus bradycardia 427.81
Tachycardia 785.0
atrial 427.89
auricular 427.89
AV nodal re-entry (re-entrant) 427.89
junctional ectopic 427.0
newborn 779.82
nodal 427.89
nonparoxysmal atrioventricular 426.89
nonparoxysmal atrioventricular (nodal) 426.89
nonsustained 427.2
paroxysmal 427.2
with sinus bradycardia 427.81
atrial (PAT) 427.0
psychogenic 316 [427.0]

Tachycardia — *continued*
paroxysmal — *continued*
atrioventricular (AV) 427.0
psychogenic 316 [427.0]
essential 427.2
junctional 427.0
nodal 427.0
psychogenic 316 [427.2]
atrial 316 [427.0]
supraventricular 316 [427.0]
ventricular 316 [427.1]
supraventricular 427.0
psychogenic 316 [427.0]
ventricular 427.1
psychogenic 316 [427.1]
postoperative 997.1
psychogenic 306.2
sick sinus 427.81
sinoauricular 427.89
sinus 427.89
supraventricular 427.89
sustained 427.2
supraventricular 427.0
ventricular 427.1
ventricular (paroxysmal) 427.1
psychogenic 316 [427.1]
Tachygastria 536.8
Tachypnea 786.06
hysterical 300.11
newborn (idiopathic) (transitory) 770.6
psychogenic 306.1
transitory, of newborn 770.6
TACO (transfusion associated circulatory overload) 276.61
Taenia (infection) (infestation) — *see also* Infestation, taenia 123.3
diminuta 123.6
echinococcal infestation (*see also* Echinococcus) 122.9
nana 123.6
saginata infestation 123.2
solium (intestinal form) 123.0
larval form 123.1
Taeniasis (intestine) — *see also* Infestation, taenia 123.3
saginata 123.2
solium 123.0
Taenzer's disease 757.4
Tag (hypertrophied skin) (infected) 701.9
adenoid 474.8
anus 455.9
endocardial (*see also* Endocarditis) 424.90
hemorrhoidal 455.9
hymen 623.8
perineal 624.8
preauricular 744.1
rectum 455.9
sentinel 455.9
skin 701.9
accessory 757.39
anus 455.9
congenital 757.39
preauricular 744.1
rectum 455.9
tonsil 474.8
urethra, urethral 599.84
vulva 624.8
Tahyna fever 062.5
Takayasu (-Onishi) disease or syndrome (pulseless disease) 446.7
Takotsubo syndrome 429.83
Talc granuloma 728.82
in operation wound 998.7
Talcosis 502
Talipes (congenital) 754.70
acquired NEC 736.79
planus 734
asymmetric 754.79
acquired 736.79
calcaneovalgus 754.62
acquired 736.76
calcaneovarus 754.59
acquired 736.76
calcaneus 754.79
acquired 736.76
cavovarus 754.59

Talipes — *continued*
cavovarus — *continued*
acquired 736.75
cavus 754.71
acquired 736.73
equinovalgus 754.69
acquired 736.72
equinovarus 754.51
acquired 736.71
equinus 754.79
acquired, NEC 736.72
percavus 754.71
acquired 736.73
planovalgus 754.69
acquired 736.79
planus (acquired) (any degree) 734
congenital 754.61
due to rickets 268.1
valgus 754.60
acquired 736.79
varus 754.50
acquired 736.79
Talma's disease 728.85
Talon noir 924.20
hand 923.20
heel 924.20
toe 924.3
Tamponade heart (Rose's) — *see also* Pericarditis 423.3
Tanapox 059.21
Tangier disease (familial high-density lipoprotein deficiency) 272.5
Tank ear 380.12
Tantrum (childhood) — *see also* Disturbance, conduct 312.1 ☑
Tapeworm (infection) (infestation) — *see also* Infestation, tapeworm 123.9
Tapia's syndrome 352.6
Tarantism 297.8
Target-oval cell anemia 285.8
with thalassemia — *see* Thalassemia
Tarlov's cyst 355.9
Tarral-Besnier disease (pityriasis rubra pilaris) 696.4
Tarsalgia 729.2
Tarsal tunnel syndrome 355.5
Tarsitis (eyelid) 373.00
syphilitic 095.8 [373.00]
tuberculous (*see also* Tuberculosis) 017.0 ☑ [373.4]
Tartar (teeth) 523.6
Tattoo (mark) 709.09
Taurodontism 520.2
Taussig-Bing defect, heart, or syndrome (transposition, aorta and overriding pulmonary artery) 745.11
Taybi's syndrome (otopalatodigital) 759.89
Tay's choroiditis 363.41
Taylor's
disease (diffuse idiopathic cutaneous atrophy) 701.8
syndrome 625.5
Tay-Sachs
amaurotic familial idiocy 330.1
disease 330.1
TBI (traumatic brain injury) — *see also* Injury, intracranial 854.0 ☑
with skull fracture — *see* Fracture, skull, by site
Tear stone 375.57
Tear, torn (traumatic) — *see also* Wound, open, by site
annular fibrosis 722.51
anus, anal (sphincter) 863.89
with open wound in cavity 863.99
complicating delivery (healed) (old) 654.8 ☑
with mucosa 664.3 ☑
not associated with third-degree perineal laceration 664.6 ☑
nontraumatic, nonpuerperal (healed) (old) 569.43
articular cartilage, old (*see also* Disorder, cartilage, articular) 718.0 ☑

☑ **Additional Digit Required** — Refer to the Tabular List for Digit Selection
◥ **Subterms under main terms may continue to next column or page**
2015 ICD-9-CM   ▶◀ Revised Text   ● New Line   ▲ Revised Code   Volume 2 — 277

Tear, torn — *see also* Wound, open, by site — *continued*
  bladder
    with
      abortion — *see* Abortion, by type, with damage to pelvic organs
      ectopic pregnancy (*see also* categories 633.0–633.9) 639.2
      molar pregnancy (*see also* categories 630–632) 639.2
    following
      abortion 639.2
      ectopic or molar pregnancy 639.2
    obstetrical trauma 665.5 ☑
  bowel
    with
      abortion — *see* Abortion, by type, with damage to pelvic organs
      ectopic pregnancy (*see also* categories 633.0–633.9) 639.2
      molar pregnancy (*see also* categories 630–632) 639.2
    following
      abortion 639.2
      ectopic or molar pregnancy 639.2
    obstetrical trauma 665.5 ☑
  broad ligament
    with
      abortion — *see* Abortion, by type, with damage to pelvic organs
      ectopic pregnancy (*see also* categories 633.0–633.9) 639.2
      molar pregnancy (*see also* categories 630–632) 639.2
    following
      abortion 639.2
      ectopic or molar pregnancy 639.2
    obstetrical trauma 665.6 ☑
  bucket handle (knee) (meniscus) — *see* Tear, meniscus
  capsule
    joint — *see* Sprain, by site
    spleen — *see* Laceration, spleen, capsule
  cartilage (*see also* Sprain, by site)
    articular, old (*see also* Disorder, cartilage, articular) 718.0 ☑
    knee — *see* Tear, meniscus
    semilunar (knee) (current injury) — *see* Tear, meniscus
  cervix
    with
      abortion — *see* Abortion, by type, with damage to pelvic organs
      ectopic pregnancy (*see also* categories 633.0–633.9) 639.2
      molar pregnancy (*see also* categories 630–632) 639.2
    following
      abortion 639.2
      ectopic or molar pregnancy 639.2
    obstetrical trauma (current) 665.3 ☑
    old 622.3
  dural 349.31
    accidental puncture or laceration during a procedure 349.31
    incidental (inadvertent) 349.31
    nontraumatic NEC 349.39
  internal organ (abdomen, chest, or pelvis) — *see* Injury, internal, by site
  ligament (*see also* Sprain, by site)
    with open wound — *see* Wound, open, by site
  meniscus (knee) (current injury) 836.2
    bucket handle 836.0
      old 717.0
    lateral 836.1
      anterior horn 836.1
        old 717.42
      bucket handle 836.1
        old 717.41
      old 717.40
      posterior horn 836.1
        old 717.43
      specified site NEC 836.1
        old 717.49
    medial 836.0

Tear, torn — *see also* Wound, open, by site — *continued*
  meniscus — *continued*
    medial — *continued*
      anterior horn 836.0
        old 717.1
      bucket handle 836.0
        old 717.0
      old 717.3
      posterior horn 836.0
        old 717.2
    old NEC 717.5
    site other than knee — *see* Sprain, by site
  muscle (*see also* Sprain, by site)
    with open wound — *see* Wound, open by site
  pelvic
    floor, complicating delivery 664.1 ☑
    organ NEC
      with
        abortion — *see* Abortion, by type, with damage to pelvic organs
        ectopic pregnancy (*see also* categories 633.0–633.9) 639.2
        molar pregnancy (*see also* categories 630–632) 639.2
      following
        abortion 639.2
        ectopic or molar pregnancy 639.2
      obstetrical trauma 665.5 ☑
  perineum (*see also* Laceration, perineum)
    obstetrical trauma 665.5 ☑
  periurethral tissue
    with
      abortion — *see* Abortion, by type, with damage to pelvic organs
      ectopic pregnancy (*see also* categories 633.0–633.9) 639.2
      molar pregnancy (*see also* categories 630–632) 639.2
    following
      abortion 639.2
      ectopic or molar pregnancy 639.2
    obstetrical trauma 664.8 ☑
  rectovaginal septum — *see* Laceration, rectovaginal septum
  retina, retinal (recent) (with detachment) 361.00
    without detachment 361.30
    dialysis (juvenile) (with detachment) 361.04
    giant (with detachment) 361.03
    horseshoe (without detachment) 361.32
    multiple (with detachment) 361.02
      without detachment 361.33
    old
      delimited (partial) 361.06
      partial 361.06
      total or subtotal 361.07
    partial (without detachment)
      giant 361.03
      multiple defects 361.02
      old (delimited) 361.06
      single defect 361.01
    round hole (without detachment) 361.31
    single defect (with detachment) 361.01
    total or subtotal (recent) 361.05
      old 361.07
  rotator cuff (traumatic) 840.4
    current injury 840.4
    degenerative 726.10
    nontraumatic (complete) 727.61
      partial 726.13
  semilunar cartilage, knee (*see also* Tear, meniscus) 836.2
    old 717.5
  tendon (*see also* Sprain, by site)
    with open wound — *see* Wound, open by site
  tentorial, at birth 767.0
  umbilical cord
    affecting fetus or newborn 772.0
    complicating delivery 663.8 ☑

Tear, torn — *see also* Wound, open, by site — *continued*
  urethra
    with
      abortion — *see* Abortion, by type, with damage to pelvic organs
      ectopic pregnancy (*see also* categories 633.0–633.9) 639.2
      molar pregnancy (*see also* categories 630–632) 639.2
    following
      abortion 639.2
      ectopic or molar pregnancy 639.2
    obstetrical trauma 665.5 ☑
  uterus — *see* Injury, internal, uterus
  vagina — *see* Laceration, vagina
  vessel, from catheter 998.2
  vulva, complicating delivery 664.0 ☑

Teething 520.7
  syndrome 520.7
Teeth, tooth — *see also* condition
  grinding 306.8
  prenatal 520.6
Tegmental syndrome 344.89
Telangiectasia, telangiectasis (verrucous) 448.9
  ataxic (cerebellar) 334.8
  familial 448.0
  hemorrhagic, hereditary (congenital) (senile) 448.0
  hereditary hemorrhagic 448.0
  retina 362.15
  spider 448.1
Telecanthus (congenital) 743.63
Telescoped bowel or intestine — *see also* Intussusception 560.0
Teletherapy, adverse effect NEC 990
Telogen effluvium 704.02
Temperature
  body, high (of unknown origin) (*see also* Pyrexia) 780.60
  cold, trauma from 991.9
    newborn 778.2
    specified effect NEC 991.8
  high
    body (of unknown origin) (*see also* Pyrexia) 780.60
    trauma from — *see* Heat
Temper tantrum (childhood) — *see also* Disturbance, conduct 312.1 ☑
Temple — *see* condition
Temporal — *see also* condition
  lobe syndrome 310.0
Temporomandibular joint-pain-dysfunction syndrome 524.60
Temporosphenoidal — *see* condition
Tendency
  bleeding (*see also* Defect, coagulation) 286.9
  homosexual, ego-dystonic 302.0
  paranoid 301.0
  suicide 300.9
Tenderness
  abdominal (generalized) (localized) 789.6 ☑
  rebound 789.6 ☑
  skin 782.0
Tendinitis, tendonitis — *see also* Tenosynovitis 726.90
  Achilles 726.71
  adhesive 726.90
    shoulder 726.0
  calcific 727.82
    shoulder 726.11
  gluteal 726.5
  patellar 726.64
  peroneal 726.79
  pes anserinus 726.61
  psoas 726.5
  tibialis (anterior) (posterior) 726.72
  trochanteric 726.5
Tendon — *see* condition
Tendosynovitis — *see* Tenosynovitis
Tendovaginitis — *see* Tenosynovitis
Tenesmus 787.99
  rectal 787.99
  vesical 788.99
Tenia — *see* Taenia

Teniasis — *see* Taeniasis
Tennis elbow 726.32
Tenonitis — *see also* Tenosynovitis
  eye (capsule) 376.04
Tenontosynovitis — *see* Tenosynovitis
Tenontothecitis — *see* Tenosynovitis
Tenophyte 727.9
Tenosynovitis (*see also* Synovitis) 727.00
  adhesive 726.90
    shoulder 726.0
  ankle 727.06
  bicipital (calcifying) 726.12
  buttock 727.09
  due to crystals — *see* Arthritis, due to crystals
  elbow 727.09
  finger 727.05
  foot 727.06
  gonococcal 098.51
  hand 727.05
  hip 727.09
  knee 727.09
  radial styloid 727.04
  shoulder 726.10
    adhesive 726.0
  specified NEC 727.09
  spine 720.1
  supraspinatus 726.10
  toe 727.06
  tuberculous — *see* Tuberculosis, tenosynovitis
  wrist 727.05
Tenovaginitis — *see* Tenosynovitis
Tension
  arterial, high (*see also* Hypertension) 401.9
    without diagnosis of hypertension 796.2
  headache 307.81
  intraocular (elevated) 365.00
  nervous 799.21
  ocular (elevated) 365.00
  pneumothorax 512.0
    iatrogenic 512.1
    postoperative 512.1
    spontaneous 512.0
  premenstrual 625.4
  state 300.9
Tentorium — *see* condition
Teratencephalus 759.89
Teratism 759.7
Teratoblastoma (malignant) (M9080/3) — *see* Neoplasm, by site, malignant
Teratocarcinoma (M9081/3) — *see also* Neoplasm, by site, malignant
  liver 155.0
Teratoma (solid) (M9080/1) — *see also* Neoplasm, by site, uncertain behavior
  adult (cystic) (M9080/0) — *see* Neoplasm, by site, benign
  and embryonal carcinoma, mixed (M9081/3) — *see* Neoplasm, by site, malignant
  benign (M9080/0) — *see* Neoplasm, by site, benign
  combined with choriocarcinoma (M9101/3) — *see* Neoplasm, by site, malignant
  cystic (adult) (M9080/0) — *see* Neoplasm, by site, benign
  differentiated type (M9080/0) — *see* Neoplasm, by site, benign
  embryonal (M9080/3) (*see also* Neoplasm, by site, malignant)
    liver 155.0
  fetal
    sacral, causing fetopelvic disproportion 653.7 ☑
  immature (M9080/3) — *see* Neoplasm, by site, malignant
  liver (M9080/3) 155.0
    adult, benign, cystic, differentiated type or mature (M9080/0) 211.5
  malignant (M9080/3) (*see also* Neoplasm, by site, malignant)
    anaplastic type (M9082/3) — *see* Neoplasm, by site, malignant
    intermediate type (M9083/3) — *see* Neoplasm, by site, malignant
    liver (M9080/3) 155.0

☑ Additional Digit Required — Refer to the Tabular List for Digit Selection ▽ Subterms under main terms may continue to next column or page

278 — Volume 2   ▶◀ Revised Text   ● New Line   ▲ Revised Code   2015 ICD-9-CM

Teratoma — see also Neoplasm, by site,
    uncertain behavior — continued
    malignant (see also Neoplasm, by site, malig-
        nant) — continued
        trophoblastic (M9102/3)
            specified site — see Neoplasm, by
                site, malignant
            unspecified site 186.9
        undifferentiated type (M9082/3) — see
            Neoplasm, by site, malignant
    mature (M9080/0) — see Neoplasm, by site,
        benign
        malignant (M9080/3) — see Neoplasm,
            by site, malignant
    ovary (M9080/0) 220
        embryonal, immature, or malignant
            (M9080/3) 183.0
        suprasellar (M9080/3) — see Neoplasm, by
            site, malignant
    testis (M9080/3) 186.9
        adult, benign, cystic, differentiated type
            or mature (M9080/0) 222.0
        undescended 186.0
Terminal care V66.7
Termination
    anomalous (see also Malposition, congeni-
        tal)
        portal vein 747.49
        right pulmonary vein 747.42
    pregnancy (legal) (therapeutic) — see
        Abortion, legal 635.9 ☑
        fetus NEC 779.6
        illegal (see also Abortion, illegal)
            636.9 ☑
Ternidens diminutus infestation 127.7
Terrors, night (child) 307.46
Terry's syndrome (see also Retinopathy of
    prematurity) 362.21
Tertiary — see condition
Tessellated fundus, retina (tigroid) 362.89
Test(s)
    adequacy
        hemodialysis V56.31
        peritoneal dialysis V56.32
    AIDS virus V72.69
    allergen V72.7
    bacterial disease NEC (see also Screening,
        by name of disease) V74.9
    basal metabolic rate V72.69
    blood
        alcohol V70.4
        drug V70.4
            for therapeutic drug monitoring
                V58.83
            for routine general physical examination
                V72.62
            prior to treatment or procedure V72.63
        typing V72.86
            Rh typing V72.86
    developmental, infant or child V20.2
    Dick V74.8
    fertility V26.21
    genetic
        female V26.32
        for genetic disease carrier status
            female V26.31
            male V26.34
        male V26.39
    hearing V72.19
        following failed hearing screening
            V72.11
        routine, for infant and child V20.2
    HIV V72.69
    human immunodeficiency virus V72.69
    immunity status V72.61
    Kveim V82.89
    laboratory V72.60
        for medicolegal reason V70.4
        ordered as part of a routine general
            medical examination V72.62
        pre-operative V72.63
        pre-procedural V72.63
        specified NEC V72.69
    male partner of female with recurrent
        pregnancy loss V26.35
    Mantoux (for tuberculosis) V74.1

Test(s) — continued
    mycotic organism V75.4
    nuchal translucency V28.89
    parasitic agent NEC V75.8
    paternity V70.4
    peritoneal equilibration V56.32
    pregnancy
        negative result V72.41
        positive result V72.42
            first pregnancy V72.42
        unconfirmed V72.40
    preoperative V72.84
        cardiovascular V72.81
        respiratory V72.82
        specified NEC V72.83
    procreative management NEC V26.29
        genetic disease carrier status
            female V26.31
            male V26.34
    Rh typing V72.86
    sarcoidosis V82.89
    Schick V74.3
    Schultz-Charlton V74.8
    skin, diagnostic
        allergy V72.7
        bacterial agent NEC (see also Screening,
            by name of disease) V74.9
        Dick V74.8
        hypersensitivity V72.7
        Kveim V82.89
        Mantoux V74.1
        mycotic organism V75.4
        parasitic agent NEC V75.8
        sarcoidosis V82.89
        Schick V74.3
        Schultz-Charlton V74.8
        tuberculin V74.1
    specified type NEC V72.85
    tuberculin V74.1
    vision V72.0
        routine, for infant and child V20.2
    Wassermann
        positive (see also Serology for syphilis,
            positive) 097.1
        false 795.6
Testicle, testicular, testis — see also condition
    feminization (syndrome) 259.51
Tetanus, tetanic (cephalic) (convulsions) 037
    with
        abortion — see Abortion, by type, with
            sepsis
        ectopic pregnancy (see also categories
            633.0–633.9) 639.0
        molar pregnancy — see categories
            630–632 639.0
    following
        abortion 639.0
        ectopic or molar pregnancy 639.0
    inoculation V03.7
        reaction (due to serum) — see Complica-
            tions, vaccination
    neonatorum 771.3
    puerperal, postpartum, childbirth 670.8 ☑
Tetany, tetanic 781.7
    alkalosis 276.3
    associated with rickets 268.0
    convulsions 781.7
        hysterical 300.11
    functional (hysterical) 300.11
    hyperkinetic 781.7
        hysterical 300.11
    hyperpnea 786.01
        hysterical 300.11
        psychogenic 306.1
    hyperventilation 786.01
        hysterical 300.11
        psychogenic 306.1
    hypocalcemic, neonatal 775.4
    hysterical 300.11
    neonatal 775.4
    parathyroid (gland) 252.1
    parathyroprival 252.1
    postoperative 252.1
    postthyroidectomy 252.1
    pseudotetany 781.7
        hysterical 300.11

Tetany, tetanic — continued
    psychogenic 306.1
        specified as conversion reaction 300.11
Tetralogy of Fallot 745.2
Tetraplegia — see Quadriplegia
Thailand hemorrhagic fever 065.4
Thalassanemia 282.40
Thalassemia (disease) 282.40
    with other hemoglobinopathy 282.49
    alpha (major) (severe) (triple gene defect)
        282.43
        silent carrier 282.46
    beta (homozygous) (major) (severe) 282.44
    delta-beta (homozygous) 282.45
    dominant 282.49
    Hb-S (without crisis) 282.41
        with
            crisis 282.42
            vaso-occlusive pain 282.42
    hemoglobin
        C (Hb-C) 282.49
        D (Hb-D) 282.49
        E (Hb-E) 282.49
        E-beta 282.47
        H (Hb-H) 282.49
        I (Hb-I) 282.49
    high fetal gene (see also Thalassemia) 282.40
    high fetal hemoglobin (see also Thalassemia)
        282.40
    intermedia 282.44
    major 282.44
    minor (alpha) (beta) 282.46
    mixed 282.49
    sickle-cell (without crisis) 282.41
        with
            crisis 282.42
            vaso-occlusive pain 282.42
    specified NEC 282.49
    trait (alpha) (beta) (delta-beta) 282.46
Thalassemic variants 282.49
Thaysen-Gee disease (nontropical sprue)
    579.0
Thecoma (M8600/0) 220
    malignant (M8600/3) 183.0
Thelarche, precocious 259.1
Thelitis 611.0
    puerperal, postpartum 675.0 ☑
Therapeutic — see condition
Therapy V57.9
    blood transfusion, without reported diagno-
        sis V58.2
    breathing V57.0
    chemotherapy, antineoplastic V58.11
        fluoride V07.31
        prophylactic NEC V07.39
    dialysis (intermittent) (treatment)
        extracorporeal V56.0
        peritoneal V56.8
        renal V56.0
        specified type NEC V56.8
    exercise NEC V57.1
        breathing V57.0
    extracorporeal dialysis (renal) V56.0
    fluoride prophylaxis V07.31
    hemodialysis V56.0
    hormone replacement (postmenopausal)
        V07.4
    immunotherapy antineoplastic V58.12
    long term oxygen therapy V46.2
    occupational V57.21
    orthoptic V57.4
    orthotic V57.81
    peritoneal dialysis V56.8
    physical NEC V57.1
    postmenopausal hormone replacement
        V07.4
    radiation V58.0
    speech (-language) V57.3
    vocational V57.22
Thermalgesia 782.0
Thermalgia 782.0
Thermanalgesia 782.0
Thermanesthesia 782.0
Thermic — see condition
Thermography (abnormal) 793.99
    breast 793.89

Thermoplegia 992.0
Thesaurismosis
    amyloid 277.39
    bilirubin 277.4
    calcium 275.40
    cystine 270.0
    glycogen (see also Disease, glycogen stor-
        age) 271.0
    kerasin 272.7
    lipoid 272.7
    melanin 255.41
    phosphatide 272.7
    urate 274.9
Thiaminic deficiency 265.1
    with beriberi 265.0
Thibierge-Weissenbach syndrome (cuta-
    neous systemic sclerosis) 710.1
Thickened endometrium 793.5
Thickening
    bone 733.99
        extremity 733.99
    breast 611.79
    hymen 623.3
    larynx 478.79
    nail 703.8
        congenital 757.5
    periosteal 733.99
    pleura (see also Pleurisy) 511.0
    skin 782.8
    subepiglottic 478.79
    tongue 529.8
    valve, heart — see Endocarditis
Thiele syndrome 724.6
Thigh — see condition
Thinning vertebra — see also Osteoporosis
    733.00
Thirst, excessive 783.5
    due to deprivation of water 994.3
Thomsen's disease 359.22
Thomson's disease (congenital poikiloderma)
    757.33
Thoracic — see also condition
    kidney 753.3
    outlet syndrome 353.0
    stomach — see Hernia, diaphragm
Thoracogastroschisis (congenital) 759.89
Thoracopagus 759.4
Thoracoschisis 756.3
**Thoracoscopic surgical procedure converted
    to open procedure** V64.42
Thorax — see condition
Thorn's syndrome — see also Disease, renal
    593.9
Thornwaldt's, Tornwaldt's
    bursitis (pharyngeal) 478.29
    cyst 478.26
    disease (pharyngeal bursitis) 478.29
Thorson-Biörck syndrome (malignant carci-
    noid) 259.2
Threadworm (infection) (infestation) 127.4
Threatened
    abortion or miscarriage 640.0 ☑
        with subsequent abortion (see also
            Abortion, spontaneous) 634.9 ☑
        affecting fetus 762.1
    labor 644.1 ☑
        affecting fetus or newborn 761.8
        premature 644.0 ☑
    miscarriage 640.0 ☑
        affecting fetus 762.1
    premature
        delivery 644.2 ☑
            affecting fetus or newborn 761.8
        labor 644.0 ☑
            before 22 completed weeks gesta-
                tion 640.0 ☑
Three-day fever 066.0
Threshers' lung 495.0
Thrix annulata (congenital) 757.4
Throat — see condition
Thrombasthenia (Glanzmann's) (hemorrhagic)
    (hereditary) 287.1
Thromboangiitis 443.1
    obliterans (general) 443.1
        cerebral 437.1

☑ Additional Digit Required — Refer to the Tabular List for Digit Selection   ▽ Subterms under main terms may continue to next column or page

2015 ICD-9-CM   ▶◀ Revised Text   ● New Line   ▲ Revised Code   Volume 2 — 279

Thromboangiitis — *continued*
  obliterans — *continued*
    vessels
      brain 437.1
      spinal cord 437.1
Thromboarteritis — *see* Arteritis
Thromboasthenia (Glanzmann's) (hemorrhagic) (hereditary) 287.1
Thrombocytasthenia (Glanzmann's) 287.1
Thrombocythemia (primary) (M9962/1) 238.71
  essential 238.71
  hemorrhagic 238.71
  idiopathic (hemorrhagic) (M9962/1) 238.71
Thrombocytopathy (dystrophic) (granulopenic) 287.1
Thrombocytopenia, thrombocytopenic 287.5
  with
    absent radii (TAR) syndrome 287.33
    giant hemangioma 287.39
  amegakaryocytic, congenital 287.33
  congenital 287.33
  cyclic 287.39
  dilutional 287.49
  due to
    drugs 287.49
    extracorporeal circulation of blood 287.49
    massive blood transfusion 287.49
    platelet alloimmunization 287.49
  essential 287.30
  fetal 678.0 ☑
  heparin-induced (HIT) 289.84
  hereditary 287.33
  Kasabach-Merritt 287.39
  neonatal, transitory 776.1
    due to
      exchange transfusion 776.1
      idiopathic maternal thrombocytopenia 776.1
      isoimmunization 776.1
  primary 287.30
  puerperal, postpartum 666.3 ☑
  purpura (*see also* Purpura, thrombocytopenic) 287.30
    thrombotic 446.6
  secondary NEC 287.49
  sex-linked 287.39
Thrombocytosis 238.71
  essential 238.71
  primary 238.71
Thromboembolism — *see* Embolism
Thrombopathy (Bernard-Soulier) 287.1
  constitutional 286.4
  Willebrand-Jürgens (angiohemophilia) 286.4
Thrombopenia — *see also* Thrombocytopenia 287.5
Thrombophlebitis 451.9
  antecubital vein 451.82
  antepartum (superficial) 671.2 ☑
    affecting fetus or newborn 760.3
    deep 671.3 ☑
  arm 451.89
    deep 451.83
    superficial 451.82
  breast, superficial 451.89
  cavernous (venous) sinus — *see* Thrombophlebitis, intracranial venous sinus
  cephalic vein 451.82
  cerebral (sinus) (vein) 325
    late effect — *see* category 326
    nonpyogenic 437.6
      in pregnancy or puerperium 671.5 ☑
      late effect — *see* Late effect(s) (of) cerebrovascular disease
  due to implanted device — *see* Complications, due to (presence of) any device, implant or graft classified to 996.0–996.5 NEC
  during or resulting from a procedure NEC 997.2
  femoral 451.11
  femoropopliteal 451.19
  following infusion, perfusion, or transfusion 999.2
  hepatic (vein) 451.89
  idiopathic, recurrent 453.1

Thrombophlebitis — *continued*
  iliac vein 451.81
  iliofemoral 451.11
  intracranial venous sinus (any) 325
    late effect — *see* category 326
    nonpyogenic 437.6
      in pregnancy or puerperium 671.5 ☑
      late effect — *see* Late effect(s) (of) cerebrovascular disease
  jugular vein 451.89
  lateral (venous) sinus — *see* Thrombophlebitis, intracranial venous sinus
  leg 451.2
    deep (vessels) 451.19
      femoral vein 451.11
      specified vessel NEC 451.19
    superficial (vessels) 451.0
      femoral vein 451.11
  longitudinal (venous) sinus — *see* Thrombophlebitis, intracranial venous sinus
  lower extremity 451.2
    deep (vessels) 451.19
      femoral vein 451.11
      specified vessel NEC 451.19
    superficial (vessels) 451.0
  migrans, migrating 453.1
  pelvic
    with
      abortion — *see* Abortion, by type, with sepsis
      ectopic pregnancy (*see also* categories 633.0–633.9) 639.0
      molar pregnancy (*see also* categories 630–632) 639.0
    following
      abortion 639.0
      ectopic or molar pregnancy 639.0
    puerperal 671.4 ☑
  popliteal vein 451.19
  portal (vein) 572.1
  postoperative 997.2
  pregnancy (superficial) 671.2 ☑
    affecting fetus or newborn 760.3
    deep 671.3 ☑
  puerperal, postpartum, childbirth (extremities) (superficial) 671.2 ☑
    deep 671.4 ☑
    pelvic 671.4 ☑
    septic 670.3 ☑
    specified site NEC 671.5 ☑
  radial vein 451.83
  saphenous (greater) (lesser) 451.0
  sinus (intracranial) — *see* Thrombophlebitis, intracranial venous sinus
    specified site NEC 451.89
  tibial vein 451.19
Thrombosis, thrombotic (maranchic) (multiple) (progressive) (vein) (vessel) 453.9
  with childbirth or during the puerperium — *see* Thrombosis, puerperal, postpartum
  antepartum — *see* Thrombosis, pregnancy
  aorta, aortic 444.1
    abdominal 444.09
      saddle 444.01
    bifurcation 444.09
      saddle 444.01
    terminal 444.09
    thoracic 444.1
    valve — *see* Endocarditis, aortic
  apoplexy (*see also* Thrombosis, brain) 434.0 ☑
    late effect — *see* Late effect(s) (of) cerebrovascular disease
  appendix, septic — *see* Appendicitis, acute
  arteriolar-capillary platelet, disseminated 446.6
  artery, arteries (postinfectional) 444.9
    auditory, internal 433.8 ☑
    basilar (*see also* Occlusion, artery, basilar) 433.0 ☑
    carotid (common) (internal) (*see also* Occlusion, artery, carotid) 433.1 ☑
      with other precerebral artery 433.3 ☑

Thrombosis, thrombotic — *continued*
  artery, arteries — *continued*
    cerebellar (anterior inferior) (posterior inferior) (superior) 433.8 ☑
    cerebral (*see also* Thrombosis, brain) 434.0 ☑
    choroidal (anterior) 433.8 ☑
    communicating posterior 433.8 ☑
    coronary (*see also* Infarct, myocardium) 410.9 ☑
      without myocardial infarction 411.81
      due to syphilis 093.89
      healed or specified as old 412
    extremities 444.22
      lower 444.22
      upper 444.21
    femoral 444.22
    hepatic 444.89
    hypophyseal 433.8 ☑
    meningeal, anterior or posterior 433.8 ☑
    mesenteric (with gangrene) 557.0
    ophthalmic (*see also* Occlusion, retina) 362.30
    pontine 433.8 ☑
    popliteal 444.22
    precerebral — *see* Occlusion, artery, precerebral NEC
    pulmonary 415.19
      iatrogenic 415.11
      personal history of V12.55
      postoperative 415.11
      septic 415.12
    renal 593.81
    retinal (*see also* Occlusion, retina) 362.30
    specified site NEC 444.89
    spinal, anterior or posterior 433.8 ☑
    traumatic (complication) (early) (*see also* Injury, blood vessel, by site) 904.9
    vertebral (*see also* Occlusion, artery, vertebral) 433.2 ☑
      with other precerebral artery 433.3 ☑
  atrial (endocardial) 424.90
    without endocarditis 429.89
    due to syphilis 093.89
  auricular (*see also* Infarct, myocardium) 410.9 ☑
  axillary (acute) (vein) 453.84
    chronic 453.74
    personal history of V12.51
  basilar (artery) (*see also* Occlusion, artery, basilar) 433.0 ☑
  bland NEC 453.9
  brain (artery) (stem) 434.0 ☑
    due to syphilis 094.89
    iatrogenic 997.02
    late effect — *see* Late effect(s) (of) cerebrovascular disease
    postoperative 997.02
    puerperal, postpartum, childbirth 674.0 ☑
    sinus (*see also* Thrombosis, intracranial venous sinus) 325
  capillary 448.9
    arteriolar, generalized 446.6
  cardiac (*see also* Infarct, myocardium) 410.9 ☑
    due to syphilis 093.89
    healed or specified as old 412
    valve — *see* Endocarditis
  carotid (artery) (common) (internal) (*see also* Occlusion, artery, carotid) 433.1 ☑
    with other precerebral artery 433.3 ☑
  cavernous sinus (venous) — *see* Thrombosis, intracranial venous sinus
  cerebellar artery (anterior inferior) (posterior inferior) (superior) 433.8 ☑
    late effect — *see* Late effect(s) (of) cerebrovascular disease
  cerebral (arteries) (*see also* Thrombosis, brain) 434.0 ☑
    late effect — *see* Late effect(s) (of) cerebrovascular disese
  coronary (artery) (*see also* Infarct, myocardium) 410.9 ☑

Thrombosis, thrombotic — *continued*
  coronary (*see also* Infarct, myocardium) — *continued*
    without myocardial infarction 411.81
    due to syphilis 093.89
    healed or specified as old 412
  corpus cavernosum 607.82
  cortical (*see also* Thrombosis, brain) 434.0 ☑
  due to (presence of) any device, implant, or graft classifiable to 996.0–996.5 — *see* Complications, due to (presence of) any device, implant, or graft classified to 996.0–996.5 NEC
  effort 453.89
  endocardial — *see* Infarct, myocardium
  eye (*see also* Occlusion, retina) 362.30
  femoral (vein) 453.6
    with inflammation or phlebitis 451.11
    artery 444.22
    deep 453.41
    personal history of V12.51
  genital organ, male 608.83
  heart (chamber) (*see also* Infarct, myocardium) 410.9 ☑
  hepatic (vein) 453.0
    artery 444.89
    infectional or septic 572.1
  iliac (acute) (vein) 453.41
    with inflammation or phlebitis 451.81
    artery (common) (external) (internal) 444.81
    chronic 453.51
    personal history of V12.51
  inflammation, vein — *see* Thrombophlebitis
  internal carotid artery (*see also* Occlusion, artery, carotid) 433.1 ☑
    with other precerebral artery 433.3 ☑
  intestine (with gangrene) 557.0
  intracranial (*see also* Thrombosis, brain) 434.0 ☑
    venous sinus (any) 325
      nonpyogenic origin 437.6
        in pregnancy or puerperium 671.5 ☑
  intramural (*see also* Infarct, myocardium) 410.9 ☑
    without
      cardiac condition 429.89
      coronary artery disease 429.89
      myocardial infarction 429.89
    healed or specified as old 412
  jugular (bulb)
    external (acute) 453.89
      chronic 453.79
    internal (acute) 453.86
      chronic 453.76
  kidney 593.81
    artery 593.81
  lateral sinus (venous) — *see* Thrombosis, intracranial venous sinus
  leg (*see also* Thrombosis, lower extremity) 453.6
    with inflammation or phlebitis — *see* Thrombophlebitis
    deep (vessels) 453.40
      acute 453.40
        lower distal 453.42
        upper (proximal) 453.41
      chronic 453.50
        lower (distal) 453.52
        upper (proximal) 453.51
      lower (distal) 453.42
      upper (proximal) 453.41
    personal history of V12.51
    superficial (vessels) 453.6
  liver (venous) 453.0
    artery 444.89
    infectional or septic 572.1
    portal vein 452
  longitudinal sinus (venous) — *see* Thrombosis, intracranial venous sinus
  lower extremity (superficial) 453.6
    deep vessels 453.40
      acute 453.40
        calf 453.42
        distal (lower leg) 453.42

☑ **Additional Digit Required — Refer to the Tabular List for Digit Selection**

✏ **Subterms under main terms may continue to next column or page**

Thrombosis, thrombotic — *continued*
  lower extremity — *continued*
    deep vessels — *continued*
      acute — *continued*
        femoral 453.41
        iliac 453.41
        lower leg 453.42
        peroneal 453.42
        popliteal 453.41
        proximal (upper leg) 453.41
        thigh 453.41
        tibial 453.42
      chronic 453.50
        calf 453.52
        distal (lower leg) 453.52
        femoral 453.51
        iliac 453.51
        lower leg 453.52
        peroneal 453.52
        popliteal 453.51
        proximal (upper leg) 453.51
        thigh 453.51
        tibial 453.52
    personal history of V12.51
    saphenous (greater) (lesser) 453.6
    superficial 453.6
  lung 415.19
    iatrogenic 415.11
    personal history of V12.55
    postoperative 415.11
    septic 415.12
  marantic, dural sinus 437.6
  meninges (brain) (*see also* Thrombosis, brain) 434.0 ☑
  mesenteric (artery) (with gangrene) 557.0
    vein (inferior) (superior) 557.0
  mitral — *see* Insufficiency, mitral
  mural (heart chamber) (*see also* Infarct, myocardium) 410.9 ☑
    without
      cardiac condition 429.89
      coronary artery disease 429.89
      myocardial infarction 429.89
    due to syphilis 093.89
    following myocardial infarction 429.79
    healed or specified as old 412
  omentum (with gangrene) 557.0
  ophthalmic (artery) (*see also* Occlusion, retina) 362.30
  pampiniform plexus (male) 608.83
    female 620.8
  parietal (*see also* Infarct, myocardium) 410.9 ☑
  penis, penile 607.82
  peripheral arteries 444.22
    lower 444.22
    upper 444.21
  platelet 446.6
  portal 452
    due to syphilis 093.89
    infectional or septic 572.1
  precerebral artery (*see also* Occlusion, artery, precerebral NEC)
  pregnancy 671.2 ☑
    deep (vein) 671.3 ☑
    superficial (vein) 671.2 ☑
  puerperal, postpartum, childbirth 671.2 ☑
    brain (artery) 674.0 ☑
      venous 671.5 ☑
    cardiac 674.8 ☑
    cerebral (artery) 674.0 ☑
      venous 671.5 ☑
    deep (vein) 671.4 ☑
    intracranial sinus (nonpyogenic) (venous) 671.5 ☑
    pelvic 671.4 ☑
    pulmonary (artery) 673.2 ☑
    specified site NEC 671.5 ☑
    superficial 671.2 ☑
  pulmonary (artery) (vein) 415.19
    iatrogenic 415.11
    personal history of V12.55
    postoperative 415.11
    septic 415.12
  renal (artery) 593.81
    vein 453.3

Thrombosis, thrombotic — *continued*
  resulting from presence of shunt or other internal prosthetic device — *see* Complications, due to (presence of) any device, implant, or graft classified to 996.0–996.5 NEC
  retina, retinal (artery) 362.30
    arterial branch 362.32
    central 362.31
    partial 362.33
    vein
      central 362.35
      tributary (branch) 362.36
  saphenous vein (greater) (lesser) 453.6
  scrotum 608.83
  seminal vesicle 608.83
  sigmoid (venous) sinus — *see* Thrombosis, intracranial venous sinus 325
  silent NEC 453.9
  sinus, intracranial (venous) (any) (*see also* Thrombosis, intracranial venous sinus) 325
  softening, brain (*see also* Thrombosis, brain) 434.0 ☑
  specified site NEC (acute) 453.89
    chronic 453.79
  spermatic cord 608.83
  spinal cord 336.1
    due to syphilis 094.89
    in pregnancy or puerperium 671.5 ☑
    pyogenic origin 324.1
      late effect — *see* category 326
  spleen, splenic 289.59
    artery 444.89
  testis 608.83
  traumatic (complication) (early) (*see also* Injury, blood vessel, by site) 904.9
  tricuspid — *see* Endocarditis, tricuspid
  tumor — *see* Neoplasm, by site
  tunica vaginalis 608.83
  umbilical cord (vessels) 663.6 ☑
    affecting fetus or newborn 762.6
  upper extremity (acute) 453.83
    chronic 453.73
      deep 453.72
      superficial 453.71
    deep 453.82
    superficial 453.81
  vas deferens 608.83
  vein
    antecubital (acute) 453.81
      chronic 453.71
    axillary (acute) 453.84
      chronic 453.74
    basilic (acute) 453.81
      chronic 453.71
    brachial (acute) 453.82
      chronic 453.72
    brachiocephalic (innominate) (acute) 453.87
      chronic 453.77
    cephalic (acute) 453.81
      chronic 453.71
    deep 453.40
      personal history of V12.51
    internal jugular (acute) 453.86
      chronic 453.76
    lower extremity — *see* Thrombosis, lower extremity
    personal history of V12.51
    radial (acute) 453.82
      chronic 453.72
    saphenous (greater) (lesser) 453.6
    specified site NEC (acute) 453.89
      chronic 453.79
    subclavian (acute) 453.85
      chronic 453.75
    superior vena cava (acute) 453.87
      chronic 453.77
    thoracic (acute) 453.87
      chronic 453.77
    ulnar (acute) 453.82
      chronic 453.72
    upper extremity — *see* Thrombosis, upper extremity

Thrombosis, thrombotic — *continued*
  vena cava
    inferior 453.2
      personal history of V12.51
    superior (acute) 453.87
      chronic 453.77
Thrombus — *see* Thrombosis
Thrush 112.0
  newborn 771.7
Thumb — *see also* condition
  gamekeeper's 842.12
  sucking (child problem) 307.9
Thygeson's superficial punctate keratitis 370.21
Thymergasia — *see also* Psychosis, affective 296.80
Thymitis 254.8
Thymoma (benign) (M8580/0) 212.6
  malignant (M8580/3) 164.0
Thymus, thymic (gland) — *see* condition
Thyrocele — *see also* Goiter 240.9
Thyroglossal — *see also* condition
  cyst 759.2
  duct, persistent 759.2
Thyroid (body) (gland) — *see also* condition
  hormone resistance 246.8
  lingual 759.2
Thyroiditis 245.9
  acute (pyogenic) (suppurative) 245.0
    nonsuppurative 245.0
  autoimmune 245.2
  chronic (nonspecific) (sclerosing) 245.8
    fibrous 245.3
    lymphadenoid 245.2
    lymphocytic 245.2
    lymphoid 245.2
  complicating pregnancy, childbirth, or puerperium 648.1 ☑
  de Quervain's (subacute granulomatous) 245.1
  fibrous (chronic) 245.3
  giant (cell) (follicular) 245.1
  granulomatous (de Quervain's) (subacute) 245.1
  Hashimoto's (struma lymphomatosa) 245.2
  iatrogenic 245.4
  invasive (fibrous) 245.3
  ligneous 245.3
  lymphocytic (chronic) 245.2
  lymphoid 245.2
  lymphomatous 245.2
  pseudotuberculous 245.1
  pyogenic 245.0
  radiation 245.4
  Riedel's (ligneous) 245.3
  subacute 245.1
  suppurative 245.0
  tuberculous (*see also* Tuberculosis) 017.5 ☑
  viral 245.1
  woody 245.3
Thyrolingual duct, persistent 759.2
Thyromegaly 240.9
Thyrotoxic
  crisis or storm (*see also* Thyrotoxicosis) 242.9 ☑
  heart failure (*see also* Thyrotoxicosis) 242.9 ☑ [425.7]
Thyrotoxicosis 242.9 ☑

Note — Use the following fifth-digit subclassification with category 242:

0   *without mention of thyrotoxic crisis or storm*

1   *with mention of thyrotoxic crisis or storm*

  with
    goiter (diffuse) 242.0 ☑
      adenomatous 242.3 ☑
        multinodular 242.2 ☑
        uninodular 242.1 ☑
      nodular 242.3 ☑
        multinodular 242.2 ☑
        uninodular 242.1 ☑
    infiltrative
      dermopathy 242.0 ☑

Thyrotoxicosis — *continued*
  with — *continued*
    infiltrative — *continued*
      ophthalmopathy 242.0 ☑
      thyroid acropachy 242.0 ☑
    complicating pregnancy, childbirth, or puerperium 648.1 ☑
  due to
    ectopic thyroid nodule 242.4 ☑
    ingestion of (excessive) thyroid material 242.8 ☑
    specified cause NEC 242.8 ☑
  factitia 242.8 ☑
  heart 242.9 ☑ [425.7]
  neonatal (transient) 775.3
TIA (transient ischemic attack) 435.9
  with transient neurologic deficit 435.9
  late effect — *see* Late effect(s) (of) cerebrovascular disease
Tibia vara 732.4
Tic 307.20
  breathing 307.20
  child problem 307.21
  compulsive 307.22
  convulsive 307.20
  degenerative (generalized) (localized) 333.3
    facial 351.8
  douloureux (*see also* Neuralgia, trigeminal) 350.1
    atypical 350.2
  habit 307.20
    chronic (motor or vocal) 307.22
    transient (of childhood) 307.21
  lid 307.20
    transient (of childhood) 307.21
  motor-verbal 307.23
  occupational 300.89
  orbicularis 307.20
    transient (of childhood) 307.21
  organic origin 333.3
  postchoreic — *see* Chorea
  psychogenic 307.20
    compulsive 307.22
  salaam 781.0
  spasm 307.20
    chronic (motor or vocal) 307.22
    transient (of childhood) 307.21
Tick-bite fever NEC 066.1
  African 087.1
  Colorado (virus) 066.1
  Rocky Mountain 082.0
Tick (-borne) fever NEC 066.1
  American mountain 066.1
  Colorado 066.1
  hemorrhagic NEC 065.3
    Crimean 065.0
    Kyasanur Forest 065.2
    Omsk 065.1
  mountain 066.1
  nonexanthematous 066.1
Tick paralysis 989.5
Tics and spasms, compulsive 307.22
Tietze's disease or syndrome 733.6
Tight, tightness
  anus 564.89
  chest 786.59
  fascia (lata) 728.9
  foreskin (congenital) 605
  hymen 623.3
  introitus (acquired) (congenital) 623.3
  rectal sphincter 564.89
  tendon 727.81
    Achilles (heel) 727.81
  urethral sphincter 598.9
Tilting vertebra 737.9
Timidity, child 313.21
Tinea (intersecta) (tarsi) 110.9
  amiantacea 110.0
  asbestina 110.0
  barbae 110.0
  beard 110.0
  black dot 110.0
  blanca 111.2
  capitis 110.0
  corporis 110.5
  cruris 110.3

☑ Additional Digit Required — Refer to the Tabular List for Digit Selection   ▽ Subterms under main terms may continue to next column or page

282 — Volume 2   ▶◀ Revised Text   ● New Line   ▲ Revised Code   2015 ICD-9-CM

Tracheopharyngitis (acute) 465.8
- chronic 478.9
  - due to external agent — *see* Condition, respiratory, chronic, due to
  - due to external agent — *see* Inflammation, respiratory, upper, due to

Tracheostenosis 519.19
- congenital 748.3

Tracheostomy
- attention to V55.0
- complication 519.00
- granuloma 519.09
- hemorrhage 519.09
- infection 519.01
- malfunctioning 519.02
- obstruction 519.09
- sepsis 519.01
- status V44.0
- stenosis 519.02

Trachoma, trachomatous 076.9
- active (stage) 076.1
- contraction of conjunctiva 076.1
- dubium 076.0
- healed or late effect 139.1
- initial (stage) 076.0
- Türck's (chronic catarrhal laryngitis) 476.0

Trachyphonia 784.49

Traction, vitreomacular 379.27

Training
- insulin pump V65.46
- orthoptic V57.4
- orthotic V57.81

Train sickness 994.6

Trait
- hemoglobin
  - abnormal NEC 282.7
    - with thalassemia 282.46
  - C (*see also* Disease, hemoglobin, C) 282.7
    - with elliptocytosis 282.7
  - S (Hb-S) 282.5
  - Lepore 282.49
    - with other abnormal hemoglobin NEC 282.49
- paranoid 301.0
- sickle-cell 282.5
  - with
    - elliptocytosis 282.5
    - spherocytosis 282.5
- thalassemia (alpha) (beta) (delta-beta) 282.46

Traits, paranoid 301.0

Tramp V60.0

Trance 780.09
- hysterical 300.13

Transaminasemia 790.4

Transfusion, blood
- without reported diagnosis V58.2
- donor V59.01
  - stem cells V59.02
- fetal twin to twin 678.0 ☑
- incompatible (*see also* Complications, transfusion) 999.80
  - ABO (*see also* Complications, transfusion) 999.60
  - minor blood group 999.89
  - non-ABO (*see also* Complications, transfusion) 999.75
  - Rh (antigen) (C) (c) (D) (E) (e) (*see also* Complications, transfusion) 999.70
- reaction or complication — *see* Complications, transfusion
- related acute lung injury (TRALI) 518.7
- syndrome
  - fetomaternal 772.0
  - twin-to-twin
    - blood loss (donor twin) 772.0
    - recipient twin 776.4
- twin to twin fetal 678.0 ☑

Transient — *see also* condition
- alteration of awareness 780.02
- blindness 368.12
- deafness (ischemic) 388.02
- global amnesia 437.7
- hyperglycemia (post-procedural) 790.29
- hypoglycemia (post-procedural) 251.2

Transient — *see also* condition — continued
- person (homeless) NEC V60.0

Transitional, lumbosacral joint of vertebra 756.19

Translocation
- autosomes NEC 758.5
  - 13-15 758.1
  - 16-18 758.2
  - 21 or 22 758.0
  - balanced in normal individual 758.4
  - D₁ 758.1
  - E₃ 758.2
  - G 758.0
- balanced autosomal in normal individual 758.4
- chromosomes NEC 758.89
- Down's syndrome 758.0

Translucency, iris 364.53

Transmission of chemical substances through the placenta (affecting fetus or newborn) 760.70
- alcohol 760.71
- anticonvulsants 760.77
- antifungals 760.74
- anti-infective agents 760.74
- antimetabolics 760.78
- cocaine 760.75
- "crack" 760.75
- diethylstilbestrol [DES] 760.76
- hallucinogenic agents 760.73
- medicinal agents NEC 760.79
- narcotics 760.72
- obstetric anesthetic or analgesic drug 763.5
- specified agent NEC 760.79
- suspected, affecting management of pregnancy 655.5 ☑

Transplant(ed)
- bone V42.4
  - marrow V42.81
- complication (*see also* Complications, due to (presence of) any device, implant, or graft classified to 996.0–996.5 NEC)
  - bone marrow 996.85
  - corneal graft NEC 996.79
    - infection or inflammation 996.69
    - reaction 996.51
    - rejection 996.51
  - organ (failure) (immune or nonimmune cause) (infection) (rejection) 996.80
    - bone marrow 996.85
    - heart 996.83
    - intestines 996.87
    - kidney 996.81
    - liver 996.82
    - lung 996.84
    - pancreas 996.86
    - specified NEC 996.89
  - previously removed due to complication, failure, rejection or infection V45.87
  - removal status V45.87
  - skin NEC 996.79
    - infection or inflammation 996.69
    - rejection 996.52
      - artificial 996.55
      - decellularized allodermis 996.55
  - stem cell(s) 996.88
    - from
      - peripheral blood 996.88
      - umbilical cord 996.88
- cornea V42.5
- hair V50.0
- heart V42.1
  - valve V42.2
- intestine V42.84
- kidney V42.0
- liver V42.7
- lung V42.6
- organ V42.9
  - specified NEC V42.89
- pancreas V42.83
- peripheral stem cells V42.82
- skin V42.3

Transplant(ed) — *continued*
- stem cells, peripheral V42.82
- tissue V42.9
  - specified NEC V42.89

Transplants, ovarian, endometrial 617.1

Transposed — *see* Transposition

Transposition (congenital) — *see also* Malposition, congenital
- abdominal viscera 759.3
- aorta (dextra) 745.11
- appendix 751.5
- arterial trunk 745.10
- colon 751.5
- great vessels (complete) 745.10
  - both originating from right ventricle 745.11
  - corrected 745.12
  - double outlet right ventricle 745.11
  - incomplete 745.11
  - partial 745.11
  - specified type NEC 745.19
- heart 746.87
  - with complete transposition of viscera 759.3
- intestine (large) (small) 751.5
- pulmonary veins 747.49
- reversed jejunal (for bypass) (status) V45.3
- scrotal 752.81
- stomach 750.7
  - with general transposition of viscera 759.3
- teeth, tooth 524.30
- vessels (complete) 745.10
  - partial 745.11
- viscera (abdominal) (thoracic) 759.3

Trans-sexualism 302.50
- with
  - asexual history 302.51
  - heterosexual history 302.53
  - homosexual history 302.52

Transverse — *see also* condition
- arrest (deep), in labor 660.3 ☑
  - affecting fetus or newborn 763.1
- lie 652.3 ☑
  - before labor, affecting fetus or newborn 761.7
  - causing obstructed labor 660.0 ☑
    - affecting fetus or newborn 763.1
  - during labor, affecting fetus or newborn 763.1

Transvestism, transvestitism (transvestic fetishism) 302.3

Trapped placenta (with hemorrhage) 666.0 ☑
- without hemorrhage 667.0 ☑

Traumatic — *see also* condition
- brain injury (TBI) (*see also* Injury, intracranial) 854.0 ☑
  - with skull fracture — *see* Fracture, skull, by site

Trauma, traumatism — *see also* Injury, by site 959.9
- birth — *see* Birth, injury NEC
- causing hemorrhage of pregnancy or delivery 641.8 ☑
- complicating
  - abortion — *see* Abortion, by type, with damage to pelvic organs
  - ectopic pregnancy (*see also* categories 633.0–633.9) 639.2
  - molar pregnancy (*see also* categories 630–632) 639.2
- during delivery NEC 665.9 ☑
- following
  - abortion 639.2
  - ectopic or molar pregnancy 639.2
- maternal, during pregnancy, affecting fetus or newborn 760.5
- neuroma — *see* Injury, nerve, by site
- previous major, affecting management of pregnancy, childbirth, or puerperium V23.89
- psychic (current) (*see also* Reaction, adjustment)
  - previous (history) V15.49
- psychologic, previous (affecting health) V15.49

Trauma, traumatism — *see also* Injury, by site — continued
- transient paralysis — *see* Injury, nerve, by site

Treacher Collins' syndrome (incomplete facial dysostosis) 756.0

Treitz's hernia — *see* Hernia, Treitz's

Trematode infestation NEC 121.9

Trematodiasis NEC 121.9

Trembles 988.8

Trembling paralysis — *see also* Parkinsonism 332.0

Tremor 781.0
- essential (benign) 333.1
- familial 333.1
- flapping (liver) 572.8
- hereditary 333.1
- hysterical 300.11
- intention 333.1
- medication-induced postural 333.1
- mercurial 985.0
- muscle 728.85
- Parkinson's (*see also* Parkinsonism) 332.0
- psychogenic 306.0
  - specified as conversion reaction 300.11
- senilis 797
- specified type NEC 333.1

Trench
- fever 083.1
- foot 991.4
- mouth 101
- nephritis — *see* Nephritis, acute

Treponema pallidum infection — *see also* Syphilis 097.9

Treponematosis 102.9
- due to
  - T. pallidum — *see* Syphilis
  - T. pertenue (yaws) (*see also* Yaws) 102.9

Triad
- Kartagener's 759.3
- Reiter's (complete) (incomplete) 099.3
- Saint's (*see also* Hernia, diaphragm) 553.3

Trichiasis 704.2
- cicatricial 704.2
- eyelid 374.05
  - with entropion (*see also* Entropion) 374.00

Trichinella spiralis (infection) (infestation) 124

Trichinelliasis 124

Trichinellosis 124

Trichiniasis 124

Trichinosis 124

Trichobezoar 938
- intestine 936
- stomach 935.2

Trichocephaliasis 127.3

Trichocephalosis 127.3

Trichocephalus infestation 127.3

Trichoclasis 704.2

Trichoepithelioma (M8100/0) — *see also* Neoplasm, skin, benign
- breast 217
- genital organ NEC — *see* Neoplasm, by site, benign
- malignant (M8100/3) — *see* Neoplasm, skin, malignant

Trichofolliculoma (M8101/0) — *see* Neoplasm, skin, benign

Tricholemmoma (M8102/0) — *see* Neoplasm, skin, benign

Trichomatosis 704.2

Trichomoniasis 131.9
- bladder 131.09
- cervix 131.09
- intestinal 007.3
- prostate 131.03
- seminal vesicle 131.09
- specified site NEC 131.8
- urethra 131.02
- urogenitalis 131.00
- vagina 131.01
- vulva 131.01
- vulvovaginal 131.01

Trichomycosis 039.0
- axillaris 039.0
- nodosa 111.2

☑ Additional Digit Required — Refer to the Tabular List for Digit Selection   ▽ Subterms under main terms may continue to next column or page

2015 ICD-9-CM   ►◄ Revised Text   ● New Line   ▲ Revised Code   Volume 2 — 283

Trichomycosis — continued
  nodularis 111.2
  rubra 039.0
Trichonocardiosis (axillaris) (palmellina) 039.0
Trichonodosis 704.2
Trichophytide — see Dermatophytosis
Trichophytid, trichophyton infection — see also Dermatophytosis 110.9
Trichophytobezoar 938
  intestine 936
  stomach 935.2
Trichophytosis — see Dermatophytosis
Trichoptilosis 704.2
Trichorrhexis (nodosa) 704.2
Trichosporosis nodosa 111.2
Trichostasis spinulosa (congenital) 757.4
Trichostrongyliasis (small intestine) 127.6
Trichostrongylosis 127.6
Trichostrongylus (instabilis) infection 127.6
Trichotillomania 312.39
Trichromat, anomalous (congenital) 368.59
Trichromatopsia, anomalous (congenital) 368.59
Trichuriasis 127.3
Trichuris trichiuria (any site) (infection) (infestation) 127.3
Tricuspid (valve) — see condition
Trifid — see also Accessory
  kidney (pelvis) 753.3
  tongue 750.13
Trigeminal neuralgia — see also Neuralgia, trigeminal 350.1
Trigeminoencephaloangiomatosis 759.6
Trigeminy 427.89
  postoperative 997.1
Trigger finger (acquired) 727.03
  congenital 756.89
Trigonitis (bladder) (chronic) (pseudomembranous) 595.3
  tuberculous (see also Tuberculosis) 016.1 ☑
Trigonocephaly 756.0
Trihexosidosis 272.7
Trilobate placenta — see Placenta, abnormal
Trilocular heart 745.8
Trimethylaminuria 270.8
Tripartita placenta — see Placenta, abnormal
Triple — see also Accessory
  kidneys 753.3
  uteri 752.2
  X female 758.81
Triplegia 344.89
  congenital or infantile 343.8
Triplet
  affected by maternal complications of pregnancy 761.5
  healthy liveborn — see Newborn, multiple
  pregnancy (complicating delivery) NEC 651.1 ☑
    with fetal loss and retention of one or more fetus(es) 651.4 ☑
    following (elective) fetal reduction 651.7 ☑
Triplex placenta — see Placenta, abnormal
Triplication — see Accessory
Trismus 781.0
  neonatorum 771.3
  newborn 771.3
Trisomy (syndrome) NEC 758.5
  13 (partial) 758.1
  16-18 758.2
  18 (partial) 758.2
  21 (partial) 758.0
  22 758.0
  autosomes NEC 758.5
  D_1 758.1
  E_3 758.2
  G (group) 758.0
  group D_1 758.1
  group E 758.2
  group G 758.0
Tritanomaly 368.53
Tritanopia 368.53
Troisier-Hanot-Chauffard syndrome (bronze diabetes) 275.01
Trombidiosis 133.8
Trophedema (hereditary) 757.0

Trophedema — continued
  congenital 757.0
Trophoblastic disease — see also Hydatidiform mole 630
  previous, affecting management of pregnancy V23.1
Tropholymphedema 757.0
Trophoneurosis NEC 356.9
  arm NEC 354.9
  disseminated 710.1
  facial 349.89
  leg NEC 355.8
  lower extremity NEC 355.8
  upper extremity NEC 354.9
Tropical — see also condition
  maceration feet (syndrome) 991.4
  wet foot (syndrome) 991.4
Trouble — see also Disease
  bowel 569.9
  heart — see Disease, heart
  intestine 569.9
  kidney (see also Disease, renal) 593.9
  nervous 799.21
  sinus (see also Sinusitis) 473.9
Trousseau's syndrome (thrombophlebitis migrans) 453.1
Truancy, childhood — see also Disturbance, conduct
  socialized 312.2 ☑
  undersocialized, unsocialized 312.1 ☑
Truncus
  arteriosus (persistent) 745.0
  common 745.0
  communis 745.0
Trunk — see condition
Trychophytide — see Dermatophytosis
Trypanosoma infestation — see Trypanosomiasis
Trypanosomiasis 086.9
  with meningoencephalitis 086.9 [323.2]
  African 086.5
    due to Trypanosoma 086.5
      gambiense 086.3
      rhodesiense 086.4
  American 086.2
    with
      heart involvement 086.0
      other organ involvement 086.1
    without mention of organ involvement 086.2
  Brazilian — see Trypanosomiasis, American
  Chagas' — see Trypanosomiasis, American
  due to Trypanosoma
    cruzi — see Trypanosomiasis, American
    gambiense 086.3
    rhodesiense 086.4
  gambiensis, Gambian 086.3
  North American — see Trypanosomiasis, American
  rhodesiensis, Rhodesian 086.4
  South American — see Trypanosomiasis, American
T-shaped incisors 520.2
Tsutsugamushi fever 081.2
Tubercle — see also Tuberculosis
  brain, solitary 013.2 ☑
  Darwin's 744.29
  epithelioid noncaseating 135
  Ghon, primary infection 010.0 ☑
Tuberculid, tuberculide (indurating) (lichenoid) (miliary) (papulonecrotic) (primary) (skin) (subcutaneous) — see also Tuberculosis 017.0 ☑
Tuberculoma — see also Tuberculosis
  brain (any part) 013.2 ☑
  meninges (cerebral) (spinal) 013.1 ☑
  spinal cord 013.4 ☑

Tuberculosis, tubercular, tuberculous (calcification) (calcified) (caseous) (chromogenic acid-fast bacilli) (congenital) (degeneration) (disease) (fibrocaseous) (fistula) (gangrene) (interstitial) (isolated circumscribed lesions) (necrosis) (parenchymatous) (ulcerative) 011.9 ☑

> Note — Use the following fifth-digit subclassification with categories 010–018:
>
> 0 unspecified
>
> 1 bacteriological or histological examination not done
>
> 2 bacteriological or histological examination unknown (at present)
>
> 3 tubercle bacilli found (in sputum) by microscopy
>
> 4 tubercle bacilli not found (in sputum) by microscopy, but found by bacterial culture
>
> 5 tubercle bacilli not found by bacteriological examination, but tuberculosis confirmed histologically
>
> 6 tubercle bacilli not found by bacteriological or histological examination, but tuberculosis confirmed by other methods [inoculation of animals]
>
> For tuberculous conditions specified as late effects or sequelae, see category 137.

  abdomen 014.8 ☑
    lymph gland 014.8 ☑
  abscess 011.9 ☑
    arm 017.9 ☑
    bone (see also Osteomyelitis, due to, tuberculosis) 015.9 ☑ [730.8] ☑
      hip 015.1 [730.85]
      knee 015.2 ☑ [730.86]
      sacrum 015.0 [730.88]
      specified site NEC 015.7 [730.88]
      spinal 015.0 [730.88]
      vertebra 015.0 [730.88]
    brain 013.3 ☑
    breast 017.9 ☑
    Cowper's gland 016.5 ☑
    dura (mater) 013.8 ☑
      brain 013.3 ☑
      spinal cord 013.5 ☑
    epidural 013.8 ☑
      brain 013.3 ☑
      spinal cord 013.5 ☑
    frontal sinus — see Tuberculosis, sinus
    genital organs NEC 016.9 ☑
      female 016.7 ☑
      male 016.5 ☑
    genitourinary NEC 016.9 ☑
    gland (lymphatic) — see Tuberculosis, lymph gland
    hip 015.1 ☑
    iliopsoas 015.0 [730.88]
    intestine 014.8 ☑
    ischiorectal 014.8 ☑
    joint 015.9 ☑
      hip 015.1 ☑
      knee 015.2 ☑
      specified joint NEC 015.8 ☑
      vertebral 015.0 [730.88]
    kidney 016.0 [590.81]
    knee 015.2 ☑
    lumbar 015.0 [730.88]
    lung 011.2 ☑
      primary, progressive 010.8 ☑
    meninges (cerebral) (spinal) 013.0 ☑
    pelvic 016.9 ☑
      female 016.7 ☑
      male 016.5 ☑
    perianal 014.8 ☑
      fistula 014.8 ☑
    perinephritic 016.0 ☑ [590.81]

Tuberculosis, tubercular, tuberculous — continued
  abscess — continued
    perineum 017.9 ☑
    perirectal 014.8 ☑
    psoas 015.0 [730.88]
    rectum 014.8 ☑
    retropharyngeal 012.8 ☑
    sacrum 015.0 [730.88]
    scrofulous 017.2 ☑
    scrotum 016.5 ☑
    skin 017.0 ☑
      primary 017.0 ☑
    spinal cord 013.5 ☑
    spine or vertebra (column) 015.0 [730.88]
    strumous 017.2 ☑
    subdiaphragmatic 014.8 ☑
    testis 016.5 ☑
    thigh 017.9 ☑
    urinary 016.3 ☑
      kidney 016.0 [590.81]
    uterus 016.7 ☑
  accessory sinus — see Tuberculosis, sinus
  Addison's disease 017.6 ☑
  adenitis (see also Tuberculosis, lymph gland) 017.2 ☑
  adenoids 012.8 ☑
  adenopathy (see also Tuberculosis, lymph gland) 017.2 ☑
    tracheobronchial 012.1 ☑
      primary progressive 010.8 ☑
  adherent pericardium 017.9 ☑ [420.0]
  adnexa (uteri) 016.7 ☑
  adrenal (capsule) (gland) 017.6 ☑
  air passage NEC 012.8 ☑
  alimentary canal 014.8 ☑
  anemia 017.9 ☑
  ankle (joint) 015.8 ☑
    bone 015.5 ☑ [730.87]
  anus 014.8 ☑
  apex (see also Tuberculosis, pulmonary) 011.9 ☑
  apical (see also Tuberculosis, pulmonary) 011.9 ☑
  appendicitis 014.8 ☑
  appendix 014.8 ☑
  arachnoid 013.0 ☑
  artery 017.9 ☑
  arthritis (chronic) (synovial) 015.9 ☑ [711.40]
    ankle 015.8 ☑ [730.87]
    hip 015.1 ☑ [711.45]
    knee 015.2 ☑ [711.46]
    specified site NEC 015.8 ☑ [711.48]
    spine or vertebra (column) 015.0 [720.81]
    wrist 015.8 ☑ [730.83]
  articular — see Tuberculosis, joint
  ascites 014.0 ☑
  asthma (see also Tuberculosis, pulmonary) 011.9 ☑
  axilla, axillary 017.2 ☑
    gland 017.2 ☑
  bilateral (see also Tuberculosis, pulmonary) 011.9 ☑
  bladder 016.1 ☑
  bone (see also Osteomyelitis, due to, tuberculosis) 015.9 ☑ [730.8] ☑
    hip 015.1 ☑ [730.85]
    knee 015.2 ☑ [730.86]
    limb NEC 015.5 ☑ [730.88]
    sacrum 015.0 ☑ [730.88]
    specified site NEC 015.7 ☑ [730.88]
    spinal or vertebral column 015.0 ☑ [730.88]
  bowel 014.8 ☑
    miliary 018.9 ☑
  brain 013.2 ☑
  breast 017.9 ☑
  broad ligament 016.7 ☑
  bronchi, bronchial, bronchus 011.3 ☑
    ectasia, ectasis 011.5 ☑
    fistula 011.3 ☑

☑ Additional Digit Required — Refer to the Tabular List for Digit Selection   ☑ Subterms under main terms may continue to next column or page

284 — Volume 2   ▶◀ Revised Text   ● New Line   ▲ Revised Code   2015 ICD-9-CM

Tuberculosis, tubercular, tuberculous — *continued*
  bronchi, bronchial, bronchus — *continued*
    fistula — *continued*
      primary, progressive 010.8 ☑
      gland 012.1 ☑
        primary, progressive 010.8 ☑
      isolated 012.2 ☑
      lymph gland or node 012.1 ☑
        primary, progressive 010.8 ☑
  bronchiectasis 011.5 ☑
  bronchitis 011.3 ☑
  bronchopleural 012.0 ☑
  bronchopneumonia, bronchopneumonic 011.6 ☑
  bronchorrhagia 011.3 ☑
  bronchotracheal 011.3 ☑
    isolated 012.2 ☑
  bronchus — *see* Tuberculosis, bronchi
  bronze disease (Addison's) 017.6 ☑
  buccal cavity 017.9 ☑
  bulbourethral gland 016.5 ☑
  bursa (*see also* Tuberculosis, joint) 015.9 ☑
  cachexia NEC (*see also* Tuberculosis, pulmonary) 011.9 ☑
  cardiomyopathy 017.9 ☑ *[425.8]*
  caries (*see also* Tuberculosis, bone) 015.9 ☑ *[730.8]*
  cartilage (*see also* Tuberculosis, bone) 015.9 ☑ *[730.8]*
    intervertebral 015.0 ☑ *[730.88]*
  catarrhal (*see also* Tuberculosis, pulmonary) 011.9 ☑
  cecum 014.8 ☑
  cellular tissue (primary) 017.0 ☑
  cellulitis (primary) 017.0 ☑
  central nervous system 013.9 ☑
    specified site NEC 013.8 ☑
  cerebellum (current) 013.2 ☑
  cerebral (current) 013.2 ☑
    meninges 013.0 ☑
  cerebrospinal 013.6 ☑
    meninges 013.0 ☑
  cerebrum (current) 013.2 ☑
  cervical 017.2 ☑
    gland 017.2 ☑
    lymph nodes 017.2 ☑
  cervicitis (uteri) 016.7 ☑
  cervix 016.7 ☑
  chest (*see also* Tuberculosis, pulmonary) 011.9 ☑
  childhood type or first infection 010.0 ☑
  choroid 017.3 ☑ *[363.13]*
  choroiditis 017.3 ☑ *[363.13]*
  ciliary body 017.3 ☑ *[364.11]*
  colitis 014.8 ☑
  colliers' 011.4 ☑
  colliquativa (primary) 017.0 ☑
  colon 014.8 ☑
    ulceration 014.8 ☑
  complex, primary 010.0 ☑
  complicating pregnancy, childbirth, or puerperium 647.3 ☑
    affecting fetus or newborn 760.2
  congenital 771.2
  conjunctiva 017.3 ☑ *[370.31]*
  connective tissue 017.9 ☑
    bone — *see* Tuberculosis, bone
  contact V01.1
  converter (tuberculin skin test) (without disease) 795.51
  cornea (ulcer) 017.3 ☑ *[370.31]*
  Cowper's gland 016.5 ☑
  coxae 015.1 ☑ *[730.85]*
  coxalgia 015.1 ☑ *[730.85]*
  cul-de-sac of Douglas 014.8 ☑
  curvature, spine 015.0 ☑ *[737.40]*
  cutis (colliquativa) (primary) 017.0 ☑
  cystitis 016.1 ☑
  cyst, ovary 016.6 ☑
  dacryocystitis 017.3 ☑ *[375.32]*
  dactylitis 015.5 ☑
  diarrhea 014.8 ☑

Tuberculosis, tubercular, tuberculous — *continued*
  diffuse (*see also* Tuberculosis, miliary) 018.9 ☑
    lung — *see* Tuberculosis, pulmonary
    meninges 013.0 ☑
  digestive tract 014.8 ☑
  disseminated (*see also* Tuberculosis, miliary) 018.9 ☑
    meninges 013.0 ☑
  duodenum 014.8 ☑
  dura (mater) 013.9 ☑
    abscess 013.8 ☑
      cerebral 013.3 ☑
      spinal 013.5 ☑
  dysentery 014.8 ☑
  ear (inner) (middle) 017.4 ☑
    bone 015.6 ☑
    external (primary) 017.0 ☑
    skin (primary) 017.0 ☑
  elbow 015.8 ☑
  emphysema — *see* Tuberculosis, pulmonary
  empyema 012.0 ☑
  encephalitis 013.6 ☑
  endarteritis 017.9 ☑
  endocarditis (any valve) 017.9 ☑ *[424.91]*
  endocardium (any valve) 017.9 ☑ *[424.91]*
  endocrine glands NEC 017.9 ☑
  endometrium 016.7 ☑
  enteric, enterica 014.8 ☑
  enteritis 014.8 ☑
  enterocolitis 014.8 ☑
  epididymis 016.4 ☑
  epididymitis 016.4 ☑
  epidural abscess 013.8 ☑
    brain 013.3 ☑
    spinal cord 013.5 ☑
  epiglottis 012.3 ☑
  episcleritis 017.3 ☑ *[379.00]*
  erythema (induratum) (nodosum) (primary) 017.1 ☑
  esophagus 017.8 ☑
  Eustachian tube 017.4 ☑
  exposure to V01.1
  exudative 012.0 ☑
    primary, progressive 010.1 ☑
  eye 017.3 ☑
  eyelid (primary) 017.0 ☑
    lupus 017.0 ☑ *[373.4]*
  fallopian tube 016.6 ☑
  fascia 017.9 ☑
  fauces 012.8 ☑
  finger 017.9 ☑
  first infection 010.0 ☑
  fistula, perirectal 014.8 ☑
  Florida 011.6 ☑
  foot 017.9 ☑
  funnel pelvis 137.3
  gallbladder 017.9 ☑
  galloping (*see also* Tuberculosis, pulmonary) 011.9 ☑
  ganglionic 015.9 ☑
  gastritis 017.9 ☑
  gastrocolic fistula 014.8 ☑
  gastroenteritis 014.8 ☑
  gastrointestinal tract 014.8 ☑
  general, generalized 018.9 ☑
    acute 018.0 ☑
    chronic 018.8 ☑
  genital organs NEC 016.9 ☑
    female 016.7 ☑
    male 016.5 ☑
  genitourinary NEC 016.9 ☑
  genu 015.2 ☑
  glandulae suprarenalis 017.6 ☑
  glandular, general 017.2 ☑
  glottis 012.3 ☑
  grinders' 011.4 ☑
  groin 017.2 ☑
  gum 017.9 ☑
  hand 017.9 ☑
  heart 017.9 ☑ *[425.8]*
  hematogenous — *see* Tuberculosis, miliary

Tuberculosis, tubercular, tuberculous — *continued*
  hemoptysis (*see also* Tuberculosis, pulmonary) 011.9 ☑
  hemorrhage NEC (*see also* Tuberculosis, pulmonary) 011.9 ☑
  hemothorax 012.0 ☑
  hepatitis 017.9 ☑
  hilar lymph nodes 012.1 ☑
    primary, progressive 010.8 ☑
  hip (disease) (joint) 015.1 ☑
    bone 015.1 ☑ *[730.85]*
  hydrocephalus 013.8 ☑
  hydropneumothorax 012.0 ☑
  hydrothorax 012.0 ☑
  hypoadrenalism 017.6 ☑
  hypopharynx 012.8 ☑
  ileocecal (hyperplastic) 014.8 ☑
  ileocolitis 014.8 ☑
  ileum 014.8 ☑
  iliac spine (superior) 015.0 ☑ *[730.88]*
  incipient NEC (*see also* Tuberculosis, pulmonary) 011.9 ☑
  indurativa (primary) 017.1 ☑
  infantile 010.0 ☑
  infection NEC 011.9 ☑
    without clinical manifestation 010.0 ☑
  infraclavicular gland 017.2 ☑
  inguinal gland 017.2 ☑
  inguinalis 017.2 ☑
  intestine (any part) 014.8 ☑
  iris 017.3 ☑ *[364.11]*
  iritis 017.3 ☑ *[364.11]*
  ischiorectal 014.8 ☑
  jaw 015.7 ☑ *[730.88]*
  jejunum 014.8 ☑
  joint 015.9 ☑
    hip 015.1 ☑
    knee 015.2 ☑
    specified site NEC 015.8 ☑
    vertebral 015.0 ☑ *[730.88]*
  keratitis 017.3 ☑ *[370.31]*
    interstitial 017.3 ☑ *[370.59]*
  keratoconjunctivitis 017.3 ☑ *[370.31]*
  kidney 016.0 ☑
  knee (joint) 015.2 ☑
  kyphoscoliosis 015.0 ☑ *[737.43]*
  kyphosis 015.0 ☑ *[737.41]*
  lacrimal apparatus, gland 017.3 ☑
  laryngitis 012.3 ☑
  larynx 012.3 ☑
  latent 795.51
  leptomeninges, leptomeningitis (cerebral) (spinal) 013.0 ☑
  lichenoides (primary) 017.0 ☑
  linguae 017.9 ☑
  lip 017.9 ☑
  liver 017.9 ☑
  lordosis 015.0 ☑ *[737.42]*
  lung — *see* Tuberculosis, pulmonary
  luposa 017.0 ☑
    eyelid 017.0 ☑ *[373.4]*
  lymphadenitis — *see* Tuberculosis, lymph gland
  lymphangitis — *see* Tuberculosis, lymph gland
  lymphatic (gland) (vessel) — *see* Tuberculosis, lymph gland
  lymph gland or node (peripheral) 017.2 ☑
    abdomen 014.8 ☑
    bronchial 012.1 ☑
      primary, progressive 010.8 ☑
    cervical 017.2 ☑
    hilar 012.1 ☑
      primary, progressive 010.8 ☑
    intrathoracic 012.1 ☑
      primary, progressive 010.8 ☑
    mediastinal 012.1 ☑
      primary, progressive 010.8 ☑
    mesenteric 014.8 ☑
    peripheral 017.2 ☑
    retroperitoneal 014.8 ☑
    tracheobronchial 012.1 ☑

Tuberculosis, tubercular, tuberculous — *continued*
  lymph gland or node — *continued*
    tracheobronchial — *continued*
      primary, progressive 010.8 ☑
    malignant NEC (*see also* Tuberculosis, pulmonary) 011.9 ☑
  mammary gland 017.9 ☑
  marasmus NEC (*see also* Tuberculosis, pulmonary) 011.9 ☑
  mastoiditis 015.6 ☑
  maternal, affecting fetus or newborn 760.2
  mediastinal (lymph) gland or node 012.1 ☑
    primary, progressive 010.8 ☑
  mediastinitis 012.8 ☑
    primary, progressive 010.8 ☑
  mediastinopericarditis 017.9 ☑ *[420.0]*
  mediastinum 012.8 ☑
    primary, progressive 010.8 ☑
  medulla 013.9 ☑
    brain 013.2 ☑
    spinal cord 013.4 ☑
  melanosis, Addisonian 017.6 ☑
  membrane, brain 013.0 ☑
  meninges (cerebral) (spinal) 013.0 ☑
  meningitis (basilar) (brain) (cerebral) (cerebrospinal) (spinal) 013.0 ☑
  meningoencephalitis 013.0 ☑
  mesentery, mesenteric 014.8 ☑
    lymph gland or node 014.8 ☑
  miliary (any site) 018.9 ☑
    acute 018.0 ☑
    chronic 018.8 ☑
    specified type NEC 018.8 ☑
  millstone makers' 011.4 ☑
  miners' 011.4 ☑
  moulders' 011.4 ☑
  mouth 017.9 ☑
  multiple 018.9 ☑
    acute 018.0 ☑
    chronic 018.8 ☑
  muscle 017.9 ☑
  myelitis 013.6 ☑
  myocarditis 017.9 ☑ *[422.0]*
  myocardium 017.9 ☑ *[422.0]*
  nasal (passage) (sinus) 012.8 ☑
  nasopharynx 012.8 ☑
  neck gland 017.2 ☑
  nephritis 016.0 ☑ *[583.81]*
  nerve 017.9 ☑
  nose (septum) 012.8 ☑
  ocular 017.3 ☑
  old NEC 137.0
    without residuals V12.01
  omentum 014.8 ☑
  oophoritis (acute) (chronic) 016.6 ☑
  optic 017.3 ☑ *[377.39]*
    nerve trunk 017.3 ☑ *[377.39]*
    papilla, papillae 017.3 ☑ *[377.39]*
  orbit 017.3 ☑
  orchitis 016.5 ☑ *[608.81]*
  organ, specified NEC 017.9 ☑
  orificialis (primary) 017.0 ☑
  osseous (*see also* Tuberculosis, bone) 015.9 ☑ *[730.8]*
  osteitis (*see also* Tuberculosis, bone) 015.9 ☑ *[730.8]*
  osteomyelitis (*see also* Tuberculosis, bone) 015.9 ☑ *[730.8]*
  otitis (media) 017.4 ☑
  ovaritis (acute) (chronic) 016.6 ☑
  ovary (acute) (chronic) 016.6 ☑
  oviducts (acute) (chronic) 016.6 ☑
  pachymeningitis 013.0 ☑
  palate (soft) 017.9 ☑
  pancreas 017.9 ☑
  papulonecrotic (primary) 017.0 ☑
  parathyroid glands 017.9 ☑
  paronychia (primary) 017.0 ☑
  parotid gland or region 017.9 ☑
  pelvic organ NEC 016.9 ☑
    female 016.7 ☑
    male 016.5 ☑

☑ **Additional Digit Required** — Refer to the Tabular List for Digit Selection   ▽ **Subterms under main terms may continue to next column or page**

2015 ICD-9-CM   ▶◀ Revised Text   ● New Line   ▲ Revised Code   Volume 2 — 285

Tuberculosis, tubercular, tuberculous — *continued*

pelvis (bony) 015.7 ✓ [730.85]
penis 016.5 ✓
peribronchitis 011.3 ✓
pericarditis 017.9 ✓ [420.0]
pericardium 017.9 ✓ [420.0]
perichondritis, larynx 012.3 ✓
perineum 017.9 ✓
periostitis (*see also* Tuberculosis, bone) 015.9 ✓ [730.8]
periphlebitis 017.9 ✓
    eye vessel 017.3 ✓ [362.18]
    retina 017.3 ✓ [362.18]
perirectal fistula 014.8 ✓
peritoneal gland 014.8 ✓
peritoneum 014.0 ✓
peritonitis 014.0 ✓
pernicious NEC (*see also* Tuberculosis, pulmonary) 011.9 ✓
pharyngitis 012.8 ✓
pharynx 012.8 ✓
phlyctenulosis (conjunctiva) 017.3 ✓ [370.31]
phthisis NEC (*see also* Tuberculosis, pulmonary) 011.9 ✓
pituitary gland 017.9 ✓
placenta 016.7 ✓
pleura, pleural, pleurisy, pleuritis (fibrinous) (obliterative) (purulent) (simple plastic) (with effusion) 012.0 ✓
    primary, progressive 010.1 ✓
pneumonia, pneumonic 011.6 ✓
pneumothorax 011.7 ✓
polyserositis 018.9 ✓
    acute 018.0 ✓
    chronic 018.8 ✓
potters' 011.4 ✓
prepuce 016.5 ✓
primary 010.9 ✓
    complex 010.0 ✓
    complicated 010.8 ✓
        with pleurisy or effusion 010.1 ✓
    progressive 010.8 ✓
        with pleurisy or effusion 010.1 ✓
    skin 017.0 ✓
proctitis 014.8 ✓
prostate 016.5 ✓ [601.4]
prostatitis 016.5 ✓ [601.4]
pulmonaris (*see also* Tuberculosis, pulmonary) 011.9 ✓
pulmonary (artery) (incipient) (malignant) (multiple round foci) (pernicious) (reinfection stage) 011.9 ✓
    cavitated or with cavitation 011.2 ✓
        primary, progressive 010.8 ✓
    childhood type or first infection 010.0 ✓
    chromogenic acid-fast bacilli 795.39
    fibrosis or fibrotic 011.4 ✓
    infiltrative 011.0 ✓
        primary, progressive 010.9 ✓
    nodular 011.1 ✓
    specified NEC 011.8 ✓
    sputum positive only 795.39
    status following surgical collapse of lung NEC 011.9 ✓
pyelitis 016.0 ✓ [590.81]
pyelonephritis 016.0 ✓ [590.81]
pyemia — *see* Tuberculosis, miliary
pyonephrosis 016.0 ✓
pyopneumothorax 012.0 ✓
pyothorax 012.0 ✓
rectum (with abscess) 014.8 ✓
    fistula 014.8 ✓
reinfection stage (*see also* Tuberculosis, pulmonary) 011.9 ✓
renal 016.0 ✓
renis 016.0 ✓
reproductive organ 016.7 ✓
respiratory NEC (*see also* Tuberculosis, pulmonary) 011.9 ✓
    specified site NEC 012.8 ✓
retina 017.3 ✓ [363.13]

Tuberculosis, tubercular, tuberculous — *continued*

retroperitoneal (lymph gland or node) 014.8 ✓
    gland 014.8 ✓
retropharyngeal abscess 012.8 ✓
rheumatism 015.9 ✓
rhinitis 012.8 ✓
sacroiliac (joint) 015.8 ✓
sacrum 015.0 ✓ [730.88]
salivary gland 017.9 ✓
salpingitis (acute) (chronic) 016.6 ✓
sandblasters' 011.4 ✓
sclera 017.3 ✓ [379.09]
scoliosis 015.0 ✓ [737.43]
scrofulous 017.2 ✓
scrotum 016.5 ✓
seminal tract or vesicle 016.5 ✓ [608.81]
senile NEC (*see also* Tuberculosis, pulmonary) 011.9 ✓
septic NEC (*see also* Tuberculosis, miliary) 018.9 ✓
shoulder 015.8 ✓
    blade 015.7 ✓ [730.8]
sigmoid 014.8 ✓
sinus (accessory) (nasal) 012.8 ✓
    bone 015.7 ✓ [730.88]
    epididymis 016.4 ✓
skeletal NEC (*see also* Osteomyelitis, due to tuberculosis) 015.9 ✓ [730.8]
skin (any site) (primary) 017.0 ✓
small intestine 014.8 ✓
soft palate 017.9 ✓
spermatic cord 016.5 ✓
spinal
    column 015.0 ✓ [730.88]
    cord 013.4 ✓
    disease 015.0 ✓ [730.88]
    medulla 013.4 ✓
    membrane 013.0 ✓
    meninges 013.0 ✓
spine 015.0 ✓ [730.88]
spleen 017.7 ✓
splenitis 017.7 ✓
spondylitis 015.0 ✓ [720.81]
spontaneous pneumothorax — *see* Tuberculosis, pulmonary
sternoclavicular joint 015.8 ✓
stomach 017.9 ✓
stonemasons' 011.4 ✓
struma 017.2 ✓
subcutaneous tissue (cellular) (primary) 017.0 ✓
subcutis (primary) 017.0 ✓
subdeltoid bursa 017.9 ✓
submaxillary 017.9 ✓
    region 017.9 ✓
supraclavicular gland 017.2 ✓
suprarenal (capsule) (gland) 017.6 ✓
swelling, joint (*see also* Tuberculosis, joint) 015.9 ✓
symphysis pubis 015.7 ✓ [730.88]
synovitis 015.9 ✓ [727.01]
    hip 015.1 ✓ [727.01]
    knee 015.2 ✓ [727.01]
    specified site NEC 015.8 ✓ [727.01]
    spine or vertebra 015.0 ✓ [727.01]
systemic — *see* Tuberculosis, miliary
tarsitis (eyelid) 017.0 ✓ [373.4]
    ankle (bone) 015.5 ✓ [730.87]
tendon (sheath) — *see* Tuberculosis, tenosynovitis
tenosynovitis 015.9 ✓ [727.01]
    hip 015.1 ✓ [727.01]
    knee 015.2 ✓ [727.01]
    specified site NEC 015.8 ✓ [727.01]
    spine or vertebra 015.0 ✓ [727.01]
testis 016.5 ✓ [608.81]
throat 012.8 ✓
thymus gland 017.9 ✓
thyroid gland 017.5 ✓
toe 017.9 ✓
tongue 017.9 ✓

Tuberculosis, tubercular, tuberculous — *continued*

tonsil (lingual) 012.8 ✓
tonsillitis 012.8 ✓
trachea, tracheal 012.8 ✓
    gland 012.1 ✓
        primary, progressive 010.8 ✓
    isolated 012.2 ✓
tracheobronchial 011.3 ✓
    glandular 012.1 ✓
        primary, progressive 010.8 ✓
    isolated 012.2 ✓
    lymph gland or node 012.1 ✓
        primary, progressive 010.8 ✓
tubal 016.6 ✓
tunica vaginalis 016.5 ✓
typhlitis 014.8 ✓
ulcer (primary) (skin) 017.0 ✓
    bowel or intestine 014.8 ✓
    specified site NEC — *see* Tuberculosis, by site
unspecified site — *see* Tuberculosis, pulmonary
ureter 016.2 ✓
urethra, urethral 016.3 ✓
urinary organ or tract 016.3 ✓
    kidney 016.0 ✓
uterus 016.7 ✓
uveal tract 017.3 ✓ [363.13]
uvula 017.9 ✓
vaccination, prophylactic (against) V03.2
vagina 016.7 ✓
vas deferens 016.5 ✓
vein 017.9 ✓
verruca (primary) 017.0 ✓
verrucosa (cutis) (primary) 017.0 ✓
vertebra (column) 015.0 ✓ [730.88]
vesiculitis 016.5 ✓ [608.81]
viscera NEC 014.8 ✓
vulva 016.7 ✓ [616.51]
wrist (joint) 015.8 ✓
    bone 015.5 ✓ [730.83]

Tuberculum
    auriculae 744.29
    occlusal 520.2
    paramolare 520.2
Tuberosity
    jaw, excessive 524.07
    maxillary, entire 524.07
Tuberous sclerosis (brain) 759.5
Tube, tubal, tubular — *see also* condition
    ligation, admission for V25.2
Tubo-ovarian — *see* condition
Tuboplasty, after previous sterilization V26.0
Tubotympanitis 381.10
Tularemia 021.9
    with
        conjunctivitis 021.3
        pneumonia 021.2
    bronchopneumonic 021.2
    conjunctivitis 021.3
    cryptogenic 021.1
    disseminated 021.8
    enteric 021.1
    generalized 021.8
    glandular 021.8
    intestinal 021.1
    oculoglandular 021.3
    ophthalmic 021.3
    pneumonia 021.2
    pulmonary 021.2
    specified NEC 021.8
    typhoidal 021.1
    ulceroglandular 021.0
    vaccination, prophylactic (against) V03.4
Tularensis conjunctivitis 021.3
Tumefaction — *see also* Swelling
    liver (*see also* Hypertrophy, liver) 789.1
Tumor (M8000/1) — *see also* Neoplasm, by site, unspecified nature
    Abrikossov's (M9580/0) (*see also* Neoplasm, connective tissue, benign)
        malignant (M9580/3) — *see* Neoplasm, connective tissue, malignant

Tumor — *see also* Neoplasm, by site, unspecified nature — *continued*

acinar cell (M8550/1) — *see* Neoplasm, by site, uncertain behavior
acinic cell (M8550/1) — *see* Neoplasm, by site, uncertain behavior
adenomatoid (M9054/0) (*see also* Neoplasm, by site, benign)
    odontogenic (M9300/0) 213.1
        upper jaw (bone) 213.0
adnexal (skin) (M8390/0) — *see* Neoplasm, skin, benign
adrenal
    cortical (benign) (M8370/0) 227.0
        malignant (M8370/3) 194.0
    rest (M8671/0) — *see* Neoplasm, by site, benign
alpha cell (M8152/0)
    malignant (M8152/3)
        pancreas 157.4
        specified site NEC — *see* Neoplasm, by site, malignant
        unspecified site 157.4
    pancreas 211.7
    specified site NEC — *see* Neoplasm, by site, benign
    unspecified site 211.7
aneurysmal (*see also* Aneurysm) 442.9
aortic body (M8691/1) 237.3
    malignant (M8691/3) 194.6
argentaffin (M8241/1) — *see* Neoplasm, by site, uncertain behavior
basal cell (M8090/1) (*see also* Neoplasm, skin, uncertain behavior)
benign (M8000/0) — *see* Neoplasm, by site, benign
beta cell (M8151/0)
    malignant (M8151/3)
        pancreas 157.4
        specified site — *see* Neoplasm, by site, malignant
        unspecified site 157.4
    pancreas 211.7
    specified site NEC — *see* Neoplasm, by site, benign
    unspecified site 211.7
blood — *see* Hematoma
Brenner (M9000/0) 220
    borderline malignancy (M9000/1) 236.2
    malignant (M9000/3) 183.0
    proliferating (M9000/1) 236.2
Brooke's (M8100/0) — *see* Neoplasm, skin, benign
brown fat (M8880/0) — *see* Lipoma, by site
Burkitt's (M9750/3) 200.2 ✓
calcifying epithelial odontogenic (M9340/0) 213.1
    upper jaw (bone) 213.0
carcinoid (M8240/1) 209.60
    benign 209.60
        appendix 209.51
        ascending colon 209.53
        bronchus 209.61
        cecum 209.52
        colon 209.50
        descending colon 209.55
        duodenum 209.41
        foregut 209.65
        hindgut 209.67
        ileum 209.43
        jejunum 209.42
        kidney 209.64
        large intestine 209.50
        lung 209.61
        midgut 209.66
        rectum 209.57
        sigmoid colon 209.56
        small intestine 209.40
        specified NEC 209.69
        stomach 209.63
        thymus 209.62
        transverse colon 209.54
    malignant (of) 209.20
        appendix 209.11
        ascending colon 209.13
        bronchus 209.21

✓ **Additional Digit Required** — Refer to the Tabular List for Digit Selection   ▽ **Subterms under main terms may continue to next column or page**

Tumor — see also Neoplasm, by site, unspecified nature — continued
  carcinoid — continued
    malignant — continued
      cecum 209.12
      colon 209.10
      descending colon 209.15
      duodenum 209.01
      foregut 209.25
      hindgut 209.27
      ileum 209.03
      jejunum 209.02
      kidney 209.24
      large intestine 209.10
      lung 209.21
      midgut 209.26
      rectum 209.17
      sigmoid colon 209.16
      small intestine 209.00
      specified NEC 209.29
      stomach 209.23
      thymus 209.22
      transverse colon 209.14
    secondary — see Tumor, neuroendocrine, secondary
  carotid body (M8692/1) 237.3
    malignant (M8692/3) 194.5
  Castleman's (mediastinal lymph node hyperplasia) 785.6
  cells (M8001/1) (see also Neoplasm, by site, unspecified nature)
    benign (M8001/0) — see Neoplasm, by site, benign
    malignant (M8001/3) — see Neoplasm, by site, malignant
    uncertain whether benign or malignant (M8001/1) — see Neoplasm, by site, uncertain nature
  cervix
    in pregnancy or childbirth 654.6 ☑
      affecting fetus or newborn 763.89
      causing obstructed labor 660.2 ☑
        affecting fetus or newborn 763.1
  chondromatous giant cell (M9230/0) — see Neoplasm, bone, benign
  chromaffin (M8700/0) (see also Neoplasm, by site, benign)
    malignant (M8700/3) — see Neoplasm, by site, malignant
  Cock's peculiar 706.2
  Codman's (benign chondroblastoma) (M9230/0) — see Neoplasm, bone, benign
  dentigerous, mixed (M9282/0) 213.1
    upper jaw (bone) 213.0
  dermoid (M9084/0) — see Neoplasm, by site, benign
    with malignant transformation (M9084/3) 183.0
  desmoid (extra-abdominal) (M8821/1) (see also Neoplasm, connective tissue, uncertain behavior)
    abdominal (M8822/1) — see Neoplasm, connective tissue, uncertain behavior
  embryonal (mixed) (M9080/1) (see also Neoplasm, by site, uncertain behavior)
    liver (M9080/3) 155.0
  endodermal sinus (M9071/3)
    specified site — see Neoplasm, by site, malignant
    unspecified site
      female 183.0
      male 186.9
  epithelial
    benign (M8010/0) — see Neoplasm, by site, benign
    malignant (M8010/3) — see Neoplasm, by site, malignant
  Ewing's (M9260/3) — see Neoplasm, bone, malignant
  fatty — see Lipoma
  fetal, causing disproportion 653.7 ☑
    causing obstructed labor 660.1 ☑
  fibroid (M8890/0) — see Leiomyoma

Tumor — see also Neoplasm, by site, unspecified nature — continued
  G cell (M8153/1)
    malignant (M8153/3)
      pancreas 157.4
      specified site NEC — see Neoplasm, by site, malignant
      unspecified site 157.4
    specified site — see Neoplasm, by site, uncertain behavior
    unspecified site 235.5
  giant cell (type) (M8003/1) (see also Neoplasm, by site, unspecified nature)
    bone (M9250/1) 238.0
      malignant (M9250/3) — see Neoplasm, bone, malignant
    chondromatous (M9230/0) — see Neoplasm, bone, benign
    malignant (M8003/3) — see Neoplasm, by site, malignant
    peripheral (gingiva) 523.8
    soft parts (M9251/1) (see also Neoplasm, connective tissue, uncertain behavior)
      malignant (M9251/3) — see Neoplasm, connective tissue, malignant
    tendon sheath 727.02
  glomus (M8711/0) (see also Hemangioma, by site)
    jugulare (M8690/1) 237.3
      malignant (M8690/3) 194.6
  gonadal stromal (M8590/1) — see Neoplasm, by site, uncertain behavior
  granular cell (M9580/0) (see also Neoplasm, connective tissue, benign)
    malignant (M9580/3) — see Neoplasm, connective tissue, malignant
  granulosa cell (M8620/1) 236.2
    malignant (M8620/3) 183.0
  granulosa cell-theca cell (M8621/1) 236.2
    malignant (M8621/3) 183.0
  Grawitz's (hypernephroma) (M8312/3) 189.0
  hazard-crile (M8350/3) 193
  hemorrhoidal — see Hemorrhoids
  hilar cell (M8660/0) 220
  Hürthle cell (benign) (M8290/0) 226
    malignant (M8290/3) 193
  hydatid (see also Echinococcus) 122.9
  hypernephroid (M8311/1) (see also Neoplasm, by site, uncertain behavior)
  interstitial cell (M8650/1) (see also Neoplasm, by site, uncertain behavior)
    benign (M8650/0) — see Neoplasm, by site, benign
    malignant (M8650/3) — see Neoplasm, by site, malignant
  islet cell (M8150/0)
    malignant (M8150/3)
      pancreas 157.4
      specified site — see Neoplasm, by site, malignant
      unspecified site 157.4
    pancreas 211.7
    specified site NEC — see Neoplasm, by site, benign
    unspecified site 211.7
  juxtaglomerular (M8361/1) 236.91
  Krukenberg's (M8490/6) 198.6
  Leydig cell (M8650/1)
    benign (M8650/0)
      specified site — see Neoplasm, by site, benign
      unspecified site
        female 220
        male 222.0
    malignant (M8650/3)
      specified site — see Neoplasm, by site, malignant
      unspecified site
        female 183.0
        male 186.9
    specified site — see Neoplasm, by site, uncertain behavior
    unspecified site
      female 236.2

Tumor — see also Neoplasm, by site, unspecified nature — continued
  Leydig cell — continued
    unspecified site — continued
      male 236.4
  lipid cell, ovary (M8670/0) 220
  lipoid cell, ovary (M8670/0) 220
  lymphomatous, benign (M9590/0) (see also Neoplasm, by site, benign)
  lysis syndrome (following antineoplastic drug therapy) (spontaneous) 277.88
  Malherbe's (M8110/0) — see Neoplasm, skin, benign
  malignant (M8000/3) (see also Neoplasm, by site, malignant)
    fusiform cell (type) (M8004/3) — see Neoplasm, by site, malignant
    giant cell (type) (M8003/3) — see Neoplasm, by site, malignant
    mixed NEC (M8940/3) — see Neoplasm, by site, malignant
    small cell (type) (M8002/3) — see Neoplasm, by site, malignant
    spindle cell (type) (M8004/3) — see Neoplasm, by site, malignant
  mast cell (M9740/1) 238.5
    malignant (M9740/3) 202.6 ☑
  melanotic, neuroectodermal (M9363/0) — see Neoplasm, by site, benign
  Merkel cell — see Carcinoma, Merkel cell
  mesenchymal
    malignant (M8800/3) — see Neoplasm, connective tissue, malignant
    mixed (M8990/1) — see Neoplasm, connective tissue, uncertain behavior
  mesodermal, mixed (M8951/3) (see also Neoplasm, by site, malignant)
    liver 155.0
  mesonephric (M9110/1) (see also Neoplasm, by site, uncertain behavior)
    malignant (M9110/3) — see Neoplasm, by site, malignant
  metastatic
    from specified site (M8000/3) — see Neoplasm, by site, malignant
    to specified site (M8000/6) — see Neoplasm, by site, malignant, secondary
  mixed NEC (M8940/0) (see also Neoplasm, by site, benign)
    malignant (M8940/3) — see Neoplasm, by site, malignant
  mucocarcinoid, malignant (M8243/3) — see Neoplasm, by site, malignant
  mucoepidermoid (M8430/1) — see Neoplasm, by site, uncertain behavior
  Müllerian, mixed (M8950/3) — see Neoplasm, by site, malignant
  myoepithelial (M8982/0) — see Neoplasm, by site, benign
  neuroendocrine 209.60
    malignant poorly differentiated 209.30
    secondary 209.70
      bone 209.73
      distant lymph nodes 209.71
      liver 209.72
      peritoneum 209.74
      site specified NEC 209.79
  neurogenic olfactory (M9520/3) 160.0
  nonencapsulated sclerosing (M8350/3) 193
  odontogenic (M9270/1) 238.0
    adenomatoid (M9300/0) 213.1
      upper jaw (bone) 213.0
    benign (M9270/0) 213.1
      upper jaw (bone) 213.0
    calcifying epithelial (M9340/0) 213.1
      upper jaw (bone) 213.0
    malignant (M9270/3) 170.1
      upper jaw (bone) 170.0
    squamous (M9312/0) 213.1
      upper jaw (bone) 213.0
  ovarian stromal (M8590/1) 236.2
  ovary
    in pregnancy or childbirth 654.4 ☑
      affecting fetus or newborn 763.89

Tumor — see also Neoplasm, by site, unspecified nature — continued
  ovary — continued
    in pregnancy or childbirth — continued
      causing obstructed labor 660.2 ☑
        affecting fetus or newborn 763.1
  pacinian (M9507/0) — see Neoplasm, skin, benign
  Pancoast's (M8010/3) 162.3
  papillary — see Papilloma
  pelvic, in pregnancy or childbirth 654.9 ☑
    affecting fetus or newborn 763.89
    causing obstructed labor 660.2 ☑
      affecting fetus or newborn 763.1
  phantom 300.11
  plasma cell (M9731/1) 238.6
    benign (M9731/0) — see Neoplasm, by site, benign
    malignant (M9731/3) 203.8 ☑
  polyvesicular vitelline (M9071/3)
    specified site — see Neoplasm, by site, malignant
    unspecified site
      female 183.0
      male 186.9
  Pott's puffy (see also Osteomyelitis) 730.2 ☑
  Rathke's pouch (M9350/1) 237.0
  regaud's (M8082/3) — see Neoplasm, nasopharynx, malignant
  rete cell (M8140/0) 222.0
  retinal anlage (M9363/0) — see Neoplasm, by site, benign
  Rokitansky's 620.2
  salivary gland type, mixed (M8940/0) (see also Neoplasm, by site, benign)
    malignant (M8940/3) — see Neoplasm, by site, malignant
  Sampson's 617.1
  Schloffer's (see also Peritonitis) 567.29
  Schmincke (M8082/3) — see Neoplasm, nasopharynx, malignant
  sebaceous (see also Cyst, sebaceous) 706.2
  secondary (M8000/6) — see Neoplasm, by site, secondary
    carcinoid — see Tumor, neuroendocrine, secondary
    neuroendocrine — see Tumor, neuroendocrine, secondary
  Sertoli cell (M8640/0)
    with lipid storage (M8641/0)
      specified site — see Neoplasm, by site, benign
      unspecified site
        female 220
        male 222.0
    specified site — see Neoplasm, by site, benign
    unspecified site
      female 220
      male 222.0
  Sertoli-Leydig cell (M8631/0)
    specified site, — see Neoplasm, by site, benign
    unspecified site
      female 220
      male 222.0
  sex cord (-stromal) (M8590/1) — see Neoplasm, by site, uncertain behavior
  skin appendage (M8390/0) — see Neoplasm, skin, benign
  soft tissue
    benign (M8800/0) — see Neoplasm, connective tissue, benign
    malignant (M8800/3) — see Neoplasm, connective tissue, malignant
  sternomastoid 754.1
  stromal
    abdomen
      benign 215.5
      malignant NEC 171.5
      uncertain behavior 238.1
    digestive system 238.1
      benign 215.5
      malignant NEC 171.5
      uncertain behavior 238.1

☑ **Additional Digit Required — Refer to the Tabular List for Digit Selection**   ▽ **Subterms under main terms may continue to next column or page**

2015 ICD-9-CM   ▶◀ Revised Text   ● New Line   ▲ Revised Code   **Volume 2 — 287**

Tumor — see also Neoplasm, by site,
    unspecified nature — continued
  stromal — continued
    endometrium (endometrial) 236.0
    gastric 238.1
      benign 215.5
      malignant 151.9
      uncertain behavior 238.1
    gastrointestinal 238.1
      benign 215.5
      malignant NEC 171.5
      uncertain behavior 238.1
    intestine (small) 238.1
      benign 215.5
      malignant 152.9
      uncertain behavior 238.1
    stomach 238.1
      benign 215.5
      malignant 151.9
      uncertain behavior 238.1
  superior sulcus (lung) (pulmonary) (syn-
    drome) (M8010/3) 162.3
  suprasulcus (M8010/3) 162.3
  sweat gland (M8400/1) (see also Neoplasm,
    skin, uncertain behavior)
    benign (M8400/0) — see Neoplasm, skin,
      benign
    malignant (M8400/3) — see Neoplasm,
      skin, malignant
  syphilitic brain 094.89
    congenital 090.49
  testicular stromal (M8590/1) 236.4
  theca cell (M8600/0) 220
  theca cell-granulosa cell (M8621/1) 236.2
  theca-lutein (M8610/0) 220
  turban (M8200/0) 216.4
  uterus
    in pregnancy or childbirth 654.1 ☑
      affecting fetus or newborn 763.89
      causing obstructed labor 660.2 ☑
        affecting fetus or newborn 763.1
  vagina
    in pregnancy or childbirth 654.7 ☑
      affecting fetus or newborn 763.89
      causing obstructed labor 660.2 ☑
        affecting fetus or newborn 763.1
  varicose (see also Varicose, vein) 454.9
  von Recklinghausen's (M9540/1) 237.71
  vulva
    in pregnancy or childbirth 654.8 ☑
      affecting fetus or newborn 763.89
      causing obstructed labor 660.2 ☑
        affecting fetus or newborn 763.1
  Warthin's (salivary gland) (M8561/0) 210.2
  white (see also Tuberculosis, arthritis)
  White-Darier 757.39
  Wilms' (nephroblastoma) (M8960/3) 189.0
  yolk sac (M9071/3)
    specified site — see Neoplasm, by site,
      malignant
    unspecified site
      female 183.0
      male 186.9
Tumorlet (M8040/1) — see Neoplasm, by site,
    uncertain behavior
Tungiasis 134.1
Tunica vasculosa lentis 743.39
Tunnel vision 368.45
Turban tumor (M8200/0) 216.4
Türck's trachoma (chronic catarrhal laryngitis)
    476.0
Türk's syndrome (ocular retraction syndrome)
    378.71
Turner's
  hypoplasia (tooth) 520.4
  syndrome 758.6
  tooth 520.4
Turner-Kieser syndrome (hereditary osteo-
    onychodysplasia) 756.89
Turner-Varny syndrome 758.6
Turricephaly 756.0
Tussis convulsiva — see also Whooping cough
    033.9
Twiddler's syndrome (due to)
  automatic implantable defibrillator 996.04
  pacemaker 996.01

Twin
  affected by maternal complications of
    pregnancy 761.5
  conjoined 759.4
    fetal 678.1 ☑
  healthy liveborn — see Newborn, twin
  pregnancy (complicating delivery) NEC
    651.0 ☑
    with fetal loss and retention of one fetus
      651.3 ☑
    conjoined 678.1 ☑
    following (elective) fetal reduction
      651.7 ☑
Twinning, teeth 520.2
Twist, twisted
  bowel, colon, or intestine 560.2
  hair (congenital) 757.4
  mesentery 560.2
  omentum 560.2
  organ or site, congenital NEC — see
    Anomaly, specified type NEC
  ovarian pedicle 620.5
    congenital 752.0
  umbilical cord — see Compression, umbili-
    cal cord
Twitch 781.0
Tylosis 700
  buccalis 528.6
  gingiva 523.8
  linguae 528.6
  palmaris et plantaris 757.39
Tympanism 787.3
Tympanites (abdominal) (intestine) 787.3
Tympanitis — see Myringitis
Tympanosclerosis 385.00
  involving
    combined sites NEC 385.09
      with tympanic membrane 385.03
    tympanic membrane 385.01
      with ossicles 385.02
        and middle ear 385.03
Tympanum — see condition
Tympany
  abdomen 787.3
  chest 786.7
Typhlitis — see also Appendicitis 541
Typhoenteritis 002.0
Typhogastric fever 002.0
Typhoid (abortive) (ambulant) (any site) (fever)
    (hemorrhagic) (infection) (intermittent)
    (malignant) (rheumatic) 002.0
  with pneumonia 002.0 [484.8]
  abdominal 002.0
  carrier (suspected) of V02.1
  cholecystitis (current) 002.0
  clinical (Widal and blood test negative)
    002.0
  endocarditis 002.0 [421.1]
  inoculation reaction — see Complications,
    vaccination
  meningitis 002.0 [320.7]
  mesenteric lymph nodes 002.0
  myocarditis 002.0 [422.0]
  osteomyelitis (see also Osteomyelitis, due
    to, typhoid) 002.0 [730.8] ☑
  perichondritis, larynx 002.0 [478.71]
  pneumonia 002.0 [484.8]
  spine 002.0 [720.81]
  ulcer (perforating) 002.0
  vaccination, prophylactic (against) V03.1
  Widal negative 002.0
Typhomalaria (fever) — see also Malaria 084.6
Typhomania 002.0
Typhoperitonitis 002.0
Typhus (fever) 081.9
  abdominal, abdominalis 002.0
  African tick 082.1
  amarillic (see also Fever, Yellow) 060.9
  brain 081.9
  cerebral 081.9
  classical 080
  endemic (flea-borne) 081.0
  epidemic (louse-borne) 080
  exanthematicus SAI 080
    brillii SAI 081.1
    Mexicanus SAI 081.0

Typhus — continued
  exanthematicus SAI — continued
    pediculo vestimenti causa 080
    typhus murinus 081.0
  exanthematic NEC 080
  flea-borne 081.0
  Indian tick 082.1
  Kenya tick 082.1
  louse-borne 080
  Mexican 081.0
    flea-borne 081.0
    louse-borne 080
    tabardillo 080
  mite-borne 081.2
  murine 081.0
  North Asian tick-borne 082.2
  petechial 081.9
  Queensland tick 082.3
  rat 081.0
  recrudescent 081.1
  recurrent (see also Fever, relapsing) 087.9
  São Paulo 082.0
  scrub (China) (India) (Malaya) (New Guinea)
    081.2
  shop (of Malaya) 081.0
  Siberian tick 082.2
  tick-borne NEC 082.9
  tropical 081.2
  vaccination, prophylactic (against) V05.8
Tyrosinemia 270.2
  neonatal 775.89
Tyrosinosis (Medes) (Sakai) 270.2
Tyrosinuria 270.2
Tyrosyluria 270.2

U

Uehlinger's syndrome (acropachyderma)
    757.39
Uhl's anomaly or disease (hypoplasia of my-
    ocardium, right ventricle) 746.84
Ulcerosa scarlatina 034.1
Ulcer, ulcerated, ulcerating, ulceration, ul-
    cerative 707.9
  with gangrene 707.9 [785.4]
  abdomen (wall) (see also Ulcer, skin) 707.8
  ala, nose 478.19
  alveolar process 526.5
  amebic (intestine) 006.9
    skin 006.6
  anastomotic — see Ulcer, gastrojejunal
  anorectal 569.41
  antral — see Ulcer, stomach
  anus (sphincter) (solitary) 569.41
    varicose — see Varicose, ulcer, anus
  aorta — see Aneuysm
  aphthous (oral) (recurrent) 528.2
    genital organ(s)
      female 616.50
      male 608.89
    mouth 528.2
  arm (see also Ulcer, skin) 707.8
  arteriosclerotic plaque — see Arteriosclero-
    sis, by site
  artery NEC 447.2
    without rupture 447.8
  atrophic NEC — see Ulcer, skin
  Barrett's (chronic peptic ulcer of esophagus)
    530.85
  bile duct 576.8
  bladder (solitary) (sphincter) 596.89
    bilharzial (see also Schistosomiasis)
      120.9 [595.4]
    submucosal (see also Cystitis) 595.1
    tuberculous (see also Tuberculosis)
      016.1 ☑
  bleeding NEC — see Ulcer, peptic, with
    hemorrhage
  bone 730.9 ☑
  bowel (see also Ulcer, intestine) 569.82
  breast 611.0
  bronchitis 491.8
  bronchus 519.19
  buccal (cavity) (traumatic) 528.9
  burn (acute) — see Ulcer, duodenum
  Buruli 031.1
  buttock (see also Ulcer, skin) 707.8

Ulcer, ulcerated, ulcerating, ulceration,
    ulcerative — continued
  buttock (see also Ulcer, skin) — contin-
    ued
    decubitus (see also Ulcer, pressure)
      707.00
  cancerous (M8000/3) — see Neoplasm, by
    site, malignant
  cardia — see Ulcer, stomach
  cardio-esophageal (peptic) 530.20
    with bleeding 530.21
  cecum (see also Ulcer, intestine) 569.82
  cervix (uteri) (trophic) 622.0
    with mention of cervicitis 616.0
  chancroidal 099.0
  chest (wall) (see also Ulcer, skin) 707.8
  Chiclero 085.4
  chin (pyogenic) (see also Ulcer, skin) 707.8
  chronic (cause unknown) (see also Ulcer,
    skin)
    penis 607.89
  Cochin-China 085.1
  colitis — see Colitis, ulcerative
  colon (see also Ulcer, intestine) 569.82
  conjunctiva (acute) (postinfectional) 372.00
  cornea (infectional) 370.00
    with perforation 370.06
    annular 370.02
    catarrhal 370.01
    central 370.03
    dendritic 054.42
    marginal 370.01
    mycotic 370.05
    phlyctenular, tuberculous (see also Tuber-
      culosis) 017.3 ☑ [370.31]
    ring 370.02
    rodent 370.07
    serpent, serpiginous 370.04
    superficial marginal 370.01
    tuberculous (see also Tuberculosis)
      017.3 ☑ [370.31]
  corpus cavernosum (chronic) 607.89
  crural — see Ulcer, lower extremity
  Curling's — see Ulcer, duodenum
  Cushing's — see Ulcer, peptic
  cystitis (interstitial) 595.1
  decubitus (unspecified site) (see also Ulcer,
    pressure) 707.00
    with gangrene 707.00 [785.4]
    ankle 707.06
    back
      lower 707.03
      upper 707.02
    buttock 707.05
    coccyx 707.03
    elbow 707.01
    head 707.09
    heel 707.07
    hip 707.04
    other site 707.09
    sacrum 707.03
    shoulder blades 707.02
  dendritic 054.42
  diabetes, diabetic (mellitus) 250.8 ☑ [707.9]
    due to secondary diabetes
      249.8 ☑ [707.9]
    lower limb 250.8 ☑ [707.10]
      ankle 250.8 ☑ [707.13]
        due to secondary diabetes
          249.8 ☑ [707.13]
      calf 250.8 ☑ [707.12]
        due to secondary diabetes
          249.8 ☑ [707.12]
      due to secondary diabetes
        249.8 ☑ [707.10]
      foot 250.8 ☑ [707.15]
        due to secondary diabetes
          249.8 ☑ [707.15]
      heel 250.8 ☑ [707.14]
        due to secondary diabetes
          249.8 ☑ [707.14]
      knee 250.8 ☑ [707.19]
        due to secondary diabetes
          249.8 ☑ [707.19]
      specified site NEC 250.8 ☑ [707.19]

☑ Additional Digit Required — Refer to the Tabular List for Digit Selection   ▽ Subterms under main terms may continue to next column or page

288 — Volume 2   ▶◀ Revised Text   ● New Line   ▲ Revised Code   2015 ICD-9-CM

Ulcer, ulcerated, ulcerating, ulceration, ulcerative — continued
diabetes, diabetic — continued
lower limb — continued
specified site — continued
due to secondary diabetes
249.8 ☑ [707.19]
thigh 250.8 ☑ [707.11]
due to secondary diabetes
249.8 ☑ [707.11]
toes 250.8 ☑ [707.15]
due to secondary diabetes
249.8 ☑ [707.15]
specified site NEC 250.8 ☑ [707.8]
due to secondary diabetes
249.8 ☑ [707.8]
Dieulafoy — see Lesion, Dieulafoy
due to
infection NEC — see Ulcer, skin
radiation, radium — see Ulcer, by site
trophic disturbance (any region) — see
Ulcer, skin
x-ray — see Ulcer, by site
duodenum, duodenal (eroded) (peptic)
532.9 ☑

Note — Use the following fifth-digit
subclassification with categories
531–534:

0   without mention of obstruction

1   with obstruction

with
hemorrhage (chronic) 532.4 ☑
and perforation 532.6 ☑
perforation (chronic) 532.5 ☑
and hemorrhage 532.6 ☑
acute 532.3 ☑
with
hemorrhage 532.0 ☑
and perforation 532.2 ☑
perforation 532.1 ☑
and hemorrhage 532.2 ☑
bleeding (recurrent) — see Ulcer, duodenum, with hemorrhage
chronic 532.7 ☑
with
hemorrhage 532.4 ☑
and perforation 532.6 ☑
perforation 532.5 ☑
and hemorrhage 532.6 ☑
penetrating — see Ulcer, duodenum,
with perforation
perforating — see Ulcer, duodenum,
with perforation
dysenteric NEC 009.0
elusive 595.1
endocarditis (any valve) (acute) (chronic)
(subacute) 421.0
enteritis — see Colitis, ulcerative
enterocolitis 556.0
epiglottis 478.79
esophagus (peptic) 530.20
with bleeding 530.21
due to ingestion
aspirin 530.20
chemicals 530.20
medicinal agents 530.20
fungal 530.20
infectional 530.20
varicose (see also Varix, esophagus) 456.1
bleeding (see also Varix, esophagus,
bleeding) 456.0
eyelid (region) 373.01
eye NEC 360.00
dendritic 054.42
face (see also Ulcer, skin) 707.8
fauces 478.29
Fenwick (-Hunner) (solitary) (see also Cystitis) 595.1
fistulous NEC — see Ulcer, skin
foot (indolent) (see also Ulcer, lower extremity) 707.15
perforating 707.15
leprous 030.1
syphilitic 094.0

Ulcer, ulcerated, ulcerating, ulceration, ulcerative — continued
foot (see also Ulcer, lower extremity) —
continued
trophic 707.15
varicose 454.0
inflamed or infected 454.2
frambesial, initial or primary 102.0
gallbladder or duct 575.8
gall duct 576.8
gangrenous (see also Gangrene) 785.4
gastric — see Ulcer, stomach
gastrocolic — see Ulcer, gastrojejunal
gastroduodenal — see Ulcer, peptic
gastroesophageal — see Ulcer, stomach
gastrohepatic — see Ulcer, stomach
gastrointestinal — see Ulcer, gastrojejunal
gastrojejunal (eroded) (peptic) 534.9 ☑

Note — Use the following fifth-digit
subclassification with categories
531–534:

0   without mention of obstruction

1   with obstruction

with
hemorrhage (chronic) 534.4 ☑
and perforation 534.6 ☑
perforation 534.5 ☑
and hemorrhage 534.6 ☑
acute 534.3 ☑
with
hemorrhage 534.0 ☑
and perforation 534.2 ☑
perforation 534.1 ☑
and hemorrhage 534.2 ☑
bleeding (recurrent) — see Ulcer, gastrojejunal, with hemorrhage
chronic 534.7 ☑
with
hemorrhage 534.4 ☑
and perforation 534.6 ☑
perforation 534.5 ☑
and hemorrhage 534.6 ☑
penetrating — see Ulcer, gastrojejunal,
with perforation
perforating — see Ulcer, gastrojejunal,
with perforation
gastrojejunocolic — see Ulcer, gastrojejunal
genital organ
female 629.89
male 608.89
gingiva 523.8
gingivitis 523.10
glottis 478.79
granuloma of pudenda 099.2
gum 523.8
gumma, due to yaws 102.4
hand (see also Ulcer, skin) 707.8
hard palate 528.9
heel (see also Ulcer, lower extremity) 707.14
decubitus (see also Ulcer, pressure)
707.07
hemorrhoids 455.8
external 455.5
internal 455.2
hip (see also Ulcer, skin) 707.8
decubitus (see also Ulcer, pressure)
707.04
Hunner's 595.1
hypopharynx 478.29
hypopyon (chronic) (subacute) 370.04
hypostaticum — see Ulcer, varicose
ileocolitis 556.1
ileum (see also Ulcer, intestine) 569.82
intestine, intestinal 569.82
with perforation 569.83
amebic 006.9
duodenal — see Ulcer, duodenum
granulocytopenic (with hemorrhage)
288.09
marginal 569.82
perforating 569.83
small, primary 569.82
stercoraceous 569.82

Ulcer, ulcerated, ulcerating, ulceration, ulcerative — continued
intestine, intestinal — continued
stercoral 569.82
tuberculous (see also Tuberculosis)
014.8 ☑
typhoid (fever) 002.0
varicose 456.8
ischemic 707.9
lower extremity (see also Ulcer, lower
extremity) 707.10
ankle 707.13
calf 707.12
foot 707.15
heel 707.14
knee 707.19
specified site NEC 707.19
thigh 707.11
toes 707.15
jejunum, jejunal — see Ulcer, gastrojejunal
keratitis (see also Ulcer, cornea) 370.00
knee — see Ulcer, lower extremity
labium (majus) (minus) 616.50
laryngitis (see also Laryngitis) 464.00
with obstruction 464.01
larynx (aphthous) (contact) 478.79
diphtheritic 032.3
leg — see Ulcer, lower extremity
lip 528.5
Lipschütz's 616.50
lower extremity (atrophic) (chronic) (neurogenic) (perforating) (pyogenic)
(trophic) (tropical) 707.10
with gangrene (see also Ulcer, lower extremity) 707.10 [785.4]
arteriosclerosis 440.24
ankle 707.13
arteriosclerotic 440.23
with gangrene 440.24
calf 707.12
decubitus (see also Ulcer, pressure)
707.00
with gangrene 707.00 [785.4]
ankle 707.06
buttock 707.05
heel 707.07
hip 707.04
foot 707.15
heel 707.14
knee 707.19
specified site NEC 707.19
thigh 707.11
toes 707.15
varicose 454.0
inflamed or infected 454.2
luetic — see Ulcer, syphilitic
lung 518.89
tuberculous (see also Tuberculosis)
011.2 ☑
malignant (M8000/3) — see Neoplasm, by
site, malignant
marginal NEC — see Ulcer, gastrojejunal
meatus (urinarius) 597.89
Meckel's diverticulum 751.0
Meleney's (chronic undermining) 686.09
Mooren's (cornea) 370.07
mouth (traumatic) 528.9
mycobacterial (skin) 031.1
nasopharynx 478.29
navel cord (newborn) 771.4
neck (see also Ulcer, skin) 707.8
uterus 622.0
neurogenic NEC — see Ulcer, skin
nose, nasal (infectional) (passage) 478.19
septum 478.19
varicose 456.8
skin — see Ulcer, skin
spirochetal NEC 104.8
oral mucosa (traumatic) 528.9
palate (soft) 528.9
penetrating NEC — see Ulcer, peptic, with
perforation
penis (chronic) 607.89

Ulcer, ulcerated, ulcerating, ulceration, ulcerative — continued
peptic (site unspecified) 533.9 ☑

Note — Use the following fifth-digit
subclassification with categories
531–534:

0   without mention of obstruction

1   with obstruction

with
hemorrhage 533.4 ☑
and perforation 533.6 ☑
perforation (chronic) 533.5 ☑
and hemorrhage 533.6 ☑
acute 533.3 ☑
with
hemorrhage 533.0 ☑
and perforation 533.2 ☑
perforation 533.1 ☑
and hemorrhage 533.2 ☑
bleeding (recurrent) — see Ulcer, peptic,
with hemorrhage
chronic 533.7 ☑
with
hemorrhage 533.4 ☑
and perforation 533.6 ☑
perforation 533.5 ☑
and hemorrhage 533.6 ☑
penetrating — see Ulcer, peptic, with
perforation
perforating NEC (see also Ulcer, peptic, with
perforation) 533.5 ☑
skin 707.9
perineum (see also Ulcer, skin) 707.8
peritonsillar 474.8
phagedenic (tropical) NEC — see Ulcer, skin
pharynx 478.29
phlebitis — see Phlebitis
plaster (see also Ulcer, pressure) 707.00
popliteal space — see Ulcer, lower extremity
postpyloric — see Ulcer, duodenum
prepuce 607.89
prepyloric — see Ulcer, stomach
pressure 707.00
with
abrasion, blister, partial thickness
skin loss involving epidermis
and/or dermis 707.22
full thickness skin loss involving
damage or necrosis of subcutaneous tissue 707.23
gangrene 707.00 [785.4]
necrosis of soft tissue through to underlying muscle, tendon, or
bone 707.24
ankle 707.06
back
lower 707.03
upper 707.02
buttock 707.05
coccyx 707.03
elbow 707.01
head 707.09
healed — omit code
healing — code to Ulcer, pressure, by
stage
heel 707.07
hip 707.04
other site 707.09
sacrum 707.03
shoulder blades 707.02
stage
I (healing) 707.21
II (healing) 707.22
III (healing) 707.23
IV (healing) 707.24
unspecified (healing) 707.20
unstageable 707.25
primary of intestine 569.82
with perforation 569.83
proctitis 556.2
with ulcerative sigmoiditis 556.3
prostate 601.8
pseudopeptic — see Ulcer, peptic
pyloric — see Ulcer, stomach

☑ Additional Digit Required — Refer to the Tabular List for Digit Selection
▽ Subterms under main terms may continue to next column or page
2015 ICD-9-CM
►◄ Revised Text
● New Line
▲ Revised Code
Volume 2 — 289

Ulcer, ulcerated, ulcerating, ulceration, ulcerative — *continued*
rectosigmoid 569.82
  with perforation 569.83
rectum (sphincter) (solitary) 569.41
  stercoraceous, stercoral 569.41
  varicose — *see* Varicose, ulcer, anus
retina (*see also* Chorioretinitis) 363.20
rodent (M8090/3) (*see also* Neoplasm, skin, malignant)
  cornea 370.07
round — *see* Ulcer, stomach
sacrum (region) (*see also* Ulcer, skin) 707.8
Saemisch's 370.04
scalp (*see also* Ulcer, skin) 707.8
sclera 379.09
scrofulous (*see also* Tuberculosis) 017.2 ☑
scrotum 608.89
  tuberculous (*see also* Tuberculosis) 016.5 ☑
  varicose 456.4
seminal vesicle 608.89
sigmoid 569.82
  with perforation 569.83
skin (atrophic) (chronic) (neurogenic) (non-healing) (perforating) (pyogenic) (trophic) 707.9
  with gangrene 707.9 [785.4]
  amebic 006.6
  decubitus (*see also* Ulcer, pressure) 707.00
    with gangrene 707.00 [785.4]
  in granulocytopenia 288.09
  lower extremity (*see also* Ulcer, lower extremity) 707.10
    with gangrene 707.10 [785.4]
      arteriosclerotic 440.24
    ankle 707.13
    arteriosclerotic 440.23
      with gangrene 440.24
    calf 707.12
    foot 707.15
    heel 707.14
    knee 707.19
    specified site NEC 707.19
    thigh 707.11
    toes 707.15
  mycobacterial 031.1
  syphilitic (early) (secondary) 091.3
  tuberculous (primary) (*see also* Tuberculosis) 017.0 ☑
  varicose — *see* Ulcer, varicose
sloughing NEC — *see* Ulcer, skin
soft palate 528.9
solitary, anus or rectum (sphincter) 569.41
sore throat 462
  streptococcal 034.0
spermatic cord 608.89
spine (tuberculous) 015.0 ☑ [730.88]
stasis (leg) (venous) 454.0
  with varicose veins 454.0
  without varicose veins 459.81
  inflamed or infected 454.2
stercoral, stercoraceous 569.82
  with perforation 569.83
  anus or rectum 569.41
stoma, stomal — *see* Ulcer, gastrojejunal
stomach (eroded) (peptic) (round) 531.9 ☑

> *Note* — Use the following fifth-digit subclassification with categories 531–534:
>
> 0   without mention of obstruction
> 1   with obstruction

  with
    hemorrhage 531.4 ☑
      and perforation 531.6 ☑
    perforation (chronic) 531.5 ☑
      and hemorrhage 531.6 ☑
  acute 531.3 ☑
    with
      hemorrhage 531.0 ☑
        and perforation 531.2 ☑
      perforation 531.1 ☑
        and hemorrhage 531.2 ☑

Ulcer, ulcerated, ulcerating, ulceration, ulcerative — *continued*
stomach — *continued*
  bleeding (recurrent) — *see* Ulcer, stomach, with hemorrhage
  chronic 531.7 ☑
    with
      hemorrhage 531.4 ☑
        and perforation 531.6 ☑
      perforation 531.5 ☑
        and hemorrhage 531.6 ☑
  penetrating — *see* Ulcer, stomach, with perforation
  perforating — *see* Ulcer, stomach, with perforation
stomatitis 528.00
stress — *see* Ulcer, peptic
strumous (tuberculous) (*see also* Tuberculosis) 017.2 ☑
submental (*see also* Ulcer, skin) 707.8
submucosal, bladder 595.1
syphilitic (any site) (early) (secondary) 091.3
  late 095.9
  perforating 095.9
    foot 094.0
testis 608.89
thigh — *see* Ulcer, lower extremity
throat 478.29
  diphtheritic 032.0
toe — *see* Ulcer, lower extremity
tongue (traumatic) 529.0
tonsil 474.8
  diphtheritic 032.0
trachea 519.19
trophic — *see* Ulcer, skin
tropical NEC (*see also* Ulcer, skin) 707.9
tuberculous — *see* Tuberculosis, ulcer
tunica vaginalis 608.89
turbinate 730.9 ☑
typhoid (fever) 002.0
  perforating 002.0
umbilicus (newborn) 771.4
unspecified site NEC — *see* Ulcer, skin
urethra (meatus) (*see also* Urethritis) 597.89
uterus 621.8
  cervix 622.0
    with mention of cervicitis 616.0
  neck 622.0
    with mention of cervicitis 616.0
vagina 616.89
valve, heart 421.0
varicose (lower extremity, any part) 454.0
  anus — *see* Varicose, ulcer, anus
  broad ligament 456.5
  esophagus (*see also* Varix, esophagus) 456.1
    bleeding (*see also* Varix, esophagus, bleeding) 456.0
  inflamed or infected 454.2
  nasal septum 456.8
  perineum 456.6
  rectum — *see* Varicose, ulcer, anus
  scrotum 456.4
  specified site NEC 456.8
  sublingual 456.3
  vulva 456.6
vas deferens 608.89
vesical (*see also* Ulcer, bladder) 596.89
vulva (acute) (infectional) 616.50
  Behçet's syndrome 136.1 [616.51]
  herpetic 054.12
  tuberculous 016.7 ☑ [616.51]
vulvobuccal, recurring 616.50
x-ray — *see* Ulcer, by site
yaws 102.4
Ulcus — *see also* Ulcer
cutis tuberculosum (*see also* Tuberculosis) 017.0 ☑
duodeni — *see* Ulcer, duodenum
durum 091.0
  extragenital 091.2
gastrojejunale — *see* Ulcer, gastrojejunal
hypostaticum — *see* Ulcer, varicose
molle (cutis) (skin) 099.0
serpens corneae (pneumococcal) 370.04
ventriculi — *see* Ulcer, stomach

Ulegyria 742.4
Ulerythema
  acneiforma 701.8
  centrifugum 695.4
  ophryogenes 757.4
Ullrich-Feichtiger syndrome 759.89
Ullrich (-Bonnevie) (-Turner) syndrome 758.6
Ulnar — *see* condition
Ulorrhagia 523.8
Ulorrhea 523.8
Umbilicus, umbilical — *see also* condition
  cord necrosis, affecting fetus or newborn 762.6
Unacceptable
  existing dental restoration
    contours 525.65
    morphology 525.65
Unavailability of medical facilities (at) V63.9
  due to
    investigation by social service agency V63.8
    lack of services at home V63.1
    remoteness from facility V63.0
    waiting list V63.2
  home V63.1
  outpatient clinic V63.0
  specified reason NEC V63.8
Uncinaria americana infestation 126.1
Uncinariasis — *see also* Ancylostomiasis 126.9
Unconscious, unconsciousness 780.09
Underdevelopment — *see also* Undeveloped
  sexual 259.0
Underfill, endodontic 526.63
Undernourishment 269.9
Undernutrition 269.9
Under observation — *see* Observation
Underweight 783.22
  for gestational age — *see* Light-for-dates
Underwood's disease (sclerema neonatorum) 778.1
Undescended — *see also* Malposition, congenital
  cecum 751.4
  colon 751.4
  testis 752.51
Undetermined diagnosis or cause 799.9
Undeveloped, undevelopment — *see also* Hypoplasia
  brain (congenital) 742.1
  cerebral (congenital) 742.1
  fetus or newborn 764.9 ☑
  heart 746.89
  lung 748.5
  testis 257.2
  uterus 259.0
Undiagnosed (disease) 799.9
Undulant fever — *see also* Brucellosis 023.9
Unemployment, anxiety concerning V62.0
Unequal leg (acquired) (length) 736.81
  congenital 755.30
Unerupted teeth, tooth 520.6
Unextracted dental root 525.3
Unguis incarnatus 703.0
Unicornis uterus 752.33
Unicornuate uterus (with or without a separate uterine horn) 752.33
Unicorporeus uterus 752.39
Uniformis uterus 752.39
Unilateral — *see also* condition
  development, breast 611.89
  organ or site, congenital NEC — *see* Agenesis
  vagina 752.49
Unilateralis uterus 752.39
Unilocular heart 745.8
Uninhibited bladder 596.54
  with cauda equina syndrome 344.61
  neurogenic — *see also* Neurogenic, bladder 596.54
Union, abnormal — *see also* Fusion
  divided tendon 727.89
  larynx and trachea 748.3
Universal
  joint, cervix 620.6
  mesentery 751.4

Unknown
  cause of death 799.9
  diagnosis 799.9
Unna's disease (seborrheic dermatitis) 690.10
Unresponsiveness, adrenocorticotropin (ACTH) 255.41
Unsatisfactory
  cytology smear
    anal 796.78
    cervical 795.08
    vaginal 795.18
  restoration, tooth (existing) 525.60
    specified NEC 525.69
Unsoundness of mind — *see also* Psychosis 298.9
Unspecified cause of death 799.9
Unstable
  back NEC 724.9
  colon 569.89
  joint — *see* Instability, joint
  lie 652.0 ☑
    affecting fetus or newborn (before labor) 761.7
    causing obstructed labor 660.0 ☑
      affecting fetus or newborn 763.1
  lumbosacral joint (congenital) 756.19
    acquired 724.6
  sacroiliac 724.6
  spine NEC 724.9
Untruthfulness, child problem — *see also* Disturbance, conduct 312.0 ☑
Unverricht (-Lundborg) disease, syndrome, or epilepsy 345.1 ☑
Unverricht-Wagner syndrome (dermatomyositis) 710.3
Upper respiratory — *see* condition
Upset
  gastric 536.8
    psychogenic 306.4
  gastrointestinal 536.8
    psychogenic 306.4
    virus (*see also* Enteritis, viral) 008.8
  intestinal (large) (small) 564.9
    psychogenic 306.4
  menstruation 626.9
  mental 300.9
  stomach 536.8
    psychogenic 306.4
Urachus — *see also* condition
  patent 753.7
  persistent 753.7
Uratic arthritis 274.00
Urbach's lipoid proteinosis 272.8
Urbach-Oppenheim disease or syndrome (necrobiosis lipoidica diabeticorum) 250.8 ☑ [709.3]
  due to secondary diabetes 249.8 ☑ [709.3]
Urbach-Wiethe disease or syndrome (lipoid proteinosis) 272.8
Urban yellow fever 060.1
Urea, blood, high — *see* Uremia
Uremia, uremic (absorption) (amaurosis) (amblyopia) (aphasia) (apoplexy) (coma) (delirium) (dementia) (dropsy) (dyspnea) (fever) (intoxication) (mania) (paralysis) (poisoning) (toxemia) (vomiting) 586
  with
    abortion — *see* Abortion, by type, with renal failure
    ectopic pregnancy (*see also* categories 633.0–633.9) 639.3
    hypertension (*see also* Hypertension, kidney) 403.91
    molar pregnancy (*see also* categories 630–632) 639.3
  chronic 585.9
  complicating
    abortion 639.3
    ectopic or molar pregnancy 639.3
    hypertension (*see also* Hypertension, kidney) 403.91
    labor and delivery 669.3 ☑
  congenital 779.89
  extrarenal 788.99
  hypertensive (chronic) (*see also* Hypertension, kidney) 403.91

☑ **Additional Digit Required** — Refer to the Tabular List for Digit Selection   ▽ **Subterms under main terms may continue to next column or page**

290 — Volume 2   ▶◀ Revised Text   ● New Line   ▲ Revised Code   2015 ICD-9-CM

Uremia, uremic — *continued*
  maternal NEC, affecting fetus or newborn 760.1
  neuropathy 585.9 *[357.4]*
  pericarditis 585.9 *[420.0]*
  prenatal 788.99
  pyelitic (*see also* Pyelitis) 590.80
Ureteralgia 788.0
Ureterectasis 593.89
Ureteritis 593.89
  cystica 590.3
  due to calculus 592.1
  gonococcal (acute) 098.19
    chronic or duration of 2 months or over 098.39
  nonspecific 593.89
Ureterocele (acquired) 593.89
  congenital 753.23
Ureterolith 592.1
Ureterolithiasis 592.1
Ureterostomy status V44.6
  with complication 997.5
Ureter, ureteral — *see* condition
Urethralgia 788.99
Urethra, urethral — *see* condition
Urethritis (abacterial) (acute) (allergic) (anterior) (chronic) (nonvenereal) (posterior) (recurrent) (simple) (subacute) (ulcerative) (undifferentiated) 597.80
  diplococcal (acute) 098.0
    chronic or duration of 2 months or over 098.2
  due to Trichomonas (vaginalis) 131.02
  gonococcal (acute) 098.0
    chronic or duration of 2 months or over 098.2
  nongonococcal (sexually transmitted) 099.40
    Chlamydia trachomatis 099.41
    Reiter's 099.3
    specified organism NEC 099.49
  nonspecific (sexually transmitted) (*see also* Urethritis, nongonococcal) 099.40
  not sexually transmitted 597.80
  Reiter's 099.3
  trichomonal or due to Trichomonas (vaginalis) 131.02
  tuberculous (*see also* Tuberculosis) 016.3 ☑
  venereal NEC (*see also* Urethritis, nongonococcal) 099.40
Urethrocele
  female 618.03
    with uterine prolapse 618.4
      complete 618.3
      incomplete 618.2
  male 599.5
Urethrolithiasis 594.2
Urethro-oculoarticular syndrome 099.3
Urethro-oculosynovial syndrome 099.3
Urethrorectal — *see* condition
Urethrorrhagia 599.84
Urethrorrhea 788.7
Urethrostomy status V44.6
  with complication 997.5

Urethrotrigonitis 595.3
Urethrovaginal — *see* condition
Urgency
  fecal 787.63
  hypertensive — *see* Hypertension
Urhidrosis, uridrosis 705.89
Uric acid
  diathesis 274.9
  in blood 790.6
Uricacidemia 790.6
Uricemia 790.6
Uricosuria 791.9
Urination
  frequent 788.41
  painful 788.1
  urgency 788.63
Urinemia — *see* Uremia
Urine, urinary — *see also* condition
  abnormality NEC 788.69
  blood in (*see also* Hematuria) 599.70
  discharge, excessive 788.42
  enuresis 788.30
    nonorganic origin 307.6
  extravasation 788.8
  frequency 788.41
  hesitancy 788.64
  incontinence 788.30
    active 788.30
    female 788.30
      stress 625.6
      and urge 788.33
    male 788.30
      stress 788.32
      and urge 788.33
    mixed (stress and urge) 788.33
    neurogenic 788.39
    nonorganic origin 307.6
    overflow 788.38
    stress (female) 625.6
      male NEC 788.32
  intermittent stream 788.61
  pus in 791.9
  retention or stasis NEC 788.20
    bladder, incomplete emptying 788.21
    psychogenic 306.53
    specified NEC 788.29
  secretion
    deficient 788.5
    excessive 788.42
    frequency 788.41
  strain 788.65
  stream
    intermittent 788.61
    slowing 788.62
    splitting 788.61
    weak 788.62
  urgency 788.63
Urinoma NEC 599.9
  bladder 596.89
  kidney 593.89
  renal 593.89
  ureter 593.89
  urethra 599.84
Uroarthritis, infectious 099.3

Urodialysis 788.5
Urolithiasis 592.9
Uronephrosis 593.89
Uropathy 599.9
  obstructive 599.60
Urosepsis 599.0
  meaning sepsis 995.91
  meaning urinary tract infection 599.0
Urticaria 708.9
  with angioneurotic edema 995.1
    hereditary 277.6
  allergic 708.0
  cholinergic 708.5
  chronic 708.8
  cold, familial 708.2
  dermatographic 708.3
  due to
    cold or heat 708.2
    drugs 708.0
    food 708.0
    inhalants 708.0
    plants 708.8
    serum 999.59
  factitial 708.3
  giant 995.1
    hereditary 277.6
  gigantea 995.1
    hereditary 277.6
  idiopathic 708.1
  larynx 995.1
    hereditary 277.6
  neonatorum 778.8
  nonallergic 708.1
  papulosa (Hebra) 698.2
  perstans hemorrhagica 757.39
  pigmentosa 757.33
  recurrent periodic 708.8
  serum 999.59
  solare 692.72
  specified type NEC 708.8
  thermal (cold) (heat) 708.2
  vibratory 708.4
Urticarioides acarodermatitis 133.9
Use of
  agents affecting estrogen receptors and estrogen levels NEC V07.59
  anastrozole (Arimidex) V07.52
  aromatase inhibitors V07.52
  estrogen receptor downregulators V07.59
  exemestane (Aromasin) V07.52
  fulvestrant (Faslodex) V07.59
  gonadotropin-releasing hormone (GnRH) agonist V07.59
  goserelin acetate (Zoladex) V07.59
  letrozole (Femara) V07.52
  leuprolide acetate (leuprorelin) (Lupron) V07.59
  megestrol acetate (Megace) V07.59
  methadone 304.00
  nonprescribed drugs (*see also* Abuse, drugs, nondependent) 305.9 ☑
  patent medicines (*see also* Abuse, drugs, nondependent) 305.9 ☑
  raloxifene (Evista) V07.51

Use of — *continued*
  selective estrogen receptor modulators (SERMs) V07.51
  tamoxifen (Nolvadex) V07.51
  toremifene (Fareston) V07.51
Usher-Senear disease (pemphigus erythematosus) 694.4
Uta 085.5
Uterine size-date discrepancy 649.6 ☑
Uteromegaly 621.2
Uterovaginal — *see* condition
Uterovesical — *see* condition
Uterus — *see also* condition
  with only one functioning horn 752.33
Utriculitis (utriculus prostaticus) 597.89
Uveal — *see* condition
Uveitis (anterior) — *see also* Iridocyclitis 364.3
  acute or subacute 364.00
    due to or associated with
      gonococcal infection 098.41
      herpes (simplex) 054.44
        zoster 053.22
    primary 364.01
    recurrent 364.02
    secondary (noninfectious) 364.04
      infectious 364.03
  allergic 360.11
  chronic 364.10
    due to or associated with
      sarcoidosis 135 *[364.11]*
      tuberculosis (*see also* Tuberculosis) 017.3 ☑ *[364.11]*
  due to
    operation 360.11
    toxoplasmosis (acquired) 130.2
      congenital (active) 771.2
  granulomatous 364.10
  heterochromic 364.21
  lens-induced 364.23
  nongranulomatous 364.00
  posterior 363.20
    disseminated — *see* Chorioretinitis, disseminated
    focal — *see* Chorioretinitis, focal
  recurrent 364.02
  sympathetic 360.11
  syphilitic (secondary) 091.50
    congenital 090.0 *[363.13]*
    late 095.8 *[363.13]*
  tuberculous (*see also* Tuberculosis) 017.3 ☑ *[364.11]*
Uveoencephalitis 363.22
Uveokeratitis — *see also* Iridocyclitis 364.3
Uveoparotid fever 135
Uveoparotitis 135
Uvula — *see* condition
Uvulitis (acute) (catarrhal) (chronic) (gangrenous) (membranous) (suppurative) (ulcerative) 528.3

V

Vaccination
- complication or reaction — *see* Complications, vaccination
- delayed V64.00
- not carried out V64.00
  - because of
    - acute illness V64.01
    - allergy to vaccine or component V64.04
    - caregiver refusal V64.05
    - chronic illness V64.02
    - guardian refusal V64.05
    - immune compromised state V64.03
    - parent refusal V64.05
    - patient had disease being vaccinated against V64.08
    - patient refusal V64.06
    - reason NEC V64.09
    - religious reasons V64.07
- prophylactic (against) V05.9
  - arthropod-borne viral
    - disease NEC V05.1
    - encephalitis V05.0
  - chickenpox V05.4
  - cholera (alone) V03.0
    - with typhoid-paratyphoid (cholera + TAB) V06.0
  - common cold V04.7
  - diphtheria (alone) V03.5
    - with
      - poliomyelitis (DTP+ polio) V06.3
      - tetanus V06.5
        - pertussis combined (DTP) (DTaP) V06.1
        - typhoid-paratyphoid (DTP + TAB) V06.2
  - disease (single) NEC V05.9
    - bacterial NEC V03.9
      - specified type NEC V03.89
    - combination NEC V06.9
      - specified type NEC V06.8
    - specified type NEC V05.8
  - encephalitis, viral, arthropod-borne V05.0
  - Hemophilus influenzae, type B [Hib] V03.81
  - hepatitis, viral V05.3
  - influenza V04.81
    - with
      - Streptococcus pneumoniae [pneumococcus] V06.6
  - leishmaniasis V05.2
  - measles (alone) V04.2
    - with mumps-rubella (MMR) V06.4
  - mumps (alone) V04.6
    - with measles and rubella (MMR) V06.4
  - pertussis alone V03.6
  - plague V03.3
  - poliomyelitis V04.0
    - with diphtheria-tetanus-pertussis (DTP + polio) V06.3
  - rabies V04.5
  - respiratory syncytial virus (RSV) V04.82
  - rubella (alone) V04.3
    - with measles and mumps (MMR) V06.4
  - smallpox V04.1
  - Streptococcus pneumoniae [pneumococcus] V03.82
    - with
      - influenza V06.6
  - tetanus toxoid (alone) V03.7
    - with diphtheria [Td] [DT] V06.5
      - with
        - pertussis (DTP) (DTaP) V06.1
          - with poliomyelitis (DTP+polio) V06.3
  - tuberculosis (BCG) V03.2
  - tularemia V03.4
  - typhoid-paratyphoid (TAB) (alone) V03.1
    - with diphtheria-tetanus-pertussis (TAB + DTP) V06.2
  - varicella V05.4

Vaccination — *continued*
- prophylactic — *continued*
  - viral
    - disease NEC V04.89
    - encephalitis, arthropod-borne V05.0
    - hepatitis V05.3
    - yellow fever V04.4

Vaccinia (generalized) 999.0
- without vaccination 051.02
- congenital 771.2
- conjunctiva 999.39
- eyelids 999.0 [373.5]
- localized 999.39
- nose 999.39
- not from vaccination 051.02
  - eyelid 051.02 [373.5]
- sine vaccinatione 051.02

Vacuum
- extraction of fetus or newborn 763.3
- in sinus (accessory) (nasal) (*see also* Sinusitis) 473.9

Vagabond V60.0
Vagabondage V60.0
Vagabonds' disease 132.1
Vaginalitis (tunica) 608.4
Vagina, vaginal — *see also* condition
- high risk human papillomavirus (HPV) DNA test positive 795.15
- low risk human papillomavirus (HPV) DNA test positive 795.19

Vaginismus (reflex) 625.1
- functional 306.51
- hysterical 300.11
- psychogenic 306.51

Vaginitis (acute) (chronic) (circumscribed) (diffuse) (emphysematous) (Hemophilus vaginalis) (nonspecific) (nonvenereal) (ulcerative) 616.10
- with
  - abortion — *see* Abortion, by type, with sepsis
  - ectopic pregnancy (*see also* categories 633.0–633.9) 639.0
  - molar pregnancy (*see also* categories 630–632) 639.0
- adhesive, congenital 752.49
- atrophic, postmenopausal 627.3
- bacterial 616.10
- blennorrhagic (acute) 098.0
  - chronic or duration of 2 months or over 098.2
- candidal 112.1
- chlamydial 099.53
- complicating pregnancy or puerperium 646.6 ☑
  - affecting fetus or newborn 760.8
- congenital (adhesive) 752.49
- due to
  - C. albicans 112.1
  - Trichomonas (vaginalis) 131.01
- following
  - abortion 639.0
  - ectopic or molar pregnancy 639.0
- gonococcal (acute) 098.0
  - chronic or duration of 2 months or over 098.2
- granuloma 099.2
- Monilia 112.1
- mycotic 112.1
- pinworm 127.4 [616.11]
- postirradiation 616.10
- postmenopausal atrophic 627.3
- senile (atrophic) 627.3
- syphilitic (early) 091.0
  - late 095.8
- trichomonal 131.01
- tuberculous (*see also* Tuberculosis) 016.7 ☑
- venereal NEC 099.8

Vaginosis — *see* Vaginitis
Vagotonia 352.3
Vagrancy V60.0
VAIN I (vaginal intraepithelial neoplasia I) 623.0
VAIN II (vaginal intraepithelial neoplasia II) 623.0
VAIN III (vaginal intraepithelial neoplasia III) 233.31

Vallecula — *see* condition
Valley fever 114.0
Valsuani's disease (progressive pernicious anemia, puerperal) 648.2 ☑
Valve, valvular (formation) — *see also* condition
- cerebral ventricle (communicating) in situ V45.2
- cervix, internal os 752.49
- colon 751.5
- congenital NEC — *see* Atresia
- formation, congenital NEC — *see* Atresia
- heart defect — *see* Anomaly, heart, valve
- ureter 753.29
  - pelvic junction 753.21
  - vesical orifice 753.22
- urethra 753.6

Valvulitis (chronic) — *see also* Endocarditis 424.90
- rheumatic (chronic) (inactive) (with chorea) 397.9
  - active or acute (aortic) (mitral) (pulmonary) (tricuspid) 391.1
- syphilitic NEC 093.20
  - aortic 093.22
  - mitral 093.21
  - pulmonary 093.24
  - tricuspid 093.23

Valvulopathy — *see* Endocarditis
van Bogaert-Nijssen (-Peiffer) disease 330.0
van Bogaert's leukoencephalitis (sclerosing) (subacute) 046.2
van Buchem's syndrome (hyperostosis corticalis) 733.3
Vancomycin (glycopeptide)
- intermediate staphylococcus aureus (VISA/GISA) V09.8 ☑
- resistant
  - enterococcus (VRE) V09.8 ☑
  - staphylococcus aureus (VRSA/GRSA) V09.8 ☑
van Creveld-von Gierke disease (glycogenosis I) 271.0
van den Bergh's disease (enterogenous cyanosis) 289.7
van der Hoeve-Halbertsma-Waardenburg syndrome (ptosis-epicanthus) 270.2
van der Hoeve-Waardenburg-Gualdi syndrome (ptosis epicanthus) 270.2
van der Hoeve's syndrome (brittle bones and blue sclera, deafness) 756.51
Vanillism 692.89
Vanishing lung 492.0
Vanishing twin 651.33
van Neck (-Odelberg) disease or syndrome (juvenile osteochondrosis) 732.1
Vapor asphyxia or suffocation NEC 987.9
- specified agent — *see* Table of Drugs and Chemicals
Vaquez's disease (M9950/1) 238.4
Vaquez-Osler disease (polycythemia vera) (M9950/1) 238.4
Variance, lethal ball, prosthetic heart valve 996.02
Variants, thalassemic 282.49
Variations in hair color 704.3
Varicella 052.9
- with
  - complication 052.8
    - specified NEC 052.7
  - pneumonia 052.1
  - vaccination and inoculation (prophylactic) V05.4
- exposure to V01.71
- vaccination and inoculation (against) (prophylactic) V05.4
Varices — *see* Varix
Varicocele (scrotum) (thrombosed) 456.4
- ovary 456.5
- perineum 456.6
- spermatic cord (ulcerated) 456.4
Varicose
- aneurysm (ruptured) (*see also* Aneurysm) 442.9
- dermatitis (lower extremity) — *see* Varicose, vein, inflamed or infected

Varicose — *continued*
- eczema — *see* Varicose, vein
- phlebitis — *see* Varicose, vein, inflamed or infected
- placental vessel — *see* Placenta, abnormal
- tumor — *see* Varicose, vein
- ulcer (lower extremity, any part) 454.0
  - anus 455.8
    - external 455.5
    - internal 455.2
  - esophagus (*see also* Varix, esophagus) 456.1
    - bleeding (*see also* Varix, esophagus, bleeding) 456.0
  - inflamed or infected 454.2
  - nasal septum 456.8
  - perineum 456.6
  - rectum — *see* Varicose, ulcer, anus
  - scrotum 456.4
  - specified site NEC 456.8
  - vein (lower extremity) (ruptured) (*see also* Varix) 454.9
    - with
      - complications NEC 454.8
      - edema 454.8
      - inflammation or infection 454.1
        - ulcerated 454.2
      - pain 454.8
      - stasis dermatitis 454.1
        - with ulcer 454.2
      - swelling 454.8
      - ulcer 454.0
        - inflamed or infected 454.2
    - anus — *see* Hemorrhoids
    - broad ligament 456.5
    - congenital (peripheral) 747.60
      - gastrointestinal 747.61
      - lower limb 747.64
      - renal 747.62
      - specified NEC 747.69
      - upper limb 747.63
    - esophagus (ulcerated) (*see also* Varix, esophagus) 456.1
      - bleeding (*see also* Varix, esophagus, bleeding) 456.0
    - inflamed or infected 454.1
      - with ulcer 454.2
    - in pregnancy or puerperium 671.0 ☑
      - vulva or perineum 671.1 ☑
    - nasal septum (with ulcer) 456.8
    - pelvis 456.5
    - perineum 456.6
      - in pregnancy, childbirth, or puerperium 671.1 ☑
    - rectum — *see* Hemorrhoids
    - scrotum (ulcerated) 456.4
    - specified site NEC 456.8
    - sublingual 456.3
    - ulcerated 454.0
      - inflamed or infected 454.2
    - umbilical cord, affecting fetus or newborn 762.6
    - urethra 456.8
    - vulva 456.6
      - in pregnancy, childbirth, or puerperium 671.1 ☑
    - vessel (*see also* Varix)
      - placenta — *see* Placenta, abnormal
Varicosis, varicosities, varicosity — *see also* Varix 454.9
Variola 050.9
- hemorrhagic (pustular) 050.0
- major 050.0
- minor 050.1
- modified 050.2
Varioloid 050.2
Variolosa, purpura 050.0
Varix (lower extremity) (ruptured) 454.9
- with
  - complications NEC 454.8
  - edema 454.8
  - inflammation or infection 454.1
    - with ulcer 454.2
  - pain 454.8
  - stasis dermatitis 454.1
    - with ulcer 454.2

Varix — continued
with — continued
swelling 454.8
ulcer 454.0
with inflammation or infection 454.2
aneurysmal (see also Aneurysm) 442.9
anus — see Hemorrhoids
arteriovenous (congenital) (peripheral) NEC
747.60
gastrointestinal 747.61
lower limb 747.64
renal 747.62
specified NEC 747.69
spinal 747.82
upper limb 747.63
bladder 456.5
broad ligament 456.5
congenital (peripheral) 747.60
esophagus (ulcerated) 456.1
bleeding 456.0
in
cirrhosis of liver 571.5 [456.20]
portal hypertension
572.3 [456.20]
congenital 747.69
in
cirrhosis of liver 571.5 [456.21]
with bleeding 571.5 [456.20]
portal hypertension
572.3 [456.21]
with bleeding 572.3 [456.20]
gastric 456.8
inflamed or infected 454.1
ulcerated 454.2
in pregnancy or puerperium 671.0 ☑
perineum 671.1 ☑
vulva 671.1 ☑
labia (majora) 456.6
orbit 456.8
congenital 747.69
ovary 456.5
papillary 448.1
pelvis 456.5
perineum 456.6
in pregnancy or puerperium 671.1 ☑
pharynx 456.8
placenta — see Placenta, abnormal
prostate 456.8
rectum — see Hemorrhoids
renal papilla 456.8
retina 362.17
scrotum (ulcerated) 456.4
sigmoid colon 456.8
specified site NEC 456.8
spinal (cord) (vessels) 456.8
spleen, splenic (vein) (with phlebolith) 456.8
sublingual 456.3
ulcerated 454.0
inflamed or infected 454.2
umbilical cord, affecting fetus or newborn
762.6
uterine ligament 456.5
vocal cord 456.8
vulva 456.6
in pregnancy, childbirth, or puerperium
671.1 ☑
Vasa previa 663.5 ☑
affecting fetus or newborn 762.6
hemorrhage from, affecting fetus or newborn 772.0
Vascular — see also condition
loop on papilla (optic) 743.57
sheathing, retina 362.13
spasm 443.9
spider 448.1
Vascularity, pulmonary, congenital 747.39
Vascularization
choroid 362.16
cornea 370.60
deep 370.63
localized 370.61
retina 362.16
subretinal 362.16
Vasculitis 447.6
allergic 287.0
cryoglobulinemic 273.2

Vasculitis — continued
disseminated 447.6
kidney 447.8
leukocytoclastic 446.29
nodular 695.2
retinal 362.18
rheumatic — see Fever, rheumatic
Vasculopathy
cardiac allograft 996.83
Vas deferens — see condition
Vas deferentitis 608.4
Vasectomy, admission for V25.2
Vasitis 608.4
nodosa 608.4
scrotum 608.4
spermatic cord 608.4
testis 608.4
tuberculous (see also Tuberculosis) 016.5 ☑
tunica vaginalis 608.4
vas deferens 608.4
Vasodilation 443.9
Vasomotor — see condition
Vasoplasty, after previous sterilization V26.0
Vasoplegia, splanchnic — see also Neuropathy, peripheral, autonomic 337.9
Vasospasm 443.9
cerebral (artery) 435.9
with transient neurologic deficit 435.9
coronary 413.1
nerve
arm NEC 354.9
autonomic 337.9
brachial plexus 353.0
cervical plexus 353.2
leg NEC 355.8
lower extremity NEC 355.8
peripheral NEC 355.9
spinal NEC 355.9
sympathetic 337.9
upper extremity NEC 354.9
peripheral NEC 443.9
retina (artery) (see also Occlusion, retinal,
artery) 362.30
Vasospastic — see condition
Vasovagal attack (paroxysmal) 780.2
psychogenic 306.2
Vater's ampulla — see condition
VATER syndrome 759.89
vCJD (variant Creutzfeldt-Jakob disease) 046.11
Vegetation, vegetative
adenoid (nasal fossa) 474.2
consciousness (persistent) 780.03
endocarditis (acute) (any valve) (chronic)
(subacute) 421.0
heart (mycotic) (valve) 421.0
state (persistent) 780.03
Veil
Jackson's 751.4
over face (causing asphyxia) 768.9
Vein, venous — see condition
Veldt sore — see also Ulcer, skin 707.9
Velo-cardio-facial syndrome 758.32
Velpeau's hernia — see Hernia, femoral
Venereal
balanitis NEC 099.8
bubo 099.1
disease 099.9
specified nature or type NEC 099.8
granuloma inguinale 099.2
lymphogranuloma (Durand-Nicolas-Favre),
any site 099.1
salpingitis 098.37
urethritis (see also Urethritis, nongonococcal) 099.40
vaginitis NEC 099.8
warts 078.11
Vengefulness, in child — see also Disturbance,
conduct 312.0 ☑
Venofibrosis 459.89
Venom, venomous
bite or sting (animal or insect) 989.5
poisoning 989.5
Venous — see condition
Ventouse delivery NEC 669.5 ☑
affecting fetus or newborn 763.3
Ventral — see condition

Ventricle, ventricular — see also condition
escape 427.69
standstill (see also Arrest, cardiac) 427.5
Ventriculitis, cerebral — see also Meningitis
322.9
Ventriculostomy status V45.2
Verbiest's syndrome (claudicatio intermittens
spinalis) 435.1
Vernet's syndrome 352.6
Verneuil's disease (syphilitic bursitis) 095.7
Verruca (filiformis) 078.10
acuminata (any site) 078.11
necrogenica (primary) (see also Tuberculosis)
017.0 ☑
peruana 088.0
peruviana 088.0
plana (juvenilis) 078.19
plantaris 078.12
seborrheica 702.19
inflamed 702.11
senilis 702.0
tuberculosa (primary) (see also Tuberculosis)
017.0 ☑
venereal 078.11
viral 078.10
specified NEC 078.19
vulgaris 078.10
Verrucosities — see also Verruca 078.10
Verrucous endocarditis (acute) (any valve)
(chronic) (subacute) 710.0 [424.91]
nonbacterial 710.0 [424.91]
Verruga
peruana 088.0
peruviana 088.0
Verse's disease (calcinosis intervertebralis)
275.49 [722.90]
Version
before labor, affecting fetus or newborn
761.7
cephalic (correcting previous malposition)
652.1 ☑
affecting fetus or newborn 763.1
cervix — see Version, uterus
uterus (postinfectional) (postpartal, old) (see
also Malposition, uterus) 621.6
forward — see Anteversion, uterus
lateral — see Lateroversion, uterus
Vertebra, vertebral — see condition
Vertigo 780.4
auditory 386.19
aural 386.19
benign paroxysmal positional 386.11
central origin 386.2
cerebral 386.2
Dix and Hallpike (epidemic) 386.12
endemic paralytic 078.81
epidemic 078.81
Dix and Hallpike 386.12
Gerlier's 078.81
Pedersen's 386.12
vestibular neuronitis 386.12
epileptic — see Epilepsy
Gerlier's (epidemic) 078.81
hysterical 300.11
labyrinthine 386.10
laryngeal 786.2
malignant positional 386.2
Ménière's (see also Disease, Ménière's)
386.00
menopausal 627.2
otogenic 386.19
paralytic 078.81
paroxysmal positional, benign 386.11
Pedersen's (epidemic) 386.12
peripheral 386.10
specified type NEC 386.19
positional
benign paroxysmal 386.11
malignant 386.2
Verumontanitis (chronic) — see also Urethritis
597.89
Vesania — see also Psychosis 298.9
Vesical — see condition
Vesicle
cutaneous 709.8
seminal — see condition

Vesicle — continued
skin 709.8
Vesicocolic — see condition
Vesicoperineal — see condition
Vesicorectal — see condition
Vesicourethrorectal — see condition
Vesicovaginal — see condition
Vesicular — see condition
Vesiculitis (seminal) 608.0
amebic 006.8
gonorrheal (acute) 098.14
chronic or duration of 2 months or over
098.34
trichomonal 131.09
tuberculous (see also Tuberculosis)
016.5 ☑ [608.81]
Vestibulitis (ear) — see also Labyrinthitis
386.30
nose (external) 478.19
vulvar 625.71
Vestibulopathy, acute peripheral (recurrent)
386.12
Vestige, vestigial — see also Persistence
branchial 744.41
structures in vitreous 743.51
Vibriosis NEC 027.9
Vidal's disease (lichen simplex chronicus)
698.3
Video display tube syndrome 723.8
Vienna-type encephalitis 049.8
Villaret's syndrome 352.6
Villous — see condition
VIN I (vulvar intraepithelial neoplasia I) 624.01
VIN II (vulvar intraepithelial neoplasia II) 624.02
VIN III (vulvar intraepithelial neoplasia III)
233.32
Vincent's
angina 101
bronchitis 101
disease 101
gingivitis 101
infection (any site) 101
laryngitis 101
stomatitis 101
tonsillitis 101
Vinson-Plummer syndrome (sideropenic
dysphagia) 280.8
Viosterol deficiency — see also Deficiency,
calciferol 268.9
Virchow's disease 733.99
Viremia 790.8
Virilism (adrenal) (female) NEC 255.2
with
3-beta-hydroxysteroid dehydrogenase
defect 255.2
11-hydroxylase defect 255.2
21-hydroxylase defect 255.2
adrenal
hyperplasia 255.2
insufficiency (congenital) 255.2
cortical hyperfunction 255.2
Virilization (female) (suprarenal) — see also
Virilism 255.2
isosexual 256.4
Virulent bubo 099.0
Virus, viral — see also condition
infection NEC (see also Infection, viral)
079.99
septicemia 079.99
yaba monkey tumor 059.22
VISA (vancomycin intermediate staphylococcus
aureus) V09.8 ☑
Viscera, visceral — see condition
Visceroptosis 569.89
Visible peristalsis 787.4
Vision, visual
binocular, suppression 368.31
blurred, blurring 368.8
hysterical 300.11
defect, defective (see also Impaired, vision)
369.9
disorientation (syndrome) 368.16
disturbance NEC (see also Disturbance, vision) 368.9
hysterical 300.11
examination V72.0

☑ **Additional Digit Required** — Refer to the Tabular List for Digit Selection

▽ **Subterms under main terms may continue to next column or page**

Vision, visual — *continued*
> field, limitation 368.40
> fusion, with defective steropsis 368.33
> hallucinations 368.16
> halos 368.16
> loss 369.9
>> both eyes (*see also* Blindness, both eyes) 369.3
>> complete (*see also* Blindness, both eyes) 369.00
>> one eye 369.8
>> sudden 368.16
> low (both eyes) 369.20
>> one eye (other eye normal) (*see also* Impaired, vision) 369.70
>>> blindness, other eye 369.10
> perception, simultaneous without fusion 368.32
> tunnel 368.45

Vitality, lack or want of 780.79
> newborn 779.89

Vitamin deficiency NEC — *see also* Deficiency, vitamin 269.2

Vitelline duct, persistent 751.0

Vitiligo 709.01
> due to pinta (carate) 103.2
> eyelid 374.53
> vulva 624.8

Vitium cordis — *see* Disease, heart

Vitreous — *see also* condition
> touch syndrome 997.99

VLCAD (long chain/very long chain acyl CoA dehydrogenase deficiency, LCAD) 277.85

Vocal cord — *see* condition

Vocational rehabilitation V57.22

Vogt's (Cecile) disease or syndrome 333.7 ☑

Vogt-Koyanagi syndrome 364.24

Vogt-Spielmeyer disease (amaurotic familial idiocy) 330.1

Voice
> change (*see also* Dysphonia) 784.49
> loss (*see also* Aphonia) 784.41

Volhard-Fahr disease (malignant nephrosclerosis) 403.00

Volhynian fever 083.1

Volkmann's ischemic contracture or paralysis (complicating trauma) 958.6

Voluntary starvation 307.1

Volvulus (bowel) (colon) (intestine) 560.2
> with
>> hernia (*see also* Hernia, by site, with obstruction)
>>> gangrenous — *see* Hernia, by site, with gangrene
>> perforation 560.2
> congenital 751.5
> duodenum 537.3
> fallopian tube 620.5
> oviduct 620.5
> stomach (due to absence of gastrocolic ligament) 537.89

Vomiting 787.03
> with nausea 787.01
> allergic 535.4 ☑
> asphyxia 933.1
> bilious (cause unknown) 787.04
>> following gastrointestinal surgery 564.3
>> newborn 779.32
> blood (*see also* Hematemesis) 578.0
> causing asphyxia, choking, or suffocation (*see also* Asphyxia, food) 933.1
> cyclical 536.2
>> associated with migraine 346.2 ☑
>> psychogenic 306.4
> epidemic 078.82
> fecal matter 569.87
> following gastrointestinal surgery 564.3
> functional 536.8
>> psychogenic 306.4
> habit 536.2
> hysterical 300.11
> nervous 306.4
> neurotic 306.4
> newborn 779.33
>> bilious 779.32
> of or complicating pregnancy 643.9 ☑

Vomiting — *continued*
> of or complicating pregnancy — *continued*
>> due to
>>> organic disease 643.8 ☑
>>> specific cause NEC 643.8 ☑
>> early — *see* Hyperemesis, gravidarum
>> late (after 22 completed weeks of gestation) 643.2 ☑
> pernicious or persistent 536.2
>> complicating pregnancy — *see* Hyperemesis, gravidarum
> psychogenic 306.4
> physiological 787.03
>> bilious 787.04
> psychic 306.4
> psychogenic 307.54
> stercoral 569.89
> uncontrollable 536.2
>> psychogenic 306.4
> uremic — *see* Uremia
> winter 078.82

von Bechterew (-Strumpell) disease or syndrome (ankylosing spondylitis) 720.0

von Bezold's abscess 383.01

von Economo's disease (encephalitis lethargica) 049.8

von Eulenburg's disease (congenital paramyotonia) 359.29

von Gierke's disease (glycogenosis I) 271.0

von Gies' joint 095.8

von Graefe's disease or syndrome 378.72

von Hippel (-Lindau) disease or syndrome (retinocerebral angiomatosis) 759.6

von Jaksch's anemia or disease (pseudoleukemia infantum) 285.8

von Recklinghausen-Applebaum disease (hemochromatosis) — *see also* Hemochromatosis 275.03

von Recklinghausen's
> disease or syndrome (nerves) (skin) (M9540/1) 237.71
>> bones (osteitis fibrosa cystica) 252.01
>> tumor (M9540/1) 237.71

von Schroetter's syndrome (intermittent venous claudication) 453.89

von Willebrand (-Jürgens) (-Minot) disease or syndrome (angiohemophilia) 286.4

von Zambusch's disease (lichen sclerosus et atrophicus) 701.0

Voorhoeve's disease or dyschondroplasia 756.4

Vossius' ring 921.3
> late effect 366.21

Voyeurism 302.82

VRE (vancomycin resistant enterococcus) V09.8 ☑

Vrolik's disease (osteogenesis imperfecta) 756.51

VRSA (vancomycin resistant staphylococcus aureus) V09.8 ☑

Vulva — *see* condition

Vulvismus 625.1

Vulvitis (acute) (allergic) (chronic) (gangrenous) (hypertrophic) (intertriginous) 616.10
> with
>> abortion — *see* Abortion, by type, with sepsis
>> ectopic pregnancy (*see also* categories 633.0–633.9) 639.0
>> molar pregnancy (*see also* categories 630–632) 639.0
> adhesive, congenital 752.49
> blennorrhagic (acute) 098.0
>> chronic or duration of 2 months or over 098.2
> chlamydial 099.53
> complicating pregnancy or puerperium 646.6 ☑
> due to Ducrey's bacillus 099.0
> following
>> abortion 639.0
>> ectopic or molar pregnancy 639.0
> gonococcal (acute) 098.0

Vulvitis — *continued*
> gonococcal — *continued*
>> chronic or duration of 2 months or over 098.2
> herpetic 054.11
> leukoplakic 624.09
> monilial 112.1
> puerperal, postpartum, childbirth 646.6 ☑
> syphilitic (early) 091.0
>> late 095.8
> trichomonal 131.01

Vulvodynia 625.70
> specified NEC 625.79

Vulvorectal — *see* condition

Vulvovaginitis — *see also* Vulvitis 616.10
> amebic 006.8
> chlamydial 099.53
> gonococcal (acute) 098.0
>> chronic or duration of 2 months or over 098.2
> herpetic 054.11
> monilial 112.1
> trichomonal (Trichomonas vaginalis) 131.01

W

Waardenburg-Klein syndrome (ptosis-epicanthus) 270.2

Waardenburg's syndrome 756.89
> meaning ptosis-epicanthus 270.2

Wagner's disease (colloid milium) 709.3

Wagner (-Unverricht) syndrome (dermatomyositis) 710.3

Waiting list, person on V63.2
> undergoing social agency investigation V63.8

Wakefulness disorder — *see also* Hypersomnia 780.54
> nonorganic origin 307.43

Waldenström's
> disease (osteochondrosis, capital femoral) 732.1
> hepatitis (lupoid hepatitis) 571.49
> hypergammaglobulinemia 273.0
> macroglobulinemia 273.3
> purpura, hypergammaglobulinemic 273.0
> syndrome (macroglobulinemia) 273.3

Waldenström-Kjellberg syndrome (sideropenic dysphagia) 280.8

Walking
> difficulty 719.7
>> psychogenic 307.9
> sleep 307.46
>> hysterical 300.13

Wall, abdominal — *see* condition

Wallenberg's syndrome (posterior inferior cerebellar artery) — *see also* Disease, cerebrovascular, acute 436

Wallgren's
> disease (obstruction of splenic vein with collateral circulation) 459.89
> meningitis (*see also* Meningitis, aseptic) 047.9

Wandering
> acetabulum 736.39
> gallbladder 751.69
> in diseases classified elsewhere V40.31
> kidney, congenital 753.3
> organ or site, congenital NEC — *see* Malposition, congenital
> pacemaker (atrial) (heart) 427.89
> spleen 289.59

Wardrop's disease (with lymphangitis) 681.9
> finger 681.02
> toe 681.11

War neurosis 300.16

Wart (digitate) (filiform) (infectious) (viral) 078.10
> common 078.19
> external genital organs (venereal) 078.11
> fig 078.19
> flat 078.19
> genital 078.11
> Hassall-Henle's (of cornea) 371.41
> Henle's (of cornea) 371.41
> juvenile 078.19
> moist 078.10

Wart — *continued*
> Peruvian 088.0
> plantar 078.12
> prosector (*see also* Tuberculosis) 017.0 ☑
> seborrheic 702.19
>> inflamed 702.11
> senile 702.0
> specified NEC 078.19
> syphilitic 091.3
> tuberculous (*see also* Tuberculosis) 017.0 ☑
> venereal (female) (male) 078.11

Warthin's tumor (salivary gland) (M8561/0) 210.2

Washerwoman's itch 692.4

Wassilieff's disease (leptospiral jaundice) 100.0

Wasting
> disease 799.4
>> due to malnutrition 261
> extreme (due to malnutrition) 261
> muscular NEC 728.2
> palsy, paralysis 335.21
> pelvic muscle 618.83

Water
> clefts 366.12
> deprivation of 994.3
> in joint (*see also* Effusion, joint) 719.0 ☑
> intoxication 276.69
> itch 120.3
> lack of 994.3
> loading 276.69
> on
>> brain — *see* Hydrocephalus
>> chest 511.89
> poisoning 276.69

Waterbrash 787.1

Water-hammer pulse — *see also* Insufficiency, aortic 424.1

Waterhouse (-Friderichsen) disease or syndrome 036.3

Water-losing nephritis 588.89

Watermelon stomach 537.82
> with hemorrhage 537.83
> without hemorrhage 537.82

Wax in ear 380.4

Waxy
> degeneration, any site 277.39
> disease 277.39
> kidney 277.39 [583.81]
> liver (large) 277.39
> spleen 277.39

Weak, weakness (generalized) 780.79
> arches (acquired) 734
>> congenital 754.61
> bladder sphincter 596.59
> congenital 779.89
> eye muscle — *see* Strabismus
> facial 781.94
> foot (double) — *see* Weak, arches
> heart, cardiac (*see also* Failure, heart) 428.9
>> congenital 746.9
> mind 317
> muscle (generalized) 728.87
> myocardium (*see also* Failure, heart) 428.9
> newborn 779.89
> pelvic fundus
>> pubocervical tissue 618.81
>> rectovaginal tissue 618.82
> pulse 785.9
> senile 797
> urinary stream 788.62
> valvular — *see* Endocarditis

Wear, worn, tooth, teeth (approximal) (hard tissues) (interproximal) (occlusal) — *see also* Attrition, teeth 521.10

Weather, weathered
> effects of
>> cold NEC 991.9
>>> specified effect NEC 991.8
>> hot (*see also* Heat) 992.9
> skin 692.74

Weber-Christian disease or syndrome (nodular nonsuppurative panniculitis) 729.30

Weber-Cockayne syndrome (epidermolysis bullosa) 757.39

Weber-Dimitri syndrome 759.6
Weber-Gubler syndrome 344.89
Weber-Leyden syndrome 344.89
Weber-Osler syndrome (familial hemorrhagic telangiectasia) 448.0
Weber's paralysis or syndrome 344.89
Web, webbed (congenital) — see also Anomaly, specified type NEC
  canthus 743.63
  digits (see also Syndactylism) 755.10
  duodenal 751.5
  esophagus 750.3
  fingers (see also Syndactylism, fingers) 755.11
  larynx (glottic) (subglottic) 748.2
  neck (pterygium colli) 744.5
  Paterson-Kelly (sideropenic dysphagia) 280.8
  popliteal syndrome 756.89
  toes (see also Syndactylism, toes) 755.13
Wedge-shaped or wedging vertebra — see also Osteoporosis 733.00
Wegener's granulomatosis or syndrome 446.4
Wegner's disease (syphilitic osteochondritis) 090.0
Weight
  gain (abnormal) (excessive) 783.1
    during pregnancy 646.1 ☑
      insufficient 646.8 ☑
  less than 1000 grams at birth 765.0 ☑
  loss (cause unknown) 783.21
Weightlessness 994.9
Weil's disease (leptospiral jaundice) 100.0
Weill-Marchesani syndrome (brachymorphism and ectopia lentis) 759.89
Weingarten's syndrome (tropical eosinophilia) 518.3
Weir Mitchell's disease (erythromelalgia) 443.82
Weiss-Baker syndrome (carotid sinus syncope) 337.01
Weissenbach-Thibierge syndrome (cutaneous systemic sclerosis) 710.1
Wen — see also Cyst, sebaceous 706.2
Wenckebach's phenomenon, heart block (second degree) 426.13
Werdnig-Hoffmann syndrome (muscular atrophy) 335.0
Werlhof-Wichmann syndrome — see also Purpura, thrombocytopenic 287.39
Werlhof's disease — see also Purpura, thrombocytopenic 287.39
Wermer's syndrome or disease (polyendocrine adenomatosis) 258.01
Werner's disease or syndrome (progeria adultorum) 259.8
Werner-His disease (trench fever) 083.1
Werner-Schultz disease (agranulocytosis) 288.09
Wernicke's encephalopathy, disease, or syndrome (superior hemorrhagic polioencephalitis) 265.1
Wernicke-Korsakoff syndrome or psychosis (nonalcoholic) 294.0
  alcoholic 291.1
Wernicke-Posadas disease — see also Coccidioidomycosis 114.9
Wesselsbron fever 066.3
West African fever 084.8
West Nile
  encephalitis 066.41
  encephalomyelitis 066.41
  fever 066.40
    with
      cranial nerve disorders 066.42
      encephalitis 066.41
      optic neuritis 066.42
      other complications 066.49
      other neurologic manifestations 066.42
      polyradiculitis 066.42
  virus 066.40
Westphal-Strümpell syndrome (hepatolenticular degeneration) 275.1

Wet
  brain (alcoholic) (see also Alcoholism) 303.9 ☑
  feet, tropical (syndrome) (maceration) 991.4
  lung (syndrome)
    adult 518.52
    newborn 770.6
Wharton's duct — see condition
Wheal 709.8
Wheelchair confinement status V46.3
Wheezing 786.07
Whiplash injury or syndrome 847.0
Whipple's disease or syndrome (intestinal lipodystrophy) 040.2
Whipworm 127.3
"Whistling face" syndrome (craniocarpotarsal dystrophy) 759.89
White — see also condition
  kidney
    large — see Nephrosis
    small 582.9
  leg, puerperal, postpartum, childbirth 671.4 ☑
    nonpuerperal 451.19
  mouth 112.0
  patches of mouth 528.6
  sponge nevus of oral mucosa 750.26
  spot lesions, teeth 521.01
White's disease (congenital) (keratosis follicularis) 757.39
Whitehead 706.2
Whitlow (with lymphangitis) 681.01
  herpetic 054.6
Whitmore's disease or fever (melioidosis) 025
Whooping cough 033.9
  with pneumonia 033.9 [484.3]
  due to
    Bordetella
      bronchoseptica 033.8
        with pneumonia 033.8 [484.3]
      parapertussis 033.1
        with pneumonia 033.1 [484.3]
      pertussis 033.0
        with pneumonia 033.0 [484.3]
    specified organism NEC 033.8
      with pneumonia 033.8 [484.3]
  vaccination, prophylactic (against) V03.6
Wichmann's asthma (laryngismus stridulus) 478.75
Widal (-Abrami) syndrome (acquired hemolytic jaundice) 283.9
Widening aorta — see also Ectasia, aortic 447.70
  with aneurysm 441.9
  ruptured 441.5
Wilkie's disease or syndrome 557.1
Wilkinson-Sneddon disease or syndrome (subcorneal pustular dermatosis) 694.1
Willan's lepra 696.1
Willan-Plumbe syndrome (psoriasis) 696.1
Willebrand (-Jürgens) syndrome or thrombopathy (angiohemophilia) 286.4
Willi-Prader syndrome (hypogenital dystrophy with diabetic tendency) 759.81
Willis' disease (diabetes mellitus) — see also Diabetes 250.0 ☑
  due to secondary diabetes 249.0 ☑
Wilms' tumor or neoplasm (nephroblastoma) (M8960/3) 189.0
Wilson's
  disease or syndrome (hepatolenticular degeneration) 275.1
  hepatolenticular degeneration 275.1
  lichen ruber 697.0
Wilson-Brocq disease (dermatitis exfoliativa) 695.89
Wilson-Mikity syndrome 770.7
Window — see also Imperfect, closure aorticopulmonary 745.0
Winged scapula 736.89
Winter — see also condition
  vomiting disease 078.82
Wise's disease 696.2
Wiskott-Aldrich syndrome (eczema-thrombocytopenia) 279.12

Withdrawal symptoms, syndrome
  alcohol 291.81
    delirium (acute) 291.0
      chronic 291.1
      newborn 760.71
  drug or narcotic 292.0
  newborn, infant of dependent mother 779.5
  steroid NEC
    correct substance properly administered 255.41
    overdose or wrong substance given or taken 962.0
Withdrawing reaction, child or adolescent 313.22
Witts' anemia (achlorhydric anemia) 280.9
Witzelsucht 301.9
Woakes' syndrome (ethmoiditis) 471.1
Wohlfart-Kugelberg-Welander disease 335.11
Woillez's disease (acute idiopathic pulmonary congestion) 518.52
Wolff-Parkinson-White syndrome (anomalous atrioventricular excitation) 426.7
Wolhynian fever 083.1
Wolman's disease (primary familial xanthomatosis) 272.7
Wood asthma 495.8
Woolly, wooly hair (congenital) (nevus) 757.4
Wool-sorters' disease 022.1
Word
  blindness (congenital) (developmental) 315.01
    secondary to organic lesion 784.61
  deafness (secondary to organic lesion) 784.69
    developmental 315.31
Worm(s) (colic) (fever) (infection) (infestation) — see also Infestation 128.9
  guinea 125.7
  in intestine NEC 127.9
Worm-eaten soles 102.3
Worn out — see also Exhaustion 780.79
  artificial heart valve 996.02
  cardiac defibrillator (with synchronous cardiac pacemaker) V53.32
  cardiac pacemaker lead or battery V53.31
  joint prosthesis (see also Complications, mechanical, device NEC, prosthetic NEC, joint) 996.46
"Worried well" V65.5
Wound, open (by cutting or piercing instrument) (by firearms) (cut) (dissection) (incised) (laceration) (penetration) (perforating) (puncture) (with initial hemorrhage, not internal) 879.8

> Note — For fracture with open wound, see Fracture.
>
> For laceration, traumatic rupture, tear or penetrating wound of internal organs, such as heart, lung, liver, kidney, pelvic organs, etc., whether or not accompanied by open wound or fracture in the same region, see Injury, internal.
>
> For contused wound, see Contusion. For crush injury, see Crush. For abrasion, insect bite (nonvenomous), blister, or scratch, see Injury, superficial.
>
> Complicated includes wounds with:
>
>   delayed healing
>
>   delayed treatment
>
>   foreign body
>
>   primary infection
>
> For late effect of open wound, see Late, effect, wound, open, by site.

  abdomen, abdominal (external) (muscle) 879.2
    complicated 879.3
    wall (anterior) 879.2
      complicated 879.3
      lateral 879.4
        complicated 879.5
  alveolar (process) 873.62

Wound, open — continued
  alveolar — continued
    complicated 873.72
  ankle 891.0
    with tendon involvement 891.2
    complicated 891.1
  anterior chamber, eye (see also Wound, open, intraocular) 871.9
  anus 863.89
  arm 884.0
    with tendon involvement 884.2
    complicated 884.1
    forearm 881.00
      with tendon involvement 881.20
      complicated 881.10
    multiple sites — see Wound, open, multiple sites, upper limb
    upper 880.03
      with tendon involvement 880.23
      complicated 880.13
      multiple sites (with axillary or shoulder regions) 880.09
        with tendon involvement 880.29
        complicated 880.19
  artery — see Injury, blood vessel, by site
  auditory
    canal (external) (meatus) 872.02
      complicated 872.12
    ossicles (incus) (malleus) (stapes) 872.62
      complicated 872.72
  auricle, ear 872.01
    complicated 872.11
  axilla 880.02
    with tendon involvement 880.22
    complicated 880.12
      with tendon involvement 880.29
    involving other sites of upper arm 880.09
      complicated 880.19
  back 876.0
    complicated 876.1
  bladder — see Injury, internal, bladder
  blood vessel — see Injury, blood vessel, by site
  brain — see Injury, intracranial, with open intracranial wound
  breast 879.0
    complicated 879.1
  brow 873.42
    complicated 873.52
  buccal mucosa 873.61
    complicated 873.71
  buttock 877.0
    complicated 877.1
  calf 891.0
    with tendon involvement 891.2
    complicated 891.1
  canaliculus lacrimalis 870.8
    with laceration of eyelid 870.2
  canthus, eye 870.8
    laceration — see also Laceration, eyelid
  cavernous sinus — see Injury, intracranial
  cerebellum — see Injury, intracranial
  cervical esophagus 874.4
    complicated 874.5
  cervix — see Injury, internal, cervix
  cheek(s) (external) 873.41
    complicated 873.51
    internal 873.61
      complicated 873.71
  chest (wall) (external) 875.0
    complicated 875.1
  chin 873.44
    complicated 873.54
  choroid 363.63
  ciliary body (eye) (see also Wound, open, intraocular) 871.9
  clitoris 878.8
    complicated 878.9
  cochlea 872.64
    complicated 872.74
  complicated 879.9
  conjunctiva — see Wound, open, intraocular
  cornea (nonpenetrating) (see also Wound, open, intraocular) 871.9
  costal region 875.0
    complicated 875.1

Wound, open — *continued*
- Descemet's membrane (*see also* Wound, open, intraocular) 871.9
- digit(s)
  - foot 893.0
    - with tendon involvement 893.2
    - complicated 893.1
  - hand 883.0
    - with tendon involvement 883.2
    - complicated 883.1
- drumhead, ear 872.61
  - complicated 872.71
- ear 872.8
  - canal 872.02
    - complicated 872.12
  - complicated 872.9
  - drum 872.61
    - complicated 872.71
  - external 872.00
    - complicated 872.10
  - multiple sites 872.69
    - complicated 872.79
  - ossicles (incus) (malleus) (stapes) 872.62
    - complicated 872.72
  - specified part NEC 872.69
    - complicated 872.79
- elbow 881.01
  - with tendon involvement 881.21
  - complicated 881.11
- epididymis 878.2
  - complicated 878.3
- epigastric region 879.2
  - complicated 879.3
- epiglottis 874.01
  - complicated 874.11
- esophagus (cervical) 874.4
  - complicated 874.5
  - thoracic — *see* Injury, internal, esophagus
- Eustachian tube 872.63
  - complicated 872.73
- extremity
  - lower (multiple) NEC 894.0
    - with tendon involvement 894.2
    - complicated 894.1
  - upper (multiple) NEC 884.0
    - with tendon involvement 884.2
    - complicated 884.1
- eye(s) (globe) — *see* Wound, open, intraocular
- eyeball NEC 871.9
  - laceration (*see also* Laceration, eyeball) 871.4
  - penetrating (*see also* Penetrating wound, eyeball) 871.7
- eyebrow 873.42
  - complicated 873.52
- eyelid NEC 870.8
  - laceration — *see* Laceration, eyelid
- face 873.40
  - complicated 873.50
  - multiple sites 873.49
    - complicated 873.59
  - specified part NEC 873.49
    - complicated 873.59
- fallopian tube — *see* Injury, internal, fallopian tube
- finger(s) (nail) (subungual) 883.0
  - with tendon involvement 883.2
  - complicated 883.1
- flank 879.4
  - complicated 879.5
- foot (any part except toe(s) alone) 892.0
  - with tendon involvement 892.2
  - complicated 892.1
- forearm 881.00
  - with tendon involvement 881.20
  - complicated 881.10
- forehead 873.42
  - complicated 873.52
- genital organs (external) NEC 878.8
  - complicated 878.9
  - internal — *see* Injury, internal, by site
- globe (eye) (*see also* Wound, open, eyeball) 871.9
- groin 879.4

Wound, open — *continued*
- groin — *continued*
  - complicated 879.5
- gum(s) 873.62
  - complicated 873.72
- hand (except finger(s) alone) 882.0
  - with tendon involvement 882.2
  - complicated 882.1
- head NEC 873.8
  - with intracranial injury — *see* Injury, intracranial
    - due to or associated with skull fracture — *see* Fracture, skull
  - complicated 873.9
  - scalp — *see* Wound, open, scalp
- heel 892.0
  - with tendon involvement 892.2
  - complicated 892.1
- high-velocity (grease gun) — *see* Wound, open, complicated, by site
- hip 890.0
  - with tendon involvement 890.2
  - complicated 890.1
- hymen 878.6
  - complicated 878.7
- hypochondrium 879.4
  - complicated 879.5
- hypogastric region 879.2
  - complicated 879.3
- iliac (region) 879.4
  - complicated 879.5
- incidental to
  - dislocation — *see* Dislocation, open, by site
  - fracture — *see* Fracture, open, by site
  - intracranial injury — *see* Injury, intracranial, with open intracranial wound
  - nerve injury — *see* Injury, nerve, by site
- inguinal region 879.4
  - complicated 879.5
- instep 892.0
  - with tendon involvement 892.2
  - complicated 892.1
- interscapular region 876.0
  - complicated 876.1
- intracranial — *see* Injury, intracranial, with open intracranial wound
- intraocular 871.9
  - with
    - partial loss (of intraocular tissue) 871.2
    - prolapse or exposure (of intraocular tissue) 871.1
    - without prolapse (of intraocular tissue) 871.0
  - laceration (*see also* Laceration, eyeball) 871.4
  - penetrating 871.7
    - with foreign body (nonmagnetic) 871.6
      - magnetic 871.5
- iris (*see also* Wound, open, eyeball) 871.9
- jaw (fracture not involved) 873.44
  - with fracture — *see* Fracture, jaw
  - complicated 873.54
- knee 891.0
  - with tendon involvement 891.2
  - complicated 891.1
- labium (majus) (minus) 878.4
  - complicated 878.5
- lacrimal apparatus, gland, or sac 870.8
  - with laceration of eyelid 870.2
- larynx 874.01
  - with trachea 874.00
    - complicated 874.10
  - complicated 874.11
- leg (multiple) 891.0
  - with tendon involvement 891.2
  - complicated 891.1
  - lower 891.0
    - with tendon involvement 891.2
    - complicated 891.1
  - thigh 890.0
    - with tendon involvement 890.2
    - complicated 890.1

Wound, open — *continued*
- leg — *continued*
  - upper 890.0
    - with tendon involvement 890.2
    - complicated 890.1
- lens (eye) (alone) (*see also* Cataract, traumatic) 366.20
  - with involvement of other eye structures — *see* Wound, open, eyeball
- limb
  - lower (multiple) NEC 894.0
    - with tendon involvement 894.2
    - complicated 894.1
  - upper (multiple) NEC 884.0
    - with tendon involvement 884.2
    - complicated 884.1
- lip 873.43
  - complicated 873.53
- loin 876.0
  - complicated 876.1
- lumbar region 876.0
  - complicated 876.1
- malar region 873.41
  - complicated 873.51
- mastoid region 873.49
  - complicated 873.59
- mediastinum — *see* Injury, internal, mediastinum
- midthoracic region 875.0
  - complicated 875.1
- mouth 873.60
  - complicated 873.70
  - floor 873.64
    - complicated 873.74
  - multiple sites 873.69
    - complicated 873.79
  - specified site NEC 873.69
    - complicated 873.79
- multiple, unspecified site(s) 879.8

> Note — Multiple open wounds of sites classifiable to the same four-digit category should be classified to that category unless they are in different limbs.
>
> Multiple open wounds of sites classifiable to different four-digit categories, or to different limbs, should be coded separately.

  - complicated 879.9
  - lower limb(s) (one or both) (sites classifiable to more than one three-digit category in 890 to 893) 894.0
    - with tendon involvement 894.2
    - complicated 894.1
  - upper limb(s) (one or both) (sites classifiable to more than one three-digit category in 880 to 883) 884.0
    - with tendon involvement 884.2
    - complicated 884.1
- muscle — *see* Sprain, by site
- nail
  - finger(s) 883.0
    - complicated 883.1
  - thumb 883.0
    - complicated 883.1
  - toe(s) 893.0
    - complicated 893.1
- nape (neck) 874.8
  - complicated 874.9
  - specified part NEC 874.8
    - complicated 874.9
- nasal (*see also* Wound, open, nose)
  - cavity 873.22
    - complicated 873.32
  - septum 873.21
    - complicated 873.31
  - sinuses 873.23
    - complicated 873.33
- nasopharynx 873.22
  - complicated 873.32
- neck 874.8
  - complicated 874.9
  - nape 874.8
    - complicated 874.9
  - specified part NEC 874.8

Wound, open — *continued*
- neck — *continued*
  - specified part — *continued*
    - complicated 874.9
  - nerve — *see* Injury, nerve, by site
- non-healing surgical 998.83
- nose 873.20
  - complicated 873.30
  - multiple sites 873.29
    - complicated 873.39
  - septum 873.21
    - complicated 873.31
  - sinuses 873.23
    - complicated 873.33
- occipital region — *see* Wound, open, scalp
- ocular NEC 871.9
  - adnexa 870.9
    - specified region NEC 870.8
  - laceration (*see also* Laceration, ocular) 871.4
  - muscle (extraocular) 870.3
    - with foreign body 870.4
    - eyelid 870.1
  - intraocular — *see* Wound, open, eyeball
  - penetrating (*see also* Penetrating wound, ocular) 871.7
- orbit 870.8
  - penetrating 870.3
    - with foreign body 870.4
- orbital region 870.9
- ovary — *see* Injury, internal, pelvic organs
- palate 873.65
  - complicated 873.75
- palm 882.0
  - with tendon involvement 882.2
  - complicated 882.1
- parathyroid (gland) 874.2
  - complicated 874.3
- parietal region — *see* Wound, open, scalp
- pelvic floor or region 879.6
  - complicated 879.7
- penis 878.0
  - complicated 878.1
- perineum 879.6
  - complicated 879.7
- periocular area 870.8
  - laceration of skin 870.0
- pharynx 874.4
  - complicated 874.5
- pinna 872.01
  - complicated 872.11
- popliteal space 891.0
  - with tendon involvement 891.2
  - complicated 891.1
- prepuce 878.0
  - complicated 878.1
- pubic region 879.2
  - complicated 879.3
- pudenda 878.8
  - complicated 878.9
- rectovaginal septum 878.8
  - complicated 878.9
- sacral region 877.0
  - complicated 877.1
- sacroiliac region 877.0
  - complicated 877.1
- salivary (ducts) (glands) 873.69
  - complicated 873.79
- scalp 873.0
  - complicated 873.1
- scalpel, fetus or newborn 767.8
- scapular region 880.01
  - with tendon involvement 880.21
  - complicated 880.11
  - involving other sites of upper arm 880.09
    - with tendon involvement 880.29
    - complicated 880.19
- sclera (*see also* Wound, open, intraocular) 871.9
- scrotum 878.2
  - complicated 878.3
- seminal vesicle — *see* Injury, internal, pelvic organs
- shin 891.0
  - with tendon involvement 891.2

☑ **Additional Digit Required** — Refer to the Tabular List for Digit Selection   ▽ᵇⁱˡ **Subterms under main terms may continue to next column or page**

2015 ICD-9-CM   ▶◀ Revised Text   ● New Line   ▲ Revised Code   **Volume 2 — 297**

Wound, open — *continued*
shin — *continued*
   complicated 891.1
  shoulder 880.00
    with tendon involvement 880.20
    complicated 880.10
    involving other sites of upper arm 880.09
      with tendon involvement 880.29
      complicated 880.19
  skin NEC 879.8
    complicated 879.9
  skull (*see also* Injury, intracranial, with open intracranial wound)
    with skull fracture — *see* Fracture, skull
  spermatic cord (scrotal) 878.2
    complicated 878.3
    pelvic region — *see* Injury, internal, spermatic cord
  spinal cord — *see* Injury, spinal
  sternal region 875.0
    complicated 875.1
  subconjunctival — *see* Wound, open, intraocular
  subcutaneous NEC 879.8
    complicated 879.9
  submaxillary region 873.44
    complicated 873.54
  submental region 873.44
    complicated 873.54
  subungual
    finger(s) (thumb) — *see* Wound, open, finger
    toe(s) — *see* Wound, open, toe
  supraclavicular region 874.8
    complicated 874.9
  supraorbital 873.42
    complicated 873.52
  surgical, non-healing 998.83
  temple 873.49
    complicated 873.59
  temporal region 873.49
    complicated 873.59
  testis 878.2
    complicated 878.3
  thigh 890.0
    with tendon involvement 890.2
    complicated 890.1
  thorax, thoracic (external) 875.0
    complicated 875.1
  throat 874.8
    complicated 874.9
  thumb (nail) (subungual) 883.0
    with tendon involvement 883.2
    complicated 883.1
  thyroid (gland) 874.2
    complicated 874.3
  toe(s) (nail) (subungual) 893.0
    with tendon involvement 893.2
    complicated 893.1
  tongue 873.64
    complicated 873.74
  tonsil — *see* Wound, open, neck
  trachea (cervical region) 874.02
    with larynx 874.00
      complicated 874.10
    complicated 874.12
    intrathoracic — *see* Injury, internal, trachea
  trunk (multiple) NEC 879.6
    complicated 879.7
    specified site NEC 879.6
      complicated 879.7

Wound, open — *continued*
  tunica vaginalis 878.2
    complicated 878.3
  tympanic membrane 872.61
    complicated 872.71
  tympanum 872.61
    complicated 872.71
  umbilical region 879.2
    complicated 879.3
  ureter — *see* Injury, internal, ureter
  urethra — *see* Injury, internal, urethra
  uterus — *see* Injury, internal, uterus
  uvula 873.69
    complicated 873.79
  vagina 878.6
    complicated 878.7
  vas deferens — *see* Injury, internal, vas deferens
  vitreous (humor) 871.2
  vulva 878.4
    complicated 878.5
  wrist 881.02
    with tendon involvement 881.22
    complicated 881.12
Wright's syndrome (hyperabduction) 447.8
  pneumonia 390 [517.1]
Wringer injury — *see* Crush injury, by site
Wrinkling of skin 701.8
Wrist — *see also* condition
  drop (acquired) 736.05
Wrong drug (given in error) NEC 977.9
  specified drug or substance — *see* Table of Drugs and Chemicals
Wry neck — *see also* Torticollis
  congenital 754.1
Wuchereria infestation 125.0
  bancrofti 125.0
  Brugia malayi 125.1
  malayi 125.1
Wuchereriasis 125.0
Wuchereriosis 125.0
Wuchernde struma langhans (M8332/3) 193

X

Xanthelasma 272.2
  eyelid 272.2 [374.51]
  palpebrarum 272.2 [374.51]
Xanthelasmatosis (essential) 272.2
Xanthelasmoidea 757.33
Xanthine stones 277.2
Xanthinuria 277.2
Xanthofibroma (M8831/0) — *see* Neoplasm, connective tissue, benign
Xanthoma(s), xanthomatosis 272.2
  with
    hyperlipoproteinemia
      type I 272.3
      type III 272.2
      type IV 272.1
      type V 272.3
  bone 272.7
  craniohypophyseal 277.89
  cutaneotendinous 272.7
  diabeticorum 250.8 ☑ [272.2]
    due to secondary diabetes 249.8 ☑ [272.2]
  disseminatum 272.7
  eruptive 272.2
  eyelid 272.2 [374.51]
  familial 272.7
  hereditary 272.7

Xanthoma(s), xanthomatosis — *continued*
  hypercholesterinemic 272.0
  hypercholesterolemic 272.0
  hyperlipemic 272.4
  hyperlipidemic 272.4
  infantile 272.7
  joint 272.7
  juvenile 272.7
  multiple 272.7
  multiplex 272.7
  primary familial 272.7
  tendon (sheath) 272.7
  tuberosum 272.2
  tuberous 272.2
  tubo-eruptive 272.2
Xanthosis 709.09
  surgical 998.81
Xenophobia 300.29
Xeroderma (congenital) 757.39
  acquired 701.1
    eyelid 373.33
  eyelid 373.33
  pigmentosum 757.33
  vitamin A deficiency 264.8
Xerophthalmia 372.53
  vitamin A deficiency 264.7
Xerosis
  conjunctiva 372.53
    with Bitôt's spot 372.53
      vitamin A deficiency 264.1
    vitamin A deficiency 264.0
  cornea 371.40
    with corneal ulceration 370.00
      vitamin A deficiency 264.3
    vitamin A deficiency 264.2
  cutis 706.8
  skin 706.8
Xerostomia 527.7
Xiphodynia 733.90
Xiphoidalgia 733.90
Xiphoiditis 733.99
Xiphopagus 759.4
XO syndrome 758.6
X-ray
  effects, adverse, NEC 990
  of chest
    for suspected tuberculosis V71.2
    routine V72.5
XXX syndrome 758.81
XXXXY syndrome 758.81
XXY syndrome 758.7
Xyloketosuria 271.8
Xylosuria 271.8
Xylulosuria 271.8
XYY syndrome 758.81

Y

Yaba monkey tumor virus 059.22
Yawning 786.09
  psychogenic 306.1
Yaws 102.9
  bone or joint lesions 102.6
  butter 102.1
  chancre 102.0
  cutaneous, less than five years after infection 102.2
  early (cutaneous) (macular) (maculopapular) (micropapular) (papular) 102.2
    frambeside 102.2
    skin lesions NEC 102.2

Yaws — *continued*
  eyelid 102.9 [373.4]
  ganglion 102.6
  gangosis, gangosa 102.5
  gumma, gummata 102.4
    bone 102.6
  gummatous
    frambeside 102.4
    osteitis 102.6
    periostitis 102.6
  hydrarthrosis 102.6
  hyperkeratosis (early) (late) (palmar) (plantar) 102.3
  initial lesions 102.0
  joint lesions 102.6
  juxta-articular nodules 102.7
  late nodular (ulcerated) 102.4
  latent (without clinical manifestations) (with positive serology) 102.8
  mother 102.0
  mucosal 102.7
  multiple papillomata 102.1
  nodular, late (ulcerated) 102.4
  osteitis 102.6
  papilloma, papillomata (palmar) (plantar) 102.1
  periostitis (hypertrophic) 102.6
  ulcers 102.4
  wet crab 102.1
Yeast infection — *see also* Candidiasis 112.9
Yellow
  atrophy (liver) 570
    chronic 571.8
    resulting from administration of blood, plasma, serum, or other biological substance (within 8 months of administration) — *see* Hepatitis, viral
  fever — *see* Fever, yellow
  jack (*see also* Fever, yellow) 060.9
  jaundice (*see also* Jaundice) 782.4
  vernix syndrome 762.2
Yersinia septica 027.8

Z

Zagari's disease (xerostomia) 527.7
Zahorsky's disease (exanthema subitum) (*see also* Exanthem subitum) 058.10
  syndrome (herpangina) 074.0
Zellweger syndrome 277.86
Zenker's diverticulum (esophagus) 530.6
Ziehen-Oppenheim disease 333.6
Zieve's syndrome (jaundice, hyperlipemia, and hemolytic anemia) 571.1
Zika fever 066.3
Zollinger-Ellison syndrome (gastric hypersecretion with pancreatic islet cell tumor) 251.5
Zona — *see also* Herpes, zoster 053.9
Zoophilia (erotica) 302.1
Zoophobia 300.29
Zoster (herpes) — *see also* Herpes, zoster 053.9
Zuelzer (-Ogden) anemia or syndrome (nutritional megaloblastic anemia) 281.2
Zygodactyly — *see also* Syndactylism 755.10
Zygomycosis 117.7
Zymotic — *see* condition

☑ Additional Digit Required — Refer to the Tabular List for Digit Selection   � Subterms under main terms may continue to next column or page

298 — Volume 2   ▶◀ Revised Text   ● New Line   ▲ Revised Code   2015 ICD-9-CM

SECTION 2

Alphabetic Index to Poisoning and External Causes of Adverse Effects of Drugs and Other Chemical Substances

TABLE OF DRUGS AND CHEMICALS

This table contains a classification of drugs and other chemical substances to identify poisoning states and external causes of adverse effects.

Each of the listed substances in the table is assigned a code according to the poisoning classification (960-989). These codes are used when there is a statement of poisoning, overdose, wrong substance given or taken, or intoxication.

The table also contains a listing of external causes of adverse effects. An adverse effect is a pathologic manifestation due to ingestion or exposure to drugs or other chemical substances (e.g., dermatitis, hypersensitivity reaction, aspirin gastritis). The adverse effect is to be identified by the appropriate code found in Section 1, Index to Diseases and Injuries. An external cause code can then be used to identify the circumstances involved. The table headings pertaining to external causes are defined below:

Accidental poisoning (E850-E869) — accidental overdose of drug, wrong substance given or taken, drug taken inadvertently, accidents in the usage of drugs and biologicals in medical and surgical procedures, and to show external causes of poisonings classifiable to 980-989.

Therapeutic use (E930-E949) — a correct substance properly administered in therapeutic or prophylactic dosage as the external cause of adverse effects.

Suicide attempt (E950-E952) — instances in which self-inflicted injuries or poisonings are involved.

Assault (E961-E962) — injury or poisoning inflicted by another person with the intent to injure or kill.

Undetermined (E980-E982) — to be used when the intent of the poisoning or injury cannot be determined whether it was intentional or accidental.

The American Hospital Formulary Service list numbers are included in the table to help classify new drugs not identified in the table by name. The AHFS list numbers are keyed to the continually revised American Hospital Formulary Service (AHFS).* These listings are found in the table under the main term **Drug**.

Excluded from the table are radium and other radioactive substances. The classification of adverse effects and complications pertaining to these substances will be found in Section 1, Index to Diseases and Injuries, and Section 3, Index to External Causes of Injuries.

Although certain substances are indexed with one or more subentries, the majority are listed according to one use or state. It is recognized that many substances may be used in various ways, in medicine and in industry, and may cause adverse effects whatever the state of the agent (solid, liquid, or fumes arising from a liquid). In cases in which the reported data indicates a use or state not in the table, or which is clearly different from the one listed, an attempt should be made to classify the substance in the form which most nearly expresses the reported facts.

*American Hospital Formulary Service, 2 vol. (Washington, D.C.: American Society of Hospital Pharmacists, 1959-)

☑ Additional Digit Required — Refer to the Tabular List for Digit Selection   ⩔ Subterms under main terms may continue to next column or page

2015 ICD-9-CM   ▶◀ Revised Text   ● New Line   ▲ Revised Code   Volume 2 — 299

	Poisoning	External Cause (E-Code)				
		Accident	Therapeutic Use	Suicide Attempt	Assault	Undetermined
1-propanol	980.3	E860.4	—	E950.9	E962.1	E980.9
2-propanol	980.2	E860.3	—	E950.9	E962.1	E980.9
2, 4-D (dichlorophenoxyacetic acid)	989.4	E863.5	—	E950.6	E962.1	E980.7
2, 4-toluene diiso-cyanate	983.0	E864.0	—	E950.7	E962.1	E980.6
2, 4, 5-T (trichlorophenoxy-acetic acid)	989.2	E863.5	—	E950.6	E962.1	E980.7
14-hydroxydihydromorphi-none	965.09	E850.2	E935.2	E950.0	E962.0	E980.0
ABOB	961.7	E857	E931.7	E950.4	E962.0	E980.4
Abrus (seed)	988.2	E865.3	—	E950.9	E962.1	E980.9
Absinthe	980.0	E860.1	—	E950.9	E962.1	E980.9
beverage	980.0	E860.0	—	E950.9	E962.1	E980.9
Acenocoumarin, aceno-coumarol	964.2	E858.2	E934.2	E950.4	E962.0	E980.4
Acepromazine	969.1	E853.0	E939.1	E950.3	E962.0	E980.3
Acetal	982.8	E862.4	—	E950.9	E962.1	E980.9
Acetaldehyde (vapor)	987.8	E869.8	—	E952.8	E962.2	E982.8
liquid	989.89	E866.8	—	E950.9	E962.1	E980.9
Acetaminophen	965.4	E850.4	E935.4	E950.0	E962.0	E980.0
Acetaminosalol	965.1	E850.3	E935.3	E950.0	E962.0	E980.0
Acetanilid(e)	965.4	E850.4	E935.4	E950.0	E962.0	E980.0
Acetarsol, acetarsone	961.1	E857	E931.1	E950.4	E962.0	E980.4
Acetazolamide	974.2	E858.5	E944.2	E950.4	E962.0	E980.4
Acetic						
acid	983.1	E864.1	—	E950.7	E962.1	E980.6
with sodium acetate (oint-ment)	976.3	E858.7	E946.3	E950.4	E962.0	E980.4
irrigating solution	974.5	E858.5	E944.5	E950.4	E962.0	E980.4
lotion	976.2	E858.7	E946.2	E950.4	E962.0	E980.4
anhydride	983.1	E864.1	—	E950.7	E962.1	E980.6
ether (vapor)	982.8	E862.4	—	E950.9	E962.1	E980.9
Acetohexamide	962.3	E858.0	E932.3	E950.4	E962.0	E980.4
Acetomenaphthone	964.3	E858.2	E934.3	E950.4	E962.0	E980.4
Acetomorphine	965.01	E850.0	E935.0	E950.0	E962.0	E980.0
Acetone (oils) (vapor)	982.8	E862.4	—	E950.9	E962.1	E980.9
Acetophenazine						
(maleate)	969.1	E853.0	E939.1	E950.3	E962.0	E980.3
Acetophenetidin	965.4	E850.4	E935.4	E950.0	E962.0	E980.0
Acetophenone	982.0	E862.4	—	E950.9	E962.1	E980.9
Acetorphine	965.09	E850.2	E935.2	E950.0	E962.0	E980.0
Acetosulfone (sodium)	961.8	E857	E931.8	E950.4	E962.0	E980.4
Acetrizoate (sodium)	977.8	E858.8	E947.8	E950.4	E962.0	E980.4
Acetylcarbromal	967.3	E852.2	E937.3	E950.2	E962.0	E980.2
Acetylcholine (chloride)	971.0	E855.3	E941.0	E950.4	E962.0	E980.4
Acetylcysteine	975.5	E858.6	E945.5	E950.4	E962.0	E980.4
Acetyldigitoxin	972.1	E858.3	E942.1	E950.4	E962.0	E980.4
Acetyldihydrocodeine	965.09	E850.2	E935.2	E950.0	E962.0	E980.0
Acetyldihydrocodeinone	965.09	E850.2	E935.2	E950.0	E962.0	E980.0
Acetylene (gas) (industri-al)	987.1	E868.1	—	E951.8	E962.2	E981.8
incomplete combustion of — see Carbon monoxide, fuel, utility						
tetrachloride (vapor)	982.3	E862.4	—	E950.9	E962.1	E980.9
Acetyliodosalicylic acid	965.1	E850.3	E935.3	E950.0	E962.0	E980.0
Acetylphenylhydrazine	965.8	E850.8	E935.8	E950.0	E962.0	E980.0
Acetylsalicylic acid	965.1	E850.3	E935.3	E950.0	E962.0	E980.0
Achromycin	960.4	E856	E930.4	E950.4	E962.0	E980.4
ophthalmic preparation	976.5	E858.7	E946.5	E950.4	E962.0	E980.4
topical NEC	976.0	E858.7	E946.0	E950.4	E962.0	E980.4
Acidifying agents	963.2	E858.1	E933.2	E950.4	E962.0	E980.4
Acids (corrosive) NEC	983.1	E864.1	—	E950.7	E962.1	E980.6
Aconite (wild)	988.2	E865.4	—	E950.9	E962.1	E980.9
Aconitine (liniment)	976.8	E858.7	E946.8	E950.4	E962.0	E980.4
Aconitum ferox	988.2	E865.4	—	E950.9	E962.1	E980.9
Acridine	983.0	E864.0	—	E950.7	E962.1	E980.6
vapor	987.8	E869.8	—	E952.8	E962.2	E982.8
Acriflavine	961.9	E857	E931.9	E950.4	E962.0	E980.4
Acrisorcin	976.0	E858.7	E946.0	E950.4	E962.0	E980.4
Acrolein (gas)	987.8	E869.8	—	E952.8	E962.2	E982.8
liquid	989.89	E866.8	—	E950.9	E962.1	E980.9
Actaea spicata	988.2	E865.4	—	E950.9	E962.1	E980.9
Acterol	961.5	E857	E931.5	E950.4	E962.0	E980.4
ACTH	962.4	E858.0	E932.4	E950.4	E962.0	E980.4
Acthar	962.4	E858.0	E932.4	E950.4	E962.0	E980.4
Actinomycin (C) (D)	960.7	E856	E930.7	E950.4	E962.0	E980.4
Adalin (acetyl)	967.3	E852.2	E937.3	E950.2	E962.0	E980.2
Adenosine (phosphate)	977.8	E858.8	E947.8	E950.4	E962.0	E980.4
ADH	962.5	E858.0	E932.5	E950.4	E962.0	E980.4
Adhesives	989.89	E866.6	—	E950.9	E962.1	E980.9

	Poisoning	External Cause (E-Code)				
		Accident	Therapeutic Use	Suicide Attempt	Assault	Undetermined
Adicillin	960.0	E856	E930.0	E950.4	E962.0	E980.4
Adiphenine	975.1	E855.6	E945.1	E950.4	E962.0	E980.4
Adjunct, pharmaceutical	977.4	E858.8	E947.4	E950.4	E962.0	E980.4
Adrenal (extract, cortex or medulla) (glucocorticoids) (hormones) (mineralocorti-coids)	962.0	E858.0	E932.0	E950.4	E962.0	E980.4
ENT agent	976.6	E858.7	E946.6	E950.4	E962.0	E980.4
ophthalmic preparation	976.5	E858.7	E946.5	E950.4	E962.0	E980.4
topical NEC	976.0	E858.7	E946.0	E950.4	E962.0	E980.4
Adrenalin	971.2	E855.5	E941.2	E950.4	E962.0	E980.4
Adrenergic blocking agents	971.3	E855.6	E941.3	E950.4	E962.0	E980.4
Adrenergics	971.2	E855.5	E941.2	E950.4	E962.0	E980.4
Adrenochrome (deriva-tives)	972.8	E858.3	E942.8	E950.4	E962.0	E980.4
Adrenocorticotropic hor-mone	962.4	E858.0	E932.4	E950.4	E962.0	E980.4
Adrenocorticotropin	962.4	E858.0	E932.4	E950.4	E962.0	E980.4
Adriamycin	960.7	E856	E930.7	E950.4	E962.0	E980.4
Aerosol spray — see Sprays						
Aerosporin	960.8	E856	E930.8	E950.4	E962.0	E980.4
ENT agent	976.6	E858.7	E946.6	E950.4	E962.0	E980.4
ophthalmic preparation	976.5	E858.7	E946.5	E950.4	E962.0	E980.4
topical NEC	976.0	E858.7	E946.0	E950.4	E962.0	E980.4
Aethusa cynapium	988.2	E865.4	—	E950.9	E962.1	E980.9
Aflatoxin	989.7	E865.9	—	E950.9	E962.1	E980.9
African boxwood	988.2	E865.4	—	E950.9	E962.1	E980.9
Agar (-agar)	973.3	E858.4	E943.3	E950.4	E962.0	E980.4
Agricultural agent NEC	989.89	E863.9	—	E950.6	E962.1	E980.7
Agrypnal	967.0	E851	E937.0	E950.1	E962.0	E980.1
Air contaminant(s), source or type not specified	987.9	E869.9	—	E952.9	E962.2	E982.9
specified type — see specific substance						
Akee	988.2	E865.4	—	E950.9	E962.1	E980.9
Akrinol	976.0	E858.7	E946.0	E950.4	E962.0	E980.4
Alantolactone	961.6	E857	E931.6	E950.4	E962.0	E980.4
Albamycin	960.8	E856	E930.8	E950.4	E962.0	E980.4
Albumin (normal human serum)	964.7	E858.2	E934.7	E950.4	E962.0	E980.4
Albuterol	975.7	E858.6	E945.7	E950.4	E962.0	E980.4
Alcohol	980.9	E860.9	—	E950.9	E962.1	E980.9
absolute	980.0	E860.1	—	E950.9	E962.1	E980.9
beverage	980.0	E860.0	E947.8	E950.9	E962.1	E980.9
amyl	980.3	E860.4	—	E950.9	E962.1	E980.9
antifreeze	980.1	E860.2	—	E950.9	E962.1	E980.9
butyl	980.3	E860.4	—	E950.9	E962.1	E980.9
dehydrated	980.0	E860.1	—	E950.9	E962.1	E980.9
beverage	980.0	E860.0	E947.8	E950.9	E962.1	E980.9
denatured	980.0	E860.1	—	E950.9	E962.1	E980.9
deterrents	977.3	E858.8	E947.3	E950.4	E962.0	E980.4
diagnostic (gastric func-tion)	977.8	E858.8	E947.8	E950.4	E962.0	E980.4
ethyl	980.0	E860.1	—	E950.9	E962.1	E980.9
beverage	980.0	E860.0	E947.8	E950.9	E962.1	E980.9
grain	980.0	E860.1	—	E950.9	E962.1	E980.9
beverage	980.0	E860.0	E947.8	E950.9	E962.1	E980.9
industrial	980.9	E860.9	—	E950.9	E962.1	E980.9
isopropyl	980.2	E860.3	—	E950.9	E962.1	E980.9
methyl	980.1	E860.2	—	E950.9	E962.1	E980.9
preparation for consump-tion	980.0	E860.0	E947.8	E950.9	E962.1	E980.9
propyl	980.3	E860.4	—	E950.9	E962.1	E980.9
secondary	980.2	E860.3	—	E950.9	E962.1	E980.9
radiator	980.1	E860.2	—	E950.9	E962.1	E980.9
rubbing	980.2	E860.3	—	E950.9	E962.1	E980.9
specified type NEC	980.8	E860.8	—	E950.9	E962.1	E980.9
surgical	980.9	E860.9	—	E950.9	E962.1	E980.9
vapor (from any type of alco-hol)	987.8	E869.8	—	E952.8	E962.2	E982.8
wood	980.1	E860.2	—	E950.9	E962.1	E980.9
Alcuronium chloride	975.2	E858.6	E945.2	E950.4	E962.0	E980.4
Aldactone	974.4	E858.5	E944.4	E950.4	E962.0	E980.4
Aldicarb	989.3	E863.2	—	E950.6	E962.1	E980.7
Aldomet	972.6	E858.3	E942.6	E950.4	E962.0	E980.4
Aldosterone	962.0	E858.0	E932.0	E950.4	E962.0	E980.4
Aldrin (dust)	989.2	E863.0	—	E950.6	E962.1	E980.7
Algeldrate	973.0	E858.4	E943.0	E950.4	E962.0	E980.4
Alidase	963.4	E858.1	E933.4	E950.4	E962.0	E980.4
Aliphatic thiocyanates	989.0	E866.8	—	E950.9	E962.1	E980.9

Nontherapeutic use substance

▽ Subterms under main terms may continue to next column or page

	External Cause (E-Code)					
	Poisoning	Accident	Therapeutic Use	Suicide Attempt	Assault	Undetermined
Alkaline antiseptic solution (aromatic)	976.6	E858.7	E946.6	E950.4	E962.0	E980.4
Alkalinizing agents (medicinal)	963.3	E858.1	E933.3	E950.4	E962.0	E980.4
Alkalis, caustic	983.2	E864.2	—	E950.7	E962.1	E980.6
Alkalizing agents (medicinal)	963.3	E858.1	E933.3	E950.4	E962.0	E980.4
Alka-seltzer	965.1	E850.3	E935.3	E950.0	E962.0	E980.0
Alkavervir	972.6	E858.3	E942.6	E950.4	E962.0	E980.4
Allegron	969.05	E854.0	E939.0	E950.3	E962.0	E980.3
Alleve — Naproxen						
Allobarbital, allobarbitone	967.0	E851	E937.0	E950.1	E962.0	E980.1
Allopurinol	974.7	E858.5	E944.7	E950.4	E962.0	E980.4
Allylestrenol	962.2	E858.0	E932.2	E950.4	E962.0	E980.4
Allylisopropylacetylurea	967.8	E852.8	E937.8	E950.2	E962.0	E980.2
Allylisopropylmalonylurea	967.0	E851	E937.0	E950.1	E962.0	E980.1
Allyltribromide	967.3	E852.2	E937.3	E950.2	E962.0	E980.2
Aloe, aloes, aloin	973.1	E858.4	E943.1	E950.4	E962.0	E980.4
Alosetron	973.8	E858.4	E943.8	E950.4	E962.0	E980.4
Aloxidone	966.0	E855.0	E936.0	E950.4	E962.0	E980.4
Aloxiprin	965.1	E850.3	E935.3	E950.0	E962.0	E980.0
Alpha-1 blockers	971.3	E855.6	E941.3	E950.4	E962.0	E980.4
Alpha amylase	963.4	E858.1	E933.4	E950.4	E962.0	E980.4
Alphaprodine (hydrochloride)	965.09	E850.2	E935.2	E950.0	E962.0	E980.0
Alpha tocopherol	963.5	E858.1	E933.5	E950.4	E962.0	E980.4
Alseroxylon	972.6	E858.3	E942.6	E950.4	E962.0	E980.4
Alum (ammonium) (potassium)	983.2	E864.2	—	E950.7	E962.1	E980.6
medicinal (astringent) NEC	976.2	E858.7	E946.2	E950.4	E962.0	E980.4
Aluminium, aluminum (gel) (hydroxide)	973.0	E858.4	E943.0	E950.4	E962.0	E980.4
acetate solution	976.2	E858.7	E946.2	E950.4	E962.0	E980.4
aspirin	965.1	E850.3	E935.3	E950.0	E962.0	E980.0
carbonate	973.0	E858.4	E943.0	E950.4	E962.0	E980.4
glycinate	973.0	E858.4	E943.0	E950.4	E962.0	E980.4
nicotinate	972.2	E858.3	E942.2	E950.4	E962.0	E980.4
ointment (surgical) (topical)	976.3	E858.7	E946.3	E950.4	E962.0	E980.4
phosphate	973.0	E858.4	E943.0	E950.4	E962.0	E980.4
subacetate	976.2	E858.7	E946.2	E950.4	E962.0	E980.4
topical NEC	976.3	E858.7	E946.3	E950.4	E962.0	E980.4
Alurate	967.0	E851	E937.0	E950.1	E962.0	E980.1
Alverine (citrate)	975.1	E858.6	E945.1	E950.4	E962.0	E980.4
Alvodine	965.09	E850.2	E935.2	E950.0	E962.0	E980.0
Amanita phalloides	988.1	E865.5	—	E950.9	E962.1	E980.9
Amantadine (hydrochloride)	966.4	E855.0	E936.4	E950.4	E962.0	E980.4
Ambazone	961.9	E857	E931.9	E950.4	E962.0	E980.4
Ambenonium	971.0	E855.3	E941.0	E950.4	E962.0	E980.4
Ambutonium bromide	971.1	E855.4	E941.1	E950.4	E962.0	E980.4
Ametazole	977.8	E858.8	E947.8	E950.4	E962.0	E980.4
Amethocaine (infiltration) (topical)	968.5	E855.2	E938.5	E950.4	E962.0	E980.4
nerve block (peripheral) (plexus)	968.6	E855.2	E938.6	E950.4	E962.0	E980.4
spinal	968.7	E855.2	E938.7	E950.4	E962.0	E980.4
Amethopterin	963.1	E858.1	E933.1	E950.4	E962.0	E980.4
Amfepramone	977.0	E858.8	E947.0	E950.4	E962.0	E980.4
Amidon	965.02	E850.1	E935.1	E950.0	E962.0	E980.0
Amidopyrine	965.5	E850.5	E935.5	E950.0	E962.0	E980.0
Aminacrine	976.0	E858.7	E946.0	E950.4	E962.0	E980.4
Aminitrozole	961.5	E857	E931.5	E950.4	E962.0	E980.4
Aminoacetic acid	974.5	E858.5	E944.5	E950.4	E962.0	E980.4
Amino acids	974.5	E858.5	E944.5	E950.4	E962.0	E980.4
Aminocaproic acid	964.4	E858.2	E934.4	E950.4	E962.0	E980.4
Aminoethylisothiourium	963.8	E858.1	E933.8	E950.4	E962.0	E980.4
Aminoglutethimide	966.3	E855.0	E936.3	E950.4	E962.0	E980.4
Aminometradine	974.3	E858.5	E944.3	E950.4	E962.0	E980.4
Aminopentamide	971.1	E855.4	E941.1	E950.4	E962.0	E980.4
Aminophenazone	965.5	E850.5	E935.5	E950.0	E962.0	E980.0
Aminophenol	983.0	E864.0	—	E950.7	E962.1	E980.6
Aminophenylpyridone	969.5	E853.8	E939.5	E950.3	E962.0	E980.3
Aminophyllin	975.7	E858.6	E945.7	E950.4	E962.0	E980.4
Aminopterin	963.1	E858.1	E933.1	E950.4	E962.0	E980.4
Aminopyrine	965.5	E850.5	E935.5	E950.0	E962.0	E980.0
Aminosalicylic acid	961.8	E857	E931.8	E950.4	E962.0	E980.4
Amiphenazole	970.1	E854.3	E940.1	E950.4	E962.0	E980.4
Amiquinsin	972.6	E858.3	E942.6	E950.4	E962.0	E980.4
Amisometradine	974.3	E858.5	E944.3	E950.4	E962.0	E980.4
Amitriptyline	969.05	E854.0	E939.0	E950.3	E962.0	E980.3
Ammonia (fumes) (gas) (vapor)	987.8	E869.8	—	E952.8	E962.2	E982.8
liquid (household) NEC	983.2	E861.4	—	E950.7	E962.1	E980.6
spirit, aromatic	970.89	E854.3	E940.8	E950.4	E962.0	E980.4
Ammoniated mercury	976.0	E858.7	E946.0	E950.4	E962.0	E980.4
Ammonium						
carbonate	983.2	E864.2	—	E950.7	E962.1	E980.6
chloride (acidifying agent)	963.2	E858.1	E933.2	E950.4	E962.0	E980.4
expectorant	975.5	E858.6	E945.5	E950.4	E962.0	E980.4
compounds (household) NEC	983.2	E861.4	—	E950.7	E962.1	E980.6
fumes (any usage)	987.8	E869.8	—	E952.8	E962.2	E982.8
industrial	983.2	E864.2	—	E950.7	E962.1	E980.6
ichthyosulfonate	976.4	E858.7	E946.4	E950.4	E962.0	E980.4
mandelate	961.9	E857	E931.9	E950.4	E962.0	E980.4
Amobarbital	967.0	E851	E937.0	E950.1	E962.0	E980.1
Amodiaquin(e)	961.4	E857	E931.4	E950.4	E962.0	E980.4
Amopyroquin(e)	961.4	E857	E931.4	E950.4	E962.0	E980.4
Amphenidone	969.5	E853.8	E939.5	E950.3	E962.0	E980.3
Amphetamine	969.72	E854.2	E939.7	E950.3	E962.0	E980.3
Amphomycin	960.8	E856	E930.8	E950.4	E962.0	E980.4
Amphotericin B	960.1	E856	E930.1	E950.4	E962.0	E980.4
topical	976.0	E858.7	E946.0	E950.4	E962.0	E980.4
Ampicillin	960.0	E856	E930.0	E950.4	E962.0	E980.4
Amprotropine	971.1	E855.4	E941.1	E950.4	E962.0	E980.4
Amygdalin	977.8	E858.8	E947.8	E950.4	E962.0	E980.4
Amyl						
acetate (vapor)	982.8	E862.4	—	E950.9	E962.1	E980.9
alcohol	980.3	E860.4	—	E950.9	E962.1	E980.9
nitrite (medicinal)	972.4	E858.3	E942.4	E950.4	E962.0	E980.4
Amylase (alpha)	963.4	E858.1	E933.4	E950.4	E962.0	E980.4
Amylene hydrate	980.8	E860.8	—	E950.9	E962.1	E980.9
Amylobarbitone	967.0	E851	E937.0	E950.1	E962.0	E980.1
Amylocaine	968.9	E855.2	E938.9	E950.4	E962.0	E980.4
infiltration (subcutaneous)	968.5	E855.2	E938.5	E950.4	E962.0	E980.4
nerve block (peripheral) (plexus)	968.6	E855.2	E938.6	E950.4	E962.0	E980.4
spinal	968.7	E855.2	E938.7	E950.4	E962.0	E980.4
topical (surface)	968.5	E855.2	E938.5	E950.4	E962.0	E980.4
Amytal (sodium)	967.0	E851	E937.0	E950.1	E962.0	E980.1
Analeptics	970.0	E854.3	E940.0	E950.4	E962.0	E980.4
Analgesics	965.9	E850.9	E935.9	E950.0	E962.0	E980.0
aromatic NEC	965.4	E850.4	E935.4	E950.0	E962.0	E980.0
non-narcotic NEC	965.7	E850.7	E935.7	E950.0	E962.0	E980.0
specified NEC	965.8	E850.8	E935.8	E950.0	E962.0	E980.0
Anamirta cocculus	988.2	E865.3	—	E950.9	E962.1	E980.9
Ancillin	960.0	E856	E930.0	E950.4	E962.0	E980.4
Androgens (anabolic congeners)	962.1	E858.0	E932.1	E950.4	E962.0	E980.4
Androstalone	962.1	E858.0	E932.1	E950.4	E962.0	E980.4
Androsterone	962.1	E858.0	E932.1	E950.4	E962.0	E980.4
Anemone pulsatilla	988.2	E865.4	—	E950.9	E962.1	E980.9
Anesthesia, anesthetic (general) NEC	968.4	E855.1	E938.4	E950.4	E962.0	E980.4
block (nerve) (plexus)	968.6	E855.2	E938.6	E950.4	E962.0	E980.4
gaseous NEC	968.2	E855.1	E938.2	E950.4	E962.0	E980.4
halogenated hydrocarbon derivatives NEC	968.2	E855.1	E938.2	E950.4	E962.0	E980.4
infiltration (intradermal) (subcutaneous) (submucosal)	968.5	E855.2	E938.5	E950.4	E962.0	E980.4
intravenous	968.3	E855.1	E938.3	E950.4	E962.0	E980.4
local NEC	968.9	E855.2	E938.9	E950.4	E962.0	E980.4
nerve blocking (peripheral) (plexus)	968.6	E855.2	E938.6	E950.4	E962.0	E980.4
rectal NEC	968.3	E855.1	E938.3	E950.4	E962.0	E980.4
spinal	968.7	E855.2	E938.7	E950.4	E962.0	E980.4
surface	968.5	E855.2	E938.5	E950.4	E962.0	E980.4
topical	968.5	E855.2	E938.5	E950.4	E962.0	E980.4
Aneurine	963.5	E858.1	E933.5	E950.4	E962.0	E980.4
Anginine — see Glyceryl trinitrate						
Angio-Conray	977.8	E858.8	E947.8	E950.4	E962.0	E980.4
Angiotensin	971.2	E855.5	E941.2	E950.4	E962.0	E980.4
Anhydrohydroxyprogesterone	962.2	E858.0	E932.2	E950.4	E962.0	E980.4
Anhydron	974.3	E858.5	E944.3	E950.4	E962.0	E980.4
Anileridine	965.09	E850.2	E935.2	E950.0	E962.0	E980.0

	External Cause (E-Code)					
	Poisoning	Accident	Therapeutic Use	Suicide Attempt	Assault	Undeter-mined
Aniline (dye) (liquid)	983.0	E864.0	—	E950.7	E962.1	E980.6
analgesic	965.4	E850.4	E935.4	E950.0	E962.0	E980.0
derivatives, therapeutic NEC	965.4	E850.4	E935.4	E950.0	E962.0	E980.0
vapor	987.8	E869.8	—	E952.8	E962.2	E982.8
Aniscoropine	971.1	E855.4	E941.1	E950.4	E962.0	E980.4
Anisindione	964.2	E858.2	E934.2	E950.4	E962.0	E980.4
Anorexic agents	977.0	E858.8	E947.0	E950.4	E962.0	E980.4
Ant (bite) (sting)	—	E905.5	—	E950.9	E962.1	E980.9
Antabuse	977.3	E858.8	E947.3	E950.4	E962.0	E980.4
Antacids	973.0	E858.4	E943.0	E950.4	E962.0	E980.4
Antazoline	963.0	E858.1	E933.0	E950.4	E962.0	E980.4
Anthralin	976.4	E858.7	E946.4	E950.4	E962.0	E980.4
Anthramycin	960.7	E856	E930.7	E950.4	E962.0	E980.4
Antiadrenergics	971.3	E855.6	E941.3	E950.4	E962.0	E980.4
Antiallergic agents	963.0	E858.1	E933.0	E950.4	E962.0	E980.4
Antianemic agents NEC	964.1	E858.2	E934.1	E950.4	E962.0	E980.4
Antiaris toxicaria	988.2	E865.4	—	E950.9	E962.1	E980.9
Antiarteriosclerotic agents	972.2	E858.3	E942.2	E950.4	E962.0	E980.4
Antiasthmatics	975.7	E858.6	E945.7	E950.4	E962.0	E980.4
Antibiotics	960.9	E856	E930.9	E950.4	E962.0	E980.4
antifungal	960.1	E856	E930.1	E950.4	E962.0	E980.4
antimycobacterial	960.6	E856	E930.6	E950.4	E962.0	E980.4
antineoplastic	960.7	E856	E930.7	E950.4	E962.0	E980.4
cephalosporin (group)	960.5	E856	E930.5	E950.4	E962.0	E980.4
chloramphenicol (group)	960.2	E856	E930.2	E950.4	E962.0	E980.4
macrolides	960.3	E856	E930.3	E950.4	E962.0	E980.4
specified NEC	960.8	E856	E930.8	E950.4	E962.0	E980.4
tetracycline (group)	960.4	E856	E930.4	E950.4	E962.0	E980.4
Anticancer agents NEC	963.1	E858.1	E933.1	E950.4	E962.0	E980.4
antibiotics	960.7	E856	E930.7	E950.4	E962.0	E980.4
Anticholinergics	971.1	E855.4	E941.1	E950.4	E962.0	E980.4
Anticholinesterase (organophosphorus) (reversible)	971.0	E855.3	E941.0	E950.4	E962.0	E980.4
Anticoagulants	964.2	E858.2	E934.2	E950.4	E962.0	E980.4
antagonists	964.5	E858.2	E934.5	E950.4	E962.0	E980.4
Anti-common cold agents NEC	975.6	E858.6	E945.6	E950.4	E962.0	E980.4
Anticonvulsants NEC	966.3	E855.0	E936.3	E950.4	E962.0	E980.4
Antidepressants	969.00	E854.0	E939.0	E950.3	E962.0	E980.3
monoamine oxidase inhibitors (MAOI)	969.01	E854.0	E939.0	E950.3	E962.0	E980.3
specified type NEC	969.09	E854.0	E939.0	E950.3	E962.0	E980.3
SSNRI (selective serotonin and norepinephrine reuptake inhibitors)	969.02	E854.0	E939.0	E950.3	E962.0	E980.3
SSRI (selective serotonin reuptake inhibitors)	969.03	E854.0	E939.0	E950.3	E962.0	E980.3
tetracyclic	969.04	E854.0	E939.0	E950.3	E962.0	E980.3
tricyclic	969.05	E854.0	E939.0	E950.3	E962.0	E980.3
Antidiabetic agents	962.3	E858.0	E932.3	E950.4	E962.0	E980.4
Antidiarrheal agents	973.5	E858.4	E943.5	E950.4	E962.0	E980.4
Antidiuretic hormone	962.5	E858.0	E932.5	E950.4	E962.0	E980.4
Antidotes NEC	977.2	E858.8	E947.2	E950.4	E962.0	E980.4
Antiemetic agents	963.0	E858.1	E933.0	E950.4	E962.0	E980.4
Antiepilepsy agent NEC	966.3	E855.0	E936.3	E950.4	E962.0	E980.4
Antifertility pills	962.2	E858.0	E932.2	E950.4	E962.0	E980.4
Antiflatulents	973.8	E858.4	E943.8	E950.4	E962.0	E980.4
Antifreeze	989.89	E866.8	—	E950.9	E962.1	E980.9
alcohol	980.1	E860.2	—	E950.9	E962.1	E980.9
ethylene glycol	982.8	E862.4	—	E950.9	E962.1	E980.9
Antifungals (nonmedicinal) (sprays)	989.4	E863.6	—	E950.6	E962.1	E980.7
medicinal NEC	961.9	E857	E931.9	E950.4	E962.0	E980.4
antibiotic	960.1	E856	E930.1	E950.4	E962.0	E980.4
topical	976.0	E858.7	E946.0	E950.4	E962.0	E980.4
Antigastric secretion agents	973.0	E858.4	E943.0	E950.4	E962.0	E980.4
Antihelmintics	961.6	E857	E931.6	E950.4	E962.0	E980.4
Antihemophilic factor (human)	964.7	E858.2	E934.7	E950.4	E962.0	E980.4
Antihistamine	963.0	E858.1	E933.0	E950.4	E962.0	E980.4
Antihypertensive agents NEC	972.6	E858.3	E942.6	E950.4	E962.0	E980.4
Anti-infectives NEC	961.9	E857	E931.9	E950.4	E962.0	E980.4
antibiotics	960.9	E856	E930.9	E950.4	E962.0	E980.4
specified NEC	960.8	E856	E930.8	E950.4	E962.0	E980.4
antihelmintic	961.6	E857	E931.6	E950.4	E962.0	E980.4
antimalarial	961.4	E857	E931.4	E950.4	E962.0	E980.4
antimycobacterial NEC	961.8	E857	E931.8	E950.4	E962.0	E980.4

	External Cause (E-Code)					
	Poisoning	Accident	Therapeutic Use	Suicide Attempt	Assault	Undeter-mined
Anti-infectives — continued						
antimycobacterial — continued						
antibiotics	960.6	E856	E930.6	E950.4	E962.0	E980.4
antiprotozoal NEC	961.5	E857	E931.5	E950.4	E962.0	—
blood	961.4	E857	E931.4	E950.4	E962.0	E980.4
antiviral	961.7	E857	E931.7	E950.4	E962.0	E980.4
arsenical	961.1	E857	E931.1	E950.4	E962.0	E980.4
ENT agents	976.6	E858.7	E946.6	E950.4	E962.0	E980.4
heavy metals NEC	961.2	E857	E931.2	E950.4	E962.0	E980.4
local	976.0	E858.7	E946.0	E950.4	E962.0	E980.4
ophthalmic preparation	976.5	E858.7	E946.5	E950.4	E962.0	E980.4
topical NEC	976.0	E858.7	E946.0	E950.4	E962.0	E980.4
Anti-inflammatory agents (topical)	976.0	E858.7	E946.0	E950.4	E962.0	E980.4
Antiknock (tetraethyl lead)	984.1	E862.1	—	E950.9	—	E980.9
Antilipemics	972.2	E858.3	E942.2	E950.4	E962.0	E980.4
Antimalarials	961.4	E857	E931.4	E950.4	E962.0	E980.4
Antimony (compounds) (vapor) NEC	985.4	E866.2	—	E950.9	E962.1	E980.9
anti-infectives	961.2	E857	E931.2	E950.4	E962.0	E980.4
pesticides (vapor)	985.4	E863.4	—	E950.6	E962.2	E980.7
potassium tartrate	961.2	E857	E931.2	E950.4	E962.0	E980.4
tartrated	961.2	E857	E931.2	E950.4	E962.0	E980.4
Antimuscarinic agents	971.1	E855.4	E941.1	E950.4	E962.0	E980.4
Antimycobacterials NEC	961.8	E857	E931.8	E950.4	E962.0	E980.4
antibiotics	960.6	E856	E930.6	E950.4	E962.0	E980.4
Antineoplastic agents	963.1	E858.1	E933.1	E950.4	E962.0	E980.4
antibiotics	960.7	E856	E930.7	E950.4	E962.0	E980.4
Anti-Parkinsonism agents	966.4	E855.0	E936.4	E950.4	E962.0	E980.4
Antiphlogistics	965.69	E850.6	E935.6	E950.0	E962.0	E980.0
Antiprotozoals NEC	961.5	E857	E931.5	E950.4	E962.0	E980.4
blood	961.4	E857	E931.4	E950.4	E962.0	E980.4
Antipruritics (local)	976.1	E858.7	E946.1	E950.4	E962.0	E980.4
Antipsychotic agents NEC	969.3	E853.8	E939.3	E950.3	E962.0	E980.3
Antipyretics	965.9	E850.9	E935.9	E950.0	E962.0	E980.0
specified NEC	965.8	E850.8	E935.8	E950.0	E962.0	E980.0
Antipyrine	965.5	E850.5	E935.5	E950.0	E962.0	E980.0
Antirabies serum (equine)	979.9	E858.8	E949.9	E950.4	E962.0	E980.4
Antirheumatics	965.69	E850.6	E935.6	E950.0	E962.0	E980.0
Antiseborrheics	976.4	E858.7	E946.4	E950.4	E962.0	E980.4
Antiseptics (external) (medicinal)	976.0	E858.7	E946.0	E950.4	E962.0	E980.4
Antistine	963.0	E858.1	E933.0	E950.4	E962.0	E980.4
Antithyroid agents	962.8	E858.0	E932.8	E950.4	E962.0	E980.4
Antitoxin, any	979.9	E858.8	E949.9	E950.4	E962.0	E980.4
Antituberculars	961.8	E857	E931.8	E950.4	E962.0	E980.4
antibiotics	960.6	E856	E930.6	E950.4	E962.0	E980.4
Antitussives	975.4	E858.6	E945.4	E950.4	E962.0	E980.4
Antivaricose agents (sclerosing)	972.7	E858.3	E942.7	E950.4	E962.0	E980.4
Antivenin (crotaline) (spider-bite)	979.9	E858.8	E949.9	E950.4	E962.0	E980.4
Antivert	963.0	E858.1	E933.0	E950.4	E962.0	E980.4
Antivirals NEC	961.7	E857	E931.7	E950.4	E962.0	E980.4
Ant poisons — see Pesticides						
Antrol	989.4	E863.4	—	E950.6	E962.1	E980.7
fungicide	989.4	E863.6	—	E950.6	E962.1	E980.7
Apomorphine hydrochloride (emetic)	973.6	E858.4	E943.6	E950.4	E962.0	E980.4
Appetite depressants, central	977.0	E858.8	E947.0	E950.4	E962.0	E980.4
Apresoline	972.6	E858.3	E942.6	E950.4	E962.0	E980.4
Aprobarbital, aprobarbitone	967.0	E851	E937.0	E950.1	E962.0	E980.1
Apronalide	967.8	E852.8	E937.8	E950.2	E962.0	E980.2
Aqua fortis	983.1	E864.1	—	E950.7	E962.1	E980.6
Arachis oil (topical)	976.3	E858.7	E946.3	E950.4	E962.0	E980.4
cathartic	973.2	E858.4	E943.2	E950.4	E962.0	E980.4
Aralen	961.4	E857	E931.4	E950.4	E962.0	E980.4
Arginine salts	974.5	E858.5	E944.5	E950.4	E962.0	E980.4
Argyrol	976.0	E858.7	E946.0	E950.4	E962.0	E980.4
ENT agent	976.6	E858.7	E946.6	E950.4	E962.0	E980.4
ophthalmic preparation	976.5	E858.7	E946.5	E950.4	E962.0	E980.4
Aristocort	962.0	E858.0	E932.0	E950.4	E962.0	E980.4
ENT agent	976.6	E858.7	E946.6	E950.4	E962.0	E980.4
ophthalmic preparation	976.5	E858.7	E946.5	E950.4	E962.0	E980.4
topical NEC	976.0	E858.7	E946.0	E950.4	E962.0	E980.4

Nontherapeutic use substance

Subterms under main terms may continue to next column or page

Substance		External Cause (E-Code)				
	Poisoning	Accident	Therapeutic Use	Suicide Attempt	Assault	Undetermined
Aromatics, corrosive	983.0	E864.0	—	E950.7	E962.1	E980.6
disinfectants	983.0	E861.4	—	E950.7	E962.1	E980.6
Arsenate of lead (insecticide)	985.1	E863.4	—	E950.8	E962.1	E980.8
herbicide	985.1	E863.5	—	E950.8	E962.1	E980.8
Arsenic, arsenicals (compounds) (dust) (fumes) (vapor) NEC	985.1	E866.3	—	E950.8	E962.1	E980.8
anti-infectives	961.1	E857	E931.1	E950.4	E962.0	E980.4
pesticide (dust) (fumes)	985.1	E863.4	—	E950.8	E962.1	E980.8
Arsine (gas)	985.1	E866.3	—	E950.8	E962.1	E980.8
Arsphenamine (silver)	961.1	E857	E931.1	E950.4	E962.0	E980.4
Arsthinol	961.1	E857	E931.1	E950.4	E962.0	E980.4
Artane	971.1	E855.4	E941.1	E950.4	E962.0	E980.4
Arthropod (venomous) NEC	989.5	E905.5	—	E950.9	E962.1	E980.9
Asbestos	989.81	E866.8	—	E950.9	E962.1	E980.9
Ascaridole	961.6	E857	E931.6	E950.4	E962.0	E980.4
Ascorbic acid	963.5	E858.1	E933.5	E950.4	E962.0	E980.4
Asiaticoside	976.0	E858.7	E946.0	E950.4	E962.0	E980.4
Aspidium (oleoresin)	961.6	E857	E931.6	E950.4	E962.0	E980.4
Aspirin	965.1	E850.3	E935.3	E950.0	E962.0	E980.0
Astringents (local)	976.2	E858.7	E946.2	E950.4	E962.0	E980.4
Atabrine	961.3	E857	E931.3	E950.4	E962.0	E980.4
Ataractics	969.5	E853.8	E939.5	E950.3	E962.0	E980.3
Atonia drug, intestinal	973.3	E858.4	E943.3	E950.4	E962.0	E980.4
Atophan	974.7	E858.5	E944.7	E950.4	E962.0	E980.4
Atropine	971.1	E855.4	E941.1	E950.4	E962.0	E980.4
Attapulgite	973.5	E858.4	E943.5	E950.4	E962.0	E980.4
Attenuvax	979.4	E858.8	E949.4	E950.4	E962.0	E980.4
Aureomycin	960.4	E856	E930.4	E950.4	E962.0	E980.4
ophthalmic preparation	976.5	E858.7	E946.5	E950.4	E962.0	E980.4
topical NEC	976.0	E858.7	E946.0	E950.4	E962.0	E980.4
Aurothioglucose	965.69	E850.6	E935.6	E950.0	E962.0	E980.0
Aurothioglycanide	965.69	E850.6	E935.6	E950.0	E962.0	E980.0
Aurothiomalate	965.69	E850.6	E935.6	E950.0	E962.0	E980.0
Automobile fuel	981	E862.1	—	E950.9	E962.1	E980.9
Autonomic nervous system agents NEC	971.9	E855.9	E941.9	E950.4	E962.0	E980.4
Avlosulfon	961.8	E857	E931.8	E950.4	E962.0	E980.4
Avomine	967.8	E852.8	E937.8	E950.2	E962.0	E980.2
Azacyclonol	969.5	E853.8	E939.5	E950.3	E962.0	E980.3
Azapetine	971.3	E855.6	E941.3	E950.4	E962.0	E980.4
Azaribine	963.1	E858.1	E933.1	E950.4	E962.0	E980.4
Azaserine	960.7	E856	E930.7	E950.4	E962.0	E980.4
Azathioprine	963.1	E858.1	E933.1	E950.4	E962.0	E980.4
Azosulfamide	961.0	E857	E931.0	E950.4	E962.0	E980.4
Azulfidine	961.0	E857	E931.0	E950.4	E962.0	E980.4
Azuresin	977.8	E858.8	E947.8	E950.4	E962.0	E980.4
Bacimycin	976.0	E858.7	E946.0	E950.4	E962.0	E980.4
ophthalmic preparation	976.5	E858.7	E946.5	E950.4	E962.0	E980.4
Bacitracin	960.8	E856	E930.8	E950.4	E962.0	E980.4
ENT agent	976.6	E858.7	E946.6	E950.4	E962.0	E980.4
ophthalmic preparation	976.5	E858.7	E946.5	E950.4	E962.0	E980.4
topical NEC	976.0	E858.7	E946.0	E950.4	E962.0	E980.4
Baking soda	963.3	E858.1	E933.3	E950.4	E962.0	E980.4
BAL	963.8	E858.1	E933.8	E950.4	E962.0	E980.4
Bamethan (sulfate)	972.5	E858.3	E942.5	E950.4	E962.0	E980.4
Bamipine	963.0	E858.1	E933.0	E950.4	E962.0	E980.4
Baneberry	988.2	E865.4	—	E950.9	E962.1	E980.9
Banewort	988.2	E865.4	—	E950.9	E962.1	E980.9
Barbenyl	967.0	E851	E937.0	E950.1	E962.0	E980.1
Barbital, barbitone	967.0	E851	E937.0	E950.1	E962.0	E980.1
Barbiturates, barbituric acid	967.0	E851	E937.0	E950.1	E962.0	E980.1
anesthetic (intravenous)	968.3	E855.1	E938.3	E950.4	E962.0	E980.4
Barium (carbonate) (chloride) (sulfate)	985.8	E866.4	—	E950.9	E962.1	E980.9
diagnostic agent	977.8	E858.8	E947.8	E950.4	E962.0	E980.4
pesticide	985.8	E863.4	—	E950.6	E962.1	E980.7
rodenticide	985.8	E863.7	—	E950.6	E962.1	E980.7
Barrier cream	976.3	E858.7	E946.3	E950.4	E962.0	E980.4
Battery acid or fluid	983.1	E864.1	—	E950.7	E962.1	E980.6
Bay rum	980.8	E860.8	—	E950.9	E962.1	E980.9
BCG vaccine	978.0	E858.8	E948.0	E950.4	E962.0	E980.4
Bearsfoot	988.2	E865.4	—	E950.9	E962.1	E980.9
Beclamide	966.3	E855.0	E936.3	E950.4	E962.0	E980.4
Bee (sting) (venom)	989.5	E905.3	—	E950.9	E962.1	E980.9
Belladonna (alkaloids)	971.1	E855.4	E941.1	E950.4	E962.0	E980.4
Bemegride	970.0	E854.3	E940.0	E950.4	E962.0	E980.4
Benactyzine	969.8	E855.8	E939.8	E950.3	E962.0	E980.3
Benadryl	963.0	E858.1	E933.0	E950.4	E962.0	E980.4

Substance		External Cause (E-Code)				
	Poisoning	Accident	Therapeutic Use	Suicide Attempt	Assault	Undetermined
Bendrofluazide	974.3	E858.5	E944.3	E950.4	E962.0	E980.4
Bendroflumethiazide	974.3	E858.5	E944.3	E950.4	E962.0	E980.4
Benemid	974.7	E858.5	E944.7	E950.4	E962.0	E980.4
Benethamine penicillin G	960.0	E856	E930.0	E950.4	E962.0	E980.4
Benisone	976.0	E858.7	E946.0	E950.4	E962.0	E980.4
Benoquin	976.8	E858.7	E946.8	E950.4	E962.0	E980.4
Benoxinate	968.5	E855.2	E938.5	E950.4	E962.0	E980.4
Bentonite	976.3	E858.7	E946.3	E950.4	E962.0	E980.4
Benzalkonium (chloride)	976.0	E858.7	E946.0	E950.4	E962.0	E980.4
ophthalmic preparation	976.5	E858.7	E946.5	E950.4	E962.0	E980.4
Benzamidosalicylate (calcium)	961.8	E857	E931.8	E950.4	E962.0	E980.4
Benzathine penicillin	960.0	E856	E930.0	E950.4	E962.0	E980.4
Benzcarbimine	963.1	E858.1	E933.1	E950.4	E962.0	E980.4
Benzedrex	971.2	E855.5	E941.2	E950.4	E962.0	E980.4
Benzedrine (amphetamine)	969.72	E854.2	E939.7	E950.3	E962.0	E980.3
Benzene (acetyl) (dimethyl) (methyl) (solvent) (vapor)	982.0	E862.4	—	E950.9	E962.1	E980.9
hexachloride (gamma) (insecticide) (vapor)	989.2	E863.0	—	E950.6	E962.1	E980.7
Benzethonium	976.0	E858.7	E946.0	E950.4	E962.0	E980.4
Benzhexol (chloride)	966.4	E855.0	E936.4	E950.4	E962.0	E980.4
Benzilonium	971.1	E855.4	E941.1	E950.4	E962.0	E980.4
Benzin(e) — see Ligroin						
Benziodarone	972.4	E858.3	E942.4	E950.4	E962.0	E980.4
Benzocaine	968.5	E855.2	E938.5	E950.4	E962.0	E980.4
Benzodiapin	969.4	E853.2	E939.4	E950.3	E962.0	E980.3
Benzodiazepines (tranquilizers) NEC	969.4	E853.2	E939.4	E950.3	E962.0	E980.3
Benzoic acid (with salicylic acid) (anti-infective)	976.0	E858.7	E946.0	E950.4	E962.0	E980.4
Benzoin	976.3	E858.7	E946.3	E950.4	E962.0	E980.4
Benzol (vapor)	982.0	E862.4	—	E950.9	E962.1	E980.9
Benzomorphan	965.09	E850.2	E935.2	E950.0	E962.0	E980.0
Benzonatate	975.4	E858.6	E945.4	E950.4	E962.0	E980.4
Benzothiadiazides	974.3	E858.5	E944.3	E950.4	E962.0	E980.4
Benzoylpas	961.8	E857	E931.8	E950.4	E962.0	E980.4
Benzperidol	969.5	E853.8	E939.5	E950.3	E962.0	E980.3
Benzphetamine	977.0	E858.8	E947.0	E950.4	E962.0	E980.4
Benzpyrinium	971.0	E855.3	E941.0	E950.4	E962.0	E980.4
Benzquinamide	963.0	E858.1	E933.0	E950.4	E962.0	E980.4
Benzthiazide	974.3	E858.5	E944.3	E950.4	E962.0	E980.4
Benztropine	971.1	E855.4	E941.1	E950.4	E962.0	E980.4
Benzyl						
acetate	982.8	E862.4	—	E950.9	E962.1	E980.9
benzoate (anti-infective)	976.0	E858.7	E946.0	E950.4	E962.0	E980.4
morphine	965.09	E850.2	E935.2	E950.0	E962.0	E980.0
penicillin	960.0	E856	E930.0	E950.4	E962.0	E980.4
Bephenium hydroxynapthoate	961.6	E857	E931.6	E950.4	E962.0	E980.4
Bergamot oil	989.89	E866.8	—	E950.9	E962.1	E980.9
Berries, poisonous	988.2	E865.3	—	E950.9	E962.1	E980.9
Beryllium (compounds) (fumes)	985.3	E866.4	—	E950.9	E962.1	E980.9
Beta-carotene	976.3	E858.7	E946.3	E950.4	E962.0	E980.4
Beta-Chlor	967.1	E852.0	E937.1	E950.2	E962.0	E980.2
Betamethasone	962.0	E858.0	E932.0	E950.4	E962.0	E980.4
topical	976.0	E858.7	E946.0	E950.4	E962.0	E980.4
Betazole	977.8	E858.8	E947.8	E950.4	E962.0	E980.4
Bethanechol	971.0	E855.3	E941.0	E950.4	E962.0	E980.4
Bethanidine	972.6	E858.3	E942.6	E950.4	E962.0	E980.4
Betula oil	976.3	E858.7	E946.3	E950.4	E962.0	E980.4
Bhang	969.6	E854.1	E939.6	E950.3	E962.0	E980.3
Bialamicol	961.5	E857	E931.5	E950.4	E962.0	E980.4
Bichloride of mercury — see Mercury, chloride						
Bichromates (calcium) (crystals) (potassium) (sodium)	983.9	E864.3	—	E950.7	E962.1	E980.6
fumes	987.8	E869.8	—	E952.8	E962.2	E982.8
Biguanide derivatives, oral	962.3	E858.0	E932.3	E950.4	E962.0	E980.4
Biligrafin	977.8	E858.8	E947.8	E950.4	E962.0	E980.4
Bilopaque	977.8	E858.8	E947.8	E950.4	E962.0	E980.4
Bioflavonoids	972.8	E858.3	E942.8	E950.4	E962.0	E980.4
Biological substance NEC	979.9	E858.8	E949.9	E950.4	E962.0	E980.4
Biperiden	966.4	E855.0	E936.4	E950.4	E962.0	E980.4
Bisacodyl	973.1	E858.4	E943.1	E950.4	E962.0	E980.4
Bishydroxycoumarin	964.2	E858.2	E934.2	E950.4	E962.0	E980.4

Nontherapeutic use substance

Subterms under main terms may continue to next column or page

	Poisoning	Accident	Therapeutic Use	Suicide Attempt	Assault	Undetermined
Bismarsen	961.1	E857	E931.1	E950.4	E962.0	E980.4
Bismuth (compounds)						
NEC	985.8	E866.4	—	E950.9	E962.1	E980.9
anti-infectives	961.2	E857	E931.2	E950.4	E962.0	E980.4
subcarbonate	973.5	E858.4	E943.5	E950.4	E962.0	E980.4
sulfarsphenamine	961.1	E857	E931.1	E950.4	E962.0	E980.4
Bisphosphonates						
intravenous	963.1	E858.1	E933.7	E950.4	E962.0	E980.4
oral	963.1	E858.1	E933.6	E950.4	E962.0	E980.4
Bithionol	961.6	E857	E931.6	E950.4	E962.0	E980.4
Bitter almond oil	989.0	E866.8	—	E950.9	E962.1	E980.9
Bittersweet	988.2	E865.4	—	E950.9	E962.1	E930.9
Black						
flag	989.4	E863.4	—	E950.6	E962.1	E980.7
henbane	988.2	E865.4	—	E950.9	E962.1	E980.9
leaf (40)	989.4	E863.4	—	E950.6	E962.1	E980.7
widow spider (bite)	989.5	E905.1	—	E950.9	E962.1	E980.9
antivenin	979.9	E858.8	E949.9	E950.4	E962.0	E980.4
Blast furnace gas (carbon monoxide from)	986	E868.8	—	E952.1	E962.2	E982.1
Bleaching solutions	983.9	E864.3	—	E950.7	E962.1	E980.6
Bleach NEC	983.9	E864.3	—	E950.7	E962.1	E980.6
Bleomycin (sulfate)	960.7	E856	E930.7	E950.4	E962.0	E980.4
Blockain	968.9	E855.2	E938.9	E950.4	E962.0	E980.4
infiltration (subcutaneous)	968.5	E855.2	E938.5	E950.4	E962.0	E980.4
nerve block (peripheral) (plexus)	968.6	E855.2	E938.6	E950.4	E962.0	E980.4
topical (surface)	968.5	E855.2	E938.5	E950.4	E962.0	E980.4
Blood (derivatives) (natural) (plasma) (whole)	964.7	E858.2	E934.7	E950.4	E962.0	E980.4
affecting agent	964.9	E858.2	E934.9	E950.4	E962.0	E980.4
specified NEC	964.8	E858.2	E934.8	E950.4	E962.0	E980.4
substitute (macromolecular)	964.8	E858.2	E934.8	E950.4	E962.0	E980.4
Blue velvet	965.09	E850.2	E935.2	E950.0	E962.0	E980.0
Bone meal	989.89	E866.5	—	E950.9	E962.1	E980.9
Bonine	963.0	E858.1	E933.0	E950.4	E962.0	E980.4
Boracic acid	976.0	E858.7	E946.0	E950.4	E962.0	E980.4
ENT agent	976.6	E858.7	E946.6	E950.4	E962.0	E980.4
ophthalmic preparation	976.5	E858.7	E946.5	E950.4	E962.0	E980.4
Borate (cleanser) (sodium)	989.6	E861.3	—	E950.9	E962.1	E980.9
Borax (cleanser)	989.6	E861.3	—	E950.9	E962.1	E980.9
Boric acid	976.0	E858.7	E946.0	E950.4	E962.0	E980.4
ENT agent	976.6	E858.7	E946.6	E950.4	E962.0	E980.4
ophthalmic preparation	976.5	E858.7	E946.5	E950.4	E962.0	E980.4
Boron hydride NEC	989.89	E866.8	—	E950.9	E962.1	E980.9
fumes or gas	987.8	E869.8	—	E952.8	E962.2	E982.8
Botox	975.3	E858.6	E945.3	E950.4	E962.0	E980.4
Brake fluid vapor	987.8	E869.8	—	E952.8	E962.2	E982.8
Brass (compounds) (fumes)	985.8	E866.4	—	E950.9	E962.1	E980.9
Brasso	981	E861.3	—	E950.9	E962.1	E980.9
Bretylium (tosylate)	972.6	E858.3	E942.6	E950.4	E962.0	E980.4
Brevital (sodium)	968.3	E855.1	E938.3	E950.4	E962.0	E980.4
British antilewisite	963.8	E858.1	E933.8	E950.4	E962.0	E980.4
Bromal (hydrate)	967.3	E852.2	E937.3	E950.2	E962.0	E980.2
Bromelains	963.4	E858.1	E933.4	E950.4	E962.0	E980.4
Bromides NEC	967.3	E852.2	E937.3	E950.2	E962.0	E980.2
Bromine (vapor)	987.8	E869.8	—	E952.8	E962.2	E982.8
compounds (medicinal)	967.3	E852.2	E937.3	E950.2	E962.0	E980.2
Bromisovalum	967.3	E852.2	E937.3	E950.2	E962.0	E980.2
Bromobenzyl cyanide	987.5	E869.3	—	E952.8	E962.2	E982.8
Bromodiphenhydramine	963.0	E858.1	E933.0	E950.4	E962.0	E980.4
Bromoform	967.3	E852.2	E937.3	E950.2	E962.0	E980.2
Bromophenol blue reagent	977.8	E858.8	E947.8	E950.4	E962.0	E980.4
Bromosalicylhydroxamic acid	961.8	E857	E931.8	E950.4	E962.0	E980.4
Bromo-seltzer	965.4	E850.4	E935.4	E950.0	E962.0	E980.0
Brompheniramine	963.0	E858.1	E933.0	E950.4	E962.0	E980.4
Bromural	967.3	E852.2	E937.3	E950.2	E962.0	E980.2
Brown spider (bite) (venom)	989.5	E905.1	—	E950.9	E962.1	E980.9
Brucia	988.2	E865.3	—	E950.9	E962.1	E980.9
Brucine	989.1	E863.7	—	E950.6	E962.1	E980.7
Brunswick green — see Copper						
Bruten — see Ibuprofen						
Bryonia (alba) (dioica)	988.2	E865.4	—	E950.9	E962.1	E980.9
Buclizine	969.5	E853.8	E939.5	E950.3	E962.0	E980.3
Bufferin	965.1	E850.3	E935.3	E950.0	E962.0	E980.0
Bufotenine	969.6	E854.1	E939.6	E950.3	E962.0	E980.3
Buphenine	971.2	E855.5	E941.2	E950.4	E962.0	E980.4
Bupivacaine	968.9	E855.2	E938.9	E950.4	E962.0	E980.4
infiltration (subcutaneous)	968.5	E855.2	E938.5	E950.4	E962.0	E980.4
nerve block (peripheral) (plexus)	968.6	E855.2	E938.6	E950.4	E962.0	E980.4
Busulfan	963.1	E858.1	E933.1	E950.4	E962.0	E980.4
Butabarbital (sodium)	967.0	E851	E937.0	E950.1	E962.0	E980.1
Butabarbitone	967.0	E851	E937.0	E950.1	E962.0	E980.1
Butabarpal	967.0	E851	E937.0	E950.1	E962.0	E980.1
Butacaine	968.5	E855.2	E938.5	E950.4	E962.0	E980.4
Butallylonal	967.0	E851	E937.0	E950.1	E962.0	E980.1
Butane (distributed in mobile container)	987.0	E868.0	—	E951.1	E962.2	E981.1
distributed through pipes	987.0	E867	—	E951.0	E962.2	E981.0
incomplete combustion of — see Carbon monoxide, butane						
Butanol	980.3	E860.4	—	E950.9	E962.1	E980.9
Butanone	982.8	E862.4	—	E950.9	E962.1	E980.9
Butaperazine	969.1	E853.0	E939.1	E950.3	E962.0	E980.3
Butazolidin	965.5	E850.5	E935.5	E950.0	E962.0	E980.0
Butethal	967.0	E851	E937.0	E950.1	E962.0	E980.1
Butethamate	971.1	E855.4	E941.1	E950.4	E962.0	E980.4
Buthalitone (sodium)	968.3	E855.1	E938.3	E950.4	E962.0	E980.4
Butisol (sodium)	967.0	E851	E937.0	E950.1	E962.0	E980.1
Butobarbital, butobarbitone	967.0	E851	E937.0	E950.1	E962.0	E980.1
Butriptyline	969.05	E854.0	E939.0	E950.3	E962.0	E980.3
Buttercups	988.2	E865.4	—	E950.9	E962.1	E980.9
Butter of antimony — see Antimony						
Butyl						
acetate (secondary)	982.8	E862.4	—	E950.9	E962.1	E980.9
alcohol	980.3	E860.4	—	E950.9	E962.1	E980.9
carbinol	980.8	E860.8	—	E950.9	E962.1	E980.9
carbitol	982.8	E862.4	—	E950.9	E962.1	E980.9
cellosolve	982.8	E862.4	—	E950.9	E962.1	E980.9
chloral (hydrate)	967.1	E852.0	E937.1	E950.2	E962.0	E980.2
formate	982.8	E862.4	—	E950.9	E962.1	E980.9
scopolammonium bromide	971.1	E855.4	E941.1	E950.4	E962.0	E980.4
Butyn	968.5	E855.2	E938.5	E950.4	E962.0	E980.4
Butyrophenone (-based tranquilizers)	969.2	E853.1	E939.2	E950.3	E962.0	E980.3
Cacodyl, cacodylic acid — see Arsenic						
Cactinomycin	960.7	E856	E930.7	E950.4	E962.0	E980.4
Cade oil	976.4	E858.7	E946.4	E950.4	E962.0	E980.4
Cadmium (chloride) (compounds) (dust) (fumes) (oxide)	985.5	E866.4	—	E950.9	E962.1	E980.9
sulfide (medicinal) NEC	976.4	E858.7	E946.4	E950.4	E962.0	E980.4
Caffeine	969.71	E854.2	E939.7	E950.3	E962.0	E980.3
Calabar bean	988.2	E865.4	—	E950.9	E962.1	E980.9
Caladium seguinium	988.2	E865.4	—	E950.9	E962.1	E980.9
Calamine (liniment) (lotion)	976.3	E858.7	E946.3	E950.4	E962.0	E980.4
Calciferol	963.5	E858.1	E933.5	E950.4	E962.0	E980.4
Calcium (salts) NEC	974.5	E858.5	E944.5	E950.4	E962.0	E980.4
acetylsalicylate	965.1	E850.3	E935.3	E950.0	E962.0	E980.0
benzamidosalicylate	961.8	E857	E931.8	E950.4	E962.0	E980.4
carbaspirin	965.1	E850.3	E935.3	E950.0	E962.0	E980.0
carbimide (citrated)	977.3	E858.8	E947.3	E950.4	E962.0	E980.4
carbonate (antacid)	973.0	E858.4	E943.0	E950.4	E962.0	E980.4
cyanide (citrated)	977.3	E858.8	E947.3	E950.4	E962.0	E980.4
dioctyl sulfosuccinate	973.2	E858.4	E943.2	E950.4	E962.0	E980.4
disodium edathamil	963.8	E858.1	E933.8	E950.4	E962.0	E980.4
disodium edetate	963.8	E858.1	E933.8	E950.4	E962.0	E980.4
EDTA	963.8	E858.1	E933.8	E950.4	E962.0	E980.4
hydrate, hydroxide	983.2	E864.2	—	E950.7	E962.1	E980.6
mandelate	961.9	E857	E931.9	E950.4	E962.0	E980.4
oxide	983.2	E864.2	—	E950.7	E962.1	E980.6
Calomel — see Mercury, chloride						
Caloric agents NEC	974.5	E858.5	E944.5	E950.4	E962.0	E980.4
Calusterone	963.1	E858.1	E933.1	E950.4	E962.0	E980.4
Camoquin	961.4	E857	E931.4	E950.4	E962.0	E980.4
Camphor (oil)	976.1	E858.7	E946.1	E950.4	E962.0	E980.4

Nontherapeutic use substance

▽ Subterms under main terms may continue to next column or page

		External Cause (E-Code)			
Poisoning	Accident	Therapeutic Use	Suicide Attempt	Assault	Undetermined

	Poisoning	Accident	Therapeutic Use	Suicide Attempt	Assault	Undetermined
Candeptin	976.0	E858.7	E946.0	E950.4	E962.0	E980.4
Candicidin	976.0	E858.7	E946.0	E950.4	E962.0	E980.4
Cannabinols	969.6	E854.1	E939.6	E950.3	E962.0	E980.3
Cannabis (derivatives) (indica) (sativa)	969.6	E854.1	E939.6	E950.3	E962.0	E980.3
Canned heat	980.1	E860.2	—	E950.9	E962.1	E980.9
Cantharides, cantharidin, cantharis	976.8	E858.7	E946.8	E950.4	E962.0	E980.4
Capillary agents	972.8	E858.3	E942.8	E950.4	E962.0	E980.4
Capreomycin	960.6	E856	E930.6	E950.4	E962.0	E980.4
Captodiame, captodiamine	969.5	E853.8	E939.5	E950.3	E962.0	E980.3
Caramiphen (hydrochloride)	971.1	E855.4	E941.1	E950.4	E962.0	E980.4
Carbachol	971.0	E855.3	E941.0	E950.4	E962.0	E980.4
Carbacrylamine resins	974.5	E858.5	E944.5	E950.4	E962.0	E980.4
Carbamate (sedative)	967.8	E852.8	E937.8	E950.2	E962.0	E980.2
herbicide	989.3	E863.5	—	E950.6	E962.1	E980.7
insecticide	989.3	E863.2	—	E950.6	E962.1	E980.7
Carbamazepine	966.3	E855.0	E936.3	E950.4	E962.0	E980.4
Carbamic esters	967.8	E852.8	E937.8	E950.2	E962.0	E980.2
Carbamide	974.4	E858.5	E944.4	E950.4	E962.0	E980.4
topical	976.8	E858.7	E946.8	E950.4	E962.0	E980.4
Carbamylcholine chloride	971.0	E855.3	E941.0	E950.4	E962.0	E980.4
Carbarsone	961.1	E857	E931.1	E950.4	E962.0	E980.4
Carbaryl	989.3	E863.2	—	E950.6	E962.1	E980.7
Carbaspirin	965.1	E850.3	E935.3	E950.0	E962.0	E980.0
Carbazochrome	972.8	E858.3	E942.8	E950.4	E962.0	E980.4
Carbenicillin	960.0	E856	E930.0	E950.4	E962.0	E980.4
Carbenoxolone	973.8	E858.4	E943.8	E950.4	E962.0	E980.4
Carbetapentane	975.4	E858.6	E945.4	E950.4	E962.0	E980.4
Carbimazole	962.8	E858.0	E932.8	E950.4	E962.0	E980.4
Carbinol	980.1	E860.2	—	E950.9	E962.1	E980.9
Carbinoxamine	963.0	E858.1	E933.0	E950.4	E962.0	E980.4
Carbitol	982.8	E862.4	—	E950.9	E962.1	E980.9
Carbocaine	968.9	E855.2	E938.9	E950.4	E962.0	E980.4
infiltration (subcutaneous)	968.5	E855.2	E938.5	E950.4	E962.0	E980.4
nerve block (peripheral) (plexus)	968.6	E855.2	E938.6	E950.4	E962.0	E980.4
topical (surface)	968.5	E855.2	E938.5	E950.4	E962.0	E980.4
Carbol-fuchsin solution	976.0	E858.7	E946.0	E950.4	E962.0	E980.4
Carbolic acid — see also Phenol	983.0	E864.0	—	E950.7	E962.1	E980.6
Carbomycin	960.8	E856	E930.8	E950.4	E962.0	E980.4
Carbon						
bisulfide (liquid) (vapor)	982.2	E862.4	—	E950.9	E962.1	E980.9
dioxide (gas)	987.8	E869.8	—	E952.8	E962.2	E982.8
disulfide (liquid) (vapor)	982.2	E862.4	—	E950.9	E962.1	E980.9
monoxide (from incomplete combustion of) (in)						
NEC	986	E868.9	—	E952.1	E962.2	E982.1
blast furnace gas	986	E868.8	—	E952.1	E962.2	E982.1
butane (distributed in mobile container)	986	E868.0	—	E951.1	E962.2	E981.1
distributed through pipes	986	E867	—	E951.0	E962.2	E981.0
charcoal fumes	986	E868.3	—	E952.1	E962.2	E982.1
coal						
gas (piped)	986	E867	—	E951.0	E962.2	E981.0
solid (in domestic stoves, fireplaces)	986	E868.3	—	E952.1	E962.2	E982.1
coke (in domestic stoves, fireplaces)	986	E868.3	—	E952.1	E962.2	E982.1
exhaust gas (motor) not in transit	986	E868.2	—	E952.0	E962.2	E982.0
combustion engine, any not in watercraft	986	E868.2	—	E952.0	E962.2	E982.0
farm tractor, not in transit	986	E868.2	—	E952.0	E962.2	E982.0
gas engine	986	E868.2	—	E952.0	E962.2	E982.0
motor pump	986	E868.2	—	E952.0	E962.2	E982.0
motor vehicle, not in transit	986	E868.2	—	E952.0	E962.2	E982.0
fuel (in domestic use)	986	E868.3	—	E952.1	E962.2	E982.1
gas (piped)	986	E867	—	E951.0	E962.2	E981.0
in mobile container	986	E868.0	—	E951.1	E962.2	E981.1
utility	986	E868.1	—	E951.8	E962.2	E981.1
in mobile container	986	E868.0	—	E951.1	E962.2	E981.1
piped (natural)	986	E867	—	E951.0	E962.2	E981.0
illuminating gas	986	E868.1	—	E951.8	E962.2	E981.8

	Poisoning	Accident	Therapeutic Use	Suicide Attempt	Assault	Undetermined
Carbon — *continued*						
monoxide — *continued*						
industrial fuels or gases, any	986	E868.8	—	E952.1	E962.2	E982.1
kerosene (in domestic stoves, fireplaces)	986	E868.3	—	E952.1	E962.2	E982.1
kiln gas or vapor	986	E868.8	—	E952.1	E962.2	E982.1
motor exhaust gas, not in transit	986	E868.2	—	E952.0	E962.2	E982.0
piped gas (manufactured) (natural)	986	E867	—	E951.0	E962.2	E981.0
producer gas	986	E868.8	—	E952.1	E962.2	E982.1
propane (distributed in mobile container)	986	E868.0	—	E951.1	E962.2	E981.1
distributed through pipes	986	E867	—	E951.0	E962.2	E981.0
specified source NEC	986	E868.8	—	E952.1	E962.2	E982.1
stove gas	986	E868.1	—	E951.8	E962.2	E981.8
piped	986	E867	—	E951.0	E962.2	E981.0
utility gas	986	E868.1	—	E951.8	E962.2	E981.8
piped	986	E867	—	E951.0	E962.2	E981.0
water gas	986	E868.1	—	E951.8	E962.2	E981.8
wood (in domestic stoves, fireplaces)	986	E868.3	—	E952.1	E962.2	E982.1
tetrachloride (vapor) NEC	987.8	E869.8	—	E952.8	E962.2	E982.8
liquid (cleansing agent) NEC	982.1	E861.3	—	E950.9	E962.1	E980.9
solvent	982.1	E862.4	—	E950.9	E962.1	E980.9
Carbonic acid (gas)	987.8	E869.8	—	E952.8	E962.2	E982.8
anhydrase inhibitors	974.2	E858.5	E944.2	E950.4	E962.0	E980.4
Carbowax	976.3	E858.7	E946.3	E950.4	E962.0	E980.4
Carbrital	967.0	E851	E937.0	E950.1	E962.0	E980.1
Carbromal (derivatives)	967.3	E852.2	E937.3	E950.2	E962.0	E980.2
Cardiac						
depressants	972.0	E858.3	E942.0	E950.4	E962.0	E980.4
rhythm regulators	972.0	E858.3	E942.0	E950.4	E962.0	E980.4
Cardiografin	977.8	E858.8	E947.8	E950.4	E962.0	E980.4
Cardio-green	977.8	E858.8	E947.8	E950.4	E962.0	E980.4
Cardiotonic glycosides	972.1	E858.3	E942.1	E950.4	E962.0	E980.4
Cardiovascular agents						
NEC	972.9	E858.3	E942.9	E950.4	E962.0	E980.4
Cardrase	974.2	E858.5	E944.2	E950.4	E962.0	E980.4
Carfusin	976.0	E858.7	E946.0	E950.4	E962.0	E980.4
Carisoprodol	968.0	E855.1	E938.0	E950.4	E962.0	E980.4
Carmustine	963.1	E858.1	E933.1	E950.4	E962.0	E980.4
Carotene	963.5	E858.1	E933.5	E950.4	E962.0	E980.4
Carphenazine (maleate)	969.1	E853.0	E939.1	E950.3	E962.0	E980.3
Carter's Little Pills	973.1	E858.4	E943.1	E950.4	E962.0	E980.4
Cascara (sagrada)	973.1	E858.4	E943.1	E950.4	E962.0	E980.4
Cassava	988.2	E865.4	—	E950.9	E962.1	E980.9
Castellani's paint	976.0	E858.7	E946.0	E950.4	E962.0	E980.4
Castor						
bean	988.2	E865.3	—	E950.9	E962.1	E980.9
oil	973.1	E858.4	E943.1	E950.4	E962.0	E980.4
Caterpillar (sting)	989.5	E905.5	—	E950.9	E962.1	E980.9
Catha (edulis)	970.89	E854.3	E940.8	E950.4	E962.0	E980.4
Cathartics NEC	973.3	E858.4	E943.3	E950.4	E962.0	E980.4
contact	973.1	E858.4	E943.1	E950.4	E962.0	E980.4
emollient	973.2	E858.4	E943.2	E950.4	E962.0	E980.4
intestinal irritants	973.1	E858.4	E943.1	E950.4	E962.0	E980.4
saline	973.3	E858.4	E943.3	E950.4	E962.0	E980.4
Cathomycin	960.8	E856	E930.8	E950.4	E962.0	E980.4
Caustic(s)	983.9	E864.4	—	E950.7	E962.1	E980.6
alkali	983.2	E864.2	—	E950.7	E962.1	E980.6
hydroxide	983.2	E864.2	—	E950.7	E962.1	E980.6
potash	983.2	E864.2	—	E950.7	E962.1	E980.6
soda	983.2	E864.2	—	E950.7	E962.1	E980.6
specified NEC	983.9	E864.3	—	E950.7	E962.1	E980.6
Ceepryn	976.0	E858.7	E946.0	E950.4	E962.0	E980.4
ENT agent	976.6	E858.7	E946.6	E950.4	E962.0	E980.4
lozenges	976.6	E858.7	E946.6	E950.4	E962.0	E980.4
Celestone	962.0	E858.0	E932.0	E950.4	E962.0	E980.4
topical	976.0	E858.7	E946.0	E950.4	E962.0	E980.4
Cellosolve	982.8	E862.4	—	E950.9	E962.1	E980.9
Cell stimulants and proliferants	976.8	E858.7	E946.8	E950.4	E962.0	E980.4
Cellulose derivatives, cathartic	973.3	E858.4	E943.3	E950.4	E962.0	E980.4
nitrates (topical)	976.3	E858.7	E946.3	E950.4	E962.0	E980.4
Centipede (bite)	989.5	E905.4	—	E950.9	E962.1	E980.9
Central nervous system						
depressants	968.4	E855.1	E938.4	E950.4	E962.0	E980.4

Nontherapeutic use substance

▽ Subterms under main terms may continue to next column or page

	Poisoning	Accident	Therapeutic Use	Suicide Attempt	Assault	Undetermined
Central nervous system —						
continued						
depressants — *continued*						
anesthetic (general)						
NEC	968.4	E855.1	E938.4	E950.4	E962.0	E980.4
gases NEC	968.2	E855.1	E938.2	E950.4	E962.0	E980.4
intravenous	968.3	E855.1	E938.3	E950.4	E962.0	E980.4
barbiturates	967.0	E851	E937.0	E950.1	E962.0	E980.1
bromides	967.3	E852.2	E937.3	E950.2	E962.0	E980.2
cannabis sativa	969.6	E854.1	E939.6	E950.3	E962.0	E980.3
chloral hydrate	967.1	E852.0	E937.1	E950.2	E962.0	E980.2
hallucinogenics	969.6	E854.1	E939.6	E950.3	E962.0	E980.3
hypnotics	967.9	E852.9	E937.9	E950.2	E962.0	E980.2
specified NEC	967.8	E852.8	E937.8	E950.2	E962.0	E980.2
muscle relaxants	968.0	E855.1	E938.0	E950.4	E962.0	E980.4
paraldehyde	967.2	E852.1	E937.2	E950.2	E962.0	E980.2
sedatives	967.9	E852.9	E937.9	E950.2	E962.0	E980.2
mixed NEC	967.6	E852.5	E937.6	E950.2	E962.0	E980.2
specified NEC	967.8	E852.8	E937.8	E950.2	E962.0	E980.2
muscle-tone depressants	968.0	E855.1	E938.0	E950.4	E962.0	E980.4
stimulants	970.9	E854.3	E940.9	E950.4	E962.0	E980.4
amphetamines	969.72	E854.2	E939.7	E950.3	E962.0	E980.3
analeptics	970.0	E854.3	E940.0	E950.4	E962.0	E980.4
antidepressants	969.00	E854.0	E939.0	E950.3	E962.0	E980.3
opiate antagonists	970.1	E854.3	E940.0	E950.4	E962.0	E980.4
specified NEC	970.89	E854.3	E940.8	E950.4	E962.0	E980.4
Cephalexin	960.5	E856	E930.5	E950.4	E962.0	E980.4
Cephaloglycin	960.5	E856	E930.5	E950.4	E962.0	E980.4
Cephaloridine	960.5	E856	E930.5	E950.4	E962.0	E980.4
Cephalosporins NEC	960.5	E856	E930.5	E950.4	E962.0	E980.4
N (adicillin)	960.0	E856	E930.0	E950.4	E962.0	E980.4
Cephalothin (sodium)	960.5	E856	E930.5	E950.4	E962.0	E980.4
Cerbera (odallam)	988.2	E865.4	—	E950.9	E962.1	E980.9
Cerberin	972.1	E858.3	E942.1	E950.4	E962.0	E980.4
Cerebral stimulants	970.9	E854.3	E940.9	E950.4	E962.0	E980.4
psychotherapeutic	969.79	E854.2	E939.7	E950.3	E962.0	E980.3
specified NEC	970.89	E854.3	E940.8	E950.4	E962.0	E980.4
Cetalkonium (chloride)	976.0	E858.7	E946.0	E950.4	E962.0	E980.4
Cetoxime	963.0	E858.1	E933.0	E950.4	E962.0	E980.4
Cetrimide	976.2	E858.7	E946.2	E950.4	E962.0	E980.4
Cetylpyridinium	976.0	E858.7	E946.0	E950.4	E962.0	E980.4
ENT agent	976.6	E858.7	E946.6	E950.4	E962.0	E980.4
lozenges	976.6	E858.7	E946.6	E950.4	E962.0	E980.4
Cevadilla — see Sabadilla						
Cevitamic acid	963.5	E858.1	E933.5	E950.4	E962.0	E980.4
Chalk, precipitated	973.0	E858.4	E943.0	E950.4	E962.0	E980.4
Charcoal						
fumes (carbon monoxide)	986	E868.3	—	E952.1	E962.2	E982.1
industrial	986	E868.8	—	E952.1	E962.2	E982.1
medicinal (activated)	973.0	E858.4	E943.0	E950.4	E962.0	E980.4
Chelating agents NEC	977.2	E858.8	E947.2	E950.4	E962.0	E980.4
Chelidonium majus	988.2	E865.4	—	E950.9	E962.1	E980.9
Chemical substance	989.9	E866.9	—	E950.9	E962.1	E980.9
specified NEC	989.89	E866.8	—	E950.9	E962.1	E980.9
Chemotherapy, antineoplastic	963.1	E858.1	E933.1	E950.4	E962.0	E980.4
Chenopodium (oil)	961.6	E857	E931.6	E950.4	E962.0	E980.4
Cherry laurel	988.2	E865.4	—	E950.9	E962.1	E980.9
Chiniofon	961.3	E857	E931.3	E950.4	E962.0	E980.4
Chlophedianol	975.4	E858.6	E945.4	E950.4	E962.0	E980.4
Chloral (betaine) (formamide) (hydrate)	967.1	E852.0	E937.1	E950.2	E962.0	E980.2
Chloralamide	967.1	E852.0	E937.1	E950.2	E962.0	E980.2
Chlorambucil	963.1	E858.1	E933.1	E950.4	E962.0	E980.4
Chloramphenicol	960.2	E856	E930.2	E950.4	E962.0	E980.4
ENT agent	976.6	E858.7	E946.6	E950.4	E962.0	E980.4
ophthalmic preparation	976.5	E858.7	E946.5	E950.4	E962.0	E980.4
topical NEC	976.0	E858.7	E946.0	E950.4	E962.0	E980.4
Chlorate(s) (potassium) (sodium) NEC	983.9	E864.3	—	E950.7	E962.1	E980.6
herbicides	989.4	E863.5	—	E950.6	E962.1	E980.7
Chlorcyclizine	963.0	E858.1	E933.0	E950.4	E962.0	E980.4
Chlordan(e) (dust)	989.2	E863.0	—	E950.6	E962.1	E980.7
Chlordantoin	976.0	E858.7	E946.0	E950.4	E962.0	E980.4
Chlordiazepoxide	969.4	E853.2	E939.4	E950.3	E962.0	E980.3
Chloresium	976.8	E858.7	E946.8	E950.4	E962.0	E980.4
Chlorethiazol	967.1	E852.0	E937.1	E950.2	E962.0	E980.2
Chlorethyl — *see* Ethyl, chloride						
Chloretone	967.1	E852.0	E937.1	E950.2	E962.0	E980.2
Chlorex	982.3	E862.4	—	E950.9	E962.1	E980.9

	Poisoning	Accident	Therapeutic Use	Suicide Attempt	Assault	Undetermined
Chlorhexadol	967.1	E852.0	E937.1	E950.2	E962.0	E980.2
Chlorhexidine (hydrochloride)	976.0	E858.7	E946.0	E950.4	E962.0	E980.4
Chlorhydroxyquinolin	976.0	E858.7	E946.0	E950.4	E962.0	E980.4
Chloride of lime (bleach)	983.9	E864.3	—	E950.7	E962.1	E980.6
Chlorinated						
camphene	989.2	E863.0	—	E950.6	E962.1	E980.7
diphenyl	989.89	E866.8	—	E950.9	E962.1	E980.9
hydrocarbons NEC	989.2	E863.0	—	E950.6	E962.1	E980.7
solvent	982.3	E862.4	—	E950.9	E962.1	E980.9
lime (bleach)	983.9	E864.3	—	E950.7	E962.1	E980.6
naphthalene — see Naphthalene						
pesticides NEC	989.2	E863.0	—	E950.6	E962.1	E980.7
soda — see Sodium, hypochlorite						
Chlorine (fumes) (gas)	987.6	E869.8	—	E952.8	E962.2	E982.8
bleach	983.9	E864.3	—	E950.7	E962.1	E980.6
compounds NEC	983.9	E864.3	—	E950.7	E962.1	E980.6
disinfectant	983.9	E861.4	—	E950.7	E962.1	E980.6
releasing agents NEC	983.9	E864.3	—	E950.7	E962.1	E980.6
Chlorisondamine	972.3	E858.3	E942.3	E950.4	E962.0	E980.4
Chlormadinone	962.2	E858.0	E932.2	E950.4	E962.0	E980.4
Chlormerodrin	974.0	E858.5	E944.0	E950.4	E962.0	E980.4
Chlormethiazole	967.1	E852.0	E937.1	E950.2	E962.0	E980.2
Chlormethylenecycline	960.4	E856	E930.4	E950.4	E962.0	E980.4
Chlormezanone	969.5	E853.8	E939.5	E950.3	E962.0	E980.3
Chloroacetophenone	987.5	E869.3	—	E952.8	E962.2	E982.8
Chloroaniline	983.0	E864.0	—	E950.7	E962.1	E980.6
Chlorobenzene, chlorobenzol	982.0	E862.4	—	E950.9	E962.1	E980.9
Chlorobutanol	967.1	E852.0	E937.1	E950.2	E962.0	E980.2
Chlorodinitrobenzene	983.0	E864.0	—	E950.7	E962.1	E980.6
dust or vapor	987.8	E869.8	—	E952.8	E962.2	E982.8
Chloroethane — see Ethyl, chloride						
Chloroform (fumes) (vapor)	987.8	E869.8	—	E952.8	E962.2	E982.8
anesthetic (gas)	968.2	E855.1	E938.2	E950.4	E962.0	E980.4
liquid NEC	968.4	E855.1	E938.4	E950.4	E962.0	E980.4
solvent	982.3	E862.4	—	E950.9	E962.1	E980.9
Chloroguanide	961.4	E857	E931.4	E950.4	E962.0	E980.4
Chloromycetin	960.2	E856	E930.2	E950.4	E962.0	E980.4
ENT agent	976.6	E858.7	E946.6	E950.4	E962.0	E980.4
ophthalmic preparation	976.5	E858.7	E946.5	E950.4	E962.0	E980.4
otic solution	976.6	E858.7	E946.6	E950.4	E962.0	E980.4
topical NEC	976.0	E858.7	E946.0	E950.4	E962.0	E980.4
Chloronitrobenzene	983.0	E864.0	—	E950.7	E962.1	E980.6
dust or vapor	987.8	E869.8	—	E952.8	E962.2	E982.8
Chlorophenol	983.0	E864.0	—	E950.7	E962.1	E980.6
Chlorophenothane	989.2	E863.0	—	E950.6	E962.1	E980.7
Chlorophyll (derivatives)	976.8	E858.7	E946.8	E950.4	E962.0	E980.4
Chloropicrin (fumes)	987.8	E869.8	—	E952.8	E962.2	E982.8
fumigant	989.4	E863.8	—	E950.6	E962.1	E980.7
fungicide	989.4	E863.6	—	E950.6	E962.1	E980.7
pesticide (fumes)	989.4	E863.4	—	E950.6	E962.1	E980.7
Chloroprocaine	968.9	E855.2	E938.9	E950.4	E962.0	E980.4
infiltration (subcutaneous)	968.5	E855.2	E938.5	E950.4	E962.0	E980.4
nerve block (peripheral) (plexus)	968.6	E855.2	E938.6	E950.4	E962.0	E980.4
Chloroptic	976.5	E858.7	E946.5	E950.4	E962.0	E980.4
Chloropurine	963.1	E858.1	E933.1	E950.4	E962.0	E980.4
Chloroquine (hydrochloride) (phosphate)	961.4	E857	E931.4	E950.4	E962.0	E980.4
Chlorothen	963.0	E858.1	E933.0	E950.4	E962.0	E980.4
Chlorothiazide	974.3	E858.5	E944.3	E950.4	E962.0	E980.4
Chlorotrianisene	962.2	E858.0	E932.2	E950.4	E962.0	E980.4
Chlorovinyldichloroarsine	985.1	E866.3	—	E950.8	E962.1	E980.8
Chloroxylenol	976.0	E858.7	E946.0	E950.4	E962.0	E980.4
Chlorphenesin (carbamate)	968.0	E855.1	E938.0	E950.4	E962.0	E980.4
topical (antifungal)	976.0	E858.7	E946.0	E950.4	E962.0	E980.4
Chlorpheniramine	963.0	E858.1	E933.0	E950.4	E962.0	E980.4
Chlorphenoxamine	966.4	E855.0	E936.4	E950.4	E962.0	E980.4
Chlorphentermine	977.0	E858.8	E947.0	E950.4	E962.0	E980.4
Chlorproguanil	961.4	E857	E931.4	E950.4	E962.0	E980.4
Chlorpromazine	969.1	E853.0	E939.1	E950.3	E962.0	E980.3
Chlorpropamide	962.3	E858.0	E932.3	E950.4	E962.0	E980.4
Chlorprothixene	969.3	E853.8	E939.3	E950.3	E962.0	E980.3
Chlorquinaldol	976.0	E858.7	E946.0	E950.4	E962.0	E980.4

Nontherapeutic use substance

▽ Subterms under main terms may continue to next column or page

	Poisoning	Accident	Therapeutic Use	Suicide Attempt	Assault	Undetermined
			External Cause (E-Code)			
Chlortetracycline	960.4	E856	E930.4	E950.4	E962.0	E980.4
Chlorthalidone	974.4	E858.5	E944.4	E950.4	E962.0	E980.4
Chlortrianisene	962.2	E858.0	E932.2	E950.4	E962.0	E980.4
Chlor-Trimeton	963.0	E858.1	E933.0	E950.4	E962.0	E980.4
Chlorzoxazone	968.0	E855.1	E938.0	E950.4	E962.0	E980.4
Choke damp	987.8	E869.8	—	E952.8	E962.2	E982.8
Cholebrine	977.8	E858.8	E947.8	E950.4	E962.0	E980.4
Cholera vaccine	978.2	E858.8	E948.2	E950.4	E962.0	E980.4
Cholesterol-lowering agents	972.2	E858.3	E942.2	E950.4	E962.0	E980.4
Cholestyramine (resin)	972.2	E858.3	E942.2	E950.4	E962.0	E980.4
Cholic acid	973.4	E858.4	E943.4	E950.4	E962.0	E980.4
Choline						
dihydrogen citrate	977.1	E858.8	E947.1	E950.4	E962.0	E980.4
salicylate	965.1	E850.3	E935.3	E950.0	E962.0	E980.0
theophyllinate	974.1	E858.5	E944.1	E950.4	E962.0	E980.4
Cholinergics	971.0	E855.3	E941.0	E950.4	E962.0	E980.4
Cholografin	977.8	E858.8	E947.8	E950.4	E962.0	E980.4
Chorionic gonadotropin	962.4	E858.0	E932.4	E950.4	E962.0	E980.4
Chromates	983.9	E864.3	—	E950.7	E962.1	E980.6
dust or mist	987.8	E869.8	—	E952.8	E962.2	E982.8
lead	984.0	E866.0	—	E950.9	E962.1	E980.9
paint	984.0	E861.5	—	E950.9	E962.1	E980.9
Chromic acid	983.9	E864.3	—	E950.7	E962.1	E980.6
dust or mist	987.8	E869.8	—	E952.8	E962.2	E982.8
Chromium	985.6	E866.4	—	E950.9	E962.1	E980.9
compounds — see Chromates						
Chromonar	972.4	E858.3	E942.4	E950.4	E962.0	E980.4
Chromyl chloride	983.9	E864.3	—	E950.7	E962.1	E980.6
Chrysarobin (ointment)	976.4	E858.7	E946.4	E950.4	E962.0	E980.4
Chrysazin	973.1	E858.4	E943.1	E950.4	E962.0	E980.4
Chymar	963.4	E858.1	E933.4	E950.4	E962.0	E980.4
ophthalmic preparation	976.5	E858.7	E946.5	E950.4	E962.0	E980.4
Chymotrypsin	963.4	E858.1	E933.4	E950.4	E962.0	E980.4
ophthalmic preparation	976.5	E858.7	E946.5	E950.4	E962.0	E980.4
Cicuta maculata or virosa	988.2	E865.4	—	E950.9	E962.1	E980.9
Cigarette lighter fluid	981	E862.1	—	E950.9	E962.1	E980.9
Cinchocaine (spinal)	968.7	E855.2	E938.7	E950.4	E962.0	E980.4
topical (surface)	968.5	E855.2	E938.5	E950.4	E962.0	E980.4
Cinchona	961.4	E857	E931.4	E950.4	E962.0	E980.4
Cinchonine alkaloids	961.4	E857	E931.4	E950.4	E962.0	E980.4
Cinchophen	974.7	E858.5	E944.7	E950.4	E962.0	E980.4
Cinnarizine	963.0	E858.1	E933.0	E950.4	E962.0	E980.4
Citanest	968.9	E855.2	E938.9	E950.4	E962.0	E980.4
infiltration (subcutaneous)	968.5	E855.2	E938.5	E950.4	E962.0	E980.4
nerve block (peripheral) (plexus)	968.6	E855.2	E938.6	E950.4	E962.0	E980.4
Citric acid	989.89	E866.8	—	E950.9	E962.1	E980.9
Citrovorum factor	964.1	E858.2	E934.1	E950.4	E962.0	E980.4
Claviceps purpurea	988.2	E865.4	—	E950.9	E962.1	E980.9
Cleaner, cleansing agent, type not specified	989.89	E861.9	—	E950.9	E962.1	E980.9
of paint or varnish	982.8	E862.9	—	E950.9	E962.1	E980.9
specified type NEC	989.89	E861.3	—	E950.9	E962.1	E980.9
Clematis vitalba	988.2	E865.4	—	E950.9	E962.1	E980.9
Clemizole	963.0	E858.1	E933.0	E950.4	E962.0	E980.4
penicillin	960.0	E856	E930.0	E950.4	E962.0	E980.4
Clidinium	971.1	E855.4	E941.1	E950.4	E962.0	E980.4
Clindamycin	960.8	E856	E930.8	E950.4	E962.0	E980.4
Cliradon	965.09	E850.2	E935.2	E950.0	E962.0	E980.0
Clocortolone	962.0	E858.0	E932.0	E950.4	E962.0	E980.4
Clofedanol	975.4	E858.6	E945.4	E950.4	E962.0	E980.4
Clofibrate	972.2	E858.3	E942.2	E950.4	E962.0	E980.4
Clomethiazole	967.1	E852.0	E937.1	E950.2	E962.0	E980.2
Clomiphene	977.8	E858.8	E947.8	E950.4	E962.0	E980.4
Clonazepam	969.4	E853.2	E939.4	E950.3	E962.0	E980.3
Clonidine	972.6	E858.3	E942.6	E950.4	E962.0	E980.4
Clopamide	974.3	E858.5	E944.3	E950.4	E962.0	E980.4
Clorazepate	969.4	E853.2	E939.4	E950.3	E962.0	E980.3
Clorexolone	974.4	E858.5	E944.4	E950.4	E962.0	E980.4
Clorox (bleach)	983.9	E864.3	—	E950.7	E962.1	E980.6
Clortermine	977.0	E858.8	E947.0	E950.4	E962.0	E980.4
Clotrimazole	976.0	E858.7	E946.0	E950.4	E962.0	E980.4
Cloxacillin	960.0	E856	E930.0	E950.4	E962.0	E980.4
Coagulants NEC	964.5	E858.2	E934.5	E950.4	E962.0	E980.4
Coal (carbon monoxide from) — see also Carbon, monoxide, coal						
oil — see Kerosene						

	Poisoning	Accident	Therapeutic Use	Suicide Attempt	Assault	Undetermined
			External Cause (E-Code)			
Coal — see also Carbon, monoxide, coal — continued						
tar NEC	983.0	E864.0	—	E950.7	E962.1	E980.6
fumes	987.8	E869.8	—	E952.8	E962.2	E982.8
medicinal (ointment)	976.4	E858.7	E946.4	E950.4	E962.0	E980.4
analgesics NEC	965.5	E850.5	E935.5	E950.0	E962.0	E980.0
naphtha (solvent)	981	E862.0	—	E950.9	E962.1	E980.9
Cobalt (fumes) (industrial)	985.8	E866.4	—	E950.9	E962.1	E980.9
Cobra (venom)	989.5	E905.0	—	E950.9	E962.1	E980.9
Coca (leaf)	970.81	E854.3	E940.8	E950.4	E962.0	E980.4
Cocaine (hydrochloride) (salt)	970.81	E854.3	E940.8	E950.4	E962.0	E980.4
topical anesthetic	968.5	E855.2	E938.5	E950.4	E962.0	E980.4
Coccidioidin	977.8	E858.8	E947.8	E950.4	E962.0	E980.4
Cocculus indicus	988.2	E865.3	—	E950.9	E962.1	E980.9
Cochineal	989.89	E866.8	—	E950.9	E962.1	E980.9
medicinal products	977.4	E858.8	E947.4	E950.4	E962.0	E980.4
Codeine	965.09	E850.2	E935.2	E950.0	E962.0	E980.0
Coffee	989.89	E866.8	—	E950.9	E962.1	E980.9
Cogentin	971.1	E855.4	E941.1	E950.4	E962.0	E980.4
Coke fumes or gas (carbon monoxide)	986	E868.3	—	E952.1	E962.2	E982.1
industrial use	986	E868.8	—	E952.1	E962.2	E982.1
Colace	973.2	E858.4	E943.2	E950.4	E962.0	E980.4
Colchicine	974.7	E858.5	E944.7	E950.4	E962.0	E980.4
Colchicum	988.2	E865.3	—	E950.9	E962.1	E980.9
Cold cream	976.3	E858.7	E946.3	E950.4	E962.0	E980.4
Colestipol	972.2	E858.3	E942.2	E950.4	E962.0	E980.4
Colistimethate	960.8	E856	E930.8	E950.4	E962.0	E980.4
Colistin	960.8	E856	E930.8	E950.4	E962.0	E980.4
Collagen	977.8	E866.8	E947.8	E950.9	E962.1	E980.9
Collagenase	976.8	E858.7	E946.8	E950.4	E962.0	E980.4
Collodion (flexible)	976.3	E858.7	E946.3	E950.4	E962.0	E980.4
Colocynth	973.1	E858.4	E943.1	E950.4	E962.0	E980.4
Coloring matter — see Dye(s)						
Combustion gas — see Carbon, monoxide						
Compazine	969.1	E853.0	E939.1	E950.3	E962.0	E980.3
Compound						
42 (warfarin)	989.4	E863.7	—	E950.6	E962.1	E980.7
269 (endrin)	989.2	E863.0	—	E950.6	E962.1	E980.7
497 (dieldrin)	989.2	E863.0	—	E950.6	E962.1	E980.7
1080 (sodium fluoroacetate)	989.4	E863.7	—	E950.6	E962.1	E980.7
3422 (parathion)	989.3	E863.1	—	E950.6	E962.1	E980.7
3911 (phorate)	989.3	E863.1	—	E950.6	E962.1	E980.7
3956 (toxaphene)	989.2	E863.0	—	E950.6	E962.1	E980.7
4049 (malathion)	989.3	E863.1	—	E950.6	E962.1	E980.7
4124 (dicapthon)	989.4	E863.4	—	E950.6	E962.1	E980.7
E (cortisone)	962.0	E858.0	E932.0	E950.4	E962.0	E980.4
F (hydrocortisone)	962.0	E858.0	E932.0	E950.4	E962.0	E980.4
Congo red	977.8	E858.8	E947.8	E950.4	E962.0	E980.4
Coniine, conine	965.7	E850.7	E935.7	E950.0	E962.0	E980.0
Conium (maculatum)	988.2	E865.4	—	E950.9	E962.1	E980.9
Conjugated estrogens (equine)	962.2	E858.0	E932.2	E950.4	E962.0	E980.4
Contac	975.6	E858.6	E945.6	E950.4	E962.0	E980.4
Contact lens solution	976.5	E858.7	E946.5	E950.4	E962.0	E980.4
Contraceptives (oral)	962.2	E858.0	E932.2	E950.4	E962.0	E980.4
vaginal	976.8	E858.7	E946.8	E950.4	E962.0	E980.4
Contrast media (roentgenographic)	977.8	E858.8	E947.8	E950.4	E962.0	E980.4
Convallaria majalis	988.2	E865.4	—	E950.9	E962.1	E980.9
Copperhead snake (bite) (venom)	989.5	E905.0	—	E950.9	E962.1	E980.9
Copper (dust) (fumes) (salts) NEC	985.8	E866.4	—	E950.9	E962.1	E980.9
arsenate, arsenite	985.1	E866.3	—	E950.8	E962.1	E980.8
insecticide	985.1	E863.4	—	E950.8	E962.1	E980.8
emetic	973.6	E858.4	E943.6	E950.4	E962.0	E980.4
fungicide	985.8	E863.6	—	E950.6	E962.1	E980.7
insecticide	985.8	E863.4	—	E950.6	E962.1	E980.7
oleate	976.0	E858.7	E946.0	E950.4	E962.0	E980.4
sulfate	983.9	E864.3	—	E950.7	E962.1	E980.6
cupric	973.6	E858.4	E943.6	E950.4	E962.0	E980.4
cuprous	983.9	E864.3	—	E950.7	E962.1	E980.6
fungicide	983.9	E863.6	—	E950.7	E962.1	E980.6
Coral (sting)	989.5	E905.6	—	E950.9	E962.1	E980.9
snake (bite) (venom)	989.5	E905.0	—	E950.9	E962.1	E980.9
Cordran	976.0	E858.7	E946.0	E950.4	E962.0	E980.4
Corn cures	976.4	E858.7	E946.4	E950.4	E962.0	E980.4
Cornhusker's lotion	976.3	E858.7	E946.3	E950.4	E962.0	E980.4

Nontherapeutic use substance

▽ Subterms under main terms may continue to next column or page

	External Cause (E-Code)							External Cause (E-Code)				
	Poisoning	Accident	Therapeutic Use	Suicide Attempt	Assault	Undeter-mined		Poisoning	Accident	Therapeutic Use	Suicide Attempt	Assault	Undeter-mined
Corn starch	976.3	E858.7	E946.3	E950.4	E962.0	E980.4	**Cupric sulfate**	973.6	E858.4	E943.6	E950.4	E962.0	E980.4
Corrosive	983.9	E864.4	—	E950.7	E962.1	E980.6	**Cuprous sulfate**	983.9	E864.3	—	E950.7	E962.1	E980.6
acids NEC	983.1	E864.1	—	E950.7	E962.1	E980.6	**Curare, curarine**	975.2	E858.6	E945.2	E950.4	E962.0	E980.4
aromatics	983.0	E864.0	—	E950.7	E962.1	E980.6	**Cyanic acid** — see Cyanide(s)						
disinfectant	983.0	E861.4	—	E950.7	E962.1	E980.6	**Cyanide(s)** (compounds) (hy-						
fumes NEC	987.9	E869.9	—	E952.9	E962.2	E982.9	drogen) (potassium) (sodi-						
specified NEC	983.9	E864.3	—	E950.7	E962.1	E980.6	um) NEC	989.0	E866.8	—	E950.9	E962.1	E980.9
sublimate — see Mercury, chloride							dust or gas (inhalation)						
Cortate	962.0	E858.0	E932.0	E950.4	E962.0	E980.4	NEC	987.7	E869.8	—	E952.8	E962.2	E982.8
Cort-Dome	962.0	E858.0	E932.0	E950.4	E962.0	E980.4	fumigant	989.0	E863.8	—	E950.6	E962.1	E980.7
ENT agent	976.6	E858.7	E946.6	E950.4	E962.0	E980.4	mercuric — see Mercury						
ophthalmic preparation	976.5	E858.7	E946.5	E950.4	E962.0	E980.4	pesticide (dust) (fumes)	989.0	E863.4	—	E950.6	E962.1	E980.7
topical NEC	976.0	E858.7	E946.0	E950.4	E962.0	E980.4	**Cyanocobalamin**	964.1	E858.2	E934.1	E950.4	E962.0	E980.4
Cortef	962.0	E858.0	E932.0	E950.4	E962.0	E980.4	**Cyanogen (chloride) (gas)**						
ENT agent	976.6	E858.7	E946.6	E950.4	E962.0	E980.4	NEC	987.8	E869.8	—	E952.8	E962.2	E982.8
ophthalmic preparation	976.5	E858.7	E946.5	E950.4	E962.0	E980.4	**Cyclaine**	968.5	E855.2	E938.5	E950.4	E962.0	E980.4
topical NEC	976.0	E858.7	E946.0	E950.4	E962.0	E980.4	**Cyclamen europaeum**	988.2	E865.4	—	E950.9	E962.1	E980.9
Corticosteroids (fluorinat-ed)	962.0	E858.0	E932.0	E950.4	E962.0	E980.4	**Cyclandelate**	972.5	E858.3	E942.5	E950.4	E962.0	E980.4
ENT agent	976.6	E858.7	E946.6	E950.4	E962.0	E980.4	**Cyclazocine**	965.09	E850.2	E935.2	E950.0	E962.0	E980.0
ophthalmic preparation	976.5	E858.7	E946.5	E950.4	E962.0	E980.4	**Cyclizine**	963.0	E858.1	E933.0	E950.4	E962.0	E980.4
topical NEC	976.0	E858.7	E946.0	E950.4	E962.0	E980.4	**Cyclobarbital, cyclobarbi-tone**	967.0	E851	E937.0	E950.1	E962.0	E980.1
Corticotropin	962.4	E858.0	E932.4	E950.4	E962.0	E980.4	**Cycloguanil**	961.4	E857	E931.4	E950.4	E962.0	E980.4
Cortisol	962.0	E858.0	E932.0	E950.4	E962.0	E980.4	**Cyclohexane**	982.0	E862.4	—	E950.9	E962.1	E980.9
ENT agent	976.6	E858.7	E946.6	E950.4	E962.0	E980.4	**Cyclohexanol**	980.8	E860.8	—	E950.9	E962.1	E980.9
ophthalmic preparation	976.5	E858.7	E946.5	E950.4	E962.0	E980.4	**Cyclohexanone**	982.8	E862.4	—	E950.9	E962.1	E980.9
topical NEC	976.0	E858.7	E946.0	E950.4	E962.0	E980.4	**Cyclomethycaine**	968.5	E855.2	E938.5	E950.4	E962.0	E980.4
Cortisone derivatives (ac-etate)	962.0	E858.0	E932.0	E950.4	E962.0	E980.4	**Cyclopentamine**	971.2	E855.5	E941.2	E950.4	E962.0	E980.4
ENT agent	976.6	E858.7	E946.6	E950.4	E962.0	E980.4	**Cyclopenthiazide**	974.3	E858.5	E944.3	E950.4	E962.0	E980.4
ophthalmic preparation	976.5	E858.7	E946.5	E950.4	E962.0	E980.4	**Cyclopentolate**	971.1	E855.4	E941.1	E950.4	E962.0	E980.4
topical NEC	976.0	E858.7	E946.0	E950.4	E962.0	E980.4	**Cyclophosphamide**	963.1	E858.1	E933.1	E950.4	E962.0	E980.4
Cortogen	962.0	E858.0	E932.0	E950.4	E962.0	E980.4	**Cyclopropane**	968.2	E855.1	E938.2	E950.4	E962.0	E980.4
ENT agent	976.6	E858.7	E946.6	E950.4	E962.0	E980.4	**Cycloserine**	960.6	E856	E930.6	E950.4	E962.0	E980.4
ophthalmic preparation	976.5	E858.7	E946.5	E950.4	E962.0	E980.4	**Cyclothiazide**	974.3	E858.5	E944.3	E950.4	E962.0	E980.4
Cortone	962.0	E858.0	E932.0	E950.4	E962.0	E980.4	**Cycrimine**	966.4	E855.0	E936.4	E950.4	E962.0	E980.4
ENT agent	976.6	E858.7	E946.6	E950.4	E962.0	E980.4	**Cymarin**	972.1	E858.3	E942.1	E950.4	E962.0	E980.4
ophthalmic preparation	976.5	E858.7	E946.5	E950.4	E962.0	E980.4	**Cyproheptadine**	963.0	E858.1	E933.0	E950.4	E962.0	E980.4
Cortril	962.0	E858.0	E932.0	E950.4	E962.0	E980.4	**Cyprolidol**	969.09	E854.0	E939.0	E950.3	E962.0	E980.3
ENT agent	976.6	E858.7	E946.6	E950.4	E962.0	E980.4	**Cytarabine**	963.1	E858.1	E933.1	E950.4	E962.0	E980.4
ophthalmic preparation	976.5	E858.7	E946.5	E950.4	E962.0	E980.4	**Cytisus**						
topical NEC	976.0	E858.7	E946.0	E950.4	E962.0	E980.4	laburnum	988.2	E865.4	—	E950.9	E962.1	E980.9
Cosmetics	989.89	E866.7	—	E950.9	E962.1	E980.9	scoparius	988.2	E865.4	—	E950.9	E962.1	E980.9
Cosyntropin	977.8	E858.8	E947.8	E950.4	E962.0	E980.4	**Cytomel**	962.7	E858.0	E932.7	E950.4	E962.0	E980.4
Cotarnine	964.5	E858.2	E934.5	E950.4	E962.0	E980.4	**Cytosine** (antineoplastic)	963.1	E858.1	E933.1	E950.4	E962.0	E980.4
Cottonseed oil	976.3	E858.7	E946.3	E950.4	E962.0	E980.4	**Cytoxan**	963.1	E858.1	E933.1	E950.4	E962.0	E980.4
Cough mixtures (antitus-sives)	975.4	E858.6	E945.4	E950.4	E962.0	E980.4	**Dacarbazine**	963.1	E858.1	E933.1	E950.4	E962.0	E980.4
containing opiates	965.09	E850.2	E935.2	E950.0	E962.0	E980.0	**Dactinomycin**	960.7	E856	E930.7	E950.4	E962.0	E980.4
expectorants	975.5	E858.6	E945.5	E950.4	E962.0	E980.4	**DADPS**	961.8	E857	E931.8	E950.4	E962.0	E980.4
Coumadin	964.2	E858.2	E934.2	E950.4	E962.0	E980.4	**Dakin's solution** (exter-nal)	976.0	E858.7	E946.0	E950.4	E962.0	E980.4
rodenticide	989.4	E863.7	—	E950.6	E962.1	E980.7	**Dalmane**	969.4	E853.2	E939.4	E950.3	E962.0	E980.3
Coumarin	964.2	E858.2	E934.2	E950.4	E962.0	E980.4	**DAM**	977.2	E858.8	E947.2	E950.4	E962.0	E980.4
Coumetarol	964.2	E858.2	E934.2	E950.4	E962.0	E980.4	**Danilone**	964.2	E858.2	E934.2	E950.4	E962.0	E980.4
Cowbane	988.2	E865.4	—	E950.9	E962.1	E980.9	**Danthron**	973.1	E858.4	E943.1	E950.4	E962.0	E980.4
Cozyme	963.5	E858.1	E933.5	E950.4	E962.0	E980.4	**Dantrolene**	975.2	E858.6	E945.2	E950.4	E962.0	E980.4
Crack	970.81	E854.3	E940.8	E950.4	E962.0	E980.4	**Daphne** (gnidium) (mez-ereum)	988.2	E865.4	—	E950.9	E962.1	E980.9
Creolin	983.0	E864.0	—	E950.7	E962.1	E980.6	berry	988.2	E865.3	—	E950.9	E962.1	E980.9
disinfectant	983.0	E861.4	—	E950.7	E962.1	E980.6	**Dapsone**	961.8	E857	E931.8	E950.4	E962.0	E980.4
Creosol (compound)	983.0	E864.0	—	E950.7	E962.1	E980.6	**Daraprim**	961.4	E857	E931.4	E950.4	E962.0	E980.4
Creosote (beechwood) (coal tar)	983.0	E864.0	—	E950.7	E962.1	E980.6	**Darnel**	988.2	E865.3	—	E950.9	E962.1	E980.9
medicinal (expectorant)	975.5	E858.6	E945.5	E950.4	E962.0	E980.4	**Darvon**	965.8	E850.8	E935.8	E950.0	E962.0	E980.0
syrup	975.5	E858.6	E945.5	E950.4	E962.0	E980.4	**Daunorubicin**	960.7	E856	E930.7	E950.4	E962.0	E980.4
Cresol	983.0	E864.0	—	E950.7	E962.1	E980.6	**DBI**	962.3	E858.0	E932.3	E950.4	E962.0	E980.4
disinfectant	983.0	E861.4	—	E950.7	E962.1	E980.6	**D-Con** (rodenticide)	989.4	E863.7	—	E950.6	E962.1	E980.7
Cresylic acid	983.0	E864.0	—	E950.7	E962.1	E980.6	**DDS**	961.8	E857	E931.8	E950.4	E962.0	E980.4
Cropropamide	965.7	E850.7	E935.7	E950.0	E962.0	E980.0	**DDT**	989.2	E863.0	—	E950.6	E962.1	E980.7
with crotethamide	970.0	E854.3	E940.0	E950.4	E962.0	E980.4	**Deadly nightshade**	988.2	E865.4	—	E950.9	E962.1	E980.9
Crotamiton	976.0	E858.7	E946.0	E950.4	E962.0	E980.4	berry	988.2	E865.3	—	E950.9	E962.1	E980.9
Crotethamide	965.7	E850.7	E935.7	E950.0	E962.0	E980.0	**Deanol**	969.79	E854.2	E939.7	E950.3	E962.0	E980.3
with cropropamide	970.0	E854.3	E940.0	E950.4	E962.0	E980.4	**Debrisoquine**	972.6	E858.3	E942.6	E950.4	E962.0	E980.4
Croton (oil)	973.1	E858.4	E943.1	E950.4	E962.0	E980.4	**Decaborane**	989.89	E866.8	—	E950.9	E962.1	E980.9
chloral	967.1	E852.0	E937.1	E950.2	E962.0	E980.2	fumes	987.8	E869.8	—	E952.8	E962.2	E982.8
Crude oil	981	E862.1	—	E950.9	E962.1	E980.9	**Decadron**	962.0	E858.0	E932.0	E950.4	E962.0	E980.4
Cryogenine	965.8	E850.8	E935.8	E950.0	E962.0	E980.0	ENT agent	976.6	E858.7	E946.6	E950.4	E962.0	E980.4
Cryolite (pesticide)	989.4	E863.4	—	E950.6	E962.1	E980.7	ophthalmic preparation	976.5	E858.7	E946.5	E950.4	E962.0	E980.4
Cryptenamine	972.6	E858.3	E942.6	E950.4	E962.0	E980.4	topical NEC	976.0	E858.7	E946.0	E950.4	E962.0	E980.4
Crystal violet	976.0	E858.7	E946.0	E950.4	E962.0	E980.4	**Decahydronaphthalene**	982.0	E862.4	—	E950.9	E962.1	E980.9
Cuckoopint	988.2	E865.4	—	E950.9	E962.1	E980.9	**Decalin**	982.0	E862.4	—	E950.9	E962.1	E980.9
Cumetharol	964.2	E858.2	E934.2	E950.4	E962.0	E980.4	**Decamethonium**	975.2	E858.6	E945.2	E950.4	E962.0	E980.4
							Decholin	973.4	E858.4	E943.4	E950.4	E962.0	E980.4
							sodium (diagnostic)	977.8	E858.8	E947.8	E950.4	E962.0	E980.4

Nontherapeutic use substance

⚥ Subterms under main terms may continue to next column or page

External Cause (E-Code)

Substance	Poisoning	Accident	Therapeutic Use	Suicide Attempt	Assault	Undeter-mined
Declomycin	960.4	E856	E930.4	E950.4	E962.0	E980.4
Deferoxamine	963.8	E858.1	E933.8	E950.4	E962.0	E980.4
Dehydrocholic acid	973.4	E858.4	E943.4	E950.4	E962.0	E980.4
Dekalin	982.0	E862.4	—	E950.9	E962.1	E980.9
Delalutin	962.2	E858.0	E932.2	E950.4	E962.0	E980.4
Delphinium	988.2	E865.3	—	E950.9	E962.1	E980.9
Deltasone	962.0	E858.0	E932.0	E950.4	E962.0	E980.4
Deltra	962.0	E858.0	E932.0	E950.4	E962.0	E980.4
Delvinal	967.0	E851	E937.0	E950.1	E962.0	E980.1
Demecarium (bromide)	971.0	E855.3	E941.0	E950.4	E962.0	E980.4
Demeclocycline	960.4	E856	E930.4	E950.4	E962.0	E980.4
Demecolcine	963.1	E858.1	E933.1	E950.4	E962.0	E980.4
Demelanizing agents	976.8	E858.7	E946.8	E950.4	E962.0	E980.4
Demerol	965.09	E850.2	E935.2	E950.0	E962.0	E980.0
Demethylchlortetracy-cline	960.4	E856	E930.4	E950.4	E962.0	E980.4
Demethyltetracycline	960.4	E856	E930.4	E950.4	E962.0	E980.4
Demeton	989.3	E863.1	—	E950.6	E962.1	E980.7
Demulcents	976.3	E858.7	E946.3	E950.4	E962.0	E980.4
Demulen	962.2	E858.0	E932.2	E950.4	E962.0	E980.4
Denatured alcohol	980.0	E860.1	—	E950.9	E962.1	E980.9
Dendrid	976.5	E858.7	E946.5	E950.4	E962.0	E980.4
Dental agents, topical	976.7	E858.7	E946.7	E950.4	E962.0	E980.4
Deodorant spray (feminine hygiene)	976.8	E858.7	E946.8	E950.4	E962.0	E980.4
Deoxyribonuclease	963.4	E858.1	E933.4	E950.4	E962.0	E980.4
Depressants						
appetite, central	977.0	E858.8	E947.0	E950.4	E962.0	E980.4
cardiac	972.0	E858.3	E942.0	E950.4	E962.0	E980.4
central nervous system (anes-thetic)	968.4	E855.1	E938.4	E950.4	E962.0	E980.4
psychotherapeutic	969.5	E853.9	E939.5	E950.3	E962.0	E980.3
Dequalinium	976.0	E858.7	E946.0	E950.4	E962.0	E980.4
Dermolate	976.2	E858.7	E946.2	E950.4	E962.0	E980.4
DES	962.2	E858.0	E932.2	E950.4	E962.0	E980.4
Desenex	976.0	E858.7	E946.0	E950.4	E962.0	E980.4
Deserpidine	972.6	E858.3	E942.6	E950.4	E962.0	E980.4
Desipramine	969.05	E854.0	E939.0	E950.3	E962.0	E980.3
Deslanoside	972.1	E858.3	E942.1	E950.4	E962.0	E980.4
Desocodeine	965.09	E850.2	E935.2	E950.0	E962.0	E980.0
Desomorphine	965.09	E850.2	E935.2	E950.0	E962.0	E980.0
Desonide	976.0	E858.7	E946.0	E950.4	E962.0	E980.4
Desoxycorticosterone derivatives	962.0	E858.0	E932.0	E950.4	E962.0	E980.4
Desoxyephedrine	969.72	E854.2	E939.7	E950.3	E962.0	E980.3
DET	969.6	E854.1	E939.6	E950.3	E962.0	E980.3
Detergents (ingested) (synthet-ic)	989.6	E861.0	—	E950.9	E962.1	E980.9
ENT agent	976.6	E858.7	E946.6	E950.4	E962.0	E980.4
external medication	976.2	E858.7	E946.2	E950.4	E962.0	E980.4
ophthalmic preparation	976.5	E858.7	E946.5	E950.4	E962.0	E980.4
topical NEC	976.0	E858.7	E946.0	E950.4	E962.0	E980.4
Deterrent, alcohol	977.3	E858.8	E947.3	E950.4	E962.0	E980.4
Detrothyronine	962.7	E858.0	E932.7	E950.4	E962.0	E980.4
Dettol (external medica-tion)	976.0	E858.7	E946.0	E950.4	E962.0	E980.4
Dexamethasone	962.0	E858.0	E932.0	E950.4	E962.0	E980.4
Dexamphetamine	969.72	E854.2	E939.7	E950.3	E962.0	E980.3
Dexedrine	969.72	E854.2	E939.7	E950.3	E962.0	E980.3
Dexpanthenol	963.5	E858.1	E933.5	E950.4	E962.0	E980.4
Dextran	964.8	E858.2	E934.8	E950.4	E962.0	E980.4
Dextriferron	964.0	E858.2	E934.0	E950.4	E962.0	E980.4
Dextroamphetamine	969.72	E854.2	E939.7	E950.3	E962.0	E980.3
Dextro calcium pantothen-ate	963.5	E858.1	E933.5	E950.4	E962.0	E980.4
Dextromethorphan	975.4	E858.6	E945.4	E950.4	E962.0	E980.4
Dextromoramide	965.09	E850.2	E935.2	E950.0	E962.0	E980.0
Dextro pantothenyl alco-hol	963.5	E858.1	E933.5	E950.4	E962.0	E980.4
topical	976.8	E858.7	E946.8	E950.4	E962.0	E980.4
Dextropropoxyphene (hy-drochloride)	965.8	E850.8	E935.8	E950.0	E962.0	E980.0
Dextrorphan	965.09	E850.2	E935.2	E950.0	E962.0	E980.0
Dextrose NEC	974.5	E858.5	E944.5	E950.4	E962.0	E980.4
Dextrothyroxin	962.7	E858.0	E932.7	E950.4	E962.0	E980.4
DFP	971.0	E855.3	E941.0	E950.4	E962.0	E980.4
DHE-45	972.9	E858.3	E942.9	E950.4	E962.0	E980.4
Diabinese	962.3	E858.0	E932.3	E950.4	E962.0	E980.4
Diacetyl monoxime	977.2	E858.8	E947.2	E950.4	E962.0	E980.4
Diacetylmorphine	965.01	E850.0	E935.0	E950.0	E962.0	E980.0
Diagnostic agents	977.8	E858.8	E947.8	E950.4	E962.0	E980.4
Dial (soap)	976.2	E858.7	E946.2	E950.4	E962.0	E980.4
Dial — continued						
sedative	967.0	E851	E937.0	E950.1	E962.0	E980.1
Diallylbarbituric acid	967.0	E851	E937.0	E950.1	E962.0	E980.1
Diaminodiphenylsulfone	961.8	E857	E931.8	E950.4	E962.0	E980.4
Diamorphine	965.01	E850.0	E935.0	E950.0	E962.0	E980.0
Diamox	974.2	E858.5	E944.2	E950.4	E962.0	E980.4
Diamthazole	976.0	E858.7	E946.0	E950.4	E962.0	E980.4
Diaphenylsulfone	961.8	E857	E931.8	E950.4	E962.0	E980.4
Diasone (sodium)	961.8	E857	E931.8	E950.4	E962.0	E980.4
Diazepam	969.4	E853.2	E939.4	E950.3	E962.0	E980.3
Diazinon	989.3	E863.1	—	E950.6	E962.1	E980.7
Diazomethane (gas)	987.8	E869.8	—	E952.8	E962.2	E982.8
Diazoxide	972.5	E858.3	E942.5	E950.4	E962.0	E980.4
Dibenamine	971.3	E855.6	E941.3	E950.4	E962.0	E980.4
Dibenzheptropine	963.0	E858.1	E933.0	E950.4	E962.0	E980.4
Dibenzyline	971.3	E855.6	E941.3	E950.4	E962.0	E980.4
Diborane (gas)	987.8	E869.8	—	E952.8	E962.2	E982.8
Dibromomannitol	963.1	E858.1	E933.1	E950.4	E962.0	E980.4
Dibucaine (spinal)	968.7	E855.2	E938.7	E950.4	E962.0	E980.4
topical (surface)	968.5	E855.2	E938.5	E950.4	E962.0	E980.4
Dibunate sodium	975.4	E858.6	E945.4	E950.4	E962.0	E980.4
Dibutoline	971.1	E855.4	E941.1	E950.4	E962.0	E980.4
Dicapthon	989.4	E863.4	—	E950.6	E962.1	E980.7
Dichloralphenazone	967.1	E852.0	E937.1	E950.2	E962.0	E980.2
Dichlorodifluo-romethane	987.4	E869.2	—	E952.8	E962.2	E982.8
Dichloroethane	982.3	E862.4	—	E950.9	E962.1	E980.9
Dichloroethylene	982.3	E862.4	—	E950.9	E962.1	E980.9
Dichloroethyl sulfide	987.8	E869.8	—	E952.8	E962.2	E982.8
Dichlorohydrin	982.3	E862.4	—	E950.9	E962.1	E980.9
Dichloromethane (solvent) (vapor)	982.3	E862.4	—	E950.9	E962.1	E980.9
Dichlorophen(e)	961.6	E857	E931.6	E950.4	E962.0	E980.4
Dichlorphenamide	974.2	E858.5	E944.2	E950.4	E962.0	E980.4
Dichlorvos	989.3	E863.1	—	E950.6	E962.1	E980.7
Diclofenac sodium	965.69	E850.6	E935.6	E950.0	E962.0	E980.0
Dicoumarin, dicumarol	964.2	E858.2	E934.2	E950.4	E962.0	E980.4
Dicyanogen (gas)	987.8	E869.8	—	E952.8	E962.2	E982.8
Dicyclomine	971.1	E855.4	E941.1	E950.4	E962.0	E980.4
Dieldrin (vapor)	989.2	E863.0	—	E950.6	E962.1	E980.7
Dienestrol	962.2	E858.0	E932.2	E950.4	E962.0	E980.4
Dietetics	977.0	E858.8	E947.0	E950.4	E962.0	E980.4
Diethazine	966.4	E855.0	E936.4	E950.4	E962.0	E980.4
Diethyl						
barbituric acid	967.0	E851	E937.0	E950.1	E962.0	E980.1
carbamazine	961.6	E857	E931.6	E950.4	E962.0	E980.4
carbinol	980.8	E860.8	—	E950.9	E962.1	E980.9
carbonate	982.8	E862.4	—	E950.9	E962.1	E980.9
dioxide	982.8	E862.4	—	E950.9	E962.1	E980.9
ether (vapor) — see Ether(s)						
glycol (monoacetate) (mo-noethyl ether)	982.8	E862.4	—	E950.9	E962.1	E980.9
propion	977.0	E858.8	E947.0	E950.4	E962.0	E980.4
stilbestrol	962.2	E858.0	E932.2	E950.4	E962.0	E980.4
Diethylene						
dioxide	982.8	E862.4	—	E950.9	E962.1	E980.9
glycol (monoacetate) (mo-noethyl ether)	982.8	E862.4	—	E950.9	E962.1	E980.9
Diethylsulfone-diethyl-methane	967.8	E852.8	E937.8	E950.2	E962.0	E980.2
Difencloxazine	965.09	E850.2	E935.2	E950.0	E962.0	E980.0
Diffusin	963.4	E858.1	E933.4	E950.4	E962.0	E980.4
Diflos	971.0	E855.3	E941.0	E950.4	E962.0	E980.4
Digestants	973.4	E858.4	E943.4	E950.4	E962.0	E980.4
Digitalin(e)	972.1	E858.3	E942.1	E950.4	E962.0	E980.4
Digitalis glycosides	972.1	E858.3	E942.1	E950.4	E962.0	E980.4
Digitoxin	972.1	E858.3	E942.1	E950.4	E962.0	E980.4
Digoxin	972.1	E858.3	E942.1	E950.4	E962.0	E980.4
Dihydrocodeine	965.09	E850.2	E935.2	E950.0	E962.0	E980.0
Dihydrocodeinone	965.09	E850.2	E935.2	E950.0	E962.0	E980.0
Dihydroergocristine	972.9	E858.3	E942.9	E950.4	E962.0	E980.4
Dihydroergotamine	972.9	E858.3	E942.9	E950.4	E962.0	E980.4
Dihydroergotoxine	972.9	E858.3	E942.9	E950.4	E962.0	E980.4
Dihydrohydroxy-codeinone	965.09	E850.2	E935.2	E950.0	E962.0	E980.0
Dihydrohydroxymorphi-none	965.09	E850.2	E935.2	E950.0	E962.0	E980.0
Dihydroisocodeine	965.09	E850.2	E935.2	E950.0	E962.0	E980.0
Dihydromorphine	965.09	E850.2	E935.2	E950.0	E962.0	E980.0
Dihydromorphinone	965.09	E850.2	E935.2	E950.0	E962.0	E980.0
Dihydrostreptomycin	960.6	E856	E930.6	E950.4	E962.0	E980.4
Dihydrotachysterol	962.6	E858.0	E932.6	E950.4	E962.0	E980.4

Subterms under main terms may continue to next column or page

Substance	Poisoning	Accident	Therapeutic Use	Suicide Attempt	Assault	Undetermined
Dihydroxyan-thraquinone	973.1	E858.4	E943.1	E950.4	E962.0	E980.4
Dihydroxycodeinone	965.09	E850.2	E935.2	E950.0	E962.0	E980.0
Diiodohydroxyquin	961.3	E857	E931.3	E950.4	E962.0	E980.4
topical	976.0	E858.7	E946.0	E950.4	E962.0	E980.4
Diiodohydroxyquinoline	961.3	E857	E931.3	E950.4	E962.0	E980.4
Dilantin	966.1	E855.0	E936.1	E950.4	E962.0	E980.4
Dilaudid	965.09	E850.2	E935.2	E950.0	E962.0	E980.0
Diloxanide	961.5	E857	E931.5	E950.4	E962.0	E980.4
Dimefline	970.0	E854.3	E940.0	E950.4	E962.0	E980.4
Dimenhydrinate	963.0	E858.1	E933.0	E950.4	E962.0	E980.4
Dimercaprol	963.8	E858.1	E933.8	E950.4	E962.0	E980.4
Dimercaptopropanol	963.8	E858.1	E933.8	E950.4	E962.0	E980.4
Dimetane	963.0	E858.1	E933.0	E950.4	E962.0	E980.4
Dimethicone	976.3	E858.7	E946.3	E950.4	E962.0	E980.4
Dimethindene	963.0	E858.1	E933.0	E950.4	E962.0	E980.4
Dimethisoquin	968.5	E855.2	E938.5	E950.4	E962.0	E980.4
Dimethisterone	962.2	E858.0	E932.2	E950.4	E962.0	E980.4
Dimethoxanate	975.4	E858.6	E945.4	E950.4	E962.0	E980.4
Dimethyl						
arsine, arsinic acid — see Arsenic						
carbinol	980.2	E860.3	—	E950.9	E962.1	E980.9
diguanide	962.3	E858.0	E932.3	E950.4	E962.0	E980.4
ketone	982.8	E862.4	—	E950.9	E962.1	E980.9
vapor	987.8	E869.8	—	E952.8	E962.2	E982.8
meperidine	965.09	E850.2	E935.2	E950.0	E962.0	E980.0
parathion	989.3	E863.1	—	E950.6	E962.1	E980.7
polysiloxane	973.8	E858.4	E943.8	E950.4	E962.0	E980.4
sulfate (fumes)	987.8	E869.8	—	E952.8	E962.2	E982.8
liquid	983.9	E864.3	—	E950.7	E962.1	E980.6
sulfoxide NEC	982.8	E862.4	—	E950.9	E962.1	E980.9
medicinal	976.4	E858.7	E946.4	E950.4	E962.0	E980.4
triptamine	969.6	E854.1	E939.6	E950.3	E962.0	E980.3
tubocurarine	975.2	E858.6	E945.2	E950.4	E962.0	E980.4
Dindevan	964.2	E858.2	E934.2	E950.4	E962.0	E980.4
Dinitrobenzene	983.0	E864.0	—	E950.7	E962.1	E980.6
vapor	987.8	E869.8	—	E952.8	E962.2	E982.8
Dinitro (-ortho-) cresol (herbicide) (spray)	989.4	E863.5	—	E950.6	E962.1	E980.7
insecticide	989.4	E863.4	—	E950.6	E962.1	E980.7
Dinitro-orthocresol (herbicide)	989.4	E863.5	—	E950.6	E962.1	E980.7
insecticide	989.4	E863.4	—	E950.6	E962.1	E980.7
Dinitrophenol (herbicide) (spray)	989.4	E863.5	—	E950.6	E962.1	E980.7
insecticide	989.4	E863.4	—	E950.6	E962.1	E980.7
Dinoprost	975.0	E858.6	E945.0	E950.4	E962.0	E980.4
Dioctyl sulfosuccinate (calcium) (sodium)	973.2	E858.4	E943.2	E950.4	E962.0	E980.4
Diodoquin	961.3	E857	E931.3	E950.4	E962.0	E980.4
Dione derivatives NEC	966.3	E855.0	E936.3	E950.4	E962.0	E980.4
Dionin	965.09	E850.2	E935.2	E950.0	E962.0	E980.0
Dioxane	982.8	E862.4	—	E950.9	E962.1	E980.9
Dioxin — see Herbicide						
Dioxyline	972.5	E858.3	E942.5	E950.4	E962.0	E980.4
Dipentene	982.8	E862.4	—	E950.9	E962.1	E980.9
Diphemanil	971.1	E855.4	E941.1	E950.4	E962.0	E980.4
Diphenadione	964.2	E858.2	E934.2	E950.4	E962.0	E980.4
Diphenhydramine	963.0	E858.1	E933.0	E950.4	E962.0	E980.4
Diphenidol	963.0	E858.1	E933.0	E950.4	E962.0	E980.4
Diphenoxylate	973.5	E858.4	E943.5	E950.4	E962.0	E980.4
Diphenylchloroarsine	985.1	E866.3	—	E950.8	E962.1	E980.8
Diphenylhydantoin (sodium)	966.1	E855.0	E936.1	E950.4	E962.0	E980.4
Diphenylpyraline	963.0	E858.1	E933.0	E950.4	E962.0	E980.4
Diphtheria						
antitoxin	979.9	E858.8	E949.9	E950.4	E962.0	E980.4
toxoid	978.5	E858.8	E948.5	E950.4	E962.0	E980.4
with tetanus toxoid	978.9	E858.8	E948.9	E950.4	E962.0	E980.4
with pertussis component	978.6	E858.8	E948.6	E950.4	E962.0	E980.4
vaccine	978.5	E858.8	E948.5	E950.4	E962.0	E980.4
Dipipanone	965.09	E850.2	E935.2	E950.0	E962.0	E980.0
Diplovax	979.5	E858.8	E949.5	E950.4	E962.0	E980.4
Diprophylline	975.1	E858.6	E945.1	E950.4	E962.0	E980.4
Dipyridamole	972.4	E858.3	E942.4	E950.4	E962.0	E980.4
Dipyrone	965.5	E850.5	E935.5	E950.0	E962.0	E980.0
Diquat	989.4	E863.5	—	E950.6	E962.1	E980.7
Disinfectant NEC	983.9	E861.4	—	E950.7	E962.1	E980.6
alkaline	983.2	E861.4	—	E950.7	E962.1	E980.6
aromatic	983.0	E861.4	—	E950.7	E962.1	E980.6
Disipal	966.4	E855.0	E936.4	E950.4	E962.0	E980.4
Disodium edetate	963.8	E858.1	E933.8	E950.4	E962.0	E980.4
Disulfamide	974.4	E858.5	E944.4	E950.4	E962.0	E980.4
Disulfanilamide	961.0	E857	E931.0	E950.4	E962.0	E980.4
Disulfiram	977.3	E858.8	E947.3	E950.4	E962.0	E980.4
Dithiazanine	961.6	E857	E931.6	E950.4	E962.0	E980.4
Dithioglycerol	963.8	E858.1	E933.8	E950.4	E962.0	E980.4
Dithranol	976.4	E858.7	E946.4	E950.4	E962.0	E980.4
Diucardin	974.3	E858.5	E944.3	E950.4	E962.0	E980.4
Diupres	974.3	E858.5	E944.3	E950.4	E962.0	E980.4
Diuretics NEC	974.4	E858.5	E944.4	E950.4	E962.0	E980.4
carbonic acid anhydrase inhibitors	974.2	E858.5	E944.2	E950.4	E962.0	E980.4
mercurial	974.0	E858.5	E944.0	E950.4	E962.0	E980.4
osmotic	974.4	E858.5	E944.4	E950.4	E962.0	E980.4
purine derivatives	974.1	E858.5	E944.1	E950.4	E962.0	E980.4
saluretic	974.3	E858.5	E944.3	E950.4	E962.0	E980.4
Diuril	974.3	E858.5	E944.3	E950.4	E962.0	E980.4
Divinyl ether	968.2	E855.1	E938.2	E950.4	E962.0	E980.4
D-lysergic acid diethylamide	969.6	E854.1	E939.6	E950.3	E962.0	E980.3
DMCT	960.4	E856	E930.4	E950.4	E962.0	E980.4
DMSO	982.8	E862.4	—	E950.9	E962.1	E980.9
DMT	969.6	E854.1	E939.6	E950.3	E962.0	E980.3
DNOC	989.4	E863.5	—	E950.6	E962.1	E980.7
DOCA	962.0	E858.0	E932.0	E950.4	E962.0	E980.4
Dolophine	965.02	E850.1	E935.1	E950.0	E962.0	E980.0
Doloxene	965.8	E850.8	E935.8	E950.0	E962.0	E980.0
DOM	969.6	E854.1	E939.6	E950.3	E962.0	E980.3
Domestic gas — see Gas, utility						
Domiphen (bromide) (lozenges)	976.6	E858.7	E946.6	E950.4	E962.0	E980.4
Dopa (levo)	966.4	E855.0	E936.4	E950.4	E962.0	E980.4
Dopamine	971.2	E855.5	E941.2	E950.4	E962.0	E980.4
Doriden	967.5	E852.4	E937.5	E950.2	E962.0	E980.2
Dormiral	967.0	E851	E937.0	E950.1	E962.0	E980.1
Dormison	967.8	E852.8	E937.8	E950.2	E962.0	E980.2
Dornase	963.4	E858.1	E933.4	E950.4	E962.0	E980.4
Dorsacaine	968.5	E855.2	E938.5	E950.4	E962.0	E980.4
Dothiepin hydrochloride	969.05	E854.0	E939.0	E950.3	E962.0	E980.3
Doxapram	970.0	E854.3	E940.0	E950.4	E962.0	E980.4
Doxepin	969.05	E854.0	E939.0	E950.3	E962.0	E980.3
Doxorubicin	960.7	E856	E930.7	E950.4	E962.0	E980.4
Doxycycline	960.4	E856	E930.4	E950.4	E962.0	E980.4
Doxylamine	963.0	E858.1	E933.0	E950.4	E962.0	E980.4
Dramamine	963.0	E858.1	E933.0	E950.4	E962.0	E980.4
Drano (drain cleaner)	983.2	E864.2	—	E950.7	E962.1	E980.6
Dromoran	965.09	E850.2	E935.2	E950.0	E962.0	E980.0
Dromostanolone	962.1	E858.0	E932.1	E950.4	E962.0	E980.4
Droperidol	969.2	E853.1	E939.2	E950.3	E962.0	E980.3
Drotrecogin alfa	964.2	E858.2	E934.2	E950.4	E962.0	E980.4
Drug	977.9	E858.9	E947.9	E950.5	E962.0	E980.5
AHFS List						
4:00 antihistamine drugs	963.0	E858.1	E933.0	E950.4	E962.0	E980.4
8:04 amebacides	961.5	E857	E931.5	E950.4	E962.0	E980.4
arsenical anti-infectives	961.1	E857	E931.1	E950.4	E962.0	E980.4
quinoline derivatives	961.3	E857	E931.3	E950.4	E962.0	E980.4
8:08 anthelmintics	961.6	E857	E931.6	E950.4	E962.0	E980.4
quinoline derivatives	961.3	E857	E931.3	E950.4	E962.0	E980.4
8:12.04 antifungal antibiotics	960.1	E856	E930.1	E950.4	E962.0	E980.4
8:12.06 cephalosporins	960.5	E856	E930.5	E950.4	E962.0	E980.4
8:12.08 chloramphenicol	960.2	E856	E930.2	E950.4	E962.0	E980.4
8:12.12 erythromycins	960.3	E856	E930.3	E950.4	E962.0	E980.4
8:12.16 penicillins	960.0	E856	E930.0	E950.4	E962.0	E980.4
8:12.20 streptomycins	960.6	E856	E930.6	E950.4	E962.0	E980.4
8:12.24 tetracyclines	960.4	E856	E930.4	E950.4	E962.0	E980.4
8:12.28 other antibiotics	960.8	E856	E930.8	E950.4	E962.0	E980.4
antimycobacterial	960.6	E856	E930.6	E950.4	E962.0	E980.4
macrolides	960.3	E856	E930.3	E950.4	E962.0	E980.4
8:16 antituberculars	961.8	E857	E931.8	E950.4	E962.0	E980.4
antibiotics	960.6	E856	E930.6	E950.4	E962.0	E980.4
8:18 antivirals	961.7	E857	E931.7	E950.4	E962.0	E980.4
8:20 plasmodicides (antimalarials)	961.4	E857	E931.4	E950.4	E962.0	E980.4
8:24 sulfonamides	961.0	E857	E931.0	E950.4	E962.0	E980.4
8:26 sulfones	961.8	E857	E931.8	E950.4	E962.0	E980.4
8:28 treponemicides	961.2	E857	E931.2	E950.4	E962.0	E980.4
8:32 trichomonacides	961.5	E857	E931.5	E950.4	E962.0	E980.4
nitrofuran derivatives	961.9	E857	E931.9	E950.4	E962.0	E980.4
quinoline derivatives	961.3	E857	E931.3	E950.4	E962.0	E980.4

Nontherapeutic use substance

Subterms under main terms may continue to next column or page

Drug — continued	Poisoning	Accident	Therapeutic Use	Suicide Attempt	Assault	Undetermined
8:36 urinary germicides	961.9	E857	E931.9	E950.4	E962.0	E980.4
quinoline derivatives	961.3	E857	E931.3	E950.4	E962.0	E980.4
8:40 other anti-infectives	961.9	E857	E931.9	E950.4	E962.0	E980.4
10:00 antineoplastic agents	963.1	E858.1	E933.1	E950.4	E962.0	E980.4
antibiotics	960.7	E856	E930.7	E950.4	E962.0	E980.4
progestogens	962.2	E858.0	E932.2	E950.4	E962.0	E980.4
12:04 parasympathomimetic (cholinergic) agents	971.0	E855.3	E941.0	E950.4	E962.0	E980.4
12:08 parasympatholytic (cholinergic-blocking) agents	971.1	E855.4	E941.1	E950.4	E962.0	E980.4
12:12 Sympathomimetic (adrenergic) agents	971.2	E855.5	E941.2	E950.4	E962.0	E980.4
12:16 sympatholytic (adrenergic-blocking) agents	971.3	E855.6	E941.3	E950.4	E962.0	E980.4
12:20 skeletal muscle relaxants						
central nervous system muscle-tone depressants	968.0	E855.1	E938.0	E950.4	E962.0	E980.4
myoneural blocking agents	975.2	E858.6	E945.2	E950.4	E962.0	E980.4
16:00 blood derivatives	964.7	E858.2	E934.7	E950.4	E962.0	E980.4
20:04.04 iron preparations	964.0	E858.2	E934.0	E950.4	E962.0	E980.4
20:04.08 liver and stomach preparations	964.1	E858.2	E934.1	E950.4	E962.0	E980.4
20:04 antianemia drugs	964.1	E858.2	E934.1	E950.4	E962.0	E980.4
20:12.04 anticoagulants	964.2	E858.2	E934.2	E950.4	E962.0	E980.4
20:12.08 antiheparin agents	964.5	E858.2	E934.5	E950.4	E962.0	E980.4
20:12.12 coagulants	964.5	E858.2	E934.5	E950.4	E962.0	E980.4
20:12.16 hemostatics NEC	964.5	E858.2	E934.5	E950.4	E962.0	E980.4
capillary active drugs	972.8	E858.3	E942.8	E950.4	E962.0	E980.4
24:04 cardiac drugs	972.9	E858.3	E942.9	E950.4	E962.0	E980.4
cardiotonic agents	972.1	E858.3	E942.1	E950.4	E962.0	E980.4
rhythm regulators	972.0	E858.3	E942.0	E950.4	E962.0	E980.4
24:06 antilipemic agents	972.2	E858.3	E942.2	E950.4	E962.0	E980.4
thyroid derivatives	962.7	E858.0	E932.7	E950.4	E962.0	E980.4
24:08 hypotensive agents	972.6	E858.3	E942.6	E950.4	E962.0	E980.4
adrenergic blocking agents	971.3	E855.6	E941.3	E950.4	E962.0	E980.4
ganglion blocking agents	972.3	E858.3	E942.3	E950.4	E962.0	E980.4
vasodilators	972.5	E858.3	E942.5	E950.4	E962.0	E980.4
24:12 vasodilating agents NEC	972.5	E858.3	E942.5	E950.4	E962.0	E980.4
coronary	972.4	E858.3	E942.4	E950.4	E962.0	E980.4
nicotinic acid derivatives	972.2	E858.3	E942.2	E950.4	E962.0	E980.4
24:16 sclerosing agents	972.7	E858.3	E942.7	E950.4	E962.0	E980.4
28:04 general anesthetics	968.4	E855.1	E938.4	E950.4	E962.0	E980.4
gaseous anesthetics	968.2	E855.1	E938.2	E950.4	E962.0	E980.4
halothane	968.1	E855.1	E938.1	E950.4	E962.0	E980.4
intravenous anesthetics	968.3	E855.1	E938.3	E950.4	E962.0	E980.4
28:08 analgesics and antipyretics	965.9	E850.9	E935.9	E950.0	E962.0	E980.0
antirheumatics	965.69	E850.6	E935.6	E950.0	E962.0	E980.0
aromatic analgesics	965.4	E850.4	E935.4	E950.0	E962.0	E980.0
non-narcotic NEC	965.7	E850.7	E935.7	E950.0	E962.0	E980.0
opium alkaloids	965.00	E850.2	E935.2	E950.0	E962.0	E980.0
heroin	965.01	E850.0	E935.0	E950.0	E962.0	E980.0
methadone	965.02	E850.1	E935.1	E950.0	E962.0	E980.0
specified type NEC	965.09	E850.2	E935.2	E950.0	E962.0	E980.0
pyrazole derivatives	965.5	E850.5	E935.5	E950.0	E962.0	E980.0
salicylates	965.1	E850.3	E935.3	E950.0	E962.0	E980.0
specified NEC	965.8	E850.8	E935.8	E950.0	E962.0	E980.0
28:10 narcotic antagonists	970.1	E854.3	E940.1	E950.4	E962.0	E980.4
28:12 anticonvulsants	966.3	E855.0	E936.3	E950.4	E962.0	E980.4
barbiturates	967.0	E851	E937.0	E950.1	E962.0	E980.1
benzodiazepine-based tranquilizers	969.4	E853.2	E939.4	E950.3	E962.0	E980.3
bromides	967.3	E852.2	E937.3	E950.2	E962.0	E980.2
hydantoin derivatives	966.1	E855.0	E936.1	E950.4	E962.0	E980.4
oxazolidine (derivatives)	966.0	E855.0	E936.0	E950.4	E962.0	E980.4
succinimides	966.2	E855.0	E936.2	E950.4	E962.0	E980.4

Drug — continued	Poisoning	Accident	Therapeutic Use	Suicide Attempt	Assault	Undetermined
28:16.04 antidepressants	969.00	E854.0	E939.0	E950.3	E962.0	E980.3
28:16.08 tranquilizers	969.5	E853.9	E939.5	E950.3	E962.0	E980.3
benzodiazepine-based	969.4	E853.2	E939.4	E950.3	E962.0	E980.3
butyrophenone-based	969.2	E853.1	E939.2	E950.3	E962.0	E980.3
major NEC	969.3	E853.8	E939.3	E950.3	E962.0	E980.3
phenothiazine-based	969.1	E853.0	E939.1	E950.3	E962.0	E980.3
28:16.12 other psychotherapeutic agents	969.8	E855.8	E939.8	E950.3	E962.0	E980.3
28:20 respiratory and cerebral stimulants	970.9	E854.3	E940.9	E950.4	E962.0	E980.4
analeptics	970.0	E854.3	E940.0	E950.4	E962.0	E980.4
anorexigenic agents	977.0	E858.8	E947.0	E950.4	E962.0	E980.4
psychostimulants	969.70	E854.2	E939.7	E950.3	E962.0	E980.3
specified NEC	970.89	E854.3	E940.8	E950.4	E962.0	E980.4
28:24 sedatives and hypnotics	967.9	E852.9	E937.9	E950.2	E962.0	E980.2
barbiturates	967.0	E851	E937.0	E950.1	E962.0	E980.1
benzodiazepine-based tranquilizers	969.4	E853.2	E939.4	E950.3	E962.0	E980.3
chloral hydrate (group)	967.1	E852.0	E937.1	E950.2	E962.0	E980.2
glutethamide group	967.5	E852.4	E937.5	E950.2	E962.0	E980.2
intravenous anesthetics	968.3	E855.1	E938.3	E950.4	E962.0	E980.4
methaqualone (compounds)	967.4	E852.3	E937.4	E950.2	E962.0	E980.2
paraldehyde	967.2	E852.1	E937.2	E950.2	E962.0	E980.2
phenothiazine-based tranquilizers	969.1	E853.0	E939.1	E950.3	E962.0	E980.3
specified NEC	967.8	E852.8	E937.8	E950.2	E962.0	E980.2
thiobarbiturates	968.3	E855.1	E938.3	E950.4	E962.0	E980.4
tranquilizer NEC	969.5	E853.9	E939.5	E950.3	E962.0	E980.3
36:04 to 36:88 diagnostic agents	977.8	E858.8	E947.8	E950.4	E962.0	E980.4
40:00 electrolyte, caloric, and water balance agents NEC	974.5	E858.5	E944.5	E950.4	E962.0	E980.4
40:04 acidifying agents	963.2	E858.1	E933.2	E950.4	E962.0	E980.4
40:08 alkalinizing agents	963.3	E858.1	E933.3	E950.4	E962.0	E980.4
40:10 ammonia detoxicants	974.5	E858.5	E944.5	E950.4	E962.0	E980.4
40:12 replacement solutions	974.5	E858.5	E944.5	E950.4	E962.0	E980.4
plasma expanders	964.8	E858.2	E934.8	E950.4	E962.0	E980.4
40:16 sodium-removing resins	974.5	E858.5	E944.5	E950.4	E962.0	E980.4
40:18 potassium-removing resins	974.5	E858.5	E944.5	E950.4	E962.0	E980.4
40:20 caloric agents	974.5	E858.5	E944.5	E950.4	E962.0	E980.4
40:24 salt and sugar substitutes	974.5	E858.5	E944.5	E950.4	E962.0	E980.4
40:28 diuretics NEC	974.4	E858.5	E944.4	E950.4	E962.0	E980.4
carbonic acid anhydrase inhibitors	974.2	E858.5	E944.2	E950.4	E962.0	E980.4
mercurials	974.0	E858.5	E944.0	E950.4	E962.0	E980.4
purine derivatives	974.1	E858.5	E944.1	E950.4	E962.0	E980.4
saluretics	974.3	E858.5	E944.3	E950.4	E962.0	E980.4
thiazides	974.3	E858.5	E944.3	E950.4	E962.0	E980.4
40:36 irrigating solutions	974.5	E858.5	E944.5	E950.4	E962.0	E980.4
40:40 uricosuric agents	974.7	E858.5	E944.7	E950.4	E962.0	E980.4
44:00 enzymes	963.4	E858.1	E933.4	E950.4	E962.0	E980.4
fibrinolysis-affecting agents	964.4	E858.2	E934.4	E950.4	E962.0	E980.4
gastric agents	973.4	E858.4	E943.4	E950.4	E962.0	E980.4
48:00 expectorants and cough preparations						
antihistamine agents	963.0	E858.1	E933.0	E950.4	E962.0	E980.4
antitussives	975.4	E858.6	E945.4	E950.4	E962.0	E980.4
codeine derivatives	965.09	E850.2	E935.2	E950.0	E962.0	E980.0
expectorants	975.5	E858.6	E945.5	E950.4	E962.0	E980.4
narcotic agents NEC	965.09	E850.2	E935.2	E950.0	E962.0	E980.0
52:04.04 antibiotics (EENT)						
ENT agent	976.6	E858.7	E946.6	E950.4	E962.0	E980.4
ophthalmic preparation	976.5	E858.7	E946.5	E950.4	E962.0	E980.4
52:04.06 antivirals (EENT)						
ENT agent	976.6	E858.7	E946.6	E950.4	E962.0	E980.4
ophthalmic preparation	976.5	E858.7	E946.5	E950.4	E962.0	E980.4
52:04.08 sulfonamides (EENT)						
ENT agent	976.6	E858.7	E946.6	E950.4	E962.0	E980.4
ophthalmic preparation	976.5	E858.7	E946.5	E950.4	E962.0	E980.4
52:04.12 miscellaneous anti-infectives (EENT)						
ENT agent	976.6	E858.7	E946.6	E950.4	E962.0	E980.4

Nontherapeutic use substance ▼ Subterms under main terms may continue to next column or page

	External Cause (E-Code)					
	Poisoning	Accident	Therapeutic Use	Suicide Attempt	Assault	Undetermined
Drug — *continued*						
52:04.12 miscellaneous anti-infectives — *continued*						
ophthalmic preparation	976.5	E858.7	E946.5	E950.4	E962.0	E980.4
52:04 anti-infectives (EENT)						
ENT agent	976.6	E858.7	E946.6	E950.4	E962.0	E980.4
ophthalmic preparation	976.5	E858.7	E946.5	E950.4	E962.0	E980.4
52:08 anti-inflammatory agents (EENT)						
ENT agent	976.6	E858.7	E946.6	E950.4	E962.0	E980.4
ophthalmic preparation	976.5	E858.7	E946.5	E950.4	E962.0	E980.4
52:10 carbonic anhydrase inhibitors	974.2	E858.5	E944.2	E950.4	E962.0	E980.4
52:12 contact lens solutions	976.5	E858.7	E946.5	E950.4	E962.0	E980.4
52:16 local anesthetics (EENT)	968.5	E855.2	E938.5	E950.4	E962.0	E980.4
52:20 miotics	971.0	E855.3	E941.0	E950.4	E962.0	E980.4
52:24 mydriatics						
adrenergics	971.2	E855.5	E941.2	E950.4	E962.0	E980.4
anticholinergics	971.1	E855.4	E941.1	E950.4	E962.0	E980.4
antimuscarinics	971.1	E855.4	E941.1	E950.4	E962.0	E980.4
parasympatholytics	971.1	E855.4	E941.1	E950.4	E962.0	E980.4
spasmolytics	971.1	E855.4	E941.1	E950.4	E962.0	E980.4
sympathomimetics	971.2	E855.5	E941.2	E950.4	E962.0	E980.4
52:28 mouth washes and gargles	976.6	E858.7	E946.6	E950.4	E962.0	E980.4
52:32 vasoconstrictors (EENT)	971.2	E855.5	E941.2	E950.4	E962.0	E980.4
52:36 unclassified agents (EENT)						
ENT agent	976.6	E858.7	E946.6	E950.4	E962.0	E980.4
ophthalmic preparation	976.5	E858.7	E946.5	E950.4	E962.0	E980.4
56:04 antacids and adsorbents	973.0	E858.4	E943.0	E950.4	E962.0	E980.4
56:08 antidiarrhea agents	973.5	E858.4	E943.5	E950.4	E962.0	E980.4
56:10 antiflatulents	973.8	E858.4	E943.8	E950.4	E962.0	E980.4
56:12 cathartics NEC	973.3	E858.4	E943.3	E950.4	E962.0	E980.4
emollients	973.2	E858.4	E943.2	E950.4	E962.0	E980.4
irritants	973.1	E858.4	E943.1	E950.4	E962.0	E980.4
56:16 digestants	973.4	E858.4	E943.4	E950.4	E962.0	E980.4
56:20 emetics and antiemetics						
antiemetics	963.0	E858.1	E933.0	E950.4	E962.0	E980.4
emetics	973.6	E858.4	E943.6	E950.4	E962.0	E980.4
56:24 lipotropic agents	977.1	E858.8	E947.1	E950.4	E962.0	E980.4
56:40 miscellaneous G.I. drugs	973.8	E858.4	E943.8	E950.4	E962.0	E980.4
60:00 gold compounds	965.69	E850.6	E935.6	E950.0	E962.0	E980.0
64:00 heavy metal antagonists	963.8	E858.1	E933.8	E950.4	E962.0	E980.4
68:04 adrenals	962.0	E858.0	E932.0	E950.4	E962.0	E980.4
68:08 androgens	962.1	E858.0	E932.1	E950.4	E962.0	E980.4
68:12 contraceptives, oral	962.2	E858.0	E932.2	E950.4	E962.0	E980.4
68:16 estrogens	962.2	E858.0	E932.2	E950.4	E962.0	E980.4
68:18 gonadotropins	962.4	E858.0	E932.4	E950.4	E962.0	E980.4
68:20.08 insulins	962.3	E858.0	E932.3	E950.4	E962.0	E980.4
68:20 insulins and antidiabetic agents	962.3	E858.0	E932.3	E950.4	E962.0	E980.4
68:24 parathyroid	962.6	E858.0	E932.6	E950.4	E962.0	E980.4
68:28 pituitary (posterior)	962.5	E858.0	E932.5	E950.4	E962.0	E980.4
anterior	962.4	E858.0	E932.4	E950.4	E962.0	E980.4
68:32 progestogens	962.2	E858.0	E932.2	E950.4	E962.0	E980.4
68:34 other corpus luteum hormones NEC	962.2	E858.0	E932.2	E950.4	E962.0	E980.4
68:36 thyroid and antithyroid						
antithyroid	962.8	E858.0	E932.8	E950.4	E962.0	E980.4
thyroid (derivatives)	962.7	E858.0	E932.7	E950.4	E962.0	E980.4
72:00 local anesthetics						
NEC	968.9	E855.2	E938.9	E950.4	E962.0	E980.4
infiltration (intradermal) (subcutaneous) (submucosal)	968.5	E855.2	E938.5	E950.4	E962.0	E980.4
nerve blocking (peripheral) (plexus) (regional)	968.6	E855.2	E938.6	E950.4	E962.0	E980.4
spinal	968.7	E855.2	E938.7	E950.4	E962.0	E980.4
topical (surface)	968.5	E855.2	E938.5	E950.4	E962.0	E980.4
76:00 oxytocics	975.0	E858.6	E945.0	E950.4	E962.0	E980.4
78:00 radioactive agents	990	—	—	—	—	—
80:04 serums NEC	979.9	E858.8	E949.9	E950.4	E962.0	E980.4
Drug — *continued*						
80:04 serums — *continued*						
immune gamma globulin (human)	964.6	E858.2	E934.6	E950.4	E962.0	E980.4
80:08 toxoids NEC	978.8	E858.8	E948.8	E950.4	E962.0	E980.4
diphtheria	978.5	E858.8	E948.5	E950.4	E962.0	E980.4
and diphtheria	978.9	E858.8	E948.9	E950.4	E962.0	E980.4
with pertussis component	978.6	E858.8	E948.6	E950.4	E962.0	E980.4
and tetanus	978.9	E858.8	E948.9	E950.4	E962.0	E980.4
with pertussis component	978.6	E858.8	E948.6	E950.4	E962.0	E980.4
tetanus	978.4	E858.8	E948.4	E950.4	E962.0	E980.4
80:12 vaccines	979.9	E858.8	E949.9	E950.4	E962.0	E980.4
bacterial NEC	978.8	E858.8	E948.8	E950.4	E962.0	E980.4
with						
other bacterial components	978.9	E858.8	E948.9	E950.4	E962.0	E980.4
pertussis component	978.6	E858.8	E948.6	E950.4	E962.0	E980.4
viral and rickettsial components	979.7	E858.8	E949.7	E950.4	E962.0	E980.4
rickettsial NEC	979.6	E858.8	E949.6	E950.4	E962.0	E980.4
with						
bacterial component	979.7	E858.8	E949.7	E950.4	E962.0	E980.4
pertussis component	978.6	E858.8	E948.6	E950.4	E962.0	E980.4
viral component	979.7	E858.8	E949.7	E950.4	E962.0	E980.4
viral NEC	979.6	E858.8	E949.6	E950.4	E962.0	E980.4
with						
bacterial component	979.7	E858.8	E949.7	E950.4	E962.0	E980.4
pertussis component	978.6	E858.8	E948.6	E950.4	E962.0	E980.4
rickettsial component	979.7	E858.8	E949.7	E950.4	E962.0	E980.4
84:04.04 antibiotics (skin and mucous membrane)	976.0	E858.7	E946.0	E950.4	E962.0	E980.4
84:04.08 fungicides (skin and mucous membrane)	976.0	E858.7	E946.0	E950.4	E962.0	E980.4
84:04.12 scabicides and pediculicides (skin and mucous membrane)	976.0	E858.7	E946.0	E950.4	E962.0	E980.4
84:04.16 miscellaneous local anti-infectives (skin and mucous membrane)	976.0	E858.7	E946.0	E950.4	E962.0	E980.4
84:06 anti-inflammatory agents (skin and mucous membrane)	976.0	E858.7	E946.0	E950.4	E962.0	E980.4
84:08 antipruritics and local anesthetics						
antipruritics	976.1	E858.7	E946.1	E950.4	E962.0	E980.4
local anesthetics	968.5	E855.2	E938.5	E950.4	E962.0	E980.4
84:12 astringents	976.2	E858.7	E946.2	E950.4	E962.0	E980.4
84:16 cell stimulants and proliferants	976.8	E858.7	E946.8	E950.4	E962.0	E980.4
84:20 detergents	976.2	E858.7	E946.2	E950.4	E962.0	E980.4
84:24 emollients, demulcents, and protectants	976.3	E858.7	E946.3	E950.4	E962.0	E980.4
84:28 keratolytic agents	976.4	E858.7	E946.4	E950.4	E962.0	E980.4
84:32 keratoplastic agents	976.4	E858.7	E946.4	E950.4	E962.0	E980.4
84:36 miscellaneous agents (skin and mucous membrane)	976.8	E858.7	E946.8	E950.4	E962.0	E980.4
86:00 spasmolytic agents	975.1	E858.6	E945.1	E950.4	E962.0	E980.4
antiasthmatics	975.7	E858.6	E945.7	E950.4	E962.0	E980.4
papaverine	972.5	E858.3	E942.5	E950.4	E962.0	E980.4
theophylline	974.1	E858.5	E944.1	E950.4	E962.0	E980.4
88:04 vitamin A	963.5	E858.1	E933.5	E950.4	E962.0	E980.4
88:08 vitamin B complex	963.5	E858.1	E933.5	E950.4	E962.0	E980.4
hematopoietic vitamin	964.1	E858.2	E934.1	E950.4	E962.0	E980.4
nicotinic acid derivatives	972.2	E858.3	E942.2	E950.4	E962.0	E980.4
88:12 vitamin C	963.5	E858.1	E933.5	E950.4	E962.0	E980.4
88:16 vitamin D	963.5	E858.1	E933.5	E950.4	E962.0	E980.4
88:20 vitamin E	963.5	E858.1	E933.5	E950.4	E962.0	E980.4
88:24 vitamin K activity	964.3	E858.2	E934.3	E950.4	E962.0	E980.4
88:28 multivitamin preparations	963.5	E858.1	E933.5	E950.4	E962.0	E980.4

Nontherapeutic use substance

⩗ Subterms under main terms may continue to next column or page

	Poisoning	Accident	Therapeutic Use	Suicide Attempt	Assault	Undetermined
Drug — *continued*						
92:00 unclassified therapeutic agents	977.8	E858.8	E947.8	E950.4	E962.0	E980.4
specified NEC	977.8	E858.8	E947.8	E950.4	E962.0	E980.4
Duboisine	971.1	E855.4	E941.1	E950.4	E962.0	E980.4
Dulcolax	973.1	E858.4	E943.1	E950.4	E962.0	E980.4
Duponol (C) (EP)	976.2	E858.7	E946.2	E950.4	E962.0	E980.4
Durabolin	962.1	E858.0	E932.1	E950.4	E962.0	E980.4
Dyclone	968.5	E855.2	E938.5	E950.4	E962.0	E980.4
Dyclonine	968.5	E855.2	E938.5	E950.4	E962.0	E980.4
Dydrogesterone	962.2	E858.0	E932.2	E950.4	E962.0	E980.4
Dyes NEC	989.89	E866.8	—	E950.9	E962.1	E980.9
diagnostic agents	977.8	E858.8	E947.8	E950.4	E962.0	E980.4
pharmaceutical NEC	977.4	E858.8	E947.4	E950.4	E962.0	E980.4
Dyfols	971.0	E855.3	E941.0	E950.4	E962.0	E980.4
Dymelor	962.3	E858.0	E932.3	E950.4	E962.0	E980.4
Dynamite	989.89	E866.8	—	E950.9	E962.1	E980.9
fumes	987.8	E869.8	—	E952.8	E962.2	E982.8
Dyphylline	975.1	E858.6	E945.1	E950.4	E962.0	E980.4
Ear preparations	976.6	E858.7	E946.6	E950.4	E962.0	E980.4
Echothiopate, ecothiopate	971.0	E855.3	E941.0	E950.4	E962.0	E980.4
Ecstasy	969.72	E854.2	E939.7	E950.3	E962.0	E980.3
Ectylurea	967.8	E852.8	E937.8	E950.2	E962.0	E980.2
Edathamil disodium	963.8	E858.1	E933.8	E950.4	E962.0	E980.4
Edecrin	974.4	E858.5	E944.4	E950.4	E962.0	E980.4
Edetate, disodium (calcium)	963.8	E858.1	E933.8	E950.4	E962.0	E980.4
Edrophonium	971.0	E855.3	E941.0	E950.4	E962.0	E980.4
Elase	976.8	E858.7	E946.8	E950.4	E962.0	E980.4
Elaterium	973.1	E858.4	E943.1	E950.4	E962.0	E980.4
Elder	988.2	E865.4	—	E950.9	E962.1	E980.9
berry (unripe)	988.2	E865.3	—	E950.9	E962.1	E980.9
Electrolytes NEC	974.5	E858.5	E944.5	E950.4	E962.0	E980.4
Electrolytic agent NEC	974.5	E858.5	E944.5	E950.4	E962.0	E980.4
Embramine	963.0	E858.1	E933.0	E950.4	E962.0	E980.4
Emetics	973.6	E858.4	E943.6	E950.4	E962.0	E980.4
Emetine (hydrochloride)	961.5	E857	E931.5	E950.4	E962.0	E980.4
Emollients	976.3	E858.7	E946.3	E950.4	E962.0	E980.4
Emylcamate	969.5	E853.8	E939.5	E950.3	E962.0	E980.3
Encyprate	969.09	E854.0	E939.0	E950.3	E962.0	E980.3
Endocaine	968.5	E855.2	E938.5	E950.4	E962.0	E980.4
Endrin	989.2	E863.0	—	E950.6	E962.1	E980.7
Enflurane	968.2	E855.1	E938.2	E950.4	E962.0	E980.4
Enovid	962.2	E858.0	E932.2	E950.4	E962.0	E980.4
ENT preparations (anti-infectives)	976.6	E858.7	E946.6	E950.4	E962.0	E980.4
Enzodase	963.4	E858.1	E933.4	E950.4	E962.0	E980.4
Enzymes NEC	963.4	E858.1	E933.4	E950.4	E962.0	E980.4
Epanutin	966.1	E855.0	E936.1	E950.4	E962.0	E980.4
Ephedra (tincture)	971.2	E855.5	E941.2	E950.4	E962.0	E980.4
Ephedrine	971.2	E855.5	E941.2	E950.4	E962.0	E980.4
Epiestriol	962.2	E858.0	E932.2	E950.4	E962.0	E980.4
Epilim — see Sodium valproate						
Epinephrine	971.2	E855.5	E941.2	E950.4	E962.0	E980.4
Epsom salt	973.3	E858.4	E943.3	E950.4	E962.0	E980.4
Equanil	969.5	E853.8	E939.5	E950.3	E962.0	E980.3
Equisetum (diuretic)	974.4	E858.5	E944.4	E950.4	E962.0	E980.4
Ergometrine	975.0	E858.6	E945.0	E950.4	E962.0	E980.4
Ergonovine	975.0	E858.6	E945.0	E950.4	E962.0	E980.4
Ergotamine (tartrate) (for migraine) NEC	972.9	E858.3	E942.9	E950.4	E962.0	E980.4
Ergotrate	975.0	E858.6	E945.0	E950.4	E962.0	E980.4
Ergot NEC	988.2	E865.4	—	E950.9	E962.1	E980.9
medicinal (alkaloids)	975.0	E858.6	E945.0	E950.4	E962.0	E980.4
Erythrityl tetranitrate	972.4	E858.3	E942.4	E950.4	E962.0	E980.4
Erythrol tetranitrate	972.4	E858.3	E942.4	E950.4	E962.0	E980.4
Erythromycin	960.3	E856	E930.3	E950.4	E962.0	E980.4
ophthalmic preparation	976.5	E858.7	E946.5	E950.4	E962.0	E980.4
topical NEC	976.0	E858.7	E946.0	E950.4	E962.0	E980.4
Eserine	971.0	E855.3	E941.0	E950.4	E962.0	E980.4
Eskabarb	967.0	E851	E937.0	E950.1	E962.0	E980.1
Eskalith	969.8	E855.8	E939.8	E950.3	E962.0	E980.3
Estradiol (cypionate) (dipropionate) (valerate)	962.2	E858.0	E932.2	E950.4	E962.0	E980.4
Estriol	962.2	E858.0	E932.2	E950.4	E962.0	E980.4
Estrogens (with progestogens)	962.2	E858.0	E932.2	E950.4	E962.0	E980.4
Estrone	962.2	E858.0	E932.2	E950.4	E962.0	E980.4
Etafedrine	971.2	E855.5	E941.2	E950.4	E962.0	E980.4
Ethacrynate sodium	974.4	E858.5	E944.4	E950.4	E962.0	E980.4

	Poisoning	Accident	Therapeutic Use	Suicide Attempt	Assault	Undetermined
Ethacrynic acid	974.4	E858.5	E944.4	E950.4	E962.0	E980.4
Ethambutol	961.8	E857	E931.8	E950.4	E962.0	E980.4
Ethamide	974.2	E858.5	E944.2	E950.4	E962.0	E980.4
Ethamivan	970.0	E854.3	E940.0	E950.4	E962.0	E980.4
Ethamsylate	964.5	E858.2	E934.5	E950.4	E962.0	E980.4
Ethanol	980.0	E860.1	—	E950.9	E962.1	E980.9
beverage	980.0	E860.0	—	E950.9	E962.1	E980.9
Ethchlorvynol	967.8	E852.8	E937.8	E950.2	E962.0	E980.2
Ethebenecid	974.7	E858.5	E944.7	E950.4	E962.0	E980.4
Ether(s) (diethyl) (ethyl) (vapor)	987.8	E869.8	—	E952.8	E962.2	E982.8
anesthetic	968.2	E855.1	E938.2	E950.4	E962.0	E980.4
petroleum — see Ligroin						
solvent	982.8	E862.4	—	E950.9	E962.1	E980.9
Ethidine chloride (vapor)	987.8	E869.8	—	E952.8	E962.2	E982.8
liquid (solvent)	982.3	E862.4	—	E950.9	E962.1	E980.9
Ethinamate	967.8	E852.8	E937.8	E950.2	E962.0	E980.2
Ethinylestradiol	962.2	E858.0	E932.2	E950.4	E962.0	E980.4
Ethionamide	961.8	E857	E931.8	E950.4	E962.0	E980.4
Ethisterone	962.2	E858.0	E932.2	E950.4	E962.0	E980.4
Ethobral	967.0	E851	E937.0	E950.1	E962.0	E980.1
Ethocaine (infiltration) (topical)	968.5	E855.2	E938.5	E950.4	E962.0	E980.4
nerve block (peripheral) (plexus)	968.6	E855.2	E938.6	E950.4	E962.0	E980.4
spinal	968.7	E855.2	E938.7	E950.4	E962.0	E980.4
Ethoheptazine (citrate)	965.7	E850.7	E935.7	E950.0	E962.0	E980.0
Ethopropazine	966.4	E855.0	E936.4	E950.4	E962.0	E980.4
Ethosuximide	966.2	E855.0	E936.2	E950.4	E962.0	E980.4
Ethotoin	966.1	E855.0	E936.1	E950.4	E962.0	E980.4
Ethoxazene	961.9	E857	E931.9	E950.4	E962.0	E980.4
Ethoxzolamide	974.2	E858.5	E944.2	E950.4	E962.0	E980.4
Ethyl						
acetate (vapor)	982.8	E862.4	—	E950.9	E962.1	E980.9
alcohol	980.0	E860.1	—	E950.9	E962.1	E980.9
beverage	980.0	E860.0	—	E950.9	E962.1	E980.9
aldehyde (vapor)	987.8	E869.8	—	E952.8	E962.2	E982.8
liquid	989.89	E866.8	—	E950.9	E962.1	E980.9
aminobenzoate	968.5	E855.2	E938.5	E950.4	E962.0	E980.4
biscoumacetate	964.2	E858.2	E934.2	E950.4	E962.0	E980.4
bromide (anesthetic)	968.2	E855.1	E938.2	E950.4	E962.0	E980.4
carbamate (antineoplastic)	963.1	E858.1	E933.1	E950.4	E962.0	E980.4
carbinol	980.3	E860.4	—	E950.9	E962.1	E980.9
chaulmoograte	961.8	E857	E931.8	E950.4	E962.0	E980.4
chloride (vapor)	987.8	E869.8	—	E952.8	E962.2	E982.8
anesthetic (local)	968.5	E855.2	E938.5	E950.4	E962.0	E980.4
inhaled	968.2	E855.1	E938.2	E950.4	E962.0	E980.4
solvent	982.3	E862.4	—	E950.9	E962.1	E980.9
estranol	962.1	E858.0	E932.1	E950.4	E962.0	E980.4
ether — see Ether(s)						
formate (solvent) NEC	982.8	E862.4	—	E950.9	E962.1	E980.9
iodoacetate	987.5	E869.3	—	E952.8	E962.2	E982.8
lactate (solvent) NEC	982.8	E862.4	—	E950.9	E962.1	E980.9
methylcarbinol	980.8	E860.8	—	E950.9	E962.1	E980.9
morphine	965.09	E850.2	E935.2	E950.0	E962.0	E980.0
Ethylene (gas)	987.1	E869.8	—	E952.8	E962.2	E982.8
anesthetic (general)	968.2	E855.1	E938.2	E950.4	E962.0	E980.4
chlorohydrin (vapor)	982.3	E862.4	—	E950.9	E962.1	E980.9
dichloride (vapor)	982.3	E862.4	—	E950.9	E962.1	E980.9
glycol(s) (any) (vapor)	982.8	E862.4	—	E950.9	E962.1	E980.9
Ethylidene						
chloride NEC	982.3	E862.4	—	E950.9	E962.1	E980.9
diethyl ether	982.8	E862.4	—	E950.9	E962.1	E980.9
Ethynodiol	962.2	E858.0	E932.2	E950.4	E962.0	E980.4
Etidocaine	968.9	E855.2	E938.9	E950.4	E962.0	E980.4
infiltration (subcutaneous)	968.5	E855.2	E938.5	E950.4	E962.0	E980.4
nerve (peripheral) (plexus)	968.6	E855.2	E938.6	E950.4	E962.0	E980.4
Etilfen	967.0	E851	E937.0	E950.1	E962.0	E980.1
Etomide	965.7	E850.7	E935.7	E950.0	E962.0	E980.0
Etorphine	965.09	E850.2	E935.2	E950.0	E962.0	E980.0
Etoval	967.0	E851	E937.0	E950.1	E962.0	E980.1
Etryptamine	969.01	E854.0	E939.0	E950.3	E962.0	E980.3
Eucaine	968.5	E855.2	E938.5	E950.4	E962.0	E980.4
Eucalyptus (oil) NEC	975.5	E858.6	E945.5	E950.4	E962.0	E980.4
Eucatropine	971.1	E855.4	E941.1	E950.4	E962.0	E980.4
Eucodal	965.09	E850.2	E935.2	E950.0	E962.0	E980.0
Euneryl	967.0	E851	E937.0	E950.1	E962.0	E980.1
Euphthalmine	971.1	E855.4	E941.1	E950.4	E962.0	E980.4
Eurax	976.0	E858.7	E946.0	E950.4	E962.0	E980.4

Nontherapeutic use substance

⌖ Subterms under main terms may continue to next column or page

	Poisoning	Accident	Therapeutic Use	Suicide Attempt	Assault	Undetermined
Euresol	976.4	E858.7	E946.4	E950.4	E962.0	E980.4
Euthroid	962.7	E858.0	E932.7	E950.4	E962.0	E980.4
Evans blue	977.8	E858.8	E947.8	E950.4	E962.0	E980.4
Evipal	967.0	E851	E937.0	E950.1	E962.0	E980.1
sodium	968.3	E855.1	E938.3	E950.4	E962.0	E980.4
Evipan	967.0	E851	E937.0	E950.1	E962.0	E980.1
sodium	968.3	E855.1	E938.3	E950.4	E962.0	E980.4
Exalgin	965.4	E850.4	E935.4	E950.0	E962.0	E980.0
Excipients, pharmaceutical	977.4	E858.8	E947.4	E950.4	E962.0	E980.4
Exhaust gas — see Carbon, monoxide						
Ex-Lax (phenolphthalein)	973.1	E858.4	E943.1	E950.4	E962.0	E980.4
Expectorants	975.5	E858.6	E945.5	E950.4	E962.0	E980.4
External medications (skin)						
(mucous membrane)	976.9	E858.7	E946.9	E950.4	E962.0	E980.4
dental agent	976.7	E858.7	E946.7	E950.4	E962.0	E980.4
ENT agent	976.6	E858.7	E946.6	E950.4	E962.0	E980.4
ophthalmic preparation	976.5	E858.7	E946.5	E950.4	E962.0	E980.4
specified NEC	976.8	E858.7	E946.8	E950.4	E962.0	E980.4
Eye agents (anti-infective)	976.5	E858.7	E946.5	E950.4	E962.0	E980.4
Factor IX complex (human)	964.5	E858.2	E934.5	E950.4	E962.0	E980.4
Fecal softeners	973.2	E858.4	E943.2	E950.4	E962.0	E980.4
Fenbutrazate	977.0	E858.8	E947.0	E950.4	E962.0	E980.4
Fencamfamin	970.89	E854.3	E940.8	E950.4	E962.0	E980.4
Fenfluramine	977.0	E858.8	E947.0	E950.4	E962.0	E980.4
Fenoprofen	965.61	E850.6	E935.6	E950.0	E962.0	E980.0
Fentanyl	965.09	E850.2	E935.2	E950.0	E962.0	E980.0
Fentazin	969.1	E853.0	E939.1	E950.3	E962.0	E980.3
Fenticlor, fentichlor	976.0	E858.7	E946.0	E950.4	E962.0	E980.4
Fer de lance (bite) (venom)	989.5	E905.0	—	E950.9	E962.1	E980.9
Ferric — see Iron						
Ferrocholinate	964.0	E858.2	E934.0	E950.4	E962.0	E980.4
Ferrous fumerate, gluconate, lactate, salt NEC, sulfate (medicinal)	964.0	E858.2	E934.0	E950.4	E962.0	E980.4
Ferrum — see Iron						
Fertilizers NEC	989.89	E866.5	—	E950.9	E962.1	E980.4
with herbicide mixture	989.4	E863.5	—	E950.6	E962.1	E980.7
Fibrinogen (human)	964.7	E858.2	E934.7	E950.4	E962.0	E980.4
Fibrinolysin	964.4	E858.2	E934.4	E950.4	E962.0	E980.4
Fibrinolysis-affecting agents	964.4	E858.2	E934.4	E950.4	E962.0	E980.4
Filix mas	961.6	E857	E931.6	E950.4	E962.0	E980.4
Fiorinal	965.1	E850.3	E935.3	E950.0	E962.0	E980.0
Fire damp	987.1	E869.8	—	E952.8	E962.2	E982.8
Fish, nonbacterial or noxious	988.0	E865.2	—	E950.9	E962.1	E980.9
shell	988.0	E865.1	—	E950.9	E962.1	E980.9
Flagyl	961.5	E857	E931.5	E950.4	E962.0	E980.4
Flavoxate	975.1	E858.6	E945.1	E950.4	E962.0	E980.4
Flaxedil	975.2	E858.6	E945.2	E950.4	E962.0	E980.4
Flaxseed (medicinal)	976.3	E858.7	E946.3	E950.4	E962.0	E980.4
Flomax	971.3	E855.6	E941.3	E950.4	E962.0	E980.1
Florantyrone	973.4	E858.4	E943.4	E950.4	E962.0	E980.4
Floraquin	961.3	E857	E931.3	E950.4	E962.0	E980.4
Florinef	962.0	E858.0	E932.0	E950.4	E962.0	E980.4
ENT agent	976.6	E858.7	E946.6	E950.4	E962.0	E980.4
ophthalmic preparation	976.5	E858.7	E946.5	E950.4	E962.0	E980.4
topical NEC	976.0	E858.7	E946.0	E950.4	E962.0	E980.4
Flowers of sulfur	976.4	E858.7	E946.4	E950.4	E962.0	E980.4
Floxuridine	963.1	E858.1	E933.1	E950.4	E962.0	E980.4
Flucytosine	961.9	E857	E931.9	E950.4	E962.0	E980.4
Fludrocortisone	962.0	E858.0	E932.0	E950.4	E962.0	E980.4
ENT agent	976.6	E858.7	E946.6	E950.4	E962.0	E980.4
ophthalmic preparation	976.5	E858.7	E946.5	E950.4	E962.0	E980.4
topical NEC	976.0	E858.7	E946.0	E950.4	E962.0	E980.4
Flumethasone	976.0	E858.7	E946.0	E950.4	E962.0	E980.4
Flumethiazide	974.3	E858.5	E944.3	E950.4	E962.0	E980.4
Flumidin	961.7	E857	E931.7	E950.4	E962.0	E980.4
Flunitrazepam	969.4	E853.2	E939.4	E950.3	E962.0	E980.3
Fluocinolone	976.0	E858.7	E946.0	E950.4	E962.0	E980.4
Fluocortolone	962.0	E858.0	E932.0	E950.4	E962.0	E980.4
Fluohydrocortisone	962.0	E858.0	E932.0	E950.4	E962.0	E980.4
ENT agent	976.6	E858.7	E946.6	E950.4	E962.0	E980.4
ophthalmic preparation	976.5	E858.7	E946.5	E950.4	E962.0	E980.4
topical NEC	976.0	E858.7	E946.0	E950.4	E962.0	E980.4
Fluonid	976.0	E858.7	E946.0	E950.4	E962.0	E980.4
Fluopromazine	969.1	E853.0	E939.1	E950.3	E962.0	E980.3

	Poisoning	Accident	Therapeutic Use	Suicide Attempt	Assault	Undetermined
Fluoracetate	989.4	E863.7	—	E950.6	E962.1	E980.7
Fluorescein (sodium)	977.8	E858.8	E947.8	E950.4	E962.0	E980.4
Fluoride(s) (pesticides) (sodium) NEC	989.4	E863.4	—	E950.6	E962.1	E980.7
hydrogen — see Hydrofluoric acid						
medicinal	976.7	E858.7	E946.7	E950.4	E962.0	E980.4
not pesticide NEC	983.9	E864.4	—	E950.7	E962.1	E980.6
stannous	976.7	E858.7	E946.7	E950.4	E962.0	E980.4
Fluorinated corticosteroids	962.0	E858.0	E932.0	E950.4	E962.0	E980.4
Fluorine (compounds) (gas)	987.8	E869.8	—	E952.8	E962.2	E982.8
salt — see Fluoride(s)						
Fluoristan	976.7	E858.7	E946.7	E950.4	E962.0	E980.4
Fluoroacetate	989.4	E863.7	—	E950.6	E962.1	E980.7
Fluorodeoxyuridine	963.1	E858.1	E933.1	E950.4	E962.0	E980.4
Fluorometholone (topical) NEC	976.0	E858.7	E946.0	E950.4	E962.0	E980.4
ophthalmic preparation	976.5	E858.7	E946.5	E950.4	E962.0	E980.4
Fluorouracil	963.1	E858.1	E933.1	E950.4	E962.0	E980.4
Fluothane	968.1	E855.1	E938.1	E950.4	E962.0	E980.4
Fluoxetine hydrochloride	969.03	E854.0	E939.0	E950.3	E962.0	E980.3
Fluoxymesterone	962.1	E858.0	E932.1	E950.4	E962.0	E980.4
Fluphenazine	969.1	E853.0	E939.1	E950.3	E962.0	E980.3
Fluprednisolone	962.0	E858.0	E932.0	E950.4	E962.0	E980.4
Flurandrenolide	976.0	E858.7	E946.0	E950.4	E962.0	E980.4
Flurazepam (hydrochloride)	969.4	E853.2	E939.4	E950.3	E962.0	E980.3
Flurbiprofen	965.61	E850.6	E935.6	E950.0	E962.0	E980.0
Flurobate	976.0	E858.7	E946.0	E950.4	E962.0	E980.4
Flurothyl	969.8	E855.8	E939.8	E950.3	E962.0	E980.3
Fluroxene	968.2	E855.1	E938.2	E950.4	E962.0	E980.4
Folacin	964.1	E858.2	E934.1	E950.4	E962.0	E980.4
Folic acid	964.1	E858.2	E934.1	E950.4	E962.0	E980.4
Follicle stimulating hormone	962.4	E858.0	E932.4	E950.4	E962.0	E980.4
Food, foodstuffs, nonbacterial or noxious	988.9	E865.9	—	E950.9	E962.1	E980.9
berries, seeds	988.2	E865.3	—	E950.9	E962.1	E980.9
fish	988.0	E865.2	—	E950.9	E962.1	E980.9
mushrooms	988.1	E865.5	—	E950.9	E962.1	E980.9
plants	988.2	E865.9	—	E950.9	E962.1	E980.9
specified type NEC	988.2	E865.4	—	E950.9	E962.1	E980.9
shellfish	988.0	E865.1	—	E950.9	E962.1	E980.9
specified NEC	988.8	E865.8	—	E950.9	E962.1	E980.9
Fool's parsley	988.2	E865.4	—	E950.9	E962.1	E980.9
Formaldehyde (solution)	989.89	E861.4	—	E950.9	E962.1	E980.9
fungicide	989.4	E863.6	—	E950.6	E962.1	E980.7
gas or vapor	987.8	E869.8	—	E952.8	E962.2	E982.8
Formalin	989.89	E861.4	—	E950.9	E962.1	E980.9
fungicide	989.4	E863.6	—	E950.6	E962.1	E980.7
vapor	987.8	E869.8	—	E952.8	E962.2	E982.8
Formic acid	983.1	E864.1	—	E950.7	E962.1	E980.6
automobile	981	E862.1	—	E950.9	E962.1	E980.9
exhaust gas, not in transit	986	E868.2	—	E952.0	E962.2	E982.0
vapor NEC	987.1	E869.8	—	E952.8	E962.2	E982.8
gas (domestic use) (see also Carbon, monoxide, fuel)						
utility	987.1	E868.1	—	E951.8	E962.2	E981.8
incomplete combustion of — see Carbon, monoxide, fuel, utility						
in mobile container	987.0	E868.0	—	E951.1	E962.2	E981.1
piped (natural)	987.1	E867	—	E951.0	E962.2	E981.0
industrial, incomplete combustion	986	E868.3	—	E952.1	E962.2	E982.1
vapor	987.8	E869.8	—	E952.8	E962.2	E982.8
Fowler's solution	985.1	E866.3	—	E950.8	E962.1	E980.8
Foxglove	988.2	E865.4	—	E950.9	E962.1	E980.9
Fox green	977.8	E858.8	E947.8	E950.4	E962.0	E980.4
Framycetin	960.8	E856	E930.8	E950.4	E962.0	E980.4
Frangula (extract)	973.1	E858.4	E943.1	E950.4	E962.0	E980.4
Frei antigen	977.8	E858.8	E947.8	E950.4	E962.0	E980.4
Freons	987.4	E869.2	—	E952.8	E962.2	E982.8
Fructose	974.5	E858.5	E944.5	E950.4	E962.0	E980.4
Frusemide	974.4	E858.5	E944.4	E950.4	E962.0	E980.4
FSH	962.4	E858.0	E932.4	E950.4	E962.0	E980.4
Fuel						
Fugillin	960.8	E856	E930.8	E950.4	E962.0	E980.4

Nontherapeutic use substance

▽ Subterms under main terms may continue to next column or page

	Poisoning	Accident	Therapeutic Use	Suicide Attempt	Assault	Undetermined
Fulminate of mercury	985.0	E866.1	—	E950.9	E962.1	E980.9
Fulvicin	960.1	E856	E930.1	E950.4	E962.0	E980.4
Fumadil	960.8	E856	E930.8	E950.4	E962.0	E980.4
Fumagillin	960.8	E856	E930.8	E950.4	E962.0	E980.4
Fumes (from)	987.9	E869.9	—	E952.9	E962.2	E982.9
carbon monoxide — see Carbon, monoxide						
charcoal (domestic use)	986	E868.3	—	E952.1	E962.2	E982.1
chloroform — see Chloroform						
coke (in domestic stoves, fireplaces)	986	E868.3	—	E952.1	E962.2	E982.1
corrosive NEC	987.8	E869.8	—	E952.8	E962.2	E982.8
ether — see Ether(s)						
freons	987.4	E869.2	—	E952.8	E962.2	E982.8
hydrocarbons	987.1	E869.8	—	E952.8	E962.2	E982.8
petroleum (liquefied)	987.0	E868.0	—	E951.1	E962.2	E981.1
distributed through pipes (pure or mixed with air)	987.0	E867	—	E951.0	E962.2	E981.0
lead — see Lead						
metals — see specified metal						
nitrogen dioxide	987.2	E869.0	—	E952.8	E962.2	E982.8
pesticides — see Pesticides						
petroleum (liquefied)	987.0	E868.0	—	E951.1	E962.2	E981.1
distributed through pipes (pure or mixed with air)	987.0	E867	—	E951.0	E962.2	E981.0
polyester	987.8	E869.8	—	E952.8	E962.2	E982.8
specified, source other (see also substance specified)	987.8	E869.8	—	E952.8	E962.2	E982.8
sulfur dioxide	987.3	E869.1	—	E952.8	E962.2	E982.8
Fumigants	989.4	E863.8	—	E950.6	E962.1	E980.7
Fungicides — see also Antifungals	989.4	E863.6	—	E950.6	E962.1	E980.7
Fungi, noxious, used as food	988.1	E865.5	—	E950.9	E962.1	E980.9
Fungizone	960.1	E856	E930.1	E950.4	E962.0	E980.4
topical	976.0	E858.7	E946.0	E950.4	E962.0	E980.4
Furacin	976.0	E858.7	E946.0	E950.4	E962.0	E980.4
Furadantin	961.9	E857	E931.9	E950.4	E962.0	E980.4
Furazolidone	961.9	E857	E931.9	E950.4	E962.0	E980.4
Furnace (coal burning) (domestic), gas from	986	E868.3	—	E952.1	E962.2	E982.1
industrial	986	E868.8	—	E952.1	E962.2	E982.1
Furniture polish	989.89	E861.2	—	E950.9	E962.1	E980.9
Furosemide	974.4	E858.5	E944.4	E950.4	E962.0	E980.4
Furoxone	961.9	E857	E931.9	E950.4	E962.0	E980.4
Fusel oil (amyl) (butyl) (propyl)	980.3	E860.4	—	E950.9	E962.1	E980.9
Fusidic acid	960.8	E856	E930.8	E950.4	E962.0	E980.4
Gallamine	975.2	E858.6	E945.2	E950.4	E962.0	E980.4
Gallotannic acid	976.2	E858.7	E946.2	E950.4	E962.0	E980.4
Gamboge	973.1	E858.4	E943.1	E950.4	E962.0	E980.4
Gamimune	964.6	E858.2	E934.6	E950.4	E962.0	E980.4
Gamma-benzene hexachloride (vapor)	989.2	E863.0	—	E950.6	E962.1	E980.7
Gamma globulin	964.6	E858.2	E934.6	E950.4	E962.0	E980.4
Gamma hydroxy butyrate (GHB)	968.4	E855.1	E938.4	E950.4	E962.0	E980.4
Gamulin	964.6	E858.2	E934.6	E950.4	E962.0	E980.4
Ganglionic blocking agents	972.3	E858.3	E942.3	E950.4	E962.0	E980.4
Ganja	969.6	E854.1	E939.6	E950.3	E962.0	E980.3
Garamycin	960.8	E856	E930.8	E950.4	E962.0	E980.4
ophthalmic preparation	976.5	E858.7	E946.5	E950.4	E962.0	E980.4
topical NEC	976.0	E858.7	E946.0	E950.4	E962.0	E980.4
Gardenal	967.0	E851	E937.0	E950.1	E962.0	E980.1
Gardepanyl	967.0	E851	E937.0	E950.1	E962.0	E980.1
Gas	987.9	E869.9	—	E952.9	E962.2	E982.9
acetylene	987.1	E868.1	—	E951.8	E962.2	E981.8
incomplete combustion of — see Carbon, monoxide, fuel, utility						
air contaminants, source or type not specified	987.9	E869.9	—	E952.9	E962.2	E982.9
anesthetic (general) NEC	968.2	E855.1	E938.2	E950.4	E962.0	E980.4
blast furnace	986	E868.8	—	E952.1	E962.2	E982.1
butane — see Butane						
carbon monoxide — see Carbon, monoxide						

	Poisoning	Accident	Therapeutic Use	Suicide Attempt	Assault	Undetermined
Gas — continued						
chlorine	987.6	E869.8	—	E952.8	E962.2	E982.8
coal — see Carbon, monoxide, coal						
cyanide	987.7	E869.8	—	E952.8	E962.2	E982.8
dicyanogen	987.8	E869.8	—	E952.8	E962.2	E982.8
domestic — see Gas, utility						
exhaust — see Carbon, monoxide, exhaust gas						
from wood- or coal-burning stove or fireplace	986	E868.3	—	E952.1	E962.2	E982.1
fuel (domestic use) (see also Carbon, monoxide, fuel)						
industrial use	986	E868.8	—	E952.1	E962.2	E982.1
utility	987.1	E868.1	—	E951.8	E962.2	E981.8
incomplete combustion of — see Carbon, monoxide, fuel, utility						
in mobile container	987.0	E868.0	—	E951.1	E962.2	E981.1
piped (natural)	987.1	E867	—	E951.0	E962.2	E981.0
garage	986	E868.2	—	E952.0	E962.2	E982.0
hydrocarbon NEC	987.1	E869.8	—	E952.8	E962.2	E982.8
incomplete combustion of — see Carbon, monoxide, fuel, utility						
liquefied (mobile container)	987.0	E868.0	—	E951.1	E962.2	E981.1
piped	987.0	E867	—	E951.0	E962.2	E981.0
hydrocyanic acid	987.7	E869.8	—	E952.8	E962.2	E982.8
illuminating — see Gas, utility						
incomplete combustion, any — see Carbon, monoxide						
kiln	986	E868.8	—	E952.1	E962.2	E982.1
lacrimogenic	987.5	E869.3	—	E952.8	E962.2	E982.8
marsh	987.1	E869.8	—	E952.8	E962.2	E982.8
motor exhaust, not in transit	986	E868.8	—	E952.1	E962.2	E982.1
mustard — see Mustard, gas						
natural	987.1	E867	—	E951.0	E962.2	E981.0
nerve (war)	987.9	E869.9	—	E952.9	E962.2	E982.9
oils	981	E862.1	—	E950.9	E962.1	E980.9
petroleum (liquefied) (distributed in mobile containers)	987.0	E868.0	—	E951.1	E962.2	E981.1
piped (pure or mixed with air)	987.0	E867	—	E951.1	E962.2	E981.1
piped (manufactured) (natural) NEC	987.1	E867	—	E951.0	E962.2	E981.0
producer	986	E868.8	—	E952.1	E962.2	E982.1
propane — see Propane						
refrigerant (freon)	987.4	E869.2	—	E952.8	E962.2	E982.8
not freon	987.9	E869.9	—	E952.9	E962.2	E982.9
sewer	987.8	E869.8	—	E952.8	E962.2	E982.8
specified source NEC (see also substance specified)	987.8	E869.8	—	E952.8	E962.2	E982.8
stove — see Gas, utility						
tear	987.5	E869.3	—	E952.8	E962.2	E982.8
utility (for cooking, heating, or lighting) (piped) NEC	987.1	E868.1	—	E951.8	E962.2	E981.8
incomplete combustion of — see Carbon, monoxide, fuel, utility						
in mobile container	987.0	E868.0	—	E951.1	E962.2	E981.1
piped (natural)	987.1	E867	—	E951.0	E962.2	E981.0
water	987.1	E868.1	—	E951.8	E962.2	E981.8
incomplete combustion of — see Carbon, monoxide, fuel, utility						
Gaseous substance — see Gas						
Gasoline, gasolene	981	E862.1	—	E950.9	E962.1	E980.9
vapor	987.1	E869.8	—	E952.8	E962.2	E982.8
Gastric enzymes	973.4	E858.4	E943.4	E950.4	E962.0	E980.4
Gastrografin	977.8	E858.8	E947.8	E950.4	E962.0	E980.4
Gastrointestinal agents	973.9	E858.4	E943.9	E950.4	E962.0	E980.4
specified NEC	973.8	E858.4	E943.8	E950.4	E962.0	E980.4
Gaultheria procumbens	988.2	E865.4	—	E950.9	E962.1	E980.9
Gelatin (intravenous)	964.8	E858.2	E934.8	E950.4	E962.0	E980.4
absorbable (sponge)	964.5	E858.2	E934.5	E950.4	E962.0	E980.4
Gelfilm	976.8	E858.7	E946.8	E950.4	E962.0	E980.4
Gelfoam	964.5	E858.2	E934.5	E950.4	E962.0	E980.4

| Nontherapeutic use substance | | ▽ Subterms under main terms may continue to next column or page |

	Poisoning	External Cause (E-Code)				
		Accident	Therapeutic Use	Suicide Attempt	Assault	Undetermined
Gelsemine	970.89	E854.3	E940.8	E950.4	E962.0	E980.9
Gelsemium (semper-virens)	988.2	E865.4	—	E950.9	E962.1	E980.9
Gemonil	967.0	E851	E937.0	E950.1	E962.0	E980.1
Gentamicin	960.8	E856	E930.8	E950.4	E962.0	E980.4
ophthalmic preparation	976.5	E858.7	E946.5	E950.4	E962.0	E980.4
topical NEC	976.0	E858.7	E946.0	E950.4	E962.0	E980.4
Gentian violet	976.0	E858.7	E946.0	E950.4	E962.0	E980.4
Gexane	976.0	E858.7	E946.0	E950.4	E962.0	E980.4
Gila monster (venom)	989.5	E905.0	—	E950.9	E962.1	E980.9
Ginger, Jamaica	989.89	E866.8	—	E950.9	E962.1	E980.9
Gitalin	972.1	E858.3	E942.1	E950.4	E962.0	E980.4
Gitoxin	972.1	E858.3	E942.1	E950.4	E962.0	E980.4
Glandular extract (medicinal) NEC	977.9	E858.9	E947.9	E950.5	E962.0	E980.5
Glaucarubin	961.5	E857	E931.5	E950.4	E962.0	E980.4
Globin zinc insulin	962.3	E858.0	E932.3	E950.4	E962.0	E980.4
Glucagon	962.3	E858.0	E932.3	E950.4	E962.0	E980.4
Glucochloral	967.1	E852.0	E937.1	E950.2	E962.0	E980.2
Glucocorticoids	962.0	E858.0	E932.0	E950.4	E962.0	E980.4
Glucose	974.5	E858.5	E944.5	E950.4	E962.0	E980.4
oxidase reagent	977.8	E858.8	E947.8	E950.4	E962.0	E980.4
Glucosulfone sodium	961.8	E857	E931.8	E950.4	E962.0	E980.4
Glue(s)	989.89	E866.6	—	E950.9	E962.1	E980.9
Glutamic acid (hydrochloride)	973.4	E858.4	E943.4	E950.4	E962.0	E980.4
Glutaraldehyde	989.89	E861.4	—	E950.9	E962.1	E980.9
Glutathione	963.8	E858.1	E933.8	E950.4	E962.0	E980.4
Glutethimide (group)	967.5	E852.4	E937.5	E950.2	E962.0	E980.2
Glycerin (lotion)	976.3	E858.7	E946.3	E950.4	E962.0	E980.4
Glycerol (topical)	976.3	E858.7	E946.3	E950.4	E962.0	E980.4
Glyceryl						
guaiacolate	975.5	E858.6	E945.5	E950.4	E962.0	E980.4
triacetate (topical)	976.0	E858.7	E946.0	E950.4	E962.0	E980.4
trinitrate	972.4	E858.3	E942.4	E950.4	E962.0	E980.4
Glycine	974.5	E858.5	E944.5	E950.4	E962.0	E980.4
Glycobiarsol	961.1	E857	E931.1	E950.4	E962.0	E980.4
Glycols (ether)	982.8	E862.4	—	E950.9	E962.1	E980.9
Glycopyrrolate	971.1	E855.4	E941.1	E950.4	E962.0	E980.4
Glymidine	962.3	E858.0	E932.3	E950.4	E962.0	E980.4
Gold (compounds) (salts)	965.69	E850.6	E935.6	E950.0	E962.0	E980.0
Golden sulfide of antimony	985.4	E866.2	—	E950.9	E962.1	E980.9
Goldylocks	988.2	E865.4	—	E950.9	E962.1	E980.9
Gonadal tissue extract	962.9	E858.0	E932.9	E950.4	E962.0	E980.4
female	962.2	E858.0	E932.2	E950.4	E962.0	E980.4
male	962.1	E858.0	E932.1	E950.4	E962.0	E980.4
Gonadotropin	962.4	E858.0	E932.4	E950.4	E962.0	E980.4
Grain alcohol	980.0	E860.1	—	E950.9	E962.1	E980.9
beverage	980.0	E860.0	—	E950.9	E962.1	E980.9
Gramicidin	960.8	E856	E930.8	E950.4	E962.0	E980.4
Gratiola officinalis	988.2	E865.4	—	E950.9	E962.1	E980.9
Grease	989.89	E866.8	—	E950.9	E962.1	E980.9
Green hellebore	988.2	E865.4	—	E950.9	E962.1	E980.9
Green soap	976.2	E858.7	E946.2	E950.4	E962.0	E980.4
Grifulvin	960.1	E856	E930.1	E950.4	E962.0	E980.4
Griseofulvin	960.1	E856	E930.1	E950.4	E962.0	E980.4
Growth hormone	962.4	E858.0	E932.4	E950.4	E962.0	E980.4
Guaiacol	975.5	E858.6	E945.5	E950.4	E962.0	E980.4
Guaiac reagent	977.8	E858.8	E947.8	E950.4	E962.0	E980.4
Guaifenesin	975.5	E858.6	E945.5	E950.4	E962.0	E980.4
Guaiphenesin	975.5	E858.6	E945.5	E950.4	E962.0	E980.4
Guanatol	961.4	E857	E931.4	E950.4	E962.0	E980.4
Guanethidine	972.6	E858.3	E942.6	E950.4	E962.0	E980.4
Guano	989.89	E866.5	—	E950.9	E962.1	E980.9
Guanochlor	972.6	E858.3	E942.6	E950.4	E962.0	E980.4
Guanoctine	972.6	E858.3	E942.6	E950.4	E962.0	E980.4
Guanoxan	972.6	E858.3	E942.6	E950.4	E962.0	E980.4
Hair treatment agent NEC	976.4	E858.7	E946.4	E950.4	E962.0	E980.4
Halcinonide	976.0	E858.7	E946.0	E950.4	E962.0	E980.4
Halethazole	976.0	E858.7	E946.0	E950.4	E962.0	E980.4
Hallucinogens	969.6	E854.1	E939.6	E950.3	E962.0	E980.3
Haloperidol	969.2	E853.1	E939.2	E950.3	E962.0	E980.3
Haloprogin	976.0	E858.7	E946.0	E950.4	E962.0	E980.4
Halotex	976.0	E858.7	E946.0	E950.4	E962.0	E980.4
Halothane	968.1	E855.1	E938.1	E950.4	E962.0	E980.4
Halquinols	976.0	E858.7	E946.0	E950.4	E962.0	E980.4
Hand sanitizer	976.0	E858.7	E946.0	E950.4	E962.0	E980.4
Harmonyl	972.6	E858.3	E942.6	E950.4	E962.0	E980.4
Hartmann's solution	974.5	E858.5	E944.5	E950.4	E962.0	E980.4
Hashish	969.6	E854.1	E939.6	E950.3	E962.0	E980.3
Hawaiian wood rose seeds	969.6	E854.1	E939.6	E950.3	E962.0	E980.3
Headache cures, drugs, powders NEC	977.9	E858.9	E947.9	E950.5	E962.0	E980.9
Heavenly Blue (morning glory)	969.6	E854.1	E939.6	E950.3	E962.0	E980.3
Heavy metal antagonists	963.8	E858.1	E933.8	E950.4	E962.0	E980.4
anti-infectives	961.2	E857	E931.2	E950.4	E962.0	E980.4
Hedaquinium	976.0	E858.7	E946.0	E950.4	E962.0	E980.4
Hedge hyssop	988.2	E865.4	—	E950.9	E962.1	E980.9
Heet	976.8	E858.7	E946.8	E950.4	E962.0	E980.4
Helenin	961.6	E857	E931.6	E950.4	E962.0	E980.4
Hellebore (black) (green) (white)	988.2	E865.4	—	E950.9	E962.1	E980.9
Hemlock	988.2	E865.4	—	E950.9	E962.1	E980.9
Hemostatics	964.5	E858.2	E934.5	E950.4	E962.0	E980.4
capillary active drugs	972.8	E858.3	E942.8	E950.4	E962.0	E980.4
Henbane	988.2	E865.4	—	E950.9	E962.1	E980.9
Heparin (sodium)	964.2	E858.2	E934.2	E950.4	E962.0	E980.4
Heptabarbital, heptabarbitone	967.0	E851	E937.0	E950.1	E962.0	E980.1
Heptachlor	989.2	E863.0	—	E950.6	E962.1	E980.7
Heptalgin	965.09	E850.2	E935.2	E950.0	E962.0	E980.0
Herbicides	989.4	E863.5	—	E950.6	E962.1	E980.7
Heroin	965.01	E850.0	E935.0	E950.0	E962.0	E980.0
Herplex	976.5	E858.7	E946.5	E950.4	E962.0	E980.4
HES	964.8	E858.2	E934.8	E950.4	E962.0	E980.4
Hetastarch	964.8	E858.2	E934.8	E950.4	E962.0	E980.4
Hexachlorocyclohexane	989.2	E863.0	—	E950.6	E962.1	E980.7
Hexachlorophene	976.2	E858.7	E946.2	E950.4	E962.0	E980.4
Hexadimethrine (bromide)	964.5	E858.2	E934.5	E950.4	E962.0	E980.4
Hexafluorenium	975.2	E858.6	E945.2	E950.4	E962.0	E980.4
Hexa-germ	976.2	E858.7	E946.2	E950.4	E962.0	E980.4
Hexahydrophenol	980.8	E860.8	—	E950.9	E962.1	E980.9
Hexalin	980.8	E860.8	—	E950.9	E962.1	E980.9
Hexamethonium	972.3	E858.3	E942.3	E950.4	E962.0	E980.4
Hexamethyleneamine	961.9	E857	E931.9	E950.4	E962.0	E980.4
Hexamine	961.9	E857	E931.9	E950.4	E962.0	E980.4
Hexanone	982.8	E862.4	—	E950.9	E962.1	E980.9
Hexapropymate	967.8	E852.8	E937.8	E950.2	E962.0	E980.2
Hexestrol	962.2	E858.0	E932.2	E950.4	E962.0	E980.4
Hexethal (sodium)	967.0	E851	E937.0	E950.1	E962.0	E980.1
Hexetidine	976.0	E858.7	E946.0	E950.4	E962.0	E980.4
Hexobarbital, hexobarbitone	967.0	E851	E937.0	E950.1	E962.0	E980.1
sodium (anesthetic)	968.3	E855.1	E938.3	E950.4	E962.0	E980.4
soluble	968.3	E855.1	E938.3	E950.4	E962.0	E980.4
Hexocyclium	971.1	E855.4	E941.1	E950.4	E962.0	E980.4
Hexoestrol	962.2	E858.0	E932.2	E950.4	E962.0	E980.4
Hexone	982.8	E862.4	—	E950.9	E962.1	E980.9
Hexylcaine	968.5	E855.2	E938.5	E950.4	E962.0	E980.4
Hexylresorcinol	961.6	E857	E931.6	E950.4	E962.0	E980.4
Hinkle's pills	973.1	E858.4	E943.1	E950.4	E962.0	E980.4
Histalog	977.8	E858.8	E947.8	E950.4	E962.0	E980.4
Histamine (phosphate)	972.5	E858.3	E942.5	E950.4	E962.0	E980.4
Histoplasmin	977.8	E858.8	E947.8	E950.4	E962.0	E980.4
Holly berries	988.2	E865.3	—	E950.9	E962.1	E980.9
Homatropine	971.1	E855.4	E941.1	E950.4	E962.0	E980.4
Homo-tet	964.6	E858.2	E934.6	E950.4	E962.0	E980.4
Hormones (synthetic substitute) NEC	962.9	E858.0	E932.9	E950.4	E962.0	E980.4
adrenal cortical steroids	962.0	E858.0	E932.0	E950.4	E962.0	E980.4
antidiabetic agents	962.3	E858.0	E932.3	E950.4	E962.0	E980.4
follicle stimulating	962.4	E858.0	E932.4	E950.4	E962.0	E980.4
gonadotropic	962.4	E858.0	E932.4	E950.4	E962.0	E980.4
growth	962.4	E858.0	E932.4	E950.4	E962.0	E980.4
ovarian (substitutes)	962.2	E858.0	E932.2	E950.4	E962.0	E980.4
parathyroid (derivatives)	962.6	E858.0	E932.6	E950.4	E962.0	E980.4
pituitary (posterior)	962.5	E858.0	E932.5	E950.4	E962.0	E980.4
anterior	962.4	E858.0	E932.4	E950.4	E962.0	E980.4
thyroid (derivative)	962.7	E858.0	E932.7	E950.4	E962.0	E980.4
Hornet (sting)	989.5	E905.3	—	E950.9	E962.1	E980.9
Horticulture agent NEC	989.4	E863.9	—	E950.6	E962.1	E980.7
Hyaluronidase	963.4	E858.1	E933.4	E950.4	E962.0	E980.4
Hyazyme	963.4	E858.1	E933.4	E950.4	E962.0	E980.4
Hycodan	965.09	E850.2	E935.2	E950.0	E962.0	E980.0
Hydantoin derivatives	966.1	E855.0	E936.1	E950.4	E962.0	E980.4
Hydeltra	962.0	E858.0	E932.0	E950.4	E962.0	E980.4
Hydergine	971.3	E855.6	E941.3	E950.4	E962.0	E980.4
Hydrabamine penicillin	960.0	E856	E930.0	E950.4	E962.0	E980.4

▽ Subterms under main terms may continue to next column or page

	External Cause (E-Code)					
	Poisoning	Accident	Therapeutic Use	Suicide Attempt	Assault	Undetermined
Hydralazine, hydralazine	972.6	E858.3	E942.6	E950.4	E962.0	E980.4
Hydrargaphen	976.0	E858.7	E946.0	E950.4	E962.0	E980.4
Hydrazine	983.9	E864.3	—	E950.7	E962.1	E980.6
Hydriodic acid	975.5	E858.6	E945.5	E950.4	E962.0	E980.4
Hydrocarbon gas	987.1	E869.8	—	E952.8	E962.2	E982.8
incomplete combustion of — see Carbon, monoxide, fuel, utility						
liquefied (mobile container)	987.0	E868.0	—	E951.1	E962.2	E981.1
piped (natural)	987.0	E867	—	E951.0	E962.2	E981.0
Hydrochloric acid (liquid)	983.1	E864.1	—	E950.7	E962.1	E980.6
medicinal	973.4	E858.4	E943.4	E950.4	E962.0	E980.4
vapor	987.8	E869.8	—	E952.8	E962.2	E982.8
Hydrochlorothiazide	974.3	E858.5	E944.3	E950.4	E962.0	E980.4
Hydrocodone	965.09	E850.2	E935.2	E950.0	E962.0	E980.0
Hydrocortisone	962.0	E858.0	E932.0	E950.4	E962.0	E980.4
ENT agent	976.6	E858.7	E946.6	E950.4	E962.0	E980.4
ophthalmic preparation	976.5	E858.7	E946.5	E950.4	E962.0	E980.4
topical NEC	976.0	E858.7	E946.0	E950.4	E962.0	E980.4
Hydrocortone	962.0	E858.0	E932.0	E950.4	E962.0	E980.4
ENT agent	976.6	E858.7	E946.6	E950.4	E962.0	E980.4
ophthalmic preparation	976.5	E858.7	E946.5	E950.4	E962.0	E980.4
topical NEC	976.0	E858.7	E946.0	E950.4	E962.0	E980.4
Hydrocyanic acid — see Cyanide(s)						
Hydroflumethiazide	974.3	E858.5	E944.3	E950.4	E962.0	E980.4
Hydrofluoric acid (liquid)	983.1	E864.1	—	E950.7	E962.1	E980.6
vapor	987.8	E869.8	—	E952.8	E962.2	E982.8
Hydrogen	987.8	E869.8	—	E952.8	E962.2	E982.8
arsenide	985.1	E866.3	—	E950.8	E962.1	E980.8
arseniureted	985.1	E866.3	—	E950.8	E962.1	E980.8
cyanide (salts)	989.0	E866.8	—	E950.9	E962.1	E980.9
gas	987.7	E869.8	—	E952.8	E962.2	E982.8
fluoride (liquid)	983.1	E864.1	—	E950.7	E962.1	E980.6
vapor	987.8	E869.8	—	E952.8	E962.2	E982.8
peroxide (solution)	976.6	E858.7	E946.6	E950.4	E962.0	E980.4
phosphureted	987.8	E869.8	—	E952.8	E962.2	E982.8
sulfide (gas)	987.8	E869.8	—	E952.8	E962.2	E982.8
arseniureted	985.1	E866.3	—	E950.8	E962.1	E980.8
sulfureted	987.8	E869.8	—	E952.8	E962.2	E982.8
Hydromorphinol	965.09	E850.2	E935.2	E950.0	E962.0	E980.0
Hydromorphinone	965.09	E850.2	E935.2	E950.0	E962.0	E980.0
Hydromorphone	965.09	E850.2	E935.2	E950.0	E962.0	E980.0
Hydromox	974.3	E858.5	E944.3	E950.4	E962.0	E980.4
Hydrophilic lotion	976.3	E858.7	E946.3	E950.4	E962.0	E980.4
Hydroquinone	983.0	E864.0	—	E950.7	E962.1	E980.6
vapor	987.8	E869.8	—	E952.8	E962.2	E982.8
Hydrosulfuric acid (gas)	987.8	E869.8	—	E952.8	E962.2	E982.8
Hydrous wool fat (lotion)	976.3	E858.7	E946.3	E950.4	E962.0	E980.4
Hydroxide, caustic	983.2	E864.2	—	E950.7	E962.1	E980.6
Hydroxocobalamin	964.1	E858.2	E934.1	E950.4	E962.0	E980.4
Hydroxyamphetamine	971.2	E855.5	E941.2	E950.4	E962.0	E980.4
Hydroxychloroquine	961.4	E857	E931.4	E950.4	E962.0	E980.4
Hydroxydihydrocodeinone	965.09	E850.2	E935.2	E950.0	E962.0	E980.0
Hydroxyethyl starch	964.8	E858.2	E934.8	E950.4	E962.0	E980.4
Hydroxyphenamate	969.5	E853.8	E939.5	E950.3	E962.0	E980.3
Hydroxyphenylbutazone	965.5	E850.5	E935.5	E950.0	E962.0	E980.0
Hydroxyprogesterone	962.2	E858.0	E932.2	E950.4	E962.0	E980.4
Hydroxyquinoline derivatives	961.3	E857	E931.3	E950.4	E962.0	E980.4
Hydroxystilbamidine	961.5	E857	E931.5	E950.4	E962.0	E980.4
Hydroxyurea	963.1	E858.1	E933.1	E950.4	E962.0	E980.4
Hydroxyzine	969.5	E853.8	E939.5	E950.3	E962.0	E980.3
Hyoscine (hydrobromide)	971.1	E855.4	E941.1	E950.4	E962.0	E980.4
Hyoscyamine	971.1	E855.4	E941.1	E950.4	E962.0	E980.4
Hyoscyamus (albus) (niger)	988.2	E865.4	—	E950.9	E962.1	E980.9
Hypaque	977.8	E858.8	E947.8	E950.4	E962.0	E980.4
Hypertussis	964.6	E858.2	E934.6	E950.4	E962.0	E980.4
Hypnotics NEC	967.9	E852.9	E937.9	E950.2	E962.0	E980.2
Hypochlorites — see Sodium, hypochlorite						
Hypotensive agents NEC	972.6	E858.3	E942.6	E950.4	E962.0	E980.4
Ibufenac	965.69	E850.6	E935.6	E950.0	E962.0	E980.0
Ibuprofen	965.61	E850.6	E935.6	E950.0	E962.0	E980.0
ICG	977.8	E858.8	E947.8	E950.4	E962.0	E980.4
Ichthammol	976.4	E858.7	E946.4	E950.4	E962.0	E980.4
Ichthyol	976.4	E858.7	E946.4	E950.4	E962.0	E980.4
Idoxuridine	976.5	E858.7	E946.5	E950.4	E962.0	E980.4

	External Cause (E-Code)					
	Poisoning	Accident	Therapeutic Use	Suicide Attempt	Assault	Undetermined
IDU	976.5	E858.7	E946.5	E950.4	E962.0	E980.4
Iletin	962.3	E858.0	E932.3	E950.4	E962.0	E980.4
Ilex	988.2	E865.4	—	E950.9	E962.1	E980.9
Illuminating gas — see Gas, utility						
Ilopan	963.5	E858.1	E933.5	E950.4	E962.0	E980.4
Ilotycin	960.3	E856	E930.3	E950.4	E962.0	E980.4
ophthalmic preparation	976.5	E858.7	E946.5	E950.4	E962.0	E980.4
topical NEC	976.0	E858.7	E946.0	E950.4	E962.0	E980.4
Imipramine	969.05	E854.0	E939.0	E950.3	E962.0	E980.3
Immu-G	964.6	E858.2	E934.6	E950.4	E962.0	E980.4
Immuglobin	964.6	E858.2	E934.6	E950.4	E962.0	E980.4
Immune serum globulin	964.6	E858.2	E934.6	E950.4	E962.0	E980.4
Immunosuppressive agents	963.1	E858.1	E933.1	E950.4	E962.0	E980.4
Immu-tetanus	964.6	E858.2	E934.6	E950.4	E962.0	E980.4
Indandione (derivatives)	964.2	E858.2	E934.2	E950.4	E962.0	E980.4
Inderal	972.0	E858.3	E942.0	E950.4	E962.0	E980.4
Indian						
hemp	969.6	E854.1	E939.6	E950.3	E962.0	E980.3
tobacco	988.2	E865.4	—	E950.9	E962.1	E980.9
Indigo carmine	977.8	E858.8	E947.8	E950.4	E962.0	E980.4
Indocin	965.69	E850.6	E935.6	E950.0	E962.0	E980.0
Indocyanine green	977.8	E858.8	E947.8	E950.4	E962.0	E980.4
Indomethacin	965.69	E850.6	E935.6	E950.0	E962.0	E980.0
Industrial						
alcohol	980.9	E860.9	—	E950.9	E962.1	E980.9
fumes	987.8	E869.8	—	E952.8	E962.2	E982.8
solvents (fumes) (vapors)	982.8	E862.9	—	E950.9	E962.1	E980.9
Influenza vaccine	979.6	E858.8	E949.6	E950.4	E962.0	E980.4
Ingested substances NEC	989.9	E866.9	—	E950.9	E962.1	E980.9
INH (isoniazid)	961.8	E857	E931.8	E950.4	E962.0	E980.4
Inhalation, gas (noxious) — see Gas						
Ink	989.89	E866.8	—	E950.9	E962.1	E980.9
Innovar	967.6	E852.5	E937.6	E950.2	E962.0	E980.2
Inositol niacinate	972.2	E858.3	E942.2	E950.4	E962.0	E980.4
Inproquone	963.1	E858.1	E933.1	E950.4	E962.0	E980.4
Insecticides — see also Pesticides	989.4	E863.4	—	E950.6	E962.1	E980.7
chlorinated	989.2	E863.0	—	E950.6	E962.1	E980.7
mixtures	989.4	E863.3	—	E950.6	E962.1	E980.7
organochlorine (compounds)	989.2	E863.0	—	E950.6	E962.1	E980.7
organophosphorus (compounds)	989.3	E863.1	—	E950.6	E962.1	E980.7
Insect (sting), venomous	989.5	E905.5	—	E950.9	E962.1	E980.9
Insular tissue extract	962.3	E858.0	E932.3	E950.4	E962.0	E980.4
Insulin (amorphous) (globin) (isophane) (Lente) (NPH) (protamine) (Semilente) (Ultralente) (zinc)	962.3	E858.0	E932.3	E950.4	E962.0	E980.4
Intranarcon	968.3	E855.1	E938.3	E950.4	E962.0	E980.4
Inulin	977.8	E858.8	E947.8	E950.4	E962.0	E980.4
Invert sugar	974.5	E858.5	E944.5	E950.4	E962.0	E980.4
Inza — see Naproxen						
Iodide NEC — see also Iodine	976.0	E858.7	E946.0	E950.4	E962.0	E980.4
mercury (ointment)	976.0	E858.7	E946.0	E950.4	E962.0	E980.4
methylate	976.0	E858.7	E946.0	E950.4	E962.0	E980.4
potassium (expectorant) NEC	975.5	E858.6	E945.5	E950.4	E962.0	E980.4
Iodinated glycerol	975.5	E858.6	E945.5	E950.4	E962.0	E980.4
Iodine (antiseptic, external) (tincture) NEC	976.0	E858.7	E946.0	E950.4	E962.0	E980.4
diagnostic	977.8	E858.8	E947.8	E950.4	E962.0	E980.4
for thyroid conditions (antithyroid)	962.8	E858.0	E932.8	E950.4	E962.0	E980.4
vapor	987.8	E869.8	—	E952.8	E962.2	E982.8
Iodized oil	977.8	E858.8	E947.8	E950.4	E962.0	E980.4
Iodobismitol	961.2	E857	E931.2	E950.4	E962.0	E980.4
Iodochlorhydroxyquin	961.3	E857	E931.3	E950.4	E962.0	E980.4
topical	976.0	E858.7	E946.0	E950.4	E962.0	E980.4
Iodoform	976.0	E858.7	E946.0	E950.4	E962.0	E980.4
Iodopanoic acid	977.8	E858.8	E947.8	E950.4	E962.0	E980.4
Iodophthalein	977.8	E858.8	E947.8	E950.4	E962.0	E980.4
Ion exchange resins	974.5	E858.5	E944.5	E950.4	E962.0	E980.4
Iopanoic acid	977.8	E858.8	E947.8	E950.4	E962.0	E980.4
Iophendylate	977.8	E858.8	E947.8	E950.4	E962.0	E980.4
Iothiouracil	962.8	E858.0	E932.8	E950.4	E962.0	E980.4
Ipecac	973.6	E858.4	E943.6	E950.4	E962.0	E980.4
Ipecacuanha	973.6	E858.4	E943.6	E950.4	E962.0	E980.4

Nontherapeutic use substance

✤ Subterms under main terms may continue to next column or page

Index — Ipodate — Lighter fluid

	External Cause (E-Code)					
	Poisoning	Accident	Therapeutic Use	Suicide Attempt	Assault	Undetermined
Ipodate	977.8	E858.8	E947.8	E950.4	E962.0	E980.4
Ipral	967.0	E851	E937.0	E950.1	E962.0	E980.1
Ipratropium	975.1	E858.6	E945.1	E950.4	E962.0	E980.4
Iproniazid	969.01	E854.0	E939.0	E950.3	E962.0	E980.3
Iron (compounds) (medicinal)						
(preparations)	964.0	E858.2	E934.0	E950.4	E962.0	E980.4
dextran	964.0	E858.2	E934.0	E950.4	E962.0	E980.4
nonmedicinal (dust) (fumes)						
NEC	985.8	E866.4	—	E950.9	E962.1	E980.9
Irritant drug	977.9	E858.9	E947.9	E950.5	E962.0	E980.5
Ismelin	972.6	E858.3	E942.6	E950.4	E962.0	E980.4
Isoamyl nitrite	972.4	E858.3	E942.4	E950.4	E962.0	E980.4
Isobutyl acetate	982.8	E862.4	—	E950.9	E962.1	E980.9
Isocarboxazid	969.01	E854.0	E939.0	E950.3	E962.0	E980.3
Isoephedrine	971.2	E855.5	E941.2	E950.4	E962.0	E980.4
Isoetharine	971.2	E855.5	E941.2	E950.4	E962.0	E980.4
Isofluorophate	971.0	E855.3	E941.0	E950.4	E962.0	E980.4
Isoniazid (INH)	961.8	E857	E931.8	E950.4	E962.0	E980.4
Isopentaquine	961.4	E857	E931.4	E950.4	E962.0	E980.4
Isophane insulin	962.3	E858.0	E932.3	E950.4	E962.0	E980.4
Isopregnenone	962.2	E858.0	E932.2	E950.4	E962.0	E980.4
Isoprenaline	971.2	E855.5	E941.2	E950.4	E962.0	E980.4
Isopropamide	971.1	E855.4	E941.1	E950.4	E962.0	E980.4
Isopropanol	980.2	E860.3	—	E950.9	E962.1	E980.9
topical (germicide)	976.0	E858.7	E946.0	E950.4	E962.0	E980.4
Isopropyl						
acetate	982.8	E862.4	—	E950.9	E962.1	E980.9
alcohol	980.2	E860.3	—	E950.9	E962.1	E980.9
topical (germicide)	976.0	E858.7	E946.0	E950.4	E962.0	E980.4
ether	982.8	E862.4	—	E950.9	E962.1	E980.9
Isoproterenol	971.2	E855.5	E941.2	E950.4	E962.0	E980.4
Isosorbide dinitrate	972.4	E858.3	E942.4	E950.4	E962.0	E980.4
Isothipendyl	963.0	E858.1	E933.0	E950.4	E962.0	E980.4
Isoxazolyl penicillin	960.0	E856	E930.0	E950.4	E962.0	E980.4
Isoxsuprine hydrochloride	972.5	E858.3	E942.5	E950.4	E962.0	E980.4
l-thyroxine sodium	962.7	E858.0	E932.7	E950.4	E962.0	E980.4
Jaborandi (pilocarpus) (extract)	971.0	E855.3	E941.0	E950.4	E962.0	E980.4
Jalap	973.1	E858.4	E943.1	E950.4	E962.0	E980.4
Jamaica						
dogwood (bark)	965.7	E850.7	E935.7	E950.0	E962.0	E980.0
ginger	989.89	E866.8	—	E950.9	E962.1	E980.9
Jatropha	988.2	E865.4	—	E950.9	E962.1	E980.9
curcas	988.2	E865.3	—	E950.9	E962.1	E980.9
Jectofer	964.0	E858.2	E934.0	E950.4	E962.0	E980.4
Jellyfish (sting)	989.5	E905.6	—	E950.9	E962.1	E980.9
Jequirity (bean)	988.2	E865.3	—	E950.9	E962.1	E980.9
Jimson weed	988.2	E865.4	—	E950.9	E962.1	E980.9
seeds	988.2	E865.3	—	E950.9	E962.1	E980.9
Juniper tar (oil) (ointment)	976.4	E858.7	E946.4	E950.4	E962.0	E980.4
Kallikrein	972.5	E858.3	E942.5	E950.4	E962.0	E980.4
Kanamycin	960.6	E856	E930.6	E950.4	E962.0	E980.4
Kantrex	960.6	E856	E930.6	E950.4	E962.0	E980.4
Kaolin	973.5	E858.4	E943.5	E950.4	E962.0	E980.4
Karaya (gum)	973.3	E858.4	E943.3	E950.4	E962.0	E980.4
Kemithal	968.3	E855.1	E938.3	E950.4	E962.0	E980.4
Kenacort	962.0	E858.0	E932.0	E950.4	E962.0	E980.4
Keratolytics	976.4	E858.7	E946.4	E950.4	E962.0	E980.4
Keratoplastics	976.4	E858.7	E946.4	E950.4	E962.0	E980.4
Kerosene, kerosine (fuel) (solvent) NEC	981	E862.1	—	E950.9	E962.1	E980.9
insecticide	981	E863.4	—	E950.6	E962.1	E980.7
vapor	987.1	E869.8	—	E952.8	E962.2	E982.8
Ketamine	968.3	E855.1	E938.3	E950.4	E962.0	E980.4
Ketobemidone	965.09	E850.2	E935.2	E950.0	E962.0	E980.0
Ketols	982.8	E862.4	—	E950.9	E962.1	E980.9
Ketone oils	982.8	E862.4	—	E950.9	E962.1	E980.9
Ketoprofen	965.61	E850.6	E935.6	E950.0	E962.0	E980.0
Kiln gas or vapor (carbon monoxide)	986	E868.8	—	E952.1	E962.2	E982.1
Konsyl	973.3	E858.4	E943.3	E950.4	E962.0	E980.4
Kosam seed	988.2	E865.3	—	E950.9	E962.1	E980.9
Krait (venom)	989.5	E905.0	—	E950.9	E962.1	E980.9
Kwell (insecticide)	989.2	E863.0	—	E950.6	E962.1	E980.7
anti-infective (topical)	976.0	E858.7	E946.0	E950.4	E962.0	E980.4
Laburnum (flowers) (seeds)	988.2	E865.3	—	E950.9	E962.1	E980.9
leaves	988.2	E865.4	—	E950.9	E962.1	E980.9
Lacquers	989.89	E861.6	—	E950.9	E962.1	E980.9
Lacrimogenic gas	987.5	E869.3	—	E952.8	E962.2	E982.8
Lactic acid	983.1	E864.1	—	E950.7	E962.1	E980.6
Lactobacillus aci-dophilus	973.5	E858.4	E943.5	E950.4	E962.0	E980.4
Lactoflavin	963.5	E858.1	E933.5	E950.4	E962.0	E980.4
Lactuca (virosa) (extract)	967.8	E852.8	E937.8	E950.2	E962.0	E980.2
Lactucarium	967.8	E852.8	E937.8	E950.2	E962.0	E980.2
Laevulose	974.5	E858.5	E944.5	E950.4	E962.0	E980.4
Lanatoside (C)	972.1	E858.3	E942.1	E950.4	E962.0	E980.4
Lanolin (lotion)	976.3	E858.7	E946.3	E950.4	E962.0	E980.4
Largactil	969.1	E853.0	E939.1	E950.3	E962.0	E980.3
Larkspur	988.2	E865.3	—	E950.9	E962.1	E980.9
Laroxyl	969.05	E854.0	E939.0	E950.3	E962.0	E980.3
Lasix	974.4	E858.5	E944.4	E950.4	E962.0	E980.4
Latex	989.82	E866.8	—	E950.9	E962.1	E980.9
Lathyrus (seed)	988.2	E865.3	—	E950.9	E962.1	E980.9
Laudanum	965.09	E850.2	E935.2	E950.0	E962.0	E980.0
Laudexium	975.2	E858.6	E945.2	E950.4	E962.0	E980.4
Laurel, black or cherry	988.2	E865.4	—	E950.9	E962.1	E980.9
Laurolinium	976.0	E858.7	E946.0	E950.4	E962.0	E980.4
Lauryl sulfoacetate	976.2	E858.7	E946.2	E950.4	E962.0	E980.4
Laxatives NEC	973.3	E858.4	E943.3	E950.4	E962.0	E980.4
emollient	973.2	E858.4	E943.2	E950.4	E962.0	E980.4
L-dopa	966.4	E855.0	E936.4	E950.4	E962.0	E980.4
Lead (dust) (fumes) (vapor) NEC	984.9	E866.0	—	E950.9	E962.1	E980.9
acetate (dust)	984.1	E866.0	—	E950.9	E962.1	E980.9
anti-infectives	961.2	E857	E931.2	E950.4	E962.0	E980.4
antiknock compound (tetraethyl)	984.1	E862.1	—	E950.9	E962.1	E980.9
arsenate, arsenite (dust) (insecticide) (vapor)	985.1	E863.4	—	E950.8	E962.1	E980.8
herbicide	985.1	E863.5	—	E950.8	E962.1	E980.8
carbonate	984.0	E866.0	—	E950.9	E962.1	E980.9
paint	984.0	E861.5	—	E950.9	E962.1	E980.9
chromate	984.0	E866.0	—	E950.9	E962.1	E980.9
paint	984.0	E861.5	—	E950.9	E962.1	E980.9
dioxide	984.0	E866.0	—	E950.9	E962.1	E980.9
inorganic (compound)	984.0	E866.0	—	E950.9	E962.1	E980.9
paint	984.0	E861.5	—	E950.9	E962.1	E980.9
iodide	984.0	E866.0	—	E950.9	E962.1	E980.9
pigment (paint)	984.0	E861.5	—	E950.9	E962.1	E980.9
monoxide (dust)	984.0	E866.0	—	E950.9	E962.1	E980.9
paint	984.0	E861.5	—	E950.9	E962.1	E980.9
organic	984.1	E866.0	—	E950.9	E962.1	E980.9
oxide	984.0	E866.0	—	E950.9	E962.1	E980.9
paint	984.0	E861.5	—	E950.9	E962.1	E980.9
paint	984.0	E861.5	—	E950.9	E962.1	E980.9
salts	984.0	E866.0	—	E950.9	E962.1	E980.9
specified compound NEC	984.8	E866.0	—	E950.9	E962.1	E980.9
tetra-ethyl	984.1	E862.1	—	E950.9	E962.1	E980.9
Lebanese red	969.6	E854.1	E939.6	E950.3	E962.0	E980.3
Lente Iletin (insulin)	962.3	E858.0	E932.3	E950.4	E962.0	E980.4
Leptazol	970.0	E854.3	E940.0	E950.4	E962.0	E980.4
Leritine	965.09	E850.2	E935.2	E950.0	E962.0	E980.0
Letter	962.7	E858.0	E932.7	E950.4	E962.0	E980.4
Lettuce opium	967.8	E852.8	E937.8	E950.2	E962.0	E980.2
Leucovorin (factor)	964.1	E858.2	E934.1	E950.4	E962.0	E980.4
Leukeran	963.1	E858.1	E933.1	E950.4	E962.0	E980.4
Levalbuterol	975.7	E858.6	E945.7	E950.4	E962.0	E980.4
Levallorphan	970.1	E854.3	E940.1	E950.4	E962.0	E980.4
Levanil	967.8	E852.8	E937.8	E950.2	E962.0	E980.2
Levarterenol	971.2	E855.5	E941.2	E950.4	E962.0	E980.4
Levodopa	966.4	E855.0	E936.4	E950.4	E962.0	E980.4
Levo-dromoran	965.09	E850.2	E935.2	E950.0	E962.0	E980.0
Levoid	962.7	E858.0	E932.7	E950.4	E962.0	E980.4
Levo-iso-methadone	965.02	E850.1	E935.1	E950.0	E962.0	E980.0
Levomepromazine	967.8	E852.8	E937.8	E950.2	E962.0	E980.2
Levoprome	967.8	E852.8	E937.8	E950.2	E962.0	E980.2
Levopropoxyphene	975.4	E858.6	E945.4	E950.4	E962.0	E980.4
Levorphan, levophanol	965.09	E850.2	E935.2	E950.0	E962.0	E980.0
Levothyroxine (sodium)	962.7	E858.0	E932.7	E950.4	E962.0	E980.4
Levsin	971.1	E855.4	E941.1	E950.4	E962.0	E980.4
Levulose	974.5	E858.5	E944.5	E950.4	E962.0	E980.4
Lewisite (gas)	985.1	E866.3	—	E950.8	E962.1	E980.8
Librium	969.4	E853.2	E939.4	E950.3	E962.0	E980.3
Lidex	976.0	E858.7	E946.0	E950.4	E962.0	E980.4
Lidocaine (infiltration) (topical)	968.5	E855.2	E938.5	E950.4	E962.0	E980.4
nerve block (peripheral) (plexus)	968.6	E855.2	E938.6	E950.4	E962.0	E980.4
spinal	968.7	E855.2	E938.7	E950.4	E962.0	E980.4
Lighter fluid	981	E862.1	—	E950.9	E962.1	E980.9

Nontherapeutic use substance

▼ Subterms under main terms may continue to next column or page

▶◀ Revised Text   ● New Line   ▲ Revised Code

	Poisoning	Accident	Therapeutic Use	Suicide Attempt	Assault	Undetermined
Lignocaine (infiltration) (topical)	968.5	E855.2	E938.5	E950.4	E962.0	E980.4
nerve block (peripheral) (plexus)	968.6	E855.2	E938.6	E950.4	E962.0	E980.4
spinal	968.7	E855.2	E938.7	E950.4	E962.0	E980.4
Ligroin(e) (solvent)	981	E862.0	—	E950.9	E962.1	E980.9
vapor	987.1	E869.8	—	E952.8	E962.2	E982.8
Ligustrum vulgare	988.2	E865.3	—	E950.9	E962.1	E980.9
Lily of the valley	988.2	E865.4	—	E950.9	E962.1	E980.9
Lime (chloride)	983.2	E864.2	—	E950.7	E962.1	E980.6
solution, sulferated	976.4	E858.7	E946.4	E950.4	E962.0	E980.4
Limonene	982.8	E862.4	—	E950.9	E962.1	E980.9
Lincomycin	960.8	E856	E930.8	E950.4	E962.0	E980.4
Lindane (insecticide) (vapor)	989.2	E863.0	—	E950.6	E962.1	E980.7
anti-infective (topical)	976.0	E858.7	E946.0	E950.4	E962.0	E980.4
Liniments NEC	976.9	E858.7	E946.9	E950.4	E962.0	E980.4
Linoleic acid	972.2	E858.3	E942.2	E950.4	E962.0	E980.4
Liothyronine	962.7	E858.0	E932.7	E950.4	E962.0	E980.4
Liotrix	962.7	E858.0	E932.7	E950.4	E962.0	E980.4
Lipancreatin	973.4	E858.4	E943.4	E950.4	E962.0	E980.4
Lipo-Lutin	962.2	E858.0	E932.2	E950.4	E962.0	E980.4
Lipotropic agents	977.1	E858.8	E947.1	E950.4	E962.0	E980.4
Liquefied petroleum gases	987.0	E868.0	—	E951.1	E962.2	E981.1
piped (pure or mixed with air)	987.0	E867	—	E951.0	E962.2	E981.0
Liquid petrolatum	973.2	E858.4	E943.2	E950.4	E962.0	E980.4
substance	989.9	E866.9	—	E950.9	E962.1	E980.9
specified NEC	989.89	E866.8	—	E950.9	E962.1	E980.9
Lirugen	979.4	E858.8	E949.4	E950.4	E962.0	E980.4
Lithane	969.8	E855.8	E939.8	E950.3	E962.0	E980.3
Lithium	985.8	E866.4	—	E950.9	E962.1	E980.9
carbonate	969.8	E855.8	E939.8	E950.3	E962.0	E980.3
Lithonate	969.8	E855.8	E939.8	E950.3	E962.0	E980.3
Liver (extract) (injection) (preparations)	964.1	E858.2	E934.1	E950.4	E962.0	E980.4
Lizard (bite) (venom)	989.5	E905.0	—	E950.9	E962.1	E980.9
LMD	964.8	E858.2	E934.8	E950.4	E962.0	E980.4
Lobelia	988.2	E865.4	—	E950.9	E962.1	E980.9
Lobeline	970.0	E854.3	E940.0	E950.4	E962.0	E980.4
Locorten	976.0	E858.7	E946.0	E950.4	E962.0	E980.4
Lolium temulentum	988.2	E865.3	—	E950.9	E962.1	E980.9
Lomotil	973.5	E858.4	E943.5	E950.4	E962.0	E980.4
Lomustine	963.1	E858.1	E933.1	E950.4	E962.0	E980.4
Lophophora williamsii	969.6	E854.1	E939.6	E950.3	E962.0	E980.3
Lorazepam	969.4	E853.2	E939.4	E950.3	E962.0	E980.3
Lotions NEC	976.9	E858.7	E946.9	E950.4	E962.0	E980.4
Lotronex	973.8	E858.4	E943.8	E950.4	E962.0	E980.4
Lotusate	967.0	E851	E937.0	E950.1	E962.0	E980.1
Lowila	976.2	E858.7	E946.2	E950.4	E962.0	E980.4
Loxapine	969.3	E853.8	E939.3	E950.3	E962.0	E980.3
Lozenges (throat)	976.6	E858.7	E946.6	E950.4	E962.0	E980.4
LSD (25)	969.6	E854.1	E939.6	E950.3	E962.0	E980.3
L-Tryptophan — see amino acid						
Lubricating oil NEC	981	E862.2	—	E950.9	E962.1	E980.9
Lucanthone	961.6	E857	E931.6	E950.4	E962.0	E980.4
Luminal	967.0	E851	E937.0	E950.1	E962.0	E980.1
Lung irritant (gas) NEC	987.9	E869.9	—	E952.9	E962.2	E982.9
Lutocylol	962.2	E858.0	E932.2	E950.4	E962.0	E980.4
Lutromone	962.2	E858.0	E932.2	E950.4	E962.0	E980.4
Lututrin	975.0	E858.6	E945.0	E950.4	E962.0	E980.4
Lye (concentrated)	983.2	E864.2	—	E950.7	E962.1	E980.6
Lygranum (skin test)	977.8	E858.8	E947.8	E950.4	E962.0	E980.4
Lymecycline	960.4	E856	E930.4	E950.4	E962.0	E980.4
Lymphogranuloma venereum antigen	977.8	E858.8	E947.8	E950.4	E962.0	E980.4
Lynestrenol	962.2	E858.0	E932.2	E950.4	E962.0	E980.4
Lyovac Sodium Edecrin	974.4	E858.5	E944.4	E950.4	E962.0	E980.4
Lypressin	962.5	E858.0	E932.5	E950.4	E962.0	E980.4
Lysergic acid (amide) (diethylamide)	969.6	E854.1	E939.6	E950.3	E962.0	E980.3
Lysergide	969.6	E854.1	E939.6	E950.3	E962.0	E980.3
Lysine vasopressin	962.5	E858.0	E932.5	E950.4	E962.0	E980.4
Lysol	983.0	E864.0	—	E950.7	E962.1	E980.6
Lytta (vitatta)	976.8	E858.7	E946.8	E950.4	E962.0	E980.4
Mace	987.5	E869.3	—	E952.8	E962.2	E982.8
Macrolides (antibiotics)	960.3	E856	E930.3	E950.4	E962.0	E980.4
Mafenide	976.0	E858.7	E946.0	E950.4	E962.0	E980.4
Magaldrate	973.0	E858.4	E943.0	E950.4	E962.0	E980.4
Magic mushroom	969.6	E854.1	E939.6	E950.3	E962.0	E980.3
Magnamycin	960.8	E856	E930.8	E950.4	E962.0	E980.4
Magnesia magma	973.0	E858.4	E943.0	E950.4	E962.0	E980.4
Magnesium (compounds) (fumes) NEC	985.8	E866.4	—	E950.9	E962.1	E980.9
antacid	973.0	E858.4	E943.0	E950.4	E962.0	E980.4
carbonate	973.0	E858.4	E943.0	E950.4	E962.0	E980.4
cathartic	973.3	E858.4	E943.3	E950.4	E962.0	E980.4
citrate	973.3	E858.4	E943.3	E950.4	E962.0	E980.4
hydroxide	973.0	E858.4	E943.0	E950.4	E962.0	E980.4
oxide	973.0	E858.4	E943.0	E950.4	E962.0	E980.4
sulfate (oral)	973.3	E858.4	E943.3	E950.4	E962.0	E980.4
intravenous	966.3	E855.0	E936.3	E950.4	E962.0	E980.4
trisilicate	973.0	E858.4	E943.0	E950.4	E962.0	E980.4
Malathion (insecticide)	989.3	E863.1	—	E950.6	E962.1	E980.7
Male fern (oleoresin)	961.6	E857	E931.6	E950.4	E962.0	E980.4
Mandelic acid	961.9	E857	E931.9	E950.4	E962.0	E980.4
Manganese compounds (fumes) NEC	985.2	E866.4		E950.9	E962.1	E980.9
Mannitol (diuretic) (medicinal) NEC	974.4	E858.5	E944.4	E950.4	E962.0	E980.4
hexanitrate	972.4	E858.3	E942.4	E950.4	E962.0	E980.4
mustard	963.1	E858.1	E933.1	E950.4	E962.0	E980.4
Mannomustine	963.1	E858.1	E933.1	E950.4	E962.0	E980.4
MAO inhibitors	969.01	E854.0	E939.0	E950.3	E962.0	E980.3
Mapharsen	961.1	E857	E931.1	E950.4	E962.0	E980.4
Marcaine	968.9	E855.2	E938.9	E950.4	E962.0	E980.4
infiltration (subcutaneous)	968.5	E855.2	E938.5	E950.4	E962.0	E980.4
nerve block (peripheral) (plexus)	968.6	E855.2	E938.6	E950.4	E962.0	E980.4
Marezine	963.0	E858.1	E933.0	E950.4	E962.0	E980.4
Marihuana, marijuana (derivatives)	969.6	E854.1	E939.6	E950.3	E962.0	E980.3
Marine animals or plants (sting)	989.5	E905.6	—	E950.9	E962.1	E980.9
Marplan	969.01	E854.0	E939.0	E950.3	E962.0	E980.3
Marsh gas	987.1	E869.8	—	E952.8	E962.2	E982.8
Marsilid	969.01	E854.0	E939.0	E950.3	E962.0	E980.3
Matulane	963.1	E858.1	E933.1	E950.4	E962.0	E980.4
Mazindol	977.0	E858.8	E947.0	E950.4	E962.0	E980.4
MDMA	969.72	E854.2	E939.7	E950.3	E962.0	E980.3
Meadow saffron	988.2	E865.3	—	E950.9	E962.1	E980.9
Measles vaccine	979.4	E858.8	E949.4	E950.4	E962.0	E980.4
Meat, noxious or nonbacterial	988.8	E865.0	—	E950.9	E962.1	E980.9
Mebanazine	969.01	E854.0	E939.0	E950.3	E962.0	E980.3
Mebaral	967.0	E851	E937.0	E950.1	E962.0	E980.1
Mebendazole	961.6	E857	E931.6	E950.4	E962.0	E980.4
Mebeverine	975.1	E858.6	E945.1	E950.4	E962.0	E980.4
Mebhydroline	963.0	E858.1	E933.0	E950.4	E962.0	E980.4
Mebrophenhydramine	963.0	E858.1	E933.0	E950.4	E962.0	E980.4
Mebutamate	969.5	E853.8	E939.5	E950.3	E962.0	E980.3
Mecamylamine (chloride)	972.3	E858.3	E942.3	E950.4	E962.0	E980.4
Mechlorethamine hydrochloride	963.1	E858.1	E933.1	E950.4	E962.0	E980.4
Meclizene (hydrochloride)	963.0	E858.1	E933.0	E950.4	E962.0	E980.4
Meclofenoxate	970.0	E854.3	E940.0	E950.4	E962.0	E980.4
Meclozine (hydrochloride)	963.0	E858.1	E933.0	E950.4	E962.0	E980.4
Medazepam	969.4	E853.2	E939.4	E950.3	E962.0	E980.3
Medicine, medicinal substance	977.9	E858.9	E947.9	E950.5	E962.0	E980.5
specified NEC	977.8	E858.8	E947.8	E950.4	E962.0	E980.4
Medinal	967.0	E851	E937.0	E950.1	E962.0	E980.1
Medomin	967.0	E851	E937.0	E950.1	E962.0	E980.1
Medroxyprogesterone	962.2	E858.0	E932.2	E950.4	E962.0	E980.4
Medrysone	976.5	E858.7	E946.5	E950.4	E962.0	E980.4
Mefenamic acid	965.7	E850.7	E935.7	E950.0	E962.0	E980.0
Megahallucinogen	969.6	E854.1	E939.6	E950.3	E962.0	E980.3
Megestrol	962.2	E858.0	E932.2	E950.4	E962.0	E980.4
Meglumine	977.8	E858.8	E947.8	E950.4	E962.0	E980.4
Meladinin	976.3	E858.7	E946.3	E950.4	E962.0	E980.4
Melanizing agents	976.3	E858.7	E946.3	E950.4	E962.0	E980.4
Melarsoprol	961.1	E857	E931.1	E950.4	E962.0	E980.4
Melia azedarach	988.2	E865.3	—	E950.9	E962.1	E980.9
Mellaril	969.1	E853.0	E939.1	E950.3	E962.0	E980.3
Meloxine	976.3	E858.7	E946.3	E950.4	E962.0	E980.4
Melphalan	963.1	E858.1	E933.1	E950.4	E962.0	E980.4
Menadiol sodium diphosphate	964.3	E858.2	E934.3	E950.4	E962.0	E980.4
Menadione (sodium bisulfite)	964.3	E858.2	E934.3	E950.4	E962.0	E980.4
Menaphthone	964.3	E858.2	E934.3	E950.4	E962.0	E980.4

Nontherapeutic use substance

Subterms under main terms may continue to next column or page

Meningococcal vaccine — Methyl

	Poisoning	Accident	Therapeutic Use	Suicide Attempt	Assault	Undetermined
Meningococcal vaccine	978.8	E858.8	E948.8	E950.4	E962.0	E980.4
Menningovax-C	978.8	E858.8	E948.8	E950.4	E962.0	E980.4
Menotropins	962.4	E858.0	E932.4	E950.4	E962.0	E980.4
Menthol NEC	976.1	E858.7	E946.1	E950.4	E962.0	E980.4
Mepacrine	961.3	E857	E931.3	E950.4	E962.0	E980.4
Meparfynol	967.8	E852.8	E937.8	E950.2	E962.0	E980.2
Mepazine	969.1	E853.0	E939.1	E950.3	E962.0	E980.3
Mepenzolate	971.1	E855.4	E941.1	E950.4	E962.0	E980.4
Meperidine	965.09	E850.2	E935.2	E950.0	E962.0	E980.0
Mephenamin(e)	966.4	E855.0	E936.4	E950.4	E962.0	E980.4
Mephenesin (carbamate)	968.0	E855.1	E938.0	E950.4	E962.0	E980.4
Mephenoxalone	969.5	E853.8	E939.5	E950.3	E962.0	E980.3
Mephentermine	971.2	E855.5	E941.2	E950.4	E962.0	E980.4
Mephenytoin	966.1	E855.0	E936.1	E950.4	E962.0	E980.4
Mephobarbital	967.0	E851	E937.0	E950.1	E962.0	E980.1
Mepiperphenidol	971.1	E855.4	E941.1	E950.4	E962.0	E980.4
Mepivacaine	968.9	E855.2	E938.9	E950.4	E962.0	E980.4
infiltration (subcutaneous)	968.5	E855.2	E938.5	E950.4	E962.0	E980.4
nerve block (peripheral) (plexus)	968.6	E855.2	E938.6	E950.4	E962.0	E980.4
topical (surface)	968.5	E855.2	E938.5	E950.4	E962.0	E980.4
Meprednisone	962.0	E858.0	E932.0	E950.4	E962.0	E980.4
Meprobam	969.5	E853.8	E939.5	E950.3	E962.0	E980.3
Meprobamate	969.5	E853.8	E939.5	E950.3	E962.0	E980.3
Mepyramine (maleate)	963.0	E858.1	E933.0	E950.4	E962.0	E980.4
Meralluride	974.0	E858.5	E944.0	E950.4	E962.0	E980.4
Merbaphen	974.0	E858.5	E944.0	E950.4	E962.0	E980.4
Merbromin	976.0	E858.7	E946.0	E950.4	E962.0	E980.4
Mercaptomerin	974.0	E858.5	E944.0	E950.4	E962.0	E980.4
Mercaptopurine	963.1	E858.1	E933.1	E950.4	E962.0	E980.4
Mercumatilin	974.0	E858.5	E944.0	E950.4	E962.0	E980.4
Mercuramide	974.0	E858.5	E944.0	E950.4	E962.0	E980.4
Mercuranin	976.0	E858.7	E946.0	E950.4	E962.0	E980.4
Mercurochrome	976.0	E858.7	E946.0	E950.4	E962.0	E980.4
Mercury, mercuric, mercurous (compounds) (cyanide) (fumes) (nonmedicinal) (vapor) NEC	985.0	E866.1	—	E950.9	E962.1	E980.9
ammoniated	976.0	E858.7	E946.0	E950.4	E962.0	E980.4
anti-infective	961.2	E857	E931.2	E950.4	E962.0	E980.4
topical	976.0	E858.7	E946.0	E950.4	E962.0	E980.4
chloride (antiseptic) NEC	976.0	E858.7	E946.0	E950.4	E962.0	E980.4
fungicide	985.0	E863.6	—	E950.6	E962.1	E980.7
diuretic compounds	974.0	E858.5	E944.0	E950.4	E962.0	E980.4
fungicide	985.0	E863.6	—	E950.6	E962.1	E980.7
organic (fungicide)	985.0	E863.6	—	E950.6	E962.1	E980.7
Merethoxylline	974.0	E858.5	E944.0	E950.4	E962.0	E980.4
Mersalyl	974.0	E858.5	E944.0	E950.4	E962.0	E980.4
Merthiolate (topical)	976.0	E858.7	E946.0	E950.4	E962.0	E980.4
ophthalmic preparation	976.5	E858.7	E946.5	E950.4	E962.0	E980.4
Meruvax	979.4	E858.8	E949.4	E950.4	E962.0	E980.4
Mescal buttons	969.6	E854.1	E939.6	E950.3	E962.0	E980.3
Mescaline (salts)	969.6	E854.1	E939.6	E950.3	E962.0	E980.3
Mesoridazine besylate	969.1	E853.0	E939.1	E950.3	E962.0	E980.3
Mestanolone	962.1	E858.0	E932.1	E950.4	E962.0	E980.4
Mestranol	962.2	E858.0	E932.2	E950.4	E962.0	E980.4
Metacresylacetate	976.0	E858.7	E946.0	E950.4	E962.0	E980.4
Metaldehyde (snail killer) NEC	989.4	E863.4	—	E950.6	E962.1	E980.7
Metals (heavy) (nonmedicinal) NEC	985.9	E866.4	—	E950.9	E962.1	E980.9
dust, fumes, or vapor NEC	985.9	E866.4	—	E950.9	E962.1	E980.9
light NEC	985.9	E866.4	—	E950.9	E962.1	E980.9
dust, fumes, or vapor NEC	985.9	E866.4	—	E950.9	E962.1	E980.9
pesticides (dust) (vapor)	985.9	E863.4	—	E950.6	E962.1	E980.7
Metamucil	973.3	E858.4	E943.3	E950.4	E962.0	E980.4
Metaphen	976.0	E858.7	E946.0	E950.4	E962.0	E980.4
Metaproterenol	975.1	E858.6	E945.1	E950.4	E962.0	E980.4
Metaraminol	972.8	E858.3	E942.8	E950.4	E962.0	E980.4
Metaxalone	968.0	E855.1	E938.0	E950.4	E962.0	E980.4
Metformin	962.3	E858.0	E932.3	E950.4	E962.0	E980.4
Methacycline	960.4	E856	E930.4	E950.4	E962.0	E980.4
Methadone	965.02	E850.1	E935.1	E950.0	E962.0	E980.0
Methallenestril	962.2	E858.0	E932.2	E950.4	E962.0	E980.4
Methamphetamine	969.72	E854.2	E939.7	E950.3	E962.0	E980.3
Methandienone	962.1	E858.0	E932.1	E950.4	E962.0	E980.4
Methandriol	962.1	E858.0	E932.1	E950.4	E962.0	E980.4
Methandrostenolone	962.1	E858.0	E932.1	E950.4	E962.0	E980.4
Methane gas	987.1	E869.8	—	E952.8	E962.2	E982.8
Methanol	980.1	E860.2	—	E950.9	E962.1	E980.9
vapor	987.8	E869.8	—	E952.8	E962.2	E982.8
Methantheline	971.1	E855.4	E941.1	E950.4	E962.0	E980.4
Methaphenilene	963.0	E858.1	E933.0	E950.4	E962.0	E980.4
Methapyrilene	963.0	E858.1	E933.0	E950.4	E962.0	E980.4
Methaqualone (compounds)	967.4	E852.3	E937.4	E950.2	E962.0	E980.2
Metharbital, metharbitone	967.0	E851	E937.0	E950.1	E962.0	E980.1
Methazolamide	974.2	E858.5	E944.2	E950.4	E962.0	E980.4
Methdilazine	963.0	E858.1	E933.0	E950.4	E962.0	E980.4
Methedrine	969.72	E854.2	E939.7	E950.3	E962.0	E980.3
Methenamine (mandelate)	961.9	E857	E931.9	E950.4	E962.0	E980.4
Methenolone	962.1	E858.0	E932.1	E950.4	E962.0	E980.4
Methergine	975.0	E858.6	E945.0	E950.4	E962.0	E980.4
Methiacil	962.8	E858.0	E932.8	E950.4	E962.0	E980.4
Methicillin (sodium)	960.0	E856	E930.0	E950.4	E962.0	E980.4
Methimazole	962.8	E858.0	E932.8	E950.4	E962.0	E980.4
Methionine	977.1	E858.8	E947.1	E950.4	E962.0	E980.4
Methisazone	961.7	E857	E931.7	E950.4	E962.0	E980.4
Methitural	967.0	E851	E937.0	E950.1	E962.0	E980.1
Methixene	971.1	E855.4	E941.1	E950.4	E962.0	E980.4
Methobarbital, methobarbitone	967.0	E851	E937.0	E950.1	E962.0	E980.1
Methocarbamol	968.0	E855.1	E938.0	E950.4	E962.0	E980.4
Methohexital, methohexitone (sodium)	968.3	E855.1	E938.3	E950.4	E962.0	E980.4
Methoin	966.1	E855.0	E936.1	E950.4	E962.0	E980.4
Methopholine	965.7	E850.7	E935.7	E950.0	E962.0	E980.0
Methorate	975.4	E858.6	E945.4	E950.4	E962.0	E980.4
Methoserpidine	972.6	E858.3	E942.6	E950.4	E962.0	E980.4
Methotrexate	963.1	E858.1	E933.1	E950.4	E962.0	E980.4
Methotrimeprazine	967.8	E852.8	E937.8	E950.2	E962.0	E980.2
Methoxa-Dome	976.3	E858.7	E946.3	E950.4	E962.0	E980.4
Methoxamine	971.2	E855.5	E941.2	E950.4	E962.0	E980.4
Methoxsalen	976.3	E858.7	E946.3	E950.4	E962.0	E980.4
Methoxybenzyl penicillin	960.0	E856	E930.0	E950.4	E962.0	E980.4
Methoxychlor	989.2	E863.0	—	E950.6	E962.1	E980.7
Methoxyflurane	968.2	E855.1	E938.2	E950.4	E962.0	E980.4
Methoxyphenamine	971.2	E855.5	E941.2	E950.4	E962.0	E980.4
Methoxypromazine	969.1	E853.0	E939.1	E950.3	E962.0	E980.3
Methoxypsoralen	976.3	E858.7	E946.3	E950.4	E962.0	E980.4
Methscopolamine (bromide)	971.1	E855.4	E941.1	E950.4	E962.0	E980.4
Methsuximide	966.2	E855.0	E936.2	E950.4	E962.0	E980.4
Methyclothiazide	974.3	E858.5	E944.3	E950.4	E962.0	E980.4
Methyl						
acetate	982.8	E862.4	—	E950.9	E962.1	E980.9
acetone	982.8	E862.4	—	E950.9	E962.1	E980.9
alcohol	980.1	E860.2	—	E950.9	E962.1	E980.9
amphetamine	969.72	E854.2	E939.7	E950.3	E962.0	E980.3
androstanolone	962.1	E858.0	E932.1	E950.4	E962.0	E980.4
atropine	971.1	E855.4	E941.1	E950.4	E962.0	E980.4
benzene	982.0	E862.4	—	E950.9	E962.1	E980.9
bromide (gas)	987.8	E869.8	—	E952.8	E962.2	E982.8
fumigant	987.8	E863.8	—	E950.6	E962.2	E980.7
butanol	980.8	E860.8	—	E950.9	E962.1	E980.9
carbinol	980.1	E860.2	—	E950.9	E962.1	E980.9
cellosolve	982.8	E862.4	—	E950.9	E962.1	E980.9
cellulose	973.3	E858.4	E943.3	E950.4	E962.0	E980.4
chloride (gas)	987.8	E869.8	—	E952.8	E962.2	E982.8
cyclohexane	982.8	E862.4	—	E950.9	E962.1	E980.9
cyclohexanone	982.8	E862.4	—	E950.9	E962.1	E980.9
dihydromorphinone	965.09	E850.2	E935.2	E950.0	E962.0	E980.0
ergometrine	975.0	E858.6	E945.0	E950.4	E962.0	E980.4
ergonovine	975.0	E858.6	E945.0	E950.4	E962.0	E980.4
ethyl ketone	982.8	E862.4	—	E950.9	E962.1	E980.9
hydrazine	983.9	E864.3	—	E950.7	E962.1	E980.6
isobutyl ketone	982.8	E862.4	—	E950.9	E962.1	E980.9
morphine NEC	965.09	E850.2	E935.2	E950.0	E962.0	E980.0
parafynol	967.8	E852.8	E937.8	E950.2	E962.0	E980.2
parathion	989.3	E863.1	—	E950.6	E962.1	E980.7
pentynol NEC	967.8	E852.8	E937.8	E950.2	E962.0	E980.2
peridol	969.2	E853.1	E939.2	E950.3	E962.0	E980.3
phenidate	969.73	E854.2	E939.7	E950.3	E962.0	E980.3
prednisolone	962.0	E858.0	E932.0	E950.4	E962.0	E980.4
ENT agent	976.6	E858.7	E946.6	E950.4	E962.0	E980.4
ophthalmic preparation	976.5	E858.7	E946.5	E950.4	E962.0	E980.4
topical NEC	976.0	E858.7	E946.0	E950.4	E962.0	E980.4
propylcarbinol	980.8	E860.8	—	E950.9	E962.1	E980.9

  Nontherapeutic use substance

Subterms under main terms may continue to next column or page

	Poisoning	Accident	Therapeutic Use	Suicide Attempt	Assault	Undetermined
Methyl — *continued*						
rosaniline NEC	976.0	E858.7	E946.0	E950.4	E962.0	E980.4
salicylate NEC	976.3	E858.7	E946.3	E950.4	E962.0	E980.4
sulfate (fumes)	987.8	E869.8	—	E952.8	E962.2	E982.8
liquid	983.9	E864.3	—	E950.7	E962.1	E980.6
sulfonal	967.8	E852.8	E937.8	E950.2	E962.0	E980.2
testosterone	962.1	E858.0	E932.1	E950.4	E962.0	E980.4
thiouracil	962.8	E858.0	E932.8	E950.4	E962.0	E980.4
Methylated spirit	980.0	E860.1	—	E950.9	E962.1	E980.9
Methyldopa	972.6	E858.3	E942.6	E950.4	E962.0	E980.4
Methylene						
blue	961.9	E857	E931.9	E950.4	E962.0	E980.4
chloride or dichloride (solvent) NEC	982.3	E862.4	—	E950.9	E962.1	E980.9
Methylhexabital	967.0	E851	E937.0	E950.1	E962.0	E980.1
Methylparaben (oph-thalmic)	976.5	E858.7	E946.5	E950.4	E962.0	E980.4
Methyprylon	967.5	E852.4	E937.5	E950.2	E962.0	E980.2
Methysergide	971.3	E855.6	E941.3	E950.4	E962.0	E980.4
Metoclopramide	963.0	E858.1	E933.0	E950.4	E962.0	E980.4
Metofoline	965.7	E850.7	E935.7	E950.0	E962.0	E980.0
Metopon	965.09	E850.2	E935.2	E950.0	E962.0	E980.0
Metronidazole	961.5	E857	E931.5	E950.4	E962.0	E980.4
Metycaine	968.9	E855.2	E938.9	E950.4	E962.0	E980.4
infiltration (subcuta-neous)	968.5	E855.2	E938.5	E950.4	E962.0	E980.4
nerve block (peripheral) (plexus)	968.6	E855.2	E938.6	E950.4	E962.0	E980.4
topical (surface)	968.5	E855.2	E938.5	E950.4	E962.0	E980.4
Metyrapone	977.8	E858.8	E947.8	E950.4	E962.0	E980.4
Mevinphos	989.3	E863.1	—	E950.6	E962.1	E980.7
Mezereon (berries)	988.2	E865.3	—	E950.9	E962.1	E980.9
Micatin	976.0	E858.7	E946.0	E950.4	E962.0	E980.4
Miconazole	976.0	E858.7	E946.0	E950.4	E962.0	E980.4
Midol	965.1	E850.3	E935.3	E950.0	E962.0	E980.0
Mifepristone	962.9	E858.0	E932.9	E950.4	E962.0	E980.4
Milk of magnesia	973.0	E858.4	E943.0	E950.4	E962.0	E980.4
Millipede (tropical) (ven-omous)	989.5	E905.4	—	E950.9	E962.1	E980.9
Miltown	969.5	E853.8	E939.5	E950.3	E962.0	E980.3
Mineral						
oil (medicinal)	973.2	E858.4	E943.2	E950.4	E962.0	E980.4
nonmedicinal	981	E862.1	—	E950.9	E962.1	E980.9
topical	976.3	E858.7	E946.3	E950.4	E962.0	E980.4
salts NEC	974.6	E858.5	E944.6	E950.4	E962.0	E980.4
spirits	981	E862.0	—	E950.9	E962.1	E980.9
Minocycline	960.4	E856	E930.4	E950.4	E962.0	E980.4
Mithramycin (antineoplas-tic)	960.7	E856	E930.7	E950.4	E962.0	E980.4
Mitobronitol	963.1	E858.1	E933.1	E950.4	E962.0	E980.4
Mitomycin (antineoplas-tic)	960.7	E856	E930.7	E950.4	E962.0	E980.4
Mitotane	963.1	E858.1	E933.1	E950.4	E962.0	E980.4
Moderil	972.6	E858.3	E942.6	E950.4	E962.0	E980.4
Mogadon — *see* Nitrazepam						
Molindone	969.3	E853.8	E939.3	E950.3	E962.0	E980.3
Monistat	976.0	E858.7	E946.0	E950.4	E962.0	E980.4
Monkshood	988.2	E865.4	—	E950.9	E962.1	E980.9
Monoamine oxidase in-hibitors	969.01	E854.0	E939.0	E950.3	E962.0	E980.3
Monochlorobenzene	982.0	E862.4	—	E950.9	E962.1	E980.9
Monosodium glutamate	989.89	E866.8	—	E950.9	E962.1	E980.9
Monoxide, carbon — *see* Carbon, monoxide						
Moperone	969.2	E853.1	E939.2	E950.3	E962.0	E980.3
Morning glory seeds	969.6	E854.1	E939.6	E950.3	E962.0	E980.3
Moroxydine (hydrochlo-ride)	961.7	E857	E931.7	E950.4	E962.0	E980.4
Morphazinamide	961.8	E857	E931.8	E950.4	E962.0	E980.4
Morphinans	965.09	E850.2	E935.2	E950.0	E962.0	E980.0
Morphine NEC	965.09	E850.2	E935.2	E950.0	E962.0	E980.0
antagonists	970.1	E854.3	E940.1	E950.4	E962.0	E980.4
Morpholinylethylmor-phine	965.09	E850.2	E935.2	E950.0	E962.0	E980.0
Morrhuate sodium	972.7	E858.3	E942.7	E950.4	E962.0	E980.4
Moth balls — *see also* Pesti-cides	989.4	E863.4	—	E950.6	E962.1	E980.7
naphthalene	983.0	E863.4	—	E950.7	E962.1	E980.6
Motor exhaust gas — *see* Carbon, monoxide, exhaust gas						
Mouth wash	976.6	E858.7	E946.6	E950.4	E962.0	E980.4

	Poisoning	Accident	Therapeutic Use	Suicide Attempt	Assault	Undetermined
Mucolytic agent	975.5	E858.6	E945.5	E950.4	E962.0	E980.4
Mucomyst	975.5	E858.6	E945.5	E950.4	E962.0	E980.4
Mucous membrane agents						
(external)	976.9	E858.7	E946.9	E950.4	E962.0	E980.4
specified NEC	976.8	E858.7	E946.8	E950.4	E962.0	E980.4
Mumps						
immune globulin (hu-man)	964.6	E858.2	E934.6	E950.4	E962.0	E980.4
skin test antigen	977.8	E858.8	E947.8	E950.4	E962.0	E980.4
vaccine	979.6	E858.8	E949.6	E950.4	E962.0	E980.4
Mumpsvax	979.6	E858.8	E949.6	E950.4	E962.0	E980.4
Muriatic acid — *see* Hydrochlo-ric acid						
Muscarine	971.0	E855.3	E941.0	E950.4	E962.0	E980.4
Muscle affecting agents						
NEC	975.3	E858.6	E945.3	E950.4	E962.0	E980.4
oxytocic	975.0	E858.6	E945.0	E950.4	E962.0	E980.4
relaxants	975.3	E858.6	E945.3	E950.4	E962.0	E980.4
central nervous system	968.0	E855.1	E938.0	E950.4	E962.0	E980.4
skeletal	975.2	E858.6	E945.2	E950.4	E962.0	E980.4
smooth	975.1	E858.6	E945.1	E950.4	E962.0	E980.4
Mushrooms, noxious	988.1	E865.5	—	E950.9	E962.1	E980.9
Mussel, noxious	988.0	E865.1	—	E950.9	E962.1	E980.9
Mustard (emetic)	973.6	E858.4	E943.6	E950.4	E962.0	E980.4
gas	987.8	E869.8	—	E952.8	E962.2	E982.8
nitrogen	963.1	E858.1	E933.1	E950.4	E962.0	E980.4
Mustine	963.1	E858.1	E933.1	E950.4	E962.0	E980.4
M-vac	979.4	E858.8	E949.4	E950.4	E962.0	E980.4
Mycifradin	960.8	E856	E930.8	E950.4	E962.0	E980.4
topical	976.0	E858.7	E946.0	E950.4	E962.0	E980.4
Mycitracin	960.8	E856	E930.8	E950.4	E962.0	E980.4
ophthalmic preparation	976.5	E858.7	E946.5	E950.4	E962.0	E980.4
Mycostatin	960.1	E856	E930.1	E950.4	E962.0	E980.4
topical	976.0	E858.7	E946.0	E950.4	E962.0	E980.4
Mydriacyl	971.1	E855.4	E941.1	E950.4	E962.0	E980.4
Myelobromal	963.1	E858.1	E933.1	E950.4	E962.0	E980.4
Myleran	963.1	E858.1	E933.1	E950.4	E962.0	E980.4
Myochrysin(e)	965.69	E850.6	E935.6	E950.0	E962.0	E980.0
Myoneural blocking agents	975.2	E858.6	E945.2	E950.4	E962.0	E980.4
Myristica fragrans	988.2	E865.3	—	E950.9	E962.1	E980.9
Myristicin	988.2	E865.3	—	E950.9	E962.1	E980.9
Mysoline	966.3	E855.0	E936.3	E950.4	E962.0	E980.4
Nafcillin (sodium)	960.0	E856	E930.0	E950.4	E962.0	E980.4
Nail polish remover	982.8	E862.4	—	E950.9	E962.1	E908.9
Nalidixic acid	961.9	E857	E931.9	E950.4	E962.0	E980.4
Nalorphine	970.1	E854.3	E940.1	E950.4	E962.0	E980.4
Naloxone	970.1	E854.3	E940.1	E950.4	E962.0	E980.4
Nandrolone (decanoate) (phenpropionate)	962.1	E858.0	E932.1	E950.4	E962.0	E980.4
Naphazoline	971.2	E855.5	E941.2	E950.4	E962.0	E980.4
Naphtha (painter's) (petroleum)	981	E862.0	—	E950.9	E962.1	E980.9
solvent	981	E862.0	—	E950.9	E962.1	E980.9
vapor	987.1	E869.8	—	E952.8	E962.2	E982.8
Naphthalene (chlorinat-ed)	983.0	E864.0	—	E950.7	E962.1	E980.6
insecticide or moth repel-lent	983.0	E863.4	—	E950.7	E962.1	E980.6
vapor	987.8	E869.8	—	E952.8	E962.2	E982.8
Naphthol	983.0	E864.0	—	E950.7	E962.1	E980.6
Naphthylamine	983.0	E864.0	—	E950.7	E962.1	E980.6
Naprosyn — *see* Naproxen						
Naproxen	965.61	E850.6	E935.6	E950.0	E962.0	E980.0
Narcotic (drug)	967.9	E852.9	E937.9	E950.2	E962.0	E980.2
analgesic NEC	965.8	E850.8	E935.8	E950.0	E962.0	E980.0
antagonist	970.1	E854.3	E940.1	E950.4	E962.0	E980.4
specified NEC	967.8	E852.8	E937.8	E950.2	E962.0	E980.2
Narcotine	975.4	E858.6	E945.4	E950.4	E962.0	E980.4
Nardil	969.01	E854.0	E939.0	E950.3	E962.0	E980.3
Natrium cyanide — *see* Cyanide(s)						
Natural						
blood (product)	964.7	E858.2	E934.7	E950.4	E962.0	E980.4
gas (piped)	987.1	E867	—	E951.0	E962.2	E981.0
incomplete combustion	986	E867	—	E951.0	E962.2	E981.0
Nealbarbital, nealbarbi-tone	967.0	E851	E937.0	E950.1	E962.0	E980.1
Nectadon	975.4	E858.6	E945.4	E950.4	E962.0	E980.4
Nematocyst (sting)	989.5	E905.6	—	E950.9	E962.1	E980.9
Nembutal	967.0	E851	E937.0	E950.1	E962.0	E980.1
Neoarsphenamine	961.1	E857	E931.1	E950.4	E962.0	E980.4

▽ Subterms under main terms may continue to next column or page

Neocinchophen — Organophosphates

Substance	Poisoning	Accident	Therapeutic Use	Suicide Attempt	Assault	Undetermined
Neocinchophen	974.7	E858.5	E944.7	E950.4	E962.0	E980.4
Neomycin	960.8	E856	E930.8	E950.4	E962.0	E980.4
ENT agent	976.6	E858.7	E946.6	E950.4	E962.0	E980.4
ophthalmic preparation	976.5	E858.7	E946.5	E950.4	E962.0	E980.4
topical NEC	976.0	E858.7	E946.0	E950.4	E962.0	E980.4
Neonal	967.0	E851	E937.0	E950.1	E962.0	E980.1
Neoprontosil	961.0	E857	E931.0	E950.4	E962.0	E980.4
Neosalvarsan	961.1	E857	E931.1	E950.4	E962.0	E980.4
Neosilversalvarsan	961.1	E857	E931.1	E950.4	E962.0	E980.4
Neosporin	960.8	E856	E930.8	E950.4	E962.0	E980.4
ENT agent	976.6	E858.7	E946.6	E950.4	E962.0	E980.4
opthalmic preparation	976.5	E858.7	E946.5	E950.4	E962.0	E980.4
topical NEC	976.0	E858.7	E946.0	E950.4	E962.0	E980.4
Neostigmine	971.0	E855.3	E941.0	E950.4	E962.0	E980.4
Neraval	967.0	E851	E937.0	E950.1	E962.0	E980.1
Neravan	967.0	E851	E937.0	E950.1	E962.0	E980.1
Nerium oleander	988.2	E865.4	—	E950.9	E962.1	E980.9
Nerve gases (war)	987.9	E869.9	—	E952.9	E962.2	E982.9
Nesacaine	968.9	E855.2	E938.9	E950.4	E962.0	E980.4
infiltration (subcutaneous)	968.5	E855.2	E938.5	E950.4	E962.0	E980.4
nerve block (peripheral) (plexus)	968.6	E855.2	E938.6	E950.4	E962.0	E980.4
Neurobarb	967.0	E851	E937.0	E950.1	E962.0	E980.1
Neuroleptics NEC	969.3	E853.8	E939.3	E950.3	E962.0	E980.3
Neuroprotective agent	977.8	E858.8	E947.8	E950.4	E962.0	E980.4
Neutral spirits	980.0	E860.1	—	E950.9	E962.1	E980.9
beverage	980.0	E860.0	—	E950.9	E962.1	E980.9
Niacin, niacinamide	972.2	E858.3	E942.2	E950.4	E962.0	E980.4
Nialamide	969.01	E854.0	E939.0	E950.3	E962.0	E980.3
Nickle (carbonyl) (compounds) (fumes) (tetracarbonyl) (vapor)	985.8	E866.4	—	E950.9	E962.1	E980.9
Niclosamide	961.6	E857	E931.6	E950.4	E962.0	E980.4
Nicomorphine	965.09	E850.2	E935.2	E950.0	E962.0	E980.0
Nicotinamide	972.2	E858.3	E942.2	E950.4	E962.0	E980.4
Nicotine (insecticide) (spray) (sulfate) NEC	989.4	E863.4	—	E950.6	E962.1	E980.7
not insecticide	989.89	E866.8	—	E950.9	E962.1	E980.9
Nicotinic acid (derivatives)	972.2	E858.3	E942.2	E950.4	E962.0	E980.4
Nicotinyl alcohol	972.2	E858.3	E942.2	E950.4	E962.0	E980.4
Nicoumalone	964.2	E858.2	E934.2	E950.4	E962.0	E980.4
Nifenazone	965.5	E850.5	E935.5	E950.0	E962.0	E980.0
Nifuraldezone	961.9	E857	E931.9	E950.4	E962.0	E980.4
Nightshade (deadly)	988.2	E865.4	—	E950.9	E962.1	E980.9
Nikethamide	970.0	E854.3	E940.0	E950.4	E962.0	E980.4
Nilstat	960.1	E856	E930.1	E950.4	E962.0	E980.4
topical	976.0	E858.7	E946.0	E950.4	E962.0	E980.4
Nimodipine	977.8	E858.8	E947.8	E950.4	E962.0	E980.4
Niridazole	961.6	E857	E931.6	E950.4	E962.0	E980.4
Nisentil	965.09	E850.2	E935.2	E950.0	E962.0	E980.0
Nitrates	972.4	E858.3	E942.4	E950.4	E962.0	E980.4
Nitrazepam	969.4	E853.2	E939.4	E950.3	E962.0	E980.3
Nitric						
acid (liquid)	983.1	E864.1	—	E950.7	E962.1	E980.6
vapor	987.8	E869.8	—	E952.8	E962.2	E982.8
oxide (gas)	987.2	E869.0	—	E952.8	E962.2	E982.8
Nitrite, amyl (medicinal) (vapor)	972.4	E858.3	E942.4	E950.4	E962.0	E980.4
Nitroaniline	983.0	E864.0	—	E950.7	E962.1	E980.6
vapor	987.8	E869.8	—	E952.8	E962.2	E982.8
Nitrobenzene, nitrobenzol	983.0	E864.0	—	E950.7	E962.1	E980.6
vapor	987.8	E869.8	—	E952.8	E962.2	E982.8
Nitrocellulose	976.3	E858.7	E946.3	E950.4	E962.0	E980.4
Nitrofuran derivatives	961.9	E857	E931.9	E950.4	E962.0	E980.4
Nitrofurantoin	961.9	E857	E931.9	E950.4	E962.0	E980.4
Nitrofurazone	976.0	E858.7	E946.0	E950.4	E962.0	E980.4
Nitrogen (dioxide) (gas) (oxide)	987.2	E869.0	—	E952.8	E962.2	E982.8
mustard (antineoplastic)	963.1	E858.1	E933.1	E950.4	E962.2	E980.4
nonmedicinal	989.89	E866.8	—	E950.9	E962.1	E980.9
fumes	987.8	E869.0	—	E952.8	E962.2	E982.8
Nitroglycerin, nitroglycerol (medicinal)	972.4	E858.3	E942.4	E950.4	E962.0	E980.4
Nitrohydrochloric acid	983.1	E864.1	—	E950.7	E962.1	E980.6
Nitromersol	976.0	E858.7	E946.0	E950.4	E962.0	E980.4
Nitronaphthalene	983.0	E864.0	—	E950.7	E962.2	E980.6
Nitrophenol	983.0	E864.0	—	E950.7	E962.2	E980.6
Nitrothiazol	961.6	E857	E931.6	E950.4	E962.0	E980.4
Nitrotoluene, nitrotoluol	983.0	E864.0	—	E950.7	E962.1	E980.6

Substance	Poisoning	Accident	Therapeutic Use	Suicide Attempt	Assault	Undetermined
Nitrotoluene, nitrotoluol — continued						
vapor	987.8	E869.8	—	E952.8	E962.2	E982.8
Nitrous	968.2	E855.1	E938.2	E950.4	E962.0	E980.4
acid (liquid)	983.1	E864.1	—	E950.7	E962.1	E980.6
fumes	987.2	E869.0	—	E952.8	E962.2	E982.8
oxide (anesthetic) NEC	968.2	E855.1	E938.2	E950.4	E962.0	E980.4
Nitrozone	976.0	E858.7	E946.0	E950.4	E962.0	E980.4
Noctec	967.1	E852.0	E937.1	E950.2	E962.0	E980.2
Noludar	967.5	E852.4	E937.5	E950.2	E962.0	E980.2
Noptil	967.0	E851	E937.0	E950.1	E962.0	E980.1
Noradrenalin	971.2	E855.5	E941.2	E950.4	E962.0	E980.4
Noramidopyrine	965.5	E850.5	E935.5	E950.0	E962.0	E980.0
Norepinephrine	971.2	E855.5	E941.2	E950.4	E962.0	E980.4
Norethandrolone	962.1	E858.0	E932.1	E950.4	E962.0	E980.4
Norethindrone	962.2	E858.0	E932.2	E950.4	E962.0	E980.4
Norethisterone	962.2	E858.0	E932.2	E950.4	E962.0	E980.4
Norethynodrel	962.2	E858.0	E932.2	E950.4	E962.0	E980.4
Norlestrin	962.2	E858.0	E932.2	E950.4	E962.0	E980.4
Norlutin	962.2	E858.0	E932.2	E950.4	E962.0	E980.4
Normison — see Benzodiazepines						
Normorphine	965.09	E850.2	E935.2	E950.0	E962.0	E980.0
Nortriptyline	969.05	E854.0	E939.0	E950.3	E962.0	E980.3
Noscapine	975.4	E858.6	E945.4	E950.4	E962.0	E980.4
Nose preparations	976.6	E858.7	E946.6	E950.4	E962.0	E980.4
Novobiocin	960.8	E856	E930.8	E950.4	E962.0	E980.4
Novocain (infiltration) (topical)	968.5	E855.2	E938.5	E950.4	E962.0	E980.4
nerve block (peripheral) (plexus)	968.6	E855.2	E938.6	E950.4	E962.0	E980.4
spinal	968.7	E855.2	E938.7	E950.4	E962.0	E980.4
Noxythiolin	961.9	E857	E931.9	E950.4	E962.0	E980.4
NPH Iletin (insulin)	962.3	E858.0	E932.3	E950.4	E962.0	E980.4
Numorphan	965.09	E850.2	E935.2	E950.0	E962.0	E980.0
Nunol	967.0	E851	E937.0	E950.1	E962.0	E980.1
Nupercaine (spinal anesthetic)	968.7	E855.2	E938.7	E950.4	E962.0	E980.4
topical (surface)	968.5	E855.2	E938.5	E950.4	E962.0	E980.4
Nutmeg oil (liniment)	976.3	E858.7	E946.3	E950.4	E962.0	E980.4
Nux vomica	989.1	E863.7	—	E950.6	E962.1	E980.7
Nydrazid	961.8	E857	E931.8	E950.4	E962.0	E980.4
Nylidrin	971.2	E855.5	E941.2	E950.4	E962.0	E980.4
Nystatin	960.1	E856	E930.1	E950.4	E962.0	E980.4
topical	976.0	E858.7	E946.0	E950.4	E962.0	E980.4
Nytol	963.0	E858.1	E933.0	E950.4	E962.0	E980.4
Oblivion	967.8	E852.8	E937.8	E950.2	E962.0	E980.2
Octyl nitrite	972.4	E858.3	E942.4	E950.4	E962.0	E980.4
Oestradiol (cypionate) (dipropionate) (valerate)	962.2	E858.0	E932.2	E950.4	E962.0	E980.4
Oestriol	962.2	E858.0	E932.2	E950.4	E962.0	E980.4
Oestrone	962.2	E858.0	E932.2	E950.4	E962.0	E980.4
Oil (of) NEC	989.89	E866.8	—	E950.9	E962.1	E980.9
bitter almond	989.0	E866.8	—	E950.9	E962.1	E980.9
camphor	976.1	E858.7	E946.1	E950.4	E962.0	E980.4
colors	989.89	E861.6	—	E950.9	E962.1	E980.9
fumes	987.8	E869.8	—	E952.8	E962.2	E982.8
lubricating	981	E862.2	—	E950.9	E962.1	E980.9
specified source, other — see substance specified						
vitriol (liquid)	983.1	E864.1	—	E950.7	E962.1	E980.6
fumes	987.8	E869.8	—	E952.8	E962.2	E982.8
wintergreen (bitter) NEC	976.3	E858.7	E946.3	E950.4	E962.0	E980.4
Ointments NEC	976.9	E858.7	E946.9	E950.4	E962.0	E980.4
Oleander	988.2	E865.4	—	E950.9	E962.1	E980.9
Oleandomycin	960.3	E856	E930.3	E950.4	E962.0	E980.4
Oleovitamin A	963.5	E858.1	E933.5	E950.4	E962.0	E980.4
Oleum ricini	973.1	E858.4	E943.1	E950.4	E962.0	E980.4
Olive oil (medicinal) NEC	973.2	E858.4	E943.2	E950.4	E962.0	E980.4
OMPA	989.3	E863.1	—	E950.6	E962.1	E980.7
Oncovin	963.1	E858.1	E933.1	E950.4	E962.0	E980.4
Ophthaine	968.5	E855.2	E938.5	E950.4	E962.0	E980.4
Ophthetic	968.5	E855.2	E938.5	E950.4	E962.0	E980.4
Opiates, opioids, opium NEC	965.00	E850.2	E935.2	E950.0	E962.0	E980.0
antagonists	970.1	E854.3	E940.1	E950.4	E962.0	E980.4
Oracon	962.2	E858.0	E932.2	E950.4	E962.0	E980.4
Oragrafin	977.8	E858.8	E947.8	E950.4	E962.0	E980.4
Oral contraceptives	962.2	E858.0	E932.2	E950.4	E962.0	E980.4
Orciprenaline	975.1	E858.6	E945.1	E950.4	E962.0	E980.4
Organidin	975.5	E858.6	E945.5	E950.4	E962.0	E980.4
Organophosphates	989.3	E863.1	—	E950.6	E962.1	E980.7

Nontherapeutic use substance

▽ Subterms under main terms may continue to next column or page

Substance	Poisoning	Accident	Therapeutic Use	Suicide Attempt	Assault	Undetermined
Orimune	979.5	E858.8	E949.5	E950.4	E962.0	E980.4
Orinase	962.3	E858.0	E932.3	E950.4	E962.0	E980.4
Orphenadrine	966.4	E855.0	E936.4	E950.4	E962.0	E980.4
Ortal (sodium)	967.0	E851	E937.0	E950.1	E962.0	E980.1
Orthoboric acid	976.0	E858.7	E946.0	E950.4	E962.0	E980.4
ENT agent	976.6	E858.7	E946.6	E950.4	E962.0	E980.4
ophthalmic preparation	976.5	E858.7	E946.5	E950.4	E962.0	E980.4
Orthocaine	968.5	E855.2	E938.5	E950.4	E962.0	E980.4
Ortho-Novum	962.2	E858.0	E932.2	E950.4	E962.0	E980.4
Orthotolidine (reagent)	977.8	E858.8	E947.8	E950.4	E962.0	E980.4
Osmic acid (liquid)	983.1	E864.1	—	E950.7	E962.1	E980.6
fumes	987.8	E869.8	—	E952.8	E962.2	E982.8
Osmotic diuretics	974.4	E858.5	E944.4	E950.4	E962.0	E980.4
Ouabain	972.1	E858.3	E942.1	E950.4	E962.0	E980.4
Ovarian hormones (synthetic substitutes)	962.2	E858.0	E932.2	E950.4	E962.0	E980.4
Ovral	962.2	E858.0	E932.2	E950.4	E962.0	E980.4
Ovulation suppressants	962.2	E858.0	E932.2	E950.4	E962.0	E980.4
Ovulen	962.2	E858.0	E932.2	E950.4	E962.0	E980.4
Oxacillin (sodium)	960.0	E856	E930.0	E950.4	E962.0	E980.4
Oxalic acid	983.1	E864.1	—	E950.7	E962.1	E980.6
Oxanamide	969.5	E853.8	E939.5	E950.3	E962.0	E980.3
Oxandrolone	962.1	E858.0	E932.1	E950.4	E962.0	E980.4
Oxaprozin	965.61	E850.6	E935.6	E950.0	E962.0	E980.0
Oxazepam	969.4	E853.2	E939.4	E950.3	E962.0	E980.3
Oxazolidine derivatives	966.0	E855.0	E936.0	E950.4	E962.0	E980.4
Ox bile extract	973.4	E858.4	E943.4	E950.4	E962.0	E980.4
Oxedrine	971.2	E855.5	E941.2	E950.4	E962.0	E980.4
Oxeladin	975.4	E858.6	E945.4	E950.4	E962.0	E980.4
Oxethazaine NEC	968.5	E855.2	E938.5	E950.4	E962.0	E980.4
Oxidizing agents NEC	983.9	E864.3	—	E950.7	E962.1	E980.6
Oxolinic acid	961.3	E857	E931.3	E950.4	E962.0	E980.4
Oxophenarsine	961.1	E857	E931.1	E950.4	E962.0	E980.4
Oxsoralen	976.3	E858.7	E946.3	E950.4	E962.0	E980.4
Oxtriphylline	975.7	E858.6	E945.7	E950.4	E962.0	E980.4
Oxybuprocaine	968.5	E855.2	E938.5	E950.4	E962.0	E980.4
Oxybutynin	975.1	E858.6	E945.1	E950.4	E962.0	E980.4
Oxycodone	965.09	E850.2	E935.2	E950.0	E962.0	E980.0
Oxygen	987.8	E869.8	—	E952.8	E962.2	E982.8
Oxylone	976.0	E858.7	E946.0	E950.4	E962.0	E980.4
ophthalmic preparation	976.5	E858.7	E946.5	E950.4	E962.0	E980.4
Oxymesterone	962.1	E858.0	E932.1	E950.4	E962.0	E980.4
Oxymetazoline	971.2	E855.5	E941.2	E950.4	E962.0	E980.4
Oxymetholone	962.1	E858.0	E932.1	E950.4	E962.0	E980.4
Oxymorphone	965.09	E850.2	E935.2	E950.0	E962.0	E980.0
Oxypertine	969.09	E854.0	E939.0	E950.3	E962.0	E980.3
Oxyphenbutazone	965.5	E850.5	E935.5	E950.0	E962.0	E980.0
Oxyphencyclimine	971.1	E855.4	E941.1	E950.4	E962.0	E980.4
Oxyphenisatin	973.1	E858.4	E943.1	E950.4	E962.0	E980.4
Oxyphenonium	971.1	E855.4	E941.1	E950.4	E962.0	E980.4
Oxyquinoline	961.3	E857	E931.3	E950.4	E962.0	E980.4
Oxytetracycline	960.4	E856	E930.4	E950.4	E962.0	E980.4
Oxytocics	975.0	E858.6	E945.0	E950.4	E962.0	E980.4
Oxytocin	975.0	E858.6	E945.0	E950.4	E962.0	E980.4
Ozone	987.8	E869.8	—	E952.8	E962.2	E982.8
PABA	976.3	E858.7	E946.3	E950.4	E962.0	E980.4
Packed red cells	964.7	E858.2	E934.7	E950.4	E962.0	E980.4
Paint NEC	989.89	E861.6	—	E950.9	E962.1	E980.9
cleaner	982.8	E862.9	—	E950.9	E962.1	E980.9
fumes NEC	987.8	E869.8	—	E952.8	E962.1	E982.8
lead (fumes)	984.0	E861.5	—	E950.9	E962.1	E980.9
solvent NEC	982.8	E862.9	—	E950.9	E962.1	E980.9
stripper	982.8	E862.9	—	E950.9	E962.1	E980.9
Palfium	965.09	E850.2	E935.2	E950.0	E962.0	E980.0
Palivizumab	979.9	E858.8	E949.6	E950.4	E962.0	E980.4
Paludrine	961.4	E857	E931.4	E950.4	E962.0	E980.4
PAM	977.2	E855.8	E947.2	E950.4	E962.0	E980.4
Pamaquine (naphthoate)	961.4	E857	E931.4	E950.4	E962.0	E980.4
Pamprin	965.1	E850.3	E935.3	E950.0	E962.0	E980.0
Panadol	965.4	E850.4	E935.4	E950.0	E962.0	E980.0
Pancreatic dornase (mucolytic)	963.4	E858.1	E933.4	E950.4	E962.0	E980.4
Pancreatin	973.4	E858.4	E943.4	E950.4	E962.0	E980.4
Pancrelipase	973.4	E858.4	E943.4	E950.4	E962.0	E980.4
Pangamic acid	963.5	E858.1	E933.5	E950.4	E962.0	E980.4
Panthenol	963.5	E858.1	E933.5	E950.4	E962.0	E980.4
topical	976.8	E858.7	E946.8	E950.4	E962.0	E980.4
Pantopaque	977.8	E858.8	E947.8	E950.4	E962.0	E980.4
Pantopon	965.00	E850.2	E935.2	E950.0	E962.0	E980.0
Pantothenic acid	963.5	E858.1	E933.5	E950.4	E962.0	E980.4
Panwarfin	964.2	E858.2	E934.2	E950.4	E962.0	E980.4
Papain	973.4	E858.4	E943.4	E950.4	E962.0	E980.4
Papaverine	972.5	E858.3	E942.5	E950.4	E962.0	E980.4
Para-aminobenzoic acid	976.3	E858.7	E946.3	E950.4	E962.0	E980.4
Para-aminophenol derivatives	965.4	E850.4	E935.4	E950.0	E962.0	E980.0
Para-aminosalicylic acid (derivatives)	961.8	E857	E931.8	E950.4	E962.0	E980.4
Paracetaldehyde (medicinal)	967.2	E852.1	E937.2	E950.2	E962.0	E980.2
Paracetamol	965.4	E850.4	E935.4	E950.0	E962.0	E980.0
Paracodin	965.09	E850.2	E935.2	E950.0	E962.0	E980.0
Paradione	966.0	E855.0	E936.0	E950.4	E962.0	E980.4
Paraffin(s) (wax)	981	E862.3	—	E950.9	E962.1	E980.9
liquid (medicinal)	973.2	E858.4	E943.2	E950.4	E962.0	E980.4
nonmedicinal (oil)	981	E862.1	—	E950.9	—	E980.9
Paraldehyde (medicinal)	967.2	E852.1	E937.2	E950.2	E962.0	E980.2
Paramethadione	966.0	E855.0	E936.0	E950.4	E962.0	E980.4
Paramethasone	962.0	E858.0	E932.0	E950.4	E962.0	E980.4
Paraquat	989.4	E863.5	—	E950.6	E962.1	E980.7
Parasympatholytics	971.1	E855.4	E941.1	E950.4	E962.0	E980.4
Parasympathomimetics	971.0	E855.3	E941.0	E950.4	E962.0	E980.4
Parathion	989.3	E863.1	—	E950.6	E962.1	E980.7
Parathormone	962.6	E858.0	E932.6	E950.4	E962.0	E980.4
Parathyroid (derivatives)	962.6	E858.0	E932.6	E950.4	E962.0	E980.4
Paratyphoid vaccine	978.1	E858.8	E948.1	E950.4	E962.0	E980.4
Paredrine	971.2	E855.5	E941.2	E950.4	E962.0	E980.4
Paregoric	965.00	E850.2	E935.2	E950.0	E962.0	E980.0
Pargyline	972.3	E858.3	E942.3	E950.4	E962.0	E980.4
Paris green	985.1	E866.3	—	E950.8	E962.1	E980.8
insecticide	985.1	E863.4	—	E950.8	E962.1	E980.8
Parnate	969.01	E854.0	E939.0	E950.3	E962.0	E980.3
Paromomycin	960.8	E856	E930.8	E950.4	E962.0	E980.4
Paroxypropione	963.1	E858.1	E933.1	E950.4	E962.0	E980.4
Parzone	965.09	E850.2	E935.2	E950.0	E962.0	E980.0
PAS	961.8	E857	E931.8	E950.4	E962.0	E980.4
PCBs	981	E862.3	—	E950.9	E962.1	E980.9
PCP (pentachlorophenol)	989.4	E863.6	—	E950.6	E962.1	E980.7
herbicide	989.4	E863.5	—	E950.6	E962.1	E980.7
insecticide	989.4	E863.4	—	E950.6	E962.1	E980.7
phencyclidine	968.3	E855.1	E938.3	E950.4	E962.0	E980.4
Peach kernel oil (emulsion)	973.2	E858.4	E943.2	E950.4	E962.0	E980.4
Peanut oil (emulsion)						
NEC	973.2	E858.4	E943.2	E950.4	E962.0	E980.4
topical	976.3	E858.7	E946.3	E950.4	E962.0	E980.4
Pearly Gates (morning glory seeds)	969.6	E854.1	E939.6	E950.3	E962.0	E980.3
Pecazine	969.1	E853.0	E939.1	E950.3	E962.0	E980.3
Pecilocin	960.1	E856	E930.1	E950.4	E962.0	E980.4
Pectin (with kaolin) NEC	973.5	E858.4	E943.5	E950.4	E962.0	E980.4
Pelletierine tannate	961.6	E857	E931.6	E950.4	E962.0	E980.4
Pemoline	969.79	E854.2	E939.7	E950.3	E962.0	E980.3
Pempidine	972.3	E858.3	E942.3	E950.4	E962.0	E980.4
Penamecillin	960.0	E856	E930.0	E950.4	E962.0	E980.4
Penethamate hydriodide	960.0	E856	E930.0	E950.4	E962.0	E980.4
Penicillamine	963.8	E858.1	E933.8	E950.4	E962.0	E980.4
Penicillin (any type)	960.0	E856	E930.0	E950.4	E962.0	E980.4
Penicillinase	963.4	E858.1	E933.4	E950.4	E962.0	E980.4
Pentachlorophenol (fungicide)	989.4	E863.6	—	E950.6	E962.1	E980.7
herbicide	989.4	E863.5	—	E950.6	E962.1	E980.7
insecticide	989.4	E863.4	—	E950.6	E962.1	E980.7
Pentaerythritol	972.4	E858.3	E942.4	E950.4	E962.0	E980.4
chloral	967.1	E852.0	E937.1	E950.2	E962.0	E980.2
tetranitrate NEC	972.4	E858.3	E942.4	E950.4	E962.0	E980.4
Pentagastrin	977.8	E858.8	E947.8	E950.4	E962.0	E980.4
Pentalin	982.3	E862.4	—	E950.9	E962.1	E980.9
Pentamethonium (bromide)	972.3	E858.3	E942.3	E950.4	E962.0	E980.4
Pentamidine	961.5	E857	E931.5	E950.4	E962.0	E980.4
Pentanol	980.8	E860.8	—	E950.9	E962.1	E980.9
Pentaquine	961.4	E857	E931.4	E950.4	E962.0	E980.4
Pentazocine	965.8	E850.8	E935.8	E950.0	E962.0	E980.0
Penthienate	971.1	E855.4	E941.1	E950.4	E962.0	E980.4
Pentobarbital, pentobarbitone (sodium)	967.0	E851	E937.0	E950.1	E962.0	E980.1
Pentolinium (tartrate)	972.3	E858.3	E942.3	E950.4	E962.0	E980.4
Pentothal	968.3	E855.1	E938.3	E950.4	E962.0	E980.4
Pentylenetetrazol	970.0	E854.3	E940.0	E950.4	E962.0	E980.4
Pentylsalicylamide	961.8	E857	E931.8	E950.4	E962.0	E980.4
Pepsin	973.4	E858.4	E943.4	E950.4	E962.0	E980.4
Peptavlon	977.8	E858.8	E947.8	E950.4	E962.0	E980.4
Percaine (spinal)	968.7	E855.2	E938.7	E950.4	E962.0	E980.4

Nontherapeutic use substance

▼ Subterms under main terms may continue to next column or page

	Poisoning	Accident	Therapeutic Use	Suicide Attempt	Assault	Undetermined
Percaine — *continued*						
topical (surface)	968.5	E855.2	E938.5	E950.4	E962.0	E980.4
Perchloroethylene (vapor)	982.3	E862.4	—	E950.9	E962.1	E980.9
medicinal	961.6	E857	E931.6	E950.4	E962.0	E980.4
Percodan	965.09	E850.2	E935.2	E950.0	E962.0	E980.0
Percogesic	965.09	E850.2	E935.2	E950.0	E962.0	E980.0
Percorten	962.0	E858.0	E932.0	E950.4	E962.0	E980.4
Pergonal	962.4	E858.0	E932.4	E950.4	E962.0	E980.4
Perhexiline	972.4	E858.3	E942.4	E950.4	E962.0	E980.4
Periactin	963.0	E858.1	E933.0	E950.4	E962.0	E980.4
Periclor	967.1	E852.0	E937.1	E950.2	E962.0	E980.2
Pericyazine	969.1	E853.0	E939.1	E950.3	E962.0	E980.3
Peritrate	972.4	E858.3	E942.4	E950.4	E962.0	E980.4
Permanganates NEC	983.9	E864.3	—	E950.7	E962.1	E980.6
potassium (topical)	976.0	E858.7	E946.0	E950.4	E962.0	E980.4
Pernocton	967.0	E851	E937.0	E950.1	E962.0	E980.1
Pernoston	967.0	E851	E937.0	E950.1	E962.0	E980.1
Peronin(e)	965.09	E850.2	E935.2	E950.0	E962.0	E980.0
Perphenazine	969.1	E853.0	E939.1	E950.3	E962.0	E980.3
Pertofrane	969.05	E854.0	E939.0	E950.3	E962.0	E980.3
Pertussis						
immune serum (human)	964.6	E858.2	E934.6	E950.4	E962.0	E980.4
vaccine (with diphtheria toxoid) (with tetanus toxoid)	978.6	E858.8	E948.6	E950.4	E962.0	E980.4
Peruvian balsam	976.8	E858.7	E946.8	E950.4	E962.0	E980.4
Pesticides (dust) (fumes) (vapor)	989.4	E863.4	—	E950.6	E962.1	E980.7
arsenic	985.1	E863.4	—	E950.8	E962.1	E980.8
chlorinated	989.2	E863.0	—	E950.6	E962.1	E980.7
cyanide	989.0	E863.4	—	E950.6	E962.1	E980.7
kerosene	981	E863.4	—	E950.6	E962.1	E980.7
mixture (of compounds)	989.4	E863.3	—	E950.6	E962.1	E980.7
naphthalene	983.0	E863.4	—	E950.7	E962.1	E980.6
organochlorine (compounds)	989.2	E863.0	—	E950.6	E962.1	E980.7
petroleum (distillate) (products) NEC	981	E863.4	—	E950.6	E962.1	E980.7
specified ingredient NEC	989.4	E863.4	—	E950.6	E962.1	E980.7
strychnine	989.1	E863.4	—	E950.6	E962.1	E980.7
thallium	985.8	E863.7	—	E950.6	E962.1	E980.7
Pethidine (hydrochloride)	965.09	E850.2	E935.2	E950.0	E962.0	E980.0
Petrichloral	967.1	E852.0	E937.1	E950.2	E962.0	E980.2
Petrol	981	E862.1	—	E950.9	E962.1	E980.9
vapor	987.1	E869.8	—	E952.8	E962.2	E982.8
Petrolatum (jelly) (ointment)	976.3	E858.7	E946.3	E950.4	E962.0	E980.4
hydrophilic	976.3	E858.7	E946.3	E950.4	E962.0	E980.4
liquid	973.2	E858.4	E943.2	E950.4	E962.0	E980.4
topical	976.3	E858.7	E946.3	E950.4	E962.0	E980.4
nonmedicinal	981	E862.1	—	E950.9	E962.1	E980.9
Petroleum (cleaners) (fuels) (products) NEC	981	E862.1	—	E950.9	E962.1	E980.9
benzin(e) — see Ligroin						
ether — see Ligroin						
jelly — see Petrolatum						
naphtha — see Ligroin						
pesticide	981	E863.4	—	E950.6	E962.1	E980.7
solids	981	E862.3	—	E950.9	E962.1	E980.9
solvents	981	E862.1	—	E950.9	E962.1	E980.9
vapor	987.1	E869.8	—	E952.8	E962.2	E982.8
Peyote	969.6	E854.1	E939.6	E950.3	E962.0	E980.3
Phanodorm, phanodorn	967.0	E851	E937.0	E950.1	E962.0	E980.1
Phanquinone, phanquone	961.5	E857	E931.5	E950.4	E962.0	E980.4
Pharmaceutical excipient or adjunct	977.4	E858.8	E947.4	E950.4	E962.0	E980.4
Phenacemide	966.3	E855.0	E936.3	E950.4	E962.0	E980.4
Phenacetin	965.4	E850.4	E935.4	E950.0	E962.0	E980.0
Phenadoxone	965.09	E850.2	E935.2	E950.0	E962.0	E980.0
Phenaglycodol	969.5	E853.8	E939.5	E950.3	E962.0	E980.3
Phenantoin	966.1	E855.0	E936.1	E950.4	E962.0	E980.4
Phenaphthazine reagent	977.8	E858.8	E947.8	E950.4	E962.0	E980.4
Phenazocine	965.09	E850.2	E935.2	E950.0	E962.0	E980.0
Phenazone	965.5	E850.5	E935.5	E950.0	E962.0	E980.0
Phenazopyridine	976.1	E858.7	E946.1	E950.4	E962.0	E980.4
Phenbenicillin	960.0	E856	E930.0	E950.4	E962.0	E980.4
Phenbutrazate	977.0	E858.8	E947.0	E950.4	E962.0	E980.4
Phencyclidine	968.3	E855.1	E938.3	E950.4	E962.0	E980.4
Phendimetrazine	977.0	E858.8	E947.0	E950.4	E962.0	E980.4
Phenelzine	969.01	E854.0	E939.0	E950.3	E962.0	E980.3
Phenergan	967.8	E852.8	E937.8	E950.2	E962.0	E980.2
Phenethicillin (potassium)	960.0	E856	E930.0	E950.4	E962.0	E980.4
Phenetsal	965.1	E850.3	E935.3	E950.0	E962.0	E980.0
Pheneturide	966.3	E855.0	E936.3	E950.4	E962.0	E980.4
Phenformin	962.3	E858.0	E932.3	E950.4	E962.0	E980.4
Phenglutarimide	971.1	E855.4	E941.1	E950.4	E962.0	E980.4
Phenicarbazide	965.8	E850.8	E935.8	E950.0	E962.0	E980.0
Phenindamine (tartrate)	963.0	E858.1	E933.0	E950.4	E962.0	E980.4
Phenindione	964.2	E858.2	E934.2	E950.4	E962.0	E980.4
Pheniprazine	969.01	E854.0	E939.0	E950.3	E962.0	E980.3
Pheniramine (maleate)	963.0	E858.1	E933.0	E950.4	E962.0	E980.4
Phenmetrazine	977.0	E858.8	E947.0	E950.4	E962.0	E980.4
Phenobal	967.0	E851	E937.0	E950.1	E962.0	E980.1
Phenobarbital	967.0	E851	E937.0	E950.1	E962.0	E980.1
Phenobarbitone	967.0	E851	E937.0	E950.1	E962.0	E980.1
Phenoctide	976.0	E858.7	E946.0	E950.4	E962.0	E980.4
Phenolphthalein	973.1	E858.4	E943.1	E950.4	E962.0	E980.4
Phenolsulfonphthalein	977.8	E858.8	E947.8	E950.4	E962.0	E980.4
Phenol (derivatives) NEC	983.0	E864.0	—	E950.7	E962.1	E980.6
disinfectant	983.0	E864.0	—	E950.7	E962.1	E980.6
pesticide	989.4	E863.4	—	E950.6	E962.1	E980.7
red	977.8	E858.8	E947.8	E950.4	E962.0	E980.4
Phenomorphan	965.09	E850.2	E935.2	E950.0	E962.0	E980.0
Phenonyl	967.0	E851	E937.0	E950.1	E962.0	E980.1
Phenoperidine	965.09	E850.2	E935.2	E950.0	E962.0	E980.0
Phenoquin	974.7	E858.5	E944.7	E950.4	E962.0	E980.4
Phenothiazines (tranquilizers) NEC	969.1	E853.0	E939.1	E950.3	E962.0	E980.3
insecticide	989.3	E863.4	—	E950.6	E962.1	E980.7
Phenoxybenzamine	971.3	E855.6	E941.3	E950.4	E962.0	E980.4
Phenoxymethyl penicillin	960.0	E856	E930.0	E950.4	E962.0	E980.4
Phenprocoumon	964.2	E858.2	E934.2	E950.4	E962.0	E980.4
Phensuximide	966.2	E855.0	E936.2	E950.4	E962.0	E980.4
Phentermine	977.0	E858.8	E947.0	E950.4	E962.0	E980.4
Phentolamine	971.3	E855.6	E941.3	E950.4	E962.0	E980.4
Phenyl						
butazone	965.5	E850.5	E935.5	E950.0	E962.0	E980.0
enediamine	983.0	E864.0	—	E950.7	E962.1	E980.6
hydrazine	983.0	E864.0	—	E950.7	E962.1	E980.6
antineoplastic	963.1	E858.1	E933.1	E950.4	E962.0	E980.4
mercuric compounds — see Mercury						
salicylate	976.3	E858.7	E946.3	E950.4	E962.0	E980.4
Phenylephrine	971.2	E855.5	E941.2	E950.4	E962.0	E980.4
Phenylethylbiguanide	962.3	E858.0	E932.3	E950.4	E962.0	E980.4
Phenylpropanolamine	971.2	E855.5	E941.2	E950.4	E962.0	E980.4
Phenylsulfthion	989.3	E863.1	—	E950.6	E962.1	E980.7
Phenyramidol, phenyramidon	965.7	E850.7	E935.7	E950.0	E962.0	E980.0
Phenytoin	966.1	E855.0	E936.1	E950.4	E962.0	E980.4
pHisoHex	976.2	E858.7	E946.2	E950.4	E962.0	E980.4
Pholcodine	965.09	E850.2	E935.2	E950.0	E962.0	E980.0
Phorate	989.3	E863.1	—	E950.6	E962.1	E980.7
Phosdrin	989.3	E863.1	—	E950.6	E962.1	E980.7
Phosgene (gas)	987.8	E869.8	—	E952.8	E962.2	E982.8
Phosphate (tricresyl)	989.89	E866.8	—	E950.9	E962.1	E980.9
organic	989.3	E863.1	—	E950.6	E962.1	E980.7
solvent	982.8	E862.4	—	E950.9	E926.1	E980.9
Phosphine	987.8	E869.8	—	E952.8	E962.2	E982.8
fumigant	987.8	E863.8	—	E950.6	E962.2	E980.7
Phospholine	971.0	E855.3	E941.0	E950.4	E962.0	E980.4
Phosphoric acid	983.1	E864.1	—	E950.7	E962.1	E980.6
Phosphorus (compounds) NEC	983.9	E864.3	—	E950.7	E962.1	E980.6
rodenticide	983.9	E863.7	—	E950.7	E962.1	E980.6
Phthalimidoglutarimide	967.8	E852.8	E937.8	E950.2	E962.0	E980.2
Phthalylsulfathiazole	961.0	E857	E931.0	E950.4	E962.0	E980.4
Phylloquinone	964.3	E858.2	E934.3	E950.4	E962.0	E980.4
Physeptone	965.02	E850.1	E935.1	E950.0	E962.0	E980.0
Physostigma venenosum	988.2	E865.4	—	E950.9	E962.1	E980.9
Physostigmine	971.0	E855.3	E941.0	E950.4	E962.0	E980.4
Phytolacca decandra	988.2	E865.4	—	E950.9	E962.1	E980.9
Phytomenadione	964.3	E858.2	E934.3	E950.4	E962.0	E980.4
Phytonadione	964.3	E858.2	E934.3	E950.4	E962.0	E980.4
Picric (acid)	983.0	E864.0	—	E950.7	E962.1	E980.6
Picrotoxin	970.0	E854.3	E940.0	E950.4	E962.0	E980.4
Pilocarpine	971.0	E855.3	E941.0	E950.4	E962.0	E980.4
Pilocarpus (jaborandi) extract	971.0	E855.3	E941.0	E950.4	E962.0	E980.4

Nontherapeutic use substance

⚐ Subterms under main terms may continue to next column or page

(Side tab: Percaine — Pilocarpus (jaborandi) extract)

External Cause (E-Code)

	Poisoning	Accident	Therapeutic Use	Suicide Attempt	Assault	Undetermined
Pimaricin	960.1	E856	E930.1	E950.4	E962.0	E980.4
Piminodine	965.09	E850.2	E935.2	E950.0	E962.0	E980.0
Pine oil, pinesol (disinfectant)	983.9	E861.4	—	E950.7	E962.1	E980.6
Pinkroot	961.6	E857	E931.6	E950.4	E962.0	E980.4
Pipadone	965.09	E850.2	E935.2	E950.0	E962.0	E980.0
Pipamazine	963.0	E858.1	E933.0	E950.4	E962.0	E980.4
Pipazethate	975.4	E858.6	E945.4	E950.4	E962.0	E980.4
Pipenzolate	971.1	E855.4	E941.1	E950.4	E962.0	E980.4
Piperacetazine	969.1	E853.0	E939.1	E950.3	E962.0	E980.3
Piperazine NEC	961.6	E857	E931.6	E950.4	E962.0	E980.4
estrone sulfate	962.2	E858.0	E932.2	E950.4	E962.0	E980.4
Piper cubeba	988.2	E865.4	—	E950.9	E962.1	E980.9
Piperidione	975.4	E858.4	E945.4	E950.4	E962.0	E980.4
Piperidolate	971.1	E855.4	E941.1	E950.4	E962.0	E980.4
Piperocaine	968.9	E855.2	E938.9	E950.4	E962.0	E980.4
infiltration (subcutaneous)	968.5	E855.2	E938.5	E950.4	E962.0	E980.4
nerve block (peripheral) (plexus)	968.6	E855.2	E938.6	E950.4	E962.0	E980.4
topical (surface)	968.5	E855.2	E938.5	E950.4	E962.0	E980.4
Pipobroman	963.1	E858.1	E933.1	E950.4	E962.0	E980.4
Pipradrol	970.89	E854.3	E940.8	E950.4	E962.0	E980.4
Piscidia (bark) (erythrina)	965.7	E850.7	E935.7	E950.0	E962.0	E980.0
Pitch	983.0	E864.0	—	E950.7	E962.1	E980.6
Pitkin's solution	968.7	E855.2	E938.7	E950.4	E962.0	E980.4
Pitocin	975.0	E858.6	E945.0	E950.4	E962.0	E980.4
Pitressin (tannate)	962.5	E858.0	E932.5	E950.4	E962.0	E980.4
Pituitary extracts (posterior)	962.5	E858.0	E932.5	E950.4	E962.0	E980.4
anterior	962.4	E858.0	E932.4	E950.4	E962.0	E980.4
Pituitrin	962.5	E858.0	E932.5	E950.4	E962.0	E980.4
Placental extract	962.9	E858.0	E932.9	E950.4	E962.0	E980.4
Placidyl	967.8	E852.8	E937.8	E950.2	E962.0	E980.2
Plague vaccine	978.3	E858.8	E948.3	E950.4	E962.0	E980.4
Plant foods or fertilizers NEC	989.89	E866.5	—	E950.9	E962.1	E980.9
mixed with herbicides	989.4	E863.5	—	E950.6	E962.1	E980.7
Plants, noxious, used as food	988.2	E865.9	—	E950.9	E962.1	E980.9
berries and seeds	988.2	E865.3	—	E950.9	E962.1	E980.9
specified type NEC	988.2	E865.4	—	E950.9	E962.1	E980.9
Plasma (blood)	964.7	E858.2	E934.7	E950.4	E962.0	E980.4
expanders	964.8	E858.2	E934.8	E950.4	E962.0	E980.4
Plasmanate	964.7	E858.2	E934.7	E950.4	E962.0	E980.4
Plegicil	969.1	E853.0	E939.1	E950.3	E962.0	E980.3
Podophyllin	976.4	E858.7	E946.4	E950.4	E962.0	E980.4
Podophyllum resin	976.4	E858.7	E946.4	E950.4	E962.0	E980.4
Poisonous berries	988.2	E865.3	—	E950.9	E962.1	E980.9
Poison NEC	989.9	E866.9	—	E950.9	E962.1	E980.9
Pokeweed (any part)	988.2	E865.4	—	E950.9	E962.1	E980.9
Poldine	971.1	E855.4	E941.1	E950.4	E962.0	E980.4
Poliomyelitis vaccine	979.5	E858.8	E949.5	E950.4	E962.0	E980.4
Poliovirus vaccine	979.5	E858.8	E949.5	E950.4	E962.0	E980.4
Polish (car) (floor) (furniture) (metal) (silver)	989.89	E861.2	—	E950.9	E962.1	E980.9
abrasive	989.89	E861.3	—	E950.9	E962.1	E980.9
porcelain	989.89	E861.3	—	E950.9	E962.1	E980.9
Poloxalkol	973.2	E858.4	E943.2	E950.4	E962.0	E980.4
Polyaminostyrene resins	974.5	E858.5	E944.5	E950.4	E962.0	E980.4
Polychlorinated biphenyl — see PCBs						
Polycycline	960.4	E856	E930.4	E950.4	E962.0	E980.4
Polyester resin hardener	982.8	E862.4	—	E950.9	E962.1	E980.9
fumes	987.8	E869.8	—	E952.8	E962.2	E982.8
Polyestradiol (phosphate)	962.2	E858.0	E932.2	E950.4	E962.0	E980.4
Polyethanolamine alkyl sulfate	976.2	E858.7	E946.2	E950.4	E962.0	E980.4
Polyethylene glycol	976.3	E858.7	E946.3	E950.4	E962.0	E980.4
Polyferose	964.0	E858.2	E934.0	E950.4	E962.0	E980.4
Polymyxin B	960.8	E856	E930.8	E950.4	E962.0	E980.4
ENT agent	976.6	E858.7	E946.6	E950.4	E962.0	E980.4
ophthalmic preparation	976.5	E858.7	E946.5	E950.4	E962.0	E980.4
topical NEC	976.0	E858.7	E946.0	E950.4	E962.0	E980.4
Polynoxylin(e)	976.0	E858.7	E946.0	E950.4	E962.0	E980.4
Polyoxymethyleneurea	976.0	E858.7	E946.0	E950.4	E962.0	E980.4
Polytetrafluoroethylene (inhaled)	987.8	E869.8	—	E952.8	E962.2	E982.8
Polythiazide	974.3	E858.5	E944.3	E950.4	E962.0	E980.4
Polyvinylpyrrolidone	964.8	E858.2	E934.8	E950.4	E962.0	E980.4
Pontocaine (hydrochloride) (infiltration) (topical)	968.5	E855.2	E938.5	E950.4	E962.0	E980.4
nerve block (peripheral) (plexus)	968.6	E855.2	E938.6	E950.4	E962.0	E980.4
spinal	968.7	E855.2	E938.7	E950.4	E962.0	E980.4
Pot	969.6	E854.1	E939.6	E950.3	E962.0	E980.3
Potash (caustic)	983.2	E864.2	—	E950.7	E962.1	E980.6
Potassic saline injection (lactated)	974.5	E858.5	E944.5	E950.4	E962.0	E980.4
Potassium (salts) NEC	974.5	E858.5	E944.5	E950.4	E962.0	E980.4
aminosalicylate	961.8	E857	E931.8	E950.4	E962.0	E980.4
arsenite (solution)	985.1	E866.3	—	E950.8	E962.1	E980.8
bichromate	983.9	E864.3	—	E950.7	E962.1	E980.6
bisulfate	983.9	E864.3	—	E950.7	E962.1	E980.6
bromide (medicinal) NEC	967.3	E852.2	E937.3	E950.2	E962.0	E980.2
carbonate	983.2	E864.2	—	E950.7	E962.1	E980.6
chlorate NEC	983.9	E864.3	—	E950.7	E962.1	E980.6
cyanide — see Cyanide						
hydroxide	983.2	E864.2	—	E950.7	E962.1	E980.6
iodide (expectorant) NEC	975.5	E858.6	E945.5	E950.4	E962.0	E980.4
nitrate	989.89	E866.8	—	E950.9	E962.1	E980.9
oxalate	983.9	E864.3	—	E950.7	E962.1	E980.6
perchlorate NEC	977.8	E858.8	E947.8	E950.4	E962.0	E980.4
antithyroid	962.8	E858.0	E932.8	E950.4	E962.0	E980.4
permanganate	976.0	E858.7	E946.0	E950.4	E962.0	E980.4
nonmedicinal	983.9	E864.3	—	E950.7	E962.1	E980.6
Povidone-iodine (anti-infective) NEC	976.0	E858.7	E946.0	E950.4	E962.0	E980.4
Practolol	972.0	E858.3	E942.0	E950.4	E962.0	E980.4
Pralidoxime (chloride)	977.2	E858.8	E947.2	E950.4	E962.0	E980.4
Pramoxine	968.5	E855.2	E938.5	E950.4	E962.0	E980.4
Prazosin	972.6	E858.3	E942.6	E950.4	E962.0	E980.4
Prednisolone	962.0	E858.0	E932.0	E950.4	E962.0	E980.4
ENT agent	976.6	E858.7	E946.6	E950.4	E962.0	E980.4
ophthalmic preparation	976.5	E858.7	E946.5	E950.4	E962.0	E980.4
topical NEC	976.0	E858.7	E946.0	E950.4	E962.0	E980.4
Prednisone	962.0	E858.0	E932.0	E950.4	E962.0	E980.4
Pregnanediol	962.2	E858.0	E932.2	E950.4	E962.0	E980.4
Pregneninolone	962.2	E858.0	E932.2	E950.4	E962.0	E980.4
Preludin	977.0	E858.8	E947.0	E950.4	E962.0	E980.4
Premarin	962.2	E858.0	E932.2	E950.4	E962.0	E980.4
Prenylamine	972.4	E858.3	E942.4	E950.4	E962.0	E980.4
Preparation H	976.8	E858.7	E946.8	E950.4	E962.0	E980.4
Preservatives	989.89	E866.8	—	E950.9	E962.1	E980.9
Pride of China	988.2	E865.3	—	E950.9	E962.1	E980.9
Prilocaine	968.9	E855.2	E938.9	E950.4	E962.0	E980.4
infiltration (subcutaneous)	968.5	E855.2	E938.5	E950.4	E962.0	E980.4
nerve block (peripheral) (plexus)	968.6	E855.2	E938.6	E950.4	E962.0	E980.4
Primaquine	961.4	E857	E931.4	E950.4	E962.0	E980.4
Primidone	966.3	E855.0	E936.3	E950.4	E962.0	E980.4
Primula (veris)	988.2	E865.4	—	E950.9	E962.1	E980.9
Prinadol	965.09	E850.2	E935.2	E950.0	E962.0	E980.0
Priscol, Priscoline	971.3	E855.6	E941.3	E950.4	E962.0	E980.4
Privet	988.2	E865.4	—	E950.9	E962.1	E980.9
Privine	971.2	E855.5	E941.2	E950.4	E962.0	E980.4
Pro-Banthine	971.1	E855.4	E941.1	E950.4	E962.0	E980.4
Probarbital	967.0	E851	E937.0	E950.1	E962.0	E980.1
Probenecid	974.7	E858.5	E944.7	E950.4	E962.0	E980.4
Procainamide (hydrochloride)	972.0	E858.3	E942.0	E950.4	E962.0	E980.4
Procaine (hydrochloride) (infiltration) (topical)	968.5	E855.2	E938.5	E950.4	E962.0	E980.4
nerve block (peripheral) (plexus)	968.6	E855.2	E938.6	E950.4	E962.0	E980.4
penicillin G	960.0	E856	E930.0	E950.4	E962.0	E980.4
spinal	968.7	E855.2	E938.7	E950.4	E962.0	E980.4
Procalmidol	969.5	E853.8	E939.5	E950.3	E962.0	E980.3
Procarbazine	963.1	E858.1	E933.1	E950.4	E962.0	E980.4
Prochlorperazine	969.1	E853.0	E939.1	E950.3	E962.0	E980.3
Procyclidine	966.4	E855.0	E936.4	E950.4	E962.0	E980.4
Producer gas	986	E868.8	—	E952.1	E962.2	E982.1
Profenamine	966.4	E855.0	E936.4	E950.4	E962.0	E980.4
Profenil	975.1	E858.6	E945.1	E950.4	E962.0	E980.4
Progesterones	962.2	E858.0	E932.2	E950.4	E962.0	E980.4
Progestin	962.2	E858.0	E932.2	E950.4	E962.0	E980.4
Progestogens (with estrogens)	962.2	E858.0	E932.2	E950.4	E962.0	E980.4
Progesterone	962.2	E858.0	E932.2	E950.4	E962.0	E980.4
Proguanil	961.4	E857	E931.4	E950.4	E962.0	E980.4
Prolactin	962.4	E858.0	E932.4	E950.4	E962.0	E980.4

Nontherapeutic use substance

Subterms under main terms may continue to next column or page

	External Cause (E-Code)				
Poisoning	Accident	Therapeutic Use	Suicide Attempt	Assault	Undetermined

Substance	Poisoning	Accident	Therapeutic Use	Suicide Attempt	Assault	Undetermined
Proloid	962.7	E858.0	E932.7	E950.4	E962.0	E980.4
Proluton	962.2	E858.0	E932.2	E950.4	E962.0	E980.4
Promacetin	961.8	E857	E931.8	E950.4	E962.0	E980.4
Promazine	969.1	E853.0	E939.1	E950.3	E962.0	E980.3
Promedol	965.09	E850.2	E935.2	E950.0	E962.0	E980.0
Promethazine	967.8	E852.8	E937.8	E950.2	E962.0	E980.2
Promin	961.8	E857	E931.8	E950.4	E962.0	E980.4
Pronestyl (hydrochloride)	972.0	E858.3	E942.0	E950.4	E962.0	E980.4
Pronetalol, pronethalol	972.0	E858.3	E942.0	E950.4	E962.0	E980.4
Prontosil	961.0	E857	E931.0	E950.4	E962.0	E980.4
Propamidine isethionate	961.5	E857	E931.5	E950.4	E962.0	E980.4
Propanal (medicinal)	967.8	E852.8	E937.8	E950.2	E962.0	E980.2
Propane (gas) (distributed in mobile container)	987.0	E868.0	—	E951.1	E962.2	E981.1
distributed through pipes	987.0	E867	—	E951.0	E962.2	E981.0
incomplete combustion of — see Carbon monoxide, Propane						
Propanidid	968.3	E855.1	E938.3	E950.4	E962.0	E980.4
Propanol	980.3	E860.4	—	E950.9	E962.1	E980.9
Propantheline	971.1	E855.4	E941.1	E950.4	E962.0	E980.4
Proparacaine	968.5	E855.2	E938.5	E950.4	E962.0	E980.4
Propatyl nitrate	972.4	E858.3	E942.4	E950.4	E962.0	E980.4
Propicillin	960.0	E856	E930.0	E950.4	E962.0	E980.4
Propiolactone (vapor)	987.8	E869.8	—	E952.8	E962.2	E982.8
Propiomazine	967.8	E852.8	E937.8	E950.2	E962.0	E980.2
Propionaldehyde (medicinal)	967.8	E852.8	E937.8	E950.2	E962.0	E980.2
Propionate compound	976.0	E858.7	E946.0	E950.4	E962.0	E980.4
Propion gel	976.0	E858.7	E946.0	E950.4	E962.0	E980.4
Propitocaine	968.9	E855.2	E938.9	E950.4	E962.0	E980.4
infiltration (subcutaneous)	968.5	E855.2	E938.5	E950.4	E962.0	E980.4
nerve block (peripheral) (plexus)	968.6	E855.2	E938.6	E950.4	E962.0	E980.4
Propoxur	989.3	E863.2	—	E950.6	E962.1	E980.7
Propoxycaine	968.9	E855.2	E938.9	E950.4	E962.0	E980.4
infiltration (subcutaneous)	968.5	E855.2	E938.5	E950.4	E962.0	E980.4
nerve block (peripheral) (plexus)	968.6	E855.2	E938.6	E950.4	E962.0	E980.4
topical (surface)	968.5	E855.2	E938.5	E950.4	E962.0	E980.4
Propoxyphene (hydrochloride)	965.8	E850.8	E935.8	E950.0	E962.0	E980.0
Propranolol	972.0	E858.3	E942.0	E950.4	E962.0	E980.4
Propyl						
alcohol	980.3	E860.4	—	E950.9	E962.1	E980.9
carbinol	980.3	E860.4	—	E950.9	E962.1	E980.9
hexadrine	971.2	E855.5	E941.2	E950.4	E962.0	E980.4
iodone	977.8	E858.8	E947.8	E950.4	E962.0	E980.4
thiouracil	962.8	E858.0	E932.8	E950.4	E962.0	E980.4
Propylene	987.1	E869.8	—	E952.8	E962.2	E982.8
Propylparaben (ophthalmic)	976.5	E858.7	E946.5	E950.4	E962.0	E980.4
Proscillaridin	972.1	E858.3	E942.1	E950.4	E962.0	E980.4
Prostaglandins	975.0	E858.6	E945.0	E950.4	E962.0	E980.4
Prostigmin	971.0	E855.3	E941.0	E950.4	E962.0	E980.4
Protamine (sulfate)	964.5	E858.2	E934.5	E950.4	E962.0	E980.4
zinc insulin	962.3	E858.0	E932.3	E950.4	E962.0	E980.4
Protectants (topical)	976.3	E858.7	E946.3	E950.4	E962.0	E980.4
Protein hydrolysate	974.5	E858.5	E944.5	E950.4	E962.0	E980.4
Prothiaden — see Dothiepin hydrochloride						
Prothionamide	961.8	E857	E931.8	E950.4	E962.0	E980.4
Prothipendyl	969.5	E853.8	E939.5	E950.3	E962.0	E980.3
Protokylol	971.2	E855.5	E941.2	E950.4	E962.0	E980.4
Protopam	977.2	E858.8	E947.2	E950.4	E962.0	E980.4
Protoveratrine(s) (A) (B)	972.6	E858.3	E942.6	E950.4	E962.0	E980.4
Protriptyline	969.05	E854.0	E939.0	E950.3	E962.0	E980.3
Provera	962.2	E858.0	E932.2	E950.4	E962.0	E980.4
Provitamin A	963.5	E858.1	E933.5	E950.4	E962.0	E980.4
Proxymetacaine	968.5	E855.2	E938.5	E950.4	E962.0	E980.4
Proxyphylline	975.1	E858.6	E945.1	E950.4	E962.0	E980.4
Prozac — see Fluoxetine hydrochloride						
Prunus						
laurocerasus	988.2	E865.4	—	E950.9	E962.1	E980.9
virginiana	988.2	E865.4	—	E950.9	E962.1	E980.9
Prussic acid	989.0	E866.8	—	E950.9	E962.1	E980.9
vapor	987.7	E869.8	—	E952.8	E962.2	E982.8
Pseudoephedrine	971.2	E855.5	E941.2	E950.4	E962.0	E980.4
Psilocin	969.6	E854.1	E939.6	E950.3	E962.0	E980.3
Psilocybin	969.6	E854.1	E939.6	E950.3	E962.0	E980.3
PSP	977.8	E858.8	E947.8	E950.4	E962.0	E980.4
Psychedelic agents	969.6	E854.1	E939.6	E950.3	E962.0	E980.3
Psychodysleptics	969.6	E854.1	E939.6	E950.3	E962.0	E980.3
Psychostimulants	969.70	E854.2	E939.7	E950.3	E962.0	E980.3
Psychotherapeutic agents	969.9	E855.9	E939.9	E950.3	E962.0	E980.3
antidepressants	969.00	E854.0	E939.0	E950.3	E962.0	E980.3
specified NEC	969.8	E855.8	E939.8	E950.3	E962.0	E980.3
tranquilizers NEC	969.5	E853.9	E939.5	E950.3	E962.0	E980.3
Psychotomimetic agents	969.6	E854.1	E939.6	E950.3	E962.0	E980.3
Psychotropic agents	969.9	E854.8	E939.9	E950.3	E962.0	E980.3
specified NEC	969.8	E854.8	E939.8	E950.3	E962.0	E980.3
Psyllium	973.3	E858.4	E943.3	E950.4	E962.0	E980.4
Pteroylglutamic acid	964.1	E858.2	E934.1	E950.4	E962.0	E980.4
Pteroyltriglutamate	963.1	E858.1	E933.1	E950.4	E962.0	E980.4
PTFE	987.8	E869.8	—	E952.8	E962.2	E982.8
Pulsatilla	988.2	E865.4	—	E950.9	E962.1	E980.9
Purex (bleach)	983.9	E864.3	—	E950.7	E962.1	E980.6
Purine diuretics	974.1	E858.5	E944.1	E950.4	E962.0	E980.4
Purinethol	963.1	E858.1	E933.1	E950.4	E962.0	E980.4
PVP	964.8	E858.2	E934.8	E950.4	E962.0	E980.4
Pyrabital	965.7	E850.7	E935.7	E950.0	E962.0	E980.0
Pyramidon	965.5	E850.5	E935.5	E950.0	E962.0	E980.0
Pyrantel (pamoate)	961.6	E857	E931.6	E950.4	E962.0	E980.4
Pyrathiazine	963.0	E858.1	E933.0	E950.4	E962.0	E980.4
Pyrazinamide	961.8	E857	E931.8	E950.4	E962.0	E980.4
Pyrazinoic acid (amide)	961.8	E857	E931.8	E950.4	E962.0	E980.4
Pyrazole (derivatives)	965.5	E850.5	E935.5	E950.0	E962.0	E980.0
Pyrazolone (analgesics)	965.5	E850.5	E935.5	E950.0	E962.0	E980.0
Pyrethrins, pyrethrum	989.4	E863.4	—	E950.6	E962.1	E980.7
Pyribenzamine	963.0	E858.1	E933.0	E950.4	E962.0	E980.4
Pyridine (liquid) (vapor)	982.0	E862.4	—	E950.9	E962.1	E980.9
aldoxime chloride	977.2	E858.8	E947.2	E950.4	E962.0	E980.4
Pyridium	976.1	E858.7	E946.1	E950.4	E962.0	E980.4
Pyridostigmine	971.0	E855.3	E941.0	E950.4	E962.0	E980.4
Pyridoxine	963.5	E858.1	E933.5	E950.4	E962.0	E980.4
Pyrilamine	963.0	E858.1	E933.0	E950.4	E962.0	E980.4
Pyrimethamine	961.4	E857	E931.4	E950.4	E962.0	E980.4
Pyrogallic acid	983.0	E864.0	—	E950.7	E962.1	E980.6
Pyroxylin	976.3	E858.7	E946.3	E950.4	E962.0	E980.4
Pyrrobutamine	963.0	E858.1	E933.0	E950.4	E962.0	E980.4
Pyrrocitine	968.5	E855.2	E938.5	E950.4	E962.0	E980.4
Pyrvinium (pamoate)	961.6	E857	E931.6	E950.4	E962.0	E980.4
PZI	962.3	E858.0	E932.3	E950.4	E962.0	E980.4
Quaalude	967.4	E852.3	E937.4	E950.2	E962.0	E980.2
Quaternary ammonium derivatives	971.1	E855.4	E941.1	E950.4	E962.0	E980.4
Quicklime	983.2	E864.2	—	E950.7	E962.1	E980.6
Quinacrine	961.3	E857	E931.3	E950.4	E962.0	E980.4
Quinaglute	972.0	E858.3	E942.0	E950.4	E962.0	E980.4
Quinalbarbitone	967.0	E851	E937.0	E950.1	E962.0	E980.1
Quinestradiol	962.2	E858.0	E932.2	E950.4	E962.0	E980.4
Quinethazone	974.3	E858.5	E944.3	E950.4	E962.0	E980.4
Quinidine (gluconate) (polygalacturonate) (salts) (sulfate)	972.0	E858.3	E942.0	E950.4	E962.0	E980.4
Quinine	961.4	E857	E931.4	E950.4	E962.0	E980.4
Quiniobine	961.3	E857	E931.3	E950.4	E962.0	E980.4
Quinolines	961.3	E857	E931.3	E950.4	E962.0	E980.4
Quotane	968.5	E855.2	E938.5	E950.4	E962.0	E980.4
Rabies						
immune globulin (human)	964.6	E858.2	E934.6	E950.4	E962.0	E980.4
vaccine	979.1	E858.8	E949.1	E950.4	E962.0	E980.4
Racemoramide	965.09	E850.2	E935.2	E950.0	E962.0	E980.0
Racemorphan	965.09	E850.2	E935.2	E950.0	E962.0	E980.0
Radiator alcohol	980.1	E860.2	—	E950.9	E962.1	E980.9
Radio-opaque (drugs) (materials)	977.8	E858.8	E947.8	E950.4	E962.0	E980.4
Ranunculus	988.2	E865.4	—	E950.9	E962.1	E980.9
Rat poison	989.4	E863.7	—	E950.6	E962.1	E980.7
Rattlesnake (venom)	989.5	E905.0	—	E950.9	E962.1	E980.9
Raudixin	972.6	E858.3	E942.6	E950.4	E962.0	E980.4
Rautensin	972.6	E858.3	E942.6	E950.4	E962.0	E980.4
Rautina	972.6	E858.3	E942.6	E950.4	E962.0	E980.4
Rautotal	972.6	E858.3	E942.6	E950.4	E962.0	E980.4
Rauwiloid	972.6	E858.3	E942.6	E950.4	E962.0	E980.4
Rauwoldin	972.6	E858.3	E942.6	E950.4	E962.0	E980.4
Rauwolfia (alkaloids)	972.6	E858.3	E942.6	E950.4	E962.0	E980.4
Realgar	985.1	E866.3	—	E950.8	E962.1	E980.8

Nontherapeutic use substance

▽ Subterms under main terms may continue to next column or page

	Poisoning	Accident	Therapeutic Use	Suicide Attempt	Assault	Undetermined
Red cells, packed	964.7	E858.2	E934.7	E950.4	E962.0	E980.4
Reducing agents, industrial NEC	983.9	E864.3	—	E950.7	E962.1	E980.6
Refrigerant gas (freon)	987.4	E869.2	—	E952.8	E962.2	E982.8
central nervous system	968.0	E855.1	E938.0	E950.4	E962.0	E980.4
not freon	987.9	E869.9	—	E952.9	E962.2	E982.9
Regroton	974.4	E858.5	E944.4	E950.4	E962.0	E980.4
Rela	968.0	E855.1	E938.0	E950.4	E962.0	E980.4
Relaxants, skeletal muscle (autonomic)	975.2	E858.6	E945.2	E950.4	E962.0	E980.4
Renese	974.3	E858.5	E944.3	E950.4	E962.0	E980.4
Renografin	977.8	E858.8	E947.8	E950.4	E962.0	E980.4
Replacement solutions	974.5	E858.5	E944.5	E950.4	E962.0	E980.4
Rescinnamine	972.6	E858.3	E942.6	E950.4	E962.0	E980.4
Reserpine	972.6	E858.3	E942.6	E950.4	E962.0	E980.4
Resorcin, resorcinol	976.4	E858.7	E946.4	E950.4	E962.0	E980.4
Respaire	975.5	E858.6	E945.5	E950.4	E962.0	E980.4
Respiratory agents NEC	975.8	E858.6	E945.8	E950.4	E962.0	E980.4
Retinoic acid	976.8	E858.7	E946.8	E950.4	E962.0	E980.4
Retinol	963.5	E858.1	E933.5	E950.4	E962.0	E980.4
Rh (D) immune globulin (human)	964.6	E858.2	E934.6	E950.4	E962.0	E980.4
Rhodine	965.1	E850.3	E935.3	E950.0	E962.0	E980.0
RhoGAM	964.6	E858.2	E934.6	E950.4	E962.0	E980.4
Riboflavin	963.5	E858.1	E933.5	E950.4	E962.0	E980.4
Ricin	989.89	E866.8	—	E950.9	E962.1	E980.9
Ricinus communis	988.2	E865.3	—	E950.9	E962.1	E980.9
Rickettsial vaccine NEC	979.6	E858.8	E949.6	E950.4	E962.1	E980.4
with viral and bacterial vaccine	979.7	E858.8	E949.7	E950.4	E962.0	E980.4
Rifampin	960.6	E856	E930.6	E950.4	E962.0	E980.4
Rimifon	961.8	E857	E931.8	E950.4	E962.0	E980.4
Ringer's injection (lactated)	974.5	E858.5	E944.5	E950.4	E962.0	E980.4
Ristocetin	960.8	E856	E930.8	E950.4	E962.0	E980.4
Ritalin	969.73	E854.2	E939.7	E950.3	E962.0	E980.3
Roach killers — see Pesticides						
Rocky Mountain spotted fever vaccine	979.6	E858.8	E949.6	E950.4	E962.0	E980.4
Rodenticides	989.4	E863.7	—	E950.6	E962.1	E980.7
Rohypnol	969.4	E853.2	E939.4	E950.3	E962.0	E980.3
Rolaids	973.0	E858.4	E943.0	E950.4	E962.0	E980.4
Rolitetracycline	960.4	E856	E930.4	E950.4	E962.0	E980.4
Romilar	975.4	E858.6	E945.4	E950.4	E962.0	E980.4
Rose water ointment	976.3	E858.7	E946.3	E950.4	E962.0	E980.4
Rosuvastatin calcium	972.1	E858.3	E942.2	E950.4	E962.0	E980.4
Rotenone	989.4	E863.7	—	E950.6	E962.1	E980.7
Rotoxamine	963.0	E858.1	E933.0	E950.4	E962.0	E980.4
Rough-on-rats	989.4	E863.7	—	E950.6	E962.1	E980.7
RU486	962.9	E858.0	E932.9	E950.4	E962.0	E980.4
Rubbing alcohol	980.2	E860.3	—	E950.9	E962.1	E980.9
Rubella virus vaccine	979.4	E858.8	E949.4	E950.4	E962.0	E980.4
Rubelogen	979.4	E858.8	E949.4	E950.4	E962.0	E980.4
Rubeovax	979.4	E858.8	E949.4	E950.4	E962.0	E980.4
Rubidomycin	960.7	E856	E930.7	E950.4	E962.0	E980.4
Rue	988.2	E865.4	—	E950.9	E962.1	E980.9
Ruta	988.2	E865.4	—	E950.9	E962.1	E980.9
Sabadilla (medicinal)	976.0	E858.7	E946.0	E950.4	E962.0	E980.4
pesticide	989.4	E863.4	—	E950.6	E962.1	E980.7
Sabin oral vaccine	979.5	E858.8	E949.5	E950.4	E962.0	E980.4
Saccharated iron oxide	964.0	E858.2	E934.0	E950.4	E962.0	E980.4
Saccharin	974.5	E858.5	E944.5	E950.4	E962.0	E980.4
Safflower oil	972.2	E858.3	E942.2	E950.4	E962.0	E980.4
Salbutamol sulfate	975.7	E858.6	E945.7	E950.4	E962.0	E980.4
Salicylamide	965.1	E850.3	E935.3	E950.0	E962.0	E980.0
Salicylate(s)	965.1	E850.3	E935.3	E950.0	E962.0	E980.0
methyl	976.3	E858.7	E946.3	E950.4	E962.0	E980.4
theobromine calcium	974.1	E858.5	E944.1	E950.4	E962.0	E980.4
Salicylazosulfapyridine	961.0	E857	E931.0	E950.4	E962.0	E980.4
Salicylhydroxamic acid	976.0	E858.7	E946.0	E950.4	E962.0	E980.4
Salicylic acid (keratolytic) NEC	976.4	E858.7	E946.4	E950.4	E962.0	E980.4
congeners	965.1	E850.3	E935.3	E950.0	E962.0	E980.0
salts	965.1	E850.3	E935.3	E950.0	E962.0	E980.0
Saliniazid	961.8	E857	E931.8	E950.4	E962.0	E980.4
Salol	976.3	E858.7	E946.3	E950.4	E962.0	E980.4
Salt (substitute) NEC	974.5	E858.5	E944.5	E950.4	E962.0	E980.4
Saluretics	974.3	E858.5	E944.3	E950.4	E962.0	E980.4
Saluron	974.3	E858.5	E944.3	E950.4	E962.0	E980.4
Salvarsan 606 (neosilver) (silver)	961.1	E857	E931.1	E950.4	E962.0	E980.4
Sambucus canadensis	988.2	E865.4	—	E950.9	E962.1	E980.9
Sambucus canadensis — continued						
berry	988.2	E865.3	—	E950.9	E962.1	E980.9
Sandril	972.6	E858.3	E942.6	E950.4	E962.0	E980.4
Sanguinaria canadensis	988.2	E865.4	—	E950.9	E962.1	E980.9
Saniflush (cleaner)	983.9	E861.3	—	E950.7	E962.1	E980.6
Santonin	961.6	E857	E931.6	E950.4	E962.0	E980.4
Santyl	976.8	E858.7	E946.8	E950.4	E962.0	E980.4
Sarkomycin	960.7	E856	E930.7	E950.4	E962.0	E980.4
Saroten	969.05	E854.0	E939.0	E950.3	E962.0	E980.3
Saturnine — see Lead						
Savin (oil)	976.4	E858.7	E946.4	E950.4	E962.0	E980.4
Scammony	973.1	E858.4	E943.1	E950.4	E962.0	E980.4
Scarlet red	976.8	E858.7	E946.8	E950.4	E962.0	E980.4
Scheele's green	985.1	E866.3	—	E950.8	E962.1	E980.8
insecticide	985.1	E863.4	—	E950.8	E962.1	E980.8
Schradan	989.3	E863.1	—	E950.6	E962.1	E980.7
Schweinfurt(h) green	985.1	E866.3	—	E950.8	E962.1	E980.8
insecticide	985.1	E863.4	—	E950.8	E962.1	E980.8
Scilla — see Squill						
Sclerosing agents	972.7	E858.3	E942.7	E950.4	E962.0	E980.4
Scopolamine	971.1	E855.4	E941.1	E950.4	E962.0	E980.4
Scouring powder	989.89	E861.3	—	E950.9	E962.1	E980.9
Sea						
anemone (sting)	989.5	E905.6	—	E950.9	E962.1	E980.9
cucumber (sting)	989.5	E905.6	—	E950.9	E962.1	E980.9
snake (bite) (venom)	989.5	E905.0	—	E950.9	E962.1	E980.9
urchin spine (puncture)	989.5	E905.6	—	E950.9	E962.1	E980.9
Secbutabarbital	967.0	E851	E937.0	E950.1	E962.0	E980.1
Secbutabarbitone	967.0	E851	E937.0	E950.1	E962.0	E980.1
Secobarbital	967.0	E851	E937.0	E950.1	E962.0	E980.1
Seconal	967.0	E851	E937.0	E950.1	E962.0	E980.1
Secretin	977.8	E858.8	E947.8	E950.4	E962.0	E980.4
Sedatives, nonbarbiturate	967.9	E852.9	E937.9	E950.2	E962.0	E980.2
specified NEC	967.8	E852.8	E937.8	E950.2	E962.0	E980.2
Sedormid	967.8	E852.8	E937.8	E950.2	E962.0	E980.2
Seed (plant)	988.2	E865.3	—	E950.9	E962.1	E980.9
disinfectant or dressing	989.89	E866.5	—	E950.9	E962.1	E980.9
Selective serotonin and norepinephrine reuptake inhibitors (SSNRI)	969.02	E854.0	E939.0	E950.3	E962.0	E980.3
Selective serotonin reuptake inhibitors (SSRI)	969.03	E854.0	E939.0	E950.3	E962.0	E980.3
Selenium (fumes) NEC	985.8	E866.4	—	E950.9	E962.1	E980.9
disulfide or sulfide	976.4	E858.7	E946.4	E950.4	E962.0	E980.4
Selsun	976.4	E858.7	E946.4	E950.4	E962.0	E980.4
Senna	973.1	E858.4	E943.1	E950.4	E962.0	E980.4
Septisol	976.2	E858.7	E946.2	E950.4	E962.0	E980.4
Serax	969.4	E853.2	E939.4	E950.3	E962.0	E980.3
Serenesil	967.8	E852.8	E937.8	E950.2	E962.0	E980.2
Serenium (hydrochloride)	961.9	E857	E931.9	E950.4	E962.0	E980.4
Serepax — see Oxazepam						
Sernyl	968.3	E855.1	E938.3	E950.4	E962.0	E980.4
Serotonin	977.8	E858.8	E947.8	E950.4	E962.0	E980.4
Serpasil	972.6	E858.3	E942.6	E950.4	E962.0	E980.4
Sewer gas	987.8	E869.8	—	E952.8	E962.2	E982.8
Shampoo	989.6	E861.0	—	E950.9	E962.1	E980.9
Shellfish, nonbacterial or noxious	988.0	E865.1	—	E950.9	E962.1	E980.9
Silicones NEC	989.83	E866.8	E947.8	E950.9	E962.1	E980.9
Silvadene	976.0	E858.7	E946.0	E950.4	E962.0	E980.4
Silver (compound) (medicinal) NEC	976.0	E858.7	E946.0	E950.4	E962.0	E980.4
anti-infectives	976.0	E858.7	E946.0	E950.4	E962.0	E980.4
arsphenamine	961.1	E857	E931.1	E950.4	E962.0	E980.4
nitrate	976.0	E858.7	E946.0	E950.4	E962.0	E980.4
ophthalmic preparation	976.5	E858.7	E946.5	E950.4	E962.0	E980.4
toughened (keratolytic)	976.4	E858.7	E946.4	E950.4	E962.0	E980.4
nonmedicinal (dust)	985.8	E866.4	—	E950.9	E962.1	E980.9
protein (mild) (strong)	976.0	E858.7	E946.0	E950.4	E962.0	E980.4
salvarsan	961.1	E857	E931.1	E950.4	E962.0	E980.4
Simethicone	973.8	E858.4	E943.8	E950.4	E962.0	E980.4
Sinequan	969.05	E854.0	E939.0	E950.3	E962.0	E980.3
Singoserp	972.6	E858.3	E942.6	E950.4	E962.0	E980.4
Sintrom	964.2	E858.2	E934.2	E950.4	E962.0	E980.4
Sitosterols	972.2	E858.3	E942.2	E950.4	E962.0	E980.4
Skeletal muscle relaxants	975.2	E858.6	E945.2	E950.4	E962.0	E980.4
Skin						
agents (external)	976.9	E858.7	E946.9	E950.4	E962.0	E980.4
specified NEC	976.8	E858.7	E946.8	E950.4	E962.0	E980.4

▽ Subterms under main terms may continue to next column or page

	Poisoning	Accident	Therapeutic Use	Suicide Attempt	Assault	Undetermined
Skin — *continued*						
test antigen	977.8	E858.8	E947.8	E950.4	E962.0	E980.4
Sleep-eze	963.0	E858.1	E933.0	E950.4	E962.0	E980.4
Sleeping draught (drug) (pill) (tablet)	967.9	E852.9	E937.9	E950.2	E962.0	E980.2
Smallpox vaccine	979.0	E858.8	E949.0	E950.4	E962.0	E980.4
Smelter fumes NEC	985.9	E866.4	—	E950.9	E962.1	E980.9
Smog	987.3	E869.1	—	E952.8	E962.2	E982.8
Smoke NEC	987.9	E869.9	—	E952.9	E962.2	E982.9
Smooth muscle relaxant	975.1	E858.6	E945.1	E950.4	E962.0	E980.4
Snail killer	989.4	E863.4	—	E950.6	E962.1	E980.7
Snake (bite) (venom)	989.5	E905.0	—	E950.9	E962.1	E980.9
Snuff	989.89	E866.8	—	E950.9	E962.1	E980.9
Soap (powder) (product)	989.6	E861.1	—	E950.9	E962.1	E980.9
bicarb	963.3	E858.1	E933.3	E950.4	E962.0	E980.4
chlorinated — see Sodium, hypochlorite						
medicinal, soft	976.2	E858.7	E946.2	E950.4	E962.0	E980.4
Soda (caustic)	983.2	E864.2	—	E950.7	E962.1	E980.6
Sodium						
acetosulfone	961.8	E857	E931.8	E950.4	E962.0	E980.4
acetrizoate	977.8	E858.8	E947.8	E950.4	E962.0	E980.4
amytal	967.0	E851	E937.0	E950.1	E962.0	E980.1
arsenate — see Arsenic						
bicarbonate	963.3	E858.1	E933.3	E950.4	E962.0	E980.4
bichromate	983.9	E864.3	—	E950.7	E962.1	E980.6
biphosphate	963.2	E858.1	E933.2	E950.4	E962.0	E980.4
bisulfate	983.9	E864.3	—	E950.7	E962.1	E980.6
borate (cleanser)	989.6	E861.3	—	E950.9	E962.1	E980.9
bromide NEC	967.3	E852.2	E937.3	E950.2	E962.0	E980.2
cacodylate (nonmedicinal)						
NEC	978.8	E858.8	E948.8	E950.4	E962.0	E980.4
anti-infective	961.1	E857	E931.1	E950.4	E962.0	E980.4
herbicide	989.4	E863.5	—	E950.6	E962.1	E980.7
calcium edetate	963.8	E858.1	E933.8	E950.4	E962.0	E980.4
carbonate NEC	983.2	E864.2	—	E950.7	E962.1	E980.6
chlorate NEC	983.9	E864.3	—	E950.7	E962.1	E980.6
herbicide	983.9	E863.5	—	E950.7	E962.1	E980.6
chloride NEC	974.5	E858.5	E944.5	E950.4	E962.0	E980.4
chromate	983.9	E864.3	—	E950.7	E962.1	E980.6
citrate	963.3	E858.1	E933.3	E950.4	E962.0	E980.4
cyanide — see Cyanide(s)						
cyclamate	974.5	E858.5	E944.5	E950.4	E962.0	E980.4
diatrizoate	977.8	E858.8	E947.8	E950.4	E962.0	E980.4
dibunate	975.4	E858.6	E945.4	E950.4	E962.0	E980.4
dioctyl sulfosuccinate	973.2	E858.4	E943.2	E950.4	E962.0	E980.4
edetate	963.8	E858.1	E933.8	E950.4	E962.0	E980.4
ethacrynate	974.4	E858.5	E944.4	E950.4	E962.0	E980.4
fluoracetate (dust) (rodenticide)	989.4	E863.7	—	E950.6	E962.1	E980.7
fluoride — see Fluoride(s)						
free salt	974.5	E858.5	E944.5	E950.4	E962.0	E980.4
glucosulfone	961.8	E857	E931.8	E950.4	E962.0	E980.4
hydroxide	983.2	E864.2	—	E950.7	E962.1	E980.6
hypochlorite (bleach)						
NEC	983.9	E864.3	—	E950.7	E962.1	E980.6
disinfectant	983.9	E861.4	—	E950.7	E962.1	E980.6
medicinal (anti-infective) (external)	976.0	E858.7	E946.0	E950.4	E962.0	E980.4
vapor	987.8	E869.8	—	E952.8	E962.2	E982.8
hyposulfite	976.0	E858.7	E946.0	E950.4	E962.0	E980.4
indigotindisulfonate	977.8	E858.8	E947.8	E950.4	E962.0	E980.4
iodide	977.8	E858.8	E947.8	E950.4	E962.0	E980.4
iothalamate	977.8	E858.8	E947.8	E950.4	E962.0	E980.4
iron edetate	964.0	E858.2	E934.0	E950.4	E962.0	E980.4
lactate	963.3	E858.1	E933.3	E950.4	E962.0	E980.4
lauryl sulfate	976.2	E858.7	E946.2	E950.4	E962.0	E980.4
L-triiodothyronine	962.7	E858.0	E932.7	E950.4	E962.0	E980.4
metrizoate	977.8	E858.8	E947.8	E950.4	E962.0	E980.4
monofluoracetate (dust) (rodenticide)	989.4	E863.7	—	E950.6	E962.1	E980.7
morrhuate	972.7	E858.3	E942.7	E950.4	E962.0	E980.4
nafcillin	960.0	E856	E930.0	E950.4	E962.0	E980.4
nitrate (oxidizing agent)	983.9	E864.3	—	E950.7	E962.1	E980.6
nitrite (medicinal)	972.4	E858.3	E942.4	E950.4	E962.0	E980.4
nitroferricyanide	972.6	E858.3	E942.6	E950.4	E962.0	E980.4
nitroprusside	972.6	E858.3	E942.6	E950.4	E962.0	E980.4
para-aminohippurate	977.8	E858.8	E947.8	E950.4	E962.0	E980.4
perborate (nonmedicinal)						
NEC	989.89	E866.8	—	E950.9	E962.1	E980.9
medicinal	976.6	E858.7	E946.6	E950.4	E962.0	E980.4
soap	989.6	E861.1	—	E950.9	E962.1	E980.9

	Poisoning	Accident	Therapeutic Use	Suicide Attempt	Assault	Undetermined
Sodium — *continued*						
percarbonate — see Sodium, perborate						
phosphate	973.3	E858.4	E943.3	E950.4	E962.0	E980.4
polystyrene sulfonate	974.5	E858.5	E944.5	E950.4	E962.0	E980.4
propionate	976.0	E858.7	E946.0	E950.4	E962.0	E980.4
psylliate	972.7	E858.3	E942.7	E950.4	E962.0	E980.4
removing resins	974.5	E858.5	E944.5	E950.4	E962.0	E980.4
salicylate	965.1	E850.3	E935.3	E950.0	E962.0	E980.0
sulfate	973.3	E858.4	E943.3	E950.4	E962.0	E980.4
sulfoxone	961.8	E857	E931.8	E950.4	E962.0	E980.4
tetradecyl sulfate	972.7	E858.3	E942.7	E950.4	E962.0	E980.4
thiopental	968.3	E855.1	E938.3	E950.4	E962.0	E980.4
thiosalicylate	965.1	E850.3	E935.3	E950.0	E962.0	E980.0
thiosulfate	976.0	E858.7	E946.0	E950.4	E962.0	E980.4
tolbutamide	977.8	E858.8	E947.8	E950.4	E962.0	E980.4
tyropanoate	977.8	E858.8	E947.8	E950.4	E962.0	E980.4
valproate	966.3	E855.0	E936.3	E950.4	E962.0	E980.4
Solanine	977.8	E858.8	E947.8	E950.4	E962.0	E980.4
Solanum dulcamara	988.2	E865.4	—	E950.9	E962.1	E980.9
Solapsone	961.8	E857	E931.8	E950.4	E962.0	E980.4
Solasulfone	961.8	E857	E931.8	E950.4	E962.0	E980.4
Soldering fluid	983.1	E864.1	—	E950.7	E962.1	E980.6
Solid substance	989.9	E866.9	—	E950.9	E962.1	E980.9
specified NEC	989.9	E866.8	—	E950.9	E962.1	E980.9
Solvents, industrial	982.8	E862.9	—	E950.9	E962.1	E980.9
naphtha	981	E862.0	—	E950.9	E962.1	E980.9
petroleum	981	E862.0	—	E950.9	E962.1	E980.9
specified NEC	982.8	E862.4	—	E950.9	E962.1	E980.9
Soma	968.0	E855.1	E938.0	E950.4	E962.0	E980.4
Somatotropin	962.4	E858.0	E932.4	E950.4	E962.0	E980.4
Sominex	963.0	E858.1	E933.0	E950.4	E962.0	E980.4
Somnos	967.1	E852.0	E937.1	E950.2	E962.0	E980.2
Somonal	967.0	E851	E937.0	E950.1	E962.0	E980.1
Soneryl	967.0	E851	E937.0	E950.1	E962.0	E980.1
Soothing syrup	977.9	E858.9	E947.9	E950.5	E962.0	E980.5
Sopor	967.4	E852.3	E937.4	E950.2	E962.0	E980.2
Soporific drug	967.9	E852.9	E937.9	E950.2	E962.0	E980.2
specified type NEC	967.8	E852.8	E937.8	E950.2	E962.0	E980.2
Sorbitol NEC	977.4	E858.8	E947.4	E950.4	E962.0	E980.4
Sotradecol	972.7	E858.3	E942.7	E950.4	E962.0	E980.4
Spacoline	975.1	E858.6	E945.1	E950.4	E962.0	E980.4
Spanish fly	976.8	E858.7	E946.8	E950.4	E962.0	E980.4
Sparine	969.1	E853.0	E939.1	E950.3	E962.0	E980.3
Sparteine	975.0	E858.6	E945.0	E950.4	E962.0	E980.4
Spasmolytics	975.1	E858.6	E945.1	E950.4	E962.0	E980.4
anticholinergics	971.1	E855.4	E941.1	E950.4	E962.0	E980.4
Spectinomycin	960.8	E856	E930.8	E950.4	E962.0	E980.4
Speed	969.72	E854.2	E939.7	E950.3	E962.0	E980.3
Spermicides	976.8	E858.7	E946.8	E950.4	E962.0	E980.4
Spider (bite) (venom)	989.5	E905.1	—	E950.9	E962.1	E980.9
antivenin	979.9	E858.8	E949.9	E950.4	E962.0	E980.4
Spigelia (root)	961.6	E857	E931.6	E950.4	E962.0	E980.4
Spiperone	969.2	E853.1	E939.2	E950.3	E962.0	E980.3
Spiramycin	960.3	E856	E930.3	E950.4	E962.0	E980.4
Spirilene	969.5	E853.8	E939.5	E950.3	E962.0	E980.3
Spirit(s) (neutral) NEC	980.0	E860.1	—	E950.9	E962.1	E980.9
beverage	980.0	E860.0	—	E950.9	E962.1	E980.9
industrial	980.9	E860.9	—	E950.9	E962.1	E980.9
mineral	981	E862.0	—	E950.9	E962.1	E980.9
of salt — see Hydrochloric acid						
surgical	980.9	E860.9	—	E950.9	E962.1	E980.9
Spironolactone	974.4	E858.5	E944.4	E950.4	E962.0	E980.4
Sponge, absorbable (gelatin)	964.5	E858.2	E934.5	E950.4	E962.0	E980.4
Sporostacin	976.0	E858.7	E946.0	E950.4	E962.0	E980.4
Sprays (aerosol)	989.89	E866.8	—	E950.9	E962.1	E980.9
cosmetic	989.89	E866.7	—	E950.9	E962.1	E980.9
medicinal NEC	977.9	E858.9	E947.9	E950.5	E962.0	E980.5
pesticides — see Pesticides						
specified content — see substance specified						
Spurge flax	988.2	E865.4	—	E950.9	E962.1	E980.9
Spurges	988.2	E865.4	—	E950.9	E962.1	E980.9
Squill (expectorant) NEC	975.5	E858.6	E945.5	E950.4	E962.0	E980.4
rat poison	989.4	E863.7	—	E950.6	E962.1	E980.7
Squirting cucumber (cathartic)	973.1	E858.4	E943.1	E950.4	E962.0	E980.4
SSNRI (selective serotonin and norepinephrine reuptake inhibitors)	969.02	E854.0	E939.0	E950.3	E962.0	E980.3

Nontherapeutic use substance   Subterms under main terms may continue to next column or page

	Poisoning	Accident	Therapeutic Use	Suicide Attempt	Assault	Undetermined
SSRI (selective serotonin reuptake inhibitors)	969.03	E854.0	E939.0	E950.3	E962.0	E980.3
Stains	989.89	E866.8	—	E950.9	E962.1	E980.9
Stannous — *see also* Tin						
fluoride	976.7	E858.7	E946.7	E950.4	E962.0	E980.4
Stanolone	962.1	E858.0	E932.1	E950.4	E962.0	E980.4
Stanozolol	962.1	E858.0	E932.1	E950.4	E962.0	E980.4
Staphisagria or stavesacre (pediculicide)	976.0	E858.7	E946.0	E950.4	E962.0	E980.4
Stelazine	969.1	E853.0	E939.1	E950.3	E962.0	E980.3
Stemetil	969.1	E853.0	E939.1	E950.3	E962.0	E980.3
Sterculia (cathartic) (gum)	973.3	E858.4	E943.3	E950.4	E962.0	E980.4
Sternutator gas	987.8	E869.8	—	E952.8	E962.2	E982.8
Steroids NEC	962.0	E858.0	E932.0	E950.4	E962.0	E980.4
ENT agent	976.6	E858.7	E946.6	E950.4	E962.0	E980.4
ophthalmic preparation	976.5	E858.7	E946.5	E950.4	E962.0	E980.4
topical NEC	976.0	E858.7	E946.0	E950.4	E962.0	E980.4
Stibine	985.8	E866.4	—	E950.9	E962.1	E980.9
Stibophen	961.2	E857	E931.2	E950.4	E962.0	E980.4
Stilbamide, stilbamidine	961.5	E857	E931.5	E950.4	E962.0	E980.4
Stilbestrol	962.2	E858.0	E932.2	E950.4	E962.0	E980.4
Stimulants (central nervous system)	970.9	E854.3	E940.9	E950.4	E962.0	E980.4
analeptics	970.0	E854.3	E940.0	E950.4	E962.0	E980.4
opiate antagonist	970.1	E854.3	E940.1	E950.4	E962.0	E980.4
psychotherapeutic NEC	969.09	E854.0	E939.0	E950.3	E962.0	E980.3
specified NEC	970.89	E854.3	E940.8	E950.4	E962.0	E980.4
Storage batteries (acid) (cells)	983.1	E864.1	—	E950.7	E962.1	E980.6
Stovaine	968.9	E855.2	E938.9	E950.4	E962.0	E980.4
infiltration (subcutaneous)	968.5	E855.2	E938.5	E950.4	E962.0	E980.4
nerve block (peripheral) (plexus)	968.6	E855.2	E938.6	E950.4	E962.0	E980.4
spinal	968.7	E855.2	E938.7	E950.4	E962.0	E980.4
topical (surface)	968.5	E855.2	E938.5	E950.4	E962.0	E980.4
Stovarsal	961.1	E857	E931.1	E950.4	E962.0	E980.4
Stove gas — *see* Gas, utility						
Stoxil	976.5	E858.7	E946.5	E950.4	E962.0	E980.4
STP	969.6	E854.1	E939.6	E950.3	E962.0	E980.3
Stramonium (medicinal) NEC	971.1	E855.4	E941.1	E950.4	E962.0	E980.4
natural state	988.2	E865.4	—	E950.9	E962.1	E980.9
Streptodornase	964.4	E858.2	E934.4	E950.4	E962.0	E980.4
Streptoduocin	960.6	E856	E930.6	E950.4	E962.0	E980.4
Streptokinase	964.4	E858.2	E934.4	E950.4	E962.0	E980.4
Streptomycin	960.6	E856	E930.6	E950.4	E962.0	E980.4
Streptozocin	960.7	E856	E930.7	E950.4	E962.0	E980.4
Stripper (paint) (solvent)	982.8	E862.9	—	E950.9	E962.1	E980.9
Strobane	989.2	E863.0	—	E950.6	E962.1	E980.7
Strophanthin	972.1	E858.3	E942.1	E950.4	E962.0	E980.4
Strophanthus hispidus or kombe	988.2	E865.4	—	E950.9	E962.1	E980.9
Strychnine (rodenticide) (salts)	989.1	E863.7	—	E950.6	E962.1	E980.7
medicinal NEC	970.89	E854.3	E940.8	E950.4	E962.0	E980.4
Strychnos (ignatii) — *see* Strychnine						
Styramate	968.0	E855.1	E938.0	E950.4	E962.0	E980.4
Styrene	983.0	E864.0	—	E950.7	E962.1	E980.6
Succinimide (anticonvulsant)	966.2	E855.0	E936.2	E950.4	E962.0	E980.4
mercuric — *see* Mercury						
Succinylcholine	975.2	E858.6	E945.2	E950.4	E962.0	E980.4
Succinylsulfathiazole	961.0	E857	E931.0	E950.4	E962.0	E980.4
Sucrose	974.5	E858.5	E944.5	E950.4	E962.0	E980.4
Sulfacetamide	961.0	E857	E931.0	E950.4	E962.0	E980.4
ophthalmic preparation	976.5	E858.7	E946.5	E950.4	E962.0	E980.4
Sulfachlorpyridazine	961.0	E857	E931.0	E950.4	E962.0	E980.4
Sulfacytine	961.0	E857	E931.0	E950.4	E962.0	E980.4
Sulfadiazine	961.0	E857	E931.0	E950.4	E962.0	E980.4
silver (topical)	976.0	E858.7	E946.0	E950.4	E962.0	E980.4
Sulfadimethoxine	961.0	E857	E931.0	E950.4	E962.0	E980.4
Sulfadimidine	961.0	E857	E931.0	E950.4	E962.0	E980.4
Sulfaethidole	961.0	E857	E931.0	E950.4	E962.0	E980.4
Sulfafurazole	961.0	E857	E931.0	E950.4	E962.0	E980.4
Sulfaguanidine	961.0	E857	E931.0	E950.4	E962.0	E980.4
Sulfamerazine	961.0	E857	E931.0	E950.4	E962.0	E980.4
Sulfameter	961.0	E857	E931.0	E950.4	E962.0	E980.4
Sulfamethizole	961.0	E857	E931.0	E950.4	E962.0	E980.4
Sulfamethoxazole	961.0	E857	E931.0	E950.4	E962.0	E980.4
Sulfamethoxydiazine	961.0	E857	E931.0	E950.4	E962.0	E980.4

	Poisoning	Accident	Therapeutic Use	Suicide Attempt	Assault	Undetermined
Sulfamethoxypyridazine	961.0	E857	E931.0	E950.4	E962.0	E980.4
Sulfamethylthiazole	961.0	E857	E931.0	E950.4	E962.0	E980.4
Sulfamylon	976.0	E858.7	E946.0	E950.4	E962.0	E980.4
Sulfan blue (diagnostic dye)	977.8	E858.8	E947.8	E950.4	E962.0	E980.4
Sulfanilamide	961.0	E857	E931.0	E950.4	E962.0	E980.4
Sulfanilylguanidine	961.0	E857	E931.0	E950.4	E962.0	E980.4
Sulfaphenazole	961.0	E857	E931.0	E950.4	E962.0	E980.4
Sulfaphenylthiazole	961.0	E857	E931.0	E950.4	E962.0	E980.4
Sulfaproxyline	961.0	E857	E931.0	E950.4	E962.0	E980.4
Sulfapyridine	961.0	E857	E931.0	E950.4	E962.0	E980.4
Sulfapyrimidine	961.0	E857	E931.0	E950.4	E962.0	E980.4
Sulfarsphenamine	961.1	E857	E931.1	E950.4	E962.0	E980.4
Sulfasalazine	961.0	E857	E931.0	E950.4	E962.0	E980.4
Sulfasomizole	961.0	E857	E931.0	E950.4	E962.0	E980.4
Sulfasuxidine	961.0	E857	E931.0	E950.4	E962.0	E980.4
Sulfinpyrazone	974.7	E858.5	E944.7	E950.4	E962.0	E980.4
Sulfisoxazole	961.0	E857	E931.0	E950.4	E962.0	E980.4
ophthalmic preparation	976.5	E858.7	E946.5	E950.4	E962.0	E980.4
Sulfomyxin	960.8	E856	E930.8	E950.4	E962.0	E980.4
Sulfonal	967.8	E852.8	E937.8	E950.2	E962.0	E980.2
Sulfonamides (mixtures)	961.0	E857	E931.0	E950.4	E962.0	E980.4
Sulfones	961.8	E857	E931.8	E950.4	E962.0	E980.4
Sulfonethylmethane	967.8	E852.8	E937.8	E950.2	E962.0	E980.2
Sulfonmethane	967.8	E852.8	E937.8	E950.2	E962.0	E980.2
Sulfonphthal, sulfonph-thol	977.8	E858.8	E947.8	E950.4	E962.0	E980.4
Sulfonylurea derivatives, oral	962.3	E858.0	E932.3	E950.4	E962.0	E980.4
Sulfoxone	961.8	E857	E931.8	E950.4	E962.0	E980.4
Sulfur, sulfureted, sulfuric, sulfurous, sulfuryl (compounds) NEC	989.89	E866.8	—	E950.9	E962.1	E980.9
acid	983.1	E864.1	—	E950.7	E962.1	E980.6
dioxide	987.3	E869.1	—	E952.8	E962.2	E982.8
ether — *see* Ether(s)						
hydrogen	987.8	E869.8	—	E952.8	E962.2	E982.8
medicinal (keratolytic) (ointment) NEC	976.4	E858.7	E946.4	E950.4	E962.0	E980.4
pesticide (vapor)	989.4	E863.4	—	E950.6	E962.1	E980.7
vapor NEC	987.8	E869.8	—	E952.8	E962.2	E982.8
Sulkowitch's reagent	977.8	E858.8	E947.8	E950.4	E962.0	E980.4
Sulphadione	961.8	E857	E931.8	E950.4	E962.0	E980.4
Sulph — *see also* Sulf-						
Sulthiame, sultiame	966.3	E855.0	E936.3	E950.4	E962.0	E980.4
Superinone	975.5	E858.6	E945.5	E950.4	E962.0	E980.4
Suramin	961.5	E857	E931.5	E950.4	E962.0	E980.4
Surfacaine	968.5	E855.2	E938.5	E950.4	E962.0	E980.4
Surital	968.3	E855.1	E938.3	E950.4	E962.0	E980.4
Sutilains	976.8	E858.7	E946.8	E950.4	E962.0	E980.4
Suxamethonium (bromide) (chloride) (iodide)	975.2	E858.6	E945.2	E950.4	E962.0	E980.4
Suxethonium (bromide)	975.2	E858.6	E945.2	E950.4	E962.0	E980.4
Sweet oil (birch)	976.3	E858.7	E946.3	E950.4	E962.0	E980.4
Sym-dichloroethyl ether	982.3	E862.4	—	E950.9	E962.1	E980.9
Sympatholytics	971.3	E855.6	E941.3	E950.4	E962.0	E980.4
Sympathomimetics	971.2	E855.5	E941.2	E950.4	E962.0	E980.4
Synagis	979.6	E858.8	E949.6	E950.4	E962.0	E980.4
Synalar	976.0	E858.7	E946.0	E950.4	E962.0	E980.4
Synthroid	962.7	E858.0	E932.7	E950.4	E962.0	E980.4
Syntocinon	975.0	E858.6	E945.0	E950.4	E962.0	—
Syrosingopine	972.6	E858.3	E942.6	E950.4	E962.0	E980.4
Systemic agents (primarily)	963.9	E858.1	E933.9	E950.4	E962.0	E980.4
specified NEC	963.8	E858.1	E933.8	E950.4	E962.0	E980.4
Tablets — *see also* specified substance	977.9	E858.9	E947.9	E950.5	E962.0	E980.5
Tace	962.2	E858.0	E932.2	E950.4	E962.0	E980.4
Tacrine	971.0	E855.3	E941.0	E950.4	E962.0	E980.4
Talbutal	967.0	E851	E937.0	E950.1	E962.0	E980.1
Talc	976.3	E858.7	E946.3	E950.4	E962.0	E980.4
Talcum	976.3	E858.7	E946.3	E950.4	E962.0	E980.4
Tamsulosin	971.3	E855.6	E941.3	E950.4	E962.0	E980.4
Tandearil, tanderil	965.5	E850.5	E935.5	E950.0	E962.0	E980.0
Tannic acid	983.1	E864.1	—	E950.7	E962.1	E980.6
medicinal (astringent)	976.2	E858.7	E946.2	E950.4	E962.0	E980.4
Tannin — *see* Tannic acid						
Tansy	988.2	E865.4	—	E950.9	E962.1	E980.9
TAO	960.3	E856	E930.3	E950.4	E962.0	E980.4
Tapazole	962.8	E858.0	E932.8	E950.4	E962.0	E980.4
Taractan	969.3	E853.8	E939.3	E950.3	E962.0	E980.3
Tarantula (venomous)	989.5	E905.1	—	E950.9	E962.1	E980.9

	External Cause (E-Code)					
	Poisoning	Accident	Therapeutic Use	Suicide Attempt	Assault	Undetermined
Tartar emetic (anti-infective)	961.2	E857	E931.2	E950.4	E962.0	E980.4
Tartaric acid	983.1	E864.1	—	E950.7	E962.1	E980.6
Tartrated antimony (anti-infective)	961.2	E857	E931.2	E950.4	E962.0	E980.4
Tar NEC	983.0	E864.0	—	E950.7	E962.1	E980.6
camphor — see Naphthalene						
fumes	987.8	E869.8	—	E952.8	E962.2	E982.8
TCA — see Trichloroacetic acid						
TDI	983.0	E864.0	—	E950.7	E962.1	E980.6
vapor	987.8	E869.8	—	E952.8	E962.2	E982.8
Tear gas	987.5	E869.3	—	E952.8	E962.2	E982.8
Teclothiazide	974.3	E858.5	E944.3	E950.4	E962.0	E980.4
Tegretol	966.3	E855.0	E936.3	E950.4	E962.0	E980.4
Telepaque	977.8	E858.8	E947.8	E950.4	E962.0	E980.4
Tellurium	985.8	E866.4	—	E950.9	E962.1	E980.9
fumes	985.8	E866.4	—	E950.9	E962.1	E980.9
TEM	963.1	E858.1	E933.1	E950.4	E962.0	E980.4
Temazepan — see Benzodiazepines						
TEPA	963.1	E858.1	E933.1	E950.4	E962.0	E980.4
TEPP	989.3	E863.1	—	E950.6	E962.1	E980.7
Terbutaline	971.2	E855.5	E941.2	E950.4	E962.0	E980.4
Teroxalene	961.6	E857	E931.6	E950.4	E962.0	E980.4
Terpin hydrate	975.5	E858.6	E945.5	E950.4	E962.0	E980.4
Terramycin	960.4	E856	E930.4	E950.4	E962.0	E980.4
Tessalon	975.4	E858.6	E945.4	E950.4	E962.0	E980.4
Testosterone	962.1	E858.0	E932.1	E950.4	E962.0	E980.4
Tetanus (vaccine)	978.4	E858.8	E948.4	E950.4	E962.0	E980.4
antitoxin	979.9	E858.8	E949.9	E950.4	E962.0	E980.4
immune globulin (human)	964.6	E858.2	E934.6	E950.4	E962.0	E980.4
toxoid	978.4	E858.8	E948.4	E950.4	E962.0	E980.4
with diphtheria toxoid	978.9	E858.8	E948.9	E950.4	E962.0	E980.4
with pertussis	978.6	E858.8	E948.6	E950.4	E962.0	E980.4
Tetrabenazine	969.5	E853.8	E939.5	E950.3	E962.0	E980.3
Tetracaine (infiltration) (topical)	968.5	E855.2	E938.5	E950.4	E962.0	E980.4
nerve block (peripheral) (plexus)	968.6	E855.2	E938.6	E950.4	E962.0	E980.4
spinal	968.7	E855.2	E938.7	E950.4	E962.0	E980.4
Tetrachlorethylene — see Tetrachloroethylene						
Tetrachlormethiazide	974.3	E858.5	E944.3	E950.4	E962.0	E980.4
Tetrachloroethane (liquid) (vapor)	982.3	E862.4	—	E950.9	E962.1	E980.9
paint or varnish	982.3	E861.6	—	E950.9	E962.1	E980.9
Tetrachloroethylene (liquid) (vapor)	982.3	E862.4	—	E950.9	E962.1	E980.9
medicinal	961.6	E857	E931.6	E950.4	E962.0	E980.4
Tetrachloromethane — see Carbon, tetrachloride						
Tetracycline	960.4	E856	E930.4	E950.4	E962.0	E980.4
ophthalmic preparation	976.5	E858.7	E946.5	E950.4	E962.0	E980.4
topical NEC	976.0	E858.7	E946.0	E950.4	E962.0	E980.4
Tetraethylammonium chloride	972.3	E858.3	E942.3	E950.4	E962.0	E980.4
Tetraethyl lead (antiknock compound)	984.1	E862.1	—	E950.9	E962.1	E980.9
Tetraethyl pyrophosphate	989.3	E863.1	—	E950.6	E962.1	E980.7
Tetraethylthiuram disulfide	977.3	E858.8	E947.3	E950.4	E962.0	E980.4
Tetrahydroaminoacridine	971.0	E855.3	E941.0	E950.4	E962.0	E980.4
Tetrahydrocannabinol	969.6	E854.1	E939.6	E950.3	E962.0	E980.3
Tetrahydronaphthalene	982.0	E862.4	—	E950.9	E962.1	E980.9
Tetrahydrozoline	971.2	E855.5	E941.2	E950.4	E962.0	E980.4
Tetralin	982.0	E862.4	—	E950.9	E962.1	E980.9
Tetramethylthiuram (disulfide) NEC	989.4	E863.6	—	E950.6	E962.1	E980.7
medicinal	976.2	E858.7	E946.2	E950.4	E962.0	E980.4
Tetronal	967.8	E852.8	E937.8	E950.2	E962.0	E980.2
Tetryl	983.0	E864.0	—	E950.7	E962.1	E980.6
Thalidomide	967.8	E852.8	E937.8	E950.2	E962.0	E980.2
Thallium (compounds) (dust) NEC	985.8	E866.4	—	E950.9	E962.1	E980.9
pesticide (rodenticide)	985.8	E863.7	—	E950.6	E962.1	E980.7
THC	969.6	E854.1	E939.6	E950.3	E962.0	E980.3
Thebacon	965.09	E850.2	E935.2	E950.0	E962.0	E980.0
Thebaine	965.09	E850.2	E935.2	E950.0	E962.0	E980.0

	External Cause (E-Code)					
	Poisoning	Accident	Therapeutic Use	Suicide Attempt	Assault	Undetermined
Theobromine (calcium salicylate)	974.1	E858.5	E944.1	E950.4	E962.0	E980.4
Theophylline (diuretic)	974.1	E858.5	E944.1	E950.4	E962.0	E980.4
ethylenediamine	975.7	E858.6	E945.7	E950.4	E962.0	E980.4
Thiabendazole	961.6	E857	E931.6	E950.4	E962.0	E980.4
Thialbarbital, thialbarbitone	968.3	E855.1	E938.3	E950.4	E962.0	E980.4
Thiamine	963.5	E858.1	E933.5	E950.4	E962.0	E980.4
Thiamylal (sodium)	968.3	E855.1	E938.3	E950.4	E962.0	E980.4
Thiazesim	969.09	E854.0	E939.0	E950.3	E962.0	E980.3
Thiazides (diuretics)	974.3	E858.5	E944.3	E950.4	E962.0	E980.4
Thiethylperazine	963.0	E858.1	E933.0	E950.4	E962.0	E980.4
Thimerosal (topical)	976.0	E858.7	E946.0	E950.4	E962.0	E980.4
ophthalmic preparation	976.5	E858.7	E946.5	E950.4	E962.0	E980.4
Thioacetazone	961.8	E857	E931.8	E950.4	E962.0	E980.4
Thiobarbiturates	968.3	E855.1	E938.3	E950.4	E962.0	E980.4
Thiobismol	961.2	E857	E931.2	E950.4	E962.0	E980.4
Thiocarbamide	962.8	E858.0	E932.8	E950.4	E962.0	E980.4
Thiocarbarsone	961.1	E857	E931.1	E950.4	E962.0	E980.4
Thiocarlide	961.8	E857	E931.8	E950.4	E962.0	E980.4
Thioguanine	963.1	E858.1	E933.1	E950.4	E962.0	E980.4
Thiomercaptomerin	974.0	E858.5	E944.0	E950.4	E962.0	E980.4
Thiomerin	974.0	E858.5	E944.0	E950.4	E962.0	E980.4
Thiopental, thiopentone (sodium)	968.3	E855.1	E938.3	E950.4	E962.0	E980.4
Thiopropazate	969.1	E853.0	E939.1	E950.3	E962.0	E980.3
Thioproperazine	969.1	E853.0	E939.1	E950.3	E962.0	E980.3
Thioridazine	969.1	E853.0	E939.1	E950.3	E962.0	E980.3
Thio-TEPA, thiotepa	963.1	E858.1	E933.1	E950.4	E962.0	E980.4
Thiothixene	969.3	E853.8	E939.3	E950.3	E962.0	E980.3
Thiouracil	962.8	E858.0	E932.8	E950.4	E962.0	E980.4
Thiourea	962.8	E858.0	E932.8	E950.4	E962.0	E980.4
Thiphenamil	971.1	E855.4	E941.1	E950.4	E962.0	E980.4
Thiram NEC	989.4	E863.6	—	E950.6	E962.1	E980.7
medicinal	976.2	E858.7	E946.2	E950.4	E962.0	E980.4
Thonzylamine	963.0	E858.1	E933.0	E950.4	E962.0	E980.4
Thorazine	969.1	E853.0	E939.1	E950.3	E962.0	E980.3
Thornapple	988.2	E865.4	—	E950.9	E962.1	E980.9
Throat preparation (lozenges) NEC	976.6	E858.7	E946.6	E950.4	E962.0	E980.4
Thrombin	964.5	E858.2	E934.5	E950.4	E962.0	E980.4
Thrombolysin	964.4	E858.2	E934.4	E950.4	E962.0	E980.4
Thymol	983.0	E864.0	—	E950.7	E962.1	E980.6
Thymus extract	962.9	E858.0	E932.9	E950.4	E962.0	E980.4
Thyroglobulin	962.7	E858.0	E932.7	E950.4	E962.0	E980.4
Thyroid (derivatives) (extract)	962.7	E858.0	E932.7	E950.4	E962.0	E980.4
Thyrolar	962.7	E858.0	E932.7	E950.4	E962.0	E980.4
Thyrothrophin, thyrotropin	977.8	E858.8	E947.8	E950.4	E962.0	E980.4
Thyroxin(e)	962.7	E858.0	E932.7	E950.4	E962.0	E980.4
Tigan	963.0	E858.1	E933.0	E950.4	E962.0	E980.4
Tigloidine	968.0	E855.1	E938.0	E950.4	E962.0	E980.4
Tinactin	976.0	E858.7	E946.0	E950.4	E962.0	E980.4
Tincture, iodine — see Iodine						
Tindal	969.1	E853.0	E939.1	E950.3	E962.0	E980.3
Tin (chloride) (dust) (oxide) NEC	985.8	E866.4	—	E950.9	E962.1	E980.9
anti-infectives	961.2	E857	E931.2	E950.4	E962.0	E980.4
Titanium (compounds) (vapor)	985.8	E866.4	—	E950.9	E962.1	E980.9
ointment	976.3	E858.7	E946.3	E950.4	E962.0	E980.4
Titroid	962.7	E858.0	E932.7	E950.4	E962.0	E980.4
TMTD — see Tetramethylthiuram disulfide						
TNT	989.89	E866.8	—	E950.9	E962.1	E980.9
fumes	987.8	E869.8	—	E952.8	E962.2	E982.8
Toadstool	988.1	E865.5	—	E950.9	E962.1	E980.9
Tobacco NEC	989.84	E866.8	—	E950.9	E962.1	E980.9
Indian	988.2	E865.4	—	E950.9	E962.1	E980.9
smoke, second-hand	987.8	E869.4	—	—	—	—
Tocopherol	963.5	E858.1	E933.5	E950.4	E962.0	E980.4
Tocosamine	975.0	E858.6	E945.0	E950.4	E962.0	E980.4
Tofranil	969.05	E854.0	E939.0	E950.3	E962.0	E980.3
Toilet deodorizer	989.89	E866.8	—	E950.9	E962.1	E980.9
Tolazamide	962.3	E858.0	E932.3	E950.4	E962.0	E980.4
Tolazoline	971.3	E855.6	E941.3	E950.4	E962.0	E980.4
Tolbutamide	962.3	E858.0	E932.3	E950.4	E962.0	E980.4
sodium	977.8	E858.8	E947.8	E950.4	E962.0	E980.4
Tolmetin	965.69	E850.6	E935.6	E950.0	E962.0	E980.0
Tolnaftate	976.0	E858.7	E946.0	E950.4	E962.0	E980.4
Tolpropamine	976.1	E858.7	E946.1	E950.4	E962.0	E980.4

		External Cause (E-Code)				
	Poisoning	Accident	Therapeutic Use	Suicide Attempt	Assault	Undeter-mined
Tolserol	968.0	E855.1	E938.0	E950.4	E962.0	E980.4
Toluene (liquid) (vapor)	982.0	E862.4	—	E950.9	E962.1	E980.9
diisocyanate	983.0	E864.0	—	E950.7	E962.1	E980.6
Toluidine	983.0	E864.0	—	E950.7	E962.1	E980.6
vapor	987.8	E869.8	—	E952.8	E962.2	E982.8
Toluol (liquid) (vapor)	982.0	E862.4	—	E950.9	E962.1	E980.9
Tolylene-2, 4-diiso-cyanate	983.0	E864.0	—	E950.7	E962.1	E980.6
Tonics, cardiac	972.1	E858.3	E942.1	E950.4	E962.0	E980.4
Toxaphene (dust) (spray)	989.2	E863.0	—	E950.6	E962.1	E980.7
Toxoids NEC	978.8	E858.8	E948.8	E950.4	E962.0	E980.4
Tractor fuel NEC	981	E862.1		E950.9	E962.1	E980.9
Tragacanth	973.3	E858.4	E943.3	E950.4	E962.0	E980.4
Tramazoline	971.2	E855.5	E941.2	E950.4	E962.0	E980.4
Tranquilizers	969.5	E853.9	E939.5	E950.3	E962.0	E980.3
benzodiazepine-based	969.4	E853.2	E939.4	E950.3	E962.0	E980.3
butyrophenone-based	969.2	E853.1	E939.2	E950.3	E962.0	E980.3
major NEC	969.3	E853.8	E939.3	E950.3	E962.0	E980.3
phenothiazine-based	969.1	E853.0	E939.1	E950.3	E962.0	E980.3
specified NEC	969.5	E853.8	E939.5	E950.3	E962.0	E980.3
Trantoin	961.9	E857	E931.9	E950.4	E962.0	E980.4
Tranxene	969.4	E853.2	E939.4	E950.3	E962.0	E980.3
Tranylcypromine (sul-fate)	969.01	E854.0	E939.0	E950.3	E962.0	E980.3
Trasentine	975.1	E858.6	E945.1	E950.4	E962.0	E980.4
Travert	974.5	E858.5	E944.5	E950.4	E962.0	E980.4
Trecator	961.8	E857	E931.8	E950.4	E962.0	E980.4
Tretinoin	976.8	E858.7	E946.8	E950.4	E962.0	E980.4
Triacetin	976.0	E858.7	E946.0	E950.4	E962.0	E980.4
Triacetyloleandomycin	960.3	E856	E930.3	E950.4	E962.0	E980.4
Triamcinolone	962.0	E858.0	E932.0	E950.4	E962.0	E980.4
ENT agent	976.6	E858.7	E946.6	E950.4	E962.0	E980.4
medicinal (keratolytic)	976.4	E858.7	E946.4	E950.4	E962.0	E980.4
ophthalmic preparation	976.5	E858.7	E946.5	E950.4	E962.0	E980.4
topical NEC	976.0	E858.7	E946.0	E950.4	E962.0	E980.4
Triamterene	974.4	E858.5	E944.4	E950.4	E962.0	E980.4
Triaziquone	963.1	E858.1	E933.1	E950.4	E962.0	E980.4
Tribromacetaldehyde	967.3	E852.2	E937.3	E950.2	E962.0	E980.2
Tribromoethanol	968.2	E855.1	E938.2	E950.4	E962.0	E980.4
Tribromomethane	967.3	E852.2	E937.3	E950.2	E962.0	E980.2
Trichlorethane	982.3	E862.4	—	E950.9	E962.1	E980.9
Trichlormethiazide	974.3	E858.5	E944.3	E950.4	E962.0	E980.4
Trichloroacetic acid	983.1	E864.1	—	E950.7	E962.1	E980.6
Trichloroethanol	967.1	E852.0	E937.1	E950.2	E962.0	E980.2
Trichloroethylene (liquid) (va-por)	982.3	E862.4	—	E950.9	E962.1	E980.9
anesthetic (gas)	968.2	E855.1	E938.2	E950.4	E962.0	E980.4
Trichloroethyl phos-phate	967.1	E852.0	E937.1	E950.2	E962.0	E980.2
Trichlorofluoromethane NEC	987.4	E869.2	—	E952.8	E962.2	E982.8
Trichlorotriethylamine	963.1	E858.1	E933.1	E950.4	E962.0	E980.4
Trichomonacides NEC	961.5	E857	E931.5	E950.4	E962.0	E980.4
Trichomycin	960.1	E856	E930.1	E950.4	E962.0	E980.4
Triclofos	967.1	E852.0	E937.1	E950.2	E962.0	E980.2
Tricresyl phosphate	989.89	E866.8	—	E950.9	E962.1	E980.9
solvent	982.8	E862.4	—	E950.9	E962.1	E980.9
Tricyclamol	966.4	E855.0	E936.4	E950.4	E962.0	E980.4
Tridesilon	976.0	E858.7	E946.0	E950.4	E962.0	E980.4
Tridihexethyl	971.1	E855.4	E941.1	E950.4	E962.0	E980.4
Tridione	966.0	E855.0	E936.0	E950.4	E962.0	E980.4
Triethanolamine NEC	983.2	E864.2	—	E950.7	E962.1	E980.6
detergent	983.2	E861.0	—	E950.7	E962.1	E980.6
trinitrate	972.4	E858.3	E942.4	E950.4	E962.0	E980.4
Triethanomelamine	963.1	E858.1	E933.1	E950.4	E962.0	E980.4
Triethylene melamine	963.1	E858.1	E933.1	E950.4	E962.0	E980.4
Triethylenephospho-ramide	963.1	E858.1	E933.1	E950.4	E962.0	E980.4
Triethylenethiophospho-ramide	963.1	E858.1	E933.1	E950.4	E962.0	E980.4
Trifluoperazine	969.1	E853.0	E939.1	E950.3	E962.0	E980.3
Trifluperidol	969.2	E853.1	E939.2	E950.3	E962.0	E980.3
Triflupromazine	969.1	E853.0	E939.1	E950.3	E962.0	E980.3
Trihexyphenidyl	971.1	E855.4	E941.1	E950.4	E962.0	E980.4
Triiodothyronine	962.7	E858.0	E932.7	E950.4	E962.0	E980.4
Trilene	968.2	E855.1	E938.2	E950.4	E962.0	E980.4
Trimeprazine	963.0	E858.1	E933.0	E950.4	E962.0	E980.4
Trimetazidine	972.4	E858.3	E942.4	E950.4	E962.0	E980.4
Trimethadione	966.0	E855.0	E936.0	E950.4	E962.0	E980.4
Trimethaphan	972.3	E858.3	E942.3	E950.4	E962.0	E980.4
Trimethidinium	972.3	E858.3	E942.3	E950.4	E962.0	E980.4
Trimethobenzamide	963.0	E858.1	E933.0	E950.4	E962.0	E980.4

		External Cause (E-Code)				
	Poisoning	Accident	Therapeutic Use	Suicide Attempt	Assault	Undeter-mined
Trimethylcarbinol	980.8	E860.8	—	E950.9	E962.1	E980.9
Trimethylpsoralen	976.3	E858.7	E946.3	E950.4	E962.0	E980.4
Trimeton	963.0	E858.1	E933.0	E950.4	E962.0	E980.4
Trimipramine	969.05	E854.0	E939.0	E950.3	E962.0	E980.3
Trimustine	963.1	E858.1	E933.1	E950.4	E962.0	E980.4
Trinitrin	972.4	E858.3	E942.4	E950.4	E962.0	E980.4
Trinitrophenol	983.0	E864.0	—	E950.7	E962.1	E980.6
Trinitrotoluene	989.89	E866.8	—	E950.9	E962.1	E980.9
fumes	987.8	E869.8	—	E952.8	E962.2	E982.8
Trional	967.8	E852.8	E937.8	E950.2	E962.0	E980.2
Trioxide of arsenic — see Arsenic						
Trioxsalen	976.3	E858.7	E946.3	E950.4	E962.0	E980.4
Tripelennamine	963.0	E858.1	E933.0	E950.4	E962.0	E980.4
Triperidol	969.2	E853.1	E939.2	E950.3	E962.0	E980.3
Triprolidine	963.0	E858.1	E933.0	E950.4	E962.0	E980.4
Trisoralen	976.3	E858.7	E946.3	E950.4	E962.0	E980.4
Troleandomycin	960.3	E856	E930.3	E950.4	E962.0	E980.4
Trolnitrate (phosphate)	972.4	E858.3	E942.4	E950.4	E962.0	E980.4
Trometamol	963.3	E858.1	E933.3	E950.4	E962.0	E980.4
Tromethamine	963.3	E858.1	E933.3	E950.4	E962.0	E980.4
Tronothane	968.5	E855.2	E938.5	E950.4	E962.0	E980.4
Tropicamide	971.1	E855.4	E941.1	E950.4	E962.0	E980.4
Troxidone	966.0	E855.0	E936.0	E950.4	E962.0	E980.4
Tryparsamide	961.1	E857	E931.1	E950.4	E962.0	E980.4
Trypsin	963.4	E858.1	E933.4	E950.4	E962.0	E980.4
Tryptizol	969.05	E854.0	E939.0	E950.3	E962.0	E980.3
Tuaminoheptane	971.2	E855.5	E941.2	E950.4	E962.0	E980.4
Tuberculin (old)	977.8	E858.8	E947.8	E950.4	E962.0	E980.4
Tubocurare	975.2	E858.6	E945.2	E950.4	E962.0	E980.4
Tubocurarine	975.2	E858.6	E945.2	E950.4	E962.0	E980.4
Turkish green	969.6	E854.1	E939.6	E950.3	E962.0	E980.3
Turpentine (spirits of) (liquid) (vapor)	982.8	E862.4	—	E950.9	E962.1	E980.9
Tybamate	969.5	E853.8	E939.5	E950.3	E962.0	E980.3
Tyloxapol	975.5	E858.6	E945.5	E950.4	E962.0	E980.4
Tymazoline	971.2	E855.5	E941.2	E950.4	E962.0	E980.4
Typhoid vaccine	978.1	E858.8	E948.1	E950.4	E962.0	E980.4
Typhus vaccine	979.2	E858.8	E949.2	E950.4	E962.0	E980.4
Tyrothricin	976.0	E858.7	E946.0	E950.4	E962.0	E980.4
ENT agent	976.6	E858.7	E946.6	E950.4	E962.0	E980.4
ophthalmic preparation	976.5	E858.7	E946.5	E950.4	E962.0	E980.4
Undecenoic acid	976.0	E858.7	E946.0	E950.4	E962.0	E980.4
Undecylenic acid	976.0	E858.7	E946.0	E950.4	E962.0	E980.4
Unna's boot	976.3	E858.7	E946.3	E950.4	E962.0	E980.4
Uracil mustard	963.1	E858.1	E933.1	E950.4	E962.0	E980.4
Uramustine	963.1	E858.1	E933.1	E950.4	E962.0	E980.4
Urari	975.2	E858.6	E945.2	E950.4	E962.0	E980.4
Urea	974.4	E858.5	E944.4	E950.4	E962.0	E980.4
topical	976.8	E858.7	E946.8	E950.4	E962.0	E980.4
Urethan(e) (antineoplastic)	963.1	E858.1	E933.1	E950.4	E962.0	E980.4
Urginea (maritima) (scilla) — see Squill						
Uric acid metabolism agents NEC	974.7	E858.5	E944.7	E950.4	E962.0	E980.4
Urokinase	964.4	E858.2	E934.4	E950.4	E962.0	E980.4
Urokon	977.8	E858.8	E947.8	E950.4	E962.0	E980.4
Urotropin	961.9	E857	E931.9	E950.4	E962.0	E980.4
Urtica	988.2	E865.4	—	E950.9	E962.1	E980.9
Utility gas — see Gas, utility						
Vaccine NEC	979.9	E858.8	E949.9	E950.4	E962.0	E980.4
bacterial NEC	978.8	E858.8	E948.8	E950.4	E962.0	E980.4
with other bacterial compo-nent	978.9	E858.8	E948.9	E950.4	E962.0	E980.4
pertussis component	978.6	E858.8	E948.6	E950.4	E962.0	E980.4
viral-rickettsial compo-nent	979.7	E858.8	E949.7	E950.4	E962.0	E980.4
mixed NEC	978.9	E858.8	E948.9	E950.4	E962.0	E980.4
BCG	978.0	E858.8	E948.0	E950.4	E962.0	E980.4
cholera	978.2	E858.8	E948.2	E950.4	E962.0	E980.4
diphtheria	978.5	E858.8	E948.5	E950.4	E962.0	E980.4
influenza	979.6	E858.8	E949.6	E950.4	E962.0	E980.4
measles	979.4	E858.8	E949.4	E950.4	E962.0	E980.4
meningococcal	978.8	E858.8	E948.8	E950.4	E962.0	E980.4
mumps	979.6	E858.8	E949.6	E950.4	E962.0	E980.4
paratyphoid	978.1	E858.8	E948.1	E950.4	E962.0	E980.4
pertussis (with diphtheria toxoid) (with tetanus tox-oid)	978.6	E858.8	E948.6	E950.4	E962.0	E980.4
plague	978.3	E858.8	E948.3	E950.4	E962.0	E980.4

Nontherapeutic use substance

▽ Subterms under main terms may continue to next column or page

Vaccine NEC — Zinc (side tab)

	External Cause (E-Code)					
	Poisoning	Accident	Therapeutic Use	Suicide Attempt	Assault	Undetermined
Vaccine — *continued*						
poliomyelitis	979.5	E858.8	E949.5	E950.4	E962.0	E980.4
poliovirus	979.5	E858.8	E949.5	E950.4	E962.0	E980.4
rabies	979.1	E858.8	E949.1	E950.4	E962.0	E980.4
respiratory syncytial virus	979.6	E858.8	E949.6	E950.4	E962.0	E980.4
rickettsial NEC	979.6	E858.8	E949.6	E950.4	E962.0	E980.4
with						
bacterial component	979.7	E858.8	E949.7	E950.4	E962.0	E980.4
pertussis component	978.6	E858.8	E948.6	E950.4	E962.0	E980.4
viral component	979.7	E858.8	E949.7	E950.4	E962.0	E980.4
Rocky mountain spotted						
fever	979.6	E858.8	E949.6	E950.4	E962.0	E980.4
rotavirus	979.6	E858.8	E949.6	E950.4	E962.0	E980.4
rubella virus	979.4	E858.8	E949.4	E950.4	E962.0	E980.4
sabin oral	979.5	E858.8	E949.5	E950.4	E962.0	E980.4
smallpox	979.0	E858.8	E949.0	E950.4	E962.0	E980.4
tetanus	978.4	E858.8	E948.4	E950.4	E962.0	E980.4
typhoid	978.1	E858.8	E948.1	E950.4	E962.0	E980.4
typhus	979.2	E858.8	E949.2	E950.4	E962.0	E980.4
viral NEC	979.6	E858.8	E949.6	E950.4	E962.0	E980.4
with						
bacterial component	979.7	E858.8	E949.7	E950.4	E962.0	E980.4
pertussis component	978.6	E858.8	E948.6	E950.4	E962.0	E980.4
rickettsial component	979.7	E858.8	E949.7	E950.4	E962.0	E980.4
yellow fever	979.3	E858.8	E949.3	E950.4	E962.0	E980.4
Vaccinia immune globulin						
(human)	964.6	E858.2	E934.6	E950.4	E962.0	E980.4
Vaginal contraceptives	976.8	E858.7	E946.8	E950.4	E962.0	E980.4
Valethamate	971.1	E855.4	E941.1	E950.4	E962.0	E980.4
Valisone	976.0	E858.7	E946.0	E950.4	E962.0	E980.4
Valium	969.4	E853.2	E939.4	E950.3	E962.0	E980.3
Valmid	967.8	E852.2	E937.8	E950.2	E962.0	E980.2
Vanadium	985.8	E866.4	—	E950.9	E962.1	E980.9
Vancomycin	960.8	E856	E930.8	E950.4	E962.0	E980.4
Vapor — *see also* Gas	987.9	E869.9	—	E952.9	E962.2	E982.9
kiln (carbon monoxide)	986	E868.8	—	E952.1	E962.2	E982.1
lead — *see* Lead						
specified source NEC (*see also*						
specific substance)	987.8	E869.8	—	E952.8	E962.2	E982.8
Varidase	964.4	E858.2	E934.4	E950.4	E962.0	E980.4
Varnish	989.89	E861.6	—	E950.9	E962.1	E980.9
cleaner	982.8	E862.9	—	E950.9	E962.1	E980.9
Vaseline	976.3	E858.7	E946.3	E950.4	E962.0	E980.4
Vasodilan	972.5	E858.3	E942.5	E950.4	E962.0	E980.4
Vasodilators NEC	972.5	E858.3	E942.5	E950.4	E962.0	E980.4
coronary	972.4	E858.3	E942.4	E950.4	E962.0	E980.4
Vasopressin	962.5	E858.0	E932.5	E950.4	E962.0	E980.4
Vasopressor drugs	962.5	E858.0	E932.5	E950.4	E962.0	E980.4
Venom, venomous (bite)						
(sting)	989.5	E905.9	—	E950.9	E962.1	E980.9
arthropod NEC	989.5	E905.5	—	E950.9	E962.1	E980.9
bee	989.5	E905.3	—	E950.9	E962.1	E980.9
centipede	989.5	E905.4	—	E950.9	E962.1	E980.9
hornet	989.5	E905.3	—	E950.9	E962.1	E980.9
lizard	989.5	E905.0	—	E950.9	E962.1	E980.9
marine animals or plants	989.5	E905.6	—	E950.9	E962.1	E980.9
millipede (tropical)	989.5	E905.4	—	E950.9	E962.1	E980.9
plant NEC	989.5	E905.7	—	E950.9	E962.1	E980.9
marine	989.5	E905.6	—	E950.9	E962.1	E980.9
scorpion	989.5	E905.2	—	E950.9	E962.1	E980.9
snake	989.5	E905.0	—	E950.9	E962.1	E980.9
specified NEC	989.5	E905.8	—	E950.9	E962.1	E980.9
spider	989.5	E905.1	—	E950.9	E962.1	E980.9
wasp	989.5	E905.3	—	E950.9	E962.1	E980.9
Ventolin — *see* Salbutamol						
sulfate						
Veramon	967.0	E851	E937.0	E950.1	E962.0	E980.1
Veratrum						
album	988.2	E865.4	—	E950.9	E962.1	E980.9
alkaloids	972.6	E858.3	E942.6	E950.4	E962.0	E980.4
viride	988.2	E865.4	—	E950.9	E962.1	E980.9
Verdigris — *see also* Cop-						
per	985.8	E866.4	—	E950.9	E962.1	E980.9
Veronal	967.0	E851	E937.0	E950.1	E962.0	E980.1
Veroxil	961.6	E857	E931.6	E950.4	E962.0	E980.4
Versidyne	965.7	E850.7	E935.7	E950.0	E962.0	E980.0
Viagra	972.5	E858.3	E942.5	E950.4	E962.0	E980.4
Vienna						
green	985.1	E866.3	—	E950.8	E962.1	E980.8
insecticide	985.1	E863.4	—	E950.6	E962.1	E980.7
red	989.89	E866.8	—	E950.9	E962.1	E980.9
pharmaceutical dye	977.4	E858.8	E947.4	E950.4	E962.0	E980.4
Vinbarbital, vinbarbi-						
tone	967.0	E851	E937.0	E950.1	E962.0	E980.1
Vinblastine	963.1	E858.1	E933.1	E950.4	E962.0	E980.4
Vincristine	963.1	E858.1	E933.1	E950.4	E962.0	E980.4
Vinesthene, vinethene	968.2	E855.1	E938.2	E950.4	E962.0	E980.4
Vinyl						
bital	967.0	E851	E937.0	E950.1	E962.0	E980.1
ether	968.2	E855.1	E938.2	E950.4	E962.0	E980.4
Vioform	961.3	E857	E931.3	E950.4	E962.0	E980.4
topical	976.0	E858.7	E946.0	E950.4	E962.0	E980.4
Viomycin	960.6	E856	E930.6	E950.4	E962.0	E980.4
Viosterol	963.5	E858.1	E933.5	E950.4	E962.0	E980.4
Viper (venom)	989.5	E905.0	—	E950.9	E962.1	E980.9
Viprynium (embonate)	961.6	E857	E931.6	E950.4	E962.0	E980.4
Virugon	961.7	E857	E931.7	E950.4	E962.0	E980.4
Visine	976.5	E858.7	E946.5	E950.4	E962.0	E980.4
Vitamins NEC	963.5	E858.1	E933.5	E950.4	E962.0	E980.4
B_{12}	964.1	E858.2	E934.1	E950.4	E962.0	E980.4
hematopoietic	964.1	E858.2	E934.1	E950.4	E962.0	E980.4
K	964.3	E858.2	E934.3	E950.4	E962.0	E980.4
Vleminckx's solution	976.4	E858.7	E946.4	E950.4	E962.0	E980.4
Voltaren — *see* Diclofenac						
sodium						
Warfarin (potassium) (sodi-						
um)	964.2	E858.2	E934.2	E950.4	E962.0	E980.4
rodenticide	989.4	E863.7	—	E950.6	E962.1	E980.7
Wasp (sting)	989.5	E905.3	—	E950.9	E962.1	E980.9
Water						
balance agents NEC	974.5	E858.5	E944.5	E950.4	E962.0	E980.4
gas	987.1	E868.1	—	E951.8	E962.2	E981.8
incomplete combustion of						
— *see* Carbon, monoxide,						
fuel, utility						
hemlock	988.2	E865.4	—	E950.9	E962.1	E980.9
moccasin (venom)	989.5	E905.0	—	E950.9	E962.1	E980.9
Wax (paraffin) (petroleum)	981	E862.3	—	E950.9	E962.1	E980.9
automobile	989.89	E861.2	—	E950.9	E962.1	E980.9
floor	981	E862.0	—	E950.9	E962.1	E980.9
Weed killers NEC	989.4	E863.5	—	E950.6	E962.1	E980.7
Welldorm	967.1	E852.0	E937.1	E950.2	E962.0	E980.2
White						
arsenic — *see* Arsenic						
hellebore	988.2	E865.4	—	E950.9	E962.1	E980.9
lotion (keratolytic)	976.4	E858.7	E946.4	E950.4	E962.0	E980.4
spirit	981	E862.0	—	E950.9	E962.1	E980.9
Whitewashes	989.89	E861.6	—	E950.9	E962.1	E980.9
Whole blood	964.7	E858.2	E934.7	E950.4	E962.0	E980.4
Wild						
black cherry	988.2	E865.4	—	E950.9	E962.1	E980.9
poisonous plants NEC	988.2	E865.4	—	E950.9	E962.1	E980.9
Window cleaning fluid	989.89	E861.3	—	E950.9	E962.1	E980.9
Wintergreen (oil)	976.3	E858.7	E946.3	E950.4	E962.0	E980.4
Witch hazel	976.2	E858.7	E946.2	E950.4	E962.0	E980.4
Wood						
alcohol	980.1	E860.2	—	E950.9	E962.1	E980.9
spirit	980.1	E860.2	—	E950.9	E962.1	E980.9
Woorali	975.2	E858.6	E945.2	E950.4	E962.0	E980.4
Wormseed, American	961.6	E857	E931.6	E950.4	E962.0	E980.4
Xanthine diuretics	974.1	E858.5	E944.1	E950.4	E962.0	E980.4
Xanthocillin	960.0	E856	E930.0	E950.4	E962.0	E980.4
Xanthotoxin	976.3	E858.7	E946.3	E950.4	E962.0	E980.4
Xigris	964.2	E858.2	E934.2	E950.4	E962.0	E980.4
Xylene (liquid) (vapor)	982.0	E862.4	—	E950.9	E962.1	E980.9
Xylocaine (infiltration) (topi-						
cal)	968.5	E855.2	E938.5	E950.4	E962.0	E980.4
nerve block (peripheral)						
(plexus)	968.6	E855.2	E938.6	E950.4	E962.0	E980.4
spinal	968.7	E855.2	E938.7	E950.4	E962.0	E980.4
Xylol (liquid) (vapor)	982.0	E862.4	—	E950.9	E962.1	E980.9
Xylometazoline	971.2	E855.5	E941.2	E950.4	E962.0	E980.4
Yellow						
fever vaccine	979.3	E858.8	E949.3	E950.4	E962.0	E980.4
jasmine	988.2	E865.4	—	E950.9	E962.1	E980.9
Yew	988.2	E865.4	—	E950.9	E962.1	E980.9
Zactane	965.7	E850.7	E935.7	E950.0	E962.0	E980.0
Zaroxolyn	974.3	E858.5	E944.3	E950.4	E962.0	E980.4
Zephiran (topical)	976.0	E858.7	E946.0	E950.4	E962.0	E980.4
ophthalmic preparation	976.5	E858.7	E946.5	E950.4	E962.0	E980.4
Zerone	980.1	E860.2	—	E950.9	E962.1	E980.9
Zinc (compounds) (fumes)						
(salts) (vapor) NEC	985.8	E866.4	—	E950.9	E962.1	E980.9
anti-infectives	976.0	E858.7	E946.0	E950.4	E962.0	E980.4

Nontherapeutic use substance   ⓇⒺⒻ Subterms under main terms may continue to next column or page

		External Cause (E-Code)				
	Poisoning	Accident	Therapeutic Use	Suicide Attempt	Assault	Undeter- mined
Zinc — *continued*						
antivaricose	972.7	E858.3	E942.7	E950.4	E962.0	E980.4
bacitracin	976.0	E858.7	E946.0	E950.4	E962.0	E980.4
chloride	976.2	E858.7	E946.2	E950.4	E962.0	E980.4
gelatin	976.3	E858.7	E946.3	E950.4	E962.0	E980.4
oxide	976.3	E858.7	E946.3	E950.4	E962.0	E980.4
peroxide	976.0	E858.7	E946.0	E950.4	E962.0	E980.4
pesticides	985.8	E863.4	—	E950.6	E962.1	E980.7
phosphide (rodenticide)	985.8	E863.7	—	E950.6	E962.1	E980.7
stearate	976.3	E858.7	E946.3	E950.4	E962.0	E980.4
sulfate (antivaricose)	972.7	E858.3	E942.7	E950.4	E962.0	E980.4
ENT agent	976.6	E858.7	E946.6	E950.4	E962.0	E980.4
ophthalmic solution	976.5	E858.7	E946.5	E950.4	E962.0	E980.4
topical NEC	976.0	E858.7	E946.0	E950.4	E962.0	E980.4
undecylenate	976.0	E858.7	E946.0	E950.4	E962.0	E980.4
Zovant	964.2	E858.2	E934.2	E950.4	E962.0	E980.4
Zoxazolamine	968.0	E855.1	E938.0	E950.4	E962.0	E980.4
Zygadenus (venenosus)	988.2	E865.4	—	E950.9	E962.1	E980.9
Zyprexa	969.3	E853.8	E939.3	E950.3	E962.0	E980.3

SECTION 3

Alphabetic Index to External Causes of Injury and Poisoning (E Code)

This section contains the index to the codes which classify environmental events, circumstances, and other conditions as the cause of injury and other adverse effects. Where a code from the section Supplementary Classification of External Causes of Injury and Poisoning (E800-E999) is applicable, it is intended that the E code shall be used in addition to a code from the main body of the classification, Chapters 1 to 17.

The alphabetic index to the E codes is organized by main terms which describe the accident, circumstance, event, or specific agent which caused the injury or other adverse effect.

Note — Transport accidents (E800-E848) include accidents involving:

- *aircraft and spacecraft (E840-E845)*
- *watercraft (E830-E838)*
- *motor vehicle (E810-E825)*
- *railway (E800-E807)*
- *other road vehicles (E826-E829)*

For definitions and examples related to transport accidents — see Volume 1 code categories E800-E848.

The fourth-digit subdivisions for use with categories E800-E848 to identify the injured person are found at the end of this section.

For identifying the place in which an accident or poisoning occurred (circumstances classifiable to categories E850-E869 and E880-E928) — see the listing in this section under "Accident, occurring."

See the Table of Drugs and Chemicals (Section 2 of this volume) for identifying the specific agent involved in drug overdose or a wrong substance given or taken in error, and for intoxication or poisoning by a drug or other chemical substance.

The specific adverse effect, reaction, or localized toxic effect to a correct drug or substance properly administered in therapeutic or prophylactic dosage should be classified according to the nature of the adverse effect (e.g., allergy, dermatitis, tachycardia) listed in Section 1 of this volume.

☑ Additional Digit Required — Refer to the Tabular List for Digit Selection   ▽ Subterms under main terms may continue to next column or page

334 — Volume 2   ▶◀ Revised Text   ● New Line   ▲ Revised Code   2015 ICD-9-CM

A

Abandonment
causing exposure to weather conditions — see Exposure
child, with intent to injure or kill E968.4
helpless person, infant, newborn E904.0
with intent to injure or kill E968.4
Abortion, criminal, injury to child E968.8
Abuse (alleged) (suspected)
adult
by
child E967.4
ex-partner E967.3
ex-spouse E967.3
father E967.0
grandchild E967.7
grandparent E967.6
mother E967.2
non-related caregiver E967.8
other relative E967.7
other specified person E967.1
partner E967.3
sibling E967.5
spouse E967.3
stepfather E967.0
stepmother E967.2
unspecified person E967.9
child
by
boyfriend of parent or guardian E967.0
child E967.4
father E967.0
female partner of parent or guardian E967.2
girlfriend of parent or guardian E967.2
grandchild E967.7
grandparent E967.6
male partner of parent or guardian E967.0
mother E967.2
non-related caregiver E967.8
other relative E967.7
other specified person(s) E967.1
sibling E967.5
stepfather E967.0
stepmother E967.2
unspecified person E967.9
Accident (to) E928.9
aircraft (in transit) (powered) E841 ☑
at landing, take-off E840 ☑
due to, caused by cataclysm — see categories E908 ☑, E909 ☑
late effect of E929.1
unpowered (see also Collision, aircraft, unpowered) E842 ☑
while alighting, boarding E843 ☑
amphibious vehicle
on
land — see Accident, motor vehicle
water — see Accident, watercraft
animal-drawn vehicle NEC E827 ☑
animal, ridden NEC E828 ☑
balloon (see also Collision, aircraft, unpowered) E842 ☑
caused by, due to
abrasive wheel (metalworking) E919.3
animal NEC E906.9
being ridden (in sport or transport) E828 ☑
avalanche NEC E909.2
band saw E919.4
bench saw E919.4
bore, earth-drilling or mining (land) (seabed) E919.1
bulldozer E919.7
cataclysmic
earth surface movement or eruption E909.9
storm E908.9
chain
hoist E919.2
agricultural operations E919.0
mining operations E919.1

Accident (to) — continued
caused by, due to — continued
chain — continued
saw E920.1
circular saw E919.4
cold (excessive) (see also Cold, exposure to) E901.9
combine E919.0
conflagration — see Conflagration
corrosive liquid, substance NEC E924.1
cotton gin E919.8
crane E919.2
agricultural operations E919.0
mining operations E919.1
cutting or piercing instrument (see also Cut) E920.9
dairy equipment E919.8
derrick E919.2
agricultural operations E919.0
mining operations E919.1
drill E920.1
earth (land) (seabed) E919.1
hand (powered) E920.1
not powered E920.4
metalworking E919.3
woodworking E919.4
earth(-)
drilling machine E919.1
moving machine E919.7
scraping machine E919.7
electric
current (see also Electric shock) E925.9
motor (see also Accident, machine, by type of machine)
current (of) — see Electric shock
elevator (building) (grain) E919.2
agricultural operations E919.0
mining operations E919.1
environmental factors NEC E928.9
excavating machine E919.7
explosive material (see also Explosion) E923.9
farm machine E919.0
firearm missile — see Shooting
fire, flames (see also Fire)
conflagration — see Conflagration
forging (metalworking) machine E919.3
forklift (truck) E919.2
agricultural operations E919.0
mining operations E919.1
gas turbine E919.5
harvester E919.0
hay derrick, mower, or rake E919.0
heat (excessive) (see also Heat) E900.9
hoist (see also Accident, caused by, due to, lift) E919.2
chain — see Accident, caused by, due to, chain
shaft E919.1
hot
liquid E924.0
caustic or corrosive E924.1
object (not producing fire or flames) E924.8
substance E924.9
caustic or corrosive E924.1
liquid (metal) NEC E924.0
specified type NEC E924.8
human bite E928.3
ignition — see Ignition
internal combustion engine E919.5
landslide NEC E909.2
lathe (metalworking) E919.3
turnings E920.8
woodworking E919.4
lift, lifting (appliances) E919.2
agricultural operations E919.0
mining operations E919.1
shaft E919.1
lightning NEC E907
machine, machinery (see also Accident, machine)
drilling, metal E919.3
manufacturing, for manufacture of beverages E919.8

Accident (to) — continued
caused by, due to — continued
machine, machinery (see also Accident, machine) — continued
manufacturing, for manufacture of — continued
clothing E919.8
foodstuffs E919.8
paper E919.8
textiles E919.8
milling, metal E919.3
moulding E919.4
power press, metal E919.3
printing E919.8
rolling mill, metal E919.3
sawing, metal E919.3
specified type NEC E919.8
spinning E919.8
weaving E919.8
natural factor NEC E928.9
overhead plane E919.4
plane E920.4
overhead E919.4
powered
hand tool NEC E920.1
saw E919.4
hand E920.1
printing machine E919.8
pulley (block) E919.2
agricultural operations E919.0
mining operations E919.1
transmission E919.6
radial saw E919.4
radiation — see Radiation
reaper E919.0
road scraper E919.7
when in transport under its own power — see categories E810-E825 ☑
roller coaster E919.8
sander E919.4
saw E920.4
band E919.4
bench E919.4
chain E920.1
circular E919.4
hand E920.4
powered E920.1
powered, except hand E919.4
radial E919.4
sawing machine, metal E919.3
shaft
hoist E919.1
lift E919.1
transmission E919.6
shears E920.4
hand E920.4
powered E920.1
mechanical E919.3
shovel E920.4
steam E919.7
spinning machine E919.8
steam (see also Burning, steam)
engine E919.5
shovel E919.7
thresher E919.0
thunderbolt NEC E907
tractor E919.0
when in transport under its own power — see categories E810-E825 ☑
transmission belt, cable, chain, gear, pinion, pulley, shaft E919.6
turbine (gas) (water driven) E919.5
under-cutter E919.1
weaving machine E919.8
winch E919.2
agricultural operations E919.0
mining operations E919.1
diving E883.0
with insufficient air supply E913.2
glider (hang) (see also Collision, aircraft, unpowered) E842 ☑
hovercraft
on
land — see Accident, motor vehicle

Accident (to) — continued
hovercraft — continued
on — continued
water — see Accident, watercraft
ice yacht (see also Accident, vehicle NEC) E848
in
medical, surgical procedure
as, or due to misadventure — see Misadventure
causing an abnormal reaction or later complication without mention of misadventure — see Reaction, abnormal
kite carrying a person (see also Collision, involving aircraft, unpowered) E842 ☑
land yacht (see also Accident, vehicle NEC) E848
late effect of — see Late effect
launching pad E845 ☑
machine, machinery (see also Accident, caused by, due to, by specific type of machine) E919.9
agricultural including animal-powered E919.0
earth-drilling E919.1
earth moving or scraping E919.7
excavating E919.7
involving transport under own power on highway or transport vehicle — see categories E810-E825 ☑, E840-E845 ☑
lifting (appliances) E919.2
metalworking E919.3
mining E919.1
prime movers, except electric motors E919.5
electric motors — see Accident, machine, by specific type of machine
recreational E919.8
specified type NEC E919.8
transmission E919.6
watercraft (deck) (engine room) (galley) (laundry) (loading) E836 ☑
woodworking or forming E919.4
motor vehicle (on public highway) (traffic) E819 ☑
due to cataclysm — see categories E908 ☑, E909 ☑
involving
collision (see also Collision, motor vehicle) E812 ☑
nontraffic, not on public highway — see categories E820-E825 ☑
not involving collision — see categories E816-E819 ☑
nonmotor vehicle NEC E829 ☑
nonroad — see Accident, vehicle NEC
road, except pedal cycle, animal-drawn vehicle, or animal being ridden E829 ☑
nonroad vehicle NEC — see Accident, vehicle NEC
not elsewhere classifiable involving
cable car (not on rails) E847
on rails E829 ☑
coal car in mine E846
hand truck — see Accident, vehicle NEC
logging car E846
sled(ge), meaning snow or ice vehicle E848
tram, mine or quarry E846
truck
mine or quarry E846
self-propelled, industrial E846
station baggage E846
tub, mine or quarry E846
vehicle NEC E848
snow and ice E848
used only on industrial premises E846
wheelbarrow E848
occurring (at) (in)
apartment E849.0
baseball field, diamond E849.4

☑ Additional Digit Required — Refer to the Tabular List for Digit Selection

▽ Subterms under main terms may continue to next column or page

Accident (to) — *continued*
  occurring — *continued*
    construction site, any E849.3
    dock E849.8
      yard E849.3
    dormitory E849.7
    factory (building) (premises) E849.3
    farm E849.1
      buildings E849.1
      house E849.0
    football field E849.4
    forest E849.8
    garage (place of work) E849.3
      private (home) E849.0
    gravel pit E849.2
    gymnasium E849.4
    highway E849.5
    home (private) (residential) E849.0
      institutional E849.7
    hospital E849.7
    hotel E849.6
    house (private) (residential) E849.0
      movie E849.6
      public E849.6
    institution, residential E849.7
    jail E849.7
    mine E849.2
    motel E849.6
    movie house E849.6
    office (building) E849.6
    orphanage E849.7
    park (public) E849.4
      mobile home E849.8
      trailer E849.8
    parking lot or place E849.8
    place
      industrial NEC E849.3
      parking E849.8
      public E849.8
        specified place NEC E849.5
      recreational NEC E849.4
      sport NEC E849.4
    playground (park) (school) E849.4
    prison E849.6
    public building NEC E849.6
    quarry E849.2
    railway
      line NEC E849.8
      yard E849.3
    residence
      home (private) E849.0
    resort (beach) (lake) (mountain)
        (seashore) (vacation) E849.4
    restaurant E849.6
    sand pit E849.2
    school (building) (private) (public) (state)
        E849.6
      reform E849.7
      riding E849.4
    seashore E849.8
      resort E849.4
    shop (place of work) E849.3
      commercial E849.6
    skating rink E849.4
    sports palace E849.4
    stadium E849.4
    store E849.6
    street E849.5
    swimming pool (public) E849.4
      private home or garden E849.0
    tennis court, public E849.4
    theatre, theater E849.6
    trailer court E849.8
    tunnel E849.8
      under construction E849.2
    warehouse E849.3
    yard
      dock E849.3
      industrial E849.3
      private (home) E849.0
      railway E849.3
  off-road type motor vehicle (not on public
      highway) NEC E821 ☑
    on public highway — *see categories*
        E810-E819 ☑
  pedal cycle E826 ☑

Accident (to) — *continued*
  railway E807 ☑
    due to cataclysm — *see categories*
        E908 ☑, E909 ☑
    involving
      avalanche E909.2
      burning by engine, locomotive, train
          (*see also* Explosion, railway
          engine) E803 ☑
      collision (*see also* Collision, railway)
          E800 ☑
      derailment (*see also* Derailment, rail-
          way) E802 ☑
      explosion (*see also* Explosion, railway
          engine) E803 ☑
      fall (*see also* Fall, from, railway rolling
          stock) E804 ☑
      fire (*see also* Explosion, railway en-
          gine) E803 ☑
      hitting by, being struck by
        object falling in, on, from, rolling
            stock, train, vehicle
            E806 ☑
        rolling stock, train, vehicle
            E805 ☑
      overturning, railway rolling stock,
          train, vehicle (*see also* Derail-
          ment, railway) E802 ☑
      running off rails, railway (*see also*
          Derailment, railway) E802 ☑
      specified circumstances NEC E806 ☑
      train or vehicle hit by
        avalanche E909.2
        falling object (earth, rock, tree)
            E806 ☑
          due to cataclysm — *see cate-
              gories*
              E908 ☑, E909 ☑
        landslide E909.2
  roller skate E885.1
  scooter (nonmotorized) E885.0
  skateboard E885.2
  ski(ing) E885.3
    jump E884.9
    lift or tow (with chair or gondola) E847
  snowboard E885.4
  snow vehicle, motor driven (not on public
      highway) E820 ☑
    on public highway — *see categories*
        E810-E819 ☑
  spacecraft E845 ☑
  specified cause NEC E928.8
  street car E829 ☑
  traffic NEC E819 ☑
  vehicle NEC (with pedestrian) E848
    battery powered
      airport passenger vehicle E846
      truck (baggage) (mail) E846
    powered commercial or industrial (with
        other vehicle or object within
        commercial or industrial premis-
        es) E846
  watercraft E838 ☑
    with
      drowning or submersion resulting
          from
        accident other than to watercraft
            E832 ☑
        accident to watercraft E830 ☑
      injury, except drowning or submer-
          sion, resulting from
        accident other than to watercraft
            — *see categories*
            E833-E838 ☑
        accident to watercraft E831 ☑
    due to, caused by cataclysm — *see cate-*
        gories E908 ☑, E909 ☑
  machinery E836 ☑
Acid throwing E961
Acosta syndrome E902.0
Activity (involving) E030
  aerobic and step exercise (class) E009.2
  alpine skiing E003.2
  animal care NEC E019.9
  arts and handcrafts NEC E012.9

Activity — *continued*
  athletics NEC E008.9
    played
      as a team or group NEC E007.9
      individually NEC E006.9
  baking E015.2
  ballet E005.0
  barbells E010.2
  baseball E007.3
  BASE (Building, Antenna, Span, Earth)
      jumping E004.2
  basketball E007.6
  bathing (personal) E013.0
  beach volleyball E007.7
  bike riding E006.4
  boogie boarding E002.7
  bowling E006.3
  boxing E008.0
  brass instrument playing E018.3
  building and construction E016.2
  bungee jumping E004.3
  calisthenics E009.1
  canoeing (in calm and turbulent water)
      E002.5
  capture the flag E007.8
  cardiorespiratory exercise NEC E009.9
  caregiving (providing) NEC E014.9
    bathing E014.0
    lifting E014.1
  cellular
    communication device E011.1
    telephone E011.1
  challenge course E009.4
  cheerleading E005.4
  circuit training E009.3
  cleaning
    floor E013.4
  climbing NEC E004.9
    mountain E004.0
    rock E004.0
    wall climbing E004.0
  combatives E008.4
  computer
    keyboarding E011.0
    technology NEC E011.9
  confidence course E009.4
  construction (building) E016.2
  cooking and baking E015.2
  cooking and grilling NEC E015.9
  cool down exercises E009.1
  cricket E007.9
  crocheting E012.0
  cross country skiing E003.3
  dancing (all types) E005.0
  digging
    dirt E016.0
  dirt digging E016.0
  dishwashing E015.0
  diving (platform) (springboard) E002.1
    underwater E002.4
  dodge ball E007.8
  downhill skiing E003.2
  drum playing E018.1
  dumbbells E010.2
  electronic
    devices NEC E011.9
      hand held interactive E011.1
    game playing (using) (with)
      interactive device E011.1
      keyboard or other stationary device
          E011.0
  elliptical machine E009.0
  exercise(s)
    machines (primarily for)
      cardiorespiratory conditioning
          E009.0
      muscle strengthening E010.0
    muscle strengthening (non-machine)
        NEC E010.9
    external motion NEC E017.9
      roller coaster E017.0
  field hockey E007.4
  figure skating (pairs) (singles) E003.0
  flag football E007.1
  floor mopping and cleaning E013.4
  food preparation and clean up E015.0

Activity — *continued*
  football (American) NOS E007.0
    flag E007.1
    tackle E007.0
    touch E007.1
  four square E007.8
  free weights E010.2
  frisbee (ultimate) E008.3
  furniture
    building E012.2
    finishing E012.2
    repair E012.2
  game playing (electronic)
    using
      interactive device E011.1
      keyboard or other stationary device
          E011.0
  gardening E016.1
  golf E006.2
  grass drills E009.5
  grilling and smoking food E015.1
  grooming and shearing an animal E019.2
  guerilla drills E009.5
  gymnastics (rhythmic) E005.2
  handball E008.2
  handcrafts NEC E012.9
  hand held interactive electronic device
      E011.1
  hang gliding E004.4
  hiking (on level or elevated terrain) E001.0
  hockey (ice) E003.1
    field E007.4
  horseback riding E006.1
  household maintenance NEC E013.9
  ice NEC E003.9
    dancing E003.0
    hockey E003.1
    skating E003.0
  inline roller skating E006.0
  ironing E013.3
  judo E008.4
  jumping jacks E009.1
  jumping rope E006.5
  jumping (off) NEC E004.9
    BASE (Building, Antenna, Span, Earth)
        E004.2
    bungee E004.3
    jacks E009.1
    rope E006.5
  karate E008.4
  kayaking (in calm and turbulent water)
      E002.5
  keyboarding (computer) E011.0
  kickball E007.8
  knitting E012.0
  lacrosse E007.4
  land maintenance NEC E016.9
  landscaping E016.1
  laundry E013.1
  machines (exercise) primarily for cardiores-
      piratory conditioning E009.0
  maintenance
    building E016.9
    household NEC E013.9
    land E016.9
    property E016.9
  marching (on level or elevated terrain)
      E001.0
  martial arts E008.4
  microwave oven E015.2
  milking an animal E019.1
  mopping (floor) E013.4
  mountain climbing E004.0
  muscle strengthening
    exercises (non-machine) NEC E010.9
    machines E010.0
  musical keyboard (electronic) playing E018.0
  nordic skiing E003.3
  obstacle course E009.4
  oven (microwave) E015.2
  packing up and unpacking in moving to a
      new residence E013.5
  parasailing E002.9
  percussion instrument playing NEC E018.1
  personal
    bathing and showering E013.0

☑ **Additional Digit Required — Refer to the Tabular List for Digit Selection**   ◹ **Subterms under main terms may continue to next column or page**

336 — Volume 2   ▶◀ **Revised Text**   ● **New Line**   ▲ **Revised Code**   **2015 ICD-9-CM**

Activity — *continued*
  personal — *continued*
    hygiene NEC E013.8
    showering E013.0
  physical
    games generally associated with school recess, summer camp and children E007.8
    training NEC E009.9
  piano playing E018.0
  pilates E010.3
  platform diving E002.1
  playing musical instrument
    brass instrument E018.3
    drum E018.1
    musical keyboard (electronic) E018.0
    percussion instrument NEC E018.1
    piano E018.0
    string instrument E018.2
    wind instrument E018.3
  property maintenance NEC E016.9
  pruning (garden and lawn) E016.1
  pull-ups E010.1
  push-ups E010.1
  racquetball E008.2
  rafting (in calm and turbulent water) E002.5
  raking (leaves) E016.0
  rappelling E004.1
  refereeing a sports activity E029.0
  residential relocation E013.5
  rhythmic
    gymnastics E005.2
    movement NEC E005.9
  riding
    horseback E006.1
    roller coaster E017.0
  rock climbing E004.0
  roller coaster riding E017.0
  roller skating (inline) E006.0
  rough housing and horseplay E029.2
  rowing (in calm and turbulent water) E002.5
  rugby E007.2
  running E001.1
  SCUBA diving E002.4
  sewing E012.1
  shoveling E016.0
    dirt E016.0
    snow E016.0
  showering (personal) E013.0
  sit-ups E010.1
  skateboarding E006.0
  skating (ice) E003.0
    roller E006.0
  skiing (alpine) (downhill) E003.2
    cross country E003.3
    nordic E003.3
  sledding (snow) E003.2
  smoking and grilling food E015.1
  snorkeling E002.4
  snow NEC E003.9
    boarding E003.2
    shoveling E016.0
    sledding E003.2
    tubing E003.2
  soccer E007.5
  softball E007.3
  specified NEC E029.9
  spectator at an event E029.1
  sports played as a team or group NEC E007.9
  sports played individually NEC E006.9
  sports NEC E008.9
  springboard diving E002.1
  squash E008.2
  stationary bike E009.0
  step (stepping) exercise (class) E009.2
  stepper machine E009.0
  stove E015.2
  string instrument playing E018.2
  surfing E002.7
  swimming E002.0
  tackle football E007.0
  tap dancing E005.0
  tennis E008.2
  tobogganing E003.2
  touch football E007.1
  track and field events (non-running) E006.6

Activity — *continued*
  track and field events — *continued*
    running E001.1
  trampoline E005.3
  treadmill E009.0
  trimming shrubs E016.1
  tubing (in calm and turbulent water) E002.5
    snow E003.2
  ultimate frisbee E008.3
  underwater diving E002.4
  unpacking in moving to a new residence E013.5
  use of stove, oven and microwave oven E015.2
  vacuuming E013.2
  volleyball (beach) (court) E007.7
  wake boarding E002.6
  walking (on level or elevated terrain) E001.0
    an animal E019.0
  walking an animal E019.0
  wall climbing E004.0
  warm up and cool down exercises E009.1
  water NEC E002.9
    aerobics E002.3
    craft NEC E002.9
    exercise E002.3
    polo E002.2
    skiing E002.6
    sliding E002.8
    survival training and testing E002.9
  weeding (garden and lawn) E016.1
  wind instrument playing E018.3
  windsurfing E002.7
  wrestling E008.1
  yoga E005.1
Activity status E000.9
  child assisting in compensated work of other family member E000.8
  civilian
    done for
      financial or other compensation E000.0
      pay or income E000.0
  family member assisting in compensated work of other family member E000.8
  for income E000.0
  hobby or leisure E000.8
  military E000.1
    off duty E000.8
  off duty military E000.8
  recreation E000.8
  specified NEC E000.8
  sport not for income E000.8
  student E000.8
  volunteer E000.2
Aeroneurosis E902.1
Aero-otitis media — *see* Effects of, air pressure
Aerosinusitis — *see* Effects of, air pressure
After-effect, late — *see* Late effect
Air
  blast
    in
      terrorism E979.2
      war operations E993.9
  embolism (traumatic) NEC E928.9
    in
      infusion or transfusion E874.1
      perfusion E874.2
    sickness E903
Alpine sickness E902.0
Altitude sickness — *see* Effects of, air pressure
Anaphylactic shock, anaphylaxis — *see also* Table of Drugs and Chemicals E947.9
  due to bite or sting (venomous) — *see* Bite, venomous
Andes disease E902.0
Apoplexy
  heat — *see* Heat
Arachnidism E905.1
Arson E968.0
Asphyxia, asphyxiation
  by
    chemical
      in
        terrorism E979.7

Asphyxia, asphyxiation — *continued*
  by — *continued*
    chemical — *continued*
      in — *continued*
        war operations E997.2
    explosion — *see* Explosion
    food (bone) (regurgitated food) (seed) E911
    foreign object, except food E912
    fumes
      in
        terrorism (chemical weapons) E979.7
        war operations E997.2
    gas (*see also* Table of Drugs and Chemicals)
      in
        terrorism E979.7
        war operations E997.2
      legal
        execution E978
        intervention (tear) E972
      tear E972
    mechanical means (*see also* Suffocation) E913.9
  from
    conflagration — *see* Conflagration
    fire (*see also* Fire) E899
      in
        terrorism E979.3
        war operations E990.9
    ignition — *see* Ignition
Aspiration
  foreign body — *see* Foreign body, aspiration
  mucus, not of newborn (with asphyxia, obstruction respiratory passage, suffocation) E912
  phlegm (with asphyxia, obstruction respiratory passage, suffocation) E912
  vomitus (with asphyxia, obstruction respiratory passage, suffocation) (*see also* Foreign body, aspiration, food) E911
Assassination (attempt) — *see also* Assault E968.9
Assault (homicidal) (by) (in) E968.9
  acid E961
    swallowed E962.1
  air gun E968.6
  BB gun E968.6
  bite NEC E968.8
    of human being E968.7
  bomb ((placed in) car or house) E965.8
    antipersonnel E965.5
    letter E965.7
    petrol E965.6
  brawl (hand) (fists) (foot) E960.0
  burning, burns (by fire) E968.0
    acid E961
      swallowed E962.1
    caustic, corrosive substance E961
      swallowed E962.1
    chemical from swallowing caustic, corrosive substance NEC E962.1
    hot liquid E968.3
    scalding E968.3
    vitriol E961
      swallowed E962.1
  caustic, corrosive substance E961
    swallowed E962.1
  cut, any part of body E966
  dagger E966
  drowning E964
  explosive(s) E965.9
    bomb (*see also* Assault, bomb) E965.8
    dynamite E965.8
  fight (hand) (fists) (foot) E960.0
    with weapon E968.9
      blunt or thrown E968.2
      cutting or piercing E966
      firearm — *see* Shooting, homicide
  fire E968.0
  firearm(s) — *see* Shooting, homicide
  garrotting E963
  gunshot (wound) — *see* Shooting, homicide
  hanging E963
  injury NEC E968.9

Assault — *continued*
  knife E966
  late effect of E969
  ligature E963
  poisoning E962.9
    drugs or medicinals E962.0
    gas(es) or vapors, except drugs and medicinals E962.2
    solid or liquid substances, except drugs and medicinals E962.1
  puncture, any part of body E966
  pushing
    before moving object, train, vehicle E968.5
    from high place E968.1
  rape E960.1
  scalding E968.3
  shooting — *see* Shooting, homicide
  sodomy E960.1
  stab, any part of body E966
  strangulation E963
  submersion E964
  suffocation E963
  transport vehicle E968.5
  violence NEC E968.9
  vitriol E961
    swallowed E962.1
  weapon E968.9
    blunt or thrown E968.2
    cutting or piercing E966
    firearm — *see* Shooting, homicide
  wound E968.9
    cutting E966
    gunshot — *see* Shooting, homicide
    knife E966
    piercing E966
    puncture E966
    stab E966
Attack by animal NEC E906.9
Avalanche E909.2
  falling on or hitting
    motor vehicle (in motion) (on public highway) E909.2
    railway train E909.2
Aviators' disease E902.1

B

Barotitis, barodontalgia, barosinusitis, barotrauma (otitic) (sinus) — *see* Effects of, air pressure
Battered
  baby or child (syndrome) — *see* Abuse, child; category E967 ☑
  person other than baby or child — *see* Assault
Bayonet wound — *see also* Cut, by bayonet E920.3
  in
    legal intervention E974
    terrorism E979.8
    war operations E995.2
Bean in nose E912
Bed set on fire NEC E898.0
Beheading (by guillotine)
  homicide E966
  legal execution E978
Bending, injury
  due to
    repetitive movement E927.3
    sudden strenuous movement E927.0
Bends E902.0
Bite
  animal NEC E906.5
    other specified (except arthropod) E906.3
    venomous NEC E905.9
  arthropod (nonvenomous) NEC E906.4
    venomous — *see* Sting
  black widow spider E905.1
  cat E906.3
  centipede E905.4
  cobra E905.0
  copperhead snake E905.0
  coral snake E905.0
  dog E906.0
  fer de lance E905.0

☑ **Additional Digit Required** — Refer to the Tabular List for Digit Selection   ▽ **Subterms under main terms may continue to next column or page**

2015 ICD-9-CM   ▶◀ Revised Text   ● New Line   ▲ Revised Code   **Volume 2 — 337**

Bite — continued
 gila monster E905.0
 human being
  accidental E928.3
  assault E968.7
 insect (nonvenomous) E906.4
  venomous — see Sting
 krait E905.0
 late effect of — see Late effect
 lizard E906.2
  venomous E905.0
 mamba E905.0
 marine animal
  nonvenomous E906.3
   snake E906.2
  venomous E905.6
   snake E905.0
 millipede E906.4
  venomous E905.4
 moray eel E906.3
 rat E906.1
 rattlesnake E905.0
 rodent, except rat E906.3
 serpent — see Bite, snake
 shark E906.3
 snake (venomous) E905.0
  nonvenomous E906.2
  sea E905.0
 spider E905.1
  nonvenomous E906.4
 tarantula (venomous) E905.1
 venomous NEC E905.9
  by specific animal — see category
   E905 ☑
 viper E905.0
 water moccasin E905.0
Blast (air)
 from nuclear explosion E996 ☑
 in
  terrorism E979.2
   from nuclear explosion E979.5
   underwater E979.0
  war operations E993.9
   from nuclear explosion — see War
    operations, injury due to, nu-
    clear weapons
   underwater E992.9
Blizzard E908.3
Blow E928.9
 by law-enforcing agent, police (on duty)
  E975
  with blunt object (baton) (nightstick)
   (stave) (truncheon) E973
Blowing up — see also Explosion E923.9
Brawl (hand) (fists) (foot) E960.0
Breakage (accidental)
 cable of cable car not on rails E847
 ladder (causing fall) E881.0
 part (any) of
  animal-drawn vehicle E827 ☑
  ladder (causing fall) E881.0
  motor vehicle
   in motion (on public highway)
    E818 ☑
    not on public highway E825 ☑
  nonmotor road vehicle, except animal-
   drawn vehicle or pedal cycle
   E829 ☑
  off-road type motor vehicle (not on
   public highway) NEC E821 ☑
   on public highway E818 ☑
  pedal cycle E826 ☑
  scaffolding (causing fall) E881.1
  snow vehicle, motor-driven (not on
   public highway) E820 ☑
   on public highway E818 ☑
  vehicle NEC — see Accident, vehicle
Broken
 glass
  fall on E888.0
  injury by E920.8
 power line (causing electric shock) E925.1
Bumping against, into (accidentally)
 object (moving) E917.9
  caused by crowd E917.1
   with subsequent fall E917.6

Bumping against, into — continued
 object — continued
  furniture E917.3
   with subsequent fall E917.7
  in
   running water E917.2
   sports E917.0
    with subsequent fall E917.5
  stationary E917.4
   with subsequent fall E917.8
 person(s) E917.9
  with fall E886.9
   in sports E886.0
  as, or caused by, a crowd E917.1
   with subsequent fall E917.6
  in sports E917.0
   with fall E886.0
Burning, burns (accidental) (by) (from) (on)
  E899
 acid (any kind) E924.1
  swallowed — see Table of Drugs and
   Chemicals
 airgun E928.7
 bedclothes (see also Fire, specified NEC)
  E898.0
 blowlamp (see also Fire, specified NEC)
  E898.1
 blowtorch (see also Fire, specified NEC)
  E898.1
 boat, ship, watercraft — see categories
  E830 ☑, E831 ☑, E837 ☑
 bonfire (controlled) E897
  uncontrolled E892
 candle (see also Fire, specified NEC) E898.1
 caustic liquid, substance E924.1
  swallowed — see Table of Drugs and
   Chemicals
 chemical E924.1
  from swallowing caustic, corrosive substance — see Table of Drugs and
   Chemicals
  in
   terrorism E979.7
   war operations E997.2
 cigar(s) or cigarette(s) (see also Fire, specified NEC) E898.1
 clothes, clothing, nightdress — see Ignition,
  clothes
  with conflagration — see Conflagration
 conflagration — see Conflagration
 corrosive liquid, substance E924.1
  swallowed — see Table of Drugs and
   Chemicals
 electric current (see also Electric shock)
  E925.9
 firearm E928.7
 fire, flames (see also Fire) E899
 flare, Verey pistol E922.8
 heat
  from appliance (electrical) E924.8
  in local application, or packing during
   medical or surgical procedure
   E873.5
 homicide (attempt) (see also Assault, burning) E968.0
 hot
  liquid E924.0
   caustic or corrosive E924.1
  object (not producing fire or flames)
   E924.8
  substance E924.9
   caustic or corrosive E924.1
   liquid (metal) NEC E924.0
   specified type NEC E924.8
  tap water E924.2
 ignition (see also Ignition)
  clothes, clothing, nightdress (see also
   Ignition, clothes)
   with conflagration — see Conflagra-
    tion
  highly inflammable material (benzine)
   (fat) (gasoline) (kerosene) (paraffin) (petrol) E894
 in
  terrorism E979.3
   from nuclear explosion E979.5

Burning, burns — continued
 in — continued
  terrorism — continued
   petrol bomb E979.3
  war operations (from fire-producing device or conventional weapon)
   E990.9
   from nuclear explosion (see also War
    operations, injury due to, nu-
    clear weapons) E996.2
   incendiary bomb E990.0
   petrol bomb E990.0
 inflicted by other person
  stated as
   homicidal, intentional (see also As-
    sault, burning) E968.0
   undetermined whether accidental or
    intentional (see also Burn,
    stated as undetermined
    whether accidental or inten-
    tional) E988.1
 internal, from swallowed caustic, corrosive
  liquid, substance — see Table of
  Drugs and Chemicals
 lamp (see also Fire, specified NEC) E898.1
 late effect of NEC E929.4
 lighter (cigar) (cigarette) (see also Fire,
  specified NEC) E898.1
 lightning E907
 liquid (boiling) (hot) (molten) E924.0
  caustic, corrosive (external) E924.1
   swallowed — see Table of Drugs and
    Chemicals
 local application of externally applied substance in medical or surgical care
  E873.5
 machinery — see Accident, machine
 matches (see also Fire, specified NEC) E898.1
 medicament, externally applied E873.5
 metal, molten E924.0
 object (hot) E924.8
  producing fire or flames — see Fire
 oven (electric) (gas) E924.8
 pipe (smoking) (see also Fire, specified NEC)
  E898.1
 radiation — see Radiation
 railway engine, locomotive, train (see also
  Explosion, railway engine) E803 ☑
 self-inflicted (unspecified whether accidental or intentional) E988.1
  caustic or corrosive substance NEC
   E988.7
  stated as intentional, purposeful E958.1
   caustic or corrosive substance NEC
    E958.7
  stated as undetermined whether accidental
   or intentional E988.1
   caustic or corrosive substance NEC
    E988.7
 steam E924.0
  pipe E924.8
 substance (hot) E924.9
  boiling or molten E924.0
  caustic, corrosive (external) E924.1
   swallowed — see Table of Drugs and
    Chemicals
 suicidal (attempt) NEC E958.1
  caustic substance E958.7
  late effect of E959
 tanning bed E926.2
 therapeutic misadventure
  overdose of radiation E873.2
 torch, welding (see also Fire, specified NEC)
  E898.1
 trash fire (see also Burning, bonfire) E897
 vapor E924.0
 vitriol E924.1
 x-rays E926.3
  in medical, surgical procedure — see
   Misadventure, failure, in dosage,
   radiation
Butted by animal E906.8

<hr>

C

Cachexia, lead or saturnine E866.0

Cachexia, lead or saturnine — continued
 from pesticide NEC (see also Table of Drugs
  and Chemicals) E863.4
Caisson disease E902.2
Capital punishment (any means) E978
Car sickness E903
Casualty (not due to war) NEC E928.9
 terrorism E979.8
 war (see also War operations) E995.9
Cat
 bite E906.3
 scratch E906.8
Cataclysmic (any injury)
 earth surface movement or eruption E909.9
  specified type NEC E909.8
 storm or flood resulting from storm E908.9
  specified type NEC E909.8
Catching fire — see Ignition
Caught
 between
  objects (moving) (stationary and moving) E918
   and machinery — see Accident, ma-
    chine
  by cable car, not on rails E847
 in
  machinery (moving parts of) — see, Accident, machine
  object E918
Cave-in (causing asphyxia, suffocation (by
  pressure)) — see also Suffocation, due
  to, cave-in E913.3
 with injury other than asphyxia or suffocation E916
  with asphyxia or suffocation (see also
   Suffocation, due to, cave-in)
   E913.3
 struck or crushed by E916
  with asphyxia or suffocation (see also
   Suffocation, due to, cave-in)
   E913.3
Change(s) in air pressure — see also Effects
  of, air pressure
 sudden, in aircraft (ascent) (descent) (causing aeroneurosis or aviators' disease)
  E902.1
Chilblains E901.0
 due to manmade conditions E901.1
Choking (on) (any object except food or vomitus) E912
 apple E911
 bone E911
 food, any type (regurgitated) E911
 mucus or phlegm E912
 seed E911
Civil insurrection — see War operations
Cloudburst E908.8
Cold, exposure to (accidental) (excessive)
  (extreme) (place) E901.9
 causing chilblains or immersion foot E901.0
 due to
  manmade conditions E901.1
  specified cause NEC E901.8
  weather (conditions) E901.0
 late effect of NEC E929.5
 self-inflicted (undetermined whether accidental or intentional) E988.3
  suicidal E958.3
 suicide E958.3
Colic, lead, painter's, or saturnine — see
  category E866 ☑
Collapse
 building E916
  burning (uncontrolled fire) E891.8
   in terrorism E979.3
   private E890.8
 dam E909.3
 due to heat — see Heat
 machinery — see Accident, machine or vehicle
 man-made structure E909.3
 postoperative NEC E878.9
 structure
  burning (uncontrolled fire) NEC E891.8
   in terrorism E979.3

☑ **Additional Digit Required** — Refer to the Tabular List for Digit Selection ☒ **Subterms under main terms may continue to next column or page**

338 — Volume 2 ▶◀ Revised Text ● New Line ▲ Revised Code 2015 ICD-9-CM

Collision (accidental)

Note — In the case of collisions between different types of vehicles, persons and objects, priority in classification is in the following order:

Aircraft

Watercraft

Motor vehicle

Railway vehicle

Pedal cycle

Animal-drawn vehicle

Animal being ridden

Streetcar or other nonmotor road vehicle

Other vehicle

Pedestrian or person using pedestrian conveyance

Object (except where falling from or set in motion by vehicle etc. listed above)

In the listing below, the combinations are listed only under the vehicle etc. having priority. For definitions, see Supplementary Classification of External Causes of Injury and Poisoning (E800-E999).

aircraft (with object or vehicle) (fixed) (movable) (moving) E841 ✓
  with
    person (while landing, taking off) (without accident to aircraft) E844 ✓
    powered (in transit) (with unpowered aircraft) E841 ✓
      while landing, taking off E840 ✓
    unpowered E842 ✓
      while landing, taking off E840 ✓
animal being ridden (in sport or transport) E828 ✓
  and
    animal (being ridden) (herded) (unattended) E828 ✓
    nonmotor road vehicle, except pedal cycle or animal-drawn vehicle E828 ✓
    object (fallen) (fixed) (movable) (moving) not falling from or set in motion by vehicle of higher priority E828 ✓
    pedestrian (conveyance or vehicle) E828 ✓
animal-drawn vehicle E827 ✓
  and
    animal (being ridden) (herded) (unattended) E827 ✓
    nonmotor road vehicle, except pedal cycle E827 ✓
    object (fallen) (fixed) (movable) (moving) not falling from or set in motion by vehicle of higher priority E827 ✓
    pedestrian (conveyance or vehicle) E827 ✓
    streetcar E827 ✓
motor vehicle (on public highway) (traffic accident) E812 ✓
  after leaving, running off, public highway (without antecedent collision) (without re-entry) E816 ✓
  with antecedent collision on public highway — see categories E810-E815 ✓
  with re-entrance collision with another motor vehicle E811 ✓
  and
    abutment (bridge) (overpass) E815 ✓
    animal (herded) (unattended) E815 ✓

Collision — continued
motor vehicle — continued
  and — continued
    animal — continued
      carrying person, property E813 ✓
    animal-drawn vehicle E813 ✓
    another motor vehicle (abandoned) (disabled) (parked) (stalled) (stopped) E812 ✓
      with, involving re-entrance (on same roadway) (across median strip) E811 ✓
    any object, person, or vehicle off the public highway resulting from a noncollision motor vehicle nontraffic accident E816 ✓
    avalanche, fallen or not moving E815 ✓
      falling E909.2
    boundary fence E815 ✓
    culvert E815 ✓
    fallen
      stone E815 ✓
      tree E815 ✓
    guard post or guard rail E815 ✓
    inter-highway divider E815 ✓
    landslide, fallen or not moving E815 ✓
      moving E909 ✓
    machinery (road) E815 ✓
    nonmotor road vehicle NEC E813 ✓
    object (any object, person, or vehicle off the public highway resulting from a noncollision motor vehicle nontraffic accident) E815 ✓
      off, normally not on, public highway resulting from a noncollision motor vehicle traffic accident E816 ✓
    pedal cycle E813 ✓
    pedestrian (conveyance) E814 ✓
    person (using pedestrian conveyance) E814 ✓
    post or pole (lamp) (light) (signal) (telephone) (utility) E815 ✓
    railway rolling stock, train, vehicle E810 ✓
    safety island E815 ✓
    street car E813 ✓
    traffic signal, sign, or marker (temporary) E815 ✓
    tree E815 ✓
    tricycle E813 ✓
    wall of cut made for road E815 ✓
  due to cataclysm — see categories E908 ✓, E909 ✓
  not on public highway, nontraffic accident E822 ✓
  and
    animal (carrying person, property) (herded) (unattended) E822 ✓
    animal-drawn vehicle E822 ✓
    another motor vehicle (moving), except off-road motor vehicle E822 ✓
      stationary E823 ✓
    avalanche, fallen, not moving E823 ✓
      moving E909.2
    landslide, fallen, not moving E823 ✓
      moving E909.2
    nonmotor vehicle (moving) E822 ✓
      stationary E823 ✓
    object (fallen) (normally) (fixed) (movable but not in motion) (stationary) E823 ✓
      moving, except when falling from, set in motion by, aircraft or cataclysm E822 ✓
    pedal cycle (moving) E822 ✓

Collision — continued
motor vehicle — continued
  not on public highway, nontraffic accident — continued
  and — continued
    pedal cycle — continued
      stationary E823 ✓
    pedestrian (conveyance) E822 ✓
    person (using pedestrian conveyance) E822 ✓
    railway rolling stock, train, vehicle (moving) E822 ✓
      stationary E823 ✓
    road vehicle (any) (moving) E822 ✓
      stationary E823 ✓
    tricycle (moving) E822 ✓
      stationary E823 ✓
  off-road type motor vehicle (not on public highway) E821 ✓
  and
    animal (being ridden) (-drawn vehicle) E821 ✓
    another off-road motor vehicle, except snow vehicle E821 ✓
    other motor vehicle, not on public highway E821 ✓
    other object or vehicle NEC, fixed or movable, not set in motion by aircraft, motor vehicle on highway, or snow vehicle, motor driven E821 ✓
    pedal cycle E821 ✓
    pedestrian (conveyance) E821 ✓
    railway train E821 ✓
  on public highway — see Collision, motor vehicle
pedal cycle E826 ✓
  and
    animal (carrying person, property) (herded) (unherded) E826 ✓
    animal-drawn vehicle E826 ✓
    another pedal cycle E826 ✓
    nonmotor road vehicle E826 ✓
    object (fallen) (fixed) (movable) (moving) not falling from or set in motion by aircraft, motor vehicle, or railway train NEC E826 ✓
    pedestrian (conveyance) E826 ✓
    person (using pedestrian conveyance) E826 ✓
    street car E826 ✓
pedestrian(s) (conveyance) E917.9
  with fall E886.9
    in sports E886.0
  and
    crowd, human stampede E917.1
      with subsequent fall E917.6
    furniture E917.3
      with subsequent fall E917.7
    machinery — see Accident, machine
    object (fallen) (moving) not falling from NEC, fixed or set in motion by any vehicle classifiable to E800-E848 ✓, E917.9
      with subsequent fall E917.6
      caused by a crowd E917.1
        with subsequent fall E917.6
      furniture E917.3
        with subsequent fall E917.7
      in
        running water E917.2
          with drowning or submersion — see Submersion
        sports E917.0
          with subsequent fall E917.5
        stationary E917.4
          with subsequent fall E917.8
    vehicle, nonmotor, nonroad E848
    in
      running water E917.2

Collision — continued
pedestrian(s) — continued
  in — continued
    running water — continued
      with drowning or submersion — see Submersion
    sports E917.0
      with fall E886.0
  person(s) (using pedestrian conveyance) (see also Collision, pedestrian) E917.9
railway (rolling stock) (train) (vehicle) (with (subsequent) derailment, explosion, fall or fire) E800 ✓
  with antecedent derailment E802 ✓
  and
    animal (carrying person) (herded) (unattended) E801 ✓
    another railway train or vehicle E800 ✓
    buffers E801 ✓
    fallen tree on railway E801 ✓
    farm machinery, nonmotor (in transport) (stationary) E801 ✓
    gates E801 ✓
    nonmotor vehicle E801 ✓
    object (fallen) (fixed) (movable) (moving) not falling from, set in motion by, aircraft or motor vehicle NEC E801 ✓
    pedal cycle E801 ✓
    pedestrian (conveyance) E805 ✓
    person (using pedestrian conveyance) E805 ✓
    platform E801 ✓
    rock on railway E801 ✓
    street car E801 ✓
snow vehicle, motor-driven (not on public highway) E820 ✓
  and
    animal (being ridden) (-drawn vehicle) E820 ✓
    another off-road motor vehicle E820 ✓
    other motor vehicle, not on public highway E820 ✓
    other object or vehicle NEC, fixed or movable, not set in motion by aircraft or motor vehicle on highway E820 ✓
    pedal cycle E820 ✓
    pedestrian (conveyance) E820 ✓
    railway train E820 ✓
  on public highway — see Collision, motor vehicle
street car(s) E829 ✓
  and
    animal, herded, not being ridden, unattended E829 ✓
    nonmotor road vehicle NEC E829 ✓
    object (fallen) (fixed) (movable) (moving) not falling from or set in motion by aircraft, animal-drawn vehicle, animal being ridden, motor vehicle, pedal cycle, or railway train E829 ✓
    pedestrian (conveyance) E829 ✓
    person (using pedestrian conveyance) E829 ✓
vehicle
  animal-drawn — see Collision, animal-drawn vehicle
  motor — see Collision, motor vehicle
  nonmotor
    nonroad E848
    and
      another nonmotor, nonroad vehicle E848

✓ Additional Digit Required — Refer to the Tabular List for Digit Selection   ▽ Subterms under main terms may continue to next column or page

2015 ICD-9-CM   ►◄ Revised Text   ● New Line   ▲ Revised Code   Volume 2 — 339

Collision — *continued*
  vehicle — *continued*
    nonmotor — *continued*
      nonroad — *continued*
        and — *continued*
          object (fallen) (fixed) (movable) (moving) not falling from or set in motion by aircraft, animal-drawn vehicle, animal being ridden, motor vehicle, nonmotor road vehicle, pedal cycle, railway train, or streetcar E848
          road, except animal being ridden, animal-drawn vehicle, or pedal cycle E829 ☑
          and
            animal, herded, not being ridden, unattended E829 ☑
            another nonmotor road vehicle, except animal being ridden, animal-drawn vehicle, or pedal cycle E829 ☑
            object (fallen) (fixed) (movable) (moving) not falling from or set in motion by, aircraft, animal-drawn vehicle, animal being ridden, motor vehicle, pedal cycle, or railway train E829 ☑
            pedestrian (conveyance) E829 ☑
            person (using pedestrian conveyance) E829 ☑
            vehicle, nonmotor, nonroad E829 ☑
    watercraft E838 ☑
      and
        person swimming or water skiing E838 ☑
      causing
        drowning, submersion E830 ☑
        injury except drowning, submersion E831 ☑
Combustion, spontaneous — *see* Ignition
Complication of medical or surgical procedure or treatment
  as an abnormal reaction — *see* Reaction, abnormal
  delayed, without mention of misadventure — *see* Reaction, abnormal
  due to misadventure — *see* Misadventure
Compression
  divers' squeeze E902.2
  trachea by
    food E911
    foreign body, except food E912
Conflagration
  building or structure, except private dwelling (barn) (church) (convalescent or residential home) (factory) (farm outbuilding) (hospital) (hotel) (institution) (educational) (domitory) (residential) (school) (shop) (store) (theater) E891.9
    with or causing (injury due to)
      accident or injury NEC E891.9
        specified circumstance NEC E891.8
      burns, burning E891.3
      carbon monoxide E891.2
      fumes E891.2
        polyvinylchloride (PVC) or similar material E891.1
      smoke E891.2
    causing explosion E891.0
    in terrorism E979.3
    not in building or structure E892

Conflagration — *continued*
  private dwelling (apartment) (boarding house) (camping place) (caravan) (farmhouse) (home (private)) (house) (lodging house) (private garage) (rooming house) (tenement) E890.9
    with or causing (injury due to)
      accident or injury NEC E890.9
        specified circumstance NEC E890.8
      burns, burning E890.3
      carbon monoxide E890.2
      fumes E890.2
        polyvinylchloride (PVC) or similar material E890.1
      smoke E890.2
    causing explosion E890.0
Constriction, external
  caused by
    hair E928.4
    other object E928.5
Contact with
  dry ice E901.1
  liquid air, hydrogen, nitrogen E901.1
Cramp(s)
  Heat — *see* Heat
  swimmers (*see also* category E910) E910.2
    not in recreation or sport E910.3
Cranking (car) (truck) (bus) (engine), injury by E917.9
Crash
  aircraft (in transit) (powered) E841 ☑
    at landing, take-off E840 ☑
    in
      terrorism E979.1
      war operations E994.9
    on runway NEC E840 ☑
    stated as
      homicidal E968.8
      suicidal E958.6
      undetermined whether accidental or intentional E988.6
    unpowered E842 ☑
  glider E842 ☑
  motor vehicle (*see also* Accident, motor vehicle)
    homicidal E968.5
    suicidal E958.5
    undetermined whether accidental or intentional E988.5
Crushed (accidentally) E928.9
  between
    boat(s), ship(s), watercraft (and dock or pier) (without accident to watercraft) E838 ☑
      after accident to, or collision, watercraft E831 ☑
    objects (moving) (stationary and moving) E918
  by
    avalanche NEC E909.2
    boat, ship, watercraft after accident to, collision, watercraft E831 ☑
    cave-in E916
      with asphyxiation or suffocation (*see also* Suffocation, due to, cave-in) E913.3
    crowd, human stampede E917.1
    falling
      aircraft (*see also* Accident, aircraft) E841 ☑
        in
          terrorism E979.1
          war operations E994.8
      earth, material E916
        with asphyxiation or suffocation (*see also* Suffocation, due to, cave-in) E913.3
      object E916
        on ship, watercraft E838 ☑
        while loading, unloading watercraft E838 ☑
    firearm E928.7
    landslide NEC E909.2
    lifeboat after abandoning ship E831 ☑
    machinery — *see* Accident, machine

Crushed — *continued*
  by — *continued*
    railway rolling stock, train, vehicle (part of) E805 ☑
    slide trigger mechanism, scope or other part of gun E928.7
    street car E829 ☑
    vehicle NEC — *see* Accident, vehicle NEC
  in
    machinery — *see* Accident, machine
    object E918
    transport accident — *see* categories E800-E848
  late effect of NEC E929.9
Cut, cutting (any part of body) (accidental) E920.9
  by
    arrow E920.8
    axe E920.4
    bayonet (*see also* Bayonet wound) E920.3
      in war operations E995.2
    blender E920.2
    broken glass E920.8
      following fall E888.0
    can opener E920.4
      powered E920.2
    chisel E920.4
    circular saw E919.4
    cutting or piercing instrument (*see also* category) E920
      following fall E888.0
      late effect of E929.8
    dagger E920.3
    dart E920.8
    drill — *see* Accident, caused by drill
    edge of stiff paper E920.8
    electric
      beater E920.2
      fan E920.2
      knife E920.2
      mixer E920.2
    firearm component E928.7
    fork E920.4
    garden fork E920.4
    hand saw or tool (not powered) E920.4
      powered E920.1
    hedge clipper E920.4
      powered E920.1
    hoe E920.4
    ice pick E920.4
    knife E920.3
      electric E920.2
      in war operations E995.2
    lathe turnings E920.8
    lawn mower E920.4
      powered E920.0
      riding E919.8
    machine — *see* Accident, machine
    meat
      grinder E919.8
      slicer E919.8
    nails E920.8
    needle E920.4
      hypodermic E920.5
    object, edged, pointed, sharp — *see* category E920 ☑
      following fall E888.0
    paper cutter E920.4
    piercing instrument (*see also* category) E920 ☑
      late effect of E929.8
    pitchfork E920.4
    powered
      can opener E920.2
      garden cultivator E920.1
        riding E919.8
      hand saw E920.1
      hand tool NEC E920.1
      hedge clipper E920.1
      household appliance or implement E920.2
      lawn mower (hand) E920.0
        riding E919.8
      rivet gun E920.1
      staple gun E920.1

Cut, cutting — *continued*
  by — *continued*
    rake E920.4
    saw
      circular E919.4
      hand E920.4
    scissors E920.4
    screwdriver E920.4
    sewing machine (electric) (powered) E920.2
      not powered E920.4
    shears E920.4
    shovel E920.4
    slide trigger mechanism, scope or other part of gun E928.7
    spade E920.4
    splinters E920.8
    sword E920.3
      in war operations E995.2
    tin can lid E920.8
    wood slivers E920.8
  homicide (attempt) E966
  inflicted by other person
    stated as
      intentional, homicidal E966
      undetermined whether accidental or intentional E986
  late effect of NEC E929.8
  legal
    execution E978
    intervention E974
  self-inflicted (unspecified whether accidental or intentional) E986
    stated as intentional, purposeful E956
    stated as undetermined whether accidental or intentional E986
  suicidal (attempt) E956
  terrorism E979.8
  war operations E995.2
Cyclone E908.1

D

Death due to injury occurring one year or more previous — *see* Late effect
Decapitation (accidental circumstances) NEC E928.9
  homicidal E966
  legal execution (by guillotine) E978
Deprivation — *see also* Privation
  homicidal intent E968.4
Derailment (accidental)
  railway (rolling stock) (train) (vehicle) (with subsequent collision) E802 ☑
    with
      collision (antecedent) (*see also* Collision, railway) E800 ☑
      explosion (subsequent) (without antecedent collision) E802 ☑
        antecedent collision E803 ☑
      fall (without collision (antecedent)) E802 ☑
      fire (without collision (antecedent)) E802 ☑
    street car E829 ☑
Descent
  parachute (voluntary) (without accident to aircraft) E844 ☑
    due to accident to aircraft — *see* categories E840-E842 ☑
Desertion
  child, with intent to injure or kill E968.4
  helpless person, infant, newborn E904.0
    with intent to injure or kill E968.4
Destitution — *see* Privation
Dirty bomb (*see also* War operations, injury due to, nuclear weapons) E996.9
Disability, late effect or sequela of injury — *see* Late effect
Disease
  Andes E902.0
  aviators' E902.1
  caisson E902.2
  range E902.0
Divers' disease, palsy, paralysis, squeeze E902.0

☑ **Additional Digit Required** — Refer to the Tabular List for Digit Selection   ▽ **Subterms under main terms may continue to next column or page**

340 — Volume 2   ▶◀ **Revised Text**   ● **New Line**   ▲ **Revised Code**   **2015 ICD-9-CM**

Dog bite E906.0
Dragged by
  cable car (not on rails) E847
    on rails E829 ☑
  motor vehicle (on highway) E814 ☑
    not on highway, nontraffic accident
      E825 ☑
  street car E829 ☑
Drinking poison (accidental) — *see* Table of
    Drugs and Chemicals
Drowning — *see* Submersion
Dust in eye E914

E

Earth falling (on) (with asphyxia or suffocation
    (by pressure)) — *see also* Suffocation,
    due to, cave-in E913.3
  as, or due to, a cataclysm (involving any
    transport vehicle) — *see* categories
    E908 ☑, E909 ☑
  not due to cataclysmic action E913.3
    motor vehicle (in motion) (on public
      highway) E813 ☑
      not on public highway E825 ☑
    nonmotor road vehicle NEC E829 ☑
    pedal cycle E826 ☑
    railway rolling stock, train, vehicle
      E806 ☑
    street car E829 ☑
  struck or crushed by E916
    with asphyxiation or suffocation
      E913.3
    with injury other than asphyxia, suf-
      focation E916
Earthquake (any injury) E909.0
Effect(s) (adverse) of
  air pressure E902.9
    at high altitude E902.9
      in aircraft E902.1
      residence or prolonged visit (causing
        conditions classifiable to
        E902.0) E902.0
    due to
      diving E902.2
      specified cause NEC E902.8
    in aircraft E902.1
  cold, excessive (exposure to) (*see also* Cold,
    exposure to) E901.9
  heat (excessive) (*see also* Heat) E900.9
  hot
    place — *see* Heat
    weather E900.0
  insulation — *see* Heat
  late — *see* Late effect of
  motion E903
  nuclear explosion or weapon
    in
      terrorism E979.5
      war operations (*see also* War opera-
        tions, injury due to, nuclear
        weapons) E996.9
  radiation — *see* Radiation
  terrorism, secondary E979.9
  travel E903
Electric shock, electrocution (accidental)
    (from exposed wire, faulty appliance,
    high voltage cable, live rail, open socket)
    (by) (in) E925.9
  appliance or wiring
    domestic E925.0
    factory E925.2
    farm (building) E925.8
    house E925.0
    home E925.0
    industrial (conductor) (control appara-
      tus) (transformer) E925.2
    outdoors E925.8
    public building E925.8
    residential institution E925.8
    school E925.8
    specified place NEC E925.8
  caused by other person
    stated as
      intentional, homicidal E968.8

Electric shock, electrocution — *continued*
  caused by other person — *continued*
    stated as — *continued*
      undetermined whether accidental or
        intentional E988.4
  electric power generating plant, distribution
    station E925.1
  electroshock gun (taser) (stun gun) E925.8
    caused by other person E968.8
      legal intervention E975
      stated as accidental E925.8
      stated as intentional E968.8
    due to legal intervention E975
    stated as intentional self-harm (suicidal
      attempt) E958.4
    stated as undetermined whether acciden-
      tal or intentional E988.4
    suicide (attempt) E958.4
  homicidal (attempt) E968.8
  legal execution E978
  lightning E907
  machinery E925.9
    domestic E925.0
    factory E925.2
    farm E925.8
    home E925.0
  misadventure in medical or surgical proce-
    dure
    in electroshock therapy E873.4
  self-inflicted (undetermined whether acci-
    dental or intentional) E988.4
    stated as intentional E958.4
    stated as undetermined whether accidental
      or intentional E988.4
  suicidal (attempt) E958.4
  transmission line E925.1
Electrocution — *see* Electric shock
Embolism
  air (traumatic) NEC — *see* Air, embolism
Encephalitis
  lead or saturnine E866.0
    from pesticide NEC E863.4
Entanglement
  in
    bedclothes, causing suffocation E913.0
    wheel of pedal cycle E826 ☑
Entry of foreign body, material, any — *see*
    Foreign body
Execution, legal (any method) E978
**Exertion, excessive physical, from pro-
    longed activity** E927.2
Exhaustion
  cold — *see* Cold, exposure to
  due to excessive exertion E927.2
  heat — *see* Heat
Explosion (accidental) (in) (of) (on) E923.9
  acetylene E923.2
  aerosol can E921.8
  aircraft (in transit) (powered) E841 ☑
    at landing, take-off E840 ☑
    in
      terrorism E979.1
      war operations
        from
          enemy fire or explosive(s)
            (device placed on air-
            craft) E994.0
          own onboard explosives
            E994.1
    unpowered E842 ☑
  air tank (compressed) (in machinery) E921.1
  anesthetic gas in operating theatre E923.2
  automobile tire NEC E921.8
    causing transport accident — *see* cate-
      gories E810-E825 ☑
  blasting (cap) (materials) E923.1
  boiler (machinery), not on transport vehicle
    E921.0
    steamship — *see* Explosion, watercraft
  bomb E923.8
    in
      terrorism E979.2
      war operations E993.8
        after cessation of hostilities
          E998.1

Explosion — *continued*
  bomb — *continued*
    in — *continued*
      war operations — *continued*
        atom, hydrogen or nuclear (*see
          also* War operations, injury
          due to, nuclear weapons)
          E996.9
        injury by fragments from E991.9
        antipersonnel bomb E991.3
  butane E923.2
  caused by
    other person
      stated as
        intentional, homicidal — *see* As-
          sault, explosive
        undetermined whether acciden-
          tal or homicidal E985.5
  coal gas E923.2
  detonator E923.1
  dynamite E923.1
  explosive (material) NEC E923.9
    gas(es) E923.2
    missile E923.8
      in
        terrorism E979.2
        war operations E993.1
          injury by fragments from
            E991.9
          antipersonnel bomb
            E991.3
    used in blasting operations E923.1
  fire-damp E923.2
  fireworks E923.0
  gas E923.2
    cylinder (in machinery) E921.1
    pressure tank (in machinery) E921.1
  gasoline (fumes) (tank) not in moving motor
    vehicle E923.2
  grain store (military) (munitions) E923.8
  grenade E923.8
    in
      terrorism E979.2
      war operations E993.8
        injury by fragments from E991.4
  homicide (attempt) — *see* Assault, explosive
  hot water heater, tank (in machinery) E921.0
  in mine (of explosive gases) NEC E923.2
  late effect of NEC E929.8
  machinery (*see also* Accident, machine)
    pressure vessel — *see* Explosion, pres-
      sure vessel
  methane E923.2
  missile E923.8
    in
      terrorism E979.2
      war operations E993.1
        injury by fragments from E991.4
  motor vehicle (part of)
    in motion (on public highway) E818 ☑
      not on public highway E825 ☑
  munitions (dump) (factory) E923.8
    in
      terrorism E979.2
      war operations E993.9
  of mine E923.8
    in
      terrorism
        at sea or in harbor E979.0
        land E979.2
        marine E979.0
      war operations
        after cessation of hostilities
          E998.0
        at sea or in harbor E992.2
        land E993.8
          after cessation of hostilities
            E998.0
          injury by fragments from
            E991.4
        marine E992.2
  own weapons
    in
      terrorism (*see also* Suicide) E979.2
      war operations E993.7
        injury by fragments from E991.9

Explosion — *continued*
  own weapons — *continued*
    in — *continued*
      war operations — *continued*
        injury by fragments from — *con-
          tinued*
          antipersonnel bomb E991.3
  pressure
    cooker E921.8
    gas tank (in machinery) E921.1
    vessel (in machinery) E921.9
      on transport vehicle — *see* cate-
        gories E800-E848 ☑
      specified type NEC E921.8
  propane E923.2
  railway engine, locomotive, train (boiler)
    (with subsequent collision, derail-
    ment, fall) E803 ☑
    with
      collision (antecedent) (*see also* Colli-
        sion, railway) E800 ☑
      derailment (antecedent) E802 ☑
      fire (without antecedent collision or
        derailment) E803 ☑
  secondary fire resulting from — *see* Fire
  self-inflicted (unspecified whether acciden-
    tal or intentional) E985.5
    stated as intentional, purposeful E955.5
  shell (artillery) E923.8
    in
      terrorism E979.2
      war operations E993.2
        injury by fragments from E991.4
  stated as undetermined whether caused
    accidentally or purposely inflicted
    E985.5
  steam or water lines (in machinery) E921.0
  suicide (attempted) E955.5
  terrorism — *see* Terrorism, explosion
  torpedo E923.8
    in
      terrorism E979.0
      war operations E992.0
  transport accident — *see* categories
    E800-E848 ☑
  war operations — *see* War operations, ex-
    plosion
  watercraft (boiler) E837 ☑
    causing drowning, submersion (after
      jumping from watercraft) E830 ☑
Exposure (weather) (conditions) (rain) (wind)
    E904.3
  with homicidal intent E968.4
  environmental
    to
      algae bloom E928.6
      blue-green algae bloom E928.6
      brown tide E928.6
      cyanobacteria bloom E928.6
      Florida red tide E928.6
      harmful alage
        and toxins E928.6
        bloom E928.6
      pfiesteria piscicida E928.6
      red tide E928.6
  excessive E904.3
    cold (*see also* Cold, exposure to) E901.9
      self-inflicted — *see* Cold, exposure
        to, self-inflicted
    heat (*see also* Heat) E900.9
  helpless person, infant, newborn due to
    abandonment or neglect E904.0
  noise E928.1
  prolonged in deep-freeze unit or refrigerator
    E901.1
  radiation — *see* Radiation
  resulting from transport accident — *see*
    categories E800-E848 ☑
  smoke from, due to
    fire — *see* Fire
    tobacco, second-hand E869.4
  vibration E928.2
External cause status E000.9
  child assisting in compensated work of
    other family member E000.8

☑ **Additional Digit Required — Refer to the Tabular List for Digit Selection**

▽ **Subterms under main terms may continue to next column or page**

External cause status — *continued*
  civilian
    done for
      financial or other compensation
        E000.0
        pay or income E000.0
    family member assisting in compensated
      work of other family member E000.8
  for income E000.0
  hobby or leisure E000.8
  military E000.1
    off duty E000.8
  off duty military E000.8
  recreation E000.8
  specified NEC E000.8
  sport not for income E000.8
  student E000.8
  volunteer E000.2

F

Fallen on by
  animal (horse) (not being ridden) E906.8
    being ridden (in sport or transport)
      E828 ☑
Fall, falling (accidental) E888.9
  building E916
    burning E891.8
      private E890.8
  down
    escalator E880.0
    ladder E881.0
      in boat, ship, watercraft E833 ☑
    staircase E880.9
    stairs, steps — *see* Fall, from, stairs
  earth (with asphyxia or suffocation (by
    pressure)) (*see also* Earth, falling)
    E913.3
  from, off
    aircraft (at landing, take-off) (in-transit)
      (while alighting, boarding)
      E843 ☑
      resulting from accident to aircraft —
        see categories E840-E842 ☑
    animal (in sport or transport) E828 ☑
    animal-drawn vehicle E827 ☑
    balcony E882
    bed E884.4
    bicycle E826 ☑
    boat, ship, watercraft (into water)
      E832 ☑
      after accident to, collision, fire on
        E830 ☑
        and subsequently struck by (part
          of) boat E831 ☑
        and subsequently struck by (part of)
          while alighting, boat E831 ☑
      burning, crushed, sinking E830 ☑
        and subsequently struck by (part
          of) boat E831 ☑
    bridge E882
    building E882
      burning (uncontrolled fire) E891.8
        in terrorism E979.3
      private E890.8
    bunk in boat, ship, watercraft E834 ☑
      due to accident to watercraft
        E831 ☑
    cable car (not on rails) E847
      on rails E829 ☑
    car — *see* Fall from motor vehicle
    chair E884.2
    cliff E884.1
    commode E884.6
    curb (sidewalk) E880.1
    elevation aboard ship E834 ☑
      due to accident to ship E831 ☑
    embankment E884.9
    escalator E880.0
    fire escape E882
    flagpole E882
    furniture NEC E884.5
    gangplank (into water) (*see also* Fall,
      from, boat) E832 ☑
      to deck, dock E834 ☑
    hammock on ship E834 ☑

Fall, falling — *continued*
  from, off — *continued*
    hammock on ship — *continued*
      due to accident to watercraft
        E831 ☑
    haystack E884.9
    heelies E885.1
    high place NEC E884.9
      stated as undetermined whether ac-
        cidental or intentional — *see*
        Jumping, from, high place
    horse (in sport or transport) E828 ☑
    in-line skates E885.1
    ladder E881.0
      in boat, ship, watercraft E833 ☑
        due to accident to watercraft
          E831 ☑
    machinery (*see also* Accident, machine)
      not in operation E884.9
    motorized
      mobility scooter E884.3
      wheelchair E884.3
    motor vehicle (in motion) (on public
      highway) E818 ☑
      not on public highway E825 ☑
        stationary, except while alighting,
          boarding, entering, leav-
          ing E884.9
        while alighting, boarding, enter-
          ing, leaving E824 ☑
      stationary, except while alighting,
        boarding, entering, leaving
        E884.9
      while alighting, boarding, entering,
        leaving, except off-road type
        motor vehicle E817 ☑
      off-road type — *see* Fall, from,
        off-road type motor vehi-
        cle
    nonmotor road vehicle (while alighting,
      boarding) NEC E829 ☑
      stationary, except while alighting,
        boarding, entering, leaving
        E884.9
    off road type motor vehicle (not on
      public highway) NEC E821 ☑
      on public highway E818 ☑
        while alighting, boarding, enter-
          ing, leaving E817 ☑
      snow vehicle — *see* Fall from snow
        vehicle, motor-driven
    one
      deck to another on ship E834 ☑
        due to accident to ship E831 ☑
      level to another NEC E884.9
        boat, ship, or watercraft E834 ☑
          due to accident to watercraft
            E831 ☑
    pedal cycle E826 ☑
    playground equipment E884.0
    railway rolling stock, train, vehicle (while
      alighting, boarding) E804 ☑
      with
        collision (*see also* Collision, rail-
          way) E800 ☑
        derailment (*see also* Derailment,
          railway) E802 ☑
        explosion (*see also* Explosion,
          railway engine) E803 ☑
    rigging (aboard ship) E834 ☑
      due to accident to watercraft
        E831 ☑
    roller skates E885.1
    scaffolding E881.1
    scooter (nonmotorized) E885.0
      motorized mobility E884.3
    sidewalk (curb) E880.1
      moving E885.9
    skateboard E885.2
    skis E885.3
    snowboard E885.4
    snow vehicle, motor-driven (not on
      public highway) E820 ☑
      on public highway E818 ☑

Fall, falling — *continued*
  from, off — *continued*
    snow vehicle, motor-driven — *contin-*
      ued
      on public highway — *continued*
        while alighting, boarding, enter-
          ing, leaving E817 ☑
    stairs, steps E880.9
      boat, ship, watercraft E833 ☑
        due to accident to watercraft
          E831 ☑
      motor bus, motor vehicle — *see* Fall,
        from, motor vehicle, while
        alighting, boarding
      street car E829 ☑
    stationary vehicle NEC E884.9
    stepladder E881.0
    street car (while boarding, alighting)
      E829 ☑
      stationary, except while boarding or
        alighting E884.9
    structure NEC E882
      burning (uncontrolled fire) E891.8
        in terrorism E979.3
    table E884.9
    toilet E884.6
    tower E882
    tree E884.9
    turret E882
    vehicle NEC (*see also* Accident, vehicle
      NEC)
      stationary E884.9
    viaduct E882
    wall E882
    wheelchair (electric) (motorized) E884.3
    wheelies E885.1
    window E882
  in, on
    aircraft (at landing, take-off) (in-transit)
      E843 ☑
      resulting from accident to aircraft —
        see categories E840-E842 ☑
    boat, ship, watercraft E835 ☑
      due to accident to watercraft
        E831 ☑
      one level to another NEC E834 ☑
      on ladder, stairs E833 ☑
    cutting or piercing instrument or ma-
      chine E888.0
    deck (of boat, ship, watercraft) E835 ☑
      due to accident to watercraft
        E831 ☑
    escalator E880.0
    gangplank E835 ☑
    glass, broken E888.0
    knife E888.0
    ladder E881.0
      in boat, ship, watercraft E833 ☑
        due to accident to watercraft
          E831 ☑
    object
      edged, pointed or sharp E888.0
      other E888.1
    pitchfork E888.0
    railway rolling stock, train, vehicle (while
      alighting, boarding) E804 ☑
      with
        collision (*see also* Collision, rail-
          way) E800 ☑
        derailment (*see also* Derailment,
          railway) E802 ☑
        explosion (see also Explosion,
          railway engine) E803 ☑
    scaffolding E881.1
    scissors E888.0
    staircase, stairs, steps (*see also* Fall, from,
      stairs) E880.9
    street car E829 ☑
    water transport (*see also* Fall, in, boat)
      E835 ☑
  into
    cavity E883.9
    dock E883.9
      from boat, ship, watercraft (*see also*
        Fall, from, boat) E832 ☑

Fall, falling — *continued*
  into — *continued*
    hold (of ship) E834 ☑
      due to accident to watercraft
        E831 ☑
    hole E883.9
    manhole E883.2
    moving part of machinery — *see* Acci-
      dent, machine
    opening in surface NEC E883.9
    pit E883.9
    quarry E883.9
    shaft E883.9
    storm drain E883.2
    tank E883.9
    water (with drowning or submersion)
      E910.9
    well E883.1
  late effect of NEC E929.3
  object (*see also* Hit by, object, falling) E916
  other E888.8
  over
    animal E885.9
    cliff E884.1
    embankment E884.9
    small object E885.9
  overboard (*see also* Fall, from, boat) E832 ☑
  resulting in striking against object E888.1
    sharp E888.0
  rock E916
  same level NEC E888.9
    aircraft (any kind) E843 ☑
      resulting from accident to aircraft —
        see categories E840-E842 ☑
    boat, ship, watercraft E835 ☑
      due to accident to, collision, water-
        craft E831 ☑
    from
      collision, pushing, shoving, by or
        with other person(s) E886.9
      as, or caused by, a crowd E917.6
        in sports E886.0
      in-line skates E885.1
      roller skates E885.1
      scooter (nonmotorized) E885.0
      skateboard E885.2
      slipping stumbling, tripping E885 ☑
      snowboard E885.4
  snowslide E916
    as avalanche E909.2
  stone E916
  through
    hatch (on ship) E834 ☑
      due to accident to watercraft
        E831 ☑
    roof E882
    window E882
  timber E916
  while alighting from, boarding, entering,
    leaving
    aircraft (any kind) E843 ☑
    motor bus, motor vehicle — *see* Fall,
      from, motor vehicle, while
      alighting, boarding
    nonmotor road vehicle NEC E829 ☑
    railway train E804 ☑
    street car E829 ☑
Fell or jumped from high place, so stated —
  see Jumping, from, high place
Felo-de-se — *see also* Suicide E958.9
Fever
  heat — *see* Heat
  thermic — *see* Heat
Fight (hand) (fist) (foot) — *see also* Assault,
  fight E960.0
Fire (accidental) (caused by great heat from
  appliance (electrical), hot object or hot
  substance) (secondary, resulting from
  explosion) E899
  conflagration — *see* Conflagration
  controlled, normal (in brazier, fireplace,
    furnace, or stove) (charcoal) (coal)
    (coke) (electric) (gas) (wood)
    bonfire E897
    brazier, not in building or structure E897

Fire, hot object or hot substance — *continued*
  controlled, normal — *continued*
    in building or structure, except private
        dwelling (barn) (church) (convalescent or residential home) (factory) (farm outbuilding) (hospital)
        (hotel) (institution (educational)
        (dormitory) (residential)) (private
        garage) (school) (shop) (store)
        (theatre) E896
    in private dwelling (apartment) (boarding house) (camping place) (caravan) (farmhouse) (home (private))
        (house) (lodging house) (rooming
        house) (tenement) E895
    not in building or structure E897
    trash E897
  forest (uncontrolled) E892
  grass (uncontrolled) E892
  hay (uncontrolled) E892
  homicide (attempt) E968.0
    late effect of E969
  in, of, on, starting in E892
    aircraft (in transit) (powered) E841 ☑
      at landing, take-off E840 ☑
      stationary E892
      unpowered (balloon) (glider)
        E842 ☑
    balloon E842 ☑
    boat, ship, watercraft — *see* categories
        E830 ☑, E831 ☑, E837 ☑
    building or structure, except private
        dwelling (barn) (church) (convalescent or residential home) (factory) (farm outbuilding) (hospital)
        (hotel) (institution (educational)
        (dormitory) (residential)) (school)
        (shop) (store) (theatre) (*see also*
        Conflagration, building or structure, except private dwelling)
        E891.9
    forest (uncontrolled) E892
    glider E842 ☑
    grass (uncontrolled) E892
    hay (uncontrolled) E892
    lumber (uncontrolled) E892
    machinery — *see* Accident, machine
    mine (uncontrolled) E892
    motor vehicle (in motion) (on public
        highway) E818 ☑
      not on public highway E825 ☑
      stationary E892
    prairie (uncontrolled) E892
    private dwelling (apartment) (boarding
        house) (camping place) (caravan)
        (farmhouse) (home (private))
        (house) (lodging house) (private
        garage) (rooming house) (tenement) (*see also* Conflagration,
        private dwelling) E890.9
    railway rolling stock, train, vehicle (*see
        also* Explosion, railway engine)
        E803 ☑
      stationary E892
    room NEC E898.1
    street car (in motion) E829 ☑
      stationary E892
  terrorism (by fire-producing device)
        E979.3
    fittings or furniture (burning building) (uncontrolled fire) E979.3
    from nuclear explosion E979.5
  transport vehicle, stationary NEC E892
  tunnel (uncontrolled) E892
  war operations (by fire-producing device
        or conventional weapon) E990.9
    from nuclear explosion (*see also* War
        operations, injury due to, nuclear weapons) E996.2
      incendiary bomb E990.0
      petrol bomb E990.0
  late effect of NEC E929.4
  lumber (uncontrolled) E892
  mine (uncontrolled) E892
  prairie (uncontrolled) E892

Fire, hot object or hot substance — *continued*
  self-inflicted (unspecified whether accidental or intentional) E988.1
    stated as intentional, purposeful E958.1
  specified NEC E898.1
    with
      conflagration — *see* Conflagration
      ignition (of)
        clothing — *see* Ignition, clothes
        highly inflammable material
            (benzine) (fat) (gasoline)
            (kerosene) (paraffin)
            (petrol) E894
  started by other person
    stated as
      with intent to injure or kill E968.0
      undetermined whether or not with
          intent to injure or kill E988.1
  suicide (attempted) E958.1
    late effect of E959
  tunnel (uncontrolled) E892
Fireball effects from nuclear explosion
  in
    terrorism E979.5
    war operations (*see also* War operations,
        injury due to, nuclear weapons)
        E996.2
Fireworks (explosion) E923.0
Flash burns from explosion — *see also* Explosion E923.9
Flood (any injury) (resulting from storm) E908.2
  caused by collapse of dam or manmade
        structure E909.3
Forced landing (aircraft) E840 ☑
Foreign body, object or material (entrance
        into) (accidental)
  air passage (causing injury) E915
    with asphyxia, obstruction, suffocation
        E912
      food or vomitus E911
    nose (with asphyxia, obstruction, suffocation) E912
    causing injury without asphyxia, obstruction, suffocation E915
  alimentary canal (causing injury) (with obstruction) E915
    with asphyxia, obstruction respiratory
        passage, suffocation E912
      food E911
  mouth E915
    with asphyxia, obstruction, suffocation E912
      food E911
  pharynx E915
    with asphyxia, obstruction, suffocation E912
      food E911
  aspiration (with asphyxia, obstruction respiratory passage, suffocation) E912
    causing injury without asphyxia, obstruction respiratory passage, suffocation E915
      food (regurgitated) (vomited) E911
    causing injury without asphyxia, obstruction respiratory passage,
        suffocation E915
  mucus (not of newborn) E912
  phlegm E912
  bladder (causing injury or obstruction) E915
  bronchus, bronchi — *see* Foreign body, air
        passages
  conjunctival sac E914
  digestive system — *see* Foreign body, alimentary canal
  ear (causing injury or obstruction) E915
  esophagus (causing injury or obstruction)
        (*see also* Foreign body, alimentary
        canal) E915
  eye (any part) E914
  eyelid E914
  hairball (stomach) (with obstruction) E915
  ingestion — *see* Foreign body, alimentary
        canal
  inhalation — *see* Foreign body, aspiration

Foreign body, object or material — *continued*
  intestine (causing injury or obstruction)
        E915
  iris E914
  lacrimal apparatus E914
  larynx — *see* Foreign body, air passage
  late effect of NEC E929.8
  lung — *see* Foreign body, air passage
  mouth — *see* Foreign body, alimentary
        canal, mouth
  nasal passage — *see* Foreign body, air passage, nose
  nose — *see* Foreign body, air passage, nose
  ocular muscle E914
  operation wound (left in) — *see* Misadventure, foreign object
  orbit E914
  pharynx — *see* Foreign body, alimentary
        canal, pharynx
  rectum (causing injury or obstruction) E915
  stomach (hairball) (causing injury or obstruction) E915
  tear ducts or glands E914
  trachea — *see* Foreign body, air passage
  urethra (causing injury or obstruction) E915
  vagina (causing injury or obstruction) E915
Found dead, injured
  from exposure (to) — *see* Exposure
  on
    public highway E819 ☑
    railway right of way E807 ☑
Fracture (circumstances unknown or unspecified) E887
  due to specified external means — *see*
        manner of accident
  late effect of NEC E929.3
  occurring in water transport NEC E835 ☑
Freezing — *see* Cold, exposure to
Frostbite E901.0
  due to manmade conditions E901.1
Frozen — *see* Cold, exposure to

G

Garrotting, homicidal (attempted) E963
Gored E906.8
Gunshot wound — *see also* Shooting E922.9

H

Hailstones, injury by E904.3
Hairball (stomach) (with obstruction) E915
Hanged himself — *see also* Hanging, self-inflicted E983.0
Hang gliding E842 ☑
Hanging (accidental) E913.8
  caused by other person
    in accidental circumstances E913.8
    stated as
      intentional, homicidal E963
      undetermined whether accidental or
          intentional E983.0
  homicide (attempt) E963
  in bed or cradle E913.0
  legal execution E978
  self-inflicted (unspecified whether accidental or intentional) E983.0
    in accidental circumstances E913.8
    stated as intentional, purposeful E953.0
  stated as undetermined whether accidental
        or intentional E983.0
  suicidal (attempt) E953.0
Heat (apoplexy) (collapse) (cramps) (effects of)
        (excessive) (exhaustion) (fever) (prostration) (stroke) E900.9
  due to
    manmade conditions (as listed in E900.1,
        except boat, ship, watercraft)
        E900.1
    weather (conditions) E900.0
  from
    electric heating apparatus causing burning E924.8
    nuclear explosion
      in
        terrorism E979.5

Heat — *continued*
  from — *continued*
    nuclear explosion — *continued*
      in — *continued*
        war operations (*see also* War operations, injury due to, nuclear weapons) E996.2
    generated in, boiler, engine, evaporator, fire
        room of boat, ship, watercraft
        E838 ☑
    inappropriate in local application or packing
        in medical or surgical procedure
        E873.5
  late effect of NEC E989
Hemorrhage
  delayed following medical or surgical
        treatment without mention of misadventure — *see* Reaction, abnormal
  during medical or surgical treatment as
        misadventure — *see* Misadventure,
        cut
High
  altitude, effects E902.9
  level of radioactivity, effects — *see* Radiation
  pressure effects (*see also* Effects of, air pressure)
    from rapid descent in water (causing
        caisson or divers' disease, palsy,
        or paralysis) E902.2
  temperature, effects — *see* Heat
Hit, hitting (accidental) by
  aircraft (propeller) (without accident to aircraft) E844 ☑
    unpowered E842 ☑
  avalanche E909.2
  being thrown against object in or part of
        motor vehicle (in motion) (on public
        highway) E818 ☑
    not on public highway E825 ☑
    nonmotor road vehicle NEC E829 ☑
    street car E829 ☑
  boat, ship, watercraft
    after fall from watercraft E838 ☑
    damaged, involved in accident
        E831 ☑
    while swimming, water skiing E838 ☑
  bullet (*see also* Shooting) E922.9
    from air gun E922.4
    in
      terrorism E979.4
      war operations E991.2
        rubber E991.0
  flare, Verey pistol (*see also* Shooting) E922.8
  hailstones E904.3
  landslide E909.2
  law-enforcing agent (on duty) E975
    with blunt object (baton) (night stick)
        (stave) (truncheon) E973
  machine — *see* Accident, machine
  missile
    firearm (*see also* Shooting) E922.9
    in
      terrorism — *see* Terrorism, missile
      war operations — *see* War operations, missile
  motor vehicle (on public highway) (traffic
        accident) E814 ☑
    not on public highway, nontraffic accident E822 ☑
  nonmotor road vehicle NEC E829 ☑
  object
    falling E916
      from, in, on
        aircraft E844 ☑
          due to accident to aircraft —
              see categories
              E840–E842 ☑
          unpowered E842 ☑
        boat, ship, watercraft E838 ☑
          due to accident to watercraft
              E831 ☑
        building E916
          burning (uncontrolled fire)
              E891.8
            in terrorism E979.3

☑ **Additional Digit Required** — Refer to the Tabular List for Digit Selection   ᵀᴮˢ **Subterms under main terms may continue to next column or page**

Hit, hitting by — continued
object — continued
falling — continued
from, in, on — continued
building — continued
burning — continued
private E890.8
cataclysmic
earth surface movement or
eruption E909.9
storm E908.9
cave-in E916
with asphyxiation or suffoca-
tion (see also Suffocation, due to, cave-in)
E913.3
earthquake E909.0
motor vehicle (in motion) (on
public highway) E818 ☑
not on public highway
E825 ☑
stationary E916
nonmotor road vehicle NEC
E829 ☑
pedal cycle E826 ☑
railway rolling stock, train, vehicle
E806 ☑
street car E829 ☑
structure, burning NEC E891.8
vehicle, stationary E916
moving NEC — see Striking against, object
projected NEC — see Striking against,
object
set in motion by
compressed air or gas, spring, striking, throwing — see Striking
against, object
explosion — see Explosion
thrown into, on, or towards
motor vehicle (in motion) (on public
highway) E818 ☑
not on public highway E825 ☑
nonmotor road vehicle NEC E829 ☑
pedal cycle E826 ☑
street car E829 ☑
off-road type motor vehicle (not on public
highway) E821 ☑
on public highway E814 ☑
other person(s) E917.9
with blunt or thrown object E917.9
in sports E917.0
with subsequent fall E917.5
intentionally, homicidal E968.2
as, or caused by, a crowd E917.1
with subsequent fall E917.6
in sports E917.0
pedal cycle E826 ☑
police (on duty) E975
with blunt object (baton) (nightstick)
(stave) (truncheon) E973
railway, rolling stock, train, vehicle (part of)
E805 ☑
shot — see Shooting
snow vehicle, motor-driven (not on public
highway) E820 ☑
on public highway E814 ☑
street car E829 ☑
vehicle NEC — see Accident, vehicle NEC
Homicide, homicidal (attempt) (justifiable) —
see also Assault E968.9
Hot
liquid, object, substance, accident caused
by (see also Accident, caused by, hot,
by type of substance)
late effect of E929.8
place, effects — see Heat
weather, effects E900.0
Humidity, causing problem E904.3
Hunger E904.1
resulting from
abandonment or neglect E904.0
transport accident — see categories
E800-E848
Hurricane (any injury) E908.0

Hypobarism, hypobaropathy — see Effects
of, air pressure
Hypothermia — see Cold, exposure to

Ictus
caloris — see Heat
solaris E900.0
Ignition (accidental)
anesthetic gas in operating theatre E923.2
bedclothes
with
conflagration — see Conflagration
ignition (of)
clothing — see Ignition, clothes
highly inflammable material
(benzine) (fat) (gasoline)
(kerosene) (paraffin)
(petrol) E894
benzine E894
clothes, clothing (from controlled fire) (in
building) E893.9
with conflagration — see Conflagration
from
bonfire E893.2
highly inflammable material E894
sources or material as listed in E893.8
trash fire E893.2
uncontrolled fire — see Conflagration
in
private dwelling E893.0
specified building or structure, except private dwelling E893.1
not in building or structure E893.2
explosive material — see Explosion
fat E894
gasoline E894
kerosene E894
material
explosive — see Explosion
highly inflammable E894
with conflagration — see Conflagration
with explosion E923.2
nightdress — see Ignition, clothes
paraffin E894
petrol E894
Immersion — see Submersion
Implantation of quills of porcupine E906.8
Inanition (from) E904.9
hunger — see Lack of, food
resulting from homicidal intent E968.4
thirst — see Lack of, water
Inattention after, at birth E904.0
homicidal, infanticidal intent E968.4
Infanticide — see also Assault
Ingestion
foreign body (causing injury) (with obstruction) — see Foreign body, alimentary
canal
poisonous substance NEC — see Table of
Drugs and Chemicals
Inhalation
excessively cold substance, manmade
E901.1
foreign body — see Foreign body, aspiration
liquid air, hydrogen, nitrogen E901.1
mucus, not of newborn (with asphyxia, obstruction respiratory passage, suffocation) E912
phlegm (with asphyxia, obstruction respiratory passage, suffocation) E912
poisonous gas — see Table of Drugs and
Chemicals
smoke from, due to
fire — see Fire
tobacco, second-hand E869.4
vomitus (with asphyxia, obstruction respiratory passage, suffocation) E911
Injury, injured (accidental(ly)) NEC E928.9
by, caused by, from
air rifle (BB gun) E922.4
animal (not being ridden) NEC E906.9
being ridden (in sport or transport)
E828 ☑

Injury, injured — continued
by, caused by, from — continued
assault (see also Assault) E968.9
avalanche E909.2
bayonet (see also Bayonet wound)
E920.3
being thrown against some part of, or
object in
motor vehicle (in motion) (on public
highway) E818 ☑
not on public highway E825 ☑
nonmotor road vehicle NEC E829 ☑
off-road motor vehicle NEC E821 ☑
railway train E806 ☑
snow vehicle, motor-driven E820 ☑
street car E829 ☑
bending
due to
repetitive movement E927.3
sudden strenuous movement
E927.0
bite, human E928.3
broken glass E920.8
bullet — see Shooting
cave-in (see also Suffocation, due to,
cave-in) E913.3
without asphyxiation or suffocation
E916
earth surface movement or eruption
E909.9
storm E908.9
cloudburst E908.8
component of firearm or air gun E928.7
cutting or piercing instrument (see also
Cut) E920.9
cyclone E908.1
earthquake E909.0
earth surface movement or eruption
E909.9
electric current (see also Electric shock)
E925.9
explosion (see also Explosion) E923.9
of gun part E928.7
fire — see Fire
flare, Verey pistol E922.8
flood E908.2
foreign body — see Foreign body
gun recoil E928.7
hailstones E904.3
hurricane E908.0
landslide E909.2
law-enforcing agent, police, in course of
legal intervention — see Legal
intervention
lightning E907
live rail or live wire — see Electric shock
machinery (see also Accident, machine)
aircraft, without accident to aircraft
E844 ☑
boat, ship, watercraft (deck) (engine
room) (galley) (laundry)
(loading) E836 ☑
mechanism of firearm or air gun E928.7
missile
explosive E923.8
firearm — see Shooting
in
terrorism — see Terrorism, missile
war operations — see War operations, missile
moving part of motor vehicle (in motion)
(on public highway) E818 ☑
not on public highway, nontraffic
accident E825 ☑
while alighting, boarding, entering,
leaving — see Fall, from, motor vehicle, while alighting,
boarding
nail E920.8
needle (sewing) E920.4
hypodermic E920.5
noise E928.1

Injury, injured — continued
by, caused by, from — continued
object
fallen on
motor vehicle (in motion) (on
public highway) E818 ☑
not on public highway
E825 ☑
falling — see Hit by, object, falling
paintball gun E922.5
radiation — see Radiation
railway rolling stock, train, vehicle (part
of) E805 ☑
door or window E806 ☑
recoil of firearm E928.7
rotating propeller, aircraft E844 ☑
rough landing of off-road type motor
vehicle (after leaving ground or
rough terrain) E821 ☑
snow vehicle E820 ☑
saber (see also Wound, saber) E920.3
shot — see Shooting
sound waves E928.1
splinter or sliver, wood E920.8
straining
due to
repetitive movement E927.3
sudden strenuous movement
E927.0
street car (door) E829 ☑
suicide (attempt) E958.9
sword E920.3
terrorism — see Terrorism
third rail — see Electric shock
thunderbolt E907
tidal wave E909.4
caused by storm E908.0
tornado E908.1
torrential rain E908.2
twisting
due to
repetitive movement E927.3
sudden strenuous movement
E927.0
vehicle NEC — see Accident, vehicle NEC
vibration E928.2
volcanic eruption E909.1
weapon burst, in war operations E993.9
weightlessness (in spacecraft, real or
simulated) E928.0
wood splinter or sliver E920.8
due to
civil insurrection — see War operations
occurring after cessation of hostilities
E998.9
terrorism — see Terrorism
war operations — see War operations
occurring after cessation of hostilities
E998.9
weapon of mass destruction [WMD]
E997.3
homicidal (see also Assault) E968.9
inflicted (by)
in course of arrest (attempted), suppression of disturbance, maintenance
of order, by law enforcing agents
— see Legal intervention
law-enforcing agent (on duty) — see
Legal intervention
other person
stated as
accidental E928.9
homicidal, intentional — see Assault
undetermined whether accidental or intentional — see
Injury, stated as undetermined
police (on duty) — see Legal intervention
in, on
civil insurrection — see War operations
fight E960.0
parachute descent (voluntary) (without
accident to aircraft) E844 ☑

☑ Additional Digit Required — Refer to the Tabular List for Digit Selection   ▽ Subterms under main terms may continue to next column or page

344 — Volume 2   ▶◀ Revised Text   ● New Line   ▲ Revised Code   2015 ICD-9-CM

Injury, injured — *continued*
in, on — *continued*
parachute descent — *continued*
with accident to aircraft — *see* categories E840-E842 ☑
public highway E819 ☑
railway right of way E807 ☑
terrorism — *see* Terrorism
war operations — *see* War operations
late effect of E929.9
purposely (inflicted) by other person(s) — *see* Assault
self-inflicted (unspecified whether accidental or intentional) E988.9
stated as
accidental E928.9
intentionally, purposely E958.9
specified cause NEC E928.8
stated as
hanging E983.0
knife E986
late effect of E989
puncture (any part of body) E986
shooting — *see* Shooting, stated as undetermined whether accidental or intentional
specified means NEC E988.8
stab (any part of body) E986
strangulation — *see* Suffocation, stated as undetermined whether accidental or intentional
submersion E984
suffocation — *see* Suffocation, stated as undetermined whether accidental or intentional
undetermined whether accidentally or purposely inflicted (by) E988.9
cut (any part of body) E986
cutting or piercing instrument (classifiable to E920) E986
drowning E984
explosive(s) (missile) E985.5
falling from high place E987.9
manmade structure, except residential E987.1
natural site E987.2
residential premises E987.0
to child due to criminal abortion E968.8
Insufficient nourishment — *see also* Lack of, food
homicidal intent E968.4
Insulation, effects — *see* Heat
Interruption of respiration by
food lodged in esophagus E911
foreign body, except food, in esophagus E912
Intervention, legal — *see* Legal intervention
Intoxication, drug or poison — *see* Table of Drugs and Chemicals
Irradiation — *see* Radiation

J

Jammed (accidentally)
between objects (moving) (stationary and moving) E918
in object E918
Jumped or fell from high place, so stated — *see* Jumping, from, high place, stated as in undetermined circumstances
Jumping
before train, vehicle or other moving object (unspecified whether accidental or intentional) E988.0
stated as
intentional, purposeful E958.0
suicidal (attempt) E958.0
from
aircraft
by parachute (voluntarily) (without accident to aircraft) E844 ☑
due to accident to aircraft — *see* categories E840-E842 ☑
boat, ship, watercraft (into water)
after accident to, fire on, watercraft E830 ☑

Jumping — *continued*
from — *continued*
boat, ship, watercraft — *continued*
after accident to, fire on, watercraft — *continued*
and subsequently struck by (part of) boat E831 ☑
burning, crushed, sinking E830 ☑
and subsequently struck by (part of) boat E831 ☑
voluntarily, without accident (to boat) with injury other than drowning or submersion E883.0
building (*see also* Jumping, from, high place)
burning (uncontrolled fire) E891.8
in terrorism E979.3
private E890.8
cable car (not on rails) E847
on rails E829 ☑
high place
in accidental circumstances or in sport — *see* categories E880-E884 ☑
stated as
with intent to injure self E957.9
man-made structures NEC E957.1
natural sites E957.2
residential premises E957.0
in undetermined circumstances E987.9
man-made structures NEC E987.1
natural sites E987.2
residential premises E987.0
suicidal (attempt) E957.9
man-made structures NEC E957.1
natural sites E957.1
residential premises E957.0
motor vehicle (in motion) (on public highway) — *see* Fall, from, motor vehicle
nonmotor road vehicle NEC E829 ☑
street car E829 ☑
structure (*see also* Jumping, from, high place)
burning NEC (uncontrolled fire) E891.8
in terrorism E979.3
into water
with injury other than drowning or submersion E883.0
drowning or submersion — *see* Submersion
from, off, watercraft — *see* Jumping, from, boat
Justifiable homicide — *see* Assault

K

Kicked by
animal E906.8
person(s) (accidentally) E917.9
with intent to injure or kill E960.0
as, or caused by a crowd E917.1
with subsequent fall E917.6
in fight E960.0
in sports E917.0
with subsequent fall E917.5
Kicking against
object (moving) E917.9
in sports E917.0
with subsequent fall E917.5
stationary E917.4
with subsequent fall E917.8
person — *see* Striking against, person
Killed, killing (accidentally) NEC — *see also* Injury E928.9
in
action — *see* War operations
brawl, fight (hand) (fists) (foot) E960.0
by weapon (*see also* Assault)
cutting, piercing E966
firearm — *see* Shooting, homicide

Killed, killing — *see also* Injury — *continued*
self
stated as
accident E928.9
suicide — *see* Suicide
unspecified whether accidental or suicidal E988.9
Knocked down (accidentally) (by) NEC E928.9
animal (not being ridden) E906.8
being ridden (in sport or transport) E828 ☑
blast from explosion (*see also* Explosion) E923.9
crowd, human stampede E917.6
late effect of — *see* Late effect
person (accidentally) E917.9
in brawl, fight E960.0
in sports E917.5
transport vehicle — *see* vehicle involved under Hit by
while boxing E917.5

L

Laceration NEC E928.9
Lack of
air (refrigerator or closed place), suffocation by E913.2
care (helpless person) (infant) (newborn) E904.0
homicidal intent E968.4
food except as result of transport accident E904.1
helpless person, infant, newborn due to abandonment or neglect E904.0
water except as result of transport accident E904.2
helpless person, infant, newborn due to abandonment or neglect E904.0
Landslide E909.2
falling on, hitting
motor vehicle (any) (in motion) (on or off public highway) E909.2
railway rolling stock, train, vehicle E909.2
Late effect of
accident NEC (accident classifiable to E928.9) E929.9
specified NEC (accident classifiable to E910–E928.8) E929.8
assault E969
fall, accidental (accident classifiable to E880–E888) E929.3
fire, accident caused by (accident classifiable to E890–E899) E929.4
homicide, attempt (any means) E969
injury due to terrorism E999.1
injury undetermined whether accidentally or purposely inflicted (injury classifiable to E980–E988) E989
legal intervention (injury classifiable to E970–E976) E977
medical or surgical procedure, test or therapy
as, or resulting in, or from
abnormal or delayed reaction or complication — *see* Reaction, abnormal
misadventure — *see* Misadventure
motor vehicle accident (accident classifiable to E810–E825) E929.0
natural or environmental factor, accident due to (accident classifiable to E900–E909) E929.5
poisoning, accidental (accident classifiable to E850–E858, E860–E869) E929.2
suicide, attempt (any means) E959
transport accident NEC (accident classifiable to E800–E807, E826–E838, E840–E848) E929.1
war operations, injury due to (injury classifiable to E990–E998) E999.0
Launching pad accident E845 ☑
Legal
execution, any method E978
intervention (by) (injury from) E976
baton E973

Legal — *continued*
intervention — *continued*
bayonet E974
blow E975
blunt object (baton) (nightstick) (stave) (truncheon) E973
cutting or piercing instrument E974
dynamite E971
execution, any method E973
explosive(s) (shell) E971
firearm(s) E970
gas (asphyxiation) (poisoning) (tear) E972
grenade E971
late effect of E977
machine gun E970
manhandling E975
mortar bomb E971
nightstick E973
revolver E970
rifle E970
specified means NEC E975
stabbing E974
stave E973
truncheon E973
Lifting, injury
due to
repetitive movement E927.3
sudden strenuous movement E927.0
Lightning (shock) (stroke) (struck by) E907
Liquid (noncorrosive) in eye E914
corrosive E924.1
Loss of control
motor vehicle (on public highway) (without antecedent collision) E816 ☑
with
antecedent collision on public highway — *see* Collision, motor vehicle
involving any object, person or vehicle not on public highway E816 ☑
not on public highway, nontraffic accident E825 ☑
with antecedent collision — *see* Collision, motor vehicle, not on public highway
on public highway — *see* Collision, motor vehicle
off-road type motor vehicle (not on public highway) E821 ☑
on public highway — *see* Loss of control, motor vehicle
snow vehicle, motor-driven (not on public highway) E820 ☑
on public highway — *see* Loss of control, motor vehicle
Lost at sea E832 ☑
with accident to watercraft E830 ☑
in war operations E995.8
Low
pressure, effects — *see* Effects of, air pressure
temperature, effects — *see* Cold, exposure to
Lying before train, vehicle or other moving object (unspecified whether accidental or intentional) E988.0
stated as intentional, purposeful, suicidal (attempt) E958.0
Lynching — *see also* Assault E968.9

M

Malfunction, atomic power plant in water transport E838 ☑
Mangled (accidentally) NEC E928.9
Manhandling (in brawl, fight) E960.0
legal intervention E975
Manslaughter (nonaccidental) — *see* Assault
Marble in nose E912
Mauled by animal E906.8
Medical procedure, complication of
delayed or as an abnormal reaction without mention of misadventure — *see* Reaction, abnormal

---

Medical procedure, complication of — *continued*
  due to or as a result of misadventure — *see* Misadventure

Melting of fittings and furniture in burning
  in terrorism E979.3

Minamata disease E865.2

Misadventure(s) to patient(s) during surgical or medical care E876.9
  contaminated blood, fluid, drug or biological substance (presence of agents and toxins as listed in E875) E875.9
    administered (by) NEC E875.9
      infusion E875.0
      injection E875.1
      specified means NEC E875.2
      transfusion E875.0
      vaccination E875.1
  cut, cutting, puncture, perforation or hemorrhage (accidental) (inadvertent) (inappropriate) (during) E870.9
    aspiration of fluid or tissue (by puncture or catheterization, except heart) E870.5
    biopsy E870.8
      needle (aspirating) E870.5
    blood sampling E870.5
    catheterization E870.5
      heart E870.6
    dialysis (kidney) E870.2
    endoscopic examination E870.4
    enema E870.7
    infusion E870.1
    injection E870.3
    lumbar puncture E870.5
    needle biopsy E870.5
    paracentesis, abdominal E870.5
    perfusion E870.2
    specified procedure NEC E870.8
    surgical operation E870.0
    thoracentesis E870.5
    transfusion E870.1
    vaccination E870.3
  excessive amount of blood or other fluid during transfusion or infusion E873.0
  failure
    in dosage E873.9
      electroshock therapy E873.4
      inappropriate temperature (too hot or too cold) in local application and packing E873.5
      infusion
        excessive amount of fluid E873.0
        incorrect dilution of fluid E873.1
      insulin-shock therapy E873.4
      nonadministration of necessary drug or medicinal E873.6
      overdose (*see also* Overdose)
        radiation, in therapy E873.2
      radiation
        inadvertent exposure of patient (receiving radiation for test or therapy) E873.3
        not receiving radiation for test or therapy — *see* Radiation
        overdose E873.2
      specified procedure NEC E873.8
      transfusion
        excessive amount of blood E873.0
    mechanical, of instrument or apparatus (during procedure) E874.9
      aspiration of fluid or tissue (by puncture or catheterization, except of heart) E874.4
      biopsy E874.8
        needle (aspirating) E874.4
      blood sampling E874.4
      catheterization E874.4
        heart E874.5
      dialysis (kidney) E874.2
      endoscopic examination E874.3
      enema E874.8
      infusion E874.1
      injection E874.8
      lumbar puncture E874.4

Misadventure(s) to patient(s) during surgical or medical care — *continued*
  failure — *continued*
    mechanical, of instrument or apparatus — *continued*
      needle biopsy E874.4
      paracentesis, abdominal E874.4
      perfusion E874.2
      specified procedure NEC E874.8
      surgical operation E874.0
      thoracentesis E874.4
      transfusion E874.1
      vaccination E874.8
    sterile precautions (during procedure) E872.9
      aspiration of fluid or tissue (by puncture or catheterization, except heart) E872.5
      biopsy E872.8
        needle (aspirating) E872.5
      blood sampling E872.5
      catheterization E872.5
        heart E872.6
      dialysis (kidney) E872.2
      endoscopic examination E872.4
      enema E872.8
      infusion E872.1
      injection E872.3
      lumbar puncture E872.5
      needle biopsy E872.5
      paracentesis, abdominal E872.5
      perfusion E872.2
      removal of catheter or packing E872.8
      specified procedure NEC E872.8
      surgical operation E872.0
      thoracentesis E872.5
      transfusion E872.1
      vaccination E872.3
    suture or ligature during surgical procedure E876.2
    to introduce or to remove tube or instrument E876.4
    foreign object left in body — *see* Misadventure, foreign object
  foreign object left in body (during procedure) E871.9
    aspiration of fluid or tissue (by puncture or catheterization, except heart) E871.5
    biopsy E871.8
      needle (aspirating) E871.5
    blood sampling E871.5
    catheterization E871.5
      heart E871.6
    dialysis (kidney) E871.2
    endoscopic examination E871.4
    enema E871.8
    infusion E871.1
    injection E871.3
    lumbar puncture E871.5
    needle biopsy E871.5
    paracentesis, abdominal E871.5
    perfusion E871.2
    removal of catheter or packing E871.7
    specified procedure NEC E871.8
    surgical operation E871.0
    thoracentesis E871.5
    transfusion E871.1
    vaccination E871.3
  hemorrhage — *see* Misadventure, cut
  inadvertent exposure of patient to radiation (being received for test or therapy) E873.3
  inappropriate
    temperature (too hot or too cold) in local application or packing E873.5
  infusion (*see also* Misadventure, by specific type, infusion)
    excessive amount of fluid E873.0
    incorrect dilution of fluid E873.1
    wrong fluid E876.1
  mismatched blood in transfusion E876.0
  nonadministration of necessary drug or medicinal E873.6
  overdose (*see also* Overdose)

Misadventure(s) to patient(s) during surgical or medical care — *continued*
  overdose (*see also* Overdose) — *continued*
    radiation, in therapy E873.2
  perforation — *see* Misadventure, cut
  performance of correct operation (procedure) on wrong
    body part E876.7
    side E876.7
    site E876.7
  performance of operation (procedure)
    intended for another patient E876.6
    on patient not scheduled for surgery E876.6
    on wrong patient E876.6
  performance of wrong operation on correct patient E876.5
  puncture — *see* Misadventure, cut
  specified type NEC E876.8
    failure
      suture or ligature during surgical operation E876.2
      to introduce or to remove tube or instrument E876.4
      foreign object left in body E871.9
    infusion of wrong fluid E876.1
    performance of inappropriate operation E876.5
    transfusion of mismatched blood E876.0
    wrong
      fluid in infusion E876.1
      placement of endotracheal tube during anesthetic procedure E876.3
  transfusion (*see also* Misadventure, by specific type, transfusion)
    excessive amount of blood E873.0
    mismatched blood E876.0
  wrong
    device implanted into correct surgical site E876.5
    drug given in error — *see* Table of Drugs and Chemicals
    fluid in infusion E876.1
    placement of endotracheal tube during anesthetic procedure E876.3
    procedure (operation) performed on the correct patient E876.5

Motion (effects) E903
  sickness E903

Mountain sickness E902.0

Mucus aspiration or inhalation, not of newborn (with asphyxia, obstruction respiratory passage, suffocation) E912

Mudslide of cataclysmic nature E909.2

Murder (attempt) — *see also* Assault E968.9

N

Nail, injury by E920.8

Needlestick (sewing needle) E920.4
  hypodermic E920.5

Neglect — *see also* Privation
  criminal E968.4
  homicidal intent E968.4

Noise (causing injury) (pollution) E928.1

Nuclear weapon — *see also* War operations, injury due to, nuclear weapons E996.9

O

Object
  falling
    from, in, on, hitting
      aircraft E844 ☑
        due to accident to aircraft — *see* categories E840-E842 ☑
      machinery (*see also* Accident, machine)
        not in operation E916
      motor vehicle (in motion) (on public highway) E818 ☑
        nonmotor road vehicle NEC E829 ☑
        not on public highway E825 ☑
        pedal cycle E826 ☑

Object — *continued*
  falling — *continued*
    from, in, on, hitting — *continued*
      motor vehicle — *continued*
        person E916
        railway rolling stock, train, vehicle E806 ☑
        stationary E916
        street car E829 ☑
        watercraft E838 ☑
          due to accident to watercraft E831 ☑
  set in motion by
    accidental explosion of pressure vessel — *see* category E921 ☑
    firearm — *see* category E922 ☑
    machine(ry) — *see* Accident, machine
    transport vehicle — *see* categories E800-E848 ☑
  thrown from, in, on, towards
    aircraft E844 ☑
    cable car (not on rails) E847
      on rails E829 ☑
    motor vehicle (in motion) (on public highway) E818 ☑
      not on public highway E825 ☑
    nonmotor road vehicle NEC E829 ☑
    pedal cycle E826 ☑
    street car E829 ☑
    vehicle NEC — *see* Accident, vehicle NEC

Obstruction
  air passages, larynx, respiratory passages
    by
      external means NEC — *see* Suffocation
      food, any type (regurgitated) (vomited) E911
      material or object, except food E912
      mucus E912
      phlegm E912
      vomitus E911
  digestive tract, except mouth or pharynx
    by
      food, any type E915
      foreign body (any) E915
  esophagus
    without asphyxia or obstruction of respiratory passage E915
    food E911
    foreign body, except food E912
  mouth or pharynx
    by
      food, any type E911
      material or object, except food E912
  respiration — *see* Obstruction, air passages

Oil in eye E914

Overdose
  anesthetic (drug) — *see* Table of Drugs and Chemicals
  drug — *see* Table of Drugs and Chemicals

Overexertion E927.9
  from
    lifting
      repetitive movement E927.3
      sudden strenuous movement E927.0
    maintaining prolonged positions E927.1
      holding E927.1
      sitting E927.1
      standing E927.1
    prolonged static position E927.1
    pulling
      repetitive movement E927.3
      sudden strenuous movement E927.0
    pushing
      repetitive movement E927.3
      sudden strenuous movement E927.0
    specified NEC E927.8
    sudden strenuous movement E927.0

Overexposure (accidental) (to)
  cold (*see also* Cold, exposure to) E901.9
    due to manmade conditions E901.1
  heat (*see also* Heat) E900.9
  radiation — *see* Radiation
  radioactivity — *see* Radiation
  sun, except sunburn E900.0
  weather — *see* Exposure

☑ **Additional Digit Required** — Refer to the Tabular List for Digit Selection   ▽ **Subterms under main terms may continue to next column or page**

Reaction, abnormal to or following — *continued*
  transplant, transplantation — *continued*
    partial organ E878.4
  ureterostomy E878.3
  vaccination E879.8
Reduction in
  atmospheric pressure (*see also* Effects of, air pressure)
    while surfacing from
      deep water diving causing caisson or divers' disease, palsy or paralysis E902.2
    underground E902.8
Repetitive movements NEC E927.8
Residual (effect) — *see* Late effect
Rock falling on or hitting (accidentally)
  motor vehicle (in motion) (on public highway) E818 ☑
    not on public highway E825 ☑
  nonmotor road vehicle NEC E829 ☑
  pedal cycle E826 ☑
  person E916
  railway rolling stock, train, vehicle E806 ☑
Running off, away
  animal (being ridden) (in sport or transport) E828 ☑
    not being ridden E906.8
  animal-drawn vehicle E827 ☑
  rails, railway (*see also* Derailment) E802 ☑
  roadway
    motor vehicle (without antecedent collision) E816 ☑
      with
        antecedent collision — *see* Collision motor vehicle
        subsequent collision
          involving any object, person or vehicle not on public highway E816 ☑
          on public highway E811 ☑
    nontraffic accident E825 ☑
      with antecedent collision — *see* Collision, motor vehicle, not on public highway
    nonmotor road vehicle NEC E829 ☑
    pedal cycle E826 ☑
Run over (accidentally) (by)
  animal (not being ridden) E906.8
    being ridden (in sport or transport) E828 ☑
  animal-drawn vehicle E827 ☑
  machinery — *see* Accident, machine
  motor vehicle (on public highway) — *see* Hit by, motor vehicle
  nonmotor road vehicle NEC E829 ☑
  railway train E805 ☑
  street car E829 ☑
  vehicle NEC E848

S

Saturnism E866.0
  from insecticide NEC E863.4
Scald, scalding (accidental) (by) (from) (in) E924.0
  acid — *see* Scald, caustic
  boiling tap water E924.2
  caustic or corrosive liquid, substance E924.1
    swallowed — *see* Table of Drugs and Chemicals
  homicide (attempt) — *see* Assault, burning
  inflicted by other person
    stated as
      intentional or homicidal E968.3
      undetermined whether accidental or intentional E988.2
  late effect of NEC E929.8
  liquid (boiling) (hot) E924.0
  local application of externally applied substance in medical or surgical care E873.5
  molten metal E924.0
  self-inflicted (unspecified whether accidental or intentional) E988.2
    stated as intentional, purposeful E958.2

Scald, scalding — *continued*
  stated as undetermined whether accidental or intentional E988.2
  steam E924.0
  tap water (boiling) E924.2
  transport accident — *see* categories E800-E848 ☑
  vapor E924.0
Scratch, cat E906.8
Sea
  sickness E903
Self-mutilation — *see* Suicide
Sequelae (of)
  in
    terrorism E999.1
    war operations E999.0
Shock
  anaphylactic (*see also* Table of Drugs and Chemicals) E947.9
    due to
      bite (venomous) — *see* Bite, venomous NEC
      sting — *see* Sting
  electric (*see also* Electric shock) E925.9
  from electric appliance or current (*see also* Electric shock) E925.9
Shooting, shot (accidental(ly)) E922.9
  air gun E922.4
  BB gun E922.4
  hand gun (pistol) (revolver) E922.0
  himself (*see also* Shooting, self-inflicted) E985.4
    hand gun (pistol) (revolver) E985.0
    military firearm, except hand gun E985.3
      hand gun (pistol) (revolver) E985.0
    rifle (hunting) E985.2
      military E985.3
    shotgun (automatic) E985.1
    specified firearm NEC E985.4
    Verey pistol E985.4
  homicide (attempt) E965.4
    air gun E968.6
    BB gun E968.6
    hand gun (pistol) (revolver) E965.0
    military firearm, except hand gun E965.3
      hand gun (pistol) (revolver) E965.0
    paintball gun E965.4
    rifle (hunting) E965.2
      military E965.3
    shotgun (automatic) E965.1
    specified firearm NEC E965.4
    Verey pistol E965.4
  in
    terrorism — *see* Terrorism, shooting
    war operations — *see* War operations, shooting
  inflicted by other person
    in accidental circumstances E922.9
      hand gun (pistol) (revolver) E922.0
      military firearm, except hand gun E922.3
        hand gun (pistol) (revolver) E922.0
      rifle (hunting) E922.2
        military E922.3
      shotgun (automatic) E922.1
      specified firearm NEC E922.8
      Verey pistol E922.8
    stated as
      intentional, homicidal E965.4
        hand gun (pistol) (revolver) E965.0
        military firearm, except hand gun E965.3
          hand gun (pistol) (revolver) E965.0
        paintball gun E965.4
        rifle (hunting) E965.2
          military E965.3
        shotgun (automatic) E965.1
        specified firearm E965.4
        Verey pistol E965.4
      undetermined whether accidental or intentional E985.4
        air gun E985.6
        BB gun E985.6

Shooting, shot — *continued*
  inflicted by other person — *continued*
    stated as — *continued*
      undetermined whether accidental or intentional — *continued*
        hand gun (pistol) (revolver) E985.0
        military firearm, except hand gun E985.3
          hand gun (pistol) (revolver) E985.0
        paintball gun E985.7
        rifle (hunting) E985.2
        shotgun (automatic) E985.1
        specified firearm NEC E985.4
        Verey pistol E985.4
  legal
    execution E978
    intervention E970
  military firearm, except hand gun E922.3
    hand gun (pistol) (revolver) E922.0
  paintball gun E922.5
  rifle (hunting) E922.2
    military E922.3
  self-inflicted (unspecified whether accidental or intentional) E985.4
    air gun E985.6
    BB gun E985.6
    hand gun (pistol) (revolver) E985.0
    military firearm, except hand gun E985.3
      hand gun (pistol) (revolver) E985.0
    paintball gun E985.7
    rifle (hunting) E985.2
      military E985.3
    shotgun (automatic) E985.1
    specified firearm NEC E985.4
    stated as
      accidental E922.9
        hand gun (pistol) (revolver) E922.0
        military firearm, except hand gun E922.3
          hand gun (pistol) (revolver) E922.0
        paintball gun E922.5
        rifle (hunting) E922.2
          military E922.3
        shotgun (automatic) E922.1
        specified firearm NEC E922.8
        Verey pistol E922.8
      intentional, purposeful E955.4
        hand gun (pistol) (revolver) E955.0
        military firearm, except hand gun E955.3
          hand gun (pistol) (revolver) E955.0
        paintball gun E955.7
        rifle (hunting) E955.2
          military E955.3
        shotgun (automatic) E955.1
        specified firearm NEC E955.4
        Verey pistol E955.4
  shotgun (automatic) E922.1
  specified firearm NEC E922.8
  stated as undetermined whether accidental or intentional E985.4
    hand gun (pistol) (revolver) E985.0
    military firearm, except hand gun E985.3
      hand gun (pistol) (revolver) E985.0
    paintball gun E985.7
    rifle (hunting) E985.2
      military E985.3
    shotgun (automatic) E985.1
    specified firearm NEC E985.4
    Verey pistol E985.4
  suicidal (attempt) E955.4
    air gun E955.6
    BB gun E955.6
    hand gun (pistol) (revolver) E955.0
    military firearm, except hand gun E955.3
      hand gun (pistol) (revolver) E955.0
    paintball gun E955.7
    rifle (hunting) E955.2
      military E955.3
    shotgun (automatic) E955.1

Shooting, shot — *continued*
  suicidal — *continued*
    specified firearm NEC E955.4
    Verey pistol E955.4
Shoving (accidentally) by other person — *see also* Pushing by other person E917.9
Sickness
  air E903
  alpine E902.0
  car E903
  motion E903
  mountain E902.0
  sea E903
  travel E903
Sinking (accidental)
  boat, ship, watercraft (causing drowning, submersion) E830 ☑
    causing injury except drowning, submersion E831 ☑
Siriasis E900.0
Skydiving E844 ☑
Slashed wrists — *see also* Cut, self-inflicted E986
Slipping (accidental)
  on
    deck (of boat, ship, watercraft) (icy) (oily) (wet) E835 ☑
    ice E885.9
    ladder of ship E833 ☑
      due to accident to watercraft E831 ☑
    mud E885.9
    oil E885.9
    snow E885.9
    stairs of ship E833 ☑
      due to accident to watercraft E831 ☑
    surface
      slippery E885 ☑
      wet E885 ☑
Sliver, wood, injury by E920.8
Smothering, smothered — *see also* Suffocation E913.9
Smouldering building or structure in terrorism E979.3
Sodomy (assault) E960.1
Solid substance in eye (any part) or adnexa E914
Sound waves (causing injury) E928.1
Splinter, injury by E920.8
Stab, stabbing E966
  accidental — *see* Cut
Starvation E904.1
  helpless person, infant, newborn — *see* Lack of food
  homicidal intent E968.4
  late effect of NEC E929.5
  resulting from accident connected with transport — *see* categories E800-E848 ☑
Stepped on
  by
    animal (not being ridden) E906.8
      being ridden (in sport or transport) E828 ☑
    crowd E917.1
    person E917.9
      in sports E917.0
  in sports E917.0
Stepping on
  object (moving) E917.9
    in sports E917.0
      with subsequent fall E917.5
    stationary E917.4
      with subsequent fall E917.8
  person E917.9
    as, or caused by a crowd E917.1
      with subsequent fall E917.6
    in sports E917.0
Sting E905.9
  ant E905.5
  bee E905.3
  caterpillar E905.5
  coral E905.6
  hornet E905.3

☑ **Additional Digit Required** — Refer to the Tabular List for Digit Selection ▼ **Subterms under main terms may continue to next column or page**

Sting — *continued*
  insect NEC E905.5
  jellyfish E905.6
  marine animal or plant E905.6
  nematocysts E905.6
  scorpion E905.2
  sea anemone E905.6
  sea cucumber E905.6
  wasp E905.3
  yellow jacket E905.3
Storm E908.9
  specified type NEC E908.8
Straining, injury
  due to
    repetitive movement E927.3
    sudden strenuous movement E927.0
Strangling — *see* Suffocation
Strangulation — *see* Suffocation
Strenuous movements (in recreational or
  other activities) NEC E927.8
Striking against
  bottom (when jumping or diving into water)
    E883.0
  object (moving) E917.9
    caused by crowd E917.1
      with subsequent fall E917.6
    furniture E917.3
      with subsequent fall E917.7
    in
      running water E917.2
        with drowning or submersion —
          see Submersion
      sports E917.0
        with subsequent fall E917.5
    stationary E917.4
      with subsequent fall E917.8
  person(s) E917.9
    with fall E886.9
      in sports E886.0
    as, or caused by, a crowd E917.1
      with subsequent fall E917.6
      in sports E917.0
        with fall E886.0
Stroke
  heat — *see* Heat
  lightning E907
Struck by — *see also* Hit by
  bullet
    in
      terrorism E979.4
      war operations E991.2
        rubber E991.0
  lightning E907
  missile
    in terrorism — *see* Terrorism, missile
  object
    falling
      from, in, on
        building
          burning (uncontrolled fire)
            in terrorism E979.3
  thunderbolt E907
**Stumbling over animal, carpet, curb, rug or
  (small) object (with fall)** E885.9
  without fall — *see* Striking against, object
Submersion (accidental) E910.8
  boat, ship, watercraft (causing drowning,
    submersion) E830 ☑
    causing injury except drowning, submer-
      sion E831 ☑
  by other person
    in accidental circumstances — *see* cate-
      gory E910 ☑
    intentional, homicidal E964
    stated as undetermined whether acciden-
      tal or intentional E984
  due to
    accident
      machinery — *see* Accident, machine
      to boat, ship, watercraft E830 ☑
      transport — *see* categories
        E800-E848 ☑
    avalanche E909.2
    cataclysmic
      earth surface movement or eruption
        E909.9

Submersion (accidental) — *continued*
  due to — *continued*
    cataclysmic — *continued*
      storm E908.9
    cloudburst E908.8
    cyclone E908.1
    fall
      from
        boat, ship, watercraft (not in-
          volved in accident)
          E832 ☑
          burning, crushed E830 ☑
          involved in accident, collision
            E830 ☑
        gangplank (into water) E832 ☑
        overboard NEC E832 ☑
    flood E908.2
    hurricane E908.0
    jumping into water E910.8
      from boat, ship, watercraft
        burning, crushed, sinking E830 ☑
        involved in accident, collision
          E830 ☑
        not involved in accident, for swim
          E910.2
      in recreational activity (without div-
        ing equipment) E910.2
        with or using diving equipment
          E910.1
      to rescue another person E910.3
  in
    bathtub E910.4
    specified activity, not sport, transport or
      recreational E910.3
    sport or recreational activity (without
      diving equipment) E910.2
      with or using diving equipment
        E910.1
      water skiing E910.0
    swimming pool NEC E910.8
    terrorism E979.8
    war operations E995.4
      intentional E995.3
    water transport E832 ☑
      due to accident to boat, ship, water-
        craft E830 ☑
  landslide E909.2
    overturning boat, ship, watercraft E909.2
    sinking boat, ship, watercraft E909.2
    submersion boat, ship, watercraft E909.2
    tidal wave E909.4
      caused by storm E908.0
    torrential rain E908.2
  late effect of NEC E929.8
  quenching tank E910.8
  self-inflicted (unspecified whether acciden-
    tal or intentional) E984
    in accidental circumstances — *see* cate-
      gory E910 ☑
    stated as intentional, purposeful E954
    stated as undetermined whether accidental
      or intentional E984
  suicidal (attempted) E954
  while
    attempting rescue of another person
      E910.3
    engaged in
      marine salvage E910.3 ●
      underwater construction or repairs ●
        E910.3 ●
    fishing, not from boat E910.2
    hunting, not from boat E910.2
    ice skating E910.2
    pearl diving E910.3
    placing fishing nets E910.3
    playing in water E910.2
    scuba diving E910.1
      nonrecreational E910.3
    skin diving E910.1
    snorkel diving E910.2
    spear fishing underwater E910.1
    surfboarding E910.2
    swimming (swimming pool) E910.2
    wading (in water) E910.2
    water skiing E910.0

Sucked
  into
    jet (aircraft) E844 ☑
Suffocation (accidental) (by external means)
  (by pressure) (mechanical) E913.9
  caused by other person
    in accidental circumstances — *see* cate-
      gory E913 ☑
    stated as
      intentional, homicidal E963
      undetermined whether accidental or
        intentional E983.9
      by, in
        hanging E983.0
        plastic bag E983.1
        specified means NEC E983.8
  due to, by
    avalanche E909.2
    bedclothes E913.0
    bib E913.0
    blanket E913.0
    cave-in E913.3
      caused by cataclysmic earth surface
        movement or eruption E909.9
    conflagration — *see* Conflagration
    explosion — *see* Explosion
    falling earth, other substance E913.3
    fire — *see* Fire
    food, any type (ingestion) (inhalation)
      (regurgitated) (vomited) E911
    foreign body, except food (ingestion)
      (inhalation) E912
    ignition — *see* Ignition
    landslide E909.2
    machine(ry) — *see* Accident, machine
    material, object except food entering by
      nose or mouth, ingested, inhaled
      E912
    mucus (aspiration) (inhalation), not of
      newborn E912
    phlegm (aspiration) (inhalation) E912
    pillow E913.0
    plastic bag — *see* Suffocation, in, plastic
      bag
    sheet (plastic) E913.0
    specified means NEC E913.8
    vomitus (aspiration) (inhalation) E911
  homicidal (attempt) E963
    in war operations E995.3
  in
    airtight enclosed place E913.2
    baby carriage E913.0
    bed E913.0
    closed place E913.2
    cot, cradle E913.0
    perambulator E913.0
    plastic bag (in accidental circumstances)
      E913.1
      homicidal, purposely inflicted by
        other person E963
      self-inflicted (unspecified whether
        accidental or intentional)
        E983.1
        in accidental circumstances
          E913.1
        intentional, suicidal E953.1
        stated as undetermined whether ac-
          cidentally or purposely inflict-
          ed E983.1
      suicidal, purposely self-inflicted
        E953.1
    refrigerator E913.2
    war operations E995.3
  self-inflicted (*see also* Suffocation, stated as
    undetermined whether accidental or
    intentional) E953.9
    in accidental circumstances — *see* cate-
      gory E913 ☑
    stated as intentional, purposeful — *see*
      Suicide, suffocation
    stated as undetermined whether accidental
      or intentional E983.9
    by, in
      hanging E983.0
      plastic bag E983.1
      specified means NEC E983.8

Suffocation — *continued*
  suicidal — *see* Suicide, suffocation
Suicide, suicidal (attempted) (by) E958.9
  burning, burns E958.1
  caustic substance E958.7
    poisoning E950.7
    swallowed E950.7
  cold, extreme E958.3
  cut (any part of body) E956
  cutting or piercing instrument (classifiable
    to E920) E956
  drowning E954
  electrocution E958.4
  explosive(s) (classifiable to E923) E955.5
  fire E958.1
  firearm (classifiable to E922) — *see* Shoot-
    ing, suicidal
  hanging E953.0
  jumping
    before moving object, train, vehicle
      E958.0
    from high place — *see* Jumping, from,
      high place, stated as, suicidal
  knife E956
  late effect of E959
  motor vehicle, crashing of E958.5
  poisoning — *see* Table of Drugs and Chem-
    icals
  puncture (any part of body) E956
  scald E958.2
  shooting — *see* Shooting, suicidal
  specified means NEC E958.8
  stab (any part of body) E956
  strangulation — *see* Suicide, suffocation
  submersion E954
  suffocation E953.9
    by, in
      hanging E953.0
      plastic bag E953.1
      specified means NEC E953.8
  wound NEC E958.9
Sunburn E926.2
Sunstroke E900.0
Supersonic waves (causing injury) E928.1
Surgical procedure, complication of
  delayed or as an abnormal reaction without
    mention of misadventure — *see* Re-
    action, abnormal
  due to or as a result of misadventure — *see*
    Misadventure
Swallowed, swallowing
  foreign body — *see* Foreign body, alimenta-
    ry canal
  poison — *see* Table of Drugs and Chemicals
  substance
    caustic — *see* Table of Drugs and
      Chemicals
    corrosive — *see* Table of Drugs and
      Chemicals
    poisonous — *see* Table of Drugs and
      Chemicals
Swimmers cramp — *see also* category E910
  E910.2
  not in recreation or sport E910.3
Syndrome, battered
  baby or child — *see* Abuse, child
  wife — *see* Assault

T

Tackle in sport E886.0
Terrorism (injury) (by) (in) E979.8
  air blast E979.2
  aircraft burned, destroyed, exploded, shot
    down E979.1
    used as a weapon E979.1
  anthrax E979.6
  asphyxia from
    chemical (weapons) E979.7
    fire, conflagration (caused by fire-produc-
      ing device) E979.3
    from nuclear explosion E979.5
    gas or fumes E979.7
  bayonet E979.8
  biological agents E979.6
  blast (air) (effects) E979.2
    from nuclear explosion E979.5

☑ Additional Digit Required — Refer to the Tabular List for Digit Selection   ▽ Subterms under main terms may continue to next column or page

2015 ICD-9-CM   ►◄ Revised Text   ● New Line   ▲ Revised Code   October 2014 • Volume 2 — 349

Sting — Terrorism

Terrorism — *continued*
blast — *continued*
  underwater E979.0
 bomb (antipersonnel) (mortar) (explosion) (fragments) E979.2
 bullet(s) (from carbine, machine gun, pistol, rifle, shotgun) E979.4
 burn from
  chemical E979.7
  fire, conflagration (caused by fire-producing device) E979.3
   from nuclear explosion E979.5
  gas E979.7
 burning aircraft E979.1
 chemical E979.7
 cholera E979.6
 conflagration E979.3
 crushed by falling aircraft E979.1
 depth-charge E979.0
 destruction of aircraft E979.1
 disability, as sequelae one year or more after injury E999.1
 drowning E979.8
 effect
  of nuclear weapon (direct) (secondary) E979.5
  secondary NEC E979.9
  sequelae E999.1
 explosion (artillery shell) (breech-block) (cannon block) E979.2
  aircraft E979.1
  bomb (antipersonnel) (mortar) E979.2
   nuclear (atom) (hydrogen) E979.5
  depth-charge E979.0
  grenade E979.2
  injury by fragments from E979.2
  land-mine E979.2
  marine weapon E979.0
  mine (land) E979.2
   at sea or in harbor E979.0
   marine E979.0
  missile (explosive) NEC E979.2
  munitions (dump) (factory) E979.2
  nuclear (weapon) E979.5
   other direct and secondary effects of E979.5
  sea-based artillery shell E979.0
  torpedo E979.0
 exposure to ionizing radiation from nuclear explosion E979.5
 falling aircraft E979.1
 firearms E979.4
 fireball effects from nuclear explosion E979.5
 fire or fire-producing device E979.3
 fragments from artillery shell, bomb NEC, grenade, guided missile, land-mine, rocket, shell, shrapnel E979.2
 gas or fumes E979.7
 grenade (explosion) (fragments) E979.2
 guided missile (explosion) (fragments) E979.2
  nuclear E979.5
 heat from nuclear explosion E979.5
 hot substances E979.3
 hydrogen cyanide E979.7
 land-mine (explosion) (fragments) E979.2
 laser(s) E979.8
 late effect of E999.1
 lewisite E979.7
 lung irritant (chemical) (fumes) (gas) E979.7
 marine mine E979.0
 mine E979.2
  at sea E979.0
  in harbor E979.0
  land (explosion) (fragments) E979.2
  marine E979.0
 missile (explosion) (fragments) (guided) E979.2
  marine E979.0
  nuclear weapons E979.5
 mortar bomb (explosion) (fragments) E979.2
 mustard gas E979.7
 nerve gas E979.7
 nuclear weapons E979.5
 pellets (shotgun) E979.4

Terrorism — *continued*
 petrol bomb E979.3
 phosgene E979.7
 piercing object E979.8
 poisoning (chemical) (fumes) (gas) E979.7
 radiation, ionizing from nuclear explosion E979.5
 rocket (explosion) (fragments) E979.2
 saber, sabre E979.8
 sarin E979.7
 screening smoke E979.7
 sequelae effect (of) E999.1
 shell (aircraft) (artillery) (cannon) (land-based) (explosion) (fragments) E979.2
  sea-based E979.0
 shooting E979.4
  bullet(s) E979.4
  pellet(s) (rifle) (shotgun) E979.4
 shrapnel E979.2
 smallpox E979.7
 stabbing object(s) E979.8
 submersion E979.8
 torpedo E979.0
 underwater blast E979.0
 vesicant (chemical) (fumes) (gas) E979.7
 weapon burst E979.2
Thermic fever E900.9
Thermoplegia E900.9
Thirst — *see also* Lack of water
 resulting from accident connected with transport — *see* categories E800-E848 ☑
Thrown (accidently)
 against object in or part of vehicle
  by motion of vehicle
   aircraft E844 ☑
   boat, ship, watercraft E838 ☑
   motor vehicle (on public highway) E818 ☑
    not on public highway E825 ☑
    off-road type (not on public highway) E821 ☑
    on public highway E818 ☑
    snow vehicle E820 ☑
     on public highway E818 ☑
   nonmotor road vehicle NEC E829 ☑
   railway rolling stock, train, vehicle E806 ☑
   street car E829 ☑
 from
  animal (being ridden) (in sport or transport) E828 ☑
  high place, homicide (attempt) E968.1
  machinery — *see* Accident, machine
  vehicle NEC — *see* Accident, vehicle NEC
 off — *see* Thrown, from
 overboard (by motion of boat, ship, watercraft) E832 ☑
  by accident to boat, ship, watercraft E830 ☑
Thunderbolt NEC E907
Tidal wave (any injury) E909.4
 caused by storm E908.0
Took
 overdose of drug — *see* Table of Drugs and Chemicals
 poison — *see* Table of Drugs and Chemicals
Tornado (any injury) E908.1
Torrential rain (any injury) E908.2
Traffic accident NEC E819 ☑
Trampled by animal E906.8
 being ridden (in sport or transport) E828 ☑
Trapped (accidently)
 between
  objects (moving) (stationary and moving) E918
 by
  door of
   elevator E918
   motor vehicle (on public highway) (while alighting, boarding) — *see* Fall, from, motor vehicle, while alighting
   railway train (underground) E806 ☑

Trapped — *continued*
 by — *continued*
  door of — *continued*
   street car E829 ☑
   subway train E806 ☑
 in object E918
Trauma
 cumulative
  from
   repetitive
    impact E927.4
    motion or movements E927.3
  sudden from strenuous movement E927.0
Travel (effects) E903
 sickness E903
Tree
 falling on or hitting E916
  motor vehicle (in motion) (on public highway) E818 ☑
   not on public highway E825 ☑
  nonmotor road vehicle NEC E829 ☑
  pedal cycle E826 ☑
  person E916
  railway rolling stock, train, vehicle E806 ☑
  street car E829 ☑
Trench foot E901.0
Tripping over animal, carpet, curb, rug, or small object (with fall) E885 ☑
 without fall — *see* Striking against, object
Tsunami E909.4
Twisting, injury
 due to
  repetitive movement E927.3
  sudden strenuous movement E927.0

V

Violence, nonaccidental — *see also* Assault E968.9
Volcanic eruption (any injury) E909.1
Vomitus in air passages (with asphyxia, obstruction or suffocation) E911

W

War operations (during hostilities) (injury) (by) (in) E995.9
 after cessation of hostilities, injury due to E998.9
 air blast E993.9
 aircraft burned, destroyed, exploded, shot down E994 ☑
 asphyxia from
  chemical E997.2
  fire, conflagration (caused by fire producing device or conventional weapon) E990.9
   from nuclear explosion (*see also* War operations, injury due to, nuclear weapons) E996.8
  incendiary bomb E990.0
  petrol bomb E990.0
  fumes E997.2
  gas E997.2
 baton (nightstick) E995.1
 battle wound NEC E995.8
 bayonet E995.2
 biological warfare agents E997.1
 blast (air) (effects) E993.9
  from nuclear explosion — *see* War operations, injury due to, nuclear weapons
  underwater E992.9
 bomb (mortar) (explosion) E993.2
  after cessation of hostilities E998.1
  fragments, injury by E991.4
   antipersonnel E991.3
 bullet(s) (from carbine, machine gun, pistol, rifle, shotgun) E991.2
  rubber E991.0
 burn from
  chemical E997.2
  fire, conflagration (caused by fire-producing device or conventional weapon) E990.9

War operations — *continued*
 burn from — *continued*
  fire, conflagration — *continued*
   from
    conventional weapon E990.3
    flamethrower E990.1
    incendiary bomb E990.0
    incendiary bullet E990.2
    nuclear explosion E996.2
   petrol bomb E990.0
  gas E997.2
 burning aircraft E994.3
 chemical E997.2
 chlorine E997.2
 conventional warfare, specified form NEC E995.8
 crushing by falling aircraft E994.8
 depth charge E992.1
 destruction of aircraft E994.9
 detonation of own munitions (ammunition) (artillery) (mortars), unintentional E993.6
 disability as sequela one year or more after injury E999.0
 discharge of own munitions launch device (autocannons) (automatic grenade launchers) (missile launchers) (small arms), unintentional E993.7
 drowning E995.4
 effect nuclear weapon (*see also* War operations, injury due to, nuclear weapons) E996.9
 explosion (breech block) (cannon shell) E993.9
  after cessation of hostilities
   bomb placed in war E998.1
   mine placed in war E998.0
  aircraft E994.1
   due to
    enemy fire or explosives E994.0
    own onboard explosives E994.1
  artillery shell E993.2
  bomb (mortar) E993.2
   aerial E993.0
   atom (*see also* War operations, injury due to, nuclear weapons) E996.9
   hydrogen (*see also* War operations, injury due to, nuclear weapons) E996.9
   injury by fragments from E991.4
    antipersonnel E991.3
   nuclear (*see also* War operations, injury due to, nuclear weapons) E996.9
  depth charge E992.1
  injury by fragments from E991.4
   antipersonnel E991.3
  marine weapon NEC E992.8
  mine
   at sea or in harbor E992.2
   land E993.8
    injury by fragments from E991.4
   marine E992.2
  missile, guided E993.1
  mortar E993.2
  munitions (accidental) (being used in war) (dump) (factory) E993.9
   own E993.7
    ammunition (artillery) (mortars) E993.6
    launch device (autocannons) (automatic grenade launchers) (missile launchers) (small arms) E993.7
  nuclear (weapon) (*see also* War operations, injury due to, nuclear weapons) E996.9
  own weapons (accidental) E993.7
   injury by fragments from E991.9
    antipersonnel E991.3
  sea-based artillery shell E992.3
  specified NEC E993.8
  torpedo E992.0

☑ **Additional Digit Required** — Refer to the Tabular List for Digit Selection | TBS **Subterms under main terms may continue to next column or page**

War operations — *continued*

exposure to ionizing radiation from nuclear explosion (*see also* War operations, injury due to, nuclear weapons) E996.3

falling aircraft E994.8

fireball effects from nuclear explosion E996.2

fire or fire-producing device E990.9
- flamethrower E990.1
- incendiary bomb E990.0
- incendiary bullet E990.2
- indirectly caused from conventional weapon E990.3
- petrol bomb E990.0

fragments from
- antipersonnel bomb E991.3
- artillery shell E991.4
- bomb NEC E991.4
- grenade E991.4
- guided missile E991.4
- land mine E991.4
- rocket E991.4
- shell E991.4
- shrapnel E991.9

fumes E997.2

gas E997.2

grenade (explosion) E993.8
- fragments, injury by E991.4

guided missile (explosion) E993.1
- fragments, injury by E991.4
- nuclear (*see also* War operations, injury due to, nuclear weapons) E996.9

heat from nuclear explosion E996.2

injury due to
- aerial bomb E993.0
- air blast E993.9
- aircraft shot down E994.0
- artillery shell E993.2
- blast E993.9
  - wave E993.9
  - wind E993.9
- bomb E993.8
- but occurring after cessation of hostilities
  - explosion of bombs E998.1
  - explosion of mines E998.0
  - specified NEC E998.8
- conventional warfare E995.9
  - specified form NEC E995.8
- depth charge E992.1
- destruction of aircraft E994.9
  - due to
    - air to air missile E994.0
    - collision with other aircraft E994.2
    - enemy fire or explosives E994.0
    - on board explosion (explosives) E994.1
    - on board fire E994.3
    - rocket propelled grenade [RPG] E994.0
    - small arms fire E994.0
    - surface to air missile E994.0
  - specified NEC E994.8
- dirty bomb (*see also* War operations, injury due to, nuclear weapons) E996.9
- drowning E995.4
- explosion (direct pressure) (indirect pressure) (due to) E993.9
  - depth charge E992.1

War operations — *continued*

injury due to — *continued*
- explosion — *continued*
  - improvised explosive device [IED]
    - person borne E993.3
    - roadside E993.5
    - specified NEC E993.5
    - transport vehicle (air) (land) (water) borne E993.4
    - vehicle (air) (land) (water) borne E993.4
  - marine mines (in harbor) (at sea) E992.2
  - marine weapons E992.9
    - specified NEC E992.8
  - sea based artillery shell E992.3
  - specified NEC E993.8
  - torpedo E992.0
  - unintentional (of own)
    - autocannons E993.7
    - automatic grenade launchers E993.7
    - launch device discharge E993.7
    - missile launchers E993.7
    - munitions detonation (ammunition) (artillery) (mortars) E993.6
    - small arms E993.7
- fragments (from) E991.9
  - artillery E991.8
  - artillery shells E991.4
  - autocannons E991.8
  - automatic grenade launchers [AGL] E991.8
  - bombs E991.4
    - antipersonnel E991.3
  - detonation of unexploded ordnance [UXO] E991.4
  - grenade E991.4
  - guided missile E991.4
  - improvised explosive device [IED]
    - person borne E991.5
    - roadside E991.7
    - specified NEC E991.7
    - transport vehicle (air) (land) (water) borne E991.6
    - vehicle (air) (land) (water) borne E991.6
  - land mine E991.4
  - missile launchers E991.8
  - mortars E991.8
  - munitions (artillery shells) (bombs) (grenades) (rockets) (shells) E991.4
  - rockets E991.4
  - shells E991.4
  - small arms E991.8
  - specified NEC E991.9
  - weapons (artillery) (autocannons) (mortars) (small arms) E991.8
- grenade E993.8
- guided missile E993.1
- hand to hand combat, unarmed E995.0
- improvised explosive device [IED]
  - person borne E993.3
  - roadside E993.5
  - specified NEC E993.5
  - transport vehicle (air) (land) (water) borne E993.4
  - vehicle (air) (land) (water) borne E993.4
- inability to surface or obtain air E995.4

War operations — *continued*

injury due to — *continued*
- land mine E993.8
- marine mines (in harbor) (at sea) E992.2
- marine weapons E992.9
  - specified NEC E992.8
- mortar E993.2
- nuclear weapons E996.9
  - beta burns E996.3
  - blast debris E996.1
  - blast pressure E996.0
  - burns due to thermal radiation E996.2
  - direct blast effect E996.0
  - fallout exposure E996.3
  - fireball effect E996.2
  - flash burns E996.2
  - heat effect E996.2
  - indirect blast effect E996.1
  - nuclear radiation effects E996.3
  - radiation exposure (acute) E996.3
  - radiation sickness E996.3
  - secondary effects E996.3
  - specified effects NEC E996.8
  - thermal radiation effect E996.2
- piercing object E995.2
- restriction of airway, intentional E995.3
- sea based artillery shell E992.3
- shrapnel E991.9
- stave E995.1
- strangulation E995.3
- strike by blunt object (baton) (nightstick) (stave) E995.1
- submersion (accidental) (unintentional) E995.4
  - intentional E995.3
- suffocation E995.3
  - accidental E995.4
- torpedo E992.0
- underwater blast E992.9
- weapon of mass destruction [WMD] E997.3

knife E995.2

lacrimator (gas) (chemical) E997.2

land mine (explosion) E993.8
- after cessation of hostilities E998.0
- fragments, injury by E991.4

laser(s) E997.0

late effect of E999.0

lewisite E997.2

lung irritant (chemical) (fumes) (gas) E997.2

marine mine E992.2

mine
- after cessation of hostilities E998.0
- at sea E992.2
- in harbor E992.2
- land (explosion) E993.8
  - fragments, injury by E991.4
- marine E992.2

missile (guided) (explosion) E993.1
- fragments, injury by E991.4
- marine E992.8
- nuclear (*see also* War operations, injury due to, nuclear weapons) E996.9

mortar bomb (explosion) E993.2
- fragments, injury by E991.4

mustard gas E997.2

nerve gas E997.2

phosgene E997.2

piercing object E995.2

poisoning (chemical) (fumes) (gas) E997.2

War operations — *continued*

radiation, ionizing from nuclear explosion (*see also* War operations, injury due to, nuclear weapons) E996.3

rocket (explosion) E993.8
- fragments, injury by E991.4

saber, sabre E995.2

screening smoke E997.8

shell (aircraft) (artillery) (cannon) (land based) (explosion) E993.2
- fragments, injury by E991.4
- sea-based E992.3

shooting E991.2
- after cessation of hostilities E998.8
- bullet(s) E991.2
  - rubber E991.0
- pellet(s) (rifle) E991.1
- shrapnel E991.9
- submersion E995 ☑
- torpedo E992 ☑

stave E995.2

strike by blunt object (baton) (nightstick) (stave) E995.1

submersion E995.4
- intentional E995.3

sword E995.2

torpedo E992.0

unconventional warfare, except by nuclear weapon E997.9
- biological (warfare) E997.1
- gas, fumes, chemicals E997.2
- laser(s) E997.0
- specified type NEC E997.8

underwater blast E992.9

vesicant (chemical) (fumes) (gas) E997.2

weapon burst E993.9

Washed
- away by flood — *see* Flood
- away by tidal wave — *see* Tidal wave
- off road by storm (transport vehicle) E908.9
- overboard E832 ☑

Weapon of mass destruction [WMD] E997.3

Weather exposure — *see also* Exposure
- cold E901.0
- hot E900.0

Weightlessness (causing injury) (effects of) (in spacecraft, real or simulated) E928.0

Wound (accidental) NEC — *see also* Injury E928.9
- battle (*see also* War operations) E995.9
- bayonet E920.3
  - in
    - legal intervention E974
    - war operations E995.2
- gunshot — *see* Shooting
- incised — *see* Cut
- saber, sabre E920.3
  - in war operations E995.2

Wrong
- body part, performance of correct operation (procedure) on E876.7
- device implanted into correct surgical site E876.5
- patient, performance of operation (procedure) on E876.6
- procedure (operation) performed on correct patient E876.5
- side, performance of correct operation (procedure) on E876.7
- site, performance of correct operation (procedure) on E876.7

☑ Additional Digit Required — Refer to the Tabular List for Digit Selection   ᵂ Subterms under main terms may continue to next column or page

Railway Accidents (E800-E807)

The following fourth-digit subdivisions are for use with categories E800-E807 to identify the injured person:

.0 **Railway employee**
Any person who by virtue of his employment in connection with a railway, whether by the railway company or not, is at increased risk of involvement in a railway accident, such as:
catering staff on train
postal staff on train
driver
railway fireman
guard
shunter
porter
sleeping car attendant

.1 **Passenger on railway**
Any authorized person traveling on a train, except a railway employee

EXCLUDES   intending passenger waiting at station (.8)
unauthorized rider on railway vehicle (.8)

.2 **Pedestrian** See definition (r), E-Codes-2

.3 **Pedal cyclist** See definition (p), E-Codes-2

.8 **Other specified person** Intending passenger waiting at station
Unauthorized rider on railway vehicle

.9 **Unspecified person**

Motor Vehicle Traffic and Nontraffic Accidents (E810-E825)

The following fourth-digit subdivisions are for use with categories E810-E819 and E820-E825 to identify the injured person:

.0 **Driver of motor vehicle other than motorcycle** See definition (1), E-Codes-2

.1 **Passenger in motor vehicle other than motorcycle** See definition (1), E-Codes-2

.2 **Motorcyclist** See definition (1), E-Codes-2

.3 **Passenger on motorcycle** See definition (1), E-Codes-2

.4 **Occupant of streetcar**

.5 **Rider of animal; occupant of animal-drawn vehicle**

.6 **Pedal cyclist** See definition (p), E-Codes-2

.7 **Pedestrian** See definition (r), E-Codes-2

.8 **Other specified person**
Occupant of vehicle other than above
Person in railway train involved in accident
Unauthorized rider of motor vehicle

.9 **Unspecified person**

Other Road Vehicle Accidents (E826-E829)

(animal-drawn vehicle, streetcar, pedal cycle, and other nonmotor road vehicle accidents)

The following fourth-digit subdivisions are for use with categories E826-E829 to identify the injured person:

.0 **Pedestrian** See definition (r), E-Codes-2

.1 **Pedal cyclist** (does not apply to codes E827, E828, E829) See definition (p), E-Codes-2

.2 **Rider of animal** (does not apply to code E829)

.3 **Occupant of animal-drawn vehicle (does not apply to codes E828, E829)**

.4 **Occupant of streetcar**

.8 **Other specified person**

.9 **Unspecified person**

Water Transport Accidents (E830-E838)

The following fourth-digit subdivisions are for use with categories E830-E838 to identify the injured person:

.0 **Occupant of small boat, unpowered**

.1 **Occupant of small boat, powered** See definition (t), E-Codes-2

EXCLUDES   water skier (.4)

.2 **Occupant of other watercraft — crew**
Persons:
engaged in operation of watercraft
providing passenger services [cabin attendants, ship's physician, catering personnel]
working on ship during voyage in other capacity [musician in band, operators of shops and beauty parlors]

.3 **Occupant of other watercraft — other than crew**
Passenger
Occupant of lifeboat, other than crew, after abandoning ship

.4 **Water skier**

.5 **Swimmer**

.6 **Dockers, stevedores**
Longshoreman employed on the dock in loading and unloading ships

.8 **Other specified person**
Immigration and custom officials on board ship
Persons:
accompanying passenger or member of crew visiting boat
Pilot (guiding ship into port)

.9 **Unspecified person**

Air and Space Transport Accidents (E840-E845)

The following fourth-digit subdivisions are for use with categories E840-E845 to identify the injured person:

.0 **Occupant of spacecraft**
Crew
Passenger (civilian)
(military)   in military aircraft [air force]
Troops   [army] [national guard] [navy]

.1 **Occupant of military aircraft, any**

EXCLUDES   occupants of aircraft operated under jurisdiction of police departments (.5) parachutist (.7)

.2 **Crew of commercial aircraft (powered) in surface to surface transport**

.3 **Other occupant of commercial aircraft (powered) in surface to surface transport**
Flight personnel:
not part of crew
on familiarization flight Passenger on aircraft

.4 **Occupant of commercial aircraft (powered) in surface to air transport**
Occupant [crew] [passenger] of aircraft (powered) engaged in activities, such as:
air drops of emergency supplies
air drops of parachutists, except from military craft
crop dusting
lowering of construction material [bridge or telephone pole]
sky writing

.5 **Occupant of other powered aircraft**
Occupant [crew] [passenger] of aircraft (powered) engaged in activities, such as:
aerial spraying (crops)(fire retardants)
aerobatic flying
aircraft racing
rescue operation
storm surveillance
traffic suveillance
Occupant of private plane NOS

.6 **Occupant of unpowered aircraft, except parachutist**
Occupant of aircraft classifiable to E842

.7 **Parachutist (military)(other)**
Person making voluntary descent
person making descent after accident to aircraft (.1-.6)

.8 **Ground crew, airline employee**
Persons employed at airfields (civil)(military) or launching pads, not occupants of aircraft

.9 **Other person**

1. Infectious and Parasitic Diseases (001-139)

NOTE Categories for "late effects" of infectious and parasitic diseases are to be found at 137-139.

INCLUDES diseases generally recognized as communicable or transmissible as well as a few diseases of unknown but possibly infectious origin

EXCLUDES acute respiratory infections (460-466)
carrier or suspected carrier of infectious organism (V02.0-V02.9)
certain localized infections
influenza (487.0-487.8, 488.01-488.19)

Intestinal Infectious Diseases (001-009)

EXCLUDES helminthiases (120.0-129)

✓4th 001 Cholera
DEF: An acute infectious enteritis caused by a potent enterotoxin produced by *Vibrio cholerae*; changes the permeability of the mucosa of the intestines and leads to diarrhea and dehydration.

001.0 Due to Vibrio cholerae   `CC`
CC Excl: 001.0-001.9

001.1 Due to Vibrio cholerae el tor   `CC`
CC Excl: See code: 001.0

001.9 Cholera, unspecified   `CC`
CC Excl: See code: 001.0

✓4th 002 Typhoid and paratyphoid fevers
DEF: Typhoid fever: an acute generalized illness caused by *Salmonella typhi*; clinical features are fever, headache, abdominal pain, cough, toxemia, leukopenia, abnormal pulse, rose spots on the skin, bacteremia, hyperplasia of intestinal lymph nodes, mesenteric lymphadenopathy, and Peyer's patches in the intestines.
DEF: Paratyphoid fever: a prolonged febrile illness, caused by salmonella serotypes other than *S. typhi*, especially *S. enteritidis* serotypes paratyphi A and B and *S. choleraesuis*.

002.0 Typhoid fever   `CC`
Typhoid (fever) (infection) [any site]
CC Excl: 002.0-002.9

002.1 Paratyphoid fever A   `CC`
CC Excl: See code: 002.0

002.2 Paratyphoid fever B   `CC`
CC Excl: See code: 002.0

002.3 Paratyphoid fever C   `CC`
CC Excl: See code: 002.0

002.9 Paratyphoid fever, unspecified   `CC`
CC Excl: See code: 002.0

✓4th 003 Other salmonella infections
INCLUDES infection or food poisoning by Salmonella [any serotype]
DEF: Infections caused by a genus of gram-negative, anaerobic bacteria of the family *Enterobacteriaceae*; major symptoms are enteric fevers, acute gastroenteritis and septicemia.

003.0 Salmonella gastroenteritis   `CC`
Salmonellosis
CC Excl: 002.0, 002.9-003.0, 004.9-005.2, 007.5, 008.00-009.0, 040.41-040.42, 536.8, 558.2-558.9, 564.1, 567.21, 567.23, 567.31-567.39, 567.89, 777.50-777.53, 777.8

003.1 Salmonella septicemia   `MCC` `HIV`
CC Excl: 03.1, 020.2, 022.3, 036.2, 038.0-038.9, 040.89-041.3, 041.41-041.85, 041.89-041.9, 054.5, 139.8, 771.81, 771.83-771.89, 995.90-995.94, V09.0-V09.91

✓5th 003.2 Localized salmonella infections

003.20 Localized salmonella infection, unspecified   `HIV`

003.21 Salmonella meningitis   `MCC` `HIV`
CC Excl: 003.21, 013.00-013.16, 036.0, 047.0-047.9, 049.0-049.1, 072.1, 078.88-078.89, 079.81, 079.88-079.99, 090.42, 091.81, 094.2, 098.89, 100.81, 112.83, 114.2, 115.01, 115.11, 115.91, 130.0, 139.8, 320.0-322.9, 349.89-349.9

003.22 Salmonella pneumonia   `MCC` `HIV`
CC Excl: 003.22, 011.00-012.16, 012.80-012.86, 017.90-017.96, 020.3-020.5, 021.3, 022.1, 031.0, 039.1, 073.0, 115.05, 115.15, 115.95, 122.1, 130.4, 136.3, 480.0-480.2, 480.8-487.1, 488.0-488.1, 495.0-495.7, 500, 502-508.9, 517.1, 517.8, 518.89, 519.8-519.9

003.23 Salmonella arthritis   `CC` `HIV`
CC Excl: 003.23, 015.80-015.96, 036.82, 056.71, 098.50-098.51, 098.59, 098.89, 711.00-714.0, 715.00, 715.09-715.10, 715.18-716.99, 718.00-718.08, 719.00-719.10, 719.18-719.69, 719.80-719.99

003.24 Salmonella osteomyelitis   `CC` `HIV`
CC Excl: 003.24, 015.50-015.56, 015.70-015.76, 015.90-015.96, 730.00-730.39, 730.80-730.99

003.29 Other   `CC` `HIV`
CC Excl: 003.29

003.8 Other specified salmonella infections   `CC` `HIV`
CC Excl: 003.8

003.9 Salmonella infection, unspecified   `CC` `HIV`
CC Excl: 003.9

✓4th 004 Shigellosis
INCLUDES bacillary dysentery
DEF: Acute infectious dysentery caused by the genus *Shigella*, of the family *Enterobacteriaceae*; affecting the colon causing blood-stained stools, tenesmus, abdominal cramps and fever.

004.0 Shigella dysenteriae   `CC`
Infection by group A Shigella (Schmitz) (Shiga)
CC Excl: 001.1, 002.0, 002.9-003.0, 004.0, 004.9-005.2, 006.0-006.2, 006.9, 007.1-007.9, 008.1-008.3, 008.5, 008.8-009.0, 014.80-014.86, 040.41-040.42, 112.85, 129, 487.8, 488.09, 488.19, 536.3, 536.8, 555.0-557.9, 558.2-558.9, 564.1, 775.0-775.7, 775.9, 777.50-777.53, 777.8

004.1 Shigella flexneri
Infection by group B Shigella

004.2 Shigella boydii
Infection by group C Shigella

004.3 Shigella sonnei
Infection by group D Shigella

004.8 Other specified Shigella infections

004.9 Shigellosis, unspecified

✓4th 005 Other food poisoning (bacterial)
EXCLUDES salmonella infections (003.0-003.9)
toxic effect of:
food contaminants (989.7)
noxious foodstuffs (988.0-988.9)
DEF: Enteritis caused by ingesting contaminated foods and characterized by diarrhea, abdominal pain, vomiting; symptoms may be mild or life threatening.

005.0 Staphylococcal food poisoning   `CC`
Staphylococcal toxemia specified as due to food
CC Excl: 001.0-009.3, 040.41-040.42

005.1 Botulism food poisoning   `CC`
Botulism NOS
Food poisoning due to Clostridium botulinum
EXCLUDES infant botulism (040.41)
wound botulism (040.42)
CC Excl: 005.0-005.2, 008.45-008.46, 040.41-040.42

005.2 Food poisoning due to Clostridium perfringens [C. welchii]   `CC`
Enteritis necroticans
CC Excl: 003.0, 004.9-005.2, 007.5, 008.00-009.0, 040.41-040.42, 487.8, 488.09, 488.19, 536.3, 536.8, 558.2-558.9, 564.1, 567.21, 567.23, 567.31-567.39, 567.89, 777.50-777.53, 777.8

005.3 Food poisoning due to other Clostridia   `CC`
CC Excl: See code: 005.0

005.4 Food poisoning due to Vibrio parahaemolyticus   `CC`
CC Excl: See code: 005.0

✓5th 005.8 Other bacterial food poisoning
EXCLUDES salmonella food poisoning (003.0-003.9)

005.81 Food poisoning due to Vibrio vulnificus   `CC`
CC Excl: See code: 005.0

005.89 Other bacterial food poisoning   `CC`
Food poisoning due to Bacillus cereus
CC Excl: See code: 005.0

005.9 Food poisoning, unspecified

√4ᵗʰ **006 Amebiasis**

INCLUDES infection due to Entamoeba histolytica

EXCLUDES *amebiasis due to organisms other than Entamoeba histolytica (007.8)*

DEF: Infection of the large intestine caused by *Entamoeba histolytica;* usually asymptomatic but symptoms may range from mild diarrhea to profound life-threatening dysentery. Extraintestinal complications include hepatic abscess, which may rupture, causing life-threatening infections.

006.0 Acute amebic dysentery without mention of abscess CC
Acute amebiasis
DEF: Sudden, severe *Entamoeba histolytica* infection causing bloody stools.
CC Excl: 006.0-006.1, 007.5

006.1 Chronic intestinal amebiasis without mention of abscess CC
Chronic:
amebiasis
amebic dysentery
CC Excl: See code: 006.0

006.2 Amebic nondysenteric colitis CC
DEF: *Entamoeba histolytica* infection with inflamed colon but no dysentery.
CC Excl: 003.0, 004.9-005.0, 005.2, 006.0-006.2, 006.9, 007.1-009.0, 129, 487.8, 488.09, 488.19, 536.3, 536.8, 555.0-557.9, 558.2-558.9, 564.1, 777.50-777.53, 777.8

006.3 Amebic liver abscess MCC
Hepatic amebiasis
CC Excl: 006.3, 572.0

006.4 Amebic lung abscess MCC
Amebic abscess of lung (and liver)
CC Excl: 006.4, 513.0

006.5 Amebic brain abscess MCC
Amebic abscess of brain (and liver) (and lung)
CC Excl: 006.5, 324.0

006.6 Amebic skin ulceration
Cutaneous amebiasis

006.8 Amebic infection of other sites CC
Amebic: Ameboma
appendicitis
balanitis
EXCLUDES *specific infections by free-living amebae (136.21-136.29)*
CC Excl: 006.0-006.5, 006.8

006.9 Amebiasis, unspecified
Amebiasis NOS

√4ᵗʰ **007 Other protozoal intestinal diseases**
INCLUDES protozoal:
colitis
diarrhea
dysentery

007.0 Balantidiasis
Infection by Balantidium coli

007.1 Giardiasis CC
Infection by Giardia lamblia
Lambliasis
CC Excl: 003.0, 004.9-005.0, 005.2, 006.0-006.2, 006.9, 007.1-009.0, 129, 487.8, 488.09, 488.19, 536.3, 536.8, 558.2-558.9, 564.1

007.2 Coccidiosis CC HIV
Infection by Isospora belli and Isospora hominis Isosporiasis
CC Excl: See code: 007.1

007.3 Intestinal trichomoniasis
DEF: Colitis, diarrhea, or dysentery caused by the protozoa *Trichomonas.*

007.4 Cryptosporidiosis CC
DEF: An intestinal infection by protozoan parasites causing intractable diarrhea in patients with AIDS and other immunosuppressed individuals.
CC Excl: See code: 007.1
AHA: 4Q, '97, 30

007.5 Cyclosporiasis CC
DEF: An infection of the small intestine by the protozoal organism, *Cyclospora cayetenanesis,* spread to humans through ingestion of contaminated water or food. Symptoms include watery diarrhea, loss of appetite, increased gas, stomach cramps, nausea, vomiting, muscle aches, low grade fever, and fatigue.
CC Excl: 003.0, 004.9-005.0, 005.2, 006.0-006.2, 006.9, 007.1-009.0, 129, 487.8, 488.09, 488.19, 536.3, 536.8, 558.2-558.9, 564.1, 567.21, 567.23, 567.31-567.39, 567.89
AHA: 4Q, '00, 38

007.8 Other specified protozoal intestinal diseases CC
Amebiasis due to organisms other than Entamoeba histolytica
CC Excl: See code: 007.1

007.9 Unspecified protozoal intestinal disease CC
Flagellate diarrhea
Protozoal dysentery NOS
CC Excl: See code: 007.1

√4ᵗʰ **008 Intestinal infections due to other organisms**
INCLUDES any condition classifiable to 009.0-009.3 with mention of the responsible organisms
EXCLUDES *food poisoning by these organisms (005.0-005.9)*

√5ᵗʰ **008.0 Escherichia coli [E. coli]**
AHA: 4Q, '92, 17

008.00 E. coli, unspecified CC
E. coli enteritis NOS
CC Excl: 003.0, 004.9-005.0, 005.2, 007.5, 008.00-009.0, 487.8, 488.09, 488.19, 536.3, 536.8, 558.2-558.9, 564.1, 567.21, 567.23, 567.31-567.39, 567.89, 777.50-777.53, 777.8

008.01 Enteropathogenic E. coli CC
DEF: *E. coli* causing inflammation of intestines.
CC Excl: See code: 008.00

008.02 Enterotoxigenic E. coli CC
DEF: A toxic reaction to *E. coli* of the intestinal mucosa, causing voluminous watery secretions.
CC Excl: See code: 008.00

008.03 Enteroinvasive E. coli CC
DEF: *E. coli* infection penetrating intestinal mucosa.
CC Excl: See code: 008.00

008.04 Enterohemorrhagic E. coli CC
DEF: *E. coli* infection penetrating the intestinal mucosa, producing microscopic ulceration and bleeding.
CC Excl: See code: 008.00
AHA: 4Q, '11, 83

008.09 Other intestinal E. coli infections CC
CC Excl: See code: 008.00

008.1 Arizona group of paracolon bacilli CC
CC Excl: See code: 008.00

008.2 Aerobacter aerogenes CC
Enterobacter aeogenes
CC Excl: See code: 008.00

008.3 Proteus (mirabilis) (morganii) CC
CC Excl: See code: 008.00

√5ᵗʰ **008.4 Other specified bacteria**
AHA: 4Q, '92, 18

008.41 Staphylococcus CC
Staphylococcal enterocolitis
CC Excl: 001.1, 002.0, 002.9-003.0, 004.9-005.2, 006.0-006.2, 006.9, 007.1-009.0, 014.80-014.86, 040.41-040.42, 112.85, 129, 487.8, 488.09, 488.19, 536.3, 536.8, 555.0-557.9, 558.2-558.9, 564.1, 775.0-775.7, 775.9, 777.50-777.53, 777.8

008.42 Pseudomonas CC
CC Excl: See code: 008.41
AHA: 2Q, '89, 10

008.43 Campylobacter CC
CC Excl: See code 008.41

008.44 Yersinia enterocolitica CC
CC Excl: See code 008.41

N Newborn Age: 0   P Pediatric Age: 0-17   M Maternity Age: 12-55   A Adult Age: 15-124   MCC Major CC Condition   CC CC Condition   HIV HIV Related Dx

2 – Volume 1   2015 ICD-9-CM

008.45 Clostridium difficile `CC`
Pseudomembranous colitis
DEF: An overgrowth of a species of bacterium that is a part of the normal colon flora in human infants and sometimes in adults; produces a toxin that causes pseudomembranous enterocolitis typically is seen in patients undergoing antibiotic therapy.
CC Excl: See code 008.41
A04.7 Enterocolitis due to clostridium difficile `I-10`

008.46 Other anaerobes `CC`
Anaerobic enteritis NOS
Bacteroides (fragilis)
Gram-negative anaerobes
CC Excl: See code 008.41

008.47 Other gram-negative bacteria `CC`
Gram-negative enteritis NOS
EXCLUDES gram-negative anaerobes (008.46)
CC Excl: See code 008.41

008.49 Other `CC`
CC Excl: See code 008.41
AHA: 2Q, '89, 10; 1Q, '88, 6

008.5 Bacterial enteritis, unspecified `CC`
CC Excl: 001.1, 002.0, 002.9-003.0, 004.9-005.0, 005.2, 006.0-006.2, 006.9, 007.1-009.0, 014.80-014.86, 112.85, 129, 487.8, 488.09, 488.19, 536.3, 536.8, 558.2-558.9, 564.1, 567.21, 567.23, 567.31-567.39, 567.89, 777.50-777.53, 777.8

√5ᵗʰ **008.6 Enteritis due to specified virus**
AHA: 4Q, '92, 18

008.61 Rotavirus `CC`
CC Excl: 003.0, 004.9-005.0, 005.2, 006.0-006.2, 006.9, 007.1-009.0, 014.80-014.86, 112.85, 129, 487.8, 488.09, 488.19, 536.3, 536.8, 558.2-558.9, 564.1, 567.21, 567.23, 567.31-567.39, 567.89, 777.50-777.53, 777.8

008.62 Adenovirus `CC`
CC Excl: See code: 008.61

008.63 Norwalk virus `CC`
Norovirus
Norwalk-like agent
CC Excl: See code: 008.61

008.64 Other small round viruses [SRVs] `CC`
Small round virus NOS
CC Excl: See code: 008.61

008.65 Calicivirus `CC`
DEF: Enteritis due to a subgroup of *Picornaviruses.*
CC Excl: See code: 008.61

008.66 Astrovirus `CC`
CC Excl: See code: 008.61

008.67 Enterovirus NEC `CC`
Coxsackie virus
Echovirus
EXCLUDES poliovirus (045.0-045.9)
CC Excl: See code: 008.61

008.69 Other viral enteritis `CC`
Torovirus
CC Excl: See code: 008.61
AHA: 1Q, '03, 10

008.8 Other organism, not elsewhere classified
Viral:
enteritis NOS
gastroenteritis
EXCLUDES influenza with involvement of gastrointestinal tract (487.8, 488.09, 488.19)
A08.4 Viral intestinal infection unspecified `I-10`

√4ᵗʰ **009 Ill-defined intestinal infections**
EXCLUDES diarrheal disease or intestinal infection due to specified organism (001.0-008.8)
diarrhea following gastrointestinal surgery (564.4)
intestinal malabsorption (579.0-579.9)
ischemic enteritis (557.0-557.9)
other noninfectious gastroenteritis and colitis (558.1-558.9)
regional enteritis (555.0-555.9)
ulcerative colitis (556)

009.0 Infectious colitis, enteritis, and gastroenteritis `CC`
Colitis
Enteritis } septic
Gastroenteritis
Dysentery: Dysentery:
NOS   hemorrhagic
catarrhal
DEF: Colitis: An inflammation of mucous membranes of the colon.
DEF: Enteritis: An inflammation of mucous membranes of the small intestine.
DEF: Gastroenteritis: An inflammation of mucous membranes of stomach and intestines.
CC Excl: 001.0-009.3, 040.41-040.42
AHA: 3Q, '99, 4
A09 Infectious gastroenteritis and colitis unspec `I-10`

009.1 Colitis, enteritis, and gastroenteritis of presumed infectious origin `CC`
EXCLUDES colitis NOS (558.9)
enteritis NOS (558.9)
gastroenteritis NOS (558.9)
CC Excl: 009.1
AHA: 3Q, '99, 6

009.2 Infectious diarrhea `CC`
Diarrhea: Infectious diarrheal disease NOS
dysenteric
epidemic
CC Excl: See code: 009.0

009.3 Diarrhea of presumed infectious origin `CC`
EXCLUDES diarrhea NOS (787.91)
CC Excl: 009.3
AHA: N-D, '87, 7

Tuberculosis (010-018)

INCLUDES infection by Mycobacterium tuberculosis (human) (bovine)
EXCLUDES congenital tuberculosis (771.2)
late effects of tuberculosis (137.0-137.4)

The following fifth-digit subclassification is for use with categories 010-018:
0 **unspecified**
1 **bacteriological or histological examination not done**
2 **bacteriological or histological examination unknown (at present)**
3 **tubercle bacilli found (in sputum) by microscopy**
4 **tubercle bacilli not found (in sputum) by microscopy, but found by bacterial culture**
5 **tubercle bacilli not found by bacteriological examination, but tuberculosis confirmed histologically**
6 **tubercle bacilli not found by bacteriological or histological examination but tuberculosis confirmed by other methods [inoculation of animals]**

DEF: An infection by *Mycobacterium tuberculosis* causing the formation of small, rounded nodules, called tubercles, that can disseminate throughout the body via lymph and blood vessels. Localized tuberculosis is most often seen in the lungs.b

010 Primary tuberculous infection
DEF: Tuberculosis of the lungs occurring when the patient is first infected.

§ √5ᵗʰ **010.0 Primary tuberculous infection** `CC` `HIV`
[0-6] *EXCLUDES* nonspecific reaction to test for tuberculosis without active tuberculosis (795.51-795.52)
positive PPD (795.51)
positive tuberculin skin test without active tuberculosis (795.51)
CC Excl: 010.00-018.96
DEF: Hilar or paratracheal lymph node enlargement in pulmonary tuberculosis.

§ Requires fifth digit. Valid digits are in [brackets] under each code. See beginning of section 010-018 for codes and definitions.

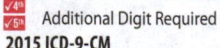

Infectious and Parasitic Diseases

010.1–014.8

§ ✓5ᵗʰ **010.1 Tuberculous pleurisy in primary progressive** `CC` `HIV`
[0-6]   **tuberculosis**
    CC Excl: See code: 010.0
    DEF: Inflammation and exudation in the lining of the tubercular lung.

§ ✓5ᵗʰ **010.8 Other primary progressive tuberculosis** `CC` `HIV`
[0-6]   **EXCLUDES** *tuberculous erythema nodosum (017.1)*
    CC Excl: See code: 010.0

§ ✓5ᵗʰ **010.9 Primary tuberculous infection, unspecified** `CC` `HIV`
[0-6]   **CC Excl:** See code: 010.0

✓4ᵗʰ **011 Pulmonary tuberculosis**
    Use additional code to identify any associated silicosis (502)

§ ✓5ᵗʰ **011.0 Tuberculosis of lung, infiltrative** `CC` `HIV`
[0-6]   **CC Excl: For code 011.00:** 011.00–012.86, 017.90–018.96, 031.0,
    031.2–031.9, 041.81–041.9, 137.0, 139.8, 480.0–480.2, 480.8–487.1,
    488.01–488.02, 488.11–488.12, 494.0–508.9, 517.1, 518.89

§ ✓5ᵗʰ **011.1 Tuberculosis of lung, nodular** `CC` `HIV`
[0-6]   **CC Excl:** See code: 011.0

§ ✓5ᵗʰ **011.2 Tuberculosis of lung with cavitation** `CC` `HIV`
[0-6]   **CC Excl:** See code: 011.0

§ ✓5ᵗʰ **011.3 Tuberculosis of bronchus** `CC` `HIV`
[0-6]   **EXCLUDES** *isolated bronchial tuberculosis (012.2)*
    CC Excl: See code: 011.0

§ ✓5ᵗʰ **011.4 Tuberculous fibrosis of lung** `CC` `HIV`
[0-6]   **CC Excl:** See code: 011.0

§ ✓5ᵗʰ **011.5 Tuberculous bronchiectasis** `CC` `HIV`
[0-6]   **CC Excl:** See code: 011.0

§ ✓5ᵗʰ **011.6 Tuberculous pneumonia [any form]** `MCC` `HIV`
[0-6]   **DEF:** Inflammatory pulmonary reaction to tuberculous cells.
    CC Excl: For codes 011.60-011.65: See code 011.0; **For code 011.66:** 011.66,
    139.8, 480.0–480.2, 480.8–487.1, 488.01–488.02, 488.11–488.12,
    494.0–508.9, 517.1, 518.89

§ ✓5ᵗʰ **011.7 Tuberculous pneumothorax** `CC` `HIV`
[0-6]   **DEF:** Spontaneous rupture of damaged tuberculous pulmonary
    tissue.
    CC Excl: See code: 011.0

§ ✓5ᵗʰ **011.8 Other specified pulmonary tuberculosis** `CC` `HIV`
[0-6]   **CC Excl:** See code: 011.0

§ ✓5ᵗʰ **011.9 Pulmonary tuberculosis, unspecified** `CC` `HIV`
[0-6]   Respiratory tuberculosis NOS
    Tuberculosis of lung NOS
    CC Excl: See code: 011.0

✓4ᵗʰ **012 Other respiratory tuberculosis**
    EXCLUDES *respiratory tuberculosis, unspecified (011.9)*

§ ✓5ᵗʰ **012.0 Tuberculous pleurisy** `CC` `HIV`
[0-6]   Tuberculosis of pleura
    Tuberculous empyema
    Tuberculous hydrothorax
    EXCLUDES *pleurisy with effusion without mention of cause*
        (511.9)
        tuberculous pleurisy in primary progressive
        tuberculosis (010.1)
    DEF: Inflammation and exudation in the lining of the tubercular lung.
    CC Excl: 011.00–012.86, 017.90–018.96, 031.0, 031.2–031.9,
    041.81–041.9, 137.0, 139.8, 480.0–480.2, 480.8–487.1, 488,
    494.0–508.9, 517.1, 518.89

§ ✓5ᵗʰ **012.1 Tuberculosis of intrathoracic lymph nodes** `CC` `HIV`
[0-6]   Tuberculosis of lymph nodes:
        hilar
        mediastinal
        tracheobronchial
    Tuberculous tracheobronchial adenopathy
    EXCLUDES *that specified as primary (010.0-010.9)*
    CC Excl: See code: 012.0

§ ✓5ᵗʰ **012.2 Isolated tracheal or bronchial tuberculosis** `CC` `HIV`
[0-6]   **CC Excl:** 010.00-014.86, 018.00-018.96

§ ✓5ᵗʰ **012.3 Tuberculous laryngitis** `CC` `CM`
[0-6]   Tuberculosis of glottis
    CC Excl: See code: 012.2

§ ✓5ᵗʰ **012.8 Other specified respiratory tuberculosis** `CC` `HIV`
[0-6]   Tuberculosis of: Tuberculosis of:
        mediastinum   nose (septum)
        nasopharynx   sinus [any nasal]
    CC Excl: See code: 012.2

✓4ᵗʰ **013 Tuberculosis of meninges and central nervous system**

§ ✓5ᵗʰ **013.0 Tuberculous meningitis** `MCC` `HIV`
[0-6]   Tuberculosis of meninges (cerebral) (spinal)
    Tuberculous:
        leptomeningitis
        meningoencephalitis
    EXCLUDES *tuberculoma of meninges (013.1)*
    CC Excl: 003.21, 013.00–013.16, 013.40–013.56, 013.80–013.96,
    017.90–017.96, 031.2–031.9, 036.0, 041.81–041.9, 047.0–047.9,
    049.0–049.1, 053.0, 054.72, 072.1, 090.42, 091.81, 094.2, 098.89,
    100.81, 112.83, 114.2, 115.01, 115.11, 115.91, 130.0, 137.1, 139.8,
    320.0–322.9, 349.89–349.9, 357.0

§ ✓5ᵗʰ **013.1 Tuberculoma of meninges** `MCC` `HIV`
[0-6]   **CC Excl:** See code: 013.0

§ ✓5ᵗʰ **013.2 Tuberculoma of brain** `MCC` `HIV`
[0-6]   Tuberculosis of brain (current disease)
    CC Excl: 013.20–013.36, 013.60–013.96, 017.90–017.96, 031.2–031.9,
    041.81–041.9, 137.1, 139.8

§ ✓5ᵗʰ **013.3 Tuberculous abscess of brain** `MCC` `HIV`
[0-6]   **CC Excl:** See code: 013.2

§ ✓5ᵗʰ **013.4 Tuberculoma of spinal cord** `MCC` `HIV`
[0-6]   **CC Excl:** 013.00–013.16, 013.40–013.56, 013.80–013.96, 017.90–017.96,
    031.2–031.9, 041.81–041.9, 137.1, 139.8

§ ✓5ᵗʰ **013.5 Tuberculous abscess of spinal cord** `MCC` `HIV`
[0-6]   **CC Excl:** See code: 013.4

§ ✓5ᵗʰ **013.6 Tuberculous encephalitis or myelitis** `MCC` `HIV`
[0-6]   **CC Excl:** See code: 013.2

§ ✓5ᵗʰ **013.8 Other specified tuberculosis of central** `MCC` `HIV`
[0-6]   **nervous system**
    CC Excl: 013.80–013.96, 017.90–017.96, 031.2–031.9, 041.81–041.9,
    137.1, 139.8

§ ✓5ᵗʰ **013.9 Unspecified tuberculosis of central nervous** `MCC` `HIV`
[0-6]   **system**
    Tuberculosis of central nervous system NOS
    CC Excl: See code: 013.8

✓4ᵗʰ **014 Tuberculosis of intestines, peritoneum, and mesenteric glands**

§ ✓5ᵗʰ **014.0 Tuberculous peritonitis** `MCC` `HIV`
[0-6]   Tuberculous ascites
    DEF: Tuberculous inflammation of the membrane lining the
    abdomen.
    CC Excl: 014.00–014.86, 017.90–017.96, 031.2–031.9, 041.81–041.9,
    139.8

§ ✓5ᵗʰ **014.8 Other** `CC` `HIV`
[0-6]   Tuberculosis (of):
        anus
        intestine (large) (small)
        mesenteric glands
        rectum
        retroperitoneal (lymph nodes)
    Tuberculous enteritis
    CC Excl: For codes 014.80, 014.82-014.86: 014.00–014.86, 017.90–017.96,
    031.2–031.9, 041.81–041.9, 139.8; **For code 014.81:** 014.81, 139.8

---

§   Requires fifth digit. Valid digits are in [brackets] under each code. See beginning of section 010-018 for codes and definitions.

`N` Newborn Age: 0   `P` Pediatric Age: 0-17   `M` Maternity Age: 12-55   `A` Adult Age: 15-124   `MCC` Major CC Condition   `CC` CC Condition   `HIV` HIV Related Dx

4 – Volume 1   **2015 ICD-9-CM**

√4th **015 Tuberculosis of bones and joints**
  Use additional code to identify manifestation, as:
    tuberculous:
      arthropathy (711.4)
      necrosis of bone (730.8)
      osteitis (730.8)
      osteomyelitis (730.8)
      synovitis (727.01)
      tenosynovitis (727.01)

§ √5th **015.0 Vertebral column**   `CC` `HIV`
  [0-6]   Pott's disease
    Use additional code to identify manifestation, as:
      curvature of spine [Pott's] (737.4)
      kyphosis (737.4)
      spondylitis (720.81)
    CC Excl: 015.00-015.06

§ √5th **015.1 Hip**   `CC` `HIV`
  [0-6]   **CC Excl:** 015.10-015.16

§ √5th **015.2 Knee**   `CC` `HIV`
  [0-6]   **CC Excl:** 015.20-015.26

§ √5th **015.5 Limb bones**   `CC` `HIV`
  [0-6]   Tuberculous dactylitis
    CC Excl: 015.10-015.56

§ √5th **015.6 Mastoid**   `CC` `HIV`
  [0-6]   Tuberculous mastoiditis
    CC Excl: 015.60-015.66

§ √5th **015.7 Other specified bone**   `CC` `HIV`
  [0-6]   **CC Excl: For code 015.70:** 015.00-015.70; **For code 015.71:** 015.00-015.66,
    015.71; **For code 015.72:** 015.00-015.66, 015.72; **For code 015.73:**
    015.00-015.66, 015.73; **For code 015.74:** 015.00-015.66, 015.74; **For
    code 015.75:** 015.00-015.66, 015.75; **For code 015.76:** 015.00-015.66,
    015.76

§ √5th **015.8 Other specified joint**   `CC` `HIV`
  [0-6]   **CC Excl:** 015.80-015.86

§ √5th **015.9 Tuberculosis of unspecified bones and joints**   `CC` `HIV`
  [0-6]   **CC Excl: For codes 015.90, 015.92-015.96:** 015.00-015.66, 015.80-015.96;
    For codes 015.91: 015.00-015.66, 015.80-015.93, 015.95-015.96

√4th **016 Tuberculosis of genitourinary system**

§ √5th **016.0 Kidney**   `CC` `HIV`
  [0-6]   Renal tuberculosis
    Use additional code to identify manifestation, as:
      tuberculous:
        nephropathy (583.81)
        pyelitis (590.81)
        pyelonephritis (590.81)
    CC Excl: 016.00-016.36, 016.90-016.96, 017.90-017.96, 031.2-031.9,
    041.81-041.9, 137.2, 139.8

§ √5th **016.1 Bladder**   `CC` `HIV`
  [0-6]   **CC Excl:** See code: 016.0

§ √5th **016.2 Ureter**   `CC` `HIV`
  [0-6]   **CC Excl:** See code: 016.0

§ √5th **016.3 Other urinary organs**   `CC` `HIV`
  [0-6]   **CC Excl:** See code: 016.0

§ √5th **016.4 Epididymis**   `CC` `HIV` ♂
  [0-6]   **CC Excl:** 016.40-016.56, 016.90-016.96, 017.90-017.96, 031.2-031.9,
    041.81-041.9, 137.2, 139.8

§ √5th **016.5 Other male genital organs**   `CC` `HIV` ♂
  [0-6]   Use additional code to identify manifestation, as:
      tuberculosis of:
        prostate (601.4)
        seminal vesicle (608.81)
        testis (608.81)
    CC Excl: See code: 016.4

§ √5th **016.6 Tuberculous oophoritis and salpingitis**   `CC` `HIV` ♀
  [0-6]   **CC Excl:** 016.60-016.96, 017.90-017.96, 031.2-031.9, 041.81-041.9,
    137.2, 139.8

§ √5th **016.7 Other female genital organs**   `CC` `HIV` ♀
  [0-6]   Tuberculous:
      cervicitis
      endometritis
    CC Excl: See code: 016.6

§ √5th **016.9 Genitourinary tuberculosis, unspecified**   `CC` `HIV`
  [0-6]   **CC Excl:** 016.90-016.96, 017.90-017.96, 031.2-031.9,
    041.81-041.9, 137.2, 139.8

√4th **017 Tuberculosis of other organs**

§ √5th **017.0 Skin and subcutaneous cellular tissue**   `CC` `HIV`
  [0-6]   Lupus: Tuberculosis:
          exedens   colliquativa
          vulgaris   cutis
          Scrofuloderma   lichenoides
                               papulonecrotica
                               verrucosa cutis

    EXCLUDES lupus erythematosus (695.4)
                  disseminated (710.0)
                lupus NOS (710.0)
                nonspecific reaction to test for tuberculosis without
                  active tuberculosis (795.51-795.52)
                positive PPD (795.51)
                positive tuberculin skin test without active
                  tuberculosis (795.51)

    CC Excl: 010.00-018.96

§ √5th **017.1 Erythema nodosum with hypersensitivity**   `HIV`
  [0-6]   **reaction in tuberculosis**
      Bazin's disease
      Erythema:
        induratum
        nodosum, tuberculous
      Tuberculosis indurativa

    EXCLUDES erythema nodosum NOS (695.2)

    DEF: Tender, inflammatory, bilateral nodules appearing on the shins
    and thought to be an allergic reaction to tuberculotoxin.

§ √5th **017.2 Peripheral lymph nodes**   `CC` `HIV`
  [0-6]   Scrofula
      Scrofulous abscess
      Tuberculous adenitis

    EXCLUDES tuberculosis of lymph nodes:
                  bronchial and mediastinal (012.1)
                  mesenteric and retroperitoneal (014.8)
                  tuberculous tracheobronchial adenopathy (012.1)

    DEF: Scrofula: Old name for tuberculous cervical lymphadenitis.
    CC Excl: 017.20-017.26, 017.90-017.96, 031.2-031.9, 041.81-041.9,
    139.8

§ √5th **017.3 Eye**   `CC` `HIV`
  [0-6]   Use additional code to identify manifestation, as:
      tuberculous:
        chorioretinitis, disseminated (363.13)
        episcleritis (379.09)
        interstitial keratitis (370.59)
        iridocyclitis, chronic (364.11)
        keratoconjunctivitis (phlyctenular) (370.31)
    CC Excl: 017.30-017.36, 017.90-017.96, 031.2-031.9, 041.81-041.9,
    139.8

§ √5th **017.4 Ear**   `CC` `HIV`
  [0-6]   Tuberculosis of ear
      Tuberculous otitis media

    EXCLUDES tuberculous mastoiditis (015.6)

    CC Excl: 017.40-017.46, 017.90-017.96, 031.2-031.9, 041.81-041.9,
    139.8

§ √5th **017.5 Thyroid gland**   `CC` `HIV`
  [0-6]   **CC Excl:** 017.50-017.56, 017.90-017.96, 031.2-031.9, 041.81-041.9,
    139.8

§ √5th **017.6 Adrenal glands**   `CC` `HIV`
  [0-6]   Addison's disease, tuberculous
    CC Excl: 017.60-017.66, 017.90-017.96, 031.2-031.9, 041.81-041.9,
    139.8

§ √5th **017.7 Spleen**   `CC` `HIV`
  [0-6]   **CC Excl:** 017.70-017.76, 017.90-017.96, 031.2-031.9, 041.81-041.9,
    139.8

§ √5th **017.8 Esophagus**   `CC` `HIV`
  [0-6]   **CC Excl:** 017.80-017.96, 031.2-031.9, 041.81-041.9, 139.8

---

§ Requires fifth digit. Valid digits are in [brackets] under each code. See beginning of section 010-018 for codes and definitions.

√4th / √5th Additional Digit Required   Unacceptable PDx   Manifestation Code   Hospital Acquired Condition   ►◄ Revised Text   ● New Code   ▲ Revised Code Title

Infectious and Parasitic Diseases

017.9–023.9

§ ✓5ᵗʰ **017.9 Other specified organs**   `CC` `HIV`
[0-6]   Use additional code to identify manifestation, as:
      tuberculosis of:
         endocardium [any valve] (424.91)
         myocardium (422.0)
         pericardium (420.0)
    CC Excl: 017.90-017.96, 031.2-031.9, 041.81-041.9, 139.8

✓4ᵗʰ **018 Miliary tuberculosis**
    INCLUDES   tuberculosis:
         disseminated
         generalized
         miliary, whether of a single specified site, multiple sites,
            or unspecified site
         polyserositis
    DEF: A form of tuberculosis caused by caseous material carried through the bloodstream planting seedlike tubercles in various body organs.

§ ✓5ᵗʰ **018.0 Acute miliary tuberculosis**   `MCC` `HIV`
[0-6]   **CC Excl:** 017.90-018.96, 031.2-031.9, 041.81-041.9, 139.8

§ ✓5ᵗʰ **018.8 Other specified miliary tuberculosis**   `MCC` `HIV`
[0-6]   **CC Excl:** See code: 018.0

§ ✓5ᵗʰ **018.9 Miliary tuberculosis, unspecified**   `MCC` `HIV`
[0-6]   **CC Excl:** See code: 018.0

Zoonotic Bacterial Diseases (020-027)

✓4ᵗʰ **020 Plague**
    INCLUDES   infection by Yersinia [Pasteurella] pestis

    020.0 Bubonic   `MCC`
      DEF: Most common acute and severe form of plague characterized by lymphadenopathy (buboes), chills, fever and headache.
      CC Excl: 020.0-020.9

    020.1 Cellulocutaneous   `MCC`
      DEF: Plague characterized by inflammation and necrosis of skin.
      CC Excl: See code: 020.0

    020.2 Septicemic   `MCC`
      DEF: Plague characterized by massive infection in the bloodstream.
      CC Excl: 020.0-020.9, 771.81, 771.83-771.89, 995.90-995.94

    020.3 Primary pneumonic   `MCC`
      DEF: Plague characterized by massive pulmonary infection.
      CC Excl: 011.00-012.16, 012.80-012.86, 017.90-017.96, 020.0-020.9, 021.3, 022.1, 031.0, 039.1, 073.0, 115.05, 115.15, 115.95, 122.1, 130.4, 136.3, 480.0-487.1, 488.01-488.02, 488.11-488.12, 495.0-495.9, 500-502

    020.4 Secondary pneumonic   `MCC`
      DEF: Lung infection as a secondary complication of plague.
      CC Excl: 011.73-011.93, 480.3

    020.5 Pneumonic, unspecified   `MCC`
      CC Excl: 020.5, 480.3

    020.8 Other specified types of plague   `MCC`
      Abortive plague   Pestis minor
      Ambulatory plague
      CC Excl: 020.8

    020.9 Plague, unspecified   `MCC`
      CC Excl: 020.9

✓4ᵗʰ **021 Tularemia**
    INCLUDES   deerfly fever
         infection by Francisella [Pasteurella] tularensis
         rabbit fever
    DEF: A febrile disease transmitted by the bites of deer flies, fleas and ticks, by inhalations of aerosolized F. tularensis or by ingestion of contaminated food or water; patients quickly develop fever, chills, weakness, headache, backache and malaise.

    021.0 Ulceroglandular tularemia   `CC`
      DEF: Lesions occur at the site Francisella tularensis organism enters body, usually the fingers or hands.
      CC Excl: 021.0

    021.1 Enteric tularemia   `CC`
      Tularemia:
        cryptogenic
        intestinal
        typhoidal
      CC Excl: 021.1

    021.2 Pulmonary tularemia   `CC`
      Bronchopneumonic tularemia
      CC Excl: 482.49-487.1, 488.01-488.02, 488.11-488.12, 495.0-495.9, 500-508.9, 517.1, 517.8, 518.89, 519.8-519.9

    021.3 Oculoglandular tularemia   `CC`
      DEF: Painful conjunctival infection by Francisella tularensis organism with possible corneal, preauricular lymph, or lacrimal involvement.
      CC Excl: 021.3, 480.3

    021.8 Other specified tularemia   `CC`
      Tularemia:
        generalized or disseminated
        glandular
      CC Excl: 021.0-021.9

    021.9 Unspecified tularemia   `CC`
      CC Excl: See code: 021.8

✓4ᵗʰ **022 Anthrax**
    DEF: A bacterial disease usually transmitted by contact with infected animals or their discharges; primary routes of inoculation are cutaneous, gastrointestinal and inhalation.
    AHA: 4Q '02, 70

    022.0 Cutaneous anthrax   `CC`
      Malignant pustule
      CC Excl: 022.0

    022.1 Pulmonary anthrax   `MCC`
      Respiratory anthrax
      Wool-sorters' disease
      CC Excl: 011.00-012.16, 012.80-012.86, 017.90-017.96, 020.3-020.5, 021.3, 022.1, 031.0, 039.1, 073.0, 115.05, 115.15, 115.95, 122.1, 130.4, 136.3, 480.0-487.1, 488.01-488.02, 488.11-488.12, 494.0-495.9, 500-508.9, 517.1, 517.8, 518.89, 519.8-519.9

    022.2 Gastrointestinal anthrax   `CC`
      CC Excl: 022.2

    022.3 Anthrax septicemia   `MCC`
      CC Excl: 003.1, 020.2, 022.3, 036.2, 038.0-038.9, 040.89-041.3, 041.41-041.9, 054.5, 139.8, 771.81, 771.83-771.89, 995.90-995.94, V09.0-V09.91

    022.8 Other specified manifestations of anthrax   `CC`
      CC Excl: 022.8

    022.9 Anthrax, unspecified   `CC`
      CC Excl: 022.0-022.9

✓4ᵗʰ **023 Brucellosis**
    INCLUDES   fever:
         Malta
         Mediterranean
         undulant
    DEF: An infectious disease caused by gram-negative, aerobic coccobacilli organisms transmitted to humans through contact with infected tissue or dairy products; fever, sweating, weakness and aching are symptoms.

    023.0 Brucella melitensis
      DEF: Infection from direct or indirect contact with infected sheep or goats.

    023.1 Brucella abortus
      DEF: Infection from direct or indirect contact with infected cattle.

    023.2 Brucella suis
      DEF: Infection from direct or indirect contact with infected swine.

    023.3 Brucella canis
      DEF: Infection from direct or indirect contact with infected dogs.

    023.8 Other brucellosis   `CC`
      Infection by more than one organism
      CC Excl: 023.0-023.9

    023.9 Brucellosis, unspecified   `CC`
      CC Excl: See code: 023.8

---

§   Requires fifth digit. Valid digits are in [brackets] under each code. See beginning of section 010-018 for codes and definitions.

N Newborn Age: 0   **P** Pediatric Age: 0-17   **M** Maternity Age: 12-55   **A** Adult Age: 15-124   `MCC` Major CC Condition   `CC` CC Condition   `HIV` HIV Related Dx

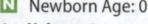 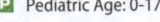

6 – Volume 1   **2015 ICD-9-CM**

024 Glanders `CC`

Infection by:
    actinobacillus mallei
    malleomyces mallei
    pseudomonas mallei
Farcy
Malleus

DEF: Equine infection causing mucosal inflammation and skin ulcers in humans.

CC Excl: 024

025 Melioidosis `CC`

Infection by:
    malleomyces pseudomallei
    pseudomonas pseudomallei
    whitmore's bacillus
Pseudoglanders

DEF: Rare infection caused by *Pseudomonas pseudomallei;* clinical symptoms range from localized infection to fatal septicemia.

CC Excl: 025

✓4ᵗʰ 026 Rat-bite fever

026.0 Spirillary fever `CC`

Rat-bite fever due to Spirillum minor [S. minus]
Sodoku

CC Excl: 026.0-026.9

026.1 Streptobacillary fever `CC`

Epidemic arthritic erythema
Haverhill fever
Rat-bite fever due to Streptobacillus moniliformis

CC Excl: See code: 026.0

026.9 Unspecified rat-bite fever `CC`

CC Excl: See code: 026.0

✓4ᵗʰ 027 Other zoonotic bacterial diseases

027.0 Listeriosis `CC`

Infection   ⎫
Septicemia ⎬ by Listeria monocytogenes

Use additional code to identify manifestation, as meningitis (320.7)

EXCLUDES *congenital listeriosis (771.2)*

CC Excl: 027.0-027.9

027.1 Erysipelothrix infection

Erysipeloid (of Rosenbach)
Infection   ⎫ by Erysipelothrix insidiosa [E.
Septicemia ⎬   rhusiopathiae]

DEF: Usually associated with handling of fish, meat, or poultry; symptoms range from localized inflammation to septicemia.

027.2 Pasteurellosis `CC`

Pasteurella pseudotuberculosis infection
Mesenteric adenitis   ⎫
Septic infection (cat ⎬ by Pasteurella multocida
   bite) (dog bite)   ⎭   [P. septica]

EXCLUDES *infection by:*
    Francisella [Pasteurella] tularensis (021.0-021.9)
    Yersinia [Pasteurella] pestis (020.0-020.9)

DEF: Swelling, abscesses, or septicemia from *Pasteurella multocida,* commonly transmitted to humans by a dog or cat scratch.

CC Excl: See code: 027.0

AHA: 3Q, '12, 13

027.8 Other specified zoonotic bacterial diseases `CC`

CC Excl: See code: 027.0

027.9 Unspecified zoonotic bacterial disease `CC`

CC Excl: See code: 027.0

Other Bacterial Diseases (030-041)

EXCLUDES *bacterial venereal diseases (098.0-099.9)*
    bartonellosis (088.0)

✓4ᵗʰ 030 Leprosy

INCLUDES Hansen's disease
infection by Mycobacterium leprae

030.0 Lepromatous [type L] `CC`

Lepromatous leprosy (macular) (diffuse) (infiltrated) (nodular) (neuritic)

DEF: Infectious, disseminated leprosy bacilli with lesions and deformities.

CC Excl: 030.0

030.1 Tuberculoid [type T] `CC`

Tuberculoid leprosy (macular) (maculoanesthetic) (major) (minor) (neuritic)

DEF: Relatively benign, self-limiting leprosy with neuralgia and scales.

CC Excl: 030.1

030.2 Indeterminate [group I] `CC`

Indeterminate [uncharacteristic] leprosy (macular) (neuritic)

DEF: Uncharacteristic leprosy, frequently an early manifestation.

CC Excl: 030.2

030.3 Borderline [group B] `CC`

Borderline or dimorphous leprosy (infiltrated) (neuritic)

DEF: Transitional form of leprosy, neither lepromatous nor tuberculoid.

CC Excl: 030.3

030.8 Other specified leprosy `CC`

CC Excl: 030.8

030.9 Leprosy, unspecified `CC`

CC Excl: 030.9

✓4ᵗʰ 031 Diseases due to other mycobacteria

031.0 Pulmonary `CC`

Battey disease
Infection by Mycobacterium:
    avium
    intracellulare [Battey bacillus]
    kansasii

CC Excl: 011.00-012.86, 017.90-017.96, 031.0, 031.2-031.9, 041.81-041.9, 137.0, 139.8, 480.0-480.2, 480.8-487.1, 488.01-488.02, 488.11-488.12, 494.0-508.9, 517.1, 518.89

AHA: ▶2Q, '13, 17◀

031.1 Cutaneous `CC`

Buruli ulcer
Infection by Mycobacterium:
    marinum [M. balnei]
    ulcerans

CC Excl: 031.0-031.9

031.2 Disseminated `CC` `HIV`

Disseminated mycobacterium avium-intracellulare complex (DMAC)
Mycobacterium avium-intracellulare complex (MAC) bacteremia

DEF: Disseminated mycobacterium avium-intracellulare complex (DMAC): A serious systemic form of MAC commonly observed in patients in the late course of AIDS.

DEF: Mycobacterium avium-intracellulare complex (MAC) bacterium: Human pulmonary disease, lymphadenitis in children and systemic disease in immunocompromised individuals caused by a slow growing, gram-positive, aerobic organism.

CC Excl: See code: 031.1

AHA: 4Q, '97, 31

031.8 Other specified mycobacterial diseases `CC` `HIV`

CC Excl: See code: 031.1

031.9 Unspecified diseases due to mycobacteria `CC` `HIV`

Atypical mycobacterium infection NOS

CC Excl: See code: 031.1

✓4ᵗʰ 032 Diphtheria

INCLUDES infection by Corynebacterium diphtheriae

032.0 Faucial diphtheria `CC`

Membranous angina, diphtheritic

DEF: Diphtheria of the throat.

CC Excl: 032.0-032.9

032.1 Nasopharyngeal diphtheria `CC`

CC Excl: See code: 032.0

032.2 Anterior nasal diphtheria `CC`

CC Excl: See code: 032.0

032.3 Laryngeal diphtheria `CC`

Laryngotracheitis, diphtheritic

CC Excl: See code: 032.0

✓5ᵗʰ 032.8 Other specified diphtheria

032.81 Conjunctival diphtheria `CC`

Pseudomembranous diphtheritic conjunctivitis

CC Excl: See code: 032.0

2015 ICD-9-CM   ✓4ᵗʰ ✓5ᵗʰ Additional Digit Required   Unacceptable PDx   Manifestation Code   Hospital Acquired Condition   ▶◀ Revised Text   ● New Code   ▲ Revised Code Title

October 2014 · Volume 1 – 7

032.82 Diphtheritic myocarditis `CC`
CC Excl: 032.82, 074.20, 074.22-074.23, 093.82, 390, 391.2-391.9, 398.0-398.90, 398.99, 422.0-422.99, 429.0, 429.71-429.79, 459.89-459.9

032.83 Diphtheritic peritonitis `CC`
CC Excl: 014.00-014.06, 032.83, 090.0, 095.2, 098.86, 099.56, 540.0-540.1, 567.0-567.1, 567.22, 567.29, 567.81, 567.9, 569.87-569.9, 577.8, 614.5-614.7, 639.0, 670.00-670.84, 777.6, 998.7

032.84 Diphtheritic cystitis `CC`
CC Excl: See code: 032.0

032.85 Cutaneous diphtheria `CC`
CC Excl: See code: 032.0
AHA: ▶1Q, '14, 5◀

032.89 Other `CC`
CC Excl: See code: 032.0

032.9 Diphtheria, unspecified `CC`
CC Excl: See code: 032.0

√4ᵗʰ 033 Whooping cough
INCLUDES   pertussis
Use additional code to identify any associated pneumonia (484.3)
DEF: An acute, highly contagious respiratory tract infection caused by *Bordetella pertussis* and *B. bronchiseptica*; characteristic paroxysmal cough.

033.0 Bordetella pertussis [B. pertussis] `CC`
CC Excl: 033.0-033.9

033.1 Bordetella parapertussis [B. parapertussis] `CC`
CC Excl: See code: 033.0

033.8 Whooping cough due to other specified organism `CC`
Bordetella bronchiseptica [B. bronchiseptica]
CC Excl: See code: 033.0

033.9 Whooping cough, unspecified organism `CC`
CC Excl: See code: 033.0

√4ᵗʰ 034 Streptococcal sore throat and scarlet fever

034.0 Streptococcal sore throat
Septic: Streptococcal:
   angina   angina
   sore throat   laryngitis
                         pharyngitis
                         tonsillitis

J02.0 Streptococcal pharyngitis `I-10`

034.1 Scarlet fever `CC`
Scarlatina
EXCLUDES   parascarlatina (057.8)
DEF: Streptococcal infection and fever with red rash spreading from trunk.
CC Excl: 034.0-035

035 Erysipelas
EXCLUDES   postpartum or puerperal erysipelas (670.8)
DEF: An acute superficial cellulitis involving the dermal lymphatics; it is often caused by group A streptococci.

√4ᵗʰ 036 Meningococcal infection

036.0 Meningococcal meningitis `MCC`
Cerebrospinal fever (meningococcal)
Meningitis:
   cerebrospinal
   epidemic
CC Excl: 003.21, 013.00-013.16, 036.0, 036.89-036.9, 041.81-041.9, 047.0-047.9, 049.0-049.1, 053.0, 054.72, 072.1, 090.42, 091.81, 094.2, 098.89, 100.81, 112.83, 114.2, 115.01, 115.11, 115.91, 130.0, 139.8, 320.0-322.9, 349.89-349.9, 357.0

036.1 Meningococcal encephalitis `MCC`
CC Excl: 036.1, 036.89-036.9, 041.81-041.9, 139.8

036.2 Meningococcemia `MCC`
Meningococcal septicemia
CC Excl: 003.1, 020.2, 036.2, 036.89-036.9, 038.0-038.9, 041.81-041.9, 054.5, 139.8, 995.90-995.94

036.3 Waterhouse-Friderichsen syndrome, meningococcal `MCC`
Meningococcal hemorrhagic adrenalitis
Meningococcic adrenal syndrome
Waterhouse-Friderichsen syndrome NOS
CC Excl: 036.3, 036.89-036.9, 041.81-041.9, 139.8

√5ᵗʰ 036.4 Meningococcal carditis

036.40 Meningococcal carditis, unspecified `MCC`
CC Excl: 036.40, 036.89-036.9, 041.81-041.9, 139.8

036.41 Meningococcal pericarditis `MCC`
DEF: Meningococcal infection of the outer membrane of the heart.
CC Excl: 036.41, 036.89-036.9, 041.81-041.9, 139.8

036.42 Meningococcal endocarditis `MCC`
DEF: Meningococcal infection of the membranes lining the cavities of the heart.
CC Excl: 036.42, 036.89-036.9, 041.81-041.9, 139.8

036.43 Meningococcal myocarditis `MCC`
DEF: Meningococcal infection of the muscle of the heart.
CC Excl: 036.43, 041.81-041.9, 139.8

√5ᵗʰ 036.8 Other specified meningococcal infections

036.81 Meningococcal optic neuritis `CC`
CC Excl: 036.81, 036.89-036.9, 041.81-041.9, 139.8

036.82 Meningococcal arthropathy `CC`
CC Excl: 036.82-036.9, 041.81-041.9, 139.8

036.89 Other `CC`
CC Excl: 036.89-036.9, 041.81-041.9, 139.8

036.9 Meningococcal infection, unspecified `CC`
Meningococcal infection NOS
CC Excl: See code: 036.89

037 Tetanus `MCC`
EXCLUDES   tetanus:
      complicating:
         abortion (634-638 with .0, 639.0)
         ectopic or molar pregnancy (639.0)
      neonatorum (771.3)
      puerperal (670.8)
DEF: An acute, often fatal, infectious disease caused by the anaerobic, spore-forming bacillus *Clostridium tetani;* the bacillus enters the body through a contaminated wound, burns, surgical wounds, or cutaneous ulcers. Symptoms: lockjaw, spasms, seizures, and paralysis.
CC Excl: 037, 139.8

√4ᵗʰ 038 Septicemia
Use additional code for systemic inflammatory response syndrome (SIRS) (995.91-995.92)
EXCLUDES   bacteremia (790.7)
      during labor (659.3)
      following ectopic or molar pregnancy (639.0)
      following infusion, injection, transfusion, or vaccination (999.3)
      postpartum, puerperal (670)
      septicemia (sepsis) of newborn (771.81)
      that complicating abortion (634-638 with .0, 639.0)
DEF: A systemic disease associated with the presence and persistence of pathogenic microorganisms or their toxins in the blood.
AHA: 3Q, '12, 11-12; 1Q, '12, 19; 2Q, '10, 4; 2Q, '04, 16; 4Q, '88, 10; 3Q, '88, 12
TIP: When septicemia is due to a complication of care, sequence the complication code first (e.g., due to device or injury).

038.0 Streptococcal septicemia `MCC` `HIV`
CC Excl: 003.1, 020.2, 036.2, 038.0-038.9, 040.82-041.3, 041.41-041.9, 054.5, 139.8, 995.90-995.94, V09.0-V09.91
AHA: 4Q, '03, 79; 2Q, '96, 5

√5ᵗʰ 038.1 Staphylococcal septicemia
AHA: 4Q, '97, 32

038.10 Staphylococcal septicemia, unspecified `MCC` `HIV`
CC Excl: See code: 038.0

038.11 Methicillin susceptible Staphylococcus aureus septicemia `MCC` `HIV`
MSSA septicemia
Staphylococcus aureus septicemia NOS
CC Excl: See code: 038.0
AHA: 4Q, '08, 69-70;1Q, '05, 7; 2Q, '00, 5; 4Q, '98, 42
A41.01 Sepsis d/t Methicillin susceptible Staphylococcus aureus `I-10`

038.12 Methicillin resistant Staphylococcus aureus septicemia `MCC` `HIV`
CC Excl: See code: 038.0
AHA: 4Q, '11, 153; 3Q, '11, 15; 4Q, '08, 69-73

N Newborn Age: 0   P Pediatric Age: 0-17   M Maternity Age: 12-55   A Adult Age: 15-124   MCC Major CC Condition   CC CC Condition   HIV HIV Related Dx

8 – Volume 1 · October 2014   2015 ICD-9-CM

038.19 Other staphylococcal septicemia `MCC` `HIV`
    CC Excl: See code: 038.0
    AHA: 2Q, '00, 5
    A41.1 Sepsis due to other specified `I-10`

038.2 Pneumococcal septicemia `MCC` `HIV`
[Streptococcus pneumoniae septicemia]
    CC Excl: See code 038.0
    AHA: 2Q, '96, 5; 1Q, '91, 13

038.3 Septicemia due to anaerobes `MCC` `HIV`
Septicemia due to bacteroides
    EXCLUDES *gas gangrene (040.0)*
        that due to anaerobic streptococci (038.0)
    DEF: Infection of blood by microorganisms that thrive without oxygen.
    CC Excl: See code 038.0

`√5ᵗʰ` **038.4 Septicemia due to other gram-negative organisms**
    DEF: Infection of blood by microorganisms categorized as gram-negative by Gram's method of staining for identification of bacteria.

038.40 Gram-negative organism, unspecified `MCC` `HIV`
Gram-negative septicemia NOS
    CC Excl: See code 038.0

038.41 Hemophilus influenzae [H. influenzae] `MCC` `HIV`
    CC Excl: See code 038.0

038.42 Escherichia coli [E. coli] `MCC` `HIV`
    CC Excl: See code 038.0
    AHA: 4Q, '03, 73
    A41.51 Sepsis due to Escherichia coli [E coli] `I-10`

038.43 Pseudomonas `MCC` `HIV`
    CC Excl: See code 038.0

038.44 Serratia `MCC` `HIV`
    CC Excl: See code 038.0

038.49 Other `MCC` `HIV`
    CC Excl: See code 038.0
    AHA: 3Q, '12, 13
    A41.59 Other Gram-negative sepsis `I-10`

038.8 Other specified septicemias `MCC` `HIV`
    EXCLUDES *septicemia (due to):*
        anthrax (022.3)
        gonococcal (098.89)
        herpetic (054.5)
        meningococcal (036.2)
        septicemic plague (020.2)
    CC Excl: See code 038.0

038.9 Unspecified septicemia `MCC` `HIV`
Septicemia NOS
    EXCLUDES *bacteremia NOS (790.7)*
    CC Excl: See code 038.0
    AHA: 4Q, '07, 97; 2Q, '05, 18-19; 2Q, '04, 16; 4Q, '03, 79; 2Q, '00, 3; 3Q, '99, 5, 9; 1Q, '98, 5; 3Q, '96, 16; 2Q, '96, 6
    TIP: Ensure that documentation includes clinical evidence of systemic infection; do not code if documentation indicates "urosepsis" only.
    A41.9 Sepsis unspecified `I-10`

`√4ᵗʰ` **039 Actinomycotic infections**
    INCLUDES actinomycotic mycetoma
        infection by Actinomycetales, such as species of
          Actinomyces, Actinomadura, Nocardia,
          Streptomyces
        maduromycosis (actinomycotic)
        schizomycetoma (actinomycotic)
    DEF: Inflammatory lesions and abscesses at site of infection by *Actinomyces israelii.*

039.0 Cutaneous `CC` `HIV`
Erythrasma
Trichomycosis axillaris
    CC Excl: 039.0, 039.8-039.9

039.1 Pulmonary `CC` `HIV`
Thoracic actinomycosis
    CC Excl: 039.1, 039.8-039.9, 480.3

039.2 Abdominal `CC` `HIV`
    CC Excl: 039.2, 039.8-039.9

039.3 Cervicofacial `CC` `HIV`
    CC Excl: 039.3, 039.8-039.9

039.4 Madura foot `CC` `HIV`
    EXCLUDES *madura foot due to mycotic infection (117.4)*
    CC Excl: 039.4-039.9

039.8 Of other specified sites `CC` `HIV`
    CC Excl: 039.0-039.9

039.9 Of unspecified site `CC` `HIV`
Actinomycosis NOS
Maduromycosis NOS
Nocardiosis NOS
    CC Excl: See code: 039.8

`√4ᵗʰ` **040 Other bacterial diseases**
    EXCLUDES *bacteremia NOS (790.7)*
        bacterial infection NOS (041.9)

040.0 Gas gangrene `MCC`
Gas bacillus infection or gangrene
Infection by Clostridium:
    histolyticum
    oedematiens
    perfringens [welchii]
    septicum
    sordellii
Malignant edema
Myonecrosis, clostridial
Myositis, clostridial
    CC Excl: 040.0, 139.8
    AHA: 1Q, '95, 11

040.1 Rhinoscleroma
    DEF: Growths on the nose and nasopharynx caused by *Klebsiella rhinoscleromatis.*

040.2 Whipple's disease `CC`
Intestinal lipodystrophy
    CC Excl: 040.2

040.3 Necrobacillosis `CC`
    DEF: Infection with *Fusobacterium necrophorum* causing abscess or necrosis.
    CC Excl: 040.3
    AHA: 4Q, '07, 85

`√5ᵗʰ` **040.4 Other specified botulism**
Non-foodborne intoxication due to toxins of Clostridium botulinum [C. botulinum]
    EXCLUDES *botulism NOS (005.1)*
        food poisoning due to toxins of Clostridium botulinum (005.1)

040.41 Infant botulism `P` `CC`
    DEF: Colonization of Clostridium botulinum spores in the large intestine; release of neurotoxins results in constipation; may progress to neuromuscular paralysis; affects infants of less than six months.
    CC Excl: 005.0-005.2, 008.45-008.46, 040.41-040.42
    AHA: 4Q, '07, 60

040.42 Wound botulism `CC`
Non-foodborne botulism NOS
    Use additional code to identify complicated open wound
    CC Excl: See code 040.41
    AHA: 4Q, '07, 60

`√5ᵗʰ` **040.8 Other specified bacterial diseases**

040.81 Tropical pyomyositis `CC`
    CC Excl: 040.81, 040.89

040.82 Toxic shock syndrome `MCC`
    Use additional code to identify the organism
    DEF: Syndrome caused by staphylococcal exotoxin that may rapidly progress to severe and intractable shock; symptoms include sunburn-like rash with peeling of skin on palms and soles, sudden onset high fever, vomiting, diarrhea, myalgia, and hypotension.
    CC Excl: 040.82, 338.0-338.4, 780.64-780.65, 780.91-780.99, 785.50-785.59, 785.9, 799.81-799.89
    AHA: ►2Q, '13, 21;◄ 4Q, '02, 44

040.89 Other
    AHA: N-D, '86, 7

✓4ᵗʰ **041 Bacterial infection in conditions classified elsewhere and of unspecified site**

> **NOTE** This category is provided to be used as an additional code to identify the bacterial agent in diseases classified elsewhere. This category will also be used to classify bacterial infections of unspecified nature or site.
>
> **EXCLUDES** septicemia (038.0-038.9)
> **AHA:** 2Q, '01, 12; J-A, '84, 19

✓5ᵗʰ **041.0 Streptococcus**

041.00 Streptococcus, unspecified

041.01 Group A
> **AHA:** 1Q, '02, 3

041.02 Group B
> **B95.1** Streptococcus group B cause of dz   I-10

041.03 Group C

041.04 Group D [Enterococcus]
> **B95.2** Enterococcus as the cause of dz class   I-10

041.05 Group G

041.09 Other Streptococcus
> **B95.4** Oth streptococcus cause of dz class elsewhere   I-10

✓5ᵗʰ **041.1 Staphylococcus**

041.10 Staphylococcus, unspecified
> **AHA:** 2Q, '06, 15

041.11 Methicillin susceptible Staphylococcus aureus
> MSSA
> Staphylococcus aureus NOS
> **AHA:** 4Q, '08, 69-70; 2Q, '06, 16; 4Q, '03, 104, 106; 2Q, '01, 11; 4Q, '98, 42, 54; 4Q, '97, 32
> **A49.01** Methicillin suscep staph infection, unsp site   I-10

041.12 Methicillin resistant Staphylococcus aureus
> Methicillin-resistant staphylococcus aureus (MRSA)
> **AHA:** 4Q, '09, 98; 4Q, '08, 69-70, 73
> **TIP:** Do not assign if combination code (with localized infection) available, or if only colonization or carrier status documented.

041.19 Other Staphylococcus
> **AHA:** 2Q, '11, 7; 2Q, '08, 3
> **B95.7** Other staphylococcus cause of dz class   I-10

041.2 Pneumococcus

041.3 Klebsiella pneumoniae
> **AHA:** 4Q, '08, 149

✓5ᵗʰ **041.4 Escherichia coli [E. coli]**
> **AHA:** 4Q, '11, 81-83

041.41 Shiga toxin-producing Escherichia coli [E. coli] (STEC) O157
> E. coli O157:H- (nonmotile) with confirmation of Shiga toxin
> E. coli O157 with confirmation of Shiga toxin when H antigen is unknown, or is not H7
> O157:H7 Escherichia coli [E.coli] with or without confirmation of Shiga toxin-production
> Shiga toxin-producing Escherichia coli [E.coli] O157:H7 with or without confirmation of Shiga toxin-production
> STEC O157:H7 with or without confirmation of Shiga toxin-production
> **AHA:** 4Q, '11, 83

041.42 Other specified Shiga toxin-producing Escherichia coli [E. coli] (STEC)
> Non-O157 Shiga toxin-producing Escherichia coli [E.coli]
> Non-O157 Shiga toxin-producing Escherichia coli [E.coli] with known O group

041.43 Shiga toxin-producing Escherichia coli [E. coli] (STEC), unspecified
> Shiga toxin-producing Escherichia coli [E. coli] with unspecified O group
> STEC NOS

041.49 Other and unspecified Escherichia coli [E. coli]
> Escherichia coli [E. coli] NOS
> Non-Shiga toxin-producing E. Coli
> **AHA:** 4Q, '11, 155
> **B96.20** Unsp Escherichia coli as cause of diseases classd elswhr   I-10

041.5 Hemophilus influenzae [H. influenzae]

041.6 Proteus (mirabilis) (morganii)

041.7 Pseudomonas
> **AHA:** 1Q, '10, 9; 4Q, '02, 45
> **B96.5** Pseudomonas as the cause of dz class elsewhere   I-10

✓5ᵗʰ **041.8 Other specified bacterial infections**

041.81 Mycoplasma
> Eaton's agent
> Pleuropneumonia-like organisms [PPLO]

041.82 Bacteroides fragilis
> **DEF:** Anaerobic gram-negative bacilli of the gastrointestinal tract; frequently implicated in intra-abdominal infection; commonly resistant to antibiotics.

041.83 Clostridium perfringens

041.84 Other anaerobes
> Gram-negative anaerobes
> **EXCLUDES** Helicobacter pylori (041.86)

041.85 Other gram-negative organisms
> Aerobacter aerogenes
> Gram-negative bacteria NOS
> Mima polymorpha
> Serratia
> **EXCLUDES** gram-negative anaerobes (041.84)
> **AHA:** 1Q, '95, 18

041.86 Helicobacter pylori [H. pylori]
> **AHA:** 4Q, '95, 60
> **B96.81** Helicobacter pylori cause of dz class elsewhere   I-10

041.89 Other specified bacteria
> **AHA:** 2Q, '06, 7; 2Q, '03, 7
> **A49.8** Other bacterial infections of unspecified site   I-10

041.9 Bacterial infection, unspecified
> **AHA:** 2Q, '91, 9

Human Immunodeficiency Virus (HIV) Infection (042)

042 Human immunodeficiency virus [HIV] disease   MCC
> Acquired immune deficiency syndrome
> Acquired immunodeficiency syndrome
> AIDS
> AIDS-like syndrome
> AIDS-related complex
> ARC
> HIV infection, symptomatic
>
> Use additional code(s) to identify all manifestations of HIV
> Use additional code to identify HIV-2 infection (079.53)
>
> **EXCLUDES** asymptomatic HIV infection status (V08)
> exposure to HIV virus (V01.79)
> nonspecific serologic evidence of HIV (795.71)
>
> **CC Excl:** 042, 139.8
> **AHA:** 3Q, '10, 13; 4Q, '07, 63; 3Q, '06, 15; 1Q, '05, 7; 2Q, '04, 11; 1Q, '04, 5; 1Q, '03, 15; 1Q, '99, 14; 4Q, '97, 30, 31; 1Q, '93, 21; 2Q, '92, 11; 3Q, '90, 17; J-A, '87, 8
> **TIP:** Code only confirmed cases of HIV infection/illness; may be coded from provider's diagnostic statement.
> **B20** Human immunodeficiency virus [HIV] disease   I-10

N Newborn Age: 0   P Pediatric Age: 0-17   M Maternity Age: 12-55   A Adult Age: 15-124   MCC Major CC Condition   CC CC Condition   HIV HIV Related Dx

10 — Volume 1   2015 ICD-9-CM

Poliomyelitis and Other Non-Arthropod-borne Viral Diseases and Prion Diseases of Central Nervous System (045-049)

√4ᵗʰ 045 Acute poliomyelitis

> **EXCLUDES** *late effects of acute poliomyelitis (138)*

> The following fifth-digit subclassification is for use with category 045:
> 0 **poliovirus, unspecified type**
> 1 **poliovirus type I**
> 2 **poliovirus type II**
> 3 **poliovirus type III**

§ √5ᵗʰ 045.0 Acute paralytic poliomyelitis specified as bulbar MCC
[0-3]
Infantile paralysis (acute)
Poliomyelitis (acute) (anterior) } specified as bulbar
Polioencephalitis (acute) (bulbar)
Polioencephalomyelitis (acute) (anterior) (bulbar)
DEF: Acute paralytic infection occurring where the brain merges with the spinal cord; affecting breathing, swallowing, and heart rate.
CC Excl: 045.00-045.13

§ √5ᵗʰ 045.1 Acute poliomyelitis with other paralysis MCC
[0-3]
Paralysis:
  acute atrophic, spinal
  infantile, paralytic
Poliomyelitis (acute)
  anterior } with paralysis except bulbar
  epidemic
DEF: Paralytic infection affecting peripheral or spinal nerves.
CC Excl: See code: 045.0

§ √5ᵗʰ 045.2 Acute nonparalytic poliomyelitis
[0-3]
Poliomyelitis (acute)
  anterior } specified as nonparalytic
  epidemic
DEF: Nonparalytic infection causing pain, stiffness, and paresthesias.

§ √5ᵗʰ 045.9 Acute poliomyelitis, unspecified
[0-3]
Infantile paralysis
Poliomyelitis (acute) } unspecified whether paralytic or
  anterior   nonparalytic
  epidemic

√4ᵗʰ 046 Slow virus infections and prion diseases of central nervous system

046.0 Kuru CC
DEF: A chronic, progressive, fatal nervous system disorder; clinical symptoms include cerebellar ataxia, trembling, spasticity and progressive dementia.
CC Excl: 046.0-046.9

√5ᵗʰ 046.1 Jakob-Creutzfeldt disease
Use additional code to identify dementia:
  with behavioral disturbance (294.11)
  without behavioral disturbance (294.10)

046.11 Variant Creutzfeldt-Jakob disease CC
vCJD
AHA: 4Q, '08, 73-75
CC Excl: 013.60-013.66, 046.0-046.9, 048-049.0, 049.8, 052.0, 052.2, 054.3, 054.74, 056.01, 057.8-058.29, 059.00-059.9, 062.0-064, 066.2-066.3, 072.2, 073.7, 079.99, 081.9, 083.9, 090.41, 094.81, 117.5, 124, 130.0, 290.12, 323.01-323.9, 341.1, 487.8, 488.09, 488.19, 771.2, 984.9

046.19 Other and unspecified Creutzfeldt-Jakob disease CC
CJD
Familial Creutzfeldt-Jakob disease
Iatrogenic Creutzfeldt-Jakob disease
Jakob-Creutzfeldt disease, unspecified
Sporadic Creutzfeldt-Jakob disease
Subacute spongiform encephalopathy
EXCLUDES *variant Creutzfeldt-Jakob disease (vCJD) (046.11)*
DEF: Communicable, progressive spongiform encephalopathy thought to be caused by an infectious particle known as a "prion" (proteinaceous infection particle); a progressive, fatal disease manifested principally by mental deterioration.
CC Excl: See code: 046.11
AHA: 4Q, '08, 73-75

046.2 Subacute sclerosing panencephalitis CC
Dawson's inclusion body encephalitis
Van Bogaert's sclerosing leukoencephalitis
CC Excl: 046.2, 139.8
DEF: Progressive viral infection causing cerebral dysfunction, blindness, dementia, and death (SSPE).

046.3 Progressive multifocal leukoencephalopathy CC HIV
Multifocal leukoencephalopathy NOS
DEF: Infection affecting cerebral cortex in patients with weakened immune systems.
CC Excl: 013.60-013.66, 046.0-046.9, 048-049.0, 049.8, 052.0, 052.2, 054.3, 054.74, 056.01, 057.8-058.29, 059.00-059.9, 062.0-064, 066.2-066.3, 072.2, 073.7, 075, 081.9, 083.9, 090.41, 094.81, 117.5, 124, 130.0, 290.12, 323.01-323.9, 341.1, 487.8, 488.09, 488.19, 771.2, 984.9

√5ᵗʰ 046.7 Other specified prion diseases of central nervous system
EXCLUDES *Creutzfeldt-Jakob disease (046.11-046.19)*
Jakob-Creutzfeldt disease (046.11-046.19)
kuru (046.0)
variant Creutzfeldt-Jakob disease (vCJD) (046.11)

046.71 Gerstmann-Sträussler-Scheinker syndrome CC HIV
GSS syndrome
AHA: 4Q, '08, 73-75
CC Excl: 046.0-046.9, 066.40-066.49, 079.82

046.72 Fatal familial insomnia CC HIV
FFI
AHA: 4Q, '08, 73-75
CC Excl: See code: 046.71

046.79 Other and unspecified prion disease of central nervous system CC HIV
CC Excl: See code: 046.71

046.8 Other specified slow virus infection of central nervous system CC HIV
CC Excl: 046.0-046.9, 066.40-066.49, 079.82

046.9 Unspecified slow virus infection of central nervous system CC HIV
CC Excl: 046.0-046.9

√4ᵗʰ 047 Meningitis due to enterovirus
INCLUDES meningitis:
  abacterial
  aseptic
  viral
EXCLUDES *meningitis due to:*
  adenovirus (049.1)
  arthropod-borne virus (060.0-066.9)
  leptospira (100.81)
  virus of:
    herpes simplex (054.72)
    herpes zoster (053.0)
    lymphocytic choriomeningitis (049.0)
    mumps (072.1)
    poliomyelitis (045.0-045.9)
  any other infection specifically classified elsewhere
AHA: J-F, '87, 6

047.0 Coxsackie virus CC
CC Excl: 003.21, 013.00-013.16, 036.0, 047.0-047.9, 049.0-049.1, 072.1, 078.88-078.89, 079.81, 079.88-079.99, 090.42, 091.81, 094.2, 098.89, 100.81, 112.83, 114.2, 115.01, 115.11, 115.91, 130.0, 139.8, 320.0-322.9, 349.89-349.9, 357.0

047.1 ECHO virus CC
Meningo-eruptive syndrome
CC Excl: See code: 047.0

047.8 Other specified viral meningitis CC
CC Excl: See code: 047.0

047.9 Unspecified viral meningitis CC
Viral meningitis NOS
CC Excl: See code: 047.0
A87.9 Viral meningitis unspecified I-10

---

§ Requires fifth digit. Valid digits are in [brackets] under each code. See category 045 for codes and definitions.

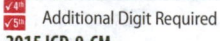

Infectious and Parasitic Diseases

048–053.12

048 Other enterovirus diseases of central nervous system `CC`
Boston exanthem
CC Excl: 013.60-013.66, 046.2, 046.71-046.8, 048-049.0, 049.8, 052.0, 052.2, 054.3, 054.74, 056.01, 057.8-058.29, 059.00-059.9, 062.0-064, 066.2-066.49, 072.2, 073.7, 075, 079.82, 079.99, 081.9, 083.9, 090.41, 094.81, 117.5, 124, 130.0, 290.12, 323.01-323.9, 341.1, 487.8, 488.09, 488.19, 771.2, 984.9

√4th **049 Other non-arthropod-borne viral diseases of central nervous system**
     EXCLUDES late effects of viral encephalitis (139.0)

   049.0 Lymphocytic choriomeningitis `CC`
Lymphocytic:
   meningitis (serous) (benign)
   meningoencephalitis (serous) (benign)
CC Excl: 003.21, 013.00-013.16, 036.0, 047.0-047.9, 049.0-049.1, 066.40-066.49, 072.1, 078.88-078.89, 079.81-079.82, 079.88-079.99, 090.42, 091.81, 094.2, 098.89, 100.81, 112.83, 114.2, 115.01, 115.11, 115.91, 130.0, 139.8, 320.0-322.9, 349.89-349.9, 357.0

   049.1 Meningitis due to adenovirus `CC`
DEF: Inflammation of lining of brain caused by Arenaviruses and usually occurring in adults in fall and winter months.
CC Excl: 003.21, 013.00-013.16, 036.0, 047.0-047.9, 049.0-049.1, 072.1, 078.88-078.89, 079.81, 079.88-079.99, 090.42, 091.81, 094.2, 098.89, 100.81, 112.83, 114.2, 115.01, 115.11, 115.91, 130.0, 139.8, 320.0-322.9, 349.89-349.9, 357.0

   049.8 Other specified non-arthropod-borne viral diseases of central nervous system `CC` `HIV`
Encephalitis: Encephalitis:
   acute: lethargica
     inclusion body   Rio Bravo
     necrotizing   von Economo's disease
     epidemic
     EXCLUDES human herpesvirus 6 encephalitis (058.21)
               other human herpesvirus encephalitis (058.29)
CC Excl: 013.60-013.66, 046.2, 046.71-046.8, 048-049.0, 049.8, 052.0, 052.2, 054.3, 054.74, 056.01, 057.8-058.29, 059.00-059.9, 062.0-064, 066.2-066.49, 072.2, 073.7, 075, 079.82, 079.99, 081.9, 083.9, 090.41, 094.81, 117.5, 124, 130.0, 290.12, 323.01-323.9, 341.1, 382.4, 487.8, 488.09, 488.19, 710.0, 771.2, 984.9

   049.9 Unspecified non-arthropod-borne viral diseases of central nervous system `CC` `HIV`
Viral encephalitis NOS
CC Excl: 013.60-013.66, 046.2, 046.71-046.8, 048-049.0, 049.8-049.9, 052.0, 052.2, 054.3, 054.74, 056.01, 057.8-058.29, 059.00-059.9, 062.0-064, 066.2-066.3, 072.2, 073.7, 075, 079.99, 081.9, 083.9, 090.41, 094.81, 117.5, 124, 130.0, 290.12, 323.01-323.9, 341.1, 382.4, 487.8, 488.09, 488.19, 710.0, 771.2, 984.9

Viral Diseases Generally Accompanied by Exanthem (050-059)
     EXCLUDES arthropod-borne viral diseases (060.0-066.9)
               Boston exanthem (048)

√4th **050 Smallpox**

   050.0 Variola major `CC`
Hemorrhagic (pustular)   Malignant smallpox
   smallpox   Purpura variolosa
DEF: Form of smallpox known for its high mortality; exists only in laboratories.
CC Excl: 050.0-052.9

   050.1 Alastrim `CC`
Variola minor
DEF: Mild form of smallpox known for its low mortality rate.
CC Excl: See code: 050.0

   050.2 Modified smallpox `CC`
Varioloid
DEF: Mild form occurring in patients with history of infection or vaccination.
CC Excl: See code: 050.0

   050.9 Smallpox, unspecified `CC`
CC Excl: See code: 050.0

√4th **051 Cowpox and paravaccinia**

√5th   **051.0 Cowpox and vaccinia not from vaccination**

     051.01 Cowpox
DEF: A disease contracted by milking infected cows; vesicles usually appear on the fingers, hands and adjacent areas and usually disappear without scarring; other symptoms: local edema, lymphangitis and regional lymphadenitis with or without fever.
AHA: 4Q, '08, 76-77

     051.02 Vaccinia not from vaccination
       EXCLUDES vaccinia (generalized) (from vaccination) (999.0)
AHA: 4Q, '08, 76-77

   051.1 Pseudocowpox
Milkers' node
DEF: Hand lesions and mild fever in dairy workers caused by exposure to paravaccinia.

   051.2 Contagious pustular dermatitis
Ecthyma contagiosum   Orf
DEF: Skin eruptions caused by exposure to poxvirus-infected sheep or goats.

   051.9 Paravaccinia, unspecified

√4th **052 Chickenpox**
DEF: Contagious infection by Varicella-zoster virus causing rash with pustules and fever.

   052.0 Postvaricella encephalitis `MCC`
Postchickenpox encephalitis
CC Excl: 051.9-052.0, 052.2-052.9, 078.88-078.89, 079.81, 079.88-079.99, 139.8

   052.1 Varicella (hemorrhagic) pneumonitis `MCC`
CC Excl: 051.9, 052.1-052.9, 078.88-078.89, 079.81, 079.88-079.99, 139.8

   052.2 Postvaricella myelitis `MCC`
Postchickenpox myelitis
CC Excl: 051.9, 052.2-052.9, 053.14, 054.74, 078.88-078.89, 079.81, 079.88-079.99, 139.8, 323.01-323.02, 323.41-323.82, 341.20-341.22
AHA: 4Q, '06, 58-63

   052.7 With other specified complications `CC`
CC Excl: 051.9, 052.2-052.9, 078.88-078.89, 079.81, 079.88-079.99, 139.8
AHA: 1Q, '02, 3

   052.8 With unspecified complication `CC`
CC Excl: See code: 052.7

   052.9 Varicella without mention of complication `CC`
Chickenpox NOS   Varicella NOS
CC Excl: See code: 052.7

√4th **053 Herpes zoster**
     INCLUDES shingles
               zona
DEF: Self-limiting infection by Varicella-zoster virus causing unilateral eruptions and neuralgia along affected nerves.

   053.0 With meningitis `MCC` `HIV`
DEF: Varicella-zoster virus infection causing inflammation of the lining of the brain and/or spinal cord.
CC Excl: 003.21, 013.00-013.16, 036.0, 047.0-047.9, 049.0-049.1, 053.0-053.19, 053.79-053.9, 054.72, 054.74-054.9, 058.81-058.89, 072.1, 078.88-078.89, 079.81, 079.88-079.99, 090.42, 091.81, 094.2, 098.89, 100.81, 112.83, 114.2, 115.01, 115.11, 115.91, 130.0, 139.8, 320.0-322.9, 349.89-349.9, 357.0

√5th   **053.1 With other nervous system complications**

     053.10 With unspecified nervous system complication `CC` `HIV`
CC Excl: 053.0-053.19, 053.79-053.9, 054.72, 054.74-054.9, 058.81-058.89, 078.88-078.89, 079.81, 079.88-079.99, 139.8

     053.11 Geniculate herpes zoster `CC` `HIV`
Herpetic geniculate ganglionitis
DEF: Unilateral eruptions and neuralgia along the facial nerve geniculum affecting face and outer and middle ear.
CC Excl: See code: 053.10

     053.12 Postherpetic trigeminal neuralgia `CC` `HIV`
DEF: Severe oral or nasal pain following a herpes zoster infection.
CC Excl: See code: 053.10

`N` Newborn Age: 0   `P` Pediatric Age: 0-17   `M` Maternity Age: 12-55   `A` Adult Age: 15-124   `MCC` Major CC Condition   `CC` CC Condition   `HIV` HIV Related Dx

053.13 Postherpetic polyneuropathy `CC` `HIV`
> **DEF:** Multiple areas of pain following a herpes zoster infection.
> **CC Excl:** See code: 053.10

053.14 Herpes zoster myelitis `MCC`
> **CC Excl:** 052.2, 053.0-053.19, 053.79-053.9, 054.72, 054.74-054.9, 058.81-058.89, 078.88-078.89, 079.81, 079.88-079.99, 139.8, 323.01-323.02, 323.41-323.82, 341.20-341.22
> **AHA:** 4Q, '06, 58-63

053.19 Other `CC` `HIV`
> **CC Excl:** See code: 053.10

√5ᵗʰ **053.2 With ophthalmic complications**

053.20 Herpes zoster dermatitis of eyelid `CC` `HIV`
> Herpes zoster ophthalmicus
> **CC Excl:** 053.20-053.29

053.21 Herpes zoster keratoconjunctivitis `CC` `HIV`
> **CC Excl:** See code: 053.20

053.22 Herpes zoster iridocyclitis `CC` `HIV`
> **CC Excl:** See code: 053.20

053.29 Other `CC` `HIV`
> **CC Excl:** See code: 053.20

√5ᵗʰ **053.7 With other specified complications**

053.71 Otitis externa due to herpes zoster `CC` `HIV`
> **CC Excl:** 053.71

053.79 Other `CC` `HIV`
> **CC Excl:** 053.0-054.71, 054.73-054.9, 058.21-058.89, 078.88-078.89, 079.81, 079.88-079.99, 139.8

053.8 With unspecified complication `CC` `HIV`
> **CC Excl:** See code: 053.79

053.9 Herpes zoster without mention of complication `HIV`
> Herpes zoster NOS
> **B02.9** Zoster without complications `I-10`

√4ᵗʰ **054 Herpes simplex**
> **EXCLUDES** congenital herpes simplex (771.2)

054.0 Eczema herpeticum `HIV`
> Kaposi's varicelliform eruption
> **DEF:** Herpes simplex virus invading site of preexisting skin inflammation.

√5ᵗʰ **054.1 Genital herpes**
> **AHA:** J-F, '87, 15, 16

054.10 Genital herpes, unspecified `HIV`
> Herpes progenitalis
> **AHA:** 2Q, '10, 10
> **A60.00** Herpesviral infection urogenital system unspec `I-10`

054.11 Herpetic vulvovaginitis `HIV` ♀

054.12 Herpetic ulceration of vulva `HIV` ♀

054.13 Herpetic infection of penis `HIV` ♂

054.19 Other `HIV`

054.2 Herpetic gingivostomatitis `CC` `HIV`
> **CC Excl:** 054.2

054.3 Herpetic meningoencephalitis `MCC` `HIV`
> Herpes encephalitis
> Simian B disease
> **EXCLUDES** human herpesvirus 6 encephalitis (058.21)
>   other human herpesvirus encephalitis (058.29)
> **DEF:** Inflammation of the brain and its lining, caused by infection of herpes simplex 1 in adults and simplex 2 in newborns.
> **CC Excl:** 054.3, 054.74-054.9, 058.21-058.89, 139.8

√5ᵗʰ **054.4 With ophthalmic complications**

054.40 With unspecified ophthalmic complication `CC` `HIV`
> **CC Excl:** 054.40-054.49, 054.79-054.9, 058.81-058.89

054.41 Herpes simplex dermatitis of eyelid `CC` `HIV`
> **CC Excl:** See code: 054.40

054.42 Dendritic keratitis `CC` `HIV`
> **CC Excl:** See code: 054.40

054.43 Herpes simplex disciform keratitis `CC` `HIV`
> **CC Excl:** See code: 054.40

054.44 Herpes simplex iridocyclitis `CC` `HIV`
> **CC Excl:** See code: 054.40

054.49 Other `CC` `HIV`
> **CC Excl:** See code: 054.40

054.5 Herpetic septicemia `MCC` `HIV`
> **CC Excl:** 003.1, 020.2, 036.2, 038.0-038.9, 054.5, 054.74-054.9, 058.81-058.89, 139.8, 995.90-995.94
> **AHA:** 2Q, '00, 5

054.6 Herpetic whitlow `HIV`
> Herpetic felon
> **DEF:** A primary infection of the terminal segment of a finger by herpes simplex; intense itching and pain start the disease, vesicles form, and tissue ultimately is destroyed.

√5ᵗʰ **054.7 With other specified complications**

054.71 Visceral herpes simplex `CC` `HIV`
> **CC Excl:** 054.71-054.72, 054.74-054.9, 058.81-058.89, 139.8

054.72 Herpes simplex meningitis `MCC` `HIV`
> **CC Excl:** 003.21, 013.00-013.16, 036.0, 047.0-047.9, 049.0-049.1, 053.0, 054.72, 054.74-054.9, 058.81-058.89, 072.1, 090.42, 091.81, 094.2, 098.89, 100.81, 112.83, 114.2, 115.01, 115.11, 115.91, 130.0, 139.8, 320.0-322.9, 349.89-349.9, 357.0

054.73 Herpes simplex otitis externa `HIV`

054.74 Herpes simplex myelitis `MCC`
> **CC Excl:** 052.2, 053.14, 054.74-054.9, 058.81-058.89, 078.88-078.89, 079.81, 079.88-079.99, 139.8, 323.01-323.02, 323.41-323.82, 341.20-341.22
> **AHA:** 4Q, '06, 58-63

054.79 Other `CC` `HIV`
> **CC Excl:** 054.74-054.9, 058.81-058.89, 078.88-078.89, 079.81, 079.88-079.99, 139.8

054.8 With unspecified complication `HIV`

054.9 Herpes simplex without mention of complication `HIV`
> **B00.9** Herpesviral infection unspecified `I-10`

√4ᵗʰ **055 Measles**
> **INCLUDES** morbilli
>   rubeola

055.0 Postmeasles encephalitis `MCC`
> **CC Excl:** 055.0, 055.79-055.9, 078.88-078.89, 079.81, 079.88-079.99, 139.8

055.1 Postmeasles pneumonia `MCC`
> **CC Excl:** 055.1, 055.79-055.9, 078.88-078.89, 079.81, 079.88-079.99, 139.8

055.2 Postmeasles otitis media

√5ᵗʰ **055.7 With other specified complications**

055.71 Measles keratoconjunctivitis `CC`
> Measles keratitis
> **CC Excl:** 055.71-055.9, 078.88-078.89, 079.81, 079.88-079.99, 139.8

055.79 Other `CC`
> **CC Excl:** 055.79-055.9, 078.88-078.89, 079.81, 079.88-079.99, 139.8

055.8 With unspecified complication

055.9 Measles without mention of complication

√4ᵗʰ **056 Rubella**
> **INCLUDES** German measles
> **EXCLUDES** congenital rubella (771.0)
> **DEF:** Acute but usually benign togavirus infection causing fever, sore throat, and rash; associated with complications to fetus as a result of maternal infection.

√5ᵗʰ **056.0 With neurological complications**

056.00 With unspecified neurological complication `CC`
> **CC Excl:** 056.00-056.09, 056.79-056.9, 078.88-078.89, 079.81, 079.88-079.99, 139.8

056.01 Encephalomyelitis due to rubella `MCC`
> Encephalitis   }
> Meningoencephalitis   } due to rubella
> **CC Excl:** See code: 056.00

√4ᵗʰ
√5ᵗʰ Additional Digit Required   Unacceptable PDx   Manifestation Code   Hospital Acquired Condition   ▶◀ Revised Text   ● New Code   ▲ Revised Code Title

2015 ICD-9-CM   **Volume 1 – 13**

Infectious and Parasitic Diseases

056.09–062.1

056.09 **Other** `CC`
CC Excl: See code: 056.00

√5th 056.7 **With other specified complications**

056.71 **Arthritis due to rubella** `CC`
CC Excl: 056.71-056.9, 078.88-078.89, 079.81, 079.88-079.99, 139.8

056.79 **Other** `CC`
CC Excl: 056.00-056.09, 056.79-056.9, 078.88-078.89, 079.81, 079.88-079.99, 139.8

056.8 **With unspecified complications**

056.9 **Rubella without mention of complication**

√4th 057 **Other viral exanthemata**
DEF: Skin eruptions or rashes and fever caused by viruses, including poxviruses.

057.0 **Erythema infectiosum [fifth disease]** `CC`
DEF: A moderately contagious, benign, epidemic disease, usually seen in children, of probable viral etiology; a red macular rash appears on face and may spread to the limbs and trunk.
CC Excl: 057.0, 079.83

057.8 **Other specified viral exanthemata**
Dukes (-Filatow) disease   Parascarlatina
Fourth disease   Pseudoscarlatina
EXCLUDES   exanthema subitum [sixth disease] (058.10-058.12)
roseola infantum (058.10-058.12)

057.9 **Viral exanthem, unspecified**

√4th 058 **Other human herpesvirus**
EXCLUDES   congenital herpes (771.2)
cytomegalovirus (078.5)
Epstein-Barr virus (075)
herpes NOS (054.0-054.9)
herpes simplex (054.0-054.9)
herpes zoster (053.0-053.9)
human herpesvirus NOS (054.0-054.9)
human herpesvirus 1 (054.0-054.9)
human herpesvirus 2 (054.0-054.9)
human herpesvirus 3 (052.0-053.9)
human herpesvirus 4 (075)
human herpesvirus 5 (078.5)
varicella (052.0-052.9)
varicella-zoster virus (052.0-053.9)
AHA: 4Q, '07, 61

√5th 058.1 **Roseola infantum**
Exanthema subitum [sixth disease]

058.10 **Roseola infantum, unspecified** `P`
Exanthema subitum [sixth disease], unspecified
AHA: 4Q, '07, 63

058.11 **Roseola infantum due to human herpesvirus 6** `P`
Exanthema subitum [sixth disease] due to human herpesvirus 6

058.12 **Roseola infantum due to human herpesvirus 7** `P`
Exanthema subitum [sixth disease] due to human herpesvirus 7

√5th 058.2 **Other human herpesvirus encephalitis**
EXCLUDES   herpes encephalitis NOS (054.3)
herpes simplex encephalitis (054.3)
human herpesvirus encephalitis NOS (054.3)
simian B herpesvirus encephalitis (054.3)

058.21 **Human herpesvirus 6 encephalitis** `MCC` `HIV`
CC Excl: 054.3, 054.74-054.9, 058.21-058.89, 139.8

058.29 **Other human herpesvirus encephalitis** `MCC` `HIV`
Human herpesvirus 7 encephalitis
CC Excl: See code: 058.21

√5th 058.8 **Other human herpesvirus infections**

058.81 **Human herpesvirus 6 infection**

058.82 **Human herpesvirus 7 infection**

058.89 **Other human herpesvirus infection**
Human herpesvirus 8 infection
Kaposi's sarcoma-associated herpesvirus infection
AHA: 4Q, '07, 63

√4th 059 **Other poxvirus infections**
EXCLUDES   contagious pustular dermatitis (051.2)
cowpox (051.01)
ecthyma contagiosum (051.2)
milker's nodule (051.1)
orf (051.2)
paravaccinia NOS (051.9)
pseudocowpox (051.1)
smallpox (050.0-050.9)
vaccinia (generalized) (from vaccination) (999.0)
vaccinia not from vaccination (051.02)
AHA: 4Q, '08, 76-78

√5th 059.0 **Other orthopoxvirus infections**

059.00 **Orthopoxvirus infection, unspecified**

059.01 **Monkeypox** `CC`
CC Excl: 051.01-051.02, 057.0-057.9, 059.00-059.9

059.09 **Other orthopoxvirus infection**

√5th 059.1 **Other parapoxvirus infections**

059.10 **Parapoxvirus infection, unspecified**

059.11 **Bovine stomatitis**

059.12 **Sealpox**

059.19 **Other parapoxvirus infections**

√5th 059.2 **Yatapoxvirus infections**

059.20 **Yatapoxvirus infection, unspecified**

059.21 **Tanapox** `CC`
CC Excl: See code: 059.01

059.22 **Yaba monkey tumor virus**

059.8 **Other poxvirus infections**

059.9 **Poxvirus infections, unspecified**

Arthropod-borne Viral Diseases (060-066)
Use additional code to identify any associated meningitis (321.2)
EXCLUDES   late effects of viral encephalitis (139.0)

√4th 060 **Yellow fever**
DEF: Fever and jaundice from infection by mosquito-borne virus of genus *Flavivirus.*

060.0 **Sylvatic** `CC`
Yellow fever: Yellow fever:
   jungle   sylvan
DEF: Yellow fever transmitted from animal to man, via mosquito.
CC Excl: 060.0-060.9

060.1 **Urban** `CC`
DEF: Yellow fever transmitted from man to man, via mosquito.
CC Excl: See code: 060.0

060.9 **Yellow fever, unspecified** `CC`
CC Excl: See code: 060.0

061 **Dengue** `CC`
Breakbone fever
EXCLUDES   hemorrhagic fever caused by dengue virus (065.4)
DEF: Acute, self-limiting infection by mosquito-borne virus characterized by fever and generalized aches.
CC Excl: 061

√4th 062 **Mosquito-borne viral encephalitis**

062.0 **Japanese encephalitis** `MCC`
Japanese B encephalitis
DEF: *Flavivirus* causing inflammation of the brain, with a wide range of clinical manifestations.
CC Excl: 013.60-013.66, 046.2, 046.71-046.8, 048-049.0, 049.8, 052.0, 052.2, 054.3, 054.74, 056.01, 057.8-058.29, 059.00-059.9, 062.0-064, 066.2-066.49, 072.2, 073.7, 075, 079.82, 079.99, 081.9, 083.9, 090.41, 094.81, 117.5, 124, 130.0, 290.12, 323.01-323.9, 341.1, 487.8, 771.2, 984.9

062.1 **Western equine encephalitis** `MCC`
DEF: Alphavirus WEE infection causing inflammation of the brain, found in areas west of the Mississippi; transmitted horse to mosquito to man.
CC Excl: See code: 062.0

N Newborn Age: 0   P Pediatric Age: 0-17   M Maternity Age: 12-55   A Adult Age: 15-124   **MCC** Major CC Condition   **CC** CC Condition   **HIV** HIV Related Dx

14 – Volume 1   2015 ICD-9-CM

062.2　Eastern equine encephalitis `MCC`
> EXCLUDES　*Venezuelan equine encephalitis (066.2)*
> **DEF:** Alphavirus EEE causing inflammation of the brain and spinal cord, found from Canada to South America and Mexico; transmitted horse to mosquito to man.
> **CC Excl:** See code: 062.0

062.3　St. Louis encephalitis `MCC`
> **DEF:** Epidemic form caused by *Flavivirus* and transmitted by mosquito, and characterized by fever, difficulty in speech, and headache.
> **CC Excl:** See code: 062.0

062.4　Australian encephalitis `MCC`
> Australian arboencephalitis
> Australian X disease
> Murray Valley encephalitis
> **DEF:** *Flavivirus* causing inflammation of the brain, occurring in Australia and New Guinea.
> **CC Excl:** See code: 062.0

062.5　California virus encephalitis `MCC`
> Encephalitis:　　　Tahyna fever
> 　California
> 　La Crosse
> **DEF:** Bunyamwere virus causing inflammation of the brain.
> **CC Excl:** See code: 062.0

062.8　Other specified mosquito-borne viral encephalitis `MCC`
> Encephalitis by Ilheus virus
> EXCLUDES　*West Nile virus (066.40-066.49)*
> **CC Excl:** See code: 062.0

062.9　Mosquito-borne viral encephalitis, unspecified `MCC`
> **CC Excl:** See code: 062.0

✓4ᵗʰ **063　Tick-borne viral encephalitis**
> INCLUDES　diphasic meningoencephalitis

063.0　Russian spring-summer [taiga] encephalitis `MCC`
> **CC Excl:** See code: 062.0

063.1　Louping ill `MCC`
> **DEF:** Inflammation of brain caused by virus transmitted sheep to tick to man; incidence usually limited to British Isles.
> **CC Excl:** See code: 062.0

063.2　Central European encephalitis `MCC`
> **DEF:** Inflammation of brain caused by virus transmitted by tick; limited to central Europe and presenting with two distinct phases.
> **CC Excl:** See code: 062.0

063.8　Other specified tick-borne viral encephalitis `MCC`
> Langat encephalitisPowassan encephalitis
> **CC Excl:** See code: 062.0

063.9　Tick-borne viral encephalitis, unspecified `MCC`
> **CC Excl:** See code: 062.0

064　Viral encephalitis transmitted by other and unspecified arthropods `MCC`
> Arthropod-borne viral encephalitis, vector unknown
> Negishi virus encephalitis
> EXCLUDES　*viral encephalitis NOS (049.9)*
> **CC Excl:** See code: 062.0

✓4ᵗʰ **065　Arthropod-borne hemorrhagic fever**

065.0　Crimean hemorrhagic fever [CHF Congo virus] `CC`
> Central Asian hemorrhagic fever
> **CC Excl:** 065.0-066.9

065.1　Omsk hemorrhagic fever `CC`
> **CC Excl:** See code: 065.0

065.2　Kyasanur Forest disease `CC`
> **CC Excl:** See code: 065.0

065.3　Other tick-borne hemorrhagic fever `CC`
> **CC Excl:** See code: 065.0

065.4　Mosquito-borne hemorrhagic fever `CC`
> Chikungunya hemorrhagic fever
> Dengue hemorrhagic fever
> EXCLUDES　*Chikungunya fever (066.3)*
> 　　　　*dengue (061)*
> 　　　　*yellow fever (060.0-060.9)*
> **CC Excl:** See code: 065.0

065.8　Other specified arthropod-borne hemorrhagic fever `CC`
> Mite-borne hemorrhagic fever
> **CC Excl:** See code: 065.0

065.9　Arthropod-borne hemorrhagic fever, unspecified `CC`
> Arbovirus hemorrhagic fever NOS
> **CC Excl:** See code: 065.0

✓4ᵗʰ **066　Other arthropod-borne viral diseases**

066.0　Phlebotomus fever `CC`
> Changuinola fever
> Sandfly fever
> **DEF:** Sandfly-borne viral infection occurring in Asia, Mideast and South America.
> **CC Excl:** See code: 065.0

066.1　Tick-borne fever `CC`
> Nairobi sheep disease　　　Tick fever:
> Tick fever:　　　　　　　　Kemerovo
> 　American mountain　　　Quaranfil
> 　Colorado
> **CC Excl:** See code: 065.0

066.2　Venezuelan equine fever `CC`
> Venezuelan equine encephalitis
> **DEF:** Alphavirus VEE infection causing inflammation of the brain, usually limited to South America, Mexico, and Florida; transmitted horse to mosquito to man.
> **CC Excl:** 013.60-013.66, 046.2, 046.71-046.8, 048-049.0, 049.8, 052.0, 052.2, 054.3, 054.74, 056.01, 057.8-058.29, 059.00-059.9, 062.0-066.9, 072.2, 073.7, 075, 079.82, 079.99, 081.9, 083.9, 090.41, 094.81, 117.5, 124, 130.0, 290.12, 323.01-323.9, 341.1, 487.8, 488.09, 488.19, 771.2, 984.9

066.3　Other mosquito-borne fever `CC`
> Fever (viral):　　　　　Fever (viral):
> 　Bunyamwera　　　　　Oropouche
> 　Bwamba　　　　　　　Pixuna
> 　Chikungunya　　　　　Rift valley
> 　Guama　　　　　　　　Ross river
> 　Mayaro　　　　　　　Wesselsbron
> 　Mucambo　　　　　　Zika
> 　O'Nyong-Nyong
> EXCLUDES　*dengue (061)*
> 　　　　*yellow fever (060.0-060.9)*
> **CC Excl:** See code: 066.2

✓5ᵗʰ **066.4　West Nile fever**
> **DEF:** Mosquito-borne fever causing fatal inflammation of the brain, the lining of the brain, or of the lining of the brain and spinal cord.
> **AHA:** 4Q, '02, 44

066.40　West Nile fever, unspecified `MCC`
> West Nile fever NOS
> West Nile fever without complications
> West Nile virus NOS
> **CC Excl:** 013.60-013.66, 046.2, 046.71-046.8, 048-049.0, 049.8, 052.0, 052.2, 054.3, 054.74, 056.01, 057.8-058.29, 059.00-059.9, 062.0-066.3, 066.8-066.9, 072.2, 073.7, 075, 079.99, 081.9, 083.9, 090.41, 094.81, 117.5, 124, 130.0, 323.01-323.9, 341.1, 487.8, 488.09, 488.19, 771.2

066.41　West Nile fever with encephalitis `MCC`
> West Nile encephalitis
> West Nile encephalomyelitis
> **CC Excl:** See code: 066.40
> **AHA:** 4Q, '04, 51

066.42　West Nile fever with other neurologic manifestation `MCC`
> Use additional code to specify the neurologic manifestation
> **CC Excl:** See code: 066.40
> **AHA:** 4Q, '04, 51

066.49　West Nile fever with other complications `MCC`
> Use additional code to specify the other conditions
> **CC Excl:** See code: 066.40

066.8　Other specified arthropod-borne viral diseases `CC`
> Chandipura fever
> Piry fever
> **CC Excl:** 065.0-066.9

066.9　Arthropod-borne viral disease, unspecified `CC`
> Arbovirus infection NOS
> **CC Excl:** 065.0-066.9

Infectious and Parasitic Diseases

070–073.0

Other Diseases Due to Viruses and Chlamydiae (070-079)

√4ᵗʰ **070 Viral hepatitis**

> INCLUDES   viral hepatitis (acute) (chronic)
>
> EXCLUDES   *cytomegalic inclusion virus hepatitis (078.5)*

> The following fifth-digit subclassification is for use with categories 070.2 and 070.3:
> - 0   acute or unspecified, without mention of hepatitis delta
> - 1   acute or unspecified, with hepatitis delta
> - 2   chronic, without mention of hepatitis delta
> - 3   chronic, with hepatitis delta

DEF: Hepatitis A: HAV infection is self-limiting with flulike symptoms; transmission, fecal-oral.
DEF: Hepatitis B: HBV infection can be chronic and systemic; transmission, bodily fluids.
DEF: Hepatitis C: HCV infection can be chronic and systemic; transmission, blood transfusion and unidentified agents.
DEF: Hepatitis D (delta): HDV occurs only in the presence of hepatitis B virus.
DEF: Hepatitis E: HEV is epidemic form; transmission and nature under investigation.
AHA: 2Q, '07, 5

070.0 Viral hepatitis A with hepatic coma   MCC
   CC Excl: 070.0-070.9, 078.88-078.89, 079.81, 079.88-079.99, 139.8

070.1 Viral hepatitis A without mention of hepatic coma   CC
   Infectious hepatitis
   CC Excl: See code: 070.0

§ √5ᵗʰ **070.2 Viral hepatitis B with hepatic coma**   MCC
   [0-3]
   CC Excl: See code: 070.0
   AHA: 4Q, '91, 28; **For code 070.20:** 2Q, '07, 6

§ √5ᵗʰ **070.3 Viral hepatitis B without mention of hepatic coma**   CC
   [0-3]
   Serum hepatitis
   CC Excl: See code: 070.0
   AHA: 1Q, '93, 28; 4Q, '91, 28
   B16.9 Acute hep B w/o delta-agent & w/o hepatic coma   I-10

√5ᵗʰ **070.4 Other specified viral hepatitis with hepatic coma**
   AHA: 4Q, '91, 28

     070.41 Acute hepatitis C with hepatic coma   MCC
       CC Excl: See code: 070.0

     070.42 Hepatitis delta without mention of active hepatitis B disease with hepatic coma   MCC
       Hepatitis delta with hepatitis B carrier state
       CC Excl: See code: 070.0

     070.43 Hepatitis E with hepatic coma   MCC
       CC Excl: See code: 070.0

     070.44 Chronic hepatitis C with hepatic coma   MCC
       CC Excl: See code: 070.0
       AHA: 2Q, '07, 5

     070.49 Other specified viral hepatitis with hepatic coma   MCC
       CC Excl: See code: 070.0

√5ᵗʰ **070.5 Other specified viral hepatitis without mention of hepatic coma**
   AHA: 4Q, '91, 28

     070.51 Acute hepatitis C without mention of hepatic coma   CC
       CC Excl: See code: 070.0

     070.52 Hepatitis delta without mention of active hepatititis B disease or hepatic coma   CC
       CC Excl: See code: 070.0

     070.53 Hepatitis E without mention of hepatic coma   CC
       CC Excl: See code: 070.0

     070.54 Chronic hepatitis C without mention of hepatic coma   CC
       AHA: 1Q, '11, 23; 4Q, '08, 120; 3Q, '07, 7; 2Q, '06, 13
       B18.2 Chronic viral hepatitis C   I-10

     070.59 Other specified viral hepatitis without mention of hepatic coma   CC
       CC Excl: See code: 070.0

070.6 Unspecified viral hepatitis with hepatic coma   MCC
   EXCLUDES   *unspecified viral hepatitis C with hepatic coma (070.71)*
   CC Excl: See code: 070.0

√5ᵗʰ **070.7 Unspecified viral hepatitis C**

     070.70 Unspecified viral hepatitis C without hepatic coma
       Unspecified viral hepatitis C NOS
       AHA: 4Q, '04, 52
       B19.20 Unspecified viral hepatits C w/o hepatic coma   I-10

     070.71 Unspecified viral hepatitis C with hepatic coma   MCC
       CC Excl: See code: 070.0
       AHA: 4Q, '04, 52

070.9 Unspecified viral hepatitis without mention of hepatic coma   CC
   Viral hepatitis NOS
   EXCLUDES   *unspecified viral hepatitis C without hepatic coma (070.70)*
   CC Excl: See code: 070.0

071 Rabies   CC
   Hydrophobia
   Lyssa
   DEF: Acute infectious disease of the CNS caused by a rhabdovirus; usually spread by bites by infected animals; progresses from fever, restlessness, and extreme excitability, to hydrophobia, seizures, confusion and death.
   CC Excl: 071

√4ᵗʰ **072 Mumps**
   DEF: Acute infectious disease caused by paramyxovirus; usually seen in children less than 15 years of age; salivary glands are typically enlarged, involves other organs, such as testes, pancreas and meninges.

   072.0 Mumps orchitis   CC ♂
     CC Excl: 072.0, 072.79-072.9, 078.88-078.89, 079.81, 079.88-079.99, 139.8

   072.1 Mumps meningitis   MCC
     CC Excl: 003.21, 013.00-013.16, 036.0, 047.0-047.9, 049.0-049.1, 053.0, 054.72, 072.1, 072.79-072.9, 078.88-078.89, 079.81, 079.88-079.99, 090.42, 091.81, 094.2, 098.89, 100.81, 112.83, 114.2, 115.01, 115.11, 115.91, 130.0, 139.8, 320.0-322.9, 349.89-349.9, 357.0

   072.2 Mumps encephalitis   MCC
     Mumps meningoencephalitis
     CC Excl: 072.2, 072.79-072.9, 078.88-078.89, 079.81, 079.88-079.99, 139.8

   072.3 Mumps pancreatitis   CC
     CC Excl: 072.3, 072.79-072.9, 078.88-078.89, 079.81, 079.88-079.99, 139.8

√5ᵗʰ   **072.7 Mumps with other specified complications**

     072.71 Mumps hepatitis   CC
       CC Excl: 072.71, 072.79-072.9, 078.88-078.89, 079.81, 079.88-079.99, 139.8

     072.72 Mumps polyneuropathy   CC
       CC Excl: 072.72-072.9, 078.88-078.89, 079.81, 079.88-079.99, 139.8

     072.79 Other   CC
       CC Excl: 072.79-072.9, 078.88-078.89, 079.81, 079.88-079.99, 139.8

   072.8 Mumps with unspecified complication   CC
     CC Excl: 072.79-072.9, 078.88-078.89, 079.81, 079.88-079.99

   072.9 Mumps without mention of complication
     Epidemic parotitis
     Infectious parotitis

√4ᵗʰ **073 Ornithosis**
   INCLUDES   parrot fever
             psittacosis
   DEF: *Chlamydia psittaci* infection often transmitted from birds to humans.

   073.0 With pneumonia   MCC
     Lobular pneumonitis due to ornithosis
     CC Excl: 011.00-012.16, 012.80-012.86, 017.90-017.96, 020.3-020.5, 021.3, 022.1, 031.0, 039.1, 073.0, 073.8-073.9, 115.05, 115.15, 115.95, 122.1, 130.4, 136.3, 480.0-487.1, 488.01-488.02, 488.11-488.12, 495.0-495.9, 500-508.9, 517.1, 517.8, 518.89, 519.8-519.9

---

§   Requires fifth digit. Valid digits are in [brackets] under each code. See category 070 for codes and definitions.

N Newborn Age: 0   P Pediatric Age: 0-17   M Maternity Age: 12-55   A Adult Age: 15-124   MCC Major CC Condition   CC CC Condition   HIV HIV Related Dx

16 – Volume 1   2015 ICD-9-CM

073.7 With other specified complications `CC`
> **CC Excl:** 013.60-013.66, 046.2, 046.71-046.8, 048-049.0, 049.8, 052.0, 052.2, 054.3, 054.74, 056.01, 057.8-058.29, 059.00-059.9, 062.0-064, 066.2-066.49, 072.2, 073.0-073.9, 079.82, 079.99, 081.9, 083.9, 090.41, 094.81, 117.5, 124, 130.0, 290.12, 323.01-323.9, 341.1, 487.8, 488.09, 488.19, 771.2, 984.9

073.8 With unspecified complication `CC`
> **CC Excl:** 073.0, 073.8-073.9

073.9 Ornithosis, unspecified `CC`
> **CC Excl:** See code: 073.8

✓4th 074 Specific diseases due to Coxsackie virus
> **EXCLUDES** Coxsackie virus:
> *infection NOS (079.2)*
> *meningitis (047.0)*

074.0 Herpangina
Vesicular pharyngitis
> **DEF:** Acute infectious coxsackie virus infection causing throat lesions, fever, and vomiting; generally affects children in summer.

074.1 Epidemic pleurodynia
Bornholm disease   Epidemic:
Devil's grip   myalgia
                    myositis
> **DEF:** Paroxysmal pain in chest, accompanied by fever and usually limited to children and young adults; caused by coxsackie virus.

✓5th 074.2 Coxsackie carditis

074.20 Coxsackie carditis, unspecified `CC`
> **CC Excl:** 074.20, 074.22-074.23, 093.82, 390, 391.2-391.9, 398.0-398.90, 398.99, 422.0-422.99, 429.0, 429.71-429.79, 459.89-459.9

074.21 Coxsackie pericarditis `CC`
> **DEF:** Coxsackie infection of the outer lining of the heart.
> **CC Excl:** 074.21, 093.81, 391.0, 393, 420.0-420.99, 423.3-423.9, 459.89-459.9

074.22 Coxsackie endocarditis `CC`
> **DEF:** Coxsackie infection within the heart's cavities.
> **CC Excl:** 002.0, 036.42, 074.22, 083.0, 093.20-093.24, 098.84, 112.81, 115.94, 116.0, 390, 391.1, 391.8-392.0, 394.0-395.9, 396.9-397.9, 398.90, 398.99, 421.0-421.9, 424.0-424.99, 425.3, 459.89-459.9, 746.09, 746.89, 996.61

074.23 Coxsackie myocarditis `CC`
Aseptic myocarditis of newborn
> **DEF:** Coxsackie infection of the muscle of the heart.
> **CC Excl:** See code: 074.20

074.3 Hand, foot, and mouth disease
Vesicular stomatitis and exanthem
> **DEF:** Mild coxsackie infection causing lesions on hands, feet and oral mucosa, most commonly seen in preschool children.

074.8 Other specified diseases due to Coxsackie virus
Acute lymphonodular pharyngitis

075 Infectious mononucleosis
Glandular fever   Pfeiffer's disease
Monocytic angina
> **DEF:** Acute infection by Epstein-Barr virus causing fever, sore throat, enlarged lymph glands and spleen, and fatigue; usually seen in teens and young adults.
> **AHA:** 3Q, '01, 13; M-A, '87, 8

✓4th 076 Trachoma
> **EXCLUDES** *late effect of trachoma (139.1)*
> **DEF:** A chronic infectious disease of the cornea and conjunctiva caused by a strain of the bacteria *Chlamydia trachomatis;* the infection can cause photophobia, pain, excessive tearing and sometimes blindness.

076.0 Initial stage
Trachoma dubium

076.1 Active stage
Granular conjunctivitis (trachomatous)
Trachomatous:
   follicular conjunctivitis
   pannus

076.9 Trachoma, unspecified
Trachoma NOS

✓4th 077 Other diseases of conjunctiva due to viruses and Chlamydiae
> **EXCLUDES** *ophthalmic complications of viral diseases classified elsewhere*

077.0 Inclusion conjunctivitis
Paratrachoma   Swimming pool conjunctivitis
> **EXCLUDES** *inclusion blennorrhea (neonatal) (771.6)*
> **DEF:** Pus in conjunctiva caused by *Chlamydiae trachomatis.*

077.1 Epidemic keratoconjunctivitis
Shipyard eye
> **DEF:** Highly contagious corneal or conjunctival infection caused by adenovirus type 8; symptoms include inflammation and corneal infiltrates.

077.2 Pharyngoconjunctival fever
Viral pharyngoconjunctivitis

077.3 Other adenoviral conjunctivitis
Acute adenoviral follicular conjunctivitis

077.4 Epidemic hemorrhagic conjunctivitis
Apollo:
   conjunctivitis
   disease
Conjunctivitis due to enterovirus type 70
Hemorrhagic conjunctivitis (acute) (epidemic)

077.8 Other viral conjunctivitis
Newcastle conjunctivitis

✓5th 077.9 Unspecified diseases of conjunctiva due to viruses and Chlamydiae

077.98 Due to Chlamydiae

077.99 Due to viruses
Viral conjunctivitis NOS
B30.9 Viral conjunctivitis, unspecified `I-10`

✓4th 078 Other diseases due to viruses and Chlamydiae
> **EXCLUDES** *viral infection NOS (079.0-079.9)*
> *viremia NOS (790.8)*

078.0 Molluscum contagiosum
> **DEF:** Benign poxvirus infection causing small bumps on the skin or conjunctiva; transmitted by close contact.

✓5th 078.1 Viral warts
Viral warts due to human papilloma virus
> **DEF:** A keratotic papilloma of the epidermis caused by the human papilloma virus; the superficial vegetative lesions last for varying durations and eventually regress spontaneously.
> **AHA:** 2Q, '97, 9; 4Q, '93, 22

078.10 Viral warts, unspecified
Verruca:
   NOS
   Vulgaris
Warts (infectious)

078.11 Condyloma acuminatum
Condyloma NOS   Genital warts NOS
> **DEF:** Clusters of mucosa or epidermal lesions on external genitalia; viral infection is sexually transmitted.

078.12 Plantar wart
Verruca plantaris
> **AHA:** 4Q, '08, 78-79

078.19 Other specified viral warts
Common wart
Flat wart
Veruca planna

078.2 Sweating fever
Miliary fever   Sweating disease
> **DEF:** A viral infection characterized by profuse sweating; various papular, vesicular and other eruptions cause the blockage of sweat glands.

078.3 Cat-scratch disease `CC`
Benign lymphoreticulosis (of inoculation)
Cat-scratch fever
> **CC Excl:** 078.3, 079.82

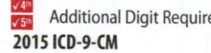

✓4th ✓5th Additional Digit Required   Unacceptable PDx   Manifestation Code   Hospital Acquired Condition   ▶◀ Revised Text   ● New Code   ▲ Revised Code Title

2015 ICD-9-CM   **Volume 1 – 17**

Infectious and Parasitic Diseases

078.4–079.99

078.4 Foot and mouth disease
Aphthous fever   Epizootic:
Epizootic: stomatitis
   aphthae
DEF: Ulcers on oral mucosa, legs, and feet after exposure to infected animal.

078.5 Cytomegaloviral disease   CC HIV
Cytomegalic inclusion disease
Salivary gland virus disease
Use additional code to identify manifestation, as:
   cytomegalic inclusion virus:
     hepatitis (573.1)
     pneumonia (484.1)
EXCLUDES congenital cytomegalovirus infection (771.1)
DEF: A herpesvirus associated with serious disease morbidity including fever, leukopenia, pneumonia, retinitis, hepatitis and organ transplant; often leads to hepatomegaly, splenomegaly and thrombocytopenia; a common post-transplant complication.
CC Excl: 078.5-078.7, 078.89-079.50, 079.59, 079.81-079.82, 079.89, 079.99
AHA: 3Q, '11, 5; 1Q, '03, 10; 3Q, '98, 4; 2Q, '93, 11; 1Q, '89, 9

078.6 Hemorrhagic nephrosonephritis   CC
Hemorrhagic fever: Hemorrhagic fever:
   epidemic   Russian
   Korean   with renal syndrome
DEF: Viral infection causing kidney dysfunction and bleeding disorders.
CC Excl: 016.00-016.06, 016.30-016.36, 016.90-016.96, 017.90-017.96, 078.6, 079.82, 098.10, 098.19, 098.30-098.31, 098.89, 112.2, 131.00, 131.8-131.9, 249.40-249.41, 249.80-249.91, 250.40-250.43, 250.80-250.93, 274.10, 274.19, 580.0-584.9, 586-591, 593.0-593.2, 593.89-593.9, 599.70-599.9

078.7 Arenaviral hemorrhagic fever   CC
Hemorrhagic fever: Hemorrhagic fever:
   Argentine   Junin virus
   Bolivian   Machupo virus
CC Excl: 078.5-079.82, 079.88-079.99

√5th 078.8 Other specified diseases due to viruses and Chlamydiae
EXCLUDES epidemic diarrhea (009.2)
              lymphogranuloma venereum (099.1)

078.81 Epidemic vertigo

078.82 Epidemic vomiting syndrome
Winter vomiting disease

078.88 Other specified diseases due to Chlamydiae
AHA: 4Q, '96, 22

078.89 Other specified diseases due to viruses
Epidemic cervical myalgia
Marburg disease

√4th 079 Viral and chlamydial infection in conditions classified elsewhere and of unspecified site
NOTE This category is provided to be used as an additional code to identify the viral agent in diseases classifiable elsewhere. This category will also be used to classify virus infection of unspecified nature or site.

079.0 Adenovirus

079.1 ECHO virus
DEF: An "orphan" enteric RNA virus, certain serotypes of which are associated with human disease, especially aseptic meningitis.

079.2 Coxsackie virus
DEF: A heterogenous group of viruses associated with aseptic meningitis, myocarditis, pericarditis, and acute onset juvenile diabetes.

079.3 Rhinovirus
DEF: Rhinoviruses affect primarily the upper respiratory tract. Over 100 distinct types infect humans.

079.4 Human papillomavirus
DEF: Viral infection caused by the genus *Papillomavirus* causing cutaneous and genital warts, including verruca vulgaris and condyloma acuminatum; certain types are associated with cervical dysplasia, cancer and other genital malignancies.
AHA: 2Q, '97, 9; 4Q, '93, 22
TIP: Do not assign for viral warts; see instead subcategory 078.1.

√5th 079.5 Retrovirus
EXCLUDES human immunodeficiency virus, type 1 [HIV-1] (042)
             human T-cell lymphotrophic virus, type III [HTLV-III] (042)
             lymphadenopathy-associated virus [LAV] (042)
DEF: A large group of RNA viruses that carry reverse transcriptase and include the leukoviruses and lentiviruses.
AHA: 4Q, '93, 22, 23

079.50 Retrovirus, unspecified

079.51 Human T-cell lymphotrophic virus, type I [HTLV-I]   CC
CC Excl: 079.51-079.59, 079.81-079.82, 079.88-079.99

079.52 Human T-cell lymphotrophic virus, type II [HTLV-II]   CC
CC Excl: 079.50-079.59, 079.81-079.82, 079.88-079.99

079.53 Human immunodeficiency virus, type 2 [HIV-2]   CC
CC Excl: 042, 079.50-079.59, 079.81-079.82, 079.88-079.99

079.59 Other specified retrovirus

079.6 Respiratory syncytial virus [RSV]
DEF: The major respiratory pathogen of young children, causing severe bronchitis and bronchopneumonia, and minor infection in adults.
AHA: 4Q, '96, 27, 28

√5th 079.8 Other specified viral and chlamydial infections
AHA: 1Q, '88, 12

079.81 Hantavirus   CC
DEF: An infection caused by the Muerto Canyon virus whose primary rodent reservoir is the deer mouse Peromyscus maniculatus; commonly characterized by fever, myalgias, headache, cough.
CC Excl: 070.70-070.71, 078.5-079.82, 079.88-079.99
AHA: 4Q, '95, 60

079.82 SARS-associated coronavirus   CC
DEF: A life-threatening respiratory disease, severe acute respiratory syndrome (SARS); etiology coronavirus; presenting symptoms may range from mild to severe forms of flu-like conditions; fever, chills, cough, headache, myalgia; diagnosis of SARS is based upon clinical, laboratory, and epidemiological criteria.
CC Excl: 011.00-012.16, 012.80-012.86, 017.90-017.96, 021.2, 031.0, 039.1, 079.82, 079.89, 115.05, 115.15, 115.95, 122.1, 130.4, 136.3, 480.0-480.2, 480.8-487.1, 488.01-488.02, 488.11-488.12, 494.0-508.9, 517.1, 517.8, 518.89, 519.8-519.9, 748.61
AHA: 4Q, '03, 46

079.83 Parvovirus B19   CC
Human parvovirus
Parvovirus NOS
EXCLUDES erythema infectiosum [fifth disease] (057.0)
DEF: The only known parvovirus to cause disease in humans; manifestation is erythema infectiosum; also associated with polyarthropathy, chronic anemia, red cell aplasia, and fetal hydrops.
CC Excl: 057.0, 079.83
AHA: 4Q, '07, 64

079.88 Other specified chlamydial infection

079.89 Other specified viral infection

√5th 079.9 Unspecified viral and chlamydial infections
EXCLUDES viremia NOS (790.8)
AHA: 2Q, '91, 8

079.98 Unspecified chlamydial infection
Chlamydial infections NOS

079.99 Unspecified viral infection
Viral infections NOS
B97.89 Other viral agents cause of dz class elsewhere   I-10

N Newborn Age: 0   P Pediatric Age: 0-17   M Maternity Age: 12-55   A Adult Age: 15-124   MCC Major CC Condition   CC CC Condition   HIV HIV Related Dx

18 – Volume 1   2015 ICD-9-CM

Rickettsioses and Other Arthropod-Borne Diseases (080-088)

EXCLUDES *arthropod-borne viral diseases (060.0-066.9)*

080 Louse-borne [epidemic] typhus ` CC `

Typhus (fever):　　　　Typhus (fever):
　classical　　　　　　　exanthematic NOS
　epidemic　　　　　　　louse-borne

DEF: *Rickettsia prowazekii;* causes severe headache, rash, high fever.
CC Excl: 080-083.9, 085.0-088.9

√4ᵗʰ 081 Other typhus

081.0 Murine [endemic] typhus ` CC `

Typhus (fever):　　Typhus (fever):
　endemic　　　　　flea-borne

DEF: Milder typhus caused by *Rickettsia typhi (mooseri);* transmitted by rat flea.
CC Excl: See code: 080

081.1 Brill's disease ` CC `

Brill-Zinsser diseaseRecrudescent typhus (fever)
CC Excl: See code: 080

081.2 Scrub typhus ` CC `

Japanese river fever　　Mite-borne typhus
Kedani fever　　　　　　Tsutsugamushi

DEF: Typhus caused by *Rickettsia tsutsugamushi* transmitted by chigger.
CC Excl: See code: 080

081.9 Typhus, unspecified ` CC `

Typhus (fever) NOS
CC Excl: 013.60-013.66, 046.2, 046.71-046.8, 048-049.0, 049.8, 052.0, 052.2, 054.3, 054.74, 056.01, 057.8-058.29, 059.00-059.9, 062.0-064, 066.2-066.49, 072.2, 073.7, 079.82, 079.99-084.0, 085.0-088.9, 090.41, 094.81, 117.5, 124, 130.0, 290.12, 323.01-323.9, 341.1, 487.8, 488.09, 488.19, 771.2, 984.9

√4ᵗʰ 082 Tick-borne rickettsioses

082.0 Spotted fevers ` CC `

Rocky mountain spotted fever
Sao Paulo fever
CC Excl: See code: 080

082.1 Boutonneuse fever ` CC `

African tick typhus　　Marseilles fever
India tick typhus　　　Mediterranean tick fever
Kenya tick typhus
CC Excl: See code: 080

082.2 North Asian tick fever ` CC `

Siberian tick typhus
CC Excl: See code: 080

082.3 Queensland tick typhus ` CC `
CC Excl: See code: 080

√5ᵗʰ 082.4 Ehrlichiosis

AHA: 3Q, '06, 11; 4Q, '00, 38

082.40 Ehrlichiosis, unspecified ` CC `
CC Excl: See code: 080

082.41 Ehrlichiosis chaffeensis [E. chaffeensis] ` CC `

DEF: A febrile illness caused by bacterial infection, also called human monocytic ehrlichiosis (HME). Causal organism is *Ehrlichia chaffeensis,* transmitted by the Lone Star tick. Symptoms include fever, chills, myalgia, nausea, vomiting, diarrhea, confusion, and severe headache occurring one week after a tick bite. Clinical findings are lymphadenopathy, rash, thrombocytopenia, leukopenia, and abnormal liver function tests.
CC Excl: See code: 080

082.49 Other ehrlichiosis ` CC `
CC Excl: See code: 080

082.8 Other specified tick-borne rickettsioses ` CC `

Lone star fever
CC Excl: See code: 080
AHA: 4Q, '99, 19

082.9 Tick-borne rickettsiosis, unspecified ` CC `

Tick-borne typhus NOS
CC Excl: See code: 080

√4ᵗʰ 083 Other rickettsioses

083.0 Q fever ` CC `

DEF: Infection of *Coxiella burnettii* usually acquired through airborne organisms.
CC Excl: See code: 080

083.1 Trench fever ` CC `

Quintan fever
Wolhynian fever
CC Excl: See code: 080

083.2 Rickettsialpox ` CC `

Vesicular rickettsiosis
DEF: Infection of *Rickettsia akari* usually acquired through a mite bite.
CC Excl: 082.0-083.9

083.8 Other specified rickettsioses ` CC `
CC Excl: See code: 083.2

083.9 Rickettsiosis, unspecified ` CC `
CC Excl: See code: 083.2

√4ᵗʰ 084 Malaria

NOTE Subcategories 084.0-084.6 exclude the listed conditions with mention of pernicious complications (084.8-084.9).
EXCLUDES *congenital malaria (771.2)*
DEF: Mosquito-borne disease causing high fever and prostration and cataloged by species of *Plasmodium: P. falciparum, P. malariae, P. ovale,* and *P. vivax.*

084.0 Falciparum malaria [malignant tertian] ` MCC `

Malaria (fever):
　by Plasmodium falciparum
　subtertian
CC Excl: 084.0-086.9

084.1 Vivax malaria [benign tertian] ` CC `

Malaria (fever) by Plasmodium vivax
CC Excl: 084.0-088.9

084.2 Quartan malaria ` CC `

Malaria (fever) by Plasmodium malariae
Malariae malaria
CC Excl: See code: 084.0

084.3 Ovale malaria ` CC `

Malaria (fever) by Plasmodium ovale
CC Excl: See code: 084.0

084.4 Other malaria ` CC `

Monkey malaria
CC Excl: See code: 084.0

084.5 Mixed malaria ` CC `

Malaria (fever) by more than one parasite
CC Excl: See code: 084.0

084.6 Malaria, unspecified ` CC `

Malaria (fever) NOS
CC Excl: 079.82, 084.0-086.9

084.7 Induced malaria ` CC `

Therapeutically induced malaria
EXCLUDES *accidental infection from syringe, blood transfusion, etc. (084.0-084.6, above, according to parasite species)*
transmission from mother to child during delivery (771.2)
CC Excl: 084.1-086.9

084.8 Blackwater fever ` CC `

Hemoglobinuric:
　fever (bilious)
　malaria
Malarial hemoglobinuria
DEF: Severe hemic and renal complication of *Plasmodium falciparum* infection.
CC Excl: See code: 084.0

084.9 Other pernicious complications of malaria ` CC `

Algid malaria
Cerebral malaria

Use additional code to identify complication, as:
　malarial:
　　hepatitis (573.2)
　　nephrosis (581.81)
CC Excl: See code: 084.0

Infectious and Parasitic Diseases

085–090.1

√4ᵗʰ **085 Leishmaniasis**

085.0 Visceral [kala-azar] CC
Dumdum fever
Infection by Leishmania:
donovani
infantum
Leishmaniasis:
dermal, post-kala-azar
Mediterranean
visceral (Indian)
CC Excl: 080-088.9

085.1 Cutaneous, urban CC
Aleppo boil
Baghdad boil
Delhi boil
Infection by Leishmania tropica (minor)
Leishmaniasis, cutaneous:
dry form
late
recurrent
ulcerating
Oriental sore
CC Excl: See code: 085.0

085.2 Cutaneous, Asian desert CC
Infection by Leishmania tropica major
Leishmaniasis, cutaneous:
acute necrotizing
rural
wet form
zoonotic form
CC Excl: See code: 085.0

085.3 Cutaneous, Ethiopian CC
Infection by Leishmania ethiopica
Leishmaniasis, cutaneous:
diffuse
lepromatous
CC Excl: See code: 085.0

085.4 Cutaneous, American CC
Chiclero ulcer
Infection by Leishmania mexicana
Leishmaniasis tegumentaria diffusa
CC Excl: See code: 085.0

085.5 Mucocutaneous (American) CC
Espundia
Infection by Leishmania braziliensis
Uta
CC Excl: See code: 085.0

085.9 Leishmaniasis, unspecified CC
CC Excl: See code: 085.0

√4ᵗʰ **086 Trypanosomiasis**
Use additional code to identify manifestations, as:
trypanosomiasis:
encephalitis (323.2)
meningitis (321.3)

086.0 Chagas' disease with heart involvement CC
American trypanosomiasis ⎱ with heart
Infection by Trypanosoma cruzi ⎰ involvement
Any condition classifiable to 086.2 with heart involvement
CC Excl: 086.0, 139.8

086.1 Chagas' disease with other organ involvement CC
American trypanosomiasis ⎱ with involvement of organ
Infection by Trypanosoma cruzi ⎰ other than heart
Any condition classifiable to 086.2 with involvement of organ
other than heart
CC Excl: 080-088.9

086.2 Chagas' disease without mention of organ involvement CC
American trypanosomiasis
Infection by Trypanosoma cruzi
CC Excl: See code: 086.1

086.3 Gambian trypanosomiasis CC
Gambian sleeping sickness
Infection by Trypanosoma gambiense
CC Excl: See code: 086.1

086.4 Rhodesian trypanosomiasis CC
Infection by Trypanosoma rhodesiense
Rhodesian sleeping sickness
CC Excl: See code: 086.1

086.5 African trypanosomiasis, unspecified CC
Sleeping sickness NOS
CC Excl: See code: 086.1

086.9 Trypanosomiasis, unspecified CC
CC Excl: 013.60-013.66, 046.2, 046.71-046.8, 048-049.0, 049.8, 052.0, 052.2, 054.3, 054.74, 056.01, 057.8-058.29, 059.00-059.9, 062.0-064, 066.2-066.3, 072.2, 073.7, 075, 078.3, 079.99-088.9, 090.41, 094.81, 117.5, 124, 130.0, 290.12, 323.01-323.9, 341.1, 382.4, 487.8, 488.09, 488.19, 771.2, 984.9

√4ᵗʰ **087 Relapsing fever**
INCLUDES recurrent fever
DEF: Infection of *Borrelia*; symptoms are episodic and include fever and arthralgia.

087.0 Louse-borne CC
CC Excl: 080-083.9, 085.0-088.9

087.1 Tick-borne CC
CC Excl: See code: 087.0

087.9 Relapsing fever, unspecified CC
CC Excl: See code: 087.0

√4ᵗʰ **088 Other arthropod-borne diseases**

088.0 Bartonellosis CC
Carrión's disease   Verruga peruana
Oroya fever
CC Excl: See code: 087.0

√5ᵗʰ **088.8 Other specified arthropod-borne diseases**

088.81 Lyme disease CC
Erythema chronicum migrans
DEF: A recurrent multisystem disorder caused by the spirochete *Borrelia burgdorferi* with the carrier being the tick; begins with lesions of erythema chronicum migrans; followed by arthritis of the large joints, myalgia, malaise, and neurological and cardiac manifestations.
CC Excl: See code: 087.0
AHA: 4Q, '91, 15; 3Q, '90, 14; 2Q, '89, 10
TIP: Do not assign if patient has been cured of Lyme disease but has residual chronic condition; refer instead to late-effect code 139.8.

088.82 Babesiosis CC
Babesiasis
DEF: A tick-borne disease caused by infection of *Babesia*, characterized by fever, malaise, listlessness, severe anemia and hemoglobinuria.
CC Excl: 080-088.9
AHA: 4Q, '93, 23

088.89 Other

088.9 Arthropod-borne disease, unspecified

Syphilis and other Venereal Diseases (090-099)

EXCLUDES nonvenereal endemic syphilis (104.0)
urogenital trichomoniasis (131.0)

√4ᵗʰ **090 Congenital syphilis**
DEF: Infection by spirochete *Treponema pallidum* acquired in utero from the infected mother.

090.0 Early congenital syphilis, symptomatic CC
Congenital syphilitic: Congenital syphilitic:
choroiditis   splenomegaly
coryza (chronic)   Syphilitic (congenital):
hepatomegaly   epiphysitis
mucous patches   osteochondritis
periostitis   pemphigus
Any congenital syphilitic condition specified as early or manifest less than two years after birth
CC Excl: 090.0-097.9

090.1 Early congenital syphilis, latent
Congenital syphilis without clinical manifestations, with positive serological reaction and negative spinal fluid test, less than two years after birth

N Newborn Age: 0   P Pediatric Age: 0-17   M Maternity Age: 12-55   A Adult Age: 15-124   MCC Major CC Condition   CC CC Condition   HIV HIV Related Dx

20 – Volume 1   2015 ICD-9-CM

090.2 Early congenital syphilis, unspecified   `CC`
Congenital syphilis NOS, less than two years after birth
CC Excl: 090.0-099.9, 139.8

090.3 Syphilitic interstitial keratitis   `CC`
Syphilitic keratitis:
parenchymatous
punctata profunda
EXCLUDES interstitial keratitis NOS (370.50)
CC Excl: See code: 090.0

√5th 090.4 Juvenile neurosyphilis
Use additional code to identify any associated mental disorder
DEF: *Treponema pallidum* infection involving the nervous system.

090.40 Juvenile neurosyphilis, unspecified   `CC`
Congenital neurosyphilis
Dementia paralytica juvenilis
Juvenile:
general paresis
tabes
taboparesis
CC Excl: 090.0-097.9, 099.40-099.9, 139.8

090.41 Congenital syphilitic encephalitis   `MCC`
DEF: Congenital *Treponema pallidum* infection involving the brain.
CC Excl: See code: 090.40

090.42 Congenital syphilitic meningitis   `MCC`
DEF: Congenital *Treponema pallidum* infection involving the lining of the brain and/or spinal cord.
CC Excl: 003.21, 013.00-013.16, 036.0, 047.0-047.9, 049.0-049.1, 053.0, 054.72, 072.1, 090.0-097.9, 098.89, 099.40-099.9, 100.81, 112.83, 114.2, 115.01, 115.11, 115.91, 130.0, 139.8, 320.0-322.9, 349.89-349.9, 357.0

090.49 Other   `CC`
CC Excl: See code: 090.40

090.5 Other late congenital syphilis, symptomatic   `CC`
Gumma due to congenital syphilis
Hutchinson's teeth
Syphilitic saddle nose
Any congenital syphilitic condition specified as late or manifest two years or more after birth
CC Excl: 090.0-097.9

090.6 Late congenital syphilis, latent
Congenital syphilis without clinical manifestations, with positive serological reaction and negative spinal fluid test, two years or more after birth

090.7 Late congenital syphilis, unspecified
Congenital syphilis NOS, two years or more after birth

090.9 Congenital syphilis, unspecified

√4th 091 Early syphilis, symptomatic
EXCLUDES early cardiovascular syphilis (093.0-093.9)
early neurosyphilis (094.0-094.9)

091.0 Genital syphilis (primary)
Genital chancre
DEF: Genital lesion at the site of initial infection by *Treponema pallidum*.

091.1 Primary anal syphilis
DEF: Anal lesion at the site of initial infection by *Treponema pallidum*.

091.2 Other primary syphilis
Primary syphilis of:
breast
fingers
lip
tonsils
DEF: Lesion at the site of initial infection by *Treponema pallidum*.

091.3 Secondary syphilis of skin or mucous membranes   `CC`
Condyloma latum
Secondary syphilis of:
anus
mouth
pharynx
skin
tonsils
vulva
DEF: Transitory or chronic lesions following initial syphilis infection.
CC Excl: 090.0-097.9

091.4 Adenopathy due to secondary syphilis   `CC`
Syphilitic adenopathy (secondary)
Syphilitic lymphadenitis (secondary)
CC Excl: 090.0-097.9

√5th 091.5 Uveitis due to secondary syphilis

091.50 Syphilitic uveitis, unspecified   `CC`
CC Excl: 090.0-097.9

091.51 Syphilitic chorioretinitis (secondary)   `CC`
DEF: Inflammation of choroid and retina as a secondary infection.
CC Excl: 090.0-097.9

091.52 Syphilitic iridocyclitis (secondary)   `CC`
DEF: Inflammation of iris and ciliary body as a secondary infection.
CC Excl: 090.0-097.9

√5th 091.6 Secondary syphilis of viscera and bone

091.61 Secondary syphilitic periostitis   `CC`
DEF: Inflammation of outer layers of bone as a secondary infection.
CC Excl: 015.90-015.96, 090.0-099.9, 102.6, 730.10-730.19, 730.30-730.39, 733.99

091.62 Secondary syphilitic hepatitis   `CC`
Secondary syphilis of liver
CC Excl: 090.0-099.9, 571.42-571.9, 573.1-573.3, 573.8-573.9

091.69 Other viscera   `CC`
CC Excl: 090.0-099.9, 139.8

091.7 Secondary syphilis, relapse   `CC`
Secondary syphilis, relapse (treated) (untreated)
DEF: Return of symptoms of syphilis following asymptomatic period.
CC Excl: 090.0-099.9, 139.8

√5th 091.8 Other forms of secondary syphilis

091.81 Acute syphilitic meningitis (secondary)   `MCC`
DEF: Sudden, severe inflammation of the lining of the brain and/or spinal cord as a secondary infection.
CC Excl: 003.21, 013.00-013.16, 036.0, 047.0-047.9, 049.0-049.1, 072.1, 078.88-078.89, 079.81, 079.88-079.99, 090.0-099.9, 100.81, 112.83, 114.2, 115.01, 115.11, 115.91, 130.0, 139.8, 320.0-322.9, 349.89-349.9, 357.0

091.82 Syphilitic alopecia   `CC`
DEF: Hair loss following initial syphilis infection.
CC Excl: 090.0-099.9

091.89 Other   `CC`
CC Excl: 090.0-099.9, 139.8

091.9 Unspecified secondary syphilis   `CC`
CC Excl: 090.0-099.9, 139.8

√4th 092 Early syphilis, latent
INCLUDES syphilis (acquired) without clinical manifestations, with positive serological reaction and negative spinal fluid test, less than two years after infection

092.0 Early syphilis, latent, serological relapse after treatment

092.9 Early syphilis, latent, unspecified

√4th 093 Cardiovascular syphilis

093.0 Aneurysm of aorta, specified as syphilitic   `CC`
Dilatation of aorta, specified as syphilitic
CC Excl: 090.0-097.9, 099.40-099.9, 139.8

093.1 Syphilitic aortitis   `CC`
DEF: Inflammation of the aorta — the main artery leading from the heart.
CC Excl: See code: 093.0

| √4th √5th Additional Digit Required | Unacceptable PDx | Manifestation Code | Hospital Acquired Condition | ►◄ Revised Text | ● New Code | ▲ Revised Code Title |

2015 ICD-9-CM   **Volume 1 – 21**

✓5th **093.2 Syphilitic endocarditis** `CC`
DEF: Inflammation of the tissues lining the cavities of the heart.

093.20 Valve, unspecified `CC`
Syphilitic ostial coronary disease
CC Excl: See code: 093.0

093.21 Mitral valve `CC`
CC Excl: See code: 093.0

093.22 Aortic valve `CC`
Syphilitic aortic incompetence or stenosis
CC Excl: See code: 093.0

093.23 Tricuspid valve `CC`
CC Excl: See code: 093.0

093.24 Pulmonary valve `CC`
CC Excl: See code: 093.0

✓5th **093.8 Other specified cardiovascular syphilis**

093.81 Syphilitic pericarditis `CC`
DEF: Inflammation of the outer lining of the heart.
CC Excl: See code: 093.0

093.82 Syphilitic myocarditis `CC`
DEF: Inflammation of the muscle of the heart.
CC Excl: See code: 093.0

093.89 Other `CC`
CC Excl: See code: 093.0

093.9 Cardiovascular syphilis, unspecified `CC`
CC Excl: See code: 093.0

✓4th **094 Neurosyphilis**
Use additional code to identify any associated mental disorder

094.0 Tabes dorsalis `CC`
Locomotor ataxia (progressive)
Posterior spinal sclerosis (syphilitic)
Tabetic neurosyphilis
Use additional code to identify manifestation, as:
neurogenic arthropathy [Charcot's joint disease] (713.5)
DEF: Progressive degeneration of nerves associated with long-term syphilis; causing pain, wasting away, incontinence, and ataxia.
CC Excl: 090.0-097.9, 099.40-099.9, 139.8
AHA: 3Q, '12, 4

094.1 General paresis `CC`
Dementia paralytica
General paralysis (of the insane) (progressive)
Paretic neurosyphilis
Taboparesis
DEF: Degeneration of brain associated with long-term syphilis, causing loss of brain function, progressive dementia, and paralysis.
CC Excl: 090.0-097.9, 099.40-099.9, 139.8

094.2 Syphilitic meningitis `MCC`
Meningovascular syphilis
EXCLUDES acute syphilitic meningitis (secondary) (091.81)
DEF: Inflammation of the lining of the brain and/or spinal cord.
CC Excl: 003.21, 013.00-013.16, 036.0, 047.0-047.9, 049.0-049.1, 053.0, 054.72, 072.1, 090.0-097.9, 098.89, 099.40-099.9, 100.81, 112.83, 114.2, 115.01, 115.11, 115.91, 130.0, 139.8, 320.0-322.9, 349.89-349.9, 357.0

094.3 Asymptomatic neurosyphilis `CC`
CC Excl: 090.0-097.9, 099.40-099.9, 139.8

✓5th **094.8 Other specified neurosyphilis**

094.81 Syphilitic encephalitis `MCC`
CC Excl: 090.0-097.9, 099.40-099.9, 139.8

094.82 Syphilitic Parkinsonism `CC`
DEF: Decreased motor function, tremors, and muscular rigidity.
CC Excl: 090.0-099.9, 332.0-333.0

094.83 Syphilitic disseminated retinochoroiditis `CC`
DEF: Inflammation of retina and choroid due to neurosyphilis.
CC Excl: 017.30-017.36, 090.0-099.9, 115.02, 115.12, 362.01, 362.12-362.13, 362.29, 362.41, 362.52, 362.76, 363.00, 363.05-363.10, 363.13-363.15, 646.80-646.84, 679.12, 679.14

094.84 Syphilitic optic atrophy `CC`
DEF: Degeneration of the eye and its nerves due to neurosyphilis.
CC Excl: 003.21, 013.00-013.16, 036.0, 047.0-047.9, 049.0-049.1, 072.1, 078.88-078.89, 079.81, 079.88-079.99, 090.0-099.9, 100.81, 112.83, 114.2, 115.01, 115.11, 115.91, 130.0, 139.8, 320.0-322.9, 349.89-349.9, 357.0

094.85 Syphilitic retrobulbar neuritis `CC`
DEF: Inflammation of the posterior optic nerve due to neurosyphilis.
CC Excl: 090.0-099.9, 377.32

094.86 Syphilitic acoustic neuritis `CC`
DEF: Inflammation of acoustic nerve due to neurosyphilis.
CC Excl: 090.0-099.9, 388.5

094.87 Syphilitic ruptured cerebral aneurysm `MCC`
CC Excl: 090.0-097.9, 099.40-099.9, 139.8

094.89 Other `CC`
CC Excl: 090.0-097.9, 099.40-099.9, 139.8

094.9 Neurosyphilis, unspecified `CC`
Gumma (syphilitic) ⎫
Syphilis (early) (late) ⎬ of central nervous system NOS
Syphiloma ⎭
CC Excl: 090.0-097.9, 099.40-099.9, 139.8

✓4th **095 Other forms of late syphilis, with symptoms**
INCLUDES gumma (syphilitic)
syphilis, late, tertiary, or unspecified stage

095.0 Syphilitic episcleritis `CC`
CC Excl: 017.30-017.36, 090.0-099.9, 379.00-379.02, 379.09

095.1 Syphilis of lung `CC`
CC Excl: 090.0-099.9

095.2 Syphilitic peritonitis `CC`
CC Excl: 014.00-014.06, 032.83, 090.0-099.9, 540.0-540.1, 567.0-567.1, 567.22, 567.29, 567.81, 567.9, 569.87-569.9, 577.8, 614.5-614.7, 639.0, 670.00-670.84, 777.6, 998.7

095.3 Syphilis of liver `CC`
CC Excl: 090.0-099.9

095.4 Syphilis of kidney `CC`
CC Excl: 090.0-099.9

095.5 Syphilis of bone `CC`
CC Excl: 090.0-099.9

095.6 Syphilis of muscle `CC`
Syphilitic myositis
CC Excl: 090.0-099.9

095.7 Syphilis of synovium, tendon, and bursa `CC`
Syphilitic:
bursitis
synovitis
CC Excl: 090.0-099.9

095.8 Other specified forms of late symptomatic syphilis `CC`
EXCLUDES cardiovascular syphilis (093.0-093.9)
neurosyphilis (094.0-094.9)
CC Excl: 090.0-099.9

095.9 Late symptomatic syphilis, unspecified `CC`
CC Excl: 090.0-099.9

096 Late syphilis, latent
Syphilis (acquired) without clinical manifestations, with positive serological reaction and negative spinal fluid test, two years or more after infection

✓4th **097 Other and unspecified syphilis**

097.0 Late syphilis, unspecified

097.1 Latent syphilis, unspecified
Positive serological reaction for syphilis

097.9 Syphilis, unspecified
Syphilis (acquired) NOS
EXCLUDES syphilis NOS causing death under two years of age (090.9)

`N` Newborn Age: 0   `P` Pediatric Age: 0-17   `M` Maternity Age: 12-55   `A` Adult Age: 15-124   `MCC` Major CC Condition   `CC` CC Condition   `HIV` HIV Related Dx

☑4ᵗʰ 098 Gonococcal infections
　　DEF: *Neisseria gonorrhoeae* infection generally acquired in utero or in sexual congress.

098.0 Acute, of lower genitourinary tract　　CC
　　Gonococcal:　　　　　Gonorrhea (acute):
　　　Bartholinitis (acute)　　NOS
　　　urethritis (acute)　　　genitourinary (tract) NOS
　　　vulvovaginitis (acute)
　　CC Excl: 098.0-098.39, 098.89, 099.40-099.9, 139.8

☑5ᵗʰ 098.1 Acute, of upper genitourinary tract

　098.10 Gonococcal infection (acute) of upper　CC
　　　genitourinary tract, site unspecified
　　　CC Excl: See code: 098.0

　098.11 Gonococcal cystitis (acute) upper　CC
　　　Gonorrhea (acute) of bladder
　　　CC Excl: See code: 098.0

　098.12 Gonococcal prostatitis (acute)　CC ♂
　　　CC Excl: See code: 098.0

　098.13 Gonococcal epididymo-orchitis (acute)　CC ♂
　　　Gonococcal orchitis (acute)
　　　DEF: Acute inflammation of the testes.
　　　CC Excl: See code: 098.0

　098.14 Gonococcal seminal vesiculitis (acute)　CC ♂
　　　Gonorrhea (acute) of seminal vesicle
　　　CC Excl: See code: 098.0

　098.15 Gonococcal cervicitis (acute)　CC ♀
　　　Gonorrhea (acute) of cervix
　　　CC Excl: See code: 098.0

　098.16 Gonococcal endometritis (acute)　CC ♀
　　　Gonorrhea (acute) of uterus
　　　CC Excl: See code: 098.0

　098.17 Gonococcal salpingitis, specified as acute　CC ♀
　　　DEF: Acute inflammation of the fallopian tubes.
　　　CC Excl: See code: 098.0

　098.19 Other　CC
　　　CC Excl: See code: 098.0

098.2 Chronic, of lower genitourinary tract
　　Gonoccocal:
　　　Bartholinitis
　　　urethritis　　　　｝specified as chronic or
　　　vulvovaginitis　　　　with duration of two
　　Gonorrhea:　　　　　　months or more
　　　NOS
　　　genitourinary (tract)
　　Any condition classifiable to 098.0 specified as chronic or with duration of two months or more

☑5ᵗʰ 098.3 Chronic, of upper genitourinary tract
　　INCLUDES any condition classifiable to 098.1 stated as chronic or with a duration of two months or more

　098.30 Chronic gonococcal infection of upper
　　　genitourinary tract, site unspecified

　098.31 Gonococcal cystitis, chronic
　　　Gonorrhea of bladder, chronic
　　　Any condition classifiable to 098.11, specified as chronic

　098.32 Gonococcal prostatitis, chronic　♂
　　　Any condition classifiable to 098.12, specified as chronic

　098.33 Gonococcal epididymo-orchitis, chronic　♂
　　　Chronic gonococcal orchitis
　　　Any condition classifiable to 098.13, specified as chronic
　　　DEF: Chronic inflammation of the testes.

　098.34 Gonococcal seminal vesiculitis, chronic　♂
　　　Gonorrhea of seminal vesicle, chronic
　　　Any condition classifiable to 098.14, specified as chronic

　098.35 Gonococcal cervicitis, chronic　♀
　　　Gonorrhea of cervix, chronic
　　　Any condition classifiable to 098.15, specified as chronic

　098.36 Gonococcal endometritis, chronic　♀
　　　Any condition classifiable to 098.16, specified as chronic
　　　DEF: Chronic inflammation of the uterus.

　098.37 Gonococcal salpingitis (chronic)　♀
　　　DEF: Chronic inflammation of the fallopian tubes.

　098.39 Other

☑5ᵗʰ 098.4 Gonococcal infection of eye

　098.40 Gonococcal conjunctivitis (neonatorum)　CC
　　　Gonococcal ophthalmia (neonatorum)
　　　DEF: Infection of conjunctiva present at birth.
　　　CC Excl: 090.0-099.9

　098.41 Gonococcal iridocyclitis　CC
　　　DEF: Inflammation and infection of iris and ciliary body.
　　　CC Excl: 090.0-099.9

　098.42 Gonococcal endophthalmia　CC
　　　DEF: Inflammation and infection of contents of eyeball.
　　　CC Excl: 090.0-099.9

　098.43 Gonococcal keratitis　CC
　　　DEF: Inflammation and infection of the cornea.
　　　CC Excl: 090.0-099.9

　098.49 Other　CC
　　　CC Excl: 090.0-099.9

☑5ᵗʰ 098.5 Gonococcal infection of joint

　098.50 Gonococcal arthritis　CC
　　　Gonococcal infection of joint NOS
　　　CC Excl: 003.23, 015.80-015.96, 017.90-017.96, 036.82, 056.71, 090.0-099.9, 711.00-714.0, 715.00, 715.09-715.10, 715.18-716.99, 718.00-718.08, 719.00-719.10, 719.18-719.69, 719.80-719.99

　098.51 Gonococcal synovitis and tenosynovitis　CC
　　　CC Excl: See code: 098.50

　098.52 Gonococcal bursitis　CC
　　　DEF: Inflammation of the sac-like cavities in a joint.
　　　CC Excl: See code: 098.50

　098.53 Gonococcal spondylitis　CC
　　　CC Excl: See code: 098.50

　098.59 Other　CC
　　　Gonococcal rheumatism
　　　CC Excl: See code: 098.50

098.6 Gonococcal infection of pharynx

098.7 Gonococcal infection of anus and rectum
　　Gonococcal proctitis

☑5ᵗʰ 098.8 Gonococcal infection of other specified sites

　098.81 Gonococcal keratosis (blennorrhagica)　CC
　　　DEF: Pustular skin lesions caused by *Neisseria gonorrhoeae.*
　　　CC Excl: 098.40-098.49, 098.81

　098.82 Gonococcal meningitis　MCC
　　　DEF: Inflammation of lining of brain and/or spinal cord.
　　　CC Excl: 003.21, 013.00-013.16, 036.0, 047.0-047.9, 049.0-049.1, 072.1, 078.88-078.89, 079.81, 079.88-079.99, 090.0-099.9, 100.81, 112.83, 114.2, 115.01, 115.11, 115.91, 130.0, 139.8, 320.0-322.9, 349.89-349.9, 357.0

　098.83 Gonococcal pericarditis　MCC
　　　DEF: Inflammation of the outer lining of the heart.
　　　CC Excl: 074.21, 090.0-099.9, 391.0, 393, 420.0-420.99, 423.3-423.9, 459.89-459.9

　098.84 Gonococcal endocarditis　MCC
　　　DEF: Inflammation of tissues lining the cavities of heart.
　　　CC Excl: 002.0, 036.42, 074.22, 083.0, 090.0-099.9, 112.81, 115.94, 116.0, 390, 391.1, 391.8-392.0, 394.0-395.9, 396.9-397.9, 398.90, 398.99, 421.0-421.9, 424.0-424.99, 425.3, 459.89-459.9, 711.00, 711.08-711.09, 746.09, 746.89, 996.61

Infectious and Parasitic Diseases

098–098.84

Infectious and Parasitic Diseases

098.85–102.2

098.85 Other gonococcal heart disease `CC`
CC Excl: 002.0, 036.42, 074.20, 074.22-074.23, 083.0, 090.0-099.9, 112.81, 115.94, 116.0, 390, 391.1-392.0, 394.0-395.9, 396.9-398.90, 398.99, 421.0-422.99, 424.0-424.99, 425.3, 429.0, 429.71-429.79, 459.89-459.9, 711.00, 711.08-711.09, 746.09, 746.89, 996.61

098.86 Gonococcal peritonitis `CC`
DEF: Inflammation of the membrane lining the abdomen.
CC Excl: 014.00-014.06, 032.83, 090.0-099.9, 540.0-540.1, 567.0-567.1, 567.22, 567.29, 567.81, 567.9, 569.89-569.9, 577.8, 614.5-614.7, 639.0, 670.00-670.04, 777.6, 998.7

098.89 Other `CC`
Gonococcemia
CC Excl: 090.0-099.9, 588.81-588.89

✓4th **099 Other venereal diseases**

099.0 Chancroid
Bubo (inguinal):
chancroidal
due to Hemophilus ducreyi
Chancre:
Ducrey's
simple
soft
Ulcus molle (cutis)(skin)
DEF: A sexually transmitted disease caused by *Haemophilus ducreyi*; identified by a painful primary ulcer at the site of inoculation (usually external genitalia) with related lymphadenitis.

099.1 Lymphogranuloma venereum
Climatic or tropical bubo
(Durand-) Nicolas-Favre disease
Esthiomene
Lymphogranuloma inguinale
DEF: Sexually transmitted infection of *Chlamydia trachomatis* causing skin lesions.

099.2 Granuloma inguinale
Donovanosis
Granuloma pudendi (ulcerating)
Granuloma venereum
Pudendal ulcer
DEF: Chronic, sexually transmitted infection of *Calymmatobacterium granulomatis* causing progressive, anogenital skin ulcers.

099.3 Reiter's disease
Reactive arthritis
Reiter's syndrome
Use additional code for associated:
arthropathy (711.1)
conjunctivitis (372.33)
DEF: A symptom complex of unknown etiology consisting of urethritis, conjunctivitis, arthritis and myocutaneous lesions; occurs most commonly in young men and patients with HIV. Also a form of reactive arthritis.

✓5th **099.4 Other nongonococcal urethritis [NGU]**

099.40 Unspecified
Nonspecific urethritis

099.41 Chlamydia trachomatis

099.49 Other specified organism

✓5th **099.5 Other venereal diseases due to Chlamydia trachomatis**
EXCLUDES *Chlamydia trachomatis infection of conjunctiva (076.0-076.9, 077.0, 077.9)*
Lymphogranuloma venereum (099.1)
DEF: Venereal diseases caused by *Chlamydia trachomatis* at other sites besides the urethra (e.g., pharynx, anus and rectum, conjunctiva and peritoneum).

099.50 Unspecified site

099.51 Pharynx

099.52 Anus and rectum

099.53 Lower genitourinary sites
Use additional code to specify site of infection, such as:
bladder (595.4)
cervix (616.0)
vagina and vulva (616.11)
EXCLUDES *urethra (099.41)*

099.54 Other genitourinary sites
Use additional code to specify site of infection, such as:
pelvic inflammatory disease NOS (614.9)
testis and epididymis (604.91)

099.55 Unspecified genitourinary site

099.56 Peritoneum `CC`
Perihepatitis
CC Excl: 014.00-014.06, 032.83, 090.0-099.9, 540.0-540.1, 567.0-567.1, 567.22, 567.29, 567.81, 567.9, 569.89-569.9, 577.8, 614.5-614.7, 639.0, 670.00-670.04, 777.6, 998.7

099.59 Other specified site

099.8 Other specified venereal diseases

099.9 Venereal disease, unspecified

Other Spirochetal Diseases (100-104)

✓4th **100 Leptospirosis**
DEF: A blood infection of any spirochete of the genus *Leptospire*; transmitted to humans by exposure to contaminated animal tissues or water. Patients present with flulike symptoms, characteristic muscle aches involving the thighs and low back.

100.0 Leptospirosis icterohemorrhagica `CC`
Leptospiral or spirochetal jaundice (hemorrhagic)
Weil's disease
CC Excl: 100.0-100.9

✓5th **100.8 Other specified leptospiral infections**

100.81 Leptospiral meningitis (aseptic) `MCC`
CC Excl: 003.21, 013.00-013.16, 036.0, 047.0-047.9, 049.0-049.1, 072.1, 078.88-078.89, 079.81, 079.88-079.99, 090.42, 091.81, 094.2, 098.89, 100.0-100.9, 112.83, 114.2, 115.01, 115.11, 115.91, 130.0, 139.8, 320.0-322.9, 349.89-349.9, 357.0

100.89 Other `CC`
Fever: Infection by Leptospira:
Fort Bragg   australis
pretibial   bataviae
swamp   pyrogenes
CC Excl: See code: 100.0

100.9 Leptospirosis, unspecified `CC`
CC Excl: See code: 100.0

101 Vincent's angina `CC`
Acute necrotizing ulcerative:
gingivitis
stomatitis
Fusospirochetal pharyngitis
Spirochetal stomatitis
Trench mouth
Vincent's:
gingivitis
infection [any site]
DEF: Painful ulceration with edema and hypermic patches of the oropharyngeal and throat membranes; it is caused by spreading of acute ulcerative gingivitis.
CC Excl: 101

✓4th **102 Yaws**
INCLUDES frambesia
pian
DEF: An infectious, endemic, tropical disease caused by *Treponema pertenue*; usually affects persons 15 years old or younger; a primary cutaneous lesion develops, then a granulomatous skin eruption, and occasionally lesions that destroy skin and bone.

102.0 Initial lesions
Chancre of yaws   Initial frambesial ulcer
Frambesia, initial or primary   Mother yaw

102.1 Multiple papillomata and wet crab yaws
Butter yaws
Frambesioma
Pianoma
Plantar or palmar papilloma of yaws

102.2 Other early skin lesions
Cutaneous yaws, less than five years after infection
Early yaws (cutaneous) (macular) (papular) (maculopapular) (micropapular)
Frambeside of early yaws

`N` Newborn Age: 0   `P` Pediatric Age: 0-17   `M` Maternity Age: 12-55   `A` Adult Age: 15-124   `MCC` Major CC Condition   `CC` CC Condition   `HIV` HIV Related Dx

24 – Volume 1   **2015 ICD-9-CM**

102.3 Hyperkeratosis
Ghoul hand
Hyperkeratosis, palmar or plantar (early) (late) due to yaws
Worm-eaten soles
DEF: Overgrowth of skin of palm or bottoms of feet, due to yaws.

102.4 Gummata and ulcers
Gummatous frambeside
Nodular late yaws (ulcerated)
DEF: Rubbery lesions and areas of dead skin caused by yaws.

102.5 Gangosa
Rhinopharyngitis mutilans
DEF: Massive, mutilating lesions of the nose and oral cavity caused by yaws.

102.6 Bone and joint lesions
Goundou
Gumma, bone   } of yaws (late)
Gummatous osteitis or periostitis

Hydrarthrosis
Osteitis   } of yaws (early) (late)
Periostitis (hypertrophic)

102.7 Other manifestations
Juxta-articular nodules of yaws
Mucosal yaws

102.8 Latent yaws
Yaws without clinical manifestations, with positive serology

102.9 Yaws, unspecified

√4ᵗʰ **103 Pinta**
DEF: A chronic form of treponematosis, endemic in areas of tropical America; it is identified by the presence of red, violet, blue, coffee-colored or white spots on the skin.

103.0 Primary lesions
Chancre (primary)
Papule (primary)   } of pinta [carate]
Pintid

103.1 Intermediate lesions
Erythematous plaques
Hyperchronic lesions   } of pinta [carate]
Hyperkeratosis

103.2 Late lesions
Cardiovascular lesions
Skin lesions:
  achromic
  cicatricial   } of pinta [carate]
  dyschromic
Vitiligo

103.3 Mixed lesions
Achromic and hyperchromic skin lesions of pinta [carate]

103.9 Pinta, unspecified

√4ᵗʰ **104 Other spirochetal infection**
104.0 Nonvenereal endemic syphilis
Bejel
Njovera
DEF: *Treponema pallidum, T. pertenue,* or *T. caroteum* infection transmitted non-sexually, causing lesions on mucosa and skin.

104.8 Other specified spirochetal infections
EXCLUDES relapsing fever (087.0-087.9)
syphilis (090.0-097.9)

104.9 Spirochetal infection, unspecified

Mycoses (110-118)
Use additional code to identify manifestation as:
arthropathy (711.6)
meningitis (321.0-321.1)
otitis externa (380.15)
EXCLUDES infection by Actinomycetales, such as species of Actinomyces, Actinomadura, Nocardia, Streptomyces (039.0-039.9)

√4ᵗʰ **110 Dermatophytosis**
INCLUDES infection by species of Epidermophyton, Microsporum, and Trichophyton
tinea, any type except those in 111
DEF: Superficial infection of the skin caused by a parasitic fungus.

110.0 Of scalp and beard
Kerion
Sycosis, mycotic
Trichophytic tinea [black dot tinea], scalp

110.1 Of nail
Dermatophytic onychia
Onychomycosis
Tinea unguium
B35.1 Tinea unguium   I-10

110.2 Of hand
Tinea manuum

110.3 Of groin and perianal area
Dhobie itch
Eczema marginatum
Tinea cruris

110.4 Of foot
Athlete's foot
Tinea pedis

110.5 Of the body
Herpes circinatus
Tinea imbricata [Tokelau]

110.6 Deep seated dermatophytosis
Granuloma trichophyticum
Majocchi's granuloma

110.8 Of other specified sites

110.9 Of unspecified site
Favus NOS
Microsporic tinea NOS
Ringworm NOS

√4ᵗʰ **111 Dermatomycosis, other and unspecified**

111.0 Pityriasis versicolor
Infection by Malassezia [Pityrosporum] furfur
Tinea flava
Tinea versicolor

111.1 Tinea nigra
Infection by Cladosporium species
Keratomycosis nigricans
Microsporosis nigra
Pityriasis nigra
Tinea palmaris nigra

111.2 Tinea blanca
Infection by Trichosporon (beigelii) cutaneum
White piedra

111.3 Black piedra
Infection by Piedraia hortai

111.8 Other specified dermatomycoses

111.9 Dermatomycosis, unspecified

√4ᵗʰ **112 Candidiasis**
INCLUDES infection by Candida species
moniliasis
EXCLUDES neonatal monilial infection (771.7)
DEF: Fungal infection caused by *Candida;* usually seen in mucous membranes or skin.

112.0 Of mouth   CC HIV
Thrush (oral)
CC Exd: 112.0-112.9, 117.9, 139.8
B37.0 Candidal stomatitis   I-10

112.1 Of vulva and vagina   ♀
> Candidal vulvovaginitis
> Monilial vulvovaginitis
> **B37.3** Candidiasis of vulva and vagina   I-10

8 **112.2 Of other urogenital sites**   CC
> Candidal balanitis
> **CC Excl:** 112.2, 112.4-112.9, 588.81-588.89
> **AHA:** 3Q, '12, 11-12; 4Q, '03, 105; 4Q, '96, 33

112.3 Of skin and nails   HIV
> Candidal intertrigo
> Candidal onychia
> Candidal perionyxis [paronychia]
> **B37.2** Candidiasis of skin and nail   I-10

112.4 Of lung   MCC HIV
> Candidal pneumonia
> **CC Excl:** See code: 112.0
> **AHA:** 2Q, '98, 7

112.5 Disseminated   MCC HIV
> Systemic candidiasis
> **CC Excl:** See code: 112.0
> **AHA:** 3Q, '12, 11-12; 2Q, '00, 5; 2Q, '89, 10
> **TIP:** Report for candidal sepsis, followed by the appropriate subcategory 995.9 code. If due to underlying candidal UTI, code also 112.2.

√5th **112.8 Of other specified sites**

112.81 Candidal endocarditis   MCC HIV
> **CC Excl:** See code: 112.0

112.82 Candidal otitis externa   CC HIV
> Otomycosis in moniliasis
> **CC Excl:** See code: 112.0

112.83 Candidal meningitis   MCC HIV
> **CC Excl:** 003.21, 013.00-013.16, 036.0, 047.0-047.9, 049.0-049.1, 053.0, 054.72, 072.1, 090.42, 091.81, 094.2, 098.89, 100.81, 112.0-112.9, 114.2, 115.01, 115.11, 115.91, 117.9, 130.0, 139.8, 320.0-322.9, 349.89-349.9, 357.0

112.84 Candidal esophagitis   CC HIV
> **CC Excl:** See code: 112.0
> **AHA:** 4Q, '92, 19
> **B37.81** Candidal esophagitis   I-10

112.85 Candidal enteritis   CC HIV
> **CC Excl:** See code: 112.0
> **AHA:** 4Q, '92, 19

112.89 Other   CC HIV
> **CC Excl:** 112.4-112.9
> **AHA:** 1Q, '92, 17; 3Q, '91, 20

112.9 Of unspecified site   HIV

√4th **114 Coccidioidomycosis**
> **INCLUDES** infection by Coccidioides (immitis)
> Posada-Wernicke disease
> **DEF:** A fungal disease caused by inhalation of dust particles containing arthrospores of *Coccidiodes immitis;* a self-limited respiratory infection; the primary form is known as San Joaquin fever, desert fever or valley fever.
> **AHA:** 4Q, '93, 23

114.0 Primary coccidioidomycosis (pulmonary)   CC HIV
> Acute pulmonary coccidioidomycosis
> Coccidioidomycotic pneumonitis
> Desert rheumatism
> Pulmonary coccidioidomycosis
> San Joaquin Valley fever
> **DEF:** Acute, self-limiting *Coccidioides immitis* infection of the lung.
> **CC Excl:** 114.0, 114.3-114.9, 117.9, 139.8
> **B38.0** Acute pulmonary coccidioidomycosis   I-10

114.1 Primary extrapulmonary coccidioidomycosis   CC HIV
> Chancriform syndrome
> Primary cutaneous coccidioidomycosis
> **DEF:** Acute, self-limiting *Coccidioides immitis* infection in nonpulmonary site.
> **CC Excl:** 114.0-114.9

114.2 Coccidioidal meningitis   MCC HIV
> **DEF:** *Coccidioides immitis* infection of the lining of the brain and/or spinal cord.
> **CC Excl:** 003.21, 013.00-013.16, 036.0, 047.0-047.9, 049.0-049.1, 053.0, 054.72, 072.1, 090.42, 091.81, 094.2, 098.89, 100.81, 112.83, 114.2-114.3, 114.9, 115.01, 115.11, 115.91, 117.9, 130.0, 139.8, 320.0-322.9, 349.89-349.9, 357.0

114.3 Other forms of progressive coccidioidomycosis   CC HIV
> Coccidioidal granuloma
> Disseminated coccidioidomycosis
> **CC Excl:** 114.3, 114.9, 117.9, 139.8

114.4 Chronic pulmonary coccidioidomycosis   CC HIV
> **CC Excl:** 114.0-115.99

114.5 Pulmonary coccidioidomycosis, unspecified   CC HIV
> **CC Excl:** See code: 114.4

114.9 Coccidioidomycosis, unspecified   CC HIV
> **CC Excl:** See code: 114.3

√4th **115 Histoplasmosis**

> The following fifth-digit subclassification is for use with category 115:
> 0 **without mention of manifestation**
> 1 **meningitis**
> 2 **retinitis**
> 3 **pericarditis**
> 4 **endocarditis**
> 5 **pneumonia**
> 9 **other**

§ √5th **115.0 Infection by Histoplasma capsulatum**   CC 2,9 HIV MCC 1, 3-5
> [0-5, 9] American histoplasmosis
> Darling's disease
> Reticuloendothelial cytomycosis
> Small form histoplasmosis
> **CC Excl: For code 115.01:** 003.21, 013.00-013.16, 036.0, 047.0-047.9, 049.0-049.1, 053.0, 054.72, 072.1, 090.42, 091.81, 094.2, 098.89, 100.81, 112.83, 114.2, 115.00-115.01, 115.09, 115.11, 115.90-115.91, 115.99, 117.9, 130.0, 139.8, 320.0-322.9, 349.89-349.9, 357.0; **For code 115.02:** 115.00, 115.02, 115.09, 115.90, 115.92, 115.99, 117.9, 139.8; **For code 115.03:** 115.00, 115.03, 115.09, 115.90, 115.93, 115.99, 117.9, 139.8; **For code 115.04:** 115.00, 115.04, 115.09, 115.90, 115.94, 115.99, 117.9, 139.8; **For code 115.05:** 115.00, 115.05-115.09, 115.90, 115.95-115.99, 117.9, 139.8, 480.0-480.2, 480.8-487.1, 488.01-488.02, 488.11-488.12, 494.0-508.9, 517.1, 518.89; **For code 115.09:** 114.0-115.09

§ √5th **115.1 Infection by Histoplasma duboisii**   CC 2,9 HIV MCC 1, 3-5
> [0-5, 9] African histoplasmosis
> Large form histoplasmosis
> **CC Excl: For code 115.11:** 003.21, 013.00-013.16, 036.0, 047.0-047.9, 049.0-049.1, 053.0, 054.72, 072.1, 090.42, 091.81, 094.2, 098.89, 100.81, 112.83, 114.2, 115.00-115.01, 115.09, 115.11, 115.90-115.91, 115.99, 117.9, 130.0, 139.8, 320.0-322.9, 349.89-349.9, 357.0; **For code 115.12:** 115.10, 115.12, 115.19-115.90, 115.92, 115.99, 117.9, 139.8; **For code 115.13:** 115.10, 115.13, 115.19-115.90, 115.93, 115.99, 117.9, 139.8; **For code 115.14:** 115.10, 115.14, 115.19-115.90, 115.94, 115.99, 117.9, 139.8; **For code 115.15:** 115.05, 115.10, 115.15-115.90, 115.95-115.99, 117.9, 139.8, 480.0-480.2, 480.8-487.1, 488.01-488.02, 488.11-488.12, 494.0-508.9, 517.1, 518.89; **For code 115.19:** 115.10, 115.19-115.90, 115.99, 117.9, 139.8

§ √5th **115.9 Histoplasmosis, unspecified**   CC 2 HIV MCC 1, 3-5
> [0-5, 9] Histoplasmosis NOS
> **CC Excl: For code 115.91:** 003.21, 013.00-013.16, 036.0, 047.0-047.9, 049.0-049.1, 053.0, 054.72, 072.1, 090.42, 091.81, 094.2, 098.89, 100.81, 112.83, 114.2, 115.01, 115.11, 115.91, 115.99, 117.9, 130.0, 139.8, 320.0-322.9, 349.89-349.9, 357.0; **For code 115.92:** 115.92, 115.99, 117.9, 139.8; **For code 115.93:** 115.93, 115.99, 117.9, 139.8; **For code 115.94:** 115.94, 115.99, 117.9, 139.8; **For code 115.95:** 115.05, 115.15, 115.95-115.99, 117.9, 139.8

√4th **116 Blastomycotic infection**

116.0 Blastomycosis   CC
> Blastomycotic dermatitis
> Chicago disease
> Cutaneous blastomycosis
> Disseminated blastomycosis
> Gilchrist's disease
> Infection by Blastomyces [Ajellomyces] dermatitidis
> North American blastomycosis
> Primary pulmonary blastomycosis
> **CC Excl:** 116.0, 117.9, 139.8

8 CC/MCC except when in combination with 996.64 and POA = N
§ Requires fifth digit. Valid digits are in [brackets] under each code. See category 115 for codes and definitions.

N Newborn Age: 0   P Pediatric Age: 0-17   M Maternity Age: 12-55   A Adult Age: 15-124   MCC Major CC Condition   CC CC Condition   HIV HIV Related Dx

26 – Volume 1   **2015 ICD-9-CM**

116.1 Paracoccidioidomycosis `CC`
Brazilian blastomycosis
Infection by Paracoccidioides [Blastomyces] brasiliensis
Lutz-Splendore-Almeida disease
Mucocutaneous-lymphangitic paracoccidioidomycosis
Pulmonary paracoccidioidomycosis
South American blastomycosis
Visceral paracoccidioidomycosis
CC Excl: 116.1, 117.9, 139.8

116.2 Lobomycosis
Infections by Loboa [Blastomyces] loboi
Keloidal blastomycosis
Lobo's disease

√4th 117 Other mycoses

117.0 Rhinosporidiosis
Infection by Rhinosporidium seeberi

117.1 Sporotrichosis
Cutaneous sporotrichosis
Disseminated sporotrichosis
Infection by Sporothrix [Sporotrichum] schenckii
Lymphocutaneous sporotrichosis
Pulmonary sporotrichosis
Sporotrichosis of the bones

117.2 Chromoblastomycosis
Chromomycosis
Infection by Cladosporidium carrionii, Fonsecaea compactum, Fonsecaea pedrosoi, Phialophora verrucosa

117.3 Aspergillosis `CC`
Infection by Aspergillus species, mainly A. fumigatus, A. flavus group, A. terreus group
CC Excl: 117.3, 117.9, 139.8
AHA: 4Q, '97, 40

117.4 Mycotic mycetomas `CC`
Infection by various genera and species of Ascomycetes and Deuteromycetes, such as Acremonium [Cephalosporium] falciforme, Neotestudina rosatii, Madurella grisea, Madurella mycetomii, Pyrenochaeta romeroi, Zopfia [Leptosphaeria] senegalensis
Madura foot, mycotic
Maduromycosis, mycotic
EXCLUDES *actinomycotic mycetomas (039.0-039.9)*
CC Excl: 117.4, 117.9, 139.8

117.5 Cryptococcosis `CC` `HIV`
Busse-Buschke's disease
European cryptococcosis
Infection by Cryptococcus neoformans
Pulmonary cryptococcosis
Systemic cryptococcosis
Torula
CC Excl: 117.5, 117.9, 139.8

117.6 Allescheriosis [Petriellidosis] `CC`
Infections by Allescheria [Petriellidium] boydii [Monosporium apiospermum]
EXCLUDES *mycotic mycetoma (117.4)*
CC Excl: 117.6, 117.9, 139.8

117.7 Zygomycosis [Phycomycosis or Mucormycosis] `MCC`
Infection by species of Absidia, Basidiobolus, Conidiobolus, Cunninghamella, Entomophthora, Mucor, Rhizopus, Saksenaea
CC Excl: 117.7, 117.9, 139.8

117.8 Infection by dematiacious fungi, [Phaehyphomycosis] `CC`
Infection by dematiacious fungi, such as Cladosporium trichoides [bantianum], Dreschlera hawaiiensis, Phialophora gougerotii, Phialophora jeanselmi
CC Excl: 117.8-117.9

117.9 Other and unspecified mycoses `CC`
CC Excl: See code: 117.8

118 Opportunistic mycoses `CC` `HIV`
Infection of skin, subcutaneous tissues, and/or organs by a wide variety of fungi generally considered to be pathogenic to compromised hosts only (e.g., infection by species of Alternaria, Dreschlera, Fusarium)
Use additional code to identify manifestation, such as:
keratitis (370.8)
CC Excl: 117.9-118, 139.8

Helminthiases (120-129)

√4th 120 Schistosomiasis [bilharziasis]
DEF: Infection caused by *Schistosoma,* a genus of flukes or trematode parasites.

120.0 Schistosoma haematobium `CC`
Vesical schistosomiasis NOS
CC Excl: 120.0-120.9

120.1 Schistosoma mansoni `CC`
Intestinal schistosomiasis NOS
CC Excl: See code: 120.0

120.2 Schistosoma japonicum `CC`
Asiatic schistosomiasis NOS
Katayama disease or fever
CC Excl: See code: 120.0

120.3 Cutaneous `CC`
Cercarial dermatitis
Infection by cercariae of Schistosoma
Schistosome dermatitis
Swimmers' itch
CC Excl: See code: 120.0

120.8 Other specified schistosomiasis `CC`
Infection by Schistosoma:
bovis
intercalatum
mattheii
spindale
Schistosomiasis chestermani
CC Excl: See code: 120.0

120.9 Schistosomiasis, unspecified `CC`
Blood flukes NOS
Hemic distomiasis
CC Excl: See code: 120.0

√4th 121 Other trematode infections

121.0 Opisthorchiasis `CC`
Infection by:
cat liver fluke
Opisthorchis (felineus) (tenuicollis) (viverrini)
CC Excl: 121.0-121.9

121.1 Clonorchiasis `CC`
Biliary cirrhosis due to clonorchiasis
Chinese liver fluke disease
Hepatic distomiasis due to Clonorchis sinensis
Oriental liver fluke disease
CC Excl: See code: 121.0

121.2 Paragonimiasis `CC`
Infection by Paragonimus
Lung fluke disease (oriental)
Pulmonary distomiasis
CC Excl: See code: 121.0

121.3 Fascioliasis `CC`
Infection by Fasciola:
gigantica
hepatica
Liver flukes NOS
Sheep liver fluke infection
CC Excl: See code: 121.0

121.4 Fasciolopsiasis `CC`
Infection by Fasciolopsis (buski)
Intestinal distomiasis
CC Excl: See code: 121.0

121.5 Metagonimiasis `CC`
Infection by Metagonimus yokogawai
CC Excl: See code: 121.0

Infectious and Parasitic Diseases

121.6–125.9

121.6 Heterophyiasis `CC`
Infection by:
Heterophyes heterophyes
Stellantchasmus falcatus
CC Excl: See code: 121.0

121.8 Other specified trematode infections `CC`
Infection by:
Dicrocoelium dendriticum
Echinostoma ilocanum
Gastrodiscoides hominis
CC Excl: See code: 121.0

121.9 Trematode infection, unspecified
Distomiasis NOS
Fluke disease NOS

✓4ᵗʰ **122 Echinococcosis**
INCLUDES echinococciasis
hydatid disease
hydatidosis
DEF: Infection caused by larval forms of tapeworms of the genus *Echinococcus.*

122.0 Echinococcus granulosus infection of liver `CC`
CC Excl: 122.0, 122.8-122.9

122.1 Echinococcus granulosus infection of lung `CC`
CC Excl: 122.1, 122.8-122.9, 480.3

122.2 Echinococcus granulosus infection of thyroid `CC`
CC Excl: 122.2, 122.8-122.9

122.3 Echinococcus granulosus infection, other `CC`
CC Excl: 122.3, 122.8-122.9

122.4 Echinococcus granulosus infection, unspecified `CC`
CC Excl: 122.4, 122.8-122.9

122.5 Echinococcus multilocularis infection of liver `CC`
CC Excl: 122.5, 122.8-122.9

122.6 Echinococcus multilocularis infection, other `CC`
CC Excl: 122.6, 122.8-122.9

122.7 Echinococcus multilocularis infection, unspecified `CC`
CC Excl: 122.7-122.9

122.8 Echinococcosis, unspecified, of liver `CC`
CC Excl: 122.8-122.9

122.9 Echinococcosis, other and unspecified `CC`
CC Excl: See code: 122.8

✓4ᵗʰ **123 Other cestode infection**

123.0 Taenia solium infection, intestinal form `CC`
Pork tapeworm (adult) (infection)
CC Excl: 001.1, 002.0, 002.9-003.0, 004.9-005.2, 006.0-006.2, 006.9, 007.1-009.0, 014.80-014.86, 040.41-040.42, 112.85, 123.0-123.9, 129, 487.8, 488.09, 488.19, 536.3, 536.8, 558.2-558.9, 564.1, 777.50-777.53, 777.8

123.1 Cysticercosis `CC`
Cysticerciasis
Infection by Cysticercus cellulosae [larval form of Taenia solium]
CC Excl: 123.0-123.9
AHA: 2Q, '97, 8

123.2 Taenia saginata infection `CC`
Beef tapeworm (infection)
Infection by Taeniarhynchus saginatus
CC Excl: See code: 123.1

123.3 Taeniasis, unspecified `CC`
CC Excl: See code: 123.1

123.4 Diphyllobothriasis, intestinal `CC`
Diphyllobothrium (adult) (latum) (pacificum) infection
Fish tapeworm (infection)
CC Excl: See code: 123.1

123.5 Sparganosis [larval diphyllobothriasis] `CC`
Infection by:
Diphyllobothrium larvae
Sparganum (mansoni) (proliferum)
Spirometra larvae
CC Excl: See code: 123.1

123.6 Hymenolepiasis `CC`
Dwarf tapeworm (infection)
Hymenolepis (diminuta) (nana) infection
Rat tapeworm (infection)
CC Excl: See code: 123.1

123.8 Other specified cestode infection `CC`
Diplogonoporus (grandis)
Dipylidium (caninum) } infection
Dog tapeworm (infection)
CC Excl: See code: 123.1

123.9 Cestode infection, unspecified
Tapeworm (infection) NOS

124 Trichinosis `CC`
Trichinella spiralis infection
Trichinellosis
Trichiniasis
DEF: Infection by *Trichinella spiralis,* the smallest of the parasitic nematodes.
CC Excl: 013.60-013.66, 046.2, 046.71-046.8, 048-049.0, 049.8, 052.0, 052.2, 054.3, 054.74, 056.01, 057.8-058.29, 059.00-059.9, 062.0-064, 066.2-066.49, 072.2, 073.7, 079.82, 079.99, 081.9, 083.9, 090.41, 094.81, 117.5, 124, 130.0, 290.12, 323.01-323.9, 341.1, 487.8, 488.09, 488.19, 771.2, 984.9

✓4ᵗʰ **125 Filarial infection and dracontiasis**

125.0 Bancroftian filariasis `CC`
Chyluria
Elephantiasis
Infection } due to Wuchereria bancrofti
Lymphadenitis
Lymphangitis
Wuchereriasis
CC Excl: 125.0-125.9

125.1 Malayan filariasis `CC`
Brugia filariasis
Chyluria
Elephantiasis
Infection } due to Wuchereria bancrofti
Lymphadenitis
Lymphangitis
CC Excl: See code: 125.0

125.2 Loiasis `CC`
Eyeworm disease of Africa
Loa loa infection
CC Excl: See code: 125.0

125.3 Onchocerciasis `CC`
Onchocerca volvulus infection
Onchocercosis
CC Excl: See code: 125.0

125.4 Dipetalonemiasis `CC`
Infection by:
Acanthocheilonema perstans
Dipetalonema perstans
CC Excl: See code: 125.0

125.5 Mansonella ozzardi infection `CC`
Filariasis ozzardi
CC Excl: See code: 125.0

125.6 Other specified filariasis `CC`
Dirofilaria infection
Infection by:
Acanthocheilonema streptocerca
Dipetalonema streptocerca
CC Excl: See code: 125.0

125.7 Dracontiasis `CC`
Guinea-worm infection
Infection by Dracunculus medinensis
CC Excl: See code: 125.0

125.9 Unspecified filariasis `CC`
CC Excl: See code: 125.0

N Newborn Age: 0   **P** Pediatric Age: 0-17   **M** Maternity Age: 12-55   **A** Adult Age: 15-124   **MCC** Major CC Condition   **CC** CC Condition   **HIV** HIV Related Dx

28 – Volume 1   **2015 ICD-9-CM**

√4th **126 Ancylostomiasis and necatoriasis**

INCLUDES cutaneous larva migrans due to Ancylostoma
hookworm (disease) (infection)
uncinariasis

126.0 Ancylostoma duodenale CC
CC Excl: 126.0-126.9

126.1 Necator americanus CC
CC Excl: See code: 126.0

126.2 Ancylostoma braziliense CC
CC Excl: See code: 126.0

126.3 Ancylostoma ceylanicum CC
CC Excl: See code: 126.0

126.8 Other specified Ancylostoma CC
CC Excl: See code: 126.0

126.9 Ancylostomiasis and necatoriasis, unspecified CC
Creeping eruption NOS
Cutaneous larva migrans NOS
CC Excl: See code: 126.0

√4th **127 Other intestinal helminthiases**

127.0 Ascariasis CC
Ascaridiasis
Infection by Ascaris lumbricoides
Roundworm infection
CC Excl: 127.0-127.9

127.1 Anisakiasis CC
Infection by Anisakis larva
CC Excl: See code: 127.0

127.2 Strongyloidiasis CC HIV
Infection by Strongyloides stercoralis
EXCLUDES trichostrongyliasis (127.6)
CC Excl: See code: 127.0

127.3 Trichuriasis CC
Infection by Trichuris trichiura
Trichocephaliasis
Whipworm (disease) (infection)
CC Excl: See code: 127.0

127.4 Enterobiasis CC
Infection by Enterobius vermicularis
Oxyuriasis
Oxyuris vermicularis infection
Pinworm (disease) (infection)
Threadworm infection
CC Excl: See code: 127.0

127.5 Capillariasis CC
Infection by Capillaria philippinensis
EXCLUDES infection by Capillaria hepatica (128.8)
CC Excl: See code: 127.0

127.6 Trichostrongyliasis CC
Infection by Trichostrongylus species
CC Excl: See code: 127.0

127.7 Other specified intestinal helminthiasis CC
Infection by:
Oesophagostomum apiostomum and related species
Ternidens diminutus
other specified intestinal helminth
Physalopteriasis
CC Excl: 127.0-129

127.8 Mixed intestinal helminthiasis CC
Infection by intestinal helminths classified to more than one
of the categories 120.0-127.7
Mixed helminthiasis NOS
CC Excl: See code: 127.7

127.9 Intestinal helminthiasis, unspecified CC
CC Excl: See code: 127.7

√4th **128 Other and unspecified helminthiases**

128.0 Toxocariasis
Larva migrans visceralis
Toxocara (canis) (cati) infection
Visceral larva migrans syndrome

128.1 Gnathostomiasis
Infection by Gnathostoma spinigerum and related species

128.8 Other specified helminthiasis
Infection by:
Angiostrongylus cantonensis
Capillaria hepatica
other specified helminth

128.9 Helminth infection, unspecified
Helminthiasis NOS
Worms NOS

129 Intestinal parasitism, unspecified

Other Infectious and Parasitic Diseases (130–136)

√4th **130 Toxoplasmosis**

INCLUDES infection by toxoplasma gondii
toxoplasmosis (acquired)
EXCLUDES congenital toxoplasmosis (771.2)

130.0 Meningoencephalitis due to toxoplasmosis MCC HIV
Encephalitis due to acquired toxoplasmosis
CC Excl: 130.0, 130.7-130.9, 139.8

130.1 Conjunctivitis due to toxoplasmosis CC HIV
CC Excl: 130.1, 130.7-130.9, 139.8

130.2 Chorioretinitis due to toxoplasmosis CC HIV
Focal retinochoroiditis due to acquired toxoplasmosis
CC Excl: 130.2, 130.7-130.9, 139.8

130.3 Myocarditis due to toxoplasmosis MCC HIV
CC Excl: 130.3, 130.7-130.9, 139.8

130.4 Pneumonitis due to toxoplasmosis MCC HIV
CC Excl: 130.4, 130.7-130.9, 139.8, 480.0-480.2, 480.8-487.1,
488.01-488.02, 488.11-488.12, 494.0-508.9, 517.1, 518.89

130.5 Hepatitis due to toxoplasmosis CC HIV
CC Excl: 130.5-130.9, 139.8

130.7 Toxoplasmosis of other specified sites CC HIV
CC Excl: 130.7-130.9, 139.8

130.8 Multisystemic disseminated toxoplasmosis MCC HIV
Toxoplasmosis of multiple sites
CC Excl: See code: 130.7

130.9 Toxoplasmosis, unspecified CC HIV
CC Excl: 130.9

√4th **131 Trichomoniasis**

INCLUDES infection due to Trichomonas (vaginalis)

√5th **131.0 Urogenital trichomoniasis**

131.00 Urogenital trichomoniasis, unspecified
Fluor (vaginalis)   ⎫ trichomonal or due to
Leukorrhea   ⎬ Trichomonas
(vaginalis)   ⎭ (vaginalis)
DEF: Trichomonas vaginalis infection of reproductive and
urinary organs, transmitted through coitus.

131.01 Trichomonal vulvovaginitis ♀
Vaginitis, trichomonal or due to Trichomonas
(vaginalis)
DEF: Trichomonas vaginalis infection of vulva and vagina;
often asymptomatic, transmitted through coitus.

131.02 Trichomonal urethritis
DEF: Trichomonas vaginalis infection of the urethra.

131.03 Trichomonal prostatitis ♂
DEF: Trichomonas vaginalis infection of the prostate.

131.09 Other

131.8 Other specified sites
EXCLUDES intestinal (007.3)

131.9 Trichomoniasis, unspecified

√4th **132 Pediculosis and phthirus infestation**

132.0 Pediculus capitis [head louse]

132.1 Pediculus corporis [body louse]

132.2 Phthirus pubis [pubic louse]
Pediculus pubis

132.3 Mixed infestation
Infestation classifiable to more than one of the categories
132.0-132.2

Infectious and Parasitic Diseases

132.9–139.8

132.9 Pediculosis, unspecified

√4ᵗʰ **133 Acariasis**

133.0 Scabies
Infestation by Sarcoptes scabiei
Norwegian scabies
Sarcoptic itch

133.8 Other acariasis
Chiggers
Infestation by:
Demodex folliculorum
Trombicula

133.9 Acariasis, unspecified
Infestation by mites NOS

√4ᵗʰ **134 Other infestation**

134.0 Myiasis
Infestation by:
Dermatobia (hominis)
fly larvae
Gasterophilus (intestinalis)
maggots
Oestrus ovis

134.1 Other arthropod infestation
Infestation by:
chigoe
sand flea
Tunga penetrans
Jigger disease
Scarabiasis
Tungiasis

134.2 Hirudiniasis
Hirudiniasis (external) (internal)
Leeches (aquatic) (land)

134.8 Other specified infestations

134.9 Infestation, unspecified
Infestation (skin) NOS
Skin parasites NOS

135 Sarcoidosis
Besnier-Boeck-Schaumann disease
Lupoid (miliary) of Boeck
Lupus pernio (Besnier)
Lymphogranulomatosis, benign (Schaumann's)
Sarcoid (any site):
NOS
Boeck
Darier-Roussy
Uveoparotid fever
DEF: A chronic, granulomatous reticulosis (abnormal increase in cells), affecting any organ or tissue; acute form has high rate of remission; chronic form is progressive.
D86.9 Sarcoidosis unspecified   `I-10`

√4ᵗʰ **136 Other and unspecified infectious and parasitic diseases**

136.0 Ainhum
Dactylolysis spontanea
DEF: A disease affecting the toes, especially the fifth digit, the fingers, mostly seen in black adult males; it is characterized by a linear constriction around the affected digit leading to spontaneous amputation of the distal part of the digit.

136.1 Behçet's syndrome
DEF: A chronic inflammatory disorder of unknown etiology involving the small blood vessels; characterized by recurrent aphthous ulceration of the oral and pharyngeal mucous membranes and the genitalia; skin lesions, severe uveitis, retinal vascularitis and optic atrophy.

√5ᵗʰ **136.2 Specific infections by free-living amebae**
AHA: 4Q, '08, 79-81

136.21 Specific infection due to acanthamoeba
Use additional code to identify manifestation, such as:
keratitis (370.8)
AHA: 4Q, '08, 81

136.29 Other specific infections by free-living amebae   `CC`
Meningoencephalitis due to Naegleria
CC Excl: 136.0-136.9

136.3 Pneumocystosis   `MCC` `HIV`
Pneumonia due to Pneumocystis carinii
Pneumonia due to Pneumocystis jiroveci
DEF: *Pneumocystis carinii* fungus causing pneumonia in immunocompromised patients; a leading cause of death among AIDS patients.
CC Excl: 136.3, 139.8, 480.0-480.2, 480.8-487.1, 488.01-488.02, 488.11-488.12, 494.0-508.9, 517.1, 518.89
AHA: 1Q, '05, 7; 1Q, '03, 15; N-D, '87, 5-6

136.4 Psorospermiasis   `CC`
CC Excl: See code: 136.2

136.5 Sarcosporidiosis   `CC`
Infection by Sarcocystis lindemanni
DEF: *Sarcocystis* infection causing muscle cysts of intestinal inflammation.
CC Excl: See code: 136.2

136.8 Other specified infectious and parasitic diseases   `HIV`
Candiru infestation

136.9 Unspecified infectious and parasitic diseases
Infectious disease NOS
Parasitic disease NOS
AHA: 2Q, '91, 8

Late Effects of Infectious and Parasitic Diseases (137-139)

√4ᵗʰ **137 Late effects of tuberculosis**
NOTE This category is to be used to indicate conditions classifiable to 010-018 as the cause of late effects, which are themselves classified elsewhere. The "late effects" include those specified as such, as sequelae, or as due to old or inactive tuberculosis, without evidence of active disease.

137.0 Late effects of respiratory or unspecified tuberculosis

137.1 Late effects of central nervous system tuberculosis

137.2 Late effects of genitourinary tuberculosis

137.3 Late effects of tuberculosis of bones and joints

137.4 Late effects of tuberculosis of other specified organs

138 Late effects of acute poliomyelitis
NOTE This category is to be used to indicate conditions classifiable to 045 as the cause of late effects, which are themselves classified elsewhere. The "late effects" include conditions specified as such, or as sequelae, or as due to old or inactive poliomyelitis, without evidence of active disease.
B91 Sequelae of poliomyelitis   `I-10`

√4ᵗʰ **139 Late effects of other infectious and parasitic diseases**
NOTE This category is to be used to indicate conditions classifiable to categories 001-009, 020-041, 046-136 as the cause of late effects, which are themselves classified elsewhere. The "late effects" include conditions specified as such; they also include sequela of diseases classifiable to the above categories if there is evidence that the disease itself is no longer present.

139.0 Late effects of viral encephalitis
Late effects of conditions classifiable to 049.8-049.9, 062-064

139.1 Late effects of trachoma
Late effects of conditions classifiable to 076

139.8 Late effects of other and unspecified infectious and parasitic diseases
AHA: 2Q, '06, 17; 4Q, '91, 15; 3Q, '90, 14; M-A, '87, 8

`N` Newborn Age: 0   `P` Pediatric Age: 0-17   `M` Maternity Age: 12-55   `A` Adult Age: 15-124   `MCC` Major CC Condition   `CC` CC Condition   `HIV` HIV Related Dx

2. Neoplasms (140-239)

NOTES

1. Content

   This chapter contains the following broad groups:

   140-195   Malignant neoplasms, stated or presumed to be primary, of specified sites, except of lymphatic and hematopoietic tissue

   196-198   Malignant neoplasms, stated or presumed to be secondary, of specified sites

   199   Malignant neoplasms, without specification of site

   200-208   Malignant neoplasms, stated or presumed to be primary, of lymphatic and hematopoietic tissue

   209   Neuroendocrine tumors

   210-229   Benign neoplasms

   230-234   Carcinoma in situ

   235-238   Neoplasms of uncertain behavior [see Note, above category 235]

   239   Neoplasms of unspecified nature

2. Functional activity

   All neoplasms are classified in this chapter, whether or not functionally active. An additional code from Chapter 3 may be used to identify such functional activity associated with any neoplasm, e.g.:

   > catecholamine-producing malignant pheochromocytoma of adrenal:
   >
   > > code 194.0, additional code 255.6
   >
   > basophil adenoma of pituitary with Cushing's syndrome:
   >
   > > code 227.3, additional code 255.0

3. Morphology [Histology]

   For those wishing to identify the histological type of neoplasms, a comprehensive coded nomenclature, which comprises the morphology rubrics of the ICD-Oncology, is given in Appendix A.

4. Malignant neoplasms overlapping site boundaries

   Categories 140-195 are for the classification of primary malignant neoplasms according to their point of origin. A malignant neoplasm that overlaps two or more subcategories within a three-digit rubric and whose point of origin cannot be determined should be classified to the subcategory .8 "Other."

   For example, "carcinoma involving tip and ventral surface of tongue" should be assigned to 141.8. On the other hand, "carcinoma of tip of tongue, extending to involve the ventral surface" should be coded to 141.2, as the point of origin, the tip, is known. Three subcategories (149.8, 159.8, 165.8) have been provided for malignant neoplasms that overlap the boundaries of three-digit rubrics within certain systems.

   Overlapping malignant neoplasms that cannot be classified as indicated above should be assigned to the appropriate subdivision of category 195 (Malignant neoplasm of other and ill-defined sites).

   > **DEF:** An abnormal growth; morphology determines behavior, i.e., whether it will remain intact (benign) or spread to adjacent tissue (malignant). The term mass is not synonymous with neoplasm, as it is often used to describe cysts and thickenings such as those occurring with hematoma or infection.
   > **AHA:** 2Q, '90, 7

Malignant Neoplasm of Lip, Oral Cavity, and Pharynx (140-149)

EXCLUDES carcinoma in situ (230.0)

√4ᵗʰ **140 Malignant neoplasm of lip**

    EXCLUDES malignant melanoma of skin of lip (172.0)
                  malignant neoplasm of skin of lip (173.00-173.09)

  140.0 Upper lip, vermilion border
      Upper lip:
         NOS
         external
         lipstick area

  140.1 Lower lip, vermilion border
      Lower lip:
         NOS
         external
         lipstick area

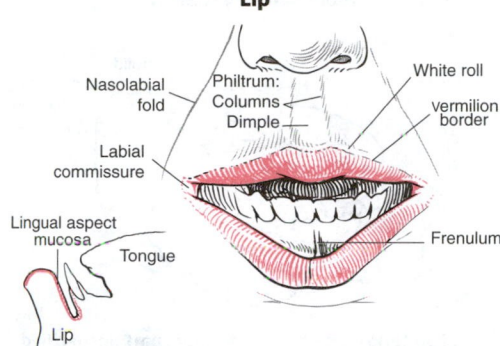

Lip

140.3 Upper lip, inner aspect
    Upper lip:
      buccal aspect
      frenulum
      mucosa
      oral aspect

140.4 Lower lip, inner aspect
    Lower lip:
      buccal aspect
      frenulum
      mucosa
      oral aspect

140.5 Lip, unspecified, inner aspect
    Lip, not specified whether upper or lower:
      buccal aspect
      frenulum
      mucosa
      oral aspect

140.6 Commissure of lip
    Labial commissure

140.8 Other sites of lip
    Malignant neoplasm of contiguous or overlapping sites of lip whose point of origin cannot be determined

140.9 Lip, unspecified, vermilion border
    Lip, not specified as upper or lower:
      NOS
      external
      lipstick area

√4ᵗʰ **141 Malignant neoplasm of tongue**

  141.0 Base of tongue
      Dorsal surface of base of tongue
      Fixed part of tongue NOS
      AHA: 4Q, '06, 90

  141.1 Dorsal surface of tongue
      Anterior two-thirds of tongue, dorsal surface
      Dorsal tongue NOS
      Midline of tongue
      EXCLUDES dorsal surface of base of tongue (141.0)

  141.2 Tip and lateral border of tongue

  141.3 Ventral surface of tongue
      Anterior two-thirds of tongue, ventral surface
      Frenulum linguae

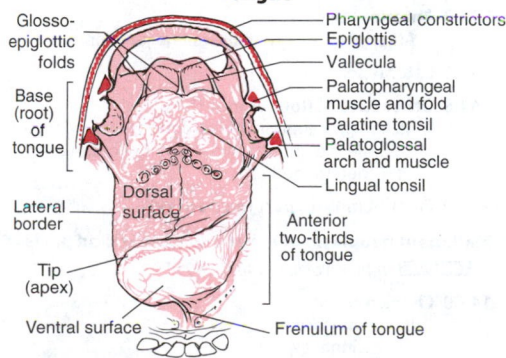

Tongue

√4ᵗʰ √5ᵗʰ Additional Digit Required   Unacceptable PDx   Manifestation Code   Hospital Acquired Condition   ▶◀ Revised Text   ● New Code   ▲ Revised Code Title

2015 ICD-9-CM   **Volume 1 – 31**

Main Salivary Glands

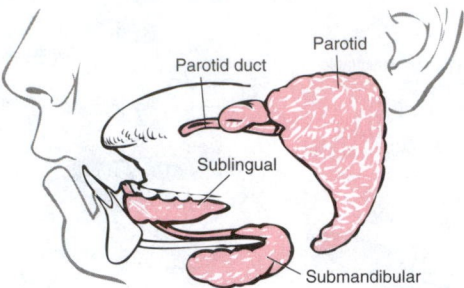

Mouth

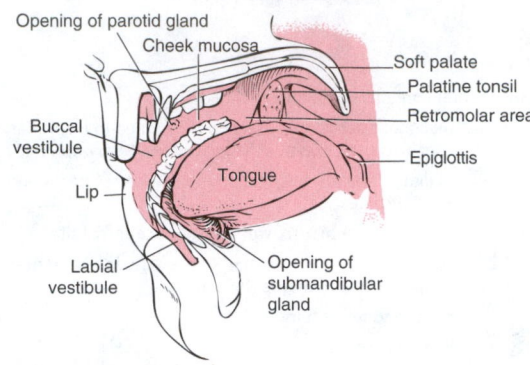

141.4 Anterior two-thirds of tongue, part unspecified
Mobile part of tongue NOS

141.5 Junctional zone
Border of tongue at junction of fixed and mobile parts at insertion of anterior tonsillar pillar

141.6 Lingual tonsil

141.8 Other sites of tongue
Malignant neoplasm of contiguous or overlapping sites of tongue whose point of origin cannot be determined

141.9 Tongue, unspecified
Tongue NOS

✓4ᵗʰ 142 Malignant neoplasm of major salivary glands
INCLUDES   salivary ducts
EXCLUDES   *malignant neoplasm of minor salivary glands:*
NOS (145.9)
buccal mucosa (145.0)
soft palate (145.3)
tongue (141.0–141.9)
tonsil, palatine (146.0)

142.0 Parotid gland

142.1 Submandibular gland
Submaxillary gland

142.2 Sublingual gland

142.8 Other major salivary glands
Malignant neoplasm of contiguous or overlapping sites of salivary glands and ducts whose point of origin cannot be determined

142.9 Salivary gland, unspecified
Salivary gland (major) NOS

✓4ᵗʰ 143 Malignant neoplasm of gum
INCLUDES   alveolar (ridge) mucosa
gingiva (alveolar) (marginal)
interdental papillae
EXCLUDES   *malignant odontogenic neoplasms (170.0–170.1)*

143.0 Upper gum

143.1 Lower gum

143.8 Other sites of gum
Malignant neoplasm of contiguous or overlapping sites of gum whose point of origin cannot be determined

143.9 Gum, unspecified

✓4ᵗʰ 144 Malignant neoplasm of floor of mouth

144.0 Anterior portion
Anterior to the premolar-canine junction

144.1 Lateral portion

144.8 Other sites of floor of mouth
Malignant neoplasm of contiguous or overlapping sites of floor of mouth whose point of origin cannot be determined

144.9 Floor of mouth, part unspecified

✓4ᵗʰ 145 Malignant neoplasm of other and unspecified parts of mouth
EXCLUDES   *mucosa of lips (140.0–140.9)*

145.0 Cheek mucosa
Buccal mucosa
Cheek, inner aspect

145.1 Vestibule of mouth
Buccal sulcus (upper) (lower)
Labial sulcus (upper) (lower)

145.2 Hard palate

145.3 Soft palate
EXCLUDES   *nasopharyngeal [posterior] [superior] surface of soft palate (147.3)*

145.4 Uvula

145.5 Palate, unspecified
Junction of hard and soft palate
Roof of mouth

145.6 Retromolar area

145.8 Other specified parts of mouth
Malignant neoplasm of contiguous or overlapping sites of mouth whose point of origin cannot be determined

145.9 Mouth, unspecified
Buccal cavity NOS
Minor salivary gland, unspecified site
Oral cavity NOS

Oropharynx

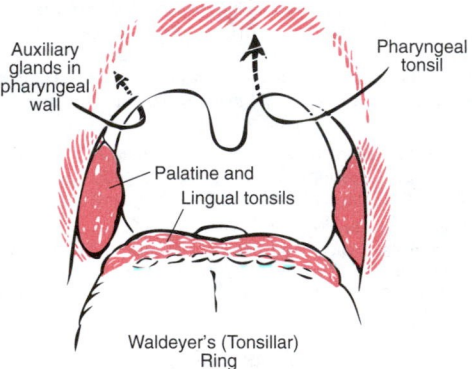

Nasopharynx

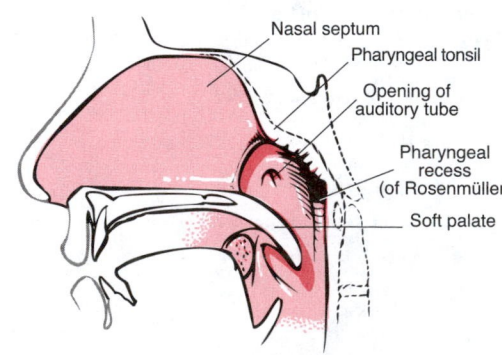

N Newborn Age: 0   P Pediatric Age: 0-17   M Maternity Age: 12-55   A Adult Age: 15-124   MCC Major CC Condition   CC CC Condition   HIV HIV Related Dx

32 – Volume 1   2015 ICD-9-CM

✓4ᵗʰ 146 Malignant neoplasm of oropharynx

146.0 Tonsil
Tonsil:
   NOS
   faucial
   palatine
   EXCLUDES *lingual tonsil (141.6)*
           pharyngeal tonsil (147.1)
    AHA: S-O, '87, 8

146.1 Tonsillar fossa

146.2 Tonsillar pillars (anterior) (posterior)
Faucial pillar
Glossopalatine fold
Palatoglossal arch
Palatopharyngeal arch

146.3 Vallecula
Anterior and medial surface of the pharyngoepiglottic fold

146.4 Anterior aspect of epiglottis
Epiglottis, free border [margin]
Glossoepiglottic fold(s)
   EXCLUDES *epiglottis:*
           NOS (161.1)
           suprahyoid portion (161.1)

146.5 Junctional region
Junction of the free margin of the epiglottis, the aryepiglottic fold, and the pharyngoepiglottic fold

146.6 Lateral wall of oropharynx

146.7 Posterior wall of oropharynx

146.8 Other specified sites of oropharynx
Branchial cleft
Malignant neoplasm of contiguous or overlapping sites of oropharynx whose point of origin cannot be determined

146.9 Oropharynx, unspecified
    AHA: 2Q, '02, 6

✓4ᵗʰ 147 Malignant neoplasm of nasopharynx

147.0 Superior wall
Roof of nasopharynx

147.1 Posterior wall
Adenoid
Pharyngeal tonsil

147.2 Lateral wall
Fossa of Rosenmüller
Opening of auditory tube
Pharyngeal recess

147.3 Anterior wall
Floor of nasopharynx
Nasopharyngeal [posterior] [superior] surface of soft palate
Posterior margin of nasal septum and choanae

147.8 Other specified sites of nasopharynx
Malignant neoplasm of contiguous or overlapping sites of nasopharynx whose point of origin cannot be determined

147.9 Nasopharynx, unspecified
Nasopharyngeal wall NOS

✓4ᵗʰ 148 Malignant neoplasm of hypopharynx

148.0 Postcricoid region

148.1 Pyriform sinus
Pyriform fossa

148.2 Aryepiglottic fold, hypopharyngeal aspect
Aryepiglottic fold or interarytenoid fold:
   NOS
   marginal zone
   EXCLUDES *aryepiglottic fold or interarytenoid fold, laryngeal aspect (161.1)*

148.3 Posterior hypopharyngeal wall

Hypopharynx

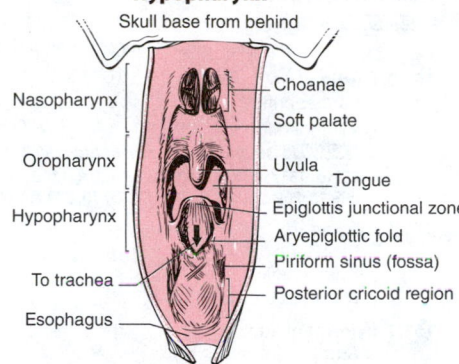

148.8 **Other specified sites of hypopharynx**
Malignant neoplasm of contiguous or overlapping sites of hypopharynx whose point of origin cannot be determined

148.9 **Hypopharynx, unspecified**
Hypopharyngeal wall NOS
Hypopharynx NOS

✓4ᵗʰ 149 Malignant neoplasm of other and ill-defined sites within the lip, oral cavity, and pharynx

149.0 **Pharynx, unspecified**

149.1 **Waldeyer's ring**

149.8 **Other**
Malignant neoplasms of lip, oral cavity, and pharynx whose point of origin cannot be assigned to any one of the categories 140-148
   EXCLUDES *"book leaf" neoplasm [ventral surface of tongue and floor of mouth] (145.8)*

149.9 **Ill-defined**

Malignant Neoplasm of Digestive Organs and Peritoneum (150-159)
   EXCLUDES *carcinoma in situ (230.1-230.9)*

✓4ᵗʰ 150 Malignant neoplasm of esophagus

150.0 **Cervical esophagus**   **CC**
   CC Excl: 150.0-150.9, 159.0, 159.8-159.9, 176.3, 195.8, 199.0-199.2, 209.20, 209.29-209.30, 209.70, 209.75, 239.0, 239.81-239.9

150.1 **Thoracic esophagus**   **CC**
   CC Excl: See code: 150.0

150.2 **Abdominal esophagus**   **CC**
   EXCLUDES *adenocarcinoma (151.0)*
           cardio-esophageal junction (151.0)
   CC Excl: See code 150.0

150.3 **Upper third of esophagus**   **CC**
Proximal third of esophagus
   CC Excl: See code 150.0

150.4 **Middle third of esophagus**   **CC**
   CC Excl: See code 150.0

150.5 **Lower third of esophagus**   **CC**
Distal third of esophagus
   EXCLUDES *adenocarcinoma (151.0)*
           cardio-esophageal junction (151.0)
   CC Excl: See code 150.0

150.8 **Other specified part**   **CC**
Malignant neoplasm of contiguous or overlapping sites of esophagus whose point of origin cannot be determined
   CC Excl: See code 150.0

150.9 **Esophagus, unspecified**   **CC**
   CC Excl: See code 150.0

Neoplasms

146–150.9

✓4ᵗʰ Additional Digit Required   ✓5ᵗʰ
Unacceptable PDx   Manifestation Code   Hospital Acquired Condition   ►◄ Revised Text   ● New Code   ▲ Revised Code Title
2015 ICD-9-CM   Volume 1 – 33

Neoplasms

151–153.9

☑4ᵗʰ **151 Malignant neoplasm of stomach**

    EXCLUDES *benign carcinoid tumor of stomach (209.63)*
                  malignant carcinoid tumor of stomach (209.23)

  151.0 Cardia `CC`
       Cardiac orifice
       Cardio-esophageal junction
       EXCLUDES *squamous cell carcinoma (150.2, 150.5)*
       CC Excl: 151.0-151.9, 159.0, 159.8-159.9, 176.3, 195.8, 199.0-199.2, 209.20, 209.23, 209.25-209.30, 209.70, 209.75, 239.0, 239.81-239.9

  151.1 Pylorus `CC`
       Prepylorus
       Pyloric canal
       CC Excl: See code 151.0

  151.2 Pyloric antrum `CC`
       Antrum of stomach NOS
       CC Excl: See code 151.0

  151.3 Fundus of stomach `CC`
       CC Excl: See code 151.0

  151.4 Body of stomach `CC`
       CC Excl: See code 151.0

  151.5 Lesser curvature, unspecified `CC`
       Lesser curvature, not classifiable to 151.1-151.4
       CC Excl: See code 151.0

  151.6 Greater curvature, unspecified `CC`
       Greater curvature, not classifiable to 151.0-151.4
       CC Excl: See code 151.0

  151.8 Other specified sites of stomach `CC`
       Anterior wall, not classifiable to 151.0-151.4
       Posterior wall, not classifiable to 151.0-151.4
       Malignant neoplasm of contiguous or overlapping sites of stomach whose point of origin cannot be determined
       CC Excl: See code 151.0

  151.9 Stomach, unspecified `CC`
       Carcinoma ventriculi
       Gastric cancer
       CC Excl: See code 151.0
       AHA: 2Q, '01, 17

☑4ᵗʰ **152 Malignant neoplasm of small intestine, including duodenum**

    EXCLUDES *benign carcinoid tumor of small intestine and duodenum (209.40-209.43)*
                  malignant carcinoid tumor of small intestine and duodenum (209.00-209.03)

  152.0 Duodenum `CC`
       CC Excl: 152.0, 152.8-152.9, 159.0, 159.8-159.9, 176.3, 195.8, 199.0-199.2, 209.00-209.01, 209.20, 209.29-209.30, 209.70, 209.75, 239.0, 239.81-239.9

  152.1 Jejunum `CC`
       CC Excl: 152.1, 152.8-152.9, 159.0, 159.8-159.9, 176.3, 195.8, 199.0-199.2, 209.00, 209.02, 209.20, 209.29-209.30, 209.70, 209.75, 239.0, 239.81-239.9

  152.2 Ileum `CC`
       EXCLUDES *ileocecal valve (153.4)*
       CC Excl: 152.2, 152.8-152.9, 159.0, 159.8-159.9, 176.3, 195.8, 199.0-199.2, 209.00, 209.03, 209.20, 209.29-209.30, 209.70, 209.75, 239.0, 239.81-239.9

  152.3 Meckel's diverticulum `CC`
       CC Excl: 152.3-152.9, 159.0, 159.8-159.9, 176.3, 195.8, 199.0-199.2, 209.00, 209.20, 209.29-209.30, 209.70, 209.75, 239.0, 239.81-239.9

  152.8 Other specified sites of small intestine `CC`
       Duodenojejunal junction
       Malignant neoplasm of contiguous or overlapping sites of small intestine whose point of origin cannot be determined
       CC Excl: 152.8-152.9, 159.0, 159.8-159.9, 176.3, 195.8, 199.0-199.2, 209.00, 209.20, 209.29-209.30, 209.70, 209.75, 239.0, 239.81-239.9

  152.9 Small intestine, unspecified `CC`
       CC Excl: See code 152.8

Colon

Anatomical distribution of large bowel cancers

☑4ᵗʰ **153 Malignant neoplasm of colon**

    EXCLUDES *benign carcinoid tumor of colon (209.50-209.56)*
                  malignant carcinoid tumor of colon (209.10-209.16)

  153.0 Hepatic flexure `CC`
       CC Excl: 153.0, 153.8-153.9, 159.0, 159.8-159.9, 176.3, 195.8, 199.0-199.2, 209.10, 209.20, 209.29-209.30, 209.70, 209.75, 239.0, 239.81-239.9

  153.1 Transverse colon `CC`
       CC Excl: 153.1, 153.8-153.9, 159.0, 159.8-159.9, 176.3, 195.8, 199.0-199.2, 209.10, 209.14, 209.20, 209.29-209.30, 209.70, 209.75, 239.0, 239.81-239.9
       AHA: ▶3Q, '13, 9◄

  153.2 Descending colon `CC`
       Left colon
       CC Excl: 153.2, 153.8-153.9, 159.0, 159.8-159.9, 176.3, 195.8, 199.0-199.2, 209.10, 209.15, 209.20, 209.29-209.30, 209.70, 209.75, 239.0, 239.81-239.9

  153.3 Sigmoid colon `CC`
       Sigmoid (flexure)
       EXCLUDES *rectosigmoid junction (154.0)*
       CC Excl: 153.3, 153.8-153.9, 159.0, 159.8-159.9, 176.3, 195.8, 199.0-199.2, 209.10, 209.16, 209.20, 209.29-209.30, 209.70, 209.75, 239.0, 239.81-239.9

  153.4 Cecum `CC`
       Ileocecal valve
       CC Excl: 153.4, 153.8-153.9, 159.0, 159.8-159.9, 176.3, 195.8, 199.0-199.2, 209.10, 209.12, 209.20, 209.29-209.30, 209.70, 209.75, 239.0, 239.81-239.9
       `C18.0` Malignant neoplasm of cecum `I-10`

  153.5 Appendix `CC`
       CC Excl: 153.5, 153.8-153.9, 159.0, 159.8-159.9, 176.3, 195.8, 199.0-199.2, 209.10-209.11, 209.20, 209.29-209.30, 209.70, 209.75, 239.0, 239.81-239.9

  153.6 Ascending colon `CC`
       Right colon
       CC Excl: 153.6, 153.8-153.9, 159.0, 159.8-159.9, 176.3, 195.8, 199.0-199.2, 209.10, 209.13, 209.20, 209.29-209.30, 209.70, 209.75, 239.0, 239.81-239.9
       `C18.2` Malignant neoplasm of ascending colon `I-10`

  153.7 Splenic flexure `CC`
       CC Excl: 153.7-153.9, 159.0, 159.8-159.9, 176.3, 195.8, 199.0-199.2, 209.10, 209.20, 209.29-209.30, 209.70, 209.75, 239.0, 239.81-239.9

  153.8 Other specified sites of large intestine `CC`
       Malignant neoplasm of contiguous or overlapping sites of colon whose point of origin cannot be determined
       EXCLUDES *ileocecal valve (153.4)*
                  rectosigmoid junction (154.0)
       CC Excl: 153.8-153.9, 159.0, 159.8-159.9, 176.3, 195.8, 199.0-199.2, 209.10, 209.20, 209.29-209.30, 209.70, 209.75, 239.0, 239.81-239.9

  153.9 Colon, unspecified `CC`
       Large intestine NOS
       CC Excl: See code: 153.8
       AHA: 2Q, '10, 12
       `C18.9` Malignant neoplasm of colon unspecified `I-10`

`N` Newborn Age: 0   `P` Pediatric Age: 0-17   `M` Maternity Age: 12-55   `A` Adult Age: 15-124   `MCC` Major CC Condition   `CC` CC Condition   `HIV` HIV Related Dx

✓4ᵗʰ **154 Malignant neoplasm of rectum, rectosigmoid junction, and anus**

EXCLUDES *benign carcinoid tumor of rectum (209.57)*
malignant carcinoid tumor of rectum (209.17)

154.0 Rectosigmoid junction   `cc`
Colon with rectum
Rectosigmoid (colon)
CC Excl: 154.0, 154.8, 159.0, 159.8-159.9, 176.3, 195.8, 199.0-199.2, 209.20, 209.29-209.30, 209.70, 209.75, 239.0, 239.81-239.9

154.1 Rectum   `cc`
Rectal ampulla
CC Excl: 154.1, 154.8, 159.0, 159.8-159.9, 176.3, 195.8, 199.0-199.2, 209.17-209.20, 209.29-209.30, 209.70, 209.75, 239.0, 239.81-239.9
C20 Malignant neoplasm of rectum   `I-10`

154.2 Anal canal   `cc`
Anal sphincter
EXCLUDES *malignant melanoma of skin of anus (172.5)*
malignant neoplasm of skin of anus (173.50-173.59)
CC Excl: 154.2-154.8, 159.0, 159.8-159.9, 176.3, 195.8, 199.0-199.2, 209.20, 209.29-209.30, 209.70, 209.75, 239.0, 239.81-239.9
AHA: 1Q, '01, 8

154.3 Anus, unspecified   `cc`
EXCLUDES *malignant melanoma of:*
anus:
margin (172.5)
skin (172.5)
perianal skin (172.5)
malignant neoplasm of:
anus:
margin (173.50-173.59)
skin (173.50-173.59)
perianal skin (173.50-173.59)
CC Excl: See code: 154.2

154.8 Other   `cc`
Anorectum
Cloacogenic zone
Malignant neoplasm of contiguous or overlapping sites of rectum, rectosigmoid junction, and anus whose point of origin cannot be determined
CC Excl: 154.8, 159.0, 159.8-159.9, 176.3, 195.8, 199.0-199.2, 209.20, 209.29-209.30, 209.70, 209.75, 239.0, 239.81-239.9

✓4ᵗʰ **155 Malignant neoplasm of liver and intrahepatic bile ducts**

155.0 Liver, primary   `cc`
Carcinoma:
liver, specified as primary
hepatocellular
liver cell
Hepatoblastoma
CC Excl: 155.0-155.2, 159.0, 159.8-159.9, 176.3, 195.8, 199.0-199.2, 209.20, 209.29-209.30, 209.70, 209.75, 239.0, 239.81-239.9
AHA: 4Q, '08, 82
C22.0 Liver cell carcinoma   `I-10`

155.1 Intrahepatic bile ducts   `cc`
Canaliculi biliferi   Intrahepatic:
Interlobular: biliary passages
  bile ducts   canaliculi
  biliary canals   gall duct
EXCLUDES *hepatic duct (156.1)*
CC Excl: See code 155.0

155.2 Liver, not specified as primary or secondary   `cc`
CC Excl: See code 155.0

✓4ᵗʰ **156 Malignant neoplasm of gallbladder and extrahepatic bile ducts**

156.0 Gallbladder   `cc`
CC Excl: 156.0, 156.8-156.9, 159.0, 159.8-159.9, 176.3, 195.8, 199.0-199.2, 209.20, 209.29-209.30, 209.70, 209.75, 239.0, 239.81-239.9

156.1 Extrahepatic bile ducts   `cc`
Biliary duct or passage NOS
Common bile duct
Cystic duct
Hepatic duct
Sphincter of Oddi
CC Excl: 156.1, 156.8-156.9, 159.0, 159.8-159.9, 176.3, 195.8, 199.0-199.2, 209.20, 209.29-209.30, 209.70, 209.75, 239.0, 239.81-239.9

156.2 Ampulla of Vater   `cc`
DEF: Malignant neoplasm in the area of dilation at the juncture of the common bile and pancreatic ducts near the opening into the lumen of the duodenum.
CC Excl: 156.2-156.9, 159.0, 159.8-159.9, 176.3, 195.8, 199.0-199.2, 209.20, 209.29-209.30, 209.70, 209.75, 239.0, 239.81-239.9

156.8 Other specified sites of gallbladder and extrahepatic bile ducts   `cc`
Malignant neoplasm of contiguous or overlapping sites of gallbladder and extrahepatic bile ducts whose point of origin cannot be determined
CC Excl: 156.8-156.9, 159.0, 159.8-159.9, 176.3, 195.8, 199.0-199.2, 209.20, 209.29-209.30, 209.70, 209.75, 239.0, 239.81-239.9

156.9 Biliary tract, part unspecified   `cc`
Malignant neoplasm involving both intrahepatic and extrahepatic bile ducts
CC Excl: See code: 156.8

✓4ᵗʰ **157 Malignant neoplasm of pancreas**
AHA: 4Q, '07, 72

157.0 Head of pancreas   `cc`
CC Excl: 157.0-157.9, 159.0, 159.8-159.9, 176.3, 195.8, 199.0-199.2, 209.20, 209.29-209.30, 209.70, 209.75, 239.0, 239.81-239.9
AHA: 2Q, '05, 9; 4Q, '00, 40

157.1 Body of pancreas   `cc`
CC Excl: See code 157.0

157.2 Tail of pancreas   `cc`
CC Excl: See code 157.0

157.3 Pancreatic duct   `cc`
Duct of:
Santorini
Wirsung
CC Excl: See code 157.0

157.4 Islets of Langerhans   `cc`
Islets of Langerhans, any part of pancreas
Use additional code to identify any functional activity
DEF: Malignant neoplasm within the structures of the pancreas that produce insulin, somatostatin and glucagon.
CC Excl: See code 157.0

157.8 Other specified sites of pancreas   `cc`
Ectopic pancreatic tissue
Malignant neoplasm of contiguous or overlapping sites of pancreas whose point of origin cannot be determined
CC Excl: See code 157.0

157.9 Pancreas, part unspecified   `cc`
CC Excl: See code 157.0
AHA: 4Q, '89, 11
C25.9 Malignant neoplasm of pancreas unspecified   `I-10`

✓4ᵗʰ **158 Malignant neoplasm of retroperitoneum and peritoneum**

158.0 Retroperitoneum   `cc`
Periadrenal tissue   Perirenal tissue
Perinephric tissue   Retrocecal tissue
CC Excl: 158.0, V58.0

158.8 Specified parts of peritoneum   `cc`
Cul-de-sac (of Douglas)
Malignant neoplasm of contiguous or overlapping sites of retroperitoneum and peritoneum whose point of origin cannot be determined
Mesentery
Mesocolon
Omentum
Peritoneum:
  parietal
  pelvic
Rectouterine pouch
CC Excl: 158.0-158.9, V58.0

158.9 Peritoneum, unspecified   `cc`
CC Excl: See code: 158.8

Neoplasms

154–158.9

Neoplasms

159–162.9

Retroperitoneum and Peritoneum

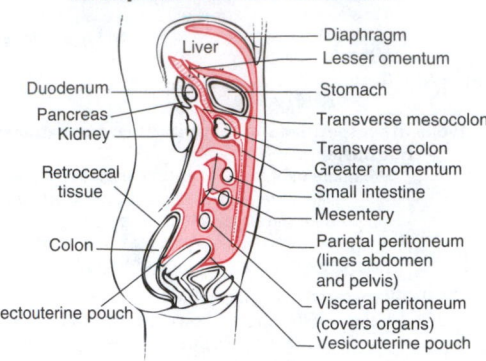

Diaphragm
Liver
Lesser omentum
Duodenum
Stomach
Pancreas
Transverse mesocolon
Kidney
Transverse colon
Greater momentum
Retrocecal tissue
Small intestine
Mesentery
Colon
Parietal peritoneum (lines abdomen and pelvis)
Visceral peritoneum (covers organs)
Rectouterine pouch
Vesicouterine pouch

☑4ᵗʰ 159 Malignant neoplasm of other and ill-defined sites within the digestive organs and peritoneum

159.0 Intestinal tract, part unspecified
Intestine NOS

159.1 Spleen, not elsewhere classified
Angiosarcoma ⎤ of spleen
Fibrosarcoma ⎦

> *EXCLUDES* Hodgkin's disease (201.0-201.9)
> lymphosarcoma (200.1)
> reticulosarcoma (200.0)

159.8 Other sites of digestive system and intra-abdominal organs
Malignant neoplasm of digestive organs and peritoneum whose point of origin cannot be assigned to any one of the categories 150-158

> *EXCLUDES* anus and rectum (154.8)
> cardio-esophageal junction (151.0)
> colon and rectum (154.0)

159.9 Ill-defined
Alimentary canal or tract NOS
Gastrointestinal tract NOS

> *EXCLUDES* abdominal NOS (195.2)
> intra-abdominal NOS (195.2)

Neoplasm of Respiratory and Intrathoracic Organs (160-165)

> *EXCLUDES* carcinoma in situ (231.0-231.9)

☑4ᵗʰ 160 Malignant neoplasm of nasal cavities, middle ear, and accessory sinuses

160.0 Nasal cavities
Cartilage of nose   Septum of nose
Conchae, nasal   Vestibule of nose
Internal nose

> *EXCLUDES* malignant melanoma of skin of nose (172.3)
> malignant neoplasm of skin of nose (173.30-173.39)
> nasal bone (170.0)
> nose NOS (195.0)
> olfactory bulb (192.0)
> posterior margin of septum and choanae (147.3)
> turbinates (170.0)

160.1 Auditory tube, middle ear, and mastoid air cells
Antrum tympanicum
Eustachian tube
Tympanic cavity

> *EXCLUDES* bone of ear (meatus) (170.0)
> cartilage of ear (171.0)
> malignant melanoma of:
>   auditory canal (external) (172.2)
>   ear (external) (skin) (172.2)
> malignant neoplasm of:
>   auditory canal (external) (173.20-173.29)
>   ear (external) (skin) (173.20-173.29)

160.2 Maxillary sinus
Antrum (Highmore) (maxillary)

160.3 Ethmoidal sinus

160.4 Frontal sinus

160.5 Sphenoidal sinus

160.8 Other
Malignant neoplasm of contiguous or overlapping sites of nasal cavities, middle ear, and accessory sinuses whose point of origin cannot be determined

160.9 Accessory sinus, unspecified

☑4ᵗʰ 161 Malignant neoplasm of larynx

161.0 Glottis
Intrinsic larynx
Laryngeal commissure (anterior) (posterior)
True vocal cord
Vocal cord NOS

161.1 Supraglottis
Aryepiglottic fold or interarytenoid fold, laryngeal aspect
Epiglottis (suprahyoid portion) NOS
Extrinsic larynx
False vocal cords
Posterior (laryngeal) surface of epiglottis
Ventricular bands

> *EXCLUDES* anterior aspect of epiglottis (146.4)
> aryepiglottic fold or interarytenoid fold:
>   NOS (148.2)
>   hypopharyngeal aspect (148.2)
>   marginal zone (148.2)

161.2 Subglottis

161.3 Laryngeal cartilages
Cartilage:
   arytenoid
   cricoid
   cuneiform
   thyroid

161.8 Other specified sites of larynx
Malignant neoplasm of contiguous or overlapping sites of larynx whose point of origin cannot be determined
AHA: 3Q, '07, 7

161.9 Larynx, unspecified

☑4ᵗʰ 162 Malignant neoplasm of trachea, bronchus, and lung

> *EXCLUDES* benign carcinoid tumor of bronchus (209.61)
> malignant carcinoid tumor of bronchus (209.21)

162.0 Trachea   `CC`
Cartilage ⎤ of trachea
Mucosa ⎦
CC Excl: 162.0-162.9, 165.8-165.9, 176.4, 195.1, 195.8, 197.0-197.1, 197.3, 199.0-199.2, 209.20-209.21, 209.29-209.30, 209.70, 209.75, 239.1, 239.81-239.9

162.2 Main bronchus   `CC`
Carina
Hilus of lung
CC Excl: 162.2, 162.8-162.9, 165.8-165.9, 176.4, 195.8, 199.0-199.2, 209.20-209.21, 209.29-209.30, 209.70, 209.75, 239.1, 239.81-239.9

162.3 Upper lobe, bronchus or lung   `CC`
CC Excl: 162.3, 162.8-162.9, 165.8-165.9, 176.4, 195.8, 199.0-199.2, 209.20-209.21, 209.29-209.30, 209.70, 209.75, 239.1, 239.81-239.9
AHA: 1Q, '04, 4
C34.10 Malig neoplasm upper lobe unspec bronchus/lung   `I-10`

162.4 Middle lobe, bronchus or lung   `CC`
CC Excl: 162.4, 162.8-162.9, 165.8-165.9, 176.4, 195.8, 199.0-199.2, 209.20-209.21, 209.29-209.30, 209.70, 209.75, 239.1, 239.81-239.9

162.5 Lower lobe, bronchus or lung   `CC`
CC Excl: 162.5-162.9, 165.8-165.9, 176.4, 195.8, 199.0-199.2, 209.20-209.21, 209.29-209.30, 209.70, 209.75, 239.1, 239.81-239.9
AHA: 3Q, '10, 3

162.8 Other parts of bronchus or lung   `CC`
Malignant neoplasm of contiguous or overlapping sites of bronchus or lung whose point of origin cannot be determined
CC Excl: 162.8-162.9, 165.8-165.9, 176.4, 195.8, 199.0-199.2, 209.20-209.21, 209.29-209.30, 209.70, 209.75, 239.1, 239.81-239.9
AHA: 3Q, '06, 7

162.9 Bronchus and lung, unspecified   `CC`
CC Excl: See code: 162.8
AHA: 2Q, '10, 14; 3Q, '06, 14-15; 2Q, '97, 3; 4Q, '96, 48
C34.90 Malig neoplasm unspec part of unspec bronchus/lung   `I-10`

`N` Newborn Age: 0   `P` Pediatric Age: 0-17   `M` Maternity Age: 12-55   `A` Adult Age: 15-124   `MCC` Major CC Condition   `CC` CC Condition   `HIV` HIV Related Dx

36 – Volume 1   **2015 ICD-9-CM**

√4ᵗʰ **163 Malignant neoplasm of pleura**

163.0 Parietal pleura `CC`
CC Excl: 163.0-163.9, 165.8-165.9, 195.8, 199.0-199.2, 209.20, 209.29-209.30, 209.70, 209.75, 239.1, 239.81-239.9

163.1 Visceral pleura `CC`
CC Excl: See code 163.0

163.8 Other specified sites of pleura `CC`
Malignant neoplasm of contiguous or overlapping sites of pleura whose point of origin cannot be determined
CC Excl: See code 163.0

163.9 Pleura, unspecified `CC`
CC Excl: See code 163.0

√4ᵗʰ **164 Malignant neoplasm of thymus, heart, and mediastinum**

164.0 Thymus `CC`
EXCLUDES benign carcinoid tumor of the thymus (209.62)
malignant carcinoid tumor of the thymus (209.22)
CC Excl: 164.0, 209.22

164.1 Heart `CC`
Endocardium
Epicardium
Myocardium
Pericardium
EXCLUDES great vessels (171.4)
CC Excl: 164.1

164.2 Anterior mediastinum `CC`
CC Excl: 164.2-164.9, 165.8-165.9, 195.8, 199.0-199.2, 209.20, 209.29-209.30, 209.70, 209.75, 239.1, 239.81-239.9

164.3 Posterior mediastinum `CC`
CC Excl: See code 164.2

164.8 Other `CC`
Malignant neoplasm of contiguous or overlapping sites of thymus, heart, and mediastinum whose point of origin cannot be determined
CC Excl: See code 164.2

164.9 Mediastinum, part unspecified `CC`
CC Excl: See code 164.2

√4ᵗʰ **165 Malignant neoplasm of other and ill-defined sites within the respiratory system and intrathoracic organs**

165.0 Upper respiratory tract, part unspecified

165.8 Other
Malignant neoplasm of respiratory and intrathoracic organs whose point of origin cannot be assigned to any one of the categories 160-164

165.9 Ill-defined sites within the respiratory system
Respiratory tract NOS
EXCLUDES intrathoracic NOS (195.1)
thoracic NOS (195.1)

Malignant Neoplasm of Bone, Connective Tissue, Skin, and Breast (170-176)

EXCLUDES carcinoma in situ:
breast (233.0)
skin (232.0-232.9)

√4ᵗʰ **170 Malignant neoplasm of bone and articular cartilage**
INCLUDES cartilage (articular) (joint)
periosteum
EXCLUDES bone marrow NOS (202.9)
cartilage:
ear (171.0)
eyelid (171.0)
larynx (161.3)
nose (160.0)
synovia (171.0-171.9)
AHA: 4Q, '06, 103
TIP: Do not assign for bone metastasis; see instead code 198.5.

Skull

Orbital rim
Frontal
Roof
Zygoma (malar)
Ethmoid
Lacrimal
Zygomatic arch
Nasal
Condylar process
Maxilla
Palate
Coronoid process
Alveolar margins
Ramus
Mandible   Body   Angle
Symphysis

170.0 Bones of skull and face, except mandible `CC`
Bone: Bone:
ethmoid   sphenoid
frontal   temporal
malar   zygomatic
nasal   Maxilla (superior)
occipital   Turbinate
orbital   Upper jaw bone
parietal   Vomer
EXCLUDES carcinoma, any type except intraosseous or odontogenic:
maxilla, maxillary (sinus) (160.2)
upper jaw bone (143.0)
jaw bone (lower) (170.1)
CC Excl: 170.0, 170.9, V58.0

170.1 Mandible `CC`
Inferior maxilla
Jaw bone NOS
Lower jaw bone
EXCLUDES carcinoma, any type except intraosseous or odontogenic:
jaw bone NOS (143.9)
lower (143.1)
upper jaw bone (170.0)
CC Excl: 170.1, 170.9, V58.0

170.2 Vertebral column, excluding sacrum and coccyx `CC`
Spinal column
Spine
Vertebra
EXCLUDES sacrum and coccyx (170.6)
CC Excl: 170.2, 170.9, V58.0

170.3 Ribs, sternum, and clavicle `CC`
Costal cartilage
Costovertebral joint
Xiphoid process
CC Excl: 170.3, 170.9, V58.0

170.4 Scapula and long bones of upper limb `CC`
Acromion
Bones NOS of upper limb
Humerus
Radius
Ulna
CC Excl: 170.4, 170.9, V58.0
AHA: 2Q, '99, 9

170.5 Short bones of upper limb `CC`
Carpal   Scaphoid (of hand)
Cuneiform, wrist   Semilunar or lunate
Metacarpal   Trapezium
Navicular, of hand Trapezoid
Phalanges of hand Unciform
Pisiform
CC Excl: 170.5, 170.9, V58.0

170.6 Pelvic bones, sacrum, and coccyx `CC`
Coccygeal vertebra
Ilium
Ischium
Pubic bone
Sacral vertebra
CC Excl: 170.6, 170.9, V58.0

170.7 Long bones of lower limb `CC`
Bones NOS of lower limb
Femur
Fibula
Tibia
CC Excl: 170.7, 170.9, V58.0

170.8 Short bones of lower limb `CC`
Astragalus [talus]   Navicular (of ankle)
Calcaneus   Patella
Cuboid   Phalanges of foot
Cuneiform, ankle   Tarsal
Metatarsal
CC Excl: 170.8-170.9, V58.0

170.9 Bone and articular cartilage, site unspecified `CC`
CC Excl: 170.0-170.9, V58.0

✓4ᵗʰ **171 Malignant neoplasm of connective and other soft tissue**
INCLUDES   blood vessel
bursa
fascia
fat
ligament, except uterine
muscle
peripheral, sympathetic, and parasympathetic nerves and ganglia
synovia
tendon (sheath)
EXCLUDES   cartilage (of):
articular (170.0-170.9)
larynx (161.3)
nose (160.0)
connective tissue:
breast (174.0-175.9)
internal organs — code to malignant neoplasm of the site [e.g., leiomyosarcoma of stomach, 151.9]
heart (164.1)
uterine ligament (183.4)

171.0 Head, face, and neck `CC`
Cartilage of:
ear
eyelid
CC Excl: V58.0
AHA: 2Q, '99, 6

171.2 Upper limb, including shoulder `CC`
Arm
Finger
Forearm
Hand
CC Excl: See code: 171.0

171.3 Lower limb, including hip `CC`
Foot
Leg
Popliteal space
Thigh
Toe
CC Excl: See code: 171.0
AHA: 3Q, '12, 7-8

171.4 Thorax `CC`
Axilla
Diaphragm
Great vessels
EXCLUDES   heart (164.1)
mediastinum (164.2-164.9)
thymus (164.0)
CC Excl: See code: 171.0

171.5 Abdomen `CC`
Abdominal wall
Hypochondrium
EXCLUDES   peritoneum (158.8)
retroperitoneum (158.0)
CC Excl: See code: 171.0

171.6 Pelvis `CC`
Buttock
Groin
Inguinal region
Perineum
EXCLUDES   pelvic peritoneum (158.8)
retroperitoneum (158.0)
uterine ligament, any (183.3-183.5)
CC Excl: See code: 171.0

171.7 Trunk, unspecified `CC`
Back NOS
Flank NOS
CC Excl: See code: 171.0

171.8 Other specified sites of connective and other soft tissue `CC`
Malignant neoplasm of contiguous or overlapping sites of connective tissue whose point of origin cannot be determined
CC Excl: See code: 171.0

171.9 Connective and other soft tissue, site unspecified `CC`
CC Excl: See code: 171.0

✓4ᵗʰ **172 Malignant melanoma of skin**
INCLUDES   melanocarcinoma
melanoma (skin) NOS
melanoma in situ of skin
EXCLUDES   skin of genital organs (184.0-184.9, 187.1-187.9)
sites other than skin — code to malignant neoplasm of the site
DEF: Malignant neoplasm of melanocytes; most common in skin, may involve oral cavity, esophagus, anal canal, vagina, leptomeninges, or conjunctiva.

172.0 Lip
EXCLUDES   vermilion border of lip (140.0-140.1, 140.9)

172.1 Eyelid, including canthus

172.2 Ear and external auditory canal
Auricle (ear)
Auricular canal, external
External [acoustic] meatus
Pinna

172.3 Other and unspecified parts of face
Cheek (external)
Chin
Eyebrow
Forehead
Nose, external
Temple

172.4 Scalp and neck

172.5 Trunk, except scrotum
Axilla   Perianal skin
Breast   Perineum
Buttock   Umbilicus
Groin
EXCLUDES   anal canal (154.2)
anus NOS (154.3)
scrotum (187.7)

172.6 Upper limb, including shoulder
Arm   Forearm
Finger   Hand

172.7 Lower limb, including hip
Ankle   Leg
Foot   Popliteal area
Heel   Thigh
Knee   Toe

172.8 Other specified sites of skin
Malignant melanoma of contiguous or overlapping sites of skin whose point of origin cannot be determined

172.9 Melanoma of skin, site unspecified

`N` Newborn Age: 0   `P` Pediatric Age: 0-17   `M` Maternity Age: 12-55   `A` Adult Age: 15-124   `MCC` Major CC Condition   `CC` CC Condition   `HIV` HIV Related Dx

38 – Volume 1   2015 ICD-9-CM

√4ᵗʰ **173　Other and unspecified malignant neoplasm of skin**

> INCLUDES　malignant neoplasm of:
> 　　　sebaceous glands
> 　　　sudoriferous, sudoriparous glands
> 　　　sweat glands
>
> EXCLUDES　Kaposi's sarcoma (176.0-176.9)
> 　　　malignant melanoma of skin (172.0-172.9)
> 　　　Merkel cell carcinoma of skin (209.31-209.36)
> 　　　skin of genital organs (184.0-184.9, 187.1-187.9)
>
> AHA: 4Q, '11, 83-87; 1Q, '00, 18; 2Q, '96, 12
> TIP: Do not assign for malignant neoplasm of skin documented as melanoma; see instead category 172.

√5ᵗʰ **173.0　Other and unspecified malignant neoplasm of skin of lip**

> EXCLUDES　vermilion border of lip (140.0-140.1, 140.9)

　173.00　Unspecified malignant neoplasm of skin of lip

　173.01　Basal cell carcinoma of skin of lip

　173.02　Squamous cell carcinoma of skin of lip

　173.09　Other specified malignant neoplasm of skin of lip

√5ᵗʰ **173.1　Other and unspecified malignant neoplasm of skin of eyelid, including canthus**

> EXCLUDES　cartilage of eyelid (171.0)

　173.10　Unspecified malignant neoplasm of eyelid, including canthus

　173.11　Basal cell carcinoma of eyelid, including canthus

　173.12　Squamous cell carcinoma of eyelid, including canthus

　173.19　Other specified malignant neoplasm of eyelid, including canthus

√5ᵗʰ **173.2　Other and unspecified malignant neoplasm of skin of ear and external auditory canal**

> Auricle (ear)
> Auricular canal, external
> External meatus
> Pinna
>
> EXCLUDES　cartilage of ear (171.0)

　173.20　Unspecified malignant neoplasm of skin of ear and external auditory canal

　173.21　Basal cell carcinoma of skin of ear and external auditory canal

　173.22　Squamous cell carcinoma of skin of ear and external auditory canal

　173.29　Other specified malignant neoplasm of skin of ear and external auditory canal

√5ᵗʰ **173.3　Other and unspecified malignant neoplasm of skin of other and unspecified parts of face**

> Cheek, external　　Forehead
> Chin　　　　　　　Nose, external
> Eyebrow　　　　　Temple
>
> AHA: 1Q, '00, 3

　173.30　Unspecified malignant neoplasm of skin of other and unspecified parts of face

　173.31　Basal cell carcinoma of skin of other and unspecified parts of face

　173.32　Squamous cell carcinoma of skin of other and unspecified parts of face

　173.39　Other specified malignant neoplasm of skin of other and unspecified parts of face

√5ᵗʰ **173.4　Other and unspecified malignant neoplasm of scalp and skin of neck**

　173.40　Unspecified malignant neoplasm of scalp and skin of neck

　173.41　Basal cell carcinoma of scalp and skin of neck

　173.42　Squamous cell carcinoma of scalp and skin of neck

　173.49　Other specified malignant neoplasm of scalp and skin of neck

√5ᵗʰ **173.5　Other and unspecified malignant neoplasm of skin of trunk, except scrotum**

> Axillary fold　　　Skin of:
> Perianal skin　　　　buttock
> Skin of:　　　　　　chest wall
> 　abdominal wall　　groin
> 　anus　　　　　　　perineum
> 　back　　　　　　　umbilicus
> 　breast
>
> EXCLUDES　anal canal (154.2)
> 　　　anus NOS (154.3)
> 　　　skin of scrotum (187.7)
>
> AHA: 1Q, '01, 8

　173.50　Unspecified malignant neoplasm of skin of trunk, except scrotum

　173.51　Basal cell carcinoma of skin of trunk, except scrotum

　173.52　Squamous cell carcinoma of skin of trunk, except scrotum

　173.59　Other specified malignant neoplasm of skin of trunk, except scrotum

√5ᵗʰ **173.6　Other and unspecified malignant neoplasm of skin of upper limb, including shoulder**

> Arm　　　　　Forearm
> Finger　　　　Hand

　173.60　Unspecified malignant neoplasm of skin of upper limb, including shoulder

　173.61　Basal cell carcinoma of skin of upper limb, including shoulder

　173.62　Squamous cell carcinoma of skin of upper limb, including shoulder

　173.69　Other specified malignant neoplasm of skin of upper limb, including shoulder

√5ᵗʰ **173.7　Other and unspecified malignant neoplasm of skin of lower limb, including hip**

> Ankle　　　　Leg
> Foot　　　　　Popliteal area
> Heel　　　　　Thigh
> Knee　　　　　Toe

　173.70　Unspecified malignant neoplasm of skin of lower limb, including hip

　173.71　Basal cell carcinoma of skin of lower limb, including hip

　173.72　Squamous cell carcinoma of skin of lower limb, including hip

　173.79　Other specified malignant neoplasm of skin of lower limb, including hip

√5ᵗʰ **173.8　Other and unspecified malignant neoplasm of other specified sites of skin**

> Malignant neoplasm of contiguous or overlapping sites of skin whose point of origin cannot be determined

　173.80　Unspecified malignant neoplasm of other specified sites of skin

　173.81　Basal cell carcinoma of other specified sites of skin

　173.82　Squamous cell carcinoma of other specified sites of skin

　173.89　Other specified malignant neoplasm of other specified sites of skin

√5ᵗʰ **173.9　Other and unspecified malignant neoplasm of skin, site unspecified**

　173.90　Unspecified malignant neoplasm of skin, site unspecified
　　　Malignant neoplasm of skin NOS

　173.91　Basal cell carcinoma of skin, site unspecified

　173.92　Squamous cell carcinoma of skin, site unspecified

　173.99　Other specified malignant neoplasm of skin, site unspecified

√4ᵗʰ / √5ᵗʰ Additional Digit Required　　Unacceptable PDx　　Manifestation Code　　Hospital Acquired Condition　　►◄ Revised Text　　● New Code　　▲ Revised Code Title

2015 ICD-9-CM　　　　　　　　　　　　　　　　　　　　　　　　　　　　　　**Volume 1 – 39**

Female Breast

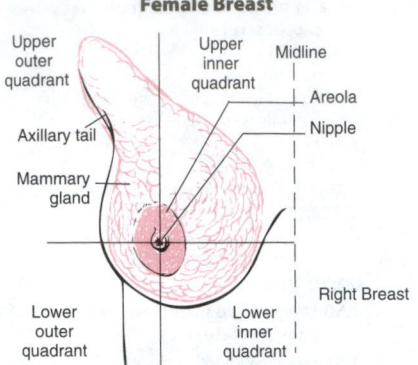

Upper outer quadrant — Upper inner quadrant — Midline — Areola — Nipple — Axillary tail — Mammary gland — Lower outer quadrant — Lower inner quadrant — Right Breast

√4ᵗʰ **174 Malignant neoplasm of female breast**

INCLUDES breast (female)
     connective tissue
     soft parts
     Paget's disease of:
       breast
       nipple

Use additional code to identify estrogen receptor status (V86.0, V86.1)

EXCLUDES *malignant melanoma of skin of breast (172.5)*
     malignant neoplasm of skin of breast (173.50-173.59)

AHA: 3Q, '97, 8; 4Q, '89, 11

TIP: For bilateral breast malignancy, do not assign two codes unless documentation indicates separate sites (i.e., different fourth digits).

174.0 Nipple and areola ♀

174.1 Central portion ♀

174.2 Upper-inner quadrant ♀

174.3 Lower-inner quadrant ♀

174.4 Upper-outer quadrant ♀
    AHA: 4Q, '08, 155; 1Q, '04, 3; '3Q, '97, 8

174.5 Lower-outer quadrant ♀

174.6 Axillary tail ♀

174.8 Other specified sites of female breast ♀
    Ectopic sites
    Inner breast
    Lower breast
    Midline of breast
    Outer breast
    Upper breast
    Malignant neoplasm of contiguous or overlapping sites of breast whose point of origin cannot be determined

174.9 Breast (female), unspecified ♀
    AHA: 3Q, '09, 3; 3Q, '05, 11; 2Q, '94, 10; 4Q, '89, 11
    C50.911 Malig neoplasm of uns site of rt female breast   I-10

√4ᵗʰ **175 Malignant neoplasm of male breast**
Use additional code to identify estrogen receptor status (V86.0, V86.1)

EXCLUDES *malignant melanoma of skin of breast (172.5)*
     malignant neoplasm of skin of breast (173.50-173.59)

175.0 Nipple and areola ♂

175.9 Other and unspecified sites of male breast ♂
    Ectopic breast tissue, male

√4ᵗʰ **176 Kaposi's sarcoma**
    AHA: 4Q, '91, 24

176.0 Skin   CC HIV
    CC Excl: 176.0, 176.8-176.9, V58.0
    AHA: 4Q, '07, 63; 4Q, '94, 29; 4Q, '91, 24

176.1 Soft tissue   CC HIV
    Blood vessel
    Connective tissue
    Fascia
    Ligament
    Lymphatic(s) NEC
    Muscle
    EXCLUDES *lymph glands and nodes (176.5)*
    CC Excl: 176.1, 176.8-176.9, V58.0

176.2 Palate   CC HIV
    CC Excl: 176.2, 176.8-176.9, V58.0

176.3 Gastrointestinal sites   CC HIV
    CC Excl: 176.3, 176.8-176.9, V58.0

176.4 Lung   CC HIV
    CC Excl: 162.8-162.9, 165.8-165.9, 176.4, 195.8, 199.0-199.2, 209.20-209.21, 209.29-209.30, 209.70, 239.1, 239.81-239.9

176.5 Lymph nodes   CC HIV
    CC Excl: 176.5, 195.8-196.9, 199.0-199.2, 209.20, 209.29-209.30, 209.70-209.71, 209.75, 239.81-239.9

176.8 Other specified sites   CC HIV
    Oral cavity NEC
    CC Excl: 176.0-176.9, V58.0

176.9 Unspecified   CC HIV
    Viscera NOS
    CC Excl: 176.0-192.9, 195.0-199.2, 209.20, 209.24, 209.29-209.30, 209.70-209.79, 230.0-237.6, 237.9-238.3, 238.8-239.9, V58.0

Malignant Neoplasm of Genitourinary Organs (179-189)

EXCLUDES *carcinoma in situ (233.1-233.9)*

179 Malignant neoplasm of uterus, part unspecified ♀

√4ᵗʰ **180 Malignant neoplasm of cervix uteri**
    INCLUDES invasive malignancy [carcinoma]
    EXCLUDES *carcinoma in situ (233.1)*

180.0 Endocervix ♀
    Cervical canal NOS
    Endocervical canal
    Endocervical gland

180.1 Exocervix ♀

180.8 Other specified sites of cervix ♀
    Cervical stump
    Squamocolumnar junction of cervix
    Malignant neoplasm of contiguous or overlapping sites of cervix uteri whose point of origin cannot be determined

180.9 Cervix uteri, unspecified ♀

181 Malignant neoplasm of placenta ♀
    Choriocarcinoma NOS
    Chorioepithelioma NOS
    EXCLUDES *chorioadenoma (destruens) (236.1)*
     hydatidiform mole (630)
      malignant (236.1)
     invasive mole (236.1)
     male choriocarcinoma NOS (186.0-186.9)

√4ᵗʰ **182 Malignant neoplasm of body of uterus**
    EXCLUDES *carcinoma in situ (233.2)*

182.0 Corpus uteri, except isthmus ♀
    Cornu
    Endometrium
    Fundus
    Myometrium
    AHA: 3Q, '09, 5
    C54.9 Malignant neoplasm of corpus uteri unspecified   I-10

182.1 Isthmus ♀
    Lower uterine segment

182.8 Other specified sites of body of uterus ♀
    Malignant neoplasm of contiguous or overlapping sites of body of uterus whose point of origin cannot be determined
    EXCLUDES *uterus NOS (179)*

N Newborn Age: 0   P Pediatric Age: 0-17   M Maternity Age: 12-55   A Adult Age: 15-124   MCC Major CC Condition   CC CC Condition   HIV HIV Related Dx

40 – Volume 1   2015 ICD-9-CM

√4ᵗʰ **183 Malignant neoplasm of ovary and other uterine adnexa**

     EXCLUDES *Douglas' cul-de-sac (158.8)*

183.0 Ovary   CC ♀

     Use additional code to identify any functional activity

     CC Excl: 183.0-183.9, 195.3, 198.6, 199.0-199.2, 209.20, 209.29-209.30, 209.70, 209.75

     AHA: 4Q, '07, 96

     C56.9 Malignant neoplasm of unspec ovary   I-10

183.2 Fallopian tube   ♀
     Oviduct
     Uterine tube

183.3 Broad ligament   ♀
     Mesovarium
     Parovarian region

183.4 Parametrium   ♀
     Uterine ligament NOS
     Uterosacral ligament

183.5 Round ligament   ♀
     AHA: 3Q, '99, 5

183.8 Other specified sites of uterine adnexa   ♀
     Tubo-ovarian
     Utero-ovarian
     Malignant neoplasm of contiguous or overlapping sites of ovary and other uterine adnexa whose point of origin cannot be determined

183.9 Uterine adnexa, unspecified   ♀

√4ᵗʰ **184 Malignant neoplasm of other and unspecified female genital organs**

     EXCLUDES *carcinoma in situ (233.30-233.39)*

184.0 Vagina   ♀
     Gartner's duct
     Vaginal vault

184.1 Labia majora   ♀
     Greater vestibular [Bartholin's] gland

184.2 Labia minora   ♀

184.3 Clitoris   ♀

184.4 Vulva, unspecified   ♀
     External female genitalia NOS
     Pudendum

184.8 Other specified sites of female genital organs   ♀
     Malignant neoplasm of contiguous or overlapping sites of female genital organs whose point of origin cannot be determined

184.9 Female genital organ, site unspecified   ♀
     Female genitourinary tract NOS

185 Malignant neoplasm of prostate   ♂

     EXCLUDES *seminal vesicles (187.8)*

     AHA: 2Q, '10, 3; 3Q, '03, 13; 3Q, '99, 5; 3Q, '92, 7

     TIP: Assign as a secondary diagnosis if patient treated for BPH and incidental finding of carcinoma of the prostate is made.

     C61 Malignant neoplasm of prostate   I-10

√4ᵗʰ **186 Malignant neoplasm of testis**

     Use additional code to identify any functional activity

186.0 Undescended testis   ♂
     Ectopic testis
     Retained testis

186.9 Other and unspecified testis   ♂
     Testis:
       NOS
       descended
       scrotal

√4ᵗʰ **187 Malignant neoplasm of penis and other male genital organs**

187.1 Prepuce   ♂
     Foreskin

187.2 Glans penis   ♂

187.3 Body of penis   ♂
     Corpus cavernosum

187.4 Penis, part unspecified   ♂
     Skin of penis NOS

187.5 Epididymis   ♂

187.6 Spermatic cord   ♂
     Vas deferens

187.7 Scrotum   ♂
     Skin of scrotum

187.8 Other specified sites of male genital organs   ♂
     Seminal vesicle
     Tunica vaginalis
     Malignant neoplasm of contiguous or overlapping sites of penis and other male genital organs whose point of origin cannot be determined

187.9 Male genital organ, site unspecified   ♂
     Male genital organ or tract NOS

√4ᵗʰ **188 Malignant neoplasm of bladder**

     EXCLUDES *carcinoma in situ (233.7)*

188.0 Trigone of urinary bladder

188.1 Dome of urinary bladder

188.2 Lateral wall of urinary bladder

188.3 Anterior wall of urinary bladder

188.4 Posterior wall of urinary bladder

188.5 Bladder neck
     Internal urethral orifice

188.6 Ureteric orifice

188.7 Urachus

188.8 Other specified sites of bladder
     Malignant neoplasm of contiguous or overlapping sites of bladder whose point of origin cannot be determined

188.9 Bladder, part unspecified
     Bladder wall NOS
     AHA: 1Q, '00, 5
     C67.9 Malignant neoplasm of bladder unspecified   I-10

√4ᵗʰ **189 Malignant neoplasm of kidney and other and unspecified urinary organs**

     EXCLUDES *benign carcinoid tumor of kidney (209.64)*
               malignant carcinoid tumor of kidney (209.24)

189.0 Kidney, except pelvis   CC
     Kidney NOS
     Kidney parenchyma
     CC Excl: 189.0-189.1, 189.8-189.9, 195.8, 199.0-199.2, 209.20, 209.24, 209.29-209.30, 209.70, 209.75, 239.5, 239.81-239.9
     AHA: 2Q, '05, 4; 2Q, '04, 4
     C64.9 Malig neoplasm unspec kidney no renal pelvis   I-10

189.1 Renal pelvis   CC
     Renal calyces   Ureteropelvic junction
     CC Excl: See code: 189.0

189.2 Ureter   CC
     EXCLUDES *ureteric orifice of bladder (188.6)*
     CC Excl: 189.2, 189.8-189.9, 195.8, 199.0-199.2, 209.20, 209.29-209.30, 209.70, 209.75, 239.5, 239.81-239.9

189.3 Urethra   CC
     EXCLUDES *urethral orifice of bladder (188.5)*
     CC Excl: 189.3-189.9, 198.82

189.4 Paraurethral glands   CC
     CC Excl: See code: 189.3

189.8 Other specified sites of urinary organs   CC
     Malignant neoplasm of contiguous or overlapping sites of kidney and other urinary organs whose point of origin cannot be determined
     CC Excl: 189.0-189.9, 195.3, 198.0-198.1, 209.24

189.9 Urinary organ, site unspecified   CC
     Urinary system NOS
     CC Excl: See code: 189.8

√4ᵗʰ ✓5ᵗʰ Additional Digit Required   Unacceptable PDx   Manifestation Code   Hospital Acquired Condition   ►◄ Revised Text   ● New Code   ▲ Revised Code Title

Neoplasms

190–194.1

Malignant Neoplasm of Other and Unspecified Sites (190-199)

EXCLUDES *carcinoma in situ (234.0-234.9)*

✓4ᵗʰ **190 Malignant neoplasm of eye**

EXCLUDES *carcinoma in situ (234.0)*
dark area on retina and choroid (239.81)
  cartilage (171.0)
malignant melanoma of eyelid (skin) (172.1)
malignant neoplasm of eyelid (skin) (173.10-173.19)
optic nerve (192.0)
orbital bone (170.0)
retinal freckle (239.81)

190.0 Eyeball, except conjunctiva, cornea, retina, and choroid
Ciliary body   Sclera
Crystalline lens   Uveal tract
Iris

190.1 Orbit
Connective tissue of orbit
Extraocular muscle
Retrobulbar
EXCLUDES *bone of orbit (170.0)*

190.2 Lacrimal gland

190.3 Conjunctiva

190.4 Cornea

190.5 Retina

190.6 Choroid

190.7 Lacrimal duct
Lacrimal sac
Nasolacrimal duct

190.8 Other specified sites of eye
Malignant neoplasm of contiguous or overlapping sites of eye whose point of origin cannot be determined

190.9 Eye, part unspecified

✓4ᵗʰ **191 Malignant neoplasm of brain**

EXCLUDES *cranial nerves (192.0)*
retrobulbar area (190.1)
AHA: 4Q, '07, 104

191.0 Cerebrum, except lobes and ventricles `CC`
Basal ganglia   Globus pallidus
Cerebral cortex   Hypothalamus
Corpus striatum   Thalamus
CC Excl: 191.0-191.1, 192.8-192.9, 195.8, 199.0-199.2, 209.20, 209.29-209.30, 209.70, 209.75, 239.6-239.9

191.1 Frontal lobe `CC`
CC Excl: See code 191.0
AHA: 4Q, '05, 118

191.2 Temporal lobe `CC`
Hippocampus   Uncus
CC Excl: See code 191.0
AHA: 3Q, '09, 8; 4Q, '06, 123

191.3 Parietal lobe `CC`
CC Excl: See code 191.0

191.4 Occipital lobe `CC`
CC Excl: See code 191.0

Brain and Meninges

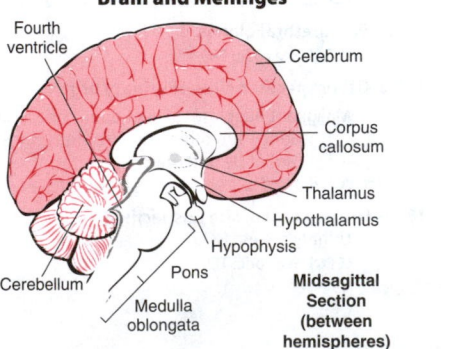

Fourth ventricle
Cerebrum
Corpus callosum
Thalamus
Hypothalamus
Hypophysis
Pons
Cerebellum
Medulla oblongata
Midsagittal Section (between hemispheres)

191.5 Ventricles `CC`
Choroid plexus
Floor of ventricle
CC Excl: See code 191.0

191.6 Cerebellum NOS `CC`
Cerebellopontine angle
CC Excl: See code 191.0

191.7 Brain stem `CC`
Cerebral peduncle
Medulla oblongata
Midbrain
Pons
CC Excl: See code 191.0

191.8 Other parts of brain `CC`
Corpus callosum
Tapetum
Malignant neoplasm of contiguous or overlapping sites of brain whose point of origin cannot be determined
CC Excl: See code 191.0

191.9 Brain, unspecified `CC`
Cranial fossa NOS
CC Excl: See code 191.0
AHA: 4Q, '09, 143

✓4ᵗʰ **192 Malignant neoplasm of other and unspecified parts of nervous system**

EXCLUDES *peripheral, sympathetic, and parasympathetic nerves and ganglia (171.0-171.9)*

192.0 Cranial nerves `CC`
Olfactory bulb
CC Excl: 192.0, 192.8-192.9, 195.8, 199.0-199.2, 209.20, 209.29-209.30, 209.70, 209.75, 239.6-239.9

192.1 Cerebral meninges `CC`
Dura (mater)   Meninges NOS
Falx (cerebelli) (cerebri)   Tentorium
CC Excl: 192.1, 192.8-192.9, 195.8, 199.0-199.2, 209.20, 209.29-209.30, 209.70, 209.75, 239.6-239.9

192.2 Spinal cord `CC`
Cauda equina
CC Excl: 192.2, 192.8-192.9, 195.8, 199.0-199.2, 209.20, 209.29-209.30, 209.70, 209.75, 239.6-239.9

192.3 Spinal meninges `CC`
CC Excl: 192.3-192.9, 195.8, 199.0-199.2, 209.20, 209.29-209.30, 209.70, 209.75, 239.6-239.9

192.8 Other specified sites of nervous system `CC`
Malignant neoplasm of contiguous or overlapping sites of other parts of nervous system whose point of origin cannot be determined
CC Excl: 191.0-192.9, 195.8, 199.0-199.2, 209.20, 209.29-209.30, 209.70, 209.75, 239.6-239.9

192.9 Nervous system, part unspecified `CC`
Nervous system (central) NOS
EXCLUDES *meninges NOS (192.1)*
CC Excl: 191.0-192.9, 195.8, 198.3-198.4, 199.0-199.2, 209.20, 209.29-209.30, 209.70, 209.75, 239.6-239.9

193 Malignant neoplasm of thyroid gland
Thyroglossal duct
Use additional code to identify any functional activity
C73 Malignant neoplasm of thyroid gland `I-10`

✓4ᵗʰ **194 Malignant neoplasm of other endocrine glands and related structures**

EXCLUDES *islets of Langerhans (157.4)*
neuroendocrine tumors (209.00-209.69)
ovary (183.0)
testis (186.0-186.9)
thymus (164.0)

194.0 Adrenal gland `CC`
Adrenal cortex   Suprarenal gland
Adrenal medulla
CC Excl: 194.0, 194.9, 195.2, 195.8, 198.7, 199.0-199.2, 209.20, 209.29-209.30, 209.70, 209.75

194.1 Parathyroid gland `CC`
CC Excl: 194.1, 194.8-194.9

N Newborn Age: 0   P Pediatric Age: 0-17   M Maternity Age: 12-55   A Adult Age: 15-124   MCC Major CC Condition   CC CC Condition   HIV HIV Related Dx

42 – Volume 1   2015 ICD-9-CM

Neoplasms

194.3 Pituitary gland and craniopharyngeal duct `CC`
Craniobuccal pouch   Rathke's pouch
Hypophysis   Sella turcica
CC Excl: 194.3, V58.0
AHA: J-A, '85, 9

194.4 Pineal gland `CC`
CC Excl: 194.4, V58.0

194.5 Carotid body `CC`
CC Excl: 194.5, 194.8-194.9

194.6 Aortic body and other paraganglia `CC`
Coccygeal body   Para-aortic body
Glomus jugulare
CC Excl: 194.5-194.9

194.8 Other `CC`
Pluriglandular involvement NOS
> **NOTE** If the sites of multiple involvements are known, they should be coded separately.

CC Excl: 194.0-194.9

194.9 Endocrine gland, site unspecified `CC`
CC Excl: See code: 194.8

✓4ᵗʰ 195 Malignant neoplasm of other and ill-defined sites
> **INCLUDES** malignant neoplasms of contiguous sites, not elsewhere classified, whose point of origin cannot be determined

> **EXCLUDES** malignant neoplasm:
> lymphatic and hematopoietic tissue (200.0-208.9)
> secondary sites (196.0-198.8)
> unspecified site (199.0-199.1)

195.0 Head, face, and neck
Cheek NOS   Nose NOS
Jaw NOS   Supraclavicular region NOS
AHA: 4Q, '03, 107

195.1 Thorax
Axilla   Intrathoracic NOS
Chest (wall) NOS

195.2 Abdomen
Intra-abdominal NOS
AHA: 2Q, '97, 3

195.3 Pelvis
Groin
Inguinal region NOS
Presacral region
Sacrococcygeal region
Sites overlapping systems within pelvis, as:
   rectovaginal (septum)
   rectovesical (septum)

195.4 Upper limb

195.5 Lower limb

195.8 Other specified sites
Back NOS   Trunk NOS
Flank NOS

Lymph Nodes

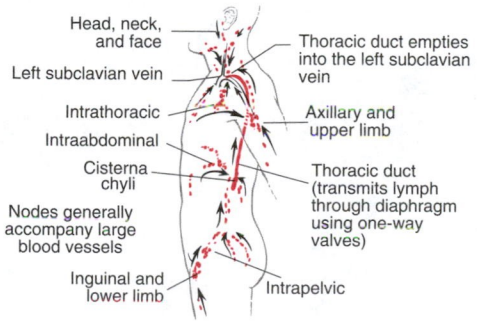

Head, neck, and face
Left subclavian vein
Intrathoracic
Intraabdominal
Cisterna chyli
Nodes generally accompany large blood vessels
Inguinal and lower limb

Thoracic duct empties into the left subclavian vein
Axillary and upper limb
Thoracic duct (transmits lymph through diaphragm using one-way valves)
Intrapelvic

✓4ᵗʰ 196 Secondary and unspecified malignant neoplasm of lymph nodes
> **EXCLUDES** any malignant neoplasm of lymph nodes, specified as primary (200.0-202.9)
> Hodgkin's disease (201.0-201.9)
> lymphosarcoma (200.1)
> other forms of lymphoma (202.0-202.9)
> reticulosarcoma (200.0)
> secondary neuroendocrine tumor of (distant) lymph nodes (209.71)

196.0 Lymph nodes of head, face, and neck `CC`
Cervical   Scalene
Cervicofacial   Supraclavicular
CC Excl: 176.5, 195.8-196.9, 199.0-199.2, 209.20, 209.29-209.30, 209.70-209.71, 239.81-239.9
AHA: 3Q, '07, 7
C77.0 Sec & uns malig neo lymph nodes head face & neck `I-10`

196.1 Intrathoracic lymph nodes `CC`
Bronchopulmonary   Mediastinal
Intercostal   Tracheobronchial
CC Excl: See code 196.0
AHA: 3Q, '06, 7

196.2 Intra-abdominal lymph nodes `CC`
Intestinal   Retroperitoneal
Mesenteric
CC Excl: See code 196.0
AHA: 4Q, '03, 111
C77.2 Sec & uns malig neoplasm intra-abd lymph nodes `I-10`

196.3 Lymph nodes of axilla and upper limb `CC`
Brachial   Infraclavicular
Epitrochlear   Pectoral
CC Excl: See code 196.0

196.5 Lymph nodes of inguinal region and lower limb `CC`
Femoral   Popliteal
Groin   Tibial
CC Excl: See code 196.0

196.6 Intrapelvic lymph nodes `CC`
Hypogastric   Obturator
Iliac   Parametrial
CC Excl: See code 196.0
AHA: 2Q, '12, 9

196.8 Lymph nodes of multiple sites `CC`
CC Excl: See code 196.0

196.9 Site unspecified `CC`
Lymph nodes NOS
CC Excl: See code 196.0

✓4ᵗʰ 197 Secondary malignant neoplasm of respiratory and digestive systems
> **EXCLUDES** lymph node metastasis (196.0-196.9)
> secondary neuroendocrine tumor of liver (209.72)
> secondary neuroendocrine tumor of respiratory organs (209.79)

AHA: M-J, '85, 3

197.0 Lung `CC`
Bronchus
CC Excl: 195.8, 197.0, 197.3, 198.89-199.2, 209.20, 209.29-209.30, 209.70, 209.75-209.79, 239.81-239.9
AHA: 3Q, '10, 3; 1Q, '06, 4; 2Q, '99, 9
C78.00 Secondary malignant neoplasm of unspec lung `I-10`

197.1 Mediastinum `CC`
CC Excl: 195.8, 197.1, 197.3, 198.89-199.2, 209.20, 209.29-209.30, 209.70, 209.75-209.79, 239.81-239.9
AHA: 3Q, '06, 7

197.2 Pleura `CC`
CC Excl: 195.8, 197.2-197.3, 198.89-199.2, 209.20, 209.29-209.30, 209.70, 209.75-209.79, 239.81-239.9, 511.81
AHA: 1Q, '08, 16; 3Q, '07, 3; 4Q, '03, 110; 4Q, '89, 11
TIP: Do not assign for malignant pleural effusion; see instead code 511.81.
C78.2 Secondary malignant neoplasm of pleura `I-10`

197.3 Other respiratory organs `CC`
Trachea
CC Excl: 195.8, 197.0-197.3, 198.89-199.2, 209.20, 209.29-209.30, 209.70, 209.75-209.79, 239.81-239.9

194.3–197.3

Neoplasms

197.4–199.2

197.4 Small intestine, including duodenum `CC`
CC Excl: 195.8, 197.4, 197.8, 198.89-199.2, 209.20, 209.29-209.30, 209.70, 209.75-209.79, 239.81-239.9

197.5 Large intestine and rectum `CC`
CC Excl: 195.8, 197.5, 197.8, 198.89-199.2, 209.20, 209.29-209.30, 209.70, 209.75-209.79, 239.81-239.9

197.6 Retroperitoneum and peritoneum `CC`
CC Excl: 195.8, 197.6, 197.8, 198.89-199.2, 209.20, 209.29-209.30, 209.70, 209.74-209.79, 239.81-239.9
AHA: 3Q, '10, 3; 2Q, '04, 4; 4Q, '89, 11
C78.6 Sec malignant neoplasm of retroperiton & periton `I-10`

197.7 Liver, specified as secondary `CC`
CC Excl: 195.8, 197.7-197.8, 198.89-199.2, 209.20, 209.29-209.30, 209.70, 209.72, 209.75-209.79, 239.81-239.9
AHA: 3Q, '10, 3; 1Q, '06, 4; 2Q, '05, 9
C78.7 Secondary malignant neoplasm of liver `I-10`

197.8 Other digestive organs and spleen `CC`
CC Excl: 195.8, 197.4-197.8, 198.89-199.2, 209.20, 209.29-209.30, 209.70, 209.72, 209.74-209.79, 239.81-239.9
AHA: 2Q, '97, 3; 2Q, '92, 3

✓4ᵗʰ 198 Secondary malignant neoplasm of other specified sites
EXCLUDES lymph node metastasis (196.0-196.9)
secondary neuroendocrine tumor of other specified sites (209.79)
AHA: M-J, '85, 3

198.0 Kidney `CC`
CC Excl: 195.8, 198.0-198.1, 198.89-199.2, 209.20, 209.29-209.30, 209.70, 209.75-209.79, 239.81-239.9

198.1 Other urinary organs `CC`
CC Excl: See code: 198.0

198.2 Skin `CC`
Skin of breast
CC Excl: 195.8, 198.2, 198.89-199.2, 209.20, 209.29-209.30, 209.70, 209.75-209.79, 239.81-239.9

198.3 Brain and spinal cord `CC`
CC Excl: 195.8, 198.3, 198.89-199.2, 209.20, 209.29-209.30, 209.70, 209.75-209.79, 239.81-239.9
AHA: 3Q, '07, 4; 3Q, '99, 7
C79.31 Secondary malignant neoplasm of brain `I-10`

198.4 Other parts of nervous system `CC`
Meninges (cerebral) (spinal)
CC Excl: 195.8, 198.4, 198.89-199.2, 209.20, 209.29-209.30, 209.70, 209.75-209.79, 239.81-239.9
AHA: J-F, '87, 7

198.5 Bone and bone marrow `CC`
CC Excl: 195.8, 198.5, 198.89-199.2, 209.20, 209.29-209.30, 209.70, 209.73, 209.75-209.79, 239.81-239.9
AHA: 1Q, '07, 6; 4Q, '03, 110; 3Q, '99, 5; 2Q, '92, 3; 1Q, '91, 16; 4Q, '89, 10
C79.51 Secondary malignant neoplasm of bone `I-10`

198.6 Ovary `CC` ♀
CC Excl: 195.8, 198.6, 198.89-199.2, 209.20, 209.29-209.30, 209.70, 209.75-209.79, 239.81-239.9

198.7 Adrenal gland `CC`
Suprarenal gland
CC Excl: 195.8, 198.7, 198.89-199.2, 209.20, 209.29-209.30, 209.70, 209.75-209.79, 239.81-239.9
C79.70 Sec malignant neoplasm of unspec adrenal gland `I-10`

✓5ᵗʰ 198.8 Other specified sites
198.81 Breast `CC`
EXCLUDES skin of breast (198.2)
CC Excl: 195.8, 198.81, 198.89-199.2, 209.20, 209.29-209.30, 209.70, 209.75-209.79, 239.81-239.9

198.82 Genital organs `CC`
CC Excl: 195.8, 198.82-199.2, 209.20, 209.29-209.30, 209.70, 209.75-209.79, 239.81-239.9

198.89 Other `CC`
EXCLUDES retroperitoneal lymph nodes (196.2)
CC Excl: 195.8, 198.89-199.2, 209.20, 209.29-209.30, 209.70, 209.75-209.79, 239.81-239.9
AHA: 2Q, '05, 4; 2Q, '97, 4
TIP: Assign for intra-abdominal metastasis when no further specificity of site is documented.
C79.89 Secondary malignant neoplasm of other spec sites `I-10`

✓4ᵗʰ 199 Malignant neoplasm without specification of site
EXCLUDES malignant carcinoid tumor of unknown primary site (209.20)
malignant (poorly differentiated) neuroendocrine carcinoma, any site (209.30)
malignant (poorly differentiated) neuroendocrine tumor, any site (209.30)
neuroendocrine carcinoma (high grade), any site (209.30)

199.0 Disseminated `CC`
Carcinomatosis
Generalized:
  cancer   } unspecified site (primary)
  malignancy   (secondary)
Multiple cancer
CC Excl: 195.8, 198.89-199.2, 209.20, 209.29-209.30, 209.70, 209.79, 239.81-239.9
AHA: 4Q, '89, 10

199.1 Other
Cancer
Carcinoma   } unspecified site (primary)
Malignancy   (secondary)
AHA: 3Q, '06, 14-15; 1Q, '06, 4
TIP: Assign if patient is assessed for a metastatic tumor but primary site is unknown.
C80.1 Malignant neoplasm unspecified `I-10`

199.2 Malignant neoplasm associated with transplanted organ `CC`
Code first complication of transplanted organ (996.80-996.89)
Use additional code for specific malignancy
CC Excl: 195.8, 198.89-199.2, 209.20, 209.29-209.30, 209.70, 209.79, 239.81-239.9
AHA: 4Q, '08, 82-83
TIP: Assign first the appropriate code from subcategory 996.8, Complications of transplanted organ; use additional code for the specific malignancy.

N Newborn Age: 0   P Pediatric Age: 0-17   M Maternity Age: 12-55   A Adult Age: 15-124   `MCC` Major CC Condition   `CC` CC Condition   `HIV` HIV Related Dx

Malignant Neoplasm of Lymphatic and Hematopoietic Tissue (200-208)

EXCLUDES *autoimmune lymphoproliferative syndrome (279.41)*
secondary and unspecified neoplasm of lymph nodes (196.0-196.9)
secondary neoplasm of:
bone marrow (198.5)
spleen (197.8)

The following fifth-digit subclassification is for use with categories 200-202:
0 **unspecified site, extranodal and solid organ sites**
1 **lymph nodes of head, face, and neck**
2 **intrathoracic lymph nodes**
3 **intra-abdominal lymph nodes**
4 **lymph nodes of axilla and upper limb**
5 **lymph nodes of inguinal region and lower limb**
6 **intrapelvic lymph nodes**
7 **spleen**
8 **lymph nodes of multiple sites**

√4th **200 Lymphosarcoma and reticulosarcoma and other specified malignant tumors of lymphatic tissue**
AHA: 4Q, '07, 65; 2Q, '92, 3; N-D, '86, 5

§ √5th **200.0 Reticulosarcoma**   CC HIV
[0-8]   Lymphoma (malignant):   Reticulum cell sarcoma:
histiocytic (diffuse):   NOS
nodular   pleomorphic cell type
pleomorphic cell type
reticulum cell type

DEF: Malignant lymphoma of primarily histolytic cells; commonly originates in reticuloendothelium of lymph nodes.
CC Excl: For code 200.00: 200.00-200.08, 239.81-239.9; **For code 200.01:** 200.00-200.01, 200.08, 239.81-239.9; **For code 200.02:** 200.00, 200.02, 200.08, 239.81-239.9; **For code 200.03:** 200.00, 200.03, 200.08, 239.81-239.9; **For code 200.04:** 200.00, 200.04, 200.08, 239.81-239.9; **For code 200.05:** 200.00, 200.05, 200.08, 239.81-239.9; **For code 200.06:** 200.00, 200.06, 200.08, 239.81-239.9; **For code 200.07:** 200.00, 200.07-200.08, 239.81-239.9; **For code 200.08:** 200.00-200.08, 239.81-239.9
AHA: For Code 200.03: 3Q, '01, 12

§ √5th **200.1 Lymphosarcoma**   CC
[0-8]   Lymphoblastoma (diffuse)
Lymphoma (malignant):
lymphoblastic (diffuse)
lymphocytic (cell type) (diffuse)
lymphosarcoma type
prolymphocytic
Lymphosarcoma:
NOS
diffuse NOS
lymphoblastic (diffuse)
lymphocytic (diffuse)
prolymphocytic

EXCLUDES *lymphosarcoma:*
follicular or nodular (202.0)
mixed cell type (200.8)
lymphosarcoma cell leukemia (207.8)

DEF: Malignant lymphoma created from anaplastic lymphoid cells resembling lymphocytes or lymphoblasts.
CC Excl: For code 200.10: 200.10-200.18, 239.81-239.9; **For code 200.11:** 200.10-200.11, 200.18, 239.81-239.9; **For code 200.12:** 200.10, 200.12, 200.18, 239.81-239.9; **For code 200.13:** 200.10, 200.13, 200.18, 239.81-239.9; **For code 200.14:** 200.10, 200.14, 200.18, 239.81-239.9; **For code 200.15:** 200.10, 200.15, 200.18, 239.81-239.9; **For code 200.16:** 200.10, 200.16, 200.18, 239.81-239.9; **For code 200.17:** 200.10, 200.17-200.18, 239.81-239.9; **For code 200.18:** 200.10-200.18, 239.81-239.9

§ √5th **200.2 Burkitt's tumor or lymphoma**   CC HIV
[0-8]   Malignant lymphoma, Burkitt's type
DEF: Large osteolytic lesion most common in jaw or as abdominal mass; usually found in central Africa but reported elsewhere.
CC Excl: For code 200.20: 200.20-200.28, 239.81-239.9; **For code 200.21:** 200.20-200.21, 200.28, 239.81-239.9; **For code 200.22:** 200.20, 200.22, 200.28, 239.81-239.9; **For code 200.23:** 200.20, 200.23, 200.28, 239.81-239.9; **For code 200.24:** 200.20, 200.24, 200.28, 239.81-239.9; **For code 200.25:** 200.20, 200.25, 200.28, 239.81-239.9; **For code 200.26:** 200.20, 200.26, 200.28, 239.81-239.9; **For code 200.27:** 200.20, 200.27-200.28, 239.81-239.9; **For code 200.28:** 200.20-200.28, 239.81-239.9

§ √5th **200.3 Marginal zone lymphoma**   CC HIV
[0-8]   Extranodal marginal zone B-cell lymphoma
Mucosa associated lymphoid tissue [MALT]
Nodal marginal zone B-cell lymphoma
Splenic marginal zone B-cell lymphoma
CC Excl: For code 200.30: 200.30-200.78, 202.70-202.90, 239.81-239.9; **For code 200.31:** 200.30-200.31, 200.38-200.41, 200.48-200.51, 200.58-200.61, 200.68-200.71, 200.78, 202.70-202.71, 202.78-202.81, 202.88, 202.91, 239.81-239.9; **For code 200.32:** 200.30, 200.32, 200.38-200.40, 200.42, 200.48-200.50, 200.52, 200.58-200.60, 200.62, 200.68-200.70, 200.72, 200.78, 202.70, 202.72, 202.78-202.80, 202.82, 202.88, 202.92, 239.81-239.9; **For code 200.33:** 200.30, 200.33, 200.38-200.40, 200.43, 200.48-200.50, 200.53, 200.58-200.60, 200.63, 200.68-200.70, 200.73, 200.78, 202.70, 202.73, 202.78-202.80, 202.83, 202.88, 202.93, 239.81-239.9; **For code 200.34:** 200.30, 200.34, 200.38-200.40, 200.44, 200.48-200.50, 200.54, 200.58-200.60, 200.64, 200.68-200.70, 200.74, 200.78, 202.70, 202.74, 202.78-202.80, 202.84, 202.88, 202.94, 239.81-239.9; **For code 200.35:** 200.30, 200.35, 200.38-200.40, 200.45, 200.48-200.50, 200.55, 200.58-200.60, 200.65, 200.68-200.70, 200.75, 200.78, 202.70, 202.75, 202.78-202.80, 202.85, 202.88, 202.95, 239.81-239.9; **For code 200.36:** 200.30, 200.36, 200.38-200.40, 200.46, 200.48-200.50, 200.56, 200.58-200.60, 200.66, 200.68-200.70, 200.76, 200.78, 202.70, 202.76, 202.78-202.80, 202.86, 202.88, 202.96, 239.81-239.9; **For code 200.37:** 200.30, 200.37-200.40, 200.47-200.50, 200.57-200.60, 200.67-200.70, 200.77-200.78, 202.70, 202.77-202.80, 202.87-202.88, 202.97, 239.81-239.9; **For code 200.38:** 200.30-200.78, 202.70-202.88, 202.98, 239.81-239.9
AHA: 4Q, '07, 65

§ √5th **200.4 Mantle cell lymphoma**   CC HIV
[0-8]   **CC Excl:** For code 200.40: 200.30-200.78, 202.70-202.90, 239.81-239.9; **For code 200.41:** 200.30-200.31, 200.38-200.41, 200.48-200.51, 200.58-200.61, 200.68-200.71, 200.78, 202.70-202.71, 202.78-202.81, 202.88, 202.91, 239.81-239.9; **For code 200.42:** 200.30, 200.32, 200.38-200.40, 200.42, 200.48-200.50, 200.52, 200.58-200.60, 200.62, 200.68-200.70, 200.72, 200.78, 202.70, 202.72, 202.78-202.80, 202.82, 202.88, 202.92, 239.81-239.9; **For code 200.43:** 200.30, 200.33, 200.38-200.40, 200.43, 200.48-200.50, 200.53, 200.58-200.60, 200.63, 200.68-200.70, 200.73, 200.78, 202.70, 202.73, 202.78-202.80, 202.83, 202.88, 202.93, 239.81-239.9; **For code 200.44:** 200.30, 200.34, 200.38-200.40, 200.44, 200.48-200.50, 200.54, 200.58-200.60, 200.64, 200.68-200.70, 200.74, 200.78, 202.70, 202.74, 202.78-202.80, 202.84, 202.88, 202.94, 239.81-239.9; **For code 200.45:** 200.30, 200.35, 200.38-200.40, 200.45, 200.48-200.50, 200.55, 200.58-200.60, 200.65, 200.68-200.70, 200.75, 200.78, 202.70, 202.75, 202.78-202.80, 202.85, 202.88, 202.95, 239.81-239.9; **For code 200.46:** 200.30, 200.36, 200.38-200.40, 200.46, 200.48-200.50, 200.56, 200.58-200.60, 200.66, 200.68-200.70, 200.76, 200.78, 202.70, 202.76, 202.78-202.80, 202.86, 202.88, 202.96, 239.81-239.9; **For code 200.47:** 200.30, 200.37-200.40, 200.47-200.50, 200.57-200.60, 200.67-200.70, 200.77-200.78, 202.70, 202.77-202.80, 202.87-202.88, 202.97, 239.81-239.9; **For code 200.48:** 200.30-200.78, 202.70-202.88, 202.98, 239.81-239.9
AHA: 4Q, '07, 65

§ √5th **200.5 Primary central nervous system lymphoma**   CC HIV
[0-8]   **CC Excl:** For code 200.50: 200.30-200.78, 202.70-202.90, 239.81-239.9; **For code 200.51:** 200.30-200.31, 200.38-200.41, 200.48-200.51, 200.58-200.61, 200.68-200.71, 200.78, 202.70-202.71, 202.78-202.81, 202.88, 202.91, 239.81-239.9; **For code 200.52:** 200.30, 200.32, 200.38-200.40, 200.42, 200.48-200.50, 200.52, 200.58-200.60, 200.62, 200.68-200.70, 200.72, 200.78, 202.70, 202.72, 202.78-202.80, 202.82, 202.88, 202.92, 239.81-239.9; **For code 200.53:** 200.30, 200.33, 200.38-200.40, 200.43, 200.48-200.50, 200.53, 200.58-200.60, 200.63, 200.68-200.70, 200.73, 200.78, 202.70, 202.73, 202.78-202.80, 202.83, 202.88, 202.93, 239.81-239.9; **For code 200.54:** 200.30, 200.34, 200.38-200.40, 200.44, 200.48-200.50, 200.54, 200.58-200.60, 200.64, 200.68-200.70, 200.74, 200.78, 202.70, 202.74, 202.78-202.80, 202.84, 202.88, 202.94, 239.81-239.9; **For code 200.55:** 200.30, 200.35, 200.38-200.40, 200.45, 200.48-200.50, 200.55, 200.58-200.60, 200.65, 200.68-200.70, 200.75, 200.78, 202.70, 202.75, 202.78-202.80, 202.85, 202.88, 202.95, 239.81-239.9; **For code 200.56:** 200.30, 200.36, 200.38-200.40, 200.46, 200.48-200.50, 200.56, 200.58-200.60, 200.66, 200.68-200.70, 200.76, 200.78, 202.70, 202.76, 202.78-202.80, 202.86, 202.88, 202.96, 239.81-239.9; **For code 200.57:** 200.30, 200.37-200.40, 200.47-200.50, 200.57-200.60, 200.67-200.70, 200.77-200.78, 202.70, 202.77-202.80, 202.87-202.88, 202.97, 239.81-239.9; **For code 200.58:** 200.30-200.78, 202.70-202.88, 202.98, 239.81-239.9
AHA: ▶1Q, '13, 4;◀ 4Q, '07, 66

§   Requires fifth digit. Valid digits are in [brackets] under each code. See beginning of section 200-208 for codes and definitions.

√4th √5th Additional Digit Required   Unacceptable PDx   Manifestation Code   Hospital Acquired Condition   ▶◀ Revised Text   ● New Code   ▲ Revised Code Title

§ ✓5th **200.6 Anaplastic large cell lymphoma** CC HIV
[0-8]   CC Excl: For code 200.60: 200.30-200.78, 202.70-202.90, 239.81-239.9;
For code 200.61: 200.30-200.31, 200.38-200.41, 200.48-200.51,
200.58-200.61, 200.68-200.71, 200.78, 202.70-202.71,
202.78-202.81, 202.88, 202.91, 239.81-239.9; For code 200.62: 200.30,
200.32, 200.38-200.40, 200.42, 200.48-200.50, 200.52,
200.58-200.60, 200.62, 200.68-200.70, 200.72, 200.78, 202.70,
202.72, 202.78-202.80, 202.82, 202.88, 202.92, 239.81-239.9; For code
200.63: 200.30, 200.33, 200.38-200.40, 200.43, 200.48-200.50, 200.53,
200.58-200.60, 200.63, 200.68-200.70, 200.73, 200.78, 202.70,
202.73, 202.78-202.80, 202.83, 202.88, 202.93, 239.81-239.9; For code
200.64: 200.30, 200.34, 200.38-200.40, 200.44, 200.48-200.50, 200.54,
200.58-200.60, 200.64, 200.68-200.70, 200.74, 200.78, 202.70,
202.74, 202.78-202.80, 202.84, 202.88, 202.94, 239.81-239.9; For code
200.65: 200.30, 200.35, 200.38-200.40, 200.45, 200.48-200.50, 200.55,
200.58-200.60, 200.65, 200.68-200.70, 200.75, 200.78, 202.70,
202.75, 202.78-202.80, 202.85, 202.88, 202.95, 239.81-239.9; For code
200.66: 200.30, 200.36, 200.38-200.40, 200.46, 200.48-200.50, 200.56,
200.58-200.60, 200.66, 200.68-200.70, 200.76, 200.78, 202.70,
202.76, 202.78-202.80, 202.86, 202.88, 202.96, 239.81-239.9; For code
200.67: 200.30, 200.37-200.40, 200.47-200.50, 200.57-200.60,
200.67-200.70, 200.77-200.78, 202.70, 202.77-202.80,
202.87-202.88, 202.97, 239.81-239.9; For code 200.68: 200.30-200.78,
202.70-202.88, 202.98, 239.81-239.9
AHA: 4Q, '07, 66

§ ✓5th **200.7 Large cell lymphoma** CC HIV
[0-8]   CC Excl: For code 200.70: 200.30-200.78, 202.70-202.90, 239.81-239.9;
For code 200.71: 200.30-200.31, 200.38-200.41, 200.48-200.51,
200.58-200.61, 200.68-200.71, 200.78, 202.70-202.71,
202.78-202.81, 202.88, 202.91, 239.81-239.9; For code 200.72: 200.30,
200.32, 200.38-200.40, 200.42, 200.48-200.50, 200.52,
200.58-200.60, 200.62, 200.68-200.70, 200.72, 200.78, 202.70,
202.72, 202.78-202.80, 202.82, 202.88, 202.92, 239.81-239.9; For code
200.73: 200.30, 200.33, 200.38-200.40, 200.43, 200.48-200.50, 200.53,
200.58-200.60, 200.63, 200.68-200.70, 200.73, 200.78, 202.70,
202.73, 202.78-202.80, 202.83, 202.88, 202.93, 239.81-239.9; For code
200.74: 200.30, 200.34, 200.38-200.40, 200.44, 200.48-200.50, 200.54,
200.58-200.60, 200.64, 200.68-200.70, 200.74, 200.78, 202.70,
202.74, 202.78-202.80, 202.84, 202.88, 202.94, 239.81-239.9; For code
200.75: 200.30, 200.35, 200.38-200.40, 200.45, 200.48-200.50, 200.55,
200.58-200.60, 200.65, 200.68-200.70, 200.75, 200.78, 202.70,
202.75, 202.78-202.80, 202.85, 202.88, 202.95, 239.81-239.9; For code
200.76: 200.30, 200.36, 200.38-200.40, 200.46, 200.48-200.50, 200.56,
200.58-200.60, 200.66, 200.68-200.70, 200.76, 200.78, 202.70,
202.76, 202.78-202.80, 202.86, 202.88, 202.96, 239.81-239.9; For code
200.77: 200.30, 200.37-200.40, 200.47-200.50, 200.57-200.60,
200.67-200.70, 200.77-200.78, 202.70, 202.77-202.80,
202.87-202.88, 202.97, 239.81-239.9; For code 200.78: 200.30-200.78,
202.70-202.88, 202.98, 239.81-239.9
AHA: 4Q, '07, 66

§ ✓5th **200.8 Other named variants** CC HIV
[0-8]   Lymphoma (malignant):
          lymphoplasmacytoid type
          mixed lymphocytic-histiocytic (diffuse)
        Lymphosarcoma, mixed cell type (diffuse)
        Reticulolymphosarcoma (diffuse)
        CC Excl: For code 200.80: 200.80-200.88, 239.81-239.9; For code 200.81:
200.80-200.81, 200.88, 239.81-239.9; For code 200.82: 200.80, 200.82,
200.88, 239.81-239.9; For code 200.83: 200.80, 200.83, 200.88,
239.81-239.9; For code 200.84: 200.80, 200.84, 200.88, 239.81-239.9;
For code 200.85: 200.80, 200.85, 239.81-239.9; For code 200.86:
200.80, 200.86, 200.88, 239.81-239.9; For code 200.87: 200.80,
200.87-200.88, 239.81-239.9; For code 200.88: 200.80-200.88,
239.81-239.9

✓4th **201 Hodgkin's disease**
        DEF: Painless, progressive enlargement of lymph nodes, spleen and general
        lymph tissue; symptoms include anorexia, lassitude, weight loss, fever,
        pruritis, night sweats, anemia.
        AHA: 2Q, '92, 3; N-D, '86, 5

§ ✓5th **201.0 Hodgkin's paragranuloma** CC
[0-8]   CC Excl: For code 201.00: 201.00-201.08, 201.90, 239.81-239.9; For code
201.01: 201.00-201.01, 201.08, 201.90-201.91, 239.81-239.9; For code
201.02: 201.00, 201.02, 201.08, 201.90, 201.92, 239.81-239.9; For code
201.03: 201.00, 201.03, 201.08, 201.90, 201.93, 239.81-239.9; For code
201.04: 201.00, 201.04, 201.08, 201.90, 201.94, 239.81-239.9; For code
201.05: 201.00, 201.05, 201.08, 201.90, 201.95, 239.81-239.9; For code
201.06: 201.00, 201.06, 201.08, 201.90, 201.96, 239.81-239.9; For code
201.07: 201.00, 201.07-201.08, 201.90, 201.97, 239.81-239.9; For code
201.08: 201.00-201.08, 201.90, 201.98, 239.81-239.9

§ ✓5th **201.1 Hodgkin's granuloma** CC
[0-8]   CC Excl: For code 201.10: 201.10-201.18, 201.90, 201.98, 239.81-239.9;
For code 201.11: 201.10-201.11, 201.18, 201.90-201.91, 201.98,
239.81-239.9; For code 201.12: 201.10-201.11, 201.18, 201.90-201.91,
201.98, 239.81-239.9; For code 201.13: 201.10, 201.13, 201.18, 201.90,
201.93, 201.98, 239.81-239.9; For code 201.14: 201.10, 201.14, 201.18,
201.90, 201.94, 201.98, 239.81-239.9; For code 201.15: 201.10, 201.15,
201.18, 201.90, 201.95, 201.98, 239.81-239.9; For code 201.16: 201.10,
201.16, 201.18, 201.90, 201.96, 201.98, 239.81-239.9; For code 201.17:
201.10, 201.17-201.18, 201.90, 201.97-201.98, 239.81-239.9; For code
201.18: 201.10-201.18, 201.90, 201.98, 239.81-239.9
AHA: 2Q, '99, 7

§ ✓5th **201.2 Hodgkin's sarcoma** CC
[0-8]   CC Excl: For code 201.20: 201.20-201.28, 201.90, 201.98, 239.81-239.9;
For code 201.21: 201.20-201.21, 201.28, 201.90-201.91, 201.98,
239.81-239.9; For code 201.22: 201.20, 201.22, 201.28, 201.90, 201.92,
201.98, 239.81-239.9; For code 201.23: 201.20, 201.23, 201.28, 201.90,
201.93, 201.98, 239.81-239.9; For code 201.24: 201.20, 201.24, 201.28,
201.90, 201.94, 201.98, 239.81-239.9; For code 201.25: 201.20, 201.25,
201.28, 201.90, 201.95, 201.98, 239.81-239.9; For code 201.26: 201.20,
201.26, 201.28, 201.90, 201.96, 201.98, 239.81-239.9; For code 201.27:
201.20, 201.27-201.28, 201.90, 201.97-201.98, 239.81-239.9; For code
201.28: 201.20-201.28, 201.90, 201.98, 239.81-239.9

§ ✓5th **201.4 Lymphocytic-histiocytic predominance** CC
[0-8]   CC Excl: For code 201.40: 201.40-201.48, 201.90, 201.98, 239.81-239.9;
For code 201.41: 201.40-201.41, 201.48, 201.90-201.91, 201.98,
239.81-239.9; For code 201.42: 201.40, 201.42, 201.48, 201.90, 201.92,
201.98, 239.81-239.9; For code 201.43: 201.40, 201.43, 201.48, 201.90,
201.93, 201.98, 239.81-239.9; For code 201.44: 201.40, 201.44, 201.48,
201.90, 201.94, 201.98, 239.81-239.9; For code 201.45: 201.40, 201.45,
201.48, 201.90, 201.95, 201.98, 239.81-239.9; For code 201.46: 201.40,
201.46, 201.48, 201.90, 201.96, 201.98, 239.81-239.9; For code 201.47:
201.40, 201.47-201.48, 201.90, 201.97-201.98, 239.81-239.9; For code
201.48: 201.40-201.48, 201.90, 201.98, 239.81-239.9

§ ✓5th **201.5 Nodular sclerosis** CC
[0-8]   Hodgkin's disease, nodular sclerosis:
          NOS
          cellular phase
        CC Excl: For code 201.50: 201.50-201.58, 201.90, 201.98, 239.81-239.9;
For code 201.51: 201.50-201.51, 201.58, 201.90-201.91, 201.98,
239.81-239.9; For code 201.52: 201.50, 201.52, 201.58, 201.90, 201.92,
201.98, 239.81-239.9; For code 201.53: 201.50, 201.53, 201.58, 201.90,
201.93, 201.98, 239.81-239.9; For code 201.54: 201.50, 201.54, 201.58,
201.90, 201.94, 201.98, 239.81-239.9; For code 201.55: 201.50, 201.55,
201.58, 201.90, 201.95, 201.98, 239.81-239.9; For code 201.56: 201.50,
201.56, 201.58, 201.90, 201.96, 201.98, 239.81-239.9; For code 201.57:
201.50, 201.57-201.58, 201.90, 201.97-201.98, 239.81-239.9; For code
201.58: 201.50-201.58, 201.90, 201.98, 239.81-239.9

§ ✓5th **201.6 Mixed cellularity** CC
[0-8]   CC Excl: For code 201.60: 201.60-201.68, 201.90, 201.98, 239.81-239.9;
For code 201.61: 201.60-201.61, 201.68, 201.90-201.91, 201.98,
239.81-239.9; For code 201.62: 201.60, 201.62, 201.68, 201.90, 201.92,
201.98, 239.81-239.9; For code 201.63: 201.60, 201.63, 201.68, 201.90,
201.93, 201.98, 239.81-239.9; For code 201.64: 201.60, 201.64, 201.68,
201.90, 201.94, 201.98, 239.81-239.9; For code 201.65: 201.60, 201.65,
201.68, 201.90, 201.95, 201.98, 239.81-239.9; For code 201.66: 201.60,
201.66, 201.68, 201.90, 201.96, 201.98, 239.81-239.9; For code 201.67:
201.60, 201.67-201.68, 201.90, 201.97-201.98, 239.81-239.9; For code
201.68: 201.60-201.68, 201.90, 201.98, 239.81-239.9

§ ✓5th **201.7 Lymphocytic depletion** CC
[0-8]   Hodgkin's disease, lymphocytic depletion:
          NOS
          diffuse fibrosis
          reticular type
        CC Excl: For code 201.70:201.70-201.90, 201.98, 239.81-239.9; For code
201.71: 201.70-201.71, 201.78, 201.91, 201.98, 239.81-239.9; For code
201.72: 201.70, 201.72, 201.78, 201.92, 201.98, 239.81-239.9; For code
201.73: 201.70, 201.73, 201.78, 201.93, 201.98, 239.81-239.9; For code
201.74: 201.70, 201.74, 201.78, 201.94, 201.98, 239.81-239.9; For code
201.75: 201.70, 201.75, 201.78, 201.95, 201.98, 239.81-239.9; For code
201.76: 201.70, 201.76, 201.78, 201.96, 201.98, 239.81-239.9; For code
201.77: 201.70, 201.77-201.78, 201.97-201.98, 239.81-239.9; For code
201.78: 201.70-201.78, 201.98, 239.81-239.9

---

§   Requires fifth digit. Valid digits are in [brackets] under each code. See beginning of section 200-208 for codes and definitions.

§ ✓5ᵗʰ **201.9 Hodgkin's disease, unspecified**   CC

[0-8]   Hodgkin's: Malignant:
       disease NOS   lymphogranuloma
       lymphoma NOS   lymphogranulomatosis

CC Excl: For code 201.90: 201.90-201.98, 239.81-239.9; **For code 201.91:** 201.90-201.91, 201.98, 239.81-239.9; **For code 201.92:** 201.90, 201.92, 201.98, 239.81-239.9; **For code 201.93:** 201.90, 201.93, 201.98, 239.81-239.9; **For code 201.94:** 201.90, 201.94, 201.98, 239.81-239.9; **For code 201.95:** 201.90, 201.95, 201.98, 239.81-239.9; **For code 201.96:** 201.90, 201.96, 201.98, 239.81-239.9; **For code 201.97:** 201.90, 201.97-201.98, 239.81-239.9; **For code 201.98:** 201.90-201.98, 239.81-239.9

✓4ᵗʰ **202 Other malignant neoplasms of lymphoid and histiocytic tissue**

     AHA: 2Q, '92, 3; N-D, '86, 5

§ ✓5ᵗʰ **202.0 Nodular lymphoma**   CC

[0-8]   Brill-Symmers disease   Lymphosarcoma:
    Lymphoma: follicular (giant)
       follicular (giant) (large cell)   nodular
       lymphocytic, nodular

DEF: Lymphomatous cells clustered into nodules within the lymph node; usually occurs in older adults and may involve all nodes and possibly extranodal sites.

CC Excl: For code 202.00: 200.30, 200.40, 200.50, 200.60, 200.70,202.00-202.08, 202.70, 202.80, 202.90, 239.8-239.9; **For code 202.01:** 200.31, 200.41, 200.51, 200.61, 200.71,202.00-202.01, 202.08, 202.71, 202.81, 202.91, 239.8-239.9; **For code 202.02:** 200.32, 200.42, 200.52, 200.62, 200.72, 202.00, 202.02, 202.08, 202.72, 202.82, 202.92, 239.8-239.9; **For code 202.03:** 200.33, 200.43, 200.53, 200.63, 200.73, 202.00, 202.03, 202.08, 202.73, 202.83, 202.93, 239.8-239.9; ; **For code 202.04:** 3Q, '09, 4; 200.34, 200.44, 200.54, 200.64, 200.74, 202.00, 202.04, 202.08, 202.74, 202.84, 202.94, 239.8-239.9; ; **For code 202.05:** 200.35, 200.45, 200.55, 200.65, 200.75, 202.00, 202.05, 202.08, 202.75, 202.85, 202.95, 239.8-239.9; **For code 202.06:** 200.36, 200.46, 200.56, 200.66, 200.76, 200.00, 202.06, 202.08, 202.76, 202.86, 202.96, 239.8-239.9; **For code 202.07:** 200.37, 200.47, 200.57, 200.67, 200.77, 202.00,202.07-202.08, 202.77, 202.87, 202.97, 239.8-239.9; **For code 202.08:** 200.38, 200.48, 200.58, 200.68, 200.78,202.00-202.08, 202.78, 202.88, 202.98, 239.8-239.9

§ ✓5ᵗʰ **202.1 Mycosis fungoides**   CC

[0-8]   *EXCLUDES* peripheral T-cell lymphoma (202.7)

DEF: Type of cutaneous T-cell lymphoma; may evolve into generalized lymphoma; formerly thought to be of fungoid origin.

CC Excl: For code 202.10: 200.30, 200.40, 200.50, 200.60, 200.70, 202.10-202.18, 202.70, 202.80, 202.90, 239.81-239.9; **For code 202.11:** 200.31, 200.41, 200.51, 200.61, 200.71, 202.10-202.11, 202.18, 202.71, 202.81, 202.91, 239.81-239.9; **For code 202.12:** 200.32, 200.42, 200.52, 200.62, 200.72, 202.10, 202.12, 202.18, 202.72, 202.82, 202.92, 239.81-239.9; **For code 202.13:** 200.33, 200.43, 200.53, 200.63, 200.73, 202.10, 202.13, 202.18, 202.73, 202.83, 202.93, 239.81-239.9; **For code 202.14:** 200.34, 200.44, 200.54, 200.64, 200.74, 202.10, 202.14, 202.18, 202.74, 202.84, 202.94, 239.81-239.9; **For code 202.15:** 200.35, 200.45, 200.55, 200.65, 200.75, 202.10, 202.15, 202.18, 202.75, 202.85, 202.95, 239.81-239.9; **For code 202.16:** 200.36, 200.46, 200.56, 200.66, 200.76, 202.10, 202.16, 202.18, 202.76, 202.86, 202.96, 239.81-239.9; **For code 202.17:** 200.37, 200.47, 200.57, 200.67, 200.77, 202.10, 202.17-202.18, 202.77, 202.87, 202.97, 239.81-239.9; **For code 202.18:** 200.38, 200.48, 200.58, 200.68, 200.78, 202.10-202.18, 202.78, 202.88, 202.98, 239.81-239.9

AHA: 2Q, '92, 4

§ ✓5ᵗʰ **202.2 Sézary's disease**   CC

[0-8]   **DEF:** Type of cutaneous T-cell lymphoma with erythroderma, intense pruritus, peripheral lymphadenopathy, abnormal hyperchromatic mononuclear cells in skin, lymph nodes and peripheral blood.

CC Excl: For code 202.20: 200.30, 200.40, 200.50, 200.60, 200.70, 202.20-202.28, 202.70, 202.80, 202.90, 239.81-239.9; **For code 202.21:** 200.31, 200.41, 200.51, 200.61, 200.71, 202.20-202.21, 202.28, 202.71, 202.81, 202.91, 239.81-239.9; **For code 202.22:** 200.32, 200.42, 200.52, 200.62, 200.72, 202.20, 202.22, 202.28, 202.72, 202.82, 202.92, 239.81-239.9; **For code 202.23:** 200.33, 200.43, 200.53, 200.63, 200.73, 202.20, 202.23, 202.28, 202.73, 202.83, 202.93, 239.81-239.9; **For code 202.24:** 200.34, 200.44, 200.54, 200.64, 200.74, 202.20, 202.24, 202.28, 202.74, 202.84, 202.94, 239.81-239.9; **For code 202.25:** 200.35, 200.45, 200.55, 200.65, 200.75, 202.20, 202.25, 202.28, 202.75, 202.85, 202.95, 239.81-239.9; **For code 202.26:** 200.36, 200.46, 200.56, 200.66, 200.76, 202.20, 202.26, 202.28, 202.76, 202.86, 202.96, 239.81-239.9; **For code 202.27:** 200.37, 200.47, 200.57, 200.67, 200.77, 202.20, 202.27-202.28, 202.77, 202.87, 202.97, 239.81-239.9; **For code 202.28:** 200.38, 200.48, 200.58, 200.68, 200.78, 202.20-202.28, 202.78, 202.88, 202.98, 239.81-239.9

AHA: 2Q, '99, 7

§ ✓5ᵗʰ **202.3 Malignant histiocytosis**   CC

[0-8]   Histiocytic medullary reticulosis
    Malignant:
       reticuloendotheliosis
       reticulosis

CC Excl: For code 202.30: 200.30, 200.40, 200.50, 200.60, 200.70, 202.30-202.38, 202.70, 202.80, 202.90, 239.81-239.9; **For code 202.31:** 200.31, 200.41, 200.51, 200.61, 200.71, 202.30-202.31, 202.38, 202.71, 202.81, 202.91, 239.81-239.9; **For code 202.32:** 200.32, 200.42, 200.52, 200.62, 200.72, 202.30, 202.32, 202.38, 202.72, 202.82, 202.92, 239.81-239.9; **For code 202.33:** 200.33, 200.43, 200.53, 200.63, 200.73, 202.30, 202.33, 202.38, 202.73, 202.83, 202.93, 239.81-239.9; **For code 202.34:** 200.34, 200.44, 200.54, 200.64, 200.74, 202.30, 202.34, 202.38, 202.74, 202.84, 202.94, 239.81-239.9; **For code 202.35:** 200.35, 200.45, 200.55, 200.65, 200.75, 202.30, 202.35, 202.38, 202.75, 202.85, 202.95, 239.81-239.9; **For code 202.36:** 200.36, 200.46, 200.56, 200.66, 200.76, 202.30, 202.36, 202.38, 202.76, 202.86, 202.96, 239.81-239.9; **For code 202.37:** 200.37, 200.47, 200.57, 200.67, 200.77, 202.30, 202.37-202.38, 202.77, 202.87, 202.97, 239.81-239.9; **For code 202.38:** 200.38, 200.48, 200.58, 200.68, 200.78, 202.30-202.38, 202.78, 202.88, 202.98, 239.81-239.9

§ ✓5ᵗʰ **202.4 Leukemic reticuloendotheliosis**   CC

[0-8]   Hairy-cell leukemia

DEF: Chronic leukemia with large, mononuclear cells with "hairy" appearance in marrow, spleen, liver, blood.

CC Excl: For code 202.40: 200.30, 200.40, 200.50, 200.60, 200.70, 202.40-202.48, 202.70, 202.80, 202.90, 239.81-239.9; **For code 202.41:** 200.31, 200.41, 200.51, 200.61, 200.71, 202.40-202.41, 202.48, 202.71, 202.81, 202.91, 239.81-239.9; **For code 202.42:** 200.32, 200.42, 200.52, 200.62, 200.72, 202.40, 202.42, 202.48, 202.72, 202.82, 202.92, 239.81-239.9; **For code 202.43:** 200.33, 200.43, 200.53, 200.63, 200.73, 202.40, 202.43, 202.48, 202.73, 202.83, 202.93, 239.81-239.9; **For code 202.44:** 200.34, 200.44, 200.54, 200.64, 200.74, 202.40, 202.44, 202.48, 202.74, 202.84, 202.94, 239.81-239.9; **For code 202.45:** 200.35, 200.45, 200.55, 200.65, 200.75, 202.40, 202.45, 202.48, 202.75, 202.85, 202.95, 239.81-239.9; **For code 202.46:** 200.36, 200.46, 200.56, 200.66, 200.76, 202.40, 202.46, 202.48, 202.76, 202.86, 202.96, 239.81-239.9; **For code 202.47:** 200.37, 200.47, 200.57, 200.67, 200.77, 202.40, 202.47-202.48, 202.77, 202.87, 202.97, 239.81-239.9; **For code 202.48:** 200.38, 200.48, 200.58, 200.68, 200.78, 202.40-202.48, 202.78, 202.88, 202.98, 239.81-239.9

§ ✓5ᵗʰ **202.5 Letterer-Siwe disease**   CC

[0-8]   Acute:
       differentiated progressive histiocytosis
       histiocytosis X (progressive)
       infantile reticuloendotheliosis
       reticulosis of infancy

    EXCLUDES adult pulmonary Langerhans cell histiocytosis (516.5)
               Hand-Schüller-Christian disease (277.89)
               histiocytosis (acute) (chronic) (277.89)
               histiocytosis X (chronic) (277.89)

DEF: A recessive reticuloendotheliosis of early childhood, with a hemorrhagic tendency, eczema-like skin eruption, hepatosplenomegaly, lymph node enlargement, and progressive anemia; often a fatal disease with no established cause.

CC Excl: For code 202.50: 200.30, 200.40, 200.50, 200.60, 200.70, 202.50-202.58, 202.70, 202.80, 202.90, 239.81-239.9; **For code 202.51:** 200.31, 200.41, 200.51, 200.61, 200.71, 202.50-202.51, 202.58, 202.71, 202.81, 202.91, 239.81-239.9; **For code 202.52:** 200.32, 200.42, 200.52, 200.62, 200.72, 202.50, 202.52, 202.58, 202.72, 202.82, 202.92, 239.81-239.9; **For code 202.53:** 200.33, 200.43, 200.53, 200.63, 200.73, 202.50, 202.53, 202.58, 202.73, 202.83, 202.93, 239.81-239.9; **For code 202.54:** 200.34, 200.44, 200.54, 200.64, 200.74, 202.50, 202.54, 202.58, 202.74, 202.84, 202.94, 239.81-239.9; **For code 202.55:** 200.35, 200.45, 200.55, 200.65, 200.75, 202.50, 202.55, 202.58, 202.75, 202.85, 202.95, 239.81-239.9; **For code 202.56:** 200.36, 200.46, 200.56, 200.66, 200.76, 202.50, 202.56, 202.58, 202.76, 202.86, 202.96, 239.81-239.9; **For code 202.57:** 200.37, 200.47, 200.57, 200.67, 200.77, 202.50, 202.57-202.58, 202.77, 202.87, 202.97, 239.81-239.9; **For code 202.58:** 200.38, 200.48, 200.58, 200.68, 200.78, 202.50-202.58, 202.78, 202.88, 202.98, 239.81-239.9

---

§   Requires fifth digit. Valid digits are in [brackets] under each code. See beginning of section 200-208 for codes and definitions.

✓4ᵗʰ/✓5ᵗʰ Additional Digit Required   Unacceptable PDx   Manifestation Code   Hospital Acquired Condition   ▶◀ Revised Text   ● New Code   ▲ Revised Code Title

Neoplasms

202.6–204.9

§ ✓5ᵗʰ **202.6 Malignant mast cell tumors**   **CC**
[0-8]

Malignant:	Mast cell sarcoma
mastocytoma	Systemic tissue mast cell disease
mastocytosis	

EXCLUDES mast cell leukemia (207.8)

CC Excl: For code 202.60: 200.30, 200.40, 200.50, 200.60, 200.70, 202.60-202.70, 202.80, 202.90, 239.81-239.9; **For code 202.61:** 200.31, 200.41, 200.51, 200.61, 200.71, 202.60-202.61, 202.68, 202.71, 202.81, 202.91, 239.81-239.9; **For code 202.62:** 200.32, 200.42, 200.52, 200.62, 200.72, 202.60, 202.62, 202.68, 202.72, 202.82, 202.92, 239.81-239.9; **For code 202.63:** 200.33, 200.43, 200.53, 200.63, 200.73, 202.60, 202.63, 202.68, 202.73, 202.83, 202.93, 239.81-239.9; **For code 202.64:** 200.34, 200.44, 200.54, 200.64, 200.74, 202.60, 202.64, 202.68, 202.74, 202.84, 202.94, 239.81-239.9; **For code 202.65:** 200.35, 200.45, 200.55, 200.65, 200.75, 202.60, 202.65, 202.68, 202.75, 202.85, 202.95, 239.81-239.9; **For code 202.66:** 200.36, 200.46, 200.56, 200.66, 200.76, 202.60, 202.66, 202.68, 202.76, 202.86, 202.96, 239.81-239.9; **For code 202.67:** 200.37, 200.47, 200.57, 200.67, 200.77, 202.60, 202.67-202.68, 202.77, 202.87, 202.97, 239.81-239.9; **For code 202.68:** 200.38, 200.48, 200.58, 200.68, 200.78, 202.60-202.68, 202.78, 202.88, 202.98, 239.81-239.9

AHA: For code 202.60: ▶2Q, '13, 12◄

§ ✓5ᵗʰ **202.7 Peripheral T-cell lymphoma**   **CC HIV**
[0-8]

CC Excl: For code 202.70: 200.30-200.78, 202.70-202.90, 239.81-239.9; **For code 202.71:** 200.30-200.31, 200.38-200.41, 200.48-200.51, 200.58-200.61, 200.68-200.71, 200.78, 202.70-202.71, 202.78-202.81, 202.88, 202.91, 239.81-239.9; **For code 202.72:** 200.30, 200.32, 200.38-200.40, 200.42, 200.48-200.50, 200.52, 200.58-200.60, 200.62, 200.68-200.70, 200.72, 200.78, 202.70, 202.72, 202.78-202.80, 202.82, 202.88, 202.92, 239.81-239.9; **For code 202.73:** 200.30, 200.33, 200.38-200.40, 200.43, 200.48-200.50, 200.53, 200.58-200.60, 200.63, 200.68-200.70, 200.73, 200.78, 202.70, 202.73, 202.78-202.80, 202.83, 202.88, 202.93, 239.81-239.9; **For code 202.74:** 200.30, 200.34, 200.38-200.40, 200.44, 200.48-200.50, 200.54, 200.58-200.60, 200.64, 200.68-200.70, 200.74, 200.78, 202.70, 202.74, 202.78-202.80, 202.84, 202.88, 202.94, 239.81-239.9; **For code 202.75:** 200.30, 200.35, 200.38-200.40, 200.45, 200.48-200.50, 200.55, 200.58-200.60, 200.65, 200.68-200.70, 200.75, 200.78, 202.70, 202.75, 202.78-202.80, 202.85, 202.88, 202.95, 239.81-239.9; **For code 202.76:** 200.30, 200.36, 200.38-200.40, 200.46, 200.48-200.50, 200.56, 200.58-200.60, 200.66, 200.68-200.70, 200.76, 200.78, 202.70, 202.76, 202.78-202.80, 202.86, 202.88, 202.96, 239.81-239.9; **For code 202.77:** 200.30, 200.37-200.40, 200.47-200.50, 200.57-200.60, 200.67-200.70, 200.77-200.78, 202.70, 202.77-202.80, 202.87-202.88, 202.97, 239.81-239.9; **For code 202.78:** 200.30-200.78, 202.70-202.88, 202.98, 239.81-239.9

AHA: 4Q, '07, 66

§ ✓5ᵗʰ **202.8 Other lymphomas**   **CC HIV**
[0-8]

Lymphoma (malignant):
  NOS
  diffuse

EXCLUDES benign lymphoma (229.0)

CC Excl: For code 202.80: 200.30-200.78, 202.70-202.90, 239.81-239.9; **For code 202.81:** 200.30-200.31, 200.38-200.41, 200.48-200.51, 200.58-200.61, 200.68-200.71, 200.78, 202.70-202.71, 202.78-202.81, 202.88, 202.91, 239.81-239.9; **For code 202.82:** 200.30, 200.32, 200.38-200.40, 200.42, 200.48-200.50, 200.52, 200.58-200.60, 200.62, 200.68-200.70, 200.72, 200.78, 202.70, 202.72, 202.78-202.80, 202.82, 202.88, 202.92, 239.81-239.9; **For code 202.83:** 200.30, 200.33, 200.38-200.40, 200.43, 200.48-200.50, 200.53, 200.58-200.60, 200.63, 200.68-200.70, 200.73, 200.78, 202.70, 202.73, 202.78-202.80, 202.83, 202.88, 202.93, 239.81-239.9; **For code 202.84:** 200.30, 200.34, 200.38-200.40, 200.44, 200.48-200.50, 200.54, 200.58-200.60, 200.64, 200.68-200.70, 200.74, 200.78, 202.70, 202.74, 202.78-202.80, 202.84, 202.88, 202.94, 239.81-239.9; **For code 202.85:** 200.30, 200.35, 200.38-200.40, 200.45, 200.48-200.50, 200.55, 200.58-200.60, 200.65, 200.68-200.70, 200.75, 200.78, 202.70, 202.75, 202.78-202.80, 202.85, 202.88, 202.95, 239.81-239.9; **For code 202.86:** 200.30, 200.36, 200.38-200.40, 200.46, 200.48-200.50, 200.56, 200.58-200.60, 200.66, 200.68-200.70, 200.76, 200.78, 202.70, 202.76, 202.78-202.80, 202.86, 202.88, 202.96, 239.81-239.9; **For code 202.87:** 200.30, 200.37-200.40, 200.47-200.50, 200.57-200.60, 200.67-200.70, 200.77-200.78, 202.70, 202.77-202.80, 202.87-202.88, 202.97, 239.81-239.9; **For code 202.88:** 200.30-200.78, 202.70-202.88, 202.98, 239.81-239.9

AHA: 4Q, '06, 135; 2Q, '06, 20-21; 2Q, '92, 4; **For code 202.80:** 4Q, '08, 83; 1Q, '08, 16; 3Q, '07, 3

C85.80 Oth spec types non-Hodgkins lymphoma unspec site   **I-10**

§ ✓5ᵗʰ **202.9 Other and unspecified malignant neoplasms**   **CC**
[0-8]   **of lymphoid and histiocytic tissue**

Follicular dendritic cell sarcoma
Interdigitating dendritic cell sarcoma
Langerhans cell sarcoma
Malignant neoplasm of bone marrow NOS

CC Excl: For code 202.90: 202.90-202.98, 239.81-239.9; **For code 202.91:** 202.90-202.91, 202.98, 239.81-239.9; **For code 202.92:** 202.90, 202.92, 202.98, 239.81-239.9; **For code 202.93:** 202.90, 202.93, 202.98, 239.81-239.9; **For code 202.94:** 202.90, 202.94, 202.98, 239.81-239.9; **For code 202.95:** 202.90, 202.95, 202.98, 239.81-239.9; **For code 202.96:** 202.90, 202.96, 202.98, 239.81-239.9; **For code 202.97:** 202.90, 202.97-202.98, 239.81-239.9; **For code 202.98:** 202.90-202.98, 239.81-239.9

✓4ᵗʰ **203 Multiple myeloma and immunoproliferative neoplasms**

AHA: 4Q, '08, 83-84; 4Q, '91, 26

The following fifth-digit subclassification is for use with category 203:
  0 without mention of having achieved remission
    Failed remission
  1 in remission
  2 in relapse

§ ✓5ᵗʰ **203.0 Multiple myeloma**   **CC**
[0-2]

Kahler's disease	Myelomatosis

EXCLUDES solitary myeloma (238.6)

CC Excl: 203.00-208.92, 239.81-239.9

AHA: 1Q, '96, 16; 4Q, '89, 10; **For code 203.00:** 3Q, '12,16; 2Q, '10, 6; 2Q, '07, 8; **For code 203.01:** 4Q, '08, 91

C90.00 Multiple myeloma not in remission   **I-10**

§ ✓5ᵗʰ **203.1 Plasma cell leukemia**   **CC**
[0-2]

Plasmacytic leukemia

CC Excl: See code 203.0

AHA: 4Q, '91, 26

§ ✓5ᵗʰ **203.8 Other immunoproliferative neoplasms**   **CC**
[0-2]

CC Excl: See code 203.0

AHA: 4Q, '90, 26; S-O, '86, 12

✓4ᵗʰ **204 Lymphoid leukemia**

INCLUDES leukemia:
  lymphatic
  lymphoblastic
  lymphocytic
  lymphogenous

AHA: 4Q, '08, 83-84; 3Q, '93, 4

The following fifth-digit subclassification is for use with category 204:
  0 without mention of having achieved remission
    Failed remission
  1 in remission
  2 in relapse

§ ✓5ᵗʰ **204.0 Acute**   **CC**
[0-2]

EXCLUDES acute exacerbation of chronic lymphoid leukemia (204.1)

CC Excl: 203.00-208.92, 239.81-239.9

AHA: 3Q, '99, 6; **For code 204.02:** 1Q, '12, 13
For code 204.00: 2Q, '11, 4

§ ✓5ᵗʰ **204.1 Chronic**   **CC**
[0-2]

CC Excl: See code: 204.0

C91.10 Chronic lymphocytic leukemia not in remission   **I-10**

§ ✓5ᵗʰ **204.2 Subacute**   **CC**
[0-2]

CC Excl: See code: 204.0

§ ✓5ᵗʰ **204.8 Other lymphoid leukemia**   **CC**
[0-2]

Aleukemic leukemia:	Aleukemic leukemia:
lymphatic	lymphoid
lymphocytic	

CC Excl: See code: 204.0

AHA: 3Q, '09, 4

TIP: Assign for T-cell large granular lymphocytic leukemia.

§ ✓5ᵗʰ **204.9 Unspecified lymphoid leukemia**   **CC**
[0-2]   **CC Excl:** See code: 204.0

---

§ Requires fifth digit. Valid digits are in [brackets] under each code. See appropriate category for codes and definitions.

N Newborn Age: 0   **P** Pediatric Age: 0-17   **M** Maternity Age: 12-55   **A** Adult Age: 15-124   **MCC** Major CC Condition   **CC** CC Condition   **HIV** HIV Related Dx

48 – Volume 1 • October 2014   2015 ICD-9-CM

☑4ᵗʰ **205 Myeloid leukemia**
INCLUDES leukemia:
granulocytic
myeloblastic
myelocytic
myelogenous
myelomonocytic
myelosclerotic
myelosis
AHA: 4Q, '08, 83-84; 3Q, '93, 3; 4Q, '91, 26; 4Q, '90, 3; M-J, '85, 18

The following fifth-digit subclassification is for use with category 205:
0 **without mention of having achieved remission**
Failed remission
1 **in remission**
2 **in relapse**

§ ☑5ᵗʰ **205.0 Acute**   CC
[0-2]   Acute promyelocytic leukemia
EXCLUDES *acute exacerbation of chronic myeloid leukemia (205.1)*
CC Excl: 203.00-208.92, 239.81-239.9
AHA: For code 205.00: 4Q, '09, 79; 2Q, '06, 20-21; For code 205.01: 2Q, '12, 16
C92.00 Acute myeloid leukemia not in remission   I-10

§ ☑5ᵗʰ **205.1 Chronic**   CC
[0-2]   Eosinophilic leukemia   Neutrophilic leukemia
CC Excl: See code: 205.0
AHA: 1Q, '00, 6; J-A, '85, 13; For code 205.10: 4Q, '08, 142

§ ☑5ᵗʰ **205.2 Subacute**   CC
[0-2]   CC Excl: See code: 205.0

§ ☑5ᵗʰ **205.3 Myeloid sarcoma**   CC
[0-2]   Chloroma   Granulocytic sarcoma
CC Excl: See code: 205.0

§ ☑5ᵗʰ **205.8 Other myeloid leukemia**   CC
[0-2]   Aleukemic leukemia: Aleukemic leukemia:
granulocytic   myeloid
myelogenous   Aleukemic myelosis
CC Excl: See code: 205.0

§ ☑5ᵗʰ **205.9 Unspecified myeloid leukemia**   CC
[0-2]   CC Excl: See code: 205.0

☑4ᵗʰ **206 Monocytic leukemia**
INCLUDES leukemia:
histiocytic
monoblastic
monocytoid
AHA: 4Q,, '08, 83-84

The following fifth-digit subclassification is for use with category 206:
0 **without mention of having achieved remission**
Failed remission
1 **in remission**
2 **in relapse**

§ ☑5ᵗʰ **206.0 Acute**   CC
[0-2]   EXCLUDES *acute exacerbation of chronic monocytic leukemia (206.1)*
CC Excl: 203.00-208.92, 239.81-239.9

§ ☑5ᵗʰ **206.1 Chronic**   CC
[0-2]   CC Excl: See code: 206.0

§ ☑5ᵗʰ **206.2 Subacute**   CC
[0-2]   CC Excl: See code: 206.0

§ ☑5ᵗʰ **206.8 Other monocytic leukemia**   CC
[0-2]   Aleukemic: Aleukemic:
monocytic leukemia   monocytoid leukemia
CC Excl: See code: 206.0

§ ☑5ᵗʰ **206.9 Unspecified monocytic leukemia**   CC
[0-2]   CC Excl: See code: 206.0

☑4ᵗʰ **207 Other specified leukemia**
EXCLUDES *leukemic reticuloendotheliosis (202.4)*
plasma cell leukemia (203.1)
AHA: 4Q, '08, 83-85

The following fifth-digit subclassification is for use with category 207:
0 **without mention of having achieved remission**
Failed remission
1 **in remission**
2 **in relapse**

§ ☑5ᵗʰ **207.0 Acute erythremia and erythroleukemia**   CC
[0-2]   Acute erythremic myelosis   Erythremic myelosis
Di Guglielmo's disease
DEF: Erythremia: polycythemia vera.
DEF: Erythroleukemia: a malignant blood dyscrasia (a myeloproliferative disorder).
CC Excl: 203.00-208.92, 239.81-239.9

§ ☑5ᵗʰ **207.1 Chronic erythremia**   CC
[0-2]   Heilmeyer-Schöner disease
CC Excl: See code: 207.0

§ ☑5ᵗʰ **207.2 Megakaryocytic leukemia**   CC
[0-2]   Megakaryocytic myelosis   Thrombocytic leukemia
CC Excl: See code: 207.0

§ ☑5ᵗʰ **207.8 Other specified leukemia**   CC
[0-2]   Lymphosarcoma cell leukemia
CC Excl: See code: 207.0

☑4ᵗʰ **208 Leukemia of unspecified cell type**
AHA: 4Q, '08, 83-85

The following fifth-digit subclassification is for use with category 208:
0 **without mention of having achieved remission**
Failed remission
1 **in remission**
2 **in relapse**

§ ☑5ᵗʰ **208.0 Acute**   CC
[0-2]   Acute leukemia NOS   Stem cell leukemia
Blast cell leukemia
EXCLUDES *acute exacerbation of chronic unspecified leukemia (208.1)*
CC Excl: 203.00-208.92, 239.81-239.9

§ ☑5ᵗʰ **208.1 Chronic**   CC
[0-2]   Chronic leukemia NOS
CC Excl: See code: 208.0

§ ☑5ᵗʰ **208.2 Subacute**   CC
[0-2]   Subacute leukemia NOS
CC Excl: See code: 208.0

§ ☑5ᵗʰ **208.8 Other leukemia of unspecified cell type** CC
[0-2]   CC Excl: See code: 208.0

§ ☑5ᵗʰ **208.9 Unspecified leukemia**   CC
[0-2]   Leukemia NOS
CC Excl: See code: 208.0
AHA: For code 208.90: 4Q, '11, 148

Neuroendocrine Tumors (209)

☑4ᵗʰ **209 Neuroendocrine tumors**
Code first any associated multiple endocrine neoplasia syndrome (258.01-258.03)
Use additional code to identify associated endocrine syndrome, such as:
carcinoid syndrome (259.2)
EXCLUDES *benign pancreatic islet cell tumors (211.7)*
malignant pancreatic islet cell tumors (157.4)
AHA: 4Q, '09, 150; 4Q, '08, 85-89

☑4ᵗʰ **209.0 Malignant carcinoid tumors of the small intestine**

209.00 Malignant carcinoid tumor of the small   CC
intestine, unspecified portion
CC Excl: 152.8-152.9, 159.0, 159.8-159.9, 176.3, 195.8, 199.0-199.2, 209.00-209.30, 209.70, 209.75, 239.0, 239.81-239.9

---

§ Requires fifth digit. Valid digits are in [brackets] under each code. See appropriate category for codes and definitions.

| ☑4ᵗʰ ☑5ᵗʰ Additional Digit Required | Unacceptable PDx | Manifestation Code | Hospital Acquired Condition | ►◄ Revised Text | ● New Code | ▲ Revised Code Title |

Neoplasms

209.01–209.69

209.01 Malignant carcinoid tumor of the duodenum `CC`
CC Excl: 152.0, 152.8-152.9, 159.0, 159.8-159.9, 176.3, 195.8, 199.0-199.2, 209.00-209.30, 209.70, 209.75, 239.0, 239.81-239.9

209.02 Malignant carcinoid tumor of the jejunum `CC`
CC Excl: 152.1, 152.8-152.9, 159.0, 159.8-159.9, 176.3, 195.8, 199.0-199.2, 209.00-209.30, 209.70, 209.75, 239.0, 239.81-239.9

209.03 Malignant carcinoid tumor of the ileum `CC`
CC Excl: 152.2, 152.8-152.9, 159.0, 159.8-159.9, 176.3, 195.8, 199.0-199.2, 209.00-209.30, 209.70, 209.75, 239.0, 239.81-239.9

✓5th **209.1 Malignant carcinoid tumors of the appendix, large intestine, and rectum**

209.10 Malignant carcinoid tumor of the large intestine, unspecified portion `CC`
Malignant carcinoid tumor of the colon NOS
CC Excl: 153.8-153.9, 159.0, 159.8-159.9, 176.3, 195.8, 199.0-199.2, 209.00-209.30, 209.70, 209.75, 239.0, 239.81-239.9

209.11 Malignant carcinoid tumor of the appendix `CC`
CC Excl: 153.5, 153.8-153.9, 159.0, 159.8-159.9, 176.3, 195.8, 199.0-199.2, 209.00-209.30, 209.70, 209.75, 239.0, 239.81-239.9

209.12 Malignant carcinoid tumor of the cecum `CC`
CC Excl: 153.4, 153.8-153.9, 159.0, 159.8-159.9, 176.3, 195.8, 199.0-199.2, 209.00-209.30, 209.70, 209.75, 239.0, 239.81-239.9

209.13 Malignant carcinoid tumor of the ascending colon `CC`
CC Excl: 153.6, 153.8-153.9, 159.0, 159.8-159.9, 176.3, 195.8, 199.0-199.2, 209.00-209.30, 209.70, 209.75, 239.0, 239.81-239.9

209.14 Malignant carcinoid tumor of the transverse colon `CC`
CC Excl: 153.1, 153.8-153.9, 159.0, 159.8-159.9, 176.3, 195.8, 199.0-199.2, 209.00-209.30, 209.70, 209.75, 239.0, 239.81-239.9

209.15 Malignant carcinoid tumor of the descending colon `CC`
CC Excl: 153.2, 153.8-153.9, 159.0, 159.8-159.9, 176.3, 195.8, 199.0-199.2, 209.00-209.30, 209.70, 209.75, 239.0, 239.81-239.9

209.16 Malignant carcinoid tumor of the sigmoid colon `CC`
CC Excl: 153.3, 153.8-153.9, 159.0, 159.8-159.9, 176.3, 195.8, 199.0-199.2, 209.00-209.30, 209.70, 209.75, 239.0, 239.81-239.9

209.17 Malignant carcinoid tumor of the rectum `CC`
CC Excl: 154.1, 154.8, 159.0, 159.8-159.9, 176.3, 195.8, 199.0-199.2, 209.00-209.30, 209.70, 209.75, 239.0, 239.81-239.9

✓5th **209.2 Malignant carcinoid tumors of other and unspecified sites**

209.20 Malignant carcinoid tumor of unknown primary site `CC`
CC Excl: 195.8, 198.89-199.2, 209.00-209.30, 209.70, 209.75-209.79, 239.81-239.9

209.21 Malignant carcinoid tumor of the bronchus and lung `CC`
CC Excl: 162.8-162.9, 165.8-165.9, 176.4, 195.8, 199.0-199.2, 209.00-209.30, 209.70, 209.75, 239.1, 239.81-239.9

209.22 Malignant carcinoid tumor of the thymus `CC`
CC Excl: 164.0, 209.00-209.30

209.23 Malignant carcinoid tumor of the stomach `CC`
CC Excl: 151.0-151.9, 159.0, 159.8-159.9, 176.3, 195.8, 199.0-199.2, 209.00-209.30, 209.70, 209.75, 239.0, 239.81-239.9
AHA: 4Q, '08, 89

209.24 Malignant carcinoid tumor of the kidney `CC`
CC Excl: 189.0-189.1, 189.8-189.9, 195.8, 199.0-199.2, 209.00-209.30, 209.70, 209.75, 239.5, 239.81-239.9

209.25 Malignant carcinoid tumor of the foregut NOS `CC`
CC Excl: 151.0-151.9, 159.0, 159.8-159.9, 176.3, 195.8, 199.0-199.2, 209.00-209.30, 209.70, 239.0, 239.81-239.9

209.26 Malignant carcinoid tumor of the midgut NOS `CC`
CC Excl: 151.0-151.9, 159.0, 159.8-159.9, 176.3, 195.8, 199.0-199.2, 209.00-209.30, 209.70, 239.0, 239.81-239.9

209.27 Malignant carcinoid tumor of the hindgut NOS `CC`
CC Excl: 151.0-151.9, 159.0, 159.8-159.9, 176.3, 195.8, 199.0-199.2, 209.00-209.30, 209.70, 239.0, 239.81-239.9

209.29 Malignant carcinoid tumor of the other sites `CC`
CC Excl: 195.8, 198.89-199.2, 209.00-209.30, 209.70, 209.79, 239.81-239.9

✓5th **209.3 Malignant poorly differentiated neuroendocrine tumors**
AHA: 4Q, '09, 73,74

209.30 Malignant poorly differentiated neuroendocrine carcinoma, any site `CC`
High grade neuroendocrine carcinoma, any site
Malignant poorly differentiated neuroendocrine tumor NOS
EXCLUDES *Merkel cell carcinoma (209.31-209.36)*
CC Excl: 195.8, 198.89-199.2, 209.00-209.30, 209.70, 209.79, 239.81-239.9
AHA: ▶1Q, '14, 5◀

209.31 Merkel cell carcinoma of the face
Merkel cell carcinoma of the ear
Merkel cell carcinoma of the eyelid, including canthus
Merkel cell carcinoma of the lip

209.32 Merkel cell carcinoma of the scalp and neck

209.33 Merkel cell carcinoma of the upper limb

209.34 Merkel cell carcinoma of the lower limb

209.35 Merkel cell carcinoma of the trunk

209.36 Merkel cell carcinoma of other sites
Merkel cell carcinoma of the buttock
Merkel cell carcinoma of the genitals
Merkel cell carcinoma NOS
AHA: 4Q, '09, 74

✓5th **209.4 Benign carcinoid tumors of the small intestine**

209.40 Benign carcinoid tumor of the small intestine, unspecified portion

209.41 Benign carcinoid tumor of the duodenum

209.42 Benign carcinoid tumor of the jejunum

209.43 Benign carcinoid tumor of the ileum

✓5th **209.5 Benign carcinoid tumors of the appendix, large intestine, and rectum**

209.50 Benign carcinoid tumor of the large intestine, unspecified portion
Benign carcinoid tumor of the colon NOS

209.51 Benign carcinoid tumor of the appendix

209.52 Benign carcinoid tumor of the cecum

209.53 Benign carcinoid tumor of the ascending colon

209.54 Benign carcinoid tumor of the transverse colon

209.55 Benign carcinoid tumor of the descending colon

209.56 Benign carcinoid tumor of the sigmoid colon

209.57 Benign carcinoid tumor of the rectum

✓5th **209.6 Benign carcinoid tumors of other and unspecified sites**

209.60 Benign carcinoid tumor of unknown primary site
Carcinoid tumor NOS
Neuroendocrine tumor NOS

209.61 Benign carcinoid tumor of the bronchus and lung
AHA: 4Q, '09, 151

209.62 Benign carcinoid tumor of the thymus

209.63 Benign carcinoid tumor of the stomach

209.64 Benign carcinoid tumor of the kidney

209.65 Benign carcinoid tumor of the foregut NOS

209.66 Benign carcinoid tumor of the midgut NOS

209.67 Benign carcinoid tumor of the hindgut NOS

209.69 Benign carcinoid tumors of other sites

| `N` Newborn Age: 0 | `P` Pediatric Age: 0-17 | `M` Maternity Age: 12-55 | `A` Adult Age: 15-124 | `MCC` Major CC Condition | `CC` CC Condition | `HIV` HIV Related Dx |

50 – Volume 1 • October 2014   2015 ICD-9-CM

☑5ᵗʰ **209.7 Secondary neuroendocrine tumors**
Secondary carcinoid tumors
AHA: 4Q, '09,74

209.70 Secondary neuroendocrine tumor, unspecified site

209.71 Secondary neuroendocrine tumor of distant CC
lymph nodes
CC Excl: 176.5, 195.8-196.9, 199.0-199.2, 209.20,
209.29-209.30, 209.70-209.79, 239.81-239.9
AHA: ▶1Q, '14, 5◀

209.72 Secondary neuroendocrine tumor of liver CC
CC Excl: 195.8, 197.7-197.8, 198.89-199.2, 209.20,
209.29-209.30, 209.70-209.79, 239.81-239.9

209.73 Secondary neuroendocrine tumor of bone CC
CC Excl: 195.8, 198.5, 198.89-199.2, 209.20, 209.29-209.30,
209.70-209.79, 239.81-239.9

209.74 Secondary neuroendocrine tumor of peritoneum CC
Mesentery metastasis of neuroendocrine tumor
CC Excl: 195.8, 197.6, 197.8, 198.89-199.2, 209.20,
209.29-209.30, 209.70-209.79, 239.81-239.9
AHA: 4Q, '11, 181; 4Q, '09, 150

209.75 Secondary Merkel cell carcinoma
Merkel cell carcinoma nodal presentation
Merkel cell carcinoma visceral metastatic
presentation
Secondary Merkel cell carcinoma, any site

209.79 Secondary neuroendocrine tumor of other sites CC
CC Excl: 195.8, 198.89-199.2, 209.20, 209.29-209.30,
209.70-209.79, 239.81-239.9
AHA: ▶1Q, '14, 5◀

Benign Neoplasms (210-229)

☑4ᵗʰ **210 Benign neoplasm of lip, oral cavity, and pharynx**
EXCLUDES cyst (of):
jaw (526.0-526.2, 526.89)
oral soft tissue (528.4)
radicular (522.8)

210.0 Lip
Frenulum labii
Lip (inner aspect) (mucosa) (vermilion border)
EXCLUDES labial commissure (210.4)
skin of lip (216.0)

210.1 Tongue
Lingual tonsil

210.2 Major salivary glands
Gland: Gland:
parotid   submandibular
sublingual
EXCLUDES benign neoplasms of minor salivary glands:
NOS (210.4)
buccal mucosa (210.4)
lips (210.0)
palate (hard) (soft) (210.4)
tongue (210.1)
tonsil, palatine (210.5)

210.3 Floor of mouth

210.4 Other and unspecified parts of mouth
Gingiva   Oral mucosa
Gum (upper) (lower)   Palate (hard) (soft)
Labial commissure   Uvula
Oral cavity NOS
EXCLUDES benign odontogenic neoplasms of bone (213.0-213.1)
developmental odontogenic cysts (526.0)
mucosa of lips (210.0)
nasopharyngeal [posterior] [superior] surface of soft
palate (210.7)

210.5 Tonsil
Tonsil (faucial) (palatine)
EXCLUDES lingual tonsil (210.1)
pharyngeal tonsil (210.7)
tonsillar:
fossa (210.6)
pillars (210.6)

210.6 Other parts of oropharynx
Branchial cleft or vestiges   Tonsillar:
Epiglottis, anterior aspect   fossa
Fauces NOS   pillars
Mesopharynx NOS   Vallecula
EXCLUDES epiglottis:
NOS (212.1)
suprahyoid portion (212.1)

210.7 Nasopharynx
Adenoid tissue   Pharyngeal tonsil
Lymphadenoid tissue   Posterior nasal septum

210.8 Hypopharynx
Arytenoid fold   Postcricoid region
Laryngopharynx   Pyriform fossa

210.9 Pharynx, unspecified
Throat NOS

☑4ᵗʰ **211 Benign neoplasm of other parts of digestive system**
EXCLUDES benign stromal tumors of digestive system (215.5)

211.0 Esophagus

211.1 Stomach
Body
Cardia   } of stomach
Fundus
Cardiac orifice
Pylorus
EXCLUDES benign carcinoid tumors of the stomach (209.63)
D13.1 Benign neoplasm of stomach   I-10

211.2 Duodenum, jejunum, and ileum
Small intestine NOS
EXCLUDES ampulla of Vater (211.5)
benign carcinoid tumors of the small intestine
(209.40-209.43)
ileocecal valve (211.3)

211.3 Colon
Appendix   Ileocecal valve
Cecum   Large intestine NOS
EXCLUDES benign carcinoid tumors of the large intestine
(209.50-209.56)
rectosigmoid junction (211.4)
AHA: ▶4Q, '13, 103, 104;◀ 2Q, '11, 9; 3Q, '05, 17;
2Q, '05, 16; 4Q, '01, 56
D12.6 Benign neoplasm of colon unspecified   I-10

211.4 Rectum and anal canal
Anal canal or sphincter   Rectosigmoid junction
Anus NOS
EXCLUDES anus:
margin (216.5)
skin (216.5)
benign carcinoid tumors of the rectum (209.57)
perianal skin (216.5)
AHA: 2Q, '11, 9

211.5 Liver and biliary passages
Ampulla of Vater   Gallbladder
Common bile duct   Hepatic duct
Cystic duct   Sphincter of Oddi

211.6 Pancreas, except islets of Langerhans

211.7 Islets of Langerhans
Islet cell tumor
Use additional code to identify any functional activity

211.8 Retroperitoneum and peritoneum
Mesentery   Omentum
Mesocolon   Retroperitoneal tissue

211.9 Other and unspecified site
Alimentary tract NOS
Digestive system NOS
Gastrointestinal tract NOS
Intestinal tract NOS
Intestine NOS
Spleen, not elsewhere classified

Neoplasms

212–216.1

✓4th **212 Benign neoplasm of respiratory and intrathoracic organs**

212.0 Nasal cavities, middle ear, and accessory sinuses

Cartilage of nose   Sinus:
Eustachian tube   ethmoidal
Nares   frontal
Septum of nose   maxillary
                 sphenoidal

EXCLUDES *auditory canal (external) (216.2)*
bone of:
     ear (213.0)
     nose [turbinates] (213.0)
cartilage of ear (215.0)
ear (external) (skin) (216.2)
nose NOS (229.8)
     skin (216.3)
olfactory bulb (225.1)
polyp of:
     accessory sinus (471.8)
     ear (385.30-385.35)
     nasal cavity (471.0)
     posterior margin of septum and choanae (210.7)

212.1 Larynx

Cartilage: Epiglottis (suprahyoid portion) NOS
   arytenoid   Glottis
   cricoid   Vocal cords (false)(true)
   cuneiform
   thyroid

EXCLUDES *epiglottis, anterior aspect (210.6)*
polyp of vocal cord or larynx (478.4)

212.2 Trachea

212.3 Bronchus and lung

Carina
Hilus of lung

EXCLUDES *benign carcinoid tumors of bronchus and lung (209.61)*

212.4 Pleura

212.5 Mediastinum

212.6 Thymus

EXCLUDES *benign carcinoid tumors of thymus (209.62)*

212.7 Heart

EXCLUDES *great vessels (215.4)*

212.8 Other specified sites

212.9 Site unspecified

Respiratory organ NOS
Upper respiratory tract NOS

EXCLUDES *intrathoracic NOS (229.8)*
thoracic NOS (229.8)

✓4th **213 Benign neoplasm of bone and articular cartilage**

INCLUDES cartilage (articular) (joint)
periosteum

EXCLUDES *cartilage of:*
     ear (215.0)
     eyelid (215.0))
     larynx (212.1)
     nose (212.0)
exostosis NOS (726.91
synovia (215.0-215.9)

213.0 Bones of skull and face

EXCLUDES *lower jaw bone (213.1)*

213.1 Lower jaw bone

213.2 Vertebral column, excluding sacrum and coccyx

213.3 Ribs, sternum, and clavicle

213.4 Scapula and long bones of upper limb

213.5 Short bones of upper limb

213.6 Pelvic bones, sacrum, and coccyx

213.7 Long bones of lower limb

213.8 Short bones of lower limb

213.9 Bone and articular cartilage, site unspecified

✓4th **214 Lipoma**

INCLUDES angiolipoma
fibrolipoma
hibernoma
lipoma (fetal) (infiltrating) (intramuscular)
myelolipoma
myxolipoma

DEF: Benign tumor frequently composed of mature fat cells; may occasionally be composed of fetal fat cells.

214.0 Skin and subcutaneous tissue of face

214.1 Other skin and subcutaneous tissue

214.2 Intrathoracic organs

214.3 Intra-abdominal organs

214.4 Spermatic cord   ♂

214.8 Other specified sites

AHA: 3Q, '94, 7

214.9 Lipoma, unspecified site

✓4th **215 Other benign neoplasm of connective and other soft tissue**

INCLUDES blood vessel
bursa
fascia
ligament
muscle
peripheral, sympathetic, and parasympathetic nerves and ganglia
synovia
tendon (sheath)

EXCLUDES *cartilage:*
     articular (213.0-213.9)
     larynx (212.1)
     nose (212.0)
connective tissue of:
     breast (217)
     internal organ, except lipoma and hemangioma — code to benign neoplasm of the site
lipoma (214.0-214.9)

215.0 Head, face, and neck

215.2 Upper limb, including shoulder

215.3 Lower limb, including hip

215.4 Thorax

EXCLUDES *heart (212.7)*
mediastinum (212.5)
thymus (212.6)

215.5 Abdomen

Abdominal wall
Benign stromal tumors of abdomen
Hypochondrium

215.6 Pelvis

Buttock   Inguinal region
Groin   Perineum

EXCLUDES *uterine:*
     leiomyoma (218.0-218.9)
     ligament, any (221.0)

215.7 Trunk, unspecified

Back NOS   Flank NOS

215.8 Other specified sites

215.9 Site unspecified

✓4th **216 Benign neoplasm of skin**

INCLUDES blue nevus
dermatofibroma
hydrocystoma
pigmented nevus
syringoadenoma
syringoma

EXCLUDES *skin of genital organs (221.0-222.9)*

AHA: 1Q, '00, 21

216.0 Skin of lip

EXCLUDES *vermilion border of lip (210.0)*

216.1 Eyelid, including canthus

EXCLUDES *cartilage of eyelid (215.0)*

N Newborn Age: 0   P Pediatric Age: 0-17   M Maternity Age: 12-55   A Adult Age: 15-124   MCC Major CC Condition   CC CC Condition   HIV HIV Related Dx

52 – Volume 1   2015 ICD-9-CM

216.2 Ear and external auditory canal
Auricle (ear)   External meatus
Auricular canal, externalPinna
EXCLUDES *cartilage of ear (215.0)*

216.3 Skin of other and unspecified parts of face
Cheek, external   Nose, external
Eyebrow   Temple

216.4 Scalp and skin of neck
AHA: 3Q, '91, 12

216.5 Skin of trunk, except scrotum
Axillary fold   Skin of:
Perianal skin   buttock
Skin of: chest wall
   abdominal wall   groin
   anus   perineum
   back   Umbilicus
   breast
EXCLUDES *anal canal (211.4)*
anus NOS (211.4)
skin of scrotum (222.4)

216.6 Skin of upper limb, including shoulder

216.7 Skin of lower limb, including hip

216.8 Other specified sites of skin

216.9 Skin, site unspecified

217 Benign neoplasm of breast
Breast (male) (female):   Breast (male) (female):
   connective tissue   soft parts
   glandular tissue
EXCLUDES *adenofibrosis (610.2)*
benign cyst of breast (610.0)
fibrocystic disease (610.1)
skin of breast (216.5)
AHA: 1Q, '00, 4

✓4ᵗʰ 218 Uterine leiomyoma
INCLUDES fibroid (bleeding) (uterine)
uterine:
   fibromyoma
   myoma
DEF: Benign tumor primarily derived from uterine smooth muscle tissue; may contain fibrous, fatty, or epithelial tissue; also called uterine fibroid or myoma.

218.0 Submucous leiomyoma of uterus ♀

218.1 Intramural leiomyoma of uterus ♀
Interstitial leiomyoma of uterus
D25.1 Intramural leiomyoma of uterus   I-10

218.2 Subserous leiomyoma of uterus ♀

218.9 Leiomyoma of uterus, unspecified ♀
AHA: 1Q, '03, 4
D25.9 Leiomyoma of uterus unspecified   I-10

✓4ᵗʰ 219 Other benign neoplasm of uterus

219.0 Cervix uteri ♀

219.1 Corpus uteri ♀
Endometrium   Myometrium
Fundus

219.8 Other specified parts of uterus ♀

219.9 Uterus, part unspecified ♀

220 Benign neoplasm of ovary ♀
Use additional code to identify any functional activity (256.0-256.1)
EXCLUDES *cyst:*
corpus albicans (620.2)
corpus luteum (620.1)
endometrial (617.1)
follicular (atretic) (620.0)
graafian follicle (620.0)
ovarian NOS (620.2)
retention (620.2)
D27.9 Benign neoplasm of unspec ovary   I-10

Types of Uterine Fibroids

✓4ᵗʰ 221 Benign neoplasm of other female genital organs
INCLUDES adenomatous polyp
benign teratoma
EXCLUDES *cyst:*
epoophoron (752.11)
fimbrial (752.11)
Gartner's duct (752.11)
parovarian (752.11)

221.0 Fallopian tube and uterine ligaments ♀
Oviduct
Parametruim
Uterine ligament (broad) (round) (uterosacral)
Uterine tube

221.1 Vagina ♀

221.2 Vulva ♀
Clitoris
External female genitalia NOS
Greater vestibular [Bartholin's] gland
Labia (majora) (minora)
Pudendum
EXCLUDES *Bartholin's (duct) (gland) cyst (616.2)*

221.8 Other specified sites of female genital organs ♀

221.9 Female genital organ, site unspecified ♀
Female genitourinary tract NOS

✓4ᵗʰ 222 Benign neoplasm of male genital organs

222.0 Testis ♂
Use additional code to identify any functional activity

222.1 Penis ♂
Corpus cavernosum   Prepuce
Glans penis

222.2 Prostate ♂
EXCLUDES *adenomatous hyperplasia of prostate*
(600.20-600.21)
prostatic:
adenoma (600.20-600.21)
enlargement (600.00-600.01)
hypertrophy (600.00-600.01)

222.3 Epididymis ♂

222.4 Scrotum ♂
Skin of scrotum

222.8 Other specified sites of male genital organs ♂
Seminal vesicle   Spermatic cord

222.9 Male genital organ, site unspecified ♂
Male genitourinary tract NOS

✓4ᵗʰ 223 Benign neoplasm of kidney and other urinary organs

223.0 Kidney, except pelvis
Kidney NOS
EXCLUDES *benign carcinoid tumors of kidney (209.64)*
renal:
calyces (223.1)
pelvis (223.1)

223.1 Renal pelvis

223.2 Ureter
EXCLUDES *ureteric orifice of bladder (223.3)*

Eyeball

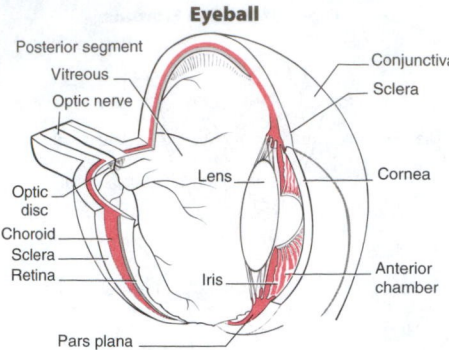

223.3 Bladder

✓5ᵗʰ **223.8 Other specified sites of urinary organs**

223.81 Urethra
EXCLUDES urethral orifice of bladder (223.3)

223.89 Other
Paraurethral glands

223.9 Urinary organ, site unspecified
Urinary system NOS

✓4ᵗʰ **224 Benign neoplasm of eye**
EXCLUDES cartilage of eyelid (215.0)
eyelid (skin) (216.1)
optic nerve (225.1)
orbital bone (213.0)

224.0 Eyeball, except conjunctiva, cornea, retina, and choroid
Ciliary body   Sclera
Iris   Uveal tract

224.1 Orbit
EXCLUDES bone of orbit (213.0)

224.2 Lacrimal gland

224.3 Conjunctiva

224.4 Cornea

224.5 Retina
EXCLUDES hemangioma of retina (228.03)

224.6 Choroid

224.7 Lacrimal duct
Lacrimal sac   Nasolacrimal duct

224.8 Other specified parts of eye

224.9 Eye, part unspecified

✓4ᵗʰ **225 Benign neoplasm of brain and other parts of nervous system**
EXCLUDES hemangioma (228.02)
neurofibromatosis (237.70-237.79)
peripheral, sympathetic, and parasympathetic nerves and ganglia (215.0-215.9)
retrobulbar (224.1)

225.0 Brain

225.1 Cranial nerves
Acoustic neuroma
AHA: 4Q, '04, 113

225.2 Cerebral meninges
Meninges NOS   Meningioma (cerebral)
D32.0 Benign neoplasm of cerebral meninges   I-10

225.3 Spinal cord
Cauda equina

225.4 Spinal meninges
Spinal meningioma

225.8 Other specified sites of nervous system

225.9 Nervous system, part unspecified
Nervous system (central) NOS
EXCLUDES meninges NOS (225.2)

226 Benign neoplasm of thyroid glands
Use additional code to identify any functional activity

✓4ᵗʰ **227 Benign neoplasm of other endocrine glands and related structures**
Use additional code to identify any functional activity
EXCLUDES ovary (220)
pancreas (211.6)
testis (222.0)

227.0 Adrenal gland
Suprarenal gland

227.1 Parathyroid gland

227.3 Pituitary gland and craniopharyngeal duct (pouch)
Craniobuccal pouch   Rathke's pouch
Hypophysis   Sella turcica

227.4 Pineal gland
Pineal body

227.5 Carotid body

227.6 Aortic body and other paraganglia
Coccygeal body   Para-aortic body
Glomus jugulare
AHA: N-D, '84, 17

227.8 Other

227.9 Endocrine gland, site unspecified

✓4ᵗʰ **228 Hemangioma and lymphangioma, any site**
INCLUDES angioma (benign) (cavernous) (congenital) NOS
cavernous nevus
glomus tumor
hemangioma (benign) (congenital)
EXCLUDES benign neoplasm of spleen, except hemangioma and lymphangioma (211.9)
glomus jugulare (227.6)
nevus:
NOS (216.0-216.9)
blue or pigmented (216.0-216.9)
vascular (757.32)
AHA: 1Q, '00, 21

✓5ᵗʰ **228.0 Hemangioma, any site**
DEF: A common benign tumor usually occurring in infancy; composed of newly formed blood vessels due to malformation of angioblastic tissue.
AHA: J-F, '85, 19

228.00 Of unspecified site

228.01 Of skin and subcutaneous tissue
AHA: 3Q, '10, 16

228.02 Of intracranial structures

228.03 Of retina

228.04 Of intra-abdominal structures
Peritoneum
Retroperitoneal tissue

228.09 Of other sites
Systemic angiomatosis
AHA: 3Q, '91, 20

228.1 Lymphangioma, any site
Congenital lymphangioma
Lymphatic nevus

✓4ᵗʰ **229 Benign neoplasm of other and unspecified sites**

229.0 Lymph nodes
EXCLUDES lymphangioma (228.1)

229.8 Other specified sites
Intrathoracic NOS
Thoracic NOS

229.9 Site unspecified

N Newborn Age: 0   P Pediatric Age: 0-17   M Maternity Age: 12-55   A Adult Age: 15-124   MCC Major CC Condition   CC CC Condition   HIV HIV Related Dx

54 – Volume 1   2015 ICD-9-CM

Carcinoma In Situ (230-234)

INCLUDES Bowen's disease
erythroplasia
Queyrat's erythroplasia

EXCLUDES *leukoplakia* — *see Alphabetic Index*

DEF: A neoplastic type; with tumor cells confined to epithelium of origin; without further invasion.

√4th **230 Carcinoma in situ of digestive organs**

230.0 Lip, oral cavity, and pharynx
Gingiva   Oropharynx
Hypopharynx   Salivary gland or duct
Mouth [any part]   Tongue
Nasopharynx
EXCLUDES *aryepiglottic fold or interarytenoid fold, laryngeal aspect (231.0)*
epiglottis:
NOS (231.0)
suprahyoid portion (231.0)
skin of lip (232.0)

230.1 Esophagus

230.2 Stomach
Body
Cardia } of stomach
Fundus
Cardiac orifice
Pylorus

230.3 Colon
Appendix
Cecum
Ileocecal valve
Large intestine NOS
EXCLUDES *rectosigmoid junction (230.4)*

230.4 Rectum
Rectosigmoid junction

230.5 Anal canal
Anal sphincter

230.6 Anus, unspecified
EXCLUDES *anus:*
margin (232.5)
skin (232.5)
perianal skin (232.5)

230.7 Other and unspecified parts of intestine
Duodenum
Ileum
Jejunum
Small intestine NOS
EXCLUDES *ampulla of Vater (230.8)*

230.8 Liver and biliary system
Ampulla of Vater
Common bile duct
Cystic duct
Gallbladder
Hepatic duct
Sphincter of Oddi

230.9 Other and unspecified digestive organs
Digestive organ NOS
Gastrointestinal tract NOS
Pancreas
Spleen

√4th **231 Carcinoma in situ of respiratory system**

231.0 Larynx
Cartilage: Epiglottis:
arytenoid   NOS
cricoid   posterior surface
cuneiform   suprahyoid portion
thyroid   Vocal cords (false)(true)
EXCLUDES *aryepiglottic fold or interarytenoid fold:*
NOS (230.0)
hypopharyngeal aspect (230.0)
marginal zone (230.0)

231.1 Trachea

231.2 Bronchus and lung
Carina   Hilus of lung

231.8 Other specified parts of respiratory system
Accessory sinuses
Middle ear
Nasal cavities
Pleura
EXCLUDES *ear (external) (skin) (232.2)*
nose NOS (234.8)
skin (232.3)

231.9 Respiratory system, part unspecified
Respiratory organ NOS

√4th **232 Carcinoma in situ of skin**
INCLUDES pigment cells
EXCLUDES *melanoma in situ of skin (172.0-172.9)*

232.0 Skin of lip
EXCLUDES *vermilion border of lip (230.0)*

232.1 Eyelid, including canthus

232.2 Ear and external auditory canal

232.3 Skin of other and unspecified parts of face

232.4 Scalp and skin of neck

232.5 Skin of trunk, except scrotum
Anus, margin   Skin of:
Axillary fold   breast
Perianal skin   buttock
Skin of: chest wall
  abdominal wall   groin
  anus   perineum
  back   Umbilicus
EXCLUDES *anal canal (230.5)*
anus NOS (230.6)
skin of genital organs (233.30-233.39, 233.5-233.6)

232.6 Skin of upper limb, including shoulder

232.7 Skin of lower limb, including hip

232.8 Other specified sites of skin

232.9 Skin, site unspecified

√4th **233 Carcinoma in situ of breast and genitourinary system**
TIP: For patients with carcinoma in situ found incidentally when admitted for treatment of another condition, sequence the 233 code as a secondary condition.

233.0 Breast
EXCLUDES *Paget's disease (174.0-174.9)*
skin of breast (232.5)
TIP: Assign for tumors specified as intraductal carcinoma.

233.1 Cervix uteri   ♀
Adenocarcinoma in situ of cervix
Cervical intraepithelial glandular neoplasia, grade III
Cervical intraepithelial neoplasia III [CIN III]
Severe dysplasia of cervix
EXCLUDES *cervical intraepithelial neoplasia II [CIN II] (622.12)*
cytologic evidence of malignancy without histologic confirmation (795.06)
high grade squamous intraepithelial lesion (HGSIL) (795.04)
moderate dysplasia of cervix (622.12)
AHA: 3Q, '92, 7; 3Q, '92, 8; 1Q, '91, 11

233.2 Other and unspecified parts of uterus   ♀

√5th **233.3 Other and unspecified female genital organs**
AHA: 4Q, '07, 67

    233.30 Unspecified female genital organ   ♀

    233.31 Vagina   ♀
    Severe dysplasia of vagina
    Vaginal intraepithelial neoplasia III [VAIN III]

    233.32 Vulva   ♀
    Severe dysplasia of vulva
    Vulvar intraepithelial neoplasia III [VIN III]

    233.39 Other female genital organ   ♀

233.4 Prostate   ♂

√4th √5th Additional Digit Required   Unacceptable PDx   Manifestation Code   Hospital Acquired Condition   ►◄ Revised Text   ● New Code   ▲ Revised Code Title

2015 ICD-9-CM   **Volume 1 – 55**

233.5   **Penis**   ♂

233.6   **Other and unspecified male genital organs**   ♂

233.7   **Bladder**
      AHA: 2Q, '12, 10

233.9   **Other and unspecified urinary organs**

✓4ᵗʰ **234   Carcinoma in situ of other and unspecified sites**

234.0   **Eye**
      EXCLUDES   *cartilage of eyelid (234.8)*
                      eyelid (skin) (232.1)
                      optic nerve (234.8)
                      orbital bone (234.8)

234.8   **Other specified sites**
      Endocrine gland [any]

234.9   **Site unspecified**
      Carcinoma in situ NOS

Neoplasms Of Uncertain Behavior (235-238)

NOTE   Categories 235–238 classify by site certain histomorphologically well-defined neoplasms, the subsequent behavior of which cannot be predicted from the present appearance.

TIP: Typically assigned for cases in which the tumor is in transition and may be undergoing malignant transformation, but continued study is required for accurate classification.

✓4ᵗʰ **235   Neoplasm of uncertain behavior of digestive and respiratory systems**
      EXCLUDES   *stromal tumors of uncertain behavior of digestive system (238.1)*

235.0   **Major salivary glands**
      Gland:
         parotid
         sublingual
         submandibular
      EXCLUDES   *minor salivary glands (235.1)*

235.1   **Lip, oral cavity, and pharynx**
      Gingiva   Nasopharynx
      Hypopharynx   Oropharynx
      Minor salivary glands   Tongue
      Mouth
      EXCLUDES   *aryepiglottic fold or interarytenoid fold, laryngeal*
                  aspect (235.6)
                  epiglottis:
                     NOS (235.6)
                     suprahyoid portion (235.6)
                  skin of lip (238.2)

235.2   **Stomach, intestines, and rectum**

235.3   **Liver and biliary passages**
      Ampulla of Vater
      Bile ducts [any]
      Gallbladder
      Liver

235.4   **Retroperitoneum and peritoneum**

235.5   **Other and unspecified digestive organs**
      Anal: Esophagus
        canal   Pancreas
        sphincter   Spleen
      Anus NOS
      EXCLUDES   *anus:*
                  margin (238.2)
                  skin (238.2)
                  perianal skin (238.2)

235.6   **Larynx**
      EXCLUDES   *aryepiglottic fold or interarytenoid fold:*
                  NOS (235.1)
                  hypopharyngeal aspect (235.1)
                  marginal zone (235.1)

235.7   **Trachea, bronchus, and lung**

235.8   **Pleura, thymus, and mediastinum**

235.9   **Other and unspecified respiratory organs**
      Accessory sinuses   Nasal cavities
      Middle ear   Respiratory organ NOS
      EXCLUDES   *ear (external) (skin) (238.2)*
                  nose (238.8)
                  skin (238.2)

✓4ᵗʰ **236   Neoplasm of uncertain behavior of genitourinary organs**

236.0   **Uterus**   ♀

236.1   **Placenta**   ♀
      Chorioadenoma (destruens)
      Invasive mole
      Malignant hydatid mole
      Malignant hydatidiform mole

236.2   **Ovary**   ♀
      Use additional code to identify any functional activity

236.3   **Other and unspecified female genital organs**   ♀

236.4   **Testis**   ♂
      Use additional code to identify any functional activity

236.5   **Prostate**   ♂

236.6   **Other and unspecified male genital organs**   ♂

236.7   **Bladder**

✓5ᵗʰ 236.9   **Other and unspecified urinary organs**

236.90   **Urinary organ, unspecified**

236.91   **Kidney and ureter**

236.99   **Other**

✓4ᵗʰ **237   Neoplasm of uncertain behavior of endocrine glands and nervous system**

237.0   **Pituitary gland and craniopharyngeal duct**
      Use additional code to identify any functional activity

237.1   **Pineal gland**

237.2   **Adrenal gland**
      Suprarenal gland
      Use additional code to identify any functional activity

237.3   **Paraganglia**
      Aortic body   Coccygeal body
      Carotid body   Glomus jugulare
      AHA: N-D, '84, 17

237.4   **Other and unspecified endocrine glands**
      Parathyroid gland   Thyroid gland

237.5   **Brain and spinal cord**

237.6   **Meninges**
      Meninges:
         NOS
         cerebral
         spinal
      AHA: ▶1Q, '14, 16◀

✓5ᵗʰ 237.7   **Neurofibromatosis**
      DEF: An inherited condition with developmental changes in the nervous system, muscles, bones and skin; multiple soft tumors (neurofibromas) distributed over the entire body.

237.70   **Neurofibromatosis, unspecified**

237.71   **Neurofibromatosis, type 1 [von Recklinghausen's disease]**
      AHA: 4Q, '10, 76

237.72   **Neurofibromatosis, type 2 [acoustic neurofibromatosis]**
      DEF: Inherited condition with cutaneous lesions, benign tumors of peripheral nerves and bilateral 8th nerve masses.
      AHA: 4Q, '10, 76

237.73   **Schwannomatosis**
      DEF: A genetic mutation (SMARCB1/INI1) causing multiple benign tumors along nerve pathways, characterized by the exception of 8th cranial nerve involvement.
      AHA: 4Q, '10, 76-77

237.79   **Other neurofibromatosis**
      AHA: 4Q, '10, 76-77

N Newborn Age: 0   P Pediatric Age: 0-17   M Maternity Age: 12-55   A Adult Age: 15-124   MCC Major CC Condition   CC CC Condition   HIV HIV Related Dx

56 – Volume 1 · October 2014   2015 ICD-9-CM

237.9 Other and unspecified parts of nervous system
Cranial nerves

EXCLUDES *peripheral, sympathetic, and parasympathetic nerves and ganglia (238.1)*

✓4th 238 Neoplasm of uncertain behavior of other and unspecified sites and tissues

238.0 Bone and articular cartilage
EXCLUDES *cartilage:*
ear (238.1)
eyelid (238.1)
larynx (235.6)
nose (235.9)
synovia (238.1)
AHA: 4Q, '04, 128

238.1 Connective and other soft tissue
Peripheral, sympathetic, and parasympathetic nerves and ganglia
Stromal tumors of digestive system
EXCLUDES *cartilage (of):*
articular (238.0)
larynx (235.6)
nose (235.9)
connective tissue of breast (238.3)

238.2 Skin
EXCLUDES *anus NOS (235.5)*
skin of genital organs (236.3, 236.6)
vermilion border of lip (235.1)
TIP: Assign when documentation indicates keratocanthoma only.

238.3 Breast
EXCLUDES *skin of breast (238.2)*

238.4 Polycythemia vera
DEF: Abnormal proliferation of all bone marrow elements, increased red cell mass and total blood volume; unknown etiology, frequently associated with splenomegaly, leukocytosis, and thrombocythemia.
D45 Polycythemia vera   I-10

238.5 Histiocytic and mast cells   CC
Mast cell tumor NOS
Mastocytoma NOS
CC Excl: 238.4-238.76, 238.79, 289.83, V58.0

238.6 Plasma cells   CC
Plasmacytoma NOS
Solitary myeloma
CC Excl: See code: 238.5

✓5th 238.7 Other lymphatic and hematopoietic tissues
EXCLUDES *acute myelogenous leukemia (205.0)*
chronic myelomonocytic leukemia (205.1)
myelosclerosis NOS (289.89)
myelosis:
NOS (205.9)
megakaryocytic (207.2)
AHA: 3Q, '01, 13; 1Q, '97, 5; 2Q, '89, 8

238.71 Essential thrombocythemia
Essential hemorrhagic thrombocythemia
Essential thrombocytosis
Idiopathic (hemorrhagic) thrombocythemia
Primary thrombocytosis
AHA: 4Q, '06, 63-66
D47.3 Essential (hemorrhagic) thrombocythemia   I-10

238.72 Low grade myelodysplastic syndrome lesions
Refractory anemia (RA)
Refractory anemia with excess blasts-1 (RAEB-1)
Refractory anemia with ringed sideroblasts (RARS)
Refractory cytopenia with multilineage dysplasia (RCMD)
Refractory cytopenia with multilineage dysplasia and ringed sideroblasts (RCMD-RS)
DEF: Refractory anemia (RA): Form of bone marrow disorder (myelodysplastic syndrome) that interferes with red blood cell production in the bone marrow; unresponsive to hematinics; characteristic normal or hypercellular marrow with abnormal erythrocyte development and reticulocytopenia.
AHA: 4Q, '06, 63-66

238.73 High grade myelodysplastic syndrome lesions   CC
Refractory anemia with excess blasts-2 (RAEB-2)
CC Excl: 202.40-202.48, 203.10-203.11, 203.80-203.81, 204.00-208.92, 238.4-238.76, 238.79-238.9
AHA: 4Q, '06, 63-66

238.74 Myelodysplastic syndrome with 5q deletion   CC
5q minus syndrome NOS
EXCLUDES *constitutional 5q deletion (758.39)*
high grade myelodysplastic syndrome with 5q deletion (238.73)
CC Excl: See code: 238.73
AHA: 4Q, '06, 63-66

238.75 Myelodysplastic syndrome, unspecified
AHA: 4Q, '06, 63-66
D46.9 Myelodysplastic syndrome unspecified   I-10

238.76 Myelofibrosis with myeloid metaplasia   CC
Agnogenic myeloid metaplasia
Idiopathic myelofibrosis (chronic)
Myelosclerosis with myeloid metaplasia
Primary myelofibrosis
EXCLUDES *myelofibrosis NOS (289.83)*
myelophthisic anemia (284.2)
myelophthisis (284.2)
secondary myelofibrosis (289.83)
CC Excl: See code: 238.73
AHA: 4Q, '06, 63-66

238.77 Post-transplant lymphoproliferative disorder [PTLD]   CC
Code first complications of transplant (996.80-996.89)
DEF: Excessive proliferation of B-cell lymphocytes following Epstein-Barr virus infection in organ transplant patients; may progress to non-Hodgkins lymphoma.
CC Excl: 238.77, 996.80, 996.87, 997.91-997.99
AHA: 4Q, '08, 90-91

238.79 Other lymphatic and hematopoietic tissues   CC
Lymphoproliferative disease (chronic) NOS
Megakaryocytic myelosclerosis
Myeloproliferative disease (chronic) NOS
Panmyelosis (acute)
CC Excl: 202.40-202.48, 203.10-203.11, 203.80-203.81, 204.00-208.92, 238.4-238.76, 238.79-238.9
AHA: 4Q, '06, 63-66

238.8 Other specified sites
Eye
Heart
EXCLUDES *eyelid (skin) (238.2)*
cartilage (238.1)

238.9 Site unspecified

Neoplasms of Unspecified Nature (239)

✓4th 239 Neoplasms of unspecified nature
NOTE Category 239 classifies by site neoplasms of unspecified morphology and behavior. The term "mass," unless otherwise stated, is not to be regarded as a neoplastic growth.
INCLUDES "growth" NOS
neoplasm NOS
new growth NOS
tumor NOS
TIP: Do not assign for inpatient cases; more information should be available.

239.0 Digestive system
EXCLUDES *anus:*
margin (239.2)
skin (239.2)
perianal skin (239.2)

239.1 Respiratory system

Neoplasms

239.2–239.9

239.2 Bone, soft tissue, and skin

> EXCLUDES   anal canal (239.0)
>   anus NOS (239.0)
>   bone marrow (202.9)
>   cartilage:
>   larynx (239.1)
>   nose (239.1)
>   connective tissue of breast (239.3)
>   skin of genital organs (239.5)
>   vermilion border of lip (239.0)

239.3 Breast

> EXCLUDES   skin of breast (239.2)

239.4 Bladder

239.5 Other genitourinary organs

239.6 Brain

> EXCLUDES   cerebral meninges (239.7)
>   cranial nerves (239.7)

239.7 Endocrine glands and other parts of nervous system

> EXCLUDES   peripheral, sympathetic, and parasympathetic nerves
>   and ganglia (239.2)

√5th **239.8 Other specified sites**

> EXCLUDES   eyelid (skin) (239.2)
>   cartilage (239.2)
>   great vessels (239.2)
>   optic nerve (239.7)

AHA: 4Q, '09, 75

239.81 Retina and choroid
Dark area on retina
Retinal freckle

TIP: Assign for documentation of retinal "freckles" or spots that may be indicative of malignant melanoma. Histologic confirmation not required.

239.89 Other specified sites

239.9 Site unspecified

N Newborn Age: 0   P Pediatric Age: 0-17   M Maternity Age: 12-55   A Adult Age: 15-124   MCC Major CC Condition   CC CC Condition   HIV HIV Related Dx

58 – Volume 1   2015 ICD-9-CM

3. Endocrine, Nutritional and Metabolic Diseases, and Immunity Disorders (240-279)

EXCLUDES *endocrine and metabolic disturbances specific to the fetus and newborn (775.0-775.9)*

NOTE All neoplasms, whether functionally active or not, are classified in Chapter 2. Codes in Chapter 3 (i.e., 242.8, 246.0, 251-253, 255-259) may be used to identify such functional activity associated with any neoplasm, or by ectopic endocrine tissue.

Disorders of Thyroid Gland (240-246)

✓4ᵗʰ 240 Simple and unspecified goiter

> **DEF:** An enlarged thyroid gland often caused by an inadequate dietary intake of iodine.

240.0 Goiter, specified as simple

> Any condition classifiable to 240.9, specified as simple

240.9 Goiter, unspecified

> Enlargement of thyroid
> Goiter or struma:
>   NOS
>   diffuse colloid
>   endemic
> Goiter or struma:
>   hyperplastic
>   nontoxic (diffuse)
>   parenchymatous
>   sporadic
>
> **EXCLUDES** *congenital (dyshormonogenic) goiter (246.1)*

✓4ᵗʰ 241 Nontoxic nodular goiter

> **EXCLUDES** *adenoma of thyroid (226)*
> *cystadenoma of thyroid (226)*

241.0 Nontoxic uninodular goiter

> Thyroid nodule   Uninodular goiter (nontoxic)
> **DEF:** Enlarged thyroid, commonly due to decreased thyroid production, with single nodule; no clinical hypothyroidism.
> **E04.1** Nontoxic single thyroid nodule   I-10

241.1 Nontoxic multinodular goiter

> Multinodular goiter (nontoxic)
> **DEF:** Enlarged thyroid, commonly due to decreased thyroid production with multiple nodules; no clinical hypothyroidism.

241.9 Unspecified nontoxic nodular goiter

> Adenomatous goiter
> Nodular goiter (nontoxic) NOS
> Struma nodosa (simplex)

✓4ᵗʰ 242 Thyrotoxicosis with or without goiter

> **EXCLUDES** *neonatal thyrotoxicosis (775.3)*
> **DEF:** A condition caused by excess quantities of thyroid hormones being introduced into the tissues
>
> The following fifth-digit subclassification is for use with categories 242:
>   **0 without mention of thyrotoxic crisis or storm**
>   **1 with mention of thyrotoxic crisis or storm**

§ ✓5ᵗʰ 242.0 Toxic diffuse goiter   MCC 1
[0-1]
> Basedow's disease
> Exophthalmic or toxic goiter NOS
> Graves' disease
> Primary thyroid hyperplasia
> **DEF:** Diffuse thyroid enlargement accompanied by hyperthyroidism, bulging eyes, and dermopathy.
> **CC Excl:** For code 242.01: 017.50-017.56, 017.90-017.96, 240.0-246.9, 259.50-259.9

§ ✓5ᵗʰ 242.1 Toxic uninodular goiter   MCC 1
[0-1]
> Thyroid nodule
> Uninodular goiter } toxic or with hyperthyroidism
> **DEF:** Symptomatic hyperthyroidism with a single nodule on the enlarged thyroid gland. Abrupt onset of symptoms; including extreme nervousness, insomnia, weight loss, tremors, and psychosis or coma.
> **CC Excl:** See code 242.0

§ ✓5ᵗʰ 242.2 Toxic multinodular goiter   MCC 1
[0-1]
> Secondary thyroid hyperplasia
> **DEF:** Symptomatic hyperthyroidism with multiple nodules on the enlarged thyroid gland. Abrupt onset of symptoms; including extreme nervousness, insomnia, weight loss, tremors, and psychosis or coma.
> **CC Excl:** See code 242.0

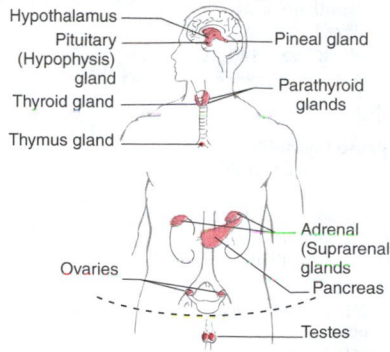

The Endocrine System

§ ✓5ᵗʰ 242.3 Toxic nodular goiter, unspecified   MCC 1
[0-1]
> Adenomatous goiter
> Nodular goiter } toxic or with hyperthyroidism
> Struma nodosa
>
> Any condition classifiable to 241.9 specified as toxic or with hyperthyroidism
> **CC Excl:** See code 242.0

§ ✓5ᵗʰ 242.4 Thyrotoxicosis from ectopic thyroid nodule   MCC 1
[0-1]   **CC Excl:** See code 242.0

§ ✓5ᵗʰ 242.8 Thyrotoxicosis of other specified origin   MCC 1
[0-1]
> Overproduction of thyroid-stimulating hormone [TSH]
> Thyrotoxicosis:
>   factitia from ingestion of excessive thyroid material
> **Use additional E code to identify cause, if drug-induced**
> **CC Excl:** See code 242.0

§ ✓5ᵗʰ 242.9 Thyrotoxicosis without mention of goiter   MCC 1
[0-1]   **or other cause**
> Hyperthyroidism NOS
> Thyrotoxicosis NOS
> **CC Excl:** See code 242.0
> **E05.90** Thyrotoxicosis uns w/o thyrotoxic crisis or storm   I-10

243 Congenital hypothyroidism

> Congenital thyroid insufficiency
> Cretinism (athyrotic) (endemic)
> **Use additional code to identify associated intellectual disabilities**
> **EXCLUDES** *congenital (dyshormonogenic) goiter (246.1)*
> **DEF:** Underproduction of thyroid hormone present from birth.

✓4ᵗʰ 244 Acquired hypothyroidism

> **INCLUDES** athyroidism (acquired)
> hypothyroidism (acquired)
> myxedema (adult) (juvenile)
> thyroid (gland) insufficiency (acquired)

244.0 Postsurgical hypothyroidism

> **DEF:** Underproduction of thyroid hormone due to surgical removal of all or part of the thyroid gland.
> **E89.0** Postprocedural hypothyroidism   I-10

244.1 Other postablative hypothyroidism

> Hypothyroidism following therapy, such as irradiation

244.2 Iodine hypothyroidism

> Hypothyroidism resulting from administration or ingestion of iodine
> **Use additional E code to identify drug**
> **EXCLUDES** *hypothyroidism resulting from administration of radioactive iodine (244.1)*

244.3 Other iatrogenic hypothyroidism

> Hypothyroidism resulting from:
>   P-aminosalicylic acid [PAS]
>   Phenylbutazone
>   Resorcinol
> Iatrogenic hypothyroidism NOS
> **Use additional E code to identify drug**

244.8 Other specified acquired hypothyroidism

> Secondary hypothyroidism NEC
> **AHA:** J-A, '85, 9

---

§   Requires fifth digit. Valid digits are in [brackets] under each code. See category 242 for codes and definitions.

| ✓4ᵗʰ ✓5ᵗʰ Additional Digit Required | Unacceptable PDx | Manifestation Code | Hospital Acquired Condition | ►◄ Revised Text | ● New Code | ▲ Revised Code Title |

Endocrine, Nutritional and Metabolic Diseases, and Immunity

244.9–249.6

244.9 Unspecified hypothyroidism
Hypothyroidism } primary or NOS
Myxedema
AHA: 3Q, '99, 19; 4Q, '96, 29
E03.9 Hypothyroidism unspecified   `I-10`

✓4ᵗʰ **245 Thyroiditis**

245.0 Acute thyroiditis   `CC`
Abscess of thyroid
Thyroiditis:
  nonsuppurative, acute
  pyogenic
  suppurative
Use additional code to identify organism
DEF: Inflamed thyroid caused by infection, with abscess and liquid puris.
CC Excl: 245.0-245.9

245.1 Subacute thyroiditis
Thyroiditis:
  de Quervain's
  giant cell
  granulomatous
  viral
DEF: Inflammation of the thyroid, characterized by fever and painful enlargement of the thyroid gland, with granulomas in the gland.

245.2 Chronic lymphocytic thyroiditis
Hashimoto's disease
Struma lymphomatosa
Thyroiditis:
  autoimmune
  lymphocytic (chronic)
DEF: Autoimmune disease of thyroid; lymphocytes infiltrate the gland and thyroid antibodies are produced; women more often affected.

245.3 Chronic fibrous thyroiditis
Struma fibrosa
Thyroiditis:
  invasive (fibrous)
  ligneous
  Riedel's
DEF: Persistent fibrosing inflammation of thyroid with adhesions to nearby structures; rare condition

245.4 Iatrogenic thyroiditis
Use additional code to identify cause
DEF: Thyroiditis resulting from treatment or intervention by physician or in a patient intervention setting.

245.8 Other and unspecified chronic thyroiditis
Chronic thyroiditis:
  NOS
  nonspecific

245.9 Thyroiditis, unspecified
Thyroiditis NOS

✓4ᵗʰ **246 Other disorders of thyroid**

246.0 Disorders of thyrocalcitonin secretion
Hypersecretion of calcitonin or thyrocalcitonin

246.1 Dyshormonogenic goiter
Congenital (dyshormonogenic) goiter
Goiter due to enzyme defect in synthesis of thyroid hormone
Goitrous cretinism (sporadic)

246.2 Cyst of thyroid
EXCLUDES cystadenoma of thyroid (226)

246.3 Hemorrhage and infarction of thyroid   `CC`
CC Excl: 246.3

246.8 Other specified disorders of thyroid
Abnormality of thyroid-binding globulin
Atrophy of thyroid
Hyper-TBG-nemia
Hypo-TBG-nemia
AHA: 2Q, '06, 5

246.9 Unspecified disorder of thyroid
E07.9 Disorder of thyroid unspecified   `I-10`

Diseases of Other Endocrine Glands (249-259)

✓4ᵗʰ **249 Secondary diabetes mellitus**
INCLUDES   diabetes mellitus (due to) (in) (secondary) (with):
    drug-induced or chemical induced
    infection
Use additional code to identify any associated insulin use (V58.67)
EXCLUDES   gestational diabetes (648.8)
    hyperglycemia NOS (790.29)
    neonatal diabetes mellitus (775.1)
    nonclinical diabetes (790.29)
    Type I diabetes — see category 250
    Type II diabetes — see category 250
AHA: 4Q, '08, 91-95
TIP: If the secondary DM is due to pancreatectomy, code first 251.3 Postsurgical hypoinsulinemia; also assign a code from category 249 and any manifestations, and code V88.1x Acquired absence of pancreas.

The following fifth-digit subclassification is for use with category 249:
  0 not stated as uncontrolled, or unspecified
  1 uncontrolled

§ ✓5ᵗʰ **249.0 Secondary diabetes mellitus without mention**
[0-1]   **of complication**
Secondary diabetes mellitus without mention of complication or manifestation classifiable to 249.1-249.9
Secondary diabetes mellitus NOS
E09.9 Drug/chemical induced diabetes mellitus w/o comp   `I-10`

§ ✓5ᵗʰ **249.1 Secondary diabetes mellitus with ketoacidosis**   `MCC`
[0-1]
Secondary diabetes mellitus with diabetic acidosis without mention of coma
Secondary diabetes mellitus with diabetic ketosis without mention of coma
CC Excl: 249.00-251.3, 259.8-259.9

§ ✓5ᵗʰ **249.2 Secondary diabetes mellitus with hyperosmolarity**   `MCC`
[0-1]
Secondary diabetes mellitus with hyperosmolar (nonketotic) coma
CC Excl: See code: 249.1

§ ✓5ᵗʰ **249.3 Secondary diabetes mellitus with other coma**   `MCC`
[0-1]
Secondary diabetes mellitus with diabetic coma (with ketoacidosis)
Secondary diabetes mellitus with diabetic hypoglycemic coma
Secondary diabetes mellitus with insulin coma NOS
EXCLUDES   secondary diabetes mellitus with hyperosmolar coma (249.2)
CC Excl: See code: 249.1

§ ✓5ᵗʰ **249.4 Secondary diabetes mellitus with renal manifestations**
[0-1]
Use additional code to identify manifestation, as:
  chronic kidney disease (585.1-585.9)
  diabetic nephropathy NOS (583.81)
  diabetic nephrosis (581.81)
  intercapillary glomerulosclerosis (581.81)
  Kimmelstiel-Wilson syndrome (581.81)

§ ✓5ᵗʰ **249.5 Secondary diabetes mellitus with ophthalmic**
[0-1]   **manifestations**
Use additional code to identify manifestation, as:
  diabetic blindness (369.00-369.9)
  diabetic cataract (366.41)
  diabetic glaucoma (365.44)
  diabetic macular edema (362.07)
  diabetic retinal edema (362.07)
  diabetic retinopathy (362.01-362.07)

§ ✓5ᵗʰ **249.6 Secondary diabetes mellitus with neurological**
[0-1]   **manifestations**
Use additional code to identify manifestation, as:
  diabetic amyotrophy (353.5)
  diabetic gastroparalysis (536.3)
  diabetic gastroparesis (536.3)
  diabetic mononeuropathy (354.0-355.9)
  diabetic neurogenic arthropathy (713.5)
  diabetic peripheral autonomic neuropathy (337.1)
  diabetic polyneuropathy (357.2)
AHA: For code 249.60: 4Q, '08, 94

---

§   Requires fifth digit. Valid digits are in [brackets] under each code. See category 249 for codes and definitions.

`N` Newborn Age: 0   `P` Pediatric Age: 0-17   `M` Maternity Age: 12-55   `A` Adult Age: 15-124   `MCC` Major CC Condition   `CC` CC Condition   `HIV` HIV Related Dx

60 – Volume 1   2015 ICD-9-CM

§ ✓5th **249.7 Secondary diabetes mellitus with peripheral**
[0-1]   **circulatory disorders**
    Use additional code to identify manifestation, as:
      diabetic gangrene (785.4)
      diabetic peripheral angiopathy (443.81)

§ ✓5th **249.8 Secondary diabetes mellitus with other**
[0-1]   **specified manifestations**
    Secondary diabetic hypoglycemia in diabetes mellitus
    Secondary hypoglycemic shock in diabetes mellitus
    Use additional code to identify manifestation, as:
      any associated ulceration (707.10-707.19, 707.8, 707.9)
      diabetic bone changes (731.8)

§ ✓5th **249.9 Secondary diabetes mellitus with unspecified complication**
[0-1]

✓4th **250 Diabetes mellitus**
    EXCLUDES   *gestational diabetes (648.8)*
       hyperglycemia NOS (790.29)
       neonatal diabetes mellitus (775.1)
       nonclinical diabetes (790.29)
       secondary diabetes (249.0-249.9)

> The following fifth-digit subclassification is for use with category 250:
> **0 type II or unspecified type, not state as uncontrolled**
>   Fifth-digit 0 is for use for type II patients, even if the patient requires insulin
>   Use additional code, if applicable, for associated long-term (current) insulin use (V58.67)
> **1 type I [juvenile type], not stated as uncontrolled**
> **2 type II or unspecified type, uncontrolled**
>   Fifth-digit 2 is for use for type II patients, even if the patient requires insulin
>   Use additional code, if applicable, for associated long-term (current) insulin use (V58.67)
> **3 type I [juvenile type], uncontrolled**

DEF: Diabetes mellitus: Inability to metabolize carbohydrates, proteins, and fats due to insufficient secretion of insulin. Symptoms may be unremarkable, with long-term complications, involving kidneys, nerves, blood vessels, and eyes.

DEF: Uncontrolled diabetes: A nonspecific term indicating that the current treatment regimen does not keep the blood sugar level of a patient within acceptable levels.

AHA: 1Q, '11, 9; 4Q, '04, 56; 2Q, '04, 17; 2Q, '02, 13; 2Q,'01, 16; 2Q,'98, 15; 4Q, '97, 32; 2Q, '97, 14; 3Q, '96, 5; 4Q, '93, 19; 2Q, '92, 5; 3Q, '91, 3; 2Q, '90, 22; N-D, '85, 11

TIP: Use of insulin does not ensure type I DM; if patient is on routine insulin, assign also V58.67 Long-term (current) use of insulin.

7 § ✓5th **250.0 Diabetes mellitus without mention of complication**
[0-3]   Diabetes mellitus without mention of complication or
      manifestation classifiable to 250.1-250.9
    Diabetes (mellitus) NOS
    AHA: 1Q, '06, 14; 4Q, '97, 32; 3Q, '91, 3, 12; N-D, '85, 11; **For code 250.00:** ▶3Q, '13, 13;◀ 2Q, '12, 19; 4Q, '09, 77; 1Q, '05, 15; 4Q, '04, 55; 4Q, '03, 105, 108; 2Q, '03, 16; 1Q, '02, 7, 11; **For code 250.01:** 4Q, '04, 55; 4Q, '03, 110; 2Q, '03, 6; **For code 250.02:** 1Q, '03, 5; **For code 250.03:** ▶3Q, '13, 9◀
    E11.9 Type 2 diabetes mellitus w/o comp   I-10

§ ✓5th **250.1 Diabetes with ketoacidosis**   MCC
[0-3]   Diabetic:
     acidosis
     ketosis } without mention of coma
    DEF: Diabetic hyperglycemic crisis causing ketone presence in body fluids.
    CC Excl: For code 250.10: 249.00-251.3, 259.8-259.9;
    For code 250.11-250.13: 249.00-251.3, 259.50-259.9
    AHA: 3Q, '91, 6; **For code 250.11:** 2Q, '06, 19-20; 4Q, '03, 82; **For code 250.13:** 2Q, '06, 19-20
    E10.10 Type 1 diabetes mellitus w/ketoacidosis w/o coma   I-10

§ ✓5th **250.2 Diabetes with hyperosmolarity**   MCC
[0-3]   Hyperosmolar (nonketotic) coma
    CC Excl: For code 250.20: 249.00-251.3, 259.8-259.9;
    For code 250.21-250.23: 249.00-251.3, 259.50-259.9
    AHA: 4Q, '93, 19; 3Q, '91, 7

§ ✓5th **250.3 Diabetes with other coma**   MCC
[0-3]   Diabetic coma (with ketoacidosis)
    Diabetic hypoglycemic coma
    Insulin coma NOS
    EXCLUDES   *diabetes with hyperosmolar coma (250.2)*
    DEF: Coma (not hyperosmolar) caused by hyperglycemia or hypoglycemia as complication of diabetes.
    CC Excl: For code 250.30: 249.00-251.3, 259.8-259.9; **For code 250.31-250.33:** 249.00-251.3, 259.50-259.9
    AHA: 3Q, '91, 7, 12

§ ✓5th **250.4 Diabetes with renal manifestations**
[0-3]   Use additional code to identify manifestation, as:
      chronic kidney disease (585.1-585.9)
      diabetic:
        nephropathy NOS (583.81)
        nephrosis (581.81)
      intercapillary glomerulosclerosis (581.81)
      Kimmelstiel-Wilson syndrome (581.81)
    AHA: 3Q, '91, 8, 12; S-O, '87, 9; S-O, '84, 3; **For code 250.40:** 2Q, '12, 19; 1Q, '03, 20; **For code 250.41:** ▶2Q, '13, 6◀
    E11.22 Type 2 diabetes mellitus w/diabetic ckd   I-10

§ ✓5th **250.5 Diabetes with ophthalmic manifestations**
[0-3]   Use additional code to identify manifestation, as:
      diabetic:
       blindness (369.00-369.9)
       cataract (366.41)
       glaucoma (365.44)
       macular edema (362.07)
       retinal edema (362.07)
       retinopathy (362.01-362.07)
    AHA: 4Q, '05, 65; 3Q, '91, 8; S-O, '85, 11; **For code 250.50:** 4Q, '05, 67
    E10.36 Type 1 diabetes mellitus with diabetic cataract   I-10

§ ✓5th **250.6 Diabetes with neurological manifestations**
[0-3]   Use additional code to identify manifestation, as:
      diabetic:
       amyotrophy (353.5)
       gastroparalysis (536.3)
       gastroparesis (536.3)
       mononeuropathy (354.0-355.9)
       neurogenic arthropathy (713.5)
       peripheral autonomic neuropathy (337.1)
       polyneuropathy (357.2)
    AHA: 4Q, '09, 151; 2Q, '09, 13, 15; 3Q, '08, 5; 2Q, '93, 6; 2Q, '92, 15; 3Q, '91, 9; N-D, '84, 9; **For code 250.60:** 4Q, '03, 105; **For code 250.61:** 2Q, '04, 7
    E11.40 Type 2 diabetes mellitus w/diab neuropathy   I-10

§ ✓5th **250.7 Diabetes with peripheral circulatory disorders**
[0-3]   Use additional code to identify manifestation, as:
      diabetic:
       gangrene (785.4)
       peripheral angiopathy (443.81)
    DEF: Blood vessel damage or disease, usually in the feet, legs, or hands, as a complication of diabetes.
    AHA: 1Q, '96, 10; 3Q, '94, 5; 2Q, '94, 17; 3Q, '91, 10, 12; 3Q, '90, 15; **For code 250.70:** 1Q, '04, 14
    E10.51 Type 1 DM w/diab periph angiopathy w/o gangrene   I-10

§ ✓5th **250.8 Diabetes with other specified manifestations**
[0-3]   Diabetic hypoglycemia NOS
    Hypoglycemic shock NOS
    Use additional code to identify manifestation, as:
      any associated ulceration (707.10-707.19, 707.8, 707.9)
      diabetic bone changes (731.8)
    AHA: 4Q, '00, 44; 4Q, '97, 43; 2Q, '97, 16; 4Q, '93, 20; 3Q, '91, 10; **For code 250.80:** 1Q, '04, 14
    TIP: Assign for diabetic osteomyelitis, along with code 731.8 and the appropriate code from category 730.
    E11.618 Type 2 DM with other diabetic arthropathy   I-10

§ ✓5th **250.9 Diabetes with unspecified complication**
[0-3]   **AHA:** 2Q, '92, 15; 3Q, '91, 7, 12
    TIP: Do not assign with any other code in category 250.
    E10.8 Type 1 diabetes mellitus with unspecified comp   I-10

---

§   Requires fifth digit. Valid digits are in [brackets] under each code. See appropriate category for codes and definitions.
7   Questionable admission when fifth-digit = 0

 Additional Digit Required   Unacceptable PDx   Manifestation Code   Hospital Acquired Condition   ▶◀ Revised Text   ● New Code   ▲ Revised Code Title

√4ᵗʰ **251 Other disorders of pancreatic internal secretion**

251.0 Hypoglycemic coma   `CC`
Iatrogenic hyperinsulinism
Non-diabetic insulin coma
Use additional E code to identify cause, if drug-induced
EXCLUDES *hypoglycemic coma in diabetes mellitus (249.3, 250.3)*
DEF: Coma induced by low blood sugar in non-diabetic patient.
CC Excl: 2249.00-251.3, 259.50-259.9
AHA: M-A, '85, 8

251.1 Other specified hypoglycemia
Hyperinsulinism:
  NOS
  ectopic
  functional
Hyperplasia of pancreatic
  islet beta cells NOS
Use additional E code to identify cause, if drug-induced.
EXCLUDES *hypoglycemia:*
  in diabetes mellitus (249.8, 250.8)
  in infant of diabetic mother (775.0)
  hypoglycemic coma (251.0)
  neonatal hypoglycemia (775.6)
DEF: Excessive production of insulin by the pancreas; associated with obesity and insulin-producing tumors.
AHA: ▶3Q, '13, 12;◀ 1Q, '03, 10

251.2 Hypoglycemia, unspecified
Hypoglycemia: Hypoglycemia:
  NOS   spontaneous
  reactive
EXCLUDES *hypoglycemia:*
  with coma (251.0)
  in diabetes mellitus (249.8, 250.8)
  leucine-induced (270.3)
AHA: M-A, '85, 8
`I-10` **E16.2** Hypoglycemia unspecified

251.3 Postsurgical hypoinsulinemia   `CC`
Hypoinsulinemia following complete or partial
  pancreatectomy
Postpancreatectomy hyperglycemia
Use additional code to identify (any associated):
  acquired absence of pancreas (V88.11-V88.12)
  insulin use (V58.67)
  secondary diabetes mellitus (249.00-249.91)
EXCLUDES *transient hyperglycemia post procedure (790.29)*
  transient hypoglycemia post procedure (251.2)
CC Excl: See code: 251.0
AHA: 3Q, '91, 6

251.4 Abnormality of secretion of glucagon
Hyperplasia of pancreatic islet alpha cells with glucagon
  excess
DEF: Production malfunction of a pancreatic hormone secreted by cells of the islets of Langerhans.

251.5 Abnormality of secretion of gastrin
Hyperplasia of pancreatic alpha cells with gastrin excess
Zollinger-Ellison syndrome

251.8 Other specified disorders of pancreatic internal secretion
AHA: 2Q, '98, 15; 3Q, '91, 6
`I-10` **E16.8** Oth spec d/o of pancreatic internal secretion

251.9 Unspecified disorder of pancreatic internal secretion
Islet cell hyperplasia NOS

√4ᵗʰ **252 Disorders of parathyroid gland**
EXCLUDES *hungry bone syndrome (275.5)*

√5ᵗʰ **252.0 Hyperparathyroidism**
EXCLUDES *ectopic hyperparathyroidism (259.3)*
DEF: Abnormally high secretion of parathyroid hormones causing bone deterioration, reduced renal function, kidney stones.

  252.00 Hyperparathyroidism, unspecified
  `I-10` **E21.3** Hyperparathyroidism unspecified

Dorsal View of Parathyroid Glands

  252.01 Primary hyperparathyroidism
  Hyperplasia of parathyroid
  DEF: Parathyroid dysfunction commonly caused by hyperplasia of two or more glands; characteristic hypercalcemia and increased parathyroid hormone levels.

  252.02 Secondary hyperparathyroidism, non-renal
  EXCLUDES *secondary hyperparathyroidism (of renal origin) (588.81)*
  DEF: Underlying disease of nonrenal origin decreases blood levels of calcium causing the parathyroid to release increased levels of parathyroid hormone; parathyroid hormone levels return to normal once underlying condition is treated and blood calcium levels are normal.
  AHA: 4Q, '04, 57-59

  252.08 Other hyperparathyroidism
  Tertiary hyperparathyroidism
  DEF: Tertiary hyperparathyroidism: chronic secondary hyperparathyroidism with adenomatous parathyroid causing irreversible abnormal production of parathyroid hormone (PTH); PTH remains high after the serum calcium levels are brought under control.

252.1 Hypoparathyroidism
Parathyroiditis (autoimmune)
Tetany:
  parathyroid
  parathyroprival
EXCLUDES *pseudohypoparathyroidism (275.4)*
  pseudopseudohypoparathyroidism (275.4)
  tetany NOS (781.7)
  transitory neonatal hypoparathyroidism (775.4)
DEF: Abnormally low secretion of parathyroid hormones which causes decreased calcium and increased phosphorus in the blood, resulting in muscle cramps, tetany, urinary frequency and cataracts.

252.8 Other specified disorders of parathyroid gland
Cyst   } of parathyroid
Hemorrhage

252.9 Unspecified disorder of parathyroid gland

√4ᵗʰ **253 Disorders of the pituitary gland and its hypothalamic control**
INCLUDES the listed conditions whether the disorder is in the pituitary or the hypothalamus
EXCLUDES *Cushing's syndrome (255.0)*

253.0 Acromegaly and gigantism
Overproduction of growth hormone
DEF: Acromegaly: chronic, middle age condition; caused by hypersecretion of the pituitary growth hormone; enlarged parts of skeleton, especially the nose, ears, jaws, fingers and toes.
DEF: Gigantism: pituitary gigantism caused by excess growth of short flat bones; men may grow 78 to 80 inches tall.

253.1 Other and unspecified anterior pituitary hyperfunction   `CC`
Forbes-Albright syndrome
EXCLUDES *overproduction of:*
  ACTH (255.3)
  thyroid-stimulating hormone [TSH] (242.8)
DEF: Spontaneous galactorrhea-amenorrhea syndrome unrelated to pregnancy; usually related to presence of pituitary tumor.
CC Excl: 253.1, 253.4, 253.6
AHA: J-A, '85, 9

`N` Newborn Age: 0   `P` Pediatric Age: 0-17   `M` Maternity Age: 12-55   `A` Adult Age: 15-124   `MCC` Major CC Condition   `CC` CC Condition   `HIV` HIV Related Dx

62 – Volume 1 · October 2014   2015 ICD-9-CM

253.2 Panhypopituitarism   `CC`
Cachexia, pituitary
Necrosis of pituitary
Pituitary insufficiency NOS
Simmonds' disease
Sheehan's syndrome (postpartum)
EXCLUDES *iatrogenic hypopituitarism (253.7)*
DEF: Damage to or absence of pituitary gland leading to impaired sexual function, weight loss, fatigue, bradycardia, hypotension, pallor, depression, and impaired growth in children; called Simmonds' disease if cachexia is prominent.
CC Excl: 253.0-253.9, 259.50-259.9

253.3 Pituitary dwarfism
Isolated deficiency of (human) growth hormone [HGH]
Lorain-Levi dwarfism
DEF: Dwarfism with infantile physical characteristics due to abnormally low secretion of growth hormone and gonadotropin deficiency.

253.4 Other anterior pituitary disorders
Isolated or partial deficiency of an anterior pituitary hormone, other than growth hormone
Prolactin deficiency
AHA: J-A, '85, 9

253.5 Diabetes insipidus   `CC`
Vasopressin deficiency
EXCLUDES *nephrogenic diabetes insipidus (588.1)*
DEF: Metabolic disorder causing insufficient antidiuretic hormone release; symptoms include frequent urination, thirst, ravenous hunger, loss of weight, fatigue.
CC Excl: 253.1-253.2, 253.4-253.9, 259.50-259.9

253.6 Other disorders of neurohypophysis   `CC`
Syndrome of inappropriate secretion of antidiuretic hormone [ADH]
EXCLUDES *ectopic antidiuretic hormone secretion (259.3)*
CC Excl: 253.0-253.9, 259.8-259.9
E22.2 Synd inappropriate secrectn antidiuretic hormone   `I-10`

253.7 Iatrogenic pituitary disorders
Hypopituitarism:
    hormone-induced
    hypophysectomy-induced
    postablative
    radiotherapy-induced
Use additional E code to identify cause
DEF: Pituitary dysfunction that results from drug therapy, radiation therapy, or surgery, causing mild to severe symptoms.

253.8 Other disorders of the pituitary and other syndromes of diencephalohypophyseal origin
Abscess of pituitary
Adiposogenital dystrophy
Cyst of Rathke's pouch
Fröhlich's syndrome
EXCLUDES *craniopharyngioma (237.0)*

253.9 Unspecified
Dyspituitarism

254 Diseases of thymus gland   `✓4ᵗʰ`
EXCLUDES *aplasia or dysplasia with immunodeficiency (279.2)*
hypoplasia with immunodeficiency (279.2)
myasthenia gravis (358.00-358.01)

254.0 Persistent hyperplasia of thymus
Hypertrophy of thymus
DEF: Continued abnormal growth of the twin lymphoid lobes that produce T lymphocytes.

254.1 Abscess of thymus   `CC`
CC Excl: 254.0-254.9, 259.50-259.9

254.8 Other specified diseases of thymus gland
Astrophy ⎫
Cyst   ⎬ of thymus
EXCLUDES *thymoma (212.6)*

254.9 Unspecified disease of thymus gland

255 Disorders of adrenal glands   `✓4ᵗʰ`
INCLUDES the listed conditions whether the basic disorder is in the adrenals or is pituitary-induced

255.0 Cushing's syndrome   `CC`
Adrenal hyperplasia due to excess ACTH
Cushing's syndrome:
    NOS
    iatrogenic
    idiopathic
    pituitary-dependent
Ectopic ACTH syndrome
Iatrogenic syndrome of excess cortisol
Overproduction of cortisol
Use additional E code to identify cause, if drug-induced
EXCLUDES *congenital adrenal hyperplasia (255.2)*
DEF: Due to adrenal cortisol oversecretion or glucocorticoid medications; may cause excess fatty tissue of the face, neck and body; osteoporosis and curvature of spine, hypertension, diabetes mellitus, female genitourinary problems, male impotence, degeneration of muscle tissues, weakness.
CC Excl: 255.0-255.2, 259.50-259.9

255.1 Hyperaldosteronism   `✓5ᵗʰ`
DEF: Oversecretion of aldosterone causing fluid retention, hypertension.
AHA: 4Q, '03, 48

255.10 Hyperaldosteronism, unspecified
Aldosteronism NOS
Primary aldosteronism, unspecified
EXCLUDES *Conn's syndrome (255.12)*

255.11 Glucocorticoid-remediable aldosteronism
Familial aldosteronism type I
EXCLUDES *Conn's syndrome (255.12)*
DEF: Rare autosomal dominant familial form of primary aldosteronism in which the secretion of aldosterone is under the influence of adrenocortiotrophic hormone (ACTH) rather than the renin-angiotensin mechanism; moderate hypersecretion of aldosterone and suppressed plasma renin activity rapidly reversed by administration of glucosteroids; symptoms include hypertension and mild hypokalemia.

255.12 Conn's syndrome
DEF: A type of primary aldosteronism caused by an adenoma of the glomerulosa cells in the adrenal cortex; presence of hypertension.

255.13 Bartter's syndrome
DEF: A cluster of symptoms caused by a defect in the ability of the kidney to reabsorb potassium; signs include alkalosis (hypokalemic alkalosis), increased aldosterone, increased plasma renin, and normal blood pressure; symptoms include muscle cramping, weakness, constipation, frequency of urination, and failure to grow; also known as urinary potassium wasting or juxtaglomerular cell hyperplasia.

255.14 Other secondary aldosteronism
AHA: 3Q, '06, 24

255.2 Adrenogenital disorders
Achard-Thiers syndrome
Adrenogenital syndromes, virilizing or feminizing, whether acquired or associated with congenital adrenal hyperplasia consequent on inborn enzyme defects in hormone synthesis
Congenital adrenal hyperplasia
Female adrenal pseudohermaphroditism
Male:
    macrogenitosomia praecox
    sexual precocity with adrenal hyperplasia
Virilization (female) (suprarenal)
EXCLUDES *adrenal hyperplasia due to excess ACTH (255.0)*
isosexual virilization (256.4)

255.3 Other corticoadrenal overactivity   `CC`
Acquired benign adrenal androgenic overactivity
Overproduction of ACTH
CC Excl: 017.60-017.66, 017.90-017.96, 255.3-255.9, 259.50-259.9

√5ᵗʰ 255.4 Corticoadrenal insufficiency
> **EXCLUDES** *tuberculous Addison's disease (017.6)*
> **DEF:** Underproduction of adrenal hormones causing low blood pressure.
> **AHA:** 4Q, '07, 68; 3Q, '06, 24

> **255.41 Glucocorticoid deficiency** `CC`
> > Addisonian crisis
> > Addison's disease NOS
> > Adrenal atrophy (autoimmune)
> > Adrenal calcification
> > Adrenal crisis
> > Adrenal hemorrhage
> > Adrenal infarction
> > Adrenal insufficiency NOS
> > Combined glucocorticoid and mineralocorticoid deficiency
> > Corticoadrenal insufficiency NOS
> > **DEF:** Decreased function of the adrenal cortex resulting in insufficient production of glucocorticoid, the hormone regulating carbohydrate, fat, and protein metabolism; manifestations: hyponatremia, hyperpigmentation, orthostatic hypotension, anemia, loss of appetite, and malaise.
> > **CC Excl:** See code: 255.3
> > **AHA:** 4Q, '07, 68, 69
> > **E27.1** Primary adrenocortical insufficiency `I-10`

> **255.42 Mineralocorticoid deficiency** `CC`
> > Hypoaldosteronism
> > **EXCLUDES** *combined glucocorticoid and mineralocorticoid deficiency (255.41)*
> > **DEF:** Decreased function of the adrenal cortex resulting in insufficient production of mineralocorticoid, which regulates electrolyte and water balance; manifestations: hyponatremia, hyperkalemia, and mild acidosis.
> > **CC Excl:** See code: 255.3

255.5 Other adrenal hypofunction `CC`
> Adrenal medullary insufficiency
> **EXCLUDES** *Waterhouse-Friderichsen syndrome (meningococcal) (036.3)*
> **CC Excl:** See code 255.3

255.6 Medulloadrenal hyperfunction `CC`
> Catecholamine secretion by pheochromocytoma
> **CC Excl:** See code 255.3

255.8 Other specified disorders of adrenal glands
> Abnormality of cortisol-binding globulin

255.9 Unspecified disorder of adrenal glands

√4ᵗʰ 256 Ovarian dysfunction
> **AHA:** 4Q, '00, 51

256.0 Hyperestrogenism ♀
> **DEF:** Excess secretion of estrogen by the ovaries; characterized by ovaries containing multiple follicular cysts filled with serous fluid.

256.1 Other ovarian hyperfunction ♀
> Hypersecretion of ovarian androgens
> **AHA:** 3Q, '95, 15

256.2 Postablative ovarian failure ♀
> Ovarian failure: Ovarian failure:
>   iatrogenic   postsurgical
>   postirradiation
> Use additional code for states associated with artificial menopause (627.4)
> **EXCLUDES** *acquired absence of ovary (V45.77)*
> *asymptomatic age-related (natural) postmenopausal status (V49.81)*
> **DEF:** Failed ovarian function after medical or surgical intervention.
> **AHA:** 2Q, '02, 12

√5ᵗʰ 256.3 Other ovarian failure
> Use additional code for states associated with natural menopause (627.2)
> **EXCLUDES** *asymptomatic age-related (natural) postmenopausal status (V49.81)*
> **AHA:** 4Q, '01, 41

> **256.31 Premature menopause** `A` ♀
> > **DEF:** Permanent cessation of ovarian function before the age of 40 occuring naturally of unknown cause.

256.39 Other ovarian failure ♀
> Delayed menarche
> Ovarian hypofunction
> Primary ovarian failure NOS

256.4 Polycystic ovaries ♀
> Isosexual virilization
> Stein-Leventhal syndrome
> **DEF:** Multiple serous filled cysts of ovary; symptoms of infertility, hirsutism, oligomenorrhea or amenorrhea.
> **E28.2** Polycystic ovarian syndrome `I-10`

256.8 Other ovarian dysfunction ♀

256.9 Unspecified ovarian dysfunction ♀

√4ᵗʰ 257 Testicular dysfunction

257.0 Testicular hyperfunction ♂
> Hypersecretion of testicular hormones

257.1 Postablative testicular hypofunction ♂
> Testicular hypofunction:
>   iatrogenic
>   postirradiation
>   postsurgical

257.2 Other testicular hypofunction
> Defective biosynthesis of testicular androgen
> Eunuchoidism:
>   NOS
>   hypogonadotropic
> Failure:
>   Leydig's cell, adult
>   seminiferous tubule, adult
> Testicular hypogonadism
> **EXCLUDES** *azoospermia (606.0)*

257.8 Other testicular dysfunction
> **EXCLUDES** *androgen insensitivity syndromes (259.50-259.52)*

257.9 Unspecified testicular dysfunction ♂

√4ᵗʰ 258 Polyglandular dysfunction and related disorders

√5ᵗʰ 258.0 Polyglandular activity in multiple endocrine adenomatosis
> Multiple endocrine neoplasia [MEN] syndromes
> Use additional codes to identify any malignancies and other conditions associated with the syndromes
> **AHA:** 4Q, '09, 150; 4Q, '07, 70

> **258.01 Multiple endocrine neoplasia [MEN] type I**
> > Wermer's syndrome
> > **DEF:** Wermer's syndrome: A rare hereditary condition characterized by the presence of adenomas or hyperplasia in more than one endocrine gland causing premature aging.
> > **AHA:** 4Q, '08, 86, 89; 4Q, '07, 70, 72

> **258.02 Multiple endocrine neoplasia [MEN] type IIA**
> > Sipple's syndrome
> > **DEF:** Sipple's syndrome: A hereditary disorder caused by a defect in the RET gene causing overactivity of the thyroid, adrenal, and parathyroid glands, resulting in adrenal pheochromocytoma and thyroid medullary carcinoma.

> **258.03 Multiple endocrine neoplasia [MEN] type IIB**

258.1 Other combinations of endocrine dysfunction
> Lloyd's syndrome
> Schmidt's syndrome

258.8 Other specified polyglandular dysfunction

258.9 Polyglandular dysfunction, unspecified

√4ᵗʰ 259 Other endocrine disorders

259.0 Delay in sexual development and puberty, not elsewhere classified
> Delayed puberty

259.1 Precocious sexual development and puberty, not elsewhere classified `P`
> Sexual precocity: Sexual precocity:
>   NOS   cryptogenic
>   constitutional   idiopathic

| `N` Newborn Age: 0 | `P` Pediatric Age: 0-17 | `M` Maternity Age: 12-55 | `A` Adult Age: 15-124 | `MCC` Major CC Condition | `CC` CC Condition | `HIV` HIV Related Dx |

259.2 Carcinoid syndrome `CC`
Hormone secretion by carcinoid tumors
DEF: Presence of carcinoid tumors that spread to liver; characterized by cyanotic flushing of skin, diarrhea, bronchospasm, acquired tricuspid and pulmonary stenosis, sudden drops in blood pressure, edema, ascites.
CC Excl: 259.2-259.3, 259.50-259.9
AHA: 4Q, '08, 85-86, 89

259.3 Ectopic hormone secretion, not elsewhere classified
Ectopic:
    antidiuretic hormone secretion [ADH]
    hyperparathyroidism
    EXCLUDES *ectopic ACTH syndrome (255.0)*
AHA: N-D, '85, 4

259.4 Dwarfism, not elsewhere classified
Dwarfism:
    NOS
    constitutional
    EXCLUDES *dwarfism:*
        achondroplastic (756.4)
        intrauterine (759.7)
        nutritional (263.2)
        pituitary (253.3)
        renal (588.0)
        progeria (259.8)

✓5th **259.5 Androgen insensitivity syndrome**
DEF: X chromosome abnormality that prohibits the body from recognizing androgen; XY genotype with ambiguous genitalia.
AHA: 4Q, '08, 95-96; 4Q, '05, 53

259.50 Androgen insensitivity, unspecified

259.51 Androgen insensitivity syndrome
Complete androgen insensitivity
de Quervain's syndrome
Goldberg-Maxwell Syndrome

259.52 Partial androgen insensitivity
Partial androgen insensitivity syndrome
Reifenstein syndrome

259.8 Other specified endocrine disorders
Pineal gland dysfunction
Progeria
Werner's syndrome

259.9 Unspecified endocrine disorder
Disturbance:
    endocrine NOS
    hormone NOS
    Infantilism NOS

Nutritional Deficiencies (260-269)

EXCLUDES *deficiency anemias (280.0-281.9)*
TIP: Assign first a code for the underlying condition (e.g., anorexia nervosa) if specified.

260 Kwashiorkor `MCC`
Nutritional edema with dyspigmentation of skin and hair
DEF: Syndrome, particularly of children; excessive carbohydrate with inadequate protein intake, inhibited growth potential, anomalies in skin and hair pigmentation, edema and liver disease.
CC Excl: 260-263.9
AHA: 3Q, '09, 6
TIP: Do not assign when documentation indicates "mild or moderate protein malnutrition" only. Kwashiorkor is a rare severe protein deficiency.
E40 Kwashiorkor `I-10`

261 Nutritional marasmus `MCC`
Nutritional atrophy
Severe calorie deficiency
Severe malnutrition NOS
DEF: Protein-calorie malabsorption or malnutrition in children; characterized by tissue wasting, dehydration, and subcutaneous fat depletion; may occur with infectious disease; also called infantile atrophy.
CC Excl: See code 260
AHA: 3Q, '12, 10; 4Q, '07, 97; 3Q, '06, 14; 2Q, '06, 12
E41 Nutritional marasmus `I-10`

262 Other severe, protein-calorie malnutrition `MCC`
Nutritional edema without mention of dyspigmentation of skin and hair
CC Excl: See code 260
AHA: 4Q, '92, 24; J-A, '85, 12

✓4th **263 Other and unspecified protein-calorie malnutrition**
AHA: 4Q, '92, 24

263.0 Malnutrition of moderate degree `CC`
DEF: Malnutrition characterized by biochemical changes in electrolytes, lipids, blood plasma.
CC Excl: See code 260
AHA: 3Q, '12, 10; 3Q, '09, 6; J-A, '85, 1

263.1 Malnutrition of mild degree `CC`
CC Excl: See code 260
AHA: J-A, '85, 1

263.2 Arrested development following protein-calorie malnutrition `CC`
Nutritional dwarfism
Physical retardation due to malnutrition
CC Excl: See code 260

263.8 Other protein-calorie malnutrition `CC`
CC Excl: See code 260

263.9 Unspecified protein-calorie malnutrition `CC`
Dystrophy due to malnutrition
Malnutrition (calorie) NOS
EXCLUDES *nutritional deficiency NOS (269.9)*
CC Excl: See code 260
AHA: 3Q, '12, 9; 4Q '03, 109; N-D, '84, 19
E46 Unspecified protein-calorie malnutrition `I-10`

✓4th **264 Vitamin A deficiency**

264.0 With conjunctival xerosis
DEF: Vitamin A deficiency with conjunctival dryness.

264.1 With conjunctival xerosis and Bitot's spot
Bitot's spot in the young child
DEF: Vitamin A deficiency with conjunctival dryness, superficial spots of keratinized epithelium.

264.2 With corneal xerosis
DEF: Vitamin A deficiency with corneal dryness.

264.3 With corneal ulceration and xerosis
DEF: Vitamin A deficiency with corneal dryness, epithelial ulceration.

264.4 With keratomalacia
DEF: Vitamin A deficiency creating corneal dryness; progresses to corneal insensitivity, softness, necrosis; usually bilateral.

264.5 With night blindness
DEF: Vitamin A deficiency causing vision failure in dim light.

264.6 With xerophthalmic scars of cornea
DEF: Vitamin A deficiency with corneal scars from dryness.

264.7 Other ocular manifestations of vitamin A deficiency
Xerophthalmia due to vitamin A deficiency

264.8 Other manifestations of vitamin A deficiency
Follicular keratosis ⎫ due to vitamin A deficiency
Xeroderma ⎭

264.9 Unspecified vitamin A deficiency
Hypovitaminosis A NOS

✓4th **265 Thiamine and niacin deficiency states**

265.0 Beriberi `CC`
DEF: Inadequate vitamin B_1 (thiamine) intake, affects heart and peripheral nerves; individual may become edematous and develop cardiac disease due to the excess fluid; affects alcoholics and people with a diet of excessive polished rice.
CC Excl: 265.0-266.9, 269.1-269.9

265.1 Other and unspecified manifestations of thiamine deficiency `CC`
Other vitamin B_1 deficiency states
CC Excl: See code: 265.0

265.2 Pellagra
Deficiency:
    niacin (-tryptophan)
    nicotinamide
    nicotinic acid
    vitamin PP
Pellagra (alcoholic)
DEF: Niacin deficiency causing dermatitis, inflammation of mucous membranes, diarrhea, and psychic disturbances.

✓4th **266   Deficiency of B-complex components**

266.0   Ariboflavinosis   CC
Riboflavin [vitamin B_2] deficiency
DEF: Vitamin B_2 (riboflavin) deficiency marked by swollen lips and tongue fissures, corneal vascularization, scaling lesions, and anemia.
CC Excl: See code: 265.0
AHA: S-O, '86, 10

266.1   Vitamin B_6 deficiency
Deficiency:
    pyridoxal
    pyridoxamine
    pyridoxine
Vitamin B_6 deficiency syndrome
    EXCLUDES   *vitamin B_6-responsive sideroblastic anemia (285.0)*
DEF: Vitamin B_6 deficiency causing skin, lip, and tongue disturbances, peripheral neuropathy; and convulsions in infants.

266.2   Other B-complex deficiencies
Deficiency:
    cyanocobalamin
    folic acid
    vitamin B_{12}
    EXCLUDES   *combined system disease with anemia (281.0-281.1)*
       deficiency anemias (281.0-281.9)
       subacute degeneration of spinal cord with anemia (281.0-281.1)
    E53.8 Deficiency of other specified B group vitamins   I-10

266.9   Unspecified vitamin B deficiency

267   Ascorbic acid deficiency
Deficiency of vitamin C
Scurvy
    EXCLUDES   *scorbutic anemia (281.8)*
DEF: Vitamin C deficiency causing swollen gums, myalgia, weight loss, and weakness.

✓4th **268   Vitamin D deficiency**
    EXCLUDES   *vitamin D-resistant:*
       osteomalacia (275.3)
       rickets (275.3)

268.0   Rickets, active   CC
    EXCLUDES   *celiac rickets (579.0)*
       renal rickets (588.0)
DEF: Inadequate vitamin D intake, usually in pediatrics, that affects bones most involved with muscular action; may cause nodules on ends and sides of bones; delayed closure of fontanels in infants; symptoms may include muscle soreness, and profuse sweating.
CC Excl: 268.0-269.9

268.1   Rickets, late effect
Any condition specified as due to rickets and stated to be a late effect or sequela of rickets
Code first the nature of late effect
DEF: Distorted or demineralized bones as a result of vitamin D deficiency.

268.2   Osteomalacia, unspecified
DEF: Softening of bones due to decrease in calcium; marked by pain, tenderness, muscular weakness, anorexia, and weight loss.

268.9   Unspecified vitamin D deficiency
Avitaminosis D

✓4th **269   Other nutritional deficiencies**

269.0   Deficiency of vitamin K
    EXCLUDES   *deficiency of coagulation factor due to vitamin K deficiency (286.7)*
       vitamin K deficiency of newborn (776.0)

269.1   Deficiency of other vitamins
Deficiency:
    vitamin E
    vitamin P

269.2   Unspecified vitamin deficiency
Multiple vitamin deficiency NOS

269.3   Mineral deficiency, not elsewhere classified
Deficiency:
    calcium, dietary
    iodine
    EXCLUDES   *deficiency:*
       calcium NOS (275.4)
       potassium (276.8)
       sodium (276.1)

269.8   Other nutritional deficiency
    EXCLUDES   *adult failure to thrive (783.7)*
       failure to thrive in childhood (783.41)
       feeding problems (783.3)
       newborn (779.31-779.34)

269.9   Unspecified nutritional deficiency

Other Metabolic and Immunity Disorders (270-279)

Use additional code to identify any associated intellectual disabilities

✓4th **270   Disorders of amino-acid transport and metabolism**
    EXCLUDES   *abnormal findings without manifest disease (790.0-796.9)*
       disorders of purine and pyrimidine metabolism (277.1-277.2)
       gout (274.00-274.9)

270.0   Disturbances of amino-acid transport   CC
Cystinosis
Cystinuria
Fanconi (-de Toni) (-Debré) syndrome
Glycinuria (renal)
Hartnup disease
CC Excl: 270.0-273.3, 273.8-273.9

270.1   Phenylketonuria [PKU]   CC
Hyperphenylalaninemia
DEF: Inherited metabolic condition causing excess phenylpyruvic and other acids in urine; results in mental retardation, neurological manifestations, including spasticity and tremors, light pigmentation, eczema, and mousy odor.
CC Excl: See code: 270.0

270.2   Other disturbances of aromatic amino-acid metabolism   CC
Albinism
Alkaptonuria
Alkaptonuric ochronosis
Disturbances of metabolism of tyrosine and tryptophan
Homogentisic acid defects
Hydroxykynureninuria
Hypertyrosinemia
Indicanuria
Kynureninase defects
Oasthouse urine disease
Ochronosis
Tyrosinosis
Tyrosinuria
Waardenburg syndrome
    EXCLUDES   *vitamin B_6-deficiency syndrome (266.1)*
CC Excl: See code: 270.0
AHA: 3Q, '99, 20

270.3   Disturbances of branched-chain amino-acid metabolism   CC
Disturbances of metabolism of leucine, isoleucine, and valine
Hypervalinemia
Intermittent branched-chain ketonuria
Leucine-induced hypoglycemia
Leucinosis
Maple syrup urine disease
CC Excl: See code: 270.0
AHA: 3Q, '00, 8

270.4   Disturbances of sulphur-bearing amino-acid metabolism   CC
Cystathioninemia
Cystathioninuria
Disturbances of metabolism of methionine, homocystine, and cystathionine
Homocystinuria
Hypermethioninemia
Methioninemia
CC Excl: See code: 270.0
AHA: ▶4Q, '13, 87;◀ 2Q, '07, 7;1Q, '04, 6

N   Newborn Age: 0   P   Pediatric Age: 0-17   M   Maternity Age: 12-55   A   Adult Age: 15-124   MCC   Major CC Condition   CC   CC Condition   HIV   HIV Related Dx

66 – Volume 1 · October 2014   2015 ICD-9-CM

270.5 Disturbances of histidine metabolism   [CC]
Carnosinemia
Histidinemia
Hyperhistidinemia
Imidazole aminoaciduria
CC Excl: See code: 270.0

270.6 Disorders of urea cycle metabolism   [CC]
Argininosuccinic aciduria
Citrullinemia
Disorders of metabolism of ornithine, citrulline,
    argininosuccinic acid, arginine, and ammonia
Hyperammonemia
Hyperornithinemia
CC Excl: See code: 270.0

270.7 Other disturbances of straight-chain amino-acid metabolism   [CC]
Glucoglycinuria
Glycinemia (with methylmalonic acidemia)
Hyperglycinemia
Hyperlysinemia
Other disturbances of metabolism of glycine, threonine,
    serine, glutamine, and lysine
Pipecolic acidemia
Saccharopinuria
CC Excl: See code: 270.0
AHA: 3Q, '00, 8

270.8 Other specified disorders of amino-acid metabolism   [CC]
Alaninemia   Iminoacidopathy
Ethanolaminuria   Prolinemia
Glycoprolinuria   Prolinuria
Hydroxyprolinemia Sarcosinemia
Hyperprolinemia
CC Excl: See code: 270.0

270.9 Unspecified disorder of amino-acid metabolism   [CC]
CC Excl: See code: 270.0

✓4ᵗʰ 271 Disorders of carbohydrate transport and metabolism
EXCLUDES abnormality of secretion of glucagon (251.4)
    diabetes mellitus (249.0-249.9, 250.0-250.9)
    hypoglycemia NOS (251.2)
    mucopolysaccharidosis (277.5)

271.0 Glycogenosis   [CC]
Amylopectinosis
Glucose-6-phosphatase deficiency
Glycogen storage disease
McArdle's disease
Pompe's disease
von Gierke's disease
CC Excl: 270.0-273.3, 273.8-273.9
AHA: 1Q, '98, 5

271.1 Galactosemia   [CC]
Galactose-1-phosphate uridyl transferase deficiency
Galactosuria
DEF: Any of three genetic disorders due to defective galactose
metabolism; symptoms include failure to thrive in infancy, jaundice,
liver and spleen damage, cataracts, and mental retardation.
CC Excl: See code: 271.0

271.2 Hereditary fructose intolerance
Essential benign fructosuria
Fructosemia
DEF: Chromosome recessive disorder of carbohydrate metabolism; in
infants, occurs after dietary sugar introduced; characterized by
enlarged spleen, yellowish cast to skin, and progressive inability to
thrive.

271.3 Intestinal disaccharidase deficiencies and disaccharide malabsorption
Intolerance or malabsorption (congenital) (of):
    glucose-galactose
    lactose
    sucrose-isomaltose
E73.9 Lactose intolerance unspecified   [I-10]

271.4 Renal glycosuria
Renal diabetes
DEF: Persistent abnormal levels of glucose in urine, with normal
blood glucose levels; caused by failure of the renal tubules to
reabsorb glucose.

271.8 Other specified disorders of carbohydrate transport and metabolism   [CC]
Essential benign pentosuria   Mannosidosis
Fucosidosis   Oxalosis
Glycolic aciduria   Xylosuria
Hyperoxaluria (primary) Xylulosuria
CC Excl: See code: 271.0

271.9 Unspecified disorder of carbohydrate transport and metabolism

✓4ᵗʰ 272 Disorders of lipoid metabolism
EXCLUDES localized cerebral lipidoses (330.1)

272.0 Pure hypercholesterolemia
Familial hypercholesterolemia
Fredrickson Type IIa hyperlipoproteinemia
Hyperbetalipoproteinemia
Hyperlipidemia, Group A
Low-density-lipoid-type [LDL] hyperlipoproteinemia
AHA: 4Q, '05, 71
E78.0 Pure hypercholesterolemia   [I-10]

272.1 Pure hyperglyceridemia
Endogenous hyperglyceridemia
Fredrickson Type IV hyperlipoproteinemia
Hyperlipidemia, Group B
Hyperprebetalipoproteinemia
Hypertriglyceridemia, essential
Very-low-density-lipoid-type [VLDL] hyperlipoproteinemia

272.2 Mixed hyperlipidemia
Broad- or floating-betalipoproteinemia
Combined hyperlipidemia
Elevated cholesterol with elevated triglycerides NEC
Fredrickson Type IIb or III hyperlipoproteinemia
Hypercholesterolemia with endogenous hyperglyceridemia
Hyperbetalipoproteinemia with prebetalipoproteinemia
Tubo-eruptive xanthoma
Xanthoma tuberosum
DEF: Elevated levels of lipoprotein, a complex of fats and proteins, in
blood due to inherited metabolic disorder.

272.3 Hyperchylomicronemia
Bürger-Grütz syndrome
Fredrickson type I or V hyperlipoproteinemia
Hyperlipidemia, Group D
Mixed hyperglyceridemia

272.4 Other and unspecified hyperlipidemia
Alpha-lipoproteinemia
Hyperlipidemia NOS
Hyperlipoproteinemia NOS
DEF: Hyperlipoproteinemia: elevated levels of transient chylomicrons
in the blood which are a form of lipoproteins that transport dietary
cholesterol and triglycerides from the small intestine to the blood.
AHA: 1Q, '05, 17
E78.4 Other hyperlipidemia   [I-10]

272.5 Lipoprotein deficiencies
Abetalipoproteinemia
Bassen-Kornzweig syndrome
High-density lipoid deficiency
Hypoalphalipoproteinemia
Hypobetalipoproteinemia (familial)
DEF: Abnormally low levels of lipoprotein, a complex of fats and
protein, in the blood.

Lipid Metabolism

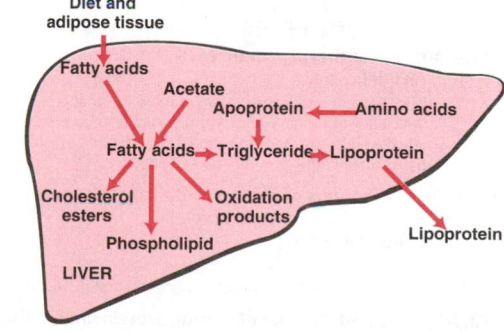

Additional Digit Required   Unacceptable PDx   Manifestation Code   Hospital Acquired Condition   ▶◀ Revised Text   ● New Code   ▲ Revised Code Title

272.6 Lipodystrophy
Barraquer-Simons disease
Progressive lipodystrophy
Use additional E code to identify cause, if iatrogenic
EXCLUDES *intestinal lipodystrophy (040.2)*
DEF: Disturbance of fat metabolism resulting in loss of fatty tissue in some areas of the body.

272.7 Lipidoses
Chemically-induced lipidosis
Disease:
  Anderson's
  Fabry's
  Gaucher's
  I cell [mucolipidosis I]
  lipoid storage NOS
  Niemann-Pick
  pseudo-Hurler's or mucolipdosis III
  triglyceride storage, Type I or II
  Wolman's or triglyceride storage, Type III
Mucolipidosis II
Primary familial xanthomatosis
EXCLUDES *cerebral lipidoses (330.1)*
Tay-Sachs disease (330.1)
DEF: Lysosomal storage diseases marked by an abnormal amount of lipids in reticuloendothelial cells.

272.8 Other disorders of lipoid metabolism
Hoffa's disease or liposynovitis prepatellaris
Launois-Bensaude's lipomatosis
Lipoid dermatoarthritis

272.9 Unspecified disorder of lipoid metabolism

✓4th **273 Disorders of plasma protein metabolism**
EXCLUDES *agammaglobulinemia and*
hypogammaglobulinemia (279.0-279.2)
coagulation defects (286.0-286.9)
hereditary hemolytic anemias (282.0-282.9)

273.0 Polyclonal hypergammaglobulinemia
Hypergammaglobulinemic purpura:
  benign primary
  Waldenström's
DEF: Elevated blood levels of gamma globulins, frequently found in patients with chronic infectious diseases.

273.1 Monoclonal paraproteinemia
Benign monoclonal hypergammaglobulinemia [BMH]
Monoclonal gammopathy:
  NOS
  associated with lymphoplasmacytic dyscrasias
  benign
Paraproteinemia:
  benign (familial)
  secondary to malignant or inflammatory disease

273.2 Other paraproteinemias
Cryoglobulinemic:
  purpura
  vasculitis
Mixed cryoglobulinemia
AHA: 2Q, '08, 17

273.3 Macroglobulinemia
Macroglobulinemia (idiopathic) (primary)
Waldenström's macroglobulinemia
DEF: Elevated blood levels of macroglobulins (plasma globulins of high weight); characterized by malignant neoplasms of bone marrow, spleen, liver, or lymph nodes; symptoms include weakness, fatigue, bleeding disorders, and vision problems.

273.4 Alpha-1-antitrypsin deficiency
AAT deficiency
DEF: Disorder of plasma protein metabolism that results in a deficiency of Alpha-1-antitrypsin, an acute-phase reactive protein, released into the blood in response to infection or injury to protect tissue against the harmful effect of enzymes.

273.8 Other disorders of plasma protein metabolism
Abnormality of transport protein
Bisalbuminemia
AHA: 2Q, '98, 11
E88.09 Other disorders of plasma-protein metablolis NEC   I-10

273.9 Unspecified disorder of plasma protein metabolism

✓4th **274 Gout**
EXCLUDES *lead gout (984.0-984.9)*
DEF: Purine and pyrimidine metabolic disorders; manifested by hyperuricemia and recurrent acute inflammatory arthritis; monosodium urate or monohydrate crystals may be deposited in and around the joints, leading to joint destruction, and severe crippling.
AHA: 2Q, '95, 4

✓5th **274.0 Gouty arthropathy**
AHA: 4Q, '09, 76-77

274.00 Gouty arthropathy, unspecified
M10.00 Idiopathic gout unspecified site   I-10

274.01 Acute gouty arthropathy
Acute gout   Gout flare
Gout attack   Podagra

274.02 Chronic gouty arthropathy without mention of tophus (tophi)
Chronic gout

274.03 Chronic gouty arthropathy with tophus (tophi)
Chronic tophaceous gout   Gout with tophi NOS
AHA: 4Q, '09, 77

✓5th **274.1 Gouty nephropathy**

274.10 Gouty nephropathy, unspecified
AHA: N-D, '85, 15

274.11 Uric acid nephrolithiasis   CC
DEF: Sodium urate stones in the kidney.
CC Excl: 016.00-016.06, 016.30-016.36, 016.90-016.96, 017.90-017.96, 078.6, 098.10, 098.19, 098.30-098.31, 098.89, 112.2, 131.00, 131.8-131.9, 249.40-249.41, 249.80-249.91, 250.40-250.43, 250.80-250.93, 274.10-274.19, 274.89, 580.0-584.9, 586-588.1, 588.9-591, 593.0-593.2, 593.89-593.9, 599.60-599.9

274.19 Other

✓5th **274.8 Gout with other specified manifestations**

274.81 Gouty tophi of ear
DEF: Chalky sodium urate deposit in the ear due to gout; produces chronic inflammation of external ear.

274.82 Gouty tophi of other sites
Gouty tophi of heart
EXCLUDES *gout with tophi NOS (274.03)*
gouty arthropathy with tophi (274.03)

274.89 Other
Use additional code to identify manifestations, as:
  gouty:
    iritis (364.11)
    neuritis (357.4)

274.9 Gout, unspecified
M10.9 Gout unspecified   I-10

✓4th **275 Disorders of mineral metabolism**
EXCLUDES *abnormal findings without manifest disease (790.0-796.9)*

✓5th **275.0 Disorders of iron metabolism**
EXCLUDES *anemia:*
iron deficiency (280.0-280.9)
sideroblastic (285.0)
AHA: 4Q, '10, 77-78; 2Q, '97, 11

275.01 Hereditary hemochromatosis
Bronzed diabetes
Pigmentary cirrhosis (of liver)
Primary (hereditary) hemochromatosis
E83.110 Hereditary hemochromatosis   I-10

275.02 Hemochromatosis due to repeated red blood cell transfusions
Iron overload due to repeated red blood cell transfusions
Transfusion (red blood cell) associated hemochromatosis
AHA: 4Q, '10, 77-78
E83.111 Hemochromatosis due to repeated red blood cell transfusions   I-10

275.03 Other hemochromatosis
Hemochromatosis NOS
E83.118 Other hemochromatosis   I-10

275.09 Other disorders of iron metabolism
E83.10 Disorder of iron-metabolism unspecified   I-10

N Newborn Age: 0   P Pediatric Age: 0-17   M Maternity Age: 12-55   A Adult Age: 15-124   MCC Major CC Condition   CC CC Condition   HIV HIV Related Dx

68 – Volume 1   **2015 ICD-9-CM**

275.1 Disorders of copper metabolism
Hepatolenticular degeneration
Wilson's disease

275.2 Disorders of magnesium metabolism
Hypermagnesemia   Hypomagnesemia
AHA: 1Q, '10, 14; 3Q, '09, 21
E83.40 Disorders of magnesium metabolism unspecified   `I-10`

275.3 Disorders of phosphorus metabolism
Familial hypophosphatemia
Hypophosphatasia
Vitamin D-resistant:
    osteomalacia
    rickets

√5ᵗʰ 275.4 Disorders of calcium metabolism
    EXCLUDES *hungry bone syndrome (275.5)*
                parathyroid disorders (252.00-252.9)
                vitamin D deficiency (268.0-268.9)
    AHA: 4Q, '97, 33

275.40 Unspecified disorder of calcium metabolism

275.41 Hypocalcemia
    DEF: Abnormally decreased blood calcium level; symptoms include hyperactive deep tendon reflexes, muscle, abdominal cramps, and carpopedal spasm.
    AHA: 3Q, '07, 5
    E83.51 Hypocalcemia   `I-10`

275.42 Hypercalcemia
    DEF: Abnormally increased blood calcium level; symptoms include muscle weakness, fatigue, nausea, depression, and constipation.
    AHA: 3Q, '12,16; 4Q, '03, 110

275.49 Other disorders of calcium metabolism
Nephrocalcinosis
Pseudohypoparathyroidism
Pseudopseudohypoparathyroidism
    DEF: Nephrocalcinosis: calcium phosphate deposits in the tubules of the kidney with resultant renal insufficiency.
    DEF: Pseudohypoparathyroidism: inherited hypoparathyroidism disorder; caused by inadequate response to parathyroid hormone, not hormonal deficiency; includes muscle cramps, tetany, urinary frequency, blurred vision due to cataracts, and dry scaly skin.
    DEF: Pseudopseudohypoparathyroidism: clinical manifestations of hypoparathyroidism without affecting blood calcium levels.

275.5 Hungry bone syndrome
    DEF: Marked and prolonged hypocalcemia; usually involves an extended history of elevated levels of parathyroid hormone, related bone demineralization causing the bone to sequester calcium.
    AHA: 4Q, '08, 96-97

275.8 Other specified disorders of mineral metabolism

275.9 Unspecified disorder of mineral metabolism

√4ᵗʰ 276 Disorders of fluid, electrolyte, and acid-base balance
    EXCLUDES *diabetes insipidus (253.5)*
                familial periodic paralysis (359.3)

276.0 Hyperosmolality and/or hypernatremia   `CC`
Sodium [Na] excess
Sodium [Na] overload
    CC Excl: 276.0-276.52, 276.61-276.9

276.1 Hyposmolality and/or hyponatremia   `CC`
Sodium [Na] deficiency
    CC Excl: See code: 276.0
    E87.1 Hypo-osmolality and hyponatremia   `I-10`

276.2 Acidosis   `CC`
Acidosis: Acidosis:
   NOS   metabolic
   lactic   respiratory
    EXCLUDES *diabetic acidosis (249.1, 250.1)*
    DEF: Disorder involves decrease of pH (hydrogen ion) concentration in blood and cellular tissues; caused by increase in acid and decrease in bicarbonate.
    CC Excl: 276.0-276.9
    AHA: J-F, '87, 15
    E87.2 Acidosis   `I-10`

276.3 Alkalosis   `CC`
Alkalosis:
   NOS
   metabolic
   respiratory
    DEF: Increased blood alkalinity (base) without relative loss of base in body fluids; caused by increased arterial plasma bicarbonate concentration or loss of carbon dioxide due to hyperventilation.
    CC Excl: See code: 276.0

276.4 Mixed acid-base balance disorder   `CC`
Hypercapnia with mixed acid-base disorder
    CC Excl: See code 276.0

√5ᵗʰ 276.5 Volume depletion
    EXCLUDES *hypovolemic shock:*
                postoperative (998.09)
                traumatic (958.4)
    AHA: 4Q, '05, 54; 2Q, '05, 9; 1Q, '03, 5, 22; 3Q, '02, 21; 4Q, '97, 30; 2Q, '88, 9

276.50 Volume depletion, unspecified
    DEF: Depletion of total body water (dehydration) and/or contraction of total intravascular plasma (hypovolemia).
    E86.9 Volume depletion unspecified   `I-10`

276.51 Dehydration
    DEF: Depletion of total body water; blood volume may be normal while fluid is pulled from other tissues.
    AHA: 1Q, '08, 10
    E86.0 Dehydration   `I-10`

276.52 Hypovolemia
Depletion of volume of plasma
    DEF: Depletion of volume plasma; depletion of total blood volume.

√6ᵗʰ 276.6 Fluid overload
    EXCLUDES *ascites (789.51-789.59)*
                localized edema (782.3)
    AHA: 4Q, '10, 79; 3Q, '07, 9; 4Q, '06, 136

276.61 Transfusion associated circulatory overload
Fluid overload due to transfusion (blood) (blood components)
TACO
    AHA: 4Q, '10, 79-80
    E87.71 Transfusion associated circulatory overload   `I-10`

276.69 Other fluid overload
Fluid retention
    E87.79 Other fluid overload   `I-10`

276.7 Hyperpotassemia
Hyperkalemia
Potassium [K]:
   excess
   intoxication
   overload
    DEF: Elevated blood levels of potassium; symptoms include abnormal EKG readings, weakness; related to defective renal excretion.
    AHA: 2Q, '11, 6; 1Q, '05, 9; 2Q,'01, 12
    E87.5 Hyperkalemia   `I-10`

276.8 Hypopotassemia
Hypokalemia
Potassium [K] deficiency
    DEF: Decreased blood levels of potassium; symptoms include neuromuscular disorders.
    E87.6 Hypokalemia   `I-10`

276.9 Electrolyte and fluid disorders not elsewhere classified
Electrolyte imbalance
Hyperchloremia
Hypochloremia
    EXCLUDES *electrolyte imbalance:*
                associated with hyperemesis gravidarum (643.1)
                complicating labor and delivery (669.0)
                following abortion and ectopic or molar pregnancy (634-638 with .4, 639.4)
    AHA: J-F, '87, 15
    E87.8 Oth disorders of electrolyte & fluid balance NEC   `I-10`

Endocrine, Nutritional and Metabolic Diseases, and Immunity

277–277.85

✓4ᵗʰ **277 Other and unspecified disorders of metabolism**

✓5ᵗʰ **277.0 Cystic fibrosis**

Fibrocystic disease of the pancreas
Mucoviscidosis

DEF: Genetic disorder of infants, children, and young adults marked by exocrine gland dysfunction; characterized by chronic pulmonary disease with excess mucus production, pancreatic deficiency, and high levels of electrolytes in the sweat.

AHA: 4Q, '90, 16; 3Q, '90, 18

TIP: Sequencing of CF is determined by circumstances of admission. If a patient is admitted for CF, sequence the CF first. If admitted for a complication of CF (e.g., pneumothorax, acute bronchitis, or acute cor pulmonale), sequence the complication first.

277.00 Without mention of meconium ileus `CC`

Cystic fibrosis NOS

CC Excl: 277.00-277.09

AHA: 2Q, '03, 12

E84.9 Cystic fibrosis unspecified `I-10`

277.01 With meconium ileus `MCC` `N`

Meconium:
    ileus (of newborn)
    obstruction of intestine in mucoviscidosis

CC Excl: See code 277.00

277.02 With pulmonary manifestations `MCC`

Cystic fibrosis with pulmonary exacerbation

Use additional code to identify any infectious organism present, such as:
    pseudomonas (041.7)

CC Excl: See code 277.00

277.03 With gastrointestinal manifestations `CC`

EXCLUDES with meconium ileus (277.01)

CC Excl: See code 277.00

AHA: 4Q, '02, 45

277.09 With other manifestations `CC`

CC Excl: See code 277.00

277.1 Disorders of porphyrin metabolism `CC`

Hematoporphyria
Hematoporphyrinuria
Hereditary coproporphyria
Porphyria
Porphyrinuria
Protocoproporphyria
Protoporphyria
Pyrroloporphyria

CC Excl: 277.1-277.2, 277.4-277.7

277.2 Other disorders of purine and pyrimidine metabolism `CC`

Hypoxanthine-guanine-phosphoribosyltransferase deficiency [HG-PRT deficiency]
Lesch-Nyhan syndrome
Xanthinuria

EXCLUDES gout (274.00-274.9)
    orotic aciduric anemia (281.4)

CC Excl: See code: 277.1

✓5ᵗʰ **277.3 Amyloidosis**

DEF: Conditions of diverse etiologies characterized by the accumulation of insoluble fibrillar proteins (amyloid) in various organs and tissues of the body, compromising vital functions.

AHA: 1Q, '96, 16

277.30 Amyloidosis, unspecified `CC`

Amyloidosis NOS

CC Excl: 277.30-277.39, 277.7

AHA: 4Q, '06, 66

277.31 Familial Mediterranean fever `CC`

Benign paroxysmal peritonitis
Hereditary amyloid nephropathy
Periodic familial polyserositis
Recurrent polyserositis

DEF: Early-life onset of recurrent attacks characterized by high fevers with pain and inflammation of chest and abdominal cavities, skin and joints, also rash or vasculitis. Etiology unknown, possibly genetic, but may be precipitated by stress, trauma or exertion.

CC Excl: See code: 277.30

AHA: 2Q, '12, 18; 4Q, '06, 66

277.39 Other amyloidosis `CC`

Hereditary cardiac amyloidosis
Inherited systemic amyloidosis
Neuropathic (Portuguese) (Swiss) amyloidosis
Secondary amyloidosis

CC Excl: See code: 277.30

AHA: 1Q, '09, 9; 2Q, '08, 8; 4Q, '06, 66

277.4 Disorders of bilirubin excretion

Hyperbilirubinemia:
    congenital
    constitutional
Syndrome:
    Crigler-Najjar
    Dubin-Johnson
    Gilbert's
    Rotor's

EXCLUDES hyperbilirubinemias specific to the perinatal period (774.0-774.7)

AHA: ▶1Q, '14, 8◄

277.5 Mucopolysaccharidosis `CC`

Gargoylism
Hunter's syndrome
Hurler's syndrome
Lipochondrodystrophy
Maroteaux-Lamy syndrome
Morquio-Brailsford disease
Osteochondrodystrophy
Sanfilippo's syndrome
Scheie's syndrome

DEF: Metabolic disorders evidenced by excretion of various mucopolysaccharides in urine and infiltration of these substances into connective tissue, with resulting defects of bone, cartilage and connective tissue.

CC Excl: 277.1-277.31, 277.4-277.7

277.6 Other deficiencies of circulating enzymes

Hereditary angioedema

AHA: 2Q, '10, 12

277.7 Dysmetabolic syndrome X

Use additional code for associated manifestation, such as:
    cardiovascular disease (414.00-414.07)
    obesity (278.00-278.03)

DEF: A specific group of metabolic disorders that are related to the state of insulin resistance (decreased cellular response to insulin) without elevated blood sugars; often related to elevated cholesterol and triglycerides, obesity, cardiovascular disease, and high blood pressure.

AHA: 4Q, '01, 42

✓5ᵗʰ **277.8 Other specified disorders of metabolism**

AHA: 4Q, '03, 50; 2Q, '01, 18; S-O, '87, 9

277.81 Primary carnitine deficiency

277.82 Carnitine deficiency due to inborn errors of metabolism

277.83 Iatrogenic carnitine deficiency

Carnitine deficiency due to:
    hemodialysis
    valproic acid therapy

277.84 Other secondary carnitine deficiency

277.85 Disorders of fatty acid oxidation `CC`

Carnitine palmitoyltransferase deficiencies (CPT1, CPT2)
Glutaric aciduria type II (type IIA, IIB, IIC)
Long chain 3-hydroxyacyl CoA dehydrogenase deficiency (LCHAD)
Long chain/very long chain acyl CoA dehydrogenase deficiency (LCAD, VLCAD)
Medium chain acyl CoA dehydrogenase deficiency (MCAD)
Short chain acyl CoA dehydrogenase deficiency (SCAD)

EXCLUDES primary carnitine deficiency (277.81)

CC Excl: 277.81-277.84, 277.86-277.87, 277.89

`N` Newborn Age: 0   `P` Pediatric Age: 0-17   `M` Maternity Age: 12-55   `A` Adult Age: 15-124   `MCC` Major CC Condition   `CC` CC Condition   `HIV` HIV Related Dx

70 – Volume 1 · October 2014   2015 ICD-9-CM

277.86 Peroxisomal disorders `CC`
Adrenomyeloneuropathy
Neonatal adrenoleukodystrophy
Rhizomelic chrondrodysplasia punctata
X-linked adrenoleukodystrophy
Zellweger syndrome
> **EXCLUDES** *infantile Refsum disease (356.3)*
> **CC Excl:** 277.4, 277.81-277.85, 277.87, 277.89

277.87 Disorders of mitochondrial metabolism `CC`
Kearns-Sayre syndrome
Mitochondrial Encephalopathy, Lactic Acidosis and Stroke-like episodes (MELAS syndrome)
Mitochondrial Neurogastrointestinal Encephalopathy syndrome (MNGIE)
Myoclonus with Epilepsy and with Ragged Red Fibers (MERRF syndrome)
Neuropathy, Ataxia and Retinitis Pigmentosa (NARP syndrome)
Use additional code for associated conditions
> **EXCLUDES** *disorders of pyruvate metabolism (271.8)*
> *Leber's optic atrophy (377.16)*
> *Leigh's subacute necrotizing encephalopathy (330.8)*
> *Reye's syndrome (331.81)*
> **CC Excl:** 277.4, 277.81-277.86, 277.89
> **AHA:** 4Q, '04, 62

277.88 Tumor lysis syndrome `MCC`
Spontaneous tumor lysis syndrome
Tumor lysis syndrome following antineoplastic drug therapy
Use additional E code to identify cause, if drug-induced
> **DEF:** A potentially fatal metabolic complication of tumor necrosis caused by either spontaneous or treatment-related accumulation of byproducts from dying cancer cells; symptoms include hyperkalemia, hyperphosphatemia, hypocalcemia, hyperuricemia, and hyperuricosuria.
> **CC Excl:** 277.88, 580.0-581.0, 581.81-581.9, 583.4-584.9
> **AHA:** 4Q, '09, 78-79

277.89 Other specified disorders of metabolism `CC`
Hand-Schüller-Christian disease
Histiocytosis (acute) (chronic)
Histiocytosis X (chronic)
> **EXCLUDES** *histiocytosis:*
> *acute differentiated progressive (202.5)*
> *adult pulmonary Langerhans cell (516.5)*
> *X, acute (progressive) (202.5)*
> **CC Excl:** 277.4, 277.81-277.87

277.9 Unspecified disorder of metabolism
Enzymopathy NOS

√4ᵗʰ **278 Overweight, obesity and other hyperalimentation**
> **EXCLUDES** *hyperalimentation NOS (783.6)*
> *poisoning by vitamins NOS (963.5)*
> *polyphagia (783.6)*

√5ᵗʰ **278.0 Overweight and obesity**
Use additional code to identify Body Mass Index (BMI), if known (V85.0-V85.54)
> **EXCLUDES** *adiposogenital dystrophy (253.8)*
> *obesity of endocrine origin NOS (259.9)*
> **AHA:** 3Q, '11, 4; 4Q, '05, 97

278.00 Obesity, unspecified
Obesity NOS
> **DEF:** BMI (body mass index) between 30.0 and 39.9.
> **AHA:** 4Q, '01, 42; 1Q, '99, 5, 6

278.01 Morbid obesity
Severe obesity
> **DEF:** BMI (body mass index) 40 or greater.
> **AHA:** 4Q, '10, 81; 2Q, '09, 11; 2Q, '06, 5-6; 3Q, '03, 6-8
> **E66.01** Morbid (severe) obesity due to excess calories `I-10`

278.02 Overweight
> **DEF:** BMI (body mass index) between 25 and 29.9.
> **AHA:** 4Q, '05, 55
> **E66.3** Overweight `I-10`

278.03 Obesity hypoventilation syndrome `CC`
Pickwickian syndrome
> **DEF:** Hypoventilation, somnolence and erythrocytosis due to excessive weight against the chest wall.
> **CC Excl:** 278.03, 416.0-416.1, 416.8-416.9
> **AHA:** 4Q, '10, 80-81
> **E66.2** Morbid obesity w/ alveolar hyperventilation `I-10`

278.1 Localized adiposity
Fat pad
> **AHA:** 2Q, '06, 10

278.2 Hypervitaminosis A

278.3 Hypercarotinemia
> **DEF:** Elevated blood carotene level due to ingesting excess carotenoids or the inability to convert carotenoids to vitamin A.

278.4 Hypervitaminosis D
> **DEF:** Weakness, fatigue, loss of weight, and other symptoms resulting from ingesting excessive amounts of vitamin D.

278.8 Other hyperalimentation
> **AHA:** 2Q, '09, 11

√4ᵗʰ **279 Disorders involving the immune mechanism**
Use additional code for associated manifestations

√5ᵗʰ **279.0 Deficiency of humoral immunity**
> **DEF:** Inadequate immune response to bacterial infections with potential reinfection by viruses due to lack of circulating immunoglobulins (acquired antibodies).

279.00 Hypogammaglobulinemia, unspecified `CC`
Agammaglobulinemia NOS
> **CC Excl:** 279.00-279.49, 279.8-279.9

279.01 Selective IgA immunodeficiency `CC`
> **CC Excl:** See code: 279.00

279.02 Selective IgM immunodeficiency `CC`
> **CC Excl:** 279.02-279.49, 279.8-279.9

279.03 Other selective immunoglobulin deficiencies `CC`
Selective deficiency of IgG
> **CC Excl:** See code: 279.02

279.04 Congenital hypogammaglobulinemia `CC`
Agammaglobulinemia:
  Bruton's type
  X-linked
> **CC Excl:** See code 279.02

279.05 Immunodeficiency with increased IgM `CC`
Immunodeficiency with hyper-IgM:
  autosomal recessive
  X-linked
> **CC Excl:** See code 279.02

279.06 Common variable immunodeficiency `CC`
Dysgammaglobulinemia (acquired) (congenital) (primary)
Hypogammaglobulinemia:
  acquired primary
  congenital non-sex-linked
  sporadic
> **CC Excl:** See code 279.02

279.09 Other `CC`
Transient hypogammaglobulinemia of infancy
> **CC Excl:** See code 279.02

√5ᵗʰ **279.1 Deficiency of cell-mediated immunity**

279.10 Immunodeficiency with predominant T-cell defect, unspecified `CC`
> **CC Excl:** See code 279.02
> **AHA:** S-O, '87, 10

279.11 DiGeorge's syndrome `CC`
Pharyngeal pouch syndrome
Thymic hypoplasia
> **DEF:** Congenital hypoplasia or aplasia of the thymus, parathyroid glands; related heart defects, anomalies of the great vessels, esophageal atresia, and abnormalities of facial structures.
> **CC Excl:** See code 279.02

√4ᵗʰ √5ᵗʰ Additional Digit Required   Unacceptable PDx   Manifestation Code   Hospital Acquired Condition   ▶◀ Revised Text   ● New Code   ▲ Revised Code Title

279.12 Wiskott-Aldrich syndrome `CC`
DEF: A disease characterized by chronic conditions, such as eczema, suppurative otitis media and anemia; results from an X-linked recessive gene and is classified as an immune deficiency syndrome.
CC Excl: See code 279.02

279.13 Nezelof's syndrome `CC`
Cellular immunodeficiency with abnormal immunoglobulin deficiency
DEF: Immune system disorder characterized by a pathological deficiency in cellular immunity and humoral antibodies resulting in inability to fight infectious diseases.
CC Excl: See code 279.02

279.19 Other `CC`
EXCLUDES ataxia-telangiectasia (334.8)
CC Excl: See code 279.02

279.2 Combined immunity deficiency `CC`
Agammaglobulinemia:
   autosomal recessive
   Swiss-type
   x-linked recessive
Severe combined immunodeficiency [SCID]
Thymic:
   alymphoplasia
   aplasia or dysplasia with immunodeficiency
EXCLUDES thymic hypoplasia (279.11)
DEF: Agammaglobulinemia: No immunoglobulins in the blood.
DEF: Thymic alymphoplasia: Severe combined immunodeficiency; result of failed lymphoid tissue development.
CC Excl: See code 279.02
AHA: 4Q, '11, 148

279.3 Unspecified immunity deficiency `CC`
CC Excl: See code 279.02

✓5ᵗʰ 279.4 Autoimmune disease, not elsewhere classified
EXCLUDES transplant failure or rejection (996.80-996.89)
AHA: 4Q, '09, 80; 3Q, 08, 5

279.41 Autoimmune lymphoproliferative syndrome
ALPS
DEF: Rare genetic alteration of the Fas protein; impairs normal cellular apoptosis (normal cell death), causing abnormal accumulation of lymphocytes in the lymph glands, liver, and spleen; symptoms include neutropenia, anemia, and thrombocytopenia.

279.49 Autoimmune disease, not elsewhere classified
Autoimmune disease NOS
AHA: 3Q, '12, 8; 2Q, '11, 15
TIP: Assign for pediatric autoimmune neuropsychiatric disorder associated with streptococcal infection (PANDAS), with additional codes to report specific neurological or psychiatric manifestations.

✓5ᵗʰ 279.5 Graft-versus-host disease
Code first underlying cause, such as:
   complication of blood transfusion (999.89)
   complication of transplanted organ (996.80-996.89)
Use additional code to identify associated manifestations, such as:
desquamative dermatitis (695.89)
diarrhea (787.91)
elevated bilirubin (782.4)
hair loss (704.09)
DEF: A complication of transplantation, most commonly bone marrow; may involve skin, GI tract, liver and cause increased susceptibility to infection; results when donor cells responsible for immune response attack the cells of the transplant recipient.
AHA: 4Q, '08, 97-99, 154

279.50 Graft-versus-host disease, unspecified `CC`
CC Excl: 279.50-279.53, 996.85, 997.91-997.99
AHA: 4Q, '08, 99

279.51 Acute graft-versus-host disease `CC`
CC Excl: See code 279.50
AHA: 4Q, '11, 148; 4Q, '08, 99

279.52 Chronic graft-versus-host disease `CC`
CC Excl: See code 279.50

279.53 Acute on chronic graft-versus-host disease `CC`
CC Excl: See code 279.50

279.8 Other specified disorders involving the immune mechanism
Single complement [C_1-C_9] deficiency or dysfunction

279.9 Unspecified disorder of immune mechanism
AHA: 3Q, '92, 13

N Newborn Age: 0   **P** Pediatric Age: 0-17   **M** Maternity Age: 12-55   **A** Adult Age: 15-124   **MCC** Major CC Condition   **CC** CC Condition   **HIV** HIV Related Dx

72 – Volume 1   2015 ICD-9-CM

4. Diseases of the Blood and Blood-Forming Organs (280-289)

EXCLUDES *anemia complicating pregnancy or the puerperium (648.2)*

✓4th 280 Iron deficiency anemias

INCLUDES anemia:
　asiderotic
　hypochromic-microcytic
　sideropenic

EXCLUDES *familial microcytic anemia (282.49)*

280.0 Secondary to blood loss (chronic)
Normocytic anemia due to blood loss
EXCLUDES *acute posthemorrhagic anemia (285.1)*
AHA: ▶3Q, '13, 4;◄ 4Q, '93, 34

280.1 Secondary to inadequate dietary iron intake

280.8 Other specified iron deficiency anemias
Paterson-Kelly syndrome
Plummer-Vinson syndrome
Sideropenic dysphagia

280.9 Iron deficiency anemia, unspecified
Anemia:
　achlorhydric
　chlorotic
　idiopathic hypochromic
　iron [Fe] deficiency NOS

✓4th 281 Other deficiency anemias

281.0 Pernicious anemia
Anemia:
　Addison's
　Biermer's
　congenital pernicious
Congenital intrinsic factor [Castle's] deficiency
EXCLUDES *combined system disease without mention of anemia (266.2)*
subacute degeneration of spinal cord without mention of anemia (266.2)
DEF: Chronic progressive anemia due to Vitamin B12 malabsorption; caused by lack of a secretion of intrinsic factor, which is produced by the gastric mucosa of the stomach.
AHA: N-D, '84, 1; S-O, '84, 16

281.1 Other vitamin B_{12} deficiency anemia
Anemia:
　vegan's
　vitamin B_{12} deficiency (dietary)
　due to selective vitamin B_{12} malabsorption with proteinuria
Syndrome:
　Imerslund's
　Imerslund-Gräsbeck
EXCLUDES *combined system disease without mention of anemia (266.2)*
subacute degeneration of spinal cord without mention of anemia (266.2)

281.2 Folate-deficiency anemia
Congenital folate malabsorption
Folate or folic acid deficiency anemia:
　NOS
　dietary
　drug-induced
Goat's milk anemia
Nutritional megaloblastic anemia (of infancy)
Use additional E code to identify drug
DEF: Macrocytic anemia resembles pernicious anemia but without absence of hydrochloric acid secretions; responsive to folic acid therapy.

281.3 Other specified megaloblastic anemias not elsewhere classified
Combined B_{12} and folate-deficiency anemia
Refractory megaloblastic anemia
DEF: Megaloblasts predominant in bone marrow with few normoblasts; rare familial type associated with proteinuria and genitourinary tract anomalies.

281.4 Protein-deficiency anemia
Amino-acid-deficiency anemia

281.8 Anemia associated with other specified nutritional deficiency
Scorbutic anemia

281.9 Unspecified deficiency anemia
Anemia:　　　　　Anemia:
　dimorphic　　　　　nutritional NOS
　macrocytic　　　　　simple chronic
　megaloblastic NOS

✓4th 282 Hereditary hemolytic anemias
DEF: Escalated rate of erythrocyte destruction; similar to all anemias, occurs when imbalance exists between blood loss and blood production.

282.0 Hereditary spherocytosis
Acholuric (familial) jaundice
Congenital hemolytic anemia (spherocytic)
Congenital spherocytosis
Minkowski-Chauffard syndrome
Spherocytosis (familial)
EXCLUDES *hemolytic anemia of newborn (773.0-773.5)*
DEF: Hereditary, chronic illness marked by abnormal red blood cell membrane; symptoms include enlarged spleen, jaundice; and anemia in severe cases.

282.1 Hereditary elliptocytosis
Elliptocytosis (congenital)
Ovalocytosis (congenital) (hereditary)
DEF: Genetic hemolytic anemia characterized by malformed, elliptical erythrocytes; there is increased destruction of red cells with resulting anemia.

282.2 Anemias due to disorders of glutathione metabolism
Anemia:
　6-phosphogluconic dehydrogenase deficiency
　enzyme deficiency, drug-induced
　erythrocytic glutathione deficiency
　glucose-6-phosphate dehydrogenase [G-6-PD] deficiency
　glutathione-reductase deficiency
　hemolytic nonspherocytic (hereditary), type I
Disorder of pentose phosphate pathway
Favism

282.3 Other hemolytic anemias due to enzyme deficiency
Anemia:
　hemolytic nonspherocytic (hereditary), type II
　hexokinase deficiency
　pyruvate kinase [PK] deficiency
　triosephosphate isomerase deficiency

✓5th 282.4 Thalassemias
EXCLUDES *sickle-cell:*
disease (282.60-282.69)
trait (282.5)
DEF: Inherited hemolytic disorders characterized by decreased production of at least one polypeptide globin chain results in defective hemoglobin synthesis; symptoms include severe anemia, expanded marrow spaces, transfusional and absorptive iron overload, impaired growth rate, thickened cranial bones, and pathologic fractures.
AHA: 4Q, '03, 51

282.40 Thalassemia, unspecified
Thalassemia NOS
AHA: 4Q, '11, 87-91

282.41 Sickle-cell thalassemia without crisis
Microdrepanocytosis
Sickle-cell thalassemia NOS
Thalassemia Hb-S disease without crisis

282.42 Sickle-cell thalassemia with crisis　　MCC
Sickle-cell thalassemia with vaso-occlusive pain
Thalassemia Hb-S disease with crisis
Use additional code for type of crisis, such as:
　acute chest syndrome (517.3)
　splenic sequestration (289.52)
CC Excl: 280.0-285.9, 286.53, 289.81-289.83, 289.89-289.9, 517.3

✓4th ✓5th Additional Digit Required　　Unacceptable PDx　　Manifestation Code　　Hospital Acquired Condition　　▶◀ Revised Text　　● New Code　　▲ Revised Code Title

2015 ICD-9-CM　　　　　**October 2014 • Volume 1 – 73**

Diseases of the Blood and Blood-Forming Organs

282.43–282.69

282.43 Alpha thalassemia
Alpha thalassemia major
Hemoglobin H Constant Spring
Hemoglobin H disease
Hydrops fetalis due to alpha thalassemia
Severe alpha thalassemia
Triple gene defect alpha thalassemia

> **EXCLUDES** *alpha thalassemia trait or minor (282.46)*
> *hydrops fetalis due to isoimmunization (773.3)*
> *hydrops fetalis not due to immune hemolysis (778.0)*

DEF: HBA1 and HBA2 genetic variant of chromosome 16 prevalent among Western African and South Asian descent; associated with a wide spectrum of anemic presentation, includes hemoglobin H disease subtypes.

AHA: 4Q, '11, 87-91

282.44 Beta thalassemia
Beta thalassemia major
Cooley's anemia
Homozygous beta thalassemia
Severe beta thalassemia
Thalassemia intermedia
Thalassemia major

> **EXCLUDES** *beta thalassemia minor (282.46)*
> *beta thalassemia trait (282.46)*
> *delta-beta thalassemia (282.45)*
> *hemoglobin E-beta thalassemia (282.47)*
> *sickle-cell beta thalassemia (282.41, 282.42)*

DEF: Diversity of mutations of HBB gene on chromosome 11 prevalent among Mediterranean and certain South Asian descent with significant cellular damage, can result in toxicity and increased disease severity (e.g., severe beta thalassemia, thalassemia major).

AHA: 4Q, '11, 87-91

282.45 Delta-beta thalassemia
Homozygous delta-beta thalassemia

> **EXCLUDES** *delta-beta thalassemia trait (282.46)*

AHA: 4Q, '11, 87-91

282.46 Thalassemia minor
Alpha thalassemia minor
Alpha thalassemia trait
Alpha thalassemia silent carrier
Beta thalassemia minor
Beta thalassemia trait
Delta-beta thalassemia trait
Thalassemia trait NOS

> **EXCLUDES** *alpha thalassemia (282.43)*
> *beta thalassemia (282.44)*
> *delta-beta thalassemia (282.45)*
> *hemoglobin E-beta thalassemia (282.47)*
> *sickle-cell trait (282.5)*

DEF: Solitary abnormal gene that identifies a carrier of the disease, yet with an absence of symptoms or a clinically mild anemic presentation.

AHA: 4Q, '11, 87-91

282.47 Hemoglobin E-beta thalassemia

> **EXCLUDES** *beta thalassemia (282.44)*
> *beta thalassemia minor (282.46)*
> *beta thalassemia trait (282.46)*
> *delta-beta thalassemia (282.45)*
> *delta-beta thalassemia trait (282.46)*
> *hemoglobin E disease (282.7)*
> *other hemoglobinopathies (282.7)*
> *sickle-cell beta thalassemia (282.41, 282.42)*

DEF: Clinically similar phenotype to B thalassemia major prevalent among Southeast Asian and certain Indian descent; results in severe transfusion-dependent anemia when present with certain B mutations.

AHA: 4Q, '11, 87-91

282.49 Other thalassemia
Dominant thalassemia
Hemoglobin C thalassemia
Hereditary leptocytosis
Mediterranean anemia (with other hemoglobinopathy)
Mixed thalassemia
Thalassemia with other hemoglobinopathy

> **EXCLUDES** *hemoglobin C disease (282.7)*
> *hemoglobin E disease (282.7)*
> *other hemoglobinopathies (282.7)*
> *sickle-cell anemias (282.60-282.69)*
> *sickle-cell beta thalassemia (282.41-282.42)*

282.5 Sickle-cell trait
Hb-AS genotype   Heterozygous:
Hemoglobin S [Hb-S] trait   hemoglobin S
              Hb-S

> **EXCLUDES** *that with other hemoglobinopathy (282.60-282.69)*
> *that with thalassemia (282.41-282.42)*

DEF: Heterozygous genetic makeup characterized by one gene for normal hemoglobin and one for sickle-cell hemoglobin; clinical disease rarely present.

AHA: 3Q, '12, 5

TIP: Report in addition to the appropriate code for the live birth (V30–V39) for a newborn with sickle cell trait.

TIP: Do not assign along with another code for sickle-cell disease or thalassemia.

√5th 282.6 Sickle-cell disease
Sickle-cell anemia

> **EXCLUDES** *sickle-cell thalassemia (282.41-282.42)*
> *sickle-cell trait (282.5)*

DEF: Inherited blood disorder; sickle-shaped red blood cells are hard and pointed, clogging blood flow; anemia characterized by periodic episodes of pain, acute abdominal discomfort, skin ulcerations of the legs, increased infections.

282.60 Sickle-cell disease, unspecified
Sickle-cell anemia NOS

AHA: 2Q, '97, 11

282.61 Hb-SS disease without crisis

282.62 Hb-SS disease with crisis   `MCC`
Hb-SS disease with vaso-occlusive pain
Sickle-cell crisis NOS

> Use additional code for type of crisis, such as:
> acute chest syndrome (517.3)
> splenic sequestration (289.52)

CC Excl: See code: 282.42

AHA: 4Q, '10, 78; 4Q, '03, 56; 2Q, '98, 8; 2Q, '91, 15

282.63 Sickle-cell/Hb-C disease without crisis
Hb-S/Hb-C disease without crisis

282.64 Sickle-cell/Hb-C disease with crisis   `MCC`
Hb-S/Hb-C disease with crisis
Sickle-cell/Hb-C disease with vaso-occlusive pain

> Use additional code for type of crisis, such as:
> acute chest syndrome (517.3)
> splenic sequestration (289.52)

CC Excl: See code: 282.42

AHA: 4Q, '03, 51

282.68 Other sickle-cell disease without crisis
Hb-S/Hb-D
Hb-S/Hb-E } diseases without
Sickle-cell/Hb-D   crisis
Sickle-cell/Hb-E

AHA: 4Q, '03, 51

282.69 Other sickle-cell disease with crisis   `MCC`
Hb-S/Hb-D
Hb-S/Hb-E } diseases with crisis
Sickle-cell/Hb-D
Sickle-cell/Hb-E
Other sickle-cell disease with vaso-occlusive pain

> Use additional code for type of crisis, such as:
> acute chest syndrome (517.3)
> splenic sequestration (289.52)

CC Excl: 280.0-285.9, 286.53, 289.81-289.83, 289.89-289.9, 517.3

`N` Newborn Age: 0   `P` Pediatric Age: 0-17   `M` Maternity Age: 12-55   `A` Adult Age: 15-124   `MCC` Major CC Condition   `CC` CC Condition   `HIV` HIV Related Dx

74 – Volume 1   **2015 ICD-9-CM**

282.7 Other hemoglobinopathies
Abnormal hemoglobin NOS
Congenital Heinz-body anemia
Disease:
hemoglobin C [Hb-C]
hemoglobin D [Hb-D]
hemoglobin E [Hb-E]
hemoglobin Zurich [Hb-Zurich]
Hemoglobinopathy NOS
Hereditary persistence of fetal hemoglobin [HPFH]
Unstable hemoglobin hemolytic disease

EXCLUDES *familial polycythemia (289.6)*
hemoglobin E-beta thalassemia (282.47)
hemoglobin M [Hb-M] disease (289.7)
high-oxygen-affinity hemoglobin (289.0)
other hemoglobinopathies with thalassemia (282.49)

DEF: Any disorder of hemoglobin due to alteration of molecular structure; may include overt anemia.

282.8 Other specified hereditary hemolytic anemias `CC`
Stomatocytosis
CC Excl: 280.0-284.2, 284.81-285.9, 289.9, 517.3, 776.5-776.6

282.9 Hereditary hemolytic anemia, unspecified `CC`
Hereditary hemolytic anemia NOS
CC Excl: See code: 282.8

√4th 283 Acquired hemolytic anemias
DEF: Non-hereditary anemia characterized by premature destruction of red blood cells; caused by infectious organisms, poisons, and physical agents.
AHA: N-D, '84, 1

283.0 Autoimmune hemolytic anemias `CC`
Autoimmune hemolytic disease (cold type) (warm type)
Chronic cold hemagglutinin disease
Cold agglutinin disease or hemoglobinuria
Hemolytic anemia:
cold type (secondary) (symptomatic)
drug-induced
warm type (secondary) (symptomatic)

Use additional E code to identify cause, if drug-induced
EXCLUDES *Evans' syndrome (287.32)*
hemolytic disease of newborn (773.0-773.5)
CC Excl: 280.0-285.9, 286.53, 289.81-289.83, 289.89-289.9, 517.3
AHA: 3Q, '08, 5

√5th 283.1 Non-autoimmune hemolytic anemias
Use additional E code to identify cause
DEF: Hemolytic anemia and thrombocytopenia with acute renal failure; relatively rare condition; 50 percent of patients require renal dialysis.
AHA: 4Q, '93, 25

283.10 Non-autoimmune hemolytic anemia, unspecified `CC`
CC Excl: See code: 283.0

283.11 Hemolytic-uremic syndrome `MCC`
Use additional code to identify associated:
E. coli infection (041.41-041.49)
Pneumococcal pnemonia (481)
Shigella dysenteriae (004.0)
CC Excl: See code: 283.0

283.19 Other non-autoimmune hemolytic anemias `CC`
Hemolytic anemia:
mechanical
microangiopathic
toxic
CC Excl: See code: 283.0

283.2 Hemoglobinuria due to hemolysis from external causes
Acute intravascular hemolysis
Hemoglobinuria:
due to other hemolysis
from exertion
march
paroxysmal (cold) (nocturnal)
Marchiafava-Micheli syndrome

Use additional E code to identify cause

283.9 Acquired hemolytic anemia, unspecified `CC`
Acquired hemolytic anemia NOS
Chronic idiopathic hemolytic anemia
CC Excl: See code: 283.0

√4th 284 Aplastic anemia and other bone marrow failure syndromes
DEF: Bone marrow failure to produce the normal amount of blood components; generally non-responsive to usual therapy.
AHA: 1Q, '91, 14; N-D, '84, 1; S-O, '84, 16

√5th 284.0 Constitutional aplastic anemia
AHA: 1Q, '91, 14

284.01 Constitutional red blood cell aplasia `CC`
Aplasia, (pure) red cell:
congenital
of infants
primary
Blackfan-Diamond syndrome
Familial hypoplastic anemia
CC Excl: 280.0-284.09, 284.81-285.9, 289.9, 776.5-776.6
AHA: 4Q, '06, 67-69

284.09 Other constitutional aplastic anemia `CC`
Fanconi's anemia
Pancytopenia with malformations
CC Excl: 280.0-284.09, 284.81-285.9, 287.30-287.39, 289.9, 776.5-776.6
AHA: 4Q, '06, 67-69

√5th 284.1 Pancytopenia
EXCLUDES *pancytopenia (due to) (with):*
aplastic anemia NOS (284.9)
bone marrow infiltration (284.2)
constitutional red blood cell aplasia (284.01)
hairy cell leukemia (202.4)
human immunodeficiency virus disease (042)
leukoerythroblastic anemia (284.2)
malformations (284.09)
myelodysplastic syndromes (238.72-238.75)
myeloproliferative disease (238.79)
other constitutional aplastic anemia (284.09)

AHA: 4Q, '11, 91-92; 4Q, '06, 67-69

284.11 Antineoplastic chemotherapy induced pancytopenia `MCC`
EXCLUDES *aplastic anemia due to antineoplastic chemotherapy (284.89)*
CC Excl: 284.11-285.9, 288.00-288.09, 288.4-288.62, 288.66-288.69, 289.9, 776.6
AHA: 4Q, '11, 92

284.12 Other drug-induced pancytopenia `MCC`
EXCLUDES *aplastic anemia due to drugs (284.89)*
CC Excl: see Code: 284.11

284.19 Other pancytopenia `CC`
CC Excl: see Code: 284.11
AHA: ►1Q, '14, 7◄

284.2 Myelophthisis `CC`
Leukoerythroblastic anemia
Myelophthisic anemia

Code first the underlying disorder, such as:
malignant neoplasm of breast (174.0-174.9, 175.0-175.9)
tuberculosis (015.0-015.9)
EXCLUDES *idiopathic myelofibrosis (238.76)*
myelofibrosis NOS (289.83)
myelofibrosis with myeloid metaplasia (238.76)
primary myelofibrosis (238.76)
secondary myelofibrosis (289.83)

DEF: A secondary disease process involving replacement of normal hematopoeitic tissue in the bone marrow with abnormal tissue, such as fibrous tissue or tumors. Occurs with advanced-stage neoplasms, granulomatous diseases such as miliary tuberculosis, and other inflammatory diseases.
CC Excl: 284.1-284.2, 284.81-285.9, 288.00-288.09, 288.4-288.62, 288.66-288.69, 289.9, 776.6
AHA: 4Q, '06, 67-69

√5th 284.8 Other specified aplastic anemias
AHA: 4Q, '07, 72; 3Q, '05, 11; 1Q, '97, 5; 1Q, '92, 15; 1Q, '91, 14

284.81 Red cell aplasia (acquired) (adult) (with thymoma) `MCC`
Red cell aplasia NOS
CC Excl: 280.0-285.9, 286.53, 289.81-289.83, 289.89-289.9, 517.3

284.89 Other specified aplastic anemias   `MCC`

Aplastic anemia (due to):
chronic systemic disease
drugs
infection
radiation
toxic (paralytic)

Use additional E code to identify cause

CC Excl: See code: 284.81

AHA: 1Q, '11, 6; 1Q, '09, 20; 2Q, '08, 6

284.9 Aplastic anemia, unspecified   `CC`

Anemia:
aplastic (idiopathic) NOS
aregenerative
hypoplastic NOS
nonregenerative
Medullary hypoplasia

EXCLUDES *refractory anemia (238.72)*

CC Excl: See code: 284.81

✓4th **285 Other and unspecified anemias**

AHA: 1Q, '91, 14; N-D, '84, 1

285.0 Sideroblastic anemia

Anemia:
hypochromic with iron loading
sideroachrestic
sideroblastic:
acquired
congenital
hereditary
primary
secondary (drug-induced) (due to disease)
sex-linked hypochromic
vitamin B6-responsive
Pyridoxine-responsive (hypochromic) anemia

Use additional E code to identify cause, if drug induced

EXCLUDES *refractory sideroblastic anemia (238.72)*

DEF: Characterized by a disruption of final heme synthesis; results in iron overload of reticuloendothelial tissues.

285.1 Acute posthemorrhagic anemia   `CC`

Anemia due to acute blood loss

EXCLUDES *anemia due to chronic blood loss (280.0)*
blood loss anemia NOS (280.0)

CC Excl: 280.0-285.9, 286.53, 289.81-289.83, 289.89-289.9, 517.3, 958.2

AHA: ▶3Q, '13, 9;◀4Q, '11, 146; 1Q, '07, 19; 2Q, '92, 15

✓5th **285.2 Anemia of chronic disease**

Anemia in (due to) (with) chronic illness

AHA: 4Q, '00, 39

285.21 Anemia in chronic kidney disease

Anemia in end stage renal disease
Erythropoietin-resistant anemia (EPO resistant anemia)

TIP: Assign also a code for the chronic kidney disease (585.X).

285.22 Anemia in neoplastic disease

EXCLUDES *anemia due to antineoplastic chemotherapy (285.3)*
aplastic anemia due to antineoplastic chemotherapy (284.89)

AHA: 4Q, '09, 81

TIP: Assign also a code for the neoplasm causing the anemia. Do not assign if anemia is caused by chemotherapy drugs, which is instead reported with 285.3.

D63.0 Anemia in neoplastic disease   `I-10`

285.29 Anemia of other chronic disease

Anemia in other chronic illness

285.3 Antineoplastic chemotherapy induced anemia

Anemia due to antineoplastic chemotherapy

EXCLUDES *anemia due to drug NEC — code to type of anemia*
anemia in neoplastic disease (285.22)
aplastic anemia due to antineoplastic chemotherapy (284.89)

DEF: Reversible adverse effect of chemotherapy, causing inhibition of bone marrow production; decrease in red blood cell production prevents adequate oxygenation of the tissues and organs causing fatigue, SOB, and exacerbation of other medical conditions.

AHA: 4Q, '09, 80-82

285.8 Other specified anemias

Anemia:
dyserythropoietic (congenital)
dyshematopoietic (congenital)
von Jaksch's
Infantile pseudoleukemia

AHA: 1Q, '91, 16

285.9 Anemia, unspecified

Anemia: Anemia:
NOS   profound
essential   progressive
normocytic, not due   secondary
to blood loss   Oligocythemia

EXCLUDES *anemia (due to):*
blood loss:
acute (285.1)
chronic or unspecified (280.0)
iron deficiency (280.0-280.9)

AHA: 1Q, '11, 16; 1Q, '09, 17, 20; 1Q. '07, 19; 1Q, '02, 14; 2Q, '92, 16; M-A, '85, 13; N-D, '84, 1

TIP: Assign for "postoperative anemia" if there is no mention of blood loss.

✓4th **286 Coagulation defects**

AHA: 2Q, '06, 17

286.0 Congenital factor VIII disorder   `MCC`

Antihemophilic globulin [AHG] deficiency
Factor VIII (functional)deficiency
Hemophilia:
NOS
A
classical
familial
hereditary
Subhemophilia

EXCLUDES *factor VIII deficiency with vascular defect (286.4)*

DEF: Hereditary, sex-linked, results in missing antihemophilic globulin (AHG) (factor VIII); causes abnormal coagulation characterized by increased bleeding, large bruises of skin, bleeding in mouth, nose, gastrointestinal tract; hemorrhages into joints, resulting in swelling and impaired function.

CC Excl: 286.0-286.4, 286.52-287.9, 289.81-289.9

286.1 Congenital factor IX disorder   `MCC`

Christmas disease
Deficiency:
factor IX (functional)
plasma thromboplastin component [PTC]
Hemophilia B

DEF: Deficiency of plasma thromboplastin component (PTC) (factor IX) and plasma thromboplastin antecedent (PTA); PTC deficiency clinically indistinguishable from classical hemophilia.

CC Excl: See code: 286.0

286.2 Congenital factor XI deficiency   `CC`

Hemophilia C
Plasma thromboplastin antecedent [PTA] deficiency
Rosenthal's disease

CC Excl: See code: 286.0

`N` Newborn Age: 0   `P` Pediatric Age: 0-17   `M` Maternity Age: 12-55   `A` Adult Age: 15-124   `MCC` Major CC Condition   `CC` CC Condition   `HIV` HIV Related Dx

286.3 Congenital deficiency of other clotting factors `CC`
　　Congenital afibrinogenemia
　　Deficiency:
　　　AC globulin factor:
　　　　I [fibrinogen]
　　　　II [prothrombin]
　　　　V [labile]
　　　　VII [stable]
　　　　X [Stuart-Prower]
　　　　XII [Hageman]
　　　　XIII [fibrin stabilizing]
　　　Laki-Lorand factor
　　　proaccelerin
　　Disease:
　　　Owren's
　　　Stuart-Prower
　　Dysfibrinogenemia (congenital)
　　Dysprothrombinemia (constitutional)
　　Hypoproconvertinemia
　　Hypoprothrombinemia (hereditary)
　　Parahemophilia
　　CC Excl: See code: 286.0
　　AHA: ▶4Q, '13, 87◀

286.4 von Willebrand's disease `CC`
　　Angiohemophilia (A) (B)
　　Constitutional thrombopathy
　　Factor VIII deficiency with vascular defect
　　Pseudohemophilia type B
　　Vascular hemophilia
　　von Willebrand's (-Jürgens') disease
　　EXCLUDES factor VIII deficiency:
　　　　　　NOS (286.0)
　　　　　　with functional defect (286.0)
　　　　　　hereditary capillary fragility (287.8)
　　DEF: Abnormal blood coagulation caused by deficient blood Factor VII; congenital; symptoms include excess or prolonged bleeding.
　　CC Excl: See code: 286.0

√5th **286.5 Hemorrhagic disorder due to intrinsic circulating anticoagulants, antibodies, or inhibitors**
　　AHA: 4Q, '11, 93-95; 3Q, '04, 7; No.5, '93, 16; 3Q, '92, 15; 3Q, '90, 14
　　TIP: Do not assign a code from subcategory 286.5 for Coumadin/warfarin toxicity, poisoning or adverse effect. Follow coding guidelines for poisoning and adverse reactions.

286.52 Acquired hemophilia `CC`
　　Autoimmune hemophilia
　　Autoimmune inhibitors to clotting factors
　　Secondary hemophilia
　　CC Excl: 286.0-286.4, 286.52-287.9, 289.81, 289.82, 289.84-289.9

286.53 Antiphospholipid antibody with hemorrhagic disorder `CC`
　　Lupus anticoagulant [LAC] with hemorrhagic disorder
　　Systemic lupus erythematosus [SLE] inhibitor with hemorrhagic disorder
　　EXCLUDES anti-phospholipid antibody, finding without diagnosis (795.79)
　　　　　　anti-phospholipid antibody syndrome (289.81)
　　　　　　anti-phospholipid antibody with hypercoagulable state (289.81)
　　　　　　lupus anticoagulant [LAC] finding without diagnosis (795.79)
　　　　　　lupus anticoagulant [LAC] with hypercoagulable state (289.81)
　　　　　　systemic lupus erythematosus [SLE] inhibitor finding without diagnosis (795.79)
　　　　　　systemic lupus erythematosus [SLE] inhibitor with hypercoagulable state (289.81)
　　CC Excl: 286.52-286.59, 288.00-288.51, 288.59- 289.9
　　TIP: When a resulting associated hypercoagulable state is present, assign code 289.81.

286.59 Other hemorrhagic disorder due to intrinsic circulating anticoagulants, antibodies, or inhibitors `CC`
　　Antithrombinemia
　　Antithromboplastinemia
　　Antithromboplastinogenemia
　　Increase in:
　　　anti-II (prothrombin)
　　　anti-VIIIa
　　　anti-IXa
　　　anti-XIa
　　CC Excl: See code: 286.52

286.6 Defibrination syndrome `MCC`
　　Afibrinogenemia, acquired
　　Consumption coagulopathy
　　Diffuse or disseminated intravascular coagulation [DIC syndrome]
　　Fibrinolytic hemorrhage, acquired
　　Hemorrhagic fibrinogenolysis
　　Pathologic fibrinolysis
　　Purpura:
　　　fibrinolytic
　　　fulminans
　　EXCLUDES that complicating:
　　　　　　abortion (634-638 with .1, 639.1)
　　　　　　pregnancy or the puerperium (641.3, 666.3)
　　　　　　disseminated intravascular coagulation in newborn (776.2)
　　DEF: Characterized by destruction of circulating fibrinogen; often precipitated by other conditions, such as injury, causing release of thromboplastic particles in blood stream.
　　CC Excl: See code: 286.0
　　AHA: 4Q, '93, 29

286.7 Acquired coagulation factor deficiency `CC`
　　Deficiency of coagulation factor due to:
　　　liver disease
　　　vitamin K deficiency
　　Hypoprothrombinemia, acquired
　　Use additional E code to identify cause, if drug induced
　　EXCLUDES vitamin K deficiency of newborn (776.0)
　　CC Excl: See code: 286.0
　　AHA: 4Q, '93, 29

286.9 Other and unspecified coagulation defects `CC`
　　Defective coagulation NOS　　　Disorder:
　　Deficiency, coagulation　　　　　coagulation
　　　factor NOS　　　　　　　　　　hemostasis
　　Delay, coagulation
　　EXCLUDES abnormal coagulation profile (790.92)
　　　　　　hemorrhagic disease of newborn (776.0)
　　　　　　that complicating:
　　　　　　　abortion (634-638 with .1, 639.1)
　　　　　　　pregnancy or the puerperium (641.3, 666.3)
　　CC Excl: See code: 286.0
　　AHA: 4Q, '99, 22; 4Q, '93, 29

√4th **287 Purpura and other hemorrhagic conditions**
　　EXCLUDES hemorrhagic thrombocythemia (238.71)
　　　　　　purpura fulminans (286.6)
　　AHA: 1Q, '91, 14

287.0 Allergic purpura `CC`
　　Peliosis rheumatica　　　　　Purpura:
　　Purpura:　　　　　　　　　　　nonthrombocytopenic:
　　　anaphylactoid　　　　　　　　idiopathic
　　　autoimmune　　　　　　　　　rheumatica
　　　Henoch's　　　　　　　　　　Schönlein-Henoch
　　　nonthrombocytopenic:　　　　vascular
　　　　hemorrhagic　　　　　　　Vasculitis, allergic
　　EXCLUDES hemorrhagic purpura (287.39)
　　　　　　purpura annularis telangiectodes (709.1)
　　DEF: Any hemorrhagic condition, thrombocytic or nonthrombocytopenic in origin, caused by a presumed allergic reaction.
　　CC Excl: See code: 286.0

Diseases of the Blood and Blood-Forming Organs

287.1–288.3

287.1 Qualitative platelet defects
Thrombasthenia (hemorrhagic) (hereditary)
Thrombocytasthenia
Thrombocytopathy (dystrophic)
Thrombopathy (Bernard-Soulier)
> **EXCLUDES** *von Willebrand's disease (286.4)*

287.2 Other nonthrombocytopenic purpuras
Purpura:
  NOS
  senile
  simplex

√5ᵗʰ **287.3 Primary thrombocytopenia**
> **EXCLUDES** *thrombotic thrombocytopenic purpura (446.6)*
> *transient thrombocytopenia of newborn (776.1)*

> **DEF:** Decrease in number of blood platelets in circulating blood and purpural skin hemorrhages.
> **AHA:** 4Q, '05, 56

287.30 Primary thrombocytopenia, unspecified
Megakaryocytic hypoplasia

287.31 Immune thrombocytopenic purpura   [CC]
Idiopathic thrombocytopenic purpura
Tidal platelet dysgenesis
> **DEF:** Tidal platelet dysgenesis: Platelet counts fluctuate from normal to very low within periods of 20 to 40 days and may involve autoimmune platelet destruction.
> **CC Excl:** See code: 286.0
> **AHA:** ▶1Q, '14, 7;◀ 4Q, '05, 57

287.32 Evans' syndrome   [CC]
> **DEF:** Combination of immunohemolytic anemia and autoimmune hemolytic anemia, sometimes with neutropenia.
> **CC Excl:** See code: 286.0

287.33 Congenital and hereditary thrombocytopenic purpura   [CC]
Congenital and hereditary thrombocytopenia
Thrombocytopenia with absent radii (TAR) syndrome
> **EXCLUDES** *Wiskott-Aldrich syndrome (279.12)*

> **DEF:** Thrombocytopenia with absent radii (TAR) syndrome: autosomal recessive syndrome characterized by thrombocytopenia and bilateral radial aplasia; manifestations include skeletal, gastrointestinal, hematologic, and cardiac system abnormalities.
> **CC Excl:** See code: 286.0

287.39 Other primary thrombocytopenia

√5ᵗʰ **287.4 Secondary thrombocytopenia**
> Use additional E code to identify cause
> **EXCLUDES** *heparin-induced thrombocytopenia (HIT) (289.84)*
> *transient thrombocytopenia of newborn (776.1)*

> **AHA:** 4Q, '10, 81-82; M-A, '85, 14

287.41 Posttransfusion purpura
Posttransfusion purpura from whole blood (fresh) or
  blood products
PTP
> **DEF:** A potentially fatal transfusion complication characterized by sudden onset of severe thrombocytopenia, fever, chills, and cutaneous hemorrhaging.

287.49 Other secondary thrombocytopenia
Thrombocytopenia (due to):
  dilutional
  drugs
  extracorporeal circulation of blood
  massive blood transfusion
  platelet alloimmunization
  secondary NOS
> **DEF:** Reduced number of platelets in circulating blood as consequence of an underlying disease or condition.

287.5 Thrombocytopenia, unspecified

287.8 Other specified hemorrhagic conditions
Capillary fragility (hereditary)
Vascular pseudohemophilia

287.9 Unspecified hemorrhagic conditions
Hemorrhagic diathesis (familial)

√4ᵗʰ **288 Diseases of white blood cells**
> **EXCLUDES** *leukemia (204.0-208.9)*
> **AHA:** 4Q, '06, 69; 1Q, '91, 14

√5ᵗʰ **288.0 Neutropenia**
Decreased absolute neutrophil count [ANC]
> Use additional code for any associated:
>   fever (780.61)
>   mucositis (478.11, 528.00-528.09, 538, 616.81)
> **EXCLUDES** *neutropenic splenomegaly (289.53)*
> *transitory neonatal neutropenia (776.7)*

> **DEF:** Sudden, severe condition characterized by reduced number of white blood cells; results in sores in the throat, stomach or skin; symptoms include chills, fever.
> **AHA:** 4Q, '06, 69-73; 3Q, '05, 11; 3Q, '99, 6; 2Q, '99, 9; 3Q, '96, 16; 2Q, '96, 6

288.00 Neutropenia, unspecified
> **AHA:** 4Q, '06, 69-73

288.01 Congenital neutropenia
Congenital agranulocytosis
Infantile genetic agranulocytosis
Kostmann's syndrome
> **AHA:** 4Q, '06, 69-73

288.02 Cyclic neutropenia
Cyclic hematopoiesis   Periodic neutropenia
> **AHA:** 4Q, '06, 69-73

288.03 Drug induced neutropenia
> Use additional E code to identify drug
> **AHA:** 4Q, '06, 69-73
> **TIP:** Assign for neutropenic fever due to chemotherapy drugs, along with codes for the fever, adverse effect, and the underlying malignancy.

288.04 Neutropenia due to infection
> **AHA:** 4Q, '06, 69-73

288.09 Other neutropenia
Agranulocytosis
Neutropenia:
  immune
  toxic
> **AHA:** 4Q, '06, 69-73

288.1 Functional disorders of polymorphonuclear neutrophils
Chronic (childhood) granulomatous disease
Congenital dysphagocytosis
Job's syndrome
Lipochrome histiocytosis (familial)
Progressive septic granulomatosis

288.2 Genetic anomalies of leukocytes
Anomaly (granulation) (granulocyte) or syndrome:
  Alder's (-Reilly)
  Chédiak-Steinbrinck (-Higashi)
  Jordan's
  May-Hegglin
  Pelger-Huet
Hereditary:
  hypersegmentation
  hyposegmentation
  leukomelanopathy

288.3 Eosinophilia
Eosinophilia:
  allergic
  hereditary
  idiopathic
  secondary
Eosinophilic leukocytosis
> **EXCLUDES** *Löffler's syndrome (518.3)*
> *pulmonary eosinophilia (518.3)*

> **DEF:** Elevated number of eosinophils in the blood; characteristic of allergic states and various parasitic infections.
> **AHA:** 3Q, '00, 11

[N] Newborn Age: 0   [P] Pediatric Age: 0-17   [M] Maternity Age: 12-55   [A] Adult Age: 15-124   [MCC] Major CC Condition   [CC] CC Condition   [HIV] HIV Related Dx

288.4 Hemophagocytic syndromes   CC
    Familial hemophagocytic lymphohistiocytosis
    Familial hemophagocytic reticulosis
    Hemophagocytic syndrome, infection-associated
    Histiocytic syndromes
    Macrophage activation syndrome
    CC Excl: 284.1-284.9, 286.6, 287.30-287.39, 287.41-288.09, 288.50,
    288.59, 289.84, 289.9
    AHA: 4Q, '06, 69-73

√5ᵗʰ 288.5 Decreased white blood cell count
    EXCLUDES *neutropenia (288.01-288.09)*

    288.50 Leukocytopenia, unspecified
        Decreased leukocytes, unspecified
        Decreased white blood cell count, unspecified
        Leukopenia NOS
        AHA: 4Q, '06, 69-73

    288.51 Lymphocytopenia
        Decreased lymphocytes
        AHA: 4Q, '06, 69-73

    288.59 Other decreased white blood cell count
        Basophilic leukopenia
        Eosinophilic leukopenia
        Monocytopenia
        Plasmacytopenia
        AHA: 4Q, '06, 69-73

√5ᵗʰ 288.6 Elevated white blood cell count
    EXCLUDES *eosinophilia (288.3)*

    288.60 Leukocytosis, unspecified
        Elevated leukocytes, unspecified
        Elevated white blood cell count, unspecified
        AHA: 4Q, '06, 69-73

    288.61 Lymphocytosis (symptomatic)
        Elevated lymphocytes
        AHA: 4Q, '06, 69-73

    288.62 Leukemoid reaction
        Basophilic leukemoid reaction
        Lymphocytic leukemoid reaction
        Monocytic leukemoid reaction
        Myelocytic leukemoid reaction
        Neutrophilic leukemoid reaction
        AHA: 4Q, '06, 69-73

    288.63 Monocytosis (symptomatic)
        EXCLUDES *infectious mononucleosis (075)*
        AHA: 4Q, '06, 69-73

    288.64 Plasmacytosis
        AHA: 4Q, '06, 69-73

    288.65 Basophilia
        AHA: 4Q, '06, 69-73

    288.66 Bandemia
        Bandemia without diagnosis of specific infection
        EXCLUDES *confirmed infection — code to infection*
            leukemia (204.00-208.9)
        DEF: Increase in early neutrophil cells, called band cells; may
        indicate infection.
        AHA: 4Q, '07, 73
        TIP: Do not assign based on lab values alone; physician
        must substantiate bandemia without evidence of
        corresponding infection.

    288.69 Other elevated white blood cell count
        AHA: 4Q, '06, 69-73

288.8 Other specified disease of white blood cells
    EXCLUDES *decreased white blood cell counts (288.50-288.59)*
           elevated white blood cell counts (288.60-288.69)
           immunity disorders (279.0-279.9)
    AHA: M-A, '87, 12

288.9 Unspecified disease of white blood cells

√4ᵗʰ 289 Other diseases of blood and blood-forming organs

289.0 Polycythemia, secondary
    High-oxygen-affinity hemoglobin   Polycythemia:
    Polycythemia: erythropoietin
        acquired   hypoxemic
        benign   nephrogenous
        due to: relative
           fall in plasma volume   spurious
           high altitude   stress
        emotional
    EXCLUDES *polycythemia:*
           neonatal (776.4)
           primary (238.4)
           vera (238.4)
    DEF: Elevated number of red blood cells in circulating blood as result
    of reduced oxygen supply to the tissues.
    D75.1 Secondary polycythemia   I-10

289.1 Chronic lymphadenitis
    Chronic:
        adenitis   } any lymph node, except
        lymphadenitis }   mesenteric
    EXCLUDES *acute lymphadenitis (683)*
           mesenteric (289.2)
           enlarged glands NOS (785.6)
    DEF: Persistent inflammation of lymph node tissue; origin of
    infection is usually elsewhere.
    I88.1 Chronic lymphadenitis except mesenteric   I-10

289.2 Nonspecific mesenteric lymphadenitis
    Mesenteric lymphadenitis (acute) (chronic)
    DEF: Inflammation of the lymph nodes in peritoneal fold that encases
    abdominal organs; disease resembles acute appendicitis; unknown
    etiology.
    I88.0 Nonspecific mesenteric lymphadenitis   I-10

289.3 Lymphadenitis, unspecified, except mesenteric
    AHA: 2Q, '12, 18; 2Q, '92, 8
    I88.9 Nonspecific lymphadenitis unspecified   I-10

289.4 Hypersplenism
    "Big spleen" syndrome   Hypersplenia
    Dyssplenism
    EXCLUDES *primary splenic neutropenia (289.53)*
    DEF: An overactive spleen causing a deficiency of the peripheral
    blood components, an increase in bone marrow cells and sometimes
    a notable increase in the size of the spleen.
    D73.1 Hypersplenism   I-10

√5ᵗʰ 289.5 Other diseases of spleen

    289.50 Disease of spleen, unspecified
        D73.9 Disease of spleen unspecified   I-10

    289.51 Chronic congestive splenomegaly
        D73.2 Chronic congestive splenomegaly   I-10

    289.52 Splenic sequestration
        Code first sickle-cell disease in crisis (282.42, 282.62,
          282.64, 282.69)
        DEF: Blood is entrapped in the spleen due to vessel occlusion;
        most often associated with sickle-cell disease; spleen
        becomes enlarged and there is a sharp drop in hemoglobin.
        AHA: 4Q, '03, 51

    289.53 Neutropenic splenomegaly
        AHA: 4Q, '06, 73
        D73.81 Neutropenic splenomegaly   I-10

    289.59 Other
        Lien migrans   Splenic:
        Perisplenitis   fibrosis
        Splenic: infarction
          abscess   rupture, nontraumatic
          atrophy   Splenitis
          cyst   Wandering spleen
        EXCLUDES *bilharzial splenic fibrosis (120.0-120.9)*
            hepatolienal fibrosis (571.5)
            splenomegaly NOS (789.2)
        AHA: ▶1Q, '14, 11◀
        D73.89 Other diseases of spleen   I-10

289.6 Familial polycythemia
    Familial: Familial:
        benign polycythemia   erythrocytosis
    DEF: Elevated number of red blood cells.

289.7 Methemoglobinemia `CC`

Congenital NADH [DPNH]-methemoglobin-
     reductase deficiency
Hemoglobin M [Hb-M] disease
Methemoglobinemia:
     NOS
     acquired (with sulfhemoglobinemia)
     hereditary
     toxic
Stokvis' disease
Sulfhemoglobinemia

Use additional E code to identify cause

DEF: Presence of blood methemoglobin, a chemically altered form of hemoglobin; causes cyanosis, headache, ataxia, dyspnea, tachycardia, nausea, stupor, and coma.

CC Excl: 282.7-283.10, 283.19-283.9, 285.3-285.9, 289.7, 289.9

D74.0 Congenital methemoglobinemia `I-10`

☑5ᵗʰ **289.8 Other specified diseases of blood and blood-forming organs**

DEF: Hypercoagulable states: a group of inherited or acquired abnormalities of specific proteins and anticoagulant factors; also called thromboembolic states or thrombotic disorders, result in abnormal development of blood clots.

AHA: 4Q, '03, 56; 1Q, '02, 16; 2Q, '89, 8; M-A, '87, 12

289.81 Primary hypercoagulable state `CC`

Activated protein C resistance
Antiphospholipid antibody syndrome
Antithrombin III deficiency
Factor V Leiden mutation
Lupus anticoagulant with hypercoagulable state
Protein C deficiency
Protein S deficiency
Prothrombin gene mutation
Systemic lupus erythematosus [SLE] inhibitor with hypercoagulable state

EXCLUDES *anti-phospholipid antibody, finding without diagnosis (795.79)*
anti-phospholipid antibody with hemorrhagic disorder (286.53)
lupus anticoagulant [LAC] finding without diagnosis (795.79)
lupus anticoagulant [LAC] with hemorrhagic disorder (286.53)
secondary activated protein C resistance (289.82)
secondary antiphospholipid antibody syndrome (289.82)
secondary lupus anticoagulant with hypercoagulable state (289.82)
secondary systemic lupus erythematosus [SLE] inhibitor with hypercoagulable state (289.82)
systemic lupus erythematosus [SLE] inhibitor finding without diagnosis (795.79)
systemic lupus erythematosus [SLE] inhibitor with hypercoagulable state (286.53)

DEF: Activated protein C resistance: decreased effectiveness of protein C to degrade factor V, necessary to inhibit clotting cascade; also called Factor V Leiden mutation.

DEF: Antithrombin III deficiency: deficiency in plasma antithrombin III one of six naturally occurring antithrombins that limit coagulation.

DEF: Factor V Leiden mutation: also called activated protein C resistance.

DEF: Lupus anticoagulant: autoimmune deficiency in a circulating anticoagulant that inhibits the conversion of prothrombin into thrombin; also called anti-phospholipid syndrome.

DEF: Protein C deficiency: deficiency of activated protein C which functions to bring the blood-clotting process into balance; same outcome as factor V Leiden mutation.

DEF: Protein S deficiency: similar to protein C deficiency; protein S is a vitamin K dependent cofactor in the activation of protein C.

DEF: Prothrombin gene mutation: increased levels of prothrombin, or factor II, a plasma protein that is converted to thrombin, which acts upon fibrinogen to form the fibrin.

CC Excl: 286.53, 288.00-288.9, 289.53, 289.81-289.83, 289.89-289.9

AHA: 4Q, '11, 93

D68.59 Other primary thrombophilia `I-10`

289.82 Secondary hypercoagulable state `CC`

EXCLUDES *heparin-induced thrombocytopenia (HIT) (289.84)*

CC Excl: See code: 289.81

D68.69 Other thrombophilia `I-10`

289.83 **Myelofibrosis** `CC`

Myelofibrosis NOS
Secondary myelofibrosis

Code first the underlying disorder, such as:
     malignant neoplasm of breast (174.0-174.9, 175.0-175.9)

Use additional code for associated therapy-related myelodysplastic syndrome, if applicable (238.72, 238.73)

Use additional external cause code if due to anti-neoplastic chemotherapy (E933.1)

EXCLUDES *idiopathic myelofibrosis (238.76)*
leukoerythroblastic anemia (284.2)
myelofibrosis with myeloid metaplasia (238.76)
myelophthisic anemia (284.2)
myelophthisis (284.2)
primary myelofibrosis (238.76)

DEF: A progressive bone marrow disease characterized by the replacement of bone marrow with the overgrowth of neoplastic stem cells and fibrotic tissue, also progressive anemia and enlarged spleen.

CC Excl: 202.40-202.48, 203.10-203.11, 203.80-203.81, 204.00-208.92, 238.4-238.76, 238.79-238.9

AHA: 4Q, '06, 73

D75.81 Myelofibrosis `I-10`

289.84 Heparin-induced thrombocytopenia [HIT]

DEF: Immune-mediated reaction to heparin therapy causing an abrupt fall in platelet count and serious complications such as pulmonary embolism, stroke, AMI or DVT.

AHA: 4Q, '08, 100-101

289.89 Other specified diseases of blood and blood-forming organs

Hypergammaglobulinemia
Pseudocholinesterase deficiency

D75.89 Oth specified dz of blood & blood-forming organs `I-10`

289.9 Unspecified diseases of blood and blood-forming organs

Blood dyscrasia NOS
Erythroid hyperplasia

AHA: M-A, '85, 14

D75.9 Disease of blood and blood-forming organs unspec `I-10`

N Newborn Age: 0   **P** Pediatric Age: 0-17   **M** Maternity Age: 12-55   **A** Adult Age: 15-124   **MCC** Major CC Condition   **CC** CC Condition   **HIV** HIV Related Dx

80 – Volume 1   **2015 ICD-9-CM**

5. Mental, Behavioral and Neurodevelopmental Disorders (290-319)

Psychoses (290-299)

EXCLUDES *intellectual disabilities (317-319)*

Organic Psychotic Conditions (290-294)

INCLUDES *psychotic organic brain syndrome*

EXCLUDES *nonpsychotic syndromes of organic etiology (310.0-310.9)*
psychoses classifiable to 295-298 and without impairment of orientation, comprehension, calculation, learning capacity, and judgment, but associated with physical disease, injury, or condition affecting the brain [eg., following childbirth] (295.0-298.8)

√4ᵗʰ **290 Dementias**

Code first the associated neurological condition

EXCLUDES *dementia due to alcohol (291.0-291.2)*
dementia due to drugs (292.82)
dementia not classified as senile, presenile, or arteriosclerotic (294.10-294.11)
psychoses classifiable to 295-298 occurring in the senium without dementia or delirium (295.0-298.8)
senility with mental changes of nonpsychotic severity (310.1)
transient organic psychotic conditions (293.0-293.9)

290.0 Senile dementia, uncomplicated `A`
Senile dementia: Senile dementia:
 NOS   simple type

EXCLUDES *mild memory disturbances, not amounting to dementia, associated with senile brain disease (310.89)*
senile dementia with:
 delirium or confusion (290.3)
 delusional [paranoid] features (290.20)
 depressive features (290.21)

AHA: 4Q, '99, 4

F03.90 Unspecif dementia w/o behavioral disturbance `I-10`

√5ᵗʰ **290.1 Presenile dementia**
Brain syndrome with presenile brain disease

EXCLUDES *arteriosclerotic dementia (290.40-290.43)*
dementia associated with other cerebral conditions (294.10-294.11)

AHA: N-D, '84, 20

290.10 Presenile dementia, uncomplicated `A` `HIV`
Presenile dementia:
 NOS
 simple type

290.11 Presenile dementia with delirium `CC` `A` `HIV`
Presenile dementia with acute confusional state
CC Excl: 290.0-290.12, 290.20-290.3, 290.8-290.9, 292.81, 293.0, V62.84
AHA: 1Q, '88, 3

290.12 Presenile dementia with delusional features `CC` `A` `HIV`
Presenile dementia, paranoid type
CC Excl: 079.82, 290.0-290.12, 290.20-290.3, 290.8-290.9, 292.81, 293.0

290.13 Presenile dementia with depressive features `CC` `A` `HIV`
Presenile dementia, depressed type
CC Excl: 290.0, 290.13-290.3, 296.21-296.24, 296.30-296.34, 296.43-296.44, 296.53-296.54, 296.63-296.64

√5ᵗʰ **290.2 Senile dementia with delusional or depressive features**
EXCLUDES *senile dementia:*
 NOS (290.0)
 with delirium and/or confusion (290.3)

290.20 Senile dementia with delusional features `CC` `A`
Senile dementia, paranoid type
Senile psychosis NOS
CC Excl: 290.0-290.20, 290.3

290.21 Senile dementia with depressive features `CC` `A`
CC Excl: 290.13, 290.21

290.3 Senile dementia with delirium `CC`
Senile dementia with acute confusional state
EXCLUDES *senile:*
 dementia NOS (290.0)
 psychosis NOS (290.20)
CC Excl: 290.10-290.20, 290.3, V62.84
AHA: 3Q, '09, 11

√5ᵗʰ **290.4 Vascular dementia**
Multi-infarct dementia or psychosis

Use additional code to identify cerebral atherosclerosis (437.0)

EXCLUDES *suspected cases with no clear evidence of arteriosclerosis (290.9)*
AHA: 1Q, '88, 3

290.40 Vascular dementia, uncomplicated `A`
Arteriosclerotic dementia:
 NOS
 simple type
F01.50 Vascular dementia without behavioral disturbance `I-10`

290.41 Vascular dementia with delirium `CC` `A`
Arteriosclerotic dementia with acute confusional state
CC Excl: 290.11-290.12, 290.20, 290.3, 290.41

290.42 Vascular dementia with delusions `CC` `A`
Arteriosclerotic dementia, paranoid type
CC Excl: 290.42

290.43 Vascular dementia with depressed mood `CC` `A`
Arteriosclerotic dementia, depressed type
CC Excl: 290.43

290.8 Other specified senile psychotic conditions `CC`
Presbyophrenic psychosis
CC Excl: 290.8-291.0, 292.11, 292.81-292.82, 295.00-295.04, 295.10-295.14, 295.21-295.24, 295.31, 295.33-295.34, 295.40-295.44, 295.53-295.54, 295.63-295.64, 295.71, 295.73-295.74, 295.80-295.84, 295.91, 295.93-295.94, 296.21-296.24, 296.30-296.34

290.9 Unspecified senile psychotic condition `CC` `A`
CC Excl: See code: 290.8

√4ᵗʰ **291 Alcohol induced mental disorders**
EXCLUDES *alcoholism without psychosis (303.0-303.9)*
AHA: 1Q, '88, 3; S-O, '86, 3

291.0 Alcohol withdrawal delirium `CC`
Alcoholic delirium
Delirium tremens
EXCLUDES *alcohol withdrawal (291.81)*
CC Excl: 291.0-294.9, 303.00-305.03, 305.20-305.93, 790.3
AHA: 2Q, '91, 11
F10.921 Alcohol use unsp w/intox delirium `I-10`

291.1 Alcohol induced persisting amnestic disorder
Alcoholic polyneuritic psychosis
Korsakoff's psychosis, alcoholic
Wernicke-Korsakoff syndrome (alcoholic)
DEF: Prominent and lasting reduced memory span, disordered time appreciation and confabulation, occurring in alcoholics, as sequel to acute alcoholic psychosis.
AHA: 1Q, '88, 3

291.2 Alcohol induced persisting dementia `CC`
Alcoholic dementia NOS
Alcoholism associated with dementia NOS
Chronic alcoholic brain syndrome
CC Excl: See code: 291.0
F10.27 Alcohol depend alcohol-induced persist dementia `I-10`

Mental, Behavioral and Neurodevelopmental Disorders

291.3–293.0

291.3 Alcohol induced psychotic disorder with hallucinations `CC`
Alcoholic:
   hallucinosis (acute)
   psychosis with hallucinosis

> **EXCLUDES** *alcohol withdrawal with delirium (291.0)*
> *schizophrenia (295.0-295.9) and paranoid states (297.0-297.9) taking the form of chronic hallucinosis with clear consciousness in an alcoholic*

DEF: Psychosis lasting less than six months with slight or no clouding of consciousness in which auditory hallucinations predominate.
CC Excl: See code: 291.0
AHA: 2Q, '91, 11

291.4 Idiosyncratic alcohol intoxication
Pathologic: Pathologic:
   alcohol intoxication   drunkenness

> **EXCLUDES** *acute alcohol intoxication (305.0)*
> *in alcoholism (303.0)*
> *simple drunkenness (305.0)*

DEF: Unique behavioral patterns, like belligerence, after intake of relatively small amounts of alcohol; behavior not due to excess consumption.

291.5 Alcohol induced psychotic disorder with delusions
Alcoholic: Alcoholic:
   paranoia   psychosis, paranoid type

> **EXCLUDES** *nonalcoholic paranoid states (297.0-297.9)*
> *schizophrenia, paranoid type (295.3)*

`√5ᵗʰ` **291.8 Other specified alcohol induced mental disorders**
AHA: 3Q, '94, 13; J-A, '85, 10

  291.81 Alcohol withdrawal `CC`
    Alcohol:
      abstinence syndrome or symptoms
      withdrawal syndrome or symptoms

> **EXCLUDES** *alcohol withdrawal:*
> *delirium (291.0)*
> *hallucinosis (291.3)*
> *delirium tremens (291.0)*

    CC Excl: See code: 291.0
    AHA: 2Q, '12, 9; 4Q, '96, 28; 2Q, '91, 11
    `F10.239` Alcohol dependence with withdrawal unspec `I-10`

  291.82 Alcohol induced sleep disorders
    Alcohol induced circadian rhythm sleep disorders
    Alcohol induced hypersomnia
    Alcohol induced insomnia
    Alcohol induced parasomnia

  291.89 Other `CC`
    Alcohol induced anxiety disorder
    Alcohol induced mood disorder
    Alcohol induced sexual dysfunction
    CC Excl: See code: 291.0

291.9 Unspecified alcohol induced mental disorders `CC`
Alcoholic:
   mania NOS
   psychosis NOS
Alcoholism (chronic) with psychosis
Alcohol related disorder NOS
CC Excl: See code: 291.0

`√4ᵗʰ` **292 Drug induced mental disorders**
> **INCLUDES** organic brain syndrome associated with consumption of drugs

Use additional code for any associated drug dependence (304.0-304.9)
Use additional E code to identify drug
AHA: 3Q, '04, 8; 2Q, '91, 11; S-O, '86, 3

292.0 Drug withdrawal `CC`
Drug:
   abstinence syndrome or symptoms
   withdrawal syndrome or symptoms
CC Excl: See code: 291.0
AHA: 1Q, '97, 12; 1Q, '88, 3
TIP: Assign only for patients who suffer mental or behavioral disturbances due to drug withdrawal, regardless of the circumstances.
`F19.939` Oth psychoactive sbstnc use uns w/withdrawal uns `I-10`

`√5ᵗʰ` **292.1 Drug induced psychotic disorders**

  292.11 Drug induced psychotic disorder with delusions `CC`
    Paranoid state induced by drugs
    CC Excl: See code: 291.0

  292.12 Drug induced psychotic disorder with hallucinations `CC`
    Hallucinatory state induced by drugs

> **EXCLUDES** *states following LSD or other hallucinogens, lasting only a few days or less ["bad trips"] (305.3)*

    CC Excl: See code: 291.0

292.2 Pathological drug intoxication
Drug reaction:
   NOS
   idiosyncratic   } resulting in brief psychotic states
   pathologic

> **EXCLUDES** *expected brief psychotic reactions to hallucinogens ["bad trips"] (305.3)*
> *physiological side-effects of drugs (e.g., dystonias)*

`√5ᵗʰ` **292.8 Other specified drug induced mental disorders**

  292.81 Drug induced delirium `CC`
    CC Excl: 291.0-294.9, 303.00-305.03, 305.20-305.93, 790.3
    AHA: 1Q, '88, 3
    `F19.921` Oth psychoactv sbstnc use uns intoxcatn delirium `I-10`

  292.82 Drug induced persisting dementia `CC`
    CC Excl: See code: 292.81

  292.83 Drug induced persisting amnestic disorder

  292.84 Drug induced mood disorder
    Depressive state induced by drugs

  292.85 Drug induced sleep disorders
    Drug induced circadian rhythm sleep disorder
    Drug induced hypersomnia
    Drug induced insomnia
    Drug induced parasomnia

  292.89 Other
    Drug induced anxiety disorder
    Drug induced organic personality syndrome
    Drug induced sexual dysfunction
    Drug intoxication

292.9 Unspecified drug induced mental disorder
Drug related disorder NOS
Organic psychosis NOS due to or associated with drugs

`√4ᵗʰ` **293 Transient mental disorders due to conditions classified elsewhere**
> **INCLUDES** transient organic mental disorders not associated with alcohol or drugs

Code first the associated physical or neurological condition

> **EXCLUDES** *confusional state or delirium superimposed on senile dementia (290.3)*
> *dementia due to:*
> *alcohol (291.0-291.9)*
> *arteriosclerosis (290.40-290.43)*
> *drugs (292.82)*
> *senility (290.0)*

293.0 Delirium due to conditions classified elsewhere `CC`
Acute:
   confusional state
   infective psychosis
   organic reaction
   posttraumatic organic psychosis
   psycho-organic syndrome
Acute psychosis associated with endocrine, metabolic, or cerebrovascular disorder
Epileptic:
   confusional state
   twilight state
CC Excl: 290.11, 290.3, 293.0, V62.84
AHA: 1Q, '88, 3
`F05` Delirium due to known physiological condition `I-10`

`N` Newborn Age: 0   `P` Pediatric Age: 0-17   `M` Maternity Age: 12-55   `A` Adult Age: 15-124   `MCC` Major CC Condition   `CC` CC Condition   `HIV` HIV Related Dx

293.1 Subacute delirium `CC`
Subacute:
  confusional state
  infective psychosis
  organic reaction
  posttraumatic organic psychosis
  psycho-organic syndrome
  psychosis associated with endocrine or metabolic disorder
CC Excl: 293.0-293.1, 293.89-293.9

√5ᵗʰ **293.8 Other specified transient mental disorders due to conditions classified elsewhere**

293.81 Psychotic disorder with delusions in conditions classified elsewhere `CC`
Transient organic psychotic condition, paranoid type
CC Excl: 291.0-294.9, 303.00-305.03, 305.20-305.93, 790.3
AHA: 1Q, '11, 12

293.82 Psychotic disorder with hallucinations in conditions classified elsewhere `CC`
Transient organic psychotic condition, hallucinatory type
CC Excl: See code: 293.81

293.83 Mood disorder in conditions classified elsewhere
Transient organic psychotic condition, depressive type

293.84 Anxiety disorder in conditions classified elsewhere
AHA: 4Q, '96, 29

293.89 Other
Catatonic disorder in conditions classified elsewhere

293.9 Unspecified transient mental disorder in conditions classified elsewhere `CC`
Organic psychosis:
  infective NOS
  posttraumatic NOS
  transient NOS
Psycho-organic syndrome
CC Excl: See code: 293.81

√4ᵗʰ **294 Persistent mental disorders due to conditions classified elsewhere**
INCLUDES organic psychotic brain syndromes (chronic), not elsewhere classified
AHA: M-A, '85, 12

294.0 Amnestic disorder in conditions classified elsewhere
Korsakoff's psychosis or syndrome (nonalcoholic)
Code first underlying condition
EXCLUDES alcoholic:
  amnestic syndrome (291.1)
  Korsakoff's psychosis (291.1)

√5ᵗʰ **294.1 Dementia in conditions classified elsewhere**
Dementia of the Alzheimer's type
Code first any underlying physical condition, as:
  Alzheimer's disease (331.0)
  cerebral lipidoses (330.1)
  dementia with Lewy bodies (331.82)
  dementia with Parkinsonism (331.82)
  epilepsy (345.0-345.9)
  frontal dementia (331.19)
  frontotemporal dementia (331.19)
  general paresis [syphilis] (094.1)
  hepatolenticular degeneration (275.1)
  Huntington's chorea (333.4)
  Jakob-Creutzfeldt disease (046.11-046.19)
  multiple sclerosis (340)
  Parkinson's disease (332.0)
  Pick's disease of the brain (331.11)
  polyarteritis nodosa (446.0)
  syphilis (094.1)
EXCLUDES dementia:
  arteriosclerotic (290.40-290.43)
  presenile (290.10-290.13)
  senile (290.0)
  epileptic psychosis NOS (294.8)
AHA: 4Q, '00, 40; 1Q, '99, 14; N-D, '85, 5

294.10 **Dementia in conditions classified elsewhere without behavioral disturbance**
Dementia in conditions classified elsewhere NOS
F02.80 Dementia in oth dz class elsw w/o behavrl disturb `I-10`

294.11 **Dementia in conditions classified elsewhere with behavioral disturbance** `CC`
Aggressive behavior   Violent behavior
Combative behavior
Use additional code, where applicable, to identify:
  wandering in conditions classified elsewhere (V40.31)
CC Excl: 294.11, 294.21
AHA: 4Q, '00, 41
TIP: Review entire medical record for documentation of behavioral disturbance (aggressive, combative, violent behavior, wandering off); requires physician substantiation.

√5ᵗʰ **294.2 Dementia, unspecified**
EXCLUDES mild memory disturbances, not amounting to dementia (310.89)
AHA: 4Q, '11, 95-96

294.20 Dementia, unspecified, without behavioral disturbance
Dementia NOS

294.21 Dementia, unspecified, with behavioral disturbance `CC`
Aggressive behavior   Violent behavior
Combative behavior
Use additional code, where applicable, to identify:
  wandering in conditions classified elsewhere (V40.31)
CC Excl: see Code: 294.11
AHA: 4Q, '11, 95

294.8 Other persistent mental disorders due to conditions classified elsewhere
Amnestic disorder NOS
Epileptic psychosis NOS
Mixed paranoid and affective organic psychotic states
Use additional code for associated epilepsy (345.0-345.9)
EXCLUDES mild memory disturbances, not amounting to dementia (310.89)
AHA: 3Q, '09, 11; 3Q, '03, 14; 1Q, '88, 5
F06.8 Oth spec mental disord d/t known physiol cond `I-10`

294.9 Unspecified persistent mental disorders due to conditions classified elsewhere `HIV`
Cognitive disorder NOS   Organic psychosis (chronic)
AHA: 2Q, '07, 4

Other Psychoses (295-299)

Use additional code to identify any associated physical disease, injury, or condition affecting the brain with psychoses classifiable to 295-298

√4ᵗʰ **295 Schizophrenic disorders**
INCLUDES schizophrenia of the types described in 295.0-295.9 occurring in children
EXCLUDES childhood type schizophrenia (299.9)
  infantile autism (299.0)

The following fifth-digit subclassification is for use with category 295:
  0 unspecified
  1 subchronic
  2 chronic
  3 subchronic with acute exacerbation
  4 chronic with acute exacerbation
  5 in remission

DEF: Group of disorders with disturbances in thought (delusions, hallucinations), mood (blunted, flattened, inappropriate affect), sense of self; also bizarre, purposeless behavior, repetitious activity, or inactivity.

§ √5ᵗʰ **295.0 Simple type** `CC 0-4`
[0-5] Schizophrenia simplex
EXCLUDES latent schizophrenia (295.5)
CC Excl: For codes 295.00-295.04: 295.00-301.9, 306.0-310.2, 310.9-315.34, 315.39-319, 339.10-339.12, 388.45, 799.23-799.24

---

§   Requires fifth digit. Valid digits are in [brackets] under each code. See category 295 for codes and definitions.

√4ᵗʰ √5ᵗʰ Additional Digit Required   Unacceptable PDx   Manifestation Code   Hospital Acquired Condition   ▶◀ Revised Text   ● New Code   ▲ Revised Code Title

§ ✓5ᵗʰ **295.1 Disorganized type**   `CC 0-4`
[0-5]   Hebephrenia
     Hebephrenic type schizophrenia
DEF: Inappropriate behavior; results in extreme incoherence and disorganization of time, place and sense of social appropriateness; withdrawal from routine social interaction may occur.
CC Excl: For codes 295.10-295.14: 295.00-301.9, 306.0-319, 339.10-339.12, 388.45, 799.23-799.24

§ ✓5ᵗʰ **295.2 Catatonic type**   `CC 0-4`
[0-5]   Catatonic (schizophrenia):
     agitation
     excitation
     excited type
     stupor
     withdrawn type
   Schizophrenic:
     catalepsy
     catatonia
     flexibilitas cerea
DEF: Extreme changes in motor activity; one extreme is decreased response or reaction to the environment and the other is spontaneous activity.
CC Excl: For codes 295.20-295.24: 295.00-301.9, 306.0-319, 339.10-339.12, 388.45, 799.23-799.24

§ ✓5ᵗʰ **295.3 Paranoid type**   `CC 0-4`
[0-5]   Paraphrenic schizophrenia
   EXCLUDES *involutional paranoid state (297.2)*
               paranoia (297.1)
               paraphrenia (297.2)
DEF: Preoccupied with delusional suspicions and auditory hallucinations related to single theme; usually hostile, grandiose, overly religious, occasionally hypochondriacal.
CC Excl: For codes 295.30-295.34: 295.00-301.9, 306.0-319, 339.10-339.12, 388.45, 799.23-799.24
F20.0 Paranoid schizophrenia   `I-10`

§ ✓5ᵗʰ **295.4 Schizophreniform disorder**   `CC 0-4`
[0-5]   Oneirophrenia   Schizophreniform:
   Schizophreniform: psychosis, confusional type
     attack
   EXCLUDES *acute forms of schizophrenia of:*
               catatonic type (295.2)
               hebephrenic type (295.1)
               paranoid type (295.3)
               simple type (295.0)
               undifferentiated type (295.8)
CC Excl: For codes 295.40-295.44: 295.00-301.9, 306.0-319, 339.10-339.12, 388.45, 799.23-799.24

§ ✓5ᵗʰ **295.5 Latent schizophrenia**   `CC 3-4`
[0-5]   Latent schizophrenic reaction
   Schizophrenia:
     borderline
     incipient
     prepsychotic
     prodromal
     pseudoneurotic
     pseudopsychopathic
   EXCLUDES *schizoid personality (301.20-301.22)*
CC Excl: For code 295.53-295.54: 295.00-295.04, 295.10-295.14, 295.21-295.24, 295.31, 295.33-295.34, 295.40-295.44, 295.53-295.54, 295.63-295.64, 295.71, 295.73-295.74, 295.80-295.84, 295.91, 295.93-295.94
AHA: For code 295.50: 1Q, '06, 10

§ ✓5ᵗʰ **295.6 Residual type**   `CC 0-4`
[0-5]   Chronic undifferentiated schizophrenia
   Restzustand (schizophrenic)
   Schizophrenic residual state
CC Excl: For codes 295.60-295.64: 295.00-301.9, 306.0-319, 339.10-339.12, 388.45, 799.23-799.24
AHA: For code 295.62: 4Q, '06, 78

§ ✓5ᵗʰ **295.7 Schizoaffective disorder**   `CC 1-4`
[0-5]   Cyclic schizophrenia
   Mixed schizophrenic and affective psychosis
   Schizo-affective psychosis
   Schizophreniform psychosis, affective type
CC Excl: For codes 295.71-295.74: 295.00-301.9, 306.0-319, 339.10-339.12, 388.45, 799.23-799.24
F25.9 Schizoaffective disorder unspecified   `I-10`

§ ✓5ᵗʰ **295.8 Other specified types of schizophrenia**   `CC 0-4`
[0-5]   Acute (undifferentiated) schizophrenia
   Atypical schizophrenia
   Cenesthopathic schizophrenia
   EXCLUDES *infantile autism (299.0)*
CC Excl: For codes 295.80-295.84: 295.00-301.9, 306.0-319, 339.10-339.12, 388.45, 799.23-799.24

§ ✓5ᵗʰ **295.9 Unspecified schizophrenia**   `CC 1-4`
[0-5]   Schizophrenia:
     NOS
     mixed NOS
     undifferentiated NOS
     undifferentiated type
   Schizophrenic reaction NOS
   Schizophreniform psychosis NOS
CC Excl: For codes 295.91-295.94: 295.00-301.9, 306.0-319, 339.10-339.12, 388.45, 799.23-799.24
AHA: 3Q, '95, 6
F20.9 Schizophrenia unspecified   `I-10`

✓4ᵗʰ **296 Episodic mood disorders**
   INCLUDES episodic affective disorders
   EXCLUDES *neurotic depression (300.4)*
               reactive depressive psychosis (298.0)
               reactive excitation (298.1)

> The following fifth-digit subclassification is for use with categories 296.0-296.6:
> **0 unspecified**
> **1 mild**
> **2 moderate**
> **3 severe, without mention of psychotic behavior**
> **4 severe, specified as with psychotic behavior**
> **5 in partial or unspecified remission**
> **6 in full remission**

AHA: M-A, '85, 14

§ ✓5ᵗʰ **296.0 Bipolar I disorder, single manic episode**   `CC 0-4`
[0-6]   Hypomania (mild) NOS
   Hypomanic psychosis
   Mania (monopolar) NOS   } single episode or unspecified
   Manic-depressive psychosis or
     reaction:
     hypomanic
     manic
   EXCLUDES *circular type, if there was a previous attack of depression (296.4)*
DEF: Mood disorder identified by hyperactivity; may show extreme agitation or exaggerated excitability; speech and thought processes may be accelerated.
CC Excl: For codes 296.00-296.02: 295.00-301.9, 306.0-319, 388.45; **For codes 296.03:** 296.03-296.04, 296.13-296.14, 296.43-296.44, 296.53-296.54, 296.63-296.64; **For codes 296.04:** 295.00-301.9, 306.0-319, 388.45

§ ✓5ᵗʰ **296.1 Manic disorder, recurrent episode**   `CC 0-4`
[0-6]   Any condition classifiable to 296.0, stated to be recurrent
   EXCLUDES *circular type, if there was a previous attack of depression (296.4)*
CC Excl: For codes 296.10-296.12: 295.00-301.9, 306.0-319, 339.10-339.12, 388.45; **For codes 296.13:** 296.13-296.14, 296.43-296.44, 296.53-296.54, 296.63-296.64; **For codes 296.14:** 295.00-301.9, 306.0-319, 339.10-339.12, 388.45

---

§   Requires fifth digit. Valid digits are in [brackets] under each code. See appropriate category for codes and definitions.

`N` Newborn Age: 0   `P` Pediatric Age: 0-17   `M` Maternity Age: 12-55   `A` Adult Age: 15-124   `MCC` Major CC Condition   `CC` CC Condition   `HIV` HIV Related Dx

84 – Volume 1   2015 ICD-9-CM

§ ✓5ᵗʰ **296.2 Major depressive disorder, single episode** `CC 0-4`
[0-6]
    Depressive psychosis
    Endogenous depression
    Involutional melancholia   single episode or
    Manic-depressive psychosis or   unspecified
      reaction, depressed type
    Monopolar depression
    Psychotic depression

    EXCLUDES *circular type, if previous attack was of manic type*
      (296.5)
      depression NOS (311)
      reactive depression (neurotic) (300.4)
      psychotic (298.0)
    DEF: Mood disorder that produces depression; may exhibit as
    sadness, low self-esteem, or guilt feelings; other manifestations may
    be withdrawal from friends and family; interrupted sleep.
    CC Excl: For code 296.20: 295.00-301.9, 306.0-319, 339.10-339.12,
    388.45; **For codes 296.21-296.24:** 296.21-296.24, 296.30-296.34
    AHA: For code 296.20: 3Q, '09, 18
    F32.9 Major depressive disorder single episode uns   `I-10`

§ ✓5ᵗʰ **296.3 Major depressive disorder, recurrent episode** `CC 0-4`
[0-6]
    Any condition classifiable to 296.2, stated to be recurrent
    EXCLUDES *circular type, if previous attack was of manic type*
      (296.5)
      depression NOS (311)
      reactive depression (neurotic) (300.4)
      psychotic (298.0)
    CC Excl: For codes 296.30-296.33: 296.21-296.24, 296.30-296.34; **For**
    codes 296.34: 295.00-301.9, 306.0-319, 339.10-339.12, 388.45
    F33.2 Maj dprsv disord recur sev w/o psychot features   `I-10`

§ ✓5ᵗʰ **296.4 Bipolar I disorder, most recent episode** `CC 0-4`
[0-6] **(or current) manic**
    Bipolar disorder, now manic
    Manic-depressive psychosis, circular type but currently manic
    EXCLUDES *brief compensatory or rebound mood swings (296.99)*
    CC Excl: For codes 296.40-296.42 and 296.44: 295.00-301.9, 306.0-319,
    339.10-339.12, 388.45; **For code 296.43:** 296.43-296.44, 296.63-296.64,
    339.10-339.12
    F31.2 Bipolar d/o currnt epis mnic sev w/psychotc features   `I-10`

§ ✓5ᵗʰ **296.5 Bipolar I disorder, most recent episode** `CC 0-4`
[0-6] **(or current) depressed**
    Bipolar disorder, now depressed
    Manic-depressive psychosis, circular type but currently
      depressed
    EXCLUDES *brief compensatory or rebound mood swings (296.99)*
    CC Excl: For codes 296.50-296.52 and 296.54: 295.00-301.9, 306.0-319,
    339.10-339.12, 388.45; **For code 296.53:** 296.43-296.44, 296.53-296.54,
    296.63-296.64
    F31.30 Bipol disord currnt epis dprsd mild/mod sev uns   `I-10`

§ ✓5ᵗʰ **296.6 Bipolar I disorder, most recent episode** `CC 0-4`
[0-6] **(or current) mixed**
    Manic-depressive psychosis, circular type, mixed
    CC Excl: For codes 296.60-296.62 and 296.64: 295.00-301.9, 306.0-319,
    339.10-339.12, 388.45; **For code 296.63:** 296.43-296.44, 296.53-296.54,
    296.63-296.64

296.7 Bipolar I disorder, most recent episode (or current)
unspecified
    Atypical bipolar affective disorder NOS
    Manic-depressive psychosis, circular type, current condition
      not specified as either manic or depressive
    DEF: Manic-depressive disorder referred to as bipolar because of the
    mood range from manic to depressive.

✓5ᵗʰ **296.8 Other and unspecified bipolar disorders**

    296.80 Bipolar disorder, unspecified
      Bipolar disorder NOS
      Manic-depressive:
        reaction NOS
        syndrome NOS
      F31.9 Bipolar disorder unspecified   `I-10`

    296.81 Atypical manic disorder

    296.82 Atypical depressive disorder

    296.89 Other `CC`
      Bipolar II disorder
      Manic-depressive psychosis, mixed type
      CC Excl: 295.00-301.9, 306.0-319, 339.10-339.12, 388.45
      F31.81 Bipolar II disorder   `I-10`

✓5ᵗʰ **296.9 Other and unspecified episodic mood disorder**
    EXCLUDES *psychogenic affective psychoses (298.0-298.8)*

    296.90 Unspecified episodic mood disorder
      Affective psychosis NOS
      Melancholia NOS
      Mood disorder NOS
      AHA: M-A, '85, 14
      F39 Unspecified mood [affective] disorder   `I-10`

    296.99 Other specified episodic mood disorder `CC`
      Mood swings:
        brief compensatory
        rebound
      CC Excl: 295.00-301.9, 306.0-319, 339.10-339.12, 388.45

✓4ᵗʰ **297 Delusional disorders**
    INCLUDES paranoid disorders
    EXCLUDES *acute paranoid reaction (298.3)*
      alcoholic jealousy or paranoid state (291.5)
      paranoid schizophrenia (295.3)

    297.0 Paranoid state, simple

    297.1 Delusional disorder
      Chronic paranoid psychosis
      Sander's disease
      Systematized delusions
      EXCLUDES *paranoid personality disorder (301.0)*
      F22 Delusional disorders   `I-10`

    297.2 Paraphrenia
      Involutional paranoid state
      Late paraphrenia
      Paraphrenia (involutional)
      DEF: Paranoid schizophrenic disorder that persists over a prolonged
      period but does not distort personality despite persistent delusions.

    297.3 Shared psychotic disorder
      Folie à deux
      Induced psychosis or paranoid disorder
      DEF: Mental disorder two people share; first person with the
      delusional disorder convinces second person because of a close
      relationship and shared experiences to accept the delusions.

    297.8 Other specified paranoid states
      Paranoia querulans
      Sensitiver Beziehungswahn
      EXCLUDES *acute paranoid reaction or state (298.3)*
      senile paranoid state (290.20)

    297.9 Unspecified paranoid state
      Paranoid:
        disorder NOS
        psychosis NOS
        reaction NOS
        state NOS
      AHA: J-A, '85, 9

✓4ᵗʰ **298 Other nonorganic psychoses**
    INCLUDES psychotic conditions due to or provoked by:
      emotional stress
      environmental factors as major part of etiology

    298.0 Depressive type psychosis `CC`
      Psychogenic depressive psychosis
      Psychotic reactive depression
      Reactive depressive psychosis
      EXCLUDES *manic-depressive psychosis, depressed type*
      (296.2-296.3)
      neurotic depression (300.4)
      reactive depression NOS (300.4)
      CC Excl: 295.00-301.9, 306.0-319, 339.10-339.12, 388.45

---

§   Requires fifth digit. Valid digits are in [brackets] under each code. See category 296 for codes and definitions.

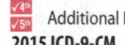

✓4ᵗʰ / ✓5ᵗʰ   Additional Digit Required   `Unacceptable PDx`   `Manifestation Code`   `Hospital Acquired Condition`   ►◄ Revised Text   ● New Code   ▲ Revised Code Title

2015 ICD-9-CM   **Volume 1 – 85**

298.1 Excitative type psychosis   `CC`
Acute hysterical psychosis
Psychogenic excitation
Reactive excitation

EXCLUDES *manic-depressive psychosis, manic type (296.0-296.1)*

DEF: Affective disorder similar to manic-depressive psychosis, in the manic phase, seemingly brought on by stress.

CC Excl: See code: 298.0

298.2 Reactive confusion
Psychogenic confusion   Psychogenic twilight state

EXCLUDES *acute confusional state (293.0)*

DEF: Confusion, disorientation, cloudiness in consciousness; brought on by severe emotional upheaval.

298.3 Acute paranoid reaction   `CC`
Acute psychogenic paranoid psychosis
Bouffée délirante

EXCLUDES *paranoid states (297.0-297.9)*

CC Excl: See code: 298.0

298.4 Psychogenic paranoid psychosis   `CC`
Protracted reactive paranoid psychosis

CC Excl: See code: 298.0

298.8 Other and unspecified reactive psychosis
Brief psychotic disorder
Brief reactive psychosis NOS
Hysterical psychosis
Psychogenic psychosis NOS
Psychogenic stupor

EXCLUDES *acute hysterical psychosis (298.1)*

298.9 Unspecified psychosis   `HIV`
Atypical psychosis   Psychotic disorder NOS
Psychosis NOS

AHA: 3Q, '06, 22

F28 Oth psych d/o not d/t sbstnc/knwn physiolog cond   `I-10`

✓4ᵗʰ 299 Pervasive developmental disorders

EXCLUDES *adult type psychoses occurring in childhood, as:*
    affective disorders (296.0-296.9)
    manic-depressive disorders (296.0-296.9)
    schizophrenia (295.0-295.9)

> The following fifth-digit subclassification is for use with category 299:
> 0   current or active state
> 1   residual state

§ ✓5ᵗʰ 299.0 Autistic disorder   `CC`
[0-1]   Childhood autism
Infantile psychosis
Kanner's syndrome

EXCLUDES *disintegrative psychosis (299.1)*
    Heller's syndrome (299.1)
    schizophrenic syndrome of childhood (299.9)

DEF: Severe mental disorder of children, results in impaired social behavior; abnormal development of communicative skills, appears to be unaware of the need for emotional support and little emotional response to family members.

CC Excl: 295.00-301.9, 306.0-319, 339.10-339.12, 388.45

AHA: For code 299.00: 3Q, '12, 19-20

§ ✓5ᵗʰ 299.1 Childhood disintegrative disorder   `CC`
[0-1]   Heller's syndrome

Use additional code to identify any associated neurological disorder

EXCLUDES *infantile autism (299.0)*
    schizophrenic syndrome of childhood (299.9)

DEF: Mental disease of children identified by impaired development of reciprocal social skills, verbal and nonverbal communication skills, imaginative play.

CC Excl: See code: 299.0

§ ✓5ᵗʰ 299.8 Other specified pervasive developmental disorders   `CC`
[0-1]   Asperger's disorder
Atypical childhood psychosis
Borderline psychosis of childhood

EXCLUDES *simple stereotypes without psychotic disturbance (307.3)*

CC Excl: See code: 299.0

---

§ ✓5ᵗʰ 299.9 Unspecified pervasive developmental disorder   `CC`
[0-1]   Child psychosis NOS
Pervasive developmental disorder NOS
Schizophrenia, childhood type NOS
Schizophrenic syndrome of childhood NOS

EXCLUDES *schizophrenia of adult type occurring in childhood (295.0-295.9)*

CC Excl: See code: 299.0

Neurotic Disorders, Personality Disorders, and Other Nonpsychotic Mental Disorders (300-316)

✓4ᵗʰ 300 Anxiety, dissociative and somatoform disorders

✓5ᵗʰ 300.0 Anxiety states

EXCLUDES *anxiety in:*
    acute stress reaction (308.0)
    transient adjustment reaction (309.24)
  neurasthenia (300.5)
  psychophysiological disorders (306.0-306.9)
  separation anxiety (309.21)

DEF: Mental disorder characterized by anxiety and avoidance behavior not particularly related to any specific situation or stimulus; symptoms include emotional instability, apprehension, fatigue.

300.00 Anxiety state, unspecified
Anxiety:
  neurosis
  reaction
  state (neurotic)
Atypical anxiety disorder

AHA: 3Q, '11, 6; 2Q, '11, 5; 1Q, '02, 6

TIP: For chest pain due to anxiety, assign chest pain code first, because chest pain is not integral to the diagnosis of anxiety.

F41.9 Anxiety disorder unspecified   `I-10`

300.01 Panic disorder without agoraphobia
Panic:
  attack
  state

EXCLUDES *panic disorder with agoraphobia (300.21)*

DEF: Neurotic disorder characterized by recurrent panic or anxiety, apprehension, fear or terror; symptoms include shortness of breath, palpitations, dizziness, shakiness; fear of dying may persist.

F41.0 Panic d/o [epis paroxysmal anxiety] w/o agoraphobia   `I-10`

300.02 Generalized anxiety disorder

300.09 Other

✓5ᵗʰ 300.1 Dissociative, conversion and factitious disorders

EXCLUDES *adjustment reaction (309.0-309.9)*
  anorexia nervosa (307.1)
  gross stress reaction (308.0-308.9)
  hysterical personality (301.50-301.59)
  psychophysiologic disorders (306.0-306.9)

300.10 Hysteria, unspecified

300.11 Conversion disorder
Astasia-abasia, hysterical
Conversion hysteria or reaction
Hysterical:
  blindness
  deafness
  paralysis

DEF: Mental disorder that impairs physical functions with no physiological basis; sensory motor symptoms include seizures, paralysis, temporary blindness; increase in stress or avoidance of unpleasant responsibilities may precipitate onset of symptoms.

AHA: 2Q, '11, 5; N-D, '85, 15

300.12 Dissociative amnesia
Hysterical amnesia

300.13 Dissociative fugue
Hysterical fugue

DEF: Dissociative hysteria; identified by loss of memory, flight from familiar surroundings; conscious activity is not associated with perception of surroundings, no later memory of episode.

---

§   Requires fifth digit. Valid digits are in [brackets] under each code. See category 299 for codes and definitions.

| `N` Newborn Age: 0 | `P` Pediatric Age: 0-17 | `M` Maternity Age: 12-55 | `A` Adult Age: 15-124 | `MCC` Major CC Condition | `CC` CC Condition | `HIV` HIV Related Dx |

300.14 Dissociative identity disorder

300.15 Dissociative disorder or reaction, unspecified

DEF: Hysterical neurotic episode; sudden but temporary changes in perceived identity, memory, consciousness, segregated memory patterns exist separate from dominant personality.

300.16 Factitious disorder with predominantly psychological signs and symptoms
Compensation neurosis
Ganser's syndrome, hysterical

DEF: A disorder characterized by the purposeful assumption of mental illness symptoms; which are acted out more often when another person is present.

300.19 Other and unspecified factitious illness
Factitious disorder (with combined psychological and physical signs and symptoms) (with predominantly physical signs and symptoms) NOS

EXCLUDES multiple operations or hospital addiction syndrome (301.51)

√5ᵗʰ 300.2 Phobic disorders

EXCLUDES anxiety state not associated with a specific situation or object (300.00-300.09)
obsessional phobias (300.3)

300.20 Phobia, unspecified
Anxiety-hysteria NOS
Phobia NOS

300.21 Agoraphobia with panic disorder
Fear of:
  open spaces
  streets   } with panic attacks
  travel
Panic disorder with agoraphobia

EXCLUDES agoraphobia without panic disorder (300.22)
panic disorder without agoraphobia (300.01)

300.22 Agoraphobia without mention of panic attacks
Any condition classifiable to 300.21 without mention of panic attacks

300.23 Social phobia
Fear of:
  eating in public
  public speaking
  washing in public

300.29 Other isolated or specific phobias
Acrophobia
Animal phobias
Claustrophobia
Fear of crowds

300.3 Obsessive-compulsive disorders
Anancastic neurosis
Compulsive neurosis
Obsessional phobia [any]

EXCLUDES obsessive-compulsive symptoms occurring in:
endogenous depression (296.2-296.3)
organic states (eg., encephalitis)
schizophrenia (295.0-295.9)

300.4 Dysthymic disorder
Anxiety depression
Depression with anxiety
Depressive reaction
Neurotic depressive state
Reactive depression

EXCLUDES adjustment reaction with depressive symptoms (309.0-309.1)
depression NOS (311)
manic-depressive psychosis, depressed type (296.2-296.3)
reactive depressive psychosis (298.0)

DEF: Depression without psychosis; less severe depression related to personal change or unexpected circumstances; also referred to as "reactional depression."
AHA: 3Q, '11, 6
F34.1 Dysthymic disorder   I-10

300.5 Neurasthenia
Fatigue neurosis
Nervous debility
Psychogenic:
  asthenia
  general fatigue
Use additional code to identify any associated physical disorder

EXCLUDES anxiety state (300.00-300.09)
neurotic depression (300.4)
psychophysiological disorders (306.0-306.9)
specific nonpsychotic mental disorders following organic brain damage (310.0-310.9)

DEF: Physical and mental symptoms caused primarily by what is known as mental exhaustion; symptoms include chronic weakness, fatigue.

300.6 Depersonalization disorder
Derealization (neurotic)
Neurotic state with depersonalization episode

EXCLUDES depersonalization associated with:
anxiety (300.00-300.09)
depression (300.4)
manic-depressive disorder or psychosis (296.0-296.9)
schizophrenia (295.0-295.9)

DEF: Dissociative disorder characterized by feelings of strangeness about self or body image; symptoms include dizziness, anxiety, fear of insanity, loss of reality of surroundings.

300.7 Hypochondriasis
Body dysmorphic disorder

EXCLUDES hypochondriasis in:
hysteria (300.10-300.19)
manic-depressive psychosis, depressed type (296.2-296.3)
neurasthenia (300.5)
obsessional disorder (300.3)
schizophrenia (295.0-295.9)

√5ᵗʰ 300.8 Somatoform disorders

300.81 Somatization disorder
Briquet's disorder
Severe somatoform disorder

300.82 Undifferentiated somatoform disorder
Atypical somatoform disorder
Somatoform disorder NOS

DEF: Disorders in which patients have symptoms that suggest an organic disease but no evidence of physical disorder after repeated testing.
AHA: 4Q, '96, 29

300.89 Other somatoform disorders
Occupational neurosis, including writers' cramp
Psychasthenia
Psychasthenic neurosis

300.9 Unspecified nonpsychotic mental disorder
Psychoneurosis NOS

√4ᵗʰ 301 Personality disorders
INCLUDES character neurosis
Use additional code to identify any associated neurosis or psychosis, or physical condition

EXCLUDES nonpsychotic personality disorder associated with organic brain syndromes (310.0-310.9)

301.0 Paranoid personality disorder
Fanatic personality
Paranoid personality (disorder)
Paranoid traits

EXCLUDES acute paranoid reaction (298.3)
alcoholic paranoia (291.5)
paranoid schizophrenia (295.3)
paranoid states (297.0-297.9)

AHA: J-A, '85, 9

√5ᵗʰ 301.1 Affective personality disorder

EXCLUDES affective psychotic disorders (296.0-296.9)
neurasthenia (300.5)
neurotic depression (300.4)

301.10 Affective personality disorder, unspecified

301.11 Chronic hypomanic personality disorder
Chronic hypomanic disorder
Hypomanic personality

301.12 Chronic depressive personality disorder
Chronic depressive disorder
Depressive character or personality

301.13 Cyclothymic disorder
Cycloid personality
Cyclothymia
Cyclothymic personality

√5th **301.2 Schizoid personality disorder**
EXCLUDES *schizophrenia (295.0-295.9)*

301.20 Schizoid personality disorder, unspecified

301.21 Introverted personality

301.22 Schizotypal personality disorder

301.3 Explosive personality disorder
Aggressive:
   personality
   reaction
Aggressiveness
Emotional instability (excessive)
Pathological emotionality
Quarrelsomeness
EXCLUDES *dyssocial personality (301.7)*
hysterical neurosis (300.10-300.19)

301.4 Obsessive-compulsive personality disorder
Anancastic personality
Obsessional personality
EXCLUDES *obsessive-compulsive disorder (300.3)*
phobic state (300.20-300.29)

√5th **301.5 Histrionic personality disorder**
EXCLUDES *hysterical neurosis (300.10-300.19)*
DEF: Extreme emotional behavior, often theatrical; often concerned about own appeal; may demand attention, exhibit seductive behavior.

301.50 Histrionic personality disorder, unspecified
Hysterical personality NOS

301.51 Chronic factitious illness with physical symptoms   CC
Hospital addiction syndrome
Multiple operations syndrome
Munchausen syndrome
CC Excl: 295.00-301.9, 306.0-319, 339.10-339.12, 388.45

301.59 Other histrionic personality disorder
Personality:
   emotionally unstable
   labile
   psychoinfantile

301.6 Dependent personality disorder
Asthenic personality
Inadequate personality
Passive personality
EXCLUDES *neurasthenia (300.5)*
passive-aggressive personality (301.84)
DEF: Overwhelming feeling of helplessness; fears of abandonment may persist; difficulty in making personal decisions without confirmation by others; low self-esteem due to irrational sensitivity to criticism.

301.7 Antisocial personality disorder
Amoral personality
Asocial personality
Dyssocial personality
Personality disorder with predominantly sociopathic or asocial manifestation
EXCLUDES *disturbance of conduct without specifiable personality disorder (312.0-312.9)*
explosive personality (301.3)
DEF: Continuous antisocial behavior that violates rights of others; social traits include extreme aggression, total disregard for traditional social rules.
AHA: S-O, '84, 16

√5th **301.8 Other personality disorders**

301.81 Narcissistic personality disorder
DEF: Grandiose fantasy or behavior, lack of social empathy, hypersensitive to the lack of others' judgment, exploits others; need for continual admiration.

301.82 Avoidant personality disorder
DEF: Personality disorder marked by feelings of social inferiority; sensitivity to criticism, emotionally restrained due to fear of rejection.

301.83 Borderline personality disorder
DEF: Personality disorder characterized by unstable moods, self-image, and interpersonal relationships; uncontrolled anger, impulsive and self-destructive acts, fears of abandonment, feelings of emptiness and boredom, recurrent suicide threats or self-mutilation.
F60.3 Borderline personality disorder   I-10

301.84 Passive-aggressive personality
DEF: Pattern of procrastination and refusal to meet standards; introduce own obstacles to success and exploit failure.

301.89 Other
Personality:
   eccentric
   "haltlose" type
   immature
   masochistic
   psychoneurotic
EXCLUDES *psychoinfantile personality (301.59)*

301.9 Unspecified personality disorder
Pathological personality NOS
Personality disorder NOS
Psychopathic:
   constitutional state
   personality (disorder)

√4th **302 Sexual and gender identity disorders**
EXCLUDES *sexual disorder manifest in:*
   organic brain syndrome (290.0-294.9, 310.0-310.9)
   psychosis (295.0-298.9)

302.0 Ego-dystonic sexual orientation
Ego-dystonic lesbianism
Sexual orientation conflict disorder
EXCLUDES *homosexual pedophilia (302.2)*

302.1 Zoophilia
Bestiality
DEF: A sociodeviant disorder marked by engaging in sexual intercourse with animals.

302.2 Pedophilia
DEF: A sociodeviant condition of adults characterized by sexual activity with children.

302.3 Transvestic fetishism
EXCLUDES *trans-sexualism (302.5)*
DEF: The desire to dress in clothing of opposite sex.

302.4 Exhibitionism
DEF: Sexual deviant behavior; exposure of genitals to strangers; behavior prompted by intense sexual urges and fantasies.

√5th **302.5 Trans-sexualism**
Sex reassignment surgery status
EXCLUDES *transvestism (302.3)*
DEF: Gender identity disturbance; overwhelming desire to change anatomic sex, due to belief that individual is a member of the opposite sex.

302.50 With unspecified sexual history

302.51 With asexual history

302.52 With homosexual history

302.53 With heterosexual history

302.6 Gender identity disorder in children
Feminism in boys
Gender identity disorder NOS
EXCLUDES *gender identity disorder in adult (302.85)*
trans-sexualism (302.50-302.53)
transvestism (302.3)

N Newborn Age: 0   P Pediatric Age: 0-17   M Maternity Age: 12-55   A Adult Age: 15-124   MCC Major CC Condition   CC CC Condition   HIV HIV Related Dx

√5ᵗʰ **302.7 Psychosexual dysfunction**

> **EXCLUDES** *impotence of organic origin (607.84)*
> *normal transient symptoms from ruptured hymen*
> *transient or occasional failures of erection due to*
> *fatigue, anxiety, alcohol, or drugs*

302.70 Psychosexual dysfunction, unspecified
Sexual dysfunction NOS

302.71 Hypoactive sexual desire disorder
> **EXCLUDES** *decreased sexual desire NOS (799.81)*

302.72 With inhibited sexual excitement
Female sexual arousal disorder
Frigidity
Impotence
Male erectile disorder

302.73 Female orgasmic disorder ♀

302.74 Male orgasmic disorder ♂

302.75 Premature ejaculation ♂

302.76 Dyspareunia, psychogenic ♀
> **DEF:** Difficult or painful sex due to psychosomatic state.

302.79 With other specified psychosexual dysfunctions
Sexual aversion disorder

√5ᵗʰ **302.8 Other specified psychosexual disorders**

302.81 Fetishism
> **DEF:** Psychosexual disorder noted for intense sexual urges and arousal precipitated by fantasies; use of inanimate objects, such as clothing, to stimulate sexual arousal, orgasm.

302.82 Voyeurism
> **DEF:** Psychosexual disorder characterized by uncontrollable impulse to observe others, without their knowledge, who are nude or engaged in sexual activity.

302.83 Sexual masochism
> **DEF:** Psychosexual disorder noted for need to achieve sexual gratification through humiliating or hurtful acts inflicted on self.

302.84 Sexual sadism
> **DEF:** Psychosexual disorder noted for need to achieve sexual gratification through humiliating or hurtful acts inflicted on someone else.

302.85 Gender identity disorder in adolescents or adults
Use additional code to identify sex reassignment surgery status (302.5)
> **EXCLUDES** *gender identity disorder NOS (302.6)*
> *gender identity disorder in children (302.6)*

302.89 Other
Frotteurism
Nymphomania
Satyriasis

302.9 Unspecified psychosexual disorder
Paraphilia NOS
Pathologic sexuality NOS
Sexual deviation NOS
Sexual disorder NOS

√4ᵗʰ **303 Alcohol dependence syndrome**
Use additional code to identify any associated condition, as:
alcoholic psychoses (291.0-291.9)
drug dependence (304.0-304.9)
physical complications of alcohol, such as:
cerebral degeneration (331.7)
cirrhosis of liver (571.2)
epilepsy (345.0-345.9)
gastritis (535.3)
hepatitis (571.1)
liver damage NOS (571.3)
> **EXCLUDES** *drunkenness NOS (305.0)*

> The following fifth-digit subclassification is for use with category 303:
> **0 unspecified**
> **1 continuous**
> **2 episodic**
> **3 in remission**

AHA: 1Q, '10, 20-21; 3Q, '95, 6; 2Q, '91, 9; 4Q, '88, 8; S-O, '86, 3
TIP: The patient has become physically addicted to alcohol and often experiences withdrawal symptoms when not drinking. Do not assign both 303.0X and 303.9X on the same encounter.

§ √5ᵗʰ **303.0 Acute alcoholic intoxication**
[0-3] Acute drunkenness in alcoholism

§ √5ᵗʰ **303.9 Other and unspecified alcohol dependence**
[0-3] Chronic alcoholism
Dipsomania
AHA: 2Q, '02, 4; 2Q, '89, 9; **For code 303.90:** 2Q, '12, 9; 2Q, '07, 6
F10.20 Alcohol dependence uncomplicated `I-10`
F10.21 Alcohol dependence in remission `I-10`

√4ᵗʰ **304 Drug dependence**
> **EXCLUDES** *nondependent abuse of drugs (305.1-305.9)*

> The following fifth-digit subclassification is for use with category 304:
> **0 unspecified**
> **1 continuous**
> **2 episodic**
> **3 in remission**

AHA: 1Q, '10, 20-21; 2Q, '91, 10; 4Q, '88, 8; S-O, '86, 3

§ √5ᵗʰ **304.0 Opioid type dependence** `CC 1`
[0-3] Heroin
Meperidine
Methadone
Morphine
Opium
Opium alkaloids and their derivatives
Synthetics with morphine-like effects
CC Excl: For code 304.01: 291.0-292.9, 303.00-305.03, 305.20-305.93, 790.3
AHA: 2Q, '06, 7; **For code 304.00:** ▶2Q, '13, 14;◀ 1Q, '11, 15: 2Q, '10, 13

§ √5ᵗʰ **304.1 Sedative, hypnotic or anxiolytic dependence** `CC 1`
[0-3] Barbiturates
Nonbarbiturate sedatives and tranquilizers with a similar effect:
chlordiazepoxide
diazepam
glutethimide
meprobamate
methaqualone
CC Excl: For code 304.11: 291.0-292.9, 303.00-305.03, 305.20-305.93, 790.3
AHA: For code 304.10: ▶2Q, '13, 14◀

§ √5ᵗʰ **304.2 Cocaine dependence** `CC 1`
[0-3] Coca leaves and derivatives
CC Excl: For code 304.21: 291.0-292.9, 303.00-305.03, 305.20-305.93, 790.3
F14.20 Cocaine dependence uncomplicated `I-10`

§ √5ᵗʰ **304.3 Cannabis dependence**
[0-3] Hashish   Marihuana
Hemp

§ √5ᵗʰ **304.4 Amphetamine and other psychostimulant** `CC 1`
[0-3] **dependence**
Methylphenidate Phenmetrazine
CC Excl: For code 304.41: 291.0-292.9, 303.00-305.03, 305.20-305.93, 790.3

---

§ Requires fifth digit. Valid digits are in [brackets] under each code. See appropriate category for codes and definitions.

√4ᵗʰ
√5ᵗʰ Additional Digit Required   Unacceptable PDx   Manifestation Code   Hospital Acquired Condition   ►◄ Revised Text   ● New Code   ▲ Revised Code Title

Mental, Behavioral and Neurodevelopmental Disorders

304.5–306.3

§ ✓5ᵗʰ **304.5 Hallucinogen dependence**   CC 1
[0-3]   Dimethyltryptamine [DMT]
     Lysergic acid diethylamide [LSD] and derivatives
     Mescaline
     Psilocybin
     CC Excl: For code 304.51: 291.0-292.9, 303.00-305.03, 305.20-305.93, 790.3

§ ✓5ᵗʰ **304.6 Other specified drug dependence**   CC 1
[0-3]   Absinthe addiction
     Glue sniffing
     Inhalant dependence
     Phencyclidine dependence
     EXCLUDES *tobacco dependence (305.1)*
     CC Excl: For code 304.61: 291.0-292.9, 303.00-305.03, 305.20-305.93, 790.3

§ ✓5ᵗʰ **304.7 Combinations of opioid type drug with any other**   CC 1
[0-3]   **CC Excl:** For code 304.71: 291.0-292.9, 303.00-305.03, 305.20-305.93, 790.3
     AHA: M-A, '86, 12

§ ✓5ᵗʰ **304.8 Combinations of drug dependence excluding**   CC 1
[0-3]   **opioid type drug**
     CC Excl: For code 304.81: 291.0-292.9, 303.00-305.03, 305.20-305.93, 790.3
     AHA: M-A, '86, 12

§ ✓5ᵗʰ **304.9 Unspecified drug dependence**   CC 1
[0-3]   Drug addiction NOS
     Drug dependence NOS
     CC Excl: For code 304.91: 291.0-292.9, 303.00-305.03, 305.20-305.93, 790.3
     AHA: For code 304.90: 2Q, '12, 16; 4Q, '03, 103

✓4ᵗʰ **305 Nondependent abuse of drugs**
     NOTE Includes cases where a person, for whom no other diagnosis is possible, has come under medical care because of the maladaptive effect of a drug on which he is not dependent and that he has taken on his own initiative to the detriment of his health or social functioning.
     EXCLUDES *alcohol dependence syndrome (303.0-303.9)*
         drug dependence (304.0-304.9)
         drug withdrawal syndrome (292.0)
         poisoning by drugs or medicinal substances (960.0-979.9)

> The following fifth-digit subclassification is for use with codes 305.0, 305.2-305.9:
>   **0 unspecified**
>   **1 continuous**
>   **2 episodic**
>   **3 in remission**

     AHA: 1Q, '10, 20-21; 2Q, '91, 10; 4Q, '88, 8; S-O, '86, 3

§ ✓5ᵗʰ **305.0 Alcohol abuse**
[0-3]   Drunkenness NOS
     Excessive drinking of alcohol NOS
     "Hangover" (alcohol)
     Inebriety NOS
     EXCLUDES *acute alcohol intoxication in alcoholism (303.0)*
         alcoholic psychoses (291.0-291.9)
     AHA: 3Q, '96, 16; For code 305.00: 4Q, '09, 112
     F10.10 Alcohol abuse uncomplicated   I-10

305.1 Tobacco use disorder
     Tobacco dependence
     EXCLUDES *history of tobacco use (V15.82)*
         smoking complicating pregnancy (649.0)
         tobacco use disorder complicating pregnancy (649.0)
     AHA: 1Q, '09, 16; 2Q, '96, 10; N-D, '84, 12
     F17.210 Nicotine dependence cigarettes uncomplicated   I-10

§ ✓5ᵗʰ **305.2 Cannabis abuse**
[0-3]   **F12.10** Cannabis abuse uncomplicated   I-10

§ ✓5ᵗʰ **305.3 Hallucinogen abuse**
[0-3]   Acute intoxication from hallucinogens ["bad trips"]
     LSD reaction

§ ✓5ᵗʰ **305.4 Sedative, hypnotic or anxiolytic abuse**
[0-3]

§ ✓5ᵗʰ **305.5 Opioid abuse**
[0-3]

§ ✓5ᵗʰ **305.6 Cocaine abuse**
[0-3]   **AHA:** For code 305.60: 1Q, '05, 6; 1Q, '93, 25
     F14.10 Cocaine abuse uncomplicated   I-10

§ ✓5ᵗʰ **305.7 Amphetamine or related acting sympathomimetic abuse**
[0-3]   **AHA:** For code 305.70: 2Q, '03, 10–11

§ ✓5ᵗʰ **305.8 Antidepressant type abuse**
[0-3]

§ ✓5ᵗʰ **305.9 Other, mixed, or unspecified drug abuse**
[0-3]   Caffeine intoxication
     Inhalant abuse
     "Laxative habit"
     Misuse of drugs NOS
     Nonprescribed use of drugs or patent medicinals
     Phencyclidine abuse
     AHA: 3Q, '99, 20

✓4ᵗʰ **306 Physiological malfunction arising from mental factors**
     INCLUDES psychogenic:
         physical symptoms ⎫
         physiological   ⎬ not involving tissue damage
            manifestations ⎭
     EXCLUDES *hysteria (300.11-300.19)*
         physical symptoms secondary to a psychiatric disorder classified elsewhere
         psychic factors associated with physical conditions involving tissue damage classified elsewhere (316)
         specific nonpsychotic mental disorders following organic brain damage (310.0-310.9)
     DEF: Functional disturbances or interruptions due to mental or psychological causes; no tissue damage sustained in these conditions.

306.0 Musculoskeletal
     Psychogenic paralysis
     Psychogenic torticollis
     EXCLUDES *Gilles de la Tourette's syndrome (307.23)*
         paralysis as hysterical or conversion reaction (300.11)
         tics (307.20-307.22)

306.1 Respiratory
     Psychogenic: Psychogenic:
        air hunger   hyperventilation
        cough   yawning
        hiccough
     EXCLUDES *psychogenic asthma (316 and 493.9)*

306.2 Cardiovascular
     Cardiac neurosis
     Cardiovascular neurosis
     Neurocirculatory asthenia
     Psychogenic cardiovascular disorder
     EXCLUDES *psychogenic paroxysmal tachycardia (316 and 427.2)*
     DEF: Neurocirculatory asthenia: functional nervous and circulatory irregularities with palpitations, dyspnea, fatigue, rapid pulse, precordial pain, fear of effort, discomfort during exercise, anxiety; also called DaCosta's syndrome, Effort syndrome, Irritable or Soldier's Heart.
     AHA: J-A, '85, 14

306.3 Skin
     Psychogenic pruritus
     EXCLUDES *psychogenic:*
         alopecia (316 and 704.00)
         dermatitis (316 and 692.9)
         eczema (316 and 691.8 or 692.9)
         urticaria (316 and 708.0-708.9)

---

§   Requires fifth digit. Valid digits are in [brackets] under each code. See appropriate category for codes and definitions.

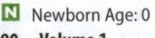 Newborn Age: 0    Pediatric Age: 0-17    Maternity Age: 12-55    Adult Age: 15-124   **MCC** Major CC Condition   **CC** CC Condition   **HIV** HIV Related Dx

306.4 Gastrointestinal
    Aerophagy
    Cyclical vomiting, psychogenic
    Diarrhea, psychogenic
    Nervous gastritis
    Psychogenic dyspepsia

> *EXCLUDES* *cyclical vomiting NOS (536.2)*
>   *associated with migraine (346.2)*
> *globus hystericus (300.11)*
> *mucous colitis (316 and 564.9)*
> *psychogenic:*
>   *cardiospasm (316 and 530.0)*
>   *duodenal ulcer (316 and 532.0-532.9)*
>   *gastric ulcer (316 and 531.0-531.9)*
>   *peptic ulcer NOS (316 and 533.0-533.9)*
>   *vomiting NOS (307.54)*

DEF: Aerophagy: excess swallowing of air, usually unconscious; related to anxiety; results in distended abdomen or belching, often interpreted by the patient as a physical disorder.
AHA: 2Q, '89, 11

√5ᵗʰ 306.5 Genitourinary

> *EXCLUDES* *enuresis, psychogenic (307.6)*
> *frigidity (302.72)*
> *impotence (302.72)*
> *psychogenic dyspareunia (302.76)*

306.50 Psychogenic genitourinary malfunction, unspecified

306.51 Psychogenic vaginismus ♀
    Functional vaginismus
    DEF: Psychogenic response resulting in painful contractions of vaginal canal muscles; can be severe enough to prevent sexual intercourse.

306.52 Psychogenic dysmenorrhea ♀

306.53 Psychogenic dysuria

306.59 Other
    AHA: M-A, '87, 11

306.6 Endocrine

306.7 Organs of special sense
> *EXCLUDES* *hysterical blindness or deafness (300.11)*
> *psychophysical visual disturbances (368.16)*

306.8 Other specified psychophysiological malfunction
    Bruxism
    Teeth grinding

306.9 Unspecified psychophysiological malfunction
    Psychophysiologic disorder NOS
    Psychosomatic disorder NOS

√4ᵗʰ 307 Special symptoms or syndromes, not elsewhere classified
> **NOTE** This category is intended for use if the psychopathology is manifested by a single specific symptom or group of symptoms which is not part of an organic illness or other mental disorder classifiable elsewhere.

> *EXCLUDES* *those due to mental disorders classified elsewhere*
> *those of organic origin*

307.0 Adult onset fluency disorder
> *EXCLUDES* *childhood onset fluency disorder (315.35)*
> *dysphasia (784.59)*
> *fluency disorder due to late effect of cerebrovascular accident (438.14)*
> *fluency disorder in conditions classified elsewhere (784.52)*
> *lisping or lalling (307.9)*
> *retarded development of speech (315.31-315.39)*

    AHA: 4Q, '10, 83

307.1 Anorexia nervosa CC
> *EXCLUDES* *eating disturbance NOS (307.50)*
> *feeding problem (783.3)*
>   *of nonorganic origin (307.59)*
> *loss of appetite (783.0)*
>   *of nonorganic origin (307.59)*

    CC Excl: 306.4, 306.8-306.9, 307.1, 307.50-307.59, 309.22
    AHA: 2Q, '06, 12; 4Q, '89, 11
    TIP: Assign an additional code for any associated malnutrition.

√5ᵗʰ 307.2 Tics
> *EXCLUDES* *nail-biting or thumb-sucking (307.9)*
> *stereotypes occurring in isolation (307.3)*
> *tics of organic origin (333.3)*

DEF: Involuntary muscle response usually confined to the face, shoulders.

307.20 Tic disorder, unspecified
    Tic disorder NOS

307.21 Transient tic disorder

307.22 Chronic motor or vocal tic disorder

307.23 Tourette's disorder
    Motor-verbal tic disorder
    DEF: Syndrome of facial and vocal tics in childhood; progresses to spontaneous or involuntary jerking, obscene utterances, other uncontrollable actions considered inappropriate.

307.3 Stereotypic movement disorder
    Body-rocking
    Head banging
    Spasmus nutans
    Stereotypes NOS
> *EXCLUDES* *tics (307.20-307.23)*
> *of organic origin (333.3)*

√5ᵗʰ 307.4 Specific disorders of sleep of nonorganic origin
> *EXCLUDES* *narcolepsy (347.00-347.11)*
> *organic hypersomnia (327.10-327.19)*
> *organic insomnia (327.00-327.09)*
> *those of unspecified cause (780.50-780.59)*

307.40 Nonorganic sleep disorder, unspecified

307.41 Transient disorder of initiating or maintaining sleep
    Adjustment insomnia
    Hyposomnia ⎫ associated with intermittent
    Insomnia   ⎬ emotional reactions
    Sleeplessness ⎭ or conflicts

307.42 Persistent disorder of initiating or maintaining sleep
    Hyposomnia, insomnia, or sleeplessness associated with:
        anxiety
        conditioned arousal
        depression (major) (minor)
        psychosis
    Idiopathic insomnia
    Paradoxical insomnia
    Primary insomnia
    Psychophysiological insomnia

307.43 Transient disorder of initiating or maintaining wakefulness
    Hypersomnia associated with acute or intermittent emotional reactions or conflicts

307.44 Persistent disorder of initiating or maintaining wakefulness
    Hypersomnia associated with depression (major) (minor)
    Insufficient sleep syndrome
    Primary hypersomnia
> *EXCLUDES* *sleep deprivation (V69.4)*

307.45 Circadian rhythm sleep disorder of nonorganic origin

307.46 Sleep arousal disorder
    Night terror disorder
    Night terrors
    Sleep terror disorder
    Sleepwalking
    Somnambulism
    DEF: Sleepwalking marked by extreme terror, panic, screaming, confusion; no recall of event upon arousal; term may refer to simply the act of sleepwalking.

Mental, Behavioral and Neurodevelopmental Disorders

307.47–309.29

307.47 Other dysfunctions of sleep stages or arousal from sleep
Nightmare disorder
Nightmares:
  NOS
  REM-sleep type
  Sleep drunkenness

307.48 Repetitive intrusions of sleep
Repetitive intrusion of sleep with:
  atypical polysomnographic features
  environmental disturbances
  repeated REM-sleep interruptions

307.49 Other
"Short-sleeper"   Subjective insomnia complaint

✓5th **307.5 Other and unspecified disorders of eating**
EXCLUDES anorexia:
nervosa (307.1)
of unspecified cause (783.0)
overeating, of unspecified cause (783.6)
vomiting:
NOS (787.03)
cyclical (536.2)
associated with migraine (346.2)
psychogenic (306.4)

307.50 Eating disorder, unspecified
Eating disorder NOS

307.51 Bulimia nervosa   CC
Overeating of nonorganic origin
DEF: Mental disorder commonly characterized by binge eating followed by self-induced vomiting; perceptions of being fat; and fear the inability to stop eating voluntarily.
CC Excl: 307.1, 307.50-307.51, 307.53-307.59
AHA: 3Q, '12, 9

307.52 Pica
Perverted appetite of nonorganic origin
DEF: Compulsive eating disorder characterized by craving for substances other than food, such as paint chips or dirt.

307.53 Rumination disorder
Regurgitation, of nonorganic origin, of food with reswallowing
EXCLUDES obsessional rumination (300.3)

307.54 Psychogenic vomiting

307.59 Other
Feeding disorder of infancy or early childhood of nonorganic origin
Infantile feeding disturbances } of nonorganic origin
Loss of appetite

307.6 Enuresis
Enuresis (primary) (secondary) of nonorganic origin
EXCLUDES enuresis of unspecified cause (788.3)
DEF: Involuntary urination past age of normal control; also called bedwetting; no trace to biological problem; focus on psychological issues.

307.7 Encopresis
Encopresis (continuous) (discontinuous) of nonorganic origin
EXCLUDES encopresis of unspecified cause (787.60-787.63)
DEF: Inability to control bowel movements; cause traced to psychological, not biological, problems.

✓5th **307.8 Pain disorders related to psychological factors**

307.80 Psychogenic pain, site unspecified

307.81 Tension headache
EXCLUDES headache:
NOS (784.0)
migraine (346.0-346.9)
syndromes (339.00-339.89)
tension type (339.10-339.12)
AHA: 4Q, '08, 103; N-D, '85, 16

307.89 Other
Code first to type or site of pain
EXCLUDES pain disorder exclusively attributed to psychological factors (307.80)
psychogenic pain (307.80)

307.9 Other and unspecified special symptoms or syndromes, not elsewhere classified
Communication disorder NOS   Masturbation
Hair plucking   Nail-biting
Lalling   Thumb-sucking
Lisping

✓4th **308 Acute reaction to stress**
INCLUDES catastrophic stress
combat and operational stress reaction
combat fatigue
gross stress reaction (acute)
transient disorders in response to exceptional physical or mental stress which usually subside within hours or days
EXCLUDES adjustment reaction or disorder (309.0-309.9)
chronic stress reaction (309.1-309.9)

308.0 Predominant disturbance of emotions
Anxiety
Emotional crisis } as acute reaction to exceptional [gross] stress
Panic state

308.1 Predominant disturbance of consciousness
Fugues as acute reaction to exceptional [gross] stress

308.2 Predominant psychomotor disturbance
Agitation states } as acute reaction to exceptional [gross] stress
Stupor

308.3 Other acute reactions to stress
Acute situational disturbance
Acute stress disorder
EXCLUDES prolonged posttraumatic emotional disturbance (309.81)

308.4 Mixed disorders as reaction to stress

308.9 Unspecified acute reaction to stress

✓4th **309 Adjustment reaction**
INCLUDES adjustment disorders
reaction (adjustment) to chronic stress
EXCLUDES acute reaction to major stress (308.0-308.9)
neurotic disorders (300.0-300.9)

309.0 Adjustment disorder with depressed mood
Grief reaction
EXCLUDES affective psychoses (296.0-296.9)
neurotic depression (300.4)
prolonged depressive reaction (309.1)
psychogenic depressive psychosis (298.0)
AHA: ▶1Q, '14, 10◀
F43.21 Adjustment disorder with depressed mood   I-10

309.1 Prolonged depressive reaction
EXCLUDES affective psychoses (296.0-296.9)
brief depressive reaction (309.0)
neurotic depression (300.4)
psychogenic depressive psychosis (298.0)

✓5th **309.2 With predominant disturbance of other emotions**

309.21 Separation anxiety disorder
DEF: Abnormal apprehension by a child when physically separated from support environment; byproduct of abnormal symbiotic child-parent relationship.

309.22 Emancipation disorder of adolescence and early adult life
DEF: Adjustment reaction of late adolescence; conflict over independence from parental supervision; symptoms include difficulty in making decisions, increased reliance on parental advice, deliberate adoption of values in opposition of parents.

309.23 Specific academic or work inhibition

309.24 Adjustment disorder with anxiety

309.28 Adjustment disorder with mixed anxiety and depressed mood
Adjustment reaction with anxiety and depression
F43.23 Adjustment d/o w/mixed anxiety & depressed mood   I-10

309.29 Other
Culture shock

N Newborn Age: 0   P Pediatric Age: 0-17   M Maternity Age: 12-55   A Adult Age: 15-124   MCC Major CC Condition   CC CC Condition   HIV HIV Related Dx

92 – Volume 1 • October 2014   2015 ICD-9-CM

309.3 Adjustment disorder with disturbance of conduct
Conduct disturbance ⎫
Destructiveness   ⎬ as adjustment reaction

> **EXCLUDES** *destructiveness in child (312.9)*
> *disturbance of conduct NOS (312.9)*
> *dyssocial behavior without manifest psychiatric*
> *disorder (V71.01-V71.02)*
> *personality disorder with predominantly sociopathic*
> *or asocial manifestations (301.7)*

309.4 Adjustment disorder with mixed disturbance of emotions and conduct

√5ᵗʰ **309.8 Other specified adjustment reactions**

309.81 Posttraumatic stress disorder
Chronic posttraumatic stress disorder
Concentration camp syndrome
Posttraumatic stress disorder NOS
Post-traumatic stress disorder (PTSD)

> **EXCLUDES** *acute stress disorder (308.3)*
> *posttraumatic brain syndrome:*
> *nonpsychotic (310.2)*
> *psychotic (293.0-293.9)*

DEF: Preoccupation with traumatic events beyond normal
experience; i.e., rape, personal assault, etc.; also recurring
flashbacks of trauma; symptoms include difficulty
remembering, sleeping, or concentrating, and guilt feelings
for surviving.
AHA: 2Q, '11, 5

309.82 Adjustment reaction with physical symptoms

309.83 Adjustment reaction with withdrawal
Elective mutism as adjustment reaction
Hospitalism (in children) NOS

309.89 Other

309.9 Unspecified adjustment reaction
Adaptation reaction NOS
Adjustment reaction NOS

√4ᵗʰ **310 Specific nonpsychotic mental disorders due to brain damage**

> **EXCLUDES** *neuroses, personality disorders, or other nonpsychotic*
> *conditions occurring in a form similar to that seen with*
> *functional disorders but in association with a physical*
> *condition (300.0-300.9, 301.0-301.9)*

310.0 Frontal lobe syndrome
Lobotomy syndrome
Postleucotomy syndrome [state]

> **EXCLUDES** *postcontusion syndrome (310.2)*

310.1 Personality change due to conditions classified elsewhere
Cognitive or personality change of other type, of
nonpsychotic severity
Organic psychosyndrome of nonpsychotic severity
Presbyophrenia NOS
Senility with mental changes of nonpsychotic severity

> **EXCLUDES** *mild cognitive impairment (331.83)*
> *postconcussion syndrome (310.2)*
> *signs and symptoms involving emotional state*
> *(799.21-799.29)*

DEF: Personality disorder caused by organic factors, such as brain
lesions, head trauma, or cerebrovascular accident (CVA).
AHA: 2Q, '05, 6

310.2 Postconcussion syndrome
Postcontusion syndrome or encephalopathy
Posttraumatic brain syndrome, nonpsychotic
Status postcommotio cerebri

Use additional code to identify associated post-traumatic
headache, if applicable (339.20-339.22)

> **EXCLUDES** *any organic psychotic conditions following head*
> *injury (293.0-294.0)*
> *frontal lobe syndrome (310.0)*
> *postencephalitic syndrome (310.89)*

DEF: Nonpsychotic disorder due to brain trauma, causes symptoms
unrelated to any disease process; symptoms include amnesia, serial
headaches, rapid heartbeat, fatigue, disrupted sleep patterns,
inability to concentrate.
AHA: 4Q, '90, 24
TIP: For treatment within 24 to 48 hours of the concussion, clarify
with physician whether the concussion is still in the acute phase; if
so, assign instead a code from 850.X subcategory.

√5ᵗʰ **310.8 Other specified nonpsychotic mental disorders following organic brain damage**
AHA: 4Q, '11, 96-97

310.81 Pseudobulbar affect
Involuntary emotional expression disorder

Code first underlying cause, if known, such as:
amyotrophic lateral sclerosis (335.20)
late effect of cerebrovascular accident (438.89)
late effect of traumatic brain injury (907.0)
mutiple sclerosis (340)

AHA: 4Q, '11, 97

310.89 Other specified nonpsychotic mental disorders following organic brain damage
Mild memory disturbance
Other focal (partial) organic psychosyndromes
Postencephalitic syndrome

> **EXCLUDES** *memory loss of unknown cause (780.93)*

310.9 Unspecified nonpsychotic mental disorder following organic brain damage   **HIV**
AHA: 4Q, '03, 103

311 Depressive disorder, not elsewhere classified
Depressive disorder NOS   Depression NOS
Depressive state NOS

> **EXCLUDES** *acute reaction to major stress with depressive symptoms*
> *(308.0)*
> *affective personality disorder (301.10-301.13)*
> *affective psychoses (296.0-296.9)*
> *brief depressive reaction (309.0)*
> *depressive states associated with stressful events*
> *(309.0-309.1)*
> *disturbance of emotions specific to childhood and*
> *adolescence, with misery and unhappiness (313.1)*
> *mixed adjustment reaction with depressive symptoms*
> *(309.4)*
> *neurotic depression (300.4)*
> *prolonged depressive adjustment reaction (309.1)*
> *psychogenic depressive psychosis (298.0)*

AHA: 3Q, '11, 6; 4Q, '03, 75

√4ᵗʰ **312 Disturbance of conduct, not elsewhere classified**

> **EXCLUDES** *adjustment reaction with disturbance of conduct (309.3)*
> *drug dependence (304.0-304.9)*
> *dyssocial behavior without manifest psychiatric disorder*
> *(V71.01-V71.02)*
> *personality disorder with predominantly sociopathic or*
> *asocial manifestations (301.7)*
> *sexual deviations (302.0-302.9)*

The following fifth-digit subclassification is for use with categories
312.0-312.2

0	unspecified	**2**	moderate
1	mild	**3**	severe

§ √5ᵗʰ **312.0 Undersocialized conduct disorder, aggressive type**
[0-3]   Aggressive outburst   Unsocialized aggressive disorder
Anger reaction

DEF: Mental condition identified by behaviors disrespectful of others'
rights and of age-appropriate social norms or rules; symptoms
include bullying, vandalism, verbal and physical abusiveness, lying,
stealing, defiance.

---

§   Requires fifth digit. Valid digits are in [brackets] under each code. See category 312 for codes and definitions.

Mental, Behavioral and Neurodevelopmental Disorders

312.1–315.2

§ √5th **312.1 Undersocialized conduct disorder, unaggressive type**
[0-3]
    Childhood truancy, unsocialized
    Solitary stealing
    Tantrums

§ √5th **312.2 Socialized conduct disorder**
[0-3]
    Childhood truancy, socialized
    Group delinquency
    EXCLUDES *gang activity without manifest psychiatric disorder (V71.01)*

√5th **312.3 Disorders of impulse control, not elsewhere classified**

    312.30 Impulse control disorder, unspecified

    312.31 Pathological gambling

    312.32 Kleptomania

    312.33 Pyromania

    312.34 Intermittent explosive disorder

    312.35 Isolated explosive disorder

    312.39 Other
        Trichotillomania

312.4 Mixed disturbance of conduct and emotions
    Neurotic delinquency
    EXCLUDES *compulsive conduct disorder (312.3)*

√5th **312.8 Other specified disturbances of conduct, not elsewhere classified**

    312.81 Conduct disorder, childhood onset type

    312.82 Conduct disorder, adolescent onset type

    312.89 Other conduct disorder
        Conduct disorder of unspecified onset

312.9 Unspecified disturbance of conduct
    Delinquency (juvenile)
    Disruptive behavior disorder NOS
    AHA: 2Q, '11, 5

√4th **313 Disturbance of emotions specific to childhood and adolescence**
    EXCLUDES *adjustment reaction (309.0-309.9)*
    emotional disorder of neurotic type (300.0-300.9)
    masturbation, nail-biting, thumbsucking, and other isolated symptoms (307.0-307.9)

313.0 Overanxious disorder
    Anxiety and fearfulness } of childhood and
    Overanxious disorder   adolescence
    EXCLUDES *abnormal separation anxiety (309.21)*
    anxiety states (300.00-300.09)
    hospitalism in children (309.83)
    phobic state (300.20-300.29)

313.1 Misery and unhappiness disorder
    EXCLUDES *depressive neurosis (300.4)*

√5th **313.2 Sensitivity, shyness, and social withdrawal disorder**
    EXCLUDES *infantile autism (299.0)*
    schizoid personality (301.20-301.22)
    schizophrenia (295.0-295.9)

    313.21 Shyness disorder of childhood
        Sensitivity reaction of childhood or adolescence

    313.22 Introverted disorder of childhood
        Social withdrawal } of childhood and
        Withdrawal reaction   adolescence

    313.23 Selective mutism
        EXCLUDES *elective mutism as adjustment reaction (309.83)*

313.3 Relationship problems
    Sibling jealousy
    EXCLUDES *relationship problems associated with aggression, destruction, or other forms of conduct disturbance (312.0-312.9)*

√5th **313.8 Other or mixed emotional disturbances of childhood or adolescence**

    313.81 Oppositional defiant disorder
        DEF: Mental disorder of children noted for pervasive opposition, defiance of authority.

    313.82 Identity disorder
        Identity problem
        DEF: Distress of adolescents caused by inability to form acceptable self-identity; uncertainty about career choice, sexual orientation, moral values.

    313.83 Academic underachievement disorder

    313.89 Other   P
        Reactive attachment disorder of infancy or early childhood

313.9 Unspecified emotional disturbance of childhood or adolescence   P
    Mental disorder of infancy, childhood or adolescence NOS

√4th **314 Hyperkinetic syndrome of childhood**
    EXCLUDES *hyperkinesis as symptom of underlying disorder — code the underlying disorder*
    TIP: These codes may be assigned for patients of any age.

√5th **314.0 Attention deficit disorder**
    Adult   Child
    DEF: A behavioral disorder usually diagnosed at an early age; characterized by the inability to focus attention for a normal period of time.

    314.00 Without mention of hyperactivity
        Predominantly inattentive type
        AHA: 1Q, '97, 8

    314.01 With hyperactivity
        Combined type
        Overactivity NOS
        Predominantly hyperactive/impulsive type
        Simple disturbance of attention with overactivity
        AHA: 3Q, '12, 19; 2Q, '11, 5; 1Q, '97, 8
        F90.1 ADHD predominantly hyperactive type   I-10

314.1 Hyperkinesis with developmental delay
    Developmental disorder of hyperkinesis
    Use additional code to identify any associated neurological disorder

314.2 Hyperkinetic conduct disorder
    Hyperkinetic conduct disorder without developmental delay
    EXCLUDES *hyperkinesis with significant delays in specific skills (314.1)*

314.8 Other specified manifestations of hyperkinetic syndrome

314.9 Unspecified hyperkinetic syndrome
    Hyperkinetic reaction of childhood or adolescence NOS
    Hyperkinetic syndrome NOS

√4th **315 Specific delays in development**
    EXCLUDES *that due to a neurological disorder (320.0-389.9)*

√5th **315.0 Specific reading disorder**

    315.00 Reading disorder, unspecified

    315.01 Alexia
        DEF: Lack of ability to understand written language; manifestation of aphasia.

    315.02 Developmental dyslexia
        DEF: Serious impairment of reading skills unexplained in relation to general intelligence and teaching processes.

    315.09 Other
        Specific spelling difficulty

315.1 Mathematics disorder
    Dyscalculia

315.2 Other specific learning difficulties
    Disorder of written expression
    EXCLUDES *specific arithmetical disorder (315.1)*
    specific reading disorder (315.00-315.09)

---

§   Requires fifth digit. Valid digits are in [brackets] under each code. See category 312 for codes and definitions.

N Newborn Age: 0   **P** Pediatric Age: 0-17   **M** Maternity Age: 12-55   **A** Adult Age: 15-124   **MCC** Major CC Condition   **CC** CC Condition   **HIV** HIV Related Dx

94 – Volume 1   2015 ICD-9-CM

√5ᵗʰ **315.3 Developmental speech or language disorder**

315.31 Expressive language disorder
Developmental aphasia
Word deafness
EXCLUDES acquired aphasia (784.3)
elective mutism (309.83, 313.0, 313.23)

315.32 Mixed receptive-expressive language disorder
Central auditory processing disorder
EXCLUDES acquired auditory processing disorder
(388.45)
AHA: 2Q, '05, 5; 4Q, '96, 30

315.34 Speech and language developmental delay due to hearing loss
AHA: 4Q, '07, 80, 81

315.35 Childhood onset fluency disorder
Cluttering NOS
Stuttering NOS
EXCLUDES adult onset fluency disorder (307.0)
fluency disorder due to late effect of
cerebrovascular accident (438.14)
fluency disorder in conditions classified
elsewhere (784.52)
AHA: 4Q, '10, 83-84
F80.81 Child onset fluency disorder   I-10

315.39 Other
Developmental articulation disorder
Dyslalia
Phonological disorder
EXCLUDES lisping and lalling (307.9)
AHA: 3Q, '07, 7

315.4 Developmental coordination disorder
Clumsiness syndrome
Dyspraxia syndrome
Specific motor development disorder

315.5 Mixed development disorder
AHA: 2Q, '02, 11

315.8 Other specified delays in development
F88 Other disorders of psychological development   I-10

315.9 Unspecified delay in development
Developmental disorder NOS
Learning disorder NOS

316 Psychic factors associated with diseases classified elsewhere
Psychologic factors in physical conditions classified elsewhere
Use additional code to identify the associated physical condition, as:
psychogenic:
asthma (493.9)
dermatitis (692.9)
duodenal ulcer (532.0-532.9)
eczema (691.8, 692.9)
gastric ulcer (531.0-531.9)
mucous colitis (564.9)
paroxysmal tachycardia (427.2)
ulcerative colitis (556)
urticaria (708.0-708.9)
psychosocial dwarfism (259.4)
EXCLUDES physical symptoms and physiological malfunctions, not
involving tissue damage, of mental origin
(306.0-306.9)

Intellectual Disabilities (317-319)

Use additional code(s) to identify any associated psychiatric or
physical condition(s)
AHA: 4Q, '11, 98

317 Mild intellectual disabilities
High-grade defect
IQ 50-70
Mild mental subnormality
F70 Mild intellectual disabilities   I-10

√4ᵗʰ **318 Other specified intellectual disabilities**

318.0 Moderate intellectual disabilities
IQ 35-49
Moderate mental subnormality

318.1 Severe intellectual disabilities   CC
IQ 20-34
Severe mental subnormality
CC Excl: 318.1-318.2

318.2 Profound intellectual disabilities   CC
IQ under 20
Profound mental subnormality
CC Excl: See code: 318.1

319 Unspecified intellectual disabilities
Mental deficiency NOS
Mental subnormality NOS
F79 Unspecified intellectual disabilities   I-10

| √4ᵗʰ √5ᵗʰ Additional Digit Required | Unacceptable PDx | Manifestation Code | Hospital Acquired Condition | ►◄ Revised Text | ● New Code | ▲ Revised Code Title |

2015 ICD-9-CM   **Volume 1 – 95**

Mental, Behavioral and Neurodevelopmental Disorders   315.3–319

6. Diseases of the Nervous System and Sense Organs (320-389)

Inflammatory Diseases of the Central Nervous System (320-326)

✓4th 320 Bacterial meningitis

INCLUDES
- arachnoiditis
- leptomeningitis
- meningitis   } bacterial
- meningoencephalitis
- meningomyelitis
- pachymeningitis

DEF: Bacterial infection causing inflammation of the lining of the brain and/or spinal cord.
AHA: J-F, '87, 6

320.0 Hemophilus meningitis   MCC
Meningitis due to Hemophilus influenzae [H. influenzae]
CC Excl: 003.21, 013.00-013.16, 036.0, 047.0-047.9, 049.0-049.1, 053.0, 054.72, 072.1, 090.42, 091.81, 094.2, 098.89, 100.81, 112.83, 114.2, 115.01, 115.11, 115.91, 130.0, 249.60-249.61, 249.80-249.91, 250.60-250.63, 250.80-250.93, 320.0-322.9, 349.89-349.9, 357.0

320.1 Pneumococcal meningitis   MCC
CC Excl: See code: 320.0

320.2 Streptococcal meningitis   MCC
CC Excl: See code: 320.0

320.3 Staphylococcal meningitis   MCC
CC Excl: See code: 320.0

320.7 *Meningitis in other bacterial diseases classified elsewhere*   MCC
Code first underlying disease, as:
- actinomycosis (039.8)
- listeriosis (027.0)
- typhoid fever (002.0)
- whooping cough (033.0-033.9)

EXCLUDES *meningitis (in):*
- *epidemic (036.0)*
- *gonococcal (098.82)*
- *meningococcal (036.0)*
- *salmonellosis (003.21)*
- *syphilis:*
  - *NOS (094.2)*
  - *congenital (090.42)*
  - *meningovascular (094.2)*
  - *secondary (091.81)*
- *tuberculous (013.0)*

CC Excl: See code: 320.0

✓5th 320.8 Meningitis due to other specified bacteria

320.81 Anaerobic meningitis   MCC
Bacteroides (fragilis)
Gram-negative anaerobes
CC Excl: See code 320.0

320.82 Meningitis due to gram-negative bacteria, not elsewhere classified   MCC
Aerobacter aerogenes pneumoniae
Escherichia coli [E. coli]
Friedländer bacillus
Klebsiella
Proteus morganii
Pseudomonas
EXCLUDES *gram-negative anaerobes (320.81)*
CC Excl: See code: 320.0
AHA: 4Q, '11, 155

320.89 Meningitis due to other specified bacteria   MCC
Bacillus pyocyaneus
CC Excl: See code: 320.0

320.9 Meningitis due to unspecified bacterium   MCC
Meningitis: Meningitis:
- bacterial NOS   pyogenic NOS
- purulent NOS   suppurative NOS
CC Excl: See code: 320.0

✓4th 321 Meningitis due to other organisms

INCLUDES
- arachnoiditis
- leptomeningitis   } due to organisms other
- meningitis   than bacterial
- pachymeningitis

DEF: Infection causing inflammation of the lining of the brain and/or spinal cord, due to organisms other than bacteria.
AHA: J-F, '87, 6

321.0 *Cryptococcal meningitis*   MCC
Code first underlying disease (117.5)
CC Excl: See code: 320.0

321.1 *Meningitis in other fungal diseases*   MCC
Code first underlying disease (110.0-118)
EXCLUDES *meningitis in:*
- *candidiasis (112.83)*
- *coccidioidomycosis (114.2)*
- *histoplasmosis (115.01, 115.11, 115.91)*
CC Excl: See code: 320.0

321.2 *Meningitis due to viruses not elsewhere classified*   MCC
Code first underlying disease, as:
- meningitis due to arbovirus (060.0-066.9)
EXCLUDES *meningitis (due to):*
- *abacterial (047.0-047.9)*
- *adenovirus (049.1)*
- *aseptic NOS (047.9)*
- *Coxsackie (virus)(047.0)*
- *ECHO virus (047.1)*
- *enterovirus (047.0-047.9)*
- *herpes simplex virus (054.72)*
- *herpes zoster virus (053.0)*
- *lymphocytic choriomeningitis virus (049.0)*
- *mumps (072.1)*
- *viral NOS (047.9)*
- *meningo-eruptive syndrome (047.1)*
CC Excl: 003.21, 013.00-013.16, 036.0, 047.0-047.9, 049.0-049.1, 053.0, 054.72, 072.1, 090.42, 091.81, 094.2, 098.89, 100.81, 112.83, 114.2, 115.01, 115.11, 115.91, 130.0, 320.0-322.9, 349.89-349.9, 357.0
AHA: 4Q, '04, 51

321.3 *Meningitis due to trypanosomiasis*   MCC
Code first underlying disease (086.0-086.9)
CC Excl: See code: 320.0

321.4 *Meningitis in sarcoidosis*   MCC
Code first underlying disease (135)
CC Excl: See code: 320.0

321.8 *Meningitis due to other nonbacterial organisms classified elsewhere*   MCC
Code first underlying disease
EXCLUDES *leptospiral meningitis (100.81)*
CC Excl: See code: 320.0

✓4th 322 Meningitis of unspecified cause

INCLUDES
- arachnoiditis
- leptomeningitis   } with no organism
- meningitis   specified as cause
- pachymeningitis

AHA: J-F, '87, 6
DEF: Infection causing inflammation of the lining of the brain and/or spinal cord, due to unspecified cause.

322.0 Nonpyogenic meningitis   MCC
Meningitis with clear cerebrospinal fluid
CC Excl: See code: 320.0

322.1 Eosinophilic meningitis   MCC
CC Excl: See code: 320.0

322.2 Chronic meningitis   CC
CC Excl: See code: 320.0

322.9 Meningitis, unspecified   MCC
CC Excl: See code: 320.0

✓4th ✓5th Additional Digit Required   Unacceptable PDx   Manifestation Code   Hospital Acquired Condition   ►◄ Revised Text   ● New Code   ▲ Revised Code Title

2015 ICD-9-CM   **Volume 1 – 97**

Diseases of the Nervous System and Sense Organs

323–323.63

√4ᵗʰ **323**   **Encephalitis, myelitis, and encephalomyelitis**

INCLUDES   acute disseminated encephalomyelitis
meningoencephalitis, except bacterial
meningomyelitis, except bacterial
myelitis:
     ascending
     transverse

EXCLUDES   *acute transverse myelitis NOS (341.20)*
acute transverse myelitis in conditions classified elsewhere
     (341.21)
bacterial:
     meningoencephalitis (320.0-320.9)
     meningomyelitis (320.0-320.9)
idiopathic transverse myelitis (341.22)

DEF: Encephalitis: inflammation of brain tissues.
DEF: Myelitis: inflammation of the spinal cord.
DEF: Encephalomyelitis: inflammation of brain and spinal cord.

√5ᵗʰ **323.0**   **Encephalitis, myelitis, and encephalomyelitis in viral diseases classified elsewhere**

Code first underlying disease, as:
     cat-scratch disease (078.3)
     human immunodeficiency virus [HIV] disease (042)
     infectious mononucleosis (075)
     ornithosis (073.7)

323.01   *Encephalitis and encephalomyelitis in viral diseases classified elsewhere*   MCC

EXCLUDES   *encephalitis (in):*
     arthropod-borne viral (062.0-064)
     herpes simplex (054.3)
     mumps (072.2)
     other viral diseases of central nervous
         system (049.8-049.9)
     poliomyelitis (045.0-045.9)
     rubella (056.01)
     slow virus infections of central nervous
         system (046.0-046.9)
     viral NOS (049.9)
     West Nile (066.41)

CC Excl: 003.21, 013.00-013.16, 013.60-013.66, 036.0, 046.2, 046.71-046.8, 047.0-049.8, 051.9-052.0, 052.7-053.13, 053.19, 053.79-053.9, 054.3, 054.72, 054.79-054.9, 056.01, 057.8-059.9, 062.0-064, 066.2-066.49, 072.1-072.2, 073.7, 075, 078.89, 079.81-079.82, 079.89, 079.99, 090.41-090.42, 091.81, 094.2, 094.81, 098.89, 100.81, 112.83, 114.2, 115.01, 115.11, 115.91, 130.0, 139.8, 290.12, 320.0-323.9, 341.1, 349.89-349.9, 357.0, 487.8, 488.09, 488.19, 771.2
AHA: 3Q, '10, 13; 4Q, '06, 58-63

323.02   *Myelitis in viral diseases classified elsewhere*   MCC

EXCLUDES   *myelitis (in):*
     herpes simplex (054.74)
     herpes zoster (053.14)
     poliomyelitis (045.0-045.9)
     rubella (056.01)
     other viral diseases of central nervous
         system (049.8-049.9)

CC Excl: See code: 323.01
AHA: 4Q, '06, 58-63

323.1   *Encephalitis, myelitis, and encephalomyelitis in rickettsial diseases classified elsewhere*   MCC

Code first underlying disease (080-083.9)
DEF: Inflammation of the brain caused by rickettsial disease carried by louse, tick, or mite.
CC Excl: 013.60-013.66, 046.2, 046.71-046.8, 048-049.0, 049.8, 052.0, 052.2, 054.3, 054.74, 056.01, 057.8-058.29, 059.00-059.9, 062.0-064, 066.2-066.49, 072.2, 073.7, 079.82, 079.99, 081.9, 083.9, 090.41, 094.81, 117.5, 124, 130.0, 290.12, 323.01-323.9, 341.1, 487.8, 771.2, 984.9

323.2   *Encephalitis, myelitis, and encephalomyelitis in protozoal diseases classified elsewhere*   MCC

Code first underlying disease, as:
     malaria (084.0-084.9)
     trypanosomiasis (086.0-086.9)
DEF: Inflammation of the brain caused by protozoal disease carried by mosquitoes and flies.
CC Excl: 013.60-013.66, 046.2, 046.71-046.8, 048-049.0, 049.8, 052.0, 052.2, 054.3, 054.74, 056.01, 057.8-058.29, 059.00-059.9, 062.0-064, 066.2-066.49, 072.2, 073.7, 079.82, 079.99, 081.9, 083.9, 084.6, 090.41, 094.81, 117.5, 124, 130.0, 290.12, 323.01-323.9, 341.1, 487.8, 488.09, 488.19, 771.2, 984.9

√5ᵗʰ **323.4**   **Other encephalitis, myelitis, and encephalomyelitis due to other infections classified elsewhere**

Code first underlying disease

323.41   *Other encephalitis and encephalomyelitis due to other infections classified elsewhere*   MCC

EXCLUDES   *encephalitis (in):*
     meningococcal (036.1)
     syphilis:
         NOS (094.81)
         congenital (090.41)
     toxoplasmosis (130.0)
     tuberculosis (013.6)
     meningoencephalitis due to free-living
         ameba [Naegleria] (136.29)

CC Excl: See code: 323.01
AHA: 4Q, '06, 58-63

323.42   *Other myelitis due to other infections classified elsewhere*   MCC

EXCLUDES   *myelitis (in):*
     syphilis (094.89)
     tuberculosis (013.6)

CC Excl: See code: 323.01
AHA: 4Q, '06, 58-63

√5ᵗʰ **323.5**   **Encephalitis, myelitis, and encephalomyelitis following immunization procedures**

Use additional E code to identify vaccine

323.51   **Encephalitis and encephalomyelitis following immunization procedures**   MCC
Encephalitis postimmunization or postvaccinal
Encephalomyelitis postimmunization or postvaccinal
CC Excl: See code: 323.01
AHA: 4Q, '06, 58-63

323.52   **Myelitis following immunization procedures**   MCC
Myelitis postimmunization or postvaccinal
CC Excl: See code: 323.01
AHA: 4Q, '06, 58-63

√5ᵗʰ **323.6**   **Postinfectious encephalitis, myelitis, and encephalomyelitis**

Code first underlying disease
DEF: Infection, inflammation of brain several weeks following the outbreak of a systemic infection.

323.61   *Infectious acute disseminated encephalomyelitis [ADEM]*   MCC
Acute necrotizing hemorrhagic encephalopathy
EXCLUDES   *noninfectious acute disseminated*
     encephalo- myelitis (ADEM) (323.81)
CC Excl: See code: 323.01
AHA: 4Q, '06, 58-63

323.62   *Other postinfectious encephalitis and encephalomyelitis*   MCC
EXCLUDES   *encephalitis:*
     postchickenpox (052.0)
     postmeasles (055.0)
CC Excl: See code: 323.01
AHA: 4Q, '06, 58-63

323.63   *Postinfectious myelitis*   MCC
EXCLUDES   *postchickenpox myelitis (052.2)*
     herpes simplex myelitis (054.74)
     herpes zoster myelitis (053.14)
CC Excl: See code: 323.01
AHA: 4Q, '06, 58-63

N Newborn Age: 0   P Pediatric Age: 0-17   M Maternity Age: 12-55   A Adult Age: 15-124   MCC Major CC Condition   CC CC Condition   HIV HIV Related Dx

98 – Volume 1   **2015 ICD-9-CM**

√5ᵗʰ **323.7 Toxic encephalitis, myelitis, and encephalomyelitis**

Code first underlying cause, as:
carbon tetrachloride (982.1)
hydroxyquinoline derivatives (961.3)
lead (984.0-984.9)
mercury (985.0)
thallium (985.8)
AHA: 2Q, '97, 8

323.71 Toxic encephalitis and encephalomyelitis `MCC`
CC Excl: See code: 323.01
AHA: 4Q, '06, 58-63

323.72 Toxic myelitis `MCC`
CC Excl: See code: 323.01
AHA: 4Q, '06, 58-63

√5ᵗʰ **323.8 Other causes of encephalitis, myelitis, and encephalomyelitis**

323.81 Other causes of encephalitis and encephalomyelitis `MCC` `HIV`
Noninfectious acute disseminated encephalomyelitis (ADEM)
CC Excl: See code: 323.01
AHA: 1Q, '11, 12; 3Q, '10, 15; 4Q, '06, 58-63

323.82 Other causes of myelitis `MCC` `HIV`
Transverse myelitis NOS
CC Excl: See code: 323.01
AHA: 4Q, '06, 58-63

323.9 Unspecified cause of encephalitis, myelitis, and encephalomyelitis `MCC` `HIV`
CC Excl: 013.60-013.66, 046.2, 046.71-046.8, 048-049.0, 049.8, 052.0, 052.2, 054.3, 054.74, 056.01, 057.8-058.29, 059.00-059.9, 062.0-064, 066.2-066.49, 072.2, 073.7, 075, 078.3, 079.82, 079.99, 081.9, 083.9, 084.6, 090.41, 094.81, 117.5, 124, 130.0, 290.12, 323.01-323.9, 341.1, 382.4, 487.8, 488.09, 488.19, 710.0, 771.2, 984.9
AHA: 1Q, '06, 8

√4ᵗʰ **324 Intracranial and intraspinal abscess**

324.0 Intracranial abscess `MCC`
Abscess (embolic):
cerebellar
cerebral
Abscess (embolic) of brain [any part]:
epidural
extradural
otogenic
subdural
EXCLUDES *tuberculous (013.3)*
CC Excl: 006.5, 013.20-013.36, 249.60-249.61, 249.80-249.91, 250.60-250.63, 250.80-250.93, 324.0-325, 348.81-348.9

324.1 Intraspinal abscess `MCC`
Abscess (embolic) of spinal cord [any part]:
epidural
extradural
subdural
EXCLUDES *tuberculous (013.5)*
CC Excl: 0006.5, 013.20-013.36, 249.60-249.61, 249.80-249.91, 250.60-250.63, 250.80-250.93, 324.1

324.9 Of unspecified site `MCC`
Extradural or subdural abscess NOS
CC Excl: 006.5, 013.20-013.36, 249.60-249.61, 249.80-249.91, 250.60-250.63, 250.80-250.93, 324.0-325

325 Phlebitis and thrombophlebitis of intracranial venous sinuses `MCC`
Embolism
Endophlebitis
Phlebitis, septic or suppurative
Thrombophlebitis
Thrombosis
} of cavernous, lateral or other intracranial or unspecified intracranial venous sinus
EXCLUDES *that specified as:*
complicating pregnancy, childbirth, or the puerperium (671.5)
of nonpyogenic origin (437.6)
DEF: Inflammation and formation of blood clot in a vein within the brain or its lining.
CC Excl: See code: 324.9

326 Late effects of intracranial abscess or pyogenic infection
`NOTE` This category is to be used to indicate conditions whose primary classification is to 320-325 [excluding 320.7, 321.0-321.8, 323.01-323.42, 323.6-323.7] as the cause of late effects, themselves classifiable elsewhere. The "late effects" include conditions specified as such, or as sequelae, which may occur at any time after the resolution of the causal condition.
Use additional code to identify condition, as:
hydrocephalus (331.4)
paralysis (342.0-342.9, 344.0-344.9)

Organic Sleep Disorders (327)

TIP: If the sleep disorder is not documented with the etiology related to an organic disease process, see instead subcategory 307.4.

√4ᵗʰ **327 Organic sleep disorders**
AHA: 4Q, '05, 59-64

√5ᵗʰ **327.0 Organic disorders of initiating and maintaining sleep [Organic insomnia]**
EXCLUDES *insomnia NOS (780.52)*
insomnia not due to a substance or known physiological condition (307.41-307.42)
insomnia with sleep apnea NOS (780.51)

327.00 Organic insomnia, unspecified

327.01 Insomnia due to medical condition classified elsewhere
Code first underlying condition
EXCLUDES *insomnia due to mental disorder (327.02)*

327.02 Insomnia due to mental disorder
Code first mental disorder
EXCLUDES *alcohol induced insomnia (291.82)*
drug induced insomnia (292.85)

327.09 Other organic insomnia

√5ᵗʰ **327.1 Organic disorder of excessive somnolence [Organic hypersomnia]**
EXCLUDES *hypersomnia NOS (780.54)*
hypersomnia not due to a substance or known physiological condition (307.43-307.44)
hypersomnia with sleep apnea NOS (780.53)

327.10 Organic hypersomnia, unspecified

327.11 Idiopathic hypersomnia with long sleep time

327.12 Idiopathic hypersomnia without long sleep time

327.13 Recurrent hypersomnia
Kleine-Levin syndrome
Menstrual related hypersomnia

327.14 Hypersomnia due to medical condition classified elsewhere
Code first underlying condition
EXCLUDES *hypersomnia due to mental disorder (327.15)*

327.15 Hypersomnia due to mental disorder
Code first mental disorder
EXCLUDES *alcohol induced hypersomnia (291.82)*
drug induced hypersomnia (292.85)

327.19 Other organic hypersomnia

√5ᵗʰ **327.2 Organic sleep apnea**
EXCLUDES *Cheyne-Stokes breathing (786.04)*
hypersomnia with sleep apnea NOS (780.53)
insomnia with sleep apnea NOS (780.51)
sleep apnea in newborn (770.81-770.82)
sleep apnea NOS (780.57)

327.20 Organic sleep apnea, unspecified

327.21 Primary central sleep apnea

327.22 High altitude periodic breathing

327.23 Obstructive sleep apnea (adult) (pediatric)
G47.33 Obstructive sleep apnea (adult) (pediatric) `I-10`

327.24 Idiopathic sleep related nonobstructive alveolar hypoventilation
Sleep related hypoxia

√4ᵗʰ
√5ᵗʰ Additional Digit Required   Unacceptable PDx   Manifestation Code   Hospital Acquired Condition   ►◄ Revised Text   ● New Code   ▲ Revised Code Title

327.25 Congenital central alveolar hypoventilation syndrome

327.26 Sleep related hypoventilation/ hypoxemia in conditions classifiable elsewhere

Code first underlying condition

327.27 Central sleep apnea in conditions classified elsewhere

Code first underlying condition

327.29 Other organic sleep apnea

✓5ᵗʰ 327.3 Circadian rhythm sleep disorder
Organic disorder of sleep wake cycle
Organic disorder of sleep wake schedule

EXCLUDES alcohol induced circadian rhythm sleep disorder (291.82)
circadian rhythm sleep disorder of nonorganic origin (307.45)
disruption of 24 hour sleep wake cycle NOS (780.55)
drug induced circadian rhythm sleep disorder (292.85)

327.30 Circadian rhythm sleep disorder, unspecified

327.31 Circadian rhythm sleep disorder, delayed sleep phase type

327.32 Circadian rhythm sleep disorder, advanced sleep phase type

327.33 Circadian rhythm sleep disorder, irregular sleep-wake type

327.34 Circadian rhythm sleep disorder, free-running type

327.35 Circadian rhythm sleep disorder, jet lag type

327.36 Circadian rhythm sleep disorder, shift work type

327.37 Circadian rhythm sleep disorder in conditions classified elsewhere

Code first underlying condition

327.39 Other circadian rhythm sleep disorder

✓5ᵗʰ 327.4 Organic parasomnia

EXCLUDES alcohol induced parasomnia (291.82)
drug induced parasomnia (292.85)
parasomnia not due to a known physiological condition (307.47)

327.40 Organic parasomnia, unspecified

327.41 Confusional arousals

327.42 REM sleep behavior disorder

327.43 Recurrent isolated sleep paralysis

327.44 Parasomnia in conditions classified elsewhere

Code first underlying condition

327.49 Other organic parasomnia

✓5ᵗʰ 327.5 Organic sleep related movement disorders

EXCLUDES restless legs syndrome (333.94)
sleep related movement disorder NOS (780.58)

327.51 Periodic limb movement disorder
Periodic limb movement sleep disorder

327.52 Sleep related leg cramps

327.53 Sleep related bruxism

327.59 Other organic sleep related movement disorders

327.8 Other organic sleep disorders
AHA: 2Q, '07, 6

Hereditary and Degenerative Diseases of the Central Nervous System (330-337)

EXCLUDES hepatolenticular degeneration (275.1)
multiple sclerosis (340)
other demyelinating diseases of central nervous system (341.0-341.9)

✓4ᵗʰ 330 Cerebral degenerations usually manifest in childhood
Use additional code to identify associated intellectual disabilities

330.0 Leukodystrophy   CC
Krabbe's disease
Leukodystrophy:
  NOS
  globoid cell
  metachromatic
Leukodystrophy:
  sudanophilic
Pelizaeus-Merzbacher disease
Sulfatide lipidosis

DEF: Hereditary disease of arylsulfatase or cerebroside sulfatase; characterized by a diffuse loss of myelin in CNS; infantile form causes blindness, motor disturbances, rigidity, mental deterioration and, occasionally, convulsions.
CC Excl: 330.0-330.9, 331.7, 348.81-348.9, 349.89-349.9

330.1 Cerebral lipidoses   CC
Amaurotic (familial) idiocy
Disease:
  Batten
  Jansky-Bielschowsky
  Kufs'
Disease:
  Spielmeyer-Vogt
  Tay-Sachs
Gangliosidosis

DEF: Genetic disorder causing abnormal lipid accumulation in the reticuloendothelial cells of the brain.
CC Excl: 330.1-331.2, 331.6, 331.7, 331.83-331.9

330.2 Cerebral degeneration in generalized lipidoses   CC

Code first underlying disease, as:
  Fabry's disease (272.7)
  Gaucher's disease (272.7)
  Niemann-Pick disease (272.7)
  sphingolipidosis (272.7)
CC Excl: See code: 330.1

330.3 Cerebral degeneration of childhood in other diseases classified elsewhere   CC

Code first underlying disease, as:
  Hunter's disease (277.5)
  mucopolysaccharidosis (277.5)
CC Excl: See code: 330.1

330.8 Other specified cerebral degenerations in childhood   CC
Alpers' disease or gray-matter degeneration
Infantile necrotizing encephalomyelopathy
Leigh's disease
Subacute necrotizing encephalopathy or encephalomyelopathy
CC Excl: See code: 330.1
AHA: N-D, '85, 5

330.9 Unspecified cerebral degeneration in childhood   CC
CC Excl: See code: 330.1

✓4ᵗʰ 331 Other cerebral degenerations
Use additional code, where applicable, to identify dementia:
with behavioral disturbance (294.11)
without behavioral disturbance (294.10)

331.0 Alzheimer's disease
DEF: Diffuse atrophy of cerebral cortex; causing a progressive decline in intellectual and physical functions, including memory loss, personality changes and profound dementia.
AHA: 4Q, '00, 41; 4Q, '99, 7; N-D, '84, 20
G30.9 Alzheimer's disease unspecified   I-10

✓5ᵗʰ 331.1 Frontotemporal dementia
DEF: Rare, progressive degenerative brain disease, similar to Alzheimer's; cortical atrophy affects the frontal and temporal lobes.
AHA: 4Q, '03, 57

331.11 Pick's disease
DEF: A progressive frontotemporal dementia with asymmetrical atrophy of the frontal and temporal regions of the cerebral cortex, abnormal rounded brain cells called Pick cells with the presence of abnormal staining of protein (called tau); symptoms include prominent apathy, behavioral changes such as disinhibition and restlessness, echolalia, impairment of language, memory, and intellect, increased carelessness, poor personal hygiene, and decreased attention span.

N Newborn Age: 0   P Pediatric Age: 0-17   M Maternity Age: 12-55   A Adult Age: 15-124   MCC Major CC Condition   CC CC Condition   HIV HIV Related Dx

100 – Volume 1   2015 ICD-9-CM

331.19 Other frontotemporal dementia
Frontal dementia

331.2 Senile degeneration of brain
EXCLUDES senility NOS (797)

331.3 Communicating hydrocephalus   `CC`
Secondary normal pressure hydrocephalus
EXCLUDES congenital hydrocephalus (742.3)
   idiopathic normal pressure hydrocephalus (331.5)
   normal pressure hydrocephalus (331.5)
   spina bifida with hydrocephalus (741.0)
DEF: Subarachnoid hemorrhage and meningitis causing excess buildup of cerebrospinal fluid in cavities due to nonabsorption of fluid back through fluid pathways.
CC Excl: 331.3-331.5
AHA: S-O, '85, 12

331.4 Obstructive hydrocephalus   `CC`
Acquired hydrocephalus NOS
EXCLUDES congenital hydrocephalus (742.3)
   idiopathic normal pressure hydrocephalus (331.5)
   normal pressure hydrocephalus (331.5)
   spina bifida with hydrocephalus (741.0)
DEF: Obstruction of cerebrospinal fluid passage from brain into spinal canal.
CC Excl: 249.60-249.61, 249.80-249.91, 250.60-250.63, 250.80-250.93, 331.3-331.7, 331.82-331.9, 348.81, 348.89-348.9, 741.00-741.03, 742.3-742.4, 742.59-742.9
AHA: 4Q, '03, 106; 1Q, '99, 9
G91.1 Obstructive hydrocephalus   `I-10`

331.5 Idiopathic normal pressure hydrocephalus [INPH]   `CC`
Normal pressure hydrocephalus NOS
EXCLUDES congenital hydrocephalus (742.3)
   secondary normal pressure hydrocephalus (331.3)
   spina bifida with hydrocephalus (741.0)
DEF: Abnormal increase of cerebrospinal fluid in the brain's ventricles; results in dementia, progressive mental impairment, gait disturbance, and impaired bladder control.
CC Excl: See code: 331.3
AHA: 4Q, '07, 74

331.6 Corticobasal degeneration
AHA: 4Q, '11, 98

331.7 Cerebral degeneration in diseases classified elsewhere
Code first underlying disease, as:
   alcoholism (303.0-303.9)
   beriberi (265.0)
   cerebrovascular disease (430-438)
   congenital hydrocephalus (741.0, 742.3)
   myxedema (244.0-244.9)
   neoplastic disease (140.0-239.9)
   vitamin B12 deficiency (266.2)
EXCLUDES cerebral degeneration in:
   Jakob-Creutzfeldt disease (046.11-046.19)
   progressive multifocal leukoencephalopathy (046.3)
   subacute spongiform encephalopathy (046.1)

√5ᵗʰ 331.8 Other cerebral degeneration

331.81 Reye's syndrome   `MCC` `P`
DEF: Rare childhood illness, often developed after a viral upper respiratory infection; characterized by vomiting, elevated serum transaminase, changes in liver and other viscera; brain swelling, disturbances of consciousness and seizures; can be fatal.
CC Excl: 331.81

331.82 Dementia with Lewy bodies
Dementia with Parkinsonism
Lewy body dementia
Lewy body disease
DEF: A cerebral dementia with neurophysiologic changes, increased hippocampal volume, hypoperfusion in the occipital lobes, and beta amyloid deposits with neurofibrillarity tangles, atrophy of cortex and brainstem; hallmark neuropsychologic characteristics are fluctuating cognition with pronounced variation in attention and alertness; recurrent hallucinations; and parkinsonism.
AHA: 4Q, '03, 57
G31.83 Dementia with Lewy bodies   `I-10`

331.83 Mild cognitive impairment, so stated
EXCLUDES altered mental status (780.97)
   cerebral degeneration (331.0-331.9)
   change in mental status (780.97)
   cognitive deficits following (late effects of) cerebral hemorrhage or infarction (438.0)
   cognitive impairment due to intracranial or head injury (850-854, 959.01)
   cognitive impairment due to late effect of intracranial injury (907.0)
   cognitive impairment due to skull fracture (800-801, 803-804)
   dementia (290.0-290.43, 294.20-294.21)
   mild memory disturbance (310.89)
   neurologic neglect syndrome (781.8)
   personality change, nonpsychotic (310.1)
AHA: 4Q, '06, 75

331.89 Other
Cerebral ataxia

331.9 Cerebral degeneration, unspecified

√4ᵗʰ 332 Parkinson's disease
EXCLUDES dementia with Parkinsonism (331.82)

332.0 Paralysis agitans
Parkinsonism or Parkinson's disease:
   NOS
   idiopathic
   primary
DEF: Form of progressive parkinsonism characterized by mask-like facial expressions, inability to stand or walk smoothly, muscle weakness, and involuntary trembling movement.
AHA: M-A, '87, 7
G20 Parkinson's disease   `I-10`

332.1 Secondary Parkinsonism   `CC`
Neuroleptic-induced Parkinsonism
Parkinsonism due to drugs
Use additional E code to identify drug, if drug-induced
EXCLUDES Parkinsonism (in):
   Huntington's disease (333.4)
   progressive supranuclear palsy (333.0)
   Shy-Drager syndrome (333.0)
   syphilitic (094.82)
CC Excl: 332.0-332.1

√4ᵗʰ 333 Other extrapyramidal disease and abnormal movement disorders
INCLUDES other forms of extrapyramidal, basal ganglia, or striatopallidal disease
EXCLUDES abnormal movements of head NOS (781.0)
   sleep related movement disorders (327.51-327.59)

333.0 Other degenerative diseases of the basal ganglia   `CC`
Atrophy or degeneration:
   olivopontocerebellar [Déjérine-Thomas syndrome]
   pigmentary pallidal [Hallervorden-Spatz disease]
   striatonigral
Parkinsonian syndrome associated with:
   idiopathic orthostatic hypotension
   symptomatic orthostatic hypotension
Progressive supranuclear ophthalmoplegia
Shy-Drager syndrome
CC Excl: 332.0-332.1, 335.23, 337.00-337.09, 348.30-348.39
AHA: 3Q, '96, 8

333.1 Essential and other specified forms of tremor
Benign essential tremor
Familial tremor
Medication-induced postural tremor
Use additional E code to identify drug, if drug-induced
EXCLUDES tremor NOS (781.0)

333.2 Myoclonus
Familial essential myoclonus
Palatal myoclonus
EXCLUDES progressive myoclonic epilepsy (345.1)
   Unverricht-Lundborg disease (345.1)
Use additional E code to identify drug, if drug-induced
DEF: Spontaneous movements or contractions of muscles.
AHA: 3Q, '97, 4; M-A, '87, 12

333.3 Tics of organic origin

Use additional E code to identify drug, if drug-induced

EXCLUDES Gilles de la Tourette's syndrome (307.23)
habit spasm (307.22)
tic NOS (307.20)

333.4 Huntington's chorea ⟨CC⟩

DEF: Genetic disease characterized by chronic progressive mental deterioration; dementia and death within 15 years of onset.
CC Excl: 332.0-332.1, 340-341.1, 341.8-341.9, 343.0-344.2, 348.1, 348.30-348.9, 349.1, 349.82-349.9, 780.72

333.5 Other choreas
Hemiballism(us)
Paroxysmal choreo-athetosis

Use additional E code to identify drug, if drug-induced

EXCLUDES Sydenham's or rheumatic chorea (392.0-392.9)

333.6 Genetic torsion dystonia
Dystonia:
deformans progressiva
musculorum deformans
(Schwalbe-) Ziehen-Oppenheim disease

DEF: Sustained muscular contractions, causing twisting and repetitive movements that result in abnormal postures of trunk and limbs; etiology unknown.

√5ᵗʰ 333.7 Acquired torsion dystonia

333.71 Athetoid cerebral palsy ⟨CC⟩
Double athetosis (syndrome)
Vogt's disease

EXCLUDES infantile cerebral palsy (343.0-343.9)

CC Excl: 332.0-332.1, 333.71, 333.90, 333.99, 343.0-343.9, 348.30-348.39
AHA: 4Q, '06, 76-78

333.72 Acute dystonia due to drugs ⟨CC⟩
Acute dystonic reaction due to drugs
Neuroleptic induced acute dystonia

Use additional E code to identify drug

EXCLUDES blepharospasm due to drugs (333.85)
orofacial dyskinesia due to drugs (333.85)
secondary Parkinsonism (332.1)
subacute dyskinesia due to drugs (333.85)
tardive dyskinesia (333.85)

CC Excl: 332.0-332.1, 333.71, 333.90, 333.99, 348.30-348.39
AHA: 4Q, '06, 76-78

333.79 Other acquired torsion dystonia ⟨CC⟩
CC Excl: See code: 333.72
AHA: 4Q, '06, 76-78

√5ᵗʰ 333.8 Fragments of torsion dystonia
Use additional E code to identify drug, if drug-induced

333.81 Blepharospasm
EXCLUDES blepharospasm due to drugs (333.85)

DEF: Uncontrolled winking or blinking due to orbicularis oculi muscle spasm.

333.82 Orofacial dyskinesia
EXCLUDES orofacial dyskinesia due to drugs (333.85)

DEF: Uncontrolled movement of mouth or facial muscles.

333.83 Spasmodic torticollis
EXCLUDES torticollis:
NOS (723.5)
hysterical (300.11)
psychogenic (306.0)

DEF: Uncontrolled movement of head due to spasms of neck muscle.

333.84 Organic writers' cramp
EXCLUDES pychogenic (300.89)

333.85 Subacute dyskinesia due to drugs
Blepharospasm due to drugs
Orofacial dyskinesia due to drugs
Tardive dyskinesia

Use additional E code to identify drug

EXCLUDES acute dystonia due to drugs (333.72)
acute dystonic reaction due to drugs (333.72)
secondary Parkinsonism (332.1)

AHA: 4Q, '06, 76-78

333.89 Other

√5ᵗʰ 333.9 Other and unspecified extrapyramidal diseases and abnormal movement disorders

333.90 Unspecified extrapyramidal disease and abnormal movement disorder ⟨CC⟩
Medication-induced movement disorders NOS

Use additional E code to identify drug, if drug-induced

CC Excl: 332.0-332.1, 333.1-333.83, 333.85-333.93, 333.99, 335.22-335.23, 340-341.1, 341.8-341.9, 343.0-344.2, 348.1, 348.30-348.9, 349.1, 349.82-349.9, 780.72

333.91 Stiff-man syndrome ⟨CC⟩
CC Excl: See code: 333.90

333.92 Neuroleptic malignant syndrome ⟨MCC⟩
Use additional E code to identify drug

EXCLUDES neuroleptic induced Parkinsonism (332.1)

CC Excl: 333.0-333.93, 333.99, 342.00-342.92, 348.2-348.39
AHA: 4Q, '94, 37

333.93 Benign shuddering attacks
AHA: 4Q, '94, 37

333.94 Restless legs syndrome [RLS]
DEF: Neurological disorder of unknown etiology with an irresistible urge to move the legs, which may temporarily relieve the symptoms, is accompanied by motor restlessness and sensations of pain, burning, prickling, or tingling.
AHA: 4Q, '06, 79
TIP: Assign an additional code if the underlying cause of the RLS is specified (e.g., iron deficiency anemia).
G25.81 Restless legs syndrome ⟨I-10⟩

333.99 Other
Neuroleptic-induced acute akathisia

Use additional E code to identify drug, if drug-induced

AHA: 4Q, '04, 95; 2Q, '04, 12; 4Q, '94, 37

√4ᵗʰ 334 Spinocerebellar disease
EXCLUDES olivopontocerebellar degeneration (333.0)
peroneal muscular atrophy (356.1)

334.0 Friedreich's ataxia ⟨CC⟩
DEF: Genetic recessive disease of children; sclerosis of dorsal, lateral spinal cord columns; characterized by ataxia, speech impairment, swaying and irregular movements, with muscle paralysis, especially of lower limbs.
CC Excl: 334.0-334.9, 348.30-348.39

334.1 Hereditary spastic paraplegia ⟨CC⟩
CC Excl: 333.0-333.93, 333.99-337.9, 340-344.9, 348.1, 348.30-348.39, 348.81-349.2, 349.82-349.9, 780.72

334.2 Primary cerebellar degeneration ⟨CC⟩
Cerebellar ataxia:
Marie's
Sanger-Brown
Dyssynergia cerebellaris myoclonica
Primary cerebellar degeneration:
NOS
hereditary
sporadic
CC Excl: 333.0-333.93, 333.99-337.9, 340-344.9, 348.0-348.1, 348.30-348.39, 348.81-348.9, 349.82-349.9, 780.72
AHA: M-A, '87, 9

334.3 Other cerebellar ataxia ⟨CC⟩
Cerebellar ataxia NOS

Use additional E code to identify drug, if drug-induced
CC Excl: See code: 334.2

334.4 *Cerebellar ataxia in diseases classified elsewhere* ⟨CC⟩
Code first underlying disease, as:
alcoholism (303.0-303.9)
myxedema (244.0-244.9)
neoplastic disease (140.0-239.9)
CC Excl: See code: 334.2

334.8 Other spinocerebellar diseases ⟨CC⟩
Ataxia-telangiectasia [Louis-Bar syndrome]
Corticostriatal-spinal degeneration
CC Excl: See code: 334.2

| N Newborn Age: 0 | P Pediatric Age: 0-17 | M Maternity Age: 12-55 | A Adult Age: 15-124 | MCC Major CC Condition | CC CC Condition | HIV HIV Related Dx |

334.9 Spinocerebellar disease, unspecified `CC`
CC Excl: 334.0-334.9

`√4th` **335 Anterior horn cell disease**

335.0 Werdnig-Hoffmann disease `CC`
Infantile spinal muscular atrophy
Progressive muscular atrophy of infancy
DEF: Spinal muscle atrophy manifested in prenatal period or shortly after birth; symptoms include hypotonia, atrophy of skeletal muscle; death occurs in infancy.
CC Excl: 249.60-249.61, 249.80-249.91, 250.60-250.63, 250.80-250.93, 334.8-337.9, 349.89-349.9

`√5th` **335.1 Spinal muscular atrophy**

335.10 Spinal muscular atrophy, unspecified `CC`
CC Excl: See code: 335.0

335.11 Kugelberg-Welander disease `CC`
Spinal muscular atrophy:
familial
juvenile
DEF: Hereditary; juvenile muscle atrophy; appears during first two decades of life; due to lesions of anterior horns of spinal cord; includes wasting, diminution of lower body muscles and twitching.
CC Excl: See code: 335.0

335.19 Other `CC`
Adult spinal muscular atrophy
CC Excl: See code: 335.0

`√5th` **335.2 Motor neuron disease**

335.20 Amyotrophic lateral sclerosis `CC` `A`
Motor neuron disease (bulbar) (mixed type)
CC Excl: See code: 335.0
AHA: 4Q, '95, 81

335.21 Progressive muscular atrophy `CC`
Duchenne-Aran muscular atrophy
Progressive muscular atrophy (pure)
CC Excl: See code: 335.0

335.22 Progressive bulbar palsy `CC`
CC Excl: See code: 335.0

335.23 Pseudobulbar palsy `CC`
CC Excl: See code: 335.0

335.24 Primary lateral sclerosis `CC`
CC Excl: See code: 335.0

335.29 Other `CC`
CC Excl: See code: 335.0

335.8 Other anterior horn cell diseases `CC`
CC Excl: See code: 335.0

335.9 Anterior horn cell disease, unspecified `CC`
CC Excl: See code: 335.0

`√4th` **336 Other diseases of spinal cord**

336.0 Syringomyelia and syringobulbia `CC`
CC Excl: 334.8-337.9, 340-344.9, 348.30-348.39, 348.81-349.2, 349.89-349.9, 780.72
AHA: 1Q, '89, 10

336.1 Vascular myelopathies `MCC`
Acute infarction of spinal cord (embolic) (nonembolic)
Arterial thrombosis of spinal cord
Edema of spinal cord
Hematomyelia
Subacute necrotic myelopathy
CC Excl: 249.60-249.61, 250.60-250.63, 334.8-337.9, 340-344.9, 348.1, 348.30-348.39, 349.0-349.2, 349.89-349.9, 780.72

336.2 *Subacute combined degeneration of spinal cord in diseases classified elsewhere* `CC`
Code first underlying disease, as:
pernicious anemia (281.0)
other vitamin B$_{12}$ deficiency anemia (281.1)
vitamin B$_{12}$ deficiency (266.2)
CC Excl: 334.8-337.9, 340-344.9, 348.1, 348.30-348.39, 349.0-349.2, 349.89-349.9, 780.72

336.3 *Myelopathy in other diseases classified elsewhere* `CC`
Code first underlying disease, as:
myelopathy in neoplastic disease (140.0-239.9)
EXCLUDES *myelopathy in:*
intervertebral disc disorder (722.70-722.73)
spondylosis (721.1, 721.41-721.42, 721.91)
CC Excl: See code: 336.1
AHA: 3Q, '99, 5

336.8 Other myelopathy `CC`
Myelopathy: Myelopathy:
drug-induced   radiation-induced
Use additonal E code to identify cause
CC Excl: See code: 336.1

336.9 Unspecified disease of spinal cord `CC` `HIV`
Cord compression NOS
Myelopathy NOS
EXCLUDES *myelitis (323.02, 323.1, 323.2, 323.42, 323.52, 323.63, 323.72, 323.82, 323.9)*
spinal (canal) stenosis (723.0, 724.00-724.09)
CC Excl: 249.60-249.61, 250.60-250.63, 334.1, 334.8-337.9, 340-344.9, 348.1, 348.30-348.39, 349.0-349.2, 349.89-349.9, 780.72

`√4th` **337 Disorders of the autonomic nervous system**
INCLUDES disorders of peripheral autonomic, sympathetic, parasympathetic, or vegetative system
EXCLUDES *familial dysautonomia [Riley-Day syndrome] (742.8)*

`√5th` **337.0 Idiopathic peripheral autonomic neuropathy**

337.00 Idiopathic peripheral autonomic neuropathy, unspecified

337.01 Carotid sinus syndrome
Carotid sinus syncope
DEF: Vagal activation caused by pressure on the carotid sinus baroreceptors; sympathetic nerve impulses may cause sinus arrest or AV block.
AHA: 4Q, '08, 101-102

337.09 Other idiopathic peripheral autonomic neuropathy
Cervical sympathetic dystrophy or paralysis

337.1 *Peripheral autonomic neuropathy in disorders classified elsewhere* `CC`
Code first underlying disease, as:
amyloidosis (277.30-277.39)
diabetes (249.6, 250.6)
CC Excl: 337.00-337.29, 337.9, 348.30-348.39
AHA: 2Q, '09, 13; 2Q, '93, 6; 3Q, '91, 9; N-D, '84, 9

`√5th` **337.2 Reflex sympathetic dystrophy**
DEF: Disturbance of the sympathetic nervous system evidenced by sweating, pain, pallor and edema following injury to nerves or blood vessels.
AHA: 4Q, '93, 24

337.20 Reflex sympathetic dystrophy, unspecified `CC`
Complex regional pain syndrome type I, unspecified
CC Excl: 337.20-337.29

337.21 Reflex sympathetic dystrophy of the upper limb `CC`
Complex regional pain syndrome type I of the upper limb
CC Excl: 249.60-249.61, 250.60-250.63, 334.8-337.9, 340-344.9, 348.1, 348.30-348.39, 349.0-349.2, 349.89-349.9, 780.72

337.22 Reflex sympathetic dystrophy of the lower limb `CC`
Complex regional pain syndrome type I of the lower limb
CC Excl: See code: 337.21

337.29 Reflex sympathetic dystrophy of other specified site `CC`
Complex regional pain syndrome type I of other specified site
CC Excl: See code: 337.21

337.3 Autonomic dysreflexia

Use additional code to identify the cause, such as:
    fecal impaction (560.32)
    pressure ulcer (707.00-707.09)
    urinary tract infection (599.0)

DEF: Noxious stimuli evokes paroxysmal hypertension, bradycardia, excess sweating, headache, pilomotor responses, facial flushing, and nasal congestion due to uncontrolled parasympathetic nerve response; occurs in patients with spinal cord injury above sympathetic outflow tract (T_6).

AHA: 4Q, '98, 37

337.9 Unspecified disorder of autonomic nervous system

Pain (338)

✓4ᵗʰ **338 Pain, not elsewhere classified**

Use additional code to identify:
    pain associated with psychological factors (307.89)

EXCLUDES   *generalized pain (780.96)*
    headache syndromes (339.00-339.89)
    localized pain, unspecified type — code to pain by site
    migraines (346.0-346.9)
    pain disorder exclusively attributed to psychological factors
      (307.80)
    vulvar vestibulitis (625.71)
    vulvodynia (625.70-625.79)

AHA: 2Q, '07, 12

TIP: Do not assign a 338 code if the pain is not specified as acute or chronic, unless post-thoracotomy, postoperative, neoplasm related or central pain syndrome.

338.0 Central pain syndrome

Déjérine-Roussy syndrome
Myelopathic pain syndrome
Thalamic pain syndrome (hyperesthetic)

AHA: 4Q, '06, 79-81

✓5ᵗʰ **338.1 Acute pain**

    338.11 Acute pain due to trauma
        AHA: 1Q, '07, 7; 4Q, '06, 79-81

    338.12 Acute post-thoracotomy pain
        Post-thoracotomy pain NOS
        AHA: 4Q, '06, 79-81

    338.18 Other acute postoperative pain
        Postoperative pain NOS
        AHA: 4Q, '06, 79-81
        G89.18 Other acute postprocedural pain   I-10

    338.19 Other acute pain
        EXCLUDES *neoplasm related acute pain (338.3)*
        AHA: 2Q, '07, 11; 4Q, '06, 79-81

✓5ᵗʰ **338.2 Chronic pain**

    EXCLUDES *causalgia (355.9)*
        lower limb (355.71)
        upper limb (354.4)
        chronic pain syndrome (338.4)
        myofascial pain syndrome (729.1)
        neoplasm related chronic pain (338.3)
        reflex sympathetic dystrophy (337.20-337.29)

    338.21 Chronic pain due to trauma
        AHA: 4Q, '06, 79-81

    338.22 Chronic post-thoracotomy pain
        AHA: 4Q, '06, 79-81

    338.28 Other chronic postoperative pain
        AHA: 4Q, '06, 79-81
        G89.28 Other chronic postprocedural pain   I-10

    338.29 Other chronic pain
        AHA: 4Q, '06, 79-81

338.3 Neoplasm related pain (acute) (chronic)

Cancer associated pain
Pain due to malignancy (primary) (secondary)
Tumor associated pain

AHA: 2Q, '07, 11; 4Q, '06, 79-81
G89.3 Neoplasm related pain (acute) (chronic)   I-10

338.4 Chronic pain syndrome

Chronic pain associated with significant psychosocial dysfunction

AHA: 2Q, '07, 11; 4Q, '06, 79-81
G89.4 Chronic pain syndrome   I-10

Other Headache Syndromes (339)

✓4ᵗʰ **339 Other headache syndromes**

EXCLUDES *headache:*
    NOS (784.0)
    due to lumbar puncture (349.0)
    migraine (346.0-346.9)

AHA: 4Q, '08, 102-105

✓5ᵗʰ **339.0 Cluster headaches and other trigeminal autonomic cephalgias**

TACS

    339.00 Cluster headache syndrome, unspecified
        Ciliary neuralgia   Lower half migraine
        Cluster headache NOS   Migrainous neuralgia
        Histamine cephalgia

    339.01 Episodic cluster headache

    339.02 Chronic cluster headache

    339.03 Episodic paroxysmal hemicrania
        Paroxysmal hemicrania NOS

    339.04 Chronic paroxysmal hemicrania

    339.05 Short lasting unilateral neuralgiform headache with conjunctival injection and tearing
        SUNCT

    339.09 Other trigeminal autonomic cephalgias

✓5ᵗʰ **339.1 Tension type headache**

    EXCLUDES *tension headache NOS (307.81)*
        tension headache related to psychological factors
          (307.81)

    AHA: 4Q, '08, 103

    339.10 Tension type headache, unspecified

    339.11 Episodic tension type headache

    339.12 Chronic tension type headache

✓5ᵗʰ **339.2 Post-traumatic headache**

    TIP: Do not assign during the acute phase of the trauma (e.g., head injury). When assigning 339.2X, report also a late effect code (e.g., 907.0 for intracranial injury).

    339.20 Post-traumatic headache, unspecified
        AHA: 4Q, '08, 108

    339.21 Acute post-traumatic headache

    339.22 Chronic post-traumatic headache

339.3 Drug induced headache, not elsewhere classified

Medication overuse headache
Rebound headache

✓5ᵗʰ **339.4 Complicated headache syndromes**

    339.41 Hemicrania continua

    339.42 New daily persistent headache
        NDPH

    339.43 Primary thunderclap headache

    339.44 Other complicated headache syndrome

✓5ᵗʰ **339.8 Other specified headache syndromes**

    339.81 Hypnic headache

    339.82 Headache associated with sexual activity
        Orgasmic headache
        Preorgasmic headache

    339.83 Primary cough headache

    339.84 Primary exertional headache

    339.85 Primary stabbing headache

    339.89 Other specified headache syndromes

N Newborn Age: 0   **P** Pediatric Age: 0-17   **M** Maternity Age: 12-55   **A** Adult Age: 15-124   **MCC** Major CC Condition   **CC** CC Condition   **HIV** HIV Related Dx

104 – Volume 1   **2015 ICD-9-CM**

Other Disorders of the Central Nervous System (340-349)

340 Multiple sclerosis

Disseminated or multiple sclerosis:
NOS
brain stem
cord
generalized
CC Excl: 250.60-250.63, 250.80-250.93, 340, 341.8-341.9
G35 Multiple sclerosis `I-10`

`√4th` **341 Other demyelinating diseases of central nervous system**

341.0 Neuromyelitis optica `CC`
CC Excl: 341.0, 348.30-348.39

341.1 Schilder's disease `CC`
Baló's concentric sclerosis   Encephalitis periaxialis:
Encephalitis periaxialis: diffusa [Schilder's]
concentrica [Baló's]
DEF: Chronic leukoencephalopathy of children and adolescents; symptoms include blindness, deafness, bilateral spasticity and progressive mental deterioration.
CC Excl: 066.40-066.49, 079.82, 348.30-348.39

`√5th` **341.2 Acute (transverse) myelitis**
EXCLUDES acute (transverse) myelitis (in) (due to):
following immunization procedures (323.52)
infection classified elsewhere (323.42)
postinfectious (323.63)
protozoal diseases classified elsewhere (323.2)
rickettsial diseases classified elsewhere (323.1)
toxic (323.72)
viral diseases classified elsewhere (323.02)
transverse myelitis NOS (323.82)

341.20 Acute (transverse) myelitis NOS `CC`
CC Excl: 003.21, 013.00-013.16, 036.0, 047.0-047.9, 049.0-049.1, 053.0-053.13, 053.19, 053.79-053.9, 054.72, 054.79-054.9, 058.81-058.89, 072.1, 078.89, 079.81, 079.89, 079.99, 090.42, 091.81, 094.2, 098.89, 100.81, 112.83, 114.2, 115.01, 115.11, 115.91, 130.0, 139.8, 249.60-249.61, 250.60-250.63, 320.0-322.9, 334.8-337.9, 340-341.1, 341.8-344.9, 348.1, 348.30-348.39, 349.0-349.2, 349.89-349.9, 357.0, 780.72
AHA: 4Q, '06, 58-63

341.21 Acute (transverse) myelitis in conditions classified elsewhere `CC`
Code first underlying condition
CC Excl: See code: 341.20
AHA: 4Q, '06, 58-63

341.22 Idiopathic transverse myelitis `CC`
CC Excl: See code: 341.20
AHA: 4Q, '06, 58-63

341.8 Other demyelinating diseases of central nervous system `CC`
Central demyelination of corpus callosum
Central pontine myelinosis
Marchiafava (-Bignami) disease
CC Excl: 333.1-333.93, 333.99-337.9, 340-344.9, 348.30-348.39, 348.81-348.9, 349.82-349.9, 780.72
AHA: N-D, '87, 6

341.9 Demyelinating disease of central nervous system, unspecified `CC` `HIV`
CC Excl: See code: 341.8

`√4th` **342 Hemiplegia and hemiparesis**
NOTE This category is to be used when hemiplegia (complete) (incomplete) is reported without further specification, or is stated to be old or long-standing but of unspecified cause. The category is also for use in multiple coding to identify these types of hemiplegia resulting from any cause.
EXCLUDES congenital (343.1)
hemiplegia due to late effect of cerebrovascular accident (438.20-438.22)
infantile NOS (343.4)

The following fifth-diits are for use with codes 342.0-342.9:
0 affecting unspecified side
1 affecting dominant side
2 affecting nondominant side

AHA: 4Q, '94, 38

§ `√5th` **342.0 Flaccid hemiplegia** `CC`
[0-2]   **CC Excl:** 334.0-337.9, 340-344.9, 348.30-348.39, 348.81-348.9, 349.82-349.9, 780.72

§ `√5th` **342.1 Spastic hemiplegia** `CC`
[0-2]   **CC Excl:** See code: 342.0

§ `√5th` **342.8 Other specified hemiplegia** `CC`
[0-2]   **CC Excl:** See code: 342.0

§ `√5th` **342.9 Hemiplegia, unspecified** `CC`
[0-2]   **CC Excl:** See code: 342.0
AHA: 3Q, '06, 5; 4Q, '98, 87
G81.90 Hemiplegia unspecified affect unspecified side `I-10`

`√4th` **343 Infantile cerebral palsy**
INCLUDES cerebral:
palsy NOS
spastic infantile paralysis
congenital spastic paralysis (cerebral)
Little's disease
paralysis (spastic) due to birth injury:
intracranial
spinal
EXCLUDES athetoid cerebral palsy (333.71)
hereditary cerebral paralysis, such as:
hereditary spastic paraplegia (334.1)
Vogt's disease (333.71)
spastic paralysis specified as noncongenital or noninfantile (344.0-344.9)

343.0 Diplegic `CC`
Congenital diplegiaCongenital paraplegia
DEF: Paralysis affecting both sides of the body simultaneously.
CC Excl: 343.0, 348.30-348.39

343.1 Hemiplegic `CC`
Congenital hemiplegia
EXCLUDES infantile hemiplegia NOS (343.4)
CC Excl: 343.1, 348.30-348.39

343.2 Quadriplegic `MCC`
Tetraplegic
CC Excl: 249.60-249.61, 249.80-249.91, 250.60-250.63, 250.80-250.93, 342.00-344.9, 348.81-348.9, 349.89-349.9, 742.59-742.9, 780.72

343.3 Monoplegic

343.4 Infantile hemiplegia `CC`
Infantile hemiplegia (postnatal) NOS
CC Excl: See code: 342.0

343.8 Other specified infantile cerebral palsy

343.9 Infantile cerebral palsy, unspecified
Cerebral palsy NOS
AHA: 4Q, '05, 89
G80.9 Cerebral palsy unspecified `I-10`

`√4th` **344 Other paralytic syndromes**
NOTE This category is to be used when the listed conditions are reported without further specification or are stated to be old or long-standing but of unspecified cause. The category is also for use in multiple coding to identify these conditions resulting from any cause.
INCLUDES paralysis (complete) (incomplete), except as classifiable to 342 and 343
EXCLUDES congenital or infantile cerebral palsy (343.0-343.9)
hemiplegia (342.0-342.9)
congenital or infantile (343.1, 343.4)

`√5th` **344.0 Quadriplegia and quadriparesis**
TIP: Assign also a code from subcategory 438.5 if late effect of CVA.

344.00 Quadriplegia unspecified `MCC`
CC Excl: See code: 343.2
AHA: 4Q, '03, 103; 4Q, '98, 38
G82.50 Quadriplegia unspecified `I-10`

344.01 C₁-C₄ complete `MCC`
CC Excl: See code: 343.2

344.02 C₁-C₄ incomplete `MCC`
CC Excl: See code: 343.2

344.03 C₅-C₇ complete `MCC`
CC Excl: See code: 343.2

---

§ Requires fifth digit. Valid digits are in [brackets] under each code. See category 342 for codes and definitions.

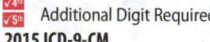

Additional Digit Required   Unacceptable PDx   Manifestation Code   Hospital Acquired Condition   ▶◀ Revised Text   ● New Code   ▲ Revised Code Title

Diseases of the Nervous System and Sense Organs

344.04–345.3

344.04 C$_5$-C$_7$ incomplete   `MCC`
CC Excl: See code: 343.2

344.09 Other   `MCC`
CC Excl: See code: 343.2
AHA: 1Q, '01, 12; 4Q, '98, 39

344.1 Paraplegia   `CC`
Paralysis of both lower limbs
Paraplegia (lower)
CC Excl: 334.0-337.9, 340-344.9, 348.30-348.39, 348.8-348.9, 349.82-349.9, 780.72
AHA: 4Q, '03, 110;M-A, '87, 10
G82.20 Paraplegia unspecified   `I-10`

344.2 Diplegia of upper limbs   `CC`
Diplegia (upper)
Paralysis of both upper limbs
CC Excl: 344.00-344.09, 344.2, 344.81-344.9, 349.89-349.9, 780.72

√5ᵗʰ **344.3 Monoplegia of lower limb**
Paralysis of lower limb
EXCLUDES *monoplegia of lower limb due to late effect of cerebrovascular accident (438.40-438.42)*

344.30 Affecting unspecified side

344.31 Affecting dominant side

344.32 Affecting nondominant side

√5ᵗʰ **344.4 Monoplegia of upper limb**
Paralysis of upper limb
EXCLUDES *monoplegia of upper limb due to late effect of cerebrovascular accident (438.30-438.32)*

344.40 Affecting unspecified side

344.41 Affecting dominant side

344.42 Affecting nondominant side

344.5 Unspecified monoplegia

√5ᵗʰ **344.6 Cauda equina syndrome**
DEF: Dull pain and paresthesias in sacrum, perineum and bladder due to compression of spinal nerve roots; pain radiates down buttocks, back of thigh, calf of leg and into foot with prickling, burning sensations.

344.60 Without mention of neurogenic bladder   `CC`
CC Excl: 344.00-344.1, 344.30-344.32, 344.60-344.9, 349.89-349.9, 780.72

344.61 With neurogenic bladder   `CC`
Acontractile bladder
Autonomic hyperreflexia of bladder
Cord bladder
Detrusor hyperreflexia
CC Excl: 334.0-337.9, 340-344.9, 348.30-348.39, 348.81-348.9, 349.82-349.9, 599.60-599.69, 780.72
AHA: M-J, '87, 12; M-A, '87, 10

√5ᵗʰ **344.8 Other specified paralytic syndromes**

344.81 Locked-in state   `MCC`
DEF: State of consciousness where patients are paralyzed and unable to respond to environmental stimuli; patients have eye movements, and stimuli can enter the brain but patients unable to respond.
CC Excl: 342.00-344.9, 348.30-348.39, 348.81-348.9, 349.82-349.9, 780.72
AHA: 4Q, '93, 24

344.89 Other specified paralytic syndrome
AHA: 2Q, '99, 4

344.9 Paralysis, unspecified

√4ᵗʰ **345 Epilepsy and recurrent seizures**

The following fifth-digit subclassification is for use with categories 345.0, .1, .4-.9:
  0 **without mention of intractable epilepsy**
  1 **with intractable epilepsy**
     pharmacoresistant (pharmacologically resistant)
     poorly controlled
     refractory (medically)
     treatment resistant

EXCLUDES *hippocampal sclerosis (348.81)*
     mesial temporal sclerosis (348.81)
     temporal sclerosis (348.81)
DEF: Brain disorder characterized by electrical-like disturbances; may include occasional impairment or loss of consciousness, abnormal motor phenomena and psychic or sensory disturbances.
AHA: 4Q, '09, 82; 1Q, '93, 24; 2Q, '92, 8; 4Q, '92, 23

§ √5ᵗʰ **345.0 Generalized nonconvulsive epilepsy**   `CC 1`
[0-1]   Absences: Pykno-epilepsy
      atonic   Seizures:
      typical   akinetic
   Minor epilepsy   atonic
   Petit mal
CC Excl: 249.60-249.61, 250.60-250.63, 345.00-345.91, 348.81-348.9, 349.89-349.9; **For code 345.01:** 249.60-249.61, 250.60-250.63, 345.00-345.91, 348.81, 348.89-348.9, 349.89-349.9, 780.33
AHA: **For code 345.00:** 1Q, '04, 18; **For code 345.01:** ▶1Q, '14, 12◀

§ √5ᵗʰ **345.1 Generalized convulsive epilepsy**   `CC 1`
[0-1]   Epileptic seizures:
     clonic
     myoclonic
     tonic
     tonic-clonic
   Grand mal
   Major epilepsy
   Progressive myoclonic epilepsy
   Unverricht-Lundborg disease
EXCLUDES *convulsions:*
     NOS (780.39)
     infantile (780.39)
     newborn (779.0)
   infantile spasms (345.6)
DEF: Convulsive seizures with tension of limbs (tonic) or rhythmic contractions (clonic).
CC Excl: **For code 345.11:** 249.60-249.61, 250.60-250.63, 345.00-345.91, 348.81-348.9, 349.89-349.9
AHA: 3Q, '97, 4

345.2 Petit mal status   `MCC`
Epileptic absence status
DEF: Minor myoclonic spasms and sudden momentary loss of consciousness in epilepsy.
CC Excl: 249.60-249.61, 249.80-249.91, 250.60-250.63, 250.80-250.93, 345.00-345.91, 348.81, 348.89-348.9, 349.89-349.9, 780.33
AHA: ▶1Q, '14, 11◀

345.3 Grand mal status   `MCC`
Status epilepticus NOS
EXCLUDES *epilepsia partialis continua (345.7)*
     status:
      psychomotor (345.7)
      temporal lobe (345.7)
DEF: Sudden loss of consciousness followed by generalized convulsions in epilepsy.
CC Excl: See code: 345.2
AHA: 3Q, '05, 12
G40.301 Gen idiopath epilep&epi syn not intractabl w/se   `I-10`

---

§   Requires fifth digit. Valid digits are in [brackets] under each code. See category 345 for codes and definitions.

§ ✓5ᵗʰ **345.4 Localization-related (focal) (partial) epilepsy** `CC`
   [0-1] **and epileptic syndromes with complex partial seizures**
      Epilepsy:
         limbic system
         partial:
            secondarily generalized
            with impairment of consciousness
            with memory and ideational disturbances
         psychomotor
         psychosensory
         temporal lobe
      Epileptic automatism
      CC Excl: For code 345.40: 345.00-345.91, 348.30-348.39, 348.9, 349.89-349.9, 780.33; **For code 345.41:** 249.60-249.61, 250.60-250.63, 345.00-345.91, 348.81-348.9, 349.89-349.9
      AHA: For code 345.41: 4Q, '09, 83

§ ✓5ᵗʰ **345.5 Localization-related (focal) (partial) epilepsy** `CC`
   [0-1] **and epileptic syndromes with simple partial seizures**
      Epilepsy:
         Bravais-Jacksonian NOS
         focal (motor) NOS
         Jacksonian NOS
         motor partial
         partial NOS:
            without impairment of consciousness
         sensory-induced
         somatomotor
         somatosensory
         visceral
         visual
      CC Excl: For code 345.50: 345.00-345.91, 348.30-348.39, 348.9, 349.89-349.9; **For code 345.51:** 249.60-249.61, 250.60-250.63, 345.00-345.91, 348.81-348.9, 349.89-349.9

§ ✓5ᵗʰ **345.6 Infantile spasms** `CC`
   [0-1] Hypsarrhythmia
      Lightning spasms
      Salaam attacks
      EXCLUDES *salaam tic (781.0)*
      CC Excl: For code 345.60: 345.00-345.91, 348.30-348.39, 348.9, 349.89-349.9; **For code 345.61:** 249.60-249.61, 250.60-250.63, 345.00-345.91, 348.81-348.9, 349.89-349.9
      AHA: N-D, '84, 12

§ ✓5ᵗʰ **345.7 Epilepsia partialis continua** `CC 0` `MCC 1`
   [0-1] Kojevnikov's epilepsy
      DEF: Continuous muscle contractions and relaxation; result of abnormal neural discharge.
      CC Excl: 249.60-249.61, 250.60-250.63, 345.00-345.91, 348.81-348.9, 349.89-349.9
      AHA: ▶1Q, '14, 11◀

§ ✓5ᵗʰ **345.8 Other forms of epilepsy and recurrent seizures** `CC`
   [0-1] Epilepsy: Epilepsy:
         cursive [running]   gelastic
      CC Excl: 249.60-249.61, 250.60-250.63, 345.00-345.91, 348.81-348.9, 349.89-349.9
      AHA: ▶1Q, '14, 11◀

§ ✓5ᵗʰ **345.9 Epilepsy, unspecified** `CC 1`
   [0-1] Epileptic convulsions, fits, or seizures NOS
      Seizure disorder NOS
      EXCLUDES *convulsion (convulsive) disorder (780.39)*
               convulsive seizure or fit NOS (780.39)
               recurrent convulsions (780.39)
      CC Excl: For code 345.91: 249.60-249.61, 250.60-250.63, 345.00-345.91, 348.81-348.9, 349.89-349.9
      AHA: 1Q, '08, 17; N-D, '87, 12; **For code 345.90:** ▶4Q, '13, 86;◀ 2Q, '12, 9; 2Q, '09, 10
      TIP: Code also alcohol withdrawal seizure with epileptic seizure when both conditions are documented by the provider. Assign a separate code for the alcohol dependence.
      G40.909 Epilepsy uns not intractbl w/o status epilepticus `I-10`

✓4ᵗʰ **346 Migraine**
      EXCLUDES *headache:*
            NOS (784.0)
            syndromes (339.00-339.89)
      AHA: 4Q, '08, 103, 105-107

      The following fifth-digit subclassification is for use with category 346:
      0 without mention of Intractable migraine without mention of status migrainosus
         without mention of refractory migraine without mention of status migrainosus
      1 with intractable migraine, so stated, without mention of status migrainosus
         with refractory migraine, so stated, without mention of status migrainosus
      2 without mention of intractable migraine with status migrainosus
         without mention of refractory migraine with status migrainosus
      3 with intractable migraine, so stated, with status migrainosus
         with refractory migraine, so stated, with status migrainosus

      DEF: Benign vascular headache of extreme pain; commonly associated with irritability, nausea, vomiting and often photophobia; premonitory visual hallucination of a crescent in the visual field (scotoma).

§ ✓5ᵗʰ **346.0 Migraine with aura**
   [0-3] Basilar migraine
      Classic migraine
      Migraine preceded or accompanied by transient focal neurological phenomena
      Migraine triggered seizures
      Migraine with acute-onset aura
      Migraine with aura without headache (migraine equivalents)
      Migraine with prolonged aura
      Migraine with typical aura
      Retinal migraine
      EXCLUDES *persistent migraine aura (346.5, 346.6)*

§ ✓5ᵗʰ **346.1 Migraine without aura**
   [0-3] Common migraine

§ ✓5ᵗʰ **346.2 Variants of migraine, not elsewhere classified**
   [0-3] Abdominal migraine
      Cyclical vomiting associated with migraine
      Ophthalmoplegic migraine
      Periodic headache syndromes in child or adolescent
      EXCLUDES *cyclical vomiting NOS (536.2)*
               psychogenic cyclical vomiting (306.4)

§ ✓5ᵗʰ **346.3 Hemiplegic migraine**
   [0-3] Familial migraine
      Sporadic migraine

§ ✓5ᵗʰ **346.4 Menstrual migraine** ♀
   [0-3] Menstrual headache   Premenstrual migraine
      Menstrually related migraine   Pure menstrual migraine
      Premenstrual headache

§ ✓5ᵗʰ **346.5 Persistent migraine aura without cerebral infarction**
   [0-3] Persistent migraine aura NOS

§ ✓5ᵗʰ **346.6 Persistent migraine aura with cerebral infarction** `CC`
   [0-3] **CC Excl:** For code 346.60: 346.60-346.63, 433.00-434.91; **For code 346.61, 346.62, 346.63:** 346.60-346.63, 433.00-434.91, 436
      AHA: For code 346.60: 4Q, '08, 108
      TIP: Assign also a code for the specific type of cerebral infarction.

§ ✓5ᵗʰ **346.7 Chronic migraine without aura**
   [0-3] Transformed migraine without aura

§ ✓5ᵗʰ **346.8 Other forms of migraine**
   [0-3]

§ ✓5ᵗʰ **346.9 Migraine, unspecified**
   [0-3] **AHA:** N-D, '85, 16
      G43.909 Migraine unspecified not intract w/o stat migran `I-10`

✓4ᵗʰ **347 Cataplexy and narcolepsy**
      DEF: Cataplexy: Sudden onset of muscle weakness with loss of tone and strength; caused by aggressive or spontaneous emotions.
      DEF: Narcolepsy: Brief, recurrent, uncontrollable episodes of sound sleep.

  ✓5ᵗʰ **347.0 Narcolepsy**

      347.00 Without cataplexy
         Narcolepsy NOS

---

§ Requires fifth digit. Valid digits are in [brackets] under each code. See appropriate category for codes and definitions.

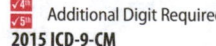 Additional Digit Required   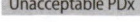 Unacceptable PDx   Manifestation Code   Hospital Acquired Condition   ▶◀ Revised Text   ● New Code   ▲ Revised Code Title

Diseases of the Nervous System and Sense Organs   **345.4–347.00**

347.01 With cataplexy

✓5ᵗʰ **347.1 Narcolepsy in conditions classified elsewhere**
Code first underlying condition

     347.10 *Without cataplexy*

     347.11 *With cataplexy*

✓4ᵗʰ **348 Other conditions of brain**

348.0 Cerebral cysts
   Arachnoid cyst   Porencephaly, acquired
   Porencephalic cyst   Pseudoporencephaly
   EXCLUDES *porencephaly (congenital) (742.4)*

348.1 Anoxic brain damage   `CC`
   Use additional E code to identify cause
   EXCLUDES *that occurring in:*
       abortion (634-638 with .7, 639.8)
       ectopic or molar pregnancy (639.8)
       labor or delivery (668.2, 669.4)
       that of newborn (767.0, 768.0-768.9, 772.1-772.2)
   DEF: Brain injury due to lack of oxygen, other than birth trauma.
   CC Excl: 249.60-249.61, 249.80-249.91, 250.60-250.63, 250.80-250.93, 348.1-348.2, 349.89-349.9
   AHA: ▶3Q, '13, 10◀
   G93.1 Anoxic brain damage not elsewhere classified   `I-10`

348.2 Benign intracranial hypertension
   Pseudotumor cerebri
   EXCLUDES *hypertensive encephalopathy (437.2)*
   DEF: Elevated pressure in brain due to fluid retention in brain cavities.

✓5ᵗʰ **348.3 Encephalopathy, not elsewhere classified**
   AHA: 4Q, '03, 58; 3Q, '97, 4

   348.30 Encephalopathy, unspecified   `MCC` `HIV`
     CC Excl: 333.92, 344.81, 348.31-348.39
     G93.40 Encephalopathy unspecified   `I-10`

   348.31 Metabolic encephalopathy   `MCC` `HIV`
     Septic encephalopathy
     EXCLUDES *toxic metabolic encephalopathy (349.82)*
     CC Excl: 333.92, 344.81, 348.30, 348.39
     TIP: Physician documentation of "acute confusional state" denotes delirium inherent to the encephalopathy. Do not report an additional code for the delirium

   348.39 Other encephalopathy   `MCC` `HIV`
     EXCLUDES *encephalopathy:*
       alcoholic (291.2)
       hepatic (572.2)
       hypertensive (437.2)
       toxic (349.82)
     CC Excl: 333.92, 344.81, 348.30-348.31

348.4 Compression of brain   `MCC`
   Compression ⎱
   Herniation ⎰ brain (stem)
   Posterior fossa compression syndrome
   DEF: Elevated pressure in brain due to blood clot, tumor, fracture, abscess, other condition.
   CC Excl: 342.90, 348.82
   AHA: ▶2Q, '13, 8; ◀3Q, '11, 11;4Q, '94, 37
   TIP: Assign for Arnold-Chiari syndrome, Type I. For Type II, III, or IV, refer to categories 741 and 742.

348.5 Cerebral edema   `MCC`
   DEF: Elevated pressure in the brain due to fluid retention in brain tissues.
   CC Excl: 348.5, 348.82
   AHA: 4Q, '11, 99; 1Q, '10, 8; 3Q, '09, 8
   G93.6 Cerebral edema   `I-10`

✓5ᵗʰ **348.8 Other conditions of brain**
   AHA: S-O, '87, 9

   348.81 Temporal sclerosis
     Hippocampal sclerosis
     Mesial temporal sclerosis
     DEF: Abnormal hardening or scarring of frontal lobe tissues due to injury, tumor, congenital anomaly, or hypoxia, resulting in loss of functional neurons; commonly associated with temporal lobe epilepsy.
     AHA: 4Q, '09, 83

348.82 Brain death   `MCC`
   CC Excl: 070.0-070.9, 249.00-249.91, 250.00-250.93, 251.0-251.3, 338.0-338.4, 348.81-349.9, ▶430-432.9, 572.2, 780.01-780.09, 780.2, 780.4, 780.64-780.65, 780.91-780.99, 799.81-799.89, 800.00-801.99, 803.00-804.96, 850.0-854.19
   AHA: 4Q, '11, 99-100

348.89 Other conditions of brain
   Cerebral:
     calcification
     fungus
   EXCLUDES *brain death (348.82)*

348.9 Unspecified condition of brain   `HIV`

✓4ᵗʰ **349 Other and unspecified disorders of the nervous system**
   AHA: 4Q, '08, 109

349.0 Reaction to spinal or lumbar puncture
   Headache following lumbar puncture
   AHA: 2Q, '99, 9; 3Q, '90, 18
   G97.1 Other reaction to spinal and lumbar puncture   `I-10`

349.1 Nervous system complications from surgically implanted device   `CC`
   EXCLUDES *immediate postoperative complications (997.00-997.09)*
       mechanical complications of nervous system device (996.2)
   CC Excl: 2249.60-249.61, 249.80-249.91, 250.60-250.63, 250.80-250.93, 349.1, 349.89-349.9

349.2 Disorders of meninges, not elsewhere classified
   Adhesions, meningeal (cerebral) (spinal)
   Cyst, spinal meninges
   Meningocele, acquired
   Pseudomeningocele, acquired
   AHA: 1Q, '06, 15; 2Q, '98, 18; 3Q, '94, 4

✓5ᵗʰ **349.3 Dural tear**

   349.31 Accidental puncture or laceration of dura during a procedure   `CC`
     Incidental (inadvertent) durotomy
     CC Excl: 349.31-349.39, 997.91-997.99, 998.2, 998.81, 998.83-998.9
     AHA: 4Q, '08, 109-110
     TIP: Do not assign code 998.2 Accidental puncture or laceration during a procedure, for an incidental dural tear.

   349.39 Other dural tear   `CC`
     CC Excl: 349.31-349.39, 997.91-997.99, 998.2, 998.81, 998.83-998.9

✓5ᵗʰ **349.8 Other specified disorders of nervous system**

   349.81 Cerebrospinal fluid rhinorrhea   `CC`
     EXCLUDES *cerebrospinal fluid otorrhea (388.61)*
     DEF: Cerebrospinal fluid discharging from the nose; caused by fracture of frontal bone with tearing of dura mater and arachnoid.
     CC Excl: 249.60-249.61, 249.80-249.91, 250.60-250.63, 250.80-250.93, 349.81, 349.89-349.9

   349.82 Toxic encephalopathy   `MCC`
     Toxic metabolic encephalopathy
     Use additional E code to identify cause
     DEF: Brain tissue degeneration due to toxic substance.
     CC Excl: 013.60-013.66, 017.90-017.96, 036.1, 049.8-049.9, 052.0, 054.3, 058.21-058.29, 062.0-063.9, 072.2, 090.41, 094.81, 130.0, 249.60-249.61, 249.80-249.91, 250.60-250.63, 250.80-250.93, 323.01-323.9, 341.20-341.22, 348.30-348.39, 348.81-348.9, 349.82-349.9
     AHA: 4Q, '93, 29
     G92 Toxic encephalopathy   `I-10`

   349.89 Other

349.9 Unspecified disorders of nervous system   `HIV`
   Disorder of nervous system (central) NOS
   AHA: 3Q, '12, 4

 Newborn Age: 0    Pediatric Age: 0-17    Maternity Age: 12-55    Adult Age: 15-124   `MCC` Major CC Condition   `CC` CC Condition   `HIV` HIV Related Dx

108 – Volume 1 · October 2014   **2015 ICD-9-CM**

Disorders of the Peripheral Nervous System (350-359)

EXCLUDES diseases of:
  acoustic [8th] nerve (388.5)
  oculomotor [3rd, 4th, 6th] nerves (378.0-378.9)
  optic [2nd] nerve (377.0-377.9)
  peripheral autonomic nerves (337.0-337.9)
  neuralgia
  neuritis } NOS or "rheumatic" (729.2)
  radiculitis
  peripheral neuritis in pregnancy (646.4)

✓4th 350 Trigeminal nerve disorders
INCLUDES disorders of 5th cranial nerve

350.1 Trigeminal neuralgia
Tic douloureux   Trigeminal neuralgia NOS
Trifacial neuralgia
EXCLUDES postherpetic (053.12)
G50.0 Trigeminal neuralgia   `I-10`

350.2 Atypical face pain

350.8 Other specified trigeminal nerve disorders

350.9 Trigeminal nerve disorder, unspecified

✓4th 351 Facial nerve disorders
INCLUDES disorders of 7th cranial nerve
EXCLUDES that in newborn (767.5)

351.0 Bell's palsy
Facial palsy
DEF: Unilateral paralysis of face due to lesion on facial nerve; produces facial distortion.
G51.0 Bell's palsy   `I-10`

351.1 Geniculate ganglionitis
Geniculate ganglionitis NOS
EXCLUDES herpetic (053.11)
DEF: Inflammation of tissue at bend in facial nerve.

351.8 Other facial nerve disorders
Facial myokymia   Melkersson's syndrome
AHA: 3Q, '02, 13

351.9 Facial nerve disorder, unspecified

✓4th 352 Disorders of other cranial nerves

352.0 Disorders of olfactory [lst] nerve

352.1 Glossopharyngeal neuralgia
DEF: Pain between throat and ear along petrosal and jugular ganglia.
AHA: 2Q, '02, 8

352.2 Other disorders of glossopharyngeal [9th] nerve

352.3 Disorders of pneumogastric [10th] nerve
Disorders of vagal nerve
EXCLUDES paralysis of vocal cords or larynx (478.30-478.34)
DEF: Nerve disorder affecting ear, tongue, pharynx, larynx, esophagus, viscera and thorax.

352.4 Disorders of accessory [11th] nerve
DEF: Nerve disorder affecting palate, pharynx, larynx, thoracic viscera, sternocleidomastoid and trapezius muscles.

352.5 Disorders of hypoglossal [12th] nerve
DEF: Nerve disorder affecting tongue muscles.

Cranial Nerves

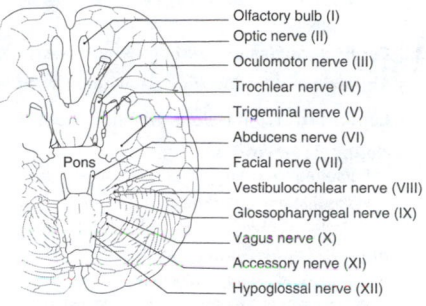

Olfactory bulb (I)
Optic nerve (II)
Oculomotor nerve (III)
Trochlear nerve (IV)
Trigeminal nerve (V)
Abducens nerve (VI)
Facial nerve (VII)
Vestibulocochlear nerve (VIII)
Glossopharyngeal nerve (IX)
Vagus nerve (X)
Accessory nerve (XI)
Hypoglossal nerve (XII)
Pons

Peripheral Nervous System

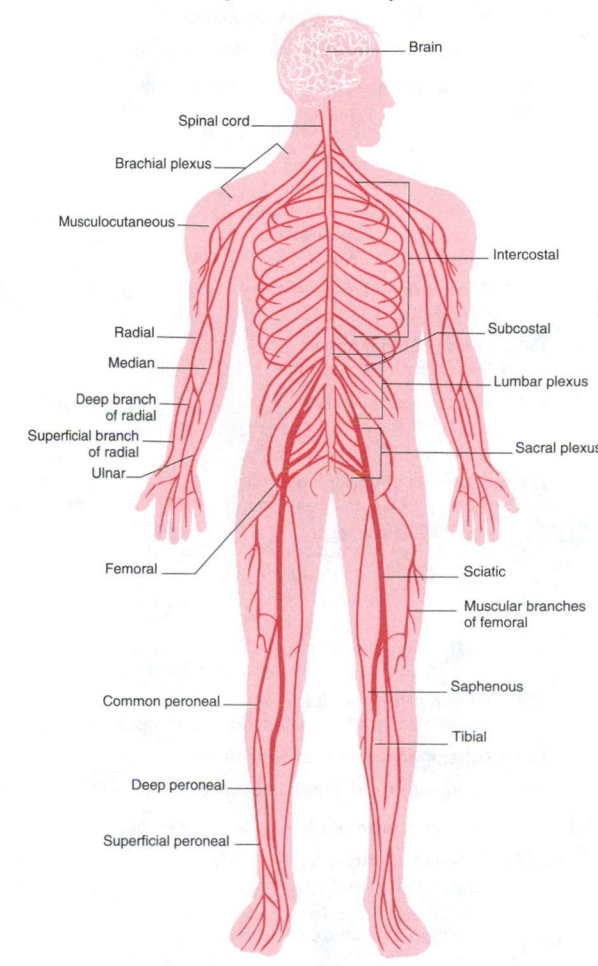

Brain
Spinal cord
Brachial plexus
Musculocutaneous
Intercostal
Radial
Subcostal
Median
Lumbar plexus
Deep branch of radial
Superficial branch of radial
Sacral plexus
Ulnar
Femoral
Sciatic
Muscular branches of femoral
Saphenous
Common peroneal
Tibial
Deep peroneal
Superficial peroneal

352.6 Multiple cranial nerve palsies
Collet-Sicard syndrome
Polyneuritis cranialis

352.9 Unspecified disorder of cranial nerves

✓4th 353 Nerve root and plexus disorders
EXCLUDES conditions due to:
  intervertebral disc disorders (722.0-722.9)
  spondylosis (720.0-721.9)
  vertebrogenic disorders (723.0-724.9)

353.0 Brachial plexus lesions
Cervical rib syndrome
Costoclavicular syndrome
Scalenus anticus syndrome
Thoracic outlet syndrome
EXCLUDES brachial neuritis or radiculitis NOS (723.4)
  that in newborn (767.6)
DEF: Acquired disorder in tissue along nerves in shoulder; causes corresponding motor and sensory dysfunction.
AHA: 3Q, '06, 12

Trigeminal and Facial Nerve Branches

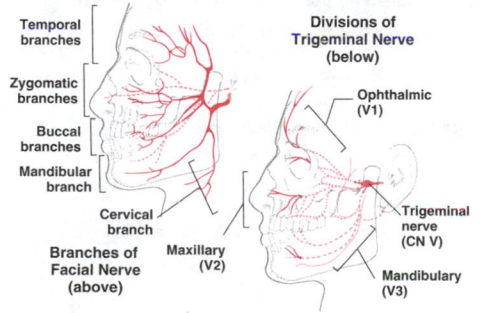

Temporal branches
Zygomatic branches
Buccal branches
Mandibular branch
Cervical branch
Branches of Facial Nerve (above)
Maxillary (V2)
Divisions of Trigeminal Nerve (below)
Ophthalmic (V1)
Trigeminal nerve (CN V)
Mandibulary (V3)

Diseases of the Nervous System and Sense Organs

353.1–357.3

353.1 Lumbosacral plexus lesions

DEF: Acquired disorder in tissue along nerves in lower back; causes corresponding motor and sensory dysfunction.

353.2 Cervical root lesions, not elsewhere classified

353.3 Thoracic root lesions, not elsewhere classified

353.4 Lumbosacral root lesions, not elsewhere classified

353.5 Neuralgic amyotrophy

Parsonage-Aldren-Turner syndrome

Code first any associated underlying disease, such as:
diabetes mellitus (249.6, 250.6)

353.6 Phantom limb (syndrome)

DEF: Abnormal tingling or a burning sensation, transient aches, and intermittent or continuous pain perceived as originating in the absent limb.

353.8 Other nerve root and plexus disorders

353.9 Unspecified nerve root and plexus disorder

✓4ᵗʰ 354 Mononeuritis of upper limb and mononeuritis multiplex

DEF: Inflammation of a single nerve; known as mononeuritis multiplex when several nerves in unrelated body areas are affected.

354.0 Carpal tunnel syndrome

Median nerve entrapment   Partial thenar atrophy

DEF: Compression of median nerve by tendons; causes pain, tingling, numbness and burning sensation in hand.

G56.00 Carpal tunnel syndrome unspec upper limb   `I-10`

354.1 Other lesion of median nerve

Median nerve neuritis

354.2 Lesion of ulnar nerve

Cubital tunnel syndrome   Tardy ulnar nerve palsy

354.3 Lesion of radial nerve

Acute radial nerve palsy

AHA: N-D, '87, 6

354.4 Causalgia of upper limb

Complex regional pain syndrome type II of the upper limb

EXCLUDES causalgia:
NOS (355.9)
lower limb (355.71)
complex regional pain syndrome type II of the lower limb (355.71)

DEF: Peripheral nerve damage, upper limb; usually due to injury; causes burning sensation and trophic skin changes.

354.5 Mononeuritis multiplex

Combinations of single conditions classifiable to 354 or 355

354.8 Other mononeuritis of upper limb

354.9 Mononeuritis of upper limb, unspecified

✓4ᵗʰ 355 Mononeuritis of lower limb

355.0 Lesion of sciatic nerve

EXCLUDES sciatica NOS (724.3)

DEF: Acquired disorder of sciatic nerve; causes motor and sensory dysfunction in back, buttock and leg.

AHA: 2Q, '89, 12

355.1 Meralgia paresthetica

Lateral cutaneous femoral nerve of thigh compression or syndrome

DEF: Inguinal ligament entraps lateral femoral cutaneous nerve; causes tingling, pain and numbness along outer thigh.

355.2 Other lesion of femoral nerve

355.3 Lesion of lateral popliteal nerve

Lesion of common peroneal nerve

355.4 Lesion of medial popliteal nerve

355.5 Tarsal tunnel syndrome

DEF: Compressed, entrapped posterior tibial nerve; causes tingling, pain and numbness in sole of foot.

355.6 Lesion of plantar nerve

Morton's metatarsalgia, neuralgia, or neuroma

✓5ᵗʰ 355.7 Other mononeuritis of lower limb

355.71 Causalgia of lower limb

EXCLUDES causalgia:
NOS (355.9)
upper limb (354.4)
complex regional pain syndrome type II of upper limb (354.4)

DEF: Dysfunction of lower limb peripheral nerve, usually due to injury; causes burning pain and trophic skin changes.

355.79 Other mononeuritis of lower limb

355.8 Mononeuritis of lower limb, unspecified

355.9 Mononeuritis of unspecified site

Causalgia NOS   Complex regional pain syndrome NOS

EXCLUDES causalgia:
lower limb (355.71)
upper limb (354.4)
complex regional pain syndrome:
lower limb (355.71)
upper limb (354.4)

G58.9 Mononeuropathy unspecified   `I-10`

✓4ᵗʰ 356 Hereditary and idiopathic peripheral neuropathy

356.0 Hereditary peripheral neuropathy

Déjérine-Sottas disease

356.1 Peroneal muscular atrophy

Charcôt-Marie-Tooth disease
Neuropathic muscular atrophy

DEF: Genetic disorder, in muscles innervated by peroneal nerves; symptoms include muscle wasting in lower limbs and locomotor difficulties.

356.2 Hereditary sensory neuropathy

DEF: Inherited disorder in dorsal root ganglia, optic nerve, and cerebellum, causing sensory losses, shooting pains, and foot ulcers.

356.3 Refsum's disease   `CC`

Heredopathia atactica polyneuritiformis

DEF: Genetic disorder of lipid metabolism; causes persistent, painful inflammation of nerves and retinitis pigmentosa.

CC Excl: 350.1-357.9

356.4 Idiopathic progressive polyneuropathy

356.8 Other specified idiopathic peripheral neuropathy

Supranuclear paralysis

356.9 Unspecified

AHA: ▶1Q, '13, 3◀

G60.9 Hereditary & idiopathic neuropathy unspecified   `I-10`

✓4ᵗʰ 357 Inflammatory and toxic neuropathy

357.0 Acute infective polyneuritis   `CC`

Guillain-Barré syndrome
Postinfectious polyneuritis

DEF: Guillain-Barré syndrome: acute demyelinating polyneuropathy preceded by viral illness (i.e., herpes, cytomegalovirus [CMV], Epstein-Barr virus [EBV]) or a bacterial illness; areflexic motor paralysis with mild sensory disturbance and acellular rise in spinal fluid protein.

CC Excl: 003.21, 013.00-013.16, 036.0, 036.89-036.9, 041.81-041.9, 047.0-047.9, 049.0-049.1, 053.0, 054.72, 072.1, 090.42, 091.81, 094.2, 098.89, 100.81, 112.83, 114.2, 115.01, 115.11, 115.91, 130.0, 139.8, 320.0-322.9, 349.89-349.9, 357.0

AHA: 2Q, '98, 12

357.1 Polyneuropathy in collagen vascular disease

Code first underlying disease, as:
disseminated lupus erythematosus (710.0)
polyarteritis nodosa (446.0)
rheumatoid arthritis (714.0)

357.2 Polyneuropathy in diabetes

Code first underlying disease (249.6, 250.6)

AHA: 4Q, '09, 151; 2Q, '09, 13, 15; 3Q, '08, 5; 4Q, '03, 105; 2Q, '92, 15; 3Q, '91, 9

357.3 Polyneuropathy in malignant disease

Code first underlying disease (140.0-208.9)

`N` Newborn Age: 0   `P` Pediatric Age: 0-17   `M` Maternity Age: 12-55   `A` Adult Age: 15-124   `MCC` Major CC Condition   `CC` CC Condition   `HIV` HIV Related Dx

110 – Volume 1 • October 2014   **2015 ICD-9-CM**

357.4 Polyneuropathy in other diseases classified elsewhere

Code first underlying disease, as:
amyloidosis (277.30-277.39)
beriberi (265.0)
chronic uremia (585.9)
deficiency of B vitamins (266.0-266.9)
diphtheria (032.0-032.9)
hypoglycemia (251.2)
pellagra (265.2)
porphyria (277.1)
sarcoidosis (135)
uremia NOS (586)

EXCLUDES *polyneuropathy in:*
herpes zoster (053.13)
mumps (072.72)

AHA: 2Q, '08, 8; 2Q, '98, 15

G63 Polyneuropathy in diseases classified elsewhere　　`I-10`

357.5 Alcoholic polyneuropathy

357.6 Polyneuropathy due to drugs

Use additional E code to identify drug

357.7 Polyneuropathy due to other toxic agents

Use additional E code to identify toxic agent

357.8 Other

AHA: 4Q, '02, 47; 2Q, '98, 12

357.81 Chronic inflammatory demyelinating polyneuritis　　`CC`

DEF: Inflammation of peripheral nerves resulting in destruction of myelin sheath; associated with diabetes mellitus, dysproteinemia, renal failure and malnutrition; symptoms include tingling, numbness, burning pain, diminished tendon reflexes, weakness, of lower extremities.

CC Excl: 351.0-353.5, 353.8-356.9, 357.81-357.89

357.82 Critical illness polyneuropathy　　`CC`

Acute motor neuropathy

DEF: An acute axonal neuropathy, both sensory and motor, that is associated with Systemic Inflammatory Response Syndrome (SIRS).

CC Excl: 351.0-353.5, 353.8-356.9, 357.81-357.9
AHA: 4Q, '03, 111

357.89 Other inflammatory and toxic neuropathy

AHA: ▶1Q, '14, 10; 1Q, '13, 3◀

357.9 Unspecified

358 Myoneural disorders

358.0 Myasthenia gravis

DEF: Autoimmune disorder of acetylcholine at neuromuscular junction; causing fatigue of voluntary muscles.
AHA: 4Q, '03, 59

358.00 Myasthenia gravis without (acute) exacerbation

Myasthenia gravis NOS

G70.00 Myathenia gravis without (acute) exacerbation　　`I-10`

358.01 Myasthenia gravis with (acute) exacerbation　　`MCC`

Myasthenia gravis in crisis

CC Excl: 249.60-249.61, 249.80-249.91, 250.60-250.63, 250.80-250.93, 349.89-349.9, 358.00-358.1, 358.30-358.39
AHA: 4Q, '07, 109; 1Q, '05, 4; 4Q, '04, 139

358.1 Myasthenic syndromes in diseases classified elsewhere　　`CC`

Code first underlying disease, as:
botulism (005.1, 040.41-040.42)
hypothyroidism (244.0-244.9)
malignant neoplasm (140.0-208.9)
pernicious anemia (281.0)
thyrotoxicosis (242.0-242.9)

CC Excl: See code: 358.01

358.2 Toxic myoneural disorders

Use additional E code to identify toxic agent

358.3 Lambert-Eaton syndrome

Eaton-Lambert syndrome
AHA: 4Q, '11, 100-101

358.30 Lambert-Eaton syndrome, unspecified　　`CC`

Lambert-Eaton syndrome NOS

CC Excl: 249.60-249.61, 249.80-249.81, 249.90-249.91, 250.60-250.63, 250.80-250.83, 250.90-250.93, 349.89-349.9, 358.00-358.1, 358.30-358.39, 359.4, 359.6, 359.81
AHA: 4Q, '11, 101

358.31 Lambert-Eaton syndrome in neoplastic disease　　`CC`

Code first the underlying neoplastic disease
CC Excl: See code: 358.30

358.39 Lambert-Eaton syndrome in other diseases classified elsewhere　　`CC`

Code first the underlying condition
CC Excl: See code: 358.30

358.8 Other specified myoneural disorders

358.9 Myoneural disorders, unspecified

AHA: 2Q, '02, 16

359 Muscular dystrophies and other myopathies

EXCLUDES *idiopathic polymyositis (710.4)*

359.0 Congenital hereditary muscular dystrophy　　`CC`

Benign congenital myopathy
Central core disease
Centronuclear myopathy
Myotubular myopathy
Nemaline body disease

EXCLUDES *arthrogryposis multiplex congenita (754.89)*

DEF: Genetic disorder; causing progressive or nonprogressive muscle weakness.

CC Excl: 249.60-249.61, 249.80-249.91, 250.60-250.63, 250.80-250.93, 349.89-349.9, 359.0-359.1

359.1 Hereditary progressive muscular dystrophy　　`CC`

Muscular dystrophy: NOS
distal
Duchenne
Erb's
fascioscapulohumeral

Muscular dystrophy: Gower's
Landouzy-Déjérine
limb-girdle
ocular
oculopharyngeal

DEF: Genetic degenerative, muscle disease; causes progressive weakness, wasting of muscle with no nerve involvement.
CC Excl: See code: 359.0

359.2 Myotonic disorders

EXCLUDES *periodic paralysis (359.3)*

DEF: Impaired movement due to spasmatic, rigid muscles.
AHA: 4Q, '07, 75

359.21 Myotonic muscular dystrophy

Dystrophia myotonica
Myotonia atrophica
Myotonic dystrophy
Proximal myotonic myopathy [PROMM]
Steinert's disease

359.22 Myotonia congenita

Acetazolamide responsive myotonia congenita
Dominant form [Thomsen's disease]
Myotonia levior
Recessive form [Becker's disease]

359.23 Myotonic chondrodystrophy

Congenital myotonic chondrodystrophy
Schwartz-Jampel disease

359.24 Drug induced myotonia

Use additional E code to identify drug

359.29 Other specified myotonic disorder

Myotonia fluctuans
Myotonia permanens
Paramyotonia congenita (of von Eulenburg)

`✓4th` `✓5th` Additional Digit Required　　Unacceptable PDx　　Manifestation Code　　Hospital Acquired Condition　　▶◀ Revised Text　　● New Code　　▲ Revised Code Title

2015 ICD-9-CM　　　　　　　　　　　　　　　　　　　　　　　　　　　　**October 2014 • Volume 1 – 111**

Diseases of the Nervous System and Sense Organs

359.3–360.31

359.3 Periodic paralysis
Familial periodic paralysis
Hypokalemic familial periodic paralysis
Hyperkalemic periodic paralysis
Hypokalemic periodic paralysis
Potassium sensitive periodic paralysis
EXCLUDES *paramyotonia congenita (of von Eulenburg) (359.29)*
DEF: Genetic disorder; characterized by rapidly progressive flaccid paralysis; attacks often occur after exercise or exposure to cold or dietary changes.

359.4 Toxic myopathy CC
Use additional E code to identify toxic agent
DEF: Muscle disorder caused by toxic agent.
CC Excl: 349.89-349.9, 358.00-359.6, 359.81-359.9
AHA: 1Q, '88, 5

359.5 *Myopathy in endocrine diseases classified elsewhere*
Code first underlying disease, as:
Addison's disease (255.41)
Cushing's syndrome (255.0)
hypopituitarism (253.2)
myxedema (244.0-244.9)
thyrotoxicosis (242.0-242.9)
DEF: Muscle disorder secondary to dysfunction in hormone secretion.

359.6 *Symptomatic inflammatory myopathy in diseases classified elsewhere* CC
Code first underlying disease, as:
amyloidosis (277.30-277.39)
disseminated lupus erythematosus (710.0)
malignant neoplasm (140.0-208.9)
polyarteritis nodosa (446.0)
rheumatoid arthritis (714.0)
sarcoidosis (135)
scleroderma (710.1)
Sjögren's disease (710.2)
CC Excl: 249.60-249.61, 249.80-249.91, 250.60-250.63, 250.80-250.93, 349.89-349.9, 358.00-359.6, 359.81-359.9

√5th **359.7 Inflammatory and immune myopathies, NEC**

359.71 Inclusion body myositis
IBM
DEF: Progressive, debilitating inflammatory muscle disease characterized by dysphagia, chronic muscle swelling, weakness, and atrophy (wasting); impairs fine motor functions.
AHA: 4Q, '09, 84

359.79 Other inflammatory and immune myopathies, NEC
Inflammatory myopathy NOS

√5th **359.8 Other myopathies**
AHA: 4Q, '02, 47; 3Q, '90, 17

359.81 Critical illness myopathy CC
Acute necrotizing myopathy
Acute quadriplegic myopathy
Intensive care (ICU) myopathy
Myopathy of critical illness
CC Excl: 358.1-359.6, 359.81-359.9

359.89 Other myopathies

359.9 Myopathy, unspecified

Disorders of the Eye and Adnexa (360-379)

Use additional external cause code, if applicable, to identify the cause of the eye condition

√4th **360 Disorders of the globe**
INCLUDES disorders affecting multiple structures of eye

√5th **360.0 Purulent endophthalmitis**
EXCLUDES *bleb associated endophthalmitis (379.63)*

360.00 Purulent endophthalmitis, unspecified CC
CC Excl: 360.00-360.04, 360.13, 360.19, 364.05

360.01 Acute endophthalmitis CC
CC Excl: See code 360.00

360.02 Panophthalmitis CC
CC Excl: See code 360.00

360.03 Chronic endophthalmitis

Eye

Sclera, Cornea, Iris, Pupil, Anterior chamber, Posterior chamber, Ciliary body, Conjunctiva, Choroid (uvea), Vitreous body, Lens, Hyaloid canal, Lamina cribosa, Optic nerve, Optic disk, Fovea, Retina — **Globe (Eyeball)**

Posterior Pole of Globe

Macula, Fovea, Optic disk — Ciliary body, Conjunctival veins, Canal of Schlemm, Trabecular mesh, Anterior chamber, Iris, Lens — **Flow of Aqueous Humor**

360.04 Vitreous abscess CC
CC Excl: 360.00-360.19

√5th **360.1 Other endophthalmitis**
EXCLUDES *bleb associated endophthalmitis (379.63)*

360.11 Sympathetic uveitis CC
DEF: Inflammation of vascular layer of uninjured eye; follows injury to other eye.
CC Excl: 360.11-360.12

360.12 Panuveitis CC
DEF: Inflammation of entire vascular layer of eye, including choroid, iris and ciliary body.
CC Excl: 360.11-360.12

360.13 Parasitic endophthalmitis NOS CC
DEF: Parasitic infection causing inflammation of the entire eye.
CC Excl: 360.00-360.04, 360.13, 360.19, 364.05

360.14 Ophthalmia nodosa
DEF: Conjunctival inflammation caused by embedded hairs.

360.19 Other CC
Phacoanaphylactic endophthalmitis
CC Excl: 360.00-360.04, 360.13, 360.19, 364.05

√5th **360.2 Degenerative disorders of globe**
AHA: 3Q, '91, 3

360.20 Degenerative disorder of globe, unspecified

360.21 Progressive high (degenerative) myopia
Malignant myopia
DEF: Severe, progressive nearsightedness in adults, complicated by serious disease of the choroid; leads to retinal detachment and blindness.

360.23 Siderosis
DEF: Iron pigment deposits within tissue of eyeball; caused by high iron content of blood.

360.24 Other metallosis
Chalcosis
DEF: Metal deposits, other than iron, within eyeball tissues.

360.29 Other
EXCLUDES *xerophthalmia (264.7)*

√5th **360.3 Hypotony of eye**

360.30 Hypotony, unspecified
DEF: Low osmotic pressure causing lack of tone, tension and strength.

360.31 Primary hypotony

N Newborn Age: 0   P Pediatric Age: 0-17   M Maternity Age: 12-55   A Adult Age: 15-124   MCC Major CC Condition   CC CC Condition   HIV HIV Related Dx

112 – Volume 1   2015 ICD-9-CM

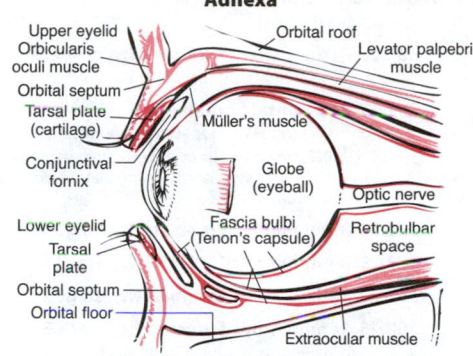

Adnexa

Upper eyelid
Orbicularis oculi muscle
Orbital septum
Tarsal plate (cartilage)
Conjunctival fornix
Lower eyelid
Tarsal plate
Orbital septum
Orbital floor
Orbital roof
Levator palpebri muscle
Müller's muscle
Globe (eyeball)
Optic nerve
Retrobulbar space
Fascia bulbi (Tenon's capsule)
Extraocular muscle

360.32 Ocular fistula causing hypotony
DEF: Low intraocular pressure due to leak through abnormal passage.

360.33 Hypotony associated with other ocular disorders

360.34 Flat anterior chamber
DEF: Low pressure behind cornea, causing compression.

√5ᵗʰ **360.4 Degenerated conditions of globe**

360.40 Degenerated globe or eye, unspecified

360.41 Blind hypotensive eye
Atrophy of globe   Phthisis bulbi
DEF: Vision loss due to extremely low intraocular pressure.

360.42 Blind hypertensive eye
Absolute glaucoma
DEF: Vision loss due to painful, high intraocular pressure.

360.43 Hemophthalmos, except current injury
EXCLUDES traumatic (871.0-871.9, 921.0-921.9)
DEF: Pool of blood within eyeball, not from current injury.

360.44 Leucocoria
DEF: Whitish mass or reflex in the pupil behind lens; also called cat's eye reflex; often indicative of retinoblastoma.

√5ᵗʰ **360.5 Retained (old) intraocular foreign body, magnetic**
Use additional code to identify foreign body (V90.11)
EXCLUDES current penetrating injury with magnetic foreign body (871.5)
retained (old) foreign body of orbit (376.6)

360.50 Foreign body, magnetic, intraocular, unspecified

360.51 Foreign body, magnetic, in anterior chamber

360.52 Foreign body, magnetic, in iris or ciliary body

360.53 Foreign body, magnetic, in lens

360.54 Foreign body, magnetic, in vitreous

360.55 Foreign body, magnetic, in posterior wall

360.59 Foreign body, magnetic, in other or multiple sites

√6ᵗʰ **360.6 Retained (old) intraocular foreign body, nonmagnetic**
Retained (old) foreign body:
NOS
nonmagnetic
Use additional code to identify foreign body (V90.01-V90.10, V90.12, V90.2-V90.9)
EXCLUDES current penetrating injury with (nonmagnetic) foreign body (871.6)
retained (old) foreign body in orbit (376.6)

360.60 Foreign body, intraocular, unspecified

360.61 Foreign body in anterior chamber

360.62 Foreign body in iris or ciliary body

360.63 Foreign body in lens

360.64 Foreign body in vitreous

360.65 Foreign body in posterior wall

360.69 Foreign body in other or multiple sites

√5ᵗʰ **360.8 Other disorders of globe**

360.81 Luxation of globe
DEF: Displacement of eyeball.

360.89 Other

360.9 Unspecified disorder of globe

√4ᵗʰ **361 Retinal detachments and defects**
DEF: Disorders of light-sensitive layer at back of eye, which separates from blood supply, disrupting vision.

√5ᵗʰ **361.0 Retinal detachment with retinal defect**
Rhegmatogenous retinal detachment
EXCLUDES detachment of retinal pigment epithelium (362.42-362.43)
retinal detachment (serous) (without defect) (361.2)

361.00 Retinal detachment with retinal defect, unspecified

361.01 Recent detachment, partial, with single defect

361.02 Recent detachment, partial, with multiple defects

361.03 Recent detachment, partial, with giant tear

361.04 Recent detachment, partial, with retinal dialysis
Dialysis (juvenile) of retina (with detachment)

361.05 Recent detachment, total or subtotal

361.06 Old detachment, partial
Delimited old retinal detachment

361.07 Old detachment, total or subtotal

√5ᵗʰ **361.1 Retinoschisis and retinal cysts**
EXCLUDES juvenile retinoschisis (362.73)
microcystoid degeneration of retina (362.62)
parasitic cyst of retina (360.13)

361.10 Retinoschisis, unspecified
DEF: Separation of retina due to degenerative process of aging; should not be confused with acute retinal detachment.

361.11 Flat retinoschisis
DEF: Slow, progressive split of retinal sensory layers.

361.12 Bullous retinoschisis
DEF: Fluid retention between split retinal sensory layers.

361.13 Primary retinal cysts

361.14 Secondary retinal cysts

361.19 Other
Pseudocyst of retina

361.2 Serous retinal detachment   CC
Retinal detachment without retinal defect
EXCLUDES central serous retinopathy (362.41)
retinal pigment epithelium detachment (362.42-362.43)
CC Excl: 361.00-361.9, 362.40-362.43

√5ᵗʰ **361.3 Retinal defects without detachment**
EXCLUDES chorioretinal scars after surgery for detachment (363.30-363.35)
peripheral retinal degeneration without defect (362.60-362.66)

361.30 Retinal defect, unspecified
Retinal break(s) NOS

361.31 Round hole of retina without detachment

361.32 Horseshoe tear of retina without detachment
Operculum of retina without mention of detachment

361.33 Multiple defects of retina without detachment

√5ᵗʰ **361.8 Other forms of retinal detachment**

361.81 Traction detachment of retina   CC
Traction detachment with vitreoretinal organization
CC Excl: 361.00-361.9, 362.40-362.43

361.89 Other   CC
CC Excl: 361.00-361.9, 362.40-362.43
AHA: 3Q, '99, 12

361.9 Unspecified retinal detachment   CC
CC Excl: 361.00-361.9, 362.40-362.43
AHA: N-D, '87, 10

✓4th 362   Other retinal disorders

> **EXCLUDES** chorioretinal scars (363.30-363.35)
> chorioretinitis (363.0-363.2)

✓5th 362.0   Diabetic retinopathy

Code first diabetes (249.5, 250.5)

DEF: Retinal changes in diabetes of long duration; causes hemorrhages, microaneurysms, waxy deposits and proliferative noninflammatory degenerative disease of retina.
AHA: 4Q, '05, 65; 3Q, '91, 8

362.01   Background diabetic retinopathy
Diabetic retinal microaneurysms
Diabetic retinopathy NOS

362.02   Proliferative diabetic retinopathy
DEF: Occurrence of the ischemic effects of vessel blockages result in neovascularization; new blood vessels begin to form to compensate for restricted blood flow; multiple areas of the retina and inner vitreous may be affected.
AHA: 3Q, '96, 5

362.03   Nonproliferative diabetic retinopathy NOS

362.04   Mild nonproliferative diabetic retinopathy
DEF: Early stages of degenerative condition of the retina due to diabetes; microaneurysm formation; small balloon-like swelling of the retinal vessels.

362.05   Moderate nonproliferative diabetic retinopathy
DEF: Stage of degenerative condition of the retina due to diabetes with pronounced microaneurysms; vessel blockages can occur.

362.06   Severe nonproliferative diabetic retinopathy
DEF: Stage of degenerative condition of the retina due to diabetes in which vascular breakdown in the retina results in multiple vascular blockages, or "beadings," with intraretinal hemorrhages.
AHA: 4Q, '05, 67

362.07   Diabetic macular edema
NOTE Code 362.07 must be used with a code for diabetic retinopathy (362.01-362.06)
Diabetic retinal edema
DEF: Leakage from retinal blood vessels causes swelling of the macula and impaired vision; exudates or plaques may develop in the posterior pole of the retina due to the breakdown of retinal vasculature.

✓5th 362.1   Other background retinopathy and retinal vascular changes

362.10   Background retinopathy, unspecified
AHA: 1Q, '06, 12

362.11   Hypertensive retinopathy
DEF: Retinal irregularities caused by systemic hypertension.
AHA: 3Q, '90, 3

362.12   Exudative retinopathy
Coats' syndrome
AHA: 3Q, '99, 12

362.13   Changes in vascular appearance
Vascular sheathing of retina
Use additional code for any associated atherosclerosis (440.8)

362.14   Retinal microaneurysms NOS
DEF: Microscopic dilation of retinal vessels in nondiabetic.

362.15   Retinal telangiectasia
DEF: Dilation of blood vessels of the retina.

362.16   Retinal neovascularization NOS
Neovascularization: Neovascularization:
   choroidal   subretinal
DEF: New and abnormal vascular growth in the retina.

362.17   Other intraretinal microvascular abnormalities
Retinal sclerosis   Retinal varices

362.18   Retinal vasculitis
Eales' disease   Retinal:
Retinal: perivasculitis
   arteritis   phlebitis
   endarteritis
DEF: Inflammation of retinal blood vessels.

✓5th 362.2   Other proliferative retinopathy
AHA: 4Q, '08, 110-111

362.20   Retinopathy of prematurity, unspecified
Retinopathy of prematurity NOS

362.21   Retrolental fibroplasia
Cicatricial retinopathy of prematurity
DEF: Fibrous tissue in vitreous, from retina to lens, causing blindness; associated with premature infants requiring high amounts of oxygen.

362.22   Retinopathy of prematurity, stage 0

362.23   Retinopathy of prematurity, stage 1

362.24   Retinopathy of prematurity, stage 2

362.25   Retinopathy of prematurity, stage 3

362.26   Retinopathy of prematurity, stage 4

362.27   Retinopathy of prematurity, stage 5

362.29   Other nondiabetic proliferative retinopathy
AHA: 3Q, '96, 5

✓5th 362.3   Retinal vascular occlusion
DEF: Obstructed blood flow to and from retina.

362.30   Retinal vascular occlusion, unspecified   `CC`
CC Excl: 362.30-362.37

362.31   Central retinal artery occlusion   `CC`
CC Excl: See code: 362.30

362.32   Arterial branch occlusion   `CC`
CC Excl: See code: 362.30

362.33   Partial arterial occlusion   `CC`
Hollenhorst plaque
Retinal microembolism
CC Excl: See code: 362.30

362.34   Transient arterial occlusion   `CC`
Amaurosis fugax
CC Excl: See code: 362.30
AHA: 1Q, '00, 16

362.35   Central retinal vein occlusion   `CC`
CC Excl: See code: 362.30
AHA: 2Q, '93, 6

362.36   Venous tributary (branch) occlusion

362.37   Venous engorgement
Occlusion:
   incipient }
   partial   } of retinal vein

✓5th 362.4   Separation of retinal layers
> **EXCLUDES** retinal detachment (serous) (361.2)
> rhegmatogenous (361.00-361.07)

362.40   Retinal layer separation, unspecified   `CC`
CC Excl: 361.00-361.9, 362.40-362.43

362.41   Central serous retinopathy
DEF: Serous-filled blister causing detachment of retina from pigment epithelium.

362.42   Serous detachment of retinal pigment epithelium   `CC`
Exudative detachment of retinal pigment epithelium
CC Excl: See code: 362.40
DEF: Blister of fatty fluid causing detachment of retina from pigment epithelium.

362.43   Hemorrhagic detachment of retinal pigment epithelium   `CC`
CC Excl: See code: 362.40
DEF: Blood-filled blister causing detachment of retina from pigment epithelium.

✓5th 362.5   Degeneration of macula and posterior pole
> **EXCLUDES** degeneration of optic disc (377.21-377.24)
> hereditary retinal degeneration [dystrophy] (362.70-362.77)

362.50   Macular degeneration (senile), unspecified

| N Newborn Age: 0 | P Pediatric Age: 0-17 | M Maternity Age: 12-55 | A Adult Age: 15-124 | MCC Major CC Condition | CC CC Condition | HIV HIV Related Dx |

362.51 Nonexudative senile macular degeneration
Senile macular degeneration:
atrophic
dry

362.52 Exudative senile macular degeneration
Kuhnt-Junius degeneration
Senile macular degeneration:
disciform
wet
DEF: Leakage in macular blood vessels with loss of visual acuity.

362.53 Cystoid macular degeneration
Cystoid macular edema
DEF: Retinal swelling and cyst formation in macula.

362.54 Macular cyst, hole, or pseudohole
AHA: 4Q, '11, 106

362.55 Toxic maculopathy
Use additional E code to identify drug, if drug induced

362.56 Macular puckering
Preretinal fibrosis

362.57 Drusen (degenerative)
DEF: White, hyaline deposits on Bruch's membrane (lamina basalis choroideae).

√5th **362.6 Peripheral retinal degenerations**
EXCLUDES hereditary retinal degeneration [dystrophy] (362.70-362.77)
retinal degeneration with retinal defect (361.00-361.07)

362.60 Peripheral retinal degeneration, unspecified

362.61 Paving stone degeneration
DEF: Degeneration of peripheral retina; causes thinning through which choroid is visible.

362.62 Microcystoid degeneration
Blessig's cysts　　　Iwanoff's cysts

362.63 Lattice degeneration
Palisade degeneration of retina
DEF: Degeneration of retina; often bilateral, usually benign; characterized by lines intersecting at irregular intervals in peripheral retina; retinal thinning and retinal holes may occur.

362.64 Senile reticular degeneration
DEF: Net-like appearance of retina; sign of degeneration.

362.65 Secondary pigmentary degeneration
Pseudoretinitis pigmentosa

362.66 Secondary vitreoretinal degenerations

√5th **362.7 Hereditary retinal dystrophies**
DEF: Genetically induced progressive changes in retina.

362.70 Hereditary retinal dystrophy, unspecified

362.71 *Retinal dystrophy in systemic or cerebroretinal lipidoses*
Code first underlying disease, as:
cerebroretinal lipidoses (330.1)
systemic lipidoses (272.7)

362.72 *Retinal dystrophy in other systemic disorders and syndromes*
Code first underlying disease, as:
Bassen-Kornzweig syndrome (272.5)
Refsum's disease (356.3)

362.73 Vitreoretinal dystrophies
Juvenile retinoschisis

362.74 Pigmentary retinal dystrophy
Retinal dystrophy, albipunctate
Retinitis pigmentosa

362.75 Other dystrophies primarily involving the sensory retina
Progressive cone(-rod) dystrophy
Stargardt's disease

362.76 Dystrophies primarily involving the retinal pigment epithelium
Fundus flavimaculatus　　　Vitelliform dystrophy

362.77 Dystrophies primarily involving Bruch's membrane
Dystrophy:
hyaline
pseudoinflammatory foveal
Hereditary drusen

√5th **362.8 Other retinal disorders**
EXCLUDES chorioretinal inflammations (363.0-363.2)
chorioretinal scars (363.30-363.35)

362.81 Retinal hemorrhage
Hemorrhage:
preretinal
retinal (deep) (superficial)
subretinal
AHA: 4Q, '96, 43

362.82 Retinal exudates and deposits

362.83 Retinal edema
Retinal:
cotton wool spots
edema (localized) (macular) (peripheral)
DEF: Retinal swelling due to fluid accumulation.

362.84 Retinal ischemia　　　cc
CC Excl: 362.81-362.89
DEF: Reduced retinal blood supply.

362.85 Retinal nerve fiber bundle defects

362.89 Other retinal disorders

362.9 Unspecified retinal disorder

√4th **363 Chorioretinal inflammations, scars, and other disorders of choroid**

√5th **363.0 Focal chorioretinitis and focal retinochoroiditis**
EXCLUDES focal chorioretinitis or retinochoroiditis in:
histoplasmosis (115.02, 115.12, 115.92)
toxoplasmosis (130.2)
congenital infection (771.2)

363.00 Focal chorioretinitis, unspecified
Focal:
choroiditis or chorioretinitis NOS
retinitis or retinochoroiditis NOS

363.01 Focal choroiditis and chorioretinitis, juxtapapillary

363.03 Focal choroiditis and chorioretinitis of other posterior pole

363.04 Focal choroiditis and chorioretinitis, peripheral

363.05 Focal retinitis and retinochoroiditis, juxtapapillary
Neuroretinitis

363.06 Focal retinitis and retinochoroiditis, macular or paramacular

363.07 Focal retinitis and retinochoroiditis of other posterior pole

363.08 Focal retinitis and retinochoroiditis, peripheral

√5th **363.1 Disseminated chorioretinitis and disseminated retinochoroiditis**
EXCLUDES disseminated choroiditis or chorioretinitis in:
secondary syphilis (091.51)
neurosyphilitic disseminated retinitis or retinochoroiditis (094.83)
retinal (peri)vasculitis (362.18)

363.10 Disseminated chorioretinitis, unspecified　　　cc
Disseminated:
choroiditis or chorioretinitis NOS
retinitis or retinochoroiditis NOS
CC Excl: 363.00-363.22

363.11 Disseminated choroiditis and chorioretinitis, posterior pole　　　cc
CC Excl: See code: 363.10

363.12 Disseminated choroiditis and chorioretinitis, peripheral　　　cc
CC Excl: See code: 363.10

363.13 Disseminated choroiditis and chorioretinitis, generalized   `CC`
Code first any underlying disease, as:
tuberculosis (017.3)
CC Excl: See code: 363.10

363.14 Disseminated retinitis and retinochoroiditis, metastatic   `CC`
CC Excl: See code: 363.10

363.15 Disseminated retinitis and retinochoroiditis, pigment epitheliopathy   `CC`
Acute posterior multifocal placoid pigment epitheliopathy
DEF: Widespread inflammation of retina and choroid; characterized by pigmented epithelium involvement.
CC Excl: See code: 363.10

√5th **363.2 Other and unspecified forms of chorioretinitis and retinochoroiditis**
EXCLUDES panophthalmitis (360.02)
sympathetic uveitis (360.11)
uveitis NOS (364.3)

363.20 Chorioretinitis, unspecified   `CC`
Choroiditis NOS
Retinitis NOS
Uveitis, posterior NOS
CC Excl: See code: 363.10

363.21 Pars planitis
Posterior cyclitis
DEF: Inflammation of peripheral retina and ciliary body; characterized by bands of white cells.

363.22 Harada's disease
DEF: Retinal detachment and bilateral widespread exudative choroiditis; symptoms include headache, vomiting, increased lymphocytes in cerebrospinal fluid; with temporary or permanent deafness.

√5th **363.3 Chorioretinal scars**
Scar (postinflammatory) (postsurgical) (posttraumatic):
choroid
retina

363.30 Chorioretinal scar, unspecified

363.31 Solar retinopathy
DEF: Retinal scarring caused by solar radiation.

363.32 Other macular scars

363.33 Other scars of posterior pole

363.34 Peripheral scars

363.35 Disseminated scars

√5th **363.4 Choroidal degenerations**

363.40 Choroidal degeneration, unspecified
Choroidal sclerosis NOS

363.41 Senile atrophy of choroid
DEF: Wasting away of choroid; due to aging.

363.42 Diffuse secondary atrophy of choroid
DEF: Wasting away of choroid in systemic disease.

363.43 Angioid streaks of choroid
DEF: Degeneration of choroid; characterized by dark brown steaks radiating from optic disc; occurs with pseudoxanthoma, elasticum or Paget's disease.

√5th **363.5 Hereditary choroidal dystrophies**
Hereditary choroidal atrophy:
partial [choriocapillaris]
total [all vessels]

363.50 Hereditary choroidal dystrophy or atrophy, unspecified

363.51 Circumpapillary dystrophy of choroid, partial

363.52 Circumpapillary dystrophy of choroid, total
Helicoid dystrophy of choroid

363.53 Central dystrophy of choroid, partial
Dystrophy, choroidal:
central areolar
circinate

363.54 Central choroidal atrophy, total
Dystrophy, choroidal: Dystrophy, choroidal:
central gyrate   serpiginous

363.55 Choroideremia
DEF: Hereditary choroid degeneration, occurs in first decade; characterized by constricted visual field and ultimately blindness in males; less debilitating in females.

363.56 Other diffuse or generalized dystrophy, partial
Diffuse choroidal sclerosis

363.57 Other diffuse or generalized dystrophy, total
Generalized gyrate atrophy, choroid

√5th **363.6 Choroidal hemorrhage and rupture**

363.61 Choroidal hemorrhage, unspecified

363.62 Expulsive choroidal hemorrhage

363.63 Choroidal rupture   `CC`
CC Excl: 363.61-363.9

√5th **363.7 Choroidal detachment**

363.70 Choroidal detachment, unspecified   `CC`
CC Excl: See code: 363.63

363.71 Serous choroidal detachment   `CC`
DEF: Detachment of choroid from sclera; due to blister of serous fluid.
CC Excl: See code: 363.63

363.72 Hemorrhagic choroidal detachment   `CC`
DEF: Detachment of choroid from sclera; due to blood-filled blister.
CC Excl: See code: 363.63

363.8 Other disorders of choroid
AHA: 1Q, '06, 12

363.9 Unspecified disorder of choroid

√4th **364 Disorders of iris and ciliary body**

√5th **364.0 Acute and subacute iridocyclitis**
Anterior uveitis
Cylitis
Iridocyclitis   } acute, subacute
Iritis

EXCLUDES gonococcal (098.41)
herpes simplex (054.44)
herpes zoster (053.22)

364.00 Acute and subacute iridocyclitis, unspecified   `CC`
CC Excl: 364.00-364.3

364.01 Primary iridocyclitis   `CC`
CC Excl: See code: 364.00

364.02 Recurrent iridocyclitis   `CC`
CC Excl: See code: 364.00

364.03 Secondary iridocyclitis, infectious   `CC`
CC Excl: See code: 364.00

364.04 Secondary iridocyclitis, noninfectious
Aqueous: Aqueous:
cells   flare
fibrin

364.05 Hypopyon
DEF: Accumulation of white blood cells between cornea and lens.

√5th **364.1 Chronic iridocyclitis**
EXCLUDES posterior cyclitis (363.21)

364.10 Chronic iridocyclitis, unspecified

364.11 Chronic iridocyclitis in diseases classified elsewhere
Code first underlying disease, as:
sarcoidosis (135)
tuberculosis (017.3)
EXCLUDES syphilitic iridocyclitis (091.52)
DEF: Persistent inflammation of iris and ciliary body; due to underlying disease or condition.

N Newborn Age: 0   P Pediatric Age: 0-17   M Maternity Age: 12-55   A Adult Age: 15-124   MCC Major CC Condition   CC CC Condition   HIV HIV Related Dx

116 – Volume 1   2015 ICD-9-CM

√5ᵗʰ **364.2 Certain types of iridocyclitis**

EXCLUDES *posterior cyclitis (363.21)*
sympathetic uveitis (360.11)

364.21 Fuchs' heterochromic cyclitis
DEF: Chronic cyclitis characterized by differences in the color of the two irises; the lighter iris appears in the inflamed eye.

364.22 Glaucomatocyclitic crises   CC
DEF: An uncommon inflammatory unilateral eye condition, characteristic recurrent episodes of high intraocular pressure accompanied by mild inflammation.
CC Excl: See code: 364.00

364.23 Lens-induced iridocyclitis
DEF: Inflammation of iris; due to immune reaction to proteins in lens following trauma or other lens abnormality.

364.24 Vogt-Koyanagi syndrome
DEF: Uveomeningitis with exudative iridocyclitis and choroiditis; causes depigmentation of hair and skin, detached retina; tinnitus and loss of hearing.

364.3 Unspecified iridocyclitis   CC
Uveitis NOS
CC Excl: See code: 364.00-364.3

√5ᵗʰ **364.4 Vascular disorders of iris and ciliary body**

364.41 Hyphema
Hemorrhage of iris or ciliary body
DEF: Hemorrhage in anterior chamber; also called hyphemia or "blood shot" eyes.

364.42 Rubeosis iridis
Neovascularization of iris or ciliary body
DEF: Blood vessel and connective tissue formation on surface of iris; symptomatic of diabetic retinopathy, central retinal vein occlusion and retinal detachment.

√6ᵗʰ **364.5 Degenerations of iris and ciliary body**

364.51 Essential or progressive iris atrophy

364.52 Iridoschisis
DEF: Splitting of the iris into two layers.

364.53 Pigmentary iris degeneration
Acquired heterochromia
Pigment dispersion syndrome ⎫ of iris
Translucency ⎭

364.54 Degeneration of pupillary margin
Atrophy of sphincter ⎫ of iris
Ectropion of pigment epithelium ⎭

364.55 Miotic cysts of pupillary margin
DEF: Serous-filled sacs in pupillary margin of iris.

364.56 Degenerative changes of chamber angle

364.57 Degenerative changes of ciliary body

364.59 Other iris atrophy
Iris atrophy (generalized) (sector shaped)

√5ᵗʰ **364.6 Cysts of iris, ciliary body, and anterior chamber**

EXCLUDES *miotic pupillary cyst (364.55)*
parasitic cyst (360.13)

364.60 Idiopathic cysts
DEF: Fluid-filled sacs in iris or ciliary body; unknown etiology.

364.61 Implantation cysts
Epithelial down-growth, anterior chamber
Implantation cysts (surgical) (traumatic)

364.62 Exudative cysts of iris or anterior chamber

364.63 Primary cyst of pars plana
DEF: Fluid-filled sacs of outermost ciliary ring.

364.64 Exudative cyst of pars plana
DEF: Protein, fatty-filled sacs of outermost ciliary ring; due to fluid leak from blood vessels.

√5ᵗʰ **364.7 Adhesions and disruptions of iris and ciliary body**

EXCLUDES *flat anterior chamber (360.34)*

364.70 Adhesions of iris, unspecified
Synechiae (iris) NOS

Plateau Iris Syndrome

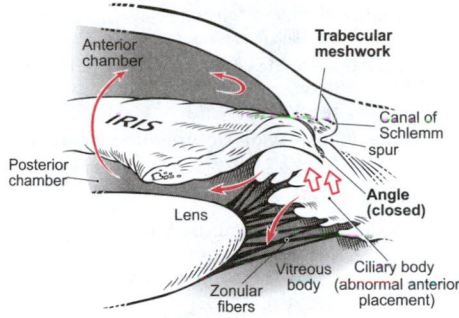

364.71 Posterior synechiae
DEF: Adhesion binding iris to lens.

364.72 Anterior synechiae
DEF: Adhesion binding the iris to cornea.

364.73 Goniosynechiae
Peripheral anterior synechiae
DEF: Adhesion binding the iris to cornea at the angle of the anterior chamber.

364.74 Pupillary membranes
Iris bombé   Pupillary:
Pupillary: seclusion
occlusion
DEF: Membrane traversing the pupil and blocking vision.

364.75 Pupillary abnormalities
Deformed pupil   Rupture of sphincter, pupil
Ectopic pupil
DEF: Separation of the iris from the ciliary body base; due to trauma or surgical accident.

364.76 Iridodialysis
DEF: Separation of the iris from the ciliary body base; due to trauma or surgical accident.

364.77 Recession of chamber angle
DEF: Receding of anterior chamber angle of the eye; restricts vision.

√5ᵗʰ **364.8 Other disorders of iris and ciliary body**
AHA: 2Q, '07, 9

364.81 Floppy iris syndrome
Intraoperative floppy iris syndrome [IFIS]
Use additional E code to identify cause, such as: sympatholytics [antiadrenergics] causing adverse effect in therapeutic use (E941.3)
DEF: Condition complicating cataract surgery for patients who have received alpha blocker treatment for urinary retention problems; iris dilator muscle fails to dilate, and the iris may billow or flap.
AHA: 4Q, '07, 77, 79

364.82 Plateau iris syndrome
DEF: A postoperative chronic angle-closure glaucoma characterized by closing of the anterior chamber angle secondary to a large or anteriorly positioned ciliary body that impairs the normal flow of aqueous fluid.
AHA: 4Q, '08, 112

364.89 Other disorders of iris and ciliary body
Prolapse of iris NOS
EXCLUDES *prolapse of iris in recent wound (871.1)*

364.9 Unspecified disorder of iris and ciliary body

√4ᵗʰ **365 Glaucoma**
EXCLUDES *blind hypertensive eye [absolute glaucoma] (360.42)*
congenital glaucoma (743.20-743.22)
DEF: Rise in intraocular pressure restricting blood flow; multiple causes.

√5ᵗʰ **365.0 Borderline glaucoma [glaucoma suspect]**
AHA: 1Q, '90, 8

365.00 Preglaucoma, unspecified

365.01 Open angle with borderline findings, low risk
Open angle, low risk
DEF: Minor block of aqueous outflow from eye.
AHA: 4Q, '11, 102

365.02 Anatomical narrow angle
Primary angle closure suspect

365.03 Steroid responders

365.04 Ocular hypertension
DEF: High fluid pressure within eye; no clear cause.

365.05 Open angle with borderline findings, high risk
Open angle, high risk
AHA: 4Q, '11, 102-103

365.06 Primary angle closure without glaucoma damage
AHA: 4Q, '11, 102-103

√5th **365.1 Open-angle glaucoma**

365.10 Open-angle glaucoma, unspecified
Wide-angle glaucoma NOS
Use additional code to identify glaucoma stage
(365.70-365.74)

365.11 Primary open angle glaucoma
Chronic simple glaucoma
Use additional code to identify glaucoma stage
(365.70-365.74)
DEF: High intraocular pressure, despite free flow of aqueous.

365.12 Low tension glaucoma
Use additional code to identify glaucoma stage
(365.70-365.74)

365.13 Pigmentary glaucoma
Use additional code to identify glaucoma stage
(365.70-365.74)
DEF: High intraocular pressure; due to iris pigment granules blocking aqueous flow.

365.14 Glaucoma of childhood
Infantile or juvenile glaucoma

365.15 Residual stage of open angle glaucoma

√5th **365.2 Primary angle-closure glaucoma**
DEF: Glaucoma caused by a shift in the position of the iris of the eye that blocks the surface of the trabecular meshwork causing impairment of the normal flow of aqueous fluid.

365.20 Primary angle-closure glaucoma, unspecified
Use additional code to identify glaucoma stage
(365.70-365.74)

365.21 Intermittent angle-closure glaucoma
Angle-closure glaucoma:
interval
subacute
DEF: Recurring attacks of high intraocular pressure; due to blocked aqueous flow.

365.22 Acute angle-closure glaucoma   CC
Acute angle-closure glaucoma attack
Acute angle-closure glaucoma crisis
DEF: Sudden, severe rise in intraocular pressure due to blockage in aqueous drainage.
CC Excl: See code: 365.22

365.23 Chronic angle-closure glaucoma
Chronic primary angle closure glaucoma
Use additional code to identify glaucoma stage
(365.70-365.74)
AHA: 2Q, '98, 16

365.24 Residual stage of angle-closure glaucoma

√5th **365.3 Corticosteroid-induced glaucoma**
DEF: Elevated intraocular pressure; due to long-term corticosteroid therapy.

365.31 Glaucomatous stage
Use additional code to identify glaucoma stage
(365.70-365.74)

365.32 Residual stage

√5th **365.4 Glaucoma associated with congenital anomalies, dystrophies, and systemic syndromes**

365.41 Glaucoma associated with chamber angle anomalies

365.42 Glaucoma associated with anomalies of iris

365.43 Glaucoma associated with other anterior segment anomalies

Normal Aqueous Flow

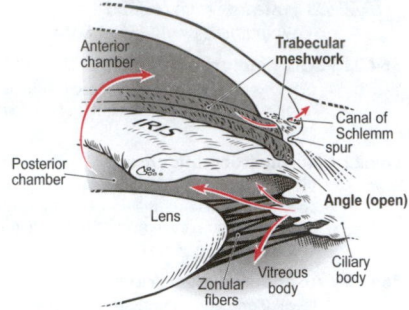

Angle-Closure Glaucoma

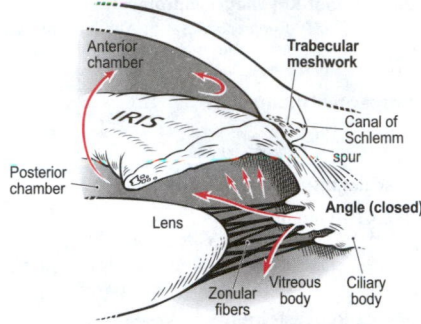

365.44 Glaucoma associated with systemic syndromes
Code first associated disease, as
neurofibromatosis (237.70-237.79)
Sturge-Weber (-Dimitri) syndrome (759.6)

√5th **365.5 Glaucoma associated with disorders of the lens**

365.51 Phacolytic glaucoma
DEF: Elevated intraocular pressure; due to lens protein blocking aqueous flow.

365.52 Pseudoexfoliation glaucoma
Use additional code to identify glaucoma stage
(365.70-365.74)
DEF: Glaucoma characterized by small grayish particles deposited on the lens.

365.59 Glaucoma associated with other lens disorders

√5th **365.6 Glaucoma associated with other ocular disorders**

365.60 Glaucoma associated with unspecified ocular disorder

365.61 Glaucoma associated with pupillary block
DEF: Acute, open-angle glaucoma caused by mature cataract; aqueous flow is blocked by lens material and macrophages.

365.62 Glaucoma associated with ocular inflammations
Use additional code to identify glaucoma stage
(365.70-365.74)

365.63 Glaucoma associated with vascular disorders
Use additional code to identify glaucoma stage
(365.70-365.74)

365.64 Glaucoma associated with tumors or cysts

365.65 Glaucoma associated with ocular trauma
Use additional code to identify glaucoma stage
(365.70-365.74)

√5th **365.7 Glaucoma stage**
Code first associated type of glaucoma (365.10-365.13, 365.20, 365.23, 365.31, 365.52, 365.62-365.63, 365.65)
AHA: 4Q, '11, 101-105
TIP: If a patient has bilateral glaucoma with different stages or the stage evolves during the encounter from one stage to another, assign one code for the highest stage documented.

365.70 Glaucoma stage, unspecified
Glaucoma stage NOS

365.71 Mild stage glaucoma
Early stage glaucoma

N Newborn Age: 0   P Pediatric Age: 0-17   M Maternity Age: 12-55   A Adult Age: 15-124   MCC Major CC Condition   CC CC Condition   HIV HIV Related Dx

118 – Volume 1   2015 ICD-9-CM

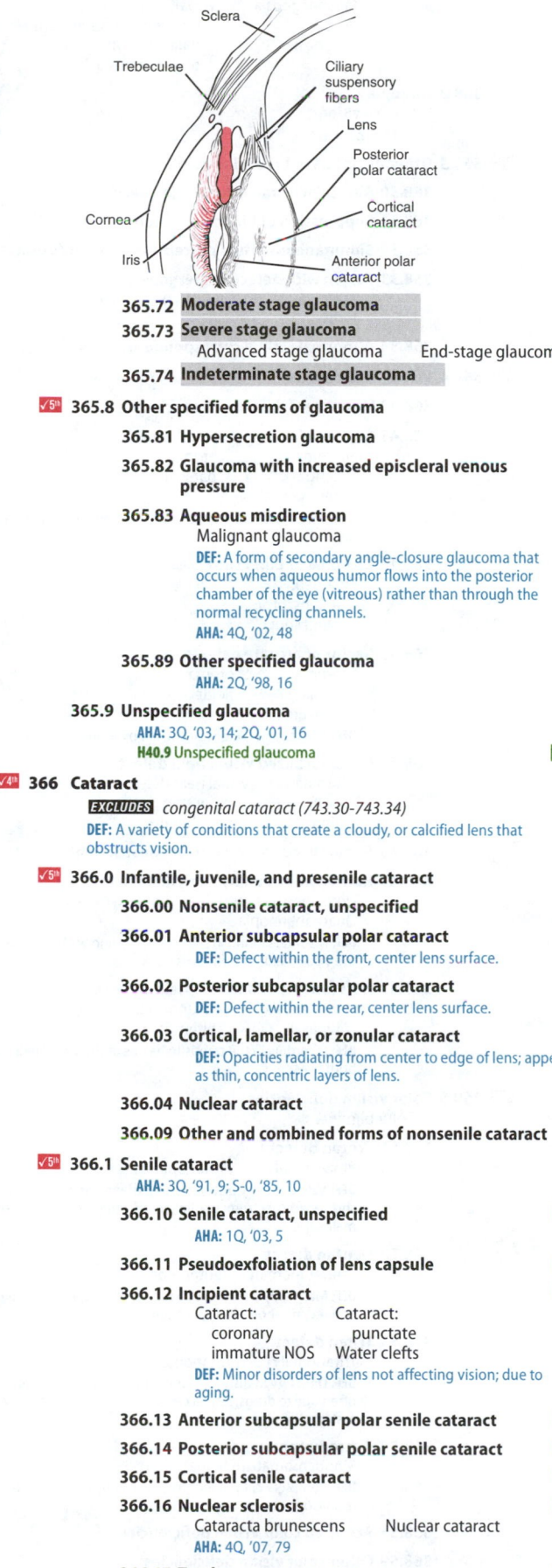

Cataract

365.72 **Moderate stage glaucoma**

365.73 **Severe stage glaucoma**
    Advanced stage glaucoma   End-stage glaucoma

365.74 **Indeterminate stage glaucoma**

✓5ᵗʰ 365.8 **Other specified forms of glaucoma**

365.81 **Hypersecretion glaucoma**

365.82 **Glaucoma with increased episcleral venous pressure**

365.83 **Aqueous misdirection**
    Malignant glaucoma
    DEF: A form of secondary angle-closure glaucoma that occurs when aqueous humor flows into the posterior chamber of the eye (vitreous) rather than through the normal recycling channels.
    AHA: 4Q, '02, 48

365.89 **Other specified glaucoma**
    AHA: 2Q, '98, 16

365.9 **Unspecified glaucoma**
    AHA: 3Q, '03, 14; 2Q, '01, 16
    H40.9 Unspecified glaucoma   `I-10`

✓4ᵗʰ **366 Cataract**
    EXCLUDES *congenital cataract (743.30-743.34)*
    DEF: A variety of conditions that create a cloudy, or calcified lens that obstructs vision.

✓5ᵗʰ 366.0 **Infantile, juvenile, and presenile cataract**

366.00 **Nonsenile cataract, unspecified**

366.01 **Anterior subcapsular polar cataract**
    DEF: Defect within the front, center lens surface.

366.02 **Posterior subcapsular polar cataract**
    DEF: Defect within the rear, center lens surface.

366.03 **Cortical, lamellar, or zonular cataract**
    DEF: Opacities radiating from center to edge of lens; appear as thin, concentric layers of lens.

366.04 **Nuclear cataract**

366.09 **Other and combined forms of nonsenile cataract**

✓5ᵗʰ 366.1 **Senile cataract**
    AHA: 3Q, '91, 9; S-0, '85, 10

366.10 **Senile cataract, unspecified**   `A`
    AHA: 1Q, '03, 5

366.11 **Pseudoexfoliation of lens capsule**   `A`

366.12 **Incipient cataract**   `A`
    Cataract: Cataract:
      coronary   punctate
      immature NOS   Water clefts
    DEF: Minor disorders of lens not affecting vision; due to aging.

366.13 **Anterior subcapsular polar senile cataract**   `A`

366.14 **Posterior subcapsular polar senile cataract**   `A`

366.15 **Cortical senile cataract**   `A`

366.16 **Nuclear sclerosis**   `A`
    Cataracta brunescens   Nuclear cataract
    AHA: 4Q, '07, 79

366.17 **Total or mature cataract**   `A`

366.18 **Hypermature cataract**   `A`
    Morgagni cataract

366.19 **Other and combined forms of senile cataract**   `A`

✓5ᵗʰ 366.2 **Traumatic cataract**

366.20 **Traumatic cataract, unspecified**

366.21 **Localized traumatic opacities**
    Vossius' ring

366.22 **Total traumatic cataract**

366.23 **Partially resolved traumatic cataract**

✓5ᵗʰ 366.3 **Cataract secondary to ocular disorders**

366.30 **Cataracta complicata, unspecified**

366.31 **Glaucomatous flecks (subcapsular)**
    Code first underlying glaucoma (365.0-365.9)

366.32 **Cataract in inflammatory disorders**
    Code first underlying condition, as:
      chronic choroiditis (363.0-363.2)

366.33 **Cataract with neovascularization**
    Code first underlying condition, as:
      chronic iridocyclitis (364.10)

366.34 **Cataract in degenerative disorders**
    Sunflower cataract
    Code first underlying condition, as:
      chalcosis (360.24)
      degenerative myopia (360.21)
      pigmentary retinal dystrophy (362.74)

✓5ᵗʰ 366.4 **Cataract associated with other disorders**

366.41 *Diabetic cataract*
    Code first diabetes (249.5, 250.5)
    AHA: 3Q, '91, 9; S-O, '85, 11

366.42 *Tetanic cataract*
    Code first underlying disease, as:
      calcinosis (275.4)
      hypoparathyroidism (252.1)

366.43 *Myotonic cataract*
    Code first underlying disorder (359.21, 359.23)

366.44 *Cataract associated with other syndromes*
    Code first underlying condition, as:
      craniofacial dysostosis (756.0)
      galactosemia (271.1)

366.45 **Toxic cataract**
    Drug-induced cataract
    Use additional E code to identify drug or other toxic substance

366.46 **Cataract associated with radiation and other physical influences**
    Use additional E code to identify cause

✓5ᵗʰ 366.5 **After-cataract**

366.50 **After-cataract, unspecified**
    Secondary cataract NOS

366.51 **Soemmering's ring**
    DEF: A donut-shaped lens remnant and a capsule behind the pupil as a result of cataract surgery or trauma.

366.52 **Other after-cataract, not obscuring vision**

366.53 **After-cataract, obscuring vision**

366.8 **Other cataract**
    Calcification of lens

366.9 **Unspecified cataract**
    AHA: 4Q, '09, 131
    H26.9 Unspecified cataract   `I-10`

✓4ᵗʰ **367 Disorders of refraction and accommodation**

367.0 **Hypermetropia**
    Far-sightedness   Hyperopia
    DEF: Refraction error, called also hyperopia, focal point is posterior to retina; abnormally short anteroposterior diameter or subnormal refractive power; causes farsightedness.

✓4ᵗʰ ✓5ᵗʰ Additional Digit Required   Unacceptable PDx   Manifestation Code   Hospital Acquired Condition   ►◄ Revised Text   ● New Code   ▲ Revised Code Title

2015 ICD-9-CM   **Volume 1 – 119**

Diseases of the Nervous System and Sense Organs

367.1–368.59

367.1 Myopia
Near-sightedness
DEF: Refraction error, focal point is anterior to retina; causes near-sightedness.

√5ᵗʰ **367.2 Astigmatism**

367.20 Astigmatism, unspecified

367.21 Regular astigmatism

367.22 Irregular astigmatism

√5ᵗʰ **367.3 Anisometropia and aniseikonia**

367.31 Anisometropia
DEF: Eyes with refractive powers that differ by at least one diopter.

367.32 Aniseikonia
DEF: Eyes with unequal retinal imaging; usually due to refractive error.

367.4 Presbyopia
DEF: Loss of crystalline lens elasticity; causes errors of accommodation; due to aging.

√5ᵗʰ **367.5 Disorders of accommodation**

367.51 Paresis of accommodation
Cycloplegia
DEF: Partial paralysis of ciliary muscle, causing focus problems.

367.52 Total or complete internal ophthalmoplegia
DEF: Total paralysis of ciliary muscle; large pupil incapable of focus.

367.53 Spasm of accommodation
DEF: Abnormal contraction of ciliary muscle; causes focus problems.

√5ᵗʰ **367.8 Other disorders of refraction and accommodation**

367.81 Transient refractive change

367.89 Other
Drug-induced ⎱ disorders of refraction and
Toxic ⎰ accommodation

367.9 Unspecified disorder of refraction and accommodation

√4ᵗʰ **368 Visual disturbances**
EXCLUDES electrophysiological disturbances (794.11-794.14)

√5ᵗʰ **368.0 Amblyopia ex anopsia**
DEF: Vision impaired due to disuse; esotropia often cause.

368.00 Amblyopia, unspecified

368.01 Strabismic amblyopia
Suppression amblyopia

368.02 Deprivation amblyopia
DEF: Decreased vision associated with suppressed retinal image of one eye.

368.03 Refractive amblyopia

√5ᵗʰ **368.1 Subjective visual disturbances**

368.10 Subjective visual disturbance, unspecified

368.11 Sudden visual loss   **CC**
CC Excl: 368.10-368.12, 368.16

368.12 Transient visual loss   **CC**
Concentric fadingScintillating scotoma
CC Excl: See code: 368.11

368.13 Visual discomfort
Asthenopia   Photophobia
Eye strain

368.14 Visual distortions of shape and size
Macropsia   Micropsia
Metamorphopsia

368.15 Other visual distortions and entoptic phenomena
Photopsia   Refractive:
Refractive: polyopia
   diplopia   Visual halos

368.16 Psychophysical visual disturbances
Prosopagnosia   Visual:
Visual: disorientation syndrome
   agnosia   hallucinations
     object agnosia

368.2 Diplopia
Double vision
H53.2 Diplopia   **I-10**

√5ᵗʰ **368.3 Other disorders of binocular vision**

368.30 Binocular vision disorder, unspecified

368.31 Suppression of binocular vision

368.32 Simultaneous visual perception without fusion

368.33 Fusion with defective stereopsis
DEF: Faulty depth perception though normal ability to focus.

368.34 Abnormal retinal correspondence

√5ᵗʰ **368.4 Visual field defects**

368.40 Visual field defect, unspecified

368.41 Scotoma involving central area
Scotoma: Scotoma:
  central   paracentral
  centrocecal
DEF: Vision loss (blind spot) in central five degrees of visual field.

368.42 Scotoma of blind spot area
Enlarged: Paracecal scotoma
  angioscotoma
  blind spot

368.43 Sector or arcuate defects
Scotoma: Scotoma:
  arcuate   Seidel
  Bjerrum
DEF: Arc-shaped blind spot caused by retinal nerve damage.

368.44 Other localized visual field defect
Scotoma: Visual field defect:
  NOS   nasal step
  ring   peripheral

368.45 Generalized contraction or constriction

368.46 Homonymous bilateral field defects
Hemianopsia (altitudinal) (homonymous)
Quadrant anopia
DEF: Disorders found in the corresponding vertical halves of the visual fields of both eyes.

368.47 Heteronymous bilateral field defects
Hemianopsia: Hemianopsia:
  binasal   bitemporal
DEF: Disorders in the opposite halves of the visual fields of both eyes.

√5ᵗʰ **368.5 Color vision deficiencies**
Color blindness

368.51 Protan defect
Protanomaly   Protanopia
DEF: Mild difficulty distinguishing green and red hues with shortened spectrum; sex-linked affecting one percent of males.

368.52 Deutan defect
Deuteranomaly   Deuteranopia
DEF: Male-only disorder; difficulty in distinguishing green and red, no shortened spectrum.

368.53 Tritan defect
Tritanomaly   Tritanopia
DEF: Difficulty in distinguishing blue and yellow; occurs often due to drugs, retinal detachment and central nervous system diseases.

368.54 Achromatopsia
Monochromatism (cone) (rod)
DEF: Complete color blindness; caused by disease, injury to retina, optic nerve or pathway.

368.55 Acquired color vision deficiencies

368.59 Other color vision deficiencies

N Newborn Age: 0   **P** Pediatric Age: 0-17   **M** Maternity Age: 12-55   **A** Adult Age: 15-124   **MCC** Major CC Condition   **CC** CC Condition   **HIV** HIV Related Dx

120 – Volume 1   2015 ICD-9-CM

√5ᵗʰ **368.6 Night blindness**
     Nyctalopia
     DEF: Nyctalopia: disorder of vision in dim light or night blindness.

368.60 Night blindness, unspecified

368.61 Congenital night blindness
     Hereditary night blindness   Oguchi's disease

368.62 Acquired night blindness
     EXCLUDES *that due to vitamin A deficiency (264.5)*

368.63 Abnormal dark adaptation curve
     Abnormal threshold } of cones or rods
     Delayed adaptation

368.69 Other night blindness

368.8 Other specified visual disturbances
     Blurred vision NOS
     AHA: 4Q, '02, 56

368.9 Unspecified visual disturbance
     AHA: 3Q, '06, 22; 1Q, '04, 15

√4ᵗʰ **369 Blindness and low vision**
     NOTE Visual impairment refers to a functional limitation of the eye (e.g., limited visual acuity or visual field). It should be distinguished from visual disability, indicating a limitation of the abilities of the individual (e.g., limited reading skills, vocational skills), and from visual handicap, indicating a limitation of personal and socioeconomic indepen- dence (e.g., limited mobility, limited employability).

     The levels of impairment defined in the table on the next page are based on the recommendations of the WHO Study Group on Prevention of Blindness (Geneva, November 6-10, 1972; WHO Technical Report Series 518), and of the International Council of Ophthalmology (1976).

     Note that definitions of blindness vary in different settings.

     For international reporting WHO defines blindness as profound impairment. This definition can be applied to blindness of one eye (369.1, 369.6) and to blindness of the individual (369.0).

     For determination of benefits in the U.S.A., the definition of legal blindness as severe impairment is often used. This definition applies to blindness of the individual only.

     EXCLUDES *correctable impaired vision due to refractive errors (367.0-367.9)*

√5ᵗʰ **369.0 Profound impairment, both eyes**

369.00 Impairment level not further specified
     Blindness:
         NOS according to WHO definition
         both eyes

369.01 Better eye: total impairment; lesser eye: total impairment

369.02 Better eye: near-total impairment; lesser eye: not further specified

369.03 Better eye: near-total impairment; lesser eye: total impairment

369.04 Better eye: near-total impairment; lesser eye: near-total impairment

369.05 Better eye: profound impairment; lesser eye: not further specified

369.06 Better eye: profound impairment; lesser eye: total impairment

369.07 Better eye: profound impairment; lesser eye: near-total impairment

369.08 Better eye: profound impairment; lesser eye: profound impairment

√4ᵗʰ **369.1 Moderate or severe impairment, better eye, profound impairment lesser eye**

369.10 Impairment level not further specified
     Blindness, one eye, low vision other eye

369.11 Better eye: severe impairment; lesser eye: blind, not further specified

369.12 Better eye: severe impairment; lesser eye: total impairment

369.13 Better eye: severe impairment; lesser eye: near-total impairment

369.14 Better eye: severe impairment; lesser eye: profound impairment

369.15 Better eye: moderate impairment; lesser eye: blind, not further specified

369.16 Better eye: moderate impairment; lesser eye: total impairment

369.17 Better eye: moderate impairment; lesser eye: near-total impairment

369.18 Better eye: moderate impairment; lesser eye: profound impairment

√5ᵗʰ **369.2 Moderate or severe impairment, both eyes**

369.20 Impairment level not further specified
     Low vision, both eyes NOS

369.21 Better eye: severe impairment; lesser eye: not further specified

369.22 Better eye: severe impairment; lesser eye: severe impairment

369.23 Better eye: moderate impairment; lesser eye: not further specified

369.24 Better eye: moderate impairment; lesser eye: severe impairment

369.25 Better eye: moderate impairment; lesser eye: moderate impairment

369.3 Unqualified visual loss, both eyes
     EXCLUDES *blindness NOS:*
         legal [U.S.A. definition] (369.4)
         WHO definition (369.00)

369.4 Legal blindness, as defined in U.S.A.
     Blindness NOS according to U.S.A. definition
     EXCLUDES *legal blindness with specification of impairment level (369.01-369.08, 369.11-369.14, 369.21-369.22)*
     H54.8 Legal blindness as defined in USA   I-10

√5ᵗʰ **369.6 Profound impairment, one eye**

369.60 Impairment level not further specified
     Blindness, one eye

369.61 One eye: total impairment; other eye: not specified

369.62 One eye: total impairment; other eye: near normal vision

369.63 One eye: total impairment; other eye: normal vision

369.64 One eye: near-total impairment; other eye: not specified

369.65 One eye: near-total impairment; other eye: near-normal vision

369.66 One eye: near-total impairment; other eye: normal vision

369.67 One eye: profound impairment; other eye: not specified

369.68 One eye: profound impairment; other eye: near-normal vision

369.69 One eye: profound impairment; other eye: normal vision

√5ᵗʰ **369.7 Moderate or severe impairment, one eye**

369.70 Impairment level not further specified
     Low vision, one eye

369.71 One eye: severe impairment; other eye: not specified

369.72 One eye: severe impairment; other eye: near-normal vision

369.73 One eye: severe impairment; other eye: normal vision

369.74 One eye: moderate impairment; other eye: not specified

369.75 One eye: moderate impairment; other eye: near-normal vision

√4ᵗʰ √5ᵗʰ Additional Digit Required   Unacceptable PDx   Manifestation Code   Hospital Acquired Condition   ▶◀ Revised Text   ● New Code   ▲ Revised Code Title

2015 ICD-9-CM   **Volume 1 – 121**

Diseases of the Nervous System and Sense Organs

369.76–370.64

Classification		LEVELS OF VISUAL IMPAIRMENT	Additional descriptors which may be encountered
"legal"	WHO	Visual acuity and/or visual field limitation (whichever is worse)	
	(N E A R-) N O R M A L V I S I O N	RANGE OF NORMAL VISION 20/10 20/13 20/16 20/20 20/25 2.0 1.6 1.25 1.0 0.8	
		NEAR-NORMAL VISION 20/30 20/40 20/50 20/60 0.7 0.6 0.5 0.4 0.3	
L E G A L B L I N D N E S S (U.S.A.) both eyes	L O W V I S I O N	MODERATE VISUAL IMPAIRMENT 20/70 20/80 20/100 20/125 20/160 0.25 0.20 0.16 0.12	Moderate low vision
		SEVERE VISUAL IMPAIRMENT 20/200 20/250 20/320 20/400 0.10 0.08 0.06 0.05 Visual field: 20 degrees or less	Severe low vision, "Legal" blindness
	B L I N D N E S S (WHO) one or both eyes	PROFOUND VISUAL IMPAIRMENT 20/500 20/630 20/800 20/1000 0.04 0.03 0.025 0.02 Count fingers at: less than 3m (10 ft.) Visual field: 10 degrees or less	Profound low vision, Moderate blindness
		NEAR-TOTAL VISUAL IMPAIRMENT Visual acuity: less than 0.02 (20/1000) Count fingers at: 1m (3 ft.) or less Hand movements: 5m (15 ft.) or less Light projection, light perception Visual field: 5 degrees or less	Severe blindness Near-total blindness
		TOTAL VISUAL IMPAIRMENT No light perception (NLP)	Total blindness

Visual acuity refers to best achievable acuity with correction.

Non-listed Snellen fractions may be classified by converting to the nearest decimal equivalent, e.g. 10/200 = 0.05, 6/30 = 0.20.

CF (count fingers) without designation of distance, may be classified to profound impairment.

HM (hand motion) without designation of distance, may be classified to near-total impairment.

Visual field measurements refer to the largest field diameter for a 1/100 white test object.

369.76 One eye: moderate impairment; other eye: normal vision

369.8 Unqualified visual loss, one eye

369.9 Unspecified visual loss
> AHA: 4Q, '02, 114; 3Q, '02, 20

√4th **370 Keratitis**

√5th **370.0 Corneal ulcer**
> EXCLUDES that due to vitamin A deficiency (264.3)

370.00 Corneal ulcer, unspecified

370.01 Marginal corneal ulcer

370.02 Ring corneal ulcer

370.03 Central corneal ulcer

370.04 Hypopyon ulcer
> Serpiginous ulcer
> DEF: Corneal ulcer with an accumulation of pus in the eye's anterior chamber.

370.05 Mycotic corneal ulcer
> DEF: Fungal infection causing corneal tissue loss.

370.06 Perforated corneal ulcer
> DEF: Tissue loss through all layers of cornea.

370.07 Mooren's ulcer
> DEF: Tissue loss, with chronic inflammation, at junction of cornea and sclera; seen in elderly.

√5th **370.2 Superficial keratitis without conjunctivitis**
> EXCLUDES dendritic [herpes simplex] keratitis (054.42)

370.20 Superficial keratitis, unspecified

370.21 Punctate keratitis
> Thygeson's superficial punctate keratitis
> DEF: Formation of cellular and fibrinous deposits (keratic precipitates) on posterior surface; deposits develop after injury or iridocyclitis.

370.22 Macular keratitis
> Keratitis: Keratitis:
> areolar   stellate
> nummular   striate

370.23 Filamentary keratitis
> DEF: Keratitis characterized by twisted filaments of mucoid material on the cornea's surface.

370.24 Photokeratitis
> Snow blindness   Welders' keratitis
> DEF: Painful, inflamed cornea; due to extended exposure to ultraviolet light.
> AHA: 3Q, '96, 6

√5th **370.3 Certain types of keratoconjunctivitis**

370.31 Phlyctenular keratoconjunctivitis
> Phlyctenulosis
> Use additional code for any associated tuberculosis (017.3)
> DEF: Miniature blister on conjunctiva or cornea; associated with tuberculosis and malnutrition disorders.

370.32 Limbar and corneal involvement in vernal conjunctivitis
> Use additional code for vernal conjunctivitis (372.13)
> DEF: Corneal itching and inflammation in conjunctivitis; often limited to lining of eyelids.

370.33 Keratoconjunctivitis sicca, not specified as Sjögren's
> EXCLUDES Sjögren's syndrome (710.2)
> DEF: Inflammation of conjunctiva and cornea; characterized by "horny" looking tissue and excess blood in these areas; decreased flow of lacrimal (tear) is a contributing factor.

370.34 Exposure keratoconjunctivitis
> DEF: Incomplete closure of eyelid causing dry, inflamed eye.
> AHA: 3Q, '96, 6

370.35 Neurotrophic keratoconjunctivitis

√5th **370.4 Other and unspecified keratoconjunctivitis**

370.40 Keratoconjunctivitis, unspecified
> Superficial keratitis with conjunctivitis NOS

370.44 *Keratitis or keratoconjunctivitis in exanthema*
> *Code first underlying condition (050.0-052.9)*
> EXCLUDES herpes simplex (054.43)
> herpes zoster (053.21)
> measles (055.71)

370.49 Other
> EXCLUDES epidemic keratoconjunctivitis (077.1)

√5th **370.5 Interstitial and deep keratitis**

370.50 Interstitial keratitis, unspecified

370.52 Diffuse interstitial keratitis
> Cogan's syndrome
> DEF: Inflammation of cornea; with deposits in middle corneal layers; may obscure vision.

370.54 Sclerosing keratitis
> DEF: Chronic corneal inflammation leading to opaque scarring.

370.55 Corneal abscess
> DEF: Pocket of pus and inflammation on the cornea.

370.59 Other
> EXCLUDES disciform herpes simplex keratitis (054.43)
> syphilitic keratitis (090.3)

√5th **370.6 Corneal neovascularization**

370.60 Corneal neovascularization, unspecified

370.61 Localized vascularization of cornea
> DEF: Limited infiltration of cornea by new blood vessels.

370.62 Pannus (corneal)
> DEF: Buildup of superficial vascularization and granulated tissue under epithelium of cornea.
> AHA: 3Q, '02, 20

370.63 Deep vascularization of cornea
> DEF: Deep infiltration of cornea by new blood vessels.

370.64 Ghost vessels (corneal)

N Newborn Age: 0   P Pediatric Age: 0-17   M Maternity Age: 12-55   A Adult Age: 15-124   MCC Major CC Condition   CC CC Condition   HIV HIV Related Dx

122 – Volume 1   **2015 ICD-9-CM**

370.8 Other forms of keratitis
Code first underlying condition, such as:
Acanthamoeba (136.21)
Fusarium (118)
AHA: 4Q, '08, 80-81; 3Q, '94, 5

370.9 Unspecified keratitis

√4ᵗʰ **371 Corneal opacity and other disorders of cornea**

√5ᵗʰ **371.0 Corneal scars and opacities**
EXCLUDES   that due to vitamin A deficiency (264.6)

371.00 Corneal opacity, unspecified
Corneal scar NOS

371.01 Minor opacity of cornea
Corneal nebula

371.02 Peripheral opacity of cornea
Corneal macula not interfering with central vision

371.03 Central opacity of cornea
Corneal:
leucoma   } interfering with central
macula   } vision

371.04 Adherent leucoma
DEF: Dense, opaque corneal growth adhering to the iris; also spelled as leukoma.

371.05 Phthisical cornea
Code first underlying tuberculosis (017.3)

√5ᵗʰ **371.1 Corneal pigmentations and deposits**

371.10 Corneal deposit, unspecified

371.11 Anterior pigmentations
Stähli's lines

371.12 Stromal pigmentations
Hematocornea

371.13 Posterior pigmentations
Krukenberg spindle

371.14 Kayser-Fleischer ring
DEF: Copper deposits forming ring at outer edge of cornea; seen in Wilson's disease and other liver disorders.

371.15 Other deposits associated with metabolic disorders

371.16 Argentous deposits
DEF: Silver deposits in cornea.

√5ᵗʰ **371.2 Corneal edema**

371.20 Corneal edema, unspecified

371.21 Idiopathic corneal edema
DEF: Corneal swelling and fluid retention of unknown cause.

371.22 Secondary corneal edema
DEF: Corneal swelling and fluid retention caused by an underlying disease, injury, or condition.

371.23 Bullous keratopathy
DEF: Corneal degeneration; characterized by recurring, rupturing epithelial "blisters;" ruptured blebs expose corneal nerves; occurs in glaucoma, iridocyclitis and Fuchs' epithelial dystrophy.

371.24 Corneal edema due to wearing of contact lenses

√5ᵗʰ **371.3 Changes of corneal membranes**

371.30 Corneal membrane change, unspecified

371.31 Folds and rupture of Bowman's membrane

371.32 Folds in Descemet's membrane

371.33 Rupture in Descemet's membrane

√5ᵗʰ **371.4 Corneal degenerations**

371.40 Corneal degeneration, unspecified

371.41 Senile corneal changes
Arcus senilis   Hassall-Henle bodies

371.42 Recurrent erosion of cornea
EXCLUDES   Mooren's ulcer (370.07)

371.43 Band-shaped keratopathy
DEF: Horizontal bands of superficial corneal calcium deposits.

371.44 Other calcerous degenerations of cornea

371.45 Keratomalacia NOS
EXCLUDES   that due to vitamin A deficiency (264.4)
DEF: Destruction of the cornea by keratinization of the epithelium with ulceration and perforation of the cornea; seen in cases of vitamin A deficiency.

371.46 Nodular degeneration of cornea
Salzmann's nodular dystrophy

371.48 Peripheral degenerations of cornea
Marginal degeneration of cornea [Terrien's]

371.49 Other
Discrete colliquative keratopathy

√5ᵗʰ **371.5 Hereditary corneal dystrophies**
DEF: Genetic disorder; leads to opacities, edema or lesions of cornea.

371.50 Corneal dystrophy, unspecified

371.51 Juvenile epithelial corneal dystrophy

371.52 Other anterior corneal dystrophies
Corneal dystrophy: Corneal dystrophy:
microscopic cystic   ring-like

371.53 Granular corneal dystrophy

371.54 Lattice corneal dystrophy

371.55 Macular corneal dystrophy

371.56 Other stromal corneal dystrophies
Crystalline corneal dystrophy

371.57 Endothelial corneal dystrophy
Combined corneal dystrophy   Fuchs' endothelial
Cornea guttata   dystrophy

371.58 Other posterior corneal dystrophies
Polymorphous corneal dystrophy

√5ᵗʰ **371.6 Keratoconus**
DEF: Bilateral bulging protrusion of anterior cornea; often due to noninflammatory thinning.

371.60 Keratoconus, unspecified

371.61 Keratoconus, stable condition

371.62 Keratoconus, acute hydrops

√5ᵗʰ **371.7 Other corneal deformities**

371.70 Corneal deformity, unspecified

371.71 Corneal ectasia
DEF: Bulging protrusion of thinned, scarred cornea.

371.72 Descemetocele
DEF: Protrusion of Descemet's membrane into cornea.

371.73 Corneal staphyloma
DEF: Protrusion of cornea into adjacent tissue.

√5ᵗʰ **371.8 Other corneal disorders**

371.81 Corneal anesthesia and hypoesthesia
DEF: Decreased or absent sensitivity of cornea.

371.82 Corneal disorder due to contact lens
EXCLUDES   corneal edema due to contact lens (371.24)
DEF: Contact lens wear causing cornea disorder, excluding swelling.

371.89 Other
AHA: 3Q, '99, 12

371.9 Unspecified corneal disorder

√4ᵗʰ **372 Disorders of conjunctiva**
EXCLUDES   keratoconjunctivitis (370.3-370.4)

√5ᵗʰ **372.0 Acute conjunctivitis**

372.00 Acute conjunctivitis, unspecified

372.01 Serous conjunctivitis, except viral
EXCLUDES   viral conjunctivitis NOS (077.9)
AHA: 3Q, '08, 6

√4ᵗʰ
√5ᵗʰ Additional Digit Required | Unacceptable PDx | Manifestation Code | Hospital Acquired Condition | ►◄ Revised Text   ● New Code   ▲ Revised Code Title

372.02 Acute follicular conjunctivitis
Conjunctival folliculosis NOS
EXCLUDES *conjunctivitis:*
adenoviral (acute follicular) (077.3)
epidemic hemorrhagic (077.4)
inclusion (077.0)
Newcastle (077.8)
epidemic keratoconjunctivitis (077.1)
pharyngoconjunctival fever (077.2)
DEF: Severe conjunctival inflammation with dense infiltrations of lymphoid tissues of inner eyelids; may be traced to a viral or chlamydial etiology.

372.03 Other mucopurulent conjunctivitis
Catarrhal conjunctivitis
EXCLUDES *blennorrhea neonatorum (gonococcal) (098.40)*
neonatal conjunctivitis(771.6)
ophthalmia neonatorum NOS (771.6)

372.04 Pseudomembranous conjunctivitis
Membranous conjunctivitis
EXCLUDES *diphtheritic conjunctivitis (032.81)*
DEF: Severe inflammation of conjunctiva; false membrane develops on inner surface of eyelid; membrane can be removed without harming epithelium, due to bacterial infections, toxic and allergic factors, and viral infections.

372.05 Acute atopic conjunctivitis
DEF: Sudden, severe conjunctivitis due to allergens.

372.06 Acute chemical conjunctivitis
Acute toxic conjunctivitis
Use additional E code to identify the chemical or toxic agent
EXCLUDES *burn of eye and adnexa (940.0-940.9)*
chemical corrosion injury of eye (940.2-940.3)
AHA: 4Q, '09, 85

√5th **372.1 Chronic conjunctivitis**

372.10 Chronic conjunctivitis, unspecified

372.11 Simple chronic conjunctivitis

372.12 Chronic follicular conjunctivitis
DEF: Persistent conjunctival inflammation with dense, localized infiltrations of lymphoid tissues of inner eyelids.

372.13 Vernal conjunctivitis
AHA: 3Q, '96, 8

372.14 Other chronic allergic conjunctivitis
AHA: 3Q, '96, 8

372.15 Parasitic conjunctivitis
Code first underlying disease, as:
filariasis (125.0-125.9)
mucocutaneous leishmaniasis (085.5)

√5th **372.2 Blepharoconjunctivitis**

372.20 Blepharoconjunctivitis, unspecified

372.21 Angular blepharoconjunctivitis
DEF: Inflammation at junction of upper and lower eyelids; may block lacrimal secretions.

372.22 Contact blepharoconjunctivitis

√5th **372.3 Other and unspecified conjunctivitis**

372.30 Conjunctivitis, unspecified
H10.9 Unspecified conjunctivitis   I-10

372.31 Rosacea conjunctivitis
Code first underlying rosacea dermatitis (695.3)

372.33 Conjunctivitis in mucocutaneous disease
Code first underlying disease, as:
erythema multiforme (695.10-695.19)
Reiter's disease (099.3)
EXCLUDES *ocular pemphigoid (694.61)*

372.34 Pingueculitis
EXCLUDES *pinguecula (372.51)*
AHA: 4Q, '08, 112-113

372.39 Other
AHA: 2Q, '07, 9

√5th **372.4 Pterygium**
EXCLUDES *pseudopterygium (372.52)*
DEF: Wedge-shaped, conjunctival thickening that advances from the inner corner of the eye toward the cornea.

372.40 Pterygium, unspecified

372.41 Peripheral pterygium, stationary

372.42 Peripheral pterygium, progressive

372.43 Central pterygium

372.44 Double pterygium

372.45 Recurrent pterygium

√5th **372.5 Conjunctival degenerations and deposits**

372.50 Conjunctival degeneration, unspecified

372.51 Pinguecula
EXCLUDES *pingueculitis (372.34)*
DEF: Proliferative spot on the bulbar conjunctiva located near the sclerocorneal junction, usually on the nasal side; it is seen in elderly people.

372.52 Pseudopterygium
DEF: Conjunctival scar joined to the cornea; it looks like a pterygium but is not attached to the tissue.

372.53 Conjunctival xerosis
EXCLUDES *conjunctival xerosis due to vitamin A deficiency (264.0, 264.1, 264.7)*
DEF: Dry conjunctiva due to vitamin A deficiency; related to Bitot's spots; may develop into xerophthalmia and keratomalacia.

372.54 Conjunctival concretions
DEF: Calculus or deposit on conjunctiva.

372.55 Conjunctival pigmentations
Conjunctival argyrosis
DEF: Color deposits in conjunctiva.

372.56 Conjunctival deposits

√5th **372.6 Conjunctival scars**

372.61 Granuloma of conjunctiva

372.62 Localized adhesions and strands of conjunctiva
DEF: Abnormal fibrous connections in conjunctiva.

372.63 Symblepharon
Extensive adhesions of conjunctiva
DEF: Adhesion of the eyelids to the eyeball.

372.64 Scarring of conjunctiva
Contraction of eye socket (after enucleation)

√5th **372.7 Conjunctival vascular disorders and cysts**

372.71 Hyperemia of conjunctiva
DEF: Conjunctival blood vessel congestion causing eye redness.

372.72 Conjunctival hemorrhage
Hyposphagma   Subconjunctival hemorrhage

372.73 Conjunctival edema
Chemosis of conjunctiva
Subconjunctival edema
DEF: Fluid retention and swelling in conjunctival tissue.

372.74 Vascular abnormalities of conjunctiva
Aneurysm(ata) of conjunctiva

372.75 Conjunctival cysts
DEF: Abnormal sacs of fluid in conjunctiva.

√5th **372.8 Other disorders of conjunctiva**

372.81 Conjunctivochalasis
AHA: 4Q, '00, 41
DEF: Bilateral condition of redundant conjunctival tissue between globe and lower eyelid margin; may cover lower punctum, interfering with normal tearing.

372.89 Other disorders of conjunctiva

372.9 Unspecified disorder of conjunctiva

✓4ᵗʰ **373 Inflammation of eyelids**

  ✓5ᵗʰ **373.0 Blepharitis**

    EXCLUDES *blepharoconjunctivitis (372.20-372.22)*

    373.00 Blepharitis, unspecified

    373.01 Ulcerative blepharitis

    373.02 Squamous blepharitis

  ✓5ᵗʰ **373.1 Hordeolum and other deep inflammation of eyelid**

    DEF: Purulent, localized, staphylococcal infection in sebaceous glands of eyelids.

    373.11 Hordeolum externum

      Hordeolum NOS   Stye

      DEF: Infection of the oil glands in the eyelash follicles.

    373.12 Hordeolum internum

      Infection of meibomian gland

      DEF: Infection of the oil gland of the eyelid margin.

    373.13 Abscess of eyelid

      Furuncle of eyelid

      DEF: Inflamed pocket of pus on the eyelid.

  373.2 Chalazion

    Meibomian (gland) cyst

    EXCLUDES *infected meibomian gland (373.12)*

    DEF: Chronic inflammation of the meibomian gland, causing an eyelid mass.

  ✓5ᵗʰ **373.3 Noninfectious dermatoses of eyelid**

    373.31 Eczematous dermatitis of eyelid

    373.32 Contact and allergic dermatitis of eyelid

    373.33 Xeroderma of eyelid

    373.34 Discoid lupus erythematosus of eyelid

  373.4 *Infective dermatitis of eyelid of types resulting in deformity*

    Code first underlying disease, as:

      leprosy (030.0-030.9)

      lupus vulgaris (tuberculous) (017.0)

      yaws (102.0-102.9)

  373.5 *Other infective dermatitis of eyelid*

    Code first underlying disease, as:

      actinomycosis (039.3)

      impetigo (684)

      mycotic dermatitis (110.0-111.9)

      vaccinia (051.0)

      postvaccination (999.0)

    EXCLUDES *herpes:*

      simplex (054.41)

      zoster (053.20)

  373.6 *Parasitic infestation of eyelid*

    Code first underlying disease, as:

      leishmaniasis (085.0-085.9)

      loiasis (125.2)

      onchocerciasis (125.3)

      pediculosis (132.0)

  373.8 Other inflammations of eyelids

  373.9 Unspecified inflammation of eyelid

✓4ᵗʰ **374 Other disorders of eyelids**

  ✓5ᵗʰ **374.0 Entropion and trichiasis of eyelid**

    DEF: Entropion: turning inward of eyelid edge toward eyeball.

    DEF: Trichiasis: ingrowing eyelashes marked by irritation with possible distortion of sight.

    374.00 Entropion, unspecified

    374.01 Senile entropion Ⓐ

    374.02 Mechanical entropion

    374.03 Spastic entropion

    374.04 Cicatricial entropion

    374.05 Trichiasis without entropion

  ✓5ᵗʰ **374.1 Ectropion**

    DEF: Turning outward (eversion) of eyelid edge; exposes palpebral conjunctiva; dryness irritation result.

    374.10 Ectropion, unspecified

Entropion and Ectropion

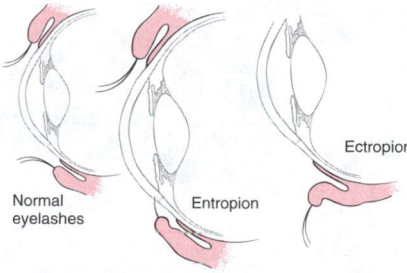

Normal eyelashes   Entropion   Ectropion

    374.11 Senile ectropion Ⓐ

    374.12 Mechanical ectropion

    374.13 Spastic ectropion

    374.14 Cicatricial ectropion

  ✓5ᵗʰ **374.2 Lagophthalmos**

    DEF: Incomplete closure of eyes; causes dry eye and other complications.

    374.20 Lagophthalmos, unspecified

    374.21 Paralytic lagophthalmos

    374.22 Mechanical lagophthalmos

    374.23 Cicatricial lagophthalmos

  ✓5ᵗʰ **374.3 Ptosis of eyelid**

    374.30 Ptosis of eyelid, unspecified

      AHA: 2Q, '96, 11

    374.31 Paralytic ptosis

      DEF: Drooping of upper eyelid due to nerve disorder.

    374.32 Myogenic ptosis

      DEF: Drooping of upper eyelid due to muscle disorder.

    374.33 Mechanical ptosis

      DEF: Outside force causes drooping of upper eyelid.

    374.34 Blepharochalasis

      Pseudoptosis

      DEF: Loss of elasticity, thickened or indurated skin of eyelids associated with recurrent episodes of idiopathic edema causing intracellular tissue atrophy.

  ✓5ᵗʰ **374.4 Other disorders affecting eyelid function**

    EXCLUDES *blepharoclonus (333.81)*

      blepharospasm (333.81)

      facial nerve palsy (351.0)

      third nerve palsy or paralysis (378.51-378.52)

      tic (psychogenic) (307.20-307.23)

      organic (333.3)

    374.41 Lid retraction or lag

    374.43 Abnormal innervation syndrome

      Jaw-blinking   Paradoxical facial movements

    374.44 Sensory disorders

    374.45 Other sensorimotor disorders

      Deficient blink reflex

    374.46 Blepharophimosis

      Ankyloblepharon

      DEF: Narrowing of palpebral fissure horizontally; caused by laterally displaced inner canthi; either acquired or congenital.

  ✓5ᵗʰ **374.5 Degenerative disorders of eyelid and periocular area**

    374.50 Degenerative disorder of eyelid, unspecified

    374.51 *Xanthelasma*

      Xanthoma (planum) (tuberosum) of eyelid

      Code first underlying condition (272.0-272.9)

      DEF: Fatty tumors of the eyelid linked to high fat content of blood.

    374.52 Hyperpigmentation of eyelid

      Chloasma   Dyspigmentation

      DEF: Excess pigment of eyelid.

✓4ᵗʰ ✓5ᵗʰ Additional Digit Required   Unacceptable PDx   Manifestation Code   Hospital Acquired Condition   ►◄ Revised Text   ● New Code   ▲ Revised Code Title

2015 ICD-9-CM   **Volume 1 – 125**

Diseases of the Nervous System and Sense Organs

374.53–376.02

Lacrimal System

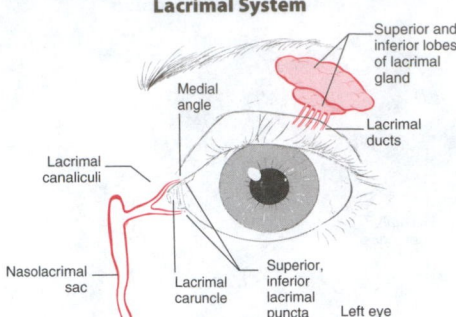

Superior and inferior lobes of lacrimal gland
Medial angle
Lacrimal ducts
Lacrimal canaliculi
Nasolacrimal sac
Lacrimal caruncle
Superior, inferior lacrimal puncta
Left eye

374.53 Hypopigmentation of eyelid
Vitiligo of eyelid
DEF: Lack of color pigment of the eyelid.

374.54 Hypertrichosis of eyelid
DEF: Excessive eyelash growth.

374.55 Hypotrichosis of eyelid
Madarosis of eyelid
DEF: Less than normal, or absent, eyelashes.

374.56 Other degenerative disorders of skin affecting eyelid

✓5ᵗʰ **374.8 Other disorders of eyelid**

374.81 Hemorrhage of eyelid
EXCLUDES black eye (921.0)

374.82 Edema of eyelid
Hyperemia of eyelid
DEF: Swelling and fluid retention in eyelid.
AHA: 4Q, '08, 131

374.83 Elephantiasis of eyelid
DEF: Filarial disease causing dermatitis and enlargement of eyelid.

374.84 Cysts of eyelids
Sebaceous cyst of eyelid

374.85 Vascular anomalies of eyelid

374.86 Retained foreign body of eyelid
Use additional code to identify foreign body (V90.01-V90.9)

374.87 Dermatochalasis
DEF: Acquired form of connective tissue disorder associated with decreased elastic tissue and abnormal elastin formation resulting in loss of elasticity of the skin of the eyelid, generally associated with aging.

374.89 Other disorders of eyelid

374.9 Unspecified disorder of eyelid

✓4ᵗʰ **375 Disorders of lacrimal system**

✓5ᵗʰ **375.0 Dacryoadenitis**

375.00 Dacryoadenitis, unspecified

375.01 Acute dacryoadenitis
DEF: Severe, sudden inflammation of the lacrimal gland.

375.02 Chronic dacryoadenitis
DEF: Persistent inflammation of the lacrimal gland.

375.03 Chronic enlargement of lacrimal gland

✓5ᵗʰ **375.1 Other disorders of lacrimal gland**

375.11 Dacryops
DEF: Overproduction and constant flow of tears; may cause distended lacrimal duct.

375.12 Other lacrimal cysts and cystic degeneration

375.13 Primary lacrimal atrophy

375.14 Secondary lacrimal atrophy
DEF: Wasting away of the lacrimal gland due to another disease.

375.15 Tear film insufficiency, unspecified
Dry eye syndrome
AHA: 3Q, '96, 6
DEF: Eye dryness and irritation from insufficient tear production.

375.16 Dislocation of lacrimal gland

✓5ᵗʰ **375.2 Epiphora**
DEF: Abnormal development of tears due to stricture of lacrimal passages.

375.20 Epiphora, unspecified as to cause

375.21 Epiphora due to excess lacrimation
DEF: Tear overflow due to overproduction.

375.22 Epiphora due to insufficient drainage
DEF: Tear overflow due to blocked drainage.

✓5ᵗʰ **375.3 Acute and unspecified inflammation of lacrimal passages**
EXCLUDES neonatal dacryocystitis (771.6)

375.30 Dacryocystitis, unspecified

375.31 Acute canaliculitis, lacrimal

375.32 Acute dacryocystitis
Acute peridacryocystitis

375.33 Phlegmonous dacryocystitis
DEF: Infection of the tear sac with pockets of pus.

✓5ᵗʰ **375.4 Chronic inflammation of lacrimal passages**

375.41 Chronic canaliculitis

375.42 Chronic dacryocystitis

375.43 Lacrimal mucocele

✓5ᵗʰ **375.5 Stenosis and insufficiency of lacrimal passages**

375.51 Eversion of lacrimal punctum
DEF: Abnormal turning outward of the tear duct.

375.52 Stenosis of lacrimal punctum
DEF: Abnormal narrowing of the tear duct.

375.53 Stenosis of lacrimal canaliculi

375.54 Stenosis of lacrimal sac
DEF: Abnormal narrowing of the tear sac.

375.55 Obstruction of nasolacrimal duct, neonatal
EXCLUDES congenital anomaly of nasola- crimal duct (743.65)
DEF: Acquired, abnormal obstruction of tear drainage system from the eye to the nose; in an infant.

375.56 Stenosis of nasolacrimal duct, acquired

375.57 Dacryolith
DEF: Concretion or stone anywhere in lacrimal system.

✓5ᵗʰ **375.6 Other changes of lacrimal passages**

375.61 Lacrimal fistula
DEF: Abnormal communication from the lacrimal system.

375.69 Other

✓5ᵗʰ **375.8 Other disorders of lacrimal system**

375.81 Granuloma of lacrimal passages
DEF: Abnormal nodules within lacrimal system.

375.89 Other

375.9 Unspecified disorder of lacrimal system

✓4ᵗʰ **376 Disorders of the orbit**

✓5ᵗʰ **376.0 Acute inflammation of orbit**

376.00 Acute inflammation of orbit, unspecified

376.01 Orbital cellulitis   CC
Abscess of orbit
DEF: Infection of tissue between the orbital bone and eyeball.
CC Excl: 376.00-376.04

376.02 Orbital periostitis   CC
DEF: Inflammation of connective tissue covering the orbital bone.
CC Excl: 003.24, 015.50-015.56, 015.70-015.76, 015.90-015.96, 017.90-017.96, 376.02, 730.00-730.39, 730.80-730.99

376.03 Orbital osteomyelitis `CC`
DEF: Inflammation of the orbital bone.
CC Excl: 003.24, 015.50-015.56, 015.70-015.76, 015.90-015.96, 017.90-017.96, 376.03, 730.00-730.39, 730.80-730.99

376.04 Tenonitis

✓5ᵗʰ **376.1 Chronic inflammatory disorders of orbit**

376.10 Chronic inflammation of orbit, unspecified

376.11 Orbital granuloma
Pseudotumor (inflammatory) of orbit
DEF: Abnormal nodule between orbital bone and eyeball.

376.12 Orbital myositis
DEF: Painful inflammation of the muscles of the eye.

376.13 Parasitic infestation of orbit
Code first underlying disease, as:
hydatid infestation of orbit (122.3, 122.6, 122.9)
myiasis of orbit (134.0)

✓5ᵗʰ **376.2 Endocrine exophthalmos**
Code first underlying thyroid disorder (242.0-242.9)

376.21 Thyrotoxic exophthalmos
DEF: Painful inflammation of eye muscles.

376.22 Exophthalmic ophthalmoplegia
DEF: Inability to rotate eye as a result of bulging eyes.

✓5ᵗʰ **376.3 Other exophthalmic conditions**

376.30 Exophthalmos, unspecified
DEF: Abnormal protrusion of eyeball.

376.31 Constant exophthalmos
DEF: Continuous, abnormal protrusion or bulging of eyeball.

376.32 Orbital hemorrhage
DEF: Bleeding behind the eyeball, causing it to bulge.

376.33 Orbital edema or congestion
DEF: Fluid retention behind eyeball, causing forward bulge.

376.34 Intermittent exophthalmos

376.35 Pulsating exophthalmos
DEF: Bulge or protrusion; associated with a carotid-cavernous fistula.

376.36 Lateral displacement of globe
DEF: Abnormal displacement of the eyeball away from nose, toward temple.

✓5ᵗʰ **376.4 Deformity of orbit**

376.40 Deformity of orbit, unspecified

376.41 Hypertelorism of orbit
DEF: Abnormal increase in interorbital distance; associated with congenital facial deformities; may be accompanied by mental deficiency.

376.42 Exostosis of orbit
DEF: Abnormal bony growth of orbit.

376.43 Local deformities due to bone disease
DEF: Acquired abnormalities of orbit; due to bone disease.

376.44 Orbital deformities associated with craniofacial deformities

376.45 Atrophy of orbit
DEF: Wasting away of bone tissue of orbit.

376.46 Enlargement of orbit

376.47 Deformity due to trauma or surgery

✓5ᵗʰ **376.5 Enophthalmos**
DEF: Recession of eyeball deep into eye socket.

376.50 Enophthalmos, unspecified as to cause

376.51 Enophthalmos due to atrophy of orbital tissue

376.52 Enophthalmos due to trauma or surgery

376.6 Retained (old) foreign body following penetrating wound of orbit
Retrobulbar foreign body
Use additional code to identify foreign body (V90.01-V90.9)

✓5ᵗʰ **376.8 Other orbital disorders**

376.81 Orbital cysts
Encephalocele of orbit
AHA: 3Q, '99, 13

376.82 Myopathy of extraocular muscles
DEF: Disease in the muscles that control eyeball movement.

376.89 Other

376.9 Unspecified disorder of orbit

✓4ᵗʰ **377 Disorders of optic nerve and visual pathways**

✓5ᵗʰ **377.0 Papilledema**

377.00 Papilledema, unspecified `CC`
CC Excl: 017.30-017.36, 017.90-017.96, 036.81, 249.50-249.51, 249.80-249.91, 250.50-250.53, 250.80-250.93, 377.00-377.03, 377.14, 377.24, 379.60-379.90, 379.99, 743.8-743.9

377.01 Papilledema associated with increased intracranial pressure `CC`
CC Excl: See code: 377.00

377.02 Papilledema associated with decreased ocular pressure

377.03 Papilledema associated with retinal disorder

377.04 Foster-Kennedy syndrome
DEF: Retrobulbar optic neuritis, central scotoma and optic atrophy; caused by tumors in frontal lobe of brain that press downward.

✓5ᵗʰ **377.1 Optic atrophy**

377.10 Optic atrophy, unspecified

377.11 Primary optic atrophy
EXCLUDES neurosyphilitic optic atrophy (094.84)

377.12 Postinflammatory optic atrophy
DEF:: Adverse effect of inflammation causing wasting away of eye.

377.13 Optic atrophy associated with retinal dystrophies
DEF: Progressive changes in retinal tissue due to metabolic disorder causing wasting away of eye.

377.14 Glaucomatous atrophy [cupping] of optic disc

377.15 Partial optic atrophy
Temporal pallor of optic disc

377.16 Hereditary optic atrophy
Optic atrophy: Optic atrophy:
    dominant hereditary   Leber's

✓5ᵗʰ **377.2 Other disorders of optic disc**

377.21 Drusen of optic disc

377.22 Crater-like holes of optic disc

377.23 Coloboma of optic disc
DEF: Ocular malformation caused by the failure of fetal fissure of optic stalk to close.

377.24 Pseudopapilledema

✓5ᵗʰ **377.3 Optic neuritis**
EXCLUDES meningococcal optic neuritis (036.81)

377.30 Optic neuritis, unspecified `CC`
CC Excl: 377.30-377.39

377.31 Optic papillitis `CC`
CC Excl: See code: 377.30
DEF: Swelling and inflammation of the optic disc.

377.32 Retrobulbar neuritis (acute) `CC`
EXCLUDES syphilitic retrobulbar neuritis (094.85)
CC Excl: See code: 377.30
DEF: Inflammation of optic nerve immediately behind the eyeball.

377.33 Nutritional optic neuropathy
DEF: Malnutrition causing optic nerve disorder.

377.34 Toxic optic neuropathy
Toxic amblyopia
DEF: Toxic substance causing optic nerve disorder.

Diseases of the Nervous System and Sense Organs

377.39–378.45

377.39 Other `CC`
> EXCLUDES *ischemic optic neuropathy (377.41)*
> CC Excl: See code: 377.30

✓5ᵗʰ **377.4 Other disorders of optic nerve**

377.41 Ischemic optic neuropathy
> DEF: Decreased blood flow affecting optic nerve.

377.42 Hemorrhage in optic nerve sheaths
> DEF: Bleeding in meningeal lining of optic nerve.

377.43 Optic nerve hypoplasia
> AHA: 4Q, '06, 81

377.49 Other
> Compression of optic nerve

✓5ᵗʰ **377.5 Disorders of optic chiasm**

377.51 Associated with pituitary neoplasms and disorders `CC`
> CC Excl: 377.51-377.63
> DEF: Abnormal pituitary growth causing disruption in nerve chain from retina to brain.

377.52 Associated with other neoplasms `CC`
> CC Excl: See code: 377.51
> DEF: Abnormal growth, other than pituitary, causing disruption in nerve chain from retina to brain.

377.53 Associated with vascular disorders `CC`
> CC Excl: See code: 377.51
> DEF: Vascular disorder causing disruption in nerve chain from retina to brain.

377.54 Associated with inflammatory disorders `CC`
> CC Excl: See code: 377.51
> DEF: Inflammatory disease causing disruption in nerve chain from retina to brain.

✓5ᵗʰ **377.6 Disorders of other visual pathways**

377.61 Associated with neoplasms `CC`
> CC Excl: See code: 377.51

377.62 Associated with vascular disorders `CC`
> CC Excl: See code: 377.51

377.63 Associated with inflammatory disorders `CC`
> CC Excl: See code: 377.51

✓5ᵗʰ **377.7 Disorders of visual cortex**
> EXCLUDES *visual:*
>   *agnosia (368.16)*
>   *hallucinations (368.16)*
>   *halos (368.15)*

377.71 Associated with neoplasms `CC`
> CC Excl: 377.71-377.9

377.72 Associated with vascular disorders `CC`
> CC Excl: See code: 377.71

377.73 Associated with inflammatory disorders `CC`
> CC Excl: See code: 377.71

377.75 Cortical blindness
> DEF: Blindness due to brain disorder, rather than eye disorder.

377.9 Unspecified disorder of optic nerve and visual pathways

✓4ᵗʰ **378 Strabismus and other disorders of binocular eye movements**
> EXCLUDES *nystagmus and other irregular eye movements (379.50-379.59)*
> DEF: Misalignment of the eyes due to imbalance in extraocular muscles.

✓5ᵗʰ **378.0 Esotropia**
> Convergent concomitant strabismus
> EXCLUDES *intermittent esotropia (378.20-378.22)*
> DEF: Visual axis deviation created by one eye fixing upon an image and the other eye deviating inward.

378.00 Esotropia, unspecified

378.01 Monocular esotropia

378.02 Monocular esotropia with A pattern

378.03 Monocular esotropia with V pattern

378.04 Monocular esotropia with other noncomitancies
> Monocular esotropia with X or Y pattern

Eye Musculature

Muscles and actions (right eye)

R.   L. Monocular (one eye only) esotropia (inward)

Monocular exotropia (outward)

Monocular hypertropia (upward)

378.05 Alternating esotropia

378.06 Alternating esotropia with A pattern

378.07 Alternating esotropia with V pattern

378.08 Alternating esotropia with other noncomitancies
> Alternating esotropia with X or Y pattern

✓5ᵗʰ **378.1 Exotropia**
> Divergent concomitant strabismus
> EXCLUDES *intermittent exotropia (378.20, 378.23-378.24)*
> DEF: Visual axis deviation created by one eye fixing upon an image and the other eye deviating outward.

378.10 Exotropia, unspecified

378.11 Monocular exotropia

378.12 Monocular exotropia with A pattern

378.13 Monocular exotropia with V pattern

378.14 Monocular exotropia with other noncomitancies
> Monocular exotropia with X or Y pattern

378.15 Alternating exotropia

378.16 Alternating exotropia with A pattern

378.17 Alternating exotropia with V pattern

378.18 Alternating exotropia with other noncomitancies
> Alternating exotropia with X or Y pattern

✓5ᵗʰ **378.2 Intermittent heterotropia**
> EXCLUDES *vertical heterotropia (intermittent) (378.31)*
> DEF: Deviation of eyes seen only at intervals; it is also called strabismus.

378.20 Intermittent heterotropia, unspecified
> Intermittent: Intermittent:
> esotropia NOS   exotropia NOS

378.21 Intermittent esotropia, monocular

378.22 Intermittent esotropia, alternating

378.23 Intermittent exotropia, monocular

378.24 Intermittent exotropia, alternating

✓5ᵗʰ **378.3 Other and unspecified heterotropia**

378.30 Heterotropia, unspecified

378.31 Hypertropia
> Vertical heterotropia (constant) (intermittent)

378.32 Hypotropia

378.33 Cyclotropia

378.34 Monofixation syndrome
> Microtropia

378.35 Accommodative component in esotropia

✓5ᵗʰ **378.4 Heterophoria**
> DEF: Deviation occurring only when the other eye is covered.

378.40 Heterophoria, unspecified

378.41 Esophoria

378.42 Exophoria

378.43 Vertical heterophoria

378.44 Cyclophoria

378.45 Alternating hyperphoria

`N` Newborn Age: 0   `P` Pediatric Age: 0-17   `M` Maternity Age: 12-55   `A` Adult Age: 15-124   `MCC` Major CC Condition   `CC` CC Condition   `HIV` HIV Related Dx

√5th **378.5 Paralytic strabismus**
    DEF: Deviation of the eye due to nerve paralysis affecting muscle.

    378.50 Paralytic strabismus, unspecified

    378.51 Third or oculomotor nerve palsy, partial
        AHA: 3Q, '91, 9

    378.52 Third or oculomotor nerve palsy, total
        AHA: 2Q, '89, 12

    378.53 Fourth or trochlear nerve palsy
        AHA: 2Q, '01, 21

    378.54 Sixth or abducens nerve palsy
        AHA: 2Q, '89, 12

    378.55 External ophthalmoplegia

    378.56 Total ophthalmoplegia

√5th **378.6 Mechanical strabismus**
    DEF: Deviation of the eye due to an outside force upon the extraocular muscles.

    378.60 Mechanical strabismus, unspecified

    378.61 Brown's (tendon) sheath syndrome
        DEF: Congenital or acquired shortening of the anterior sheath of superior oblique muscle; eye is unable to move upward and inward; usually unilateral.

    378.62 Mechanical strabismus from other musculofascial disorders

    378.63 Limited duction associated with other conditions

√5th **378.7 Other specified strabismus**

    378.71 Duane's syndrome
        DEF: Congenital, affects one eye; due to abnormal fibrous bands attached to rectus muscle; inability to abduct affected eye with retraction of globe.

    378.72 Progressive external ophthalmoplegia
        DEF: Paralysis progressing from one eye muscle to another.

    378.73 Strabismus in other neuromuscular disorders

√5th **378.8 Other disorders of binocular eye movements**
    EXCLUDES *nystagmus (379.50-379.56)*

    378.81 Palsy of conjugate gaze
        DEF: Paralysis progressing from one eye muscle to another.

    378.82 Spasm of conjugate gaze
        DEF: Muscle contractions impairing parallel movement of eye.

    378.83 Convergence insufficiency or palsy

    378.84 Convergence excess or spasm

    378.85 Anomalies of divergence

    378.86 Internuclear ophthalmoplegia
        DEF: Eye movement anomaly due to brainstem lesion.

    378.87 Other dissociated deviation of eye movements
        Skew deviation

    378.9 Unspecified disorder of eye movements
        Ophthalmoplegia NOS   Strabismus NOS
        AHA: 2Q, '01, 21

√4th **379 Other disorders of eye**

√5th **379.0 Scleritis and episcleritis**
    EXCLUDES *syphilitic episcleritis (095.0)*

    379.00 Scleritis, unspecified
        Episcleritis NOS

    379.01 Episcleritis periodica fugax
        DEF: Hyperemia (engorgement) of the sclera and overlying conjunctiva characterized by a sudden onset and short duration.

    379.02 Nodular episcleritis
        DEF: Inflammation of the outermost layer of the sclera, with formation of nodules.

    379.03 Anterior scleritis

    379.04 Scleromalacia perforans
        DEF: Scleral thinning, softening and degeneration; seen with rheumatoid arthritis.

    379.05 Scleritis with corneal involvement
        Scleroperikeratitis

    379.06 Brawny scleritis
        DEF: Severe scleral inflammation with thickening corneal margins.

    379.07 Posterior scleritis
        Sclerotenonitis

    379.09 Other
        Scleral abscess

√5th **379.1 Other disorders of sclera**
    EXCLUDES *blue sclera (743.47)*

    379.11 Scleral ectasia
        Scleral staphyloma NOS
        DEF: Protrusion of the contents of the eyeball where the sclera has thinned.

    379.12 Staphyloma posticum
        DEF: Ring-shaped protrusion or bulging of sclera and uveal tissue at posterior pole of eye.

    379.13 Equatorial staphyloma
        DEF: Ring-shaped protrusion or bulging of sclera and uveal tissue midway between front and back of eye.

    379.14 Anterior staphyloma, localized

    379.15 Ring staphyloma

    379.16 Other degenerative disorders of sclera

    379.19 Other

√5th **379.2 Disorders of vitreous body**
    DEF: Disorder of clear gel that fills space between retina and lens.

    379.21 Vitreous degeneration
        Vitreous: Vitreous:
          cavitation   liquefaction
          detachment

    379.22 Crystalline deposits in vitreous
        Asteroid hyalitis   Synchysis scintillans

    379.23 Vitreous hemorrhage
        AHA: 3Q, '91, 15

    379.24 Other vitreous opacities
        Vitreous floaters

    379.25 Vitreous membranes and strands

    379.26 Vitreous prolapse
        DEF: Slipping of vitreous from normal position.

    379.27 Vitreomacular adhesion   ▲
        Vitreomacular traction
        EXCLUDES *traction detachment with vitreoretinal organization (361.81)*
        AHA: 4Q, '11, 105-106

    379.29 Other disorders of vitreous
        EXCLUDES *vitreous abscess (360.04)*
        AHA: 1Q, '99, 11

√5th **379.3 Aphakia and other disorders of lens**
    EXCLUDES *after-cataract (366.50-366.53)*

    379.31 Aphakia
        EXCLUDES *cataract extraction status (V45.61)*
        DEF: Absence of eye's crystalline lens.

    379.32 Subluxation of lens

    379.33 Anterior dislocation of lens
        DEF: Lens displaced toward iris.

    379.34 Posterior dislocation of lens
        DEF: Lens displaced backward toward vitreous.

    379.39 Other disorders of lens

√5th **379.4 Anomalies of pupillary function**

    379.40 Abnormal pupillary function, unspecified

    379.41 Anisocoria
        DEF: Unequal pupil diameter.

    379.42 Miosis (persistent), not due to miotics
        DEF: Abnormal contraction of pupil less than 2 mil.

√4th √5th Additional Digit Required   Unacceptable PDx   Manifestation Code   Hospital Acquired Condition   ►◄ Revised Text   ● New Code   ▲ Revised Code Title

379.43 Mydriasis (persistent), not due to mydriatics
DEF: Morbid dilation of pupil.

379.45 Argyll Robertson pupil, atypical
Argyll Robertson phenomenon or pupil, nonsyphilitic
EXCLUDES *Argyll Robertson pupil (syphilitic) (094.89)*
DEF: Failure of pupil to respond to light; affects both eyes; may be caused by diseases such as syphilis of the central nervous system or miosis.

379.46 Tonic pupillary reaction
Adie's pupil or syndrome

379.49 Other
Hippus   Pupillary paralysis

√5th **379.5 Nystagmus and other irregular eye movements**

379.50 Nystagmus, unspecified
AHA: 4Q, '02, 68; 2Q, '01, 21
DEF: Involuntary, rapid, rhythmic movement of eyeball; vertical, horizontal, rotatory or mixed; cause may be congenital, acquired, physiological, neurological, myopathic, or due to ocular diseases.

379.51 Congenital nystagmus

379.52 Latent nystagmus

379.53 Visual deprivation nystagmus

379.54 Nystagmus associated with disorders of the vestibular system

379.55 Dissociated nystagmus

379.56 Other forms of nystagmus

379.57 Deficiencies of saccadic eye movements
Abnormal optokinetic response
DEF: Saccadic eye movements; small, rapid, involuntary movements by both eyes simultaneously, due to changing point of fixation on visualized object.

379.58 Deficiencies of smooth pursuit movements

379.59 Other irregularities of eye movements
Opsoclonus

√5th **379.6 Inflammation (infection) of postprocedural bleb**
Postprocedural blebitis

379.60 Inflammation (infection) of postprocedural bleb, unspecified
AHA: 4Q, '06, 82

379.61 Inflammation (infection) of postprocedural bleb, stage 1
AHA: 4Q, '06, 82

379.62 Inflammation (infection) of postprocedural bleb, stage 2
AHA: 4Q, '06, 82

379.63 Inflammation (infection) of postprocedural bleb, stage 3
Bleb associated endophthalmitis
AHA: 4Q, '06, 82

379.8 Other specified disorders of eye and adnexa

√5th **379.9 Unspecified disorder of eye and adnexa**

379.90 Disorder of eye, unspecified

379.91 Pain in or around eye

379.92 Swelling or mass of eye

379.93 Redness or discharge of eye

379.99 Other ill-defined disorders of eye
EXCLUDES *blurred vision NOS (368.8)*

Diseases of the Ear and Mastoid Process (380-389)
Use additional external cause code, if applicable, to identify the cause of the ear condition

√4th **380 Disorders of external ear**

√5th **380.0 Perichondritis and chondritis of pinna**
Chondritis of auricle   Perichondritis of auricle

380.00 Perichondritis of pinna, unspecified

380.01 Acute perichondritis of pinna

Ear and Mastoid Process

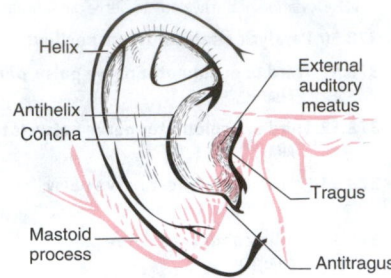

Helix — External auditory meatus — Antihelix — Concha — Tragus — Mastoid process — Antitragus

380.02 Chronic perichondritis of pinna

380.03 Chondritis of pinna
AHA: 4Q, '04, 76
DEF: Infection that has progressed into the cartilage; presents as indurated and edematous skin over the pinna; vascular compromise occurs with tissue necrosis and deformity.

√5th **380.1 Infective otitis externa**

380.10 Infective otitis externa, unspecified
Otitis externa (acute):   Otitis externa (acute):
   NOS   hemorrhagica
   circumscribed   infective NOS
   diffuse

380.11 Acute infection of pinna
EXCLUDES *furuncular otitis externa (680.0)*

380.12 Acute swimmers' ear
Beach ear   Tank ear
DEF: Otitis externa due to swimming.

380.13 *Other acute infections of external ear*
Code first underlying disease, as:
   erysipelas (035)
   impetigo (684)
   seborrheic dermatitis (690.10-690.18)
EXCLUDES *herpes simplex (054.73)*
herpes zoster (053.71)

380.14 Malignant otitis externa   CC
CC Excl: 380.14, 383.00-383.1
DEF: Severe necrotic otitis externa; due to bacteria.

380.15 *Chronic mycotic otitis externa*
Code first underlying disease, as:
   aspergillosis (117.3)
   otomycosis NOS (111.9)
EXCLUDES *candidal otitis externa (112.82)*

380.16 Other chronic infective otitis externa
Chronic infective otitis externa NOS

√5th **380.2 Other otitis externa**

380.21 Cholesteatoma of external ear
Keratosis obturans of external ear (canal)
EXCLUDES *cholesteatoma NOS (385.30-385.35)*
postmastoidectomy (383.32)
DEF: Cystlike mass filled with debris, including cholesterol; rare, congenital condition.

380.22 Other acute otitis externa
Acute otitis externa: Acute otitis externa:
   actinic   eczematoid
   chemical   reactive
   contact

380.23 Other chronic otitis externa
Chronic otitis externa NOS

√5th **380.3 Noninfectious disorders of pinna**

380.30 Disorder of pinna, unspecified

380.31 Hematoma of auricle or pinna

380.32 Acquired deformities of auricle or pinna
EXCLUDES *cauliflower ear (738.7)*
AHA: 3Q, '03, 12

380.39 Other
EXCLUDES *gouty tophi of ear (274.81)*

N Newborn Age: 0   P Pediatric Age: 0-17   M Maternity Age: 12-55   A Adult Age: 15-124   MCC Major CC Condition   CC CC Condition   HIV HIV Related Dx

130 – Volume 1   2015 ICD-9-CM

380.4 Impacted cerumen
  Wax in ear

√5ᵗʰ **380.5 Acquired stenosis of external ear canal**
  Collapse of external ear canal

  380.50 Acquired stenosis of external ear canal, unspecified as to cause

  380.51 Secondary to trauma
    DEF: Narrowing of the external ear canal; due to trauma.

  380.52 Secondary to surgery
    DEF: Postsurgical narrowing of the external ear canal.

  380.53 Secondary to inflammation
    DEF: Narrowing of the external ear canal; due to chronic inflammation.

√5ᵗʰ **380.8 Other disorders of external ear**

  380.81 Exostosis of external ear canal

  380.89 Other

380.9 Unspecified disorder of external ear

√4ᵗʰ **381 Nonsuppurative otitis media and Eustachian tube disorders**

√5ᵗʰ **381.0 Acute nonsuppurative otitis media**
  Acute tubotympanic catarrh
  Otitis media, acute or subacute:
    catarrhal
    exudative
    transudative
    with effusion
    EXCLUDES otitic barotrauma (993.0)

  381.00 Acute nonsuppurative otitis media, unspecified

  381.01 Acute serous otitis media
    Acute or subacute secretory otitis media
    DEF: Sudden, severe infection of the middle ear.

  381.02 Acute mucoid otitis media
    Acute or subacute seromucinous otitis media
    Blue drum syndrome
    DEF: Sudden, severe infection of the middle ear, with mucous.

  381.03 Acute sanguinous otitis media
    DEF: Sudden, severe infection of the middle ear, with blood.

  381.04 Acute allergic serous otitis media

  381.05 Acute allergic mucoid otitis media

  381.06 Acute allergic sanguinous otitis media

√5ᵗʰ **381.1 Chronic serous otitis media**
  Chronic tubotympanic catarrh

  381.10 Chronic serous otitis media, simple or unspecified
    DEF: Persistent infection of the middle ear, without pus.

  381.19 Other
    Serosanguinous chronic otitis media

√5ᵗʰ **381.2 Chronic mucoid otitis media**
  Glue ear
  EXCLUDES adhesive middle ear disease (385.10-385.19)
  DEF: Chronic condition; characterized by viscous fluid in middle ear; due to obstructed Eustachian tube.

  381.20 Chronic mucoid otitis media, simple or unspecified

  381.29 Other
    Mucosanguinous chronic otitis media

381.3 Other and unspecified chronic nonsuppurative otitis media
  Otitis media, chronic: Otitis media, chronic:
    allergic   seromucinous
    exudative   transudative
    secretory   with effusion

381.4 Nonsuppurative otitis media, not specified as acute or chronic
  Otitis media: Otitis media:
    allergic   secretory
    catarrhal   seromucinous
    exudative   serous
    mucoid   transudative
                           with effusion

√5ᵗʰ **381.5 Eustachian salpingitis**

  381.50 Eustachian salpingitis, unspecified

  381.51 Acute Eustachian salpingitis
    DEF: Sudden, severe inflammation of the Eustachian tube.

  381.52 Chronic Eustachian salpingitis
    DEF: Persistent inflammation of the Eustachian tube.

√5ᵗʰ **381.6 Obstruction of Eustachian tube**
  Stenosis }
  Stricture } of Eustachian tube

  381.60 Obstruction of Eustachian tube, unspecified

  381.61 Osseous obstruction of Eustachian tube
    Obstruction of Eustachian tube from cholesteatoma, polyp, or other osseous lesion

  381.62 Intrinsic cartilaginous obstruction of Eustachian tube
    DEF: Blockage of Eustachian tube; due to cartilage overgrowth.

  381.63 Extrinsic cartilaginous obstruction of Eustachian tube
    Compression of Eustachian tube

381.7 Patulous Eustachian tube
  DEF: Distended, oversized Eustachian tube.

√5ᵗʰ **381.8 Other disorders of Eustachian tube**

  381.81 Dysfunction of Eustachian tube

  381.89 Other

381.9 Unspecified Eustachian tube disorder

√4ᵗʰ **382 Suppurative and unspecified otitis media**

√5ᵗʰ **382.0 Acute suppurative otitis media**
  Otitis media, acute: Otitis media, acute:
    necrotizing NOS   purulent

  382.00 Acute suppurative otitis media without spontaneous rupture of ear drum
    DEF: Sudden, severe inflammation of middle ear, with pus.

  382.01 Acute suppurative otitis media with spontaneous rupture of ear drum
    DEF: Sudden, severe inflammation of middle ear, with pressure tearing ear drum tissue.

  382.02 *Acute suppurative otitis media in diseases classified elsewhere*
    Code first underlying disease, as:
      influenza (487.8, 488.09, 488.19)
      scarlet fever (034.1)
    EXCLUDES postmeasles otitis (055.2)

382.1 Chronic tubotympanic suppurative otitis media
  Benign chronic suppurative } (with anterior
    otitis media   } perforation of
  Chronic tubotympanic disease } ear drum)

  DEF: Inflammation of tympanic cavity and auditory tube; with pus formation.

382.2 Chronic atticoantral suppurative otitis media
  Chronic atticoantral disease } (with posterior or superior
  Persistent mucosal disease   } maginal perforation of
                               } ear drum)

  DEF: Inflammation of upper tympanic membrane and mastoid antrum with pus formation.

382.3 Unspecified chronic suppurative otitis media
  Chronic purulent otitis media
  EXCLUDES tuberculous otitis media (017.4)

382.4 Unspecified suppurative otitis media
  Purulent otitis media NOS

382.9 Unspecified otitis media
  Otitis media: Otitis media:
    NOS   chronic NOS
    acute NOS
  AHA: N-D, '84, 16
  H66.93 Otitis media unspecified bilateral

I-10

(side tab) Diseases of the Nervous System and Sense Organs — **380.4–382.9**

✓4th **383 Mastoiditis and related conditions**

✓5th **383.0 Acute mastoiditis**
Abscess of mastoid   Empyema of mastoid

383.00 Acute mastoiditis without complications CC
DEF: Sudden, severe inflammation of mastoid air cells.
CC Excl: 015.60-015.66, 017.40-017.46, 017.90-017.96, 383.00-383.9, 388.71-388.9, 744.00, 744.02, 744.09, 744.29-744.3

383.01 Subperiosteal abscess of mastoid CC
DEF: Pocket of pus within the mastoid bone.
CC Excl: See code: 383.00

383.02 Acute mastoiditis with other complications CC
Gradenigo's syndrome
CC Excl: See code: 383.00

383.1 Chronic mastoiditis
Caries of mastoid   Fistula of mastoid
EXCLUDES tuberculous mastoiditis (015.6)
DEF: Persistent inflammation of the mastoid air cells.

✓5th **383.2 Petrositis**
Coalescing osteitis
Inflammation   } of petrous bone
Osteomyelitis

383.20 Petrositis, unspecified

383.21 Acute petrositis
DEF: Sudden, severe inflammation of dense bone behind the ear.

383.22 Chronic petrositis
DEF: Persistent inflammation of dense bone behind the ear.

✓5th **383.3 Complications following mastoidectomy**

383.30 Postmastoidectomy complication, unspecified

383.31 Mucosal cyst of postmastoidectomy cavity
DEF: Mucous-lined cyst cavity following removal of mastoid bone.

383.32 Recurrent cholesteatoma of postmastoidectomy cavity
DEF: Cystlike mass of cell debris in cavity following removal of mastoid bone.

383.33 Granulations of postmastoidectomy cavity
Chronic inflammation of postmastoidectomy cavity
DEF: Granular tissue in cavity following removal of mastoid bone.

✓5th **383.8 Other disorders of mastoid**

383.81 Postauricular fistula
DEF: Abnormal passage behind mastoid cavity.

383.89 Other

383.9 Unspecified mastoiditis

✓4th **384 Other disorders of tympanic membrane**

✓5th **384.0 Acute myringitis without mention of otitis media**

384.00 Acute myringitis, unspecified
Acute tympanitis NOS
DEF: Sudden, severe inflammation of ear drum.

384.01 Bullous myringitis
Myringitis bullosa hemorrhagica
DEF: Type of viral otitis media characterized by the appearance of serous or hemorrhagic blebs on the tympanic membrane.

384.09 Other

384.1 Chronic myringitis without mention of otitis media
Chronic tympanitis
DEF: Persistent inflammation of ear drum; with no evidence of middle ear infection.

✓5th **384.2 Perforation of tympanic membrane**
Perforation of ear drum:
NOS
persistent posttraumatic
postinflammatory
EXCLUDES otitis media with perforation of tympanic membrane (382.00-382.9)
traumatic perforation [current injury] (872.61)

Middle and Inner Ear

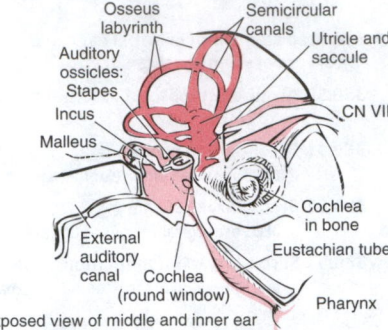

Osseus labyrinth
Semicircular canals
Utricle and saccule
Auditory ossicles:
Stapes
Incus
Malleus
CN VIII
Cochlea in bone
External auditory canal
Cochlea (round window)
Eustachian tube
Pharynx
Exposed view of middle and inner ear

Cholesteatoma

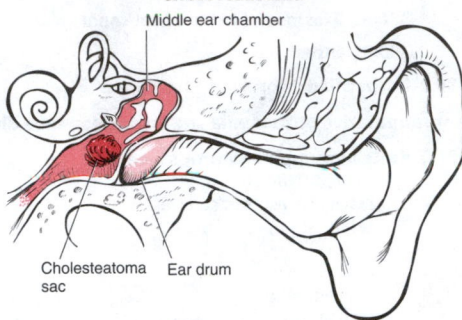

Middle ear chamber
Cholesteatoma sac
Ear drum

384.20 Perforation of tympanic membrane, unspecified

384.21 Central perforation of tympanic membrane

384.22 Attic perforation of tympanic membrane
Pars flaccida

384.23 Other marginal perforation of tympanic membrane

384.24 Multiple perforations of tympanic membrane

384.25 Total perforation of tympanic membrane

✓5th **384.8 Other specified disorders of tympanic membrane**

384.81 Atrophic flaccid tympanic membrane
Healed perforation of ear drum

384.82 Atrophic nonflaccid tympanic membrane

384.9 Unspecified disorder of tympanic membrane

✓4th **385 Other disorders of middle ear and mastoid**
EXCLUDES mastoiditis (383.0-383.9)

✓5th **385.0 Tympanosclerosis**

385.00 Tympanosclerosis, unspecified as to involvement

385.01 Tympanosclerosis involving tympanic membrane only
DEF: Tough, fibrous tissue impeding functions of ear drum.

385.02 Tympanosclerosis involving tympanic membrane and ear ossicles
DEF: Tough, fibrous tissue impeding functions of middle ear bones (stapes, malleus, incus).

385.03 Tympanosclerosis involving tympanic membrane, ear ossicles, and middle ear
DEF: Tough, fibrous tissue impeding functions of ear drum, middle ear bones and middle ear canal.

385.09 Tympanosclerosis involving other combination of structures

✓5th **385.1 Adhesive middle ear disease**
Adhesive otitis   Otitis media:
Otitis media: fibrotic
chronic adhesive
EXCLUDES glue ear (381.20-381.29)
DEF: Adhesions of middle ear structures.

385.10 Adhesive middle ear disease, unspecified as to involvement

385.11 Adhesions of drum head to incus

385.12 Adhesions of drum head to stapes

N Newborn Age: 0   P Pediatric Age: 0-17   M Maternity Age: 12-55   A Adult Age: 15-124   MCC Major CC Condition   CC CC Condition   HIV HIV Related Dx

132 – Volume 1   2015 ICD-9-CM

385.13 Adhesions of drum head to promontorium

385.19 Other adhesions and combinations

√5th **385.2 Other acquired abnormality of ear ossicles**

385.21 Impaired mobility of malleus
Ankylosis of malleus

385.22 Impaired mobility of other ear ossicles
Ankylosis of ear ossicles, except malleus

385.23 Discontinuity or dislocation of ear ossicles
DEF: Disruption in auditory chain; created by malleus, incus and stapes.

385.24 Partial loss or necrosis of ear ossicles
DEF: Tissue loss in malleus, incus and stapes.

√5th **385.3 Cholesteatoma of middle ear and mastoid**
Cholesterosis
Epidermosis   } of (middle) ear
Keratosis
Polyp

EXCLUDES cholesteatoma:
external ear canal (380.21)
recurrent of postmastoidectomy cavity (383.32)
DEF: Cystlike mass of middle ear and mastoid antrum filled with debris, including cholesterol.

385.30 Cholesteatoma, unspecified

385.31 Cholesteatoma of attic

385.32 Cholesteatoma of middle ear

385.33 Cholesteatoma of middle ear and mastoid
DEF: Cystlike mass of cell debris in middle ear and mastoid air cells behind ear.
AHA: 3Q, '00, 10

385.35 Diffuse cholesteatosis

√5th **385.8 Other disorders of middle ear and mastoid**

385.82 Cholesterin granuloma
DEF: Granuloma formed of fibrotic tissue; contains cholesterol crystals surrounded by foreign-body cells; found in the middle ear and mastoid area.

385.83 Retained foreign body of middle ear
Use additional code to identify foreign body (V90.01-V90.9)
AHA: 3Q, '94, 7; N-D, '87, 9

385.89 Other

385.9 Unspecified disorder of middle ear and mastoid

√4th **386 Vertiginous syndromes and other disorders of vestibular system**
EXCLUDES vertigo NOS (780.4)
AHA: M-A, '85, 12

√5th **386.0 Ménière's disease**
Endolymphatic hydrops
Lermoyez's syndrome
Ménière's syndrome or vertigo
DEF: Distended membranous labyrinth of middle ear from endolymphatic hydrops; causes ischemia, failure of nerve function; hearing and balance dysfunction; symptoms include fluctuating deafness, ringing in ears and dizziness.

386.00 Ménière's disease, unspecified
Ménière's disease (active)
H81.03 Ménière's disease bilateral   I-10

386.01 Active Ménière's disease, cochleovestibular

386.02 Active Ménière's disease, cochlear

386.03 Active Ménière's disease, vestibular

386.04 Inactive Ménière's disease
Ménière's disease in remission

√5th **386.1 Other and unspecified peripheral vertigo**
EXCLUDES epidemic vertigo (078.81)

386.10 Peripheral vertigo, unspecified

386.11 Benign paroxysmal positional vertigo
Benign paroxysmal positional nystagmus

386.12 Vestibular neuronitis
Acute (and recurrent) peripheral vestibulopathy
DEF: Transient benign vertigo, unknown cause; characterized by response to caloric stimulation on one side, nystagmus with rhythmic movement of eyes; normal auditory function present.

386.19 Other
Aural vertigo   Otogenic vertigo

386.2 Vertigo of central origin
Central positional nystagmus   Malignant positional vertigo

√5th **386.3 Labyrinthitis**

386.30 Labyrinthitis, unspecified

386.31 Serous labyrinthitis
Diffuse labyrinthitis
DEF: Inflammation of labyrinth; with fluid buildup.

386.32 Circumscribed labyrinthitis
Focal labyrinthitis

386.33 Suppurative labyrinthitis
Purulent labyrinthitis
DEF: Inflammation of labyrinth; with pus.

386.34 Toxic labyrinthitis
DEF: Inflammation of labyrinth; due to toxic reaction.

386.35 Viral labyrinthitis

√5th **386.4 Labyrinthine fistula**

386.40 Labyrinthine fistula, unspecified

386.41 Round window fistula

386.42 Oval window fistula

386.43 Semicircular canal fistula

386.48 Labyrinthine fistula of combined sites

√5th **386.5 Labyrinthine dysfunction**

386.50 Labyrinthine dysfunction, unspecified

386.51 Hyperactive labyrinth, unilateral
DEF: Abnormal increased sensitivity of labyrinth to stimuli such as sound, pressure or gravitational change, affecting one ear.

386.52 Hyperactive labyrinth, bilateral
DEF: Abnormal increased sensitivity of labyrinth to stimuli such as sound, pressure or gravitational change, affecting both ears.

386.53 Hypoactive labyrinth, unilateral
DEF: Abnormal decreased sensitivity of labyrinth to stimuli such as sound, pressure or gravitational change, affecting one ear.

386.54 Hypoactive labyrinth, bilateral
DEF: Abnormal decreased sensitivity of labyrinth to stimuli such as sound, pressure or gravitational change, affecting both ears.

386.55 Loss of labyrinthine reactivity, unilateral
DEF: Decreased function of the labyrinth sensors, affecting one ear

386.56 Loss of labyrinthine reactivity, bilateral
DEF: Decreased function of the labyrinth sensors, affecting both ears

386.58 Other forms and combinations

386.8 Other disorders of labyrinth
AHA: 1Q, '11, 6

386.9 Unspecified vertiginous syndromes and labyrinthine disorders

√4th **387 Otosclerosis**
INCLUDES otospongiosis
DEF: Synonym for otospongiosis, spongy bone formation in the labyrinth bones of the ear; it causes progressive hearing impairment.

387.0 Otosclerosis involving oval window, nonobliterative
DEF: Tough, fibrous tissue impeding functions of oval window.

387.1 Otosclerosis involving oval window, obliterative
DEF: Tough, fibrous tissue blocking oval window.

√4th
√5th Additional Digit Required   Unacceptable PDx   Manifestation Code   Hospital Acquired Condition   ▶◀ Revised Text   ● New Code   ▲ Revised Code Title

387.2 Cochlear otosclerosis
Otosclerosis involving: Otosclerosis involving:
otic capsule   round window
DEF: Tough, fibrous tissue impeding functions of cochlea.

387.8 Other otosclerosis

387.9 Otosclerosis, unspecified

√4th **388 Other disorders of ear**

√5th **388.0 Degenerative and vascular disorders of ear**

388.00 Degenerative and vascular disorders, unspecified

388.01 Presbyacusis
DEF: Progressive, bilateral perceptive hearing loss caused by advancing age; it is also known as presbycusis.

388.02 Transient ischemic deafness
DEF: Restricted blood flow to auditory organs causing temporary hearing loss.

√5th **388.1 Noise effects on inner ear**

388.10 Noise effects on inner ear, unspecified

388.11 Acoustic trauma (explosive) to ear
Otitic blast injury

388.12 Noise-induced hearing loss

388.2 Sudden hearing loss, unspecified

√5th **388.3 Tinnitus**
DEF: Abnormal noises in ear; may be heard by others beside the affected individual; noises include ringing, clicking, roaring and buzzing.

388.30 Tinnitus, unspecified

388.31 Subjective tinnitus

388.32 Objective tinnitus

√5th **388.4 Other abnormal auditory perception**

388.40 Abnormal auditory perception, unspecified

388.41 Diplacusis
DEF: Perception of a single auditory sound as two sounds at two different levels of intensity.

388.42 Hyperacusis
DEF: Exceptionally acute sense of hearing caused by such conditions as Bell's palsy; this term may also refer to painful sensitivity to sounds.

388.43 Impairment of auditory discrimination
DEF: Impaired ability to distinguish tone of sound.

388.44 Recruitment
DEF: Perception of abnormally increased loudness caused by a slight increase in sound intensity; it is a term used in audiology.

388.45 Acquired auditory processing disorder
Auditory processing disorder NOS
EXCLUDES central auditory processing disorder (315.32)
DEF: Difficulty in recognizing and interpreting sounds; a failure of the brain to process auditory information; due to neurological problems due to injury, infection, and degenerative conditions.
AHA: 4Q, '07, 79

388.5 Disorders of acoustic nerve
Acoustic neuritis
Degeneration   } of acoustic or eighth nerve
Disorder
EXCLUDES acoustic neuroma (225.1)
syphilitic acoustic neuritis (094.86)
AHA: M-A, '87, 8

√5th **388.6 Otorrhea**

388.60 Otorrhea, unspecified
Discharging ear NOS

388.61 Cerebrospinal fluid otorrhea `CC`
EXCLUDES cerebrospinal fluid rhinorrhea (349.81)
DEF: Spinal fluid leakage from ear.
CC Excl: 388.61-388.69
AHA: ▶2Q, '13, 8◀

388.69 Other
Otorrhagia

√5th **388.7 Otalgia**

388.70 Otalgia, unspecified
Earache NOS

388.71 Otogenic pain

388.72 Referred pain

388.8 Other disorders of ear

388.9 Unspecified disorder of ear

√4th **389 Hearing loss**

√5th **389.0 Conductive hearing loss**
Conductive deafness
EXCLUDES mixed conductive and sensorineural hearing loss (389.20-389.22)
DEF: Dysfunction in sound-conducting structures of external or middle ear causing hearing loss.
AHA: 4Q, '07, 80; 4Q, '89, 5

389.00 Conductive hearing loss, unspecified
AHA: ▶2Q, '13, 8◀

389.01 Conductive hearing loss, external ear

389.02 Conductive hearing loss, tympanic membrane

389.03 Conductive hearing loss, middle ear

389.04 Conductive hearing loss, inner ear

389.05 Conductive hearing loss, unilateral

389.06 Conductive hearing loss, bilateral
AHA: 4Q, '07, 81

389.08 Conductive hearing loss of combined types

√5th **389.1 Sensorineural hearing loss**
Perceptive hearing loss or deafness
EXCLUDES abnormal auditory perception (388.40-388.44)
mixed conductive and sensorineural hearing loss (389.20-389.22)
psychogenic deafness (306.7)
DEF: Nerve conduction causing hearing loss.
AHA: 4Q, '07, 80; 4Q, '89, 5

389.10 Sensorineural hearing loss, unspecified
AHA: 1Q, '93, 29

389.11 Sensory hearing loss, bilateral

389.12 Neural hearing loss, bilateral

389.13 Neural hearing loss, unilateral

389.14 Central hearing loss

389.15 Sensorineural hearing loss, unilateral
AHA: 4Q, '06, 84

389.16 Sensorineural hearing loss, asymmetrical
AHA: 4Q, '06, 84

389.17 Sensory hearing loss, unilateral

389.18 Sensorineural hearing loss, bilateral
AHA: 4Q, '06, 84

√5th **389.2 Mixed conductive and sensorineural hearing loss**
Deafness or hearing loss of type classifiable to 389.00-389.08 with type classifiable to 389.10-389.18
AHA: 4Q, '07, 80

389.20 Mixed hearing loss, unspecified

389.21 Mixed hearing loss, unilateral

389.22 Mixed hearing loss, bilateral

389.7 Deaf, non-speaking, not elsewhere classifiable

389.8 Other specified forms of hearing loss

389.9 Unspecified hearing loss
Deafness NOS
AHA: 1Q, '04, 15
H91.93 Unspecified hearing loss bilateral   `I-10`

| `N` Newborn Age: 0 | `P` Pediatric Age: 0-17 | `M` Maternity Age: 12-55 | `A` Adult Age: 15-124 | `MCC` Major CC Condition | `CC` CC Condition | `HIV` HIV Related Dx |

7. Diseases of the Circulatory System (390-459)

Acute Rheumatic Fever (390-392)

DEF: Febrile disease occurs mainly in children or young adults following throat infection by group A streptococci; symptoms include fever, joint pain, lesions of heart, blood vessels and joint connective tissue, abdominal pain, skin changes, and chorea.

390   Rheumatic fever without mention of heart involvement
Arthritis, rheumatic, acute or subacute
Rheumatic fever (active) (acute)
Rheumatism, articular, acute or subacute
EXCLUDES   *that with heart involvement (391.0-391.9)*

✓4ᵗʰ 391   Rheumatic fever with heart involvement
EXCLUDES   *chronic heart diseases of rheumatic origin (393-398.99)*
                 unless rheumatic fever is also present or there is
                 evidence of recrudescence or activity of the rheumatic
                 process

391.0   Acute rheumatic pericarditis   `cc`
Rheumatic:
    fever (active) (acute) with pericarditis
    pericarditis (acute)
Any condition classifiable to 390 with pericarditis
EXCLUDES   *that not specified as rheumatic (420.0-420.9)*
DEF: Sudden, severe inflammation of heart lining due to rheumatic fever.
CC Excl: 074.21, 093.81, 391.0, 393, 420.0-420.99, 423.3-423.9, 459.89-459.9

391.1   Acute rheumatic endocarditis   `cc`
Rheumatic:
    endocarditis, acute
    fever (active) (acute) with endocarditis or valvulitis
    valvulitis acute
Any condition classifiable to 390 with endocarditis or valvulitis
DEF: Sudden, severe inflammation of heart cavities due to rheumatic fever.
CC Excl: 002.0, 036.42, 074.22, 083.0, 093.20-093.24, 098.84, 112.81, 115.94, 390, 391.1, 391.8-392.0, 394.0-395.9, 396.9-397.9, 398.90, 398.99, 421.0-421.9, 424.0-424.99, 425.3, 459.89-459.9, 746.09, 746.89, 996.61

391.2   Acute rheumatic myocarditis   `cc`
Rheumatic fever (active) (acute) with myocarditis
Any condition classifiable to 390 with myocarditis
DEF: Sudden, severe inflammation of heart muscles due to rheumatic fever.
CC Excl: 074.20, 074.22-074.23, 093.82, 390, 391.2-391.9, 398.0-398.90, 398.99, 422.0-422.99, 429.0, 429.71-429.79, 459.89-459.9

391.8   Other acute rheumatic heart disease   `cc`
Rheumatic:
    fever (active) (acute) with other or multiple types of heart involvement
    pancarditis, acute
Any condition classifiable to 390 with other or multiple types of heart involvement
CC Excl: 391.0-398.99, 428.20-428.43

391.9   Acute rheumatic heart disease, unspecified   `cc`
Rheumatic:
    carditis, acute
    fever (active) (acute) with unspecified type of heart involvement
    heart disease, active or acute
Any condition classifiable to 390 with unspecified type of heart involvement
CC Excl: 391.0-398.99

✓4ᵗʰ 392   Rheumatic chorea
INCLUDES   Sydenham's chorea
EXCLUDES   *chorea:*
         NOS (333.5)
         Huntington's (333.4)
DEF: Childhood disease linked with rheumatic fever and streptococcal infections; symptoms include spasmodic, involuntary movements of limbs or facial muscles, psychic symptoms, and irritability.

392.0   With heart involvement   `cc`
Rheumatic chorea with heart involvement of any type classifiable to 391
CC Excl: See code: 391.8

392.9   Without mention of heart involvement   `cc`
CC Excl: See code: 391.9

Chronic Rheumatic Heart Disease (393-398)

393   Chronic rheumatic pericarditis   `cc`
Adherent pericardium, rheumatic
Chronic rheumatic:
    mediastinopericarditis
    myopericarditis
EXCLUDES   *pericarditis NOS or not specified as rheumatic (423.0-423.9)*
DEF: Persistent inflammation of heart lining due to rheumatic heart disease.
CC Excl: 074.21, 093.81, 391.0, 393, 420.0-420.99, 423.3-423.9, 459.89-459.9

✓4ᵗʰ 394   Diseases of mitral valve
EXCLUDES   *that with aortic valve involvement (396.0-396.9)*

394.0   Mitral stenosis
Mitral (valve):
    obstruction (rheumatic)
    stenosis NOS
DEF: Narrowing, of mitral valve between left atrium and left ventricle; due to rheumatic heart disease.
TIP: Assign when documentation indicates mitral valve stenosis or obstruction with no further specification of cause.

394.1   Rheumatic mitral insufficiency
Rheumatic mitral:
    incompetence
    regurgitation
EXCLUDES   *that not specified as rheumatic (424.0)*
DEF: Malfunction of mitral valve between left atrium and left ventricle; due to rheumatic heart disease.
AHA: 2Q, '05, 14

394.2   Mitral stenosis with insufficiency
Mitral stenosis with incompetence or regurgitation
DEF: A narrowing or stricture of the mitral valve situated between the left atrium and left ventricle; valve does not completely close, is insufficient (inadequate) in preventing regurgitation into the atrium; also called incompetence.
AHA: 1Q, '07, 11

394.9   Other and unspecified mitral valve diseases
Mitral (valve):
    disease (chronic)
    failure

✓4ᵗʰ 395   Diseases of aortic valve
EXCLUDES   *that not specified as rheumatic (424.1)*
           that with mitral valve involvement (396.0-396.9)

395.0   Rheumatic aortic stenosis
Rheumatic aortic (valve) obstruction
DEF: Narrowing of the aortic valve; results in backflow into ventricle; due to rheumatic heart disease.
AHA: 4Q, '88, 8

395.1   Rheumatic aortic insufficiency
Rheumatic aortic:
    incompetence
    regurgitation
DEF: Malfunction of the aortic valve; results in backflow into left ventricle; due to rheumatic heart disease.

395.2   Rheumatic aortic stenosis with insufficiency
Rheumatic aortic stenosis with incompetence or regurgitation
DEF: Malfunction and narrowing, of the aortic valve; results in backflow into left ventricle; due to rheumatic heart disease.

395.9   Other and unspecified rheumatic aortic diseases
Rheumatic aortic (valve) disease

Diseases of the Circulatory System

396–402.91

√4ʰ **396 Diseases of mitral and aortic valves**

> **INCLUDES** involvement of both mitral and aortic valves, whether specified as rheumatic or not

> AHA: N-D, '87, 8

396.0 Mitral valve stenosis and aortic valve stenosis
> Atypical aortic (valve) stenosis
> Mitral and aortic (valve) obstruction (rheumatic)

396.1 Mitral valve stenosis and aortic valve insufficiency

396.2 Mitral valve insufficiency and aortic valve stenosis
> AHA: 2Q, '09, 17; 1Q, '09, 18; 2Q, '00, 16

396.3 Mitral valve insufficiency and aortic valve insufficiency
> Mitral and aortic (valve):
>> incompetence
>> regurgitation
> I08.0 Rheumatic d/o of both mitral & aortic valves   I-10

396.8 Multiple involvement of mitral and aortic valves
> Stenosis and insufficiency of mitral or aortic valve with stenosis or insufficiency, or both, of the other valve

396.9 Mitral and aortic valve diseases, unspecified

√4ʰ **397 Diseases of other endocardial structures**

397.0 Diseases of tricuspid valve
> Tricuspid (valve) (rheumatic):
>> disease
>> insufficiency
>> obstruction
>> regurgitation
>> stenosis
> **DEF:** Malfunction of the valve between right atrium and right ventricle; due to rheumatic heart disease.
> AHA: 3Q, '06, 7; 2Q, '00, 16
> I07.2 Rheumatic tricuspid stenosis and insufficiency   I-10

397.1 Rheumatic diseases of pulmonary valve
> **EXCLUDES** that not specified as rheumatic (424.3)

397.9 Rheumatic diseases of endocardium, valve unspecified
> Rheumatic:
>> endocarditis (chronic)
>> valvulitis (chronic)
> **EXCLUDES** that not specified as rheumatic (424.90-424.99)

√4ʰ **398 Other rheumatic heart disease**

398.0 Rheumatic myocarditis   CC
> Rheumatic degeneration of myocardium
> **EXCLUDES** myocarditis not specified as rheumatic (429.0)
> **DEF:** Chronic inflammation of heart muscle; due to rheumatic heart disease.
> **CC Excl:** 390, 391.2-391.9, 398.0-398.90, 398.99, 422.0-422.99, 429.0, 429.71-429.79, 459.89-459.9

√5ʰ **398.9 Other and unspecified rheumatic heart diseases**

398.90 Rheumatic heart disease, unspecified
> Rheumatic: Rheumatic:
> carditis   heart disease NOS
> **EXCLUDES** carditis not specified as rheumatic (429.89)
>> heart disease NOS not specified as rheumatic (429.9)

398.91 Rheumatic heart failure (congestive)   CC
> Rheumatic left ventricular failure
> **DEF:** Decreased cardiac output, edema and hypertension; due to rheumatic heart disease.
> **CC Excl:** 398.90-398.99, 402.01, 402.11, 402.91, 428.0-428.9, 459.89-459.9
> AHA: 2Q, '05, 14; 1Q, '95, 6; 3Q, '88, 3
> I09.81 Rheumatic heart failure   I-10

398.99 Other

Hypertensive Disease (401-405)

> **EXCLUDES** that complicating pregnancy, childbirth, or the puerperium (642.0-642.9)
>> that involving coronary vessels (410.00-414.9)
> AHA: 3Q, '90, 3; 2Q, '89, 12; S-O, '87, 9; J-A, '84, 11

√4ʰ **401 Essential hypertension**

> **INCLUDES** high blood pressure
>> hyperpiesia
>> hyperpiesis
>> hypertension (arterial) (essential) (primary) (systemic)
>> hypertensive vascular:
>>> degeneration
>>> disease
> **EXCLUDES** elevated blood pressure without diagnosis of hypertension (796.2)
>> pulmonary hypertension (416.0-416.9)
>> that involving vessels of:
>>> brain (430-438)
>>> eye (362.11)
> **DEF:** Hypertension that occurs without apparent organic cause; idiopathic.
> AHA: 2Q, '92, 5

401.0 Malignant   CC
> **DEF:** Severe high arterial blood pressure; results in necrosis in kidney, retina, etc.; hemorrhages occur and death commonly due to uremia or rupture of cerebral vessel.
> **CC Excl:** 401.0-405.99, 459.89-459.9
> AHA: M-J, '85, 19

401.1 Benign
> **DEF:** Mildly elevated arterial blood pressure.

401.9 Unspecified
> AHA: 1Q, '12, 14; 4Q, '10,124,125, 135; 4Q, '09, 77, 129; 1Q, '09, 16; 2Q, '08, 16; 4Q, '05, 71; 3Q, '05, 8; 4Q, '04, 78; 4Q, '03, 105, 108, 111; 3Q, '03, 14; 2Q, '03, 16; 4Q, '97, 37
> I10 Essential (primary) hypertension   I-10

√4ʰ **402 Hypertensive heart disease**

> **INCLUDES** hypertensive:
>> cardiomegaly
>> cardiopathy
>> cardiovascular disease
>> heart (disease) (failure)
>> any condition classifiable to 429.0-429.3, 429.8, 429.9 due to hypertension
> Use additional code to specify type of heart failure (428.0-428.43), if known
> AHA: 4Q, '02, 49; 2Q, '93, 9; N-D, '84, 18
> **TIP:** Assign when a cardiac condition is stated (due to hypertension) or implied (hypertensive).

√5ʰ **402.0 Malignant**

402.00 Without heart failure   CC
> **CC Excl:** See code: 401.0

402.01 With heart failure   CC
> **CC Excl:** 398.91, 401.0-405.99, 428.0-428.9, 459.89-459.9
> AHA: 4Q, '08, 180

√5ʰ **402.1 Benign**

402.10 Without heart failure

402.11 With heart failure

√5ʰ **402.9 Unspecified**

402.90 Without heart failure
> I11.9 Hypertensive heart disease without heart failure   I-10

402.91 With heart failure
> AHA: 4Q, '02, 52; 1Q, '93, 19; 2Q, '89, 12

N Newborn Age: 0   P Pediatric Age: 0-17   M Maternity Age: 12-55   A Adult Age: 15-124   MCC Major CC Condition   CC CC Condition   HIV HIV Related Dx

136 – Volume 1   2015 ICD-9-CM

√4ᵗʰ **403 Hypertensive chronic kidney disease**

INCLUDES   arteriolar nephritis
arteriosclerosis of:
     kidney
     renal arterioles
arteriosclerotic nephritis (chronic) (interstitial)
hypertensive:
     nephropathy
     renal failure
     uremia (chronic)
nephrosclerosis
renal sclerosis with hypertension

     any condition classifiable to 585 and 587 with any condition classifiable to 401

EXCLUDES   acute kidney failure (584.5-584.9)
renal disease stated as not due to hypertension
renovascular hypertension (405.0-405.9 with fifth-digit 1)

> The following fifth-digit subclassification is for use with category 403:
> **0 with chronic kidney disease stage I through stage IV, or unspecified**
>   Use additional code to identify the stage of chronic kidney disease (585.1-585.4, 585.9)
> **1 with chronic kidney disease stage V or end stage renal disease**
>   Use additional code to identify the stage of chronic kidney disease (585.5, 585.6)

AHA: 4Q, '06, 84-86; 4Q, '05, 68; 4Q, '92, 22; 2Q, '92, 5

TIP: Assign whenever a patient has both chronic kidney disease and hypertension (presumed cause-and-effect relationship).

§ √5ᵗʰ **403.0 Malignant**   CC
[0-1]   **CC Excl:** 401.0-405.99, 459.89-459.9

§ √5ᵗʰ **403.1 Benign**   CC 1
[0-1]   **CC Excl: For code 403.11:** See code 403.0
       AHA: For code 403.11: 3Q,'10, 12

§ √5ᵗʰ **403.9 Unspecified**   CC 1
[0-1]   **CC Excl: For code 403.91:** 401.0-405.99, 459.89-459.9, 585.6
       AHA: For code 403.90: 4Q, '10, 137; 1Q, '08, 10; 2Q, '07, 3; 4Q, '06, 86;
       For code 403.91: 4Q, '10, 137; 1Q, '08, 7; 4Q, '05, 69; 1Q, '04, 14; 1Q, '03, 20; 2Q, '01, 11; 3Q, '91, 8
       I12.9 HTN CKD w/stage I thru IV CKD/UNS CKD   I-10

√4ᵗʰ **404 Hypertensive heart and chronic kidney disease**

INCLUDES   disease:
     cardiorenal
     cardiovascular renal

     any condition classifiable to 402 with any condition classifiable to 403

Use additional code to specify type of heart failure (428.0-428.43), if known

> The following fifth-digit subclassification is for use with category 404:
> **0 without heart failure and with chronic kidney disease stage I through stage IV, or unspecified**
>   Use additional code to identify the stage of chronic kidney disease (585.1-585.4, 585.9)
> **1 with heart failure and with chronic kidney disease stage I through stage IV, or unspecified**
>   Use additional code to identify the stage of chronic kidney disease (585.1-585.4, 585.9)
> **2 without heart failure and with chronic kidney disease stage V or end stage renal disease**
>   Use additional code to identify the stage of chronic kidney disease (585.5, 585.6)
> **3 with heart failure and chronic kidney disease stage V or end stage renal disease**
>   Use additional code to identify the stage of chronic kidney disease (585.5, 585.6)

AHA: 4Q, '06, 84-86; 4Q, '05, 68; 4Q, '02, 49; 3Q, '90, 3; J-A, '84, 14

§ √5ᵗʰ **404.0 Malignant**   CC
[0-3]   **CC Excl:** 401.0-405.99, 459.89-459.9

§ √5ᵗʰ **404.1 Benign**   CC 1-3
[0-3]   **CC Excl: For codes 404.11-404.13:** 401.0-405.99, 459.89-459.9

§ √5ᵗʰ **404.9 Unspecified**   CC 1-3
[0-3]   **CC Excl: For codes 404.91-404.93:** 401.0-405.99, 459.89-459.9
       I13.0 HTN heart & CKD HF & stage I thru IV CKD/UNS CKD   I-10

√4ᵗʰ **405 Secondary hypertension**

DEF: High arterial blood pressure due to or with a variety of primary diseases, such as renal disorders, CNS disorders, endocrine, and vascular diseases.
AHA: 3Q, '90, 3; S-O, '87, 9, 11; J-A, '84, 14

√5ᵗʰ **405.0 Malignant**

     405.01 Renovascular   CC
       CC Excl: See code: 404.0

     405.09 Other   CC
       CC Excl: See code: 404.0

√5ᵗʰ **405.1 Benign**

     405.11 Renovascular

     405.19 Other

√5ᵗʰ **405.9 Unspecified**

     405.91 Renovascular

     405.99 Other
       AHA: 3Q, '00, 4

Ischemic Heart Disease (410-414)

INCLUDES   that with mention of hypertension

Use additional code to identify presence of hypertension (401.0-405.9)
AHA: 3Q, '91, 10; J-A, '84, 5

√4ᵗʰ **410 Acute myocardial infarction**

INCLUDES   cardiac infarction
coronary (artery):
     embolism
     occlusion
     rupture
     thrombosis
infarction of heart, myocardium, or ventricle
rupture of heart, myocardium, or ventricle
ST elevation (STEMI) and non-ST elevation (NSTEMI)
     myocardial infarction

     any condition classifiable to 414.1-414.9 specified as acute or with a stated duration of 8 weeks or less

> The following fifth-digit subclassification is for use with category 410:
> **0 episode of care unspecified**
>   Use when the source document does not contain sufficient information for the assigment of fifth-digit 1 or 2.
> **1 initial episode of care**
>   Use fifth-digit 1 to designate the first episode of care (regardless of facility site) for a newly diagnosed myocardial infarction. The fifth-digit 1 is assigned regardless of the number of times a patient may be transferred during the initial episode of care.
> **2 subsequent episode of care**
>   Use fifth-digit 2 to designate an episode of care following the initial episode when the patient is admitted for further observation, evaluation or treatment for a myocardial infarction that has received initial treatment, but is still less than 8 weeks old.

DEF: A sudden insufficiency of blood supply to an area of the heart muscle; usually due to a coronary artery occlusion.
AHA: 1Q, '12, 7; 2Q, '06, 9; 4Q, '05, 69; 3Q, '01, 21; 3Q, '98, 15; 4Q, '97, 37; 3Q, '95, 9; 4Q, 92, 24; 1Q, '92, 10; 3Q, '91, 18; 1Q, '91, 14; 3Q, '89, 3
TIP: Assign an acute MI code with a fifth digit of "1," initial episode of care, for all care provided before the AMI has resolved, regardless of type or number of transfers between facilities.

§ √5ᵗʰ **410.0 Of anterolateral wall**   MCC 1
[0-2]   ST elevation myocardial infarction (STEMI) of anterolateral wall
       CC Excl: For code 410.01 410.00-410.92, 459.89-459.9
       AHA: For code 410.01: 4Q, '09, 129; 4Q, '08, 72

§ √5ᵗʰ **410.1 Of other anterior wall**   MCC 1
[0-2]   Infarction:
     anterior (wall) NOS   } (with contiguous portion of
     anteroapical   intraventricular
     anteroseptal   septum)
     ST elevation myocardial infarction (STEMI) of other anterior wall
       CC Excl: For code 410.11: See code 410.0
       AHA: For code 410.11: 3Q, '03, 10

---

§   Requires fifth digit. Valid digits are in [brackets] under each code. See appropriate category for codes and definitions.

√4ᵗʰ √5ᵗʰ Additional Digit Required   Unacceptable PDx   Manifestation Code   Hospital Acquired Condition   ▶◀ Revised Text   ● New Code   ▲ Revised Code Title

2015 ICD-9-CM   **Volume 1 – 137**

Diseases of the Circulatory System

410.2–413.1

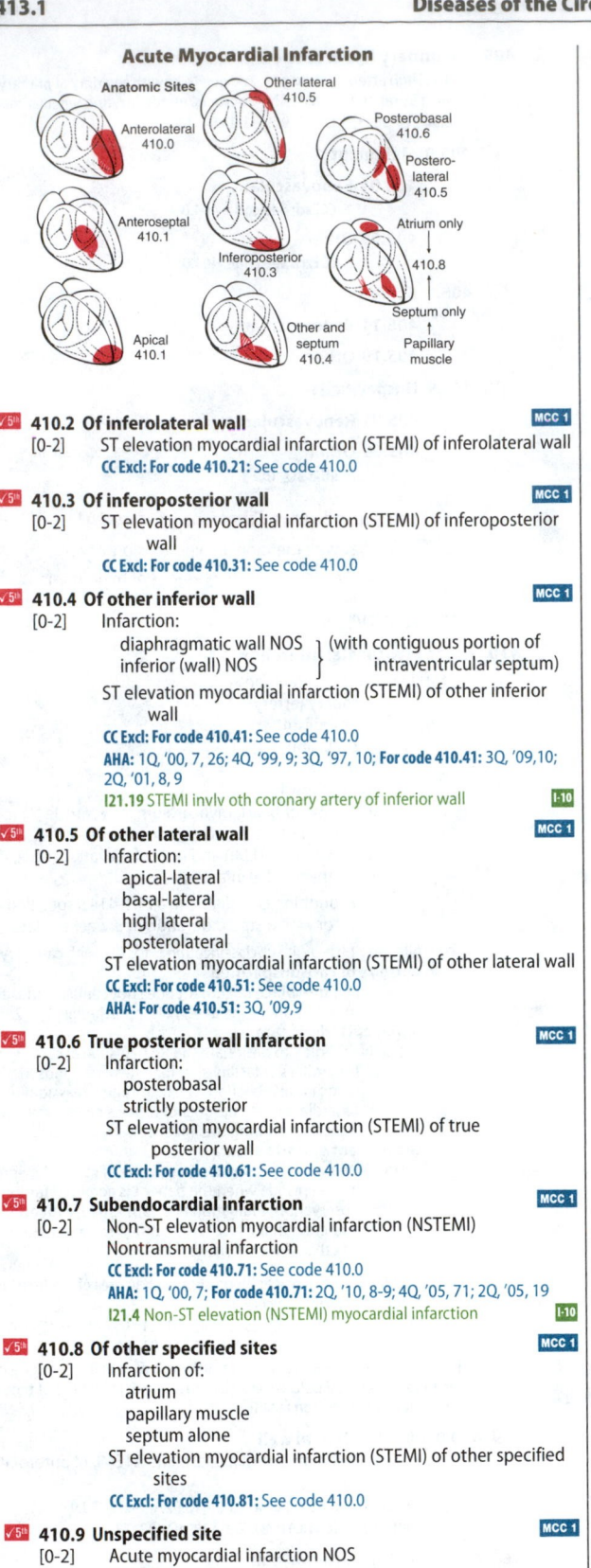

Acute Myocardial Infarction

Anatomic Sites

Anterolateral 410.0

Other lateral 410.5

Anteroseptal 410.1

Inferoposterior 410.3

Posterobasal 410.6

Postero-lateral 410.5

Apical 410.1

Other and septum 410.4

Atrium only 410.8

Septum only

Papillary muscle

§ ✓5ᵗʰ **410.2 Of inferolateral wall**   MCC 1
[0-2]   ST elevation myocardial infarction (STEMI) of inferolateral wall
CC Excl: For code 410.21: See code 410.0

§ ✓5ᵗʰ **410.3 Of inferoposterior wall**   MCC 1
[0-2]   ST elevation myocardial infarction (STEMI) of inferoposterior wall
CC Excl: For code 410.31: See code 410.0

§ ✓5ᵗʰ **410.4 Of other inferior wall**   MCC 1
[0-2]   Infarction:
diaphragmatic wall NOS } (with contiguous portion of
inferior (wall) NOS   intraventricular septum)
ST elevation myocardial infarction (STEMI) of other inferior wall
CC Excl: For code 410.41: See code 410.0
AHA: 1Q, '00, 7, 26; 4Q, '99, 9; 3Q, '97, 10; **For code 410.41:** 3Q, '09,10; 2Q, '01, 8, 9
I21.19 STEMI invlv oth coronary artery of inferior wall   I-10

§ ✓5ᵗʰ **410.5 Of other lateral wall**   MCC 1
[0-2]   Infarction:
apical-lateral
basal-lateral
high lateral
posterolateral
ST elevation myocardial infarction (STEMI) of other lateral wall
CC Excl: For code 410.51: See code 410.0
AHA: For code 410.51: 3Q, '09,9

§ ✓5ᵗʰ **410.6 True posterior wall infarction**   MCC 1
[0-2]   Infarction:
posterobasal
strictly posterior
ST elevation myocardial infarction (STEMI) of true posterior wall
CC Excl: For code 410.61: See code 410.0

§ ✓5ᵗʰ **410.7 Subendocardial infarction**   MCC 1
[0-2]   Non-ST elevation myocardial infarction (NSTEMI)
Nontransmural infarction
CC Excl: For code 410.71: See code 410.0
AHA: 1Q, '00, 7; **For code 410.71:** 2Q, '10, 8-9; 4Q, '05, 71; 2Q, '05, 19
I21.4 Non-ST elevation (NSTEMI) myocardial infarction   I-10

§ ✓5ᵗʰ **410.8 Of other specified sites**   MCC 1
[0-2]   Infarction of:
atrium
papillary muscle
septum alone
ST elevation myocardial infarction (STEMI) of other specified sites
CC Excl: For code 410.81: See code 410.0

§ ✓5ᵗʰ **410.9 Unspecified site**   MCC 1
[0-2]   Acute myocardial infarction NOS
Coronary occlusion NOS
Myocardial infarction NOS
CC Excl: For code 410.91: See code 410.0
AHA: 1Q, '96, 17; 1Q, '92, 9; **For code 410.91:** 2Q, '05, 18; 3Q, '02, 5
I21.3 ST elevation myocardial infarction of uns site   I-10

✓4ᵗʰ **411 Other acute and subacute forms of ischemic heart disease**
AHA: 4Q, '94, 55; 3Q, '91, 24

411.0 Postmyocardial infarction syndrome   CC
Dressler's syndrome
DEF: Complication developing several days/weeks after myocardial infarction; symptoms include fever, leukocytosis, chest pain, pericarditis, pleurisy, and pneumonitis; tendency to recur.
CC Excl: 411.0, 411.81-411.89, 459.89-459.9

411.1 Intermediate coronary syndrome   CC
Impending infarction
Preinfarction angina
Preinfarction syndrome
Unstable angina
EXCLUDES angina (pectoris) (413.9)
decubitus (413.0)
DEF: A condition representing an intermediate stage between angina of effort and acute myocardial infarction. It is often documented by the physician as "unstable angina."
CC Excl: 398.91, 402.01, 402.11, 402.91, 404.01, 404.03, 404.11, 404.13, 404.91, 404.93, 410.00-410.92, 411.1-411.89, 413.0-414.00, 414.2-414.9, 428.0-428.1, 428.9, 459.89-459.9, 785.50-785.51
AHA: 3Q, '07, 9; 4Q, '05, 105; 2Q, '04, 3; 1Q, '03, 12; 3Q, '01, 15; 2Q, '01, 7, 9; 4Q, '98, 86; 2Q, '96, 10; 3Q, '91, 24; 1Q, '91, 14; 3Q, '90, 6; 4Q, '89, 10
TIP: Do not assign code 411.1 on the same episode of care as an acute myocardial infarction (category 410). Assign 411.1 for accelerated angina.
I20.0 Unstable angina   I-10

✓5ᵗʰ **411.8 Other**
AHA: 3Q, '91, 18; 3Q, '89, 4

411.81 Acute coronary occlusion without myocardial infarction   CC
Acute coronary (artery):
embolism
obstruction   } without or not resulting in
occlusion   myocardial infarction
thrombosis
EXCLUDES obstruction without infarction due to atherosclerosis (414.00-414.07)
occlusion without infarction due to atherosclerosis (414.00-414.07)
DEF: Interrupted blood flow to a portion of the heart; without tissue death.
CC Excl: 410.00-411.89, 413.0-413.9, 414.8-414.9, 459.89-459.9
AHA: 3Q, '91, 24; 1Q, '91, 14

411.89 Other   CC
Coronary insufficiency (acute)
Subendocardial ischemia
CC Excl: See code: 411.81
AHA: 3Q, '01, 14; 1Q, '92, 9

412 Old myocardial infarction
Healed myocardial infarction
Past myocardial infarction diagnosed on ECG [EKG] or other special investigation, but currently presenting no symptoms
AHA: 2Q, '03, 10; 2Q, '01, 9; 3Q, '98, 15; 2Q, '91, 22; 3Q, '90, 7
TIP: Assign for any acute myocardial infarction stated to be older than 8 weeks.
I25.2 Old myocardial infarction   I-10

✓4ᵗʰ **413 Angina pectoris**
DEF: Severe constricting pain in the chest, often radiating from the precordium to the left shoulder and down the arm, due to ischemia of the heart muscle; usually caused by coronary disease; pain is often precipitated by effort or excitement.

413.0 Angina decubitus   CC
Nocturnal angina
DEF: Angina occurring only in the recumbent position.
CC Excl: 410.00-410.92, 411.1-411.89, 413.0-413.9, 414.8-414.9, 459.89-459.9

413.1 Prinzmetal angina   CC
Variant angina pectoris
DEF: Angina occurring when patient is recumbent; associated with ST-segment elevations.
CC Excl: See code: 413.0
AHA: 3Q, '06, 23

---

§ Requires fifth digit. Valid digits are in [brackets] under each code. See category 410 for codes and definitions.

N Newborn Age: 0   P Pediatric Age: 0-17   M Maternity Age: 12-55   A Adult Age: 15-124   MCC Major CC Condition   CC CC Condition   HIV HIV Related Dx

413.9 Other and unspecified angina pectoris

Angina:
NOS
cardiac
equivalent
of effort

Anginal syndrome
Status anginosus
Stenocardia
Syncope anginosa

Use additional code(s) for symptoms associated with angina equivalent

EXCLUDES *preinfarction angina (411.1)*

AHA: 2Q, '08, 16; 3Q, '02, 4; 3Q, '91, 16; 3Q, '90, 6

TIP: For patients with both angina and coronary artery disease, sequence the CAD (subcategory 414.0) code first.

I20.9 Angina pectoris unspecified I-10

✓4th **414 Other forms of chronic ischemic heart disease**

EXCLUDES *arteriosclerotic cardiovascular disease [ASCVD] (429.2)*
cardiovascular:
arteriosclerosis or sclerosis (429.2)
degeneration or disease (429.2)

✓5th **414.0 Coronary atherosclerosis**

Arteriosclerotic heart disease [ASHD]
Atherosclerotic heart disease
Coronary (artery):
arteriosclerosis
arteritis or endarteritis
atheroma
sclerosis
stricture

Use additional code, if applicable, to identify chronic total occlusion of coronary artery (414.2)

EXCLUDES *embolism of graft (996.72)*
occlusion NOS of graft (996.72)
thrombus of graft (996.72)

DEF: A chronic condition marked by thickening and loss of elasticity of the coronary artery; caused by deposits of plaque containing cholesterol, lipoid material and lipophages.

AHA: 2Q, '97, 13; 2Q, '95, 17; 4Q, '94, 49; 2Q, '94, 13; 1Q, '94, 6; 3Q, '90, 7

414.00 Of unspecified type of vessel, native or graft A

AHA: 1Q, '04, 24; 2Q, '03, 16; 3Q, '01, 15; 4Q, '99, 4; 3Q, '97, 15; 4Q, '96, 31

414.01 Of native coronary artery A

DEF: Plaque deposits in natural heart vessels.

AHA: 3Q, '12, 17; 3Q, '09, 9, 10; 3Q, '08, 10; 2Q, '08, 16; 3Q, '06, 25; 4Q, '05, 71; 2Q, '04, 3; 4Q, '03, 108; 3Q, '03, 9, 14; 3Q, '02, 4-9; 3Q, '01, 15; 2Q, '01, 8, 9; 3Q, '97, 15; 2Q, '96, 10; 4Q, '96, 31

TIP: Assign for documentation of CAD NOS in a patient with no history of coronary artery bypass procedure.

I25.10 ASHD of native cor artery w/o angina pectoris I-10

414.02 Of autologous vein bypass graft CC A

DEF: Plaque deposit in grafted vein originating within patient.

AHA: 2Q, '10, 8-9

CC Excl: 414.00-414.05, 414.07, 414.2-414.3

414.03 Of nonautologous biological bypass graft CC A

DEF: Plaque deposits in grafted vessel originating outside patient.

CC Excl: See code: 414.02

414.04 Of artery bypass graft CC A

Internal mammary artery

DEF: Plaque deposits in grafted artery originating within patient.

CC Excl: See code: 414.02

AHA: 4Q, '96, 31

414.05 Of unspecified type of bypass graft A

Bypass graft NOS

AHA: 3Q, '97, 15; 4Q, '96, 31

414.06 Of native coronary artery of transplanted heart CC

CC Excl: 414.00-414.07, 414.2-414.3

AHA: 4Q, '03, 60; 4Q, '02, 53

414.07 Of bypass graft (artery) (vein) of transplanted heart CC A

CC Excl: 414.00-414.06, 414.2-414.3

Arteries of the Heart

Aortic valve
Right coronary artery
Marginal branches
Descending branch (posterior interventricular artery)
Left coronary artery
Circumflex branch
Descending branch (anterior interventricular artery)

✓5th **414.1 Aneurysm and dissection of heart**

AHA: 4Q, '02, 54

414.10 Aneurysm of heart (wall) CC

Aneurysm (arteriovenous):
mural
ventricular

CC Excl: 414.10-414.11, 414.19

414.11 Aneurysm of coronary vessels

Aneurysm (arteriovenous) of coronary vessels

DEF: Dilatation of all three-vessel wall layers forming a sac filled with blood.

AHA: 2Q, '10, 8-9; 3Q, '03, 10; 1Q, '99, 17

414.12 Dissection of coronary artery MCC

DEF: A tear in the intimal arterial wall of a coronary artery resulting in the sudden intrusion of blood within the layers of the wall.

CC Excl: 414.12, 443.29, 447.2, 447.5-447.6, 447.8-447.9

AHA: 1Q, '11, 3-4

414.19 Other aneurysm of heart CC

Arteriovenous fistula, acquired, of heart

CC Excl: See code: 414.10

414.2 Chronic total occlusion of coronary artery

Complete occlusion of coronary artery
Total occlusion of coronary artery

Code first coronary atherosclerosis (414.00-414.07)

EXCLUDES *acute coronary occlusion with myocardial infarction (410.00-410.92)*
acute coronary occlusion without myocardial infarction (411.81)

DEF: Complete blockage of coronary artery due to plaque accumulation over an extended period of time; results in substantial reduction of blood flow.

AHA: 4Q, '07, 82

414.3 Coronary atherosclerosis due to lipid rich plaque A

Code first coronary atherosclerosis (414.00-414.07)

AHA: 4Q, '08, 113

414.4 Coronary atherosclerosis due to calcified coronary lesion

Coronary atherosclerosis due to severely calcified coronary lesion

Code first coronary atherosclerosis (414.00-414.07)

AHA: 4Q, '11, 107

414.8 Other specified forms of chronic ischemic heart disease

Chronic coronary insufficiency
Ischemia, myocardial (chronic)

Any condition classifiable to 410 specified as chronic, or presenting with symptoms after 8 weeks from date of infarction

EXCLUDES *coronary insufficiency (acute) (411.89)*

AHA: ▶4Q, '13, 102;◀ 3Q, '01, 15; 1Q, '92, 10; 3Q, '90, 7, 15; 2Q, '90, 19

I25.89 Other forms of chronic ischemic heart disease I-10

414.9 Chronic ischemic heart disease, unspecified

Ischemic heart disease NOS

2015 ICD-9-CM

✓4th ✓5th Additional Digit Required Unacceptable PDx Manifestation Code Hospital Acquired Condition ▶◀ Revised Text ● New Code ▲ Revised Code Title

October 2014 • Volume 1 – 139

Diseases of the Circulatory System

Diseases of Pulmonary Circulation (415-417)

√4ᵗʰ 415   Acute pulmonary heart disease

415.0   Acute cor pulmonale   `MCC`

   EXCLUDES cor pulmonale NOS (416.9)

   DEF: A heart-lung disease marked by dilation and failure of the right side of heart; due to pulmonary embolism; ventilatory function is impaired and pulmonary hypertension results.

   CC Excl: 415.0, 416.8-416.9, 459.89-459.9

√5ᵗʰ 415.1   Pulmonary embolism and infarction

   Pulmonary (artery) (vein):   Pulmonary (artery) (vein):
      apoplexy   infarction (hemorrhagic)
      embolism   thrombosis

   EXCLUDES chronic pulmonary embolism (416.2)
      personal history of pulmonary embolism (V12.55)
      that complicating:
         abortion (634-638 with .6, 639.6)
         ectopic or molar pregnancy (639.6)
         pregnancy, childbirth, or the puerperium
            (673.0-673.8)

   DEF: Embolism: Closure of the pulmonary artery or branch; due to thrombosis (blood clot).

   DEF: Infarction: Necrosis of lung tissue; due to obstructed arterial blood supply, most often by pulmonary embolism.

   AHA: 4Q, '90, 25

¹¹415.11   Iatrogenic pulmonary embolism and infarction   `MCC`

   Use additional code for associated septic pulmonary embolism, if applicable, 415.12

   CC Excl: 415.11-415.19, 416.2, 444.01-444.09, 459.89-459.9

   AHA: 4Q, '95, 58

   TIP: Do not report code 997.39 Other respiratory complications, with code 415.11.

415.12   Septic pulmonary embolism   `MCC`

   Septic embolism NOS

   Code first underlying infection, such as:
      septicemia (038.0-038.9)

   EXCLUDES septic arterial embolism (449)

   CC Excl: See code: 415.11

   AHA: 4Q, '07, 84-86

¹¹415.13   Saddle embolus of pulmonary artery   `MCC`

   CC Excl: See code 415.11

   AHA: 4Q, '11, 107-108

¹¹415.19   Other   `MCC`

   CC Excl: See code: 415.11

   AHA: 3Q, '10, 10; 4Q, '09, 86

   I26.99 Other pulmonary emb w/o acute cor pulmonale   `I-10`

√4ᵗʰ 416   Chronic pulmonary heart disease

416.0   Primary pulmonary hypertension   `CC`

   Idiopathic pulmonary arteriosclerosis
   Pulmonary hypertension (essential) (idiopathic) (primary)

   EXCLUDES pulmonary hypertension NOS (416.8)
      secondary pulmonary hypertension (416.8)

   DEF: A rare increase in pulmonary circulation, often resulting in right ventricular failure or fatal syncope.

   CC Excl: 278.03, 416.0, 416.8-416.9, 417.8-417.9, 459.89-459.9

   I27.0 Primary pulmonary hypertension   `I-10`

416.1   Kyphoscoliotic heart disease   `CC`

   DEF: High blood pressure within the lungs as a result of curvature of the spine.

   CC Excl: 278.03, 416.0-416.1, 416.8-416.9

416.2   Chronic pulmonary embolism   `CC`

   Use additional code, if applicable, for associated long-term (current) use of anticoagulants (V58.61)

   EXCLUDES personal history of pulmonary embolism (V12.55)

   DEF: A long-standing condition commonly associated with pulmonary hypertension in which small blood clots travel to the lungs repeatedly over many weeks, months, or years, requiring continuation of established anticoagulant or thrombolytic therapy.

   CC Excl: 415.11-415.19, 416.2, 444.01-444.09, 459.89-459.9

   AHA: 4Q, '09, 85, 86

416.8   Other chronic pulmonary heart diseases

   Pulmonary hypertension NOS
   Pulmonary hypertension, secondary

   AHA: 1Q, '12, 17; 1Q, '11, 10; 2Q, '10,10

   I27.89 Other specified pulmonary heart diseases   `I-10`

416.9   Chronic pulmonary heart disease, unspecified

   Chronic cardiopulmonary disease
   Cor pulmonale (chronic) NOS

√4ᵗʰ 417   Other diseases of pulmonary circulation

417.0   Arteriovenous fistula of pulmonary vessels   `CC`

   EXCLUDES congenital arteriovenous fistula (747.32)

   DEF: Abnormal communication between blood vessels within lung.

   CC Excl: 417.0-417.9

417.1   Aneurysm of pulmonary artery   `CC`

   EXCLUDES congenital aneurysm (747.39)
      congenital arteriovenous aneurysm (747.32)

   CC Excl: See code: 417.0

417.8   Other specified diseases of pulmonary circulation

   Pulmonary: Pulmonary:
      arteritis   endarteritis
   Rupture   }
   Stricture   of pulmonary vessel

417.9   Unspecified disease of pulmonary circulation

Other Forms of Heart Disease (420-429)

√4ᵗʰ 420   Acute pericarditis

   INCLUDES acute:
      mediastinopericarditis
      myopericarditis
      pericardial effusion
      pleuropericarditis
      pneumopericarditis

   EXCLUDES acute rheumatic pericarditis (391.0)
      postmyocardial infarction syndrome [Dressler's] (411.0)

   DEF: Inflammation of the pericardium (heart sac); pericardial friction rub results from this inflammation and is heard as a scratchy or leathery sound.

420.0   Acute pericarditis in diseases classified elsewhere   `CC`

   Code first underlying disease, as:
      actinomycosis (039.8)
      amebiasis (006.8)
      chronic uremia (585.9)
      nocardiosis (039.8)
      tuberculosis (017.9)
      uremia NOS (586)

   EXCLUDES pericarditis (acute) (in):
      Coxsackie (virus) (074.21)
      gonococcal (098.83)
      histoplasmosis (115.0-115.9 with fifth-digit 3)
      meningococcal infection (036.41)
      syphilitic (093.81)

   CC Excl: 391.0, 393, 420.0-420.99, 423.3-423.9, 459.89-459.9

√5ᵗʰ 420.9   Other and unspecified acute pericarditis

420.90   Acute pericarditis, unspecified   `CC`

   Pericarditis (acute):   Pericarditis (acute):
      NOS   sicca
      infective NOS

   CC Excl: See code: 420.0

   AHA: 2Q, '89, 12

420.91   Acute idiopathic pericarditis   `CC`

   Pericarditis, acute: Pericarditis, acute:
      benign   viral
      nonspecific

   CC Excl: See code: 420.0

---

¹¹ HAC when reported with procedure codes 00.85-00.87, 81.51, 81.52, 81.54 and POA = N

`N` Newborn Age: 0   `P` Pediatric Age: 0-17   `M` Maternity Age: 12-55   `A` Adult Age: 15-124   `MCC` Major CC Condition   `CC` CC Condition   `HIV` HIV Related Dx

140 – Volume 1   **2015 ICD-9-CM**

Anatomy

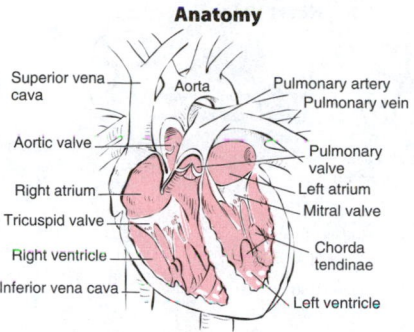

Superior vena cava · Aorta · Pulmonary artery · Pulmonary vein · Aortic valve · Pulmonary valve · Right atrium · Left atrium · Tricuspid valve · Mitral valve · Right ventricle · Chorda tendinae · Inferior vena cava · Left ventricle

Blood Flow

420.99 Other   `CC`
Pericarditis (acute):
    pneumococcal
    purulent
    staphylococcal
    streptococcal
    suppurative
Pneumopyopericardium
Pyopericardium

EXCLUDES pericarditis in diseases classified elsewhere (420.0)
CC Excl: See code: 420.0

✓4ᵗʰ 421 Acute and subacute endocarditis
DEF: Bacterial inflammation of the endocardium (intracardiac area); major symptoms include fever, fatigue, heart murmurs, splenomegaly, embolic episodes and areas of infarction.

421.0 Acute and subacute bacterial endocarditis   `MCC` `HIV`
Endocarditis (acute)(chronic) (subacute):
    bacterial
    infective NOS
    lenta
    malignant
    purulent
    septic
    ulcerative
    vegetative
Infective aneurysm
Subacute bacterial endocarditis [SBE]

Use additional code to identify infectious organism [e.g., Streptococcus 041.0, Staphylococcus 041.1]
CC Excl: 391.1, 397.9, 421.0-421.9, 424.90-424.99, 459.89-459.9
AHA: 4Q, '08, 73; 1Q, '99, 12; 1Q, '91, 15
`I-10` I33.0 Acute and subacute infective endocarditis

421.1 Acute and subacute infective endocarditis in diseases classified elsewhere   `MCC`

Code first underlying disease, as:
    blastomycosis (116.0)
    Q fever (083.0)
    typhoid (fever) (002.0)
EXCLUDES endocarditis (in):
    Coxsackie (virus) (074.22)
    gonococcal (098.84)
    histoplasmosis (115.0-115.9 with fifth-digit 4)
    meningococcal infection (036.42)
    monilial (112.81)
CC Excl: See code: 421.0

421.9 Acute endocarditis, unspecified   `MCC` `HIV`
Endocarditis
Myoendocarditis ⎫ acute or subacute
Periendocarditis ⎭

EXCLUDES acute rheumatic endocarditis (391.1)
CC Excl: See code: 421.0

✓4ᵗʰ 422 Acute myocarditis
EXCLUDES acute rheumatic myocarditis (391.2)
DEF: Acute inflammation of the muscular walls of the heart (myocardium).

422.0 Acute myocarditis in diseases classified elsewhere   `MCC`
Code first underlying disease, as:
    myocarditis (acute):
        influenzal (487.8, 488.09, 488.19)
        tuberculous (017.9)
EXCLUDES *myocarditis (acute) (due to):*
        aseptic, of newborn (074.23)
        Coxsackie (virus) (074.23)
        diphtheritic (032.82)
        meningococcal infection (036.43)
        syphilitic (093.82)
        toxoplasmosis (130.3)
CC Excl: 391.2, 398.0, 422.0-422.99, 429.0, 429.71-429.79, 459.89-459.9

✓5ᵗʰ 422.9 Other and unspecified acute myocarditis

422.90 Acute myocarditis, unspecified   `MCC` `HIV`
Acute or subacute (interstitial) myocarditis
CC Excl: See code: 422.0

422.91 Idiopathic myocarditis   `MCC` `HIV`
Myocarditis (acute or subacute):
    Fiedler's
    giant cell
    isolated (diffuse) (granulomatous)
    nonspecific granulomatous
CC Excl: See code: 422.0

422.92 Septic myocarditis   `MCC` `HIV`
Myocarditis, acute or subacute:
    pneumococcal
    staphylococcal

Use additional code to identify infectious organism [e.g., Staphylococcus 041.1]
EXCLUDES *myocarditis, acute or subacute:*
        in bacterial diseases classified elsewhere (422.0)
        streptococcal (391.2)
CC Excl: See code 422.0

422.93 Toxic myocarditis   `MCC` `HIV`
DEF: Inflammation of the heart muscle due to an adverse reaction to certain drugs or chemicals reaching the heart through the bloodstream.
CC Excl: See code: 422.0

422.99 Other   `MCC` `HIV`
CC Excl: See code: 422.0

✓4ᵗʰ 423 Other diseases of pericardium
EXCLUDES that specified as rheumatic (393)

423.0 Hemopericardium   `CC`
DEF: Blood in the pericardial sac (pericardium).
CC Excl: 423.0-423.9, 459.89-459.9

423.1 Adhesive pericarditis   `CC`
Adherent pericardium   Pericarditis:
Fibrosis of pericardium   adhesive
Milk spots   obliterative
                Soldiers' patches
DEF: Two layers of serous pericardium adhere to each other by fibrous adhesions.
CC Excl: See code: 423.0

423.2 Constrictive pericarditis   `CC`
Concato's disease   Pick's disease of heart (and liver)
DEF: Inflammation identified by a rigid, thickened and sometimes calcified pericardium; ventricles of the heart not adequately filled; congestive heart failure may result.
CC Excl: See code: 423.0

Diseases of the Circulatory System

423.3–425.0

Cardiac Tamponade

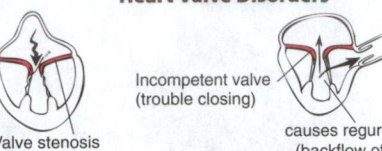

Normal   Cardiac Tamponade

- Fibrous pericardium
- Serous pericardium (visceral layer)
- Pericardial space (potential)
- Serous pericardium (parietal layer)
- Excessive fluid in pericardial space
- ▨ --constricted areas

Heart Valve Disorders

- Valve stenosis (trouble opening)
- Incompetent valve (trouble closing)
- causes regurgitation (backflow of blood)
- Insufficient valve (unable to close completely)
- Shortened, fused chorda tendinae
- Ventricular hypertrophy

Normal Heart Valve Function

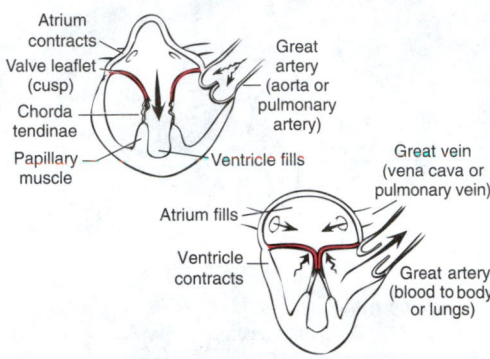

- Atrium contracts
- Valve leaflet (cusp)
- Chorda tendinae
- Papillary muscle
- Great artery (aorta or pulmonary artery)
- Ventricle fills
- Great vein (vena cava or pulmonary vein)
- Atrium fills
- Ventricle contracts
- Great artery (blood to body or lungs)

423.3 Cardiac tamponade   `CC`

Code first the underlying cause

DEF: Life-threatening condition in which fluid or blood accumulates between the muscle of the heart (myocardium) and the outer sac (pericardium), resulting in compression of the heart, which decreases cardiac output.

CC Excl: 074.21, 093.81, 391.0, 393, 420.0-420.99, 423.3-423.9, 459.89-459.9

AHA: 4Q, '07, 86, 87

423.8 Other specified diseases of pericardium   `CC`

Calcification ⎱
Fistula   ⎰ of pericardium

CC Excl: See code: 423.3

AHA: 2Q, '89, 12

423.9 Unspecified disease of pericardium   `CC`

CC Excl: See code: 423.3

AHA: 1Q, '07, 11

✓4ᵗʰ **424 Other diseases of endocardium**

EXCLUDES bacterial endocarditis (421.0-421.9)
rheumatic endocarditis (391.1, 394.0-397.9)
syphilitic endocarditis (093.20-093.24)

424.0 Mitral valve disorders

Mitral (valve):
incompetence ⎱
insufficiency ⎰ NOS of specified cause,
regurgitation   except rheumatic

EXCLUDES mitral (valve):
disease (394.9)
failure (394.9)
stenosis (394.0)
the listed conditions:
specified as rheumatic (394.1)
unspecified as to cause but with mention of:
diseases of aortic valve (396.0-396.9)
mitral stenosis or obstruction (394.2)

AHA: 3Q, '06, 7; 2Q, '00, 16; 3Q, '98, 11; N-D, '87, 8; N-D, '84, 8

I34.8 Other nonrheumatic mitral valve disorders   `I-10`

424.1 Aortic valve disorders

Aortic (valve):
incompetence ⎱
insufficiency ⎱ NOS of specified cause,
regurgitation ⎰ except rheumatic
stenosis

EXCLUDES hypertrophic subaortic stenosis (425.11)
that specified as rheumatic (395.0-395.9)
that of unspecified cause but with mention of diseases of mitral valve (396.0-396.9)

AHA: 4Q, '11, 152; 4Q, '08, 179; 4Q, '88, 8; N-D, '87, 8

424.2 Tricuspid valve disorders, specified as nonrheumatic

Tricuspid valve:
incompetence ⎱
insufficiency ⎱ of specified cause, except
regurgitation ⎰ rheumatic
stenosis

EXCLUDES rheumatic or of unspecified cause (397.0)

424.3 Pulmonary valve disorders

Pulmonic: Pulmonic:
incompetence NOS   regurgitation NOS
insufficiency NOS   stenosis NOS

EXCLUDES that specified as rheumatic (397.1)

✓5ᵗʰ **424.9 Endocarditis, valve unspecified**

424.90 Endocarditis, valve unspecified, unspecified cause   `CC`

Endocarditis (chronic):
NOS
nonbacterial thrombotic
Valvular:
incompetence ⎱
insufficiency ⎱ of unspecified valve,
regurgitation ⎰ unspecified cause
stenosis
Valvulitis (chronic)

CC Excl: 424.90-424.99, 459.89-459.9

I38 Endocarditis valve unspecified   `I-10`

424.91 Endocarditis in diseases classified elsewhere   `CC`

Code first underlying disease as:
atypical verrucous endocarditis [Libman-Sacks] (710.0)
disseminated lupus erythematosus (710.0)
tuberculosis (017.9)

EXCLUDES syphilitic (093.20-093.24)

CC Excl: See code: 424.90

424.99 Other   `CC`

Any condition classifiable to 424.90 with specified cause, except rheumatic

EXCLUDES endocardial fibroelastosis (425.3)
that specified as rheumatic (397.9)

CC Excl: See code: 424.90

✓4ᵗʰ **425 Cardiomyopathy**

INCLUDES myocardiopathy

AHA: J-A, '85, 15

425.0 Endomyocardial fibrosis   `CC`

CC Excl: 398.91, 402.01, 402.11, 402.91, 404.01, 404.03, 404.11, 404.13, 404.91, 404.93, 414.00-414.07, 414.2-414.9, 425.0-425.9, 426.10-426.13, 426.50-426.54, 426.81-426.89, 427.31-427.42, 427.60-427.89, 428.0-428.1, 428.9, 459.89-459.9, 746.86, 785.0-785.1, 785.50-785.51

`N` Newborn Age: 0   `P` Pediatric Age: 0-17   `M` Maternity Age: 12-55   `A` Adult Age: 15-124   `MCC` Major CC Condition   `CC` CC Condition   `HIV` HIV Related Dx

√5ᵗʰ **425.1 Hypertrophic cardiomyopathy**

EXCLUDES *ventricular hypertrophy (429.3)*

DEF: Cardiomyopathy marked by left ventricle hypertrophy, enlarged septum; results in obstructed blood flow.

AHA: 4Q, '11, 109-110

425.11 Hypertrophic obstructive cardiomyopathy `CC`

Hypertrophic subaortic stenosis (idiopathic)

CC Excl: see Code: 425.0

AHA: ▶3Q, '13, 10◀

425.18 Other hypertrophic cardiomyopathy `CC`

Nonobstructive hypertrophic cardiomyopathy

CC Excl: see Code: 425.0

425.2 Obscure cardiomyopathy of Africa `CC`

Becker's disease

Idiopathic mural endomyocardial disease

CC Excl: See code: 425.0

425.3 Endocardial fibroelastosis `CC`

Elastomyofibrosis

DEF: A condition marked by left ventricle hypertrophy and conversion of the endocardium into a thick fibroelastic coat; capacity of the ventricle may be reduced, but is often increased.

CC Excl: See code: 425.0

425.4 Other primary cardiomyopathies `CC`

Cardiomyopathy:
  NOS
  congestive
  constrictive
  familial

Cardiomyopathy:
  idiopathic
  obstructive
  restrictive
  Cardiovascular collagenosis

CC Excl: See code: 425.0

AHA: 4Q, '11, 109-110; 4Q, '09, 141; 1Q, '07, 20; 2Q, '05, 14; 1Q, '00, 22; 4Q, '97, 55; 2Q, '90, 19

TIP: For congestive cardiomyopathy, assign first a code for the CHF (category 428) if the treatment is directed toward the CHF.

I42.8 Other cardiomyopathies `I-10`

425.5 Alcoholic cardiomyopathy `CC`

DEF: Heart disease as result of excess alcohol consumption.

CC Excl: See code: 425.0

AHA: S-O, '85, 15

425.7 Nutritional and metabolic cardiomyopathy `CC`

Code first underlying disease, as:
  amyloidosis (277.30-277.39)
  beriberi (265.0)
  cardiac glycogenosis (271.0)
  mucopolysaccharidosis (277.5)
  thyrotoxicosis (242.0-242.9)

EXCLUDES *gouty tophi of heart (274.82)*

CC Excl: See code 425.0

425.8 Cardiomyopathy in other diseases classified elsewhere `CC`

Code first underlying disease, as:
  Friedreich's ataxia (334.0)
  myotonia atrophica (359.21)
  progressive muscular dystrophy (359.1)
  sarcoidosis (135)

EXCLUDES *cardiomyopathy in Chagas' disease (086.0)*

CC Excl: See code 425.0

AHA: 2Q, '93, 9

I43 Cardiomyopathy in diseases classified elsewhere `I-10`

425.9 Secondary cardiomyopathy, unspecified `CC`

CC Excl: See code 425.0

√4ᵗʰ **426 Conduction disorders**

DEF: Disruption or disturbance in the electrical impulses that regulate heartbeats.

426.0 Atrioventricular block, complete `CC`

Third degree atrioventricular block

CC Excl: 426.0-427.5, 427.89, 459.89-459.9

AHA: 2Q, '06, 14

TIP: Assign if documentation indicates intermittent complete heart block.

√5ᵗʰ **426.1 Atrioventricular block, other and unspecified**

TIP: Assign separate codes for each type of AV block documented.

426.10 Atrioventricular block, unspecified

Atrioventricular [AV] block (incomplete) (partial)

AHA: 2Q, '06, 14

Nerve Conduction of the Heart

Sinoatrial node (pacemaker)
Internodal tracts:
  Anterior
  Middle
  Posterior
Atrioventricular node
Common bundle (of His)
Atrioventricular block
Accessory bundle (of Kent)
Right bundle branch
Right bundle branch block
Moderator band
Bachmann's bundle
Left bundle branch block
Left bundle branch:
  Anterior fascicle
  Posterior fascicle
Left bundle branch hemiblock
Purkinje fibers

426.11 First degree atrioventricular block

Incomplete atrioventricular block, first degree
Prolonged P-R interval NOS

I44.0 Atrioventricular block first degree `I-10`

426.12 Mobitz (type) II atrioventricular block `CC`

Incomplete atrioventricular block:
  Mobitz (type) II
  second degree, Mobitz (type) II

DEF: Impaired conduction of excitatory impulse from cardiac atrium to ventricle through AV node.

CC Excl: See code: 426.0

426.13 Other second degree atrioventricular block

Incomplete atrioventricular block:
  Mobitz (type) I [Wenckebach's]
  second degree:
    NOS
    Mobitz (type) I
    with 2:1 atrioventricular response [block]
  Wenckebach's phenomenon

DEF: Wenckebach's phenomenon: impulses generated at constant rate to sinus node, P-R interval lengthens; results in cycle of ventricular inadequacy and shortened P-R interval; second-degree A-V block commonly called "Mobitz type 1."

426.2 Left bundle branch hemiblock

Block:
  left anterior fascicular
  left posterior fascicular

426.3 Other left bundle branch block

Left bundle branch block:
  NOS
  anterior fascicular with posterior fascicular
  complete
  main stem

I44.7 Left bundle-branch block unspecified `I-10`

426.4 Right bundle branch block

AHA: 3Q, '00, 3

I45.10 Unspecified right bundle-branch block `I-10`

√5ᵗʰ **426.5 Bundle branch block, other and unspecified**

426.50 Bundle branch block, unspecified

426.51 Right bundle branch block and left posterior fascicular block

426.52 Right bundle branch block and left anterior fascicular block

426.53 Other bilateral bundle branch block `CC`

Bifascicular block NOS
Bilateral bundle branch block NOS
Right bundle branch with left bundle branch block (incomplete) (main stem)

CC Excl: 426.0-427.5, 427.89, 459.89-459.9

426.54 Trifascicular block `CC`

CC Excl: 426.0-427.5, 427.89, 459.89-459.9

426.6 Other heart block

Intraventricular block:
  NOS
  diffuse
  myofibrillar

Sinoatrial block
Sinoauricular block

√4ᵗʰ√5ᵗʰ Additional Digit Required   Unacceptable PDx   Manifestation Code   Hospital Acquired Condition   ▶◀ Revised Text   ● New Code   ▲ Revised Code Title

Normal and Long QT Electrocardiogram

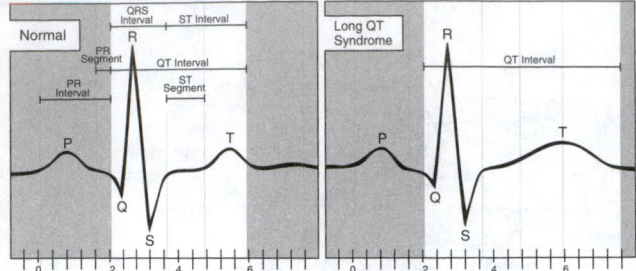

426.7 Anomalous atrioventricular excitation
Atrioventricular conduction:
    accelerated
    accessory
    pre-excitation
Ventricular pre-excitation
Wolff-Parkinson-White syndrome
DEF: Wolff-Parkinson-White: normal conduction pathway is bypassed; results in short P-R interval on EKG; tendency to supraventricular tachycardia.

√5ᵗʰ 426.8 Other specified conduction disorders

  426.81 Lown-Ganong-Levine syndrome
    Syndrome of short P-R interval, normal QRS complexes, and supraventricular tachycardias

  426.82 Long QT syndrome
    DEF: Condition characterized by recurrent syncope, malignant arrhythmias, and sudden death; characteristic prolonged Q-T interval on electrocardiogram.
    AHA: 4Q, '05, 72

  426.89 Other   `CC`
    Dissociation:
      atrioventricular [AV]
      interference
      isorhythmic
    Nonparoxysmal AV nodal tachycardia
    CC Excl: 426.0-426.5, 427.89, 459.89-459.9
    AHA: ▶2Q, '13, 25◀

426.9 Conduction disorder, unspecified
Heart block NOS
Stokes-Adams syndrome

√4ᵗʰ 427 Cardiac dysrhythmias
  EXCLUDES *that complicating:*
      abortion (634-638 with .7, 639.8)
      ectopic or molar pregnancy (639.8)
      labor or delivery (668.1, 669.4)
  DEF: Disruption or disturbance in the rhythm of heartbeats.
  AHA: J-A, '85, 15

  427.0 Paroxysmal supraventricular tachycardia   `CC`
    Paroxysmal tachycardia: Paroxysmal tachycardia:
      atrial [PAT]   junctional
      atrioventricular [AV]   nodal
    DEF: Rapid atrial rhythm.
    CC Excl: See code: 426.89

  427.1 Paroxysmal ventricular tachycardia   `CC`
    Ventricular tachycardia (paroxysmal)
    DEF: Rapid ventricular rhythm.
    CC Excl: See code: 426.89
    AHA: ▶3Q, '13, 6; 1Q, '13, 10;◀ 2Q, '09, 14; 1Q, '08, 14; 2Q, '06, 15-16; 3Q, '95, 9; M-A, '86, 11
    TIP: If a ventricular tachycardia is documented as sustained or nonsustained but is induced during an EP study, assign 427.1.
    I47.2 Ventricular tachycardia   `I-10`

  427.2 Paroxysmal tachycardia, unspecified
    Bouveret-Hoffmann syndrome
    Paroxysmal tachycardia:
      essential
      NOS

√5ᵗʰ 427.3 Atrial fibrillation and flutter
  TIP: Assign V58.61 Long-term (current) use of anticoagulants, as a secondary diagnosis if the patient is maintained on Coumadin.

  427.31 Atrial fibrillation
    DEF: Irregular, rapid atrial contractions.
    AHA: ▶4Q, '13, 98, 101;◀ 1Q, '12, 7; 4Q, '08, 135; 3Q, '05, 8; 4Q, '04, 78, 121; 3Q, '04, 7; 4Q, '03, 95, 105; 1Q, '03, 8; 2Q, '99, 17; 3Q, '95, 8
    I48.0 Atrial fibrillation   `I-10`

  427.32 Atrial flutter   `CC`
    DEF: Regular, rapid atrial contractions.
    CC Excl: See code: 426.89
    AHA: 4Q, '03, 94
    I48.1 Atrial flutter   `I-10`

√5ᵗʰ 427.4 Ventricular fibrillation and flutter

  ¹ **427.41 Ventricular fibrillation**   `MCC`
    DEF: Irregular, rapid ventricular contractions.
    CC Excl: See code: 426.89
    AHA: 2Q, '09, 14-15; 3Q, '02, 5

  427.42 Ventricular flutter   `MCC`
    DEF: Regular, rapid, ventricular contractions.
    CC Excl: See code: 426.89

¹ **427.5 Cardiac arrest**   `MCC`
  Cardiorespiratory arrest
  CC Excl: 427.0-427.5, 459.89-459.9
  AHA: ▶1Q, '13, 9-11;◀ 3Q, '02, 5; 2Q, '00, 12; 3Q, '95, 8; 2Q, '88, 8
  I46.9 Cardiac arrest cause unspecified   `I-10`

√5ᵗʰ 427.6 Premature beats

  427.60 Premature beats, unspecified
    Ectopic beats
    Extrasystoles
    Extrasystolic arrhythmia
    Premature contractions or systoles NOS

  427.61 Supraventricular premature beats
    Atrial premature beats, contractions, or systoles

  427.69 Other
    Ventricular premature beats, contractions, or systoles
    AHA: 4Q, '93, 42

√5ᵗʰ 427.8 Other specified cardiac dysrhythmias

  427.81 Sinoatrial node dysfunction
    Sinus bradycardia:
      persistent
      severe
    Syndrome:
      sick sinus
      tachycardia-bradycardia
    EXCLUDES *sinus bradycardia NOS (427.89)*
    DEF: Complex cardiac arrhythmia; appears as severe sinus bradycardia, sinus bradycardia with tachycardia, or sinus bradycardia with atrioventricular block.
    AHA: 4Q, '11, 168; 3Q, '10, 9; 3Q, '00, 8
    I49.5 Sick sinus syndrome   `I-10`

  427.89 Other
    Rhythm disorder:
      coronary sinus
      ectopic
      nodal
    Wandering (atrial) pacemaker
    EXCLUDES *carotid sinus syncope (337.0)*
      neonatal bradycardia (779.81)
      neonatal tachycardia (779.82)
      reflex bradycardia (337.0)
      tachycardia NOS (785.0)
    AHA: 3Q, '12, 9
    I49.8 Other specified cardiac arrhythmias   `I-10`

427.9 Cardiac dysrhythmia, unspecified
  Arrhythmia (cardiac) NOS
  AHA: 2Q, '89, 10

---

¹ MCC = Only if patient is discharged alive.

N Newborn Age: 0   P Pediatric Age: 0-17   M Maternity Age: 12-55   A Adult Age: 15-124   `MCC` Major CC Condition   `CC` CC Condition   `HIV` HIV Related Dx

144 – Volume 1 · October 2014   2015 ICD-9-CM

√4ᵗʰ **428 Heart failure**

Code, if applicable, heart failure due to hypertension first (402.0-402.9, with fifth-digit 1 or 404.0-404.9 with fifth-digit 1 or 3)

EXCLUDES *following cardiac surgery (429.4)*
rheumatic (398.91)
that complicating:
abortion (634-638 with .7, 639.8)
ectopic or molar pregnancy (639.8)
labor or delivery (668.1, 669.4)

AHA: 4Q, '02, 49; 3Q, '98, 5; 2Q, '90, 16; 2Q, '90, 19; 2Q, '89, 10; 3Q, '88, 3

428.0 Congestive heart failure, unspecified

Congestive heart disease
Right heart failure (secondary to left heart failure)

EXCLUDES *fluid overload NOS (276.69)*

DEF: Mechanical inadequacy; caused by inability of heart to pump and circulate blood; results in fluid collection in lungs, hypertension, congestion and edema of tissue.

AHA: 3Q, '12, 9; 4Q, '09, 141; 1Q, '09, 8, 18; 4Q, '08, 72, 180, 182; 3Q, '08, 12; 3Q, '07, 9; 1Q, 07, 20; 3Q, '06, 7; 4Q, '05, 120; 3Q, '05, 8; 1Q, '05, 5, 9; 1Q, '05, 5, 9; 4Q, '04, 140; 3Q, '04, 7;4Q, '03, 109; 1Q, '03, 9; 4Q, '02, 52; 2Q, '01, 13; 4Q, '00, 48; 2Q, '00, 16; 1Q, '00, 22; 4Q, '99, 4; 1Q, '99, 11; 4Q, '97, 55; 3Q, '97, 10; 3Q, '96, 9; 3Q, '91, 18; 3Q, '91, 19; 2Q, '89, 12

TIP: Assign additional code(s) from subcategory 428.2, 428.3, or 428.4 to specify the type of heart failure.

I50.9 Heart failure unspecified   `I-10`

428.1 Left heart failure   `CC`

Acute edema of lung ⎱ with heart disease NOS or
Acute pulmonary edema ⎰ heart failure
Cardiac asthma
Left ventricular failure

DEF: Mechanical inadequacy of left ventricle; causing fluid in lungs.

CC Excl: 398.91, 402.01, 402.11, 402.91, 428.0-428.9, 459.89-459.9

√5ᵗʰ **428.2 Systolic heart failure**

EXCLUDES *combined systolic and diastolic heart failure (428.40-428.43)*

DEF: Heart failure due to a defect in expulsion of blood caused by an abnormality in systolic function, or ventricular contractile dysfunction.

428.20 Unspecified   `CC`

CC Excl: 398.91, 402.01, 402.11, 402.91, 428.0-428.9, 459.89-459.9, 518.4

I50.20 Unspecified systolic congestive heart failure   `I-10`

428.21 Acute   `MCC`

CC Excl: See code: 428.20

I50.21 Acute systolic congestive heart failure   `I-10`

428.22 Chronic   `CC`

CC Excl: See code: 428.20

AHA: 4Q, '05, 120

428.23 Acute on chronic   `MCC`

CC Excl: See code: 428.20

AHA: 1Q, '09, 8, 18; 1Q, '03, 9

Echocardiography of Heart Failure

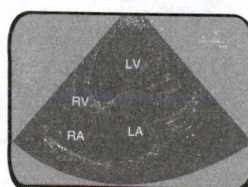

Systolic dysfunction
with dilated LV

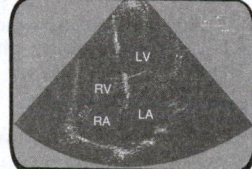

Diastolic dysfunction
with LV hypertrophy

Four-chamber echocardiograms,
two-dimensional views.
LV: Left ventricle
RV: Right ventricle
RA: Right atrium
LA: Left atrium

√5ᵗʰ **428.3 Diastolic heart failure**

EXCLUDES *combined systolic and diastolic heart failure (428.40-428.43)*

DEF: Heart failure due to resistance to ventricular filling caused by an abnormality in the diastolic function.

AHA: 1Q, '12, 7

428.30 Unspecified   `CC`

CC Excl: See code: 428.20

AHA: 4Q, '02, 52

I50.30 Unspecified diastolic congestive heart failure   `I-10`

428.31 Acute   `MCC`

CC Excl: See code: 428.20

428.32 Chronic   `CC`

CC Excl: See code: 428.20

AHA: 3Q, '08, 12

I50.32 Chronic diastolic congestive heart failure   `I-10`

428.33 Acute on chronic   `MCC`

CC Excl: See code: 428.20

AHA: 4Q, '09, 141; 3Q, '08, 12;1Q, '07, 20

I50.33 Acute on chronic diastolic heart failure   `I-10`

√5ᵗʰ **428.4 Combined systolic and diastolic heart failure**

428.40 Unspecified   `CC`

CC Excl: See code: 428.20

428.41 Acute   `MCC`

CC Excl: See code: 428.20

AHA: 4Q, '04, 140

428.42 Chronic   `CC`

CC Excl: See code: 428.20

428.43 Acute on chronic   `MCC`

CC Excl: See code: 428.20

AHA: 3Q, '06, 7; 4Q, '02, 52

428.9 Heart failure, unspecified

Cardiac failure NOS
Heart failure NOS
Myocardial failure NOS
Weak heart

AHA: 2Q, '89, 10; N-D, '85, 14

√4ᵗʰ **429 Ill-defined descriptions and complications of heart disease**

429.0 Myocarditis, unspecified

Myocarditis:
NOS
chronic (interstitial ⎱ (with mention of
fibroid   ⎰ arteriosclerosis)
senile

Use additional code to Identify presence of arteriosclerosis

EXCLUDES *acute or subacute (422.0-422.9)*
rheumatic (398.0)
acute (391.2)
that due to hypertension (402.0-402.9)

429.1 Myocardial degeneration

Degeneration of heart or
myocardium:
fatty
mural   ⎱ (with mention of
muscular   ⎰ arteriosclerosis)
Myocardial:
degeneration
disease

Use additional code to identify presence of arteriosclerosis

EXCLUDES *that due to hypertension (402.0-402.9)*

429.2 Cardiovascular disease, unspecified

Arteriosclerotic cardiovascular disease [ASCVD]
Cardiovascular arteriosclerosis
Cardiovascular:
degeneration ⎱ (with mention of
disease   ⎰ arteriosclerosis)
sclerosis

Use additional code to identify presence of arteriosclerosis

EXCLUDES *that due to hypertension (402.0-402.9)*

AHA: 3Q, '12, 17

√4ᵗʰ / √5ᵗʰ Additional Digit Required   Unacceptable PDx   Manifestation Code   Hospital Acquired Condition   ▶◀ Revised Text   ● New Code   ▲ Revised Code Title

Diseases of the Circulatory System

429.3–432.9

429.3 Cardiomegaly
Cardiac:
dilatation
hypertrophy
Ventricular dilatation
> **EXCLUDES** *that due to hypertension (402.0-402.9)*
>
> `I-10` I51.7 Cardiomegaly

429.4 Functional disturbances following cardiac surgery
Cardiac insufficiency ⎫ following cardiac surgery or
Heart failure   ⎬   due to prosthesis
Postcardiotomy syndrome
Postvalvulotomy syndrome
> **EXCLUDES** *cardiac failure in the immediate postoperative period (997.1)*

AHA: 2Q, '02, 12; N-D, '85, 6

429.5 Rupture of chordae tendineae `MCC`
DEF: Torn tissue, between heart valves and papillary muscles.
CC Excl: 429.5, 429.71-429.79, 459.89-459.9

429.6 Rupture of papillary muscle `MCC`
DEF: Torn muscle, between chordae tendineae and heart wall.
CC Excl: 429.6-429.81, 459.89-459.9

✓5th 429.7 Certain sequelae of myocardial infarction, not elsewhere classified
Use additional code to identify the associated myocardial infarction:
with onset of 8 weeks or less (410.00-410.92)
with onset of more than 8 weeks (414.8)
> **EXCLUDES** *congenital defects of heart (745, 746)*
> *coronary aneurysm (414.11)*
> *disorders of papillary muscle (429.6, 429.81)*
> *postmyocardial infarction syndrome (411.0)*
> *rupture of chordae tendineae (429.5)*

AHA: 3Q, '89, 5

429.71 Acquired cardiac septal defect `CC` `A`
> **EXCLUDES** *acute septal infarction (410.00-410.92)*

DEF: Abnormal communication, between opposite heart chambers; due to defect of septum; not present at birth.
CC Excl: 422.0-422.99, 429.0, 429.4-429.82, 459.89-459.9, 745.0-745.9, 746.89-746.9, 747.83-747.9, 759.7-759.89

429.79 Other `CC` `A`
Mural thrombus (atrial) (ventricular), acquired, following myocardial infarction
CC Excl: See code: 429.71
AHA: 1Q, '92, 10

✓5th 429.8 Other ill-defined heart diseases

429.81 Other disorders of papillary muscle `CC`
Papillary muscle:
atrophy
degeneration
dysfunction
incompetence
incoordination
scarring
CC Excl: 429.6-429.81, 459.89-459.9

429.82 Hyperkinetic heart disease `CC`
DEF: Condition of unknown origin in young adults; marked by increased cardiac output at rest, increased rate of ventricular ejection; may lead to heart failure.
CC Excl: 429.71-429.79, 429.82, 459.89-459.9

429.83 Takotsubo syndrome `CC`
Broken heart syndrome
Reversible left ventricular dysfunction following sudden emotional stress
Stress induced cardiomyopathy
Transient left ventricular apical ballooning syndrome
CC Excl: 398.91, 402.01, 402.11, 402.91, 428.0-428.9, 429.83, 429.9, 459.89-459.9
AHA: 4Q, '06, 87

429.89 Other
Carditis
> **EXCLUDES** *that due to hypertension (402.0-402.9)*

AHA: 2Q, '06, 18; 3Q, '05, 14; 1Q, '92, 10

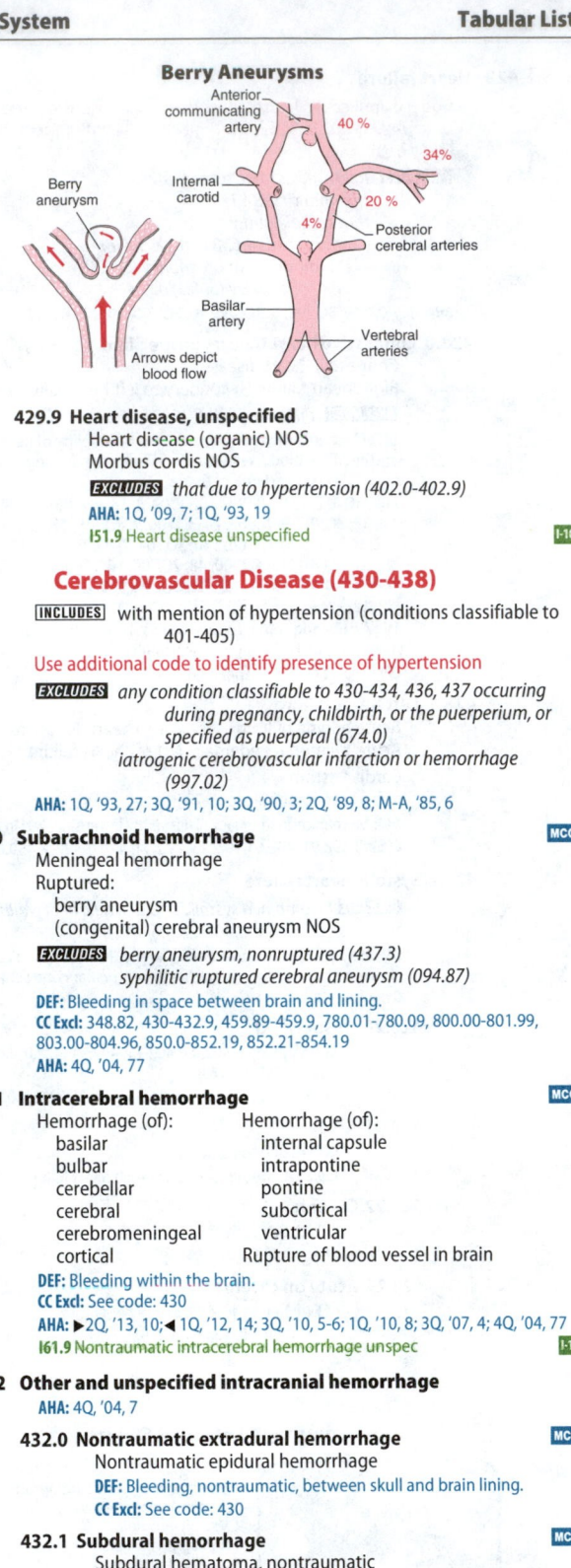

Berry Aneurysms

429.9 Heart disease, unspecified
Heart disease (organic) NOS
Morbus cordis NOS
> **EXCLUDES** *that due to hypertension (402.0-402.9)*

AHA: 1Q, '09, 7; 1Q, '93, 19
`I-10` I51.9 Heart disease unspecified

Cerebrovascular Disease (430-438)
> **INCLUDES** with mention of hypertension (conditions classifiable to 401-405)

Use additional code to identify presence of hypertension
> **EXCLUDES** *any condition classifiable to 430-434, 436, 437 occurring during pregnancy, childbirth, or the puerperium, or specified as puerperal (674.0)*
> *iatrogenic cerebrovascular infarction or hemorrhage (997.02)*

AHA: 1Q, '93, 27; 3Q, '91, 10; 3Q, '90, 3; 2Q, '89, 8; M-A, '85, 6

430 Subarachnoid hemorrhage `MCC`
Meningeal hemorrhage
Ruptured:
berry aneurysm
(congenital) cerebral aneurysm NOS
> **EXCLUDES** *berry aneurysm, nonruptured (437.3)*
> *syphilitic ruptured cerebral aneurysm (094.87)*

DEF: Bleeding in space between brain and lining.
CC Excl: 348.82, 430-432.9, 459.89-459.9, 780.01-780.09, 800.00-801.99, 803.00-804.96, 850.0-852.19, 852.21-854.19
AHA: 4Q, '04, 77

431 Intracerebral hemorrhage `MCC`
Hemorrhage (of):   Hemorrhage (of):
basilar   internal capsule
bulbar   intrapontine
cerebellar   pontine
cerebral   subcortical
cerebromeningeal   ventricular
cortical   Rupture of blood vessel in brain
DEF: Bleeding within the brain.
CC Excl: See code: 430
AHA: ▶2Q, '13, 10;◀ 1Q, '12, 14; 3Q, '10, 5-6; 1Q, '10, 8; 3Q, '07, 4; 4Q, '04, 77
`I-10` I61.9 Nontraumatic intracerebral hemorrhage unspec

✓4th 432 Other and unspecified intracranial hemorrhage
AHA: 4Q, '04, 7

432.0 Nontraumatic extradural hemorrhage `MCC`
Nontraumatic epidural hemorrhage
DEF: Bleeding, nontraumatic, between skull and brain lining.
CC Excl: See code: 430

432.1 Subdural hemorrhage `MCC`
Subdural hematoma, nontraumatic
DEF: Bleeding, between outermost and other layers of brain lining.
CC Excl: See code: 430

432.9 Unspecified intracranial hemorrhage `CC`
Intracranial hemorrhage NOS
CC Excl: See code: 430

`N` Newborn Age: 0   `P` Pediatric Age: 0-17   `M` Maternity Age: 12-55   `A` Adult Age: 15-124   `MCC` Major CC Condition   `CC` CC Condition   `HIV` HIV Related Dx

Cerebrovascular Arteries

✓4ᵗʰ 433 Occlusion and stenosis of precerebral arteries

INCLUDES embolism
narrowing
obstruction } of basilar, carotid, and vertebral arteries
thrombosis

Use additional code, if applicable, to identify status post administration of tPA (rtPA) in a different facility within the last 24 hours prior to admission to current facility (V45.88)

EXCLUDES insufficiency NOS of precerebral arteries (435.0-435.9)

The following fifth-digit subclassification is for use with category 433:
0 without mention of cerebral infarction
1 with cerebral infarction

DEF: Blockage, stricture, arteries branching into brain.
AHA: 2Q, '95, 14; 3Q, '90, 16

§ ✓5ᵗʰ **433.0 Basilar artery**   MCC 1
[0-1]   CC Excl: For code 433.01: 249.70-249.91, 250.70-250.93, 346.60-346.63, 433.00-433.91, 435.0, 459.89-459.9

§ ✓5ᵗʰ **433.1 Carotid artery**   MCC 1
[0-1]   CC Excl: For code 433.11: 249.70-249.91, 250.70-250.93, 346.60-346.63, 433.00-433.91, 459.89-459.9
AHA: 1Q, '00, 16; For code 433.10: 1Q, '06, 17; 1Q, '02, 7, 10
I65.29 Occlusion and stenosis of unspec carotid artery   I-10

§ ✓5ᵗʰ **433.2 Vertebral artery**   MCC 1
[0-1]   CC Excl: For code 433.21: 249.70-249.91, 250.70-250.93, 346.60-346.63, 433.00-433.91, 435.1, 459.89-459.9

§ ✓5ᵗʰ **433.3 Multiple and bilateral**   MCC 1
[0-1]   CC Excl: For code 433.31: 249.70-249.91, 250.70-250.93, 346.60-346.63, 433.00-433.91, 459.89-459.9
AHA: 2Q, '02, 19

§ ✓5ᵗʰ **433.8 Other specified precerebral artery**   MCC 1
[0-1]   CC Excl: For code 433.81: 249.70-249.91, 250.70-250.93, 346.60-346.63, 433.00-433.91, 435.0, 459.89-459.9

§ ✓5ᵗʰ **433.9 Unspecified precerebral artery**   MCC 1
[0-1]   Precerebral artery NOS
CC Excl: For code 433.91: 249.70-249.91, 250.70-250.93, 346.60-346.63, 433.00-433.91, 435.0, 459.89-459.9

✓4ᵗʰ 434 Occlusion of cerebral arteries

Use additional code, if applicable, to identify status post administration of tPA (rtPA) in a different facility within the last 24 hours prior to admission to current facility (V45.88)

The following fifth-digit subclassification is for use with category 434:
0 without mention of cerebral infarction
1 with cerebral infarction

AHA: 2Q, '95, 14

§§ ✓5ᵗʰ **434.0 Cerebral thrombosis**   MCC 1
[0-1]   Thrombosis of cerebral arteries
CC Excl: For code 434.01: 249.70-249.91, 250.70-250.93, 346.60-346.63, 434.00-434.91, 436, 459.89-459.9
AHA: For code 434.01: 4Q, '04, 77

§§ ✓5ᵗʰ **434.1 Cerebral embolism**   MCC 1
[0-1]   CC Excl: For code 434.11: 249.70-249.91, 250.70-250.93, 346.60-346.63, 433.00-433.91, 435.0, 459.89-459.9
AHA: For code 434.11: 4Q, '04, 77; 3Q, '97, 11
I63.449 Cerbral infarct d/t embo of uns cerebellar art   I-10

§§ ✓5ᵗʰ **434.9 Cerebral artery occlusion, unspecified**   MCC 1
[0-1]   CC Excl: For code 434.91: 249.70-249.91, 250.70-250.93, 346.60-346.63, 433.00-433.91, 435.0, 459.89-459.9
AHA: For code 434.91: ▶2Q, '13, 10;◀ 3Q, '10, 5-6; 4Q, '08, 108; 3Q, '07, 9; 1Q, '07, 23; 4Q, '04, 77-78; 4Q, '98, 87

✓4ᵗʰ 435 Transient cerebral ischemia

INCLUDES cerebrovascular insufficiency (acute) with trans-ient focal neurological signs and symptoms
insufficiency of basilar, carotid, and vertebral arteries
spasm of cerebral arteries

EXCLUDES acute cerebrovascular insufficiency NOS (437.1)
that due to any condition classifiable to 433 (433.0-433.9)

435.0 Basilar artery syndrome   CC
CC Excl: 249.70-249.91, 250.70-250.93, 433.00-433.91, 435.0-435.9, 459.89-459.9

435.1 Vertebral artery syndrome   CC
CC Excl: See code: 435.0

435.2 Subclavian steal syndrome   CC
DEF: Cerebrovascular insufficiency, due to occluded subclavian artery; symptoms include pain in mastoid and posterior head regions, flaccid paralysis of arm and diminished or absent radial pulse on affected side.
CC Excl: See code: 435.0

435.3 Vertebrobasilar artery syndrome   CC
DEF: Transient ischemic attack; due to brainstem dysfunction; symptoms include confusion, vertigo, binocular blindness, diplopia, unilateral or bilateral weakness and paresthesis of extremities.
CC Excl: See code: 435.0
AHA: 4Q, '95, 60

435.8 Other specified transient cerebral ischemias   CC
CC Excl: See code: 435.0

435.9 Unspecified transient cerebral ischemia   CC
Impending cerebrovascular accident
Intermittent cerebral ischemia
Transient ischemic attack [TIA]
DEF: Temporary restriction of blood flow to arteries branching into brain.
CC Excl: See code: 435.0
AHA: N-D, '85, 12
G45.9 Transient cerebral ischemic attack unspecified   I-10

436 Acute, but ill-defined, cerebrovascular disease   CC

Apoplexy, apoplectic:
NOS
attack
cerebral
seizure
Cerebral seizure

EXCLUDES any condition classifiable to categories 430-435
cerebrovascular accident (434.91)
CVA (ischemic) (434.91)
embolic (434.11)
hemorrhagic (430, 431, 432.0-432.9)
thrombotic (434.01)
postoperative cerebrovascular accident (997.02)
stroke (ischemic) (434.91)
embolic (434.11)
hemorrhagic (430, 431, 432.0-432.9)
thrombotic (434.01)

CC Excl: 249.70-249.91, 250.70-250.93, 346.60-346.63, 348.82, 430-432.9, 434.00-434.91, 436, 459.89-459.9, 780.01-780.09, 800.00-801.99, 803.00-804.96, 850.0-852.19, 852.21-854.19
AHA: 4Q, '04, 77; 4Q, '99, 3
TIP: Do not assign when documentation indicates "CVA, stroke, or cerebral infarction." See instead default code 434.91.

✓4ᵗʰ 437 Other and ill-defined cerebrovascular disease

437.0 Cerebral atherosclerosis   A
Atheroma of cerebral arteries
Cerebral arteriosclerosis
AHA: 3Q, '10, 15
I67.2 Cerebral atherosclerosis   I-10

---

§   Requires fifth digit. Valid digits are in [brackets] under each code. See category 433 for codes and definitions.
§§ Requires fifth digit. Valid digits are in [brackets] under each code. See category 434 for codes and definitions.

✓4ᵗʰ ✓5ᵗʰ Additional Digit Required   Unacceptable PDx   Manifestation Code   Hospital Acquired Condition   ▶◀ Revised Text   ● New Code   ▲ Revised Code Title

Diseases of the Circulatory System

437.1–438.83

437.1 Other generalized ischemic cerebrovascular disease `CC`
Acute cerebrovascular insufficiency NOS
Cerebral ischemia (chronic)
CC Excl: 249.70-249.91, 250.70-250.93, 430-432.9, 434.00-436, 437.1, 459.89-459.9
AHA: 1Q, '09, 8

437.2 Hypertensive encephalopathy `CC`
DEF: Cerebral manifestations (such as visual disturbances and headache) due to high blood pressure.
CC Excl: 249.70-249.91, 250.70-250.93, 437.2, 459.89-459.9
AHA: J-A, '84, 14

437.3 Cerebral aneurysm, nonruptured
Internal carotid artery, intracranial portion
Internal carotid artery NOS
EXCLUDES congenital cerebral aneurysm, nonruptured (747.81)
internal carotid artery, extracranial portion (442.81)
AHA: ▶4Q, '13, 92;◄ 2Q, '09, 12

437.4 Cerebral arteritis `CC`
DEF: Inflammation of a cerebral artery or arteries.
CC Excl: 249.70-249.91, 250.70-250.93, 437.4, 459.89-459.9
AHA: 4Q, '99, 21

437.5 Moyamoya disease `CC`
DEF: Cerebrovascular ischemia; vessels occlude and rupture causing tiny hemorrhages at base of brain; predominantly affects Japanese.
CC Excl: 249.70-249.91, 250.70-250.93, 437.5, 459.89-459.9

437.6 Nonpyogenic thrombosis of intracranial venous sinus `CC`
EXCLUDES pyogenic (325)
CC Excl: 249.70-249.91, 250.70-250.93, 437.6, 459.89-459.9

437.7 Transient global amnesia
DEF: Episode of short-term memory loss, not often recurrent; pathogenesis unknown; with no signs or symptoms of neurological disorder.
AHA: 4Q, '92, 20

437.8 Other
AHA: ▶2Q, '13, 10◄

437.9 Unspecified
Cerebrovascular disease or lesion NOS
AHA: 1Q, '09, 9

`√4th` **438 Late effects of cerebrovascular disease**
NOTE This category is to be used to indicate conditions in 430-437 as the cause of late effects. The "late effects" include conditions specified as such, as sequelae, which may occur at any time after the onset of the causal condition.
EXCLUDES personal history of:
cerebral infarction without residual deficits (V12.54)
PRIND [Prolonged reversible ischemic neurologic deficit] (V12.54)
RIND [Reversible ischemic neurological deficit] (V12.54)
transient ischemic attack [TIA] (V12.54)
AHA: 3Q, '06, 3-4, 6; 4Q, '99, 4, 6, 7; 4Q, '98, 39, 88; 4Q, '97, 35, 37; 4Q, '92, 21;N-D,'86, 12; M-A, '86, 7
TIP: Assign instead code V12.54 TIA and cerebral infarction without residual effects, if no residual deficits are present.

438.0 Cognitive deficits

`√5th` **438.1 Speech and language deficits**

438.10 Speech and language deficit, unspecified

438.11 Aphasia
DEF: Impairment or absence of the ability to communicate by speech, writing or signs or to comprehend the spoken or written language due to disease or injury to the brain.
AHA: 4Q, '03, 105; 4Q, '97, 36

438.12 Dysphasia
DEF: Impaired speech; marked by inability to sequence language.
AHA: 4Q, '99, 3, 9

438.13 Dysarthria
DEF: Speech disorder caused by paralysis, spasticity, or other nerve damage resulting in difficulty expressing words or sounds; characterized by slurring, interrupted rhythm of speech, or distorted vowel sounds.
AHA: 4Q, '09, 87-88
TIP: If dysarthria or other speech disturbances are not due to underlying cerebrovascular disease, see subcategory 784.5 codes.

438.14 Fluency disorder
Stuttering due to late effect of cerebrovascular accident
DEF: Interruption in the flow of speech that significantly interferes with communication; characterized by primary sound and syllable repetitions, articulatory fixations, and abnormal prolongation of speech sounds.
AHA: 4Q, '10, 83; 4Q, '09, 87-88

438.19 Other speech and language deficits

`√5th` **438.2 Hemiplegia/hemiparesis**
DEF: Paralysis of one side of the body.
AHA: 1Q, '10, 5

438.20 Hemiplegia affecting unspecified side `CC`
CC Excl: 438.20
AHA: 4Q, '07, 94; 4Q, '03, 105; 4Q, '99, 3, 9
I69.959 Hempl & hemiparesis flw uns CVD affect uns side `I-10`

438.21 Hemiplegia affecting dominant side `CC`
CC Excl: 438.21

438.22 Hemiplegia affecting nondominant side `CC`
CC Excl: 438.22
AHA: 4Q, '03, 105; 1Q, '02, 16

`√5th` **438.3 Monoplegia of upper limb**
DEF: Paralysis of one limb or one muscle group.

438.30 Monoplegia of upper limb affecting unspecified side

438.31 Monoplegia of upper limb affecting dominant side

438.32 Monoplegia of upper limb affecting nondominant side

`√5th` **438.4 Monoplegia of lower limb**

438.40 Monoplegia of lower limb affecting unspecified side

438.41 Monoplegia of lower limb affecting dominant side

438.42 Monoplegia of lower limb affecting nondominant side

`√5th` **438.5 Other paralytic syndrome**
Use additional code to identify type of paralytic syndrome, such as:
locked-in state (344.81)
quadriplegia (344.00-344.09)
EXCLUDES late effects of cerebrovascular accident with:
hemiplegia/hemiparesis (438.20-438.22)
monoplegia of lower limb (438.40-438.42)
monoplegia of upper limb (438.30-438.32)

438.50 Other paralytic syndrome affecting unspecified side

438.51 Other paralytic syndrome affecting dominant side

438.52 Other paralytic syndrome affecting nondominant side

438.53 Other paralytic syndrome, bilateral
AHA: 4Q, '98, 39

438.6 Alterations of sensations
Use additional code to identify the altered sensation

438.7 Disturbances of vision
Use additional code to identify the visual disturbance
AHA: 4Q, '02, 56

`√5th` **438.8 Other late effects of cerebrovascular disease**

438.81 Apraxia
DEF: Inability to activate learned movements; no known sensory or motor impairment.

438.82 Dysphagia
Use additional code to identify the type of dysphagia, if known (787.20-787.29)
DEF: Inability or difficulty in swallowing.
AHA: 4Q, '07, 94
I69.991 Dysphagia following uns cerebrovascular disease `I-10`

438.83 Facial weakness
Facial droop

`N` Newborn Age: 0   `P` Pediatric Age: 0-17   `M` Maternity Age: 12-55   `A` Adult Age: 15-124   `MCC` Major CC Condition   `CC` CC Condition   `HIV` HIV Related Dx

148 – Volume 1 • October 2014   2015 ICD-9-CM

438.84 Ataxia
    AHA: 4Q, '02, 56

438.85 Vertigo

438.89 Other late effects of cerebrovascular disease
    Use additional code to identify the late effect
    AHA: 2Q, '09, 10; 1Q, '05, 13; 4Q, '98, 39
    TIP: Assign 438.89 and 728.87 Muscle weakness, for residual weakness secondary to late effect of CVA.
    I69.998 Other sequelae flw uns cerebrovascular disease   `I-10`

438.9 Unspecified late effects of cerebrovascular disease

Diseases of Arteries, Arterioles, and Capillaries (440-449)

✓4th 440 Atherosclerosis
    INCLUDES arteriolosclerosis
                  arteriosclerosis (obliterans) (senile)
                  arteriosclerotic vascular disease
                  atheroma
                  degeneration:
                    arterial
                    arteriovascular
                    vascular
                  endarteritis deformans or obliterans
                  senile:
                    arteritis
                    endarteritis
    EXCLUDES atheroembolism (445.01-445.89)
                  atherosclerosis of bypass graft of the extremities (440.30-440.32)
    DEF: Stricture and reduced elasticity of an artery; due to plaque deposits.

440.0 Of aorta   `A`
    AHA: 2Q, '93, 7; 2Q, '93, 8; 4Q, '88, 8

440.1 Of renal artery   `A`
    EXCLUDES atherosclerosis of renal arterioles (403.00-403.91)

✓5th 440.2 Of native arteries of the extremities
    Use additional code, if applicable, to identify chronic total occlusion of artery of the extremities (440.4)
    EXCLUDES atherosclerosis of bypass graft of the extremities (440.30-440.32)
    AHA: 4Q, '94, 49; 4Q, '93, 27; 4Q, '92, 25; 3Q, '90, 15; M-A, '87, 6
    TIP: Codes are listed in order of increasing severity; all patients who have gangrene (regardless of whether ulceration, rest pain, and/or intermittent claudication are present) are coded to 440.24. Patients without gangrene, but with ulceration (regardless of whether they also suffer from rest pain or intermittent claudication) are coded to 440.23.

    440.20 Atherosclerosis of the extremities, unspecified   `A`
        I70.209 Uns atherosclero natv art of extrem uns extrem   `I-10`

    440.21 Atherosclerosis of the extremities with intermittent claudication   `A`
        DEF: Atherosclerosis; marked by pain, tension and weakness after walking; no symptoms while at rest.
        I70.219 Atherosclerosis native arteries ext w/interm claud uns ext   `I-10`

    440.22 Atherosclerosis of the extremities with rest pain   `A`
        INCLUDES any condition classifiable to 440.21
        DEF: Atherosclerosis, marked by pain, tension and weakness while at rest.

440.23 Atherosclerosis of the extremities with ulceration   `A`
    INCLUDES any condition classifiable to 440.21 and 440.22
    Use additional code for any associated ulceration (707.10-707.19, 707.8, 707.9)
    AHA: 4Q, '00, 44
    I70.249 Atherosclero natv art lt leg ulceration uns site   `I-10`

440.24 Atherosclerosis of the extremities with gangrene   `CC`
    INCLUDES any condition classifiable to 440.21, 440.22, and 440.23 with ischemic gangrene 785.4
    Use additional code for any associated ulceration (707.10-707.19, 707.8, 707.9)
    EXCLUDES gas gangrene (040.0)
    CC Excl: 338.0-338.4, 440.24, 780.64-780.65, 780.91-780.99, 785.4, 799.81-799.89
    AHA: 4Q, '03, 109; 3Q, '03, 14; 4Q, '95, 54; 1Q, '95, 11

440.29 Other   `A`

✓5th 440.3 Of bypass graft of extremities
    EXCLUDES atherosclerosis of native arteries of the extremities (440.21-440.24)
                  embolism [occlusion NOS] [thrombus] of graft (996.74)
    AHA: 4Q, '94, 49

    440.30 Of unspecified graft   `A`

    440.31 Of autologous vein bypass graft   `A`

    440.32 Of nonautologous biological bypass graft   `A`

440.4 Chronic total occlusion of artery of the extremities   `CC`
    Complete occlusion of artery of the extremities
    Total occlusion of artery of the extremities
    Code first atherosclerosis of arteries of the extremities (440.20-440.29, 440.30-440.32)
    EXCLUDES acute occlusion of artery of extremity (444.21-444.22)
    CC Excl: 440.4, 443.81-443.89, 447.0-447.2, 447.5-447.73, 449

440.8 Of other specified arteries   `A`
    EXCLUDES basilar (433.0)
                  carotid (433.1)
                  cerebral (437.0)
                  coronary (414.00-414.07)
                  mesenteric (557.1)
                  precerebral (433.0-433.9)
                  pulmonary (416.0)
                  vertebral (433.2)
    AHA: 3Q, '09, 9
    TIP: Assign for arteriosclerosis of the iliac artery.

440.9 Generalized and unspecified atherosclerosis   `A`
    Arteriosclerotic vascular disease NOS
    EXCLUDES arteriosclerotic cardiovascular disease [ASCVD] (429.2)
    I70.91 Generalized atherosclerosis   `I-10`

✓4th ✓5th Additional Digit Required   Unacceptable PDx   Manifestation Code   Hospital Acquired Condition   ►◄ Revised Text   ● New Code   ▲ Revised Code Title

Diseases of the Circulatory System

441–441.9

Map of Major Arteries

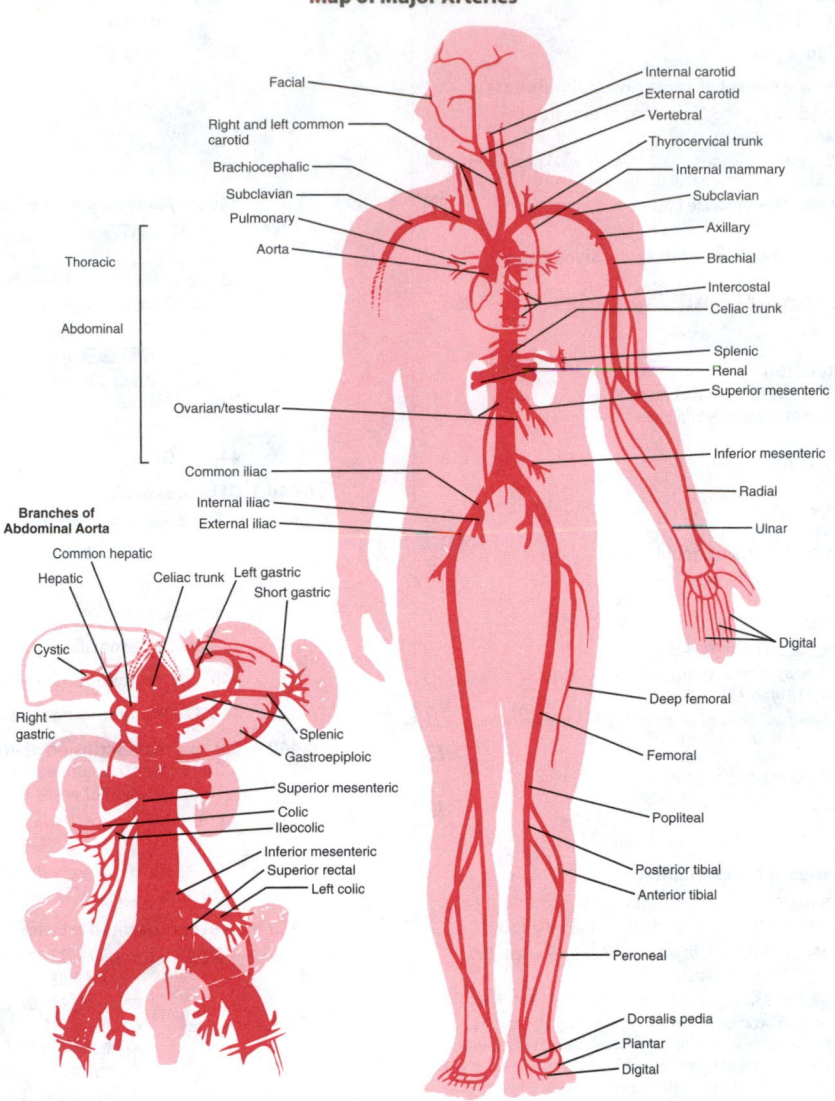

✓4th 441 Aortic aneurysm and dissection

EXCLUDES aortic ectasia (447.70-447.73)
syphilitic aortic aneurysm (093.0)
traumatic aortic aneurysm (901.0, 902.0)

✓5th 441.0 Dissection of aorta

AHA: 4Q, '89, 10

DEF: Dissection or splitting of wall of the aorta; due to blood entering through intimal tear or interstitial hemorrhage.

441.00 Unspecified site   MCC

CC Excl: 249.70-249.91, 250.70-250.93, 441.00-441.9, 447.70-447.73, 459.89-459.9

441.01 Thoracic   MCC

CC Excl: See code: 441.00

AHA: ▶4Q, '13, 92;◀ 1Q, '09, 16; 4Q, '07, 87

441.02 Abdominal   MCC

CC Excl: See code: 441.00

441.03 Thoracoabdominal   MCC

CC Excl: See code: 441.00

441.1 Thoracic aneurysm, ruptured   MCC

CC Excl: See code: 441.00

441.2 Thoracic aneurysm without mention of rupture

AHA: 3Q, '92, 10

I71.2 Thoracic aortic aneurysm without rupture   I-10

441.3 Abdominal aneurysm, ruptured   MCC

CC Excl: See code: 441.00

I71.3 Abdominal aortic aneurysm, ruptured   I-10

441.4 Abdominal aneurysm without mention of rupture

AHA: 4Q, '00, 64; 1Q, '99, 15, 16, 17; 3Q, '92, 10

I71.4 Abdominal aortic aneurysm without rupture   I-10

441.5 Aortic aneurysm of unspecified site, ruptured   MCC

Rupture of aorta NOS

CC Excl: See code: 441.00

441.6 Thoracoabdominal aneurysm, ruptured   MCC

CC Excl: See code: 441.00

441.7 Thoracoabdominal aneurysm, without mention of rupture

AHA: 2Q, '06, 16

441.9 Aortic aneurysm of unspecified site without mention of rupture

Aneurysm
Dilatation   } of aorta
Hyaline necrosis

AHA: 4Q, '10, 84

N Newborn Age: 0   **P** Pediatric Age: 0-17   **M** Maternity Age: 12-55   **A** Adult Age: 15-124   **MCC** Major CC Condition   **CC** CC Condition   **HIV** HIV Related Dx

150 – Volume 1 · October 2014   2015 ICD-9-CM

Thoracic and Abdominal Aortic Aneurysm

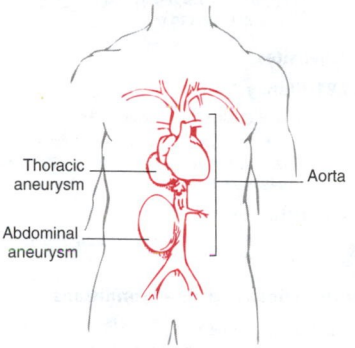

Thoracic aneurysm

Abdominal aneurysm

Aorta

✓4ᵗʰ **442 Other aneurysm**

INCLUDES aneurysm (ruptured) (cirsoid) (false) (varicose)
aneurysmal varix

EXCLUDES arteriovenous aneurysm or fistula:
acquired (447.0)
congenital (747.60-747.69)
traumatic (900.0-904.9)

DEF: Dissection or splitting of arterial wall; due to blood entering through intimal tear or interstitial hemorrhage.

442.0 Of artery of upper extremity

442.1 Of renal artery

442.2 Of iliac artery
AHA: 1Q, '99, 16, 17

442.3 Of artery of lower extremity
Aneurysm:
femoral artery
popliteal artery
AHA: 2Q, '08, 13; 3Q, '02, 24-26; 1Q, '99, 16

✓5ᵗʰ **442.8 Of other specified artery**

442.81 Artery of neck
Aneurysm of carotid artery (common) (external)
(internal, extracranial portion)
EXCLUDES internal carotid artery, intracranial portion
(437.3)

442.82 Subclavian artery

442.83 Splenic artery

442.84 Other visceral artery
Aneurysm:
celiac
gastroduodenal
gastroepiploic   } artery
hepatic
pancreaticoduodenal
superior mesenteric

442.89 Other
Aneurysm:
mediastinal artery
spinal artery
EXCLUDES cerebral (nonruptured) (437.3)
congenital (747.81)
ruptured (430)
coronary (414.11)
heart (414.10)
pulmonary (417.1)

442.9 Of unspecified site

✓4ᵗʰ **443 Other peripheral vascular disease**

443.0 Raynaud's syndrome
Raynaud's:
disease
phenomenon (secondary)
Use additional code to identify gangrene (785.4)
DEF: Constriction of the arteries, due to cold or stress; bilateral ischemic attacks of fingers, toes, nose or ears; symptoms include pallor, paresthesia and pain.
I73.00 Raynaud's syndrome without gangrene   I-10

443.1 Thromboangiitis obliterans [Buerger's disease]
Presenile gangrene
DEF: Inflammatory disease of extremity blood vessels, mainly the lower; occurs primarily in young men and leads to tissue ischemia and gangrene.

✓5ᵗʰ **443.2 Other arterial dissection**
EXCLUDES dissection of aorta (441.00-441.03)
dissection of coronary arteries (414.12)
AHA: 4Q, '02, 54

443.21 Dissection of carotid artery   MCC
CC Excl: 447.2, 447.5-447.6, 447.8-447.9
AHA: ▶4Q, '13, 92◀

443.22 Dissection of iliac artery   MCC
CC Excl: See code: 443.21

443.23 Dissection of renal artery   MCC
CC Excl: See code: 443.21

443.24 Dissection of vertebral artery   MCC
CC Excl: See code: 443.21

443.29 Dissection of other artery   MCC
CC Excl: See code: 443.21

✓5ᵗʰ **443.8 Other specified peripheral vascular diseases**

443.81 Peripheral angiopathy in diseases classified elsewhere
Code first underlying disease, as:
diabetes mellitus (249.7, 250.7)
AHA: 1Q, '04, 14; 3Q, '91, 10
I79.8 Oth d/o art arterioles & cap in dz class elsw   I-10

443.82 Erythromelalgia
DEF: Rare syndrome of paroxysmal vasodilation; maldistribution of blood flow causes redness, pain, increased skin temperature, and burning sensations in various parts of the body.
AHA: 4Q, '05, 73

443.89 Other
Acrocyanosis
Acroparesthesia:
simple [Schultze's type]
vasomotor [Nothnagel's type]
Erythrocyanosis
EXCLUDES chilblains (991.5)
frostbite (991.0-991.3)
immersion foot (991.4)
AHA: 4Q, '07, 124
I73.89 Other specified peripheral vascular disease   I-10

443.9 Peripheral vascular disease, unspecified
Intermittent claudication NOS
Peripheral:
angiopathy NOS
vascular disease NOS
Spasm of artery
EXCLUDES atherosclerosis of the arteries of the extremities
(440.20-440.22)
spasm of cerebral artery (435.0-435.9)
AHA: 4Q, '92, 25; 3Q, '91, 10
I73.9 Peripheral vascular disease unspecified   I-10

Arterial Diseases and Disorders

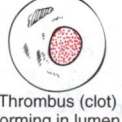

Lipids
Calcium deposits

Atherosclerosis narrowing lumen

Thrombus (clot) forming in lumen

Organization of thrombus and recanalization

Intimal proliferation

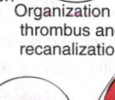

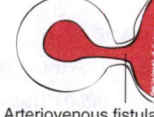

Embolus (from elsewhere) occluding lumen

...bulges from arterial wall

Aneurysm bypasses lumen or...

Arteriovenous fistula

✓4ᵗʰ ✓5ᵗʰ Additional Digit Required   Unacceptable PDx   Manifestation Code   Hospital Acquired Condition   ▶◀ Revised Text   ● New Code   ▲ Revised Code Title

2015 ICD-9-CM   **October 2014 • Volume 1 – 151**

√4ᵗʰ **444 Arterial embolism and thrombosis**

INCLUDES   infarction:
     embolic
     thrombotic
     occlusion

EXCLUDES   *atheroembolism (445.01-445.89)*
     that complicating:
       abortion (634-638 with .6, 639.6)
       ectopic or molar pregnancy (639.6)
       pregnancy, childbirth, or the pueperium (673.0-673.8)
     septic arterial embolism (449)

AHA: 2Q, '92, 11; 4Q, '90, 27

√5ᵗʰ **444.0 Of abdominal aorta**
   CC Excl: 249.70-249.91, 250.70-250.93, 444.0, 444.89-444.9, 449, 459.89-459.9
   AHA: 4Q, '11, 107-109; 2Q, '93, 7; 4Q, '90, 27

444.01 Saddle embolus of abdominal aorta   MCC
   CC Excl: 415.11-415.19, 416.2, 444.01-444.09, 459.89-459.9
   AHA: 4Q, '11, 108

444.09 Other arterial embolism and thrombosis of abdominal aorta   CC
   Aortic bifurcation syndrome
   Aortoiliac obstruction
   Leriche's syndrome
   CC Excl: See code 444.01

444.1 Of thoracic aorta   CC
   Embolism or thrombosis of aorta (thoracic)
   CC Excl: 249.70-249.91, 250.70-250.93, 444.1, 444.89-444.9, 449, 459.89-459.9

√5ᵗʰ **444.2 Of arteries of the extremities**
   AHA: M-A, '87, 6

444.21 Upper extremity   CC
   CC Excl: 249.70-249.91, 250.70-250.93, 444.21, 444.89-444.9, 449, 459.89-459.9

444.22 Lower extremity   CC
   Arterial embolism or thrombosis:
     femoral
     peripheral NOS
     popliteal
   EXCLUDES   *iliofemoral (444.81)*
   CC Excl: 249.70-249.91, 250.70-250.93, 444.22, 444.89-444.9, 449, 459.89-459.9
   AHA: 2Q, '11, 8; 4Q, '07, 85; 3Q, '03, 10; 1Q, '03, 17; 3Q, '90, 16
   I74.3 Embo & thromb of arteries of the low extremities   I-10

√5ᵗʰ **444.8 Of other specified artery**

444.81 Iliac artery   CC
   CC Excl: 249.70-249.91, 250.70-250.93, 444.81-444.9, 449, 459.89-459.9
   AHA: 1Q, '03, 16

444.89 Other   CC
   EXCLUDES   *basilar (433.0)*
     carotid (433.1)
     cerebral (434.0-434.9)
     coronary (410.00-410.92)
     mesenteric (557.0)
     ophthalmic (362.30-362.34)
     precerebral (433.0-433.9)
     pulmonary (415.11-415.19)
     renal (593.81)
     retinal (362.30-362.34)
     vertebral (433.2)
   CC Excl: 249.70-249.91, 250.70-250.93, 444.89-444.9, 449, 459.89-459.9

444.9 Of unspecified artery   CC
   CC Excl: See code: 444.89

√4ᵗʰ **445 Atheroembolism**

INCLUDES   atherothrombotic microembolism
   cholesterol embolism

AHA: 4Q, '02, 57

√5ᵗʰ **445.0 Of extremities**

445.01 Upper extremity   CC
   CC Excl: 249.70-249.91, 250.70-250.93, 444.89-445.01, 449, 459.89-459.9

445.02 Lower extremity   CC
   CC Excl: 249.70-249.91, 250.70-250.93, 444.89-444.9, 445.02, 449, 459.89-459.9

√5ᵗʰ **445.8 Of other sites**

445.81 Kidney   CC
   Use additional code for any associated acute kidney failure or chronic kidney disease (584, 585)
   CC Excl: 249.70-249.91, 250.70-250.93, 444.89-444.9, 445.81, 449, 459.89-459.9

445.89 Other site   CC
   CC Excl: 249.70-249.91, 250.70-250.93, 444.89-444.9, 445.89, 449, 459.89-459.9

√4ᵗʰ **446 Polyarteritis nodosa and allied conditions**

446.0 Polyarteritis nodosa   CC
   Disseminated necrotizing periarteritis
   Necrotizing angiitis
   Panarteritis (nodosa)
   Periarteritis (nodosa)
   DEF: Inflammation of small and mid-size arteries; symptoms related to involved arteries in kidneys, muscles, gastrointestinal tract and heart; results in tissue death.
   CC Excl: 249.70-249.91, 250.70-250.93, 446.0-446.7, 459.89-459.9

446.1 Acute febrile mucocutaneous lymph node syndrome [MCLS]   CC
   Kawasaki disease
   DEF: Acute febrile disease of children; marked by erythema of conjunctiva and mucous membranes of upper respiratory tract, skin eruptions and edema.
   CC Excl: 446.0-446.29, 446.4-446.7, 459.89-459.9

√5ᵗʰ **446.2 Hypersensitivity angiitis**

EXCLUDES   *antiglomerular basement membrane disease without pulmonary hemorrhage (583.89)*

446.20 Hypersensitivity angiitis, unspecified   CC
   CC Excl: See code: 446.0

446.21 Goodpasture's syndrome   CC
   Antiglomerular basement membrane antibody-mediated nephritis with pulmonary hemorrhage
   Use additional code to identify renal disease (583.81)
   DEF: Glomerulonephritis associated with hematuria, progresses rapidly; results in death from renal failure.
   CC Excl: See code: 446.0

446.29 Other specified hypersensitivity angiitis   CC
   CC Excl: See code: 446.0
   AHA: 1Q, '95, 3

446.3 Lethal midline granuloma   CC
   Malignant granuloma of face
   DEF: Granulomatous lesion; in nose or paranasal sinuses; often fatal; occurs chiefly in males.
   CC Excl: See code: 446.0

446.4 Wegener's granulomatosis   CC
   Necrotizing respiratory granulomatosis
   Wegener's syndrome
   DEF: A disease occurring mainly in men; marked by necrotizing granulomas and ulceration of the upper respiratory tract; cause is a vasculitis affecting small vessels due to an immune disorder.
   CC Excl: See code: 446.0
   AHA: 3Q, '00, 11

446.5 Giant cell arteritis
   Bagratuni's syndrome   Horton's disease
   Cranial arteritis   Temporal arteritis
   DEF: Inflammation of arteries; due to giant cells affecting carotid artery branches, resulting in occlusion; symptoms include fever, headache and neurological problems.
   M31.6 Other giant cell arteritis   I-10

446.6 Thrombotic microangiopathy   MCC
   Moschcowitz's syndrome
   Thrombotic thrombocytopenic purpura
   DEF: Blockage of small blood vessels; due to hyaline deposits; symptoms include purpura, CNS disorders; results in protracted disease or rapid death.
   CC Excl: See code: 446.0

N Newborn Age: 0   P Pediatric Age: 0-17   M Maternity Age: 12-55   A Adult Age: 15-124   MCC Major CC Condition   CC CC Condition   HIV HIV Related Dx

446.7 Takayasu's disease `CC`
  Aortic arch arteritis   Pulseless disease
  DEF: Progressive obliterative arteritis of brachiocephalic trunk, left subclavian, and left common carotid arteries above aortic arch; results in ischemia in brain, heart and arm.
  CC Excl: See code: 446.0

`√4th` **447 Other disorders of arteries and arterioles**

447.0 Arteriovenous fistula, acquired
  Arteriovenous aneurysm, acquired
  EXCLUDES *cerebrovascular (437.3)*
       coronary (414.19)
       pulmonary (417.0)
       surgically created arteriovenous shunt or fistula:
         complication (996.1, 996.61-996.62)
         status or presence (V45.11)
         traumatic (900.0-904.9)
  DEF: Communication between an artery and vein caused by error in healing.

447.1 Stricture of artery
  AHA: 2Q, '93, 8; M-A, '87, 6
  `I-10` I77.1 Stricture of artery

447.2 Rupture of artery `CC`
  Erosion
  Fistula, except arteriovenous } of artery
  Ulcer
  EXCLUDES *traumatic rupture of artery (900.0-904.9)*
  CC Excl: 249.70-249.91, 250.70-250.93, 446.0-446.7, 459.89-459.9

447.3 Hyperplasia of renal artery
  Fibromuscular hyperplasia of renal artery
  DEF: Overgrowth of cells in muscular lining of renal artery.

447.4 Celiac artery compression syndrome `CC`
  Celiac axis syndrome   Marable's syndrome
  CC Excl: 447.4

447.5 Necrosis of artery `CC`
  CC Excl: 447.5

447.6 Arteritis, unspecified
  Aortitis NOS   Endarteritis NOS
  EXCLUDES *arteritis, endarteritis:*
       aortic arch (446.7)
       cerebral (437.4)
       coronary (414.00-414.07)
       deformans (440.0-440.9)
       obliterans (440.0-440.9)
       pulmonary (417.8)
       senile (440.0-440.9)
     polyarteritis NOS (446.0)
     syphilitic aortitis (093.1)
  AHA: 1Q, '95, 3

`√5th` **447.7 Aortic ectasia**
  Ectasis aorta
  EXCLUDES *aortic aneurysm and dissection (441.00-441.9)*
  DEF: A diffuse, irregular dilation of the aorta less than 3 cm in diameter; increases the patient's risk of developing an aortic aneurysm.
  AHA: 4Q, '10, 84-85

  447.70 Aortic ectasia, unspecified site
  447.71 Thoracic aortic ectasia
  447.72 Abdominal aortic ectasia
  447.73 Thoracoabdominal aortic ectasia

447.8 Other specified disorders of arteries and arterioles
  Fibromuscular hyperplasia of arteries, except renal

447.9 Unspecified disorders of arteries and arterioles

`√4th` **448 Disease of capillaries**

448.0 Hereditary hemorrhagic telangiectasia
  Rendu-Osler-Weber disease
  DEF: Genetic disease with onset after puberty; results in multiple telangiectases, dilated venules on skin and mucous membranes; recurrent bleeding may occur.

448.1 Nevus, non-neoplastic
  Nevus: Nevus:
    araneus   spider
    senile   stellar
  EXCLUDES *neoplastic (216.0-216.9)*
       port wine (757.32)
       strawberry (757.32)
  DEF: Enlarged or malformed blood vessels of skin; results in reddish swelling, skin patch, or birthmark.

448.9 Other and unspecified capillary diseases
  Capillary:
    hemorrhage
    hyperpermeability
    thrombosis
  EXCLUDES *capillary fragility (hereditary) (287.8)*

449 Septic arterial embolism `CC`
  Code first underlying infection, such as:
    infective endocarditis (421.0)
    lung abscess (513.0)
  Use additional code to identify the site of the embolism (433.0-433.9, 444.01-444.9)
  EXCLUDES *septic pulmonary embolism (415.12)*
  CC Excl: 249.70-249.91, 250.70-250.93, 444.89-444.9, 449, 459.89-459.9
  AHA: 4Q, '07, 84-85

Diseases of Veins And Lymphatics, and Other Diseases of Circulatory System (451-459)

`√4th` **451 Phlebitis and thrombophlebitis**
  INCLUDES endophlebitis
       inflammation, vein
       periphlebitis
       suppurative phlebitis
  Use additional E code to identify drug, if drug-induced
  EXCLUDES *that complicating:*
       abortion (634-638 with .7, 639.8)
       ectopic or molar pregnancy (639.8)
       pregnancy, childbirth, or the puerperium (671.0-671.9)
     that due to or following:
       implant or catheter device (996.61-996.62)
       infusion, perfusion, or transfusion (999.2)
  DEF: Inflammation of a vein (phlebitis) with formation of a thrombus (thrombophlebitis).
  AHA: ▶2Q, '13, 3;◀ 1Q, '11, 19; 1Q, '92, 16
  TIP: Assign an additional code from category 453 for thrombosis; if both conditions are present, assign codes from categories 451 and 453.

451.0 Of superficial vessels of lower extremities
  Saphenous vein (greater) (lesser)
  AHA: 3Q, '91, 16

`√5th` **451.1 Of deep vessels of lower extremities**
  AHA: 3Q, '91, 16

  451.11 Femoral vein (deep) (superficial) `CC`
    CC Excl: 249.70-249.91, 250.70-250.93, 451.0-451.9, 459.89-459.9

  451.19 Other `CC`
    Femoropopliteal vein
    Popliteal vein
    Tibial vein
    CC Excl: 249.70-249.91, 250.70-250.93, 451.0-451.9, 459.89-459.9

451.2 Of lower extremities, unspecified
  AHA: 4Q, '04, 80

`√5th` **451.8 Of other sites**
  EXCLUDES *intracranial venous sinus (325)*
       nonpyogenic (437.6)
       portal (vein) (572.1)

  451.81 Iliac vein `CC`
    CC Excl: See code: 451.19

  451.82 Of superficial veins of upper extremities
    Antecubital vein
    Basilic vein
    Cephalic vein

`√4th` `√5th` Additional Digit Required   Unacceptable PDx   Manifestation Code   Hospital Acquired Condition   ▶◀ Revised Text   ● New Code   ▲ Revised Code Title

451.83 Of deep veins of upper extremities `CC`
Brachial vein   Ulnar vein
Radial vein
CC Excl: 451.0-451.2, 451.83, 451.89-451.9

451.84 Of upper extremities, unspecified

451.89 Other `CC`
Axillary vein
Jugular vein
Subclavian vein
Thrombophlebitis of breast (Mondor's disease)
CC Excl: 451.0-451.2, 451.89-451.9

451.9 Of unspecified site

452 Portal vein thrombosis `MCC`
Portal (vein) obstruction
EXCLUDES hepatic vein thrombosis (453.0)
phlebitis of portal vein (572.1)
DEF: Formation of a blood clot in main vein of liver.
CC Excl: 249.70-249.91, 250.70-250.93, 452, 453.40-453.9, 459.89-459.9

✓4ᵗʰ **453 Other venous embolism and thrombosis**
EXCLUDES that complicating:
abortion (634-638 with .7, 639.8)
ectopic or molar pregnancy (639.8)
pregnancy, childbirth, or the puerperium (671.0-671.9)
AHA: 1Q, '11, 19-21; 1Q, '92, 16

453.0 Budd-Chiari syndrome `MCC`
Hepatic vein thrombosis
DEF: Thrombosis or other obstruction of hepatic vein; symptoms include enlarged liver, extensive collateral vessels, intractable ascites and severe portal hypertension.
CC Excl: 249.70-249.91, 250.70-250.93, 453.0, 453.40-453.9, 459.89-459.9

453.1 Thrombophlebitis migrans `CC`
DEF: Slow, advancing thrombophlebitis; appearing first in one vein then another.
CC Excl: 249.70-249.91, 250.70-250.93, 453.1, 453.40-453.9, 459.89-459.9

453.2 Of inferior vena cava `MCC`
CC Excl: 249.70-249.91, 250.70-250.93, 453.2, 453.40-453.9, 459.89-459.9

453.3 Of renal vein `CC`
CC Excl: 249.70-249.91, 250.70-250.93, 453.3-453.9, 459.89-459.9

✓5ᵗʰ **453.4 Acute venous embolism and thrombosis of deep vessels of lower extremity**
AHA: 4Q, '09, 88-92; 3Q, '08, 16

[11] **453.40 Acute venous embolism and thrombosis of unspecified deep vessels of lower extremity** `CC`
Deep vein thrombosis NOS   DVT NOS
CC Excl: 249.70-249.91, 250.70-250.93, 453.40-453.9, 459.89-459.9
AHA: 1Q, '12, 18
TIP: Assign as the default code for "deep vein thrombosis," whether documented as acute or subacute.
I82.409 Ac embo & thrombo of uns deep veins of unsp lower ext `I-10`

Map of Major Veins

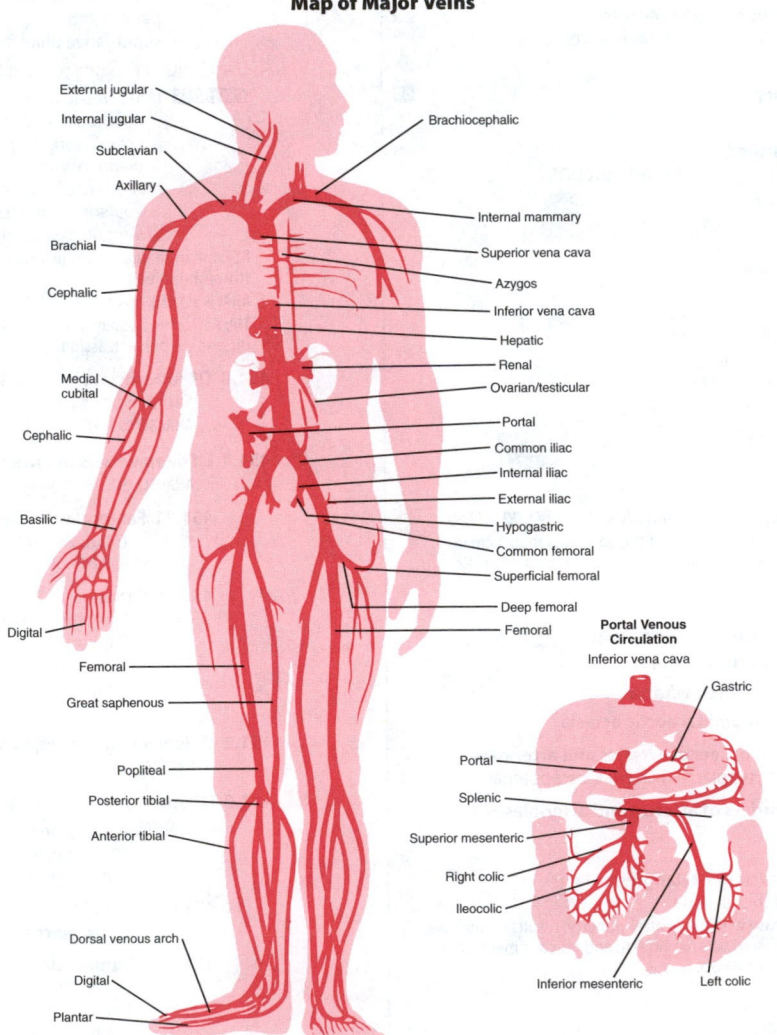

Portal Venous Circulation

---

[11] HAC when reported with procedure codes 00.85-00.87, 81.51, 81.52, 81.54 and POA = N

`N` Newborn Age: 0   `P` Pediatric Age: 0-17   `M` Maternity Age: 12-55   `A` Adult Age: 15-124   `MCC` Major CC Condition   `CC` CC Condition   `HIV` HIV Related Dx

[11]**453.41 Acute venous embolism and thrombosis of deep vessels of proximal lower extremity** `CC`
Femoral
Iliac
Popliteal
Thigh
Upper leg NOS
CC Excl: See code: 453.40
AHA: 4Q, '04, 79

[11]**453.42 Acute venous embolism and thrombosis of deep vessels of distal lower extremity** `CC`
Calf
Lower leg NOS
Peroneal
Tibial
CC Excl: See code: 453.40

√5ᵗʰ **453.5 Chronic venous embolism and thrombosis of deep vessels of lower extremity**
Use additional code, if applicable, for associated long-term (current) use of anticoagulants (V58.61)
EXCLUDES *personal history of venous thrombosis and embolism (V12.51)*
AHA: 4Q, '09, 88-92

453.50 Chronic venous embolism and thrombosis of unspecified deep vessels of lower extremity `CC`
CC Excl: See code: 453.40

453.51 Chronic venous embolism and thrombosis of deep vessels of proximal lower extremity `CC`
Femoral   Thigh
Iliac   Upper leg NOS
Popliteal
CC Excl: See code: 453.40

453.52 Chronic venous embolism and thrombosis of deep vessels of distal lower extremity `CC`
Calf   Peroneal
Lower leg NOS   Tibial
CC Excl: See code: 453.40

453.6 Venous embolism and thrombosis of superficial vessels of lower extremity `CC`
Saphenous vein (greater) (lesser)
Use additional code, if applicable, for associated long-term (current) use of anticoagulants (V58.61)
CC Excl: See code: 453.40
AHA: 4Q, '09, 88-92

√5ᵗʰ **453.7 Chronic venous embolism and thrombosis of other specified vessels**
Use additional code, if applicable, for associated long-term (current) use of anticoagulants (V58.61)
EXCLUDES *personal history of venous thrombosis and embolism (V12.51)*
AHA: 4Q, '09, 88-92

453.71 Chronic venous embolism and thrombosis of superficial veins of upper extremity `CC`
Antecubital vein Cephalic vein
Basilic vein
CC Excl: See code: 453.40

Veins of the Head and Neck

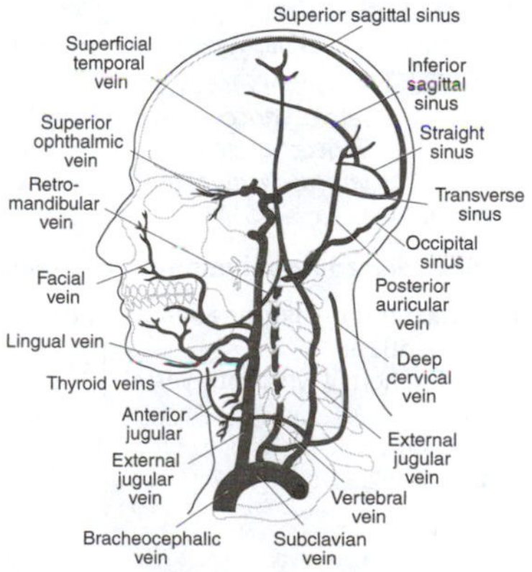

Superior sagittal sinus
Superficial temporal vein
Inferior sagittal sinus
Straight sinus
Superior ophthalmic vein
Retro-mandibular vein
Transverse sinus
Occipital sinus
Facial vein
Posterior auricular vein
Lingual vein
Deep cervical vein
Thyroid veins
Anterior jugular
External jugular vein
External jugular vein
Vertebral vein
Bracheocephalic vein
Subclavian vein

453.72 Chronic venous embolism and thrombosis of deep veins of upper extremity `CC`
Brachial vein
Radial vein
Ulnar vein
CC Excl: 249.70-249.91, 250.70-250.93, 453.40-453.79, 453.81-453.9, 459.89-459.9

453.73 Chronic venous embolism and thrombosis of upper extremity, unspecified `CC`
CC Excl: See code: 453.72

453.74 Chronic venous embolism and thrombosis of axillary veins `CC`
CC Excl: See code: 453.72

453.75 Chronic venous embolism and thrombosis of subclavian veins `CC`
CC Excl: See code: 453.72

453.76 Chronic venous embolism and thrombosis of internal jugular veins `CC`
CC Excl: See code: 453.72

453.77 Chronic venous embolism and thrombosis of other thoracic veins `CC`
Brachiocephalic (innominate)
Superior vena cava
CC Excl: See code: 453.72

453.79 Chronic venous embolism and thrombosis of other specified veins `CC`
CC Excl: See code: 453.72

√5ᵗʰ **453.8 Acute venous embolism and thrombosis of other specified veins**
EXCLUDES *cerebral (434.0-434.9)*
coronary (410.00-410.92)
intracranial venous sinus (325)
* nonpyogenic (437.6)*
mesenteric (557.0)
portal (452)
precerebral (433.0-433.9)
pulmonary (415.19)
AHA: 4Q, '09, 88-92; 3Q, '91, 16; M-A, '87, 6

453.81 Acute venous embolism and thrombosis of superficial veins of upper extremity `CC`
Antecubital vein
Basilic vein
Cephalic vein
CC Excl: 249.70-249.91, 250.70-250.93, 453.40-453.79, 453.81-453.9, 459.89-459.9

453.82 Acute venous embolism and thrombosis of deep veins of upper extremity `CC`
Brachial vein
Radial vein
Ulnar vein
CC Excl: See code: 453.81

453.83 Acute venous embolism and thrombosis of upper extremity, unspecified `CC`
CC Excl: See code: 453.81

453.84 Acute venous embolism and thrombosis of axillary veins `CC`
CC Excl: See code: 453.81

453.85 Acute venous embolism and thrombosis of subclavian veins `CC`
CC Excl: See code: 453.81

453.86 Acute venous embolism and thrombosis of internal jugular veins `CC`
CC Excl: See code: 453.81

453.87 Acute venous embolism and thrombosis of other thoracic veins `CC`
Brachiocephalic (innominate)
Superior vena cava
CC Excl: See code: 453.81

453.89 Acute venous embolism and thrombosis of other specified veins `CC`
CC Excl: See code: 453.81
I82.890 Ac embolism and thrombosis of unspec deep vein of unspec lower ext `I-10`

---

[11] HAC when reported with procedure codes 00.85-00.87, 81.51, 81.52, 81.54 and POA = N

453.9 Of unspecified site `CC`
Embolism of vein
Thrombosis (vein)
CC Excl: See code: 453.81
AHA: 1Q, '12, 18

`√4th` **454 Varicose veins of lower extremities**
EXCLUDES *that complicating pregnancy, childbirth, or the puerperium (671.0)*
DEF: Dilated leg veins; due to incompetent vein valves that allow reversed blood flow and cause tissue erosion or weakness of wall; may be painful.
AHA: 2Q, '91, 20

454.0 With ulcer `A`
Varicose ulcer (lower extremity, any part)
Varicose veins with ulcer of lower extremity [any part] or of unspecified site
Any condition classifiable to 454.9 with ulcer or specified as ulcerated
AHA: 4Q, '99, 18

454.1 With inflammation `A`
Stasis dermatitis
Varicose veins with inflammation of lower extremity [any part] or of unspecified site
Any condition classifiable to 454.9 with inflammation or specified as inflamed

454.2 With ulcer and inflammation `CC` `A`
Varicose veins with ulcer and inflammation of lower extremity [any part] or of unspecified site
Any condition classifiable to 454.9 with ulcer and inflammation
CC Excl: 454.0-454.2, 454.9

454.8 With other complications
Edema
Pain
Swelling
AHA: 4Q, '02, 58

454.9 Asymptomatic varicose veins `A`
Phlebectasia ⎫
Varicose veins ⎬ of lower extremity [any part]
Varix ⎭ or of unspecified site
Varicose veins NOS
AHA: 4Q, '02, 58
TIP: Do not assign if patient seen for surgical treatment of varicose veins; query physician for specific symptom (inflammation, pain, edema, swelling).

`√4th` **455 Hemorrhoids**
INCLUDES hemorrhoids (anus) (rectum)
piles
varicose veins, anus or rectum
EXCLUDES *that complicating pregnancy, childbirth, or the puerperium (671.8)*
DEF: Varicose condition of external hemorrhoidal veins causing painful swellings at the anus.

455.0 Internal hemorrhoids without mention of complication
AHA: 3Q, '05, 17
`K64.0` First degree hemorrhoids `I-10`

455.1 Internal thrombosed hemorrhoids

455.2 Internal hemorrhoids with other complication
Internal hemorrhoids:
bleeding
prolapsed
strangulated
ulcerated
AHA: 3Q, '05, 17; 1Q, '03, 8
`K64.2` Third degree hemorrhoid `I-10`

455.3 External hemorrhoids without mention of complication
AHA: 1Q, '07, 13; 3Q, '05, 17
`K64.4` Residual hemorrhoidal skin tags `I-10`

455.4 External thrombosed hemorrhoids

455.5 External hemorrhoids with other complication
External hemorrhoids:
bleeding
prolapsed
strangulated
ulcerated
AHA: 3Q, '05, 17; 1Q, '03, 8

455.6 Unspecified hemorrhoids without mention of complication
Hemorrhoids NOS

455.7 Unspecified thrombosed hemorrhoids
Thrombosed hemorrhoids, unspecified whether internal or external

455.8 Unspecified hemorrhoids with other complication
Hemorrhoids, unspecified whether internal or external:
bleeding
prolapsed
strangulated
ulcerated

455.9 Residual hemorrhoidal skin tags
Skin tags, anus or rectum

`√4th` **456 Varicose veins of other sites**

456.0 Esophageal varices with bleeding `MCC`
DEF: Distended, tortuous, veins of lower esophagus, usually due to portal hypertension.
CC Excl: 251.5, 456.0, 456.20, 459.89-459.9, 530.20-530.21, 530.7, 530.82, 530.85, 531.00-534.91, 535.01, 535.11, 535.21, 535.31, 535.41, 535.51, 535.61, 535.71, 537.83, 562.02-562.03, 562.12-562.13, 569.3, 569.85, 578.0-578.9

456.1 Esophageal varices without mention of bleeding `CC`
CC Excl: 251.5, 456.0-456.20, 459.89-459.9, 530.7, 530.82, 531.00-534.91, 535.01, 535.11, 535.21, 535.31, 535.41, 535.51, 535.61, 535.71, 537.83, 578.0-578.9

`√5th` **456.2 Esophageal varices in diseases classified elsewhere**
Code first underlying cause, as:
cirrhosis of liver (571.0-571.9)
portal hypertension (572.3)

456.20 With bleeding `MCC`
CC Excl: 456.0, 456.20, 459.89-459.9, 530.82
AHA: N-D, '85, 14
`I85.11` Secondary esophageal varices with bleeding `I-10`

456.21 Without mention of bleeding `CC`
CC Excl: 251.5, 456.0, 456.20-456.21, 459.89-459.9, 530.7, 530.82, 531.00-534.91, 535.01, 535.11, 535.21, 535.31, 535.41, 535.51, 535.61, 535.71, 537.83, 578.0-578.9
AHA: 3Q, '05, 15; 2Q, '02, 4

456.3 Sublingual varices
DEF: Distended, tortuous veins beneath tongue.

456.4 Scrotal varices ♂
Varicocele

456.5 Pelvic varices
Varices of broad ligament

456.6 Vulval varices ♀
Varices of perineum
EXCLUDES *that complicating pregnancy, childbirth, or the puerperium (671.1)*

456.8 Varices of other sites
Varicose veins of nasal septum (with ulcer)
EXCLUDES *placental varices (656.7)*
retinal varices (362.17)
varicose ulcer of unspecified site (454.0)
varicose veins of unspecified site (454.9)
AHA: 2Q, '02, 4

`√4th` **457 Noninfectious disorders of lymphatic channels**

457.0 Postmastectomy lymphedema syndrome `A`
Elephantiasis ⎫
Obliteration of lymphatic vessel ⎬ due to mastectomy
DEF: Reduced lymphatic circulation following mastectomy; symptoms include swelling of the arm on the operative side.
AHA: 2Q, '02, 12

`N` Newborn Age: 0   `P` Pediatric Age: 0-17   `M` Maternity Age: 12-55   `A` Adult Age: 15-124   `MCC` Major CC Condition   `CC` CC Condition   `HIV` HIV Related Dx

156 – Volume 1
2015 ICD-9-CM

457.1 Other lymphedema
Elephantiasis (nonfilarial) NOS
Lymphangiectasis
Lymphedema:
    acquired (chronic)
    praecox
    secondary
Obliteration, lymphatic vessel

> EXCLUDES *elephantiasis (nonfilarial):*
>   *congenital (757.0)*
>   *eyelid (374.83)*
>   *vulva (624.8)*

DEF: Fluid retention due to reduced lymphatic circulation; due to other than mastectomy.
AHA: 3Q, '04, 5
I89.0 Lymphedema not elsewhere classified   I-10

457.2 Lymphangitis
Lymphangitis:
    NOS
    chronic
    subacute

> EXCLUDES *acute lymphangitis (682.0-682.9)*

457.8 Other noninfectious disorders of lymphatic channels
Chylocele (nonfilarial)   Lymph node or vessel:
Chylous: fistula
    ascites   infarction
    cyst   rupture

> EXCLUDES *chylocele:*
>   *filarial (125.0-125.9)*
>   *tunica vaginalis (nonfilarial) (608.84)*

AHA: 1Q, '04, 5; 3Q, '03, 17

457.9 Unspecified noninfectious disorder of lymphatic channels

✓4th 458 Hypotension
INCLUDES hypopiesis

> EXCLUDES *cardiovascular collapse (785.50)*
>   *maternal hypotension syndrome (669.2)*
>   *shock (785.50-785.59)*
>   *Shy-Drager syndrome (333.0)*

458.0 Orthostatic hypotension
Hypotension:
    orthostatic (chronic)
    postural
DEF: Low blood pressure; occurs when standing.
AHA: 3Q, '00, 8; 3Q, '91, 9
I95.1 Orthostatic hypotension   I-10

458.1 Chronic hypotension
Permanent idiopathic hypotension
DEF: Persistent low blood pressure.

✓5th 458.2 Iatrogenic hypotension
DEF: Abnormally low blood pressure; due to medical treatment.
AHA: 4Q, '03, 60; 3Q, '02, 12; 4Q, '95, 57

458.21 Hypotension of hemodialysis
Intra-dialytic hypotension
AHA: 4Q, '03, 61

458.29 Other iatrogenic hypotension
Postoperative hypotension
I95.81 Postprocedural hypotension   I-10

458.8 Other specified hypotension
AHA: 4Q, '97, 37

458.9 Hypotension, unspecified
Hypotension (arterial) NOS
I95.9 Hypotension unspecified   I-10

✓4th 459 Other disorders of circulatory system

459.0 Hemorrhage, unspecified
Rupture of blood vessel NOS
Spontaneous hemorrhage NEC

> EXCLUDES *hemorrhage:*
>   *gastrointestinal NOS (578.9)*
>   *in newborn NOS (772.9)*
>   *secondary or recurrent following trauma (958.2)*
>   *traumatic rupture of blood vessel (900.0-904.9)*
>   *nontraumatic hematoma of soft tissue (729.92)*

AHA: 4Q, '90, 26
R58 Hemorrhage not elsewhere classified   I-10

✓5th 459.1 Postphlebitic syndrome
Chronic venous hypertension due to deep vein thrombosis

> EXCLUDES *chronic venous hypertension without deep vein thrombosis (459.30-459.39)*

DEF: Various conditions following deep vein thrombosis; including edema, pain, stasis dermatitis, cellulitis, varicose veins and ulceration of the lower leg.
AHA: 4Q, '02, 58; 2Q, '91, 20

459.10 Postphlebitic syndrome without complications
Asymptomatic postphlebitic syndrome
Postphlebitic syndrome NOS

459.11 Postphlebitic syndrome with ulcer   CC
CC Excl: 451.0-451.9

459.12 Postphlebitic syndrome with inflammation

459.13 Postphlebitic syndrome with ulcer and inflammation   CC
CC Excl: See code: 459.11

459.19 Postphlebitic syndrome with other complication

459.2 Compression of vein   CC
Stricture of vein
Vena cava syndrome (inferior) (superior)
CC Excl: 459.2

✓5th 459.3 Chronic venous hypertension (idiopathic)
Stasis edema

> EXCLUDES *chronic venous hypertension due to deep vein thrombosis (459.10-459.9)*
>   *varicose veins (454.0-454.9)*

AHA: 4Q, '02, 59

459.30 Chronic venous hypertension without complications
Asymptomatic chronic venous hypertension
Chronic venous hypertension NOS

459.31 Chronic venous hypertension with ulcer   CC
CC Excl: 454.0-454.2, 454.9, 459.81-459.9
AHA: 4Q, '02, 43

459.32 Chronic venous hypertension with inflammation

459.33 Chronic venous hypertension with ulcer and inflammation   CC
CC Excl: See code: 459.31

459.39 Chronic venous hypertension with other complication

✓5th 459.8 Other specified disorders of circulatory system

459.81 Venous (peripheral) insufficiency, unspecified
Chronic venous insufficiency NOS

Use additional code for any associated ulceration (707.10-707.19, 707.8, 707.9)

DEF: Insufficient drainage, venous blood, any part of body, results in edema or dermatosis.
AHA: 3Q, '04, 5; 2Q, '91, 20; M-A, '87, 6
TIP: Assign for stasis dermatitis without varicose veins or past DVT.
I87.2 Venous insufficiency (chronic) (peripheral)   I-10

459.89 Other
Collateral circulation (venous), any site
Phlebosclerosis
Venofibrosis

459.9 Unspecified circulatory system disorder
AHA: ▶1Q, '13, 7◀

| ✓4th ✓5th Additional Digit Required | Unacceptable PDx | Manifestation Code | Hospital Acquired Condition | ▶◀ Revised Text | ● New Code | ▲ Revised Code Title |

8. Diseases of the Respiratory System (460-519)

Use additional code to identify infectious organism

Acute Respiratory Infections (460-466)

EXCLUDES pneumonia and influenza (480.0-488.19)

460 Acute nasopharyngitis [common cold]
Coryza (acute)
Nasal catarrh, acute
Nasopharyngitis:
  NOS
  acute
  infective NOS
Rhinitis:
  acute
  infective

EXCLUDES nasopharyngitis, chronic (472.2)
  pharyngitis:
    acute or unspecified (462)
    chronic (472.1)
  rhinitis:
    allergic (477.0-477.9)
    chronic or unspecified (472.0)
  sore throat:
    acute or unspecified (462)
    chronic (472.1)

DEF: Acute inflammation of mucous membranes; extends from nares to pharynx.
AHA: 1Q, '88, 12

√4ᵗʰ 461 Acute sinusitis
INCLUDES abscess
  empyema
  infection   } acute, of sinus
  inflammation   (accessory) (nasal)
  suppuration

EXCLUDES chronic or unspecified sinusitis (473.0-473.9)

461.0 Maxillary
Acute antritis

461.1 Frontal

461.2 Ethmoidal

461.3 Sphenoidal

461.8 Other acute sinusitis
Acute pansinusitis

461.9 Acute sinusitis, unspecified
Acute sinusitis NOS
J01.90 Acute sinusitis unspecified   `I-10`

462 Acute pharyngitis
Acute sore throat NOS   Pharyngitis (acute):
Pharyngitis (acute):   staphylococcal
  NOS   suppurative
  gangrenous   ulcerative
  infective   Sore throat (viral) NOS
  phlegmonous   Viral pharyngitis
  pneumococcal

EXCLUDES abscess:
    peritonsillar [quinsy] (475)
    pharyngeal NOS (478.29)
    retropharyngeal (478.24)
  chronic pharyngitis (472.1)
  infectious mononucleosis (075)
  that specified as (due to):
    Coxsackie (virus) (074.0)
    gonococcus (098.6)
    herpes simplex (054.79)
    influenza (487.1, 488.02, 488.12)
    septic (034.0)
    streptococcal (034.0)

AHA: 2Q, '12, 18; 4Q, '99, 26; S-O, '85, 8
J02.9 Acute pharyngitis unspecified   `I-10`

Respiratory System

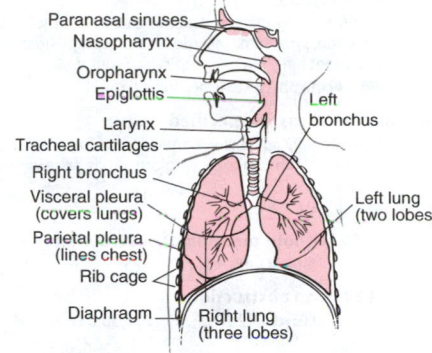

Paranasal sinuses
Nasopharynx
Oropharynx
Epiglottis
Larynx
Tracheal cartilages
Right bronchus
Visceral pleura (covers lungs)
Parietal pleura (lines chest)
Rib cage
Diaphragm
Left bronchus
Left lung (two lobes)
Right lung (three lobes)

463 Acute tonsillitis
Tonsillitis (acute):   Tonsillitis (acute):
  NOS   septic
  follicular   staphylococcal
  gangrenous   suppurative
  infective   ulcerative
  pneumococcal   viral

EXCLUDES chronic tonsillitis (474.0)
  hypertrophy of tonsils (474.1)
  peritonsillar abscess [quinsy] (475)
  sore throat:
    acute or NOS (462)
    septic (034.0)
  streptococcal tonsillitis (034.0)

AHA: N-D, '84, 16

√4ᵗʰ 464 Acute laryngitis and tracheitis
EXCLUDES that associated with influenza (487.1, 488.02, 488.12)
  that due to Streptococcus (034.0)

√5ᵗʰ 464.0 Acute laryngitis
Laryngitis (acute):
  NOS
  edematous
  Hemophilus influenzae [H. influenzae]
  pneumococcal
  septic
  suppurative
  ulcerative

EXCLUDES chronic laryngitis (476.0-476.1)
  influenzal laryngitis (487.1, 488.02, 488.12)

464.00 Without mention of obstruction

464.01 With obstruction   `MCC`
CC Excl: 012.20-012.86, 464.00-464.31, 579.8-519.9

√5ᵗʰ 464.1 Acute tracheitis
Tracheitis (acute):   Tracheitis (acute):
  NOS   viral
  catarrhal

EXCLUDES chronic tracheitis (491.8)

464.10 Without mention of obstruction

464.11 With obstruction   `MCC`
CC Excl: 012.20-012.86, 017.90-017.96, 464.00-464.31, 519.8-519.9

√5ᵗʰ 464.2 Acute laryngotracheitis
Laryngotracheitis (acute)
Tracheitis (acute) with laryngitis (acute)

EXCLUDES chronic laryngotracheitis (476.1)

464.20 Without mention of obstruction

464.21 With obstruction   `MCC`
CC Excl: See code 464.11

√5ᵗʰ 464.3 Acute epiglottitis
Viral epiglottitis

EXCLUDES epiglottitis, chronic (476.1)

464.30 Without mention of obstruction   `CC`
CC Excl: 464.01, 464.30-464.31, 464.51

464.31 With obstruction   `MCC`
CC Excl: See code 464.11

Diseases of the Respiratory System

464.4–472.2

464.4 Croup

Croup syndrome

DEF: Acute laryngeal obstruction due to allergy, foreign body or infection; symptoms include barking cough, hoarseness and harsh, persistent high-pitched respiratory sound.

J05.0 Acute obstructive laryngitis [croup]   **I-10**

✓5ᵗʰ **464.5 Supraglottitis, unspecified**

DEF: A rapidly advancing generalized upper respiratory infection of the lingual tonsillar area, epiglottic folds, false vocal cords, and the epiglottis.

AHA: 4Q, '01, 42

     464.50 Without mention of obstruction

         AHA: 4Q, '01, 43

     464.51 With obstruction   **MCC**

         CC Excl: 012.20-012.86, 017.90-017.96, 464.00-464.31, 519.8-519.9

✓4ᵗʰ **465 Acute upper respiratory infections of multiple or unspecified sites**

   EXCLUDES upper respiratory infection due to:
       influenza (487.1, 488.02, 488.12)
       Streptococcus (034.0)

   465.0 Acute laryngopharyngitis

     DEF: Acute infection of the vocal cords and pharynx.

   465.8 Other multiple sites

     Multiple URI
     AHA: 4Q, '07, 85

   465.9 Unspecified site

     Acute URI NOS
     Upper respiratory infection (acute)
     J06.9 Acute upper respiratory infection unspecified   **I-10**

✓4ᵗʰ **466 Acute bronchitis and bronchiolitis**

   INCLUDES that with:
       bronchospasm
       obstruction

   466.0 Acute bronchitis

     Bronchitis, acute or subacute:
       fibrinous
       membranous
       pneumococcal
       purulent
       septic
       viral
       with tracheitis
     Croupous bronchitis
     Tracheobronchitis, acute

     EXCLUDES acute bronchitis with chronic obstructive pulmonary disease (491.22)

     DEF: Acute inflammation of main branches of bronchial tree due to infectious or irritant agents; symptoms include cough with a varied production of sputum, fever, substernal soreness, and lung rales.

     AHA: 4Q, '04, 137; 1Q, '04, 3; 4Q, '02, 46; 4Q, '96, 28; 4Q, '91, 24; 1Q, '88, 12

     TIP: If documented with COPD, assign only 491.22 Obstructive chronic bronchitis with acute bronchitis.

     J20.9 Acute bronchitis unspecified   **I-10**

✓5ᵗʰ **466.1 Acute bronchiolitis**

     Bronchiolitis (acute)   Capillary pneumonia

     EXCLUDES respiratory bronchiolitis interstitial lung disease (516.34)

     DEF: Acute inflammation of the smallest branches of bronchial tree due to infectious or irritant agents; symptoms include cough, tachycardia, labored breathing, and lung crackles.

     466.11 Acute bronchiolitis due to respiratory syncytial virus (RSV)   **CC**

         CC Excl: 466.11
         AHA: 1Q, '05, 10; 4Q, '96, 27
         J21.0 Acute bronchiolitis d/t resp syncytial virus   **I-10**

     466.19 Acute bronchiolitis due to other infectious organisms   **CC**

         Use additional code to identify organism
         CC Excl: 466.0-466.19
         J21.8 Acute bronchiolitis d/t oth specified organisms   **I-10**

Upper Respiratory System

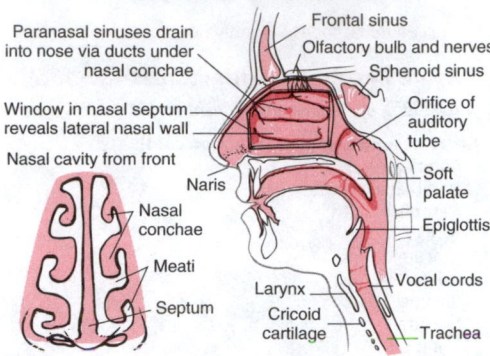

Paranasal sinuses drain into nose via ducts under nasal conchae

Window in nasal septum reveals lateral nasal wall

Nasal cavity from front

Frontal sinus

Olfactory bulb and nerves

Sphenoid sinus

Orifice of auditory tube

Soft palate

Naris

Nasal conchae

Epiglottis

Meati

Vocal cords

Larynx

Septum

Cricoid cartilage

Trachea

Other Diseases of the Upper Respiratory Tract (470-478)

470 Deviated nasal septum

Deflected septum (nasal) (acquired)

EXCLUDES congenital (754.0)

✓4ᵗʰ **471 Nasal polyps**

EXCLUDES adenomatous polyps (212.0)

   471.0 Polyp of nasal cavity

     Polyp:
       choanal
       nasopharyngeal

   471.1 Polypoid sinus degeneration

     Woakes' syndrome or ethmoiditis

   471.8 Other polyp of sinus

     Polyp of sinus:
       accessory
       ethmoidal
       maxillary
       sphenoidal

   471.9 Unspecified nasal polyp

     Nasal polyp NOS

✓4ᵗʰ **472 Chronic pharyngitis and nasopharyngitis**

   472.0 Chronic rhinitis

     Ozena   Rhinitis:
     Rhinitis: hypertrophic
       NOS   obstructive
       atrophic   purulent
       granulomatous   ulcerative

     EXCLUDES allergic rhinitis (477.0-477.9)

     DEF: Persistent inflammation of mucous membranes of nose.

   472.1 Chronic pharyngitis

     Chronic sore throat   Pharyngitis:
     Pharyngitis: granular (chronic)
       atrophic   hypertrophic

   472.2 Chronic nasopharyngitis

     EXCLUDES acute or unspecified nasopharyngitis (460)

     DEF: Persistent inflammation of mucous membranes extending from nares to pharynx.

Paranasal Sinuses

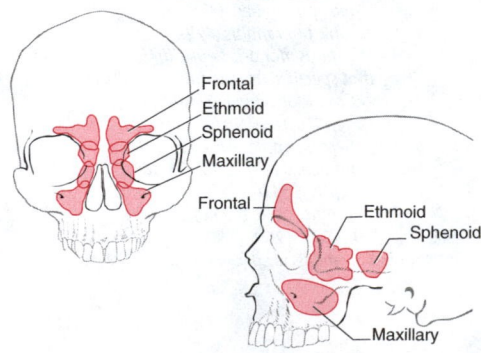

Frontal
Ethmoid
Sphenoid
Maxillary
Frontal

Frontal
Ethmoid
Sphenoid
Maxillary

N Newborn Age: 0   **P** Pediatric Age: 0-17   **M** Maternity Age: 12-55   **A** Adult Age: 15-124   **MCC** Major CC Condition   **CC** CC Condition   **HIV** HIV Related Dx

160 – Volume 1   2015 ICD-9-CM

✓4ᵗʰ **473 Chronic sinusitis**

INCLUDES abscess
empyema
infection   (chronic) of sinus (accessory)
suppuration   (nasal)

EXCLUDES *acute sinusitis (461.0-461.9)*

473.0 Maxillary
Antritis (chronic)
J32.0 Chronic maxillary sinusitis   I-10

473.1 Frontal

473.2 Ethmoidal
EXCLUDES *Woakes' ethmoiditis (471.1)*

473.3 Sphenoidal

473.8 Other chronic sinusitis
Pansinusitis (chronic)

473.9 Unspecified sinusitis (chronic)
Sinusitis (chronic) NOS
J32.9 Chronic sinusitis unspecified   I-10

✓4ᵗʰ **474 Chronic disease of tonsils and adenoids**

✓5ᵗʰ **474.0 Chronic tonsillitis and adenoiditis**
EXCLUDES *acute or unspecified tonsillitis (463)*
AHA: 4Q, '97, 38

474.00 Chronic tonsillitis

474.01 Chronic adenoiditis

474.02 Chronic tonsillitis and adenoiditis

✓5ᵗʰ **474.1 Hypertrophy of tonsils and adenoids**
Enlargement
Hyperplasia   of tonsils or adenoids
Hypertrophy

EXCLUDES *that with:*
adenoiditis (474.01)
adenoiditis and tonsillitis (474.02)
tonsillitis (474.00)

474.10 Tonsils with adenoids
AHA: 2Q, '05, 16

474.11 Tonsils alone

474.12 Adenoids alone

474.2 Adenoid vegetations
DEF: Fungus-like growth of lymph tissue between the nares and pharynx.

474.8 Other chronic disease of tonsils and adenoids
Amygdalolith   Tonsillar tag
Calculus, tonsil   Ulcer, tonsil
Cicatrix of tonsil (and adenoid)

474.9 Unspecified chronic disease of tonsils and adenoids
Disease (chronic) of tonsils (and adenoids)

475 Peritonsillar abscess   CC
Abscess of tonsil   Quinsy
Peritonsillar cellulitis
EXCLUDES *tonsillitis:*
acute or NOS (463)
chronic (474.0)
CC Excl: 475, 519.8-519.9
J36 Peritonsillar abscess   I-10

✓4ᵗʰ **476 Chronic laryngitis and laryngotracheitis**

476.0 Chronic laryngitis
Laryngitis:
catarrhal
hypertrophic
sicca

476.1 Chronic laryngotracheitis
Laryngitis, chronic, with tracheitis (chronic)
Tracheitis, chronic, with laryngitis
EXCLUDES *chronic tracheitis (491.8)*
laryngitis and tracheitis, acute or unspecified
(464.00-464.51)

✓4ᵗʰ **477 Allergic rhinitis**

INCLUDES allergic rhinitis (nonseasonal) (seasonal)
hay fever
spasmodic rhinorrhea

EXCLUDES *allergic rhinitis with asthma (bronchial) (493.0)*

DEF: True immunoglobulin E (IgE)-mediated allergic reaction of nasal mucosa; seasonal (typical hay fever) or perennial (year-round allergens; dust, food, dander).

477.0 Due to pollen
Pollinosis

477.1 Due to food
AHA: 4Q, '00, 42

477.2 Due to animal (cat) (dog) hair and dander

477.8 Due to other allergen

477.9 Cause unspecified
AHA: 2Q, '97, 9
J30.9 Allergic rhinitis unspecified   I-10

✓4ᵗʰ **478 Other diseases of upper respiratory tract**

478.0 Hypertrophy of nasal turbinates
DEF: Overgrowth, enlargement of shell-shaped bones in nasal cavity.

✓5ᵗʰ **478.1 Other diseases of nasal cavity and sinuses**
EXCLUDES *varicose ulcer of nasal septum (456.8)*

478.11 Nasal mucositis (ulcerative)
Use additional E code to identify adverse effects of therapy, such as:
antineoplastic and immunosuppressive drugs (E930.7, E933.1)
radiation therapy (E879.2)
AHA: 4Q, '06, 88-90

478.19 Other diseases of nasal cavity and sinuses
Abscess
Necrosis   of nose (septum)
Ulcer

Cyst or mucocele of sinus (nasal)
Rhinolith
AHA: 4Q, '06, 88-90
J34.1 Cyst and mucocele of nose and nasal sinus   I-10

✓5ᵗʰ **478.2 Other diseases of pharynx, not elsewhere classified**

478.20 Unspecified disease of pharynx

478.21 Cellulitis of pharynx or nasopharynx   CC
CC Excl: 478.20-478.24, 519.8-519.9

478.22 Parapharyngeal abscess   CC
CC Excl: See code: 478.21

478.24 Retropharyngeal abscess   CC
DEF: Purulent infection, behind pharynx and front of precerebral fascia.
CC Excl: See code 478.21

478.25 Edema of pharynx or nasopharynx

478.26 Cyst of pharynx or nasopharynx

478.29 Other
Abscess of pharynx or nasopharynx
EXCLUDES *ulcerative pharyngitis (462)*

✓5ᵗʰ **478.3 Paralysis of vocal cords or larynx**
DEF: Loss of motor ability of vocal cords or larynx; due to nerve or muscle damage.

478.30 Paralysis, unspecified
Laryngoplegia Paralysis of glottis

478.31 Unilateral, partial

478.32 Unilateral, complete

478.33 Bilateral, partial

478.34 Bilateral, complete   CC
CC Excl: 478.30-478.34, 478.5, 478.70, 519.8-519.9

478.4 Polyp of vocal cord or larynx
EXCLUDES *adenomatous polyps (212.1)*

| ✓4ᵗʰ ✓5ᵗʰ Additional Digit Required | Unacceptable PDx | Manifestation Code | Hospital Acquired Condition | ►◄ Revised Text | ● New Code | ▲ Revised Code Title |

2015 ICD-9-CM   **Volume 1 – 161**

478.5 Other diseases of vocal cords

Abscess
Cellulitis
Granuloma } of vocal cords
Leukoplakia

Chorditis (fibrinous) (nodosa) (tuberosa)
Singers' nodes

478.6 Edema of larynx

Edema (of):   Edema (of):
   glottis   supraglottic
   subglottic

✓5ᵗʰ 478.7 Other diseases of larynx, not elsewhere classified

478.70 Unspecified disease of larynx

478.71 Cellulitis and perichondritis of larynx `CC`
DEF: Inflammation of deep soft tissues or lining of bone of the larynx.
CC Excl: 478.70-478.71, 478.79

478.74 Stenosis of larynx

478.75 Laryngeal spasm
Laryngismus (stridulus)
DEF: Involuntary muscle contraction of the larynx.

478.79 Other
Abscess
Necrosis
Obstruction } of larynx
Pachyderma
Ulcer
EXCLUDES *ulcerative laryngitis (464.00-464.01)*
AHA: 3Q, '91, 20

478.8 Upper respiratory tract hypersensitivity reaction, site unspecified

EXCLUDES *hypersensitivity reaction of lower respiratory tract, as:*
extrinsic allergic alveolitis (495.0-495.9)
pneumoconiosis (500-505)

478.9 Other and unspecified diseases of upper respiratory tract

Abscess } of trachea
Cicatrix

Pneumonia and Influenza (480-488)

EXCLUDES *pneumonia:*
allergic or eosinophilic (518.3)
aspiration:
  NOS (507.0)
  newborn (770.18)
  solids and liquids (507.0-507.8)
congenital (770.0)
lipoid (507.1)
passive (514)
rheumatic (390)
ventilator-associated (997.31)

✓4ᵗʰ 480 Viral pneumonia

480.0 Pneumonia due to adenovirus `MCC`
CC Excl: 011.00-012.16, 012.80-012.86, 017.90-017.96, 020.3-020.5, 021.3, 022.1, 031.0, 039.1, 073.0, 115.05, 115.15, 115.95, 122.1, 130.4, 136.3, 480.0-487.1, 488.01-488.02, 488.11-488.12, 495.0-495.9, 500-508.9, 517.1, 517.8, 518.89, 519.8-519.9

480.1 Pneumonia due to respiratory syncytial virus `MCC`
CC Excl: See code: 480.0
AHA: 4Q, '10, 98; 4Q, '96, 28; 1Q, '88, 12

480.2 Pneumonia due to parainfluenza virus `MCC`
CC Excl: See code: 480.0

480.3 Pneumonia due to SARS-associated coronavirus `MCC` `HIV`
DEF: A severe adult respiratory syndrome caused by the coronavirus, specified as inflammation of the lungs with consolidation.
CC Excl: 011.00-012.16, 012.80-012.86, 017.90-017.96, 021.2, 031.0, 039.1, 115.05, 115.15, 115.95, 122.1, 130.4, 136.3, 480.0-487.1, 488.01-488.02, 488.11-488.12, 494.0-508.9, 517.1, 517.8, 518.89, 519.8-519.9, 748.61
AHA: 4Q, '03, 46-47

Lungs

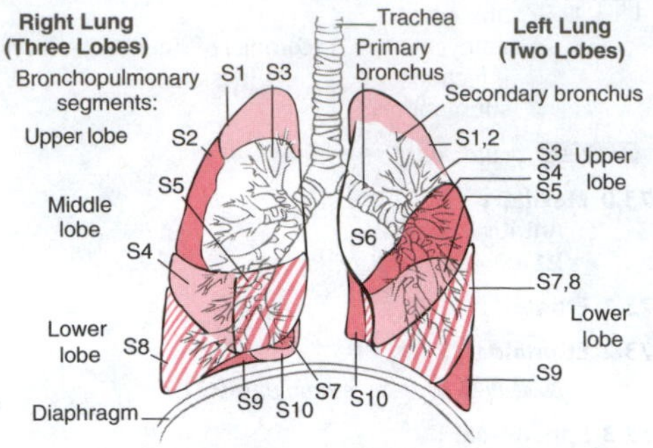

Right Lung (Three Lobes) — Bronchopulmonary segments: — Upper lobe — Middle lobe — Lower lobe — Diaphragm — S1 S3 S2 S5 S4 S8 S9 S10 S7 S10 — Trachea — Primary bronchus — Secondary bronchus — Left Lung (Two Lobes) — S1,2 S3 S4 S5 Upper lobe — S6 — S7,8 — Lower lobe — S9

480.8 Pneumonia due to other virus not elsewhere classified `MCC` `HIV`
EXCLUDES *congenital rubella pneumonitis (771.0)*
pneumonia complicating viral diseases classified elsewhere (484.1-484.8)
CC Excl: See code: 480.0

480.9 Viral pneumonia, unspecified `MCC` `HIV`
CC Excl: See code: 480.0
AHA: 3Q, '98, 5

481 Pneumococcal pneumonia [Streptococcus pneumoniae pneumonia] `MCC` `HIV`

Lobar pneumonia, organism unspecified
CC Excl: 011.00-012.16, 012.80-012.86, 017.90-017.96, 021.2, 031.0, 039.1, 115.05, 115.15, 115.95, 122.1, 130.4, 136.3, 480.0-480.2, 480.8-487.1, 488.01-488.02, 488.11-488.12, 494.0-508.9, 517.1, 517.8, 518.89, 519.8-519.9, 748.61
AHA: 2Q, '98, 7; 4Q, '92, 19; 1Q, '92, 18; 1Q, '91, 13; 1Q, '88, 13; M-A, '85, 6

✓4ᵗʰ 482 Other bacterial pneumonia

AHA: 4Q, '93, 39

482.0 Pneumonia due to Klebsiella pneumoniae `MCC` `HIV`
CC Excl: See code 481

482.1 Pneumonia due to Pseudomonas `MCC` `HIV`
CC Excl: See code 481

482.2 Pneumonia due to Hemophilus influenzae [H. influenzae] `MCC` `HIV`
CC Excl: See code 481
AHA: 2Q, '05, 19

✓5ᵗʰ 482.3 Pneumonia due to Streptococcus

EXCLUDES *Streptococcus pneumoniae (481)*
AHA: 1Q, '88, 13

482.30 Streptococcus, unspecified `MCC` `HIV`
CC Excl: See code 481

482.31 Group A `MCC` `HIV`
CC Excl: See code 481

482.32 Group B `MCC` `HIV`
CC Excl: See code 481

482.39 Other Streptococcus `MCC` `HIV`
CC Excl: See code 481

✓5ᵗʰ 482.4 Pneumonia due to Staphylococcus

AHA: 3Q, '91, 16

482.40 Pneumonia due to Staphylococcus, unspecified `MCC` `HIV`
CC Excl: See code 481

482.41 Methicillin susceptible pneumonia due to Staphylococcus aureus `MCC` `HIV`
Staphylococcus aureus
MSSA pneumonia
Pneumonia due to Staphylococcus aureus NOS
CC Excl: See code 481
J15.211 Pneumonia d/t methicillin suscep staph `I-10`

482.42 Methicillin resistant pneumonia due to Staphylococcus aureus `MCC` `HIV`
CC Excl: See code 481
AHA: 4Q, '08, 69, 71, 72

482.49 Other Staphylococcus pneumonia `MCC` `HIV`
CC Excl: See code 481
AHA: ▶2Q, '13, 21◀

`N` Newborn Age: 0   `P` Pediatric Age: 0-17   `M` Maternity Age: 12-55   `A` Adult Age: 15-124   `MCC` Major CC Condition   `CC` CC Condition   `HIV` HIV Related Dx

162 – Volume 1 • October 2014   2015 ICD-9-CM

☑5ᵗʰ **482.8 Pneumonia due to other specified bacteria**

> **EXCLUDES** *pneumonia, complicating infectious disease classified elsewhere (484.1-484.8)*

AHA: 3Q, '88, 11

482.81 Anaerobes   MCC HIV
Bacteroides (melaninogenicus)
Gram-negative anaerobes
CC Excl: See code 481

482.82 Escherichia coli [E. coli]   MCC HIV
CC Excl: See code 481

482.83 Other gram-negative bacteria   MCC HIV
Gram-negative pneumonia   Proteus
    NOS   Serratia marcescens
> **EXCLUDES** *gram-negative anaerobes (482.81)*
> *Legionnaires' disease (482.84)*

CC Excl: See code 481
AHA: 2Q, '98, 5; 3Q, '94, 9
TIP: Do not assign based solely on laboratory findings of gram-negative bacteria on gram-stain. Physician substantiation is required.
J15.6 Pneumonia d/t oth aerobic Gram-negative bacteria   I-10

482.84 Legionnaires' disease   MCC HIV
DEF: Severe and often fatal infection by Legionella pneumophilia; symptoms include high fever, gastrointestinal pain, headache, myalgia, dry cough, and pneumonia; usually transmitted airborne via air conditioning systems.
CC Excl: See code 481
AHA: 4Q, '97, 38

482.89 Other specified bacteria   MCC HIV
CC Excl: See code 481
AHA: ▶2Q, '13, 17;◀ 2Q, '97, 6
TIP: Do not assign based on documentation of "mixed bacterial pneumonia" or "gram-positive pneumonia." See instead 482.9.

482.9 Bacterial pneumonia unspecified   MCC HIV
CC Excl: See code 481
AHA: 2Q, '98, 6; 2Q, '97, 6; 1Q, '94, 17
J15.9 Unspecified bacterial pneumonia   I-10

☑4ᵗʰ **483 Pneumonia due to other specified organism**
AHA: N-D, '87, 5
TIP: Do not assign if pneumonia due to candidiasis; see instead code 112.4.

483.0 Mycoplasma pneumoniae   MCC
Eaton's agent   Pleuropneumonia-like organism [PPLO]
CC Excl: See code 481

483.1 Chlamydia   MCC
CC Excl: See code 481
AHA: 4Q, '96, 31

483.8 Other specified organism   MCC
CC Excl: See code 481

☑4ᵗʰ **484 Pneumonia in infectious diseases classified elsewhere**

484.1 Pneumonia in cytomegalic inclusion disease   MCC
Code first underlying disease (078.5)
CC Excl: See code 481

484.3 Pneumonia in whooping cough   MCC
Code first underlying disease (033.0-033.9)
CC Excl: See code 481

484.5 Pneumonia in anthrax   MCC
Code first underlying disease (022.1)
CC Excl: See code 481

484.6 Pneumonia in aspergillosis   MCC
Code first underlying disease (117.3)
CC Excl: See code 481
AHA: 4Q, '97, 40

484.7 Pneumonia in other systemic mycoses   MCC
Code first underlying disease
> **EXCLUDES** *pneumonia in:*
> *candidiasis (112.4)*
> *coccidioidomycosis (114.0)*
> *histoplasmosis (115.0-115.9 with fifth-digit 5)*

CC Excl: See code 481

484.8 Pneumonia in other infectious diseases classified elsewhere   MCC
Code first underlying disease, as:
Q fever (083.0)
typhoid fever (002.0)
> **EXCLUDES** *pneumonia in:*
> *actinomycosis (039.1)*
> *measles (055.1)*
> *nocardiosis (039.1)*
> *ornithosis (073.0)*
> *Pneumocystis carinii (136.3)*
> *salmonellosis (003.22)*
> *toxoplasmosis (130.4)*
> *tuberculosis (011.6)*
> *tularemia (021.2)*
> *varicella (052.1)*

CC Excl: See code 481

485 Bronchopneumonia, organism unspecified   MCC
Bronchopneumonia: Pneumonia:
    hemorrhagic   lobular
    terminal   segmental
Pleurobronchopneumonia
> **EXCLUDES** *bronchiolitis (acute) (466.11-466.19)*
> *chronic (491.8)*
> *lipoid pneumonia (507.1)*

CC Excl: See code 481

486 Pneumonia, organism unspecified   MCC HIV
> **EXCLUDES** *hypostatic or passive pneumonia (514)*
> *inhalation or aspiration pneumonia due to foreign materials (507.0-507.8)*
> *pneumonitis due to fumes and vapors (506.0)*

CC Excl: 011.00-012.16, 012.80-012.86, 017.90-017.96, 021.2, 031.0, 039.1, 115.05, 115.15, 115.95, 122.1, 130.4, 136.3, 480.0-480.2, 480.8-487.1, 488, 494.0-508.9, 517.1, 517.8, 518.89, 519.8-519.9, 748.61
AHA: 4Q, '10, 135; 1Q, '10, 3, 12; 3Q, '09, 16; 4Q, '08, 142; 4Q, '99, 6; 3Q, '99, 9; 3Q, '98, 7; 2Q, '98, 4, 5; 1Q, '98, 8; 3Q, '97, 9; 3Q, '94, 10; 3Q, '88, 11
TIP: Never assume a causal organism based on laboratory or radiology findings alone.
J18.9 Pneumonia unspecified organism   I-10

☑4ᵗʰ **487 Influenza**
Influenza caused by unspecified influenza virus
> **EXCLUDES** *Hemophilus influenzae [H. influenzae]:*
> *infection NOS (041.5)*
> *influenza due to identified avian influenza virus (488.01-488.09)*
> *influenza due to 2009 H1N1 [swine] influenza virus (488.11-488.19)*
> *influenza due to identified (novel) 2009 H1N1 influenza virus (488.11-488.19)*
> *laryngitis (464.00-464.01)*
> *meningitis (320.0)*

487.0 With pneumonia   MCC
Influenza with pneumonia,   Influenzal:
    any form   pneumonia
                    bronchopneumonia
Use additional code to identify the type of pneumonia (480.0-480.9, 481, 482.0-482.9, 483.0-483.8, 485)
CC Excl: See code 486
AHA: 1Q, '06, 18; 2Q, '05, 18
TIP: Selection of the principal diagnosis will be dependent on the circumstances of admission.

487.1 With other respiratory manifestations
Influenza NEC   Influenzal:
Influenza NOS   pharyngitis
Influenzal: respiratory infection (upper) (acute)
    laryngitis
AHA: 4Q, '11, 114; 1Q, '10, 4; 1Q, '06, 18; 2Q, '05, 18; 4Q, '99, 26
J10.1 Influenza d/t oth influenza virus w/resp manifestations   I-10

487.8 With other manifestations
Encephalopathy due to influenza
Influenza with involvement of gastrointestinal tract
> **EXCLUDES** *"intestinal flu" [viral gastroenteritis] (008.8)*

☑4ᵗʰ Additional Digit Required   ▨ Unacceptable PDx   ▨ Manifestation Code   ▨ Hospital Acquired Condition   ▶◀ Revised Text   ● New Code   ▲ Revised Code Title
☑5ᵗʰ

2015 ICD-9-CM   **October 2014 · Volume 1 – 163**

√4ᵗʰ **488 Influenza due to certain identified influenza viruses**

> **EXCLUDES** *influenza caused by unspecified or seasonal influenza viruses (487.0-487.8)*
>
> **AHA:** 4Q, '09, 92-93
>
> **TIP:** Do not assign a code from this category unless the specified influenza virus is confirmed.

√5ᵗʰ **488.0 Influenza due to identified avian influenza virus**

> Avian influenza   Influenza A/H5N1
> Bird flu
>
> **DEF:** Infection caused by contact with bird influenza viruses; results in flu-like symptoms that may progress to other severe and life-threatening complications.
>
> **AHA:** 4Q, '10, 85-87; 4Q, '07, 87

488.01 Influenza due to identified avian influenza virus with pneumonia `MCC` `HIV`

> Avian influenzal:
>   bronchopneumonia
>   pneumonia
> Influenza due to identified avian influenza virus with pneumonia, any form
>
> Use additional code to identify the type of pneumonia (480.0- 480.9, 481, 482.0-482.9, 483.0-483.8, 485)
>
> **CC Excl:** 011.00-012.16, 012.80-012.86, 017.90-017.96, 021.2, 031.0, 039.1, 115.05, 115.15, 115.95, 122.1, 130.4, 136.3, 480.0-480.2, 480.8-487.1, 488.01-488.19, 491.21-491.22, 493.01-493.02, 493.11-493.12, 493.21-493.22, 493.91-508.9, 517.1, 517.8, 518.89, 519.8-519.9, 748.61
>
> **J09.X1** Influenza d/t ident novel influenza A virus w/pneumonia   `I-10`

488.02 Influenza due to identified avian influenza virus with other respiratory manifestations `CC`

> Avian influenzal:
>   laryngitis
>   pharyngitis
>   respiratory infection (acute) (upper)
> Identified avian influenza NOS
>
> **CC Excl:** 488.01-488.19, 491.21-491.22, 493.01-493.02, 493.11-493.12, 493.21-493.22, 493.91-493.92, 494.1
>
> **J09.X2** Flu d/t ident novel influenza A virus w/oth resp manifest   `I-10`

488.09 Influenza due to identified avian influenza virus with other manifestations `CC`

> Avian influenza with involvement of gastrointestinal tract
> Encephalopathy due to identified avian influenza
>
> **EXCLUDES** *"intestinal flu" [viral gastroenteritis] (008.8)*
>
> **CC Excl:** 488.01-488.19, 491.21-491.22, 493.01-493.02, 493.11-493.12, 493.21-493.22, 493.91-493.92, 494.1

√5ᵗʰ **488.1 Influenza due to identified 2009 H1N1 influenza virus**

> 2009 H1N1 swine influenza virus
> (Novel) 2009 influenza H1N1
> Novel H1N1 influenza
> Novel influenza A/H1N1
>
> **EXCLUDES** *bird influenza virus infection (488.01-488.09)*
> *influenza A/H5N1 (488.01-488.09)*
> *other human infection with influenza virus of animal origin (488.81-488.89)*
> *swine influenza virus infection (488.81-488.89)*
>
> **AHA:** 4Q, '11, 110-112, 114; 4Q, '10, 85-87; 1Q, '10, 3-4

488.11 Influenza due to identified 2009 H1N1 influenza virus with pneumonia `MCC`

> Influenza due to identified (novel) 2009 H1N1 with pneumonia, any form
> (Novel) 2009 H1N1 influenzal:
>   bronchopneumonia
>   pneumonia
>
> Use additional code to identify the type of pneumonia (480.0- 480.9, 481, 482.0-482.9, 483.0-483.8, 485)
>
> **CC Excl:** 011.00-012.16, 012.80-012.86, 017.90-017.96, 021.2, 031.0, 039.1, 115.05, 115.15, 115.95, 122.1, 130.4, 136.3, 480.0-480.2, 480.8-487.1, 488.01-488.19, 491.21-491.22, 493.01-493.02, 493.11-493.12, 493.21-493.22, 493.91-508.9, 517.1, 517.8, 518.89, 519.8-519.9, 748.61
>
> **J10.08** Influenza d/t oth ident influenza virus w/oth pneumonia   `I-10`

488.12 Influenza due to identified 2009 H1N1 influenza virus with other respiratory manifestations

> (Novel) 2009 H1N1 influenza NOS
> (Novel) 2009 H1N1 influenzal:
>   laryngitis
>   pharyngitis
>   respiratory infection (acute) (upper)
>
> **J10.1** Flu d/t oth ident influenza virus w/oth resp manifest   `I-10`

488.19 Influenza due to identified 2009 H1N1 influenza virus with other manifestations

> Encephalopathy due to identified (novel) 2009 H1N1 influenza
> (Novel) 2009 H1N1 influenza with involvement of gastrointestinal tract
>
> **EXCLUDES** *"intestinal flu" [viral gastroenteritis] (008.8)*

√5ᵗʰ **488.8 Influenza due to novel influenza A**

> Influenza due to animal origin influenza virus
> Infection with influenza viruses occurring in pigs or other animals
> Other novel influenza A viruses not previously found in humans
>
> **EXCLUDES** *bird influenza virus infection (488.01-488.09)*
> *influenza A/H5N1 (488.01-488.09)*
> *influenza due to identified 2009 H1N1 influenza virus (488.11- 488.19)*
>
> **AHA:** 4Q, '11, 110-114

488.81 Influenza due to identified novel influenza A virus with pneumonia `MCC`

> Influenza due to animal origin influenza virus with pneumonia, any form
> Novel influenza A:
>   bronchopneumonia
>   pneumonia
>
> Use additional code to identify the type of pneumonia (480.0-480.9, 481, 482.0-482.9, 483.0-483.8, 485)
>
> **CC Excl:** 011.00-012.16, 012.80-012.86, 017.90-017.96, 021.2, 031.0, 039.1, 115.05, 115.15, 115.95, 122.1, 130.4, 136.3, 480.0-480.2, 480.8-487.1, 488.01-488.02, 488.11-488.12, 488.81-488.82, 494.0-508.1, 508.8-508.9, 517.1, 517.8, 518.89, 519.8-519.9, 748.61, 793.11

488.82 Influenza due to identified novel influenza A virus with other respiratory manifestations

> Influenza due to animal origin influenza A virus with other respiratory manifestations
> Novel influenza A:
>   laryngitis
>   pharyngitis
>   respiratory infection (acute) (upper)

488.89 Influenza due to identified novel influenza A virus with other manifestations

> Encephalopathy due to novel influenza A
> Influenza due to animal origin influenza virus with encephalopathy
> Influenza due to animal origin influenza virus with involvement of gastrointestinal tract
> Novel influenza A with involvement of gastrointestinal tract
>
> **EXCLUDES** *"intestinal flu" [viral gastroenteritis] (008.8)*

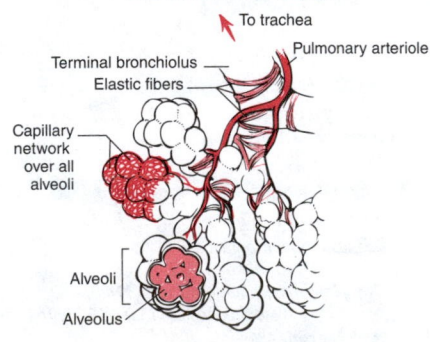

Bronchioli and Alveoli

To trachea
Pulmonary arteriole
Terminal bronchiolus
Elastic fibers
Capillary network over all alveoli
Alveoli
Alveolus

`N` Newborn Age: 0   `P` Pediatric Age: 0-17   `M` Maternity Age: 12-55   `A` Adult Age: 15-124   `MCC` Major CC Condition   `CC` CC Condition   `HIV` HIV Related Dx

Interrelationship Between Chronic Airway Obstruction, Chronic Bronchitis, and Emphysema

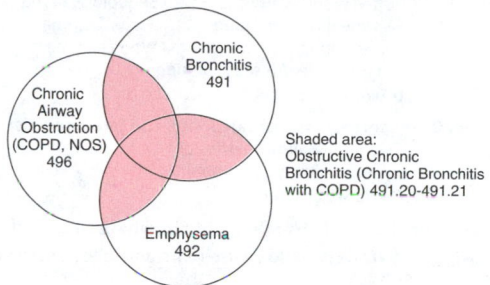

Chronic Bronchitis 491

Chronic Airway Obstruction (COPD, NOS) 496

Emphysema 492

Shaded area: Obstructive Chronic Bronchitis (Chronic Bronchitis with COPD) 491.20-491.21

Chronic Obstructive Pulmonary Disease and Allied Conditions (490-496)

AHA: 3Q, '88, 5

TIP: Due to the overlapping nature of conditions that make up COPD, it's essential that the coder review all instructional notes carefully.

490 Bronchitis, not specified as acute or chronic

Bronchitis NOS: Tracheobronchitis NOS
  catarrhal
  with tracheitis NOS

EXCLUDES bronchitis:
    allergic NOS (493.9)
    asthmatic NOS (493.9)
    due to fumes and vapors (506.0)

J40 Bronchitis not specified as acute or chronic I-10

√4th **491 Chronic bronchitis**

EXCLUDES *chronic obstructive asthma (493.2)*

491.0 Simple chronic bronchitis

Catarrhal bronchitis, chronic
Smokers' cough

J41.0 Simple chronic bronchitis I-10

491.1 Mucopurulent chronic bronchitis

Bronchitis (chronic) (recurrent):
    fetid
    mucopurulent
    purulent

DEF: Chronic bronchial infection characterized by both mucus and pus secretions in the bronchial tree; recurs after asymptomatic periods; signs are coughing, expectoration and secondary changes in the lung.

AHA: 3Q, '88, 12

√5th **491.2 Obstructive chronic bronchitis**

Bronchitis: Bronchitis with:
    emphysematous chronic airway obstruction
    obstructive (chronic) emphysema
    (diffuse)

EXCLUDES *asthmatic bronchitis (acute) NOS (493.9)*
    chronic obstructive asthma (493.2)

AHA: 3Q, '97, 9; 4Q, '91, 25; 2Q, '91, 21

491.20 Without exacerbation

Emphysema with chronic bronchitis

AHA: 3Q, '97, 9

J44.9 Chronic obst pulmonary disease, unspecified I-10

491.21 With (acute) exacerbation CC

Acute exacerbation of chronic obstructive pulmonary disease [COPD]
Decompensated chronic obstructive pulmonary disease [COPD]
Decompensated chronic obstructive pulmonary disease [COPD] with exacerbation

EXCLUDES *chronic obstructive asthma with acute exacerbation (493.22)*

CC Excl: 488.01-488.11, 491.1-491.9, 493.20-493.21

AHA: 1Q, '10, 12; 1Q, '04, 3; 3Q, '02, 18, 19; 4Q, '01, 43; 2Q, '96, 10

J44.1 Chronic obst pulmonary disease with exacerbation I-10

491.22 With acute bronchitis CC

CC Excl: See code 491.21

AHA: 3Q, '06, 20; 4Q, '04, 82

J44.0 Chronic obst pulm dz acute lower respiratory inf I-10

491.8 Other chronic bronchitis

Chronic: Chronic:
    tracheitis tracheobronchitis

491.9 Unspecified chronic bronchitis

J42 Unspecified chronic bronchitis I-10

√4th **492 Emphysema**

AHA: 2Q, '91, 21

492.0 Emphysematous bleb

Giant bullous emphysema Tension pneumatocele
Ruptured emphysematous bleb Vanishing lung

DEF: Formation of vesicle or bulla in emphysematous lung, more than one millimeter; contains serum or blood.

AHA: 2Q, '93, 3

492.8 Other emphysema

Emphysema (lung or pulmonary): MacLeod's syndrome
    NOS Swyer-James syndrome
    centriacinar Unilateral hyperlucent
    centrilobular lung
    obstructive
    panacinar
    panlobular
    unilateral
    vesicular

EXCLUDES *emphysema:*
    with chronic bronchitis (491.20-491.22)
    compensatory (518.2)
    due to fumes and vapors (506.4)
    interstitial (518.1)
        newborn (770.2)
    mediastinal (518.1)
    surgical (subcutaneous) (998.81)
    traumatic (958.7)

AHA: 4Q, '08, 175; 1Q, '05, 4; 4Q, '93, 41; J-A, '84, 17

J43.9 Emphysema unspecified I-10

√4th **493 Asthma**

EXCLUDES *wheezing NOS (786.07)*

The following fifth-digit subclassification is for use with codes 493.0-493.2, 493.9:
    0 unspecified
    1 with status asthmaticus
    2 with (acute) exacerbation

DEF: Status asthmaticus: severe, intractable episode of asthma unresponsive to normal therapeutic measures.

AHA: 4Q, '04, 137; 4Q, '03, 62; 4Q, '01, 43; 4Q, '00, 42; 1Q, '91, 13; 3Q, '88, 9; J-A, '85, 8; N-D, '84, 17

TIP: If documentation indicates both exacerbation and status asthmaticus, assign only the code for status asthmaticus.

§ √5th **493.0 Extrinsic asthma** CC 1-2
[0-2]

Asthma: Asthma:
    allergic with stated cause hay
    atopic platinum
    childhood Hay fever with asthma

EXCLUDES *asthma:*
    allergic NOS (493.9)
    detergent (507.8)
    miners' (500)
    wood (495.8)

DEF: Transient stricture of airway diameters of bronchi; due to environmental factor; also called allergic (bronchial) asthma.

CC Excl: For code 493.01 and 493.02: 488.01-488.11, 493.00-493.92, 517.8, 518.89, 519.8-519.9

J45.20 Mild intermittent asthma uncomplicated I-10

§ √5th **493.1 Intrinsic asthma** CC 1-2
[0-2]

Late-onset asthma

DEF: Transient stricture of airway diameters of bronchi; due to pathophysiological disturbances.

CC Excl: For code 493.11 and 493.12: See code 493.01

AHA: 3Q, '88, 9; M-A, '85, 7

---

§ Requires fifth digit. Valid digits are in [brackets] under each code. See category 493 for codes and definitions.

√4th √5th Additional Digit Required Unacceptable PDx Manifestation Code Hospital Acquired Condition ►◄ Revised Text ● New Code ▲ Revised Code Title

Diseases of the Respiratory System
493.2–506.0

§ ✓5ᵗʰ **493.2 Chronic obstructive asthma**   CC 1-2
[0-2]
     Asthma with chronic obstructive pulmonary disease [COPD]
     Chronic asthmatic bronchitis

     EXCLUDES *acute bronchitis (466.0)*
                   chronic obstructive bronchitis (491.20-491.22)

     DEF: Persistent narrowing of airway diameters in the bronchial tree, restricting airflow and causing constant labored breathing.
     CC Excl: For code 493.21: 488.01-488.11, 491.1-493.92, 517.8, 518.89, 519.8-519.9; **For code 493.22:** 493.00-493.92, 517.8, 518.89, 519.8-519.9
     AHA: 2Q, '91, 21; 2Q, '90, 20; **For code 493.20:** 4Q, '03, 108; **For code 493.22:** 1Q, '09, 17; 3Q, '06, 20

✓5ᵗʰ **493.8 Other forms of asthma**
     AHA: 4Q, '03, 62

     493.81 Exercise induced bronchospasm

     493.82 Cough variant asthma

§ ✓5ᵗʰ **493.9 Asthma, unspecified**   CC 1-2
[0-2]
     Asthma (bronchial) (allergic NOS)   Bronchitis:
     Bronchitis: asthmatic
       allergic

     CC Excl: For code 493.91 and 493.92: 493.00-493.92, 517.8, 518.89, 519.8-519.9
     AHA: 4Q, '97, 40, **For code 493.90:** 4Q, '04, 137; 4Q, '03, 108; 4Q, '99, 25; 1Q, '97, 7; **For code 493.91:** 1Q, '05, 5; **For code 493.92:** 1Q, '03, 9
     J45.909 Unspecified asthma uncomplicated   I-10
     J45.901 Unspecified asthma with acute exacerbation   I-10

✓4ᵗʰ **494 Bronchiectasis**
     Bronchiectasis (fusiform) (postinfectious) (recurrent)
     Bronchiolectasis

     EXCLUDES *congenital (748.61)*
                   tuberculous bronchiectasis (current disease) (011.5)

     DEF: Dilation of bronchi; due to infection or chronic conditions; causes decreased lung capacity and recurrent infections of lungs.
     AHA: 4Q, '00, 42
     J47.9 Bronchiectasis uncomplicated   I-10

     494.0 Bronchiectasis without acute exacerbation
         J47.9 Bronchiectasis uncomplicated   I-10

     494.1 Bronchiectasis with acute exacerbation   CC
         CC Excl: 017.90-017.96, 487.1, 488.01-488.12, 494.1, 496, 506.1, 506.4-506.9, 748.61

✓4ᵗʰ **495 Extrinsic allergic alveolitis**
     INCLUDES allergic alveolitis and pneumonitis due to inhaled organic dust particles of fungal, thermophilic actinomycete, or other origin

     DEF: Pneumonitis due to particles inhaled into lung, often at workplace; symptoms include cough, chills, fever, increased heart and respiratory rates; develops within hours of exposure.

     495.0 Farmers' lung

     495.1 Bagassosis

     495.2 Bird-fanciers' lung
         Budgerigar-fanciers' disease or lung
         Pigeon-fanciers' disease or lung

     495.3 Suberosis
         Cork-handlers' disease or lung

     495.4 Malt workers' lung
         Alveolitis due to Aspergillus clavatus

     495.5 Mushroom workers' lung

     495.6 Maple bark-strippers' lung
         Alveolitis due to Cryptostroma corticale

     495.7 "Ventilation" pneumonitis   CC
         Allergic alveolitis due to fungal, thermophilic actinomycete, and other organisms growing in ventilation [air conditioning] systems
         CC Excl: 011.00-012.16, 012.80-012.86, 017.90-017.96, 021.2, 031.0, 039.1, 115.05, 115.15, 115.95, 122.1, 130.4, 136.3, 480.0-480.2, 480.8-487.1, 488, 494.0-508.9, 517.1, 517.8, 518.89, 519.8-519.9, 748.61

495.8 Other specified allergic alveolitis and pneumonitis   CC
     Cheese-washers' lung   Pituitary snuff-takers' disease
     Coffee workers' lung   Sequoiosis or red-cedar
     Fish-meal workers' lung   asthma
     Furriers' lung   Wood asthma
     Grain-handlers' disease or lung
     CC Excl: See code 495.7

495.9 Unspecified allergic alveolitis and pneumonitis   CC
     Alveolitis, allergic (extrinsic)
     Hypersensitivity pneumonitis
     CC Excl: See code 495.7

496 Chronic airway obstruction, not elsewhere classified
     NOTE This code is not to be used with any code from categories 491-493
     Chronic: Chronic:
       nonspecific lung disease   obstructive pulmonary disease
       obstructive lung disease   [COPD] NOS

     EXCLUDES *chronic obstructive lung disease [COPD] specified (as) (with):*
                   allergic alveolitis (495.0-495.9)
                   asthma (493.20-493.22)
                   bronchiectasis (494.0-494.1)
                   bronchitis (491.20-491.22)
                      with emphysema (491.20-491.22)
                   decompensated (491.21)
                   emphysema (492.0-492.8)

     AHA: 1Q, '10, 5, 18; 1Q, '09, 16; 3Q, '07, 10; 4Q, '03, 109; 2Q, '00, 15; 2Q, '92, 16; 2Q, '91, 21; 3Q, '88, 56
     TIP: COPD is a nonspecific term that encompasses many different respiratory conditions; review medical record and query physician for more specific documentation of emphysema, bronchitis, asthma, etc.
     J44.9 Chronic obstructive pulmonary disease unspec   I-10

Pneumoconioses and Other Lung Diseases Due to External Agents (500-508)

DEF: Permanent deposits of particulate matter, within lungs; due to occupational or environmental exposure; results in chronic induration and fibrosis. (See specific listings in 500-508 code range)

500 Coal workers' pneumoconiosis   A
     Anthracosilicosis   Coal workers' lung
     Anthracosis   Miner's asthma
     Black lung disease

501 Asbestosis   A

502 Pneumoconiosis due to other silica or silicates
     Pneumoconiosis due to talc   Silicosis (simple) (complicated)
     Silicotic fibrosis (massive) of lung

503 Pneumoconiosis due to other inorganic dust
     Aluminosis (of lung)   Graphite fibrosis (of lung)
     Baritosis   Siderosis
     Bauxite fibrosis (of lung)   Stannosis
     Berylliosis

504 Pneumonopathy due to inhalation of other dust
     Byssinosis   Flax-dressers' disease
     Cannabinosis

     EXCLUDES *allergic alveolitis (495.0-495.9)*
                   asbestosis (501)
                   bagassosis (495.1)
                   farmers' lung (495.0)

505 Pneumoconiosis, unspecified

✓4ᵗʰ **506 Respiratory conditions due to chemical fumes and vapors**
     Use additional E code to identify cause
     Use additional code to identify associated respiratory conditions, such as:
     acute respiratory failure (518.81)

     506.0 Bronchitis and pneumonitis due to fumes and vapors   CC
         Chemical bronchitis (acute)
         CC Excl: 011.00-012.16, 012.80-012.86, 017.90-017.96, 021.2, 031.0, 039.1, 115.05, 115.15, 115.95, 122.1, 130.4, 136.3, 480.0-480.2, 480.8-487.1, 488, 494.0-508.9, 517.1, 517.8, 518.89, 519.8-519.9, 748.61
         AHA: 3Q. '10, 19; 3Q, '08, 7

---

§   Requires fifth digit. Valid digits are in [brackets] under each code. See category 493 for codes and definitions.

N Newborn Age: 0   P Pediatric Age: 0-17   M Maternity Age: 12-55   A Adult Age: 15-124   MCC Major CC Condition   CC CC Condition   HIV HIV Related Dx

506.1 Acute pulmonary edema due to fumes and vapors   `MCC`
Chemical pulmonary edema (acute)
EXCLUDES *acute pulmonary edema NOS (518.4)*
chronic or unspecified pulmonary edema (514)
CC Excl: See code 506.0
AHA: 3Q, '88, 4

506.2 Upper respiratory inflammation due to fumes and vapors
AHA: 3Q, '05, 10

506.3 Other acute and subacute respiratory conditions due to fumes and vapors
AHA: 3Q, '10, 19

506.4 Chronic respiratory conditions due to fumes and vapors
Emphysema (diffuse) (chronic)
Obliterative bronchiolitis   } due to inhalation of
(chronic) (subacute)   chemical fumes and
Pulmonary fibrosis (chronic) vapors

506.9 Unspecified respiratory conditions due to fumes and vapors
Silo-fillers' disease

✓4ᵗʰ **507 Pneumonitis due to solids and liquids**
EXCLUDES *fetal aspiration pneumonitis (770.18)*
postprocedural pneumonitis (997.32)
AHA: 3Q, '91, 16

507.0 Due to inhalation of food or vomitus   `MCC`
Aspiration pneumonia (due to):
NOS
food (regurgitated)
gastric secretions
milk
saliva
vomitus
CC Excl: See code 506.0
AHA: 4Q, '11, 150; 1Q, '11, 16; 1Q, '08, 18;1Q, '89, 10
TIP: If postprocedural or postoperative aspiration pneumonia is specified, assign instead 997.32.
J69.0 Pneumonitis due to inhalation of food and vomit   `I-10`

507.1 Due to inhalation of oils and essences   `MCC`
Lipoid pneumonia (exogenous)
EXCLUDES *endogenous lipoid pneumonia (516.8)*
CC Excl: See code 506.0

507.8 Due to other solids and liquids   `MCC`
Detergent asthma
CC Excl: See code 506.0

✓4ᵗʰ **508 Respiratory conditions due to other and unspecified external agents**
Use additional E code to identify cause
Use additional code to identify associated respiratory conditions, such as:
acute respiratory failure (518.81)

508.0 Acute pulmonary manifestations due to radiation   `CC`
Radiation pneumonitis
CC Excl: See code 506.0
AHA: 2Q, '88, 4

508.1 Chronic and other pulmonary manifestations due to radiation   `CC`
Fibrosis of lung following radiation
CC Excl: See code 506.0

508.2 Respiratory conditions due to smoke inhalation
Smoke inhalation NOS
EXCLUDES *smoke inhalation due to chemical fumes and vapors (506.9)*
AHA: 4Q, '11, 114-115
TIP: Assign for smoke inhalation, along with the appropriate E code describing the source of the smoke and fumes.

508.8 Respiratory conditions due to other specified external agents

508.9 Respiratory conditions due to unspecified external agent

Other Diseases of Respiratory System (510-519)

✓4ᵗʰ **510 Empyema**
Use additional code to identify infectious organism (041.0-041.9)
EXCLUDES *abscess of lung (513.0)*
DEF: Purulent infection within pleural space.

510.0 With fistula   `MCC`
Fistula: Fistula:
bronchocutaneous   mediastinal
bronchopleural   pleural
hepatopleural   thoracic
Any condition classifiable to 510.9 with fistula
DEF: Purulent infection of respiratory cavity, with communication from cavity to another structure.
CC Excl: 510.0-510.9, 517.8, 518.89, 519.8-519.9

510.9 Without mention of fistula   `MCC`
Abscess: Pleurisy:
pleura   septic
thorax   seropurulent
Empyema (chest) (lung) (pleura)   suppurative
Fibrinopurulent pleurisy   Pyopneumothorax
Pleurisy: Pyothorax
purulent
CC Excl: See code: 510.0
AHA: 4Q, '07, 113; 3Q, '94, 6
J86.9 Pyothorax without fistula   `I-10`

✓4ᵗʰ **511 Pleurisy**
EXCLUDES *pleurisy with mention of tuberculosis, current disease (012.0)*
DEF: Inflammation of serous membrane of lungs and lining of thoracic cavity; causes exudation in cavity or membrane surface.

511.0 Without mention of effusion or current tuberculosis
Adhesion, lung or pleura   Pleurisy:
Calcification of pleura   NOS
Pleurisy (acute) (sterile):   pneumococcal
diaphragmatic   staphylococcal
fibrinous   streptococcal
interlobar   Thickening of pleura
AHA: 3Q, '94, 5

511.1 With effusion, with mention of a bacterial cause other than tuberculosis   `MCC`
Pleurisy with effusion (exudative) (serous):
other specified nontuberculous bacterial cause
pneumococcal
staphylococcal
streptococcal
CC Excl: 011.00-012.16, 012.80-012.86, 017.90-017.96, 511.0-511.9, 517.8, 518.89, 519.8-519.9

✓5ᵗʰ **511.8 Other specified forms of effusion, except tuberculous**
EXCLUDES *traumatic (860.2-860.5, 862.29, 862.39)*
AHA: 4Q, '08, 113-114;1Q, '97, 10

511.81 Malignant pleural effusion   `CC`
Code first malignant neoplasm, if known
CC Excl: 195.8, 197.2-197.3, 198.89-199.2, 209.20, 209.29-209.30, 209.70, 209.75-209.79, 239.81-239.9, 511.81-511.89
J91.0 Malignant pleural effusion   `I-10`

511.89 Other specified forms of effusion, except tuberculous   `CC`
Encysted pleurisy   Hydropneumothorax
Hemopneumothorax   Hydrothorax
Hemothorax
CC Excl: 011.00-012.16, 012.80-012.86, 017.90-017.96, 511.0-511.9, 517.8, 518.89, 519.8-519.9

511.9 Unspecified pleural effusion   `CC`
Pleural effusion NOS   Pleurisy:
Pleurisy: serous
exudative   with effusion NOS
serofibrinous
CC Excl: 011.00-012.16, 012.80-012.86, 017.90-017.96, 511.0-511.9, 517.8, 518.89, 519.8-519.9
AHA: 2Q, '03, 7; 3Q, '91, 19; 4Q, '89, 11
TIP: Do not assign when the pleural effusion is a symptom of CHF and no therapeutic treatment (e.g., thoracentesis) is directed towards the pleural effusion.
J90 Pleural effusion not elsewhere classified   `I-10`

✓4ᵗʰ ✓5ᵗʰ Additional Digit Required   Unacceptable PDx   Manifestation Code   Hospital Acquired Condition   ►◄ Revised Text   ● New Code   ▲ Revised Code Title

Diseases of the Respiratory System

512–516.37

✓4th **512 Pneumothorax and air leak**
DEF: Collapsed lung; due to gas or air in pleural space.
AHA: 4Q, '11, 115-116

512.0 Spontaneous tension pneumothorax `MCC`
DEF: Leaking air from lung into lining causing collapse.
CC Excl: 512.0-512.89, 517.8, 518.89, 519.8-519.9, 793.11
AHA: 3Q, '94, 5

[16] **512.1 Iatrogenic pneumothorax** `CC`
Postoperative pneumothorax
DEF: Air trapped in the lining of the lung following surgery.
CC Excl: See code 512.0
AHA: 1Q, '11, 14; 4Q, '94, 40
TIP: Pneumothorax is a known risk associated with most thoracic surgery; do not assign based on radiology findings alone, without physician substantiation.
J95.811 Postprocedural pneumothorax `I-10`

512.2 Postoperative air leak `CC`
CC Excl: see Code: 512.0
AHA: 4Q, '11, 115-117

✓5th **512.8 Other pneumothorax and air leak**
EXCLUDES pneumothorax:
congenital (770.2)
traumatic (860.0-860.1, 860.4-860.5)
tuberculous, current disease (011.7)
AHA: 4Q, '11, 115-117; 2Q, '93, 3

512.81 Primary spontaneous pneumothorax `CC`
CC Excl: see Code: 512.0
J93.11 Primary spontaneous pneumothorax `I-10`

512.82 Secondary spontaneous pneumothorax `CC`
Code first underlying condition, such as:
cancer metastatic to lung (197.0)
catamenial pneumothorax due to endometriosis (617.8)
cystic fibrosis (277.02)
eosinophilic pneumonia (518.3)
lymphangioleiomyomatosis (516.4)
Marfan syndrome (759.82)
pneumocystis carinii pneumonia (136.3)
primary lung cancer (162.3-162.9)
spontaneous rupture of the esophagus (530.4)
CC Excl: see Code: 512.0

512.83 Chronic pneumothorax `CC`
CC Excl: see Code: 512.0

512.84 Other air leak `CC`
Persistent air leak
CC Excl: see Code: 512.0

512.89 Other pneumothorax `CC`
Acute pneumothorax
Pneumothorax NOS
Spontaneous pneumothorax NOS
CC Excl: see Code: 512.0
J93.9 Pneumothorax unspecified `I-10`

✓4th **513 Abscess of lung and mediastinum**

513.0 Abscess of lung `MCC`
Abscess (multiple) of lung
Gangrenous or necrotic pneumonia
Pulmonary gangrene or necrosis
CC Excl: 006.4, 011.00-012.16, 012.80-012.86, 017.90-017.96, 513.0, 519.8-519.9
AHA: 4Q, '07, 85; 2Q, '98, 7

513.1 Abscess of mediastinum `MCC`
CC Excl: 513.1, 519.8-519.9

514 Pulmonary congestion and hypostasis `CC`
Hypostatic:
bronchopneumonia
pneumonia
Passive pneumonia
Pulmonary congestion (chronic) (passive)
Pulmonary edema:
NOS
chronic
EXCLUDES acute pulmonary edema:
NOS (518.4)
with mention of heart disease or failure (428.1)
hypostatic pneumonia due to or specified as a specific type of pneumonia — code to the type of pneumonia (480.0-480.9, 481, 482.0-482.9, 483.0-483.8, 487.0, 488.01, 488.11)
DEF: Excessive retention of interstitial fluid in the lungs and pulmonary vessels due to poor circulation.
CC Excl: 514, 517.8, 518.89, 519.8-519.9
AHA: 2Q, '98, 6; 3Q, '88, 5
J81.1 Chronic pulmonary edema `I-10`

515 Postinflammatory pulmonary fibrosis
Cirrhosis of lung
Fibrosis of lung (atrophic) (confluent) (massive) (perialveolar) (peribronchial)
Induration of lung
} chronic or unspecified
DEF: Fibrosis and scarring of the lungs due to inflammatory reaction.
J84.10 Pulmonary fibrosis, unspecified `I-10`

✓4th **516 Other alveolar and parietoalveolar pneumonopathy**

516.0 Pulmonary alveolar proteinosis `CC`
DEF: Reduced ventilation due to proteinaceous deposits on alveoli; symptoms include dyspnea, cough, chest pain, and hemoptysis.
CC Excl: 011.00-012.16, 012.80-012.86, 017.90-017.96, 494.0-508.1, 508.8-508.9, 515-516.2, 516.30-516.5, 516.8-516.9, 517.2, 517.8, 518.89, 519.8-519.9, 748.61, 793.11

516.1 Idiopathic pulmonary hemosiderosis `CC`
Code first underlying disease (275.01-275.09)
Essential brown induration of lung
EXCLUDES acute idiopathic pulmonary hemorrhage in infants [AIPHI] (786.31)
DEF: Fibrosis of alveolar walls; marked by abnormal amounts hemosiderin in lungs; primarily affects children; symptoms include anemia, fluid in lungs, and blood in sputum; etiology unknown.
CC Excl: See code 516.0

516.2 Pulmonary alveolar microlithiasis `CC`
DEF: Small calculi in pulmonary alveoli resembling sand-like particles on x-ray.
CC Excl: See code 516.0

✓5th **516.3 Idiopathic interstitial pneumonia**
AHA: 4Q, '11, 117-119

516.30 Idiopathic interstitial pneumonia, not otherwise specified
Idiopathic fibrosing alveolitis

516.31 Idiopathic pulmonary fibrosis
Cryptogenic fibrosing alveolitis
DEF: Chronic disease of unknown causation characterized by scarring and thickening of the lungs.

516.32 Idiopathic non-specific interstitial pneumonitis
EXCLUDES non-specific interstitial pneumonia NOS, or due to known underlying cause (516.8)

516.33 Acute interstitial pneumonitis `CC`
Hamman Rich syndrome
EXCLUDES pneumocystis pneumonia (136.3)
CC Excl: see Code: 516.0

516.34 Respiratory bronchiolitis interstitial lung disease

516.35 Idiopathic lymphoid interstitial pneumonia `CC`
Idiopathic lymphocytic interstitial pneumonitis
EXCLUDES lymphoid interstitial pneumonia NOS, or due to known underlying cause (516.8)
pneumocystis pneumonia (136.3)
CC Excl: See code 516.0

516.36 Cryptogenic organizing pneumonia `CC`
EXCLUDES organizing pneumonia NOS, or due to known underlying cause (516.8)
CC Excl: See code 516.0

516.37 Desquamative interstitial pneumonia `CC`
CC Excl: See code 516.0

---

[16] HAC when reported with procedure code 38.93 and POA = N.

`N` Newborn Age: 0   `P` Pediatric Age: 0-17   `M` Maternity Age: 12-55   `A` Adult Age: 15-124   `MCC` Major CC Condition   `CC` CC Condition   `HIV` HIV Related Dx

516.4 Lymphangioleiomyomatosis ♀ MCC
Lymphangiomyomatosis
CC Excl: See Code: 516.0
AHA: 4Q, '11, 119

516.5 Adult pulmonary Langerhans cell histiocytosis A CC
Adult PLCH
CC Excl: See code 516.0
AHA: 4Q, '11, 119

√5th **516.6 Interstitial lung diseases of childhood**
AHA: 4Q, '11, 120-123

516.61 Neuroendocrine cell hyperplasia of infancy MCC
CC Excl: 516.61-516.69, 768.5-768.9, 769-770.9, 779.81-779.89

516.62 Pulmonary interstitial glycogenosis MCC
CC Excl: see code 516.61

516.63 Surfactant mutations of the lung MCC
CC Excl: see code 516.61
DEF: Group of genetic disorders resulting in potentially fatal pediatric lung disease with onset typically within the perinatal period; leading indication for pediatric lung transplantation.

516.64 Alveolar capillary dysplasia with vein misalignment MCC
CC Excl: see code 516.61

516.69 Other interstitial lung diseases of childhood MCC
CC Excl: see code 516.61

516.8 Other specified alveolar and parietoalveolar pneumonopathies CC
Endogenous lipoid pneumonia
Interstitial pneumonia
Lymphoid interstitial pneumonia due to known underlying cause
Lymphoid interstitial pneumonia NOS
Non-specific interstitial pneumonia due to known underlying cause
Non-specific interstitial pneumonia NOS
Organizing pneumonia due to known underlying cause
Organizing pneumonia NOS

Code first, if applicable, underlying cause of pneumonopathy, if known

Use additional E code, if applicable, for drug-induced or toxic pneumonopathy

EXCLUDES *cryptogenic organizing pneumonia (516.36)*
idiopathic lymphoid interstitial pneumonia (516.35)
idiopathic non-specific interstitial pneumonitis (516.32)
lipoid pneumonia, exogenous or unspecified (507.1)
CC Excl: 011.00-012.16, 012.80-012.86, 017.90-017.96, 494.0-508.9, 515-516.9, 517.2, 517.8, 518.89, 519.8-519.9, 748.61
AHA: 1Q, '11, 16; 1Q, '10, 6; 2Q, '06, 20; 1Q, '92, 12

516.9 Unspecified alveolar and parietoalveolar pneumonopathy CC
CC Excl: See code: 516.0

√4th **517 Lung involvement in conditions classified elsewhere**
EXCLUDES *rheumatoid lung (714.81)*

517.1 Rheumatic pneumonia CC
Code first underlying disease (390)
CC Excl: 011.00-012.16, 012.80-012.86, 017.90-017.96, 480.0-480.2, 480.8-487.1, 488.01-488.02, 488.11-488.12, 494.0-508.9, 515-516.2, 516.30-516.5, 516.8-517.2, 517.8, 518.89, 519.8-519.9, 748.61

517.2 Lung involvement in systemic sclerosis CC
Code first underlying disease (710.1)
CC Excl: 011.00-012.16, 012.80-012.86, 017.90-017.96, 494.0-508.9, 515-516.9, 517.2, 517.8, 518.89, 519.8-519.9, 748.61

517.3 Acute chest syndrome CC
Code first sickle-cell disease in crisis (282.42, 282.62, 282.64, 282.69)
CC Excl: 280.0-282.3, 282.5-282.63, 282.69-284.2, 284.81-285.9, 289.9, 776.5-776.6
AHA: 4Q, '03, 51, 56

517.8 Lung involvement in other diseases classified elsewhere
Code first underlying disease, as:
amyloidosis (277.30-277.39)
polymyositis (710.4)
sarcoidosis (135)
Sjögren's disease (710.2)
systemic lupus erythematosus (710.0)
EXCLUDES *syphilis (095.1)*
AHA: 2Q, '03, 7

√4th **518 Other diseases of lung**

518.0 Pulmonary collapse CC
Atelectasis   Middle lobe syndrome
Collapse of lung
EXCLUDES *atelectasis:*
congenital (partial) (770.5)
primary (770.4)
tuberculous, current disease (011.8)
CC Excl: 518.0, 519.8-519.9
AHA: 4Q, '90, 25
J98.11 Atelectasis I-10

518.1 Interstitial emphysema
Mediastinal emphysema
EXCLUDES *surgical (subcutaneous) emphysema (998.81)*
that in fetus or newborn (770.2)
traumatic emphysema (958.7)
DEF: Escaped air from the alveoli trapped in the interstices of the lung; trauma or cough may cause the disease.

518.2 Compensatory emphysema
DEF: Distention of all or part of the lung due to disease processes or surgical intervention that decreased volume in other parts of lung.

518.3 Pulmonary eosinophilia CC
Eosinophilic asthma   Pneumonia:
Löffler's syndrome   eosinophilic
Pneumonia: Tropical eosinophilia
allergic
EXCLUDES *pulmonary infiltrate NOS (793.19)*
DEF: Infiltration, into pulmonary parenchyma of eosinophils; results in cough, fever, and dyspnea.
CC Excl: 011.00-012.16, 012.80-012.86, 017.90-017.96, 020.3-020.5, 021.3, 022.1, 031.0, 039.1, 073.0, 115.05, 115.15, 115.95, 122.1, 130.4, 136.3, 480.0-480.2, 480.8-487.1, 488.01-488.02, 488.11-488.12, 494.0-495.9, 500-508.9, 517.1, 517.8, 518.3, 518.89, 519.8-519.9, 748.61
AHA: 4Q, '11, 139

518.4 Acute edema of lung, unspecified MCC
Acute pulmonary edema NOS
Pulmonary edema, postoperative
EXCLUDES *pulmonary edema:*
acute, with mention of heart disease or failure (428.1)
chronic or unspecified (514)
due to external agents (506.0-508.9)
DEF: Severe, sudden fluid retention within lung tissues.
CC Excl: 398.91, 428.0-428.9, 518.4, 519.8-519.9
TIP: Do not assign separately if associated with CHF or heart disease; it is incorporated into those codes.

√5th **518.5 Pulmonary insufficiency following trauma and surgery**
EXCLUDES *adult respiratory distress syndrome associated with other conditions (518.82)*
pneumonia:
aspiration (507.0)
hypostatic (514)
respiratory failure in other conditions (518.81, 518.83-518.84)
AHA: 4Q, '11, 123-125; 3Q, '10, 19; 4Q, '04, 139; 3Q, '88, 3; 3Q, '88, 7; S-O, '87, 1

518.51 Acute respiratory failure following trauma and surgery MCC
Respiratory failure, not otherwise specified, following trauma and surgery
EXCLUDES *acute respiratory failure in other conditions (518.81)*
CC Excl: 518.5, 519.8-519.9
J95.821 Acute postprocedural respiratory failure I-10

√4th √5th Additional Digit Required | Unacceptable PDx | Manifestation Code | Hospital Acquired Condition | ►◄ Revised Text | ● New Code | ▲ Revised Code Title

Diseases of the Respiratory System

518.52–519.9

518.52 Other pulmonary insufficiency, not elsewhere classified, following trauma and surgery `MCC`
Adult respiratory distress syndrome
Pulmonary insufficiency following surgery
Pulmonary insufficiency following trauma
Shock lung related to trauma and surgery
EXCLUDES *adult respiratory distress syndrome associated with other conditions (518.82)*
aspiration pneumonia (507.0)
hypostatic pneumonia (514)
shock lung, not related to trauma or surgery (518.82)
CC Excl: see code 518.51

518.53 Acute and chronic respiratory failure following trauma and surgery `MCC`
EXCLUDES *acute and chronic respiratory failure in other conditions (518.84)*
CC Excl: see code 518.51

518.6 Allergic bronchopulmonary aspergillosis `CC`
DEF: Noninvasive hypersensitive reaction; due to allergic reaction to *Aspergillus fumigatus* (mold).
CC Excl: 518.6, 519.8-519.9
AHA: 4Q, '97, 39

518.7 Transfusion related acute lung injury [TRALI] `CC`
DEF: A relatively rare, but serious pulmonary complication of blood transfusion, with acute respiratory distress, noncardiogenic pulmonary edema, cyanosis, hypoxemia, hypotension, fever and chills.
CC Excl: 518.7, 997.31-997.39, 997.91-997.99, 998.81, 998.83-998.9
AHA: 4Q, '06, 91

✓5ᵗʰ **518.8 Other diseases of lung**

518.81 Acute respiratory failure `MCC`
Respiratory failure NOS
EXCLUDES *acute and chronic respiratory failure (518.84)*
acute respiratory distress (518.82)
acute respiratory failure following trauma and surgery (518.51)
chronic respiratory failure (518.83)
respiratory arrest (799.1)
respiratory failure, newborn (770.84)
CC Excl: 518.81-518.84, 519.8-519.9, 799.1
AHA: 3Q, '12, 21-22; 4Q, '10, 80; 1Q, '10, 18-19; 3Q, '09, 14; 2Q, '09, 11; 1Q, '08, 18; 3Q, '07, 6; 2Q, '06, 25; 4Q, '05, 96; 2Q, '05, 19; 1Q, '05, 3-8; 1Q, '05, 3-8; 4Q, '04, 139; 1Q, '03, 15; 4Q, '98, 41; 3Q, '91, 14; 2Q, '91, 3; 4Q, '90, 25; 2Q, '90, 20; 3Q, '88, 7; 3Q, '88, 10; S-O, '87, 1
TIP: If both respiratory failure and another acute condition are equally responsible for admission, either may be sequenced as principal diagnosis in the absence of chapter-specific guidelines to the contrary.
`J96.01` Acute respiratory failure with hypoxia `I-10`

518.82 Other pulmonary insufficiency, not elsewhere classified `CC`
Acute respiratory distress
Acute respiratory insufficiency
Adult respiratory distress syndrome NEC
EXCLUDES *acute interstitial pneumonitis (516.33)*
adult respiratory distress syndrome associated with trauma or surgery (518.52)
pulmonary insufficiency following trauma or surgery (518.52)
respiratory distress:
NOS (786.09)
newborn (770.89)
syndrome, newborn (769)
CC Excl: See code: 518.81
AHA: 4Q, '03, 105; 2Q, '91, 21; 3Q, '88, 7
`J80` Acute respiratory distress syndrome `I-10`

518.83 Chronic respiratory failure `CC`
CC Excl: See code: 518.81
AHA: 4Q, '05, 96; 4Q, '03, 103, 111
`J96.10` Chronic respiratory failure, unsp whth w/hypox or hypercap `I-10`

518.84 Acute and chronic respiratory failure `MCC`
Acute on chronic respiratory failure
EXCLUDES *acute and chronic respiratory failure following trauma or surgery (518.53)*
CC Excl: See code: 518.81
AHA: 2Q, '11, 7
`J96.20` Ac & chr resp failure unsp whth w/hypox or hypercap `I-10`

518.89 Other diseases of lung, not elsewhere classified
Broncholithiasis   Lung disease NOS
Calcification of lung   Pulmolithiasis
DEF: Broncholithiasis: calculi in lumen of transbronchial tree.
DEF: Pulmolithiasis: calculi in lung.
AHA: 3Q, '90, 18; 4Q, '88, 6
TIP: Do not assign for solitary lung nodule; see instead code 793.11.
`J98.4` Other disorders of lung `I-10`

✓4ᵗʰ **519 Other diseases of respiratory system**

✓5ᵗʰ **519.0 Tracheostomy complications**

519.00 Tracheostomy complication, unspecified `CC`
CC Excl: 519.00-519.19, 519.8-519.9

519.01 Infection of tracheostomy `CC`
Use additional code to identify type of infection, such as:
abscess or cellulitis of neck (682.1)
septicemia (038.0-038.9)
Use additional code to identify organism (041.00-041.9)
CC Excl: See code 519.00
AHA: 4Q, '98, 41

519.02 Mechanical complication of tracheostomy `CC`
Tracheal stenosis due to tracheostomy
CC Excl: See code 519.00

519.09 Other tracheostomy complications `CC`
Hemorrhage due to tracheostomy
Tracheoesophageal fistula due to tracheostomy
CC Excl: See code 519.00

✓5ᵗʰ **519.1 Other diseases of trachea and bronchus, not elsewhere classified**
AHA: 3Q, '02, 18; 3Q, '88, 6

519.11 Acute bronchospasm
Bronchospasm NOS
EXCLUDES *acute bronchitis with bronchospasm (466.0)*
asthma (493.00-493.92)
exercise induced bronchospasm (493.81)
AHA: 4Q, '06, 92

519.19 Other diseases of trachea and bronchus
Calcification ⎫
Stenosis   ⎬ of bronchus or trachea
Ulcer   ⎭
AHA: 4Q, '06, 92

⁹ **519.2 Mediastinitis** `MCC`
DEF: Inflammation of tissue between organs behind sternum.
CC Excl: 519.2-519.3, 519.8-519.9

519.3 Other diseases of mediastinum, not elsewhere classified
Fibrosis ⎫
Hernia   ⎬ of mediastinum
Retraction ⎭

519.4 Disorders of diaphragm
Diaphragmitis   Relaxation of diaphragm
Paralysis of diaphragm
EXCLUDES *congenital defect of diaphragm (756.6)*
diaphragmatic hernia (551-553 with .3)
congenital (756.6)

519.8 Other diseases of respiratory system, not elsewhere classified
AHA: 4Q, '89, 12

519.9 Unspecified disease of respiratory system
Respiratory disease (chronic) NOS

---

⁹ HAC = when in combination with a procedure code from 36.10-36.19.

`N` Newborn Age: 0   `P` Pediatric Age: 0-17   `M` Maternity Age: 12-55   `A` Adult Age: 15-124   `MCC` Major CC Condition   `CC` CC Condition   `HIV` HIV Related Dx

9. Diseases of the Digestive System (520-579)

Diseases of Oral Cavity, Salivary Glands, and Jaws (520-529)

✓4ᵗʰ 520 Disorders of tooth development and eruption

520.0 Anodontia
Absence of teeth (complete) (congenital) (partial)
Hypodontia
Oligodontia
> **EXCLUDES** *acquired absence of teeth (525.10-525.19)*

520.1 Supernumerary teeth
Distomolar	Paramolar
Fourth molar	Supplemental teeth
Mesiodens	
> **EXCLUDES** *supernumerary roots (520.2)*

520.2 Abnormalities of size and form
Concrescence ⎫
Fusion ⎬ of teeth
Gemination ⎭

Dens evaginatus
Dens in dente
Dens invaginatus
Enamel pearls
Macrodontia
Microdontia
Peg-shaped [conical] teeth
Supernumerary roots
Taurodontism
Tuberculum paramolare
> **EXCLUDES** *that due to congenital syphilis (090.5)*
> *tuberculum Carabelli, which is regarded as a normal variation*

520.3 Mottled teeth
Mottling of enamel
Dental fluorosis
Nonfluoride enamel opacities

Digestive System

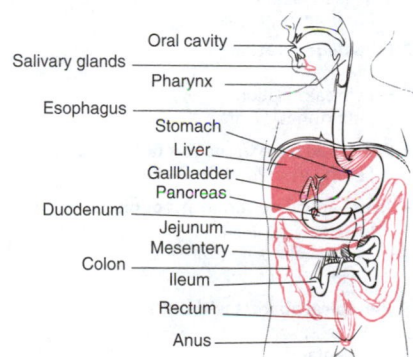

The Oral Cavity

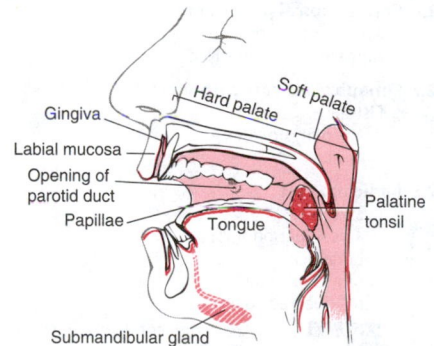

Teeth

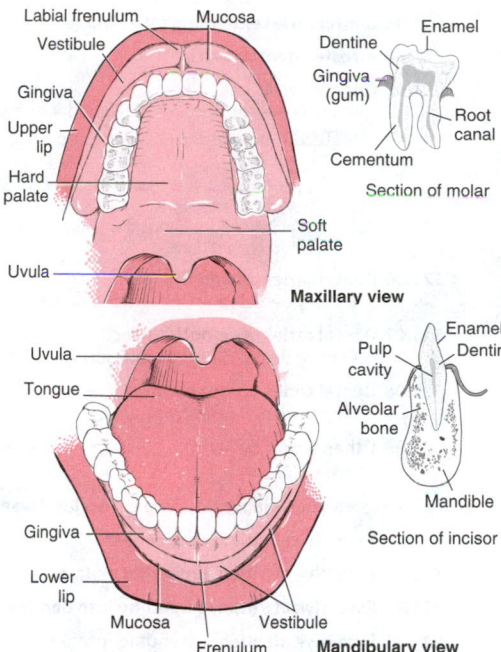

Maxillary view

Mandibulary view

520.4 Disturbances of tooth formation
Aplasia and hypoplasia of cementum
Dilaceration of tooth
Enamel hypoplasia (neonatal) (postnatal) (prenatal)
Horner's teeth
Hypocalcification of teeth
Regional odontodysplasia
Turner's tooth
> **EXCLUDES** *Hutchinson's teeth and mulberry molars in congenital syphilis (090.5)*
> *mottled teeth (520.3)*

520.5 Hereditary disturbances in tooth structure, not elsewhere classified
Amelogensis ⎫
Dentinogenesis ⎬ imperfecta
Odontogenesis ⎭

Dentinal dysplasia
Shell teeth

520.6 Disturbances in tooth eruption
Teeth:	Tooth eruption:
embedded	late
impacted	obstructed
natal	premature
neonatal	
prenatal	
primary [deciduous]:	
persistent	
shedding, premature	
> **EXCLUDES** *exfoliation of teeth (attributable to disease of surrounding tissues) (525.0-525.19)*

AHA: 1Q, '06, 18; 2Q, '05, 15

520.7 Teething syndrome

520.8 Other specified disorders of tooth development and eruption
Color changes during tooth formation
Pre-eruptive color changes
> **EXCLUDES** *posteruptive color changes (521.7)*

520.9 Unspecified disorder of tooth development and eruption

✓4ᵗʰ 521 Diseases of hard tissues of teeth

✓5ᵗʰ 521.0 Dental caries
AHA: 4Q, '01, 44

521.00 Dental caries, unspecified

✓4ᵗʰ
✓5ᵗʰ
Additional Digit Required   Unacceptable PDx   Manifestation Code   Hospital Acquired Condition   ▶◀ Revised Text   ● New Code   ▲ Revised Code Title

2015 ICD-9-CM   **Volume 1 – 171**

521.01 Dental caries limited to enamel
Initial caries   White spot lesion

521.02 Dental caries extending into dentine

521.03 Dental caries extending into pulp

521.04 Arrested dental caries

521.05 Odontoclasia
Infantile melanodontia   Melanodontoclasia
EXCLUDES *internal and external resorption of teeth (521.40-521.49)*
DEF: A pathological dental condition described as stained areas, loss of tooth substance, and hypoplasia linked to nutritional deficiencies during tooth development and to cariogenic oral conditions.

521.06 Dental caries pit and fissure
Primary dental caries, pit and fissure origin

521.07 Dental caries of smooth surface
Primary dental caries, smooth surface origin

521.08 Dental caries of root surface
Primary dental caries, root surface

521.09 Other dental caries
AHA: 3Q, '02, 14

✓5ᵗʰ **521.1 Excessive attrition (approximal wear) (occlusal wear)**

521.10 Excessive attrition, unspecified

521.11 Excessive attrition, limited to enamel

521.12 Excessive attrition, extending into dentine

521.13 Excessive attrition, extending into pulp

521.14 Excessive attrition, localized

521.15 Excessive attrition, generalized

✓5ᵗʰ **521.2 Abrasion**
Abrasion:
dentifrice
habitual
occupational } of teeth
ritual
traditional
Wedge defect NOS

521.20 Abrasion, unspecified

521.21 Abrasion, limited to enamel

521.22 Abrasion, extending into dentine

521.23 Abrasion, extending into pulp

521.24 Abrasion, localized

521.25 Abrasion, generalized

✓5ᵗʰ **521.3 Erosion**
Erosion of teeth:
NOS
due to:
medicine
persistent vomiting
idiopathic
occupational

521.30 Erosion, unspecified

521.31 Erosion, limited to enamel

521.32 Erosion, extending into dentine

521.33 Erosion, extending into pulp

521.34 Erosion, localized

521.35 Erosion, generalized

✓5ᵗʰ **521.4 Pathological resorption**
DEF: Loss of dentin and cementum due to disease process.

521.40 Pathological resorption, unspecified

521.41 Pathological resorption, internal

521.42 Pathological resorption, external

521.49 Other pathological resorption
Internal granuloma of pulp

521.5 Hypercementosis
Cementation hyperplasia
DEF: Excess deposits of cementum, on tooth root.

521.6 Ankylosis of teeth
DEF: Adhesion of tooth to surrounding bone.

521.7 Intrinsic posteruptive color changes
Staining [discoloration] of teeth:
NOS
due to:
drugs
metals
pulpal bleeding
EXCLUDES *accretions [deposits] on teeth (523.6)*
extrinsic color changes (523.6)
pre-eruptive color changes (520.8)

✓5ᵗʰ **521.8 Other specified diseases of hard tissues of teeth**

521.81 Cracked tooth
EXCLUDES *asymptomatic craze lines in enamel — omit code*
broken tooth due to trauma (873.63, 873.73)
fractured tooth due to trauma (873.63, 873.73)

521.89 Other specified diseases of hard tissues of teeth
Irradiated enamel
Sensitive dentin

521.9 Unspecified disease of hard tissues of teeth

✓4ᵗʰ **522 Diseases of pulp and periapical tissues**

522.0 Pulpitis   `CC`
Pulpal:
abscess
polyp
Pulpitis:
acute
chronic (hyperplastic) (ulcerative)
suppurative
CC Excl: 520.0-525.9

522.1 Necrosis of the pulp
Pulp gangrene
DEF: Death of pulp tissue.

522.2 Pulp degeneration
Denticles
Pulp calcifications
Pulp stones

522.3 Abnormal hard tissue formation in pulp
Secondary or irregular dentin

522.4 Acute apical periodontitis of pulpal origin   `CC`
DEF: Severe inflammation of periodontal ligament due to pulpal inflammation or necrosis.
CC Excl: See code: 522.0

522.5 Periapical abscess without sinus
Abscess:
dental
dentoalveolar
EXCLUDES *periapical abscess with sinus (522.7)*

522.6 Chronic apical periodontitis
Apical or periapical granuloma
Apical periodontitis NOS

522.7 Periapical abscess with sinus
Fistula:
alveolar process
dental

522.8 Radicular cyst
Cyst:
apical (periodontal)
periapical
radiculodental
residual radicular
EXCLUDES *lateral developmental or lateral periodontal cyst (526.0)*
DEF: Cyst in tissue around tooth apex due to chronic infection of granuloma around root.

N Newborn Age: 0   P Pediatric Age: 0-17   M Maternity Age: 12-55   A Adult Age: 15-124   MCC Major CC Condition   CC CC Condition   HIV HIV Related Dx

172 – Volume 1   **2015 ICD-9-CM**

522.9 Other and unspecified diseases of pulp and periapical tissues

✓4ᵗʰ **523 Gingival and periodontal diseases**

✓5ᵗʰ **523.0 Acute gingivitis**

EXCLUDES *acute necrotizing ulcerative gingivitis (101)*
            herpetic gingivostomatitis (054.2)

523.00 Acute gingivitis, plaque induced
Acute gingivitis NOS

523.01 Acute gingivitis, non-plaque induced

✓5ᵗʰ **523.1 Chronic gingivitis**
Gingivitis (chronic):
  desquamative
  hyperplastic
  simple marginal
  ulcerative
EXCLUDES *herpetic gingivostomatitis (054.2)*

523.10 Chronic gingivitis, plaque induced
Chronic gingivitis NOS
Gingivitis NOS

523.11 Chronic gingivitis, non-plaque induced

✓5ᵗʰ **523.2 Gingival recession**
Gingival recession (postinfective) (postoperative)

523.20 Gingival recession, unspecified

523.21 Gingival recession, minimal

523.22 Gingival recession, moderate

523.23 Gingival recession, severe

523.24 Gingival recession, localized

523.25 Gingival recession, generalized

✓5ᵗʰ **523.3 Aggressive and acute periodontitis**
Acute:
  pericementitis
  pericoronitis
EXCLUDES *acute apical periodontitis (522.4)*
            periapical abscess (522.5, 522.7)
DEF: Severe inflammation of tissues supporting teeth.

523.30 Aggressive periodontitis, unspecified

523.31 Aggressive periodontitis, localized
Periodontal abscess

523.32 Aggressive periodontitis, generalized

523.33 Acute periodontitis

✓5ᵗʰ **523.4 Chronic periodontitis**
Chronic pericoronitis
Pericementitis (chronic)
Periodontitis:
  complex
  simplex
  NOS
EXCLUDES *chronic apical periodontitis (522.6)*

523.40 Chronic periodontitis, unspecified

523.41 Chronic periodontitis, localized

523.42 Chronic periodontitis, generalized

523.5 Periodontosis

523.6 Accretions on teeth
Dental calculus:
  subgingival
  supragingival
Deposits on teeth:
  betel
  materia alba
  soft
  tartar
  tobacco
Extrinsic discoloration of teeth
EXCLUDES *intrinsic discoloration of teeth (521.7)*
DEF: Foreign material on tooth surface, usually plaque or calculus.

523.8 Other specified periodontal diseases
Giant cell:
  epulis
  peripheral granuloma
Gingival:
  cysts
  enlargement NOS
  fibromatosis
Gingival polyp
Periodontal lesions due to traumatic occlusion
Peripheral giant cell granuloma
EXCLUDES *leukoplakia of gingiva (528.6)*

523.9 Unspecified gingival and periodontal disease
AHA: 3Q, '02, 14

✓4ᵗʰ **524 Dentofacial anomalies, including malocclusion**

✓5ᵗʰ **524.0 Major anomalies of jaw size**
EXCLUDES *hemifacial atrophy or hypertrophy (754.0)*
            unilateral condylar hyperplasia or hypoplasia of
            mandible (526.89)

524.00 Unspecified anomaly
DEF: Unspecified deformity of jaw size.

524.01 Maxillary hyperplasia
DEF: Overgrowth or over development of upper jaw bone.

524.02 Mandibular hyperplasia
DEF: Overgrowth or over development of lower jaw bone.

524.03 Maxillary hypoplasia
DEF: Incomplete or underdeveloped upper jaw bone.

524.04 Mandibular hypoplasia
DEF: Incomplete or underdeveloped lower jaw bone.
AHA: 2Q, '12, 17

524.05 Macrogenia
DEF: Enlarged jaw, especially chin; affects bone, soft tissue, or both.

524.06 Microgenia
DEF: Underdeveloped mandible, characterized by an extremely small chin.

524.07 Excessive tuberosity of jaw
Entire maxillary tuberosity

524.09 Other specified anomaly

✓5ᵗʰ **524.1 Anomalies of relationship of jaw to cranial base**

524.10 Unspecified anomaly
Prognathism
Retrognathism
DEF: Prognathism: protrusion of lower jaw.
DEF: Retrognathism: jaw is located posteriorly to a normally positioned jaw; backward position of mandible.

524.11 Maxillary asymmetry
DEF: Absence of symmetry of maxilla.

524.12 Other jaw asymmetry

524.19 Other specified anomaly

✓5ᵗʰ **524.2 Anomalies of dental arch relationship**
Anomaly of dental arch
EXCLUDES *hemifacial atrophy or hypertrophy (754.0)*
            soft tissue impingement (524.81-524.82)
            unilateral condylar hyperplasia or hypoplasia of
            mandible (526.89)

524.20 Unspecified anomaly of dental arch relationship

524.21 Malocclusion, Angle's class I
Neutro-occlusion

524.22 Malocclusion, Angle's class II
Disto-occlusion Division I
Disto-occlusion Division II

524.23 Malocclusion, Angle's class III
Mesio-occlusion

524.24 Open anterior occlusal relationship
Anterior open bite

524.25 Open posterior occlusal relationship
Posterior open bite

✓4ᵗʰ / ✓5ᵗʰ Additional Digit Required   Unacceptable PDx   Manifestation Code   Hospital Acquired Condition   ►◄ Revised Text   ● New Code   ▲ Revised Code Title

2015 ICD-9-CM   Volume 1 – 173

Diseases of the Digestive System

524.26–525.25

Angle's Classification of Malocclusion

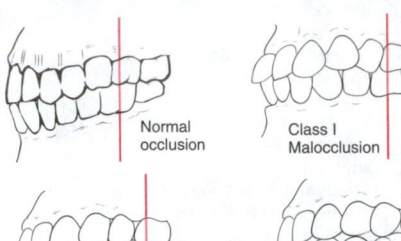

Normal occlusion   Class I Malocclusion

Class II Malocclusion   Class III Malocclusion

524.26 Excessive horizontal overlap
Excessive horizontal overjet

524.27 Reverse articulation
Anterior articulation   Posterior articulation
Crossbite

524.28 Anomalies of interarch distance
Excessive interarch distance
Inadequate interarch distance

524.29 Other anomalies of dental arch relationship
Other anomalies of dental arch

√5ᵗʰ **524.3 Anomalies of tooth position of fully erupted teeth**
EXCLUDES *impacted or embedded teeth with abnormal position of such teeth or adjacent teeth (520.6)*

524.30 Unspecified anomaly of tooth position
Diastema of teeth NOS
Displacement of teeth NOS
Transposition of teeth NOS

524.31 Crowding of teeth

524.32 Excessive spacing of teeth

524.33 Horizontal displacement of teeth
Tipped teeth   Tipping of teeth

524.34 Vertical displacement of teeth
Extruded tooth   Intruded tooth
Infraeruption of teeth   Supraeruption of teeth

524.35 Rotation of tooth/teeth

524.36 Insufficient interocclusal distance of teeth (ridge)
Lack of adequate intermaxillary vertical dimension

524.37 Excessive interocclusal distance of teeth
Excessive intermaxillary vertical dimension
Loss of occlusal vertical dimension

524.39 Other anomalies of tooth position

524.4 Malocclusion, unspecified
DEF: Malposition of top and bottom teeth; interferes with chewing.

√5ᵗʰ **524.5 Dentofacial functional abnormalities**

524.50 Dentofacial functional abnormality, unspecified

524.51 Abnormal jaw closure

524.52 Limited mandibular range of motion

524.53 Deviation in opening and closing of the mandible

524.54 Insufficient anterior guidance
Insufficient anterior occlusal guidance

524.55 Centric occlusion maximum intercuspation discrepancy
Centric occlusion of teeth discrepancy

524.56 Non-working side interference
Balancing side interference

524.57 Lack of posterior occlusal support

524.59 Other dentofacial functional abnormalities
Abnormal swallowing
Mouth breathing
Sleep postures
Tongue, lip, or finger habits

√5ᵗʰ **524.6 Temporomandibular joint disorders**
EXCLUDES *current temporomandibular joint:*
dislocation (830.0-830.1)
strain (848.1)

524.60 Temporomandibular joint disorders, unspecified
Temporomandibular joint-pain-dysfunction syndrome [TMJ]

524.61 Adhesions and ankylosis (bony or fibrous)
DEF: Stiffening or union of temporomandibular joint due to bony or fibrous union across joint.

524.62 Arthralgia of temporomandibular joint
DEF: Pain in temporomandibular joint; not inflammatory in nature.

524.63 Articular disc disorder (reducing or non-reducing)

524.64 Temporomandibular joint sounds on opening and/or closing the jaw

524.69 Other specified temporomandibular joint disorders

√5ᵗʰ **524.7 Dental alveolar anomalies**

524.70 Unspecified alveolar anomaly

524.71 Alveolar maxillary hyperplasia
DEF: Excessive tissue formation in the dental alveoli of upper jaw.

524.72 Alveolar mandibular hyperplasia
DEF: Excessive tissue formation in the dental alveoli of lower jaw.

524.73 Alveolar maxillary hypoplasia
DEF: Incomplete or underdeveloped alveolar tissue of upper jaw.

524.74 Alveolar mandibular hypoplasia
DEF: Incomplete or underdeveloped alveolar tissue of lower jaw.

524.75 Vertical displacement of alveolus and teeth
Extrusion of alveolus and teeth

524.76 Occlusal plane deviation

524.79 Other specified alveolar anomaly

√5ᵗʰ **524.8 Other specified dentofacial anomalies**

524.81 Anterior soft tissue impingement

524.82 Posterior soft tissue impingement

524.89 Other specified dentofacial anomalies

524.9 Unspecified dentofacial anomalies

√4ᵗʰ **525 Other diseases and conditions of the teeth and supporting structures**

525.0 Exfoliation of teeth due to systemic causes
DEF: Deterioration of teeth and surrounding structures due to systemic disease.

√5ᵗʰ **525.1 Loss of teeth due to trauma, extraction, or periodontal disease**
Code first class of edentulism (525.40-525.44, 525.50-525.54)
AHA: 4Q, '05, 74; 4Q, '01, 44

525.10 Acquired absence of teeth, unspecified
Tooth extraction status, NOS

525.11 Loss of teeth due to trauma

525.12 Loss of teeth due to periodontal disease

525.13 Loss of teeth due to caries

525.19 Other loss of teeth

√5ᵗʰ **525.2 Atrophy of edentulous alveolar ridge**

525.20 Unspecified atrophy of edentulous alveolar ridge
Atrophy of the mandible NOS
Atrophy of the maxilla NOS

525.21 Minimal atrophy of the mandible

525.22 Moderate atrophy of the mandible

525.23 Severe atrophy of the mandible

525.24 Minimal atrophy of the maxilla

525.25 Moderate atrophy of the maxilla

N Newborn Age: 0   P Pediatric Age: 0-17   M Maternity Age: 12-55   A Adult Age: 15-124   MCC Major CC Condition   CC CC Condition   HIV HIV Related Dx

525.26 **Severe atrophy of the maxilla**

525.3 **Retained dental root**

✓5ᵗʰ 525.4 **Complete edentulism**
Use additional code to identify cause of edentulism (525.10-525.19)
AHA: 4Q, '05, 74

525.40 **Complete edentulism, unspecified**
Edentulism NOS

525.41 **Complete edentulism, class I**

525.42 **Complete edentulism, class II**

525.43 **Complete edentulism, class III**

525.44 **Complete edentulism, class IV**

✓5ᵗʰ 525.5 **Partial edentulism**
Use additional code to identify cause of edentulism (525.10-525.19)
AHA: 4Q, '05, 74

525.50 **Partial edentulism, unspecified**

525.51 **Partial edentulism, class I**

525.52 **Partial edentulism, class II**

525.53 **Partial edentulism, class III**

525.54 **Partial edentulism, class IV**

✓5ᵗʰ 525.6 **Unsatisfactory restoration of tooth**
Defective bridge, crown, fillings
Defective dental restoration
EXCLUDES *dental restoration status (V45.84)*
unsatisfactory endodontic treatment (526.61-526.69)

525.60 **Unspecified unsatisfactory restoration of tooth**
Unspecified defective dental restoration

525.61 **Open restoration margins**
Dental restoration failure of marginal integrity
Open margin on tooth restoration

525.62 **Unrepairable overhanging of dental restorative materials**
Overhanging of tooth restoration

525.63 **Fractured dental restorative material without loss of material**
EXCLUDES *cracked tooth (521.81)*
fractured tooth (873.63, 873.73)

525.64 **Fractured dental restorative material with loss of material**
EXCLUDES *cracked tooth (521.81)*
fractured tooth (873.63, 873.73)

525.65 **Contour of existing restoration of tooth biologically incompatible with oral health**
Dental restoration failure of periodontal anatomical integrity
Unacceptable contours of existing restoration
Unacceptable morphology of existing restoration

525.66 **Allergy to existing dental restorative material**
Use additional code to identify the specific type of allergy

525.67 **Poor aesthetics of existing restoration**
Dental restoration aesthetically inadequate or displeasing

525.69 **Other unsatisfactory restoration of existing tooth**

✓5ᵗʰ 525.7 **Endosseous dental implant failure**

525.71 **Osseointegration failure of dental implant**
Failure of dental implant due to infection
Failure of dental implant due to unintentional loading
Failure of dental implant osseointegration due to premature loading
Failure of dental implant to osseointegrate prior to intentional prosthetic loading
Hemorrhagic complications of dental implant placement
Iatrogenic osseointegration failure of dental implant
Osseointegration failure of dental implant due to complications of systemic disease
Osseointegration failure of dental implant due to poor bone quality
Pre-integration failure of dental implant NOS
Pre-osseointegration failure of dental implant

525.72 **Post-osseointegration biological failure of dental implant**
Failure of dental implant due to lack of attached gingiva
Failure of dental implant due to occlusal trauma (caused by poor prosthetic design)
Failure of dental implant due to parafunctional habits
Failure of dental implant due to periodontal infection (peri-implantitis)
Failure of dental implant due to poor oral hygiene
Failure of dental implant to osseointegrate following intentional prosthetic loading
Iatrogenic post-osseointegration failure of dental implant
Post-osseointegration failure of dental implant due to complications of systemic disease

525.73 **Post-osseointegration mechanic failure of dental implant**
Failure of dental prosthesis causing loss of dental implant
Fracture of dental implant
Mechanical failure of dental implant NOS
EXCLUDES *cracked tooth (521.81)*
fractured dental restorative material with loss of material (525.64)
fractured dental restorative material without loss of material (525.63)
fractured tooth (873.63, 873.73)

525.79 **Other endosseous dental implant failure**
Dental implant failure NOS

525.8 **Other specified disorders of the teeth and supporting structures**
Enlargement of alveolar ridge NOS
Irregular alveolar process

525.9 **Unspecified disorder of the teeth and supporting structures**

✓4ᵗʰ 526 **Diseases of the jaws**

526.0 **Developmental odontogenic cysts**
Cyst: Cyst:
  dentigerous   lateral periodontal
  eruption   primordial
  follicular   Keratocyst
  lateral developmental
EXCLUDES *radicular cyst (522.8)*

526.1 **Fissural cysts of jaw**
Cyst: Cyst:
  globulomaxillary   median palatal
  incisor canal   nasopalatine
  median anterior maxillary   palatine of papilla
EXCLUDES *cysts of oral soft tissues (528.4)*

526.2 **Other cysts of jaws**
Cyst of jaw: Cyst of jaw:
  NOS   hemorrhagic
  aneurysmal   traumatic

526.3 **Central giant cell (reparative) granuloma**
EXCLUDES *peripheral giant cell granuloma (523.8)*

526.4 Inflammatory conditions

Abscess
Osteitis
Osteomyelitis (neonatal)
Periostitis } of jaw (acute) (chronic) (suppurative)

Sequestrum of jaw bone
EXCLUDES *alveolar osteitis (526.5)*
osteonecrosis of jaw (733.45)

526.5 Alveolitis of jaw
Alveolar osteitis   Dry socket
DEF: Inflammation of alveoli or tooth socket.

√5ᵗʰ **526.6 Periradicular pathology associated with previous endodontic treatment**

526.61 Perforation of root canal space

526.62 Endodontic overfill

526.63 Endodontic underfill

526.69 Other periradicular pathology associated with previous endodontic treatment

√5ᵗʰ **526.8 Other specified diseases of the jaws**

526.81 Exostosis of jaw
Torus mandibularis   Torus palatinus
DEF: Spur or bony outgrowth on the jaw.

526.89 Other
Cherubism
Fibrous dysplasia
Latent bone cyst
Osteoradionecrosis } of jaw(s)

Unilateral condylar hyperplasia or hypoplasia of mandible

526.9 Unspecified disease of the jaws
AHA: 4Q, '10, 93-94

√4ᵗʰ **527 Diseases of the salivary glands**

527.0 Atrophy
DEF: Wasting away, necrosis of salivary gland tissue.

527.1 Hypertrophy
DEF: Overgrowth or overdeveloped salivary gland tissue.

527.2 Sialoadenitis
Parotitis: Sialoangitis
  NOS   Sialodochitis
  allergic
  toxic
EXCLUDES *epidemic or infectious parotitis (072.0-072.9)*
uveoparotid fever (135)
DEF: Inflammation of salivary gland.

527.3 Abscess   `CC`
CC Excl: 527.0-527.9, 537.89-538

527.4 Fistula   `CC`
EXCLUDES *congenital fistula of salivary gland (750.24)*
CC Excl: See code: 527.3

527.5 Sialolithiasis
Calculus
Stone } of salivary gland or duct

Sialodocholithiasis

527.6 Mucocele
Mucous:
  extravasation cyst of salivary gland
  retention cyst of salivary gland
Ranula
DEF: Dilated salivary gland cavity filled with mucous.

527.7 Disturbance of salivary secretion
Hyposecretion   Sialorrhea
Ptyalism   Xerostomia

527.8 Other specified diseases of the salivary glands
Benign lymphoepithelial lesion of salivary gland
Sialectasia
Sialosis
Stenosis
Stricture } of salivary duct

527.9 Unspecified disease of the salivary glands

√4ᵗʰ **528 Diseases of the oral soft tissues, excluding lesions specific for gingiva and tongue**

√5ᵗʰ **528.0 Stomatitis and mucositis (ulcerative)**
EXCLUDES *cellulitis and abscess of mouth (528.3)*
diphtheritic stomatitis (032.0)
epizootic stomatitis (078.4)
gingivitis (523.0-523.1)
oral thrush (112.0)
Stevens-Johnson syndrome (695.13)
stomatitis:
  acute necrotizing ulcerative (101)
  aphthous (528.2)
  gangrenous (528.1)
  herpetic (054.2)
  Vincent's (101)
DEF: Stomatitis: Inflammation of oral mucosa; labial and buccal mucosa, tongue, palate, floor of the mouth, and gingivae.
AHA: 2Q, '99, 9
TIP: Do not assign if documented as fungal oral thrush, or as due to candidiasis. See instead 112.0.

528.00 Stomatitis and mucositis, unspecified
Mucositis NOS
Ulcerative mucositis NOS
Ulcerative stomatitis NOS
Vesicular stomatitis NOS
AHA: 4Q, '06, 88-90

528.01 Mucositis (ulcerative) due to antineoplastic therapy
Use additional E code to identify adverse effects of therapy, such as:
  antineoplastic and immunosuppressive drugs (E930.7, E933.1)
  radiation therapy (E879.2)
AHA: 4Q, '06, 88-90

528.02 Mucositis (ulcerative) due to other drugs
Use additional E code to identify drug
AHA: 4Q, '06, 88-90

528.09 Other stomatitis and mucositis (ulcerative)
AHA: 4Q, '06, 88-90

528.1 Cancrum oris
Gangrenous stomatitis   Noma
DEF: A severely gangrenous lesion of mouth due to fusospirochetal infection; destroys buccal, labial and facial tissues; can be fatal; found primarily in debilitated and malnourished children.

528.2 Oral aphthae
Aphthous stomatitis
Canker sore
Periadenitis mucosa necrotica recurrens
Recurrent aphthous ulcer
Stomatitis herpetiformis
EXCLUDES *herpetic stomatitis (054.2)*
DEF: Small oval or round ulcers of the mouth marked by a grayish exudate and a red halo effect.
AHA: 2Q, '12, 18

528.3 Cellulitis and abscess   `CC`
Cellulitis of mouth (floor)   Oral fistula
Ludwig's angina
EXCLUDES *abscess of tongue (529.0)*
cellulitis or abscess of lip (528.5)
fistula (of):
  dental (522.7)
  lip (528.5)
gingivitis (523.00-523.11)
CC Excl: 528.00-528.09, 528.3, 529.0, 529.2

528.4 Cysts
Dermoid cyst
Epidermoid cyst
Epstein's pearl
Lymphoepithelial cyst
Nasoalveolar cyst
Nasolabial cyst } or mouth

EXCLUDES *cyst:*
  gingiva (523.8)
  tongue (529.8)

 Newborn Age: 0    Pediatric Age: 0-17    Maternity Age: 12-55    Adult Age: 15-124   `MCC` Major CC Condition   `CC` CC Condition   `HIV` HIV Related Dx

176 – Volume 1   2015 ICD-9-CM

528.5 Diseases of lips
Abscess
Cellulitis
Fistula } of lips
Hypertrophy

Cheilitis:
  NOS
  angular
Cheilodynia
Cheilosis
  EXCLUDES *actinic cheilitis (692.79)*
    congenital fistula of lip (750.25)
    leukoplakia of lips (528.6)
  AHA: S-O, '86, 10

528.6 Leukoplakia of oral mucosa, including tongue
Leukokeratosis of oral mucosa   Leukoplakia of:
Leukoplakia of: lips
  gingiva   tongue
  EXCLUDES *carcinoma in situ (230.0, 232.0)*
    leukokeratosis nicotina palati (528.79)
  DEF: Thickened white patches of epithelium on mucous membranes of mouth.

√5ᵗʰ 528.7 Other disturbances of oral epithelium, including tongue
  EXCLUDES *carcinoma in situ (230.0, 232.0)*
    leukokeratosis NOS (702.8)

528.71 Minimal keratinized residual ridge mucosa
Minimal keratinization of alveolar ridge mucosa

528.72 Excessive keratinized residual ridge mucosa
Excessive keratinization of alveolar ridge mucosa

528.79 Other disturbances of oral epithelium, including tongue
Erythroplakia of mouth or tongue
Focal epithelial hyperplasia of mouth or tongue
Leukoedema of mouth or tongue
Leukokeratosis nicotina palate
Other oral epithelium disturbances

528.8 Oral submucosal fibrosis, including of tongue

528.9 Other and unspecified diseases of the oral soft tissues
Cheek and lip biting
Denture sore mouth
Denture stomatitis
Melanoplakia
Papillary hyperplasia of palate
Eosinophilic granuloma
Irritative hyperplasisa } of oral mucosa
Pyogenic granuloma
Ulcer (traumatic)

√4ᵗʰ 529 Diseases and other conditions of the tongue

529.0 Glossitis
Abscess
Ulceration (traumatic) } of tongue
  EXCLUDES *glossitis:*
    benign migratory (529.1)
    Hunter's (529.4)
    median rhomboid (529.2)
    Moeller's (529.4)

529.1 Geographic tongue
Benign migratory glossitis   Glossitis areata exfoliativa
  DEF: Chronic glossitis; marked by filiform papillae atrophy and inflammation; no known etiology.

529.2 Median rhomboid glossitis
  DEF: A noninflammatory, congenital disease characterized by rhomboid-like lesions at the middle third of the tongue's dorsal surface.

529.3 Hypertrophy of tongue papillae
Black hairy tongue   Hypertrophy of foliate papillae
Coated tongue   Lingua villosa nigra

529.4 Atrophy of tongue papillae
Bald tongue   Glossitis:
Glazed tongue   Moeller's
Glossitis: Glossodynia exfoliativa
  Hunter's   Smooth atrophic tongue

529.5 Plicated tongue
Fissured
Furrowed } tongue
Scrotal
  EXCLUDES *fissure of tongue, congenital (750.13)*
  DEF: Cracks, fissures or furrows, on dorsal surface of tongue.

529.6 Glossodynia
Glossopyrosis
Painful tongue
  EXCLUDES *glossodynia exfoliativa (529.4)*

529.8 Other specified conditions of the tongue
Atrophy
Crenated
Enlargement } (of) tongue
Hypertrophy

Glossocele
Glossoptosis
  EXCLUDES *erythroplasia of tongue (528.79)*
    leukoplakia of tongue (528.6)
    macroglossia (congenital) (750.15)
    microglossia (congenital) (750.16)
    oral submucosal fibrosis (528.8)

529.9 Unspecified condition of the tongue

Diseases of Esophagus, Stomach, and Duodenum (530-539)

√4ᵗʰ 530 Diseases of esophagus
  EXCLUDES *esophageal varices (456.0-456.2)*

530.0 Achalasia and cardiospasm
Achalasia (of cardia)   Megaesophagus
Aperistalsis of esophagus
  EXCLUDES *congenital cardiospasm (750.7)*
  DEF: Failure of smooth muscle fibers to relax at gastrointestinal junctures; such as esophagogastric sphincter when swallowing.

√5ᵗʰ 530.1 Esophagitis
Esophagitis: Esophagitis:
  chemical   postoperative
  peptic   regurgitant
  Use additional E code to identify cause, if induced by chemical
  EXCLUDES *tuberculous esophagitis (017.8)*
  AHA: 4Q, '93, 27; 1Q, '92, 17; 3Q, '91, 20
  TIP: Do not assign if esophagitis due to candidiasis; see instead code 112.84.

530.10 Esophagitis, unspecified
Esophagitis NOS
  AHA: 3Q, '05, 17

530.11 Reflux esophagitis
  DEF: Inflammation of lower esophagus; due to regurgitated gastric acid.
  AHA: 4Q, '95, 82
  K21.0 Gastro-esophageal reflux disease w/esophagitis **I-10**

530.12 Acute esophagitis
  DEF: An acute inflammation of the mucous lining or submucosal coat of the esophagus.
  CC Excl: 530.10-530.21, 530.4, 530.7, 530.82, 530.85-530.89
  AHA: 4Q, '01, 45

530.13 Eosinophilic esophagitis
  AHA: 4Q, '08, 115-116

Esophagus

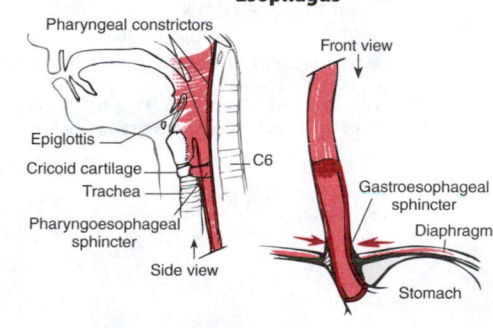

Pharyngeal constrictors
Front view
Epiglottis
Cricoid cartilage
C6
Trachea
Pharyngoesophageal sphincter
Gastroesophageal sphincter
Diaphragm
Side view
Stomach

530.19 **Other esophagitis**
Abscess of esophagus
AHA: 3Q, '01, 10
K20.8 Other esophagitis I-10

√5th **530.2 Ulcer of esophagus**
Ulcer of esophagus:
fungal
peptic
Ulcer of esophagus due to ingestion of:
aspirin
chemicals
medicines
Use additional E code to identify cause, if induced by chemical or drug
AHA: 4Q, '03, 63

530.20 Ulcer of esophagus without bleeding CC
Ulcer of esophagus NOS
CC Excl: 530.21, 530.89-530.9, 537.84

530.21 Ulcer of esophagus with bleeding MCC
EXCLUDES *bleeding esophageal varices (456.0, 456.20)*
CC Excl: 251.5, 456.0, 530.20-530.21, 530.7, 530.82, 530.85, 531.00-534.91, 535.01, 535.11, 535.21, 535.31, 535.41, 535.51, 535.61, 535.71, 537.83, 537.89-538, 562.02-562.03, 562.12-562.13, 569.3, 569.85, 578.0-578.9

530.3 Stricture and stenosis of esophagus
Compression of esophagus
Obstruction of esophagus
EXCLUDES *congenital stricture of esophagus (750.3)*
AHA: 1Q, '12, 15; 2Q, '01, 4; 2Q, '97, 3; 1Q, '88, 13
TIP: If esophageal obstruction is due to impacted foreign body, such as meat or other substance, assign instead code 935.1.
K22.2 Esophageal obstruction I-10

530.4 Perforation of esophagus MCC
Rupture of esophagus
EXCLUDES *traumatic perforation of esophagus (862.22, 862.32, 874.4-874.5)*
CC Excl: 530.4, 530.7-530.81, 530.83-530.84, 530.89-530.9

530.5 Dyskinesia of esophagus
Corkscrew esophagus
Curling esophagus
Esophagospasm
Spasm of esophagus
EXCLUDES *cardiospasm (530.0)*
DEF: Difficulty performing voluntary esophageal movements.
AHA: 1Q, '88, 13; N-D, '84, 19

530.6 Diverticulum of esophagus, acquired
Diverticulum, acquired:
epiphrenic
pharyngoesophageal
pulsion
subdiaphragmatic
Diverticulum, acquired:
traction
Zenker's (hypopharyngeal)
Esophageal pouch, acquired
Esophagocele, acquired
EXCLUDES *congenital diverticulum of esophagus (750.4)*
AHA: J-F, '85, 3

530.7 Gastroesophageal laceration-hemorrhage syndrome MCC
Mallory-Weiss syndrome
DEF: Laceration of distal esophagus and proximal stomach due to vomiting, hiccups or other sustained activity.
CC Excl: 251.5, 456.0, 530.20-530.21, 530.4, 530.7-530.85, 530.89-534.91, 535.01, 535.11, 535.21, 535.31, 535.41, 535.51, 535.61, 535.71, 537.83, 562.02-562.03, 562.12-562.13, 569.3, 569.85, 578.0-578.9

√5th **530.8 Other specified disorders of esophagus**

530.81 Esophageal reflux
Gastroesophageal reflux
EXCLUDES *reflux esophagitis (530.11)*
DEF: Regurgitation of the gastric contents into esophagus and possibly pharynx.
AHA: 4Q, '10, 97; 2Q, '01, 4; 1Q, '95, 7; 4Q, '92, 27
K21.9 Gastro-esophageal reflux dz w/o esophagitis I-10

530.82 Esophageal hemorrhage MCC
EXCLUDES *hemorrhage due to esophageal varices (456.0-456.2)*
CC Excl: 251.5, 456.0, 456.20, 459.89-459.9, 530.20-530.21, 530.7, 530.82, 530.85, 531.00-534.91, 535.01, 535.11, 535.21, 535.31, 535.41, 535.51, 535.61, 537.83, 562.02-562.03, 562.12-562.13, 569.3, 569.85, 578.0-578.9
AHA: 1Q, '05, 17

530.83 Esophageal leukoplakia

530.84 Tracheoesophageal fistula MCC
EXCLUDES *congenital tracheoesophageal fistula (750.3)*
CC Excl: 530.4, 530.7-530.81, 530.83-530.84, 530.89-530.9

530.85 Barrett's esophagus
DEF: A metaplastic disorder in which specialized columnar epithelial cells replace the normal squamous epithelial cells; secondary to chronic gastroesophageal reflux damage to the mucosa; increases risk of developing adenocarcinoma.
AHA: 4Q, '03, 63
K22.70 Barrett's esophagus w/o dysphagia I-10

530.86 Infection of esophagostomy CC
Use additional code to specify infection
CC Excl: 530.86-530.87, 536.40-536.49, 539.01-539.89, 569.71-569.79, 997.41-997.49, 997.71, 997.91-997.99, 998.81, 998.83-998.9

530.87 Mechanical complication of esophagostomy CC
Malfunction of esophagostomy
CC Excl: See code: 530.86

530.89 Other
EXCLUDES *Paterson-Kelly syndrome (280.8)*

530.9 Unspecified disorder of esophagus

√4th **531 Gastric ulcer**
INCLUDES ulcer (peptic):
prepyloric
pylorus
stomach
Use additional E code to identify drug, if drug-induced
EXCLUDES *peptic ulcer NOS (533.0-533.9)*

The following fifth-digit subclassification is for use with category 531:
0 without mention of obstruction
1 with obstruction

DEF: Destruction of tissue in lumen of stomach due to action of gastric acid and pepsin on gastric mucosa decreasing resistance to ulcers.
AHA: 1Q, '91, 15; 4Q, '90, 27

§ √5th **531.0 Acute with hemorrhage** MCC
[0-1] **CC Excl:** 251.5, 456.0, 530.20-530.21, 530.7, 530.82, 530.85, 531.00-534.91, 535.01, 535.11, 535.21, 535.31, 535.41, 535.51, 535.61, 537.83, 537.89-538, 562.02-562.03, 562.12-562.13, 569.3, 569.85, 578.0-578.9
AHA: N-D, '84, 15

§ √5th **531.1 Acute with perforation** MCC
[0-1] **CC Excl:** See code 531.0

§ √5th **531.2 Acute with hemorrhage and perforation** MCC
[0-1] **CC Excl:** See code 531.0

§ √5th **531.3 Acute without mention of hemorrhage or perforation** MCC 1 CC 0
[0-1] **CC Excl:** See code 531.0

§ √5th **531.4 Chronic or unspecified with hemorrhage** MCC
[0-1] **CC Excl:** See code 531.0
AHA: 4Q, '90, 22
K25.4 Chronic/unspecified gastric ulcer w/hemorrhage I-10

§ √5th **531.5 Chronic or unspecified with perforation** MCC
[0-1] **CC Excl:** See code 531.0

§ √5th **531.6 Chronic or unspecified with hemorrhage and perforation** MCC
[0-1] **CC Excl:** See code 531.0

§ √5th **531.7 Chronic without mention of hemorrhage or perforation** MCC 1
[0-1] **CC Excl:** For code 531.71: see code 531.0

§ Requires fifth digit. Valid digits are in [brackets] under each code. See category 531 for codes and definitions.

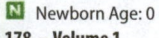

N Newborn Age: 0 P Pediatric Age: 0-17 M Maternity Age: 12-55 A Adult Age: 15-124 MCC Major CC Condition CC CC Condition HIV HIV Related Dx

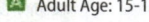

Stomach

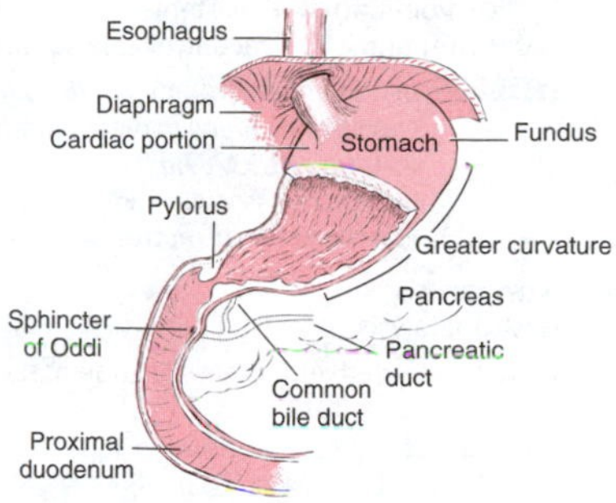

Esophagus
Diaphragm
Cardiac portion
Fundus
Stomach
Pylorus
Greater curvature
Pancreas
Sphincter of Oddi
Pancreatic duct
Common bile duct
Proximal duodenum

§ ✓5ᵗʰ **531.9 Unspecified as acute or chronic, without** `MCC 1`
[0-1] **mention of hemorrhage or perforation**
CC Excl: For code 531.91: see code 531.0
K25.9 Gastric ulcer uns acute/chronic w/o hem/perf `I-10`

✓4ᵗʰ **532 Duodenal ulcer**
INCLUDES   erosion (acute) of duodenum
ulcer (peptic):
duodenum
postpyloric

Use additional E code to identify drug, if drug-induced

EXCLUDES peptic ulcer NOS (533.0-533.9)

The following fifth-digit subclassification is for use with category 532:
0 without mention of obstruction
1 with obstruction

DEF: Ulcers in duodenum due to action of gastric acid and pepsin on mucosa decreasing resistance to ulcers.
AHA: 4Q, '90, 27; 1Q, '91, 15

§ ✓5ᵗʰ **532.0 Acute with hemorrhage** `MCC`
[0-1]   For code 532.00: 251.5, 456.0, 530.20-530.21, 530.7, 530.82, 530.85, 531.00-534.91, 535.01, 535.11, 535.21, 535.31, 535.41, 535.51, 535.61, 535.71, 537.3, 537.83, 537.89-538, 562.02-562.03, 562.12-562.13, 569.3, 569.85, 578.0-578.9
AHA: 4Q, '90, 22

§ ✓5ᵗʰ **532.1 Acute with perforation** `MCC`
[0-1]   CC Excl: See code 532.0

§ ✓5ᵗʰ **532.2 Acute with hemorrhage and perforation** `MCC`
[0-1]   CC Excl: See code 532.0

§ ✓5ᵗʰ **532.3 Acute without mention of hemorrhage or** `MCC 1` `CC 0`
[0-1] **perforation**
For code 532.30: 251.5, 456.0, 530.7, 530.82, 531.00-534.91, 535.01, 535.11, 535.21, 535.31, 535.41, 535.51, 535.61, 535.71, 537.3, 537.83-538, 562.02-562.03, 562.12-562.13, 569.3, 569.85, 578.0-578.9; For code 532.31: 251.5, 456.0, 530.20-530.21, 530.7, 530.82, 530.85, 531.00-534.91, 535.01, 535.11, 535.21, 535.31, 535.41, 535.51, 535.61, 537.3, 537.83, 537.89-538, 562.02-562.03, 562.12-562.13, 569.3, 569.85, 578.0-578.9

§ ✓5ᵗʰ **532.4 Chronic or unspecified with hemorrhage** `MCC`
[0-1]   CC Excl: See code 532.0
K26.4 Chronic/unspecified duodenal ulcer w/hemorrhage `I-10`

§ ✓5ᵗʰ **532.5 Chronic or unspecified with perforation** `MCC`
[0-1]   CC Excl: See code 532.0

§ ✓5ᵗʰ **532.6 Chronic or unspecified with hemorrhage and** `MCC`
[0-1] **perforation**
CC Excl: See code 532.0

§ ✓5ᵗʰ **532.7 Chronic without mention of hemorrhage or** `MCC 1`
[0-1] **peforation**
CC Excl: For code 532.71: See code 532.0

§ ✓5ᵗʰ **532.9 Unspecified as acute or chronic, without mention of** `MCC 1`
[0-1] **hemorrhage or perforation**
CC Excl: For code 532.91: See code 532.0
K26.9 Duodenal ulcer uns acute/chronic w/o hem/perf `I-10`

✓4ᵗʰ **533 Peptic ulcer, site unspecified**
INCLUDES   gastroduodenal ulcer NOS
peptic ulcer NOS
stress ulcer NOS

Use additional E code to identify drug, if drug-induced

EXCLUDES peptic ulcer:
duodenal (532.0-532.9)
gastric (531.0-531.9)

The following fifth-digit subclassification is for use with category 533:
0 without mention of obstruction
1 with obstruction

DEF: Ulcer of mucous membrane of esophagus, stomach or duodenum due to gastric acid secretion.
AHA: 1Q, '91, 15; 4Q, '90, 27

§ ✓5ᵗʰ **533.0 Acute with hemorrhage** `MCC`
[0-1]   CC Excl: See code 532.0

§ ✓5ᵗʰ **533.1 Acute with perforation** `MCC`
[0-1]   CC Excl: See code 533.0

§ ✓5ᵗʰ **533.2 Acute with hemorrhage and perforation** `MCC`
[0-1]   CC Excl: See code 533.0

§ ✓5ᵗʰ **533.3 Acute without mention of hemorrhage** `MCC 1` `CC 0`
[0-1] **and perforation**
CC Excl: See code: 533.0

§ ✓5ᵗʰ **533.4 Chronic or unspecified with hemorrhage** `MCC`
[0-1]   CC Excl: See code 533.0

§ ✓5ᵗʰ **533.5 Chronic or unspecified with perforation** `MCC`
[0-1]   CC Excl: See code 533.0

§ ✓5ᵗʰ **533.6 Chronic or unspecified with hemorrhage** `MCC`
[0-1] **and perforation**
CC Excl: See code 533.0

§ ✓5ᵗʰ **533.7 Chronic without mention of hemorrhage or** `MCC 1`
[0-1] **perforation**
CC Excl: For code 533.71: See code 533.0
AHA: 2Q, '89, 16

§ ✓5ᵗʰ **533.9 Unspecified as acute or chronic, without** `MCC 1`
[0-1] **mention of hemorrhage or perforation**
CC Excl: For code 533.91: See code 533.0

✓4ᵗʰ **534 Gastrojejunal ulcer**
INCLUDES   ulcer (peptic) or erosion:
anastomotic
gastrocolic
gastrointestinal
gastrojejunal
jejunal
marginal
stomal

EXCLUDES primary ulcer of small intestine (569.82)

The following fifth-digit subclassification is for use with category 534:
0 without mention of obstruction
1 with obstruction

AHA: 1Q, '91, 15; 4Q, '90, 27

§ ✓5ᵗʰ **534.0 Acute with hemorrhage** `MCC`
[0-1]   CC Excl: 251.5, 456.0, 530.20-530.21, 530.7, 530.82, 530.85, 531.00-534.91, 535.01, 535.11, 535.21, 535.31, 535.41, 535.51, 535.61, 537.83, 537.89-538, 562.02-562.03, 562.12-562.13, 569.3, 569.85, 578.0-578.9

§ ✓5ᵗʰ **534.1 Acute with perforation** `MCC`
[0-1]   CC Excl: See code 534.0

§ ✓5ᵗʰ **534.2 Acute with hemorrhage and perforation** `MCC`
[0-1]   CC Excl: See code 534.0

§ ✓5ᵗʰ **534.3 Acute without mention of hemorrhage** `MCC 1` `CC 0`
[0-1] **or perforation**
CC Excl:: See code 534.0

§ ✓5ᵗʰ **534.4 Chronic or unspecified with hemorrhage** `MCC`
[0-1]   CC Excl: See code 534.0

§ ✓5ᵗʰ **534.5 Chronic or unspecified with perforation** `MCC`
[0-1]   CC Excl: See code 534.0

---

§ Requires fifth digit. Valid digits are in [brackets] under each code. See appropriate category for codes and definitions.

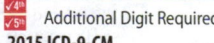

✓4ᵗʰ ✓5ᵗʰ Additional Digit Required   Unacceptable PDx   `Manifestation Code`   `Hospital Acquired Condition`   ►◄ Revised Text   ● New Code   ▲ Revised Code Title

§ ✓5ᵗʰ **534.6 Chronic or unspecified with hemorrhage** `MCC`
[0-1] **and perforation**
CC Excl: See code 534.0

§ ✓5ᵗʰ **534.7 Chronic without mention of hemorrhage or** `MCC 1`
[0-1] **perforation**
CC Excl: For code 534.71: See code 534.0

§ ✓5ᵗʰ **534.9 Unspecified as acute or chronic, without** `MCC 1`
[0-1] **mention of hemorrhage or perforation**
CC Excl: For code 534.91: See code 534.0

✓4ᵗʰ **535 Gastritis and duodenitis**

The following fifth-digit subclassification is for use with category 535:
0 **without mention of hemorrhage**
1 **with hemorrhage**

AHA: 2Q, '92, 9; 4Q, '91, 25

§ ✓5ᵗʰ **535.0 Acute gastritis** `MCC 1`
[0-1] For code 532.01: 251.5, 456.0, 530.20-530.21, 530.7, 530.82, 530.85, 531.00-534.91, 535.01, 535.11, 535.21, 535.31, 535.41, 535.51, 535.61, 535.71, 537.83, 562.02-562.03, 562.12-562.13, 569.3, 569.85, 578.0-578.9
AHA: 2Q, '92, 8; N-D, '86, 9

§ ✓5ᵗʰ **535.1 Atrophic gastritis** `MCC 1`
[0-1] Gastritis: Gastritis:
atrophic-hyperplastic   chronic (atrophic)
DEF: Inflammation of stomach, with mucous membrane atrophy and peptic gland destruction.
CC Excl: For code 535.11: See code 535.01
AHA: 1Q, '94, 18
K29.50 Unspecified chronic gastritis without bleeding `I-10`

§ ✓5ᵗʰ **535.2 Gastric mucosal hypertrophy** `MCC 1`
[0-1] Hypertrophic gastritis
CC Excl: For code 535.21: See code 535.01

§ ✓5ᵗʰ **535.3 Alcoholic gastritis** `MCC 1`
[0-1] CC Excl: For code 535.31: See code 535.01

§ ✓5ᵗʰ **535.4 Other specified gastritis** `MCC 1`
[0-1] Gastritis: Gastritis:
allergic   superficial
bile induced   toxic
irritant
EXCLUDES eosinophilic gastritis (535.7)
CC Excl: For code 535.41: See code 535.01
AHA: 4Q, '90, 27

§ ✓5ᵗʰ **535.5 Unspecified gastritis and gastroduodenitis** `MCC 1`
[0-1] CC Excl: For code 535.51: See code 535.01
AHA: For code 535.50: 3Q, '05, 17; 4Q, '99, 25

§ ✓5ᵗʰ **535.6 Duodenitis** `MCC 1`
[0-1] DEF: Inflammation of intestine, between pylorus and jejunum.
CC Excl: For code 535.61: See code 535.01
AHA: For code 535.60: 3Q, '05, 17
K29.80 Duodenitis without bleeding `I-10`

§ ✓5ᵗʰ **535.7 Eosinophilic gastritis** `MCC 1`
[0-1] CC Excl: For code 535.71: 251.5, 456.0, 530.20-530.21, 530.7, 530.82, 530.85, 531.00-534.91, 535.01, 535.11, 535.21, 535.31, 535.41, 535.51, 535.61-535.71, 537.83, 558.41, 562.02-562.03, 562.12-562.13, 569.3, 569.85, 578.0-578.9
AHA: 4Q, '08, 115-116

✓4ᵗʰ **536 Disorders of function of stomach**
EXCLUDES functional disorders of stomach specified as psychogenic (306.4)

536.0 Achlorhydria
DEF: Absence of gastric acid due to gastric mucosa atrophy; unresponsive to histamines; also known as gastric anacidity.

536.1 Acute dilatation of stomach `CC`
Acute distention of stomach
CC Excl: 536.1

536.2 Persistent vomiting
Cyclical vomiting   Persistent vomiting [not of pregnancy]
Habit vomiting   Uncontrollable vomiting
EXCLUDES bilious emesis (vomiting) (787.04)
excessive vomiting in pregnancy (643.0-643.9)
vomiting NOS (787.03)
cyclical, associated with migraine (346.2)
vomiting of fecal matter (569.87)

536.3 Gastroparesis
Gastroparalysis
Code first underlying disease, if known, such as:
diabetes mellitus (249.6, 250.6)
DEF: Slight degree of paralysis within muscular coat of stomach.
AHA: 4Q, '08, 94; 2Q, '04, 7; 2Q, '01, 4; 4Q, '94, 42

✓5ᵗʰ **536.4 Gastrostomy complications**
AHA: 4Q, '98, 42
TIP: Do not assign code 997.4 Digestive system complications, for any gastrostomy complications.

536.40 Gastrostomy complication, unspecified

536.41 Infection of gastrostomy `CC`
Use additional code to specify type of infection, such as:
abscess or cellulitis of abdomen (682.2)
septicemia (038.0-038.9)
Use additional code to identify organism (041.00-041.9)
CC Excl: 530.86-530.87, 536.40-536.49, 539.01-539.89, 569.71-569.79, 997.41-997.49, 997.71, 997.91-997.99, 998.81, 998.83-998.9
AHA: 4Q, '98, 42

536.42 Mechanical complication of gastrostomy `CC`
CC Excl: See code 536.41

536.49 Other gastrostomy complications
AHA: 4Q, '98, 42

536.8 Dyspepsia and other specified disorders of function of stomach
Achylia gastrica   Hyperchlorhydria
Hourglass contraction   Hypochlorhydria
of stomach   Indigestion
Hyperacidity   Tachygastria
EXCLUDES achlorhydria (536.0)
heartburn (787.1)
AHA: 2Q, '93, 6; 2Q, '89, 16; N-D, '84, 9
K30 Functional dyspepsia `I-10`

536.9 Unspecified functional disorder of stomach
Functional gastrointestinal: Functional gastrointestinal:
disorder   irritation
disturbance

✓4ᵗʰ **537 Other disorders of stomach and duodenum**

537.0 Acquired hypertrophic pyloric stenosis `CC`
Constriction ⎫
Obstruction   ⎬ of pylorus, acquired or adult
Stricture   ⎭
EXCLUDES congenital or infantile pyloric stenosis (750.5)
CC Excl: 536.3, 536.8-537.0, 537.3, 750.5, 750.8-750.9, 751.1, 751.5
AHA: 2Q, '01, 4; J-F, '85, 14

537.1 Gastric diverticulum
EXCLUDES congenital diverticulum of stomach (750.7)
DEF: Herniated sac or pouch within stomach or duodenum.
AHA: J-F, '85, 4

537.2 Chronic duodenal ileus
DEF: Persistent obstruction between pylorus and jejunum.

537.3 Other obstruction of duodenum `CC`
Cicatrix   ⎫
Stenosis   ⎬ of duodenum
Stricture ⎪
Volvulus   ⎭
EXCLUDES congenital obstruction of duodenum (751.1)
CC Excl: 537.3, 750.8-750.9, 751.1, 751.5

---

§ Requires fifth digit. Valid digits are in [brackets] under each code. See appropriate category for codes and definitions.

`N` Newborn Age: 0   `P` Pediatric Age: 0-17   `M` Maternity Age: 12-55   `A` Adult Age: 15-124   `MCC` Major CC Condition   `CC` CC Condition   `HIV` HIV Related Dx

180 – Volume 1   **2015 ICD-9-CM**

Duodenum

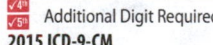

537.4 Fistula of stomach or duodenum `CC`
Gastrocolic fistula   Gastrojejunocolic fistula
CC Excl: 537.4, 750.8-750.9, 751.5
AHA: 1Q, '12, 10
TIP: Assign when a previous G-tube site has failed to spontaneously close and requires further treatment.

537.5 Gastroptosis
DEF: Downward displacement of stomach.

537.6 Hourglass stricture or stenosis of stomach
Cascade stomach
EXCLUDES *congenital hourglass stomach (750.7)*
hourglass contraction of stomach (536.8)

√5ᵗʰ **537.8 Other specified disorders of stomach and duodenum**
AHA: 4Q, '91, 25

537.81 Pylorospasm
EXCLUDES *congenital pylorospasm (750.5)*
DEF: Spasm of the pyloric sphincter.

537.82 Angiodysplasia of stomach and duodenum (without mention of hemorrhage)
AHA: 2Q, '07, 7; 3Q, '96, 10; 4Q, '90, 4

537.83 Angiodysplasia of stomach and duodenum with hemorrhage `MCC`
CC Excl: 251.5, 456.0, 530.20-530.21, 530.7, 530.82, 530.85, 531.00-534.91, 535.01, 535.11, 535.21, 535.31, 535.41, 535.51, 535.61, 537.83, 562.02- 562.03, 562.12-562.13, 569.3, 569.85, 578.0-578.9
DEF: Bleeding of stomach and duodenum due to vascular abnormalities.
AHA: 2Q, '07, 7

537.84 Dieulafoy lesion (hemorrhagic) of stomach and duodenum `MCC`
CC Excl: 251.5, 456.0, 530.20-530.21, 530.7, 530.82, 530.85, 531.00-534.91, 535.01, 535.11, 535.21, 535.31, 535.41, 535.51, 535.61, 535.71, 537.83-537.84, 562.02-562.03, 562.12-562.13, 569.3, 569.85, 578.0-578.9
DEF: An abnormally large and convoluted submucosal artery protruding through a defect in the mucosa in the stomach or intestines that can erode the epithelium causing hemorrhaging.
AHA: 4Q, '02, 60

537.89 Other
Gastric or duodenal:
prolapse
rupture
Intestinal metaplasia of gastric mucosa
Passive congestion of stomach
EXCLUDES *diverticula of duodenum (562.00-562.01)*
gastrointestinal hemorrhage (578.0-578.9)
AHA: 1Q, '11, 10-11; 3Q, '05, 15; N-D, '84, 7
TIP: Assign for congestive portal gastropathy or portal hypertensive gastropathy.

537.9 Unspecified disorder of stomach and duodenum

538 Gastrointestinal mucositis (ulcerative) `CC`
Use additional E code to identify adverse effects of therapy, such as:
antineoplastic and immunosuppressive drugs (E930.7, E933.1)
radiation therapy (E879.2)
EXCLUDES *mucositis (ulcerative) of mouth and oral soft tissue (528.00-528.09)*
CC Excl: 251.5, 456.0, 530.20-530.21, 530.7, 530.82, 530.85, 531.00-534.91, 535.01, 535.11, 535.21, 535.31, 535.41, 535.51, 535.61, 537.83, 537.89-538, 562.02-562.03, 562.12-562.13, 569.3, 569.85, 578.0-578.9
AHA: 4Q, '06, 88-90

√4ᵗʰ **539 Complications of bariatric procedures**
TIP: If associated dumping syndrome is documented, assign also code 564.2.

√5ᵗʰ **539.0 Complications of gastric band procedure**
AHA: 4Q, '11, 125-127

¹⁴**539.01 Infection due to gastric band procedure** `CC`
Use additional code to specify type of infection, such as:
abscess or cellulitis of abdomen (682.2)
septicemia (038.0-038.9)
Use additional code to identify organism (041.00-041.9)
CC Excl: 530.86-530.87, 536.40-536.49, 539.01-539.89, 569.71-569.79, 997.41-997.49, 997.71, 997.91-997.99, 998.81, 998.83-998.9
AHA: 4Q, '11, 127

539.09 Other complications of gastric band procedure `CC`
Use additional code(s) to further specify the complication
CC Excl: See code 539.01

√5ᵗʰ **539.8 Complications of other bariatric procedure**
EXCLUDES *complications of gastric band procedure (539.01-539.09)*
AHA: 4Q, '11, 125-127

¹⁴**539.81 Infection due to other bariatric procedure** `CC`
Use additional code to specify type of infection, such as:
abscess or cellulitis of abdomen (682.2)
septicemia (038.0-038.9)
Use additional code to identify organism (041.00-041.9)
CC Excl: 530.86-530.87, 536.40-536.49, 539.01-539.89, 569.71-569.79, 997.41-997.49, 997.71, 997.91-997.99, 998.81, 998.83-998.9

539.89 Other complications of other bariatric procedure `CC`
Use additional code(s) to further specify the complication
CC Excl: See code 539.81
AHA: ►3Q, '13, 12◄

Appendicitis (540-543)

√4ᵗʰ **540 Acute appendicitis**
DEF: Inflammation of vermiform appendix due to fecal obstruction, neoplasm or foreign body of appendiceal lumen; causes infection, edema and infarction of appendiceal wall; may result in mural necrosis, and perforation.
AHA: N-D, '84, 19

540.0 With generalized peritonitis `MCC`
Appendicitis (acute) with: perforation, peritonitis (generalized), rupture — fulminating, gangrenous, obstructive
Cecitis (acute) with perforation, peritonitis (generalized), rupture
Rupture of appendix
EXCLUDES *acute appendicitis with peritoneal abscess (540.1)*
CC Excl: 537.89-543.9
K35.2 Acute appendicitis w/generalized peritonitis `I-10`

540.1 With peritoneal abscess `MCC`
Abscess of appendix   With generalized peritonitis
CC Excl: See code 540.0
AHA: N-D, '84, 19

---

¹⁴ HAC = when in combination with principal diagnosis 278.01 and procedure code 44.38, 44.39, or 44.95.

√4ᵗʰ √5ᵗʰ Additional Digit Required   Unacceptable PDx   Manifestation Code   Hospital Acquired Condition   ►◄ Revised Text   ● New Code   ▲ Revised Code Title

Appendix

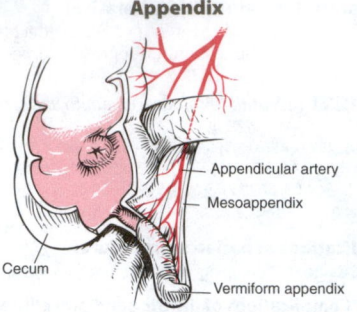

Appendicular artery
Mesoappendix
Cecum
Vermiform appendix

540.9 Without mention of peritonitis `CC`
Acute appendicitis without mention of perforation, peritonitis, or rupture:
fulminating
gangrenous
inflamed
obstructive
Acute cecitis without mention of perforation, peritonitis, or rupture
CC Excl: See code 540.0
AHA: ▶2Q, '13, 7;◀1Q, '01, 15; 4Q, '97, 52
K35.80 Unspecified acute appendicitis `I-10`

541 Appendicitis, unqualified
AHA: 2Q, '90, 26
TIP: Do not assign for normal appendix found at appendectomy. Assign instead symptom code (e.g., abdominal pain).

542 Other appendicitis
Appendicitis: Appendicitis:
chronic   relapsing
recurrent   subacute
EXCLUDES hyperplasia (lymphoid) of appendix (543.0)
AHA: 1Q, '01, 15

√4ᵗʰ 543 Other diseases of appendix

543.0 Hyperplasia of appendix (lymphoid)
DEF: Proliferation of cells in appendix tissue.

543.9 Other and unspecified diseases of appendix
Appendicular or appendiceal:
colic
concretion
fistula
Diverticulum
Fecalith
Intussusception } of appendix
Mucocele
Stercolith

Hernia of Abdominal Cavity (550-553)

INCLUDES hernia:
acquired
congenital, except diaphragmatic or hiatal

√4ᵗʰ 550 Inguinal hernia
INCLUDES bubonocele
inguinal hernia (direct) (double) (indirect) (oblique) (sliding)
scrotal hernia

The following fifth-digit subclassification is for use with category 550:
0 **unilateral or unspecified (not specified as recurrent)**
Unilateral NOS
1 **unilateral or unspecified, recurrent**
2 **bilateral (not specified as recurrent)**
Bilateral NOS
3 **bilateral, recurrent**

DEF: Hernia protrusion of an abdominal organ or tissue through inguinal canal.
DEF: Indirect inguinal hernia: (external or oblique) leaves abdomen through deep inguinal ring, passes through inguinal canal lateral to the inferior epigastric artery.
DEF: Direct inguinal hernia: (internal) emerges between inferior epigastric artery and rectus muscle edge.
AHA: N-D, '85, 12

Hernias of Abdominal Cavity

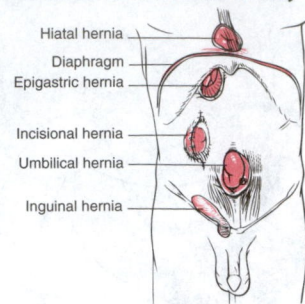

Hiatal hernia
Diaphragm
Epigastric hernia
Incisional hernia
Umbilical hernia
Inguinal hernia

§ √5ᵗʰ 550.0 Inguinal hernia, with gangrene `MCC`
[0-3] Inguinal hernia with gangrene (and obstruction)
CC Excl: 537.89-538, 550.0-550.93, 552.8-552.9, 553.8-553.9

§ √5ᵗʰ 550.1 Inguinal hernia, with obstruction, without `CC`
[0-3] **mention of gangrene**
Inguinal hernia with mention of incarceration, irreducibility, or strangulation
CC Excl: See code 550.0

§ √5ᵗʰ 550.9 Inguinal hernia, without mention of obstruction or
[0-3] **gangrene**
Inguinal hernia NOS
AHA: For code 550.91: 3Q, '03, 10; 1Q, '03, 4
K40.90 Uni ingin hernia w/o obst/gangrene not spec recur `I-10`

√4ᵗʰ 551 Other hernia of abdominal cavity, with gangrene
INCLUDES that with gangrene (and obstruction)

√5ᵗʰ 551.0 Femoral hernia with gangrene

551.00 Unilateral or unspecified (not specified `MCC`
as recurrent)
Femoral hernia NOS with gangrene
CC Excl: 537.89-538, 551.00-551.03, 552.8-553.03, 553.8-553.9

551.01 Unilateral or unspecified, recurrent `MCC`
CC Excl: See code 551.00

551.02 Bilateral (not specified as recurrent) `MCC`
CC Excl: See code 551.00

551.03 Bilateral, recurrent `MCC`
CC Excl: See code 551.00

551.1 Umbilical hernia with gangrene `MCC`
Parumbilical hernia specified as gangrenous
CC Excl: 537.89-538, 551.1-551.29, 552.1-552.29, 552.8-552.9, 553.1-553.29, 553.8-553.9

√5ᵗʰ 551.2 Ventral hernia with gangrene

551.20 Ventral, unspecified, with gangrene `MCC`
CC Excl: See code 551.1

551.21 Incisional, with gangrene `MCC`
Hernia:
postoperative } specified as
recurrent, ventral } gangrenous
CC Excl: See code 551.1

551.29 Other `MCC`
Epigastric hernia specified as gangrenous
CC Excl: See code 551.1

551.3 Diaphragmatic hernia with gangrene `MCC`
Hernia:
hiatal (esophageal) (sliding) } specified as
paraesophageal } gangrenous
Thoracic stomach
EXCLUDES congenital diaphragmatic hernia (756.6)
CC Excl: 551.3, 552.3-552.9, 553.3-553.9

551.8 Hernia of other specified sites, with gangrene `MCC`
Any condition classifiable to 553.8 if specified as gangrenous
CC Excl: 537.89-538, 550.00-553.9

551.9 Hernia of unspecified site, with gangrene `MCC`
Any condition classifiable to 553.9 if specified as gangrenous
CC Excl: See code 551.8

---

§ Requires fifth digit. Valid digits are in [brackets] under each code. See category 550 for codes and definitions.

N Newborn Age: 0   **P** Pediatric Age: 0-17   **M** Maternity Age: 12-55   **A** Adult Age: 15-124   **MCC** Major CC Condition   **CC** CC Condition   **HIV** HIV Related Dx

Inguinal Hernias

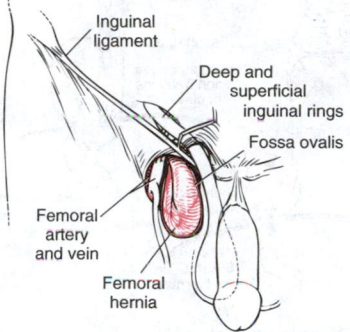

Femoral Hernia

552.3 Diaphragmatic hernia with obstruction `CC`
Hernia:
hiatal (esophageal) ⎫ specified as caracerated,
(sliding)   ⎬ irreducible,
paraesophageal   ⎪ strangulated, or
Thoracic stomach   ⎭ causing obstruction
EXCLUDES *congenital diaphragmatic hernia (756.6)*
CC Excl: 551.3, 552.3-552.9, 553.3-553.9

552.8 Hernia of other specified sites, with obstruction `CC`
Any condition classifiable to 553.8 if specified as incarcerated,
irreducible, strangulated, or causing obstruction
CC Excl: 550.00-553.9
AHA: 1Q, '04, 10

552.9 Hernia of unspecified site, with obstruction `CC`
Any condition classifiable to 553.9 if specified as incarcerated,
irreducible, strangulated, or causing obstruction
CC Excl: See code: 552.8

√4ᵗʰ **553 Other hernia of abdominal cavity without mention of
obstruction or gangrene**
EXCLUDES *the listed conditions with mention of:
gangrene (and obstruction) (551.0-551.9)
obstruction (552.0-552.9)*

√5ᵗʰ **553.0 Femoral hernia**

**553.00 Unilateral or unspecified (not specified as
recurrent)**
Femoral hernia NOS

553.01 Unilateral or unspecified, recurrent

553.02 Bilateral (not specified as recurrent)

553.03 Bilateral, recurrent

553.1 Umbilical hernia
Parumbilical hernia
K42.9 Umbilical hernia without obstruction/gangrene `I-10`

√5ᵗʰ **553.2 Ventral hernia**

553.20 Ventral, unspecified
AHA: 2Q, '06, 10; 3Q, '03, 6

553.21 Incisional
Hernia:
postoperative
recurrent, ventral
AHA: 3Q, '03, 6
K43.2 Incisional hernia w/o obstruction or gangrene `I-10`

553.29 Other
Hernia:
epigastric
spigelian

√4ᵗʰ **552 Other hernia of abdominal cavity, with obstruction, but without
mention of gangrene**
EXCLUDES *that with mention of gangrene (551.0-551.9)*

√5ᵗʰ **552.0 Femoral hernia with obstruction**
Femoral hernia specified as incarcerated, irreducible,
strangulated, or causing obstruction

**552.00 Unilateral or unspecified (not specified
as recurrent)** `CC`
CC Excl: 537.89-538, 551.00-551.03, 552.00-552.03,
552.8-553.03, 553.8-553.9

552.01 Unilateral or unspecified, recurrent `CC`
CC Excl: See code 552.00

552.02 Bilateral (not specified as recurrent) `CC`
CC Excl: See code 552.00

552.03 Bilateral, recurrent `CC`
CC Excl: See code 552.00

552.1 Umbilical hernia with obstruction `CC`
Parumbilical hernia specified as incarcerated, irreducible,
strangulated, or causing obstruction
CC Excl: 551.1-551.29, 552.1-552.29, 552.8-552.9, 553.8-553.9

√5ᵗʰ **552.2 Ventral hernia with obstruction**
Ventral hernia specified as incarcerated, irreducible,
strangulated, or causing obstruction

552.20 Ventral, unspecified, with obstruction `CC`
CC Excl: See code 552.1
AHA: 2Q, '11, 18

552.21 Incisional, with obstruction `CC`
Hernia:
postoperative ⎫ specified as incarcerated,
recurrent,   ⎬ irreducible, strangulated,
ventral   ⎭ or causing obstruction
CC Excl: See code 552.1
AHA: 1Q, '12, 8; 3Q, '03, 11

552.29 Other `CC`
Epigastric hernia specified as incarcerated,
irreducible, strangulated, or causing
obstruction
CC Excl: See code 552.1

Diseases of the Digestive System

553.3–557.1

Diaphragmatic Hernias

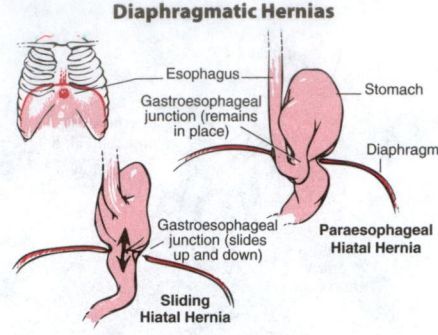

Esophagus

Gastroesophageal junction (remains in place)

Stomach

Diaphragm

Gastroesophageal junction (slides up and down)

Paraesophageal Hiatal Hernia

Sliding Hiatal Hernia

553.3 Diaphragmatic hernia

Hernia: Thoracic stomach
   hiatal (esophageal) (sliding)
   paraesophageal

EXCLUDES *congenital:*
     diaphragmatic hernia (756.6)
     hiatal hernia (750.6)
     esophagocele (530.6)

AHA: 2Q, '01, 6; 1Q, '00, 6

K44.9 Diaphragmatic hernia w/o obstruction/gangrene   `I-10`

553.8 Hernia of other specified sites

Hernia: Hernia:
   ischiatic   pudendal
   ischiorectal   retroperitoneal
   lumbar   sciatic
   obturator
Other abdominal hernia of specified site

EXCLUDES *vaginal enterocele (618.6)*

553.9 Hernia of unspecified site

Enterocele   Hernia:
Epiplocele   intestinal
Hernia: intra-abdominal
   NOS   Rupture (nontraumatic)
   interstitial   Sarcoepiplocele

Noninfectious Enteritis and Colitis (555-558)

✓4ᵗʰ 555 Regional enteritis

INCLUDES Crohn's disease
          granulomatous enteritis

EXCLUDES *ulcerative colitis (556)*

DEF: Inflammation of intestine; classified to site.

TIP: Assign separate code for fistula, if present. Sequence 555 code as first-listed/principal diagnosis (if underlying cause of fistula).

555.0 Small intestine   `CC`

Ileitis: Regional enteritis or Crohn's disease of:
   regional   duodenum
   segmental   ileum
   terminal   jejunum

CC Excl: 555.0-556.9

555.1 Large intestine   `CC`

Colitis: Regional enteritis or Crohn's disease of:
   granulmatous   colon
   regional   large bowel
   transmural   rectum

CC Excl: See code: 555.0

AHA: 3Q, '99, 8

Large Intestine

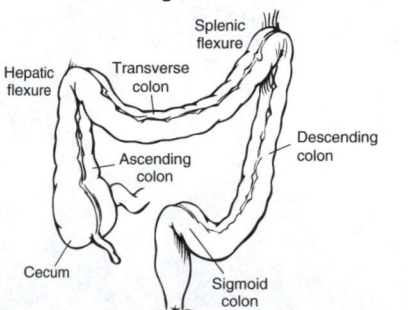

Splenic flexure

Transverse colon

Hepatic flexure

Descending colon

Ascending colon

Cecum

Sigmoid colon

555.2 Small intestine with large intestine   `CC`

Regional ileocolitis

CC Excl: See code: 555.0

AHA: 1Q, '03, 18

555.9 Unspecified site   `CC`

Crohn's disease NOS   Regional enteritis NOS

CC Excl: 555.0-555.9

AHA: 1Q, '09, 5; 2Q, '05, 11; 3Q, '99, 8; 4Q, '97, 42; 2Q, '97, 3

K50.90 Crohns disease unspecified w/o complications   `I-10`

✓4ᵗʰ 556 Ulcerative colitis

DEF: Chronic inflammation of mucosal lining of intestinal tract; may be single area or entire colon.

AHA: 3Q, '99, 8

556.0 Ulcerative (chronic) enterocolitis   `CC`

CC Excl: 555.0-556.9

556.1 Ulcerative (chronic) ileocolitis   `CC`

CC Excl: 555.0-556.9

556.2 Ulcerative (chronic) proctitis   `CC`

CC Excl: 555.0-556.9

556.3 Ulcerative (chronic) proctosigmoiditis   `CC`

CC Excl: 555.0-556.9

556.4 Pseudopolyposis of colon   `CC`

CC Excl: 555.0-556.9

556.5 Left-sided ulcerative (chronic) colitis   `CC`

CC Excl: 555.0-556.9

556.6 Universal ulcerative (chronic) colitis   `CC`

Pancolitis

CC Excl: 555.0-556.9

556.8 Other ulcerative colitis   `CC`

CC Excl: 555.0-556.9

556.9 Ulcerative colitis, unspecified   `CC`

Ulcerative enteritis NOS

CC Excl: 555.0-556.9

AHA: 1Q, '03, 10

K51.90 Ulcerative colitis unspecified w/o complications   `I-10`

✓4ᵗʰ 557 Vascular insufficiency of intestine

EXCLUDES *necrotizing enterocolitis of the newborn (777.50-777.53)*

DEF: Inadequacy of intestinal vessels.

557.0 Acute vascular insufficiency of intestine   `MCC`

Acute:
   hemorrhagic enterocolitis
   ischemic colitis, enteritis, or enterocolitis
   massive necrosis of intestine
Bowel infarction
Embolism of mesenteric artery
Fulminant enterocolitis
Hemorrhagic necrosis of intestine
Infarction of appendices epiploicae
Intestinal gangrene
Intestinal infarction (acute) (agnogenic) (hemorrhagic) (nonocclusive)
Mesenteric infarction (embolic) (thrombotic)
Necrosis of intestine
Terminal hemorrhagic enteropathy
Thrombosis of mesenteric artery

CC Excl: 557.0-557.1

AHA: 3Q, '11, 11; 2Q, '08, 15; 4Q, '01, 53

TIP: Do not assign an additional code for GI bleeding; it is inherent in 557.0.

K55.0 Acute vascular disorders of intestine   `I-10`

557.1 Chronic vascular insufficiency of intestine   `CC`

Angina, abdominal
Chronic ischemic colitis, enteritis, or enterocolitis
Ischemic stricture of intestine
Mesenteric:
   angina
   artery syndrome (superior)
   vascular insufficiency

CC Excl: 557.0-557.9

AHA: 3Q, '96, 9; 4Q, '90, 4; N-D, '86, 11; N-D, '84, 7

`N` Newborn Age: 0   `P` Pediatric Age: 0-17   `M` Maternity Age: 12-55   `A` Adult Age: 15-124   `MCC` Major CC Condition   `CC` CC Condition   `HIV` HIV Related Dx

184 – Volume 1   2015 ICD-9-CM

557.9 Unspecified vascular insufficiency of intestine `CC`
Alimentary pain due to vascular insufficiency
Ischemic colitis, enteritis, or enterocolitis NOS
CC Excl: 557.0-557.9
K55.9 Vascular disorder of intestine unspecified `I-10`

✓4th **558 Other and unspecified noninfectious gastroenteritis and colitis**
EXCLUDES infectious:
colitis, enteritis, or gastroenteritis (009.0-009.1)
diarrhea (009.2-009.3)

558.1 Gastroenteritis and colitis due to radiation `CC`
Radiation enterocolitis
CC Excl: 558.1

558.2 Toxic gastroenteritis and colitis `CC`
Use additional E code to identify cause
CC Excl: 558.2

558.3 Allergic gastroenteritis and colitis
Use additional code to identify type of food allergy
(V15.01-V15.05)
DEF: True immunoglobulin E (IgE)-mediated allergic reaction of the lining of the stomach, intestines, or colon to food proteins; causes nausea, vomiting, diarrhea, and abdominal cramping.
AHA: 4Q, '08, 116; 1Q, '03, 12; 4Q, '00, 42

✓5th **558.4 Eosinophilic gastroenteritis and colitis**
AHA: 4Q, '08, 115-116

558.41 Eosinophilic gastroenteritis
Eosinophilic enteritis

558.42 Eosinophilic colitis

558.9 Other and unspecified noninfectious gastroenteritis and colitis

Colitis
Enteritis
Gastroenteritis } NOS, dietetic, or
Ileitis } noninfectious
Jejunitis
Sigmoiditis

AHA: 3Q, '11, 11; 2Q, '08, 10; 1Q, '08, 10; 3Q, '99, 4, 6; N-D, '87, 7
K52.9 Noninfective gastroenteritis & colitis unspec `I-10`

Other Diseases of Intestines and Peritoneum (560-569)

✓4th **560 Intestinal obstruction without mention of hernia**
EXCLUDES duodenum (537.2-537.3)
inguinal hernia with obstruction (550.1)
intestinal obstruction complicating hernia (552.0-552.9)
mesenteric:
embolism (557.0)
infarction (557.0)
thrombosis (557.0)
neonatal intestinal obstruction (277.01, 777.1-777.2, 777.4)
TIP: If intestinal obstruction is due to abdominal carcinomatosis or Crohn's disease, sequence that condition first.

560.0 Intussusception `CC`
Intussusception (colon) (intestine) (rectum)
Invagination of intestine or colon
EXCLUDES intussusception of appendix (543.9)
CC Excl: 560.0-560.31, 560.39-560.9, 569.87-569.9
AHA: 4Q, '98, 82

560.1 Paralytic ileus `CC`
Adynamic ileus
Ileus (of intestine) (of bowel) (of colon)
Paralysis of intestine or colon
EXCLUDES gallstone ileus (560.31)
DEF: Obstruction of ileus due to inhibited bowel motility.
CC Excl: See code 560.0
AHA: 1Q, '12, 6; J-F, '87, 13
K56.0 Paralytic ileus `I-10`

560.2 Volvulus `MCC`

Knotting
Strangulation } if intestine, bowel, or colon
Torsion
Twist

DEF: Entanglement of bowel; causes obstruction; may compromise bowel circulation.
CC Excl: See code 560.0

✓5th **560.3 Impaction of intestine**

560.30 Impaction of intestine, unspecified `CC`
Impaction of colon
CC Excl: See code 560.0

560.31 Gallstone ileus `CC`
Obstruction of intestine by gallstone
CC Excl: See code 560.0

560.32 Fecal impaction
EXCLUDES constipation (564.00-564.09)
incomplete defecation (787.61)
AHA: 4Q, '10, 87-89
K56.41 Fecal impaction `I-10`

560.39 Other `CC`
Concretion of intestine
Enterolith
CC Excl: See code 560.0
AHA: 4Q, '98, 38
K56.49 Other impaction of intestine `I-10`

✓5th **560.8 Other specified intestinal obstruction**

560.81 Intestinal or peritoneal adhesions with obstruction (postoperative) (postinfection) `CC`
EXCLUDES adhesions without obstruction (568.0)
DEF: Obstruction of peritoneum or intestine due to abnormal union of tissues.
CC Excl: See code 560.0
AHA: 1Q, '10, 11; 4Q, '95, 55; 3Q, '95, 6; N-D, '87, 9
TIP: Do not assign additional code 997.4 Digestive system complications.
K56.5 Intestinal adhes [bands] w/obst (postproc) (postinfec) `I-10`

560.89 Other `CC`
Acute pseudo-obstruction of intestine
Mural thickening causing obstruction
EXCLUDES ischemic stricture of intestine (557.1)
CC Excl: See code 560.0
AHA: 2Q, '97, 3; 1Q, '88, 6

560.9 Unspecified intestinal obstruction `CC`
Enterostenosis

Obstruction
Occlusion } of intestine or colon
Stenosis
Stricture

EXCLUDES congenital stricture or stenosis of intestine (751.1-751.2)
CC Excl: See code 560.0
K56.60 Unspecified intestinal obstruction `I-10`

✓4th **562 Diverticula of intestine**
Use additional code to identify any associated:
peritonitis (567.0-567.9)
EXCLUDES congenital diverticulum of colon (751.5)
diverticulum of appendix (543.9)
Meckel's diverticulum (751.0)
AHA: 4Q, '91, 25; J-Γ, '85, 1

✓5th **562.0 Small intestine**

562.00 Diverticulosis of small intestine (without mention of hemorrhage)
Diverticulosis:
duodenum
ileum } without mention of
jejunum } diverticulitis
DEF: Saclike herniations of mucous lining of small intestine.

562.01 Diverticulitis of small intestine (without mention of hemorrhage) `CC`
Diverticulitis (with diverticulosis):
duodenum
ileum
jejunum
small intestine
DEF: Inflamed saclike herniations of mucous lining of small intestine
CC Excl: 562.00-562.03

Diseases of the Digestive System

562.02–566

562.02 Diverticulosis of small intestine with hemorrhage `MCC`
CC Excl: 251.5, 456.0, 530.20-530.21, 530.7, 530.82, 530.85, 531.00-534.91, 535.01, 535.11, 535.21, 535.31, 535.41, 535.51, 535.61, 537.83, 562.02-562.03, 562.12-562.13, 569.3, 569.85, 578.0-578.9

562.03 Diverticulitis of small intestine with hemorrhage `MCC`
CC Excl: See code 562.02

✓5ᵗʰ **562.1 Colon**

562.10 Diverticulosis of colon (without mention of hemorrhage)
Diverticulosis:
  NOS } without mention of
  intestine (large) } diverticulitis
Diverticular disease (colon) without mention of diverticulitis
DEF: Saclike herniations of mucous lining of large intestine.
AHA: 3Q, '05, 17; 3Q, '02, 15; 4Q, '90, 21; J-F, '85, 5
K57.30 Divrticulos lg intest uns w/o perf/absc w/o bldg `I-10`

562.11 Diverticulitis of colon (without mention of hemorrhage) `CC`
Diverticulitis (with diverticulosis):
  NOS
  colon
  intestine (large)
DEF: Inflamed saclike herniations of mucosal lining of large intestine.
CC Excl: 562.10-562.13
AHA: 1Q, '96, 14; J-F, '85, 5
K57.32 Divrticulit lg intest uns w/o perf/absc w/o bldg `I-10`

562.12 Diverticulosis of colon with hemorrhage `MCC`
CC Excl: See code 562.02

562.13 Diverticulitis of colon with hemorrhage `MCC`
CC Excl: See code 562.02

✓4ᵗʰ **564 Functional digestive disorders, not elsewhere classified**
EXCLUDES functional disorders of stomach (536.0-536.9)
  those specified as psychogenic (306.4)

✓5ᵗʰ **564.0 Constipation**
EXCLUDES fecal impaction (560.32)
  incomplete defecation (787.61)
AHA: 4Q, '01, 45

564.00 Constipation, unspecified
K59.00 Constipation unspecified `I-10`

564.01 Slow transit constipation
DEF: Delay in the transit of fecal material through the colon secondary to smooth muscle dysfunction or decreased peristaltic contractions along the colon; also called colonic inertia or delayed transit.

564.02 Outlet dysfunction constipation
DEF: Failure to relax the paradoxical contractions of the striated pelvic floor muscles during the attempted defecation.

564.09 Other constipation

564.1 Irritable bowel syndrome
Irritable colon   Spastic colon
DEF: Functional gastrointestinal disorder (FGID); symptoms include diarrhea, constipation, abdominal pain, gas, distended abdomen, nausea, vomiting, emotional distress, and depression.
AHA: 1Q, '88, 6
K58.9 Irritable bowel syndrome without diarrhea `I-10`

564.2 Postgastric surgery syndromes
Dumping syndrome   Postgastrectomy syndrome
Jejunal syndrome   Postvagotomy syndrome
EXCLUDES malnutrition following gastrointestinal surgery (579.3)
  postgastrojejunostomy ulcer (534.0-534.9)
AHA: 1Q, '95, 11

564.3 Vomiting following gastrointestinal surgery
Vomiting (bilious) following gastrointestinal surgery

564.4 Other postoperative functional disorders
Diarrhea following gastrointestinal surgery
EXCLUDES colostomy and enterostomy complications (569.60-569.69)

564.5 Functional diarrhea
EXCLUDES diarrhea:
  NOS (787.91)
  psychogenic (306.4)
DEF: Diarrhea with no detectable organic cause.

564.6 Anal spasm
Proctalgia fugax

564.7 Megacolon, other than Hirschsprung's `CC`
Dilatation of colon
EXCLUDES megacolon:
  congenital [Hirschsprung's] (751.3)
  toxic (556)
DEF: Enlarged colon; congenital or acquired; can occur acutely or become chronic.
CC Excl: 564.1-564.9

✓5ᵗʰ **564.8 Other specified functional disorders of intestine**
EXCLUDES malabsorption (579.0-579.9)
AHA: 1Q, '88, 6

564.81 Neurogenic bowel `CC`
DEF: Disorder of bowel due to spinal cord lesion above conus medullaris; symptoms include precipitous micturition, nocturia, headache, sweating, nasal obstruction and spastic contractions.
CC Excl: See code: 564.7
AHA: 1Q, '01, 12; 4Q, '98, 45

564.89 Other functional disorders of intestine
Atony of colon
AHA: 3Q, '12, 22
TIP: Assign for visceral hypersensitivity; an overstimulation response causing extreme pain.

564.9 Unspecified functional disorder of intestine

✓4ᵗʰ **565 Anal fissure and fistula**

565.0 Anal fissure
EXCLUDES anal sphincter tear (healed) (non-traumatic) (old) (569.43)
  traumatic (863.89, 863.99)
DEF: Ulceration of cleft at anal mucosa; causes pain, itching, bleeding, infection, and sphincter spasm; may occur with hemorrhoids.

565.1 Anal fistula
Fistula: Fistula:
  anorectal   rectum to skin
  rectal
EXCLUDES fistula of rectum to internal organs—see Alphabetic Index
  ischiorectal fistula (566)
  rectovaginal fistula (619.1)
DEF: Abnormal opening on cutaneous surface near anus; may lack connection with rectum.
AHA: 1Q, '07, 13

566 Abscess of anal and rectal regions `CC`
Abscess: Cellulitis:
  ischiorectal   anal
  perianal   perirectal
  perirectal   rectal
               Ischiorectal fistula
CC Excl: 566

Anal Fistula and Abscess

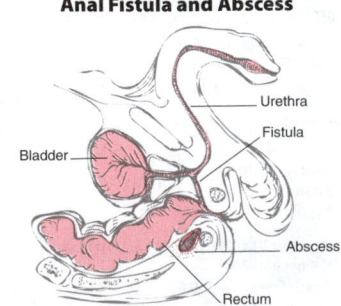

Urethra
Fistula
Bladder
Abscess
Rectum

`N` Newborn Age: 0   `P` Pediatric Age: 0-17   `M` Maternity Age: 12-55   `A` Adult Age: 15-124   `MCC` Major CC Condition   `CC` CC Condition   `HIV` HIV Related Dx

186 – Volume 1   **2015 ICD-9-CM**

Diseases of the Digestive System

567–569.1

✓4th 567 Peritonitis and retroperitoneal infections

EXCLUDES peritonitis:
- benign paroxysmal (277.31)
- pelvic, female (614.5, 614.7)
- periodic familial (277.31)
- puerperal (670.8)
- with or following:
  - abortion (634-638 with .0, 639.0)
  - appendicitis (540.0-540.1)
  - ectopic or molar pregnancy (639.0)

DEF: Inflammation of the peritoneal cavity.

567.0 Peritonitis in infectious diseases classified elsewhere   `MCC`

Code first underlying disease

EXCLUDES peritonitis:
- gonococcal (098.86)
- syphilitic (095.2)
- tuberculous (014.0)

CC Excl: 567.0-567.29, 567.38-567.9, 569.87-569.9

567.1 Pneumococcal peritonitis   `MCC`
CC Excl: See code: 567.0

✓5th 567.2 Other suppurative peritonitis
AHA: 4Q, '05, 74; 2Q, '01, 11, 12; 3Q, '99, 9; 2Q, '98, 19

567.21 Peritonitis (acute) generalized   `MCC`
Pelvic peritonitis, male
CC Excl: See code 567.0
TIP: For pelvic peritonitis in a female patient, refer to code 614.5.

567.22 Peritoneal abscess   `MCC`
Abscess (of):
- abdominopelvic
- mesenteric
- omentum
- peritoneum

Abscess (of):
- retrocecal
- subdiaphragmatic
- subhepatic
- subphrenic

CC Excl: See code 567.0
K65.1 Peritoneal abscess   `I-10`

567.23 Spontaneous bacterial peritonitis   `MCC`
EXCLUDES bacterial peritonitis NOS (567.29)
CC Excl: See code 567.0

567.29 Other suppurative peritonitis   `MCC`
Subphrenic peritonitis
AHA: 2Q, '10, 4
CC Excl: See code 567.0

✓5th 567.3 Retroperitoneal infections
AHA: 4Q, '05, 74

567.31 Psoas muscle abscess   `MCC`
DEF: Infection that extends into or around the psoas muscle that connects the lumbar vertebrae to the femur.
CC Excl: 567.31, 728.0, 728.11-728.3, 728.81, 728.86

567.38 Other retroperitoneal abscess   `MCC`
AHA: 4Q, '05, 77
CC Excl: See code 567.0

567.39 Other retroperitoneal infections   `MCC`
CC Excl: See code 567.0

Psoas Muscle Abscess

✓5th 567.8 Other specified peritonitis
AHA: 4Q, '05, 74

567.81 Choleperitonitis   `MCC`
Peritonitis due to bile
DEF: Inflammation or infection due to presence of bile in the peritoneum resulting from rupture of the bile passages or gallbladder.
CC Excl: See code 567.0

567.82 Sclerosing mesenteritis   `CC`
Fat necrosis of peritoneum
(Idiopathic) sclerosing mesenteric fibrosis
Mesenteric lipodystrophy
Mesenteric panniculitis
Retractile mesenteritis
DEF: Inflammatory processes involving the mesenteric fat; progresses to fibrosis and necrosis of tissue.
CC Excl: See code 567.0
AHA: 4Q, '05, 77

567.89 Other specified peritonitis   `MCC`
Chronic proliferative peritonitis
Mesenteric saponification
Peritonitis due to urine
CC Excl: See code 567.0

567.9 Unspecified peritonitis   `MCC`
Peritonitis NOS   Peritonitis of unspecified cause
CC Excl: See code 567.0
AHA: ▶2Q, '13, 3;◀ 1Q, '04, 10

✓4th 568 Other disorders of peritoneum

568.0 Peritoneal adhesions (postoperative) (postinfection)
Adhesions (of):
- abdominal (wall)
- diaphragm
- intestine
- male pelvis

Adhesions (of):
- mesenteric
- omentum
- stomach
- Adhesive bands

EXCLUDES adhesions:
- pelvic, female (614.6)
- with obstruction:
  - duodenum (537.3)
  - intestine (560.81)

DEF: Abnormal union of tissues in peritoneum.
AHA: 1Q, '12, 8; 2Q, '11, 18; 3Q, '03, 7, 11; 4Q, '95, 55; 3Q, '95, 7; S-O, '85, 11
TIP: Do not assign additional code from subcategory 997.4 Digestive system complications.
K66.0 Peritoneal adhesns (postprocedural) (postinfection)   `I-10`

✓5th 568.8 Other specified disorders of peritoneum

568.81 Hemoperitoneum (nontraumatic)   `MCC`
CC Excl: 568.81

568.82 Peritoneal effusion (chronic)   `CC`
EXCLUDES ascites NOS (789.51-789.59)
DEF: Persistent leakage of fluid within peritoneal cavity.
CC Excl: 568.82

568.89 Other
Peritoneal:
- cyst

Peritoneal:
- granuloma

568.9 Unspecified disorder of peritoneum

✓4th 569 Other disorders of intestine

569.0 Anal and rectal polyp
Anal and rectal polyp NOS
EXCLUDES adenomatous anal and rectal polyp (211.4)

569.1 Rectal prolapse
Procidentia:
- anus (sphincter)
- rectum (sphincter)
Proctoptosis

Prolapse:
- anal canal
- rectal mucosa

EXCLUDES prolapsed hemorrhoids (455.2, 455.5)

✓4th ✓5th   Additional Digit Required   Unacceptable PDx   Manifestation Code   Hospital Acquired Condition   ▶◀ Revised Text   ● New Code   ▲ Revised Code Title

2015 ICD-9-CM   **October 2014 • Volume 1 – 187**

Diseases of the Digestive System

569.2–569.84

Rectum and Anus

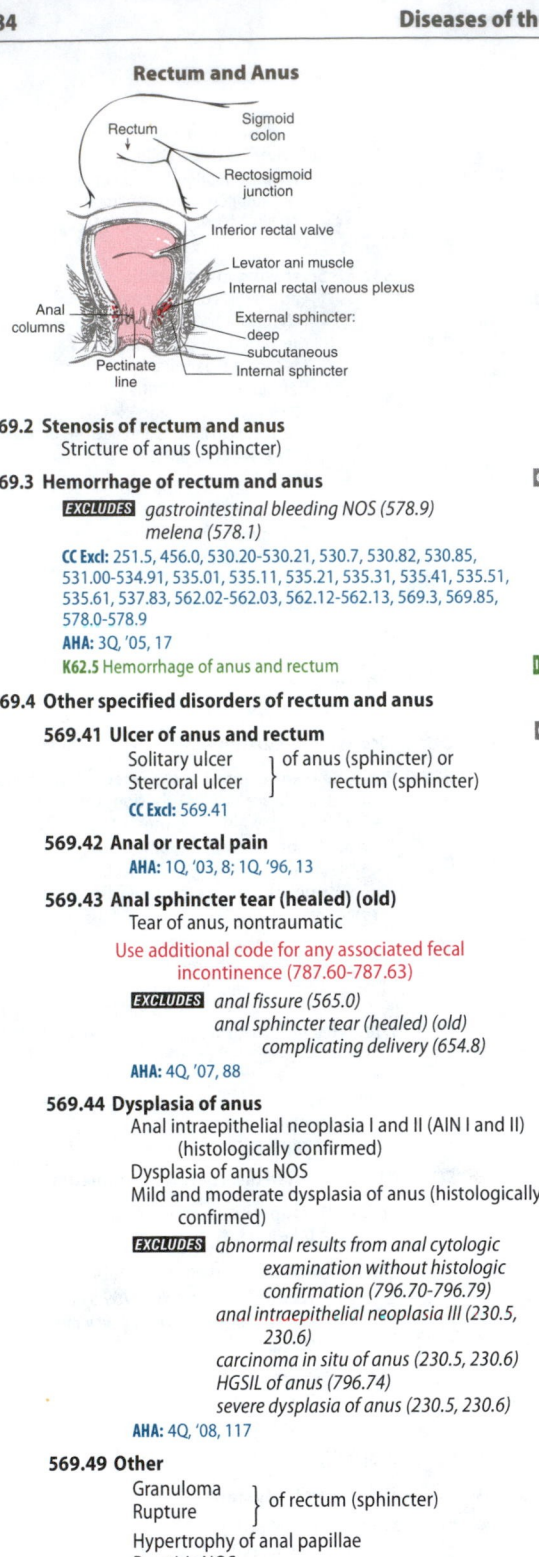

Sigmoid colon
Rectum
Rectosigmoid junction
Inferior rectal valve
Levator ani muscle
Internal rectal venous plexus
External sphincter:
— deep
— subcutaneous
— Internal sphincter
Anal columns
Pectinate line

569.2 Stenosis of rectum and anus
Stricture of anus (sphincter)

569.3 Hemorrhage of rectum and anus   `CC`
> EXCLUDES gastrointestinal bleeding NOS (578.9)
> melena (578.1)

CC Excl: 251.5, 456.0, 530.20-530.21, 530.7, 530.82, 530.85, 531.00-534.91, 535.01, 535.11, 535.21, 535.31, 535.41, 535.51, 535.61, 537.83, 562.02-562.03, 562.12-562.13, 569.3, 569.85, 578.0-578.9
AHA: 3Q, '05, 17

K62.5 Hemorrhage of anus and rectum   `I-10`

`√5th` **569.4 Other specified disorders of rectum and anus**

569.41 Ulcer of anus and rectum   `CC`
> Solitary ulcer } of anus (sphincter) or
> Stercoral ulcer } rectum (sphincter)

CC Excl: 569.41

569.42 Anal or rectal pain
AHA: 1Q, '03, 8; 1Q, '96, 13

569.43 Anal sphincter tear (healed) (old)
Tear of anus, nontraumatic
> Use additional code for any associated fecal incontinence (787.60-787.63)

> EXCLUDES anal fissure (565.0)
> anal sphincter tear (healed) (old) complicating delivery (654.8)

AHA: 4Q, '07, 88

569.44 Dysplasia of anus
Anal intraepithelial neoplasia I and II (AIN I and II) (histologically confirmed)
Dysplasia of anus NOS
Mild and moderate dysplasia of anus (histologically confirmed)
> EXCLUDES abnormal results from anal cytologic examination without histologic confirmation (796.70-796.79)
> anal intraepithelial neoplasia III (230.5, 230.6)
> carcinoma in situ of anus (230.5, 230.6)
> HGSIL of anus (796.74)
> severe dysplasia of anus (230.5, 230.6)

AHA: 4Q, '08, 117

569.49 Other
> Granuloma } of rectum (sphincter)
> Rupture   }
Hypertrophy of anal papillae
Proctitis NOS
> Use additional code for any associated fecal incontinence (787.60-787.63)

> EXCLUDES fistula of rectum to:
> internal organs — see Alphabetic Index
> skin (565.1)
> hemorrhoids (455.0-455.9)

569.5 Abscess of intestine   `CC`
> EXCLUDES appendiceal abscess (540.1)

CC Excl: 569.5
K63.0 Abscess of intestine   `I-10`

`√5th` **569.6 Colostomy and enterostomy complications**
> **DEF:** Complication in a surgically created opening, from intestine to surface skin.
> **AHA:** 4Q, '95, 58
> **TIP:** Do not assign additional code from subcategory 997.4 Digestive system complications.

569.60 Colostomy and enterostomy complication, unspecified

569.61 Infection of colostomy or enterostomy   `CC`
> Use additional code to identify organism (041.00-041.9)
> Use additional code to specify type of infection, such as:
> abscess or cellulitis of abdomen (682.2)
> septicemia (038.0-038.9)

CC Excl: 569.60-569.69

569.62 Mechanical complication of colostomy and enterostomy   `CC`
Malfunction of colostomy and enterostomy
CC Excl: 530.86-530.87, 536.40-536.49, 539.01-539.89, 569.60-569.79, 997.41-997.49, 997.71, 997.91-997.99, 998.81, 998.83-998.9
AHA: 2Q, '05, 11 ; 1Q, '03, 10; 4Q, '98, 44

569.69 Other complication   `CC`
> Fistula   Prolapse
> Hernia
CC Excl: See code: 569.61
AHA: 3Q, '98, 16

`√5th` **569.7 Complications of intestinal pouch**
> **TIP:** Do not assign code from subcategory 997.4 Digestive system complications in addition to a code from this subcategory.

569.71 Pouchitis   `CC`
Inflammation of internal ileoanal pouch
> **DEF:** Inflammatory complication of an existing surgically created ileoanal pouch, resulting in multiple GI complaints, including diarrhea, abdominal pain, rectal bleeding, fecal urgency, or incontinence.
CC Excl: 530.86-530.87, 536.40-536.49, 539.01-539.89, 569.60-569.79, 997.41-997.49, 997.71, 997.91-997.99, 998.81, 998.83-998.9
AHA: 4Q, '09, 94

569.79 Other complications of intestinal pouch   `CC`
CC Excl: See code: 569.71

`√5th` **569.8 Other specified disorders of intestine**
AHA: 4Q, '91, 25

569.81 Fistula of intestine, excluding rectum and anus   `CC`
> Fistula: Fistula:
> abdominal wall   enteroenteric
> enterocolic   ileorectal
> EXCLUDES fistula of intestine to internal organs — see Alphabetic Index
> persistent postoperative fistula (998.6)

CC Excl: 569.81
AHA: 3Q, '99, 8

569.82 Ulceration of intestine   `CC`
> Primary ulcer of intestine   Ulceration of colon
> EXCLUDES that with perforation (569.83)

CC Excl: 569.82

569.83 Perforation of intestine   `MCC`
CC Excl: 569.83
AHA: 2Q, '12, 5

569.84 Angiodysplasia of intestine (without mention of hemorrhage)
> **DEF:** Small vascular abnormalities of the intestinal tract without bleeding problems.
AHA: 3Q, '96, 10; 4Q, '90, 4; 4Q, '90, 21
> **TIP:** Assign code 569.84 or 569.85 for documentation of either intestinal arteriovenous (AV) malformation or angiodysplasia.

`N` Newborn Age: 0   `P` Pediatric Age: 0-17   `M` Maternity Age: 12-55   `A` Adult Age: 15-124   `MCC` Major CC Condition   `CC` CC Condition   `HIV` HIV Related Dx

188 – Volume 1   **2015 ICD-9-CM**

569.85 Angiodysplasia of intestine with hemorrhage `MCC`

DEF: Small vascular abnormalities of the intestinal tract with bleeding problems.

CC Excl: 251.5, 456.0, 530.20-530.21, 530.7, 530.82, 530.85, 531.00-534.91, 535.01, 535.11, 535.21, 535.31, 535.41, 535.51, 535.61, 537.83, 562.02-562.03, 562.12-562.13, 569.3, 569.85, 578.0-578.9

AHA: 3Q, '96, 9

569.86 Dieulafoy lesion (hemorrhagic) of intestine `MCC`

CC Excl: 251.5, 456.0, 530.20-530.21, 530.7, 530.82, 530.85, 531.00-534.91, 535.01, 535.11, 535.21, 535.31, 535.41, 535.51, 535.61, 535.71, 537.83, 562.02-562.03, 562.12-562.13, 569.3, 569.85-569.86, 578.0-578.9

AHA: 4Q, '02, 60-61

569.87 Vomiting of fecal matter

DEF: Spasmodic expulsion of partially digested substance with similar odor to fecal matter; often suggestive of bowel obstruction or other underlying causal pathology.

AHA: 4Q, '09, 105

569.89 Other

Enteroptosis

Granuloma

Prolapse   } of intestine

Pericolitis

Perisigmoiditis

Visceroptosis

EXCLUDES *gangrene of intestine, mesentery, or omentum (557.0)*
hemorrhage of intestine NOS (578.9)
obstruction of intestine (560.0-560.9)

AHA: ▶2Q, '13, 3;◀ 3Q, '96, 9

569.9 Unspecified disorder of intestine

Other Diseases of Digestive System (570-579)

570 Acute and subacute necrosis of liver `MCC`

Acute hepatic failure

Acute or subacute hepatitis, not specified as infective

Necrosis of liver (acute) (diffuse) (massive) (subacute)

Parenchymatous degeneration of liver

Yellow atrophy (liver) (acute) (subacute)

EXCLUDES *icterus gravis of newborn (773.0-773.2)*
serum hepatitis (070.2-070.3)
that with:
    abortion (634-638 with .7, 639.8)
    ectopic or molar pregnancy (639.8)
    pregnancy, childbirth, or the puerperium (646.7)
    viral hepatitis (070.0-070.9)

CC Excl: 570, 573.4-573.9

AHA: 2Q, '05, 9; 1Q, '00, 22

K72.00 Acute and subacute hepatic failure without coma `I-10`

571 Chronic liver disease and cirrhosis

571.0 Alcoholic fatty liver `A`

571.1 Acute alcoholic hepatitis `A`

Acute alcoholic liver disease

AHA: 2Q, '02, 4

Liver

571.2 Alcoholic cirrhosis of liver `A`

Florid cirrhosis   Laennec's cirrhosis (alcoholic)

DEF: Fibrosis and dysfunction of liver; due to alcoholic liver disease.

AHA: 1Q, '11, 23; 3Q, '07, 7; 2Q, '07, 6; 2Q, '02, 4; 1Q, '02, 3; N-D, '85, 14

TIP: For a patient admitted for bleeding esophageal varices due to alcoholic liver cirrhosis, sequence the liver cirrhosis first.

K70.30 Alcoholic cirrhosis of liver without ascites `I-10`

571.3 Alcoholic liver damage, unspecified `A`

571.4 Chronic hepatitis

EXCLUDES *viral hepatitis (acute) (chronic) (070.0-070.9)*

571.40 Chronic hepatitis, unspecified

571.41 Chronic persistent hepatitis

571.42 Autoimmune hepatitis

AHA: 4Q, '08, 120

571.49 Other

Chronic hepatitis: Recurrent hepatitis
active
aggressive

AHA: 3Q, '99, 19; N-D, '85, 14

571.5 Cirrhosis of liver without mention of alcohol

Cirrhosis of liver: Cirrhosis of liver:
NOS   posthepatitic
cryptogenic   postnecrotic
macronodular   Healed yellow atrophy (liver)
micronodular   Portal cirrhosis

Code first, if applicable, viral hepatitis (acute) (chronic) (070.0-070.9)

DEF: Fibrosis and dysfunction of liver; not alcohol related.

AHA: 1Q, '11, 23; 3Q, '07, 7; 2Q, '07, 5

TIP: For a patient admitted for bleeding esophageal varices due to liver cirrhosis, sequence the liver cirrhosis first.

571.6 Biliary cirrhosis

Chronic nonsuppurative   Cirrhosis:
     destructive cholangitis   cholangitic
                       cholestatic

571.8 Other chronic nonalcoholic liver disease

Chronic yellow atrophy (liver)

Fatty liver, without mention of alcohol

AHA: 2Q, '96, 12

571.9 Unspecified chronic liver disease without mention of alcohol

572 Liver abscess and sequelae of chronic liver disease

572.0 Abscess of liver `MCC`

EXCLUDES *amebic liver abscess (006.3)*

CC Excl: 006.3, 572.0-572.1, 573.8-573.9

572.1 Portal pyemia `MCC`

Phlebitis of portal vein   Pylephlebitis
Portal thrombophlebitis   Pylethrombophlebitis

DEF: Inflammation of portal vein or branches; may be due to intestinal disease; symptoms include fever, chills, jaundice, sweating, and abscess in various body parts.

CC Excl: See code 572.0

572.2 Hepatic encephalopathy `MCC`

Hepatic coma   Portal-systemic encephalopathy
Hepatocerebral intoxication

EXCLUDES *hepatic coma associated with viral hepatitis — see category 070*

CC Excl: 572.2, 573.8-573.9

AHA: 2Q, '07, 5; 2Q, '05, 9; 1Q, '02, 3; 3Q, '95, 14

TIP: Do not assign if hepatic coma is documented with viral hepatitis; see category 070 with fourth digit indicating hepatic coma.

K72.91 Hepatic failure unspecified with coma `I-10`

572.3 Portal hypertension `CC`

Use additional code for any associated complications, such as: portal hypertensive gastropathy (537.89)

DEF: Abnormally high blood pressure in the portal vein.

CC Excl: 572.2-572.3, 573.8-573.9

AHA: 3Q, '05, 15

K76.6 Portal hypertension `I-10`

√4ᵗʰ √5ᵗʰ Additional Digit Required   Unacceptable PDx   Manifestation Code   Hospital Acquired Condition   ▶◀ Revised Text   ● New Code   ▲ Revised Code Title

2015 ICD-9-CM   **October 2014 • Volume 1 – 189**

Diseases of the Digestive System

572.4 Hepatorenal syndrome `MCC`

> **EXCLUDES** *that following delivery (674.8)*
> **DEF:** Hepatic and renal failure characterized by cirrhosis with ascites or obstructive jaundice, oliguria, and low sodium concentration.
> **CC Excl:** 572.4, 573.8-573.9
> **AHA:** 3Q, '93, 15

572.8 Other sequelae of chronic liver disease

> **EXCLUDES** *hepatopulmonary syndrome (573.5)*

✓4th **573 Other disorders of liver**

> **EXCLUDES** *amyloid or lardaceous degeneration of liver (277.39)*
> *congenital cystic disease of liver (751.62)*
> *glycogen infiltration of liver (271.0)*
> *hepatomegaly NOS (789.1)*
> *portal vein obstruction (452)*

573.0 Chronic passive congestion of liver

> **DEF:** Blood accumulation in liver tissue.

573.1 Hepatitis in viral diseases classified elsewhere `CC`

> **Code first underlying disease as:**
> Coxsackie virus disease (074.8)
> cytomegalic inclusion virus disease (078.5)
> infectious mononucleosis (075)
> **EXCLUDES** *hepatitis (in):*
> *mumps (072.71)*
> *viral (070.0-070.9)*
> *yellow fever (060.0-060.9)*
> **CC Excl:** 573.1-573.3, 573.8-573.9

573.2 Hepatitis in other infectious diseases classified elsewhere `CC`

> **Code first underlying disease, as:**
> malaria (084.9)
> **EXCLUDES** *hepatitis in:*
> *late syphilis (095.3)*
> *secondary syphilis (091.62)*
> *toxoplasmosis (130.5)*
> **CC Excl:** See code: 573.1

573.3 Hepatitis, unspecified
> Toxic (noninfectious) hepatitis
> Use additional E code to identify cause
> **AHA:** 3Q, '98, 3, 4; 4Q, '90, 26
> **K75.9** Inflammatory liver disease unspecified `I-10`

573.4 Hepatic infarction `MCC`
> **CC Excl:** 570, 573.4-573.9

573.5 Hepatopulmonary syndrome
> **Code first underlying liver disease, such as:**
> alcoholic cirrhosis of liver (571.2)
> cirrhosis of liver without mention of alcohol (571.5)
> **AHA:** 4Q, '11, 127-128

573.8 Other specified disorders of liver
> Hepatoptosis
> **AHA:** ▶1Q, '14, 8◀

573.9 Unspecified disorder of liver

✓4th **574 Cholelithiasis**

> The following fifth-digit subclassification is for use with category 574:
> **0 without mention of obstruction**
> **1 with obstruction**
> **EXCLUDES** *retained cholelithiasis following cholecystectomy (997.41)*

§ ✓5th **574.0 Calculus of gallbladder with acute cholecystitis** `CC`
[0-1]
> Biliary calculus ⎫
> Calculus of cystic duct ⎬ with acute cholecystitis
> Cholelithiasis ⎭
> Any condition classifiable to 574.2 with acute cholecystitis
> **CC Excl: For code 574.00:** 574.00-574.21, 574.40, 574.60-574.61, 574.80-574.81, 575.0-575.12, 575.9, 576.8-576.9; **For code 574.01:** 574.00-574.21, 574.60-574.61, 574.80-574.81, 575.0-575.12, 575.9, 576.8-576.9
> **AHA:** 4Q, '96, 32
> **K80.00** Calculus of GB w/acute cholecystitis w/o obst `I-10`

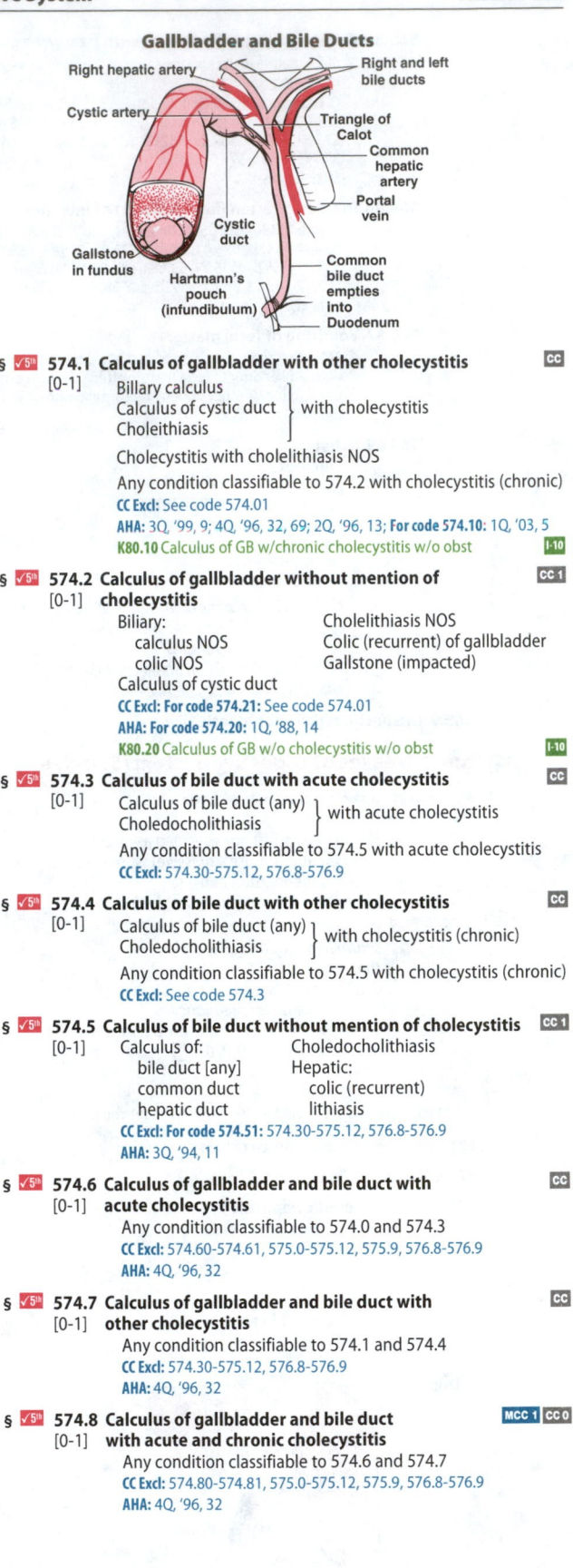

§ ✓5th **574.1 Calculus of gallbladder with other cholecystitis** `CC`
[0-1]
> Biliary calculus ⎫
> Calculus of cystic duct ⎬ with cholecystitis
> Choleithiasis ⎭
> Cholecystitis with cholelithiasis NOS
> Any condition classifiable to 574.2 with cholecystitis (chronic)
> **CC Excl:** See code 574.01
> **AHA:** 3Q, '99, 9; 4Q, '96, 32, 69; 2Q, '96, 13; **For code 574.10:** 1Q, '03, 5
> **K80.10** Calculus of GB w/chronic cholecystitis w/o obst `I-10`

§ ✓5th **574.2 Calculus of gallbladder without mention of** `CC 1`
[0-1] **cholecystitis**
> Biliary: Cholelithiasis NOS
>   calculus NOS   Colic (recurrent) of gallbladder
>   colic NOS   Gallstone (impacted)
> Calculus of cystic duct
> **CC Excl: For code 574.21:** See code 574.01
> **AHA: For code 574.20:** 1Q, '88, 14
> **K80.20** Calculus of GB w/o cholecystitis w/o obst `I-10`

§ ✓5th **574.3 Calculus of bile duct with acute cholecystitis** `CC`
[0-1]
> Calculus of bile duct (any) ⎫
> Choledocholithiasis ⎬ with acute cholecystitis
> Any condition classifiable to 574.5 with acute cholecystitis
> **CC Excl:** 574.30-575.12, 576.8-576.9

§ ✓5th **574.4 Calculus of bile duct with other cholecystitis** `CC`
[0-1]
> Calculus of bile duct (any) ⎫
> Choledocholithiasis ⎬ with cholecystitis (chronic)
> Any condition classifiable to 574.5 with cholecystitis (chronic)
> **CC Excl:** See code 574.3

§ ✓5th **574.5 Calculus of bile duct without mention of cholecystitis** `CC 1`
[0-1]
> Calculus of: Choledocholithiasis
>   bile duct [any]   Hepatic:
>   common duct   colic (recurrent)
>   hepatic duct   lithiasis
> **CC Excl: For code 574.51:** 574.30-575.12, 576.8-576.9
> **AHA:** 3Q, '94, 11

§ ✓5th **574.6 Calculus of gallbladder and bile duct with** `CC`
[0-1] **acute cholecystitis**
> Any condition classifiable to 574.0 and 574.3
> **CC Excl:** 574.60-574.61, 575.0-575.12, 575.9, 576.8-576.9
> **AHA:** 4Q, '96, 32

§ ✓5th **574.7 Calculus of gallbladder and bile duct with** `CC`
[0-1] **other cholecystitis**
> Any condition classifiable to 574.1 and 574.4
> **CC Excl:** 574.30-575.12, 576.8-576.9
> **AHA:** 4Q, '96, 32

§ ✓5th **574.8 Calculus of gallbladder and bile duct** `MCC 1` `CC 0`
[0-1] **with acute and chronic cholecystitis**
> Any condition classifiable to 574.6 and 574.7
> **CC Excl:** 574.80-574.81, 575.0-575.12, 575.9, 576.8-576.9
> **AHA:** 4Q, '96, 32

---

§   Requires fifth digit. Valid digits are in [brackets] under each code. See category 574 for codes and definitions.

`N` Newborn Age: 0   `P` Pediatric Age: 0-17   `M` Maternity Age: 12-55   `A` Adult Age: 15-124   `MCC` Major CC Condition   `CC` CC Condition   `HIV` HIV Related Dx

§ ✓5ᵗʰ **574.9 Calculus of gallbladder and bile duct**   CC 1
[0-1]   **without cholecystitis**
     Any condition classifiable to 574.2 and 574.5
     CC Excl: For code 574.91: 574.30-575.12, 576.8-576.9
     AHA: 4Q, '96, 32

✓4ᵗʰ **575 Other disorders of gallbladder**
     TIP: Do not assign a separate cholecystitis code from category 575 with a code from category 574.

     575.0 Acute cholecystitis   CC
       Abscess of gallbladder ⎫
       Angiocholecystitis   ⎪
       Cholecystitis: ⎪
         emphysematous (acute) ⎬ without mention of
         gangrenous   ⎪   calculus
         suppurative   ⎪
       Empyema of gallbladder ⎪
       Gangrene of gallbladder ⎭

       EXCLUDES *that with:*
         acute and chronic cholecystitis (575.12)
         choledocholithiasis (574.3)
         choledocholithiasis and cholelithiasis (574.6)
         cholelithiasis (574.0)
       CC Excl: 574.60-574.61, 574.80-574.81, 575.0-575.12, 575.9, 576.8-576.9
       AHA: 3Q, '91, 17
       K81.0 Acute cholecystitis   I-10

     ✓5ᵗʰ **575.1 Other cholecystitis**
       Cholecystitis: ⎫
         NOS   ⎬ without mention of calculus
         chronic ⎭

       EXCLUDES *that with:*
         choledocholithiasis (574.4)
         choledocholithiasis and cholelithiasis (574.8)
         cholelithiasis (574.1)
       AHA: 4Q, '96, 32

       575.10 Cholecystitis, unspecified
         Cholecystitis NOS

       575.11 Chronic cholecystitis
         K81.1 Chronic cholecystitis   I-10

       575.12 Acute and chronic cholecystitis   CC
         CC Excl: 575.0-575.12, 575.9, 576.8-576.9
         AHA: 4Q, '97, 52; 4Q, '96, 32

     575.2 Obstruction of gallbladder   CC
       Occlusion ⎫
       Stenosis ⎬ of cystic duct or gallbladder without
       Stricture ⎭   mention of calculus

       EXCLUDES *that with calculus (574.0-574.2 with fifth-digit 1)*
       CC Excl: 575.2-575.9, 576.8-576.9

     575.3 Hydrops of gallbladder   CC
       Mucocele of gallbladder
       DEF: Serous fluid accumulation in bladder.
       CC Excl: See code 575.2
       AHA: 2Q, '89, 13

     575.4 Perforation of gallbladder   MCC
       Rupture of cystic duct or gallbladder
       CC Excl: See code 575.2

     575.5 Fistula of gallbladder   CC
       Fistula: Fistula:
         cholecystoduodenal   cholecystoenteric
       CC Excl: See code 575.2

     575.6 Cholesterolosis of gallbladder
       Strawberry gallbladder
       DEF: Cholesterol deposits in gallbladder tissue.
       AHA: 4Q, '90, 17

     575.8 Other specified disorders of gallbladder
       Adhesions   ⎫
       Atrophy   ⎪
       Cyst   ⎬ of cystic duct or gallbladder
       Hypertrophy   ⎪
       Nonfunctioning ⎪
       Ulcer   ⎭
       Biliary dyskinesia
       EXCLUDES *Hartmann's pouch of intestine (V44.3)*
         nonvisualization of gallbladder (793.3)
       AHA: 4Q, '90, 26; 2Q, '89, 13

     575.9 Unspecified disorder of gallbladder

✓4ᵗʰ **576 Other disorders of biliary tract**
     EXCLUDES *that involving the:*
       cystic duct (575.0-575.9)
       gallbladder (575.0-575.9)

     576.0 Postcholecystectomy syndrome
       DEF: Jaundice or abdominal pain following cholecystectomy.
       AHA: 1Q, '88, 10
       TIP: Do not assign additional code from subcategory 997.4 Digestive system complications.

     576.1 Cholangitis   CC
       Cholangitis: Cholangitis:
         NOS   recurrent
         acute   sclerosing
         ascending   secondary
         chronic   stenosing
         primary   suppurative
       CC Excl: 576.1, 576.8-576.9
       AHA: 2Q, '99, 13
       K83.0 Cholangitis   I-10

     576.2 Obstruction of bile duct   MCC
       Occlusion ⎫
       Stenosis ⎬ of bile duct, except cystic duct, without
       Stricture ⎭   mention of calculus

       EXCLUDES *congenital (751.61)*
         that with calculus (574.3-574.5 with fifth-digit 1)
       CC Excl: 574.31, 574.41, 574.51, 576.2, 576.8-576.9, 751.61
       AHA: 3Q, '03, 17-18; 1Q, '01, 8; 2Q, '99, 13
       K83.1 Obstruction of bile duct   I-10

     576.3 Perforation of bile duct   MCC
       Rupture of bile duct, except cystic duct
       CC Excl: 576.3-576.4, 576.8-576.9

     576.4 Fistula of bile duct   CC
       Choledochoduodenal fistula
       CC Excl: See code: 576.3

     576.5 Spasm of sphincter of Oddi

     576.8 Other specified disorders of biliary tract
       Adhesions   ⎫
       Atrophy   ⎪
       Cyst   ⎬ of bile duct (any)
       Hypertrophy   ⎪
       Nonfunctioning ⎪
       Ulcer   ⎭
       EXCLUDES *congenital choledochal cyst (751.69)*
       AHA: ▶1Q, '14, 8;◀ 3Q, '03, 17; 2Q, '99, 14

     576.9 Unspecified disorder of biliary tract

---

§   Requires fifth digit. Valid digits are in [brackets] under each code. See category 574 for codes and definitions.

✓4ᵗʰ ✓5ᵗʰ Additional Digit Required   Unacceptable PDx   Manifestation Code   Hospital Acquired Condition   ▶◀ Revised Text   ● New Code   ▲ Revised Code Title

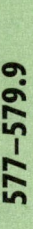

Diseases of the Digestive System

577–579.9

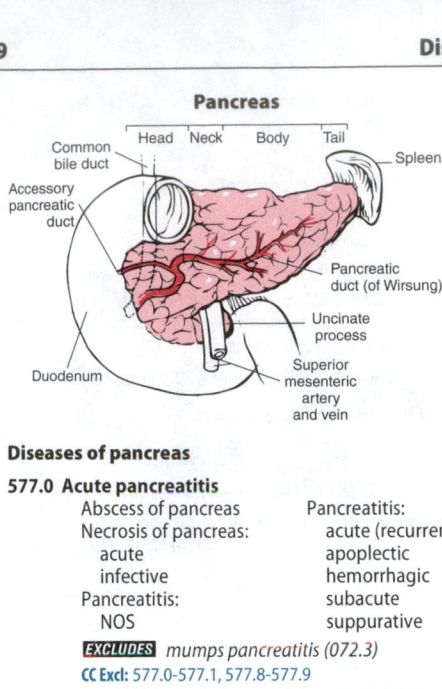

Pancreas

Head   Neck   Body   Tail

Common bile duct

Accessory pancreatic duct

Spleen

Pancreatic duct (of Wirsung)

Uncinate process

Duodenum

Superior mesenteric artery and vein

√4ᵗʰ **577   Diseases of pancreas**

577.0   Acute pancreatitis   `MCC`

Abscess of pancreas   Pancreatitis:
Necrosis of pancreas: acute (recurrent)
   acute   apoplectic
   infective   hemorrhagic
Pancreatitis: subacute
   NOS   suppurative

EXCLUDES   *mumps pancreatitis (072.3)*

CC Excl: 577.0-577.1, 577.8-577.9

AHA: 3Q, '99, 9; 2Q, '98, 19; 2Q, '96, 13; 2Q, '89, 9

K85.0 Idiopathic acute pancreatitis   `I-10`

577.1   Chronic pancreatitis   `CC`

Chronic pancreatitis: Pancreatitis:
   NOS   painless
   infectious   recurrent
   interstitial   relapsing

CC Excl: 251.8, 577.0-577.9

AHA: 1Q, '01, 8; 2Q, '96, 13; 3Q, '94, 11

K86.1 Other chronic pancreatitis   `I-10`

577.2   Cyst and pseudocyst of pancreas   `CC`

CC Excl: 577.2-577.9

K86.2 Cyst of pancreas   `I-10`

577.8   Other specified diseases of pancreas

Atrophy
Calculus
Cirrhosis   } of pancreas
Fibrosis

Pancreatic: Pancreatolithiasis
   infantilism
   necrosis:
     NOS
     aseptic
     fat

EXCLUDES   *fibrocystic disease of pancreas(277.00-277.09)*
         islet cell tumor of pancreas (211.7)
         pancreatic steatorrhea (579.4)

AHA: 1Q, '01, 8

577.9   Unspecified disease of pancreas

√4ᵗʰ **578   Gastrointestinal hemorrhage**

EXCLUDES   *that with mention of:*
     angiodysplasia of stomach and duodenum (537.83)
     angiodysplasia of intestine (569.85)
     diverticulitis, intestine:
       large (562.13)
       small (562.03)
     diverticulosis, intestine:
       large (562.12)
       small (562.02)
     gastritis and duodenitis (535.0-535.6)
     ulcer:
       duodenal, gastric, gastrojejunal or peptic
       (531.00-534.91)

AHA: 2Q, '92, 9; 4Q, '90, 20

578.0   Hematemesis   `CC`

Vomiting of blood

CC Excl: 251.5, 456.0, 530.20-530.21, 530.7, 530.82, 530.85, 531.00-534.91, 535.01, 535.11, 535.21, 535.31, 535.41, 535.51, 535.61, 537.83, 562.02-562.03, 562.12-562.13, 569.3, 569.85, 578.0-578.9

AHA: 2Q, '02, 4

578.1   Blood in stool   `CC`

Melena

EXCLUDES   *melena of the newborn (772.4, 777.3)*
         occult blood (792.1)

CC Excl: See code 578.0

AHA: ▶4Q, '13, 83; 3Q, '13, 9;◄ 2Q, '06, 17; 2Q, '92, 8

K92.1 Melena   `I-10`

578.9   Hemorrhage of gastrointestinal tract, unspecified   `CC`

Gastric hemorrhage   Intestinal hemorrhage

CC Excl: See code 578.0

AHA: 4Q, '06, 91; 3Q, '05, 17; N-D, '86, 9

TIP: Assign 578.9 if the physician does not establish a causal link between GI bleeding and any possible causes found on endoscopy.

K92.2 Gastrointestinal hemorrhage unspecified   `I-10`

√4ᵗʰ **579   Intestinal malabsorption**

579.0   Celiac disease

Celiac: Gee (-Herter) disease
   crisis   Gluten enteropathy
   infantilism   Idiopathic steatorrhea
   rickets   Nontropical sprue

DEF: Malabsorption syndrome due to gluten consumption; symptoms include fetid, bulky, frothy, oily stools, distended abdomen, gas, asthenia, electrolyte depletion and vitamin B, D and K deficiency.

579.1   Tropical sprue   `CC`

Sprue: Tropical steatorrhea
   NOS
   tropical

DEF: Diarrhea, occurs in tropics; may be due to enteric infection and malnutrition.

CC Excl: 277.03, 579.0-579.9

579.2   Blind loop syndrome   `CC`

Postoperative blind loop syndrome

DEF: Obstruction or impaired passage in small intestine due to alterations, from strictures or surgery; causes stasis, abnormal bacterial flora, diarrhea, weight loss, multiple vitamin deficiency, and megaloblastic anemia.

CC Excl: See code: 579.1

TIP: Do not assign additional code from subcategory 997.4 Digestive system complications.

579.3   Other and unspecified postsurgical nonabsorption   `CC`

Hypoglycemia   } following gastrointestinal
Malnutrition   surgery

CC Excl: 579.3-579.9

AHA: 4Q, '03, 104

579.4   Pancreatic steatorrhea   `CC`

DEF: Excess fat in feces due to absence of pancreatic secretions in intestine.

CC Excl: See code: 579.1

579.8   Other specified intestinal malabsorption   `CC`

Enteropathy: Steatorrhea (chronic)
   exudative
   protein-losing

CC Excl: See code: 579.1

AHA: 1Q, '88, 6

579.9   Unspecified intestinal malabsorption   `CC`

Malabsorption syndrome NOS

CC Excl: See code: 579.1

AHA: 2Q, '11, 15; 4Q, '04, 59

`N` Newborn Age: 0   `P` Pediatric Age: 0-17   `M` Maternity Age: 12-55   `A` Adult Age: 15-124   `MCC` Major CC Condition   `CC` CC Condition   `HIV` HIV Related Dx

10. Diseases of the Genitourinary System (580-629)

Nephritis, Nephrotic Syndrome, and Nephrosis (580-589)

EXCLUDES hypertensive chronic kidney disease (403.00-403.91, 404.00-404.93)

☑4ᵗʰ **580 Acute glomerulonephritis**

    INCLUDES acute nephritis

    DEF: Acute, severe inflammation in tuft of capillaries that filter the kidneys.

    580.0 With lesion of proliferative glomerulonephritis   `MCC`

        Acute (diffuse) proliferative glomerulonephritis
        Acute poststreptococcal glomerulonephritis

        CC Excl: 016.00-016.06, 016.30-016.36, 016.90-016.96, 017.90-017.96, 098.10, 098.19, 098.30-098.31, 098.89, 112.2, 131.00, 131.8-131.9, 249.40-249.41, 249.80-249.91, 250.40-250.43, 250.80-250.93, 274.10, 274.19, 277.88, 580.0-591, 593.0-593.2, 593.89-593.9, 599.70-599.9

    580.4 With lesion of rapidly progressive glomerulonephritis   `MCC`

        Acute nephritis with lesion of necrotizing glomerulitis

        DEF: Acute glomerulonephritis; progresses to ESRD with diffuse epithelial proliferation.

        CC Excl: See code 580.0

☑5ᵗʰ   **580.8 With other specified pathological lesion in kidney**

        580.81 *Acute glomerulonephritis in diseases classified elsewhere*   `MCC`

            Code first underlying disease, as:
                infectious hepatitis (070.0-070.9)
                mumps (072.79)
                subacute bacterial endocarditis (421.0)
                typhoid fever (002.0)

            CC Excl: See code 580.0

        580.89 Other   `MCC`

            Glomerulonephritis, acute, with lesion of:
                exudative nephritis
                interstitial (diffuse) (focal) nephritis

            CC Excl: 016.00-016.06, 016.30-016.36, 016.90-016.96, 017.90-017.96, 098.10, 098.19, 098.30-098.31, 098.89, 112.2, 131.00, 131.8-131.9, 274.10, 274.19, 277.88, 580.0-591, 593.0-593.2, 593.89-593.9, 599.70-599.9

    580.9 Acute glomerulonephritis with unspecified pathological lesion in kidney   `MCC`

        Glomerulonephritis
          NOS
          hemorrhagic   } specified as acute
        Nephritis
        Nephropathy

        CC Excl: See code: 580.0

☑4ᵗʰ **581 Nephrotic syndrome**

    DEF: Disease process marked by symptoms such as extensive edema, notable proteinuria, hypoalbuminemia, and susceptibility to intercurrent infections.

    581.0 With lesion of proliferative glomerulonephritis   `CC`

        CC Excl: 016.00-016.06, 016.30-016.36, 016.90-016.96, 017.90-017.96, 098.10, 098.19, 098.30-098.31, 098.89, 112.2, 131.00, 131.8-131.9, 249.40-249.41, 249.80-249.91, 250.40-250.43, 250.80-250.93, 274.10, 274.19, 277.88, 580.0-591, 593.0-593.2, 593.89-593.9, 599.70-599.9

Kidney

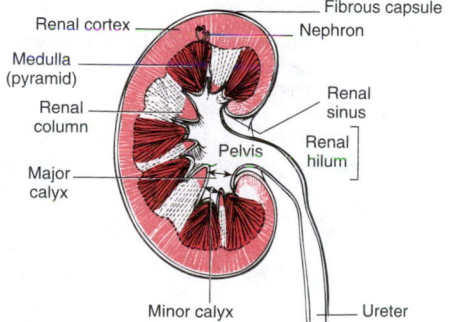

581.1 With lesion of membranous glomerulonephritis   `CC`

    Epimembranous nephritis
    Idiopathic membranous glomerular disease
    Nephrotic syndrome with lesion of:
        focal glomerulosclerosis
        sclerosing membranous glomerulonephritis
        segmental hyalinosis

    CC Excl: See code: 581.0

581.2 With lesion of membranoproliferative glomerulonephritis   `CC`

    Nephrotic syndrome with lesion (of):
        endothelial
        hypocomplementemic persistent
        lobular   } glomerulonephritis
        mesangiocapillary
        mixed membranous and proliferative

    DEF: Glomerulonephritis combined with clinical features of nephrotic syndrome; characterized by uneven thickening of glomerular capillary walls and mesangial cell increase; slowly progresses to ESRD.

    CC Excl: See code: 581.0

581.3 With lesion of minimal change glomerulonephritis   `CC`

    Foot process disease
    Lipoid nephrosis
    Minimal change:
        glomerular disease
        glomerulitis
        nephrotic syndrome

    CC Excl: See code: 581.0

    AHA: 1Q, '07, 23

☑5ᵗʰ **581.8 With other specified pathological lesion in kidney**

    581.81 *Nephrotic syndrome in diseases classified elsewhere*   `CC`

        Code first underlying disease, as:
            amyloidosis (277.30-277.39)
            diabetes mellitus (249.4, 250.4)
            malaria (084.9)
            polyarteritis (446.0)
            systemic lupus erythematosus (710.0)

        EXCLUDES nephrosis in epidemic hemorrhagic fever (078.6)

        CC Excl: See code: 581.0

        AHA: 3Q, '91, 8, 12; S-O, '85, 3

    581.89 Other   `CC`

        Glomerulonephritis with edema and lesion of:
            exudative nephritis
            interstitial (diffuse) (focal) nephritis

        CC Excl: See code: 581.0

581.9 Nephrotic syndrome with unspecified pathological lesion in kidney   `CC`

    Glomerulonephritis with edema NOS
    Nephritis:
        nephrotic NOS
        with edema NOS
    Nephrosis NOS
    Renal disease with edema NOS

    CC Excl: See code: 581.0

Nephron

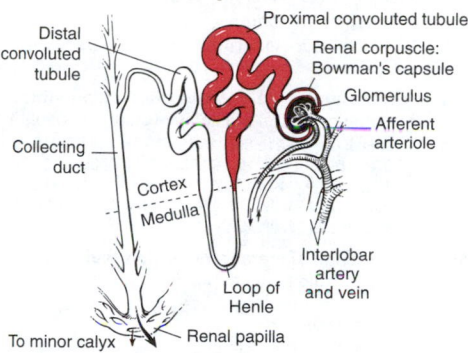

☑4ᵗʰ ☑5ᵗʰ Additional Digit Required   Unacceptable PDx   Manifestation Code   Hospital Acquired Condition   ►◄ Revised Text   ● New Code   ▲ Revised Code Title

2015 ICD-9-CM   **Volume 1 – 193**

Diseases of the Genitourinary System

582–583.9

√4ᵗʰ **582   Chronic glomerulonephritis**

INCLUDES   chronic nephritis

DEF: Slow progressive type of nephritis characterized by inflammation of the capillary loops in the glomeruli of the kidney, which leads to renal failure.

582.0   With lesion of proliferative glomerulonephritis   CC

Chronic (diffuse) proliferative glomerulonephritis

CC Excl: 016.00-016.06, 016.30-016.36, 016.90-016.96, 017.90-017.96, 078.6, 098.10, 098.19, 098.30-098.31, 098.89, 112.2, 131.00, 131.8-131.9, 249.40-249.41, 249.80-249.91, 250.40-250.43, 250.80-250.93, 274.10, 274.19, 580.0-584.9, 586-591, 593.0-593.2, 593.89-593.9, 599.70-599.9

582.1   With lesion of membranous glomerulonephritis   CC

Chronic glomerulonephritis:

     membranous

     sclerosing

Focal glomerulosclerosis

Segmental hyalinosis

CC Excl: See code: 582.0

AHA: S-O, '84, 16

582.2   With lesion of membranoproliferative glomerulonephritis   CC

Chronic glomerulonephritis:

     endothelial

     hypocomplementemic persistent

     lobular

     membranoproliferative

     mesangiocapillary

     mixed membranous and proliferative

DEF: Chronic glomerulonephritis with mesangial cell proliferation.

CC Excl: See code: 582.0

582.4   With lesion of rapidly progressive glomerulonephritis   CC

Chronic nephritis with lesion of necrotizing glomerulitis

DEF: Chronic glomerulonephritisrapidly progresses to ESRD; marked by diffuse epithelial proliferation.

CC Excl: See code: 582.0

√5ᵗʰ **582.8   With other specified pathological lesion in kidney**

582.81   *Chronic glomerulonephritis in diseases classified elsewhere*   CC

Code first underlying disease, as:

     amyloidosis (277.30-277.39)

     systemic lupus erythematosus (710.0)

CC Excl: See code: 582.0

582.89   Other   CC

Chronic glomerulonephritis with lesion of:

     exudative nephritis

     interstitial (diffuse) (focal) nephritis

CC Excl: See code: 582.0

582.9   Chronic glomerulonephritis with unspecified pathological lesion in kidney   CC

Glomerulonephritis:

     NOS

     hemorrhagic   } specified as chronic

Nephritis

Nephropathy

CC Excl: See code: 582.0

AHA: 2Q, '01, 12

√4ᵗʰ **583   Nephritis and nephropathy, not specified as acute or chronic**

INCLUDES   "renal disease" so stated, not specified as acute or chronic but with stated pathology or cause

583.0   With lesion of proliferative glomerulonephritis   CC

Proliferative:

     glomerulonephritis (diffuse) NOS

     nephritis NOS

     nephropathy NOS

CC Excl: See code: 582.0

583.1   With lesion of membranous glomerulonephritis   CC

Membranous:

     glomerulonephritis NOS

     nephritis NOS

Membranous nephropathy NOS

DEF: Kidney inflammation or dysfunction with deposits on glomerular capillary basement membranes.

CC Excl: See code: 582.0

N05.2   Uns nephritic syndr w/ diffuse membranous gln   I-10

583.2   With lesion of membranoproliferative glomerulonephritis   CC

Membranoproliferative:

     glomerulonephritis NOS

     nephritis NOS

     nephropathy NOS

Nephritis NOS, with lesion of:

     hypocomplementemic

       persistent

     lobular

     mesangiocapillary   } glomerulonephritis

     mixed membranous and

       proliferative

DEF: Kidney inflammation or dysfunction with mesangial cell proliferation.

CC Excl: See code: 582.0

583.4   With lesion of rapidly progressive glomerulonephritis   MCC

Necrotizing or rapidly progressive:

     glomerulitis NOS

     glomerulonephritis NOS

     nephritis NOS

     nephropathy NOS

Nephritis, unspecified, with lesion of necrotizing glomerulitis

DEF: Kidney inflammation or dysfunction; rapidly progresses to ESRD marked by diffuse epithelial proliferation.

CC Excl: 016.00-016.06, 016.30-016.36, 016.90-016.96, 017.90-017.96, 098.10, 098.19, 098.30-098.31, 098.89, 112.2, 131.00, 131.8-131.9, 249.40-249.41, 249.80-249.91, 250.40-250.43, 250.80-250.93, 274.10, 274.19, 277.88, 580.0-591, 593.0-593.2, 593.89-593.9, 599.70-599.9

583.6   With lesion of renal cortical necrosis   MCC

Nephritis, NOS   } with (renal) cortical necrosis

Nephropathy NOS

Renal cortical necrosis NOS

CC Excl: 277.88, 583.6, 588.81-588.89

583.7   With lesion of renal medullary necrosis   CC

Nephritis, NOS   } with (renal) medullary

Nephropathy NOS   [papillary] necrosis

CC Excl: 277.88, 583.7, 588.81-588.89

√5ᵗʰ **583.8   With other specified pathological lesion in kidney**

583.81   *Nephritis and nephropathy, not specified as acute or chronic, in diseases classified elsewhere*

Code first underlying disease, as:

     amyloidosis (277.30-277.39)

     diabetes mellitus (249.4, 250.4)

     gonococcal infection (098.19)

     Goodpasture's syndrome (446.21)

     systemic lupus erythematosus (710.0)

     tuberculosis (016.0)

EXCLUDES   *gouty nephropathy (274.10)*

     syphilitic nephritis (095.4)

AHA: ▶2Q, '13, 6;◄ 2Q, '12, 19; 2Q, '03, 7; 3Q, '91, 8; S-O, '85, 3

583.89   Other

Glomerulitis

Glomerulonephritis   } with lesions of:

Nephritis   exudative nephritis

Nephropathy   interstitial nephritis

Renal disease

583.9   With unspecified pathological lesion in kidney

Glomerulitis

Glomerulonephritis   } NOS

Nephritis

Nephropathy

EXCLUDES   *nephropathy complicating pregnancy, labor, or the puerperium (642.0-642.9, 646.2)*

     renal disease NOS with no stated cause (593.9)

N   Newborn Age: 0   P   Pediatric Age: 0-17   M   Maternity Age: 12-55   A   Adult Age: 15-124   MCC   Major CC Condition   CC   CC Condition   HIV   HIV Related Dx

☑4ᵗʰ **584 Acute kidney failure**

INCLUDES acute renal failure

EXCLUDES *following labor and delivery (669.3)*
posttraumatic (958.5)
that complicating:
abortion (634-638 with .3, 639.3)
ectopic or molar pregnancy (639.3)

DEF: State resulting from increasing urea and related substances from the blood (azotemia), often with urine output of less than 500 ml per day.
AHA: 2Q, '11, 15; 3Q, '10, 15; 1Q, '93, 18; 2Q, '92, 5; 4Q, '92, 22
TIP: Report acute renal failure separately when documented in addition to or association with hypertensive renal disease.

584.5 Acute kidney failure with lesion of tubular necrosis MCC
Lower nephron nephrosis
Renal failure with (acute) tubular necrosis
Tubular necrosis:
NOS
acute

DEF: Acute decline in kidney efficiency with destruction of tubules.
CC Excl: 249.40-249.41, 249.80-249.91, 250.40-250.43, 250.80-250.93, 274.10, 274.19, 277.88, 580.0-591, 593.0-593.2, 593.89-593.9, 599.70-599.9, 753.0-753.3, 753.9

N17.0 Acute renal failure with tubular necrosis I-10

584.6 Acute kidney failure with lesion of renal cortical necrosis MCC

DEF: Acute decline in kidney efficiency with destruction of renal tissues that filter blood.
CC Excl: See code: 584.5

584.7 Acute kidney failure with lesion of renal medullary [papillary] necrosis MCC
Necrotizing renal papillitis

DEF: Acute decline in kidney efficiency with destruction of renal tissues that collect urine.
CC Excl: See code: 584.5

584.8 Acute kidney failure with other specified pathological lesion in kidney CC

CC Excl: 249.40-249.41, 249.80-249.91, 250.40-250.43, 250.80-250.93, 274.10, 274.19, 277.88, 580.0-591, 593.0-593.2, 593.89-593.9, 599.70-599.9
AHA: 3Q, '11, 16-17; N-D, '85, 1

584.9 Acute kidney failure, unspecified CC
Acute kidney injury (nontraumatic)

EXCLUDES *traumatic kidney injury (866.00-866.13)*

CC Excl: See code: 584.5
AHA: 3Q, '11, 16-17; 4Q, '09, 98; 4Q, '08, 192; 4Q, '07, 97; 2Q, '05, 18; 2Q, '03, 7; 1Q, '03, 22; 3Q, '02, 21, 28; 2Q, '01, 14; 1Q, '00, 22; 3Q, '96, 9; 4Q, '88, 1

N17.9 Acute renal failure unspecified I-10

☑4ᵗʰ **585 Chronic kidney disease [CKD]**
Chronic uremia

Code first hypertensive chronic kidney disease, if applicable, (403.00-403.91, 404.00-404.93)

Use additional code to identify kidney transplant status, if applicable (V42.0)

Use additional code to identify manifestation as:
uremic:
neuropathy (357.4)
pericarditis (420.0)

AHA: 4Q, '06, 84-86; 4Q, '05, 68, 77; 1Q, '04, 5; 4Q, '03, 61, 111; 2Q, '03, 7; 2Q, '01, 12, 13; 1Q, '01, 3; 4Q, '98, 55; 3Q, '98, 6, 7; 2Q, '98, 20; 3Q, '96, 9; 1Q, '93, 18; 3Q, '91, 8; 4Q, '89, 1; N-D, '85, 15; S-O, '84, 3

585.1 Chronic kidney disease, Stage I
DEF: Some kidney damage; normal or slightly increased GFR (> 90).

585.2 Chronic kidney disease, Stage II (mild)
DEF: Kidney damage with mild decrease in GFR (60–89).

585.3 Chronic kidney disease, Stage III (moderate)
DEF: Kidney damage with moderate decrease in GFR (30–59).
AHA: ▶2Q, '13, 13;◀ 4Q, '05, 69
N18.3 Chronic kidney disease stage 3 (moderate) I-10

585.4 Chronic kidney disease, Stage IV (severe) CC
DEF: Kidney damage with severe decrease in GFR (15–29).
CC Excl: See code: 584.5
N18.4 Chronic kidney disease stage 4 (severe) I-10

585.5 Chronic kidney disease, Stage V CC
EXCLUDES *chronic kidney disease, stage V requiring chronic dialysis (585.6)*
DEF: Kidney failure with GFR value of less than 15.
AHA: ▶2Q, '13, 6;◀ 4Q, '10, 137
CC Excl: See code 584.5

585.6 End stage renal disease MCC
Chronic kidney disease requiring chronic dialysis
DEF: Federal government indicator of a stage V CKD patient undergoing treatment by dialysis or transplantation.
CC Excl: 249.40-249.41, 249.80-249.91, 250.40-250.43, 250.80-250.93, 274.10, 274.19, 403.90, 580.0-591, 593.0-593.2, 593.89-593.9, 599.70-599.9, 753.0-753.3, 753.9
AHA: ▶2Q, '13, 5;◀ 3Q, '11,15; 2Q, '11, 6; 3Q '10, 12, 15; 4Q, '08, 193; 1Q, '08, 7; 4Q, '07, 86; 3Q, '07, 5, 9; 4Q, '06, 136; 4Q, '05, 79
N18.6 End stage renal disease I-10

585.9 Chronic kidney disease, unspecified
Chronic renal disease
Chronic renal failure NOS
Chronic renal insufficiency
AHA: 1Q, '08, 10; 2Q, '07, 3; 4Q, '06, 86; 4Q, '05, 79
N18.9 Chronic kidney disease unspecified I-10

586 Renal failure, unspecified
Uremia NOS

EXCLUDES *following labor and delivery (669.3)*
posttraumatic renal failure (958.5)
that complicating:
abortion (634-638 with .3, 639.3)
ectopic or molar pregnancy (639.3)
uremia:
extrarenal (788.9)
prerenal (788.9)

DEF: Renal failure: kidney functions cease; malfunction may be due to inability to excrete metabolized substances or retain level of electrolytes.
DEF: Uremia: excess urea, creatinine and other nitrogenous products of protein and amino acid metabolism in blood due to reduced excretory function in bilateral kidney disease; also called azotemia.
AHA: 3Q, '98, 6; 1Q, '93, 18; 1Q, '88, 3
N19 Unspecified renal failure I-10

587 Renal sclerosis, unspecified
Atrophy of kidney
Contracted kidney
Renal:
cirrhosis
fibrosis
AHA: 4Q, '10, 137

☑4ᵗʰ **588 Disorders resulting from impaired renal function**

588.0 Renal osteodystrophy
Azotemic osteodystrophy
Phosphate-losing tubular disorders
Renal:
dwarfism
infantilism
rickets

DEF: Condition resulting from chronic renal failure results in osteomalacia, osteoporosis or osteosclerosis; an abnormal level of phosphorus in the blood and impaired stimulation of the parathyroid.

588.1 Nephrogenic diabetes insipidus CC
EXCLUDES *diabetes insipidus NOS (253.5)*
DEF: Type of diabetes due to renal tubules inability to reabsorb water; not responsive to vasopressin; may develop into chronic renal insufficiency.
CC Excl: 016.00-016.06, 016.30-016.36, 016.90-016.96, 017.90-017.96, 078.6, 098.10, 098.19, 098.30-098.31, 098.89, 112.2, 131.00, 131.8-131.9, 249.40-249.41, 249.80-249.91, 250.40-250.43, 250.80-250.93, 274.10, 274.19, 580.0-584.9, 585.3-585.6, 586-591, 593.0-593.2, 593.89-593.9, 599.70-599.9

√5th **588.8 Other specified disorders resulting from impaired renal function**

> *EXCLUDES*   *secondary hypertension (405.0-405.9)*

588.81 Secondary hyperparathyroidism (of renal origin)   `CC`

Secondary hyperparathyroidism NOS

DEF: Parathyroid dysfunction caused by chronic renal failure; phosphate clearance is impaired, phosphate is released from bone, vitamin D is not produced, intestinal calcium absorption is low, and blood levels of calcium are lowered causing excessive production of parathyroid hormone.

CC Excl: 016.00-016.06, 016.30-016.36, 016.90-016.96, 017.90-017.96, 078.6, 098.10, 098.19, 098.30-098.31, 098.89, 112.2, 131.00, 131.8-131.9, 249.40-249.41, 249.80-249.91, 250.40-250.43, 250.80-250.93, 274.10, 274.19, 580.0-584.9, 586-588.1, 588.89-591, 593.0-593.2, 593.89-593.9, 599.70-599.9

AHA: 4Q, '04, 58-59

N25.81 Secondary hyperparathyroidism of renal origin   `I-10`

588.89 Other specified disorders resulting from impaired renal function

Hypokalemic nephropathy

588.9 Unspecified disorder resulting from impaired renal function

√4th **589 Small kidney of unknown cause**

589.0 Unilateral small kidney

589.1 Bilateral small kidneys

589.9 Small kidney, unspecified

Other Diseases of Urinary System (590-599)

√4th **590 Infections of kidney**

Use additional code to identify organism, such as Escherichia coli [E. coli] (041.41-041.49)

√5th **590.0 Chronic pyelonephritis**

Chronic pyelitis
Chronic pyonephrosis

Code if applicable, any casual condition first

590.00 Without lesion of renal medullary necrosis

590.01 With lesion of renal medullary necrosis   `CC`

CC Excl: 016.00-016.06, 016.30-016.36, 016.90-016.96, 017.90-017.96, 078.6, 098.10, 098.19, 098.30-098.31, 098.89, 112.2, 131.00, 131.8-131.9, 249.40-249.41, 249.80-249.91, 250.40-250.43, 250.80-250.93, 274.10, 274.19, 580.0-584.9, 586-591, 593.0-593.2, 593.89-593.9, 599.70-599.9, 646.61-646.64

√5th **590.1 Acute pyelonephritis**

Acute pyelitis
Acute pyonephrosis

8 **590.10 Without lesion of renal medullary necrosis**   `CC`

CC Excl: 016.00-016.06, 016.30-016.36, 016.90-016.96, 017.90-017.96, 098.10, 098.19, 098.30-098.31, 098.89, 112.2, 131.00, 131.8-131.9, 249.40-249.41, 249.80-249.91, 250.40-250.43, 250.80-250.93, 274.10, 274.19, 580-591, 593.0-593.2, 593.89-593.9, 599.0, 599.70-599.9

Genitourinary System

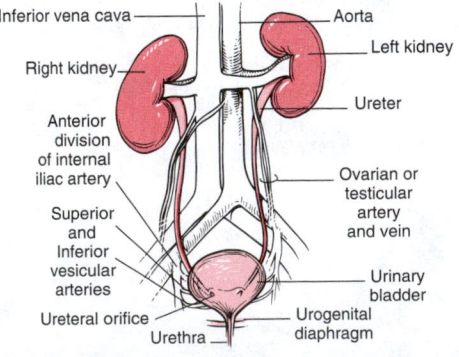

Inferior vena cava — Aorta
Right kidney — Left kidney
Anterior division of internal iliac artery — Ureter
Superior and Inferior vesicular arteries — Ovarian or testicular artery and vein
Ureteral orifice — Urinary bladder
Urethra — Urogenital diaphragm

---

8 **590.11 With lesion of renal medullary necrosis**   `MCC`

CC Excl: See code 590.10

8 **590.2 Renal and perinephric abscess**   `MCC`

Abscess: Carbuncle of kidney
   kidney
   nephritic
   perirenal

CC Excl: See code 590.10

8 **590.3 Pyeloureteritis cystica**   `CC`

Infection of renal pelvis and ureter
Ureteritis cystica

DEF: Inflammation and formation of submucosal cysts in the kidney, pelvis, and ureter.

CC Excl: 016.00-016.06, 016.30-016.36, 016.90-016.96, 017.90-017.96, 098.10, 098.19, 098.30-098.31, 098.89, 112.2, 131.00, 131.8-131.9, 274.10, 274.19, 580.0-591, 593.0-593.2, 593.89-593.9, 599.0, 599.70-599.9

√5th **590.8 Other pyelonephritis or pyonephrosis, not specified as acute or chronic**

8 **590.80 Pyelonephritis, unspecified**   `CC`

Pyelitis NOS
Pyelonephritis NOS

CC Excl: See code 590.3

AHA: 1Q, '98, 10; 4Q, '97, 40

N11.9 Chronic tubulo-interstitial nephritis uns   `I-10`

8 **590.81 *Pyelitis or pyelonephritis in diseases classified elsewhere***   `CC`

Code first underlying disease, as:
tuberculosis (016.0)

CC Excl: See code 590.3

590.9 Infection of kidney, unspecified

> *EXCLUDES*   *urinary tract infection NOS (599.0)*

591 Hydronephrosis   `CC`

Hydrocalycosis   Hydroureteronephrosis
Hydronephrosis

> *EXCLUDES*   *congenital hydronephrosis (753.29)*
>   *hydroureter (593.5)*

DEF: Distention of kidney and pelvis, with urine build-up due to ureteral obstruction; pyonephrosis may result.

CC Excl: See code 590.3

AHA: 3Q, '12, 11-12; 2Q, '98, 9

TIP: Hydronephrosis is not inherent in urinary obstructions and should be coded separately.

N13.30 Unspecified hydronephrosis   `I-10`

√4th **592 Calculus of kidney and ureter**

> *EXCLUDES*   *nephrocalcinosis (275.4)*

592.0 Calculus of kidney

Nephrolithiasis NOS   Staghorn calculus
Renal calculus or stone   Stone in kidney

> *EXCLUDES*   *uric acid nephrolithiasis (274.11)*

AHA: 3Q, '12, 11-12; 1Q, '00, 4

N20.0 Calculus of kidney   `I-10`

592.1 Calculus of ureter   `CC`

Ureteric stone
Ureterolithiasis

CC Excl: 592.0-592.9, 593.3-593.5, 593.89-594.9, 599.60-599.9

AHA: 2Q, '98, 9; 1Q, '98, 10; 1Q, '91, 11

N20.1 Calculus of ureter   `I-10`

592.9 Urinary calculus, unspecified

AHA: 1Q, '98, 10; 4Q, '97, 40

√4th **593 Other disorders of kidney and ureter**

593.0 Nephroptosis

Floating kidney
Mobile kidney

593.1 Hypertrophy of kidney

---

8   CC/MCC except when in combination with 996.64 and POA = N

`N` Newborn Age: 0   `P` Pediatric Age: 0-17   `M` Maternity Age: 12-55   `A` Adult Age: 15-124   `MCC` Major CC Condition   `CC` CC Condition   `HIV` HIV Related Dx

196 – Volume 1   **2015 ICD-9-CM**

593.2 Cyst of kidney, acquired

Cyst (multiple) (solitary) of kidney, not congenital

Peripelvic (lymphatic) cyst

> **EXCLUDES** calyceal or pyelogenic cyst of kidney (591)
> congenital cyst of kidney (753.1)
> polycystic (disease of) kidney (753.1)

DEF: Abnormal, fluid-filled sac in the kidney, not present at birth.

AHA: 4Q, '90, 3

N28.1 Cyst of kidney acquired   I-10

593.3 Stricture or kinking of ureter

Angulation ⎫
            ⎬ of ureter (post-operative)
Constriction ⎭

Stricture of pelviureteric junction

DEF: Stricture or knot in tube connecting kidney to bladder.

AHA: 2Q, '98, 9

593.4 Other ureteric obstruction   CC

Idiopathic retroperitoneal fibrosis

Occlusion NOS of ureter

> **EXCLUDES** that due to calculus (592.1)

CC Excl: 593.3-593.5, 593.89-593.9, 595.0-595.9, 596.89-596.9, 599.0, 599.60-599.9, 753.4-753.5, 753.9, V45.74

AHA: 1Q, '10, 9; 2Q, '97, 4

593.5 Hydroureter   CC

> **EXCLUDES** congenital hydroureter (753.22)
> hydroureteronephrosis (591)

CC Excl: 593.3-593.5, 593.89-593.9, 595.0-595.9, 596.89-596.9, 599.0, 599.60-599.9, 753.4-753.5, 753.9

593.6 Postural proteinuria

Benign postural proteinuria

Orthostatic proteinuria

> **EXCLUDES** proteinuria NOS (791.0)

DEF: Excessive amounts of serum protein in the urine caused by the body position, e.g., orthostatic and lordotic.

√5th 593.7 Vesicoureteral reflux

DEF: Backflow of urine, from bladder into ureter due to obstructed bladder neck.

AHA: 4Q, '94, 42

593.70 Unspecified or without reflux nephropathy

593.71 With reflux nephropathy, unilateral

593.72 With reflux nephropathy, bilateral

593.73 With reflux nephropathy NOS

√5th 593.8 Other specified disorders of kidney and ureter

593.81 Vascular disorders of kidney   CC

Renal (artery):   Renal (artery):
  embolism   thrombosis
  hemorrhage   Renal infarction

CC Excl: 593.70-593.81, 593.9

593.82 Ureteral fistula   CC

Intestinoureteral fistula

> **EXCLUDES** fistula between ureter and female genital
> tract (619.0)

DEF: Abnormal communication, between tube connecting kidney to bladder and another structure.

CC Excl: 593.82-593.9

593.89 Other

Adhesions, kidney or ureter

Periureteritis

Polyp of ureter

Pyelectasia

Ureterocele

> **EXCLUDES** tuberculosis of ureter (016.2)
> ureteritis cystica (590.3)

593.9 Unspecified disorder of kidney and ureter

Acute renal disease   Renal disease NOS

Acute renal insufficiency   Salt-losing nephritis or syndrome

> **EXCLUDES** chronic renal insufficiency (585.9)
> cystic kidney disease (753.1)
> nephropathy, so stated (583.0-583.9)
> renal disease:
>   arising in pregnancy or the puerperium
>   (642.1-642.2, 642.4-642.7, 646.2)
>   not specified as acute or chronic, but with stated
>   pathology or cause (583.0-583.9)

AHA: 4Q, '05, 79; 1Q, '93, 17

N28.9 Disorder of kidney and ureter unspecified   I-10

√4th 594 Calculus of lower urinary tract

594.0 Calculus in diverticulum of bladder

DEF: Stone or mineral deposit in abnormal sac on the bladder wall.

594.1 Other calculus in bladder

Urinary bladder stone

> **EXCLUDES** staghorn calculus (592.0)

DEF: Stone or mineral deposit in bladder.

594.2 Calculus in urethra

DEF: Stone or mineral deposit in tube that empties urine from bladder.

594.8 Other lower urinary tract calculus

AHA: J-F, '85, 16

594.9 Calculus of lower urinary tract, unspecified

> **EXCLUDES** calculus of urinary tract NOS (592.9)

√4th 595 Cystitis

Use additional code to identify organism, such as Escherichia coli [E. coli] (041.41-041.49)

> **EXCLUDES** prostatocystitis (601.3)

8 595.0 Acute cystitis   CC

> **EXCLUDES** trigonitis (595.3)

DEF: Acute inflammation of bladder.

CC Excl: 016.10-016.16, 016.30-016.36, 016.90-016.96, 017.90-017.96, 098.0, 098.11, 098.2, 098.39, 098.89, 112.2, 131.00, 131.8-131.9, 593.3-593.5, 593.89-593.9, 595.0-595.9, 596.89-596.9, 599.0, 599.60-599.9

AHA: 2Q, '99, 15

N30.00 Acute cystitis without hematuria   I-10

595.1 Chronic interstitial cystitis

Hunner's ulcer   Submucous cystitis

Panmural fibrosis of bladder

DEF: Inflamed lesion affecting bladder wall; symptoms include urinary frequency, pain on bladder filling, nocturia, and distended bladder.

595.2 Other chronic cystitis

Chronic cystitis NOS Subacute cystitis

> **EXCLUDES** trigonitis (595.3)

DEF: Persistent inflammation of bladder.

595.3 Trigonitis

Follicular cystitis   Urethrotrigonitis

Trigonitis (acute) (chronic)

DEF: Inflammation of the triangular area of the bladder called the trigonum vesicae.

595.4 Cystitis in diseases classified elsewhere

Code first underlying disease, as:
  actinomycosis (039.8)
  amebiasis (006.8)
  bilharziasis (120.0-120.9)
  Echinococcus infestation (122.3, 122.6)

> **EXCLUDES** cystitis:
>   diphtheritic (032.84)
>   gonococcal (098.11, 098.31)
>   monilial (112.2)
>   trichomonal (131.09)
>   tuberculous (016.1)

√5th 595.8 Other specified types of cystitis

595.81 Cystitis cystica

DEF: Inflammation of the bladder characterized by formation of multiple cysts.

---

8 CC/MCC except when in combination with 996.64 and POA = N

 √4th / √5th Additional Digit Required   Unacceptable PDx   Manifestation Code   Hospital Acquired Condition   ►◄ Revised Text   ● New Code   ▲ Revised Code Title

2015 ICD-9-CM   **Volume 1 – 197**

595.82 Irradiation cystitis   `CC`
Use additional E code to identify cause
DEF: Inflammation of the bladder due to effects of radiation.
CC Excl: see code 595.0

595.89 Other
Abscess of bladder   Cystitis:
Cystitis: emphysematous
  bullous   glandularis

595.9 Cystitis, unspecified

`✓4th` **596 Other disorders of bladder**
Use additional code to identify urinary incontinence (625.6, 788.30-788.39)
AHA: M-A, '87, 10

596.0 Bladder neck obstruction
Contracture (acquired) ⎫ of bladder neck or
Obstruction (acquired) ⎬ vesicourethral
Stenosis (acquired)   ⎭ orifice
EXCLUDES congenital (753.6)
DEF: Bladder outlet and vesicourethral obstruction; occurs as a consequence of benign prostatic hypertrophy or prostatic cancer; may also occur in either sex due to strictures, following radiation, cystoscopy, catheterization, injury, infection, blood clots, bladder cancer, impaction or disease compressing bladder neck.
AHA: 3Q, '02, 28; 2Q, '01, 14; N-D, '86, 10
N32.0 Bladder-neck obstruction   `I-10`

596.1 Intestinovesical fistula   `CC`
Fistula: Fistula:
  enterovesical   vesicoenteric
  vesicocolic   vesicorectal
DEF: Abnormal communication, between intestine and bladder.
CC Excl: 098.0, 098.2, 098.39, 098.89, 596.1-596.2, 596.89-596.9, 599.70-599.9, 788.1

596.2 Vesical fistula, not elsewhere classified   `CC`
Fistula: Fistula:
  bladder NOS   vesicocutaneous
  urethrovesical   vesicoperineal
EXCLUDES fistula between bladder and female genital tract (619.0)
DEF: Abnormal communication between bladder and another structure.
CC Excl: See code: 596.1

596.3 Diverticulum of bladder
Diverticulitis   ⎫ of bladder
Diverticulum (acquired) (false) ⎭
EXCLUDES that with calculus in diverticulum of bladder (594.0)
DEF: Abnormal pouch in bladder wall.

Bladder

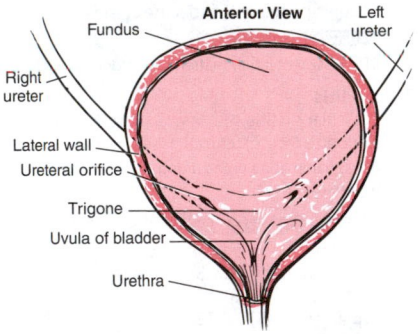

Anterior View
Fundus
Left ureter
Right ureter
Lateral wall
Ureteral orifice
Trigone
Uvula of bladder
Urethra

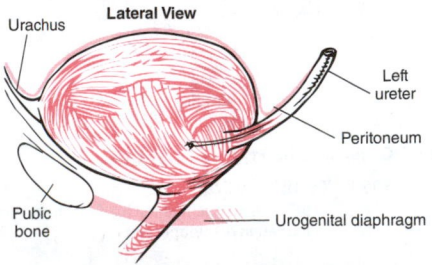

Lateral View
Urachus
Left ureter
Peritoneum
Pubic bone
Urogenital diaphragm

596.4 Atony of bladder
High compliance bladder
Hypotonicity ⎫ of bladder
Inertia   ⎭
EXCLUDES neurogenic bladder (596.54)
DEF: Distended, bladder with loss of expulsive force; linked to CNS disease.

`✓5th` **596.5 Other functional disorders of bladder**
EXCLUDES cauda equina syndrome with neurogenic bladder (344.61)

596.51 Hypertonicity of bladder
Hyperactivity   Overactive bladder
DEF: Abnormal tension of muscular wall of bladder; may appear after surgery of voluntary nerve.
N32.81 Overactive bladder   `I-10`

596.52 Low bladder compliance
DEF: Low bladder capacity; causes increased pressure and frequent urination.

596.53 Paralysis of bladder
DEF: Impaired bladder motor function due to nerve or muscle damage.

596.54 Neurogenic bladder NOS
DEF: Unspecified dysfunctional bladder due to lesion of central, peripheral nervous system; may result in incontinence, residual urine retention, urinary infection, stones and renal failure.
AHA: 1Q, '01, 12
N31.9 Neuromuscular dysfunction of bladder unspecified   `I-10`

596.55 Detrusor sphincter dyssynergia
DEF: Instability of the urinary bladder sphincter muscle associated with urinary incontinence.

596.59 Other functional disorder of bladder
Detrusor instability
DEF: Detrusor instability: instability of bladder; marked by uninhibited contractions often leading to incontinence.

596.6 Rupture of bladder, nontraumatic   `MCC`
CC Excl: 596.6-596.7, 596.89-596.9, 599.70-599.9, 788.1

596.7 Hemorrhage into bladder wall   `CC`
Hyperemia of bladder
EXCLUDES acute hemorrhagic cystitis (595.0)
CC Excl: See code: 596.6

`✓5th` **596.8 Other specified disorders of bladder**
EXCLUDES cystocele, female (618.01-618.02, 618.09, 618.2-618.4)
hernia or prolapse of bladder, female (618.01-618.02, 618.09, 618.2-618.4)
AHA: 4Q, '11, 128-129; J-F, '85, 8

596.81 Infection of cystostomy   `CC`
Use additional code to specify type of infection, such as:
abscess or cellulitis of abdomen (682.2)
septicemia (038.0-038.9)
Use additional code to identify organism (041.00-041.9)
CC Excl: 596.81-596.89, 599.0, 996.30, 996.39, 996.56-996.60, 996.64-996.65, 996.68-996.70, 996.76, 996.79, 997.91-997.99, 998.81, 998.83-998.9
AHA: 4Q, '11, 129

596.82 Mechanical complication of cystostomy   `CC`
Malfunction of cystostomy
CC Excl: 596.81-596.89, 996.39, 996.64-996.65, 996.76, 997.91-997.99, 998.81, 998.83-998.9

596.83 Other complication of cystostomy   `CC`
Fistula
Hernia
Prolapse
CC Excl: 596.81-596.89, 996.30, 996.39, 996.52, 996.55-996.60, 996.64-996.65, 996.68-996.70, 996.76, 996.79, 997.91-997.99, 998.81, 998.83-998.9

596.89 Other specified disorders of bladder
Bladder hemorrhage   Calcified bladder
Bladder hypertrophy   Contracted bladder
AHA: ▶1Q, '13, 5◄

`N` Newborn Age: 0   `P` Pediatric Age: 0-17   `M` Maternity Age: 12-55   `A` Adult Age: 15-124   `MCC` Major CC Condition   `CC` CC Condition   `HIV` HIV Related Dx

198 – Volume 1 • October 2014   2015 ICD-9-CM

596.9 Unspecified disorder of bladder
　　AHA: J-F, '85, 8

✓4ᵗʰ **597 Urethritis, not sexually transmitted, and urethral syndrome**
　　EXCLUDES *nonspecific urethritis, so stated (099.4)*

⁸ **597.0 Urethral abscess**   CC
　　Abscess: Abscess of:
　　　periurethral   Cowper's gland
　　　urethral (gland)   Littré's gland
　　Abscess of: Periurethral cellulitis
　　　bulbourethral gland
　　　　EXCLUDES *urethral caruncle (599.3)*
　　DEF: Pocket of pus in tube that empties urine from the bladder.
　　CC Excl: 098.0, 098.2, 098.39, 098.89, 099.40-099.49, 112.2, 131.00,
　　131.02, 131.8-131.9, 597.0-598.01, 598.8-599.0, 599.60-599.9,
　　607.1-607.83, 607.85-607.9, 608.4-608.81, 608.85, 608.87-608.89,
　　752.61-752.69, 752.81-752.9, 753.6-753.9, 788.1

✓5ᵗʰ **597.8 Other urethritis**

597.80 Urethritis, unspecified

597.81 Urethral syndrome NOS

597.89 Other
　　Adenitis, Skene's glands   Ulcer, urethra (meatus)
　　Cowperitis   Verumontanitis
　　Meatitis, urethral
　　　EXCLUDES *trichomonal (131.02)*

✓4ᵗʰ **598 Urethral stricture**
　　Use additional code to identify urinary incontinence (625.6,
　　　788.30-788.39)
　　INCLUDES pinhole meatus
　　　stricture of urinary meatus
　　EXCLUDES *congenital stricture of urethra and urinary meatus (753.6)*
　　DEF: Narrowing of tube that empties urine from bladder.

✓5ᵗʰ **598.0 Urethral stricture due to infection**

598.00 Due to unspecified infection

598.01 Due to infective diseases classified elsewhere
　　Code first underlying disease, as:
　　　gonococcal infection (098.2)
　　　schistosomiasis (120.0-120.9)
　　　syphilis (095.8)

598.1 Traumatic urethral stricture
　　Stricture of urethra:
　　　late effect of injury
　　　postobstetric
　　　EXCLUDES *postoperative following surgery on genitourinary
　　　　tract (598.2)*

598.2 Postoperative urethral stricture
　　Postcatheterization stricture of urethra
　　AHA: 3Q, '97, 6

598.8 Other specified causes of urethral stricture
　　AHA: N-D, '84, 9

598.9 Urethral stricture, unspecified

✓4ᵗʰ **599 Other disorders of urethra and urinary tract**

⁸ **599.0 Urinary tract infection, site not specified**   CC
　　Use additional code to identify organism, such as Escherichia
　　　coli [E. coli] (041.41-041.49)
　　EXCLUDES *candidiasis of urinary tract (112.2)*
　　　urinary tract infection of newborn (771.82)
　　CC Excl: 098.2, 098.39, 098.89, 099.40-099.49, 112.2, 131.00,
　　131.8-131.9, 590.10-591, 593.89-593.9, 595.0-595.9, 596.81, 599.0,
　　599.60-599.9, 788.1, 996.64
　　AHA: 2Q, '12, 20; 1Q, '12, 11;4Q, '11, 129; 1Q, '10, 9; 3Q, '09, 10-11; 3Q,
　　'05, 12; 2Q, '04, 13; 4Q, '03, 79; 4Q, '99, 6; 2Q, '99, 15;1Q, '98, 5; 2Q, '96,
　　7; 4Q, '96, 33; 2Q, '95, 7; 1Q, '92, 13
　　N39.0 Urinary tract infection site not specified   I-10

599.1 Urethral fistula   CC
　　Fistula: Urinary fistula NOS
　　　urethroperineal
　　　urethrorectal
　　　EXCLUDES *fistula:*
　　　　urethroscrotal (608.89)
　　　　urethrovaginal (619.0)
　　　　urethrovesicovaginal (619.0)
　　CC Excl: 597.0-598.9, 599.1-599.9, 607.1-607.83, 607.85-607.9,
　　608.4-608.81, 608.85, 608.87-608.89, 752.61-752.69, 752.81-752.9,
　　753.9, 788.1
　　AHA: 2Q, '11, 13; 3Q, '97, 6

599.2 Urethral diverticulum
　　DEF: Abnormal pouch in urethral wall.

599.3 Urethral caruncle
　　Polyp of urethra

599.4 Urethral false passage
　　DEF: Abnormal opening in urethra due to surgery; trauma or disease.

599.5 Prolapsed urethral mucosa
　　Prolapse of urethra   Urethrocele
　　　EXCLUDES *urethrocele, female (618.03, 618.09, 618.2-618.4)*

✓5ᵗʰ **599.6 Urinary obstruction**
　　Use additional code to identify urinary incontinence (625.6,
　　　788.30-788.39)
　　EXCLUDES *obstructive nephropathy NOS (593.89)*
　　AHA: 4Q, '05, 80

599.60 Urinary obstruction, unspecified
　　Obstructive uropathy NOS
　　Urinary (tract) obstruction NOS
　　N13.9 Obstructive and reflux uropathy unspec   I-10

599.69 Urinary obstruction, not elsewhere classified
　　Code, if applicable, any causal condition first, such as:
　　　hyperplasia of prostate (600.0-600.9 with
　　　　fifth-digit 1)
　　AHA: 4Q, '06, 93

✓5ᵗʰ **599.7 Hematuria**
　　Hematuria (benign) (essential)
　　　EXCLUDES *hemoglobinuria (791.2)*
　　AHA: 4Q, '08, 121; 1Q, '00, 5; 3Q, '95, 8

599.70 Hematuria, unspecified
　　R31.9 Hematuria unspecified   I-10

599.71 Gross hematuria
　　AHA: 2Q, '10, 3

599.72 Microscopic hematuria

✓5ᵗʰ **599.8 Other specified disorders of urethra and urinary tract**
　　Use additional code to identify urinary incontinence (625.6,
　　　788.30-788.39), if present
　　EXCLUDES *symptoms and other conditions classifiable to
　　　　788.0-788.2, 788.4-788.9, 791.0-791.9*

599.81 Urethral hypermobility
　　DEF: Hyperactive urethra.

599.82 Intrinsic (urethral) sphincter deficiency [ISD]
　　DEF: Malfunctioning urethral sphincter.
　　AHA: 2Q, '96, 15

599.83 Urethral instability
　　DEF: Inconsistent functioning of urethra.

599.84 Other specified disorders of urethra
　　Rupture of urethra   Urethral:
　　　(nontraumatic)   cyst
　　　　　　　　　　　　　　　　granuloma
　　DEF: Rupture of urethra due to herniation or breaking down
　　of tissue; not due to trauma.
　　DEF: Urethral cyst: abnormal sac in urethra; usually fluid
　　filled.
　　DEF: Granuloma: inflammatory cells forming small nodules
　　in urethra.
　　AHA: 1Q, '09, 15

599.89 Other specified disorders of urinary tract

599.9 Unspecified disorder of urethra and urinary tract

---

⁸ CC/MCC except when in combination with 996.64 and POA = N

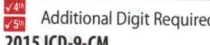

Additional Digit Required   Unacceptable PDx   Manifestation Code   Hospital Acquired Condition   ▶◀ Revised Text   ● New Code   ▲ Revised Code Title

Diseases of the Genitourinary System

600–601.9

Male Pelvic Organs

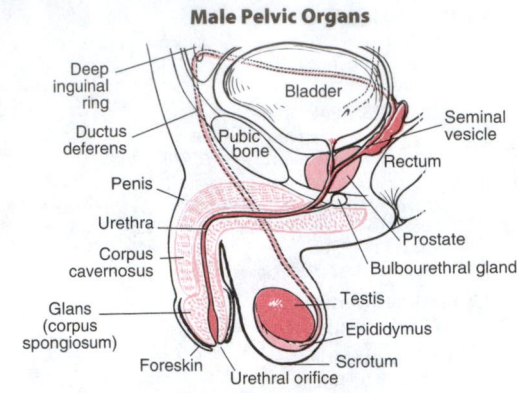

Deep inguinal ring
Bladder
Ductus deferens
Pubic bone
Seminal vesicle
Penis
Rectum
Urethra
Prostate
Corpus cavernosus
Bulbourethral gland
Glans (corpus spongiosum)
Testis
Epididymus
Foreskin
Scrotum
Urethral orifice

Diseases of Male Genital Organs (600-608)

√4th 600 Hyperplasia of prostate

> INCLUDES enlarged prostate
>
> DEF: Fibrostromal proliferation in periurethral glands, causes blood in urine; etiology unknown.
>
> AHA: 3Q, '05, 20; 4Q, '00, 43; 3Q, '94, 12; 3Q, '92, 7; N-D, '86, 10

√5th 600.0 Hypertrophy (benign) of prostate

> Benign prostatic hypertrophy   Smooth enlarged prostate
> Enlargement of prostate   Soft enlarged prostate
>
> AHA: 4Q, '06, 93-95; 3Q, '05, 20; 4Q, '03, 63; 1Q, '03, 6; 3Q, '02, 28; 2Q, '01, 14

> **600.00 Hypertrophy (benign) of prostate without urinary obstruction and other lower urinary tract symptoms [LUTS]** A ♂
>
> > Hypertrophy (benign) of prostate NOS
> >
> > I-10 N40.0 Enlarged prostate without LUTS

> **600.01 Hypertrophy (benign) of prostate with urinary obstruction and other lower urinary tract symptoms [LUTS]** A ♂
>
> > Hypertrophy (benign) of prostate with urinary retention
> >
> > Use additional code to identify symptoms:
> > incomplete bladder emptying (788.21)
> > nocturia (788.43)
> > straining on urination (788.65)
> > urinary frequency (788.41)
> > urinary hesitancy (788.64)
> > urinary incontinence (788.30-788.39)
> > urinary obstruction (599.69)
> > urinary retention (788.20)
> > urinary urgency (788.63)
> > weak urinary stream (788.62)
> >
> > AHA: 4Q, '06, 93-95; 4Q, '03, 64

√5th 600.1 Nodular prostate

> Hard, firm prostate
> Multinodular prostate
>
> EXCLUDES malignant neoplasm of prostate (185)
>
> DEF: Hard, firm nodule in prostate.
>
> AHA: 4Q, '03, 63

> **600.10 Nodular prostate without urinary obstruction** A ♂
>
> > Nodular prostate NOS

> **600.11 Nodular prostate with urinary obstruction** A ♂
>
> > Nodular prostate with urinary retention

√5th 600.2 Benign localized hyperplasia of prostate

> Adenofibromatous hypertrophy of prostate
> Adenoma of prostate
> Fibroadenoma of prostate
> Fibroma of prostate
> Myoma of prostate
> Polyp of prostate
>
> EXCLUDES benign neoplasms of prostate (222.2)
> hypertrophy of prostate (600.00-600.01)
> malignant neoplasm of prostate (185)
>
> DEF: Benign localized hyperplasia clearly defined epithelial tumor.
>
> AHA: 4Q, '06, 93-95; 4Q, '03, 63

> **600.20 Benign localized hyperplasia of prostate without urinary obstruction and other lower urinary tract symptoms [LUTS]** A ♂
>
> > Benign localized hyperplasia of prostate NOS

> **600.21 Benign localized hyperplasia of prostate with urinary obstruction and other lower urinary tract symptoms [LUTS]** A ♂
>
> > Benign localized hyperplasia of prostate with urinary retention
> >
> > Use additional code to identify symptoms:
> > incomplete bladder emptying (788.21)
> > nocturia (788.43)
> > straining on urination (788.65)
> > urinary frequency (788.41)
> > urinary hesitancy (788.64)
> > urinary incontinence (788.30-788.39)
> > urinary obstruction (599.69)
> > urinary retention (788.20)
> > urinary urgency (788.63)
> > weak urinary stream (788.62)

600.3 Cyst of prostate A ♂

> DEF: Sacs of fluid, which differentiate this from either nodular or adenomatous tumors.

√5th 600.9 Hyperplasia of prostate, unspecified

> Median bar
> Prostatic obstruction NOS
>
> AHA: 4Q, '06, 93-95; 4Q, '03, 63

> **600.90 Hyperplasia of prostate, unspecified, without urinary obstruction and other lower urinary tract symptoms [LUTS]** A ♂
>
> > Hyperplasia of prostate NOS

> **600.91 Hyperplasia of prostate, unspecified, with urinary obstruction and other lower urinary tract symptoms [LUTS]** A ♂
>
> > Hyperplasia of prostate, unspecified, with urinary retention
> >
> > Use additional code to identify symptoms:
> > incomplete bladder emptying (788.21)
> > nocturia (788.43)
> > straining on urination (788.65)
> > urinary frequency (788.41)
> > urinary hesitancy (788.64)
> > urinary incontinence (788.30-788.39)
> > urinary obstruction (599.69)
> > urinary retention (788.20)
> > urinary urgency (788.63)
> > weak urinary stream (788.62)

√4th 601 Inflammatory diseases of prostate

> Use additional code to identify organism, such as Staphylococcus (041.1), or Streptococcus (041.0)

601.0 Acute prostatitis CC A ♂

> CC Excl: 098.12, 098.32, 098.89, 112.2, 131.00, 131.03, 131.8-131.9, 600.00-602.9

601.1 Chronic prostatitis A ♂

601.2 Abscess of prostate CC A ♂

> CC Excl: See code: 601.0

601.3 Prostatocystitis A ♂

601.4 *Prostatitis in diseases classified elsewhere* A ♂

> Code first underlying disease, as:
> actinomycosis (039.8)
> blastomycosis (116.0)
> syphilis (095.8)
> tuberculosis (016.5)
>
> EXCLUDES prostatitis:
> gonococcal (098.12, 098.32)
> monilial (112.2)
> trichomonal (131.03)

601.8 Other specified inflammatory diseases of prostate A ♂

> Prostatitis:
> cavitary
> diverticular
> granulomatous

601.9 Prostatitis, unspecified A ♂

> Prostatitis NOS

N Newborn Age: 0   P Pediatric Age: 0-17   M Maternity Age: 12-55   A Adult Age: 15-124   MCC Major CC Condition   CC CC Condition   HIV HIV Related Dx

Common Inguinal Canal Anomalies

✓4ᵗʰ **602 Other disorders of prostate**

602.0 Calculus of prostate 　Ⓐ ♂
　　Prostatic stone
　　DEF: Stone or mineral deposit in prostate.

602.1 Congestion or hemorrhage of prostate 　Ⓐ ♂
　　DEF: Bleeding or fluid collection in prostate.

602.2 Atrophy of prostate 　Ⓐ ♂

602.3 Dysplasia of prostate 　♂
　　Prostatic intraepithelial neoplasia I (PIN I)
　　Prostatic intraepithelial neoplasia II (PIN II)
　　　EXCLUDES *prostatic intraepithelial neoplasia III (PIN III) (233.4)*
　　DEF: Abnormality of shape and size of the intraepithelial tissues of
　　the prostate; premalignant condition characterized by stalks and
　　absence of a basilar cell layer; synonyms are intraductal dysplasia,
　　large acinar atypical hyperplasia, atypical primary hyperplasia,
　　hyperplasia with malignant changes, marked atypia, or duct-acinar
　　dysplasia.
　　AHA: 4Q, '01, 46

602.8 Other specified disorders of prostate 　Ⓐ ♂
　　Fistula
　　Infarction 　} of prostate
　　Stricture
　　Periprostatic adhesions

602.9 Unspecified disorder of prostate 　Ⓐ ♂

✓4ᵗʰ **603 Hydrocele**
　　INCLUDES hydrocele of spermatic cord, testis or tunica vaginalis
　　EXCLUDES *congenital (778.6)*
　　DEF: Circumscribed collection of fluid in tunica vaginalis, spermatic cord or
　　testis.

603.0 Encysted hydrocele 　♂

603.1 Infected hydrocele 　CC ♂
　　Use additional code to identify organism
　　CC Excl: 112.2, 131.00, 131.8-131.9, 603.0-603.9

603.8 Other specified types of hydrocele 　♂

603.9 Hydrocele, unspecified 　♂

✓4ᵗʰ **604 Orchitis and epididymitis**
　　Use additional code to identify organism, such as:
　　　Escherichia coli [E. coli] (041.41-041.49)
　　　Staphylococcus (041.10-041.19)
　　　Streptococcus (041.00-041.09)

604.0 Orchitis, epididymitis, and epididymoorchitis, 　CC ♂
　　with abscess
　　Abscess of epididymis or testis
　　CC Excl: 072.0, 098.13-098.14, 098.33-098.34, 098.89, 112.2, 131.00,
　　131.8-131.9, 604.0-604.99

✓5ᵗʰ **604.9 Other orchitis, epididymitis, and epididymo-orchitis,**
　　without mention of abscess

　　604.90 Orchitis and epididymitis, unspecified 　♂

　　604.91 Orchitis and epididymitis in diseases classified 　♂
　　　elsewhere
　　　Code first underlying disease, as:
　　　　diphtheria (032.89)
　　　　filariasis (125.0-125.9)
　　　　syphilis (095.8)
　　　　　EXCLUDES *orchitis:*
　　　　　　gonococcal (098.13, 098.33)
　　　　　　mumps (072.0)
　　　　　　tuberculous (016.5)
　　　　　　tuberculous epididymitis (016.4)

　　604.99 Other 　♂

605 Redundant prepuce and phimosis 　♂
　　Adherent prepuce　　　Phimosis (congenital)
　　Paraphimosis　　　　　Tight foreskin
　　DEF: Constriction of preputial orifice causing inability of the prepuce to be
　　drawn back over the glans; it may be congenital or caused by infection.
　　AHA: 3Q, '08, 9

✓4ᵗʰ **606 Infertility, male**
　　AHA: 2Q, '96, 9

606.0 Azoospermia 　Ⓐ ♂
　　Absolute infertility
　　Infertility due to:
　　　germinal (cell) aplasia
　　　spermatogenic arrest (complete)
　　DEF: Absence of spermatozoa in the semen or inability to produce
　　spermatozoa.

606.1 Oligospermia 　Ⓐ ♂
　　Infertility due to:
　　　germinal cell desquamation
　　　hypospermatogenesis
　　　incomplete spermatogenic arrest
　　DEF: Insufficient number of sperm in semen.

606.8 Infertility due to extratesticular causes 　Ⓐ ♂
　　Infertility due to:
　　　drug therapy
　　　infection
　　　obstruction of efferent ducts
　　　radiation
　　　systemic disease

606.9 Male infertility, unspecified 　Ⓐ ♂

✓4ᵗʰ **607 Disorders of penis**
　　EXCLUDES *phimosis (605)*

607.0 Leukoplakia of penis 　♂
　　Kraurosis of penis
　　　EXCLUDES *carcinoma in situ of penis (233.5)*
　　　　　　erythroplasia of Queyrat (233.5)
　　DEF: White, thickened patches on glans penis.

607.1 Balanoposthitis 　♂
　　Balanitis
　　Use additional code to identify organism
　　DEF: Inflammation of glans penis and prepuce.

607.2 Other inflammatory disorders of penis 　♂
　　Abscess
　　Boil
　　Carbuncle 　} of corpus cavernosum or
　　Cellulitis 　　　　penis
　　Cavernitis (penis)
　　Use additional code to identify organism
　　　EXCLUDES *herpetic infection (054.13)*

607.3 Priapism 　CC ♂
　　Painful erection
　　DEF: Prolonged penile erection without sexual stimulation.
　　CC Excl: 607.0-607.9

✓5ᵗʰ **607.8 Other specified disorders of penis**

　　607.81 Balanitis xerotica obliterans 　♂
　　　Induratio penis plastica
　　　DEF: Inflammation of the glans penis, caused by stricture of
　　　the opening of the prepuce.

✓4ᵗʰ ✓5ᵗʰ Additional Digit Required　　Unacceptable PDx　　Manifestation Code　　Hospital Acquired Condition　　▶◀ Revised Text　　● New Code　　▲ Revised Code Title

607.82 Vascular disorders of penis   `CC` ♂

Embolisim
Hematoma
  (nontraumatic) } of corpus
Hemorrhage   cavernosum
Thrombosis   or penis

CC Excl: 607.82-607.83

607.83 Edema of penis   ♂
DEF: Fluid retention within penile tissues.

607.84 Impotence of organic origin   `A` ♂
EXCLUDES nonorganic (302.72)
DEF: Physiological cause interfering with erection.
AHA: 3Q, '91, 11
TIP: If impotence is a result of previous radical prostatectomy, report code 997.99 first.

607.85 Peyronie's disease   ♂
DEF: A severe curvature of the erect penis due to fibrosis of the cavernous sheaths.
AHA: 4Q, '03, 64

607.89 Other   ♂
Atrophy
Fibrosis   } of corpus
Hypertrophy   cavernosum
Ulcer (chronic)   or penis

607.9 Unspecified disorder of penis   ♂

608 Other disorders of male genital organs

608.0 Seminal vesiculitis   ♂
Abscess
Cellulitis } of seminal vesicle

Vesiculitis (seminal)
Use additional code to identify organism
EXCLUDES gonococcal infection (098.14, 098.34)
DEF: Inflammation of seminal vesicle.

608.1 Spermatocele   ♂
DEF: Cystic enlargement of the epididymis or the testis; the cysts contain spermatozoa.

608.2 Torsion of testis
DEF: Twisted or rotated testis; may compromise blood flow.

608.20 Torsion of testis, unspecified   `CC` ♂
CC Excl: 608.20-608.24
AHA: 4Q, '06, 95

608.21 Extravaginal torsion of spermatic cord   `CC` ♂
DEF: Torsion of the spermatic cord just below the tunica vaginalis attachments.
CC Excl: See code: 608.20
AHA: 4Q, '06, 95

608.22 Intravaginal torsion of spermatic cord   `CC` ♂
Torsion of spermatic cord NOS
DEF: Torsion within the tunica vaginalis also called the "bell-clapper" anomaly. It usually occurs in older children.
CC Excl: See code: 608.20
AHA: 4Q, '06, 95

608.23 Torsion of appendix testis   `CC` ♂
DEF: Torsion of small solid projection of tissue on the upper outer surface of the testis (hydatid of Morgagni); a remnant of the embryologic Müllerian duct.
CC Excl: See code: 608.20
AHA: 4Q, '06, 95

608.24 Torsion of appendix epididymis   `CC` ♂
DEF: Torsion of small stalked appendage of the head of the epididymis (pedunculated hydatid); a detached embryologic efferent duct.
CC Excl: See code: 608.20
AHA: 4Q, '06, 95

608.3 Atrophy of testis   ♂

608.4 Other inflammatory disorders of male genital organs   ♂
Abscess
Boil   } of scrotum, spermatic cord, testis
Carbuncle   [except abscess], tunica
Cellulitis   vaginalis, or vas deferens
Vasitis
Use additional code to identify organism
EXCLUDES abscess of testis (604.0)

608.8 Other specified disorders of male genital organs

608.81 *Disorders of male genital organs in diseases classified elsewhere*   ♂
Code first underlying disease, as:
  filariasis (125.0-125.9)
  tuberculosis (016.5)

608.82 Hematospermia   ♂
DEF: Presence of blood in the ejaculate; relatively common, affecting men of any age after puberty; cause is often the result of a viral or bacterial infection and inflammation.
AHA: 4Q, '01, 46

608.83 Vascular disorders   ♂
Hematoma (non-   } of seminal vessel, spermatic
  traumatic)   cord, testis, scrotum,
Hemorrhage   tunica vaginalis, or vas
Thrombosis   deferens

Hematocele NOS, male
AHA: 4Q, '03, 110
TIP: Assign for Fournier's gangrene, which is a result of an infection in the genital area.

608.84 Chylocele of tunica vaginalis   ♂
DEF: Chylous effusion into tunica vaginalis; due to infusion of lymphatic fluids.

608.85 Stricture   ♂
Stricture of: Stricture of:
  spermatic cord   vas deferens
  tunica vaginalis

608.86 Edema   ♂

608.87 Retrograde ejaculation   ♂
DEF: Condition where the semen travels to the bladder rather than out through the urethra due to damaged nerves causing the bladder neck to remain open during ejaculation.
AHA: 4Q, '01, 46

608.89 Other   ♂
Atrophy
Fibrosis   } of seminal vessel, spermatic
Hypertrophy   cord, testis, scrotum,
Ulcer   tunica vaginalis, or vas
            deferens
EXCLUDES atrophy of testis (608.3)

608.9 Unspecified disorder of male genital organs   ♂

Disorders of Breast (610-612)

610 Benign mammary dysplasias

610.0 Solitary cyst of breast
Cyst (solitary) of breast

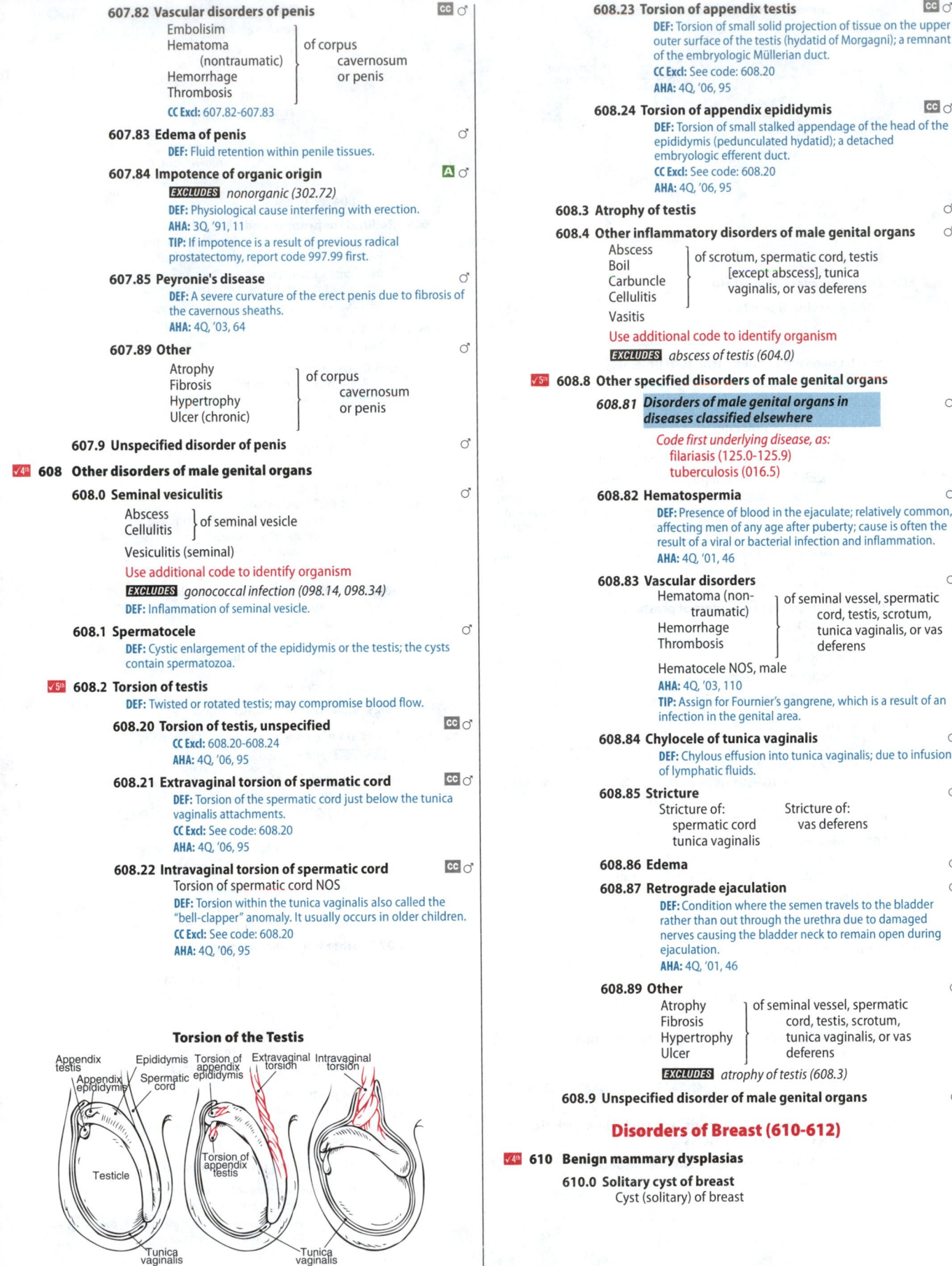

Torsion of the Testis

Appendix testis · Epididymis · Torsion of appendix epididymis · Extravaginal torsion · Intravaginal torsion
Appendix epididymis · Spermatic cord
Testicle
Torsion of appendix testis
Tunica vaginalis · Tunica vaginalis

`N` Newborn Age: 0   `P` Pediatric Age: 0-17   `M` Maternity Age: 12-55   `A` Adult Age: 15-124   `MCC` Major CC Condition   `CC` CC Condition   `HIV` HIV Related Dx

202 – Volume 1   2015 ICD-9-CM

610.1 Diffuse cystic mastopathy   [A]
Chronic cystic mastitis
Cystic breast
Fibrocystic disease of
breast
DEF: Extensive formation of nodular cysts in breast tissue; symptoms include tenderness, change in size and hyperplasia of ductal epithelium.
AHA: 2Q, '06, 10
TIP: Assign in addition to screening mammography V code; is a normal variant, commonly found in normal breasts and not a pathological condition.

610.2 Fibroadenosis of breast
Fibroadenosis of breast: Fibroadenosis of breast:
   NOS   diffuse
   chronic   periodic
   cystic   segmental
DEF: Non-neoplastic nodular condition of breast.

610.3 Fibrosclerosis of breast
DEF: Fibrous tissue in breast.

610.4 Mammary duct ectasia
Comedomastitis   Mastitis:
Duct ectasia   periductal
   plasma cell
DEF: Atrophy of duct epithelium; causes distended collecting ducts of mammary gland, drying up of breast secretion, intraductal inflammation and periductal and interstitial chronic inflammatory reaction.

610.8 Other specified benign mammary dysplasias
Mazoplasia   Sebaceous cyst of breast
AHA: 2Q, '09, 9

610.9 Benign mammary dysplasia, unspecified

✓4ᵗʰ 611 Other disorders of breast
EXCLUDES *that associated with lactation or the puerperium (675.0-676.9)*

611.0 Inflammatory disease of breast
Abscess (acute) (chronic) (nonpuerperal) of:
   areola
   breast
Mammillary fistula
Mastitis (acute) (subacute) (nonpuerperal):
   NOS
   infective
   retromammary
   submammary
EXCLUDES *carbuncle of breast (680.2)*
chronic cystic mastitis (610.1)
neonatal infective mastitis (771.5)
thrombophlebitis of breast [Mondor's disease] (451.89)
AHA: ▶2Q, '13, 23◀

611.1 Hypertrophy of breast
Gynecomastia
Hypertrophy of breast:
   NOS
   massive pubertal
EXCLUDES *breast engorgement in newborn (778.7)*
disproportion of reconstructed breast (612.1)

611.2 Fissure of nipple

611.3 Fat necrosis of breast
Fat necrosis (segmental) of breast
Code first breast necrosis due to breast graft (996.79)
DEF: Splitting of neutral fats in adipose tissue cells as a result of trauma; a firm circumscribed mass is then formed in the breast.

611.4 Atrophy of breast

611.5 Galactocele
DEF: Milk-filled cyst in breast due to blocked duct.

611.6 Galactorrhea not associated with childbirth
DEF: Flow of milk not associated with childbirth or pregnancy.

✓5ᵗʰ 611.7 Signs and symptoms in breast
611.71 Mastodynia
Pain in breast

611.72 Lump or mass in breast
AHA: 4Q, '09, 106; 2Q, '03, 4-5
TIP: Do not assign if the underlying cause of the breast lump or mass is determined and documented during the episode of care.

611.79 Other
Induration of breast
Inversion of nipple
Nipple discharge
Retraction of nipple

✓5ᵗʰ 611.8 Other specified disorders of breast
AHA: 4Q, '08, 121-122

611.81 Ptosis of breast   [A]
EXCLUDES *ptosis of native breast in relation to reconstructed breast (612.1)*

611.82 Hypoplasia of breast   [A]
Micromastia
EXCLUDES *congenital absence of breast (757.6)*
hypoplasia of native breast in relation to reconstructed breast (612.1)

611.83 Capsular contracture of breast implant   [A]
TIP: Do not assign additional code from category 996 Complications peculiar to certain specified procedures.

611.89 Other specified disorders of breast
Hematoma (nontraumatic) of breast
Infarction of breast
Occlusion of breast duct
Subinvolution of breast (postlactational) (postpartum)

611.9 Unspecified breast disorder

✓4ᵗʰ 612 Deformity and disproportion of reconstructed breast
AHA: 4Q, '08, 123

612.0 Deformity of reconstructed breast   [A]
Contour irregularity in reconstructed breast
Excess tissue in reconstructed breast
Misshapen reconstructed breast

612.1 Disproportion of reconstructed breast   [A]
Breast asymmetry between native breast and reconstructed breast
Disproportion between native breast and reconstructed breast

Inflammatory Disease of Female Pelvic Organs (614-616)
Use additional code to identify organism, such as Staphylococcus (041.1), or Streptococcus (041.0)
EXCLUDES *that associated with pregnancy, abortion, childbirth, or the puerperium (630-676.9)*

✓4ᵗʰ 614 Inflammatory disease of ovary, fallopian tube, pelvic cellular tissue, and peritoneum
EXCLUDES *endometritis (615.0-615.9)*
major infection following delivery (670.0-670.8)
that complicating:
abortion (634-638 with .0, 639.0)
ectopic or molar pregnancy (639.0)
pregnancy or labor (646.6)

614.0 Acute salpingitis and oophoritis   [CC] ♀
Any condition classifiable to 614.2, specified as acute or subacute
DEF: Acute inflammation of ovary and fallopian tube.
CC Excl: 016.60-016.96, 017.90-017.96, 098.15-098.17, 098.35-098.37, 098.89, 112.2, 131.00, 131.8-131.9, 614.0-615.9, 616.81-616.9, 625.70, 625.79-625.9, 629.20-629.9, 752.81-752.9

614.1 Chronic salpingitis and oophoritis   ♀
Hydrosalpinx
Salpingitis:
   follicularis
   isthmica nodosa
Any condition classifiable to 614.2, specified as chronic
DEF: Persistent inflammation of ovary and fallopian tube.

614.2 Salpingitis and oophoritis not specified as acute, subacute, or chronic ♀

Abscess (of):
  fallopian tube
  ovary
  tubo-ovarian
Oophoritis
Perioophoritis

Perisalpingitis
Pyosalpinx
Salpingitis
Salpingo-oophoritis
Tubo-ovarian inflammatory disease

EXCLUDES gonococcal infection (chronic) (098.37)
    acute (098.17)
    tuberculous (016.6)

AHA: 2Q, '91, 5

614.3 Acute parametritis and pelvic cellulitis CC ♀
Acute inflammatory pelvic disease
Any condition classifiable to 614.4, specified as acute

DEF: Parametritis: inflammation of the parametrium; pelvic cellulitis is a synonym for parametritis.

CC Excl: See code 614.0

614.4 Chronic or unspecified parametritis and pelvic cellulitis ♀

Abscess (of):
  broad ligament
  parametrium
  pelvis, femal
  pouch of Douglas } chronic or NOS

Chronic inflammatory pelvic disease
Pelvic cellulitis, female

EXCLUDES tuberculous (016.7)

614.5 Acute or unspecified pelvic peritonitis, female MCC ♀

CC Excl: See code 614.0

AHA: 4Q, '05, 74

TIP: For pelvic peritonitis in a male patient, refer to code 567.21.

614.6 Pelvic peritoneal adhesions, female (postoperative) (postinfection) ♀

Adhesions:
  peritubal
  tubo-ovarian

Use additional code to identify any associated infertility (628.2)

DEF: Fibrous scarring abnormally joining structures within abdomen.

AHA: 2Q, '11, 19; 3Q, '03, 6; 1Q, '03, 4; 3Q, '95, 7; 3Q, '94, 12

N73.6 Female pelvic peritoneal adhesions (postinfective) I-10

614.7 Other chronic pelvic peritonitis, female CC ♀

EXCLUDES tuberculous (016.7)

CC Excl: See code: 614.0

614.8 Other specified inflammatory disease of female pelvic organs and tissues ♀

614.9 Unspecified inflammatory disease of female pelvic organs and tissues ♀
Pelvic infection or inflammation, female NOS
Pelvic inflammatory disease [PID]

√4th **615 Inflammatory diseases of uterus, except cervix**

EXCLUDES following delivery (670.0-670.8)
    hyperplastic endometritis (621.30-621.35)
    that complicating:
      abortion (634-638 with .0, 639.0)
      ectopic or molar pregnancy (639.0)
      pregnancy or labor (646.6)

615.0 Acute CC ♀
Any condition classifiable to 615.9, specified as acute or subacute

CC Excl: 016.60-016.96, 017.90-017.96, 098.15-098.17, 098.35-098.37, 098.89, 112.2, 131.00, 131.8-131.9, 614.0-616.0, 616.81-616.9, 621.8-621.9, 625.70, 625.79-625.9, 629.20-629.9, 752.81-752.9

615.1 Chronic ♀
Any condition classifiable to 615.9, specified as chronic

615.9 Unspecified inflammatory disease of uterus ♀
Endometritis
Endomyometritis
Intrauterine infection
Metritis

Myometritis
Perimetritis
Pyometra
Uterine abscess

N71.9 Inflammatory disease of uterus unspecified I-10

√4th **616 Inflammatory disease of cervix, vagina, and vulva** ♀

EXCLUDES that complicating:
    abortion (634-638 with .0, 639.0)
    ectopic or molar pregnancy (639.0)
    pregnancy, childbirth, or the puerperium (646.6)

616.0 Cervicitis and endocervicitis ♀
Cervicitis
Endocervicitis } with or without mention of erosion or ectropion
Nabothian (gland) cyst or follicle

EXCLUDES erosion or ectropion without mention of cervicitis (622.0)

N72 Inflammatory disease of cervix uteri I-10

√5th **616.1 Vaginitis and vulvovaginitis**

EXCLUDES vulvar vestibulitis (625.71)

DEF: Inflammation or infection of vagina or external female genitalia.

616.10 Vaginitis and vulvovaginitis, unspecified ♀
Vaginitis:
  NOS
  postirradiation

Vulvitis NOS
Vulvovaginitis NOS

Use additional code to identify organism, such as:
  Escherichia coli [E. coli] (041.41-041.49)
  Staphylococcus (041.10-041.19)
  Streptococcus (041.00-041.09)

EXCLUDES noninfective leukorrhea (623.5)
    postmenopausal or senile vaginitis (627.3)

616.11 Vaginitis and vulvovaginitis in diseases classified elsewhere ♀

Code first underlying disease, as:
  pinworm vaginitis (127.4)

EXCLUDES herpetic vulvovaginitis (054.11)
    monilial vulvovaginitis (112.1)
    trichomonal vaginitis or vulvovaginitis (131.01)

616.2 Cyst of Bartholin's gland ♀
Bartholin's duct cyst

DEF: Fluid-filled sac within gland of vaginal orifice.

616.3 Abscess of Bartholin's gland CC ♀
Vulvovaginal gland abscess

CC Excl: 016.70-016.96, 017.90-017.96, 112.1-112.2, 131.00-131.01, 131.8-131.9, 616.10-616.9, 624.3-624.9, 625.70-625.9, 629.20-629.9, 752.81-752.9

616.4 Other abscess of vulva CC ♀
Abscess
Carbuncle } of vulva
Furuncle

CC Excl: See code 616.3

√5th **616.5 Ulceration of vulva**

616.50 Ulceration of vulva, unspecified ♀
Ulcer NOS of vulva

616.51 Ulceration of vulva in diseases classified elsewhere ♀

Code first underlying disease, as:
  Behçet's syndrome (136.1)
  tuberculosis (016.7)

EXCLUDES vulvar ulcer (in):
    gonococcal (098.0)
    herpes simplex (054.12)
    syphilitic (091.0)

Female Genitourinary System

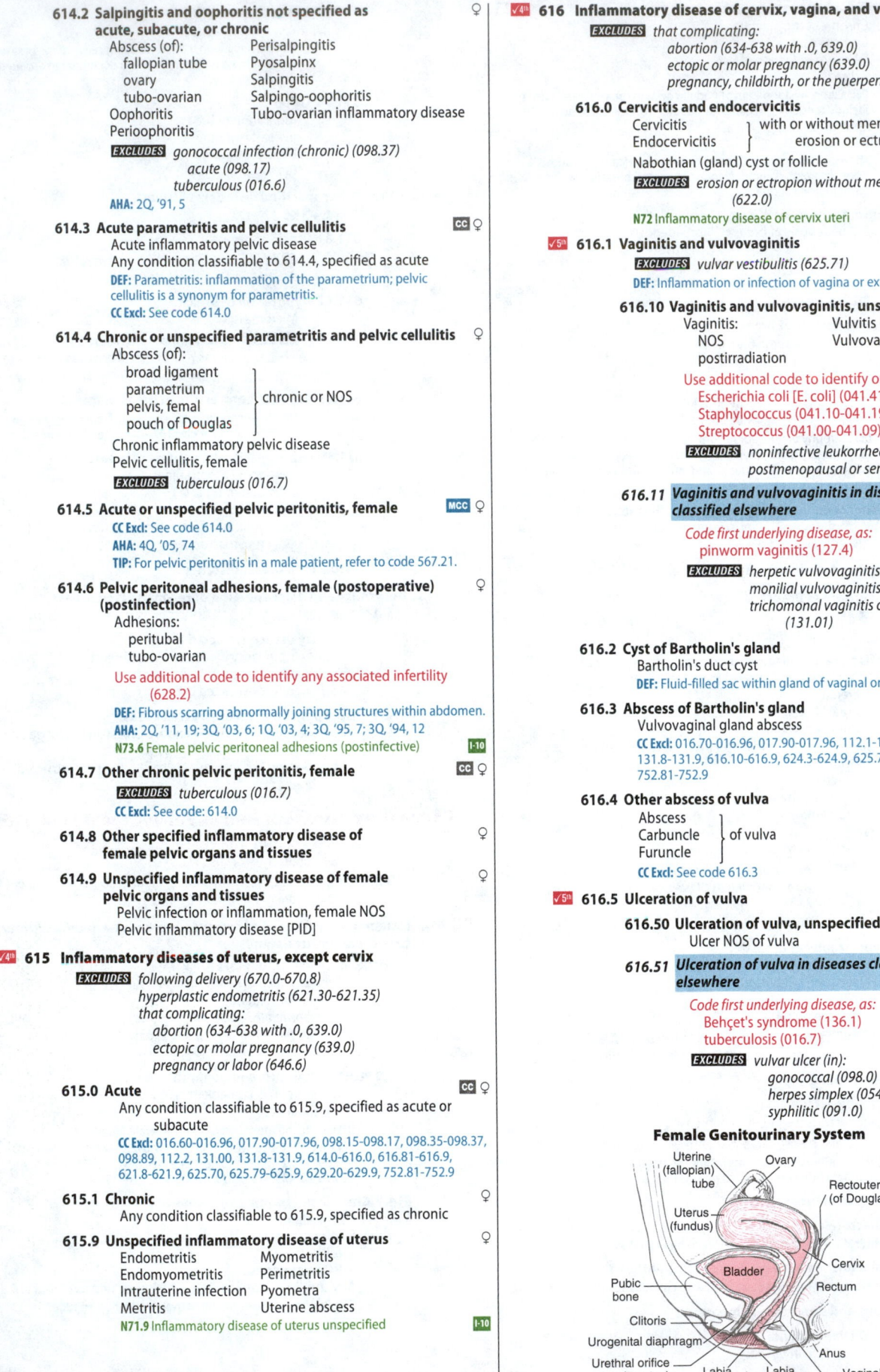

Uterine (fallopian) tube
Ovary
Rectouterine pouch (of Douglas)
Uterus (fundus)
Cervix
Bladder
Rectum
Pubic bone
Clitoris
Urogenital diaphragm
Anus
Urethral orifice (meatus)
Labia minora
Labia majora
Vaginal canal

N Newborn Age: 0   P Pediatric Age: 0-17   M Maternity Age: 12-55   A Adult Age: 15-124   MCC Major CC Condition   CC CC Condition   HIV HIV Related Dx

204 – Volume 1

2015 ICD-9-CM

Diseases of the Genitourinary System

616.8–618.05

Common Sites of Endometriosis

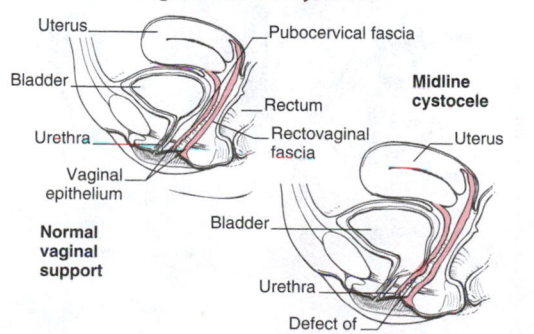

Common sites of endometriosis, in descending order of frequency:
(1) ovary
(2) cul de sac
(3) uterosacral ligaments
(4) broad ligaments
(5) fallopian tube
(6) uterovesical fold
(7) round ligament
(8) vermiform appendix
(9) vagina
(10) rectovaginal septum

✓5ᵗʰ **616.8 Other specified inflammatory diseases of cervix, vagina, and vulva**

> EXCLUDES noninflammatory disorders of:
> cervix (622.0-622.9)
> vagina (623.0-623.9)
> vulva (624.0-624.9)

616.81 Mucositis (ulcerative) of cervix, vagina, and vulva [CC] ♀

Use additional E code to identify adverse effects of therapy, such as:
antineoplastic and immunosuppressive drugs (E930.7, E933.1)
radiation therapy (E879.2)
CC Excl: 616.0, 616.81-616.9
AHA: 4Q, '06, 88-90

616.89 Other inflammatory disease of cervix, vagina, and vulva ♀
Caruncle, vagina or labium
Ulcer, vagina
AHA: 4Q, '06, 88-90

616.9 Unspecified inflammatory disease of cervix, vagina, and vulva ♀

Other Disorders of Female Genital Tract (617-629)

✓4ᵗʰ **617 Endometriosis**

617.0 Endometriosis of uterus ♀
Adenomyosis   Endometriosis:
Endometriosis: internal
  cervix   myometrium

> EXCLUDES stromal endometriosis (236.0)

DEF: Aberrant uterine mucosal tissue; creating products of menses and inflamed uterine tissues.
AHA: 3Q, '92, 7
N80.0 Endometriosis of uterus [I-10]

617.1 Endometriosis of ovary ♀
Chocolate cyst of ovary
Endometrial cystoma of ovary
DEF: Aberrant uterine tissue; creating products of menses and inflamed ovarian tissues.
N80.1 Endometriosis of ovary [I-10]

617.2 Endometriosis of fallopian tube ♀
DEF: Aberrant uterine tissue; creating products of menses and inflamed tissues of fallopian tubes.

Vaginal Midline Cystocele

Uterus — Pubocervical fascia
Bladder
— Rectum
Urethra — Rectovaginal fascia
Vaginal epithelium
Midline cystocele
Uterus
Bladder
Normal vaginal support
Urethra
Defect of pubocervical fascia

Vaginal Lateral Cystocele

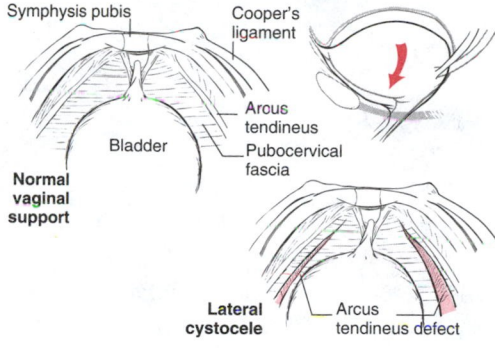

Symphysis pubis   Cooper's ligament
Bladder   Arcus tendineus
Normal vaginal support   Pubocervical fascia
Lateral cystocele   Arcus tendineus defect

617.3 Endometriosis of pelvic peritoneum ♀
Endometriosis:
broad ligament
cul-de-sac (Douglas')
parametrium
round ligament
DEF: Aberrant uterine tissue; creating products of menses and inflamed peritoneum tissues.

617.4 Endometriosis of rectovaginal septum and vagina ♀
DEF: Aberrant uterine tissue; creating products of menses and inflamed tissues in and behind vagina.

617.5 Endometriosis of intestine ♀
Endometriosis: Endometriosis:
appendix   rectum
colon
DEF: Aberrant uterine tissue; creating products of menses and inflamed intestinal tissues.

617.6 Endometriosis in scar of skin ♀

617.8 Endometriosis of other specified sites ♀
Endometriosis:
bladder
lung
umbilicus
vulva

617.9 Endometriosis, site unspecified ♀

✓4ᵗʰ **618 Genital prolapse**

Use additional code to identify urinary incontinence (625.6, 788.31, 788.33-788.39)

> EXCLUDES that complicating pregnancy, labor, or delivery (654.4)

✓5ᵗʰ **618.0 Prolapse of vaginal walls without mention of uterine prolapse**

> EXCLUDES that with uterine prolapse (618.2-618.4)
> enterocele (618.6)
> vaginal vault prolapse following hysterectomy (618.5)

618.00 Unspecified prolapse of vaginal walls ♀
Vaginal prolapse NOS

618.01 Cystocele, midline ♀
Cystocele NOS
DEF: Defect in the pubocervical fascia, the supportive layer of the bladder, causing bladder drop and herniated into the vagina along the midline.
N81.11 Cystocele midline [I-10]

618.02 Cystocele, lateral ♀
Paravaginal
DEF: Loss of support of the lateral attachment of the vagina at the arcus tendinous results in bladder drop; bladder herniates into the vagina laterally.

618.03 Urethrocele ♀

618.04 Rectocele ♀
Proctocele
Use additional code for any associated fecal incontinence (787.60-787.63)
N81.6 Rectocele [I-10]

618.05 Perineocele ♀

Diseases of the Genitourinary System

618.09–620.4

Types of Vaginal Hernias

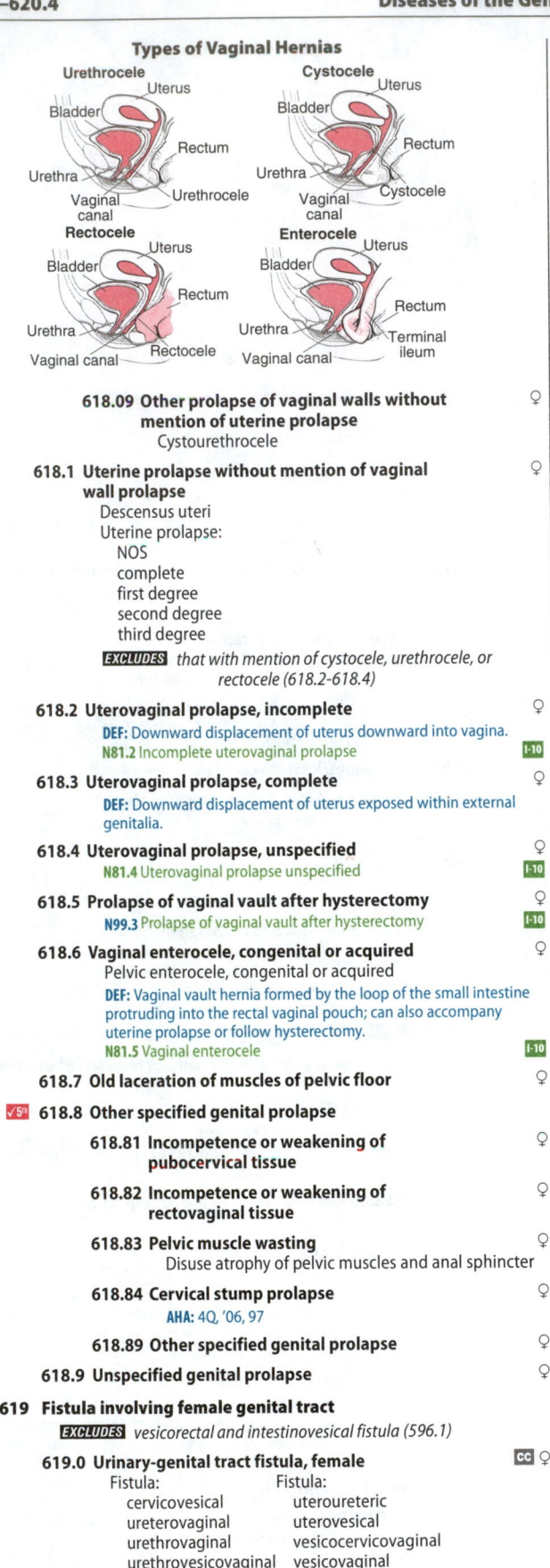

Urethrocele — Uterus, Bladder, Rectum, Urethra, Urethrocele, Vaginal canal

Cystocele — Uterus, Bladder, Rectum, Urethra, Cystocele, Vaginal canal

Rectocele — Uterus, Bladder, Rectum, Urethra, Rectocele, Vaginal canal

Enterocele — Uterus, Bladder, Rectum, Urethra, Terminal ileum, Vaginal canal

618.09 Other prolapse of vaginal walls without mention of uterine prolapse ♀
Cystourethrocele

618.1 Uterine prolapse without mention of vaginal wall prolapse ♀
Descensus uteri
Uterine prolapse:
  NOS
  complete
  first degree
  second degree
  third degree
> **EXCLUDES** *that with mention of cystocele, urethrocele, or rectocele (618.2-618.4)*

618.2 Uterovaginal prolapse, incomplete ♀
DEF: Downward displacement of uterus downward into vagina.
N81.2 Incomplete uterovaginal prolapse   **I-10**

618.3 Uterovaginal prolapse, complete ♀
DEF: Downward displacement of uterus exposed within external genitalia.

618.4 Uterovaginal prolapse, unspecified ♀
N81.4 Uterovaginal prolapse unspecified   **I-10**

618.5 Prolapse of vaginal vault after hysterectomy ♀
N99.3 Prolapse of vaginal vault after hysterectomy   **I-10**

618.6 Vaginal enterocele, congenital or acquired ♀
Pelvic enterocele, congenital or acquired
DEF: Vaginal vault hernia formed by the loop of the small intestine protruding into the rectal vaginal pouch; can also accompany uterine prolapse or follow hysterectomy.
N81.5 Vaginal enterocele   **I-10**

618.7 Old laceration of muscles of pelvic floor ♀

√5ᵗʰ **618.8 Other specified genital prolapse**

  618.81 Incompetence or weakening of pubocervical tissue ♀

  618.82 Incompetence or weakening of rectovaginal tissue ♀

  618.83 Pelvic muscle wasting ♀
  Disuse atrophy of pelvic muscles and anal sphincter

  618.84 Cervical stump prolapse ♀
  AHA: 4Q, '06, 97

  618.89 Other specified genital prolapse ♀

618.9 Unspecified genital prolapse ♀

√4ᵗʰ **619 Fistula involving female genital tract**
> **EXCLUDES** *vesicorectal and intestinovesical fistula (596.1)*

  619.0 Urinary-genital tract fistula, female **CC** ♀
  Fistula:
    cervicovesical
    ureterovaginal
    urethrovaginal
    urethrovesicovaginal
  Fistula:
    uteroureteric
    uterovesical
    vesicocervicovaginal
    vesicovaginal
  CC Excl: 619.0-619.9

619.1 Digestive-genital tract fistula, female **CC** ♀
Fistula:
  intestinouterine
  intestinovaginal
  rectovaginal
Fistula:
  rectovulval
  sigmoidovaginal
  uterorectal
CC Excl: See code: 619.0

619.2 Genital tract-skin fistula, female **CC** ♀
Fistula:
  uterus to abdominal wall
  vaginoperineal
CC Excl: See code: 619.0

619.8 Other specified fistulas involving female genital tract **CC** ♀
Fistula:
  cervix
  cul-de-sac (Douglas')
  uterus
  vagina
CC Excl: See code: 619.0

619.9 Unspecified fistula involving female genital tract **CC** ♀
CC Excl: see code 619.0

√4ᵗʰ **620 Noninflammatory disorders of ovary, fallopian tube, and broad ligament**
> **EXCLUDES** *hydrosalpinx (614.1)*

620.0 Follicular cyst of ovary ♀
Cyst of graafian follicle
DEF: Fluid-filled, encapsulated cyst due to occluded follicle duct that secretes hormones into ovaries.
N83.0 Follicular cyst of ovary   **I-10**

620.1 Corpus luteum cyst or hematoma ♀
Corpus luteum hemorrhage or rupture
Lutein cyst
DEF: Fluid-filled cyst due to serous developing from corpus luteum or clotted blood.
N83.1 Corpus luteum cyst   **I-10**

620.2 Other and unspecified ovarian cyst ♀
Cyst:
  NOS
  corpus albicans
  retention NOS } of ovary
  serous
  theca-lutein
Simple cystoma of ovary
> **EXCLUDES** *cystadenoma (benign) (serous) (220)*
> *developmental cysts (752.0)*
> *neoplastic cysts (220)*
> *polycystic ovaries (256.4)*
> *Stein-Leventhal syndrome (256.4)*

N83.20 Unspecified ovarian cysts   **I-10**

620.3 Acquired atrophy of ovary and fallopian tube ♀
Senile involution of ovary

620.4 Prolapse or hernia of ovary and fallopian tube ♀
Displacement of ovary and fallopian tube
Salpingocele

Uterus and Ovaries

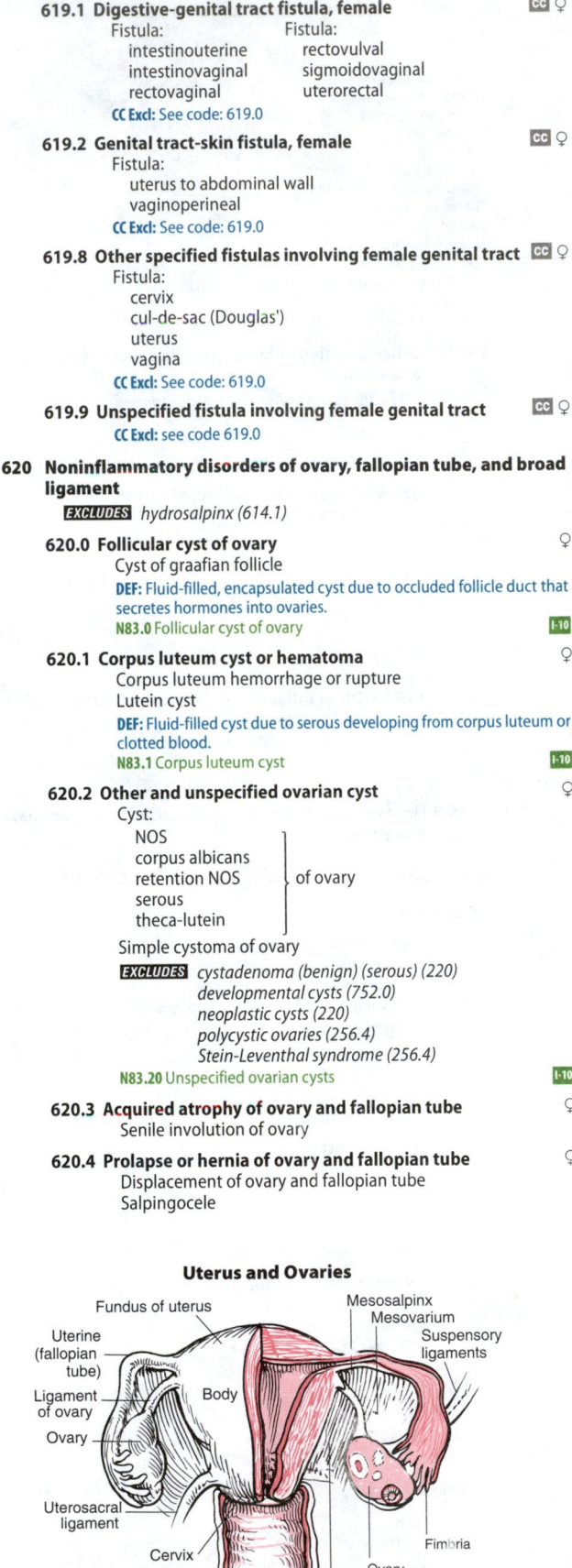

Fundus of uterus, Uterine (fallopian tube), Ligament of ovary, Ovary, Uterosacral ligament, Cervix, Vagina, Body, Mesosalpinx, Mesovarium, Suspensory ligaments, Fimbria, Ovary, Broad ligament

---

 Newborn Age: 0    **Pediatric Age: 0-17**   **M** Maternity Age: 12-55   **A** Adult Age: 15-124   **MCC** Major CC Condition   **CC** CC Condition   **HIV** HIV Related Dx

206 – Volume 1   2015 ICD-9-CM

620.5 Torsion of ovary, ovarian pedicle, or fallopian tube `CC` ♀
Torsion:
  accessory tube
  hydatid of Morgagni
CC Excl: 620.0-620.9

620.6 Broad ligament laceration syndrome ♀
Masters-Allen syndrome

620.7 Hematoma of broad ligament ♀
Hematocele, broad ligament
DEF: Blood within peritoneal fold that supports uterus.

620.8 Other noninflammatory disorders of ovary, fallopian tube, and broad ligament ♀
Cyst } of broad ligament or
Polyp } fallopian tube

Infarction }
Rupture } of ovary or fallopian tube
Hematosalpinx

EXCLUDES hematosalpinx in ectopic pregnancy (639.2)
  peritubal adhesions (614.6)
  torsion of ovary, ovarian pedicle, or fallopian tube (620.5)

620.9 Unspecified noninflammatory disorder of ovary, fallopian tube, and broad ligament ♀

✓4ᵗʰ **621 Disorders of uterus, not elsewhere classified**

621.0 Polyp of corpus uteri ♀
Polyp: Polyp:
  endometrium   uterus NOS
EXCLUDES cervical polyp NOS (622.7)
`N84.0` Polyp of corpus uteri `I-10`

621.1 Chronic subinvolution of uterus ♀
EXCLUDES puerperal (674.8)
DEF: Abnormal size of uterus after delivery; the uterus does not return to its normal size after the birth of a child.
AHA: 1Q, '91, 11

621.2 Hypertrophy of uterus ♀
Bulky or enlarged uterus
EXCLUDES puerperal (674.8)

✓5ᵗʰ **621.3 Endometrial hyperplasia**
DEF: Abnormal cystic overgrowth of endometrial tissue.

  621.30 Endometrial hyperplasia, unspecified ♀
Endometrial hyperplasia NOS
Hyperplasia (adenomatous) (cystic) (glandular) of endometrium
Hyperplastic endometritis

  621.31 Simple endometrial hyperplasia without atypia ♀
EXCLUDES benign endometrial hyperplasia (621.34)

  621.32 Complex endometrial hyperplasia without atypia ♀
EXCLUDES benign endometrial hyperplasia (621.34)

  621.33 Endometrial hyperplasia with atypia ♀
EXCLUDES endometrial intraepithelial neoplasia [EIN] (621.35)

  621.34 Benign endometrial hyperplasia ♀
DEF: Excessive cell growth of the endometrium due to primary hormonal changes (menopause) that result in secondary effects to the endometrial stroma and associated structures.
AHA: 4Q, '09, 95-96

  621.35 Endometrial intraepithelial neoplasia [EIN] ♀
EXCLUDES malignant neoplasm of endometrium with endometrial intraepithelial neoplasia [EIN] (182.0)
DEF: Abnormal premalignant neoplastic changes of the endometrial glands prone to malignant transformation.
AHA: 4Q, '09, 95-96
TIP: Do not confuse (EIN) with unrelated serous intraepithelial carcinoma (serous EIC), which is an early phase of (Type II) papillary serous adenocarcinoma of the endometrium.

621.4 Hematometra ♀
Hemometra
EXCLUDES that in congenital anomaly (752.2-752.39)
DEF: Accumulated blood in uterus.

621.5 Intrauterine synechiae ♀
Adhesions of uterus
Band(s) of uterus

621.6 Malposition of uterus ♀
Anteversion }
Retroflexion } of uterus
Retroversion }
EXCLUDES malposition complicating pregnancy, labor, or delivery (654.3-654.4)

621.7 Chronic inversion of uterus ♀
EXCLUDES current obstetrical trauma (665.2)
  prolapse of uterus (618.1-618.4)

621.8 Other specified disorders of uterus, not elsewhere classified ♀
Atrophy, acquired }
Cyst }
Fibrosis NOS } of uterus
Old laceration (postpartum) }
Ulcer }
EXCLUDES bilharzial fibrosis (120.0-120.9)
  endometriosis (617.0)
  fistulas (619.0-619.8)
  inflammatory diseases (615.0-615.9)

621.9 Unspecified disorder of uterus ♀

✓4ᵗʰ **622 Noninflammatory disorders of cervix**
EXCLUDES abnormality of cervix complicating pregnancy, labor, or delivery (654.5-654.6)
  fistula (619.0-619.8)

622.0 Erosion and ectropion of cervix ♀
Eversion }
Ulcer } of cervix
EXCLUDES that in chronic cervicitis (616.0)
DEF: Ulceration or turning outward of uterine cervix.

✓5ᵗʰ **622.1 Dysplasia of cervix (uteri)**
EXCLUDES abnormal results from cervical cytologic examination without histologic confirmation (795.00-795.09)
  carcinoma in situ of cervix (233.1)
  cervical intraepithelial neoplasia III [CIN III] (233.1)
  HGSIL of cervix (795.04)
DEF: Abnormal cell structures in portal between uterus and vagina.
AHA: 1Q, '91, 11

  622.10 Dysplasia of cervix, unspecified ♀
Anaplasia of cervix
Cervical atypism
Cervical dysplasia NOS

  622.11 Mild dysplasia of cervix ♀
Cervical intraepithelial neoplasia I [CIN I]

  622.12 Moderate dysplasia of cervix ♀
Cervical intraepithelial neoplasia II [CIN II]
EXCLUDES carcinoma in situ of cervix (233.1)
  cervical intraepithelial neoplasia III [CIN III] (233.1)
  severe dysplasia (233.1)

622.2 Leukoplakia of cervix (uteri) ♀
EXCLUDES carcinoma in situ of cervix (233.1)
DEF: Thickened, white patches on portal between uterus and vagina.

622.3 Old laceration of cervix ♀
Adhesions }
Band(s) } of cervix
Cicatrix (postpartum) }
EXCLUDES current obstetrical trauma (665.3)
DEF: Scarring or other evidence of old wound on cervix.

622.4 Stricture and stenosis of cervix ♀

Atresia (acquired)
Contracture — of cervix
Occlusion

Pinpoint os uteri

EXCLUDES congenital (752.49)
that complicating labor (654.6)

622.5 Incompetence of cervix ♀

EXCLUDES complicating pregnancy (654.5)
that affecting fetus or newborn (761.0)

DEF: Inadequate functioning of cervix; marked by abnormal widening during pregnancy; causing miscarriage.

622.6 Hypertrophic elongation of cervix ♀

DEF: Overgrowth of cervix tissues extending down into vagina.

622.7 Mucous polyp of cervix ♀

Polyp NOS of cervix

EXCLUDES adenomatous polyp of cervix (219.0)

622.8 Other specified noninflammatory disorders of cervix ♀

Atrophy (senile)
Cyst — of cervix
Fibrosis
Hemorrhage

EXCLUDES endometriosis (617.0)
fistula (619.0-619.8)
inflammatory diseases (616.0)

622.9 Unspecified noninflammatory disorder of cervix ♀

√4ᵗʰ **623 Noninflammatory disorders of vagina**

EXCLUDES abnormality of vagina complicating pregnancy, labor, or delivery (654.7)
congenital absence of vagina (752.49)
congenital diaphragm or bands (752.49)
fistulas involving vagina (619.0-619.8)

623.0 Dysplasia of vagina ♀

Mild and moderate dysplasia of vagina
Vaginal intraepithelial neoplasia I and II [VAIN I and II]

EXCLUDES abnormal results from vaginal cytological examination without histologic confirmation (795.10-795.19)
carcinoma in situ of vagina (233.31)
HGSIL of vagina (795.14)
severe dysplasia of vagina (233.31)
vaginal intraepithelial neoplasia III [VAIN III] (233.31)

623.1 Leukoplakia of vagina ♀

DEF: Thickened white patches on vaginal canal.

623.2 Stricture or atresia of vagina ♀

Adhesions (postoperative) (postradiation) of vagina
Occlusion of vagina
Stenosis, vagina

Use additional E code to identify any external cause

EXCLUDES congenital atresia or stricture (752.49)

623.3 Tight hymenal ring ♀

Rigid hymen
Tight hymenal ring — acquired or congenital
Tight introitus

EXCLUDES imperforate hymen (752.42)

623.4 Old vaginal laceration ♀

EXCLUDES old laceration involving muscles of pelvic floor (618.7)

DEF: Scarring or other evidence of old wound on vagina.

623.5 Leukorrhea, not specified as infective ♀

Leukorrhea NOS of vagina
Vaginal discharge NOS

EXCLUDES trichomonal (131.00)

DEF: Viscid whitish discharge from vagina.

623.6 Vaginal hematoma ♀

EXCLUDES current obstetrical trauma (665.7)

623.7 Polyp of vagina ♀

623.8 Other specified noninflammatory disorders of vagina ♀

Cyst — of vagina
Hemorrhage

623.9 Unspecified noninflammatory disorder of vagina ♀

√4ᵗʰ **624 Noninflammatory disorders of vulva and perineum**

EXCLUDES abnormality of vulva and perineum complicating pregnancy, labor, or delivery (654.8)
condyloma acuminatum (078.11)
fistulas involving:
perineum — see Alphabetic Index
vulva (619.0-619.8)
vulval varices (456.6)
vulvar involvement in skin conditions (690-709.9)

√5ᵗʰ **624.0 Dystrophy of vulva**

EXCLUDES carcinoma in situ of vulva (233.32)
severe dysplasia of vulva (233.32)
vulvar intraepithelial neoplasia III [VIN III] (233.32)

AHA: 4Q, '07, 90

624.01 Vulvar intraepithelial neoplasia I [VIN I] ♀

Mild dysplasia of vulva

624.02 Vulvar intraepithelial neoplasia II [VIN II] ♀

Moderate dysplasia of vulva

AHA: 4Q, '07, 91

624.09 Other dystrophy of vulva ♀

Kraurosis of vulva
Leukoplakia of vulva

624.1 Atrophy of vulva ♀

624.2 Hypertrophy of clitoris ♀

EXCLUDES that in endocrine disorders (255.2, 256.1)

624.3 Hypertrophy of labia ♀

Hypertrophy of vulva NOS

DEF: Overgrowth of fleshy folds on either side of vagina.

624.4 Old laceration or scarring of vulva ♀

DEF: Scarring or other evidence of old wound on external female genitalia.

624.5 Hematoma of vulva ♀

EXCLUDES that complicating delivery (664.5)

DEF: Blood in tissue of external genitalia.

624.6 Polyp of labia and vulva ♀

624.8 Other specified noninflammatory disorders of vulva and perineum ♀

Cyst
Edema — of vulva
Stricture

AHA: 1Q, '03, 13; 1Q, '95, 8

624.9 Unspecified noninflammatory disorder of vulva and perineum ♀

√4ᵗʰ **625 Pain and other symptoms associated with female genital organs**

625.0 Dyspareunia ♀

EXCLUDES psychogenic dyspareunia (302.76)

DEF: Difficult or painful sexual intercourse.

625.1 Vaginismus ♀

Colpospasm
Vulvismus

EXCLUDES psychogenic vaginismus (306.51)

DEF: Vaginal spasms; due to involuntary contraction of musculature; prevents intercourse.

625.2 Mittelschmerz ♀

Intermenstrual pain
Ovulation pain

DEF: Pain occurring between menstrual periods.

625.3 Dysmenorrhea ♀

Painful menstruation

EXCLUDES psychogenic dysmenorrhea (306.52)

AHA: 2Q, '94, 12

N94.6 Dysmenorrhea unspecified `I-10`

625.4 Premenstrual tension syndromes ♀

Menstrual molimen
Premenstrual dysphoric disorder
Premenstrual syndrome
Premenstrual tension NOS

EXCLUDES menstrual migraine (346.4)

AHA: 4Q, '03, 116

N Newborn Age: 0 **P** Pediatric Age: 0-17 **M** Maternity Age: 12-55 **A** Adult Age: 15-124 **MCC** Major CC Condition **CC** CC Condition **HIV** HIV Related Dx

208 – Volume 1

2015 ICD-9-CM

625.5 Pelvic congestion syndrome ♀
Congestion-fibrosis syndrome
Taylor's syndrome
DEF: Excessive accumulation of blood in vessels of pelvis; may occur after orgasm; causes abnormal menstruation, lower back pain and vaginal discharge.

625.6 Stress incontinence, female ♀
EXCLUDES *mixed incontinence (788.33)*
stress incontinence, male (788.32)
DEF: Involuntary leakage of urine due to insufficient sphincter control; occurs upon sneezing, laughing, coughing, sudden movement or lifting.
N39.3 Stress incontinence (female) (male)   `I-10`

√5ᵗʰ **625.7 Vulvodynia**
DEF: Vulvar pain without an identifiable cause that persists for three months or longer.
AHA: 4Q, '08, 124

625.70 Vulvodynia, unspecified ♀
Vulvodynia NOS

625.71 Vulvar vestibulitis ♀

625.79 Other vulvodynia ♀

625.8 Other specified symptoms associated with female genital organs ♀
AHA: N-D, '85, 16

625.9 Unspecified symptom associated with female genital organs ♀
AHA: 4Q, '06, 110
R10.2 Pelvic and perineal pain   `I-10`

√4ᵗʰ **626 Disorders of menstruation and other abnormal bleeding from female genital tract**
EXCLUDES *menopausal and premenopausal bleeding (627.0)*
pain and other symptoms associated with menstrual cycle (625.2-625.4)
postmenopausal bleeding (627.1)
precocious puberty (259.1)

626.0 Absence of menstruation ♀
Amenorrhea (primary) (secondary)

626.1 Scanty or infrequent menstruation ♀
Hypomenorrhea   Oligomenorrhea

626.2 Excessive or frequent menstruation ♀
Heavy periods
Menometrorrhagia
Menorrhagia
Plymenorrhea
EXCLUDES *premenopausal (627.0)*
that in puberty (626.3)
AHA: 4Q, '11, 146
N92.0 Excess & frequent menstruation w/regular cycle   `I-10`

626.3 Puberty bleeding ♀
Excessive bleeding associated with onset of menstrual periods
Pubertal menorrhagia

626.4 Irregular menstrual cycle ♀
Irregular:
bleeding NOS
menstruation
periods

626.5 Ovulation bleeding ♀
Regular intermenstrual bleeding

626.6 Metrorrhagia ♀
Bleeding unrelated to menstrual cycle
Irregular intermenstrual bleeding

626.7 Postcoital bleeding ♀
DEF: Bleeding from vagina after sexual intercourse.

626.8 Other ♀
Dysfunctional or functional uterine hemorrhage NOS
Menstruation:
retained
suppression of
N92.5 Other specified irregular menstruation   `I-10`

626.9 Unspecified ♀

√4ᵗʰ **627 Menopausal and postmenopausal disorders**
EXCLUDES *asymptomatic age-related (natural) postmenopausal status (V49.81)*

627.0 Premenopausal menorrhagia ♀
Excessive bleeding associated with onset of menopause
Menorrhagia:
climacteric
menopausal
preclimacteric

627.1 Postmenopausal bleeding ♀
N95.0 Postmenopausal bleeding   `I-10`

627.2 Symptomatic menopausal or female climacteric states ♀
Symptoms, such as flushing, sleeplessness, headache, lack of concentration, associated with the menopause

627.3 Postmenopausal atrophic vaginitis ♀
Senile (atrophic) vaginitis

627.4 Symptomatic states associated with artificial menopause ♀
Postartificial menopause syndromes
Any condition classifiable to 627.1, 627.2, or 627.3 which follows induced menopause
DEF: Conditions arising after hysterectomy.

627.8 Other specified menopausal and postmenopausal disorders ♀
EXCLUDES *premature menopause NOS (256.31)*

627.9 Unspecified menopausal and postmenopausal disorder ♀

√4ᵗʰ **628 Infertility, female**
INCLUDES primary and secondary sterility
DEF: Infertility: inability to conceive for at least one year with regular intercourse.
DEF: Primary infertility: occurring in patients who have never conceived.
DEF: Secondary infertility: occurring in patients who have previously conceived.
AHA: 2Q, '96, 9; 1Q, '95, 7

628.0 Associated with anovulation ♀
Anovulatory cycle
Use additional code for any associated Stein-Leventhal syndrome (256.4)

628.1 *Of pituitary-hypothalamic origin* ♀
Code first underlying cause, as:
adiposogenital dystrophy (253.8)
anterior pituitary disorder (253.0-253.4)

628.2 Of tubal origin ♀
Infertility associated with congenital anomaly of tube
Tubal:
block
occlusion
stenosis
Use additional code for any associated peritubal adhesions (614.6)

628.3 Of uterine origin ♀
Infertility associated with congenital anomaly of uterus
Nonimplantation
Use additional code for any associated tuberculous endometritis (016.7)

628.4 Of cervical or vaginal origin ♀
Infertility associated with:
anomaly of cervical mucus
congenital structural anomaly
dysmucorrhea

628.8 Of other specified origin ♀

628.9 Of unspecified origin ♀

√4ᵗʰ **629 Other disorders of female genital organs**

629.0 Hematocele, female, not elsewhere classified ♀
EXCLUDES *hematocele or hematoma:*
broad ligament (620.7)
fallopian tube (620.8)
that associated with ectopic pregnancy (633.00-633.91)
uterus (621.4)
vagina (623.6)
vulva (624.5)

Diseases of the Genitourinary System

629.1–629.9

629.1 Hydrocele, canal of Nuck ♀
Cyst of canal of Nuck (acquired)
EXCLUDES congenital (752.41)

√5ᵗʰ **629.2 Female genital mutilation status**
Female circumcision status
Female genital cutting
AHA: 4Q, '04, 88

629.20 Female genital mutilation status, unspecified ♀
Female genital cutting status, unspecified
Female genital mutilation status NOS

629.21 Female genital mutilation Type I status ♀
Clitorectomy status
Female genital cutting Type I status
DEF: Female genital mutilation involving clitorectomy, with part or all of the clitoris removed.

629.22 Female genital mutilation Type II status ♀
Clitorectomy with excision of labia minora status
Female genital cutting Type II status
DEF: Female genital mutilation involving clitoris and the labia minora amputation.
AHA: 4Q, '04, 90

629.23 Female genital mutilation Type III status ♀
Female genital cutting Type III status
Infibulation status
DEF: Female genital mutilation involving removal, most or all of the labia minora excised, labia majora incised which is then made into a hood of skin over the urethral and vaginal opening.
AHA: 4Q, '04, 90

629.29 Other female genital mutilation status ♀
Female genital cutting Type IV status
Female genital mutilation Type IV status
Other female genital cutting status
AHA: 4Q, '06, 97

√5ᵗʰ **629.3 Complication of implanted vaginal mesh and other prosthetic materials**
AHA: 4Q, '11, 130-131

629.31 Erosion of implanted vaginal mesh and other prosthetic materials to surrounding organ or tissue ♀
Erosion of implanted vaginal mesh and other prosthetic materials into pelvic floor muscles

629.32 Exposure of implanted vaginal mesh and other prosthetic materials into vagina ♀
Exposure of vaginal mesh and other prosthetic materials through vaginal wall

√5ᵗʰ **629.8 Other specified disorders of female genital organs**

629.81 Recurrent pregnancy loss without current pregnancy ♀
EXCLUDES recurrent pregnancy loss with current pregnancy (646.3)
AHA: 4Q, '06, 98

629.89 Other specified disorders of female genital organs ♀
AHA: 4Q, '06, 98

629.9 Unspecified disorder of female genital organs ♀

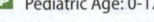 Newborn Age: 0    Pediatric Age: 0-17    Maternity Age: 12-55    Adult Age: 15-124   **MCC** Major CC Condition   **CC** CC Condition   **HIV** HIV Related Dx

210 – Volume 1   **2015 ICD-9-CM**

11. Complications of Pregnancy, Childbirth, and the Puerperium (630-679)

Ectopic and Molar Pregnancy (630-633)

Use additional code from category 639 to identify any complications

630 Hydatidiform mole   M♀

Trophoblastic disease NOS   Vesicular mole

EXCLUDES   chorioadenoma (destruens) (236.1)
chorionepithelioma (181)
malignant hydatidiform mole (236.1)

DEF: Abnormal product of pregnancy; marked by mass of cysts resembling bunch of grapes due to chorionic villi proliferation, and dissolution; must be surgically removed.

√4ᵗʰ **631 Other abnormal product of conception**

AHA: 4Q, '11, 131-132

631.0 Inappropriate change in quantitative human chorionic gonadotropin (hCG) in early pregnancy   M♀

Biochemical pregnancy
Chemical pregnancy
Inappropriate level of quantitative human chorionic gonadotropin (hCG) for gestational age in early pregnancy

EXCLUDES   blighted ovum (631.8)
molar pregnancy (631.8)

631.8 Other abnormal products of conception   M♀

Blighted ovum

632 Missed abortion   M♀

Early fetal death before completion of 22 weeks' gestation with retention of dead fetus
Retained products of conception, not following spontaneous or induced abortion or delivery

EXCLUDES   failed induced abortion (638.0-638.9)
fetal death (intrauterine) (late) (656.4)
missed delivery (656.4)
that with hydatidiform mole (630)
that with other abnormal products of conception (631.8)

AHA: 1Q, '01, 5

002.1 Missed abortion   I-10

√4ᵗʰ **633 Ectopic pregnancy**

INCLUDES   ruptured ectopic pregnancy

DEF: Fertilized egg develops outside uterus.

AHA: 4Q, '02, 61

√5ᵗʰ **633.0 Abdominal pregnancy**

Intraperitoneal pregnancy

633.00 Abdominal pregnancy without intrauterine pregnancy   CC M♀

CC Excl: 633.01, 633.11-633.91

633.01 Abdominal pregnancy with intrauterine pregnancy   CC M♀

CC Excl: 633.00-633.91

√5ᵗʰ **633.1 Tubal pregnancy**

Fallopian pregnancy
Rupture of (fallopian) tube due to pregnancy
Tubal abortion

AHA: 2Q, '90, 27

633.10 Tubal pregnancy without intrauterine pregnancy   CC M♀

CC Excl: See code: 633.01

000.1 Tubal pregnancy   I-10

633.11 Tubal pregnancy with intrauterine pregnancy   CC M♀

CC Excl: See code: 633.01

√5ᵗʰ **633.2 Ovarian pregnancy**

633.20 Ovarian pregnancy without intrauterine pregnancy   CC M♀

CC Excl: See code: 633.01

633.21 Ovarian pregnancy with intrauterine pregnancy   CC M♀

CC Excl: See code: 633.01

√5ᵗʰ **633.8 Other ectopic pregnancy**

Pregnancy: Pregnancy:
cervical   intraligamentous
combined   mesometric
cornual   mural

633.80 Other ectopic pregnancy without intrauterine pregnancy   CC M♀

CC Excl: See code: 633.01

633.81 Other ectopic pregnancy with intrauterine pregnancy   CC M♀

CC Excl: See code: 633.01

√5ᵗʰ **633.9 Unspecified ectopic pregnancy**

633.90 Unspecified ectopic pregnancy without intrauterine pregnancy   CC M♀

CC Excl: See code: 633.01

633.91 Unspecified ectopic pregnancy with intrauterine pregnancy   CC M♀

CC Excl: See code: 633.01

Other Pregnancy with Abortive Outcome (634-639)

The following fourth-digit subdivisions are for use with categories 634-638:

.0 Complicated by genital tract and pelvic infection
Endometritis
Salpingo-oophoritis
Sepsis NOS
Septicemia NOS

Any condition classifiable to 639.0 with condition classifiable to 634-638
EXCLUDES urinary tract infection (634-638 with .7)

.1 Complicated by delayed or excessive hemorrhage
Afibrinogenemia
Defibrination syndrome
Intravascular hemolysis

Any condition classifiable to 639.1 with condition classifiable to 634-638

.2 Complicated by damage to pelvic organs and tissues
Laceration, perforation, or tear of:
bladder
uterus

Any condition classifiable to 639.2 with condition classifiable to 634-638

.3 Complicated by renal failure
Oliguria   Uremia

Any condition classifiable to 639.3, with condition classifiable to 634-638

.4 Complicated by metabolic disorder
Electrolyte imbalance with conditions classfiable to 634-638

.5 Complicated by shock
Circulatory collapse
Shock (postoperative) (septic)

Any condition classifiable to 639.5 with condition classifiable to 634-638

.6 Complicated by embolism
Embolism: Embolism:
NOS   pulmonary
amniotic fluid

Any condition classifiable to 639.6, with condition classifiable to 634-638

.7 With other specified complications
Cardiac arrest or failure
Urinary tract infection

Any condition classiable to 639.8 with condition classifiable to 634-638

.8 With unspecified complication

.9 Without mention of complication

§ √4ᵗʰ **634 Spontaneous abortion**

Requires fifth digit to identify stage:
  0 unspecified
  1 incomplete
  2 complete

INCLUDES   miscarriage
spontaneous abortion

DEF: Spontaneous premature expulsion of the products of conception from the uterus.

AHA: 4Q, '11, 181; 2Q, '91, 16

§§ √5ᵗʰ **634.0 Complicated by genital tract and pelvic infection**   CC M♀
[0-2]   **CC Excl:** 634.00-638.9, 640.00-641.23, 646.80-646.93, 648.90-649.64, 650, 669.40-669.44, 669.80-669.94, 679.00-679.04, 679.12, 679.14

---

§   See beginning of section 634-639 for fourth-digit definitions.
§§ Requires fifth digit. Valid digits are in [brackets] under each code. See appropriate category for codes and definitions.

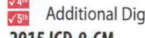

√4ᵗʰ √5ᵗʰ   Additional Digit Required   Unacceptable PDx   Manifestation Code   Hospital Acquired Condition   ►◄ Revised Text   ● New Code   ▲ Revised Code Title

Complications of Pregnancy, Childbirth, and the Puerperium

634.1–637

Ectopic Pregnancy Sites

§§ ✓5th **634.1 Complicated by delayed or excessive hemorrhage**   M ♀
[0-2]
AHA: For Code 634.11: 1Q, '03, 6

§§ ✓5th **634.2 Complicated by damage to pelvic organs or tissues**   CC M ♀
[0-2]
CC Excl: See code: 634.0

§§ ✓5th **634.3 Complicated by renal failure**   MCC M ♀
[0-2]
CC Excl: See code: 634.0

§§ ✓5th **634.4 Complicated by metabolic disorder**   CC M ♀
[0-2]
CC Excl: See code: 634.0

§§ ✓5th **634.5 Complicated by shock**   MCC M ♀
[0-2]
CC Excl: See code: 634.0

§§ ✓5th **634.6 Complicated by embolism**   MCC 1-2 CC 0 M ♀
[0-2]
CC Excl: See code: 634.0

§§ ✓5th **634.7 With other specified complications**   CC M ♀
[0-2]
CC Excl: See code: 634.0

§§ ✓5th **634.8 With unspecified complication**   CC M ♀
[0-2]
CC Excl: See code: 634.0

§§ ✓5th **634.9 Without mention of complication**   M ♀
[0-2]

§ ✓4th **635 Legally induced abortion**

Requires fifth digit to identify stage:
0 unspecified
1 incomplete
2 complete

INCLUDES   abortion or termination of pregnancy:
elective
legal
therapeutic

EXCLUDES   menstrual extraction or regulation (V25.3)
DEF: Intentional expulsion of products of conception from uterus performed by medical professionals inside boundaries of law.
AHA: 4Q, '11, 181; 2Q, '94, 14

§§ ✓5th **635.0 Complicated by genital tract and pelvic infection**   CC M ♀
[0-2]
CC Excl: 634.00-635.02, 635.20-635.22, 635.70-638.9, 640.00-641.23, 646.80-646.93, 648.90-649.64, 650, 669.40-669.44, 669.80-669.94, 679.00-679.04, 679.12, 679.14

§§ ✓5th **635.1 Complicated by delayed or excessive hemorrhage**   M ♀
[0-2]

§§ ✓5th **635.2 Complicated by damage to pelvic organs or tissues**   CC M ♀
[0-2]
CC Excl: For code 635.20: 634.00-638.9, 640.00-641.23, 646.80-646.93, 648.90-649.64, 650, 669.40-669.44, 669.80-669.94, 679.00-679.04, 679.12, 679.14; For code 635.21: 634.00-635.62, 638.5-638.9, 640.00-641.00; For code 635.22: 635.22

§§ ✓5th **635.3 Complicated by renal failure**   MCC M ♀
[0-2]
CC Excl: For code 635.30: 635.30-635.32; For code 635.31: 635.30-635.32, 637.11-638.9, 640.00-641.23, 646.80-646.93, 648.90-649.64, 650, 669.40-669.44, 669.80-669.94, 679.00-679.04, 679.12, 679.14; For code 635.32: 634.00-634.92, 635.30-635.32, 635.70-638.9, 640.00-641.23, 646.80-646.93, 648.90-649.64, 650, 669.40-669.44, 669.80-669.94, 679.00-679.04, 679.12, 679.144

§§ ✓5th **635.4 Complicated by metabolic disorder**   CC M ♀
[0-2]
CC Excl: 634.00-638.9, 640.00-641.23, 646.80-646.93, 648.90-649.64, 650, 669.40-669.44, 669.80-669.94, 679.00-679.04, 679.12, 679.14

§§ ✓5th **635.5 Complicated by shock**   MCC M ♀
[0-2]
CC Excl: 634.00-634.92, 635.50-635.52, 635.70-638.9, 640.00-641.23, 646.80-646.93, 648.90-649.64, 650, 669.40-669.44, 669.80-669.94, 679.00-679.04, 679.12, 679.14

§§ ✓5th **635.6 Complicated by embolism**   MCC M ♀
[0-2]
CC Excl: 634.00-634.92, 635.60-638.9, 640.00-641.23, 646.80-646.93, 648.90-649.64, 650, 669.40-669.44, 669.80-669.94, 679.00-679.04, 679.12, 679.14

§§ ✓5th **635.7 With other specified complications**   CC M ♀
[0-2]
CC Excl: 634.00-638.9, 640.00-641.23, 646.80-646.93, 648.90-649.64, 650, 669.40-669.44, 669.80-669.94, 679.00-679.04, 679.12, 679.14

§§ ✓5th **635.8 With unspecified complication**   CC M ♀
[0-2]
CC Excl: 634.00-638.9, 640.00-641.23, 646.80-646.93, 648.90-649.64, 650, 669.40-669.44, 669.80-669.94, 679.00-679.04, 679.12, 679.14

§§ ✓5th **635.9 Without mention of complication**   M ♀
[0-2]
AHA: For code 635.92: 2Q, '10, 6-7; 2Q, '94, 14

§ ✓4th **636 Illegally induced abortion**

Requires fifth digit to identify stage:
0 unspecified
1 incomplete
2 complete

INCLUDES   abortion:
criminal
illegal
self-induced

DEF: Intentional expulsion of products of conception from uterus; outside boundaries of law.
AHA: 4Q, '11, 181

§§ ✓5th **636.0 Complicated by genital tract and pelvic infection**   CC M ♀
[0-2]
CC Excl: 634.00-636.02, 636.70-638.9, 640.00-641.23, 646.80-646.93, 648.90-649.64, 650, 669.40-669.44, 669.80-669.94, 679.00-679.04, 679.12, 679.14

§§ ✓5th **636.1 Complicated by delayed or excessive hemorrhage**   M ♀
[0-2]

§§ ✓5th **636.2 Complicated by damage to pelvic organs or tissues**   CC M ♀
[0-2]
CC Excl: 634.00-638.9, 640.00-641.23, 646.80-646.93, 648.90-649.64, 650, 669.40-669.44, 669.80-669.94, 679.00-679.04, 679.12, 679.14

§§ ✓5th **636.3 Complicated by renal failure**   MCC M ♀
[0-2]
CC Excl: 634.00-635.92, 636.30-636.32, 636.70-638.9, 640.00-641.23, 646.80-646.93, 648.90-649.64, 650, 669.40-669.44, 669.80-669.94, 679.00-679.04, 679.12, 679.14

§§ ✓5th **636.4 Complicated by metabolic disorder**   CC M ♀
[0-2]
CC Excl: 634.00-635.92, 636.30-636.32, 636.70-638.9, 640.00-641.23, 646.80-646.93, 648.90-649.64, 650, 669.40-669.44, 669.80-669.94, 679.00-679.04, 679.12, 679.14

§§ ✓5th **636.5 Complicated by shock**   MCC M ♀
[0-2]
CC Excl: For codes 636.50 and 636.51: 634.00-635.92, 636.50-636.52, 636.70-638.9, 640.00-641.23, 646.80-646.93, 648.90-649.64, 650, 669.40-669.44, 669.80-669.94, 679.00-679.04, 679.12, 679.14; For code 636.52: 634.00-635.92, 636.50-636.52, 636.70-636.92, 637.50-637.52, 637.70-637.92, 638.5, 638.7-638.9, 640.00-641.23, 646.80-646.93, 648.90- 649.64, 650, 669.40-669.44, 669.80-669.94, 679.00-679.04, 679.12, 679.14

§§ ✓5th **636.6 Complicated by embolism**   MCC M ♀
[0-2]
CC Excl: 634.00-635.92, 636.60-638.9, 640.00-641.23, 646.80-646.93, 648.90-649.64, 650, 669.40-669.44, 669.80-669.94, 679.00-679.04, 679.12, 679.14

§§ ✓5th **636.7 With other specified complications**   CC M ♀
[0-2]
CC Excl: 634.00-641.23, 646.80-646.93, 648.90-649.64, 650, 669.40-669.44, 669.80-669.94, 679.00-679.04, 679.12, 679.14

§§ ✓5th **636.8 With unspecified complication**   CC M ♀
[0-2]
CC Excl: See code: 636.2

§§ ✓5th **636.9 Without mention of complication**   M ♀
[0-2]

§ ✓4th **637 Unspecified abortion**

Requires fifth digit to identify stage:
0 unspecified
1 incomplete
2 complete

INCLUDES   abortion NOS
retained products of conception following abortion, not classifiable elsewhere

AHA: 4Q, '11, 181

---

§   See beginning of section 634-639 for fourth-digit definitions.
§§ Requires fifth digit. Valid digits are in [brackets] under each code. See appropriate category for codes and definitions.

N Newborn Age: 0   P Pediatric Age: 0-17   M Maternity Age: 12-55   A Adult Age: 15-124   MCC Major CC Condition   CC CC Condition   HIV HIV Related Dx

§§ ✓5ʰ **637.0 Complicated by genital tract and pelvic infection** CC M♀
[0-2] CC Excl: 634.00-637.02, 637.70-638.9, 640.00-641.23, 646.80-646.93, 650, 669.40-669.44, 669.80-669.94, 679.00-679.04, 679.12, 679.14

§§ ✓5ʰ **637.1 Complicated by delayed or excessive hemorrhage** M♀
[0-2]

§§ ✓5ʰ **637.2 Complicated by damage to pelvic organs or tissues** CC M♀
[0-2] CC Excl: 634.00-636.92, 637.30-637.32, 637.70-638.9, 640.00-641.23, 646.80-646.93, 648.90-649.64, 650, 669.40-669.44, 669.80-669.94, 679.00-679.04, 679.12, 679.14

§§ ✓5ʰ **637.3 Complicated by renal failure** MCC M♀
[0-2] CC Excl: 634.00-636.92, 637.30-637.32, 637.70-638.9, 640.00-641.23, 646.80-646.93, 648.90-649.64, 650, 669.40-669.44, 669.80-669.94, 679.00-679.04, 679.12, 679.14

§§ ✓5ʰ **637.4 Complicated by metabolic disorder** CC M♀
[0-2] CC Excl: See code: 637.2

§§ ✓5ʰ **637.5 Complicated by shock** MCC M♀
[0-2] CC Excl: 634.00-636.92, 637.50-637.52, 637.70-638.9, 640.00-641.23, 646.80-646.93, 648.90-649.64, 650, 669.40-669.44, 669.80-669.94, 679.00-679.04, 679.12, 679.14

§§ ✓5ʰ **637.6 Complicated by embolism** MCC M♀
[0-2] CC Excl: For codes 637.60 and 637.61: 634.00-636.92, 637.60-638.9, 640.00-641.23, 646.80-646.93, 648.90-649.64, 650, 669.40-669.44, 669.80-669.94, 679.00-679.04, 679.12, 679.14; For code 637.62: 634.00-636.92, 637.60-638.9, 640.00-641.23, 646.80-646.93, 648.90-649.64, 650, 669.40-669.44, 669.80-669.94, 679.00-679.04, 679.12, 679.14

§§ ✓5ʰ **637.7 With other specified complications** CC M♀
[0-2] CC Excl: See code: 637.2

§§ ✓5ʰ **637.8 With unspecified complication** CC M♀
[0-2] CC Excl: For codes 637.80 and 637.82: 634.00-638.9, 640.00-641.23, 646.80-646.93, 648.90-649.64, 650, 669.40-669.44, 669.80-669.94, 679.00-679.04, 679.12, 679.14; For code 637.81: 634.00-635.32, 635.41-638.9, 640.00-641.23, 646.80-646.93, 648.90-649.64, 650, 669.40-669.44, 669.80-669.94, 679.00-679.04, 679.12, 679.14

§§ ✓5ʰ **637.9 Without mention of complication** M♀
[0-2]

§ ✓4ʰ **638 Failed attempted abortion**
INCLUDES failure of attempted induction of (legal) abortion
EXCLUDES incomplete abortion (634.0-637.9)
DEF: Continued pregnancy despite an attempted legal abortion.

638.0 Complicated by genital tract and pelvic infection CC M♀
CC Excl: 634.00-638.0, 638.7-638.9, 640.00-641.23, 646.80-646.93, 648.90-649.64, 650, 669.40-669.44, 669.80-669.94, 679.00-679.04, 679.12, 679.14

638.1 Complicated by delayed or excessive hemorrhage CC M♀
CC Excl: 634.00-637.92, 638.1, 638.7-638.9, 640.00-641.23, 646.80-646.93, 648.90-649.64, 650, 669.40-669.44, 669.80-669.94, 679.00-679.04, 679.12, 679.14

638.2 Complicated by damage to pelvic organs or tissues CC M♀
CC Excl: 634.00-637.92, 638.2, 638.7-638.9, 640.00-641.23, 646.80-646.93, 648.90-649.64, 650, 669.40-669.44, 669.80-669.94, 679.00-679.04, 679.12, 679.14

638.3 Complicated by renal failure MCC M♀
CC Excl: 634.00-637.92, 638.3, 638.7-638.9, 640.00-641.23, 646.80-646.93, 648.90-649.64, 650, 669.40-669.44, 669.80-669.94, 679.00-679.04, 679.12, 679.14

638.4 Complicated by metabolic disorder CC M♀
CC Excl: 634.00-638.9, 640.00-641.23, 646.80-646.93, 648.90-649.64, 650, 669.40-669.44, 669.80-669.94, 679.00-679.04, 679.12, 679.14

638.5 Complicated by shock MCC M♀
CC Excl: 634.00-637.12, 637.21-637.92, 638.4-638.5, 638.7-638.9, 640.00-641.23, 646.80-646.93, 648.90-649.64, 650, 669.40-669.44, 669.80-669.94, 679.00-679.04, 679.12, 679.14

638.6 Complicated by embolism MCC M♀
CC Excl: 634.00-637.92, 638.6-638.9, 640.00-641.23, 646.80-646.93, 648.90-649.64, 650, 669.40-669.44, 669.80-669.94, 679.00-679.04, 679.12, 679.14

638.7 With other specified complications CC M♀
CC Excl: See code: 638.4

638.8 With unspecified complication CC M♀
CC Excl: See code: 638.4

638.9 Without mention of complication M♀

✓4ʰ **639 Complications following abortion and ectopic and molar pregnancies**
NOTE This category is provided for use when it is required to classify separately the complications classifiable to the fourth-digit level in categories 634-638; for example:
a) when the complication itself was responsible for an episode of medical care, the abortion, ectopic or molar pregnancy itself having been dealt with at a previous episode
b) when these conditions are immediate complications of ectopic or molar pregnancies classifiable to 630-633 where they cannot be identified at fourth-digit level.

639.0 Genital tract and pelvic infection CC M♀
Endometritis
Parametritis
Pelvic peritonitis
Salpingitis   following conditions
Salpingo-oophoritis   classifiable to 630-638
Sepsis NOS
Septicemia NOS
EXCLUDES urinary tract infection (639.8)
CC Excl: 639.0, 639.2-641.23, 646.80-646.93, 648.90-649.64, 650, 669.40-669.44, 669.80-669.94, 679.00-679.04, 679.12, 679.14

639.1 Delayed or excessive hemorrhage CC M♀
Afibrinogenemia   following conditions
Defibrination syndrome   classfiable to 630-638
Intravascular
CC Excl: 639.1-641.23, 646.80-646.93, 648.90-649.64, 650, 669.40-669.44, 669.80-669.94, 679.00-679.04, 679.12, 679.14

639.2 Damage to pelvic organs and tissues CC M♀
Laceration, perforation, or tear of:
bladder
bowel
broad ligament
cervix   following conditions
periurethral tissue   classifiable to 630-638
uterus
vagina
CC Excl: 639.2-641.23, 646.80-646.93, 648.90-649.64, 650, 669.40-669.44, 669.80-669.94, 679.00-679.04, 679.12, 679.14

639.3 Kidney failure MCC M♀
Oliguria
Renal (kidney):
failure (acute)   following conditions
shutdown   classifiable to 630-638
tubular necrosis
Uremia
CC Excl: See code: 639.2

639.4 Metabolic disorders CC M♀
Electrolyte imbalance following conditions classifiable to 630-638
CC Excl: See code: 639.2

639.5 Shock MCC M♀
Circulatory collapse   following conditions
Shock (postoperative) (septic) classifiable to 630-638
CC Excl: See code: 639.2

639.6 Embolism MCC M♀
Embolism:
NOS
air
amniotic fluid
blood-clot
fat   following conditions
pulmonary   classifiable to 630-638
pyemic
septic
soap
CC Excl: See code: 639.2

---

§ See beginning of section 634-639 for fourth-digit definitions.
§§ Requires fifth digit. Valid digits are in [brackets] under each code. See appropriate category for codes and definitions.

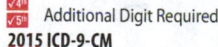

✓4ʰ
✓5ʰ Additional Digit Required   Unacceptable PDx   Manifestation Code   Hospital Acquired Condition   ►◄ Revised Text   ● New Code   ▲ Revised Code Title

639.8 Other specified complications following abortion or ectopic and molar pregnancy CC M ♀

Acute yellow atrophy or
   necrosis of liver   following conditons
Cardiac arrest or failure   classifiable to
Cerebral anoxia   630-638
Urinary tract infection

CC Excl: See code: 639.2

639.9 Unspecified complication following abortion or ectopic and molar pregnancy CC M ♀

Complication(s) not further specified following conditions classifiable to 630-638

CC Excl: See code: 639.2

Complications Mainly Related to Pregnancy (640-649)

INCLUDES   the listed conditions even if they arose or were present during labor, delivery, or the puerperium

AHA: 2Q, '90, 11

The following fifth-digit subclassification is for use with categories 640-649 to denote the current episode of care. Valid fifth-digits are in [brackets] under each code.

0 unspecified as to episode of care or not applicable
1 delivered, with or without mention of antepartum condition
    Antepartum condition with delivery
    Delivery NOS (with mention of antepartum complication during current episode of care)
    Intrapartum obstetric condition (with mention of antepartum complication during current episode of care)
    Pregnancy, delivered (with mention of antepartum complication during current episode of care)
2 delivered, with mention of postpartum complication
    Delivery with mention of puerperal complication during current episode of care
3 antepartum condition or complication
    Antepartum obstetric condtion, not delivered during the current episode of care
4 postpartum condition or complication
    Postpartum or puerperal obstetric condition or complication following delivery that occurred:
       during previous episode of care
       outside hospital, with subsequent admission for observation or care

✓4th **640 Hemorrhage in early pregnancy**

INCLUDES hemorrhage before completion of 22 weeks' gestation

§ ✓5th **640.0 Threatened abortion** CC 1,3 M ♀
[0,1,3]   **DEF:** Bloody discharge during pregnancy; cervix may be dilated and pregnancy is threatened, but the pregnancy is not terminated.
    CC Excl: For codes 640.01 and 640.03: 640.00-641.13, 646.80-646.93, 648.90-649.64, 650, 669.40-669.44, 669.80-669.94, 679.00-679.04, 679.12, 679.14

§ ✓5th **640.8 Other specified hemorrhage in early pregnancy** M ♀
[0,1,3]

§ ✓5th **640.9 Unspecified hemorrhage in early pregnancy** CC 3 M ♀
[0,1,3]   **CC Excl:** For code 640.93: 640.00-641.13, 646.80-646.93, 648.90-649.64, 650, 669.40-669.44, 669.80-669.94, 679.00-679.04, 679.12, 679.14

✓4th **641 Antepartum hemorrhage, abruptio placentae, and placenta previa**

§ ✓5th **641.0 Placenta previa without hemorrhage** CC 1,3 M ♀
[0,1,3]

Low implantation of placenta
Placenta previa noted: without
    during pregnancy   hemorrhage
    before labor (and delivered
       by caesarean delivery

DEF: Placenta implanted in lower segment of uterus; commonly causes hemorrhage in the last trimester of pregnancy.
CC Excl: For codes 641.01 and 641.03: 640.00-641.13, 646.80-646.93, 648.90-649.64, 650, 669.40-669.44, 669.80-669.94, 679.00-679.04, 679.12, 679.14

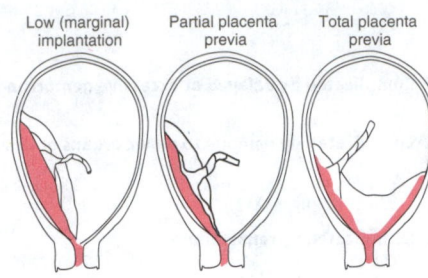

Placenta Previa

Low (marginal)   Partial placenta   Total placenta
implantation   previa   previa

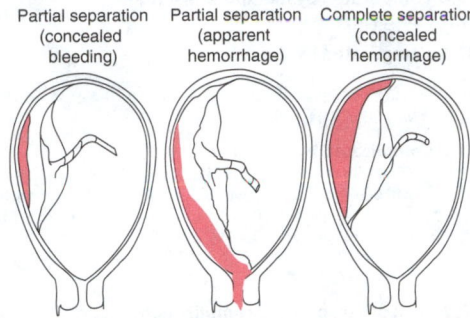

Abruptio Placentae

Partial separation   Partial separation   Complete separation
(concealed   (apparent   (concealed
bleeding)   hemorrhage)   hemorrhage)

§ ✓5th **641.1 Hemorrhage from placenta previa** MCC 1,3 M ♀
[0,1,3]
Low-lying placenta
Placenta previa   NOS or with hemorrhage
    incomplete   (intrapartum)
    marginal
    partial
    total

EXCLUDES hemorrhage from vasa previa (663.5)
CC Excl: For codes 641.11 and 641.13: 640.00-641.13, 646.80-646.93, 648.90-649.64, 650, 669.40-669.44, 669.80-669.94, 679.00-679.04, 679.12, 679.14

§ ✓5th **641.2 Premature separation of placenta** MCC 1 CC 3 M ♀
[0,1,3]
Ablatio placentae
Abruptio placentae
Accidental antepartum hemorrhage
Couvelaire uterus
Detachment of placenta (premature)
Premature separation of normally implanted placenta
DEF: Abruptio placentae: premature detachment of the placenta, characterized by shock, oliguria and decreased fibrinogen.
CC Excl: For code 641.21: 640.00-641.13, 641.21, 646.80-646.93, 648.90-649.64, 650, 669.40-669.44, 669.80-669.94, 679.00-679.04, 679.12, 679.14; For code 641.23: 640.00-641.13, 641.23, 646.80-646.93, 648.90-649.64, 650, 669.40-669.44, 669.80-669.94, 679.00-679.04, 679.12, 679.14
045.90 Premature sep of placenta unspec, uns trimester I-10

§ ✓5th **641.3 Antepartum hemorrhage associated** MCC 1,3 M ♀
[0,1,3] **with coagulation defects**
Antepartum or intrapartum hemorrhage associated with:
    afibrinogenemia
    hyperfibrinolysis
    hypofibrinogenemia
EXCLUDES coagulation defects not associated with antepartum hemorrhage (649.3)
DEF: Uterine hemorrhage prior to delivery.
CC Excl: For codes 641.31 and 641.33: 641.30-641.93, 646.80-646.93, 648.90-649.64, 650, 669.40-669.44, 669.80-669.94, 679.00-679.04, 679.12, 679.14

§ ✓5th **641.8 Other antepartum hemorrhage** M ♀
[0,1,3]
Antepartum or intrapartum hemorrhage associated with:
    trauma
    uterine leiomyoma

§ ✓5th **641.9 Unspecified antepartum hemorrhage** M ♀
[0,1,3]
Hemorrhage: Hemorrhage:
    antepartum NOS   of pregnancy NOS
    intrapartum NOS

---

§   Requires fifth digit. Valid digits are in [brackets] under each code. See beginning of section 640-649 for codes and definitions.

N Newborn Age: 0   **P** Pediatric Age: 0-17   **M** Maternity Age: 12-55   **A** Adult Age: 15-124   **MCC** Major CC Condition   **CC** CC Condition   **HIV** HIV Related Dx

214 – Volume 1   2015 ICD-9-CM

✓4ᵗʰ **642 Hypertension complicating pregnancy, childbirth, and the puerperium**

§ ✓5ᵗʰ **642.0 Benign essential hypertension complicating**   CC 1-3 Ⓜ♀
[0-4] **pregnancy, childbirth, and the puerperium**

Hypertension
  benign essential
  chronic NOS | specified as complicating, or as reason for obstetric care during pregnancy, childbirth, or the puerperium
  essential
  pre-existing NOS

CC Excl: For codes 642.01, 642.02, 642.03: 642.00-642.94, 646.10-646.14, 646.80-646.93, 648.90-649.64, 650, 669.40-669.44, 669.80-669.94, 679.00-679.04, 679.12, 679.14

010.02 Pre-exist essential hypertension comp childbirth   I-10

§ ✓5ᵗʰ **642.1 Hypertension secondary to renal disease,**   MCC 1-2 CC 3-4 ♀
[0-4] **complicating pregnancy, childbirth, and the puerperium**

Hypertension secondary to renal disease, specified as complicating, or as a reason for obstetric care during pregnancy, childbirth, or the puerperium

CC Excl: For codes 642.11-642.14: See code: 642.01

§ ✓5ᵗʰ **642.2 Other pre-existing hypertension complicating**   Ⓜ♀
[0-4] **pregnancy, childbirth, and the puerperium**

Hypertensive
  chronic kidney disease
  heart and chronic | specified as complicating, or as a reason for obstetric care
      kidney disease | during pregnancy, childbirth, or the
  heart disease | puerperium
  Malignant hypertension

§ ✓5ᵗʰ **642.3 Transient hypertension of pregnancy**   CC 1-2 Ⓜ♀
[0-4]

Gestational hypertension
Transient hypertension, so described, in pregnancy, childbirth, or the puerperium

CC Excl: For codes 642.31, 642.32: See code: 642.01
AHA: 3Q, '90, 4

013.9 Gestatnl pg-inducd HTN w/o sig protnuria uns tri   I-10

§ ✓5ᵗʰ **642.4 Mild or unspecified pre-eclampsia**   MCC 2 CC 1, 3, 4 Ⓜ♀
[0-4]

Hypertension in pregnancy, childbirth, or the puerperium, not specified as pre-existing, with either albuminuria or edema, or both; mild or unspecified
Pre-eclampsia:
  NOS
  mild
Toxemia (pre-eclamptic):
  NOS
  mild

EXCLUDES albuminuria in pregnancy, without mention of hypertension (646.2)
edema in pregnancy, without mention of hypertension (646.1)

CC Excl: For codes 642.41-642.44: See code: 642.01
AHA: For code 642.41: 4Q, '09, 153

014.00 Mild to moderate pre-eclampsia unspec trimester   I-10

§ ✓5ᵗʰ **642.5 Severe pre-eclampsia**   MCC 1-4 Ⓜ♀
[0-4]

Hypertension in pregnancy, childbirth, or the puerperium, not specified as pre-existing, with either albuminuria or edema, or both; specified as severe
Pre-eclampsia, severe
Toxemia (pre-eclamptic), severe

CC Excl: For codes 642.51-642.54: See code: 642.01
AHA: N-D, '85, 3

§ ✓5ᵗʰ **642.6 Eclampsia**   MCC 1-4 Ⓜ♀
[0-4]

Toxemia:
  eclamptic
  with convulsions

CC Excl: For codes 642.61-642.64: See code: 642.01

§ ✓5ᵗʰ **642.7 Pre-eclampsia or eclampsia superimposed**   MCC 1-4 Ⓜ♀
[0-4] **on pre-existing hypertension**

Conditions classifiable to 642.4-642.6, with conditions classifiable to 642.0-642.2

CC Excl: For codes 642.71-642.74: See code: 642.01

§ ✓5ᵗʰ **642.9 Unspecified hypertension complicating**   CC 1-4 Ⓜ♀
[0-4] **pregnancy, childbirth, or the puerperium**

Hypertension NOS, without mention of albuminuria or edema, complicating pregnancy, childbirth, or the puerperium

CC Excl: For codes 642.91, 642.92: 640.00-641.13, 646.80-646.93, 648.90-649.64, 650, 669.40-669.44, 669.80-669.94, 679.00-679.04, 679.12, 679.14; For codes 642.93, 642.94: 642.01-642.44, 642.61-642.94
AHA: For code 642.94: 1Q, '09, 17

✓4ᵗʰ **643 Excessive vomiting in pregnancy**

INCLUDES hyperemesis
vomiting:
  persistent | arising during pregnancy
  vicious
hyperemesis gravidarum

§ ✓5ᵗʰ **643.0 Mild hyperemesis gravidarum**   Ⓜ♀
[0,1,3]

Hyperemesis gravidarum, mild or unspecified, starting before the end of the 22nd week of gestation

DEF: Detrimental vomiting and nausea.

§ ✓5ᵗʰ **643.1 Hyperemesis gravidarum with metabolic disturbance**   Ⓜ♀
[0,1,3]

Hyperemesis gravidarum, starting before the end of the 22nd week of gestation, with metabolic disturbance, such as:
carbohydrate depletion
dehydration
electrolyte imbalance

§ ✓5ᵗʰ **643.2 Late vomiting of pregnancy**   Ⓜ♀
[0,1,3]

Excessive vomiting starting after 22 completed weeks of gestation

§ ✓5ᵗʰ **643.8 Other vomiting complicating pregnancy**   Ⓜ♀
[0,1,3]

Vomiting due to organic disease or other cause, specified as complicating pregnancy, or as a reason for obstetric care during pregnancy

Use additional code to specify cause

§ ✓5ᵗʰ **643.9 Unspecified vomiting of pregnancy**   Ⓜ♀
[0,1,3]

Vomiting as a reason for care during pregnancy, length of gestation unspecified

✓4ᵗʰ **644 Early or threatened labor**

§ ✓5ᵗʰ **644.0 Threatened premature labor**   MCC 3 Ⓜ♀
[0,3]

Premature labor after 22 weeks, but before 37 completed weeks of gestation without delivery

EXCLUDES that occurring before 22 completed weeks of gestation (640.0)

CC Excl: For code 644.03: 644.00-644.21, 646.80-646.93, 648.90-649.64, 650, 669.40-669.44, 669.80-669.94, 679.00-679.04, 679.12, 679.14

060.00 Preterm labor without delivery unspec trimester   I-10

§ ✓5ᵗʰ **644.1 Other threatened labor**   CC 3 Ⓜ♀
[0,3]

False labor:
  NOS
  after 37 completed weeks | without delivery
      of gestation
Threatened labor NOS

CC Excl: For code 644.13: See code 644.03

§ ✓5ᵗʰ **644.2 Early onset of delivery**   MCC 1 CC 0 Ⓜ♀
[0,1]

Onset (spontaneous) of delivery | before 37 completed
Premature labor with onset of | weeks of
      delivery | gestation

CC Excl: See code: 644.03
AHA: ▶1Q, '14, 19; 2Q, '13, 27;◀ For code 644.21: 3Q, '11, 3; 2Q, '91, 16
TIP: Assign if an attempted termination of pregnancy results in a liveborn fetus.

060.14x0 Pt labor 3rd tri w/pt del 3rd tri not applic/uns   I-10

✓4ᵗʰ **645 Late pregnancy**

AHA: 4Q, '00, 43; 4Q, '91, 26

§ ✓5ᵗʰ **645.1 Post term pregnancy**   Ⓜ♀
[0,1,3]

Pregnancy over 40 completed weeks to 42 completed weeks gestation

048.0 Post-term pregnancy   I-10

§ ✓5ᵗʰ **645.2 Prolonged pregnancy**   Ⓜ♀
[0,1,3]

Pregnancy which has advanced beyond 42 completed weeks gestation

---

§ Requires fifth digit. Valid digits are in [brackets] under each code. See beginning of section 640-649 for codes and definitions.

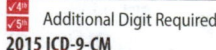

✓4ᵗʰ
✓5ᵗʰ Additional Digit Required   Unacceptable PDx   Manifestation Code   Hospital Acquired Condition   ▶◀ Revised Text   ● New Code   ▲ Revised Code Title

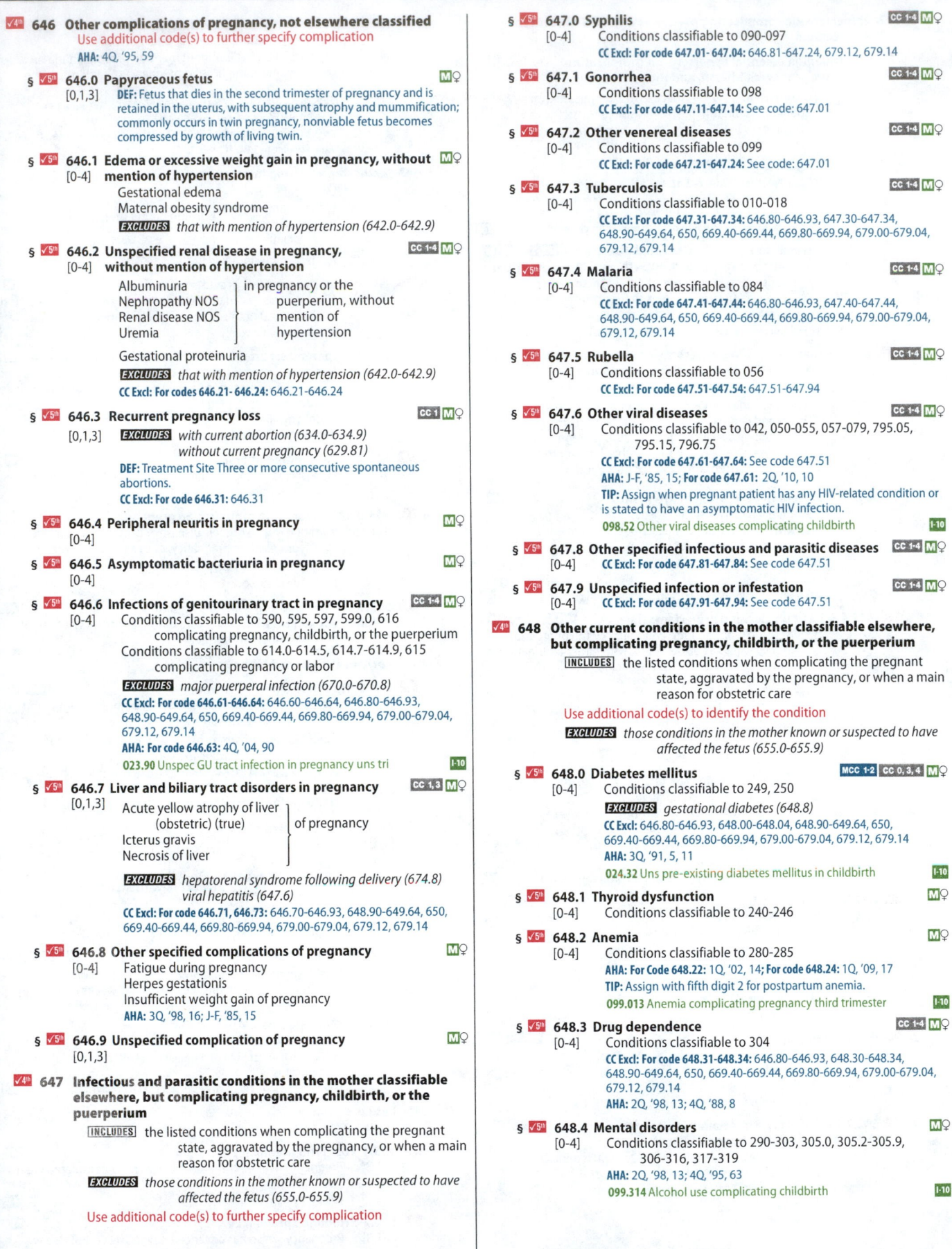

Complications of Pregnancy, Childbirth, and the Puerperium

646–648.4

√4ᵗʰ **646 Other complications of pregnancy, not elsewhere classified**
Use additional code(s) to further specify complication
AHA: 4Q, '95, 59

§ √5ᵗʰ **646.0 Papyraceous fetus** Ⓜ♀
[0,1,3]   **DEF:** Fetus that dies in the second trimester of pregnancy and is retained in the uterus, with subsequent atrophy and mummification; commonly occurs in twin pregnancy, nonviable fetus becomes compressed by growth of living twin.

§ √5ᵗʰ **646.1 Edema or excessive weight gain in pregnancy, without** Ⓜ♀
[0-4]   **mention of hypertension**
Gestational edema
Maternal obesity syndrome
EXCLUDES that with mention of hypertension (642.0-642.9)

§ √5ᵗʰ **646.2 Unspecified renal disease in pregnancy,** CC 1-4 Ⓜ♀
[0-4]   **without mention of hypertension**
Albuminuria ⎤ in pregnancy or the
Nephropathy NOS ⎥ puerperium, without
Renal disease NOS ⎥ mention of
Uremia ⎦ hypertension

Gestational proteinuria
EXCLUDES that with mention of hypertension (642.0-642.9)
CC Excl: For codes 646.21- 646.24: 646.21-646.24

§ √5ᵗʰ **646.3 Recurrent pregnancy loss** CC 1 Ⓜ♀
[0,1,3]   *EXCLUDES* with current abortion (634.0-634.9)
        without current pregnancy (629.81)
DEF: Treatment Site Three or more consecutive spontaneous abortions.
CC Excl: For code 646.31: 646.31

§ √5ᵗʰ **646.4 Peripheral neuritis in pregnancy** Ⓜ♀
[0-4]

§ √5ᵗʰ **646.5 Asymptomatic bacteriuria in pregnancy** Ⓜ♀
[0-4]

§ √5ᵗʰ **646.6 Infections of genitourinary tract in pregnancy** CC 1-4 Ⓜ♀
[0-4]   Conditions classifiable to 590, 595, 597, 599.0, 616
      complicating pregnancy, childbirth, or the puerperium
Conditions classifiable to 614.0-614.5, 614.7-614.9, 615
      complicating pregnancy or labor
EXCLUDES major puerperal infection (670.0-670.8)
CC Excl: For code 646.61-646.64: 646.60-646.64, 646.80-646.93, 648.90-649.64, 650, 669.40-669.44, 669.80-669.94, 679.00-679.04, 679.12, 679.14
AHA: For code 646.63: 4Q, '04, 90

023.90 Unspec GU tract infection in pregnancy uns tri I-10

§ √5ᵗʰ **646.7 Liver and biliary tract disorders in pregnancy** CC 1,3 Ⓜ♀
[0,1,3]   Acute yellow atrophy of liver ⎤
     (obstetric) (true) ⎥ of pregnancy
Icterus gravis ⎥
Necrosis of liver ⎦
EXCLUDES hepatorenal syndrome following delivery (674.8)
      viral hepatitis (647.6)
CC Excl: For code 646.71, 646.73: 646.70-646.93, 648.90-649.64, 650, 669.40-669.44, 669.80-669.94, 679.00-679.04, 679.12, 679.14

§ √5ᵗʰ **646.8 Other specified complications of pregnancy** Ⓜ♀
[0-4]   Fatigue during pregnancy
Herpes gestationis
Insufficient weight gain of pregnancy
AHA: 3Q, '98, 16; J-F, '85, 15

§ √5ᵗʰ **646.9 Unspecified complication of pregnancy** Ⓜ♀
[0,1,3]

√4ᵗʰ **647 Infectious and parasitic conditions in the mother classifiable elsewhere, but complicating pregnancy, childbirth, or the puerperium**
INCLUDES the listed conditions when complicating the pregnant state, aggravated by the pregnancy, or when a main reason for obstetric care
EXCLUDES those conditions in the mother known or suspected to have affected the fetus (655.0-655.9)
Use additional code(s) to further specify complication

§ √5ᵗʰ **647.0 Syphilis** CC 1-4 Ⓜ♀
[0-4]   Conditions classifiable to 090-097
CC Excl: For code 647.01- 647.04: 646.81-647.24, 679.12, 679.14

§ √5ᵗʰ **647.1 Gonorrhea** CC 1-4 Ⓜ♀
[0-4]   Conditions classifiable to 098
CC Excl: For code 647.11-647.14: See code: 647.01

§ √5ᵗʰ **647.2 Other venereal diseases** CC 1-4 Ⓜ♀
[0-4]   Conditions classifiable to 099
CC Excl: For code 647.21-647.24: See code: 647.01

§ √5ᵗʰ **647.3 Tuberculosis** CC 1-4 Ⓜ♀
[0-4]   Conditions classifiable to 010-018
CC Excl: For code 647.31-647.34: 646.80-646.93, 647.30-647.34, 648.90-649.64, 650, 669.40-669.44, 669.80-669.94, 679.00-679.04, 679.12, 679.14

§ √5ᵗʰ **647.4 Malaria** CC 1-4 Ⓜ♀
[0-4]   Conditions classifiable to 084
CC Excl: For code 647.41-647.44: 646.80-646.93, 647.40-647.44, 648.90-649.64, 650, 669.40-669.44, 669.80-669.94, 679.00-679.04, 679.12, 679.14

§ √5ᵗʰ **647.5 Rubella** CC 1-4 Ⓜ♀
[0-4]   Conditions classifiable to 056
CC Excl: For code 647.51-647.54: 647.51-647.94

§ √5ᵗʰ **647.6 Other viral diseases** CC 1-4 Ⓜ♀
[0-4]   Conditions classifiable to 042, 050-055, 057-079, 795.05, 795.15, 796.75
CC Excl: For code 647.61-647.64: See code 647.51
AHA: J-F, '85, 15; For code 647.61: 2Q, '10, 10
TIP: Assign when pregnant patient has any HIV-related condition or is stated to have an asymptomatic HIV infection.
098.52 Other viral diseases complicating childbirth I-10

§ √5ᵗʰ **647.8 Other specified infectious and parasitic diseases** CC 1-4 Ⓜ♀
[0-4]   CC Excl: For code 647.81-647.84: See code 647.51

§ √5ᵗʰ **647.9 Unspecified infection or infestation** CC 1-4 Ⓜ♀
[0-4]   CC Excl: For code 647.91-647.94: See code 647.51

√4ᵗʰ **648 Other current conditions in the mother classifiable elsewhere, but complicating pregnancy, childbirth, or the puerperium**
INCLUDES the listed conditions when complicating the pregnant state, aggravated by the pregnancy, or when a main reason for obstetric care
Use additional code(s) to identify the condition
EXCLUDES those conditions in the mother known or suspected to have affected the fetus (655.0-655.9)

§ √5ᵗʰ **648.0 Diabetes mellitus** MCC 1-2 CC 0,3,4 Ⓜ♀
[0-4]   Conditions classifiable to 249, 250
EXCLUDES gestational diabetes (648.8)
CC Excl: 646.80-646.93, 648.00-648.04, 648.90-649.64, 650, 669.40-669.44, 669.80-669.94, 679.00-679.04, 679.12, 679.14
AHA: 3Q, '91, 5, 11
024.32 Uns pre-existing diabetes mellitus in childbirth I-10

§ √5ᵗʰ **648.1 Thyroid dysfunction** Ⓜ♀
[0-4]   Conditions classifiable to 240-246

§ √5ᵗʰ **648.2 Anemia** Ⓜ♀
[0-4]   Conditions classifiable to 280-285
AHA: For Code 648.22: 1Q, '02, 14; For code 648.24: 1Q, '09, 17
TIP: Assign with fifth digit 2 for postpartum anemia.
099.013 Anemia complicating pregnancy third trimester I-10

§ √5ᵗʰ **648.3 Drug dependence** CC 1-4 Ⓜ♀
[0-4]   Conditions classifiable to 304
CC Excl: For code 648.31-648.34: 646.80-646.93, 648.30-648.34, 648.90-649.64, 650, 669.40-669.44, 669.80-669.94, 679.00-679.04, 679.12, 679.14
AHA: 2Q, '98, 13; 4Q, '88, 8

§ √5ᵗʰ **648.4 Mental disorders** Ⓜ♀
[0-4]   Conditions classifiable to 290-303, 305.0, 305.2-305.9, 306-316, 317-319
AHA: 2Q, '98, 13; 4Q, '95, 63
099.314 Alcohol use complicating childbirth I-10

---

§   Requires fifth digit. Valid digits are in [brackets] under each code. See beginning of section 640-649 for codes and definitions.

Ⓝ Newborn Age: 0   Ⓟ Pediatric Age: 0-17   Ⓜ Maternity Age: 12-55   Ⓐ Adult Age: 15-124   **MCC** Major CC Condition   **CC** CC Condition   **HIV** HIV Related Dx

§ ✓5th **648.5 Congenital cardiovascular disorders**   CC 1-4 M♀
[0-4]   Conditions classifiable to 745-747
CC Excl: For code 648.51, 648.52, 648.53, 648.54: 646.80-646.93,
648.50-648.64, 648.90-649.64, 650, 669.40-669.44, 669.80-669.94,
679.00-679.04, 679.12, 679.14

§ ✓5th **648.6 Other cardiovascular diseases**   CC 1-4 M♀
[0-4]   Conditions classifiable to 390-398, 410-429
EXCLUDES *cerebrovascular disorders in the puerperium (674.0)*
peripartum cardiomyopathy (674.5)
venous complications (671.0-671.9)
CC Excl: For code 648.61, 648.62, 648.63, 648.64: 646.80-646.93,
648.50-648.64, 648.90-649.64, 650, 669.40-669.44, 669.80-669.94,
679.00-679.04, 679.12, 679.14
AHA: 3Q, '98, 11; For code 648.64: 3Q, '12, 9

§ ✓5th **648.7 Bone and joint disorders of back, pelvis, and**   CC 1-4 M♀
[0-4]   **lower limbs**
     Conditions classifiable to 720-724, and those classifiable to
711-719 or 725-738, specified as affecting the lower
limbs
CC Excl: For code 648.71, 648.72, 648.73, 648.74: 648.71-648.74

§ ✓5th **648.8 Abnormal glucose tolerance**   M♀
[0-4]   Conditions classifiable to 790.21-790.29
     Gestational diabetes
**Use additional code, if applicable, for associated long-term
(current) insulin use (V58.67)**
DEF: Glucose intolerance arising in pregnancy, resolving at end of
pregnancy.
AHA: 3Q, '91, 5; For code 648.83: 4Q, '04, 56
TIP: Do not assign if patient was diabetic before becoming pregnant;
should never be assigned in combination with code 648.0x.
024.429 Gestational diab mellitus childbirth uns cntrl   I-10

§ ✓5th **648.9 Other current conditions classifiable elsewhere**   M♀
[0-4]   Conditions classifiable to 440-459, 795.01-795.04, 795.06,
795.10-795.14, 795.16, 796.70-796.74, 796.76
     Nutritional deficiencies [conditions classifiable to 260-269]
AHA: 3Q, '06, 14; 4Q, '04, 88; N-D, '87, 10; For code 648.91: 1Q, '02, 14;
For code 648.93: 4Q, '04, 90; For code 648.94: 1Q, '09, 17
TIP: Assign for group B streptococcus carrier patients, along with
code V02.51 Carrier or suspected carrier of infectious diseases.

✓4th **649 Other conditions or status of the mother complicating
pregnancy, childbirth, or the puerperium**
AHA: 4Q, '06, 99

§ ✓5th **649.0 Tobacco use disorder complicating pregnancy,**   M♀
[0-4]   **childbirth, or the puerperium**
     Smoking complicating pregnancy, childbirth, or the
puerperium
AHA: 4Q, '06, 99
099.334 Smoking tobacco complicating childbirth   I-10

§ ✓5th **649.1 Obesity complicating pregnancy, childbirth, or the**   M♀
[0-4]   **puerperium**
Use additional code to identify the obesity (278.00- 278.03)
AHA: 4Q, '06, 99
099.214 Obesity complicating childbirth   I-10

§ ✓5th **649.2 Bariatric surgery status complicating pregnancy,**   M♀
[0-4]   **childbirth, or the puerperium**
     Gastric banding status complicating pregnancy, childbirth, or
the puerperium
     Gastric bypass status for obesity complicating pregnancy,
childbirth, or the puerperium
     Obesity surgery status complicating pregnancy, childbirth, or
the puerperium
AHA: 4Q, '06, 99, 118

§ ✓5th **649.3 Coagulation defects complicating pregnancy,**   CC M♀
[0-4]   **childbirth, or the puerperium**
     Conditions classifiable to 286, 287, 289
**Use additional code to identify the specific coagulation defect
(286.0-286.9, 287.0-287.9, 289.0-289.9)**
EXCLUDES *coagulation defects causing antepartum
hemorrhage (641.3)*
postpartum coagulation defects (666.3)
CC Excl: For code 649.30: 648.90; For codes 649.31, 649.32, 649.33, 649.34:
648.91-648.94
AHA: 4Q, '06, 99

§ ✓5th **649.4 Epilepsy complicating pregnancy, childbirth, or**   CC 1-4 M♀
[0-4]   **the puerperium**
     Conditions classifiable to 345
**Use additional code to identify specific type of epilepsy
(345.00-345.91)**
EXCLUDES *eclampsia (642.6)*
CC Excl: For codes 649.41, 649.42, 649.43, 649.44: 648.91-648.94
AHA: 4Q, '06, 99

§ ✓5th **649.5 Spotting complicating pregnancy**   M♀
[0,1,3]   **EXCLUDES** *antepartum hemorrhage (641.0-641.9)*
hemorrhage in early pregnancy (640.0-640.9)
AHA: 4Q, '06, 99

§ ✓5th **649.6 Uterine size date discrepancy**   M♀
[0-4]   **EXCLUDES** *suspected problem with fetal growth not found
(V89.04)*
AHA: 4Q, '06, 99

§ ✓5th **649.7 Cervical shortening**   M CC
[0,1,3]   **EXCLUDES** *suspected cervical shortening not found (V89.05)*
DEF: A cervix that has shortened to < 25 mm in length by the 16th
week of pregnancy; warning sign for impending premature delivery;
treated by cervical cerclage placement or progesterone.
CC Excl: For code 649.70, 649.71, 649.73: 649.70-649.73, 654.51-654.54
AHA: 4Q, '08, 124-125; For Code 649.73: 4Q '08, 125

§ ✓5th **649.8 Onset (spontaneous) of labor after 37 completed**   M♀
[1,2]   **weeks of gestation but before 39 completed weeks
gestation, with delivery by (planned) cesarean section**
     Delivery by (planned) cesarean section occurring after 37
completed weeks of gestation but before 39 completed
weeks gestation due to (spontaneous) onset of labor
**Use additional code to specify reason for planned cesarean
section such as:
cephalopelvic disproportion (normally formed fetus)
(653.4)
previous cesarean delivery (654.2)**
AHA: 4Q, '11, 132-133; For code 649.81: 4Q, '11, 133

Normal Delivery, and Other Indications for Care in Pregnancy, Labor, and Delivery (650-659)

The following fifth-digit subclassification is for use with categories
651-659 to denote the current episode of care. Valid fifth-digits are in
[brackets] under each code.
  0   unspecified as to episode of care or not applicable
  1   delivered, with or without mention of antepartum condition
  2   delivered, with mention of postpartum complication
  3   antepartum condition or complication
  4   postpartum condition or complication

650 Normal delivery   M♀
NOTE Delivery requiring minimal or no assistance, with or without
episiotomy, without fetal manipulation [e.g., rotation version]
or instrumentation [forceps] of spontaneous, cephalic, vaginal,
full-term, single, live-born infant. This code is for use as a single
diagnosis code and is not to be used with any other code in the
range 630-676.
Use additional code to indicate outcome of delivery (V27.0)
EXCLUDES *breech delivery (assisted) (spontaneous) NOS (652.2)*
*delivery by vacuum extractor, forceps, cesarean section, or
breech extraction, without specified complication
(669.5-669.7)*
AHA: 2Q, '02, 10; 3Q, '01, 12; 3Q, '00, 5; 4Q, '95, 28, 59
TIP: Code 650 is to be assigned only for the episode of care during which the
patient delivers and may be assigned if the patient is admitted for induction
of labor.
O80 Encounter for full-term uncomplicated delivery   I-10

✓4th **651 Multiple gestation**
Use additional code to specify placenta status (V91.00-V91.99)

§ ✓5th **651.0 Twin pregnancy**   CC 1 M♀
[0,1,3]   **EXCLUDES** *fetal conjoined twins (678.1)*
CC Excl: For code 651.01: 650-651.63, 651.71-652.20, 652.23-652.93
AHA: 3Q, '06, 16
O30.009 Twin preg unspec numb of placenta & unspec
numb amniotic sacs unspec tri   I-10

---

§   Requires fifth digit. Valid digits are in [brackets] under each code. See beginning of section 640-649 for codes and definitions.

✓4th
✓5th   Additional Digit Required   Unacceptable PDx   Manifestation Code   Hospital Acquired Condition   ▶◀ Revised Text   ● New Code   ▲ Revised Code Title
2015 ICD-9-CM   **Volume 1 – 217**

Malposition and Malpresentation

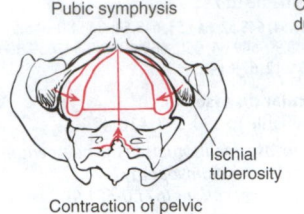

Breech

Mother's pelvis

Shoulder (arm prolapse)

Face (mentum)

Compound (extremity together with head)

Oblique

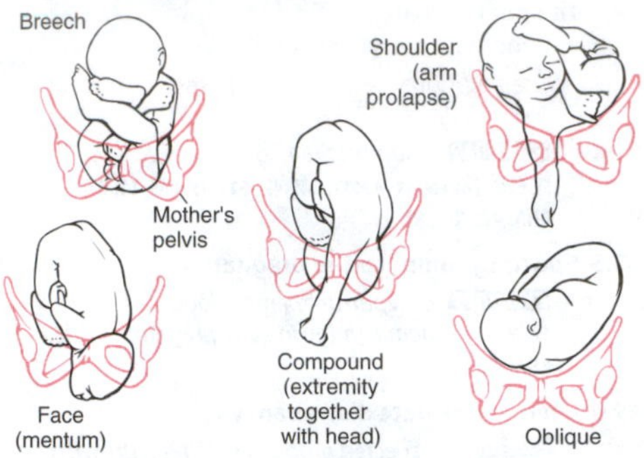

§ √5th **651.1 Triplet pregnancy**   CC 1,3 M♀
    [0,1,3]   CC Excl: For code 651.11, 651.13: 650-651.63, 651.71-652.93

§ √5th **651.2 Quadruplet pregnancy**   CC 1,3 M♀
    [0,1,3]   CC Excl: For code 651.21, 651.23: See code 651.11

§ √5th **651.3 Twin pregnancy with fetal loss and retention of one**   M♀
    [0,1,3] **fetus**
        Vanishing twin syndrome (651.33)

§ √5th **651.4 Triplet pregnancy with fetal loss and retention of**   CC 1,3 M♀
    [0,1,3] **one or more fetus(es)**
        CC Excl: For code 651.41, 651.43: See code 651.11

§ √5th **651.5 Quadruplet pregnancy with fetal loss and**   CC 1,3 M♀
    [0,1,3] **retention of one or more fetus(es)**
        CC Excl: For code 651.51, 651.53: See code 651.11

§ √5th **651.6 Other multiple pregnancy with fetal loss and retention**   M♀
    [0,1,3] **of one or more fetus(es)**

§ √5th **651.7 Multiple gestation following (elective) fetal reduction**   M♀
    [0,1,3]   Fetal reduction of multiple fetuses reduced to single fetus
        AHA: 3Q, '06, 18; For code 651.71: 4Q, '05, 81

§ √5th **651.8 Other specified multiple gestation**   CC 1,3 M♀
    [0,1,3]   CC Excl: For code 651.81, 651.83: See code 651.11

§ √5th **651.9 Unspecified multiple gestation**   M♀
    [0,1,3]

√4th **652 Malposition and malpresentation of fetus**
    Code first any associated obstructed labor (660.0)

§ √5th **652.0 Unstable lie**   M♀
    [0,1,3] **DEF:** Changing fetal position.

§ √5th **652.1 Breech or other malpresentation successfully**   M♀
    [0,1,3] **converted to cephalic presentation**
        Cephalic version NOS

§ √5th **652.2 Breech presentation without mention of version**   M♀
    [0,1,3]   Breech delivery (assisted) (spontaneous) NOS
        Buttocks presentation
        Complete breech
        Frank breech
        EXCLUDES *footling presentation (652.8)*
                     incomplete breech (652.8)
        AHA: For code 652.21: ▶3Q, '13, 7◀
        DEF: Fetal presentation of buttocks or feet at birth canal.
        032.1xx0 Maternal care breech presentation not applic/uns   I-10

§ √5th **652.3 Transverse or oblique presentation**   M♀
    [0,1,3]   Oblique lie   Transverse lie
        EXCLUDES *transverse arrest of fetal head (660.3)*
        DEF: Delivery of fetus, shoulder first.

§ √5th **652.4 Face or brow presentation**   M♀
    [0,1,3]   Mentum presentation

§ √5th **652.5 High head at term**   M♀
    [0,1,3]   Failure of head to enter pelvic brim
        AHA: For code 652.51: ▶3Q, '13, 8◀
        032.4xx0 Maternal care high head at term not applic/uns   I-10

§ √5th **652.6 Multiple gestation with malpresentation of one**   M♀
    [0,1,3] **fetus or more**

§ √5th **652.7 Prolapsed arm**   M♀
    [0,1,3]

Cephalopelvic Disproportion

Pubic symphysis

Cephalopelvic disproportion due to: Contraction of pelvic inlet, or large fetus, or hydrocephalus

Ischial tuberosity

Contraction of pelvic outlet (from below)

Pubic symphysis

Pelvic inlet from above

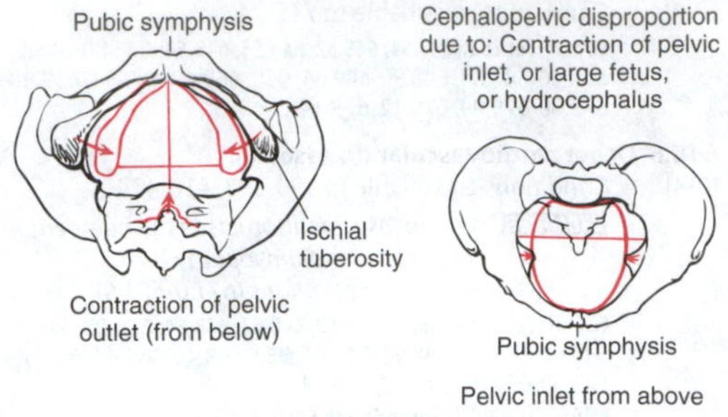

§ √5th **652.8 Other specified malposition or malpresentation**   M♀
    [0,1,3]   Compound presentation

§ √5th **652.9 Unspecified malposition or malpresentation**   M♀
    [0,1,3]

√4th **653 Disproportion**
    Code first any associated obstructed labor (660.1)

§ √5th **653.0 Major abnormality of bony pelvis, not further**   M♀
    [0,1,3] **specified**
        Pelvic deformity NOS

§ √5th **653.1 Generally contracted pelvis**   M♀
    [0,1,3]   Contracted pelvis NOS

§ √5th **653.2 Inlet contraction of pelvis**   M♀
    [0,1,3]   Inlet contraction (pelvis)

§ √5th **653.3 Outlet contraction of pelvis**   M♀
    [0,1,3]   Outlet contraction (pelvis)

§ √5th **653.4 Fetopelvic disproportion**   M♀
    [0,1,3]   Cephalopelvic disproportion NOS
        Disproportion of mixed maternal and fetal origin, with
            normally formed fetus
        033.4xx0 Mtrn care dispropor mtrn&fetal orig not applic   I-10

§ √5th **653.5 Unusually large fetus causing disproportion**   M♀
    [0,1,3]   Disproportion of fetal origin with normally formed fetus
        Fetal disproportion NOS
        EXCLUDES *that when the reason for medical care was concern*
                 for the fetus (656.6)

§ √5th **653.6 Hydrocephalic fetus causing disproportion**   M♀
    [0,1,3]   **EXCLUDES** *that when the reason for medical care was concern*
                 for the fetus (655.0)

§ √5th **653.7 Other fetal abnormality causing disproportion**   M♀
    [0,1,3]   Fetal: Fetal:
          ascites   sacral teratoma
          hydrops   tumor
          myelomeningocele
        EXCLUDES *conjoined twins causing disproportion (678.1)*

§ √5th **653.8 Disproportion of other origin**   M♀
    [0,1,3]   **EXCLUDES** *shoulder (girdle) dystocia (660.4)*

§ √5th **653.9 Unspecified disproportion**   M♀
    [0,1,3]

√4th **654 Abnormality of organs and soft tissues of pelvis**
    INCLUDES the listed conditions during pregnancy, childbirth, or the
                  puerperium
    Code first any associated obstructed labor (660.2)
    EXCLUDES *trauma to perineum and vulva complicating current delivery*
                 (664.0-664.9)

§ √5th **654.0 Congenital abnormalities of uterus**   M♀
    [0-4]   Double uterus
        Uterus bicornis

§ √5th **654.1 Tumors of body of uterus**   M♀
    [0-4]   Uterine fibroids

§ √5th **654.2 Previous cesarean delivery**   M♀
    [0,1,3]   Uterine scar from previous cesarean delivery
        AHA: 1Q, '92, 8; **For code 654.21:** ▶3Q, '13, 6;◀ 4Q, '11, 133
        034.21 Maternal care for scar from prev cesarean del   I-10

---

§   Requires fifth digit. Valid digits are in [brackets] under each code. See beginning of section 640-649 for codes and definitions.

N Newborn Age: 0   P Pediatric Age: 0-17   M Maternity Age: 12-55   A Adult Age: 15-124   MCC Major CC Condition   CC CC Condition   HIV HIV Related Dx

§ √5ᵗʰ **654.3 Retroverted and incarcerated gravid uterus** Ⓜ♀
[0-4]
  DEF: Treatment Site Retroverted: tilted back uterus; no change in angle of longitudinal axis.
  DEF: Treatment Site Incarcerated: immobile, fixed uterus.

§ √5ᵗʰ **654.4 Other abnormalities in shape or position** Ⓜ♀
[0-4] **of gravid uterus and of neighboring structures**
  Cystocele   Prolapse of gravid uterus
  Pelvic floor repair   Rectocele
  Pendulous abdomen   Rigid pelvic floor
  Prolapse of gravid uterus

§ √5ᵗʰ **654.5 Cervical incompetence** MCC 1-4 Ⓜ♀
[0-4]
  Presence of Shirodkar suture with or without mention of cervical incompetence
  DEF: Abnormal cervix; tendency to dilate in second trimester; causes premature fetal expulsion.
  DEF: Shirodkar suture: purse-string suture used to artificially close incompetent cervix.
  CC Excl: For code 654.51-654.54: 649.70-649.73, 654.51-654.54

§ √5ᵗʰ **654.6 Other congenital or acquired abnormality** Ⓜ♀
[0-4] **of cervix**
  Cicatricial cervix
  Polyp of cervix
  Previous surgery to cervix
  Rigid cervix (uteri)
  Stenosis or stricture of cervix
  Tumor of cervix

§ √5ᵗʰ **654.7 Congenital or acquired abnormality of vagina** Ⓜ♀
[0-4]
  Previous surgery to vagina
  Septate vagina
  Stenosis of vagina (acquired) (congenital)
  Stricture of vagina
  Tumor of vagina

§ √5ᵗʰ **654.8 Congenital or acquired abnormality of vulva** Ⓜ♀
[0-4]
  Anal sphincter tear (healed) (old) complicating delivery
  Fibrosis of perineum
  Persistent hymen
  Previous surgery to perineum or vulva
  Rigid perineum
  Tumor of vulva
  EXCLUDES anal sphincter tear (healed) (old) not associated with delivery (569.43)
           varicose veins of vulva (671.1)
  AHA: 1Q, '03, 14

§ √5ᵗʰ **654.9 Other and unspecified** Ⓜ♀
[0-4] Uterine scar NEC

√4ᵗʰ **655 Known or suspected fetal abnormality affecting management of mother**
  INCLUDES the listed conditions in the fetus as a reason for observation or obstetrical care of the mother, or for termination of pregnancy
  AHA: 3Q, '90, 4
  TIP: Only assign when the fetal condition affects the management of the mother. Assign on mother's chart when in utero procedures are performed on the fetus.

§ √5ᵗʰ **655.0 Central nervous system malformation in fetus** Ⓜ♀
[0,1,3] Fetal or suspected fetal:
        anencephaly
        hydrocephalus
        spina bifida (with myelomeningocele)

§ √5ᵗʰ **655.1 Chromosomal abnormality in fetus** Ⓜ♀
[0,1,3]

§ √5ᵗʰ **655.2 Hereditary disease in family possibly affecting fetus** Ⓜ♀

§ √5ᵗʰ **655.3 Suspected damage to fetus from viral disease in** Ⓜ♀
[0,1,3] **the mother**
        Suspected damage to fetus from maternal rubella

§ √5ᵗʰ **655.4 Suspected damage to fetus from other disease in** Ⓜ♀
[0,1,3] **the mother**
        Suspected damage to fetus from maternal:
        alcohol addiction
        listeriosis
        toxoplasmosis

§ √5ᵗʰ **655.5 Suspected damage to fetus from drugs** Ⓜ♀
[0,1,3]

§ √5ᵗʰ **655.6 Suspected damage to fetus from radiation** Ⓜ♀
[0,1,3]

§ √5ᵗʰ **655.7 Decreased fetal movements** Ⓜ♀
[0,1,3] **AHA:** 4Q, '97, 41

§ √5ᵗʰ **655.8 Other known or suspected fetal abnormality, not** Ⓜ♀
[0,1,3] **elsewhere classified**
        Suspected damage to fetus from:
          environmental toxins
          intrauterine contraceptive device
        AHA: 3Q, '06, 16, 18

§ √5ᵗʰ **655.9 Unspecified** Ⓜ♀
[0,1,3] **AHA:** For code 655.93: 2Q, '10, 6-7

√4ᵗʰ **656 Other known or suspected fetal and placental problems affecting management of mother**
  EXCLUDES fetal hematologic conditions (678.0)
           suspected placental problems not found (V89.02)

§ √5ᵗʰ **656.0 Fetal-maternal hemorrhage** Ⓜ♀
[0,1,3] Leakage (microscopic) of fetal blood into maternal circulation

§ √5ᵗʰ **656.1 Rhesus isoimmunization** CC 3 Ⓜ♀
[0,1,3] Anti-D [Rh] antibodies
        Rh incompatibility
        DEF: Antibodies developing against Rh factor; mother with Rh negative develops antibodies against Rh positive fetus.
        CC Excl: For code 656.13: 656.11-656.13
        036.0190 Mtrn care anti-D Rh antibods uns tri not applic I-10

§ √5ᵗʰ **656.2 Isoimmunization from other and unspecified blood-** Ⓜ♀
[0,1,3] **group incompatibility**
        ABO isoimmunization
        AHA: 4Q, '06, 135

§ √5ᵗʰ **656.3 Fetal distress** CC 1 Ⓜ♀
[0,1,3] Fetal metabolic acidemia
        EXCLUDES abnormal fetal acid-base balance (656.8)
                 abnormality in fetal heart rate or rhythm (659.7)
                 fetal bradycardia (659.7)
                 fetal tachycardia (659.7)
                 meconium in liquor (656.8)
        DEF: Life-threatening disorder; fetal anoxia, hemolytic disease and other miscellaneous diseases cause fetal distress.
        CC Excl: For code 656.31: 656.31-656.33, 659.71, 763.82
        AHA: N-D, '86, 4

§ √5ᵗʰ **656.4 Intrauterine death** CC 1,3 Ⓜ♀
[0,1,3] Fetal death:
          NOS
          after completion of 22 weeks' gestation
          late
        Missed delivery
        EXCLUDES missed abortion (632)
        CC Excl: For code 656.41: 656.41-656.43; For code 656.43: 656.43

§ √5ᵗʰ **656.5 Poor fetal growth** CC 1 Ⓜ♀
[0,1,3] "Light-for-dates"
        "Placental insufficiency"
        "Small-for-dates"
        CC Excl: For code 656.51: 656.51-656.53
        036.5190 Mtrn care known/spct placental insuff uns tri I-10

§ √5ᵗʰ **656.6 Excessive fetal growth** Ⓜ♀
[0,1,3] "Large-for-dates"
        036.60x0 Mtrn care excess fetl grwth uns tri not applic I-10

§ √5ᵗʰ **656.7 Other placental conditions** Ⓜ♀
[0,1,3] Abnormal placenta
        Placental infarct
        EXCLUDES placental polyp (674.4)
                 placentitis (658.4)

§ Requires fifth digit. Valid digits are in [brackets] under each code. See beginning of section 640-649 for codes and definitions.

√4ᵗʰ / √5ᵗʰ Additional Digit Required | Unacceptable PDx | Manifestation Code | Hospital Acquired Condition | ►◄ Revised Text | ● New Code | ▲ Revised Code Title

2015 ICD-9-CM   Volume 1 – 219

Complications of Pregnancy, Childbirth, and the Puerperium

654.3–656.7

§ ✓5th **656.8 Other specified fetal and placental problems**   M ♀
[0,1,3]
Abnormal acid-base balance
Intrauterine acidosis
Lithopedian
Meconium in liquor
Subchorionic hematoma
DEF: Lithopedion: Calcified fetus; not expelled by mother.
036.20x0 Mtrn care hydrops fetalis uns tri not applic/uns   I-10

§ ✓5th **656.9 Unspecified fetal and placental problem**   M ♀
[0,1,3]

✓4th **657 Polyhydramnios**   CC 1 M ♀
[0,1,3]

§ ✓5th Use 0 as fourth-digit for this category

Hydramnios
EXCLUDES suspected polyhydramnios not found (V89.01)
DEF: Excess amniotic fluid.
CC Excl: For code 657.01: 657.01-657.03
AHA: 3Q, '06, 16; 4Q, '91, 26
040.9xx0 Polyhydraminos uns trimester not applicable/uns   I-10

✓4th **658 Other problems associated with amniotic cavity and membranes**
EXCLUDES amniotic fluid embolism (673.1)
suspected problems with amniotic cavity and membranes not found (V89.01)

§ ✓5th **658.0 Oligohydramnios**   CC 1,3 M ♀
[0,1,3]
Oligohydramnios without mention of
rupture of membranes
DEF: Deficient amount of amniotic fluid.
CC Excl: For code 658.01, 658.03: 658.01-658.03
AHA: 3Q, '06, 16
041.00x0 Oligohydraminos uns trimester not applicable/uns   I-10

§ ✓5th **658.1 Premature rupture of membranes**   M ♀
[0,1,3]
Rupture of amniotic sac less than 24
hours prior to the onset of labor
AHA: For code 658.13: 1Q, '01, 5; 4Q, '98, 77
042.00 Prmat rom ool w/in 24 hrs of rup uns wks gestatn   I-10

§ ✓5th **658.2 Delayed delivery after spontaneous or unspecified**   M ♀
[0,1,3] **rupture of membranes**
Prolonged rupture of membranes NOS
Rupture of amniotic sac 24 hours or more prior to the onset of labor
AHA: For code 658.21: ▶1Q, '14, 19◀

§ ✓5th **658.3 Delayed delivery after artificial rupture**   M ♀
[0,1,3] **of membranes**

§ ✓5th **658.4 Infection of amniotic cavity**   MCC 1,3 M ♀
[0,1,3]
Amnionitis
Chorioamnionitis
Membranitis
Placentitis
CC Excl: For code 658.41, 658.43: 658.41-658.43
041.1090 Inf amniotic sac & memb uns tri not applic/uns   I-10

§ ✓5th **658.8 Other**   CC 1 M ♀
[0,1,3]
Amnion nodosum
Amniotic cyst
CC Excl: For code 658.81: 658.81

§ ✓5th **658.9 Unspecified**   M ♀
[0,1,3]

✓4th **659 Other indications for care or intervention related to labor and delivery, not elsewhere classified**

§ ✓5th **659.0 Failed mechanical induction**   M ♀
[0,1,3] Failure of induction of labor by surgical
or other instrumental methods

§ ✓5th **659.1 Failed medical or unspecified induction**   M ♀
[0,1,3] Failed induction NOS
Failure of induction of labor by medical
methods, such as oxytocic drugs
061.9 Failed induction of labor unspecified   I-10

§ ✓5th **659.2 Maternal pyrexia during labor, unspecified**   CC 1 M ♀
[0,1,3] **DEF:** Fever during labor.
CC Excl: For code 659.21: 659.21-659.23
075.2 Pyrexia during labor not elsewhere classified   I-10

§ ✓5th **659.3 Generalized infection during labor**   MCC 1,3 M ♀
[0,1,3] Septicemia during labor
CC Excl: For code 659.31, 659.33: 646.80-646.93, 648.90-649.64, 650, 659.30-659.33, 669.40-669.44, 669.80-669.94, 679.00-679.04, 679.12, 679.14

§ ✓5th **659.4 Grand multiparity**   M ♀
[0,1,3] **EXCLUDES** supervision only, in pregnancy (V23.3)
without current pregnancy (V61.5)
DEF: Having borne six or more children previously.

§ ✓5th **659.5 Elderly primigravida**   M ♀
[0,1,3] First pregnancy in a woman who will be 35 years of age or
older at expected date of delivery
EXCLUDES supervision only, in pregnancy (V23.81)
AHA: 3Q, '01, 12
009.519 Supervisn of elderly primigravida uns trimester   I-10

§ ✓5th **659.6 Elderly multigravida**   M ♀
[0,1,3] Second or more pregnancy in a woman who will be
35 years of age or older at expected date of delivery
EXCLUDES elderly primigravida 659.5
supervision only, in pregnancy (V23.82)
AHA: 3Q, '01, 12
009.529 Supervisn of elderly multigravida uns trimester   I-10

§ ✓5th **659.7 Abnormality in fetal heart rate or rhythm**   M ♀
[0,1,3] Depressed fetal heart tones
Fetal:
bradycardia
tachycardia
Fetal heart rate decelerations
Non-reassuring fetal heart rate or rhythm
AHA: 4Q, '98, 48; For code 659.71: ▶1Q, '14, 14◀
076 Abn in fetal heart rate & rhythm comp L&D   I-10

§ ✓5th **659.8 Other specified indications for care or intervention**   M ♀
[0,1,3] **related to labor and delivery**
Pregnancy in a female less than 16 years old at expected
date of delivery
Very young maternal age
AHA: 3Q, '01, 12

§ ✓5th **659.9 Unspecified indication for care or**   M ♀
[0,1,3] **intervention related to labor and delivery**

Complications Occurring Mainly in the Course of Labor and Delivery (660-669)

The following fifth-digit subclassification is for use with categories 660-669 to denote the current episode of care. Valid fifth-digits are in [brackets] under each code.
 0 unspecified as to episode of care or not applicable
 1 delivered, with or without mention of antepartum condition
 2 delivered, with mention of postpartum complication
 3 antepartum condition or complication
 4 postpartum condition or complication

✓4th **660 Obstructed labor**
AHA: 3Q, '95, 10

§ ✓5th **660.0 Obstruction caused by malposition of fetus at**   CC 3 M ♀
[0,1,3] **onset of labor**
Any condition classifiable to 652, causing obstruction during
labor
Use additional code from 652.0-652.9 to identify condition
CC Excl: For code 660.03: 646.80-646.93, 648.90-649.64, 650,
655.70-655.73, 660.03, 665.00-665.11, 665.50-665.54,
665.80-665.94, 669.40-669.44, 669.80-669.94, 679.00-679.04,
679.12, 679.14
AHA: For code 660.01: ▶3Q, '13, 7, 8◀

§ ✓5th **660.1 Obstruction by bony pelvis**   M ♀
[0,1,3] Any condition classifiable to 653, causing obstruction during
labor
Use additional code from 653.0-653.9 to identify condition

---

§   Requires fifth digit. Valid digits are in [brackets] under each code. See beginning of section 640-649 for codes and definitions.

N Newborn Age: 0   P Pediatric Age: 0-17   M Maternity Age: 12-55   A Adult Age: 15-124   MCC Major CC Condition   CC CC Condition   HIV HIV Related Dx

220 – Volume 1 · October 2014   2015 ICD-9-CM

§ √5ᵗʰ **660.2 Obstruction by abnormal pelvic soft tissues** Ⓜ♀
[0,1,3]   Prolapse of anterior lip of cervix
Any condition classifiable to 654, causing obstruction during labor
Use additional code from 654.0-654.9 to identify condition

§ √5ᵗʰ **660.3 Deep transverse arrest and persistent** Ⓜ♀
[0,1,3] **occipitoposterior position**
O64.0xx0 Obst labor incpl rotat of fetal head not applic   I-10

§ √5ᵗʰ **660.4 Shoulder (girdle) dystocia** Ⓜ♀
[0,1,3]   Impacted shoulders
DEF: Obstructed labor due to impacted fetal shoulders.
O66.0 Obstructed labor due to shoulder dystocia   I-10

§ √5ᵗʰ **660.5 Locked twins** Ⓜ♀
[0,1,3]

§ √5ᵗʰ **660.6 Failed trial of labor, unspecified** Ⓜ♀
[0,1,3]   Failed trial of labor, without mention of condition or suspected condition

§ √5ᵗʰ **660.7 Failed forceps or vacuum extractor, unspecified** Ⓜ♀
[0,1,3]   Application of ventouse or forceps, without mention of condition

§ √5ᵗʰ **660.8 Other causes of obstructed labor** Ⓜ♀
[0,1,3]   Use additional code to identify condition
AHA: 4Q, '04, 88

§ √5ᵗʰ **660.9 Unspecified obstructed labor** Ⓜ♀
[0,1,3]   Dystocia:
NOS
fetal NOS
maternal NOS

√4ᵗʰ **661 Abnormality of forces of labor**

§ √5ᵗʰ **661.0 Primary uterine inertia** Ⓜ♀
[0,1,3]   Failure of cervical dilation
Hypotonic uterine dysfunction, primary
Prolonged latent phase of labor
DEF: Lack of efficient contractions during labor causing prolonged labor.
O62.0 Primary inadequate contractions   I-10

§ √5ᵗʰ **661.1 Secondary uterine inertia** Ⓜ♀
[0,1,3]   Arrested active phase of labor
Hypotonic uterine dysfunction, secondary
O62.1 Secondary uterine inertia   I-10

§ √5ᵗʰ **661.2 Other and unspecified uterine inertia** Ⓜ♀
[0,1,3]   Atony of uterus without hemorrhage
Desultory labor
Irregular labor
Poor contractions
Slow slope active phase of labor
EXCLUDES atony of uterus with hemorrhage (666.1)
postpartum atony of uterus without hemorrhage (669.8)

§ √5ᵗʰ **661.3 Precipitate labor** Ⓜ♀
[0,1,3]   **DEF:** Rapid labor and delivery.

§ √5ᵗʰ **661.4 Hypertonic, incoordinate, or prolonged** Ⓜ♀
[0,1,3] **uterine contractions**
Cervical spasm
Contraction ring (dystocia)
Dyscoordinate labor
Hourglass contraction of uterus
Hypertonic uterine dysfunction
Incoordinate uterine action
Retraction ring (Bandl's) (pathological)
Tetanic contractions
Uterine dystocia NOS
Uterine spasm

§ √5ᵗʰ **661.9 Unspecified abnormality of labor** Ⓜ♀
[0,1,3]

√4ᵗʰ **662 Long labor**

§ √5ᵗʰ **662.0 Prolonged first stage** Ⓜ♀
[0,1,3]

Perineal Lacerations

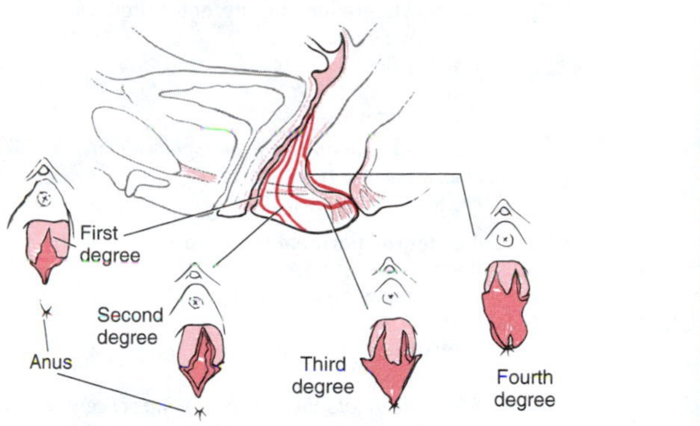

§ √5ᵗʰ **662.1 Prolonged labor, unspecified** CC 1 Ⓜ♀
[0,1,3]   **CC Excl:** For code 662.11: 646.80-646.93, 648.90-649.64, 650, 655.70-655.73, 662.11, 665.00-665.11, 665.50-665.54, 665.80-665.94, 669.40-669.44, 669.80-669.94, 679.00-679.04, 679.12, 679.14

§ √5ᵗʰ **662.2 Prolonged second stage** Ⓜ♀
[0,1,3]

§ √5ᵗʰ **662.3 Delayed delivery of second twin, triplet, etc.** Ⓜ♀
[0,1,3]

√4ᵗʰ **663 Umbilical cord complications**

§ √5ᵗʰ **663.0 Prolapse of cord** Ⓜ♀
[0,1,3]   Presentation of cord
DEF: Abnormal presentation of fetus; marked by protruding umbilical cord during labor; can cause fetal death.

§ √5ᵗʰ **663.1 Cord around neck, with compression** Ⓜ♀
[0,1,3]   Cord tightly around neck
O69.1xx0 L&D comp by cord arnd neck with comprs not applic/uns   I-10

§ √5ᵗʰ **663.2 Other and unspecified cord entanglement,** Ⓜ♀
[0,1,3] **with compression**
Entanglement of cords of twins in mono-amniotic sac
Knot in cord (with compression)

§ √5ᵗʰ **663.3 Other and unspecified cord entanglement,** Ⓜ♀
[0,1,3] **without mention of compression**
AHA: For code 663.31: 2Q, '03, 9
O69.82x0 L&D comp by oth cord entanglement w/o comprs unsp fetus   I-10

§ √5ᵗʰ **663.4 Short cord** Ⓜ♀
[0,1,3]

§ √5ᵗʰ **663.5 Vasa previa** Ⓜ♀
[0,1,3]   **DEF:** Abnormal presentation of fetus marked by blood vessels of umbilical cord in front of fetal head.

§ √5ᵗʰ **663.6 Vascular lesions of cord** Ⓜ♀
[0,1,3]   Bruising of cord   Thrombosis of vessels of cord
Hematoma of cord

§ √5ᵗʰ **663.8 Other umbilical cord complications** Ⓜ♀
[0,1,3]   Velamentous insertion of umbilical cord

§ √5ᵗʰ **663.9 Unspecified umbilical cord complication** Ⓜ♀
[0,1,3]

√4ᵗʰ **664 Trauma to perineum and vulva during delivery**
INCLUDES damage from instruments
that from extension of episiotomy
AHA: 1Q, '92, 11; N-D, '84, 10

§ √5ᵗʰ **664.0 First-degree perineal laceration** Ⓜ♀
[0,1,4]   Perineal laceration, rupture, or tear involving:
fourchette
hymen
labia
skin
vagina
vulva
O70.0 First degree perineal laceration during delivery   I-10

---

§   Requires fifth digit. Valid digits are in [brackets] under each code. See beginning of section 640-649 for codes and definitions.

√4ᵗʰ √5ᵗʰ Additional Digit Required   Unacceptable PDx   Manifestation Code   Hospital Acquired Condition   ▶◀ Revised Text   ● New Code   ▲ Revised Code Title

2015 ICD-9-CM   **Volume 1 – 221**

§ ✓5th **664.1 Second-degree perineal laceration** M♀
[0,1,4]   Perineal laceration, rupture, or tear (following episiotomy)
     involving:
      pelvic floor
      perineal muscles
      vaginal muscles
   EXCLUDES *that involving anal sphincter (664.2)*
   AHA: For code 664.11: 4Q, '08, 192
   070.1 Second degree perineal laceration dur delivery **I-10**

§ ✓5th **664.2 Third-degree perineal laceration** CC 1 M♀
[0,1,4]   Perineal laceration, rupture, or tear
     (following episiotomy) involving:
      anal sphincter
      rectovaginal septum
      sphincter NOS
   EXCLUDES *anal sphincter tear during delivery not associated*
     with third-degree perineal laceration (664.6)
     that with anal or rectal mucosal laceration (664.3)
   CC Excl: For code 664.21: 646.80-646.93, 648.90-649.64, 650,
   655.70-655.73, 664.21, 664.61, 665.00-665.11, 665.50-665.54,
   665.80- 665.94, 669.40-669.44, 669.80-669.94, 679.00-679.04,
   679.12, 679.14
   070.2 Third degree perineal laceration during delivery **I-10**

§ ✓5th **664.3 Fourth-degree perineal laceration** CC 1 M♀
[0,1,4]   Perineal laceration, rupture, or tear as
     classifiable to 664.2 and involving also:
      anal mucosa
      rectal mucosa
   CC Excl: For code 664.31: 646.80-646.93, 648.90-649.64, 650,
   655.70-655.73, 664.31, 665.00-665.11, 665.50-665.54,
   665.80-665.94, 669.40-669.44, 669.80-669.94, 679.00-679.04,
   679.12, 679.14

§ ✓5th **664.4 Unspecified perineal laceration** M♀
[0,1,4]   Central laceration
   AHA: 1Q, '92, 8

§ ✓5th **664.5 Vulval and perineal hematoma** M♀
[0,1,4]   **AHA:** N-D, '84, 10

§ ✓5th **664.6 Anal sphincter tear complicating delivery,** CC 1,4 M♀
[0,1,4] **not associated with third-degree perineal laceration**
   EXCLUDES *third-degree perineal laceration (664.2)*
   CC Excl: For code 664.61, 664.64: 646.80-646.93, 648.90-649.64, 650,
   655.70-655.73, 664.21, 664.60-664.64, 665.00-665.11,
   665.50-665.54, 665.80-665.94, 669.40-669.44, 669.80-669.94,
   679.00-679.04, 679.12, 679.14
   AHA: For code 664.61: 4Q, '07, 88, 90

§ ✓5th **664.8 Other specified trauma to perineum and vulva** M♀
[0,1,4]   Periurethral trauma
   AHA: For code 664.81: 4Q, '07, 125
   TIP: Assign when documentation indicates periurethral laceration
   only.

§ ✓5th **664.9 Unspecified trauma to perineum and vulva** M♀
[0,1,4]

✓4th **665 Other obstetrical trauma**
   INCLUDES damage from instruments

§ ✓5th **665.0 Rupture of uterus before onset of labor** MCC 1, 3 M♀
[0,1,3]   **CC Excl: For code 665.01, 665.03:** 646.80-646.93, 648.90-649.64, 650,
   655.70-655.73, 665.00-665.11, 665.50-665.54, 665.80-665.94,
   669.40-669.44, 669.80-669.94, 679.00-679.04, 679.12, 679.14

§ ✓5th **665.1 Rupture of uterus during labor** MCC 1 M♀
[0,1]   Rupture of uterus NOS
   CC Excl: For code 665.11: See code 665.01

§ ✓5th **665.2 Inversion of uterus** CC 2 M♀
[0,2,4]   **CC Excl: For code 665.22:** 646.80-646.93, 648.90-649.64, 650,
   655.70-655.73, 665.00-665.11, 665.22, 665.50-665.54,
   665.80-665.94, 669.40-669.44, 669.80-669.94, 679.00-679.04,
   679.12, 679.14

§ ✓5th **665.3 Laceration of cervix** CC 1 M♀
[0,1,4]   **CC Excl: For code 665.31:** 646.80-646.93, 648.90-649.64, 650,
   655.70-655.73, 665.00-665.11, 665.31, 665.50-665.54,
   665.80-665.94, 669.40-669.44, 669.80-669.94, 679.00-679.04,
   679.12, 679.14

§ ✓5th **665.4 High vaginal laceration** CC 1 M♀
[0,1,4]   Laceration of vaginal wall or sulcus without mention of
     perineal laceration
   CC Excl: For code 665.41: 646.80-646.93, 648.90-649.64, 650,
   655.70-655.73, 665.00-665.11, 665.41, 665.50-665.54,
   665.80-665.94, 669.40-669.44, 669.80-669.94, 679.00-679.04,
   679.12, 679.14
   071.4 Obstetric high vaginal laceration alone **I-10**

§ ✓5th **665.5 Other injury to pelvic organs** CC 1 M♀
[0,1,4]   Injury to:
      bladder
      urethra
   EXCLUDES *periurethral trauma (664.8)*
   CC Excl: For code 665.51: See code 665.01
   AHA: M-A, '87, 10
   071.5 Other obstetric injury to pelvic organs **I-10**

§ ✓5th **665.6 Damage to pelvic joints and ligaments** CC 1 M♀
[0,1,4]   Avulsion of inner symphyseal cartilage
      Damage to coccyx
      Separation of symphysis (pubis)
   CC Excl: For code 665.61: 646.80-646.93, 648.90-649.64, 650,
   655.70-655.73, 665.00-665.11, 665.50-665.54, 665.61,
   665.80-665.94, 669.40-669.44, 669.80-669.94, 679.00-679.04,
   679.12, 679.14
   AHA: N-D, '84, 12

§ ✓5th **665.7 Pelvic hematoma** CC 1-2 M♀
[0,1,2,4]   Hematoma of vagina
   CC Excl: For code 665.71: 646.80-646.93, 648.90-649.64, 650,
   655.70-655.73, 665.00-665.11, 665.50-665.54, 665.71,
   665.80-665.94, 669.40-669.44, 669.80-669.94, 679.00-679.04,
   679.12, 679.14; **For code 665.72:** 646.80-646.93, 648.90-649.64, 650,
   655.70-655.73, 665.00-665.11, 665.50-665.54, 665.72,
   665.80-665.94, 669.40-669.44, 669.80-669.94, 679.00-679.04,
   679.12, 679.14

§ ✓5th **665.8 Other specified obstetrical trauma** M♀
[0-4]

§ ✓5th **665.9 Unspecified obstetrical trauma** M♀
[0-4]

✓4th **666 Postpartum hemorrhage**
   AHA: 1Q, '88, 14

§ ✓5th **666.0 Third-stage hemorrhage** CC 2, 4 M♀
[0,2,4]   Hemorrhage associated with retained,
     trapped, or adherent placenta
   Retained placenta NOS
   CC Excl: For code 666.02: 646.80-646.93, 648.90-649.64, 650,
   655.70-655.73, 665.00-665.11, 665.50-665.54, 665.80-665.94,
   666.02, 669.40-669.44, 669.80-669.94, 679.00-679.04, 679.12,
   679.14; **For code 666.04:** 646.80-646.93, 648.90-649.64, 650,
   655.70-655.73, 665.00-665.11, 665.50-665.54, 665.80-665.94,
   666.04, 669.40-669.44, 669.80-669.94, 679.00-679.04, 679.12, 679.14

§ ✓5th **666.1 Other immediate postpartum hemorrhage** CC 2, 4 M♀
[0,2,4]   Atony of uterus with hemorrhage
   Hemorrhage within the first 24 hours following delivery of
     placenta
   Postpartum atony of uterus with hemorrhage
   Postpartum hemorrhage (atonic) NOS
   EXCLUDES *atony of uterus without hemorrhage (661.2)*
     postpartum atony of uterus without hemorrhage
     (669.8)
   CC Excl: For code 666.12: 646.80-646.93, 648.90-649.64, 650,
   655.70-655.73, 665.00-665.11, 665.50-665.54, 665.80- 665.94,
   666.12, 669.40-669.44, 669.80-669.94, 679.00-679.04, 679.12,
   679.14; **For code 666.14:** 666.10-666.14
   072.1 Other immediate postpartum hemorrhage **I-10**

§ ✓5th **666.2 Delayed and secondary postpartum hemorrhage** CC 2, 4 M♀
[0,2,4]   Hemorrhage:
      after the first 24 hours following delivery
      associated with retained portions of placenta or
        membranes
   Postpartum hemorrhage specified as delayed or secondary
   Retained products of conception NOS, following delivery
   CC Excl: For code 666.22: 646.80-646.93, 648.90-649.64, 650,
   655.70-655.73, 665.00-665.11, 665.50-665.54, 665.80- 665.94,
   666.22, 669.40-669.44, 669.80-669.94, 679.00-679.04, 679.12,
   679.14; **For code 666.24:** 666.20-666.24

---

§   Requires fifth digit. Valid digits are in [brackets] under each code. See beginning of section 640-649 for codes and definitions.

N Newborn Age: 0   **P** Pediatric Age: 0-17   **M** Maternity Age: 12-55   **A** Adult Age: 15-124   **MCC** Major CC Condition   **CC** CC Condition   **HIV** HIV Related Dx

222 – Volume 1   **2015 ICD-9-CM**

§ ✓5ᵗʰ **666.3 Postpartum coagulation defects**   `CC2` M♀
[0,2,4]   Postpartum:
    afibrinogenemia
    fibrinolysis
   CC Excl: For code 666.32: 646.80-646.93, 648.90-649.64, 650, 666.00-666.34, 669.40-669.44, 669.80-669.94, 679.00-679.04, 679.12, 679.14

✓4ᵗʰ **667 Retained placenta or membranes, without hemorrhage**
   DEF: Postpartum condition resulting from failure to expel placental membrane tissues due to failed contractions of uterine wall.
   AHA: 1Q, '88, 14
   TIP: A retained placenta is one that has not separated or been expelled within one hour after completion of the second stage of labor (birth of the fetus).

§ ✓5ᵗʰ **667.0 Retained placenta without hemorrhage**   M♀
[0,2,4]   Placenta accreta
    Retained placenta:
     NOS   } without hemorrhage
     total
   073.0 Retained placenta without hemorrhage   `I-10`

§ ✓5ᵗʰ **667.1 Retained portions of placenta or membranes,**   M♀
[0,2,4] **without hemorrhage**
    Retained products of conception following delivery, without hemorrhage

✓4ᵗʰ **668 Complications of the administration of anesthetic or other sedation in labor and delivery**
   `INCLUDES` complications arising from the administration of a general or local anesthetic, analgesic, or other sedation in labor and delivery
   Use additional code(s) to further specify complication
   `EXCLUDES` *reaction to spinal or lumbar puncture (349.0)*
      spinal headache (349.0)

§ ✓5ᵗʰ **668.0 Pulmonary complications**   M♀
[0-4]   Inhalation (aspiration) of
     stomach contents or   following anesthesia or
     secretions   other sedation in
    Mendelson's syndrome   labor or delivery
    Pressure collapse of lung

§ ✓5ᵗʰ **668.1 Cardiac complications**   M♀
[0-4]   Cardiac arrest or failure following anesthesia or other sedation in labor and delivery

§ ✓5ᵗʰ **668.2 Central nervous system complications**   M♀
[0-4]   Cerebral anoxia following anesthesia or other sedation in labor and delivery

§ ✓5ᵗʰ **668.8 Other complications of anesthesia or other**   M♀
[0-4] **sedation in labor and delivery**
   AHA: 2Q, '99, 9

§ ✓5ᵗʰ **668.9 Unspecified complication of anesthesia**   M♀
[0-4] **and other sedation**

✓4ᵗʰ **669 Other complications of labor and delivery, not elsewhere classified**

§ ✓5ᵗʰ **669.0 Maternal distress**   M♀
[0-4]   Metabolic disturbance in labor and delivery

§ ✓5ᵗʰ **669.1 Shock during or following labor and delivery**   `MCC 1-4` M♀
[0-4]   Obstetric shock
   CC Excl: For codes 669.11-669.14: 646.80-646.93, 648.90-649.64, 650, 669.10-669.14, 669.40-669.44, 669.80-669.94, 679.00-679.04, 679.12, 679.14

§ ✓5ᵗʰ **669.2 Maternal hypotension syndrome**   `MCC 1-2` `CC 4` M♀
[0-4]   **DEF:** Low arterial blood pressure in mother during labor and delivery.
   CC Excl: For code 669.21: 646.80-646.93, 648.90-649.64, 650, 669.10-669.14, 669.21, 669.40-669.44, 669.80-669.94, 679.00-679.04, 679.12, 679.14; **For code 669.22:** 646.80-646.93, 648.90-649.64, 650, 669.10-669.14, 669.22, 669.40-669.44, 669.80-669.94, 679.00-679.04, 679.12, 679.14; **For code 669.24:** 646.80-646.93, 648.90-649.64, 650, 669.10-669.14, 669.24, 669.40-669.44, 669.80-669.94, 679.00-679.04, 679.12, 679.14

§ ✓5ᵗʰ **669.3 Acute kidney failure following labor**   `MCC 2,4` M♀
[0,2,4] **and delivery**
   CC Excl: For codes 669.32, 669.34: 646.80-646.93, 648.90-649.64, 650, 669.30-669.44, 669.80-669.94, 679.00-679.04, 679.12, 679.14

§ ✓5ᵗʰ **669.4 Other complications of obstetrical surgery**   M♀
[0-4] **and procedures**
   Cardiac:
    arrest   } following cesarean or other
    failure   obstetrical surgery or
   Cerebral   procedure, including
    anoxia   delivery NOS
    `EXCLUDES` *complications of obstetrical surgical wounds (674.1-674.3)*
   AHA: For code 669.42: ▶1Q, '14, 14◀

§ ✓5ᵗʰ **669.5 Forceps or vacuum extractor delivery**   M♀
[0,1] **without mention of indication**
    Delivery by ventouse, without mention of indication

§ ✓5ᵗʰ **669.6 Breech extraction, without mention of indication**   M♀
[0,1]   `EXCLUDES` *breech delivery NOS (652.2)*

§ ✓5ᵗʰ **669.7 Cesarean delivery, without mention of indication**   M♀
[0,1]   **AHA: For code 669.71:** 1Q, '01, 11
   082 Encounter for cesarean delivery w/o indication   `I-10`

§ ✓5ᵗʰ **669.8 Other complications of labor and delivery**   M♀
[0-4]   **AHA:** 4Q, '06, 135

§ ✓5ᵗʰ **669.9 Unspecified complication of labor and delivery**   M♀
[0-4]

Complications of the Puerperium (670-677)

   `NOTE` Categories 671 and 673-676 include the listed conditions even if they occur during pregnancy or childbirth.

> The following fifth-digit subclassification is for use with categories 670-676 to denote the current episode of care. Valid fifth-digits are in [brackets] under each code.
> 0 unspecified as to episode of care or not applicable
> 1 delivered, with or without mention of antepartum condition
> 2 delivered, with mention of postpartum complication
> 3 antepartum condition or complication
> 4 postpartum condition or complication

✓4ᵗʰ **670 Major puerperal infection**
   `EXCLUDES` *infection following abortion (639.0)*
     minor genital tract infection following delivery (646.6)
     puerperal pyrexia NOS (672)
     puerperal fever NOS (672)
     puerperal pyrexia of unknown origin (672)
     urinary tract infection following delivery (646.6)
   DEF: Infection and inflammation following childbirth.
   AHA: 4Q, '91, 26; 2Q, '91, 7

§ ✓5ᵗʰ **670.0 Major puerperal infection, unspecified**   `MCC 2,4` M♀
[0,2,4]   **AHA: For code 670.02:** 3Q, '07, 8
   CC Excl: 646.80-646.93, 648.90-649.64, 650, 669.40-669.44, 669.80-670.84, 679.00-679.04, 679.12, 679.14

§ ✓5ᵗʰ **670.1 Puerperal endometritis**   `CC` M♀
[0,2,4]   **CC Excl: See code:** 670.0

§ ✓5ᵗʰ **670.2 Puerperal sepsis**   `CC 0` `MCC 2,4` M♀
[0,2,4]   Puerperal pyemia
   Use additional code to identify severe sepsis (995.92) and any associated acute organ dysfunction, if applicable
   CC Excl: See code: 670.0
   AHA: For code 670.24: 4Q, '09, 98
   TIP: Do not assign a code from category 038 or 995.91 Sepsis, along with a code from this subcategory. If applicable, assign additional codes to indicate severe sepsis (995.92), and any associated acute organ dysfunction.

§ ✓5ᵗʰ **670.3 Puerperal septic thrombophlebitis**   `CC 0` `MCC 2,4` M♀
[0,2,4]   **CC Excl: See code:** 670.0

§ ✓5ᵗʰ **670.8 Other major puerperal infection**   `MCC` M♀
[0,2,4]   Puerperal:
    pelvic cellulitis
    peritonitis
    salpingitis
   CC Excl: See code: 670.0

---

§   Requires fifth digit. Valid digits are in [brackets] under each code. See beginning of section 640-649 for codes and definitions.

✓4ᵗʰ ✓5ᵗʰ Additional Digit Required   `Unacceptable PDx`   `Manifestation Code`   `Hospital Acquired Condition`   ▶◀ Revised Text   ● New Code   ▲ Revised Code Title

2015 ICD-9-CM   **October 2014 • Volume 1 – 223**

√4th **671 Venous complications in pregnancy and the puerperium**

> EXCLUDES *personal history of venous complications prior to pregnancy, such as:*
> *thrombophlebitis (V12.52)*
> *thrombosis and embolism (V12.51)*

§ √5th **671.0 Varicose veins of legs**   M♀
[0-4]   Varicose veins NOS
> DEF: Distended, tortuous veins on legs associated with pregnancy.

§ √5th **671.1 Varicose veins of vulva and perineum**   M♀
[0-4]   DEF: Distended, tortuous veins on external female genitalia associated with pregnancy.

§ √5th **671.2 Superficial thrombophlebitis**   CC M♀
[0-4]   Phlebitis NOS
Thrombophlebitis (superficial)
Thrombosis NOS
> Use additional code to identify the superficial thrombophlebitis (453.6, 453.71, 453.81)
> CC Excl: 646.80-646.93, 648.90-649.64, 650, 669.40-669.44, 669.80-669.94, 671.20-671.94, 679.00-679.04, 679.12, 679.14

§ √5th **671.3 Deep phlebothrombosis, antepartum**   MCC 1, 3 CC 0 M♀
[0,1,3]   Deep vein thrombosis antepartum
> Use additional code to identify the deep vein thrombosis (453.40-453.42, 453.50-453.52, 453.72-453.79, 453.82-453.89)
> Use additional code for long term (current) use of anticoagulants, if applicable (V58.61)
> CC Excl: See code: 671.2

§ √5th **671.4 Deep phlebothrombosis, postpartum**   MCC 2, 4 CC 0 M♀
[0,2,4]   Deep-vein thrombosis, postpartum
Pelvic thrombophlebitis, postpartum
Phlegmasia alba dolens (puerperal)
> Use additional code to identify the deep vein thrombosis (453.40-453.42, 453.50-453.52, 453.72-453.79, 453.82-453.89)
> Use additional code for long term (current) use of anticoagulants, if applicable (V58.61)
> CC Excl: See code: 671.2

§ √5th **671.5 Other phlebitis and thrombosis**   CC M♀
[0-4]   Cerebral venous thrombosis
Thrombosis of intracranial venous sinus
> CC Excl: See code: 671.2

§ √5th **671.8 Other venous complications**   CC M♀
[0-4]   Hemorrhoids
> CC Excl: For codes 671.80-671.83: 646.80-646.93, 648.90-649.64, 650, 669.40-669.44, 669.80-669.94, 671.20-671.94, 679.00-679.04, 679.14; For code 671.84: 671.80-671.84

§ √5th **671.9 Unspecified venous complication**   CC 0-2 M♀
[0-4]   CC Excl: For code 671.90-671.92: 646.80-646.93, 648.90-649.64, 650, 669.40-669.44, 669.80-669.94, 671.20-671.94, 679.00-679.04, 679.12, 679.14

√4th **672 Pyrexia of unknown origin during the puerperium**   CC 2, 4 M♀
[0,2,4]

§ √5th Use 0 as fourth-digit for this category

Postpartum fever NOS
Puerperal fever NOS
Puerperal pyrexia NOS
> DEF: Fever of unknown origin experienced by the mother after childbirth.
> CC Excl: For code 672.02: 646.80-646.93, 648.90-649.64, 650, 669.40-669.44, 669.80-669.94, 671.20, 671.23-671.30, 671.33-671.40, 671.50, 671.53-671.80, 671.83-671.90, 671.93-671.94, 672.02, 679.00-679.04, 679.12, 679.14; For code 672.04: 672.02-672.04
> AHA: 4Q, '91, 26
> 086.4 Pyrexia of unknown origin following delivery   I-10

√4th **673 Obstetrical pulmonary embolism**

> INCLUDES *pulmonary emboli in pregnancy, childbirth, or the puerperium, or specified as puerperal*
> EXCLUDES *embolism following abortion (639.6)*

§ √5th **673.0 Obstetrical air embolism**   MCC 1-4 M♀
[0-4]   DEF: Sudden blocking of pulmonary artery with air or nitrogen bubbles during puerperium.
> CC Excl: 646.80-646.93, 648.90-649.64, 650, 669.40-669.44, 669.80-669.94, 673.00-673.84, 679.00-679.04, 679.12, 679.14

§ √5th **673.1 Amniotic fluid embolism**   MCC 1-4 M♀
[0-4]   DEF: Sudden onset of pulmonary artery blockage from amniotic fluid entering the mother's circulation near the end of pregnancy due to strong uterine contractions.
> CC Excl: For code 673.11-673.14: See code: 673.0

§ √5th **673.2 Obstetrical blood-clot embolism**   MCC 1-4 M♀
[0-4]   Puerperal pulmonary embolism NOS
> DEF: Blood clot blocking artery in the lung; associated with pregnancy.
> CC Excl: For code 673.21-673.24: See code: 673.0
> AHA: For code 673.24: 1Q, '05, 6
> TIP: If a pregnant or postpartum patient develops a pulmonary embolism that progresses to acute respiratory failure, the code for the pregnancy/delivery complication (673.2x) should be sequenced first.

§ √5th **673.3 Obstetrical pyemic and septic embolism**   MCC 1-4 CC 0 M♀
[0-4]   CC Excl: See code: 673.0

§ √5th **673.8 Other pulmonary embolism**   MCC 1-4 M♀
[0-4]   Fat embolism
> CC Excl: For code 673.81-673.84: See code: 673.0

√4th **674 Other and unspecified complications of the puerperium, not elsewhere classified**

§ √5th **674.0 Cerebrovascular disorders in the puerperium**   MCC 1 CC 2-4 M♀
[0-4]
Any condition classifiable to 430-434, 436-437 occurring during pregnancy, childbirth, or the puerperium, or specified as puerperal
> EXCLUDES *intracranial venous sinus thrombosis (671.5)*
> CC Excl: For code 674.01-674.04: 646.80-646.93, 648.90-649.64, 650, 669.40-669.44, 669.80-669.94, 674.00-674.04, 674.50-674.54, 679.00-679.04, 679.12, 679.14

§ √5th **674.1 Disruption of cesarean wound**   M♀
[0,2,4]   Dehiscence or disruption of uterine wound
> EXCLUDES *uterine rupture before onset of labor (665.0)*
> *uterine rupture during labor (665.1)*
> AHA: ▶3Q, '13, 6◀

§ √5th **674.2 Disruption of perineal wound**   M♀
[0,2,4]   Breakdown of perineum
Disruption of wound of:
   episiotomy
   perineal laceration
Secondary perineal tear
> AHA: For code 674.24: 1Q, '97, 9

§ √5th **674.3 Other complications of obstetrical surgical wounds**   M♀
[0,2,4]   Hematoma ⎤
Hemorrhage ⎬ of cesarean section or perineal wound
Infection ⎦
> EXCLUDES *damage from instruments in delivery (664.0-665.9)*
> AHA: For code 674.32: 2Q, '91, 7; For code 674.34: 4Q, '09, 98

§ √5th **674.4 Placental polyp**   M♀
[0,2,4]

§ √5th **674.5 Peripartum cardiomyopathy**   MCC M♀
[0-4]   Postpartum cardiomyopathy
> DEF: Any structural or functional abnormality of the ventricular myocardium, non-inflammatory disease of obscure or unknown etiology with onset during the postpartum period.
> CC Excl: See code: 674.01
> AHA: 4Q, '03, 65; For code 674.54: 3Q, '12, 9

§ √5th **674.8 Other**   M♀
[0,2,4]   Hepatorenal syndrome, following delivery
Postpartum:
   subinvolution of uterus
   uterine hypertrophy
> AHA: 3Q, '98, 16

§ √5th **674.9 Unspecified**   M♀
[0,2,4]   Sudden death of unknown cause during the puerperium

√4th **675 Infections of the breast and nipple associated with childbirth**

> INCLUDES *the listed conditions during pregnancy, childbirth, or the puerperium*

§ √5th **675.0 Infections of nipple**   M♀
[0-4]   Abscess of nipple

---

§   Requires fifth digit. Valid digits are in [brackets] under each code. See beginning of section 640-649 for codes and definitions.

N Newborn Age: 0   **P** Pediatric Age: 0-17   **M** Maternity Age: 12-55   **A** Adult Age: 15-124   **MCC** Major CC Condition   **CC** CC Condition   **HIV** HIV Related Dx

224 – Volume 1 • October 2014   2015 ICD-9-CM

§ ✓5ᵗʰ **675.1 Abscess of breast**   CC 1-2 M♀
[0-4]   Abscess:
     mammary
     subareolar
     submammary
     purulent
     retromammary
     submammary
   CC Excl: For codes 675.11-675.12: 646.80-646.93, 648.90-649.64, 650, 669.40-669.44, 669.80-669.94, 675.00-675.94, 679.00-679.04, 679.12, 679.14

§ ✓5ᵗʰ **675.2 Nonpurulent mastitis**   M♀
[0-4]   Lymphangitis of breast
   Mastitis:
     NOS
     interstitial
     parenchymatous

§ ✓5ᵗʰ **675.8 Other specified infections of the breast and nipple**   M♀
[0-4]

§ ✓5ᵗʰ **675.9 Unspecified infection of the breast and nipple**   M♀
[0-4]

✓4ᵗʰ **676 Other disorders of the breast associated with childbirth and disorders of lactation**
   INCLUDES the listed conditions during pregnancy, the puerperium, or lactation

§ ✓5ᵗʰ **676.0 Retracted nipple**   M♀
[0-4]

§ ✓5ᵗʰ **676.1 Cracked nipple**   M♀
[0-4]   Fissure of nipple

§ ✓5ᵗʰ **676.2 Engorgement of breasts**   M♀
[0-4]   **DEF:** Abnormal accumulation of milk in ducts of breast.

§ ✓5ᵗʰ **676.3 Other and unspecified disorder of breast**   M♀
[0-4]

§ ✓5ᵗʰ **676.4 Failure of lactation**   M♀
[0-4]   Agalactia
   DEF: Abrupt ceasing of milk secretion by breast.

§ ✓5ᵗʰ **676.5 Suppressed lactation**   M♀
[0-4]

§ ✓5ᵗʰ **676.6 Galactorrhea**   M♀
[0-4]   **EXCLUDES** *galactorrhea not associated with childbirth (611.6)*
   DEF: Excessive or persistent milk secretion by breast; may be in absence of nursing.

§ ✓5ᵗʰ **676.8 Other disorders of lactation**   M♀
[0-4]   Galactocele
   DEF: Galactocele: Obstructed mammary gland, creating retention cyst, results in milk-filled cysts enlarging mammary gland.
   AHA: 3Q, '12, 7

§ ✓5ᵗʰ **676.9 Unspecified disorder of lactation**   M♀
[0-4]

Lactation Process: Ejection Reflex Arc

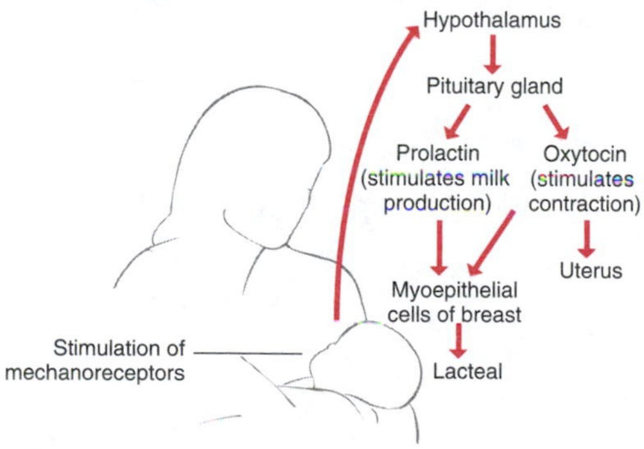

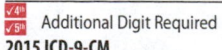

677 Late effect of complication of pregnancy, childbirth, and the puerperium   ♀
   NOTE This category is to be used to indicate conditions in 632-648.9 and 651-676.9 as the cause of the late effect, themselves classifiable elsewhere. The "late effects" include conditions specified as such, or as sequelae, which may occur at any time after puerperium.
   Code first any sequelae
   AHA: ▶3Q, '13, 6;◀ 1Q, '97, 9; 4Q, '94, 42
   TIP: Sequence as a secondary diagnosis, after the code for the late effect complication. May be assigned at any time after the initial postpartum period (six weeks following delivery).

Other Maternal and Fetal Complications (678-679)

The following fifth-digit subclassification is for use with categories 678-679 to denote the current episode of care. Valid fifth-digits are in [brackets] under each code.
   0 unspecified as to episode of care or not applicable
   1 delivered, with or without mention of antepartum condition
   2 delivered, with mention of postpartum complication
   3 antepartum condition or complication
   4 postpartum condition or complication

✓4ᵗʰ **678 Other fetal conditions**

§ ✓5ᵗʰ **678.0 Fetal hematologic conditions**   M♀
[0,1,3]   Fetal anemia
   Fetal thrombocytopenia
   Fetal twin to twin transfusion
   EXCLUDES *fetal and neonatal hemorrhage (772.0-772.9)*
     fetal hematologic disorders affecting newborn (776.0-776.9)
     fetal-maternal hemorrhage (656.00-656.03)
     isoimmunization incompatibility (656.10-656.13, 656.20-656.23)
   AHA: 4Q, '08, 125-127

§ ✓5ᵗʰ **678.1 Fetal conjoined twins**   M♀
[0,1,3]   **AHA:** 4Q, '08, 125-127

✓4ᵗʰ **679 Complications of in utero procedures**
   AHA: 4Q, '08, 127-128, 158

§ ✓5ᵗʰ **679.0 Maternal complications from in utero procedure**   M♀
[0-4]   **EXCLUDES** *maternal history of in utero procedure during previous pregnancy (V23.86)*

§ ✓5ᵗʰ **679.1 Fetal complications from in utero procedure**   M♀
[0-4]   Fetal complications from amniocentesis
   EXCLUDES *newborn affected by in utero procedure (760.61-760.64)*
   TIP: Assign only on the mother's record. Although there is a fetal complication, it affects the mother's pregnancy.

§ Requires fifth digit. Valid digits are in [brackets] under each code. See beginning of section 640-649 for codes and definitions.

✓4ᵗʰ ✓5ᵗʰ Additional Digit Required   Unacceptable PDx   Manifestation Code   Hospital Acquired Condition   ▶◀ Revised Text   ● New Code   ▲ Revised Code Title

2015 ICD-9-CM   **October 2014 • Volume 1 – 225**

12. Diseases of the Skin and Subcutaneous Tissue (680-709)

Infections of Skin and Subcutaneous Tissue (680-686)

EXCLUDES *certain infections of skin classified under "Infectious and Parasitic Diseases," such as:*
erysipelas (035)
erysipeloid of Rosenbach (027.1)
herpes:
  simplex (054.0-054.9)
  zoster (053.0-053.9)
molluscum contagiosum (078.0)
viral warts (078.10-078.19)

✓4ᵗʰ 680 Carbuncle and furuncle

INCLUDES boil
furunculosis

DEF: Carbuncle: necrotic boils in skin and subcutaneous tissue of neck or back mainly due to staphylococcal infection.
DEF: Furuncle: circumscribed inflammation of corium and subcutaneous tissue due to staphylococcal infection.

680.0 Face
Ear [any part]
Face [any part, except eye]
Nose (septum)
Temple (region)
EXCLUDES *eyelid (373.13)*
lacrimal apparatus (375.31)
orbit (376.01)

680.1 Neck

680.2 Trunk
Abdominal wall
Back [any part, except buttocks]
Breast
Chest wall
Flank
Groin
Pectoral region
Perineum
Umbilicus
EXCLUDES *buttocks (680.5)*
external genital organs:
  female (616.4)
  male (607.2, 608.4)

680.3 Upper arm and forearm
Arm [any part, except hand]
Axilla
Shoulder

680.4 Hand
Finger [any]
Thumb
Wrist

680.5 Buttock
Anus
Gluteal region

680.6 Leg, except foot
Ankle
Hip
Knee
Thigh

680.7 Foot
Heel
Toe

680.8 Other specified sites
Head [any part, except face]
Scalp
EXCLUDES *external genital organs:*
  female (616.4)
  male (607.2, 608.4)

680.9 Unspecified site
Boil NOS
Carbuncle NOS
Furuncle NOS

Skin and Subcutaneous Layer

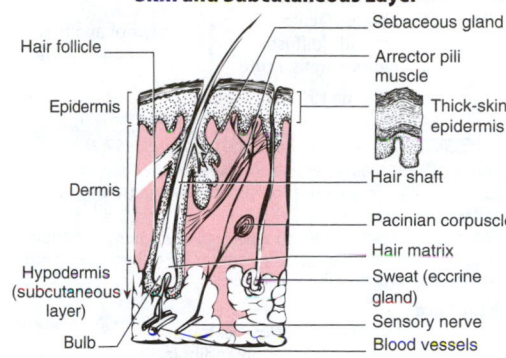

✓4ᵗʰ 681 Cellulitis and abscess of finger and toe

INCLUDES that with lymphangitis

Use additional code to identify organism, such as Staphylococcus (041.1)

DEF: Acute suppurative inflammation and edema in subcutaneous tissue or muscle of finger or toe.
AHA: 2Q, '91, 5; J-F, '87, 12
TIP: Coding of cellulitis due to superficial injury, burn, or frostbite requires two codes, one for the injury and one for the cellulitis. Sequencing depends on the circumstances of the admission.

✓5ᵗʰ 681.0 Finger

681.00 Cellulitis and abscess, unspecified
L03.019 Cellulitis of unspecified finger   `I-10`

681.01 Felon
Pulp abscess
Whitlow
EXCLUDES *herpetic whitlow (054.6)*
DEF: Painful abscess of fingertips caused by infection in the closed space of terminal phalanx.

681.02 Onychia and paronychia of finger
Panaritium } of finger
Perionychia }
DEF: Onychia: inflammation of nail matrix; causes nail loss.
DEF: Paronychia: inflammation of tissue folds around nail.

✓5ᵗʰ 681.1 Toe

681.10 Cellulitis and abscess, unspecified
AHA: 1Q, '05, 14
L03.039 Cellulitis of unspecified toe   `I-10`

681.11 Onychia and paronychia of toe
Panaritium } of toe
Perionychia }

681.9 Cellulitis and abscess of unspecified digit
Infection of nail NOS

Lymphatic System of Head and Neck

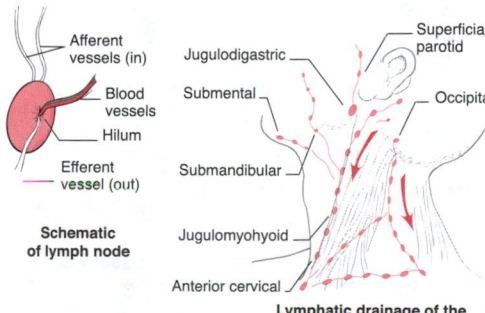

Lymphatic drainage of the head, neck, and face

Diseases of the Skin and Subcutaneous Tissue

682–685.1

✔4ᵗʰ 682 Other cellulitis and abscess

INCLUDES   abscess (acute   } (with lymphangitis) except
       cellulitis (diffuse)   of finger or toe
       lymphangitis, acute

Use additional code to identify organism, such as Staphylococcus (041.1)

EXCLUDES   lymphangitis (chronic) (subacute) (457.2)

DEF: Cellulitis: Acute suppurative inflammation of deep subcutaneous tissue and sometimes muscle due to infection of wound, burn or other lesion.

AHA: 2Q, '91, 5; J-F, '87, 12; S-O, '85, 10

TIP: Coding of cellulitis due to superficial injury, burn, or frostbite requires two codes, one for the injury and one for the cellulitis. Sequencing depends on the circumstances of the admission.

682.0 Face   CC

Cheek, external   Nose, external
Chin   Submandibular
Forehead   Temple (region)

EXCLUDES   ear [any part] (380.10-380.16)
           eyelid (373.13)
           lacrimal apparatus (375.31)
           lip (528.5)
           mouth (528.3)
           nose (internal) (478.1)
           orbit (376.01)

CC Excl: 017.00-017.06, 017.90-017.96, 040.82-041.9, 682.0, 682.8-682.9, 686.00-686.9, 705.83, 709.8, V09.0-V09.91

AHA: ▶4Q, '13, 98◀

L03.211 Cellulitis of face   I-10

682.1 Neck   CC

CC Excl: 017.00-017.06, 017.90-017.96, 040.82-041.9, 682.1, 682.8-682.9, 686.00-686.9, 705.83, 709.8, V09.0-V09.91

L03.221 Cellulitis of neck   I-10

682.2 Trunk   CC

Abdominal wall
Back [any part, except buttock]
Chest wall
Flank
Groin
Pectoral region
Perineum
Umbilicus, except newborn

EXCLUDES   anal and rectal regions (566)
           breast:
               NOS (611.0)
               puerperal (675.1)
           external genital organs:
               female (616.3-616.4)
               male (604.0, 607.2, 608.4)
           umbilicus, newborn (771.4)

CC Excl: 017.00-017.06, 017.90-017.96, 040.82-041.9, 682.2, 682.8-682.9, 686.00-686.9, 705.83, 709.8, V09.0-V09.91

AHA: 4Q, '98, 42

L03.319 Cellulitis of trunk unspecified   I-10

682.3 Upper arm and forearm   CC

Arm [any part, except hand]
Axilla
Shoulder

EXCLUDES   hand (682.4)

CC Excl: 017.00-017.06, 017.90-017.96, 040.82-041.9, 682.3, 682.8-682.9, 686.00-686.9, 705.83, 709.8, V09.0-V09.91

AHA: 2Q, '03, 7

L03.113 Cellulitis of right upper limb   I-10

682.4 Hand, except fingers and thumb   CC

Wrist

EXCLUDES   finger and thumb (681.00-681.02)

CC Excl: 017.00-017.06, 017.90-017.96, 040.82-041.9, 682.4, 682.8-682.9, 686.00-686.9, 705.83, 709.8, V09.0-V09.91

682.5 Buttock   CC

Gluteal region

EXCLUDES   anal and rectal regions (566)

CC Excl: 017.00-017.06, 017.90-017.96, 040.82-041.9, 682.5, 682.8-682.9, 686.00-686.9, 705.83, 709.8, V09.0-V09.91

L03.317 Cellulitis of buttock   I-10

682.6 Leg, except foot   CC

Ankle
Hip
Knee
Thigh

CC Excl: 017.00-017.06, 017.90-017.96, 040.82-041.9, 682.6, 682.8-682.9, 686.00-686.9, 705.83, 709.8, V09.0-V09.91

AHA: 3Q, '12, 13; 1Q, '09, 10; 3Q, '04, 5; 4Q, '03, 108

L03.115 Cellulitis of right lower limb   I-10

682.7 Foot, except toes   CC

Heel

EXCLUDES   toe (681.10-681.11)

CC Excl: 017.00-017.06, 017.90-017.96, 040.82-041.9, 682.7-682.9, 686.00-686.9, 705.83, 709.8, V09.0-V09.91

682.8 Other specified sites   CC

Head [except face]
Scalp

EXCLUDES   face (682.0)

CC Excl: 017.00-017.06, 017.90-017.96, 040.82-041.9, 682.8-682.9, 686.00-686.9, 705.83, 709.8, V09.0-V09.91

682.9 Unspecified site   CC

Abscess NOS
Cellulitis NOS
Lymphangitis, acute NOS

EXCLUDES   lymphangitis NOS (457.2)

CC Excl: See code: 682.8

683 Acute lymphadenitis

Abscess (acute)   } lymph gland or node,
Adenitis, acute   except mesenteric
Lymphadenitis, acute

Use additional code to identify organism, such as Staphylococcus (041.1)

EXCLUDES   enlarged glands NOS (785.6)
           lymphadenitis:
               chronic or subacute, except mesenteric (289.1)
               mesenteric (acute) (chronic) (subacute) (289.2)
               unspecified (289.3)

DEF: Acute inflammation of lymph nodes due to primary infection located elsewhere in the body.

684 Impetigo

Impetiginization of other dermatoses
Impetigo (contagiosa) [any site] [any organism]:
     bullous
     circinate
     neonatorum
     simplex
Pemphigus neonatorum

EXCLUDES   impetigo herpetiformis (694.3)

DEF: Infectious skin disease commonly occurring in children; caused by group A streptococci or *Staphylococcus aureus;* skin lesions usually appear on the face and consist of subcorneal vesicles and bullae that burst and form yellow crusts.

✔4ᵗʰ 685 Pilonidal cyst

INCLUDES   fistula   } coccygeal or pilonidal
          sinus

DEF: Hair-containing cyst or sinus in the tissues of the sacrococcygeal area; often drains through opening at the postanal dimple.

685.0 With abscess   CC

CC Excl: 685.0-685.1, 709.8

685.1 Without mention of abscess

AHA: 3Q, '11, 9

Stages of Pilonidal Disease

Normal follicle
Stretched follicle
Infected follicle
Acute abscess
Chronic abscess
Epithelial tube

N Newborn Age: 0   P Pediatric Age: 0-17   M Maternity Age: 12-55   A Adult Age: 15-124   MCC Major CC Condition   CC CC Condition   HIV HIV Related Dx

228 – Volume 1 • October 2014   2015 ICD-9-CM

✓4ᵗʰ **686　Other local infections of skin and subcutaneous tissue**

Use additional code to identify any infectious organism (041.0-041.8)

✓5ᵗʰ **686.0　Pyoderma**

Dermatitis:
　purulent
　septic
　suppurative

DEF: Nonspecific purulent skin disease related most to furuncles, pustules, or possibly carbuncles.

686.00　Pyoderma, unspecified

686.01　Pyoderma gangrenosum　　`CC`

DEF: Persistent debilitating skin disease, characterized by irregular, boggy, blue-red ulcerations, with central healing and undermined edges.

CC Excl: 686.00-686.09

AHA: 4Q, '97, 42

686.09　Other pyoderma

686.1　Pyogenic granuloma

Granuloma:
　septic
　suppurative
　telangiectaticum

EXCLUDES　pyogenic granuloma of oral mucosa (528.9)

DEF: Solitary polypoid capillary hemangioma often associated with local irritation, trauma, and superimposed inflammation; located on the skin and gingival or oral mucosa.

686.8　Other specified local infections of skin and subcutaneous tissue

Bacterid (pustular)
Dermatitis vegetans
Ecthyma
Perlèche

EXCLUDES　dermatitis infectiosa eczematoides (690.8)
　　　　　　panniculitis (729.30-729.39)

686.9　Unspecified local infection of skin and subcutaneous tissue

Fistula of skin NOS
Skin infection NOS

EXCLUDES　fistula to skin from internal organs — see Alphabetic Index

Other Inflammatory Conditions of Skin and Subcutaneous Tissue (690-698)

EXCLUDES　panniculitis (729.30-729.39)

✓4ᵗʰ **690　Erythematosquamous dermatosis**

EXCLUDES　eczematous dermatitis of eyelid (373.31)
　　　　　　parakeratosis variegata (696.2)
　　　　　　psoriasis (696.0-696.1)
　　　　　　seborrheic keratosis (702.11-702.19)

✓5ᵗʰ **690.1　Seborrheic dermatitis**

AHA: 4Q, '95, 58

690.10　Seborrheic dermatitis, unspecified

Seborrheic dermatitis NOS

L21.9 Seborrheic dermatitis unspecified　　`I-10`

690.11　Seborrhea capitis　　`P`

Cradle cap

690.12　Seborrheic infantile dermatitis　　`P`

690.18　Other seborrheic dermatitis

690.8　Other erythematosquamous dermatosis

✓4ᵗʰ **691　Atopic dermatitis and related conditions**

DEF: Atopic dermatitis: chronic, pruritic, inflammatory skin disorder found on the face and antecubital and popliteal fossae; often accompanied by allergic rhinitis, hay fever, asthma, and extreme itching; also called allergic dermatitis, or disseminated neurodermatitis.

691.0　Diaper or napkin rash

Ammonia dermatitis
Diaper or napkin:
　dermatitis
　erythema
　rash
Psoriasiform napkin eruption

691.8　Other atopic dermatitis and related conditions

Atopic dermatitis
Besnier's prurigo
Eczema:
　atopic
　flexural
　intrinsic (allergic)
Neurodermatitis:
　atopic
　diffuse (of Brocq)

✓4ᵗʰ **692　Contact dermatitis and other eczema**

INCLUDES　dermatitis:
　　　　　　NOS
　　　　　　contact
　　　　　　occupational
　　　　　　venenata
　　　　　eczema (acute) (chronic):
　　　　　　NOS
　　　　　　allergic
　　　　　　erythematous
　　　　　　occupational

EXCLUDES　allergy NOS (995.3)
　　　　　　contact dermatitis of eyelids (373.32)
　　　　　　dermatitis due to substances taken internally (693.0-693.9)
　　　　　　eczema of external ear (380.22)
　　　　　　perioral dermatitis (695.3)
　　　　　　urticarial reactions (708.0-708.9, 995.1)

DEF: Contact dermatitis: acute or chronic dermatitis caused by initial irritant effect of a substance, or by prior sensitization to a substance coming once again in contact with skin.

692.0　Due to detergents

692.1　Due to oils and greases

692.2　Due to solvents

Dermatitis due to solvents of:

chlorocompound ⎫
cyclohexane 　⎪
ester 　　　　⎬ group
glycol 　　　 ⎪
hydrocarbon 　⎪
ketone 　　　 ⎭

692.3　Due to drugs and medicines in contact with skin

Dermatitis (allergic) (contact) due to:
　arnica
　fungicides
　iodine
　keratolytics
　mercurials
　neomycin
　pediculocides
　phenols
　scabicides
　any drug applied to skin
Dermatitis medicamentosa due to drug applied to skin

Use additional E code to identify drug

EXCLUDES　allergy NOS due to drugs (995.27)
　　　　　　dermatitis due to ingested drugs (693.0)
　　　　　　dermatitis medicamentosa NOS (693.0)

692.4　Due to other chemical products

Dermatitis due to:
　acids
　adhesive plaster
　alkalis
　caustics
　dichromate
　insecticide
　nylon
　plastic
　rubber

AHA: 3Q, '08, 6-7; 2Q, '89, 16

✓4ᵗʰ ✓5ᵗʰ Additional Digit Required　　　Unacceptable PDx　　　Manifestation Code　　　Hospital Acquired Condition　　　▶◀ Revised Text　　　● New Code　　　▲ Revised Code Title

2015 ICD-9-CM　　**Volume 1 – 229**

692.5 Due to food in contact with skin
Dermatitis, contact, due to:
    cereals
    fish
    flour
    fruit
    meat
    milk

> **EXCLUDES** *dermatitis due to:*
>   *dyes (692.89)*
>   *ingested foods (693.1)*
>   *preservatives (692.89)*

692.6 Due to plants [except food]
Dermatitis due to:
    lacquer tree [Rhus verniciflua]
    poison:
        ivy [Rhus toxicodendron]
        oak [Rhus diversiloba]
        sumac [Rhus venenata]
        vine [Rhus radicans]
    primrose [Primula]
    ragweed [Senecio jacobae]
    other plants in contact with the skin

> **EXCLUDES** *allergy NOS due to pollen (477.0)*
>   *nettle rash (708.8)*

√5ᵗʰ 692.7 Due to solar radiation

> **EXCLUDES** *sunburn due to other ultraviolet radiation exposure (692.82)*

692.70 Unspecified dermatitis due to sun

692.71 Sunburn
First degree sunburn
Sunburn NOS

AHA: 4Q, '01, 47

TIP: Do not assign if sunburn is due to tanning bed use; see instead code 692.82.

692.72 Acute dermatitis due to solar radiation
Acute solar skin damage NOS
Berlogue dermatitis
Photoallergic response
Phototoxic response
Polymorphus light eruption

Use additional E code to identify drug, if drug induced

> **EXCLUDES** *sunburn (692.71, 692.76-692.77)*

DEF: Berloque dermatitis: Phytophotodermatitis due to sun exposure after use of a product containing bergamot oil; causes red patches, that turn brown.
DEF: Photoallergic response: Dermatitis due to hypersensitivity to the sun; causes papulovesicular, eczematous or exudative eruptions.
DEF: Phototoxic response: Chemically induced sensitivity to sun causes burn-like reaction, occasionally vesiculation and subsequent hyperpigmentation.
DEF: Polymorphous light eruption: Inflammatory skin eruptions due to sunlight exposure; eruptions differ in size and shape.
DEF: Acute solar skin damage (NOS): Rapid, unspecified injury to skin from sun.

692.73 Actinic reticuloid and actinic granuloma

DEF: Actinic reticuloid: Dermatosis aggravated by light, causes chronic eczema-like eruption on exposed skin which extends to other unexposed surfaces; occurs in the elderly.
DEF: Actinic granuloma: Inflammatory response of skin to sun causing small nodule of microphages.

692.74 Other chronic dermatitis due to solar radiation
Chronic solar skin damage NOS
Solar elastosis

> **EXCLUDES** *actinic [solar] keratosis (702.0)*

DEF: Solar elastosis: Premature aging of skin of light-skinned people; causes inelasticity, thinning or thickening, wrinkling, dryness, scaling and hyperpigmentation.
DEF: Chronic solar skin damage (NOS): Chronic skin impairment due to exposure to the sun, not otherwise specified.

692.75 Disseminated superficial actinic porokeratosis [DSAP]

DEF: Autosomal dominant skin condition occurring in skin that has been overexposed to the sun; characterized by superficial annular, keratotic, brownish-red spots or thickenings with depressed centers and sharp, ridged borders, may evolve into squamous cell carcinoma.
AHA: 4Q, '00, 43

692.76 Sunburn of second degree

AHA: 4Q, '01, 47
TIP: Do not assign if sunburn is due to tanning bed use; see instead code 692.82.

692.77 Sunburn of third degree

AHA: 4Q, '01, 47
TIP: Do not assign if sunburn is due to tanning bed use; see instead code 692.82.

692.79 Other dermatitis due to solar radiation
Hydroa aestivale
Photodermatitis   }
Photosensitiveness   } (due to sun)
Solar skin damage NOS

√5ᵗʰ 692.8 Due to other specified agents

692.81 Dermatitis due to cosmetics

692.82 Dermatitis due to other radiation
Infrared rays
Light, except from sun
Radiation NOS
Tanning bed
Ultraviolet rays, except from sun
X-rays

> **EXCLUDES** *solar radiation (692.70-692.79)*

AHA: 4Q, '01, 47; 3Q, '00, 5

692.83 Dermatitis due to metals
Jewelry

692.84 Due to animal (cat) (dog) dander
Due to animal (cat) (dog) hair

692.89 Other
Dermatitis due to: Dermatitis due to:
  cold weather   hot weather
  dyes   preservatives

> **EXCLUDES** *allergy (NOS) (rhinitis) due to animal hair or dander (477.2)*
>   *allergy to dust (477.8)*
>   *sunburn (692.71, 692.76-692.77)*

692.9 Unspecified cause
Dermatitis:
  NOS
  contact NOS
  venenata NOS
Eczema NOS
L23.9 Allergic contact dermatitis unspecified cause   **I-10**

√4ᵗʰ 693 Dermatitis due to substances taken internally

> **EXCLUDES** *adverse effect NOS of drugs and medicines (995.20)*
>   *allergy NOS (995.3)*
>   *contact dermatitis (692.0-692.9)*
>   *urticarial reactions (708.0-708.9, 995.1)*

DEF: Inflammation of skin due to ingested substance.

693.0 Due to drugs and medicines
Dermatitis medicamentosa NOS

Use additional E code to identify drug

> **EXCLUDES** *that due to drugs in contact with skin (692.3)*

AHA: 2Q, '07, 8
TIP: Assign for palmar plantar erythrodysesthesia (PPE) or hand-foot syndrome due to chemotherapy drugs.
L27.0 Gen skin eruption d/t Rx & med taken internally   **I-10**

693.1 Due to food

693.8 Due to other specified substances taken internally

693.9 Due to unspecified substance taken internally

> **EXCLUDES** *dermatitis NOS (692.9)*

N Newborn Age: 0   **P** Pediatric Age: 0-17   **M** Maternity Age: 12-55   **A** Adult Age: 15-124   **MCC** Major CC Condition   **CC** CC Condition   **HIV** HIV Related Dx

230 – Volume 1   2015 ICD-9-CM

✓4th **694 Bullous dermatoses**

694.0 Dermatitis herpetiformis
Dermatosis herpetiformisHydroa herpetiformis
Duhring's disease
EXCLUDES *herpes gestationis (646.8)*
dermatitis herpetiformis:
juvenile (694.2)
senile (694.5)

DEF: Chronic, multisystem disease manifested in the cutaneous system; seen as an extremely pruritic eruption of various lesions that frequently heal leaving hyperpigmentation or hypopigmentation and occasionally scarring; usually associated with an asymptomatic gluten-sensitive enteropathy, and immunogenic factors .

694.1 Subcorneal pustular dermatosis
Sneddon-Wilkinson disease or syndrome
DEF: Chronic relapses of sterile pustular blebs beneath the horny skin layer of the trunk and skin folds; resembles dermatitis herpetiformis.

694.2 Juvenile dermatitis herpetiformis
Juvenile pemphigoid

694.3 Impetigo herpetiformis
DEF: Rare dermatosis associated with pregnancy; marked by itching pustules in third trimester, hypocalcemia, tetany, fever and lethargy; may result in maternal or fetal death.

694.4 Pemphigus `CC`
Pemphigus: Pemphigus:
  NOS   malignant
  erythematosus   vegetans
  foliaceus   vulgaris
EXCLUDES *pemphigus neonatorum (684)*
CC Excl: 694.4-694.9, 709.8
DEF: Chronic, relapsing, sometimes fatal skin diseases; causes vesicles, bullae; autoantibodies against intracellular connections cause acantholysis.

694.5 Pemphigoid `CC`
Benign pemphigus NOS
Bullous pemphigoid
Herpes circinatus bullosus
Senile dermatitis herpetiformis
CC Excl: See code 694.4

✓5th **694.6 Benign mucous membrane pemphigoid**
Cicatricial pemphigoid
Mucosynechial atrophic bullous dermatitis

694.60 Without mention of ocular involvement

694.61 With ocular involvement
Ocular pemphigus
DEF: Mild self-limiting, subepidermal blistering of mucosa including the conjunctiva, seen predominantly in the elderly, produces adhesions and scarring.

694.8 Other specified bullous dermatoses
EXCLUDES *herpes gestationis (646.8)*

694.9 Unspecified bullous dermatoses

✓4th **695 Erythematous conditions**

695.0 Toxic erythema `CC`
Erythema venenatum
CC Excl: 695.0-695.4, 709.8

✓5th **695.1 Erythema multiforme**
Use additional code to identify associated manifestations, such as:
arthropathy associated with dermatological disorders (713.3)
conjunctival edema (372.73)
conjunctivitis (372.04, 372.33)
corneal scars and opacities (371.00-371.05)
corneal ulcer (370.00-370.07)
edema of eyelid (374.82)
inflammation of eyelid (373.8)
keratoconjunctivitis sicca (370.33)
mechanical lagophthalmos (374.22)
mucositis (478.11, 528.00, 538, 616.81)
stomatitis (528.00)
symblepharon (372.63)
Use additional E code to identify drug, if drug-induced
Use additional code to identify percentage of skin exfoliation (695.50-695.59)
EXCLUDES *(Staphylococcal) scalded skin syndrome (695.81)*
DEF: Symptom complex with varied skin eruption pattern of macular, bullous, papular, nodose, or vesicular lesions on the neck, face, and legs; gastritis and rheumatic pains; secondary to number of factors, including infections, ingestants, physical agents, malignancy and pregnancy.
AHA: 4Q, '08, 128-130

695.10 Erythema multiforme, unspecified
Erythema iris
Herpes iris

695.11 Erythema multiforme minor

695.12 Erythema multiforme major `CC`
CC Excl: 695.0-695.4, 695.81-695.9, 709.8

695.13 Stevens-Johnson syndrome `CC`
CC Excl: See code 695.12

695.14 Stevens-Johnson syndrome-toxic epidermal necrolysis overlap syndrome `CC`
SJS-TEN overlap syndrome
CC Excl: See code 695.12
AHA: 4Q, '08, 131

695.15 Toxic epidermal necrolysis `CC`
Lyell's syndrome
CC Excl: See code 695.12

695.19 Other erythema multiforme

695.2 Erythema nodosum
EXCLUDES *tuberculous erythema nodosum (017.1)*
DEF: Panniculitis (an inflammatory reaction of the subcutaneous fat) of women, usually seen as a hypersensitivity reaction to infections, drugs, sarcoidosis, and specific enteropathies; the acute stage associated with fever, malaise, and arthralgia; the lesions are pink to blue in color as tender nodules found on the front of the legs below the knees.

695.3 Rosacea
Acne: Perioral dermatitis
  erythematosa   Rhinophyma
  rosacea
DEF: Chronic skin disease, usually of the face, characterized by persistent erythema and telangiectasis with acute episodes of edema, engorgement papules, and pustules.

695.4 Lupus erythematosus
Lupus:
  erythematodes (discoid)
  erythematosus (discoid), not disseminated
EXCLUDES *lupus (vulgaris) NOS (017.0)*
systemic [disseminated] lupus erythematosus (710.0)
DEF: Group of connective tissue disorders occurring as various cutaneous diseases of unknown origin; it primarily affects women between the ages of 20 and 40.

√5ᵗʰ **695.5 Exfoliation due to erythematous conditions according to extent of body surface involved**

Code first erythematous condition causing exfoliation, such as:
Ritter's disease (695.81)
(Staphylococcal) scalded skin syndrome (695.81)
Stevens-Johnson syndrome (695.13)
Stevens-Johnson syndrome-toxic epidermal necrolysis overlap syndrome (695.14)
toxic epidermal necrolysis (695.15)
AHA: 4Q, '08, 128-131

695.50 Exfoliation due to erythematous condition involving less than 10 percent of body surface
Exfoliation due to erythematous condition NOS

695.51 Exfoliation due to erythematous condition involving 10-19 percent of body surface

695.52 Exfoliation due to erythematous condition involving 20-29 percent of body surface

695.53 Exfoliation due to erythematous condition involving 30-39 percent of body surface `CC`
CC Excl: 695.53
AHA: 4Q, '08, 131

695.54 Exfoliation due to erythematous condition involving 40-49 percent of body surface `CC`
CC Excl: 695.54

695.55 Exfoliation due to erythematous condition involving 50-59 percent of body surface `CC`
CC Excl: 695.55

695.56 Exfoliation due to erythematous condition involving 60-69 percent of body surface `CC`
CC Excl: 695.56

695.57 Exfoliation due to erythematous condition involving 70-79 percent of body surface `CC`
CC Excl: 695.57

695.58 Exfoliation due to erythematous condition involving 80-89 percent of body surface `CC`
CC Excl: 695.58

695.59 Exfoliation due to erythematous condition involving 90 percent or more of body surface `CC`
CC Excl: 695.59

√5ᵗʰ **695.8 Other specified erythematous conditions**

695.81 Ritter's disease
Dermatitis exfoliativa neonatorum
(Staphylococcal) Scalded skin syndrome
Use additional code to identify percentage of skin exfoliation (695.50-695.59)
DEF: Infectious skin disease of young children marked by eruptions ranging from a localized bullous to widespread easily ruptured fine vesicles and bullae; results in exfoliation of large planes of skin and leaves raw areas.

695.89 Other
Erythema intertrigo
Intertrigo
Pityriasis rubra (Hebra)
EXCLUDES mycotic intertrigo (111.0-111.9)
AHA: S-O, '86, 10

695.9 Unspecified erythematous condition
Erythema NOS   Erythroderma (secondary)

√4ᵗʰ **696 Psoriasis and similar disorders**

696.0 Psoriatic arthropathy
DEF: Psoriasis associated with inflammatory arthritis; often involves interphalangeal joints.

696.1 Other psoriasis
Acrodermatitis continua   Psoriasis:
Dermatitis repens   NOS
Psoriasis: any type, except arthropathic
EXCLUDES psoriatic arthropathy (696.0)
L40.9 Psoriasis unspecified   `I-10`

696.2 Parapsoriasis
Parakeratosis variegata
Parapsoriasis lichenoides chronica
Pityriasis lichenoides et varioliformis
DEF: Erythrodermas similar to lichen, planus and psoriasis; symptoms include redness and itching; resistant to treatment.

696.3 Pityriasis rosea
Pityriasis circinata (et maculata)
DEF: Common, self-limited rash of unknown etiology marked by a solitary erythematous, salmon or fawn-colored herald plaque on the trunk, arms or thighs; followed by development of papular or macular lesions that tend to peel and form a scaly collarette.

696.4 Pityriasis rubra pilaris
Devergie's disease   Lichen ruber acuminatus
EXCLUDES pityriasis rubra (Hebra) (695.89)
DEF: Inflammatory disease of hair follicles; marked by firm, red lesions topped by horny plugs; may form patches; occurs on fingers elbows, knees.

696.5 Other and unspecified pityriasis
Pityriasis: Pityriasis:
NOS   streptogenes
alba
EXCLUDES pityriasis:
simplex (690.18)
versicolor (111.0)

696.8 Other

√4ᵗʰ **697 Lichen**
EXCLUDES lichen:
obtusus corneus (698.3)
pilaris (congenital) (757.39)
ruber acuminatus (696.4)
sclerosus et atrophicus (701.0)
scrofulosus (017.0)
simplex chronicus (698.3)
spinulosus (congenital) (757.39)
urticatus (698.2)

697.0 Lichen planus
Lichen: Lichen:
planopilaris   ruber planus
DEF: Inflammatory, pruritic skin disease; marked by angular, flat-top, violet-colored papules; may be acute and widespread or chronic and localized.

697.1 Lichen nitidus
Pinkus' disease
DEF: Chronic, inflammatory, asymptomatic skin disorder, characterized by numerous glistening, flat-topped, discrete, skin-colored micropapules most often on penis, lower abdomen, inner thighs, wrists, forearms, breasts and buttocks.

697.8 Other lichen, not elsewhere classified
Lichen: Lichen:
ruber moniliforme   striata

697.9 Lichen, unspecified

√4ᵗʰ **698 Pruritus and related conditions**
EXCLUDES pruritus specified as psychogenic (306.3)
DEF: Pruritus: Intense, persistent itching due to irritation of sensory nerve endings from organic or psychogenic causes.

698.0 Pruritus ani
Perianal itch

698.1 Pruritus of genital organs

698.2 Prurigo
Lichen urticatus   Prurigo:
Prurigo: mitis
NOS   simplex
Hebra's   Urticaria papulosa (Hebra)
EXCLUDES prurigo nodularis (698.3)

698.3 Lichenification and lichen simplex chronicus
Hyde's disease
Neurodermatitis (circumscripta) (local)
Prurigo nodularis
EXCLUDES *neurodermatitis, diffuse (of Brocq) (691.8)*
DEF: Lichenification: thickening of skin due to prolonged rubbing or scratching.
DEF: Lichen simplex chronicus: eczematous dermatitis, of face, neck, extremities, scrotum, vulva, and perianal region due to repeated itching, rubbing and scratching; spontaneous or evolves with other dermatoses.

698.4 Dermatitis factitia [artefacta]
Dermatitis ficta　　　Neurotic excoriation
Use additional code to identify any associated mental disorder
DEF: Various types of self-inflicted skin lesions characterized in appearance as an erythema to a gangrene.

698.8 Other specified pruritic conditions
Pruritus:　　　　　Winter itch
　hiemalis
　senilis

698.9 Unspecified pruritic disorder
Itch NOS　　　　　Pruritus NOS
L29.9 Pruritus unspecified　　　　　**I-10**

Other Diseases of Skin and Subcutaneous Tissue (700-709)

EXCLUDES *conditions confined to eyelids (373.0-374.9)*
congenital conditions of skin, hair, and nails (757.0-757.9)

700　Corns and callosities
Callus
Clavus
DEF: Corns: Conical or horny thickening of skin on toes, due to friction, pressure from shoes and hosiery; pain and inflammation may develop.
DEF: Callosities: Localized overgrowth (hyperplasia) of the horny epidermal layer due to pressure or friction.

√4th **701　Other hypertrophic and atrophic conditions of skin**
EXCLUDES *dermatomyositis (710.3)*
hereditary edema of legs (757.0)
scleroderma (generalized) (710.1)

701.0 Circumscribed scleroderma
Addison's keloid
Dermatosclerosis, localized
Lichen sclerosus et atrophicus
Morphea
Scleroderma, circumscribed or localized
DEF: Thickened, hardened, skin and subcutaneous tissue; may involve musculoskeletal system.

701.1 Keratoderma, acquired
Acquired:
　ichthyosis
　keratoderma palmaris et plantaris
Elastosis perforans serpiginosa
Hyperkeratosis:
　NOS
　follicularis in cutem penetrans
　palmoplantaris climacterica
Keratoderma:
　climactericum
　tylodes, progressive
Keratosis (blennorrhagica)
EXCLUDES *Darier's disease [keratosis follicularis] (congenital) (757.39)*
keratosis:
*　arsenical (692.4)*
*　gonococcal (098.81)*
AHA: 4Q, '94, 48

701.2 Acquired acanthosis nigricans
Keratosis nigricans
DEF: Diffuse velvety hyperplasia of the spinous skin layer of the axilla and other body folds marked by gray, brown, or black pigmentation; in adult form often associated with malignant acanthosis nigricans in a benign, nevoid form relatively generalized.

701.3 Striae atrophicae
Atrophic spots of skin
Atrophoderma maculatum
Atrophy blanche (of Milian)
Degenerative colloid atrophy
Senile degenerative atrophy
Striae distensae
DEF: Bands of atrophic, depressed, wrinkled skin associated with stretching of skin from pregnancy, obesity, or rapid growth during puberty.

701.4 Keloid scar
Cheloid
Hypertrophic scar
Keloid
DEF: Overgrowth of scar tissue due to excess amounts of collagen during connective tissue repair; occurs mainly on upper trunk, face.

701.5 Other abnormal granulation tissue
Excessive granulation

701.8 Other specified hypertrophic and atrophic conditions of skin
Acrodermatitis atrophicans chronica
Atrophia cutis senilis
Atrophoderma neuriticum
Confluent and reticulate papillomatosis
Cutis laxa senilis
Elastosis senilis
Folliculitis ulerythematosa reticulata
Gougerot-Carteaud syndrome or disease
AHA: 1Q, '08, 7
TIP: Assign for nephrogenic fibrosing dermopathy (NFD) or nephrogenic systemic dermopathy (NSD), a systemic condition occurring only in patients with kidney disease.

701.9 Unspecified hypertrophic and atrophic conditions of skin
Atrophoderma
Skin tag

√4th **702　Other dermatoses**
EXCLUDES *carcinoma in situ (232.0-232.9)*

702.0 Actinic keratosis
DEF: Wart-like growth, red or skin-colored; may form a cutaneous horn.
AHA: 1Q, '92, 18

√5th **702.1 Seborrheic keratosis**
DEF: Common, benign, lightly pigmented, warty growth composed of basaloid cells.

702.11 Inflamed seborrheic keratosis
AHA: 4Q, '94, 48

702.19 Other seborrheic keratosis
Seborrheic keratosis NOS

702.8 Other specified dermatoses

√4th **703　Diseases of nail**
EXCLUDES *congenital anomalies (757.5)*
onychia and paronychia (681.02, 681.11)

703.0 Ingrowing nail
Ingrowing nail with infection
Unguis incarnatus
EXCLUDES *infection, nail NOS (681.9)*

703.8 Other specified diseases of nail
Dystrophia unguium
Hypertrophy of nail
Koilonychia
Leukonychia (punctata) (striata)
Onychauxis
Onychogryposis
Onycholysis

703.9 Unspecified disease of nail

Diseases of the Skin and Subcutaneous Tissue

704–706.0

✓4ᵗʰ **704   Diseases of hair and hair follicles**

> EXCLUDES *congenital anomalies (757.4)*

✓5ᵗʰ **704.0   Alopecia**

> EXCLUDES *madarosis (374.55)*
> *syphilitic alopecia (091.82)*
>
> **DEF:** Lack of hair, especially on scalp; often called baldness; may be partial or total; occurs at any age.

704.00   Alopecia, unspecified
  Baldness
  Loss of hair

704.01   Alopecia areata
  Ophiasis
> **DEF:** Alopecia areata: usually reversible, inflammatory, patchy hair loss found in beard or scalp.
> **DEF:** Ophiasis: alopecia areata of children; marked by band around temporal and occipital scalp margins.

704.02   Telogen effluvium
> **DEF:** Shedding of hair from premature telogen development in follicles due to stress, including shock, childbirth, surgery, drugs or weight loss.

704.09   Other
  Folliculitis decalvans
  Hypotrichosis:
    NOS
    postinfectional NOS
  Pseudopelade

704.1   Hirsutism
  Hypertrichosis:
    NOS
    lanuginosa, acquired
  Polytrichia
> EXCLUDES *hypertrichosis of eyelid (374.54)*
> **DEF:** Excess hair growth; often in unexpected places and amounts.

704.2   Abnormalities of the hair
  Atrophic hair
  Clastothrix
  Fragilitas crinium
  Trichiasis:
    NOS
    cicatrical
  Trichorrhexis (nodosa)
> EXCLUDES *trichiasis of eyelid (374.05)*

704.3   Variations in hair color
  Canities (premature)
  Grayness, hair (premature)
  Heterochromia of hair
  Poliosis:
    NOS
    circumscripta, acquired

✓5ᵗʰ **704.4   Pilar and trichilemmal cysts**
  AHA: 4Q, '11, 134-135

704.41   Pilar cyst

704.42   Trichilemmal cyst
  Trichilemmal proliferating cyst
  AHA: 4Q, '11, 135

704.8   Other specified diseases of hair and hair follicles
  Folliculitis:
    NOS
    abscedens et suffodiens
    pustular
  Perifolliculitis:
    NOS
    capitis abscedens et suffodiens
    scalp
  Sycosis:
    NOS
    barbae [not parasitic]
    lupoid
    vulgaris
  AHA: 1Q, '11, 8

704.9   Unspecified disease of hair and hair follicles

✓4ᵗʰ **705   Disorders of sweat glands**

705.0   Anhidrosis
  Hypohidrosis
  Oligohidrosis
> **DEF:** Lack or deficiency of ability to sweat.

705.1   Prickly heat
  Heat rash
  Miliaria rubra (tropicalis)
  Sudamina

✓5ᵗʰ **705.2   Focal hyperhidrosis**
> EXCLUDES *generalized (secondary) hyperhidrosis (780.8)*

705.21   Primary focal hyperhidrosis
  Focal hyperhidrosis NOS
  Hyperhidrosis NOS
  Hyperhidrosis of:
    axilla
    face
    palms
    soles
> **DEF:** A rare disorder of the sweat glands resulting in excessive production of sweat; occurs in the absence of any underlying condition, almost always focal, confined to one or more specific areas of the body.
> AHA: 4Q, '04, 91

705.22   Secondary focal hyperhidrosis
  Frey's syndrome
> **DEF:** Secondary focal hyperhidrosis: a symptom of an underlying disease process resulting in excessive sweating beyond what the body requires to maintain thermal control, confined to one or more specific areas of the body.
> **DEF:** Frey's syndrome: an auriculotemporal syndrome due to lesion on the parotid gland; characteristic redness and excessive sweating on the cheek in connection with eating.
> AHA: 4Q, '04, 91

✓5ᵗʰ **705.8   Other specified disorders of sweat glands**

705.81   Dyshidrosis
  Cheiropompholyx
  Pompholyx
> **DEF:** Vesicular eruption, on hands, feet causing itching and burning.

705.82   Fox-Fordyce disease
> **DEF:** Chronic, usually pruritic disease evidenced by small follicular papular eruptions, especially in the axillary and pubic areas; develops from the closure and rupture of the affected apocrine glands' intraepidermal portion of the ducts.

705.83   Hidradenitis
  Hidradenitis suppurativa
> **DEF:** Inflamed sweat glands.

705.89   Other
  Bromhidrosis
  Chromhidrosis
  Granulosis rubra nasi
  Urhidrosis
> EXCLUDES *generalized hyperhidrosis (780.8)*
> *hidrocystoma (216.0-216.9)*
>
> **DEF:** Bromhidrosis: foul-smelling axillary sweat due to decomposed bacteria.
> **DEF:** Chromhidrosis: secretion of colored sweat.
> **DEF:** Granulosis rubra nasi: idiopathic condition of children; causes redness, sweating around nose, face and chin; tends to end by puberty.
> **DEF:** Urhidrosis: urinous substance, such as uric acid, in sweat; occurs in uremia.

705.9   Unspecified disorder of sweat glands
  Disorder of sweat glands NOS

✓4ᵗʰ **706   Diseases of sebaceous glands**

706.0   Acne varioliformis
  Acne: Acne:
    frontalis   necrotica
> **DEF:** Rare form of acne characterized by persistent brown papulo-pustules usually on the brow and temporoparietal part of the scalp.

N Newborn Age: 0   P Pediatric Age: 0-17   M Maternity Age: 12-55   A Adult Age: 15-124   MCC Major CC Condition   CC CC Condition   HIV HIV Related Dx

706.1 Other acne
Acne: Blackhead
   NOS   Comedo
   conglobata
   cystic
   pustular
   vulgaris
EXCLUDES *acne rosacea (695.3)*

706.2 Sebaceous cyst
Atheroma, skin
Keratin cyst
Wen
EXCLUDES *pilar cyst (704.41)*
trichilemmal (proliferating) cyst (704.42)
DEF: Benign epidermal cyst, contains sebum and keratin; presents as firm, circumscribed nodule.

706.3 Seborrhea
EXCLUDES *seborrhea:*
capitis (690.11)
sicca (690.18)
seborrheic
dermatitis (690.10)
keratosis (702.11-702.19)
DEF: Seborrheic dermatitis marked by excessive secretion of sebum; the sebum forms an oily coating, crusts, or scales on the skin; it is also called hypersteatosis.

706.8 Other specified diseases of sebaceous glands
Asteatosis (cutis)
Xerosis cutis

706.9 Unspecified disease of sebaceous glands

✔4ᵗʰ **707 Chronic ulcer of skin**
INCLUDES non-infected sinus of skin
non-healing ulcer
EXCLUDES *varicose ulcer (454.0, 454.2)*
AHA: 4Q, '04, 92

✔5ᵗʰ **707.0 Pressure ulcer**
Bed sore   Plaster ulcer
Decubitus ulcer
Use additional code to identify pressure ulcer stage (707.20-707.25)
AHA: 4Q, '08, 132-133; 1Q, '04, 14; 4Q, '03, 110; 4Q, '99, 20; 1Q, '96, 15; 3Q, '90, 15; N-D, '87, 9

707.00 Unspecified site

707.01 Elbow

707.02 Upper back
Shoulder blades

707.03 Lower back
Coccyx
Sacrum
AHA: 3Q, '08, 17; 1Q, '05, 16
L89.159 Pressure ulcer of sacral region uns stage   I-10

707.04 Hip
L89.209 Pressure ulcer of unspecified hip uns stage   I-10

707.05 Buttock
AHA: 2Q, '12, 3
L89.309 Pressure ulcer of unspecified buttock uns stage   I-10

707.06 Ankle

Four Stages of Pressure Ulcers

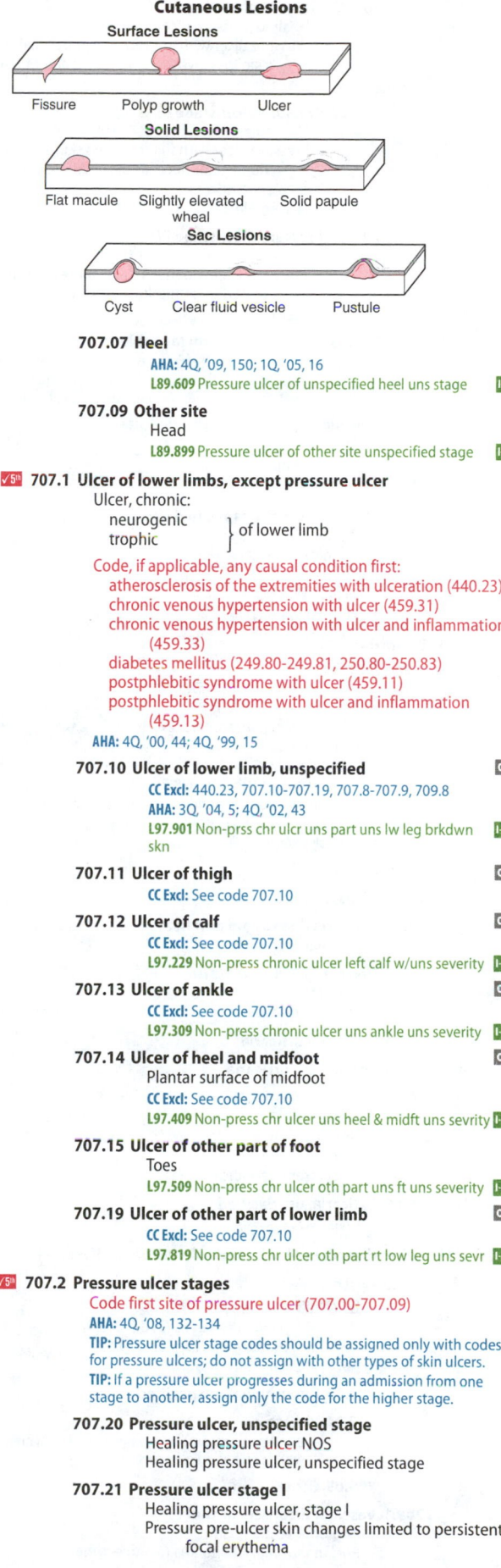

First Stage
Persistent focal erythema

Second Stage
Partial thickness skin loss involving epidermis, dermis, or both

Third Stage
Full thickness skin loss extending through subcutaneous tissue

Fourth Stage
Necrosis of soft tissue extending to muscle and bone

Cutaneous Lesions

Surface Lesions

Fissure   Polyp growth   Ulcer

Solid Lesions

Flat macule   Slightly elevated wheal   Solid papule

Sac Lesions

Cyst   Clear fluid vesicle   Pustule

707.07 Heel
AHA: 4Q, '09, 150; 1Q, '05, 16
L89.609 Pressure ulcer of unspecified heel uns stage   I-10

707.09 Other site
Head
L89.899 Pressure ulcer of other site unspecified stage   I-10

✔5ᵗʰ **707.1 Ulcer of lower limbs, except pressure ulcer**
Ulcer, chronic:
  neurogenic   } of lower limb
  trophic
Code, if applicable, any causal condition first:
atherosclerosis of the extremities with ulceration (440.23)
chronic venous hypertension with ulcer (459.31)
chronic venous hypertension with ulcer and inflammation (459.33)
diabetes mellitus (249.80-249.81, 250.80-250.83)
postphlebitic syndrome with ulcer (459.11)
postphlebitic syndrome with ulcer and inflammation (459.13)
AHA: 4Q, '00, 44; 4Q, '99, 15

707.10 Ulcer of lower limb, unspecified   CC
CC Excl: 440.23, 707.10-707.19, 707.8-707.9, 709.8
AHA: 3Q, '04, 5; 4Q, '02, 43
L97.901 Non-prss chr ulcr uns part uns lw leg brkdwn skn   I-10

707.11 Ulcer of thigh   CC
CC Excl: See code 707.10

707.12 Ulcer of calf   CC
CC Excl: See code 707.10
L97.229 Non-press chronic ulcer left calf w/uns severity   I-10

707.13 Ulcer of ankle   CC
CC Excl: See code 707.10
L97.309 Non-press chronic ulcer uns ankle uns severity   I-10

707.14 Ulcer of heel and midfoot   CC
Plantar surface of midfoot
CC Excl: See code 707.10
L97.409 Non-press chr ulcer uns heel & midft uns sevrity   I-10

707.15 Ulcer of other part of foot
Toes
L97.509 Non-press chr ulcr oth part uns ft uns severity   I-10

707.19 Ulcer of other part of lower limb   CC
CC Excl: See code 707.10
L97.819 Non-press chr ulcr oth part rt low leg uns sevr   I-10

✔5ᵗʰ **707.2 Pressure ulcer stages**
Code first site of pressure ulcer (707.00-707.09)
AHA: 4Q, '08, 132-134
TIP: Pressure ulcer stage codes should be assigned only with codes for pressure ulcers; do not assign with other types of skin ulcers.
TIP: If a pressure ulcer progresses during an admission from one stage to another, assign only the code for the higher stage.

707.20 Pressure ulcer, unspecified stage
Healing pressure ulcer NOS
Healing pressure ulcer, unspecified stage

707.21 Pressure ulcer stage I
Healing pressure ulcer, stage I
Pressure pre-ulcer skin changes limited to persistent focal erythema

Diseases of the Skin and Subcutaneous Tissue

707.22–709.9

707.22 Pressure ulcer stage II
Healing pressure ulcer, stage II
Pressure ulcer with abrasion, blister, partial thickness
    skin loss involving epidermis and/or dermis
AHA: 2Q, '12, 3

707.23 Pressure ulcer stage III   `MCC`
Healing pressure ulcer, stage III
Pressure ulcer with full thickness skin loss involving
    damage or necrosis of subcutaneous tissue
CC Excl: 707.10-707.9
AHA: 4Q, '09, 150

707.24 Pressure ulcer stage IV   `MCC`
Healing pressure ulcer, stage IV
Pressure ulcer with necrosis of soft tissues through to
    underlying muscle, tendon, or bone
CC Excl: See code 707.23

707.25 Pressure ulcer, unstageable
TIP: Assign only if ulcer is covered by eschar, has been
treated with skin or other graft, or is documented as a deep
tissue injury but not documented as due to trauma.

707.8 Chronic ulcer of other specified sites
Ulcer, chronic:
    neurogenic   } of other specified sites
    trophic

707.9 Chronic ulcer of unspecified site
Chronic ulcer NOS
Trophic ulcer NOS
Tropical ulcer NOS
Ulcer of skin NOS
L98.499 Non-press chr ulcer skin oth sites uns severity   `I-10`

√4ᵗʰ **708 Urticaria**
EXCLUDES edema:
    angioneurotic (995.1)
    Quincke's (995.1)
    hereditary angioedema (277.6)
    urticaria:
       giant (995.1)
       papulosa (Hebra) (698.2)
       pigmentosa (juvenile) (congenital) (757.33)
DEF: Skin disorder marked by raised edematous patches of skin or mucous
membrane with intense itching; also called hives.

708.0 Allergic urticaria

708.1 Idiopathic urticaria

708.2 Urticaria due to cold and heat
Thermal urticaria

708.3 Dermatographic urticaria
Dermatographia
Factitial urticaria

708.4 Vibratory urticaria

708.5 Cholinergic urticaria

708.8 Other specified urticaria
Nettle rash
Urticaria:
    chronic
    recurrent periodic

708.9 Urticaria, unspecified
Hives NOS

√4ᵗʰ **709 Other disorders of skin and subcutaneous tissue**

√5ᵗʰ **709.0 Dyschromia**
EXCLUDES albinism (270.2)
    pigmented nevus (216.0-216.9)
    that of eyelid (374.52-374.53)
DEF: Pigment disorder of skin or hair.

709.00 Dyschromia, unspecified

709.01 Vitiligo
DEF: Persistent, progressive development of nonpigmented
white patches on otherwise normal skin.

709.09 Other

709.1 Vascular disorders of skin
Angioma serpiginosum
Purpura (primary)annularis telangiectodes

709.2 Scar conditions and fibrosis of skin
Adherent scar (skin)
Cicatrix
Disfigurement (due to scar)
Fibrosis, skin NOS
Scar NOS
EXCLUDES keloid scar (701.4)
AHA: N-D, '84, 19

709.3 Degenerative skin disorders
Calcinosis:
    circumscripta
    cutis
Colloid milium
Degeneration, skin
Deposits, skin
Senile dermatosis NOS
Subcutaneous calcification

709.4 Foreign body granuloma of skin and subcutaneous tissue
Use additional code to identify foreign body (V90.01-V90.9)
EXCLUDES residual foreign body without granuloma of skin and
    subcutaneous tissue (729.6)
    that of muscle (728.82)

709.8 Other specified disorders of skin
Epithelial hyperplasia
Menstrual dermatosis
Vesicular eruption
DEF: Epithelial hyperplasia: increased number of epithelial cells.
DEF: Vesicular eruption: liquid-filled structures appearing through
skin.
AHA: ►2Q, '13, 9;◄ 4Q, '08, 99; N-D, '87, 6
L98.8 Other spec disorders skin & subcutaneous tissue   `I-10`

709.9 Unspecified disorder of skin and subcutaneous tissue
Dermatosis NOS

N Newborn Age: 0   **P** Pediatric Age: 0-17   **M** Maternity Age: 12-55   **A** Adult Age: 15-124   `MCC` Major CC Condition   `CC` CC Condition   `HIV` HIV Related Dx

236 – Volume 1 • October 2014   **2015 ICD-9-CM**

13. Diseases of the Musculoskeletal System and Connective Tissue (710-739)

Use additional external cause code, if applicable, to identify the cause of the musculoskeletal condition

The following fifth-digit subclassification is for use with categories 711-712, 715-716, 718-719, and 730:

0 site unspecified

1 shoulder region
   Acromioclavicular joint(s)
   Clavicle
   Glenohumeral joint(s)
   Scapula
   Sternoclavicular joint(s)

2 upper arm
   Elbow joint
   Humerus

3 forearm
   Radius
   Ulna
   Wrist joint

4 hand
   Carpus
   Metacarpus
   Phalanges [fingers]

5 pelvic region and thigh
   Buttock
   Femur
   Hip (joint)

6 lower leg
   Fibula
   Knee joint
   Patella
   Tibia

7 ankle and foot
   Ankle joint
   Digits [toes]
   Metatarsus
   Phalanges, foot
   Tarsus
   Other joints in foot

8 other specified sites
   Head
   Neck
   Ribs
   Skull
   Trunk
   Vertebral column

9 multiple sites

Arthropathies and Related Disorders (710-719)

EXCLUDES *disorders of spine (720.0-724.9)*

✓4ᵗʰ **710 Diffuse diseases of connective tissue**

INCLUDES all collagen diseases whose effects are not mainly confined to a single system

EXCLUDES *those affecting mainly the cardiovascular system, i.e., polyarteritis nodosa and allied conditions (446.0-446.7)*

710.0 Systemic lupus erythematosus
   Disseminated lupus erythematosus   Libman-Sacks disease

Use additional code to identify manifestation, as:
   endocarditis (424.91)
   nephritis (583.81)
       chronic (582.81)
   nephrotic syndrome (581.81)

EXCLUDES *lupus erythematosus (discoid) NOS (695.4)*

DEF: A chronic multisystemic inflammatory disease affecting connective tissue; marked by anemia, leukopenia, muscle and joint pains, fever, rash of a butterfly pattern around cheeks and forehead area; of unknown etiology.
AHA: 2Q, '03, 7-8; 2Q, '97, 8
M32.9 Systemic lupus erythematosus unspecified   I-10

710.1 Systemic sclerosis
   Acrosclerosis   Progressive systemic sclerosis
   CRST syndrome   Scleroderma

Use additional code to identify manifestation, as:
   lung involvement (517.2)
   myopathy (359.6)

EXCLUDES *circumscribed scleroderma (701.0)*

DEF: Systemic disease, involving excess fibrotic collagen build-up; symptoms include thickened skin, fibrotic degenerative changes in various organs, and vascular abnormalities; condition occurs more often in females.
AHA: 1Q, '88, 6

710.2 Sicca syndrome
   Keratoconjunctivitis sicca   Sjögren's disease
   DEF: Autoimmune disease; associated with keratoconjunctivitis, laryngopharyngitis, rhinitis, dry mouth, enlarged parotid gland, and chronic polyarthritis.

710.3 Dermatomyositis   cc
   Poikilodermatomyositis   Polymyositis with skin involvement
   DEF: Polymyositis characterized by flat-top purple papules on knuckles; upper eyelid rash, edema of eyelids and orbit area, red rash on forehead, neck, shoulders, trunk and arms; symptoms include fever, weight loss, aching muscles; visceral cancer.
   CC Excl: 710.3

710.4 Polymyositis   cc
   DEF: Chronic, progressive, inflammatory skeletal muscle disease; causes weakness of limb girdles, neck, pharynx; may precede or follow scleroderma, Sjogren's disease, systemic lupus erythematosus, arthritis, or malignancy.
   CC Excl: 710.4

710.5 Eosinophilia myalgia syndrome   cc
   Toxic oil syndrome

   Use additional E code to identify drug, if drug induced

   DEF: Eosinophilia myalgia syndrome (EMS): inflammatory, multisystem fibrosis; associated with ingesting elementary L-tryptophan; symptoms include myalgia, weak limbs and bulbar muscles, distal sensory loss, areflexia, arthralgia, cough, fever, fatigue, skin rashes, myopathy, and eosinophil counts greater than 1000/microliter.
   DEF: Toxic oil syndrome: syndrome similar to EMS due to ingesting contaminated cooking oil.
   CC Excl: 292.0-293.9, 710.5
   AHA: 4Q, '92, 21

710.8 Other specified diffuse diseases of connective tissue   cc
   Multifocal fibrosclerosis (idiopathic) NEC
   Systemic fibrosclerosing syndrome
   CC Excl: 359.71-359.79, 710.8
   AHA: M-A, '87, 12

710.9 Unspecified diffuse connective tissue disease
   Collagen disease NOS

✓4ᵗʰ **711 Arthropathy associated with infections**

INCLUDES arthritis
   arthropathy   } associated with conditions
   polyarthritis   classifiable below
   polyarthropathy

EXCLUDES *rheumatic fever (390)*

The following fifth-digit subclassification is for use with category 711; valid digits are in [brackets] under each code. See list at beginning of chapter for definitions.
   0 site unspecified
   1 shoulder region
   2 upper arm
   3 forearm
   4 hand
   5 pelvic region and thigh
   6 lower leg
   7 ankle and foot
   8 other specified sites
   9 multiple sites

AHA: 1Q, '92, 17

§ ✓5ᵗʰ **711.0 Pyogenic arthritis**   cc
[0-9]   Arthritis or polyarthritis (due to):
   coliform [Escherichia coli]
   Hemophilus influenzae [H. influenzae]
   pneumococcal
   Pseudomonas
   staphylococcal
   streptococcal
   Pyarthrosis

   Use additional code to identify infectious organism (041.0-041.8)

   DEF: Infectious arthritis caused by various bacteria; marked by inflamed synovial membranes, and purulent effusion in joints.
   CC Excl: For codes 711.00, 711.08-711.09: 015.80-015.96, 017.90-017.96, 036.82, 056.71, 098.50-098.51, 098.59, 098.89, 711.00-714.0, 715.00, 715.09-715.10, 715.18-716.99, 718.00-718.08, 719.00-719.10, 719.18-719.99; **For code 711.01:** 015.80-015.96, 017.90-017.96, 036.82, 056.71, 098.50-098.51, 098.59, 098.89, 711.00-711.01, 711.08-711.11, 711.18-711.21, 711.28-711.31, 711.38-711.41, 711.48-

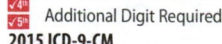

711.51, 711.58-711.61, 711.68-711.71, 711.78-711.81, 711.88-711.91, 711.98-712.11, 712.18-712.21, 712.28-712.31, 712.38-712.81, 712.88-712.91, 712.98-714.0, 715.00, 715.09-715.11, 715.18-715.21, 715.28-715.31, 715.38-715.91, 715.98-716.01, 716.08-716.11, 716.18-716.21, 716.28-716.31, 716.38-716.41, 716.48-716.51, 716.58-716.61, 716.68-716.81, 716.88-716.91, 716.98-716.99, 718.00-718.01, 718.08, 719.00-719.01, 719.08-719.11, 719.18-719.21, 719.28-719.31, 719.38-719.41, 719.48-719.51, 719.58-719.61, 719.68-719.81, 719.88-719.91, 719.98-719.99; **For code 711.02:** 015.80-015.96, 017.90-017.96, 036.82, 056.71, 098.50-098.51, 098.59, 098.89, 711.00, 711.02, 711.08-711.10, 711.12, 711.18-711.20, 711.22, 711.28-711.30, 711.32, 711.38-711.40, 711.42, 711.48-711.50, 711.52, 711.58-711.60, 711.62, 711.68-711.70, 711.72, 711.78-711.80, 711.82, 711.88-711.90, 711.92, 711.98-712.10, 712.12, 712.18-712.20, 712.22, 712.28-712.30, 712.32, 712.38-712.80, 712.82, 712.88-712.90, 712.92, 712.98-714.0, 715.00, 715.09-715.10, 715.12, 715.18-715.20, 715.22, 715.28-715.30, 715.32, 715.38-715.90, 715.92, 715.98-716.00, 716.02, 716.08-716.10, 716.12, 716.18-716.20, 716.22, 716.28-716.30, 716.32, 716.38-716.40, 716.42, 716.48-716.50, 716.52, 716.58-716.60, 716.62, 716.68-716.80, 716.82, 716.88-716.90, 716.92, 716.98-716.99, 718.00, 718.02, 718.08, 719.00, 719.02, 719.08-719.10, 719.12, 719.18-719.20, 719.22, 719.28-719.30, 719.32, 719.38-719.40, 719.42, 719.48-719.50, 719.52, 719.58-719.60, 719.62, 719.68-719.80, 719.82, 719.88-719.90, 719.92, 719.98-719.99; **For code 711.03:** 015.80-015.96, 017.90-017.96, 036.82, 056.71, 098.50-098.51, 098.59, 098.89, 711.00, 711.03, 711.08-711.10, 711.13, 711.18-711.20, 711.23, 711.28-711.30, 711.33, 711.38-711.40, 711.43, 711.48-711.50, 711.53, 711.58-711.60, 711.63, 711.68-711.70, 711.73, 711.78-711.80, 711.83, 711.88-711.90, 711.93, 711.98-712.10, 712.13, 712.18-712.20, 712.23, 712.28-712.30, 712.33, 712.38-712.80, 712.83, 712.88-712.90, 712.93, 712.98-714.0, 715.00, 715.09-715.10, 715.13, 715.18-715.20, 715.23, 715.28-715.30, 715.33, 715.38-715.90, 715.93, 715.98-716.00, 716.03, 716.08-716.10, 716.13, 716.18-716.20, 716.23, 716.28-716.30, 716.33, 716.38-716.40, 716.43, 716.48-716.50, 716.53, 716.58-716.60, 716.63, 716.68-716.80, 716.83, 716.88-716.90, 716.93, 716.98-716.99, 718.00, 718.03, 718.08, 719.00, 719.03, 719.08-719.10, 719.13, 719.18-719.20, 719.23, 719.28-719.30, 719.33, 719.38-719.40, 719.43, 719.48-719.50, 719.53, 719.58-719.60, 719.63, 719.68-719.80, 719.83, 719.88-719.90, 719.93, 719.98-719.99; **For code 711.04:** 015.80-015.96, 017.90-017.96, 036.82, 056.71, 098.50-098.51, 098.59, 098.89, 711.00, 711.04, 711.08-711.10, 711.14, 711.18-711.20, 711.24, 711.28-711.30, 711.34, 711.38-711.40, 711.44, 711.48-711.50, 711.54, 711.58-711.60, 711.64, 711.68-711.70, 711.74, 711.78-711.80, 711.84, 711.88-711.90, 711.94, 711.98-712.10, 712.14, 712.18-712.20, 712.24, 712.28-712.30, 712.34, 712.38-712.80, 712.84, 712.88-712.90, 712.94, 712.98-714.0, 715.00-715.10, 715.14, 715.18-715.20, 715.24, 715.28-715.30, 715.34, 715.38-715.90, 715.94, 715.98-716.00, 716.04, 716.08-716.10, 716.14, 716.18-716.20, 716.24, 716.28-716.30, 716.34, 716.38-716.40, 716.44, 716.48-716.50, 716.54, 716.58-716.60, 716.64, 716.68-716.80, 716.84, 716.88-716.90, 716.94, 716.98-716.99, 718.00, 718.04, 718.08, 719.00, 719.04, 719.08-719.10, 719.14, 719.18-719.20, 719.24, 719.28-719.30, 719.34, 719.38-719.40, 719.44, 719.48-719.50, 719.54, 719.58-719.60, 719.64, 719.68-719.80, 719.84, 719.88-719.90, 719.94, 719.98-719.99; **For code 711.05:** 015.80-015.96, 017.90-017.96, 036.82, 056.71, 098.50-098.51, 098.59, 098.89, 711.00, 711.05, 711.08-711.10, 711.15, 711.18-711.20, 711.25, 711.28-711.30, 711.35, 711.38-711.40, 711.45, 711.48-711.50, 711.55, 711.58-711.60, 711.65, 711.68-711.70, 711.75, 711.78-711.80, 711.85, 711.88-711.90, 711.95, 711.98-712.10, 712.15, 712.18-712.20, 712.25, 712.28-712.30, 712.35, 712.38-712.80, 712.85, 712.88-712.90, 712.95, 712.98-714.0, 715.00, 715.09-715.10, 715.15, 715.18-715.20, 715.25, 715.28-715.30, 715.35, 715.38-715.90, 715.95, 715.98-716.00, 716.05, 716.08-716.10, 716.15, 716.18-716.20, 716.25, 716.28-716.30, 716.35, 716.38-716.40, 716.45, 716.48-716.50, 716.55, 716.58-716.60, 716.65, 716.68-716.80, 716.85, 716.88-716.90, 716.95, 716.98-716.99, 718.00, 718.05, 718.08, 719.00, 719.05, 719.08-719.10, 719.15, 719.18-719.20, 719.25, 719.28-719.30, 719.35, 719.38-719.40, 719.45, 719.48-719.50, 719.55, 719.58-719.60, 719.65, 719.68-719.80, 719.85, 719.88-719.90, 719.95, 719.98-719.99; **For code 711.06:** 015.80-015.96, 017.90-017.96, 036.82, 056.71, 098.50-098.51, 098.59, 098.89, 711.00, 711.06, 711.08-711.10, 711.16, 711.18-711.20, 711.26, 711.28-711.30, 711.36, 711.38-711.40, 711.46, 711.48-711.50, 711.56, 711.58-711.60, 711.66, 711.68-711.70, 711.76, 711.78-711.80, 711.86, 711.88-711.90, 711.96, 711.98-712.10, 712.16, 712.18-712.20, 712.26, 712.28-712.30, 712.36, 712.38-712.80, 712.86, 712.88-712.90, 712.96, 712.98-714.0, 715.00, 715.09-715.10, 715.16, 715.18-715.20, 715.26, 715.28-715.30, 715.36, 715.38-715.90, 715.96, 715.98-716.00, 716.06, 716.08-716.10, 716.16, 716.18-716.20, 716.26, 716.28-716.30, 716.36, 716.38-716.40, 716.46, 716.48-716.50, 716.56, 716.58-716.60, 716.66, 716.68-716.80, 716.86, 716.88-716.90, 716.96, 716.98-719.00, 718.00, 718.08, 719.00, 719.06,

719.08-719.10, 719.16, 719.18-719.20, 719.26, 719.28-719.30, 719.36, 719.38-719.40, 719.46, 719.48-719.50, 719.56, 719.58-719.60, 719.66, 719.68-719.80, 719.86, 719.88-719.90, 719.98-719.99; **For code 711.07:** 015.80-015.96, 056.71, 098.50-098.51, 098.59, 098.89, 711.00, 711.07-711.10, 711.17-711.20, 711.27-711.30, 711.37-711.40, 711.47-711.50, 711.57-711.60, 711.67-711.70, 711.77-711.80, 711.87-711.90, 711.97-712.10, 712.17-712.20, 712.27-712.30, 712.37-712.80, 712.87-712.90, 712.97-714.0, 715.00, 715.09-715.10, 715.17-715.20, 715.27-715.30, 715.37-715.90, 715.97-716.00, 716.07-716.10, 716.17-716.20, 716.27-716.30, 716.37-716.40, 716.47-716.50, 716.57-716.60, 716.67-716.80, 716.87-716.90, 716.97-716.99, 718.00, 718.07-718.08, 719.00, 719.07-719.10, 719.17-719.20, 719.27-719.30, 719.37-719.40, 719.47-719.50, 719.57-719.60, 719.67-719.80, 719.87-719.90, 719.97-719.99

AHA: 1Q, '92, 16; 1Q, '91, 15

M00.869 Arthritis due to other bacteria unspecified knee `I-10`

§ ✓5ᵗʰ **711.1** *Arthropathy associated with Reiter's disease and* `CC`
[0-9] *nonspecific urethritis*

Code first underlying disease as:
nonspecific urethritis (099.4)
Reiter's disease (099.3)

DEF: Reiter's disease: joint disease marked by diarrhea, urethritis, conjunctivitis, keratosis and arthritis; of unknown etiology; affects young males.

DEF: Urethritis: inflamed urethra.

CC Excl: 003.23, 015.80-015.96, 017.90-017.96, 036.82, 056.71, 098.50-098.51, 098.59, 098.89, 711.00-714.0, 715.00, 715.09-715.10, 715.18-716.99, 718.00-718.08, 719.00-719.10, 719.18-719.69, 719.80-719.99

§ ✓5ᵗʰ **711.2** *Arthropathy in Behçet's syndrome* `CC`
[0-9]
Code first underlying disease (136.1)

DEF: Behçet's syndrome: Chronic inflammatory disorder, of unknown etiology; affects small blood vessels; causes ulcers of oral and pharyngeal mucous membranes and genitalia, skin lesions, retinal vasculitis, optic atrophy and severe uveitis.

CC Excl: 003.23, 015.80-015.96, 017.90-017.96, 036.82, 056.71, 098.50-098.51, 098.59, 098.89, 711.00-714.0, 715.00, 715.09-715.10, 715.18-716.99, 718.00-718.08, 719.00-719.10, 719.18-719.69, 719.80-719.99

§ ✓5ᵗʰ **711.3** *Postdysenteric arthropathy* `CC`
[0-9]
Code first underlying disease as:
dysentery (009.0)
enteritis, infectious (008.0-009.3)
paratyphoid fever (002.1-002.9)
typhoid fever (002.0)

EXCLUDES *salmonella arthritis (003.23)*

CC Excl: For codes 711.30-711.35, 711.37, and 711.39: 003.23, 015.80-015.96, 017.90-017.96, 036.82, 056.71, 098.50-098.51, 098.59, 098.89, 711.00-714.0, 715.00, 715.09-715.10, 715.18-716.99, 718.00-718.08, 719.00-719.10, 719.18-719.69, 719.80-719.99; **For code 711.36:** 003.23, 015.80-015.96, 017.90-017.96, 036.82, 056.71, 098.50-098.51, 098.59, 098.89, 711.00-714.0, 715.00, 715.09-715.10, 715.18-716.07, 716.09-716.99, 718.00-718.08, 719.00-719.10, 719.18-719.69, 719.80-719.99; **For code 711.38:** 003.23, 015.80-015.96, 017.90-017.96, 036.82, 056.71, 098.50-098.51, 098.59, 098.89, 711.00-714.0, 715.00, 715.09-715.10, 715.18-716.57, 716.59-716.99, 718.00-718.08, 719.00-719.10, 719.18-719.69, 719.80-719.99

§ ✓5ᵗʰ **711.4** *Arthropathy associated with other bacterial diseases* `CC`
[0-9]
Code first underlying disease as:
diseases classifiable to 010-040, 090-099, except as in 711.1, 711.3, and 713.5
leprosy (030.0-030.9)
tuberculosis (015.0-015.9)

EXCLUDES *gonococcal arthritis (098.50)*
meningococcal arthritis (036.82)

CC Excl: For codes 711.40, 711.42-711.49: 003.23, 015.80-015.96, 017.90-017.96, 036.82, 056.71, 098.50-098.51, 098.59, 098.89, 711.00-714.0, 715.00, 715.09-715.10, 715.18-716.99, 718.00-718.08, 719.00-719.10, 719.18-719.69, 719.80-719.99; **For code 711.41:** 003.23, 015.80-015.96, 017.90-017.96, 036.82, 056.71, 098.50-098.51, 098.59, 098.89, 711.00-714.0, 715.00, 715.09-715.10, 715.18-716.99, 718.00-718.08, 719.00-719.10, 719.18-719.39, 719.41-719.69, 719.80-719.99

---

§ Requires fifth digit. Valid digits are in [brackets] under each code. See beginning of section 710-739 for codes and defintions.

`N` Newborn Age: 0   `P` Pediatric Age: 0-17   `M` Maternity Age: 12-55   `A` Adult Age: 15-124   `MCC` Major CC Condition   `CC` CC Condition   `HIV` HIV Related Dx

238 – Volume 1   **2015 ICD-9-CM**

Joint Structures

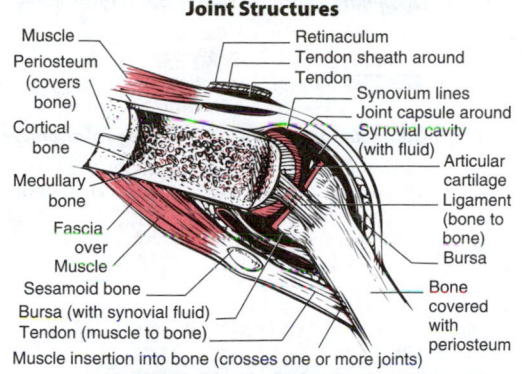

Muscle
Periosteum (covers bone)
Cortical bone
Medullary bone
Fascia over Muscle
Sesamoid bone
Bursa (with synovial fluid)
Tendon (muscle to bone)
Muscle insertion into bone (crosses one or more joints)
Retinaculum
Tendon sheath around
Tendon
Synovium lines
Joint capsule around
Synovial cavity (with fluid)
Articular cartilage
Ligament (bone to bone)
Bursa
Bone covered with periosteum

§ ✓5ᵗʰ **711.5** **Arthropathy associated with other viral diseases**   CC
[0-9]
Code first underlying disease as:
   diseases classifiable to 045-049, 050-079, 480, 487
   O'nyong nyong (066.3)

EXCLUDES *that due to rubella (056.71)*

CC Excl: 003.23, 015.80-015.96, 017.90-017.96, 036.82, 056.71, 098.50-098.51, 098.59, 098.89, 711.00-714.0, 715.00, 715.09-715.10, 715.18-716.99, 718.00-718.08, 719.00-719.10, 719.18-719.69, 719.80-719.99

§ ✓5ᵗʰ **711.6** **Arthropathy associated with mycoses**   CC
[0-9]
Code first underlying disease (110.0-118)
CC Excl: For codes 711.60, 711.68-711.69: 015.80-015.96, 017.90-017.96, 036.82, 056.71, 098.50-098.51, 098.59, 098.89, 711.00-714.0, 715.00, 715.09-715.10, 715.18-716.99, 718.00-718.08, 719.00-719.10, 719.18-719.99; **For code 711.61:** 015.80-015.96, 017.90-017.96, 036.82, 056.71, 098.50-098.51, 098.59, 098.89, 711.00-714.0, 715.00, 715.09-715.10, 715.18-716.99, 718.00-718.08, 719.00-719.10, 719.18-719.99; **For code 711.62:** 015.80-015.96, 017.90-017.96, 036.82, 056.71, 098.50-098.51, 098.59, 098.89, 711.00-711.01, 711.08-711.11, 711.18-711.21, 711.28-711.31, 711.38-711.41, 711.48-711.51, 711.58-711.61, 711.68-711.71, 711.78-711.81, 711.88-711.91, 711.98-712.11, 712.18-712.21, 712.28-712.31, 712.38-712.81, 712.88-712.91, 712.98-714.0, 715.00, 715.09-715.11, 715.18-715.21, 715.28-715.31, 715.38-715.91, 715.98-716.01, 716.08-716.11, 716.18-716.21, 716.28-716.31, 716.38-716.41, 716.48-716.51, 716.58-716.61, 716.68-716.81, 716.88-716.91, 716.98-716.99, 718.00-718.01, 718.08-719.01, 719.08-719.11, 719.18-719.21, 719.28-719.31, 719.38-719.41, 719.48-719.51, 719.58-719.61, 719.68-719.81, 719.88-719.91, 719.98-719.99; **For code 711.63:** 015.80-015.96, 017.90-017.96, 036.82, 056.71, 098.50-098.51, 098.59, 098.89, 711.00, 711.02, 711.08-711.10, 711.12, 711.18-711.20, 711.22, 711.28-711.30, 711.32, 711.38-711.40, 711.42, 711.48-711.50, 711.52, 711.58-711.60, 711.62, 711.68-711.70, 711.72, 711.78-711.80, 711.82, 711.88-711.90, 711.92, 711.98-712.10, 712.12, 712.18-712.20, 712.22, 712.28-712.30, 712.32, 712.38-712.80, 712.82, 712.88-712.90, 712.92, 712.98-714.0, 715.00, 715.09-715.10, 715.12, 715.18-715.20, 715.22, 715.28-715.30, 715.32, 715.38-715.90, 715.92, 715.98-716.00, 716.02, 716.08-716.10, 716.12, 716.18-716.20, 716.22, 716.28-716.30, 716.32, 716.38-716.40, 716.42, 716.48-716.50, 716.52, 716.58-716.60, 716.62, 716.68-716.80, 716.82, 716.88-716.90, 716.92, 716.98-716.99, 718.00, 718.02, 718.08, 719.00, 719.02, 719.08-719.10, 719.12, 719.18-719.20, 719.22, 719.28-719.30, 719.32, 719.38-719.40, 719.42, 719.48-719.50, 719.52, 719.58-719.60, 719.62, 719.68-719.80, 719.82, 719.88-719.90, 719.92, 719.98-719.99; **For code 711.64:** 015.80-015.96, 017.90-017.96, 036.82, 056.71, 098.50-098.51, 098.59, 098.89, 711.00, 711.03, 711.08-711.10, 711.13, 711.18-711.20, 711.23, 711.28-711.30, 711.33, 711.38-711.40, 711.43, 711.48-711.50, 711.53, 711.58-711.60, 711.63, 711.68-711.70, 711.73, 711.78-711.80, 711.83, 711.88-711.90, 711.93, 711.98-712.10, 712.13, 712.18-712.20, 712.23, 712.28-712.30, 712.33, 712.38-712.80, 712.83, 712.88-712.90, 712.93, 712.98-714.0, 715.00, 715.09-715.10, 715.13, 715.18-715.20, 715.23, 715.28-715.30, 715.33, 715.38-715.90, 715.93, 715.98-716.00, 716.03, 716.08-716.10, 716.13, 716.18-716.20, 716.23, 716.28-716.30, 716.33, 716.38-716.40, 716.43, 716.48-716.50, 716.53, 716.58-716.60, 716.63, 716.68-716.80, 716.83, 716.88-716.90, 716.93, 716.98-716.99, 718.00, 718.03, 718.08, 718.08, 719.00, 719.03, 719.08-719.10, 719.13, 719.18-719.20, 719.23, 719.28-719.30, 719.33, 719.38-719.40, 719.43, 719.48-719.50, 719.53, 719.58-719.60, 719.63, 719.68-719.80, 719.83, 719.88-719.90, 719.93, 719.98-719.99; **For code 711.65:** 015.80-015.96, 017.90-017.96, 036.82, 056.71, 098.50-098.51, 098.59, 098.89, 711.00, 711.04, 711.08-711.10, 711.14, 711.18-711.20, 711.24, 711.28-711.30, 711.34, 711.38-711.40, 711.44, 711.48-711.50, 711.54, 711.58-711.60, 711.64, 711.68-711.70, 711.74, 711.78-711.80, 711.84, 711.88-711.90, 711.94, 711.98-712.10, 712.14, 712.18-712.20, 712.24, 712.28-712.30, 712.34, 712.38-712.80, 712.84, 712.88-

712.90, 712.94, 712.98-714.0, 715.00-715.10, 715.14, 715.18-715.20, 715.24, 715.28-715.30, 715.34, 715.38-715.90, 715.94, 715.98-716.00, 716.04, 716.08-716.10, 716.14, 716.18-716.20, 716.24, 716.28-716.30, 716.34, 716.38-716.40, 716.44, 716.48-716.50, 716.54, 716.58-716.60, 716.64, 716.68-716.80, 716.84, 716.88-716.90, 716.94, 716.98-716.99, 718.00, 718.04, 718.08-719.00, 719.04, 719.08-719.10, 719.14, 719.18-719.20, 719.24, 719.28-719.30, 719.34, 719.38-719.40, 719.44, 719.48-719.50, 719.54, 719.58-719.60, 719.64, 719.68-719.80, 719.84, 719.88-719.90, 719.94, 719.98-719.99; **For code 711.66:** 015.80-015.96, 017.90-017.96, 036.82, 056.71, 098.50-098.51, 098.59, 098.89, 711.00, 711.05, 711.08-711.10, 711.15, 711.18-711.20, 711.25, 711.28-711.30, 711.35, 711.38-711.40, 711.45, 711.48-711.50, 711.55, 711.58-711.60, 711.65, 711.68-711.70, 711.75, 711.78-711.80, 711.85, 711.88-711.90, 711.95, 711.98-712.10, 712.15, 712.18-712.20, 712.25, 712.28-712.30, 712.35, 712.38-712.80, 712.85, 712.88-712.90, 712.95, 712.98-714.0, 715.00, 715.09-715.10, 715.15, 715.18-715.20, 715.25, 715.28-715.30, 715.35, 715.38-715.90, 715.95, 715.98-716.00, 716.05, 716.08-716.10, 716.15,

716.18-716.20, 716.25, 716.28-716.30, 716.35, 716.38-716.40, 716.45, 716.48-716.50, 716.55, 716.58-716.60, 716.65, 716.68-716.80, 716.85, 716.88-716.90, 716.95, 716.98-716.99, 718.00, 718.05, 718.08, 719.00, 719.05, 719.08-719.10, 719.15, 719.18-719.20, 719.25, 719.28-719.30, 719.35, 719.38-719.40, 719.45, 719.48-719.50, 719.55, 719.58-719.60, 719.65, 719.68-719.80, 719.85, 719.88-719.90, 719.95, 719.98-719.99; **For code 711.67:** 015.80-015.96, 017.90-017.96, 036.82, 056.71, 098.50-098.51, 098.59, 098.89, 711.00, 711.06, 711.08-711.10, 711.16, 711.18-711.20, 711.26, 711.28-711.30, 711.36, 711.38-711.40, 711.46, 711.48-711.50, 711.56, 711.58-711.60, 711.66, 711.68-711.70, 711.76, 711.78-711.80, 711.86, 711.88-711.90, 711.96, 711.98-712.10, 712.16, 712.18-712.20, 712.26, 712.28-712.30, 712.36, 712.38-712.80, 712.86, 712.88-712.90, 712.96, 712.98-714.0, 715.00, 715.09-715.10, 715.16, 715.18-715.20, 715.26, 715.28-715.30, 715.36, 715.38-715.90, 715.96, 715.98-716.00, 716.06, 716.08-716.10, 716.16, 716.18-716.20, 716.26, 716.28-716.30, 716.36, 716.38-716.40, 716.46, 716.48-716.50, 716.56, 716.58-716.60, 716.66, 716.68-716.80, 716.86, 716.88-716.90, 716.96, 716.98-716.99, 718.00, 718.08, 719.00, 719.06, 719.08-719.10, 719.16, 719.18-719.20, 719.26, 719.28-719.30, 719.36, 719.38-719.40, 719.46, 719.48-719.50, 719.56, 719.58-719.60, 719.66, 719.68-719.80, 719.86, 719.88-719.90, 719.96, 719.98-719.99 **For code 711.68:** 015.80-015.96, 017.90-017.96, 036.82, 056.71, 098.50-098.51, 098.59, 098.89, 711.00-711.99, 712.10-712.99, 713.0-713.8, 714.0, 715.00, 715.09-715.10, 715.18-715.98, 716.00-716.99, 718.00-718.08, 719.00-719.10, 719.18-719.99 **For code 711.69:** See code 711.68

§ ✓5ᵗʰ **711.7** **Arthropathy associated with helminthiasis**   CC
[0-9]
Code first underlying disease as:
   filariasis (125.0-125.9)
CC Excl: For codes 711.70-711.74, 711.76, 711.78-711.79: 003.23, 015.80-015.96, 017.90-017.96, 036.82, 056.71, 098.50-098.51, 098.59, 098.89, 711.00-714.0, 715.00, 715.09-715.10, 715.18-716.99, 718.00-718.08, 719.00-719.10, 719.18-719.69, 719.80-719.99; **For code 711.75:** 003.23, 015.80-015.96, 017.90-017.96, 036.82, 056.71, 098.50-098.51, 098.59, 098.89, 711.00-714.0, 715.00, 715.09-715.10, 715.18-716.99, 718.00-718.08, 719.00-719.10, 719.18-719.43, 719.45-719.69, 719.80-719.99; **For code 711.77:** 003.23, 015.80-015.96, 017.90-017.96, 036.82, 056.71, 098.50-098.51, 098.59, 098.89, 711.00-714.0, 715.00, 715.09-715.10, 715.18-716.99, 718.00-718.08, 719.00-719.10, 719.18-719.69, 719.80-719.97, 719.99

§ ✓5ᵗʰ **711.8** **Arthropathy associated with other infectious and parasitic diseases**   CC
[0-9]

Code first underlying disease as:
   diseases classifiable to 080-088, 100-104, 130-136
EXCLUDES *arthropathy associated with sarcoidosis (713.7)*
CC Excl: For codes 711.80, 711.82-711.89: 003.23, 015.80-015.96, 017.90-017.96, 036.82, 056.71, 098.50-098.51, 098.59, 098.89, 711.00-714.0, 715.00, 715.09-715.10, 715.18-716.99, 718.00-718.08, 719.00-719.10, 719.18-719.69, 719.80-719.99; **For code 711.81:** 003.23, 015.80-015.96, 017.90-017.96, 036.82, 056.71, 098.50-098.51, 098.59, 098.89, 711.00-711.41, 711.43-714.0, 715.00, 715.09-715.10, 715.18-716.99, 718.00-718.08, 719.00-719.10, 719.18-719.69, 719.80-719.99
AHA: 4Q, '91, 15; 3Q, '90, 14

§ ✓5ᵗʰ **711.9** **Unspecified infective arthritis**   CC
[0-9]
Infective arthritis or polyarthritis (acute) (chronic) (subacute) NOS
CC Excl: 003.23, 015.80-015.96, 017.90-017.96, 036.82, 056.71, 098.50-098.51, 098.59, 098.89, 711.00-714.0, 715.00, 715.09-715.10, 715.18-716.99, 718.00-718.08, 719.00-719.10, 719.18-719.69, 719.80-719.99

---

§   Requires fifth digit. Valid digits are in [brackets] under each code. See beginning of section 710-739 for codes and defintions.

✓4ᵗʰ ✓5ᵗʰ Additional Digit Required   Unacceptable PDx   Manifestation Code   Hospital Acquired Condition   ►◄ Revised Text   ● New Code   ▲ Revised Code Title

Diseases of the Musculoskeletal System and Connective Tissue

712–714.32

√4ᵗʰ **712 Crystal arthropathies**

> INCLUDES crystal-induced arthritis and synovitis
> EXCLUDES *gouty arthropathy (274.00-274.03)*
> **DEF:** Joint disease due to urate crystal deposit in joints or synovial membranes.

> The following fifth-digit subclassification is for use with category 712; valid digits are in [brackets] under each code. See list at beginning of chapter for definitions.
>   **0 site unspecified**
>   **1 shoulder region**
>   **2 upper arm**
>   **3 forearm**
>   **4 hand**
>   **5 pelvic region and thigh**
>   **6 lower leg**
>   **7 ankle and foot**
>   **8 other specified sites**
>   **9 multiple sites**

§ √5ᵗʰ **712.1 Chondrocalcinosis due to dicalcium phosphate crystals**
[0-9]   Chondrocalcinosis due to dicalcium phosphate crystals (with other crystals)
  Code first underlying disease (275.4)

§ √5ᵗʰ **712.2 Chondrocalcinosis due to pyrophosphate crystals**
[0-9]   *Code first underlying disease (275.4)*

§ √5ᵗʰ **712.3 Chondrocalcinosis, unspecified**
[0-9]   *Code first underlying disease (275.4)*

§ √5ᵗʰ **712.8 Other specified crystal arthropathies**
[0-9]

§ √5ᵗʰ **712.9 Unspecified crystal arthropathy**
[0-9]

√4ᵗʰ **713 Arthropathy associated with other disorders classified elsewhere**

> INCLUDES arthritis
>   arthropathy   } associated with conditions
>   polyarthritis   classifiable below
>   polyarthropathy

713.0 Arthropathy associated with other endocrine and metabolic disorders

> *Code first underlying disease as:*
>   acromegaly (253.0)
>   hemochromatosis (275.01-275.09)
>   hyperparathyroidism (252.00-252.08)
>   hypogammaglobulinemia (279.00-279.09)
>   hypothyroidism (243-244.9)
>   lipoid metabolism disorder (272.0-272.9)
>   ochronosis (270.2)
> EXCLUDES *arthropathy associated with:*
>   *amyloidosis (713.7)*
>   *crystal deposition disorders, except gout (712.1-712.9)*
>   *diabetic neuropathy (713.5)*
>   *gout (274.00-274.03)*

713.1 Arthropathy associated with gastrointestinal conditions other than infections

> *Code first underlying disease as:*
>   regional enteritis (555.0-555.9)
>   ulcerative colitis (556)

713.2 Arthropathy associated with hematological disorders

> *Code first underlying disease as:*
>   hemoglobinopathy (282.4-282.7)
>   hemophilia (286.0-286.2)
>   leukemia (204.0-208.9)
>   malignant reticulosis (202.3)
>   multiple myelomatosis (203.0)
> EXCLUDES *arthropathy associated with Henoch-Schönlein purpura (713.6)*

713.3 Arthropathy associated with dermatological disorders

> *Code first underlying disease as:*
>   erythema multiforme (695.10-695.19)
>   erythema nodosum (695.2)
> EXCLUDES *psoriatic arthropathy (696.0)*

713.4 Arthropathy associated with respiratory disorders

> *Code first underlying disease as:*
>   diseases classifiable to 490-519
> EXCLUDES *arthropathy associated with respiratory infections (711.0, 711.4-711.8)*

713.5 Arthropathy associated with neurological disorders

> Charcôt's arthropathy   } associated with diseases
> Neuropathic arthritis   classifiable elsewhere
> *Code first underlying disease as:*
>   neuropathic joint disease [Charcôt's joints]:
>   NOS (094.0)
>   diabetic (249.6, 250.6)
>   syringomyelic (336.0)
>   tabetic [syphilitic] (094.0)
> **AHA:** 3Q, '12, 4

713.6 Arthropathy associated with hypersensitivity reaction

> *Code first underlying disease as:*
>   Henoch (-Schönlein) purpura (287.0)
>   serum sickness (999.51-999.59)
> EXCLUDES *allergic arthritis NOS (716.2)*

713.7 Other general diseases with articular involvement

> *Code first underlying disease as:*
>   amyloidosis (277.30-277.39)
>   familial Mediterranean fever (277.31)
>   sarcoidosis (135)
> **AHA:** 2Q, '97, 12

713.8 Arthropathy associated with other condition classifiable elsewhere

> *Code first underlying disease as:*
>   conditions classifiable elsewhere except as in 711.1-711.8, 712, and 713.0-713.7

√4ᵗʰ **714 Rheumatoid arthritis and other inflammatory polyarthropathies**

> EXCLUDES *rheumatic fever (390)*
>   *rheumatoid arthritis of spine NOS (720.0)*
> **AHA:** 2Q, '95, 3

714.0 Rheumatoid arthritis

> Arthritis or polyarthritis: Arthritis or polyarthritis:
>   atrophic   rheumatic (chronic)
> *Use additional code to identify manifestation, as:*
>   myopathy (359.6)
>   polyneuropathy (357.1)
> EXCLUDES *juvenile rheumatoid arthritis NOS (714.30)*
> **DEF:** Chronic systemic disease principally of joints, manifested by inflammatory changes in articular structures and synovial membranes, atrophy, and loss in bone density.
> **AHA:** 2Q, '06, 20; 1Q, '90, 5
> **M06.9** Rheumatoid arthritis unspecified   I-10

714.1 Felty's syndrome

> Rheumatoid arthritis with splenoadenomegaly and leukopenia
> **DEF:** Syndrome marked by rheumatoid arthritis, splenomegaly, leukopenia, pigmented spots on lower extremity skin, anemia, and thrombocytopenia.

714.2 Other rheumatoid arthritis with visceral or systemic involvement

> Rheumatoid carditis

√5ᵗʰ **714.3 Juvenile chronic polyarthritis**

> **DEF:** Rheumatoid arthritis of more than one joint; lasts longer than six weeks in age 17 or younger; symptoms include fever, erythematous rash, weight loss, lymphadenopathy, hepatosplenomegaly and pericarditis.

714.30 Polyarticular juvenile rheumatoid arthritis, chronic or unspecified

> Juvenile rheumatoid arthritis NOS
> Still's disease

714.31 Polyarticular juvenile rheumatoid arthritis, acute   CC

> **CC Excl:** 036.82, 056.71, 711.00-714.4, 715.00, 715.09-715.10, 715.18-716.99, 718.00-718.08, 719.00-719.10, 719.18-719.99

714.32 Pauciarticular juvenile rheumatoid arthritis

---

§   Requires fifth digit. Valid digits are in [brackets] under each code. See beginning of section 710-739 for codes and defintions.

N Newborn Age: 0   P Pediatric Age: 0-17   M Maternity Age: 12-55   A Adult Age: 15-124   MCC Major CC Condition   CC CC Condition   HIV HIV Related Dx

714.33 Monoarticular juvenile rheumatoid arthritis

714.4 Chronic postrheumatic arthropathy
Chronic rheumatoid nodular fibrositis
Jaccoud's syndrome
DEF: Persistent joint disorder; follows previous rheumatic infection.

√5ᵗʰ **714.8 Other specified inflammatory polyarthropathies**

714.81 Rheumatoid lung
Caplan's syndrome
Diffuse interstitial rheumatoid disease of lung
Fibrosing alveolitis, rheumatoid
DEF: Lung disorders associated with rheumatoid arthritis.

714.89 Other

714.9 Unspecified inflammatory polyarthropathy
Inflammatory polyarthropathy or polyarthritis NOS
EXCLUDES polyarthropathy NOS (716.5)

√4ᵗʰ **715 Osteoarthrosis and allied disorders**
NOTE Localized, in the subcategories below, includes bilateral involvement of the same site.
INCLUDES arthritis or polyarthritis:
　degenerative
　hypertrophic
degenerative joint disease
osteoarthritis
EXCLUDES Marie-Strümpell spondylitis (720.0)
osteoarthrosis [osteoarthritis] of spine (721.0-721.9)

The following fifth-digit subclassification is for use with category 715; valid digits are in [brackets] under each code. See list at beginning of chapter for definitions.
　0 site unspecified
　1 shoulder region
　2 upper arm
　3 forearm
　4 hand
　5 pelvic region and thigh
　6 lower leg
　7 ankle and foot
　8 other specified sites
　9 multiple sites

§ √5ᵗʰ **715.0 Osteoarthrosis, generalized**
[0,4,9] Degenerative joint disease, involving multiple joints
Primary generalized hypertrophic osteoarthrosis
DEF: Chronic noninflammatory arthritis; marked by degenerated articular cartilage and enlarged bone; symptoms include pain and stiffness with activity.

§ √5ᵗʰ **715.1 Osteoarthrosis, localized, primary**
[0-8] Localized osteoarthropathy, idiopathic
M17.0 Bilateral primary osteoarthritis of knee [I-10]

§ √5ᵗʰ **715.2 Osteoarthrosis, localized, secondary**
[0-8] Coxae malum senilis

§ √5ᵗʰ **715.3 Osteoarthrosis, localized, not specified whether**
[0-8] **primary or secondary**
Otto's pelvis
AHA: For code 715.35: 3Q, '04, 12; 2Q, '04, 15; **For code 715.36:** 4Q, '03, 118; 2Q, '95, 5
M16.9 Osteoarthritis of hip unspecified [I-10]

§ √5ᵗʰ **715.8 Osteoarthrosis involving, or with mention of**
[0,9] **more than one site, but not specified as generalized**

§ √5ᵗʰ **715.9 Osteoarthrosis, unspecified whether generalized or**
[0-8] **localized**
AHA: For code 715.90: 2Q, '97, 12
M19.90 Unspecified osteoarthritis unspecified site [I-10]
M17.9 Osteoarthritis of knee unspecified [I-10]

√4ᵗʰ **716 Other and unspecified arthropathies**
EXCLUDES cricoarytenoid arthropathy (478.79)

The following fifth-digit subclassification is for use with category 716; valid digits are in [brackets] under each code. See list at beginning of chapter for definitions.
　0 site unspecified
　1 shoulder region
　2 upper arm
　3 forearm
　4 hand
　5 pelvic region and thigh
　6 lower leg
　7 ankle and foot
　8 other specified sites
　9 multiple sites

AHA: 2Q, '95, 3

§ √5ᵗʰ **716.0 Kaschin-Beck disease**
[0-9] Endemic polyarthritis
DEF: Chronic degenerative disease of spine and peripheral joints; occurs in eastern Siberian, northern Chinese, and Korean youth; may be a mycotoxicosis caused by eating cereals infected with fungus.

§ √5ᵗʰ **716.1 Traumatic arthropathy**
[0-9] **AHA: For Code 716.11:** 1Q, '02, 9; **For Code 716.15:** 2Q, '09, 11

§ √5ᵗʰ **716.2 Allergic arthritis**
[0-9] **EXCLUDES** arthritis associated with Henoch-Schönlein purpura or serum sickness (713.6)

§ √5ᵗʰ **716.3 Climacteric arthritis** ♀
[0-9] Menopausal arthritis
DEF: Ovarian hormone deficiency; causes pain in small joints, shoulders, elbows or knees; affects females at menopause; also called arthropathia ovaripriva.

§ √5ᵗʰ **716.4 Transient arthropathy**
[0-9] **EXCLUDES** palindromic rheumatism (719.3)

§ √5ᵗʰ **716.5 Unspecified polyarthropathy or polyarthritis**
[0-9]

§ √5ᵗʰ **716.6 Unspecified monoarthritis**
[0-8] Coxitis

§ √5ᵗʰ **716.8 Other specified arthropathy**
[0-9]

§ √5ᵗʰ **716.9 Arthropathy, unspecified**
[0-9] Arthritis ⎤
Arthropathy ⎦ (acute) (chronic) (subacute)
Articular rheumatism (chronic)
Inflammation of joint NOS
M12.9 Arthropathy unspecified [I-10]

√4ᵗʰ **717 Internal derangement of knee**
INCLUDES degeneration ⎤
rupture, old ⎬ of articular cartilage or
tear, old ⎦ meniscus of knee

EXCLUDES acute derangement of knee (836.0-836.6)
ankylosis (718.5)
contracture (718.4)
current injury (836.0-836.6)
deformity (736.4-736.6)
recurrent dislocation (718.3)

717.0 Old bucket handle tear of medial meniscus
Old bucket handle tear of unspecified cartilage

Disruption and Tears of Meniscus

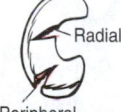

Bucket-handle　　Flap-type　　Peripheral / Radial

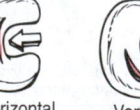

Horizontal cleavage　　Vertical　　Congenital discoid meniscus

---

§　Requires fifth digit. Valid digits are in [brackets] under each code. See beginning of section 710-739 for codes and defintions.

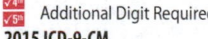 Additional Digit Required　　Unacceptable PDx　　Manifestation Code　　Hospital Acquired Condition　　►◄ Revised Text　　● New Code　　▲ Revised Code Title

Internal Derangements of Knee

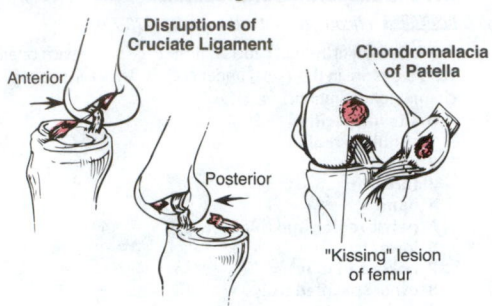

717.1 Derangement of anterior horn of medial meniscus

717.2 Derangement of posterior horn of medial meniscus

717.3 Other and unspecified derangement of medial meniscus
Degeneration of internal semilunar cartilage

√5th **717.4 Derangement of lateral meniscus**

    717.40 Derangement of lateral meniscus, unspecified

    717.41 Bucket handle tear of lateral meniscus

    717.42 Derangement of anterior horn of lateral meniscus

    717.43 Derangement of posterior horn of lateral meniscus

    717.49 Other

717.5 Derangement of meniscus, not elsewhere classified
Congenital discoid meniscus
Cyst of semilunar cartilage
Derangement of semilunar cartilage NOS

717.6 Loose body in knee
Joint mice, knee
Rice bodies, knee (joint)
DEF: The presence in the joint synovial area of a small, frequently calcified, loose body created from synovial membrane, organized fibrin fragments of articular cartilage or arthritis osteophytes.

717.7 Chondromalacia of patella
Chondromalacia patellae
Degeneration [softening] of articular cartilage of patella
DEF: Softened patella cartilage.
AHA: M-A, '85, 14; N-D, '84, 9

√5th **717.8 Other internal derangement of knee**

    717.81 Old disruption of lateral collateral ligament

    717.82 Old disruption of medial collateral ligament

    717.83 Old disruption of anterior cruciate ligament

    717.84 Old disruption of posterior cruciate ligament

    717.85 Old disruption of other ligaments of knee
    Capsular ligament of knee

    717.89 Other
    Old disruption of ligaments NOS

717.9 Unspecified internal derangement of knee
Derangement NOS of knee

Joint Derangements and Disorders

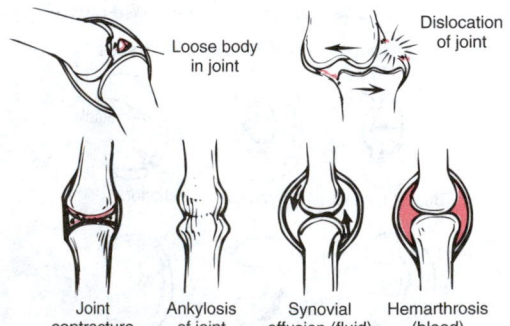

Joint contracture   Ankylosis of joint   Synovial effusion (fluid)   Hemarthrosis (blood)

√4th **718 Other derangement of joint**
    EXCLUDES current injury (830.0-848.9)
           jaw (524.60-524.69)

> The following fifth-digit subclassification is for use with category 718; valid digits are in [brackets] under each code. See list at beginning of chapter for definitions.
>   0 site unspecified
>   1 shoulder region
>   2 upper arm
>   3 forearm
>   4 hand
>   5 pelvic region and thigh
>   6 lower leg
>   7 ankle and foot
>   8 other specified sites
>   9 multiple sites

§ √5th **718.0 Articular cartilage disorder**
[0-5,7-9] Meniscus:
    disorder
    rupture, old
    tear, old
Old rupture of ligament(s) of joint NOS
    EXCLUDES articular cartilage disorder:
         in ochronosis (270.2)
         knee (717.0-717.9)
         chondrocalcinosis (275.4)
         metastatic calcification (275.4)

§ √5th **718.1 Loose body in joint**
[0-5,7-9] Joint mice
    EXCLUDES knee (717.6)
    DEF: Calcified loose bodies in synovial fluid; due to arthritic osteophytes.
    AHA: For code 718.17: 2Q, '01, 15

§ √5th **718.2 Pathological dislocation**
[0-9]   Dislocation or displacement of joint, not recurrent and not current injury
        Spontaneous dislocation (joint)

§ √5th **718.3 Recurrent dislocation of joint**
[0-9]   **AHA:** N-D, '87, 7

§ √5th **718.4 Contracture of joint**
[0-9]   **AHA:** 4Q, '98, 40
    TIP: Assign an additional code from category 438 if the contracture is a result of a CVA.

§ √5th **718.5 Ankylosis of joint**
[0-9]   Ankylosis of joint (fibrous) (osseous)
    EXCLUDES spine (724.9)
         stiffness of joint without mention of ankylosis (719.5)
    DEF: Immobility and solidification of joint; due to disease, injury or surgical procedure.

§ √5th **718.6 Unspecified intrapelvic protrusion of acetabulum**
[5]   Protrusio acetabuli, unspecified
    DEF: Sinking of the floor of acetabulum, causing femoral head to protrude, limits hip movement; of unknown etiology.

§ √5th **718.7 Developmental dislocation of joint**
[0-9]   **EXCLUDES** congenital dislocation of joint (754.0-755.8)
         traumatic dislocation of joint (830-839)
    AHA: 4Q, '01, 48

§ √5th **718.8 Other joint derangement, not elsewhere classified**
[0-9]   Flail joint (paralytic)Instability of joint
    EXCLUDES deformities classifiable to 736 (736.0-736.9)
    AHA: For code 718.81: 2Q, '00, 14
    TIP: Assign 718.81 for multidirectional shoulder instability.

§ √5th **718.9 Unspecified derangement of joint**
[0-5,7-9] **EXCLUDES** knee (717.9)

---

§ Requires fifth digit. Valid digits are in [brackets] under each code. See beginning of section 710-739 for codes and definitions.

N Newborn Age: 0   P Pediatric Age: 0-17   M Maternity Age: 12-55   A Adult Age: 15-124   MCC Major CC Condition   CC CC Condition   HIV HIV Related Dx

242 – Volume 1   2015 ICD-9-CM

✓4th **719 Other and unspecified disorders of joint**

> **EXCLUDES** *jaw (524.60-524.69)*

> The following fifth-digit subclassification is for use with codes 719.0-719.6, 719.8-719.9; valid digits are in [brackets] under each code. See list at beginning of chapter for definitions.
> 0 site unspecified
> 1 shoulder region
> 2 upper arm
> 3 forearm
> 4 hand
> 5 pelvic region and thigh
> 6 lower leg
> 7 ankle and foot
> 8 other specified sites
> 9 multiple sites

§ ✓5th **719.0 Effusion of joint**
[0-9]   Hydrarthrosis
     Swelling of joint, with or without pain
> **EXCLUDES** *intermittent hydrarthrosis (719.3)*
> **M25.469** Effusion unspecified knee   `I-10`

§ ✓5th **719.1 Hemarthrosis**   `CC`
[0-9]   **EXCLUDES** *current injury (840.0-848.9)*
     CC Excl: For codes: 719.10, 719.15, 719.18-719.19: 719.10-719.19, 958.91-958.92; For code 719.11: 719.10-719.13, 719.18-719.19, 958.91; For code 719.12: 719.10-719.12, 719.18-719.19, 958.91; For code 719.13: 719.10, 719.12-719.14, 719.18-719.19, 958.91; For code 719.14: 719.10, 719.13-719.14, 719.18-719.19, 958.91; For codes 719.16-719.17: 719.10, 719.16-719.19, 958.92

§ ✓5th **719.2 Villonodular synovitis**
[0-9]   **DEF:** Overgrowth of synovial tissue, especially at knee joint; due to macrophage infiltration of giant cells in synovial villi and fibrous nodules.

§ ✓5th **719.3 Palindromic rheumatism**
[0-9]   Hench-Rosenberg syndrome
     Intermittent hydrarthrosis
     DEF: Recurrent episodes of afebrile arthritis and periarthritis marked by their complete disappearance after a few days or hours; causes swelling, redness, and disability usually affecting only one joint; no known cause.

§ ✓5th **719.4 Pain in joint**
[0-9]   Arthralgia
     AHA: For code 719.46: 1Q, '01, 3
     TIP: Assign 719.46 for patellofemoral syndrome, a chronic knee pain common among athletes.
     M25.519 Pain in unspecified shoulder   `I-10`
     M25.552 Pain in left hip   `I-10`

§ ✓5th **719.5 Stiffness of joint, not elsewhere classified**
[0-9]

§ ✓5th **719.6 Other symptoms referable to joint**
[0-9]   Joint crepitus
     Snapping hip
     AHA: 1Q, '94, 15; For code 719.66: 2Q, '07, 6
     TIP: Assign 719.66 for patellar clunk syndrome, which is a fibrous reaction caused by chronic pressure on the patella, S/P knee replacement surgery.

719.7 Difficulty in walking
> **EXCLUDES** *abnormality of gait (781.2)*
> **AHA:** 2Q, '04, 15; 4Q, '03, 66
> **R26.2** Difficulty in walking not elsewhere classified   `I-10`

§ ✓5th **719.8 Other specified disorders of joint**
[0-9]   Calcification of joint
     Fistula of joint
> **EXCLUDES** *temporomandibular joint-pain-dysfunction syndrome [Costen's syndrome] (524.60)*

§ ✓5th **719.9 Unspecified disorder of joint**
[0-9]

Dorsopathies (720-724)

> **EXCLUDES** *curvature of spine (737.0-737.9)*
> *osteochondrosis of spine (juvenile) (732.0)*
> *adult (732.8)*

✓4th **720 Ankylosing spondylitis and other inflammatory spondylopathies**

720.0 Ankylosing spondylitis
   Rheumatoid arthritis of spine NOS
   Spondylitis:
     Marie-Strümpell
     rheumatoid
   DEF: Rheumatoid arthritis of spine and sacroiliac joints; fusion and deformity in spine follows; affects mainly males; cause unknown.

720.1 Spinal enthesopathy
   Disorder of peripheral ligamentous or muscular attachments of spine
   Romanus lesion
   DEF: Tendinous or muscular vertebral bone attachment abnormality.

720.2 Sacroiliitis, not elsewhere classified
   Inflammation of sacroiliac joint NOS
   DEF: Pain due to inflammation in joint, at juncture of sacrum and hip.

✓5th **720.8 Other inflammatory spondylopathies**

   720.81 Inflammatory spondylopathies in diseases classified elsewhere
     Code first underlying disease as:
       tuberculosis (015.0)

   720.89 Other

720.9 Unspecified inflammatory spondylopathy
   Spondylitis NOS

✓4th **721 Spondylosis and allied disorders**
   DEF: Degenerative changes in spinal joint.
   AHA: 2Q, '89, 14

721.0 Cervical spondylosis without myelopathy
   Cervical or cervicodorsal:
     arthritis
     osteoarthritis
     spondylarthritis

721.1 Cervical spondylosis with myelopathy   `CC`
   Anterior spinal artery compression syndrome
   Spondylogenic compression of cervical spinal cord
   Vertebral artery compression syndrome
   CC Excl: 721.0-721.1
   M47.12 Other spondylosis w/myelopathy cervical region   `I-10`

721.2 Thoracic spondylosis without myelopathy
   Thoracic: Thoracic:
     arthritis   spondylarthritis
     osteoarthritis

721.3 Lumbosacral spondylosis without myelopathy
   Lumbar or lumbosacral:
     arthritis
     osteoarthritis
     spondylarthritis
   AHA: 4Q, '02, 107
   M47.817 Spondylosis w/o myelopath/radiculopath lumboscrl   `I-10`

✓5th **721.4 Thoracic or lumbar spondylosis with myelopathy**

   721.41 Thoracic region   `CC`
     Spondylogenic compression of thoracic spinal cord
     CC Excl: 721.41

   721.42 Lumbar region   `CC`
     CC Excl: 721.3, 721.42, 722.10, 722.2, 722.32, 722.52-722.70, 722.73, 722.83-722.90, 722.93

721.5 Kissing spine
   Baastrup's syndrome
   DEF: Compression of spinous processes of adjacent vertebrae; due to mutual contact.

721.6 Ankylosing vertebral hyperostosis

721.7 Traumatic spondylopathy   `CC`
   Kümmell's disease or spondylitis
   CC Excl: 721.7

---

§   Requires fifth digit. Valid digits are in [brackets] under each code. See beginning of section 710-739 for codes and defintions.

| ✓4th ✓5th Additional Digit Required | Unacceptable PDx | Manifestation Code | Hospital Acquired Condition | ►◄ Revised Text | ● New Code | ▲ Revised Code Title |

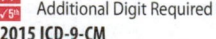

721.8 Other allied disorders of spine

√5th **721.9 Spondylosis of unspecified site**

721.90 Without mention of myelopathy
Spinal:
  arthritis (deformans) (degenerative) (hypertrophic)
  osteoarthritis NOS
  Spondylarthrosis NOS

721.91 With myelopathy `CC`
Spondylogenic compression of spinal cord NOS
CC Excl: 721.0-721.91, 724.03

√4th **722 Intervertebral disc disorders**
AHA: 1Q, '88, 10

722.0 Displacement of cervical intervertebral disc without myelopathy
Neuritis (brachial) or radiculitis due to displacement or rupture of cervical intervertebral disc
Any condition classifiable to 722.2 of the cervical or cervicothoracic intervertebral disc
M50.20 Other cerv disc displacement uns cerv region `I-10`

√5th **722.1 Displacement of thoracic or lumbar intervertebral disc without myelopathy**

722.10 Lumbar intervertebral disc without myelopathy
Lumbago or sciatica due to displacement of intervertebral disc
Neuritis or radiculitis due to displacement or rupture of lumbar intervertebral disc
Any condition classifiable to 722.2 of the lumbar or lumbosacral intervertebral disc
AHA: 4Q, '08, 184; 1Q, '07, 9; 3Q, '03, 12; 1Q, '03, 7; 4Q, '02, 107
M51.26 Oth intervertebral disc displcmnt lumbar region `I-10`

722.11 Thoracic intervertebral disc without myelopathy
Any condition classifiable to 722.2 of thoracic intervertebral disc

Anatomy of Vertebral Disc

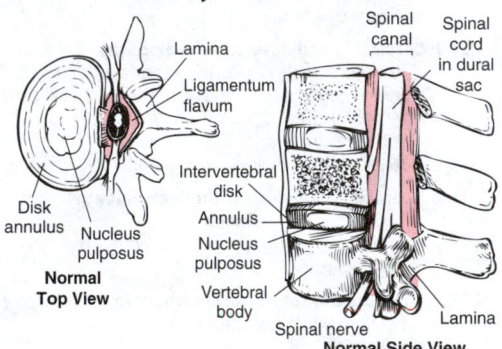

Lamina · Ligamentum flavum · Spinal canal · Spinal cord in dural sac · Intervertebral disk · Annulus · Nucleus pulposus · Vertebral body · Spinal nerve · Lamina · Disk annulus · Nucleus pulposus

Normal Top View   **Normal Side View**

Derangement of Vertebral Disc

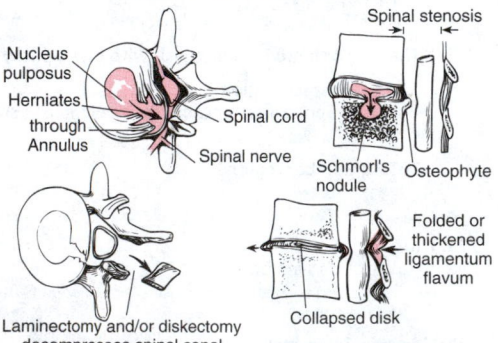

Nucleus pulposus · Herniates through Annulus · Spinal cord · Spinal nerve · Spinal stenosis · Schmorl's nodule · Osteophyte · Folded or thickened ligamentum flavum · Collapsed disk · Laminectomy and/or diskectomy decompresses spinal canal

722.2 Displacement of intervertebral disc, site unspecified, without myelopathy
Discogenic syndrome NOS
Herniation of nucleus pulposus NOS
Intervertebral disc NOS:
  extrusion
  prolapse
  protrusion
  rupture
Neuritis or radiculitis due to displacement or rupture of intervertebral disc

√5th **722.3 Schmorl's nodes**
DEF: Irregular bone defect in the margin of the vertebral body; causes herniation into end plate of vertebral body.

722.30 Unspecified region

722.31 Thoracic region

722.32 Lumbar region

722.39 Other

722.4 Degeneration of cervical intervertebral disc
Degeneration of cervicothoracic intervertebral disc
M50.30 Other cerv disc degeneration uns cerv region `I-10`

√5th **722.5 Degeneration of thoracic or lumbar intervertebral disc**

722.51 Thoracic or thoracolumbar intervertebral disc
AHA: 2Q, '11, 8

722.52 Lumbar or lumbosacral intervertebral disc
AHA: 2Q, '06, 18; 4Q, '04, 133
M51.37 Oth intervertebral disc degen lumbosacral region `I-10`

722.6 Degeneration of intervertebral disc, site unspecified
Degenerative disc disease NOS
Narrowing of intervertebral disc or space NOS

√5th **722.7 Intervertebral disc disorder with myelopathy**

722.70 Unspecified region

722.71 Cervical region `CC`
CC Excl: 722.0, 722.71

722.72 Thoracic region `CC`
CC Excl: 722.11, 722.72

722.73 Lumbar region `CC`
CC Excl: 722.11, 722.73, 724.03

√5th **722.8 Postlaminectomy syndrome**
DEF: Spinal disorder due to spinal laminectomy surgery.
AHA: J-F, '87, 7
TIP: Assign if documentation indicates that pain is due to scar tissue formation following disc surgery.

722.80 Unspecified region

722.81 Cervical region

722.82 Thoracic region

722.83 Lumbar region
AHA: 2Q, '97, 15
M96.1 Postlaminectomy syndrome NEC `I-10`

√5th **722.9 Other and unspecified disc disorder**
Calcification of intervertebral cartilage or disc
Discitis

722.90 Unspecified region
AHA: N-D, '84, 19

722.91 Cervical region

722.92 Thoracic region

722.93 Lumbar region
M51.86 Other intervertebral disc disorder lumbar region `I-10`

√4th **723 Other disorders of cervical region**
EXCLUDES conditions due to:
  intervertebral disc disorders (722.0-722.9)
  spondylosis (721.0-721.9)
AHA: 3Q, '94, 14; 2Q, '89, 14

723.0 Spinal stenosis in cervical region
AHA: 4Q, '03, 101
M48.02 Spinal stenosis cervical region `I-10`

`N` Newborn Age: 0   `P` Pediatric Age: 0-17   `M` Maternity Age: 12-55   `A` Adult Age: 15-124   `MCC` Major CC Condition   `CC` CC Condition   `HIV` HIV Related Dx

723.1 Cervicalgia
Pain in neck
DEF: Pain in cervical spine or neck region.
M54.2 Cervicalgia   `I-10`

723.2 Cervicocranial syndrome
Barré-Liéou syndrome
Posterior cervical sympathetic syndrome
DEF: Neurologic disorder of upper cervical spine and nerve roots.

723.3 Cervicobrachial syndrome (diffuse)
DEF: Complex of symptoms due to scalenus anterior muscle compressing the brachial plexus; pain radiates from shoulder to arm or back of neck.
AHA: N-D, '85, 12

723.4 Brachial neuritis or radiculitis NOS
Cervical radiculitis   Radicular syndrome of upper limbs

723.5 Torticollis, unspecified
Contracture of neck
> **EXCLUDES** congenital (754.1)
> due to birth injury (767.8)
> hysterical (300.11)
> ocular torticollis (781.93)
> psychogenic (306.0)
> spasmodic (333.83)
> traumatic, current (847.0)

DEF: Abnormally positioned neck relative to head due to cervical muscle or fascia contractions; also called wryneck.
AHA: 2Q, '01, 21; 1Q, '95, 7

723.6 Panniculitis specified as affecting neck
DEF: Inflammation of the panniculus adiposus (subcutaneous fat) in the neck.

723.7 Ossification of posterior longitudinal ligament in cervical region

723.8 Other syndromes affecting cervical region
Cervical syndrome NEC   Occipital neuralgia
Klippel's disease
AHA: 1Q, '00, 7

723.9 Unspecified musculoskeletal disorders and symptoms referable to neck
Cervical (region) disorder NOS

√4ᵗʰ **724 Other and unspecified disorders of back**
> **EXCLUDES** collapsed vertebra (code to cause, e.g., osteoporosis, 733.00-733.09)
> conditions due to:
> intervertebral disc disorders (722.0-722.9)
> spondylosis (721.0-721.9)

AHA: 2Q, '89, 14

√5ᵗʰ **724.0 Spinal stenosis, other than cervical**

724.00 Spinal stenosis, unspecified region
M48.00 Spinal stenosis site unspecified   `I-10`

724.01 Thoracic region

724.02 Lumbar region, without neurogenic claudication
Lumbar region NOS
AHA: 4Q, '08, 109; 4Q, '07, 120; 1Q, '07, 10, 20; 4Q, '99, 13
M48.06 Spinal stenosis lumbar region   `I-10`

724.03 Lumbar region, with neurogenic claudication
DEF: Spinal canal narrowing with nerve root compression causing muscle pain, fatigue, and weakness during extension of the lumbar spine; pain is relieved by sitting or bending.
AHA: 2Q, '11, 10; 4Q, '10, 89

724.09 Other

724.1 Pain in thoracic spine

724.2 Lumbago
Low back pain
Low back syndrome
Lumbalgia
AHA: 2Q, '07, 11; N-D, '85, 12
M54.5 Low back pain   `I-10`

724.3 Sciatica
Neuralgia or neuritis of sciatic nerve
> **EXCLUDES** specified lesion of sciatic nerve (355.0)
AHA: 2Q, '89, 12
M54.30 Sciatica unspecified side   `I-10`

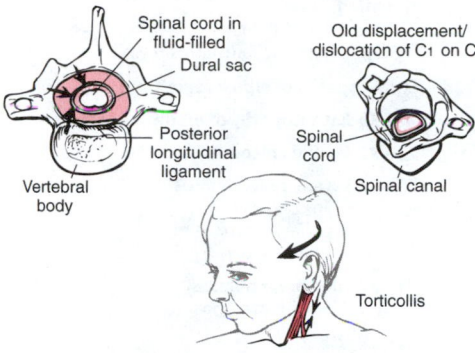

Stenosis in Cervical Region

724.4 Thoracic or lumbosacral neuritis or radiculitis, unspecified
Radicular syndrome of lower limbs
AHA: 2Q, '99, 3
M51.14 Intervertebral disc d/o w/radiculopathy thoracic   `I-10`

724.5 Backache, unspecified
Vertebrogenic (pain) syndrome NOS
M54.9 Dorsalgia unspecified   `I-10`

724.6 Disorders of sacrum
Ankylosis ⎫
Instability ⎬ lumbosacral or sacroiliac (joint)

√5ᵗʰ **724.7 Disorders of coccyx**

724.70 Unspecified disorder of coccyx

724.71 Hypermobility of coccyx

724.79 Other
Coccygodynia

724.8 Other symptoms referable to back
Ossification of posterior longitudinal ligament NOS
Panniculitis specified as sacral or affecting back

724.9 Other unspecified back disorders
Ankylosis of spine NOS
Compression of spinal nerve root NEC
Spinal disorder NOS
> **EXCLUDES** sacroiliitis (720.2)

Rheumatism, Excluding the Back (725-729)

> **INCLUDES** disorders of muscles and tendons and their attachments, and of other soft tissues

725 Polymyalgia rheumatica
DEF: Joint and muscle pain, pelvis, and shoulder girdle stiffness, high sedimentation rate and temporal arteritis; occurs in elderly.
M35.3 Polymyalgia rheumatica   `I-10`

√4ᵗʰ **726 Peripheral enthesopathies and allied syndromes**
> **NOTE** Enthesopathies are disorders of peripheral ligamentous or muscular attachments.
> **EXCLUDES** spinal enthesopathy (720.1)

726.0 Adhesive capsulitis of shoulder

√5ᵗʰ **726.1 Rotator cuff syndrome of shoulder and allied disorders**

726.10 Disorders of bursae and tendons in shoulder region, unspecified
Rotator cuff syndrome NOS
Supraspinatus syndrome NOS
AHA: 2Q, '01, 11
M75.50 Bursitis of unspecified shoulder   `I-10`

726.11 Calcifying tendinitis of shoulder

726.12 Bicipital tenosynovitis

726.13 Partial tear of rotator cuff
> **EXCLUDES** complete rupture of rotator cuff, nontraumatic (727.61)
AHA: 4Q, '11, 135-136

726.19 Other specified disorders
> **EXCLUDES** complete rupture of rotator cuff, nontraumatic (727.61)

Diseases of the Musculoskeletal System and Connective Tissue

726.2–727.41

726.2 Other affections of shoulder region, not elsewhere classified
Periarthritis of shoulder
Scapulohumeral fibrositis

√5ᵗʰ **726.3 Enthesopathy of elbow region**

726.30 Enthesopathy of elbow, unspecified

726.31 Medial epicondylitis

726.32 Lateral epicondylitis
Epicondylitis NOS
Golfers' elbow
Tennis elbow

726.33 Olecranon bursitis
Bursitis of elbow

726.39 Other

726.4 Enthesopathy of wrist and carpus
Bursitis of hand or wrist
Periarthritis of wrist

726.5 Enthesopathy of hip region
Bursitis of hip
Gluteal tendinitis
Iliac crest spur
Psoas tendinitis
Trochanteric tendinitis

√5ᵗʰ **726.6 Enthesopathy of knee**

726.60 Enthesopathy of knee, unspecified
Bursitis of knee NOS

726.61 Pes anserinus tendinitis or bursitis
DEF: Inflamed tendons of sartorius, gracilis and semitendinosus muscles of medial aspect of knee.

726.62 Tibial collateral ligament bursitis
Pellegrini-Stieda syndrome

726.63 Fibular collateral ligament bursitis

726.64 Patellar tendinitis

726.65 Prepatellar bursitis
AHA: 2Q, '06, 15

726.69 Other
Bursitis:
infrapatellar
subpatellar

√5ᵗʰ **726.7 Enthesopathy of ankle and tarsus**

726.70 Enthesopathy of ankle and tarsus, unspecified
Metatarsalgia NOS
EXCLUDES Morton's metatarsalgia (355.6)

726.71 Achilles bursitis or tendinitis

726.72 Tibialis tendinitis
Tibialis (anterior) (posterior) tendinitis

726.73 Calcaneal spur
DEF: Overgrowth of calcaneus bone; causes pain on walking; due to chronic avulsion injury of plantar fascia from calcaneus.

726.79 Other
Peroneal tendinitis

726.8 Other peripheral enthesopathies

√5ᵗʰ **726.9 Unspecified enthesopathy**

726.90 Enthesopathy of unspecified site
Capsulitis NOS   Tendinitis NOS
Periarthritis NOS

726.91 Exostosis of unspecified site
Bone spur NOS
AHA: 2Q, '01, 15

√4ᵗʰ **727 Other disorders of synovium, tendon, and bursa**

√5ᵗʰ **727.0 Synovitis and tenosynovitis**

727.00 Synovitis and tenosynovitis, unspecified
Synovitis NOS
Tenosynovitis NOS
M65.9 Synovitis and tenosynovitis unspecified   I-10

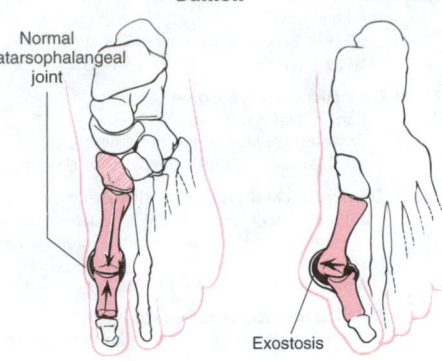

Bunion

Normal metatarsophalangeal joint

Exostosis

727.01 Synovitis and tenosynovitis in diseases classified elsewhere
Code first underlying disease as:
tuberculosis (015.0-015.9)
EXCLUDES crystal-induced (275.4)
gonococcal (098.51)
gout (274.00-274.03)
syphilitic (095.7)

727.02 Giant cell tumor of tendon sheath

727.03 Trigger finger (acquired)
DEF: Stenosing tenosynovitis or nodule in flexor tendon; cessation of flexion or extension movement in finger, followed by snapping into place.

727.04 Radial styloid tenosynovitis
de Quervain's disease

727.05 Other tenosynovitis of hand and wrist

727.06 Tenosynovitis of foot and ankle

727.09 Other

727.1 Bunion
DEF: Enlarged first metatarsal head due to inflamed bursa; results in laterally displaced great toe.

727.2 Specific bursitides often of occupational origin
Beat: Chronic crepitant synovitis of wrist
   elbow   Miners':
   hand   elbow
   knee   knee

727.3 Other bursitis
Bursitis NOS
EXCLUDES bursitis:
gonococcal (098.52)
subacromial (726.19)
subcoracoid (726.19)
subdeltoid (726.19)
syphilitic (095.7)
"frozen shoulder" (726.0)

√5ᵗʰ **727.4 Ganglion and cyst of synovium, tendon, and bursa**

727.40 Synovial cyst, unspecified
EXCLUDES that of popliteal space (727.51)
AHA: 2Q, '97, 6

727.41 Ganglion of joint

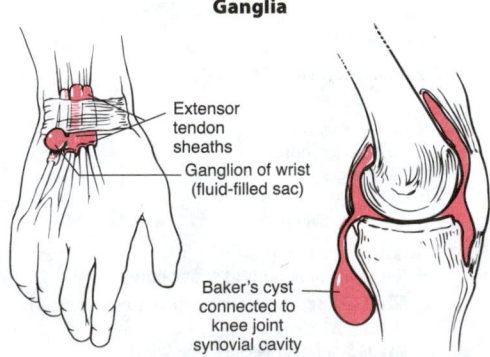

Ganglia

Extensor tendon sheaths
Ganglion of wrist (fluid-filled sac)

Baker's cyst connected to knee joint synovial cavity

N Newborn Age: 0	**P** Pediatric Age: 0-17	**M** Maternity Age: 12-55	**A** Adult Age: 15-124	**MCC** Major CC Condition	**CC** CC Condition **HIV** HIV Related Dx

727.42 Ganglion of tendon sheath

727.43 Ganglion, unspecified

727.49 Other
Cyst of bursa

√5ᵗʰ **727.5 Rupture of synovium**

727.50 Rupture of synovium, unspecified

727.51 Synovial cyst of popliteal space
Baker's cyst (knee)

727.59 Other

√5ᵗʰ **727.6 Rupture of tendon, nontraumatic**

727.60 Nontraumatic rupture of unspecified tendon

727.61 Complete rupture of rotator cuff
EXCLUDES *partial tear of rotator cuff (726.13)*
AHA: 4Q, '11, 136

727.62 Tendons of biceps (long head)

727.63 Extensor tendons of hand and wrist

727.64 Flexor tendons of hand and wrist

727.65 Quadriceps tendon

727.66 Patellar tendon

727.67 Achilles tendon

727.68 Other tendons of foot and ankle

727.69 Other

√5ᵗʰ **727.8 Other disorders of synovium, tendon, and bursa**

727.81 Contracture of tendon (sheath)
Short Achilles tendon (acquired)

727.82 Calcium deposits in tendon and bursa
Calcification of tendon NOS
Calcific tendinitis NOS
EXCLUDES *peripheral ligamentous or muscular attachments (726.0-726.9)*

727.83 Plica syndrome
Plica knee
DEF: A fold in the synovial tissue formed before birth, creating a septum between two pockets of synovial tissue; most common are the medial patellar plica and the suprapatellar plica. Plica syndrome, or plica knee, refers to symptomatic plica.
AHA: 4Q, '00, 44

727.89 Other
Abscess of bursa or tendon
EXCLUDES *xanthomatosis localized to tendons (272.7)*
AHA: 2Q, '89, 15

727.9 Unspecified disorder of synovium, tendon, and bursa

√4ᵗʰ **728 Disorders of muscle, ligament, and fascia**
EXCLUDES *enthesopathies (726.0-726.9)*
muscular dystrophies (359.0-359.1)
myoneural disorders (358.00-358.9)
myopathies (359.2-359.9)
nontraumatic hematoma of muscle (729.92)
old disruption of ligaments of knee (717.81-717.89)

728.0 Infective myositis   CC
Myositis: Myositis:
purulent   suppurative
EXCLUDES *myositis:*
epidemic (074.1)
interstitial (728.81)
syphilitic (095.6)
tropical (040.81)
CC Excl: 567.31, 728.0, 728.11-728.3, 728.81, 728.86
DEF: Inflamed connective septal tissue of muscle.

√5ᵗʰ **728.1 Muscular calcification and ossification**

728.10 Calcification and ossification, unspecified
Massive calcification (paraplegic)

728.11 Progressive myositis ossificans
DEF: Progressive myositic disease; marked by bony tissue formed by voluntary muscle; occurs among very young.

728.12 Traumatic myositis ossificans
Myositis ossificans (circumscripta)

728.13 Postoperative heterotopic calcification
DEF: Abnormal formation of calcium deposits in muscular tissue after surgery, marked by a corresponding loss of muscle tone and tension.

728.19 Other
Polymyositis ossificans

728.2 Muscular wasting and disuse atrophy, not elsewhere classified
Amyotrophia NOS   Myofibrosis
EXCLUDES *neuralgic amyotrophy (353.5)*
pelvic muscle wasting and disuse atrophy (618.83)
progressive muscular atrophy (335.0-335.9)

728.3 Other specific muscle disorders
Arthrogryposis
Immobility syndrome (paraplegic)
EXCLUDES *arthrogryposis multiplex congenita (754.89)*
stiff-man syndrome (333.91)

728.4 Laxity of ligament

728.5 Hypermobility syndrome

728.6 Contracture of palmar fascia   A
Dupuytren's contracture
DEF: Dupuytren's contracture: flexion deformity of finger, due to shortened, thickened fibrosing of palmar fascia; cause unknown; associated with long-standing epilepsy.

√5ᵗʰ **728.7 Other fibromatoses**

728.71 Plantar fascial fibromatosis
Contracture of plantar fascia
Plantar fasciitis (traumatic)
DEF: Plantar fascia fibromatosis; causes nodular swelling and pain; not associated with contractures.

728.79 Other
Garrod's or knuckle pads
Nodular fasciitis
Pseudosarcomatous fibromatosis (proliferative) (subcutaneous)
DEF: Knuckle pads: Pea-size nodules on dorsal surface of interphalangeal joints; new growth of fibrous tissue with thickened dermis and epidermis.

√5ᵗʰ **728.8 Other disorders of muscle, ligament, and fascia**

728.81 Interstitial myositis
DEF: Inflammation of septal connective parts of muscle tissue.

728.82 Foreign body granuloma of muscle
Talc granuloma of muscle
Use additional code to identify foreign body (V90.01-V90.9)

728.83 Rupture of muscle, nontraumatic

728.84 Diastasis of muscle
Diastasis recti (abdomen)
EXCLUDES *diastasis recti complicating pregnancy, labor, and delivery (665.8)*
DEF: Muscle separation, such as recti abdominis after repeated pregnancies.

728.85 Spasm of muscle
M62.838 Other muscle spasm   I-10

728.86 Necrotizing fasciitis   MCC
Use additional code to identify:
gangrene (785.4), if applicable
infectious organism (041.00-041.89)
DEF: Fulminating infection begins with extensive cellulitis, spreads to superficial and deep fascia; causes thrombosis of subcutaneous vessels, and gangrene of underlying tissue.
CC Excl: 567.31, 728.0, 728.11-728.3, 728.81, 728.86
AHA: 4Q, '95, 54

728.87 Muscle weakness (generalized)
EXCLUDES *generalized weakness (780.79)*
AHA: 1Q, '05, 13; 4Q, '03, 66
TIP: Assign an additional code from category 438 if the weakness is a result of a CVA.

√4ᵗʰ/√5ᵗʰ Additional Digit Required   Unacceptable PDx   Manifestation Code   Hospital Acquired Condition   ►◄ Revised Text   ● New Code   ▲ Revised Code Title

Diseases of the Musculoskeletal System and Connective Tissue   727.42–728.87

728.88 Rhabdomyolysis `CC`

DEF: A disintegration or destruction of muscle; an acute disease characterized by the excretion of myoglobin into the urine.

CC Excl: 567.31, 728.0, 728.11-728.3, 728.81, 728.86, 728.88

AHA: 4Q, '03, 66

728.89 Other

Eosinophilic fasciitis

Use additional E code to identify drug, if drug induced

DEF: Eosinophilic fasciitis: inflammation of fascia of extremities associated with eosinophilia, edema, and swelling; occurs alone or as part of myalgia syndrome.

AHA: 3Q, '06, 13; 3Q, '02, 28; 2Q, '01, 14, 15

728.9 Unspecified disorder of muscle, ligament, and fascia

`√4th` **729 Other disorders of soft tissues**

EXCLUDES acroparesthesia (443.89)
carpal tunnel syndrome (354.0)
disorders of the back (720.0-724.9)
entrapment syndromes (354.0-355.9)
palindromic rheumatism (719.3)
periarthritis (726.0-726.9)
psychogenic rheumatism (306.0)

729.0 Rheumatism, unspecified and fibrositis

DEF: General term describes diseases of muscle, tendon, nerve, joint, or bone; symptoms include pain and stiffness.

729.1 Myalgia and myositis, unspecified

Fibromyositis NOS

DEF: Myalgia: muscle pain.

DEF: Myositis: inflamed voluntary muscle.

DEF: Fibromyositis: inflamed fibromuscular tissue.

M79.1 Myalgia `I-10`

729.2 Neuralgia, neuritis, and radiculitis, unspecified

EXCLUDES brachial radiculitis (723.4)
cervical radiculitis (723.4)
lumbosacral radiculitis (724.4)
mononeuritis (354.0-355.9)
radiculitis due to intervertebral disc involvement (722.0-722.2, 722.7)
sciatica (724.3)

DEF: Neuralgia: paroxysmal pain along nerve; symptoms include brief pain and tenderness at point nerve exits.

DEF: Neuritis: inflamed nerve, symptoms include paresthesia, paralysis and loss of reflexes at nerve site.

DEF: Radiculitis: inflamed nerve root.

`√5th` **729.3 Panniculitis, unspecified**

DEF: Inflammatory reaction of subcutaneous fat; causes nodules; often develops in abdominal region.

729.30 Panniculitis, unspecified site

Weber-Christian disease

DEF: Febrile, nodular, nonsuppurative, relapsing inflammation of subcutaneous fat.

729.31 Hypertrophy of fat pad, knee

Hypertrophy of infrapatellar fat pad

729.39 Other site

EXCLUDES panniculitis specified as (affecting):
back (724.8)
neck (723.6)
sacral (724.8)

AHA: 2Q, '11, 3

729.4 Fasciitis, unspecified

EXCLUDES necrotizing fasciitis (728.86)
nodular fasciitis (728.79)

AHA: 2Q, '94, 13

729.5 Pain in limb

AHA: 2Q, '07, 11

M79.609 Pain in unspecified limb `I-10`

729.6 Residual foreign body in soft tissue

Use additional code to identify foreign body (V90.01-V90.9)

EXCLUDES foreign body granuloma:
muscle (728.82)
skin and subcutaneous tissue (709.4)

`√5th` **729.7 Nontraumatic compartment syndrome**

Code first, if applicable, postprocedural complication (998.89)

EXCLUDES compartment syndrome NOS (958.90)
traumatic compartment syndrome (958.90-958.99)

DEF: Compression of nerves and blood vessels within an enclosed space, leading to impaired blood flow and muscle and nerve damage.

729.71 Nontraumatic compartment syndrome of upper extremity `CC`

Nontraumatic compartment syndrome of shoulder, arm, forearm, wrist, hand, and fingers

CC Excl: 729.81, 729.89-729.99, 903.8, 904.9

AHA: 4Q, '06, 100-102

729.72 Nontraumatic compartment syndrome of lower extremity `CC`

Nontraumatic compartment syndrome of hip, buttock, thigh, leg, foot, and toes

CC Excl: 729.81, 729.89-729.99, 904.7, 904.9

AHA: 4Q, '06, 100-102

729.73 Nontraumatic compartment syndrome of abdomen `CC`

CC Excl: 863.0-867.3, 867.5-868.14, 869.0-869.1, 879.2-879.9, 929.0-929.9, 958.8, 959.8-959.9

AHA: 4Q, '06, 100-102

729.79 Nontraumatic compartment syndrome of other sites `CC`

CC Excl: 868.03-868.10, 868.13-869.1

AHA: 4Q, '06, 100-102

`√5th` **729.8 Other musculoskeletal symptoms referable to limbs**

729.81 Swelling of limb

AHA: 4Q, '88, 6

TIP: Assign for hyperalgesic pseudothrombophlebitis, which involves painful swelling of the lower extremity and mimics deep vein thrombosis (DVT).

729.82 Cramp

729.89 Other

EXCLUDES abnormality of gait (781.2)
tetany (781.7)
transient paralysis of limb (781.4)

AHA: 4Q, '88, 12

R29.898 Oth symptoms & signs involv musculoskeletal system `I-10`

`√5th` **729.9 Other and unspecified disorders of soft tissue**

AHA: 4Q, '08, 134-136

729.90 Disorders of soft tissue, unspecified

729.91 Post-traumatic seroma

EXCLUDES seroma complicating a procedure (998.13)

729.92 Nontraumatic hematoma of soft tissue

Nontraumatic hematoma of muscle

AHA: ▶2Q, '13, 8;◀ 4Q, '08, 135

TIP: Assign an additional E code for a drug adverse effect if caused by Coumadin or other anticoagulants.

729.99 Other disorders of soft tissue

Polyalgia

N Newborn Age: 0   P Pediatric Age: 0-17   M Maternity Age: 12-55   A Adult Age: 15-124   MCC Major CC Condition   CC CC Condition   HIV HIV Related Dx

248 – Volume 1 • October 2014   2015 ICD-9-CM

Osteopathies, Chondropathies, and Acquired Musculoskeletal Deformities (730-739)

✓4th 730 Osteomyelitis, periostitis, and other infections involving bone

EXCLUDES jaw (526.4-526.5)
petrous bone (383.2)

Use additional code to identify organism, such as Staphylococcus (041.1)

> The following fifth-digit subclassification is for use with category 730; valid digits are in [brackets] under each code. See list at beginning of chapter for definitions.
> - 0 site unspecified
> - 1 shoulder region
> - 2 upper arm
> - 3 forearm
> - 4 hand
> - 5 pelvic region and thigh
> - 6 lower leg
> - 7 ankle and foot
> - 8 other specified sites
> - 9 multiple sites

DEF: Osteomyelitis: bacterial inflammation of bone tissue and marrow.
DEF: Periostitis: inflammation of specialized connective tissue; causes swelling of bone and aching pain.
AHA: 4Q, '97, 43

§ ✓5th 730.0 Acute osteomyelitis [0-9] CC

Abscess of any bone except accessory sinus, jaw, or mastoid
Acute or subacute osteomyelitis, with or without mention of periostitis

Use additional code to identify major osseous defect, if applicable (731.3)

CC Excl: For code 730.00: 015.50-015.56, 015.70-015.76, 015.90-015.96, 017.90-017.96, 730.00-730.39, 730.80-730.99 For code 730.01: 015.50-015.56, 015.70-015.76, 015.90-015.96, 017.90-017.96, 730.00, 730.08-730.11, 730.18-730.21, 730.28-730.31, 730.38-730.39, 730.80-730.81, 730.88-730.91, 730.98-730.99 For code 730.02: 015.50-015.56, 015.70-015.76, 015.90-015.96, 017.90-017.96, 730.00, 730.08-730.10, 730.12, 730.18-730.20, 730.22, 730.28-730.30, 730.32, 730.38-730.39, 730.80, 730.82, 730.88-730.90, 730.92, 730.98-730.99 For code 730.03: 015.50-015.56, 015.70-015.76, 015.90-015.96, 017.90-017.96, 730.00, 730.08-730.10, 730.13, 730.18-730.20, 730.23, 730.28-730.30, 730.33, 730.38-730.39, 730.80, 730.83, 730.88-730.90, 730.93, 730.98-730.99; **For code 730.04:** 015.50-015.56, 015.70-015.76, 015.90-015.96, 017.90-017.96, 730.00, 730.08-730.10, 730.14, 730.18-730.20, 730.24, 730.28-730.30, 730.34, 730.38-730.39, 730.80, 730.84, 730.88-730.90, 730.94, 730.98-730.99 **For code 730.05:** 015.10-015.16, 015.50-015.56, 015.70-015.76, 015.90-015.96, 017.90-017.96, 730.00, 730.08-730.10, 730.15, 730.18-730.20, 730.25, 730.28-730.30, 730.35, 730.38-730.39, 730.80, 730.85, 730.88-730.90, 730.95, 730.98-730.99; **For code 730.06:** 015.20-015.56, 015.70-015.96, 015.90-015.96, 017.90-017.96, 730.00, 730.08-730.10, 730.16, 730.18-730.20, 730.26, 730.28-730.30, 730.36, 730.38-730.39, 730.80, 730.86, 730.88-730.90, 730.96, 730.98-730.99; **For code 730.07:** 015.50-015.56, 015.70-015.76, 015.90-015.96, 017.90-017.96, 730.00, 730.08-730.10, 730.17-730.20, 730.27-730.30, 730.37-730.39, 730.80, 730.87-730.90, 730.97-730.99 **For code 730.08:** 015.00-015.06, 015.50-015.56, 015.70-015.76, 015.90-015.96, 017.90-017.96, 730.00-730.39, 730.80-730.99 **For code 730.09:** 015.50-015.56, 015.70-015.76, 015.90-015.96, 017.90-017.96, 730.00-730.39, 730.80-730.99
AHA: 4Q, '06, 103; **For code 730.06:** 1Q, '02, 4; **For code 730.07:** 1Q, '04, 14

§ ✓5th 730.1 Chronic osteomyelitis [0-9] CC

Brodie's abscess
Chronic or old osteomyelitis, with or without mention of periostitis
Sclerosing osteomyelitis of Garré
Sequestrum of bone

Use additional code to identify major osseous defect, if applicable (731.3)

EXCLUDES aseptic necrosis of bone (733.40-733.49)
CC Excl: For code 730.10: 730.10-730.39, 730.80-731.1; **For codes 730.11-730.19:** 003.24, 015.50-015.56, 015.70-015.76, 015.90-015.96, 017.90-017.96, 730.00-730.39, 730.80-730.99
AHA: 4Q, '06, 103; **For code 730.17:** 3Q, '11, 15; 3Q, '00, 4

§ ✓5th 730.2 Unspecified osteomyelitis [0-9] CC

Osteitis or osteomyelitis NOS, with or without mention of periostitis

Use additional code to identify major osseous defect, if applicable (731.3)

CC Excl: For code 730.20: 730.10-730.39, 730.80-731.1; **For codes 730.21-730.29:** 003.24, 015.50-015.56, 015.70-015.76, 015.90-015.96, 017.90-017.96, 730.00-730.39, 730.80-730.99
AHA: 4Q, '06, 103;
M86.9 Osteomyelitis unspecified   I-10

§ ✓5th 730.3 Periostitis without mention of osteomyelitis [0-9]

Abscess of periosteum ⎫ without mention of
Periostosis   ⎬ osteomyelitis

EXCLUDES that in secondary syphilis (091.61)

§ ✓5th 730.7 Osteopathy resulting from poliomyelitis [0-9]

Code first underlying disease (045.0-045.9)

§ ✓5th 730.8 Other infections involving bone in diseases classified elsewhere [0-9] CC

Code first underlying disease as:
tuberculosis (015.0-015.9)
typhoid fever (002.0)

EXCLUDES syphilis of bone NOS (095.5)

CC Excl: For codes 730.80, 730.89: 015.50-015.56, 015.70-015.76, 015.90-015.96, 017.90-017.96, 730.00-730.39, 730.80-730.99; **For code 730.81:** 015.50-015.56, 015.70-015.76, 015.90-015.96, 017.90-017.96, 730.00-730.01, 730.08-730.11, 730.18-730.21, 730.28-730.31, 730.38-730.39, 730.80, 730.88-730.91, 730.98-730.99;

For code 730.82: 015.50-015.56, 015.70-015.76, 015.90-015.96, 017.90-017.96, 730.00, 730.02, 730.08-730.10, 730.12, 730.18-730.20, 730.22, 730.28-730.30, 730.32, 730.38-730.39, 730.80, 730.88-730.90, 730.92, 730.98-730.99; **For code 730.83:** 015.50-015.56, 015.70-015.76, 015.90-015.96, 017.90-017.96, 730.00, 730.03, 730.08-730.10, 730.13, 730.18-730.20, 730.23, 730.28-730.30, 730.33, 730.38-730.39, 730.80, 730.88-730.90, 730.93, 730.98-730.99; **For code 730.84:** 015.50-015.56, 015.70-015.76, 015.90-015.96, 017.90-017.96, 730.00, 730.04, 730.08-730.10, 730.14, 730.18-730.20, 730.24, 730.28-730.30, 730.34, 730.38-730.39, 730.80, 730.88-730.90, 730.94, 730.98-730.99; **For code 730.85:** 015.10-015.16, 015.50-015.56, 015.70-015.76, 015.90-015.96, 017.90-017.96, 730.00, 730.05, 730.08-730.10, 730.15, 730.18-730.20, 730.25, 730.28-730.30, 730.35, 730.38-730.39, 730.80, 730.88-730.90, 730.95, 730.98-730.99; **For code 730.86:** 015.20-015.56, 015.70-015.76, 015.90-015.96, 017.90-017.96, 730.00, 730.06, 730.08-730.10, 730.16, 730.18-730.20, 730.26, 730.28-730.30, 730.36, 730.38-730.39, 730.80, 730.88-730.90, 730.96, 730.98-730.99; **For code 730.87:** 015.50-015.56, 015.70-015.76, 015.90-015.96, 017.90-017.96, 730.00, 730.07-730.10, 730.17-730.20, 730.27-730.30, 730.37-730.39, 730.80, 730.88-730.90, 730.97-730.99; **For code 730.88:** 015.00-015.06, 015.50-015.56, 015.70-015.76, 015.90-015.96, 017.90-017.96, 730.00-730.39, 730.80-730.99

AHA: 2Q, '97, 16; 3Q, '91, 10

§ ✓5th 730.9 Unspecified infection of bone [0-9] CC

CC Excl: For codes 730.90, 730.99: 015.50-015.56, 015.70-015.76, 015.90-015.96, 017.90-017.96, 730.00-730.39, 730.80-730.99; **For code 730.91:** 015.50-015.56, 015.70-015.76, 015.90-015.96, 017.90-017.96, 730.00-730.01, 730.08-730.11, 730.18-730.21, 730.28-730.31, 730.38-730.39, 730.80-730.81, 730.88-730.90, 730.98-730.99; **For code 730.92:** 015.50-015.56, 015.70-015.76, 015.90-015.96, 017.90-017.96, 730.00, 730.02, 730.08-730.10, 730.12, 730.18-730.20, 730.22, 730.28-730.30, 730.32, 730.38-730.39, 730.80, 730.82, 730.88-730.90, 730.98-730.99; **For code 730.93:** 015.50-015.56, 015.70-015.76, 015.90-015.96, 017.90-017.96, 730.00, 730.03, 730.08-730.10, 730.13, 730.18-730.20, 730.23, 730.28-730.30, 730.33, 730.38-730.39, 730.80, 730.83, 730.88-730.90, 730.98-730.99; **For code 730.94:** 015.50-015.56, 015.70-015.76, 015.90-015.96, 017.90-017.96, 730.00, 730.04, 730.08-730.10, 730.14, 730.18-730.20, 730.24, 730.28-730.30, 730.34, 730.38-730.39, 730.80, 730.84, 730.88-730.90, 730.98-730.99; **For code 730.95:** 015.10-015.16, 015.50-015.56, 015.70-015.76, 015.90-015.96, 017.90-017.96, 730.00, 730.05, 730.08-730.10, 730.15, 730.18-730.20, 730.25, 730.28-730.30, 730.35, 730.38-730.39, 730.80, 730.85, 730.88-730.90, 730.98-730.99; **For code 730.96:** 015.20-015.56, 015.70-015.76, 015.90-015.96, 017.90-017.96, 730.00, 730.06, 730.08-730.10, 730.16, 730.18-730.20, 730.26, 730.28-730.30, 730.36, 730.38-730.39, 730.80, 730.86, 730.88-730.90, 730.98-730.99; **For code 730.97:** 015.50-015.56, 015.70-015.76, 015.90-015.96, 017.90-017.96, 730.00, 730.07-730.10, 730.17-730.20, 730.27-730.30, 730.37-730.39, 730.80, 730.87-730.90, 730.98-730.99; **For code 730.98:** 0015.00-015.06, 015.50-015.56, 015.70-015.76, 015.90-015.96, 017.90-017.96, 730.00-730.39, 730.80-730.99

§ Requires fifth digit. Valid digits are in [brackets] under each code. See beginning of section 710-739 for codes and defintions.

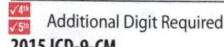

Additional Digit Required   Unacceptable PDx   Manifestation Code   Hospital Acquired Condition   ▶◀ Revised Text   ● New Code   ▲ Revised Code Title
2015 ICD-9-CM   **Volume 1 – 249**

Diseases of the Musculoskeletal System and Connective Tissue

731–733.09

☑4th 731 Osteitis deformans and osteopathies associated with other disorders classified elsewhere

> **DEF:** Osteitis deformans: Bone disease marked by episodes of increased bone loss, excessive repair attempts; causes weakened, deformed bones with increased mass, bowed long bones, deformed flat bones, pain and pathological fractures; may be fatal if associated with congestive heart failure, giant cell tumors or bone sarcoma; also called Paget's disease.

731.0 Osteitis deformans without mention of bone tumor
> Paget's disease of bone

731.1 Osteitis deformans in diseases classified elsewhere
> Code first underlying disease as:
>> malignant neoplasm of bone (170.0-170.9)

731.2 Hypertrophic pulmonary osteoarthropathy
> Bamberger-Marie disease
> **DEF:** Clubbing of fingers and toes; related to enlarged ends of long bones, due to chronic lung and heart disease.

731.3 Major osseous defects
> Code first underlying disease, if known, such as:
>> aseptic necrosis (733.40-733.49)
>> malignant neoplasm of bone (170.0-170.9)
>> osteomyelitis (730.00-730.29)
>> osteoporosis (733.00-733.09)
>> peri-prosthetic osteolysis (996.45)
> **AHA:** 4Q, '06, 103

731.8 Other bone involvement in diseases classified elsewhere
> Code first underlying disease as:
>> diabetes mellitus (249.8, 250.8)
> Use additional code to specify bone condition, such as:
>> acute osteomyelitis (730.00-730.09)
> **AHA:** 2Q, '10, 6; 1Q, '04, 14; 4Q, '97, 43; 2Q, '97, 16
> **TIP:** For diabetic osteomyelitis, assign a total of three codes: 250.8X, 731.8, and a code from category 730.
> **M90.89** Osteopathy dz classified elsewhere multiple site   `I-10`

☑4th 732 Osteochondropathies
> **DEF:** Conditions related to both bone and cartilage, or conditions in which cartilage is converted to bone (enchondral ossification).

732.0 Juvenile osteochondrosis of spine
> Juvenile osteochondrosis (of):
>> marginal or vertebral epiphysis (of Scheuermann)
>> spine NOS
> Vertebral epiphysitis
> **EXCLUDES** adolescent postural kyphosis (737.0)

732.1 Juvenile osteochondrosis of hip and pelvis
> Coxa plana
> Ischiopubic synchondrosis (of van Neck)
> Osteochondrosis (juvenile) of:
>> acetabulum
>> head of femur (of Legg-Calvé-Perthes)
>> iliac crest (of Buchanan)
>> symphysis pubis (of Pierson)
> Pseudocoxalgia

732.2 Nontraumatic slipped upper femoral epiphysis
> Slipped upper femoral epiphysis NOS

732.3 Juvenile osteochondrosis of upper extremity
> Osteochondrosis (juvenile) of:
>> capitulum of humerus (of Panner)
>> carpal lunate (of Kienbock)
>> hand NOS
>> head of humerus (of Haas)
>> heads of metacarpals (of Mauclaire)
>> lower ulna (of Burns)
>> radial head (of Brailsford)
>> upper extremity NOS

732.4 Juvenile osteochondrosis of lower extremity, excluding foot
> Osteochondrosis (juvenile) of:
>> lower extremity NOS
>> primary patellar center (of Köhler)
>> proximal tibia (of Blount)
>> secondary patellar center (of Sinding-Larsen)
>> tibial tubercle (of Osgood-Schlatter)
> Tibia vara

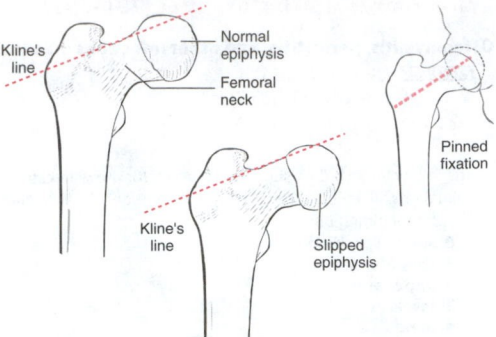

Slipped Femoral Epiphysis

Kline's line — Normal epiphysis — Femoral neck — Kline's line — Slipped epiphysis — Pinned fixation

732.5 Juvenile osteochondrosis of foot
> Calcaneal apophysitis
> Epiphysitis, os calcis
> Osteochondrosis (juvenile) of:
>> astragalus (of Diaz)
>> calcaneum (of Sever)
>> foot NOS
>> metatarsal
>>> second (of Freiberg)
>>> fifth (of Iselin)
>> os tibiale externum (of Haglund)
>> tarsal navicular (of Köhler)

732.6 Other juvenile osteochondrosis
> Apophysitis
> Epiphysitis   } specified as juvenile, of other
> Osteochondritis   site, or site NOS
> Osteochondrosis

732.7 Osteochondritis dissecans

732.8 Other specified forms of osteochondropathy
> Adult osteochondrosis of spine

732.9 Unspecified osteochondropathy
> Apophysitis   } NOS
> Epiphysitis   not specified as adult or
> Osteochondritis   juvenile, of unspecified
> Osteochondrosis   site

☑4th 733 Other disorders of bone and cartilage
> **EXCLUDES** bone spur (726.91)
>> cartilage of, or loose body in, joint (717.0-717.9, 718.0-718.9)
>> giant cell granuloma of jaw (526.3)
>> osteitis fibrosa cystica generalisata (252.01)
>> osteomalacia (268.2)
>> polyostotic fibrous dysplasia of bone (756.54)
>> prognathism, retrognathism (524.1)
>> xanthomatosis localized to bone (272.7)

☑5th 733.0 Osteoporosis
> Use additional code to identify major osseous defect, if applicable (731.3)
> Use additional code to identify personal history of pathologic (healed) fracture (V13.51)
> **DEF:** Bone mass reduction that ultimately results in fractures after minimal trauma; dorsal kyphosis or loss of height often occur.
> **AHA:** 4Q, '06, 103

733.00 Osteoporosis, unspecified
> Wedging of vertebra NOS
> **AHA:** 4Q, '07, 92;1Q, '07, 22; 3Q, '01, 19; 2Q, '98, 12
> **M81.0** Age-related osteoporosis w/o curr path fx   `I-10`

733.01 Senile osteoporosis
> Postmenopausal osteoporosis
> **AHA:** 1Q, '07, 5, 6

733.02 Idiopathic osteoporosis
> **M81.8** Other osteoporosis w/o current pathological fx   `I-10`

733.03 Disuse osteoporosis

733.09 Other
> Drug-induced osteoporosis
> Use additional E code to identify drug
> **AHA:** 4Q, '03, 108

N Newborn Age: 0   **P** Pediatric Age: 0-17   **M** Maternity Age: 12-55   **A** Adult Age: 15-124   **MCC** Major CC Condition   **CC** CC Condition   **HIV** HIV Related Dx

√5ᵗʰ **733.1 Pathologic fracture**
Chronic fracture
Spontaneous fracture
EXCLUDES *stress fracture (733.93-733.95)*
traumatic fracture (800-829)
DEF: Fracture due to bone structure weakening by pathological processes (e.g., osteoporosis, neoplasms and osteomalacia).
AHA: 4Q, '08, 158; 1Q, '07, 3-4; 4Q, '93, 25; N-D, '86, 10; N-D, '85, 16
TIP: Assign only for newly diagnosed fractures; refer to V code aftercare categories if patient is receiving routine care during healing or recovery phase.

733.10 Pathologic fracture, unspecified site CC
CC Excl: 733.10-733.19, 733.93-733.98

733.11 Pathologic fracture of humerus CC
CC Excl: See code 733.10
AHA: 2Q, '10, 6

733.12 Pathologic fracture of distal radius and ulna CC
Wrist NOS
CC Excl: See code 733.10

733.13 Pathologic fracture of vertebrae CC
Collapse of vertebra NOS
CC Excl: See code 733.10
AHA: 3Q, '08, 4; 1Q, '07, 5, 6, 22; 3Q, '99, 5
TIP: Assign for a chronic vertebral pathological fracture for which the patient is receiving medication.
M48.53xA Collasped vertebra NEC cervicothorac initial enc I-10

733.14 Pathologic fracture of neck of femur CC
Femur NOS
Hip NOS
CC Excl: See code 733.10
AHA: 1Q, '01, 1; 1Q, '96, 16

733.15 Pathologic fracture of other specified part of femur CC
CC Excl: See code 733.10
AHA: 2Q, '98, 12

733.16 Pathologic fracture of tibia or fibula CC
Ankle NOS
CC Excl: See code 733.10

733.19 Pathologic fracture of other specified site CC
CC Excl: See code 733.10

√5ᵗʰ **733.2 Cyst of bone**

733.20 Cyst of bone (localized), unspecified

733.21 Solitary bone cyst
Unicameral bone cyst

733.22 Aneurysmal bone cyst
DEF: Solitary bone lesion, bulges into periosteum; marked by calcified rim.

733.29 Other
Fibrous dysplasia (monostotic)
EXCLUDES *cyst of jaw (526.0-526.2, 526.89)*
osteitis fibrosa cystica (252.01)
polyostotic fibrousdyplasia of bone (756.54)

733.3 Hyperostosis of skull
Hyperostosis interna frontalis
Leontiasis ossium
DEF: Abnormal bone growth on inner aspect of cranial bones.

√5ᵗʰ **733.4 Aseptic necrosis of bone**
Use additional code to identify major osseous defect, if applicable (731.3)
EXCLUDES *osteochondropathies (732.0-732.9)*
DEF: Infarction of bone tissue due to a noninfectious etiology, such as a fracture, ischemic disorder or administration of immunosuppressive drugs; leads to degenerative joint disease or nonunion of fractures.
AHA: 4Q, '06, 103

733.40 Aseptic necrosis of bone, site unspecified CC
CC Excl: 733.40-733.49

733.41 Head of humerus CC
CC Excl: 733.40-733.41, 733.45-733.49

733.42 Head and neck of femur CC
Femur NOS
EXCLUDES *Legg-Calvé-Perthes disease (732.1)*
CC Excl: 733.40, 733.42, 733.45-733.49
M87.256 Osteonecrosis due to previous trauma uns femur I-10

733.43 Medial femoral condyle CC
CC Excl: 733.40, 733.43, 733.45-733.49

733.44 Talus CC
CC Excl: 733.40, 733.44-733.49

733.45 Jaw CC
Use additional E code to identify drug, if drug-induced
EXCLUDES *osteoradionecrosis of jaw (526.89)*
CC Excl: See code: 733.40
AHA: 4Q, '07, 91

733.49 Other CC
CC Excl: See code: 733.40

733.5 Osteitis condensans
Piriform sclerosis of ilium
DEF: Idiopathic condition marked by low back pain; associated with oval or triangular sclerotic, opaque bone next to sacroiliac joints in the ileum.

733.6 Tietze's disease
Costochondral junction syndrome
Costochondritis
DEF: Painful, idiopathic, nonsuppurative, swollen costal cartilage sometimes confused with cardiac symptoms because the anterior chest pain resembles that of coronary artery disease.
M94.0 Chondrocostal junction syndrome (Tietze dz) I-10

733.7 Algoneurodystrophy
Disuse atrophy of bone
Sudeck's atrophy

√5ᵗʰ **733.8 Malunion and nonunion of fracture**
AHA: 2Q, '94, 5

733.81 Malunion of fracture CC
CC Excl: 733.81-733.82

733.82 Nonunion of fracture CC
Pseudoarthrosis (bone)
CC Excl: See code: 733.81

√5ᵗʰ **733.9 Other unspecified disorders of bone and cartilage**
AHA: 4Q, '08, 136-137

733.90 Disorder of bone and cartilage
M89.9 Disorder of bone, unspecified I-10

733.91 Arrest of bone development or growth
Epiphyseal arrest

733.92 Chondromalacia
Chondromalacia: Chondromalacia:
NOS   systemic
localized, except patella   tibial plateau
EXCLUDES *chondromalacia of patella (717.7)*
DEF: Articular cartilage softening.

733.93 Stress fracture of tibia or fibula
Stress reaction of tibia or fibula
Use additional external cause code(s) to identify the cause of the stress fracture
AHA: 4Q, '08, 158; 4Q, '01, 48

733.94 Stress fracture of the metatarsals
Stress reaction of metatarsals
Use additional external cause code(s) to identify the cause of the stress fracture
AHA: 4Q, '08, 158; 4Q, '01, 48

733.95 Stress fracture of other bone
Stress reaction of other bone
Use additional external cause code(s) to identify the cause of the stress fracture
EXCLUDES *stress fracture of:*
femoral neck (733.96)
fibula (733.93)
metatarsals (733.94)
pelvis (733.98)
shaft of femur (733.97)
tibia (733.93)
AHA: 4Q, '08, 158; 4Q, '01, 48

733.96 Stress fracture of femoral neck
Stress reaction of femoral neck
Use additional external cause code(s) to identify the cause of the stress fracture
AHA: 4Q, '08, 158

733.97 Stress fracture of shaft of femur
Stress reaction of shaft of femur
Use additional external cause code(s) to identify the cause of the stress fracture
AHA: 4Q, '08, 158

733.98 Stress fracture of pelvis
Stress reaction of pelvis
Use additional external cause code(s) to identify the cause of the stress fracture
AHA: 4Q, '08, 158

733.99 Other
Diaphysitis   Relapsing polychondritis
Hypertrophy of bone
AHA: 1Q, '11, 6; J-F, '87, 14

734   Flat foot
Pes planus (acquired)
Talipes planus (acquired)
EXCLUDES *congenital (754.61)*
rigid flat foot (754.61)
spastic (everted) flat foot (754.61)

✓4ᵗʰ 735   Acquired deformities of toe
EXCLUDES *congenital (754.60-754.69, 755.65-755.66)*

735.0 Hallux valgus (acquired)
DEF: Angled displacement of the great toe, causing it to ride over or under other toes.

Acquired Deformities of Toe

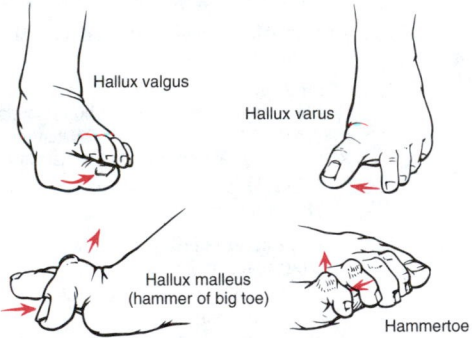

Hallux valgus

Hallux varus

Hallux malleus (hammer of big toe)

Hammertoe

Acquired Deformities of Forearm

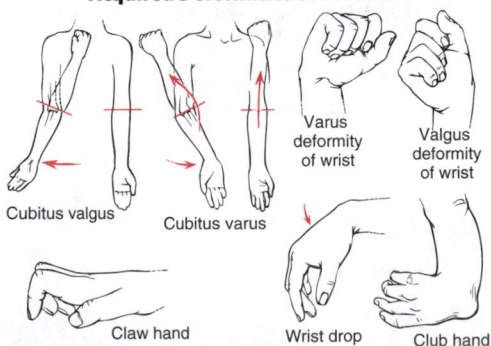

Cubitus valgus

Cubitus varus

Varus deformity of wrist

Valgus deformity of wrist

Claw hand

Wrist drop

Club hand

735.1 Hallux varus (acquired)
DEF: Angled displacement of the great toe toward the body midline, away from the other toes.

735.2 Hallux rigidus
DEF: Limited flexion movement at metatarsophalangeal joint of great toe; due to degenerative joint disease.

735.3 Hallux malleus
DEF: Extended proximal phalanx, flexed distal phalanges of great toe; foot resembles claw or hammer.

735.4 Other hammer toe (acquired)

735.5 Claw toe (acquired)
DEF: Hyperextended proximal phalanges, flexed middle and distal phalanges

735.8 Other acquired deformities of toe
AHA: 4Q, '07, 123
TIP: Assign for hallux limitus, a deformity of the first metatarsophalangeal joint, which restricts the range of motion and can lead to stiffness and pain in the joint.

735.9 Unspecified acquired deformity of toe

✓4ᵗʰ 736   Other acquired deformities of limbs
EXCLUDES *congenital (754.3-755.9)*

✓5ᵗʰ 736.0 Acquired deformities of forearm, excluding fingers

736.00 Unspecified deformity
Deformity of elbow, forearm, hand, or wrist (acquired) NOS

736.01 Cubitus valgus (acquired)
DEF: Deviation of the elbow away from the body midline upon extension; it occurs when the palm is turning outward.

736.02 Cubitus varus (acquired)
DEF: Elbow joint displacement angled laterally; when the forearm is extended, it is deviated toward the midline of the body; also called "gun stock" deformity.

736.03 Valgus deformity of wrist (acquired)
DEF: Abnormal angulation away from the body midline.

736.04 Varus deformity of wrist (acquired)
DEF: Abnormal angulation toward the body midline.

736.05 Wrist drop (acquired)
DEF: Inability to extend the hand at the wrist due to extensor muscle paralysis.

736.06 Claw hand (acquired)
DEF: Flexion and atrophy of the hand and fingers; found in ulnar nerve lesions, syringomyelia, and leprosy.

736.07 Club hand, acquired
DEF: Twisting of the hand out of shape or position; caused by the congenital absence of the ulna or radius.

736.09 Other

736.1 Mallet finger
DEF: Permanently flexed distal phalanx.

✓5ᵗʰ 736.2 Other acquired deformities of finger

736.20 Unspecified deformity
Deformity of finger (acquired) NOS

736.21 Boutonniere deformity
DEF: A deformity of the finger caused by flexion of the proximal interphalangeal joint and hyperextension of the distal joint; also called buttonhole deformity.

736.22 Swan-neck deformity
DEF: Flexed distal and hyperextended proximal interphalangeal joint.

736.29 Other
EXCLUDES *trigger finger (727.03)*
AHA: 2Q, '05, 7; 2Q, '89, 13

✓5ᵗʰ 736.3 Acquired deformities of hip

736.30 Unspecified deformity
Deformity of hip (acquired) NOS

736.31 Coxa valga (acquired)
DEF: Increase of at least 140 degrees in the angle formed by the axis of the head and the neck of the femur, and the axis of its shaft.

N Newborn Age: 0   **P** Pediatric Age: 0-17   **M** Maternity Age: 12-55   **A** Adult Age: 15-124   **MCC** Major CC Condition   **CC** CC Condition   **HIV** HIV Related Dx

252 – Volume 1   2015 ICD-9-CM

Deformities of Lower Limb

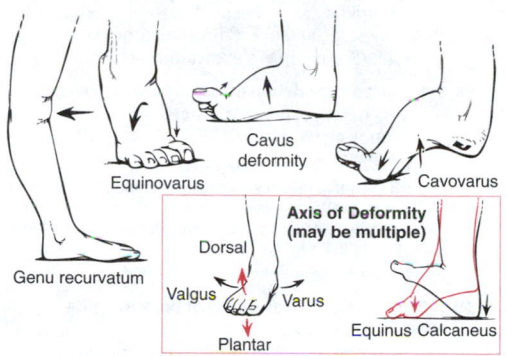

Equinovarus

Cavus deformity

Cavovarus

Genu recurvatum

Axis of Deformity (may be multiple)

Dorsal

Valgus — Varus

Plantar

Equinus Calcaneus

736.32 Coxa vara (acquired)
DEF: The bending downward of the neck of the femur, causing difficulty in movement; a right angle or less may be formed by the axis of the head and neck of the femur and the axis of its shaft.

736.39 Other
AHA: 4Q, '11, 156; 2Q, '08, 4; 2Q, '91, 18
TIP: Do not assign as principal diagnosis for patient encounters for joint replacement following previous explantation of joint prosthesis, assign code V54.82 instead.

√5th 736.4 Genu valgum or varum (acquired)

736.41 Genu valgum (acquired)
DEF: Abnormally close together and an abnormally large space between the ankles; also called "knock-knees."

736.42 Genu varum (acquired)
DEF: Abnormally separated knees and the inward bowing of the legs; it is also called "bowlegs."

736.5 Genu recurvatum (acquired)
DEF: Hyperextended knees; also called "backknee."

736.6 Other acquired deformities of knee
Deformity of knee (acquired) NOS

√5th 736.7 Other acquired deformities of ankle and foot
EXCLUDES   deformities of toe (acquired) (735.0-735.9)
pes planus (acquired) (734)

736.70 Unspecified deformity of ankle and foot, acquired

736.71 Acquired equinovarus deformity
Clubfoot, acquired
EXCLUDES   clubfoot not specified as acquired (754.5-754.7)

736.72 Equinus deformity of foot, acquired
DEF: A plantar flexion deformity that forces people to walk on their toes.

736.73 Cavus deformity of foot
EXCLUDES   that with claw foot (736.74)
DEF: Abnormally high longitudinal arch of the foot.

736.74 Claw foot, acquired
DEF: High foot arch with hyperextended toes at metatarsophalangeal joint and flexed toes at distal joints; also called "main en griffe."

Acquired Deformities of Hip

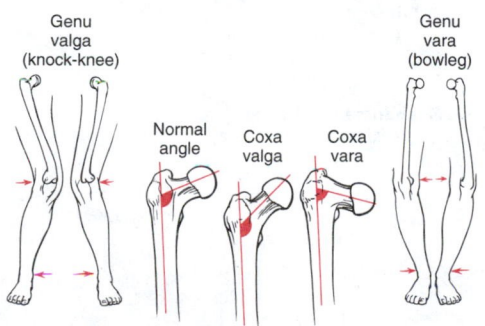

Genu valga (knock-knee)

Genu vara (bowleg)

Normal angle

Coxa valga

Coxa vara

736.75 Cavovarus deformity of foot, acquired
DEF: Inward turning of the heel from the midline of the leg and an abnormally high longitudinal arch.

736.76 Other calcaneus deformity

736.79 Other
Acquired:
pes   } not elsewhere classified
talipes

√5th 736.8 Acquired deformities of other parts of limbs

736.81 Unequal leg length (acquired)

736.89 Other
Deformity (acquired):
arm or leg, not elsewhere classified
shoulder
AHA: 4Q, '11, 156; 2Q, '08, 5
TIP: Do not assign as principal diagnosis for patient encounters for joint replacement following previous explantation of joint prosthesis, assign code V54.82 instead.

736.9 Acquired deformity of limb, site unspecified

√4th 737 Curvature of spine
EXCLUDES   congenital (754.2)

737.0 Adolescent postural kyphosis
EXCLUDES   osteochondrosis of spine (juvenile) (732.0)
adult (732.8)

√5th 737.1 Kyphosis (acquired)

737.10 Kyphosis (acquired) (postural)
M40.05 Postural kyphosis thoracolumbar region   I-10

737.11 Kyphosis due to radiation

737.12 Kyphosis, postlaminectomy
AHA: J-F, '87, 7
M96.3 Postlaminectomy kyphosis   I-10

737.19 Other
EXCLUDES   that associated with conditions classifiable elsewhere (737.41)
AHA: 1Q, '07, 20

Kyphosis and Lordosis

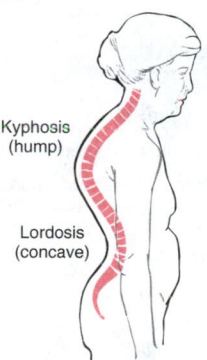

Kyphosis (hump)

Lordosis (concave)

Scoliosis and Kyphoscoliosis

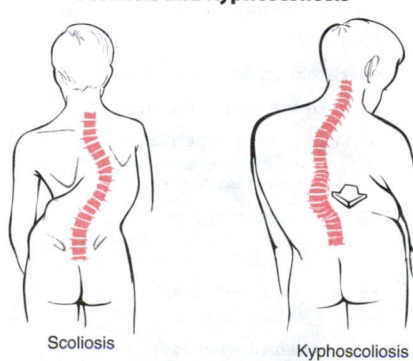

Scoliosis

Kyphoscoliosis

| √4th √5th Additional Digit Required | Unacceptable PDx | Manifestation Code | Hospital Acquired Condition | ▶◀ Revised Text | ● New Code | ▲ Revised Code Title |

2015 ICD-9-CM   **Volume 1 – 253**

✓5ᵗʰ **737.2 Lordosis (acquired)**
> **DEF:** Swayback appearance created by an abnormally increased spinal curvature; it is also referred to as "hollow back" or "saddle back."

737.20 Lordosis (acquired) (postural)

737.21 Lordosis, postlaminectomy

737.22 Other postsurgical lordosis

737.29 Other
> **EXCLUDES** *that associated with conditions classifiable elsewhere (737.42)*

✓5ᵗʰ **737.3 Kyphoscoliosis and scoliosis**
> **DEF:** Kyphoscoliosis: backward and lateral curvature of the spinal column; it is found in vertebral osteochondrosis.
> **DEF:** Scoliosis: an abnormal deviation of the spine to the left or right of the midline.

737.30 Scoliosis [and kyphoscoliosis], idiopathic
> **AHA:** 3Q, '03, 19
> **M41.115** Juvenile idiopathic scoliosis thoracolumbar region   `I-10`

737.31 Resolving infantile idiopathic scoliosis

737.32 Progressive infantile idiopathic scoliosis
> **AHA:** 3Q, '02, 12

737.33 Scoliosis due to radiation

737.34 Thoracogenic scoliosis

737.39 Other
> **EXCLUDES** *that associated with conditions classifiable elsewhere (737.43)*
> *that in kyphoscoliotic heart disease (416.1)*
> **AHA:** 2Q, '02, 16

✓5ᵗʰ **737.4 Curvature of spine associated with other conditions**
> *Code first associated condition as:*
> Charcôt-Marie-Tooth disease (356.1)
> mucopolysaccharidosis (277.5)
> neurofibromatosis (237.70-237.79)
> osteitis deformans (731.0)
> osteitis fibrosa cystica (252.01)
> osteoporosis (733.00-733.09)
> poliomyelitis (138)
> tuberculosis [Pott's curvature] (015.0)

737.40 Curvature of spine, unspecified

737.41 Kyphosis

737.42 Lordosis

737.43 Scoliosis

737.8 Other curvatures of spine

737.9 Unspecified curvature of spine
> Curvature of spine (acquired) (idiopathic) NOS
> Hunchback, acquired
> **EXCLUDES** *deformity of spine NOS (738.5)*

✓4ᵗʰ **738 Other acquired deformity**
> **EXCLUDES** *congenital (754.0-756.9, 758.0-759.9)*
> *dentofacial anomalies (524.0-524.9)*

738.0 Acquired deformity of nose
> Deformity of nose (acquired)
> Overdevelopment of nasal bones
> **EXCLUDES** *deflected or deviated nasal septum (470)*

✓5ᵗʰ **738.1 Other acquired deformity of head**

738.10 Unspecified deformity

738.11 Zygomatic hyperplasia
> **DEF:** Abnormal enlargement of the zygoma (processus zygomaticus temporalis).

738.12 Zygomatic hypoplasia
> **DEF:** Underdevelopment of the zygoma (processus zygomaticus temporalis).

738.19 Other specified deformity
> **AHA:** 1Q, '06, 6; 2Q, '03, 13

738.2 Acquired deformity of neck

738.3 Acquired deformity of chest and rib
> Deformity: Pectus:
> chest (acquired)   carinatum, acquired
> rib (acquired)   excavatum, acquired

738.4 Acquired spondylolisthesis
> Degenerative spondylolisthesis
> Spondylolysis, acquired
> **EXCLUDES** *congenital (756.12)*
> **DEF:** Vertebra displaced forward over another; due to bilateral defect in vertebral arch, eroded articular surface of posterior facets and elongated pedicle between fifth lumbar vertebra and sacrum.
> **AHA:** 4Q, '07, 120; 1Q, '07, 10
> **M43.10** Spondylolisthesis site unspecified   `I-10`

738.5 Other acquired deformity of back or spine
> Deformity of spine NOS
> **EXCLUDES** *curvature of spine (737.0-737.9)*
> **AHA:** 1Q, '08, 11
> **TIP:** Assign for post procedural flat back syndrome, which may be the result of a previous spinal fusion surgery. Do not assign a surgical complication code.

738.6 Acquired deformity of pelvis
> Pelvic obliquity
> **EXCLUDES** *intrapelvic protrusion of acetabulum (718.6)*
> *that in relation to labor and delivery (653.0-653.4, 653.8-653.9)*
> **DEF:** Pelvic obliquity: slanting or inclination of the pelvis at an angle between 55 and 60 degrees between the plane of the pelvis and the horizontal plane.

738.7 Cauliflower ear
> **DEF:** Abnormal external ear; due to injury, subsequent perichondritis.

738.8 Acquired deformity of other specified site
> Deformity of clavicle
> **AHA:** 2Q, '01, 15

738.9 Acquired deformity of unspecified site

✓4ᵗʰ **739 Nonallopathic lesions, not elsewhere classified**
> **INCLUDES** segmental dysfunction
> somatic dysfunction
> **DEF:** Disability, loss of function or abnormality of a body part that is neither classifiable to a particular system nor brought about therapeutically to counteract another disease.

739.0 Head region
> Occipitocervical region

739.1 Cervical region
> Cervicothoracic region

739.2 Thoracic region
> Thoracolumbar region

739.3 Lumbar region
> Lumbosacral region

739.4 Sacral region
> Sacrococcygeal region
> Sacroiliac region

739.5 Pelvic region
> Hip region
> Pubic region

739.6 Lower extremities

739.7 Upper extremities
> Acromioclavicular region
> Sternoclavicular region

739.8 Rib cage
> Costochondral region
> Costovertebral region
> Sternochondral region

739.9 Abdomen and other
> **AHA:** 2Q, '89, 14

N Newborn Age: 0   **P** Pediatric Age: 0-17   **M** Maternity Age: 12-55   **A** Adult Age: 15-124   **MCC** Major CC Condition   **CC** CC Condition   **HIV** HIV Related Dx

254 – Volume 1   **2015 ICD-9-CM**

14. Congenital Anomalies (740-759)

AHA: 2Q, '12, 17

TIP: Codes from chapter 14 may be assigned throughout the life of the patient, whenever the congenital anomaly is diagnosed.

✓4ᵗʰ 740 Anencephalus and similar anomalies

740.0 Anencephalus   `MCC`
Acrania
Amyelencephalus
Hemicephaly
Hemianencephaly
DEF: Fetus without cerebrum, cerebellum and flat bones of skull.
CC Excl: 740.0-740.2

740.1 Craniorachischisis   `MCC`
DEF: Congenital slit in cranium and vertebral column.
CC Excl: See code: 740.0

740.2 Iniencephaly   `MCC`
DEF: Spinal cord passes through enlarged occipital bone (foramen magnum); absent vertebral bone layer and spinal processes; resulting in both reduction in number and proper fusion of the vertebrae.
CC Excl: See code: 740.0

✓4ᵗʰ 741 Spina bifida

EXCLUDES spina bifida occulta (756.17)

The following fifth-digit subclassification is for use with category 741:
  0 unspecified region
  1 cervical region
  2 dorsal [thoracic] region
  3 lumbar region

DEF: Lack of closure of spinal cord's bony encasement; marked by cord protrusion into lumbosacral area; evident by elevated alpha-fetoprotein of amniotic fluid.
AHA: 3Q, '94, 7
TIP: For Arnold-Chiari syndrome, Type I, refer to code 348.4.

§ ✓5ᵗʰ 741.0 With hydrocephalus   `CC`
[0-3]   Arnold-Chiari syndrome, type II
Chiari malformation, type II
Any condition classifiable to 741.9 with any condition classifiable to 742.3
CC Excl: 741.00-741.93, 742.59-742.9, 759.7-759.89
AHA: 4Q, '97, 51; 4Q, '94, 37; S-O, '87, 10
Q05.4 Unspecified spina bifida with hydrocephalus   `I-10`

§ ✓5ᵗʰ 741.9 Without mention of hydrocephalus
[0-3]   Hydromeningocele (spinal)
Hydromyelocele
Meningocele (spinal)
Meningomyelocele
Myelocele
Myelocystocele
Rachischisis
Spina bifida (aperta)
Syringomyelocele
Q05.8 Sacral spina bifida without hydrocephalus   `I-10`

✓4ᵗʰ 742 Other congenital anomalies of nervous system

EXCLUDES congenital central alveolar hypoventilation syndrome (327.25)

742.0 Encephalocele   `CC`
Encephalocystocele
Encephalomyelocele
Hydroencephalocele
Hydromeningocele, cranial
Meningocele, cerebral
Meningoencephalocele
DEF: Brain tissue protrudes through skull defect.
CC Excl: 742.0-742.2, 742.4
AHA: 4Q, '94, 37

742.1 Microcephalus
Hydromicrocephaly
Micrencephaly
DEF: Extremely small head or brain.

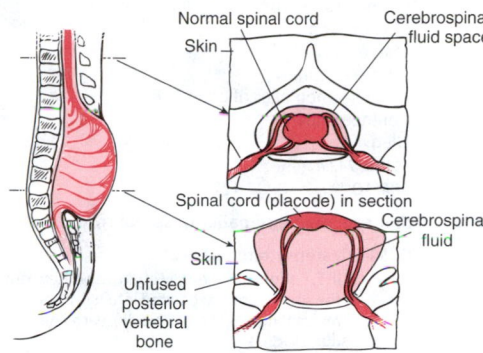

Spina Bifida

Normal spinal cord — Skin — Cerebrospinal fluid space

Spinal cord (placode) in section — Cerebrospinal fluid

Skin — Unfused posterior vertebral bone

742.2 Reduction deformities of brain   `MCC`
Absence
Agenesis   } of part of brain
Aplasia
Hypoplasia
Agyria
Arhinencephaly
Holoprosencephaly
Microgyria
CC Excl: See code 742.0
AHA: 3Q, '03, 15; 4Q, '94, 37
TIP: Assign for septo-optic dysplasia.

742.3 Congenital hydrocephalus
Aqueduct of Sylvius:
  anomaly
  obstruction, congenital
  stenosis
Atresia of foramina of Magendie and Luschka
Hydrocephalus in newborn
EXCLUDES hydrocephalus:
  acquired (331.3-331.4)
  due to congenital toxoplasmosis (771.2)
  with any condition classifiable to 741.9 (741.0)
DEF: Fluid accumulation within the skull; involves subarachnoid (external) or ventricular (internal) brain spaces.
AHA: 4Q, '05, 83
Q03.9 Congenital hydrocephalus unspecified   `I-10`

Normal Ventricles and Hydrocephalus

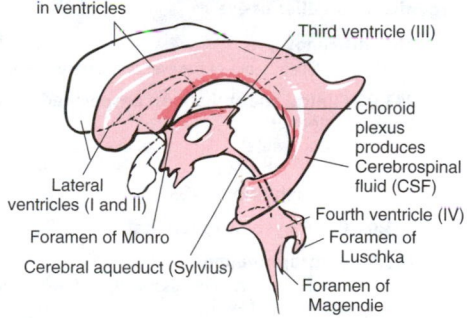

Cerebrospinal fluid in ventricles   **Normal Ventricles**
Third ventricle (III)
Choroid plexus produces Cerebrospinal fluid (CSF)
Lateral ventricles (I and II)
Foramen of Monro
Cerebral aqueduct (Sylvius)
Fourth ventricle (IV)
Foramen of Luschka
Foramen of Magendie

Hydrocephalus

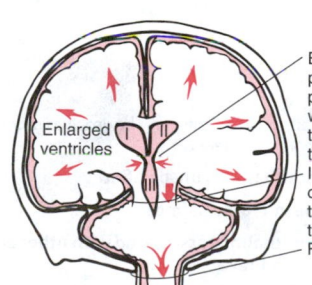

Enlarged ventricles
Blockage of any CSF passage increases pressure in skull, which may push tissue through the Incisura tentorii or through the Foramen magnum

---

§   Requires fifth digit. Valid digits are in [brackets] under each code. See category 741 for codes and defintions.

✓4ᵗʰ ✓5ᵗʰ Additional Digit Required   Unacceptable PDx   Manifestation Code   Hospital Acquired Condition   ►◄ Revised Text   ● New Code   ▲ Revised Code Title

2015 ICD-9-CM   **Volume 1 – 255**

742.4 Other specified anomalies of brain `CC`
Congenital cerebral cyst
Macroencephaly
Macrogyria
Megalencephaly
Multiple anomalies of brain NOS
Porencephaly
Ulegyria
CC Excl: 742.4
AHA: 1Q, '99, 9; 3Q, '92, 12

✓5ᵗʰ **742.5 Other specified anomalies of spinal cord**

742.51 Diastematomyelia
DEF: Congenital anomaly often associated with spina bifida; the spinal cord is separated into halves by a bony tissue resembling a "spike" (a spicule), each half surrounded by a dural sac.

742.53 Hydromyelia
Hydrorhachis
DEF: Dilated central spinal cord canal; characterized by increased fluid accumulation.

742.59 Other
Amyelia
Atelomyelia
Congenital anomaly of spinal meninges
Defective development of cauda equina
Hypoplasia of spinal cord
Myelatelia
Myelodysplasia
AHA: 2Q, '91, 14; 1Q, '89, 10
TIP: Assign for tethered spinal cord syndrome, regardless of when it is diagnosed.

742.8 Other specified anomalies of nervous system
Agenesis of nerve
Displacement of brachial plexus
Familial dysautonomia
Jaw-winking syndrome
Marcus-Gunn syndrome
Riley-Day syndrome
EXCLUDES *neurofibromatosis (237.70-237.79)*

742.9 Unspecified anomaly of brain, spinal cord, and nervous system
Anomaly
Congenital:
  disease   of: { brain
  lesion   nervous system
  Deformity   spinal cord

✓4ᵗʰ **743 Congenital anomalies of eye**

✓5ᵗʰ **743.0 Anophthalmos**
DEF: Complete absence of the eyes or the presence of vestigial eyes.

743.00 Clinical anophthalmos, unspecified
Agenesis
Congenital } of eye
  absence
Anophthalmos NOS

743.03 Cystic eyeball, congenital

743.06 Cryptophthalmos
DEF: Skin is continuous over eyeball, results in apparent absence of eyelids.

✓5ᵗʰ **743.1 Microphthalmos**
Dysplasia } of eye
Hypoplasia
Rudimentary eye
DEF: Abnormally small eyeballs, may be opacities of cornea and lens, scarring of choroid and retina.

743.10 Microphthalmos, unspecified

743.11 Simple microphthalmos

743.12 Microphthalmos associated with other anomalies of eye and adnexa

✓5ᵗʰ **743.2 Buphthalmos**
Glaucoma:
  congenital
  newborn
Hydrophthalmos
EXCLUDES *glaucoma of childhood (365.14)*
  traumatic glaucoma due to birth injury (767.8)
DEF: Distended, enlarged fibrous coats of eye; due to intraocular pressure of congenital glaucoma.

743.20 Buphthalmos, unspecified

743.21 Simple buphthalmos

743.22 Buphthalmos associated with other ocular anomalies
Keratoglobus, congenital } associated with
Megalocornea   buphthalmos

✓5ᵗʰ **743.3 Congenital cataract and lens anomalies**
EXCLUDES *infantile cataract (366.00-366.09)*
DEF: Opaque eye lens.

743.30 Congenital cataract, unspecified

743.31 Capsular and subcapsular cataract

743.32 Cortical and zonular cataract

743.33 Nuclear cataract

743.34 Total and subtotal cataract, congenital

743.35 Congenital aphakia
Congenital absence of lens

743.36 Anomalies of lens shape
Microphakia
Spherophakia

743.37 Congenital ectopic lens

743.39 Other

✓5ᵗʰ **743.4 Coloboma and other anomalies of anterior segment**
DEF: Coloboma: ocular tissue defect associated with defect of ocular fetal intraocular fissure; may cause small pit on optic disk, major defects of iris, ciliary body, choroid, and retina.

743.41 Anomalies of corneal size and shape
Microcornea
EXCLUDES *that associated with buphthalmos (743.22)*

743.42 Corneal opacities, interfering with vision, congenital

743.43 Other corneal opacities, congenital

743.44 Specified anomalies of anterior chamber, chamber angle, and related structures
Anomaly:
  Axenfeld's
  Peters'
  Rieger's

743.45 Aniridia
DEF: Incompletely formed or absent iris; affects both eyes; dominant trait; also called congenital absence of iris.
AHA: 2Q, '10, 4-5; 3Q, '02, 20

743.46 Other specified anomalies of iris and ciliary body
Anisocoria, congenital   Coloboma of iris
Atresia of pupil   Corectopia

743.47 Specified anomalies of sclera

743.48 Multiple and combined anomalies of anterior segment

743.49 Other

✓5ᵗʰ **743.5 Congenital anomalies of posterior segment**

743.51 Vitreous anomalies
Congenital vitreous opacity

743.52 Fundus coloboma
DEF: Absent retinal and choroidal tissue; occurs in lower fundus; a bright white ectatic zone of exposed sclera extends into and changes the optic disk.

743.53 Chorioretinal degeneration, congenital

743.54 Congenital folds and cysts of posterior segment

743.55 Congenital macular changes

`N` Newborn Age: 0   `P` Pediatric Age: 0-17   `M` Maternity Age: 12-55   `A` Adult Age: 15-124   `MCC` Major CC Condition   `CC` CC Condition   `HIV` HIV Related Dx

256 – Volume 1   2015 ICD-9-CM

743.56 Other retinal changes, congenital
AHA: 3Q, '99, 12

743.57 Specified anomalies of optic disc
Coloboma of optic disc (congenital)

743.58 Vascular anomalies
Congenital retinal aneurysm

743.59 Other

√5ᵗʰ **743.6 Congenital anomalies of eyelids, lacrimal system, and orbit**

    743.61 Congenital ptosis
      DEF: Drooping of eyelid.

    743.62 Congenital deformities of eyelids
      Ablepharon
      Absence of eyelid
      Accessory eyelid
      Congenital:
        ectropion
        entropion
      AHA: 1Q, '00, 22
      TIP: Assign for epiblepharon, in which a redundant horizontal skin fold under the eyelid causes an abnormal vertical orientation of the eyelashes; may result in the eyelashes touching the eyeball.

    743.63 Other specified congenital anomalies of eyelid
      Absence, agenesis, of cilia

    743.64 Specified congenital anomalies of lacrimal gland

    743.65 Specified congenital anomalies of lacrimal passages
      Absence, agenesis of:
        lacrimal apparatus
        punctum lacrimale
      Accessory lacrimal canal

    743.66 Specified congenital anomalies of orbit

    743.69 Other
      Accessory eye muscles

743.8 Other specified anomalies of eye
    EXCLUDES *congenital nystagmus (379.51)*
      ocular albinism (270.2)
      optic nerve hypoplasia (377.43)
      retinitis pigmentosa (362.74)

743.9 Unspecified anomaly of eye
  Congenital:
  anomaly NOS   } of eye (any part)
  deformity NOS

√4ᵗʰ **744 Congenital anomalies of ear, face, and neck**
  EXCLUDES *anomaly of:*
    cervical spine (754.2, 756.10-756.19)
    larynx (748.2-748.3)
    nose (748.0-748.1)
    parathyroid gland (759.2)
    thyroid gland (759.2)
    cleft lip (749.10-749.25)

√5ᵗʰ **744.0 Anomalies of ear causing impairment of hearing**
    EXCLUDES *congenital deafness without mention of cause (389.0-389.9)*

    744.00 Unspecified anomaly of ear with impairment of hearing

    744.01 Absence of external ear
      Absence of:
        auditory canal (external)
        auricle (ear) (with stenosis or atresia of auditory canal)

    744.02 Other anomalies of external ear with impairment of hearing
      Atresia or stricture of auditory canal (external)

    744.03 Anomaly of middle ear, except ossicles
      Atresia or stricture of osseous meatus (ear)

    744.04 Anomalies of ear ossicles
      Fusion of ear ossicles

744.05 Anomalies of inner ear
  Congenital anomaly of:
    membranous labyrinth
    organ of Corti

744.09 Other
  Absence of ear, congenital

744.1 Accessory auricle
  Accessory tragus
  Polyotia
  Preauricular appendage
  Supernumerary:
    ear
    lobule
  DEF: Redundant tissue or structures of ear.

√5ᵗʰ **744.2 Other specified anomalies of ear**
    EXCLUDES *that with impairment of hearing (744.00-744.09)*

    744.21 Absence of ear lobe, congenital

    744.22 Macrotia
      DEF: Abnormally large pinna of ear.

    744.23 Microtia
      DEF: Hypoplasia of pinna; associated with absent or closed auditory canal.

    744.24 Specified anomalies of Eustachian tube
      Absence of Eustachian tube

    744.29 Other
      Bat ear
      Darwin's tubercle
      Pointed ear
      Prominence of auricle
      Ridge ear
      EXCLUDES *preauricular sinus (744.46)*

744.3 Unspecified anomaly of ear
  Congenital:
  anomaly NOS   } of ear, not elsewhere
  deformity NOS   classified

√6ᵗʰ **744.4 Branchial cleft cyst or fistula; preauricular sinus**

    744.41 Branchial cleft sinus or fistula
      Branchial:
        sinus (external) (internal)
        vestige
      DEF: Cyst due to failed closure of embryonic branchial cleft.

    744.42 Branchial cleft cyst

    744.43 Cervical auricle

    744.46 Preauricular sinus or fistula

    744.47 Preauricular cyst

    744.49 Other
      Fistula (of):
        auricle, congenital
        cervicoaural

744.5 Webbing of neck
  Pterygium colli
  DEF: Thick, triangular skinfold, stretches from lateral side of neck across shoulder; associated with Turner's and Noonan's syndromes.

√5ᵗʰ **744.8 Other specified anomalies of face and neck**

    744.81 Macrocheilia
      Hypertrophy of lip, congenital
      DEF: Abnormally large lips.

    744.82 Microcheilia
      DEF: Abnormally small lips.

    744.83 Macrostomia
      DEF: Bilateral or unilateral anomaly of mouth due to malformed maxillary and mandibular processes; results in mouth extending toward ear.

    744.84 Microstomia
      DEF: Abnormally small mouth.

    744.89 Other
      EXCLUDES *congenital fistula of lip (750.25)*
        musculoskeletal anomalies (754.0-754.1, 756.0)

√4ᵗʰ √5ᵗʰ Additional Digit Required   Unacceptable PDx   Manifestation Code   Hospital Acquired Condition   ▶◀ Revised Text   ● New Code   ▲ Revised Code Title

2015 ICD-9-CM   **Volume 1 – 257**

Congenital Anomalies

744.9–746.1

744.9 Unspecified anomalies of face and neck
Congenital:
anomaly NOS } of face [any part] or neck [any
deformity NOS } part]

√4ᵗʰ **745 Bulbus cordis anomalies and anomalies of cardiac septal closure**

745.0 Common truncus `MCC`
Absent septum } between aorta and
Communication (abnormal) } pulmonary artery
Aortic septal defect
Common aortopulmonary trunk
Persistent truncus arteriosus
CC Excl: 429.71–429.79, 745.0–745.9, 746.89–746.9, 747.83–747.9, 759.7–759.89

√5ᵗʰ **745.1 Transposition of great vessels**

745.10 Complete transposition of great vessels `MCC`
Transposition of great vessels:
NOS
classical
CC Excl: See code 745.0

745.11 Double outlet right ventricle `MCC`
Dextratransposition of aorta
Incomplete transposition of great vessels
Origin of both great vessels from right ventricle
Taussig-Bing syndrome or defect
CC Excl: See code 745.0

745.12 Corrected transposition of great vessels `CC`
CC Excl: See code 745.0

745.19 Other `MCC`
CC Excl: See code 745.0

745.2 Tetralogy of Fallot `MCC`
Fallot's pentalogy
Ventricular septal defect with pulmonary stenosis or atresia,
dextraposition of aorta, and hypertrophy of right
ventricle
EXCLUDES Fallot's triad (746.09)
DEF: Obstructed cardiac outflow causes pulmonary stenosis,
interventricular septal defect and right ventricular hypertrophy.
CC Excl: See code 745.0

745.3 Common ventricle `MCC`
Cor triloculare biatriatum
Single ventricle
CC Excl: See code 745.0

745.4 Ventricular septal defect `CC`
Eisenmenger's defect or complex
Gerbo dedefect
Interventricular septal defect
Left ventricular-right atrial communication
Roger's disease
EXCLUDES common atrioventricular canal type (745.69)
single ventricle (745.3)
CC Excl: See code 745.0
Q21.0 Ventricular septal defect `I-10`

Heart Defects

Atrial septal defect

Aortic stenosis

Patent ductus arteriosus

Transposition of the great vessels

Ventricular septal defect

Pulmonary stenosis

Tetralogy of Fallot

745.5 Ostium secundum type atrial septal defect `CC`
Defect:
atrium secundum
fossa ovalis
Lutembacher's syndrome
Patent or persistent:
foramen ovale
ostium secundum
DEF: Opening in atrial septum due to failure of the septum
secundum and the endocardial cushions to fuse; there is a rim of
septum surrounding the defect.
CC Excl: 429.71–429.79, 745.0–745.3, 745.5–745.9, 746.89–746.9,
747.89–747.9, 759.7, 759.89
AHA: 2Q, '12, 3; 3Q, '09, 17
Q21.1 Atrial septal defect `I-10`

√5ᵗʰ **745.6 Endocardial cushion defects**
DEF: Atrial and/or ventricular septal defects causing abnormal fusion
of cushions in atrioventricular canal.

745.60 Endocardial cushion defect, unspecified type `CC`
DEF: Septal defect due to imperfect fusion of endocardial
cushions.
CC Excl: See code 745.0

745.61 Ostium primum defect `CC`
Persistent ostium primum
DEF: Opening in low, posterior septum primum; causes cleft
in basal portion of atrial septum; associated with cleft
mitral valve.
CC Excl: See code: 745.0

745.69 Other `CC`
Absence of atrial septum
Atrioventricular canal type ventricular septal defect
Common atrioventricular canal
Common atrium
CC Excl: See code 745.0

745.7 Cor biloculare `MCC`
Absence of atrial and ventricular septa
DEF: Atrial and ventricular septal defect; marked by heart with two
cardiac chambers (one atrium, one ventricle), and one
atrioventricular valve.
CC Excl: See code 745.0

745.8 Other

745.9 Unspecified defect of septal closure
Septal defect NOS

√4ᵗʰ **746 Other congenital anomalies of heart**
EXCLUDES endocardial fibroelastosis (425.3)

√5ᵗʰ **746.0 Anomalies of pulmonary valve**
EXCLUDES infundibular or subvalvular pulmonic stenosis
(746.83)
tetralogy of Fallot (745.2)

746.00 Pulmonary valve anomaly, unspecified `CC`
CC Excl: 746.00–746.09, 746.89–746.9, 747.89–747.9, 759.7, 759.89

746.01 Atresia, congenital `MCC`
Congenital absence of pulmonary valve
CC Excl: 746.00–746.09, 746.89–746.9, 747.89–747.9, 759.7, 759.89

746.02 Stenosis, congenital `CC`
DEF: Stenosis of opening between pulmonary artery and
right ventricle; causes obstructed blood outflow from right
ventricle.
CC Excl: See code 746.01
AHA: 1Q, '04, 16

746.09 Other `CC`
Congenital insufficiency of pulmonary valve
Fallot's triad or trilogy
CC Excl: See code: 746.00

746.1 Tricuspid atresia and stenosis, congenital `MCC`
Absence of tricuspid valve
CC Excl: 746.1–746.7, 746.89–746.9, 747.83–747.9, 759.7–759.89

`N` Newborn Age: 0   `P` Pediatric Age: 0-17   `M` Maternity Age: 12-55   `A` Adult Age: 15-124   `MCC` Major CC Condition   `CC` CC Condition   `HIV` HIV Related Dx

746.2 Ebstein's anomaly `MCC`

DEF: Malformation of the tricuspid valve characterized by septal and posterior leaflets attaching to the wall of the right ventricle; causing the right ventricle to fuse with the atrium into a large right atrium and a small ventricle; causes heart failure and abnormal cardiac rhythm.

CC Excl: See code 746.1

746.3 Congenital stenosis of aortic valve `CC`

Congenital aortic stenosis

EXCLUDES congenital:
subaortic stenosis (746.81)
supravalvular aortic stenosis (747.22)

DEF: Stenosis of orifice of aortic valve; obstructs blood outflow from left ventricle.

CC Excl: See code 746.1

AHA: 4Q, '88, 8

746.4 Congenital insufficiency of aortic valve `CC`

Bicuspid aortic valve
Congenital aortic insufficiency

DEF: Impaired functioning of aortic valve due to incomplete closure; causes backflow (regurgitation) of blood from aorta to left ventricle.

CC Excl: See code 746.1

Q23.1 Congenital insufficiency of aortic valve `I-10`

746.5 Congenital mitral stenosis `CC`

Fused commissure
Parachute deformity　}　of mitral valve
Supernumerary cusps

DEF: Stenosis of left atrioventricular orifice.

CC Excl: See code 746.1

AHA: 3Q, '07, 3

746.6 Congenital mitral insufficiency `CC`

DEF: Impaired functioning of mitral valve due to incomplete closure; causes backflow of blood from left ventricle to left atrium.

CC Excl: See code 746.1

746.7 Hypoplastic left heart syndrome `MCC`

Atresia, or marked hypoplasia, of aortic orifice or valve, with hypoplasia of ascending aorta and defective development of left ventricle (with mitral valve atresia)

CC Excl: See code 746.1

√5ᵗʰ **746.8 Other specified anomalies of heart**

746.81 Subaortic stenosis `MCC`

DEF: Stenosis, of left ventricular outflow tract due to fibrous tissue ring or septal hypertrophy below aortic valve.

CC Excl: 746.81-746.84, 746.89-746.9, 747.83-747.9, 759.7-759.89

AHA: 3Q, '07, 3

746.82 Cor triatriatum `MCC`

DEF: Transverse septum divides left atrium due to failed resorption of embryonic common pulmonary vein; results in three atrial chambers.

CC Excl: See code 746.81

746.83 Infundibular pulmonic stenosis `CC`

Subvalvular pulmonic stenosis

DEF: Stenosis of right ventricle outflow tract within infundibulum due to fibrous diaphragm below valve or long, narrow fibromuscular channel.

CC Excl: See code 746.81

746.84 Obstructive anomalies of heart, not elsewhere classified `MCC`

Shone's syndrome　　　　　Uhl's disease

Use additional code for associated anomalies, such as:
coarctation of aorta (747.10)
congenital mitral stenosis (746.5)
subaortic stenosis (746.81)

CC Excl: See code: 746.81

AHA: 2Q, '12, 3

746.85 Coronary artery anomaly `CC`

Anomalous origin or communication of coronary artery
Arteriovenous malformation of coronary artery
Coronary artery:
absence
arising from aorta or pulmonary trunk
single

CC Excl: 746.85, 746.89-746.9

AHA: N-D, '85, 3

746.86 Congenital heart block `MCC`

Complete or incomplete atrioventricular [AV] block

DEF: Impaired conduction of electrical impulses; due to maldeveloped junctional tissue.

CC Excl: 746.86, 746.89-746.9, 747.83-747.9, 759.7-759.89

746.87 Malposition of heart and cardiac apex `CC`

Abdominal heart
Dextrocardia
Ectopia cordis
Levocardia (isolated)
Mesocardia

EXCLUDES dextrocardia with complete transposition of viscera (759.3)

CC Excl: 746.81-746.84, 746.87-746.9, 747.89-747.9, 759.7, 759.89

746.89 Other

Atresia　　　}　of cardiac vein
Hypoplasia

Congenital:
cardiomegaly
diverticulum, left ventricle
pericardial defect

AHA: 3Q, '00, 3; 1Q, '99, 11; J-F, '85, 3

TIP: Assign for Brugada syndrome. Additional codes may be required.

Q24.8 Other specified congenital malformations of heart `I-10`

746.9 Unspecified anomaly of heart

Congenital:
anomaly of heart NOS
heart disease NOS

√4ᵗʰ **747 Other congenital anomalies of circulatory system**

747.0 Patent ductus arteriosus `CC`

Patent ductus Botalli
Persistent ductus arteriosus

DEF: Open lumen in ductus arteriosus causes arterial blood recirculation in lungs; inhibits blood supply to aorta; symptoms such as shortness of breath more noticeable upon activity.

CC Excl: 747.0, 747.89

AHA: 3Q, '09, 17

Q25.0 Patent ductus arteriosus `I-10`

√5ᵗʰ **747.1 Coarctation of aorta**

DEF: Localized deformity of aortic media seen as a severe constriction of the vessel lumen; major symptom is high blood pressure in the arms and low pressure in the legs; may result in a CVA, rupture of the aorta, bacterial endocarditis or congestive heart failure.

747.10 Coarctation of aorta (preductal) (postductal) `CC`

Hypoplasia of aortic arch

CC Excl: 747.10-747.22, 747.89-747.9, 759.7, 759.89

AHA: 3Q, '07, 3; 1Q, '99, 11; 4Q, '88, 8

747.11 Interruption of aortic arch `MCC`

CC Excl: 747.10-747.22, 747.83-747.9, 759.7-759.89

√5ᵗʰ **747.2 Other anomalies of aorta**

747.20 Anomaly of aorta, unspecified `CC`

CC Excl: 747.10-747.22, 747.89-747.9, 759.7, 759.89

747.21 Anomalies of aortic arch `CC`

Anomalous origin, right subclavian artery
Dextraposition of aorta
Double aortic arch
Kommerell's diverticulum
Overriding aorta
Persistent:
convolutions, aortic arch
right aortic arch
Vascular ring

EXCLUDES hypoplasia of aortic arch (747.10)

CC Excl: See code: 747.20

AHA: 1Q, '03, 15

√4ᵗʰ
√5ᵗʰ
Additional Digit Required　　Unacceptable PDx　　Manifestation Code　　Hospital Acquired Condition　　►◄ Revised Text　　● New Code　　▲ Revised Code Title

2015 ICD-9-CM　　　　　　　　　　　　　　　　　　　　　　　　　　　　　　　　**Volume 1 – 259**

Congenital Anomalies

747.22–747.83

747.22 Atresia and stenosis of aorta `CC`

Absence
Aplasia   } of aorta
Hypoplasia
Stricture

Supra (valvular)-aortic stenosis

EXCLUDES *congenital aortic (valvular) stenosis or*
stricture, so stated (746.3)
hypoplasia of aorta in hypoplastic left heart
syndrome (746.7)

CC Excl: 747.10-747.22, 747.83-747.9, 759.7-759.89

747.29 Other `CC`

Aneurysm of sinus of Valsalva
Congenital:

aneurysm   } of aorta
dilation

CC Excl: 747.10-747.29, 747.89-747.9, 759.7, 759.89

✓5ᵗʰ **747.3 Anomalies of pulmonary artery**

AHA: 4Q, '11, 137-138

747.31 Pulmonary artery coarctation and atresia `MCC`

Agenesis of pulmonary artery
Atresia of pulmonary artery
Coarctation of pulmonary artery
Hypoplasia of pulmonary artery
Stenosis of pulmonary artery

CC Excl: 747.31-747.39, 747.89-747.9
AHA: 2Q, '12, 3

747.32 Pulmonary arteriovenous malformation `MCC`

Pulmonary arteriovenous aneurysm

EXCLUDES *acquired pulmonary arteriovenous fistula*
(417.0)

CC Excl: See code 747.31
AHA: 4Q, '11, 138

747.39 Other anomalies of pulmonary artery and `MCC`
pulmonary circulation

Anomaly of pulmonary artery

CC Excl: See code 747.31
AHA: 3Q, '10, 9; 3Q, '09, 17, 18; 1Q, '04, 16; 1Q, '94, 15;
4Q, '88, 8

TIP: Assign for peripheral pulmonary stenosis (PPS)
murmur.

Q25.7 Oth congenital malformations pulmonary artery `I-10`

✓5ᵗʰ **747.4 Anomalies of great veins**

747.40 Anomaly of great veins, unspecified `CC`

Anomaly NOS of:
pulmonary veins
vena cava

CC Excl: 747.40, 747.89-747.9

747.41 Total anomalous pulmonary venous connection `CC`

Total anomalous pulmonary venous return [TAPVR]:
subdiaphragmatic
supradiaphragmatic

CC Excl: 747.41, 747.89-747.9

747.42 Partial anomalous pulmonary venous `CC`
connection

Partial anomalous pulmonary venous return

CC Excl: 747.42, 747.89-747.9

747.49 Other anomalies of great veins `CC`

Absence   } of vena cava (inferior)
Congenital stenosis } (superior)

Persistent:
left posterior cardinal vein
left superior vena cava

Scimitar syndrome
Transposition of pulmonary veins NOS

CC Excl: 747.49, 747.89-747.9

747.5 Absence or hypoplasia of umbilical artery

Single umbilical artery

✓5ᵗʰ **747.6 Other anomalies of peripheral vascular system**

Absence   }
Anomaly   } of artery or vein, NEC
Atresia

Arteriovenous aneurysm (peripheral)
Arteriovenous malformation of the peripheral vascular system
Congenital:
aneurysm (peripheral)
phlebectasia
stricture, artery
varix

Multiple renal arteries

EXCLUDES *anomalies of:*
cerebral vessels (747.81)
pulmonary artery (747.39)
congenital retinal aneurysm (743.58)
hemangioma (228.00-228.09)
lymphangioma (228.1)

747.60 Anomaly of the peripheral vascular system,
unspecified site

747.61 Gastrointestinal vessel anomaly

AHA: 3Q, '96, 10

TIP: Do not assign for gastric or intestinal AV malformation
or angiodysplasia not stated to be congenital. See instead
code 537.82, 537.83, 569.84, or 569.85.

747.62 Renal vessel anomaly

747.63 Upper limb vessel anomaly

747.64 Lower limb vessel anomaly

747.69 Anomalies of other specified sites of peripheral
vascular system

✓5ᵗʰ **747.8 Other specified anomalies of circulatory system**

747.81 Anomalies of cerebrovascular system `MCC`

Arteriovenous malformation of brain
Cerebral arteriovenous aneurysm, congenital
Congenital anomalies of cerebral vessels

EXCLUDES *ruptured cerebral (arteriovenous) aneurysm*
(430)

CC Excl: 747.81, 747.89-747.9
Q28.3 Other malformations of cerebral vessels `I-10`

747.82 Spinal vessel anomaly `CC`

Arteriovenous malformation of spinal vessel

CC Excl: 747.82, 747.89-747.9
AHA: 3Q, '95, 5

747.83 Persistent fetal circulation `MCC` `N`

Persistent pulmonary hypertension
Primary pulmonary hypertension of newborn

DEF: A return to fetal circulation due to constriction of
pulmonary arterioles and opening of the ductus arteriosus
and foramen ovale, right-to-left shunting, oxygenation of
the blood does not occur, and the lungs remain constricted
after birth; is seen in term or post-term infants; causes
include asphyxiation, meconium aspiration syndrome,
acidosis, sepsis, and developmental immaturity.

CC Excl: 416.0, 416.8-416.9
AHA: 4Q, '02, 62

Persistent Fetal Circulation

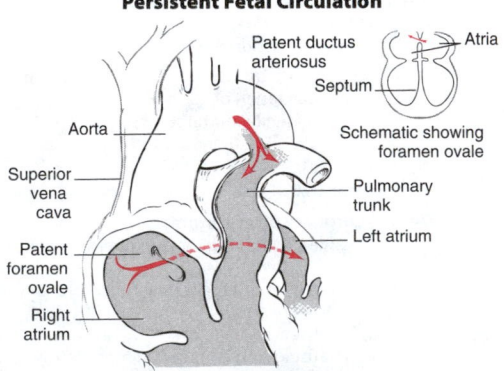

Patent ductus arteriosus — Atria
Septum
Schematic showing foramen ovale
Aorta
Superior vena cava
Pulmonary trunk
Left atrium
Patent foramen ovale
Right atrium

`N` Newborn Age: 0   `P` Pediatric Age: 0-17   `M` Maternity Age: 12-55   `A` Adult Age: 15-124   `MCC` Major CC Condition   `CC` CC Condition   `HIV` HIV Related Dx

260 – Volume 1   2015 ICD-9-CM

747.89 Other　　　　　　　　　　　　　　　　`CC`
Aneurysm, congenital, specified site not elsewhere classified
　　　EXCLUDES *congenital aneurysm:*
　　　　　　coronary (746.85)
　　　　　　peripheral (747.6)
　　　　　　pulmonary (747.39)
　　　　　　　arteriovenous (747.32)
　　　　　　retinal (743.58)
　　　CC Excl: 745.0-745.9, 747.89
　　　AHA: 4Q, '02, 63

747.9 Unspecified anomaly of circulatory system　`CC`
　　　CC Excl: 745.0-747.29, 747.31-747.82, 747.89-747.9

✓4ᵗʰ **748 Congenital anomalies of respiratory system**
　　　EXCLUDES *congenital central alveolar hypoventilation syndrome (327.25)*
　　　　　　congenital defect of diaphragm (756.6)

748.0 Choanal atresia
　Atresia
　Congenital stenosis } of nares (anterior) (posterior)
　　　DEF: Occluded posterior nares (choana), bony or membranous due to failure of embryonic bucconasal membrane to rupture.

748.1 Other anomalies of nose
　Absent nose
　Accessory nose
　Cleft nose
　Congenital:
　　deformity of nose
　　notching of tip of nose
　　perforation of wall of nasal sinus
　Deformity of wall of nasal sinus
　　　EXCLUDES *congenital deviation of nasal septum (754.0)*

748.2 Web of larynx
　Web of larynx:　　Web of larynx:
　　NOS　　　　　　subglottic
　　glottic
　　　DEF: Malformed larynx; marked by thin, translucent, or thick, fibrotic spread between vocal folds; affects speech.

748.3 Other anomalies of larynx, trachea, and bronchus　`CC`
　Absence or agenesis of:　Congenital:
　　bronchus　　　　　　　dilation, trachea
　　larynx　　　　　　　　stenosis:
　　trachea　　　　　　　　　larynx
　Anomaly (of):　　　　　　　　trachea
　　cricoid cartilage　　　　tracheocele
　　epiglottis　　　　　　Diverticulum:
　　thyroid cartilage　　　　bronchus
　　tracheal cartilage　　　　trachea
　Atresia (of):　　　　　Fissure of epiglottis
　　epiglottis　　　　　Laryngocele
　　glottis　　　　　　Posterior cleft of cricoid
　　larynx　　　　　　　　cartilage (congenital)
　　trachea　　　　　Rudimentary tracheal bronchus
　Cleft thyroid, cartilage,　Stridor, laryngeal, congenital
　　congenital
　　　CC Excl: 493.81, 519.19, 748.3, 748.8-748.9
　　　AHA: 1Q, '99, 14
　　　Q32.4 Other congenital malformations of bronchus　`I-10`

748.4 Congenital cystic lung　　　　　　　　`CC`
　Disease, lung:
　　cystic, congenital
　　polycystic, congenital
　Honeycomb lung, congenital
　　　EXCLUDES *acquired or unspecified cystic lung (518.89)*
　　　DEF: Enlarged air spaces of lung parenchyma.
　　　CC Excl: 748.4-748.9

748.5 Agenesis, hypoplasia, and dysplasia of lung　`MCC`
　Absence of lung (fissures) (lobe) (lobe)
　Aplasia of lung
　Hypoplasia of lung
　Sequestration of lung
　　　CC Excl: See code 748.4

✓5ᵗʰ **748.6 Other anomalies of lung**

　　748.60 Anomaly of lung, unspecified

748.61 Congenital bronchiectasis　　　　`CC`
　　　CC Excl: 494.0-494.1, 496, 506.1,506.4-506.9, 748.61

748.69 Other
　Accessory lung (lobe)
　Azygos lobe (fissure), lung

748.8 Other specified anomalies of respiratory system
　Abnormal communication between pericardial and pleural sacs
　Anomaly, pleural folds
　Atresia of nasopharynx
　Congenital cyst of mediastinum

748.9 Unspecified anomaly of respiratory system
　Anomaly of respiratory system NOS

✓4ᵗʰ **749 Cleft palate and cleft lip**
　　　AHA: 2Q, '12, 17

✓5ᵗʰ **749.0 Cleft palate**

　　749.00 Cleft palate, unspecified

　　749.01 Unilateral, complete

　　749.02 Unilateral, incomplete
　　　Cleft uvula

　　749.03 Bilateral, complete

　　749.04 Bilateral, incomplete

✓5ᵗʰ **749.1 Cleft lip**
　Cheiloschisis
　Congenital fissure of lip
　Harelip
　Labium leporinum

　　749.10 Cleft lip, unspecified

　　749.11 Unilateral, complete

　　749.12 Unilateral, incomplete

　　749.13 Bilateral, complete

　　749.14 Bilateral, incomplete

✓5ᵗʰ **749.2 Cleft palate with cleft lip**
　Cheilopalatoschisis

　　749.20 Cleft palate with cleft lip, unspecified

　　749.21 Unilateral, complete

　　749.22 Unilateral, incomplete

　　749.23 Bilateral, complete
　　　AHA: 1Q, '96, 14

　　749.24 Bilateral, incomplete

　　749.25 Other combinations

Cleft Lip and Palate

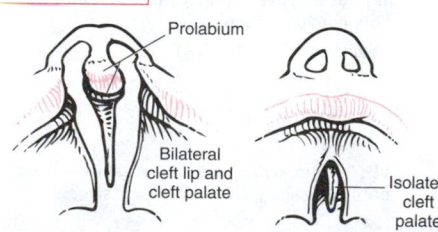

Unilateral cleft lip　　　　　　Cleft lip with cleft alveolar ridge
No cleft palate　　　　　　　　No cleft palate
　　　　　　　　　Unilateral cleft lip and cleft palate
　　　　　　　　　Alveolar ridge
　　　　　　　　　Cleft palate
Prolabium
Bilateral cleft lip and cleft palate
Isolated cleft palate

Congenital Anomalies

750–751.3

✔4ᵗʰ **750 Other congenital anomalies of upper alimentary tract**

EXCLUDES *dentofacial anomalies (524.0-524.9)*

750.0 Tongue tie
Ankyloglossia
DEF: Restricted tongue movement due to lingual frenum extending toward tip of tongue. Tongue may be fused to mouth floor affecting speech.

✔5ᵗʰ **750.1 Other anomalies of tongue**

750.10 Anomaly of tongue, unspecified

750.11 Aglossia
DEF: Absence of tongue.

750.12 Congenital adhesions of tongue

750.13 Fissure of tongue
Bifid tongue
Double tongue

750.15 Macroglossia
Congenital hypertrophy of tongue

750.16 Microglossia
Hypoplasia of tongue

750.19 Other

✔5ᵗʰ **750.2 Other specified anomalies of mouth and pharynx**

750.21 Absence of salivary gland

750.22 Accessory salivary gland

750.23 Atresia, salivary duct
Imperforate salivary duct

750.24 Congenital fistula of salivary gland

750.25 Congenital fistula of lip
Congenital (mucus) lip pits

750.26 Other specified anomalies of mouth
Absence of uvula

750.27 Diverticulum of pharynx
Pharyngeal pouch

750.29 Other specified anomalies of pharynx
Imperforate pharynx

750.3 Tracheoesophageal fistula, esophageal atresia and stenosis   `MCC`
Absent esophagus
Atresia of esophagus
Congenital:
  esophageal ring
  stenosis of esophagus
  stricture of esophagus
Congenital fistula:
  esophagobronchial
  esophagotracheal
Imperforate esophagus
Webbed esophagus
CC Excl: 530.84, 750.3-750.4, 751.8-751.9
AHA: 1Q, '12, 15

750.4 Other specified anomalies of esophagus   `CC`
Dilatation, congenital
Displacement, congenital
Diverticulum   } (of) esophagus
Duplication
Giant

Esophageal pouch
EXCLUDES *congenital hiatus hernia (750.6)*
CC Excl: 750.4, 751.8-751.9
AHA: J-F, '85, 3

750.5 Congenital hypertrophic pyloric stenosis
Congenital or infantile:
  constriction
  hypertrophy
  spasm   } of pylorus
  stenosis
  stricture

DEF: Obstructed pylorus due to overgrowth of pyloric muscle.
Q40.0 Congenital hypertrophic pyloric stenosis   `I-10`

750.6 Congenital hiatus hernia
Displacement of cardia through esophageal hiatus
EXCLUDES *congenital diaphragmatic hernia (756.6)*

750.7 Other specified anomalies of stomach
Congenital:
  cardiospasm
  hourglass stomach
Displacement of stomach
Diverticulum of stomach, congenital
Duplication of stomach
Megalogastria
Microgastria
Transposition of stomach

750.8 Other specified anomalies of upper alimentary tract

750.9 Unspecified anomaly of upper alimentary tract
Congenital:
  anomaly NOS   } of upper alimentary tract [any
  deformity NOS   }   part, except tongue]

✔4ᵗʰ **751 Other congenital anomalies of digestive system**

751.0 Meckel's diverticulum
Meckel's diverticulum (displaced) (hypertrophic)
Persistent:
  omphalomesenteric duct
  vitelline duct
DEF: Malformed sacs or appendages of ileum of small intestine; can cause strangulation, volvulus and intussusception.
AHA: 1Q, '04, 10
TIP: Assign for mesodiverticular band, a fibrous band connecting the tip of the diverticulum to the mesentery; can cause small bowel herniation and obstruction.

751.1 Atresia and stenosis of small intestine   `CC`
Atresia of:
  duodenum
  ileum
  intestine NOS
Congenital:
  absence
  obstruction   } of small intestine or intestine
  stenosis   }   NOS
  stricture
Imperforate jejunum
CC Excl: 751.1, 751.8-751.9

751.2 Atresia and stenosis of large intestine rectum, and anal canal   `CC`
Absence:
  anus (congenital)
  appendix, congenital
  large intestine, congenital
  rectum
Atresia of:
  anus
  colon
  rectum
Congenital or infantile:
  obstruction of large intestine
  occlusion of anus
  stricture of anus
Imperforate:
  anus
  rectum
Stricture of rectum, congenital
CC Excl: 751.2, 751.8-751.9
AHA: 2Q, '11, 13; 2Q, '98, 16

751.3 Hirschsprung's disease and other congenital functional disorders of colon   `CC`
Aganglionosis
Congenital dilation of colon
Congenital megacolon
Macrocolon
DEF: Hirschsprung's disease: enlarged or dilated colon (megacolon), with absence of ganglion cells in the narrowed wall distally; causes inability to defecate.
CC Excl: 751.3, 751.8-751.9

N Newborn Age: 0   **P** Pediatric Age: 0-17   **M** Maternity Age: 12-55   **A** Adult Age: 15-124   **MCC** Major CC Condition   **CC** CC Condition   **HIV** HIV Related Dx

262 – Volume 1   2015 ICD-9-CM

751.4 Anomalies of intestinal fixation `CC`
Congenital adhesions:
  omental, anomalous
  peritoneal
Jackson's membrane
Malrotation of colon
Rotation of cecum or colon:
  failure of
  incomplete
  insufficient
Universal mesentery
CC Excl: 751.4-751.5

751.5 Other anomalies of intestine `CC`
Congenital diverticulum, colon   Megaloappendix
Dolichocolon   Megaloduodenum
Duplication of: Microcolon
  anus   Persistent cloaca
  appendix   Transposition of:
  cecum   appendix
  intestine   colon
Ectopic anus   intestine
CC Excl: 751.0-751.5
AHA: ▶2Q, '13, 3;◀ 2Q, '10, 12; 3Q, '02, 11; 3Q, '01, 8
Q43.9 Congenital malformation of intestine unspecified `I-10`

√5th **751.6 Anomalies of gallbladder, bile ducts, and liver**

751.60 Unspecified anomaly of gallbladder, bile ducts, and liver `CC`
CC Excl: 751.60

751.61 Biliary atresia `MCC`
Congenital:
  absence
  hypoplasia   of bile duct (common) of
  obstruction   passage
  stricture
CC Excl: 751.61, 751.8-751.9
AHA: S-O, '87, 8

751.62 Congenital cystic disease of liver `CC`
Congenital polycystic disease of liver
Fibrocystic disease of liver
CC Excl: 751.62-751.69

751.69 Other anomalies of gallbladder, bile ducts, and liver `CC`
Absence of:
  gallbladder, congenital
  liver (lobe)
Accessory:
  hepatic ducts
  liver
Congenital:
  choledochal cyst
  hepatomegaly
Duplication of:
  biliary duct
  cystic duct
  gallbladder
  liver
Floating:
  gallbladder
  liver
Intrahepatic gallbladder
CC Excl: 751.60-751.69
AHA: S-O, '87, 8

751.7 Anomalies of pancreas `CC`
Absence
Accessory
Agenesis   (of) pancreas
Annular
Hypoplasia
Ectopic pancreatic tissue
Pancreatic heterotopia
EXCLUDES *diabetes mellitus (249.0-249.9, 250.0-250.9)*
fibrocystic disease of pancreas (277.00-277.09)
neonatal diabetes mellitus (775.1)
CC Excl: 751.7-751.9

751.8 Other specified anomalies of digestive system
Absence (complete) (partial) of alimentary tract NOS
Duplication   } of digestive organs NOS
Malposition, congenital
EXCLUDES *congenital diaphragmatic hernia (756.6)*
congenital hiatus hernia (750.6)

751.9 Unspecified anomaly of digestive system
Congenital:
  anomaly NOS   } of digestive system NOS
  deformity NOS

√4th **752 Congenital anomalies of genital organs**
EXCLUDES *syndromes associated with anomalies in the number and*
form of chromosomes (758.0-758.9)

752.0 Anomalies of ovaries ♀
Absence, congenital
Accessory   } (of) ovary
Ectopic
Streak

√5th **752.1 Anomalies of fallopian tubes and broad ligaments**

752.10 Unspecified anomaly of fallopian tubes and broad ligaments ♀

752.11 Embryonic cyst of fallopian tubes and broad ligaments ♀
Cyst: Cyst:
  epoophoron   parovarian
  fimbrial
AHA: S-O, '85, 13

752.19 Other ♀
Absence
Accessory   } (of) fallopian tube or broad
Atresia   ligament

752.2 Doubling of uterus ♀
Didelphic uterus
Doubling of uterus [any degree] (associated with doubling of cervix and vagina)

√5th **752.3 Other anomalies of uterus**
AHA: 4Q, '10, 90-91; 3Q, '06, 18

752.31 Agenesis of uterus ♀
Congenital absence of uterus
Q51.0 Congenital absence of uterus `I-10`

752.32 Hypoplasia of uterus ♀
Q51.811 Hypoplasia of uterus `I-10`

752.33 Unicornuate uterus ♀
Unicornuate uterus with or without a separate uterine horn
Uterus with only one functioning horn
Q51.4 Unicornuate uterus `I-10`

752.34 Bicornuate uterus ♀
Bicornuate uterus, complete or partial
Q51.3 Bicornuate uterus `I-10`

752.35 Septate uterus ♀
Septate uterus, complete or partial

752.36 Arcuate uterus ♀
Q51.810 Arcuate uterus `I-10`

752.39 Other anomalies of uterus ♀
Aplasia of uterus NOS
Müllerian anomaly of the uterus, NEC
EXCLUDES *anomaly of uterus due to exposure to*
diethylstilbestrol [DES] in utero
(760.76)
didelphic uterus (752.2)
doubling of uterus (752.2)
DEF: Müllerian anomalies: The failure or disruption of female embryonic Müllerian ducts to transform into the upper vagina, cervix uterus, and oviducts, resulting in anomalous organ development.

√5th **752.4 Anomalies of cervix, vagina, and external female genitalia**

752.40 Unspecified anomaly of cervix, vagina, and external female genitalia ♀

Congenital Anomalies

752.41–753.13

752.41 Embryonic cyst of cervix, vagina, and external female genitalia ♀

Cyst of:
   canal of Nuck, congenital
   Gartner's duct

Cyst of:
   vagina, embryonal
   vulva, congenital

DEF: Embryonic fluid-filled cysts of cervix, vagina or external female genitalia.

752.42 Imperforate hymen ♀

DEF: Complete closure of membranous fold around external opening of vagina.

752.43 Cervical agenesis ♀
Cervical hypoplasia
AHA: 4Q, '10, 90-92
Q51.5 Agenesis and aplasia of cervix   `I-10`

752.44 Cervical duplication ♀
AHA: 4Q, '10, 90-92

752.45 Vaginal agenesis ♀
Agenesis of vagina, total or partial
AHA: 4Q, '10, 90-92
Q52.0 Congenital absence of vagina   `I-10`

752.46 Transverse vaginal septum ♀
AHA: 4Q, '10, 90-92

752.47 Longitudinal vaginal septum ♀
Longitudinal vaginal septum with or without obstruction
AHA: 4Q, '10, 90-92

752.49 Other anomalies of cervix, vagina, and external female genitalia ♀
Absence of clitoris or vulva
Agenesis of clitoris or vulva
Anomalies of cervix, NEC
Anomalies of hymen, NEC
Congenital stenosis or stricture of:
   cervical canal
   vagina
Müllerian anomalies of the cervix and vagina, NEC
EXCLUDES double vagina associated with total duplication (752.2)
AHA: 3Q, '06, 18

✓5ᵗʰ **752.5 Undescended and retractile testicle**
AHA: 4Q, '96, 33

752.51 Undescended testis ♂
Cryptorchism
Ectopic testis
Q53.20 Undescended testicle unspecified bilateral   `I-10`

752.52 Retractile testis ♂

✓5ᵗʰ **752.6 Hypospadias and epispadias and other penile anomalies**
AHA: 4Q, '96, 34, 35

752.61 Hypospadias ♂
DEF: Abnormal opening of urethra on the ventral surface of the penis or perineum.
AHA: 4Q, '03, 67-68; 3Q, '97, 6
Q54.1 Hypospadias penile   `I-10`

752.62 Epispadias ♂
Anaspadias
DEF: Urethra opening on dorsal surface of penis.

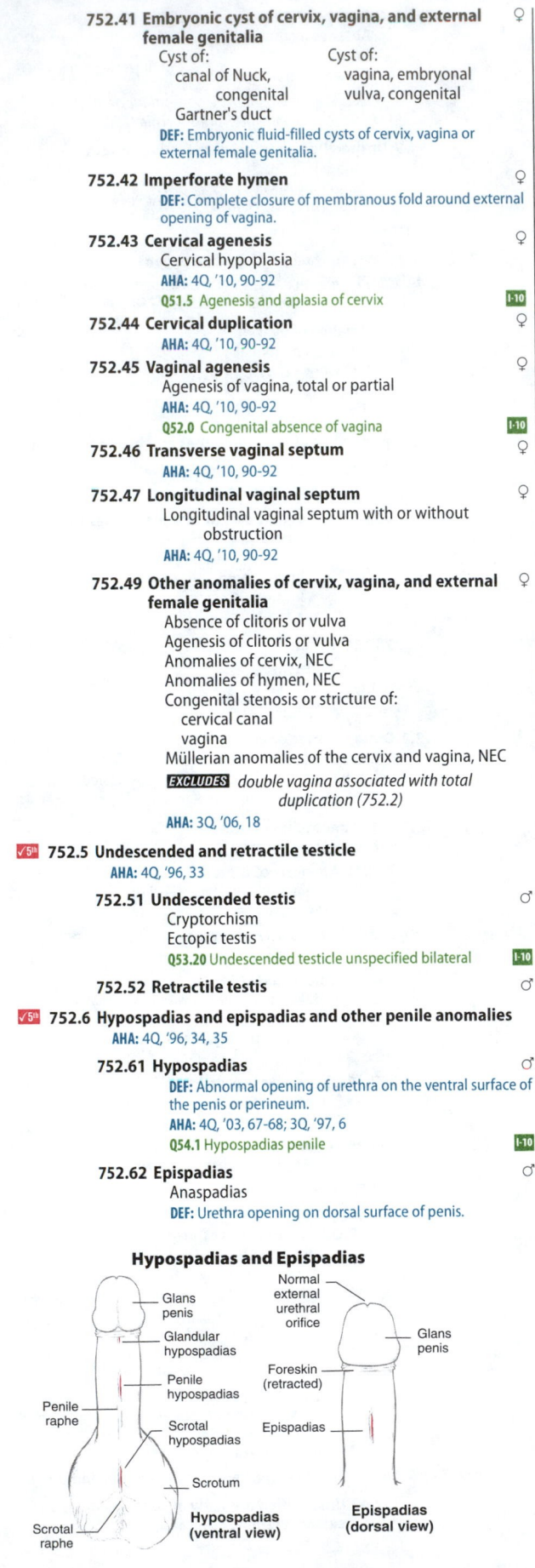

Hypospadias and Epispadias

Glans penis
Glandular hypospadias
Penile hypospadias
Penile raphe
Scrotal hypospadias
Scrotum
Scrotal raphe

Hypospadias (ventral view)

Normal external urethral orifice
Glans penis
Foreskin (retracted)
Epispadias

Epispadias (dorsal view)

752.63 Congenital chordee ♂
DEF: Ventral bowing of penis due to fibrous band along corpus spongiosum; occurs with hypospadias.

752.64 Micropenis ♂

752.65 Hidden penis ♂

752.69 Other penile anomalies ♂

752.7 Indeterminate sex and pseudohermaphroditism
Gynandrism
Hermaphroditism
Ovotestis
Pseudohermaphroditism (male) (female)
Pure gonadal dysgenesis
EXCLUDES androgen insensitivity (259.50-259.52)
   pseudohermaphroditism:
     female, with adrenocortical disorder (255.2)
     male, with gonadal disorder (257.8)
     with specified chromosomal anomaly (758.0-758.9)
   testicular feminization syndrome (259.50-259.52)
DEF: Pseudohermaphroditism: presence of gonads of one sex and external genitalia of other sex.

✓5ᵗʰ **752.8 Other specified anomalies of genital organs**
EXCLUDES congenital hydrocele (778.6)
   penile anomalies (752.61-752.69)
   phimosis or paraphimosis (605)

752.81 Scrotal transposition ♂
AHA: 4Q, '03, 67-68

752.89 Other specified anomalies of genital organs
Absence of:
   prostate
   spermatic cord
   vas deferens
Anorchism
Aplasia (congenital) of:
   prostate
   round ligament
   testicle
Atresia of:
   ejaculatory duct
   vas deferens
Fusion of testes
Hypoplasia of testis
Monorchism
Polyorchism

752.9 Unspecified anomaly of genital organs
Congenital:
   anomaly NOS } of genital organ, not
   deformity NOS } elsewhere classified

✓4ᵗʰ **753 Congenital anomalies of urinary system**

753.0 Renal agenesis and dysgenesis `CC`
Atrophy of kidney:
   congenital
   infantile
Congenital absence of kidney(s)
Hypoplasia of kidney(s)
CC Excl: 599.60-599.69, 753.0
Q60.2 Renal agenesis unspecified   `I-10`

✓5ᵗʰ **753.1 Cystic kidney disease**
EXCLUDES acquired cyst of kidney (593.2)
AHA: 4Q, '90, 3

753.10 Cystic kidney disease, unspecified `CC`
CC Excl: 599.60-599.69, 753.10
Q61.9 Cystic kidney disease unspecified   `I-10`

753.11 Congenital single renal cyst `CC`
CC Excl: 599.60-599.69, 753.11

753.12 Polycystic kidney, unspecified type `CC`
CC Excl: 599.60-599.69, 753.12-753.14
AHA: ▶3Q, '13, 6◄
Q61.3 Polycystic kidney unspecified   `I-10`

753.13 Polycystic kidney, autosomal dominant `CC`
DEF: Slow progressive disease characterized by bilateral cysts causing increased kidney size and impaired function.
CC Excl: See code: 753.12

`N` Newborn Age: 0   `P` Pediatric Age: 0-17   `M` Maternity Age: 12-55   `A` Adult Age: 15-124   `MCC` Major CC Condition   `CC` CC Condition   `HIV` HIV Related Dx

753.14 Polycystic kidney, autosomal recessive `CC`
    DEF: Rare disease characterized by multiple cysts involving kidneys and liver, producing renal and hepatic failure in childhood or adolescence.
    CC Excl: See code: 753.12

753.15 Renal dysplasia `CC`
    CC Excl: 599.60-599.69, 753.15

753.16 Medullary cystic kidney `CC`
    Nephronopthisis
    DEF: Diffuse kidney disease results in uremia onset prior to age 20.
    CC Excl: 599.60-599.69, 753.16-753.19

753.17 Medullary sponge kidney `CC`
    DEF: Dilated collecting tubules; usually asymptomatic but calcinosis in tubules may cause renal insufficiency.
    CC Excl: See code: 753.16

753.19 Other specified cystic kidney disease `CC`
    Multicystic kidney
    CC Excl: See code: 753.16

√5ᵗʰ **753.2 Obstructive defects of renal pelvis and ureter**
    AHA: 4Q, '96, 35

753.20 Unspecified obstructive defect of renal pelvis and ureter `CC`
    CC Excl: 599.60-599.69, 753.20-753.22, 753.29

753.21 Congenital obstruction of ureteropelvic junction `CC`
    DEF: Stricture at junction of ureter and renal pelvis.
    CC Excl: See code: 753.20

753.22 Congenital obstruction of ureterovesical junction `CC`
    Adynamic ureter
    Congenital hydroureter
    DEF: Stricture at junction of ureter and bladder.
    CC Excl: See code: 753.20

753.23 Congenital ureterocele `CC`
    CC Excl: See code: 753.20

753.29 Other `CC`
    CC Excl: See code: 753.20
    Q62.11 Congen occlusion of ureteropelvic junct `I-10`

753.3 Other specified anomalies of kidney
    Accessory kidney
    Congenital:
      calculus of kidney
      displaced kidney
    Discoid kidney
    Double kidney with double pelvis
    Ectopic kidney
    Fusion of kidneys
    Giant kidney
    Horseshoe kidney
    Hyperplasia of kidney
    Lobulation of kidney
    Malrotation of kidney
    Trifid kidney (pelvis)
    AHA: 1Q, '07, 23
    TIP: Assign for Finnish-type congenital nephrosis, along with code 581.3 Nephrotic syndrome.
    Q63.8 Oth specified congenital malformations of kidney `I-10`

753.4 Other specified anomalies of ureter
    Absent ureter
    Accessory ureter
    Deviation of ureter
    Displaced ureteric orifice
    Double ureter
    Ectopic ureter
    Implantation, anomalous of ureter

753.5 Exstrophy of urinary bladder `CC`
    Ectopia vesicae
    Extroversion of bladder
    DEF: Absence of lower abdominal and anterior bladder walls with posterior bladder wall protrusion.
    CC Excl: 599.60-599.69, 753.5, 753.9

753.6 Atresia and stenosis of urethra and bladder neck `CC`
    Congenital obstruction:
      bladder neck
      urethra
    Congenital stricture of:
      urethra (valvular)
      urinary meatus
      vesicourethral orifice
    Imperforate urinary meatus
    Impervious urethra
    Urethral valve formation
    CC Excl: 599.60-599.69, 753.6, 753.9

753.7 Anomalies of urachus
    Cyst
    Fistula   } (of) urachussinus
    Patent
    Persistent umbilical sinus

753.8 Other specified anomalies of bladder and urethra
    Absence, congenital of:
      bladder
      urethra
    Accessory:
      bladder
      urethra
    Congenital:
      diverticulum of bladder
      hernia of bladder
      urethrorectal fistula
      prolapse of:
        bladder (mucosa)
        urethra
    Double:
      urethra
      urinary meatus

753.9 Unspecified anomaly of urinary system
    Congenital:
      anomaly NOS   } of urinary system [any part,
      deformity NOS   except urachus]
    AHA: 2Q, '11, 6

√4ᵗʰ **754 Certain congenital musculoskeletal deformities**
    INCLUDES nonteratogenic deformities which are considered to be due to intrauterine malposition and pressure

754.0 Of skull, face, and jaw
    Asymmetry of face
    Compression facies
    Depressions in skull
    Deviation of nasal septum, congenital
    Dolichocephaly
    Plagiocephaly
    Potter's facies
    Squashed or bent nose, congenital
    EXCLUDES dentofacial anomalies (524.0-524.9)
        syphilitic saddle nose (090.5)

754.1 Of sternocleidomastoid muscle
    Congenital sternomastoid torticollis
    Congenital wryneck
    Contracture of sternocleidomastoid (muscle)
    Sternomastoid tumor

754.2 Of spine `CC`
    Congenital postural:
      lordosis
      scoliosis
    CC Excl: 754.2

√5ᵗʰ **754.3 Congenital dislocation of hip**

754.30 Congenital dislocation of hip, unilateral
    Congenital dislocation of hip NOS

754.31 Congenital dislocation of hip, bilateral

754.32 Congenital subluxation of hip, unilateral
    Congenital flexion deformity, hip or thigh
    Predislocation status of hip at birth
    Preluxation of hip, congenital

754.33 Congenital subluxation of hip, bilateral

754.35 Congenital dislocation of one hip with subluxation of other hip

√4ᵗʰ √5ᵗʰ Additional Digit Required   Unacceptable PDx   Manifestation Code   Hospital Acquired Condition   ►◄ Revised Text   ● New Code   ▲ Revised Code Title

2015 ICD-9-CM   **Volume 1 – 265**

✓5th **754.4 Congenital genu recurvatum and bowing of long bones of leg**

754.40 Genu recurvatum
  DEF: Backward curving of knee joint.

754.41 Congenital dislocation of knee (with genu recurvatum)

754.42 Congenital bowing of femur

754.43 Congenital bowing of tibia and fibula

754.44 Congenital bowing of unspecified long bones of leg

✓5th **754.5 Varus deformities of feet**
  EXCLUDES acquired (736.71, 736.75, 736.79)

754.50 Talipes varus
  Congenital varus deformity of foot, unspecified
  Pes varus
  DEF: Inverted foot marked by outer sole resting on ground.

754.51 Talipes equinovarus
  Equinovarus (congenital)
  DEF: Elevated, outward rotation of heel; also called clubfoot.

754.52 Metatarsus primus varus
  DEF: Malformed first metatarsal bone, with bone angled toward body.

754.53 Metatarsus varus

754.59 Other
  Talipes calcaneovarus

✓5th **754.6 Valgus deformities of feet**
  EXCLUDES valgus deformity of foot (acquired) (736.79)

754.60 Talipes valgus
  Congenital valgus deformity of foot, unspecified

754.61 Congenital pes planus
  Congenital rocker bottom flat foot
  Flat foot, congenital
  EXCLUDES pes planus (acquired) (734)

754.62 Talipes calcaneovalgus

754.69 Other
  Talipes:
    equinovalgus
    planovalgus

✓5th **754.7 Other deformities of feet**
  EXCLUDES acquired (736.70-736.79)

754.70 Talipes, unspecified
  Congenital deformity of foot NOS

754.71 Talipes cavus
  Cavus foot (congenital)

754.79 Other
  Asymmetric talipes
  Talipes:
    calcaneus
    equinus

✓5th **754.8 Other specified nonteratogenic anomalies**

754.81 Pectus excavatum
  Congenital funnel chest

754.82 Pectus carinatum
  Congenital pigeon chest [breast]

754.89 Other CC
  Club hand (congenital)
  Congenital:
    deformity of chest wall
    dislocation of elbow
  Generalized flexion contractures of lower limb joints, congenital
  Spade-like hand (congenital)
  CC Excl: 754.81-754.89

✓4th **755 Other congenital anomalies of limbs**
  EXCLUDES those deformities classifiable to 754.0-754.8

✓5th **755.0 Polydactyly**

755.00 Polydactyly, unspecified digits
  Supernumerary digits

755.01 Of fingers
  Accessory fingers

755.02 Of toes
  Accessory toes

✓5th **755.1 Syndactyly**
  Symphalangy
  Webbing of digits

755.10 Of multiple and unspecified sites

755.11 Of fingers without fusion of bone

755.12 Of fingers with fusion of bone

755.13 Of toes without fusion of bone

755.14 Of toes with fusion of bone

✓5th **755.2 Reduction deformities of upper limb**

755.20 Unspecified reduction deformity of upper limb
  Ectromelia NOS
  Hemimelia NOS } of upper limb
  Shortening of arm, congenital

755.21 Transverse deficiency of upper limb
  Amelia of upper limb
  Congenital absence of:
    fingers, all (complete or partial)
    forearm, including hand and fingers
    upper limb, complete
  Congenital amputation of upper limb
  Transverse hemimelia of upper limb

755.22 Longitudinal deficiency of upper limb, not elsewhere classified
  Phocomelia NOS of upper limb
  Rudimentary arm

755.23 Longitudinal deficiency, combined, involving humerus, radius, and ulna (complete or incomplete)
  Congenital absence of arm and forearm (complete or incomplete) with or without metacarpal deficiency and/or phalangeal deficiency, incomplete
  Phocomelia, complete, of upper limb

755.24 Longitudinal deficiency, humeral, complete or partial (with or without distal deficiencies, incomplete)
  Congenital absence of humerus (with or without absence of some [but not all] distal elements)
  Proximal phocomelia of upper limb

755.25 Longitudinal deficiency, radioulnar, complete or partial (with or without distal deficiencies, incomplete)
  Congenital absence of radius and ulna (with or without absence of some [but not all] distal elements)
  Distal phocomelia of upper limb

755.26 Longitudinal deficiency, radial, complete or partial (with or without distal deficiencies, incomplete)
  Agenesis of radius
  Congenital absence of radius (with or without absence of some [but not all] distal elements)

755.27 Longitudinal deficiency, ulnar, complete or partial (with or without distal deficiencies, incomplete)
  Agenesis of ulna
  Congenital absence of ulna (with or without absence of some [but not all] distal elements)

755.28 Longitudinal deficiency, carpals or metacarpals, complete or partial (with or without incomplete phalangeal deficiency)

755.29 Longitudinal deficiency, phalanges, complete or partial
  Absence of finger, congenital
  Aphalangia of upper limb, terminal, complete or partial
  EXCLUDES terminal deficiency of all five digits (755.21)
    transverse deficiency of phalanges (755.21)

N Newborn Age: 0   P Pediatric Age: 0-17   M Maternity Age: 12-55   A Adult Age: 15-124   MCC Major CC Condition   CC CC Condition   HIV HIV Related Dx

266 – Volume 1   2015 ICD-9-CM

✓5ᵗʰ **755.3 Reduction deformities of lower limb**

    755.30 Unspecified reduction deformity of lower limb

       Ectromelia NOS ⎫
       Hemimelia NOS ⎬ of lower limb
       Shortening of leg, congenital

    755.31 Transverse deficiency of lower limb

       Amelia of lower limb
       Congenital absence of:
         foot
         leg, including foot and toes
         lower limb, complete
         toes, all, complete
       Transverse hemimelia of lower limb

    755.32 Longitudinal deficiency of lower limb, not elsewhere classified

       Phocomelia NOS of lower limb

    755.33 Longitudinal deficiency, combined, involving femur, tibia, and fibula (complete or incomplete)

       Congenital absence of thigh and (lower) leg (complete or incomplete) with or without metacarpal deficiency and/or phalangeal deficiency, incomplete
       Phocomelia, complete, of lower limb

    755.34 Longitudinal deficiency, femoral, complete or partial (with or without distal deficiencies, incomplete)

       Congenital absence of femur (with or without absence of some [but not all] distal elements)
       Proximal phocomelia of lower limb

    755.35 Longitudinal deficiency, tibiofibular, complete or partial (with or without distal deficiencies, incomplete)

       Congenital absence of tibia and fibula (with or without absence of some [but not all] distal elements)
       Distal phocomelia of lower limb

    755.36 Longitudinal deficiency, tibia, complete or partial (with or without distal deficiencies, incomplete)

       Agenesis of tibia
       Congenital absence of tibia (with or without absence of some [but not all] distal elements)

    755.37 Longitudinal deficiency, fibular, complete or partial (with or without distal deficiencies, incomplete)

       Agenesis of fibula
       Congenital absence of fibula (with or without absence of some [but not all] distal elements)

    755.38 Longitudinal deficiency, tarsals or metatarsals, complete or partial (with or without incomplete phalangeal deficiency)

    755.39 Longitudinal deficiency, phalanges, complete or partial

       Absence of toe, congenital
       Aphalangia of lower limb, terminal, complete or partial
       EXCLUDES *terminal deficiency of all five digits (755.31)*
                   transverse deficiency of phalanges (755.31)

755.4 Reduction deformities, unspecified limb

    Absence, congenital (complete or partial) of limb NOS
    Amelia ⎫
    Ectromelia ⎬
    Hemimelia ⎬ of unspecified limb
    Phocomelia ⎭

✓5ᵗʰ **755.5 Other anomalies of upper limb, including shoulder girdle**

    755.50 Unspecified anomaly of upper limb

    755.51 Congenital deformity of clavicle

    755.52 Congenital elevation of scapula

       Sprengel's deformity

    755.53 Radioulnar synostosis

       DEF: Osseous adhesion of radius and ulna.

    755.54 Madelung's deformity

       DEF: Distal ulnar overgrowth or radial shortening; also called carpus curvus.

    755.55 Acrocephalosyndactyly `MCC`

       Apert's syndrome
       DEF: Premature cranial suture fusion (craniostenosis); marked by cone-shaped or pointed (acrocephaly) head and webbing of the fingers (syndactyly); similar to craniofacial dysostosis.
       CC Excl: 755.50, 755.55, 755.59

    755.56 Accessory carpal bones

    755.57 Macrodactylia (fingers)

       DEF: Abnormally large fingers, toes.

    755.58 Cleft hand, congenital

       Lobster-claw hand
       DEF: Extended separation between fingers into metacarpus; also may refer to large fingers and absent middle fingers of hand.

    755.59 Other

       Cleidocranial dysostosis
       Cubitus:
         valgus, congenital
         varus, congenital
       EXCLUDES *club hand (congenital) (754.89)*
                  congenital dislocation of elbow (754.89)

✓5ᵗʰ **755.6 Other anomalies of lower limb, including pelvic girdle**

    755.60 Unspecified anomaly of lower limb

    755.61 Coxa valga, congenital

       DEF: Abnormally wide angle between the neck and shaft of the femur.

    755.62 Coxa vara, congenital

       DEF: Diminished angle between neck and shaft of femur.

    755.63 Other congenital deformity of hip (joint)

       Congenital anteversion of femur (neck)
       EXCLUDES *congenital dislocation of hip (754.30-754.35)*
       AHA: 1Q, '94, 15; S-O, '84, 15
       Q65.9 Congenital deformity of hip unspecified `I-10`

    755.64 Congenital deformity of knee (joint)

       Congenital:
         absence of patella
         genu valgum [knock-knee]
         genu varum [bowleg]
       Rudimentary patella

    755.65 Macrodactylia of toes

       DEF: Abnormally large toes.

    755.66 Other anomalies of toes

       Congenital:
         hallux valgus
         hallux varus
         hammer toe

    755.67 Anomalies of foot, not elsewhere classified

       Astragaloscaphoid synostosis
       Calcaneonavicular bar
       Coalition of calcaneus
       Talonavicular synostosis
       Tarsal coalitions

    755.69 Other

       Congenital:
         angulation of tibia
         deformity (of):
           ankle (joint)
           sacroiliac (joint)
         fusion of sacroiliac joint

755.8 Other specified anomalies of unspecified limb

755.9 Unspecified anomaly of unspecified limb

    Congenital:
      anomaly NOS ⎫
      deformity NOS ⎬ of unspecified limb
    EXCLUDES *reduction deformity of unspecified limb (755.4)*

✓4ᵗʰ   Additional Digit Required   Unacceptable PDx   Manifestation Code   Hospital Acquired Condition   ▶◀ Revised Text   ● New Code   ▲ Revised Code Title

2015 ICD-9-CM

Volume 1 – 267

✓4ᵗʰ 756 Other congenital musculoskeletal anomalies

EXCLUDES *congenital myotonic chondrodystrophy (359.23)*
those deformities classifiable to 754.0-754.8

756.0 Anomalies of skull and face bones

Absence of skull bones
Acrocephaly
Congenital deformity of forehead
Craniosynostosis
Crouzon's disease
Hypertelorism
Imperfect fusion of skull
Oxycephaly
Platybasia
Premature closure of cranial sutures
Tower skull
Trigonocephaly

EXCLUDES *acrocephalosyndactyly [Apert's syndrome] (755.55)*
dentofacial anomalies (524.0-524.9)
skull defects associated with brain anomalies, such as:
    anencephalus (740.0)
    encephalocele (742.0)
    hydrocephalus (742.3)
    microcephalus (742.1)

AHA: 2Q, '12, 17; 3Q, '98, 9; 3Q, '96, 15

TIP: Assign for Nager syndrome (preaxial acrofacial dysostosis), along with codes for any additional features that are not captured in the code.

Q75.8 Other spec cong malformations skull & face bones   I-10

✓5ᵗʰ 756.1 Anomalies of spine

756.10 Anomaly of spine, unspecified

756.11 Spondylolysis, lumbosacral region

Prespondylolisthesis (lumbosacral)

DEF: Bilateral or unilateral defect through the pars interarticularis of a vertebra causes spondylolisthesis.

756.12 Spondylolisthesis

DEF: Downward slipping of lumbar vertebra over next vertebra; usually related to pelvic deformity.

Q76.2 Congenital spondylolisthesis   I-10

756.13 Absence of vertebra, congenital   CC

CC Excl: 756.10-756.19

756.14 Hemivertebra

DEF: Incomplete development of one side of a vertebra.

756.15 Fusion of spine [vertebra], congenital

756.16 Klippel-Feil syndrome

DEF: Short, wide neck; limits range of motion due to abnormal number of cervical vertebra or fused hemivertebrae.

756.17 Spina bifida occulta

EXCLUDES *spina bifida (aperta) (741.0-741.9)*

DEF: Spina bifida marked by a bony spinal canal defect without a protrusion of the cord or meninges; it is diagnosed by radiography and has no symptoms.

756.19 Other

Platyspondylia
Supernumerary vertebra

756.2 Cervical rib

Supernumerary rib in the cervical region

DEF: Costa cervicalis: extra rib attached to cervical vertebra.

756.3 Other anomalies of ribs and sternum   CC

Congenital absence of:
  rib
  sternum
Congenital:
  fissure of sternum
  fusion of ribs
Sternum bifidum

EXCLUDES *nonteratogenic deformity of chest wall (754.81-754.89)*

CC Excl: 756.2-756.3

756.4 Chondrodystrophy

Achondroplasia   Enchondromatosis
Chondrodystrophia (fetalis)   Ollier's disease
Dyschondroplasia

EXCLUDES *congenital myotonic chondrodystrophy (359.23)*
lipochondrodystrophy [Hurler's syndrome] (277.5)
Morquio's disease (277.5)

DEF: Abnormal development of cartilage.

AHA: 2Q, '02, 16; S-O, '87, 10

TIP: Assign for Jeune's syndrome, and also for cartilage-hair syndrome (cartilage-hair hypoplasia).

✓5ᵗʰ 756.5 Osteodystrophies

756.50 Osteodystrophy, unspecified

756.51 Osteogenesis imperfecta   CC

Fragilitas ossium
Osteopsathyrosis

DEF: A collagen disorder commonly characterized by brittle, osteoporotic, easily fractured bones, hypermobility of joints, blue sclerae, and a tendency to hemorrhage.

CC Excl: 756.50-756.59

756.52 Osteopetrosis   CC

DEF: Abnormally dense bone, optic atrophy, hepatosplenomegaly, deafness; sclerosing depletes bone marrow and nerve foramina of skull; often fatal.

CC Excl: See code: 756.51

756.53 Osteopoikilosis

DEF: Multiple sclerotic foci on ends of long bones, stippling in round, flat bones; identified by x-ray.

756.54 Polyostotic fibrous dysplasia of bone

DEF: Fibrous tissue displaces bone results in segmented ragged-edge café-au-lait spots; occurs in girls of early puberty.

756.55 Chondroectodermal dysplasia

Ellis-van Creveld syndrome

DEF: Inadequate enchondral bone formation; impaired development of hair and teeth, polydactyly, and cardiac septum defects.

756.56 Multiple epiphyseal dysplasia

756.59 Other

Albright (-McCune)-Sternberg syndrome

756.6 Anomalies of diaphragm   MCC

Absence of diaphragm   Eventration of diaphragm
Congenital hernia:
  diaphragmatic
  foramen of Morgagni

EXCLUDES *congenital hiatus hernia (750.6)*

CC Excl: 750.6, 756.6

✓5ᵗʰ 756.7 Anomalies of abdominal wall

756.70 Anomaly of abdominal wall, unspecified   MCC

CC Excl: 756.70-756.79

756.71 Prune belly syndrome   MCC

Eagle-Barrett syndrome
Prolapse of bladder mucosa

DEF: Prune belly syndrome: absence of lower rectus abdominis muscle and lower and medial oblique muscles; results in dilated bladder and ureters, dysplastic kidneys and hydronephrosis; common in male infants with undescended testicles.

CC Excl: See code: 756.70

AHA: 4Q, '97, 44

756.72 Omphalocele   MCC

Exomphalos

DEF: Exomphalos: umbilical hernia prominent navel.

DEF: Omphalocele: hernia of umbilicus due to impaired abdominal wall; results in membrane-covered intestine protruding through peritoneum and amnion.

CC Excl: See code: 756.70

AHA: 4Q, '09, 98-99

756.73 Gastroschisis   MCC

DEF: Fissure of abdominal wall, results in protruding small or large intestine.

CC Excl: See code: 756.70

AHA: 4Q, '09, 98-99

N Newborn Age: 0   P Pediatric Age: 0-17   M Maternity Age: 12-55   A Adult Age: 15-124   MCC Major CC Condition   CC CC Condition   HIV HIV Related Dx

268 – Volume 1   2015 ICD-9-CM

Omphalocele

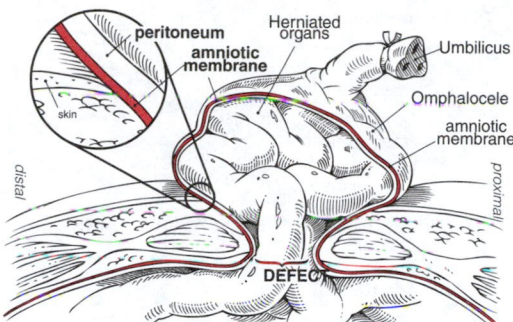

Gastroschisis

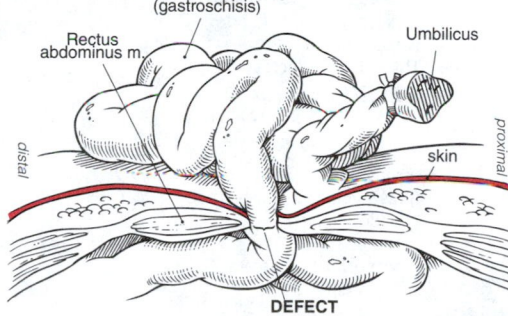

756.79 Other congenital anomalies of abdominal wall `MCC`

> **EXCLUDES** umbilical hernia (551-553 with .1)
> **CC Excl:** See code: 756.70

√5ᵗʰ 756.8 Other specified anomalies of muscle, tendon, fascia, and connective tissue

756.81 Absence of muscle and tendon
Absence of muscle (pectoral)
AHA: 1Q, '10, 13

756.82 Accessory muscle

756.83 Ehlers-Danlos syndrome `CC`
DEF: Danlos syndrome: connective tissue disorder causes hyperextended skin and joints; results in fragile blood vessels with bleeding, poor wound healing and subcutaneous pseudotumors.
CC Excl: 756.83-756.89

756.89 Other
Amyotrophia congenita
Congenital shortening of tendon
AHA: 3Q, '99, 16
TIP: Assign for Stickler's syndrome, a hereditary progressive arthro-ophthalmopathy, along with codes for the specific manifestations.

756.9 Other and unspecified anomalies of musculoskeletal system
Congenital:
  anomaly NOS ⎱ of musculoskeletal system,
  deformity NOS ⎰ not elsewhere classified

√4ᵗʰ 757 Congenital anomalies of the integument
INCLUDES anomalies of skin, subcutaneous tissue, hair, nails, and breast
EXCLUDES hemangioma (228.00-228.09)
pigmented nevus (216.0-216.9)

757.0 Hereditary edema of legs
Congenital lymphedema
Hereditary trophedema
Milroy's disease

757.1 Ichthyosis congenita
Congenital ichthyosis   Ichthyosiform erythroderma
Harlequin fetus
DEF: Overproduction of skin cells causes scaling of skin; may result in stillborn fetus or death soon after birth.

757.2 Dermatoglyphic anomalies
Abnormal palmar creases
DEF: Abnormal skin-line patterns of fingers, palms, toes and soles; initial finding of possible chromosomal abnormalities.

√5ᵗʰ 757.3 Other specified anomalies of skin

757.31 Congenital ectodermal dysplasia
DEF: Tissues and structures originate in embryonic ectoderm; includes anhidrotic and hidrotic ectodermal dysplasia and EEC syndrome.

757.32 Vascular hamartomas
Birthmarks
Port-wine stain
Strawberry nevus
DEF: Benign tumor of blood vessels; due to malformed angioblastic tissues.
AHA: 2Q, '12, 7
TIP: Assign for nevus flammeus, which may be associated with increased risk for seizure or glaucoma. Further testing may be required.
Q82.5 Congenital non-neoplastic nevus `I-10`

757.33 Congenital pigmentary anomalies of skin
Congenital poikiloderma
Urticaria pigmentosa
Xeroderma pigmentosum
EXCLUDES albinism (270.2)
AHA: ▶1Q, '13, 14◀
Q82.2 Mastocytosis `I-10`

757.39 Other
Accessory skin tags, congenital
Congenital scar
Epidermolysis bullosa
Keratoderma (congenital)
EXCLUDES pilonidal cyst (685.0-685.1)
AHA: ▶1Q, '13, 15◀
Q82.8 Other specified congenital malformations of skin `I-10`

757.4 Specified anomalies of hair
Congenital:
  alopecia
  atrichosis
  beaded hair
  hypertrichosis
  monilethrix
  Persistent lanugo

757.5 Specified anomalies of nails
Anonychia   Congenital:
Congenital: leukonychia
  clubnail   onychauxis
  koilonychia   pachyonychia

757.6 Specified congenital anomalies of breast
Accessory
Congenital absent ⎱ breast or nipple
Supernumerary
EXCLUDES absence of pectoral muscle (756.81)
hypoplasia of breast (611.82)
micromastia (611.82)

757.8 Other specified anomalies of the integument

757.9 Unspecified anomaly of the integument
Congenital:
  anomaly NOS ⎱ of integument
  deformity NOS ⎰

√4ᵗʰ 758 Chromosomal anomalies
INCLUDES syndromes associated with anomalies in the number and form of chromosomes
Use additional codes for conditions associated with the chromosomal anomalies

758.0 Down's syndrome
Mongolism
Translocation Down's syndrome
Trisomy:
  21 or 22
  G
Q90.9 Down's syndrome unspecified `I-10`

Congenital Anomalies

758.1–759.7

758.1 Patau's syndrome `CC`
Trisomy:
13
D₁
DEF: Trisomy of 13th chromosome; characteristic failure to thrive, severe mental impairment, seizures, abnormal eyes, low-set ears and sloped forehead.
CC Excl: 758.0-758.9

758.2 Edwards' syndrome `CC`
Trisomy:
18
E₃
DEF: Trisomy of 18th chromosome; characteristic mental and physical impairments; mainly affects females.
CC Excl: See code: 758.1

√5ᵗʰ **758.3 Autosomal deletion syndromes**

   758.31 Cri-du-chat syndrome `CC`
   Deletion 5p
   DEF: Hereditary congenital syndrome caused by a microdeletion of short arm of chromosome 5; characterized by catlike cry in newborn, microencephaly, severe mental deficiency, and hypertelorism.
   CC Excl: 758.0-758.2, 758.32-758.9

   758.32 Velo-cardio-facial syndrome `MCC`
   Deletion 22q11.2
   DEF: Microdeletion syndrome affecting multiple organs; characteristic cleft palate, heart defects, elongated face with almond-shaped eyes, wide nose, small ears, weak immune systems, weak musculature, hypothyroidism, short stature, and scoliosis; deletion at q11.2 on the long arm of the chromosome 22.
   CC Excl: 758.0-758.31, 758.33-758.9

   758.33 Other microdeletions `CC`
   Miller-Dieker syndrome
   Smith-Magenis syndrome
   DEF: Miller-Dieker syndrome: deletion from the short arm of chromosome 17; characteristic mental retardation, speech and motor development delays, neurological complications, and multiple abnormalities affecting the kidneys, heart, gastrointestinal tract; death in infancy or early childhood.
   DEF: Smith-Magenis syndrome: deletion in a certain area of chromosome 17 that results in craniofacial changes, speech delay, hoarse voice, hearing loss, and behavioral problems, such as self-destructive head banging, wrist biting, and tearing at nails.
   CC Excl: 758.0-758.32, 758.39-758.9

   758.39 Other autosomal deletions `CC`
   CC Excl: 758.0-758.33, 758.4-758.9

758.4 Balanced autosomal translocation in normal individual

758.5 Other conditions due to autosomal anomalies
Accessory autosomes NEC

758.6 Gonadal dysgenesis
Ovarian dysgenesis
Turner's syndrome
XO syndrome
EXCLUDES *pure gonadal dysgenesis (752.7)*

758.7 Klinefelter's syndrome ♂
XXY syndrome
DEF: Impaired embryonic development of seminiferous tubes; results in small testes, azoospermia, infertility and enlarged mammary glands.

√5ᵗʰ **758.8 Other conditions due to chromosome anomalies**

   758.81 Other conditions due to sex chromosome anomalies

   758.89 Other
   Q99.8 Other specified chromosome abnormalities `I-10`

758.9 Conditions due to anomaly of unspecified chromosome

√4ᵗʰ **759 Other and unspecified congenital anomalies**

759.0 Anomalies of spleen `CC`
Aberrant ⎫
Absent ⎬ spleen
Accessory ⎭
Congenital splenomegaly
Ectopic spleen
Lobulation of spleen
CC Excl: 759.0, 759.9

759.1 Anomalies of adrenal gland
Aberrant ⎫
Absent ⎬ adrenal gland
Accessory ⎭
EXCLUDES *adrenogenital disorders (255.2)*
congenital disorders of steroid metabolism (255.2)

759.2 Anomalies of other endocrine glands
Absent parathyroid gland
Accessory thyroid gland
Persistent thyroglossal or thyrolingual duct
Thyroglossal (duct) cyst
EXCLUDES *congenital:*
   goiter (246.1)
   hypothyroidism (243)

759.3 Situs inversus `CC`
Situs inversus or transversus:
   abdominalis
   thoracis
Transposition of viscera:
   abdominal
   thoracic
EXCLUDES *dextrocardia without mention of complete transposition (746.87)*
DEF: Laterally transposed thoracic and abdominal viscera.
CC Excl: 759.3, 759.7, 759.9

759.4 Conjoined twins `MCC`
Craniopagus
Dicephalus
Pygopagus
Thoracopagus
Xiphopagus
CC Excl: 759.4, 759.7, 759.9

759.5 Tuberous sclerosis `CC`
Bourneville's disease
Epiloia
DEF: Hamartomas of brain, retina and viscera, impaired mental ability, seizures and adenoma sebaceum.
CC Excl: 759.5-759.7, 759.9

759.6 Other hamartoses, not elsewhere classified `CC`
Syndrome:
   Peutz-Jeghers
   Sturge-Weber (-Dimitri)
   von Hippel-Lindau
EXCLUDES *neurofibromatosis (237.70-237.79)*
DEF: Peutz-Jeghers: hereditary syndrome characterized by hamartomas of small intestine.
DEF: Sturge-Weber: congenital syndrome characterized by unilateral port-wine stain over trigeminal nerve, underlying meninges and cerebral cortex.
DEF: von Hipple-Lindau: hereditary syndrome of congenital angiomatosis of the retina and cerebellum.
CC Excl: 759.6, 759.9
AHA: 3Q, '92, 12

759.7 Multiple congenital anomalies, so described `CC`
Congenital:
   anomaly, multiple NOS
   deformity, multiple NOS
CC Excl: See code: 759.3

`N` Newborn Age: 0   `P` Pediatric Age: 0-17   `M` Maternity Age: 12-55   `A` Adult Age: 15-124   `MCC` Major CC Condition   `CC` CC Condition   `HIV` HIV Related Dx

270 – Volume 1   2015 ICD-9-CM

√5ᵗʰ **759.8 Other specified anomalies**
    AHA: S-O, '87, 9; S-O, '85, 11

    759.81 Prader-Willi syndrome   CC
        CC Excl: 759.6-759.9

    759.82 Marfan syndrome   CC
        CC Excl: See code: 759.81
        AHA: 3Q, '93, 11

    759.83 Fragile X syndrome
        AHA: 4Q, '94, 41

759.89 Other   CC
    Congenital malformation syndromes affecting
        multiple systems, not elsewhere classified
    Laurence-Moon-Biedl syndrome
    CC Excl: 759.81-759.89
    AHA: ▶4Q, '13, 92;◀ 2Q, '12, 3; 3Q, '08, 3; 3Q, '06, 21; 2Q, '05,
    17; 2Q, '04, 12; 1Q, '01, 3; 3Q, '99, 17, 18; 3Q, '98, 8
    TIP: Assign for the following syndromes:
        Alagille s.
        Alport's s.
        Antley-Bixler s.
        branchio-oto-renal ((BOR) s.
        Borjeson-Forsmann-Lehmann s.
        cardiofaciocutaneous (CFC) s.
        Costello s.
        fasciocutaneoskeletal (FCS)s.
        mutliple pterygium s.
        Noonan's s.
        Startle s.
        Williams s.
    Assign additional codes for any documented
    manifestations.

759.9 Congenital anomaly, unspecified

√4ᵗʰ
√5ᵗʰ   Additional Digit Required   Unacceptable PDx   Manifestation Code   Hospital Acquired Condition   ▶◀ Revised Text   ● New Code   ▲ Revised Code Title

2015 ICD-9-CM   **October 2014 · Volume 1 – 271**

15. Certain Conditions Originating in the Perinatal Period (760-779)

INCLUDES conditions which have their origin in the perinatal period, before birth through the first 28 days after birth, even though death or morbidity occurs later

Use additional code(s) to further specify condition

TIP: A newborn condition is clinically significant when it has implications for the newborn's *future* health care. This is an exception to the UHDDS guidelines.

Maternal Causes of Perinatal Morbidity and Mortality (760-763)

AHA: 2Q, '89, 14; 3Q, '90, 5

√4th 760 Fetus or newborn affected by maternal conditions which may be unrelated to present pregnancy

INCLUDES the listed maternal conditions only when specified as a cause of mortality or morbidity of the fetus or newborn

EXCLUDES maternal endocrine and metabolic disorders affecting fetus or newborn (775.0-775.9)

AHA: 1Q, '94, 8; 2Q, '92, 12; N-D, '84, 11

TIP: Do not assign unless the mother's condition has actually affected the fetus or newborn.

760.0 Maternal hypertensive disorders
Fetus or newborn affected by maternal conditions classifiable to 642

760.1 Maternal renal and urinary tract diseases
Fetus or newborn affected by maternal conditions classifiable to 580-599

760.2 Maternal infections
Fetus or newborn affected by maternal infectious disease classifiable to 001-136 and 487, but fetus or newborn not manifesting that disease
EXCLUDES congenital infectious diseases (771.0-771.8)
maternal genital tract and other localized infections (760.8)

760.3 Other chronic maternal circulatory and respiratory diseases
Fetus or newborn affected by chronic maternal conditions classifiable to 390-459, 490-519, 745-748

760.4 Maternal nutritional disorders
Fetus or newborn affected by:
maternal disorders classifiable to 260-269
maternal malnutrition NOS
EXCLUDES fetal malnutrition (764.10-764.29)

760.5 Maternal injury
Fetus or newborn affected by maternal conditions classifiable to 800-995

√5th 760.6 Surgical operation on mother and fetus
EXCLUDES cesarean section for present delivery (763.4)
damage to placenta from amniocentesis, cesarean section, or surgical induction (762.1)
AHA: 4Q, '08, 137-138
TIP: These codes include existing conditions present at the time of birth that are related to procedures performed before the time of delivery.

760.61 Newborn affected by amniocentesis
EXCLUDES fetal complications from amniocentesis (679.1)

760.62 Newborn affected by other in utero procedure
EXCLUDES fetal complications of in utero procedure (679.1)

760.63 Newborn affected by other surgical operations on mother during pregnancy
EXCLUDES newborn affected by previous surgical procedure on mother not associated with pregnancy (760.64)

760.64 Newborn affected by previous surgical procedure on mother not associated with pregnancy

√5th 760.7 Noxious influences affecting fetus or newborn via placenta or breast milk
Fetus or newborn affected by noxious substance transmitted via placenta or breast milk
EXCLUDES anesthetic and analgesic drugs administered during labor and delivery (763.5)
drug withdrawal syndrome in newborn (779.5)
AHA: 3Q, '91, 21

760.70 Unspecified noxious substance
Fetus or newborn affected by:
Drug NEC

760.71 Alcohol
Fetal alcohol syndrome

760.72 Narcotics

760.73 Hallucinogenic agents

760.74 Anti-infectives
Antibiotics
Antifungals

760.75 Cocaine
AHA: 3Q, '94, 6; 2Q, '92, 12; 4Q, '91, 26
TIP: If documentation indicates drug withdrawal in the newborn, also assign code 779.5 Drug withdrawal syndrome in newborn.

760.76 Diethylstilbestrol [DES]
AHA: 4Q, '94, 45

760.77 Anticonvulsants   N
Carbamazepine
Phenobarbital
Phenytoin
Valproic acid
AHA: 4Q, '05, 82

760.78 Antimetabolic agents   N
Methotrexate
Retinoic acid
Statins
AHA: 4Q, '05, 82-83

760.79 Other
Fetus or newborn affected by:
immune sera
medicinal agents NEC } transmitted via placenta or breast
toxic substance NEC
AHA: 1Q, '10, 14; 3Q, '09, 21
P04.8 Newborn (suspected) affected by oth   I-10
maternl noxious substnce

760.8 Other specified maternal conditions affecting fetus or newborn
Maternal genital tract and other localized infection affecting fetus or newborn, but fetus or newborn not manifesting that disease
EXCLUDES maternal urinary tract infection affecting fetus or newborn (760.1)

760.9 Unspecified maternal condition affecting fetus or newborn

√4th 761 Fetus or newborn affected by maternal complications of pregnancy
INCLUDES the listed maternal conditions only when specified as a cause of mortality or morbidity of the fetus or newborn

761.0 Incompetent cervix
DEF: Inadequate functioning of uterine cervix.

761.1 Premature rupture of membranes

761.2 Oligohydramnios
EXCLUDES that due to premature rupture of membranes (761.1)
DEF: Deficient amniotic fluid.

761.3 Polyhydramnios
Hydramnios (acute) (chronic)
DEF: Excess amniotic fluid.

761.4 Ectopic pregnancy
Pregnancy: Pregnancy:
abdominal   tubal
intraperitoneal

√4th **√5th** Additional Digit Required   Unacceptable PDx   Manifestation Code   Hospital Acquired Condition   ►◄ Revised Text   ● New Code   ▲ Revised Code Title

2015 ICD-9-CM   **Volume 1 – 273**

761.5 Multiple pregnancy
Triplet (pregnancy)
Twin (pregnancy)

761.6 Maternal death

761.7 Malpresentation before labor
Breech presentation
External version
Oblique lie ⎱
Transverse lie ⎰ before labor
Unstable lie

761.8 Other specified maternal complications of pregnancy affecting fetus or newborn
Spontaneous abortion, fetus

761.9 Unspecified maternal complication of pregnancy affecting fetus or newborn

✓4ᵗʰ **762 Fetus or newborn affected by complications of placenta, cord, and membranes**
INCLUDES the listed maternal conditions only when specified as a cause of mortality or morbidity in the fetus or newborn
AHA: 1Q, '94, 8

762.0 Placenta previa
DEF: Placenta developed in lower segment of uterus; causes hemorrhaging in last trimester.

762.1 Other forms of placental separation and hemorrhage N
Abruptio placentae
Antepartum hemorrhage
Damage to placenta from amniocentesis, cesarean section, or surgical induction
Maternal blood loss
Premature separation of placenta
Rupture of marginal sinus

762.2 Other and unspecified morphological and functional abnormalities of placenta N
Placental: Placental:
dysfunction   insufficiency
infarction

762.3 Placental transfusion syndromes N
Placental and cord abnormality resulting in twin-to-twin or other transplacental transfusion
Use additional code to indicate resultant condition in newborn:
fetal blood loss (772.0)
polycythemia neonatorum (776.4)

762.4 Prolapsed cord N
Cord presentation

762.5 Other compression of umbilical cord N
Cord around neck   Knot in cord
Entanglement of cord   Torsion of cord
AHA: 2Q, '03, 9
TIP: Assign only if the cord compression or entanglement was documented as having affected the fetus/newborn.
P02.5 Newborn (suspected) affected by oth compression umb cord   I·10

762.6 Other and unspecified conditions of umbilical cord N
Short cord
Thrombosis ⎫
Varices ⎬ of umbilical cord
Velamentous insertion ⎪
Vasa previa ⎭
EXCLUDES infection of umbilical cord (771.4)
single umbilical artery (747.5)
P02.69 Newborn (suspected) affected by oth cond umbili cord   I·10

762.7 Chorioamnionitis N
Amnionitis   Placentitis
Membranitis
DEF: Inflamed fetal membrane.

762.8 Other specified abnormalities of chorion and amnion N

762.9 Unspecified abnormality of chorion and amnion N

✓4ᵗʰ **763 Fetus or newborn affected by other complications of labor and delivery**
INCLUDES the listed conditions only when specified as a cause of mortality or morbidity in the fetus or newborn
EXCLUDES newborn affected by surgical procedures on mother (760.61-760.64)
AHA: 1Q, '94, 8

763.0 Breech delivery and extraction N

763.1 Other malpresentation, malposition, and disproportion during labor and delivery N
Fetus or newborn affected by:
abnormality of bony pelvis
contracted pelvis
persistent occipitoposterior position
shoulder presentation
transverse lie
Fetus or newborn affected by conditions classifiable to 652, 653, and 660

763.2 Forceps delivery N
Fetus or newborn affected by forceps extraction

763.3 Delivery by vacuum extractor N

763.4 Cesarean delivery N
EXCLUDES placental separation or hemorrhage from cesarean section (762.1)

763.5 Maternal anesthesia and analgesia N
Reactions and intoxications from maternal opiates and tranquilizers during labor and delivery
EXCLUDES drug withdrawal syndrome in newborn (779.5)

763.6 Precipitate delivery N
Rapid second stage

763.7 Abnormal uterine contractions N
Fetus or newborn affected by:
contraction ring
hypertonic labor
hypotonic uterine dysfunction
uterine inertia or dysfunction
Fetus or newborn affected by conditions classifiable to 661, except 661.3

✓5ᵗʰ **763.8 Other specified complications of labor and delivery affecting fetus or newborn**
AHA: 4Q, '98, 46

763.81 Abnormality in fetal heart rate or rhythm before the onset of labor N

763.82 Abnormality in fetal heart rate or rhythm during labor N
AHA: 4Q, '98, 46

763.83 Abnormality in fetal heart rate or rhythm, unspecified as to time of onset N

763.84 Meconium passage during delivery N
EXCLUDES meconium aspiration (770.11, 770.12)
meconium staining (779.84)
DEF: Fetal intestinal activity that increases in response to a distressed state during delivery; anal sphincter relaxes, and meconium is passed into the amniotic fluid.
AHA: ▶4Q, '13, 94, 95;◀ 4Q, '05, 83
TIP: If the meconium was documented as aspirated or had any effect on the newborn, see codes 770.11 and 770.12.

763.89 Other specified complications of labor and delivery affecting fetus or newborn N
Fetus or newborn affected by:
abnormality of maternal soft tissues
destructive operation on live fetus to facilitate delivery
induction of labor (medical)
other procedures used in labor and delivery
Fetus or newborn affected by other conditions classifiable to 650-699

763.9 Unspecified complication of labor and delivery affecting fetus or newborn N

N Newborn Age: 0   P Pediatric Age: 0-17   M Maternity Age: 12-55   A Adult Age: 15-124   MCC Major CC Condition   CC CC Condition   HIV HIV Related Dx

274 – Volume 1 · October 2014   2015 ICD-9-CM

Other Conditions Originating in the Perinatal Period (764–779)

The following fifth-digit subclassification is for use with category 764 and codes 765.0-765.1 to denote birthweight:

0   **unspecified [weight]**
1   **less than 500 grams**
2   **500-749 grams**
3   **750-999 grams**
4   **1,000-1,249 grams**
5   **1,250-1,499 grams**
6   **1,500-1,749 grams**
7   **1,750-1,999 grams**
8   **2,000-2,499 grams**
9   **2,500 grams and over**

✓4th **764 Slow fetal growth and fetal malnutrition**
     AHA: 1Q, '09, 13; 3Q, '04, 4; 4Q, '02, 63; 1Q,'94, 8; 2Q, '91, 19; 2Q, '89, 15

§ ✓5th **764.0 "Light-for-dates" without mention of fetal** N
[0-9]   **malnutrition**
     Infants underweight for gestational age
     "Small-for-dates"
     P05.00 Newborn light for gest age unsp weight   I-10

§ ✓5th **764.1 "Light-for-dates" with signs of fetal malnutrition** N
[0-9]   Infants "light-for-dates" classifiable to 764.0, who in addition
     show signs of fetal malnutrition, such as dry peeling
     skin and loss of subcutaneous tissue

§ ✓5th **764.2 Fetal malnutrition without mention of** N
[0-9]   **"light-for-dates"**
     Infants, not underweight for gestational age, showing signs of
     fetal malnutrition, such as dry peeling skin and loss of
     subcutaneous tissue
     Intrauterine malnutrition

§ ✓5th **764.9 Fetal growth retardation, unspecified** N
[0-9]   Intrauterine growth retardation
     AHA: For code 764.97: 1Q, '97, 6

✓4th **765 Disorders relating to short gestation and low birthweight**
     INCLUDES the listed conditions, without further specification, as
     causes of mortality, morbidity, or additional care, in
     fetus or newborn
     AHA: 1Q, '97, 6; 1Q, '94, 8; 2Q, '91, 19; 2Q, '89, 15

§ ✓5th **765.0 Extreme immaturity** N
[0-9]   NOTE Usually implies a birthweight of less than 1000 grams.
     Use additional code for weeks of gestation (765.20-765.29)
     AHA: 1Q, '09, 13 3Q '04, 4; 4Q, '02, 63; For code 765.01: ▶ 1Q, '14, 16;◀
     For code 765.03: 4Q, '01, 51

§ ✓5th **765.1 Other preterm infants** N
[0-9]   NOTE Usually implies a birthweight of 1000-2499 grams.
     Prematurity NOS
     Prematurity or small size, not classifiable to 765.0 or as
     "light-for-dates" in 764
     Use additional code for weeks of gestation (765.20-765.29)
     AHA: 1Q, '09, 13; 3Q, '04, 4; 4Q, '02, 63; For code 765.10: 1Q, '09, 15; 1Q,
     '94, 14; For code 765.17: 4Q, '08, 139; 1Q, '97, 6; For code 765.18: 4Q, '02,
     64
     P07.10 Other low birth weight newborn uns weight   I-10

✓5th **765.2 Weeks of gestation**
     AHA: 3Q, '04, 4; 4Q, '02, 63
     TIP: Assign as an additional code with category 764 and codes from
     765.0 and 765.1, as documented by the provider.

     765.20 Unspecified weeks of gestation N

     765.21 Less than 24 completed weeks of gestation N
         AHA: ▶1Q, '14, 16◀

     765.22 24 completed weeks of gestation N

     765.23 25-26 completed weeks of gestation N
         AHA: 1Q, '09, 14

     765.24 27-28 completed weeks of gestation N

     765.25 29-30 completed weeks of gestation N
         P07.32 Preterm newborn, gestl age 29 compl wks   I-10

     765.26 31-32 completed weeks of gestation N
         AHA: 1Q, '09, 14; 4Q, '08, 139

     765.27 33-34 completed weeks of gestation N
         AHA: 4Q, '10, 97

     765.28 35-36 completed weeks of gestation N
         AHA: 4Q, '02, 64
         P07.38 Preterm newborn, gestl age 35 compl wks   I-10

     765.29 37 or more completed weeks of gestation N

✓4th **766 Disorders relating to long gestation and high birthweight**
     INCLUDES the listed conditions, without further specification, as
     causes of mortality, morbidity, or additional care, in
     fetus or newborn

     766.0 Exceptionally large baby N
         NOTE Usually implies a birthweight of 4500 grams or more.

     766.1 Other "heavy-for-dates" infants N
         Other fetus or infant "heavy-" or "large-for-dates" regardless
         of period of gestation
         P08.1 Other heavy for gestational age newborn   I-10

✓5th **766.2 Late infant, not "heavy-for-dates"** N
         AHA: 2Q, '06, 12
         TIP: May be assigned based on gestational age alone, without
         documentation of any related specific condition or disorder.

     766.21 Post-term infant N
         Infant with gestation period over 40 completed
         weeks to 42 completed weeks
         AHA: 1Q, '09, 12; 4Q, '03, 69
         P08.21 Post-term newborn   I-10

     766.22 Prolonged gestation of infant N
         Infant with gestation period over 42 completed
         weeks
         Postmaturity NOS
         AHA: 1Q, '09, 12

✓4th **767 Birth trauma**

     767.0 Subdural and cerebral hemorrhage MCC N
         Subdural and cerebral hemorrhage, whether described as due
         to birth trauma or to intrapartum anoxia or hypoxia
         Subdural hematoma (localized)
         Tentorial tear
         Use additional code to identify cause
         EXCLUDES intraventricular hemorrhage (772.10-772.14)
              subarachnoid hemorrhage (772.2)
         CC Excl: 767.0, 767.8-767.9, 779.81-779.84, 779.89

✓5th **767.1 Injuries to scalp**
         AHA: 4Q, '03, 69

     767.11 Epicranial subaponeurotic hemorrhage CC N
         (massive)
         Subgaleal hemorrhage
         DEF: A hemorrhage that occurs within the space between
         the galea aponeurotica, or epicranial aponeurosis, a thin
         tendinous structure that is attached to the skull laterally,
         and the periosteum of the skull.
         CC Excl: 767.0-767.11, 767.8-767.9, 779.81-779.84, 779.89

     767.19 Other injuries to scalp N
         Caput succedaneum
         Cephalhematoma
         Chignon (from vacuum extraction)
         P12.89 Other birth injuries to scalp   I-10

     767.2 Fracture of clavicle N

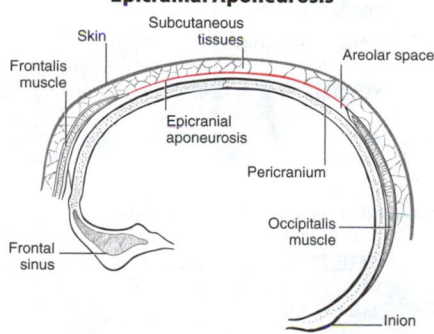

Epicranial Aponeurosis

Skin
Subcutaneous tissues
Areolar space
Frontalis muscle
Epicranial aponeurosis
Pericranium
Occipitalis muscle
Frontal sinus
Inion

---

§   Requires fifth digit. Valid digits are in [brackets] under each code. See beginning of section 764-779 for fifth digit definitions.

✓4th ✓5th Additional Digit Required   Unacceptable PDx   Manifestation Code   Hospital Acquired Condition   ▶◀ Revised Text   ● New Code   ▲ Revised Code Title

767.3 Other injuries to skeleton   N
Fracture of:
long bones
skull
EXCLUDES *congenital dislocation of hip (754.30-754.35)*
fracture of spine, congenital (767.4)

767.4 Injury to spine and spinal cord   N
Dislocation
Fracture ⎱ of spine or spinal cord due to
Laceration ⎰   birth trauma
Rupture

767.5 Facial nerve injury   N
Facial palsy

767.6 Injury to brachial plexus   N
Palsy or paralysis:
brachial
Erb (-Duchenne)
Klumpke (-Déjérine)

767.7 Other cranial and peripheral nerve injuries   N
Phrenic nerve paralysis

767.8 Other specified birth trauma   N
Eye damage   Rupture of:
Hematoma of: liver
   liver (subcapsular)   spleen
   testes   Scalpel wound
   vulva   Traumatic glaucoma
EXCLUDES *hemorrhage classifiable to 772.0-772.9*

767.9 Birth trauma, unspecified   N
Birth injury NOS

√4ᵗʰ **768 Intrauterine hypoxia and birth asphyxia**
NOTE Use only when associated with newborn morbidity classifiable
elsewhere
EXCLUDES *acidemia NOS of newborn (775.81)*
acidosis NOS of newborn (775.81)
cerebral ischemia NOS (779.2)
hypoxia NOS of newborn (770.88)
mixed metabolic and respiratory acidosis of newborn
(775.81)
respiratory arrest of newborn (770.87)
DEF: Oxygen intake insufficiency due to interrupted placental circulation or
premature separation of placenta.
AHA: 4Q, '92, 20

768.0 Fetal death from asphyxia or anoxia before   N
onset of labor or at unspecified time

768.1 Fetal death from asphyxia or anoxia during labor   N

768.2 Fetal distress before onset of labor, in liveborn infant   N
Fetal metabolic acidemia before onset of labor, in liveborn
infant

768.3 Fetal distress first noted during labor and   N
delivery, in liveborn infant
Fetal metabolic acidemia first noted during labor and
delivery, in liveborn infant

768.4 Fetal distress, unspecified as to time of onset,   N
in liveborn infant
Fetal metabolic acidemia unspecified as to time of onset, in
liveborn infant
CC Excl: 516.61-516.69, 768.5-768.6, 768.9-770.86, 770.89-770.9,
779.81-779.84, 779.89
AHA: N-D, '86, 10

768.5 Severe birth asphyxia   MCC N
Birth asphyxia with neurologic involvement
EXCLUDES *hypoxic-ischemic encephalopathy [HIE]*
(768.70-768.73)
CC Excl: 516.61-516.69, 768.5-768.6, 768.9-770.86, 770.89-770.9,
779.81-779.84, 779.89
AHA: N-D, '86, 3

768.6 Mild or moderate birth asphyxia   N
Birth asphyxia (without mention of neurologic involvement)
EXCLUDES *hypoxic-ischemic encephalopathy [HIE]*
(768.70-768.73)
AHA: N-D, '86, 3

√5ᵗʰ **768.7 Hypoxic-ischemic encephalopathy [HIE]**
AHA: 4Q, '09, 99-101; 4Q, '06, 104

768.70 Hypoxic-ischemic encephalopathy,   CC N
unspecified
CC Excl: 768.5-768.9

768.71 Mild hypoxic-ischemic encephalopathy   CC N
CC Excl: See code: 768.70

768.72 Moderate hypoxic-ischemic encephalopathy   CC N
CC Excl: See code: 768.70
AHA: 4Q, '09,101

768.73 Severe hypoxic-ischemic encephalopathy   MCC N
CC Excl: See code: 768.70

768.9 Unspecified birth asphyxia in liveborn infant   N
Anoxia ⎱ NOS, in liveborn infant
Asphyxia ⎰

769 Respiratory distress syndrome   MCC N
Cardiorespiratory distress syndrome of newborn
Hyaline membrane disease (pulmonary)
Idiopathic respiratory distress syndrome [IRDS or RDS] of newborn
Pulmonary hypoperfusion syndrome
EXCLUDES *transient tachypnea of newborn (770.6)*
DEF: Severe chest contractions upon air intake and expiratory grunting;
infant appears blue due to oxygen deficiency and has rapid respiratory rate;
formerly called hyaline membrane disease.
CC Excl: 516.61-516.69, 768.5-768.6, 768.9-770.86, 770.89-770.9,
779.81-779.84, 779.89
AHA: 1Q, '89, 10; N-D, '86, 6
TIP: Do not assign if documentation specifies Type II respiratory distress syn-
drome, which usually resolves within six to 24 hours after birth; see instead
770.6.
P22.0 Respiratory distress syndrome of newborn   I-10

√4ᵗʰ **770 Other respiratory conditions of fetus and newborn**

770.0 Congenital pneumonia   MCC N
Infective pneumonia acquired prenatally
EXCLUDES *pneumonia from infection acquired after birth*
(480.0-486)
CC Excl: 516.61-516.69, 768.5-768.6, 768.9-770.86, 770.89-770.9,
779.81-779.84, 779.89
AHA: 1Q, '05, 10

√5ᵗʰ **770.1 Fetal and newborn aspiration**
EXCLUDES *aspiration of postnatal stomach contents (770.85,*
770.86)
meconium passage during delivery (763.84)
meconium staining (779.84)
AHA: 4Q, '05, 83

770.10 Fetal and newborn aspiration, unspecified   N

770.11 Meconium aspiration without respiratory   N
symptoms
Meconium aspiration NOS

770.12 Meconium aspiration with respiratory   MCC N
symptoms
Meconium aspiration pneumonia
Meconium aspiration pneumonitis
Meconium aspiration syndrome NOS
Use additional code to identify any secondary
pulmonary hypertension (416.8), if applicable
DEF: Meconium aspiration syndrome: aspiration of fetal
intestinal material during or prior to delivery, usually a
complication of placental insufficiency, causing
pneumonitis and bronchial obstruction (inflammatory
reaction of lungs).
CC Excl: See code: 770.0

770.13 Aspiration of clear amniotic fluid without   N
respiratory symptoms
Aspiration of clear amniotic fluid NOS

770.14 Aspiration of clear amniotic   MCC N
fluid with respiratory symptoms
Aspiration of clear amniotic fluid with pneumonia
Aspiration of clear amniotic fluid with pneumonitis
Use additional code to identify any secondary
pulmonary hypertension (416.8), if applicable
CC Excl: See code: 770.0

N Newborn Age: 0   P Pediatric Age: 0-17   M Maternity Age: 12-55   A Adult Age: 15-124   MCC Major CC Condition   CC CC Condition   HIV HIV Related Dx

770.15 Aspiration of blood without respiratory symptoms `N`
Aspiration of blood NOS

770.16 Aspiration of blood with respiratory symptoms `MCC` `N`
Aspiration of blood with pneumonia
Aspiration of blood with pneumonitis
Use additional code to identify any secondary pulmonary hypertension (416.8), if applicable
CC Excl: See code: 770.0

770.17 Other fetal and newborn aspiration without respiratory symptoms `N`

770.18 Other fetal and newborn aspiration with respiratory symptoms `MCC` `N`
Other aspiration pneumonia
Other aspiration pneumonitis
Use additional code to identify any secondary pulmonary hypertension (416.8), if applicable
CC Excl: See code: 770.0

770.2 Interstitial emphysema and related conditions `MCC` `N`
Pneumomediastinum ⎫
Pneumopericardium ⎬ originating in the perinatal
Pneumothorax ⎭ period
CC Excl: See code: 770.0
P25.0 Interstitial emphysema origin perinatal period `I-10`

770.3 Pulmonary hemorrhage `MCC` `N`
Hemorrhage:
alveolar (lung) ⎫
intra-alveolar (lung) ⎬ originating in the
massive pulmonary ⎭ perinatal period
CC Excl: See code: 770.0

770.4 Primary atelectasis `CC` `N`
Pulmonary immaturity NOS
DEF: Alveoli fail to expand causing insufficient air intake by newborn.
CC Excl: See code: 770.0

770.5 Other and unspecified atelectasis `CC` `N`
Atelectasis:
NOS ⎫
partial ⎬ originating in the perinatal
secondary ⎭ period
Pulmonary collapse
CC Excl: See code: 770.0

770.6 Transitory tachypnea of newborn `N`
Idiopathic tachypnea of newborn
Wet lung syndrome
EXCLUDES *respiratory distress syndrome (769)*
DEF: Quick, shallow breathing of newborn; short-term problem.
AHA: 4Q, '95, 4; 1Q, '94, 12; 3Q, '93, 7; 1Q, '89, 10; N-D, '86, 6
P22.1 Transient tachypnea of newborn `I-10`

770.7 Chronic respiratory disease arising in the perinatal period `MCC`
Bronchopulmonary dysplasia
Interstitial pulmonary fibrosis of prematurity
Wilson-Mikity syndrome
CC Excl: See code: 770.0
AHA: 1Q, '11, 16; 2Q, '91, 19; N-D, '86, 11
P27.8 Other chronic resp dz origin perinatal period `I-10`

✓5ᵗʰ **770.8 Other respiratory problems after birth**
EXCLUDES *mixed metabolic and respiratory acidosis of newborn (775.81)*
AHA: 4Q, '02, 65; 2Q, '98, 10; 2Q, '96, 10

770.81 Primary apnea of newborn `CC` `N`
Apneic spells of newborn NOS
Essential apnea of newborn
Sleep apnea of newborn
DEF: Cessation of breathing when a neonate makes no respiratory effort for 15 seconds, resulting in cyanosis and bradycardia.
CC Excl: 770.82-770.83, 770.87-770.9, 786.03
P28.3 Primary sleep apnea of newborn `I-10`

770.82 Other apnea of newborn `CC` `N`
Obstructive apnea of newborn
CC Excl: 770.81-770.83, 770.87-770.9, 786.03

770.83 Cyanotic attacks of newborn `CC` `N`
CC Excl: 770.81-770.83, 770.87-770.9, 782.5, 786.03

770.84 Respiratory failure of newborn `MCC` `N`
EXCLUDES *respiratory distress syndrome (769)*
CC Excl: 516.61-516.69, 768.5-768.6, 768.9-770.86, 770.89-770.9, 779.81-779.84, 779.89
AHA: 4Q, '08, 99

770.85 Aspiration of postnatal stomach contents without respiratory symptoms `N`
Aspiration of postnatal stomach contents NOS
AHA: 4Q, '05, 83

770.86 Aspiration of postnatal stomach contents with respiratory symptoms `MCC` `N`
Aspiration of postnatal stomach contents with pneumonia
Aspiration of postnatal stomach contents with pneumonitis
Use additional code to identify any secondary pulmonary hypertension (416.8), if applicable
CC Excl: See code: 770.84
AHA: 4Q, '05, 83

770.87 Respiratory arrest of newborn `MCC` `N`
CC Excl: 770.11, 770.13, 770.15, 770.17, 770.6, 770.81-770.85, 770.88-770.9, 779.85, 786.03, 799.1
AHA: 4Q, '06, 104-106

770.88 Hypoxemia of newborn `N`
Hypoxia NOS of newborn
AHA: 4Q, '06, 104-106

770.89 Other respiratory problems after birth `N`
AHA: 3Q, '09, 20
P28.89 Oth specified respiratory conditions of newborn `I-10`

770.9 Unspecified respiratory condition of fetus and newborn `N`

✓4ᵗʰ **771 Infections specific to the perinatal period**
INCLUDES infections acquired before or during birth or via the umbilicus or during the first 28 days after birth
EXCLUDES *congenital pneumonia (770.0)*
congenital syphilis (090.0-090.9)
infant botulism (040.41)
maternal infectious disease as a cause of mortality or morbidity in fetus or newborn, but fetus or newborn not manifesting the disease (760.2)
ophthalmia neonatorum due to gonococcus (098.40)
other infections not specifically classified to this category
AHA: N-D, '85, 4

771.0 Congenital rubella `CC` `N`
Congenital rubella pneumonitis
CC Excl: 771.0-771.2, 779.81-779.84, 779.89

771.1 Congenital cytomegalovirus infection `MCC` `N`
Congenital cytomegalic inclusion disease
CC Excl: See code: 771.0

771.2 Other congenital infections `MCC` `N`
Congenital: Congenital:
herpes simplex   toxoplasmosis
listeriosis   tuberculosis
malaria
CC Excl: 013.60-013.66, 046.2, 046.71-046.8, 048-049.0, 049.8, 052.0, 052.2, 054.3, 054.74, 056.01, 057.8-058.29, 059.00-059.9, 062.0-064, 066.2-066.49, 072.2, 073.7, 075, 078.3, 079.82, 079.99, 081.9, 083.9, 084.6, 090.41, 094.81, 117.5, 124, 130.0, 290.12, 323.01-323.9, 341.1, 382.4, 487.8, 710.0, 771.2, 984.9

771.3 Tetanus neonatorum `MCC` `N`
Tetanus omphalitis
EXCLUDES *hypocalcemic tetany (775.4)*
DEF: Severe infection of central nervous system; due to exotoxin of tetanus bacillus from navel infection prompted by nonsterile technique during umbilical ligation.
CC Excl: 771.3, 779.81-779.84, 779.89

✓4ᵗʰ ✓5ᵗʰ Additional Digit Required   Unacceptable PDx   Manifestation Code   Hospital Acquired Condition   ▶◀ Revised Text   ● New Code   ▲ Revised Code Title

2015 ICD-9-CM   **Volume 1 – 277**

771.4 Omphalitis of the newborn 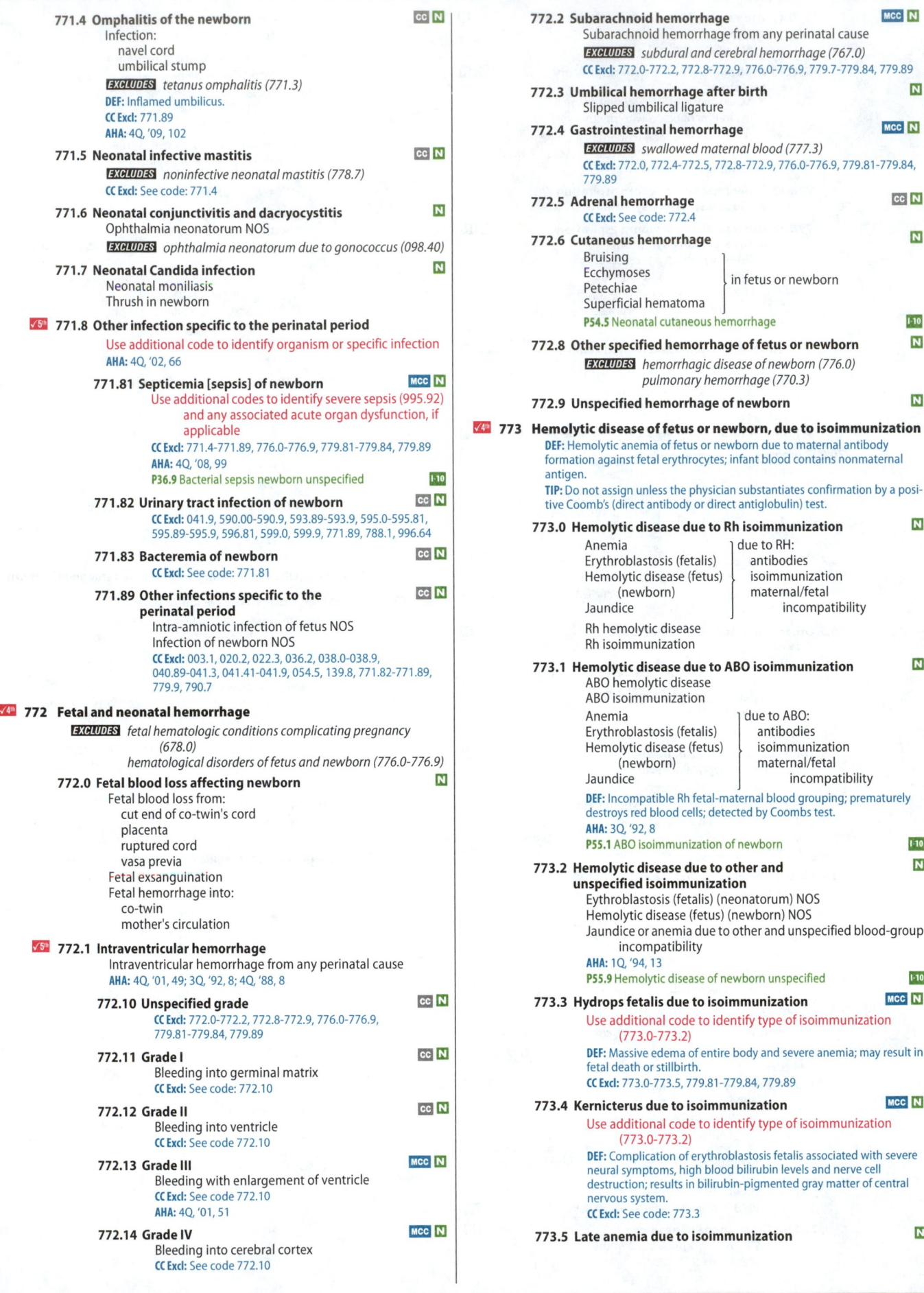 `CC` `N`
Infection:
navel cord
umbilical stump
> *EXCLUDES* tetanus omphalitis (771.3)

DEF: Inflamed umbilicus.
CC Excl: 771.89
AHA: 4Q, '09, 102

771.5 Neonatal infective mastitis `CC` `N`
> *EXCLUDES* noninfective neonatal mastitis (778.7)

CC Excl: See code: 771.4

771.6 Neonatal conjunctivitis and dacryocystitis `N`
Ophthalmia neonatorum NOS
> *EXCLUDES* ophthalmia neonatorum due to gonococcus (098.40)

771.7 Neonatal Candida infection `N`
Neonatal moniliasis
Thrush in newborn

√5ᵗʰ **771.8 Other infection specific to the perinatal period**
Use additional code to identify organism or specific infection
AHA: 4Q, '02, 66

771.81 Septicemia [sepsis] of newborn `MCC` `N`
Use additional codes to identify severe sepsis (995.92) and any associated acute organ dysfunction, if applicable
CC Excl: 771.4-771.89, 776.0-776.9, 779.81-779.84, 779.89
AHA: 4Q, '08, 99
P36.9 Bacterial sepsis newborn unspecified `I-10`

771.82 Urinary tract infection of newborn `CC` `N`
CC Excl: 041.9, 590.00-590.9, 593.89-593.9, 595.0-595.81, 595.89-595.9, 596.81, 599.0, 599.9, 771.89, 788.1, 996.64

771.83 Bacteremia of newborn `CC` `N`
CC Excl: See code: 771.81

771.89 Other infections specific to the perinatal period `CC` `N`
Intra-amniotic infection of fetus NOS
Infection of newborn NOS
CC Excl: 003.1, 020.2, 022.3, 036.2, 038.0-038.9, 040.89-041.3, 041.41-041.9, 054.5, 139.8, 771.82-771.89, 779.9, 790.7

√4ᵗʰ **772 Fetal and neonatal hemorrhage**
> *EXCLUDES* fetal hematologic conditions complicating pregnancy (678.0)
> hematological disorders of fetus and newborn (776.0-776.9)

772.0 Fetal blood loss affecting newborn `N`
Fetal blood loss from:
cut end of co-twin's cord
placenta
ruptured cord
vasa previa
Fetal exsanguination
Fetal hemorrhage into:
co-twin
mother's circulation

√5ᵗʰ **772.1 Intraventricular hemorrhage**
Intraventricular hemorrhage from any perinatal cause
AHA: 4Q, '01, 49; 3Q, '92, 8; 4Q, '88, 8

772.10 Unspecified grade `CC` `N`
CC Excl: 772.0-772.2, 772.8-772.9, 776.0-776.9, 779.81-779.84, 779.89

772.11 Grade I `CC` `N`
Bleeding into germinal matrix
CC Excl: See code: 772.10

772.12 Grade II `CC` `N`
Bleeding into ventricle
CC Excl: See code 772.10

772.13 Grade III `MCC` `N`
Bleeding with enlargement of ventricle
CC Excl: See code 772.10
AHA: 4Q, '01, 51

772.14 Grade IV `MCC` `N`
Bleeding into cerebral cortex
CC Excl: See code 772.10

772.2 Subarachnoid hemorrhage `MCC` `N`
Subarachnoid hemorrhage from any perinatal cause
> *EXCLUDES* subdural and cerebral hemorrhage (767.0)

CC Excl: 772.0-772.2, 772.8-772.9, 776.0-776.9, 779.7-779.84, 779.89

772.3 Umbilical hemorrhage after birth `N`
Slipped umbilical ligature

772.4 Gastrointestinal hemorrhage `MCC` `N`
> *EXCLUDES* swallowed maternal blood (777.3)

CC Excl: 772.0, 772.4-772.5, 772.8-772.9, 776.0-776.9, 779.81-779.84, 779.89

772.5 Adrenal hemorrhage `CC` `N`
CC Excl: See code: 772.4

772.6 Cutaneous hemorrhage `N`
Bruising ⎫
Ecchymoses ⎬ in fetus or newborn
Petechiae ⎪
Superficial hematoma ⎭
P54.5 Neonatal cutaneous hemorrhage `I-10`

772.8 Other specified hemorrhage of fetus or newborn `N`
> *EXCLUDES* hemorrhagic disease of newborn (776.0)
> pulmonary hemorrhage (770.3)

772.9 Unspecified hemorrhage of newborn `N`

√4ᵗʰ **773 Hemolytic disease of fetus or newborn, due to isoimmunization**
DEF: Hemolytic anemia of fetus or newborn due to maternal antibody formation against fetal erythrocytes; infant blood contains nonmaternal antigen.
TIP: Do not assign unless the physician substantiates confirmation by a positive Coomb's (direct antibody or direct antiglobulin) test.

773.0 Hemolytic disease due to Rh isoimmunization `N`
Anemia ⎫ due to RH:
Erythroblastosis (fetalis) ⎪ antibodies
Hemolytic disease (fetus) ⎬ isoimmunization
(newborn) ⎪ maternal/fetal
Jaundice ⎭ incompatibility
Rh hemolytic disease
Rh isoimmunization

773.1 Hemolytic disease due to ABO isoimmunization `N`
ABO hemolytic disease
ABO isoimmunization
Anemia ⎫ due to ABO:
Erythroblastosis (fetalis) ⎪ antibodies
Hemolytic disease (fetus) ⎬ isoimmunization
(newborn) ⎪ maternal/fetal
Jaundice ⎭ incompatibility
DEF: Incompatible Rh fetal-maternal blood grouping; prematurely destroys red blood cells; detected by Coombs test.
AHA: 3Q, '92, 8
P55.1 ABO isoimmunization of newborn `I-10`

773.2 Hemolytic disease due to other and unspecified isoimmunization `N`
Eythroblastosis (fetalis) (neonatorum) NOS
Hemolytic disease (fetus) (newborn) NOS
Jaundice or anemia due to other and unspecified blood-group incompatibility
AHA: 1Q, '94, 13
P55.9 Hemolytic disease of newborn unspecified `I-10`

773.3 Hydrops fetalis due to isoimmunization `MCC` `N`
Use additional code to identify type of isoimmunization (773.0-773.2)
DEF: Massive edema of entire body and severe anemia; may result in fetal death or stillbirth.
CC Excl: 773.0-773.5, 779.81-779.84, 779.89

773.4 Kernicterus due to isoimmunization `MCC` `N`
Use additional code to identify type of isoimmunization (773.0-773.2)
DEF: Complication of erythroblastosis fetalis associated with severe neural symptoms, high blood bilirubin levels and nerve cell destruction; results in bilirubin-pigmented gray matter of central nervous system.
CC Excl: See code: 773.3

773.5 Late anemia due to isoimmunization `N`

`N` Newborn Age: 0   `P` Pediatric Age: 0-17   `M` Maternity Age: 12-55   `A` Adult Age: 15-124   `MCC` Major CC Condition   `CC` CC Condition   `HIV` HIV Related Dx

✓4ᵗʰ **774 Other perinatal jaundice**

774.0 *Perinatal jaundice from hereditary hemolytic anemias* N
Code first underlying disease (282.0-282.9)

774.1 Perinatal jaundice from other excessive hemolysis N
Fetal or neonatal jaundice from:
bruising
drugs or toxins transmitted from mother
infection
polycythemia
swallowed maternal blood
Use additional code to identify cause
EXCLUDES *jaundice due to isoimmunization (773.0-773.2)*

774.2 Neonatal jaundice associated with preterm delivery N
Hyperbilirubinemia of prematurity
Jaundice due to delayed conjugation associated with preterm
delivery
AHA: 3Q, '91, 21
P59.0 Neonatal jaundice associated w/preterm delivery I-10

✓5ᵗʰ **774.3 Neonatal jaundice due to delayed conjugation from other causes**

774.30 Neonatal jaundice due to delayed conjugation, cause unspecified N
DEF: Jaundice of newborn with abnormal bilirubin metabolism; causes excess accumulated unconjugated bilirubin in blood.

774.31 *Neonatal jaundice due to delayed conjugation in diseases classified elsewhere* N
Code first underlying diseases as:
congenital hypothyroidism (243)
Crigler-Najjar syndrome (277.4)
Gilbert's syndrome (277.4)

774.39 Other N
Jaundice due to delayed conjugation from causes,
such as:
breast milk inhibitors
delayed development of conjugating system

774.4 Perinatal jaundice due to hepatocellular damage MCC N
Fetal or neonatal hepatitis
Giant cell hepatitis
Inspissated bile syndrome
CC Excl: 774.0-774.7, 779.81-779.84, 779.89

774.5 *Perinatal jaundice from other causes* N
Code first underlying cause as:
congenital obstruction of bile duct (751.61)
galactosemia (271.1)
mucoviscidosis (277.00-277.09)

774.6 Unspecified fetal and neonatal jaundice N
Icterus neonatorum
Neonatal hyperbilirubinemia (transient)
Physiologic jaundice NOS in newborn
EXCLUDES *that in preterm infants (774.2)*
AHA: 1Q, '94, 13; 2Q, '89, 15
P59.9 Neonatal jaundice unspecified I-10

774.7 Kernicterus not due to isoimmunization MCC N
Bilirubin encephalopathy
Kernicterus of newborn NOS
EXCLUDES *kernicterus due to isoimmunization (773.4)*
CC Excl: See code: 774.4

✓4ᵗʰ **775 Endocrine and metabolic disturbances specific to the fetus and newborn**
INCLUDES transitory endocrine and metabolic disturbances caused
by the infant's response to maternal endocrine and
metabolic factors, its removal from them, or its
adjustment to extrauterine existence

775.0 Syndrome of "infant of a diabetic mother" N
Maternal diabetes mellitus affecting fetus or newborn (with
hypoglycemia)
AHA: 1Q, '04, 7-8; 3Q, '91, 5
TIP: Do not assign if the infant has no manifestations or symptoms of
the syndrome; refer instead to code V18.0 Family history, diabetes
mellitus.
P70.1 Syndrome of infant of diabetic mother I-10

775.1 Neonatal diabetes mellitus CC N
Diabetes mellitus syndrome in newborn infant
CC Excl: 775.0-775.7, 775.9, 779.81-779.84, 779.89
AHA: 3Q, '91, 6

775.2 Neonatal myasthenia gravis CC N
CC Excl: See code: 775.1

775.3 Neonatal thyrotoxicosis CC N
Neonatal hyperthydroidism (transient)
CC Excl: See code 775.1

775.4 Hypocalcemia and hypomagnesemia of newborn CC N
Cow's milk hypocalcemia
Hypocalcemic tetany, neonatal
Neonatal hypoparathyroidism
Phosphate-loading hypocalcemia
CC Excl: See code 775.1

775.5 Other transitory neonatal electrolyte disturbances N
Dehydration, neonatal
AHA: 1Q, '10, 14; 3Q, '09, 21; 1Q, '05, 9
TIP: If the patient has neonatal hyperkalemia, assign also code 276.7
Hyperpotassemia.
P74.1 Dehydration of newborn I-10

775.6 Neonatal hypoglycemia N
EXCLUDES *infant of mother with diabetes mellitus (775.0)*
AHA: 1Q, '94, 8
P70.4 Other neonatal hypoglycemia I-10

775.7 Late metabolic acidosis of newborn MCC N
CC Excl: See code 775.1

✓5ᵗʰ **775.8 Other neonatal endocrine and metabolic disturbances**

775.81 Other acidosis of newborn CC N
Acidemia NOS of newborn
Acidosis of newborn NOS
Mixed metabolic and respiratory acidosis of newborn
CC Excl: 775.5, 775.7, 775.9
AHA: 4Q, '06, 104-106

775.89 Other neonatal endocrine and metabolic disturbances CC N
Amino-acid metabolic disorders described as
transitory
CC Excl: 775.0-775.7, 775.9
AHA: 4Q, '06, 104-106

775.9 Unspecified endocrine and metabolic disturbances specific to the fetus and newborn N

✓4ᵗʰ **776 Hematological disorders of newborn**
INCLUDES disorders specific to the newborn though possibly
originating in utero
EXCLUDES *fetal hematologic conditions (678.0)*

776.0 Hemorrhagic disease of newborn CC N
Hemorrhagic diathesis of newborn
Vitamin K deficiency of newborn
EXCLUDES *fetal or neonatal hemorrhage (772.0-772.9)*
CC Excl: 776.0-776.9, 779.81-779.84, 779.89

776.1 Transient neonatal thrombocytopenia MCC N
Neonatal thrombocytopenia due to:
exchange transfusion
idiopathic maternal thrombocytopenia
isoimmunization
DEF: Temporary decrease in blood platelets of newborn.
CC Excl: See code 776.0
P61.0 Transient neonatal thrombocytopenia I-10

776.2 Disseminated intravascular coagulation in newborn MCC N
DEF: Disseminated intravascular coagulation of newborn: clotting
disorder due to excess thromboplastic agents in blood as a result of
disease or trauma; causes blood clotting within vessels and reduces
available elements necessary for blood coagulation.
CC Excl: See code 776.0

776.3 Other transient neonatal disorders of coagulation CC N
Transient coagulation defect, newborn
CC Excl: See code 776.0

✓4ᵗʰ / ✓5ᵗʰ Additional Digit Required   Unacceptable PDx   Manifestation Code   Hospital Acquired Condition   ►◄ Revised Text   ● New Code   ▲ Revised Code Title

Certain Conditions Originating in the Perinatal Period

776.4–779.2

776.4 Polycythemia neonatorum   N
Plethora of newborn
Polycythemia due to:
   donor twin transfusion
   maternal-fetal transfusion
DEF: Abnormal increase of total red blood cells of newborn.

776.5 Congenital anemia   CC N
Anemia following fetal blood loss
EXCLUDES   *anemia due to isoimmunization (773.0–773.2, 773.5)*
              hereditary hemolytic anemias (282.0–282.9)
CC Excl: 280.0–282.3, 282.5–284.2, 284.81–285.9, 289.9, 517.3, 776.5–776.6

776.6 Anemia of prematurity   CC N
CC Excl: See code: 776.5
P61.2 Anemia of prematurity   I-10

776.7 Transient neonatal neutropenia   MCC N
Isoimmune neutropenia
Maternal transfer neutropenia
EXCLUDES   *congenital neutropenia (nontransient) (288.01)*
DEF: Decreased neutrophilic leukocytes in blood of newborn.
CC Excl: 280.1–281.9, 282.5–282.63, 282.69–282.7, 283.0, 283.11, 284.01–284.2, 284.81–285.0, 285.21–285.9, 289.9, 776.7–776.9

776.8 Other specified transient hematological disorders   N

776.9 Unspecified hematological disorder specific to newborn   N

√4ᵗʰ **777 Perinatal disorders of digestive system**
INCLUDES   disorders specific to the fetus and newborn
EXCLUDES   *intestinal obstruction classifiable to 560.0–560.9*

777.1 Meconium obstruction   N
Congenital fecaliths
Delayed passage of meconium
Meconium ileus NOS
Meconium plug syndrome
EXCLUDES   *meconium ileus in cystic fibrosis (277.01)*
DEF: Meconium blocked digestive tract of newborn.

777.2 Intestinal obstruction due to inspissated milk   N

777.3 Hematemesis and melena due to swallowed maternal blood   N
Swallowed blood syndrome in newborn
EXCLUDES   *that not due to swallowed maternal blood (772.4)*

777.4 Transitory ileus of newborn   CC N
EXCLUDES   *Hirschsprung's disease (751.3)*
CC Excl: 777.1–777.9

√5ᵗʰ **777.5 Necrotizing enterocolitis in newborn**
DEF: Serious intestinal infection and inflammation in preterm infants; severity is measured by stages and may progress to life-threatening perforation or peritonitis; resection surgical treatment may be necessary.
AHA: 4Q, '08, 138–140

777.50 Necrotizing enterocolitis in newborn, unspecified   MCC N
Necrotizing enterocolitis in newborn, NOS
CC Excl: 777.1–777.9, 779.81–779.84, 779.89

777.51 Stage I necrotizing enterocolitis in newborn   MCC N
Necrotizing enterocolitis without pneumatosis, without perforation
DEF: Broad-spectrum symptoms with non-specific signs including feeding intolerance, sepsis, gastroenteritis, ileus, metabolic abnormalities.
CC Excl: 777.1–777.9, 779.81–779.84, 779.89

777.52 Stage II necrotizing enterocolitis in newborn   MCC N
Necrotizing enterocolitis with pneumatosis, without perforation
DEF: Radiographic confirmation of necrotizing enterocolitis showing intestinal dilatation, fixed loops of bowels, pneumatosis intestinalis, metabolic acidosis, and thrombocytopenia.
CC Excl: 777.1–777.9, 779.81–779.84, 779.89

777.53 Stage III necrotizing enterocolitis in newborn   MCC N
Necrotizing enterocolitis with perforation
Necrotizing enterocolitis with pneumatosis and perforation
DEF: Advanced stage in which infant demonstrates signs of bowel perforation, septic shock, metabolic acidosis, ascites, disseminated intravascular coagulopathy, neutropenia.
CC Excl: 777.1–777.9, 779.81–779.84, 779.89
AHA: 4Q, '08, 139

777.6 Perinatal intestinal perforation   MCC N
Meconium peritonitis
CC Excl: See code: 777.50

777.8 Other specified perinatal disorders of digestive system   N
AHA: 4Q, '10, 97

777.9 Unspecified perinatal disorder of digestive system   N

√4ᵗʰ **778 Conditions involving the integument and temperature regulation of fetus and newborn**

778.0 Hydrops fetalis not due to isoimmunization   MCC N
Idiopathic hydrops
EXCLUDES   *hydrops fetalis due to isoimmunization (773.3)*
DEF: Edema of entire body, unrelated to immune response.
CC Excl: 778.0, 779.81–779.84, 779.89

778.1 Sclerema neonatorum   CC N
Subcutaneous fat necrosis
DEF: Diffuse, rapidly progressing white, waxy, nonpitting hardening of tissue, usually of legs and feet, life-threatening; found in preterm or debilitated infants; unknown etiology.
CC Excl: 778.1, 778.5

778.2 Cold injury syndrome of newborn   N

778.3 Other hypothermia of newborn   N

778.4 Other disturbances of temperature regulation of newborn   N
Dehydration fever in newborn
Environmentally-induced pyrexia
Hyperthermia in newborn
Transitory fever of newborn
P81.9 Disturbance of temp regulation newborn uns   I-10

778.5 Other and unspecified edema of newborn   CC N
Edema neonatorum
CC Excl: 778.1–778.5

778.6 Congenital hydrocele
Congenital hydrocele of tunica vaginalis
P83.5 Congenital hydrocele   I-10

778.7 Breast engorgement in newborn   N
Noninfective mastitis of newborn
EXCLUDES   *infective mastitis of newborn (771.5)*

778.8 Other specified conditions involving the integument of fetus and newborn   N
Urticaria neonatorum
EXCLUDES   *impetigo neonatorum (684)*
              pemphigus neonatorum (684)
P83.8 Oth spec conditions integument specific to newborn   I-10

778.9 Unspecified condition involving the integument and temperature regulation of fetus and newborn   N

√4ᵗʰ **779 Other and ill-defined conditions originating in the perinatal period**

779.0 Convulsions in newborn   MCC N
Fits
Seizures   } in newborn
CC Excl: 779.0–779.1, 779.81–779.84, 779.89
AHA: N-D, '84, 11
TIP: Clarify with the physician that convulsions are not actually infantile spasms; if so, refer to subcategory 345.6.

779.1 Other and unspecified cerebral irritability in newborn   N

779.2 Cerebral depression, coma, and other abnormal cerebral signs   MCC N
Cerebral ischemia NOS of newborn
CNS dysfunction in newborn NOS
EXCLUDES   *cerebral ischemia due to birth trauma (767.0)*
              intrauterine cerebral ischemia (768.2–768.9)
              intraventricular hemorrhage (772.10–772.14)
CC Excl: 779.0–779.2

N Newborn Age: 0   P Pediatric Age: 0-17   M Maternity Age: 12-55   A Adult Age: 15-124   MCC Major CC Condition   CC CC Condition   HIV HIV Related Dx

280 – Volume 1   **2015 ICD-9-CM**

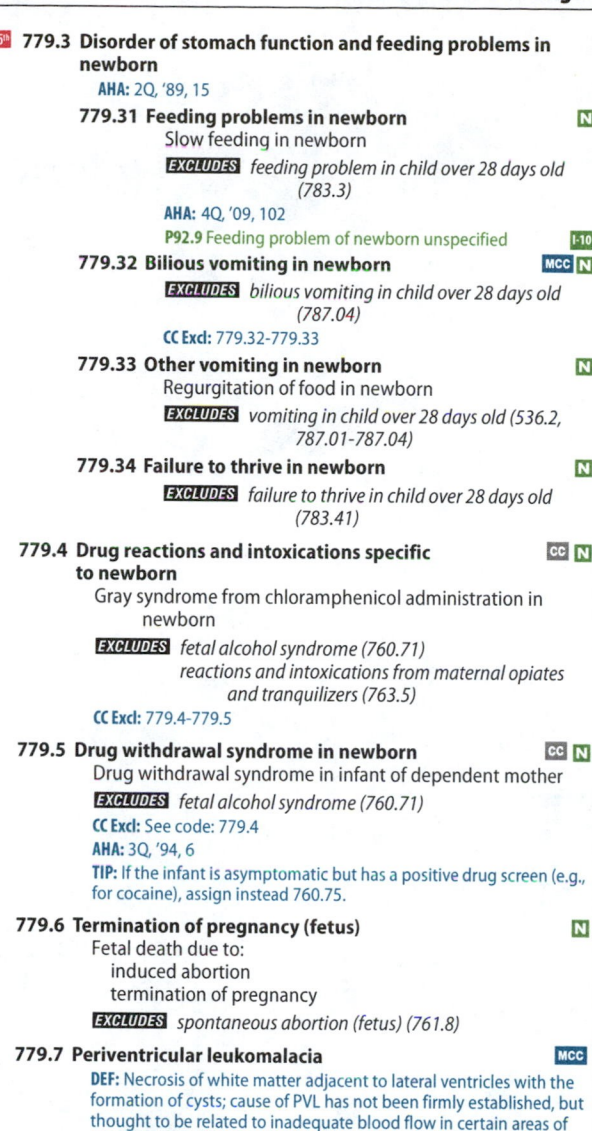

☑5th **779.3 Disorder of stomach function and feeding problems in newborn**
AHA: 2Q, '89, 15

779.31 Feeding problems in newborn   N
Slow feeding in newborn
EXCLUDES *feeding problem in child over 28 days old (783.3)*
AHA: 4Q, '09, 102
P92.9 Feeding problem of newborn unspecified   I-10

779.32 Bilious vomiting in newborn   MCC N
EXCLUDES *bilious vomiting in child over 28 days old (787.04)*
CC Excl: 779.32-779.33

779.33 Other vomiting in newborn   N
Regurgitation of food in newborn
EXCLUDES *vomiting in child over 28 days old (536.2, 787.01-787.04)*

779.34 Failure to thrive in newborn   N
EXCLUDES *failure to thrive in child over 28 days old (783.41)*

779.4 Drug reactions and intoxications specific to newborn   CC N
Gray syndrome from chloramphenicol administration in newborn
EXCLUDES *fetal alcohol syndrome (760.71)*
reactions and intoxications from maternal opiates and tranquilizers (763.5)
CC Excl: 779.4-779.5

779.5 Drug withdrawal syndrome in newborn   CC N
Drug withdrawal syndrome in infant of dependent mother
EXCLUDES *fetal alcohol syndrome (760.71)*
CC Excl: See code: 779.4
AHA: 3Q, '94, 6
TIP: If the infant is asymptomatic but has a positive drug screen (e.g., for cocaine), assign instead 760.75.

779.6 Termination of pregnancy (fetus)   N
Fetal death due to:
induced abortion
termination of pregnancy
EXCLUDES *spontaneous abortion (fetus) (761.8)*

779.7 Periventricular leukomalacia   MCC
DEF: Necrosis of white matter adjacent to lateral ventricles with the formation of cysts; cause of PVL has not been firmly established, but thought to be related to inadequate blood flow in certain areas of the brain.
CC Excl: 772.0-772.2, 772.8-772.9, 776.0-776.9, 779.7-779.84, 779.89
AHA: 4Q, '01, 50, 51

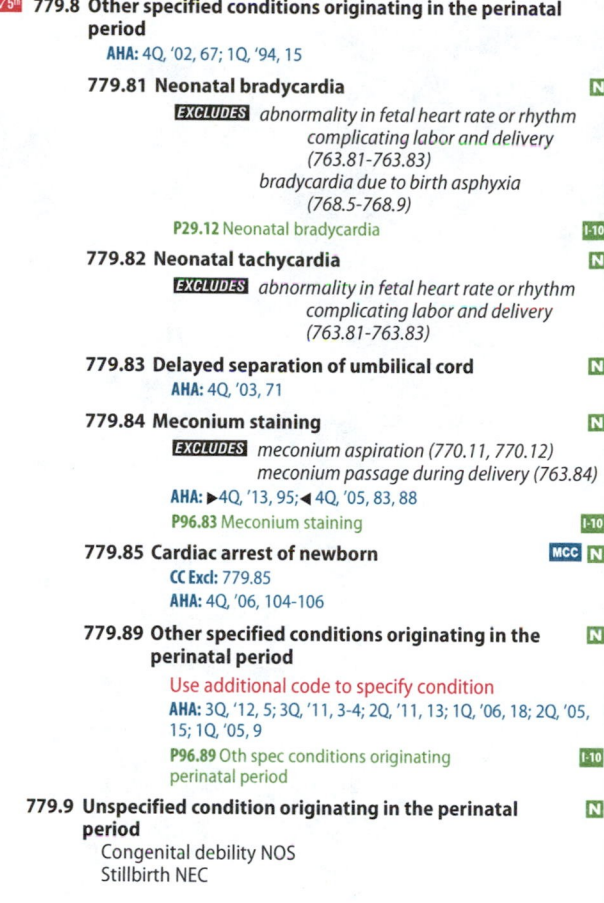

☑5th **779.8 Other specified conditions originating in the perinatal period**
AHA: 4Q, '02, 67; 1Q, '94, 15

779.81 Neonatal bradycardia   N
EXCLUDES *abnormality in fetal heart rate or rhythm complicating labor and delivery (763.81-763.83)*
bradycardia due to birth asphyxia (768.5-768.9)
P29.12 Neonatal bradycardia   I-10

779.82 Neonatal tachycardia   N
EXCLUDES *abnormality in fetal heart rate or rhythm complicating labor and delivery (763.81-763.83)*

779.83 Delayed separation of umbilical cord   N
AHA: 4Q, '03, 71

779.84 Meconium staining   N
EXCLUDES *meconium aspiration (770.11, 770.12)*
meconium passage during delivery (763.84)
AHA: ▶4Q, '13, 95;◀ 4Q, '05, 83, 88
P96.83 Meconium staining   I-10

779.85 Cardiac arrest of newborn   MCC N
CC Excl: 779.85
AHA: 4Q, '06, 104-106

779.89 Other specified conditions originating in the perinatal period   N
Use additional code to specify condition
AHA: 3Q, '12, 5; 3Q, '11, 3-4; 2Q, '11, 13; 1Q, '06, 18; 2Q, '05, 15; 1Q, '05, 9
P96.89 Oth spec conditions originating perinatal period   I-10

779.9 Unspecified condition originating in the perinatal period   N
Congenital debility NOS
Stillbirth NEC

16. Symptoms, Signs, and Ill-Defined Conditions (780-799)

This section includes symptoms, signs, abnormal results of laboratory or other investigative procedures, and ill-defined conditions regarding which no diagnosis classifiable elsewhere is recorded.

Signs and symptoms that point rather definitely to a given diagnosis are assigned to some category in the preceding part of the classification. In general, categories 780-796 include the more ill-defined conditions and symptoms that point with perhaps equal suspicion to two or more diseases or to two or more systems of the body, and without the necessary study of the case to make a final diagnosis. Practically all categories in this group could be designated as "not otherwise specified," or as "unknown etiology," or as "transient." The Alphabetic Index should be consulted to determine which symptoms and signs are to be allocated here and which to more specific sections of the classification; the residual subcategories numbered .9 are provided for other relevant symptoms which cannot be allocated elsewhere in the classification.

The conditions and signs or symptoms included in categories 780-796 consist of: (a) cases for which no more specific diagnosis can be made even after all facts bearing on the case have been investigated; (b) signs or symptoms existing at the time of initial encounter that proved to be transient and whose causes could not be determined; (c) provisional diagnoses in a patient who failed to return for further investigation or care; (d) cases referred elsewhere for investigation or treatment before the diagnosis was made; (e) cases in which a more precise diagnosis was not available for any other reason; (f) certain symptoms which represent important problems in medical care and which it might be desired to classify in addition to a known cause.

AHA: 3Q, '11, 12

Symptoms (780-789)

AHA: 1Q, '91, 12; 2Q, '90, 3; 2Q, '90, 5; 2Q, '90, 15; M-A, '85, 3

√4ᵗʰ **780 General symptoms**

√5ᵗʰ **780.0 Alteration of consciousness**

EXCLUDES alteration of consciousness due to:
intracranial injuries (850.0-854.19)
skull fractures (800.00-801.99, 803.00-804.99)
coma:
diabetic (249.2-249.3, 250.2-250.3)
hepatic (572.2)
originating in the perinatal period (779.2)

AHA: 4Q, '92, 20

780.01 Coma　　　　　`MCC`
DEF: State of unconsciousness from which the patient cannot be awakened.
CC Excl: 070.0-070.9, 249.00-251.3, 338.0-338.4, 348.81-348.9, 349.89-349.9, 430-432.9, 572.2, 780.01-780.09, 780.2, 780.4, 780.64-780.65, 780.91-780.99, 799.81-799.89, 800.00-801.99, 803.00-804.96, 850.0-852.19, 852.21-854.19
AHA: ▶3Q, '13, 10;◀ 1Q, '12, 14; 3Q, '96, 16
TIP: Although found in the symptoms and signs chapter, coma is not inherent in other conditions and should be reported whenever appropriately documented.

780.02 Transient alteration of awareness
DEF: Temporary, recurring spells of reduced consciousness.

780.03 Persistent vegetative state　　　　`CC`
DEF: Persistent wakefulness without consciousness due to nonfunctioning cerebral cortex.
CC Excl: See code: 780.01

780.09 Other
Drowsiness　　　Stupor
Semicoma　　　　Unconsciousness
Somnolence
R40.1 Stupor　　　　　`I-10`

780.1 Hallucinations　　　　　`CC`
Hallucinations:　　　　　　Hallucinations:
NOS　　　　　　　　　　　olfactory
auditory　　　　　　　　　tactile
gustatory

EXCLUDES those associated with mental disorders, as functional psychoses (295.0-298.9)
organic brain syndromes (290.0-294.9, 310.0-310.9)
visual hallucinations (368.16)

DEF: Perception of external stimulus in absence of stimulus; inability to distinguish between real and imagined.
CC Excl: 338.0-338.4, 780.1, 780.4, 780.64-780.65, 780.91-780.99, 799.81-799.89

780.2 Syncope and collapse
Blackout　　　　　　(Near) (Pre) syncope
Fainting　　　　　　Vasovagal attack

EXCLUDES carotid sinus syncope (337.0)
heat syncope (992.1)
neurocirculatory asthenia (306.2)
orthostatic hypotension (458.0)
shock NOS (785.50)

DEF: Sudden unconsciousness due to reduced blood flow to brain.
AHA: 1Q, '02, 6; 3Q, '00, 12; 4Q, '95, 42; 3Q, '95, 14; N-D, '85, 12
R55 Syncope and collapse　　　　　`I-10`

√5ᵗʰ **780.3 Convulsions**

EXCLUDES convulsions:
epileptic (345.10-345.91)
in newborn (779.0)

DEF: Sudden, involuntary contractions of the muscles.
AHA: 2Q, '12, 9; 2Q, '97, 8; 1Q, '97, 12; 3Q, '94, 9; 1Q, '93, 24; 4Q, '92, 23; N-D, '87, 12

780.31 Febrile convulsions (simple), unspecified　`CC`
Febrile seizure NOS
CC Excl: 338.0-338.4, 345.00-345.91, 348.81, 348.89-348.9, 349.89-349.9, 779.0-779.1, 780.31-780.39, 780.64-780.65, 780.91-780.99, 799.81-799.89
AHA: 4Q, '97, 45

780.32 Complex febrile convulsions　　　　　`CC`
Febrile seizure:
atypical
complex
complicated
EXCLUDES status epilepticus (345.3)
CC Excl: See code: 780.31
AHA: 4Q, '06, 106

780.33 Post traumatic seizures　　　　　`CC`
EXCLUDES post traumatic epilepsy (345.00-345.91)
CC Excl: 249.60-249.61, 250.60-250.63, 345.00-345.91, 348.81-348.9, 349.89-349.9, 780.33
AHA: ▶4Q, '13, 86;◀ 4Q, '10, 92-93

780.39 Other convulsions
Convulsive disorder NOS
Fit NOS
Recurrent convulsions NOS
Seizure NOS
AHA: ▶4Q, '13, 89;◀ 2Q, '12, 9; 2Q, '11, 5; 1Q, '08, 17; 3Q, '06, 22; 4Q, '04, 51; 1Q, '03, 7; 2Q, '99, 17; 4Q, '98, 39
R56.9 Unspecified convulsions　　　　　`I-10`

780.4 Dizziness and giddiness
Light-headedness　　　　Vertigo NOS
EXCLUDES Ménière's disease and other specified vertiginous syndromes (386.0-386.9)
DEF: Whirling sensations in head with feeling of falling.
AHA: 2Q, '03, 11; 3Q, '00, 12; 2Q, '97, 9; 2Q, '91, 17
R42 Dizziness and giddiness　　　　　`I-10`

√5ᵗʰ **780.5 Sleep disturbances**

EXCLUDES circadian rhythm sleep disorders (327.30-327.39)
organic hypersomnia (327.10-327.19)
organic insomnia (327.00-327.09)
organic sleep apnea (327.20-327.29)
organic sleep related movement disorders (327.51-327.59)
parasomnias (327.40-327.49)
that of nonorganic origin (307.40-307.49)

AHA: 4Q, '05, 59

780.50 Sleep disturbance, unspecified

Symptoms, Signs, and Ill-Defined Conditions

780.51–780.92

780.51 Insomnia with sleep apnea, unspecified
   DEF: Transient cessation of breathing disturbing sleep.

780.52 Insomnia, unspecified
   DEF: Inability to maintain adequate sleep cycle.
   `G47.00` Insomnia unspecified   `I-10`

780.53 Hypersomnia with sleep apnea, unspecified
   DEF: Autonomic response inhibited during sleep; causes insufficient oxygen intake, acidosis and pulmonary hypertension.
   AHA: 1Q, '93, 28; N-D, '85, 4

780.54 Hypersomnia, unspecified
   DEF: Prolonged sleep cycle.

780.55 Disruptions of 24 hour sleep wake cycle, unspecified

780.56 Dysfunctions associated with sleep stages or arousal from sleep

780.57 Unspecified sleep apnea
   AHA: 1Q, '01, 6 ; 1Q, '97, 5; 1Q, '93, 28
   `G47.30` Sleep apnea unspecified   `I-10`

780.58 Sleep related movement disorder, unspecified
   EXCLUDES *restless legs syndrome (333.94)*
   AHA: 4Q, '04, 95

780.59 Other

✓5th **780.6 Fever and other physiologic disturbances of temperature regulation**
   EXCLUDES *effects of reduced environmental temperature (991.0-991.9)*
      effects of heat and light (992.0-992.9)
      fever, chills or hypothermia associated with confirmed infection — code to infection
   AHA: 4Q, '08, 140-142; 3Q, '05, 16; 3Q, '00,13; 4Q, '99, 26; 2Q, '91, 8

780.60 Fever, unspecified
   Chills with fever
   Fever NOS
   Fever of unknown origin (FUO)
   Hyperpyrexia NOS
   Pyrexia NOS
   Pyrexia of unknown origin
   EXCLUDES *chills without fever (780.64)*
      neonatal fever (778.4)
      pyrexia of unknown origin (during):
        in newborn (778.4)
        labor (659.2)
        the puerperium (672)
   `R50.9` Fever unspecified   `I-10`

780.61 *Fever presenting with conditions classified elsewhere*
   Code first underlying condition when associated fever is present, such as with:
      leukemia (conditions classifiable to 204-208)
      neutropenia (288.00-288.09)
      sickle-cell disease (282.60-282.69)
   AHA: 2Q, '12, 18; 4Q, '08, 142

780.62 Postprocedural fever
   EXCLUDES *posttransfusion fever (780.66)*
      postvaccination fever (780.63)
   TIP: Do not assign a code from category 998 for post-procedural fever.

780.63 Postvaccination fever
   Postimmunization fever

780.64 Chills (without fever)
   Chills NOS
   EXCLUDES *chills with fever (780.60)*

780.65 Hypothermia not associated with low environmental temperature
   EXCLUDES *hypothermia:*
      associated with low environmental temperature (991.6)
      due to anesthesia (995.89)
      of newborn (778.2, 778.3)

780.66 Febrile nonhemolytic transfusion reaction
   FNHTR
   Posttransfusion fever
   AHA: 4Q, '10, 99-100

✓5th **780.7 Malaise and fatigue**
   EXCLUDES *debility, unspecified (799.3)*
      fatigue (during):
        combat (308.0-308.9)
        heat (992.6)
        pregnancy (646.8)
      neurasthenia (300.5)
      senile asthenia (797)
   AHA: 4Q, '88, 12; M-A, '87, 8

780.71 Chronic fatigue syndrome
   DEF: Persistent fatigue, symptoms include weak muscles, sore throat, lymphadenitis, headache, depression and mild fever; no known cause; also called chronic mononucleosis, benign myalgic encephalomyelitis, Iceland disease and neurosthenia.
   AHA: 4Q, '98, 48

780.72 Functional quadriplegia   `MCC`
   Complete immobility due to severe physical disability or frailty
   EXCLUDES *hysterical paralysis (300.11)*
      immobility syndrome (728.3)
      neurologic quadriplegia (344.00-344.09)
      quadriplegia NOS (344.00)
   DEF: Inability to move due to another condition such as dementia, severe contractures, or arthritis, not a physiologic one; no mental ability to move independently; typically found in severely demented patients.
   CC Excl: 249.60-249.61, 249.80-249.91, 250.60-250.63, 250.80-250.93, 342.00-344.9, 348.8-348.9, 349.89-349.9, 742.59-742.9, 780.72
   AHA: 4Q, '08, 143
   TIP: The functional quadriplegic patient typically has severe dementia and the quadriplegia will be due to a nonneurologic condition.

780.79 Other malaise and fatigue
   Asthenia NOS
   Lethargy
   Postviral (asthenic) syndrome
   Tiredness
   DEF: Asthenia: Any weakness, lack of strength or loss of energy, especially neuromuscular.
   DEF: Lethargy: Listlessness, drowsiness, stupor and apathy.
   DEF: Malaise: Vague feeling of debility or lack of good health.
   DEF: Postviral (asthenic) syndrome: Listlessness, drowsiness, stupor and apathy; follows acute viral infection.
   DEF: Tiredness: General exhaustion or fatigue.
   AHA: 4Q, '04, 78; 1Q, '00, 6; 4Q, '99, 26
   `R53.83` Other fatigue   `I-10`

780.8 Generalized hyperhidrosis
   Diaphoresis   Secondary hyperhidrosis
   Excessive sweating
   EXCLUDES *focal (localized) (primary) (secondary) hyperhidrosis (705.21-705.22)*
      Frey's syndrome (705.22)
   DEF: Excessive sweating, appears as droplets on skin; general or localized.

✓5th **780.9 Other general symptoms**
   EXCLUDES *hypothermia:*
      NOS (accidental) (991.6)
      due to anesthesia (995.89)
      of newborn (778.2-778.3)
      memory disturbance as part of a pattern of mental disorder
   AHA: 4Q, '02, 67; 4Q, '99, 10; 3Q, '93, 11; N-D, '85, 12

780.91 Fussy infant (baby)   `P`

780.92 Excessive crying of infant (baby)   `N`
   EXCLUDES *excessive crying of child, adolescent or adult (780.95)*

`N` Newborn Age: 0   `P` Pediatric Age: 0-17   `M` Maternity Age: 12-55   `A` Adult Age: 15-124   `MCC` Major CC Condition   `CC` CC Condition   `HIV` HIV Related Dx

284 – Volume 1   2015 ICD-9-CM

780.93 Memory loss
Amnesia (retrograde)
Memory loss NOS
> **EXCLUDES** memory loss due to:
>   intracranial injuries (850.0-854.19)
>   skull fractures (800.00-801.99,
>   803.00-804.99)
>   mild memory disturbance due to organic
>   brain damage (310.89)
>   transient global amnesia (437.7)

  AHA: 4Q, '03, 71

780.94 Early satiety
> **DEF:** The premature feeling of being full; mechanism of satiety is multifactorial.

  AHA: 4Q, '03, 72

780.95 Excessive crying of child, adolescent, or adult
> **EXCLUDES** excessive crying of infant (baby) (780.92)

  AHA: 4Q, '05, 89

780.96 Generalized pain
Pain NOS

  AHA: 4Q, '06, 79-81

  TIP: For pain syndromes, refer to category 338; if site is specified, refer to index.

780.97 Altered mental status
Change in mental status
> **EXCLUDES** altered level of consciousness
>   (780.01-780.09)
>   altered mental status due to known
>   condition — code to condition
>   delirium NOS (780.09)

  AHA: 4Q, '06, 107

  R41.82 Altered mental status unspecified   `I-10`

780.99 Other general symptoms
  AHA: 4Q, '03, 103

√4ᵗʰ 781 Symptoms involving nervous and musculoskeletal systems
> **EXCLUDES** depression NOS (311)
> disorders specifically relating to:
>   back (724.0-724.9)
>   hearing (388.0-389.9)
>   joint (718.0-719.9)
>   limb (729.0-729.9)
>   neck (723.0-723.9)
>   vision (368.0-369.9)
> pain in limb (729.5)

781.0 Abnormal involuntary movements
Abnormal head movements
Fasciculation
Spasms NOS
Tremor NOS
> **EXCLUDES** abnormal reflex (796.1)
> chorea NOS (333.5)
> infantile spasms (345.60-345.61)
> spastic paralysis (342.1, 343.0-344.9)
> specified movement disorders classifiable to 333
>   (333.0-333.9)
> that of nonorganic origin (307.2-307.3)

  R25.9 Unspecified abnormal involuntary movements   `I-10`

781.1 Disturbances of sensation of smell and taste
Anosmia
Parageusia
Parosmia
> **DEF:** Anosmia: loss of sense of smell due to organic factors, including loss of olfactory nerve conductivity, cerebral disease, nasal fossae formation and peripheral olfactory nerve diseases; can also be psychological disorder.
> **DEF:** Parageusia: distorted sense of taste, or bad taste in mouth.
> **DEF:** Parosmia: distorted sense of smell.

781.2 Abnormality of gait
Gait:
     ataxic
     paralytic
     spastic
     staggering
> **EXCLUDES** ataxia:
>   NOS (781.3)
>   locomotor (progressive) (094.0)
>   difficulty in walking (719.7)

  DEF: Abnormal, asymmetric gait.

  AHA: 1Q, '11, 9; 2Q, '05, 6; 2Q, '04, 15

  TIP: If the patient's gait abnormality is due to a joint problem, refer to code 719.7 Difficulty in walking.

  R26.9 Unspecified abnormalities of gait and mobility   `I-10`

781.3 Lack of coordination
Ataxia NOS
Muscular incoordination
> **EXCLUDES** ataxic gait (781.2)
> cerebellar ataxia (334.0-334.9)
> difficulty in walking (719.7)
> vertigo NOS (780.4)

  AHA: 4Q, '04, 51; 3Q, '97, 12

781.4 Transient paralysis of limb   `CC`
Monoplegia, transient NOS
> **EXCLUDES** paralysis (342.0-344.9)

  CC Excl: 781.4, 781.94

781.5 Clubbing of fingers
> **DEF:** Enlarged soft tissue of distal fingers.

781.6 Meningismus   `CC`
Dupré's syndrome
Meningism
> **DEF:** Condition with signs and symptoms that resemble meningeal irritation; it is associated with febrile illness and dehydration with no evidence of infection.

  CC Excl: 781.4, 781.94

  AHA: 3Q, '00,13; J-F, '87, 7

781.7 Tetany   `CC`
Carpopedal spasm
> **EXCLUDES** tetanus neonatorum (771.3)
> tetany:
>   hysterical (300.11)
>   newborn (hypocalcemic) (775.4)
>   parathyroid (252.1)
>   psychogenic (306.0)

  DEF: Nerve and muscle hyperexcitability; symptoms include muscle spasms, twitching, cramps, laryngospasm with inspiratory stridor, hyperreflexia and choreiform movements.

  CC Excl: 037, 332.0-333.93, 333.99-334.4, 338.0-338.4, 342.10-342.12, 771.3, 780.64-780.65, 780.91-780.99, 781.7, 799.81-799.89

781.8 Neurologic neglect syndrome   `CC`
Asomatognosia
Hemi-akinesia
Hemi-inattention
Hemispatial neglect
Left-sided neglect
Sensory extinction
Sensory neglect
Visuospatial neglect
> **EXCLUDES** visuospatial deficit (799.53)

  CC Excl: 781.8-781.92, 781.94-781.99

  AHA: 4Q, '94, 37

  TIP: If documented as sequelae of a CVA, assign also a code from category 438.

√5ᵗʰ 781.9 Other symptoms involving nervous and musculoskeletal systems
  AHA: 4Q, '00, 45

781.91 Loss of height
> **EXCLUDES** osteoporosis (733.00-733.09)

781.92 Abnormal posture

781.93 Ocular torticollis
> **DEF:** Abnormal head posture as a result of a contracted state of cervical muscles to correct a visual disturbance; either double vision or a visual field defect.

  AHA: 4Q, '02, 68

√4ᵗʰ / √5ᵗʰ Additional Digit Required   Unacceptable PDx   Manifestation Code   Hospital Acquired Condition   ►◄ Revised Text   ● New Code   ▲ Revised Code Title

2015 ICD-9-CM   **Volume 1 – 285**

781.94 Facial weakness
Facial droop
EXCLUDES *facial weakness due to late effect of*
cerebrovascular accident (438.83)
AHA: 4Q, '03, 72
TIP: Do not assign if facial droop or weakness is due to Bell's palsy; see instead code 351.0.
R29.810 Facial weakness [I-10]

781.99 Other symptoms involving nervous and musculoskeletal systems

✓4th **782 Symptoms involving skin and other integumentary tissue**
EXCLUDES *symptoms relating to breast (611.71-611.79)*

782.0 Disturbance of skin sensation
Anesthesia of skin
Burning or prickling sensation
Hyperesthesia
Hypoesthesia
Numbness
Paresthesia
Tingling
R20.9 Unspecified disturbances of skin sensation [I-10]

782.1 Rash and other nonspecific skin eruption
Exanthem
EXCLUDES *vesicular eruption (709.8)*
AHA: 4Q, '08, 99

782.2 Localized superficial swelling, mass, or lump
Subcutaneous nodules
EXCLUDES *localized adiposity (278.1)*

782.3 Edema
Anasarca   Localized edema NOS
Dropsy
EXCLUDES *ascites (789.51-789.59)*
edema of:
newborn NOS (778.5)
pregnancy (642.0-642.9, 646.1)
fluid retention (276.69)
hydrops fetalis (773.3, 778.0)
hydrothorax (511.81-511.89)
nutritional edema (260, 262)
DEF: Edema: excess fluid in intercellular body tissue.
DEF: Anasarca: massive edema in all body tissues.
DEF: Dropsy: serous fluid accumulated in body cavity or cellular tissue.
DEF: Localized edema: edema in specific body areas.
AHA: 2Q, '00, 18
R60.9 Edema unspecified [I-10]

782.4 Jaundice, unspecified, not of newborn [CC]
Cholemia NOS
Icterus NOS
EXCLUDES *jaundice in newborn (774.0-774.7)*
due to isoimmunization (773.0-773.2, 773.4)
DEF: Bilirubin deposits of skin, causing yellow cast.
CC Excl: 774.0-774.7, 782.4, 782.9
R17 Unspecified jaundice [I-10]

782.5 Cyanosis
EXCLUDES *newborn (770.83)*
DEF: Deficient oxygen of blood; causes blue cast to skin.

✓5th **782.6 Pallor and flushing**

782.61 Pallor

782.62 Flushing
Excessive blushing

782.7 Spontaneous ecchymoses
Petechiae
EXCLUDES *ecchymosis in fetus or newborn (772.6)*
purpura (287.0-287.9)
DEF: Hemorrhagic spots of skin; resemble freckles.

782.8 Changes in skin texture
Induration ⎫
Thickening ⎭ of skin

782.9 Other symptoms involving skin and integumentary tissues

✓4th **783 Symptoms concerning nutrition, metabolism, and development**

783.0 Anorexia
Loss of appetite
EXCLUDES *anorexia nervosa (307.1)*
loss of appetite of nonorganic origin (307.59)
R63.0 Anorexia [I-10]

783.1 Abnormal weight gain
EXCLUDES *excessive weight gain in pregnancy (646.1)*
obesity (278.00)
morbid (278.01)

✓5th **783.2 Abnormal loss of weight and underweight**
Use additional code to identify Body Mass Index (BMI), if known (V85.0-V85.54)
AHA: 4Q, '00, 45

783.21 Loss of weight
AHA: 4Q, '05, 96
R63.4 Abnormal weight loss [I-10]

783.22 Underweight
AHA: 4Q, '05, 96

783.3 Feeding difficulties and mismanagement
Feeding problem (elderly) (infant)
EXCLUDES *feeding disturbance or problems:*
in newborn (779.31-779.34)
of nonorganic origin (307.50-307.59)
AHA: 3Q, '97, 12

✓5th **783.4 Lack of expected normal physiological development in childhood**
EXCLUDES *delay in sexual development and puberty (259.0)*
gonadal dysgenesis (758.6)
pituitary dwarfism (253.3)
slow fetal growth and fetal malnutrition (764.00-764.99)
specific delays in mental development (315.0-315.9)
AHA: 4Q, '00, 45; 3Q, '97, 4

783.40 Lack of normal physiological development, unspecified
Inadequate development
Lack of development

783.41 Failure to thrive [P]
Failure to gain weight
EXCLUDES *failure to thrive in newborn (779.34)*
DEF: Organic failure to thrive: acute or chronic illness that interferes with nutritional intake, absorption, metabolism excretion and energy requirements. Nonorganic FTT is symptom of neglect or abuse.
AHA: 1Q, '03, 12

783.42 Delayed milestones [P]
Late talker
Late walker

783.43 Short stature
Growth failure
Growth retardation
Lack of growth
Physical retardation
DEF: Constitutional short stature: stature inconsistent with chronological age. Genetic short stature is when skeletal maturation matches chronological age.

783.5 Polydipsia
Excessive thirst

783.6 Polyphagia
Excessive eating
Hyperalimentation NOS
EXCLUDES *disorders of eating of nonorganic origin (307.50-307.59)*

783.7 Adult failure to thrive [A]
R62.7 Adult failure to thrive [I-10]

[N] Newborn Age: 0   [P] Pediatric Age: 0-17   [M] Maternity Age: 12-55   [A] Adult Age: 15-124   [MCC] Major CC Condition   [CC] CC Condition   [HIV] HIV Related Dx

286 – Volume 1   **2015 ICD-9-CM**

783.9 Other symptoms concerning nutrition, metabolism, and development
Hypometabolism

> EXCLUDES   abnormal basal metabolic rate (794.7)
> dehydration (276.51)
> other disorders of fluid, electrolyte, and acid-base balance (276.0-276.9)

AHA: 2Q, '04, 3

√4th **784 Symptoms involving head and neck**

> EXCLUDES   encephalopathy NOS (348.30)
> specific symptoms involving neck classifiable to 723 (723.0-723.9)

784.0 Headache
Facial pain
Pain in head NOS

> EXCLUDES   atypical face pain (350.2)
> migraine (346.0-346.9)
> tension headache (307.81)

AHA: 3Q, '06, 22; 2Q, '06, 17; 3Q, '00, 13; 1Q, '90, 4; 3Q, '92, 14
TIP: Do not assign if headache syndrome has been diagnosed, refer to category 339.
R51 Headache   I-10

784.1 Throat pain

> EXCLUDES   dysphagia (787.20-787.29)
> neck pain (723.1)
> sore throat (462)
> chronic (472.1)

784.2 Swelling, mass, or lump in head and neck
Space-occupying lesion, intracranial NOS
AHA: 1Q, '03, 8

784.3 Aphasia   CC

> EXCLUDES   aphasia due to late effects of cerebrovascular disease (438.11)
> developmental aphasia (315.31)

DEF: Inability to communicate through speech, written word, or sign language.
CC Excl: 315.31, 315.35, 432.0-434.91, 436, 784.3-784.59
AHA: 3Q, '10, 5; 4Q, '04, 78; 4Q, '98, 87; 3Q, '97, 12
R47.01 Aphasia   I-10

√5th **784.4 Voice and resonance disorders**
AHA: 4Q, '09, 102-103

784.40 Voice and resonance disorder, unspecified

784.41 Aphonia
Loss of voice

784.42 Dysphonia
Hoarseness

784.43 Hypernasality

784.44 Hyponasality

784.49 Other voice and resonance disorders
Change in voice

√5th **784.5 Other speech disturbance**

> EXCLUDES   speech disorder due to late effect of cerebrovascular accident (438.10-438.19)
> stuttering (315.35)

AHA: 4Q, '09, 87-88

784.51 Dysarthria

> EXCLUDES   dysarthria due to late effect of cerebrovascular accident (438.13)

784.52 Fluency disorder in conditions classified elsewhere
Stuttering in conditions classified elsewhere
Code first underlying disease or condition, such as:
Parkinson's disease (332.0)

> EXCLUDES   adult onset fluency disorder (307.0)
> childhood onset fluency disorder (315.35)
> fluency disorder due to late effect of cerebrovascular accident (438.14)

AHA: 4Q, '10, 83-84

784.59 Other speech disturbance
Dysphasia
Slurred speech
Speech disturbance NOS
R47.89 Other speech disturbances   I-10

√5th **784.6 Other symbolic dysfunction**

> EXCLUDES   developmental learning delays (315.0-315.9)

784.60 Symbolic dysfunction, unspecified

784.61 Alexia and dyslexia
Alexia (with agraphia)
DEF: Alexia: Inability to understand written word due to central brain lesion.
DEF: Dyslexia: Ability to recognize letters but inability to read, spell, and write words; genetic.

784.69 Other
Acalculia   Agraphia NOS
Agnosia   Apraxia

784.7 Epistaxis
Hemorrhage from nose
Nosebleed
AHA: 3Q, '04, 7
R04.0 Epistaxis   I-10

784.8 Hemorrhage from throat

> EXCLUDES   hemoptysis (786.30-786.39)

√5th **784.9 Other symptoms involving head and neck**

784.91 Postnasal drip
AHA: 4Q, '06, 108

784.92 Jaw pain
Mandibular pain
Maxilla pain

> EXCLUDES   temporomandibular joint arthralgia (524.62)

AHA: 4Q, '10, 83-84
R68.84 Jaw pain   I-10

784.99 Other symptoms involving head and neck
Choking sensation
Feeling of foreign body in throat
Halitosis
Mouth breathing
Sneezing

> EXCLUDES   foreign body in throat (933.0)

AHA: 4Q, '06, 108

√4th **785 Symptoms involving cardiovascular system**

> EXCLUDES   heart failure NOS (428.9)

785.0 Tachycardia, unspecified
Rapid heart beat

> EXCLUDES   neonatal tachycardia (779.82)
> paroxysmal tachycardia (427.0-427.2)

DEF: Excessively rapid heart rate.
AHA: 2Q, '03, 11
R00.0 Tachycardia unspecified   I-10

785.1 Palpitations
Awareness of heart beat

> EXCLUDES   specified dysrhythmias (427.0-427.9)

R00.2 Palpitations   I-10

785.2 Undiagnosed cardiac murmurs
Heart murmurs NOS
AHA: 4Q, '92, 16
R01.1 Cardiac murmur unspecified   I-10

785.3 Other abnormal heart sounds
Cardiac dullness, increased or decreased
Friction fremitus, cardiac
Precordial friction

785.4 Gangrene   `CC`

Gangrene:
   NOS
   spreading cutaneous
Gangrenous cellulitis
Phagedena

Code first any associated underlying condition

EXCLUDES   *gangrene of certain sites — see Alphabetic Index*
    gangrene with atherosclerosis of the extremities
      (440.24)
    gas gangrene (040.0)

DEF: Gangrene: necrosis of skin tissue due to bacterial infection, diabetes, embolus and vascular supply loss.

DEF: Gangrenous cellulitis: group A streptococcal infection; begins with severe cellulitis, spreads to superficial and deep fascia; produces gangrene of underlying tissues.

CC Excl: 338.0-338.4, 440.24, 780.91-780.99, 785.4, 799.81-799.89

AHA: ▶4Q, '13, 83;◀ 1Q, '04, 14; 3Q, '91, 12; 3Q, '90, 15; M-A, '86, 12

I96 Gangrene not elsewhere classified   `I-10`

✓5ᵗʰ 785.5 Shock without mention of trauma

785.50 Shock, unspecified   `CC`

Failure of peripheral circulation

DEF: Peripheral circulatory failure due to heart insufficiencies.

CC Excl: 338.0-338.4, 780.64-780.65, 780.91-780.99, 785.50-785.59, 785.9, 799.81-799.89

AHA: 2Q, '96, 10

¹ 785.51 Cardiogenic shock   `MCC`

DEF: Shock syndrome: associated with myocardial infarction, cardiac tamponade and massive pulmonary embolism; symptoms include mental confusion, reduced blood pressure, tachycardia, pallor and cold, clammy skin.

CC Excl: See code: 785.50

AHA: 4Q, '08, 182; 3Q, '05, 14

R57.0 Cardiogenic shock   `I-10`

785.52 Septic shock   `MCC`

Shock:
   endotoxic
   gram-negative

Code first underlying infection
Use additional code, if applicable, to identify systemic inflammatory response syndrome due to infectious process with organ dysfunction (995.92)

CC Excl: See code 785.50

AHA: ▶2Q, '13, 21;◀ 2Q, '10, 4; 4Q, '08, 99; 4Q, '06, 113; 2Q, '05, 18-19; 4Q, '03, 73, 79

TIP: The diagnosis of septic shock indicates the presence of severe sepsis; code 785.52 should not be assigned without first assigning code 995.92.

¹ 785.59 Other   `MCC`

Shock:
   hypovolemic

EXCLUDES   *shock (due to):*
    anesthetic (995.4)
    anaphylactic (995.0)
      due to serum (999.41-999.49)
    electric (994.8)
    following abortion (639.5)
    lightning (994.0)
    obstetrical (669.1)
    postoperative (998.00-998.09)
    traumatic (958.4)

CC Excl: see code 785.50

AHA: 2Q, '00, 3

785.6 Enlargement of lymph nodes

Lymphadenopathy
"Swollen glands"

EXCLUDES   *lymphadenitis (chronic) (289.1-289.3)*
    acute (683)

R59.9 Enlarged lymph nodes unspecified   `I-10`

785.9 Other symptoms involving cardiovascular system

Bruit (arterial)
Weak pulse

✓4ᵗʰ 786 Symptoms involving respiratory system and other chest symptoms

✓5ᵗʰ 786.0 Dyspnea and respiratory abnormalities

786.00 Respiratory abnormality, unspecified

786.01 Hyperventilation

EXCLUDES   *hyperventilation, psychogenic (306.1)*

DEF: Rapid breathing causes carbon dioxide loss from blood.

786.02 Orthopnea

DEF: Difficulty breathing except in upright position.

786.03 Apnea

EXCLUDES   *apnea of newborn (770.81, 770.82)*
    sleep apnea (780.51, 780.53, 780.57)

DEF: Cessation of breathing.

AHA: 4Q, '98, 50

786.04 Cheyne-Stokes respiration   `CC`

DEF: Rhythmic increase of depth and frequency of breathing with apnea; occurs in frontal lobe and diencephalic dysfunction.

CC Excl: 518.81-518.84, 519.8-519.9, 786.03-786.04, 799.1

AHA: 4Q, '98, 50

786.05 Shortness of breath

DEF: Inability to take in sufficient oxygen.

AHA: 4Q, '99, 25; 1Q, '99, 6; 4Q, '98, 50

R06.02 Shortness of breath   `I-10`

786.06 Tachypnea

EXCLUDES   *transitory tachypnea of newborn (770.6)*

DEF: Abnormal rapid respiratory rate; called hyperventilation.

AHA: 1Q, '11, 16-17; 4Q, '98, 50

786.07 Wheezing

EXCLUDES   *asthma (493.00-493.92)*

DEF: Stenosis of respiratory passageway; causes whistling sound; due to asthma, coryza, croup, emphysema, hay fever, edema, and pleural effusion.

AHA: 4Q, '98, 50

786.09 Other

Respiratory: Respiratory:
   distress   insufficiency

EXCLUDES   *respiratory distress:*
    following trauma and surgery (518.52)
    newborn (770.89)
    syndrome (newborn) (769)
      adult (518.52)
    respiratory failure (518.81, 518.83-518.84)
      newborn (770.84)

AHA: 4Q, '05, 90; 2Q, '98, 10; 1Q, '97, 7; 1Q, '90, 9

R06.00 Dyspnea, unspecified   `I-10`

786.1 Stridor

EXCLUDES   *congenital laryngeal stridor (748.3)*

DEF: Obstructed airway causes harsh sound.

786.2 Cough

EXCLUDES   *cough:*
    psychogenic (306.1)
    smokers' (491.0)
    with hemorrhage (786.39)

AHA: 4Q, '99, 26

R05 Cough   `I-10`

✓5ᵗʰ 786.3 Hemoptysis

DEF: Coughing up blood or blood-stained sputum.

AHA: 3Q, '11, 12; 4Q, '10, 94-95; 2Q, '06, 17; 4Q, '90, 26

786.30 Hemoptysis, unspecified   `CC`

Pulmonary hemorrhage NOS

CC Excl: 786.30-786.4, 799.82

AHA: ▶4Q, '13, 83◀

R04.2 Hemoptysis   `I-10`

---

¹ MCC = Only if patient discharged alive.

`N` Newborn Age: 0   `P` Pediatric Age: 0-17   `M` Maternity Age: 12-55   `A` Adult Age: 15-124   `MCC` Major CC Condition   `CC` CC Condition   `HIV` HIV Related Dx

786.31 Acute idiopathic pulmonary hemorrhage in infants [AIPHI]   `CC` `P`

Acute idiopathic pulmonary hemorrhage in infant over 28 days old

EXCLUDES pulmonary hemorrhage of newborn under 28 days old (770.3)
von Willebrand's disease (286.4)

CC Excl: See code: 786.30

DEF: An abrupt onset of bleeding or blood in the airway with acute respiratory distress or failure in a patient with no prior history of an identifiable causal condition.

R04.81 Acute idiopathic pulmonary hemorrhage in infants   `I-10`

786.39 Other hemoptysis   `CC`

Cough with hemorrhage

CC Excl: See code: 786.30

R04.89 Hemorrhage from othr site in resp passages   `I-10`

786.4 Abnormal sputum

Abnormal:

amount
color   } sputum
odor

Excessive septum

786.5 Chest pain   `√5th`

786.50 Chest pain, unspecified

AHA: 1Q, '07, 19; 2Q, '06, 7; 1Q, '03, 6; 1Q, '02, 4; 4Q, '99, 25

R07.9 Chest pain unspecified   `I-10`

786.51 Precordial pain

DEF: Chest pain over heart and lower thorax.

786.52 Painful respiration

Pain: Pleurodynia
anterior chest wall
pleuritic

EXCLUDES epidemic pleurodynia (074.1)

AHA: N-D, '84, 17

TIP: Assign for musculoskeletal chest pain with no indication of underlying cause.

R07.1 Chest pain on breathing   `I-10`

786.59 Other

Discomfort
Pressure   } in chest
Tightness

EXCLUDES pain in breast (611.71)

AHA: 1Q, '02, 6

TIP: Assign for chest pain due to anxiety, along with an additional code for anxiety. Chest pain is not integral to the diagnosis of anxiety.

R07.89 Other chest pain   `I-10`

786.6 Swelling, mass, or lump in chest

EXCLUDES lump in breast (611.72)

R22.2 Localized swelling, mass, lump, trunk   `I-10`

786.7 Abnormal chest sounds

Abnormal percussion, chest   Rales
Friction sounds, chest   Tympany, chest

EXCLUDES wheezing (786.07)

786.8 Hiccough

EXCLUDES psychogenic hiccough (306.1)

786.9 Other symptoms involving respiratory system and chest

Breath-holding spell

Phases of Swallowing

Oral phase   Oropharyngeal phase

Pharyngeal phase   Pharyngoesophageal phase

787 Symptoms involving digestive system   `√4th`

EXCLUDES constipation (564.00-564.09)
pylorospasm (537.81)
congenital (750.5)

787.0 Nausea and vomiting   `√5th`

Emesis

EXCLUDES hematemesis NOS (578.0)
vomiting:
bilious, following gastrointestinal surgery (564.3)
cyclical (536.2)
associated with migraine (346.2)
psychogenic (306.4)
excessive, in pregnancy (643.0-643.9)
fecal matter (569.87)
habit (536.2)
of newborn (779.32, 779.33)
persistent (536.2)
psychogenic NOS (307.54)

AHA: M-A, '85, 11

787.01 Nausea with vomiting

AHA: 1Q, '03, 5

R11.2 Nausea with vomiting, unspecified   `I-10`

787.02 Nausea alone

AHA: 3Q, '00, 12; 2Q, '97, 9

R11.0 Nausea alone   `I-10`

787.03 Vomiting alone

787.04 Bilious emesis

Bilious vomiting

EXCLUDES bilious emesis (vomiting) in newborn (779.32)

AHA: 4Q, '09, 103-104

787.1 Heartburn

Pyrosis
Waterbrash

EXCLUDES dyspepsia or indigestion (536.8)

AHA: 2Q, '01, 6

787.2 Dysphagia   `√5th`

Code first, if applicable, dysphagia due to late effect of cerebrovascular accident (438.82)

AHA: 4Q, '07, 92-94; 3Q, '07, 7; 4Q, '03, 103, 109; 2Q, '01, 4

787.20 Dysphagia, unspecified

Difficulty in swallowing NOS

787.21 Dysphagia, oral phase

787.22 Dysphagia, oropharyngeal phase

AHA: 4Q, '07, 94

787.23 Dysphagia, pharyngeal phase

787.24 Dysphagia, pharyngoesophageal phase

787.29 Other dysphagia

Cervical dysphagia
Neurogenic dysphagia

R13.19 Other dysphagia   `I-10`

787.3 Flatulence, eructation, and gas pain

Abdominal distention (gaseous)
Bloating
Tympanites (abdominal) (intestinal)

EXCLUDES aerophagy (306.4)

DEF: Flatulence: excess air or gas in intestine or stomach.

DEF: Eructation: belching, expelling gas through mouth.

DEF: Gas pain: gaseous pressure affecting gastrointestinal system.

787.4 Visible peristalsis

Hyperperistalsis

DEF: Increase in involuntary movements of intestines.

787.5 Abnormal bowel sounds

Absent bowel sounds
Hyperactive bowel sounds

`√4th` `√5th` Additional Digit Required   Unacceptable PDx   Manifestation Code   Hospital Acquired Condition   ►◄ Revised Text   ● New Code   ▲ Revised Code Title

Symptoms, Signs, and Ill-Defined Conditions

787.6–788.62

√5ᵗʰ **787.6 Incontinence of feces**
Encopresis NOS
Incontinence of sphincter ani
EXCLUDES *that of nonorganic origin (307.7)*
AHA: 4Q, '10, 87-89; 1Q, '97, 9

787.60 Full incontinence of feces
Fecal incontinence NOS
R15.9 Full incontinence of feces   I-10

787.61 Incomplete defecation
EXCLUDES *constipation (564.00-564.09)*
fecal impaction (560.32)

787.62 Fecal smearing
Fecal soiling

787.63 Fecal urgency
R15.2 Fecal urgency   I-10

787.7 Abnormal feces
Bulky stools
EXCLUDES *abnormal stool content (792.1)*
melena:
NOS (578.1)
newborn (772.4, 777.3)

√5ᵗʰ **787.9 Other symptoms involving digestive system**
EXCLUDES *gastrointestinal hemorrhage (578.0-578.9)*
intestinal obstruction (560.0-560.9)
specific functional digestive disorders:
esophagus (530.0-530.9)
stomach and duodenum (536.0-536.9)
those not elsewhere classified (564.00-564.9)

787.91 Diarrhea
Diarrhea NOS
AHA: 2Q, '10, 12; 4Q, '08, 99; 4Q, '95, 54
R19.7 Diarrhea unspecified   I-10

787.99 Other
Change in bowel habits
Tenesmus (rectal)
DEF: Tenesmus: Painful, ineffective straining at the rectum with limited passage of fecal matter.

√4ᵗʰ **788 Symptoms involving urinary system**
EXCLUDES *hematuria (599.70-599.72)*
nonspecific findings on examination of the urine (791.0-791.9)
small kidney of unknown cause (589.0-589.9)
uremia NOS (586)
urinary obstruction (599.60, 599.69)

788.0 Renal colic
Colic (recurrent) of:
kidney
ureter
DEF: Kidney pain.
AHA: 3Q, '04, 8
TIP: Do not assign if renal colic is due to calculus; see category 592.

788.1 Dysuria
Painful urination
Strangury

√5ᵗʰ **788.2 Retention of urine**
Code, if applicable, any causal condition first, such as:
hyperplasia of prostate (600.0-600.9 with fifth-digit 1)
DEF: Accumulation of urine in the bladder due to inability to void.

788.20 Retention of urine, unspecified
AHA: ▶1Q, '13, 5;◄ 4Q, '06, 93, 95; 2Q, '04, 18; 3Q, '03, 12-13; 1Q, '03, 6; 3Q, '96, 10
R33.9 Retention of urine unspecified   I-10

788.21 Incomplete bladder emptying
AHA: 4Q, '06, 93

788.29 Other specified retention of urine

√5ᵗʰ **788.3 Urinary incontinence**
Code, if applicable, any causal condition first, such as:
congenital ureterocele (753.23)
genital prolapse (618.00-618.9)
hyperplasia of prostate (600.0-600.9 with fifth-digit 1)
EXCLUDES *functional urinary incontinence (788.91)*
that of nonorganic origin (307.6)
urinary incontinence associated with cognitive impairment (788.91)
AHA: 4Q, '06, 93; 4Q, '92, 22

788.30 Urinary incontinence, unspecified
Enuresis NOS
AHA: 1Q, '09, 15
R32 Unspecified urinary incontinence   I-10

788.31 Urge incontinence
DEF: Inability to control urination, upon urge to urinate.
AHA: 1Q, '00, 19

788.32 Stress incontinence, male   ♂
EXCLUDES *stress incontinence, female (625.6)*
DEF: Inability to control urination associated with weak sphincter in males.

788.33 Mixed incontinence, (male) (female)
Urge and stress
DEF: Urge, stress incontinence: involuntary discharge of urine due to anatomic displacement.

788.34 Incontinence without sensory awareness
DEF: Involuntary discharge of urine without sensory warning.

788.35 Post-void dribbling
DEF: Involuntary discharge of residual urine after voiding.

788.36 Nocturnal enuresis
DEF: Involuntary discharge of urine during the night.

788.37 Continuous leakage
DEF: Continuous, involuntary urine seepage.

788.38 Overflow incontinence
DEF: Leakage caused by pressure of retained urine in the bladder after the bladder has fully contracted due to weakened bladder muscles or an obstruction of the urethra.

788.39 Other urinary incontinence

√5ᵗʰ **788.4 Frequency of urination and polyuria**
Code, if applicable, any causal condition first, such as:
hyperplasia of prostate (600.0-600.9 with fifth-digit 1)

788.41 Urinary frequency
Frequency of micturition
AHA: 4Q, '06, 93

788.42 Polyuria
DEF: Excessive urination.

788.43 Nocturia
DEF: Urination affecting sleep patterns.
AHA: 4Q, '06, 93

788.5 Oliguria and anuria
Deficient secretion of urine
Suppression of urinary secretion
EXCLUDES *that complicating:*
abortion (634-638 with .3, 639.3)
ectopic or molar pregnancy (639.3)
pregnancy, childbirth, or the puerperium (642.0-642.9, 646.2)
DEF: Oliguria: diminished urinary secretion related to fluid intake.
DEF: Anuria: lack of urinary secretion due to renal failure or obstructed urinary tract.

√5ᵗʰ **788.6 Other abnormality of urination**
Code, if applicable, any causal condition first, such as:
hyperplasia of prostate (600.0-600.9 with fifth-digit 1)

788.61 Splitting of urinary stream
Intermittent urinary stream

788.62 Slowing of urinary stream
Weak stream
AHA: 4Q, '06, 93

N Newborn Age: 0   P Pediatric Age: 0-17   M Maternity Age: 12-55   A Adult Age: 15-124   **MCC** Major CC Condition   **CC** CC Condition   **HIV** HIV Related Dx

788.63 Urgency of urination
> **EXCLUDES** *urge incontinence (788.31, 788.33)*
> **DEF:** Feeling of intense need to urinate; abrupt sensation of imminent urination.
> **AHA:** 4Q, '06, 93; 4Q, '03, 74

788.64 Urinary hesitancy
> **AHA:** 4Q, '06, 93, 109

788.65 Straining on urination
> **AHA:** 4Q, '06, 93, 109

788.69 Other

788.7 Urethral discharge
> Penile discharge
> Urethrorrhea

788.8 Extravasation of urine `CC`
> **DEF:** Leaking or infiltration of urine into tissues.
> **CC Excl:** 788.8-788.99

✔5ᵗʰ **788.9 Other symptoms involving urinary system**
> **AHA:** 1Q, '05, 12; 4Q, '88, 1

788.91 Functional urinary incontinence
> Urinary incontinence due to cognitive impairment, or severe physical disability or immobility
> **EXCLUDES** *urinary incontinence due to physiologic condition (788.30-788.39)*
> **AHA:** 4Q, '08, 144-145

788.99 Other symptoms involving urinary system
> Extrarenal uremia   Vesical:
> Vesical: tenesmus
>   pain

✔4ᵗʰ **789 Other symptoms involving abdomen and pelvis**
> **EXCLUDES** *symptoms referable to genital organs:*
> *female (625.0-625.9)*
> *male (607.0-608.9)*
> *psychogenic (302.70-302.79))*

> The following fifth-digit subclassification is to be used for codes 789.0, 789.3, 789.4, 789.6:
>   **0 unspecified site**
>   **1 right upper quadrant**
>   **2 left upper quadrant**
>   **3 right lower quadrant**
>   **4 left lower quadrant**
>   **5 periumbilic**
>   **6 epigastric**
>   **7 generalized**
>   **9 other specified site**
>   Multiple sites

§ ✔5ᵗʰ **789.0 Abdominal pain**
> [0-7, 9]   Cramps, abdominal
> **AHA:** 1Q, '95, 3; **For code 789.06:** 1Q, '02, 5
> **R10.9** Unspecified abdominal pain `I-10`
> **R10.31** Right lower quadrant pain `I-10`
> **R10.13** Epigastric pain `I-10`
> **R10.84** Generalized abdominal pain `I-10`

789.1 Hepatomegaly
> Enlargement of liver

789.2 Splenomegaly
> Enlargement of spleen

§ ✔5ᵗʰ **789.3 Abdominal or pelvic swelling, mass, or lump**
> [0-7, 9]   Diffuse or generalized swelling or mass:
>   abdominal NOS
>   umbilical
> **EXCLUDES** *abdominal distention (gaseous) (787.3)*
> *ascites (789.51-789.59)*

§ ✔5ᵗʰ **789.4 Abdominal rigidity**
> [0-7, 9]

✔5ᵗʰ **789.5 Ascites**
> Fluid in peritoneal cavity
> **DEF:** Serous fluid effusion and accumulation in abdominal cavity.
> **AHA:** 4Q, '07, 95; 2Q, '05, 8; 4Q, '89, 11

789.51 Malignant ascites `CC`
> *Code first malignancy, such as:*
> *malignant neoplasm of ovary (183.0)*
> *secondary malignant neoplasm of retroperitoneum and peritoneum (197.6)*
> **AHA:** 4Q, '07, 96
> **CC Excl:** 338.0-338.4, 780.64-780.65, 780.91-780.99, 789.30-789.59, 789.9, 799.81-799.89
> **R18.0** Malignant ascites `I-10`

789.59 Other ascites `CC`
> **CC Excl:** See code: 789.51
> **AHA:** 4Q, '08, 99
> **R18.8** Other ascites `I-10`

§ ✔5ᵗʰ **789.6 Abdominal tenderness**
> [0-7, 9]   Rebound tenderness

789.7 Colic `P`
> Colic NOS
> Infantile colic
> **EXCLUDES** *colic in adult and child over 12 months old (789.0)*
> *renal colic (788.0)*
> **DEF:** Inconsolable crying in an otherwise well-fed and healthy infant for more than three hours a day, three days a week, for more than three weeks.
> **AHA:** 4Q, '09, 104-105

789.9 Other symptoms involving abdomen and pelvis
> Umbilical:
>   bleeding
>   discharge

Nonspecific Abnormal Findings (790-796)
> **AHA:** 3Q, '11, 4; 2Q, '90, 16

✔4ᵗʰ **790 Nonspecific findings on examination of blood**
> **EXCLUDES** *abnormality of:*
> *platelets (287.0-287.9)*
> *thrombocytes (287.0-287.9)*
> *white blood cells (288.00-288.9)*

✔5ᵗʰ **790.0 Abnormality of red blood cells**
> **EXCLUDES** *anemia:*
> *congenital (776.5)*
> *newborn, due to isoimmunization (773.0-773.2, 773.5)*
> *of premature infant (776.6)*
> *other specified types (280.0-285.9)*
> *hemoglobin disorders (282.5-282.7)*
> *polycythemia:*
> *familial (289.6)*
> *neonatorum (776.4)*
> *secondary (289.0)*
> *vera (238.4)*
> **AHA:** 4Q, '00, 46

790.01 Precipitous drop in hematocrit `CC`
> Drop in hematocrit
> Drop in hemoglobin
> **CC Excl:** 285.1, 285.3-285.9
> **TIP:** Typically reported as a reason for encounter at a dialysis center.

790.09 Other abnormality of red blood cells
> Abnormal red cell morphology NOS
> Abnormal red cell volume NOS
> Anisocytosis
> Poikilocytosis

790.1 Elevated sedimentation rate

---

§   Requires fifth digit. Valid digits are in [brackets] under each code. See category 789 for codes and definitions.

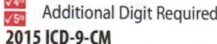

✔4ᵗʰ
✔5ᵗʰ Additional Digit Required   Unacceptable PDx   Manifestation Code   Hospital Acquired Condition   ►◄ Revised Text   ● New Code   ▲ Revised Code Title

2015 ICD-9-CM   **Volume 1 – 291**

Symptoms, Signs, and Ill-Defined Conditions

790.2–791.9

√5ᵗʰ **790.2 Abnormal glucose**

> **EXCLUDES** *diabetes mellitus (249.00-249.91, 250.00-250.93)*
> *dysmetabolic syndrome X (277.7)*
> *gestational diabetes (648.8)*
> *glycosuria (791.5)*
> *hypoglycemia (251.2)*
> *that complicating pregnancy, childbirth, or*
> *puerperium (648.8)*
>
> **AHA:** 1Q, '11, 9; 4Q, '03, 74; 3Q, '91, 5
>
> **TIP:** These codes are typically assigned on encounters before a patient is diagnosed with diabetes mellitus.

790.21 Impaired fasting glucose
> Elevated fasting glucose

790.22 Impaired glucose tolerance test (oral)
> Elevated glucose tolerance test

790.29 Other abnormal glucose
> Abnormal glucose NOS
> Abnormal non-fasting glucose
> Hyperglycemia NOS
> Pre-diabetes NOS
>
> **AHA:** 1Q, '12, 17; 3Q, '09, 5;2Q, '05, 21
>
> **TIP:** Assign for any stress hyperglycemia for which no causal condition is determined including postoperative hyperglycemia that is not specifically documented as a complication of the procedure.
>
> R73.09 Other abnormal glucose   I-10

790.3 Excessive blood level of alcohol
> Elevated blood-alcohol
>
> **AHA:** S-O, '86, 3

790.4 Nonspecific elevation of levels of transaminase or lactic acid dehydrogenase [LDH]
> R74.0 Nonspecific elevation levels transaminase & LDH   I-10

790.5 Other nonspecific abnormal serum enzyme levels
> Abnormal serum level of:
> acid phosphatase
> alkaline phosphatase
> amylase
> lipase
>
> **EXCLUDES** *deficiency of circulating enzymes (277.6)*
>
> R74.8 Abnormal levels of other serum enzymes   I-10

790.6 Other abnormal blood chemistry
> Abnormal blood level of: Abnormal blood level of:
> cobalt   lithium
> copper   magnesium
> iron   mineral
> lead   zinc
>
> **EXCLUDES** *abnormality of electrolyte or acid-base balance*
> *(276.0-276.9)*
> *hypoglycemia NOS (251.2)*
> *lead poisoning (984.0-984.9)*
> *specific finding indicating abnormality of:*
> *amino-acid transport and metabolism*
> *(270.0-270.9)*
> *carbohydrate transport and metabolism*
> *(271.0-271.9)*
> *lipid metabolism (272.0-272.9)*
> *uremia NOS (586)*
>
> **AHA:** ▶2Q, '13, 13;◀ 4Q, '88, 1
>
> **TIP:** If only azotemia is documented (indexed to 790.6), clarify with physician; if due to uremia or renal failure, code to those conditions instead.
>
> R78.89 Finding oth spec substances not norm found blood   I-10

790.7 Bacteremia   CC
> **EXCLUDES** *bacteremia of newborn (771.83)*
> *septicemia (038)*
>
> Use additional code to identify organism (041)
>
> **DEF:** Laboratory finding of bacteria in the blood in the absence of two or more signs of sepsis; transient in nature, progresses to septicemia with severe infectious process.
>
> **CC Excl:** 338.0-338.4, 780.64-780.65, 780.91-780.99, 790.7-790.99, 799.81-799.89
>
> **AHA:** ▶1Q, '14, 18;◀ 2Q, '11, 7; 2Q, '03, 7; 4Q, '93, 29; 3Q, '88, 12
>
> **TIP:** If clinical signs or symptoms indicating systemic disease exist, query physician for the presence of sepsis; code to category 038 if documented.

790.8 Viremia, unspecified
> **DEF:** Presence of a virus in the blood stream.
> **AHA:** 4Q, '88, 10

√5ᵗʰ **790.9 Other nonspecific findings on examination of blood**
> **AHA:** 4Q, '93, 29

790.91 Abnormal arterial blood gases

790.92 Abnormal coagulation profile
> Abnormal or prolonged:
> bleeding time
> coagulation time
> partial thromboplastin time [PTT]
> prothrombin time [PT]
>
> **EXCLUDES** *coagulation (hemorrhagic) disorders*
> *(286.0-286.9)*
>
> R79.1 Abnormal coagulaton profile   I-10

790.93 Elevated prostate specific antigen, [PSA]   A ♂

790.94 Euthyroid sick syndrome
> **DEF:** Transient alteration of thyroid hormone metabolism due to nonthyroid illness or stress.
> **AHA:** 4Q, '97, 45

790.95 Elevated C-reactive protein [CRP]
> **DEF:** Inflammation in an arterial wall results in elevated C-reactive protein (CRP) in the blood; CRP is a recognized risk factor in cardiovascular disease.

790.99 Other
> **AHA:** 3Q, '12, 18; 3Q, '11, 4; 2Q, '03, 14
>
> **TIP:** Assign for documentation of secondary thrombocytosis as clinically significant but without other reportable underlying cause.

√4ᵗʰ **791 Nonspecific findings on examination of urine**
> **EXCLUDES** *hematuria NOS (599.70-599.72)*
> *specific findings indicating abnormality of:*
> *amino-acid transport and metabolism (270.0-270.9)*
> *carbohydrate transport and metabolism (271.0-271.9)*

791.0 Proteinuria
> Albuminuria   Bence-Jones proteinuria
>
> **EXCLUDES** *postural proteinuria (593.6)*
> *that arising during pregnancy or the puerperium*
> *(642.0-642.9, 646.2)*
>
> **DEF:** Excess protein in urine.
> **AHA:** 2Q, '12, 19; 3Q, '91, 8

791.1 Chyluria   CC
> **EXCLUDES** *filarial (125.0-125.9)*
> **DEF:** Excess chyle in urine.
> **CC Excl:** 338.0-338.4, 780.64-780.65, 780.91-780.99, 791.1, 791.9, 799.81-799.89

791.2 Hemoglobinuria
> **DEF:** Free hemoglobin in blood due to rapid hemolysis of red blood cells.

791.3 Myoglobinuria   CC
> **DEF:** Myoglobin (oxygen-transporting pigment) in urine.
> **CC Excl:** 338.0-338.4, 780.64-780.65, 780.91-780.99, 791.2-791.3, 791.9, 799.81-799.89

791.4 Biliuria
> **DEF:** Bile pigments in urine.

791.5 Glycosuria
> **EXCLUDES** *renal glycosuria (271.4)*
> **DEF:** Sugar in urine.

791.6 Acetonuria
> Ketonuria
> **DEF:** Excess acetone in urine.

791.7 Other cells and casts in urine

791.9 Other nonspecific findings on examination of urine
> Crystalluria   Elevated urine levels of:
> Elevated urine levels of: indolacetic acid
>   17-ketosteroids   vanillylmandelic acid [VMA]
>   catecholamines   Melanuria
>
> **AHA:** 1Q, '05, 12

| N Newborn Age: 0 | P Pediatric Age: 0-17 | M Maternity Age: 12-55 | A Adult Age: 15-124 | MCC Major CC Condition | CC CC Condition | HIV HIV Related Dx |

✓4th 792 Nonspecific abnormal findings in other body substances
> **EXCLUDES** *that in chromosomal analysis (795.2)*

792.0 Cerebrospinal fluid

792.1 Stool contents
Abnormal stool color   Occult stool
Fat in stool   Pus in stool
Mucus in stool
> **EXCLUDES** *blood in stool [melena] (578.1)*
> *newborn (772.4, 777.3)*

AHA: 2Q, '92, 9

792.2 Semen ♂
Abnormal spermatozoa
> **EXCLUDES** *azoospermia (606.0)*
> *oligospermia (606.1)*

792.3 Amniotic fluid Ⓜ ♀
DEF: Nonspecific abnormal findings in amniotic fluid.
AHA: N-D, '86, 4

792.4 Saliva
> **EXCLUDES** *that in chromosomal analysis (795.2)*

792.5 Cloudy (hemodialysis) (peritoneal) dialysis effluent
AHA: 4Q, '00, 46

792.9 Other nonspecific abnormal findings in body substances
Peritoneal fluid   Synovial fluid
Pleural fluid   Vaginal fluids

✓4th 793 Nonspecific (abnormal) findings on radiological and other examination of body structure
> **INCLUDES** nonspecific abnormal findings of:
> thermography
> ultrasound examination [echogram]
> x-ray examination
> **EXCLUDES** *abnormal results of function studies and radioisotope scans (794.0-794.9)*

793.0 Skull and head
> **EXCLUDES** *nonspecific abnormal echoencephalogram (794.01)*

AHA: 3Q, '06, 22

✓5th 793.1 Lung field
AHA: 4Q, '11, 138-139

793.11 Solitary pulmonary nodule
Coin lesion lung
Solitary pulmonary nodule, subsegmental branch of the bronchial tree

793.19 Other nonspecific abnormal finding of lung field
Pulmonary infiltrate NOS
Shadow, lung
AHA: 4Q, '11, 139

793.2 Other intrathoracic organ
Abnormal:
echocardiogram
heart shadow
ultrasound cardiogram
Mediastinal shift
AHA: 1Q, '12, 17

793.3 Biliary tract
Nonvisualization of gallbladder

793.4 Gastrointestinal tract

793.5 Genitourinary organs
Filling defect:
bladder
kidney
ureter

793.6 Abdominal area, including retroperitoneum

793.7 Musculoskeletal system

✓5th 793.8 Breast
AHA: 4Q, '01, 51

793.80 Abnormal mammogram, unspecified

793.81 Mammographic microcalcification
> **EXCLUDES** *mammographic calcification (793.89)*
> *mammographic calculus (793.89)*

DEF: Calcium and cellular debris deposits in the breast that cannot be felt but can be detected on a mammogram; can be a sign of cancer, benign conditions, or changes in the breast tissue as a result of inflammation, injury, or obstructed duct.

793.82 Inconclusive mammogram
Dense breasts NOS
Inconclusive mammogram NEC
Inconclusive mammography due to dense breasts
Inconclusive mammography NEC
AHA: 4Q, '09, 105-106

793.89 Other (abnormal) findings on radiological examination of breast
Mammographic calcification
Mammographic calculus

✓5th 793.9 Other
> **EXCLUDES** *abnormal finding by radioisotope localization of placenta (794.9)*

TIP: Sequence a code for the sign or symptom that was the reason for the imaging or radiological test first.

793.91 Image test inconclusive due to excess body fat
Use additional code to identify Body Mass Index (BMI), if known (V85.0-V85.54)
AHA: 4Q, '06, 109

793.99 Other nonspecific (abnormal) findings on radiological and other examinations of body structure
Abnormal:
placental finding by x-ray or ultrasound method
radiological findings in skin and subcutaneous tissue
AHA: 4Q, '06, 109

✓4th 794 Nonspecific abnormal results of function studies
> **INCLUDES** radioisotope:
> scans
> uptake studies
> scintiphotography

✓5th 794.0 Brain and central nervous system

794.00 Abnormal function study, unspecified

794.01 Abnormal echoencephalogram

794.02 Abnormal electroencephalogram [EEG]

794.09 Other
Abnormal brain scan

✓5th 794.1 Peripheral nervous system and special senses

794.10 Abnormal response to nerve stimulation, unspecified

794.11 Abnormal retinal function studies
Abnormal electroretinogram [ERG]

794.12 Abnormal electro-oculogram [EOG]

794.13 Abnormal visually evoked potential

794.14 Abnormal oculomotor studies

794.15 Abnormal auditory function studies
AHA: 1Q, '04, 15-16
TIP: If the reason for the encounter was for a hearing examination, sequence a code from subcategory V72.1 first. When nonspecific hearing loss is documented, assign 389.9 instead of 794.15.

794.16 Abnormal vestibular function studies

794.17 Abnormal electromyogram [EMG]
> **EXCLUDES** *that of eye (794.14)*

794.19 Other

794.2 Pulmonary
Abnormal lung scan
Reduced:
ventilatory capacity
vital capacity

Additional Digit Required   Unacceptable PDx   Manifestation Code   Hospital Acquired Condition   ►◄ Revised Text   ● New Code   ▲ Revised Code Title

2015 ICD-9-CM   **Volume 1 – 293**

√5ᵗʰ **794.3 Cardiovascular**

  794.30 Abnormal function study, unspecified

  794.31 Abnormal electrocardiogram [ECG] [EKG]
      EXCLUDES *long QT syndrome (426.82)*
      R94.31 Abnormal electrocardiogram [ECG]   `I-10`

  794.39 Other
    Abnormal:
      ballistocardiogram
      phonocardiogram
      vectorcardiogram
    R94.39 Abnormal result oth cardiovasculr function   `I-10`
    study

794.4 Kidney
  Abnormal renal function test

794.5 Thyroid
  Abnormal thyroid:
    scan
    uptake

794.6 Other endocrine function study

794.7 Basal metabolism
  Abnormal basal metabolic rate [BMR]

794.8 Liver
  Abnormal liver scan
  R94.5 Abnormal results of liver function studies   `I-10`

794.9 Other
  Bladder   Placenta
  Pancreas   Spleen

√4ᵗʰ **795 Other and nonspecific abnormal cytological, histological, immunological and DNA test findings**
    EXCLUDES *abnormal cytologic smear of anus and anal HPV*
        (796.70-796.79)
      nonspecific abnormalities of red blood cells (790.01-790.09)

√5ᵗʰ **795.0 Abnormal Papanicolaou smear of cervix and cervical HPV**
  Abnormal thin preparation smear of cervix
  Abnormal cervical cytology
    EXCLUDES *abnormal cytologic smear of vagina and vaginal HPV*
        (795.10-795.19)
      carcinoma in situ of cervix (233.1)
      cervical intraepithelial neoplasia I (CIN I) (622.11)
      cervical intraepithelial neoplasia II (CIN II) (622.12)
      cervical intraepithelial neoplasia III (CIN III) (233.1)
      dysplasia (histologically confirmed) of cervix (uteri) NOS (622.10)
      mild cervical dysplasia (histologically confirmed) (622.11)
      moderate cervical dysplasia (histologically confirmed) (622.12)
      severe cervical dysplasia (histologically confirmed) (233.1)
    AHA: 4Q, '08, 145-146; 4Q, '02, 69

  795.00 Abnormal glandular Papanicolaou smear of   ♀
    cervix
    Atypical endocervical cells NOS
    Atypical endometrial cells NOS
    Atypical cervical glandular cells NOS

  795.01 Papanicolaou smear of cervix with atypical   ♀
    squamous cells of undetermined significance [ASC-US]
    AHA: 2Q, '06, 4

  795.02 Papanicolaou smear of cervix with atypical   ♀
    squamous cells cannot exclude high grade squamous intraepithelial lesion [ASC-H]

  795.03 Papanicolaou smear of cervix with low   ♀
    grade squamous intraepithelial lesion [LGSIL]

  795.04 Papanicolaou smear of cervix with high   ♀
    grade squamous intraepithelial lesion [HGSIL]

  795.05 Cervical high risk human papillomavirus   ♀
    [HPV] DNA test positive

  795.06 Papanicolaou smear of cervix with cytologic   ♀
    evidence of malignancy
    AHA: 4Q, '06, 110

  795.07 Satisfactory cervical smear but lacking   ♀
    transformation zone

  795.08 Unsatisfactory cervical cytology smear   ♀
    Inadequate cervical cytology sample
    AHA: 2Q, '06, 4

  795.09 Other abnormal Papanicolaou smear of cervix   ♀
    and cervical HPV
    Cervical low risk human papillomavirus (HPV) DNA
    test positive
    Use additional code for associated human
      papillomavirus (079.4)
      EXCLUDES *encounter for Papanicolaou cervical smear*
        to confirm findings of recent normal
        smear following initial abnormal
        smear (V72.32)

√5ᵗʰ **795.1 Abnormal Papanicolaou smear of vagina and vaginal HPV**
  Abnormal thin preparation smear of vagina NOS
  Abnormal vaginal cytology NOS
  Use additional code to identify acquired absence of uterus
    and cervix, if applicable (V88.01-V88.03)
    EXCLUDES *abnormal cytologic smear of cervix and cervical HPV*
        (795.00-795.09)
      carcinoma in situ of vagina (233.31)
      carcinoma in situ of vulva (233.32)
      dysplasia (histologically confirmed) of vagina NOS
        (623.0, 233.31)
      dysplasia (histologically confirmed) of vulva NOS
        (624.01, 624.02, 233.32)
      mild vaginal dysplasia (histologically confirmed)
        (623.0)
      mild vulvar dysplasia (histologically confirmed)
        (624.01)
      moderate vaginal dysplasia (histologically
        confirmed) (623.0)
      moderate vulvar dysplasia (histologically confirmed)
        (624.02)
      severe vaginal dysplasia (histologically confirmed)
        (233.31)
      severe vulvar dysplasia (histologically confirmed)
        (233.32)
      vaginal intraepithelial neoplasia I (VAIN I) (623.0)
      vaginal intraepithelial neoplasia II (VAIN II) (623.0)
      vaginal intraepithelial neoplasia III (VAIN III) (233.31)
      vulvar intraepithelial neoplasia I (VIN I) (624.01)
      vulvar intraepithelial neoplasia II (VIN II) (624.02)
      vulvar intraepithelial neoplasia III (VIN III) (233.32)
  AHA: 4Q, '08, 145-148

  795.10 Abnormal glandular Papanicolaou smear   ♀
    of vagina
    Atypical vaginal glandular cells NOS

  795.11 Papanicolaou smear of vagina with atypical   ♀
    squamous cells of undetermined significance [ASC-US]

  795.12 Papanicolaou smear of vagina with atypical   ♀
    squamous cells cannot exclude high grade squamous intraepithelial lesion [ASC-H]

  795.13 Papanicolaou smear of vagina with low   ♀
    grade squamous intraepithelial lesion [LGSIL]

  795.14 Papanicolaou smear of vagina with high   ♀
    grade squamous intraepithelial lesion [HGSIL]

  795.15 Vaginal high risk human   ♀
    papillomavirus [HPV] DNA test positive
      EXCLUDES *condyloma acuminatum (078.11)*
        genital warts (078.11)

  795.16 Papanicolaou smear of vagina with cytologic   ♀
    evidence of malignancy

  795.18 Unsatisfactory vaginal cytology smear   ♀
    Inadequate vaginal cytology sample

  795.19 Other abnormal Papanicolaou smear of vagina   ♀
    and vaginal HPV
    Vaginal low risk human papillomavirus (HPV) DNA
    test positive
    Use additional code for associated human
      papillomavirus (079.4)

`N` Newborn Age: 0   `P` Pediatric Age: 0-17   `M` Maternity Age: 12-55   `A` Adult Age: 15-124   `MCC` Major CC Condition   `CC` CC Condition   `HIV` HIV Related Dx

795.2 Nonspecific abnormal findings on chromosomal analysis
Abnormal karyotype

√5ᵗʰ **795.3 Nonspecific positive culture findings**
Positive culture findings in:
nose
throat
sputum
wound
EXCLUDES that of:
blood (790.7-790.8)
urine (791.9)

795.31 Nonspecific positive findings for anthrax
Positive findings by nasal swab
AHA: 4Q, '02, 70
TIP: If the patient has been exposed only to anthrax, assign instead V01.81. If a patient has not been exposed but fears anthrax and tests negative, assign instead V71.82.

795.39 Other nonspecific positive culture findings
EXCLUDES colonization status (V02.0-V02.9)

795.4 Other nonspecific abnormal histological findings

√5ᵗʰ **795.5 Nonspecific reaction to test for tuberculosis**
AHA: 4Q, '11, 140-141

795.51 Nonspecific reaction to tuberculin skin test without active tuberculosis
Abnormal result of Mantoux test
PPD positive
Tuberculin (skin test) positive
Tuberculin (skin test) reactor
EXCLUDES nonspecific reaction to cell mediated immunity measurement of gamma interferon antigen response without active tuberculosis (795.52)
AHA: 4Q, '11, 182
TIP: Assign when documentation indicates "latent tuberculosis."

795.52 Nonspecific reaction to cell mediated immunity measurement of gamma interferon antigen response without active tuberculosis
Nonspecific reaction to QuantiFERON-TB test (QFT) without active tuberculosis
EXCLUDES nonspecific reaction to tuberculin skin test without active tuberculosis (795.51)
positive tuberculin skin test (795.51)

795.6 False positive serological test for syphilis
False positive Wassermann reaction

√5ᵗʰ **795.7 Other nonspecific immunological findings**
EXCLUDES abnormal tumor markers (795.81-795.89)
elevated prostate specific antigen [PSA] (790.93)
elevated tumor associated antigens (795.81-795.89)
isoimmunization, in pregnancy (656.1-656.2)
affecting fetus or newborn (773.0-773.2)
AHA: 2Q, '93, 6

795.71 Nonspecific serologic evidence of human immunodeficiency virus [HIV]
Inclusive human immunodeficiency [HIV] test (adult) (infant)
NOTE This code is **only** to be used when a test finding is reported as nonspecific. Asymptomatic positive findings are coded to V08. If any HIV infection symptom or condition is present, see code 042. Negative findings are not coded.
EXCLUDES acquired immunodeficiency syndrome [AIDS] (042)
asymptomatic human immunodeficiency virus, [HIV] infection status (V08)
HIV infection, symptomatic (042)
human immunodeficiency virus [HIV] disease (042)
positive (status) NOS (V08)
AHA: 2Q, '04, 11; 1Q, '93, 21; 1Q, '93, 22; 2Q, '92, 11; J-A, '87, 24

795.79 Other and unspecified nonspecific immunological findings
Raised antibody titer
Raised level of immunoglobulins
AHA: 4Q, '11, 93

√5ᵗʰ **795.8 Abnormal tumor markers**
Elevated tumor associated antigens [TAA]
Elevated tumor specific antigens [TSA]
EXCLUDES elevated prostate specific antigen [PSA] (790.93)

795.81 Elevated carcinoembryonic antigen [CEA]
AHA: 4Q, '06, 111

795.82 Elevated cancer antigen 125 [CA 125] ♀
AHA: 4Q, '06, 111

795.89 Other abnormal tumor markers
AHA: 4Q, '06, 111

√4ᵗʰ **796 Other nonspecific abnormal findings**

796.0 Nonspecific abnormal toxicological findings
Abnormal levels of heavy metals or drugs in blood, urine, or other tissue
Use additional code for retained foreign body, if applicable, (V90.01-V90.9)
EXCLUDES excessive blood level of alcohol (790.3)
AHA: 1Q, '97, 16

796.1 Abnormal reflex

796.2 Elevated blood pressure reading without diagnosis of hypertension
NOTE This category is to be used to record an episode of elevated blood pressure in a patient in whom no formal diagnosis of hypertension has been made, or as an incidental finding.
AHA: 2Q, '03, 11; 3Q, '90, 4; J-A, '84, 12
TIP: Assign an additional E code for poisoning or adverse effect of a drug if the documentation indicates it's the underlying cause of the elevated blood pressure.
R03.0 Elevated blood-pressure reading without dx HTN I-10

796.3 Nonspecific low blood pressure reading

796.4 Other abnormal clinical findings
AHA: 1Q, '97, 16

796.5 Abnormal finding on antenatal screening M♀
AHA: 4Q, '97, 46

796.6 Abnormal findings on neonatal screening N
EXCLUDES nonspecific serologic evidence of human immunodeficiency virus [HIV] (795.71)
AHA: 4Q, '04, 99

√5ᵗʰ **796.7 Abnormal cytologic smear of anus and anal HPV**
EXCLUDES abnormal cytologic smear of cervix and cervical HPV (795.00-795.09)
abnormal cytologic smear of vagina and vaginal HPV (795.10-795.19)
anal intraepithelial neoplasia I (AIN I) (569.44)
anal intraepithelial neoplasia II (AIN II) (569.44)
anal intraepithelial neoplasia III (AIN III) (230.5, 230.6)
carcinoma in situ of anus (230.5, 230.6)
dysplasia (histologically confirmed) of anus NOS (569.44)
mild anal dysplasia (histologically confirmed) (569.44)
moderate anal dysplasia (histologically confirmed) (569.44)
severe anal dysplasia (histologically confirmed) (230.5, 230.6)
AHA: 4Q, '08, 117-119

796.70 Abnormal glandular Papanicolaou smear of anus
Atypical anal glandular cells NOS

796.71 Papanicolaou smear of anus with atypical squamous cells of undetermined significance [ASC-US]

796.72 Papanicolaou smear of anus with atypical squamous cells cannot exclude high grade squamous intraepithelial lesion [ASC-H]

796.73 Papanicolaou smear of anus with low grade squamous intraepithelial lesion [LGSIL]

796.74 Papanicolaou smear of anus with high grade squamous intraepithelial lesion [HGSIL]

796.75 Anal high risk human papillomavirus [HPV] DNA test positive

796.76 Papanicolaou smear of anus with cytologic evidence of malignancy

796.77 Satisfactory anal smear but lacking transformation zone

796.78 Unsatisfactory anal cytology smear
Inadequate anal cytology sample

796.79 Other abnormal Papanicolaou smear of anus and anal HPV
Anal low risk human papillomavirus (HPV) DNA test positive
Use additional code for associated human papillomavirus (079.4)

796.9 Other

Ill-Defined and Unknown Causes of Morbidity and Mortality (797-799)

797 Senility without mention of psychosis
Frailty
Old age
Senescence
Senile asthenia
Senile:
debility
exhaustion
EXCLUDES senile psychoses (290.0-290.9)

√4th **798 Sudden death, cause unknown**

798.0 Sudden infant death syndrome   P
Cot death
Crib death
Sudden death of nonspecific cause in infancy
DEF: Death of infant under age one due to nonspecific cause.

798.1 Instantaneous death

798.2 Death occurring in less than 24 hours from onset of symptoms, not otherwise explained
Death known not to be violent or instantaneous, for which no cause could be discovered
Died without sign of disease

798.9 Unattended death
Death in circumstances where the body of the deceased was found and no cause could be discovered
Found dead

√4th **799 Other ill-defined and unknown causes of morbidity and mortality**

√5th **799.0 Asphyxia and hypoxemia**
EXCLUDES asphyxia and hypoxemia (due to):
carbon monoxide (986)
hypercapnia (786.09)
inhalation of food or foreign body (932-934.9)
newborn (768.0-768.9)
traumatic (994.7)

799.01 Asphyxia   CC
DEF: Lack of oxygen in inspired air, causing a deficiency of oxygen in tissues (hypoxia) and elevated levels of arterial carbon dioxide (hypercapnia).
CC Excl: 338.0-338.4, 518.81-518.84, 780.64-780.65, 780.91-780.99, 798.0, 799.01-799.1, 799.81-799.89
AHA: 4Q, '05, 90

799.02 Hypoxemia
DEF: Deficient oxygenation of the blood.
AHA: 3Q, '09, 20; 2Q, '06, 24, 25; 4Q, '05, 90
TIP: Hypoxia is not inherent in COPD (496) and may be assigned in addition, if applicable.
R09.02 Hypoxemia   I-10

---

[1] **799.1 Respiratory arrest**   MCC
Cardiorespiratory failure
EXCLUDES cardiac arrest (427.5)
failure of peripheral circulation (785.50)
respiratory distress:
NOS (786.09)
acute (518.82)
following trauma and surgery (518.52)
newborn (770.89)
syndrome (newborn) (769)
adult (following trauma and surgery) (518.52)
other (518.82)
respiratory failure (518.81, 518.83-518.84)
newborn (770.84)
respiratory insufficiency (786.09)
acute (518.82)
CC Excl: See code: 799.01

√5th **799.2 Signs and symptoms involving emotional state**
EXCLUDES anxiety (293.84, 300.00-300.09)
depression (311)
AHA: 4Q, '09,107
TIP: If associated with underlying history of traumatic brain injury (TBI), assign in addition to a code for the late effect of TBI (e.g., 905.0 or 907.0).

799.21 Nervousness
Nervous
AHA: 4Q, '09, 108

799.22 Irritability
Irritable
AHA: 4Q, '09, 108

799.23 Impulsiveness
Impulsive
EXCLUDES impulsive neurosis (300.3)

799.24 Emotional lability

799.25 Demoralization and apathy
Apathetic

799.29 Other signs and symptoms involving emotional state

799.3 Debility, unspecified
EXCLUDES asthenia (780.79)
nervous debility (300.5)
neurasthenia (300.5)
senile asthenia (797)

799.4 Cachexia   CC
Wasting disease
Code first underlying condition, if known
DEF: General ill health and poor nutrition.
CC Excl: 338.0-338.4, 780.64-780.65, 780.91-780.99, 799.3-799.4, 799.81-799.89
AHA: ▶1Q, '13, 13;◀ 3Q, '06, 14, 15; 3Q, '90, 17
TIP: Assign an additional code for any associated malnutrition, if documented.
R64 Cachexia   I-10

√5th **799.5 Signs and symptoms involving cognition**
EXCLUDES amnesia (780.93)
amnestic syndrome (294.0)
attention deficit disorder (314.00-314.01)
late effects of cerebrovascular disease (438.0)
memory loss (780.93)
mild cognitive impairment, so stated (331.83)
specific problems in developmental delay (315.00-315.9)
transient global amnesia (437.7)
visuospatial neglect (781.8)
AHA: 3Q, '12, 19-20; 4Q, '10, 95-96
TIP: Report as additional diagnoses not integral to a known condition to describe the nature or type of deficit due to unknown or unrelated cause.

799.51 Attention or concentration deficit
AHA: 3Q, '12, 20

799.52 Cognitive communication deficit
AHA: 3Q, '12, 19-21

799.53 Visuospatial deficit

---

[1] MCC = Only if patient discharged alive.

N Newborn Age: 0   P Pediatric Age: 0-17   M Maternity Age: 12-55   A Adult Age: 15-124   MCC Major CC Condition   CC CC Condition   HIV HIV Related Dx

296 – Volume 1 • October 2014   **2015 ICD-9-CM**

799.54 **Psychomotor deficit**
　　　　AHA: 4Q, '10, 95-97

799.55 **Frontal lobe and executive function deficit**
　　　　AHA: 3Q, '12, 20

799.59 **Other signs and symptoms involving cognition**

√5ᵗʰ **799.8 Other ill-defined conditions**

799.81 **Decreased libido**　　　　　　　　　　　　　Ａ
　　　　Decreased sexual desire
　　　　EXCLUDES psychosexual dysfunction with inhibited
　　　　　　　　　　sexual desire (302.71)
　　　　AHA: 4Q, '03, 75

799.82 **Apparent life threatening event in infant**　Ｐ
　　　　ALTE
　　　　Apparent life threatening event in newborn and
　　　　　infant
　　　　Code first confirmed diagnosis, if known
　　　　Use additional code(s) for associated signs and
　　　　　symptoms if no confirmed diagnosis
　　　　　established, or if signs and symptoms are not
　　　　　associated routinely with confirmed diagnosis,
　　　　　or provide additional information for cause of
　　　　　ALTE
　　　　AHA: 4Q, '10, 97-98; 4Q, '09, 109

799.89 **Other ill-defined conditions**

799.9 **Other unknown and unspecified cause**
　　　　Undiagnosed disease, not specified as to site or system
　　　　　involved
　　　　Unknown cause of morbidity or mortality
　　　　AHA: 1Q, '98,.4; 1Q, '90, 20

17. Injury and Poisoning (800-999)

Use E code(s) to identify the cause and intent of the injury or poisoning (E800-E999)

Use additional code for retained foreign body, if applicable, (V90.01-V90.9)

NOTE

1. The principle of multiple coding of injuries should be followed wherever possible. Combination categories for multiple injuries are provided for use when there is insufficient detail as to the nature of the individual conditions, or for primary tabulation purposes when it is more convenient to record a single code; otherwise, the component injuries should be coded separately.

   Where multiple sites of injury are specified in the titles, the word "with" indicates involvement of both sites, and the word "and" indicates involvement of either or both sites. The word "finger" includes thumb.

2. Categories for "late effect" of injuries are to be found at 905-909.

Fractures (800-829)

EXCLUDES   malunion (733.81)
      nonunion (733.82)
      pathological or spontaneous fracture (733.10-733.19)
      stress fractures (733.93-733.95)

NOTE The terms "condyle," "coronoid process," "ramus," and "symphysis" indicate the portion of the bone fractured, not the name of the bone involved.

The descriptions "closed" and "open" used in the fourth-digit subdivisions include the following terms:

closed (with or without delayed healing):

comminuted	impacted
depressed	linear
elevated	simple
fissured	slipped epiphysis
fracture NOS	spiral
greenstick	

open (with or without delayed healing):

compound	puncture
infected	with foreign body
missile	

A fracture not indicated as closed or open should be classified as closed.

AHA: 4Q, '08, 158;1Q, '07, 3-4; 4Q, '90, 26; 3Q, '90, 5; 3Q, '90, 13; 2Q, '90, 7; 2Q, '89, 15, S-O, '85, 3

TIP: Assign the acute fracture codes only while the patient is receiving active treatment for the fracture, such as during surgical care, an ED encounter, or evaluation and treatment by a new physician. Otherwise, refer to aftercare category V54.

Fracture of Skull (800-804)

INCLUDES   traumatic brain injury due to fracture of skull

The following fifth-digit subclassification is for use with the appropriate codes in category 800, 801, 803, and 804:

0 unspecified state of consciousness
1 with no loss of consciousness
2 with brief [less than one hour] loss of consciousness
3 with moderate [1-24 hours] loss of consciousness
4 with prolonged [more than 24 hours] loss of consciousness and return to pre-existing conscious level
5 with prolonged [more than 24 hours] loss of consciousness, without return to pre-existing conscious level
     Use fifth-digit 5 to designate when a patient is unconscious and dies before regaining consciousness, regardless of the duration of the loss of consciousness
6 with loss of consciousness of unspecified duration
9 with concussion, unspecified

√4th **800 Fracture of vault of skull**

     INCLUDES   frontal bone
                   parietal bone

     DEF: Fracture of bone that forms skull dome and protects brain.
     AHA: 4Q,'96, 36

§ √5th **800.0 Closed without mention of intracranial**   `CC 0-2, 6, 9`   `MCC 3-5`
[0-6, 9] **injury**

         CC Excl: 800.00-801.99, 803.00-804.99, 829.0-829.1, 850.0-852.19, 852.21-854.19, 873.8-873.9, 879.8-879.9, 905.0, 925.1-925.2, 929.0-929.9, 958.8-959.09, 959.8-959.9

Fractures

§ √5th **800.1 Closed with cerebral laceration and contusion**   `MCC`
[0-6, 9]   **CC Excl:** See code 800.0

§ √5th **800.2 Closed with subarachnoid, subdural, and**   `MCC`
[0-6, 9] **extradural hemorrhage**
         CC Excl: See code 800.0

§ √5th **800.3 Closed with other and unspecified**   `MCC`
[0-6, 9] **intracranial hemorrhage**
         CC Excl: See code 800.0

§ √5th **800.4 Closed with intracranial injury of other**   `CC 0-2, 6, 9`   `MCC 3-5`
[0-6, 9] **and unspecified nature**
         CC Excl: See code 800.0

§ √5th **800.5 Open without mention of intracranial injury**   `MCC`
[0-6, 9]   **CC Excl:** See code 800.0

§ √5th **800.6 Open with cerebral laceration and contusion**   `MCC`
[0-6, 9]   **CC Excl:** See code 800.0

§ √5th **800.7 Open with subarachnoid, subdural, and**   `MCC`
[0-6, 9] **extradural hemorrhage**
         CC Excl: See code 800.0

§ √5th **800.8 Open with other and unspecified intracranial**   `MCC`
[0-6, 9] **hemorrhage**
         CC Excl: See code 800.0

§ √5th **800.9 Open with intracranial injury of other and**   `MCC`
[0-6, 9] **unspecified nature**
         CC Excl: See code 800.0

√4th **801 Fracture of base of skull**

     INCLUDES   fossa:
                anterior
                middle
                posterior
        occiput bone
        orbital roof
        sinus:
                ethmoid
                frontal
        sphenoid bone
        temporal bone

     DEF: Fracture of bone that forms skull floor.
     AHA: 4Q, '96, 36

§ √5th **801.0 Closed without mention of intracranial**   `CC 0-2, 6, 9`   `MCC 3-5`
[0-6, 9] **injury**

         CC Excl: 800.00-801.99, 803.00-804.99, 829.0-829.1, 850.0-852.19, 852.21-854.19, 873.8-873.9, 879.8-879.9, 905.0, 925.1-925.2, 929.0-929.9, 958.8-959.09, 959.8-959.9

§ √5th **801.1 Closed with cerebral laceration and contusion**   `MCC`
[0-6, 9]   **CC Excl:** See code: 801.0
         AHA: 4Q, '96, 36

§ √5th **801.2 Closed with subarachnoid, subdural, and**   `MCC`
[0-6, 9] **extradural hemorrhage**
         CC Excl: See code: 801.0

§ √5th **801.3 Closed with other and unspecified**   `MCC`
[0-6, 9] **intracranial hemorrhage**
         CC Excl: See code: 801.0

§ √5th **801.4 Closed with intracranial injury of other**   `CC 0-2, 6, 9`   `MCC 3-5`
[0-6, 9] **and unspecified nature**
         CC Excl: See code: 801.0

---

§   Requires fifth digit. Valid digits are in [brackets] under each code. See beginning of section 800-804 for codes and definitions.

√4th Additional Digit Required   Unacceptable PDx   Manifestation Code   Hospital Acquired Condition   ►◄ Revised Text   ● New Code   ▲ Revised Code Title
√5th

Skull

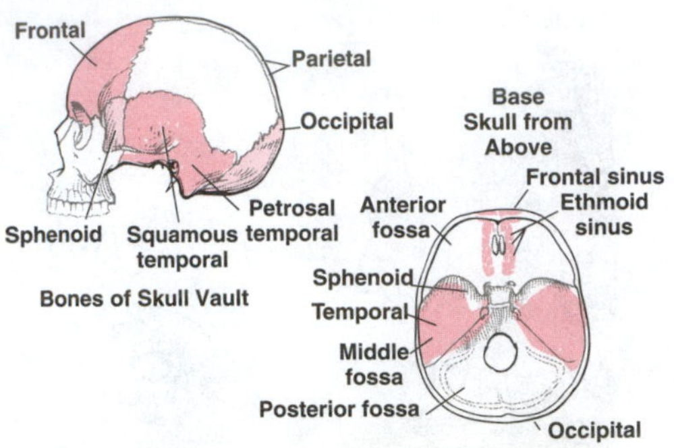

Frontal
Parietal
Occipital
Base Skull from Above
Frontal sinus
Ethmoid sinus
Anterior fossa
Sphenoid
Petrosal
Squamous temporal
Sphenoid temporal
Temporal
Bones of Skull Vault
Middle fossa
Posterior fossa
Occipital

Facial Fracture

Frontal bone
Nasal bone
LeFort Fracture Types
Type III
Orbital floor
Zygomatic bone (malar) and arch
Type II
Subcondylar
Type I
Body
Angle
Maxilla
Symphysis
Parasymphysis
Common Fracture Sites of Mandible

§ ✓5th **801.5 Open without mention of intracranial injury**   `MCC`
[0-6, 9] CC Excl: See code: 801.0

§ ✓5th **801.6 Open with cerebral laceration and contusion**   `MCC`
[0-6, 9] CC Excl: See code: 801.0

§ ✓5th **801.7 Open with subarachnoid, subdural, and**   `MCC`
[0-6, 9] **extradural hemorrhage**
    CC Excl: See code: 801.0

§ ✓5th **801.8 Open with other and unspecified**   `MCC`
[0-6, 9] **intracranial hemorrhage**
    CC Excl: See code: 801.0

§ ✓5th **801.9 Open with intracranial injury of other and**   `MCC`
[0-6, 9] **unspecified nature**
    CC Excl: See code: 801.0

✓4th **802 Fracture of face bones**
    AHA: 4Q, '96, 36

    802.0 Nasal bones, closed
      S02.2xxA Fracture nasal bones initial encounter closed fx   `I-10`

    802.1 Nasal bones, open   `CC`
      CC Excl: 800.00-802.1, 803.00-804.99, 829.0-829.1, 850.0-852.19, 852.21-854.19, 873.8-873.9, 879.8-879.9, 905.0, 925.1-925.2, 929.0-929.9, 958.8-959.09, 959.8-959.9

✓5th **802.2 Mandible, closed**
     Inferior maxilla
     Lower jaw (bone)

     802.20 Unspecified site   `CC`
       CC Excl: 800.00-801.99, 802.20-802.5, 803.00-804.99, 829.0-830.1, 850.0-852.19, 852.21-854.19, 873.8-873.9, 879.8-879.9, 905.0, 925.1-925.2, 929.0-929.9, 958.8-959.09, 959.8-959.9

     802.21 Condylar process   `CC`
       CC Excl: See code 802.20

     802.22 Subcondylar   `CC`
       CC Excl: See code 802.20

     802.23 Coronoid process   `CC`
       CC Excl: See code 802.20

     802.24 Ramus, unspecified   `CC`
       CC Excl: See code 802.20

     802.25 Angle of jaw   `CC`
       CC Excl: See code 802.20

     802.26 Symphysis of body   `CC`
       CC Excl: See code 802.20

     802.27 Alveolar border of body   `CC`
       CC Excl: See code 802.20

     802.28 Body, other and unspecified   `CC`
       CC Excl: See code 802.20

     802.29 Multiple sites   `CC`
       CC Excl: See code 802.20

✓5th **802.3 Mandible, open**

     802.30 Unspecified site   `CC`
       CC Excl: See code 802.20

     802.31 Condylar process   `CC`
       CC Excl: See code 802.20

     802.32 Subcondylar   `CC`
       CC Excl: See code 802.20

     802.33 Coronoid process   `CC`
       CC Excl: See code 802.20

     802.34 Ramus, unspecified   `CC`
       CC Excl: See code 802.20

     802.35 Angle of jaw   `CC`
       CC Excl: See code 802.20

     802.36 Symphysis of body   `CC`
       CC Excl: See code 802.20

     802.37 Alveolar border of body   `CC`
       CC Excl: See code 802.20

     802.38 Body, other and unspecified   `CC`
       CC Excl: See code 802.20

     802.39 Multiple sites   `CC`
       CC Excl: See code 802.20

    802.4 Malar and maxillary bones, closed   `CC`
      Superior maxilla   Zygoma
      Upper jaw (bone)   Zygomatic arch
      CC Excl: See code 802.20
      S02.400A Malar fx uns initial enc closed fx   `I-10`
      S02.401A Maxillary fx uns initial enc closed fx   `I-10`
      S02.402A Zygomatic fx uns initial enc closed fx   `I-10`

    802.5 Malar and maxillary bones, open   `CC`
      CC Excl: See code 802.20

    802.6 Orbital floor (blow-out), closed   `CC`
      CC Excl: 800.00-801.99, 802.6-804.99, 829.0-829.1, 850.0-852.19, 852.21-854.19, 873.8-873.9, 879.8-879.9, 905.0, 925.1-925.2, 929.0-929.9, 958.8-959.09, 959.8-959.9
      S02.3xxA Fracture orbital floor initial encounter clos fx   `I-10`

    802.7 Orbital floor (blow-out), open   `CC`
      CC Excl: See code 802.6

    802.8 Other facial bones, closed   `CC`
      Alveolus   Palate
      Orbit:
        NOS
        part other than roof or floor
      EXCLUDES orbital:
          floor (802.6)
          roof (801.0-801.9)
      CC Excl: See code 802.6
      S0242xA Fx of alveolus of maxilla initial enc closed fx   `I-10`

    802.9 Other facial bones, open   `CC`
      CC Excl: See code 802.6

✓4th **803 Other and unqualified skull fractures**
    `INCLUDES` skull NOS
          skull multiple NOS
    AHA: 4Q, '96, 36

§ ✓5th **803.0 Closed without mention of**   `MCC 3-5` `CC 0-2,6,9`
[0-6, 9] **intracranial injury**
    CC Excl: 800.00-801.99, 803.00-804.99, 829.0-829.1, 850.0-852.19, 852.21-854.19, 873.8-873.9, 879.8-879.9, 905.0, 925.1-925.2, 929.0-929.9, 958.8-959.09, 959.8-959.9

§   Requires fifth digit. Valid digits are in [brackets] under each code. See beginning of section 800-804 for codes and definitions.

`N` Newborn Age: 0   `P` Pediatric Age: 0-17   `M` Maternity Age: 12-55   `A` Adult Age: 15-124   `MCC` Major CC Condition   `CC` CC Condition   `HIV` HIV Related Dx

300 – Volume 1   2015 ICD-9-CM

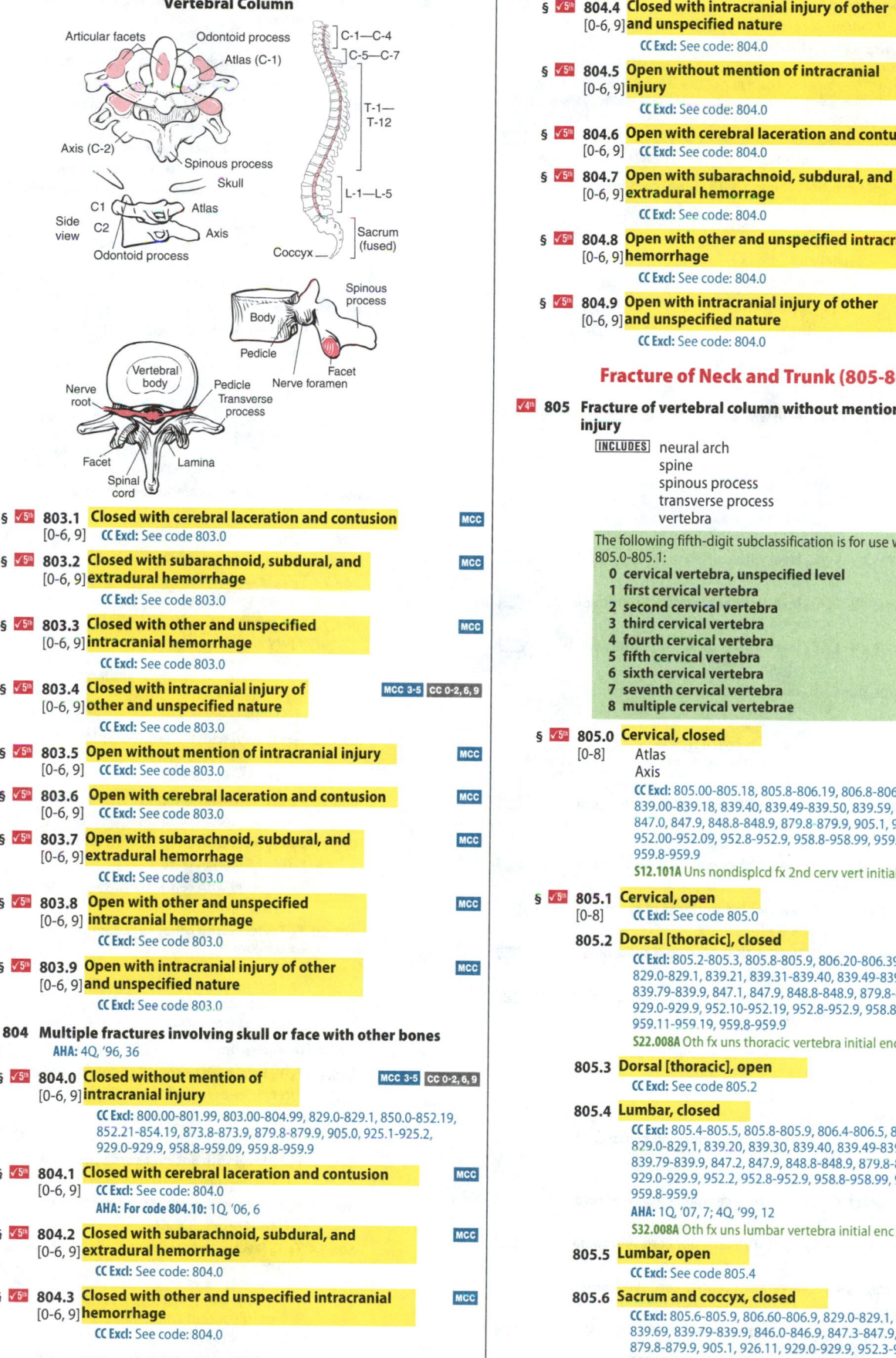

Vertebral Column

§ ✓5th **803.1** **Closed with cerebral laceration and contusion**   MCC
[0-6, 9]   CC Excl: See code 803.0

§ ✓5th **803.2** **Closed with subarachnoid, subdural, and**   MCC
[0-6, 9] **extradural hemorrhage**
   CC Excl: See code 803.0

§ ✓5th **803.3** **Closed with other and unspecified**   MCC
[0-6, 9] **intracranial hemorrhage**
   CC Excl: See code 803.0

§ ✓5th **803.4** **Closed with intracranial injury of**   MCC 3-5   CC 0-2, 6, 9
[0-6, 9] **other and unspecified nature**
   CC Excl: See code 803.0

§ ✓5th **803.5** **Open without mention of intracranial injury**   MCC
[0-6, 9]   CC Excl: See code 803.0

§ ✓5th **803.6** **Open with cerebral laceration and contusion**   MCC
[0-6, 9]   CC Excl: See code 803.0

§ ✓5th **803.7** **Open with subarachnoid, subdural, and**   MCC
[0-6, 9] **extradural hemorrhage**
   CC Excl: See code 803.0

§ ✓5th **803.8** **Open with other and unspecified**   MCC
[0-6, 9] **intracranial hemorrhage**
   CC Excl: See code 803.0

§ ✓5th **803.9** **Open with intracranial injury of other**   MCC
[0-6, 9] **and unspecified nature**
   CC Excl: See code 803.0

✓4th **804** **Multiple fractures involving skull or face with other bones**
   AHA: 4Q, '96, 36

§ ✓5th **804.0** **Closed without mention of**   MCC 3-5   CC 0-2, 6, 9
[0-6, 9] **intracranial injury**
   CC Excl: 800.00-801.99, 803.00-804.99, 829.0-829.1, 850.0-852.19,
   852.21-854.19, 873.8-873.9, 879.8-879.9, 905.0, 925.1-925.2,
   929.0-929.9, 958.8-959.09, 959.8-959.9

§ ✓5th **804.1** **Closed with cerebral laceration and contusion**   MCC
[0-6, 9]   CC Excl: See code 804.0
   AHA: For code 804.10: 1Q, '06, 6

§ ✓5th **804.2** **Closed with subarachnoid, subdural, and**   MCC
[0-6, 9] **extradural hemorrhage**
   CC Excl: See code 804.0

§ ✓5th **804.3** **Closed with other and unspecified intracranial**   MCC
[0-6, 9] **hemorrhage**
   CC Excl: See code 804.0

§ ✓5th **804.4** **Closed with intracranial injury of other**   MCC 3-5   CC 0-2, 6, 9
[0-6, 9] **and unspecified nature**
   CC Excl: See code: 804.0

§ ✓5th **804.5** **Open without mention of intracranial**   MCC 3-5   CC 0-2, 6, 9
[0-6, 9] **injury**
   CC Excl: See code: 804.0

§ ✓5th **804.6** **Open with cerebral laceration and contusion**   MCC
[0-6, 9]   CC Excl: See code: 804.0

§ ✓5th **804.7** **Open with subarachnoid, subdural, and**   MCC
[0-6, 9] **extradural hemorrage**
   CC Excl: See code: 804.0

§ ✓5th **804.8** **Open with other and unspecified intracranial**   MCC
[0-6, 9] **hemorrhage**
   CC Excl: See code: 804.0

§ ✓5th **804.9** **Open with intracranial injury of other**   MCC 3-5   CC 0-2, 6, 9
[0-6, 9] **and unspecified nature**
   CC Excl: See code: 804.0

Fracture of Neck and Trunk (805-809)

✓4th **805** **Fracture of vertebral column without mention of spinal cord injury**

   INCLUDES   neural arch
        spine
        spinous process
        transverse process
        vertebra

The following fifth-digit subclassification is for use with codes 805.0-805.1:
   0   cervical vertebra, unspecified level
   1   first cervical vertebra
   2   second cervical vertebra
   3   third cervical vertebra
   4   fourth cervical vertebra
   5   fifth cervical vertebra
   6   sixth cervical vertebra
   7   seventh cervical vertebra
   8   multiple cervical vertebrae

§ ✓5th **805.0** **Cervical, closed**   CC
[0-8]   Atlas
     Axis
   CC Excl: 805.00-805.18, 805.8-806.19, 806.8-806.9, 829.0-829.1,
   839.00-839.18, 839.40, 839.49-839.50, 839.59, 839.69, 839.79-839.9,
   847.0, 847.9, 848.8-848.9, 879.8-879.9, 905.1, 926.11, 929.0-929.9,
   952.00-952.09, 952.8-952.9, 958.8-958.99, 959.11-959.19,
   959.8-959.9
   S12.101A Uns nondisplcd fx 2nd cerv vert initial enc clos   I-10

§ ✓5th **805.1** **Cervical, open**   MCC
[0-8]   CC Excl: See code 805.0

     805.2 **Dorsal [thoracic], closed**   CC
   CC Excl: 805.2-805.3, 805.8-805.9, 806.20-806.39, 806.8-806.9,
   829.0-829.1, 839.21, 839.31-839.40, 839.49-839.50, 839.59, 839.69,
   839.79-839.9, 847.1, 847.9, 848.8-848.9, 879.8-879.9, 905.1, 926.11,
   929.0-929.9, 952.10-952.19, 952.8-952.9, 958.8-958.99,
   959.11-959.19, 959.8-959.9
   S22.008A Oth fx uns thoracic vertebra initial enc clos fx   I-10

     805.3 **Dorsal [thoracic], open**   MCC
   CC Excl: See code 805.2

     805.4 **Lumbar, closed**   CC
   CC Excl: 805.4-805.5, 805.8-805.9, 806.4-806.5, 806.8-806.9,
   829.0-829.1, 839.20, 839.30, 839.40, 839.49-839.50, 839.59, 839.69,
   839.79-839.9, 847.2, 847.9, 848.8-848.9, 879.8-879.9, 905.1, 926.11,
   929.0-929.9, 952.2, 952.8-952.9, 958.8-958.99, 959.11-959.19,
   959.8-959.9
   AHA: 1Q, '07, 7; 4Q, '99, 12
   S32.008A Oth fx uns lumbar vertebra initial enc closed fx   I-10

     805.5 **Lumbar, open**   MCC
   CC Excl: See code 805.4

     805.6 **Sacrum and coccyx, closed**   CC
   CC Excl: 805.6-805.9, 806.60-806.9, 829.0-829.1, 839.40-839.59,
   839.69, 839.79-839.9, 846.0-846.9, 847.3-847.9, 848.5-848.9,
   879.8-879.9, 905.1, 926.11, 929.0-929.9, 952.3-952.9, 958.8-958.99,
   959.11-959.19, 959.8-959.9
   S32.19xA Other fx of sacrum initial encounter closed fx   I-10

---

§   Requires fifth digit. Valid digits are in [brackets] under each code. See appropriate category for codes and definitions.

✓4th ✓5th   Additional Digit Required   Unacceptable PDx   Manifestation Code   Hospital Acquired Condition   ▶◄ Revised Text   ● New Code   ▲ Revised Code Title

Injury and Poisoning

805.7–806.35

805.7   **Sacrum and coccyx, open**   `MCC`
CC Excl: See code 805.6

805.8   **Unspecified, closed**   `CC`
CC Excl: See code 733.10-733.19, 733.93-733.98, 805.00-806.9, 829.0-829.1, 839.00-839.59, 839.69, 839.79-839.9, 846.0-847.9, 848.5-848.9, 879.8-879.9, 905.1, 926.11, 929.0-929.9, 952.00-952.9, 958.8-958.99, 959.11-959.19, 959.8-959.9

805.9   **Unspecified, open**   `MCC`
CC Excl: See code 805.8

√4th **806**   **Fracture of vertebral column with spinal cord injury**
INCLUDES   any condition classifiable to 805 with:
     complete or incomplete transverse lesion (of cord)
     hematomyelia
     injury to:
       cauda equina
       nerve
     paralysis
     paraplegia
     quadriplegia
     spinal concussion

√5th **806.0**   **Cervical, closed**

806.00 C_1-C_4 **level with unspecified spinal cord injury**   `MCC`
Cervical region NOS with spinal cord injury NOS
CC Excl: 733.10-733.19, 733.93-733.98, 805.00-805.18, 805.8-806.19, 806.8-806.9, 829.0-829.1, 839.00-839.18, 839.40, 839.49-839.50, 839.59, 839.69, 839.79-839.9, 847.9, 848.8-848.9, 879.8-879.9, 905.1, 926.11, 929.0-929.9, 952.00-952.09, 952.8-952.9, 958.8-958.99, 959.11-959.19, 959.8-959.9

806.01 C_1-C_4 **level with complete lesion of cord**   `MCC`
CC Excl: See code 806.00

806.02 C_1-C_4 **level with anterior cord syndrome**   `MCC`
CC Excl: See code 806.00

806.03 C_1-C_4 **level with central cord syndrome**   `MCC`
CC Excl: See code 806.00

806.04 C_1-C_4 **level with other specified spinal cord injury**   `MCC`
C_1-C_4 level with:
     incomplete spinal cord lesion NOS
     posterior cord syndrome
CC Excl: See code 806.00

806.05 C_5-C_7 **level with unspecified spinal cord injury**   `MCC`
CC Excl: See code 806.00

806.06 C_5-C_7 **level with complete lesion of cord**   `MCC`
CC Excl: See code 806.00

806.07 C_5-C_7 **level with anterior cord syndrome**   `MCC`
CC Excl: See code 806.00

806.08 C_5-C_7 **level with central cord syndrome**   `MCC`
CC Excl: See code 806.00

806.09 C_5-C_7 **level with other specified spinal cord injury**   `MCC`
C_5-C_7 level with:
     incomplete spinal cord lesion NOS
     posterior cord syndrome
CC Excl: See code 806.00

√5th **806.1**   **Cervical, open**

806.10 C_1-C_4 **level with unspecified spinal cord injury**   `MCC`
CC Excl: See code 806.00

806.11 C_1-C_4 **level with complete lesion of cord**   `MCC`
CC Excl: See code 806.00

806.12 C_1-C_4 **level with anterior cord syndrome**   `MCC`
CC Excl: See code 806.00

806.13 C_1-C_4 **level with central cord syndrome**   `MCC`
CC Excl: See code 806.00

806.14 C_1-C_4 **level with other specified spinal cord injury**   `MCC`
C_1-C_4 level with:
     incomplete spinal cord lesion NOS
     posterior cord syndrome
CC Excl: See code 806.00

806.15 C_5-C_7 **level with unspecified spinal cord injury**   `MCC`
CC Excl: See code 806.00

806.16 C_5-C_7 **level with complete lesion of cord**   `MCC`
CC Excl: See code 806.00

806.17 C_5-C_7 **level with anterior cord syndrome**   `MCC`
CC Excl: See code 806.00

806.18 C_5-C_7 **level with central cord syndrome**   `MCC`
CC Excl: See code 806.00

806.19 C_5-C_7 **level with other specified spinal cord injury**   `MCC`
C_5-C_7 level with:
     incomplete spinal cord lesion NOS
     posterior cord syndrome
CC Excl: See code 806.00

√5th **806.2**   **Dorsal [thoracic], closed**

806.20 T_1-T_6 **level with unspecified spinal cord injury**   `MCC`
Thoracic region NOS with spinal cord injury NOS
CC Excl: 733.10-733.19, 733.93-733.98, 805.2-805.3, 805.8-805.9, 806.20-806.39, 806.8-806.9, 829.0-829.1, 839.21, 839.31-839.40, 839.49-839.50, 839.59, 839.69, 839.79-839.9, 847.1, 847.9, 848.8-848.9, 879.8-879.9, 905.1, 926.11, 929.0-929.9, 952.10-952.19, 952.8-952.9, 958.8-958.99, 959.11-959.19, 959.8-959.9

806.21 T_1-T_6 **level with complete lesion of cord**   `MCC`
CC Excl: See code 806.20

806.22 T_1-T_6 **level with anterior cord syndrome**   `MCC`
CC Excl: See code 806.20

806.23 T_1-T_6 **level with central cord syndrome**   `MCC`
CC Excl: See code 806.20

806.24 T_1-T_6 **level with other specified spinal cord injury**   `MCC`
T_1-T_6 level with:
     incomplete spinal cord lesion NOS
     posterior cord syndrome
CC Excl: See code 806.20

806.25 T_7-T_{12} **level with unspecified spinal cord injury**   `MCC`
CC Excl: See code 806.20

806.26 T_7-T_{12} **level with complete lesion of cord**   `MCC`
CC Excl: See code 806.20

806.27 T_7-T_{12} **level with anterior cord syndrome**   `MCC`
CC Excl: See code 806.20

806.28 T_7-T_{12} **level with central cord syndrome**   `MCC`
CC Excl: See code 806.20

806.29 T_7-T_{12} **level with other specified spinal cord injury**   `MCC`
T_7-T_{12} level with:
     incomplete spinal cord lesion NOS
     posterior cord syndrome
CC Excl: See code 806.20

√5th **806.3**   **Dorsal [thoracic], open**

806.30 T_1-T_6 **level with unspecified spinal cord injury**   `MCC`
CC Excl: See code 806.20

806.31 T_1-T_6 **level with complete lesion of cord**   `MCC`
CC Excl: See code 806.20

806.32 T_1-T_6 **level with anterior cord syndrome**   `MCC`
CC Excl: See code 806.20

806.33 T_1-T_6 **level with central cord syndrome**   `MCC`
CC Excl: See code 806.20

806.34 T_1-T_6 **level with other specified spinal cord injury**   `MCC`
T_1-T_6 level with:
     incomplete spinal cord lesion NOS
     posterior cord syndrome
CC Excl: See code 806.20

806.35 T_7-T_{12} **level with unspecified spinal cord injury**   `MCC`
CC Excl: See code 806.20

N Newborn Age: 0   P Pediatric Age: 0-17   M Maternity Age: 12-55   A Adult Age: 15-124   `MCC` Major CC Condition   `CC` CC Condition   `HIV` HIV Related Dx

302 – Volume 1   2015 ICD-9-CM

806.36 T_7-T_{12} **level with complete lesion of cord** `MCC`
CC Excl: See code 806.20

806.37 T_7-T_{12} **level with anterior cord syndrome** `MCC`
CC Excl: See code 806.20

806.38 T_7-T_{12} **level with central cord syndrome** `MCC`
CC Excl: See code 806.20

806.39 T_7-T_{12} **level with other specified spinal cord injury** `MCC`
T_7-T_{12} level with:
     incomplete spinal cord lesion NOS
     posterior cord syndrome
CC Excl: See code 806.20

806.4 Lumbar, closed `MCC`
CC Excl: 733.10-733.19, 733.93-733.98, 805.4-805.5, 805.8-805.9,
806.4-806.5, 806.8-806.9, 829.0-829.1, 839.20, 839.30, 839.40,
839.49-839.50, 839.59, 839.69, 839.79-839.9, 847.2, 847.9,
848.8-848.9, 879.8-879.9, 905.1, 926.11, 929.0-929.9, 952.2,
952.8-952.9, 958.8-958.99, 959.11-959.19, 959.8-959.9
AHA: 4Q, '99, 11, 13

806.5 Lumbar, open `MCC`
CC Excl: See code 806.4

√5ᵗʰ **806.6 Sacrum and coccyx, closed**

806.60 With unspecified spinal cord injury `MCC`
CC Excl: 733.10-733.19, 733.93-733.98, 805.6-805.9,
806.60-806.9, 829.0-829.1, 839.40-839.59, 839.69,
839.79-839.9, 846.0-847.0, 847.3-847.9, 848.5-848.9,
879.8-879.9, 905.1, 926.11, 929.0-929.9, 952.3-952.9,
958.8-958.99, 959.11-959.19, 959.8-959.9

806.61 With complete cauda equina lesion `MCC`
CC Excl: See code 806.60

806.62 With other cauda equina injury `MCC`
CC Excl: See code 806.60

806.69 With other spinal cord injury `MCC`
CC Excl: See code 806.60

√5ᵗʰ **806.7 Sacrum and coccyx, open**

806.70 With unspecified spinal cord injury `MCC`
CC Excl: See code 806.60

806.71 With complete cauda equina lesion `MCC`
CC Excl: See code 806.60

806.72 With other cauda equina injury `MCC`
CC Excl: See code 806.60

806.79 With other spinal cord injury `MCC`
CC Excl: See code 806.60

806.8 Unspecified, closed `MCC`
CC Excl: 733.10-733.19, 733.93-733.95, 805.00-806.9, 829.0-829.1,
839.00-839.59, 839.69, 839.79-839.9, 846.0-847.9, 848.5-848.9,
879.8-879.9, 905.1, 926.11, 929.0-929.9, 952.00-952.9, 958.8-958.99,
959.11-959.19, 959.8-959.9

806.9 Unspecified, open `MCC`
CC Excl: See code 806.

Ribs, Sternum, Larynx, and Trachea

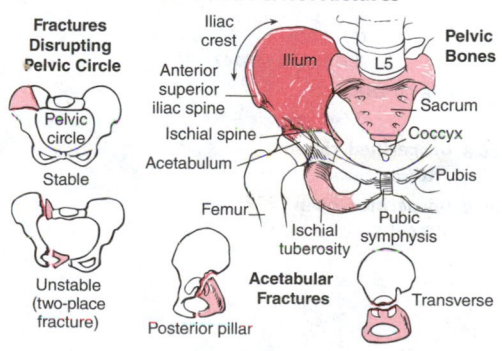

√4ᵗʰ **807 Fracture of rib(s), sternum, larynx, and trachea**

The following fifth-digit subclassification is for use with codes
807.0-807.1:
  0 rib(s) unspecifed
  1 one rib
  2 two ribs
  3 three ribs
  4 four ribs
  5 five ribs
  6 six ribs
  7 seven ribs
  8 eight or more ribs
  9 multiple ribs, unspecified

§ √5ᵗʰ **807.0 Rib(s), closed** `CC`
[0-9]
CC Excl: **For codes 807.00-807.02:** 807.00-807.4, 819.0-819.1,
828.0-829.1, 848.8-848.9, 879.8-879.9, 929.0-929.9, 958.8-958.99,
959.8-959.9; **For code 807.03:** 807.00-807.19, 807.4, 819.0-819.1,
828.0-829.1, 848.8-848.9, 879.8-879.9, 929.0-929.9, 958.8,
959.8-959.9; **For codes 807.04-807.09:** 807.00-807.19, 807.4,
819.0-819.1, 828.0-829.1, 848.8-848.9, 879.8-879.9, 929.0-929.9,
958.8-958.99, 959.8-959.9

AHA: **For codes 807.00-807.02:** ▶1Q, '13, 15◄

S22.31xA Fracture one rib right side, initial encounter closed fx `I-10`

§ √5ᵗʰ **807.1 Rib(s), open** `MCC`
[0-9]
CC Excl: 807.00-807.19, 807.4, 819.0-819.1, 828.0-829.1, 848.8-848.9,
879.8-879.9, 929.0-929.9, 958.8-958.99, 959.8-959.9

807.2 Sternum, closed `CC`
DEF: Break in flat bone (breast bone) in anterior thorax.
CC Excl: 807.2-807.4, 829.0-829.1, 848.8-848.9, 879.8-879.9,
929.0-929.9, 958.8-958.99, 959.8-959.9

807.3 Sternum, open `MCC`
DEF: Break, with open wound, in flat bone in mid anterior thorax.
CC Excl: See code: 807.2

807.4 Flail chest `MCC`
CC Excl: 807.00-807.4, 829.0-829.1, 848.8-848.9, 879.8-879.9,
929.0-929.9, 958.8-958.99, 959.8-959.9

807.5 Larynx and trachea, closed `MCC`
Hyoid bone
Thyroid cartilage
Trachea
CC Excl: 807.5-807.6, 829.0-829.1, 848.8-848.9, 879.8-879.9,
929.0-929.9, 958.8-958.99, 959.8-959.9

807.6 Larynx and trachea, open `MCC`
CC Excl: See code 807.5

√4ᵗʰ **808 Fracture of pelvis**

808.0 Acetabulum, closed `MCC`
CC Excl: 733.10-733.19, 733.93-733.98, 808.0-808.1, 808.43-808.49,
808.53-809.1, 829.0-829.1, 835.00-835.13, 843.0-843.9, 846.0-846.9,
848.5-848.9, 879.8-879.9, 929.0-929.9, 958.8-958.99, 959.6,
959.8-959.9

808.1 Acetabulum, open `MCC`
CC Excl: 808.0-808.1, 808.43-808.49, 808.53-809.1, 829.0-829.1,
835.00-835.13, 843.0-843.9, 846.0-846.9, 848.5-848.9, 879.8-879.9,
929.0-929.9, 958.8-958.99, 959.6, 959.8-959.9

Pelvis and Pelvic Fractures

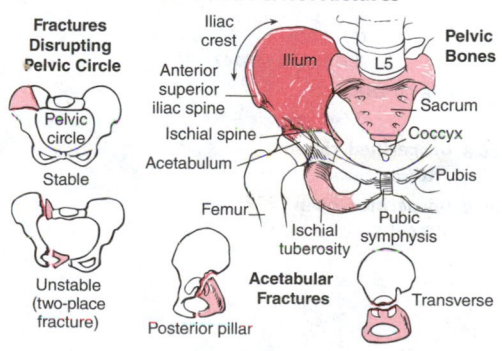

---

§   Requires fifth digit. Valid digits are in [brackets] under each code. See category 807 for codes and definitions.

Injury and Poisoning

808.2–812.02

808.2 **Pubis, closed** `CC`

  CC Excl: 733.10-733.19, 733.93-733.98, 808.2-808.3, 808.43-808.49, 808.53-809.1, 829.0-829.1, 835.00-835.13, 843.0-843.9, 846.0-846.9, 848.5-848.9, 879.8-879.9, 929.0-929.9, 958.8-958.99, 959.6, 959.8-959.9

  AHA: 1Q, '08, 9

  S32.509A Unspec fx unspec pubis initial encounter clsd fx `I-10`

808.3 **Pubis, open** `MCC`

  CC Excl: See code 808.2

√5ᵗʰ 808.4 **Other specified part, closed**

  808.41 **Ilium** `CC`

    CC Excl: 733.10, 733.19, 808.0-809.1, 829.0-829.1, 835.00-835.13, 843.0-843.9, 846.0-846.9, 848.5-848.9, 879.8-879.9, 929.0-929.9, 958.8, 958.99, 959.6, 959.8-959.9

  808.42 **Ischium** `CC`

    CC Excl: 808.42

  808.43 **Multiple closed pelvic fractures with disruption of pelvic circle** `CC`

    Multiple closed pelvic fractures with disruption of pelvic ring

    CC Excl: 733.10-733.19, 733.93-733.98, 808.0-809.1, 829.0-829.1, 835.00-835.13, 843.0-843.9, 846.0-846.9, 848.5-848.9, 879.8-879.9, 929.0-929.9, 958.8-958.99, 959.6, 959.8-959.9

    AHA: 1Q, '08, 9

    TIP: To assign, documentation must indicate multiple pelvic fractures with complete disruption of the pelvic circle.

  808.44 **Multiple closed pelvic fractures without disruption of pelvic circle** `CC`

    Multiple closed pelvic fractures without disruption of pelvic ring

    CC Excl: 808.49

    AHA: 4Q, '11, 141-142

  808.49 **Other** `CC`

    Innominate bone
    Pelvic rim

    CC Excl: See code: 808.43

√5ᵗʰ 808.5 **Other specified part, open**

  808.51 **Ilium** `MCC`

    CC Excl: 733.10-733.19, 733.93-733.98, 808.41, 808.43-808.51, 808.53-809.1, 829.0-829.1, 835.00-835.13, 843.0-843.9, 846.0-846.9, 848.5-848.9, 879.8-879.9, 929.0-929.9, 958.8-958.99, 959.6, 959.8-959.9

  808.52 **Ischium** `MCC`

    CC Excl: 733.10-733.19, 733.93-733.98, 808.42-808.49, 808.52-809.1, 829.0-829.1, 835.00-835.13, 843.0-843.9, 846.0-846.9, 848.5-848.9, 879.8-879.9, 929.0-929.9, 958.8-958.99, 959.6, 959.8-959.9

  808.53 **Multiple open pelvic fractures with disruption of pelvic circle** `MCC`

    Multiple open pelvic fractures with disruption of pelvic ring

    CC Excl: See code: 808.43

  808.54 **Multiple open pelvic fractures without disruption of pelvic circle** `MCC`

    Multiple open pelvic fractures without disruption of pelvic ring

    CC Excl: 808.49

    AHA: 4Q, '11, 141-142

  808.59 **Other** `MCC`

    CC Excl: See code: 808.43

808.8 **Unspecified, closed** `CC`

  CC Excl: See code: 808.43

808.9 **Unspecified, open** `MCC`

  CC Excl: See code: 808.43

Right Clavicle and Scapula, Anterior View

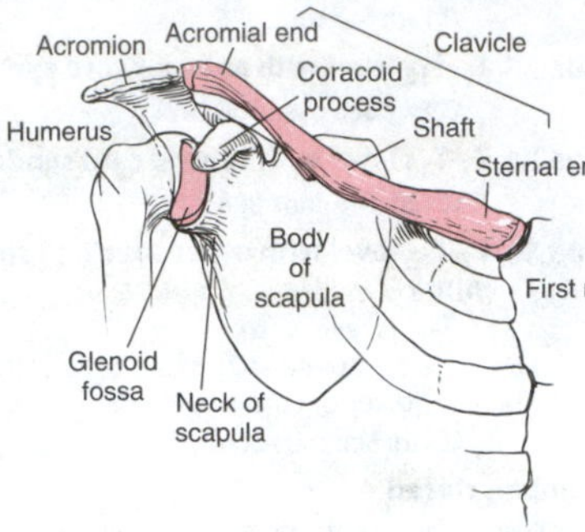

Acromion — Acromial end — Clavicle
Coracoid process
Humerus — Shaft
Sternal end
Body of scapula
First rib
Glenoid fossa — Neck of scapula

√4ᵗʰ 809 **Ill-defined fractures of bones of trunk**

  INCLUDES   bones of trunk with other bones except those of skull and face
        multiple bones of trunk

  EXCLUDES   *multiple fractures of:*
        pelvic bones alone (808.0-808.9)
        ribs alone (807.0-807.1, 807.4)
        ribs or sternum with limb bones (819.0-819.1, 828.0-828.1)
        skull or face with other bones (804.0-804.9)

  809.0 **Fracture of bones of trunk, closed** `CC`

    CC Excl: 733.10, 733.19, 808.0-809.1, 829.0-829.1, 835.00-835.13, 843.0-843.9, 846.0-846.9, 848.5-848.9, 879.8-879.9, 929.0-929.9, 958.8, 958.99, 959.6, 959.8-959.9

  809.1 **Fracture of bones of trunk, open** `MCC`

    CC Excl: See code: 809.0

Fracture of Upper Limb (810-819)

√4ᵗʰ 810 **Fracture of clavicle**

  INCLUDES   collar bone
        interligamentous part of clavicle

  The following fifth-digit subclassification is for use with category 810:
    0 **unspecified part**
       Clavicle NOS
    1 **sternal end of clavicle**
    2 **shaft of clavicle**
    3 **acromial end of clavicle**

  § √5ᵗʰ 810.0 **Closed**
    [0-3]

  § √5ᵗʰ 810.1 **Open** `CC`
    [0-3]   **CC Excl:** 810.00-810.13, 818.0-819.1

√4ᵗʰ 811 **Fracture of scapula**

  INCLUDES   shoulder blade

  The following fifth-digit subclassification is for use with category 811:
    0 **unspecified part**
    1 **acromial process**
       Acromion (process)
    2 **coracoid process**
    3 **glenoid cavity and neck of scapula**
    9 **other**

  § √5ᵗʰ 811.0 **Closed**
    [0-3, 9]

  § √5ᵗʰ 811.1 **Open** `CC`
    [0-3, 9]   **CC Excl:** 811.00-811.19, 818.0-819.1

√4ᵗʰ 812 **Fracture of humerus**

  √5ᵗʰ 812.0 **Upper end, closed**

    812.00 **Upper end, unspecified part** `CC`
       Proximal end   Shoulder
       CC Excl: 812.00-812.59, 819.0-819.1

    812.01 **Surgical neck** `CC`
       Neck of humerus NOS
       CC Excl: See code: 812.00
       S42.214A Uns nondsplcd fx surg neck rt humerus inital clo fx `I-10`

    812.02 **Anatomical neck** `CC`
       CC Excl: See code: 812.00

---

§   Requires fifth digit. Valid digits are in [brackets] under each code. See appropriate category for codes and definitions.

N Newborn Age: 0   **P** Pediatric Age: 0-17   **M** Maternity Age: 12-55   **A** Adult Age: 15-124   `MCC` Major CC Condition   `CC` CC Condition   **HIV** HIV Related Dx

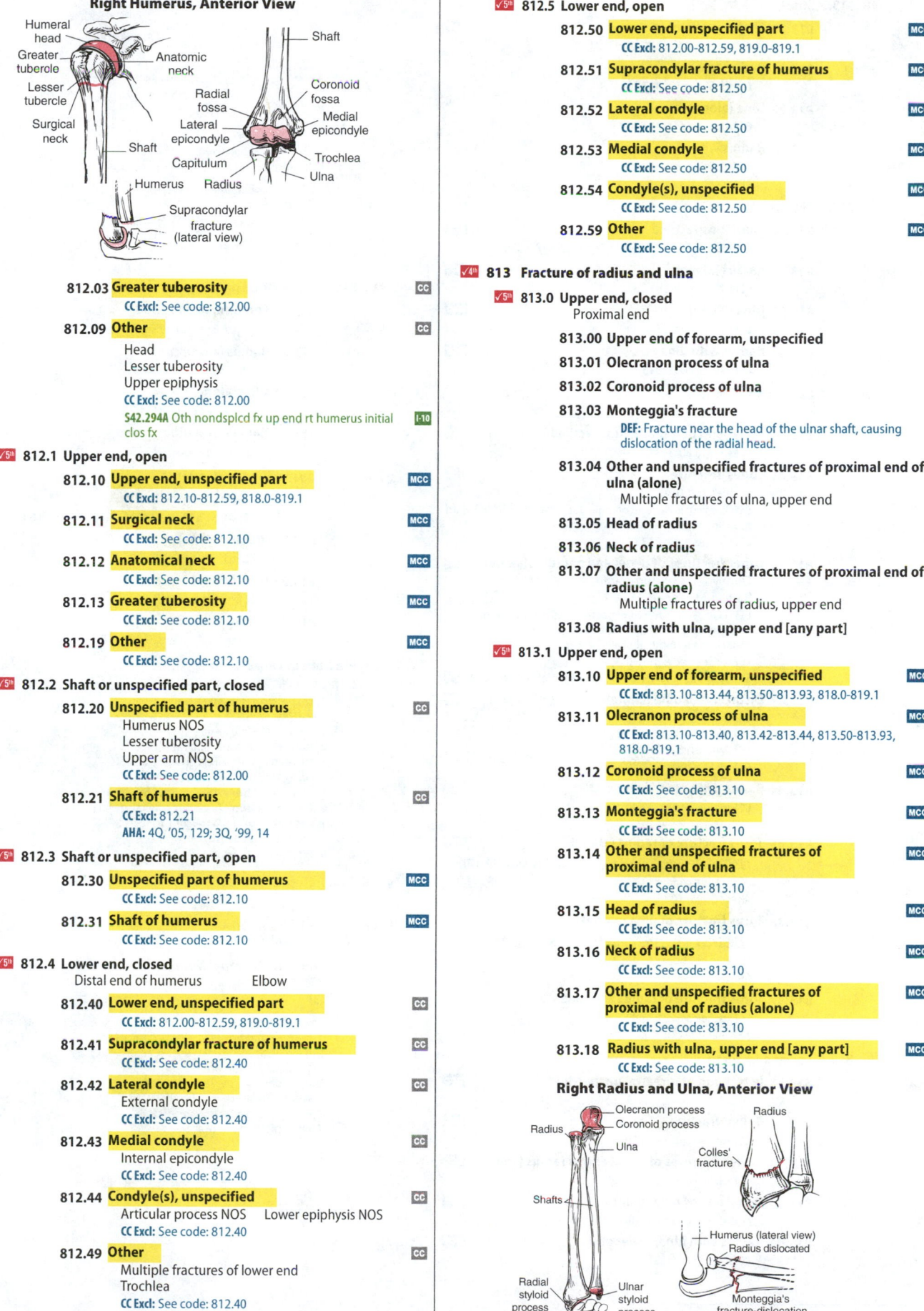

Right Humerus, Anterior View

812.03 Greater tuberosity `CC`
CC Excl: See code: 812.00

812.09 Other `CC`
Head
Lesser tuberosity
Upper epiphysis
CC Excl: See code: 812.00
S42.294A Oth nondsplcd fx up end rt humerus initial clos fx `I-10`

√5th **812.1 Upper end, open**

812.10 Upper end, unspecified part `MCC`
CC Excl: 812.10-812.59, 818.0-819.1

812.11 Surgical neck `MCC`
CC Excl: See code: 812.10

812.12 Anatomical neck `MCC`
CC Excl: See code: 812.10

812.13 Greater tuberosity `MCC`
CC Excl: See code: 812.10

812.19 Other `MCC`
CC Excl: See code: 812.10

√5th **812.2 Shaft or unspecified part, closed**

812.20 Unspecified part of humerus `CC`
Humerus NOS
Lesser tuberosity
Upper arm NOS
CC Excl: See code: 812.00

812.21 Shaft of humerus `CC`
CC Excl: 812.21
AHA: 4Q, '05, 129; 3Q, '99, 14

√5th **812.3 Shaft or unspecified part, open**

812.30 Unspecified part of humerus `MCC`
CC Excl: See code: 812.10

812.31 Shaft of humerus `MCC`
CC Excl: See code: 812.10

√5th **812.4 Lower end, closed**
Distal end of humerus   Elbow

812.40 Lower end, unspecified part `CC`
CC Excl: 812.00-812.59, 819.0-819.1

812.41 Supracondylar fracture of humerus `CC`
CC Excl: See code: 812.40

812.42 Lateral condyle `CC`
External condyle
CC Excl: See code: 812.40

812.43 Medial condyle `CC`
Internal epicondyle
CC Excl: See code: 812.40

812.44 Condyle(s), unspecified `CC`
Articular process NOS   Lower epiphysis NOS
CC Excl: See code: 812.40

812.49 Other `CC`
Multiple fractures of lower end
Trochlea
CC Excl: See code: 812.40

√5th **812.5 Lower end, open**

812.50 Lower end, unspecified part `MCC`
CC Excl: 812.00-812.59, 819.0-819.1

812.51 Supracondylar fracture of humerus `MCC`
CC Excl: See code: 812.50

812.52 Lateral condyle `MCC`
CC Excl: See code: 812.50

812.53 Medial condyle `MCC`
CC Excl: See code: 812.50

812.54 Condyle(s), unspecified `MCC`
CC Excl: See code: 812.50

812.59 Other `MCC`
CC Excl: See code: 812.50

√4th **813 Fracture of radius and ulna**

√5th **813.0 Upper end, closed**
Proximal end

813.00 Upper end of forearm, unspecified

813.01 Olecranon process of ulna

813.02 Coronoid process of ulna

813.03 Monteggia's fracture
DEF: Fracture near the head of the ulnar shaft, causing dislocation of the radial head.

813.04 Other and unspecified fractures of proximal end of ulna (alone)
Multiple fractures of ulna, upper end

813.05 Head of radius

813.06 Neck of radius

813.07 Other and unspecified fractures of proximal end of radius (alone)
Multiple fractures of radius, upper end

813.08 Radius with ulna, upper end [any part]

√5th **813.1 Upper end, open**

813.10 Upper end of forearm, unspecified `MCC`
CC Excl: 813.10-813.44, 813.50-813.93, 818.0-819.1

813.11 Olecranon process of ulna `MCC`
CC Excl: 813.10-813.40, 813.42-813.44, 813.50-813.93, 818.0-819.1

813.12 Coronoid process of ulna `MCC`
CC Excl: See code: 813.10

813.13 Monteggia's fracture `MCC`
CC Excl: See code: 813.10

813.14 Other and unspecified fractures of proximal end of ulna `MCC`
CC Excl: See code: 813.10

813.15 Head of radius `MCC`
CC Excl: See code: 813.10

813.16 Neck of radius `MCC`
CC Excl: See code: 813.10

813.17 Other and unspecified fractures of proximal end of radius (alone) `MCC`
CC Excl: See code: 813.10

813.18 Radius with ulna, upper end [any part] `MCC`
CC Excl: See code: 813.10

Right Radius and Ulna, Anterior View

√4th √5th Additional Digit Required   Unacceptable PDx   Manifestation Code   Hospital Acquired Condition   ▶◀ Revised Text   ● New Code   ▲ Revised Code Title

✓5th **813.2 Shaft, closed**

    813.20 Shaft, unspecified `CC`
       CC Excl: 813.00-813.93, 819.0-819.1

    813.21 Radius (alone) `CC`
       CC Excl: See code: 813.20

    813.22 Ulna (alone) `CC`
       CC Excl: See code: 813.20

    813.23 Radius with ulna `CC`
       CC Excl: See code: 813.20
       AHA: 4Q, '09, 120

✓5th **813.3 Shaft, open**

    813.30 Shaft, unspecified `MCC`
       CC Excl: 813.10-813.44, 813.50-813.93, 818.0-819.1

    813.31 Radius (alone) `MCC`
       CC Excl: See code: 813.30

    813.32 Ulna (alone) `MCC`
       CC Excl: See code: 813.30

    813.33 Radius with ulna `MCC`
       CC Excl: See code: 813.30

✓5th **813.4 Lower end, closed**
    Distal end

    813.40 Lower end of forearm, unspecified `CC`
       CC Excl: 813.00-813.93, 819.0-819.1

    813.41 Colles' fracture `CC`
       Smith's fracture
       DEF: Break of lower end of radius; associated with backward movement of the radius lower section.
       CC Excl: See code: 813.40

    813.42 Other fractures of distal end of radius (alone) `CC`
       Dupuytren's fracture, radius
       Radius, lower end
       DEF: Dupuytren's fracture: fracture and dislocation of the forearm; the fracture is of the radius above wrist, and the dislocation is of the ulna at lower end.
       CC Excl: See code: 813.40
       S52.501A Uns fx lower end rt radius initial enc closed fx `I-10`

    813.43 Distal end of ulna (alone) `CC`
       Ulna: Ulna:
         head   lower epiphysis
         lower end   styloid process
       CC Excl: See code: 813.40

    813.44 Radius with ulna, lower end `CC`
       CC Excl: See code: 813.40
       AHA: 1Q, '07, 7

    813.45 Torus fracture of radius (alone) `CC`
       EXCLUDES *torus fracture of radius and ulna (813.47)*
       CC Excl: See code: 813.40
       AHA: 4Q, '02, 70

    813.46 Torus fracture of ulna (alone) `CC`
       EXCLUDES *torus fracture of radius and ulna (813.47)*
       CC Excl: See code: 813.40
       AHA: 4Q, '09, 110

    813.47 Torus fracture of radius and ulna `CC`
       CC Excl: See code: 813.40
       AHA: 4Q, '09, 110

✓5th **813.5 Lower end, open**

    813.50 Lower end of forearm, unspecified `MCC`
       CC Excl: 813.10-813.44, 813.50-813.93, 818.0-819.1

    813.51 Colles' fracture `MCC`
       CC Excl: See code: 813.50

    813.52 Other fractures of distal end of radius (alone) `MCC`
       CC Excl: See code: 813.50

    813.53 Distal end of ulna (alone) `MCC`
       CC Excl: See code: 813.50

    813.54 Radius with ulna, lower end `MCC`
       CC Excl: See code: 813.50

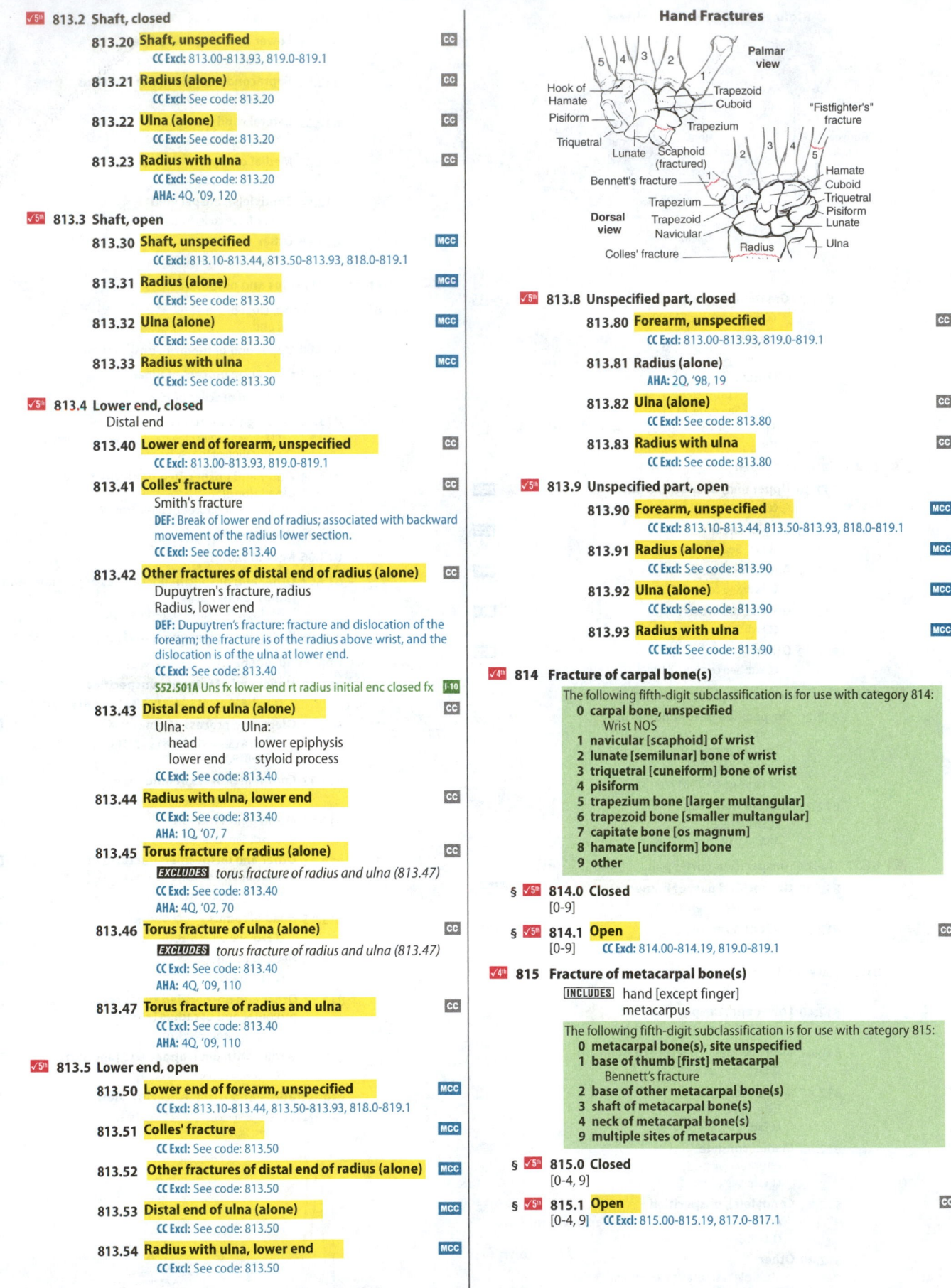

Hand Fractures

✓5th **813.8 Unspecified part, closed**

    813.80 Forearm, unspecified `CC`
       CC Excl: 813.00-813.93, 819.0-819.1

    813.81 Radius (alone)
       AHA: 2Q, '98, 19

    813.82 Ulna (alone) `CC`
       CC Excl: See code: 813.80

    813.83 Radius with ulna `CC`
       CC Excl: See code: 813.80

✓5th **813.9 Unspecified part, open**

    813.90 Forearm, unspecified `MCC`
       CC Excl: 813.10-813.44, 813.50-813.93, 818.0-819.1

    813.91 Radius (alone) `MCC`
       CC Excl: See code: 813.90

    813.92 Ulna (alone) `MCC`
       CC Excl: See code: 813.90

    813.93 Radius with ulna `MCC`
       CC Excl: See code: 813.90

✓4th **814 Fracture of carpal bone(s)**

    The following fifth-digit subclassification is for use with category 814:
      0 carpal bone, unspecified
        Wrist NOS
      1 navicular [scaphoid] of wrist
      2 lunate [semilunar] bone of wrist
      3 triquetral [cuneiform] bone of wrist
      4 pisiform
      5 trapezium bone [larger multangular]
      6 trapezoid bone [smaller multangular]
      7 capitate bone [os magnum]
      8 hamate [unciform] bone
      9 other

§ ✓5th **814.0 Closed**
    [0-9]

§ ✓5th **814.1 Open** `CC`
    [0-9]   **CC Excl:** 814.00-814.19, 819.0-819.1

✓4th **815 Fracture of metacarpal bone(s)**

    INCLUDES   hand [except finger]
               metacarpus

    The following fifth-digit subclassification is for use with category 815:
      0 metacarpal bone(s), site unspecified
      1 base of thumb [first] metacarpal
        Bennett's fracture
      2 base of other metacarpal bone(s)
      3 shaft of metacarpal bone(s)
      4 neck of metacarpal bone(s)
      9 multiple sites of metacarpus

§ ✓5th **815.0 Closed**
    [0-4, 9]

§ ✓5th **815.1 Open** `CC`
    [0-4, 9] **CC Excl:** 815.00-815.19, 817.0-817.1

---

§   Requires fifth digit. Valid digits are in [brackets] under each code. See appropriate category for codes and definitions.

`N` Newborn Age: 0   `P` Pediatric Age: 0-17   `M` Maternity Age: 12-55   `A` Adult Age: 15-124   `MCC` Major CC Condition   `CC` CC Condition   `HIV` HIV Related Dx

306 – Volume 1   **2015 ICD-9-CM**

✓4th **816 Fracture of one or more phalanges of hand**

INCLUDES finger(s)
thumb

> The following fifth-digit subclassification is for use with category 816:
> 0 phalanx or phalanges, unspecified
> 1 middle or proximal phalanx or phalanges
> 2 distal phalanx or phalanges
> 3 multiple sites

TIP: If phalangeal fracture(s) are due to crushing injury, sequence that code (927.3) first.

§ ✓5th **816.0 Closed**
[0-3]

§ ✓5th **816.1 Open** `CC`
[0-3] **CC Excl:** For codes 816.10-816.12: 816.00-817.1; For code 816.13: 816.00-816.13, 818.0-819.1
AHA: For code 816.12: 4Q, '03, 77

✓4th **817 Multiple fractures of hand bones**

INCLUDES metacarpal bone(s) with phalanx or phalanges of same hand

817.0 Closed

817.1 Open `CC`
CC Excl: 814.00-819.1

✓4th **818 Ill-defined fractures of upper limb**

INCLUDES arm NOS
multiple bones of same upper limb

EXCLUDES multiple fractures of:
metacarpal bone(s) with phalanx or phalanges (817.0-817.1)
phalanges of hand alone (816.0-816.1)
radius with ulna (813.0-813.9)

818.0 Closed

818.1 Open `CC`
CC Excl: 812.00-813.44, 813.50-819.1

✓4th **819 Multiple fractures involving both upper limbs, and upper limb with rib(s) and sternum**

INCLUDES arm(s) with rib(s) or sternum
both arms [any bones]

819.0 Closed `CC`
CC Excl: 807.00-807.4, 812.00-813.44, 813.50-819.1

819.1 Open `CC`
CC Excl: See code: 819.0

Fracture of Lower Limb (820-829)

✓4th **820 Fracture of neck of femur**

✓5th **820.0 Transcervical fracture, closed**

820.00 Intracapsular section, unspecified `MCC`
CC Excl: 733.10-733.19, 733.93-733.98, 820.00-821.39, 827.0-829.1, 843.0-843.9, 848.8-848.9, 879.8-879.9, 929.0-929.9, 958.8-958.99, 959.6, 959.8-959.9

820.01 Epiphysis (separation) (upper) `MCC`
Transepiphyseal
CC Excl: See code 820.00

820.02 Midcervical section `MCC`
Transcervical NOS
CC Excl: See code 820.00
AHA: 3Q, '03, 12

820.03 Base of neck `MCC`
Cervicotrochanteric section
CC Excl: See code 820.00

820.09 Other `MCC`
Head of femur
Subcapital
CC Excl: See code 820.00
S72.064A Nondsplcd art fx head rt femur initial enc clos fx `I-10`

✓5th **820.1 Transcervical fracture, open**

820.10 Intracapsular section, unspecified `MCC`
CC Excl: See code 820.00

820.11 Epiphysis (separation) (upper) `MCC`
CC Excl: See code 820.00

820.12 Midcervical section `MCC`
CC Excl: See code 820.00

820.13 Base of neck `MCC`
CC Excl: See code 820.00

820.19 Other `MCC`
CC Excl: See code 820.00

✓5th **820.2 Pertrochanteric fracture, closed**

820.20 Trochanteric section, unspecified `MCC`
Trochanter: Trochanter:
NOS   lesser
greater
CC Excl: See code 820.00

820.21 Intertrochanteric section `MCC`
CC Excl: See code 820.00

820.22 Subtrochanteric section `MCC`
CC Excl: See code 820.00
S72.25xA Nondsplcd subtrochant fx lt femur inital enc clo fx `I-10`

✓5th **820.3 Pertrochanteric fracture, open**

820.30 Trochanteric section, unspecified `MCC`
CC Excl: See code 820.00

820.31 Intertrochanteric section `MCC`
CC Excl: See code 820.00

820.32 Subtrochanteric section `MCC`
CC Excl: See code 820.00

820.8 Unspecified part of neck of femur, closed `MCC`
Hip NOS   Neck of femur NOS
CC Excl: See code 820.00
S72.002A Fx uns part neck left femur initial enc clos fx `I-10`

820.9 Unspecified part of neck of femur, open `MCC`
CC Excl: See code 820.00

✓4th **821 Fracture of other and unspecified parts of femur**

✓5th **821.0 Shaft or unspecified part, closed**

821.00 Unspecified part of femur `MCC`
Thigh
Upper leg
EXCLUDES hip NOS (820.8)
CC Excl: 733.10-733.19, 733.93-733.95, 820.00-821.39, 827.0-829.1, 843.0-843.9, 848.8-848.9, 879.8-879.9, 929.0-929.9, 958.8-958.99, 959.6, 959.8-959.9

821.01 Shaft `MCC`
CC Excl: See code: 821.00
AHA: 1Q, '07, 4; 1Q, '99, 5
S72.331A Displaced obl fx shaft rt femur initl enc clos fx `I-10`

✓5th **821.1 Shaft or unspecified part, open**

821.10 Unspecified part of femur `MCC`
CC Excl: See code: 821.00

821.11 Shaft `MCC`
CC Excl: See code: 821.00

Right Femur, Anterior View

Greater trochanter — Head
Intertrochanteric line
Lesser trochanter — Neck
Shaft
Lateral epicondyle — Medial epicondyle
Articular cartilage

---

§ Requires fifth digit. Valid digits are in [brackets] under each code. See appropriate category for codes and definitions.

✓4th ✓5th Additional Digit Required | Unacceptable PDx | Manifestation Code | Hospital Acquired Condition | ►◄ Revised Text | ● New Code | ▲ Revised Code Title

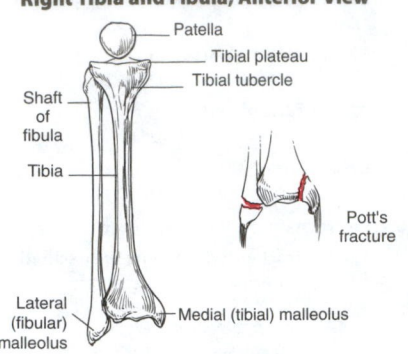

Right Tibia and Fibula, Anterior View

- Patella
- Tibial plateau
- Tibial tubercle
- Shaft of fibula
- Tibia
- Pott's fracture
- Lateral (fibular) malleolus
- Medial (tibial) malleolus

✓5ᵗʰ **821.2 Lower end, closed**
Distal end

   821.20 Lower end, unspecified part   CC
     CC Excl: 733.10, 733.14-733.15, 733.19, 820.00-821.39, 827.0-829.1, 843.0-843.9, 848.8-848.9, 879.8-879.9, 929.0-929.9, 958.8, 958.99, 959.6, 959.8-959.9

   821.21 Condyle, femoral   CC
     CC Excl: See code: 821.20

   821.22 Epiphysis, lower (separation)   CC
     CC Excl: See code: 821.20

   821.23 Supracondylar fracture of femur   CC
     CC Excl: See code: 821.20

   821.29 Other   CC
     Multiple fractures of lower end
     CC Excl: See code: 821.20

✓5ᵗʰ **821.3 Lower end, open**

   821.30 Lower end, unspecified part   MCC
     CC Excl: See code: 821.20

   821.31 Condyle, femoral   MCC
     CC Excl: See code: 821.20

   821.32 Epiphysis, lower (separation)   MCC
     CC Excl: See code: 821.20

   821.33 Supracondylar fracture of femur   MCC
     CC Excl: See code: 821.20

   821.39 Other   MCC
     CC Excl: 733.10, 733.14-733.15, 733.19, 821.39-822.1, 827.0-829.1, 843.0-843.9, 848.8-848.9, 879.8-879.9, 929.0-929.9, 958.8, 958.99, 959.6, 959.8-959.9

✓4ᵗʰ **822 Fracture of patella**

   822.0 Closed   CC

     CC Excl: 822.0-822.1, 828.0-828.1
     S82.001A Uns fx right patella initial encounter closed fx   I-10

   822.1 Open   CC
     CC Excl: 733.10, 733.19, 822.1-823.32, 823.80-823.92, 827.0-829.1, 843.0-843.9, 848.8-848.9, 879.8-879.9, 929.0-929.9, 958.8, 958.99, 959.6, 959.8-959.9

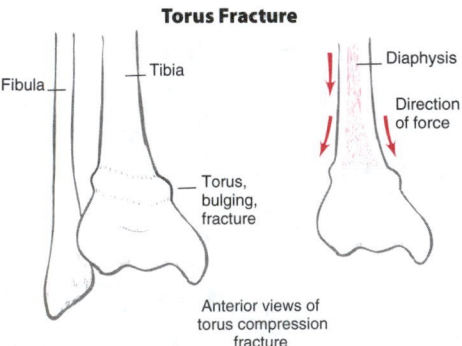

Torus Fracture

- Fibula
- Tibia
- Diaphysis
- Direction of force
- Torus, bulging, fracture

Anterior views of torus compression fracture

✓4ᵗʰ **823 Fracture of tibia and fibula**

   EXCLUDES *Dupuytren's fracture (824.4-824.5)*
      ankle (824.4-824.5)
      radius (813.42, 813.52)
      Pott's fracture (824.4-824.5)
      that involving ankle (824.0-824.9)

> The following fifth-digit subclassification is for use with category 823:
>   **0 tibia alone**
>   **1 fibula alone**
>   **2 fibula with tibia**

¹⁰§ ✓5ᵗʰ **823.0 Upper end, closed**   CC 0,2
  [0-2]   Head   Tibia:
         Proximal end   condyles
                       tuberosity
     CC Excl: For codes 823.00, 823.02: 733.10, 733.16-733.19, 823.00-823.32, 823.80-823.92, 827.0-829.1, 843.0-843.9, 848.8-848.9, 879.8-879.9, 929.0-929.9, 958.8, 958.99, 959.6, 959.8-959.9
     S82.121A Displcd fx lat condyle rt tibia initial enc clos fx   I-10

§ ✓5ᵗʰ **823.1 Upper end, open**   MCC
  [0-2]   **CC Excl:** See code: 823.00

¹⁰§ ✓5ᵗʰ **823.2 Shaft, closed**   CC 0,2
  [0-2]   **CC Excl:** See code: 823.00

§ ✓5ᵗʰ **823.3 Shaft, open**   MCC
  [0-2]   **CC Excl:** See code: 823.00

¹⁰§ ✓5ᵗʰ **823.4 Torus fracture**   CC 0,2
  [0-2]   **DEF:** A bone deformity in children, occurring commonly in the tibia and fibula, in which the bone bends and buckles but does not fracture.
     CC Excl: See code: 823.00
     AHA: 4Q, '02, 70

¹⁰§ ✓5ᵗʰ **823.8 Unspecified part, closed**   CC 0,2
  [0-2]   Lower leg NOS
     CC Excl: For code 823.80: 823.00-823.92; For code 823.82: 733.10, 733.16-733.19, 823.00-823.32, 823.80-823.92, 827.0-829.1, 843.0-843.9, 848.8-848.9, 879.8-879.9, 929.0-929.9, 958.8, 958.99, 959.6, 959.8-959.9
     AHA: For code 823.82: 1Q, '97, 8

§ ✓5ᵗʰ **823.9 Unspecified part, open**   MCC
  [0-2]   **CC Excl:** See code: 823.00\

✓4ᵗʰ **824 Fracture of ankle**
   TIP: If ankle fracture also includes syndesmotic injury, assign also code 845.03 Sprains and strains of tibiofibular (ligament), distal.

   824.0 Medial malleolus, closed
     Tibia involving: Tibia involving:
       ankle   malleolus
     AHA: 1Q, '04, 9

   824.1 Medial malleolus, open   CC
     CC Excl: 733.10, 733.16-733.19, 824.1-824.9, 827.0-829.1, 843.0-843.9, 848.8-848.9, 879.8-879.9, 929.0-929.9, 958.8, 958.99, 959.6, 959.8-959.9

   824.2 Lateral malleolus, closed
     Fibula involving: Fibula involving:
       ankle   malleolus
     AHA: 2Q, '02, 3

   824.3 Lateral malleolus, open   CC
     CC Excl: See code: 824.1

   824.4 Bimalleolar, closed
     Dupuytren's fracture, fibula   Pott's fracture
     DEF: Bimalleolar, closed: Breaking of both nodules (malleoli) on either side of ankle joint, without an open wound.
     DEF: Dupuytren's fracture (Pott's fracture): The breaking of the farthest end of the lower leg bone (fibula), with injury to the farthest end joint of the other lower leg bone (tibia).
     AHA: 2Q, '12, 11
     S82.841A Displcd bimalleolar fx rt lw leg intial enc clos fx   I-10

   824.5 Bimalleolar, open   CC
     CC Excl: See code: 824.1

   824.6 Trimalleolar, closed
     Lateral and medial malleolus with anterior or posterior lip of tibia
     S82.855A Nondispl trimalleolar fx of left lower leg, init   I-10

---

¹⁰   HAC = only for valid CC or MCC codes.
§   Requires fifth digit. Valid digits are in [brackets] under each code. See category 823 for codes and definitions.

N Newborn Age: 0   P Pediatric Age: 0-17   M Maternity Age: 12-55   A Adult Age: 15-124   MCC Major CC Condition   CC CC Condition   HIV HIV Related Dx

Right Foot, Dorsal

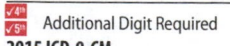

824.7 Trimalleolar, open `CC`
CC Excl: See code: 824.1

824.8 Unspecified, closed
Ankle NOS
AHA: 3Q, '00, 12
S89.302A Uns physeal fx low end lt fibula initial enc clo fx `I-10`

824.9 Unspecified, open `CC`
CC Excl: See code: 824.1

√4th **825 Fracture of one or more tarsal and metatarsal bones**

825.0 Fracture of calcaneus, closed
Heel bone Os calcis

825.1 Fracture of calcaneus, open `CC`
CC Excl: 733.10, 733.16-733.19, 825.1-825.39, 827.0-829.1,
843.0-843.9, 848.8-848.9, 879.8-879.9, 929.0-929.9, 958.8, 958.99,
959.6, 959.8-959.9

√5th **825.2 Fracture of other tarsal and metatarsal bones, closed**

825.20 Unspecified bone(s) of foot [except toes]
Instep

825.21 Astragalus
Talus

825.22 Navicular [scaphoid], foot

825.23 Cuboid

825.24 Cuneiform, foot

825.25 Metatarsal bone(s)

825.29 Other
Tarsal with metatarsal bone(s) only
EXCLUDES calcaneus (825.0)

√5th **825.3 Fracture of other tarsal and metatarsal bones, open**

825.30 Unspecified bone(s) of foot [except toes] `CC`
CC Excl: 825.0-826.1

825.31 Astragalus `CC`
CC Excl: 733.10, 733.19, 825.1-825.39, 827.0-829.1,
843.0-843.9, 848.8-848.9, 879.8-879.9, 929.0-929.9, 958.8,
958.99, 959.6, 959.8-959.9

825.32 Navicular [scaphoid], foot `CC`
CC Excl: See code: 825.31

825.33 Cuboid `CC`
CC Excl: See code: 825.31

825.34 Cuneiform, foot `CC`
CC Excl: See code: 825.31

825.35 Metatarsal bone(s) `CC`
CC Excl: See code: 825.31

825.39 Other `CC`
CC Excl: See code: 825.31

√4th **826 Fracture of one or more phalanges of foot**
INCLUDES toe(s)

826.0 Closed

826.1 Open

√4th **827 Other, multiple, and ill-defined fractures of lower limb**
INCLUDES leg NOS
multiple bones of same lower limb
EXCLUDES multiple fractures of:
ankle bones alone (824.4-824.9)
phalanges of foot alone (826.0-826.1)
tarsal with metatarsal bones (825.29, 825.39)
tibia with fibula (823.0-823.9 with fifth-digit 2)

827.0 Closed

827.1 Open `CC`
CC Excl: 820.00-823.32, 823.80-829.1

√4th **828 Multiple fractures involving both lower limbs, lower with upper limb, and lower limb(s) with rib(s) and sternum**
INCLUDES arm(s) with leg(s) [any bones]
both legs [any bones]
leg(s) with rib(s) or sternum

828.0 Closed `MCC`
CC Excl: See code: 827.1

828.1 Open `MCC`
CC Excl: See code: 827.1

√4th **829 Fracture of unspecified bones**

829.0 Unspecified bone, closed

829.1 Unspecified bone, open

Dislocation (830-839)

INCLUDES displacement
subluxation
EXCLUDES congenital dislocation (754.0-755.8)
pathological dislocation (718.2)
recurrent dislocation (718.3)

NOTE The descriptions "closed" and "open," used in the fourth-digit subdivisions, include the following terms:

closed:	open:
complete	compound
dislocation NOS	infected
partial	with foreign body
simple	
uncomplicated	

A dislocation not indicated as closed or open should be classified as closed.
AHA: 3Q, '90, 12
TIP: Do not assign if documentation indicates developmental dislocation; see instead subcategory 718.7.
Unless otherwise directed, dislocations that occur with fractures of the same site should not be coded separately; assign only the fracture code.

√4th **830 Dislocation of jaw**
INCLUDES jaw (cartilage) (meniscus)
mandible
maxilla (inferior)
temporomandibular (joint)

830.0 Closed dislocation

830.1 Open dislocation `CC`
CC Excl: 830.0-830.1, 839.69, 839.79-839.9

√4th **831 Dislocation of shoulder**
EXCLUDES sternoclavicular joint (839.61, 839.71)
sternum (839.61, 839.71)

The following fifth-digit subclassification is for use with category 831:
0 shoulder, unspecified
Humerus NOS
1 anterior dislocation of humerus
2 posterior dislocation of humerus
3 inferior dislocation of humerus
4 acromioclavicular (joint)
Clavicle
9 other
Scapula

TIP: Do not assign if documentation indicates recurrent shoulder dislocation; see instead code 718.31.

§ √5th **831.0 Closed dislocation**
[0-4, 9]

§ Requires fifth digit. Valid digits are in [brackets] under each code. See category 831 for codes and definitions.

√4th
√5th Additional Digit Required Unacceptable PDx Manifestation Code Hospital Acquired Condition ▶◀ Revised Text ● New Code ▲ Revised Code Title

Injury and Poisoning

831.1–837.1

§ ✓5ᵗʰ **831.1 Open dislocation**   CC
[0-4, 9]   CC Excl: For code 831.10: 831.10, 839.69, 839.79-839.9; For code 831.11: 831.11, 839.69, 839.79-839.9; For code 831.12: 831.12, 839.69, 839.79-839.9; For code 831.13: 831.13, 839.69, 839.79-839.9; For code 831.14: 831.14, 839.69, 839.79-839.9; For code 831.19: 831.19, 839.69, 839.79-839.9

✓4ᵗʰ **832 Dislocation of elbow**

> The following fifth-digit subclassification is for use with subcategories 832.0 and 832.1:
> 0   elbow, unspecified
> 1   anterior dislocation of elbow
> 2   posterior dislocation of elbow
> 3   medial dislocation of elbow
> 4   lateral dislocation of elbow
> 9   other

§ ✓5ᵗʰ **832.0 Closed dislocation**
[0-4, 9]

§ ✓5ᵗʰ **832.1 Open dislocation**   CC
[0-4, 9]   CC Excl: For code 832.10: 832.10; For code 832.11: 832.11; For code 832.12: 832.12; For code 832.13: 832.13; For code 832.14: 832.14; For code 832.19: 832.19

832.2 Nursemaid's elbow
Subluxation of radial head
AHA: 4Q, '09, 110-111

✓4ᵗʰ **833 Dislocation of wrist**

> The following fifth-digit subclassification is for use with category 833:
> 0   wrist unspecified part
>   Carpal (bone)
>   Radius, distal end
> 1   radioulnar (joint), distal
> 2   radiocarpal (joint)
> 3   midcarpal (joint)
> 4   carpometacarpal (joint)
> 5   metacarpal (bone), proximal end
> 9   other
>   Ulna, distal end

§ ✓5ᵗʰ **833.0 Closed dislocation**
[0-5, 9]

§ ✓5ᵗʰ **833.1 Open dislocation**   CC
[0-5, 9]   CC Excl: For codes 833.10, 833.13-833.19: 833.00-833.19; For code 833.11: 833.11; For code 833.12: 833.12

✓4ᵗʰ **834 Dislocation of finger**
INCLUDES   finger(s)
         phalanx of hand
         thumb

> The following fifth-digit subclassification is for use with category 834:
> 0   finger unspecified part
> 1   metacarpophalangeal (joint)
>   Metacarpal (bone), distal end
> 2   interphalangeal (joint), hand

§ ✓5ᵗʰ **834.0 Closed dislocation**
[0-2]

§ ✓5ᵗʰ **834.1 Open dislocation**
[0-2]

✓4ᵗʰ **835 Dislocation of hip**

> The following fifth-digit subclassification is for use with category 835:
> 0   dislocation of hip, unspecified
> 1   posterior dislocation
> 2   obturator dislocation
> 3   other anterior dislocation

§ ✓5ᵗʰ **835.0 Closed dislocation**   CC
[0-3]   CC Excl: For code 835.00: 835.00, 839.69, 839.79-839.9; For code 835.01: 835.01, 839.69, 839.79-839.9; For code 835.02: 835.02, 839.69, 839.79-839.9; For code 835.03: 835.03, 839.69, 839.79-839.9

§ ✓5ᵗʰ **835.1 Open dislocation**   MCC
[0-3]   CC Excl: For code 835.10: 835.10, 839.69, 839.79-839.9; For code 835.11: 835.11, 839.69, 839.79-839.9; For code 835.12: 835.12, 839.69, 839.79-839.9; For code 835.13: 835.13, 839.69, 839.79-839.9

✓4ᵗʰ **836 Dislocation of knee**
EXCLUDES   dislocation of knee:
       old or pathological (718.2)
       recurrent (718.3)
       internal derangement of knee joint (717.0-717.5, 717.8-717.9)
       old tear of cartilage or meniscus of knee (717.0-717.5, 717.8-717.9)

836.0 Tear of medial cartilage or meniscus of knee, current
Bucket handle tear:
   NOS   } current injury
   medial meniscus

836.1 Tear of lateral cartilage or meniscus of knee, current

836.2 Other tear of cartilage or meniscus of knee, current
Tear of:
   cartilage (semilunar) } current injury, not specified
   meniscus   as medial or lateral

836.3 Dislocation of patella, closed

836.4 Dislocation of patella, open   CC
CC Excl: 836.3-836.4

✓5ᵗʰ **836.5 Other dislocation of knee, closed**

836.50 Dislocation of knee, unspecified

836.51 Anterior dislocation of tibia, proximal end
Posterior dislocation of femur, distal end, closed

836.52 Posterior dislocation of tibia, proximal end
Anterior dislocation of femur, distal end, closed

836.53 Medial dislocation of tibia, proximal end

836.54 Lateral dislocation of tibia, proximal end

836.59 Other

✓5ᵗʰ **836.6 Other dislocation of knee, open**

836.60 Dislocation of knee, unspecified   CC
CC Excl: 717.0-717.9, 718.26, 718.36, 836.60, 839.69, 839.79-839.9

836.61 Anterior dislocation of tibia, proximal end   CC
Posterior dislocation of femur, distal end, open
CC Excl: 836.61, 839.69, 839.79-839.9

836.62 Posterior dislocation of tibia, proximal end   CC
Anterior dislocation of femur, distal end, open
CC Excl: 836.62, 839.69, 839.79-839.9

836.63 Medial dislocation of tibia, proximal end   CC
CC Excl: 836.63, 839.69, 839.79-839.9

836.64 Lateral dislocation of tibia, proximal end   CC
CC Excl: 836.64, 839.69, 839.79-839.9

836.69 Other   CC
CC Excl: 836.69, 839.69, 839.79-839.9

✓4ᵗʰ **837 Dislocation of ankle**
INCLUDES   astragalus
         fibula, distal end
         navicular, foot
         scaphoid, foot
         tibia, distal end

837.0 Closed dislocation

837.1 Open dislocation   CC
CC Excl: 837.1, 839.69, 839.79-839.9

---

§   Requires fifth digit. Valid digits are in [brackets] under each code. See appropriate category for codes and definitions.

N Newborn Age: 0   P Pediatric Age: 0-17   M Maternity Age: 12-55   A Adult Age: 15-124   MCC Major CC Condition   CC CC Condition   HIV HIV Related Dx

310 – Volume 1   **2015 ICD-9-CM**

√4ᵗʰ **838 Dislocation of foot**

> The following fifth-digit subclassification is for use with category 838:
> 0 foot unspecified
> 1 tarsal (bone), joint unspecified
> 2 midtarsal (joint)
> 3 tarsometatarsal (joint)
> 4 metatarsal (bone), joint unspecified
> 5 metatarsophalangeal (joint)
> 6 interphalangeal (joint), foot
> 9 other
>   Phalanx of foot
>   Toe(s)

§ √5ᵗʰ **838.0 Closed dislocation**
     [0-6, 9]

§ √5ᵗʰ **838.1 Open dislocation**
     [0-6, 9]

√4ᵗʰ **839 Other, multiple, and ill-defined dislocations**

√5ᵗʰ **839.0 Cervical vertebra, closed**
     Cervical spine
     Neck

     839.00 Cervical vertebra, unspecified `CC`
        CC Excl: 805.00-805.18, 806.00-806.19, 806.8-806.9, 839.00-839.18, 847.0, 848.8-848.9, 879.8-879.9, 929.0-929.9, 952.00-952.09, 958.8-958.99, 959.8-959.9

     839.01 First cervical vertebra `CC`
        CC Excl: See code 839.00

     839.02 Second cervical vertebra `CC`
        CC Excl: See code 839.00

     839.03 Third cervical vertebra `CC`
        CC Excl: See code 839.00

     839.04 Fourth cervical vertebra `CC`
        CC Excl: See code 839.00

     839.05 Fifth cervical vertebra `CC`
        CC Excl: See code 839.00

     839.06 Sixth cervical vertebra `CC`
        CC Excl: See code 839.00

     839.07 Seventh cervical vertebra `CC`
        CC Excl: See code 839.00

     839.08 Multiple cervical vertebrae `CC`
        CC Excl: See code 839.00

√5ᵗʰ **839.1 Cervical vertebra, open**

     839.10 Cervical vertebra, unspecified `MCC`
        CC Excl: See code 839.00

     839.11 First cervical vertebra `MCC`
        CC Excl: See code 839.00

     839.12 Second cervical vertebra `MCC`
        CC Excl: See code 839.00

     839.13 Third cervical vertebra `MCC`
        CC Excl: See code 839.00

     839.14 Fourth cervical vertebra `MCC`
        CC Excl: See code 839.00

     839.15 Fifth cervical vertebra `MCC`
        CC Excl: See code 839.00

     839.16 Sixth cervical vertebra `MCC`
        CC Excl: See code 839.00

     839.17 Seventh cervical vertebra `MCC`
        CC Excl: See code 839.00

     839.18 Multiple cervical vertebrae `MCC`
        CC Excl: See code 839.00

√5ᵗʰ **839.2 Thoracic and lumbar vertebra, closed**

     839.20 Lumbar vertebra

     839.21 Thoracic vertebra
        Dorsal [thoracic] vertebra

√5ᵗʰ **839.3 Thoracic and lumbar vertebra, open**

     839.30 Lumbar vertebra `MCC`
        CC Excl: 839.30

     839.31 Thoracic vertebra `MCC`
        CC Excl: 839.21, 839.31

√5ᵗʰ **839.4 Other vertebra, closed**

     839.40 Vertebra, unspecified site
        Spine NOS

     839.41 Coccyx

     839.42 Sacrum
        Sacroiliac (joint)

     839.49 Other

√5ᵗʰ **839.5 Other vertebra, open**

     839.50 Vertebra, unspecified site `MCC`
        CC Excl: 839.10-839.18, 839.30-839.31, 839.50-839.59, 839.79, 839.9

     839.51 Coccyx `CC`
        CC Excl: 839.51

     839.52 Sacrum `CC`
        CC Excl: 839.52

     839.59 Other `MCC`
        CC Excl: See code: 839.50

√5ᵗʰ **839.6 Other location, closed**

     839.61 Sternum `CC`
        Sternoclavicular joint
        CC Excl: 839.61, 839.71

     839.69 Other
        Pelvis

√5ᵗʰ **839.7 Other location, open**

     839.71 Sternum `MCC`
        CC Excl: See code: 839.61

     839.79 Other `CC`
        CC Excl: 830.1, 831.10-831.19, 832.10-832.19, 833.10-833.19, 834.10-834.12, 835.10-835.13, 836.4, 836.60-836.69, 837.1, 838.10-838.19, 839.10-839.18, 839.30-839.31, 839.50-839.59, 839.71-839.79, 839.9

     839.8 Multiple and ill-defined, closed
        Arm
        Back
        Hand
        Multiple locations, except fingers or toes alone
        Other ill-defined locations
        Unspecified location

     839.9 Multiple and ill-defined, open `CC`
        CC Excl: See code: 839.79

Sprains and Strains of Joints and Adjacent Muscles (840-848)

INCLUDES
avulsion
hemarthrosis   of:
laceration   joint capsule
rupture   ligament
sprain   muscle
strain   tendon
tear

EXCLUDES *laceration of tendon in open wounds (880-884 and 890-894 with .2)*

√4ᵗʰ **840 Sprains and strains of shoulder and upper arm**

     840.0 Acromioclavicular (joint) (ligament)

     840.1 Coracoclavicular (ligament)

     840.2 Coracohumeral (ligament)

     840.3 Infraspinatus (muscle) (tendon)

     840.4 Rotator cuff (capsule)
        EXCLUDES *complete rupture of rotator cuff, nontraumatic (727.61)*

     840.5 Subscapularis (muscle)

     840.6 Supraspinatus (muscle) (tendon)

---

§ Requires fifth digit. Valid digits are in [brackets] under each code. See appropriate category for codes and definitions.

√4ᵗʰ √5ᵗʰ Additional Digit Required   `Unacceptable PDx`   `Manifestation Code`   `Hospital Acquired Condition`   ►◄ Revised Text   ● New Code   ▲ Revised Code Title

Injury and Poisoning

840.7–848.9

840.7 Superior glenoid labrum lesion
SLAP lesion
DEF: Detachment injury of the superior aspect of the glenoid labrum which is the ring of fibrocartilage attached to the rim of the glenoid cavity of the scapula.
AHA: 2Q, '12, 15; 4Q, '01, 52

840.8 Other specified sites of shoulder and upper arm

840.9 Unspecified site of shoulder and upper arm
Arm NOS   Shoulder NOS

✓4th **841 Sprains and strains of elbow and forearm**

    841.0 Radial collateral ligament

    841.1 Ulnar collateral ligament

    841.2 Radiohumeral (joint)

    841.3 Ulnohumeral (joint)

    841.8 Other specified sites of elbow and forearm

    841.9 Unspecified site of elbow and forearm
Elbow NOS

✓4th **842 Sprains and strains of wrist and hand**

  ✓5th **842.0 Wrist**

      842.00 Unspecified site

      842.01 Carpal (joint)

      842.02 Radiocarpal (joint) (ligament)

      842.09 Other
Radioulnar joint, distal

  ✓5th **842.1 Hand**

      842.10 Unspecified site

      842.11 Carpometacarpal (joint)

      842.12 Metacarpophalangeal (joint)

      842.13 Interphalangeal (joint)

      842.19 Other
Midcarpal (joint)

✓4th **843 Sprains and strains of hip and thigh**

    843.0 Iliofemoral (ligament)

    843.1 Ischiocapsular (ligament)

    843.8 Other specified sites of hip and thigh

    843.9 Unspecified site of hip and thigh
Hip NOS   Thigh NOS

✓4th **844 Sprains and strains of knee and leg**

    844.0 Lateral collateral ligament of knee

    844.1 Medial collateral ligament of knee

    844.2 Cruciate ligament of knee

    844.3 Tibiofibular (joint) (ligament), superior

    844.8 Other specified sites of knee and leg

    844.9 Unspecified site of knee and leg
Knee NOS   Leg NOS

✓4th **845 Sprains and strains of ankle and foot**

  ✓5th **845.0 Ankle**

      845.00 Unspecified site
AHA: 2Q, '02, 3

      845.01 Deltoid (ligament), ankle
Internal collateral (ligament), ankle

      845.02 Calcaneofibular (ligament)

      845.03 Tibiofibular (ligament), distal
AHA: 1Q, '04, 9

      845.09 Other
Achilles tendon

  ✓5th **845.1 Foot**

      845.10 Unspecified site

      845.11 Tarsometatarsal (joint) (ligament)

      845.12 Metatarsophalangeal (joint)

      845.13 Interphalangeal (joint), toe

      845.19 Other

✓4th **846 Sprains and strains of sacroiliac region**

    846.0 Lumbosacral (joint) (ligament)

    846.1 Sacroiliac ligament

    846.2 Sacrospinatus (ligament)

    846.3 Sacrotuberous (ligament)

    846.8 Other specified sites of sacroiliac region

    846.9 Unspecified site of sacroiliac region

✓4th **847 Sprains and strains of other and unspecified parts of back**
EXCLUDES lumbosacral (846.0)

    847.0 Neck
Anterior longitudinal (ligament), cervical
Atlanto-axial (joints)
Atlanto-occipital (joints)
Whiplash injury
EXCLUDES neck injury NOS (959.0)
               thyroid region (848.2)
S13.4xxA Sprain ligaments cervical spine initial encounter   I-10

    847.1 Thoracic

    847.2 Lumbar

    847.3 Sacrum
Sacrococcygeal (ligament)

    847.4 Coccyx

    847.9 Unspecified site of back
Back NOS

✓4th **848 Other and ill-defined sprains and strains**

    848.0 Septal cartilage of nose

    848.1 Jaw
Temporomandibular (joint) (ligament)

    848.2 Thyroid region
Cricoarytenoid (joint) (ligament)
Cricothyroid (joint) (ligament)
Thyroid cartilage

    848.3 Ribs
Chondrocostal (joint)   } without mention of injury
Costal cartilage   to sternum

  ✓5th **848.4 Sternum**

      848.40 Unspecified site

      848.41 Sternoclavicular (joint) (ligament)

      848.42 Chondrosternal (joint)

      848.49 Other
Xiphoid cartilage

    848.5 Pelvis
Symphysis pubis
EXCLUDES that in childbirth (665.6)

    848.8 Other specified sites of sprains and strains

    848.9 Unspecified site of sprain and strain

N Newborn Age: 0   P Pediatric Age: 0-17   M Maternity Age: 12-55   A Adult Age: 15-124   MCC Major CC Condition   CC CC Condition   HIV HIV Related Dx

312 – Volume 1   2015 ICD-9-CM

Intracranial Injury, Excluding Those With Skull Fracture (850-854)

INCLUDES traumatic brain injury without skull fracture
open wound of head without intracranial injury (870.0-873.9)
skull fracture alone (800-801 and 803-804 with .0, .5)

EXCLUDES *intracranial injury with skull fracture (800-801 and 803-804, except .0 and .5)*

NOTE The description "with open intracranial wound," used in the fourth-digit subdivisions, includes those specified as open or with mention of infection or foreign body.

The following fifth-digit subclassification is for use with categories 851-854:
0 unspecified state of consciousness
1 with no loss of consciousness
2 with brief [less than one hour] loss of consciousness
3 with moderate [1-24 hours] loss of consciousness
4 with prolonged [more than 24 hours] loss of consciousness and return to pre-existing conscious level
5 with prolonged [more than 24 hours] loss of consciousness without return to pre-existing conscious level
Use fifth-digit 5 to designate when a patient is unconscious and dies before regaining consciousness, regardless of the duration of the loss of consciousness
6 with loss of consciousness of unspecified duration
9 with concussion, unspecified

AHA: 1Q, '93, 22

TIP: If documentation specifies only "head injury," with no further specificity, and is self-limiting, assign instead code 959.01 Head injury, unspecified.

850 Concussion

INCLUDES commotio cerebri

EXCLUDES *concussion with:*
cerebral laceration or contusion (851.0-851.9)
cerebral hemorrhage (852-853)
head injury NOS (959.01)

AHA: 2Q, '96, 6; 4Q, '90, 24

TIP: When a patient is treated for symptoms within 24 to 48 hours of the concussion, clarify with the physician whether the concussion is still in the acute phase or is a postconcussion syndrome; if so, assign instead code 310.2.

850.0 With no loss of consciousness
Concussion with mental confusion or disorientation, without loss of consciousness

✓5ᵗʰ 850.1 With brief loss of consciousness
Loss of consciousness for less than one hour
AHA: 4Q, '03, 76; 1Q, '99, 10; 2Q, '92, 5

850.11 With loss of consciousness of 30 minutes or less   **CC**
CC Excl: 800.00-801.99, 803.00-804.99, 850.0-852.19, 852.21-854.19, 873.8-873.9, 879.8-879.9, 905.0, 925.1-925.2, 929.0-929.9, 958.8-959.09, 959.8-959.9
S06.0x1A Concussion w/loc 30 min/less initial encounter **I-10**

850.12 With loss of consciousness from 31 to 59 minutes   **CC**
CC Excl: See code: 850.11
AHA: 4Q, '10, 111

850.2 With moderate loss of consciousness   **CC**
Loss of consciousness for 1-24 hours
CC Excl: See code: 850.11

850.3 With prolonged loss of consciousness and return to pre-existing conscious level   **CC**
Loss of consciousness for more than 24 hours with complete recovery
CC Excl: See code: 850.11

850.4 With prolonged loss of consciousness, without return to pre-existing conscious level   **MCC**
CC Excl: See code: 850.11

850.5 With loss of consciousness of unspecified duration   **CC**
CC Excl: See code: 850.11
S06.0x9A Concussion w/loc uns duration initial encounter **I-10**

850.9 Concussion, unspecified

Brain

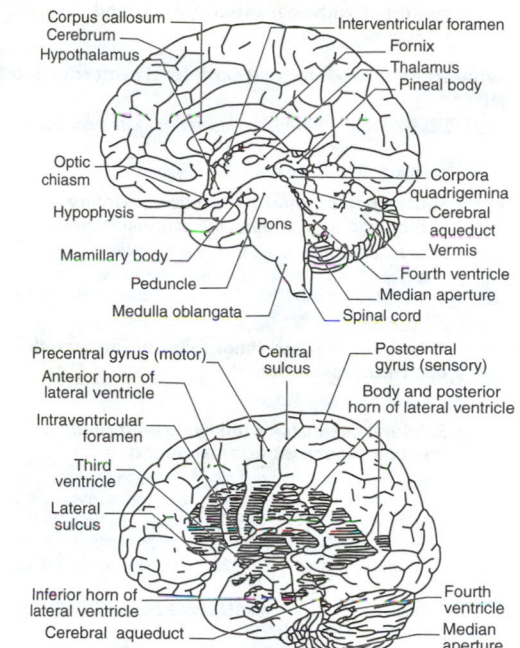

851 Cerebral laceration and contusion
AHA: 4Q, '96, 36; 1Q, '93, 22; 4Q, '90, 24

10 § ✓5ᵗʰ 851.0 Cortex (cerebral) contusion without mention of open intracranial wound   **MCC 5** **CC 2-4, 6**
[0-6, 9]
CC Excl: For codes 851.02-851.06: 800.00-801.99, 803.00-804.99, 850.0-852.19, 852.21-854.19, 873.8-873.9, 879.8-879.9, 905.0, 925.1-925.2, 929.0-929.9, 958.8-959.09, 959.8-959.9
AHA: For code 851.00: 4Q, '10, 93

§ ✓5ᵗʰ 851.1 Cortex (cerebral) contusion with open intracranial wound   **MCC**
[0-6, 9]
CC Excl: 800.00-801.99, 803.00-804.99, 850.0-852.19, 852.21-854.19, 873.8-873.9, 879.8-879.9, 905.0, 925.1-925.2, 929.0-929.9, 958.8-959.09, 959.8-959.9
AHA: 1Q, '92, 9

§ ✓5ᵗʰ 851.2 Cortex (cerebral) laceration without mention of open intracranial wound   **MCC**
[0-6, 9]
CC Excl: See code: 851.1
S06.330A Contus/lac cereb, w/o loss of consciousness, init **I-10**

§ ✓5ᵗʰ 851.3 Cortex (cerebral) laceration with open intracranial wound   **MCC**
[0-6, 9]
CC Excl: See code: 851.1

10 § ✓5ᵗʰ 851.4 Cerebellar or brain stem contusion without mention of open intracranial wound   **MCC 5** **CC 2-4, 6**
CC Excl: For codes 851.42-851.46: 800.00-801.99, 803.00-804.99, 850.0-852.19, 852.21-854.19, 873.8 873.9, 879.8-879.9, 905.0, 925.1-925.2, 929.0-929.9, 958.8-959.09, 959.8-959.9

§ ✓5ᵗʰ 851.5 Cerebellar or brain stem contusion with open intracranial wound   **MCC**
[0-6, 9]
CC Excl: See code: 851.1

§ ✓5ᵗʰ 851.6 Cerebellar or brain stem laceration without mention of open intracranial wound   **MCC**
[0-6, 9]
CC Excl: See code: 851.1

§ ✓5ᵗʰ 851.7 Cerebellar or brain stem laceration with open intracranial wound   **MCC**
[0-6, 9]
CC Excl: See code: 851.1

§ ✓5ᵗʰ 851.8 Other and unspecified cerebral laceration and contusion, without mention of open intracranial wound   **MCC**
[0-6, 9]
Brain (membrane) NOS
CC Excl: See code: 851.1
AHA: 4Q, '96, 37

---

10 HAC = only for valid CC or MCC codes.
§ Requires fifth digit. Valid digits are in [brackets] under each code. See beginning of section 850–854 for codes and definitions.

✓4ᵗʰ
✓5ᵗʰ Additional Digit Required   Unacceptable PDx   Manifestation Code   Hospital Acquired Condition   ▶◀ Revised Text   ● New Code   ▲ Revised Code Title

Injury and Poisoning

851.9–861.11

§ ✓5th **851.9 Other and unspecified cerebral laceration and contusion, with open intracranial wound** `MCC`
[0-6, 9]
     CC Excl: See code: 851.1

✓4th **852 Subarachnoid, subdural, and extradural hemorrhage, following injury**
     EXCLUDES *cerebral contusion or laceration (with hemorrhage) (851.0-851.9)*
     DEF: Bleeding from lining of brain; due to injury.

§ ✓5th **852.0 Subarachnoid hemorrhage following injury without mention of open intracranial wound** `MCC`
[0-6, 9]
     Middle meningeal hemorrhage following injury
     CC Excl: 800.00-801.99, 803.00-804.99, 850.0-852.19, 852.21-854.19, 873.8-873.9, 879.8-879.9, 905.0, 925.1-925.2, 929.0-929.9, 958.8-959.09, 959.8-959.9

§ ✓5th **852.1 Subarachnoid hemorrhage following injury with open intracranial wound** `MCC`
[0-6, 9]
     CC Excl: See code: 852.0

§ ✓5th **852.2 Subdural hemorrhage following injury without mention of open intracranial wound** `MCC`
[0-6, 9]
     CC Excl: **For code 852.20:** 800.00-801.99, 803.00-804.99, 850.0-854.19, 873.8-873.9, 879.8-879.9, 905.0, 925.1-925.2, 929.0-929.9, 958.8-959.09, 959.8-959.9; **For codes 852.21-852.29:** 800.00-801.99, 803.00-804.99, 850.0-852.19, 852.21-854.19, 873.8-873.9, 879.8-879.9, 905.0, 925.1-925.2, 929.0-929.9, 958.8-959.09, 959.8-959.9
     AHA: 4Q, '96, 43; **For codes 852.21-852.29:** 4Q, '07, 107; **For code 852.25:** 4Q, '11, 99
     S06.5x0A Traumatic subdurl hemorrhage w/o loc initial enc `I-10`

§ ✓5th **852.3 Subdural hemorrhage following injury with open intracranial wound** `MCC`
[0-6, 9]
     CC Excl: See code: 852.0

§ ✓5th **852.4 Extradural hemorrhage following injury without mention of open intracranial wound** `MCC`
[0-6, 9]
     Epidural hematoma following injury
     CC Excl: See code: 852.0

§ ✓5th **852.5 Extradural hemorrhage following injury with open intracranial wound** `MCC`
[0-6, 9]
     CC Excl: See code: 852.0

✓4th **853 Other and unspecified intracranial hemorrhage following injury**

§ ✓5th **853.0 Without mention of open intracranial wound** `MCC`
[0-6, 9]
     Cerebral compression due to injury
     Intracranial hematoma following injury
     Traumatic cerebral hemorrhage
     CC Excl: 800.00-801.99, 803.00-804.99, 850.0-852.19, 852.21-854.19, 873.8-873.9, 879.8-879.9, 905.0, 925.1-925.2, 929.0-929.9, 958.8-959.09, 959.8-959.9
     AHA: 3Q, '90, 14

§ ✓5th **853.1 With open intracranial wound** `MCC`
[0-6, 9]   CC Excl: See code: 853.0

✓4th **854 Intracranial injury of other and unspecified nature**
     INCLUDES injury:
       brain NOS
       cavernous sinus
       intracranial
       traumatic brain NOS
     EXCLUDES *any condition classifiable to 850-853 head injury NOS (959.01)*
     AHA: 1Q, '99, 10; 2Q, '92, 6
     TIP: Assign a code from category 854 for traumatic brain injury (TBI) with diffuse axonal injury (DAI), also known as a shear injury.

10 § ✓5th **854.0 Without mention of open intracranial wound** `MCC 5` `CC 2-4, 6`
[0-6, 9]
     CC Excl: **For codes 854.02-854.06:** 800.00-801.99, 803.00-804.99, 850.0-852.19, 852.21-854.19, 873.8-873.9, 879.8-879.9, 905.0, 925.1-925.2, 929.0-929.9, 958.8-959.09, 959.8-959.9
     AHA: **For code 854.00:** 4Q, '09, 108; 2Q, '05, 6

§ ✓5th **854.1 With open intracranial wound** `MCC`
[0-6, 9]   CC Excl: 800.00-801.99, 803.00-804.99, 850.0-852.19, 852.21-854.19, 873.8-873.9, 879.8-879.9, 905.0, 925.1-925.2, 929.0-929.9, 958.8-959.9

Internal Injury of Thorax, Abdomen, and Pelvis (860-869)

INCLUDES   blast injuries
     blunt trauma
     bruise
     concussion injuries (except cerebral)
     crushing } of internal organs
     hematoma
     laceration
     puncture
     tear
     traumatic rupture

EXCLUDES *concussion NOS (850.0-850.9)*
     flail chest (807.4)
     foreign body entering through orifice (930.0-939.9)
     injury to blood vessels (901.0-902.9)

NOTE The description "with open wound," used in the fourth-digit subdivisions, includes those with mention of infection or foreign body.

✓4th **860 Traumatic pneumothorax and hemothorax**
     DEF: Traumatic pneumothorax: air or gas leaking into pleural space of lung due to trauma.
     DEF: Traumatic hemothorax: blood buildup in pleural space of lung due to trauma.
     AHA: 2Q, '93, 4
     TIP: If there's no mention of trauma associated with pneumothorax, see instead category 512.

     860.0 Pneumothorax without mention of open wound into thorax `CC`
       CC Excl: 860.0-860.5, 861.20-861.32, 862.29, 862.39-862.9, 875.0-875.1, 879.8-879.9, 929.0-929.9, 958.7-958.99, 959.8-959.9
       S27.0xxA Traumatic pneumothorax initial encounter `I-10`

     860.1 Pneumothorax with open wound into thorax `MCC`
       CC Excl: See code 860.0

     860.2 Hemothorax without mention of open wound into thorax `MCC`
       CC Excl: See code 860.0

     860.3 Hemothorax with open wound into thorax `MCC`
       CC Excl: See code 860.0

     860.4 Pneumohemothorax without mention of open wound into thorax `MCC`
       CC Excl: See code 860.0

     860.5 Pneumohemothorax with open wound into thorax `MCC`
       CC Excl: See code 860.0

✓4th **861 Injury to heart and lung**
     EXCLUDES *injury to blood vessels of thorax (901.0-901.9)*

     ✓5th **861.0 Heart, without mention of open wound into thorax**
       AHA: 1Q, '92, 9

       861.00 Unspecified injury `CC`
         CC Excl: 861.00-861.13, 862.29, 862.39-862.9, 959.9

       861.01 Contusion `CC`
         Cardiac contusion
         Myocardial contusion
         DEF: Bruising within the pericardium with no mention of open wound.
         CC Excl: 861.00-861.13, 862.29, 862.39-862.9, 875.0-875.1, 879.8-879.9, 929.0-929.9, 958.7-958.99, 959.8-959.9

       861.02 Laceration without penetration of heart chambers `MCC`
         DEF: Tearing injury of heart tissue, without penetration of chambers; no open wound.
         CC Excl: See code 861.01

       861.03 Laceration with penetration of heart chambers `MCC`
         CC Excl: See code 861.01

     ✓5th **861.1 Heart, with open wound into thorax**

       861.10 Unspecified injury `MCC`
         CC Excl: See code 861.01

       861.11 Contusion `MCC`
         CC Excl: See code 861.01

---

10   HAC = only for valid CC or MCC codes.
§   Requires fifth digit. Valid digits are in [brackets] under each code. See beginning of section 850–854 for codes and definitions.

`N` Newborn Age: 0   `P` Pediatric Age: 0-17   `M` Maternity Age: 12-55   `A` Adult Age: 15-124   `MCC` Major CC Condition   `CC` CC Condition   `HIV` HIV Related Dx

314 – Volume 1   **2015 ICD-9-CM**

861.12 Laceration without penetration of heart chambers `MCC`
CC Excl: See code 861.01

861.13 Laceration with penetration of heart chambers `MCC`
CC Excl: See code 861.01

√5th **861.2 Lung, without mention of open wound into thorax**

861.20 Unspecified injury `CC`
CC Excl: 861.20-861.32, 862.29, 862.39-862.9, 875.0-875.1, 879.8-879.9, 929.0-929.9, 958.7-958.8, 958.99, 959.8-959.9

861.21 Contusion `CC`
DEF: Bruising of lung without mention of open wound.
CC Excl: See code: 861.20
S27.321A Contusion of lung unilateral initial encounter `I-10`

861.22 Laceration `MCC`
CC Excl: 861.20-861.32, 862.29, 862.39-862.9, 875.0-875.1, 879.8-879.9, 929.0-929.9, 958.7-958.99, 959.8-959.9

√5th **861.3 Lung, with open wound into thorax**

861.30 Unspecified injury `MCC`
CC Excl: See code 861.22

861.31 Contusion `MCC`
CC Excl: See code 861.22

861.32 Laceration `MCC`
CC Excl: See code 861.22

√4th **862 Injury to other and unspecified intrathoracic organs**
EXCLUDES injury to blood vessels of thorax (901.0-901.9)

862.0 Diaphragm, without mention of open wound into cavity `CC`
CC Excl: 862.0-862.1, 862.29, 862.39-862.9, 875.0-875.1, 879.8-879.9, 929.0-929.9, 958.7-958.8, 958.99, 959.8-959.9

862.1 Diaphragm, with open wound into cavity `MCC`
CC Excl: 862.0-862.1, 862.29, 862.39-862.9, 875.0-875.1, 879.8-879.9, 929.0-929.9, 958.7-958.99, 959.8-959.9

862.2 Other specified intrathoracic organs, without mention of open wound into cavity

862.21 Bronchus `MCC`
CC Excl: 862.21, 862.29-862.31, 862.39-862.9, 875.0-875.1, 879.8-879.9, 929.0-929.9, 958.7-958.99, 959.8-959.9

862.22 Esophagus `MCC`
CC Excl: 862.22-862.29, 862.32-862.9, 875.0-875.1, 879.8-879.9, 929.0-929.9, 958.7-958.99, 959.8-959.9

862.29 Other `CC`
Pleura   Thymus gland
CC Excl: 862.29, 862.39-862.9, 875.0-875.1, 879.8-879.9, 929.0-929.9, 958.7-958.99, 959.8-959.9

√5th **862.3 Other specified intrathoracic organs, with open wound into cavity**

862.31 Bronchus `MCC`
CC Excl: See code: 862.21

862.32 Esophagus `MCC`
CC Excl: See code: 862.22

862.39 Other `MCC`
CC Excl: See code: 862.29

862.8 Multiple and unspecified intrathoracic organs, without mention of open wound into cavity `CC`
Crushed chest
Multiple intrathoracic organs
CC Excl: 862.29, 862.39-862.9, 875.0-875.1, 879.8-879.9, 929.0-929.9, 958.7-958.8, 958.93-958.99, 959.8-959.9

862.9 Multiple and unspecified intrathoracic organs, with open wound into cavity `MCC`
CC Excl: See code: 862.29

√4th **863 Injury to gastrointestinal tract**
EXCLUDES anal sphincter laceration during delivery (664.2)
bile duct (868.0-868.1 with fifth-digit 2)
gallbladder (868.0-868.1 with fifth-digit 2)

863.0 Stomach, without mention of open wound into cavity `CC`
CC Excl: 729.73, 863.0-863.1, 863.80, 863.89-863.90, 863.99, 868.00, 868.03-868.10, 868.13-869.1, 879.2-879.9, 929.0-929.9, 958.8, 958.93-958.99, 959.8-959.9

863.1 Stomach, with open wound into cavity `MCC`
CC Excl: 863.0-863.1, 863.80, 863.89-863.90, 863.99, 868.00, 868.03-868.10, 868.13-869.1, 879.2-879.9, 929.0-929.9, 958.8-958.99, 959.8-959.9

√5th **863.2 Small intestine, without mention of open wound into cavity**

863.20 Small intestine, unspecified site `CC`
CC Excl: 729.73, 863.20-863.39, 863.80, 863.89-863.90, 863.99, 868.00, 868.03-868.10, 868.13-869.1, 879.2-879.9, 929.0-929.9, 958.8, 958.93-958.99, 959.8-959.9

863.21 Duodenum `CC`
CC Excl: See code: 863.20

863.29 Other `CC`
CC Excl: See code: 863.20

√5th **863.3 Small intestine, with open wound into cavity**

863.30 Small intestine, unspecified site `MCC`
CC Excl: 863.20-863.39, 863.80, 863.89-863.90, 863.99, 868.00, 868.03-868.10, 868.13-869.1, 879.2-879.9, 929.0-929.9, 958.8-958.99, 959.8-959.9

863.31 Duodenum `MCC`
CC Excl: 863.21, 863.31-863.39, 863.80, 863.89-863.90, 863.99, 868.00, 868.03-868.10, 868.13-869.1, 879.2-879.9, 929.0-929.9, 958.8-958.99, 959.8-959.9

863.39 Other `MCC`
CC Excl: See code: 863.30

√5th **863.4 Colon or rectum, without mention of open wound into cavity**

863.40 Colon, unspecified site `CC`
CC Excl: 729.73, 863.40-863.80, 863.89-863.90, 863.99, 868.00, 868.03-868.10, 868.13-869.1, 879.2-879.9, 929.0-929.9, 958.8, 958.93-958.99, 959.8-959.9

863.41 Ascending [right] colon `CC`
CC Excl: See code: 863.40

863.42 Transverse colon `CC`
CC Excl: See code: 863.40

863.43 Descending [left] colon `CC`
CC Excl: See code: 863.40

863.44 Sigmoid colon `CC`
CC Excl: See code: 863.40

863.45 Rectum `CC`
CC Excl: See code: 863.40

863.46 Multiple sites in colon and rectum `CC`
CC Excl: See code: 863.40

863.49 Other `CC`
CC Excl: See code: 863.40

√5th **863.5 Colon or rectum, with open wound into cavity**

863.50 Colon, unspecified site `MCC`
CC Excl: 863.40-863.80, 863.89-863.90, 863.99, 868.00, 868.03-868.10, 868.13-869.1, 879.2-879.9, 929.0-929.9, 958.8-958.99, 959.8-959.9

863.51 Ascending [right] colon `MCC`
CC Excl: See code 863.50

863.52 Transverse colon `MCC`
CC Excl: See code 863.50

863.53 Descending [left] colon `MCC`
CC Excl: See code 863.50

863.54 Sigmoid colon `MCC`
CC Excl: See code 863.50

863.55 Rectum `MCC`
CC Excl: See code 863.50

863.56 Multiple sites in colon and rectum `MCC`
CC Excl: See code 863.50

√4th √5th Additional Digit Required   Unacceptable PDx   Manifestation Code   Hospital Acquired Condition   ►◄ Revised Text   ● New Code   ▲ Revised Code Title

863.59 Other
CC Excl: See code 863.50

√5th **863.8 Other and unspecified gastrointestinal sites, without mention of open wound into cavity**

863.80 Gastrointestinal tract, unspecified site `CC`
CC Excl: 729.73, 863.0-863.80, 863.89-863.90, 863.99, 868.00, 868.03-868.10, 868.13-869.1, 879.2-879.9, 929.0-929.9, 958.8, 958.93-958.99, 959.8-959.9

863.81 Pancreas, head `CC`
CC Excl: 729.73, 863.80-863.84, 863.91-863.94, 863.99, 868.00, 868.03-868.10, 868.13-869.1, 879.2-879.9, 929.0-929.9, 958.8, 958.93-958.99, 959.8-959.9

863.82 Pancreas, body `CC`
CC Excl: See code: 863.81

863.83 Pancreas, tail `CC`
CC Excl: See code: 863.81

863.84 Pancreas, multiple and unspecified sites `CC`
CC Excl: See code: 863.81

863.85 Appendix `CC`
CC Excl: 729.73, 863.40-863.80, 863.85-863.90, 863.99, 868.00, 868.03-868.10, 868.13-869.1, 879.2-879.9, 929.0-929.9, 958.8, 958.93-958.99, 959.8-959.9

863.89 Other `CC`
Intestine NOS
CC Excl: 729.73, 863.0-863.84, 863.89-863.94, 863.99, 868.00, 868.03-868.10, 868.13-869.1, 879.2-879.9, 929.0-929.9, 958.8-958.90, 958.93-958.99, 959.8-959.9

√5th **863.9 Other and unspecified gastrointestinal sites, with open wound into cavity**

863.90 Gastrointestinal tract, unspecified site `MCC`
CC Excl: 863.80-863.84, 863.89-863.94, 863.99, 868.00, 868.03-868.10, 868.13-869.1, 879.2-879.9, 929.0-929.9, 958.8-958.99, 959.8-959.9

863.91 Pancreas, head `MCC`
CC Excl: 863.80-863.84, 863.91-863.94, 863.99, 868.00, 868.03-868.10, 868.13-869.1, 879.2-879.9, 929.0-929.9, 958.8-958.99, 959.8-959.9

863.92 Pancreas, body `MCC`
CC Excl: See code 863.91

863.93 Pancreas, tail `MCC`
CC Excl: See code 863.91

863.94 Pancreas, multiple and unspecified sites `MCC`
CC Excl: See code 863.91

863.95 Appendix `MCC`
CC Excl: 863.80, 863.85, 863.95-863.99, 868.00, 868.03-868.10, 868.13-869.1, 879.2-879.9, 929.0-929.9, 958.8-958.99, 959.8-959.9

863.99 Other `MCC`
CC Excl: 863.80, 863.99, 868.00, 868.03-868.10, 868.13-869.1, 879.2-879.9, 929.0-929.9, 958.8-958.99, 959.8-959.9

√4th **864 Injury to liver**

The following fifth-digit subclassification is for use with category 864:
0 unspecified injury
1 hematoma and contusion
2 laceration, minor
   Laceration involving capsule only, or without significant involvement of hepatic parenchyma [i.e., less than 1 cm deep]
3 laceration, moderate
   Laceration involving parenchyma but without major disruption of parenchyma [i.e., less than 10 cm long and less than 3 cm deep]
4 laceration, major
   Laceration with significant disruption of hepatic parenchyma [i.e., 10 cm long and 3 cm deep]
   Multiple moderate lacerations, with or without hematoma
   Stellate lacerations of liver
5 laceration, unspecified
9 other

§ √5th **864.0 Without mention of open wound** `MCC 3-4` `CC 0-2, 5, 9`
[0-5, 9] **into cavity**
CC Excl: 863.80, 863.99-864.19, 868.00, 868.03-868.10, 868.13-869.1, 879.2-879.9, 929.0-929.9, 958.8-958.99, 959.8-959.9

§ √5th **864.1 With open wound into cavity** `MCC`
[0-5, 9] CC Excl: See code 864.0

√4th **865 Injury to spleen**

The following fifth-digit subclassification is for use with category 865:
0 unspecified injury
1 hematoma without rupture of capsule
2 capsular tears, without major disruption of parenchyma
3 laceration extending into parenchyma
4 massive parenchymal disruption
9 other

§ √5th **865.0 Without mention of wound into** `MCC 3-4` `CC 0-2, 9`
[0-4, 9] **cavity**
CC Excl: 865.00-865.19, 868.00, 868.03-868.10, 879.2-879.9, 929.0-929.9, 958.8-958.99, 959.8-959.9

§ √5th **865.1 With open wound into cavity** `MCC`
[0-4, 9] CC Excl: See code 865.0

√4th **866 Injury to kidney**
EXCLUDES *acute kidney injury (nontraumatic) (584.9)*
AHA: 4Q, '08, 192

The following fifth-digit subclassification is for use with category 866:
0 unspecified injury
1 hematoma without rupture of capsule
2 laceration
3 complete disruption of kidney parenchyma

§ √5th **866.0 Without mention of open wound** `MCC 3` `CC 0-2`
[0-3] **into cavity**
CC Excl: 866.00-866.13, 868.00, 868.03-868.10, 868.13-869.1, 879.2-879.9, 929.0-929.9, 958.8-958.99, 959.8-959.9

§ √5th **866.1 With open wound into cavity** `MCC`
[0-3] CC Excl: See code 866.0

√4th **867 Injury to pelvic organs**
EXCLUDES *injury during delivery (664.0-665.9)*

867.0 Bladder and urethra, without mention of open wound into cavity `CC`
CC Excl: 867.0-867.1, 867.6-868.00, 868.03-868.10, 868.13-869.1, 879.2-879.9, 929.0-929.9, 958.8-958.99, 959.8-959.9
AHA: ▶1Q, '14, 12;◀ N-D, '85, 15
TIP: Assign for urethral injury due to senile patient's pulling out indwelling urinary catheter.
S37.20xA Unspecified injury of bladder initial encounter `I-10`

867.1 Bladder and urethra, with open wound into cavity `MCC`
CC Excl: See code 867.0

867.2 Ureter, without mention of open wound into cavity `CC`
CC Excl: 867.2-867.3, 867.6-868.00, 868.03-868.10, 868.13-869.1, 879.2-879.9, 929.0-929.9, 958.8-958.99, 959.8-959.9

867.3 Ureter, with open wound into cavity `MCC`
CC Excl: See code 867.2

867.4 Uterus, without mention of open wound into cavity `CC` ♀
CC Excl: 867.4-868.00, 868.03-868.10, 868.13-869.1, 879.2-879.9, 929.0-929.9, 958.8-958.99, 959.8-959.9

867.5 Uterus, with open wound into cavity `MCC` ♀
CC Excl: See code 867.4

867.6 Other specified pelvic organs, without mention of open wound into cavity `CC`
Fallopian tube   Seminal vesicle
Ovary   Vas deferens
Prostate
CC Excl: 867.6-868.00, 868.03-868.10, 868.13-869.1, 879.2-879.9, 929.0-929.9, 958.8-958.99, 959.8-959.9

867.7 Other specified pelvic organs, with open wound into cavity `MCC`
CC Excl: See code 867.6

867.8 Unspecified pelvic organ, without mention of open wound into cavity `CC`
CC Excl: See code 867.6

867.9 Unspecified pelvic organ, with open wound into cavity `MCC`
CC Excl: See code 867.6

---

§   Requires fifth digit. Valid digits are in [brackets] under each code. See appropriate category for codes and definitions.

`N` Newborn Age: 0   `P` Pediatric Age: 0-17   `M` Maternity Age: 12-55   `A` Adult Age: 15-124   `MCC` Major CC Condition   `CC` CC Condition   `HIV` HIV Related Dx

✓4ᵗʰ **868 Injury to other intra-abdominal organs**

> The following fifth-digit subclassification is for use with category 868:
> 0 unspecified intra-abdominal organ
> 1 adrenal gland
> 2 bile duct and gallbladder
> 3 peritoneum
> 4 retroperitoneum
> 9 other and multiple intra-abdominal organs

§ ✓5ᵗʰ **868.0 Without mention of open wound into cavity** CC
[0-4, 9]   **CC Excl:** For codes 868.00, 868.03-863.09: 868.00, 868.03-868.10, 868.13-869.1, 879.2-879.9, 929.0-929.9, 958.8-958.99, 959.8-959.9; **For code 868.01:** 868.00-868.01, 868.03-868.11, 868.13-869.1, 879.2-879.9, 929.0-929.9, 958.8-958.99, 959.8-959.9; **For code 868.02:** 868.00, 868.02-868.10, 868.13-869.1, 879.2-879.9, 929.0-929.9, 958.8-958.99, 959.8-959.9

§ ✓5ᵗʰ **868.1 With open wound into cavity** MCC
[0-4, 9]   **CC Excl:** For codes 868.10, 868.13-868.19: 868.00, 868.03-868.10, 868.13-869.1, 879.2-879.9, 929.0-929.9, 958.8-958.99, 959.8-959.9; **For code 868.11:** 868.00-868.01, 868.03-868.11, 868.13-869.1, 879.2-879.9, 929.0-929.9, 958.8-958.99, 959.8-959.9; **For code 868.12:** 868.00, 868.03-868.10, 868.12-869.1, 879.2-879.9, 929.0-929.9, 958.8-958.99, 959.8-959.9

✓4ᵗʰ **869 Internal injury to unspecified or ill-defined organs**

> **INCLUDES** internal injury NOS
> multiple internal injury NOS

869.0 Without mention of open wound into cavity CC
  CC Excl: 868.00, 868.03-868.10, 868.13-869.1, 879.2-879.9, 929.0-929.9, 958.8-958.99, 959.8-959.9

869.1 With open wound into cavity MCC
  CC Excl: See code: 869.0
  AHA: 2Q, '89, 15

Open Wound (870-897)

> **INCLUDES** animal bite
> avulsion
> cut
> laceration
> puncture wound
> traumatic amputation
>
> **EXCLUDES** burn (940.0-949.5)
> crushing (925-929.9)
> puncture of internal organs (860.0-869.1)
> superficial injury (910.0-919.9)
> that incidental to:
>   dislocation (830.0-839.9)
>   fracture (800.0-829.1)
>   internal injury (860.0-869.1)
>   intracranial injury (851.0-854.1)

NOTE The description "complicated" used in the fourth-digit subdivisions includes those with mention of delayed healing, delayed treatment, foreign body, or infection.

AHA: 4Q, '01, 52

TIP: Do not assign a code designated as "complicated" based only on physician documentation of complicated. For coding purposes, there must be indications of delayed healing, delayed treatment, infection, or foreign body.

Open Wound of Head, Neck, and Trunk (870-879)

✓4ᵗʰ **870 Open wound of ocular adnexa**

870.0 Laceration of skin of eyelid and periocular area

870.1 Laceration of eyelid, full-thickness, not involving lacrimal passages

870.2 Laceration of eyelid involving lacrimal passages CC
  CC Excl: 870.0-871.9, 879.8-879.9, 929.0-929.9, 958.8, 959.8-959.9

870.3 Penetrating wound of orbit, without mention of foreign body CC
  CC Excl: 870.0-871.9, 879.8-879.9, 929.0-929.9, 958.8-958.99, 959.8-959.9

870.4 Penetrating wound of orbit with foreign body CC
  EXCLUDES retained (old) foreign body in orbit (376.6)
  CC Excl: See code 870.3

870.8 Other specified open wounds of ocular adnexa CC
  CC Excl: See code 870.3

870.9 Unspecified open wound of ocular adnexa CC
  CC Excl: See code 870.3

✓4ᵗʰ **871 Open wound of eyeball**

> **EXCLUDES** 2nd cranial nerve [optic] injury (950.0-950.9)
> 3rd cranial nerve [oculomotor] injury (951.0)

871.0 Ocular laceration without prolapse of intraocular tissue CC
  DEF: Tear in ocular tissue without displacing structures.
  CC Excl: See code 870.3
  AHA: 3Q, '96, 7

871.1 Ocular laceration with prolapse or exposure of intraocular tissue CC
  CC Excl: See code 870.3

871.2 Rupture of eye with partial loss of intraocular tissue CC
  DEF: Forcible tearing of eyeball, with tissue loss.
  CC Excl: See code 870.3

871.3 Avulsion of eye CC
  Traumatic enucleation
  DEF: Traumatic extraction of eyeball from socket.
  CC Excl: See code 870.3

871.4 Unspecified laceration of eye

871.5 Penetration of eyeball with magnetic foreign body CC
  EXCLUDES retained (old) magnetic foreign body in globe (360.50-360.59)
  CC Excl: 870.0-871.9, 879.8-879.9, 929.0-929.9, 958.8, 959.8-959.9

871.6 Penetration of eyeball with (nonmagnetic) foreign body CC
  EXCLUDES retained (old) (nonmagnetic) foreign body in globe (360.60-360.69)
  CC Excl: 870.0-871.9, 879.8-879.9, 929.0-929.9, 958.8, 959.8-959.9

871.7 Unspecified ocular penetration

871.9 Unspecified open wound of eyeball CC
  CC Excl: See code: 870.3

✓4ᵗʰ **872 Open wound of ear**

✓5ᵗʰ **872.0 External ear, without mention of complication**

872.00 External ear, unspecified site

872.01 Auricle, ear
  Pinna
  DEF: Open wound of fleshy, outer ear.

872.02 Auditory canal
  DEF: Open wound of passage from external ear to eardrum.

✓5ᵗʰ **872.1 External ear, complicated**

872.10 External ear, unspecified site

872.11 Auricle, ear

872.12 Auditory canal CC
  CC Excl: 872.00-872.9, 879.8-879.9, 929.0-929.9, 958.8, 959.8-959.9

✓5ᵗʰ **872.6 Other specified parts of ear, without mention of complication**

872.61 Ear drum CC
  Drumhead
  Tympanic membrane
  CC Excl: See code: 872.12

872.62 Ossicles CC
  CC Excl: See code: 872.12

872.63 Eustachian tube CC
  DEF: Open wound of channel between nasopharynx and tympanic cavity.
  CC Excl: See code: 872.12

872.64 Cochlea CC
  DEF: Open wound of snail shell shaped tube of inner ear.
  CC Excl: See code: 872.12

872.69 Other and multiple sites CC
  CC Excl: See code 872.12

✓5ᵗʰ **872.7 Other specified parts of ear, complicated**

872.71 Ear drum CC
  CC Excl: See code: 872.12

---

§ Requires fifth digit. Valid digits are in [brackets] under each code. See category 868 for codes and definitions.

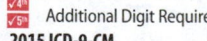

Injury and Poisoning

872.72–875.1

872.72 Ossicles `CC`
    CC Excl: 872.00-872.9, 879.8-879.9, 929.0-929.9,
    958.8-958.99, 959.8-959.9

872.73 Eustachian tube `CC`
    CC Excl: See code 872.72

872.74 Cochlea `CC`
    CC Excl: See code 872.72

872.79 Other and multiple sites `CC`
    CC Excl: See code: 872.12

872.8 Ear, part unspecified, without mention of complication
    Ear NOS

872.9 Ear, part unspecified, complicated

✓4th **873 Other open wound of head**

873.0 Scalp, without mention of complication
    S01.01xA Laceration w/o foreign body scalp initial enc `I-10`

873.1 Scalp, complicated

✓5th **873.2 Nose, without mention of complication**

    873.20 Nose, unspecified site

    873.21 Nasal septum
        DEF: Open wound between nasal passages.

    873.22 Nasal cavity
        DEF: Open wound of nostrils.

    873.23 Nasal sinus `CC`
        DEF: Open wound of mucous-lined respiratory cavities.
        CC Excl: 873.20-873.39, 879.8-879.9, 929.0-929.9, 958.8,
        959.8-959.9

    873.29 Multiple sites

✓5th **873.3 Nose, complicated**

    873.30 Nose, unspecified site

    873.31 Nasal septum

    873.32 Nasal cavity

    873.33 Nasal sinus `CC`
        CC Excl: 873.20-873.39, 879.8-879.9, 929.0-929.9,
        958.8-958.99, 959.8-959.9

    873.39 Multiple sites

✓5th **873.4 Face, without mention of complication**

    873.40 Face, unspecified site

    873.41 Cheek

    873.42 Forehead
        Eyebrow
        AHA: 4Q, '96, 43
        S01.81xA Laceration w/o FB other part head initial enc `I-10`

    873.43 Lip

    873.44 Jaw

    873.49 Other and multiple sites

✓5th **873.5 Face, complicated**

    873.50 Face, unspecified site

    873.51 Cheek

    873.52 Forehead

    873.53 Lip

    873.54 Jaw

    873.59 Other and multiple sites

✓5th **873.6 Internal structures of mouth, without mention of complication**

    873.60 Mouth, unspecified site

    873.61 Buccal mucosa
        DEF: Open wound of inside of cheek.

    873.62 Gum (alveolar process)

    873.63 Tooth (broken) (fractured) (due to trauma)
        EXCLUDES *cracked tooth (521.81)*
        AHA: 1Q, '04, 17

    873.64 Tongue and floor of mouth

873.65 Palate
    DEF: Open wound of roof of mouth.

873.69 Other and multiple sites

✓5th **873.7 Internal structures of mouth, complicated**

    873.70 Mouth, unspecified site

    873.71 Buccal mucosa

    873.72 Gum (alveolar process)

    873.73 Tooth (broken) (fractured) (due to trauma)
        EXCLUDES *cracked tooth (521.81)*
        AHA: 1Q, '04, 17

    873.74 Tongue and floor of mouth

    873.75 Palate

    873.79 Other and multiple sites

873.8 Other and unspecified open wound of head without mention of complication
    Head NOS

873.9 Other and unspecified open wound of head, complicated

✓4th **874 Open wound of neck**

✓5th **874.0 Larynx and trachea, without mention of complication**

    874.00 Larynx with trachea `MCC`
        CC Excl: 847.0, 874.00-874.12, 874.8-874.9,
        879.8-879.9, 929.0-929.9, 958.8-958.99, 959.8-959.9

    874.01 Larynx `MCC`
        CC Excl: See code 874.00

    874.02 Trachea `MCC`
        CC Excl: See code 874.00

✓5th **874.1 Larynx and trachea, complicated**

    874.10 Larynx with trachea `MCC`
        CC Excl: See code 874.00

    874.11 Larynx `MCC`
        CC Excl: See code 874.00

    874.12 Trachea `MCC`
        CC Excl: See code 874.00

874.2 Thyroid gland, without mention of complication `CC`
    CC Excl: 847.0, 874.2-874.3, 874.8-874.9, 879.8-879.9, 929.0-929.9,
    958.8, 959.8-959.9

874.3 Thyroid gland, complicated `CC`
    CC Excl: 847.0, 874.2-874.3, 874.8-874.9, 879.8-879.9,
    929.0-929.9, 958.8-958.99, 959.8-959.9

874.4 Pharynx, without mention of complication `CC`
    Cervical esophagus
    CC Excl: 847.0, 874.4-874.9, 879.8-879.9, 929.0-929.9, 958.8,
    959.8-959.9

874.5 Pharynx, complicated `CC`
    CC Excl: 847.0, 874.4-874.9, 879.8-879.9, 929.0-929.9, 958.8-958.99,
    959.8-959.9

874.8 Other and unspecified parts, without mention of complication
    Nape of neck
    Supraclavicular region
    Throat NOS

874.9 Other and unspecified parts, complicated

✓4th **875 Open wound of chest (wall)**
    EXCLUDES *open wound into thoracic cavity (860.0-862.9)*
            traumatic pneumothorax and hemothorax (860.1, 860.3,
            860.5)
    AHA: 3Q, '95, 17; 3Q, '93, 17

875.0 Without mention of complication `CC`
    CC Excl: 847.1, 862.29, 862.39-862.9, 875.0-875.1,
    879.8-879.9, 929.0-929.9, 958.7-958.99, 959.8-959.9

875.1 Complicated `CC`
    CC Excl: See code 875.0

`N` Newborn Age: 0   `P` Pediatric Age: 0-17   `M` Maternity Age: 12-55   `A` Adult Age: 15-124   `MCC` Major CC Condition   `CC` CC Condition   `HIV` HIV Related Dx

318 – Volume 1   2015 ICD-9-CM

√4ᵗʰ **876 Open wound of back**

> INCLUDES   loin
>   lumbar region
>
> EXCLUDES   *open wound into thoracic cavity (860.0-862.9)*
>   *traumatic pneumothorax and hemothorax (860.1, 860.3,*
>   *860.5)*

  876.0 Without mention of complication

  876.1 Complicated

√4ᵗʰ **877 Open wound of buttock**

> INCLUDES   sacroiliac region

  877.0 Without mention of complication

  877.1 Complicated

√4ᵗʰ **878 Open wound of genital organs (external), including traumatic amputation**

> EXCLUDES   *injury during delivery (664.0-665.9)*
>   *internal genital organs (867.0-867.9)*

  878.0 Penis, without mention of complication   ♂

  878.1 Penis, complicated   ♂

  878.2 Scrotum and testes, without mention of complication   ♂

  878.3 Scrotum and testes, complicated   ♂

  878.4 Vulva, without mention of complication   ♀
       Labium (majus) (minus)

  878.5 Vulva, complicated   ♀

  878.6 Vagina, without mention of complication   ♀

  878.7 Vagina, complicated   ♀

  878.8 Other and unspecified parts, without mention of complication

  878.9 Other and unspecified parts, complicated

√4ᵗʰ **879 Open wound of other and unspecified sites, except limbs**

  879.0 Breast, without mention of complication

  879.1 Breast, complicated

  879.2 Abdominal wall, anterior, without mention of complication
       Abdominal wall NOS
       Epigastric region
       Hypogastric region
       Pubic region
       Umbilical region
       AHA: 2Q, '91, 22; 3Q, '90, 5
       TIP: If the abdominal wall open wound results in aortic rupture, sequence code 902.0 first.

  879.3 Abdominal wall, anterior, complicated

  879.4 Abdominal wall, lateral, without mention of complication
       Flank
       Groin
       Hypochondrium
       Iliac (region)
       Inguinal region

  879.5 Abdominal wall, lateral, complicated

  879.6 Other and unspecified parts of trunk, without mention of complication
       Pelvic region
       Perineum
       Trunk NOS

  879.7 Other and unspecified parts of trunk, complicated

  879.8 Open wound(s) (multiple) of unspecified site(s) without mention of complication
       Multiple open wounds NOS
       Open wound NOS

  879.9 Open wound(s) (multiple) of unspecified site(s), complicated

Open Wound of Upper Limb (880-887)

AHA: N-D, '85, 5

TIP: For degloving injuries, assign code for open wound of the specified site, most often involving extremities.

√4ᵗʰ **880 Open wound of shoulder and upper arm**

> The following fifth-digit subclassification is for use with category 880:
>   **0 shoulder region**
>   **1 scapular region**
>   **2 axillary region**
>   **3 upper arm**
>   **9 multiple sites**

§ √5ᵗʰ **880.0 Without mention of complication**
       [0-3,9]

§ √5ᵗʰ **880.1 Complicated**
       [0-3,9]   AHA: For code 880.13: 2Q, '06, 7

§ √5ᵗʰ **880.2 With tendon involvement**   CC
       [0-3,9]   CC Excl: 880.00-880.29

√4ᵗʰ **881 Open wound of elbow, forearm, and wrist**

> The following fifth-digit subclassification is for use with category 881:
>   **0 forearm**
>   **1 elbow**
>   **2 wrist**

§ √5ᵗʰ **881.0 Without mention of complication**
       [0-2]

§ √5ᵗʰ **881.1 Complicated**
       [0-2]

§ √5ᵗʰ **881.2 With tendon involvement**   CC
       [0-2]   CC Excl: 881.00-881.22

√4ᵗʰ **882 Open wound of hand except finger(s) alone**

  882.0 Without mention of complication

  882.1 Complicated
       AHA: 4Q, '08, 152

  882.2 With tendon involvement   CC
       CC Excl: 882.0-882.2

√4ᵗʰ **883 Open wound of finger(s)**

> INCLUDES   fingernail
>   thumb (nail)

  883.0 Without mention of complication

  883.1 Complicated

  883.2 With tendon involvement   CC
       CC Excl: 883.0-883.2

√4ᵗʰ **884 Multiple and unspecified open wound of upper limb**

> INCLUDES   arm NOS
>   multiple sites of one upper limb
>   upper limb NOS

  884.0 Without mention of complication

  884.1 Complicated

  884.2 With tendon involvement   CC
       CC Excl: 884.0-884.2

√4ᵗʰ **885 Traumatic amputation of thumb (complete) (partial)**

> INCLUDES   thumb(s) (with finger(s) of either hand)

  885.0 Without mention of complication
       AHA: 1Q, '03, 7

  885.1 Complicated

√4ᵗʰ **886 Traumatic amputation of other finger(s) (complete) (partial)**

> INCLUDES   finger(s) of one or both hands, without mention of thumb(s)

  886.0 Without mention of complication

  886.1 Complicated

√4ᵗʰ **887 Traumatic amputation of arm and hand (complete) (partial)**

  887.0 Unilateral, below elbow, without mention of complication   CC
       CC Excl: 880.00-887.7, 929.0-929.9, 958.8-958.99, 959.8-959.9

---

§   Requires fifth digit. Valid digits are in [brackets] under each code. See appropriate category for codes and definitions.

√4ᵗʰ √5ᵗʰ Additional Digit Required   Unacceptable PDx   Manifestation Code   Hospital Acquired Condition   ▶◀ Revised Text   ● New Code   ▲ Revised Code Title

2015 ICD-9-CM   **Volume 1 – 319**

Injury and Poisoning

887.1–900.9

887.1 Unilateral, below elbow, complicated `CC`
CC Excl: See code 887.0

887.2 Unilateral, at or above elbow, without mention of complication `CC`
CC Excl: See code 887.0

887.3 Unilateral, at or above elbow, complicated `CC`
CC Excl: See code 887.0

887.4 Unilateral, level not specified, without mention of complication `CC`
CC Excl: See code 887.0

887.5 Unilateral, level not specified, complicated `CC`
CC Excl: See code 887.0

887.6 Bilateral [any level], without mention of complication `MCC`
One hand and other arm
CC Excl: See code 887.0

887.7 Bilateral [any level], complicated `MCC`
CC Excl: See code 887.0

Open Wound of Lower Limb (890-897)

AHA: N-D, '85, 5

✓4th **890 Open wound of hip and thigh**

890.0 Without mention of complication

890.1 Complicated

890.2 With tendon involvement `CC`
CC Excl: 890.0-890.2

✓4th **891 Open wound of knee, leg [except thigh], and ankle**
INCLUDES leg NOS
multiple sites of leg, except thigh
EXCLUDES that of thigh (890.0-890.2)
with multiple sites of lower limb (894.0-894.2)

891.0 Without mention of complication
S81.031A Puncture wound w/o FB rt knee initial encounter `I-10`

891.1 Complicated

891.2 With tendon involvement `CC`
CC Excl: 891.0-891.2

✓4th **892 Open wound of foot except toe(s) alone**
INCLUDES heel

892.0 Without mention of complication

892.1 Complicated

892.2 With tendon involvement `CC`
CC Excl: 892.0-892.2

✓4th **893 Open wound of toe(s)**
INCLUDES toenail

893.0 Without mention of complication

893.1 Complicated
AHA: 4Q, '08, 73

893.2 With tendon involvement `CC`
CC Excl: 893.0-893.2

✓4th **894 Multiple and unspecified open wound of lower limb**
INCLUDES lower limb NOS
multiple sites of one lower limb, with thigh

894.0 Without mention of complication

894.1 Complicated

894.2 With tendon involvement `CC`
CC Excl: 894.0-894.2

✓4th **895 Traumatic amputation of toe(s) (complete) (partial)**
INCLUDES toe(s) of one or both feet

895.0 Without mention of complication

895.1 Complicated

✓4th **896 Traumatic amputation of foot (complete) (partial)**

896.0 Unilateral, without mention of complication `CC`
CC Excl: 890.0-897.7, 929.0-929.9, 958.8-958.99, 959.8-959.9

896.1 Unilateral, complicated `CC`
CC Excl: See code 896.0

896.2 Bilateral, without mention of complication `MCC`
EXCLUDES one foot and other leg (897.6-897.7)
CC Excl: See code 896.0

896.3 Bilateral, complicated `MCC`
CC Excl: See code 896.0

✓4th **897 Traumatic amputation of leg(s) (complete) (partial)**

897.0 Unilateral, below knee, without mention of complication `CC`
CC Excl: See code 896.0

897.1 Unilateral, below knee, complicated `CC`
CC Excl: See code 896.0

897.2 Unilateral, at or above knee, without mention of complication `CC`
CC Excl: See code 896.0

897.3 Unilateral, at or above knee, complicated `CC`
CC Excl: See code 896.0

897.4 Unilateral, level not specified, without mention of complication `CC`
CC Excl: See code 896.0

897.5 Unilateral, level not specified, complicated `CC`
CC Excl: See code 896.0

897.6 Bilateral [any level], without mention of complication `MCC`
One foot and other leg
CC Excl: See code 896.0

897.7 Bilateral [any level], complicated `MCC`
CC Excl: See code 896.0
AHA: 3Q, '90, 5

Injury to Blood Vessels (900-904)

INCLUDES   arterial hematoma
   avulsion
   cut   of blood vessel
   laceration   secondary to other
   rupture   injuries, e.g.;
   traumatic aneurysm or fistula   fracture or open
   (arteriovenous)   wound

EXCLUDES   accidental puncture or laceration during medical procedure (998.2)
intracranial hemorrhage following injury (851.0-854.1)

AHA: 3Q, '90, 5

✓4th **900 Injury to blood vessels of head and neck**

✓5th **900.0 Carotid artery**

900.00 Carotid artery, unspecified `CC`
CC Excl: 900.00, 900.82-900.9, 904.9, 929.0-929.9, 958.8-958.99, 959.8-959.9
AHA: ▶1Q, '14, 20; 4Q, '13, 92◀

900.01 Common carotid artery `CC`
CC Excl: See code 900.00

900.02 External carotid artery `CC`
CC Excl: See code 900.00

900.03 Internal carotid artery `CC`
CC Excl: See code 900.00
AHA: ▶1Q, '14, 20◀

900.1 Internal jugular vein `CC`
CC Excl: 900.82-900.9, 904.9, 929.0-929.9, 958.8-958.99, 959.8-959.9

✓5th **900.8 Other specified blood vessels of head and neck**

900.81 External jugular vein `CC`
Jugular vein NOS
CC Excl: See code 900.1

900.82 Multiple blood vessels of head and neck `CC`
CC Excl: See code 900.1

900.89 Other `CC`
CC Excl: See code 900.1

900.9 Unspecified blood vessel of head and neck `CC`
CC Excl: See code 900.1

`N` Newborn Age: 0   `P` Pediatric Age: 0-17   `M` Maternity Age: 12-55   `A` Adult Age: 15-124   `MCC` Major CC Condition   `CC` CC Condition   `HIV` HIV Related Dx

√4th **901 Injury to blood vessels of thorax**
  EXCLUDES *traumatic hemothorax (860.2-860.5)*

  901.0 Thoracic aorta `MCC`
    CC Excl: 901.0, 904.9, 929.0-929.9, 958.8-958.99, 959.8-959.9
    AHA: ▶4Q, '13, 92◀

  901.1 Innominate and subclavian arteries `MCC`
    CC Excl: 901.1, 904.9, 929.0-929.9, 958.8-958.99, 959.8-959.9

  901.2 Superior vena cava `MCC`
    CC Excl: 901.2, 904.9, 929.0-929.9, 958.8-958.99, 959.8-959.9

  901.3 Innominate and subclavian veins `MCC`
    CC Excl: 901.3, 904.9, 929.0-929.9, 958.8-958.99, 959.8-959.9

  √5th **901.4 Pulmonary blood vessels**

    901.40 Pulmonary vessel(s), unspecified `MCC`
      CC Excl: 901.40-901.41, 904.9, 929.0-929.9, 958.8-958.90, 958.99, 959.8-959.9

    901.41 Pulmonary artery `MCC`
      CC Excl: 901.40-901.41, 904.9, 929.0-929.9, 958.8-958.99, 959.8-959.9

    901.42 Pulmonary vein `MCC`
      CC Excl: 901.40, 901.42, 904.9, 929.0-929.9, 958.8-958.99, 959.8-959.9

  √5th **901.8 Other specified blood vessels of thorax**

    901.81 Intercostal artery or vein `CC`
      CC Excl: 901.81, 901.83-901.89

    901.82 Internal mammary artery or vein `CC`
      CC Excl: 901.82-901.89

    901.83 Multiple blood vessels of thorax `MCC`
      CC Excl: 904.9, 929.0-929.9, 958.8-958.99, 959.8-959.9

    901.89 Other `CC`
      Azygos vein
      Hemiazygos vein
      CC Excl: 901.0-901.9

  901.9 Unspecified blood vessel of thorax `CC`
    CC Excl: See code: 901.89

√4th **902 Injury to blood vessels of abdomen and pelvis**

  902.0 Abdominal aorta `MCC`
    CC Excl: 902.0, 902.87-902.9, 904.9, 929.0-929.9, 958.8-958.99, 959.8-959.9

  √5th **902.1 Inferior vena cava**

    902.10 Inferior vena cava, unspecified `MCC`
      CC Excl: 902.10, 902.87-902.9, 904.9, 929.0-929.9, 958.8-958.99, 959.8-959.9

    902.11 Hepatic veins `MCC`
      CC Excl: 902.11, 902.87-902.9, 904.9, 929.0-929.9, 958.8-958.99, 959.8-959.9

    902.19 Other `MCC`
      CC Excl: 902.19, 902.87-902.9, 904.9, 929.0-929.9, 958.8-958.99, 959.8-959.9

  √5th **902.2 Celiac and mesenteric arteries**

    902.20 Celiac and mesenteric arteries, unspecified `MCC`
      CC Excl: 902.20, 902.87-902.9, 904.9, 929.0-929.9, 958.8-958.99, 959.8-959.9

    902.21 Gastric artery `MCC`
      CC Excl: 902.21, 902.87-902.9, 904.9, 929.0-929.9, 958.8-958.90, 958.93-958.99, 959.8-959.9

    902.22 Hepatic artery `MCC`
      CC Excl: 902.22, 902.87-902.9, 904.9, 929.0-929.9, 958.8-958.99, 959.8-959.9

    902.23 Splenic artery `MCC`
      CC Excl: 902.23, 902.87-902.9, 904.9, 929.0-929.9, 958.8-958.99, 959.8-959.9

    902.24 Other specified branches of celiac axis `MCC`
      CC Excl: 902.24, 902.87-902.9, 904.9, 929.0-929.9, 958.8-958.99, 959.8-959.9

    902.25 Superior mesenteric artery (trunk) `MCC`
      CC Excl: 902.25, 902.87-902.9, 904.9, 929.0-929.9, 958.8-958.99, 959.8-959.9

    902.26 Primary branches of superior mesenteric artery `MCC`
      Ileocolic artery
      CC Excl: 902.26, 902.87-902.9, 904.9, 929.0-929.9, 958.8-958.99, 959.8-959.9

    902.27 Inferior mesenteric artery `MCC`
      CC Excl: 902.27, 902.87-902.9, 904.9, 929.0-929.9, 958.8-958.99, 959.8-959.9

    902.29 Other `MCC`
      CC Excl: 902.29, 902.87-902.9, 904.9, 929.0-929.9, 958.8-958.99, 959.8-959.9

  √5th **902.3 Portal and splenic veins**

    902.31 Superior mesenteric vein and primary subdivisions `MCC`
      Ileocolic vein
      CC Excl: 902.31, 902.87-902.9, 904.9, 929.0-929.9, 958.8-958.99, 959.8-959.9

    902.32 Inferior mesenteric vein `MCC`
      CC Excl: 902.32, 902.87-902.9, 904.9, 929.0-929.9, 958.8-958.99, 959.8-959.9

    902.33 Portal vein `MCC`
      CC Excl: 902.33, 902.87-902.9, 904.9, 929.0-929.9, 958.8-958.99, 959.8-959.9

    902.34 Splenic vein `MCC`
      CC Excl: 902.34, 902.87-902.9, 904.9, 929.0-929.9, 958.8-958.99, 959.8-959.9

    902.39 Other `MCC`
      Cystic vein
      Gastric vein
      CC Excl: 902.39, 902.87-902.9, 904.9, 929.0-929.9, 958.8-958.99, 959.8-959.9

  √5th **902.4 Renal blood vessels**

    902.40 Renal vessel(s), unspecified `MCC`
      CC Excl: 902.40, 902.87-902.9, 904.9, 929.0-929.9, 958.8-958.99, 959.8-959.9

    902.41 Renal artery `MCC`
      CC Excl: 902.41, 902.87-902.9, 904.9, 929.0-929.9, 958.8-958.99, 959.8-959.9

    902.42 Renal vein `MCC`
      CC Excl: 902.42, 902.87-902.9, 904.9, 929.0-929.9, 958.8-958.99, 959.8-959.9

    902.49 Other `MCC`
      Suprarenal arteries
      CC Excl: 902.49, 902.87-902.9, 904.9, 929.0-929.9, 958.8-958.99, 959.8-959.9

  √5th **902.5 Iliac blood vessels**

    902.50 Iliac vessel(s), unspecified `MCC`
      CC Excl: 902.50, 902.53-902.54, 902.59, 902.87-902.9, 904.9, 929.0-929.9, 958.8-958.99, 959.8-959.9

    902.51 Hypogastric artery `MCC`
      CC Excl: 902.51, 902.87-902.9, 904.9, 929.0-929.9, 958.8-958.99, 959.8-959.9

    902.52 Hypogastric vein `MCC`
      CC Excl: 902.52, 902.87-902.9, 904.9, 929.0-929.9, 958.8-958.99, 959.8-959.9

    902.53 Iliac artery `MCC`
      CC Excl: 902.50, 902.53, 902.59, 902.87-902.9, 904.9, 929.0-929.9, 958.8-958.99, 959.8-959.9

    902.54 Iliac vein `MCC`
      CC Excl: 902.50, 902.54, 902.59, 902.87-902.9, 904.9, 929.0-929.9, 958.8-958.99, 959.8-959.9

    902.55 Uterine artery `CC` ♀
      CC Excl: 902.55, 902.59, 902.87-902.9, 904.9, 929.0-929.9, 958.8-958.90, 958.93-958.99, 959.8-959.9

    902.56 Uterine vein `CC` ♀
      CC Excl: 902.56-902.59, 902.87-902.9, 904.9, 929.0-929.9, 958.8-958.90, 958.93-958.99, 959.8-959.9

    902.59 Other `MCC`
      CC Excl: See code: 902.50

√4th √5th Additional Digit Required   Unacceptable PDx   Manifestation Code   Hospital Acquired Condition   ▶◀ Revised Text   ● New Code   ▲ Revised Code Title

√5th **902.8 Other specified blood vessels of abdomen and pelvis** `CC`

     902.81 Ovarian artery `CC` ♀
        CC Excl: 902.81, 902.87-902.9, 904.9, 929.0-929.9, 958.8-958.90, 958.93-958.99, 959.8-959.9

     902.82 Ovarian vein `CC` ♀
        CC Excl: 902.82-902.9, 904.9, 929.0-929.9, 958.8-958.90, 958.93-958.99, 959.8-959.9

     902.87 Multiple blood vessels of abdomen and pelvis `MCC`
        CC Excl: 902.87-902.9, 904.9, 929.0-929.9, 958.8-958.99, 959.8-959.9

     902.89 Other `CC`
        CC Excl: 902.87-902.9, 904.9, 929.0-929.9, 958.8-958.90, 958.93-958.99, 959.8-959.9

902.9 Unspecified blood vessel of abdomen and pelvis `CC`
    CC Excl: 902.0-902.9, 904.9, 929.0-929.9, 958.8-958.90, 958.93-958.99, 959.8-959.9

√4th **903 Injury to blood vessels of upper extremity**

√5th **903.0 Axillary blood vessels**

     903.00 Axillary vessel(s), unspecified `MCC`
        CC Excl: 903.00-903.02, 903.8-903.9, 904.9

     903.01 Axillary artery `MCC`
        CC Excl: 903.00-903.01, 903.8-903.9, 904.9

     903.02 Axillary vein `MCC`
        CC Excl: 903.00, 903.02, 903.8-903.9, 904.9

903.1 Brachial blood vessels `CC`
    CC Excl: 903.1, 903.8-903.9, 904.9

903.2 Radial blood vessels `CC`
    CC Excl: 903.2, 903.8-903.9, 904.9

903.3 Ulnar blood vessels `CC`
    CC Excl: 903.3, 903.8-903.9, 904.9

903.4 Palmar artery `CC`
    CC Excl: 903.4, 903.8-903.9, 904.9

903.5 Digital blood vessels `CC`
    CC Excl: 903.5-903.9, 904.9

903.8 Other specified blood vessels of upper extremity `CC`
    Multiple blood vessels of upper extremity
    CC Excl: 903.3-903.9, 904.9

903.9 Unspecified blood vessel of upper extremity `CC`
    CC Excl: See code: 903.8

√4th **904 Injury to blood vessels of lower extremity and unspecified sites**

904.0 Common femoral artery `MCC`
    Femoral artery above profunda origin
    CC Excl: 904.0, 904.7-904.9

904.1 Superficial femoral artery `MCC`
    CC Excl: 904.1, 904.7-904.9

904.2 Femoral veins `MCC`
    CC Excl: 904.2, 904.7-904.9

904.3 Saphenous veins `CC`
    Saphenous vein (greater) (lesser)
    CC Excl: 904.3, 904.7-904.9

√5th **904.4 Popliteal blood vessels**

     904.40 Popliteal vessel(s), unspecified `MCC`
        CC Excl: 904.40, 904.7-904.9

     904.41 Popliteal artery `MCC`
        CC Excl: 904.41, 904.7-904.9

     904.42 Popliteal vein `MCC`
        CC Excl: 904.42, 904.7-904.9

√5th **904.5 Tibial blood vessels**

     904.50 Tibial vessel(s), unspecified `CC`
        CC Excl: 904.50, 904.7-904.9

     904.51 Anterior tibial artery `CC`
        CC Excl: 904.51, 904.7-904.9

     904.52 Anterior tibial vein `CC`
        CC Excl: 904.52, 904.7-904.9

     904.53 Posterior tibial artery `CC`
        CC Excl: 904.53, 904.7-904.9

     904.54 Posterior tibial vein `CC`
        CC Excl: 904.54, 904.7-904.9

904.6 Deep plantar blood vessels `CC`
    CC Excl: 904.6-904.9

904.7 Other specified blood vessels of lower extremity `CC`
    Multiple blood vessels of lower extremity
    CC Excl: 729.72, 904.0-904.9

904.8 Unspecified blood vessel of lower extremity `CC`
    CC Excl: See code: 904.7

904.9 Unspecified site `CC`
    Injury to blood vessel NOS
    CC Excl: 729.71-729.72, 900.00-904.9

Late Effects Of Injuries, Poisonings, Toxic Effects, and Other External Causes (905-909)

NOTE These categories are to be used to indicate conditions classifiable to 800-999 as the cause of late effects, which are themselves classified elsewhere. The "late effects" include those specified as such, or as sequelae, which may occur at any time after the acute injury.

√4th **905 Late effects of musculoskeletal and connective tissue injuries**
    AHA: 1Q, '95, 10; 2Q, '94, 3

905.0 Late effect of fracture of skull and face bones
    Late effect of injury classifiable to 800-804
    AHA: ▶2Q, '13, 8;◀ 3Q, '97, 12

905.1 Late effect of fracture of spine and trunk without mention of spinal cord lesion
    Late effect of injury classifiable to 805, 807-809
    AHA: 1Q, '07, 20

905.2 Late effect of fracture of upper extremities
    Late effect of injury classifiable to 810-819

905.3 Late effect of fracture of neck of femur
    Late effect of injury classifiable to 820

905.4 Late effect of fracture of lower extremities
    Late effect of injury classifiable to 821-827
    S79.001S Uns physeal fx upper end right femur sequela `I-10`

905.5 Late effect of fracture of multiple and unspecified bones
    Late effect of injury classifiable to 828-829

905.6 Late effect of dislocation
    Late effect of injury classifiable to 830-839

905.7 Late effect of sprain and strain without mention of tendon injury
    Late effect of injury classifiable to 840-848, except tendon injury

905.8 Late effect of tendon injury
    Late effect of tendon injury due to:
       open wound [injury classifiable to 880-884 with .2, 890-894 with .2]
       sprain and strain [injury classifiable to 840-848]
    AHA: 2Q, '89, 13; 2Q, '89, 15

905.9 Late effect of traumatic amputation
    Late effect of injury classifiable to 885-887, 895-897
    EXCLUDES late amputation stump complication (997.60-997.69)

√4th **906 Late effects of injuries to skin and subcutaneous tissues**

906.0 Late effect of open wound of head, neck, and trunk
    Late effect of injury classifiable to 870-879

906.1 Late effect of open wound of extremities without mention of tendon injury
    Late effect of injury classifiable to 880-884, 890-894 except .2

906.2 Late effect of superficial injury
    Late effect of injury classifiable to 910-919

906.3 Late effect of contusion
    Late effect of injury classifiable to 920-924

906.4 Late effect of crushing
    Late effect of injury classifiable to 925-929

906.5 Late effect of burn of eye, face, head, and neck
    Late effect of injury classifiable to 940-941
    AHA: 4Q, '04, 76

N Newborn Age: 0   **P** Pediatric Age: 0-17   **M** Maternity Age: 12-55   **A** Adult Age: 15-124   **MCC** Major CC Condition   **CC** CC Condition   **HIV** HIV Related Dx

322 – Volume 1 · October 2014   2015 ICD-9-CM

906.6 Late effect of burn of wrist and hand
Late effect of injury classifiable to 944
AHA: 4Q, '94, 22

906.7 Late effect of burn of other extremities
Late effect of injury classifiable to 943 or 945
AHA: 4Q, '94, 22

906.8 Late effect of burns of other specified sites
Late effect of injury classifiable to 942, 946-947
AHA: 4Q, '94, 22

906.9 Late effect of burn of unspecified site
Late effect of injury classifiable to 948-949
AHA: 4Q, '94, 22

√4ᵗʰ **907 Late effects of injuries to the nervous system**

907.0 Late effect of intracranial injury without mention of skull fracture
Late effect of injury classifiable to 850-854
AHA: ▶4Q, '13, 86;◀ 3Q, '12, 20; 4Q, '11, 97; 4Q, '10, 96; 4Q, '09, 108; 4Q, '08, 108; 4Q, '03, 103; 3Q, '90, 14
S06.2x1S Diffuse traumatic brain inj loc 30 min/less seq   I-10

907.1 Late effect of injury to cranial nerve
Late effect of injury classifiable to 950-951

907.2 Late effect of spinal cord injury
Late effect of injury classifiable to 806, 952
AHA: 4Q, '03, 103; 4Q, '98, 38
S34.114S Complete lesion L4 of lumbar spinal cord sequela   I-10

907.3 Late effect of injury to nerve root(s), spinal plexus(es), and other nerves of trunk
Late effect of injury classifiable to 953-954
AHA: 2Q, '07, 11

907.4 Late effect of injury to peripheral nerve of shoulder girdle and upper limb
Late effect of injury classifiable to 955

907.5 Late effect of injury to peripheral nerve of pelvic girdle and lower limb
Late effect of injury classifiable to 956

907.9 Late effect of injury to other and unspecified nerve
Late effect of injury classifiable to 957

√4ᵗʰ **908 Late effects of other and unspecified injuries**

908.0 Late effect of internal injury to chest
Late effect of injury classifiable to 860-862

908.1 Late effect of internal injury to intra-abdominal organs
Late effect of injury classifiable to 863-866, 868

908.2 Late effect of internal injury to other internal organs
Late effect of injury classifiable to 867 or 869

908.3 Late effect of injury to blood vessel of head, neck, and extremities
Late effect of injury classifiable to 900, 903-904

908.4 Late effect of injury to blood vessel of thorax, abdomen, and pelvis
Late effect of injury classifiable to 901-902

908.5 Late effect of foreign body in orifice
Late effect of injury classifiable to 930-939

908.6 Late effect of certain complications of trauma
Late effect of complications classifiable to 958

908.9 Late effect of unspecified injury
Late effect of injury classifiable to 959
AHA: 3Q, '00, 4

√4ᵗʰ **909 Late effects of other and unspecified external causes**

909.0 Late effect of poisoning due to drug, medicinal or biological substance
Late effect of conditions classifiable to 960-979
EXCLUDES late effect of adverse effect of drug, medicinal or biological substance (909.5)
AHA: 4Q, '03, 103

909.1 Late effect of toxic effects of nonmedical substances
Late effect of conditions classifiable to 980-989

909.2 Late effect of radiation
Late effect of conditions classifiable to 990

909.3 Late effect of complications of surgical and medical care
Late effect of conditions classifiable to 996-999
AHA: 1Q, '93, 29

909.4 Late effect of certain other external causes
Late effect of conditions classifiable to 991-994

909.5 Late effect of adverse effect of drug, medical or biological substance
EXCLUDES late effect of poisoning due to drug, medicinal or biological substance (909.0)
AHA: 4Q, '94, 48

909.9 Late effect of other and unspecified external causes

Superficial Injury (910-919)

EXCLUDES burn (blisters) (940.0-949.5)
contusion (920-924.9)
foreign body:
  granuloma (728.82)
  inadvertently left in operative wound (998.4)
  residual in soft tissue (729.6)
insect bite, venomous (989.5)
open wound with incidental foreign body (870.0-897.7)

AHA: 2Q, '89, 15
TIP: Do not code separately when associated with more severe injuries of the same site.

√4ᵗʰ **910 Superficial injury of face, neck, and scalp except eye**
INCLUDES   cheek
         ear
         gum
         lip
         nose
         throat
EXCLUDES eye and adnexa (918.0-918.9)

910.0 Abrasion or friction burn without mention of infection
S00.01xA Abrasion of scalp initial encounter   I-10

910.1 Abrasion or friction burn, infected

910.2 Blister without mention of infection

910.3 Blister, infected

910.4 Insect bite, nonvenomous, without mention of infection

910.5 Insect bite, nonvenomous, infected

910.6 Superficial foreign body (splinter) without major open wound and without mention of infection

910.7 Superficial foreign body (splinter) without major open wound, infected

910.8 Other and unspecified superficial injury of face, neck, and scalp without mention of infection

910.9 Other and unspecified superficial injury of face, neck, and scalp, infected

√4ᵗʰ **911 Superficial injury of trunk**
INCLUDES   abdominal wall   interscapular region
         anus   labium (majus) (minus)
         back   penis
         breast   perineum
         buttock   scrotum
         chest wall   testis
         flank   vagina
         groin   vulva
EXCLUDES hip (916.0-916.9)
scapular region (912.0-912.9)

911.0 Abrasion or friction burn without mention of infection
AHA: 3Q, '01, 10

911.1 Abrasion or friction burn, infected

911.2 Blister without mention of infection

911.3 Blister, infected

911.4 Insect bite, nonvenomous, without mention of infection

911.5 Insect bite, nonvenomous, infected

911.6 Superficial foreign body (splinter) without major open wound and without mention of infection

911.7 Superficial foreign body (splinter) without major open wound, infected

√4ᵗʰ
√5ᵗʰ
2015 ICD-9-CM

Additional Digit Required   Unacceptable PDx   Manifestation Code   Hospital Acquired Condition   ▶◀ Revised Text   ● New Code   ▲ Revised Code Title

October 2014 • Volume 1 – 323

Injury and Poisoning

911.8–919.3

911.8 Other and unspecified superficial injury of trunk without mention of infection

911.9 Other and unspecified superficial injury of trunk, infected

✓4th **912 Superficial injury of shoulder and upper arm**

INCLUDES   axilla
          scapular region

912.0 Abrasion or friction burn without mention of infection

912.1 Abrasion or friction burn, infected

912.2 Blister without mention of infection

912.3 Blister, infected

912.4 Insect bite, nonvenomous, without mention of infection

912.5 Insect bite, nonvenomous, infected

912.6 Superficial foreign body (splinter) without major open wound and without mention of infection

912.7 Superficial foreign body (splinter) without major open wound, infected

912.8 Other and unspecified superficial injury of shoulder and upper arm without mention of infection

912.9 Other and unspecified superficial injury of shoulder and upper arm, infected

✓4th **913 Superficial injury of elbow, forearm, and wrist**

913.0 Abrasion or friction burn without mention of infection

913.1 Abrasion or friction burn, infected

913.2 Blister without mention of infection

913.3 Blister, infected

913.4 Insect bite, nonvenomous, without mention of infection

913.5 Insect bite, nonvenomous, infected

913.6 Superficial foreign body (splinter) without major open wound and without mention of infection

913.7 Superficial foreign body (splinter) without major open wound, infected

913.8 Other and unspecified superficial injury of elbow, forearm, and wrist without mention of infection

913.9 Other and unspecified superficial injury of elbow, forearm, and wrist, infected

✓4th **914 Superficial injury of hand(s) except finger(s) alone**

914.0 Abrasion or friction burn without mention of infection

914.1 Abrasion or friction burn, infected

914.2 Blister without mention of infection

914.3 Blister, infected

914.4 Insect bite, nonvenomous, without mention of infection

914.5 Insect bite, nonvenomous, infected

914.6 Superficial foreign body (splinter) without major open wound and without mention of infection

914.7 Superficial foreign body (splinter) without major open wound, infected

914.8 Other and unspecified superficial injury of hand without mention of infection

914.9 Other and unspecified superficial injury of hand, infected

✓4th **915 Superficial injury of finger(s)**

INCLUDES   fingernail
          thumb (nail)

915.0 Abrasion or friction burn without mention of infection

915.1 Abrasion or friction burn, infected

915.2 Blister without mention of infection

915.3 Blister, infected

915.4 Insect bite, nonvenomous, without mention of infection

915.5 Insect bite, nonvenomous, infected

915.6 Superficial foreign body (splinter) without major open wound and without mention of infection

915.7 Superficial foreign body (splinter) without major open wound, infected

915.8 Other and unspecified superficial injury of fingers without mention of infection
AHA: 3Q, '01, 10

915.9 Other and unspecified superficial injury of fingers, infected

✓4th **916 Superficial injury of hip, thigh, leg, and ankle**

916.0 Abrasion or friction burn without mention of infection
S80.812A Abrasion left lower leg initial encounter   I-10

916.1 Abrasion or friction burn, infected

916.2 Blister without mention of infection

916.3 Blister, infected

916.4 Insect bite, nonvenomous, without mention of infection

916.5 Insect bite, nonvenomous, infected

916.6 Superficial foreign body (splinter) without major open wound and without mention of infection

916.7 Superficial foreign body (splinter) without major open wound, infected

916.8 Other and unspecified superficial injury of hip, thigh, leg, and ankle without mention of infection

916.9 Other and unspecified superficial injury of hip, thigh, leg, and ankle, infected

✓4th **917 Superficial injury of foot and toe(s)**

INCLUDES   heel
          toenail

917.0 Abrasion or friction burn without mention of infection

917.1 Abrasion or friction burn, infected

917.2 Blister without mention of infection

917.3 Blister, infected

917.4 Insect bite, nonvenomous, without mention of infection

917.5 Insect bite, nonvenomous, infected

917.6 Superficial foreign body (splinter) without major open wound and without mention of infection

917.7 Superficial foreign body (splinter) without major open wound, infected

917.8 Other and unspecified superficial injury of foot and toes without mention of infection
AHA: 1Q, '03, 13

917.9 Other and unspecified superficial injury of foot and toes, infected
AHA: 1Q, '03, 13
TIP: Assign for hair strangulation of toe, with infection.

✓4th **918 Superficial injury of eye and adnexa**

EXCLUDES   burn (940.0-940.9)
          foreign body on external eye (930.0-930.9)

918.0 Eyelids and periocular area
Abrasion
Insect bite
Superficial foreign body (splinter)

918.1 Cornea
Corneal abrasion
Superficial laceration
EXCLUDES   corneal injury due to contact lens (371.82)

918.2 Conjunctiva

918.9 Other and unspecified superficial injuries of eye
Eye (ball) NOS

✓4th **919 Superficial injury of other, multiple, and unspecified sites**

EXCLUDES   multiple sites classifiable to the same three-digit category (910.0-918.9)

919.0 Abrasion or friction burn without mention of infection

919.1 Abrasion or friction burn, infected

919.2 Blister without mention of infection

919.3 Blister, infected

N Newborn Age: 0   P Pediatric Age: 0-17   M Maternity Age: 12-55   A Adult Age: 15-124   MCC Major CC Condition   CC CC Condition   HIV HIV Related Dx

919.4 Insect bite, nonvenomous, without mention of infection

919.5 Insect bite, nonvenomous, infected

919.6 Superficial foreign body (splinter) without major open wound and without mention of infection

919.7 Superficial foreign body (splinter) without major open wound, infected

919.8 Other and unspecified superficial injury without mention of infection

919.9 Other and unspecified superficial injury, infected

Contusion with Intact Skin Surface (920-924)

| INCLUDES | bruise | ⎫ without fracture or open |
| | hematoma | ⎬ wound |

EXCLUDES concussion (850.0-850.9)
hemarthrosis (840.0-848.9)
internal organs (860.0-869.1)
that incidental to:
   crushing injury (925-929.9)
   dislocation (830.0-839.9)
   fracture (800.0-829.1)
   internal injury (860.0-869.1)
   intracranial injury (850.0-854.1)
   nerve injury (950.0-957.9)
   open wound (870.0-897.7)

920 Contusion of face, scalp, and neck except eye(s)
Cheek	Mandibular joint area
Ear (auricle)	Nose
Gum	Throat
Lip	

   S00.33xA Contusion of nose initial encounter   I-10

✓4ᵗʰ 921 Contusion of eye and adnexa

921.0 Black eye, not otherwise specified

921.1 Contusion of eyelids and periocular area

921.2 Contusion of orbital tissues

921.3 Contusion of eyeball
   AHA: J-A, '85, 16
   TIP: If iridodialysis (rupture of the root of the iris) is present and is due to the eyeball contusion, assign also code 364.76.

921.9 Unspecified contusion of eye
   Injury of eye NOS

✓4ᵗʰ 922 Contusion of trunk

922.0 Breast

922.1 Chest wall
   S20.212A Contusion left front wall thorax initial enc   I-10

922.2 Abdominal wall
   Flank
   Groin

✓5ᵗʰ 922.3 Back
   AHA: 4Q, '96, 39

    922.31 Back
      EXCLUDES interscapular region (922.33)
      AHA: 3Q, '99, 14

    922.32 Buttock

    922.33 Interscapular region

922.4 Genital organs
Labium (majus) (minus)	Testis
Penis	Vagina
Perineum	Vulva
Scrotum	

922.8 Multiple sites of trunk

922.9 Unspecified part
   Trunk NOS

✓4ᵗʰ 923 Contusion of upper limb

✓5ᵗʰ 923.0 Shoulder and upper arm

    923.00 Shoulder region

    923.01 Scapular region

    923.02 Axillary region

    923.03 Upper arm

    923.09 Multiple sites

✓5ᵗʰ 923.1 Elbow and forearm

    923.10 Forearm

    923.11 Elbow

✓5ᵗʰ 923.2 Wrist and hand(s), except finger(s) alone

    923.20 Hand(s)

    923.21 Wrist

    923.3 Finger
      Fingernail
      Thumb (nail)

923.8 Multiple sites of upper limb

923.9 Unspecified part of upper limb
   Arm NOS

✓4ᵗʰ 924 Contusion of lower limb and of other and unspecified sites

✓5ᵗʰ 924.0 Hip and thigh

    924.00 Thigh
      AHA: 1Q, '09, 10

    924.01 Hip
      S70.02xA Contusion of left hip initial encounter   I-10

✓5ᵗʰ 924.1 Knee and lower leg

    924.10 Lower leg

    924.11 Knee

✓5ᵗʰ 924.2 Ankle and foot, excluding toe(s)

    924.20 Foot
      Heel

    924.21 Ankle

924.3 Toe
   Toenail

924.4 Multiple sites of lower limb

924.5 Unspecified part of lower limb
   Leg NOS

924.8 Multiple sites, not elsewhere classified
   AHA: 1Q, '03, 7
   S70.10xA Contusion of unspecified thigh initial encounter   I-10

924.9 Unspecified site

Crushing Injury (925-929)

Use additional code to identify any associated injuries, such as:
   fractures (800-829)
   internal injuries (860.0-869.1)
   intracranial injuries (850.0-854.1)
   AHA: 4Q, '03, 77; 2Q, '93, 7

✓4ᵗʰ 925 Crushing injury of face, scalp, and neck
Cheek	Pharynx
Ear	Throat
Larynx	

    925.1 Crushing injury of face and scalp   CC
      Cheek
      Ear
      CC Excl: 873.8-873.9, 905.0, 925.1-925.2, 929.0-929.9, 958.8-959.09, 959.8-959.9

    925.2 Crushing injury of neck   CC
      Larynx   Throat
      Pharynx
      CC Excl: See code: 925.1

✓4ᵗʰ 926 Crushing injury of trunk

    926.0 External genitalia
    | Labium (majus) (minus) | Testis |
    | Penis | Vulva |
    | Scrotum | |

✓5ᵗʰ 926.1 Other specified sites

    926.11 Back

    926.12 Buttock

| ✓4ᵗʰ ✓5ᵗʰ Additional Digit Required | Unacceptable PDx | Manifestation Code | Hospital Acquired Condition | ◄► Revised Text | ● New Code | ▲ Revised Code Title |

Injury and Poisoning

926.19–939.9

926.19 **Other**
Breast

926.8 **Multiple sites of trunk**

926.9 **Unspecified site**
Trunk NOS

✓4th 927 **Crushing injury of upper limb**

  ✓5th 927.0 **Shoulder and upper arm**

    927.00 **Shoulder region**

    927.01 **Scapular region**

    927.02 **Axillary region**

    927.03 **Upper arm**

    927.09 **Multiple sites**

  ✓5th 927.1 **Elbow and forearm**

    927.10 **Forearm**

    927.11 **Elbow**

  ✓5th 927.2 **Wrist and hand(s), except finger(s) alone**

    927.20 **Hand(s)**

    927.21 **Wrist**

  927.3 **Finger(s)**
AHA: 4Q, '03, 77

  927.8 **Multiple sites of upper limb**

  927.9 **Unspecified site**
Arm NOS

✓4th 928 **Crushing injury of lower limb**

  ✓5th 928.0 **Hip and thigh**

    928.00 **Thigh**   `CC`
    CC Excl: 928.00, 928.8-929.9

    928.01 **Hip**   `CC`
    CC Excl: 928.01, 928.8-929.9

  ✓5th 928.1 **Knee and lower leg**

    928.10 **Lower leg**

    928.11 **Knee**

  ✓5th 928.2 **Ankle and foot, excluding toe(s) alone**

    928.20 **Foot**
    Heel

    928.21 **Ankle**

  928.3 **Toe(s)**

  928.8 **Multiple sites of lower limb**

  928.9 **Unspecified site**
Leg NOS

✓4th 929 **Crushing injury of multiple and unspecified sites**

  929.0 **Multiple sites, not elsewhere classified**

  929.9 **Unspecified site**

Effects of Foreign Body Entering Through Orifice (930-939)

EXCLUDES foreign body:
  granuloma (728.82)
  inadvertently left in operative wound (998.4, 998.7)
  in open wound (800-839, 851-897)
  residual in soft tissues (729.6)
  superficial without major open wound (910-919
    with .6 or .7)

✓4th 930 **Foreign body on external eye**

EXCLUDES foreign body in penetrating wound of:
  eyeball (871.5-871.6)
    retained (old) (360.5-360.6)
  ocular adnexa (870.4)
    retained (old) (376.6)

  930.0 **Corneal foreign body**

  930.1 **Foreign body in conjunctival sac**

  930.2 **Foreign body in lacrimal punctum**

930.8 **Other and combined sites**

930.9 **Unspecified site**
External eye NOS

931 **Foreign body in ear**
Auditory canal
Auricle

932 **Foreign body in nose**
Nasal sinus
Nostril

✓4th 933 **Foreign body in pharynx and larynx**

  933.0 **Pharynx**
Nasopharynx
Throat NOS

  933.1 **Larynx**
Asphyxia due to foreign body
Choking due to:
  food (regurgitated)
  phlegm
TIP: Assign for mucous plug causing asphyxia; otherwise, for tracheobronchial, refer to code 519.19 Other diseases of trachea and bronchus.

✓4th 934 **Foreign body in trachea, bronchus, and lung**

  934.0 **Trachea**   `CC`
  CC Excl: 934.0

  934.1 **Main bronchus**   `CC`
  CC Excl: 934.0-934.9
  AHA: 3Q, '02, 18

  934.8 **Other specified parts**   `CC`
Bronchioles
Lung
  CC Excl: See code: 934.1

  934.9 **Respiratory tree, unspecified**
Inhalation of liquid or vomitus, lower respiratory tract NOS

✓4th 935 **Foreign body in mouth, esophagus, and stomach**

  935.0 **Mouth**

  935.1 **Esophagus**
  AHA: 1Q, '88, 13
  TIP: If esophageal obstruction is due to stenosis, caustic stricture (e.g., lye ingestion), or tumor, assign instead code 530.3.

  935.2 **Stomach**

936 **Foreign body in intestine and colon**

937 **Foreign body in anus and rectum**
Rectosigmoid (junction)

938 **Foreign body in digestive system, unspecified**
Alimentary tract NOS
Swallowed foreign body

✓4th 939 **Foreign body in genitourinary tract**

  939.0 **Bladder and urethra**

  939.1 **Uterus, any part**   ♀
EXCLUDES intrauterine contraceptive device:
  complications from (996.32, 996.65)
  presence of (V45.51)

  939.2 **Vulva and vagina**   ♀

  939.3 **Penis**   ♂

  939.9 **Unspecified site**

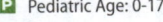
`N` Newborn Age: 0   `P` Pediatric Age: 0-17   `M` Maternity Age: 12-55   `A` Adult Age: 15-124   `MCC` Major CC Condition   `CC` CC Condition   `HIV` HIV Related Dx

326 – Volume 1   2015 ICD-9-CM

Burns (940-949)

INCLUDES   burns from:
  electrical heating appliance
  electricity
  flame
  hot object
  lightning
  radiation
  chemical burns (external) (internal)
  scalds

EXCLUDES   *friction burns (910-919 with .0, .1)*
  sunburn (692.71, 692.76-692.77)

AHA: 4Q, 94, 22; 2Q, '90, 7; 4Q, '88, 3; M-A, '86, 9
TIP: Nonhealing burns are coded as acute burns, as is necrosis of burned skin. Assign code 958.3 for any documented infected burn site.

✓4th **940 Burn confined to eye and adnexa**

940.0 Chemical burn of eyelids and periocular area

940.1 Other burns of eyelids and periocular area

940.2 Alkaline chemical burn of cornea and conjunctival sac

940.3 Acid chemical burn of cornea and conjunctival sac

940.4 Other burn of cornea and conjunctival sac

940.5 Burn with resulting rupture and destruction of eyeball [CC]
  CC Excl: No exclusion

940.9 Unspecified burn of eye and adnexa

✓4th **941 Burn of face, head, and neck**

EXCLUDES   *mouth (947.0)*

The following fifth-digit subclassification is for use with category 941:
  0 face and head, unspecified site
  1 ear [any part]
  2 eye (with other parts of face, head, and neck)
  3 lip(s)
  4 chin
  5 nose (septum)
  6 scalp [any part]
    Temple (region)
  7 forehead and cheek
  8 neck
  9 multiple sites [except with eye] of face, head, and neck

AHA: 4Q, '94, 22; M-A, '86, 9

§ ✓5th **941.0 Unspecified degree**
  [0-9]

§ ✓5th **941.1 Erythema [first degree]**
  [0-9]   **AHA: For code 941.19:** 3Q, '10, 19; 3Q, '05, 10

§ ✓5th **941.2 Blisters, epidermal loss [second degree]**
  [0-9]

§ ✓5th **941.3 Full-thickness skin loss [third degree NOS]** [CC]
  [0-9]   **CC Excl: For code 941.30:** 941.30, 941.39; **For code 941.31:** 941.31, 941.39; **For code 941.32:** 941.32, 941.39; **For code 941.33:** 941.33, 941.39; **For code 941.34:** 941.34, 941.39; **For code 941.35:** 941.35, 941.39; **For code 941.36:** 941.36, 941.39; **For code 941.37:** 941.37, 941.39; **For code 941.38:** 941.38-941.39; **For code 941.39:** 941.30-941.39

§ ✓5th **941.4 Deep necrosis of underlying tissues [deep third degree] without mention of loss of a body part** [CC]
  [0-9]
  CC Excl: For code 941.40, 941.49: 941.40, 941.49; **For code 941.41:** 941.40-941.41, 941.49; **For code 941.42:** 941.40, 941.42, 941.49; **For code 941.43:** 941.40, 941.43, 941.49; **For code 941.44:** 941.40, 941.44, 941.49; **For code 941.45:** 941.40, 941.45, 941.49; **For code 941.46:** 941.40, 941.46, 941.49; **For code 941.47:** 941.40, 941.47, 941.49; **For code 941.48:** 941.40, 941.48-941.49

§ ✓5th **941.5 Deep necrosis of underlying tissues [deep third degree] with loss of a body part** [CC]
  [0-9]
  CC Excl: For code 941.50, 941.59: 941.50, 941.59; **For code 941.51:** 941.50-941.51, 941.59; **For code 941.52:** 941.50, 941.52, 941.59; **For code 941.53:** 941.50, 941.53, 941.59; **For code 941.54:** 941.50, 941.54, 941.59; **For code 941.55:** 941.50, 941.55, 941.59; **For code 941.56:** 941.50, 941.56, 941.59; **For code 941.57:** 941.50, 941.57, 941.59; **For code 941.58:** 941.50, 941.58-941.59

✓4th **942 Burn of trunk**

EXCLUDES   *scapular region (943.0-943.5 with fifth-digit 6)*

The following fifth-digit subclassificaiton is for use with category 942:
  0 trunk, unspecified
  1 breast
  2 chest wall, excluding breast and nipple
  3 abdominal wall
    Flank
    Groin
  4 back [any part]
    Buttock
    Interscapular region
  5 genitalia
    Labium (majus) (minus)
    Penis
    Perineum
    Scrotum
    Testis
    Vulva
  9 other and multiple sites of trunk

AHA: 4Q, '94, 22; M-A, '86, 9

§ ✓5th **942.0 Unspecified degree**
  [0-5, 9]

§ ✓5th **942.1 Erythema [first degree]**
  [0-5, 9]

§ ✓5th **942.2 Blisters, epidermal loss [second degree]**
  [0-5, 9]

§ ✓5th **942.3 Full-thickness skin loss [third degree NOS]** [CC]
  [0-5, 9]   **CC Excl: For code 942.30, 942.39:** 942.30, 942.39; **For code 942.31:** 942.30-942.31, 942.39; **For code 942.32:** 942.30, 942.32, 942.39; **For code 942.33:** 942.30, 942.33, 942.39; **For code 942.34:** 942.30, 942.34, 942.39; **For code 942.35:** 942.30, 942.35-942.39

§ ✓5th **942.4 Deep necrosis of underlying tissues [deep third degree] without mention of loss of a body part** [CC]
  [0-5, 9]
  CC Excl: For code 942.40: 942.40, 942.49; **For code 942.41:** 942.40-942.41, 942.49; **For code 942.42:** 942.40, 942.42, 942.49; **For code 942.43:** 942.40, 942.43, 942.49; **For code 942.44:** 942.40, 942.44, 942.49; **For code 942.45:** 942.40, 942.45-942.49; **For code 942.49:** 942.40-942.49

§ ✓5th **942.5 Deep necrosis of underlying tissues [deep third degree] with loss of a body part** [CC]
  [0-5, 9]
  CC Excl: For code 942.50: 942.50, 942.59; **For code 942.51:** 942.50-942.51, 942.59; **For code 942.52:** 942.50, 942.52, 942.59; **For code 942.53:** 942.50, 942.53, 942.59; **For code 942.54:** 942.50, 942.54, 942.59; **For code 942.55:** 942.50, 942.55-942.59; **For code 942.59:** 942.50, 942.59

✓4th **943 Burn of upper limb, except wrist and hand**

The following fifth-digit subclassificaiton is for use with category 943:
  0 upper limb, unspecified site
  1 forearm
  2 elbow
  3 upper arm
  4 axilla
  5 shoulder
  6 scapular region
  9 multiple sites of upper limb, except wrist and hand

AHA: 4Q, '94, 22; M-A, '86, 9

§ ✓5th **943.0 Unspecified degree**
  [0-6, 9]   **AHA: For code 943.00:** 3Q, '10, 19

§ ✓5th **943.1 Erythema [first degree]**
  [0-6, 9]

§ ✓5th **943.2 Blisters, epidermal loss [second degree]**
  [0-6, 9]

§ ✓5th **943.3 Full-thickness skin loss [third degree NOS]** [CC]
  [0-6, 9]   **CC Excl: For code 943.30, 943.39:** 943.30, 943.39; **For code 943.31:** 943.30-943.31, 943.39; **For code 943.32:** 943.30, 943.32, 943.39; **For code 943.33:** 943.30, 943.33, 943.39; **For code 943.34:** 943.30, 943.34, 943.39; **For code 943.35:** 943.30, 943.35, 943.39; **For code 943.36:** 943.30, 943.36-943.39

§ ✓5th **943.4 Deep necrosis of underlying tissues [deep third degree] without mention of loss of a body part** [CC]
  [0-6, 9]
  CC Excl: For code 943.40, 943.49: 943.40, 943.49; **For code 943.41:** 943.40-943.41, 943.49; **For code 943.42:** 943.40, 943.42, 943.49; **For code 943.43:** 943.40, 943.43, 943.49; **For code 943.44:** 943.40, 943.44, 943.49; **For code 943.45:** 943.40, 943.45, 943.49; **For code 943.46:** 943.40, 943.46-943.49

---

§   Requires fifth digit. Valid digits are in [brackets] under each code. See appropriate category for codes and definitions.

✓4th / ✓5th   Additional Digit Required   Unacceptable PDx   Manifestation Code   Hospital Acquired Condition   ▶◀ Revised Text   ● New Code   ▲ Revised Code Title

§ ✓5th **943.5** **Deep necrosis of underlying tissues [deep third degree] with loss of a body part** `CC`
[0-6, 9]

> **CC Excl:** For code 943.50, 943.59: 943.50, 943.59; For code 943.51: 943.50-943.51, 943.59; For code 943.52: 943.50, 943.52, 943.59; For code 943.53: 943.50, 943.53, 943.59; For code 943.54: 943.50, 943.54, 943.59; For code 943.55: 943.50, 943.55, 943.59; For code 943.56: 943.50, 943.56-943.59

✓4th **944** **Burn of wrist(s) and hand(s)**

> The following fifth-digit subclassification is for use with category 944:
> 0   hand, unspecified site
> 1   single digit [finger (nail)] other than thumb
> 2   thumb (nail)
> 3   two or more digits, not including thumb
> 4   two or more digits including thumb
> 5   palm
> 6   back of hand
> 7   wrist
> 8   multiple sites of wrist(s) and hand(s)

§ ✓5th **944.0** **Unspecified degree**
[0-8]

§ ✓5th **944.1** **Erythema [first degree]**
[0-8]

§ ✓5th **944.2** **Blisters, epidermal loss [second degree]**
[0-8]

§ ✓5th **944.3** **Full-thickness skin loss [third degree NOS]** `CC`
[0-8]

> **CC Excl:** For code 944.30, 944.38: 944.30, 944.38; For code 944.31: 944.30-944.31, 944.38; For code 944.32: 944.30, 944.32, 944.38; For code 944.33: 944.30, 944.33, 944.38; For code 944.34: 944.30, 944.34, 944.38; For code 944.35: 944.30, 944.35, 944.38; For code 944.36: 944.30, 944.36, 944.38; For code 944.37: 944.30, 944.37-944.38

§ ✓5th **944.4** **Deep necrosis of underlying tissues [deep third degree] without mention of loss of a body part** `CC`
[0-8]

> **CC Excl:** For code 944.40, 944.48: 944.40, 944.48; For code 944.41: 944.40-944.41, 944.48; For code 944.42: 944.40, 944.42, 944.48; For code 944.43: 944.40, 944.43, 944.48; For code 944.44: 944.40, 944.44, 944.48; For code 944.45: 944.40, 944.45, 944.48; For code 944.46: 944.40, 944.46, 944.48; For code 944.47: 944.40, 944.47-944.48

§ ✓5th **944.5** **Deep necrosis of underlying tissues [deep third degree] with loss of a body part** `CC`
[0-8]

> **CC Excl:** For code 944.50, 944.58: 944.50, 944.58; For code 944.51: 944.50-944.51, 944.58; For code 944.52: 944.50, 944.52, 944.58; For code 944.53: 944.50, 944.53, 944.58; For code 944.54: 944.50, 944.54, 944.58; For code 944.55: 944.50, 944.55, 944.58; For code 944.56: 944.50, 944.56, 944.58; For code 944.57: 944.50, 944.57-944.58

✓4th **945** **Burn of lower limb(s)**

> The following fifth-digit subclassification is for use with category 945:
> 0   lower limb [leg], unspecified site
> 1   toe(s) (nail)
> 2   foot
> 3   ankle
> 4   lower leg
> 5   knee
> 6   thigh [any part]
> 9   multiple sites of lower limb(s)

> **AHA:** 4Q, '94, 22; M-A, '86, 9

§ ✓5th **945.0** **Unspecified degree**
[0-6, 9]

§ ✓5th **945.1** **Erythema [first degree]**
[0-6, 9]

§ ✓5th **945.2** **Blisters, epidermal loss [second degree]**
[0-6, 9]

§ ✓5th **945.3** **Full-thickness skin loss [third degree NOS]** `CC`
[0-6, 9]

> **CC Excl:** For code 945.30, 945.39: 945.30, 945.39; For code 945.31: 945.30-945.31, 945.39; For code 945.32: 945.30, 945.32, 945.39; For code 945.33: 945.30, 945.33, 945.39; For code 945.34: 945.30, 945.34, 945.39; For code 945.35: 945.30, 945.35, 945.39; For code 945.36: 945.30, 945.36-945.39

§ ✓5th **945.4** **Deep necrosis of underlying tissues [deep third degree] without mention of loss of a body part** `CC`
[0-6, 9]

> **CC Excl:** For code 945.40, 945.49: 945.40, 945.49; For code 945.41: 945.40-945.41, 945.49; For code 945.42: 945.40, 945.42, 945.49; For code 945.43: 945.40, 945.43, 945.49; For code 945.44: 945.40, 945.44, 945.49; For code 945.45: 945.40, 945.45, 945.49; For code 945.46: 945.40, 945.46-945.49

§ ✓5th **945.5** **Deep necrosis of underlying tissues [deep third degree] with loss of a body part** `CC`
[0-6, 9]

> **CC Excl:** For code 945.50, 945.59: 945.50, 945.59; For code 945.51: 945.50-945.51, 945.59; For code 945.52: 945.50, 945.52, 945.59; For code 945.53: 945.50, 945.53, 945.59; For code 945.54: 945.50, 945.54, 945.59; For code 945.55: 945.50, 945.55, 945.59; For code 945.56: 945.50, 945.56-945.59

✓4th **946** **Burns of multiple specified sites**

> **INCLUDES** burns of sites classifiable to more than one three-digit category in 940-945
> **EXCLUDES** multiple burns NOS (949.0-949.5)
> **AHA:** 4Q, '94, 22; M-A, '86, 9
> **TIP:** Only assign if the specific sites of the multiple burns are not specified.

946.0 **Unspecified degree**

946.1 **Erythema [first degree]**

946.2 **Blisters, epidermal loss [second degree]**

946.3 **Full-thickness skin loss [third degree NOS]** `CC`

> **CC Excl:** 946.3

946.4 **Deep necrosis of underlying tissues [deep third degree] without mention of loss of a body part** `CC`

> **CC Excl:** 946.4

946.5 **Deep necrosis of underlying tissues [deep third degree] with loss of a body part** `CC`

> **CC Excl:** 946.5

✓4th **947** **Burn of internal organs**

> **INCLUDES** burns from chemical agents (ingested)
> **AHA:** 4Q, '94, 22; M-A, '86, 9

947.0 **Mouth and pharynx**
> Gum   Tongue

947.1 **Larynx, trachea, and lung** `CC`

> **CC Excl:** 947.1, 947.8-947.9

947.2 **Esophagus** `CC`

> **CC Excl:** 947.2, 947.8-947.9

947.3 **Gastrointestinal tract** `CC`

> Colon   Small intestine
> Rectum   Stomach
> **CC Excl:** 947.3, 947.8-947.9
> **AHA:** 2Q, '12, 8

947.4 **Vagina and uterus** `CC` ♀

> **CC Excl:** 947.4-947.9

947.8 **Other specified sites**

947.9 **Unspecified site**

✓4th **948** **Burns classified according to extent of body surface involved**

> **NOTE** This category is to be used when the site of the burn is unspecified, or with categories 940-947 when the site is specified.
> **EXCLUDES** sunburn (692.71, 692.76-692.77)

> The following fifth-digit subclassification is for use with category 948 to indicate the percent of body surface with third degree burn; valid digits are in [brackets] under each code:
> 0   **less than 10 percent or unspecified**
> 1   10-19%
> 2   20-29%
> 3   30-39%
> 4   40-49%
> 5   50-59%
> 6   60-69%
> 7   70-79%
> 8   80-89%
> 9   **90% or more of body surface**

> **AHA:** 4Q, '94, 22; 4Q, '88, 3; M-A, '86, 9; N-D, '84, 13

§ ✓5th **948.0** **Burn [any degree] involving less than 10 percent of body surface**
[0]

> T31.0 Burns involving less than 10% of body surface `I-10`

---

§   Requires fifth digit. Valid digits are in [brackets] under each code. See appropriate category for codes and definitions.

`N` Newborn Age: 0   `P` Pediatric Age: 0-17   `M` Maternity Age: 12-55   `A` Adult Age: 15-124   `MCC` Major CC Condition   `CC` CC Condition   `HIV` HIV Related Dx

328 – Volume 1   **2015 ICD-9-CM**

Burns
Degrees of Burns

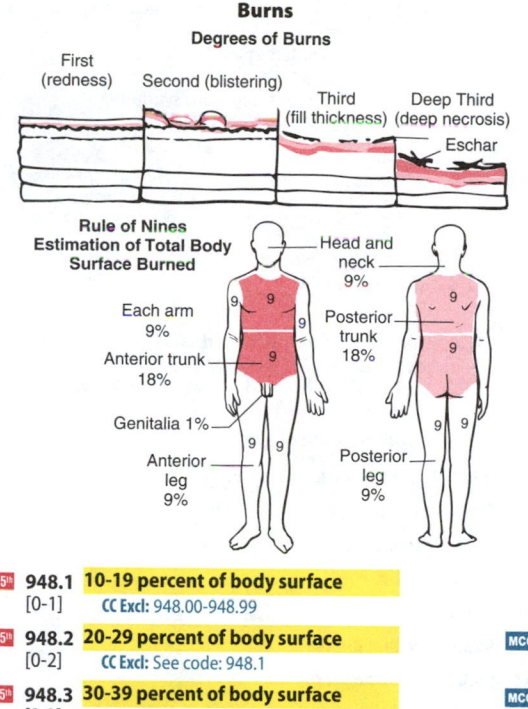

First (redness)
Second (blistering)
Third (fill thickness)
Deep Third (deep necrosis)
Eschar

Rule of Nines
Estimation of Total Body Surface Burned

Head and neck 9%
Each arm 9%
Anterior trunk 18%
Genitalia 1%
Anterior leg 9%
Posterior trunk 18%
Posterior leg 9%

---

[10] § ✓5th **948.1** **10-19 percent of body surface**   `CC 0-1`
[0-1]   CC Excl: 948.00-948.99

[10] § ✓5th **948.2** **20-29 percent of body surface**   `MCC 1-2` `CC 0`
[0-2]   CC Excl: See code: 948.1

[10] § ✓5th **948.3** **30-39 percent of body surface**   `MCC 1-3` `CC 0`
[0-3]   CC Excl: See code: 948.1

[10] § ✓5th **948.4** **40-49 percent of body surface**   `MCC 1-4` `CC 0`
[0-4]   CC Excl: See code: 948.1

[10] § ✓5th **948.5** **50-59 percent of body surface**   `MCC 1-5` `CC 0`
[0-5]   CC Excl: See code: 948.1

[10] § ✓5th **948.6** **60-69 percent of body surface**   `MCC 1-6` `CC 0`
[0-6]   CC Excl: See code: 948.1

[10] § ✓5th **948.7** **70-79 percent of body surface**   `MCC 1-7` `CC 0`
[0-7]   CC Excl: See code: 948.1

[10] § ✓5th **948.8** **80-89 percent of body surface**   `MCC 1-8` `CC 0`
[0-8]   CC Excl: See code: 948.1

[10] § ✓5th **948.9** **90 percent or more of body surface**   `MCC 1-9` `CC 0`
[0-9]   CC Excl: See code: 948.1

✓4th **949** **Burn, unspecified**

INCLUDES   burn NOS
        multiple burns NOS

EXCLUDES   burn of unspecified site but with statement of the extent of body surface involved (948.0-948.9)

AHA: 4Q, '94, 22; M-A, '86, 9

949.0 **Unspecified degree**

949.1 **Erythema [first degree]**

949.2 **Blisters, epidermal loss [second degree]**

949.3 **Full-thickness skin loss [third degree NOS]**   `CC`
CC Excl: 941.30-941.39, 942.30-942.39, 944.30-944.38, 945.30-945.39, 946.3, 949.3

949.4 **Deep necrosis of underlying tissues [deep third degree] without mention of loss of a body part**   `CC`
CC Excl: 941.40-941.49, 942.40-942.49, 944.40-944.48, 945.40-945.49, 946.4, 949.4

949.5 **Deep necrosis of underlying tissues [deep third degree] with loss of a body part**   `CC`
CC Excl: 946.5, 949.5

Injury to Nerves and Spinal Cord (950-957)

INCLUDES   division of nerve
        lesion in continuity   } (with open wound)
        traumatic neuroma
        traumatic transient paralysis

EXCLUDES   accidental puncture or laceration during medical procedure (998.2)

✓4th **950** **Injury to optic nerve and pathways**

950.0 **Optic nerve injury**   `CC`
   Second cranial nerve
   CC Excl: 950.0-950.9, 951.8-951.9

950.1 **Injury to optic chiasm**   `CC`
   CC Excl: See code: 950.0

950.2 **Injury to optic pathways**   `CC`
   CC Excl: See code: 950.0

950.3 **Injury to visual cortex**   `CC`
   CC Excl: See code: 950.0

950.9 **Unspecified**   `CC`
   Traumatic blindness NOS
   CC Excl: See code: 950.0

✓4th **951** **Injury to other cranial nerve(s)**

951.0 **Injury to oculomotor nerve**   `CC`
   Third cranial nerve
   CC Excl: 951.0, 951.8-951.9

951.1 **Injury to trochlear nerve**   `CC`
   Fourth cranial nerve
   CC Excl: 951.1, 951.8-951.9

951.2 **Injury to trigeminal nerve**   `CC`
   Fifth cranial nerve
   CC Excl: 951.2, 951.8-951.9

951.3 **Injury to abducens nerve**   `CC`
   Sixth cranial nerve
   CC Excl: 951.3, 951.8-951.9

951.4 **Injury to facial nerve**   `CC`
   Seventh cranial nerve
   CC Excl: 951.4, 951.8-951.9

951.5 **Injury to acoustic nerve**   `CC`
   Auditory nerve
   Eighth cranial nerve
   Traumatic deafness NOS
   CC Excl: 951.5, 951.8-951.9

951.6 **Injury to accessory nerve**   `CC`
   Eleventh cranial nerve
   CC Excl: 951.6, 951.8-951.9

951.7 **Injury to hypoglossal nerve**   `CC`
   Twelfth cranial nerve
   CC Excl: 951.7-951.9

951.8 **Injury to other specified cranial nerves**   `CC`
   Glossopharyngeal [9th cranial] nerve
   Olfactory [1st cranial] nerve
   Pneumogastric [10th cranial] nerve
   Traumatic anosmia NOS
   Vagus [10th cranial] nerve
   CC Excl: 951.8-951.9

951.9 **Injury to unspecified cranial nerve**   `CC`
   CC Excl: See code: 951.8

✓4th **952** **Spinal cord injury without evidence of spinal bone injury**

✓5th **952.0** **Cervical**

952.00 **C$_1$-C$_4$ level with unspecified spinal cord injury**   `MCC`
   Spinal cord injury, cervical region NOS
   CC Excl: 805.00-805.18, 805.8-806.19, 806.8-806.9, 839.00-839.18, 839.40, 839.49-839.50, 839.59, 839.69, 839.79-839.9, 847.9, 905.1, 926.11, 952.00-952.09, 952.8-952.9, 958.8-958.99, 959.11-959.19, 959.8-959.9

952.01 **C$_1$-C$_4$ level with complete lesion of spinal cord**   `MCC`
   CC Excl: See code 952.00

---

[10] HAC = only for valid CC or MCC codes.
§   Requires fifth digit. Valid digits are in [brackets] under each code. See appropriate category for codes and definitions.

✓4th ✓5th   Additional Digit Required   Unacceptable PDx   Manifestation Code   Hospital Acquired Condition   ▶◀ Revised Text   ● New Code   ▲ Revised Code Title

Injury and Poisoning

952.02–957.1

952.02 C₁-C₄ level with anterior cord syndrome `MCC`
CC Excl: See code 952.00

952.03 C₁-C₄ level with central cord syndrome `MCC`
CC Excl: See code 952.00

952.04 C₁-C₄ level with other specified spinal cord injury `MCC`
Incomplete spinal cord lesion at C₁-C₄ level:
NOS
with posterior cord syndrome
CC Excl: See code 952.00

952.05 C₅-C₇ level with unspecified spinal cord injury `MCC`
CC Excl: See code 952.00

952.06 C₅-C₇ level with complete lesion of spinal cord `MCC`
CC Excl: See code 952.00

952.07 C₅-C₇ level with anterior cord syndrome `MCC`
CC Excl: See code 952.00

952.08 C₅-C₇ level with central cord syndrome `MCC`
CC Excl: See code 952.00

952.09 C₅-C₇ level with other specified spinal cord injury `MCC`
Incomplete spinal cord lesion at C₅-C₇ level:
NOS
with posterior cord syndrome
CC Excl: See code 952.00

√5ᵗʰ **952.1 Dorsal [thoracic]**

952.10 T₁-T₆ level with unspecified spinal cord injury `MCC`
Spinal cord injury, thoracic region NOS
CC Excl: 805.8-805.9, 806.20-806.39, 839.40, 839.49-839.50,
839.59, 839.69, 839.79-839.9, 847.9, 905.1, 926.11,
952.10-952.19, 952.8-952.9, 958.8-958.99, 959.11-959.19,
959.8-959.9

952.11 T₁-T₆ level with complete lesion of spinal cord `MCC`
CC Excl: See code 952.10

952.12 T₁-T₆ level with anterior cord syndrome `MCC`
CC Excl: See code 952.10

952.13 T₁-T₆ level with central cord syndrome `MCC`
CC Excl: See code 952.10

952.14 T₁-T₆ level with other specified spinal cord injury `MCC`
Incomplete spinal cord lesion at T₁-T₆ level:
NOS
with posterior cord syndrome
CC Excl: See code 952.10

952.15 T₇-T₁₂ level with unspecified spinal cord injury `MCC`
CC Excl: See code 952.10

952.16 T₇-T₁₂ level with complete lesion of spinal cord `MCC`
CC Excl: See code 952.10

952.17 T₇-T₁₂ level with anterior cord syndrome `MCC`
CC Excl: See code 952.10

952.18 T₇-T₁₂ level with central cord syndrome `MCC`
CC Excl: See code 952.10

952.19 T₁-T₁₂ level with other specified spinal cord injury `MCC`
Incomplete spinal cord lesion at T₇-T₁₂ level:
NOS
with posterior cord syndrome
CC Excl: See code 952.10

952.2 Lumbar `MCC`
CC Excl: 805.8-805.9, 806.4-806.5, 839.40, 839.49-839.50, 839.59,
839.69, 839.79-839.9, 847.9, 905.1, 926.11, 952.2,
952.8-952.9,958.8-958.99, 959.11-959.19, 959.8-959.9

952.3 Sacral `MCC`

952.4 Cauda equina `MCC`
CC Excl: See code 952.3

952.8 Multiple sites of spinal cord `MCC`
CC Excl: 805.8-805.9, 839.40, 839.49-839.50, 839.59, 839.69,
839.79-839.9, 847.9, 905.1, 926.11, 952.8-952.9, 958.8-958.99,
959.11-959.19, 959.8-959.9

952.9 Unspecified site of spinal cord

√4ᵗʰ **953 Injury to nerve roots and spinal plexus**

953.0 Cervical root

953.1 Dorsal root

953.2 Lumbar root

953.3 Sacral root

953.4 Brachial plexus

953.5 Lumbosacral plexus

953.8 Multiple sites

953.9 Unspecified site

√4ᵗʰ **954 Injury to other nerve(s) of trunk, excluding shoulder and pelvic girdles**

954.0 Cervical sympathetic

954.1 Other sympathetic
Celiac ganglion or plexus
Inferior mesenteric plexus
Splanchnic nerve(s)
Stellate ganglion

954.8 Other specified nerve(s) of trunk

954.9 Unspecified nerve of trunk

√4ᵗʰ **955 Injury to peripheral nerve(s) of shoulder girdle and upper limb**

955.0 Axillary nerve

955.1 Median nerve

955.2 Ulnar nerve

955.3 Radial nerve

955.4 Musculocutaneous nerve

955.5 Cutaneous sensory nerve, upper limb

955.6 Digital nerve

955.7 Other specified nerve(s) of shoulder girdle and upper limb

955.8 Multiple nerves of shoulder girdle and upper limb

955.9 Unspecified nerve of shoulder girdle and upper limb

√4ᵗʰ **956 Injury to peripheral nerve(s) of pelvic girdle and lower limb**

956.0 Sciatic nerve

956.1 Femoral nerve

956.2 Posterior tibial nerve

956.3 Peroneal nerve

956.4 Cutaneous sensory nerve, lower limb

956.5 Other specified nerve(s) of pelvic girdle and lower limb

956.8 Multiple nerves of pelvic girdle and lower limb

956.9 Unspecified nerve of pelvic girdle and lower limb

√4ᵗʰ **957 Injury to other and unspecified nerves**

957.0 Superficial nerves of head and neck

957.1 Other specified nerve(s)

Spinal Nerve Roots

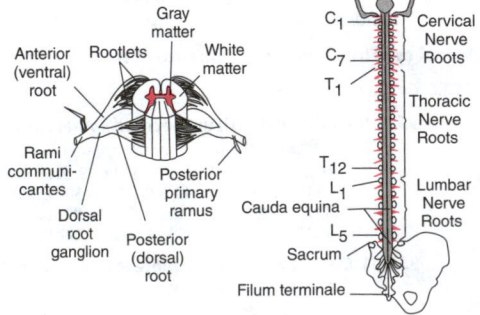

Gray matter
Anterior (ventral) root
Rootlets
White matter
Rami communi-cantes
Dorsal root ganglion
Posterior primary ramus
Posterior (dorsal) root

C₁
C₇
T₁
T₁₂
L₁
L₅
Cervical Nerve Roots
Thoracic Nerve Roots
Cauda equina
Lumbar Nerve Roots
Sacrum
Filum terminale

`N` Newborn Age: 0   `P` Pediatric Age: 0-17   `M` Maternity Age: 12-55   `A` Adult Age: 15-124   `MCC` Major CC Condition   `CC` CC Condition   `HIV` HIV Related Dx

957.8 Multiple nerves in several parts
Multiple nerve injury NOS

957.9 Unspecified site
Nerve injury NOS

Certain Traumatic Complications and Unspecified Injuries (958-959)

√4ᵗʰ **958 Certain early complications of trauma**
> EXCLUDES   adult respiratory distress syndrome (518.52)
> flail chest (807.4)
> post-traumatic seroma (729.91)
> shock lung related to trauma and surgery (518.52)
> that occurring during or following medical procedures (996.0-999.9)

958.0 Air embolism   `MCC`
Pneumathemia
> EXCLUDES   that complicating:
> abortion (634-638 with .6, 639.6)
> ectopic or molar pregnancy (639.6)
> pregnancy, childbirth, or the puerperium (673.0)

DEF: Arterial obstruction due to introduction of air bubbles into the veins following surgery or trauma.
CC Excl: 958.0, 958.8-958.99, 959.8-959.9, 997.91-997.99, 998.81, 998.83-998.9, 999.1

958.1 Fat embolism   `MCC`
> EXCLUDES   that complicating:
> abortion (634-638 with .6, 639.6)
> pregnancy, childbirth, or the puerperium (673.8)

DEF: Arterial blockage due to the entrance of fat in circulatory system, after fracture of large bones or administration of corticosteroids.
CC Excl: 958.1, 958.8-958.99, 959.8-959.9, 997.91-997.99, 998.81, 998.83-998.9

958.2 Secondary and recurrent hemorrhage   `CC`
CC Excl: 958.2, 958.8-958.99, 959.8-959.9, 997.91-997.99, 998.81, 998.83-998.9

958.3 Posttraumatic wound infection, not elsewhere classified   `CC`
> EXCLUDES   infected open wounds — code to complicated open wound of site

CC Excl: 958.3, 958.8-958.99, 959.8-959.9, 997.91-997.99, 998.81, 998.83-998.9
AHA: 4Q, '01, 53; S-O, '85, 10
TIP: Do not assign if the infection is documented as due to cellulitis; see instead categories 681 and 682 and complicated wound codes.

958.4 Traumatic shock   `MCC`
Shock (immediate) (delayed) following injury
> EXCLUDES   shock:
> anaphylactic (995.0)
> due to serum (999.41-999.49)
> anesthetic (995.4)
> electric (994.8)
> following abortion (639.5)
> lightning (994.0)
> nontraumatic NOS (785.50)
> obstetric (669.1)
> postoperative (998.00-998.09)

DEF: Shock, immediate or delayed following injury.
CC Excl: 958.4, 958.8-958.99, 959.8-959.9, 997.91-997.99, 998.81, 998.83-998.9

958.5 Traumatic anuria   `MCC`
Crush syndrome
Renal failure following crushing
> EXCLUDES   that due to a medical procedure (997.5)

DEF: Complete suppression of urinary secretion by kidneys due to trauma.
CC Excl: 958.5, 958.8-958.99, 959.8-959.9, 995.4, 997.91-998.13, 998.81, 998.83-998.9

958.6 Volkmann's ischemic contracture
Posttraumatic muscle contracture
DEF: Muscle deterioration due to loss of blood supply from injury or tourniquet; causes muscle contraction and results in inability to extend the muscles fully.

958.7 Traumatic subcutaneous emphysema   `CC`
> EXCLUDES   subcutaneous emphysema resulting from a procedure (998.81)

CC Excl: 860.0-860.5, 861.20-862.1, 862.29-862.9, 875.0-875.1, 958.7-958.99, 959.8-959.9, 997.91-997.99, 998.81, 998.83-998.9

958.8 Other early complications of trauma
AHA: 2Q, '92, 13

√5ᵗʰ **958.9 Traumatic compartment syndrome**
> EXCLUDES   nontraumatic compartment syndrome (729.71-729.79)

DEF: Compression of nerves and blood vessels within an enclosed space due to previous trauma, which leads to impaired blood flow and muscle and nerve damage.
TIP: If the compartment syndrome is specified as chronic or exercise-induced, see instead subcategory 729.7.

958.90 Compartment syndrome, unspecified   `CC`
CC Excl: 868.03-868.10, 868.13-869.1
AHA: 4Q, '06, 100-102

958.91 Traumatic compartment syndrome of upper extremity   `CC`
Traumatic compartment syndrome of shoulder, arm, forearm, wrist, hand, and fingers
CC Excl: 729.81, 729.89-729.99
AHA: 4Q, '06, 100-102

958.92 Traumatic compartment syndrome of lower extremity   `CC`
Traumatic compartment syndrome of hip, buttock, thigh, leg, foot, and toes
CC Excl: See code: 958.91
AHA: 4Q, '06, 100-102

958.93 Traumatic compartment syndrome of abdomen   `CC`
CC Excl: 863.0-867.3, 867.5-869.1, 879.2-879.9, 929.0-929.9, 958.8, 959.8-959.9
AHA: 4Q, '06, 100-102

958.99 Traumatic compartment syndrome of other sites   `CC`
CC Excl: 868.03-868.10, 868.13-869.1
AHA: 4Q, '06, 100-102

√4ᵗʰ **959 Injury, other and unspecified**
> INCLUDES   injury NOS
> EXCLUDES   injury NOS of:
> blood vessels (900.0-904.9)
> eye (921.0-921.9)
> internal organs (860.0-869.1)
> intracranial sites (854.0-854.1)
> nerves (950.0-951.9, 953.0-957.9)
> spinal cord (952.0-952.9)

√5ᵗʰ **959.0 Head, face and neck**

959.01 Head injury, unspecified
> EXCLUDES   concussion (850.1-850.9)
> with head injury NOS (850.1-850.9)
> head injury NOS with loss of consciousness (850.1-850.5)
> specified intracranial injuries (850.0-854.1)

AHA: 4Q, '08, 108; 4Q, '97, 46
S09.90xA Unspecified injury of head initial encounter   `I-10`

959.09 Injury of face and neck
Cheek   Mouth
Ear   Nose
Eyebrow   Throat
Lip
AHA: 4Q, '97, 46

√5ᵗʰ **959.1 Trunk**
> EXCLUDES   scapular region (959.2)

AHA: 4Q, '03, 78; 1Q, '99, 10

959.11 Other injury of chest wall

959.12 Other injury of abdomen

959.13 Fracture of corpus cavernosum penis   ♂

959.14 Other injury of external genitals

959.19 Other injury of other sites of trunk
Injury of trunk NOS

√4ᵗʰ √5ᵗʰ Additional Digit Required   Unacceptable PDx   Manifestation Code   Hospital Acquired Condition   ►◄ Revised Text   ● New Code   ▲ Revised Code Title

Injury and Poisoning

959.2–962.2

959.2 Shoulder and upper arm
Axilla
Scapular region

959.3 Elbow, forearm, and wrist
AHA: 1Q, '97, 8

959.4 Hand, except finger

959.5 Finger
Fingernail
Thumb (nail)

959.6 Hip and thigh
Upper leg

959.7 Knee, leg, ankle, and foot

959.8 Other specified sites, including multiple
EXCLUDES   multiple sites classifiable to the same four-digit
category (959.0-959.7)

959.9 Unspecified site

Poisoning by Drugs, Medicinal and Biological Substances (960-979)

INCLUDES   overdose of these substances
wrong substance given or taken in error

Use additional code to specify the effects of the poisoning

EXCLUDES   adverse effects ["hypersensitivity," "reaction," etc.] of correct
substance properly administered. Such cases are to be
classified according to the nature of the adverse effect,
such as:
adverse effect NOS (995.20)
allergic lymphadenitis (289.3)
aspirin gastritis (535.4)
blood disorders (280.0-289.9)
dermatitis:
contact (692.0-692.9)
due to ingestion (693.0-693.9)
nephropathy (583.9)
[The drug giving rise to the adverse effect may be identified
by use of categories E930-E949.]
drug dependence (304.0-304.9)
drug reaction and poisoning affecting the newborn
(760.0-779.9)
nondependent abuse of drugs (305.0-305.9)
pathological drug intoxication (292.2)

AHA: 2Q, '90, 11

TIP: Assign a poisoning code for interaction between prescribed drug and
alcohol or prescribed drug and other nonprescribed drug or medicinal
agent. Sequence poisoning code first, then code for manifestation of poisoning.
If respiratory failure is due to a poisoning, the poisoning code must be
sequenced first.

√4ᵗʰ **960 Poisoning by antibiotics**
EXCLUDES   antibiotics:
ear, nose, and throat (976.6)
eye (976.5)
local (976.0)

960.0 Penicillins
Ampicillin   Cloxacillin
Carbenicillin   Penicillin G

960.1 Antifungal antibiotics
Amphotericin B   Nystatin
Griseofulvin   Trichomycin
EXCLUDES   preparations intended for topical use (976.0-976.9)

960.2 Chloramphenicol group
Chloramphenicol
Thiamphenicol

960.3 Erythromycin and other macrolides
Oleandomycin
Spiramycin

960.4 Tetracycline group
Doxycycline   Oxytetracycline
Minocycline

960.5 Cephalosporin group
Cephalexin   Cephaloridine
Cephaloglycin   Cephalothin

960.6 Antimycobacterial antibiotics
Cycloserine   Rifampin
Kanamycin   Streptomycin

960.7 Antineoplastic antibiotics
Actinomycin such as: Actinomycin such as:
Bleomycin   Daunorubicin
Cactinomycin   Mitomycin
Dactinomycin

960.8 Other specified antibiotics

960.9 Unspecified antibiotic

√4ᵗʰ **961 Poisoning by other anti-infectives**
EXCLUDES   anti-infectives:
ear, nose, and throat (976.6)
eye (976.5)
local (976.0)

961.0 Sulfonamides
Sulfadiazine   Sulfamethoxazole
Sulfafurazole

961.1 Arsenical anti-infectives

961.2 Heavy metal anti-infectives
Compounds of: Compounds of:
antimony   lead
bismuth   mercury
EXCLUDES   mercurial diuretics (974.0)

961.3 Quinoline and hydroxyquinoline derivatives
Chiniofon
Diiodohydroxyquin
EXCLUDES   antimalarial drugs (961.4)

961.4 Antimalarials and drugs acting on other blood protozoa
Chloroquine   Proguanil [chloroguanide]
Cycloguanil   Pyrimethamine
Primaquine   Quinine

961.5 Other antiprotozoal drugs
Emetine

961.6 Anthelmintics
Hexylresorcinol   Thiabendazole
Piperazine

961.7 Antiviral drugs
Methisazone
EXCLUDES   amantadine (966.4)
cytarabine (963.1)
idoxuridine (976.5)

961.8 Other antimycobacterial drugs
Ethambutol
Ethionamide
Isoniazid
Para-aminosalicylic acid derivatives
Sulfones

961.9 Other and unspecified anti-infectives
Flucytosine
Nitrofuran derivatives

√4ᵗʰ **962 Poisoning by hormones and synthetic substitutes**
EXCLUDES   oxytocic hormones (975.0)

962.0 Adrenal cortical steroids
Cortisone derivatives
Desoxycorticosterone derivatives
Fluorinated corticosteroids

962.1 Androgens and anabolic congeners
Methandriol   Oxymetholone
Nandrolone   Testosterone

962.2 Ovarian hormones and synthetic substitutes
Contraceptives, oral
Estrogens
Estrogens and progestogens, combined
Progestogens

N   Newborn Age: 0   P   Pediatric Age: 0-17   M   Maternity Age: 12-55   A   Adult Age: 15-124   MCC   Major CC Condition   CC   CC Condition   HIV   HIV Related Dx

962.3 Insulins and antidiabetic agents
Acetohexamide
Biguanide derivatives, oral
Chlorpropamide
Glucagon
Insulin
Phenformin
Sulfonylurea derivatives, oral
Tolbutamide
AHA: 4Q, '93, 19; M-A, '85, 8
TIP: Assign only if documentation indicates overdose of insulin; if due to diabetic adjusting dosage, assign instead 250.8x or 249.8x and E932.3 for adverse reaction to insulin, if applicable.

962.4 Anterior pituitary hormones
Corticotropin
Gonadotropin
Somatotropin [growth hormone]

962.5 Posterior pituitary hormones
Vasopressin
EXCLUDES *oxytocic hormones (975.0)*

962.6 Parathyroid and parathyroid derivatives

962.7 Thyroid and thyroid derivatives
Dextrothyroxin   Liothyronine
Levothyroxine sodium   Thyroglobulin

962.8 Antithyroid agents
Iodides
Thiouracil
Thiourea

962.9 Other and unspecified hormones and synthetic substitutes

✓4th **963 Poisoning by primarily systemic agents**

963.0 Antiallergic and antiemetic drugs
Antihistamines   Diphenylpyraline
Chlorpheniramine   Thonzylamine
Diphenhydramine   Tripelennamine
EXCLUDES *phenothiazine-based tranquilizers (969.1)*

963.1 Antineoplastic and immunosuppressive drugs
Azathioprine   Cytarabine
Busulfan   Fluorouracil
Chlorambucil   Mercaptopurine
Cyclophosphamidethio-TEPA
EXCLUDES *antineoplastic antibiotics (960.7)*

963.2 Acidifying agents

963.3 Alkalizing agents

963.4 Enzymes, not elsewhere classified
Penicillinase

963.5 Vitamins, not elsewhere classified
Vitamin A
Vitamin D
EXCLUDES *nicotinic acid (972.2)*
vitamin K (964.3)

963.8 Other specified systemic agents
Heavy metal antagonists

963.9 Unspecified systemic agent

✓4th **964 Poisoning by agents primarily affecting blood constituents**

964.0 Iron and its compounds
Ferric salts
Ferrous sulfate and other ferrous salts

964.1 Liver preparations and other antianemic agents
Folic acid

964.2 Anticoagulants
Coumarin   Phenindione
Heparin   Warfarin sodium
AHA: 1Q, '94, 22
TIP: If documentation indicates an adverse reaction to Coumadin, assign instead manifestation (e.g., hematuria or epistaxis), code 790.92 if abnormal coagulation profile is documented, and E934.2.

964.3 Vitamin K [phytonadione]

964.4 Fibrinolysis-affecting drugs
Aminocaproic acid   Streptokinase
Streptodornase   Urokinase

964.5 Anticoagulant antagonists and other coagulants
Hexadimethrine
Protamine sulfate

964.6 Gamma globulin

964.7 Natural blood and blood products
Blood plasma   Packed red cells
Human fibrinogen   Whole blood
EXCLUDES *transfusion reactions (999.41-999.8)*

964.8 Other specified agents affecting blood constituents
Macromolecular blood substitutes
Plasma expanders

964.9 Unspecified agent affecting blood constituents

✓4th **965 Poisoning by analgesics, antipyretics, and antirheumatics**
EXCLUDES *drug dependence (304.0-304.9)*
nondependent abuse (305.0-305.9)

✓5th **965.0 Opiates and related narcotics**

965.00 Opium (alkaloids), unspecified
AHA: 3Q, '07, 6

965.01 Heroin
Diacetylmorphine

965.02 Methadone

965.09 Other
Codeine [methylmorphine]
Meperidine [pethidine]
Morphine
AHA: 3Q, '07, 6
T40.4x1A Poisoning oth synthetic narc accidnt initial enc `I-10`

965.1 Salicylates
Acetylsalicylic acid [aspirin]
Salicylic acid salts
AHA: N-D, '94, 15

965.4 Aromatic analgesics, not elsewhere classified
Acetanilid
Paracetamol [acetaminophen]
Phenacetin [acetophenetidin]

965.5 Pyrazole derivatives
Aminophenazone [aminopyrine]
Phenylbutazone

✓5th **965.6 Antirheumatics [antiphlogistics]**
EXCLUDES *salicylates (965.1)*
steroids (962.0-962.9)
AHA: 4Q, '98, 50

965.61 Propionic acid derivatives
Fenoprofen   Ketoprofen
Flurbiprofen   Naproxen
Ibuprofen   Oxaprozin
AHA: 4Q, '98, 50

965.69 Other antirheumatics
Gold salts
Indomethacin

965.7 Other non-narcotic analgesics
Pyrabital

965.8 Other specified analgesics and antipyretics
Pentazocine

965.9 Unspecified analgesic and antipyretic

✓4th **966 Poisoning by anticonvulsants and anti-Parkinsonism drugs**

966.0 Oxazolidine derivatives
Paramethadione
Trimethadione

966.1 Hydantoin derivatives
Phenytoin

966.2 Succinimides
Ethosuximide
Phensuximide

966.3 Other and unspecified anticonvulsants
Primidone
EXCLUDES *barbiturates (967.0)*
sulfonamides (961.0)

966.4 Anti-Parkinsonism drugs
Amantadine
Ethopropazine [profenamine]
Levodopa [L-dopa]

✓4ᵗʰ **967 Poisoning by sedatives and hypnotics**
EXCLUDES drug dependence (304.0-304.9)
nondependent abuse (305.0-305.9)

967.0 Barbiturates
Amobarbital [amylobarbitone]
Barbital [barbitone]
Butabarbital [butabarbitone]
Pentobarbital [pentobarbitone]
Phenobarbital [phenobarbitone]
Secobarbital [quinalbarbitone]
EXCLUDES thiobarbiturate anesthetics (968.3)

967.1 Chloral hydrate group

967.2 Paraldehyde

967.3 Bromine compounds
Bromide
Carbromal (derivatives)

967.4 Methaqualone compounds

967.5 Glutethimide group

967.6 Mixed sedatives, not elsewhere classified

967.8 Other sedatives and hypnotics

967.9 Unspecified sedative or hypnotic
Sleeping:
drug
pill } NOS
tablet

✓4ᵗʰ **968 Poisoning by other central nervous system depressants and anesthetics**
EXCLUDES drug dependence (304.0-304.9)
nondependent abuse (305.0-305.9)

968.0 Central nervous system muscle-tone depressants
Chlorphenesin (carbamate)
Mephenesin
Methocarbamol

968.1 Halothane

968.2 Other gaseous anesthetics
Ether
Halogenated hydrocarbon derivatives, except halothane
Nitrous oxide

968.3 Intravenous anesthetics
Ketamine
Methohexital [methohexitone]
Thiobarbiturates, such as thiopental sodium

968.4 Other and unspecified general anesthetics

968.5 Surface (topical) and infiltration anesthetics
Cocaine (topical)
Lidocaine (lignocaine)
Procaine
Tetracaine
EXCLUDES poisoning by cocaine used as a central nervous system stimulant (970.81)
AHA: 1Q, '93, 25

968.6 Peripheral nerve- and plexus-blocking anesthetics

968.7 Spinal anesthetics

968.9 Other and unspecified local anesthetics
T41.44xA Poisoning uns anesthetic undetermind initial enc I-10

✓4ᵗʰ **969 Poisoning by psychotropic agents**
EXCLUDES drug dependence (304.0-304.9)
nondependent abuse (305.0-305.9)

✓5ᵗʰ **969.0 Antidepressants**
AHA: 4Q, '09, 111-112

969.00 Antidepressant, unspecified
AHA: 3Q, '07, 6; #5, '94, 9; 3Q, '91, 14; N-D, '84, 14

969.01 Monoamine oxidase inhibitors
MAOI

969.02 Selective serotonin and norepinephrine reuptake inhibitors
SSNRI antidepressants
TIP: Assign for serotonin syndrome due to poisoning, along with 333.99 and E854.0, for accidental poisoning.

969.03 Selective serotonin reuptake inhibitors
SSRI antidepressants
TIP: Assign for serotonin syndrome due to poisoning, along with 333.99 and E854.0, for accidental poisoning.

969.04 Tetracyclic antidepressants

969.05 Tricyclic antidepressants
AHA: 4Q, '09, 112

969.09 Other antidepressants

969.1 Phenothiazine-based tranquilizers
Chlorpromazine   Prochlorperazine
Fluphenazine   Promazine

969.2 Butyrophenone-based tranquilizers
Haloperidol
Spiperone
Trifluperidol

969.3 Other antipsychotics, neuroleptics, and major tranquilizers

969.4 Benzodiazepine-based tranquilizers
Chlordiazepoxide
Diazepam
Flurazepam
Lorazepam
Medazepam
Nitrazepam
AHA: 4Q, '09, 112
T42.4X1A Poisoning by benzodiazepines, accidental, init I-10

969.5 Other tranquilizers
Hydroxyzine
Meprobamate

969.6 Psychodysleptics [hallucinogens]
Cannabis (derivatives)
Lysergide [LSD]
Marihuana (derivatives)
Mescaline
Psilocin
Psilocybin
AHA: ▶2Q, '13, 16◀

✓5ᵗʰ **969.7 Psychostimulants**
EXCLUDES central appetite depressants (977.0)
AHA: 4Q, '09, 113-114

969.70 Psychostimulant, unspecified
AHA: 2Q, '03, 11

969.71 Caffeine

969.72 Amphetamines
Methamphetamines
TIP: Assign for overdose and poisoning by the club drug ecstasy.

969.73 Methylphenidate

969.79 Other psychostimulants

969.8 Other specified psychotropic agents

969.9 Unspecified psychotropic agent

✓4ᵗʰ **970 Poisoning by central nervous system stimulants**

970.0 Analeptics
Lobeline   Nikethamide

970.1 Opiate antagonists
Levallorphan
Nalorphine
Naloxone

✓5ᵗʰ **970.8 Other specified central nervous system stimulants**
AHA: 1Q, '05, 6

970.81 Cocaine
Crack

970.89 Other central nervous system stimulants
AHA: ▶2Q, '13, 15◀

970.9 Unspecified central nervous system stimulant

N Newborn Age: 0   P Pediatric Age: 0-17   M Maternity Age: 12-55   A Adult Age: 15-124   MCC Major CC Condition   CC CC Condition   HIV HIV Related Dx

334 – Volume 1 • October 2014   2015 ICD-9-CM

√4th **971 Poisoning by drugs primarily affecting the autonomic nervous system**

971.0 Parasympathomimetics [cholinergics]
Acetylcholine
Anticholinesterase:
   organophosphorus
   reversible
Pilocarpine

971.1 Parasympatholytics [anticholinergics and antimuscarinics] and spasmolytics
Atropine
Homatropine
Hyoscine [scopolamine]
Quaternary ammonium derivatives
> EXCLUDES *papaverine (972.5)*

971.2 Sympathomimetics [adrenergics]
Epinephrine [adrenalin]
Levarterenol [noradrenalin]

971.3 Sympatholytics [antiadrenergics]
Phenoxybenzamine
Tolazoline hydrochloride

971.9 Unspecified drug primarily affecting autonomic nervous system

√4th **972 Poisoning by agents primarily affecting the cardiovascular system**

972.0 Cardiac rhythm regulators
Practolol
Procainamide
Propranolol
Quinidine
> EXCLUDES *lidocaine (968.5)*

972.1 Cardiotonic glycosides and drugs of similar action
Digitalis glycosides
Digoxin
Strophanthins

972.2 Antilipemic and antiarteriosclerotic drugs
Clofibrate
Nicotinic acid derivatives

972.3 Ganglion-blocking agents
Pentamethonium bromide

972.4 Coronary vasodilators
Dipyridamole
Nitrates [nitroglycerin]
Nitrites

972.5 Other vasodilators
Cyclandelate
Diazoxide
Papaverine
> EXCLUDES *nicotinic acid (972.2)*

972.6 Other antihypertensive agents
Clonidine
Guanethidine
Rauwolfia alkaloids
Reserpine

972.7 Antivaricose drugs, including sclerosing agents
Sodium morrhuate
Zinc salts

972.8 Capillary-active drugs
Adrenochrome derivatives
Metaraminol

972.9 Other and unspecified agents primarily affecting the cardiovascular system

√4th **973 Poisoning by agents primarily affecting the gastrointestinal system**

973.0 Antacids and antigastric secretion drugs
Aluminum hydroxide
Magnesium trisilicate
AHA: 1Q, '03, 19

973.1 Irritant cathartics
Bisacodyl
Castor oil
Phenolphthalein

973.2 Emollient cathartics
Dioctyl sulfosuccinates

973.3 Other cathartics, including intestinal atonia drugs
Magnesium sulfate

973.4 Digestants
Pancreatin
Papain
Pepsin

973.5 Antidiarrheal drugs
Kaolin
Pectin
> EXCLUDES *anti-infectives (960.0-961.9)*

973.6 Emetics

973.8 Other specified agents primarily affecting the gastrointestinal system

973.9 Unspecified agent primarily affecting the gastrointestinal system

√4th **974 Poisoning by water, mineral, and uric acid metabolism drugs**

974.0 Mercurial diuretics
Chlormerodrin   Mersalyl
Mercaptomerin

974.1 Purine derivative diuretics
Theobromine
Theophylline
> EXCLUDES *aminophylline [theophylline ethylenediamine] (975.7)*
>   *caffeine (969.71)*

974.2 Carbonic acid anhydrase inhibitors
Acetazolamide

974.3 Saluretics
Benzothiadiazides
Chlorothiazide group

974.4 Other diuretics
Ethacrynic acid
Furosemide

974.5 Electrolytic, caloric, and water-balance agents

974.6 Other mineral salts, not elsewhere classified

974.7 Uric acid metabolism drugs
Allopurinol   Probenecid
Colchicine

√4th **975 Poisoning by agents primarily acting on the smooth and skeletal muscles and respiratory system**

975.0 Oxytocic agents
Ergot alkaloids
Oxytocin
Prostaglandins

975.1 Smooth muscle relaxants
Adiphenine
Metaproterenol [orciprenaline]
> EXCLUDES *papaverine (972.5)*

975.2 Skeletal muscle relaxants

975.3 Other and unspecified drugs acting on muscles

975.4 Antitussives
Dextromethorphan
Pipazethate

975.5 Expectorants
Acetylcysteine
Guaifenesin
Terpin hydrate

975.6 Anti-common cold drugs

975.7 Antiasthmatics
Aminophylline [theophylline ethylenediamine]

975.8 Other and unspecified respiratory drugs

√4th Additional Digit Required   Unacceptable PDx   Manifestation Code   Hospital Acquired Condition   ►◄ Revised Text   ● New Code   ▲ Revised Code Title
√5th

2015 ICD-9-CM   **Volume 1 – 335**

Injury and Poisoning

976–983.1

☑4ᵗʰ **976 Poisoning by agents primarily affecting skin and mucous membrane, ophthalmological, otorhinolaryngological, and dental drugs**

976.0 Local anti-infectives and anti-inflammatory drugs

976.1 Antipruritics

976.2 Local astringents and local detergents

976.3 Emollients, demulcents, and protectants

976.4 Keratolytics, keratoplastics, other hair treatment drugs and preparations

976.5 Eye anti-infectives and other eye drugs
Idoxuridine

976.6 Anti-infectives and other drugs and preparations for ear, nose, and throat

976.7 Dental drugs topically applied
> EXCLUDES *anti-infectives (976.0)*
> *local anesthetics (968.5)*

976.8 Other agents primarily affecting skin and mucous membrane
Spermicides [vaginal contraceptives]

976.9 Unspecified agent primarily affecting skin and mucous membrane

☑4ᵗʰ **977 Poisoning by other and unspecified drugs and medicinal substances**

977.0 Dietetics
Central appetite depressants

977.1 Lipotropic drugs

977.2 Antidotes and chelating agents, not elsewhere classified

977.3 Alcohol deterrents

977.4 Pharmaceutical excipients
Pharmaceutical adjuncts

977.8 Other specified drugs and medicinal substances
Contrast media used for diagnostic x-ray procedures
Diagnostic agents and kits

977.9 Unspecified drug or medicinal substance

☑4ᵗʰ **978 Poisoning by bacterial vaccines**

978.0 BCG

978.1 Typhoid and paratyphoid

978.2 Cholera

978.3 Plague

978.4 Tetanus

978.5 Diphtheria

978.6 Pertussis vaccine, including combinations with a pertussis component

978.8 Other and unspecified bacterial vaccines

978.9 Mixed bacterial vaccines, except combinations with a pertussis component

☑4ᵗʰ **979 Poisoning by other vaccines and biological substances**
> EXCLUDES *gamma globulin (964.6)*

979.0 Smallpox vaccine

979.1 Rabies vaccine

979.2 Typhus vaccine

979.3 Yellow fever vaccine

979.4 Measles vaccine

979.5 Poliomyelitis vaccine

979.6 Other and unspecified viral and rickettsial vaccines
Mumps vaccine

979.7 Mixed viral-rickettsial and bacterial vaccines, except combinations with a pertussis component
> EXCLUDES *combinations with a pertussis component (978.6)*

979.9 Other and unspecified vaccines and biological substances

Toxic Effects of Substances Chiefly Nonmedicinal as to Source (980–989)

Use additional code to identify:
personal history of retained foreign body fully removed (V15.53)
retained foreign body status, if applicable, (V90.01-V90.9)
Use additional code to specify the nature of the toxic effect
> EXCLUDES *burns from chemical agents (ingested) (947.0-947.9)*
> *localized toxic effects indexed elsewhere (001.0-799.9)*
> *respiratory conditions due to external agents (506.0-508.9)*
> *respiratory conditions due to smoke inhalation NOS (508.2)*

AHA: 3Q, '10, 19

☑4ᵗʰ **980 Toxic effect of alcohol**

980.0 Ethyl alcohol
Denatured alcohol   Grain alcohol
Ethanol
Use additional code to identify any associated:
acute alcohol intoxication (305.0)
in alcoholism (303.0)
drunkenness (simple) (305.0)
pathological (291.4)
AHA: 4Q, '09, 112; 3Q, '96, 16
T51.0x1A Toxic effect ethanol accidental initial encountr   I-10

980.1 Methyl alcohol
Methanol
Wood alcohol

980.2 Isopropyl alcohol
Dimethyl carbinol
Isopropanol
Rubbing alcohol

980.3 Fusel oil
Alcohol:
amyl
butyl
propyl

980.8 Other specified alcohols

980.9 Unspecified alcohol

981 Toxic effect of petroleum products
Benzine
Gasoline
Kerosene
Paraffin wax
Petroleum:
ether
naphtha
spirit

☑4ᵗʰ **982 Toxic effect of solvents other than petroleum-based**

982.0 Benzene and homologues

982.1 Carbon tetrachloride

982.2 Carbon disulfide
Carbon bisulfide

982.3 Other chlorinated hydrocarbon solvents
Tetrachloroethylene
Trichloroethylene
> EXCLUDES *chlorinated hydrocarbon preparations other than*
> *solvents (989.2)*

AHA: 3Q, '08, 6-7

982.4 Nitroglycol

982.8 Other nonpetroleum-based solvents
Acetone

☑4ᵗʰ **983 Toxic effect of corrosive aromatics, acids, and caustic alkalis**

983.0 Corrosive aromatics
Carbolic acid or phenol   Cresol

983.1 Acids
Acid:
hydrochloric
nitric
sulfuric

N Newborn Age: 0   P Pediatric Age: 0-17   M Maternity Age: 12-55   A Adult Age: 15-124   MCC Major CC Condition   CC CC Condition   HIV HIV Related Dx

983.2 Caustic alkalis
　　　Lye
　　　Potassium hydroxide
　　　Sodium hydroxide

983.9 Caustic, unspecified

√4th **984 Toxic effect of lead and its compounds (including fumes)**
　　INCLUDES　that from all sources except medicinal substances

984.0 Inorganic lead compounds
　　　Lead dioxide
　　　Lead salts

984.1 Organic lead compounds
　　　Lead acetate
　　　Tetraethyl lead

984.8 Other lead compounds

984.9 Unspecified lead compound

√4th **985 Toxic effect of other metals**
　　INCLUDES　that from all sources except medicinal substances

985.0 Mercury and its compounds
　　　Minamata disease

985.1 Arsenic and its compounds

985.2 Manganese and its compounds

985.3 Beryllium and its compounds

985.4 Antimony and its compounds

985.5 Cadmium and its compounds

985.6 Chromium

985.8 Other specified metals
　　　Brass fumes　　　Iron compounds
　　　Copper salts　　　Nickel compounds
　　　AHA: 1Q, '88, 5
　　　TIP: Assign for aluminum overloading or excessive concentration of aluminum in the body, along with E879.1 if due to renal dialysis and E879.8 if due to total parenteral nutrition.

985.9 Unspecified metal

986 Toxic effect of carbon monoxide
　　　Carbon monoxide from any source

√4th **987 Toxic effect of other gases, fumes, or vapors**

987.0 Liquefied petroleum gases
　　　Butane
　　　Propane

987.1 Other hydrocarbon gas

987.2 Nitrogen oxides
　　　Nitrogen dioxide
　　　Nitrous fumes

987.3 Sulfur dioxide

987.4 Freon
　　　Dichloromonofluoromethane

987.5 Lacrimogenic gas
　　　Bromobenzyl cyanide
　　　Chloroacetophenone
　　　Ethyliodoacetate

987.6 Chlorine gas

987.7 Hydrocyanic acid gas

987.8 Other specified gases, fumes, or vapors
　　　Phosgene
　　　Polyester fumes

987.9 Unspecified gas, fume, or vapor
　　　AHA: 4Q, '11, 114; 3Q, '05, 10
　　　TIP: Do not assign for conditions due to smoke inhalation; assign instead code 508.2.

√4th **988 Toxic effect of noxious substances eaten as food**
　　EXCLUDES　allergic reaction to food, such as:
　　　　gastroenteritis (558.3)
　　　　rash (692.5, 693.1)
　　　food poisoning (bacterial) (005.0-005.9)
　　　toxic effects of food contaminants, such as:
　　　　aflatoxin and other mycotoxin (989.7)
　　　　mercury (985.0)

988.0 Fish and shellfish

988.1 Mushrooms

988.2 Berries and other plants

988.8 Other specified noxious substances eaten as food

988.9 Unspecified noxious substance eaten as food

√4th **989 Toxic effect of other substances, chiefly nonmedicinal as to source**

989.0 Hydrocyanic acid and cyanides
　　　Potassium cyanide
　　　Sodium cyanide
　　　EXCLUDES　gas and fumes (987.7)

989.1 Strychnine and salts

989.2 Chlorinated hydrocarbons
　　　Aldrin
　　　Chlordane
　　　DDT
　　　Dieldrin
　　　EXCLUDES　chlorinated hydrocarbon solvents (982.0-982.3)

989.3 Organophosphate and carbamate
　　　Carbaryl
　　　Dichlorvos
　　　Malathion
　　　Parathion
　　　Phorate
　　　Phosdrin

989.4 Other pesticides, not elsewhere classified
　　　Mixtures of insecticides

989.5 Venom
　　　Bites of venomous snakes, lizards, and spiders
　　　Tick paralysis

989.6 Soaps and detergents

989.7 Aflatoxin and other mycotoxin [food contaminants]

√5th **989.8 Other substances, chiefly nonmedicinal as to source**
　　　AHA: 4Q, '95, 60

　　989.81 Asbestos
　　　　EXCLUDES　asbestosis (501)
　　　　　exposure to asbestos (V15.84)

　　989.82 Latex

　　989.83 Silicone
　　　　EXCLUDES　silicone used in medical devices, implants and grafts (996.00-996.79)

　　989.84 Tobacco

　　989.89 Other

989.9 Unspecified substance, chiefly nonmedicinal as to source

Other and Unspecified Effects of External Causes (990-995)

990 Effects of radiation, unspecified
　　　Complication of:
　　　　phototherapy
　　　　radiation therapy
　　　Radiation sickness
　　　[The type of radiation giving rise to the adverse effect may be identified by use of the E codes.]
　　　EXCLUDES　specified adverse effects of radiation. Such conditions are to be classified according to the nature of the adverse effect, as:
　　　　burns (940.0-949.5)
　　　　dermatitis (692.7-692.8)
　　　　leukemia (204.0-208.9)
　　　　pneumonia (508.0)
　　　　sunburn (692.71, 692.76-692.77)

√4th √5th Additional Digit Required　　Unacceptable PDx　　Manifestation Code　　Hospital Acquired Condition　　▶◀ Revised Text　　● New Code　　▲ Revised Code Title

2015 ICD-9-CM　　　　　　　　　　　　　　　　　　　　　　　　　　　　　**Volume 1 – 337**

Injury and Poisoning

991–994.9

☑4ᵗʰ 991 Effects of reduced temperature

991.0 Frostbite of face   `CC`
CC Excl: 991.0, 991.3

991.1 Frostbite of hand   `CC`
CC Excl: 991.1, 991.3

991.2 Frostbite of foot   `CC`
CC Excl: 991.2-991.3

991.3 Frostbite of other and unspecified sites   `CC`
CC Excl: 991.0-991.4

991.4 Immersion foot   `CC`
Trench foot
DEF: Paresthesia, edema, blotchy cyanosis of foot, the skin is soft (macerated), pale and wrinkled, and the sole is swollen with surface ridging and following sustained immersion in water.
CC Excl: 991.3-991.4

991.5 Chilblains
Erythema pernio
Perniosis
DEF: Red, swollen, itchy skin; follows damp cold exposure; also associated with pruritus and a burning feeling in hands, feet, ears, and face in children, legs and toes in women, and hands and fingers in men.

991.6 Hypothermia
Hypothermia (accidental)
EXCLUDES hypothermia following anesthesia (995.89)
hypothermia not associated with low environmental temperature (780.65)
DEF: Reduced body temperature due to low environmental temperatures.

991.8 Other specified effects of reduced temperature

991.9 Unspecified effect of reduced temperature
Effects of freezing or excessive cold NOS

☑4ᵗʰ 992 Effects of heat and light

EXCLUDES burns (940.0-949.5)
diseases of sweat glands due to heat (705.0-705.9)
malignant hyperpyrexia following anesthesia (995.86)
sunburn (692.71, 692.76-692.77)

992.0 Heat stroke and sunstroke   `CC`
Heat apoplexy
Heat pyrexia
Ictus solaris
Siriasis
Thermoplegia
Use additional code(s) to identify any associated complication of heat stroke, such as:
alterations of consciousness (780.01-780.09)
systemic inflammatory response syndrome (995.93-995.94)
DEF: Headache, vertigo, cramps and elevated body temperature due to high environmental temperatures.
CC Excl: 992.0-992.9

992.1 Heat syncope
Heat collapse

992.2 Heat cramps

992.3 Heat exhaustion, anhydrotic
Heat prostration due to water depletion
EXCLUDES that associated with salt depletion (992.4)

992.4 Heat exhaustion due to salt depletion
Heat prostration due to salt (and water) depletion

992.5 Heat exhaustion, unspecified
Heat prostration NOS

992.6 Heat fatigue, transient

992.7 Heat edema
DEF: Fluid retention due to high environmental temperatures.

992.8 Other specified heat effects

992.9 Unspecified

☑4ᵗʰ 993 Effects of air pressure

993.0 Barotrauma, otitic
Aero-otitis media
Effects of high altitude on ears
DEF: Ringing ears, deafness, pain and vertigo due to air pressure changes.

993.1 Barotrauma, sinus
Aerosinusitis
Effects of high altitude on sinuses

993.2 Other and unspecified effects of high altitude
Alpine sickness
Andes disease
Anoxia due to high altitude
Hypobaropathy
Mountain sickness
AHA: 3Q, '88, 4

993.3 Caisson disease   `CC`
Bends
Compressed-air disease
Decompression sickness
Divers' palsy or paralysis
DEF: Rapid reduction in air pressure while breathing compressed air; symptoms include skin lesions, joint pains, respiratory and neurological problems.
CC Excl: 993.3-993.9

993.4 Effects of air pressure caused by explosion

993.8 Other specified effects of air pressure

993.9 Unspecified effect of air pressure

☑4ᵗʰ 994 Effects of other external causes

EXCLUDES certain adverse effects not elsewhere classified (995.0-995.8)

994.0 Effects of lightning
Shock from lightning
Struck by lightning NOS
EXCLUDES burns (940.0-949.5)

994.1 Drowning and nonfatal submersion   `CC`
Bathing cramp
Immersion
CC Excl: 994.1
AHA: ▶3Q, '13, 10;◀ 3Q, '09, 14; 3Q, '88, 4
TIP: When near-drowning results in acute respiratory edema, assign also code 518.5 Post-traumatic pulmonary insufficiency.

994.2 Effects of hunger
Deprivation of food
Starvation

994.3 Effects of thirst
Deprivation of water

994.4 Exhaustion due to exposure

994.5 Exhaustion due to excessive exertion
Exhaustion due to overexertion

994.6 Motion sickness
Air sickness
Seasickness
Travel sickness

994.7 Asphyxiation and strangulation   `CC`
Suffocation (by):   Suffocation (by):
bedclothes   plastic bag
cave-in   pressure
constriction   strangulation
mechanical
EXCLUDES asphyxia from:
carbon monoxide (986)
inhalation of food or foreign body (932-934.9)
other gases, fumes, and vapors (987.0-987.9)
CC Excl: 994.7

994.8 Electrocution and nonfatal effects of electric current
Shock from electric current
Shock from electroshock gun (taser)
EXCLUDES electric burns (940.0-949.5)

994.9 Other effects of external causes
Effects of:
abnormal gravitational [G] forces or states
weightlessness

| N Newborn Age: 0 | P Pediatric Age: 0-17 | M Maternity Age: 12-55 | A Adult Age: 15-124 | MCC Major CC Condition | CC CC Condition | HIV HIV Related Dx |

338 – Volume 1 • October 2014   2015 ICD-9-CM

☑️4ᵗʰ **995 Certain adverse effects not elsewhere classified**

> **EXCLUDES** *complications of surgical and medical care (996.0-999.9)*

995.0 Other anaphylactic reaction   CC

     Allergic shock

     Anaphylactic reaction

     Anaphylactic shock NOS or due to adverse effect of correct medicinal substance properly administered

     Anaphylactoid reaction, NOS

     Anaphylaxis

     Use additional E code to identify external cause, such as: adverse effects of correct medicinal substance properly administered [E930-E949]

> **EXCLUDES** *anaphylactic reaction to serum (999.41-999.49)*
> *anaphylactic shock or reaction due to adverse food reaction (995.60-995.69)*

     DEF: Immediate sensitivity response after exposure to specific antigen; results in life-threatening respiratory distress; usually followed by vascular collapse, shock, urticaria, angioedema and pruritus.

     CC Excl: 995.60-995.69

     AHA: ▶2Q, '13, 12;◀ 4Q, '93, 30

995.1 Angioneurotic edema

     Allergic angioedema

     Giant urticaria

> **EXCLUDES** *urticaria:*
> *due to serum (999.51-999.59)*
> *other specified (698.2, 708.0-708.9, 757.33)*

     DEF: Circulatory response of deep dermis, subcutaneous or submucosal tissues; causes localized edema and wheals.

☑️5ᵗʰ **995.2 Other and unspecified adverse effect of drug, medicinal and biological substance**

> **EXCLUDES** *pathological drug intoxication (292.2)*

     AHA: 2Q, '97, 12; 3Q, '95, 13; 3Q, '92, 16

     TIP: Codes from this subcategory should not be assigned for inpatient cases; their use is limited to certain outpatient cases in which there is no documentation of specific symptoms associated with the adverse effect.

995.20 Unspecified adverse effect of unspecified drug, medicinal and biological substance

     Unspecified adverse effect of unspecified medicinal substance properly administered

     AHA: 4Q, '06, 112

995.21 Arthus phenomenon

     Arthus reaction

     AHA: 4Q, '06, 112

995.22 Unspecified adverse effect of anesthesia

     AHA: 4Q, '06, 112

995.23 Unspecified adverse effect of insulin

     AHA: 4Q, '06, 112

995.24 Failed moderate sedation during procedure

     Failed conscious sedation during procedure

     AHA: 4Q, '09, 114

     TIP: If documentation indicates a personal history of failed moderate sedation, assign instead code V15.80 History of failed moderate sedation.

995.27 Other drug allergy

     Allergic reaction NEC (due) to correct medical substance properly administered

     Drug allergy NOS

     Drug hypersensitivity NOS

     Hypersensitivity (due) to correct medical substance properly administered

     AHA: 4Q, '06, 112

995.29 Unspecified adverse effect of other drug, medicinal and biological substance

     Unspecified adverse effect of medicinal substance NEC properly administered

     AHA: 4Q, '06, 112

995.3 Allergy, unspecified

     Allergic reaction NOS   Idiosyncrasy NOS

     Hypersensitivity NOS

> **EXCLUDES** *allergic reaction NOS to correct medicinal substance properly administered (995.27)*
> *allergy to existing dental restorative materials (525.66)*
> *specific types of allergic reaction, such as:*
> *allergic diarrhea (558.3)*
> *dermatitis (691.0-693.9)*
> *hayfever (477.0-477.9)*

995.4 Shock due to anesthesia   CC

     Shock due to anesthesia in which the correct substance was properly administered

> **EXCLUDES** *complications of anesthesia in labor or delivery (668.0-668.9)*
> *overdose or wrong substance given (968.0-969.9)*
> *postoperative shock NOS (998.00)*
> *specified adverse effects of anesthesia classified elsewhere, such as:*
> *anoxic brain damage (348.1)*
> *hepatitis (070.0-070.9), etc.*
> *unspecified adverse effect of anesthesia (995.22)*

     CC Excl: 958.4, 995.4, 997.91-998.13, 998.81, 998.83-998.9

☑️5ᵗʰ **995.5 Child maltreatment syndrome**

     Use additional code(s), if applicable, to identify any associated injuries

     Use additional E code to identify:

       nature of abuse (E960-E968)

       perpetrator (E967.0-E967.9)

     AHA: 2Q, '12, 12; 1Q, '98, 11

     TIP: Although separate codes for any associated injuries should be assigned, codes from this subcategory may be assigned alone if there are no documented injuries or associated conditions.

995.50 Child abuse, unspecified   CC P

     CC Excl: 995.50-995.59, 995.80-995.85

995.51 Child emotional/psychological abuse   CC P

     CC Excl: See code: 995.50

     AHA: 4Q, '96, 38, 40

995.52 Child neglect (nutritional)   CC P

     CC Excl: See code: 995.50

     AHA: 4Q, '96, 38, 40

995.53 Child sexual abuse   CC P

     CC Excl: See code: 995.50

     AHA: 4Q, '96, 39, 40

995.54 Child physical abuse   CC P

     Battered baby or child syndrome

> **EXCLUDES** *shaken infant syndrome (995.55)*

     CC Excl: See code: 995.50

     AHA: 3Q, '99, 14; 4Q, '96, 39, 40

995.55 Shaken infant syndrome   CC P

     Use additional code(s) to identify any associated injuries

     CC Excl: See code: 995.50

     AHA: 4Q, '96, 40, 43

995.59 Other child abuse and neglect   CC P

     Multiple forms of abuse

     CC Excl: See code: 995.50

☑️5ᵗʰ **995.6 Anaphylactic reaction due to food**

     Anaphylactic reaction due to adverse food reaction

     Anaphylactic shock or reaction due to nonpoisonous foods

     Anaphylactoid reaction due to food

     AHA: 4Q, '11, 142-145; 4Q, '93, 30

     TIP: Codes from this subcategory may be assigned not only for anaphylactic shock, but also for any documentation of anaphylactic reaction to food.

995.60 Anaphylactic reaction due to unspecified food   CC

     CC Excl: 995.60-995.69

995.61 Anaphylactic reaction due to peanuts   CC

     CC Excl: See code: 995.60

995.62 Anaphylactic reaction due to crustaceans   CC

     CC Excl: See code: 995.60

☑️4ᵗʰ ☑️5ᵗʰ Additional Digit Required   Unacceptable PDx   Manifestation Code   Hospital Acquired Condition   ▶◀ Revised Text   ● New Code   ▲ Revised Code Title

2015 ICD-9-CM   **October 2014 • Volume 1 – 339**

Injury and Poisoning

995.63–995.92

995.63 Anaphylactic reaction due to fruits and vegetables `CC`
     CC Excl: See code: 995.60

995.64 Anaphylactic reaction due to tree nuts and seeds `CC`
     AHA: 1Q, '08, 12
     CC Excl: See code: 995.60

995.65 Anaphylactic reaction due to fish `CC`
     CC Excl: See code: 995.60

995.66 Anaphylactic reaction due to food additives `CC`
     CC Excl: See code: 995.60

995.67 Anaphylactic reaction due to milk products `CC`
     CC Excl: See code: 995.60

995.68 Anaphylactic reaction due to eggs `CC`
     CC Excl: See code: 995.60

995.69 Anaphylactic reaction due to other specified food `CC`
     CC Excl: See code: 995.60

995.7 Other adverse food reactions, not elsewhere classified
     Use additional code to identify the type of reaction, such as:
       hives (708.0)
       wheezing (786.07)
     EXCLUDES anaphylactic reaction or shock due to adverse food reaction (995.60-995.69)
         asthma (493.0, 493.9)
         dermatitis due to food (693.1)
           in contact with skin (692.5)
         gastroenteritis and colitis due to food (558.3)
         rhinitis due to food (477.1)

√5ᵗʰ 995.8 Other specified adverse effects, not elsewhere classified

995.80 Adult maltreatment, unspecified `CC` `A`
     Abused person NOS
     Use additional code to identify:
       any associated injury
       perpetrator (E967.0-E967.9)
     CC Excl: 995.80
     AHA: 2Q, '12, 12; 4Q, '96, 41, 43

995.81 Adult physical abuse `CC` `A`
     Battered: Battered:
       person syndrome NEC   spouse
       man   woman
     Use additional code to identify:
       any association injury
       nature of abuse (E960-E968)
       perpetrator (E967.0-E967.9)
     CC Excl: 995.50-995.59, 995.80-995.85
     AHA: 2Q, '12, 12; 4Q, '96, 42, 43

995.82 Adult emotional/psychological abuse `A`
     Use additional E code to identify perpetrator (E967.0-E967.9)
     AHA: 2Q, '12, 12

995.83 Adult sexual abuse `CC` `A`
     Use additional code(s) to identify:
       any associated injury
       perpetrator (E967.0-E967.9)
     CC Excl: See code: 995.81
     AHA: 2Q, '12, 12

995.84 Adult neglect (nutritional) `CC` `A`
     Use additional code(s) to identify:
       intent of neglect (E904.0, E968.4)
       perpetrator (E967.0-E967.9)
     CC Excl: See code: 995.81
     AHA: 2Q, '12, 12

995.85 Other adult abuse and neglect `CC` `A`
     Multiple forms of abuse and neglect
     Use additional code(s) to identify
       any associated injury
       intent of neglect (E904.0, E968.4)
       nature of abuse (E960-E968)
       perpetrator (E967.0-E967.9)
     CC Excl: See code: 995.81
     AHA: 2Q, '12, 12

Continuum of Illness Due to Infection

Bacteremia → Septicemia → Sepsis

Severe Sepsis with Septic Shock ← Severe Sepsis ← Severe Sepsis

↓

MODS (Multiple Organ Dysfunction Syndrome) → Death

995.86 Malignant hyperthermia `CC`
     Malignant hyperpyrexia due to anesthesia
     CC Excl: 958.4, 995.4, 995.86, 997.91-998.13, 998.81, 998.83-998.9
     AHA: 4Q, '98, 51

995.89 Other
     Hypothermia due to anesthesia
     AHA: 2Q, '04, 18; 3Q, '03, 12

√5ᵗʰ 995.9 Systemic inflammatory response syndrome (SIRS)
     DEF: Clinical response to infection or trauma that can trigger an acute inflammatory reaction and progresses to coagulation, impaired fibrinolysis, and organ failure; manifested by two or more of the following symptoms: fever, tachycardia, tachypnea, leukocytosis or leukopenia.
     AHA: 4Q, '06, 113-116; 2Q, '04, 16; 4Q, '02, 71
     TIP: Coding these conditions requires a minimum of two codes: the underlying cause (e.g., infection or trauma) is sequenced first, followed by a code from subcategory 995.9.

995.90 Systemic inflammatory response syndrome, unspecified `CC`
     SIRS NOS
     CC Excl: 003.1, 020.2, 036.2, 038.0-038.9, 040.82-041.9, 054.5, 139.8, 995.90-995.94, V09.0-V09.91

995.91 Sepsis `MCC`
     Systemic inflammatory response syndrome due to infectious process without acute organ dysfunction
     Code first underlying infection
     EXCLUDES sepsis with acute organ dysfunction (995.92)
         sepsis with multiple organ dysfunction (995.92)
         severe sepsis (995.92)
     CC Excl: See code 995.90
     AHA: 3Q, '12, 11,13; 2Q, '12, 21; 3Q, '11, 15;4Q, '08, 72; 4Q, '07, 86; 4Q, '06, 113-116; 2Q, '04, 16; 4Q, '03, 79

995.92 Severe sepsis `MCC`
     Sepsis with acute organ dysfunction
     Sepsis with multiple organ dysfunction (MOD)
     Systemic inflammatory response syndrome due to infectious process with acute organ dysfunction
     Code first underlying infection
     Use additional code to specify acute organ dysfunction, such as:
       acute kidney failure (584.5-584.9)
       acute respiratory failure (518.81)
       critical illness myopathy (359.81)
       critical illness polyneuropathy (357.82)
       disseminated intravascular coagulopathy [DIC] (286.6)
       encephalopathy (348.31)
       hepatic failure (570)
       septic shock (785.52)
     CC Excl: See code 995.90
     AHA: ▶2Q, '13, 21;◀3Q, '12, 11; 4Q, '11, 153; 2Q, '10, 4; 4Q, '09, 98; 4Q, '08, 99; 4Q, '07, 97; 4Q, '06, 113-116; 2Q, '05, 18-19; 1Q, '05, 7; 1Q, '05, 7; 2Q, '04, 16; 4Q, '03, 73, 79
     R65.21 Severe sepsis with septic shock `I-10`

`N` Newborn Age: 0   `P` Pediatric Age: 0-17   `M` Maternity Age: 12-55   `A` Adult Age: 15-124   `MCC` Major CC Condition   `CC` CC Condition   `HIV` HIV Related Dx

340 – Volume 1 • October 2014   **2015 ICD-9-CM**

995.93 Systemic inflammatory response syndrome due to noninfectious process without acute organ dysfunction `CC`

Code first underlying conditions, such as:
    acute pancreatitis (577.0)
    trauma

EXCLUDES   systemic inflammatory response syndrome due to noninfectious process with acute organ dysfunction (995.94)

CC Excl: See code 995.90
AHA: 1Q, '11, 22; 1Q, '10, 10-11; 4Q, '06, 113-116

995.94 Systemic inflammatory response syndrome due to noninfectious process with acute organ dysfunction `MCC`

Code first underlying conditions, such as:
    acute pancreatitis (577.0)
    heat stroke (992.0)
    trauma

Use additional code to specify acute organ dysfunction, such as:
    acute kidney failure (584.5-584.9)
    acute respiratory failure (518.81)
    critical illness myopathy (359.81)
    critical illness polyneuropathy (357.82)
    disseminated intravascular coagulopathy [DIC] syndrome (286.6)
    encephalopathy (348.31)
    hepatic failure (570)

EXCLUDES   severe sepsis (995.92)

CC Excl: See code 995.90
AHA: 1Q, '10, 10; 4Q, '06, 113-116; 4Q, '03, 79

Complications of Surgical and Medical Care, Not Elsewhere Classified (996-999)

EXCLUDES   adverse effects of medicinal agents (001.0-799.9, 995.0-995.8)
burns from local applications and irradiation (940.0-949.5)
complications of:
    conditions for which the procedure was performed
    surgical procedures during abortion, labor, and delivery (630-676.9)
poisoning and toxic effects of drugs and chemicals (960.0-989.9)
postoperative conditions in which no complications are present, such as:
    artificial opening status (V44.0-V44.9)
    closure of external stoma (V55.0-V55.9)
    fitting of prosthetic device (V52.0-V52.9)
specified complications classified elsewhere
    anesthetic shock (995.4)
    electrolyte imbalance (276.0-276.9)
    postlaminectomy syndrome (722.80-722.83)
    postmastectomy lymphedema syndrome (457.0)
    postoperative psychosis (293.0-293.9)
    any other condition classified elsewhere in the Alphabetic Index when described as due to a procedure

AHA: 2Q, '12, 5, 8

TIP: Assign additional codes to further specify the nature of the complication unless the complication code provides a complete description of the condition.

√4th **996 Complications peculiar to certain specified procedures**

INCLUDES   complications, not elsewhere classified, in the use of artificial substitutes [e.g., Dacron, metal, Silastic, Teflon] or natural sources [e.g., bone] involving:
anastomosis (internal)
graft (bypass) (patch)
implant
internal device:
    catheter
    electronic
    fixation
    prosthetic
reimplant
transplant

EXCLUDES   accidental puncture or laceration during procedure (998.2)
capsular contracture of breast implant (611.83)
complications of internal anastomosis of:
    gastrointestinal tract (997.49)
    urinary tract (997.5)
endosseous dental implant failures (525.71-525.79)
intraoperative floppy iris syndrome [IFIS] (364.81)
mechanical complication of respirator (V46.14)
other specified complications classified elsewhere, such as:
    hemolytic anemia (283.1)
    functional cardiac disturbances (429.4)
    serum hepatitis (070.2-070.3)

AHA: 1Q, '94, 3

√5th **996.0 Mechanical complication of cardiac device, implant, and graft**

Breakdown (mechanical)	Obstruction, mechanical
Displacement	Perforation
Leakage	Protrusion

AHA: 2Q, '08, 9; 2Q, '93, 9
TIP: If the documentation indicates that the cardiac device (e.g., pacemaker, heart valve prosthesis) has reached its normally occurring end of life, do not assign a complication code; see instead subcategory V53.3.

996.00 Unspecified device, implant, and graft `CC`
CC Excl: 996.00, 996.04, 996.61-996.62, 996.70-996.74, 997.91-997.99, 998.81, 998.83-998.9

996.01 Due to cardiac pacemaker (electrode) `CC`
CC Excl: 996.01, 997.91-997.99, 998.81, 998.83-998.9
AHA: 2Q, '06, 15; 2Q, '99, 11
T82.120A Displacement cardiac electrode initial encounter `I-10`

996.02 Due to heart valve prosthesis `CC`
CC Excl: 996.02, 997.91-997.99, 998.81, 998.83-998.9

996.03 Due to coronary bypass graft `CC`
EXCLUDES   atherosclerosis of graft (414.02, 414.03)
embolism [occlusion NOS] [thrombus] of graft (996.72)
CC Excl: 996.03, 997.91-997.99, 998.81, 998.83-998.9
AHA: 2Q, '95, 17; N-D, '86, 5

996.04 Due to automatic implantable cardiac defibrillator `CC`
CC Excl: 996.04, 997.91-997.99, 998.81, 998.83-998.9
AHA: 2Q, '05, 3

996.09 Other `CC`
CC Excl: 996.09, 997.91-997.99, 998.81, 998.83-998.9
AHA: ▶1Q, '13, 4;◀ 2Q, '93, 9

√4th √5th Additional Digit Required   Unacceptable PDx   Manifestation Code   Hospital Acquired Condition   ▶◀ Revised Text   ● New Code   ▲ Revised Code Title

2015 ICD-9-CM   **October 2014 • Volume 1 — 341**

Injury and Poisoning

996.1–996.54

996.1 Mechanical complication of other vascular device, implant, and graft `CC`
Mechanical complications involving:
aortic (bifurcation) graft (replacement)
arteriovenous:
   dialysis catheter ⎫
   fistula   ⎬ surgically created
   shunt   ⎭
balloon (counterpulsation) device, intra-aortic
carotid artery bypass graft
femoral-popliteal bypass graft
umbrella device, vena cava
> **EXCLUDES** *atherosclerosis of biological graft (440.30-440.32)*
> *embolism [occlusion NOS] [thrombus] of (biological) (synthetic) graft (996.74)*
> *peritoneal dialysis catheter (996.56)*

CC Excl: 996.1, 997.91-997.99, 998.81, 998.83-998.9
AHA: 1Q, '12, 18;1Q, '11, 5; 1Q, '06, 10; 2Q, '05, 8; 1Q, '02, 13; 1Q, '95, 3
TIP: Assign for a nonmaturing AV fistula and also for postprocedural reduction in transjugular intrahepatic portosystemic shunt flow in a patient with a TIPS catheter.
   T82.330A Leakage aortic bifurcation graft initial enc `I-10`

996.2 Mechanical complication of nervous system device, implant, and graft `CC`
Mechanical complications involving:
dorsal column stimulator
electrodes implanted in brain [brain "pacemaker"]
peripheral nerve graft
ventricular (communicating) shunt
CC Excl: 996.2, 996.63, 996.75, 997.91-997.99, 998.81, 998.83-998.9
AHA: 2Q, '99, 4; S-O, '87, 10

√5th **996.3 Mechanical complication of genitourinary device, implant, and graft**
AHA: 3Q, '01, 13; S-O, '85, 3

996.30 Unspecified device, implant, and graft `CC`
CC Excl: 596.81, 596.83, 996.30, 996.64-996.65, 996.76, 997.91-997.99, 998.81, 998.83-998.9

996.31 Due to urethral [indwelling] catheter

996.32 Due to intrauterine contraceptive device ♀

996.39 Other `CC`
Prosthetic reconstruction of vas deferens
Repair (graft) of ureter without mention of resection
> **EXCLUDES** *complications due to:*
> *external stoma of urinary tract (596.81-596.83)*
> *internal anastomosis of urinary tract (997.5)*

CC Excl: 596.81-596.83, 996.39, 996.64-996.65, 996.76, 997.91-997.99, 998.81, 998.83-998.9

√5th **996.4 Mechanical complication of internal orthopedic device, implant, and graft**
Mechanical complications involving:
external (fixation) device utilizing internal screw(s), pin(s) or other methods of fixation
grafts of bone, cartilage, muscle, or tendon
internal (fixation) device such as nail, plate, rod, etc.
Use additional code to identify prosthetic joint with mechanical complication (V43.60-V43.69)
> **EXCLUDES** *complications of external orthopedic device, such as: pressure ulcer due to cast (707.00-707.09)*

AHA: 4Q, '05, 91; 2Q, '99, 10; 2Q, '98, 19; 2Q, '96, 11; 3Q, '95, 16; N-D, '85, 11
TIP: Since these codes may be used for any joint device complications, assign an additional code from subcategory V43.6 to specify the joint involved.

996.40 Unspecified mechanical complication of internal orthopedic device, implant, and graft `CC`
CC Excl: 996.40-996.49, 996.66-996.67, 996.77-996.78, 997.91-997.99, 998.81, 998.83-998.9

996.41 Mechanical loosening of prosthetic joint `CC`
Aseptic loosening
CC Excl: See code: 996.40
AHA: 4Q, '05, 112
   T84.031A Mech loosening int lt hip prosth jnt initial enc `I-10`

996.42 Dislocation of prosthetic joint `CC`
Instability of prosthetic joint
Subluxation of prosthetic joint
CC Excl: See code 996.40
   T84.020A Disloc of internal rt hip prosthesis, init encntr `I-10`

996.43 Broken prosthetic joint implant `CC`
Breakage (fracture) of prosthetic joint
CC Excl: See code 996.40

996.44 Peri-prosthetic fracture around prosthetic joint `CC`
CC Excl: See code 996.40
AHA: 4Q, '05, 93

996.45 Peri-prosthetic osteolysis `CC`
Use additional code to identify major osseous defect, if applicable (731.3)
CC Excl: See code 996.40
AHA: 4Q, '06, 103

996.46 Articular bearing surface wear of prosthetic joint `CC`
CC Excl: See code 996.40

996.47 Other mechanical complication of prosthetic joint implant `CC`
Mechanical complication of prosthetic joint NOS
Prosthetic joint implant failure NOS
CC Excl: See code 996.40

996.49 Other mechanical complication of other internal orthopedic device, implant, and graft `CC`
Breakage of internal fixation device in bone
Dislocation of internal fixation device in bone
> **EXCLUDES** *mechanical complication of prosthetic joint implant (996.41-996.47)*

CC Excl: See code 996.40
AHA: ▶2Q, '13, 22;◀ 1Q, '10, 7

√5th **996.5 Mechanical complication of other specified prosthetic device, implant, and graft**
Mechanical complications involving:
nonabsorbable surgical material NOS
other graft, implant, and internal device, not elsewhere classified
prosthetic implant in:
   bile duct
   breast
   chin
   orbit of eye
AHA: 1Q, '98, 11

996.51 Due to corneal graft `CC`
CC Excl: 996.51, 997.91-997.99
AHA: 2Q, '10, 4-5

996.52 Due to graft of other tissue, not elsewhere classified `CC`
Skin graft failure or rejection
> **EXCLUDES** *failure of artificial skin graft (996.55)*
> *failure of decellularized allodermis (996.55)*
> *sloughing of temporary skin allografts or xenografts (pigskin) — omit code*

CC Excl: 996.52, 996.55, 997.91-997.99
AHA: 3Q, '12, 6; 1Q, '96, 10
TIP: Assign for failure of living biological wound care materials used to treat nonhealing wounds recalcitrant to conventional therapy (e.g., Apligraft, CelTx, Dermagraft).

996.53 Due to ocular lens prosthesis `CC`
> **EXCLUDES** *contact lenses — code to condition*

CC Excl: 996.53, 997.91-997.99
AHA: 1Q, '00, 9

996.54 Due to breast prosthesis `CC`
Breast capsule (prosthesis)
Mammary implant
CC Excl: 996.54, 997.91-997.99
AHA: 2Q, '98, 14; 3Q, '92, 4
TIP: If documentation indicates capsular contracture of breast implant, see instead code 611.83.

`N` Newborn Age: 0   `P` Pediatric Age: 0-17   `M` Maternity Age: 12-55   `A` Adult Age: 15-124   `MCC` Major CC Condition   `CC` CC Condition   `HIV` HIV Related Dx

996.55 Due to artificial skin graft and decellularized allodermis `CC`
Dislodgement
Displacement
Failure
Non-adherence
Poor incorporation
Shearing
CC Excl: 996.52, 996.55-996.60, 996.68-996.70, 996.79, 997.91-997.99
AHA: 4Q, '98, 52

996.56 Due to peritoneal dialysis catheter `CC`
EXCLUDES *mechanical complication of arteriovenous dialysis catheter (996.1)*
CC Excl: 996.56-996.60, 996.68-996.70, 996.79, 997.91-997.99
AHA: 4Q, '98, 54

996.57 Due to insulin pump `CC`
CC Excl: 596.81-596.83, 996.00-996.30, 996.39-996.79, 997.91-997.99, 998.81, 998.83-998.9
AHA: 4Q, '03, 81-82

996.59 Due to other implant and internal device, not elsewhere classified `CC`
Nonabsorbable surgical material NOS
Prosthetic implant in:
  bile duct
  chin
  orbit of eye
CC Excl: See code: 996.56
AHA: ▶2Q, '13, 11;◀ 1Q, '11, 10-11; 2Q, '99, 13; 3Q, '94, 7
TIP: Assign for clogged biliary stent and also for nonfunctioning pressure equalization (PE) tubes.

✓5th **996.6 Infection and inflammatory reaction due to internal prosthetic device, implant, and graft**
Infection (causing obstruction) ⎱ due to (presence of) any device,
Inflammation ⎰ implant, and graft classifiable to 996.0-996.5
Use additional code to identify specified infections
AHA: 2Q, '89, 16; J-F, '87, 14; 4Q, '11, 156
TIP: Do not assign as principal diagnosis for patient encounters for joint replacement following previous explantation of joint prosthesis, assign code V54.82 instead.

996.60 Due to unspecified device, implant, and graft `CC`
CC Excl: 596.81-596.83, 996.00-996.79, 997.91-997.99, 998.81, 998.83-998.9

15 **996.61 Due to cardiac device, implant, and graft** `CC`
Cardiac pacemaker or defibrillator:
  electrode(s), lead(s)
  pulse generator
  subcutaneous pocket
Coronary artery bypass graft
Heart valve prosthesis
CC Excl: 996.00-996.1, 996.52, 996.55-996.62, 996.68-996.74, 996.79, 997.91-997.99, 998.81, 998.83-998.9

996.62 Due to other vascular device, implant, and graft `CC`
Arterial graft
Arteriovenous fistula or shunt
Infusion pump
Vascular catheter (arterial) (dialysis) (peripheral venous)
EXCLUDES *infection due to:*
    central venous catheter (999.31-999.32)
    Hickman catheter (999.31-999.32)
    peripherally inserted central catheter [PICC] (999.31-999.32)
    portacath (port-a-cath) (999.31-999.32)
    triple lumen catheter (999.31-999.32)
    umbilical venous catheter (999.31-999.32)
CC Excl: See code 996.61
AHA: 2Q, '10, 8; 4Q, '07, 86; 2Q, '04, 16; 1Q, '04, 5; 4Q, '03, 107, 111; 2Q, '03, 7; 2Q, '94, 13
T82.7xxA Inf & inflam react oth card vasc dev gft initial enc `I-10`

996.63 Due to nervous system device, implant, and graft `CC`
Electrodes implanted in brain
Peripheral nerve graft
Spinal canal catheter
Ventricular (communicating) shunt (catheter)
CC Excl: 996.2, 996.52, 996.55-996.60, 996.63, 996.68-996.69, 996.70, 996.75, 996.79, 997.91-997.99, 998.81, 998.83-998.9

996.64 Due to indwelling urinary catheter `CC`
Use additional code to identify specified infections, such as:
  cystitis (595.0-595.9)
  sepsis (038.0-038.9)
EXCLUDES *complications due to:*
    external stoma of urinary tract (596.81-596.83)
CC Excl: 596.81-596.83, 599.0, 996.30, 996.39, 996.56-996.59, 996.60, 996.64, 996.65, 996.68, 996.69, 996.70, 996.76, 996.79, 998.81, 998.83-998.9
AHA: 2Q, '12, 20; 1Q, '12, 11; 3Q, '09,10-11; 3Q, '93, 6
TIP: Assign for documented infection due to the presence of an indwelling urinary catheter, whether Foley, suprapubic, or other type.
T83.51XA Infect/inflm reaction d/t indwell urinary catheter, init `I-10`

996.65 Due to other genitourinary device, implant, and graft `CC`
Intrauterine contraceptive device
CC Excl: 596.81-596.83, 996.30, 996.39, 996.52, 996.55-996.59, 996.60, 996.64, 996.65, 996.68, 996.69, 996.70, 996.76, 996.79, 998.81, 998.83-998.9
AHA: 1Q, '00, 15

996.66 Due to internal joint prosthesis `CC`
Use additional code to identify infected prosthetic joint (V43.60-V43.69)
CC Excl: 996.40-996.49, 996.52, 996.55-996.59, 996.60, 996.66-996.69, 996.70, 996.77-996.79, 997.91-997.99, 998.81, 998.83-998.9
AHA: ▶1Q, '14, 5;◀ 4Q, '11, 156; 2Q, '08, 3-5; 2Q, '07, 7; 4Q, '05, 91, 113; 2Q, '91, 18
TIP: Do not assign as principal diagnosis for patient encounters for joint replacement following previous explantation of joint prosthesis, assign code V54.82 instead.
T84.51xA Inf & inflam reaction int rt hip pros initial enc `I-10`

12 **996.67 Due to other internal orthopedic device, implant, and graft** `CC`
Bone growth stimulator (electrode)
Internal fixation device (pin) (rod) (screw)
CC Excl: 996.40-996.49, 996.52, 996.55-996.59, 996.60, 996.66-996.69, 996.70, 996.77-996.79, 997.91-997.99, 998.81, 998.83-998.9

996.68 Due to peritoneal dialysis catheter `CC`
Exit-site infection or inflammation
CC Excl: 996.56-996.59, 996.60, 996.68, 996.69, 996.70, 996.79, 997.91-997.99
AHA: 4Q, '98, 54

996.69 Due to other internal prosthetic device, implant, and graft `CC`
Breast prosthesis
Ocular lens prosthesis
Prosthetic orbital implant
CC Excl: See code 996.60
AHA: 1Q, '11, 10; 2Q, '08, 11; 4Q, '03, 108; 4Q, '98, 52

---

12 HAC when reported with procedure codes 81.01-81.08, 81.23-81.24, 81.31-81.38, 81.83, or 81.85 and POA = N
15 HAC when reported with procedure codes 00.50-00.54, 37.74-37.77, 37.79, 37.80-37.89, 37.94, 37.96, or 37.98 and POA = N

✓4th ✓5th Additional Digit Required | Unacceptable PDx | Manifestation Code | Hospital Acquired Condition | ▶◀ Revised Text | ● New Code | ▲ Revised Code Title

Injury and Poisoning

996.7–996.94

√5ᵗʰ **996.7 Other complications of internal (biological) (synthetic) prosthetic device, implant, and graft**

Complication NOS
Occlusion NOS
Embolism
Fibrosis   } due to (presence of) any device, implant, and graft classifiable to 996.0-996.5
Hemorrhage
Pain
Stenosis
Thrombus

Use additional code to identify complication, such as:
    pain due to presence of device, implant or graft (338.18-338.19, 338.28-338.29)
    venous embolism and thrombosis (453.2-453.9)

EXCLUDES   disruption (dehiscence) of internal suture material (998.31)
     transplant rejection (996.80-996.89)

AHA: 2Q, '12, 5; 2Q, '07, 12; 4Q, '05, 94; 1Q, '89, 9; N-D, '86, 5

996.70 Due to unspecified device, implant, and graft

996.71 Due to heart valve prosthesis CC
CC Excl: 996.00, 996.02, 996.09-996.1, 996.52, 996.55-996.62, 996.68-996.74, 996.79, 997.91-997.99, 998.81, 998.83-998.9

996.72 Due to other cardiac device, implant, and graft CC
Cardiac pacemaker or defibrillator:
    electrode(s), lead(s)
    subcutaneous pocket
Coronary artery bypass (graft)
    EXCLUDES   occlusion due to atherosclerosis (414.02-414.06)
CC Excl: 996.00-996.02, 996.04-996.1, 996.52, 996.55-996.62, 996.68-996.74, 996.79, 997.91-997.99, 998.81, 998.83-998.9
AHA: 2Q, '10, 8-9; 3Q, '08, 10; 3Q, '06, 8, 25; 3Q, '01, 20
TIP: Assign for in-stent stenosis of previously placed coronary artery stent.
T82.847A Pain cardiac prosth devc impl graft initial enc   I-10

996.73 Due to renal dialysis device, implant, and graft CC
CC Excl: 996.1, 996.52, 996.55-996.60, 996.68-996.70, 996.73, 996.79, 997.91-997.99, 998.81, 998.83-998.9
AHA: 2Q, '91, 18
T82.858A Stenosis vasc prosth devc impl graft initial enc   I-10

996.74 Due to other vascular device, implant, and graft CC
    EXCLUDES   occlusion of biological graft due to atherosclerosis (440.30-440.32)
CC Excl: 996.00-996.1, 996.52, 996.55-996.62, 996.68-996.74, 996.79, 997.91-997.99, 998.81, 998.83-998.9
AHA: ▶2Q, '13, 3;◀ 1Q, '12, 18; 2Q, '11, 8; 1Q, '03, 16, 17
TIP: Assign for clotted peripherally inserted central catheter (PICC) line.

996.75 Due to nervous system device, implant, and graft CC
CC Excl: 996.2, 996.52, 996.55-996.60, 996.63, 996.68-996.70, 996.75, 996.79, 997.91-997.99, 998.81, 998.83-998.9

996.76 Due to genitourinary device, implant, and graft CC
    EXCLUDES   complications of implanted vaginal mesh (629.31-629.32)
CC Excl: 596.81-596.83, 996.30, 996.39, 996.52, 996.55-996.59, 996.60, 996.64-996.65, 996.68-996.69, 996.70, 996.76, 996.79, 998.81, 998.83-998.9
AHA: 1Q, '09, 15; 1Q, '00, 15
T83.83xA Hemorrhage GU prosth devc impl graft initial enc   I-10

996.77 Due to internal joint prosthesis CC
Use additional code to identify prosthetic joint (V43.60-V43.69)
CC Excl: 996.40-996.49, 996.52, 996.55-996.60, 996.66-996.70, 996.77-996.79, 997.91-997.99, 998.81, 998.83-998.9
AHA: 4Q, '05, 91
T84.84xA Pain int ortho prosth devc impl gft initial enc   I-10

996.78 Due to other internal orthopedic device, implant, and graft CC
CC Excl: 996.40-996.49, 996.52, 996.55-996.60, 996.66-996.70, 996.77-996.79, 997.91-997.99, 998.81, 998.83-998.9
AHA: 2Q, '03, 14

996.79 Due to other internal prosthetic device, implant, and graft CC
CC Excl: 596.81-596.83, 996.00- 996.79, 997.91-997.99, 998.81, 998.83-998.9
AHA: 2Q, '04, 7; 1Q,'01, 8; 3Q, '95, 14; 3Q, '92, 4

√5ᵗʰ **996.8 Complications of transplanted organ**
Transplant failure or rejection
Use additional code to identify nature of complication, such as:
    cytomegalovirus (CMV) infection (078.5)
    graft-versus-host disease (279.50-279.53)
    malignancy associated with organ transplant (199.2)
    post-transplant lymphoproliferative disorder (PTLD) (238.77)
AHA: 4Q, '08, 82-83; 3Q, '01, 12; 3Q, '93, 3, 4; 2Q, '93, 11; 1Q, '93, 24
TIP: Assign only if the complication affects the function of the transplanted organ. Assign also a code for the specific complication.

996.80 Transplanted organ, unspecified CC
CC Excl: 238.77, 996.80, 996.87, 997.91-997.99

996.81 Kidney CC
CC Excl: 996.81, 997.91-997.99
AHA: 2Q, '12, 6; 2Q, '11, 6; 1Q, '10, 9; 4Q, '08, 83; 3Q, '03, 16; 3Q, '98, 6, 7; 3Q, '94, 8; 2Q, '94, 9; 1Q, '93, 24
TIP: Do not assign for chronic kidney disease (CKD) status following kidney transplant. The provider must indicate transplant failure, rejection, or other complication to support assignment of this code.
T86.11 Kidney transplant rejection   I-10

996.82 Liver CC
CC Excl: 996.82, 997.91-997.99
AHA: 4Q, '08, 82, 99; 3Q, '03, 17; 3Q, '98, 3, 4

996.83 Heart CC
CC Excl: 996.83, 997.91-997.99
AHA: 3Q, '03, 16; 4Q, '02, 53; 3Q, '98, 5

996.84 Lung CC
CC Excl: 996.84, 997.91-997.99
AHA: 2Q, '03, 12; 3Q, '98, 5

996.85 Bone marrow CC
CC Excl: 279.50-279.53, 996.85, 997.91-997.99
AHA: 1Q, '12, 13;4Q, '08, 91; 4Q, '90, 4
TIP: Do not assign for recurrence or relapse of hematopoietic or lymphatic malignancy following bone marrow/stem cell transplant.

996.86 Pancreas CC
CC Excl: 996.86, 997.91-997.99

996.87 Intestine CC
CC Excl: 238.77, 996.80, 996.87, 997.91-997.99

996.88 Stem cell CC
Complications from stem cells from:
    peripheral blood
    umbilical cord
CC Excl: 996.88-996.89, 997.91- 997.99
AHA: 4Q, '11, 147-148

996.89 Other specified transplanted organ CC
CC Excl: 996.88-996.89, 997.91- 997.99
AHA: 1Q, '11, 8; 3Q, '94, 5

√5ᵗʰ **996.9 Complications of reattached extremity or body part**

996.90 Unspecified extremity CC
CC Excl: 996.90, 997.91-997.99, 998.81, 998.83-998.9

996.91 Forearm CC
CC Excl: 996.91, 997.91-997.99, 998.81, 998.83-998.9

996.92 Hand CC
CC Excl: 996.92, 997.91-997.99, 998.81, 998.83-998.9

996.93 Finger(s) CC
CC Excl: 996.93, 997.91-997.99, 998.81, 998.83-998.9

996.94 Upper extremity, other and unspecified CC
CC Excl: 996.94, 997.91-997.99, 998.81, 998.83-998.9

N Newborn Age: 0   P Pediatric Age: 0-17   M Maternity Age: 12-55   A Adult Age: 15-124   MCC Major CC Condition   CC CC Condition   HIV HIV Related Dx

996.95 Foot and toe(s) `CC`
CC Excl: 996.95, 997.91-997.99, 998.81, 998.83-998.9

996.96 Lower extremity, other and unspecified `CC`
CC Excl: 996.96, 997.91-997.99, 998.81, 998.83-998.9

996.99 Other specified body part `CC`
CC Excl: 996.99, 997.91-997.99, 998.81, 998.83-998.9

√4ᵗʰ 997 Complications affecting specified body systems, not elsewhere classified

Use additional code to identify complications

EXCLUDES the listed conditions when specified as:
causing shock (998.00-998.09)
complications of:
anesthesia:
adverse effect (001.0-799.9, 995.0-995.8)
in labor or delivery (668.0-668.9)
poisoning (968.0-969.9)
implanted device or graft (996.0-996.9)
obstetrical procedures (669.0-669.4)
reattached extremity (996.90-996.96)
transplanted organ (996.80-996.89)

AHA: 1Q, '94, 4; 1Q, '93, 26

√5ᵗʰ 997.0 Nervous system complications

997.00 Nervous system complication, unspecified

997.01 Central nervous system complication `CC`
Anoxic brain damage
Cerebral hypoxia
EXCLUDES cerebrovascular hemorrhage or infarction (997.02)
CC Excl: 997.00-997.09, 997.91-997.99, 998.81, 998.83-998.9
AHA: 1Q, '07, 22; 1Q, '06, 15
TIP: Assign for hyperperfusion syndrome, a complication of carotid endarterectomy.

997.02 Iatrogenic cerebrovascular infarction or hemorrhage `CC`
Postoperative stroke
CC Excl: See code: 997.01
AHA: 3Q, '10, 5; 3Q, '06, 6; 2Q, '04, 8; 4Q, '95, 57
TIP: Assign an additional code to specify the type of postoperative stroke involved.
I97.810 Intraop cerebrvascular infarct during card surg `I-10`

997.09 Other nervous system complications `CC`
CC Excl: See code: 997.01
G97.0 Cerebrospinal fluid leak from spinal puncture `I-10`

997.1 Cardiac complications `CC`
Cardiac:
arrest
insufficiency } during or resulting from a procedure
Cardiorespiratory failure
Heart failure
EXCLUDES the listed conditions as long-term effects of cardiac surgery or due to the presence of cardiac prosthetic device (429.4)
CC Excl: 997.1, 997.91-997.99, 998.81, 998.83-998.9
AHA: ▶4Q, '13, 98; 1Q, '13, 11;◀ 1Q, '11, 3-4; 4Q, '08, 179; 2Q, '02, 12
I97.711 Intraoperative cardiac arrest during oth surgery `I-10`

997.2 Peripheral vascular complications `CC`
Phlebitis or thrombophlebitis during or resulting from a procedure
EXCLUDES the listed conditions due to:
implant or catheter device (996.62)
infusion, perfusion, or transfusion (999.2)
complications affecting blood vessels (997.71-997.79)
CC Excl: 997.2, 997.79-997.99, 998.81, 998.83-998.9
AHA: 1Q, '03, 6; 3Q, '02, 24-26
T81.72xA Complication of vein following a procedure NEC intl enc `I-10`

√5ᵗʰ 997.3 Respiratory complications
EXCLUDES iatrogenic [postoperative] pneumothorax (512.1)
iatrogenic pulmonary embolism (415.11)
specified complications classified elsewhere, such as:
adult respiratory distress syndrome (518.52)
pulmonary edema, postoperative (518.4)
respiratory insufficiency, acute, postoperative (518.52)
shock lung related to trauma and surgery (518.52)
tracheostomy complications (519.00-519.09)
transfusion related acute lung injury [TRALI] (518.7)
AHA: 4Q, '11, 148-150; 1Q, '97, 10; 2Q, '93, 3; 2Q, '93, 9; 4Q, '90, 25

997.31 Ventilator associated pneumonia `CC`
Ventilator associated pneumonitis
Use additional code to identify organism
CC Excl: 518.7, 997.31-997.39, 997.91-997.99, 998.81, 998.83-998.9
AHA: 4Q, '08, 148-149
TIP: Do not assign unless the provider has documented the relationship between the pneumonia and ventilation status.

997.32 Postprocedural aspiration pneumonia `CC`
Chemical pneumonitis resulting from a procedure
Mendelson's syndrome resulting from a procedure
EXCLUDES aspiration pneumonia during labor and delivery (668.0)
CC Excl: See code 997.31
DEF: Mendelson's syndrome: acid pneumonitis due to aspiration of gastric acids, may occur after anesthesia or sedation.
AHA: 4Q, '11, 150
TIP: Do not assign code 507.0 in additition to 997.32; aspiration pneumonia due to a procedure is fully captured with this code.

997.39 Other respiratory complications `CC`
CC Excl: See code 997.31
AHA: 1Q, '11, 16
J95.4 Chem pneumonitis d/t anesthesia [Mendelson's syndrm] `I-10`

√5ᵗʰ 997.4 Digestive system complications
Complications of:
intestinal (internal) anastomosis and bypass, not elsewhere classified, except that involving urinary tract
Hepatic failure
Hepatorenal syndrome } specified as due to a procedure
Intestinal obstruction NOS
EXCLUDES complications of gastric band procedure (539.01-539.09)
complications of other bariatric procedure (539.81-539.89)
gastrostomy complications (536.40-536.49)
specified gastrointestinal complications classified elsewhere, such as:
blind loop syndrome (579.2)
colostomy and enterostomy complications (569.60-569.69)
complications of intestinal pouch (569.71-569.79)
gastrojejunal ulcer (534.0-534.9)
infection of esophagostomy (530.86)
infection of external stoma (569.61)
mechanical complication of esophagostomy (530.87)
pelvic peritoneal adhesions, female (614.6)
peritoneal adhesions (568.0)
peritoneal adhesions with obstruction (560.81)
postcholecystectomy syndrome (576.0)
postgastric surgery syndromes (564.2)
pouchitis (569.71)
vomiting following gastrointestinal surgery (564.3)
AHA: 4Q, '11, 125, 148-150; 2Q, '01, 4-6; 3Q, '99, 4; 2Q, '99, 14; 3Q, '97, 7; 1Q, '97, 11; 2Q, '95, 7; 1Q, '93, 26; 3Q, '92, 15; 2Q, '89, 15; 1Q, '88, 14

997.41 Retained cholelithiasis following cholecystectomy `CC`
CC Excl: 530.86-530.87, 536.40-536.49, 539.01-539.89, 569.62, 569.71-569.79, 997.41-997.49, 997.71, 997.91-997.99, 998.81, 998.83-998.9

√4ᵗʰ √5ᵗʰ Additional Digit Required   Unacceptable PDx   Manifestation Code   Hospital Acquired Condition   ▶◀ Revised Text   ● New Code   ▲ Revised Code Title

Injury and Poisoning

997.49 Other digestive system complications `CC`

CC Excl: See code 997.41

AHA: 1Q, '12, 6

TIP: Assign for ileus following gastrointestinal surgery; physician documentation of the cause-and-effect relationship is not required.

K91.89 Oth postproc comp & disorder of digest syst `I-10`

997.5 Urinary complications

Complications of:
internal anastomosis and bypass of urinary tract, including that involving intestinal tract

Oliguria or anuria
Renal (kidney):
   failure (acute)
   insufficiency (acute)   } specified as due to procedure
Tubular necrosis (acute)

EXCLUDES *complications of cystostomy (596.81-596.83)*
complications of external stoma of urinary tract (596.81-596.83)
specified complications classified elsewhere, such as:
postoperative stricture of:
ureter (593.3)
urethra (598.2)

AHA: ▶1Q, '14, 12;◀ 1Q, '12, 11; 3Q, '03, 13; 3Q, '96, 10, 15; 4Q, '95, 73; 1Q, '92, 13; 2Q, '89, 16; M-A, '87, 10; S-O, '85, 3

TIP: If a urinary tract infection is specified as a postoperative complication, assign both 997.5 and 599.0.

TIP: Assign for a urostomy-associated urinary tract infection with poor self-catheterization technique/hygiene.

N99.0 Postprocedural (acute) (chronic) renal failure `I-10`

✓5th 997.6 Amputation stump complication

EXCLUDES *admission for treatment for a current traumatic amputation — code to complicated traumatic amputation*
phantom limb (syndrome) (353.6)

AHA: 4Q, '95, 82

997.60 Unspecified complication

997.61 Neuroma of amputation stump

DEF: Hyperplasia generated nerve cell mass following amputation.

997.62 Infection (chronic) `CC`

Use additional code to identify the organism

CC Excl: 997.60, 997.62-997.69, 997.91-997.99, 998.81, 998.83-998.9

AHA: 1Q, '05, 15 4Q, '96, 46

TIP: If cellulitis is specified as a manifestation of the infection, assign an additional code from category 681 or 682.

T87.43 Infection amputation stump right lower extremity `I-10`

997.69 Other

AHA: 1Q, '05, 15

✓5th 997.7 Vascular complications of other vessels

EXCLUDES *peripheral vascular complications (997.2)*

997.71 Vascular complications of mesenteric artery `CC`

CC Excl: 997.2, 997.71-997.99, 998.81, 998.83-998.9

AHA: 4Q, '01, 53

TIP: For postoperative mesenteric artery embolism, assign also code 557.0 Acute vascular insufficiency of intestine.

997.72 Vascular complications of renal artery `CC`

CC Excl: See code 997.71

997.79 Vascular complications of other vessels `CC`

CC Excl: See code 997.71

✓5th 997.9 Complications affecting other specified body systems, not elsewhere classified

EXCLUDES *specified complications classified elsewhere, such as:*
broad ligament laceration syndrome (620.6)
postartificial menopause syndrome (627.4)
postoperative stricture of vagina (623.2)

997.91 Hypertension

EXCLUDES *essential hypertension (401.0-401.9)*

AHA: 4Q, '95, 57

997.99 Other `CC`

Vitreous touch syndrome

DEF: Vitreous touch syndrome: vitreous protruding through pupil and attaches to corneal epithelium; causes aqueous fluid in vitreous body; marked by corneal edema, loss of lucidity; complication of cataract surgery.

CC Excl: 997.91-997.99, 998.81, 998.83-998.9

AHA: 2Q, '94, 12; 1Q, '94, 17

✓4th 998 Other complications of procedures, not elsewhere classified

EXCLUDES *fluid overload due to transfusion (blood) (276.61)*
TACO (276.61)
transfusion associated circulatory overload (276.61)

AHA: 1Q, '94, 4

✓5th 998.0 Postoperative shock

Shock during or resulting from a surgical procedure

EXCLUDES *shock:*
anaphylactic due to serum (999.41-999.49)
anesthetic (995.4)
electric (994.8)
following abortion (639.5)
obstetric (669.1)
traumatic (958.4)

AHA: 4Q, '11, 150-153

998.00 Postoperative shock, unspecified `CC`

Collapse, not otherwise specified, during or resulting from a surgical procedure
Failure of peripheral circulation, postoperative

CC Excl: 958.4, 995.4, 997.91-998.13, 998.81, 998.83-998.9

998.01 Postoperative shock, cardiogenic `MCC`

CC Excl: see Code: 998.00

AHA: 4Q, '11, 152

998.02 Postoperative shock, septic `MCC`

Postoperative endotoxic shock
Postoperative gram-negative shock

Code first underlying infection

Use additional code, to identify severe sepsis (995.92) and any associated acute organ dysfunction, if applicable

CC Excl: see Code: 998.00

AHA: 4Q, '11, 153

998.09 Postoperative shock, other `MCC`

Postoperative hypovolemic shock

CC Excl: see Code: 998.00

✓5th 998.1 Hemorrhage or hematoma or seroma complicating a procedure

EXCLUDES *hemorrhage, hematoma, or seroma:*
complicating cesarean section or puerperal perineal wound (674.3)
due to implanted device or graft (996.70-996.79)

998.11 Hemorrhage complicating a procedure `CC`

CC Excl: 456.0, 456.20, 530.81-530.83, 530.89, 531.00-531.01, 531.20-531.21, 531.40-531.41, 531.60-531.61, 532.00-532.01, 532.20-532.21, 532.40-532.41, 532.60-532.61, 533.00-533.01, 533.20-533.21, 533.40-533.41, 533.60-533.61, 534.00-534.01, 534.20-534.21, 534.40-534.41, 534.60-534.61, 535.01, 535.11, 535.21, 535.31, 535.41, 535.51, 535.61, 535.71, 537.83, 562.02-562.03, 562.12-562.13, 569.3, 569.85, 578.0-578.9, 772.4, 997.91-998.13, 998.81, 998.89-998.9

AHA: 1Q, '11, 13; 3Q, '03, 13; 1Q, '03, 4; 4Q, '97, 52; 1Q, '97, 10

I97.410 Intraop hemorrhage circ sys organ comp card cath `I-10`

998.12 Hematoma complicating a procedure `CC`

CC Excl: see code 998.11

AHA: 1Q, '11, 13; 3Q, '06, 12; 1Q, '03, 6; 3Q, '02, 24, 26

998.13 Seroma complicating a procedure `CC`

CC Excl: See code 998.11

AHA: 4Q, '96, 46; 1Q, '93, 26; 2Q, '92, 15; S-O, '87, 8

`N` Newborn Age: 0   `P` Pediatric Age: 0-17   `M` Maternity Age: 12-55   `A` Adult Age: 15-124   `MCC` Major CC Condition   `CC` CC Condition   `HIV` HIV Related Dx

998.2 Accidental puncture or laceration during a procedure `CC`
Accidental perforation by catheter or other instrument during a procedure on:

blood vessel   organ
nerve

> **EXCLUDES** *iatrogenic [postoperative] pneumothorax (512.1)*
> *puncture or laceration caused by implanted device intentionally left in operation wound (996.0-996.5)*
> *specified complications classified elsewhere, such as:*
> *broad ligament laceration syndrome (620.6)*
> *dural tear (349.31)*
> *incidental durotomy (349.31)*
> *trauma from instruments during delivery (664.0-665.9)*

CC Excl: 349.31-349.39, 997.91-997.99, 998.2, 998.81, 998.83-998.9
AHA: 2Q, '12, 5; 1Q, '10, 8, 11; 2Q, '07, 9; 1Q, '06, 15; 3Q, '02, 24, 26; 3Q, '94, 6; 3Q, '90, 17; 3Q, '90, 18
TIP: Assign an additional code to describe the nature or site (e.g., organ) of the perforation.
I97.51 Accidentl punct lac circ sys organ dur circ proc   `I-10`

✓5ᵗʰ 998.3 Disruption of wound
Dehiscence ⎫
Rupture   ⎬ of operation wound

Disruption of any suture materials or other closure method

> **EXCLUDES** *disruption of:*
> *cesarean wound (674.1)*
> *perineal wound, puerperal (674.2)*

AHA: 4Q, '08,149-152; 4Q, '02, 73; 1Q, '93, 19

998.30 Disruption of wound, unspecified `CC`
Disruption of wound NOS
CC Excl: 997.91-997.99, 998.30-998.33, 998.81, 998.83-998.9

998.31 Disruption of internal operation (surgical) wound `CC`
Disruption or dehiscence of closure of:
fascia, superficial or muscular
internal organ
muscle or muscle flap
ribs or rib cage
skull or craniotomy
sternum or sternotomy
tendon or ligament
Deep disruption or dehiscence of operation wound NOS

> **EXCLUDES** *complications of internal anastomosis of:*
> *gastrointestinal tract (997.49)*
> *urinary tract (997.5)*

CC Excl: See code 998.30
AHA: 4Q, '10, 131

998.32 Disruption of external operation (surgical) wound `CC`
Disruption of operation wound NOS
Disruption or dehiscence of closure of:
cornea
mucosa
skin
subcutaneous tissue
Full-thickness skin disruption or dehiscence
Superficial disruption or dehiscence of operation wound

CC Excl: See code 998.30
AHA: ▶1Q, '14, 5;◀ 1Q, '06, 8; 1Q, '05, 11; 4Q, '03, 104, 106
T81.31xA Disruption ext operation wound NEC initial enc   `I-10`

998.33 Disruption of traumatic injury wound repair `CC`
Disruption or dehiscence of closure of traumatic laceration (external) (internal)
CC Excl: See code 998.30
AHA: 4Q, '08, 151, 152

998.4 Foreign body accidentally left during a procedure `CC`
Adhesions ⎫ due to foreign body accidentally left in
Obstruction ⎬ operative wound or body cavity
Perforation ⎭ during a procedure

> **EXCLUDES** *obstruction or perforation caused by implanted device intentionally left in body (996.0-996.5)*

CC Excl: 997.91-997.99, 998.4, 998.81, 998.83-998.9
AHA: ▶1Q, '14, 14;◀ 1Q, '12, 12; 1Q, '11, 5-6; 1Q, '09,18 1Q, '89, 9
TIP: Report for an unintended retention of a foreign object following any type of procedure, in any type of setting.

✓5ᵗʰ 998.5 Postoperative infection
> **EXCLUDES** *bleb associated endophthalmitis (379.63)*
> *infection due to:*
> *implanted device (996.60-996.69)*
> *infusion, perfusion, or transfusion (999.31-999.39)*
> *postoperative obstetrical wound infection (674.3)*

998.51 Infected postoperative seroma `CC`
Use additional code to identify organism
CC Excl: 997.91-997.99, 998.51-998.59, 998.81, 998.89-998.9
AHA: 4Q, '96, 46

13, 14, 15 998.59 Other postoperative infection `CC`
Abscess:
intra-abdominal ⎫
stitch   ⎬ postoperative
subphrenic   ⎪
wound   ⎭
Septicemia

Use additional code to identify infection
CC Excl: See code: 998.51
AHA: 4Q, '11, 153; 2Q, '06, 23; 4Q, '04, 76; 4Q, '03, 104, 106-107; 3Q, '98, 3; 3Q, '95, 5; 2Q, '95, 7; 3Q, '94, 6; 1Q, '93, 19; J-F, '87, 14
TIP: Do not assign if the infection is related to an internal prosthetic device, implant, or graft; see instead subcategory 996.6.
T81.4xxA Infection following procedure initial encounter   `I-10`

998.6 Persistent postoperative fistula `CC`
CC Excl: 997.91-997.99, 998.6, 998.81, 998.83-998.9
AHA: J-F, '87, 14
T81.83XA Persistent postprocedural fistula, init encntr   `I-10`

998.7 Acute reaction to foreign substance accidentally left during a procedure `CC`
Peritonitis:
aseptic
chemical
CC Excl: 997.91-997.99, 998.7-998.81, 998.83-998.9

✓5ᵗʰ 998.8 Other specified complications of procedures, not elsewhere classified
AHA: 4Q, '94, 46; 1Q, '89, 9

998.81 Emphysema (subcutaneous) (surgical) resulting from a procedure

998.82 Cataract fragments in eye following cataract surgery

998.83 Non-healing surgical wound `CC`
CC Excl: 997.91-997.99, 998.81, 998.83-998.9
AHA: 4Q, '96, 47

998.89 Other specified complications
AHA: ▶4Q, '13, 90;◀ 2Q, '12, 8; 2Q, '09, 11; 3Q, '06, 9; 3Q, '05, 16; 3Q, '99, 13; 2Q, '98, 16
TIP: Assign for cases in which a procedure is performed on the wrong body site (e.g., right leg versus left leg), along with E876.5-E876.7.
T81.89xA Other complications of procedures NEC, init enc   `I-10`

998.9 Unspecified complication of procedure, not elsewhere classified
Postoperative complication NOS

> **EXCLUDES** *complication NOS of obstetrical, surgery or procedure (669.4)*

AHA: 4Q, '93, 37

---

[13] HAC when reported with procedure codes 81.01-81.08, 81.23-81.24, 81.31-81.38, 81.83, 81.85, and POA = N
[14] HAC when reported with principal diagnosis 278.01 and with procedure code 44.38, 44.39, or 44.95 and POA = N
[15] HAC when reported with procedure codes 00.50-00.54, 37.74-37.77, 37.79, 37.80-37.89, 37.94, 37.96, or 37.98 and POA = N

✓4ᵗʰ ✓5ᵗʰ Additional Digit Required   Unacceptable PDx   Manifestation Code   Hospital Acquired Condition   ▶◀ Revised Text   ● New Code   ▲ Revised Code Title

Injury and Poisoning

999–999.41

√4ᵗʰ **999 Complications of medical care, not elsewhere classified**

INCLUDES complications, not elsewhere classified, of:
dialysis (hemodialysis) (peritoneal) (renal)
extracorporeal circulation
hyperalimentation therapy
immunization
infusion
inhalation therapy
injection
inoculation
perfusion
transfusion
vaccination
ventilation therapy

Use additional code, where applicable, to identify specific complication

EXCLUDES specified complications classified elsewhere such as:
complications of implanted device (996.0-996.9)
contact dermatitis due to drugs (692.3)
dementia dialysis (294.8)
transient (293.9)
dialysis disequilibrium syndrome (276.0-276.9)
poisoning and toxic effects of drugs and chemicals (960.0-989.9)
postvaccinal encephalitis (323.51)
water and electrolyte imbalance (276.0-276.9)

999.0 Generalized vaccinia   CC

EXCLUDES vaccinia not from vaccine (051.02)

DEF: Skin eruption, self-limiting; follows vaccination; due to transient viremia with virus localized in skin.

CC Excl: 999.0

999.1 Air embolism   MCC

Air embolism to any site following infusion, perfusion, or transfusion

EXCLUDES embolism specified as:
complicating:
abortion (634-638 with .6, 639.6)
ectopic or molar pregnancy (639.6)
pregnancy, childbirth, or the puerperium (673.0)
due to implanted device (996.7)
traumatic (958.0)

CC Excl: 958.0, 999.1

999.2 Other vascular complications   CC

Phlebitis
Thromboembolism } following infusion, perfusion, or transfusion
Thrombophlebitis

EXCLUDES extravasation of vesicant drugs (999.81, 999.82)
the listed conditions when specified as:
due to implanted device (996.61-996.62, 996.72-996.74)
postoperative NOS (997.2, 997.71-997.79)

CC Excl: 999.2, 999.81-999.82, 999.88

AHA: 2Q, '97, 5

TIP: Do not assign for IV infiltration; if the infiltration is severe enough to cause other complications, a code for the specific complication should be assigned. For chemotherapy extravasation, see code 999.81.

T80.1xxA Vasc comp follw inf transfusn tx inj initial enc   I-10

√5ᵗʰ **999.3 Other infection**

Infection
Sepsis } following infusion, injection, transfusion, or vaccination
Septicemia

Use additional code to identify the specified infection, such as:
septicemia (038.0-038.9)

EXCLUDES the listed conditions when specified as:
due to implanted device (996.60-996.69)
postoperative NOS (998.51-998.59)

AHA: 4Q, '07, 96; 2Q, '01, 11, 12; 2Q, '97, 5; J-F, '87, 14

999.31 Other and unspecified infection due to central venous catheter   CC

Central line-associated infection
Infection due to:
central venous catheter NOS
Hickman catheter
peripherally inserted central catheter (PICC)
triple lumen catheter
umbilical venous catheter

EXCLUDES infection due to:
arterial catheter (996.62)
catheter NOS (996.69)
peripheral venous catheter (996.62)
urinary catheter (996.64)

CC Excl: 996.62, 999.31-999.39

AHA: ▶1Q, '14, 18;◄ 2Q, '12, 16; 2Q, '11, 7; 2Q, '10, 8; 4Q, '08, 72, 193; 4Q, '07, 97

999.32 Bloodstream infection due to central venous catheter   CC

Bloodstream infection due to:
Hickman catheter
peripherally inserted central catheter (PICC)
portacath (port-a-cath)
triple lumen catheter
umbilical venous catheter
Catheter-related bloodstream infection (CRBSI) NOS
Central line-associated bloodstream infection (CLABSI)

CC Excl: See code 999.31

AHA: ▶1Q, '14, 18;◄ 4Q, '11, 153-155

999.33 Local infection due to central venous catheter   CC

Local infection due to:
Hickman catheter
peripherally inserted central catheter (PICC)
portacath (port-a-cath)
triple lumen catheter
umbilical venous catheter
Port or reservoir infection
Tunnel infection

CC Excl: See code 999.31

AHA: 4Q, '11, 153-155

999.34 Acute infection following transfusion, infusion, or injection of blood and blood products   CC

CC Excl: See code 999.31

AHA: 4Q, '11, 153-155

TIP: If the acute infection transmitted via transfusion, infusion, or injection is HIV, sequence code 042 first.

999.39 Infection following other infusion, injection, transfusion, or vaccination   CC

CC Excl: 996.62, 999.31-999.39

AHA: 4Q, '08, 99

√5ᵗʰ **999.4 Anaphylactic reaction due to serum**

Allergic shock
Anaphylactic shock due to serum
Anaphylactoid reaction due to serum
Anaphylaxis

EXCLUDES ABO incompatibility reaction due to transfusion of blood or blood products (999.60-999.69)
reaction:
allergic NOS (995.0)
anaphylactic:
NOS (995.0)
due to drugs and chemicals (995.0)
other serum (999.51-999.59)
shock:
allergic NOS (995.0)
anaphylactic:
NOS (995.0)
due to drugs and chemicals (995.0)

DEF: Life-threatening hypersensitivity to foreign serum; causes respiratory distress, vascular collapse, and shock.

AHA: 4Q, '11, 142-147

999.41 Anaphylactic reaction due to administration of blood and blood products   CC

CC Excl: 999.41-999.49, 999.51-999.59

AHA: 4Q, '11, 146

N Newborn Age: 0   P Pediatric Age: 0-17   M Maternity Age: 12-55   A Adult Age: 15-124   MCC Major CC Condition   CC CC Condition   HIV HIV Related Dx

348 – Volume 1 • October 2014   2015 ICD-9-CM

999.42 Anaphylactic reaction due to vaccination `CC`
    CC Excl: See code 999.41

999.49 Anaphylactic reaction due to other serum `CC`
    CC Excl: See code 999.41

☑5ᵗʰ **999.5 Other serum reaction**
    Intoxication by serum
    Protein sickness
    Serum rash
    Serum sickness
    Urticaria due to serum
    EXCLUDES serum hepatitis (070.2-070.3)
    DEF: Serum sickness: Hypersensitivity to foreign serum; causes fever, hives, swelling, and lymphadenopathy.
    AHA: 4Q, '11, 142-146

999.51 Other serum reaction due to administration of blood and blood products `CC`
    CC Excl: 999.41-999.49, 999.51-999.59

999.52 Other serum reaction due to vaccination `CC`
    CC Excl: See code 999.51

999.59 Other serum reaction `CC`
    CC Excl: 999.51-999.59

☑5ᵗʰ **999.6 ABO incompatibility reaction due to transfusion of blood or blood products**
    EXCLUDES minor blood group antigens reactions (Duffy) (E) (K(ell)) (Kidd) (Lewis) (M) (N) (P) (S) (999.75-999.79)

999.60 ABO incompatibility reaction, unspecified `CC`
    ABO incompatible blood transfusion NOS
    Reaction to ABO incompatibility from transfusion NOS
    CC Excl: 999.60-999.69, 999.70-999.80, 999.83-999.85, 999.89

999.61 ABO incompatibility with hemolytic transfusion reaction not specified as acute or delayed `CC`
    ABO incompatibility with hemolytic transfusion reaction at unspecified time after transfusion
    Hemolytic transfusion reaction (HTR) due to ABO incompatibility
    CC Excl: See code: 999.60

999.62 ABO incompatibility with acute hemolytic transfusion reaction `CC`
    ABO incompatibility with hemolytic transfusion reaction less than 24 hours after transfusion
    Acute hemolytic transfusion reaction (AHTR) due to ABO incompatibility
    CC Excl: See code: 999.60

999.63 ABO incompatibility with delayed hemolytic transfusion reaction `CC`
    ABO incompatibility with hemolytic transfusion reaction 24 hours or more after transfusion
    Delayed hemolytic transfusion reaction (DHTR) due to ABO incompatibility
    CC Excl: See code: 999.60

999.69 Other ABO incompatibility reaction `CC`
    Delayed serologic transfusion reaction (DSTR) from ABO incompatibility
    Other ABO incompatible blood transfusion
    Other reaction to ABO incompatibility from transfusion
    CC Excl: See code: 999.60

☑5ᵗʰ **999.7 Rh and other non-ABO incompatibility reaction due to transfusion of blood or blood products**
    Elevation of Rh titer
    AHA: 4Q, '10, 99-100,102-105

999.70 Rh incompatibility reaction, unspecified `CC`
    Reaction due to Rh factor in transfusion NOS
    Rh incompatible blood transfusion NOS
    Unspecified reaction due to incompatibility related to Rh antigens (C) (c) (D) (E) (e)
    Unspecified reaction to Rh incompatibility
    CC Excl: See code: 999.60

999.71 Rh incompatibility with hemolytic transfusion reaction not specified as acute or delayed `CC`
    Hemolytic transfusion reaction (HTR) due to Rh incompatibility
    HTR due to incompatibility related to Rh antigens (C) (c) (D) (E) (e), not specified as acute or delayed
    Rh incompatibility with hemolytic transfusion reaction at unspecified time after transfusion
    CC Excl: See code: 999.60

999.72 Rh incompatibility with acute hemolytic transfusion reaction `CC`
    Acute hemolytic transfusion reaction (AHTR) due to Rh incompatibility
    AHTR due to incompatibility related to Rh antigens (C) (c) (D) (E) (e)
    Rh incompatibility with hemolytic transfusion reaction less than 24 hours after transfusion
    CC Excl: See code: 999.60

999.73 Rh incompatibility with delayed hemolytic transfusion reaction `CC`
    Delayed hemolytic transfusion reaction (DHTR) due to Rh incompatibility
    DHTR due to incompatibility related to Rh antigens (C) (c) (D) (E) (e)
    Rh incompatibility with hemolytic transfusion reaction 24 hours or more after transfusion
    CC Excl: See code: 999.60

999.74 Other Rh incompatibility reaction `CC`
    Delayed serologic transfusion reaction (DSTR) from Rh incompatibility
    Other reaction due to incompatibility related to Rh antigens (C) (c) (D) (E) (e)
    Other reaction to Rh incompatible blood transfusion
    CC Excl: 999.60-999.69, 999.70-999.73, 999.79-999.80, 999.83-999.85, 999.89

999.75 Non-ABO incompatibility reaction, unspecified `CC`
    Non-ABO incompatible blood transfusion NOS
    Reaction to non-ABO antigen incompatibility from transfusion NOS
    Unspecified reaction due to incompatibility related to minor antigens (Duffy) (Kell) (Kidd) (Lewis) (M) (N) (P) (S)
    CC Excl: See code: 999.74

999.76 Non-ABO incompatibility with hemolytic transfusion reaction not specified as acute or delayed `CC`
    Hemolytic transfusion reaction (HTR) due to non-ABO incompatibility
    HTR from incompatibility related to minor antigens (Duffy) (Kell) (Kidd) (Lewis) (M) (N) (P) (S)
    Non-ABO incompatibility with hemolytic transfusion reaction at unspecified time after transfusion
    CC Excl: See code: 999.74

999.77 Non-ABO incompatibility with acute hemolytic transfusion reaction `CC`
    Acute hemolytic transfusion reaction (AHTR) due to non-ABO incompatibility
    AHTR from incompatibility related to minor antigens (Duffy) (Kell) (Kidd) (Lewis) (M) (N) (P) (S)
    Non-ABO incompatibility with hemolytic transfusion reaction less than 24 hours after transfusion
    CC Excl: See code: 999.74

999.78 Non-ABO incompatibility with delayed hemolytic transfusion reaction `CC`
    Delayed hemolytic transfusion reaction (DHTR) due to non-ABO incompatibility
    DHTR from incompatibility related to minor antigens (Duffy) (Kell) (Kidd) (Lewis) (M) (N) (P) (S)
    Non-ABO incompatibility with hemolytic transfusion reaction 24 hours or more after transfusion
    CC Excl: See code: 999.74

☑4ᵗʰ ☑5ᵗʰ Additional Digit Required   Unacceptable PDx   Manifestation Code   Hospital Acquired Condition   ►◄ Revised Text   ● New Code   ▲ Revised Code Title

2015 ICD-9-CM   **Volume 1 – 349**

999.79 Other non-ABO incompatibility reaction `CC`
> Delayed serologic transfusion reaction (DSTR) from non-ABO incompatibility
> Other non-ABO incompatible blood transfusion
> Other reaction due to incompatibility related to minor antigens (Duffy) (Kell) (Kidd) (Lewis) (M) (N) (P) (S)
> Other reaction to non-ABO incompatibility from transfusion
>
> **CC Excl:** 999.60-999.69, 999.70-999.80, 999.83-999.85, 999.89

✓5ᵗʰ **999.8 Other and unspecified infusion and transfusion reaction**
> *EXCLUDES*   ABO incompatibility reactions (999.60-999.69)
>   febrile nonhemolytic transfusion reaction (FNHTR) (780.66)
>   hemochromatosis due to repeated red blood cell transfusions (275.02)
>   non-ABO incompatibility reactions (999.70-999.79)
>   postoperative shock (998.00-998.09)
>   posttransfusion purpura (287.41)
>   Rh incompatibility reactions (999.70-999.74)
>   transfusion associated circulatory overload (TACO) (276.61)
>   transfusion related acute lung injury [TRALI] (518.7)
>
> **AHA:** 4Q, '08, 152-155; 3Q, '00, 9

999.80 Transfusion reaction, unspecified
> Incompatible blood transfusion NOS
> Reaction to blood group incompatibility in infusion or transfusion NOS
>
> **AHA:** 4Q, '10, 99-100, 106-107

999.81 Extravasation of vesicant chemotherapy `CC`
> Infiltration of vesicant chemotherapy
> **CC Excl:** 999.2, 999.81-999.88
> **AHA:** 4Q, '08, 155

999.82 Extravasation of other vesicant agent `CC`
> Infiltration of other vesicant agent
> **CC Excl:** 999.2, 999.81-999.88

999.83 Hemolytic transfusion reaction, incompatibility unspecified `CC`
> Hemolytic transfusion reaction (HTR) with antigen incompatibility unspecified, not specified as acute or delayed
> HTR with incompatibility unspecified at unspecified time after transfusion
> **CC Excl:** 999.60-999.69, 999.70-999.80, 999.83-999.85, 999.89
> **AHA:** 4Q, '10, 99-100, 106-107

999.84 Acute hemolytic transfusion reaction, incompatibility unspecified `CC`
> Acute hemolytic transfusion reaction (AHTR) with antigen incompatibility unspecified
> AHTR, incompatibility unspecified
> **CC Excl:** 999.60-999.69, 999.70-999.80, 999.83-999.85, 999.89
> **AHA:** 4Q, '10, 99-100, 106-107

999.85 Delayed hemolytic transfusion reaction, incompatibility unspecified `CC`
> Delayed hemolytic transfusion reaction (DHTR) with antigen incompatibility unspecified
> DHTR, incompatibility unspecified
> **CC Excl:** 999.60-999.69, 999.70-999.80, 999.83-999.85, 999.89
> **AHA:** 4Q, '10, 99-100, 106-107

999.88 Other infusion reaction

999.89 Other transfusion reaction
> Delayed serologic transfusion reaction (DSTR), incompatibility unspecified
> Use additional code to identify graft-versus-host reaction (279.5)
> **AHA:** 4Q, '08, 99, 154

999.9 Other and unspecified complications of medical care, not elsewhere classified
> Complications, not elsewhere classified, of:
>   electroshock
>   inhalation   ⎫
>   ultrasound   ⎬ therapy
>   ventilation   ⎭
>
> Unspecified misadventure of medical care
> *EXCLUDES*   unspecified complication of:
>   phototherapy (990)
>   radiation therapy (999)
>   ventilator associated pneumonia (997.31)
>
> **AHA:** 3Q, '06, 25; 1Q, '03, 19; 2Q, '97, 5

`N` Newborn Age: 0   `P` Pediatric Age: 0-17   `M` Maternity Age: 12-55   `A` Adult Age: 15-124   `MCC` Major CC Condition   `CC` CC Condition   `HIV` HIV Related Dx

350 – Volume 1   2015 ICD-9-CM

Supplementary Classification of Factors Influencing Health Status and Contact with Health Services (V01-V91)

This classification is provided to deal with occasions when circumstances other than a disease or injury classifiable to categories 001-999 (the main part of ICD) are recorded as "diagnoses" or "problems." This can arise mainly in three ways:

a) When a person who is not currently sick encounters the health services for some specific purpose, such as to act as a donor of an organ or tissue, to receive prophylactic vaccination, or to discuss a problem which is in itself not a disease or injury. This will be a fairly rare occurrence among hospital inpatients, but will be relatively more common among hospital outpatients and patients of family practitioners, health clinics, etc.

b) When a person with a known disease or injury, whether it is current or resolving, encounters the health care system for a specific treatment of that disease or injury (e.g., dialysis for renal disease; chemotherapy for malignancy; cast change).

c) When some circumstance or problem is present which influences the person's health status but is not in itself a current illness or injury. Such factors may be elicited during population surveys, when the person may or may not be currently sick, or be recorded as an additional factor to be borne in mind when the person is receiving care for some current illness or injury classifiable to categories 001-999.

In the latter circumstances the V code should be used only as a supplementary code and should not be the one selected for use in primary, single cause tabulations. Examples of these circumstances are a personal history of certain diseases, or a person with an artificial heart valve in situ.

AHA: J-F, '87, 8

Persons with Potential Health Hazards Related to Communicable Diseases (V01-V06)

EXCLUDES *family history of infectious and parasitic diseases (V18.8)*
personal history of infectious and parasitic diseases (V12.0)

√4th **V01 Contact with or exposure to communicable diseases**

TIP: Do not assign if the patient shows signs or symptoms of the disease to which he or she was exposed.

V01.0 Cholera
Conditions classifiable to 001

V01.1 Tuberculosis
Conditions classifiable to 010-018

V01.2 Poliomyelitis
Conditions classifiable to 045

V01.3 Smallpox
Conditions classifiable to 050

V01.4 Rubella
Conditions classifiable to 056

V01.5 Rabies
Conditions classifiable to 071

V01.6 Venereal diseases
Conditions classifiable to 090-099
AHA: 4Q, '07, 125

√5th **V01.7 Other viral diseases**
Conditions classifiable to 042-078 and V08, except as above
AHA: 2Q, '92, 11

² **V01.71 Varicella**

² **V01.79 Other viral diseases**

√5th **V01.8 Other communicable diseases**
Conditions classifiable to 001-136, except as above
AHA: J-A, '87, 24

V01.81 Anthrax
AHA: 4Q, '02, 70, 78

² **V01.82 Exposure to SARS-associated coronavirus**
AHA: 4Q, '03, 46-47

² **V01.83 Escherichia coli (E. coli)**

² **V01.84 Meningococcus**
Z20.811 Contact with and exposure to meningococcus **I-10**

V01.89 Other communicable diseases

V01.9 Unspecified communicable diseases

√4th **V02 Carrier or suspected carrier of infectious diseases**
INCLUDES colonization status
AHA: 3Q, '95, 18; 3Q, '94, 4

V02.0 Cholera

V02.1 Typhoid

V02.2 Amebiasis

V02.3 Other gastrointestinal pathogens

V02.4 Diphtheria

√5th **V02.5 Other specified bacterial diseases**

V02.51 Group B streptococcus
AHA: 3Q, '06, 14; 1Q, '02, 14; 4Q, '98, 56

V02.52 Other streptococcus

V02.53 Methicillin susceptible Staphylococcus aureus
MSSA colonization
AHA: 4Q, '08, 69, 71, 156

V02.54 Methicillin resistant Staphylococcus aureus
MRSA colonization
AHA: 4Q, '08, 69, 71, 72, 156

V02.59 Other specified bacterial diseases
Meningococcal   Staphylococcal

√5th **V02.6 Viral hepatitis**
Hepatitis Australian-antigen [HAA] [SH] carrier
Serum hepatitis carrier

V02.60 Viral hepatitis carrier, unspecified
AHA: 4Q, '97, 47

V02.61 Hepatitis B carrier
AHA: 4Q, '97, 47
Z22.51 Carrier of viral hepatitis B **I-10**

V02.62 Hepatitis C carrier
AHA: 4Q, '97, 47

V02.69 Other viral hepatitis carrier
AHA: 4Q, '97, 47

V02.7 Gonorrhea

V02.8 Other veneral diseases

V02.9 Other specified infectious organism
AHA: 3Q, '95, 18; 1Q, '93, 22; J-A, '87, 24

√4th **V03 Need for prophylactic vaccination and inoculation against bacterial diseases**
EXCLUDES *vaccination not carried out (V64.00-V64.09)*
vaccines against combinations of diseases (V06.0-V06.9)

V03.0 Cholera alone

V03.1 Typhoid-paratyphoid alone [TAB]

V03.2 Tuberculosis [BCG]

V03.3 Plague

V03.4 Tularemia

V03.5 Diphtheria alone

V03.6 Pertussis alone

V03.7 Tetanus toxoid alone

√5th **V03.8 Other specified vaccinations against single bacterial diseases**

V03.81 Hemophilus influenza, type B [Hib]

V03.82 Streptococcus pneumoniae [pneumococcus]

V03.89 Other specified vaccination
AHA: 2Q, '00, 9
TIP: Assign for vaccination against Lyme disease.

V03.9 Unspecified single bacterial disease

√4th **V04 Need for prophylactic vaccination and inoculation against certain viral diseases**
EXCLUDES *vaccines against combinations of diseases (V06.0-V06.9)*

V04.0 Poliomyelitis

---

² These V codes may be used as principal diagnosis on Medicare patients.

√4th √5th Additional Digit Required   Unacceptable PDx   Manifestation Code   Hospital Acquired Condition   ►◄ Revised Text   ● New Code   ▲ Revised Code Title

2015 ICD-9-CM   **Volume 1 – 351**

V04.1 Smallpox

V04.2 Measles alone

V04.3 Rubella alone

V04.4 Yellow fever

V04.5 Rabies

V04.6 Mumps alone

V04.7 Common cold

√5th **V04.8** Other viral diseases
AHA: 4Q, '03, 83

V04.81 Influenza

V04.82 Respiratory syncytial virus (RSV)
AHA: 1Q, '09, 14

V04.89 Other viral diseases
AHA: 2Q, '07, 9
TIP: Assign for vaccination against human papilloma virus (HPV).

√4th **V05** Need for other prophylactic vaccination and inoculation against single diseases
EXCLUDES vaccines against combinations of diseases (V06.0-V06.9)

V05.0 Arthropod-borne viral encephalitis

V05.1 Other arthropod-borne viral diseases

V05.2 Leshmaniasis

V05.3 Viral hepatitis

V05.4 Varicella
Chickenpox

V05.8 Other specified disease
AHA: 1Q, '01, 4; 3Q, '91, 20

V05.9 Unspecified single disease

√4th **V06** Need for prophylactic vaccination and inoculation against combinations of diseases
NOTE Use additional single vaccination codes from categories V03-V05 to identify any vaccinations not included in a combination code.

V06.0 Cholera with typhoid-paratyphoid [cholera+TAB]

V06.1 Diphtheria-tetanus-pertussis, combined [DTP] [DTaP]
AHA: 4Q, '03, 83; 3Q, '98, 13

V06.2 Diphtheria-tetanus-pertussis with typhoid-paratyphoid [DTP+TAB]

V06.3 Diphtheria-tetanus-pertussis with poliomyelitis [DTP+polio]

V06.4 Measles-mumps-rubella [MMR]

V06.5 Tetanus-diphtheria [Td] [DT]
AHA: 4Q, '03, 83

V06.6 Streptococcus pneumoniae [pneumococcus] and influenza

V06.8 Other combinations
EXCLUDES multiple single vaccination codes (V03.0-V05.9)
AHA: 1Q, '12, 11; 1Q, '94, 19

V06.9 Unspecified combined vaccine

Persons with Need for Isolation, Other Potential Health Hazards and Prophylactic Measures (V07-V09)

√4th **V07** Need for isolation and other prophylactic or treatment measures
EXCLUDES long-term (current) (prophylactic) use of certain specific drugs (V58.61-V58.69)
prophylactic organ removal (V50.41-V50.49)

² **V07.0** Isolation
Admission to protect the individual from his surroundings or for isolation of individual after contact with infectious diseases

V07.1 Desensitization to allergens

V07.2 Prophylactic immunotherapy
Administration of:
antivenin
immune sera [gamma globulin]
RhoGAM
tetanus antitoxin

√5th **V07.3** Other prophylactic chemotherapy

V07.31 Prophylactic fluoride administration

² **V07.39** Other prophylactic chemotherapy
EXCLUDES maintenance chemotherapy following disease (V58.11)

V07.4 Hormone replacement therapy (postmenopausal) ♀
Z79.890 Hormone replacement therapy postmenopausal ┃ I-10 ┃

√5th **V07.5** Use of agents affecting estrogen receptors and estrogen levels
Code first, if applicable:
malignant neoplasm of breast (174.0-174.9, 175.0-175.9)
malignant neoplasm of prostate (185)
Use additional code, if applicable, to identify:
estrogen receptor positive status (V86.0)
family history of breast cancer (V16.3)
genetic susceptibility to cancer (V84.01-V84.09)
personal history of breast cancer (V10.3)
personal history of prostate cancer (V10.46)
postmenopausal status (V49.81)
EXCLUDES hormone replacement therapy (postmenopausal) (V07.4)
AHA: 4Q, '10, 108; 4Q, '08, 156

V07.51 Use of selective estrogen receptor modulators [SERMs]
Use of:
raloxifene (Evista)
tamoxifen (Nolvadex)
toremifene (Fareston)
Z79.810 Lng term sel estrogen receptor modulators SERMS ┃ I-10 ┃

V07.52 Use of aromatase inhibitors
Use of:
anastrozole (Arimidex)
exemestane (Aromasin)
letrozole (Femara)

V07.59 Use of other agents affecting estrogen receptors and estrogen levels
Use of:
estrogen receptor downregulators
fulvestrant (Faslodex)
gonadotropin-releasing hormone (GnRH) agonist
goserelin acetate (Zoladex)
leuprolide acetate (leuprorelin) (Lupron)
megestrol acetate (Megace)

² **V07.8** Other specified prophylactic or treatment measure
AHA: ▶1Q, '13, 8;◀ 2Q, '10, 6, 14; 1Q, '92, 11
TIP: Assign for patients having prophylactic breast removal because of a strong family history of breast cancer, along with code V16.3 Family history of breast cancer.

V07.9 Unspecified prophylactic or treatment measure

V08 Asymptomatic human immunodeficiency virus [HIV] infection status
HIV positive NOS
NOTE This code is only to be used when no HIV infection symptoms or conditions are present. If any HIV infection symptoms or conditions are present, see code 042.
EXCLUDES AIDS (042)
human immunodeficiency virus [HIV] disease (042)
exposure to HIV (V01.79)
nonspecific serologic evidence of HIV (795.71)
symptomatic human immunodeficiency virus [HIV] infection (042)
AHA: 2Q, '04, 11; 2Q, '99, 8; 3Q, '95, 18
Z21 Asymptomatic HIV infection status ┃ I-10 ┃

---

² These V codes may be used as principal diagnosis on Medicare patients.

N Newborn Age: 0 ┃ P Pediatric Age: 0-17 ┃ M Maternity Age: 12-55 ┃ A Adult Age: 15-124 ┃ MCC Major CC Condition ┃ CC CC Condition ┃ HIV HIV Related Dx

352 – Volume 1 • October 2014

2015 ICD-9-CM

✓4ᵗʰ **V09** **Infection with drug-resistant microorganisms**
> **NOTE** This category is intended for use as an additional code for infectious conditions classified elsewhere to indicate the presence of drug-resistance of the infectious organism.
> **AHA:** 3Q, '94, 4; 4Q, '93, 22

V09.0 Infection with microorganisms resistant to penicillins
> **AHA:** 2Q, '06, 16; 4Q, '03, 104, 106

V09.1 Infection with microorganisms resistant to cephalosporins and other B-lactam antibiotics

V09.2 Infection with microorganisms resistant to macrolides

V09.3 Infection with microorganisms resistant to tetracyclines

V09.4 Infection with microorganisms resistant to aminoglycosides

✓5ᵗʰ **V09.5** Infection with microorganisms resistant to quinolones and fluoroquinolones

V09.50 Without mention of resistance to multiple quinolones and fluoroquinoles

V09.51 With resistance to multiple quinolones and fluoroquinoles

V09.6 Infection with microorganisms resistant to sulfonamides

✓5ᵗʰ **V09.7** Infection with microorganisms resistant to other specified antimycobacterial agents
> **EXCLUDES** *Amikacin (V09.4)*
> *Kanamycin (V09.4)*
> *Streptomycin [SM] (V09.4)*

V09.70 Without mention of resistance to multiple antimycobacterial agents

V09.71 With resistance to multiple antimycobacterial agents

✓5ᵗʰ **V09.8** Infection with microorganisms resistant to other specified drugs
> Vancomycin (glycopeptide) intermediate staphylococcus aureus (VISA/GISA)
> Vancomycin (glycopeptide) resistant enterococcus (VRE)
> Vancomycin (glycopeptide) resistant staphylococcus aureus (VRSA/GRSA)

V09.80 Without mention of resistance to multiple drugs

V09.81 With resistance to multiple drugs

✓5ᵗʰ **V09.9** Infection with drug-resistant microorganisms, unspecified
> Drug resistance, NOS

V09.90 Without mention of multiple drug resistance
> **Z16.30** Resist to unspec antimicrobial drugs **I-10**

V09.91 With multiple drug resistance
> Multiple drug resistance NOS

Persons with Potential Health Hazards Related to Personal and Family History (V10-V19)

> **EXCLUDES** *obstetric patients where the possibility that the fetus might be affected is the reason for observation or management during pregnancy (655.0-655.9)*
> **AHA:** J-F, '87, 1

✓4ᵗʰ **V10** **Personal history of malignant neoplasm**
> **AHA:** 4Q, '02, 80; 4Q, '98, 69; 1Q, '95, 4; 3Q, '92, 5; M-J, '85, 10; 2Q, '90, 9
> **TIP:** Assign the codes in this category only for a personal history of primary malignancy (not metastatic malignancies).

✓5ᵗʰ **V10.0** Gastrointestinal tract
> History of conditions classifiable to 140-159
> **EXCLUDES** *personal history of malignant carcinoid tumor (V10.91)*
> *personal history of malignant neuroendocrine tumor (V10.91)*

V10.00 Gastrointestinal tract, unspecified

V10.01 Tongue

V10.02 Other and unspecified oral cavity and pharynx

V10.03 Esophagus

V10.04 Stomach

V10.05 Large intestine
> **AHA:** 3Q, '99, 7; 1Q, '95, 4
> **Z85.038** Personal hx othr malig neoplasm lrg intestine **I-10**

V10.06 Rectum, rectosigmoid junction, and anus

V10.07 Liver

V10.09 Other
> **AHA:** 4Q, '03, 111

✓5ᵗʰ **V10.1** Trachea, bronchus, and lung
> History of conditions classifiable to 162
> **EXCLUDES** *personal history of malignant carcinoid tumor (V10.91)*
> *personal history of malignant neuroendocrine tumor (V10.91)*

V10.11 Bronchus and lung
> **AHA:** ▶1Q, '13, 8◀

V10.12 Trachea

✓5ᵗʰ **V10.2** Other respiratory and intrathoracic organs
> History of conditions classifiable to 160, 161, 163-165

V10.20 Respiratory organ, unspecified

V10.21 Larynx
> **AHA:** 4Q, '03, 108, 110

V10.22 Nasal cavities, middle ear, and accessory sinuses

V10.29 Other

V10.3 Breast
> History of conditions classifiable to 174 and 175
> **AHA:** 1Q, '12, 11; 2Q, '11, 12; 3Q, '07, 4; 1Q, '07, 6; 2Q, '03, 5; 4Q, '01, 66; 4Q, '98, 65; 4Q, '97, 50; 1Q, '91, 16; 1Q, '90, 21
> **TIP:** Do not assign for personal history of ductal carcinoma in situ (DCIS); assign code V13.89.
> **Z85.3** Personal history primary malig neoplasm breast **I-10**

✓5ᵗʰ **V10.4** Genital organs
> History of conditions classifiable to 179-187

V10.40 Female genital organ, unspecfied ♀

V10.41 Cervix uteri ♀
> **AHA:** 4Q, '07, 99

V10.42 Other parts of uterus ♀

V10.43 Ovary ♀

V10.44 Other female genital organs ♀

V10.45 Male genital organ, unspecfied ♂

V10.46 Prostate ♂
> **AHA:** 1Q, '09,15

V10.47 Testis ♂
> **Z85.47** Personal history primary malig neoplasm testis **I-10**

V10.48 Epididymis ♂

V10.49 Other male genital organs ♂

✓5ᵗʰ **V10.5** Urinary organs
> History of conditions classifiable to 188 and 189
> **EXCLUDES** *personal history of malignant carcinoid tumor (V10.91)*
> *personal history of malignant neuroendocrine tumor (V10.91)*

V10.50 Urinary organ, unspecified

V10.51 Bladder

V10.52 Kidney
> **AHA:** 2Q, '04, 4
> **EXCLUDES** *renal pelvis (V10.53)*

V10.53 Renal pelvis
> **AHA:** 4Q, '01, 55

V10.59 Other

✓5ᵗʰ **V10.6** Leukemia
> Conditions classifiable to 204-208
> **EXCLUDES** *leukemia in remission (204-208)*
> **AHA:** 2Q, '92, 13; 4Q, '91, 26; 4Q, '90, 3

V10.60 Leukemia, unspecified

V10.61 Lymphoid leukemia

| ✓4ᵗʰ ✓5ᵗʰ Additional Digit Required | Unacceptable PDx | Manifestation Code | Hospital Acquired Condition | ▶◀ Revised Text | ● New Code | ▲ Revised Code Title |

2015 ICD-9-CM

October 2014 · Volume 1 — 353

V10.62 Myeloid leukemia

V10.63 Monocytic leukemia

V10.69 Other

✓5ᵗʰ **V10.7 Other lymphatic and hematopoietic neoplasms**
Conditions classifiable to 200-203
EXCLUDES *listed conditions in 200-203 in remission*
AHA: M-J, '85, 18

V10.71 Lymphosarcoma and reticulosarcoma

V10.72 Hodgkin's disease

V10.79 Other

✓5ᵗʰ **V10.8 Personal history of malignant neoplasm of other sites**
History of conditions classifiable to 170-173, 190-195
EXCLUDES *personal history of malignant carcinoid tumor (V10.91)*
personal history of malignant neuroendocrine tumor (V10.91)

V10.81 Bone
AHA: 2Q, '03, 13

V10.82 Malignant melanoma of skin

V10.83 Other malignant neoplasm of skin

V10.84 Eye

V10.85 Brain
AHA: 1Q, '01, 6

V10.86 Other parts of the nervous system
EXCLUDES *peripheral sympathetic, and parasympathetic nerves (V10.89)*

V10.87 Thyroid

V10.88 Other endocrine glands and related structures

V10.89 Other

✓5ᵗʰ **V10.9 Other and unspecified personal history of malignant neoplasm**
AHA: 4Q, '09, 115

V10.90 Personal history of unspecified malignant neoplasm
Personal history of malignant neoplasm NOS
EXCLUDES *personal history of malignant carcinoid tumor (V10.91)*
personal history of malignant neuroendocrine tumor (V10.91)
personal history of Merkel cell carcinoma (V10.91)

V10.91 Personal history of malignant neuroendocrine tumor
Personal history of malignant carcinoid tumor NOS
Personal history of malignant neuroendocrine tumor NOS
Personal history of Merkel cell carcinoma NOS
Code first any continuing functional activity, such as: carcinoid syndrome (259.2)

✓4ᵗʰ **V11 Personal history of mental disorder**

V11.0 Schizophrenia
EXCLUDES *that in remission (295.0-295.9 with fifth-digit 5)*

V11.1 Affective disorders
Personal history of manic-depressive psychosis
EXCLUDES *that in remission (296.0-296.6 with fifth-digit 5, 6)*

V11.2 Neurosis

V11.3 Alcoholism

V11.4 Combat and operational stress reaction A
AHA: 4Q, '10, 108

V11.8 Other mental disorders

V11.9 Unspecified mental disorder

✓4ᵗʰ **V12 Personal history of certain other diseases**
AHA: 3Q, '92, 11

✓5ᵗʰ **V12.0 Infectious and parasitic diseases**
EXCLUDES *personal history of infectious diseases specific to a body system*

V12.00 Unspecified infectious and parasitic disease

V12.01 Tuberculosis

V12.02 Poliomyelitis
Z86.12 Personal history of poliomyelitis I-10

V12.03 Malaria

V12.04 Methicillin resistant Staphylococcus aureus
MRSA
AHA: 4Q, '08, 69, 71

V12.09 Other

V12.1 Nutritional deficiency

✓5ᵗʰ **V12.2 Endocrine, metabolic, and immunity disorders**
AHA: 4Q, '11, 156

V12.21 Gestational diabetes ♀

V12.29 Other endocrine, metabolic, and immunity disorders

V12.3 Diseases of blood and blood-forming organs

✓5ᵗʰ **V12.4 Disorders of nervous system and sense organs**

V12.40 Unspecified disorder of nervous system and sense organs

V12.41 Benign neoplasm of the brain
AHA: 4Q, '97, 48
TIP: Benign neoplasms of the brain are tracked separately because, besides being potentially life-threatening, they often recur and can be difficult to treat.

V12.42 Infections of the central nervous system
Encephalitis Meningitis
AHA: 4Q, '05, 95

V12.49 Other disorders of nervous system and sense organs
AHA: 4Q, '98, 59

✓5ᵗʰ **V12.5 Diseases of circulatory system**
EXCLUDES *history of anaphylactic shock (V13.81)*
old myocardial infarction (412)
postmyocardial infarction syndrome (411.0)
AHA: 4Q, '95, 61

V12.50 Unspecified circulatory disease

V12.51 Venous thrombosis and embolism
EXCLUDES *pulmonary embolism (V12.55)*
AHA: 1Q, '11, 20; 3Q, '06, 12; 4Q, '03, 108; 1Q, '02, 15

V12.52 Thrombophlebitis

V12.53 Sudden cardiac arrest
Sudden cardiac death successfully resuscitated
AHA: 4Q, '07, 98

V12.54 Transient ischemic attack [TIA], and cerebral infarction without residual deficits
Prolonged reversible ischemic neurological deficit [PRIND]
Reversible ischemic neurologic deficit [RIND]
Stroke NOS without residual deficits
EXCLUDES *history of traumatic brain injury (V15.52)*
late effects of cerebrovascular disease (438.0-438.9)
AHA: 4Q, '07, 98
TIP: Assign for old CVA for which the patient has no residual deficits; if deficits are present, see category 438.
Z86.73 Personal hx TIA & cerebral infarct w/o deficits I-10

V12.55 Pulmonary embolism
AHA: ▶4Q, '13, 83;◄ 4Q, '11, 156

V12.59 Other
AHA: ▶4Q, '13, 101;◄ 2Q, '07, 3; 4Q, '99, 4; 4Q, '98, 88; 4Q, '97, 37

N Newborn Age: 0   P Pediatric Age: 0-17   M Maternity Age: 12-55   A Adult Age: 15-124   MCC Major CC Condition   CC CC Condition   HIV HIV Related Dx

354 – Volume 1 · October 2014   2015 ICD-9-CM

✓5th **V12.6 Diseases of respiratory system**
    EXCLUDES   *tuberculosis (V12.01)*
    V12.60 Unspecified disease of respiratory system
    V12.61 Pneumonia (recurrent)
       AHA: 4Q, '05, 95
    V12.69 Other diseases of respiratory system

✓5th **V12.7 Diseases of digestive system**
    AHA: 1Q, '95, 3; 2Q, '89, 16
    V12.70 Unspecified digestive disease
    V12.71 Peptic ulcer disease
    V12.72 Colonic polyps
       AHA: ▶4Q, '13, 104, 105;◀ 3Q, '02, 15
       Z86.010 Personal history of colonic polyps   I-10
    V12.79 Other

✓4th **V13 Personal history of other diseases**

✓5th **V13.0 Disorders of urinary system**
    V13.00 Unspecified urinary disorder
    V13.01 Urinary calculi
    V13.02 Urinary (tract) infection
       AHA: 4Q, '05, 95
    V13.03 Nephrotic syndrome
       AHA: 4Q, '05, 95
    V13.09 Other

V13.1 Trophoblastic disease ♀
    EXCLUDES   *supervision during a current pregnancy (V23.1)*

✓5th **V13.2 Other genital system and obstetric disorders**
    EXCLUDES   *recurrent pregnancy loss (646.3)*
            without current pregnancy (629.81)
            supervision during a current pregnancy of a woman
              with poor obstetric history (V23.0-V23.9)
    V13.21 Personal history of pre-term labor ♀
       EXCLUDES   *current pregnancy with history of pre-term*
             labor (V23.41)
       AHA: 4Q, '02, 78
    V13.22 Personal history of cervical dysplasia ♀
       Personal history of conditions classifiable to
           622.10-622.12
       EXCLUDES   *personal history of malignant neoplasm of*
             cervix uteri (V10.41)
       AHA: 4Q, '07, 98
    V13.23 Personal history of vaginal dysplasia ♀
       Personal history of conditions classifiable to 623.0
       EXCLUDES   *personal history of malignant neoplasm of*
             vagina (V10.44)
       AHA: 4Q, '10, 108
    V13.24 Personal history of vulvar dysplasia ♀
       Personal history of conditions classifiable to
           624.01-624.02
       EXCLUDES   *personal history of malignant neoplasm of*
             vulva (V10.44)
       AHA: 4Q, '10, 108
    V13.29 Other genital system and obstetric disorders ♀

V13.3 Diseases of skin and subcutaneous tissue

V13.4 Arthritis

✓5th **V13.5 Other musculoskeletal disorders**
    AHA: 4Q, '08, 158
    TIP: Personal histories of pathological, stress, or traumatic fractures
    are separately classified because a patient with such a history is at
    much higher risk of refracture of the same site.
    V13.51 Pathologic fracture
       Healed pathologic fracture
       EXCLUDES   *personal history of traumatic fracture*
             (V15.51)

    V13.52 Stress fracture
       Healed stress fracture
       EXCLUDES   *personal history of traumatic fracture*
             (V15.51)
    V13.59 Other musculoskeletal disorders

✓5th **V13.6 Congenital (corrected) malformations**
    AHA: 4Q, '10, 108, 136; 4Q, '98, 63
    V13.61 Personal history of (corrected) hypospadias ♂
    V13.62 Personal history of other (corrected) congenital malformations of genitourinary system
    V13.63 Personal history of (corrected) congenital malformations of nervous system
    V13.64 Personal history of (corrected) congenital malformations of eye, ear, face and neck
       Corrected cleft lip and palate
    V13.65 Personal history of (corrected) congenital malformations of heart and circulatory system
    V13.66 Personal history of (corrected) congenital malformations of respiratory system
    V13.67 Personal history of (corrected) congenital malformations of digestive system
    V13.68 Personal history of (corrected) congenital malformations of integument, limbs, and musculoskeletal systems
    V13.69 Personal history of other (corrected) congenital malformations
       AHA: 4Q, '10, 108; 1Q, '04, 16

V13.7 Perinatal problems
    EXCLUDES   *low birth weight status (V21.30-V21.35)*

✓5th **V13.8 Other specified diseases**
    AHA: 4Q, '11, 156
    V13.81 Anaphylaxis
    V13.89 Other specified diseases
       AHA: 1Q, '12, 11

V13.9 Unspecified disease
    AHA: 4Q, '06, 117

✓4th **V14 Personal history of allergy to medicinal agents**
    V14.0 Penicillin
       Z88.0 Allergy status to penicillin   I-10
    V14.1 Other antibiotic agent
    V14.2 Sulfonamides
    V14.3 Other anti-infective agent
    V14.4 Anesthetic agent
    V14.5 Narcotic agent
    V14.6 Analgesic agent
    V14.7 Serum or vaccine
    V14.8 Other specified medicinal agents
    V14.9 Unspecified medicinal agent

✓4th **V15 Other personal history presenting hazards to health**
    EXCLUDES   *personal history of drug therapy (V87.41-V87.49)*

✓5th **V15.0 Allergy, other than to medicinal agents**
    EXCLUDES   *allergy to food substance used as base for medicinal*
            agent (V14.0-V14.9)
    AHA: 4Q, '00, 42, 49
    TIP: A person who has had an allergic episode to a substance in the
    past should always be considered allergic to the substance.
    V15.01 Allergy to peanuts
       Z91.010 Allergy to peanuts   I-10
    V15.02 Allergy to milk products
       EXCLUDES   *lactose intolerance (271.3)*
       AHA: 1Q, '03, 12
    V15.03 Allergy to eggs
    V15.04 Allergy to seafood
       Seafood (octopus) (squid) ink   Shellfish

✓4th ✓5th Additional Digit Required   Unacceptable PDx   Manifestation Code   Hospital Acquired Condition   ▶◀ Revised Text   ● New Code   ▲ Revised Code Title

V15.05 Allergy to other foods
    Food additives   Nuts other than peanuts

V15.06 Allergy to insects and arachnids
    Bugs
    Insect bites and stings
    Spiders

V15.07 Allergy to latex
    Latex sensitivity

V15.08 Allergy to radiographic dye
    Contrast media used for diagnostic x-ray procedures

V15.09 Other allergy, other than to medicinal agents

V15.1 Surgery to heart and great vessels
    EXCLUDES replacement by transplant or other means
        (V42.1-V42.2, V43.2-V43.4)
    AHA: 1Q, '04, 16

✓5th **V15.2 Surgery to other organs**
    EXCLUDES replacement by transplant or other means
        (V42.0-V43.8)
    AHA: 4Q, '08, 158

V15.21 Personal history of undergoing in utero procedure during pregnancy ♀
    AHA: 4Q, '08, 158

V15.22 Personal history of undergoing in utero procedure while a fetus
    AHA: 4Q, '08, 158

V15.29 Surgery to other organs

V15.3 Irradiation
    Previous exposure to therapeutic or other ionizing radiation
    AHA: 2Q, '11, 12;

✓5th **V15.4 Psychological trauma**
    EXCLUDES history of condition classifiable to 290-316
        (V11.0-V11.9)

V15.41 History of physical abuse
    Rape
    AHA: 3Q, '99, 15

V15.42 History of emotional abuse
    Neglect
    AHA: 3Q, '99, 15

V15.49 Other
    AHA: 3Q, '99, 15

✓5th **V15.5 Injury**
    AHA: 4Q, '08, 158

V15.51 Traumatic fracture
    Healed traumatic fracture
    EXCLUDES personal history of pathologic and stress
        fracture (V13.51, V13.52)
    TIP: Personal histories of pathological, stress, or traumatic fractures are separately classified because a patient with such a history is at much higher risk of refracture of the same site.

V15.52 History of traumatic brain injury
    EXCLUDES personal history of cerebrovascular accident
        (cerebral infarction) without residual
        deficits (V12.54)
    AHA: 4Q, '09, 115

V15.53 Personal history of retained foreign body fully removed
    AHA: 4Q, '10, 108

V15.59 Other injury

V15.6 Poisoning

V15.7 Contraception
    EXCLUDES current contraceptive management (V25.0-V25.4)
        presence of intrauterine contraceptive device as
        incidental finding (V45.5)

✓5th **V15.8 Other specified personal history presenting hazards to health**
    EXCLUDES contact with and (suspected) exposure to:
        aromatic compounds and dyes (V87.11-V87.19)
        arsenic and other metals (V87.01-V87.09)
        molds (V87.31)
    AHA: 4Q, '95, 62

V15.80 History of failed moderate sedation
    History of failed conscious sedation
    AHA: 4Q, '09, 115

V15.81 Noncompliance with medical treatment
    EXCLUDES noncompliance with renal dialysis (V45.12)
    AHA: 2Q, '12, 16; 3Q, '07, 9; 4Q, '06, 136; 2Q, '03, 7; 2Q, '01, 11, 12, 13; 2Q, '99, 17; 2Q, '97, 11; 1Q, '97, 12; 3Q, '96, 9

V15.82 History of tobacco use
    EXCLUDES tobacco dependence (305.1)
    AHA: 1Q, '09, 17
    Z87.891 Personal history of nicotine dependence   I-10

V15.83 Underimmunization status
    Delinquent immunization status
    Lapsed immunization schedule status
    AHA: 4Q, '09, 115

V15.84 Contact with and (suspected) exposure to asbestos
    AHA: 4Q, '09, 116

V15.85 Contact with and (suspected) exposure to potentially hazardous body fluids
    AHA: 4Q, '09, 116

V15.86 Contact with and (suspected) exposure to lead
    AHA: 4Q, '09, 116

V15.87 History of extracorporeal membrane oxygenation [ECMO]
    AHA: 4Q, '03, 84

V15.88 History of fall
    At risk for falling
    AHA: 4Q, '05, 95
    Z91.81 History of falling   I-10

V15.89 Other
    EXCLUDES contact with and (suspected) exposure to
        other potentially hazardous:
        chemicals (V87.2)
        substances (V87.39)
    AHA: 3Q, '08, 7; 3Q, '07, 5; 1Q, '90, 21; N-D, '84, 12

V15.9 Unspecified personal history presenting hazards to health

✓4th **V16 Family history of malignant neoplasm**

V16.0 Gastrointestinal tract
    Family history of condition classifiable to 140-159
    AHA: 1Q, '99, 4
    TIP: Family history of colon cancer is a condition that meets the criteria of "high risk" for a screening colonoscopy.

V16.1 Trachea, bronchus, and lung
    Family history of condition classifiable to 162

V16.2 Other respiratory and intrathoracic organs
    Family history of condition classifiable to 160-161, 163-165

V16.3 Breast
    Family history of condition classifiable to 174
    AHA: 4Q, '04, 107; 2Q, '03, 4; 2Q, '00, 8; 1Q, '92, 11
    Z80.3 Family history of malignant neoplasm of breast   I-10

✓5th **V16.4 Genital organs**
    Family history of condition classifiable to 179-187
    AHA: 4Q, '97, 48

V16.40 Genital organ, unspecified

V16.41 Ovary
    AHA: 3Q, '09, 5

V16.42 Prostate
    Z80.42 Family history of malignant neoplasm of prostate   I-10

V16.43 Testis

N Newborn Age: 0   P Pediatric Age: 0-17   M Maternity Age: 12-55   A Adult Age: 15-124   MCC Major CC Condition   CC CC Condition   HIV HIV Related Dx

356 – Volume 1   2015 ICD-9-CM

V16.49 **Other**
> AHA: 2Q, '06, 2

✓5th V16.5 **Urinary organs**
> Family history of condition classifiable to 188-189

V16.51 **Kidney**

V16.52 **Bladder**
> AHA: 4Q, '07, 98

V16.59 **Other**

V16.6 **Leukemia**
> Family history of condition classifiable to 204-208

V16.7 **Other lymphatic and hematopoietic neoplasms**
> Family history of condition classifiable to 200-203

V16.8 **Other specified malignant neoplasm**
> Family history of other condition classifiable to 140-199

V16.9 **Unspecified malignant neoplasm**

✓4th V17 **Family history of certain chronic disabling diseases**

V17.0 **Psychiatric condition**
> EXCLUDES *family history of intellectual disabilities (V18.4)*

V17.1 **Stroke (cerebrovascular)**
> Z82.3 Family history of stroke   I-10

V17.2 **Other neurological diseases**
> Epilepsy   Huntington's chorea

V17.3 **Ischemic heart disease**

✓5th V17.4 **Other cardiovascular diseases**
> AHA: 1Q, '04, 6

V17.41 **Family history of sudden cardiac death [SCD]**
> EXCLUDES *family history of ischemic heart disease (V17.3)*
> *family history of myocardial infarction (V17.3)*
> AHA: 4Q, '07, 98

V17.49 **Family history of other cardiovascular diseases**
> Family history of cardiovascular disease NOS

V17.5 **Asthma**

V17.6 **Other chronic respiratory conditions**

V17.7 **Arthritis**

✓5th V17.8 **Other musculoskeletal diseases**

V17.81 **Osteoporosis**
> AHA: 4Q, '05, 95

V17.89 **Other musculoskeletal diseases**

✓4th V18 **Family history of certain other specific conditions**

V18.0 **Diabetes mellitus**
> AHA: 1Q, '04, 8
> TIP: Assign for a normal infant born to a diabetic mother who presents with no manifestations of the syndrome.

✓5th V18.1 **Other endocrine and metabolic diseases**

V18.11 **Multiple endocrine neoplasia [MEN] syndrome**
> AHA: 4Q, '07, 98, 100

V18.19 **Other endocrine and metabolic diseases**

V18.2 **Anemia**

V18.3 **Other blood disorders**

V18.4 **Intellectual disabilities**

✓5th V18.5 **Digestive disorders**

V18.51 **Colonic polyps**
> EXCLUDES *family history of malignant neoplasm of gastrointestinal tract (V16.0)*
> AHA: 4Q, '06, 117
> Z83.71 Family history of colonic polyps   I-10

V18.59 **Other digestive disorders**

✓5th V18.6 **Kidney diseases**

V18.61 **Polycystic kidney**

V18.69 **Other kidney diseases**

V18.7 **Other genitourinary diseases**

V18.8 **Infectious and parasitic diseases**

V18.9 **Genetic disease carrier**
> AHA: 4Q, '05, 95

✓4th V19 **Family history of other conditions**

V19.0 **Blindness or visual loss**

✓5th V19.1 **Other eye disorders**
> AHA: 4Q, '11, 156

V19.11 **Glaucoma**

V19.19 **Other specified eye disorder**

V19.2 **Deafness or hearing loss**

V19.3 **Other ear disorders**

V19.4 **Skin conditions**

V19.5 **Congenital anomalies**

V19.6 **Allergic disorders**

V19.7 **Consanguinity**

V19.8 **Other condition**

Persons Encountering Health Services in Circumstances Related to Reproduction and Development (V20-V29)

✓4th V20 **Health supervision of infant or child**

2 V20.0 **Foundling**   P

V20.1 **Other healthy infant or child receiving care**   P
> Medical or nursing care supervision of healthy infant in cases of:
> maternal illness, physical or psychiatric
> socioeconomic adverse condition at home
> too many children at home preventing or interfering with normal care
> AHA: 1Q, '00, 25; 3Q, '89, 14

V20.2 **Routine infant or child health check**   P
> Developmental testing of infant or child
> Health check for child over 28 days old
> Immunizations appropriate for age
> Routine vision and hearing testing
> Use additional code(s) to identify:
> special screening examination(s) performed (V73.0-V82.9)
> EXCLUDES *health check for child under 29 days old (V20.31-V20.32)*
> *newborn health supervision (V20.31-V20.32)*
> *special screening for developmental handicaps (V79.3)*
> AHA: 4Q, '09, 115; 1Q, '09, 15; 1Q, '04, 15

✓5th V20.3 **Newborn health supervision**
> Health check for child under 29 days old
> EXCLUDES *health check for child over 28 days old (V20.2)*
> AHA: 4Q, '09, 117

V20.31 **Health supervision for newborn under 8 days old**   N
> Health check for newborn under 8 days old

V20.32 **Health supervision for newborn 8 to 28 days old**   N
> Health check for newborn 8 to 28 days old
> Newborn weight check
> AHA: 4Q, '09, 102,117

✓4th V21 **Constitutional states in development**

V21.0 **Period of rapid growth in childhood**

V21.1 **Puberty**

V21.2 **Other adolecsence**

✓5th V21.3 **Low birth weight status**
> EXCLUDES *history of perinatal problems*
> AHA: 4Q, '00, 51
> TIP: There are no age restrictions on these V codes after the perinatal period; assign for patients without the initial condition who may continue to manifest the consequences of it.

V21.30 **Low birth weight status, unspecified**

✓4th ✓5th   Additional Digit Required   Unacceptable PDx   Manifestation Code   Hospital Acquired Condition   ►◄ Revised Text   ● New Code   ▲ Revised Code Title

V Codes

V21.31–V25.2

V21.31 Low birth weight status, less than 500 grams

V21.32 Low birth weight status, 500-999 grams

V21.33 Low birth weight status, 1000-1499 grams

V21.34 Low birth weight status, 1500-1999 grams

V21.35 Low birth weight status, 2000-2500 grams

V21.8 Other specified constitutional states in development

V21.9 Unspecified constitutional state in development

√4ᵗʰ **V22 Normal pregnancy**

     EXCLUDES   *pregnancy examination or test, pregnancy unconfirmed (V72.40)*

     AHA: 1Q, '12, 10;4Q, '07, 125

     TIP: Do not assign with any code from chapter 11, "Complications of Pregnancy, Childbirth, and the Puerperium."

V22.0 Supervision of normal first pregnancy   ♀

     AHA: 3Q, '99, 16

     Z34.00 Encounter suprvisn norm 1 pregnancy uns trimestr   I-10

V22.1 Supervision of other normal pregnancy   ♀

     AHA: 3Q, '99, 16

V22.2 Pregnant state, incidental   ♀

     Pregnant state NOS

√4ᵗʰ **V23 Supervision of high-risk pregnancy**

     AHA: 1Q, '12, 10;1Q, '90, 10

V23.0 Pregnancy with history of infertility   M ♀

V23.1 Pregnancy with history of trophoblastic disease   M ♀

     Pregnancy with history of:

         hydatidiform mole

         vesicular mole

     EXCLUDES   *that without current pregnancy (V13.1)*

V23.2 Pregnancy with history of abortion   M ♀

     Pregnancy with history of conditions classifiable to 634-638

     EXCLUDES   *recurrent pregnancy loss:*

         care during pregnancy (646.3)

         that without current pregnancy (629.81)

V23.3 Grand multiparity   M ♀

     EXCLUDES   *care in relation to labor and delivery (659.4)*

         that without current pregnancy (V61.5)

√5ᵗʰ **V23.4 Pregnancy with other poor obstetric history**

     Pregnancy with history of other conditions classifiable to 630-676

V23.41 Pregnancy with history of pre-term labor   M ♀

     AHA: 4Q, '02, 79

V23.42 Pregnancy with history of ectopic pregnancy   M ♀

     AHA: 4Q, '11, 157

V23.49 Pregnancy with other poor obstetric history   M ♀

V23.5 Pregnancy with other poor reproductive history   M ♀

     Pregnancy with history of stillbirth or neonatal death

V23.7 Insufficient prenatal care   M ♀

     History of little or no prenatal care

√5ᵗʰ **V23.8 Other high-risk pregnancy**

     AHA: 4Q, '08, 158; 4Q, '98, 56, 63

V23.81 Elderly primigravida   M ♀

     First pregnancy in a woman who will be 35 years of age or older at expected date of delivery

     EXCLUDES   *elderly primigravida complicating pregnancy (659.5)*

V23.82 Elderly multigravida   M ♀

     Second or more pregnancy in a woman who will be 35 years of age or older at expected date of delivery

     EXCLUDES   *elderly multigravida complicating pregnancy (659.6)*

     AHA: 4Q, '11, 133

V23.83 Young primigravida   M ♀

     First pregnancy in a female less than 16 years old at expected date of delivery

     EXCLUDES   *young primigravida complicating pregnancy (659.8)*

V23.84 Young multigravida   M ♀

     Second or more pregnancy in a female less than 16 years old at expected date of delivery

     EXCLUDES   *young multigravida complicating pregnancy (659.8)*

V23.85 Pregnancy resulting from assisted reproductive technology   A M ♀

     Pregnancy resulting from in vitro fertilization

     AHA: 4Q, '08, 160

V23.86 Pregnancy with history of in utero procedure during previous pregnancy   M ♀

     EXCLUDES   *management of pregnancy affected by in utero procedure during current pregnancy (679.0-679.1)*

     AHA: 4Q, '08, 158, 160

V23.87 Pregnancy with inconclusive fetal viability   M ♀

     Encounter to determine fetal viability of pregnancy

     AHA: 4Q, '11, 157

V23.89 Other high-risk pregnancy   M ♀

     AHA: 3Q, '06, 14

V23.9 Unspecified high-risk pregnancy   M ♀

√4ᵗʰ **V24 Postpartum care and examination**

² **V24.0 Immediately after delivery**   M ♀

     Care and observation in uncomplicated cases

     AHA: 3Q, '06, 11

V24.1 Lactating mother   ♀

     Supervision of lactation

     AHA: 3Q, '12, 7

V24.2 Routine postpartum follow-up   ♀

√4ᵗʰ **V25 Encounter for contraceptive management**

     AHA: 4Q, '92, 24

√5ᵗʰ **V25.0 General counseling and advice**

V25.01 Prescription of oral contraceptives   ♀

V25.02 Initiation of other contraceptive measures

     Fitting of diaphragm

     Prescription of foams, creams, or other agents

     AHA: 3Q, '97, 7

V25.03 Encounter for emergency contraceptive counseling and prescription

     Encounter for postcoital contraceptive counseling and prescription

     AHA: 4Q, '03, 84

V25.04 Counseling and instruction in natural family planning to avoid pregnancy

     AHA: 4Q, '07, 99

     Z30.02 Counsel & instruct natural family plan avoid pg   I-10

V25.09 Other

     Family planning advice

√5ᵗʰ **V25.1 Encounter for insertion or removal of intrauterine contraceptive device**

     EXCLUDES   *encounter for routine checking of intrauterine contraceptive device (V25.42)*

     AHA: 4Q, '10, 109

V25.11 Encounter for insertion of intrauterine contraceptive device   ♀

V25.12 Encounter for removal of intrauterine contraceptive device   ♀

V25.13 Encounter for removal and reinsertion of intrauterine contraceptive device   ♀

     Encounter for replacement of intrauterine contraceptive device

² **V25.2 Sterilization**

     Admission for interruption of fallopian tubes or vas deferens

---

² These V codes may be used as principal diagnosis on Medicare patients.

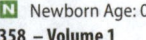 Newborn Age: 0    Pediatric Age: 0-17   M Maternity Age: 12-55   A Adult Age: 15-124   MCC Major CC Condition   CC CC Condition   HIV HIV Related Dx

358 – Volume 1   2015 ICD-9-CM

[2] **V25.3 Menstrual extraction** ♀
    Menstrual regulation

√5th **V25.4 Surveillance of previously prescribed contraceptive methods**
    Checking, reinsertion, or removal of contraceptive device
    Repeat prescription for contraceptive method
    Routine examination in connection with contraceptive maintenance

    V25.40 Contraceptive surveillance, unspecified

    V25.41 Contraceptive pill ♀

    V25.42 Intrauterine contraceptive device ♀
        Checking of intrauterine device
        EXCLUDES *insertion or removal of intrauterine contraceptive device (V25.11-V25.13)*
        presence of intrauterine contraceptive device as incidental finding (V45.51)
        AHA: 4Q, '10, 109-110;

    V25.43 Implantable subdermal contraceptive ♀

    V25.49 Other contraceptive method ♀
        AHA: 3Q, '97, 7

V25.5 Insertion of implantable subdermal contraceptive ♀
    AHA: 3Q, '92, 9

V25.8 Other specified contraceptive management
    Postvasectomy sperm count
    EXCLUDES *sperm count following sterilization reversal (V26.22)*
    sperm count for fertility testing (V26.21)
    AHA: 3Q, '96, 9

V25.9 Unspecified contraceptive management

√4th **V26 Procreative management**

[2] **V26.0 Tuboplasty or vasoplasty after previous sterilization**
    AHA: 2Q, '95, 10
    TIP: Assign for encounters for tubal ligation or vasectomy reversal procedures.

V26.1 Artificial insemination ♀

√5th **V26.2 Investigation and testing**
    EXCLUDES *postvasectomy sperm count (V25.8)*
    AHA: 4Q, '00, 56

    V26.21 Fertility testing
        Fallopian insufflation
        Sperm count for fertility testing
        EXCLUDES *genetic counseling and testing (V26.31-V26.39)*

    V26.22 Aftercare following sterilization reversal
        Fallopian insufflation following sterilization reversal
        Sperm count following sterilization reversal

    V26.29 Other investigation and testing
        AHA: 2Q, '96, 9; N-D, '85, 15

√5th **V26.3 Genetic counseling and testing**
    EXCLUDES *fertility testing (V26.21)*
    nonprocreative genetic screening (V82.71, V82.79)
    AHA: 4Q, '05, 96

    V26.31 Testing of female for genetic disease carrier status ♀
        AHA: 4Q, '06, 117

    V26.32 Other genetic testing of female ♀
        Use additional code to identify recurrent pregnancy loss (629.81, 646.3)
        AHA: 4Q, '06, 117
        Z31.438 Encounter oth genetic test female procreative mngmnt   I-10

    V26.33 Genetic counseling

    V26.34 Testing of male for genetic disease carrier status ♂
        AHA: 4Q, '06, 117

    V26.35 Encounter for testing of male partner of female with recurrent pregnancy loss ♂
        AHA: 4Q, '06, 117

    V26.39 Other genetic testing of male ♂
        AHA: 4Q, '06, 117

√5th **V26.4 General counseling and advice**

    V26.41 Procreative counseling and advice using natural family planning
        AHA: 4Q, '07, 99

    V26.42 Encounter for fertility preservation counseling
        Encounter for fertility preservation counseling prior to cancer therapy
        Encounter for fertility preservation counseling prior to surgical removal of gonads
        AHA: 4Q, '09, 117

    V26.49 Other procreative management, counseling and advice

√5th **V26.5 Sterilization status**

    V26.51 Tubal ligation status ♀
        EXCLUDES *infertility not due to previous tubal ligation (628.0-628.9)*
        Z98.51 Tubal ligation status   I-10

    V26.52 Vasectomy status ♂

√5th **V26.8 Other specified procreative management**

    V26.81 Encounter for assisted reproductive fertility procedure cycle ♀
        Patient undergoing in vitro fertilization cycle
        Use additional code to identify the type of infertility
        EXCLUDES *pre-cycle diagnosis and testing — code to reason for encounter*
        AHA: 4Q, '07, 99

    V26.82 Encounter for fertility preservation procedure
        Encounter for fertility preservation procedure prior to cancer therapy
        Encounter for fertility preservation procedure prior to surgical removal of gonads
        AHA: 4Q, '09, 117

    V26.89 Other specified procreative management

    V26.9 Unspecified procreative management

√4th **V27 Outcome of delivery**
    NOTE This category is intended for the coding of the outcome of delivery on the mother's record.
    AHA: 2Q, '91, 16
    TIP: Assign on the maternal chart for every admission during which a delivery occurs.

    V27.0 Single liveborn M ♀
        AHA: ▶1Q, '14, 14;◀ 4Q, '11, 133; 4Q, '08, 192; 4Q, '05, 81; 2Q, '03, 9; 2Q, '02, 10; 1Q, '01, 10; 3Q, '00, 5; 4Q, '98, 77; 4Q, '95, 59; 1Q, '92, 9
        Z37.0 Single live birth   I-10

    V27.1 Single stillborn M ♀

    V27.2 Twins, both liveborn M ♀
        Z37.2 Twins both liveborn   I-10

    V27.3 Twins, one liveborn and one stillborn M ♀

    V27.4 Twins, both stillborn M ♀

    V27.5 Other multiple birth, all liveborn M ♀

    V27.6 Other multiple birth, some liveborn M ♀

    V27.7 Other multiple birth, all stillborn M ♀

    V27.9 Unspecified outcome of delivery M ♀
        Single birth ⎫
        Multiple birth ⎭ outcome to infant unspecified

√4th **V28 Encounter for antenatal screening of mother**
    EXCLUDES *abnormal findings on screening — code to findings*
    routine prenatal care (V22.0-V23.9)
    suspected fetal conditions affecting management of pregnancy (655.00-655.93, 656.00-656.93, 657.00-657.03, 658.00, 658.93)
    suspected fetal conditions not found (V89.01-V89.09)
    AHA: 4Q, '06, 117; 1Q, '04, 11

    V28.0 Screening for chromosomal anomalies by amniocentesis M ♀

---

[2] These V codes may be used as principal diagnosis on Medicare patients.

√4th √5th Additional Digit Required   Unacceptable PDx   Manifestation Code   Hospital Acquired Condition   ▶◀ Revised Text   ● New Code   ▲ Revised Code Title

2015 ICD-9-CM   **October 2014 · Volume 1 – 359**

V28.1 **Screening for raised alpha-fetoprotein levels in amniotic fluid** M ♀

V28.2 **Other screening based on amniocentesis** M ♀

V28.3 **Encounter for routine screening for malformation using ultrasonics** ♀
Encounter for routine fetal ultrasound NOS
EXCLUDES *encounter for fetal anatomic survey (V28.81)*
genetic counseling and testing (V26.31-V26.39)

V28.4 **Screening for fetal growth retardation using ultrasonics** ♀

V28.5 **Screening for isoimmunization** ♀

V28.6 **Screening for Streptococcus B** M ♀
AHA: 4Q, '97, 46

√5th V28.8 **Other specified antenatal screening**
AHA: 4Q, '08, 159; 3Q, '99, 16

V28.81 **Encounter for fetal anatomic survey** M ♀

V28.82 **Encounter for screening for risk of pre-term labor** M ♀

V28.89 **Other specified antenatal screening** M ♀
Chorionic villus sampling
Genomic screening
Nuchal translucency testing
Proteomic screening

V28.9 **Unspecified antenatal screening** ♀

√4th V29 **Observation and evaluation of newborns and infants for suspected condition not found**
NOTE This category is to be used for newborns, within the neonatal period, (the first 28 days of life) who are suspected of having an abnormal condition resulting from exposure from the mother or the birth process, but without signs or symptoms, and, which after examination and observation, is found not to exist.
EXCLUDES *suspected fetal conditions not found (V89.01-V89.09)*
AHA: 1Q, '00, 25; 4Q, '94, 47; 1Q, '94, 9; 4Q, '92, 21
TIP: Do not assign if the infant shows any signs or symptoms.

[2] V29.0 **Observation for suspected infectious condition** N
AHA: 1Q, '01, 10

[2] V29.1 **Observation for suspected neurological condition** N

[2] V29.2 **Observation for suspected respiratory condition** N

V29.3 **Observation for suspected genetic or metabolic condition** N
AHA: 2Q, '05, 21; 4Q, '98, 59, 68

[2] V29.8 **Observation for other specified suspected condition** N
AHA: 2Q, '03, 15

V29.9 **Observation for unspecified suspected condition** N
AHA: 1Q, '02, 6

Liveborn Infants According to Type of Birth (V30-V39)

NOTE These categories are intended for the coding of liveborn infants who are consuming health care [e.g., crib or bassinet occupancy].

The following fourth digit subdivisions are for use with categories V30-V39

√5th 0 **Born in hospital** N
1 **Born before admission to hospital** N
2 **Born outside hospital and not hospitalized**
The following two fifth digits are for use with the fourth digit .0, Born in hospital:
0 **delivered without mention of cesarean delivery**
1 **delivered by cesarean delivery**

AHA: 1Q, '01, 10

[3] § √4th V30 **Single liveborn**
AHA: 2Q, '12, 17; 2Q, '03, 9; 4Q, '98, 46, 59; 1Q, '94, 9; **For code V30.00:** 3Q, '12, 5; 1Q, '04, 8, 16; 4Q, '03, 68; **For code V30.01:** 4Q, '09, 101; 4Q, '05, 88; **For code V30.10:** 3Q, '06, 10
Z38.00 Single liveborn infant delivered vaginally I-10

[3] § √4th V31 **Twin, mate liveborn**
AHA: 3Q, '92, 10
Z38.31 Twin liveborn infant delivered by cesarean I-10

[3] § √4th V32 **Twin, mate stillborn**

[3] § √4th V33 **Twin, unspecified**

[3] § √4th V34 **Other multiple, mates all liveborn**

[3] § √4th V35 **Other multiple, mates all stillborn**

[3] § √4th V36 **Other multiple, mates live and stillborn**

[3] § √4th V37 **Other multiple, unspecified**

[4] § √4th V39 **Unspecified**

Persons with a Condition Influencing their Health Status (V40-V49)

NOTE These categories are intended for use when these conditions are recorded as "diagnoses" or "problems."
TIP: Includes patients with a carrier status or who have sequelae or residual of a past condition or disease, which may affect current or future treatment.

√4th V40 **Mental and behavioral problems**

V40.0 **Problems with learning**

V40.1 **Problems with communication [including speech]**

V40.2 **Other mental problems**

√5th V40.3 **Other behavioral problems**
AHA: 4Q, '11, 158

V40.31 *Wandering in diseases* **classified elsewhere**
Code first underlying disorder such as:
Alzheimer's disease (331.0)
autism or pervasive developmental disorder (299.0-299.9)
dementia, unspecified, with behavioral disturbance (294.21)
intellectual disabilities (317-319)

V40.39 **Other specified behavioral problem**

V40.9 **Unspecified mental or behavioral problem**

√4th V41 **Problems with special senses and other special functions**

V41.0 **Problems with sight**

V41.1 **Other eye problems**

V41.2 **Problems with hearing**

V41.3 **Other ear problems**

V41.4 **Problems with voice production**

V41.5 **Problems with smell and taste**

V41.6 **Problems with swallowing and mastication**

V41.7 **Problems with sexual function**
EXCLUDES *marital problems (V61.10)*
psychosexual disorders (302.0-302.9)

V41.8 **Other problems with special functions**

V41.9 **Unspecified problem with special functions**

√4th V42 **Organ or tissue replaced by transplant**
INCLUDES *homologous or heterologous (animal) (human) transplant organ status*
AHA: 3Q, '11, 5; 3Q, '98, 3, 4
TIP: Do not assign if the patient has a complication of the transplanted organ; the code from subcategory 996.8 provides the information.

V42.0 **Kidney** CC
CC Excl: 238.77, 996.80-996.81, 996.87, V42.0, V42.89-V42.9
AHA: ▶3Q, '13, 6;◀ 1Q, '08, 10; 1Q, '03, 10; 3Q, '01, 12
Z94.0 Kidney transplant status I-10

---

[2] These V codes may be used as principal diagnosis on Medicare patients.
[3] These codes with a fourth digit of 0 or 1 may be used as a principal diagnosis for Medicare patients
[4] These codes with a fourth digit of 0 may be used as a principal diagnosis for Medicare patients
§ Requires fourth and fifth digit. See beginning of section V30-V39 for codes and definitions.

N Newborn Age: 0   P Pediatric Age: 0-17   M Maternity Age: 12-55   A Adult Age: 15-124   MCC Major CC Condition   CC CC Condition   HIV HIV Related Dx

V42.1 Heart `CC`
    CC Excl: 238.77, 996.80, 996.83, 996.87, V42.1, V42.89-V42.9
    AHA: 3Q, '03, 16; 3Q, '01, 13

V42.2 Heart valve

V42.3 Skin

V42.4 Bone

V42.5 Cornea

V42.6 Lung `CC`
    CC Excl: 238.77, 996.80, 996.84, 996.87, V42.6, V42.89-V42.9

V42.7 Liver `CC`
    CC Excl: 238.77, 996.80, 996.82, 996.87, V42.7, V42.89-V42.9
    AHA: 3Q, '11, 5
    Z94.4 Liver transplant status `I-10`

✓5th **V42.8 Other specified organ or tissue**
    AHA: 4Q, '98, 64; 4Q, '97, 49

    V42.81 Bone marrow `CC`
        CC Excl: 238.77, 279.50-279.53, 996.80, 996.85, 996.87, V42.9
        AHA: 1Q, '12, 13

    V42.82 Peripheral stem cells `CC`
        CC Excl: 238.77, 996.80, 996.87, V42.9

    V42.83 Pancreas `CC`
        CC Excl: 238.77, 996.80, 996.86-996.87, V42.83, V42.9
        AHA: 1Q, '03, 10; 2Q, '01, 16

    V42.84 Intestines `CC`
        CC Excl: 238.77, 996.80, 996.89, V42.84-V42.9
        AHA: 4Q, '00, 48, 50

    V42.89 Other

V42.9 Unspecified organ or tissue

✓4th **V43 Organ or tissue replaced by other means**
    INCLUDES organ or tissue assisted by other means
        replacement of organ by:
           artificial device
           mechanical device
           prosthesis
    EXCLUDES *cardiac pacemaker in situ (V45.01)*
        fitting and adjustment of prosthetic device (V52.0-V52.9)
        renal dialysis status (V45.11)

V43.0 Eye globe

V43.1 Lens
    Pseudophakos
    AHA: 4Q, '98, 65

✓5th **V43.2 Heart**
    AHA: 4Q, '03, 85

    V43.21 Heart assist device `CC`
        CC Excl: 238.77, 996.80, 996.83, 996.87, V42.1, V43.21-V43.22

    V43.22 Fully implantable artificial heart `CC`
        CC Excl: See code: V43.21

V43.3 Heart valve
    AHA: 3Q, '06, 7; 3Q, '02, 13, 14
    TIP: If the status post heart valve replacement information includes "porcine" or mention of other homologous or heterologous tissue, assign instead V42.2.
    Z95.2 Presence of prosthetic heart valve `I-10`

V43.4 Blood vessel

V43.5 Bladder

✓5th **V43.6 Joint**
    AHA: 4Q, '05, 91

    V43.60 Unspecified joint

    V43.61 Shoulder

    V43.62 Elbow

    V43.63 Wrist

    V43.64 Hip
        AHA: 1Q, '09, 6; 2Q, '08, 3-5; 3Q, '06, 4, 5; 4Q, '05, 93, 112; 2Q, '04, 15
        Z96.641 Presence of right artificial hip joint `I-10`

    V43.65 Knee
        AHA: ►1Q, '14, 5;◄ 3Q, '06, 5

V43.66 Ankle

V43.69 Other

V43.7 Limb

✓5th **V43.8 Other organ or tissue**

    V43.81 Larynx
        AHA: 4Q, '95, 55

    V43.82 Breast
        AHA: 4Q, '95, 55
        Z98.82 Breast implant status `I-10`

    V43.83 Artificial skin

    V43.89 Other

✓4th **V44 Artificial opening status**
    EXCLUDES *artificial openings requiring attention or management (V55.0-V55.9)*
    TIP: Do not assign if the patient has a complication of the artificial opening, such as infection or obstruction; assign only the complication code.

V44.0 Tracheostomy
    AHA: 4Q, '03, 103, 107, 111; 1Q, '01, 6

V44.1 Gastrostomy
    AHA: 4Q, '03, 103, 107-108, 110; 1Q, '01, 12; 3Q, '97, 12; 1Q, '93, 26

V44.2 Ileostomy

V44.3 Colostomy
    AHA: 4Q, '03, 110
    Z93.3 Colostomy status `I-10`

V44.4 Other artificial opening of gastrointestinal tract

✓5th **V44.5 Cystostomy**

    V44.50 Cystostomy, unspecified

    V44.51 Cutaneous-vesicostomy

    V44.52 Appendico-vesicostomy

    V44.59 Other cystostomy

V44.6 Other artificial opening of urinary tract
    Nephrostomy   Urethrostomy
    Ureterostomy
    AHA: 3Q, '12, 11-12

V44.7 Artificial vagina

V44.8 Other artificial opening status

V44.9 Unspecified artificial opening status

✓4th **V45 Other postprocedural states**
    EXCLUDES *aftercare management (V51-V58.9)*
        malfunction or other complication — code to condition
    AHA: 4Q, '03, 85

✓5th **V45.0 Cardiac device in situ**
    EXCLUDES *artificial heart (V43.22)*
        heart assist device (V43.21)

    V45.00 Unspecified cardiac device

    V45.01 Cardiac pacemaker
        EXCLUDES *cardiac defibrillator with synchronous cardiac pacemaker (V45.02)*

    V45.02 Automatic implantable cardiac defibrillator
        With synchronous cardiac pacemaker
        Z95.810 Presence auto implantable cardiac defibrillator `I-10`

    V45.09 Other specified cardiac device
        Carotid sinus pacemaker in situ

✓5th **V45.1 Renal dialysis status**
    EXCLUDES *admission for dialysis treatment or session (V56.0)*
    AHA: 4Q, '08, 157; 1Q, '08, 10; 4Q, '07, 86; 3Q, '07, 9; 4Q, '06, 136; 4Q, '05, 96; 2Q, '03, 7; 2Q, '01, 12, 13

    V45.11 Renal dialysis status
        Hemodialysis status
        Patient requiring intermittent renal dialysis
        Peritoneal dialysis status
        Presence of arterial-venous shunt (for dialysis)
        AHA: 3Q, '11, 15; 4Q, '08, 157, 193
        Z99.2 Dependence on renal dialysis `I-10`

    V45.12 Noncompliance with renal dialysis

✓4th ✓5th Additional Digit Required   Unacceptable PDx   Manifestation Code   Hospital Acquired Condition   ►◄ Revised Text   ● New Code   ▲ Revised Code Title

V45.2 **Presence of cerebrospinal fluid drainage device**
Cerebral ventricle (communicating) shunt, valve, or device in situ
EXCLUDES *malfunction (996.2)*
AHA: 4Q, '03, 106

V45.3 **Intestinal bypass or anastomosis status**
EXCLUDES *bariatric surgery status (V45.86)*
gastric bypass status (V45.86)
obesity surgery status (V45.86)

V45.4 **Arthrodesis status**
AHA: ▶2Q, '13, 22;◀ N-D, '84, 18
TIP: If there is a complication of the fusion graft site that requires refusion or revision, assign instead a code from subcategory 996.4.

☑5ᵗʰ **V45.5** **Presence of contraceptive device**

V45.51 **Intrauterine contraceptive device** ♀
EXCLUDES *checking of device (V25.42)*
complication from device (996.32)
insertion and removal of device (V25.11-V25.13)
Z97.5 Presence of intrauterine contraceptive device **I-10**

V45.52 **Subdermal contraceptive implant**

V45.59 **Other**

☑5ᵗʰ **V45.6** **States following surgery of eye and adnexa**
Cataract extraction ⎫
Filtering bleb ⎬ state following eye surgery
Surgical eyelid adhesion ⎭
EXCLUDES *aphakia (379.31)*
artificial eye globe (V43.0)
AHA: 4Q, '98, 65; 4Q, '97, 49

V45.61 **Cataract extraction status**
Use additional code for associated artificial lens status (V43.1)

V45.69 **Other states following surgery of eye and adnexa**
AHA: 2Q, '01, 16; 1Q, '98, 10; 4Q, '97, 19

☑5ᵗʰ **V45.7** **Acquired absence of organ**
AHA: 4Q, '98, 65; 4Q, '97, 50

² **V45.71** **Acquired absence of breast and nipple**
EXCLUDES *congenital absence of breast and nipple (757.6)*
AHA: 4Q, '08, 159; 4Q, '01, 66; 4Q, '97, 50

V45.72 **Acquired absence of intestine (large) (small)**

V45.73 **Acquired absence of kidney**

V45.74 **Other parts of urinary tract**
Bladder
AHA: 4Q, '00, 51

V45.75 **Stomach**
AHA: 4Q, '00, 51

V45.76 **Lung**
AHA: 4Q, '00, 51

V45.77 **Genital organs**
EXCLUDES *acquired absence of cervix and uterus (V88.01-V88.03)*
female genital mutilation status (629.20-629.29)
AHA: 1Q, '03, 13, 14; 4Q, '00, 51

V45.78 **Eye**
AHA: 4Q, '00, 51

V45.79 **Other acquired absence of organ**
EXCLUDES *acquired absence of pancreas (V88.11-V88.12)*
AHA: 4Q, '00, 51

☑5ᵗʰ **V45.8** **Other postprocedural status**

V45.81 **Aortocoronary bypass status**
AHA: 4Q, '11, 153; 4Q, '10, 131; 4Q, '03, 105; 3Q, '01, 15; 3Q, '97, 16

V45.82 **Percutaneous transluminal coronary angioplasty status**

V45.83 **Breast implant removal status**
AHA: 4Q, '95, 55

V45.84 **Dental restoration status**
Dental crowns status
Dental fillings status
AHA: 4Q, '01, 54

V45.85 **Insulin pump status**

V45.86 **Bariatric surgery status**
Gastric banding status
Gastric bypass status for obesity
Obesity surgery status
EXCLUDES *bariatric surgery status complicating pregnancy, childbirth or the puerperium (649.2)*
intestinal bypass or anastomosis status (V45.3)
AHA: 2Q, '09, 10; 4Q, '06, 118
Z98.84 Bariatric surgery status **I-10**

V45.87 **Transplanted organ removal status**
Transplanted organ previously removed due to complication, failure, rejection or infection
EXCLUDES *encounter for removal of transplanted organ — code to complication of transplanted organ (996.80-996.89)*
AHA: 4Q, '08, 157

V45.88 **Status post administration of tPA (rtPA) in a different facility within the last 24 hours prior to admission to current facility**
Code first condition requiring tPA administration, such as:
acute cerebral infarction (433.0-433.9 with fifth-digit 1, 434.0-434.9 with fifth digit 1)
acute myocardial infarction (410.00-410.92)
AHA: ▶4Q, '13, 99;◀ 4Q, '08, 157
TIP: Assign only on receiving facility record; assign even if the patient is still receiving tPA at the time of transfer.

V45.89 **Other**
Presence of neuropacemaker or other electronic device
EXCLUDES *artificial heart valve in situ (V43.3)*
vascular prosthesis in situ (V43.4)
AHA: 1Q, '95, 11

☑4ᵗʰ **V46** **Other dependence on machines and devices**

V46.0 **Aspirator**

☑5ᵗʰ **V46.1** **Respirator [Ventilator]**
Iron lung
AHA: 4Q, '05, 96; 4Q, '03, 103; 1Q, '01, 12; J-F, '87, 7 3

² **V46.11** **Dependence on respirator, status** **CC**
CC Excl: V46.0-V46.2, V46.8-V46.9
AHA: ▶2Q, '13, 25;◀ 4Q, '04, 100
Z99.11 Dependence on respirator ventilator status **I-10**

² **V46.12** **Encounter for respirator dependence during power failure** **CC**
CC Excl: See code V46.11
AHA: 4Q, '04, 100

² **V46.13** **Encounter for weaning from respirator [ventilator]** **CC**
CC Excl: See code V46.11

² **V46.14** **Mechanical complication of respirator [ventilator]** **CC**
Mechanical failure of respirator [ventilator]
CC Excl: See code V46.11

V46.2 **Supplemental oxygen**
Long-term oxygen therapy
AHA: 4Q, '03, 108; 4Q, '02, 79

---

² These V codes may be used as principal diagnosis on Medicare patients.

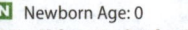

N Newborn Age: 0   **P** Pediatric Age: 0-17   **M** Maternity Age: 12-55   **A** Adult Age: 15-124   **MCC** Major CC Condition   **CC** CC Condition   **HIV** HIV Related Dx

V46.3 Wheelchair dependence
Wheelchair confinement status
Code first cause of dependence, such as:
   muscular dystrophy (359.1)
   obesity (278.00-278.03)
AHA: 4Q, '08, 157

V46.8 Other enabling machines
Hyperbaric chamber
Possum [Patient-Operated-Selector-Mechanism]
EXCLUDES   *cardiac pacemaker (V45.0)*
          kidney dialysis machine (V45.11)

V46.9 Unspecified machine dependence
AHA: 4Q, '06, 117

✓4th **V47 Other problems with internal organs**

V47.0 Deficiencies of internal organs

V47.1 Mechanical and motor problems with internal organs

V47.2 Other cardiorespiratory problems
Cardiovascular exercise intolerance with pain (with):
   at rest
   less than ordinary activity
   ordinary activity

V47.3 Other digestive problems

V47.4 Other urinary problems

V47.5 Other genital problems

V47.9 Unspecified

✓4th **V48 Problems with head, neck, and trunk**

V48.0 Deficiencies of head
EXCLUDES   *deficiencies of ears, eyelids, and nose (V48.8)*

V48.1 Deficiencies of neck and trunk

V48.2 Mechanical and motor problems with head

V48.3 Mechanical and motor problems with neck and trunk

V48.4 Sensory problem with head

V48.5 Sensory problem with neck and trunk

V48.6 Disfigurements of head

V48.7 Disfigurements of neck and trunk

V48.8 Other problems with head, neck, and trunk

V48.9 Unspecified problem with head, neck, or trunk

✓4th **V49 Other conditions influencing health status**

V49.0 Deficiencies of limbs

V49.1 Mechanical problems with limbs

V49.2 Motor problems with limbs

V49.3 Sensory problems with limbs

V49.4 Disfigurements of limbs

V49.5 Other problems of limbs

✓5th **V49.6 Upper limb amputation status**
AHA: 4Q, '05, 94; 4Q, '98, 42; 4Q, '94, 39

   V49.60 Unspecified level
      Z89.201 Acquired absence of right upper limb uns level   I-10

   V49.61 Thumb

   V49.62 Other finger(s)
      AHA: 2Q, '05, 7

   V49.63 Hand

   V49.64 Wrist
      Disarticulation of wrist

   V49.65 Below elbow

   V49.66 Above elbow
      Disarticulation of elbow

   V49.67 Shoulder
      Disarticulation of shoulder

✓5th **V49.7 Lower limb amputation status**
AHA: 3Q, '06, 5; 4Q, '05, 94; 4Q, '98, 42; 4Q, '94, 39

   V49.70 Unspecified level

   V49.71 Great toe

   V49.72 Other toe(s)

   V49.73 Foot

   V49.74 Ankle
      Disarticulation of ankle

   V49.75 Below knee
      Z89.512 Acq absence of lt leg below knee   I-10

   V49.76 Above knee
      Disarticulation of knee
      AHA: 2Q, '05, 14

   V49.77 Hip
      Disarticulation of hip

✓5th **V49.8 Other specified conditions influencing health status**
AHA: 4Q, '00, 51

   V49.81 Asymptomatic postmenopausal status (age-related) (natural)   A ♀
      EXCLUDES   *menopausal and premenopausal disorder (627.0-627.9)*
          postsurgical menopause (256.2)
          premature menopause (256.31)
          symptomatic menopause (627.0-627.9)
      AHA: 4Q, '09,106; 4Q, '02, 79; 4Q, '00, 54

   V49.82 Dental sealant status
      AHA: 4Q, '01, 54

   V49.83 Awaiting organ transplant status

   V49.84 Bed confinement status
      AHA: 4Q, '05, 96

   V49.85 Dual sensory impairment
      Blindness with deafness
      Combined visual hearing impairment
      Code first:
         hearing impairment (389.00-389.9)
         visual impairment (369.00-369.9)
      AHA: 4Q, '07, 100

   V49.86 Do not resuscitate status
      AHA: 1Q, '12, 14; 4Q, '10, 108
      Z66 Do not resuscitate   I-10

   V49.87 Physical restraints status
      AHA: 4Q, '10, 108-109
      EXCLUDES   *restraint due to a procedure – omit code*

   V49.89 Other specified conditions influencing health status
      AHA: 4Q, '05, 94

V49.9 Unspecified

Persons Encountering Health Services for Specific Procedures and Aftercare (V50-V59)

NOTE Categories V51-V59 are intended for use to indicate a reason for care in patients who may have already been treated for some disease or injury not now present, or who are receiving care to consolidate the treatment, to deal with residual states, or to prevent recurrence.

EXCLUDES   *follow-up examination for medical surveillance following treatment (V67.0-V67.9)*

✓4th **V50 Elective surgery for purposes other than remedying health states**

  2 **V50.0 Hair transplant**

  2 **V50.1 Other plastic surgery for unacceptable cosmetic appearance**
     Breast augmentation or reduction
     Face-lift
     EXCLUDES   *encounter for breast reduction (611.1)*
          plastic surgery following healed injury or operation (V51.0-V51.8)

---

2   These V codes may be used as principal diagnosis on Medicare patients.

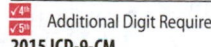

Additional Digit Required   Unacceptable PDx   Manifestation Code   Hospital Acquired Condition   ▶◀ Revised Text   ● New Code   ▲ Revised Code Title

2015 ICD-9-CM   **Volume 1 – 363**

[2] **V50.2 Routine or ritual circumcision** ♂
Circumcision in the absence of significant medical indication

V50.3 Ear piercing

√5th **V50.4 Prophylactic organ removal**
EXCLUDES *organ donations (V59.0-V59.9)*
therapeutic organ removal — code to condition
AHA: 4Q, '94, 44
TIP: Assign an additional code, such as one from category V16 Family history of malignant neoplasm, to indicate the reason for the prophylactic organ removal.

[2] **V50.41 Breast**
AHA: 2Q, '11, 12; 4Q, '04, 107

[2] **V50.42 Ovary** ♀
AHA: 3Q, '09, 5

[2] **V50.49 Other**
AHA: 3Q, '09, 5

V50.8 Other
Z40.8 Encounter for other prophylactic surgery   I-10

V50.9 Unspecified

√4th **V51 Aftercare involving the use of plastic surgery**
Plastic surgery following healed injury or operation
EXCLUDES *cosmetic plastic surgery (V50.1)*
plastic surgery as treatment for current condtion or injury — code to condition or injury
repair of scarred tissue — code to scar
AHA: 4Q, '08, 159

[2] **V51.0 Encounter for breast reconstruction following mastectomy**   A
EXCLUDES *deformity and disproportion of reconstructed breast (612.0-612.1)*
AHA: 4Q, '08, 159-160

[2] **V51.8 Other aftercare involving the use of plastic surgery**

√4th **V52 Fitting and adjustment of prosthetic device and implant**
INCLUDES *removal of device*
EXCLUDES *malfunction or complication of prosthetic device (996.0-996.7)*
status only, without need for care (V43.0-V43.8)
AHA: 4Q, '05, 94; 4Q, '95, 55 ; 1Q, '90, 7

[2] **V52.0 Artificial arm (complete) (partial)**

[2] **V52.1 Artificial leg (complete) (partial)**

[2] **V52.2 Artificial eye**

[2] **V52.3 Dental prosthetic device**

[2] **V52.4 Breast prosthesis and implant** ♀
Elective implant exchange (different material) (different size)
Removal of tissue expander without synchronous insertion of permanent implant
EXCLUDES *admission for initial breast implant insertion for breast augmentation (V50.1)*
complications of breast implant (996.54, 996.69, 996.79)
encounter for breast reconstruction following mastectomy (V51.0)
AHA: 4Q, '95, 80, 81

[2] **V52.8 Other specified prosthetic device**
AHA: 2Q, '02, 12, 16

V52.9 Unspecified prosthetic device

√4th **V53 Fitting and adjustment of other device**
INCLUDES *removal of device*
replacement of device
EXCLUDES *status only, without need for care (V45.0-V45.8)*

√5th **V53.0 Devices related to nervous system and special senses**
AHA: 4Q, '98, 66; 4Q, '97, 51

[2] **V53.01 Fitting and adjustment of cerebral ventricular (communicating) shunt**
AHA: 4Q, '97, 51

[2] **V53.02 Neuropacemaker (brain) (peripheral nerve) (spinal cord)**

[2] **V53.09 Fitting and adjustment of other devices related to nervous system and special senses**
Auditory substitution device
Visual substitution device
AHA: 2Q, '99, 4

V53.1 Spectacles and contact lenses

V53.2 Hearing aid

√5th **V53.3 Cardiac device**
Reprogramming
AHA: 3Q, '92, 3; 1Q, '90, 7; M-J, '87, 8 ; N-D, '84, 18
TIP: Assign for cardiac device replacement when the device has reached normal end-of-life parameters.

V53.31 Cardiac pacemaker
EXCLUDES *automatic implantable cardiac defibrillator with synchronous cardiac pacemaker (V53.32)*
mechanical complication of cardiac pacemaker (996.01)
AHA: 3Q, '10, 9; 1Q, '02, 3

V53.32 Automatic implantable cardiac defibrillator
With synchronous cardiac pacemaker
AHA: 3Q, '05, 8

V53.39 Other cardiac device
AHA: 4Q, '10, 124,125; 2Q, '08, 9; 1Q, '07, 20

V53.4 Orthodontic devices

√5th **V53.5 Other gastrointestinal appliance and device**
EXCLUDES *colostomy (V55.3)*
ileostomy (V55.2)
other artificial opening of digestive tract (V55.4)
AHA: 4Q, '09, 116

V53.50 Fitting and adjustment of intestinal appliance and device

V53.51 Fitting and adjustment of gastric lap band

V53.59 Fitting and adjustment of other gastrointestinal appliance and device

V53.6 Urinary devices
Urinary catheter
EXCLUDES *cystostomy (V55.5)*
nephrostomy (V55.6)
ureterostomy (V55.6)
urethrostomy (V55.6)

V53.7 Orthopedic devices
Orthopedic: Orthopedic:
   brace   corset
   cast   shoes
EXCLUDES *other orthopedic aftercare (V54)*
AHA: ▶4Q, '13, 101◀

V53.8 Wheelchair

√5th **V53.9 Other and unspecified device**
AHA: 2Q, '03, 6

V53.90 Unspecified device

V53.91 Fitting and adjustment of insulin pump
Insulin pump titration

V53.99 Other device
AHA: 2Q, '09, 10

√4th **V54 Other orthopedic aftercare**
EXCLUDES *fitting and adjustment of orthopedic devices (V53.7)*
malfunction of internal orthopedic device (996.40-996.49)
other complication of nonmechanical nature (996.60-996.79)
AHA: 4Q, '08, 158; 1Q, '07, 3-4; 3Q, '95, 3

√5th **V54.0 Aftercare involving internal fixation device**
EXCLUDES *malfunction of internal orthopedic device (996.40-996.49)*
other complication of nonmechanical nature (996.60-996.79)
removal of external fixation device (V54.89)
AHA: 4Q, '03, 87

---

[2] These V codes may be used as principal diagnosis on Medicare patients.

N Newborn Age: 0   P Pediatric Age: 0-17   M Maternity Age: 12-55   A Adult Age: 15-124   MCC Major CC Condition   CC CC Condition   HIV HIV Related Dx

364 – Volume 1 • October 2014   **2015 ICD-9-CM**

² **V54.01 Encounter for removal of internal fixation device**

² **V54.02 Encounter for lengthening/adjustment of growth rod**

² **V54.09 Other aftercare involving internal fixation device**

√5ᵗʰ **V54.1 Aftercare for healing traumatic fracture**
> **EXCLUDES** *aftercare following joint replacement (V54.81)*
> *aftercare for amputation stump (V54.89)*
>
> **AHA:** 4Q, '02, 80
>
> **TIP:** Assign for follow-up and treatment during the healing phase of the fracture; an aftercare code should be used for all subsequent encounters after the initial encounter for care of a fracture.

² **V54.10 Aftercare for healing traumatic fracture of arm, unspecified**

² **V54.11 Aftercare for healing traumatic fracture of upper arm**

² **V54.12 Aftercare for healing traumatic fracture of lower arm**
> **AHA:** 1Q, '07, 7

² **V54.13 Aftercare for healing traumatic fracture of hip**
> **AHA:** 1Q, '09, 6; 4Q, '03, 103, 105; 2Q, '03, 16

² **V54.14 Aftercare for healing traumatic fracture of leg, unspecified**

² **V54.15 Aftercare for healing traumatic fracture of upper leg**
> **EXCLUDES** *aftercare for healing traumatic fracture of hip (V54.13)*
>
> **AHA:** 3Q, '06, 6

² **V54.16 Aftercare for healing traumatic fracture of lower leg**

² **V54.17 Aftercare for healing traumatic fracture of vertebrae**

² **V54.19 Aftercare for healing traumatic fracture of other bone**
> **AHA:** 1Q, '05, 13; 4Q, '02, 80

√5ᵗʰ **V54.2 Aftercare for healing pathologic fracture**
> **EXCLUDES** *aftercare following joint replacement (V54.81)*
>
> **AHA:** 4Q, '02, 80

² **V54.20 Aftercare for healing pathologic fracture of arm, unspecified**

² **V54.21 Aftercare for healing pathologic fracture of upper arm**

² **V54.22 Aftercare for healing pathologic fracture of lower arm**

² **V54.23 Aftercare for healing pathologic fracture of hip**

² **V54.24 Aftercare for healing pathologic fracture of leg, unspecified**

² **V54.25 Aftercare for healing pathologic fracture of upper leg**
> **EXCLUDES** *aftercare for healing pathologic fracture of hip (V54.23)*

² **V54.26 Aftercare for healing pathologic fracture of lower leg**

² **V54.27 Aftercare for healing pathologic fracture of vertebrae**
> **AHA:** 1Q, '07, 6; 4Q, '03, 108

² **V54.29 Aftercare for healing pathologic fracture of other bone**
> **AHA:** 4Q, '02, 80

√5ᵗʰ **V54.8 Other orthopedic aftercare**
> **AHA:** 3Q, '01, 19; 4Q, '99, 5

² **V54.81 Aftercare following joint replacement**
> Use additional code to identify joint replacement site (V43.60-V43.69)
>
> **AHA:** 1Q, '11, 9; 1Q, '09, 6; 3Q, '06, 4; 2Q, '04, 15; 4Q, '02, 80

² **V54.82 Aftercare following explantation of joint prosthesis**
> Aftercare following explantation of joint prosthesis, staged procedure
> Encounter for joint prosthesis insertion following prior explantation of joint prosthesis
>
> **AHA:** 4Q, '11, 156
>
> **TIP:** Assign also a code from subcategory V88.2 to identify the specific joint.

² **V54.89 Other orthopedic aftercare**
> Aftercare for healing fracture NOS

V54.9 Unspecified orthopedic aftercare

√4ᵗʰ **V55 Attention to artificial openings**
> **INCLUDES** adjustment or repositioning of catheter
> closure
> passage of sounds or bougies
> reforming
> removal or replacement of catheter
> toilet or cleansing
>
> **EXCLUDES** *complications of external stoma (519.00-519.09, 569.60-569.69, 596.81-596.83, 997.49)*
> *status only, without need for care (V44.0-V44.9)*

² **V55.0 Tracheostomy**

² **V55.1 Gastrostomy**   **CC**
> **CC Excl:** V55.1
> **AHA:** 4Q, '99, 9; 3Q, '97, 7, 8; 1Q, '96, 14; 3Q, '95, 13
> **TIP:** Assign for gastrostomy or PEG tube that has been dislodged or clogged, for which simple irrigation or replacement is performed.

² **V55.2 Ileostomy**

² **V55.3 Colostomy**
> **AHA:** 1Q, '09, 5; 2Q, '05, 4; 3Q, '97, 9
> **Z43.3** Encounter for attention to colostomy   **I-10**

² **V55.4 Other artificial opening of digestive tract**
> **AHA:** 2Q, '05, 14; 1Q, '03, 10

² **V55.5 Cystostomy**

² **V55.6 Other artificial opening of urinary tract**
> Nephrostomy   Urethrostomy
> Ureterostomy

² **V55.7 Artificial vagina**

² **V55.8 Other specified artificial opening**

V55.9 Unspecified artificial opening

√4ᵗʰ **V56 Encounter for dialysis and dialysis catheter care**
> Use additional code to identify the associated condition
>
> **EXCLUDES** *dialysis preparation — code to condition*
> **AHA:** 4Q, '98, 66; 1Q, '93, 29

² **V56.0 Extracorporeal dialysis**
> Dialysis (renal) NOS
> **EXCLUDES** *dialysis status (V45.11)*
> **AHA:** 4Q, '05, 79; 1Q, '04, 23; 4Q, '00, 40; 3Q, '98, 6; 2Q, '98, 20

² **V56.1 Fitting and adjustment of extracorporeal dialysis catheter**
> Removal or replacement of catheter
> Toilet or cleansing
> Use additional code for any concurrent extracorporeal dialysis (V56.0)
> **AHA:** 2Q, '98, 20

V56.2 Fitting and adjustment of peritoneal dialysis catheter
> Use additional code for any concurrent peritoneal dialysis (V56.8)
> **AHA:** 4Q, '98, 55

√5ᵗʰ **V56.3 Encounter for adequacy testing for dialysis**
> **AHA:** 4Q, '00, 55

V56.31 Encounter for adequacy testing for hemodialysis

V56.32 Encounter for adequacy testing for peritoneal dialysis
> Peritoneal equilibration test

² **V56.8 Other dialysis**
> Peritoneal dialysis
> **AHA:** 4Q, '98, 55

---

² These V codes may be used as principal diagnosis on Medicare patients.

√4ᵗʰ √5ᵗʰ Additional Digit Required   Unacceptable PDx   Manifestation Code   Hospital Acquired Condition   ►◄ Revised Text   ● New Code   ▲ Revised Code Title

V Codes

V57–V58.68

☑4ᵗʰ **V57 Care involving use of rehabilitation procedures**
Use additional code to identify underlying condition
AHA: 3Q, '06, 3; 1Q, '02, 19; 3Q, '97, 12; 1Q, '90, 6; S–O, '86, 3
TIP: Assign codes from V57 for episodes of care related to rehabilitation.

    V57.0 Breathing exercises

⁵ **V57.1 Other physical therapy**
    Therapeutic and remedial exercises, except breathing
    AHA: 3Q, '06, 4; 2Q, '04, 15; 4Q, '02, 56; 4Q, '99, 5

☑5ᵗʰ **V57.2 Occupational therapy and vocational rehabilitation**

    ⁵ **V57.21 Encounter for occupational therapy**
        AHA: 4Q, '99, 7

    ⁵ **V57.22 Encounter for vocational therapy**

⁵ **V57.3 Speech-language therapy**
    AHA: 4Q, '97, 36

    V57.4 Orthoptic training

☑5ᵗʰ **V57.8 Other specified rehabilitation procedure**

    V57.81 Orthotic training
        Gait training in the use of artificial limbs

    ⁵ **V57.89 Other**
        Multiple training or therapy
        AHA: 4Q, '07, 94; 3Q, '06, 6; 4Q, '03, 105-106, 108; 2Q, '03, 16;
        1Q '02, 16; 3Q, '01, 21; 3Q, '97, 11, 12; S–O, '86, 4

⁵ **V57.9 Unspecified rehabilitation procedure**

☑4ᵗʰ **V58 Encounter for other and unspecified procedures and aftercare**
    EXCLUDES *convalescence and palliative care (V66)*
    TIP: If a patient is admitted for both radiation therapy and chemotherapy, either code V58.0 or V58.11 may be sequenced as the principal diagnosis.

    ² **V58.0 Radiotherapy**
        Encounter or admission for radiotherapy
        EXCLUDES *encounter for radioactive implant — code to condition*
        radioactive iodine therapy — code to condition
        AHA: ▶1Q, '13, 8;◀ 3Q, '92, 5; 2Q, '90, 7; J–F, '87, 13
        Z51.0 Encounter for antineoplastic radiation therapy   I-10

☑5ᵗʰ **V58.1 Encounter for antineoplastic chemotherapy and immunotherapy**
    Encounter or admission for chemotherapy
    EXCLUDES *chemotherapy and immunotherapy for nonneoplastic conditions — code to condition*
    AHA: 1Q, '04, 13; 2Q, '03, 16; 3Q, '93, 4; 2Q, '92, 6; 2Q, '91, 17; 2Q, '90, 7; S–O, '84, 5

    ² **V58.11 Encounter for antineoplastic chemotherapy**
        AHA: 1Q, '12, 13; 2Q, '11, 4; 4Q, '09, 79; 4Q, '08, 82, 155; 4Q, '07, 104; 2Q, '06, 20-21; 4Q, '05, 98
        Z51.11 Encounter for antineoplastic chemotherapy   I-10

    ² **V58.12 Encounter for antineoplastic immunotherapy**
        AHA: 4Q, '05, 98

    V58.2 Blood transfusion, without reported diagnosis

☑5ᵗʰ **V58.3 Attention to dressings and sutures**
    Change or removal of wound packing
    EXCLUDES *attention to drains (V58.49)*
    planned postoperative wound closure (V58.41)
    AHA: 2Q, '05, 14

    V58.30 Encounter for change or removal of nonsurgical wound dressing
        Encounter for change or removal of wound dressing NOS
        AHA: 4Q, '09, 150; 4Q, '06, 117

    V58.31 Encounter for change or removal of surgical wound dressing
        AHA: 4Q, '06, 117
        Z48.01 Encounter change/removal surgical wound dress I-10

    V58.32 Encounter for removal of sutures
        Encounter for removal of staples
        AHA: 4Q, '06, 117
        Z48.02 Encounter for removal of sutures   I-10

☑5ᵗʰ **V58.4 Other aftercare following surgery**
    NOTE Codes from this subcategory should be used in conjunction with other aftercare codes to fully identify the reason for the aftercare encounter
    EXCLUDES *aftercare following sterilization reversal surgery (V26.22)*
    attention to artificial openings (V55.0-V55.9)
    orthopedic aftercare (V54.0-V54.9)
    AHA: 4Q, '99, 9; N-D, '87, 9

    ⁶ **V58.41 Encounter for planned postoperative wound closure**
        EXCLUDES *disruption of operative wound (998.31-998.32)*
        encounter for dressings and suture aftercare (V58.30-V58.32)
        AHA: 4Q, '99, 15

    ⁶ **V58.42 Aftercare following surgery for neoplasm**
        Conditions classifiable to 140-239
        AHA: 4Q, '02, 80

    ⁶ **V58.43 Aftercare following surgery for injury and trauma**
        Conditions classifiable to 800-999
        EXCLUDES *aftercare for healing traumatic fracture (V54.10-V54.19)*
        AHA: 4Q, '02, 80

    ⁶ **V58.44 Aftercare following organ transplant**
        Use additional code to identify the organ transplanted (V42.0-V42.9)
        AHA: 3Q, '11, 5; 4Q, '04, 101

    ⁶ **V58.49 Other specified aftercare following surgery**
        Change or removal of drains
        AHA: 1Q, '96, 8, 9

    ⁶ **V58.5 Orthodontics**
        EXCLUDES *fitting and adjustment of orthodontic device (V53.4)*

☑5ᵗʰ **V58.6 Long-term (current) drug use**
    Long-term (current) prophylactic drug use
    EXCLUDES *drug abuse and dependence complicating pregnancy (648.3-648.4)*
    drug abuse (305.00-305.93)
    drug dependence (304.00-304.93)
    hormone replacement therapy (postmenopausal) (V07.4)
    use of agents affecting estrogen receptors and estrogen levels (V07.51-V07.59)
    AHA: 1Q, '11, 15; 4Q, '08, 159; 4Q, '03, 85; 4Q, '02, 84; 3Q, '02, 15; 4Q, '95, 61
    TIP: Do not assign for patients on detoxification drugs or maintenance programs to prevent withdrawal symptoms related to drug dependence; assign instead drug dependence code(s).

    ⁶ **V58.61 Long-term (current) use of anticoagulants**
        EXCLUDES *long-term (current) use of aspirin (V58.66)*
        AHA: ▶4Q, '13, 101;◀ 4Q, '08, 135; 3Q, '06, 13; 3Q, '04, 7; 4Q, '03, 108; 3Q, '02, 13-16; 1Q, '02, 15, 16
        Z79.01 Long term (current) use of anticoagulants   I-10

    V58.62 Long-term (current) use of antibiotics
        AHA: 4Q, '98, 59

    V58.63 Long-term (current) use of antiplatelets/antithrombotics
        EXCLUDES *long-term (current) use of aspirin (V58.66)*

    V58.64 Long-term (current) use of non-steroidal anti-inflammatories (NSAID)
        EXCLUDES *long-term (current) use of aspirin (V58.66)*

    V58.65 Long-term (current) use of steroids
        Z79.52 Long term (current) use of systemic steroids   I-10

    ⁶ **V58.66 Long-term (current) use of aspirin**
        AHA: 4Q, '04, 102

    ⁶ **V58.67 Long-term (current) use of insulin**
        AHA: ▶3Q, '13, 9;◀ 4Q, '04, 55-56, 103
        Z79.4 Long term (current) use of insulin   I-10

    V58.68 Long term (current) use of bisphosphonates
        AHA: 4Q, '11, 157

---

² These V codes may be used as principal diagnosis on Medicare patients.
⁵ Rehabilitation codes acceptable as a principal diagnosis when accompanied by a secondary diagnosis reflecting the condition treated.
⁶ These V codes are acceptable as principal diagnosis and group to DRGs 949-950.

N Newborn Age: 0   **P** Pediatric Age: 0-17   **M** Maternity Age: 12-55   **A** Adult Age: 15-124   **MCC** Major CC Condition   **CC** CC Condition   **HIV** HIV Related Dx

⁶ V58.69 Long-term (current) use of other medications
Other high-risk medications
Long term current use of methadone for pain control
Long term current use of opiate analgesic
> **EXCLUDES** *methadone maintenance NOS (304.00)*
> *methadone use NOS (304.00)*
> AHA: ▶2Q, '13, 13, 14;◀ 2Q, '11, 7; 2Q, '10, 10, 13; 4Q, '09, 83; 3Q, '09, 3; 4Q, '08, 156; 2Q, '04, 10; 1Q, '04, 13; 1Q, '03, 11; 2Q, '00, 8; 3Q, '99, 13; 2Q, '99, 17; 1Q, '97, 12; 2Q, '96, 7

✓5ᵗʰ V58.7 Aftercare following surgery to specified body systems, not elsewhere classified
> **NOTE** Codes from this subcategory should be used in conjunction with other aftercare codes to fully identify the reason for the aftercare encounter
> **EXCLUDES** *aftercare following organ transplant (V58.44)*
> *aftercare following surgery for neoplasm (V58.42)*
> AHA: 4Q, '03, 104; 4Q, '02, 80

⁶ V58.71 Aftercare following surgery of the sense organs, NEC
Conditions classifiable to 360-379, 380-389
> AHA: ▶2Q, '13, 11◀

⁶ V58.72 Aftercare following surgery of the nervous system, NEC
Conditions classifiable to 320-359
> **EXCLUDES** *aftercare following surgery of the sense organs, NEC (V58.71)*

⁶ V58.73 Aftercare following surgery of the circulatory system, NEC
Conditions classifiable to 390-459
> AHA: 2Q, '09, 12; 4Q, '03, 105

⁶ V58.74 Aftercare following surgery of the respiratory system, NEC
Conditions classifiable to 460-519

⁶ V58.75 Aftercare following surgery of the teeth, oral cavity and digestive system, NEC
Conditions classifiable to 520-579
> AHA: 2Q, '05, 14

⁶ V58.76 Aftercare following surgery of the genitourinary system, NEC
Conditions classifiable to 580-629
> **EXCLUDES** *aftercare following sterilization reversal (V26.22)*
> AHA: 1Q, '05, 11-12

⁶ V58.77 Aftercare following surgery of the skin and subcutaneous tissue, NEC
Conditions classifiable to 680-709

⁶ V58.78 Aftercare following surgery of the musculoskeletal system, NEC
Conditions classifiable to 710-739
> **EXCLUDES** *orthopedic aftercare (V54.01-V54.9)*

✓6ᵗʰ V58.8 Other specified procedures and aftercare
> AHA: 4Q, '94, 45; 2Q, '94, 8

⁶ V58.81 Fitting and adjustment of vascular catheter
Removal or replacement of catheter
Toilet or cleansing
> **EXCLUDES** *complication of renal dialysis (996.73)*
> *complication of vascular catheter (996.74)*
> *dialysis preparation — code to condition*
> *encounter for dialysis (V56.0-V56.8)*
> *fitting and adjustment of dialysis catheter (V56.1)*
> AHA: 2Q, '11, 4

⁶ V58.82 Fitting and adjustment of nonvascular catheter, NEC
Removal or replacement of catheter
Toilet or cleansing
> **EXCLUDES** *fitting and adjustment of peritoneal dialysis catheter (V56.2)*
> *fitting and adjustment of urinary catheter (V53.6)*

⁶ V58.83 Encounter for therapeutic drug monitoring
Use additional code for any associated long- term (current) drug use (V58.61-V58.69)
> **EXCLUDES** *blood-drug testing for medicolegal reasons (V70.4)*
> **DEF:** Drug monitoring: Measurement of the level of a specific drug in the body or measurement of a specific function to assess effectiveness of a drug.
> AHA: 4Q, '08, 156; 2Q, '04, 10; 1Q, '04, 13;4Q, '03, 85; 4Q, '02, 84; 3Q, '02, 13-16

⁶ V58.89 Other specified aftercare
> AHA: 4Q, '98, 59

⁶ V58.9 Unspecified aftercare

✓4ᵗʰ V59 Donors
> **EXCLUDES** *examination of potential donor (V70.8)*
> *self-donation of organ or tissue — code to condition*
> AHA: 4Q, '95, 62; 1Q, '90, 10; N-D, '84, 8
> **TIP:** Assign only for living donations to other individuals, not for self-donation or for cadaveric donations.

✓5ᵗʰ V59.0 Blood
> **V59.01** Whole blood
> **V59.02** Stem cells
> **V59.09** Other

² V59.1 Skin

² V59.2 Bone

² V59.3 Bone marrow

² V59.4 Kidney

² V59.5 Cornea

² V59.6 Liver

✓5ᵗʰ V59.7 Egg (oocyte) (ovum)
> AHA: 4Q, '05, 99
>
> **V59.70** Egg (oocyte) (ovum) donor, unspecified   ♀
> **V59.71** Egg (oocyte) (ovum) donor, under age 35, anonymous recipient   ♀
>   Egg donor, under age 35 NOS
> **V59.72** Egg (oocyte) (ovum) donor, under age 35, designated recipient   ♀
> **V59.73** Egg (oocyte) (ovum) donor, age 35 and over, anonymous recipient   ♀
>   Egg donor, age 35 and over NOS
> **V59.74** Egg (oocyte) (ovum) donor, age 35 and over, designated recipient   ♀

² V59.8 Other specified organ or tissue
> AHA: 3Q, '02, 20

² V59.9 Unspecified organ or tissue

Persons Encountering Health Services in Other Circumstances (V60-V69)

✓4ᵗʰ V60 Housing, household, and economic circumstances

V60.0 Lack of housing
Hobos	Transients
Social migrants	Vagabonds
Tramps	

V60.1 Inadequate housing
Lack of heating
Restriction of space
Technical defects in home preventing adequate care

V60.2 Inadequate material resources
Economic problem
Poverty NOS

V60.3 Person living alone

---

² These V codes may be used as principal diagnosis on Medicare patients.
⁶ These V codes are acceptable as principal diagnosis and group to DRGs 949-950.

2015 ICD-9-CM   ✓4ᵗʰ ✓5ᵗʰ Additional Digit Required   Unacceptable PDx   Manifestation Code   Hospital Acquired Condition   ▶◀ Revised Text   ● New Code   ▲ Revised Code Title

October 2014 • Volume 1 – 367

V60.4 No other household member able to render care

Person requiring care (has) (is):
family member too handicapped, ill, or otherwise unsuited
to render care
partner temporarily away from home
temporarily away from usual place of abode

EXCLUDES   *holiday relief care (V60.5)*

V60.5 Holiday relief care

Provision of health care facilities to a person normally cared
for at home, to enable relatives to take a vacation

V60.6 Person living in residential institution

Boarding school resident

✓5ᵗʰ **V60.8 Other specified housing or economic circumstances**

AHA: 4Q, '09, 118

V60.81 Foster care (status)

V60.89 Other specified housing or economic circumstances

V60.9 Unspecified housing or economic circumstance

✓4ᵗʰ **V61 Other family circumstances**

INCLUDES   when these circumstances or fear of them, affecting the
person directly involved or others, are mentioned as
the reason, justified or not, for seeking or receiving
medical advice or care

AHA: 1Q, '90, 9

✓5ᵗʰ **V61.0 Family disruption**

AHA: 4Q, '08, 160

V61.01 Family disruption due to family member on military deployment

Individual or family affected by other family member
being on deployment

EXCLUDES   *family disruption due to family member on non-military extended absence from home (V61.08)*

V61.02 Family disruption due to return of family member from military deployment

Individual or family affected by other family member
having returned from deployment (current or
past conflict)

V61.03 Family disruption due to divorce or legal separation

V61.04 Family disruption due to parent-child estrangement

EXCLUDES   *other family estrangement (V61.09)*

V61.05 Family disruption due to child in welfare custody

V61.06 Family disruption due to child in foster care or in care of non-parental family member

V61.07 Family disruption due to death of family member

EXCLUDES   *bereavement (V62.82)*

AHA: 4Q, '09, 117

V61.08 Family disruption due to other extended absence of family member

EXCLUDES   *family disruption due to family member on military deployment (V61.01)*

AHA: 4Q, '09, 117

V61.09 Other family disruption

Family estrangement NOS

✓5ᵗʰ **V61.1 Counseling for marital and partner problems**

EXCLUDES   *problems related to:*
psychosexual disorders (302.0-302.9)
sexual function (V41.7)

V61.10 Counseling for marital and partner problems, unspecified

Marital conflict
Marital relationship problem
Partner conflict
Partner relationship problem

V61.11 Counseling for victim of spousal and partner abuse

EXCLUDES   *encounter for treatment of current injuries due to abuse (995.80-995.85)*

V61.12 Counseling for perpetrator of spousal and partner abuse

✓5ᵗʰ **V61.2 Parent-child problems**

V61.20 Counseling for parent-child problem, unspecified

Concern about behavior of child
Parent-child conflict
Parent-child relationship problem

[2] **V61.21 Counseling for victim of child abuse**

Child battering
Child neglect

EXCLUDES   *current injuries due to abuse (995.50-995.59)*

V61.22 Counseling for perpetrator of parental child abuse

EXCLUDES   *counseling for non-parental abuser (V62.83)*

V61.23 Counseling for parent-biological child problem

Concern about behavior of biological child
Parent-biological child conflict
Parent-biological child relationship problem

AHA: 4Q, '09, 117

V61.24 Counseling for parent-adopted child problem

Concern about behavior of adopted child
Parent-adopted child conflict
Parent-adopted child relationship problem

AHA: 4Q, '09, 117

V61.25 Counseling for parent (guardian)-foster child problem

Concern about behavior of foster child
Parent (guardian)-foster child conflict
Parent (guardian)-foster child relationship problem

AHA: 4Q, '09, 117

V61.29 Other parent-child problems

AHA: 3Q, '99, 16

V61.3 Problems with aged parents or in-laws

✓5ᵗʰ **V61.4 Health problems within family**

V61.41 Alcoholism in family

V61.42 Substance abuse in family

AHA: 4Q, '09, 117

V61.49 Other

Care of   } sick or handicapped person
Presence of   } in family or household

V61.5 Multiparity

V61.6 Illegitimacy or illegitimate pregnancy   M ♀

V61.7 Other unwanted pregnancy   M ♀

V61.8 Other specified family circumstances

Problems with family members NEC
Sibling relationship problem

V61.9 Unspecified family circumstance

✓4ᵗʰ **V62 Other psychosocial circumstances**

INCLUDES   those circumstances or fear of them, affecting the person
directly involved or others, mentioned as the reason,
justified or not, for seeking or receiving medical
advice or care

EXCLUDES   *previous psychological trauma (V15.41-V15.49)*

V62.0 Unemployment

EXCLUDES   *circumstances when main problem is economic inadequacy or poverty (V60.2)*

V62.1 Adverse effects of work environment

N Newborn Age: 0   P Pediatric Age: 0-17   M Maternity Age: 12-55   A Adult Age: 15-124   MCC Major CC Condition   CC CC Condition   HIV HIV Related Dx

368 – Volume 1   2015 ICD-9-CM

√5ᵗʰ **V62.2 Other occupational circumstances or maladjustment**
AHA: 4Q, '08, 160

V62.21 Personal current military deployment status [A]
Individual (civilian or military) currently deployed in theater or in support of military war, peacekeeping and humanitarian operations

V62.22 Personal history of return from military deployment [A]
Individual (civilian or military) with past history of military war, peacekeeping and humanitarian deployment (current or past conflict)

V62.29 Other occupational circumstances or maladjustment [A]
Career choice problem
Dissatisfaction with employment
Occupational problem

V62.3 Educational circumstances
Academic problem
Dissatisfaction with school environment
Educational handicap

V62.4 Social maladjustment
Acculturation problem
Cultural deprivation
Political, religious, or sex discrimination
Social: isolation persecution

V62.5 Legal circumstances
Imprisonment   Litigation
Legal investigation   Prosecution

V62.6 Refusal of treatment for reasons of religion or conscience

√5ᵗʰ **V62.8 Other psychological or physical stress, not elsewhere classified**

V62.81 Interpersonal problems, not elsewhere classified
Relational problem NOS

V62.82 Bereavement, uncomplicated
EXCLUDES family disruption due to death of family member (V61.07)

V62.83 Counseling for perpetrator of physical/sexual abuse
EXCLUDES counseling for perpetrator of parental child abuse (V61.22)
counseling for perpetrator of spousal and partner abuse (V61.12)

² **V62.84 Suicidal ideation** [CC]
EXCLUDES suicidal tendencies (300.9)
DEF: Thoughts of committing suicide; no actual attempt of suicide has been made.
CC Excl: 290.11, 290.3, 293.0
AHA: 4Q, '05, 96
TIP: Assign patients who have not attempted suicide, and who may not be considered a suicide risk, but who have indicated thoughts about suicide.
R45.851 Suicidal ideations [I-10]

V62.85 Homicidal ideation
AHA: 4Q, '10, 110
R45.850 Homicidal ideations [I-10]

V62.89 Other
Borderline intellectual functioning
Life circumstance problems
Phase of life problems
Religious or spiritual problem

V62.9 Unspecified psychosocial circumstance

√4ᵗʰ **V63 Unavailability of other medical facilities for care**
AHA: 1Q, '91, 21

V63.0 Residence remote from hospital or other health care facility

V63.1 Medical services in home not available
EXCLUDES no other household member able to render care (V60.4)
AHA: 4Q, '01, 67; 1Q, '01, 12

V63.2 Person awaiting admission to adequate facility elsewhere

V63.8 Other specified reasons for unavailability of medical facilities
Person on waiting list undergoing social agency investigation

V63.9 Unspecified reason for unavailability of medical facilities

√4ᵗʰ **V64 Persons encountering health services for specific procedures, not carried out**

√5ᵗʰ **V64.0 Vaccination not carried out**
AHA: 4Q, '05, 99

V64.00 Vaccination not carried out, unspecified reason

V64.01 Vaccination not carried out because of acute illness

V64.02 Vaccination not carried out because of chronic illness or condition

V64.03 Vaccination not carried out because of immune compromised state

V64.04 Vaccination not carried out because of allergy to vaccine or component
Z28.04 Immunization not carried out pt allergy vaccine [I-10]

V64.05 Vaccination not carried out because of caregiver refusal
Guardian refusal   Parent refusal
EXCLUDES vaccination not carried out because of caregiver refusal for religious reasons (V64.07)
AHA: ▶3Q, '13, 4;◀ 4Q, '09, 115; 1Q, '07, 12

V64.06 Vaccination not carried out because of patient refusal

V64.07 Vaccination not carried out for religious reasons

V64.08 Vaccination not carried out because patient had disease being vaccinated against

V64.09 Vaccination not carried out for other reason

V64.1 Surgical or other procedure not carried out because of contraindication
TIP: Assign an additional code to indicate the contraindication (reason the surgery or other procedure was canceled).

V64.2 Surgical or other procedure not carried out because of patient's decision
AHA: 2Q, '01, 8

V64.3 Procedure not carried out for other reasons

√5ᵗʰ **V64.4 Closed surgical procedure converted to open procedure**
AHA: 4Q, '03, 87; 4Q, '98, 68; 4Q, '97, 52

V64.41 Laparoscopic surgical procedure converted to open procedure
AHA: 1Q, '11, 14-15

V64.42 Thoracoscopic surgical procedure converted to open procedure

V64.43 Arthroscopic surgical procedure converted to open procedure

√4ᵗʰ **V65 Other persons seeking consultation**

² **V65.0 Healthy person accompanying sick person**
Boarder

√5ᵗʰ **V65.1 Person consulting on behalf of another person**
Advice or treatment for nonttending third party
EXCLUDES concern (normal) about sick person in family (V61.41-V61.49)
AHA: 4Q, '03, 84

V65.11 Pediatric pre-birth visit for expectant parent(s)
Pre-adoption visit for adoptive parent(s)

V65.19 Other person consulting on behalf of another person

---

² These V codes may be used as principal diagnosis on Medicare patients.

√4ᵗʰ √5ᵗʰ Additional Digit Required   Unacceptable PDx   Manifestation Code   Hospital Acquired Condition   ▶◀ Revised Text   ● New Code   ▲ Revised Code Title

2015 ICD-9-CM   **October 2014 · Volume 1 – 369**

2 V65.2 Person feigning illness
    Malingerer   Peregrinating patient
    AHA: 3Q, '99, 20
    TIP: Assign for patients engaged in
        what is documented as "drug- seeking behavior."

V65.3 Dietary surveillance and counseling
    Dietary surveillance and counseling (in):
        NOS
        colitis
        diabetes mellitus
        food allergies or intolerance
        gastritis
        hypercholesterolemia
        hypoglycemia
        obesity
    Use additional code to identify Body Mass Index (BMI), if
        known (V85.0-V85.54)
    AHA: 4Q, '05, 96

√5th V65.4 Other counseling, not elsewhere classified
    Health: Health:
      advice   instruction
      education
    EXCLUDES counseling (for):
        contraception (V25.40-V25.49)
        genetic (V26.31-V26.39)
        on behalf of third party (V65.11-V65.19)
        procreative management (V26.41-V26.49)

V65.40 Counseling NOS

V65.41 Exercise counseling

V65.42 Counseling on substance use and abuse
    Z71.6 Tobacco abuse counseling   I-10

V65.43 Counseling on injury prevention

V65.44 Human immunodeficiency virus [HIV] counseling

V65.45 Counseling on other sexually transmitted diseases

V65.46 Encounter for insulin pump training
    Z46.81 Encounter for fitting & adjustment insulin pump   I-10

V65.49 Other specified counseling
    AHA: 4Q, '08, 156; 2Q, '00, 8

V65.5 Person with feared complaint in whom no diagnosis was made
    Feared condition not demonstrated
    Problem was normal state
    "Worried well"

V65.8 Other reasons for seeking consultation
    EXCLUDES specified symptoms
    AHA: 3Q, '92, 4

V65.9 Unspecified reason for consultation

√4th V66 Convalescence and palliative care

2 V66.0 Following surgery

2 V66.1 Following radiotherapy

2 V66.2 Following chemotherapy

2 V66.3 Following psychotherapy and other treatment for mental disorder

2 V66.4 Following treatment of fracture

V66.5 Following other treatment

2 V66.6 Following combined treatment

V66.7 Encounter for palliative care
    End of life care   Terminal care
    Hospice care
    Code first underlying disease
    AHA: 3Q, '12, 16; 1Q, '12, 14; 3Q, '10, 18; 3Q, '08, 13; 2Q, '05, 9; 4Q, '03,
    107; 1Q, '98, 11; 4Q, '96, 47, 48
    TIP: Assign as secondary diagnosis when treatment is focused on
      management of pain and symptoms in a patient with an incurable
      disease.
    Z51.5 Encounter for palliative care   I-10

V66.9 Unspecified convalescence
    AHA: 4Q, '99, 8

√4th V67 Follow-up examination
    INCLUDES surveillance only following completed treatment
    EXCLUDES surveillance of contraception (V25.40-V25.49)
    AHA: 4Q, '08, 157; 2Q, '03, 5

√5th V67.0 Following surgery
    AHA: 4Q, '00, 56; 4Q, '98, 69; 4Q, '97, 50; 2Q, '95, 8;1Q, '95, 4;
    3Q, '92, 11

6 V67.00 Following surgery, unspecified

6 V67.01 Follow-up vaginal pap smear   ♀
    Vaginal pap-smear, status-post hysterectomy for
      malignant condition
    Use additional code to identify:
      acquired absence of uterus (V88.01-V88.03)
      personal history of malignant neoplasm
        (V10.40-V10.44)
    EXCLUDES vaginal pap smear status-post hysterectomy
        for non-malignant condition (V76.47)
    AHA: 4Q, '08, 157

6 V67.09 Following other surgery
    EXCLUDES sperm count following sterilization reversal
        (V26.22)
        sperm count for fertility testing
        (V26.21)
    AHA: ▶4Q, '13, 105;◀ 3Q, '08, 6; 3Q, '03, 16; 3Q, '02, 15

2 V67.1 Following radiotherapy

2 V67.2 Following chemotherapy
    Cancer chemotherapy follow-up

2 V67.3 Following psychotherapy and other treatment for mental disorder

6 V67.4 Following treatment of healed fracture
    EXCLUDES current (healing) fracture aftercare (V54.0-V54.9)
    AHA: 1Q, '09, 6; 1Q, '90, 7

√5th V67.5 Following other treatment

2 V67.51 Following completed treatment with high-risk medications, not elsewhere classified
    EXCLUDES long-term (current) drug use
        (V58.61-V58.69)
    AHA: 1Q, '99, 5, 6; 4Q, '95, 61; 1Q, '90, 18

2 V67.59 Other

2 V67.6 Following combined treatment

V67.9 Unspecified follow-up examination

√4th V68 Encounters for administrative purposes

√5th V68.0 Issue of medical certificates
    EXCLUDES encounter for general medical examination
        (V70.0-V70.9)

V68.01 Disability examination
    Use additional code(s) to identify specific
      examination(s), screening and testing
      performed (V72.0-V82.9)
    AHA: 4Q, '07, 101

V68.09 Other issue of medical certificates

V68.1 Issue of repeat prescriptions
    Issue of repeat prescription for:
      appliance
      glasses
      medications
    EXCLUDES repeat prescription for contraceptives
        (V25.41-V25.49)

V68.2 Request for expert evidence

√5th V68.8 Other specified administrative purpose

V68.81 Referral of patient without examination or treatment

V68.89 Other

V68.9 Unspecified administrative purpose

---

2 These V codes may be used as principal diagnosis on Medicare patients.
6 These V codes are acceptable as principal diagnosis and group to DRGs 949-950.

N Newborn Age: 0   P Pediatric Age: 0-17   M Maternity Age: 12-55   A Adult Age: 15-124   MCC Major CC Condition   CC CC Condition   HIV HIV Related Dx

✓4th **V69 Problems related to lifestyle**
    AHA: 4Q, '94, 48

V69.0 Lack of physical exercise

V69.1 Inappropriate diet and eating habits
    EXCLUDES *anorexia nervosa (307.1)*
        bulimia (783.6)
        malnutrition and other nutritional deficiencies
          (260-269.9)
        other and unspecified eating disorders
          (307.50-307.59)

V69.2 High-risk sexual behavior

V69.3 Gambling and betting
    EXCLUDES *pathological gambling (312.31)*

2 **V69.4 Lack of adequate sleep**
    Sleep deprivation
    EXCLUDES *insomnia (780.52)*

V69.5 Behavioral insomnia of childhood   P
    DEF: Behaviors on the part of the child or caregivers that cause
    negative compliance with a child's sleep schedule; results in lack of
    adequate sleep.
    AHA: 4Q, '05, 99

V69.8 Other problems related to lifestyle
    Self-damaging behavior

V69.9 Problem related to lifestyle, unspecified

Persons Without Reported Diagnosis Encountered During Examination and Investigation of Individuals and Populations (V70-V82)

    NOTE Nonspecific abnormal findings disclosed at the time of these
    examinations are classifiable to categories 790-796.

✓4th **V70 General medical examination**
    Use additional code(s) to identify any special screening
    examination(s) performed (V73.0-V82.9)

V70.0 Routine general medical examination at a health care facility
    Health checkup
    EXCLUDES *health checkup of infant or child over 28 days old*
        (V20.2)
        health supervision of newborn 8 to 28 days old
          (V20.32)
        health supervision of newborn under 8 days old
          (V20.31)
        pre-procedural general physical examination
          (V72.83)
    AHA: ▶4Q, '13, 101◀

2 **V70.1 General psychiatric examination, requested by the authority**

V70.2 General psychiatric examination, other and unspecified

V70.3 Other medical examination for administrative purposes
    General medical examination for:
      admission to old age home
      adoption
      camp
      driving license
      immigration and naturalization
      insurance certification
      marriage
      prison
      school admission
      sports competition
    EXCLUDES *attendance for issue of medical certificates (V68.0)*
        pre-employment screening (V70.5)
    AHA: 3Q, '08, 6; 1Q, '90, 6
    Z02.6 Encounter for exam for insurance purposes   I-10

2 **V70.4 Examination for medicolegal reasons**
    Blood-alcohol tests   Paternity testing
    Blood-drug tests
    EXCLUDES *examination and observation following:*
        accidents (V71.3, V71.4)
        assault (V71.6)
        rape (V71.5)

2 **V70.5 Health examination of defined subpopulations**
    Armed forces personnel   Prisoners
    Inhabitants of institutions   Prostitutes
    Occupational health examinations   Refugees
    Pre-employment screening   School children
    Preschool children   Students

V70.6 Health examination in population surveys
    EXCLUDES *special screening (V73.0-V82.9)*

2 **V70.7 Examination of participant in clinical trial**
    Examination of participant or control in clinical research
    AHA: 2Q, '06, 5-6; 4Q, '01, 55

V70.8 Other specified general medical examinations
    Examination of potential donor of organ or tissue

V70.9 Unspecified general medical examination

✓4th **V71 Observation and evaluation for suspected conditions not found**
    INCLUDES This category is to be used when persons without a
    diagnosis are suspected of having an abnormal
    condition, without signs or symptoms, which
    requires study, but after examination and
    observation, is found not to exist. This category is
    also for use for administrative and legal observation
    status.
    EXCLUDES *suspected maternal and fetal conditions not found*
        (V89.01-V89.09)
    AHA: 4Q, '94, 47; 2Q, '90, 5; M-A, '87, 1
    TIP: Assign observation codes only as principal/first-listed diagnosis and only
    if there is no documentation of any signs or symptoms.

✓5th **V71.0 Observation for suspected mental condition**

2 **V71.01 Adult antisocial behavior**   A
    Dyssocial behavior or gang activity in adult without
      manifest psychiatric disorder

2 **V71.02 Childhood or adolescent antisocial behavior**
    Dyssocial behavior or gang activity in child or
      adolescent without manifest psychiatric
      disorder

2 **V71.09 Other suspected mental condition**

2 **V71.1 Observation for suspected malignant neoplasm**

2 **V71.2 Observation for suspected tuberculosis**

2 **V71.3 Observation following accident at work**

2 **V71.4 Observation following other accident**
    Examination of individual involved in motor vehicle traffic
      accident
    AHA: 1Q, '06, 9

2 **V71.5 Observation following alleged rape or seduction**
    Examination of victim or culprit

2 **V71.6 Observation following other inflicted injury**
    Examination of victim or culprit

2 **V71.7 Observation for suspected cardiovascular disease**
    AHA: 1Q, '04, 6; 3Q, '90, 10; S-O, '87, 10

✓5th **V71.8 Observation and evaluation for other specified suspected conditions**
    EXCLUDES *contact with and (suspected) exposure to*
        (potentially) hazardous substances
        (V15.84-V15.86, V87.0-V87.31)
    AHA: 4Q, '00, 54 ; 1Q, '90, 19

2 **V71.81 Abuse and neglect**
    EXCLUDES *adult abuse and neglect (995.80-995.85)*
        child abuse and neglect (995.50-995.59)
    AHA: 4Q, '00, 55

2 **V71.82 Observation and evaluation for suspected exposure to anthrax**
    AHA: 4Q, '02, 70, 85

---

2   These V codes may be used as principal diagnosis on Medicare patients.

✓4th / ✓5th   Additional Digit Required   Unacceptable PDx   Manifestation Code   Hospital Acquired Condition   ▶◀ Revised Text   ● New Code   ▲ Revised Code Title

V Codes

V71.83–V74.1

[2] **V71.83 Observation and evaluation for suspected exposure to other biological agent**
AHA: 4Q, '03, 47

[2] **V71.89 Other specified suspected conditions**
AHA: 2Q, '11, 4; 3Q, '08, 7; 2Q, '03, 15

V71.9 Observation for unspecified suspected condition
AHA: 1Q, '02, 6

✓4th **V72 Special investigations and examinations**
INCLUDES routine examination of specific system
Use additional code(s) to identify any special screening examination(s) performed (V73.0-V82.9)
EXCLUDES general medical examination (V70.0-V70.4)
general screening examination of defined population groups (V70.5, V70.6, V70.7)
health supervision of newborn 8 to 28 days old (V20.32)
health supervision of newborn under 8 days old (V20.31)
routine examination of infant or child over 28 days old (V20.2)

[2] **V72.0 Examination of eyes and vision**
AHA: 1Q, '04, 15

✓5th **V72.1 Examination of ears and hearing**
AHA: 1Q, '04, 15

V72.11 Encounter for hearing examination following failed hearing screening
AHA: 3Q, '11, 3; 4Q, '06, 118
Z01.110 Encounter hearing exam follow failed hearing scr   I-10

V72.12 Encounter for hearing conservation and treatment
AHA: 4Q, '07, 100

V72.19 Other examination of ears and hearing

V72.2 Dental examination

✓5th **V72.3 Gynecological examination**
EXCLUDES cervical Papanicolaou smear without general gynecological examination (V76.2)
routine examination in contraceptive management (V25.40-V25.49)

[2] **V72.31 Routine gynecological examination** ♀
General gynecological examination with or without Papanicolaou cervical smear
Pelvic examination (annual) (periodic)
Use additional code to identify:
human papillomavirus (HPV) screening (V73.81)
routine vaginal Papanicolaou smear (V76.47)
AHA: 2Q, '06, 2-3; 4Q, '05, 9

[2] **V72.32 Encounter for Papanicolaou cervical smear to confirm findings of recent normal smear following initial abnormal smear** ♀
AHA: 2Q, '06, 4

✓5th **V72.4 Pregnancy examination or test**
AHA: 4Q, '05, 98

[2] **V72.40 Pregnancy examination or test, pregnancy unconfirmed** ♀
Possible pregnancy, not (yet) confirmed

[2] **V72.41 Pregnancy examination or test, negative result** ♀

[2] **V72.42 Pregnancy examination or test, positive result** ♀ M

V72.5 Radiological examination, not elsewhere classified
Routine chest x-ray
EXCLUDES radiologic examinations as part of pre-procedural testing (V72.81-V72.84)
AHA: 1Q, '90, 19

✓5th **V72.6 Laboratory examination**
Encounters for blood and urine testing
AHA: 4Q, '09, 117-118; 2Q, '06, 4; 1Q, '90, 22

V72.60 Laboratory examination, unspecified

V72.61 Antibody response examination
Immunity status testing
EXCLUDES encounter for allergy testing (V72.7)

V72.62 Laboratory examination ordered as part of a routine general medical examination
Blood tests for routine general physical examination

V72.63 Pre-procedural laboratory examination
Blood tests prior to treatment or procedure
Pre-operative laboratory examination

V72.69 Other laboratory examination

V72.7 Diagnostic skin and sensitization tests
Allergy tests
Skin tests for hypersensitivity
EXCLUDES diagnostic skin tests for bacterial diseases (V74.0-V74.9)

✓5th **V72.8 Other specified examinations**
EXCLUDES pre-procedural laboratory examinations (V72.63)

[2] **V72.81 Pre-operative cardiovascular examination**
Pre-procedural cardiovascular examination
Z01.810 Encounter for preprocedural cardiovascular exam   I-10

[2] **V72.82 Pre-operative respiratory examination**
Pre-procedural respiratory examination
AHA: 3Q, '96, 14

[2] **V72.83 Other specified pre-operative examination**
Examination prior to chemotherapy
Other pre-procedural examination
Pre-procedural general physical examination
EXCLUDES routine general medical examination (V70.0)
AHA: ▶2Q, '13, 11;◀ 3Q, '96, 14

V72.84 Pre-operative examination, unspecified
Pre-procedural examination, unspecified

V72.85 Other specified examination
AHA: 1Q, '12, 10; 4Q, '05, 96; 1Q, '04, 12

V72.86 Encounter for blood typing

V72.9 Unspecified examination
AHA: 4Q, '06, 117

✓4th **V73 Special screening examination for viral and chlamydial diseases**
AHA: 1Q, '04, 11

V73.0 Poliomyelitis

V73.1 Smallpox

V73.2 Measles

V73.3 Rubella

V73.4 Yellow fever

V73.5 Other arthropod-borne viral diseases
Dengue fever   Viral encephalitis:
Hemorrhagic fever   tick-borne
Viral encephalitis:
mosquito-borne

V73.6 Trachoma

✓5th **V73.8 Other specified viral and chlamydial diseases**

V73.81 Human papillomavirus [HPV]
AHA: 4Q, '07, 100

V73.88 Other specified chlamydial diseases
AHA: 4Q, '07, 124

V73.89 Other specified viral diseases

✓5th **V73.9 Unspecified viral and chlamydial disease**

V73.98 Unspecified chlamydial disease

V73.99 Unspecified viral disease

✓4th **V74 Special screening examination for bacterial and spirochetal diseases**
INCLUDES diagnostic skin tests for these diseases
AHA: 1Q, '04, 11

V74.0 Cholera

V74.1 Pulmonary tuberculosis

---

[2] These V codes may be used as principal diagnosis on Medicare patients.

N Newborn Age: 0   P Pediatric Age: 0-17   M Maternity Age: 12-55   A Adult Age: 15-124   MCC Major CC Condition   CC CC Condition   HIV HIV Related Dx

372 – Volume 1 • October 2014   2015 ICD-9-CM

V74.2 Leprosy [Hansen's disease]

V74.3 Diphtheria

V74.4 Bacterial conjunctivitis

V74.5 Venereal disease

Screening for bacterial and spirochetal sexually transmitted diseases

Screening for sexually transmitted diseases NOS

> **EXCLUDES** special screening for nonbacterial sexually transmitted diseases (V73.81-V73.89, V75.4, V75.8)

AHA: 4Q, '07, 124

V74.6 Yaws

V74.8 Other specified bacterial and spirochetal diseases

Brucellosis   Tetanus
Leptospirosis   Whooping cough
Plague

V74.9 Unspecified bacterial and spirochetal disease

√4th **V75 Special screening examination for other infectious diseases**

AHA: 1Q, '04, 11

V75.0 Rickettsial diseases

V75.1 Malaria

V75.2 Leishmaniasis

V75.3 Trypanosomiasis

Chagas' disease
Sleeping sickness

V75.4 Mycotic infections

V75.5 Schistosomiasis

V75.6 Filariasis

V75.7 Intestinal helminthiasis

V75.8 Other specified parasitic infections

V75.9 Unspecified infectious disease

√4th **V76 Special screening for malignant neoplasms**

AHA: 1Q, '04, 11

TIP: Whenever a screening examination is performed, the screening code is the first-listed code, regardless of the findings or any procedure that is performed as a result of the findings.

V76.0 Respiratory organs

√5th **V76.1 Breast**

AHA: 4Q, '98, 67

V76.10 Breast screening, unspecified

V76.11 Screening mammogram for high-risk patient ♀

AHA: 2Q, '03, 4

V76.12 Other screening mammogram

AHA: 4Q, '09, 106; 2Q, '06, 10; 2Q, '03, 3-4

V76.19 Other screening breast examination

V76.2 Cervix ♀

Routine cervical Papanicolaou smear

> **EXCLUDES** special screening for human papillomavirus (V73.81) that as part of a general gynecological examination (V72.31)

V76.3 Bladder

√5th **V76.4 Other sites**

V76.41 Rectum

V76.42 Oral cavity

V76.43 Skin

[2] **V76.44 Prostate** ♂

Z12.5 Encounter screening malignant neoplasm prostate   I-10

V76.45 Testis ♂

V76.46 Ovary ♀

AHA: 4Q, '00, 52

V76.47 Vagina ♀

Vaginal pap smear status-post hysterectomy for non-malignant condition

Use additional code to identify acquired absence of uterus (V88.01-V88.03)

> **EXCLUDES** vaginal pap smear status-post hysterectomy for malignant condition (V67.01)

AHA: 4Q, '08, 157; 4Q, '00, 52

V76.49 Other sites

AHA: 1Q, '99, 4

√5th **V76.5 Intestine**

AHA: 4Q, '00, 52

V76.50 Intestine, unspecified

V76.51 Colon

Screening colonoscopy NOS

> **EXCLUDES** rectum (V76.41)

AHA: ▶4Q, '13, 103, 104;◀ 4Q, '01, 56

Z12.11 Enc screening malignant neoplasm of colon   I-10

V76.52 Small intestine

√5th **V76.8 Other neoplasm**

AHA: 4Q, '00, 52

V76.81 Nervous system

V76.89 Other neoplasm

V76.9 Unspecified

√4th **V77 Special screening for endocrine, nutritional, metabolic, and immunity disorders**

AHA: 1Q, '04, 11

V77.0 Thyroid disorders

V77.1 Diabetes mellitus

V77.2 Malnutrition

V77.3 Phenylketonuria [PKU]

V77.4 Galactosemia

V77.5 Gout

V77.6 Cystic fibrosis

Screening for mucoviscidosis

V77.7 Other inborn errors of metabolism

V77.8 Obesity

√5th **V77.9 Other and unspecified endocrine, nutritional, metabolic, and immunity disorders**

AHA: 4Q, '00, 53

V77.91 Screening for lipoid disorders

Screening for cholesterol level
Screening for hypercholesterolemia
Screening for hyperlipidemia

V77.99 Other and unspecified endocrine, nutritional, metabolic, and immunity disorders

√4th **V78 Special screening for disorders of blood and blood-forming organs**

AHA: 1Q, '04, 11

V78.0 Iron deficiency anemia

V78.1 Other and unspecified deficiency anemia

V78.2 Sickle cell disease or trait

V78.3 Other hemoglobinopathies

V78.8 Other disorders of blood and blood-forming organs

V78.9 Unspecified disorder of blood and blood-forming organs

√4th **V79 Special screening for mental disorders and developmental handicaps**

AHA: 1Q, '04, 11

V79.0 Depression

V79.1 Alcoholism

V79.2 Intellectual disabilities

---

[2] These V codes may be used as principal diagnosis on Medicare patients.

√4th √5th Additional Digit Required   Unacceptable PDx   Manifestation Code   Hospital Acquired Condition   ▶◀ Revised Text   ● New Code   ▲ Revised Code Title

2015 ICD-9-CM   **October 2014 • Volume 1 – 373**

V Codes

V79.3   Developmental handicaps in early childhood

V79.8   Other specified mental disorders and developmental handicaps

V79.9   Unspecified mental disorder and developmental handicap

✓4th **V80**   **Special screening for neurological, eye, and ear diseases**
     AHA: 1Q, '04, 11

  ✓5th **V80.0**   **Neurological conditions**
       AHA: 4Q, '09, 116

     V80.01   Traumatic brain injury

     V80.09   Other neurological conditions

   V80.1   Glaucoma

   V80.2   **Other eye conditions**
     Screening for: Screening for:
       cataract   senile macular
       congenital anomaly of eye   lesions
       EXCLUDES   general vision examination (V72.0)

   V80.3   **Ear diseases**
       EXCLUDES   general hearing examination (V72.11-V72.19)

✓4th **V81**   **Special screening for cardiovascular, respiratory, and genitourinary diseases**
     AHA: 1Q, '04, 11

   V81.0   Ischemic heart disease

   V81.1   Hypertension

   V81.2   Other and unspecified cardiovascular conditions

   V81.3   Chronic bronchitis and emphysema

   V81.4   **Other and unspecified respiratory conditions**
       EXCLUDES   screening for:
           lung neoplasm (V76.0)
           pulmonary tuberculosis (V74.1)

   V81.5   **Nephropathy**
     Screening for asymptomatic bacteriuria

   V81.6   Other and unspecified genitourinary conditions

✓4th **V82**   **Special screening for other conditions**
     AHA: 1Q, '04, 11

   V82.0   Skin conditions

   V82.1   Rheumatoid arthritis

   V82.2   Other rheumatic disorders

   V82.3   Congenital dislocation of hip

   V82.4   **Maternal postnatal screening for chromosomal anomalies** ♀
       EXCLUDES   antenatal screening by amniocentesis (V28.0)

   V82.5   **Chemical poisoning and other contamination**
     Screening for:
       heavy metal poisoning
       ingestion of radioactive substance
       poisoning from contaminated water supply
       radiation exposure

   V82.6   Multiphasic screening

  ✓5th **V82.7**   **Genetic screening**
       EXCLUDES   genetic testing for procreative management (V26.31-V26.39)

     V82.71   **Screening for genetic disease carrier status**
       AHA: 4Q, '06, 118

     V82.79   **Other genetic screening**
       AHA: 4Q, '06, 118

  ✓5th **V82.8**   **Other specified conditions**
       AHA: 4Q, '00, 53

     V82.81   **Osteoporosis**
       Use additional code to identify:
           hormone replacement therapy (postmenopausal) status (V07.4)
           postmenopausal (age-related) (natural) status (V49.81)
       AHA: 4Q, '00, 54

     V82.89   Other specified conditions

   V82.9   Unspecified condition

Genetics (V83-V84)

✓4th **V83**   **Genetic carrier status**
     AHA: 4Q, '02, 79; 4Q, '01, 54
     TIP: The patient does not have the disease or carry a risk of developing it, but may genetically pass it to offspring who then may develop it.

  ✓5th **V83.0**   **Hemophilia A carrier**

     V83.01   Asymptomatic hemophilia A carrier

     V83.02   Symptomatic hemophilia A carrier

  ✓5th **V83.8**   **Other genetic carrier status**

     V83.81   Cystic fibrosis gene carrier

     V83.89   Other genetic carrier status

✓4th **V84**   **Genetic susceptibility to disease**
     INCLUDES   confirmed abnormal gene
     EXCLUDES   chromosomal anomalies (758.0-758.9)
     Use additional code, if applicable, for any associated family history of the disease (V16-V19)
     AHA: 4Q, '04, 106
     TIP: The patient has a gene that increases the risk of developing a specific disease; assign only as a secondary condition.

  ✓5th **V84.0**   **Genetic susceptibility to malignant neoplasm**
     Code first, if applicable, any current malignant neoplasms (140.0-195.8, 200.0-208.9, 230.0-234.9)
     Use additional code, if applicable, for any personal history of malignant neoplasm (V10.0-V10.9)

     V84.01   **Genetic susceptibility to malignant neoplasm of breast**
       AHA: 2Q, '11, 12; 4Q, '04, 107
       Z15.01 Genetic susceptibility malignant neoplasm breast   [I-10]

     V84.02   **Genetic susceptibility to malignant neoplasm of ovary** ♀

     V84.03   **Genetic susceptibility to malignant neoplasm of prostate** ♂

     V84.04   **Genetic susceptibility to malignant neoplasm of endometrium** ♀

     V84.09   **Genetic susceptibility to other malignant neoplasm**
       AHA: ▶2Q, '13, 15◀

  ✓5th **V84.8**   **Genetic susceptibility to other disease**

     V84.81   **Genetic susceptibility to multiple endocrine neoplasia [MEN]**
       EXCLUDES   multiple endocrine neoplasia [MEN] syndromes (258.01-258.03)
       AHA: 4Q, '07, 100

     V84.89   **Genetic susceptibility to other disease**
       AHA: ▶4Q, '13, 87◀

Body Mass Index (V85)

✓4th **V85**   **Body Mass Index [BMI]**
     Kilograms per meters squared
     NOTE BMI adult codes are for use for persons over 20 years old
     AHA: 3Q, '11, 4-5; 2Q, '10, 15; 4Q, '08, 191; 4Q, '05, 97
     TIP: While BMI may be coded from dietician or other caregiver documentation, the diagnosis of being overweight or obese must be coded from physician documentation.

   V85.0   **Body Mass Index less than 19, adult**   [CC] [A]
     CC Excl: 278.00-278.01, 278.03, V77.8, V85.0-V85.39, V85.41-V85.54

   V85.1   Body Mass Index between 19-24, adult   [A]

  ✓5th **V85.2**   Body Mass Index between 25-29, adult

     V85.21   Body Mass Index 25.0-25.9, adult   [A]

     V85.22   Body Mass Index 26.0-26.9, adult   [A]

     V85.23   Body Mass Index 27.0-27.9, adult   [A]

     V85.24   Body Mass Index 28.0-28.9, adult   [A]

[N] Newborn Age: 0   [P] Pediatric Age: 0-17   [M] Maternity Age: 12-55   [A] Adult Age: 15-124   [MCC] Major CC Condition   [CC] CC Condition   [HIV] HIV Related Dx

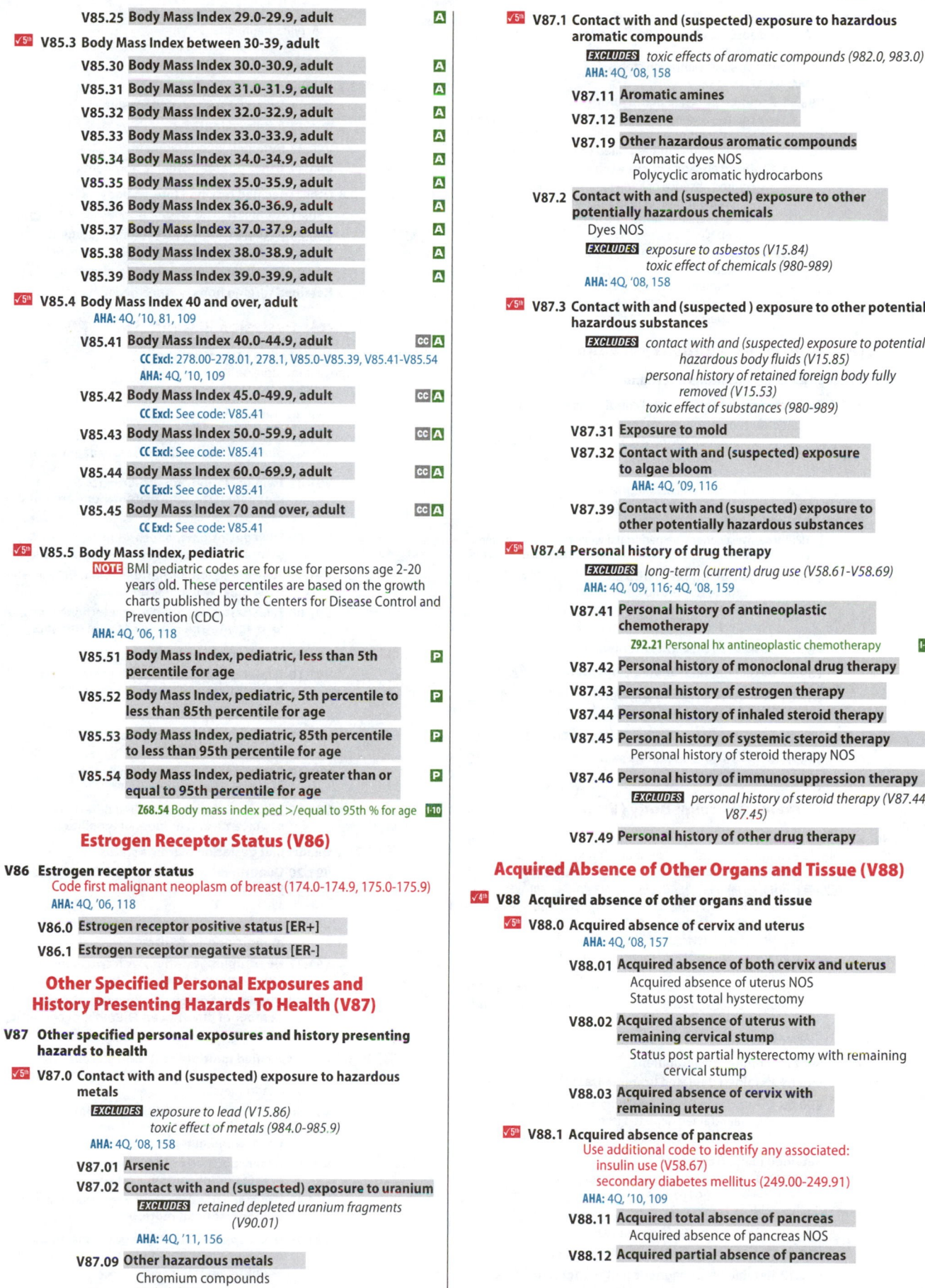

V85.25 Body Mass Index 29.0-29.9, adult   `A`

✓5ᵗʰ V85.3 Body Mass Index between 30-39, adult

    V85.30 Body Mass Index 30.0-30.9, adult   `A`

    V85.31 Body Mass Index 31.0-31.9, adult   `A`

    V85.32 Body Mass Index 32.0-32.9, adult   `A`

    V85.33 Body Mass Index 33.0-33.9, adult   `A`

    V85.34 Body Mass Index 34.0-34.9, adult   `A`

    V85.35 Body Mass Index 35.0-35.9, adult   `A`

    V85.36 Body Mass Index 36.0-36.9, adult   `A`

    V85.37 Body Mass Index 37.0-37.9, adult   `A`

    V85.38 Body Mass Index 38.0-38.9, adult   `A`

    V85.39 Body Mass Index 39.0-39.9, adult   `A`

✓5ᵗʰ V85.4 Body Mass Index 40 and over, adult
    AHA: 4Q, '10, 81, 109

    V85.41 Body Mass Index 40.0-44.9, adult   `CC` `A`
        CC Excl: 278.00-278.01, 278.1, V85.0-V85.39, V85.41-V85.54
        AHA: 4Q, '10, 109

    V85.42 Body Mass Index 45.0-49.9, adult   `CC` `A`
        CC Excl: See code: V85.41

    V85.43 Body Mass Index 50.0-59.9, adult   `CC` `A`
        CC Excl: See code: V85.41

    V85.44 Body Mass Index 60.0-69.9, adult   `CC` `A`
        CC Excl: See code: V85.41

    V85.45 Body Mass Index 70 and over, adult   `CC` `A`
        CC Excl: See code: V85.41

✓5ᵗʰ V85.5 Body Mass Index, pediatric
    NOTE BMI pediatric codes are for use for persons age 2-20 years old. These percentiles are based on the growth charts published by the Centers for Disease Control and Prevention (CDC)
    AHA: 4Q, '06, 118

    V85.51 Body Mass Index, pediatric, less than 5th percentile for age   `P`

    V85.52 Body Mass Index, pediatric, 5th percentile to less than 85th percentile for age   `P`

    V85.53 Body Mass Index, pediatric, 85th percentile to less than 95th percentile for age   `P`

    V85.54 Body Mass Index, pediatric, greater than or equal to 95th percentile for age   `P`
        Z68.54 Body mass index ped >/equal to 95th % for age   `I-10`

Estrogen Receptor Status (V86)

✓4ᵗʰ V86 Estrogen receptor status
    Code first malignant neoplasm of breast (174.0-174.9, 175.0-175.9)
    AHA: 4Q, '06, 118

    V86.0 Estrogen receptor positive status [ER+]

    V86.1 Estrogen receptor negative status [ER-]

Other Specified Personal Exposures and History Presenting Hazards To Health (V87)

✓4ᵗʰ V87 Other specified personal exposures and history presenting hazards to health

✓5ᵗʰ V87.0 Contact with and (suspected) exposure to hazardous metals
    EXCLUDES exposure to lead (V15.86)
           toxic effect of metals (984.0-985.9)
    AHA: 4Q, '08, 158

    V87.01 Arsenic

    V87.02 Contact with and (suspected) exposure to uranium
        EXCLUDES retained depleted uranium fragments (V90.01)
        AHA: 4Q, '11, 156

    V87.09 Other hazardous metals
        Chromium compounds
        Nickel dust

✓5ᵗʰ V87.1 Contact with and (suspected) exposure to hazardous aromatic compounds
    EXCLUDES toxic effects of aromatic compounds (982.0, 983.0)
    AHA: 4Q, '08, 158

    V87.11 Aromatic amines

    V87.12 Benzene

    V87.19 Other hazardous aromatic compounds
        Aromatic dyes NOS
        Polycyclic aromatic hydrocarbons

V87.2 Contact with and (suspected) exposure to other potentially hazardous chemicals
    Dyes NOS
    EXCLUDES exposure to asbestos (V15.84)
           toxic effect of chemicals (980-989)
    AHA: 4Q, '08, 158

✓5ᵗʰ V87.3 Contact with and (suspected) exposure to other potentially hazardous substances
    EXCLUDES contact with and (suspected) exposure to potentially hazardous body fluids (V15.85)
           personal history of retained foreign body fully removed (V15.53)
           toxic effect of substances (980-989)

    V87.31 Exposure to mold

    V87.32 Contact with and (suspected) exposure to algae bloom
        AHA: 4Q, '09, 116

    V87.39 Contact with and (suspected) exposure to other potentially hazardous substances

✓5ᵗʰ V87.4 Personal history of drug therapy
    EXCLUDES long-term (current) drug use (V58.61-V58.69)
    AHA: 4Q, '09, 116; 4Q, '08, 159

    V87.41 Personal history of antineoplastic chemotherapy
        Z92.21 Personal hx antineoplastic chemotherapy   `I-10`

    V87.42 Personal history of monoclonal drug therapy

    V87.43 Personal history of estrogen therapy

    V87.44 Personal history of inhaled steroid therapy

    V87.45 Personal history of systemic steroid therapy
        Personal history of steroid therapy NOS

    V87.46 Personal history of immunosuppression therapy
        EXCLUDES personal history of steroid therapy (V87.44, V87.45)

    V87.49 Personal history of other drug therapy

Acquired Absence of Other Organs and Tissue (V88)

✓4ᵗʰ V88 Acquired absence of other organs and tissue

✓5ᵗʰ V88.0 Acquired absence of cervix and uterus
    AHA: 4Q, '08, 157

    V88.01 Acquired absence of both cervix and uterus   ♀
        Acquired absence of uterus NOS
        Status post total hysterectomy

    V88.02 Acquired absence of uterus with remaining cervical stump   ♀
        Status post partial hysterectomy with remaining cervical stump

    V88.03 Acquired absence of cervix with remaining uterus   ♀

✓5ᵗʰ V88.1 Acquired absence of pancreas
    Use additional code to identify any associated:
        insulin use (V58.67)
        secondary diabetes mellitus (249.00-249.91)
    AHA: 4Q, '10, 109

    V88.11 Acquired total absence of pancreas
        Acquired absence of pancreas NOS

    V88.12 Acquired partial absence of pancreas

✓4ᵗʰ ✓5ᵗʰ Additional Digit Required   Unacceptable PDx   Manifestation Code   Hospital Acquired Condition   ▶◀ Revised Text   ● New Code   ▲ Revised Code Title

2015 ICD-9-CM   **Volume 1 – 375**

V Codes

V85.25–V88.12

☑5th **V88.2 Acquired absence of joint**
Acquired absence of joint following prior explantation of joint prosthesis
Joint prosthesis explantation status
AHA: 4Q, '11, 156-157

V88.21 Acquired absence of hip joint
Acquired absence of hip joint following explantation of joint prosthesis, with or without presence of antibiotic-impregnated cement spacer

V88.22 Acquired absence of knee joint
Acquired absence of knee joint following explantation of joint prosthesis, with or without presence of antibiotic-impregnated cement spacer

V88.29 Acquired absence of other joint
Acquired absence of other joint following explantation of joint prosthesis, with or without presence of antibiotic-impregnated cement spacer

Other Suspected Conditions Not Found (V89)

☑4th **V89 Other suspected conditions not found**

☑5th **V89.0 Suspected maternal and fetal conditions not found**
EXCLUDES known or suspected fetal anomalies affecting management of mother, not ruled out (655.00, 655.93, 656.00-656.93, 657.00-657.03, 658.00-658.93)
newborn and perinatal conditions — code to condition
AHA: 4Q, '08, 159
TIP: These investigations are performed while the fetus is in utero; the codes should be assigned only on the mother's medical record.

V89.01 Suspected problem with amniotic cavity and membrane not found M♀
Suspected oligohydramnios not found
Suspected polyhydramnios not found

V89.02 Suspected placental problem not found M♀

V89.03 Suspected fetal anomaly not found M♀

V89.04 Suspected problem with fetal growth not found M♀

V89.05 Suspected cervical shortening not found M♀

V89.09 Other suspected maternal and fetal condition not found M♀

Retained Foreign Body (V90)

☑4th **V90 Retained foreign body**
Embedded fragment (status)   Retained foreign body status
Embedded splinter (status)
EXCLUDES artificial joint prosthesis status (V43.60-V43.69)
foreign body accidentally left during a procedure (998.4)
foreign body entering through orifice (930.0-939.9)
in situ cardiac devices (V45.00-V45.09)
organ or tissue replaced by other means (V43.0-V43.89)
organ or tissue replaced by transplant (V42.0-V42.9)
personal history of retained foreign body removed (V15.53)
superficial foreign body (splinter) (categories 910-917 and 919 with 4th character 6 or 7, 918.0)
AHA: 4Q, '10, 109

☑5th **V90.0 Retained radioactive fragment**
V90.01 Retained depleted uranium fragments
V90.09 Other retained radioactive fragments
Other retained depleted isotope fragments
Retained nontherapeutic radioactive fragments

☑5th **V90.1 Retained metal fragments**
EXCLUDES retained radioactive metal fragments (V90.01-V90.09)
V90.10 Retained metal fragments, unspecified
Retained metal fragment NOS
V90.11 Retained magnetic metal fragments
V90.12 Retained nonmagnetic metal fragments

V90.2 Retained plastic fragments
Acrylics fragments
Diethylhexylphthalates fragments
Isocyanate fragments

☑5th **V90.3 Retained organic fragments**
V90.31 Retained animal quills or spines
V90.32 Retained tooth
V90.33 Retained wood fragments
V90.39 Other retained organic fragments

☑5th **V90.8 Other specified retained foreign body**
V90.81 Retained glass fragments
V90.83 Retained stone or crystalline fragments
Retained concrete or cement fragments
V90.89 Other specified retained foreign body
V90.9 Retained foreign body, unspecified material

Multiple Gestation Placenta Status (V91)

☑4th **V91 Multiple gestation placenta status**
Code first multiple gestation (651.0-651.9)
AHA: 4Q, '10, 110

☑5th **V91.0 Twin gestation placenta status**
V91.00 Twin gestation, unspecified number of placenta, unspecified number of amniotic sacs M♀
V91.01 Twin gestation, monochorionic/monoamniotic (one placenta, one amniotic sac) M♀
V91.02 Twin gestation, monochorionic/diamniotic (one placenta, two amniotic sacs) M♀
V91.03 Twin gestation, dichorionic/diamniotic (two placentae, two amniotic sacs) M♀
V91.09 Twin gestation, unable to determine number of placenta and number of amniotic sacs M♀

☑5th **V91.1 Triplet gestation placenta status**
V91.10 Triplet gestation, unspecified number of placenta and unspecified number of amniotic sacs M♀
V91.11 Triplet gestation, with two or more monochorionic fetuses M♀
V91.12 Triplet gestation, with two or more monoamniotic fetuses M♀
V91.19 Triplet gestation, unable to determine number of placenta and number of amniotic sacs M♀

☑5th **V91.2 Quadruplet gestation placenta status**
V91.20 Quadruplet gestation, unspecified number of placenta and unspecified number of amniotic sacs M♀
V91.21 Quadruplet gestation, with two or more monochorionic fetuses M♀
V91.22 Quadruplet gestation, with two or more monoamniotic fetuses M♀
V91.29 Quadruplet gestation, unable to determine number of placenta and number of amniotic sacs M♀

☑5th **V91.9 Other specified multiple gestation placenta status**
Placenta status for multiple gestations greater than quadruplets
V91.90 Other specified multiple gestation, unspecified number of placenta and unspecified number of amniotic sacs M♀
V91.91 Other specified multiple gestation, with two or more monochorionic fetuses M♀
V91.92 Other specified multiple gestation, with two or more monoamniotic fetuses M♀
V91.99 Other specified multiple gestation, unable to determine number of placenta and number of amniotic sacs M♀

N Newborn Age: 0   P Pediatric Age: 0-17   M Maternity Age: 12-55   A Adult Age: 15-124   MCC Major CC Condition   CC CC Condition   HIV HIV Related Dx

376 – Volume 1   2015 ICD-9-CM

Supplementary Classification of External Causes of Injury and Poisoning (E000-E999)

This section is provided to permit the classification of environmental events, circumstances, and conditions as the cause of injury, poisoning, and other adverse effects. Where a code from this section is applicable, it is intended that it shall be used in addition to a code from one of the main chapters of ICD-9-CM, indicating the nature of the condition. Certain other conditions which may be stated to be due to external causes are classified in Chapters 1 to 16 of ICD-9-CM. For these, the "E" code classification should be used as an additional code for more detailed analysis.

Machinery accidents [other than those connected with transport] are classifiable to category E919, in which the fourth digit allows a broad classification of the type of machinery involved.

Categories for "late effects" of accidents and other external causes are to be found at E929, E959, E969, E977, E989, and E999.

External Cause Status (E000)

NOTE A code from category E000 may be used in conjunction with the external cause code(s) assigned to a record to indicate the status of the person at the time the event occurred. A single code from category E000 should be assigned for an encounter.

√4th **E000　External cause status**

　E000.0　Civilian activity done for income or pay
　　　Civilian activity done for financial or other compensation
　　　EXCLUDES　*military activity (E000.1)*

　E000.2　Volunteer activity
　　　EXCLUDES　*activity of child or other family member assisting in compensated work of other family member (E000.8)*

　E000.1　Military activity
　　　EXCLUDES　*activity of off-duty military personnel (E000.8)*

　E000.8　Other external cause status
　　　Activity of child or other family member assisting in compensated work of other family member
　　　Activity NEC
　　　Hobby not done for income
　　　Leisure activity
　　　Off-duty activity of military personnel
　　　Recreation or sport not for income or while a student
　　　Student activity
　　　EXCLUDES　*civilian activity done for income or compensation (E000.0)*
　　　　　　　　military activity (E000.1)

　E000.9　Unspecified external cause status

Activity (E001-E030)

NOTE Categories E001 to E030 are provided for use to indicate the activity of the person seeking healthcare for an injury or health condition, such as a heart attack while shoveling snow, which resulted from, or was contributed to, by the activity. These codes are appropriate for use for both acute injuries, such as those from chapter 17, and conditions that are due to the long-term, cumulative affects of an activity, such as those from chapter 13. They are also appropriate for use with external cause codes for cause and intent if identifying the activity provides additional information on the event.

These codes should be used in conjunction with other external cause codes for external cause status (E000) and place of occurrence (E849).

This section contains the following broad activity categories:

E001　Activities involving walking and running
E002　Activities involving water and water craft
E003　Activities involving ice and snow
E004　Activities involving climbing, rappelling, and jumping off
E005　Activities involving dancing and other rhythmic movement
E006　Activities involving other sports and athletics played individually
E007　Activities involving other sports and athletics played as a team or group
E008　Activities involving other specified sports and athletics
E009　Activity involving other cardiorespiratory exercise
E010　Activity involving other muscle strengthening exercises
E011　Activities involving computer technology and electronic devices
E012　Activities involving arts and handcrafts
E013　Activities involving personal hygiene and household maintenance
E014　Activities involving person providing caregiving
E015　Activities involving food preparation, cooking and grilling
E016　Activities involving property and land maintenance, building and construction
E017　Activities involving roller coasters and other types of external motion
E018　Activities involving playing musical instrument
E019　Activities involving animal care
E029　Other activity
E030　Unspecified activity

√4th **E001　Activities involving walking and running**
　　　EXCLUDES　*walking an animal (E019.0)*
　　　　　　　　walking or running on a treadmill (E009.0)

　E001.0　Walking, marching and hiking
　　　Walking, marching and hiking on level or elevated terrain
　　　EXCLUDES　*mountain climbing (E004.0)*

　E001.1　Running

√4th **E002　Activities involving water and water craft**
　　　EXCLUDES　*activities involving ice (E003.0-E003.9)*
　　　　　　　　boating and other watercraft transport accidents (E830-E838)

　E002.0　Swimming

　E002.1　Springboard and platform diving

　E002.2　Water polo

　E002.3　Water aerobics and water exercise

　E002.4　Underwater diving and snorkeling
　　　SCUBA diving

　E002.5　Rowing, canoeing, kayaking, rafting and tubing
　　　Canoeing, kayaking, rafting and tubing in calm and turbulent water

　E002.6　Water skiing and wake boarding

　E002.7　Surfing, windsurfing and boogie boarding

　E002.8　Water sliding

　E002.9　Other activity involving water and watercraft
　　　Activity involving water NOS
　　　Parasailing
　　　Water survival training and testing

√4th **E003　Activities involving ice and snow**
　　　EXCLUDES　*shoveling ice and snow (E016.0)*

　E003.0　Ice skating
　　　Figure skating (singles) (pairs)
　　　Ice dancing
　　　EXCLUDES　*ice hockey (E003.1)*

　E003.1　Ice hockey

　E003.2　Snow (alpine) (downhill) skiing, snow boarding, sledding, tobogganing and snow tubing
　　　EXCLUDES　*cross country skiing (E003.3)*

　E003.3　Cross country skiing
　　　Nordic skiing

　E003.9　Other activity involving ice and snow
　　　Activity involving ice and snow NOS

√4th **E004　Activities involving climbing, rappelling, and jumping off**
　　　EXCLUDES　*hiking on level or elevated terrain (E001.0)*
　　　　　　　　jumping rope (E006.5)
　　　　　　　　sky diving (E840-E844)
　　　　　　　　trampoline jumping (E005.3)

　E004.0　Mountain climbing, rock climbing and wall climbing

　E004.1　Rappelling

　E004.2　BASE jumping
　　　Building, Antenna, Span, Earth jumping

　E004.3　Bungee jumping

　E004.4　Hang gliding

　E004.9　Other activity involving climbing, rappelling and jumping off

✓4ᵗʰ **E005 Activities involving dancing and other rhythmic movement**
     EXCLUDES *martial arts (E008.4)*

     E005.0 Dancing

     E005.1 Yoga

     E005.2 Gymnastics
         Rhythmic gymnastics
         EXCLUDES *trampoline (E005.3)*

     E005.3 Trampoline

     E005.4 Cheerleading

     E005.9 Other activity involving dancing and other rhythmic movements

✓4ᵗʰ **E006 Activities involving other sports and athletics played individually**
     EXCLUDES *dancing (E005.0)*
                 gymnastic (E005.2)
                 trampoline (E005.3)
                 yoga (E005.1)

     E006.0 Roller skating (inline) and skateboarding

     E006.1 Horseback riding

     E006.2 Golf

     E006.3 Bowling

     E006.4 Bike riding
         EXCLUDES *transport accident involving bike riding (E800-E829)*

     E006.5 Jumping rope

     E006.6 Non-running track and field events
         EXCLUDES *running (any form) (E001.1)*

     E006.9 Other activity involving other sports and athletics played individually
         EXCLUDES *activities involving climbing, rappelling, and jumping (E004.0-E004.9)*
                 activities involving ice and snow (E003.0-E003.9)
                 activities involving walking and running (E001.0-E001.9)
                 activities involving water and watercraft (E002.0-E002.9)

✓4ᵗʰ **E007 Activities involving other sports and athletics played as a team or group**
     EXCLUDES *ice hockey (E003.1)*
                 water polo (E002.2)

     E007.0 American tackle football
         Football NOS

     E007.1 American flag or touch football

     E007.2 Rugby

     E007.3 Baseball
         Softball

     E007.4 Lacrosse and field hockey

     E007.5 Soccer

     E007.6 Basketball

     E007.7 Volleyball (beach) (court)

     E007.8 Physical games generally associated with school recess, summer camp and children
         Capture the flag   Four square
         Dodge ball   Kickball

     E007.9 Other activity involving other sports and athletics played as a team or group
         Cricket

✓4ᵗʰ **E008 Activities involving other specified sports and athletics**

     E008.0 Boxing

     E008.1 Wrestling

     E008.2 Racquet and hand sports
         Handball   Squash
         Racquetball   Tennis

     E008.3 Frisbee
         Ultimate frisbee

     E008.4 Martial arts
         Combatives

     E008.9 Other specified sports and athletics activity
         EXCLUDES *sports and athletics activities specified in categories E001-E007*

✓4ᵗʰ **E009 Activity involving other cardiorespiratory exercise**
     Activity involving physical training

     E009.0 Exercise machines primarily for cardiorespiratory conditioning
         Elliptical and stepper machines
         Stationary bike
         Treadmill

     E009.1 Calisthenics
         Jumping jacks   Warm up and cool down

     E009.2 Aerobic and step exercise

     E009.3 Circuit training

     E009.4 Obstacle course
         Challenge course   Confidence course

     E009.5 Grass drills
         Guerilla drills

     E009.9 Other activity involving cardiorespiratory exercise
         EXCLUDES *activities involving cardiorespiratory exercise specified in categories E001-E008*

✓4ᵗʰ **E010 Activity involving other muscle strengthening exercises**

     E010.0 Exercise machines primarily for muscle strengthening

     E010.1 Push-ups, pull-ups, sit-ups

     E010.2 Free weights
         Barbells
         Dumbbells

     E010.3 Pilates

     E010.9 Other activity involving other muscle strengthening exercises
         EXCLUDES *activities involving muscle strengthening specified in categories E001-E009*

✓4ᵗʰ **E011 Activities involving computer technology and electronic devices**
     EXCLUDES *electronic musical keyboard or instruments (E018.0)*

     E011.0 Computer keyboarding
         Electronic game playing using keyboard or other stationary device

     E011.1 Hand held interactive electronic device
         Cellular telephone and communication device
         Electronic game playing using interactive device
         EXCLUDES *electronic game playing using keyboard or other stationary device (E011.0)*

     E011.9 Other activity involving computer technology and electronic devices

✓4ᵗʰ **E012 Activities involving arts and handcrafts**
     EXCLUDES *activities involving playing musical instrument (E018.0-E018.3)*

     E012.0 Knitting and crocheting

     E012.1 Sewing

     E012.2 Furniture building and finishing
         Furniture repair

     E012.9 Activity involving other arts and handcrafts

✓4ᵗʰ **E013 Activities involving personal hygiene and household maintenance**
     EXCLUDES *activities involving cooking and grilling (E015.0-E015.9)*
                 activities involving property and land maintenance, building and construction (E016.0-E016.9)
                 activity involving persons providing caregiving (E014.0-E014.9)
                 dishwashing (E015.0)
                 food preparation (E015.0)
                 gardening (E016.1)

     E013.0 Personal bathing and showering

     ✓4ᵗʰ Fourth-digit Required   ▶◀ Revised Text   ● New Code   ▲ Revised Code Title

E013.1 Laundry

E013.2 Vacuuming

E013.3 Ironing

E013.4 Floor mopping and cleaning

E013.5 Residential relocation
　　Packing up and unpacking involved in moving to a new residence

E013.8 Other personal hygiene activity

E013.9 Other household maintenance

✓4th **E014 Activities involving person providing caregiving**

E014.0 Caregiving involving bathing

E014.1 Caregiving involving lifting

E014.9 Other activity involving person providing caregiving

✓4th **E015 Activities involving food preparation, cooking and grilling**

E015.0 Food preparation and clean up
　　Dishwasing

E015.1 Grilling and smoking food

E015.2 Cooking and baking
　　Use of stove, oven and microwave oven

E015.9 Other activity involving cooking and grilling

✓4th **E016 Activities involving property and land maintenance, building and construction**

E016.0 Digging, shoveling and raking
　　Dirt digging
　　Raking leaves
　　Snow shoveling

E016.1 Gardening and landscaping
　　Pruning, trimming shrubs, weeding

E016.2 Building and construction

E016.9 Other activity involving property and land maintenance, building and construction

✓4th **E017 Activities involving roller coasters and other types of external motion**

E017.0 Roller coaster riding

E017.9 Other activity involving external motion

✓4th **E018 Activities involving playing musical instrument**
Activity involving playing electric musical instrument

E018.0 Piano playing
　　Musical keyboard (electronic) playing

E018.1 Drum and other percussion instrument playing

E018.2 String instrument playing

E018.3 Wind and brass instrument playing

✓4th **E019 Activities involving animal care**
　EXCLUDES horseback riding (E006.1)

E019.0 Walking an animal

E019.1 Milking an animal

E019.2 Grooming and shearing an animal

E019.9 Other activity involving animal care

✓4th **E029 Other activity**

E029.0 Refereeing a sports activity

E029.1 Spectator at an event

E029.2 Rough housing and horseplay

E029.9 Other activity

E030 Unspecified activity

Transport Accidents (E800-E848)

Definitions and Examples Related to Transport Accidents

(a) A **transport accident** (E800-E848) is any accident involving a device designed primarily for, or being used at the time primarily for, conveying persons or goods from one place to another.

INCLUDES accidents involving:
　　aircraft and spacecraft (E840-E845)
　　watercraft (E830-E838)
　　motor vehicle (E810-E825)
　　railway (E800-E807)
　　other road vehicles (E826-E829)

In classifying accidents which involve more than one kind of transport, the above order of precedence of transport accidents should be used.

Accidents involving agricultural and construction machines, such as tractors, cranes, and bulldozers, are regarded as transport accidents only when these vehicles are under their own power on a highway [otherwise the vehicles are regarded as machinery]. Vehicles which can travel on land or water, such as hovercraft and other amphibious vehicles, are regarded as watercraft when on the water, as motor vehicles when on the highway, and as off-road motor vehicles when on land, but off the highway.

EXCLUDES accidents:
　　in sports which involve the use of transport but where the transport vehicle itself was not involved in the accident
　　involving vehicles which are part of industrial equipment used entirely on industrial premises
　　occurring during transportation but unrelated to the hazards associated with the means of transportation [e.g., injuries received in a fight on board ship; transport vehicle involved in a cataclysm such as an earthquake]
　　to persons engaged in the maintenance or repair of transport equipment or vehicle not in motion, unlesss injured by another vehicle in motion

(b) A **railway accident** is a transport accident involving a railway train or other railway vehicle operated on rails, whether in motion or not.

EXCLUDES accidents:
　　in repair shops
　　in roundhouse or on turntable
　　on railway premises but not involving a train or other railway vehicle

(c) A **railway train** or **railway vehicle** is any device with or without cars coupled to it, desiged for traffic on a railway.

INCLUDES interurban:
　　electric car
　　street car (operated chiefly on its own right-of-way, not open to other traffic)
　　railway train, any power [diesel] [electric] [steam]:
　　funicular
　　monorail or two-rail
　　subterranean or elevated
　　other vehicle designed to run on a railway track

EXCLUDES interurban electric cars [streetcars] specified to be operating on a right-of-way that forms part of the public street or highway [definition (h)]

(d) A **railway** or **railroad** is a right-of-way designed for traffic on rails, which is used by carriages or wagons transporting passengers or freight, and by other rolling stock, and which is not open to other public vehicular traffic.

(e) A **motor vehicle accident** is a transport accident involving a motor vehicle. It is defined as a motor vehicle traffic accident or as a motor vehicle nontraffic accident according to whether the accident occurs on a public highway or elsewhere.

EXCLUDES injury or damage due to cataclysm
　　injury or damage while a motor vehicle, not under its own power, is being loaded on, or unloaded from, another conveyance

(f) A **motor vehicle traffic accident** is any motor vehicle accident occurring on a public highway [i.e., originating, terminating, or involving a vehicle partially on the highway]. A motor vehicle accident is assumed to have occurred on the highway unless another place is specified, except in the case of accidents involving only off-road motor vehicles which are classified as nontraffic accidents unless the contrary is stated.

(g) A **motor vehicle nontraffic accident** is any motor vehicle accident which occurs entirely in any place other than a public highway.

E Codes

E030–E030

(h) A **public highway [trafficway]** or **street** is the entire width between property lines [or other boundary lines] of every way or place, of which any part is open to the use of the public for purposes of vehicular traffic as a matter of right or custom. A **roadway** is that part of the public highway designed, improved, and ordinarily used, for vehicular travel.

INCLUDES　approaches (public) to:
　　　　　docks
　　　　　public building
　　　　　station

EXCLUDES　driveway (private)
　　　　　parking lot
　　　　　ramp
　　　　　roads in:
　　　　　　airfield
　　　　　　farm
　　　　　　industrial premises
　　　　　　mine
　　　　　　private grounds
　　　　　　quarry

(i) A **motor vehicle** is any mechanically or electrically powered device, not operated on rails, upon which any person or property may be transported or drawn upon a highway. Any object such as a trailer, coaster, sled, or wagon being towed by a motor vehicle is considered a part of the motor vehicle.

INCLUDES　automobile [any type]
　　　　　bus
　　　　　construction machinery, farm and industrial machinery, steam
　　　　　　roller, tractor, army tank, highway grader, or similar vehicle
　　　　　　on wheels or treads, while in transport under own power
　　　　　fire engine (motorized)
　　　　　motorcycle
　　　　　motorized bicycle [moped] or scooter
　　　　　trolley bus not operating on rails
　　　　　truck
　　　　　van

EXCLUDES　devices used solely to move persons or materials within the confines
　　　　　　of a building and its premises, such as:
　　　　　building elevator
　　　　　coal car in mine
　　　　　electric baggage or mail truck used solely within a railroad station
　　　　　electric truck used solely within an industrial plant
　　　　　moving overhead crane

(j) A **motorcycle** is a two-wheeled motor vehicle having one or two riding saddles and sometimes having a third wheel for the support of a sidecar. The sidecar is considered part of the motorcycle.

INCLUDES　motorized:
　　　　　bicycle [moped]
　　　　　scooter
　　　　　tricycle

(k) An **off-road motor vehicle** is a motor vehicle of special design, to enable it to negotiate rough or soft terrain or snow. Examples of special design are high construction, special wheels and tires, driven by treads, or support on a cushion of air.

INCLUDES　all terrain vehicle [ATV]
　　　　　army tank
　　　　　hovercraft, on land or swamp
　　　　　snowmobile

(l) A **driver** of a motor vehicle is the occupant of the motor vehicle operating it or intending to operate it. A **motorcyclist** is the driver of a motorcycle. Other authorized occupants of a motor vehicle are **passengers**.

(m) An **other road vehicle** is any device, except a motor vehicle, in, on, or by which any person or property may be transported on a highway.

INCLUDES　animal carrying a person or goods
　　　　　animal-drawn vehicles
　　　　　animal harnessed to conveyance
　　　　　bicycle [pedal cycle]
　　　　　streetcar
　　　　　tricycle (pedal)

EXCLUDES　pedestrian conveyance [definition (q)]

(n) A **streetcar** is a device designed and used primarily for transporting persons within a municipality, running on rails, usually subject to normal traffic control signals, and operated principally on a right-of-way that forms part of the traffic way. A trailer being towed by a streetcar is considered a part of the streetcar.

INCLUDES　interurban or intraurban electric or streetcar, when specified to be
　　　　　　operating on a street or public highway
　　　　　tram (car)
　　　　　trolley (car)

(o) A **pedal cycle** is any road transport vehicle operated solely by pedals.

INCLUDES　bicycle
　　　　　pedal cycle
　　　　　tricycle

EXCLUDES　motorized bicycle [definition (j)]

(p) A **pedal cyclist** is any person riding on a pedal cycle or in a sidecar attached to such a vehicle.

(q) A **pedestrian conveyance** is any human powered device by which a pedestrian may move other than by walking or by which a walking person may move another pedestrian.

INCLUDES　baby carriage
　　　　　coaster wagon
　　　　　heelies, wheelies
　　　　　ice skates
　　　　　motorized mobility scooter
　　　　　perambulator
　　　　　pushcart
　　　　　pushchair
　　　　　roller skates
　　　　　scooter
　　　　　skateboard
　　　　　skis
　　　　　sled
　　　　　wheelchair (electric)

(r) A **pedestrian** is any person involved in an accident who was not at the time of the accident riding in or on a motor vehicle, railroad train, streetcar, animal-drawn or other vehicle, or on a bicycle or animal.

INCLUDES　person:
　　　　　changing tire of vehicle
　　　　　in or operating a pedestrian conveyance
　　　　　making adjustment to motor of vehicle
　　　　　on foot

(s) A **watercraft** is any device for transporting passengers or goods on the water.

(t) A **small boat** is any watercraft propelled by paddle, oars, or small motor, with a passenger capacity of less than ten.

INCLUDES　boat NOS
　　　　　canoe
　　　　　coble
　　　　　dinghy
　　　　　punt
　　　　　raft
　　　　　rowboat
　　　　　rowing shell
　　　　　scull
　　　　　skiff
　　　　　small motorboat

EXCLUDES　barge
　　　　　lifeboat (used after abandoning ship)
　　　　　raft (anchored) being used as a diving platform
　　　　　yacht

(u) An **aircraft** is any device for transporting passengers or goods in the air.

INCLUDES　airplane [any type]
　　　　　balloon
　　　　　bomber
　　　　　dirigible
　　　　　glider (hang)
　　　　　military aircraft
　　　　　parachute

(v) A **commercial transport aircraft** is any device for collective passenger or freight transportation by air, whether run on commercial lines for profit or by government authorities, with the exception of military craft.

✓4th Fourth-digit Required　　▶◀ Revised Text　　● New Code　　▲ Revised Code Title

Railway Accidents (E800-E807)

NOTE For definitions of railway accident and related terms see definitions (a) to (d).

EXCLUDES *accidents involving railway train and:*
aircraft (E840.0-E845.9)
motor vehicle (E810.0-E825.9)
watercraft (E830.0-E838.9)

The following fourth digit subdivisions are for use with categories E800-E807 to identify the injured person:

.0 Railway employee
Any person who by virtue of his employment in connection with a railway, whether by the railway company or not, is at increased risk of involvement in a railway accident, such as:
catering staff of train
driver
guard
porter
postal staff on train
railway fireman
shunter
sleeping car attendant
.1 Passenger on railway
Any authorized person traveling on a train, except a railway employee.
EXCLUDES *intending passenger waiting at station (.8)*
unauthorized rider on railway vehicle (.8)
.2 Pedestrian
See definition (r)
.3 Pedal cyclist
See definition (p)
.8 Other specified person
Intending passenger or bystander waiting at station
Unauthorized rider on railway vehicle
.9 Unspecified person

§ ✓4ᵗʰ **E800 Railway accident involving collision with rolling stock**
INCLUDES collision between railway trains or railway vehicles, any kind
collision NOS on railway
derailment with antecedent collision with rolling stock or NOS

§ ✓4ᵗʰ **E801 Railway accident involving collision with other object**
INCLUDES collision of railway train with:
buffers
fallen tree on railway
gates
platform
rock on railway
streetcar
other nonmotor vehicle
other object
EXCLUDES *collision with:*
aircraft (E840.0-E842.9)
motor vehicle (E810.0-E810.9, E820.0-E822.9)

§ ✓4ᵗʰ **E802 Railway accident involving derailment without antecedent collision**

§ ✓4ᵗʰ **E803 Railway accident involving explosion, fire, or burning**
EXCLUDES *explosion or fire, with antecedent derailment (E802.0-E802.9)*
explosion or fire, with mention of antecedent collision (E800.0-E801.9)

§ ✓4ᵗʰ **E804 Fall in, on, or from railway train**
INCLUDES fall while alighting from or boarding railway train
EXCLUDES *fall related to collision, derailment, or explosion of railway train (E800.0-E803.9)*

§ ✓4ᵗʰ **E805 Hit by rolling stock**
INCLUDES crushed
injured
killed } by railway train or part
knocked down
run over
EXCLUDES *pedestrian hit by object set in motion by railway train (E806.0-E806.9)*

§ ✓4ᵗʰ **E806 Other specified railway accident**
INCLUDES hit by object falling in railway train
injured by door or window on railway train
nonmotor road vehicle or pedestrian hit by object set in motion by railway train
railway train hit by falling:
earth NOS
rock
tree
other object
EXCLUDES *railway accident due to cataclysm (E908-E909)*

§ ✓4ᵗʰ **E807 Railway accident of unspecified nature**
INCLUDES found dead
injured } on railway right-of-way NOS
railway accident NOS

Motor Vehicle Traffic Accidents (E810-E819)

NOTE For definitions of motor vehicle traffic accident, and related terms, see definitions (e) to (k).

EXCLUDES *accidents involving motor vehicle and aircraft (E840.0-E845.9)*

The following fourth digit subdivisions are for use with categories E810-E819 to identify the injured person:

.0 Driver of motor vehicle other than motorcycle
See definition (l)
.1 Passenger in motor vehicle other than motorcycle
See definition (l)
.2 Motorcyclist
See definition (l)
.3 Passenger on motorcycle
See definition (l)
.4 Occupant of streetcar
.5 Rider of animal; occupant of animal-drawn vehicle
.6 Pedal cyclist
See definition (p)
.7 Pedestrian
See definition (r)
.8 Other specified person
Occupant of vehicle other than above
Person in railway train involved in accident
Unauthorized rider of motor vehicle
.9 Unspecified person

§ ✓4ᵗʰ **E810 Motor vehicle traffic accident involving collision with train**
EXCLUDES *motor vehicle collision with object set in motion by railway train (E815.0-E815.9)*
railway train hit by object set in motion by motor vehicle (E818.0-E818.9)

§ ✓4ᵗʰ **E811 Motor vehicle traffic accident involving re-entrant collision with another motor vehicle**
INCLUDES collision between motor vehicle which accidentally leaves the roadway then re-enters the same roadway, or the opposite roadway on a divided highway, and another motor vehicle
EXCLUDES *collision on the same roadway when none of the motor vehicles involved have left and re-entered the highway (E812.0-E812.9)*

§ ✓4ᵗʰ **E812 Other motor vehicle traffic accident involving collision with motor vehicle**
INCLUDES collision with another motor vehicle parked, stopped, stalled, disabled, or abandoned on the highway
motor vehicle collision NOS
EXCLUDES *collision with object set in motion by another motor vehicle (E815.0-E815.9)*
re-entrant collision with another motor vehicle (E811.0-E811.9)

---

§ Requires fourth digit. See beginning of appropriate section for codes and definitions.

✓4ᵗʰ Fourth-digit Required   ◄► Revised Text   ● New Code   ▲ Revised Code Title

§ ✓4ᵗʰ **E813** **Motor vehicle traffic accident involving collision with other vehicle**

> INCLUDES   collision between motor vehicle, any kind, and:
> other road (nonmotor transport) vehicle, such as:
>   animal carrying a person
>   animal-drawn vehicle
>   pedal cycle
>   streetcar

> EXCLUDES   *collision with:*
> *object set in motion by nonmotor road vehicle (E815.0-E815.9)*
> *pedestrian (E814.0-E814.9)*
> *nonmotor road vehicle hit by object set in motion by motor vehicle (E818.0-E818.9)*

§ ✓4ᵗʰ **E814** **Motor vehicle traffic accident involving collision with pedestrian**

> INCLUDES   collision between motor vehicle, any kind, and pedestrian
> pedestrian dragged, hit, or run over by motor vehicle, any kind

> EXCLUDES   *pedestrian hit by object set in motion by motor vehicle (E818.0-E818.9)*

§ ✓4ᵗʰ **E815** **Other motor vehicle traffic accident involving collision on the highway**

> INCLUDES   collision (due to loss of control) (on highway) between motor vehicle, any kind, and:
>   abutment (bridge) (overpass)
>   animal (herded) (unattended)
>   fallen stone, traffic sign, tree, utility pole
>   guard rail or boundary fence
>   interhighway divider
>   landslide (not moving)
>   object set in motion by railway train or road vehicle (motor) (nonmotor)
>   object thrown in front of motor vehicle
>   other object, fixed, movable, or moving
>   safety island
>   temporary traffic sign or marker
>   wall of cut made for road

> EXCLUDES   *collision with:*
> *any object off the highway (resulting from loss of control) (E816.0-E816.9)*
> *any object which normally would have been off the highway and is not stated to have been on it (E816.0-E816.9)*
> *motor vehicle parked, stopped, stalled, disabled, or abandoned on highway (E812.0-E812.9)*
> *moving landslide (E909)*
> *motor vehicle hit by object:*
>   *set in motion by railway train or road vehicle (motor) (nonmotor) (E818.0-E818.9)*
>   *thrown into or on vehicle (E818.0-E818.9)*

§ ✓4ᵗʰ **E816** **Motor vehicle traffic accident due to loss of control, without collision on the highway**

> INCLUDES   motor vehicle:
>   failing to make curve
>   going out of control (due to):
>   blowout
>   burst tire
>   driver falling asleep
>   drive inattention
>   excessive speed
>   failure of mechanical part
> and:
>   coliding with object
>   off the highway
>   overturning
>   stopping abruptly off the highway

> EXCLUDES   *collision on highway following loss of control (E810.0-E815.9)*
> *loss of control of motor vehicle following collision on the highway (E810.0-E815.9)*

§ ✓4ᵗʰ **E817** **Noncollision motor vehicle traffic accident while boarding or alighting**

> INCLUDES   fall down stairs of motor bus
> fall from car in street
> injured by moving part of the vehicle
> trapped by door of motor bus
> } while boarding or alighting

§ ✓4ᵗʰ **E818** **Other noncollision motor vehicle traffic accident**

> INCLUDES   accidental poisoning from exhaust gas generated by
> breakage of any part of
> explosion of any part of
> fall, jump, or being accidentally pushed from
> fire starting in
> hit by object thrown into or on
> injured by being thrown against some part of, or object in
> injury from moving part of
> object falling in or on
> object thrown on
> } motor vehicle while in motion

> collision of railway train or road vehicle except motor vehicle, with object set in motion by motor vehicle
> motor vehicle hit by object set in motion by railway train or road vehicle (motor) (nonmotor)
> pedestrian, railway train, or road vehicle (motor) (nonmotor) hit by object set in motion by motor vehicle

> EXCLUDES   *collision between motor vehicle and:*
> *object set in motion by railway train or road vehicle (motor) (nonmotor) (E815.0-E815.9)*
> *object thrown towards the motor vehicle (E815.0-E815.9)*
> *person overcome by carbon monoxide generated by stationary motor vehicle off the roadway with motor running (E868.2)*

§ ✓4ᵗʰ **E819** **Motor vehicle traffic accident of unspecified nature**

> INCLUDES   motor vehicle traffic accident NOS
> traffic accident NOS

Motor Vehicle Nontraffic Accidents (E820-E825)

> NOTE   For definitions of motor vehicle nontraffic accident and related terms see definition (a) to (k).

> INCLUDES   accidents involving motor vehicles being used in recreational or sporting activities off the highway
> collision and noncollision motor vehicle accidents occurring entirely off the highway

> EXCLUDES   *accidents involving motor vehicle and:*
> *aircraft (E840.0-E845.9)*
> *watercraft (E830.0-E838.9)*
> *accidents, not on the public highway, involving agricultural and construction machinery but not involving another motor vehicle (E919.0, E919.2, E919.7)*

The following fourth digit subdivisions are for use with categories E820-E825 to identify the injured person:

.0 Driver of motor vehicle other than motorcycle
   See definition (l)
.1 Passenger in motor vehicle other than motorcycle
   See definition (l)
.2 Motorcyclist
   See definition (l)
.3 Passenger on motorcycle
   See definition (l)
.4 Occupant of streetcar
.5 Rider of animal; occupant of animal-drawn vehicle
.6 Pedal cyclist
   See definition (p)
.7 Pedestrian
   See definition (r)
.8 Other specified person
   Occupant of vehicle other than above
   Person in railway train involved in accident
   Unauthorized rider of motor vehicle
.9 Unspecified person

§   Requires fourth digit. See beginning of appropriate section for codes and definitions.

✓4ᵗʰ Fourth-digit Required   ▶◀ Revised Text   ● New Code   ▲ Revised Code Title

6 — E Codes   2015 ICD-9-CM

§ ✓4ᵗʰ **E820 Nontraffic accident involving motor-driven snow vehicle**

INCLUDES
breakage of part of
fall from
hit by   } motor-driven snow
overturning of   vehicle (not on
run over or dragged by   public highway)

collision of motor-driven snow vehicle with:
  animal (being ridden) (-drawn vehicle)
  another off-road motor vehicle
  other motor vehicle, not on public highway
  railway train
  other object, fixed or movable
injury caused by rough landing of motor-driven snow
  vehicle (after leaving ground on rough terrain)

EXCLUDES *accident on the public highway involving motor driven snow vehicle (E810.0-E819.9)*

§ ✓4ᵗʰ **E821 Nontraffic accident involving other off-road motor vehicle**

INCLUDES
breakage of part of
fall from
hit by   } off-road motorvehicle
overturning of   except snow
run over or dragged by   vehicle (not on
thrown against some part   public highway
  of or object in

collision with:
  animal (being ridden) (-drawn vehicle)
  another off-road motor vehicle, except snow vehicle
  other motor vehicle, not on public highway
  other object, fixed or movable

EXCLUDES *accident on public highway involving off-road motor*
  vehicle (E810.0-E819.9)
collision between motor driven snow vehicle and other
  off-road motor vehicle (E820.0-E820.9)
hovercraft accident on water (E830.0-E838.9)

§ ✓4ᵗʰ **E822 Other motor vehicle nontraffic accident involving collision with moving object**

INCLUDES collision, not on public highway, between motor vehicle,
  except off-road motor vehicle and:
  animal
  nonmotor vehicle
  other motor vehicle, except off-road motor vehicle
  pedestrian
  railway train
  other moving object

EXCLUDES *collision with:*
motor-driven snow vehicle (E820.0-E820.9)
other off-road motor vehicle (E821.0-E821.9)

§ ✓4ᵗʰ **E823 Other motor vehicle nontraffic accident involving collision with stationary object**

INCLUDES collision, not on public highway, between motor vehicle,
  except off-road motor vehicle, and any object,
  fixed or movable, but not in motion

§ ✓4ᵗʰ **E824 Other motor vehicle nontraffic accident while boarding and alighting**

INCLUDES
fall
injury from oving part   } while boarding or alighting
  of motor   from motor vehicle,
  vehicle   except off-road motor
trapped by door of   vehicle, not on public
  motor vehhicle   highway

§ ✓4ᵗʰ **E825 Other motor vehicle nontraffic accident of other and unspecified nature**

INCLUDES
accidental poisoning from carbon
  monoxide generated by
breakage of any part of
explosion of any part of
fall, jump, or being accidentally
  pushed from   } motor vehicle
fire starting in   while in
hit by object thrown into, towards,   motion, not
  or on   on public
injured by being thrown against   highway
  some part of, or object in
injury from moving part of
object falling in or on
motor vehicle nontraffic accident NOS

EXCLUDES *fall from or in stationary motor vehicle (E884.9, E885.9)*
overcome by carbon monoxide or exhaust gas generated by
  stationary motor vehicle off the roadway with motor
  running (E868.2)
struck by falling object from or in stationary motor vehicle
  (E916)

Other Road Vehicle Accidents (E826-E829)

NOTE Other road vehicle accidents are transport accidents involving road
vehicles other than motor vehicles. For definitions of other road
vehicle and related terms see definitions (m) to (o).

INCLUDES accidents involving other road vehicles being used in recreational
  or sporting activities

EXCLUDES *collision of other road vehicle [any] with:*
aircraft (E840.0-E845.9)
motor vehicle (E813.0-E813.9, E820.0-E822.9)
railway train (E801.0-E801.9))

> The following fourth digit subdivisions are for use with categories E826-E829
> to identify the injured person:
> **.0 Pedestrian**
>   See definition (r)
> **.1 Pedal cyclist**
>   See definition (p)
> **.2 Rider of animal**
> **.3 Occupant of animal-drawn vehicle**
> **.4 Occupant of streetcar**
> **.8 Other specified person**
> **.9 Unspecified person**

§ ✓4ᵗʰ **E826 Pedal cycle accident**

[0-9] INCLUDES breakage of any part of pedal cycle
collision between pedal cycle and:
  animal (being ridden) (herded) (unattended)
  another pedal cycle
  any pedestrian
  nonmotor road vehicle
  other object, fixed, movable, or moving, not set in
    motion by motor vehicle, railway train, or aircraft
entanglement in wheel of pedal cycle
fall from pedal cycle
hit by object falling or thrown on the pedal cycle
pedal cycle accident NOS
pedal cycle overturned

§ ✓4ᵗʰ **E827 Animal-drawn vehicle accident**

[0,2,4,8,9] INCLUDES breakage of any part of vehicle
collision between animal-drawn vehicle and:
  animal (being ridden) (herded) (unattended)
  nonmotor road vehicle, except pedal cycle
  pedestrian, pedestrian conveyance, or pedestrian
    vehicle
  other object, fixed, movable, or moving, not set in
    motion by motor vehicle, railway train, or aircraft

fall from
knocked down by
overturning of   } animal drawn vehicle
running over by
thrown from

EXCLUDES *collision of animal-drawn vehicle with pedal cycle*
  (E826.0-E826.9)

§ Requires fourth digit. See beginning of appropriate section for codes and definitions.

✓4ᵗʰ Fourth-digit Required   ▶◀ Revised Text   ● New Code   ▲ Revised Code Title

§ ☑4ᵗʰ **E828 Accident involving animal being ridden**

[0,2,4,8,9] INCLUDES collision between animal being ridden and:

another animal
nonmotor road vehicle, except pedal cycle, and animal-drawn vehicle
pedestrian, pedestrian conveyance, or pedestrian vehicle
other object, fixed, movable, or moving, not set in motion by motor vehicle, railway train, or aircraft

fall from
knocked down by ⎤
thrown from ⎬ animal being ridden
trampled by ⎦

ridden animal stumbled and fell

EXCLUDES *collision of animal being ridden with:*
animal-drawn vehicle (E827.0-E827.9)
pedal cycle (E826.0-E826.9)

§ ☑4ᵗʰ **E829 Other road vehicle accidents**

[0,4,8,9] INCLUDES accident while boarding ⎤
or alighting from ⎮
blow from object in ⎮ streetcar
breakage of any part of ⎮ nonmotor road vehicle
caught in door of ⎬ not classifiable to
derailment of ⎮ E826-E828
fall in, on, or from ⎮
fire in ⎦

collision between streetcar or nonmotor road vehicle, except as in E826-E828, and:
animal (not being ridden)
another nonmotor road vehicle not classifiable to E826-E828
pedestrian
other object, fixed, movable, or moving, not set in motion by motor vehicle, railway train, or aircraft
nonmotor road vehicle accident NOS
streetcar accident NOS

EXCLUDES *collision with:*
animal being ridden (E828.0-E828.9)
animal-drawn vehicle (E827.0-E827.9)
pedal cycle (E826.0-E826.9)

Water Transport Accidents (E830-E838)

NOTE For definitions of water transport accident and related terms see definitions (a), (s), and (t).

INCLUDES watercraft accidents in the course of recreational activities

EXCLUDES *accidents involving both aircraft, including objects set in motion by aircraft, and watercraft (E840.0-E845.9)*

The following fourth digit subdivisions are for use with categories E830-E838 to identify the injured person:

.0 Occupant of small boat, unpowered
.1 Occupant of small boat, powered
See definition (t)
EXCLUDES *water skier (.4)*
.2 Occupant of other watercraft — crew
Persons:
engaged in operation of watercraft
providing passenger services [cabin attendants, ship's physician, catering personnel]
working on ship during voyage in other capacity [musician in band, operators of shops and beauty parlors
.3 Occupant of other watercraft — other than crew
Passenger
Occupant of lifeboat, other than crew, after abandoning ship
.4 Water skier
.5 Swimmer
.6 Dockers, stevedores
Longshoreman employed on the dock in loading and unloading ships
.7 Occupant of military watercraft, any type
.8 Other specified person
Immigration and custom officials on board ship
Person:
accompanying passenger or member of crew visiting boat
Pilot (guiding ship into port)
.9 Unspecified person

§ ☑4ᵗʰ **E830 Accident to watercraft causing submersion**

INCLUDES submersion and drowning due to:
boat overturning
boat submerging
falling or jumping from burning ship
falling or jumping from crushed watercraft
ship sinking
other accident to watercraft

§ ☑4ᵗʰ **E831 Accident to watercraft causing other injury**

INCLUDES any injury, except submersion and drowning, as a result of an accident to watercraft
burned while ship on fire
crushed between ships in collision
crushed by lifeboat after abandoning ship
fall due to collision or other accident to watercraft
hit by falling object due to accident to watercraft
injured in watercraft accident involving collision
struck by boat or part thereof after fall or jump from damaged boat

EXCLUDES *burns from localized fire or explosion on board ship (E837.0-E837.9)*

§ ☑4ᵗʰ **E832 Other accidental submersion or drowning in water transport accident**

INCLUDES submersion or drowning as a result of an accident other than accident to the watercraft, such as:
fall:
from gangplank
from ship
overboard
thrown overboard by motion of ship
washed overboard

EXCLUDES *submersion or drowning of swimmer or diver who voluntarily jumps from boat not involved in an accident (E910.0-E910.9)*

§ ☑4ᵗʰ **E833 Fall on stairs or ladders in water transport**

EXCLUDES *fall due to accident to watercraft (E831.0-E831.9)*

§ ☑4ᵗʰ **E834 Other fall from one level to another in water transport**

EXCLUDES *fall due to accident to watercraft (E831.0-E831.9)*

§ ☑4ᵗʰ **E835 Other and unspecified fall in water transport**

EXCLUDES *fall due to accident to watercraft (E831.0-E831.9)*

§ ☑4ᵗʰ **E836 Machinery accident in water transport**

INCLUDES injuries in water transport caused by:
deck ⎤
engine room ⎮
galley ⎬ machinery
laundry ⎮
loading ⎦

§ ☑4ᵗʰ **E837 Explosion, fire, or burning in watercraft**

INCLUDES explosion of boiler on steamship
localized fire on ship

EXCLUDES *burning ship (due to collision or explosion) resulting in:*
submersion or drowning (E830.0-E830.9)
other injury (E831.0-E831.9)

§ ☑4ᵗʰ **E838 Other and unspecified water transport accident**

INCLUDES accidental poisoning by gases or fumes on ship
atomic power plant malfunction in watercraft
crushed between ship and stationary object [wharf]
crushed between ships without accident to watercraft
crushed by falling object on ship or while loading or unloading
hit by boat while water skiing
struck by boat or part thereof (after fall from boat)
watercraft accident NOS

---

§ Requires fourth digit. Valid digits are in [brackets] under each code. See beginning of appropriate section for codes and definitions.

☑4ᵗʰ Fourth-digit Required   ►◄ Revised Text   ● New Code   ▲ Revised Code Title

Air and Space Transport Accidents (E840-E845)

NOTE For definition of aircraft and related terms see definitions (u) and (v).

The following fourth digit subdivisions are for use with categories E840-E845 to identify the injured person. Valid fourth digits are in [brackets] under codes E842-E845:

.0 Occupant of spacecraft

.1 Occupant of military aircraft, any
　　Crew in military aircraft [air force] [army] [national guard] [navy]
　　Passenger (civilian) (military) in military aircraft [air force] [army] [national guard] [navy]
　　Troops in military aircraft [air force] [army] [national guard] [navy]
　　　EXCLUDES *occupants of aircraft operated under jurisdiction of police departments (.5)*
　　　　　parachutist (.7)

.2 Crew of commercial aircraft (powered) in surface to surface transport

.3 Other occupant of commercial aircraft (powered) in surface to surface transport
　　Flight personnel:
　　　not part of crew
　　　on familiarization flight
　　Passenger on aircraft (powered) NOS

.4 Occupant of commercial aircraft (powered) in surface to air transport
　　Occupant [crew] [passenger] of aircraft (powered) engaged in activities, such as:
　　　aerial spraying (crops) (fire retardants)
　　　air drops of emergency supplies
　　　air drops of parachutists, except from military craft
　　　crop dusting
　　　lowering of construction material [bridge or telephone pole]
　　　sky writing

.5 Occupant of other powered aircraft
　　Occupant [crew] [passenger] of aircraft (powered) engaged in activities, such as:
　　　aerobatic flying
　　　aircraft racing
　　　rescue operation
　　　storm surveillance
　　　traffic surveillance
　　Occupant of private plane NOS

.6 Occupant of unpowered aircraft, except parachutist
　　Occupant of aircraft classifiable to E842

.7 Parachutist (military) (other)
　　Person making voluntary descent
　　　EXCLUDES *person making descent after accident to aircraft (.1-.6)*

.8 Ground crew, airline employee
　　Persons employed at airfields (civil) (military) or launching pads, not occupants of aircraft

.9 Other person

§ ✓4ᵗʰ **E840　Accident to powered aircraft at takeoff or landing**
　　INCLUDES　collision of aircraft with any object, fixed, movable, or moving ⎫
　　　　　crash ⎪ while taking off or
　　　　　explosion on aircraft ⎬ landing
　　　　　fire on aircraft ⎪
　　　　　forced landing ⎭

§ ✓4ᵗʰ **E841　Accident to powered aircraft, other and unspecified**
　　INCLUDES　aircraft accident NOS
　　　　　aircraft crash or wreck NOS
　　　　　any accident to powered aircraft while in transit or when not specified whether in transit, taking off, or landing
　　　　　collision of aircraft with another aircraft, bird, or any object, while in transit
　　　　　explosion on aircraft while in transit
　　　　　fire on aircraft while in transit

§ ✓4ᵗʰ **E842　Accident to unpowered aircraft**
　　[6-9]　**INCLUDES**　any accident, except collision with powered aircraft, to:
　　　　　balloon
　　　　　glider
　　　　　hang glider
　　　　　kite carrying a person
　　　　　hit by object falling from unpowered aircraft

§ ✓4ᵗʰ **E843　Fall in, on, or from aircraft**
　　[0-9]　**INCLUDES**　accident in boarding or alighting from aircraft, any kind
　　　　　fall in, on, or from aircraft [any kind], while in transit, taking off, or landing, except when as a result of an accident to aircraft

§ ✓4ᵗʰ **E844　Other specified air transport accidents**
　　[0-9]　**INCLUDES**　hit by:
　　　　　　aircraft
　　　　　　object falling from aircraft
　　　　injury by or from: ⎫
　　　　　machinery of aircraft ⎪ without
　　　　　rotating propeller ⎬ accident
　　　　　voluntary parachute descent ⎪ to aircraft
　　　　poisoning by carbon monoxide from aircraft while in transit ⎪
　　　　sucked into jet ⎭
　　　　any accident involving other transport vehicle (motor) (nonmotor) due to being hit by object set in motion by aircraft (powered)
　　　EXCLUDES *air sickness (E903)*
　　　　　effects of:
　　　　　　high altitude (E902.0-E902.1)
　　　　　　pressure change (E902.0-E902.1)
　　　　　injury in parachute descent due to accident to aircraft (E840.0-E842-9)

§ ✓4ᵗʰ **E845　Accident involving spacecraft**
　　[0,8,9]　**INCLUDES**　launching pad accident
　　　　　EXCLUDES *effects of weightlessness in spacecraft (E928.0)*

Vehicle Accidents Not Elsewhere Classifiable (E846-E848)

E846　Accidents involving powered vehicles used solely within the buildings and premises of industrial or commercial establishment
　　Accident to, on, or involving:
　　　battery powered airport passenger vehicle
　　　battery powered trucks (baggage) (mail)
　　　coal car in mine
　　　logging car
　　　self propelled truck, industrial
　　　station baggage truck (powered)
　　　tram, truck, or tub (powered) in mine or quarry
　　Collision with:
　　　pedestrian
　　　other vehicle or object within premises
　　Explosion of ⎫
　　Fall from ⎪ powered vehicle, industrial or
　　Overturning of ⎬ commercial
　　Struck by ⎭
　　　EXCLUDES *accidental poisoning by exhaust gas from vehicle not elsewhere classifiable (E868.2)*
　　　　　injury by crane, lift (fork), or elevator (E919.2)

E847　Accidents involving cable cars not running on rails
　　Accident to, on, or involving:
　　　cable car, not on rails
　　　ski chair-lift
　　　ski-lift with gondola
　　　téléférique
　　Breakage of cable
　　Caught or dragged by ⎫
　　Fall or jump from ⎬ cable car, not on rails
　　Object thrown from or in ⎭

E848　Accidents involving other vehicles, not elsewhere classifiable
　　Accident to, on, or involving:
　　　ice yacht
　　　land yacht
　　　nonmotor, nonroad vehicle NOS

---

§　Requires fourth digit. See beginning of appropriate section for codes and definitions.

E Codes

E849–E851

Place of Occurrence (E849)

✓4ᵗʰ **E849   Place of Occurrence**

NOTE   The following category is for use to denote the place where the injury or poisoning occurred.

E849.0   Home

Apartment
Boarding house
Farm house
Home premises
House (residential)
Noninstitutional place
   of residence
Private:
   driveway

Private:
   garage
   garden
   home
   walk
Swimming pool in private
   house or garden
Yard of home

EXCLUDES   home under construction but not yet occupied
          (E849.3)
       institutional place of residence (E849.7)

E849.1   Farm

Farm:
   buildings
   land under cultivation

EXCLUDES   farm house and home premises of farm (E849.0)

E849.2   Mine and quarry

Gravel pit
Sand pit

Tunnel under construction

E849.3   Industrial place and premises

Building under construction
Dockyard
Dry dock
Factory
   building
   premises
Garage (place of work)

Industrial yard
Loading platform (factory)
   (store)
Plant, industrial
Railway yard
Shop (place of work)
Warehouse
Workhouse

E849.4   Place for recreation and sport

Amusement park
Baseball field
Basketball court
Beach resort
Cricket ground
Fives court
Football field
Golf course
Gymnasium
Hockey field
Holiday camp
Ice palace
Lake resort
Mountain resort

Playground, including school
   playground
Public park
Racecourse
Resort NOS
Riding school
Rifle range
Seashore resort
Skating rink
Sports palace
Stadium
Swimming pool, public
Tennis court
Vacation resort

EXCLUDES   that in private house or garden (E849.0)

E849.5   Street and highway

E849.6   Public building

Building (including adjacent grounds) used by the general
     public or by a particular group of the public, such as:

airport
bank
café
casino
church
cinema
clubhouse
courthouse
dance hall
garage building
   (for car storage)
hotel
market (grocery or
   other commodity)
movie house

music hall
nightclub
office
office building
opera house
post office
public hall
radio broadcasting station
restaurant
school (state) (public) (private)
shop, commercial
station (bus) (railway)
store
theater

EXCLUDES   home garage (E849.0)
       industrial building or workplace (E849.3)

E849.7   Residential institution

Children's home
Dormitory
Hospital
Jail

Old people's home
Orphanage
Prison
Reform school

E849.8   Other specified places

Beach NOS
Canal
Caravan site NOS
Derelict house
Desert
Dock
Forest
Harbor
Hill
Lake NOS
Mountain
Parking lot
Parking place

Pond or pool (natural)
Prairie
Public place NOS
Railway line
Reservoir
River
Sea
Seashore NOS
Stream
Swamp
Trailer court
Woods

E849.9   Unspecified place

Accidental Poisoning by Drugs, Medicinal Substances, and Biologicals (E850-E858)

INCLUDES   accidental overdose of drug, wrong drug given or taken
       in error, and drug taken inadvertently
       accidents in the use of drugs and biologicals in medical
       and surgical procedures

EXCLUDES   administration with suicidal or homicidal intent or intent to
       harm, or in circumstances classifiable to E980-E989
       (E950.0-E950.5, E962.0, E980.0-E980.5)
       correct drug properly administered in therapeutic or
       prophylactic dosage, as the cause of adverse effect
       (E930.0-E949.9)

NOTE   See Alphabetic Index for more complete list of specific drugs
       to be classified under the fourth digit subdivisions. The
       American Hospital Formulary numbers can be used to
       classify new drugs listed by the American Hospital
       Formulary Service (AHFS). See Appendix C.

✓4ᵗʰ **E850   Accidental poisoning by analgesics, antipyretics, and
       antirheumatics**

E850.0   Heroin
     Diacetylmorphine

E850.1   Methadone

E850.2   Other opiates and related narcotics
     Codeine [methylmorphine]
     Meperidine [pethidine]
     Morphine
     Opium (alkaloids)

E850.3   Salicylates
     Acetylsalicylic acid [aspirin]
     Amino derivatives of salicylic acid
     Salicylic acid salts

E850.4   Aromatic analgesics, not elsewhere classified
     Acetanilid
     Paracetamol [acetaminophen]
     Phenacetin [acetophenetidin]

E850.5   Pyrazole derivatives
     Aminophenazone [amidopyrine]
     Phenylbutazone

E850.6   Antirheumatics [antiphlogistics]
     Gold salts
     Indomethacin
     EXCLUDES   salicylates (E850.3)
               steroids (E858.0)

E850.7   Other non-narcotic analgesics
     Pyrabital

E850.8   Other specified analgesics and antipyretics
     Pentazocine

E850.9   Unspecified analgesic or antipyretic

E851   Accidental poisoning by barbiturates
     Amobarbital [amylobarbitone]
     Barbital [barbitone]
     Butabarbital [butabarbitone]
     Pentobarbital [pentobarbitone]
     Phenobarbital [phenobarbitone]
     Secobarbital [quinalbarbitone]
     EXCLUDES   thiobarbiturates (E855.1)

☑4ᵗʰ **E852 Accidental poisoning by other sedatives and hypnotics**

E852.0 Chloral hydrate group

E852.1 Paraldehyde

E852.2 Bromine compounds
Bromides
Carbromal (derivatives)

E852.3 Methaqualone compounds

E852.4 Glutethimide group

E852.5 Mixed sedatives, not elsewhere classified

E852.8 Other specified sedatives and hypnotics

E852.9 Unspecified sedative or hypnotic
Sleeping:
drug ⎫
pill ⎬ NOS
tablet ⎭

☑4ᵗʰ **E853 Accidental poisoning by tranquilizers**

E853.0 Phenothiazine-based tranquilizers
Chlorpromazine   Prochlorperazine
Fluphenazine   Promazine

E853.1 Butyrophenone-based tranquilizers
Haloperidol   Trifluperidol
Spiperone

E853.2 Benzodiazepine-based tranquilizers
Chlordiazepoxide   Lorazepam
Diazepam   Medazepam
Flurazepam   Nitrazepam

E853.8 Other specified tranquilizers
Hydroxyzine   Meprobamate

E853.9 Unspecified tranquilizer

☑4ᵗʰ **E854 Accidental poisoning by other psychotropic agents**

E854.0 Antidepressants
Amitriptyline
Imipramine
Monoamine oxidase [MAO] inhibitors

E854.1 Psychodysleptics [hallucinogens]
Cannabis derivatives   Mescaline
Lysergide [LSD]   Psilocin
Marihuana (derivatives) Psilocybin

E854.2 Psychostimulants
Amphetamine
Caffeine
EXCLUDES *central appetite depressants (E858.8)*

E854.3 Central nervous system stimulants
Analeptics
Opiate antagonists

E854.8 Other psychotropic agents

☑4ᵗʰ **E855 Accidental poisoning by other drugs acting on central and autonomic nervous system**

E855.0 Anticonvulsant and anti-Parkinsonism drugs
Amantadine
Hydantoin derivatives
Levodopa [L-dopa]
Oxazolidine derivatives [paramethadione] [trimethadione]
Succinimides

E855.1 Other central nervous system depressants
Ether
Gaseous anesthetics
Halogenated hydrocarbon derivatives
Intravenous anesthetics
Thiobarbiturates, such as thiopental sodium

E855.2 Local anesthetics
Cocaine   Procaine
Lidocaine [lignocaine] Tetracaine

E855.3 Parasympathomimetics [cholinergics]
Acetylcholine   Anticholinesterase:
Anticholinesterase: reversible
   organophosphorus   Pilocarpine

E855.4 Parasympatholytics [anticholinergics and antimuscarinics] and spasmolytics
Atropine   Hyoscine [scopolamine]
Homatropine   Quaternary ammonium derivatives

E855.5 Sympathomimetics [adrenergics]
Epinephrine [adrenalin]
Levarterenol [noradrenalin]

E855.6 Sympatholytics [antiadrenergics]
Phenoxybenzamine
Tolazoline hydrochloride

E855.8 Other specified drugs acting on central and autonomic nervous systems

E855.9 Unspecified drug acting on central and autonomic nervous systems

E856 Accidental poisoning by antibiotics

E857 Accidental poisoning by other anti-infectives

☑4ᵗʰ **E858 Accidental poisoning by other drugs**

E858.0 Hormones and synthetic substitutes

E858.1 Primarily systemic agents

E858.2 Agents primarily affecting blood constituents

E858.3 Agents primarily affecting cardiovascular system

E858.4 Agents primarily affecting gastrointestinal system

E858.5 Water, mineral, and uric acid metabolism drugs

E858.6 Agents primarily acting on the smooth and skeletal muscles and respiratory system

E858.7 Agents primarily affecting skin and mucous membrane, ophthalmological, otorhinolaryngological, and dental drugs

E858.8 Other specified drugs
Central appetite depressants

E858.9 Unspecified drug

Accidental Poisoning by Other Solid and Liquid Substances, Gases, and Vapors (E860-E869)

NOTE Categories in this section are intended primarily to indicate the external cause of poisoning states classifiable to 980-989. They may also be used to indicate external causes of localized effects classifiable to 001-799.

☑4ᵗʰ **E860 Accidental poisoning by alcohol, not elsewhere classified**

E860.0 Alcoholic beverages
Alcohol in preparations intended for consumption

E860.1 Other and unspecified ethyl alcohol and its products
Denatured alcohol   Grain alcohol NOS
Ethanol NOS   Methylated spirit

E860.2 Methyl alcohol
Methanol   Wood alcohol

E860.3 Isopropyl alcohol
Dimethyl carbinol   Rubbing alcohol subsitute
Isopropanol   Secondary propyl alcohol

E860.4 Fusel oil
Alcohol: Alcohol:
   amyl   propyl
   butyl

E860.8 Other specified alcohols

E860.9 Unspecified alcohol

☑4ᵗʰ **E861 Accidental poisoning by cleansing and polishing agents, disinfectants, paints, and varnishes**

E861.0 Synthetic detergents and shampoos

E861.1 Soap products

E861.2 Polishes

E861.3 Other cleansing and polishing agents
Scouring powders

☑4ᵗʰ Fourth-digit Required   ▶◀ Revised Text   ● New Code   ▲ Revised Code Title

E861.4 Disinfectants

Household and other disinfectants not ordinarily used on the person

EXCLUDES *carbolic acid or phenol (E864.0)*

E861.5 Lead paints

E861.6 Other paints and varnishes

Lacquers   Paints, other than lead
Oil colors   White washes

E861.9 Unspecified

✓4th **E862 Accidental poisoning by petroleum products, other solvents and their vapors, not elsewhere classified**

E862.0 Petroleum solvents

Petroleum: Petroleum:
  ether   naphtha
  benzine

E862.1 Petroleum fuels and cleaners

Antiknock additives to petroleum fuels
Gas oils
Gasoline or petrol
Kerosene

EXCLUDES *kerosene insecticides (E863.4)*

E862.2 Lubricating oils

E862.3 Petroleum solids

Paraffin wax

E862.4 Other specified solvents

Benzene

E862.9 Unspecified solvent

✓4th **E863 Accidental poisoning by agricultural and horticultural chemical and pharmaceutical preparations other than plant foods and fertilizers**

EXCLUDES *plant foods and fertilizers (E866.5)*

E863.0 Insecticides of organochlorine compounds

Benzene hexachloride   Dieldrin
Chlordane   Endrine
DDT   Toxaphene

E863.1 Insecticides of organophosphorus compounds

Demeton   Parathion
Diazinon   Phenylsulphthion
Dichlorvos   Phorate
Malathion   Phosdrin
Methyl parathion

E863.2 Carbamates

Aldicarb   Propoxur
Carbaryl

E863.3 Mixtures of insecticides

E863.4 Other and unspecified insecticides

Kerosene insecticides

E863.5 Herbicides

2, 4-Dichlorophenoxyacetic acid [2, 4-D]
2, 4, 5-Trichlorophenoxyacetic acid [2, 4, 5-T]
Chlorates
Diquat
Mixtures of plant foods and fertilizers with herbicides
Paraquat

E863.6 Fungicides

Organic mercurials (used in seed dressing)
Pentachlorophenols

E863.7 Rodenticides

Fluoroacetates   Warfarin
Squill and derivatives   Zinc phosphide
Thallium

E863.8 Fumigants

Cyanides   Phosphine
Methyl bromide

E863.9 Other and unspecified

✓4th **E864 Accidental poisoning by corrosives and caustics, not elsewhere classified**

EXCLUDES *those as components of disinfectants (E861.4)*

E864.0 Corrosive aromatics

Carbolic acid or phenol

E864.1 Acids

Acid:
  hydrochloric
  nitric
  sulfuric

E864.2 Caustic alkalis

Lye

E864.3 Other specified corrosives and caustics

E864.4 Unspecified corrosives and caustics

✓4th **E865 Accidental poisoning from poisonous foodstuffs and poisonous plants**

INCLUDES   any meat, fish, or shellfish
           plants, berries, and fungi eaten as, or in mistake for, food, or by a child

EXCLUDES   *anaphylactic shock due to adverse food reaction (995.60-995.69)*
           food poisoning (bacterial) (005.0-005.9)
           poisoning and toxic reactions to venomous plants (E905.6-E905.7)

E865.0 Meat

E865.1 Shellfish

E865.2 Other fish

E865.3 Berries and seeds

E865.4 Other specified plants

E865.5 Mushrooms and other fungi

E865.8 Other specified foods

E865.9 Unspecified foodstuff or poisonous plant

✓4th **E866 Accidental poisoning by other and unspecified solid and liquid substances**

EXCLUDES   *these substances as a component of:*
           medicines (E850.0-E858.9)
           paints (E861.5-E861.6)
           pesticides (E863.0-E863.9)
           petroleum fuels (E862.1)

E866.0 Lead and its compounds and fumes

E866.1 Mercury and its compounds and fumes

E866.2 Antimony and its compounds and fumes

E866.3 Arsenic and its compounds and fumes

E866.4 Other metals and their compounds and fumes

Beryllium (compounds)   Iron (compounds)
Brass fumes   Manganese (compounds)
Cadmium (compounds)   Nickel (compounds)
Copper salts   Thallium (compounds)

E866.5 Plant foods and fertilizers

EXCLUDES *mixtures with herbicides (E863.5)*

E866.6 Glues and adhesives

E866.7 Cosmetics

E866.8 Other specified solid or liquid substances

E866.9 Unspecified solid or liquid substance

E867 Accidental poisoning by gas distributed by pipeline

Carbon monoxide from incomplete combustion of piped gas
Coal gas NOS
Liquefied petroleum gas distributed through pipes (pure or mixed with air)
Piped gas (natural) (manufactured)

☑4ᵗʰ **E868 Accidental poisoning by other utility gas and other carbon monoxide**

    E868.0 Liquefied petroleum gas distributed in mobile containers

        Butane   or carbon monoxide
        Liquefied hydrocarbon gas   from incomplete
          NOS   conbustion of
        Propane   these gases

    E868.1 Other and unspecified utility gas

        Acetylene   or carbon monoxide
        Gas NOS used for lighting,   from incomplete
          heating, or cooking   conbustion of
        Water gas   these gases

    E868.2 Motor vehicle exhaust gas

        Exhaust gas from:
          any type of combustion engine not in watercraft
          farm tractor, not in transit
          gas engine
          motor pump
          motor vehicle, not in transit

        EXCLUDES *poisoning by carbon monoxide from:*
          aircraft while in transit (E844.0-E844.9)
          motor vehicle while in transit (E818.0-E818.9)
          watercraft whether or not in transit
            (E838.0-E838.9)

    E868.3 Carbon monoxide from incomplete combustion of other domestic fuels

        Carbon monoxide from incomplete combustion of:
          coal
          coke   in domestic stove or fireplace
          kerosene
          wood

        EXCLUDES *carbon monoxide from smoke and fumes due to conflagration (E890.0-E893.9)*

    E868.8 Carbon monoxide from other sources

        Carbon monoxide from:
          blast furnace gas
          incomplete combustion of fuels in industrial use
          kiln vapor

    E868.9 Unspecified carbon monoxide

☑4ᵗʰ **E869 Accidental poisoning by other gases and vapors**

        EXCLUDES *effects of gases used as anesthetics (E855.1, E938.2)*
          fumes from heavy metals (E866.0-E866.4)
          smoke and fumes due to conflagration or explosion
            (E890.0-E899)

    E869.0 Nitrogen oxides

    E869.1 Sulfur dioxide

    E869.2 Freon

    E869.3 Lacrimogenic gas [tear gas]

        Bromobenzyl cyanide
        Chloroacetophenone
        Ethyliodoacetate

    E869.4 Second-hand tobacco smoke

    E869.8 Other specified gases and vapors

        Chlorine
        Hydrocyanic acid gas

    E869.9 Unspecified gases and vapors

Misadventures to Patients During Surgical and Medical Care (E870-E876)

  EXCLUDES *accidental overdose of drug and wrong drug given in error*
    (E850.0-E858.9)
    surgical and medical procedures as the cause of abnormal reaction by
    the patient, without mention of misadventure at the time of
    procedure (E878.0-E879.9)

☑4ᵗʰ **E870 Accidental cut, puncture, perforation, or hemorrhage during medical care**

    E870.0 Surgical operation

    E870.1 Infusion or transfusion

    E870.2 Kidney dialysis or other perfusion

    E870.3 Injection or vaccination

    E870.4 Endoscopic examination

    E870.5 Aspiration of fluid or tissue, puncture, and catheterization

        Abdominal paracentesis
        Aspirating needle biopsy
        Blood sampling
        Lumbar puncture
        Thoracentesis

        EXCLUDES *heart catheterization (E870.6)*

    E870.6 Heart catheterization

    E870.7 Administration of enema

    E870.8 Other specified medical care

    E870.9 Unspecified medical care

☑4ᵗʰ **E871 Foreign object left in body during procedure**

    E871.0 Surgical operation

    E871.1 Infusion or transfusion

    E871.2 Kidney dialysis or other perfusion

    E871.3 Injection or vaccination

    E871.4 Endoscopic examination

    E871.5 Aspiration of fluid or tissue, puncture, and catheterization

        Abdominal paracentesis
        Aspiration needle biopsy
        Blood sampling
        Lumbar puncture
        Thoracentesis

        EXCLUDES *heart catheterization (E871.6)*

    E871.6 Heart catheterization

    E871.7 Removal of catheter or packing

    E871.8 Other specified procedures

    E871.9 Unspecified procedure

☑4ᵗʰ **E872 Failure of sterile precautions during procedure**

    E872.0 Surgical operation

    E872.1 Infusion or transfusion

    E872.2 Kidney dialysis and other perfusion

    E872.3 Injection or vaccination

    E872.4 Endoscopic examination

    E872.5 Aspiration of fluid or tissue, puncture, and catheterization

        Abdominal paracentesis   Lumbar puncture
        Aspiration needle biopsy   Thoracentesis
        Blood sampling

        EXCLUDES *heart catheterization (E872.6)*

    E872.6 Heart catheterization

    E872.8 Other specified procedures

    E872.9 Unspecified procedure

☑4ᵗʰ **E873 Failure in dosage**

        EXCLUDES *accidental overdose of drug, medicinal or*
          biological substance (E850.0-E858.9)

    E873.0 Excessive amount of blood or other fluid during transfusion or infusion

    E873.1 Incorrect dilution of fluid during infusion

    E873.2 Overdose of radiation in therapy

    E873.3 Inadvertent exposure of patient to radiation during medical care

    E873.4 Failure in dosage in electroshock or insulin-shock therapy

    E873.5 Inappropriate [too hot or too cold] temperature in local application and packing

    E873.6 Nonadministration of necessary drug or medicinal substance

    E873.8 Other specified failure in dosage

    E873.9 Unspecified failure in dosage

☑4ᵗʰ Fourth-digit Required   ▶◀ Revised Text   ● New Code   ▲ Revised Code Title

✓4ᵗʰ **E874 Mechanical failure of instrument or apparatus during procedure**

    E874.0 Surgical operation

    E874.1 Infusion and transfusion
        Air in system

    E874.2 Kidney dialysis and other perfusion

    E874.3 Endoscopic examination

    E874.4 Aspiration of fluid or tissue, puncture, and catheterization
        Abdominal paracentesis   Lumbar puncture
        Aspiration needle biopsy   Thoracentesis
        Blood sampling
        EXCLUDES *heart catheterization (E874.5)*

    E874.5 Heart catheterization

    E874.8 Other specified procedures

    E874.9 Unspecified procedure

✓4ᵗʰ **E875 Contaminated or infected blood, other fluid, drug, or biological substance**
      INCLUDES presence of:
          bacterial pyrogens
          endotoxin-producing bacteria
          serum hepatitis-producing agent

    E875.0 Contaminated substance transfused or infused

    E875.1 Contaminated substance injected or used for vaccination

    E875.2 Contaminated drug or biological substance administered by other means

    E875.8 Other

    E875.9 Unspecified

✓4ᵗʰ **E876 Other and unspecified misadventures during medical care**

    E876.0 Mismatched blood in transfusion

    E876.1 Wrong fluid in infusion

    E876.2 Failure in suture and ligature during surgical operation

    E876.3 Endotracheal tube wrongly placed during anesthetic procedure

    E876.4 Failure to introduce or to remove other tube or instrument
        EXCLUDES *foreign object left in body during procedure (E871.0-E871.9)*

*   **E876.5 Performance of wrong operation (procedure) on correct patient**
        Wrong device implanted into correct surgical site
        EXCLUDES *correct operation (procedure) performed on wrong body part (E876.7)*

*   **E876.6 Performance of operation (procedure) on patient not scheduled for surgery**
        Performance of operation (procedure) intended for another patient
        Performance of operation (procedure) on wrong patient

*   **E876.7 Performance of correct operation (procedure) on wrong side/body part**
        Performance of correct operation (procedure) on wrong side
        Performance of correct operation (procedure) on wrong site

    E876.8 Other specified misadventures during medical care
        Performance of inappropriate treatment NEC

    E876.9 Unspecified misadventure during medical care

Surgical and Medical Procedures as the Cause of Abnormal Reaction of Patient or Later Complication, Without Mention of Misadventure at the Time of Procedure (E878-E879)

  INCLUDES procedures as the cause of abnormal reaction, such as:
        displacement or malfunction of prosthetic device
        hepatorenal failure, postoperative
        malfunction of external stoma
        postoperative intestinal obstruction
        rejection of transplanted organ
  EXCLUDES *anesthetic management properly carried out as the cause of adverse effect (E937.0-E938.9)*
      infusion and transfusion, without mention of misadventure in the technique of procedure (E930.0-E949.9)

✓4ᵗʰ **E878 Surgical operation and other surgical procedures as the cause of abnormal reaction of patient, or of later complication, without mention of misadventure at the time of operation**

    E878.0 Surgical operation with transplant of whole organ
        Transplantation of:
          heart
          kidney
          liver

    E878.1 Surgical operation with implant of artificial internal device
        Cardiac pacemaker
        Electrodes implanted in brain
        Heart valve prosthesis
        Internal orthopedic device

    E878.2 Surgical operation with anastomosis, bypass, or graft, with natural or artificial tissues used as implant
        Anastomosis:
          arteriovenous
          gastrojejunal
        Graft of blood vessel, tendon, or skin
        EXCLUDES *external stoma (E878.3)*

    E878.3 Surgical operation with formation of external stoma
        Colostomy   Gastrostomy
        Cystostomy   Ureterostomy
        Duodenostomy

    E878.4 Other restorative surgery

    E878.5 Amputation of limb(s)

    E878.6 Removal of other organ (partial) (total)

    E878.8 Other specified surgical operations and procedures

    E878.9 Unspecified surgical operations and procedures

✓4ᵗʰ **E879 Other procedures, without mention of misadventure at the time of procedure, as the cause of abnormal reaction of patient, or of later complication**

    E879.0 Cardiac catheterization

    E879.1 Kidney dialysis

    E879.2 Radiological procedure and radiotherapy
        EXCLUDES *radio-opaque dyes for diagnostic x-ray procedures (E947.8)*

    E879.3 Shock therapy
        Electroshock therapy
        Insulin-shock therapy

    E879.4 Aspiration of fluid
        Lumbar puncture
        Thoracentesis

    E879.5 Insertion of gastric or duodenal sound

    E879.6 Urinary catheterization

    E879.7 Blood sampling

    E879.8 Other specified procedures
        Blood transfusion

    E879.9 Unspecified procedure

---

* Wrong surgery (MCE) edit applies.

Accidental Falls (E880-E888)

EXCLUDES *falls (in or from):*
burning building (E890.8, E891.8)
into fire (E890.0-E899)
into water (with submersion or drowning)
(E910.0-E910.9)
machinery (in operation) (E919.0-E919.9)
on edged, pointed, or sharp object (E920.0-E920.9)
transport vehicle (E800.0-E845.9)
vehicle not elsewhere classifiable (E846-E848)

✓4ᵗʰ **E880 Fall on or from stairs or steps**

E880.0 Escalator

E880.1 Fall on or from sidewalk curb
EXCLUDES *fall from moving sidewalk (E885.9)*

E880.9 Other stairs or steps

✓4ᵗʰ **E881 Fall on or from ladders or scaffolding**

E881.0 Fall from ladder

E881.1 Fall from scaffolding

E882 Fall from or out of building or other structure
Fall from: Fall from:
balcony   turret
bridge   viaduct
building   wall
flagpole   window
tower   Fall through roof
EXCLUDES *collapse of a building or structure (E916)*
fall or jump from burning building (E890.8, E891.8)

✓4ᵗʰ **E883 Fall into hole or other opening in surface**
INCLUDES fall into: fall into:
cavity   shaft
dock   swimming pool
hole   tank
pit   well
quarry
EXCLUDES *fall into water NOS (E910.9)*
that resulting in drowning or submersion without mention
of injury (E910.0-E910.9)

E883.0 Accident from diving or jumping into water [swimming pool]
Strike or hit:
against bottom when jumping or diving into water
wall or board of swimming pool
water surface
EXCLUDES *diving with insufficient air supply (E913.2)*
effects of air pressure from diving (E902.2)

E883.1 Accidental fall into well

E883.2 Accidental fall into storm drain or manhole

E883.9 Fall into other hole or other opening in surface

✓4ᵗʰ **E884 Other fall from one level to another**

E884.0 Fall from playground equipment
EXCLUDES *recreational machinery (E919.8)*

E884.1 Fall from cliff

E884.2 Fall from chair

E884.3 Fall from wheelchair
Fall from motorized mobility scooter
Fall from motorized wheelchair

E884.4 Fall from bed

E884.5 Fall from other furniture

E884.6 Fall from commode
Toilet

E884.9 Other fall from one level to another
Fall from: Fall from:
embankment   stationary vehicle
haystack   tree

✓4ᵗʰ **E885 Fall on same level from slipping, tripping, or stumbling**

E885.0 Fall from (nonmotorized) scooter
EXCLUDES *fall from motorized mobility scooter (E884.3)*

E885.1 Fall from roller skates
Heelies   Wheelies
In-line skates

E885.2 Fall from skateboard

E885.3 Fall from skis

E885.4 Fall from snowboard

E885.9 Fall from other slipping, tripping, or stumbling
Fall on moving sidewalk

✓4ᵗʰ **E886 Fall on same level from collision, pushing, or shoving, by or with other person**
EXCLUDES *crushed or pushed by a crowd or human stampede (E917.1,*
E917.6)

E886.0 In sports
Tackles in sports
EXCLUDES *kicked, stepped on, struck by object, in sports*
(E917.0, E917.5)

E886.9 Other and unspecified
Fall from collision of pedestrian (conveyance) with another
pedestrian (conveyance)

E887 Fracture, cause unspecified

✓4ᵗʰ **E888 Other and unspecified fall**
Accidental fall NOS
Fall on same level NOS

E888.0 Fall resulting in striking against sharp object
Use additional external cause code to identify object (E920)

E888.1 Fall resulting in striking against other object

E888.8 Other fall

E888.9 Unspecified fall
Fall NOS

Accidents Caused by Fire and Flames (E890-E899)

INCLUDES asphyxia or poisoning due to conflagration or ignition
burning by fire
secondary fires resulting from explosion
EXCLUDES *arson (E968.0)*
fire in or on:
machinery (in operation) (E919.0-E919.9)
transport vehicle other than stationary vehicle
(E800.0-E845.9)
vehicle not elsewhere classifiable (E846-E848)

✓4ᵗʰ **E890 Conflagration in private dwelling**
INCLUDES conflagration in:
apartment
boarding house
camping place
caravan
farmhouse
house
lodging house
mobile home
private garage
rooming house
tenement
conflagration originating from sources classifiable to
E893-E898 in the above buildings

E890.0 Explosion caused by conflagration

E890.1 Fumes from combustion of polyvinylchloride [PVC] and similar material in conflagration

E890.2 Other smoke and fumes from conflagration
Carbon monoxide ⎫
Fumes NOS   ⎬ from conflagration in private
Smoke NOS   ⎭ building

E890.3 Burning caused by conflagration

E890.8 Other accident resulting from conflagration
Collapse of   ⎫
Fall from   ⎬ burning private
Hit by object falling from ⎪ building
Jump from   ⎭

E890.9 Unspecified accident resulting from conflagration in private dwelling

✓4ᵗʰ Fourth-digit Required   ►◄ Revised Text   ● New Code   ▲ Revised Code Title

☑4ᵗʰ **E891 Conflagration in other and unspecified building or structure**

Conflagration in:
- barn
- church
- convalescent and other residential home
- dormitory of educational institution
- factory
- farm outbuildings
- hospital
- hotel
- school
- store
- theater

Conflagration originating from sources classifiable to E893-E898, in the above buildings

E891.0 Explosion caused by conflagration

E891.1 Fumes from combustion of polyvinylchloride [PVC] and similar material in conflagration

E891.2 Other smoke and fumes from conflagration

Carbon monoxide ⎫
Fumes NOS ⎬ from conflagration in private
Smoke NOS ⎭ building or structure

E891.3 Burning caused by conflagration

E891.8 Other accident resulting from conflagration

Collapse of ⎫
Fall from ⎬ burning private
Hit by object falling from ⎬ building or
Jump from ⎭ structure

E891.9 Unspecified accident resulting from conflagration of other and unspecified building or structure

E892 Conflagration not in building or structure

Fire (uncontrolled) (in) (of):
- forest
- grass
- hay
- lumber
- mine

Fire (uncontrolled) (in) (of):
- prairie
- transport vehicle [any], except while in transit
- tunnel

☑4ᵗʰ **E893 Accident caused by ignition of clothing**

> **EXCLUDES** *ignition of clothing:*
> *from highly inflammable material (E894)*
> *with conflagration (E890.0-E892)*

E893.0 From controlled fire in private dwelling

Ignition of clothing from:
- normal fire (charcoal) (coal) (electric) (gas) (wood) in: ⎫
- brazier ⎬ in private dwelling
- fireplace ⎬ (as listed in
- furnace ⎬ E890)
- stove ⎭

E893.1 From controlled fire in other building or structure

Ignition of clothing from:
- normal fire (charcoal) (coal) (electric) (gas) (wood) in: ⎫
- brazier ⎬ in other building or
- fireplace ⎬ structure (as
- furnace ⎬ listed in E891)
- stove ⎭

E893.2 From controlled fire not in building or structure

Ignition of clothing from:
- bonfire (controlled)
- brazier fire (controlled), not in building or structure
- trash fire (controlled)

> **EXCLUDES** *conflagration not in building (E892)*
> *trash fire out of control (E892)*

E893.8 From other specified sources

Ignition of clothing from:
- blowlamp
- blowtorch
- burning bedspread
- candle
- cigar

Ignition of clothing from:
- cigarette
- lighter
- matches
- pipe
- welding torch

E893.9 Unspecified source

Ignition of clothing (from controlled fire NOS) (in building NOS) NOS

E894 Ignition of highly inflammable material

Ignition of:
- benzine ⎫
- gasoline ⎬
- fat ⎬ (with ignition of clothing)
- kerosene ⎬
- paraffin ⎬
- petrol ⎭

> **EXCLUDES** *ignition of highly inflammable material with:*
> *conflagration (E890.0-E892)*
> *explosion (E923.0-E923.9)*

E895 Accident caused by controlled fire in private dwelling

Burning by (flame of) normal fire (charcoal) (coal) (electric) (gas) (wood) in:
- brazier ⎫
- fireplace ⎬ in private dwelling (as listed in E890)
- furnace ⎬
- stove ⎭

> **EXCLUDES** *burning by hot objects not producing fire or flames (E924.0-E924.9)*
> *ignition of clothing from these sources (E893.0)*
> *poisoning by carbon monoxide from incomplete combustion of fuel (E867-E868.9)*
> *that with conflagration (E890.0-E890.9)*

E896 Accident caused by controlled fire in other and unspecified building or structure

Burning by (flame of) normal fire (charcoal) (coal)(electric)(gas)(wood) in:
- brazier ⎫
- fireplace ⎬ in other building or structure (as
- furnace ⎬ listed in E891)
- stove ⎭

> **EXCLUDES** *burning by hot objects not producing fire or flames (E924.0-E924.9)*
> *ignition of clothing from these sources (E893.1)*
> *poisoning by carbon monoxide from incomplete combustion of fuel (E867-E868.9)*
> *that with conflagration (E891.0-E891.9)*

E897 Accident caused by controlled fire not in building or structure

Burns from flame of:
- bonfire ⎫
- brazier fire, not in building or structure ⎬ controlled
- trash fire ⎭

> **EXCLUDES** *ignition of clothing from these sources (E893.2)*
> *trash fire out of control (E892)*
> *that with conflagration (E892)*

☑4ᵗʰ **E898 Accident caused by other specified fire and flames**

> **EXCLUDES** *conflagration (E890.0-E892)*
> *that with ignition of:*
> *clothing (E893.0-E893.9)*
> *highly inflammable material (E894)*

E898.0 Burning bedclothes

Bed set on fire NOS

E898.1 Other

Burning by:
- blowlamp
- blowtorch
- candle
- cigar
- cigarette
- fire in room NOS

Burning by:
- lamp
- lighter
- matches
- pipe
- welding torch

E899 Accident caused by unspecified fire

Burning NOS

Accidents Due to Natural and Environmental Factors (E900-E909)

☑️4ᵗʰ **E900 Excessive heat**

E900.0 Due to weather conditions
Excessive heat as the external cause of:
   ictus solaris
   siriasis
   sunstroke

E900.1 Of man-made origin
Heat (in):	Heat (in):
boiler room	furnace room
drying room	generated in transport vehicle
factory	kitchen

E900.9 Of unspecified origin

☑️4ᵗʰ **E901 Excessive cold**

E901.0 Due to weather conditions
Excessive cold as the cause of:
   chilblains NOS
   immersion foot

E901.1 Of man-made origin
Contact with or inhalation of:	Prolonged exposure in:
dry ice	deep freeze unit
liquid air	refrigerator
liquid hydrogen	
liquid nitrogen	

E901.8 Other specified origin

E901.9 Of unspecified origin

☑️4ᵗʰ **E902 High and low air pressure and changes in air pressure**

E902.0 Residence or prolonged visit at high altitude
Residence or prolonged visit at high altitude as the cause of:
   Acosta syndrome
   Alpine sickness
   altitude sickness
   Andes disease
   anoxia, hypoxia
   barotitis, barodontalgia, barosinusitis, otitic barotrauma
   hypobarism, hypobaropathy
   mountain sickness
   range disease

E902.1 In aircraft
Sudden change in air pressure in aircraft during ascent or descent as the cause of:
   aeroneurosis
   aviators' disease

E902.2 Due to diving
High air pressure from rapid descent in water
Reduction in atmospheric pressure while surfacing from deep water diving
   as the cause of:
   caisson disease
   divers' disease
   divers' palsy or paralysis

E902.8 Due to other specified causes
Reduction in atmospheric pressure while surfacing from underground

E902.9 Unspecified cause

E903 Travel and motion

☑️4ᵗʰ **E904 Hunger, thirst, exposure, and neglect**
> *EXCLUDES* *any condition resulting from homicidal intent (E968.0-E968.9)*
> *hunger, thirst, and exposure resulting from accidents connected with transport (E800.0-E848)*

E904.0 Abandonment or neglect of infants and helpless persons
Exposure to weather conditions
Hunger or thirst
   resulting from abandonment or neglect
Desertion of newborn
Inattention at or after birth
Lack of care (helpless person) (infant)
> *EXCLUDES* *criminal [purposeful] neglect (E968.4)*

E904.1 Lack of food
Lack of food as the cause of:
   inanition
   insufficient nourishment
   starvation
> *EXCLUDES* *hunger resulting from abandonment or neglect (E904.0)*

E904.2 Lack of water
Lack of water as the cause of:
   dehydration
   inanition
> *EXCLUDES* *dehydration due to acute fluid loss (276.51)*

E904.3 Exposure (to weather conditions), not elsewhere classifiable
Exposure NOS	Struck by hailstones
Humidity	
> *EXCLUDES* *struck by lightning (E907)*

E904.9 Privation, unqualified
Destitution

☑️4ᵗʰ **E905 Venomous animals and plants as the cause of poisoning and toxic reactions**
> *INCLUDES* chemical released by animal
> insects
> release of venom through fangs, hairs, spines, tentacles, and other venom apparatus
> *EXCLUDES* *eating of poisonous animals or plants (E865.0-E865.9)*

E905.0 Venomous snakes and lizards
Cobra	Mamba
Copperhead snake	Rattlesnake
Coral snake	Sea snake
Fer de lance	Snake (venomous)
Gila monster	Viper
Krait	Water moccasin
> *EXCLUDES* *bites of snakes and lizards known to be nonvenomous (E906.2)*

E905.1 Venomous spiders
Black widow spider	Tarantula (venomous)
Brown spider	

E905.2 Scorpion

E905.3 Hornets, wasps, and bees
Yellow jacket

E905.4 Centipede and venomous millipede (tropical)

E905.5 Other venomous arthropods
Sting of:
   ant
   caterpillar

E905.6 Venomous marine animals and plants
Puncture by sea urchin spine	Sting of:
Sting of:	sea anemone
coral	sea cucumber
jelly fish	other marine animal
nematocysts	or plant
> *EXCLUDES* *bites and other injuries caused by nonvenomous marine animal (E906.2-E906.8)*
> *bite of sea snake (venomous) (E905.0)*

E905.7 Poisoning and toxic reactions caused by other plants
Injection of poisons or toxins into or through skin by plant thorns, spines, or other mechanisms
> *EXCLUDES* *puncture wound NOS by plant thorns or spines (E920.8)*

E905.8 Other specified

E905.9 Unspecified
Sting NOS
Venomous bite NOS

☑️4ᵗʰ **E906 Other injury caused by animals**
> *EXCLUDES* *poisoning and toxic reactions caused by venomous animals and insects (E905.0-E905.9)*
> *road vehicle accident involving animals (E827.0-E828.9)*
> *tripping or falling over an animal (E885.9)*

E906.0 Dog bite

E906.1 Rat bite

☑️4ᵗʰ Fourth-digit Required   ▶◀ Revised Text   ● New Code   ▲ Revised Code Title

E Codes

E906.2–E911

E906.2 Bite of nonvenomous snakes and lizards

E906.3 Bite of other animal except arthropod
Cats   Rodents, except rats
Moray eel   Shark

E906.4 Bite of nonvenomous arthropod
Insect bite NOS

E906.5 Bite by unspecified animal
Animal bite NOS

E906.8 Other specified injury caused by animal
Butted by animal
Fallen on by horse or other animal, not being ridden
Gored by animal
Implantation of quills of porcupine
Pecked by bird
Run over by animal, not being ridden
Stepped on by animal, not being ridden
> *EXCLUDES injury by animal being ridden (E828.0-E828.9)*

E906.9 Unspecified injury caused by animal

E907 Lightning
> *EXCLUDES injury from:*
> *fall of tree or other object caused by lightning (E916)*
> *fire caused by lightning (E890.0-E892)*

✓4th E908 Cataclysmic storms, and floods resulting from storms
> *EXCLUDES collapse of dam or man-made structure causing flood (E909.3)*

E908.0 Hurricane
Storm surge
"Tidal wave" caused by storm action
Typhoon

E908.1 Tornado
Cyclone
Twisters

E908.2 Floods
Torrential rainfall
Flash flood
> *EXCLUDES collapse of dam or man-made structure causing flood (E909.3)*

E908.3 Blizzard (snow)(ice)

E908.4 Dust storm

E908.8 Other cataclysmic storms
Cloudburst

E908.9 Unspecified cataclysmic storms, and floods resulting from storms
Storm NOS

✓4th E909 Cataclysmic earth surface movements and eruptions

E909.0 Earthquakes

E909.1 Volcanic eruptions
Burns from lava
Ash inhalation

E909.2 Avalanche, landslide, or mudslide

E909.3 Collapse of dam or man-made structure

E909.4 Tidalwave caused by earthquake
Tidalwave NOS
Tsunami
> *EXCLUDES tidalwave caused by tropical storm (E908.0)*

E909.8 Other cataclysmic earth surface movements and eruptions

E909.9 Unspecified cataclysmic earth surface movements and eruptions

Accidents Caused by Submersion, Suffocation, and Foreign Bodies (E910-E915)

✓4th E910 Accidental drowning and submersion
> INCLUDES   immersion
> swimmers' cramp
> *EXCLUDES diving accident (NOS) (resulting in injury except drowning) (E883.0)*
> *diving with insufficient air supply (E913.2)*
> *drowning and submersion due to:*
> *cataclysm (E908-E909)*
> *machinery accident (E919.0-E919.9)*
> *transport accident (E800.0-E845.9)*
> *effect of high and low air pressure (E902.2)*
> *injury from striking against objects while in running water (E917.2)*

E910.0 While water-skiing
Fall from water skis with submersion or drowning
> *EXCLUDES accident to water-skier involving a watercraft and resulting in submersion or other injury (E830.4, E831.4)*

E910.1 While engaged in other sport or recreational activity with diving equipment
Scuba diving NOS
Skin diving NOS
Underwater spear fishing NOS

E910.2 While engaged in other sport or recreational activity without diving equipment
Fishing or hunting, except from boat or with diving equipment
Ice skating
Playing in water
Surfboarding
Swimming NOS
Voluntarily jumping from boat, not involved in accident, for swim NOS
Wading in water
> *EXCLUDES jumping into water to rescue another person (E910.3)*

E910.3 While swimming or diving for purposes other than recreation or sport
Marine salvage
Pearl diving
Placement of fishing nets   } (with diving equipment)
Rescue (attempt) of another person
Underwater construction or repairs

E910.4 In bathtub

E910.8 Other accidental drowning or submersion
Drowning in:
quenching tank
swimming pool

E910.9 Unspecified accidental drowning or submersion
Accidental fall into water NOS
Drowning NOS

E911 Inhalation and ingestion of food causing obstruction of respiratory tract or suffocation
Aspiration and inhalation of food [any] (into respiratory tract) NOS
Asphyxia by
Choked on   } food [including bone, seed in food, regurgitated food]
Suffocation by
Compression of trachea
Interruption of respiration   } by food lodged in esophagus
Obstruction of respiration
Obstruction of pharynx by food (bolus)
> *EXCLUDES injury, except asphyxia and obstruction of respiratory passage, caused by food (E915)*
> *obstruction of esophagus by food without mention of asphyxia or obstruction of respiratory passage (E915)*

E912 Inhalation and ingestion of other object causing obstruction of respiratory tract or suffocation

Aspiration and inhalation of foreign body except food (into respiratory tract) NOS
Foreign object [bean] [marble] in nose
Obstruction of pharynx by foreign body
Compression ⎫
Interruption of respiration ⎬ by foreign body in esophagus
Obstruction of respiration ⎭

> EXCLUDES injury, except asphyxia and obstruction of respiratory passage, caused by foreign body (E915)
> obstruction of esophagus by foreign body without mention of asphyxia or obstruction in respiratory passage (E915)

☑4ᵗʰ E913 Accidental mechanical suffocation

> EXCLUDES mechanical suffocation from or by:
> accidental inhalation or ingestion of:
> food (E911)
> foreign object (E912)
> cataclysm (E908-E909)
> explosion (E921.0-E921.9, E923.0-E923.9)
> machinery accident (E919.0-E919.9)

E913.0 In bed or cradle
> EXCLUDES suffocation by plastic bag (E913.1)

E913.1 By plastic bag

E913.2 Due to lack of air (in closed place)
Accidentally closed up in refrigerator or other airtight enclosed space
Diving with insufficient air supply
> EXCLUDES suffocation by plastic bag (E913.1)

E913.3 By falling earth or other substance
Cave-in NOS
> EXCLUDES cave-in caused by cataclysmic earth surface movements and eruptions (E909)
> struck by cave-in without asphyxiation or suffocation (E916)

E913.8 Other specified means
Accidental hanging, except in bed or cradle

E913.9 Unspecified means
Asphyxia, mechanical NOS
Strangulation NOS
Suffocation NOS

E914 Foreign body accidentally entering eye and adnexa
> EXCLUDES corrosive liquid (E924.1)

E915 Foreign body accidentally entering other orifice
> EXCLUDES aspiration and inhalation of foreign body, any, (into respiratory tract) NOS (E911-E912)

Other Accidents (E916-E928)

E916 Struck accidentally by falling object
Collapse of building, except on fire
Falling:
rock
snowslide NOS
stone
tree
Object falling from:
machine, not in operation
stationary vehicle

Code first:
collapse of building on fire (E890.0-E891.9)
falling object in:
cataclysm (E908-E909)
machinery accidents (E919.0-E919.9)
transport accidents (E800.0-E845.9)
vehicle accidents not elsewhere classifiable (E846-E848)
object set in motion by:
explosion (E921.0-E921.9, E923.0-E923.9)
firearm (E922.0-E922.9)
projected object (E917.0-E917.9)

☑4ᵗʰ E917 Striking against or struck accidentally by objects or persons

> INCLUDES bumping into or against ⎫
> colliding with ⎬ object (moving) (projected) (stationary)
> kicking against ⎪ pedestrian conveyance
> stepping on ⎪ person
> struck by ⎭

> EXCLUDES fall from:
> collision with another person, except when caused by a crowd (E886.0-E886.9)
> stumbling over object (E885.9)
> fall resulting in striking against object (E888.0, E888.1)
> injury caused by:
> assault (E960.0-E960.1, E967.0-E967.9)
> cutting or piercing instrument (E920.0-E920.9)
> explosion (E921.0-E921.9, E923.0-E923.9)
> firearm (E922.0-E922.9)
> machinery (E919.0-E919.9)
> transport vehicle (E800.0-E845.9)
> vehicle not elsewhere classifiable (E846-E848)

E917.0 In sports without subsequent fall
Kicked or stepped on during game (football) (rugby)
Struck by hit or thrown ball
Struck by hockey stick or puck

E917.1 Caused by a crowd, by collective fear or panic without subsequent fall
Crushed ⎫
Pushed ⎬ by crowd or human stampede
Stepped on ⎭

E917.2 In running water without subsequent fall
> EXCLUDES drowning or submersion (E910.0-E910.9)
> that in sports (E917.0, E917.5)

E917.3 Furniture without subsequent fall
> EXCLUDES fall from furniture (E884.2, E884.4-E884.5)

E917.4 Other stationary object without subsequent fall
Bath tub
Fence
Lamp-post

E917.5 Object in sports with subsequent fall
Knocked down while boxing

E917.6 Caused by a crowd, by collective fear or panic with subsequent fall

E917.7 Furniture with subsequent fall
> EXCLUDES fall from furniture (E884.2, E884.4-E884.5)

E917.8 Other stationary object with subsequent fall
Bath tub
Fence
Lamp-post

E917.9 Other striking against with or without subsequent fall

E918 Caught accidentally in or between objects
Caught, crushed, jammed, or pinched in or between moving or stationary objects, such as:
escalator
folding object
hand tools, appliances, or implements
sliding door and door frame
under packing crate
washing machine wringer
> EXCLUDES injury caused by:
> cutting or piercing instrument (E920.0-E920.9)
> machinery (E919.0-E919.9)
> mechanism or component of firearm and air gun (E928.7)
> transport vehicle (E800.0-E845.9)
> vehicle not elsewhere classifiable (E846-E848)
> struck accidentally by:
> falling object (E916)
> object (moving) (projected) (E917.0-E917.9)

☑4ᵗʰ Fourth-digit Required   ►◄ Revised Text   ● New Code   ▲ Revised Code Title

✓4ᵗʰ **E919** **Accidents caused by machinery**

INCLUDES
burned by
caught in (moving parts of)
collapse of
crushed by
cut or pierced by
drowning or submersion caused by
expolosion of, on, in
fall from or into moving part of
fire starting in or on   machinery
mechanical suffocation caused by   (accident)
object falling from, on, in motion
    by
overturning of
pinned under
run over by
struck by
thrown from

caught between machinery and other object
machinery accident NOS

EXCLUDES accidents involving machinery, not in operation (E884.9,
    E916-E918)
    injury caused by:
        electric current in connection with machinery
            (E925.0-E925.9)
        escalator (E880.0, E918)
        explosion of pressure vessel in connection with
            machinery (E921.0-E921.9)
        mechanism or component of firearm and air gun
            (E928.7)
        moving sidewalk (E885.9)
        powered hand tools, appliances, and implements
            (E916-E918, E920.0-E921.9, E923.0-E926.9)
        transport vehicle accidents involving machinery
            (E800.0-E848)
        poisoning by carbon monoxide generated by machine
            (E868.8)

E919.0 Agricultural machines
Animal-powered   Farm tractor
    agricultural machine   Harvester
Combine   Hay mower or rake
Derrick, hay   Reaper
Farm machinery NOS   Thresher
EXCLUDES that in transport under own power on the highway
    (E810.0-E819.9)
    that being towed by another vehicle on the
        highway (E810.0-E819.9, E827.0-E827.9,
        E829.0-E829.9)
    that involved in accident classifiable to E820-E829
        (E820.0-E829.9)

E919.1 Mining and earth-drilling machinery
Bore or drill (land) (seabed)
Shaft hoist
Shaft lift
Under-cutter
EXCLUDES coal car, tram, truck, and tub in mine (E846)

E919.2 Lifting machines and appliances
Chain hoist
Crane
Derrick
Elevator (building) (grain)   except in agricultural
Forklift truck   or mining
Lift   operations
Pulley block
Winch
EXCLUDES that being towed by another vehicle on the
    highway (E810.0-E819.9, E827.0-E827.9,
    E829.0-829.9)
    that in transport under own power on the highway
        (E810.0-E819.9)
    that involved in accident classifiable to E820-E829
        (E820.0-E829.9)

E919.3 Metalworking machines
Abrasive wheel   Metal:
Forging machine   milling machine
Lathe   power press
Mechanical shears   rolling-mill
Metal: sawing machine
    drilling machine

E919.4 Woodworking and forming machines
Band saw   Overhead plane
Bench saw   Powered saw
Circular saw   Radial saw
Molding machine   Sander
EXCLUDES hand saw (E920.1)

E919.5 Prime movers, except electrical motors
Gas turbine
Internal combustion engine
Steam engine
Water driven turbine
EXCLUDES that being towed by other vehicle on the highway
    (E810.0-E819.9, E827.0-E827.9,
    E829.0-E829.9)
    that in transport under own power on the highway
        (E810.0-E819.9)

E919.6 Transmission machinery
Transmission: Transmission:
    belt   pinion
    cable   pulley
    chain   shaft
    gear

E919.7 Earth moving, scraping, and other excavating machines
Bulldozer   Steam shovel
Road scraper
EXCLUDES that being towed by other vehicle on the highway
    (E810.0-E819.9, E827.0-E827.9,
    E829.0-E829.9)
    that in transport under own power on the highway
        (E810.0-E819.9)

E919.8 Other specified machinery
Machines for manufacture of:
    clothing
    foodstuffs and beverages
    paper
Printing machine
Recreational machinery
Spinning, weaving, and textile machines

E919.9 Unspecified machinery

✓4ᵗʰ **E920** **Accidents caused by cutting and piercing instruments or
objects**

INCLUDES
accidental injury (by) object   edged
                                 pointed
                                 sharp
EXCLUDES injury caused by mechanism or component of firearm and
    air gun (E928.7)

E920.0 Powered lawn mower

E920.1 Other powered hand tools
Any powered hand tool [compressed air] [electric]
    [explosive cartridge] [hydraulic power], such as:
    drill
    hand saw
    hedge clipper
    rivet gun
    snow blower
    staple gun
EXCLUDES band saw (E919.4)
    bench saw (E919.4)

E920.2 Powered household appliances and implements
Blender   Electric:
Electric: knife
    beater or mixer   sewing machine
    can opener   Garbage disposal appliance
    fan

E920.3 Knives, swords, and daggers

E920.4 Other hand tools and implements

Axe	Paper cutter
Can opener NOS	Pitchfork
Chisel	Rake
Fork	Scissors
Hand saw	Screwdriver
Hoe	Sewing machine, not powered
Ice pick	Shovel
Needle (sewing)	

E920.5 Hypodermic needle
    Contaminated needle
    Needle stick

E920.8 Other specified cutting and piercing instruments or objects

Arrow	Nail
Broken glass	Plant thorn
Dart	Splinter
Edge of stiff paper	Tin can lid
Lathe turnings	

> **EXCLUDES** *animal spines or quills (E906.8)*
> *flying glass due to explosion (E921.0-E923.9)*

E920.9 Unspecified cutting and piercing instrument or object

☑4ᵗʰ **E921 Accident caused by explosion of pressure vessel**

> **INCLUDES** accidental explosion of pressure vessels, whether or not part of machinery

> **EXCLUDES** *explosion of pressure vessel on transport vehicle (E800.0-E845.9)*

E921.0 Boilers

E921.1 Gas cylinders
    Air tank   Pressure gas tank

E921.8 Other specified pressure vessels
    Aerosol can   Tin can lid
    Automobile tire

E921.9 Unspecified pressure vessel

☑4ᵗʰ **E922 Accident caused by firearm, and air gun missile**

> **EXCLUDES** *injury caused by mechanism or component of firearm and air gun (E928.7)*

E922.0 Handgun
    Pistol   Revolver

> **EXCLUDES** *Verey pistol (E922.8)*

E922.1 Shotgun (automatic)

E922.2 Hunting rifle

E922.3 Military firearms
    Army rifle   Machine gun

E922.4 Air gun
    BB gun   Pellet gun

E922.5 Paintball gun

E922.8 Other specified firearm missile
    Verey pistol [flare]

E922.9 Unspecified firearm missile
    Gunshot wound NOS
    Shot NOS

☑4ᵗʰ **E923 Accident caused by explosive material**

> **INCLUDES** flash burns and other injuries resulting from explosion of explosive material
> ignition of highly explosive material with explosion

> **EXCLUDES** *explosion:*
> *in or on machinery (E919.0-E919.9)*
> *on any transport vehicle, except stationary motor vehicle (E800.0-E848)*
> *with conflagration (E890.0, E891.0,E892)*
> *injury caused by mechanism or component of firearm and air gun (E928.7)*
> *secondary fires resulting from explosion (E890.0-E899)*

E923.0 Fireworks

E923.1 Blasting materials

Blasting cap	Dynamite
Detonator	Explosive [any] used in blasting operations

E923.2 Explosive gases

Acetylene	Fire damp
Butane	Gasoline fumes
Coal gas	Methane
Explosion in mine NOS	Propane

E923.8 Other explosive materials

Bomb	Torpedo
Explosive missile	Explosion in munitions:
Grenade	dump
Mine	factory
Shell	

E923.9 Unspecified explosive material
    Explosion NOS

☑4ᵗʰ **E924 Accident caused by hot substance or object, caustic or corrosive material, and steam**

> **EXCLUDES** *burning NOS (E899)*
> *chemical burn resulting from swallowing a corrosive substance (E860.0-E864.4)*
> *fire caused by these substances and objects (E890.0-E894)*
> *radiation burns (E926.0-E926.9)*
> *therapeutic misadventures (E870.0-E876.9)*

E924.0 Hot liquids and vapors, including steam
    Burning or scalding by:
        boiling water
        hot or boiling liquids not primarily caustic or corrosive
        liquid metal
        steam
        other hot vapor

> **EXCLUDES** *hot (boiling) tap water (E924.2)*

E924.1 Caustic and corrosive substances
    Burning by:
        acid [any kind]
        ammonia
        caustic oven cleaner or other substance
        corrosive substance
        lye
        vitriol

E924.2 Hot (boiling) tap water

E924.8 Other
    Burning by:
        heat from electric heating appliance
        hot object NOS
        light bulb
        steam pipe

E924.9 Unspecified

☑4ᵗʰ **E925 Accident caused by electric current**

> **INCLUDES** electric current from exposed wire, faulty appliance, high voltage cable, live rail, or open electric socket as the cause of:
>   burn
>   cardiac fibrillation
>   convulsion
>   electric shock
>   electrocution
>   puncture wound
>   respiratory paralysis

> **EXCLUDES** *burn by heat from electrical appliance (E924.8)*
> *lightning (E907)*

E925.0 Domestic wiring and appliances

E925.1 Electric power generating plants, distribution stations, transmission lines
    Broken power line

E925.2 Industrial wiring, appliances, and electrical machinery
    Conductors
    Control apparatus
    Electrical equipment and machinery
    Transformers

E925.8 Other electric current
    Wiring and appliances in or on:
        farm [not farmhouse]
        outdoors
        public building
        residential institutions
        schools

☑4ᵗʰ Fourth-digit Required   ▶◀ Revised Text   ● New Code   ▲ Revised Code Title

E925.9 Unspecified electric current
Burns or other injury from electric current NOS
Electric shock NOS
Electrocution NOS

✓4th E926 Exposure to radiation

EXCLUDES *abnormal reaction to or complication of treatment without mention of misadventure (E879.2)*
atomic power plant malfunction in water transport (E838.0-E838.9)
misadventure to patient in surgical and medical procedures (E873.2-E873.3)
use of radiation in war operations (E996-E997.9)

E926.0 Radiofrequency radiation

Overexposure to: | from:
microwave radiation | high-powered radio and
radar radiation | television transmitters
radiofrequency | industrial radiofrequency
radiofrequency | induction heaters
  radiation [any] | radar installations

E926.1 Infrared heaters and lamps
Exposure to infrared radiation from heaters and lamps as the cause of:
blistering
burning
charring
inflammatory change
EXCLUDES *physical contact with heater or lamp (E924.8)*

E926.2 Visible and ultraviolet light sources
Arc lamps
Black light sources
Electrical welding arc
Oxygas welding torch
Sun rays
Tanning bed
EXCLUDES *excessive heat from these sources (E900.1-E900.9)*

E926.3 X-rays and other electromagnetic ionizing radiation
Gamma rays
X-rays (hard) (soft)

E926.4 Lasers

E926.5 Radioactive isotopes
Radiobiologicals
Radiopharmaceuticals

E926.8 Other specified radiation
Artificially accelerated beams of ionized particles generated by:
betatrons
synchrotrons

E926.9 Unspecified radiation
Radiation NOS

✓4th E927 Overexertion and strenuous and repetitive movements or loads

Use additional code to identify activity (E001-E030)

E927.0 Overexertion from sudden strenuous movement
Sudden trauma from strenuous movement

E927.1 Overexertion from prolonged static position
Overexertion from maintaining prolonged positions, such as:
holding
sitting
standing

E927.2 Excessive physical exertion from prolonged activity

E927.3 Cumulative trauma from repetitive motion
Cumulative trauma from repetitive movements

E927.4 Cumulative trauma from repetitive impact

E927.8 Other overexertion and strenuous and repetitive movements or loads

E927.9 Unspecified overexertion and strenuous and repetitive movements or loads

✓4th E928 Other and unspecified environmental and accidental causes

E928.0 Prolonged stay in weightless environment
Weightlessness in spacecraft (simulator)

E928.1 Exposure to noise
Noise (pollution)
Sound waves
Supersonic waves

E928.2 Vibration

E928.3 Human bite

E928.4 External constriction caused by hair

E928.5 External constriction caused by other object

E928.6 Environmental exposure to harmful algae and toxins
Algae bloom NOS   Florida red tide
Blue-green algae bloom   Harmful algae bloom
Brown tide   Pfiesteria piscicida
Cyanobacteria bloom   Red tide

E928.7 Mechanism or component of firearm and air gun
Injury due to:
explosion of gun parts
recoil
Pierced, cut, crushed, or pinched by slide, trigger mechanism, scope, or other gun part
Powder burn from firearm or air gun
EXCLUDES *accident caused by firearm and air gun missile (E922.0-E922.9)*

E928.8 Other

E928.9 Unspecified accident
Accident NOS
Blow NOS | stated as accidentally
Casualty (not due to war) | inflicted
Decapitation

Knocked down
Killed | stated as accidentally
Injury [any part of body, or | inflicted, but not
  unspecified] | otherwise
Mangled | specified
Wound
EXCLUDES *fracture, cause unspecified (E887)*
injuries undetermined whether accidentally or purposely inflicted (E980.0-E989)

Late Effects Of Accidental Injury (E929)

NOTE This category is to be used to indicate accidental injury as the cause of death or disability from late effects, which are themselves classifiable elsewhere. The "late effects" include conditions reported as such, or as sequelae which may occur at any time after the attempted suicide or self-inflicted injury.

✓4th E929 Late effects of accidental injury

EXCLUDES *late effects of:*
surgical and medical procedures (E870.0-E879.9)
therapeutic use of drugs and medicines (E930.0-E949.9)

E929.0 Late effects of motor vehicle accident
Late effects of accidents classifiable to E810-E825

E929.1 Late effects of other transport accident
Late effects of accidents classifiable to E800-E807, E826-E838, E840-E848

E929.2 Late effects of accidental poisoning
Late effects of accidents classifiable to E850-E858, E860-E869

E929.3 Late effects of accidental fall
Late effects of accidents classifiable to E880-E888

E929.4 Late effects of accident caused by fire
Late effects of accidents classifiable to E890-E899

E929.5 Late effects of accident due to natural and environmental factors
Late effects of accidents classifiable to E900-E909

E929.8 Late effects of other accidents
Late effects of accidents classifiable to E910-E928.8

E929.9 Late effects of unspecified accident
Late effects of accidents classifiable to E928.9

✓4th Fourth-digit Required   ▶◄ Revised Text   ● New Code   ▲ Revised Code Title

Drugs, Medicinal And Biological Substances Causing Adverse Effects In Therapeutic Use (E930-E949)

INCLUDES correct drug properly administered in therapeutic or prophylactic dosage, as the cause of any adverse effect including allergic or hypersensitivity reactions

EXCLUDES accidental overdose of drug and wrong drug given or taken in error (E850.0-E858.9)
accidents in the technique of administration of drug or biological substance, such as accidental puncture during injection, or contamination of drug (E870.0-E876.9)
administration with suicidal or homicidal intent or intent to harm, or in circumstances classifiable to E950.0-E950.5, E962.0, E980.0-E980.5

NOTE See Alphabetic Index for more complete list of specific drugs to be classified under the fourth digit subdivisions. The American Hospital Formulary numbers can be used to classify new drugs listed by the American Hospital Formulary Service (AHFS). See Appendix C.

✓4th **E930 Antibiotics**

EXCLUDES that used as eye, ear, nose, and throat [ENT], and local anti-infectives (E946.0-E946.9)

E930.0 Penicillins
Natural
Synthetic
Semisynthetic, such as:
  ampicillin
Semisynthetic, such as:
  cloxacillin
  nafcillin
  oxacillin

E930.1 Antifungal antibiotics
Amphotericin B
Griseofulvin
Hachimycin [trichomycin]
Nystatin

E930.2 Chloramphenicol group
Chloramphenicol
Thiamphenicol

E930.3 Erythromycin and other macrolides
Oleandomycin
Spiramycin

E930.4 Tetracycline group
Doxycycline
Minocycline
Oxytetracycline

E930.5 Cephalosporin group
Cephalexin
Cephaloglycin
Cephaloridine
Cephalothin

E930.6 Antimycobacterial antibiotics
Cycloserine
Kanamycin
Rifampin
Streptomycin

E930.7 Antineoplastic antibiotics
Actinomycins, such as:
  Bleomycin
  Cactinomycin
  Dactinomycin
Actinomycins, such as:
  Daunorubicin
  Mitomycin

EXCLUDES other antineoplastic drugs (E933.1)

E930.8 Other specified antibiotics

E930.9 Unspecified antibiotic

✓4th **E931 Other anti-infectives**

EXCLUDES ENT, and local anti-infectives (E946.0-E946.9)

E931.0 Sulfonamides
Sulfadiazine
Sulfafurazole
Sulfamethoxazole

E931.1 Arsenical anti-infectives

E931.2 Heavy metal anti-infectives
Compounds of:
  antimony
  bismuth
Compounds of:
  lead
  mercury

EXCLUDES mercurial diuretics (E944.0)

E931.3 Quinoline and hydroxyquinoline derivatives
Chiniofon
Diiodohydroxyquin

EXCLUDES antimalarial drugs (E931.4)

E931.4 Antimalarials and drugs acting on other blood protozoa
Chloroquine phosphate
Cycloguanil
Primaquine
Proguanil [chloroguanide]
Pyrimethamine
Quinine (sulphate)

E931.5 Other antiprotozoal drugs
Emetine

E931.6 Anthelmintics
Hexylresorcinol
Male fern oleoresin
Piperazine
Thiabendazole

E931.7 Antiviral drugs
Methisazone

EXCLUDES amantadine (E936.4)
cytarabine (E933.1)
idoxuridine (E946.5)

E931.8 Other antimycobacterial drugs
Ethambutol
Ethionamide
Isoniazid
Para-aminosalicylic acid derivatives
Sulfones

E931.9 Other and unspecified anti-infectives
Flucytosine
Nitrofuranderivatives

✓4th **E932 Hormones and synthetic substitutes**

E932.0 Adrenal cortical steroids
Cortisone derivatives
Desoxycorticosterone derivatives
Fluorinated corticosteroid

E932.1 Androgens and anabolic congeners
Nandrolone phenpropionate
Oxymetholone
Testosterone and preparations

E932.2 Ovarian hormones and synthetic substitutes
Contraceptives, oral
Estrogens
Estrogens and progestogens combined
Progestogens

E932.3 Insulins and antidiabetic agents
Acetohexamide
Biguanide derivatives, oral
Chlorpropamide
Glucagon
Insulin
Phenformin
Sulfonylurea derivatives, oral
Tolbutamide

EXCLUDES adverse effect of insulin administered for shock therapy (E879.3)

E932.4 Anterior pituitary hormones
Corticotropin
Gonadotropin
Somatotropin [growth hormone]

E932.5 Posterior pituitary hormones
Vasopressin

EXCLUDES oxytocic agents (E945.0)

E932.6 Parathyroid and parathyroid derivatives

E932.7 Thyroid and thyroid derivatives
Dextrothyroxine
Levothyroxine sodium
Liothyronine
Thyroglobulin

E932.8 Antithyroid agents
Iodides
Thiouracil
Thiourea

E932.9 Other and unspecified hormones and synthetic substitutes

✓4th **E933 Primarily systemic agents**

E933.0 Antiallergic and antiemetic drugs
Antihistamines
Chlorpheniramine
Diphenhydramine
Diphenylpyraline
Thonzylamine
Tripelennamine

EXCLUDES phenothiazine-based tranquilizers (E939.1)

E933.1 Antineoplastic and immunosuppressive drugs
Azathioprine
Busulfan
Chlorambucil
Cyclophosphamide
Cytarabine
Fluorouracil
Mechlorethamine hydrochloride
Mercaptopurine
Triethylenethiophosphoramide [thio-TEPA]

EXCLUDES antineoplastic antibiotics (E930.7)

E933.2 Acidifying agents

E933.3 Alkalizing agents

E933.4 Enzymes, not elsewhere classified
Penicillinase

E933.5 Vitamins, not elsewhere classified
Vitamin A
Vitamin D
EXCLUDES nicotinic acid (E942.2)
vitamin K (E934.3)

E933.6 Oral bisphosphonates

E933.7 Intravenous bisphosphonates

E933.8 Other systemic agents, not elsewhere classified
Heavy metal antagonists

E933.9 Unspecified systemic agent

✓4th **E934 Agents primarily affecting blood constituents**

E934.0 Iron and its compounds
Ferric salts
Ferrous sulphate and other ferrous salts

E934.1 Liver preparations and other antianemic agents
Folic acid

E934.2 Anticoagulants
Coumarin   Prothrombin synthesis inhibitor
Heparin   Warfarin sodium
Phenindione

E934.3 Vitamin K [phytonadione]

E934.4 Fibrinolysis-affecting drugs
Aminocaproic acid   Streptokinase
Streptodornase   Urokinase

E934.5 Anticoagulant antagonists and other coagulants
Hexadimethrine bromide
Protamine sulfate

E934.6 Gamma globulin

E934.7 Natural blood and blood products
Blood plasma   Packed red cells
Human fibrinogen   Whole blood

E934.8 Other agents affecting blood constituents
Macromolecular blood substitutes

E934.9 Unspecified agent affecting blood constituents

✓4th **E935 Analgesics, antipyretics, and antirheumatics**

E935.0 Heroin
Diacetylmorphine

E935.1 Methadone

E935.2 Other opiates and related narcotics
Codeine [methylmorphine]
Meperidine [pethidine]
Morphine
Opium (alkaloids)

E935.3 Salicylates
Acetylsalicylic acid [aspirin]
Amino derivatives of salicylic acid
Salicylic acid salts

E935.4 Aromatic analgesics, not elsewhere classified
Acetanilid
Paracetamol [acetaminophen]
Phenacetin [acetophenetidin]

E935.5 Pyrazole derivatives
Aminophenazone [aminopyrine]
Phenylbutazone

E935.6 Antirheumatics [antiphlogistics]
Gold salts   Indomethacin
EXCLUDES salicylates (E935.3)
steroids (E932.0)

E935.7 Other non-narcotic analgesics
Pyrabital

E935.8 Other specified analgesics and antipyretics
Pentazocine

E935.9 Unspecified analgesic and antipyretic

✓4th **E936 Anticonvulsants and anti-Parkinsonism drugs**

E936.0 Oxazolidine derivatives
Paramethadione   Trimethadione

E936.1 Hydantoin derivatives
Phenytoin

E936.2 Succinimides
Ethosuximide   Phensuximide

E936.3 Other and unspecified anticonvulsants
Beclamide
Primidone

E936.4 Anti-Parkinsonism drugs
Amantadine
Ethopropazine [profenamine]
Levodopa [L-dopa]

✓4th **E937 Sedatives and hypnotics**

E937.0 Barbiturates
Amobarbital [amylobarbitone]
Barbital [barbitone]
Butabarbital [butabarbitone]
Pentobarbital [pentobarbitone]
Phenobarbital [phenobarbitone]
Secobarbital [quinalbarbitone]
EXCLUDES thiobarbiturates (E938.3)

E937.1 Chloral hydrate group

E937.2 Paraldehyde

E937.3 Bromine compounds
Bromide
Carbromal (derivatives)

E937.4 Methaqualone compounds

E937.5 Glutethimide group

E937.6 Mixed sedatives, not elsewhere classified

E937.8 Other sedatives and hypnotics

E937.9 Unspecified
Sleeping:
drug
pill } NOS
tablet

✓4th **E938 Other central nervous system depressants and anesthetics**

E938.0 Central nervous system muscle-tone depressants
Chlorphenesin (carbamate)
Mephenesin
Methocarbamol

E938.1 Halothane

E938.2 Other gaseous anesthetics
Ether
Halogenated hydrocarbon derivatives, except halothane
Nitrous oxide

E938.3 Intravenous anesthetics
Ketamine
Methohexital [methohexitone]
Thiobarbiturates, such as thiopental sodium

E938.4 Other and unspecified general anesthetics

E938.5 Surface and infiltration anesthetics
Cocaine
Lidocaine [lignocaine]
Procaine
Tetracaine

E938.6 Peripheral nerve- and plexus-blocking anesthetics

E938.7 Spinal anesthetics

E938.9 Other and unspecified local anesthetics

✓4th **E939 Psychotropic agents**

E939.0 Antidepressants
Amitriptyline   Monoamine oxidase
Imipramine   [MAO] inhibitors

E939.1 Phenothiazine-based tranquilizers
Chlorpromazine   Prochlorperazine
Fluphenazine   Promazine
Phenothiazine

E939.2 Butyrophenone-based tranquilizers
Haloperidol   Trifluperidol
Spiperone

✓4th Fourth-digit Required   ▶◀ Revised Text   ● New Code   ▲ Revised Code Title

E939.3 Other antipsychotics, neuroleptics, and major tranquilizers

E939.4 Benzodiazepine-based tranquilizers
Chlordiazepoxide   Lorazepam
Diazepam   Medazepam
Flurazepam   Nitrazepam

E939.5 Other tranquilizers
Hydroxyzine   Meprobamate

E939.6 Psychodysleptics [hallucinogens]
Cannabis (derivatives)   Mescaline
Lysergide [LSD]   Psilocin
Marihuana (derivatives)   Psilocybin

E939.7 Psychostimulants
Amphetamine   Caffeine
EXCLUDES *central appetite depressants (E947.0)*

E939.8 Other psychotropic agents

E939.9 Unspecified psychotropic agent

✓4th **E940 Central nervous system stimulants**

E940.0 Analeptics
Lobeline   Nikethamide

E940.1 Opiate antagonists
Levallorphan   Naloxone
Nalorphine

E940.8 Other specified central nervous system stimulants

E940.9 Unspecified central nervous system stimulant

✓4th **E941 Drugs primarily affecting the autonomic nervous system**

E941.0 Parasympathomimetics [cholinergics]
Acetylcholine
Anticholinesterase:
  organophosphorus
  reversible
Pilocarpine

E941.1 Parasympatholytics [anticholinergics and antimuscarinics] and spasmolytics
Atropine   Hyoscine [scopolamine]
Homatropine   Quaternary ammonium derivatives
EXCLUDES *papaverine (E942.5)*

E941.2 Sympathomimetics [adrenergics]
Epinephrine [adrenalin]
Levarterenol [noradrenalin]

E941.3 Sympatholytics [antiadrenergics]
Phenoxybenzamine
Tolazolinehydrochloride

E941.9 Unspecified drug primarily affecting the autonomic nervous system

✓4th **E942 Agents primarily affecting the cardiovascular system**

E942.0 Cardiac rhythm regulators
Practolol   Propranolol
Procainamide   Quinidine

E942.1 Cardiotonic glycosides and drugs of similar action
Digitalis glycosides   Strophanthins
Digoxin

E942.2 Antilipemic and antiarteriosclerotic drugs
Cholestyramine   Nicotinic acid derivatives
Clofibrate   Sitosterols
EXCLUDES *dextrothyroxine (E932.7)*

E942.3 Ganglion-blocking agents
Pentamethonium bromide

E942.4 Coronary vasodilators
Dipyridamole   Nitrites
Nitrates [nitroglycerin] Prenylamine

E942.5 Other vasodilators
Cyclandelate   Hydralazine
Diazoxide   Papaverine

E942.6 Other antihypertensive agents
Clonidine   Rauwolfia alkaloids
Guanethidine   Reserpine

E942.7 Antivaricose drugs, including sclerosing agents
Monoethanolamine   Zinc salts

E942.8 Capillary-active drugs
Adrenochrome derivatives Metaraminol
Bioflavonoids

E942.9 Other and unspecified agents primarily affecting the cardiovascular system

✓4th **E943 Agents primarily affecting gastrointestinal system**

E943.0 Antacids and antigastric secretion drugs
Aluminum hydroxide   Magnesium trisilicate

E943.1 Irritant cathartics
Bisacodyl   Phenolphthalein
Castor oil

E943.2 Emollient cathartics
Sodium dioctyl sulfosuccinate

E943.3 Other cathartics, including intestinal atonia drugs
Magnesium sulfate

E943.4 Digestants
Pancreatin   Pepsin
Papain

E943.5 Antidiarrheal drugs
Bismuth subcarbonate   Kaolin
Pectin
EXCLUDES *anti-infectives (E930.0-E931.9)*

E943.6 Emetics

E943.8 Other specified agents primarily affecting the gastrointestinal system

E943.9 Unspecified agent primarily affecting the gastrointestinal system

✓4th **E944 Water, mineral, and uric acid metabolism drugs**

E944.0 Mercurial diuretics
Chlormerodrin   Mercurophylline
Mercaptomerin   Mersalyl

E944.1 Purine derivative diuretics
Theobromine
Theophylline
EXCLUDES *aminophylline [theophylline ethylenediamine] (E945.7)*

E944.2 Carbonic acid anhydrase inhibitors
Acetazolamide

E944.3 Saluretics
Benzothiadiazides   Chlorothiazide group

E944.4 Other diuretics
Ethacrynic acid   Furosemide

E944.5 Electrolytic, caloric, and water-balance agents

E944.6 Other mineral salts, not elsewhere classified

E944.7 Uric acid metabolism drugs
Cinchophen and congeners Phenoquin
Colchicine   Probenecid

✓4th **E945 Agents primarily acting on the smooth and skeletal muscles and respiratory system**

E945.0 Oxytocic agents
Ergot alkaloids   Prostaglandins

E945.1 Smooth muscle relaxants
Adiphenine
Metaproterenol [orciprenaline]
EXCLUDES *papaverine (E942.5)*

E945.2 Skeletal muscle relaxants
Alcuronium chloride
Suxamethonium chloride

E945.3 Other and unspecified drugs acting on muscles

E945.4 Antitussives
Dextromethorphan
Pipazethate hydrochloride

E945.5 **Expectorants**
Acetylcysteine
Cocillana
Guaifenesin [glyceryl guaiacolate]
Ipecacuanha
Terpin hydrate

E945.6 **Anti-common cold drugs**

E945.7 **Antiasthmatics**
Aminophylline [theophylline ethylenediamine]

E945.8 **Other and unspecified respiratory drugs**

✓4th **E946 Agents primarily affecting skin and mucous membrane, ophthalmological, otorhinolaryngological, and dental drugs**

E946.0 **Local anti-infectives and anti-inflammatory drugs**

E946.1 **Antipruritics**

E946.2 **Local astringents and local detergents**

E946.3 **Emollients, demulcents, and protectants**

E946.4 **Keratolytics, kerstoplastics, other hair treatment drugs and preparations**

E946.5 **Eye anti-infectives and other eye drugs**
Idoxuridine

E946.6 **Anti-infectives and other drugs and preparations for ear, nose, and throat**

E946.7 **Dental drugs topically applied**

E946.8 **Other agents primarily affecting skin and mucous membrane**
Spermicides

E946.9 **Unspecified agent primarily affecting skin and mucous membrane**

✓4th **E947 Other and unspecified drugs and medicinal substances**

E947.0 **Dietetics**

E947.1 **Lipotropic drugs**

E947.2 **Antidotes and chelating agents, not elsewhere classified**

E947.3 **Alcohol deterrents**

E947.4 **Pharmaceutical excipients**

E947.8 **Other drugs and medicinal substances**
Contrast media used for diagnostic x-ray procedures
Diagnostic agents and kits

E947.9 **Unspecified drug or medicinal substance**

✓4th **E948 Bacterial vaccines**

E948.0 **BCG vaccine**

E948.1 **Typhoid and paratyphoid**

E948.2 **Cholera**

E948.3 **Plague**

E948.4 **Tetanus**

E948.5 **Diphtheria**

E948.6 **Pertussis vaccine, including combinations with a pertussis component**

E948.8 **Other and unspecified bacterial vaccines**

E948.9 **Mixed bacterial vaccines, except combinations with a pertussis component**

✓4th **E949 Other vaccines and biological substances**
EXCLUDES *gamma globulin (E934.6)*

E949.0 **Smallpox vaccine**

E949.1 **Rabies vaccine**

E949.2 **Typhus vaccine**

E949.3 **Yellow fever vaccine**

E949.4 **Measles vaccine**

E949.5 **Poliomyelitis vaccine**

E949.6 **Other and unspecified viral and rickettsial vaccines**
Mumps vaccine

E949.7 **Mixed viral-rickettsial and bacterial vaccines, except combinations with a pertussis component**
EXCLUDES *combinations with a pertussis component (E948.6)*

E949.9 **Other and unspecified vaccines and biological substances**

Suicide and Self-inflicted Injury (E950-E959)

INCLUDES   injuries in suicide and attempted suicide
self-inflicted injuries specified as intentional

✓4th **E950 Suicide and self-inflicted poisoning by solid or liquid substances**

E950.0 **Analgesics, antipyretics, and antirheumatics**

E950.1 **Barbiturates**

E950.2 **Other sedatives and hypnotics**

E950.3 **Tranquilizers and other psychotropic agents**

E950.4 **Other specified drugs and medicinal substances**

E950.5 **Unspecified drug or medicinal substance**

E950.6 **Agricultural and horticultural chemical and pharmaceutical preparations other than plant foods and fertilizers**

E950.7 **Corrosive and caustic substances**
Suicide and self-inflicted poisoning by substances classifiable to E864

E950.8 **Arsenic and its compounds**

E950.9 **Other and unspecified solid and liquid substances**

✓4th **E951 Suicide and self-inflicted poisoning by gases in domestic use**

E951.0 **Gas distributed by pipeline**

E951.1 **Liquefied petroleum gas distributed in mobile containers**

E951.8 **Other utility gas**

✓4th **E952 Suicide and self-inflicted poisoning by other gases and vapors**

E952.0 **Motor vehicle exhaust gas**

E952.1 **Other carbon monoxide**

E952.8 **Other specified gases and vapors**

E952.9 **Unspecified gases and vapors**

✓4th **E953 Suicide and self-inflicted injury by hanging, strangulation, and suffocation**

E953.0 **Hanging**

E953.1 **Suffocation by plastic bag**

E953.8 **Other specified means**

E953.9 **Unspecified means**

E954 Suicide and self-inflicted injury by submersion [drowning]

✓4th **E955 Suicide and self-inflicted injury by firearms, air guns and explosives**

E955.0 **Handgun**

E955.1 **Shotgun**

E955.2 **Hunting rifle**

E955.3 **Military firearms**

E955.4 **Other and unspecified firearm**
Gunshot NOS
Shot NOS

E955.5 **Explosives**

E955.6 **Air gun**
BB gun
Pellet gun

E955.7 **Paintball gun**

E955.9 **Unspecified**

E956 Suicide and self-inflicted injury by cutting and piercing instrument

✓4th **E957 Suicide and self-inflicted injuries by jumping from high place**

E957.0 **Residential premises**

✓4th Fourth-digit Required   ▶◀ Revised Text   ● New Code   ▲ Revised Code Title

E957.1 Other man-made structures

E957.2 Natural sites

E957.9 Unspecified

✓4ᵗʰ **E958 Suicide and self-inflicted injury by other and unspecified means**

E958.0 Jumping or lying before moving object

E958.1 Burns, fire

E958.2 Scald

E958.3 Extremes of cold

E958.4 Electrocution

E958.5 Crashing of motor vehicle

E958.6 Crashing of aircraft

E958.7 Caustic substances, except poisoning
> **EXCLUDES** *poisoning by caustic substance (E950.7)*

E958.8 Other specified means

E958.9 Unspecified means

E959 Late effects of self-inflicted injury
> **NOTE** This category is to be used to indicate circumstances classifiable to E950-E958 as the cause of death or disability from late effects, which are themselves classifiable elsewhere. The "late effects" include conditions reported as such, or as sequelae which may occur at any time after the attempted suicide or self-inflicted injury.

Homicide and Injury Purposely Inflicted by Other Persons (E960-E969)

> **INCLUDES** injuries inflicted by another person with intent to injure or kill, by any means

> **EXCLUDES** *injuries due to:*
> *legal intervention (E970-E978)*
> *operations of war (E990-E999)*
> *terrorism (E979)*

✓4ᵗʰ **E960 Fight, brawl, rape**

E960.0 Unarmed fight or brawl
> Beatings NOS
> Brawl or fight with hands, fists, feet
> Injured or killed in fight NOS
> **EXCLUDES** *homicidal:*
> *injury by weapons (E965.0-E966, E969)*
> *strangulation (E963)*
> *submersion (E964)*

E960.1 Rape

E961 Assault by corrosive or caustic substance, except poisoning
> Injury or death purposely caused by corrosive or caustic substance, such as:
> acid [any]
> corrosive substance
> vitriol
> **EXCLUDES** *burns from hot liquid (E968.3)*
> *chemical burns from swallowing a corrosive substance (E962.0-E962.9)*

✓4ᵗʰ **E962 Assault by poisoning**

E962.0 Drugs and medicinal substances
> Homicidal poisoning by any drug or medicinal substance

E962.1 Other solid and liquid substances

E962.2 Other gases and vapors

E962.9 Unspecified poisoning

E963 Assault by hanging and strangulation
> Homicidal (attempt):   Homicidal (attempt):
> garrotting or ligature   strangulation
> hanging   suffocation

E964 Assault by submersion [drowning]

✓4ᵗʰ **E965 Assault by firearms and explosives**

E965.0 Handgun
> Pistol   Revolver

E965.1 Shotgun

E965.2 Hunting rifle

E965.3 Military firearms

E965.4 Other and unspecified firearm

E965.5 Antipersonnel bomb

E965.6 Gasoline bomb

E965.7 Letter bomb

E965.8 Other specified explosive
> Bomb NOS (placed in):
> car
> house
> Dynamite

E965.9 Unspecified explosive

E966 Assault by cutting and piercing instrument
> Assassination (attempt), homicide (attempt) by any instrument classifiable under E920
> Homicidal:
> cut
> puncture   } any part of the body
> stab
> Stabbed any part of the body

✓4ᵗʰ **E967 Perpetrator of child and adult abuse**
> **NOTE** Selection of the correct perpetrator code is based on the relationship between the perpetrator and the victim

E967.0 By father, stepfather, or boyfriend
> Male partner of child's parent or guardian

E967.1 By other specified person

E967.2 By mother, stepmother, or girlfriend
> Female partner of child's parent or guardian

E967.3 By spouse or partner
> Abuse of spouse or partner by ex-spouse or ex-partner

E967.4 By child

E967.5 By sibling

E967.6 By grandparent

E967.7 By other relative

E967.8 By non-related caregiver

E967.9 By unspecified person

✓4ᵗʰ **E968 Assault by other and unspecified means**

E968.0 Fire
> Arson   Homicidal burns NOS
> **EXCLUDES** *burns from hot liquid (E968.3)*

E968.1 Pushing from a high place

E968.2 Striking by blunt or thrown object

E968.3 Hot liquid
> Homicidal burns by scalding

E968.4 Criminal neglect
> Abandonment of child, infant, or other helpless person with intent to injure or kill

E968.5 Transport vehicle
> Being struck by other vehicle or run down with intent to injure
> Pushed in front of, thrown from, or dragged by moving vehicle with intent to injure

E968.6 Air gun
> BB gun
> Pellet gun

E968.7 Human bite

E968.8 Other specified means

E968.9 Unspecified means
> Assassination (attempt) NOS
> Homicidal (attempt):
> injury NOS
> wound NOS
> Manslaughter (nonaccidental)
> Murder (attempt) NOS
> Violence, non-accidental

✓4ᵗʰ Fourth-digit Required   ▶◀ Revised Text   ● New Code   ▲ Revised Code Title

E969   Late effects of injury purposely inflicted by other person

> **NOTE**   This category is to be used to indicate circumstances classifiable to E960-E968 as the cause of death or disability from late effects, which are themselves classifiable elsewhere. The "late effects" include conditions reported as such, or as sequelae which may occur at any time after injury purposely inflicted by another person.

Legal Intervention (E970-E978)

> **INCLUDES**   injuries inflicted by the police or other law-enforcing agents, including military on duty, in the course of arresting or attempting to arrest lawbreakers, suppressing disturbances, maintaining order, and other legal action
> legal execution
>
> **EXCLUDES**   *injuries caused by civil insurrections (E990.0-E999)*

E970   Injury due to legal intervention by firearms

Gunshot wound
Injury by:
    machine gun
    revolver
Injury by:
    rifle pellet or rubber bullet
    shot NOS

E971   Injury due to legal intervention by explosives

Injury by:
    dynamite
    explosive shell
Injury by:
    grenade
    mortar bomb

E972   Injury due to legal intervention by gas

Asphyxiation by gas
Injury by tear gas
Poisoning by gas

E973   Injury due to legal intervention by blunt object

Hit, struck by:
    baton (nightstick)
    blunt object
Hit, struck by:
    stave

E974   Injury due to legal intervention by cutting and piercing instrument

Cut
Incised wound
Injured by bayonet
Stab wound

E975   Injury due to legal intervention by other specified means

Blow
Manhandling

E976   Injury due to legal intervention by unspecified means

E977   Late effects of injuries due to legal intervention

> **NOTE**   This category is to be used to indicate circumstances classifiable to E970-E976 as the cause of death or disability from late effects, which are themselves classifiable elsewhere. The "late effects" include conditions reported as such, or as sequelae, which may occur at any time after the injury due to legal intervention.

E978   Legal execution

All executions performed at the behest of the judiciary or ruling authority [whether permanent or temporary] as:

asphyxiation by gas
beheading, decapitation (by guillotine)
capital punishment
electrocution
hanging
poisoning
shooting
other specified means

Terrorism (E979)

✓4ᵗʰ E979   Terrorism

Injuries resulting from the unlawful use of force or violence against persons or property to intimidate or coerce a Government, the civilian population, or any segment thereof, in furtherance of political or social objective

E979.0   Terrorism involving explosion of marine weapons

Depth-charge
Marine mine
Mine NOS, at sea or in harbour
Sea-based artillery shell
Torpedo
Underwater blast

E979.1   Terrorism involving destruction of aircraft

Aircraft used as a weapon
Aircraft:
    burned
    exploded
Aircraft:
    shot down
Crushed by falling aircraft

E979.2   Terrorism involving other explosions and fragments

Antipersonnel bomb
    (fragments)
Blast NOS
Explosion (of):
    artillery shell
    breech-block
    cannon block
    mortar bomb
    munitions being used
       in terrorism
    NOS
Fragments from:
    artillery shell
    bomb
    grenade
    guided missile
    land-mine
    rocket
    shell
    shrapnel
Mine NOS

E979.3   Terrorism involving fires, conflagration and hot substances

Burning building or
    structure:
    collapse of
    fall from
    hit by falling object in
    jump from
Conflagration NOS
Fire (causing):
    Asphyxia
    Burns
Fire (causing):
    NOS
    Other injury
Melting of fittings and
    furniture in burning
Petrol bomb
Smouldering building
    or structure

E979.4   Terrorism involving firearms

Bullet:
    carbine
    machine gun
    pistol
Bullet:
    rifle
    rubber (rifle)
Pellets (shotgun)

E979.5   Terrorism involving nuclear weapons

Blast effects
Exposure to ionizing radiation from nuclear weapon
Fireball effects
Heat from nuclear weapon
Other direct and secondary effects of nuclear weapons

E979.6   Terrorism involving biological weapons

Anthrax
Cholera
Smallpox

E979.7   Terrorism involving chemical weapons

Gases, fumes, chemicals
Hydrogen cyanide
Phosgene
Sarin

E979.8   Terrorism involving other means

Drowning and submersion
Lasers
Piercing or stabbing instruments
Terrorism NOS

E979.9   Terrorism, secondary effects

> **NOTE**   This code is for use to identify conditions occurring subsequent to a terrorist attack not those that are due to the initial terrorist act
>
> **EXCLUDES**   *late effect of terrorist attack (E999.1)*

Injury Undetermined Whether Accidentally or Purposely Inflicted (E980-E989)

> **NOTE**   Categories E980-E989 are for use when it is unspecified or it cannot be determined whether the injuries are accidental (unintentional), suicide (attempted), or assault.

✓4ᵗʰ E980   Poisoning by solid or liquid substances, undetermined whether accidentally or purposely inflicted

E980.0   Analgesics, antipyretics, and antirheumatics

E980.1   Barbiturates

E980.2   Other sedatives and hypnotics

E980.3   Tranquilizers and other psychotropic agents

E980.4   Other specified drugs and medicinal substances

E980.5   Unspecified drug or medicinal substance

E980.6   Corrosive and caustic substances

Poisoning, undetermined whether accidental or purposeful, by substances classifiable to E864

E980.7   Agricultural and horticultural chemical and pharmaceutical preparations other than plant foods and fertilizers

E980.8   Arsenic and its compounds

E980.9 Other and unspecified solid and liquid substances

☑4ᵗʰ **E981 Poisoning by gases in domestic use, undetermined whether accidentally or purposely inflicted**

E981.0 Gas distributed by pipeline

E981.1 Liquefied petroleum gas distributed in mobile containers

E981.8 Other utility gas

☑4ᵗʰ **E982 Poisoning by other gases, undetermined whether accidentally or purposely inflicted**

E982.0 Motor vehicle exhaust gas

E982.1 Other carbon monoxide

E982.8 Other specified gases and vapors

E982.9 Unspecified gases and vapors

☑4ᵗʰ **E983 Hanging, strangulation, or suffocation, undetermined whether accidentally or purposely inflicted**

E983.0 Hanging

E983.1 Suffocation by plastic bag

E983.8 Other specified means

E983.9 Unspecified means

E984 Submersion [drowning], undetermined whether accidentally or purposely inflicted

☑4ᵗʰ **E985 Injury by firearms, air guns and explosives, undetermined whether accidentally or purposely inflicted**

E985.0 Handgun

E985.1 Shotgun

E985.2 Hunting rifle

E985.3 Military firearms

E985.4 Other and unspecified firearm

E985.5 Explosives

E985.6 Air gun
    BB gun   Pellet gun

E985.7 Paintball gun

E986 Injury by cutting and piercing instruments, undetermined whether accidentally or purposely inflicted

☑4ᵗʰ **E987 Falling from high place, undetermined whether accidentally or purposely inflicted**

E987.0 Residential premises

E987.1 Other man-made structures

E987.2 Natural sites

E987.9 Unspecified site

☑4ᵗʰ **E988 Injury by other and unspecified means, undetermined whether accidentally or purposely inflicted**

E988.0 Jumping or lying before moving object

E988.1 Burns, fire

E988.2 Scald

E988.3 Extremes of cold

E988.4 Electrocution

E988.5 Crashing of motor vehicle

E988.6 Crashing of aircraft

E988.7 Caustic substances, except poisoning

E988.8 Other specified means

E988.9 Unspecified means

E989 Late effects of injury, undetermined whether accidentally or purposely inflicted

NOTE This category is to be used to indicate circumstances classifiable to E980-E988 as the cause of death or disability from late effects, which are themselves classifiable elsewhere. The "late effects" include conditions reported as such, or as sequelae, which may occur at any time after injury, undetermined whether accidentally or purposely inflicted.

Injury Resulting from Operations of War (E990-E999)

INCLUDES injuries to military personnel and civilians caused by war and civil insurrections and occurring during the time of war and insurrection, and peacekeeping missions

EXCLUDES *accidents during training of military personnel manufacture of war material and transport, unless attributable to enemy action*

☑4ᵗʰ **E990 Injury due to war operations by fires and conflagrations**

INCLUDES asphyxia, burns, or other injury originating from fire caused by a fire-producing device or indirectly by any conventional weapon

E990.0 From gasoline bomb
    Incendiary bomb

E990.1 From flamethrower

E990.2 From incendiary bullet

E990.3 From fire caused indirectly from conventional weapon
    EXCLUDES *fire aboard military aircraft (E994.3)*

E990.9 From other and unspecified source

☑4ᵗʰ **E991 Injury due to war operations by bullets and fragments**

EXCLUDES *injury due to bullets and fragments due to war operations, but occurring after cessation of hostilities (E998.0)*
    injury due to explosion of artillery shells and mortars (E993.2)
    injury due to explosion of improvised explosive device [IED] (E993.3-E993.5)
    injury due to sea-based artillery shell (E992.3)

E991.0 Rubber bullets (rifle)

E991.1 Pellets (rifle)

E991.2 Other bullets
    Bullet [any, except rubber bullets and pellets]:
    carbine
    machine gun
    pistol
    rifle
    shotgun

E991.3 Antipersonnel bomb (fragments)

E991.4 Fragments from munitions
Fragments from:	Fragments from:
artillery shell	guided missile
bombs, except antipersonnel	land mine
detonation of unexploded ordnance [UXO]	rockets
grenade	shell

E991.5 Fragments from person-borne improvised explosive device [IED]

E991.6 Fragments from vehicle-borne improvised explosive device [IED]
    IED borne by land, air, or water transport vehicle

E991.7 Fragments from other improvised explosive device [IED]
    Roadside IED

E991.8 Fragments from weapons
Fragments from:	Fragments from:
artillery	missile launchers
autocannons	mortars
automatic grenade launchers	small arms

E991.9 Other and unspecified fragments
    Shrapnel NOS

☑4ᵗʰ **E992 Injury due to war operations by explosion of marine weapons**

E992.0 Torpedo

E992.1 Depth charge

E992.2 Marine mines
    Marine mines at sea or in harbor

E992.3 Sea-based artillery shell

E992.8 Other marine weapons

E992.9 Unspecified marine weapon
    Underwater blast NOS

✓4th **E993 Injury due to war operations by other explosion**
Injuries due to direct or indirect pressure or air blast of an explosion occurring during war operations

> EXCLUDES injury due to fragments resulting from an explosion (E991.0-E991.9)
> injury due to detonation of unexploded ordnance but occurring after cessation of hostilities (E998.0-E998.9)
> injury due to nuclear weapons (E996.0-E996.9)

E993.0 Aerial bomb

E993.1 Guided missile

E993.2 Mortar
Artillery shell

E993.3 Person-borne improvised explosive device [IED]

E993.4 Vehicle-borne improvised explosive device [IED]
IED borne by land, air, or water transport vehicle

E993.5 Other improvised explosive device [IED]
Roadside IED

E993.6 Unintentional detonation of own munitions
Unintentional detonation of own ammunition (artillery) (mortars)

E993.7 Unintentional discharge of own munitions launch device
Unintentional explosion of own:
   autocannons
   automatic grenade launchers
   missile launchers
   small arms

E993.8 Other specified explosion
Bomb   Land mine
Grenade

E993.9 Unspecified explosion
Air blast NOS   Blast wind NOS
Blast NOS   Explosion NOS
Blast wave NOS

✓4th **E994 Injury due to war operations by destruction of aircraft**

E994.0 Destruction of aircraft due to enemy fire or explosives
Air to air missile   Rocket propelled grenade [RPG]
Explosive device placed   Small arms fire
   on aircraft   Surface to air missile

E994.1 Unintentional destruction of aircraft due to own onboard explosives

E994.2 Destruction of aircraft due to collision with other aircraft

E994.3 Destruction of aircraft due to onboard fire

E994.8 Other destruction of aircraft

E994.9 Unspecified destruction of aircraft

✓4th **E995 Injury due to war operations by other and unspecified forms of conventional warfare**

E995.0 Unarmed hand-to-hand combat
> EXCLUDES intentional restriction of airway (E995.3)

E995.1 Struck by blunt object
Baton (nightstick)
Stave

E995.2 Piercing object
Bayonet
Knife
Sword

E995.3 Intentional restriction of air and airway
Intentional submersion
Strangulation
Suffocation

E995.4 Unintentional drowning due to inability to surface or obtain air
Submersion

E995.8 Other forms of conventional warfare

E995.9 Unspecified form of conventional warfare

✓4th **E996 Injury due to war operations by nuclear weapons**
Dirty bomb NOS

> EXCLUDES late effects of injury due to nuclear weapons (E999.0, E999.1)

E996.0 Direct blast effect of nuclear weapon
Injury to bodily organs due to blast pressure

E996.1 Indirect blast effect of nuclear weapon
Injury due to being thrown by blast
Injury due to being struck or crushed by blast debris

E996.2 Thermal radiation effect of nuclear weapon
Burns due to thermal radiation
Fireball effects
Flash burns
Heat effects

E996.3 Nuclear radiation effects
Acute radiation exposure
Beta burns
Fallout exposure
Radiation sickness
Secondary effects of nuclear weapons

E996.8 Other effects of nuclear weapons

E996.9 Unspecified effect of nuclear weapon

✓4th **E997 Injury due to war operations by other forms of unconventional warfare**

E997.0 Lasers

E997.1 Biological warfare

E997.2 Gases, fumes, and chemicals

E997.3 Weapon of mass destruction [WMD], unspecified

E997.8 Other specified forms of unconventional warfare

E997.9 Unspecified form of unconventional warfare

✓4th **E998 Injury due to war operations but occurring after cessation of hostilities**
Injuries due to operations of war but occurring after cessation of hostilities by any means classifiable under E990-E997
Injuries by explosion of bombs or mines placed in the course of operations of war, if the explosion occurred after cessation of hostilities

E998.0 Explosion of mines

E998.1 Explosion of bombs

E998.8 Injury due to other war operations but occurring after cessation of hostilities

E998.9 Injury due to unspecified war operations but occurring after cessation of hostilities

✓4th **E999 Late effect of injury due to war operations and terrorism**
> NOTE This category is to be used to indicate circumstances classifiable to E979, E990-E998 as the cause of death or disability from late effects, which are themselves classifiable elsewhere. The "late effects" include conditions reported as such, or as sequelae, which may occur at any time after the injury, resulting from operations of war or terrorism

E999.0 Late effect of injury due to war operations

E999.1 Late effect of injury due to terrorism

✓4th Fourth-digit Required   ►◄ Revised Text   ● New Code   ▲ Revised Code Title

Appendix A: Morphology of Neoplasms

The World Health Organization has published an adaptation of the International Classification of Diseases for oncology (ICD-O). It contains a coded nomenclature for the morphology of neoplasms, which is reproduced here for those who wish to use it in conjunction with Chapter 2 of the International Classification of Diseases, 9th Revision, Clinical Modification.

The morphology code numbers consist of five digits; the first four identify the histological type of the neoplasm and the fifth indicates its behavior. The one-digit behavior code is as follows:

/0	Benign
/1	Uncertain whether benign or malignant Borderline malignancy
/2	Carcinoma in situ Intraepithelial Noninfiltrating Noninvasive
/3	Malignant, primary site
/6	Malignant, metastatic site Secondary site
/9	Malignant, uncertain whether primary or metastatic site

In the nomenclature below, the morphology code numbers include the behavior code appropriate to the histological type of neoplasm, but this behavior code should be changed if other reported information makes this necessary. For example, "chordoma (M9370/3)" is assumed to be malignant; the term "benign chordoma" should be coded M9370/0. Similarly, "superficial spreading adenocarcinoma (M8143/3)" described as "noninvasive" should be coded M8143/2 and "melanoma (M8720/3)" described as "secondary" should be coded M8720/6.

The following table shows the correspondence between the morphology code and the different sections of Chapter 2:

Morphology Code Histology/Behavior		ICD-9-CM Chapter 2	
Any	0	210-229	Benign neoplasms
M8000-M8004	1	239	Neoplasms of unspecified nature
M8010+	1	235-238	Neoplasms of uncertain behavior
Any	2	230-234	Carcinoma in situ
Any	3	140-195 200-208	Malignant neoplasms, stated or presumed to be primary
Any	6	196-198	Malignant neoplasms, stated or presumed to be secondary

The ICD-O behavior digit /9 is inapplicable in an ICD context, since all malignant neoplasms are presumed to be primary (/3) or secondary (/6) according to other information on the medical record. Only the first-listed term of the full ICD-O morphology nomenclature appears against each code number in the list below. The ICD-9-CM Alphabetical Index (Volume 2), however, includes all the ICD-O synonyms as well as a number of other morphological names still likely to be encountered on medical records but omitted from ICD-O as outdated or otherwise undesirable.

A coding difficulty sometimes arises where a morphological diagnosis contains two qualifying adjectives that have different code numbers. An example is "transitional cell epidermoid carcinoma." "Transitional cell carcinoma NOS" is M8120/3 and "epidermoid carcinoma NOS" is M8070/3. In such circumstances, the higher number (M8120/3 in this example) should be used, as it is usually more specific.

Coded Nomenclature for Morphology of Neoplasms

M800	Neoplasms NOS
M8000/0	Neoplasm, benign
M8000/1	Neoplasm, uncertain whether benign or malignant
M8000/3	Neoplasm, malignant
M8000/6	Neoplasm, metastatic
M8000/9	Neoplasm, malignant, uncertain whether primary or metastatic
M8001/0	Tumor cells, benign
M8001/1	Tumor cells, uncertain whether benign or malignant
M8001/3	Tumor cells, malignant
M8002/3	Malignant tumor, small cell type
M8003/3	Malignant tumor, giant cell type
M8004/3	Malignant tumor, fusiform cell type

M801-M804	Epithelial neoplasms NOS
M8010/0	Epithelial tumor, benign
M8010/2	Carcinoma in situ NOS
M8010/3	Carcinoma NOS
M8010/6	Carcinoma, metastatic NOS
M8010/9	Carcinomatosis
M8011/0	Epithelioma, benign
M8011/3	Epithelioma, malignant
M8012/3	Large cell carcinoma NOS
M8020/3	Carcinoma, undifferentiated type NOS
M8021/3	Carcinoma, anaplastic type NOS
M8022/3	Pleomorphic carcinoma
M8030/3	Giant cell and spindle cell carcinoma
M8031/3	Giant cell carcinoma
M8032/3	Spindle cell carcinoma
M8033/3	Pseudosarcomatous carcinoma
M8034/3	Polygonal cell carcinoma
M8035/3	Spheroidal cell carcinoma
M8040/1	Tumorlet
M8041/3	Small cell carcinoma NOS
M8042/3	Oat cell carcinoma
M8043/3	Small cell carcinoma, fusiform cell type

M805-M808	Papillary and squamous cell neoplasms
M8050/0	Papilloma NOS (except Papilloma of urinary bladder M8120/1)
M8050/2	Papillary carcinoma in situ
M8050/3	Papillary carcinoma NOS
M8051/0	Verrucous papilloma
M8051/3	Verrucous carcinoma NOS
M8052/0	Squamous cell papilloma
M8052/3	Papillary squamous cell carcinoma
M8053/0	Inverted papilloma
M8060/0	Papillomatosis NOS
M8070/2	Squamous cell carcinoma in situ NOS
M8070/3	Squamous cell carcinoma NOS
M8070/6	Squamous cell carcinoma, metastatic NOS
M8071/3	Squamous cell carcinoma, keratinizing type NOS
M8072/3	Squamous cell carcinoma, large cell, nonkeratinizing type
M8073/3	Squamous cell carcinoma, small cell, nonkeratinizing type
M8074/3	Squamous cell carcinoma, spindle cell type
M8075/3	Adenoid squamous cell carcinoma
M8076/2	Squamous cell carcinoma in situ with questionable stromal invasion
M8076/3	Squamous cell carcinoma, microinvasive
M8080/2	Queyrat's erythroplasia
M8081/2	Bowen's disease
M8082/3	Lymphoepithelial carcinoma

M809-M811	Basal cell neoplasms
M8090/1	Basal cell tumor
M8090/3	Basal cell carcinoma NOS
M8091/3	Multicentric basal cell carcinoma
M8092/3	Basal cell carcinoma, morphea type
M8093/3	Basal cell carcinoma, fibroepithelial type
M8094/3	Basosquamous carcinoma
M8095/3	Metatypical carcinoma
M8096/0	Intraepidermal epithelioma of Jadassohn
M8100/0	Trichoepithelioma
M8101/0	Trichofolliculoma
M8102/0	Tricholemmoma
M8110/0	Pilomatrixoma

M812-M813	Transitional cell papillomas and carcinomas
M8120/0	Transitional cell papilloma NOS
M8120/1	Urothelial papilloma
M8120/2	Transitional cell carcinoma in situ
M8120/3	Transitional cell carcinoma NOS
M8121/0	Schneiderian papilloma
M8121/1	Transitional cell papilloma, inverted type
M8121/3	Schneiderian carcinoma
M8122/3	Transitional cell carcinoma, spindle cell type
M8123/3	Basaloid carcinoma
M8124/3	Cloacogenic carcinoma
M8130/3	Papillary transitional cell carcinoma

M814-M838	Adenomas and adenocarcinomas
M8140/0	Adenoma NOS
M8140/1	Bronchial adenoma NOS
M8140/2	Adenocarcinoma in situ
M8140/3	Adenocarcinoma NOS
M8140/6	Adenocarcinoma, metastatic NOS
M8141/3	Scirrhous adenocarcinoma
M8142/3	Linitis plastica
M8143/3	Superficial spreading adenocarcinoma
M8144/3	Adenocarcinoma, intestinal type
M8145/3	Carcinoma, diffuse type
M8146/0	Monomorphic adenoma
M8147/0	Basal cell adenoma
M8150/0	Islet cell adenoma
M8150/3	Islet cell carcinoma
M8151/0	Insulinoma NOS
M8151/3	Insulinoma, malignant
M8152/0	Glucagonoma NOS
M8152/3	Glucagonoma, malignant
M8153/1	Gastrinoma NOS
M8153/3	Gastrinoma, malignant
M8154/3	Mixed islet cell and exocrine adenocarcinoma
M8160/0	Bile duct adenoma
M8160/3	Cholangiocarcinoma

M8161/0	Bile duct cystadenoma
M8161/3	Bile duct cystadenocarcinoma
M8170/0	Liver cell adenoma
M8170/3	Hepatocellular carcinoma NOS
M8180/0	Hepatocholangioma, benign
M8180/3	Combined hepatocellular carcinoma and cholangiocarcinoma
M8190/0	Trabecular adenoma
M8190/3	Trabecular adenocarcinoma
M8191/0	Embryonal adenoma
M8200/0	Eccrine dermal cylindroma
M8200/3	Adenoid cystic carcinoma
M8201/3	Cribriform carcinoma
M8210/0	Adenomatous polyp NOS
M8210/3	Adenocarcinoma in adenomatous polyp
M8211/0	Tubular adenoma NOS
M8211/3	Tubular adenocarcinoma
M8220/0	Adenomatous polyposis coli
M8220/3	Adenocarcinoma in adenomatous polyposis coli
M8221/0	Multiple adenomatous polyps
M8230/3	Solid carcinoma NOS
M8231/3	Carcinoma simplex
M8240/1	Carcinoid tumor NOS
M8240/3	Carcinoid tumor, malignant
M8241/1	Carcinoid tumor, argentaffin NOS
M8241/3	Carcinoid tumor, argentaffin, malignant
M8242/1	Carcinoid tumor, nonargentaffin NOS
M8242/3	Carcinoid tumor, nonargentaffin, malignant
M8243/3	Mucocarcinoid tumor, malignant
M8244/3	Composite carcinoid
M8250/1	Pulmonary adenomatosis
M8250/3	Bronchiolo-alveolar adenocarcinoma
M8251/0	Alveolar adenoma
M8251/3	Alveolar adenocarcinoma
M8260/0	Papillary adenoma NOS
M8260/3	Papillary adenocarcinoma NOS
M8261/1	Villous adenoma NOS
M8261/3	Adenocarcinoma in villous adenoma
M8262/3	Villous adenocarcinoma
M8263/0	Tubulovillous adenoma
M8270/0	Chromophobe adenoma
M8270/3	Chromophobe carcinoma
M8280/0	Acidophil adenoma
M8280/3	Acidophil carcinoma
M8281/0	Mixed acidophil-basophil adenoma
M8281/3	Mixed acidophil-basophil carcinoma
M8290/0	Oxyphilic adenoma
M8290/3	Oxyphilic adenocarcinoma
M8300/0	Basophil adenoma
M8300/3	Basophil carcinoma
M8310/0	Clear cell adenoma
M8310/3	Clear cell adenocarcinoma NOS
M8311/1	Hypernephroid tumor
M8312/3	Renal cell carcinoma
M8313/0	Clear cell adenofibroma
M8320/3	Granular cell carcinoma
M8321/0	Chief cell adenoma
M8322/0	Water-clear cell adenoma
M8322/3	Water-clear cell adenocarcinoma
M8323/0	Mixed cell adenoma
M8323/3	Mixed cell adenocarcinoma
M8324/0	Lipoadenoma
M8330/0	Follicular adenoma
M8330/3	Follicular adenocarcinoma NOS
M8331/3	Follicular adenocarcinoma, well differentiated type
M8332/3	Follicular adenocarcinoma, trabecular type

M8333/0	Microfollicular adenoma
M8334/0	Macrofollicular adenoma
M8340/3	Papillary and follicular adenocarcinoma
M8350/3	Nonencapsulated sclerosing carcinoma
M8360/1	Multiple endocrine adenomas
M8361/1	Juxtaglomerular tumor
M8370/0	Adrenal cortical adenoma NOS
M8370/3	Adrenal cortical carcinoma
M8371/0	Adrenal cortical adenoma, compact cell type
M8372/0	Adrenal cortical adenoma, heavily pigmented variant
M8373/0	Adrenal cortical adenoma, clear cell type
M8374/0	Adrenal cortical adenoma, glomerulosa cell type
M8375/0	Adrenal cortical adenoma, mixed cell type
M8380/0	Endometrioid adenoma NOS
M8380/1	Endometrioid adenoma, borderline malignancy
M8380/3	Endometrioid carcinoma
M8381/0	Endometrioid adenofibroma NOS
M8381/1	Endometrioid adenofibroma, borderline malignancy
M8381/3	Endometrioid adenofibroma, malignant

M839-M842 Adnexal and skin appendage neoplasms

M8390/0	Skin appendage adenoma
M8390/3	Skin appendage carcinoma
M8400/0	Sweat gland adenoma
M8400/1	Sweat gland tumor NOS
M8400/3	Sweat gland adenocarcinoma
M8401/0	Apocrine adenoma
M8401/3	Apocrine adenocarcinoma
M8402/0	Eccrine acrospiroma
M8403/0	Eccrine spiradenoma
M8404/0	Hidrocystoma
M8405/0	Papillary hydradenoma
M8406/0	Papillary syringadenoma
M8407/0	Syringoma NOS
M8410/0	Sebaceous adenoma
M8410/3	Sebaceous adenocarcinoma
M8420/0	Ceruminous adenoma
M8420/3	Ceruminous adenocarcinoma

M843 Mucoepidermoid neoplasms

M8430/1	Mucoepidermoid tumor
M8430/3	Mucoepidermoid carcinoma

M844-M849 Cystic, mucinous, and serous neoplasms

M8440/0	Cystadenoma NOS
M8440/3	Cystadenocarcinoma NOS
M8441/0	Serous cystadenoma NOS
M8441/1	Serous cystadenoma, borderline malignancy
M8441/3	Serous cystadenocarcinoma NOS
M8450/0	Papillary cystadenoma NOS
M8450/1	Papillary cystadenoma, borderline malignancy
M8450/3	Papillary cystadenocarcinoma NOS
M8460/0	Papillary serous cystadenoma NOS
M8460/1	Papillary serous cystadenoma, borderline malignancy
M8460/3	Papillary serous cystadenocarcinoma
M8461/0	Serous surface papilloma NOS
M8461/1	Serous surface papilloma, borderline malignancy
M8461/3	Serous surface papillary carcinoma
M8470/0	Mucinous cystadenoma NOS
M8470/1	Mucinous cystadenoma, borderline malignancy

M8470/3	Mucinous cystadenocarcinoma NOS
M8471/0	Papillary mucinous cystadenoma NOS
M8471/1	Papillary mucinous cystadenoma, borderline malignancy
M8471/3	Papillary mucinous cystadenocarcinoma
M8480/0	Mucinous adenoma
M8480/3	Mucinous adenocarcinoma
M8480/6	Pseudomyxoma peritonei
M8481/3	Mucin-producing adenocarcinoma
M8490/3	Signet ring cell carcinoma
M8490/6	Metastatic signet ring cell carcinoma

M850-M854 Ductal, lobular, and medullary neoplasms

M8500/2	Intraductal carcinoma, noninfiltrating NOS
M8500/3	Infiltrating duct carcinoma
M8501/2	Comedocarcinoma, noninfiltrating
M8501/3	Comedocarcinoma NOS
M8502/3	Juvenile carcinoma of the breast
M8503/0	Intraductal papilloma
M8503/2	Noninfiltrating intraductal papillary adenocarcinoma
M8504/0	Intracystic papillary adenoma
M8504/2	Noninfiltrating intracystic carcinoma
M8505/0	Intraductal papillomatosis NOS
M8506/0	Subareolar duct papillomatosis
M8510/3	Medullary carcinoma NOS
M8511/3	Medullary carcinoma with amyloid stroma
M8512/3	Medullary carcinoma with lymphoid stroma
M8520/2	Lobular carcinoma in situ
M8520/3	Lobular carcinoma NOS
M8521/3	Infiltrating ductular carcinoma
M8530/3	Inflammatory carcinoma
M8540/3	Paget's disease, mammary
M8541/3	Paget's disease and infiltrating duct carcinoma of breast
M8542/3	Paget's disease, extramammary (except Paget's disease of bone)

M855 Acinar cell neoplasms

M8550/0	Acinar cell adenoma
M8550/1	Acinar cell tumor
M8550/3	Acinar cell carcinoma

M856-M858 Complex epithelial neoplasms

M8560/3	Adenosquamous carcinoma
M8561/0	Adenolymphoma
M8570/3	Adenocarcinoma with squamous metaplasia
M8571/3	Adenocarcinoma with cartilaginous and osseous metaplasia
M8572/3	Adenocarcinoma with spindle cell metaplasia
M8573/3	Adenocarcinoma with apocrine metaplasia
M8580/0	Thymoma, benign
M8580/3	Thymoma, malignant

M859-M867 Specialized gonadal neoplasms

M8590/1	Sex cord-stromal tumor
M8600/0	Thecoma NOS
M8600/3	Theca cell carcinoma
M8610/0	Luteoma NOS
M8620/1	Granulosa cell tumor NOS
M8620/3	Granulosa cell tumor, malignant
M8621/1	Granulosa cell-theca cell tumor
M8630/0	Androblastoma, benign
M8630/1	Androblastoma NOS
M8630/3	Androblastoma, malignant
M8631/0	Sertoli-Leydig cell tumor

M8632/1	Gynandroblastoma
M8640/0	Tubular androblastoma NOS
M8640/3	Sertoli cell carcinoma
M8641/1	Tubular androblastoma with lipid storage
M8650/0	Leydig cell tumor, benign
M8650/1	Leydig cell tumor NOS
M8650/3	Leydig cell tumor, malignant
M8660/0	Hilar cell tumor
M8670/0	Lipid cell tumor of ovary
M8671/0	Adrenal rest tumor

M868-M871 Paragangliomas and glomus tumors

M8680/1	Paraganglioma NOS
M8680/3	Paraganglioma, malignant
M8681/1	Sympathetic paraganglioma
M8682/1	Parasympathetic paraganglioma
M8690/1	Glomus jugulare tumor
M8691/1	Aortic body tumor
M8692/1	Carotid body tumor
M8693/1	Extra-adrenal paraganglioma NOS
M8693/3	Extra-adrenal paraganglioma, malignant
M8700/0	Pheochromocytoma NOS
M8700/3	Pheochromocytoma, malignant
M8710/3	Glomangiosarcoma
M8711/0	Glomus tumor
M8712/0	Glomangioma

M872-M879 Nevi and melanomas

M8720/0	Pigmented nevus NOS
M8720/3	Malignant melanoma NOS
M8721/3	Nodular melanoma
M8722/0	Balloon cell nevus
M8722/3	Balloon cell melanoma
M8723/0	Halo nevus
M8724/0	Fibrous papule of the nose
M8725/0	Neuronevus
M8726/0	Magnocellular nevus
M8730/0	Nonpigmented nevus
M8730/3	Amelanotic melanoma
M8740/0	Junctional nevus
M8740/3	Malignant melanoma in junctional nevus
M8741/2	Precancerous melanosis NOS
M8741/3	Malignant melanoma in precancerous melanosis
M8742/2	Hutchinson's melanotic freckle
M8742/3	Malignant melanoma in Hutchinson's melanotic freckle
M8743/3	Superficial spreading melanoma
M8750/0	Intradermal nevus
M8760/0	Compound nevus
M8761/1	Giant pigmented nevus
M8761/3	Malignant melanoma in giant pigmented nevus
M8770/0	Epithelioid and spindle cell nevus
M8771/3	Epithelioid cell melanoma
M8772/3	Spindle cell melanoma NOS
M8773/3	Spindle cell melanoma, type A
M8774/3	Spindle cell melanoma, type B
M8775/3	Mixed epithelioid and spindle cell melanoma
M8780/0	Blue nevus NOS
M8780/3	Blue nevus, malignant
M8790/0	Cellular blue nevus

M880 Soft tissue tumors and sarcomas NOS

M8800/0	Soft tissue tumor, benign
M8800/3	Sarcoma NOS
M8800/9	Sarcomatosis NOS
M8801/3	Spindle cell sarcoma
M8802/3	Giant cell sarcoma (except of bone M9250/3)
M8803/3	Small cell sarcoma
M8804/3	Epithelioid cell sarcoma

M881-M883 Fibromatous neoplasms

M8810/0	Fibroma NOS
M8810/3	Fibrosarcoma NOS
M8811/0	Fibromyxoma
M8811/3	Fibromyxosarcoma
M8812/0	Periosteal fibroma
M8812/3	Periosteal fibrosarcoma
M8813/0	Fascial fibroma
M8813/3	Fascial fibrosarcoma
M8814/3	Infantile fibrosarcoma
M8820/0	Elastofibroma
M8821/1	Aggressive fibromatosis
M8822/1	Abdominal fibromatosis
M8823/1	Desmoplastic fibroma
M8830/0	Fibrous histiocytoma NOS
M8830/1	Atypical fibrous histiocytoma
M8830/3	Fibrous histiocytoma, malignant
M8831/0	Fibroxanthoma NOS
M8831/1	Atypical fibroxanthoma
M8831/3	Fibroxanthoma, malignant
M8832/0	Dermatofibroma NOS
M8832/1	Dermatofibroma protuberans
M8832/3	Dermatofibrosarcoma NOS

M884 Myxomatous neoplasms

M8840/0	Myxoma NOS
M8840/3	Myxosarcoma

M885-M888 Lipomatous neoplasms

M8850/0	Lipoma NOS
M8850/3	Liposarcoma NOS
M8851/0	Fibrolipoma
M8851/3	Liposarcoma, well differentiated type
M8852/0	Fibromyxolipoma
M8852/3	Myxoid liposarcoma
M8853/3	Round cell liposarcoma
M8854/3	Pleomorphic liposarcoma
M8855/3	Mixed type liposarcoma
M8856/0	Intramuscular lipoma
M8857/0	Spindle cell lipoma
M8860/0	Angiomyolipoma
M8860/3	Angiomyoliposarcoma
M8861/0	Angiolipoma NOS
M8861/1	Angiolipoma, infiltrating
M8870/0	Myelolipoma
M8880/0	Hibernoma
M8881/0	Lipoblastomatosis

M889-M892 Myomatous neoplasms

M8890/0	Leiomyoma NOS
M8890/1	Intravascular leiomyomatosis
M8890/3	Leiomyosarcoma NOS
M8891/1	Epithelioid leiomyoma
M8891/3	Epithelioid leiomyosarcoma
M8892/1	Cellular leiomyoma
M8893/0	Bizarre leiomyoma
M8894/0	Angiomyoma
M8894/3	Angiomyosarcoma
M8895/0	Myoma
M8895/3	Myosarcoma
M8900/0	Rhabdomyoma NOS
M8900/3	Rhabdomyosarcoma NOS
M8901/3	Pleomorphic rhabdomyosarcoma
M8902/3	Mixed type rhabdomyosarcoma
M8903/0	Fetal rhabdomyoma
M8904/0	Adult rhabdomyoma
M8910/3	Embryonal rhabdomyosarcoma
M8920/3	Alveolar rhabdomyosarcoma

M893-M899 Complex mixed and stromal neoplasms

M8930/3	Endometrial stromal sarcoma
M8931/1	Endolymphatic stromal myosis
M8932/0	Adenomyoma
M8940/0	Pleomorphic adenoma
M8940/3	Mixed tumor, malignant NOS
M8950/3	Mullerian mixed tumor
M8951/3	Mesodermal mixed tumor
M8960/1	Mesoblastic nephroma
M8960/3	Nephroblastoma NOS
M8961/3	Epithelial nephroblastoma
M8962/3	Mesenchymal nephroblastoma
M8970/3	Hepatoblastoma
M8980/3	Carcinosarcoma NOS
M8981/3	Carcinosarcoma, embryonal type
M8982/0	Myoepithelioma
M8990/0	Mesenchymoma, benign
M8990/1	Mesenchymoma NOS
M8990/3	Mesenchymoma, malignant
M8991/3	Embryonal sarcoma

M900-M903 Fibroepithelial neoplasms

M9000/0	Brenner tumor NOS
M9000/1	Brenner tumor, borderline malignancy
M9000/3	Brenner tumor, malignant
M9010/0	Fibroadenoma NOS
M9011/0	Intracanalicular fibroadenoma NOS
M9012/0	Pericanalicular fibroadenoma
M9013/0	Adenofibroma NOS
M9014/0	Serous adenofibroma
M9015/0	Mucinous adenofibroma
M9020/0	Cellular intracanalicular fibroadenoma
M9020/1	Cystosarcoma phyllodes NOS
M9020/3	Cystosarcoma phyllodes, malignant
M9030/0	Juvenile fibroadenoma

M904 Synovial neoplasms

M9040/0	Synovioma, benign
M9040/3	Synovial sarcoma NOS
M9041/3	Synovial sarcoma, spindle cell type
M9042/3	Synovial sarcoma, epithelioid cell type
M9043/3	Synovial sarcoma, biphasic type
M9044/3	Clear cell sarcoma of tendons and aponeuroses

M905 Mesothelial neoplasms

M9050/0	Mesothelioma, benign
M9050/3	Mesothelioma, malignant
M9051/0	Fibrous mesothelioma, benign
M9051/3	Fibrous mesothelioma, malignant
M9052/0	Epithelioid mesothelioma, benign
M9052/3	Epithelioid mesothelioma, malignant
M9053/0	Mesothelioma, biphasic type, benign
M9053/3	Mesothelioma, biphasic type, malignant
M9054/0	Adenomatoid tumor NOS

M906-M909 Germ cell neoplasms

M9060/3	Dysgerminoma
M9061/3	Seminoma NOS
M9062/3	Seminoma, anaplastic type
M9063/3	Spermatocytic seminoma
M9064/3	Germinoma
M9070/3	Embryonal carcinoma NOS
M9071/3	Endodermal sinus tumor
M9072/3	Polyembryoma
M9073/1	Gonadoblastoma
M9080/0	Teratoma, benign
M9080/1	Teratoma NOS
M9080/3	Teratoma, malignant NOS
M9081/3	Teratocarcinoma

M9082/3	*Malignant teratoma, undifferentiated type*
M9083/3	*Malignant teratoma, intermediate type*
M9084/0	*Dermoid cyst*
M9084/3	*Dermoid cyst with malignant transformation*
M9090/0	*Struma ovarii NOS*
M9090/3	*Struma ovarii, malignant*
M9091/1	*Strumal carcinoid*
M910	**Trophoblastic neoplasms**
M9100/0	*Hydatidiform mole NOS*
M9100/1	*Invasive hydatidiform mole*
M9100/3	*Choriocarcinoma*
M9101/3	*Choriocarcinoma combined with teratoma*
M9102/3	*Malignant teratoma, trophoblastic*
M911	**Mesonephromas**
M9110/0	*Mesonephroma, benign*
M9110/1	*Mesonephric tumor*
M9110/3	*Mesonephroma, malignant*
M9111/1	*Endosalpingioma*
M912-M916	**Blood vessel tumors**
M9120/0	*Hemangioma NOS*
M9120/3	*Hemangiosarcoma*
M9121/0	*Cavernous hemangioma*
M9122/0	*Venous hemangioma*
M9123/0	*Racemose hemangioma*
M9124/3	*Kupffer cell sarcoma*
M9130/0	*Hemangioendothelioma, benign*
M9130/1	*Hemangioendothelioma NOS*
M9130/3	*Hemangioendothelioma, malignant*
M9131/0	*Capillary hemangioma*
M9132/0	*Intramuscular hemangioma*
M9140/3	*Kaposi's sarcoma*
M9141/0	*Angiokeratoma*
M9142/0	*Verrucous keratotic hemangioma*
M9150/0	*Hemangiopericytoma, benign*
M9150/1	*Hemangiopericytoma NOS*
M9150/3	*Hemangiopericytoma, malignant*
M9160/0	*Angiofibroma NOS*
M9161/1	*Hemangioblastoma*
M917	**Lymphatic vessel tumors**
M9170/0	*Lymphangioma NOS*
M9170/3	*Lymphangiosarcoma*
M9171/0	*Capillary lymphangioma*
M9172/0	*Cavernous lymphangioma*
M9173/0	*Cystic lymphangioma*
M9174/0	*Lymphangiomyoma*
M9174/1	*Lymphangiomyomatosis*
M9175/0	*Hemolymphangioma*
M918-M920	**Osteomas and osteosarcomas**
M9180/0	*Osteoma NOS*
M9180/3	*Osteosarcoma NOS*
M9181/3	*Chondroblastic osteosarcoma*
M9182/3	*Fibroblastic osteosarcoma*
M9183/3	*Telangiectatic osteosarcoma*
M9184/3	*Osteosarcoma in Paget's disease of bone*
M9190/3	*Juxtacortical osteosarcoma*
M9191/0	*Osteoid osteoma NOS*
M9200/0	*Osteoblastoma*
M921-M924	**Chondromatous neoplasms**
M9210/0	*Osteochondroma*
M9210/1	*Osteochondromatosis NOS*
M9220/0	*Chondroma NOS*
M9220/1	*Chondromatosis NOS*
M9220/3	*Chondrosarcoma NOS*
M9221/0	*Juxtacortical chondroma*

M9221/3	*Juxtacortical chondrosarcoma*
M9230/0	*Chondroblastoma NOS*
M9230/3	*Chondroblastoma, malignant*
M9240/3	*Mesenchymal chondrosarcoma*
M9241/0	*Chondromyxoid fibroma*
M925	**Giant cell tumors**
M9250/1	*Giant cell tumor of bone NOS*
M9250/3	*Giant cell tumor of bone, malignant*
M9251/1	*Giant cell tumor of soft parts NOS*
M9251/3	*Malignant giant cell tumor of soft parts*
M926	**Miscellaneous bone tumors**
M9260/3	*Ewing's sarcoma*
M9261/3	*Adamantinoma of long bones*
M9262/0	*Ossifying fibroma*
M927-M934	**Odontogenic tumors**
M9270/0	*Odontogenic tumor, benign*
M9270/1	*Odontogenic tumor NOS*
M9270/3	*Odontogenic tumor, malignant*
M9271/0	*Dentinoma*
M9272/0	*Cementoma NOS*
M9273/0	*Cementoblastoma, benign*
M9274/0	*Cementifying fibroma*
M9275/0	*Gigantiform cementoma*
M9280/0	*Odontoma NOS*
M9281/0	*Compound odontoma*
M9282/0	*Complex odontoma*
M9290/0	*Ameloblastic fibro-odontoma*
M9290/3	*Ameloblastic odontosarcoma*
M9300/0	*Adenomatoid odontogenic tumor*
M9301/0	*Calcifying odontogenic cyst*
M9310/0	*Ameloblastoma NOS*
M9310/3	*Ameloblastoma, malignant*
M9311/0	*Odontoameloblastoma*
M9312/0	*Squamous odontogenic tumor*
M9320/0	*Odontogenic myxoma*
M9321/0	*Odontogenic fibroma NOS*
M9330/0	*Ameloblastic fibroma*
M9330/3	*Ameloblastic fibrosarcoma*
M9340/0	*Calcifying epithelial odontogenic tumor*
M935-M937	**Miscellaneous tumors**
M9350/1	*Craniopharyngioma*
M9360/1	*Pinealoma*
M9361/1	*Pineocytoma*
M9362/3	*Pineoblastoma*
M9363/0	*Melanotic neuroectodermal tumor*
M9370/3	*Chordoma*
M938-M948	**Gliomas**
M9380/3	*Glioma, malignant*
M9381/3	*Gliomatosis cerebri*
M9382/3	*Mixed glioma*
M9383/1	*Subependymal glioma*
M9384/1	*Subependymal giant cell astrocytoma*
M9390/0	*Choroid plexus papilloma NOS*
M9390/3	*Choroid plexus papilloma, malignant*
M9391/3	*Ependymoma NOS*
M9392/3	*Ependymoma, anaplastic type*
M9393/1	*Papillary ependymoma*
M9394/1	*Myxopapillary ependymoma*
M9400/3	*Astrocytoma NOS*
M9401/3	*Astrocytoma, anaplastic type*
M9410/3	*Protoplasmic astrocytoma*
M9411/3	*Gemistocytic astrocytoma*
M9420/3	*Fibrillary astrocytoma*
M9421/3	*Pilocytic astrocytoma*
M9422/3	*Spongioblastoma NOS*
M9423/3	*Spongioblastoma polare*
M9430/3	*Astroblastoma*

M9440/3	*Glioblastoma NOS*
M9441/3	*Giant cell glioblastoma*
M9442/3	*Glioblastoma with sarcomatous component*
M9443/3	*Primitive polar spongioblastoma*
M9450/3	*Oligodendroglioma NOS*
M9451/3	*Oligodendroglioma, anaplastic type*
M9460/3	*Oligodendroblastoma*
M9470/3	*Medulloblastoma NOS*
M9471/3	*Desmoplastic medulloblastoma*
M9472/3	*Medullomyoblastoma*
M9480/3	*Cerebellar sarcoma NOS*
M9481/3	*Monstrocellular sarcoma*
M949-M952	**Neuroepitheliomatous neoplasms**
M9490/0	*Ganglioneuroma*
M9490/3	*Ganglioneuroblastoma*
M9491/0	*Ganglioneuromatosis*
M9500/3	*Neuroblastoma NOS*
M9501/3	*Medulloepithelioma NOS*
M9502/3	*Teratoid medulloepithelioma*
M9503/3	*Neuroepithelioma NOS*
M9504/3	*Spongioneuroblastoma*
M9505/1	*Ganglioglioma*
M9506/0	*Neurocytoma*
M9507/0	*Pacinian tumor*
M9510/3	*Retinoblastoma NOS*
M9511/3	*Retinoblastoma, differentiated type*
M9512/3	*Retinoblastoma, undifferentiated type*
M9520/3	*Olfactory neurogenic tumor*
M9521/3	*Esthesioneurocytoma*
M9522/3	*Esthesioneuroblastoma*
M9523/3	*Esthesioneuroepithelioma*
M953	**Meningiomas**
M9530/0	*Meningioma NOS*
M9530/1	*Meningiomatosis NOS*
M9530/3	*Meningioma, malignant*
M9531/0	*Meningotheliomatous meningioma*
M9532/0	*Fibrous meningioma*
M9533/0	*Psammomatous meningioma*
M9534/0	*Angiomatous meningioma*
M9535/0	*Hemangioblastic meningioma*
M9536/0	*Hemangiopericytic meningioma*
M9537/0	*Transitional meningioma*
M9538/1	*Papillary meningioma*
M9539/3	*Meningeal sarcomatosis*
M954-M957	**Nerve sheath tumor**
M9540/0	*Neurofibroma NOS*
M9540/1	*Neurofibromatosis NOS*
M9540/3	*Neurofibrosarcoma*
M9541/0	*Melanotic neurofibroma*
M9550/0	*Plexiform neurofibroma*
M9560/0	*Neurilemmoma NOS*
M9560/1	*Neurinomatosis*
M9560/3	*Neurilemmoma, malignant*
M9570/0	*Neuroma NOS*
M958	**Granular cell tumors and alveolar soft part sarcoma**
M9580/0	*Granular cell tumor NOS*
M9580/3	*Granular cell tumor, malignant*
M9581/3	*Alveolar soft part sarcoma*
M959-M963	**Lymphomas, NOS or diffuse**
M9590/0	*Lymphomatous tumor, benign*
M9590/3	*Malignant lymphoma NOS*
M9591/3	*Malignant lymphoma, non Hodgkin's type*
M9600/3	*Malignant lymphoma, undifferentiated cell type NOS*
M9601/3	*Malignant lymphoma, stem cell type*

M9602/3	Malignant lymphoma, convoluted cell type NOS
M9610/3	Lymphosarcoma NOS
M9611/3	Malignant lymphoma, lymphoplasmacytoid type
M9612/3	Malignant lymphoma, immunoblastic type
M9613/3	Malignant lymphoma, mixed lymphocytic-histiocytic NOS
M9614/3	Malignant lymphoma, centroblastic-centrocytic, diffuse
M9615/3	Malignant lymphoma, follicular center cell NOS
M9620/3	Malignant lymphoma, lymphocytic, well differentiated NOS
M9621/3	Malignant lymphoma, lymphocytic, intermediate differentiation NOS
M9622/3	Malignant lymphoma, centrocytic
M9623/3	Malignant lymphoma, follicular center cell, cleaved NOS
M9630/3	Malignant lymphoma, lymphocytic, poorly differentiated NOS
M9631/3	Prolymphocytic lymphosarcoma
M9632/3	Malignant lymphoma, centroblastic type NOS
M9633/3	Malignant lymphoma, follicular center cell, noncleaved NOS

M964 **Reticulosarcomas**

M9640/3	Reticulosarcoma NOS
M9641/3	Reticulosarcoma, pleomorphic cell type
M9642/3	Reticulosarcoma, nodular

M965-M966 **Hodgkin's disease**

M9650/3	Hodgkin's disease NOS
M9651/3	Hodgkin's disease, lymphocytic predominance
M9652/3	Hodgkin's disease, mixed cellularity
M9653/3	Hodgkin's disease, lymphocytic depletion NOS
M9654/3	Hodgkin's disease, lymphocytic depletion, diffuse fibrosis
M9655/3	Hodgkin's disease, lymphocytic depletion, reticular type
M9656/3	Hodgkin's disease, nodular sclerosis NOS
M9657/3	Hodgkin's disease, nodular sclerosis, cellular phase
M9660/3	Hodgkin's paragranuloma
M9661/3	Hodgkin's granuloma
M9662/3	Hodgkin's sarcoma

M969 **Lymphomas, nodular or follicular**

M9690/3	Malignant lymphoma, nodular NOS
M9691/3	Malignant lymphoma, mixed lymphocytic-histiocytic, nodular
M9692/3	Malignant lymphoma, centroblastic-centrocytic, follicular
M9693/3	Malignant lymphoma, lymphocytic, well differentiated, nodular
M9694/3	Malignant lymphoma, lymphocytic, intermediate differentiation, nodular
M9695/3	Malignant lymphoma, follicular center cell, cleaved, follicular
M9696/3	Malignant lymphoma, lymphocytic, poorly differentiated, nodular
M9697/3	Malignant lymphoma, centroblastic type, follicular
M9698/3	Malignant lymphoma, follicular center cell, noncleaved, follicular

M970 **Mycosis fungoides**

M9700/3	Mycosis fungoides
M9701/3	Sezary's disease

M971-M972 **Miscellaneous reticuloendothelial neoplasms**

M9710/3	Microglioma
M9720/3	Malignant histiocytosis
M9721/3	Histiocytic medullary reticulosis
M9722/3	Letterer-Siwe's disease

M973 **Plasma cell tumors**

M9730/3	Plasma cell myeloma
M9731/0	Plasma cell tumor, benign
M9731/1	Plasmacytoma NOS
M9731/3	Plasma cell tumor, malignant

M974 **Mast cell tumors**

M9740/1	Mastocytoma NOS
M9740/3	Mast cell sarcoma
M9741/3	Malignant mastocytosis

M975 **Burkitt's tumor**

M9750/3	Burkitt's tumor

M980-M994 **Leukemias NOS**

M9800/3	Leukemias NOS
M9800/3	Leukemia NOS
M9801/3	Acute leukemia NOS
M9802/3	Subacute leukemia NOS
M9803/3	Chronic leukemia NOS
M9804/3	Aleukemic leukemia NOS

M981 **Compound leukemias**

M9810/3	Compound leukemia

M982 **Lymphoid leukemias**

M9820/3	Lymphoid leukemia NOS
M9821/3	Acute lymphoid leukemia
M9822/3	Subacute lymphoid leukemia
M9823/3	Chronic lymphoid leukemia
M9824/3	Aleukemic lymphoid leukemia
M9825/3	Prolymphocytic leukemia

M983 **Plasma cell leukemias**

M9830/3	Plasma cell leukemia

M984 **Erythroleukemias**

M9840/3	Erythroleukemia
M9841/3	Acute erythremia
M9842/3	Chronic erythremia

M985 **Lymphosarcoma cell leukemias**

M9850/3	Lymphosarcoma cell leukemia

M986 **Myeloid leukemias**

M9860/3	Myeloid leukemia NOS
M9861/3	Acute myeloid leukemia
M9862/3	Subacute myeloid leukemia
M9863/3	Chronic myeloid leukemia
M9864/3	Aleukemic myeloid leukemia
M9865/3	Neutrophilic leukemia
M9866/3	Acute promyelocytic leukemia

M987 **Basophilic leukemias**

M9870/3	Basophilic leukemia

M988 **Eosinophilic leukemias**

M9880/3	Eosinophilic leukemia

M989 **Monocytic leukemias**

M9890/3	Monocytic leukemia NOS
M9891/3	Acute monocytic leukemia
M9892/3	Subacute monocytic leukemia
M9893/3	Chronic monocytic leukemia
M9894/3	Aleukemic monocytic leukemia

M990-M994 **Miscellaneous leukemias**

M9900/3	Mast cell leukemia
M9910/3	Megakaryocytic leukemia
M9920/3	Megakaryocytic myelosis
M9930/3	Myeloid sarcoma
M9940/3	Hairy cell leukemia

M995-M997 **Miscellaneous myeloproliferative and lymphoproliferative disorders**

M9950/1	Polycythemia vera
M9951/1	Acute panmyelosis
M9960/1	Chronic myeloproliferative disease
M9961/1	Myelosclerosis with myeloid metaplasia
M9962/1	Idiopathic thrombocythemia
M9970/1	Chronic lymphoproliferative disease

Appendix B: Glossary of Mental Disorders

was officially deleted October 1, 2004

Appendix C: Classification of Drugs by American Hospital Formulary Service List Number and Their ICD-9-CM Equivalents

The coding of adverse effects of drugs is keyed to the continually revised Hospital Formulary of the American Hospital Formulary Service (AHFS) published under the direction of the American Society of Hospital Pharmacists.

The following section gives the ICD-9-CM diagnosis code for each AHFS list.

AHFS* List		ICD-9-CM Dx Code
4:00	ANTIHISTAMINE DRUGS	963.0
8:00	ANTI-INFECTIVE AGENTS	
8:04	Amebacides	961.5
	hydroxyquinoline derivatives	961.3
	arsenical anti-infectives	961.1
	quinoline derivatives	961.3
8:12.04	Antifungal Antibiotics	960.1
	nonantibiotics	961.9
8:12.06	Cephalosporins	960.5
8:12.08	Chloramphenicol	960.2
8:12.12	The Erythromycins	960.3
8:12.16	The Penicillins	960.0
8:12.20	The Streptomycins	960.6
8:12.24	The Tetracyclines	960.4
8:12.28	Other Antibiotics	960.8
	antimycobacterial antibiotics	960.6
	macrolides	960.3
8:16	Antituberculars	961.8
	antibiotics	960.6
8:18	Antivirals	961.7
8:20	Plasmodicides (antimalarials)	961.4
8:24	Sulfonamides	961.0
8:26	The Sulfones	961.8
8:28	Treponemicides	961.2
8:32	Trichomonacides	961.5
	hydroxyquinoline derivatives	961.3
	nitrofuran derivatives	961.9
8:36	Urinary Germicides	961.9
	quinoline derivatives	961.3
8:40	Other Anti-Infectives	961.9
10:00	ANTINEOPLASTIC AGENTS	963.1
	antibiotics	960.7
	progestogens	962.2
12:00	AUTONOMIC DRUGS	
12:04	Parasympathomimetic (Cholinergic) Agents	971.0
12:08	Parasympatholytic (Cholinergic Blocking Agents	971.1
12:12	Sympathomimetic (Adrenergic) Agents	971.2
12:16	Sympatholytic (Adrenergic Blocking) Agents	971.3
12:20	Skeletal Muscle Relaxants	975.2
	central nervous system	
	muscle-tone depressants	968.0
16:00	BLOOD DERIVATIVES	964.7
20:00	BLOOD FORMATION AND COAGULATION	
20:04	Antianemia Drugs	964.1
20:04.04	Iron Preparations	964.0
20:04.08	Liver and Stomach Preparations	964.1
20:12.04	Anticoagulants	964.2
20:12.08	Antiheparin Agents	964.5
20:12.12	Coagulants	964.5
20.12.16	Hemostatics	964.5
	capillary-active drugs	972.8
	fibrinolysis-affecting agents	964.4
	natural products	964.7
24:00	CARDIOVASCULAR DRUGS	
24:04	Cardiac Drugs	972.9
	cardiotonic agents	972.1
	rhythm regulators	972.0
24:06	Antilipemic Agents	972.2
	thyroid derivatives	962.7

AHFS* List		ICD-9-CM Dx Code
24:08	Hypotensive Agents	972.6
	adrenergic blocking agents	971.3
	ganglion-blocking agents	972.3
	vasodilators	972.5
24:12	Vasodilating Agents	972.5
	coronary	972.4
	nicotinic acid derivatives	972.2
24:16	Sclerosing Agents	972.7
28:00	CENTRAL NERVOUS SYSTEM DRUGS	
28:04	General Anesthetics	968.4
	gaseous anesthetics	968.2
	halothane	968.1
	intravenous anesthetics	968.3
28:08	Analgesics and Antipyretics	965.9
	antirheumatics	965.61-965.69
	aromatic analgesics	965.4
	non-narcotics NEC	965.7
	opium alkaloids	965.00
	heroin	965.01
	methadone	965.02
	specified type NEC	965.09
	pyrazole derivatives	965.5
	salicylates	965.1
	specified type NEC	965.8
28:10	Narcotic Antagonists	970.1
28:12	Anticonvulsants	966.3
	barbiturates	967.0
	benzodiazepine-based tranquilizers	969.4
	bromides	967.3
	hydantoin derivatives	966.1
	oxazolidine derivative	966.0
	succinimides	966.2
28:16.04	Antidepressants	969.00-969.09
28:16.08	Tranquilizers	969.5
	benzodiazepine-based	969.4
	butyrophenone-based	969.2
	major NEC	969.3
	phenothiazine-based	969.1
28:16.12	Other Psychotherapeutic Agents	969.8
28:20	Respiratory and Cerebral Stimulants	970.9
	analeptics	970.0
	anorexigenic agents	977.0
	psychostimulants	969.70-969.79
	specified type NEC	970.81-970.89
28:24	Sedatives and Hypnotics	967.9
	barbiturates	967.0
	benzodiazepine-based tranquilizers	969.4
	chloral hydrate group	967.1
	glutethamide group	967.5
	intravenous anesthetics	968.3
	methaqualone	967.4
	paraldehyde	967.2
	phenothiazine-based tranquilizers	969.1
	specified type NEC	967.8
	thiobarbiturates	968.3
	tranquilizer NEC	969.5
36:00	DIAGNOSTIC AGENTS	977.8
40:00	ELECTROLYTE, CALORIC, AND WATER BALANCE AGENTS NEC	974.5
40:04	Acidifying Agents	963.2
40:08	Alkalinizing Agents	963.3
40:10	Ammonia Detoxicants	974.5
40:12	Replacement Solutions NEC	974.5
	plasma volume expanders	964.8
40:16	Sodium-Removing Resins	974.5
40:18	Potassium-Removing Resins	974.5
40:20	Caloric Agents	974.5
40:24	Salt and Sugar Substitutes	974.5
40:28	Diuretics NEC	974.4
	carbonic acid anhydrase inhibitors	974.2
	mercurials	974.0
	purine derivatives	974.1
	saluretics	974.3

AHFS* List	ICD-9-CM Dx Code	AHFS* List	ICD-9-CM Dx Code
40:36 Irrigating Solutions	974.5	68:34 Other Corpus Luteum Hormones	962.2
40:40 Uricosuric Agents	974.7	68:36 Thyroid and Antithyroid	
44:00 ENZYMES NEC	963.4	antithyroid	962.8
fibrinolysis-affecting agents	964.4	thyroid	962.7
gastric agents	973.4	72:00 LOCAL ANESTHETICS NEC	968.9
48:00 EXPECTORANTS AND COUGH PREPARATIONS		topical (surface) agents	968.5
antihistamine agents	963.0	infiltrating agents (intradermal)	
antitussives	975.4	(subcutaneous) (submucosal)	968.5
codeine derivatives	965.09	nerve blocking agents (peripheral) (plexus) (regional)	968.6
expectorants	975.5	spinal	968.7
narcotic agents NEC	965.09	76:00 OXYTOCICS	975.0
52:00 EYE, EAR, NOSE, AND THROAT PREPARATIONS		78:00 RADIOACTIVE AGENTS	990
52:04 Anti-Infectives		80:00 SERUMS, TOXOIDS, AND VACCINES	
ENT	976.6	80:04 Serums	979.9
ophthalmic	976.5	immune globulin (gamma) (human)	964.6
52:04.04 Antibiotics		80:08 Toxoids NEC	978.8
ENT	976.6	diphtheria	978.5
ophthalmic	976.5	and tetanus	978.9
52:04.06 Antivirals		with pertussis component	978.6
ENT	976.6	tetanus	978.4
ophthalmic	976.5	and diphtheria	978.9
52:04.08 Sulfonamides		with pertussis component	978.6
ENT	976.6	80:12 Vaccines NEC	979.9
ophthalmic	976.5	bacterial NEC	978.8
52:04.12 Miscellaneous Anti-Infectives		with other bacterial component	978.9
ENT	976.6	pertussis component	978.6
ophthalmic	976.5	viral and rickettsial component	979.7
52:08 Anti-Inflammatory Agents		rickettsial NEC	979.6
ENT	976.6	with bacterial component	979.7
ophthalmic	976.5	pertussis component	978.6
52:10 Carbonic Anhydrase Inhibitors	974.2	viral component	979.7
52:12 Contact Lens Solutions	976.5	viral NEC	979.6
52:16 Local Anesthetics	968.5	with bacterial component	979.7
52:20 Miotics	971.0	pertussis component	978.6
52:24 Mydriatics		rickettsial component	979.7
adrenergics	971.2	84:00 SKIN AND MUCOUS MEMBRANE PREPARATIONS	
anticholinergics	971.1	84:04 Anti-Infectives	976.0
antimuscarinics	971.1	84:04.04 Antibiotics	976.0
parasympatholytics	971.1	84:04.08 Fungicides	976.0
spasmolytics	971.1	84:04.12 Scabicides and Pediculicides	976.0
sympathomimetics	971.2	84:04.16 Miscellaneous Local Anti-Infectives	976.0
52:28 Mouth Washes and Gargles	976.6	84:06 Anti-Inflammatory Agents	976.0
52:32 Vasoconstrictors	971.2	84:08 Antipruritics and Local Anesthetics	
52:36 Unclassified Agents		antipruritics	976.1
ENT	976.6	local anesthetics	968.5
ophthalmic	976.5	84:12 Astringents	976.2
56:00 GASTROINTESTINAL DRUGS		84:16 Cell Stimulants and Proliferants	976.8
56:04 Antacids and Absorbents	973.0	84:20 Detergents	976.2
56:08 Anti-Diarrhea Agents	973.5	84:24 Emollients, Demulcents, and Protectants	976.3
56:10 Antiflatulents	973.8	84:28 Keratolytic Agents	976.4
56:12 Cathartics NEC	973.3	84:32 Keratoplastic Agents	976.4
emollients	973.2	84:36 Miscellaneous Agents	976.8
irritants	973.1	86:00 SPASMOLYTIC AGENTS	975.1
56:16 Digestants	973.4	antiasthmatics	975.7
56:20 Emetics and Antiemetics		papaverine	972.5
antiemetics	963.0	theophyllin	974.1
emetics	973.6	88:00 VITAMINS	
56:24 Lipotropic Agents	977.1	88:04 Vitamin A	963.5
60:00 GOLD COMPOUNDS	965.69	88:08 Vitamin B Complex	963.5
64:00 HEAVY METAL ANTAGONISTS	963.8	hematopoietic vitamin	964.1
68:00 HORMONES AND SYNTHETIC SUBSTITUTES		nicotinic acid derivatives	972.2
68:04 Adrenals	962.0	88:12 Vitamin C	963.5
68:08 Androgens	962.1	88:16 Vitamin D	963.5
68:12 Contraceptives	962.2	88:20 Vitamin E	963.5
68:16 Estrogens	962.2	88:24 Vitamin K Activity	964.3
68:18 Gonadotropins	962.4	88:28 Multivitamin Preparations	963.5
68:20 Insulins and Antidiabetic Agents	962.3	92:00 UNCLASSIFIED THERAPEUTIC AGENTS	977.8
68:20.08 Insulins	962.3	* American Hospital Formulary Service	
68:24 Parathyroid	962.6		
68:28 Pituitary			
anterior	962.4		
posterior	962.5		
68:32 Progestogens	962.2		

Appendix D: Classification of Industrial Accidents According to Agency

Annex B to the Resolution concerning Statistics of Employment Injuries adopted by the Tenth International Conference of Labor Statisticians on 12 October 1962

1 Machines

11	Prime-Movers, except Electrical Motors
111	Steam engines
112	Internal combustion engines
119	Others
12	Transmission Machinery
121	Transmission shafts
122	Transmission belts, cables, pulleys, pinions, chains, gears
129	Others
13	Metalworking Machines
131	Power presses
132	Lathes
133	Milling machines
134	Abrasive wheels
135	Mechanical shears
136	Forging machines
137	Rolling-mills
139	Others
14	Wood and Assimilated Machines
141	Circular saws
142	Other saws
143	Molding machines
144	Overhand planes
149	Others
15	Agricultural Machines
151	Reapers (including combine reapers)
152	Threshers
159	Others
16	Mining Machinery
161	Under-cutters
169	Others
19	Other Machines Not Elsewhere Classified
191	Earth-moving machines, excavating and scraping machines, except means of transport
192	Spinning, weaving and other textile machines
193	Machines for the manufacture of food- stuffs and beverages
194	Machines for the manufacture of paper
195	Printing machines
199	Others

2 Means of Transport and Lifting Equipment

21	Lifting Machines and Appliances
211	Cranes
212	Lifts and elevators
213	Winches
214	Pulley blocks
219	Others
22	Means of Rail Transport
221	Inter-urban railways
222	Rail transport in mines, tunnels, quarries, industrial establishments, docks, etc.
229	Others
23	Other Wheeled Means of Transport, Excluding Rail Transport
231	Tractors
232	Lorries
233	Trucks
234	Motor vehicles, not elsewhere classified
235	Animal-drawn vehicles
236	Hand-drawn vehicles
239	Others
24	Means of Air Transport
25	Means of Water Transport
251	Motorized means of water transport
252	Non-motorized means of water transport
26	Other Means of Transport
261	Cable-cars
262	Mechanical conveyors, except cable-cars
269	Others

3 Other Equipment

31	Pressure Vessels
311	Boilers
312	Pressurized containers
313	Pressurized piping and accessories
314	Gas cylinders
315	Caissons, diving equipment
319	Others
32	Furnaces, Ovens, Kilns
321	Blast furnaces
322	Refining furnaces
323	Other furnaces
324	Kilns
325	Ovens
33	Refrigerating Plants
34	Electrical Installations, Including Electric Motors, but Excluding Electric Hand Tools
341	Rotating machines
342	Conductors
343	Transformers
344	Control apparatus
349	Others
35	Electric Hand Tools
36	Tools, Implements, and Appliances, Except Electric Hand Tools
361	Power-driven hand tools, except electric hand tools
362	Hand tools, not power-driven
369	Others
37	Ladders, Mobile Ramps
38	Scaffolding
39	Other Equipment, Not Elsewhere Classified

4 Materials, Substances and Radiations

41	Explosives
42	Dusts, Gases, Liquids and Chemicals, Excluding Explosives
421	Dusts
422	Gases, vapors, fumes
423	Liquids, not elsewhere classified
424	Chemicals, not elsewhere classified
43	Flying Fragments
44	Radiations
441	Ionizing radiations
449	Others
49	Other Materials and Substances Not Elsewhere Classified

5 Working Environment

51	Outdoor
511	Weather
512	Traffic and working surfaces
513	Water
519	Others
52	Indoor
521	Floors
522	Confined quarters
523	Stairs
524	Other traffic and working surfaces
525	Floor openings and wall openings
526	Environmental factors (lighting, ventilation, temperature, noise, etc.)
529	Others
53	Underground
531	Roofs and faces of mine roads and tunnels, etc.
532	Floors of mine roads and tunnels, etc.
533	Working-faces of mines, tunnels, etc.
534	Mine shafts
535	Fire
536	Water
539	Others

6 Other Agencies, Not Elsewhere Classified

61	Animals
611	Live animals
612	Animal products
69	Other Agencies, Not Elsewhere Classified

7 Agencies Not Classified for Lack of Sufficient Data

Appendix E: List of Three-digit Categories

1. Infectious and Parasitic Diseases

Intestinal infectious diseases (001-009)
001　Cholera
002　Typhoid and paratyphoid fevers
003　Other salmonella infections
004　Shigellosis
005　Other food poisoning (bacterial)
006　Amebiasis
007　Other protozoal intestinal diseases
008　Intestinal infections due to other organisms
009　Ill-defined intestinal infections

Tuberculosis (010-018)
010　Primary tuberculous infection
011　Pulmonary tuberculosis
012　Other respiratory tuberculosis
013　Tuberculosis of meninges and central nervous system
014　Tuberculosis of intestines, peritoneum, and mesenteric glands
015　Tuberculosis of bones and joints
016　Tuberculosis of genitourinary system
017　Tuberculosis of other organs
018　Miliary tuberculosis

Zoonotic bacterial diseases (020-027)
020　Plague
021　Tularemia
022　Anthrax
023　Brucellosis
024　Glanders
025　Melioidosis
026　Rat-bite fever
027　Other zoonotic bacterial diseases

Other bacterial diseases (030-041)
030　Leprosy
031　Diseases due to other mycobacteria
032　Diphtheria
033　Whooping cough
034　Streptococcal sore throat and scarlet fever
035　Erysipelas
036　Meningococcal infection
037　Tetanus
038　Septicemia
039　Actinomycotic infections
040　Other bacterial diseases
041　Bacterial infection in conditions classified elsewhere and of unspecified site

Human immunodeficiency virus (042)
042　Human immunodeficiency virus [HIV] disease

Poliomyelitis and other non-arthropod-borne viral diseases and prion diseases of central nervous system (045-049)
045　Acute poliomyelitis
046　Slow virus infections and prion diseases of central nervous system
047　Meningitis due to enterovirus
048　Other enterovirus diseases of central nervous system
049　Other non-arthropod-borne viral diseases of central nervous system

Viral diseases generally accompanied by exanthem (050-059)
050　Smallpox
051　Cowpox and paravaccinia
052　Chickenpox
053　Herpes zoster
054　Herpes simplex
055　Measles
056　Rubella
057　Other viral exanthemata
058　Other human herpesvirus
059　Other poxvirus infections

Arthropod-borne viral diseases (060-066)
060　Yellow fever
061　Dengue
062　Mosquito-borne viral encephalitis
063　Tick-borne viral encephalitis
064　Viral encephalitis transmitted by other and unspecified arthropods
065　Arthropod-borne hemorrhagic fever
066　Other arthropod-borne viral diseases

Other diseases due to viruses and Chlamydiae (070-079)
070　Viral hepatitis
071　Rabies
072　Mumps
073　Ornithosis
074　Specific diseases due to Coxsackie virus
075　Infectious mononucleosis
076　Trachoma
077　Other diseases of conjunctiva due to viruses and Chlamydiae
078　Other diseases due to viruses and Chlamydiae
079　Viral and chlamydial infection in conditions classified elsewhere and of unspecified site

Rickettsioses and other arthropod-borne diseases (080-088)
080　Louse-borne [epidemic] typhus
081　Other typhus
082　Tick-borne rickettsioses
083　Other rickettsioses
084　Malaria
085　Leishmaniasis
086　Trypanosomiasis
087　Relapsing fever
088　Other arthropod-borne diseases

Syphilis and other venereal diseases (090-099)
090　Congenital syphilis
091　Early syphilis, symptomatic
092　Early syphilis, latent
093　Cardiovascular syphilis
094　Neurosyphilis
095　Other forms of late syphilis, with symptoms
096　Late syphilis, latent
097　Other and unspecified syphilis
098　Gonococcal infections
099　Other venereal diseases

Other spirochetal diseases (100-104)
100　Leptospirosis
101　Vincent's angina
102　Yaws
103　Pinta
104　Other spirochetal infection

Mycoses (110-118)
110　Dermatophytosis
111　Dermatomycosis, other and unspecified
112　Candidiasis
114　Coccidioidomycosis
115　Histoplasmosis
116　Blastomycotic infection
117　Other mycoses
118　Opportunistic mycoses

Helminthiases (120-129)
120　Schistosomiasis [bilharziasis]
121　Other trematode infections
122　Echinococcosis
123　Other cestode infection
124　Trichinosis
125　Filarial infection and dracontiasis
126　Ancylostomiasis and necatoriasis
127　Other intestinal helminthiases
128　Other and unspecified helminthiases
129　Intestinal parasitism, unspecified

Other infectious and parasitic diseases (130-136)
130　Toxoplasmosis
131　Trichomoniasis
132　Pediculosis and phthirus infestation
133　Acariasis
134　Other infestation
135　Sarcoidosis
136　Other and unspecified infectious and parasitic diseases

Late effects of infectious and parasitic diseases (137-139)
137　Late effects of tuberculosis
138　Late effects of acute poliomyelitis
139　Late effects of other infectious and parasitic diseases

2. Neoplasms

Malignant neoplasm of lip, oral cavity, and pharynx (140-149)
140　Malignant neoplasm of lip
141　Malignant neoplasm of tongue
142　Malignant neoplasm of major salivary glands
143　Malignant neoplasm of gum
144　Malignant neoplasm of floor of mouth
145　Malignant neoplasm of other and unspecified parts of mouth
146　Malignant neoplasm of oropharynx
147　Malignant neoplasm of nasopharynx
148　Malignant neoplasm of hypopharynx
149　Malignant neoplasm of other and ill-defined sites within the lip, oral cavity, and pharynx

Malignant neoplasm of digestive organs and peritoneum (150-159)
150　Malignant neoplasm of esophagus
151　Malignant neoplasm of stomach
152　Malignant neoplasm of small intestine, including duodenum
153　Malignant neoplasm of colon
154　Malignant neoplasm of rectum, rectosigmoid junction, and anus
155　Malignant neoplasm of liver and intrahepatic bile ducts
156　Malignant neoplasm of gallbladder and extrahepatic bile ducts
157　Malignant neoplasm of pancreas
158　Malignant neoplasm of retroperitoneum and peritoneum
159　Malignant neoplasm of other and ill-defined sites within the digestive organs and peritoneum

Malignant neoplasm of respiratory and intrathoracic organs (160-165)
160　Malignant neoplasm of nasal cavities, middle ear, and accessory sinuses
161　Malignant neoplasm of larynx
162　Malignant neoplasm of trachea, bronchus, and lung
163　Malignant neoplasm of pleura
164　Malignant neoplasm of thymus, heart, and mediastinum
165　Malignant neoplasm of other and ill-defined sites within the respiratory system and intrathoracic organs

Malignant neoplasm of bone, connective tissue, skin, and breast (170-176)
170　Malignant neoplasm of bone and articular cartilage
171　Malignant neoplasm of connective and other soft tissue
172　Malignant melanoma of skin
173　Other and unspecified malignant neoplasm of skin
174　Malignant neoplasm of female breast
175　Malignant neoplasm of male breast
176　Kaposi's sarcoma

Malignant neoplasm of genitourinary organs (179-189)
179 Malignant neoplasm of uterus, part unspecified
180 Malignant neoplasm of cervix uteri
181 Malignant neoplasm of placenta
182 Malignant neoplasm of body of uterus
183 Malignant neoplasm of ovary and other uterine adnexa
184 Malignant neoplasm of other and unspecified female genital organs
185 Malignant neoplasm of prostate
186 Malignant neoplasm of testis
187 Malignant neoplasm of penis and other male genital organs
188 Malignant neoplasm of bladder
189 Malignant neoplasm of kidney and other unspecified urinary organs

Malignant neoplasm of other and unspecified sites (190-199)
190 Malignant neoplasm of eye
191 Malignant neoplasm of brain
192 Malignant neoplasm of other and unspecified parts of nervous system
193 Malignant neoplasm of thyroid gland
194 Malignant neoplasm of other endocrine glands and related structures
195 Malignant neoplasm of other and ill-defined sites
196 Secondary and unspecified malignant neoplasm of lymph nodes
197 Secondary malignant neoplasm of respiratory and digestive systems
198 Secondary malignant neoplasm of other specified sites
199 Malignant neoplasm without specification of site

Malignant neoplasm of lymphatic and hematopoietic tissue (200-208)
200 Lymphosarcoma and reticulosarcoma and other specified malignant tumors of lymphatic tissue
201 Hodgkin's disease
202 Other malignant neoplasm of lymphoid and histiocytic tissue
203 Multiple myeloma and immunoproliferative neoplasms
204 Lymphoid leukemia
205 Myeloid leukemia
206 Monocytic leukemia
207 Other specified leukemia
208 Leukemia of unspecified cell type

Neuroendocrine tumors (209)
209 Neuroendocrine tumors

Benign neoplasms (210-229)
210 Benign neoplasm of lip, oral cavity, and pharynx
211 Benign neoplasm of other parts of digestive system
212 Benign neoplasm of respiratory and intrathoracic organs
213 Benign neoplasm of bone and articular cartilage
214 Lipoma
215 Other benign neoplasm of connective and other soft tissue
216 Benign neoplasm of skin
217 Benign neoplasm of breast
218 Uterine leiomyoma
219 Other benign neoplasm of uterus
220 Benign neoplasm of ovary
221 Benign neoplasm of other female genital organs
222 Benign neoplasm of male genital organs
223 Benign neoplasm of kidney and other urinary organs
224 Benign neoplasm of eye
225 Benign neoplasm of brain and other parts of nervous system
226 Benign neoplasm of thyroid gland

227 Benign neoplasm of other endocrine glands and related structures
228 Hemangioma and lymphangioma, any site
229 Benign neoplasm of other and unspecified sites

Carcinoma in situ (230-234)
230 Carcinoma in situ of digestive organs
231 Carcinoma in situ of respiratory system
232 Carcinoma in situ of skin
233 Carcinoma in situ of breast and genitourinary system
234 Carcinoma in situ of other and unspecified sites

Neoplasms of uncertain behavior (235-238)
235 Neoplasm of uncertain behavior of digestive and respiratory systems
236 Neoplasm of uncertain behavior of genitourinary organs
237 Neoplasm of uncertain behavior of endocrine glands and nervous system
238 Neoplasm of uncertain behavior of other and unspecified sites and tissues

Neoplasms of unspecified nature (239)
239 Neoplasm of unspecified nature

3. Endocrine, Nutritional and Metabolic Diseases, and Immunity Disorders

Disorders of thyroid gland (240-246)
240 Simple and unspecified goiter
241 Nontoxic nodular goiter
242 Thyrotoxicosis with or without goiter
243 Congenital hypothyroidism
244 Acquired hypothyroidism
245 Thyroiditis
246 Other disorders of thyroid

Diseases of other endocrine glands (249-259)
249 Secondary diabetes mellitus
250 Diabetes mellitus
251 Other disorders of pancreatic internal secretion
252 Disorders of parathyroid gland
253 Disorders of the pituitary gland and its hypothalamic control
254 Diseases of thymus gland
255 Disorders of adrenal glands
256 Ovarian dysfunction
257 Testicular dysfunction
258 Polyglandular dysfunction and related disorders
259 Other endocrine disorders

Nutritional deficiencies (260-269)
260 Kwashiorkor
261 Nutritional marasmus
262 Other severe protein-calorie malnutrition
263 Other and unspecified protein-calorie malnutrition
264 Vitamin A deficiency
265 Thiamine and niacin deficiency states
266 Deficiency of B-complex components
267 Ascorbic acid deficiency
268 Vitamin D deficiency
269 Other nutritional deficiencies

Other metabolic disorders and immnity disorders (270-279)
270 Disorders of amino-acid transport and metabolism
271 Disorders of carbohydrate transport and metabolism
272 Disorders of lipoid metabolism
273 Disorders of plasma protein metabolism
274 Gout
275 Disorders of mineral metabolism
276 Disorders of fluid, electrolyte, and acid-base balance
277 Other and unspecified disorders of metabolism

278 Overweight, obesity and other hyperalimentation
279 Disorders involving the immune mechanism

4. Diseases of Blood and Blood-forming Organs (280-289)
280 Iron deficiency anemias
281 Other deficiency anemias
282 Hereditary hemolytic anemias
283 Acquired hemolytic anemias
284 Aplastic anemia and other bone marrow failure syndromes
285 Other and unspecified anemias
286 Coagulation defects
287 Purpura and other hemorrhagic conditions
288 Diseases of white blood cells
289 Other diseases of blood and blood-forming organs

5. Mental, Behavioral and Neurodevelopmental Disorders

Organic psychotic conditions (290-294)
290 Dementias
291 Alcoholic induced mental disorders
292 Drug induced mental disorders
293 Transient mental disorders due to conditions classified elsewhere
294 Persistent mental disorders due to conditions classified elsewhere

Other psychoses (295-299)
295 Schizophrenic disorders
296 Episodic mood disorders
297 Delusional disorders
298 Other nonorganic psychoses
299 Pervasive developmental disorders

Neurotic disorders, personality disorders, and other nonpsychotic mental disorders (300-316)
300 Anxiety, dissociative and somatoform disorders
301 Personality disorders
302 Sexual and gender identity disorders
303 Alcohol dependence syndrome
304 Drug dependence
305 Nondependent abuse of drugs
306 Physiological malfunction arising from mental factors
307 Special symptoms or syndromes, not elsewhere classified
308 Acute reaction to stress
309 Adjustment reaction
310 Specific nonpsychotic mental disorders due to brain damage
311 Depressive disorder, not elsewhere classified
312 Disturbance of conduct, not elsewhere classified
313 Disturbance of emotions specific to childhood and adolescence
314 Hyperkinetic syndrome of childhood
315 Specific delays in development
316 Psychic factors associated with diseases classified elsewhere

Intellectual Disabilities (317-319)
317 Mild intellectual disabilities
318 Other specified intellectual disabilities
319 Unspecified intellectual disabilities

6. Diseases of the Nervous System and Sense Organs

Inflammatory diseases of the central nervous system (320-326)
320 Bacterial meningitis
321 Meningitis due to other organisms
322 Meningitis of unspecified cause
323 Encephalitis, myelitis, and encephalomyelitis

324   Intracranial and intraspinal abscess
325   Phlebitis and thrombophlebitis of intracranial venous sinuses
326   Late effects of intracranial abscess or pyogenic infection

Organic Sleep Disorders (327)
327   Organic sleep disorders

Hereditary and degenerative diseases of the central nervous system (330-337)
330   Cerebral degenerations usually manifest in childhood
331   Other cerebral degenerations
332   Parkinson's disease
333   Other extrapyramidal diseases and abnormal movement disorders
334   Spinocerebellar disease
335   Anterior horn cell disease
336   Other diseases of spinal cord
337   Disorders of the autonomic nervous system

Pain (338)
338   Pain, not elsewhere classified

Other headache syndromes (339)
339   Other headache syndromes

Other disorders of the central nervous system (340-349)
340   Multiple sclerosis
341   Other demyelinating diseases of central nervous system
342   Hemiplegia and hemiparesis
343   Infantile cerebral palsy
344   Other paralytic syndromes
345   Epilepsy and recurrent seizures
346   Migraine
347   Cataplexy and narcolepsy
348   Other conditions of brain
349   Other and unspecified disorders of the nervous system

Disorders of the peripheral nervous system (350-359)
350   Trigeminal nerve disorders
351   Facial nerve disorders
352   Disorders of other cranial nerves
353   Nerve root and plexus disorders
354   Mononeuritis of upper limb and mononeuritis multiplex
355   Mononeuritis of lower limb
356   Hereditary and idiopathic peripheral neuropathy
357   Inflammatory and toxic neuropathy
358   Myoneural disorders
359   Muscular dystrophies and other myopathies

Disorders of the eye and adnexa (360-379)
360   Disorders of the globe
361   Retinal detachments and defects
362   Other retinal disorders
363   Chorioretinal inflammations and scars and other disorders of choroid
364   Disorders of iris and ciliary body
365   Glaucoma
366   Cataract
367   Disorders of refraction and accommodation
368   Visual disturbances
369   Blindness and low vision
370   Keratitis
371   Corneal opacity and other disorders of cornea
372   Disorders of conjunctiva
373   Inflammation of eyelids
374   Other disorders of eyelids
375   Disorders of lacrimal system
376   Disorders of the orbit
377   Disorders of optic nerve and visual pathways
378   Strabismus and other disorders of binocular eye movements
379   Other disorders of eye

Diseases of the ear and mastoid process (380-389)
380   Disorders of external ear
381   Nonsuppurative otitis media and Eustachian tube disorders
382   Suppurative and unspecified otitis media
383   Mastoiditis and related conditions
384   Other disorders of tympanic membrane
385   Other disorders of middle ear and mastoid
386   Vertiginous syndromes and other disorders of vestibular system
387   Otosclerosis
388   Other disorders of ear
389   Hearing loss

7. Diseases of the Circulatory System

Acute rheumatic fever (390-392)
390   Rheumatic fever without mention of heart involvement
391   Rheumatic fever with heart involvement
392   Rheumatic chorea

Chronic rheumatic heart disease (393-398)
393   Chronic rheumatic pericarditis
394   Diseases of mitral valve
395   Diseases of aortic valve
396   Diseases of mitral and aortic valves
397   Diseases of other endocardial structures
398   Other rheumatic heart disease

Hypertensive disease (401-405)
401   Essential hypertension
402   Hypertensive heart disease
403   Hypertensive chronic kidney disease
404   Hypertensive heart and chronic kidney disease
405   Secondary hypertension

Ischemic heart disease (410-414)
410   Acute myocardial infarction
411   Other acute and subacute forms of ischemic heart disease
412   Old myocardial infarction
413   Angina pectoris
414   Other forms of chronic ischemic heart disease

Diseases of pulmonary circulation (415-417)
415   Acute pulmonary heart disease
416   Chronic pulmonary heart disease
417   Other diseases of pulmonary circulation

Other forms of heart disease (420-429)
420   Acute pericarditis
421   Acute and subacute endocarditis
422   Acute myocarditis
423   Other diseases of pericardium
424   Other diseases of endocardium
425   Cardiomyopathy
426   Conduction disorders
427   Cardiac dysrhythmias
428   Heart failure
429   Ill-defined descriptions and complications of heart disease

Cerebrovascular disease (430-438)
430   Subarachnoid hemorrhage
431   Intracerebral hemorrhage
432   Other and unspecified intracranial hemorrhage
433   Occlusion and stenosis of precerebral arteries
434   Occlusion of cerebral arteries
435   Transient cerebral ischemia
436   Acute, but ill-defined, cerebrovascular disease
437   Other and ill-defined cerebrovascular disease
438   Late effects of cerebrovascular disease

Diseases of arteries, arterioles, and capillaries (440-449)
440   Atherosclerosis
441   Aortic aneurysm and dissection
442   Other aneurysm
443   Other peripheral vascular disease
444   Arterial embolism and thrombosis
445   Atheroembolism
446   Polyarteritis nodosa and allied conditions
447   Other disorders of arteries and arterioles
448   Diseases of capillaries
449   Septic arterial embolism

Diseases of veins and lymphatics, and other diseases of circulatory system (451-459)
451   Phlebitis and thrombophlebitis
452   Portal vein thrombosis
453   Other venous embolism and thrombosis
454   Varicose veins of lower extremities
455   Hemorrhoids
456   Varicose veins of other sites
457   Noninfectious disorders of lymphatic channels
458   Hypotension
459   Other disorders of circulatory system

8. Diseases of the Respiratory System

Acute respiratory infections (460-466)
460   Acute nasopharyngitis [common cold]
461   Acute sinusitis
462   Acute pharyngitis
463   Acute tonsillitis
464   Acute laryngitis and tracheitis
465   Acute upper respiratory infections of multiple or unspecified sites
466   Acute bronchitis and bronchiolitis

Other diseases of upper respiratory tract (470-478)
470   Deviated nasal septum
471   Nasal polyps
472   Chronic pharyngitis and nasopharyngitis
473   Chronic sinusitis
474   Chronic disease of tonsils and adenoids
475   Peritonsillar abscess
476   Chronic laryngitis and laryngotracheitis
477   Allergic rhinitis
478   Other diseases of upper respiratory tract

Pneumonia and influenza (480-488)
480   Viral pneumonia
481   Pneumococcal pneumonia [Streptococcus pneumoniae pneumonia]
482   Other bacterial pneumonia
483   Pneumonia due to other specified organism
484   Pneumonia in infectious diseases classified elsewhere
485   Bronchopneumonia, organism unspecified
486   Pneumonia, organism unspecified
487   Influenza
488   Influenza due to certain identified influenza viruses

Chronic obstructive pulmonary disease and allied conditions (490-496)
490   Bronchitis, not specified as acute or chronic
491   Chronic bronchitis
492   Emphysema
493   Asthma
494   Bronchiectasis
495   Extrinsic allergic alveolitis
496   Chronic airways obstruction, not elsewhere classified

Pneumoconioses and other lung diseases due to external agents (500-508)
500   Coal workers' pneumoconiosis
501   Asbestosis
502   Pneumoconiosis due to other silica or silicates
503   Pneumoconiosis due to other inorganic dust
504   Pneumopathy due to inhalation of other dust
505   Pneumoconiosis, unspecified
506   Respiratory conditions due to chemical fumes and vapors
507   Pneumonitis due to solids and liquids
508   Respiratory conditions due to other and unspecified external agents

Other diseases of respiratory system (510-519)
510 Empyema
511 Pleurisy
512 Pneumothorax and air leak
513 Abscess of lung and mediastinum
514 Pulmonary congestion and hypostasis
515 Postinflammatory pulmonary fibrosis
516 Other alveolar and parietoalveolar pneumopathy
517 Lung involvement in conditions classified elsewhere
518 Other diseases of lung
519 Other diseases of respiratory system

9. Diseases of the Digestive System

Diseases of oral cavity, salivary glands, and jaws (520-529)
520 Disorders of tooth development and eruption
521 Diseases of hard tissues of teeth
522 Diseases of pulp and periapical tissues
523 Gingival and periodontal diseases
524 Dentofacial anomalies, including malocclusion
525 Other diseases and conditions of the teeth and supporting structures
526 Diseases of the jaws
527 Diseases of the salivary glands
528 Diseases of the oral soft tissues, excluding lesions specific for gingiva and tongue
529 Diseases and other conditions of the tongue

Diseases of esophagus, stomach, and duodenum (530-539)
530 Diseases of esophagus
531 Gastric ulcer
532 Duodenal ulcer
533 Peptic ulcer, site unspecified
534 Gastrojejunal ulcer
535 Gastritis and duodenitis
536 Disorders of function of stomach
537 Other disorders of stomach and duodenum
538 Gastrointestinal mucositis (ulcerative)
539 Complications of bariatric procedures

Appendicitis (540-543)
540 Acute appendicitis
541 Appendicitis, unqualified
542 Other appendicitis
543 Other diseases of appendix

Hernia of abdominal cavity (550-553)
550 Inguinal hernia
551 Other hernia of abdominal cavity, with gangrene
552 Other hernia of abdominal cavity, with obstruction, but without mention of gangrene
553 Other hernia of abdominal cavity without mention of obstruction or gangrene

Noninfective enteritis and colitis (555-558)
555 Regional enteritis
556 Ulcerative colitis
557 Vascular insufficiency of intestine
558 Other noninfective gastroenteritis and colitis

Other diseases of intestines and peritoneum (560-569)
560 Intestinal obstruction without mention of hernia
562 Diverticula of intestine
564 Functional digestive disorders, not elsewhere classified
565 Anal fissure and fistula
566 Abscess of anal and rectal regions
567 Peritonitis and retroperitoneal infections
568 Other disorders of peritoneum
569 Other disorders of intestine

Other diseases of digestive system (570-579)
570 Acute and subacute necrosis of liver
571 Chronic liver disease and cirrhosis
572 Liver abscess and sequelae of chronic liver disease
573 Other disorders of liver
574 Cholelithiasis
575 Other disorders of gallbladder
576 Other disorders of biliary tract
577 Diseases of pancreas
578 Gastrointestinal hemorrhage
579 Intestinal Malabsorption

10. Diseases of the Genitourinary System

Nephritis, nephrotic syndrome, and nephrosis (580-589)
580 Acute gloerulonephritis
581 Nephrotic syndrome
582 Chronic glomerulonephritis
583 Nephritis and nephropathy, not specified as acute or chronic
584 Acute kidney failure
585 Chronic kidney disease (CKD)
586 Renal failure, unspecified
587 Renal sclerosis, unspecified
588 Disorders resulting from impaired renal function
589 Small kidney of unknown cause

Other diseases of urinary system (590-599)
590 Infections of kidney
591 Hydronephrosis
592 Calculus of kidney and ureter
593 Other disorders of kidney and ureter
594 Calculus of lower urinary tract
595 Cystitis
596 Other disorders of bladder
597 Urethritis, not sexually transmitted, and urethral syndrome
598 Urethral stricture
599 Other disorders of urethra and urinary tract

Diseases of male genital organs (600-608)
600 Hyperplasia of prostate
601 Inflammatory diseases of prostate
602 Other disorders of prostate
603 Hydrocele
604 Orchitis and epididymitis
605 Redundant prepuce and phimosis
606 Infertility, male
607 Disorders of penis
608 Other disorders of male genital organs

Disorders of breast (610-612)
610 Benign mammary dysplasias
611 Other disorders of breast
612 Deformity and disproportion of reconstructed breast

Inflammatory disease of female pelvic organs (614-616)
614 Inflammatory disease of ovary, fallopian tube, pelvic cellular tissue, and peritoneum
615 Inflammatory diseases of uterus, except cervix
616 Inflammatory disease of cervix, vagina, and vulva

Other disorders of female genital tract (617-629)
617 Endometriosis
618 Genital prolapse
619 Fistula involving female genital tract
620 Noninflammatory disorders of ovary, fallopian tube, and broad ligament
621 Disorders of uterus, not elsewhere classified
622 Noninflammatory disorders of cervix
623 Noninflammatory disorders of vagina
624 Noninflammatory disorders of vulva and perineum
625 Pain and other symptoms associated with female genital organs
626 Disorders of menstruation and other abnormal bleeding from female genital tract
627 Menopausal and postmenopausal disorders
628 Infertility, female
629 Other disorders of female genital organs

11. Complications of Pregnancy, Childbirth and the Puerperium

Ectopic and molar pregnancy (630-633)
630 Hydatidiform mole
631 Other abnormal product of conception
632 Missed abortion
633 Ectopic pregnancy

Other pregnancy with abortive outcome (634-639)
634 Spontaneous abortion
635 Legally induced abortion
636 Illegally induced abortion
637 Unspecified abortion
638 Failed attempted abortion
639 Complications following abortion and ectopic and molar pregnancies

Complications mainly related to pregnancy (640-649)
640 Hemorrhage in early pregnancy
641 Antepartum hemorrhage, abruptio placentae, and placenta previa
642 Hypertension complicating pregnancy, childbirth, and the puerperium
643 Excessive vomiting in pregnancy
644 Early or threatened labor
645 Late pregnancy
646 Other complications of pregnancy, not elsewhere classified
647 Infectious and parasitic conditions in the mother classifiable elsewhere, but complicating pregnancy, childbirth, and the puerperium
648 Other current conditions in the mother classifiable elsewhere, but complicating pregnancy, childbirth, and the puerperium
649 Other conditions or status of the mother complicating pregnancy, childbirth, or the puerperium

Normal delivery, and other indications for care in pregnancy, labor, and delivery (650-659)
650 Normal delivery
651 Multiple gestation
652 Malposition and malpresentation of fetus
653 Disproportion
654 Abnormality of organs and soft tissues of pelvis
655 Known or suspected fetal abnormality affecting management of mother
656 Other known or suspected fetal and placental problems affecting management of mother
657 Polyhydramnios
658 Other problems associated with amniotic cavity and membranes
659 Other indications for care or intervention related to labor and delivery, not elsewhere classified

Complications occurring mainly in the course of labor and delivery (660-669)
660 Obstructed labor
661 Abnormality of forces of labor
662 Long labor
663 Umbilical cord complications
664 Trauma to perineum and vulva during delivery
665 Other obstetrical trauma
666 Postpartum hemorrhage
667 Retained placenta or membranes, without hemorrhage
668 Complications of the administration of anesthetic or other sedation in labor and delivery
669 Other complications of labor and delivery, not elsewhere classified

Complications of the puerperium (670-677)
670 Major puerperal infection

671 Venous complications in pregnancy and the puerperium
672 Pyrexia of unknown origin during the puerperium
673 Obstetrical pulmonary embolism
674 Other and unspecified complications of the puerperium, not elsewhere classified
675 Infections of the breast and nipple associated with childbirth
676 Other disorders of the breast associated with childbirth, and disorders of lactation
677 Late effect of complication of pregnancy, childbirth, and the puerperium

Other maternal and fetal complications (678-679)
678 Other fetal conditions
679 Complications of in utero procedures

12. Diseases of the Skin and Subcutaneous Tissue

Infections of skin and subcutaneous tissue (680-686)
680 Carbuncle and furuncle
681 Cellulitis and abscess of finger and toe
682 Other cellulitis and abscess
683 Acute lymphadenitis
684 Impetigo
685 Pilonidal cyst
686 Other local infections of skin and subcutaneous tissue

Other inflammatory conditions of skin and subcutaneous tissue (690-698)
690 Erythematosquamous dermatosis
691 Atopic dermatitis and related conditions
692 Contact dermatitis and other eczema
693 Dermatitis due to substances taken internally
694 Bullous dermatoses
695 Erythematous conditions
696 Psoriasis and similar disorders
697 Lichen
698 Pruritus and related conditions

Other diseases of skin and subcutaneous tissue (700-709)
700 Corns and callosities
701 Other hypertrophic and atrophic conditions of skin
702 Other dermatoses
703 Diseases of nail
704 Diseases of hair and hair follicles
705 Disorders of sweat glands
706 Diseases of sebaceous glands
707 Chronic ulcer of skin
708 Urticaria
709 Other disorders of skin and subcutaneous tissue

13. Diseases of the Musculoskeletal System and Connective Tissue

Arthropathies and related disorders (710-719)
710 Diffuse diseases of connective tissue
711 Arthropathy associated with infections
712 Crystal arthropathies
713 Arthropathy associated with other disorders classified elsewhere
714 Rheumatoid arthritis and other inflammatory polyarthropathies
715 Osteoarthrosis and allied disorders
716 Other and unspecified arthropathies
717 Internal derangement of knee
718 Other derangement of joint
719 Other and unspecified disorder of joint

Dorsopathies (720-724)
720 Ankylosing spondylitis and other inflammatory spondylopathies
721 Spondylosis and allied disorders

722 Intervertebral disc disorders
723 Other disorders of cervical region
724 Other and unspecified disorders of back

Rheumatism, excluding the back (725-729)
725 Polymyalgia rheumatica
726 Peripheral enthesopathies and allied syndromes
727 Other disorders of synovium, tendon, and bursa
728 Disorders of muscle, ligament, and fascia
729 Other disorders of soft tissues

Osteopathies, chondropathies, and acquired musculoskeletal deformities (730-739)
730 Osteomyelitis, periostitis, and other infections involving bone
731 Osteitis deformans and osteopathies associated with other disorders classified elsewhere
732 Osteochondropathies
733 Other disorders of bone and cartilage
734 Flat foot
735 Acquired deformities of toe
736 Other acquired deformities of limbs
737 Curvature of spine
738 Other acquired deformity
739 Nonallopathic lesions, not elsewhere classified

14. Congenital Anomalies

740 Anencephalus and similar anomalies
741 Spina bifida
742 Other congenital anomalies of nervous system
743 Congenital anomalies of eye
744 Congenital anomalies of ear, face, and neck
745 Bulbus cordis anomalies and anomalies of cardiac septal closure
746 Other congenital anomalies of heart
747 Other congenital anomalies of circulatory system
748 Congenital anomalies of respiratory system
749 Cleft palate and cleft lip
750 Other congenital anomalies of upper alimentary tract
751 Other congenital anomalies of digestive system
752 Congenital anomalies of genital organs
753 Congenital anomalies of urinary system
754 Certain congenital musculoskeletal deformities
755 Other congenital anomalies of limbs
756 Other congenital musculoskeletal anomalies
757 Congenital anomalies of the integument
758 Chromosomal anomalies
759 Other and unspecified congenital anomalies

15. Certain Conditions Originating in the Perinatal Period

Maternal causes of perinatal morbidity and mortality (760-763)
760 Fetus or newborn affected by maternal conditions which may be unrelated to present pregnancy
761 Fetus or newborn affected by maternal complications of pregnancy
762 Fetus or newborn affected by complications of placenta, cord, and membranes
763 Fetus or newborn affected by other complications of labor and delivery

Other conditions originating in the perinatal period (764-779)
764 Slow fetal growth and fetal malnutrition
765 Disorders relating to short gestation and unspecified low birthweight
766 Disorders relating to long gestation and high birthweight
767 Birth trauma
768 Intrauterine hypoxia and birth asphyxia
769 Respiratory distress syndrome
770 Other respiratory conditions of fetus and newborn

771 Infections specific to the perinatal period
772 Fetal and neonatal hemorrhage
773 Hemolytic disease of fetus or newborn, due to isoimmunization
774 Other perinatal jaundice
775 Endocrine and metabolic disturbances specific to the fetus and newborn
776 Hematological disorders of newborn
777 Perinatal disorders of digestive system
778 Conditions involving the integument and temperature regulation of fetus and newborn
779 Other and ill-defined conditions originating in the perinatal period

16. Symptoms, Signs, and Ill-defined Conditions

Symptoms (780-789)
780 General symptoms
781 Symptoms involving nervous and musculoskeletal systems
782 Symptoms involving skin and other integumentary tissue
783 Symptoms concerning nutrition, metabolism, and development
784 Symptoms involving head and neck
785 Symptoms involving cardiovascular system
786 Symptoms involving respiratory system and other chest symptoms
787 Symptoms involving digestive system
788 Symptoms involving urinary system
789 Other symptoms involving abdomen and pelvis

Nonspecific abnormal findings (790-796)
790 Nonspecific findings on examination of blood
791 Nonspecific findings on examination of urine
792 Nonspecific abnormal findings in other body substances
793 Nonspecific (abnormal) findings on radiological and other examination of body structure
794 Nonspecific abnormal results of function studies
795 Other and nonspecific abnormal cystological, histological, immunological and DNA test findings
796 Other nonspecific abnormal findings

Ill-defined and unknown causes of morbidity and mortality (797-799)
797 Senility without mention of psychosis
798 Sudden death, cause unknown
799 Other ill-defined and unknown causes of morbidity and mortality

17. Injury and Poisoning

Fracture of skull (800-804)
800 Fracture of vault of skull
801 Fracture of base of skull
802 Fracture of face bones
803 Other and unqualified skull fractures
804 Multiple fractures involving skull or face with other bones

Fracture of spine and trunk (805-809)
805 Fracture of vertebral column without mention of spinal cord injury
806 Fracture of vertebral column with spinal cord injury
807 Fracture of rib(s), sternum, larynx, and trachea
808 Fracture of pelvis
809 Ill-defined fractures of bones of trunk

Fracture of upper limb (810-819)
810 Fracture of clavicle
811 Fracture of scapula
812 Fracture of humerus
813 Fracture of radius and ulna
814 Fracture of carpal bone(s)
815 Fracture of metacarpal bone(s)

816 Fracture of one or more phalanges of hand
817 Multiple fractures of hand bones
818 Ill-defined fractures of upper limb
819 Multiple fractures involving both upper limbs, and upper limb with rib(s) and sternum

Fracture of lower limb (820-829)
820 Fracture of neck of femur
821 Fracture of other and unspecified parts of femur
822 Fracture of patella
823 Fracture of tibia and fibula
824 Fracture of ankle
825 Fracture of one or more tarsal and metatarsal bones
826 Fracture of one or more phalanges of foot
827 Other, multiple, and ill-defined fractures of lower limb
828 Multiple fractures involving both lower limbs, lower with upper limb, and lower limb(s) with rib(s) and sternum
829 Fracture of unspecified bones

Dislocation (830-839)
830 Dislocation of jaw
831 Dislocation of shoulder
832 Dislocation of elbow
833 Dislocation of wrist
834 Dislocation of finger
835 Dislocation of hip
836 Dislocation of knee
837 Dislocation of ankle
838 Dislocation of foot
839 Other, multiple, and ill-defined dislocations

Sprains and strains of joints and adjacent muscles (840-848)
840 Sprains and strains of shoulder and upper arm
841 Sprains and strains of elbow and forearm
842 Sprains and strains of wrist and hand
843 Sprains and strains of hip and thigh
844 Sprains and strains of knee and leg
845 Sprains and strains of ankle and foot
846 Sprains and strains of sacroiliac region
847 Sprains and strains of other and unspecified parts of back
848 Other and ill-defined sprains and strains

Intracranial injury, excluding those with skull fracture (850-854)
850 Concussion
851 Cerebral laceration and contusion
852 Subarachnoid, subdural, and extradural hemorrhage, following injury
853 Other and unspecified intracranial hemorrhage following injury
854 Intracranial injury of other and unspecified nature

Internal injury of thorax, abdomen, and pelvis (860-869)
860 Traumatic pneumothorax and hemothorax
861 Injury to heart and lung
862 Injury to other and unspecified intrathoracic organs
863 Injury to gastrointestinal tract
864 Injury to liver
865 Injury to spleen
866 Injury to kidney
867 Injury to pelvic organs
868 Injury to other intra-abdominal organs
869 Internal injury to unspecified or ill-defined organs

Open wound of head, neck, and trunk (870-879)
870 Open wound of ocular adnexa
871 Open wound of eyeball
872 Open wound of ear
873 Other open wound of head
874 Open wound of neck
875 Open wound of chest (wall)

876 Open wound of back
877 Open wound of buttock
878 Open wound of genital organs (external), including traumatic amputation
879 Open wound of other and unspecified sites, except limbs

Open wound of upper limb (880-887)
880 Open wound of shoulder and upper arm
881 Open wound of elbow, forearm, and wrist
882 Open wound of hand except finger(s) alone
883 Open wound of finger(s)
884 Multiple and unspecified open wound of upper limb
885 Traumatic amputation of thumb (complete) (partial)
886 Traumatic amputation of other finger(s) (complete) (partial)
887 Traumatic amputation of arm and hand (complete) (partial)

Open wound of lower limb (890-897)
890 Open wound of hip and thigh
891 Open wound of knee, leg [except thigh], and ankle
892 Open wound of foot except toe(s) alone
893 Open wound of toe(s)
894 Multiple and unspecified open wound of lower limb
895 Traumatic amputation of toe(s) (complete) (partial)
896 Traumatic amputation of foot (complete) (partial)
897 Traumatic amputation of leg(s) (complete) (partial)

Injury to blood vessels (900-904)
900 Injury to blood vessels of head and neck
901 Injury to blood vessels of thorax
902 Injury to blood vessels of abdomen and pelvis
903 Injury to blood vessels of upper extremity
904 Injury to blood vessels of lower extremity and unspecified sites

Late effects of injuries, poisonings, toxic effects, and other external causes (905-909)
905 Late effects of musculoskeletal and connective tissue injuries
906 Late effects of injuries to skin and subcutaneous tissues
907 Late effects of injuries to the nervous system
908 Late effects of other and unspecified injuries
909 Late effects of other and unspecified external causes

Superficial injury (910-919)
910 Superficial injury of face, neck, and scalp except eye
911 Superficial injury of trunk
912 Superficial injury of shoulder and upper arm
913 Superficial injury of elbow, forearm, and wrist
914 Superficial injury of hand(s) except finger(s) alone
915 Superficial injury of finger(s)
916 Superficial injury of hip, thigh, leg, and ankle
917 Superficial injury of foot and toe(s)
918 Superficial injury of eye and adnexa
919 Superficial injury of other, multiple, and unspecified sites

Contusion with intact skin surface (920-924)
920 Contusion of face, scalp, and neck except eye(s)
921 Contusion of eye and adnexa
922 Contusion of trunk
923 Contusion of upper limb
924 Contusion of lower limb and of other and unspecified sites

Crushing injury (925-929)
925 Crushing injury of face, scalp, and neck
926 Crushing injury of trunk

927 Crushing injury of upper limb
928 Crushing injury of lower limb
929 Crushing injury of multiple and unspecified sites

Effects of foreign body entering through orifice (930-939)
930 Foreign body on external eye
931 Foreign body in ear
932 Foreign body in nose
933 Foreign body in pharynx and larynx
934 Foreign body in trachea, bronchus, and lung
935 Foreign body in mouth, esophagus, and stomach
936 Foreign body in intestine and colon
937 Foreign body in anus and rectum
938 Foreign body in digestive system, unspecified
939 Foreign body in genitourinary tract

Burns (940-949)
940 Burn confined to eye and adnexa
941 Burn of face, head, and neck
942 Burn of trunk
943 Burn of upper limb, except wrist and hand
944 Burn of wrist(s) and hand(s)
945 Burn of lower limb(s)
946 Burns of multiple specified sites
947 Burn of internal organs
948 Burns classified according to extent of body surface involved
949 Burn, unspecified

Injury to nerves and spinal cord (950-957)
950 Injury to optic nerve and pathways
951 Injury to other cranial nerve(s)
952 Spinal cord injury without evidence of spinal bone injury
953 Injury to nerve roots and spinal plexus
954 Injury to other nerve(s) of trunk excluding shoulder and pelvic girdles
955 Injury to peripheral nerve(s) of shoulder girdle and upper limb
956 Injury to peripheral nerve(s) of pelvic girdle and lower limb
957 Injury to other and unspecified nerves

Certain traumatic complications and unspecified injuries (958-959)
958 Certain early complications of trauma
959 Injury, other and unspecified

Poisoning by drugs, medicinals and biological substances (960-979)
960 Poisoning by antibiotics
961 Poisoning by other anti-infectives
962 Poisoning by hormones and synthetic substitutes
963 Poisoning by primarily systemic agents
964 Poisoning by agents primarily affecting blood constituents
965 Poisoning by analgesics, antipyretics, and antirheumatics
966 Poisoning by anticonvulsants and anti-Parkinsonism drugs
967 Poisoning by sedatives and hypnotics
968 Poisoning by other central nervous system depressants and anesthetics
969 Poisoning by psychotropic agents
970 Poisoning by central nervous system stimulants
971 Poisoning by drugs primarily affecting the autonomic nervous system
972 Poisoning by agents primarily affecting the cardiovascular system
973 Poisoning by agents primarily affecting the gastrointestinal system
974 Poisoning by water, mineral, and uric acid metabolism drugs
975 Poisoning by agents primarily acting on the smooth and skeletal muscles and respiratory system

976 Poisoning by agents primarily affecting skin and mucous membrane, ophthalmological, otorhinolaryngological, and dental drugs
977 Poisoning by other and unspecified drugs and medicinals
978 Poisoning by bacterial vaccines
979 Poisoning by other vaccines and biological substances

Toxic effects of substances chiefly nonmedicinal as to source (980-989)
980 Toxic effect of alcohol
981 Toxic effect of petroleum products
982 Toxic effect of solvents other than petroleum-based
983 Toxic effect of corrosive aromatics, acids, and caustic alkalis
984 Toxic effect of lead and its compounds (including fumes)
985 Toxic effect of other metals
986 Toxic effect of carbon monoxide
987 Toxic effect of other gases, fumes, or vapors
988 Effect of noxious substances eaten as food
989 Toxic effect of other substances, chiefly nonmedicinal as to source

Other and unspecified effects of external causes (990-995)
990 Effects of radiation, unspecified
991 Effects of reduced temperature
992 Effects of heat and light
993 Effects of air pressure
994 Effects of other external causes
995 Certain adverse effects, not elsewhere classified

Complications of surgical and medical care, not elsewhere classified (996-999)
996 Complications peculiar to certain specified procedures
997 Complications affecting specified body systems, not elsewhere classified
998 Other complications of procedures, not elsewhere classified
999 Complications of medical care, not elsewhere classified

Supplementary Classification of Factors Influencing Health Status and Contact With Health Services

Persons with potential health hazards related to communicable diseases (V01-V06)
V01 Contact with or exposure to communicable diseases
V02 Carrier or suspected carrier of infectious diseases
V03 Need for prophylactic vaccination and inoculation against bacterial diseases
V04 Need for prophylactic vaccination and inoculation against certain viral diseases
V05 Need for other prophylactic vaccination and inoculation against single diseases
V06 Need for prophylactic vaccination and inoculation against combinations of diseases

Persons with need for isolation, other potential health hazards, and prophylactic measures (V07-V09)
V07 Need for isolation and other prophylactic or treatment measures
V08 Asymptomatic human immunodeficiency virus [HIV] infection status
V09 Infection with drug-resistant microorganisms

Persons with potential health hazards related to personal and family history (V10-V19)
V10 Personal history of malignant neoplasm
V11 Personal history of mental disorder
V12 Personal history of certain other diseases

V13 Personal history of other diseases
V14 Personal history of allergy to medicinal agents
V15 Other personal history presenting hazards to health
V16 Family history of malignant neoplasm
V17 Family history of certain chronic disabling diseases
V18 Family history of certain other specific conditions
V19 Family history of other conditions

Persons encountering health services in circumstances related to reproduction and development (V20-V29)
V20 Health supervision of infant or child
V21 Constitutional states in development
V22 Normal pregnancy
V23 Supervision of high-risk pregnancy
V24 Postpartum care and examination
V25 Encounter for contraceptive management
V26 Procreative management
V27 Outcome of delivery
V28 Encounter for antenatal screening of mother
V29 Observation and evaluation of newborns and infants for suspected condition not found

Liveborn infants according to type of birth (V30-V39)
V30 Single liveborn
V31 Twin, mate liveborn
V32 Twin, mate stillborn
V33 Twin, unspecified
V34 Other multiple, mates all liveborn
V35 Other multiple, mates all stillborn
V36 Other multiple, mates live and stillborn
V37 Other multiple, unspecified
V39 Unspecified

Persons with a condition influencing their health status (V40-V49)
V40 Mental and behavioral problems
V41 Problems with special senses and other special functions
V42 Organ or tissue replaced by transplant
V43 Organ or tissue replaced by other means
V44 Artificial opening status
V45 Other postprocedural states
V46 Other dependence on machines and devices
V47 Other problems with internal organs
V48 Problems with head, neck, and trunk
V49 Other conditions influencing health status

Persons encountering health services for specific procedures and aftercare (V50-V59)
V50 Elective surgery for purposes other than remedying health states
V51 Aftercare involving the use of plastic surgery
V52 Fitting and adjustment of prosthetic device and implant
V53 Fitting and adjustment of other device
V54 Other orthopedic aftercare
V55 Attention to artificial openings
V56 Encounter for dialysis and dialysis catheter care
V57 Care involving use of rehabilitation procedures
V58 Encounter for other and unspecified procedures and aftercare
V59 Donors

Persons encountering health services in other circumstances (V60-V69)
V60 Housing, household, and economic circumstances
V61 Other family circumstances
V62 Other psychosocial circumstances
V63 Unavailability of other medical facilities for care
V64 Persons encountering health services for specific procedures, not carried out
V65 Other persons seeking consultation
V66 Convalescence and palliative care
V67 Follow-up examination

V68 Encounters for administrative purposes
V69 Problems related to lifestyle

Persons without reported diagnosis encountered during examination and investigation of individuals and populations (V70-V82)
V70 General medical examination
V71 Observation and evaluation for suspected conditions not found
V72 Special investigations and examinations
V73 Special screening examination for viral and chlamydial diseases
V74 Special screening examination for bacterial and spirochetal diseases
V75 Special screening examination for other infectious diseases
V76 Special screening for malignant neoplasms
V77 Special screening for endocrine, nutritional, metabolic, and immunity disorders
V78 Special screening for disorders of blood and blood-forming organs
V79 Special screening for mental disorders and developmental handicaps
V80 Special screening for neurological, eye, and ear diseases
V81 Special screening for cardiovascular, respiratory, and genitourinary diseases
V82 Special screening for other conditions

Genetics (V83-V84)
V83 Genetic carrier status
V84 Genetic susceptibility to disease

Body mass index (V85)
V85 Body Mass Index [BMI]

Estrogen receptor status (V86)
V86 Estrogen receptor status

Other specified personal exposures and history presenting hazards to health (V87)
V87 Other specified personal exposures and history presenting hazards to health

Acquired absence of other organs and tissue (V88)
V88 Acquired absence of other organs and tissue

Other suspected conditions not found (V89)
V89 Other suspected conditions not found

Retained Foreign Body (V90)
V90 Retained foreign body

Multiple Gestation Placenta Status (V91)
V91 Multiple gestation placenta status

Supplementary Classification of External Causes of Injury and Poisoning

External Cause Status (E000)
E000 External cause status

Activity (E001-E030)
E001 Activities involving walking and running
E002 Activities involving water and water craft
E003 Activities involving ice and snow
E004 Activities involving climbing, rappelling, and jumping off
E005 Activities involving dancing and other rhythmic movement
E006 Activities involving other sports and athletics played individually
E007 Activities involving other sports and athletics played as a team or group
E008 Activities involving other specified sports and athletics
E009 Activity involving other cardiorespiratory exercise
E010 Activity involving other muscle strengthening exercises

E011   Activities involving computer technology and electronic devices
E012   Activities involving arts and handcrafts
E013   Activities involving personal hygiene and household maintenance
E014   Activities involving person providing caregiving
E015   Activities involving food preparation, cooking and grilling
E016   Activities involving property and land maintenance, building and construction
E017   Activities involving roller coasters and other types of external motion
E018   Activities involving playing musical instrument
E019   Activities involving animal care
E029   Other activity
E030   Unspecified activity

Transport Accidents (E800-E848)

Railway accidents (E800-E807)
E800   Railway accident involving collision with roling stock
E801   Railway accident involving collision with other object
E802   Railway accident involving derailment without antecedent collision
E803   Railway accident involving explosion, fire, or burning
E804   Fall in, on, or from railway train
E805   Hit by rolling stock
E806   Other specified railway accident
E807   Railway accident of unspecified nature

Motor vehicle traffic accidents (E810-E819)
E810   Motor vehicle traffic accident involving collision with train
E811   Motor vehicle traffic accident involving re-entrant collision with another motor vehicle
E812   Other motor vehicle traffic accident involving collision with another motor vehicle
E813   Motor vehicle traffic accident involving collision with other vehicle
E814   Motor vehicle traffic accident involving collision with pedestrian
E815   Other motor vehicle traffic accident involving collision on the highway
E816   Motor vehicle traffic accident due to loss of control, without collision on the highway
E817   Noncollision motor vehicle traffic accident while boarding or alighting
E818   Other noncollision motor vehicle traffic accident
E819   Motor vehicle traffic accident of unspecified nature

Motor vehicle nontraffic accidents (E820-E825)
E820   Nontraffic accident involving motor-driven snow vehicle
E821   Nontraffic accident involving other off-road motor vehicle
E822   Other motor vehicle nontraffic accident involving collision with moving object
E823   Other motor vehicle nontraffic accident involving collision with stationary object
E824   Other motor vehicle nontraffic accident while boarding and alighting
E825   Other motor vehicle nontraffic accident of other and unspecified nature

Other road vehicle accidents (E826-E829)
E826   Pedal cycle accident
E827   Animal-drawn vehicle accident
E828   Accident involving animal being ridden
E829   Other road vehicle accidents

Water transport accidents (E830-E838)
E830   Accident to watercraft causing submersion
E831   Accident to watercraft causing other injury
E832   Other accidental submersion or drowning in water transport accident

E833   Fall on stairs or ladders in water transport
E834   Other fall from one level to another in water transport
E835   Other and unspecified fall in water transport
E836   Machinery accident in water transport
E837   Explosion, fire, or burning in watercraft
E838   Other and unspecified water transport accident

Air and space transport accidents (E840-E845)
E840   Accident to powered aircraft at takeoff or landing
E841   Accident to powered aircraft, other and unspecified
E842   Accident to unpowered aircraft
E843   Fall in, on, or from aircraft
E844   Other specified air transport accidents
E845   Accident involving spacecraft

Vehicle accidents, not elsewhere classfiable (E846-E849)
E846   Accidents involving powered vehicles used solely within the buildings and premises of an industrial or commercial establishment
E847   Accidents involving cable cars not running on rails
E848   Accidents involving other vehicles, not elsewhere classifiable
E849   Place of occurrence

Accidental poisoning by drugs, medicinal substances, and biologicals (E850-E858)
E850   Accidental poisoning by analgesics, antipyretics, and antirheumatics
E851   Accidental poisoning by barbiturates
E852   Accidental poisoning by other sedatives and hypnotics
E853   Accidental poisoning by tranquilizers
E854   Accidental poisoning by other psychotropic agents
E855   Accidental poisoning by other drugs acting on central and autonomic nervous systems
E856   Accidental poisoning by antibiotics
E857   Accidental poisoning by anti-infectives
E858   Accidental poisoning by other drugs

Accidental poisoning by other solid and liquid substances, gases, and vapors (E860-E869)
E860   Accidental poisoning by alcohol, not elsewhere classified
E861   Accidental poisoning by cleansing and polishing agents, disinfectants, paints, and varnishes
E862   Accidental poisoning by petroleum products, other solvents and their vapors, not elsewhere classified
E863   Accidental poisoning by agricultural and horticultural chemical and pharmaceutical preparations other than plant foods and fertilizers
E864   Accidental poisoning by corrosives and caustics, not elsewhere classified
E865   Accidental poisoning from poisonous foodstuffs and poisonous plants
E866   Accidental poisoning by other and unspecified solid and liquid substances
E867   Accidental poisoning by gas distributed by pipeline
E868   Accidental poisoning by other utility gas and other carbon monoxide
E869   Accidental poisoning by other gases and vapors

Misadventures to patients during surgical and medical care (E870-E876)
E870   Accidental cut, puncture, perforation, or hemorrhage during medical care
E871   Foreign object left in body during procedure
E872   Failure of sterile precautions during procedure
E873   Failure in dosage
E874   Mechanical failure of instrument or apparatus during procedure

E875   Contaminated or infected blood, other fluid, drug, or biological substance
E876   Other and unspecified misadventures during medical care

Surgical and medical procedures as the cause of abnormal reaction of patient or later complication, without mention of misadventure at the time of procedure (E878-E879)
E878   Surgical operation and other surgical procedures as the cause of abnormal reaction of patient, or of later complication, without mention of misadventure at the time of operation
E879   Other procedures, without mention of misadventure at the time of procedure, as the cause of abnormal reaction of patient, or of later complication

Accidental falls (E880-E888)
E880   Fall on or from stairs or steps
E881   Fall on or from ladders or scaffolding
E882   Fall from or out of building or other structure
E883   Fall into hole or other opening in surface
E884   Other fall from one level to another
E885   Fall on same level from slipping, tripping, or stumbling
E886   Fall on same level from collision, pushing or shoving, by or with other person
E887   Fracture, cause unspecified
E888   Other and unspecified fall

Accidents caused by fire and flames (E890-E899)
E890   Conflagration in private dwelling
E891   Conflagration in other and unspecified building or structure
E892   Conflagration not in building or structure
E893   Accident caused by ignition of clothing
E894   Ignition of highly inflammable material
E895   Accident caused by controlled fire in private dwelling
E896   Accident caused by controlled fire in other and unspecified building or structure
E897   Accident caused by controlled fire not in building or structure
E898   Accident caused by other specified fire and flames
E899   Accident caused by unspecified fire

Accidents due to natural and environmental factors (E900-E909)
E900   Excessive heat
E901   Excessive cold
E902   High and low air pressure and changes in air pressure
E903   Travel and motion
E904   Hunger, thirst, exposure, and neglect
E905   Venomous animals and plants as the cause of poisoning and toxic reactions
E906   Other injury caused by animals
E907   Lightning
E908   Cataclysmic storms, and floods resulting from storms
E909   Cataclysmic earth surface movements and eruptions

Accidents caused by submersion, suffocation, and foreign bodies (E910-E915)
E910   Accidental drowning and submersion
E911   Inhalation and ingestion of food causing obstruction of respiratory tract or suffocation
E912   Inhalation and ingestion of other object causing obstruction of respiratory tract or suffocation
E913   Accidental mechanical suffocation
E914   Foreign body accidentally entering eye and adnexa
E915   Foreign body accidentally entering other orifice

Other accidents (E916-E928)
E916   Struck accidentally by falling object

Appendix E: List of Three-digit Categories

E917 Striking against or struck accidentally by objects or persons
E918 Caught accidentally in or between objects
E919 Accidents caused by machinery
E920 Accidents caused by cutting and piercing instruments or objects
E921 Accident caused by explosion of pressure vessel
E922 Accident caused by firearm and air gun missile
E923 Accident caused by explosive material
E924 Accident caused by hot substance or object, caustic or corrosive material, and steam
E925 Accident caused by electric current
E926 Exposure to radiation
E927 Overexertion and strenuous and repetitive movements or loads
E928 Other and unspecified environmental and accidental causes

Late effects of accidental injury (E929)
E929 Late effects of accidental injury

Drugs, medicinal and biological substances causing adverse effects in therapeutic use (E930-E949)
E930 Antibiotics
E931 Other anti-infectives
E932 Hormones and synthetic substitutes
E933 Primarily systemic agents
E934 Agents primarily affecting blood constituents
E935 Analgesics, antipyretics, and antirheumatics
E936 Anticonvulsants and anti-Parkinsonism drugs
E937 Sedatives and hypnotics
E938 Other central nervous system depressants and anesthetics
E939 Psychotropic agents
E940 Central nervous system stimulants
E941 Drugs primarily affecting the autonomic nervous system
E942 Agents primarily affecting the cardiovascular system
E943 Agents primarily affecting gastrointestinal system
E944 Water, mineral, and uric acid metabolism drugs
E945 Agents primarily acting on the smooth and skeletal muscles and respiratory system
E946 Agents primarily affecting skin and mucous membrane, ophthalmological, otorhinolaryngological, and dental drugs
E947 Other and unspecified drugs and medicinal substances
E948 Bacterial vaccines
E949 Other vaccines and biological substances

Suicide and self-inflicted injury (E950-E959)
E950 Suicide and self-inflicted poisoning by solid or liquid substances
E951 Suicide and self-inflicted poisoning by gases in domestic use
E952 Suicide and self-inflicted poisoning by other gases and vapors
E953 Suicide and self-inflicted injury by hanging, strangulation, and suffocation
E954 Suicide and self-inflicted injury by submersion [drowning]
E955 Suicide and self-inflicted injury by firearms, air guns and explosives
E956 Suicide and self-inflicted injury by cutting and piercing instruments
E957 Suicide and self-inflicted injuries by jumping from high place
E958 Suicide and self-inflicted injury by other and unspecified means
E959 Late effects of self-inflicted injury

Homicide and injury purposely inflicted by other persons (E960-E969)
E960 Fight, brawl, and rape
E961 Assault by corrosive or caustic substance, except poisoning
E962 Assault by poisoning
E963 Assault by hanging and strangulation
E964 Assault by submersion [drowning]
E965 Assault by firearms and explosives
E966 Assault by cutting and piercing instrument
E967 Perpetrator of child and adult abuse
E968 Assault by other and unspecified means
E969 Late effects of injury purposely inflicted by other person

Legal intervention (E970-E978)
E970 Injury due to legal intervention by firearms
E971 Injury due to legal intervention by explosives
E972 Injury due to legal intervention by gas
E973 Injury due to legal intervention by blunt object
E974 Injury due to legal intervention by cutting and piercing instruments
E975 Injury due to legal intervention by other specified means
E976 Injury due to legal intervention by unspecified means
E977 Late effects of injuries due to legal intervention
E978 Legal execution

Terrorism (E979)
E979 Terrorism

Injury undetermined whether accidentally or purposely inflicted (E980-E989)
E980 Poisoning by solid or liquid substances, undetermined whether accidentally or purposely inflicted
E981 Poisoning by gases in domestic use, undetermined whether accidentally or purposely inflicted
E982 Poisoning by other gases, undetermined whether accidentally or purposely inflicted
E983 Hanging, strangulation, or suffocation, undetermined whether accidentally or purposely inflicted
E984 Submersion [drowning], undetermined whether accidentally or purposely inflicted
E985 Injury by firearms and explosives, undetermined whether accidentally or purposely inflicted
E986 Injury by cutting and piercing instruments, undetermined whether accidentally or purposely inflicted
E987 Falling from high place, undetermined whether accidentally or purposely inflicted
E988 Injury by other and unspecified means, undetermined whether accidentally or purposely inflicted
E989 Late effects of injury, undetermined whether accidentally or purposely inflicted

Injury resulting from operations of war (E990-E999)
E990 Injury due to war operations by fires and conflagrations
E991 Injury due to war operations by bullets and fragments
E992 Injury due to war operations by explosion of marine weapons
E993 Injury due to war operations by other explosion
E994 Injury due to war operations by destruction of aircraft
E995 Injury due to war operations by other and unspecified forms of conventional warfare
E996 Injury due to war operations by nuclear weapons
E997 Injury due to war operations by other forms of unconventional warfare
E998 Injury due to war operations but occurring after cessation of hostilities
E999 Late effects of injury due to war operations and terrorism

A

Abbe operation
- construction of vagina 70.61
  - with graft or prosthesis 70.63
- intestinal anastomosis — see Anastomosis, intestine

Abciximab, infusion 99.20
Abdominocentesis 54.91
Abdominohysterectomy 68.49
- laparoscopic 68.41
Abdominoplasty 86.83
Abdominoscopy 54.21
Abdominouterotomy 68.0
- obstetrical 74.99
Abduction, arytenoid 31.69
AbioCor® total replacement heart 37.52
Ablation
- biliary tract (lesion) by ERCP 51.64
- endometrial (hysteroscopic) 68.23
- inner ear (cryosurgery) (ultrasound) 20.79
  - by injection 20.72
- lesion
  - esophagus 42.39
    - endoscopic 42.33
  - heart
    - by peripherally inserted catheter 37.34
    - endovascular approach 37.34
    - maze procedure (Cox-maze)
      - endovascular approach 37.34
      - open approach 37.33
      - thoracoscopic approach 37.37
    - thoracoscopic approach 37.37
  - intestine
    - large 45.49
      - endoscopic 45.43
  - large intestine 45.49
    - endoscopic 45.43
  - liver 50.26
    - laparoscopic 50.25
    - open 50.23
    - percutaneous 50.24
  - lung 32.26
    - bronchoscopic thermoplasty 32.27
    - open 32.23
    - percutaneous 32.24
    - thoracoscopic 32.25
  - renal 55.35
    - laparoscopic 55.34
    - open 55.32
    - percutaneous 55.33
- pituitary 07.69
  - by
    - Cobalt 60 92.32
    - implantation (strontium-yttrium) (Y) NEC 07.68
      - transfrontal approach 07.64
      - transsphenoidal approach 07.65
    - proton beam (Bragg peak) 92.33
- prostate
  - by
    - cryoablation 60.62
    - laser, transurethral 60.21
    - radical cryosurgical ablation (RCSA) 60.62
    - radiofrequency thermotherapy 60.97
    - transurethral needle ablation (TUNA) 60.97
- tissue
  - heart — see Ablation, lesion, heart
  - liver — see Ablation, lesion, liver
  - lung — see Ablation, lesion, lung
  - renal — see Ablation, lesion, renal
Abortion, therapeutic 69.51
- by
  - aspiration curettage 69.51
  - dilation and curettage 69.01
  - hysterectomy — see Hysterectomy
  - hysterotomy 74.91
  - insertion
    - laminaria 69.93
    - prostaglandin suppository 96.49
  - intra-amniotic injection (saline) 75.0
Abrasion
- corneal epithelium 11.41
  - for smear or culture 11.21

Abrasion — continued
- epicardial surface 36.39
- pleural 34.6
- skin 86.25
Abscission, cornea 11.49
Absorptiometry
- photon (dual) (single) 88.98
Aburel operation (intra-amniotic injection for abortion) 75.0
Accouchement forcé 73.99
Acetabulectomy 77.85
Acetabuloplasty NEC 81.40
- with prosthetic implant 81.52
Achillorrhaphy 83.64
- delayed 83.62
Achillotenotomy 83.11
- plastic 83.85
Achillotomy 83.11
- plastic 83.85
Acid peel, skin 86.24
Acromionectomy 77.81
Acromioplasty 81.83
- for recurrent dislocation of shoulder 81.82
- partial replacement 81.81
- total replacement, NEC 81.80
  - other 81.80
  - reverse 81.88
Actinotherapy 99.82
Activities of daily living (ADL)
- therapy 93.83
- training for the blind 93.78
Acupuncture 99.92
- with smouldering moxa 93.35
- for anesthesia 99.91
Adams operation
- advancement of round ligament 69.22
- crushing of nasal septum 21.88
- excision of palmar fascia 82.35
Adenectomy — see also Excision, by site
- prostate NEC 60.69
  - retropubic 60.4
Adenoidectomy (without tonsillectomy) 28.6
- with tonsillectomy 28.3
Adhesiolysis — see also Lysis, adhesions
- for collapse of lung 33.39
- middle ear 20.23
Adipectomy 86.83
Adjustment
- cardiac pacemaker program (reprogramming) — omit code
- cochlear prosthetic device (external components) 95.49
- dental 99.97
- gastric restrictive device (laparoscopic) 44.98
- occlusal 24.8
- orthopedic device (noninvasive)
  - external fixator — omit code
- spectacles 95.31
Administration (of) — see also Injection
- Activase® 99.10
- adhesion barrier substance 99.77
- Alteplase (tPA, generic) 99.10
- Anistreplase (tPA, generic) 99.10
- antitoxins NEC 99.58
  - botulism 99.57
  - diphtheria 99.58
  - gas gangrene 99.58
  - scarlet fever 99.58
  - tetanus 99.56
- Bender Visual-Motor Gestalt test 94.02
- Benton Visual Retention test 94.02
- DrotAA 00.11
- Eminase® 99.10
- inhaled nitric oxide 00.12
- intelligence test or scale (Stanford-Binet) (Wechsler) (adult) (children) 94.01
- Minnesota Multiphasic Personality Inventory (MMPI) 94.02
- MMPI (Minnesota Multiphasic Personality Inventory) 94.02
- neuroprotective agent 99.75
- Proleukin® (low-dose) 99.28
  - high-dose 00.15
- psychologic test 94.02
- Retavase® 99.10

Administration — see also Injection — continued
- Reteplase (tPA, generic) 99.10
- Stanford-Binet test 94.01
- Streptase® 99.10
- Streptokinase (tPA, generic) 99.10
- Tenecteplase (tPA, generic) 99.10
- TNKase™ 99.10
- toxoid
  - diphtheria 99.36
    - with tetanus and pertussis, combined (DTP) 99.39
  - tetanus 99.38
    - with diphtheria and pertussis, combined (DTP) 99.39
- vaccine (see also Vaccination)
  - BCG 99.33
  - measles-mumps-rubella (MMR) 99.48
  - poliomyelitis 99.41
  - TAB 99.32
- Wechsler
  - Intelligence Scale (adult) (children) 94.01
  - Memory Scale 94.02
- Xigris® 00.11
Adrenalectomy (unilateral) 07.22
- with partial removal of remaining gland 07.29
- bilateral 07.3
  - partial 07.29
  - subtotal 07.29
- complete 07.3
- partial NEC 07.29
- remaining gland 07.3
- subtotal NEC 07.29
- total 07.3
Adrenalorrhaphy 07.44
Adrenalotomy (with drainage) 07.41
Advancement
- extraocular muscle 15.12
  - multiple (with resection or recession) 15.3
- eyelid muscle 08.59
- eye muscle 15.12
  - multiple (with resection or recession) 15.3
- graft — see Graft
- leaflet (heart) 35.10
- pedicle (flap) 86.72
- profundus tendon (Wagner) 82.51
- round ligament 69.22
- tendon 83.71
  - hand 82.51
  - profundus (Wagner) 82.51
- Wagner (profundus tendon) 82.51
AESOP® (Automated Endoscopic System for Optimal Positioning) — see category 17.4 ☑
Albee operation
- bone peg, femoral neck 78.05
- graft for slipping patella 78.06
- sliding inlay graft, tibia 78.07
Aibert operation (arthrodesis of knee) 81.22
Aldridge (-Studdiford) operation (urethral sling) 59.5
Alexander-Adams operation (shortening of round ligaments) 69.22
Alexander operation
- prostatectomy
  - perineal 60.62
  - suprapubic 60.3
- shortening of round ligaments 69.22
Alimentation, parenteral 99.29
Allograft — see Graft
Almoor operation (extrapetrosal drainage) 20.22
Altemeier operation (perineal rectal pull-through) 48.49
Alveolectomy (interradicular) (intraseptal) (radical) (simple) (with graft) (with implant) 24.5
Alveoloplasty (with graft or implant) 24.5
Alveolotomy (apical) 24.0
Ambulatory cardiac monitoring (ACM) 89.50
Ammon operation (dacryocystotomy) 09.53
Amniocentesis (transuterine) (diagnostic) 75.1
- with intra-amniotic injection of saline 75.0

Amniography 87.81
Amnioinfusion 75.37
Amnioscopy, internal 75.31
Amniotomy 73.09
- to induce labor 73.01
Amputation (cineplastic) (closed flap) (guillotine) (kineplastic) (open) 84.91
- abdominopelvic 84.19
- above-elbow 84.07
- above-knee (AK) 84.17
- ankle (disarticulation) 84.13
  - through malleoli of tibia and fibula 84.14
- arm NEC 84.00
  - through
    - carpals 84.03
    - elbow (disarticulation) 84.06
    - forearm 84.05
    - humerus 84.07
    - shoulder (disarticulation) 84.08
    - wrist (disarticulation) 84.04
  - upper 84.07
- Batch-Spittler-McFaddin (knee disarticulation) 84.16
- below-knee (BK) NEC 84.15
  - conversion into above-knee amputation 84.17
- Boyd (hip disarticulation) 84.18
- Burgess operation (amputation of ankle) 84.14
- Callander's (knee disarticulation) 84.16
- carpals 84.03
- cervix 67.4
- Chopart's (midtarsal) 84.12
- clitoris 71.4
- Dieffenbach (hip disarticulation) 84.18
- Dupuytren's (shoulder disarticulation) 84.08
- ear, external 18.39
- elbow (disarticulation) 84.06
- finger, except thumb 84.01
  - thumb 84.02
- foot (middle) 84.12
- forearm 84.05
- forefoot 84.12
- forequarter 84.09
- Gordon-Taylor (hindquarter) 84.19
- Gritti-Stokes (knee disarticulation) 84.16
- Guyon (ankle) 84.13
- hallux 84.11
- hand 84.03
- Hey's (foot) 84.12
- hindquarter 84.19
- hip (disarticulation) 84.18
- humerus 84.07
- interscapulothoracic 84.09
- interthoracoscapular 84.09
- King-Steelquist (hindquarter) 84.19
- Kirk (thigh) 84.17
- knee (disarticulation) 84.16
- Kutler (revision of current traumatic amputation of finger) 84.01
- Larry (shoulder disarticulation) 84.08
- leg NEC 84.10
  - above knee (AK) 84.17
  - below knee (BK) 84.15
  - through
    - ankle (disarticulation) 84.13
    - femur (AK) 84.17
    - foot 84.12
    - hip (disarticulation) 84.18
    - tibia and fibula (BK) 84.15
- Lisfranc
  - foot 84.12
  - shoulder (disarticulation) 84.08
- Littlewood (forequarter) 84.09
- lower limb NEC (see also Amputation, leg) 84.10
- Mazet (knee disarticulation) 84.16
- metacarpal 84.03
- metatarsal 84.11
  - head (bunionectomy) 77.59
- metatarsophalangeal (joint) 84.11
- midtarsal 84.12
- nose 21.4
- penis (circle) (complete) (flap) (partial) (radical) 64.3

Amputation — *continued*
  Pirogoff's (ankle amputation through malleoli of tibia and fibula) 84.14
  ray
    finger 84.01
    foot 84.11
    toe (metatarsal head) 84.11
  root (tooth) (apex) 23.73
    with root canal therapy 23.72
  shoulder (disarticulation) 84.08
  Sorondo-Ferré (hindquarter) 84.19
  S.P. Rogers (knee disarticulation) 84.16
  supracondyler, above-knee 84.17
  supramalleolar, foot 84.14
  Syme's (ankle amputation through malleoli of tibia and fibula) 84.14
  thigh 84.17
  thumb 84.02
  toe (through metatarsophalangeal joint) 84.11
  transcarpal 84.03
  transmetatarsal 84.12
  upper limb NEC (*see also* Amputation, arm) 84.00
  wrist (disarticulation) 84.04
Amygdalohippocampectomy 01.59
Amygdalohippocampotomy 01.39
Amygdalotomy 01.39
Analysis
  cardiac rhythm device (CRT-D) (CRT-P) (AICD) (pacemaker) — *see* Interrogation
  character 94.03
  gastric 89.39
  psychologic 94.31
  transactional
    group 94.44
    individual 94.39
Anastomosis
  abdominal artery to coronary artery 36.17
  accessory-facial nerve 04.72
  accessory-hypoglossal nerve 04.73
  anus (with formation of endorectal ileal pouch) 45.95
  aorta (descending)-pulmonary (artery) 39.0
  aorta-renal artery 39.24
  aorta-subclavian artery 39.22
  aortoceliac 39.26
  aorto(ilio)femoral 39.25
  aortomesenteric 39.26
  appendix 47.99
  arteriovenous NEC 39.29
    for renal dialysis 39.27
  artery (suture of distal to proximal end) 39.31
    with
      bypass graft 39.29
        extracranial-intracranial [EC-IC] 39.28
      excision or resection of vessel — *see* Arteriectomy, with anastomosis, by site
    revision 39.49
  bile ducts 51.39
  bladder NEC 57.88
    with
      isolated segment of intestine 57.87 [45.50]
        colon (sigmoid) 57.87 [45.52]
        ileum 57.87 [45.51]
      open loop of ileum 57.87 [45.51]
      to intestine 57.88
        ileum 57.87 [45.51]
  bowel (*see also* Anastomosis, intestine) 45.90
  bronchotracheal 33.48
  bronchus 33.48
  carotid-subclavian artery 39.22
  caval-mesenteric vein 39.1
  caval-pulmonary artery 39.21
  cervicoesophageal 42.59
  colohypopharyngeal (intrathoracic) 42.55
    antesternal or antethoracic 42.65
  common bile duct 51.39
  common pulmonary trunk and left atrium (posterior wall) 35.82

Anastomosis — *continued*
  cystic bile duct 51.39
  cystocolic 57.88
  epididymis to vas deferens 63.83
  esophagocolic (intrathoracic) NEC 42.56
    with interposition 42.55
    antesternal or antethoracic NEC 42.66
      with interposition 42.65
  esophagocologastric (intrathoracic) 42.55
    antesternal or antethoracic 42.65
  esophagoduodenal (intrathoracic) NEC 42.54
    with interposition 42.53
  esophagoenteric (intrathoracic) NEC (*see also* Anastomosis, esophagus, to intestinal segment) 42.54
    antesternal or antethoracic NEC (*see also* Anastomosis, esophagus, antesternal, to intestinal segment) 42.64
  esophagoesophageal (intrathoracic) 42.51
    antesternal or antethoracic 42.61
  esophagogastric (intrathoracic) 42.52
    antesternal or antethoracic 42.62
  esophagus (intrapleural) (intrathoracic) (retrosternal) NEC 42.59
    with
      gastrectomy (partial) 43.5
        complete or total 43.99
      interposition (of) NEC 42.58
        colon 42.55
        jejunum 42.53
        small bowel 42.53
    antesternal or antethoracic NEC 42.69
      with
        interposition (of) NEC 42.68
          colon 42.65
          jejunal loop 42.63
          small bowel 42.63
          rubber tube 42.68
      to intestinal segment NEC 42.64
        with interposition 42.68
        colon NEC 42.66
          with interposition 42.65
        small bowel NEC 42.64
          with interposition 42.63
    to intestinal segment (intrathoracic) NEC 42.54
      with interposition 42.58
      antesternal or antethoracic NEC 42.64
        with interposition 42.68
      colon (intrathoracic) NEC 42.56
        with interposition 42.55
        antesternal or antethoracic 42.66
          with interposition 42.65
      small bowel NEC 42.54
        with interposition 42.53
        antesternal or antethoracic 42.64
          with interposition 42.63
  facial-accessory nerve 04.72
  facial-hypoglossal nerve 04.71
  fallopian tube 66.73
    by reanastomosis 66.79
  gallbladder 51.35
    to
      hepatic ducts 51.31
      intestine 51.32
      pancreas 51.33
      stomach 51.34
  gastroepiploic artery to coronary artery 36.17
  hepatic duct 51.39
  hypoglossal-accessory nerve 04.73
  hypoglossal-facial nerve 04.71
  ileal loop to bladder 57.87 [45.51]
  ileoanal 45.95
  ileorectal 45.93
  inferior vena cava and portal vein 39.1
  internal mammary artery (to)
    coronary artery (single vessel) 36.15
      double vessel 36.16
    myocardium 36.2
  intestine 45.90
    large-to-anus 45.95
    large-to-large 45.94
    large-to-rectum 45.94

Anastomosis — *continued*
  intestine — *continued*
    large-to-small 45.93
    small-to-anus 45.95
    small-to-large 45.93
    small-to-rectal stump 45.92
    small-to-small 45.91
  intrahepatic 51.79
  intrathoracic vessel NEC 39.23
  kidney (pelvis) 55.86
  lacrimal sac to conjunctiva 09.82
  left-to-right (systemic-pulmonary artery) 39.0
  lymphatic (channel) (peripheral) 40.9
  mesenteric-caval 39.1
  mesocaval 39.1
  nasolacrimal 09.81
  nerve (cranial) (peripheral) NEC 04.74
    accessory-facial 04.72
    accessory-hypoglossal 04.73
    hypoglossal-facial 04.71
  pancreas (duct) (to) 52.96
    bile duct 51.39
    gall bladder 51.33
    intestine 52.96
    jejunum 52.96
    stomach 52.96
  pleurothecal (with valve) 03.79
  portacaval 39.1
  portal vein to inferior vena cava 39.1
  pulmonary-aortic (Pott's) 39.0
  pulmonary artery and superior vena cava 39.21
  pulmonary-innominate artery (Blalock) 39.0
  pulmonary-subclavian artery (Blalock-Taussig) 39.0
  pulmonary vein and azygos vein 39.23
  pyeloileocutaneous 56.51
  pyeloureterovesical 55.86
  radial artery 36.19
  rectum, rectal NEC 48.74
    stump to small intestine 45.92
  renal (pelvis) 55.86
    vein and splenic vein 39.1
  renoportal 39.1
  salpingothecal (with valve) 03.79
  splenic to renal vein 39.1
  splenorenal (venous) 39.1
    arterial 39.26
  subarachnoid-peritoneal (with valve) 03.71
  subarachnoid-ureteral (with valve) 03.72
  subclavian-aortic 39.22
  superior vena cava to pulmonary artery 39.21
  systemic-pulmonary artery 39.0
  thoracic artery (to)
    coronary artery (single) 36.15
      double 36.16
    myocardium 36.2
  ureterocalyceal 55.86
  ureterocolic 56.71
  ureterovesical 56.74
  ureter (to) NEC 56.79
    bladder 56.74
    colon 56.71
    ileal pouch (bladder) 56.51
    ileum 56.71
    intestine 56.71
    skin 56.61
  urethra (end-to-end) 58.44
  vas deferens 63.82
  veins (suture of proximal to distal end) (with bypass graft) 39.29
    with excision or resection of vessel — *see* Phlebectomy, with anastomosis, by site
    mesenteric to vena cava 39.1
    portal to inferior vena cava 39.1
    revision 39.49
    splenic and renal 39.1
  ventricle, ventricular (intracerebral) (with valve) (*see also* Shunt, ventricular) 02.22
  ventriculoatrial (with valve) 02.32
  ventriculocaval (with valve) 02.32
  ventriculomastoid (with valve) 02.31

Anastomosis — *continued*
  ventriculopleural (with valve) 02.33
  vesicle — *see* Anastomosis, bladder
Anderson operation (tibial lengthening) 78.37
Anel operation (dilation of lacrimal duct) 09.42
Anesthesia
  acupuncture for 99.91
  cryoanalgesia, nerve (cranial) (peripheral) 04.2
  spinal — *omit code*
Aneurysmectomy 38.60
  with
    anastomosis 38.30
      abdominal
        artery 38.36
        vein 38.37
      aorta (arch) (ascending) (descending) 38.34
      head and neck NEC 38.32
      intracranial NEC 38.31
      lower limb
        artery 38.38
        vein 38.39
      thoracic NEC 38.35
      upper limb (artery) (vein) 38.33
    graft replacement (interposition) 38.40
      abdominal
        aorta
          endovascular approach 39.71
            fenestrated (branching) graft 39.78
          open approach 38.44
          Zenith® Renu™ AAA graft 39.71
        artery 38.46
        vein 38.47
      aorta (arch) (ascending) (descending) (thoracic)
        abdominal 38.44
        thoracic 38.45
        thoracoabdominal 38.45 [38.44]
      head and neck NEC 38.42
      intracranial NEC 38.41
      lower limb
        artery 38.48
        vein 38.49
      thoracic NEC 38.45
      upper limb (artery) (vein) 38.43
  abdominal
    artery 38.66
    vein 38.67
  aorta (arch) (ascending) (descending) 38.64
  atrial, auricular 37.32
  head and neck NEC 38.62
  heart 37.32
  intracranial NEC 38.61
  lower limb
    artery 38.68
    vein 38.69
  sinus of Valsalva 35.39
  thoracic NEC 38.65
  upper limb (artery) (vein) 38.63
  ventricle (myocardium) 37.32
Aneurysmoplasty — *see* Aneurysmorrhaphy
Aneurysmorrhaphy NEC 39.52
  by or with
    anastomosis — *see* Aneurysmectomy, with anastomosis, by site
    clipping 39.51
    coagulation 39.52
    electrocoagulation 39.52
    endovascular graft
      abdominal aorta 39.71
        fenestrated (branching) graft 39.78
      lower extremity artery(s) 39.79
      thoracic aorta 39.73
      upper extremity artery(s) 39.79
    excision or resection (*see also* Aneurysmectomy, by site)
      with
        anastomosis — *see* Aneurysmectomy, with anastomosis, by site

☑ Additional Digit Required — Refer to the Tabular List for Digit Selection   ▽ Subterms under main terms may continue to next column or page

2 — Volume 3   ▶◀ Revised Text   ● New Line   ▲ Revised Code   2015 ICD-9-CM

Amputation — Aneurysmorrhaphy

Aneurysmorrhaphy — continued
  by or with — continued
    excision or resection (see also Aneurys-
      mectomy, by site) — contin-
      ued
      with — continued
        graft replacement — see
          Aneurysmectomy, with
          graft replacement, by site
    filipuncture 39.52
    graft replacement — see Aneurysmecto-
      my, with graft replacement, by
      site
    methyl methacrylate 39.52
    suture 39.52
    wiring 39.52
    wrapping 39.52
  Matas' 39.52
Aneurysmotomy — see Aneurysmectomy
Angiectomy
  with
    anastomosis 38.30
      abdominal
        artery 38.36
        vein 38.37
      aorta (arch) (ascending) (descending)
        38.34
      head and neck NEC 38.32
      intracranial NEC 38.31
      lower limb
        artery 38.38
        vein 38.39
      thoracic vessel NEC 38.35
      upper limb (artery) (vein) 38.33
    graft replacement (interposition) 38.40
      abdominal
        aorta 38.44
        artery 38.46
        vein 38.47
      aorta (arch) (ascending) (descending
        thoracic)
        abdominal 38.44
        thoracic 38.45
        thoracoabdominal 38.45 [38.44]
      head and neck NEC 38.42
      intracranial NEC 38.41
      lower limb
        artery 38.48
        vein 38.49
      thoracic vessel NEC 38.45
      upper limb (artery) (vein) 38.43
Angiocardiography (selective) 88.50
  carbon dioxide (negative contrast) 88.58
  combined right and left heart 88.54
  intra-operative coronary fluorescence vas-
    cular 88.59
  left heart (aortic valve) (atrium) (ventricle)
    (ventricular outflow tract) 88.53
    combined with right heart 88.54
  right heart (atrium) (pulmonary valve)
    (ventricle) (ventricular outflow tract)
    88.52
    combined with left heart 88.54
  SPY, coronary 88.59
  vena cava (inferior) (superior) 88.51
Angiography (arterial) — see also Arteriogra-
    phy 88.40
  by C.A.T. — see Scan, C.A.T., by site
  by computed tomography — see Scan,
    C.A.T., by site
  by magnetic resonance — see Imaging,
    magnetic resonance, by site
  by radioisotope — see Scan, radioisotope,
    by site
  by ultrasound — see Ultrasonography, by
    site
  basilar 88.41
  brachial 88.49
  carotid (internal) 88.41
  celiac 88.47
  cerebral (posterior circulation) 88.41
  coronary NEC 88.57
    intra-operative fluorescence vascular
      88.59
  eye (fluorescein) 95.12
  femoral 88.48

Angiography — see also Arteriography —
    continued
  heart 88.50
  intra-abdominal NEC 88.47
  intracranial 88.41
  intrathoracic vessels NEC 88.44
  lower extremity NEC 88.48
  neck 88.41
  non-coronary, intra-operative fluorescence
    17.71
  placenta 88.46
  pulmonary 88.43
  renal 88.45
  specified artery NEC 88.49
  transfemoral 88.48
  upper extremity NEC 88.49
  veins — see Phlebography
  vertebral 88.41
Angioplasty (laser) — see also Repair, blood
    vessel

  Note — Also use 00.40, 00.41, 00.42,
  or 00.43 to show the total number of
  vessels treated. Use code 00.44 once to
  show procedure on a bifurcated vessel.
  In addition, use 00.45, 00.46, 00.47, or
  00.48 to show the number of vascular
  stents inserted.

  balloon (percutaneous transluminal) NEC
    39.50
    coronary artery 00.66
      multiple vessels
  coronary 36.09
    open chest approach 36.03
    percutaneous transluminal (balloon)
      00.66
  percutaneous transluminal (balloon)
    basilar 00.62
    carotid 00.61
    cerebrovascular
      extracranial 00.61
      intracranial 00.62
        carotid 00.61
    coronary (balloon) 00.66
    extracranial 00.61
    femoropopliteal 39.50
    iliac 39.50
    intracranial 00.62
    lower extremity NOS 39.50
    mesenteric 39.50
    peripheral NEC 39.50
    renal 39.50
    subclavian 39.50
    upper extremity NOS 39.50
    vertebral 00.61
      intracranial portion 00.62
  specified site 39.50
    cerebrovascular
      extracranial 00.61
      intracranial 00.62
      peripheral 39.50
Angiorrhaphy 39.30
  artery 39.31
  vein 39.32
Angioscopy, percutaneous 38.22
  eye (fluorescein) 95.12
Angiotomy 38.00
  abdominal
    artery 38.06
    vein 38.07
  aorta (arch) (ascending) (descending) 38.04
  head and neck NEC 38.02
  intracranial NEC 38.01
  lower limb
    artery 38.08
    vein 38.09
  thoracic NEC 38.05
  upper limb (artery) (vein) 38.03
Angiotripsy 39.98
Ankylosis, production of — see Arthrodesis
Annuloplasty (heart) (posteromedial) 35.33
Anoplasty 49.79
  with hemorrhoidectomy 49.46
Anoscopy 49.21
Antibiogram — see Examination, microscopic
Antiembolic filter, vena cava 38.7
Antiphobic treatment 94.39

Antrectomy
  mastoid 20.49
  maxillary 22.39
    radical 22.31
  pyloric 43.6
Antrostomy — see Antrotomy
Antrotomy (exploratory) (nasal sinus) 22.2
  Caldwell-Luc (maxillary sinus) 22.39
    with removal of membrane lining 22.31
  intranasal 22.2
    with external approach (Caldwell-Luc)
      22.39
      radical 22.31
  maxillary (simple) 22.2
    with Caldwell-Luc approach 22.39
      with removal of membrane lining
        22.31
    external (Caldwell-Luc approach) 22.39
      with removal of membrane lining
        22.31
    radical (with removal of membrane lin-
      ing) 22.31
Antrum window operation — see Antrotomy,
    maxillary
Aorticopulmonary window operation 39.59
Aortogram, aortography (abdominal) (retro-
    grade) (selective) (translumbar) 88.42
Aortoplasty (aortic valve) (gusset type) 35.11
Aortotomy 38.04
Apexcardiogram (with ECG lead) 89.57
Apheresis, therapeutic — see category
    99.7 ☑
Apicectomy
  lung 32.39
    thoracoscopic 32.30
  petrous pyramid 20.59
  tooth (root) 23.73
    with root canal therapy 23.72
Apicoectomy 23.73
  with root canal therapy 23.72
Apicolysis (lung) 33.39
Apicostomy, alveolar 24.0
Aponeurectomy 83.42
  hand 82.33
Aponeurorrhaphy — see also Suture, tendon
    83.64
  hand (see also Suture, tendon, hand) 82.45
Aponeurotomy 83.13
  hand 82.11
Appendectomy (with drainage) 47.09
  incidental 47.19
    laparoscopic 47.11
  laparoscopic 47.01
Appendicectomy (with drainage) 47.09
  Incidental 47.19
    laparoscopic 47.11
  laparoscopic 47.01
Appendicocecostomy 47.91
Appendicoenterostomy 47.91
Appendicolysis 54.59
  with appendectomy 47.09
    laparoscopic 47.01
    other 47.09
  laparoscopic 54.51
Appendicostomy 47.91
  closure 47.92
Appendicotomy 47.2
Application
  adhesion barrier substance 99.77
  anti-shock trousers 93.58
  arch bars (orthodontic) 24.7
    for immobilization (fracture) 93.55
  barrier substance, adhesion 99.77
  Barton's tongs (skull) (with synchronous
    skeletal traction) 02.94
  bone growth stimulator (surface) (transcu-
    taneous) 99.86
  bone morphogenetic protein (Infuse™) (OP-
    1™) (recombinant) (rhBMP) 84.52
  Bryant's traction 93.44
    with reduction of fracture or dislocation
      — see Reduction, fracture and
      Reduction, dislocation
  Buck's traction 93.46
  caliper tongs (skull) (with synchronous
    skeletal traction) 02.94

Application — continued
  cast (fiberglass) (plaster) (plastic) NEC 93.53
    with reduction of fracture or dislocation
      — see Reduction, fracture and
      Reduction, dislocation
    spica 93.51
  cervical collar 93.52
    with reduction of fracture or dislocation
      — see Reduction, fracture and
      Reduction, dislocation
  clamp, cerebral aneurysm (Crutchfield) (Sil-
    verstone) 39.51
  croupette, croup tent 93.94
  crown (artificial) 23.41
  Crutchfield tongs (skull) (with synchronous
    skeletal traction) 02.94
  Dunlop's traction 93.44
    with reduction of fracture or dislocation
      — see Reduction, fracture and
      Reduction, dislocation
  elastic stockings 93.59
  electronic gaiter 93.59
  external fixator device (bone) 78.10
    carpal, metacarpal 78.14
    clavicle 78.11
    computer assisted (dependent) 84.73
    femur 78.15
    fibula 78.17
    humerus 78.12
    hybrid device or system 84.73
    Ilizarov type 84.72
    monoplanar system or device 84.71
    patella 78.16
    pelvic 78.19
    phalanges (foot) (hand) 78.19
    radius 78.13
    ring device or system 84.72
    scapula 78.11
    Sheffield type 84.72
    specified site NEC 78.19
    tarsal, metatarsal 78.18
    thorax (ribs) (sternum) 78.11
    tibia 78.17
    ulna 78.13
    vertebrae 78.19
  forceps, with delivery — see Delivery, for-
    ceps
  graft — see Graft
  gravity (G-) suit 93.59
  intermittent pressure device 93.59
  Jewett extension brace 93.59
  Jobst pumping unit (reduction of edema)
    93.59
  Lyman Smith traction 93.44
    with reduction of fracture or dislocation
      — see Reduction, fracture and
      Reduction, dislocation
  MAST (military anti-shock trousers) 93.58
  Minerva jacket 93.52
  minifixator device (bone) — see category
    78.1 ☑
  neck support (molded) 93.52
  obturator (orthodontic) 24.7
  orthodontic appliance (obturator) (wiring)
    24.7
  pelvic sling 93.44
    with reduction of fracture or dislocation
      — see Reduction, fracture and
      Reduction, dislocation
  peridontal splint (orthodontic) 24.7
  plaster jacket 93.51
    Minerva 93.52
  pressure
    dressing (bandage) (Gibney) (Robert
      Jones') (Shanz) 93.56
    trousers (anti-shock) (MAST) 93.58
  prosthesis for missing ear 18.71
  Russell's traction 93.44
    with reduction of fracture or dislocation
      — see Reduction, fracture and
      Reduction, dislocation
  splint, for immobilization (plaster) (pneumat-
    ic) (tray) 93.54
    with fracture reduction — see Reduction,
      fracture
  stereotactic head frame 93.59

☑ **Additional Digit Required** — Refer to the Tabular List for Digit Selection   ▽ **Subterms under main terms may continue to next column or page**

2015 ICD-9-CM   ►◄ Revised Text   ● New Line   ▲ Revised Code   **Volume 3 — 3**

Application — *continued*
  strapping (non-traction) 93.59
  substance, adhesion barrier 99.77
  Thomas collar 93.52
    with reduction of fracture or dislocation
      — *see* Reduction, fracture *and*
      Reduction, dislocation
  traction
    with reduction of fracture or dislocation
      — *see* Reduction, fracture *and*
      Reduction, dislocation
    adhesive tape (skin) 93.46
    boot 93.46
    Bryant's 93.44
    Buck's 93.46
    Cotrel's 93.42
    Dunlop's 93.44
    gallows 93.46
    Lyman Smith 93.44
    Russell's 93.44
    skeletal NEC 93.44
      intermittent 93.43
    skin, limbs NEC 93.46
    spinal NEC 93.42
      with skull device (halo) (caliper)
        (Crutchfield) (Gardner-Wells)
        (Vinke) (tongs) 93.41
        with synchronous insertion 02.94
    Thomas' splint 93.45
  Unna's paste boot 93.53
  vasopneumatic device 93.58
  Velpeau dressing 93.59
  Vinke tongs (skull) (with synchronous
    skeletal traction) 02.94
  wound dressing NEC 93.57
Aquapheresis 99.78
Arc lamp — *see* Photocoagulation
Arcuplasty 81.66
Arrest
  bone growth (epiphyseal) 78.20
    by stapling — *see* Stapling, epiphyseal
      plate
    femur 78.25
    fibula 78.27
    humerus 78.22
    radius 78.23
    tibia 78.27
    ulna 78.23
  cardiac, induced (anoxic) (circulatory) 39.63
  circulatory, induced (anoxic) 39.63
  hemorrhage — *see* Control, hemorrhage
Arslan operation (fenestration of inner ear)
  20.61
Arteriectomy 38.60
  with
    anastomosis 38.30
      abdominal 38.36
      aorta (arch) (ascending) (descending
        thoracic) 38.34
      head and neck NEC 38.32
      intracranial NEC 38.31
      lower limb 38.38
      thoracic NEC 38.35
      upper limb 38.33
    graft replacement (interposition) 38.40
      abdominal
        aorta 38.44
      aorta (arch) (ascending) (descending
        thoracic)
        abdominal 38.44
        thoracic 38.45
        thoracoabdominal 38.45 *[38.44]*
      head and neck NEC 38.42
      intracranial NEC 38.41
      lower limb 38.48
      thoracic NEC 38.45
      upper limb 38.43
  abdominal 38.66
  aorta (arch) (ascending) (descending) 38.64
  head and neck NEC 38.62
  intracranial NEC 38.61
  lower limb 38.68
  thoracic NEC 38.65
  upper limb 38.63
Arteriography (contrast) (fluoroscopic) (retrograde) 88.40

Arteriography — *continued*
  by
    radioisotope — *see* Scan, radioisotope
    ultrasound (Doppler) — *see* Ultrasonog-
      raphy, by site
  aorta (arch) (ascending) (descending) 88.42
  basilar 88.41
  brachial 88.49
  carotid (internal) 88.41
  cerebral (posterior circulation) 88.41
  coronary (direct) (selective) NEC 88.57
    double catheter technique (Judkins)
      (Ricketts and Abrams) 88.56
    intra-operative fluorescence vascular
      88.59
    single catheter technique (Sones) 88.55
  Doppler (ultrasonic) — *see* Ultrasonography,
    by site
  femoral 88.48
  head and neck 88.41
  intra-abdominal NEC 88.47
  intrathoracic NEC 88.44
  lower extremity 88.48
  placenta 88.46
  pulmonary 88.43
  radioisotope — *see* Scan, radioisotope
  renal 88.45
  specified site NEC 88.49
  SPY, coronary 88.59
  superior mesenteric artery 88.47
  transfemoral 88.48
  ultrasound — *see* Ultrasonography, by site
  upper extremity 88.49
Arterioplasty — *see* Repair, artery
Arteriorrhaphy 39.31
Arteriotomy 38.00
  abdominal 38.06
  aorta (arch) (ascending) (descending) 38.04
  head and neck NEC 38.02
  intracranial NEC 38.01
  lower limb 38.08
  thoracic NEC 38.05
  upper limb 38.03
Arteriovenostomy 39.29
  for renal dialysis 39.27
Arthrectomy 80.90
  ankle 80.97
  elbow 80.92
  foot and toe 80.98
  hand and finger 80.94
  hip 80.95
  intervertebral disc — *see* category 80.5 ☑
  knee 80.96
    semilunar cartilage 80.6
  shoulder 80.91
  specified site NEC 80.99
  spine NEC 80.99
  wrist 80.93
Arthrocentesis 81.91
  for arthrography — *see* Arthrogram
Arthrodesis (compression) (extra-articular)
  (intra-articular) (with bone graft) (with
  fixation device) 81.20
  ankle 81.11
  carporadial 81.25
  cricoarytenoid 31.69
  elbow 81.24
  finger 81.28
  foot NEC 81.17
  hip 81.21
  interphalangeal
    finger 81.28
    toe NEC 77.58
      claw toe repair 77.57
      hammer toe repair 77.56
  ischiofemoral 81.21
  knee 81.22
  lumbosacral, lumbar NEC 81.08
    ALIF (anterior lumbar interbody fusion)
      81.06
    anterior column (interbody)
      anterolateral (anterior) technique
        81.06
      posterior technique 81.08
    axial lumbar interbody fusion (AxiaLIF®)
      81.08

Arthrodesis — *continued*
  lumbosacral, lumbar — *continued*
    direct lateral interbody fusion (DLIF)
      81.06
    extreme lateral interbody fusion (XLIF®)
      81.06
    facet 81.07
    lateral transverse process technique
      81.07
    PLIF (posterior lumbar interbody fusion)
      81.08
    TLIF (transforaminal lumbar interbody
      fusion) 81.08
  McKeever (metatarsophalangeal) 81.16
  metacarpocarpal 81.26
  metacarpophalangeal 81.27
  metatarsophalangeal 81.16
  midtarsal 81.14
  pantalar 81.11
  sacroiliac 81.08
  shoulder 81.23
  specified joint NEC 81.29
  spinal (see also Fusion, spinal) 81.00
  subtalar 81.13
  tarsometatarsal 81.15
  tibiotalar 81.11
  toe NEC 77.58
    claw toe repair 77.57
    hammer toe repair 77.56
  triple 81.12
  wrist 81.26
Arthroendoscopy — *see* Arthroscopy
Arthroereisis, subtalar joint 81.18
Arthrogram, arthrography 88.32
  temporomandibular 87.13
Arthrolysis 93.26
Arthroplasty (with fixation device) (with traction) 81.96
  ankle 81.49
  carpals 81.75
    with prosthetic implant 81.74
  carpocarpal, carpometacarpal 81.75
    with prosthetic implant 81.74
  Carroll and Taber (proximal interphalangeal
    joint) 81.72
  cup (partial hip) 81.52
  Curtis (interphalangeal joint) 81.72
  elbow 81.85
    with prosthetic replacement (partial)
      (total) 81.84
  femoral head NEC 81.40
    with prosthetic implant 81.52
  finger(s) 81.72
    with prosthetic implant 81.71
  foot (metatarsal) with joint replacement
    81.57
  Fowler (metacarpophalangeal joint) 81.72
  hand (metacarpophalangeal) (interpha-
    langeal) 81.72
    with prosthetic implant 81.71
  hip (with bone graft) 81.40
    cup (partial hip) 81.52
    femoral head NEC 81.40
      with prosthetic implant 81.52
        with total replacement 81.51
    partial replacement 81.52
    total replacement 81.51
  interphalangeal joint 81.72
    with prosthetic implant 81.71
  Kessler (carpometacarpal joint) 81.74
  knee (see also Repair, knee) 81.47
    prosthetic replacement (bicompartmen-
      tal) (hemijoint) (partial) (total)
      (tricompartmental) (unicompart-
      mental) 81.54
    revision 81.55
  metacarpophalangeal joint 81.72
    with prosthetic implant 81.71
  shoulder 81.83
    for recurrent dislocation 81.82
    prosthetic replacement (partial) 81.81
      total, NEC 81.80
        other 81.80
        reverse 81.88
  temporomandibular 76.5
  toe NEC 77.58

Arthroplasty — *continued*
  toe — *continued*
    with prosthetic replacement 81.57
    for hallux valgus repair 77.59
  wrist 81.75
    with prosthetic implant 81.74
      total replacement 81.73
Arthroscopy 80.20
  ankle 80.27
  elbow 80.22
  finger 80.24
  foot 80.28
  hand 80.24
  hip 80.25
  knee 80.26
  shoulder 80.21
  specified site NEC 80.29
  toe 80.28
  wrist 80.23
Arthrostomy — *see also* Arthrotomy 80.10
Arthrotomy 80.10
  as operative approach — *omit code*
  with
    arthrography — *see* Arthrogram
    arthroscopy — *see* Arthroscopy
    injection of drug 81.92
    removal of prosthesis without replace-
      ment (*see* Removal, prosthesis,
      joint structures)
  ankle 80.17
  elbow 80.12
  foot and toe 80.18
  hand and finger 80.14
  hip 80.15
  knee 80.16
  shoulder 80.11
  specified site NEC 80.19
  spine 80.19
  wrist 80.13
Artificial
  heart 37.52
    AbioCor® 37.52
    CardioWest™ (TAH-t) 37.52
  insemination 69.92
  kidney 39.95
  rupture of membranes 73.09
Arytenoidectomy 30.29
Arytenoidopexy 31.69
Asai operation (larynx) 31.75
Aspiration
  abscess — *see* Aspiration, by site
  anterior chamber, eye (therapeutic) 12.91
    diagnostic 12.21
  aqueous (eye) (humor) (therapeutic) 12.91
    diagnostic 12.21
  ascites 54.91
  Bartholin's gland (cyst) (percutaneous) 71.21
  biopsy — *see* Biopsy, by site
  bladder (catheter) 57.0
    percutaneous (needle) 57.11
  bone marrow (for biopsy) 41.31
    from donor for transplant 41.91
    stem cell 99.79
  branchial cleft cyst 29.0
  breast 85.91
  bronchus 96.05
    with lavage 96.56
  bursa (percutaneous) 83.94
    hand 82.92
  calculus, bladder 57.0
  cataract 13.3
    with
      phacoemulsification 13.41
      phacofragmentation 13.43
        posterior route 13.42
  chest 34.91
  cisternal 01.01
  cranial (puncture) 01.09
  craniobuccal pouch 07.72
  craniopharyngioma 07.72
  cul-de-sac (abscess) 70.0
  curettage, uterus 69.59
    after abortion or delivery 69.52
    diagnostic 69.59
    to terminate pregnancy 69.51
  cyst — *see* Aspiration, by site

☑ **Additional Digit Required** — Refer to the Tabular List for Digit Selection   ⬆ **Subterms under main terms may continue to next column or page**

4 — Volume 3   ▶◀ Revised Text   ● New Line   ▲ Revised Code   2015 ICD-9-CM

☑ **Additional Digit Required** — Refer to the Tabular List for Digit Selection
▽ **Subterms under main terms may continue to next column or page**

2015 ICD-9-CM · ▶◀ Revised Text · ● New Line · ▲ Revised Code · Volume 3 — 5

Biopsy — *continued*
  duodenum — *continued*
    closed (endoscopic) 45.14
    open 45.15
  ear (external) 18.12
    middle or inner 20.32
  endocervix 67.11
  endometrium NEC 68.16
    by
      aspiration curettage 69.59
      dilation and curettage 69.09
    closed (endoscopic) 68.16
    open 68.13
  epididymis 63.01
  esophagus 42.24
    closed (endoscopic) 42.24
    open 42.25
  extraocular muscle or tendon 15.01
  eye 16.23
    muscle (oblique) (rectus) 15.01
  eyelid 08.11
  fallopian tube 66.11
  fascia 83.21
  fetus 75.33
  gallbladder 51.12
    closed (endoscopic) 51.14
    open 51.13
    percutaneous (needle) 51.12
  ganglion (cranial) (peripheral) NEC 04.11
    closed 04.11
    open 04.12
    percutaneous (needle) 04.11
    sympathetic nerve 05.11
  gum 24.11
  heart 37.25
  hypophysis (*see also* Biopsy, pituitary gland) 07.15
  ileum 45.14
    brush 45.14
    closed (endoscopic) 45.14
    open 45.15
  intestine NEC 45.27
    large 45.25
      brush 45.25
      closed (endoscopic) 45.25
      open 45.26
    small 45.14
      brush 45.14
      closed (endoscopic) 45.14
      open 45.15
  intra-abdominal mass 54.24
    closed 54.24
    percutaneous (needle) 54.24
  iris 12.22
  jejunum 45.14
    brush 45.14
    closed (endoscopic) 45.14
    open 45.15
  joint structure (aspiration) 80.30
    ankle 80.37
    elbow 80.32
    foot and toe 80.38
    hand and finger 80.34
    hip 80.35
    knee 80.36
    shoulder 80.31
    specified site NEC 80.39
    spine 80.39
    wrist 80.33
  kidney 55.23
    closed 55.23
    open 55.24
    percutaneous (aspiration) (needle) 55.23
  labia 71.11
  lacrimal
    gland 09.11
    sac 09.12
  larynx 31.43
    brush 31.43
    closed (endoscopic) 31.43
    open 31.45
  lip 27.23
  liver 50.11
    closed 50.11
    laparoscopic 50.14
    open 50.12

Biopsy — *continued*
  liver — *continued*
    percutaneous (aspiration) (needle) 50.11
    transjugular 50.13
    transvenous 50.13
  lung NEC 33.27
    brush 33.24
    closed (percutaneous) (needle) 33.26
      brush 33.24
      endoscopic 33.27
        brush 33.24
    endoscopic 33.27
      brush 33.24
    open 33.28
    thoracoscopic 33.20
    transbronchial 33.27
    transthoracic 33.26
  lymphatic structure (channel) (node) (vessel) 40.11
  mediastinum NEC 34.25
    closed 34.25
    open 34.26
    percutaneous (needle) 34.25
  meninges (cerebral) NEC 01.11
    closed 01.11
    open 01.12
    percutaneous (needle) 01.11
    spinal 03.32
  mesentery 54.23
  mouth NEC 27.24
  muscle 83.21
    extraocular 15.01
    ocular 15.01
  nasopharynx 29.12
  nerve (cranial) (peripheral) NEC 04.11
    closed 04.11
    open 04.12
    percutaneous (needle) 04.11
    sympathetic 05.11
  nose, nasal 21.22
    sinus 22.11
      closed (endoscopic) (needle) 22.11
      open 22.12
  ocular muscle or tendon 15.01
  omentum
    closed 54.24
    open 54.23
    percutaneous (needle) 54.24
  orbit 16.23
    by aspiration 16.22
  ovary 65.12
    by aspiration 65.11
    laparoscopic 65.13
  palate (bony) 27.21
    soft 27.22
  pancreas 52.11
    closed (endoscopic) 52.11
    open 52.12
    percutaneous (aspiration) (needle) 52.11
  pancreatic duct 52.14
    closed (endoscopic) 52.14
  parathyroid gland 06.13
  penis 64.11
  perianal tissue 49.22
  pericardium 37.24
  periprostatic 60.15
  perirectal tissue 48.26
  perirenal tissue 59.21
  peritoneal implant
    closed 54.24
    open 54.23
    percutaneous (needle) 54.24
  peritoneum
    closed 54.24
    open 54.23
    percutaneous (needle) 54.24
  periurethral tissue 58.24
  perivesical tissue 59.21
  pharynx, pharyngeal 29.12
  pineal gland 07.17
  pituitary gland 07.15
    transfrontal approach 07.13
    transsphenoidal approach 07.14
  pleura, pleural 34.24
    thoracoscopic 34.20
  prostate NEC 60.11

Biopsy — *continued*
  prostate — *continued*
    closed (transurethral) 60.11
    open 60.12
    percutaneous (needle) 60.11
    transrectal 60.11
  rectum 48.24
    brush 48.24
    closed (endoscopic) 48.24
    open 48.25
  retroperitoneal tissue 54.24
  salivary gland or duct 26.11
    closed (needle) 26.11
    open 26.12
  scrotum 61.11
  seminal vesicle NEC 60.13
    closed 60.13
    open 60.14
    percutaneous (needle) 60.13
  sigmoid colon 45.25
    brush 45.25
    closed (endoscopic) 45.25
    open 45.26
  sinus, nasal 22.11
    closed (endoscopic) (needle) 22.11
    open 22.12
  skin (punch) 86.11
  skull 01.15
  soft palate 27.22
  soft tissue NEC 86.11
    closed (needle) (punch) 86.11
    open 83.21
  spermatic cord 63.01
  sphincter of Oddi 51.14
    closed (endoscopic) 51.14
    open 51.13
  spinal cord (meninges) 03.32
  spleen 41.32
    closed 41.32
    open 41.33
    percutaneous (aspiration) (needle) 41.32
  stomach 44.14
    brush 44.14
    closed (endoscopic) 44.14
    open 44.15
  subcutaneous tissue (punch) 86.11
  supraglottic mass 29.12
  sympathetic nerve 05.11
  tendon 83.21
    extraocular 15.01
    ocular 15.01
  testis NEC 62.11
    closed 62.11
    open 62.12
    percutaneous (needle) 62.11
  thymus 07.16
  thyroid gland NEC 06.11
    closed 06.11
    open 06.12
    percutaneous (aspiration) (needle) 06.11
  tongue 25.01
    closed (needle) 25.01
    open 25.02
  tonsil 28.11
  trachea 31.44
    brush 31.44
    closed (endoscopic) 31.44
    open 31.45
  tunica vaginalis 61.11
  umbilicus 54.22
  ureter 56.33
    closed (percutaneous) 56.32
      endoscopic 56.33
      open 56.34
    transurethral 56.33
  urethra 58.23
  uterus, uterine (endometrial) 68.16
    by
      aspiration curettage 69.59
      dilation and curettage 69.09
    closed (endoscopic) 68.16
    ligaments 68.15
      closed (endoscopic) 68.15
      open 68.14
    open 68.13
  uvula 27.22

Biopsy — *continued*
  vagina 70.24
  vas deferens 63.01
  vein (any site) 38.21
  vulva 71.11
BiPAP 93.90
  delivered by
    endotracheal tube — *see category* 96.7 ☑
    tracheostomy — *see category* 96.7 ☑
Bischoff operation (spinal myelotomy) 03.29
Bischoff operation (ureteroneocystostomy) 56.74
Bisection — *see also* Excision
  hysterectomy 68.39
    laparoscopic 68.31
  ovary 65.29
    laparoscopic 65.25
  stapes foot plate 19.19
    with incus replacement 19.11
BIS (bispectral index) **monitoring** 00.94 *[89.14]*
Blalock-Hanlon operation (creation of atrial septal defect) 35.42
Blalock operation (systemic-pulmonary anastomosis) 39.0
Blalock-Taussig operation (subclavian-pulmonary anastomosis) 39.0
Blascovic operation (resection and advancement of levator palpebrae superioris) 08.33
Blepharectomy 08.20
Blepharoplasty — *see also* Reconstruction, eyelid 08.70
  extensive 08.44
Blepharorrhaphy 08.52
  division or severing 08.02
Blepharotomy 08.09
Blind rehabilitation therapy NEC 93.78
Block
  caudal — *see* Injection, spinal
  celiac ganglion or plexus 05.31
  dissection
    breast
      bilateral 85.46
      unilateral 85.45
    bronchus 32.6
    larynx 30.3
    lymph nodes 40.50
    neck 40.40
    vulva 71.5
  epidural, spinal — *see* Injection, spinal
  gasserian ganglion 04.81
  intercostal nerves 04.81
  intrathecal — *see* Injection, spinal
  nerve (cranial) (peripheral) NEC 04.81
  paravertebral stellate ganglion 05.31
  peripheral nerve 04.81
  spinal nerve root (intrathecal) — *see* Injection, spinal
  stellate (ganglion) 05.31
  subarachnoid, spinal — *see* Injection, spinal
  sympathetic nerve 05.31
  trigeminal nerve 04.81
Blood
  flow study, Doppler-type (ultrasound) — *see* Ultrasonography
  patch, spine (epidural) 03.95
  transfusion
    antihemophilic factor 99.06
    autologous
      collected prior to surgery 99.02
      intraoperative 99.00
      perioperative 99.00
      postoperative 99.00
      previously collected 99.02
      salvage 99.00
    blood expander 99.08
    blood surrogate 99.09
    coagulation factors 99.06
    exchange 99.01
    granulocytes 99.09
    hemodilution 99.03
    other substance 99.09
    packed cells 99.04
    plasma 99.07
    platelets 99.05

☑ Additional Digit Required — Refer to the Tabular List for Digit Selection　　　　▽ Subterms under main terms may continue to next column or page

6 — Volume 3　　▶◀ Revised Text　　● New Line　　▲ Revised Code　　2015 ICD-9-CM

☑ **Additional Digit Required** — Refer to the Tabular List for Digit Selection   ⟲ **Subterms under main terms may continue to next column or page**

8 — Volume 3   ▶◀ Revised Text   ● New Line   ▲ Revised Code   2015 ICD-9-CM

Chordotomy — *continued*
  stereotactic 03.21
Ciliarotomy 12.55
Ciliectomy (ciliary body) 12.44
  eyelid margin 08.20
Cinch, cinching
  for scleral buckling (*see also* Buckling, scleral) 14.49
  ocular muscle (oblique) (rectus) 15.22
    multiple (two or more muscles) 15.4
Cineangiocardiography — *see also* Angiocardiography 88.50
Cineplasty, cineplastic prosthesis
  amputation — *see* Amputation
  arm 84.44
  biceps 84.44
  extremity 84.40
    lower 84.48
    upper 84.44
  leg 84.48
Cineradiograph — *see* Radiography
Cingulumotomy (brain) (percutaneous radiofrequency) 01.32
Circumcision (male) 64.0
  female 71.4
CISH (classic infrafascial SEMM hysterectomy) 68.31
Clagett operation (closure of chest wall following open flap drainage) 34.72
Clamp and cautery, hemorrhoids 49.43
Clamping
  aneurysm (cerebral) 39.51
  blood vessel — *see* Ligation, blood vessel
  ventricular shunt 02.43
Clavicotomy 77.31
  fetal 73.8
Claviculectomy (partial) 77.81
  total 77.91
Clayton operation (resection of metatarsal heads and bases of phalanges) 77.88
Cleaning, wound 96.59
Clearance
  bladder (transurethral) 57.0
  pelvic
    female 68.8
    male 57.71
  prescalene fat pad 40.21
  renal pelvis (transurethral) 56.0
  ureter (transurethral) 56.0
Cleft lift 86.21
Cleidotomy 77.31
  fetal 73.8
Clipping
  aneurysm (basilar) (carotid) (cerebellar) (cerebellopontine) (communicating artery) (vertebral) 39.51
  arteriovenous fistula 39.53
  frenulum, frenum
    labia (lips) 27.91
    lingual (tongue) 25.91
  left atrial appendage 37.36
  tip of uvula 27.72
Clitoridectomy 71.4
Clitoridotomy 71.4
Clivogram 87.02
Closure — *see also* Repair
  abdominal wall 54.63
    delayed (granulating wound) 54.62
    secondary 54.61
    tertiary 54.62
  amputation stump, secondary 84.3
  anular disc 80.54
  anulus fibrosus 80.54
    with graft or prosthesis 80.53
  aorticopulmonary fenestration (fistula) 39.59
  appendicostomy 47.92
  artificial opening
    bile duct 51.79
    bladder 57.82
    bronchus 33.42
    common duct 51.72
    esophagus 42.83
    gallbladder 51.92
    hepatic duct 51.79

Closure — *see also* Repair — *continued*
  artificial opening — *continued*
    intestine 46.50
      large 46.52
      small 46.51
    kidney 55.82
    larynx 31.62
    rectum 48.72
    stomach 44.62
    thorax 34.72
    trachea 31.72
    ureter 56.83
    urethra 58.42
  atrial septal defect (*see also* Repair, atrial septal defect) 35.71
    with umbrella device (King-Mills type) 35.52
    combined with repair of valvular and ventricular septal defects — *see* Repair, endocardial cushion defect
  bronchostomy 33.42
  cecostomy 46.52
  cholecystostomy 51.92
  cleft hand 82.82
  colostomy 46.52
  cystostomy 57.82
  diastema (alveolar) (dental) 24.8
  disrupted abdominal wall (postoperative) 54.61
  duodenostomy 46.51
  encephalocele 02.12
  endocardial cushion defect (*see also* Repair, endocardial cushion defect) 35.73
  enterostomy 46.50
  esophagostomy 42.83
  fenestration
    aorticopulmonary 39.59
    septal, heart (*see also* Repair, heart, septum) 35.70
  filtering bleb, corneoscleral (postglaucoma) 12.66
  fistula
    abdominothoracic 34.83
    anorectal 48.73
    anovaginal 70.73
    antrobuccal 22.71
    anus 49.73
    aorticopulmonary (fenestration) 39.59
    aortoduodenal 39.59
    appendix 47.92
    biliary tract 51.79
    bladder NEC 57.84
    branchial cleft 29.52
    bronchocutaneous 33.42
    bronchoesophageal 33.42
    bronchomediastinal 34.73
    bronchopleural 34.73
    bronchopleurocutaneous 34.73
    bronchopleuromediastinal 34.73
    bronchovisceral 33.42
    bronchus 33.42
    cecosigmoidal 46.76
    cerebrospinal fluid 02.12
    cervicoaural 18.79
    cervicosigmoidal 67.62
    cervicovesical 57.84
    cervix 67.62
    cholecystocolic 51.93
    cholecystoduodenal 51.93
    cholecystoenteric 51.93
    cholecystogastric 51.93
    cholecystojejunal 51.93
    cisterna chyli 40.63
    colon 46.76
    colovaginal 70.72
    common duct 51.72
    cornea 11.49
      with lamellar graft (homograft) 11.62
      autograft 11.61
    diaphragm 34.83
    duodenum 46.72
    ear drum 19.4
    ear, middle 19.9
    enterocolic 46.74
    enterocutaneous 46.74

Closure — *see also* Repair — *continued*
  fistula — *continued*
    enterouterine 69.42
    enterovaginal 70.74
    enterovesical 57.83
    esophagobronchial 33.42
    esophagocutaneous 42.84
    esophagopleurocutaneous 34.73
    esophagotracheal 31.73
    esophagus NEC 42.84
    fecal 46.79
    gallbladder 51.93
    gastric NEC 44.63
    gastrocolic 44.63
    gastroenterocolic 44.63
    gastroesophageal 42.84
    gastrojejunal 44.63
    gastrojejunocolic 44.63
    heart valve — *see* Repair, heart, valve
    hepatic duct 51.79
    hepatopleural 34.73
    hepatopulmonary 34.73
    ileorectal 46.74
    ileosigmoidal 46.74
    ileovesical 57.83
    ileum 46.74
    in ano 49.73
    intestine 46.79
      large 46.76
      small NEC 46.74
    intestinocolonic 46.74
    intestinoureteral 56.84
    intestinouterine 69.42
    intestinovaginal 70.74
    intestinovesical 57.83
    jejunum 46.74
    kidney 55.83
    lacrimal 09.99
    laryngotracheal 31.62
    larynx 31.62
    lymphatic duct, left (thoracic) 40.63
    mastoid (antrum) 19.9
    mediastinobronchial 34.73
    mediastinocutaneous 34.73
    mouth (external) 27.53
    nasal 21.82
      sinus 22.71
    nasolabial 21.82
    nasopharyngeal 21.82
    oroantral 22.71
    oronasal 21.82
    oval window (ear) 20.93
    pancreaticoduodenal 52.95
    perilymph 20.93
    perineorectal 48.73
    perineosigmoidal 46.76
    perineourethroscrotal 58.43
    perineum 71.72
    perirectal 48.73
    pharyngoesophageal 29.53
    pharynx NEC 29.53
    pleura, pleural NEC 34.93
    pleurocutaneous 34.73
    pleuropericardial 37.49
    pleuroperitoneal 34.83
    pulmonoperitoneal 34.83
    rectolabial 48.73
    rectoureteral 56.84
    rectourethral 58.43
    rectovaginal 70.73
    rectovesical 57.83
    rectovesicovaginal 57.83
    rectovulvar 48.73
    rectum NEC 48.73
    renal 55.83
    reno-intestinal 55.83
    round window 20.93
    salivary (gland) (duct) 26.42
    scrotum 61.42
    sigmoidovaginal 70.74
    sigmoidovesical 57.83
    splenocolic 41.95
    stomach NEC 44.63
    thoracic duct 40.63
    thoracoabdominal 34.83
    thoracogastric 34.83

Closure — *see also* Repair — *continued*
  fistula — *continued*
    thoracointestinal 34.83
    thorax NEC 34.73
    trachea NEC 31.73
    tracheoesophageal 31.73
    tympanic membrane (*see also* Tympanoplasty) 19.4
    umbilicourinary 57.51
    ureter 56.84
    ureterocervical 56.84
    ureterorectal 56.84
    ureterosigmoidal 56.84
    ureterovaginal 56.84
    ureterovesical 56.84
    urethra 58.43
    urethroperineal 58.43
    urethroperineovesical 57.84
    urethrorectal 58.43
    urethroscrotal 58.43
    urethrovaginal 58.43
    uteroenteric 69.42
    uterointestinal 69.42
    uterorectal 69.42
    uteroureteric 56.84
    uterovaginal 69.42
    uterovesical 57.84
    vagina 70.75
    vaginocutaneous 70.75
    vaginoenteric 70.74
    vaginoperineal 70.75
    vaginovesical 57.84
    vesicocervicovaginal 57.84
    vesicocolic 57.83
    vesicocutaneous 57.84
    vesicoenteric 57.83
    vesicometrorectal 57.83
    vesicoperineal 57.84
    vesicorectal 57.83
    vesicosigmoidal 57.83
    vesicosigmoidovaginal 57.83
    vesicoureteral 56.84
    vesicoureterovaginal 56.84
    vesicourethral 57.84
    vesicourethrorectal 57.83
    vesicouterine 57.84
    vesicovaginal 57.84
    vulva 71.72
    vulvorectal 48.73
  foramen ovale (patent) 35.71
    with
      prosthesis (open heart technique) 35.51
        closed heart technique 35.52
      tissue graft 35.61
  gastroduodenostomy 44.5
  gastrojejunostomy 44.5
  gastrostomy 44.62
  ileostomy 46.51
  jejunostomy 46.51
  laceration (*see also* Suture, by site)
    liver 50.61
  laparotomy, delayed 54.62
  meningocele (spinal) 03.51
    cerebral 02.12
  myelomeningocele 03.52
  nephrostomy 55.82
  palmar cleft 82.82
  patent ductus arteriosus 38.85
  pelviostomy 55.82
  peptic ulcer (bleeding) (perforated) 44.40
  perforation
    ear drum (*see also* Tympanoplasty) 19.4
    esophagus 42.82
    nasal septum 21.88
    tympanic membrane (*see also* Tympanoplasty) 19.4
  proctostomy 48.72
  punctum, lacrimal (papilla) 09.91
  pyelostomy 55.82
  rectostomy 48.72
  septum defect (heart) (*see also* Repair, heart, septum) 35.70
  sigmoidostomy 46.52
  skin (V-Y type) 86.59

Chordotomy — Closure

☑ **Additional Digit Required** — Refer to the Tabular List for Digit Selection   ▽ **Subterms under main terms may continue to next column or page**

2015 ICD-9-CM   ▶◀ Revised Text   ● New Line   ▲ Revised Code   **Volume 3 — 9**

☑ Additional Digit Required — Refer to the Tabular List for Digit Selection | ⬇ Subterms under main terms may continue to next column or page

10 — Volume 3 | ▶◀ Revised Text | ● New Line | ▲ Revised Code | 2015 ICD-9-CM

Cordotomy
spinal (bilateral) NEC 03.29
percutaneous 03.21
vocal 31.3
Corectomy 12.12
Corelysis 12.35
Coreoplasty 12.35
Corneoconjunctivoplasty 11.53
Corpectomy, (vertebral) 80.99
with diskectomy 80.99
Correction — see also Repair
atresia
esophageal 42.85
by magnetic forces 42.99
external meatus (ear) 18.6
nasopharynx, nasopharyngeal 29.4
rectum 48.0
tricuspid 35.94
atrial septal defect (see also Repair, atrial
septal defect) 35.71
combined with repair of valvular and
ventricular septal defects — see
Repair, endocardial cushion defect
blepharoptosis (see also Repair, blepharoptosis) 08.36
bunionette (with osteotomy) 77.54
chordee 64.42
claw toe 77.57
cleft
lip 27.54
palate 27.62
clubfoot NEC 83.84
coarctation of aorta
with
anastomosis 38.34
graft replacement 38.44
cornea NEC 11.59
refractive NEC 11.79
epikeratophakia 11.76
keratomileusis 11.71
keratophakia 11.72
radial keratotomy 11.75
esophageal atresia 42.85
by magnetic forces 42.99
everted lacrimal punctum 09.71
eyelid
ptosis (see also Repair, blepharoptosis)
08.36
retraction 08.38
fetal defect 75.36
forcible, of musculoskeletal deformity NEC
93.29
hammer toe 77.56
hydraulic pressure, open surgery for penile
inflatable prosthesis 64.99
urinary artificial sphincter 58.99
intestinal malrotation 46.80
large 46.82
small 46.81
inverted uterus — see Repair, inverted
uterus
lymphedema (of limb) 40.9
excision with graft 40.9
obliteration of lymphatics 40.9
transplantation of autogenous lymphatics 40.9
nasopharyngeal atresia 29.4
overlapping toes 77.58
palate (cleft) 27.62
prognathism NEC 76.64
prominent ear 18.5
punctum (everted) 09.71
spinal pseudarthrosis — see Refusion, spinal
syndactyly 86.85
tetralogy of Fallot
one-stage 35.81
partial — see specific procedure
total 35.81
total anomalous pulmonary venous connection
one-stage 35.82
partial — see specific procedure
total 35.82
transposition, great arteries, total 35.84
tricuspid atresia 35.94

Correction — see also Repair — continued
truncus arteriosus
one-stage 35.83
partial — see specific procedure
total 35.83
ureteropelvic junction 55.87
ventricular septal defect (see also Repair,
ventricular septal defect) 35.72
combined with repair of valvular and
atrial septal defects — see Repair,
endocardial cushion defect
Costectomy 77.91
with lung excision — see Excision, lung
associated with thoracic operation — omit
code
Costochondrectomy 77.91
associated with thoracic operation — omit
code
Costosternoplasty (pectus excavatum repair)
34.74
Costotomy 77.31
Costotransversectomy 77.91
associated with thoracic operation — omit
code
Counseling (for) NEC 94.49
alcoholism 94.46
drug addiction 94.45
employers 94.49
family (medical) (social) 94.49
marriage 94.49
ophthalmologic (with instruction) 95.36
pastoral 94.49
Countershock, cardiac NEC 99.62
Coventry operation (tibial wedge osteotomy)
77.27
CPAP (continuous positive airway pressure)
93.90
delivered by
endotracheal tube — see category
96.7 ☑
tracheostomy — see category 96.7 ☑
Craniectomy 01.25
linear (opening of cranial suture) 02.01
reopening of site 01.23
strip (opening of cranial suture) 02.01
Cranioclasis, fetal 73.8
Cranioplasty 02.06
with synchronous repair of encephalocele
02.12
Craniotomy 01.24
as operative approach — omit code
fetal 73.8
for decompression of fracture 02.02
reopening of site 01.23
Craterization, bone — see also Excision, lesion,
bone 77.60
Crawford operation (tarso-frontalis sling of
eyelid) 08.32
Creation — see also Formation
cardiac device (defibrillator) (pacemaker)
pocket
with initial insertion of cardiac device —
omit code
new site (skin) (subcutaneous) 37.79
conduit
apical-aortic (AAC) 35.93
ileal (urinary) 56.51
left ventricle and aorta 35.93
right atrium and pulmonary artery 35.94
right ventricle and pulmonary (distal)
artery 35.92
in repair of
pulmonary artery atresia 35.92
transposition of great vessels
35.92
truncus arteriosus 35.83
endorectal ileal pouch (J-pouch) (H-pouch)
(S-pouch) (with anastomosis to anus)
45.95
esophagogastric sphincteric competence
NEC 44.66
laparoscopic 44.67
Hartmann pouch — see Colectomy, by site
interatrial fistula 35.42
pericardial window 37.12
pleural window, for drainage 34.09

Creation — see also Formation —
continued
pocket
cardiac device (defibrillator) (pacemaker)
with initial insertion of cardiac device
— omit code
new site (skin) (subcutaneous) 37.79
loop recorder 37.79
thalamic stimulator pulse generator
with initial insertion of battery package — omit code
new site (skin) (subcutaneous) 86.09
shunt (see also Shunt)
arteriovenous fistula, for dialysis 39.93
left-to-right (systemic to pulmonary circulation) 39.0
subcutaneous tunnel for esophageal anastomosis 42.86
with anastomosis — see Anastomosis,
esophagus, antesternal
syndactyly (finger) (toe) 86.89
thalamic stimulator pulse generator pocket
with initial insrtion of battery package
— omit code
new site (skin) (subcutaneous) 86.09
tracheoesophageal fistula 31.95
window
pericardial 37.12
pleura, for drainage 34.09
Credé maneuver 73.59
Cricoidectomy 30.29
Cricothyreotomy (for assistance in breathing)
31.1
Cricothyroidectomy 30.29
Cricothyrostomy 31.1
Cricothyrotomy (for assistance in breathing)
31.1
Cricotomy (for assistance in breathing) 31.1
Cricotracheotomy (for assistance in breathing)
31.1
Crisis intervention 94.35
Croupette, croup tent 93.94
Crown, dental (ceramic) (gold) 23.41
Crushing
bone — see category 78.4 ☑
calculus
bile (hepatic) passage 51.49
endoscopic 51.88
bladder (urinary) 57.0
pancreatic duct 52.09
endoscopic 52.94
fallopian tube (see also Ligation, fallopian
tube) 66.39
ganglion — see Crushing, nerve
hemorrhoids 49.45
nasal septum 21.88
nerve (cranial) (peripheral) NEC 04.03
acoustic 04.01
auditory 04.01
phrenic 04.03
for collapse of lung 33.31
sympathetic 05.0
trigeminal 04.02
vestibular 04.01
vas deferens 63.71
Cryoablation — see Ablation
Cryoanalgesia
nerve (cranial) (peripheral) 04.2
Cryoconization, cervix 67.33
Cryodestruction — see Destruction, lesion, by
site
Cryoextraction, lens — see also Extraction,
cataract, intracapsular 13.19
Cryohypophysectomy (complete) (total) —
see also Hypophysectomy 07.69
Cryoleucotomy 01.32
Cryopexy, retinal — see Cryotherapy, retina
Cryoprostatectomy 60.62
Cryoretinopexy (for)
reattachment 14.52
repair of tear or defect 14.32
Cryosurgery — see Cryotherapy
Cryothalamectomy 01.41
Cryotherapy — see also Destruction, lesion,
by site
bladder 57.59

Cryotherapy — see also Destruction, lesion, by
site — continued
brain 01.59
cataract 13.19
cervix 67.33
choroid — see Cryotherapy, retina
ciliary body 12.72
corneal lesion (ulcer) 11.43
to reshape cornea 11.79
ear
external 18.29
inner 20.79
esophagus 42.39
endoscopic 42.33
eyelid 08.25
hemorrhoids 49.44
iris 12.41
nasal turbinates 21.61
palate (bony) 27.31
prostate 60.62
retina (for)
destruction of lesion 14.22
reattachment 14.52
repair of tear 14.32
skin 86.3
stomach 43.49
endoscopic 43.41
subcutaneous tissue 86.3
turbinates (nasal) 21.61
warts 86.3
genital 71.3
Cryptectomy (anus) 49.39
endoscopic 49.31
Cryptorchidectomy (unilateral) 62.3
bilateral 62.41
Cryptotomy (anus) 49.39
endoscopic 49.31
Cuirass 93.99
Culdocentesis 70.0
Culdoplasty 70.92
with graft or prosthesis 70.93
Culdoscopy (exploration) (removal of foreign
body or lesion) 70.22
Culdotomy 70.12
Culp-Deweerd operation (spiral flap pyeloplasty) 55.87
Culp-Scardino operation (ureteral flap
pyeloplasty) 55.87
Culture (and sensitivity) — see Examination,
microscopic
Curettage (with packing) (with secondary closure) — see also Dilation and curettage
adenoids 28.6
anus 49.39
endoscopic 49.31
bladder 57.59
transurethral 57.49
bone (see also Excision, lesion, bone) 77.60
brain 01.59
bursa 83.39
hand 82.29
cartilage (see also Excision, lesion, joint)
80.80
cerebral meninges 01.51
chalazion 08.25
conjunctiva (trachoma follicles) 10.33
corneal epithelium 11.41
for smear or culture 11.21
ear, external 18.29
eyelid 08.25
joint (see also Excision, lesion, joint) 80.80
meninges (cerebral) 01.51
spinal 03.4
muscle 83.32
hand 82.22
nerve (peripheral) 04.07
sympathetic 05.29
sclera 12.84
skin 86.3
spinal cord (meninges) 03.4
subgingival 24.31
tendon 83.39
sheath 83.31
hand 82.21
uterus (with dilation) 69.09
aspiration (diagnostic) NEC 69.59

☑ **Additional Digit Required** — Refer to the Tabular List for Digit Selection   ▽ **Subterms under main terms may continue to next column or page**

Curettage — *see also* Dilation and curettage — *continued*
  uterus — *continued*
    aspiration — *continued*
      after abortion or delivery 69.52
      to terminate pregnancy 69.51
      following delivery or abortion 69.02
Curette evacuation, lens 13.2
Curtis operation (interphalangeal joint arthroplasty) 81.72
Cutaneolipectomy 86.83
Cutdown, venous 38.94
Cutting
  nerve (cranial) (peripheral) NEC 04.03
    acoustic 04.01
    auditory 04.01
    root, spinal 03.1
    sympathetic 05.0
    trigeminal 04.02
    vestibular 04.01
  pedicle (flap) graft 86.71
  pylorus (with wedge resection) 43.3
  spinal nerve root 03.1
  ureterovesical orifice 56.1
  urethral sphincter 58.5
CVP (central venous pressure monitoring) 89.62
Cyclectomy (ciliary body) 12.44
  eyelid margin 08.20
Cyclicotomy 12.55
Cycloanemization 12.74
Cyclocryotherapy 12.72
Cyclodialysis (initial) (subsequent) 12.55
Cyclodiathermy (penetrating) (surface) 12.71
Cycloelectrolysis 12.71
Cyclophotocoagulation 12.73
Cyclotomy 12.55
Cystectomy — *see also* Excision, lesion, by site
  gallbladder — *see* Cholecystectomy
  urinary (partial) (subtotal) 57.6
    complete (with urethrectomy) 57.79
      radical 57.71
        with pelvic exenteration (female) 68.8
    total (with urethrectomy) 57.79
Cystocolostomy 57.88
Cystogram, cystography NEC 87.77
Cystolitholapaxy 57.0
Cystolithotomy 57.19
Cystometrogram 89.22
Cystopexy NEC 57.89
Cystoplasty NEC 57.89
Cystoproctostomy 57.88
Cystoprostatectomy, radical 57.71
Cystopyelography 87.74
Cystorrhaphy 57.81
Cystoscopy (transurethral) 57.32
  for
    control of hemorrhage
      bladder 57.93
      prostate 60.94
    retrograde pyelography 87.74
  with biopsy 57.33
  ileal conduit 56.35
  through stoma (artificial) 57.31
Cystostomy
  closed (suprapubic) (percutaneous) 57.17
  open (suprapubic) 57.18
  percutaneous (closed) (suprapubic) 57.17
  suprapubic
    closed 57.17
    open 57.18
Cystotomy (open) (for removal of calculi) 57.19
Cystourethrogram (retrograde) (voiding) 87.76
Cystourethropexy (by) 59.79
  levator muscle sling 59.71
  retropubic suspension 59.5
  suprapubic suspension 59.4
Cystourethroplasty 57.85
Cystourethroscopy 57.32
  with biopsy
    bladder 57.33
    ureter 56.33
Cytology — *see* Examination, microscopic

D

Dacryoadenectomy 09.20
  partial 09.22
  total 09.23
Dacryoadenotomy 09.0
Dacryocystectomy (complete) (partial) 09.6
Dacryocystogram 87.05
Dacryocystorhinostomy (DCR) (by intubation) (external) (intranasal) 09.81
Dacryocystostomy 09.53
Dacryocystosyringotomy 09.53
Dacryocystotomy 09.53
Dahlman operation (excision of esophageal diverticulum) 42.31
Dana operation (posterior rhizotomy) 03.1
Danforth operation (fetal) 73.8
Darrach operation (ulnar resection) 77.83
da Vinci® (S HD) Surgical System — *see* category 17.4 ☑
Davis operation (intubated ureterotomy) 56.2
Deaf training 95.49
Debridement, NOS 86.28
  excisional, NOS 86.22
    abdominal wall 54.3
    bone (*see also* Excision, lesion, bone) 77.60
      fracture — *see* Debridement, open fracture
    brain 01.59
    burn (skin) 86.22
    bursa 83.5
    cerebral meninges 01.51
    fascia 83.44
    flap graft 86.75
    graft (flap) (pedicle) 86.75
    heart valve (calcified) — *see* Valvuloplasty, heart
    infection (skin) 86.22
      nail bed or fold 86.27
    joint — *see* Excision, lesion, joint
    meninges (cerebral) 01.51
      spinal 03.4
    muscle 83.45
      hand 82.36
    nail 86.27
    nerve (peripheral) 04.07
    open fracture (compound) 79.60
      arm NEC 79.62
      carpal, metacarpal 79.63
      facial bone 76.2
      femur 79.65
      fibula 79.66
      foot NEC 79.67
      hand NEC 79.63
      humerus 79.61
      leg NEC 79.66
      phalanges
        foot 79.68
        hand 79.64
      radius 79.62
      specified site NEC 79.69
      tarsal, metatarsal 79.67
      tibia 79.66
      ulna 79.62
    patella 77.66
    pedicle graft 86.75
    skin or subcutaneous tissue (burn) (infection) (wound) 86.22
      cardioverter/defibrillator (automatic) pocket 37.79
      graft 86.75
      nail, nail bed, nail fold 86.27
      pacemaker pocket 37.79
      pocket
        cardiac device NEC 37.79
        cardiac pacemaker 37.79
        cardioverter/defibrillator (automatic) 37.79
    skull 01.25
      compound fracture 02.02
    spinal cord (meninges) 03.4
    tendon 83.39
    wound (skin) 86.22
  nonexcisional, NOS 86.28
    burn (skin) 86.28
    dental 96.54

Debridement, — *continued*
  nonexcisional, — *continued*
    infection (skin) 86.28
    skin or subcutaneous tissue (burn) (infection) (wound) 86.28
    ultrasonic, ultrasound 86.28
    VersaJet™ 86.28
    wound (skin) 86.28
Decapitation, fetal 73.8
Decapsulation, kidney 55.91
Declotting — *see also* Removal, thrombus
  arteriovenous cannula or shunt 39.49
Decompression
  anus (imperforate) 48.0
  biliary tract 51.49
    by intubation 51.43
      endoscopic 51.87
      percutaneous 51.98
  brain 01.24
  carpal tunnel 04.43
  cauda equina 03.09
  chamber 83.97
  colon 96.08
    by incision 45.03
    endoscopic (balloon) 46.85
  common bile duct 51.42
    by intubation 51.43
      endoscopic 51.87
      percutaneous 51.98
  cranial 01.24
    for skull fracture 02.02
  endolymphatic sac 20.79
  ganglion (peripheral) NEC 04.49
    cranial NEC 04.42
  gastric 96.07
  heart 37.0
  intestine 96.08
    by incision 45.00
    endoscopic (balloon) 46.85
  intracranial 01.24
  labyrinth 20.79
  laminectomy 03.09
  laminotomy 03.09
  median nerve 04.43
  muscle 83.02
    hand 82.02
  nerve (peripheral) NEC 04.49
    auditory 04.42
    cranial NEC 04.42
    median 04.43
    trigeminal (root) 04.41
  orbit (*see also* Orbitotomy) 16.09
  pancreatic duct 52.92
    endoscopic 52.93
  pericardium 37.0
  rectum 48.0
  skull fracture 02.02
  spinal cord (canal) 03.09
  tarsal tunnel 04.44
  tendon (sheath) 83.01
    hand 82.01
  thoracic outlet
    by
      myotomy (division of scalenus anticus muscle) 83.19
      tenotomy 83.13
  trigeminal (nerve root) 04.41
Decortication
  arterial 05.25
  brain 01.51
  cerebral meninges 01.51
  heart 37.31
  kidney 55.91
  lung (partial) (total) 34.51
    thoracoscopic 34.52
  nasal turbinates — *see* Turbinectomy
  nose 21.89
  ovary 65.29
    laparoscopic 65.25
  periarterial 05.25
  pericardium 37.31
  ventricle, heart (complete) 37.31
Decoy, E2F 00.16
Deepening
  alveolar ridge 24.5
  buccolabial sulcus 24.91

Deepening — *continued*
  lingual sulcus 24.91
Defatting, flap or pedicle graft 86.75
Defibrillation, electric (external) (internal) 99.62
  automatic cardioverter/defibrillator — *see* category 37.9 ☑
de Grandmont operation (tarsectomy) 08.35
Delaying of pedicle graft 86.71
Delivery (with)
  assisted spontaneous 73.59
  breech extraction (assisted) 72.52
    partial 72.52
      with forceps to aftercoming head 72.51
    total 72.54
      with forceps to aftercoming head 72.53
    unassisted (spontaneous delivery) — *omit code*
  cesarean section — *see* Cesarean section
  Credé maneuver 73.59
  De Lee maneuver 72.4
  forceps 72.9
    application to aftercoming head (Piper) 72.6
    with breech extraction
      partial 72.51
      total 72.53
    Barton's 72.4
    failed 73.3
    high 72.39
      with episiotomy 72.31
    low (outlet) 72.0
      with episiotomy 72.1
    mid 72.29
      with episiotomy 72.21
    outlet (low) 72.0
      with episiotomy 72.1
    rotation of fetal head 72.4
    trial 73.3
  instrumental NEC 72.9
    specified NEC 72.8
  key-in-lock rotation 72.4
  Kielland rotation 72.4
  Malström's extraction 72.79
    with episiotomy 72.71
  manually assisted (spontaneous) 73.59
  spontaneous (unassisted) 73.59
    assisted 73.59
  vacuum extraction 72.79
    with episiotomy 72.71
Delorme operation
  pericardiectomy 37.31
  proctopexy 48.76
  repair of prolapsed rectum 48.76
  thoracoplasty 33.34
Denervation
  aortic body 39.89
  carotid body 39.89
  facet, percutaneous (radiofrequency) 03.96
  ovarian 65.94
  paracervical uterine 69.3
  uterosacral 69.3
Denker operation (radical maxillary antrotomy) 22.31
Dennis-Barco operation — *see* Repair, hernia, femoral
Denonvillier operation (limited rhinoplasty) 21.86
Densitometry, bone (serial) (radiographic) 88.98
Depilation, skin 86.92
Derlacki operation (tympanoplasty) 19.4
Dermabond 86.59
Dermabrasion (laser) 86.25
  for wound debridement 86.28
Derotation — *see* Reduction, torsion
Desensitization
  allergy 99.12
  psychologic 94.33
Desmotomy — *see also* Division, ligament 80.40
Destruction
  breast 85.20

Index

Curettage — Destruction

Destruction — *continued*
    chorioretinopathy (*see also* Destruction, lesion, choroid) 14.29
    ciliary body 12.74
    epithelial downgrowth, anterior chamber 12.93
    fallopian tube 66.39
        with
            crushing (and ligation) 66.31
                by endoscopy (laparoscopy) 66.21
            division (and ligation) 66.32
                by endoscopy (culdoscopy) (hysteroscopy) (laparoscopy) (peritoneoscopy) 66.22
            ligation 66.39
                with
                    crushing 66.31
                        by endoscopy (laparoscopy) 66.21
                    division 66.32
                        by endoscopy (culdoscopy) (hysteroscopy) (laparoscopy) (peritoneoscopy) 66.22
    fetus 73.8
    hemorrhoids 49.49
        by
            cryotherapy 49.44
            sclerotherapy 49.42
    inner ear NEC 20.79
        by injection 20.72
    intervertebral disc (NOS) 80.50
        by injection 80.52
        by other specified method 80.59
        herniated (nucleus pulposus) 80.51
    LAA 37.36
    lacrimal sac 09.6
    left atrial appendage 37.36
    lesion (local)
        anus 49.39
            endoscopic 49.31
        Bartholin's gland 71.24
            by
                aspiration 71.21
                excision 71.24
                incision 71.22
                marsupialization 71.23
        biliary ducts 51.69
            endoscopic 51.64
        bladder 57.59
            transurethral 57.49
        bone — *see* Excision, lesion, bone
        bowel — *see* Destruction, lesion, intestine
        brain (transtemporal approach) NEC 01.59
            by stereotactic radiosurgery 92.30
                cobalt 60 92.32
                linear accelerator (LINAC) 92.31
                multi-source 92.32
                particle beam 92.33
                particulate 92.33
                radiosurgery NEC 92.39
                single source photon 92.31
        breast NEC 85.20
        bronchus NEC 32.09
            endoscopic 32.01
        cerebral NEC 01.59
            meninges 01.51
        cervix 67.39
            by
                cauterization 67.32
                cryosurgery, cryoconization 67.33
                electroconization 67.32
        choroid 14.29
            by
                cryotherapy 14.22
                diathermy 14.21
                implantation of radiation source 14.27
                photocoagulation 14.25
                    laser 14.24
                    xenon arc 14.23
                radiation therapy 14.26

Destruction — *continued*
    lesion — *continued*
        ciliary body (nonexcisional) 12.43
            by excision 12.44
        conjunctiva 10.32
            by excision 10.31
        cornea NEC 11.49
            by
                cryotherapy 11.43
                electrocauterization 11.42
                thermocauterization 11.42
        cul-de-sac 70.32
        duodenum NEC 45.32
            by excision 45.31
            endoscopic 45.30
        endoscopic 45.30
        esophagus (chemosurgery) (cryosurgery) (electroresection) (fulguration) NEC 42.39
            by excision 42.32
            endoscopic 42.33
        endoscopic 42.33
        eyebrow 08.25
        eyelid 08.25
            excisional — *see* Excision, lesion, eyelid
        eye NEC 16.93
        heart
            by catheter ablation 37.34
            by endovascular approach 37.34
            by open approach 37.33
            by thoracoscopic approach 37.37
            left atrial appendage 37.36
        intestine (large) 45.49
            by excision 45.41
                endoscopic 45.43
                    polypectomy 45.42
            endoscopic 45.43
                polypectomy 45.42
            small 45.34
                by excision 45.33
        intranasal 21.31
        iris (nonexcisional) NEC 12.41
            by excision 12.42
        kidney 55.39
            by marsupialization 55.31
        lacrimal sac 09.6
        larynx 30.09
        liver 50.29
        lung 32.29
            endoscopic 32.28
        meninges (cerebral) 01.51
            spinal 03.4
        nerve (peripheral) 04.07
            sympathetic 05.29
        nose 21.30
            intranasal 21.31
            specified NEC 21.32
        ovary
            by
                aspiration 65.91
                excision 65.29
                    laparoscopic 65.25
            cyst by rupture (manual) 65.93
        palate (bony) (local) 27.31
            wide 27.32
        pancreas 52.22
            by marsupialization 52.3
            endoscopic 52.21
        pancreatic duct 52.22
            endoscopic 52.21
        penis 64.2
        pharynx (excisional) NEC 29.39
        pituitary gland
            by stereotactic radiosurgery 92.30
                cobalt 60 92.32
                linear accelerator (LINAC) 92.31
                multi-source 92.32
                particle beam 92.33
                particulate 92.33
                radiosurgery NEC 92.39
                single source photon 92.31
        rectum (local) 48.32
            by
                cryosurgery 48.34
                electrocoagulation 48.32

Destruction — *continued*
    lesion — *continued*
        rectum — *continued*
            by — *continued*
                excision 48.35
                fulguration 48.32
                laser (Argon) 48.33
            polyp 48.36
            radical 48.31
        retina 14.29
            by
                cryotherapy 14.22
                diathermy 14.21
                implantation of radiation source 14.27
                photocoagulation 14.25
                    laser 14.24
                    xenon arc 14.23
                radiation therapy 14.26
        salivary gland NEC 26.29
            by marsupialization 26.21
        sclera 12.84
        scrotum 61.3
        skin NEC 86.3
        sphincter of Oddi 51.69
            endoscopic 51.64
        spinal cord (meninges) 03.4
        spleen 41.42
            by marsupialization 41.41
        stomach NEC 43.49
            by excision 43.42
                endoscopic 43.41
            endoscopic 43.41
        subcutaneous tissue NEC 86.3
        testis 62.2
        tongue 25.1
        urethra (excisional) 58.39
            endoscopic 58.31
        uterus 68.29
    nerve (cranial) (peripheral) (by cryoanalgesia) by radiofrequency 04.2
        sympathetic, by injection of neurolytic agent 05.32
    neuroma
        acoustic 04.01
            by craniotomy 04.01
            by stereotactic radiosurgery 92.30
                cobalt 60 92.32
                linear accelerator (LINAC) 92.31
                multi-source 92.32
                particle beam 92.33
                particulate 92.33
                radiosurgery NEC 92.39
                single source photon 92.31
        cranial 04.07
            Morton's 04.07
        peripheral
            Morton's 04.07
    prostate (prostatic tissue)
        by
            cryotherapy 60.62
            microwave 60.96
            radiofrequency 60.97
            transurethral microwave thermotherapy (TUMT) 60.96
            transurethral needle ablation (TUNA) 60.97
            TULIP (transurethral (ultrasound) guided laser induced prostatectomy) 60.21
            TUMT (transurethral microwave thermotherapy) 60.96
            TUNA (transurethral needle ablation) 60.97
    semicircular canals, by injection 20.72
    tissue of heart — *see* Excision, lesion, heart
    vestibule, by injection 20.72
Detachment, uterosacral ligaments 69.3
Determination
    mental status (clinical) (medicolegal) (psychiatric) NEC 94.11
    psychologic NEC 94.09
    vital capacity (pulmonary) 89.37
Detorsion
    intestine (twisted) (volvulus) 46.80
        large 46.82

Detorsion — *continued*
    intestine — *continued*
        large — *continued*
            endoscopic (balloon) 46.85
        small 46.81
    kidney 55.84
    ovary 65.95
    spermatic cord 63.52
        with orchiopexy 62.5
    testis 63.52
        with orchiopexy 62.5
    volvulus 46.80
        endoscopic (balloon) 46.85
Detoxification therapy 94.25
    alcohol 94.62
        with rehabilitation 94.63
            combined alcohol and drug 94.68
                with rehabilitation 94.69
    drug 94.65
        with rehabilitation 94.66
            combined alcohol and drug 94.68
                with rehabilitation 94.69
Devascularization, stomach 44.99
Device
    CorCap™ 37.41
    external fixator — *see* Fixator, external
Dewebbing
    esophagus 42.01
    syndactyly (fingers) (toes) 86.85
Dextrorotation — *see* Reduction, torsion
Dialysis
    hemodiafiltration, hemofiltration (extracorporeal) 39.95
    kidney (extracorporeal) 39.95
    liver 50.92
    peritoneal 54.98
    renal (extracorporeal) 39.95
Diaphanoscopy
    nasal sinuses 89.35
    skull (newborn) 89.16
Diaphysectomy — *see* category 77.8 ☑
Diathermy 93.34
    choroid — *see* Diathermy, retina
    nasal turbinates 21.61
    retina
        for
            destruction of lesion 14.21
            reattachment 14.51
            repair of tear 14.31
    surgical — *see* Destruction, lesion, by site
    turbinates (nasal) 21.61
Dickson-Diveley operation (tendon transfer and arthrodesis to correct claw toe) 77.57
Dickson operation (fascial transplant) 83.82
Dieffenbach operation (hip disarticulation) 84.18
Dilation
    achalasia 42.92
    ampulla of Vater 51.81
        endoscopic 51.84
    anus, anal (sphincter) 96.23
    biliary duct
        endoscopic 51.84
        pancreatic duct 52.99
            endoscopic 52.98
        percutaneous (endoscopy) 51.98
        sphincter
            of Oddi 51.81
                endoscopic 51.84
            pancreatic 51.82
                endoscopic 51.85
    bladder 96.25
        neck 57.92
    bronchus 33.91
    cervix (canal) 67.0
        obstetrical 73.1
        to assist delivery 73.1
    choanae (nasopharynx) 29.91
    colon (endoscopic) (balloon) 46.85
        with insertion of colonic stent
            endoscopic 46.86
            other 46.87
    colostomy stoma 96.24
    duodenum (endoscopic) (balloon) 46.85

☑ Additional Digit Required — Refer to the Tabular List for Digit Selection
Subterms under main terms may continue to next column or page
2015 ICD-9-CM   ▶◀ Revised Text   ● New Line   ▲ Revised Code   Volume 3 — 13

Dilation — *continued*
  duodenum — *continued*
    with insertion of colonic stent
      endoscopic 46.86
      other 46.87
  endoscopic — *see* Dilation, by site
  enterostomy stoma 96.24
  esophagus (by bougie) (by sound) 42.92
  fallopian tube 66.96
  foreskin (newborn) 99.95
  frontonasal duct 96.21
  gastrojejunostomy site, endoscopic 44.22
  heart valve — *see* Valvulotomy, heart
  ileostomy stoma 96.24
  ileum (endoscopic) (balloon) 46.85
    with insertion of colonic stent
      endoscopic 46.86
      other 46.87
  intestinal stoma (artificial) 96.24
  intestine (endoscopic) (balloon) 46.85
    with insertion of colonic stent
      endoscopic 46.86
      other 46.87
  jejunum (endoscopic) (balloon) 46.85
    with insertion of colonic stent
      endoscopic 46.86
      other 46.87
  lacrimal
    duct 09.42
    punctum 09.41
  larynx 31.98
  lymphatic structure(s) (peripheral) 40.9
  nares 21.99
  nasolacrimal duct (retrograde) 09.43
    with insertion of tube or stent 09.44
  nasopharynx 29.91
  pancreatic duct 52.99
    endoscopic 52.98
  pharynx 29.91
  prostatic urethra (transurethral) (balloon)
    60.95
  punctum, lacrimal papilla 09.41
  pylorus
    by incision 44.21
    endoscopic 44.22
  rectum 96.22
  salivary duct 26.91
  sphenoid ostia 22.52
  sphincter
    anal 96.23
    cardiac 42.92
    of Oddi 51.81
      endoscopic 51.84
    pancreatic 51.82
      endoscopic 51.85
    pylorus, endoscopic 44.22
      by incision 44.21
  Stenson's duct 26.91
  trachea 31.99
  ureter 59.8
    meatus 56.91
  ureterovesical orifice 59.8
  urethra 58.6
    prostatic (transurethral) (balloon) 60.95
  urethrovesical junction 58.6
  vagina (instrumental) (manual) NEC 96.16
  vesical neck 57.92
  Wharton's duct 26.91
  Wirsung's duct 52.99
    endoscopic 52.98
Dilation and curettage, uterus (diagnostic)
  69.09
  after
    abortion 69.02
    delivery 69.02
  to terminate pregnancy 69.01
Diminution, ciliary body 12.74
Disarticulation 84.91
  ankle 84.13
  elbow 84.06
  finger, except thumb 84.01
    thumb 84.02
  hip 84.18
  knee 84.16
  shoulder 84.08
  thumb 84.02

Disarticulation — *continued*
  toe 84.11
  wrist 84.04
Discectomy — *see* Diskectomy
Discission
  capsular membrane 13.64
  cataract (Wheeler knife) (Ziegler knife) 13.2
    congenital 13.69
    secondary membrane 13.64
  iris 12.12
  lens (capsule) (Wheeler knife) (Ziegler knife)
    (with capsulotomy) 13.2
  orbitomaxillary, radical 16.51
  pupillary 13.2
  secondary membrane (after cataract) 13.64
  vitreous strands (posterior approach) 14.74
    anterior approach 14.73
Discogram, diskogram 87.21
Discolysis (by injection) 80.52
Diskectomy (discectomy), intervertebral
  80.51
  with corpectomy 80.99
  herniated (nucleus pulposus) 80.51
  percutaneous 80.59
Dispensing (with fitting)
  contact lens 95.32
  low vision aids NEC 95.33
  spectacles 95.31
Disruption
  blood brain barrier via infusion [BBBD] 00.19
Dissection — *see also* Excision
  aneurysm 38.60
  artery-vein-nerve bundle 39.91
  branchial cleft fistula or sinus 29.52
  bronchus 32.1
  femoral hernia 53.29
  groin, radical 40.54
  larynx block (en bloc) 30.3
  mediastinum with pneumonectomy 32.59
    thoracoscopic 32.50
  neck, radical 40.40
    with laryngectomy 30.4
    bilateral 40.42
    unilateral 40.41
  orbital fibrous bands 16.92
  pterygium (with reposition) 11.31
  radical neck — *see* Dissection, neck, radical
  retroperitoneal NEC 59.00
  thoracic structures (block) (en bloc) (radical)
    (brachial plexus, bronchus, lobe of
    lung, ribs, and sympathetic nerves)
    32.6
  vascular bundle 39.91
Distention, bladder (therapeutic) (intermittent) 96.25
Diversion
  biliopancreatic (BPD) 43.7 *[45.51] [45.91]*
    with duodenal switch
      43.89 *[45.51] [45.91]*
  urinary
    cutaneous 56.61
    ileal conduit 56.51
    internal NEC 56.71
    uretero-ileostomy 56.51
    ureter to
      intestine 56.71
      skin 56.61
Diversional therapy 93.81
Diverticulectomy
  bladder (suprapubic) 57.59
    transurethral approach 57.49
  duodenum 45.31
    endoscopic 45.30
  esophagomyotomy 42.7
  esophagus 42.31
    endoscopic 42.33
  hypopharyngeal (by cricopharyngeal myoto-
    my) 29.32
  intestine
    large 45.41
      endoscopic 45.43
    small 45.33
  kidney 55.39
  Meckel's 45.33
  pharyngeal (by cricopharyngeal myotomy)
    29.32

Diverticulectomy — *continued*
  pharyngoesophageal (by cricopharyngeal
    myotomy) 29.32
  stomach 43.42
    endoscopic 43.41
  urethra 58.39
    endoscopic 58.31
Division
  Achilles tendon 83.11
  adductor tendon (hip) 83.12
  adhesions — *see* Lysis, adhesions
  angle of mandible (open) 76.62
    closed 76.61
  anterior synechiae 12.32
  aponeurosis 83.13
  arcuate ligament (spine) — *omit code*
  arteriovenous fistula (with ligation) 39.53
  artery (with ligation) 38.80
    abdominal 38.86
    aorta (arch) (ascending) (descending)
      38.84
    head and neck NEC 38.82
    intracranial NEC 38.81
    lower limb 38.88
    thoracic NEC 38.85
    upper limb 38.83
  bladder neck 57.91
  blepharorrhaphy 08.02
  blood vessels, cornea 10.1
  bone (*see also* Osteotomy) 77.30
  brain tissue 01.32
    cortical adhesions 02.91
  canaliculus 09.52
  canthorrhaphy 08.02
  cartilage 80.40
    ankle 80.47
    elbow 80.42
    foot and toe 80.48
    hand and finger 80.44
    hip 80.45
    knee 80.46
    shoulder 80.41
    specified site NEC 80.49
    spine 80.49
    wrist 80.43
  cerebral tracts 01.32
  chordae tendineae 35.32
  common wall between posterior left atrium
    and coronary sinus (with roofing of
    resultant defect with patch graft)
    35.82
  congenital web
    larynx 31.98
    pharynx 29.54
  endometrial synechiae 68.21
  fallopian tube — *see* Ligation, fallopian tube
  fascia 83.14
    hand 82.12
  frenulum, frenum
    labial 27.91
    lingual 25.91
    tongue 25.91
  ganglion, sympathetic 05.0
  glossopharyngeal nerve 29.92
  goniosynechiae 12.31
  hypophyseal stalk (*see also* Hypophysecto-
    my, partial) 07.63
  iliotibial band 83.14
  isthmus
    horseshoe kidney 55.85
    thyroid 06.91
  joint capsule 80.40
    ankle 80.47
    elbow 80.42
    foot and toe 80.48
    hand and finger 80.44
    hip 80.45
    knee 80.46
    shoulder 80.41
    specified site NEC 80.49
    wrist 80.43
  labial frenum 27.91
  lacrimal ductules 09.0
  laryngeal nerve (external) (recurrent) (supe-
    rior) 31.91
  ligament 80.40

Division — *continued*
  ligament — *continued*
    ankle 80.47
    arcuate (spine) — *omit code*
    canthal 08.36
    elbow 80.42
    foot and toe 80.48
    hand and finger 80.44
    hip 80.45
    knee 80.46
    palpebrae 08.36
    shoulder 80.41
    specified site NEC 80.49
    spine 80.49
      arcuate — *omit code*
      flavum — omit code
    uterosacral 69.3
    wrist 80.43
  ligamentum flavum (spine) — *omit code*
  meninges (cerebral) 01.31
  muscle 83.19
    hand 82.19
  nasolacrimal duct stricture (with drainage)
    09.59
  nerve (cranial) (peripheral) NEC 04.03
    acoustic 04.01
    adrenal gland 07.42
    auditory 04.01
    glossopharyngeal 29.92
    lacrimal branch 05.0
    laryngeal (external) (recurrent) (superior)
      31.91
    phrenic 04.03
      for collapse of lung 33.31
    root, spinal or intraspinal 03.1
    sympathetic 05.0
    tracts
      cerebral 01.32
      spinal cord 03.29
        percutaneous 03.21
    trigeminal 04.02
    vagus (*see also* Vagotomy) 44.00
    vestibular 04.01
  otosclerotic process or material, middle ear
    19.0
  papillary muscle (heart) 35.31
  patent ductus arteriosus 38.85
  penile adhesions 64.93
  posterior synechiae 12.33
  pylorus (with wedge resection) 43.3
  rectum (stricture) 48.91
  scalenus anticus muscle 83.19
  Skene's gland 71.3
  soft tissue NEC 83.19
    hand 82.19
  sphincter
    anal (external) (internal) 49.59
      left lateral 49.51
      posterior 49.52
    cardiac 42.7
    of Oddi 51.82
      endoscopic 51.85
    pancreatic 51.82
      endoscopic 51.85
  spinal
    cord tracts 03.29
      percutaneous 03.21
    nerve root 03.1
  symblepharon (with insertion of conformer)
    10.5
  synechiae
    endometrial 68.21
    iris (posterior) 12.33
      anterior 12.32
  tarsorrhaphy 08.02
  tendon 83.13
    Achilles 83.11
    adductor (hip) 83.12
    hand 82.11
  trabeculae carneae cordis (heart) 35.35
  tympanum 20.23
  uterosacral ligaments 69.3
  vaginal septum 70.14
  vas deferens 63.71
  vein (with ligation) 38.80
    abdominal 38.87

☑ **Additional Digit Required — Refer to the Tabular List for Digit Selection**   ▽ **Subterms under main terms may continue to next column or page**

☑ **Additional Digit Required** — Refer to the Tabular List for Digit Selection   ▽ **Subterms under main terms may continue to next column or page**

Electrocardiogram — continued
rhythm (with one to three leads) 89.51
Electrocautery — see also Cauterization
cervix 67.32
corneal lesion (ulcer) 11.42
esophagus 42.39
endoscopic 42.33
Electrocoagulation — see also Destruction,
lesion, by site
aneurysm (cerebral) (peripheral vessels)
39.52
cervix 67.32
cystoscopic 57.49
ear
external 18.29
inner 20.79
middle 20.51
fallopian tube (lesion) 66.61
for tubal ligation — see Ligation, fallopian tube
gasserian ganglion 04.02
nasal turbinates 21.61
nose, for epistaxis (with packing) 21.03
ovary 65.29
laparoscopic 65.25
prostatic bed 60.94
rectum (polyp) 48.32
radical 48.31
retina (for)
destruction of lesion 14.21
reattachment 14.51
repair of tear 14.31
round ligament 69.19
semicircular canals 20.79
urethrovesical junction, transurethral 57.49
uterine ligament 69.19
uterosacral ligament 69.19
uterus 68.29
vagina 70.33
vulva 71.3
Electrocochleography 20.31
Electroconization, cervix 67.32
Electroconvulsive therapy (ECT) 94.27
Electroencephalogram (EEG) 89.14
monitoring (radiographic) (video) 89.19
intraoperative 00.94
Electrogastrogram 44.19
Electrokeratotomy 11.49
Electrolysis
ciliary body 12.71
hair follicle 86.92
retina (for)
destruction of lesion 14.21
reattachment 14.51
repair of tear 14.31
skin 86.92
subcutaneous tissue 86.92
Electromyogram, electromyography (EMG)
(muscle) 93.08
eye 95.25
urethral sphincter 89.23
Electronarcosis 94.29
Electronic gaiter 93.59
Electronystagmogram (ENG) 95.24
Electro-oculogram (EOG) 95.22
Electroresection — see also Destruction, lesion, by site
bladder neck (transurethral) 57.49
esophagus 42.39
endoscopic 42.33
prostate (transurethral) 60.29
stomach 43.49
endoscopic 43.41
Electroretinogram (ERG) 95.21
Electroshock therapy (EST) 94.27
subconvulsive 94.26
Elevation
bone fragments (fractured)
orbit 76.79
sinus (nasal)
frontal 22.79
maxillary 22.79
skull (with debridement) 02.02
spinal 03.53
pedicle graft 86.71

Elliot operation (scleral trephination with iridectomy) 12.61
Ellis Jones operation (repair of peroneal tendon) 83.88
Ellison operation (reinforcement of collateral
ligament) 81.44
Elmslie-Cholmeley operation (tarsal wedge
osteotomy) 77.28
Eloesser operation
thoracoplasty 33.34
thoracostomy 34.09
Elongation — see Lengthening
Embolectomy 38.00
with endarterectomy — see Endarterectomy
abdominal
artery 38.06
vein 38.07
aorta (arch) (ascending) (descending) 38.04
arteriovenous shunt or cannula 39.49
bovine graft 39.49
head and neck NEC 38.02
intracranial NEC 38.01
lower limb
artery 38.08
vein 38.09
mechanical
endovascular
head and neck 39.74
pulmonary (artery) (vein) 38.05
thoracic NEC 38.05
upper limb (artery) (vein) 38.03
Embolization (transcatheter)
adhesive (glue) 39.79
head and neck 39.72
arteriovenous fistula 39.53
endovascular 39.72
artery (selective) 38.80
by
endovascular approach 39.79
head and neck vessels
bare coils 39.75
bioactive coils 39.76
partial occlusion (balloon) (temporary) 39.77
percutaneous transcatheter infusion
99.29
abdominal NEC 38.86
duodenal (transcatheter) 44.44
gastric (transcatheter) 44.44
renal (transcatheter) 38.86
aorta (arch) (ascending) (descending)
38.84
temporary therapeutic endovascular
(balloon) (partial occlusion)
39.77
duodenal (transcatheter) 44.44
gastric (transcatheter) 44.44
head and neck NEC 38.82
intracranial NEC 38.81
lower limb 38.88
renal (transcatheter) 38.86
thoracic NEC 38.85
upper limb 38.83
uterine (gelatin sponge) (gelfoam) (microspheres) (PVA) (spherical embolics) (without coil(s)) 68.25
AVM, intracranial, endovascular approach
39.72
carotid cavernous fistula 39.53
chemoembolization 99.25
coil, endovascular 39.79
head and neck 39.75
bare coils 39.75
bioactive coils 39.76
uterine artery 68.24
vein (selective) 38.80
by
endovascular approach 39.79
head and neck 39.72
partial occlusion (balloon) (temporary) 39.77
abdominal NEC 38.87
duodenal (transcatheter) 44.44
gastric (transcatheter) 44.44
duodenal (transcatheter) 44.44
gastric (transcatheter) 44.44

Embryotomy 73.8
EMG — see Electromyogram
Emmet operation (cervix) 67.61
Encephalocentesis — see also Puncture 01.09
fetal head, transabdominal 73.8
Encephalography (cisternal puncture) (frac-
tional) (lumbar) (pneumoencephalo-
gram) 87.01
Encephalopuncture 01.09
Encircling procedure — see also Cerclage
sclera, for buckling 14.49
with implant 14.41
Endarterectomy (gas) (with patch graft) 38.10
abdominal 38.16
aorta (arch) (ascending) (descending) 38.14
coronary artery — see category 36.0 ☑
open chest approach 36.03
head and neck (open) NEC 38.12

Note — Also use 00.40, 00.41, 00.42,
or 00.43 to show the total number of
vessels treated. Use code 00.44 once to
show procedure on a bifurcated vessel.
In addition, use 00.45, 00.46, 00.47, or
00.48 to show the number of vascular
stents inserted.

percutaneous approach, extracranial
vessel(s) 00.61
percutaneous approach, intracranial
vessel(s) 00.62
intracranial (open) NEC 38.11

Note — Also use 00.40, 00.41, 00.42,
or 00.43 to show the total number of
vessels treated. Use code 00.44 once to
show prcoedure on a bifurcated vessel.
In addition, use 00.45, 00.46, 00.47, or
00.48 to show the number of vascular
stents inserted.

percutaneous approach, intracranial
vessel(s) 00.62
lower limb 38.18
thoracic NEC 38.15
upper limb 38.13
Endoaneurysmorrhaphy — see also
Aneurysmorrhaphy 39.52
by or with
endovascular graft
abdominal aorta 39.71
fenestrated (branching) graft
39.78
lower extremity artery(s) 39.79
thoracic aorta 39.73
upper extremity artery(s) 39.79
Endolymphatic (-subarachnoid) shunt 20.71
Endometrectomy (uterine) (internal) 68.29
bladder 57.59
cul-de-sac 70.32
Endoprosthesis
bile duct 51.87
femoral head (bipolar) 81.52
Endoscopy
with biopsy — see Biopsy, by site, closed
anus 49.21
biliary tract (operative) 51.11
by retrograde cholangiography (ERC)
51.11
by retrograde cholangiopancreatography (ERCP) 51.10
intraoperative 51.11
percutaneous (via T-tube or other tract)
51.98
with removal of common duct stones
51.96
bladder 57.32
through stoma (artificial) 57.31
bronchus NEC 33.23
with biopsy 33.24
fiberoptic 33.22
through stoma (artificial) 33.21
colon 45.23
through stoma (artificial) 45.22
transabdominal (operative) 45.21
cul-de-sac 70.22
ear 18.11
esophagus NEC 42.23
through stoma (artificial) 42.22

Endoscopy — continued
esophagus — continued
transabdominal (operative) 42.21
ileum 45.13
through stoma (artificial) 45.12
transabdominal (operative) 45.11
intestine NEC 45.24
large 45.24
fiberoptic (flexible) 45.23
through stoma (artificial) 45.22
transabdominal (intraoperative)
45.21
small 45.13
esophagogastroduodenoscopy (EGD)
45.13
with closed biopsy 45.16
through stoma (artificial) 45.12
transabdominal (operative) 45.11
jejunum 45.13
through stoma (artificial) 45.12
transabdominal (operative) 45.11
kidney 55.21
larynx 31.42
through stoma (artificial) 31.41
lung — see Bronchoscopy
mediastinum (transpleural) 34.22
nasal sinus 22.19
nose 21.21
pancreatic duct 52.13
pelvis 55.22
peritoneum 54.21
pharynx 29.11
rectum 48.23
through stoma (artificial) 48.22
transabdominal (operative) 48.21
sinus, nasal 22.19
stomach NEC 44.13
through stoma (artificial) 44.12
transabdominal (operative) 44.11
thorax (transpleural) 34.21
trachea NEC 31.42
through stoma (artificial) 31.41
transpleural
mediastinum 34.22
thorax 34.21
ureter 56.31
urethra 58.22
uterus 68.12
vagina 70.21
Enema (transanal) NEC 96.39
for removal of impacted feces 96.38
ENG (electronystagmogram) 95.24
Enlargement
aortic lumen, thoracic 38.14
atrial septal defect (pre-existing) 35.41
in repair of total anomalous pulmonary
venous connection 35.82
eye socket 16.64
foramen ovale (pre-existing) 35.41
in repair of total anomalous pulmonary
venous connection 35.82
intestinal stoma 46.40
large intestine 46.43
small intestine 46.41
introitus 96.16
orbit (eye) 16.64
palpebral fissure 08.51
punctum 09.41
sinus tract (skin) 86.89
Enterectomy NEC 45.63
Enteroanastomosis
large-to-large intestine 45.94
small-to-large intestine 45.93
small-to-small intestine 45.91
Enterocelectomy 53.9
female 70.92
with graft or prosthesis 70.93
vaginal 70.92
with graft or prosthesis 70.93
Enterocentesis 45.00
duodenum 45.01
large intestine 45.03
small intestine NEC 45.02
Enterocholecystostomy 51.32
Enteroclysis (small bowel) 96.43
Enterocolectomy NEC 45.79

☑ Additional Digit Required — Refer to the Tabular List for Digit Selection ⓥ Subterms under main terms may continue to next column or page

16 — Volume 3 ▶◀ Revised Text ● New Line ▲ Revised Code 2015 ICD-9-CM

Enterocolostomy 45.93
Enteroenterectomy 46.99
Enteroenterostomy 45.90
　small-to-large intestine 45.93
　small-to-small intestine 45.91
Enterogastrostomy 44.39
　laparoscopic 44.38
Enterolithotomy 45.00
Enterolysis 54.59
　laparoscopic 54.51
Enteropancreatostomy 52.96
Enterorrhaphy 46.79
　large intestine 46.75
　small intestine 46.73
Enterostomy NEC 46.39
　cecum (see also Colostomy) 46.10
　colon (transverse) (see also Colostomy) 46.10
　　loop 46.03
　delayed opening 46.31
　duodenum 46.39
　　loop 46.01
　feeding NEC 46.39
　　percutaneous (endoscopic) 46.32
　ileum (Brooke) (Dragstedt) 46.20
　　loop 46.01
　jejunum (feeding) 46.39
　　loop 46.01
　　percutaneous (endoscopic) 46.32
　sigmoid colon (see also Colostomy) 46.10
　　loop 46.03
　transverse colon (see also Colostomy) 46.10
　　loop 46.03
Enterotomy 45.00
　large intestine 45.03
　small intestine 45.02
Enucleation — see also Excision, lesion, by site
　cyst
　　broad ligament 69.19
　　dental 24.4
　　liver 50.29
　　ovarian 65.29
　　　laparoscopic 65.25
　　parotid gland 26.29
　　salivary gland 26.29
　　skin 86.3
　　subcutaneous tissue 86.3
　eyeball 16.49
　　with implant (into Tenon's capsule) 16.42
　　　with attachment of muscles 16.41
EOG (electro-oculogram) 95.22
Epicardiectomy 36.39
Epididymectomy 63.4
　with orchidectomy (unilateral) 62.3
　　bilateral 62.41
Epididymogram 87.93
Epididymoplasty 63.59
Epididymorrhaphy 63.81
Epididymotomy 63.92
Epididymovasostomy 63.83
Epiglottidectomy 30.21
Epikeratophakia 11.76
Epilation
　eyebrow (forceps) 08.93
　　cryosurgical 08.92
　　electrosurgical 08.91
　eyelid (forceps) NEC 08.93
　　cryosurgical 08.92
　　electrosurgical 08.91
　skin 86.92
Epiphysiodesis — see also Arrest, bone growth
　— see category 78.2 ☑
Epiphysiolysis — see also Arrest, bone growth
　— see category 78.2 ☑
Epiploectomy 54.4
Epiplopexy 54.74
Epiplorrhaphy 54.74
Episioperineoplasty 71.79
Episioperineorrhaphy 71.71
　obstetrical 75.69
Episioplasty 71.79
Episioproctotomy 73.6
Episiorrhaphy 71.71
　following episiotomy — see Episiotomy
　for obstetrical laceration 75.69

Episiotomy (with subsequent episiorrhaphy) 73.6
　high forceps 72.31
　low forceps 72.1
　mid forceps 72.21
　nonobstetrical 71.09
　outlet forceps 72.1
EPS (electrophysiologic stimulation)
　as part of intraoperative testing — omit code
　catheter based invasive electrophysiologic testing 37.26
　device interrogation only without arrhythmia induction (bedside check) 89.45-89.49
　noninvasive programmed electrical stimulation (NIPS) 37.20
Eptifibatide, infusion 99.20
Equalization, leg
　lengthening — see category 78.3 ☑
　shortening — see category 78.2 ☑
Equilibration (occlusal) 24.8
Equiloudness balance 95.43
ERC (endoscopic retrograde cholangiography) 51.11
ERCP (endoscopic retrograde cholangiopancreatography) 51.10
　cannulation of pancreatic duct 52.93
ERG (electroretinogram) 95.21
ERP (endoscopic retrograde pancreatography) 52.13
Eruption, tooth, surgical 24.6
Erythrocytapheresis, therapeutic 99.73
Escharectomy 86.22
Escharotomy 86.09
Esophageal voice training (post-laryngectomy) 93.73
Esophagectomy 42.40
　abdominothoracocervical (combined) (synchronous) 42.42
　partial or subtotal 42.41
　total 42.42
Esophagocologastrostomy (intrathoracic) 42.55
　antesternal or antethoracic 42.65
Esophagocolostomy (intrathoracic) NEC 42.56
　with interposition of colon 42.55
　antesternal or antethoracic NEC 42.66
　　with interposition of colon 42.65
Esophagoduodenostomy (intrathoracic) NEC 42.54
　with
　　complete gastrectomy 43.99
　　interposition of small bowel 42.53
Esophagoenterostomy (intrathoracic) NEC — see also Anastomosis, esophagus, to intestinal segment 42.54
　antesternal or antethoracic (see also Anastomosis, esophagus, antesternal, to intestinal segment) 42.64
Esophagoesophagostomy (intrathoracic) 42.51
　antesternal or antethoracic 42.61
Esophagogastrectomy 43.99
Esophagogastroduodenoscopy (EGD) 45.13
　with closed biopsy 45.16
　through stoma (artificial) 45.12
　transabdominal (operative) 45.11
Esophagogastromyotomy 42.7
Esophagogastropexy 44.65
Esophagogastroplasty 44.65
Esophagogastroscopy NEC 44.13
　through stoma (artificial) 44.12
　transabdominal (operative) 44.11
Esophagogastrostomy (intrathoracic) 42.52
　with partial gastrectomy 43.5
　antesternal or antethoracic 42.62
Esophagoileostomy (intrathoracic) NEC 42.54
　with interposition of small bowel 42.53
　antesternal or antethoracic NEC 42.64
　　with interposition of small bowel 42.63
Esophagojejunostomy (intrathoracic) NEC 42.54
　with
　　complete gastrectomy 43.99
　　interposition of small bowel 42.53

Esophagojejunostomy — continued
　antesternal or antethoracic NEC 42.64
　　with interposition of small bowel 42.63
Esophagomyotomy 42.7
Esophagoplasty NEC 42.89
Esophagorrhaphy 42.82
Esophagoscopy NEC 42.23
　by incision (operative) 42.21
　with closed biopsy 42.24
　through stoma (artificial) 42.22
　transabdominal (operative) 42.21
Esophagostomy 42.10
　cervical 42.11
　thoracic 42.19
Esophagotomy NEC 42.09
Estes operation (ovary) 65.72
　laparoscopic 65.75
Estlander operation (thoracoplasty) 33.34
ESWL (extracorporeal shockwave lithotripsy)
　NEC 98.59
　bile duct 98.52
　bladder 98.51
　gallbladder 98.52
　kidney 98.51
　Kock pouch (urinary diversion) 98.51
　renal pelvis 98.51
　specified site NEC 98.59
　ureter 98.51
Ethmoidectomy 22.63
Ethmoidotomy 22.51
Evacuation
　abscess — see Drainage, by site
　anterior chamber (eye) (aqueous) (hyphema) 12.91
　cyst (see also Excision, lesion, by site)
　　breast 85.91
　　kidney 55.01
　　liver 50.29
　hematoma (see also Incision, hematoma)
　　obstetrical 75.92
　　　incisional 75.91
　hemorrhoids (thrombosed) 49.47
　pelvic blood clot (by incision) 54.19
　　by
　　　culdocentesis 70.0
　　　culdoscopy 70.22
　retained placenta
　　with curettage 69.02
　　manual 75.4
　streptothrix from lacrimal duct 09.42
Evaluation (of)
　audiological 95.43
　cardiac rhythm device (CRT-D) (CRT-P) (AICD) (pacemaker) — see Interrogation
　criminal responsibility, psychiatric 94.11
　functional (physical therapy) 93.01
　hearing NEC 95.49
　orthotic (for brace fitting) 93.02
　prosthetic (for artificial limb fitting) 93.03
　psychiatric NEC 94.19
　　commitment 94.13
　psychologic NEC 94.08
　testimentary capacity, psychiatric 94.11
Evans operation (release of clubfoot) 83.84
Evisceration
　eyeball 16.39
　　with implant (into scleral shell) 16.31
　ocular contents 16.39
　　with implant (into scleral shell) 16.31
　orbit (see also Exenteration, orbit) 16.59
　pelvic (anterior) (posterior) (partial) (total) (female) 68.8
　　male 57.71
Evulsion
　nail (bed) (fold) 86.23
　skin 86.3
　subcutaneous tissue 86.3
Examination (for)
　breast
　　manual 89.36
　　radiographic NEC 87.37
　　thermographic 88.85
　　ultrasonic 88.73
　cervical rib (by x-ray) 87.43
　colostomy stoma (digital) 89.33

Examination — continued
　dental (oral mucosa) (peridontal) 89.31
　　radiographic NEC 87.12
　enterostomy stoma (digital) 89.33
　eye 95.09
　　color vision 95.06
　　comprehensive 95.02
　　dark adaptation 95.07
　　limited (with prescription of spectacles) 95.01
　　under anesthesia 95.04
　fetus, intrauterine 75.35
　general physical 89.7
　glaucoma 95.03
　gynecological 89.26
　hearing 95.47
　microscopic (specimen) (of) 91.9 ☑

> Note — Use the following fourth-digit subclassification with categories 90–91 to identify type of examination:
>
> 1　bacterial smear
> 2　culture
> 3　culture and sensitivity
> 4　parasitology
> 5　toxicology
> 6　cell block and Papanicolaou smear
> 9　other microsopic examination

　adenoid 90.3 ☑
　adrenal gland 90.1 ☑
　amnion 91.4 ☑
　anus 90.9 ☑
　appendix 90.9 ☑
　bile ducts 91.0 ☑
　bladder 91.3 ☑
　blood 90.5 ☑
　bone 91.5 ☑
　　marrow 90.6 ☑
　brain 90.0 ☑
　breast 91.6 ☑
　bronchus 90.4 ☑
　bursa 91.5 ☑
　cartilage 91.5 ☑
　cervix 91.4 ☑
　chest wall 90.4 ☑
　chorion 91.4 ☑
　colon 90.9 ☑
　cul-de-sac 91.1 ☑
　dental 90.8 ☑
　diaphragm 90.4 ☑
　duodenum 90.8 ☑
　ear 90.3 ☑
　endocrine gland NEC 90.1 ☑
　esophagus 90.8 ☑
　eye 90.2 ☑
　fallopian tube 91.4 ☑
　fascia 91.5 ☑
　female genital tract 91.4 ☑
　fetus 91.4 ☑
　gallbladder 91.0 ☑
　hair 91.6 ☑
　ileum 90.9 ☑
　jejunum 90.9 ☑
　joint fluid 91.5 ☑
　kidney 91.2 ☑
　large intestine 90.9 ☑
　larynx 90.3 ☑
　ligament 91.5 ☑
　liver 91.0 ☑
　lung 90.4 ☑
　lymph (node) 90.7 ☑
　meninges 90.0 ☑
　mesentery 91.1 ☑
　mouth 90.8 ☑
　muscle 91.5 ☑
　musculoskeletal system 91.5 ☑
　nails 91.6 ☑
　nerve 90.0 ☑
　nervous system 90.0 ☑
　nose 90.3 ☑

☑ **Additional Digit Required** — Refer to the Tabular List for Digit Selection　　　　☟ **Subterms under main terms may continue to next column or page**

2015 ICD-9-CM　　▶◀ Revised Text　　● New Line　　▲ Revised Code　　**Volume 3 — 17**

Examination — *continued*
microscopic — *continued*
omentum 91.1 ☑
operative wound 91.7 ☑
ovary 91.4 ☑
pancreas 91.0 ☑
parathyroid gland 90.1 ☑
penis 91.3 ☑
perirenal tissue 91.2 ☑
peritoneum (fluid) 91.1 ☑
periureteral tissue 91.2 ☑
perivesical (tissue) 91.3 ☑
pharynx 90.3 ☑
pineal gland 90.1 ☑
pituitary gland 90.1 ☑
placenta 91.4 ☑
pleura (fluid) 90.4 ☑
prostate 91.3 ☑
rectum 90.9 ☑
retroperitoneum 91.1 ☑
semen 91.3 ☑
seminal vesicle 91.3 ☑
sigmoid 90.9 ☑
skin 91.6 ☑
small intestine 90.9 ☑
specified site NEC 91.8 ☑
spinal fluid 90.0 ☑
spleen 90.6 ☑
sputum 90.4 ☑
stomach 90.8 ☑
stool 90.9 ☑
synovial membrane 91.5 ☑
tendon 91.5 ☑
thorax NEC 90.4 ☑
throat 90.3 ☑
thymus 90.1 ☑
thyroid gland 90.1 ☑
tonsil 90.3 ☑
trachea 90.4 ☑
ureter 91.2 ☑
urethra 91.3 ☑
urine 91.3 ☑
uterus 91.4 ☑
vagina 91.4 ☑
vas deferens 91.3 ☑
vomitus 90.8 ☑
vulva 91.4 ☑
neurologic 89.13
neuro-ophthalmology 95.03
ophthalmoscopic 16.21
panorex, mandible 87.12
pelvic (manual) 89.26
instrumental (by pelvimeter) 88.25
pelvimetric 88.25
physical, general 89.7
postmortem 89.8
rectum (digital) 89.34
endoscopic 48.23
through stoma (artificial) 48.22
transabdominal 48.21
retinal disease 95.03
specified type (manual) NEC 89.39
thyroid field, postoperative 06.02
uterus (digital) 68.11
endoscopic 68.12
vagina 89.26
endoscopic 70.21
visual field 95.05
Exchange transfusion 99.01
intrauterine 75.2
Excision
aberrant tissue — *see* Excision, lesion, by site of tissue origin
abscess — *see* Excision, lesion, by site
accessory tissue (*see also* Excision, lesion, by site of tissue origin)
lung 32.29
endoscopic 32.28
thoracoscopic 32.20
spleen 41.93
adenoids (tag) 28.6
with tonsillectomy 28.3
adenoma — *see* Excision, lesion, by site
adrenal gland (*see also* Adrenalectomy) 07.22

Excision — *continued*
ampulla of Vater (with reimplantation of common duct) 51.62
anal papilla 49.39
endoscopic 49.31
aneurysm (arteriovenous) (*see also* Aneurysmectomy) 38.60
coronary artery 36.91
heart 37.32
myocardium 37.32
sinus of Valsalva 35.39
ventricle (heart) 37.32
anus (complete) (partial) 49.6
aortic subvalvular ring 35.35
apocrine gland 86.3
aponeurosis 83.42
hand 82.33
appendage, left atrial 37.36
appendiceal stump 47.09
laparoscopic 47.01
appendices epiploicae 54.4
appendix (*see also* Appendectomy) 47.01, 47.09
epididymis 63.3
testis 62.2
arcuate ligament (spine) — omit code
arteriovenous fistula (*see also* Aneurysmectomy) 38.60
artery (*see also* Arteriectomy) 38.60
Baker's cyst, knee 83.39
Bartholin's gland 71.24
basal ganglion 01.59
bile duct 51.69
endoscopic 51.64
bladder (*see also* Cystectomy)
bleb (emphysematous), lung 32.29
endoscopic 32.28
thoracoscopic 32.20
blood vessel (*see also* Angiectomy) 38.60
bone (ends) (partial), except facial — *see* category 77.8 ☑
facial NEC 76.39
total 76.45
with reconstruction 76.44
for graft (autograft) (homograft) — *see* category 77.7 ☑
fragments (chips) (*see also* Incision, bone) 77.10
joint (*see also* Arthrotomy) 80.10
necrotic (*see also* Sequestrectomy, bone) 77.00
heterotopic, from
muscle 83.32
hand 82.22
skin 86.3
tendon 83.31
hand 82.21
mandible 76.31
with arthrodesis — *see* Arthrodesis
total 76.42
with reconstruction 76.41
spur — *see* Excision, lesion, bone
total, except facial — *see* category 77.9 ☑
facial NEC 76.45
with reconstruction 76.44
mandible 76.42
with reconstruction 76.41
brain 01.59
hemisphere 01.52
lobe 01.53
branchial cleft cyst or vestige 29.2
breast (*see also* Mastectomy) 85.41
aberrant tissue 85.24
accessory 85.24
ectopic 85.24
nipple 85.25
accessory 85.24
segmental 85.23
supernumerary 85.24
wedge 85.21
broad ligament 69.19
bronchogenic cyst 32.09
endoscopic 32.01
bronchus (wide sleeve) NEC 32.1
buccal mucosa 27.49

Excision — *continued*
bulbourethral gland 58.92
bulbous tuberosities (mandible) (maxilla) (fibrous) (osseous) 24.31
bunion (*see also* Bunionectomy) 77.59
bunionette (with osteotomy) 77.54
bursa 83.5
hand 82.31
canal of Nuck 69.19
cardioma 37.33
carotid body (lesion) (partial) (total) 39.89
cartilage (*see also* Chondrectomy) 80.90
intervertebral — *see* category 80.5 ☑
knee (semilunar) 80.6
larynx 30.29
nasal (submucous) 21.5
caruncle, urethra 58.39
endoscopic 58.31
cataract (*see also* Extraction, cataract) 13.19
secondary membrane (after cataract) 13.65
cervical
rib 77.91
stump 67.4
cervix (stump) NEC 67.4
cold (knife) 67.2
conization 67.2
cryoconization 67.33
electroconizaton 67.32
chalazion (multiple) (single) 08.21
cholesteatoma — *see* Excision, lesion, by site
choroid plexus 02.14
cicatrix (skin) 86.3
cilia base 08.20
ciliary body, prolapsed 12.98
clavicle (head) (partial) 77.81
total (complete) 77.91
clitoris 71.4
coarctation of aorta (end-to-end anastomosis) 38.64
with
graft replacement (interposition)
abdominal 38.44
thoracic 38.45
thoracoabdominal 38.45 [38.44]
common
duct 51.63
wall between posterior and coronary sinus (with roofing of resultant defect with patch graft) 35.82
condyle — *see* category 77.8 ☑
mandible 76.5
conjunctival ring 10.31
cornea 11.49
epithelium (with chemocauterization) 11.41
for smear or culture 11.21
costal cartilage 80.99
cul-de-sac (Douglas') 70.92
with graft or prosthesis 70.93
cusp, heart valve 35.10
aortic 35.11
mitral 35.12
tricuspid 35.14
cyst (*see also* Excision, lesion, by site)
apical (tooth) 23.73
with root canal therapy 23.72
Baker's (popliteal) 83.39
breast 85.21
broad ligament 69.19
bronchogenic 32.09
endoscopic 32.01
cervix 67.39
dental 24.4
dentigerous 24.4
epididymis 63.2
fallopian tube 66.61
Gartner's duct 70.33
hand 82.29
labia 71.3
lung 32.29
endoscopic 32.28
thoracoscopic 32.20
mesonephric duct 69.19

Excision — *continued*
cyst (*see also* Excision, lesion, by site) — *continued*
Morgagni
female 66.61
male 62.2
Müllerian duct 60.73
nasolabial 27.49
nasopalatine 27.31
by wide excision 27.32
ovary 65.29
laparoscopic 65.25
parovarian 69.19
pericardium 37.31
periodontal (apical) (lateral) 24.4
popliteal (Baker's), knee 83.39
radicular 24.4
spleen 41.42
synovial (membrane) 83.39
thyroglossal (with resection of hyoid bone) 06.7
urachal (bladder) 57.51
abdominal wall 54.3
vagina (Gartner's duct) 70.33
cystic
duct remnant 51.61
hygroma 40.29
dentinoma 24.4
diaphragm 34.81
disc, intervertebral (NOS) 80.50
herniated (nucleus pulposus) 80.51
other specified (diskectomy) 80.51
diverticulum
ampulla of Vater 51.62
anus 49.39
endoscopic 49.31
bladder 57.59
transurethral 57.49
duodenum 45.31
endoscopic 45.30
esophagus (local) 42.31
endoscopic 42.33
hypopharyngeal (by cricopharyngeal myotomy) 29.32
intestine
large 45.41
endoscopic 45.43
small NEC 45.33
Meckel's 45.33
pharyngeal (by cricopharyngeal myotomy) 29.32
pharyngoesophageal (by cricopharyngeal myotomy) 29.32
stomach 43.42
endoscopic 43.41
urethra 58.39
endoscopic 58.31
ventricle, heart 37.33
duct
Müllerian 69.19
paramesonephric 69.19
thyroglossal (with resection of hyoid bone) 06.7
ear, external (complete) NEC 18.39
partial 18.29
radical 18.31
ectopic
abdominal fetus 74.3
tissue (*see also* Excision, lesion, by site of tissue origin)
bone, from muscle 83.32
breast 85.24
lung 32.29
endoscopic 32.28
thoracoscopic 32.20
spleen 41.93
empyema pocket, lung 34.09
epididymis 63.4
epiglottis 30.21
epithelial downgrowth, anterior chamber (eye) 12.93
epulis (gingiva) 24.31
esophagus (*see also* Esophagectomy) 42.40
exostosis (*see also* Excision, lesion, bone) 77.60
auditory canal, external 18.29

☑ **Additional Digit Required — Refer to the Tabular List for Digit Selection** ▽ **Subterms under main terms may continue to next column or page**

Excision — *continued*
  exostosis (*see also* Excision, lesion, bone) —
      continued
    facial bone 76.2
    first metatarsal (hallux valgus repair) —
        see Bunionectomy
  eye 16.49
    with implant (into Tenon's capsule)
        16.42
      with attachment of muscles 16.41
  eyelid 08.20
    redundant skin 08.86
  falciform ligament 54.4
  fallopian tube — *see* Salpingectomy
  fascia 83.44
    for graft 83.43
      hand 82.34
    hand 82.35
      for graft 82.34
  fat pad NEC 86.3
    knee (infrapatellar) (prepatellar) 86.3
    scalene 40.21
  fibroadenoma, breast 85.21
  fissure, anus 49.39
    endoscopic 49.31
  fistula (*see also* Fistulectomy)
    anal 49.12
    arteriovenous (*see also* Aneurysmecto-
        my) 38.60
    ileorectal 46.74
    lacrimal
      gland 09.21
      sac 09.6
    rectal 48.73
    vesicovaginal 57.84
  frenulum, frenum
    labial (lip) 27.41
    lingual (tongue) 25.92
  ganglion (hand) (tendon sheath) (wrist)
      82.21
    gasserian 04.05
    site other than hand or nerve 83.31
    sympathetic nerve 05.29
    trigeminal nerve 04.05
  gastrocolic ligament 54.4
  gingiva 24.31
  glomus jugulare tumor 20.51
  goiter — *see* Thyroidectomy
  gum 24.31
  hallux valgus (*see also* Bunionectomy)
    with prosthetic implant 77.59
  hamartoma, mammary 85.21
  heart assist system — *see* Removal
  hematocele, tunica vaginalis 61.92
  hematoma — *see* Drainage, by site
  hemorrhoids (external) (internal) (tag) 49.46
  heterotopic bone, from
    muscle 83.32
      hand 82.22
    skin 86.3
    tendon 83.31
      hand 82.21
  hydatid cyst, liver 50.29
  hydatid of Morgagni
    female 66.61
    male 62.2
  hydrocele
    canal of Nuck (female) 69.19
    male 63.1
    round ligament 69.19
    spermatic cord 63.1
    tunica vaginalis 61.2
  hygroma, cystic 40.29
  hymen (tag) 70.31
  hymeno-urethral fusion 70.31
  intervertebral disc — *see* Excision, disc, in-
      tervertebral (NOS) 80.50
  intestine (*see also* Resection, intestine)
    for interposition 45.50
      large 45.52
      small 45.51
    large (total)
      for interposition 45.52
      laparoscopic 45.81
      local 45.41
        endoscopic 45.43

intestine (*see also* Resection, intestine) —
      continued
    large — *continued*
      open 45.82
      other 45.83
      segmental
        laparoscopic 17.39
        multiple
          laparoscopic 17.31
          open and other 45.71
        open and other 45.79
      unspecified 45.83
    small (total) 45.63
      for interposition 45.51
      local 45.33
      partial 45.62
      segmental 45.62
        multiple 45.61
  intraductal papilloma 85.21
  iris prolapse 12.13
  joint (*see also* Arthrectomy) 80.90
  keloid (scar), skin 86.3
  LAA 37.36
  labia — *see* Vulvectomy
  lacrimal
    gland 09.20
      partial 09.22
      total 09.23
    passage 09.6
    sac 09.6
  left atrial appendage 37.36
  lesion (local)
    abdominal wall 54.3
    accessory sinus — *see* Excision, lesion,
        nasal sinus
    adenoids 28.92
    adrenal gland(s) 07.21
    alveolus 24.4
    ampulla of Vater 51.62
    anterior chamber (eye) NEC 12.40
    anus 49.39
      endoscopic 49.31
    apocrine gland 86.3
    artery 38.60
      abdominal 38.66
      aorta (arch) (ascending) (descending
          thoracic) 38.64
        with end-to-end anastomosis
            38.45
        abdominal 38.44
        thoracic 38.45
        thoracoabdominal
            38.45 [38.44]
        with graft interposition graft re-
            placement 38.45
        abdominal 38.44
        thoracic 38.45
        thoracoabdominal
            38.45 [38.44]
      head and neck NEC 38.62
      intracranial NEC 38.61
      lower limb 38.68
      thoracic NEC 38.65
      upper limb 38.63
    atrium 37.33
    auditory canal or meatus, external 18.29
      radical 18.31
    auricle, ear 18.29
      radical 18.31
    biliary ducts 51.69
      endoscopic 51.64
    bladder (transurethral) 57.49
      open 57.59
      suprapubic 57.59
    blood vessel 38.60
      abdominal
        artery 38.66
        vein 38.67
      aorta (arch) (ascending) (descending)
          38.64
      head and neck NEC 38.62
      intracranial NEC 38.61
      lower limb
        artery 38.68
        vein 38.69

Excision — *continued*
  lesion — *continued*
    blood vessel — *continued*
      thoracic NEC 38.65
      upper limb (artery) (vein) 38.63
    bone 77.60
      carpal, metacarpal 77.64
      clavicle 77.61
      facial 76.2
      femur 77.65
      fibula 77.67
      humerus 77.62
      jaw 76.2
        dental 24.4
      patella 77.66
      pelvic 77.69
      phalanges (foot) (hand) 77.69
      radius 77.63
      scapula 77.61
      skull 01.6
      specified site NEC 77.69
      tarsal, metatarsal 77.68
      thorax (ribs) (sternum) 77.61
      tibia 77.67
      ulna 77.63
      vertebrae 77.69
    brain (transtemporal approach) NEC
        01.59
      by stereotactic radiosurgery 92.30
        cobalt 60 92.32
        linear accelerator (LINAC) 92.31
        multi-source 92.32
        particle beam 92.33
        particulate 92.33
        radiosurgery NEC 92.39
        single source photon 92.31
    breast (segmental) (wedge) 85.21
    broad ligament 69.19
    bronchus NEC 32.09
      endoscopic 32.01
    cerebral (cortex) NEC 01.59
      meninges 01.51
    cervix (myoma) 67.39
    chest wall 34.4
    choroid plexus 02.14
    ciliary body 12.44
    colon 45.41
      endoscopic NEC 45.43
        polypectomy 45.42
    conjunctiva 10.31
    cornea 11.49
    cranium 01.6
    cul-de-sac (Douglas') 70.32
    dental (jaw) 24.4
    diaphragm 34.81
    duodenum (local) 45.31
      endoscopic 45.30
    ear, external 18.29
      radical 18.31
    endometrium 68.29
    epicardium 37.31
    epididymis 63.3
    epiglottis 30.09
    esophagus NEC 42.32
      endoscopic 42.33
    eyebrow (skin) 08.20
    eye, eyeball 16.93
      anterior segment NEC 12.40
    eyelid 08.20
      by
        halving procedure 08.24
        wedge resection 08.24
      major
        full-thickness 08.24
        partial-thickness 08.23
      minor 08.22
    fallopian tube 66.61
    fascia 83.39
      hand 82.29
    groin region (abdominal wall) (inguinal)
        54.3
    skin 86.3
      subcutaneous tissue 86.3
    gum 24.31
    heart 37.34
      Cox-maze, open 37.33

Excision — *continued*
  lesion — *continued*
    heart — *continued*
      maze, modified, endovascular 37.34
      maze, modified, open 37.33
      open 37.33
      other approach, closed 37.34
    hepatic duct 51.69
    inguinal canal 54.3
    intestine
      large 45.41
        endoscopic NEC 45.43
          polypectomy 45.42
      small NEC 45.33
    intracranial NEC 01.59
    intranasal 21.31
    intraspinal 03.4
    iris 12.42
    jaw 76.2
      dental 24.4
    joint 80.80
      ankle 80.87
      elbow 80.82
      foot and toe 80.88
      hand and finger 80.84
      hip 80.85
      knee 80.86
      shoulder 80.81
      specified site NEC 80.89
      spine 80.89
      wrist 80.83
    kidney 55.39
      with partial nephrectomy 55.4
    labia 71.3
    lacrimal
      gland (frontal approach) 09.21
      passage 09.6
      sac 09.6
    larynx 30.09
    ligament (joint) (*see also* Excision, lesion,
        joint) 80.80
      broad 69.19
      round 69.19
      uterosacral 69.19
    lip 27.43
      by wide excision 27.42
    liver 50.29
    lung NEC 32.29
      by lung volume reduction surgery
          32.22
      by wide excision 32.39
        thoracoscopic 32.30
      endoscopic 32.28
      thoracoscopic 32.20
    lymph structure(s) (channel) (vessel) NEC
        40.29
      node — *see* Excision, lymph, node
    mammary duct 85.21
    mastoid (bone) 20.49
    mediastinum 34.3
    meninges (cerebral) 01.51
      spinal 03.4
    mesentery 54.4
    middle ear 20.51
    mouth NEC 27.49
    muscle 83.32
      hand 82.22
      ocular 15.13
    myocardium 37.33
    nail 86.23
    nasal sinus 22.60
      antrum 22.62
        with Caldwell-Luc approach 22.61
        specified approach NEC 22.62
      ethmoid 22.63
      frontal 22.42
      maxillary 22.62
        with Caldwell-Luc approach 22.61
        specified approach NEC 22.62
      sphenoid 22.64
    nasopharynx 29.3 ☑
    nerve (cranial) (peripheral) 04.07
      sympathetic 05.29
    nonodontogenic 24.31
    nose 21.30
      intranasal 21.31

☑ **Additional Digit Required — Refer to the Tabular List for Digit Selection**   ▽ **Subterms under main terms may continue to next column or page**

2015 ICD-9-CM   ►◄ Revised Text   ● New Line   ▲ Revised Code   **Volume 3 — 19**

Excision — Excision

Excision — *continued*
  lesion — *continued*
    nose — *continued*
      polyp 21.31
      skin 21.32
      specified site NEC 21.32
    odontogenic 24.4
    omentum 54.4
    orbit 16.92
    ovary 65.29
      by wedge resection 65.22
        laparoscopic 65.24
      that by laparoscope 65.25
    palate (bony) 27.31
      by wide excision 27.32
      soft 27.49
    pancreas (local) 52.22
      endoscopic 52.21
    parathyroid 06.89
    parotid gland or duct NEC 26.29
    pelvic wall 54.3
    pelvirectal tissue 48.82
    penis 64.2
    pericardium 37.31
    perineum (female) 71.3
      male 86.3
    periprostatic tissue 60.82
    perirectal tissue 48.82
    perirenal tissue 59.91
    peritoneum 54.4
    perivesical tissue 59.91
    pharynx 29.39
      diverticulum 29.32
    pineal gland 07.53
    pinna 18.29
      radical 18.31
    pituitary (gland) (*see also* Hypophysecto-
        my, partial) 07.63
      by stereotactic radiosurgery 92.30
        cobalt 60 92.32
        linear accelerator (LINAC) 92.31
        multi-source 92.32
        particle beam 92.33
        particulate 92.33
        radiosurgery NEC 92.39
        single source photon 92.31
    pleura 34.59
    pouch of Douglas 70.32
    preauricular (ear) 18.21
    presacral 54.4
    prostate (transurethral) 60.61
    pulmonary (fibrosis) 32.29
      endoscopic 32.28
      thoracoscopic 32.20
    rectovaginal septum 48.82
    rectum 48.35
      polyp (endoscopic) 48.36
    retroperitoneum 54.4
    salivary gland or duct NEC 26.29
      en bloc 26.32
    sclera 12.84
    scrotum 61.3
    sinus (nasal) — *see* Excision, lesion, nasal
        sinus
    Skene's gland 71.3
    skin 86.3
      breast 85.21
      nose 21.32
      radical (wide) (involving underlying
          or adjacent structure) (with
          flap closure) 86.4
        scrotum 61.3
    skull 01.6
    soft tissue NEC 83.39
      hand 82.29
    spermatic cord 63.3
    sphincter of Oddi 51.62
      endoscopic 51.64
    spinal cord (meninges) 03.4
    spleen (cyst) 41.42
    stomach NEC 43.42
      endoscopic 43.41
        polyp 43.41
      polyp (endoscopic) 43.41
    subcutaneous tissue 86.3
      breast 85.21

Excision — *continued*
  lesion — *continued*
    subgingival 24.31
    sweat gland 86.3
    tendon 83.39
      hand 82.29
      ocular 15.13
      sheath 83.31
        hand 82.21
    testis 62.2
    thorax 34.4
    thymus
      partial (open) (other) 07.81
        thoracoscopic 07.83
      total (open) (other) 07.82
        thoracoscopic 07.84
    thyroid 06.31
      substernal or transsternal route 06.51
    tongue 25.1
    tonsil 28.92
    trachea 31.5
    tunica vaginalis 61.92
    ureter 56.41
    urethra 58.39
      endoscopic 58.31
    uterine ligament 69.19
    uterosacral ligament 69.19
    uterus 68.29
    vagina 70.33
    vein 38.60
      abdominal 38.67
      head and neck NEC 38.62
      intracranial NEC 38.61
      lower limb 38.69
      thoracic NEC 38.65
      upper limb 38.63
    ventricle (heart) 37.33
    vocal cords 30.09
    vulva 71.3
  ligament (*see also* Arthrectomy) 80.90
    broad 69.19
    round 69.19
    uterine 69.19
    uterosacral 69.19
  ligamentum flavum (spine) — omit code
  lingual tonsil 28.5
  lip 27.43
  liver (partial) 50.22
  loose body
    bone — *see* Sequestrectomy, bone
    joint 80.10
  lung (with mediastinal dissection) 32.59
    accessory or ectopic tissue 32.29
      endoscopic 32.28
      thoracoscopic 32.20
    segmental 32.39
      thoracoscopic 32.30
    specified type NEC 32.29
      endoscopic 32.28
      thoracoscopic 32.20
    thoracoscopic 32.50
    volume reduction surgery 32.22
      biologic lung volume reduction
          (BLVR) — *see* category
          33.7 ☑
    wedge 32.29
      thoracoscopic 32.20
  lymphangioma (simple) (*see also* Excision,
      lymph, lymphatic node) 40.29
  lymph, lymphatic
    drainage area 40.29
      radical — *see* Excision, lymph, node,
          radical
      regional (with lymph node, skin,
          subcutaneous tissue, and fat)
          40.3
    node (simple) NEC 40.29
      with
        lymphatic drainage area (includ-
            ing skin, subcutaneous tis-
            sue, and fat) 40.3
        mastectomy — *see* Mastectomy,
            radical
        muscle and deep fascia — *see*
            Excision, lymph, node,
            radical

Excision — *continued*
  lymph, lymphatic — *continued*
    node — *continued*
      axillary 40.23
        radical 40.51
        regional (extended) 40.3
      cervical (deep) (with excision of sca-
          lene fat pad) 40.21
        with laryngectomy 30.4
        radical (including muscle and
            deep fascia) 40.40
          bilateral 40.42
          unilateral 40.41
        regional (extended) 40.3
        superficial 40.29
      groin 40.24
        radical 40.54
        regional (extended) 40.3
      iliac 40.29
        radical 40.53
        regional (extended) 40.3
      inguinal (deep) (superficial) 40.24
        radical 40.54
        regional (extended) 40.3
      jugular — *see* Excision, lymph, node,
          cervical
      mammary (internal) 40.22
        external 40.29
          radical 40.59
          regional (extended) 40.3
        radical 40.59
          regional (extended) 40.3
      paratracheal — *see* Excision, lymph,
          node, cervical
      periaortic 40.29
        radical 40.52
        regional (extended) 40.3
      radical 40.50
        with mastectomy — *see* Mastec-
            tomy, radical
        specified site NEC 40.59
      regional (extended) 40.3
      sternal — *see* Excision, lymph, node,
          mammary
      structure(s) (simple) NEC 40.29
        radical 40.59
        regional (extended) 40.3
    lymphocele 40.29
    mastoid (*see also* Mastoidectomy) 20.49
    median bar, transurethral approach 60.29
    meibomian gland 08.20
    meniscus (knee) 80.6
      acromioclavicular 80.91
      jaw 76.5
      sternoclavicular 80.91
      temporomandibular (joint) 76.5
      wrist 80.93
    müllerian duct cyst 60.73
    muscle 83.45
      for graft 83.43
        hand 82.34
      hand 82.36
        for graft 82.34
    myositis ossificans 83.32
      hand 82.22
    nail (bed) (fold) 86.23
    nasolabial cyst 27.49
    nasopalatine cyst 27.31
      by wide excision 27.32
    neoplasm — *see* Excision, lesion, by site
    nerve (cranial) (peripheral) NEC 04.07
      sympathetic 05.29
    neuroma (Morton's) (peripheral nerve) 04.07
      acoustic
        by craniotomy 04.01
        by stereotactic radiosurgery 92.30
          cobalt 60 92.32
          linear accelerator (LINAC) 92.31
          multi-source 92.32
          particle beam 92.33
          particulate 92.33
          radiosurgery NEC 92.39
          single source photon 92.31
      sympathetic nerve 05.29
    nipple 85.25
      accessory 85.24

Excision — *continued*
  odontoma 24.4
  orbital contents (*see also* Exenteration, orbit)
      16.59
  osteochondritis dissecans (*see also* Excision,
      lesion, joint) 80.80
  ovary (*see also* Oophorectomy)
    partial 65.29
      by wedge resection 65.22
        laparoscopic 65.24
      that by laparoscope 65.25
  Pancoast tumor (lung) 32.6
  pancreas (total) (with synchronous duo-
      denectomy) 52.6
    partial NEC 52.59
      distal (tail) (with part of body) 52.52
      proximal (head) (with part of body)
          (with synchronous duodenec-
          tomy) 52.51
      radical subtotal 52.53
    radical (one-stage) (two-stage) 52.7
    subtotal 52.53
  paramesonephric duct 69.19
  parathyroid gland (partial) (subtotal) NEC
      (*see also* Parathyroidectomy) 06.89
  parotid gland (*see also* Excision, salivary
      gland) 26.30
  parovarian cyst 69.19
  patella (complete) 77.96
    partial 77.86
  pelvirectal tissue 48.82
  perianal tissue 49.04
    skin tags 49.03
  pericardial adhesions 37.31
  periprostatic tissue 60.82
  perirectal tissue 48.82
  perirenal tissue 59.91
  periurethral tissue 58.92
  perivesical tissue 59.91
  petrous apex cells 20.59
  pharyngeal bands 29.54
  pharynx (partial) 29.33
  pilonidal cyst or sinus (open) (with partial
      closure) 86.21
  pineal gland (complete) (total) 07.54
    partial 07.53
  pituitary gland (complete) (total) (*see also*
      Hypophysectomy) 07.69
  pleura NEC 34.59
  polyp (*see also* Excision, lesion, by site)
    esophagus 42.32
      endoscopic 42.33
    large intestine 45.41
      endoscopic 45.42
    nose 21.31
    rectum (endoscopic) 48.36
    stomach (endoscopic) 43.41
  preauricular
    appendage (remnant) 18.29
    cyst, fistula, or sinus (congenital) 18.21
    remnant 18.29
  prolapsed iris (in wound) 12.13
  prostate — *see* Prostatectomy
  pterygium (simple) 11.39
    with corneal graft 11.32
  radius (head) (partial) 77.83
    total 77.93
  ranula, salivary gland NEC 26.29
  rectal mucosa 48.35
  rectum — *see* Resection, rectum
  redundant mucosa
    colostomy 45.41
      endoscopic 45.43
    duodenostomy 45.31
      endoscopic 45.30
    ileostomy 45.33
    jejunostomy 45.33
    perineum 71.3
    rectum 48.35
    vulva 71.3
  renal vessel, aberrant 38.66
  rib (cervical) 77.91
  ring of conjunctiva around cornea 10.31
  round ligament 69.19
  salivary gland 26.30
    complete 26.32

☑ **Additional Digit Required — Refer to the Tabular List for Digit Selection**

▽ **Subterms under main terms may continue to next column or page**

☑ **Additional Digit Required** — Refer to the Tabular List for Digit Selection   ▽ **Subterms under main terms may continue to next column or page**
2015 ICD-9-CM   ▶◀ **Revised Text**   ● **New Line**   ▲ **Revised Code**   **Volume 3 — 21**

Excision — Exploration

Exploration — *see also* Incision — *continued*
- spinal (canal) (nerve root) 03.09
- spleen 41.2
- stomach (by incision) 43.0
  - endoscopic — *see* Gastroscopy
- subcutaneous tissue 86.09
- subdiaphragmatic space 54.11
- superficial fossa 86.09
- tarsal tunnel 04.44
- tendon (sheath) 83.01
  - hand 82.01
- testes 62.0
- thymus (gland) 07.92
  - field 07.91
  - thoracoscopic 07.95
- thyroid (field) (gland) (by incision) 06.09
  - postoperative 06.02
- trachea (by incision) 31.3
  - endoscopic — *see* Tracheoscopy
- tunica vaginalis 61.0
- tympanum 20.09
  - transtympanic route 20.23
- ureter (by incision) 56.2
  - endoscopic 56.31
- urethra (by incision) 58.0
  - endoscopic 58.22
- uterus (corpus) 68.0
  - cervix 69.95
  - digital 68.11
  - postpartal, manual 75.7
- vagina (by incision) 70.14
  - endoscopic 70.21
- vas deferens 63.6
- vein 38.00
  - abdominal 38.07
  - head and neck NEC 38.02
  - intracranial NEC 38.01
  - lower limb 38.09
  - thoracic NEC 38.05
  - upper limb 38.03
- vulva (by incision) 71.09

Exposure — *see also* Incision, by site
- tooth (for orthodontic treatment) 24.6

Expression, trachoma follicles 10.33

Exsanguination transfusion 99.01

Extension
- buccolabial sulcus 24.91
- limb, forced 93.25
- lingual sulcus 24.91
- mandibular ridge 76.43

Exteriorization
- esophageal pouch 42.12
- intestine 46.03
  - large 46.03
  - small 46.01
- maxillary sinus 22.9
- pilonidal cyst or sinus (open excision) (with partial closure) 86.21

Extirpation — *see also* Excision, by site
- aneurysm — *see* Aneurysmectomy
- arteriovenous fistula — *see* Aneurysmectomy
- lacrimal sac 09.6
- larynx 30.3
  - with radical neck dissection (with synchronous thyroidectomy) (with synchronous tracheostomy) 30.4
- nerve, tooth (*see also* Therapy, root canal) 23.70
- varicose vein (peripheral) (lower limb) 38.59
  - upper limb 38.53

Extracorporeal
- circulation (regional), except hepatic 39.61
  - hepatic 50.92
  - percutaneous 39.66
- hemodialysis 39.95
- membrane oxygenation (ECMO) 39.65
- photopheresis, therapeutic 99.88
- shockwave lithotripsy (ESWL) NEC 98.59
  - bile duct 98.52
  - bladder 98.51
  - gallbladder 98.52
  - kidney 98.51
  - renal pelvis 98.51
  - specified site NEC 98.59

Extracorporeal — *continued*
- shockwave lithotripsy — *continued*
  - ureter 98.51

Extracranial-intracranial bypass [EC-IC] 39.28

Extraction
- breech (partial) 72.52
  - with forceps to aftercoming head 72.51
  - total 72.54
    - with forceps to aftercoming head 72.53
- cataract 13.19
  - after cataract (by)
    - capsulectomy 13.65
    - capsulotomy 13.64
    - discission 13.64
    - excision 13.65
    - iridocapsulectomy 13.65
    - mechanical fragmentation 13.66
    - needling 13.64
    - phacofragmentation (mechanical) 13.66
  - aspiration (simple) (with irrigation) 13.3
  - cryoextraction (intracapsular approach) 13.19
    - temporal inferior route (in presence of fistulization bleb) 13.11
  - curette evacuation (extracapsular approach) 13.2
  - emulsification (and aspiration) 13.41
  - erysiphake (intracapsular approach) 13.19
    - temporal inferior route (in presence of fistulization bleb) 13.11
  - extracapsular approach (with iridectomy) NEC 13.59
    - by temporal inferior route (in presence of fistulization bleb) 13.51
    - aspiration (simple) (with irrigation) 13.3
    - curette evacuation 13.2
    - emulsification (and aspiration) 13.41
    - linear extraction 13.2
    - mechanical fragmentation with aspiration by
      - posterior route 13.42
      - specified route NEC 13.43
    - phacoemulsification (ultrasonic) (with aspiration) 13.41
    - phacofragmentation (mechanical) with aspiration by
      - posterior route 13.42
      - specified route NEC 13.43
    - ultrasonic (with aspiration) 13.41
    - rotoextraction (mechanical) with aspiration by
      - posterior route 13.42
      - specified route NEC 13.43
  - intracapsular (combined) (simple) (with iridectomy) (with suction) (with zonulolysis) 13.19
    - by temporal inferior route (in presence of fistulization bleb) 13.11
  - linear extraction (extracapsular approach) 13.2
  - phacoemulsification (and aspiration) 13.41
  - phacofragmentation (mechanical)
    - with aspiration by
      - posterior route 13.42
      - specified route NEC 13.43
    - ultrasonic 13.41
  - rotoextraction (mechanical)
    - with aspiration by
      - posterior route 13.42
      - specified route NEC 13.43
  - secondary membranous (after cataract) (by)
    - capsulectomy 13.65
    - capsulotomy 13.64
    - discission 13.64
    - excision 13.65
    - iridocapsulectomy 13.65
    - mechanical fragmentation 13.66
    - needling 13.64

Extraction — *continued*
- cataract — *continued*
  - secondary membranous — *continued*
    - phacofragmentation (mechanical) 13.66
  - common duct stones (percutaneous) (through sinus tract) (with basket) 51.96
  - fat for graft or banking 86.90
  - foreign body — *see* Removal, foreign body
  - kidney stone(s), percutaneous 55.03
    - with fragmentation procedure 55.04
  - lens (eye) (*see also* Extraction, cataract) 13.19
  - Malström's 72.79
    - with episiotomy 72.71
  - menstrual, menses 69.6
  - milk from lactating breast (manual) (pump) 99.98
  - tooth (by forceps) (multiple) (single) NEC 23.09
    - with mucoperiosteal flap elevation 23.19
    - deciduous 23.01
    - surgical NEC (*see also* Removal, tooth, surgical) 23.19
  - vacuum, fetus 72.79
    - with episiotomy 72.71
  - vitreous (*see also* Removal, vitreous) 14.72

Face lift 86.82

Facetectomy 77.89

Facilitation, intraocular circulation NEC 12.59

Failed (trial) forceps 73.3

Family
- counselling (medical) (social) 94.49
- therapy 94.42

Farabeuf operation (ischiopubiotomy) 77.39

Fasanella-Servatt operation (blepharoptosis repair) 08.35

Fasciaplasty — *see* Fascioplasty

Fascia sling operation — *see* Operation, sling

Fasciectomy 83.44
- for graft 83.43
- hand 82.34
  - hand 82.35
    - for graft 82.34
- palmar (release of Dupuytren's contracture) 82.35

Fasciodesis 83.89
- hand 82.89

Fascioplasty — *see also* Repair, fascia 83.89
- hand (*see also* Repair, fascia, hand) 82.89

Fasciorrhaphy — *see* Suture, fascia

Fasciotomy 83.14
- Dupuytren's 82.12
  - with excision 82.35
- Dwyer 83.14
- hand 82.12
- Ober-Yount 83.14
- orbital (*see also* Orbitotomy) 16.09
- palmar (release of Dupuytren's contracture) 82.12
  - with excision 82.35

Fenestration
- aneurysm (dissecting), thoracic aorta 39.54
- aortic aneurysm 39.54
- cardiac valve 35.10
- chest wall 34.01
- ear
  - inner (with graft) 20.61
    - revision 20.62
  - tympanic 19.55
- labyrinth (with graft) 20.61
- Lempert's (endaural) 19.9
- operation (aorta) 39.54
- oval window, ear canal 19.55
- palate 27.1
- pericardium 37.12
- semicircular canals (with graft) 20.61
- stapes foot plate (with vein graft) 19.19
  - with incus replacement 19.11
- tympanic membrane 19.55
- vestibule (with graft) 20.61

Ferguson operation (hernia repair) 53.00

Fetography 87.81

Fetoscopy 75.31

Fiberoscopy — *see* Endoscopy, by site

Fibroidectomy, uterine 68.29

Fick operation (perforation of foot plate) 19.0

Filipuncture (aneurysm) (cerebral) 39.52

Filleting
- hammer toe 77.56
- pancreas 52.3

Filling, tooth (amalgam) (plastic) (silicate) 23.2
- root canal (*see also* therapy, root canal) 23.70

Fimbriectomy — *see also* Salpingectomy, partial 66.69
- Uchida (with tubal ligation) 66.32

Finney operation (pyloroplasty) 44.29

Fissurectomy, anal 49.39
- endoscopic 49.31
- skin (subcutaneous tissue) 49.04

Fistulectomy — *see also* Closure, fistula, by site
- abdominothoracic 34.83
- abdominouterine 69.42
- anus 49.12
- appendix 47.92
- bile duct 51.79
- biliary tract NEC 51.79
- bladder (transurethral approach) 57.84
- bone (*see also* Excision, lesion, bone) 77.60
- branchial cleft 29.52
- bronchocutaneous 33.42
- bronchoesophageal 33.42
- bronchomediastinal 34.73
- bronchopleural 34.73
- bronchopleurocutaneous 34.73
- bronchopleuromediastinal 34.73
- bronchovisceral 33.42
- cervicosigmoidal 67.62
- cholecystogastroenteric 51.93
- cornea 11.49
- diaphragm 34.83
- enterouterine 69.42
- esophagopleurocutaneous 34.73
- esophagus NEC 42.84
- fallopian tube 66.73
- gallbladder 51.93
- gastric NEC 44.63
- hepatic duct 51.79
- hepatopleural 34.73
- hepatopulmonary 34.73
- intestine
  - large 46.76
  - small 46.74
- intestinouterine 69.42
- joint (*see also* Excision, lesion, joint) 80.80
- lacrimal
  - gland 09.21
  - sac 09.6
- laryngotracheal 31.62
- larynx 31.62
- mediastinocutaneous 34.73
- mouth NEC 27.53
- nasal 21.82
  - sinus 22.71
- nasolabial 21.82
- nasopharyngeal 21.82
- oroantral 22.71
- oronasal 21.82
- pancreas 52.95
- perineorectal 71.72
- perineosigmoidal 71.72
- perirectal, not opening into rectum 48.93
- pharyngoesophageal 29.53
- pharynx NEC 29.53
- pleura 34.73
- rectolabial 71.72
- rectourethral 58.43
- rectouterine 69.42
- rectovaginal 70.73
- rectovesical 57.83
- rectovulvar 71.72
- rectum 48.73
- salivary (duct) (gland) 26.42
- scrotum 61.42
- skin 86.3
- stomach NEC 44.63

☑ **Additional Digit Required** — Refer to the Tabular List for Digit Selection

▽ **Subterms under main terms may continue to next column or page**

Fistulectomy — see also Closure, fistula, by site
— continued
  subcutaneous tissue 86.3
  thoracoabdominal 34.83
  thoracogastric 34.83
  thoracointestinal 34.83
  thorax NEC 34.73
  trachea NEC 31.73
  tracheoesophageal 31.73
  ureter 56.84
  urethra 58.43
  uteroenteric 69.42
  uterointestinal 69.42
  uterorectal 69.42
  uterovaginal 69.42
  vagina 70.75
  vesicosigmoidovaginal 57.83
  vocal cords 31.62
  vulvorectal 71.72
Fistulization
  appendix 47.91
  arteriovenous 39.27
  cisterna chyli 40.62
  endolymphatic sac (for decompression) 20.79
  esophagus, external 42.10
    cervical 42.11
    specified technique NEC 42.19
  interatrial 35.41
  labyrinth (for decompression) 20.79
  lacrimal sac into nasal cavity 09.81
  larynx 31.29
  lymphatic duct, left (thoracic) 40.62
  orbit 16.09
  peritoneal 54.93
  salivary gland 26.49
  sclera 12.69
    by trephination 12.61
    with iridectomy 12.65
  sinus, nasal NEC 22.9
  subarachnoid space 02.22
  thoracic duct 40.62
  trachea 31.29
  tracheoesophageal 31.95
  urethrovaginal 58.0
  ventricle, cerebral (see also Shunt, ventricular) 02.22
Fistulogram
  abdominal wall 88.03
  chest wall 87.38
  retroperitoneum 88.14
  specified site NEC 88.49
Fistulotomy, anal 49.11
Fitting
  arch bars (orthodontic) 24.7
    for immobilization (fracture) 93.55
  artificial limb 84.40
  contact lens 95.32
  denture (total) 99.97
    bridge (fixed) 23.42
      removable 23.43
    partial (fixed) 23.42
      removable 23.43
  hearing aid 95.48
  obturator (orthodontic) 24.7
  ocular prosthetics 95.34
  orthodontic
    appliance 24.7
    obturator 24.7
    wiring 24.7
  orthotic device 93.23
  periodontal splint (orthodontic) 24.7
  prosthesis, prosthetic device
    above knee 84.45
    arm 84.43
      lower (and hand) 84.42
      upper (and shoulder) 84.41
    below knee 84.46
    hand (and lower arm) 84.42
    leg 84.47
      above knee 84.45
      below knee 84.46
    limb NEC 84.40
    ocular 95.34
    penis (external) 64.94
    shoulder (and upper arm) 84.41

Fitting — continued
  spectacles 95.31
Five-in-one repair, knee 81.42
Fixation
  bone
    external, without reduction 93.59
      with fracture reduction — see Reduction, fracture
      cast immobilization NEC 93.53
      external fixator — see Fixator, external
      splint 93.54
      traction (skeletal) NEC 93.44
        intermittent 93.43
    internal (without fracture reduction) 78.50
      with fracture reduction — see Reduction, fracture
      carpal, metacarpal 78.54
      clavicle 78.51
      femur 78.55
      fibula 78.57
      humerus 78.52
      patella 78.56
      pelvic 78.59
      phalanges (foot) (hand) 78.59
      radius 78.53
      scapula 78.51
      specified site NEC 78.59
      tarsal, metatarsal 78.58
      thorax (ribs) (sternum) 78.51
        sternal fixation device with rigid plates 84.94
      tibia 78.57
      ulna 78.53
      vertebrae 78.59
  breast (pendulous) 85.6
  cardinal ligaments 69.22
  cervical collar 93.52
  duodenum 46.62
    to abdominal wall 46.61
  external (without manipulation for reduction) 93.59
    with fracture reduction — see Reduction, fracture
    cast immobilization NEC 93.53
    pressure dressing 93.56
    splint 93.54
    strapping (non-traction) 93.59
    traction (skeletal) NEC 93.44
      intermittent 93.43
  hip 81.40
  ileum 46.62
    to abdominal wall 46.61
  internal
    with fracture reduction — see Reduction, fracture
    without fracture reduction — see Fixation, bone, internal
  intestine 46.60
    large 46.64
      to abdominal wall 46.63
    small 46.62
      to abdominal wall 46.61
    to abdominal wall 46.60
  iris (bombé) 12.11
  jejunum 46.62
    to abdominal wall 46.61
  joint — see Arthroplasty
  kidney 55.7
  ligament
    cardinal 69.22
    palpebrae 08.36
  omentum 54.74
  parametrial 69.22
  plaster jacket 93.51
    other cast 93.53
  rectum (sling) 48.76
  spine, with fusion (see also Fusion, spinal) 81.00
  spleen 41.95
  splint 93.54
  tendon 83.88
    hand 82.85
  testis in scrotum 62.5
  tongue 25.59

Fixation — continued
  urethrovaginal (to Cooper's ligament) 70.77
    with graft or prosthesis 70.78
  uterus (abdominal) (vaginal) (ventrofixation) 69.22
  vagina 70.77
    with graft or prosthesis 70.78
Fixator, external
  computer assisted (dependent) 84.73
  hybrid device or system 84.73
  Ilizarov type 84.72
  monoplanar system 84.71
  ring device or system 84.72
  Sheffield type 84.72
Flooding (psychologic desensitization) 94.33
Flowmetry, Doppler (ultrasonic) — see also Ultrasonography
  aortic arch 88.73
  head and neck 88.71
  heart 88.72
  thorax NEC 88.73
Fluoroscopy — see Radiography
Fog therapy (respiratory) 93.94
Folding, eye muscle 15.22
  multiple (two or more muscles) 15.4
Foley operation (pyeloplasty) 55.87
Fontan operation (creation of conduit between right atrium and pulmonary artery) 35.94
Foraminotomy 03.09
Forced extension, limb 93.25
Forceps delivery — see Delivery, forceps
Formation
  adhesions
    pericardium 36.39
    pleura 34.6
  anus, artificial — see Colostomy
    duodenostomy 46.39
    ileostomy — see Ileostomy
    jejunostomy 46.39
      percutaneous (endoscopic) (PEJ) 46.32
  arteriovenous fistula (for kidney dialysis) (peripheral) (shunt) 39.27
    external cannula 39.93
  bone flap, cranial 02.03
  cardiac device (defibrillator) (pacemaker) pocket
    with initial insertion of cardiac device — omit code
    new site (skin) (subcutaneous) 37.79
  colostomy — see Colostomy
  conduit
    apical-aortic (AAC) 35.93
    ileal (urinary) 56.51
    left ventricle and aorta 35.93
    right atrium and pulmonary artery 35.94
    right ventricle and pulmonary (distal) artery 35.92
      in repair of
        pulmonary artery atresia 35.92
        transposition of great vessels 35.92
        truncus arteriosus 35.83
  endorectal ileal pouch (J-pouch) (H-pouch) (S-pouch) (with anastomosis to anus) 45.95
  fistula
    arteriovenous (for kidney dialysis) (peripheral shunt) 39.27
      external cannula 39.93
    bladder to skin NEC 57.18
      with bladder flap 57.21
      percutaneous 57.17
    cutaneoperitoneal 54.93
    gastric 43.19
      percutaneous (endoscopic) (transabdominal) 43.11
    mucous — see Colostomy
    rectovaginal 48.99
    tracheoesophageal 31.95
    tubulovalvular (Beck-Jianu) (Frank's) (Janeway) (Spivack's) (Ssabanejew-Frank) 43.19
    urethrovaginal 58.0

Formation — continued
  ileal
    bladder
      closed 57.87 [45.51]
      open 56.51
    conduit 56.51
  interatrial fistula 35.42
  mucous fistula — see Colostomy
  pericardial
    baffle, interatrial 35.91
    window 37.12
  pleural window (for drainage) 34.09
  pocket
    cardiac device (defibrillator) (pacemaker)
      with initial insertion of cardiac device — omit code
      new site (skin) (subcutaneous) 37.79
    loop recorder 37.79
    thalamic stimulator pulse generator
      with initial insertion of battery package — omit code
      new site (skin) (subcutaneous) 86.09
  pupil 12.39
    by iridectomy 12.14
  rectovaginal fistula 48.99
  reversed gastric tube (intrathoracic) (retrosternal) 42.58
    antesternal or antethoracic 42.68
  septal defect, interatrial 35.42
  shunt
    abdominovenous 54.94
    arteriovenous 39.93
    peritoneojugular 54.94
    peritoneo-vascular 54.94
    pleuroperitoneal 34.05
    transjugular intrahepatic portosystemic [TIPS] 39.1
  subcutaneous tunnel
    esophageal 42.86
      with anastomosis — see Anastomosis, esophagus, antesternal
    pulse generator lead wire 86.99
      with initial procedure — omit code
    thalamic stimulator pulse generator pocket
      with initial insertion of battery package — omit code
      new site (skin) (subcutaneous) 86.09
  syndactyly (finger) (toe) 86.89
  tracheoesophageal 31.95
  tubulovalvular fistula (Beck-Jianu) (Frank's) (Janeway) (Spivack's) (Ssabanejew-Frank) 43.19
  uretero-ileostomy, cutaneous 56.51
  ureterostomy, cutaneous 56.61
    ileal 56.51
  urethrovaginal fistula 58.0
  window
    pericardial 37.12
    pleural (for drainage) 34.09
    thoracoscopic 34.06
Fothergill (-Donald) operation (uterine suspension) 69.22
Fowler operation
  arthroplasty of metacarpophalangeal joint 81.72
  release (mallet finger repair) 82.84
  tenodesis (hand) 82.85
  thoracoplasty 33.34
Fox operation (entropion repair with wedge resection) 08.43
Fracture, surgical — see also Osteoclasis 78.70
  turbinates (nasal) 21.62
Fragmentation
  lithotriptor — see Lithotripsy
  mechanical
    cataract (with aspiration) 13.43
      posterior route 13.42
      secondary membrane 13.66
    secondary membrane (after cataract) 13.66
  ultrasonic
    cataract (with aspiration) 13.41
    stones, urinary (Kock pouch) 59.95
    urinary stones 59.95
      percutaneous nephrostomy 55.04

Franco operation (suprapubic cystotomy) 57.18
Frank operation 43.19
Frazier (-Spiller) operation (subtemporal trigeminal rhizotomy) 04.02
Fredet-Ramstedt operation (pyloromyotomy) (with wedge resection) 43.3
Freeing
adhesions — see Lysis, adhesions
anterior synechiae (with injection of air or liquid) 12.32
artery-vein-nerve bundle 39.91
extraocular muscle, entrapped 15.7
goniosynechiae (with injection of air or liquid) 12.31
intestinal segment for interposition 45.50
large 45.52
small 45.51
posterior synechiae 12.33
synechiae (posterior) 12.33
anterior (with injection of air or liquid) 12.32
vascular bundle 39.91
vessel 39.91
Freezing
gastric 96.32
prostate 60.62
Frenckner operation (intrapetrosal drainage) 20.22
Frenectomy
labial 27.41
lingual 25.92
lip 27.41
maxillary 27.41
tongue 25.92
Frenotomy
labial 27.91
lingual 25.91
Frenulumectomy — see Frenectomy
Frickman operation (abdominal proctopexy) 48.75
Frommel operation (shortening of uterosacral ligaments) 69.22
Fulguration — see also Electrocoagulation and Destruction, lesion, by site
adenoid fossa 28.7
anus 49.39
endoscopic 49.31
bladder (transurethral) 57.49
suprapubic 57.59
choroid 14.21
duodenum 45.32
endoscopic 45.30
esophagus 42.39
endoscopic 42.33
large intestine 45.49
endoscopic 45.43
polypectomy 45.42
penis 64.2
perineum, female 71.3
prostate, transurethral 60.29
rectum 48.32
radical 48.31
retina 14.21
scrotum 61.3
Skene's gland 71.3
skin 86.3
small intestine NEC 45.34
duodenum 45.32
endoscopic 45.30
stomach 43.49
endoscopic 43.41
subcutaneous tissue 86.3
tonsillar fossa 28.7
urethra 58.39
endoscopic 58.31
vulva 71.3
Function
study (see also Scan, radioisotope)
gastric 89.39
muscle 93.08
ocular 95.25
nasal 89.12
pulmonary — see categories 89.37-89.38
renal 92.03
thyroid 92.01

Function — continued
study (see also Scan, radioisotope) — continued
urethral sphincter 89.23
Fundectomy, uterine 68.39
Fundoplication (esophageal) (Nissen's) 44.66
laparoscopic 44.67
Fundusectomy, gastric 43.89
Fusion
atlas-axis (spine) — see Fusion, spinal, atlas-axis
bone (see also Osteoplasty) 78.40
cervical (spine) (C₂ level or below) — see Fusion, spinal, cervical
claw toe 77.57
craniocervical — see Fusion, spinal, craniocervical
dorsal, dorsolumbar — see Fusion, spinal, dorsal, dorsolumbar
epiphyseal-diaphyseal (see also Arrest, bone growth) 78.20
epiphysiodesis (see also Arrest, bone growth) 78.20
hammertoe 77.56
joint (with bone graft) (see also Arthrodesis) 81.20
ankle 81.11
claw toe 77.57
foot NEC 81.17
hip 81.21
interphalangeal, finger 81.28
ischiofemoral 81.21
metatarsophalangeal 81.16
midtarsal 81.14
overlapping toe(s) 77.58
pantalar 81.11
spinal (see also Fusion, spinal) 81.00
subtalar 81.13
tarsal joints NEC 81.17
tarsometatarsal 81.15
tibiotalar 81.11
toe NEC 77.58
claw toe 77.57
hammer toe 77.56
overlapping toe(s) 77.58
lip to tongue 25.59
lumbar, lumbosacral — see Fusion, spinal, lumbar, lumbosacral
occiput — C₂ (spinal) — see Fusion, spinal, occiput
spinal, NOS (with graft) (with internal fixation) (with instrumentation) 81.00

Note: Also use either 81.62, 81.63, or 81.64 as an additional code to show the total number of vertebrae fused

anterior lumbar interbody fusion (ALIF) 81.06
atlas-axis (anterior transoral) (posterior) 81.01
for pseudarthrosis 81.31
axial lumbar interbody fusion (AxiaLIF®) 81.08
cervical (C₂ level or below) NEC 81.02
anterior column (interbody), anterolateral (anterior) technique 81.02
for pseudarthrosis 81.32
C₁-C₂ level (anterior) (posterior) 81.01
for pseudarthrosis 81.31
posterior column, posterolateral (posterior) technique 81.03
for pseudarthrosis 81.33
craniocervical (anterior) (transoral) (posterior) 81.01
for pseudarthrosis 81.31
direct lateral interbody fusion (DLIF) 81.06
dorsal, dorsolumbar NEC 81.05
anterior column (interbody), anterolateral (anterior) (extracavitary) technique 81.04
for pseudarthrosis 81.34
for pseudarthrosis 81.35

Fusion — continued
spinal, — continued
dorsal, dorsolumbar — continued
posterior column, posterolateral (posterior) technique 81.05
for pseudarthrosis 81.35
extreme lateral interbody fusion (XLIF®) 81.06
facet 81.07
lumbar, lumbosacral NEC 81.08
anterior column (interbody)
anterolateral (anterior) technique 81.06
for pseudarthrosis 81.36
posterior technique 81.08
for pseudarthrosis 81.38
for pseudarthrosis 81.38
lateral transverse process technique 81.07
for pseudarthrosis 81.37
posterior column, posterior (posterolateral) (transverse process) technique 81.07
posterior (interbody), posterolateral technique 81.08
for pseudarthrosis 81.38
number of vertebrae — see codes 81.62-81.64
occiput — C₂ (anterior transoral) (posterior) 81.01
for pseudarthrosis 81.31
posterior lumbar interbody fusion (PLIF) 81.08
transforaminal lumbar interbody fusion (TLIF) 81.08
tongue (to lip) 25.59

G

Gabriel operation (abdominoperitoneal resection of rectum) 48.5 ☑
Gait training 93.22
Galeaplasty 86.89
Galvanoionization 99.27
Games
competitive 94.39
organized 93.89
Gamma irradiation, stereotactic 92.32
Ganglionectomy
gasserian 04.05
lumbar sympathetic 05.23
nerve (cranial) (peripheral) NEC 04.06
sympathetic 05.29
sphenopalatine (Meckel's) 05.21
tendon sheath (wrist) 82.21
site other than hand 83.31
trigeminal 04.05
Ganglionotomy, trigeminal (radiofrequency) 04.02
Gant operation (wedge osteotomy of trochanter) 77.25
Garceau operation (tibial tendon transfer) 83.75
Gardner operation (spinal meningocele repair) 03.51
Gas endarterectomy 38.10
abdominal 38.16
aorta (arch) (ascending) (descending) 38.14
coronary artery 36.09
head and neck NEC 38.12
intracranial NEC 38.11
lower limb 38.18
thoracic NEC 38.15
upper limb 38.13
Gastrectomy (partial) (sleeve) (subtotal) NEC 43.89
with
anastomosis (to) NEC 43.89
duodenum 43.6
esophagus 43.5
gastrogastric 43.89
jejunum 43.7
esophagogastrostomy 43.5
gastroduodenostomy (bypass) 43.6
gastroenterostomy (bypass) 43.7
gastrogastrostomy (bypass) 43.89
gastrojejunostomy (bypass) 43.7

Gastrectomy — continued
with — continued
jejunal transposition 43.81
complete NEC 43.99
with intestinal interposition 43.91
distal 43.6
Hofmeister 43.7
laparoscopic, vertical (sleeve) 43.82
Polya 43.7
proximal 43.5
radical NEC 43.99
with intestinal interposition 43.91
sleeve
laparoscopic 43.82
total NEC 43.99
with intestinal interposition 43.91
Gastrocamera 44.19
Gastroduodenectomy — see Gastrectomy
Gastroduodenoscopy 45.13
through stoma (artificial) 45.12
transabdominal (operative) 45.11
Gastroduodenostomy (bypass) (Jaboulay's) 44.39
with partial gastrectomy 43.6
laparoscopic 44.38
Gastroenterostomy (bypass) NEC 44.39
with partial gastrectomy 43.7
laparoscopic 44.38
Gastrogastrostomy (bypass) 44.39
with partial gastrectomy 43.89
laparoscopic 44.38
Gastrojejunostomy (bypass) 44.39
with partial gastrectomy 43.7
laparoscopic 44.38
percutaneous (endoscopic)
for bypass 44.32
for feeding tube placement 46.32
Gastrolysis 54.59
laparoscopic 54.51
Gastropexy 44.64
Gastroplasty NEC 44.69
laparoscopic 44.68
vertical banded gastroplasty (VBG) 44.68
Gastroplication 44.69
laparoscopic 44.68
Gastropylorectomy 43.6
Gastrorrhaphy 44.61
Gastroscopy NEC 44.13
through stoma (artificial) 44.12
transabdominal (operative) 44.11
Gastrostomy (Brunschwig's) (decompression) (fine caliber tube) (Kader) (permanent) (Stamm) (Stamm-Kader) (temporary) (tube) (Witzel) 43.19
Beck-Jianu 43.19
Frank's 43.19
Janeway 43.19
percutaneous (endoscopic) (PEG) 43.11
Spivack's 43.19
Ssabanejew-Frank 43.19
Gastrotomy 43.0
for control of hemorrhage 44.49
Gavage, gastric 96.35
Gelman operation (release of clubfoot) 83.84
Genioplasty (augmentation) (with graft) (with implant) 76.68
reduction 76.67
Ghormley operation (hip fusion) 81.21
Gifford operation
destruction of lacrimal sac 09.6
keratotomy (delimiting) 11.1
radial (refractive) 11.75
Gilliam operation (uterine suspension) 69.22
Gill operation
arthrodesis of shoulder 81.23
laminectomy 03.09
Gill-Stein operation (carporadial arthrodesis) 81.25
Gingivectomy 24.31
Gingivoplasty (with bone graft) (with soft tissue graft) 24.2
Girdlestone operation
laminectomy with spinal fusion 81.00
muscle transfer for claw toe repair 77.57
resection of femoral head and neck (without insertion of joint prosthesis) 77.85

☑ Additional Digit Required — Refer to the Tabular List for Digit Selection
▽ Subterms under main terms may continue to next column or page

24 — Volume 3
▶◀ Revised Text
● New Line
▲ Revised Code
2015 ICD-9-CM

☑ **Additional Digit Required** — Refer to the Tabular List for Digit Selection   ▽ **Subterms under main terms may continue to next column or page**

2015 ICD-9-CM   ►◄ **Revised Text**   ● **New Line**   ▲ **Revised Code**   **Volume 3 — 25**

Index   Girdlestone operation — Graft, grafting

Graft, grafting — continued
vein — continued
with — continued
tissue patch (vein) (autogenous)
(homograft) 39.56
vermilion border (lip) 27.56
Grattage, conjunctiva 10.31
Green operation (scapulopexy) 78.41
Grice operation (subtalar arthrodesis) 81.13
Grip, strength 93.04
Gritti-Stokes operation (knee disarticulation)
84.16
Gross operation (herniorrhaphy)
laparoscopic 53.43
with graft or prosthesis 53.42
other and open with graft or prosthesis
53.41
other open 53.49
Group therapy 94.44
Guttering, bone — see also Excision, lesion,
bone 77.60
Guyon operation (amputation of ankle) 84.13

H

Hagner operation (epididymotomy) 63.92
Halsted operation — see Repair, hernia, inguinal
Hampton operation (anastomosis small intestine to rectal stump) 45.92
Hanging hip operation (muscle release) 83.19
Harelip operation 27.54
Harrison-Richardson operation (vaginal suspension) 70.77
with graft or prosthesis 70.78
Hartmann resection (of intestine) (with pouch)
— see Colectomy, by site
Harvesting
bone marrow 41.91
fat for grafting or banking 86.90
stem cells 99.79
Hauser operation
achillotenotomy 83.11
bunionectomy with adductor tendon
transfer 77.53
stabilization of patella 81.44
Heaney operation (vaginal hysterectomy)
68.59
laparoscopically assisted (LAVH) 68.51
Hearing aid (with battery replacement) 95.49
Hearing test 95.47
HeartMate® II left ventricular assist system
[LVAS] 37.66
HeartMate® implantable heart assist system
37.66
Hegar operation (perineorrhaphy) 71.79
Heineke-Mikulicz operation (pyloroplasty)
44.29
Heine operation (cyclodialysis) 12.55
Helier operation (esophagomyotomy) 42.7
Hellström operation (transplantation of
aberrant renal vessel) 39.55
Hemicolectomy
left
laparoscopic 17.35
open and other 45.75
right (extended)
laparoscopic 17.33
open and other 45.73
Hemicystectomy 57.6
Hemigastrectomy — see Gastrectomy
Hemiglossectomy 25.2
Hemilaminectomy (decompression) (exploration) 03.09
Hemilaryngectomy (anterior) (lateral) (vertical)
30.1
Hemimandibulectomy 76.31
Hemimastectomy (radical) 85.23
Hemimaxillectomy (with bone graft) (with
prosthesis) 76.39
Heminephrectomy 55.4
Hemipelvectomy 84.19
Hemispherectomy (cerebral) 01.52
Hemithyroidectomy (with removal of isthmus)
(with removal of portion of remaining
lobe) 06.2
Hemodiafiltration (extracorporeal) 39.95

Hemodialysis (extracorporeal) 39.95
Hemodilution 99.03
Hemofiltration (extracorporeal) 39.95
Hemorrhage control — see Control, hemorrhage
Hemorrhoidectomy 49.46
by
cautery, cauterization 49.43
crushing 49.45
cryotherapy, cryosurgery 49.44
excision 49.46
injection 49.42
ligation 49.45
Hemostasis — see Control, hemorrhage
Henley operation (jejunal transposition) 43.81
Hepatectomy (complete) (total) 50.4
partial or subtotal 50.22
Hepatic assistance, extracorporeal 50.92
Hepaticocholangiojejunostomy 51.37
Hepaticocystoduodenostomy 51.37
Hepaticodochotomy 51.59
Hepaticoduodenostomy 51.37
Hepaticojejunostomy 51.37
Hepaticolithectomy 51.49
endoscopic 51.88
Hepaticolithotomy 51.49
endoscopic 51.88
Hepaticostomy 51.59
Hepaticotomy 51.59
Hepatocholangiocystoduodenostomy 51.37
Hepatocholedochostomy 51.43
endoscopic 51.87
Hepatoduodenostomy 50.69
Hepatogastrostomy 50.69
Hepatojejunostomy 50.69
Hepatolithotomy
hepatic duct 51.49
liver 50.0
Hepatopexy 50.69
Hepatorrhaphy 50.61
Hepatostomy (external) (internal) 50.69
Hepatotomy (with packing) 50.0
Hernioplasty — see Repair, hernia
Herniorrhaphy — see Repair, hernia
Herniotomy — see Repair, hernia
Heterograft — see Graft
Heterotransplant, heterotransplantation
— see Transplant
Hey-Groves operation (reconstruction of anterior cruciate ligament) 81.45
Heyman-Herndon (-Strong) operation (correction of metatarsus varus) 80.48
Heymen operation (soft tissue release for
clubfoot) 83.84
Hey operation (amputation of foot) 84.12
Hibbs operation (lumbar spinal fusion) — see
Fusion, lumbar
Higgins operation — see Repair, hernia,
femoral
High forceps delivery 72.39
with episiotomy 72.31
Hill-Allison operation (hiatal hernia repair,
transpleural approach) 53.80
Hinging, mitral valve 35.12
His bundle recording 37.29
Hitchcock operation (anchoring tendon of
biceps) 83.88
Hofmeister operation (gastrectomy) 43.7
Hoke operation
midtarsal fusion 81.14
triple arthrodesis 81.12
Holth operation
iridencleisis 12.63
sclerectomy 12.65
Homan operation (correction of lymphedema)
40.9
Homograft — see Graft
Homotransplant, homotransplantation —
see Transplant
Hosiery, elastic 93.59
Hutch operation (ureteroneocystostomy)
56.74
Hybinette-Eden operation (glenoid bone
block) 78.01
Hydrocelectomy
canal of Nuck (female) 69.19

Hydrocelectomy — continued
canal of Nuck — continued
male 63.1
round ligament 69.19
spermatic cord 63.1
tunica vaginalis 61.2
Hydrotherapy 93.33
assisted exercise in pool 93.31
whirlpool 93.32
Hymenectomy 70.31
Hymenoplasty 70.76
Hymenorrhaphy 70.76
Hymenotomy 70.11
Hyperalimentation (parenteral) 99.15
Hyperbaric oxygenation 93.95
wound 93.59
Hyperextension, joint 93.25
Hyperthermia NEC 93.35
for cancer treatment (interstitial) (local) (radiofrequency) (regional) (ultrasound)
(whole-body) 99.85
Hypnodrama, psychiatric 94.32
Hypnosis (psychotherapeutic) 94.32
for anesthesia — omit code
Hypnotherapy 94.32
Hypophysectomy (complete) (total) 07.69
partial or subtotal 07.63
transfrontal approach 07.61
transsphenoidal approach 07.62
specified approach NEC 07.68
transfrontal approach (complete) (total)
07.64
partial 07.61
transsphenoidal approach (complete) (total)
07.65
partial 07.62
Hypothermia (central) (local) 99.81
gastric (cooling) 96.31
freezing 96.32
systemic (in open heart surgery) 39.62
Hypotympanotomy 20.23
Hysterectomy, NOS 68.9
abdominal
laparoscopic (total) (TLH) 68.41
other (total) 68.49
partial or subtotal (supracervical)
(supravaginal) 68.39
radical (modified) (Wertheim's) 68.69
laparoscopic (total) (TLRH) 68.61
supracervical 68.39
classic infrafascial SEMM hysterectomy (CISH) 68.31
laparoscopically assisted (LASH)
68.31
laparoscopic
abdominal
radical (total) (TLRH) 68.61
total (TLH) 68.41
supracervical (LASH) (LSH) 68.31
total (TLH) 68.41
vaginal, assisted (LAVH) 68.51
radical (LRVH) 68.71
radical
abdominal
laparoscopic 68.61
other (modified) (Wertheim's) 68.69
vaginal
laparoscopic (LRVH) 68.71
other 68.79
vaginal (complete) (partial) (subtotal) (total)
68.59
laparoscopically assisted (LAVH) 68.51
radical (Schauta) 68.79
laparoscopic (LRVH) 68.71
Hysterocolpectomy (radical) (vaginal) 68.79
abdominal 68.69
laparoscopic 68.61
laparoscopic 68.71
Hysterogram NEC 87.85
percutaneous 87.84
Hysterolysis 54.59
laparoscopic 54.51
Hysteromyomectomy 68.29
Hysteropexy 69.22
Hysteroplasty 69.49
Hysterorrhaphy 69.41

Hysterosalpingography gas (contrast) 87.82
opaque dye (contrast) 87.83
Hysterosalpingostomy 66.74
Hysteroscopy 68.12
with
ablation
endometrial 68.23
biopsy 68.16
Hysterotomy (with removal of foreign body)
(with removal of hydatidiform mole) 68.0
for intrauterine transfusion 75.2
obstetrical 74.99
for termination of pregnancy 74.91
Hysterotrachelectomy 67.4
Hysterotracheloplasty 69.49
Hysterotrachelorrhaphy 69.41
Hysterotrachelotomy 69.95

I

IAEMT (intraoperative anesthetic effect monitoring and titration) 00.94 [89.14]
ICCE (intracapsular cataract extraction) 13.19
Ileal
bladder
closed 57.87 [45.51]
open (ileoureterostomy) 56.51
conduit (ileoureterostomy) 56.51
Ileocecostomy 45.93
Ileocolectomy
laparoscopic 17.33
open and other 45.73
Ileocolostomy 45.93
Ileocolotomy 45.00
Ileocystoplasty (isolated segment anastomosis) (open loop) 57.87 [45.51]
Ileoduodenotomy 45.01
Ileoectomy (partial) 45.62
with cecectomy
laparoscopic 17.32
open and other 45.72
Ileoentectropy 46.99
Ileoesophagostomy 42.54
Ileoileostomy 45.91
proximal to distal segment 45.62
Ileoloopogram 87.78
Ileopancreatostomy 52.96
Ileopexy 46.61
Ileoproctostomy 45.93
Ileorectostomy 45.93
Ileorrhaphy 46.73
Ileoscopy 45.13
through stoma (artificial) 45.12
transabdominal (operative) 45.11
Ileosigmoidostomy 45.93
Ileostomy 46.20
continent (permanent) 46.22
for urinary diversion 56.51
delayed opening 46.24
Hendon (temporary) 46.21
loop 46.01
Paul (temporary) 46.21
permanent 46.23
continent 46.22
repair 46.41
revision 46.41
tangential (temporary) 46.21
temporary 46.21
transplantation to new site 46.23
tube (temporary) 46.21
ureteral
external 56.51
internal 56.71
Ileotomy 45.02
Ileotransversostomy 45.93
Ileoureterostomy (Bricker's) (ileal bladder)
56.51
Imaging (diagnostic)
by
optical coherence tomography (OCT) —
see OCT and Tomography, optical
coherence
diagnostic, not elsewhere classified 88.90
endovascular ultrasound — see Imaging,
intravascular ultrasound

Implant, implantation — *continued*
heart — *continued*
  assist system — *continued*
    temporary non-implantable circulatory assist device — *see* Insertion, circulatory support device
    that for destination therapy (DT) 37.66
  auxiliary ventricle 37.62
  cardiac support device (CSD) 37.41
  circulatory assist system — *see* Implant, heart, assist system
  CorCap™ 37.41
  epicardial support device 37.41
  pacemaker (*see also* Implant, pacemaker, cardiac) 37.80
  prosthetic cardiac support device 37.41
  total internal biventricular replacement system 37.52
  valve(s)
    prosthesis or synthetic device (partial) (synthetic) (total) 35.20
      aortic 35.22
      mitral 35.24
      pulmonary 35.26
      tricuspid 35.28
    tissue graft 35.20
      aortic 35.21
      mitral 35.23
      pulmonary 35.25
      tricuspid 35.27
  ventricular support device 37.41
inert material
  breast (for augmentation) (bilateral) 85.54
    unilateral 85.53
  larynx 31.0
  nose 21.85
  orbit (eye socket) 16.69
    reinsertion 16.62
  scleral shell (cup) (with evisceration of eyeball) 16.31
    reinsertion 16.62
  Tenon's capsule (with enucleation of eyeball) 16.42
    with attachment of muscles 16.41
    reinsertion 16.62
  urethra 59.79
  vocal cord(s) 31.0
infusion pump 86.06
interbody spinal fusion device 84.51
intracardiac or great vessel hemodynamic monitor, subcutaneous 00.57
joint (prosthesis) (silastic) (Swanson type) NEC 81.96
  ankle (total) 81.56
    revision 81.59
  carpocarpal, carpometacarpal 81.74
  elbow (total) 81.84
    revision 81.97
  extremity (bioelectric) (cineplastic) (kineplastic) 84.40
    lower 84.48
      revision 81.59
    upper 84.44
      revision 81.97
  femoral (bipolar endoprosthesis) 81.52
    revision NOS 81.53
      acetabular and femoral components (total) 00.70
      acetabular component only 00.71
      acetabular liner and/or femoral head only 00.73
      femoral component only 00.72
      femoral head only and/or acetabular liner 00.73
      total (acetabular and femoral components) 00.70
  finger 81.71
  hand (metacarpophalangeal) (interphalangeal) 81.71
    revision 81.97
  hip (partial) 81.52
    revision NOS 81.53

Implant, implantation — *continued*
joint — *continued*
  hip — *continued*
    revision — *continued*
      acetabular and femoral components (total) 00.70
      acetabular component only 00.71
      acetabular liner and/or femoral head only 00.73
      femoral component only 00.72
      femoral head only and/or acetabular liner 00.73
      partial
        acetabular component only 00.71
        acetabular liner and/or femoral head only 00.73
        femoral component only 00.72
        femoral head only and/or acetabular liner 00.73
      total (acetabular and femoral components) 00.70
    total 81.51
      revision (acetabular and femoral components) 00.70
  interphalangeal 81.71
    revision 81.97
  knee (partial) (total) 81.54
    revision NOS 81.55
      femoral component 00.82
      partial
        femoral component 00.82
        patellar component 00.83
        tibial component 00.81
        tibial insert 00.84
      patellar component 00.83
      tibial component 00.81
      tibial insert 00.84
      total (all components) 00.80
  metacarpophalangeal 81.71
    revision 81.97
  shoulder (partial) 81.81
    revision 81.97
    total replacement, NEC 81.80
      other 81.80
      reverse 81.88
  toe 81.57
    for hallux valgus repair 77.59
    revision 81.59
  wrist (partial) 81.74
    revision 81.97
    total replacement 81.73
kidney, mechanical 55.97
Lap-Band™ 44.95
larynx 31.0
leads (cardiac) — *see* Implant, electrode(s), cardiac
limb lengthening device, internal (NOS) 84.54
  with kinetic distraction 84.53
mammary artery
  in ventricle (Vineberg) 36.2
  to coronary artery (single vessel) 36.15
    double vessel 36.16
M-Brace™ 84.82
Mulligan hood, fallopian tube 66.93
nerve (peripheral) 04.79
neuropacemaker — *see* Implant, neurostimulator, by site
neurostimulator
  brain 02.93
  electrodes
    brain 02.93
    gastric 04.92
    intracranial 02.93
    peripheral nerve 04.92
    sacral nerve 04.92
    spine 03.93
  intracranial 02.93
  peripheral nerve 04.92
  pulse generator (subcutaneous) 86.96
    cranial 01.20
    multiple array 86.95
      rechargeable 86.98

Implant, implantation — *continued*
neurostimulator — *continued*
  pulse generator — *continued*
    single array 86.94
      rechargeable 86.97
  spine 03.93
nose 21.85
Ommaya reservoir 02.22
orbit 16.69
  reinsertion 16.62
outflow tract prosthesis (heart) (gusset type) in
  pulmonary valvuloplasty 35.26
  total repair of tetralogy of Fallot 35.81
ovary into uterine cavity 65.72
  laparoscopic 65.75
pacemaker
  brain — *see* Implant, neurostimulator, brain
  cardiac (device) (initial) (permanent) (replacement) 37.80
    dual-chamber device (initial) 37.83
      replacement 37.87
    resynchronization device (biventricular pacemaker) (BiV pacemaker) (CRT-P)
      device only (initial) (replacement) 00.53
      total system (device and one or more leads) 00.50
      transvenous lead into left ventricular coronary venous system 00.52
    single-chamber device (initial) 37.81
      rate responsive 37.82
      replacement 37.85
        rate responsive 37.86
    temporary transvenous pacemaker system 37.78
      during and immediately following cardiac surgery 39.64
  carotid sinus 39.89
  diaphragm 34.85
  gastric 04.92
  intracranial — *see* Implant, neurostimulator, intracranial
  neural — *see* Implant, neurostimulator, by site
  peripheral nerve — *see* Implant, neurostimulator, peripheral nerve
  spine — *see* Implant, neurostimulator, spine
pancreas (duct) 52.96
penis, prosthesis (internal)
  inflatable 64.97
  non-inflatable 64.95
port, vascular access device 86.07
premaxilla 76.68
progesterone (subdermal) 99.23
prosthesis, prosthetic device
  acetabulum (Aufranc-Turner) 81.52
  ankle (total) 81.56
  arm (bioelectric) (cineplastic) (kineplastic) 84.44
  breast (Cronin) (Dow-Corning) (Perras-Pappillon) (bilateral) 85.54
    unilateral 85.53
  cardiac support device (CSD) (CorCap™) 37.41
  cochlear 20.96
    channel (single) 20.97
      multiple 20.98
  epiretinal visual 14.81
  extremity (bioelectric) (cineplastic) (kineplastic) 84.40
    lower 84.48
    upper 84.44
  fallopian tube (Mulligan hood) (stent) 66.93
  femoral head (Austin-Moore) (bipolar) (Eicher) (Thompson) 81.52
    revision NOS 81.53
      acetabular and femoral components (total) 00.70
      acetabular component only 00.71

Implant, implantation — *continued*
prosthesis, prosthetic device — *continued*
  femoral head — *continued*
    revision — *continued*
      acetabular liner and/or femoral head only 00.73
      femoral component only 00.72
      femoral head only and/or acetabular liner 00.73
      partial
        acetabular component only 00.71
        acetabular liner and/or femoral head only 00.73
        femoral component only 00.72
        femoral head only and/or acetabular liner 00.73
      total (acetabular and femoral components) 00.70
  joint (Swanson type) NEC 81.96
  ankle (total) 81.56
  carpocarpal, carpometacarpal 81.74
  elbow (total) 81.84
  finger 81.71
  hand (metacarpophalangeal) (interphalangeal) 81.71
  hip (partial) 81.52
    revision NOS 81.53
      acetabular and femoral components (total) 00.70
      acetabular component only 00.71
      acetabular liner and/or femoral head only 00.73
      femoral component only 00.72
      femoral head only and/or acetabular liner 00.73
      partial
        acetabular component only 00.71
        acetabular liner and/or femoral head only 00.73
        femoral component only 00.72
        femoral head only and/or acetabular liner 00.73
      total (acetabular and femoral components) 00.70
    total 81.51
      revision (acetabular and femoral components) 00.70
  interphalangeal 81.71
  knee (partial) (total) 81.54
    revision NOS 81.55
      femoral component 00.82
      partial
        femoral component 00.82
        patellar component 00.83
        tibial component 00.81
        tibial insert 00.84
      patellar component 00.83
      tibial component 00.81
      tibial insert 00.84
      total (all components) 00.80
  metacarpophalangeal 81.71
  shoulder (partial) 81.81
    total, NEC 81.80
      other 81.80
      reverse 81.88
  spine NEC 84.59
    interspinous process decompression device
  toe 81.57
    for hallux valgus repair 77.59
  wrist (partial) 81.74
    total 81.73
  leg (bioelectric) (cineplastic) (kineplastic) 84.48

☑ **Additional Digit Required** — Refer to the Tabular List for Digit Selection

▽ **Subterms under main terms may continue to next column or page**

Implant, implantation — *continued*
  prosthesis, prosthetic device — *continued*
    lens 13.91
    outflow tract (heart) (gusset type)
      in
        pulmonary valvuloplasty 35.26
        total repair of tetralogy of Fallot 35.81
    penis (internal) (non-inflatable) 64.95
      inflatable (internal) 64.97
    skin (dermal regenerative) (matrix) 86.67
    testicular (bilateral) (unilateral) 62.7
  pulsation balloon (phase-shift) 37.61
  pump, infusion 86.06
  radial artery 36.19
  radioactive isotope 92.27
  radium (radon) 92.27
  retinal attachment 14.41
    with buckling 14.41
  Rheos™ carotid sinus baroreflex activation
    device 39.81
  Rickham reservoir 02.22
  silicone
    breast (bilateral) 85.54
      unilateral 85.53
    skin (for filling of defect) 86.02
      for augmentation NEC 86.89
  spine NEC 84.59
    facet replacement device(s) 84.84
    interspinous process decompression
      device 84.80
    pedicle-based dynamic stabilization de-
      vice(s) 84.82
    posterior motion preservation device(s)
      — *see* category 84.8
  stimoceiver — *see* Implant, neurostimulator,
    by site
  stimulator
    electrodes
      carotid sinus (baroflex activation de-
        vice) 39.82
        with synchronous pulse genera-
          tor implantation (total
          system) 39.81
    pulse generator
      carotid sinus (baroreflex activation
        device) 39.83
        with synchronous electrode(s)
          implantation (total sys-
          tem) 39.81
    subdural
      grids 02.93
      strips 02.93
  Swanson prosthesis (joint) (silastic) NEC
    81.96
    carpocarpal, carpometacarpal 81.74
    finger 81.71
    hand (metacarpophalangeal) (interpha-
      langeal) 81.71
    interphalangeal 81.71
    knee (partial) (total) 81.54
      revision 81.55
    metacarpophalangeal 81.71
    toe 81.57
      for hallux valgus repair 77.59
    wrist (partial) 81.74
      total 81.73
  systemic arteries into myocardium
    (Vineberg type operation) 36.2
  Tandem™ heart 37.68
  telescope (IMT) (miniature) 13.91
  testicular prosthesis (bilateral) (unilateral)
    62.7
  tissue expander (skin) NEC 86.93
    breast 85.95
  tissue mandril (for vascular graft) 39.99
    with
      blood vessel repair 39.56
      vascular bypass or shunt — *see* By-
        pass, vascular
  tooth (bud) (germ) 23.5
    prosthetic 23.6
  umbrella, vena cava 38.7
  ureters into
    bladder 56.74

Implant, implantation — *continued*
  ureters into — *continued*
    intestine 56.71
      external diversion 56.51
    skin 56.61
  urethra
    for repair of urinary stress incontinence
      collagen 59.72
      fat 59.72
      polytef 59.72
  urethral sphincter, artificial (inflatable) 58.93
  urinary sphincter, artificial (inflatable) 58.93
  valve(s)
    endovascular — *see* Replacement, heart
      valve, by site
  vascular access device 86.07
  vitreous (silicone) 14.75
    for retinal reattachment 14.41
      with buckling 14.41
  vocal cord(s) (paraglottic) 31.98
  X Stop™ 84.80
Implosion (psychologic desensitization) 94.33
Incision (and drainage)
  with
    exploration — *see* Exploration
    removal of foreign body — *see* Removal,
      foreign body
  abdominal wall 54.0
    as operative approach — *omit code*
  abscess (*see also* Incision, by site)
    antecubital fossa 86.04
    appendix 47.2
      with appendectomy 47.09
        laparoscopic 47.01
    axilla 86.04
    cheek 86.04
    extraperitoneal 54.0
    face 86.04
    gluteal 86.04
    groin region (abdominal wall) (inguinal)
      54.0
      skin 86.04
      subcutaneous tissue 86.04
    hair follicle 86.04
    ischiorectal 49.01
    lip 27.0
    nailbed or nailfold 86.04
    neck 86.04
    omental 54.19
    paronychia 86.04
    perianal 49.01
    perigastric 54.19
    perineum (female) 71.09
      male 86.04
    perisplenic 54.19
    peritoneal NEC 54.19
      pelvic (female) 70.12
    popliteal space 86.04
    retroperitoneal 54.0
    sclera 12.89
    skin 86.04
    subcutaneous tissue 86.04
    subdiaphragmatic 54.19
    subhepatic 54.19
    submaxillary 86.04
    subphrenic 54.19
    supraclavicular fossa 86.04
    vas deferens 63.6
  adrenal gland 07.41
  alveolus, alveolar bone 24.0
  antecubital fossa 86.09
  anus NEC 49.93
    fistula 49.11
    septum 49.91
  appendix 47.2
  artery 38.00
    abdominal 38.06
      aorta (arch) (ascending) (descending)
        38.04
    head and neck NEC 38.02
    intracranial NEC 38.01
    lower limb 38.08
    thoracic NEC 38.05
    upper limb 38.03
  atrium (heart) 37.11
  auditory canal or meatus, external 18.02

Incision — *continued*
  auricle 18.09
  axilla 86.09
  Bartholin's gland or cyst 71.22
  bile duct (with T or Y tube insertion) NEC
    51.59
    for
      exploration 51.59
      relief of obstruction 51.49
    common (exploratory) 51.51
      for
        relief of obstruction NEC 51.42
        removal of calculus 51.41
  bladder 57.19
    neck (transurethral) 57.91
    percutaneous suprapubic (closed) 57.17
    suprapubic NEC 57.18
  blood vessel (*see also* Angiotomy) 38.00
  bone 77.10
    alveolus, alveolar 24.0
    carpals, metacarpals 77.14
    clavicle 77.11
    facial 76.09
    femur 77.15
    fibula 77.17
    humerus 77.12
    patella 77.16
    pelvic 77.19
    phalanges (foot) (hand) 77.19
    radius 77.13
    scapula 77.11
    skull 01.24
    specified site NEC 77.19
    tarsals, metatarsals 77.18
    thorax (ribs) (sternum) 77.11
    tibia 77.17
    ulna 77.13
    vertebrae 77.19
  brain 01.39
    cortical adhesions 02.91
  breast (skin) 85.0
    with removal of tissue expander 85.96
  bronchus 33.0
  buccal space 27.0
  bulbourethral gland 58.91
  bursa 83.03
    hand 82.03
    pharynx 29.0
  carotid body 39.89
  cerebral (meninges) 01.39
    epidural or extradural space 01.24
    subarachnoid or subdural space 01.31
  cerebrum 01.39
  cervix 69.95
    to
      assist delivery 73.93
      replace inverted uterus 75.93
  chalazion 08.09
    with removal of capsule 08.21
  cheek 86.09
  chest wall (for extrapleural drainage) (for
    removal of foreign body) 34.01
    as operative approach — *omit code*
  common bile duct (for exploration) 51.51
    for
      relief of obstruction 51.42
      removal of calculus 51.41
  common wall between posterior left atrium
    and coronary sinus (with roofing of
    resultant defect with patch graft)
    35.82
  conjunctiva 10.1
  cornea 11.1
    radial (refractive) 11.75
  cranial sinus 01.21
  craniobuccal pouch 07.72
  cul-de-sac 70.12
  cyst
    dentigerous 24.0
    radicular (apical) (periapical) 24.0
  Dührssen's (cervix, to assist delivery) 73.93
  duodenum 45.01
  ear
    external 18.09
    inner 20.79
    middle 20.23

Incision — *continued*
  endocardium 37.11
  endolymphatic sac 20.79
  epididymis 63.92
  epidural space, cerebral 01.24
  epigastric region 54.0
    intra-abdominal 54.19
  esophagus, esophageal NEC 42.09
    web 42.01
  exploratory — *see* Exploration
  extradural space (cerebral) 01.24
  extrapleural 34.01
  eyebrow 08.09
  eyelid 08.09
    margin (trichiasis) 08.01
  face 86.09
  fallopian tube 66.01
  fascia 83.09
    with division 83.14
      hand 82.12
    hand 82.09
      with division 82.12
  fascial compartments, head and neck 27.0
  fistula, anal 49.11
  flank 54.0
  furuncle — *see* Incision, by site
  gallbladder 51.04
  gingiva 24.0
  gluteal 86.09
  groin region (abdominal wall) (inguinal)
    54.0
    skin 86.09
    subcutaneous tissue 86.09
  gum 24.0
  hair follicles 86.09
  heart 37.10
    valve — *see* Valvulotomy
  hematoma (*see also* Incision, by site)
    axilla 86.04
    broad ligament 69.98
    ear 18.09
    episiotomy site 75.91
    fossa (superficial) NEC 86.04
    groin region (abdominal wall) (inguinal)
      54.0
      skin 86.04
      subcutaneous tissue 86.04
    laparotomy site 54.12
    mediastinum 34.1
    perineum (female) 71.09
      male 86.04
    popliteal space 86.04
    scrotum 61.0
    skin 86.04
    space of Retzius 59.19
    subcutaneous tissue 86.04
    vagina (cuff) 70.14
      episiotomy site 75.91
      obstetrical NEC 75.92
  hepatic ducts 51.59
  hordeolum 08.09
  hygroma (*see also* Incision, by site)
    cystic 40.0
  hymen 70.11
  hypochondrium 54.0
    intra-abdominal 54.19
  hypophysis 07.72
  iliac fossa 54.0
  infratemporal fossa 27.0
  ingrown nail 86.09
  intestine 45.00
    large 45.03
    small 45.02
  intracerebral 01.39
  intracranial (epidural space) (extradural
    space) 01.24
    subarachnoid or subdural space 01.31
  intraperitoneal 54.19
  ischiorectal tissue 49.02
    abscess 49.01
  joint structures (*see also* Arthrotomy) 80.10
  kidney 55.01
    pelvis 55.11
  labia 71.09
  lacrimal
    canaliculus 09.52

☑ **Additional Digit Required** — Refer to the Tabular List for Digit Selection   ℗ **Subterms under main terms may continue to next column or page**

2015 ICD-9-CM   ▶◀ **Revised Text**   ● **New Line**   ▲ **Revised Code**   **Volume 3 — 29**

Incision — *continued*
lacrimal — *continued*
  gland 09.0
  passage NEC 09.59
  punctum 09.51
  sac 09.53
larynx NEC 31.3
ligamentum flavum (spine) — *omit code*
liver 50.0
lung 33.1
lymphangioma 40.0
lymphatic structure (channel) (node) (vessel) 40.0
mastoid 20.21
mediastinum 34.1
meibomian gland 08.09
meninges (cerebral) 01.31
  spinal 03.09
midpalmar space 82.04
mouth NEC 27.92
  floor 27.0
muscle 83.02
  with division 83.19
    hand 82.19
  hand 82.02
    with division 82.19
myocardium 37.11
nailbed or nailfold 86.09
nasolacrimal duct (stricture) 09.59
neck 86.09
nerve (cranial) (peripheral) NEC 04.04
  root (spinal) 03.1
nose 21.1
omentum 54.19
orbit (*see also* Orbitotomy) 16.09
ovary 65.09
  laparoscopic 65.01
palate 27.1
palmar space (middle) 82.04
pancreas 52.09
pancreatic sphincter 51.82
  endoscopic 51.85
parapharyngeal (oral) (transcervical) 28.0
paronychia 86.09
parotid
  gland or duct 26.0
  space 27.0
pelvirectal tissue 48.81
penis 64.92
perianal (skin) (tissue) 49.02
  abscess 49.01
perigastric 54.19
perineum (female) 71.09
  male 86.09
peripheral vessels
  lower limb
    artery 38.08
    vein 38.09
  upper limb (artery) (vein) 38.03
periprostatic tissue 60.81
perirectal tissue 48.81
perirenal tissue 59.09
perisplenic 54.19
peritoneum 54.95
  by laparotomy 54.19
  pelvic (female) 70.12
    male 54.19
periureteral tissue 59.09
periurethral tissue 58.91
perivesical tissue 59.19
petrous pyramid (air cells) (apex) (mastoid) 20.22
pharynx, pharyngeal (bursa) 29.0
  space, lateral 27.0
pilonidal sinus (cyst) 86.03
pineal gland 07.52
pituitary (gland) 07.72
pleura NEC 34.09
popliteal space 86.09
postzygomatic space 27.0
pouch of Douglas 70.12
prostate (perineal approach) (transurethral approach) 60.0
pterygopalatine fossa 27.0
pulp canal (tooth) 24.0
Rathke's pouch 07.72

Incision — *continued*
rectovaginal septum 48.81
rectum 48.0
  stricture 48.91
renal pelvis 55.11
retroperitoneum 54.0
retropharyngeal (oral) (transcervical) 28.0
salivary gland or duct 26.0
sclera 12.89
scrotum 61.0
sebaceous cyst 86.04
seminal vesicle 60.72
sinus — *see* Sinusotomy
Skene's duct or gland 71.09
skin 86.09
  with drainage 86.04
  breast 85.0
  cardiac pacemaker pocket, new site 37.79
  ear 18.09
  nose 21.1
  subcutaneous tunnel for pulse generator lead wire 86.99
    with initial procedure — *omit code*
  thalamic stimulator pulse generator pocket, new site 86.09
    with initial insertion of battery package — *omit code*
  tunnel, subcutaneous for pulse generator lead wire 86.99
    with initial procedure — *omit code*
skull (bone) 01.24
soft tissue NEC 83.09
  with division 83.19
    hand 82.19
  hand 82.09
    with division 82.19
space of Retzius 59.19
spermatic cord 63.93
sphincter of Oddi 51.82
  endoscopic 51.85
spinal
  cord 03.09
  nerve root 03.1
spleen 41.2
stomach 43.0
stye 08.09
subarachnoid space, cerebral 01.31
subcutaneous tissue 86.09
  with drainage 86.04
  tunnel
    esophageal 42.86
      with anastomosis — *see* Anastomosis, esophagus, antesternal
    pulse generator lead wire 86.99
      with initial procedure — *omit code*
subdiaphragmatic space 54.19
subdural space, cerebral 01.31
sublingual space 27.0
submandibular space 27.0
submaxillary 86.09
  with drainage 86.04
submental space 27.0
subphrenic space 54.19
supraclavicular fossa 86.09
  with drainage 86.04
sweat glands, skin 86.04
temporal pouches 27.0
tendon (sheath) 83.01
  with division 83.13
    hand 82.11
  hand 82.01
    with division 82.11
testis 62.0
thenar space 82.04
thymus (open) (other) 07.92
  thoracoscopic 07.95
thyroid (field) (gland) NEC 06.09
  postoperative 06.02
tongue NEC 25.94
  for tongue tie 25.91
tonsil 28.0
trachea NEC 31.3
tunica vaginalis 61.0

Incision — *continued*
umbilicus 54.0
urachal cyst 54.0
ureter 56.2
urethra 58.0
uterus (corpus) 68.0
  cervix 69.95
  for termination of pregnancy 74.91
  septum (congenital) 68.22
uvula 27.71
vagina (cuff) (septum) (stenosis) 70.14
  for
    incisional hematoma (episiotomy) 75.91
    obstetrical hematoma NEC 75.92
    pelvic abscess 70.12
vas deferens 63.6
vein 38.00
  abdominal 38.07
  head and neck NEC 38.02
  intracranial NEC 38.01
  lower limb 38.09
  thoracic NEC 38.05
  upper limb 38.03
vertebral column 03.09
vulva 71.09
  obstetrical 75.92
web, esophageal 42.01
Incudectomy NEC 19.3
  with
    stapedectomy (*see also* Stapedectomy) 19.19
    tympanoplasty — *see* Tympanoplasty
Incudopexy 19.19
Incudostapediopexy 19.19
  with incus replacement 19.11
Indentation, sclera, for buckling — *see also* Buckling, scleral 14.49
Indicator dilution flow measurement 89.68
Induction
  abortion
    by
      D and C 69.01
      insertion of prostaglandin suppository 96.49
      intra-amniotic injection (prostaglandin) (saline) 75.0
    labor
      medical 73.4
      surgical 73.01
        intra- and extra-amniotic injection 73.1
      stripping of membranes 73.1
Inflation
  belt wrap 93.99
  Eustachian tube 20.8
  fallopian tube 66.8
    with injection of therapeutic agent 66.95
Infolding, sclera, for buckling — *see* also Buckling, scleral 14.49
Infraction, turbinates (nasal) 21.62
Infundibulectomy
  hypophyseal (*see also* Hypophysectomy, partial) 07.63
  ventricle (heart) (right) 35.34
    in total repair of tetralogy of Fallot 35.81
Infusion (intra-arterial) (intravenous)
  with
    disruption of blood brain barrier [BBBD] 00.19
  4-Factor Prothrombin Complex Concentrate 00.96
  Abciximab 99.20
  antibiotic
    oxazolidinone class 00.14
  antineoplastic agent (chemotherapeutic) 99.25
    biological response modifier [BRM] 99.28
    cintredekin besudotox 99.28
    CLO 17.70
    clofarabine 17.70
    CLOLAR® 17.70
    high-dose interleukin-2 00.15
    low-dose interleukin-2 99.28
    biological response modifier [BRM], antineoplastic agent 99.28

Infusion — *continued*
  biological response modifier [BRM], antineoplastic agent — *continued*
    cintredekin besudotox 99.28
    high-dose interleukin-2 00.15
    low-dose interleukin-2 99.28
  cancer chemotherapy agent NEC 99.25
  cintredekin besudotox 99.28
  CLO 17.70
  clofarabine 17.70
  CLOLAR® 17.70
  drotrecogin alfa (activated) 00.11
  electrolytes 99.18
  enzymes, thrombolytic (streptokinase) (tissue plasminogen activator) (TPA) (urokinase)
    direct coronary artery 36.04
    intravenous 99.10
  Eptifibatide 99.20
  gamma globulin 99.14
  glucarpidase 00.95
  GP IIb/IIIa inhibitor 99.20
  hormone substance NEC 99.24
  human B-type natriuretic peptide (hBNP) 00.13
  IgG (immunoglobulin) 99.14
  immunoglobulin (IgG) (IVIG) (IVIg) 99.14
  immunosuppressive antibody therapy 00.18
  interleukin-2
    high-dose 00.15
    low-dose 99.28
  IVIG (immunoglobulin) (IVIg) 99.14
  Kcentra™ 00.96
  lymphocyte 99.09
  nesiritide 00.13
  neuroprotective agent 99.75
  nimodipine 99.75
  nutritional substance — *see* Nutrition
  platelet inhibitor
    direct coronary artery 36.04
    intravenous 99.20
  Proleukin (low-dose) 99.28
    high-dose 00.15
  prophylactic substance NEC 99.29
  radioimmunoconjugate 92.28
  radioimmunotherapy 92.28
  radioisotope (liquid brachytherapy) (liquid I-125) 92.20
  recombinant protein 00.11
  reteplase 99.10
  therapeutic substance NEC 99.29
  thrombolytic agent (enzyme) (streptokinase) 99.10
    with percutaneous transluminal angioplasty

Note: Also use 00.40, 00.41, 00.42, or 00.43 to show the total number of vessels treated.

        coronary 00.66
        non-coronary vessel(s) 39.50
        specified site NEC 39.50
        direct intracoronary artery 36.04
  tirofiban (HCl) 99.20
  vaccine
    tumor 99.28
  vasopressor 00.17
  Voraxaze® 00.95
Injection (into) (hypodermically) (intramuscularly) (intravenously) (acting locally or systemically)
  Actinomycin D, for cancer chemotherapy 99.25
  adhesion barrier substance 99.77
  alcohol
    nerve — *see* Injection, nerve
    spinal 03.8
  anterior chamber, eye (air) (liquid) (medication) 12.92
  antibiotic 99.21
    oxazolidinone class 00.14
  anticoagulant 99.19
  anti-D (Rhesus) globulin 99.11
  antidote NEC 99.16
  anti-infective NEC 99.22
  antineoplastic agent (chemotherapeutic) NEC 99.25

☑ **Additional Digit Required** — Refer to the Tabular List for Digit Selection

2015 ICD-9-CM

▶◀ Revised Text

● New Line

▲ Revised Code

▽ Subterms under main terms may continue to next column or page

Volume 3 — 31

Index

Injection — Insertion

Insertion — *continued*
catheter — *continued*
  spinal canal space (epidural) (subarach-
      noid) (subdural) for infusion of
      therapeutic or palliative sub-
      stances 03.90
  Swan-Ganz (pulmonary) 89.64
  temporary occlusion, abdominal aorta
      39.77
  transtracheal for oxygenation 31.99
  vein NEC 38.93
      for renal dialysis 38.95
chest tube 34.04
  thoracoscopic 34.06
choledochohepatic tube (for decompres-
    sion) 51.43
  endoscopic 51.87
circulatory support device
  CentriMag® 37.62
  external heart assist device
      biventricular 37.60
      Impella® 37.68
      percutaneous 37.68
      temporary 37.62
      non-implantable 37.62
      pVAD (percutaneous VAD) 37.68
      TandemHeart® 37.68
      temporary non-implantable circulatory
          assist device 37.62
cochlear prosthetic device — *see* Implant,
    cochlear prosthetic device
contraceptive device (intrauterine) 69.7
CorCap™ 37.41
cordis cannula 54.98
coronary (artery)

*Note: Also use 00.40, 00.41, 00.42, or
00.43 to show the total number of vessels treated. Use code 00.44 once to
show procedure on a bifurcated vessel.
In addition, use 00.45, 00.46, 00.47, or
00.48 to show the number of vascular
stents inserted.*

  stent, drug-eluting 36.07
  stent, non-drug-eluting 36.06
Crosby-Cooney button 54.98
CRT-D (biventricular defibrillator) (BiV ICD)
    (BiV pacemaker with defibrillator)
    (BiV pacing with defibrillator) (car-
    diac resynchronization defibrillator)
    (device and one or more leads) 00.51
  left ventricular coronary venous lead
      only 00.52
  pulse generator only 00.54
CRT-P (biventricular pacemaker) (BiV pace-
    maker) (cardiac resynchronization
    pacemaker) (device and one or more
    leads) 00.50
  left ventricular coronary venous lead
      only 00.52
  pulse generator only 00.53
Crutchfield tongs (skull) (with synchronous
    skeletal traction) 02.94
Davidson button 54.98
denture (total) 99.97
device
  adjustable gastric band and port 44.95
  bronchial device NOS 33.79
  bronchial substance NOS 33.79
  bronchial valve(s)
      multiple lobes 33.73
      single lobe 33.71
  cardiac resynchronization — *see* Inser-
      tion, cardiac resynchronization
      device
  cardiac support device (CSD) 37.41
  CorCap™ 37.41
  epicardial support device 37.41
  Lap-Band™ 44.95
  left atrial appendage 37.90
  left atrial filter 37.90
  left atrial occluder 37.90
  MitraClip® mitral leaflet clip 35.97
  prosthetic cardiac support device 37.41
  sternal fixation device with rigid plates
      84.94
  vascular access 86.07

Insertion — *continued*
device — *continued*
  ventricular support device 37.41
diaphragm, vagina 96.17
drainage tube
  kidney 55.02
  pelvis 55.12
  renal pelvis 55.12
Dynesys® 84.82
elbow prosthesis (total) 81.84
  revision 81.97
electrode(s)
  bone growth stimulator (invasive) (per-
      cutaneous) (semi-invasive) — *see*
      category 78.9 ☑
  brain 02.93
      depth 02.93
      foramen ovale 02.93
      sphenoidal 02.96
  depth 02.93
  foramen ovale 02.93
  gastric 04.92
  heart (initial) (transvenous) 37.70
      atrium (initial) 37.73
          replacement 37.76
      atrium and ventricle (initial) 37.72
          replacement 37.76
      epicardium (sternotomy or thoraco-
          tomy approach) 37.74
      left ventricular coronary venous sys-
          tem 00.52
      temporary transvenous pacemaker
          system 37.78
          during and immediately follow-
              ing cardiac surgery 39.64
      ventricle (initial) 37.71
          replacement 37.76
  intracranial 02.93
  osteogenic (for bone growth stimula-
      tion) — *see* category 78.9 ☑
  peripheral nerve 04.92
  sacral nerve 04.92
  sphenoidal 02.96
  spine 03.93
electroencephalographic receiver — *see*
    Implant, electroencephalographic
    receiver, by site
electronic stimulator — *see* Implant, elec-
    tronic stimulator, by site
electrostimulator — *see* Implant, electronic
    stimulator, by site
endograft(s), endovascular graft(s)
  endovascular, abdominal aorta 39.71
      fenestrated (branching) 39.78
  endovascular, head and neck vessels
      39.72
  endovascular, other vessels (for
      aneurysm) 39.79
  endovascular, thoracic aorta 39.73
endoprosthesis
  bile duct 51.87
  femoral head (bipolar) 81.52
  pancreatic duct 52.93
envelope, antimicrobial 17.81
epidural pegs 02.93
external fixation device (bone) — *see* cate-
    gory 78.1 ☑
eye valve implant 12.67
facial bone implant (alloplastic) (synthetic)
    76.92
filling material, skin (filling of defect) 86.02
filter
  vena cava (inferior) (superior) (transve-
      nous) 38.7
fixator, mini device (bone) — *see* category
    78.1 ☑
frame (stereotactic)
  for radiosurgery 93.59
Gardner Wells tongs (skull) (with syn-
    chronous skeletal traction) 02.94
gastric bubble (balloon) 44.93
globe, into eye socket 16.69
Greenfield filter 38.7
halo device (skull) (with synchronous
    skeletal traction) 02.94

Insertion — *continued*
Harrington rod (*see also* Fusion, spinal, by
    level)
  with dorsal, dorsolumbar fusion 81.05
Harris pin 79.15
heart
  assist system — *see* Implant, heart assist
      system
  cardiac support device (CSD) 37.41
  circulatory assist system — *see* Implant,
      heart assist system
  CorCap™ 37.41
  epicardial support device 37.41
  Impella® 37.68
  pacemaker — *see* Insertion, pacemaker,
      cardiac
  prosthetic cardiac support device 37.41
  pump (Kantrowitz) 37.62
  valve — *see* Replacement, heart valve
  ventricular support device 37.41
hip prosthesis (partial) 81.52
  revision NOS 81.53
      acetabular and femoral components
          (total) 00.70
      acetabular component only 00.71
      acetabular liner and/or femoral head
          only 00.73
      femoral component only 00.72
      femoral head only and/or acetabular
          liner 00.73
      partial
          acetabular component only 00.71
          acetabular liner and/or femoral
              head only 00.73
          femoral component only 00.72
          femoral head only and/or acetab-
              ular liner 00.73
      total (acetabular and femoral compo-
          nents) 00.70
  total 81.51
      revision
          acetabular and femoral compo-
              nents (total) 00.70
          total (acetabular and femoral
              components) 00.70
Holter valve 02.22
Hufnagel valve — *see* Replacement, heart
    valve
implant — *see* Insertion, prosthesis
infusion pump 86.06
interbody spinal fusion device 84.51
intercostal catheter (with water seal), for
    drainage 34.04
  revision (with lysis of adhesions) 34.04
  thoracoscopic 34.06
intra-arterial blood gas monitoring system
    89.60
intrauterine
  contraceptive device 69.7
  radium (intracavitary) 69.91
  tamponade (nonobstetric) 69.91
Kantrowitz
  heart pump 37.62
  pulsation balloon (phase-shift) 37.61
keratoprosthesis 11.73
King-Mills umbrella device (heart) 35.52
Kirschner wire 93.44
  with reduction of fracture or dislocation
      — *see* Reduction, fracture *and*
      Reduction, dislocation
knee prosthesis (partial) (total) 81.54
  revision NOS 81.55
      femoral component 00.82
      partial
          femoral component 00.82
          patellar component 00.83
          tibial component 00.81
          tibial insert 00.84
      patellar component 00.83
      tibial component 00.81
      tibial insert 00.84
      total (all components) 00.80
laminaria, cervix 69.93
Lap-Band™ 44.95
larynx, valved tube 31.75
leads — *see* Insertion, electrode(s)

Insertion — *continued*
lens, prosthetic (intraocular) 13.70
  with cataract extraction, one-stage 13.71
  secondary (subsequent to cataract extrac-
      tion) 13.72
limb lengthening device, internal, NOS 84.54
  with kinetic distraction 84.53
loop recorder 37.79
M-Brace™ 84.82
metal staples into epiphyseal plate (*see also*
    Stapling, epiphyseal plate) 78.20
minifixator device (bone) — *see* category
    78.1 ☑
Mobitz-Uddin umbrella, vena cava 38.7
mold, vagina 96.15
Moore (cup) 81.52
Myringotomy device (button) (tube) 20.01
  with intubation 20.01
nasobiliary drainage tube (endoscopic)
    51.86
nasogastric tube
  for
      decompression, intestinal 96.07
      feeding 96.6
naso-intestinal tube 96.08
nasolacrimal tube or stent 09.44
nasopancreatic drainage tube (endoscopic)
    52.97
neuropacemaker — *see* Implant, neurostim-
    ulator, by site
neurostimulator — *see* Implant, neurostim-
    ulator, by site
non-coronary vessel
  stent(s) (stent graft)

*Note: Also use 00.40, 00.41, 00.42, or
00.43 to show the total number of vessels treated. Use code 00.44 once to
show procedure on a bifurcated vessel.
In addition, use 00.45, 00.46, 00.47, or
00.48 to show the number of vascular
stents inserted.*

  with
      angioplasty 39.50
      atherectomy 17.56
      basilar 00.64
      bypass — *omit code*
      carotid 00.63
      extracranial 00.64
      intracranial 00.65
      peripheral 39.90
          bare, drug-coated 39.90
          drug-eluting 00.55
      vertebral 00.64
  non-invasive (transcutaneous) (surface)
      stimulator 99.86
obturator (orthodontic) 24.7
ocular implant
  with synchronous
      enucleation 16.42
          with muscle attachment to im-
              plant 16.41
          evisceration 16.31
      following or secondary to enucleation
          16.61
      evisceration 16.61
Ommaya reservoir 02.22
orbital implant (stent) (outside muscle cone)
    16.69
  with orbitotomy 16.02
orthodontic appliance (obturator) (wiring)
    24.7
outflow tract prosthesis (gusset type) (heart)
    in
      pulmonary valvuloplasty 35.26
      total repair of tetralogy of Fallot
          35.81
pacemaker
  brain — *see* Implant, neurostimulator,
      brain
  cardiac (device) (initial) (permanent)
      (replacement) 37.80
      dual-chamber device (initial) 37.83
          replacement 37.87
      during and immediately following
          cardiac surgery 39.64

Insertion — *continued*
- pacemaker — *continued*
  - cardiac — *continued*
    - resynchronization (biventricular pacemaker) (BiV pacemaker) (CRT-P) (device)
      - device only (initial) (replacement) 00.53
      - total system (device and one or more leads) 00.50
      - transvenous lead into left ventricular coronary venous system 00.52
    - single-chamber device (initial) 37.81
      - rate responsive 37.82
      - replacement 37.85
        - rate responsive 37.86
    - temporary transvenous pacemaker system 37.78
      - during and immediately following cardiac surgery 39.64
  - carotid 39.89
  - gastric 04.92
  - heart — *see* Insertion, pacemaker, cardiac
  - intracranial — *see* Implant, neurostimulator, intracranial
  - neural — *see* Implant, neurostimulator, by site
  - peripheral nerve — *see* Implant, neurostimulator, peripheral nerve
  - spine — *see* Implant, neurostimulator, spine
- pacing catheter — *see* Insertion, pacemaker, cardiac
- pack
  - auditory canal, external 96.11
  - cervix (nonobstetrical) 67.0
    - after delivery or abortion 75.8
    - to assist delivery or induce labor 73.1
  - rectum 96.19
  - sella turcica 07.79
  - vagina (nonobstetrical) 96.14
    - after delivery or abortion 75.8
- palatal implant 27.64
- penile prosthesis (non-inflatable) (internal) 64.95
  - inflatable (internal) 64.97
- peridontal splint (orthodontic) 24.7
- peripheral blood vessel — *see* non-coronary
- pessary
  - cervix 96.18
    - to assist delivery or induce labor 73.1
  - vagina 96.18
- pharyngeal valve, artificial 31.75
- port, vascular access 86.07
- prostaglandin suppository (for abortion) 96.49
- prosthesis, prosthetic device
  - acetabulum (partial) 81.52
    - hip 81.52
      - revision NOS 81.53
        - acetabular and femoral components (total) 00.70
        - acetabular component only 00.71
        - acetabular liner and/or femoral head only 00.73
        - femoral component only 00.72
        - femoral head only and/or acetabular liner 00.73
        - partial
          - acetabular component only 00.71
          - acetabular liner and/or femoral head only 00.73
          - femoral component only 00.72
          - femoral head only and/or acetabular liner 00.73
        - total (acetabular and femoral components) 00.70

Insertion — *continued*
- prosthesis, prosthetic device — *continued*
  - acetabulum — *continued*
    - revision 81.53
  - ankle (total) 81.56
  - arm (bioelectric) (cineplastic) (kineplastic) 84.44
  - biliary tract 51.99
  - breast (bilateral) 85.54
    - unilateral 85.53
  - cardiac support device (CSD) (CorCap™) 37.41
  - chin (polyethylene) (silastic) 76.68
  - elbow (total) 81.84
    - revision 81.97
  - extremity (bioelectric) (cineplastic) (kineplastic) 84.40
    - lower 84.48
    - upper 84.44
  - fallopian tube 66.93
  - femoral head (Austin-Moore) (bipolar) (Eicher) (Thompson) 81.52
  - hip (partial) 81.52
    - revision NOS 81.53
      - acetabular and femoral components (total) 00.70
      - acetabular component only 00.71
      - acetabular liner and/or femoral head only 00.73
      - femoral component only 00.72
      - femoral head only and/or acetabular liner 00.73
      - partial
        - acetabular component only 00.71
        - acetabular liner and/or femoral head only 00.73
        - femoral component only 00.72
        - femoral head only and/or acetabular liner 00.73
      - total (acetabular and femoral components) 00.70
    - total 81.51
      - revision
        - acetabular and femoral components (total) 00.70
        - total (acetabular and femoral components) 00.70
  - joint — *see* Arthroplasty
  - knee (partial) (total) 81.54
    - revision NOS 81.55
      - femoral component 00.82
      - partial
        - femoral component 00.82
        - patellar component 00.83
        - tibial component 00.81
        - tibial insert 00.84
      - patellar component 00.83
      - tibial component 00.81
      - tibial insert 00.84
      - total (all components) 00.80
  - leg (bioelectric) (cineplastic) (kineplastic) 84.48
  - lens 13.91
  - ocular (secondary) 16.61
    - with orbital exenteration 16.42
  - outflow tract (gusset type) (heart)
    - in
      - pulmonary valvuloplasty 35.26
      - total repair of tetralogy of Fallot 35.81
  - penis (internal) (noninflatable) 64.95
    - with
      - construction 64.43
      - reconstruction 64.44
    - inflatable (internal) 64.97
  - Rosen (for urinary incontinence) 59.79
  - shoulder
    - partial 81.81
    - revision 81.97
    - total, NEC 81.80
      - other 81.80
      - reverse 81.88

Insertion — *continued*
- prosthesis, prosthetic device — *continued*
  - spine
    - artificial disc, NOS 84.60
      - cervical 84.62
        - nucleus 84.61
        - partial 84.61
        - total 84.62
      - lumbar, lumbosacral 84.65
        - nucleus 84.64
        - partial 84.64
        - total 84.65
      - thoracic (partial) (total) 84.63
    - other device 84.59
  - testicular (bilateral) (unilateral) 62.7
  - toe 81.57
    - hallux valgus repair 77.59
  - vagina
    - synthetic 70.95
- pseudophakos (*see also* Insertion, lens) 13.70
- pump, infusion 86.06
- radioactive isotope 92.27
- radium 92.27
- radon seeds 92.27
- Reuter bobbin (with intubation) 20.01
- Rickham reservoir 02.22
- Rosen prosthesis (for urinary incontinence) 59.79
- Scribner shunt 39.93
- Sengstaken-Blakemore tube 96.06
- sensor (lead)
  - intra-aneurysm sac pressure monitoring device 00.58
  - intra-arterial, for continuous blood gas monitoring 89.60
  - intracardiac or great vessel hemodynamic monitoring
    - with lead 00.56
    - without lead 38.26
- shunt — *see* Shunt
- sieve, vena cava 38.7
- skeletal muscle stimulator 83.92
- skull
  - plate 02.05
  - stereotactic frame 93.59
  - tongs (Barton) (caliper) (Garder Wells) (Vinke) (with synchronous skeletal traction) 02.94
- spacer (cement) (joint) (methylmethacrylate) 84.56
  - spine 84.51
- sphenoidal electrodes 02.96
- spine
  - bone void filler
    - that with percutaneous vertebral augmentation 81.66
    - that with percutaneous vertebroplasty 81.65
  - cage (BAK) 84.51
  - facet replacement device(s) 84.84
  - interbody spinal fusion device 84.51
  - interspinous process decompression device 84.80
  - non-fusion stabilization device — *see* category 84.8
  - pedicle-based dynamic stabilization device(s) 84.82
  - posterior motion preservation device(s) — *see* category 84.8
  - spacer 84.51
- Spitz-Holter valve 02.2 ☑
- Steinmann pin 93.44
  - with reduction of fracture or dislocation — *see* Reduction, fracture *and* Reduction, dislocation
- stent(s) (stent graft)
  - aqueous drainage 12.67

Insertion — *continued*
- stent(s) — *continued*
  - artery (bare) (bonded) (drug-coated) (non-drug-eluting)

    Note — Also use 00.40, 00.41, 00.42, or 00.43 to show the total number of vessels treated. Use code 00.44 once to show procedure on a bifurcated vessel. In addition, use 00.45, 00.46, 00.47, or 00.48 to show the number of vascular stents inserted.

    - basilar 00.64
    - carotid 00.63
    - cerebrovascular
      - cerebral (intracranial) 00.65
      - precerebral (extracranial) 00.64
        - carotid 00.63
    - coronary (bare) (bonded) (drug-coated) (non-drug-eluting) 36.06
      - drug-eluting 36.07
    - extracranial 00.64
      - carotid 00.63
    - femoral artery, superficial 39.90
      - drug-eluting 00.60
      - non-drug-eluting 39.90
    - intracranial 00.65
    - non-coronary vessel
      - basilar 00.64
      - carotid 00.63
      - extracranial 00.64
      - intracranial 00.65
      - peripheral 39.90
        - bare, drug-coated 39.90
        - drug-eluting 00.55
      - vertebral 00.64
  - bile duct 51.43
    - endoscopic 51.87
    - percutaneous transhepatic 51.98
  - colon
    - endoscopic (fluoroscopic guidance) 46.86
    - other 46.87
  - coronary (artery) (bare) (bonded) (drug-coated) (non-drug-eluting) 36.06

    Note — Also use 00.40, 00.41, 00.42, or 00.43 to show the total number of vessels treated. Use code 00.44 once to show procedure on a bifurcated vessel. In addition, use 00.45, 00.46, 00.47, or 00.48 to show the number of vascular stents inserted.

    - drug-eluting 36.07
  - esophagus (endoscopic) (fluoroscopic) 42.81
  - mesenteric 39.90
    - bare, drug-coated 39.90
    - drug-eluting 00.55
  - non-coronary vessel

    Note — Also use 00.40, 00.41, 00.42, or 00.43 to show the total number of vessels treated. Use code 00.44 once to show procedure on a bifurcated vessel. In addition, use 00.45, 00.46, 00.47, or 00.48 to show the number of vascular stents inserted.

    - with angioplasty or atherectomy 39.50
    - with bypass — *omit code*
    - basilar 00.64
    - carotid 00.63
    - extracranial 00.64
    - femoral artery, superficial 39.90
      - drug-eluting 00.60
      - non-drug-eluting 39.90
    - intracranial 00.65
    - mesenteric 39.90
      - bare, drug-coated 39.90
      - drug-eluting 00.55
    - peripheral 39.90
      - bare, drug-coated 39.90
      - drug-eluting 00.55
    - renal 39.90
      - bare, drug-coated 39.90

☑ Additional Digit Required — Refer to the Tabular List for Digit Selection

Subterms under main terms may continue to next column or page

2015 ICD-9-CM

▶◀ Revised Text ● New Line ▲ Revised Code

Volume 3 — 33

Insertion — Insertion

Insertion — *continued*
  stent(s) — *continued*
    non-coronary vessel — *continued*
      renal — *continued*
        drug-eluting 00.55
      vertebral 00.64
    pancreatic duct 52.92
      endoscopic 52.93
    peripheral vessel 39.90

> *Note* — *Also use 00.40, 00.41, 00.42, or 00.43 to show the total number of vessels treated. Use code 00.44 once to show procedure on a bifurcated vessel. In addition, use 00.45, 00.46, 00.47, or 00.48 to show the number of vascular stents inserted.*

      bare, drug-coated 39.90
      drug-eluting 00.55
      femoral artery, superficial, drug-eluting 00.60
      precerebral 00.64

> *Note* — *Also use 00.40, 00.41, 00.42, or 00.43 to show the total number of vessels treated. Use code 00.44 once to show procedure on a bifurcated vessel. In addition, use 00.45, 00.46, 00.47, or 00.48 to show the number of vascular stents inserted.*

    renal 39.90
      bare, drug-coated 39.90
      drug-eluting 00.55
    subclavian 39.90

> *Note* — *Also use 00.40, 00.41, 00.42, or 00.43 to show the total number of vessels treated. Use code 00.44 once to show procedure on a bifurcated vessel In addition, use 00.45, 00.46, 00.47, or 00.48 to show the number of vascular stents inserted.*

      bare, drug-coated 39.90
      drug-eluting 00.55
    tracheobronchial 96.05
    vertebral 00.64

> *Note* — *Also use 00.40, 00.41, 00.42, or 00.43 to show the total number of vessels treated. Use code 00.44 once to show procedure on a bifurcated vessel. In addition, use 00.45, 00.46, 00.47, or 00.48 to show the number of vascular stents inserted.*

  sternal fixation device with rigid plates 84.94
  stimoceiver — *see* Implant, neurostimulator, by site
  stimulator for bone growth — *see* category 78.9 ☑
  subdural
    grids 02.93
    strips 02.93
  suppository
    prostaglandin (for abortion) 96.49
    vagina 96.49
  Swan-Ganz catheter (pulmonary) 89.64
  tampon
    esophagus 96.06
    uterus 69.91
    vagina 96.14
      after delivery or abortion 75.8
  Tandem™ heart 37.68
  telescope (IMT) (miniature) 13.91
  testicular prosthesis (bilateral) (unilateral) 62.7
  tissue expander (skin) NEC 86.93
    breast 85.95
  tissue mandril (peripheral vessel) (Dacron) (Spark's type) 39.99
    with
      blood vessel repair 39.56
      vascular bypass or shunt — *see* Bypass, vascular
  tongs, skull (with synchronous skeletal traction) 02.94

Insertion — *continued*
  totally implanted device for bone growth (invasive) — *see* category 78.9 ☑
  tube (*see also* Catheterization and Intubation)
    bile duct 51.43
      endoscopic 51.87
    chest 34.04
      revision (with lysis of adhesions) 34.04
        thoracoscopic 34.06
      thoracoscopic 34.06
    endotracheal 96.04
    esophagus (nonoperative) (Sengstaken) 96.06
      permanent (silicone) (Souttar) 42.81
    feeding
      esophageal 42.81
      gastric 96.6
      nasogastric 96.6
    gastric
      by gastrostomy — *see* category 43.1 ☑
      for
        decompression, intestinal 96.07
        feeding 96.6
    intercostal catheter (with water seal), for drainage 34.04
      revision (with lysis of adhe-sions) 34.04
        thoracoscopic 34.06
      thoracoscopic 34.06
    Miller-Abbott (for intestinal decompression) 96.08
    nasobiliary (drainage) 51.86
    nasogastric (for intestinal decompression) NEC 96.07
    naso-intestinal 96.08
    nasopancreatic drainage (endoscopic) 52.97
    pancreatic duct 52.92
      endoscopic 52.93
    rectum 96.09
    stomach (nasogastric) (for intestinal de-compression) NEC 96.07
      for feeding 96.6
    tracheobronchial 96.05
  umbrella device
    atrial septum (King-Mills) 35.52
    vena cava (Mobitz-Uddin) 38.7
  ureteral stent (transurethral) 59.8
    with ureterotomy 59.8 [56.2]
  urinary sphincter, artificial (AUS) (inflatable) 58.93
  vaginal mold 96.15
  valve(s)
    bronchus
      multiple lobes 33.73
      single lobe 33.71
    Holter 02.22
    Hufnagel — *see* Replacement, heart valve
    pharyngeal (artificial) 31.75
    Spitz-Holter 02.22
    vas deferens 63.95
  vascular access device, totally implantable 86.07
  vena cava sieve or umbrella 38.7
  Vinke tongs (skull) (with synchronous skeletal traction) 02.94
  X Stop™ 84.80

Instillation
  bladder 96.49
  digestive tract, except gastric gavage 96.43
  genitourinary NEC 96.49
  radioisotope (intracavitary) (intravenous) 92.28
  thoracic cavity 34.92

Insufflation
  Eustachian tube 20.8
  fallopian tube (air) (dye) (gas) (saline) 66.8
    for radiography — *see* Hysterosalpingography
    therapeutic substance 66.95
  lumbar retroperitoneal, bilateral 88.15

Intercricothyroidotomy (for assistance in breathing) 31.1
Interleukin-2, infusion
  high-dose 00.15
  low-dose 99.28
Intermittent positive pressure breathing (IPPB) 93.91
Interposition operation
  antesternal or antethoracic NEC (*see also* Anastomosis, esophagus, antesternal, with, interposition) 42.68
  esophageal reconstruction (intrathoracic) (retrosternal) NEC (*see also* Anastomosis, esophagus, with, interposition) 42.58
  uterine suspension 69.21
Interrogation
  cardioverter-defibrillator, automatic (AICD)
    with catheter based invasive electrophysiologic testing 37.26
    with NIPS (arrhythmia induction) 37.20
    interrogation only (bedside device check) 89.49
  CRT-D (cardiac resynchronization defibrillator)
    with catheter based invasive electrophysiologic testing 37.26
    with NIPS (arrhythmia induction) 37.20
    interrogation only (bedside device check) 89.49
  CRT-P (cardiac resynchronization pacemaker)
    with catheter based invasive electrophysiologic testing 37.26
    with NIPS (arrhythmia induction) 37.20
    interrogation only (bedside device check) 89.45
  pacemaker
    with catheter based invasive electrophysiologic testing 37.26
    with NIPS (arrhythmia induction) 37.20
    interrogation only (bedside device check) 89.45
Interruption
  vena cava (inferior) (superior) 38.7
Interview (evaluation) (diagnostic)
  medical, except psychiatric 89.05
    brief (abbreviated history) 89.01
    comprehensive (history and evaluation of new problem) 89.03
    limited (interval history) 89.02
    specified type NEC 89.04
  psychiatric NEC 94.19
    follow-up 94.19
    initial 94.19
    pre-commitment 94.13
Intimectomy 38.10
  abdominal 38.16
  aorta (arch) (ascending) (descending) 38.14
  head and neck NEC 38.12
  intracranial NEC 38.11
  lower limb 38.18
  thoracic NEC 38.15
  upper limb 38.13
Intraoperative anesthetic effect monitoring and titration (IAEMT) 00.94 [89.14]
Introduction
  orthodontic appliance 24.7
  therapeutic substance (acting locally or systemically) NEC 99.29
    bursa 83.96
      hand 82.94
    fascia 83.98
      hand 82.96
    heart 37.92
    joint 81.92
      temporomandibular 76.96
    ligament (joint) 81.92
    pericardium 37.93
    soft tissue NEC 83.98
      hand 82.96
    tendon 83.97
      hand 82.95
    vein 39.92
Intubation — *see also* Catheterization and Insertion

Intubation — *see also* Catheterization and Insertion — *continued*
  bile duct(s) 51.59
    common 51.51
      endoscopic 51.87
    endoscopic 51.87
  esophagus (nonoperative) (Sengstaken) 96.06
    permanent tube (silicone) (Souttar) 42.81
  Eustachian tube 20.8
  intestine (for decompression) 96.08
  lacrimal for
    dilation 09.42
    tear drainage, intranasal 09.81
  larynx 96.05
  nasobiliary (drainage) 51.86
  nasogastric
    for
      decompression, intestinal 96.07
      feeding 96.6
  naso-intestinal 96.08
  nasolacrimal (duct) (with irrigation) 09.44
  nasopancreatic drainage (endoscopic) 52.97
  respiratory tract NEC 96.05
  small intestine (Miller-Abbott) 96.08
  stomach (nasogastric) (for intestinal decompression) NEC 96.07
    for feeding 96.6
  trachea 96.04
  ventriculocisternal 02.22
Invagination, diverticulum
  gastric 44.69
    laparoscopic 44.68
  pharynx 29.59
  stomach 44.69
    laparoscopic 44.68
Inversion
  appendix 47.99
  diverticulum
    gastric 44.69
      laparoscopic 44.68
    intestine
      large 45.49
        endoscopic 45.43
      small 45.34
    stomach 44.69
      laparoscopic 44.68
  tunica vaginalis 61.49
IOERT (intra-operative electron radiation therapy) 92.41
IOM (intra-operative neurophysiologic monitoring) 00.94
Ionization, medical 99.27
Iontherapy 99.27
Iontophoresis 99.27
Iridectomy (basal) (buttonhole) (optical) (peripheral) (total) 12.14
  with
    capsulectomy 13.65
    cataract extraction — *see* Extraction, cataract
    filtering operation (for glaucoma) NEC 12.65
    scleral
      fistulization 12.65
      thermocauterization 12.62
      trephination 12.61
Iridencleisis 12.63
Iridesis 12.63
Irido-capsulectomy 13.65
Iridocyclectomy 12.44
Iridocystectomy 12.42
Iridodesis 12.63
Iridoplasty NEC 12.39
Iridosclerectomy 12.65
Iridosclerotomy 12.69
Iridotasis 12.63
Iridotomy 12.12
  by photocoagulation 12.12
  with transfixion 12.11
  for iris bombé 12.11
  specified type NEC 12.12
Iron lung 93.99
Irradiation
  gamma, stereotactic 92.32

☑ **Additional Digit Required** — Refer to the Tabular List for Digit Selection
           ⬇ **Subterms under main terms may continue to next column or page**

☑ Additional Digit Required — Refer to the Tabular List for Digit Selection
    Subterms under main terms may continue to next column or page

36 — Volume 3
▶◀ Revised Text
● New Line
▲ Revised Code
2015 ICD-9-CM

Index

Lengthening — Lysis

Lysis — *continued*
　adhesions — *continued*
　　intestines — *continued*
　　　laparoscopic 54.51
　　iris (posterior) 12.33
　　　anterior 12.32
　　joint (capsule) (structure) (*see also* Division, joint capsule) 80.40
　　kidney 59.02
　　　laparoscopic 59.03
　　labia (vulva) 71.01
　　larynx 31.92
　　liver 54.59
　　　laparoscopic 54.51
　　lung (for collapse of lung) 33.39
　　mediastinum 34.99
　　meninges (spinal) 03.6
　　　cortical 02.91
　　middle ear 20.23
　　muscle 83.91
　　　by stretching or manipulation 93.27
　　　extraocular 15.7
　　　hand 82.91
　　　　by stretching or manipulation 93.26
　　nasopharynx 29.54
　　nerve (peripheral) NEC 04.49
　　　cranial NEC 04.42
　　　roots, spinal 03.6
　　　trigeminal 04.41
　　nose, nasal 21.91
　　ocular muscle 15.7
　　ovary 65.89
　　　laparoscopic 65.81
　　pelvic 54.59
　　　laparoscopic 54.51
　　penile 64.93
　　pericardium 37.12
　　perineal (female) 71.01
　　peripheral vessels 39.91
　　perirectal 48.81
　　perirenal 59.02
　　　laparoscopic 59.03
　　peritoneum (pelvic) 54.59
　　　laparoscopic 54.51
　　periureteral 59.02
　　　laparoscopic 59.03
　　perivesical 59.11
　　　laparoscopic 59.12
　　pharynx 29.54
　　pleura (for collapse of lung) 33.39
　　spermatic cord 63.94
　　spinal (cord) (meninges) (nerve roots) 03.6
　　spleen 54.59
　　　laparoscopic 54.51
　　tendon 83.91
　　　by stretching or manipulation 93.27
　　　hand 82.91
　　　　by stretching or manipulation 93.26
　　thorax 34.99
　　tongue 25.93
　　trachea 31.92
　　tubo-ovarian 65.89
　　　laparoscopic 65.81
　　ureter 59.02
　　　with freeing or repositioning of ureter 59.02
　　　intraluminal 56.81
　　　laparoscopic 59.03
　　urethra (intraluminal) 58.5
　　uterus 54.59
　　　intraluminal 68.21
　　　laparoscopic 54.51
　　　peritoneal 54.59
　　　　laparoscopic 54.51
　　vagina (intraluminal) 70.13
　　vitreous (posterior approach) 14.74
　　　anterior approach 14.73
　　vulva 71.01
　goniosynechiae (with injection of air or liquid) 12.31
　synechiae (posterior) 12.33
　　anterior (with injection of air or liquid) 12.32

M

Madlener operation (tubal ligation) 66.31
Magnet extraction
　foreign body
　　anterior chamber, eye 12.01
　　choroid 14.01
　　ciliary body 12.01
　　conjunctiva 98.22
　　cornea 11.0
　　eye, eyeball NEC 98.21
　　　anterior segment 12.01
　　　posterior segment 14.01
　　intraocular (anterior segment) 12.01
　　iris 12.01
　　lens 13.01
　　orbit 98.21
　　retina 14.01
　　sclera 12.01
　　vitreous 14.01
Magnetic resonance imaging (nuclear) — *see* Imaging, magnetic resonance
Magnuson (-Stack) operation (arthroplasty for recurrent shoulder dislocation) 81.82
Mako Tactile Guidance System™ [TSG] — *see* category 17.4 ☑
Malleostapediopexy 19.19
　with incus replacement 19.11
Malström's vacuum extraction 72.79
　with episiotomy 72.71
Mammaplasty — *see* Mammoplasty
Mammectomy — *see also* Mastectomy
　subcutaneous (unilateral) 85.34
　　with synchronous implant 85.35
　　bilateral 85.36
Mammilliplasty 85.87
Mammography NEC 87.37
Mammoplasty 85.89
　with
　　full-thickness graft 85.83
　　muscle flap 85.85
　　pedicle graft 85.84
　　split-thickness graft 85.82
　amputative (reduction) (bilateral) 85.32
　　unilateral 85.31
　augmentation 85.50
　　with
　　　breast implant (bilateral) 85.54
　　　　unilateral 85.53
　　　injection into breast (bilateral) 85.52
　　　　unilateral 85.51
　reduction (bilateral) 85.32
　　unilateral 85.31
　revision 85.89
　size reduction (gynecomastia) (bilateral) 85.32
　　unilateral 85.31
Mammotomy 85.0
Manchester (-Donald) (-Fothergill) operation (uterine suspension) 69.22
Mandibulectomy (partial) 76.31
　total 76.42
　　with reconstruction 76.41
Maneuver (method)
　Bracht 72.52
　Credé 73.59
　De Lee (key-in-lock) 72.4
　Kristeller 72.54
　Lovest's (extraction of arms in breech birth) 72.52
　Mauriceau (-Smellie-Veit) 72.52
　Pinard (total breech extraction) 72.54
　Prague 72.52
　Ritgen 73.59
　Scanzoni (rotation) 72.4
　Van Hoorn 72.52
　Wigand-Martin 72.52
Manipulation
　with reduction of fracture or dislocation — *see* Reduction, fracture *and* Reduction, dislocation
　enterostomy stoma (with dilation) 96.24
　intestine (intra-abdominal) 46.80
　　large 46.82
　　small 46.81
　joint
　　adhesions 93.26

Manipulation — *continued*
　joint — *continued*
　　adhesions — *continued*
　　　temporomandibular 76.95
　　dislocation — *see* Reduction, dislocation
　lacrimal passage (tract) NEC 09.49
　muscle structures 93.27
　musculoskeletal (physical therapy) NEC 93.29
　nasal septum, displaced 21.88
　osteopathic NEC 93.67
　　for general mobilization (general articulation) 93.61
　　high-velocity, low-amplitude forces (thrusting) 93.62
　　indirect forces 93.65
　　isotonic, isometric forces 93.64
　　low-velocity, high-amplitude forces (springing) 93.63
　　to move tissue fluids 93.66
　rectum 96.22
　salivary duct 26.91
　stomach, intraoperative 44.92
　temporomandibular joint NEC 76.95
　ureteral calculus by catheter
　　with removal 56.0
　　without removal 59.8
　uterus NEC 69.98
　　gravid 75.99
　　inverted
　　　manual replacement (following delivery) 75.94
　　　surgical — *see* Repair, inverted uterus
Manometry
　esophageal 89.32
　spinal fluid 89.15
　urinary 89.21
Manual arts therapy 93.81
Mapping
　cardiac (electrophysiologic) 37.27
　　doppler (flow) 88.72
　electrocardiogram only 89.52
Marckwald operation (cervical os repair) 67.59
Marshall-Marchetti (-Krantz) operation (retropubic urethral suspension) 59.5
Marsupialization — *see also* Destruction, lesion, by site
　cyst
　　Bartholin's 71.23
　　brain 01.59
　　cervical (nabothian) 67.31
　　dental 24.4
　　dentigerous 24.4
　　kidney 55.31
　　larynx 30.01
　　liver 50.21
　　ovary 65.21
　　　laparoscopic 65.23
　　pancreas 52.3
　　pilonidal (open excision) (with partial closure) 86.21
　　salivary gland 26.21
　　spinal (intraspinal) (meninges) 03.4
　　spleen, splenic 41.41
　lesion
　　brain 01.59
　　cerebral 01.59
　　liver 50.21
　pilonidal cyst or sinus (open excision) (with partial closure) 86.21
　pseudocyst, pancreas 52.3
　ranula, salivary gland 26.21
Massage
　cardiac (external) (manual) (closed) 99.63
　　open 37.91
　prostatic 99.94
　rectal (for levator spasm) 99.93
MAST (military anti-shock trousers) 93.58
Mastectomy (complete) (prophylactic) (simple) (unilateral) 85.41
　with
　　excision of regional lymph nodes 85.43
　　　bilateral 85.44
　　preservation of skin and nipple 85.34
　　　with synchronous implant 85.33
　　　bilateral 85.36

Mastectomy — *continued*
　with — *continued*
　　preservation of skin and nipple — *continued*
　　　bilateral — *continued*
　　　　with synchronous implant 85.35
　bilateral 85.42
　extended
　　radical (Urban) (unilateral) 85.47
　　　bilateral 85.48
　　simple (with regional lymphadenectomy) (unilateral) 85.43
　　　bilateral 85.44
　modified radical (unilateral) 85.43
　　bilateral 85.44
　partial 85.23
　radical (Halsted) (Meyer) (unilateral) 85.45
　　bilateral 85.46
　　extended (Urban) (unilateral) 85.47
　　　bilateral 85.48
　modified (unilateral) 85.43
　　bilateral 85.44
　subcutaneous 85.34
　　with synchronous implant 85.33
　　bilateral 85.36
　　　with synchronous implant 85.35
　subtotal 85.23
Masters' stress test (two-step) 89.42
Mastoidectomy (cortical) (conservative) 20.49
　complete (simple) 20.41
　modified radical 20.49
　radical 20.42
　　modified 20.49
　simple (complete) 20.41
Mastoidotomy 20.21
Mastoidotympanectomy 20.42
Mastopexy 85.6
Mastoplasty — *see* Mammoplasty
Mastorrhaphy 85.81
Mastotomy 85.0
Matas operation (aneurysmorrhaphy) 39.52
Mayo operation
　bunionectomy 77.59
　herniorrhaphy
　　laparoscopic 53.43
　　　with graft or prosthesis 53.42
　　　other and open with graft or prosthesis 53.41
　　other open 53.49
　vaginal hysterectomy 68.59
　　laparoscopically assisted (LAVH) 68.51
Maze procedure
　Cox-maze, open 37.33
　maze, modified, endovascular 37.34
　maze, modified, open 37.33
Mazet operation (knee disarticulation) 84.16
McBride operation (bunionectomy with soft tissue correction) 77.53
McBurney operation — *see* Repair, hernia, inguinal
McCall operation (enterocele repair) 70.92
McCauley operation (release of clubfoot) 83.84
McDonald operation (encirclement suture, cervix) 67.59
McIndoe operation (vaginal construction) 70.61
　with graft or prosthesis 70.63
McKeever operation (fusion of first metatarsophalangeal joint for hallux valgus repair) 77.52
McKissock operation (breast reduction) 85.33
McReynolds operation (transposition of pterygium) 11.31
McVay operation
　femoral hernia — *see* Repair, hernia, femoral
　inguinal hernia — *see* Repair, hernia, inguinal
Measurement
　airway resistance 89.38
　anatomic NEC 89.39
　arterial blood gases 89.65
　basal metabolic rate (BMR) 89.39
　blood gases
　　arterial 89.65
　　　continuous intra-arterial 89.60
　　venous 89.66

☑ **Additional Digit Required** — Refer to the Tabular List for Digit Selection　　　　　　　　　▽ **Subterms under main terms may continue to next column or page**

2015 ICD-9-CM　　　　▶◀ Revised Text　　　　● New Line　　　　▲ Revised Code　　　　Volume 3 — 37

☑ **Additional Digit Required** — Refer to the Tabular List for Digit Selection
ⓝᵉʷ **Subterms under main terms may continue to next column or page**
38 — Volume 3   ▶◀ **Revised Text**   ● **New Line**   ▲ **Revised Code**   2015 ICD-9-CM

Nephrostomy — *continued*
  percutaneous — *continued*
    with fragmentation (ultrasound) 55.04
Nephrotomogram, nephrotomography NEC 87.72
Nephrotomy 55.01
Nephroureterectomy (with bladder cuff) 55.51
Nephroureterocystectomy 55.51 [57.79]
Nerve block (cranial) (peripheral) NEC — *see also* Block, by site 04.81
Neurectasis (cranial) (peripheral) 04.91
Neurectomy (cranial) (infraorbital) (occipital) (peripheral) (spinal) NEC 04.07
  gastric (vagus) (see also Vagotomy) 44.00
  opticociliary 12.79
  paracervical 05.22
  presacral 05.24
  retrogasserian 04.07
  sympathetic — *see* Sympathectomy
  trigeminal 04.07
  tympanic 20.91
Neurexeresis NEC 04.07
Neuroablation
  radiofrequency 04.2
Neuroanastomosis (cranial) (peripheral) NEC 04.74
  accessory-facial 04.72
  accessory-hypoglossal 04.73
  hypoglossal-facial 04.71
NeuroFlo™ catheter for partial (temporary) **abdominal aorta occlusion** 39.77
Neurolysis (peripheral nerve) NEC 04.49
  carpal tunnel 04.43
  cranial nerve NEC 04.42
  spinal (cord) (nerve roots) 03.6
  tarsal tunnel 04.44
  trigeminal nerve 04.41
Neuromonitoring
  intra-operative 00.94
Neuroplasty (cranial) (peripheral) NEC 04.79
  of old injury (delayed repair) 04.76
  revision 04.75
Neurorrhaphy (cranial) (peripheral) 04.3
Neurotomy (cranial) (peripheral) (spinal) NEC 04.04
  acoustic 04.01
  glossopharyngeal 29.92
  lacrimal branch 05.0
  retrogasserian 04.02
  sympathetic 05.0
  vestibular 04.01
Neurotripsy (peripheral) NEC 04.03
  trigeminal 04.02
Nicola operation (tenodesis for recurrent dislocation of shoulder) 81.82
Nimodipine, infusion 99.75
NIPS (non-invasive programmed electrical stimulation) 37.20
Nissen operation (fundoplication of stomach) 44.66
  laparoscopic 44.67
Noble operation (plication of small intestine) 46.62
Norman Miller operation (vaginopexy) 70.77
  with graft or prosthesis 70.78
Norton operation (extraperitoneal cesarean section) 74.2
Nuclear magnetic resonance imaging — *see* Imaging, magnetic resonance
Nutrition, concentrated substances
  enteral infusion (of) 96.6
  parenteral, total 99.15
  peripheral parenteral 99.15

O

Ober (-Yount) operation (gluteal-iliotibial fasciotomy) 83.14
Obliteration
  bone cavity (*see also* Osteoplasty) 78.40
  calyceal diverticulum 55.39
  canaliculi 09.6
  cerebrospinal fistula 02.12
  cul-de-sac 70.92
    with graft or prosthesis 70.93
  frontal sinus (with fat) 22.42
  lacrimal punctum 09.91

Obliteration — *continued*
  lumbar pseudomeningocele 03.51
  lymphatic structure(s) (peripheral) 40.9
  maxillary sinus 22.31
  meningocele (sacral) 03.51
  pelvic 68.8
  pleural cavity 34.6
  sacral meningocele 03.51
  Skene's gland 71.3
  tympanomastoid cavity 19.9
  vagina, vaginal (partial) (total) 70.4
  vault 70.8
Occlusal molds (dental) 89.31
Occlusion
  artery
    by embolization — *see* Embolization, artery
    by endovascular approach — *see* Embolization, artery
    by ligation — *see* Ligation, artery
  fallopian tube — *see* Ligation, fallopian tube
  patent ductus arteriosus (PDA) 38.85
  vein
    by embolization — *see* Embolization, vein
    by endovascular approach — *see* Embolization, vein
    by ligation — *see* Ligation, vein
  vena cava (surgical) 38.7
Occupational therapy 93.83
OCT (optical coherence tomography) (intravascular imaging)
  coronary vessel(s) 38.24
  non-coronary vessel(s) 38.25
O'Donoghue operation (triad knee repair) 81.43
Odontectomy NEC — *see also* Removal, tooth, surgical 23.19
Oleothorax 33.39
Olshausen operation (uterine suspension) 69.22
Omentectomy 54.4
Omentofixation 54.74
Omentopexy 54.74
Omentoplasty 54.74
Omentorrhaphy 54.74
Omentotomy 54.19
Omphalectomy 54.3
Onychectomy 86.23
Onychoplasty 86.86
Onychotomy 86.09
  with drainage 86.04
Oophorectomy (unilateral) 65.39
  with salpingectomy 65.49
    laparoscopic 65.41
  bilateral (same operative episode) 65.51
    with salpingectomy 65.61
      laparoscopic 65.63
    laparoscopic 65.53
  laparoscopic 65.31
  partial 65.29
    laparoscopic 65.25
    wedge 65.22
      that by laparoscope 65.24
  remaining ovary 65.52
    with tube 65.62
      laparoscopic 65.64
    laparoscopic 65.54
Oophorocystectomy 65.29
  laparoscopic 65.25
Oophoropexy 65.79
Oophoroplasty 65.79
Oophororrhaphy 65.71
  laparoscopic 65.74
Oophorostomy 65.09
  laparoscopic 65.01
Oophorotomy 65.09
  laparoscopic 65.01
Opening
  bony labyrinth (ear) 20.79
  cranial suture 02.01
  heart valve
    closed heart technique — *see* Valvulotomy, by site
    open heart technique — *see* Valvuloplasty, by site

Opening — *continued*
  spinal dura 03.09
Operation
  Abbe
    construction of vagina 70.61
      with graft or prosthesis 70.63
    intestinal anastomosis — *see* Anastomosis, intestine
  abdominal (region) NEC 54.99
  abdominoperineal, NOS 48.50
    laparoscopic 48.51
    open 48.52
    other 48.59
  Aburel (intra-amniotic injection for abortion) 75.0
  Adams
    advancement of round ligament 69.22
    crushing of nasal septum 21.88
    excision of palmar fascia 82.35
  adenoids NEC 28.99
  adrenal (gland) (nerve) (vessel) NEC 07.49
  Albee
    bone peg, femoral neck 78.05
    graft for slipping patella 78.06
    sliding inlay graft, tibia 78.07
  Albert (arthrodesis, knee) 81.22
  Aldridge (-Studdiford) (urethral sling) 59.5
  Alexander
    prostatectomy
      perineal 60.62
      suprapubic 60.3
    shortening of round ligaments of uterus 69.22
  Alexander-Adams (shortening of round ligaments of uterus) 69.22
  Almoor (extrapetrosal drainage) 20.22
  Alteimer (perineal rectal pull-through) 48.49
  Ammon (dacryocystotomy) 09.53
  Anderson (tibial lengthening) 78.37
  Anel (dilation of lacrimal duct) 09.42
  anterior chamber (eye) NEC 12.99
  anti-incontinence NEC 59.79
  antrum window (nasal sinus) 22.2
    with Caldwell-Luc approach 22.39
  anus NEC 49.99
  aortic body NEC 39.89
  aorticopulmonary window 39.59
  appendix NEC 47.99
  Arslan (fenestration of inner ear) 20.61
  artery NEC 39.99
  Asai (larynx) 31.75
  Baffes (interatrial transposition of venous return) 35.91
  Baldy-Webster (uterine suspension) 69.22
  Ball
    herniorrhaphy — *see* Repair, hernia, inguinal
    undercutting 49.02
  Bankhart (capsular repair into glenoid, for shoulder dislocation) 81.82
  Bardenheurer (ligation of innominate artery) 38.85
  Barkan (goniotomy) 12.52
    with goniopuncture 12.53
  Barr (transfer of tibialis posterior tendon) 83.75
  Barsky (closure of cleft hand) 82.82
  Bassett (vulvectomy with inguinal lymph node dissection) 71.5 [40.3]
  Bassini (herniorrhaphy) — *see* Repair, hernia, inguinal
  Batch-Spittler-McFaddin (knee disarticulation) 84.16
  Batista (partial ventriculectomy) (ventricular reduction) (ventricular remodeling) 37.35
  Beck I (epicardial poudrage) 36.39
  Beck II (aorta-coronary sinus shunt) 36.39
  Beck-Jianu (permanent gastrostomy) 43.19
  Bell-Beuttner (subtotal abdominal hysterectomy) 68.39
  Belsey (esophagogastric sphincter) 44.65
  Benenenti (rotation of bulbous urethra) 58.49
  Berke (levator resection eyelid) 08.33

Operation — *continued*
  Biesenberger (size reduction of breast, bilateral) 85.32
    unilateral 85.31
  Bigelow (litholapaxy) 57.0
  biliary (duct) (tract) NEC 51.99
  Billroth I (partial gastrectomy with gastroduodenostomy) 43.6
  Billroth II (partial gastrectomy with gastrojejunostomy) 43.7
  Binnie (hepatopexy) 50.69
  Bischoff (ureteroneocystostomy) 56.74
  bisection hysterectomy 68.39
    laparoscopic 68.31
  Bishoff (spinal myelotomy) 03.29
  bladder NEC 57.99
    flap 56.74
  Blalock (systemic-pulmonary anastomosis) 39.0
  Blalock-Hanlon (creation of atrial septal defect) 35.42
  Blalock-Taussig (subclavian-pulmonary anastomosis) 39.0
  Blascovic (resection and advancement of levator palpebrae superioris) 08.33
  blood vessel NEC 39.99
  Blount
    by epiphyseal stapling 78.25
    femoral shortening (with blade plate) 78.25
  Boari (bladder flap) 56.74
  Bobb (cholelithotomy) 51.04
  bone NEC — *see* category 78.4 ☑
    facial 76.99
    injury NEC — *see* category 79.9 ☑
    marrow NEC 41.98
    skull NEC 02.99
  Bonney (abdominal hysterectomy) 68.49
    laparoscopic 68.41
  Borthen (iridotasis) 12.63
  Bost
    plantar dissection 80.48
    radiocarpal fusion 81.26
  Bosworth
    arthroplasty for acromioclavicular separation 81.83
    fusion of posterior lumbar spine 81.08
      for pseudarthrosis 81.38
    resection of radial head ligaments (for tennis elbow) 80.92
    shelf procedure, hip 81.40
  Bottle (repair of hydrocele of tunica vaginalis) 61.2
  Boyd (hip disarticulation) 84.18
  brain NEC 02.99
  Brauer (cardiolysis) 37.10
  breast NEC 85.99
  Bricker (ileoureterostomy) 56.51
  Bristow (repair of shoulder dislocation) 81.82
  Brock (pulmonary valvulotomy) 35.03
  Brockman (soft tissue release for clubfoot) 83.84
  bronchus NEC 33.98
  Browne (-Denis) (hypospadias repair) 58.45
  Brunschwig (temporary gastrostomy) 43.19
  buccal cavity NEC 27.99
  Bunnell (tendon transfer) 82.56
  Burch procedure (retropubic urethral suspension for urinary stress incontinence) 59.5
  Burgess (amputation of ankle) 84.14
  bursa NEC 83.99
    hand 82.99
  bypass — *see* Bypass
  Caldwell (sulcus extension) 24.91
  Caldwell-Luc (maxillary sinusotomy) 22.39
    with removal of membrane lining 22.31
  Callander (knee disarticulation) 84.16
  Campbell
    bone block, ankle 81.11
    fasciotomy (iliac crest) 83.14
    reconstruction of anterior cruciate ligaments 81.45
  canthus NEC 08.99
  cardiac NEC 37.99

☑ **Additional Digit Required** — Refer to the Tabular List for Digit Selection

▽ **Subterms under main terms may continue to next column or page**

Operation — Operation

☑ **Additional Digit Required** — Refer to the Tabular List for Digit Selection   ▽ **Subterms under main terms may continue to next column or page**

42 — Volume 3   ▶◀ Revised Text   ● New Line   ▲ Revised Code   2015 ICD-9-CM

☑ **Additional Digit Required** — Refer to the Tabular List for Digit Selection   ⬇ **Subterms under main terms may continue to next column or page**

2015 ICD-9-CM   ▶◀ Revised Text   ● New Line   ▲ Revised Code   Volume 3 — 43

☑ Additional Digit Required — Refer to the Tabular List for Digit Selection   ▽ Subterms under main terms may continue to next column or page

☑ Additional Digit Required — Refer to the Tabular List for Digit Selection   ▽ Subterms under main terms may continue to next column or page

46 — Volume 3   ▶◀ Revised Text   ● New Line   ▲ Revised Code   2015 ICD-9-CM

Reattachment — continued

extremity — continued
  forearm 84.23
  hand 84.23
  leg (lower) NEC 84.27
  thigh 84.28
  thumb 84.21
  toe 84.25
  wrist 84.23
finger 84.22
  thumb 84.21
foot 84.26
forearm 84.23
hand 84.23
joint capsule (see also Arthroplasty) 81.96
leg (lower) NEC 84.27
ligament (see also Arthroplasty)
  uterosacral 69.22
muscle 83.74
  hand 82.54
  papillary (heart) 35.31
nerve (peripheral) 04.79
nose (amputated) 21.89
papillary muscle (heart) 35.31
penis (amputated) 64.45
retina (and choroid) NEC 14.59
  by
    cryotherapy 14.52
    diathermy 14.51
    electrocoagulation 14.51
    photocoagulation 14.55
      laser 14.54
      xenon arc 14.53
tendon (to tendon) 83.73
  hand 82.53
  to skeletal attachment 83.88
    hand 82.85
thigh 84.28
thumb 84.21
toe 84.25
tooth 23.5
uterosacral ligament(s) 69.22
vessels (peripheral) 39.59
  renal, aberrant 39.55
wrist 84.23

Recession

extraocular muscle 15.11
  multiple (two or more muscles) (with advancement or resection) 15.3
gastrocnemius tendon (Strayer operation) 83.72
levator palpebrae (superioris) muscle 08.38
prognathic jaw 76.64
tendon 83.72
  hand 82.52

Reclosure — see also Closure
  disrupted abdominal wall (postoperative) 54.61

Reconstruction (plastic) — see also Construction and Repair, by site
  alveolus, alveolar (process) (ridge) (with graft or implant) 24.5
  artery (graft) — see Graft, artery
  artificial stoma, intestine 46.40
  auditory canal (external) 18.6
  auricle (ear) 18.71
  bladder 57.87
    with
      ileum 57.87 [45.51]
      sigmoid 57.87 [45.52]
  bone, except facial (see also Osteoplasty) 78.40
  facial NEC 76.46
    with total ostectomy 76.44
  mandible 76.43
    with total mandibulectomy 76.41
  breast, total NOS 85.70
    deep inferior epigastric artery perforator (DIEP) flap, free 85.74
    gluteal artery perforator (GAP) flap, free 85.76
    latissimus dorsi myocutaneous flap 85.71
    other 85.79
    superficial inferior epigastric artery (SIEA) flap, free 85.75

Reconstruction — see also Construction and Repair, by site — continued

breast, total — continued
  transverse rectus abdominis musculocutaneous (TRAM) flap, free 85.73
  transverse rectus abdominis myocutaneous (TRAM) flap, pedicled 85.72
bronchus 33.48
canthus (lateral) 08.59
cardiac annulus 35.33
chest wall (mesh) (silastic) 34.79
cleft lip 27.54
conjunctival cul-de-sac 10.43
  with graft (buccal mucous membrane) (free) 10.42
cornea NEC 11.79
diaphragm 34.84
ear (external) (auricle) 18.71
  external auditory canal 18.6
  meatus (new) (osseous skin-lined) 18.6
  ossicles 19.3
  prominent or protruding 18.5
eyebrow 08.70
eyelid 08.70
  with graft or flap 08.69
    hair follicle 08.63
    mucous membrane 08.62
    skin 08.61
    tarsoconjunctival (one-stage) (two-stage) 08.64
  full-thickness 08.74
    involving lid margin 08.73
  partial-thickness 08.72
    involving lid margin 08.71
eye socket 16.64
  with graft 16.63
fallopian tube 66.79
foot and toes (with fixation device) 81.57
  with prosthetic implant 81.57
frontonasal duct 22.79
hip (total) (with prosthesis) 81.51
intraoral 27.59
joint — see Arthroplasty
lymphatic (by transplantation) 40.9
mandible 76.43
  with total mandibulectomy 76.41
mastoid cavity 19.9
mouth 27.59
nipple NEC 85.87
nose (total) (with arm flap) (with forehead flap) 21.83
ossicles (graft) (prosthesis) NEC 19.3
  with
    stapedectomy 19.19
    tympanoplasty 19.53
pelvic floor 71.79
penis (rib graft) (skin graft) (myocutaneous flap) 64.44
pharynx 29.4
scrotum (with pedicle flap) (with rotational flap) 61.49
skin (plastic) (without graft) NEC 86.89
  with graft — see Graft, skin
subcutaneous tissue (plastic) (without skin graft) NEC 86.89
  with graft — see Graft, skin
tendon pulley — (with graft) (with local tissue) 83.83
  for opponensplasty 82.71
  hand 82.71
thumb (osteoplastic) (with bone graft) (with skin graft) 82.69
trachea (with graft) 31.75
umbilicus
  laparoscopic 53.43
    with graft or prosthesis 53.42
  other and open with graft or prosthesis 53.41
  other open 53.49
ureteropelvic junction 55.87
urethra 58.46
vagina 70.62
  with graft or prosthesis 70.64
vas deferens, surgically divided 63.82
Recontour, gingiva 24.2
Recreational therapy 93.81

Rectectomy — see also Resection, rectum 48.69

Rectopexy (Delorme) 48.76
  abdominal (Ripstein) 48.75
Rectoplasty 48.79
Rectorectostomy 48.74
Rectorrhaphy 48.71
Rectosigmoidectomy — see also Resection, rectum 48.69
  transsacral 48.61
Rectosigmoidostomy 45.94
Rectostomy 48.1
  closure 48.72
Red cell survival studies 92.05
Reduction
  adipose tissue 86.83
  batwing arms 86.83
  breast (bilateral) 85.32
    unilateral 85.31
  bulbous tuberosities (mandible) (maxilla) (fibrous) (osseous) 24.31
  buttocks 86.83
  diastasis, ankle mortise (closed) 79.77
    open 79.87
  dislocation (of joint) (manipulation) (with cast) (with splint) (with traction device) (closed) 79.70
    with fracture — see Reduction, fracture, by site
    ankle (closed) 79.77
      open 79.87
    elbow (closed) 79.72
      open 79.82
    finger (closed) 79.74
      open 79.84
    foot (closed) 79.78
      open 79.88
    hand (closed) 79.74
      open 79.84
    hip (closed) 79.75
      open 79.85
    knee (closed) 79.76
      open 79.86
    open (with external fixation) (with internal fixation) 79.80
      specified site NEC 79.89
    shoulder (closed) 79.71
      open 79.81
    specified site (closed) NEC 79.79
      open 79.89
    temporomandibular (closed) 76.93
      open 76.94
    toe (closed) 79.78
      open 79.88
    wrist (closed) 79.73
      open 79.83
  elephantiasis, scrotum 61.3
  epistaxis (see also Control, epistaxis) 21.00
  fracture (bone) (with cast) (with splint) (with traction device) (closed) 79.00
    with internal fixation 79.10
    alveolar process (with stabilization of teeth)
      mandible (closed) 76.75
        open 76.77
      maxilla (closed) 76.73
        open 76.77
    ankle — see Reduction, fracture, leg
    arm (closed) NEC 79.02
      with internal fixation 79.12
      open 79.22
        with internal fixation 79.32
    blow-out — see Reduction, fracture, orbit
    carpal, metacarpal (closed) 79.03
      with internal fixation 79.13
      open 79.23
        with internal fixation 79.33
    epiphysis — see Reduction, separation
    facial (bone) NEC 76.70
      closed 76.78
      open 76.79
    femur (closed) 79.05
      with internal fixation 79.15
      open 79.25

Reduction — continued

fracture — continued
  femur — continued
    open — continued
      with internal fixation 79.35
  fibula (closed) 79.06
    with internal fixation 79.16
    open 79.26
      with internal fixation 79.36
  foot (closed) NEC 79.07
    with internal fixation 79.17
    open 79.27
      with internal fixation 79.37
  hand (closed) NEC 79.03
    with internal fixation 79.13
    open 79.23
      with internal fixation 79.33
  humerus (closed) 79.01
    with internal fixation 79.11
    open 79.21
      with internal fixation 79.31
  jaw (lower) (see also Reduction, fracture, mandible)
    upper — see Reduction, fracture, maxilla
  larynx 31.64
  leg (closed) NEC 79.06
    with internal fixation 79.16
    open 79.26
      with internal fixation 79.36
  malar (closed) 76.71
    open 76.72
  mandible (with dental wiring) (closed) 76.75
    open 76.76
  maxilla (with dental wiring) (closed) 76.73
    open 76.74
  nasal (closed) 21.71
    open 21.72
  open 79.20
    with internal fixation 79.30
    specified site NEC 79.29
      with internal fixation 79.39
  orbit (rim) (wall) (closed) 76.78
    open 76.79
  patella (open) (with internal fixation) 79.36
  phalanges
    foot (closed) 79.08
      with internal fixation 79.18
      open 79.28
        with internal fixation 79.38
    hand (closed) 79.04
      with internal fixation 79.14
      open 79.24
        with internal fixation 79.34
  radius (closed) 79.02
    with internal fixation 79.12
    open 79.22
      with internal fixation 79.32
  skull 02.02
  specified site (closed) NEC 79.09
    with internal fixation 79.19
    open 79.29
      with internal fixation 79.39
  spine 03.53
  tarsal, metatarsal (closed) 79.07
    with internal fixation 79.17
    open 79.27
      with internal fixation 79.37
  tibia (closed) 79.06
    with internal fixation 79.16
    open 79.26
      with internal fixation 79.36
  ulna (closed) 79.02
    with internal fixation 79.12
    open 79.22
      with internal fixation 79.32
  vertebra 03.53
  zygoma, zygomatic arch (closed) 76.71
    open 76.72
fracture-dislocation — see Reduction, fracture
heart volume 37.35
hemorrhoids (manual) 49.41

☑ **Additional Digit Required** — Refer to the Tabular List for Digit Selection

2015 ICD-9-CM

▶◀ Revised Text   ● New Line   ▲ Revised Code

🞃 **Subterms under main terms may continue to next column or page**

Volume 3 — 47

Reattachment — Reduction

Removal — *see also* Excision — *continued*
  calcareous deposit — *continued*
    tendon, intratendinous — *continued*
      hand 82.29
  calcification, heart valve leaflets — *see*
    Valvuloplasty, heart
  calculus
    bile duct (by incision) 51.49
      endoscopic 51.88
      laparoscopic 51.88
      percutaneous 51.98
    bladder (by incision) 57.19
      without incision 57.0
    common duct (by incision) 51.41
      endoscopic 51.88
      laparoscopic 51.88
      percutaneous 51.96
    gallbladder 51.04
      endoscopic 51.88
      laparoscopic 51.88
    kidney (by incision) 55.01
      without incision (transurethral) 56.0
      percutaneous 55.03
        with fragmentation (ultrasound) 55.04
    renal pelvis (by incision) 55.11
      percutaneous nephrostomy 55.03
        with fragmentation 55.04
      transurethral 56.0
    lacrimal
      canaliculi 09.42
        by incision 09.52
      gland 09.3
        by incision 09.0
      passage(s) 09.49
        by incision 09.59
      punctum 09.41
        by incision 09.51
      sac 09.49
        by incision 09.53
    pancreatic duct (by incision) 52.09
      endoscopic 52.94
    perirenal tissue 59.09
    pharynx 29.39
    prostate 60.0
    salivary gland (by incision) 26.0
      by probe 26.91
    ureter (by incision) 56.2
      without incision 56.0
    urethra (by incision) 58.0
      without incision 58.6
  caliper tongs (skull) 02.95
  cannula
    for extracorporeal membrane
      oxygenation (ECMO) — *omit code*
  cardiac pacemaker (device) (initial) (permanent) (cardiac resynchronization device, CRT-P) 37.89
    with replacement
      cardiac resynchronization pacemaker (CRT-P)
        device only 00.53
        total system 00.50
      dual-chamber 37.87
      single-chamber device 37.85
        rate responsive 37.86
  cardioverter/defibrillator pulse generator
    without replacement (cardiac resynchronization defibrillator device (CRT-D) 37.79
  cast 97.88
    with reapplication 97.13
      lower limb 97.12
      upper limb 97.11
  catheter (indwelling) (*see also* Removal, tube)
    bladder 97.64
    cranial cavity 01.27
    middle ear (tympanum) 20.1
    ureter 97.62
    urinary 97.64
  CCM (cardiac contractility modulation)
    without replacement (rechargeable pulse generator) (total system) 37.79
  cerclage material, cervix 69.96
  cerumen, ear 96.52

Removal — *see also* Excision — *continued*
  corneal epithelium 11.41
    for smear or culture 11.21
  coronary artery obstruction (thrombus) 36.09
    direct intracoronary artery infusion 36.04
    open chest approach 36.03
    percutaneous transluminal (balloon) 00.66

> *Note* — *Also use 00.40, 00.41, 00.42, or 00.43 to show the total number of vessels treated. Use code 00.44 once to show procedure on a bifurcated vessel. In addition, use 00.45, 00.46, 00.47, or 00.48 to show the number of vascular stents inserted.*

  Crutchfield tongs (skull) 02.95
    with synchronous replacement 02.94
  cyst (*see also* Excision, lesion, by site)
    dental 24.4
    lung 32.29
      endoscopic 32.28
      thoracoscopic 32.20
  cystic duct remnant 51.61
  decidua (by)
    aspiration curettage 69.52
    curettage (D and C) 69.02
    manual 75.4
  dental wiring (immobilization device) 97.33
    orthodontic 24.8
  device (therapeutic) NEC 97.89
    abdomen NEC 97.86
    bronchus 33.78
      valve 33.78
    digestive system NEC 97.59
    drainage — *see* Removal, tube
    external fixation device 97.88
      mandibular NEC 97.36
      minifixator (bone) — *see* category 78.6 ☑
    for musculoskeletal immobilization NEC 97.88
    genital tract NEC 97.79
    head and neck NEC 97.39
    intrauterine contraceptive 97.71
    spine 80.09
    thorax NEC 97.49
    trunk NEC 97.87
    urinary system NEC 97.69
  diaphragm, vagina 97.73
  drainage device — *see* Removal, tube
  dye, spinal canal 03.31
  ectopic fetus (from) 66.02
    abdominal cavity 74.3
    extraperitoneal (intraligamentous) 74.3
    fallopian tube (by salpingostomy) 66.02
      by salpingotomy 66.01
      with salpingectomy 66.62
    intraligamentous 74.3
    ovarian 74.3
    peritoneal (following uterine or tubal rupture) 74.3
    site NEC 74.3
    tubal (by salpingostomy) 66.02
      by salpingotomy 66.01
      with salpingectomy 66.62
  electrodes
    bone growth stimulator — *see* category 78.6 ☑
    brain 01.22
      depth 01.22
        with synchronous replacement 02.93
      foramen ovale 01.22
        with synchronous replacement 02.93
      sphenoidal — *omit code*
        with synchronous replacement 02.96
    cardiac pacemaker (atrial) (transvenous) (ventricular) 37.77
      with replacement 37.76
    carotid sinus 39.87
      with synchronous pulse generator removal (total system) 39.86
      with synchronous replacement 39.82

Removal — *see also* Excision — *continued*
  electrodes — *continued*
    depth 01.22
      with synchronous replacement 02.93
    epicardial (myocardial) 37.77
      with replacement (by)
        atrial and/or ventricular lead(s) (electrode) 37.76
        epicardial lead 37.74
    epidural pegs 01.22
      with synchronous replacement 02.93
    foramen ovale 01.22
      with synchronous replacement 02.93
    gastric 04.93
      with synchronous replacement 04.92
    intracranial 01.22
      with synchronous replacement 02.93
    peripheral nerve 04.93
      with synchronous replacement 04.92
    sacral nerve 04.93
    sphenoidal — *omit code*
      with synchronous replacement 02.96
    spinal 03.94
      with synchronous replacement 03.93
    temporary transvenous pacemaker system — *omit code*
  electroencephalographic receiver (brain) (intracranial) 01.22
    with synchronous replacement 02.93
  electronic
    stimulator — *see* Removal, neurostimulator, by site
      bladder 57.98
      bone 78.6 ☑
      skeletal muscle 83.93
        with synchronous replacement 83.92
      ureter 56.94
  electrostimulator — *see* Removal, electronic, stimulator, by site
  embolus 38.00
    with endarterectomy — *see* Endarterectomy
    abdominal
      artery 38.06
      vein 38.07
    aorta (arch) (ascending) (descending) 38.04
    arteriovenous shunt or cannula 39.49
    bovine graft 39.49
    head and neck vessel
      endovascular approach 39.74
      open approach, intracranial vessels 38.01
      open approach, other vessels of head and neck 38.02
    intracranial vessel
      endovascular approach 39.74
      open approach, intracranial vessels 38.01
      open approach, other vessels of head and neck 38.02
    lower limb
      artery 38.08
      vein 38.09
    pulmonary (artery) (vein) 38.05
    thoracic vessel NEC 38.05
    upper limb (artery) (vein) 38.03
  embryo — *see* Removal, ectopic fetus
  encircling tube, eye (episcleral) 14.6
  epithelial downgrowth, anterior chamber 12.93
  external fixation device 97.88
    mandibular NEC 97.36
    minifixator (bone) — *see* category 78.6 ☑
  extrauterine embryo — *see* Removal, ectopic fetus
  eyeball 16.49
    with implant 16.42
      with attachment of muscles 16.41
  fallopian tube — *see* Salpingectomy
  feces (impacted) (by flushing) (manual) 96.38
  fetus, ectopic — *see* Removal, ectopic fetus
  fingers, supernumerary 86.26

Removal — *see also* Excision — *continued*
  fixation device
    external 97.88
      mandibular NEC 97.36
      minifixator (bone) — *see* category 78.6 ☑
    internal 78.60
      carpal, metacarpal 78.64
      clavicle 78.61
      facial (bone) 76.97
      femur 78.65
      fibula 78.67
      humerus 78.62
      patella 78.66
      pelvic 78.69
      phalanges (foot) (hand) 78.69
      radius 78.63
      scapula 78.61
      specified site NEC 78.69
      tarsal, metatarsal 78.68
      thorax (ribs) (sternum) 78.61
      tibia 78.67
      ulna 78.63
      vertebrae 78.69
  foreign body NEC (*see also* Incision, by site) 98.20
    abdominal (cavity) 54.92
      wall 54.0
    adenoid 98.13
      by incision 28.91
    alveolus, alveolar bone 98.22
      by incision 24.0
    antecubital fossa 98.27
      by incision 86.05
    anterior chamber 12.00
      by incision 12.02
        with use of magnet 12.01
    anus (intraluminal) 98.05
      by incision 49.93
    artifical stoma (intraluminal) 98.18
    auditory canal, external 18.02
    axilla 98.27
      by incision 86.05
    bladder (without incision) 57.0
      by incision 57.19
    bone, except fixation device (*see also* Incision, bone) 77.10
      alveolus, alveolar 98.22
        by incision 24.0
    brain 01.39
      without incision into brain 01.24
    breast 85.0
    bronchus (intraluminal) 98.15
      by incision 33.0
    bursa 83.03
      hand 82.03
    canthus 98.22
      by incision 08.51
    cerebral meninges 01.31
    cervix (intraluminal) NEC 98.16
      penetrating 69.97
    choroid (by incision) 14.00
      with use of magnet 14.01
      without use of magnet 14.02
    ciliary body (by incision) 12.00
      with use of magnet 12.01
      without use of magnet 12.02
    conjunctiva (by magnet) 98.22
      by incision 10.0
    cornea 98.21
      by
        incision 11.1
        magnet 11.0
    duodenum 98.03
      by incision 45.01
    ear (intraluminal) 98.11
      with incision 18.09
    epididymis 63.92
    esophagus (intraluminal) 98.02
      by incision 42.09
    extrapleural (by incision) 34.01
    eye, eyeball (by magnet) 98.21
      anterior segment (by incision) 12.00
        with use of magnet 12.01
        without use of magnet 12.02
      posterior segment (by incision) 14.00

☑ **Additional Digit Required** — Refer to the Tabular List for Digit Selection

⬏ **Subterms under main terms may continue to next column or page**

☑ Additional Digit Required — Refer to the Tabular List for Digit Selection
▽ Subterms under main terms may continue to next column or page
50 — Volume 3
▶◀ Revised Text
● New Line
▲ Revised Code
2015 ICD-9-CM

Index

Removal — Removal

Removal — see also Excision — continued

osteocartilagenous loose body, joint structures (see also Arthrotomy) 80.10
outer attic wall (middle ear) 20.59
ovo-testis (unilateral) 62.3
  bilateral 62.41
pacemaker
  brain (intracranial) — see Removal, neurostimulator
  cardiac (device) (initial) (permanent) 37.89
    with replacement
      dual-chamber device 37.87
      single-chamber device 37.85
        rate responsive 37.86
    electrodes (atrial) (transvenous) (ventricular) 37.77
      with replacement 37.76
    epicardium (myocardium) 37.77
      with replacement (by)
        atrial and/or ventricular lead(s) (electrode) 37.76
        epicardial lead 37.74
    temporary transvenous pacemaker system — omit code
  intracranial — see Removal, neurostimulator
  neural — see Removal, neurostimulator
  peripheral nerve — see Removal, neurostimulator
  spine — see Removal, neurostimulator
pack, packing
  dental 97.34
  intrauterine 97.72
  nasal 97.32
  rectum 97.59
  trunk NEC 97.85
  vagina 97.75
  vulva 97.75
pantopaque dye, spinal canal 03.31
patella (complete) 77.96
  partial 77.86
pectus deformity implant device 34.01
pelvic viscera, en masse (female) 68.8
  male 57.71
pessary, vagina NEC 97.74
pharynx (partial) 29.33
phlebolith — see Removal, embolus
placenta (by)
  aspiration curettage 69.52
  D and C 69.02
  manual 75.4
plaque, dental 96.54
plate, skull 02.07
  with synchronous replacement 02.05
polyp (see also Excision, lesion, by site)
  esophageal 42.32
    endoscopic 42.33
  gastric (endoscopic) 43.41
  intestine 45.41
    endoscopic 45.42
  nasal 21.31
prosthesis
  bile duct 51.95
    nonoperative 97.55
  cochlear prosthetic device 20.99
  dental 97.35
  epiretinal visual 14.82
  eye 97.31
  facial bone 76.99
  fallopian tube 66.94
    with synchronous replacement 66.93
  joint structures
    with replacement — see Revision, joint replacement, by site
    without replacement
      ankle 80.07
      elbow 80.02
      foot and toe 80.08
      hand and finger 80.04
      hip 80.05
      knee 80.06
      shoulder 80.01
      specified site NEC 80.09
      spine 80.09

Removal — see also Excision — continued

prosthesis — continued
  joint structures — continued
    without replacement — continued
      unspecified site 80.00
        wrist 80.03
  lens 13.8
  penis (internal) without replacement 64.96
  Rosen (urethra) 59.99
  testicular, by incision 62.0
  urinary sphincter, artificial 58.99
    with replacement 58.93
pseudophakos 13.8
pterygium 11.39
  with corneal graft 11.32
pulse generator
  cardiac pacemaker 37.86
  cardioverter/defibrillator 37.79
  carotid sinus 39.88
    with synchronous electrode removal (total system) 39.86
    with synchronous replacement 39.83
  neurostimulator — see Removal, neurostimulator, pulse generator
pump assist device, heart 37.64
  with replacement 37.63
  nonoperative 97.44
radioactive material — see Removal, foreign body, by site
redundant skin, eyelid 08.86
rejected organ
  kidney 55.53
  testis 62.42
reservoir, ventricular (Ommaya) (Rickham) 02.43
  with synchronous replacement 02.42
retained placenta (by)
  aspiration curettage 69.52
  D and C 69.02
  manual 75.4
retinal implant 14.6
Rheos™ carotid sinus baroreflex activation device 86.05
rhinolith 21.31
rice bodies, tendon sheaths 83.01
  hand 82.01
Roger-Anderson minifixator device (bone) — see category 78.6 ☑
root, residual (tooth) (buried) (retained) 23.11
Rosen prosthesis (urethra) 59.99
scleral buckle or implant 14.6
Scribner shunt 39.43
secondary membranous cataract (with iridectomy) 13.65
secundines (by)
  aspiration curettage 69.52
  D and C 69.02
  manual 75.4
sequestrum — see Sequestrectomy
seton, anus 49.93
Shepard's tube (ear) 20.1
Shirodkar suture, cervix 69.96
shunt
  arteriovenous 39.43
    with creation of new shunt 39.42
  lumbar-subarachnoid NEC 03.98
  pleurothecal 03.98
  salpingothecal 03.98
  spinal (thecal) NEC 03.98
  subarachnoid-peritoneal 03.98
  subarachnoid-ureteral 03.98
silastic tubes
  ear 20.1
  fallopian tubes 66.94
    with synchronous replacement 66.93
skin
  necrosis or slough 86.28
    excisional 86.22
    superficial layer (by dermabrasion) 86.25
skull tongs 02.95
  with synchronous replacement 02.94

Removal — see also Excision — continued

spacer (cement) (joint) (methylmethacrylate) 84.57
splint 97.88
stent
  bile duct 97.55
  larynx 31.98
  ureteral 97.62
  urethral 97.65
stimoceiver — see Removal, neurostimulator
subdural
  grids 01.22
  strips 01.22
supernumerary digit(s) 86.26
suture(s) NEC 97.89
  by incision — see Incision, by site
  abdominal wall 97.83
  genital tract 97.79
  head and neck 97.38
  thorax 97.43
  trunk NEC 97.84
symblepharon — see Repair, symblepharon
temporary transvenous pacemaker system — omit code
testis (unilateral) 62.3
  bilateral 62.41
  remaining or solitary 62.42
thrombus 38.00
  with endarterectomy — see Endarterectomy
  abdominal
    artery 38.06
    vein 38.07
  aorta (arch) (ascending) (descending) 38.04
  arteriovenous shunt or cannula 39.49
  bovine graft 39.49
  coronary artery 36.09
  head and neck vessel NEC 38.02
  intracranial vessel NEC 38.01
  lower limb
    artery 38.08
    vein 38.09
  pulmonary (artery) (vein) 38.05
  thoracic vessel NEC 38.05
  upper limb (artery) (vein) 38.03
tissue expander (skin) NEC 86.05
  breast 85.96
toes, supernumerary 86.26
tongs, skull 02.95
  with synchronous replacement 02.94
tonsil tag 28.4
tooth (by forceps) (multiple) (single) NEC 23.09
  deciduous 23.01
  surgical NEC 23.19
    impacted 23.19
    residual root 23.11
    root apex 23.73
      with root canal therapy 23.72
trachoma follicles 10.33
T-tube (bile duct) 97.55
tube
  appendix 97.53
  bile duct (T-tube) NEC 97.55
  cholecystostomy 97.54
  cranial cavity 01.27
  cystostomy 97.63
  ear (button) 20.1
  gastrostomy 97.51
  large intestine 97.53
  liver 97.55
  mediastinum 97.42
  nephrostomy 97.61
  pancreas 97.56
  peritoneum 97.82
  pleural cavity 97.41
  pyelostomy 97.61
  retroperitoneum 97.81
  small intestine 97.52
  thoracotomy 97.41
  tracheostomy 97.37
  tympanostomy 20.1
  tympanum 20.1
  ureterostomy 97.62

Removal — see also Excision — continued

ureteral splint (stent) 97.62
urethral sphincter, artificial 58.99
  with replacement 58.93
urinary sphincter, artificial 58.99
  with replacement 58.93
utricle 20.79
valve
  vas deferens 63.85
  ventricular (cerebral) 02.43
vascular graft or prosthesis 39.49
ventricular shunt or reservoir 02.43
  with synchronous replacement 02.42
Vinke tongs (skull) 02.95
  with synchronous replacement 02.94
vitreous (with replacement) 14.72
  anterior approach (partial) 14.71
  open sky technique 14.71
Wagner-Brooker minifixator device (bone) — see category 78.6 ☑
wiring, dental (immobilization device) 97.33
  orthodontic 24.8

Renipuncture (percutaneous) 55.92
Renogram 92.03
Renotransplantation NEC 55.69

> Note — To report donor source:
> cadaver 00.93
> live non-related donor 00.92
> live related donor 00.91
> live unrelated donor 00.92

Reopening — see also Incision, by site
  blepharorrhaphy 08.02
  canthorrhaphy 08.02
  cilia base 08.71
  craniotomy or craniectomy site 01.23
  fallopian tube (divided) 66.79
  iris in anterior chambers 12.97
  laminectomy or laminotomy site 03.02
  laparotomy site 54.12
  osteotomy site (see also Incision, bone) 77.10
    facial bone 76.09
  tarsorrhaphy 08.02
  thoracotomy site (for control of hemorrhage) (for examination) (for exploration) 34.03
  thyroid field wound (for control of hemorrhage) (for examination) (for exploration) (for removal of hematoma) 06.02

Repacking — see Replacement, pack, by site
Repair
  abdominal wall 54.72
  adrenal gland 07.44
  alveolus, alveolar (process) (ridge) (with graft) (with implant) 24.5
  anal sphincter 49.79
    artificial sphincter
      implantation 49.75
      revision 49.75
    laceration (by suture) 49.71
      obstetric (current) 75.62
      old 49.79
  aneurysm (false) (true) 39.52
    by or with
      clipping 39.51
      coagulation 39.52
      coil, NEC (endovascular approach) 39.79
        head and neck
          bare coils 39.75
          bioactive coils 39.76
      electrocoagulation 39.52
      with
        anastomosis — see Aneurysmectomy, with anastomosis, by site
        graft replacement — see Aneurysmectomy, with graft replacement, by site
        excision or resection of vessel (see also Aneurysmectomy, by site)
      endovascular graft 39.79
        abdominal aorta 39.71

☑ Additional Digit Required — Refer to the Tabular List for Digit Selection   ⟱ Subterms under main terms may continue to next column or page

2015 ICD-9-CM   ▶◀ Revised Text   ● New Line   ▲ Revised Code   Volume 3 — 51

Repair — continued
aneurysm — continued
  by or with — continued
    endovascular graft — continued
      abdominal aorta — continued
        fenestrated (branching) 39.78
      head and neck 39.72
      lower extremity artery(s) 39.79
      thoracic aorta 39.73
      upper extremity artery(s) 39.79
    filipuncture 39.52
    graft replacement — see Aneurys-
      mectomy, with graft replace-
      ment, by site
    ligation 39.52
    liquid tissue adhesive (glue) 39.79
      endovascular approach 39.79
        head and neck 39.72
    methyl methacrylate 39.52
      endovascular approach 39.79
        head and neck 39.72
    occlusion 39.52
      endovascular approach 39.79
        head and neck 39.72
    suture 39.52
    trapping 39.52
    wiring 39.52
    wrapping (gauze) (methyl
      methacrylate) (plastic) 39.52
  coronary artery 36.91
  heart 37.32
  sinus of Valsalva 35.39
  thoracic aorta (dissecting), by fenestra-
    tion 39.54
anomalous pulmonary venous connection
  (total)
  one-stage 35.82
  partial — see specific procedure
  total 35.82
anular disc 80.54
  with graft or prosthesis 80.53
anulus fibrosus 80.54
  with graft or prosthesis 80.53
anus 49.79
  laceration (by suture) 49.71
    obstetric (current) 75.62
      old 49.79
aorta 39.31
aorticopulmonary window 39.59
arteriovenous fistula 39.53
  by or with
    clipping 39.53
    coagulation 39.53
    coil, NEC (endovascular approach)
      39.79
      head and neck vessels
        bare coils 39.75
        bioactive coils 39.76
    division 39.53
    excision or resection (see also
      Aneurysmectomy, by site)
      with
        anastomosis — see Aneurys-
          mectomy, with anasto-
          mosis, by site
        graft replacement — see
          Aneurysmectomy, with
          graft replacement, by
          site
    ligation 39.53
      coronary artery 36.99
    occlusion 39.53
      endovascular approach 39.79
        head and neck 39.72
    suture 39.53
artery NEC 39.59
  by
    endovascular approach
      abdominal aorta 39.71
        fenestrated (branching) graft
          39.78
      head and neck (total emboliza-
        tion or occlusion) 39.72
      other repair (of aneurysm) 39.79

Repair — continued
artery — continued
  by — continued
    endovascular approach — contin-
      ued
      percutaneous repair of extracra-
        nial vessel(s) (for stent in-
        sertion) 00.61

> Note — Also use 00.40, 00.41, 00.42,
> or 00.43 to show the total number of
> vessels treated. Use code 00.44 once to
> show procedure on a bifurcated vessel.
> In addition, use 00.45, 00.46, 00.47, or
> 00.48 to show the number of vascular
> stents inserted.

      percutaneous repair of intracra-
        nial vessel(s) (for stent in-
        sertion) 00.62

> Note — Also use 00.40, 00.41, 00.42,
> or 00.43 to show the total number of
> vessels treated. Use code 00.44 once to
> show procedure on a bifurcated vessel.
> In addition, use 00.45, 00.46, 00.47, or
> 00.48 to show the number of vascular
> stents inserted.

      thoracic aorta 39.73
    non-coronary percutaneous translu-
      minal approach

> Note — Also use 00.40, 00.41, 00.42,
> or 00.43 to show the total number of
> vessels treated. Use code 00.44 once to
> show procedure on a bifurcated vessel.
> In addition, use 00.45, 00.46, 00.47, or
> 00.48 to show the number of vascular
> stents inserted.

    angioplasty
      basilar 00.62
      carotid 00.61
      femoropopliteal 39.50
      iliac 39.50
      lower extremity NOS 39.50
      mesenteric 39.50
      renal 39.50
      upper extremity 39.50
      vertebral 00.61
        intracranial portion 00.62
    atherectomy 17.56
  with
    patch graft 39.58
      with excision or resection of ves-
        sel — see Arteriectomy,
        with graft replacement, by
        site
      synthetic (Dacron) (Teflon) 39.57
      tissue (vein) (autogenous) (homo-
        graft) 39.56
    suture 39.31
  coronary NEC 36.99
    by angioplasty — see Angioplasty,
      coronary
    by atherectomy
      percutaneous transluminal 17.55
  artificial opening — see Repair, stoma
  atrial septal defect 35.71
    with
      prosthesis (open heart technique)
        35.51
      closed heart technique 35.52
      tissue graft 35.61
    combined with repair of valvular and
      ventricular septal defects — see
      Repair, endocardial cushion de-
      fect
    in total repair of total anomalous pul-
      monary venous connection 35.82
  atrioventricular canal defect (any type) 35.73
    with
      prosthesis 35.54
      tissue graft 35.63
  bifid digit (finger) 82.89
  bile duct NEC 51.79
    laceration (by suture) NEC 51.79
      common bile duct 51.71
  bladder NEC 57.89

Repair — continued
bladder — continued
  exstrophy 57.86
  for stress incontinence — see Repair,
    stress incontinence
  laceration (by suture) 57.81
    obstetric (current) 75.61
      old 57.89
  neck 57.85
blepharophimosis 08.59
blepharoptosis 08.36
  by
    frontalis muscle technique (with)
      fascial sling 08.32
      suture 08.31
    levator muscle technique 08.34
      with resection or advancement 08.33
    orbicularis oculi muscle sling 08.36
    tarsal technique 08.35
blood vessel NEC 39.59
  with
    patch graft 39.58
      with excision or resection — see
        Angiectomy, with graft re-
        placement
      synthetic (Dacron) (Teflon) 39.57
      tissue (vein) (autogenous) (homo-
        graft) 39.56
    resection — see Angiectomy
    suture 39.30
  coronary artery NEC 36.99
    by angioplasty — see Angioplasty,
      coronary
    by atherectomy
      percutaneous transluminal 17.55
  peripheral vessel NEC 39.59
    by angioplasty 39.50

> Note — Also use 00.40, 00.41, 00.42,
> or 00.43 to show the total number of
> vessels treated. Use code 00.44 once to
> show procedure on a bifurcated vessel.
> In addition, use 00.45, 00.46, 00.47, or
> 00.48 to show the number of vascular
> stents inserted.

    by atherectomy 17.56

> Note — Also use 00.40, 00.41, 00.42,
> or 00.43 to show the total number of
> vessels treated. Use code 00.44 once to
> show procedure on a bifurcated vessel.
> In addition, use 00.45, 00.46, 00.47, or
> 00.48 to show the number of vascular
> stents inserted.

    by endovascular approach 39.79
  bone NEC (see also Osteoplasty) — see cate-
    gory) 78.4 ☑
    by synostosis technique — see
      Arthrodesis
    accessory sinus 22.79
    cranium NEC 02.06
      with
        flap (bone) 02.03
        graft (bone) 02.04
    for malunion, nonunion, or delayed
      union of fracture — see Repair,
      fracture, malunion or nonunion
    nasal 21.89
    skull NEC 02.06
      with
        flap (bone) 02.03
        graft (bone) 02.04
  bottle, hydrocele of tunica vaginalis 61.2
  brain (trauma) NEC 02.92
  breast (plastic) (see also Mammoplasty)
    85.89
  broad ligament 69.29
  bronchus NEC 33.48
    laceration (by suture) 33.41
  bunionette (with osteotomy) 77.54
  canaliculus, lacrimal 09.73
  canthus (lateral) 08.59
  cardiac pacemaker NEC 37.89
    electrode (lead) 37.75
  cardioverter/defibrillator (automatic) pocket
    (skin) (subcutaneous) 37.99
  cerebral meninges 02.12

Repair — continued
cervix 67.69
  internal os 67.59
    transabdominal 67.51
    transvaginal 67.59
  laceration (by suture) 67.61
    obstetric (current) 75.51
      old 67.69
chest wall (mesh) (silastic) NEC 34.79
chordae tendineae 35.32
choroid NEC 14.9
  with retinal repair — see Repair, retina
cisterna chyli 40.69
claw toe 77.57
cleft
  hand 82.82
  laryngotracheal 31.69
  lip 27.54
  palate 27.62
    secondary or subsequent 27.63
coarctation of aorta — see Excision, coarctation of aorta
cochlear prosthetic device 20.99
  external components only 95.49
cockup toe 77.58
colostomy 46.43
conjunctiva NEC 10.49
  with scleral repair 12.81
  laceration 10.6
    with repair of sclera 12.81
  late effect of trachoma 10.49
cornea NEC 11.59
  with
    conjunctival flap 11.53
    transplant — see Keratoplasty
  postoperative dehiscence 11.52
coronary artery NEC 36.99
  by angioplasty — see Angioplasty,
    coronary
  by atherectomy
    percutaneous transluminal 17.55
cranium NEC 02.06
  with
    flap (bone) 02.03
    graft (bone) 02.04
cusp, valve — see Repair, heart, valve
cystocele 70.51
  with graft or prosthesis 70.54
  and rectocele 70.50
    with graft or prosthesis 70.53
dental arch 24.8
diaphragm NEC 34.84
diastasis recti 83.65
diastematomyelia 03.59
ear (external) 18.79
  auditory canal or meatus 18.6
  auricle NEC 18.79
  cartilage NEC 18.79
  laceration (by suture) 18.4
  lop ear 18.79
  middle NEC 19.9
  prominent or protruding 18.5
ectropion 08.49
  by or with
    lid reconstruction 08.44
    suture (technique) 08.42
    thermocauterization 08.41
    wedge resection 08.43
encephalocele (cerebral) 02.12
endocardial cushion defect 35.73
  with
    prosthesis (grafted to septa) 35.54
    tissue graft 35.63
enterocele (female) 70.92
  with graft or prosthesis 70.93
  male 53.9
enterostomy 46.40
entropion 08.49
  by or with
    lid reconstruction 08.44
    suture (technique) 08.42
    thermocauterization 08.41
    wedge resection 08.43
epicanthus (fold) 08.59
epididymis (and spermatic cord) NEC 63.59
  with vas deferens 63.89

☑ **Additional Digit Required** — Refer to the Tabular List for Digit Selection

▽ **Subterms under main terms may continue to next column or page**

☑ **Additional Digit Required** — Refer to the Tabular List for Digit Selection   ▼ **Subterms under main terms may continue to next column or page**

2015 ICD-9-CM   ▶◀ **Revised Text**   ● **New Line**   ▲ **Revised Code**   **Volume 3 — 53**

Repair — continued
  hernia — continued
    inguinal — continued
      bilateral — continued
        direct
          laparoscopic with graft or prosthesis 17.21
          other and open laparoscopic without graft or prosthesis 53.11
            with prosthesis or graft 53.14
        direct and indirect
          laparoscopic with graft or prosthesis 17.23
          other and open (laparoscopic without graft or prosthesis) 53.13
            with prosthesis or graft 53.16
        indirect
          laparoscopic with graft or prosthesis 17.22
          other and open (laparoscopic without graft or prosthesis) 53.12
            with prosthesis or graft 53.15
      direct (unilateral)
        with prosthesis or graft 53.03
        and indirect (unilateral)
          laparoscopic with graft or prosthesis 17.11
          other and open (laparoscopic without graft or prosthesis) 53.01
            with prosthesis or graft 53.03
        laparoscopic with graft or prosthesis 17.11
        other and open (laparoscopic without graft or prosthesis) 53.01
          with prosthesis or graft 53.03
      indirect (unilateral)
        laparoscopic with graft or prosthesis 17.12
        other and open (laparoscopic without graft or prosthesis) 53.02
          with prosthesis or graft 53.04
  internal 53.9
  ischiatic 53.9
  ischiorectal 53.9
  laparoscopic with graft or prosthesis, NOS 17.13
  lumbar 53.9
  manual 96.27
  obturator 53.9
  omental 53.9
  paraesophageal
    laparoscopic 53.71
    other and open 53.72
    unspecified 53.75
  parahiatal
    laparoscopic 53.71
    other and open 53.72
    unspecified 53.75
  paraileostomy 46.41
  parasternal 53.82
  paraumbilical
    laparoscopic 53.43
      with graft or prosthesis 53.42
    other and open with graft or prosthesis 53.41
    other open 53.49
  pericolostomy 46.42
  perineal (enterocele) 53.9
  preperitoneal 53.29
  pudendal 53.9
  retroperitoneal 53.9
  sciatic 53.9
  scrotal — see Repair, hernia, inguinal
  spigelian 53.59
    with prosthesis or graft 53.69

Repair — continued
  hernia — continued
    umbilical
      laparoscopic 53.43
        with graft or prosthesis 53.42
        other and open with graft or prosthesis 53.41
        other open 53.49
      uveal 12.39
      ventral (laparoscopic without graft or prosthesis) 53.59
        with prosthesis or graft
          laparoscopic 53.63
          other and open 53.69
        incisional 53.51
          (laparoscopic without graft or prosthesis) 53.59
          other open with prosthesis or graft 53.61
  hydrocele
    round ligament 69.19
    spermatic cord 63.1
    tunica vaginalis 61.2
  hymen 70.76
  hypospadias 58.45
  ileostomy 46.41
  ingrown toenail 86.23
  intestine, intestinal NEC 46.79
    fistula — see Closure, fistula, intestine
    laceration
      large intestine 46.75
      small intestine NEC 46.73
    stoma — see Repair, stoma
  inverted uterus NEC 69.29
    manual
      nonobstetric 69.94
      obstetric 75.94
    obstetrical
      manual 75.94
      surgical 75.93
    vaginal approach 69.23
  iris (rupture) NEC 12.39
  jejunostomy 46.41
  joint (capsule) (cartilage) NEC (see also Arthroplasty) 81.96
  kidney NEC 55.89
  knee (joint) NEC 81.47
    collateral ligaments 81.46
    cruciate ligaments 81.45
    five-in-one 81.42
    triad 81.43
  labia — see Repair, vulva
  laceration — see Suture, by site
  lacrimal system NEC 09.99
    canaliculus 09.73
    punctum 09.72
      for eversion 09.71
  laryngostomy 31.62
  laryngotracheal cleft 31.69
  larynx 31.69
    fracture 31.64
    laceration 31.61
  leads (cardiac) NEC 37.75
  ligament (see also Arthroplasty) 81.96
    broad 69.29
    collateral, knee NEC 81.46
    cruciate, knee NEC 81.45
    round 69.29
    uterine 69.29
  lip NEC 27.59
    cleft 27.54
    laceration (by suture) 27.51
  liver NEC 50.69
    laceration 50.61
  lop ear 18.79
  lung NEC 33.49
  lymphatic (channel) (peripheral) NEC 40.9
    duct, left (thoracic) NEC 40.69
  macrodactyly 82.83
  mallet finger 82.84
  mandibular ridge 76.64
  mastoid (antrum) (cavity) 19.9
  meninges (cerebral) NEC 02.12
    spinal NEC 03.59
      meningocele 03.51
      myelomeningocele 03.52

Repair — continued
  meningocele (spinal) 03.51
    cranial 02.12
  mesentery 54.75
  mouth NEC 27.59
    laceration NEC 27.52
  muscle NEC 83.87
    by
      graft or implant (fascia) (muscle) 83.82
        hand 82.72
      tendon 83.81
        hand 82.79
      suture (direct) 83.65
        hand 82.46
      transfer or transplantation (muscle) 83.77
        hand 82.58
    hand 82.89
      by
        graft or implant NEC 82.79
          fascia 82.72
        suture (direct) 82.46
        transfer or transplantation (muscle) 82.58
  musculotendinous cuff, shoulder 83.63
  myelomeningocele 03.52
  nasal
    septum (perforation) NEC 21.88
    sinus NEC 22.79
      fistula 22.71
  nasolabial flaps (plastic) 21.86
  nasopharyngeal atresia 29.4
  nerve (cranial) (peripheral) NEC 04.79
    old injury 04.76
    revision 04.75
    sympathetic 05.81
  nipple NEC 85.87
  nose (external) (internal) (plastic) NEC (see also Rhinoplasty) 21.89
    laceration (by suture) 21.81
  notched lip 27.59
  omentum 54.74
  omphalocele
    laparoscopic 53.43
      with graft or prosthesis 53.42
    other and open with graft or prosthesis 53.41
    other open 53.49
  orbit 16.89
    wound 16.81
  ostium
    primum defect 35.73
      with
        prosthesis 35.54
        tissue graft 35.63
    secundum defect 35.71
      with
        prosthesis (open heart technique) 35.51
          closed heart technique 35.52
        tissue graft 35.61
  ovary 65.79
    with tube 65.73
      laparoscopic 65.76
  overlapping toe 77.58
  pacemaker
    cardiac
      device (permanent) 37.89
      electrode(s) (leads) NEC 37.75
      pocket (skin) (subcutaneous) 37.79
  palate NEC 27.69
    cleft 27.62
      secondary or subsequent 27.63
    laceration (by suture) 27.61
  pancreas NEC 52.95
    Wirsung's duct 52.99
  papillary muscle (heart) 35.31
  patent ductus arteriosus 38.85
  pectus deformity (chest) (carinatum) (excavatum) 34.74
  pelvic floor NEC 70.79
    obstetric laceration (current) 75.69
      old 70.79
  penis NEC 64.49
    for epispadias or hypospadias 58.45

Repair — continued
  penis — continued
    inflatable prosthesis 64.99
    laceration 64.41
  pericardium 37.49
  perineum (female) 71.79
    laceration (by suture) 71.71
      obstetric (current) 75.69
        old 71.79
    male NEC 86.89
      laceration (by suture) 86.59
  peritoneum NEC 54.73
    by suture 54.64
  pharynx NEC 29.59
    laceration (by suture) 29.51
    plastic 29.4
  pleura NEC 34.93
  postcataract wound dehiscence 11.52
    with conjunctival flap 11.53
  pouch of Douglas 70.52
  primum ostium defect 35.73
    with
      prosthesis 35.54
      tissue graft 35.63
  prostate 60.93
  ptosis, eyelid — see Repair, blepharoptosis
  punctum, lacrimal NEC 09.72
    for correction of eversion 09.71
  quadriceps (mechanism) 83.86
  rectocele (posterior colporrhaphy) 70.52
    with graft or prosthesis 70.55
    and cystocele 70.50
      with graft or prosthesis 70.53
  rectum NEC 48.79
    laceration (by suture) 48.71
    prolapse NEC 48.76
      abdominal, approach 48.75
    STARR procedure 48.74
  retina, retinal
    detachment 14.59
      by
        cryotherapy 14.52
        diathermy 14.51
        photocoagulation 14.55
          laser 14.54
          xenon arc 14.53
        scleral buckling (see also Buckling, scleral) 14.49
    tear or defect 14.39
      by
        cryotherapy 14.32
        diathermy 14.31
        photocoagulation 14.35
          laser 14.34
          xenon arc 14.33
  retroperitoneal tissue 54.73
  rotator cuff (graft) (suture) 83.63
  round ligament 69.29
  ruptured tendon NEC 83.88
    hand 82.86
  salivary gland or duct NEC 26.49
  sclera, scleral 12.89
    fistula 12.82
    staphyloma NEC 12.86
      with graft 12.85
  scrotum 61.49
  sinus
    nasal NEC 22.79
    of Valsalva (aneurysm) 35.39
  skin (plastic) (without graft) 86.89
    laceration (by suture) 86.59
  skull NEC 02.06
    with
      flap (bone) 02.03
      graft (bone) 02.04
  spermatic cord NEC 63.59
    laceration (by suture) 63.51
  sphincter ani 49.79
    laceration (by suture) 49.71
      obstetric (current) 75.62
        old 49.79
  spina bifida NEC 03.59
    meningocele 03.51
    myelomeningocele 03.52
  spinal (cord) (meninges) (structures) NEC 03.59

☑ Additional Digit Required — Refer to the Tabular List for Digit Selection   ▽ Subterms under main terms may continue to next column or page

54 — Volume 3   ▶◀ Revised Text   ● New Line   ▲ Revised Code   2015 ICD-9-CM

Repair — continued
spinal — continued
  meningocele 03.51
  myelomeningocele 03.52
spleen 41.95
sternal defect 78.41
stoma
  bile duct 51.79
  bladder 57.22
  bronchus 33.42
  common duct 51.72
  esophagus 42.89
  gallbladder 51.99
  hepatic duct 51.79
  intestine 46.40
    large 46.43
    small 46.41
  kidney 55.89
  larynx 31.63
  rectum 48.79
  stomach 44.69
    laparoscopic 44.68
  thorax 34.79
  trachea 31.74
  ureter 56.62
  urethra 58.49
stomach NEC 44.69
  laceration (by suture) 44.61
  laparoscopic 44.68
stress incontinence (urinary) NEC 59.79
  by
    anterior urethropexy 59.79
    Burch 59.5
    cystourethropexy (with levator mus-
      cle sling) 59.71
    injection of implant (collagen) (fat)
      (polytef) 59.72
    paraurethral suspension (Pereyra)
      59.6
    periurethral suspension 59.6
    plication of urethrovesical junction
      59.3
    pubococcygeal sling 59.71
    retropubic urethral suspension 59.5
    suprapubic sling 59.4
    tension free vaginal tape 59.79
    urethrovesical suspension 59.4
      gracilis muscle transplant 59.71
      levator muscle sling 59.71
  subcutaneous tissue (plastic) (without
    skin graft) 86.89
    laceration (by suture) 86.59
supracristal defect (heart) 35.72
  with
    prosthesis (open heart technique)
      35.53
    closed heart technique 35.55
    tissue graft 35.62
symblepharon NEC 10.49
  by division (with insertion of conformer)
    10.5
  with free graft 10.41
syndactyly 86.85
synovial membrane, joint — see Arthroplasty
telecanthus 08.59
tendon 83.88
  by or with
    arthroplasty — see Arthroplasty
    graft or implant (tendon) 83.81
      fascia 83.82
        hand 82.72
      hand 82.79
      muscle 83.82
        hand 82.72
    suture (direct) (immediate) (primary)
      (see also Suture, tendon) 83.64
      hand 82.45
    transfer or transplantation (tendon)
      83.75
      hand 82.56
  hand 82.86
    by
      graft or implant (tendon) 82.79

Repair — continued
tendon — continued
  hand — continued
    by — continued
      suture (direct) (immediate) (pri-
        mary) (see also Suture,
        tendon, hand) 82.45
      transfer or transplantation (ten-
        don) 82.56
    rotator cuff (direct suture) 83.63
    ruptured NEC 83.88
      hand 82.86
    sheath (direct suture) 83.61
      hand 82.41
testis NEC 62.69
tetralogy of Fallot
  partial — see specific procedure
  total (one-stage) 35.81
thoracic duct NEC 40.69
thoracostomy 34.72
thymus (gland) 07.93
tongue NEC 25.59
tooth NEC 23.2
  by
    crown (artificial) 23.41
    filling (amalgam) (plastic) (silicate)
      23.2
    inlay 23.3
total anomalous pulmonary venous connection
  partial — see specific procedure
  total (one-stage) 35.82
trachea NEC 31.79
  laceration (by suture) 31.71
tricuspid atresia 35.94
truncus arteriosus
  partial — see specific procedure
  total (one-stage) 35.83
tunica vaginalis 61.49
  laceration (by suture) 61.41
tympanum — see Tympanoplasty
ureterocele 56.89
ureter NEC 56.89
  laceration (by suture) 56.82
urethra NEC 58.49
  laceration (by suture) 58.41
    obstetric (current) 75.61
    old 58.49
  meatus 58.47
urethrocele (anterior colporrhaphy) (female)
  70.51
  with graft or prosthesis 70.54
  and rectocele 70.50
    with graft or prosthesis 70.53
urinary sphincter, artificial (component)
  58.99
urinary stress incontinence — see Repair,
  stress incontinence
uterus, uterine 69.49
  inversion — see Repair, inverted uterus
  laceration (by suture) 69.41
    obstetric (current) 75.50
    old 69.49
  ligaments 69.29
    by
      interposition 69.21
      plication 69.22
uvula 27.73
  with synchronous cleft palate repair
    27.62
vagina, vaginal (cuff) (wall) NEC 70.79
  anterior 70.51
    with graft or prosthesis 70.54
    with posterior repair 70.50
      with graft or prosthesis 70.53
  cystocele 70.51
    with graft or prosthesis 70.54
    and rectocele 70.50
      with graft or prosthesis 70.53
  enterocele 70.92
    with graft or prosthesis 70.93
  laceration (by suture) 70.71
    obstetric (current) 75.69
    old 70.79
  posterior 70.52
    with anterior repair 70.50

Repair — continued
vagina, vaginal — continued
  posterior — continued
    with anterior repair — continued
      with graft or prosthesis 70.53
    rectocele 70.52
      with graft or prosthesis 70.55
      and cystocele 70.50
        with graft or prosthesis 70.53
    urethrocele 70.51
      with graft or prosthesis 70.54
      and rectocele 70.50
        with graft or prosthesis 70.53
  varicocele 63.1
  vas deferens 63.89
    by
      anastomosis 63.82
        to epididymis 63.83
      reconstruction 63.82
    laceration (by suture) 63.81
  vein NEC 39.59
    by
      endovascular approach
        head and neck (embolization or
          occlusion) 39.72
    with
      patch graft 39.58
        with excision or resection of ves-
          sel — see Phlebectomy,
          with graft replacement, by
          site
        synthetic (Dacron) (Teflon)
          39.57
        tissue (vein) (autogenous)
          (homograft) 39.56
      suture 39.32
  ventricular septal defect 35.72
    with
      prosthesis (open heart technique)
        35.53
      closed heart technique 35.55
      in total repair of tetralogy of Fal-
        lot 35.81
      tissue graft 35.62
    combined with repair of valvular and
      atrial septal defects — see Repair,
      endocardial cushion defect
    in total repair of
      tetralogy of Fallot 35.81
      truncus arteriosus 35.83
  vertebral arch defect (spina bifida) 03.59
  vulva NEC 71.79
    laceration (by suture) 71.71
      obstetric (current) 75.69
      old 71.79
  Wirsung's duct 52.99
  wound (skin) (without graft) 86.59
    abdominal wall 54.63
    dehiscence 54.61
    postcataract dehiscence (corneal) 11.52

Replacement
acetabulum (with prosthesis) 81.52
ankle, total 81.56
  revision 81.59
aortic valve, NOS 35.22
  with
    prosthesis 35.22
    tissue graft 35.21
    endovascular 35.05
    endovascular (TAVI) (TAVR) (transarteri-
      al) (transcatheter) (transfemoral)
      (with tissue graft) 35.05
    transapical (intercostal) (transcatheter)
      (transthoracic) (transventricular)
      (with tissue graft) 35.06
artery — see Graft, artery
bag — see Replacement, pack or bag
Barton's tongs (skull) 02.94
bladder
  with
    ileal loop 57.87 [45.51]
    sigmoid 57.87 [45.52]
  sphincter, artificial 58.93
bronchial device NOS 33.79
bronchial substance NOS 33.79

Replacement — continued
bronchial valve(s)
  multiple lobes 33.73
  single lobe 33.71
caliper tongs (skull) 02.94
cannula
  arteriovenous shunt 39.94
  pancreatic duct 97.05
  vessel-to-vessel (arteriovenous) 39.94
cardiac contractility modulation (CCM)
  rechargeable pulse generator only 17.52
  total system 17.51
cardiac resynchronization device
  defibrillator (biventricular defibrillator)
    (BiV ICD) (BiV pacemaker with
    defibrillator) (BiV pacing with de-
    fibrillator) (CRT-D) (device and
    one or more leads) (total system)
    00.51
    left ventricular coronary venous lead
      only 00.52
    pulse generator only 00.54
  pacemaker (biventricular pacemaker)
    (BiV pacemaker) (CRT-P) (device
    and one or more leads) (total
    system) 00.50
    left ventricular coronary venous lead
      only 00.52
    pulse generator only 00.53
cardioverter/defibrillator (total system)
  37.94
  leads only (electrodes) (sensing) (pacing)
    37.97
  pulse generator only 37.98
cast NEC 97.13
  lower limb 97.12
  upper limb 97.11
catheter
  bladder (indwelling) 57.95
  cystostomy 59.94
  external ventricular drain 02.21
  ventricular shunt (cerebral) 02.42
  wound 97.15
CCM (cardiac contractility modulation)
  rechargeable pulse generator only 17.52
  total system 17.51
CRT-D (biventricular defibrillator) (BiV ICD)
  (BiV pacemaker with defibrillator)
  (BiV pacing with defibrillator) (cardiac resynchronization defibrillator)
  (device and one or more leads) 00.51
  left ventricular coronary venous lead
    only 00.52
  pulse generator only 00.54
CRT-P (biventricular pacemaker) (BiV pacemaker) (cardiac resynchronization
  pacemaker) (device and one or more
  leads) 00.50
  left ventricular coronary venous lead
    only 00.52
  pulse generator only 00.53
Crutchfield tongs (skull) 02.94
cystostomy tube (catheter) 59.94
device
  subcutaneous for intracardiac or great
    vessel hemodynamic monitoring
    00.57
diaphragm, vagina 97.24
disc — see Replacement, intervertebral disc
drain (see also Replacement, tube)
  vagina 97.26
  vulva 97.26
  wound, musculoskeletal or skin 97.16
ear (prosthetic) 18.71
elbow (joint), total 81.84
electrode(s) — see Implant, electrode or
  lead by site or name of device
  brain
    depth 02.93
    foramen ovale 02.93
    sphenoidal 02.96
  carotid sinus 39.82
    with synchronous pulse generator
      replacement (total system)
      39.81
  depth 02.93

☑ Additional Digit Required — Refer to the Tabular List for Digit Selection   Subterms under main terms may continue to next column or page

2015 ICD-9-CM   ▶◀ Revised Text   ● New Line   ▲ Revised Code   Volume 3 — 55

Repair — Replacement

Replacement — *continued*

electrode(s) — *see* Implant, electrode or lead
by site or name of device — *continued*
foramen ovale 02.93
gastric 04.92
intracranial 02.93
pacemaker — *see* Replacement, pacemaker, electrode(s)
peripheral nerve 04.92
sacral nerve 04.92
sphenoidal 02.96
spine 03.93
electroencephalographic receiver (brain)
(intracranial) 02.93
electronic
cardioverter/defibrillator — *see* Replacement, cardioverter/defibrillator
leads (electrode) (s) — *see* Replacement,
electrode(s)
stimulator (*see also* Implant, electronic
stimulator, by site)
bladder 57.97
muscle (skeletal) 83.92
ureter 56.93
electrostimulator — *see* Implant, electronic
stimulator by site
enterostomy device (tube)
large intestine 97.04
small intestine 97.03
epidural pegs 02.93
femoral head, by prosthesis 81.52
revision 81.53
Gardner Wells tongs (skull) 02.94
gastric band, laparoscopic 44.96
gastric port device (subcutaneous) 44.96
graft — *see* Graft
halo traction device (skull) 02.94
Harrington rod (with refusion of spine) —
see Refusion, spinal
heart
artificial
total internal biventricular replacement system 37.52
implantable battery 37.54
implantable controller 37.54
thoracic unit 37.53
transcutaneous energy transfer
(TET) device 37.54
total internal biventricular replacement
system 37.52
implantable battery 37.54
implantable controller 37.54
thoracic unit 37.53
transcutaneous energy transfer (TET)
device 37.54
valve, NOS (with prosthesis) (with tissue
graft) 35.20
aortic, NOS 35.22
with
prosthesis 35.22
tissue graft 35.21
endovascular 35.05
endovascular (TAVI) (TAVR)
(transarterial) (tran-
scatheter) (transfemoral)
(with tissue graft) 35.05
transapical (intercostal) (transcatheter) (transthoracic)
(transventricular) (with
tissue graft) 35.06
endovascular, NOS 35.09
mitral, NOS 35.24
with
prosthesis 35.24
tissue graft 35.23
poppet (prosthetic) 35.95
pulmonary, NOS 35.26
with
prosthesis 35.26
tissue graft 35.25
endovascular (percutaneous)
(PPVI) (TPVR) (tran-
scatheter) (transfemoral)
(transvenous) 35.07

Replacement — *continued*

heart — *continued*
valve, — *continued*
pulmonary, — *continued*
in total repair of tetralogy of Fallot 35.81
transapical (intercostal) (transcatheter) (transthoracic)
(transventricular) 35.08
tricuspid, NOS 35.28
with
prosthesis 35.28
tissue graft 35.27
hip (partial) (with fixation device) (with
prosthesis) (with traction) 81.52
acetabulum 81.52
revision 81.53
femoral head 81.52
revision 81.53
total 81.51
revision 81.53
intervertebral disc
artificial, NOS 84.60
cervical 84.62
nucleus 84.61
partial 84.61
total 84.62
lumbar, lumbosacral 84.65
nucleus 84.64
partial 84.64
total 84.65
thoracic (partial) (total) 84.63
inverted uterus — *see* Repair, inverted
uterus
iris NEC 12.39
kidney, mechanical 55.97
knee (bicompartmental) (hemijoint) (partial)
(total) (tricompartmental) (unicompartmental) 81.54
revision 81.55
laryngeal stent 31.93
leads (electrode) (s) — *see* Replacement,
electrode(s)
mechanical kidney 55.97
mitral valve, NOS 35.24
with
prosthesis 35.24
tissue graft 35.23
Mulligan hood, fallopian tube 66.93
muscle stimulator (skeletal) 83.92
nephrostomy tube 55.93
neuropacemaker — *see* Implant, neurostimulator, by site
neurostimulator — *see* Implant, neurostimulator, by site
skeletal muscle 83.92
pacemaker
brain — *see* Implant, neurostimulator,
brain
cardiac device (initial) (permanent)
dual-chamber device 37.87
resynchronization — *see* Replacement, CRT-P
single-chamber device 37.85
rate responsive 37.86
electrode(s), cardiac (atrial) (transvenous) (ventricular) 37.76
epicardium (myocardium) 37.74
left ventricular coronary venous system 00.52
gastric — *see* Implant, neurostimulator,
gastric
intracranial — *see* Implant, neurostimulator, intracranial
neural — *see* Implant, neurostimulator,
by site
peripheral nerve — *see* Implant, neurostimulator, peripheral nerve
sacral nerve — *see* Implant, neurostimulator, sacral nerve
spine — *see* Implant, neurostimulator,
spine
temporary transvenous pacemaker system 37.78
pack or bag
nose 97.21

Replacement — *continued*

pack or bag — *continued*
teeth, tooth 97.22
vagina 97.26
vulva 97.26
wound 97.16
pessary, vagina NEC 97.25
prosthesis
acetabulum 81.53
arm (bioelectric) (cineplastic) (kineplastic) 84.44
biliary tract 51.99
channel (single) 20.97
multiple 20.98
cochlear 20.96
elbow 81.97
epiretinal visual 14.83
extremity (bioelectric) (cineplastic)
(kineplastic) 84.40
lower 84.48
upper 84.44
fallopian tube (Mulligan hood) (stent)
66.93
femur 81.53
knee 81.55
leg (bioelectric) (cineplastic) (kineplastic)
84.48
penis (internal) (non-inflatable) 64.95
inflatable (internal) 64.97
pulmonary valve, NOS 35.26
with
prosthesis 35.26
tissue graft 35.25
endovascular (percutaneous) (PPVI)
(TPVR) (transcatheter) (transfemoral) (transvenous) 35.07
in total repair of tetralogy of Fallot 35.81
transapical (intercostal) (transcatheter)
(transthoracic) (transventricular)
35.08
pyelostomy tube 55.94
rectal tube 96.09
Rheos™ carotid sinus baroreflex activation
device 39.81
sensor (lead)
intracardiac or great vessel hemodynamic monitoring 00.56
shoulder NEC 81.83
partial 81.81
total, NEC 81.80
other 81.80
reverse 81.88
skull
plate 02.05
tongs 02.94
spacer (cement) (joint) (methylmethacrylate) 84.56
specified appliance or device NEC 97.29
spinal motion preservation device
facet replacement device(s) 84.84
interspinous process device(s) 84.80
pedicle-based dynamic stabilization de-
vice(s) 84.82
splint 97.14
stent
bile duct 97.05
fallopian tube 66.93
larynx 31.93
pancreatic duct 97.05
trachea 31.93
stimoceiver — *see* Implant, stimoceiver, by
site
stimulator
electrode(s)
carotid sinus 39.82
with synchronous pulse generator replacement (total system) 39.81
pulse generator
carotid sinus 39.83
with synchronous electrode(s)
replacement (total system)
39.81
subdural
grids 02.93
strips 02.93

Replacement — *continued*

testis in scrotum 62.5
tongs, skull 02.94
tracheal stent 31.93
tricuspid valve (with prosthesis) 35.28
with tissue graft 35.27
tube
bile duct 97.05
bladder 57.95
cystostomy 59.94
esophagostomy 97.01
gastrostomy 97.02
large intestine 97.04
nasogastric 97.01
nephrostomy 55.93
pancreatic duct 97.05
pyelostomy 55.94
rectal 96.09
small intestine 97.03
tracheostomy 97.23
ureterostomy 59.93
ventricular (cerebral) 02.42
umbilical cord, prolapsed 73.92
ureter (with)
bladder flap 56.74
ileal segment implanted into bladder
56.89 [45.51]
ureterostomy tube 59.93
urethral sphincter, artificial 58.93
urinary sphincter, artificial 58.93
valve
heart (*see also* Replacement, heart valve)
poppet (prosthetic) 35.95
ventricular (cerebral) 02.42
ventricular shunt (valve) 02.42
Vinke tongs (skull) 02.94
vitreous (silicone) 14.75
for retinal reattachment 14.59
Replant, replantation — *see also* Reattachment
extremity — *see* Reattachment, extremity
penis 64.45
scalp 86.51
tooth 23.5
Reposition
cardiac pacemaker
electrode(s) (atrial) (transvenous) (ventricular) 37.75
pocket 37.79
cardiac resynchronization defibrillator (CRT-
D) — *see* Revision, cardiac resynchronization defibrillator
cardiac resynchronization pacemaker (CRT-
P) — *see* Revision, cardiac resynchronization pacemaker
cardioverter/defibrillator (automatic)
lead(s) (sensing) (pacing) (epicardial
patch) 37.75
pocket 37.79
pulse generator 37.79
cilia base 08.71
implantable hemodynamic sensor (lead)
and monitor device 37.79
iris 12.39
neurostimulator
leads
subcutaneous, without device replacement 86.09
within brain 02.93
within or over gastric nerve 04.92
within or over peripheral nerve 04.92
within or over sacral nerve 04.92
within spine 03.93
pulse generator
subcutaneous, without device replacement 86.09
renal vessel, aberrant 39.55
subcutaneous device pocket NEC 86.09
thyroid tissue 06.94
tricuspid valve (with plication) 35.14
Resection — *see also* Excision, by site
abdominoendorectal (combined), NOS
48.50
laparoscopic 48.51
open 48.52
other 48.59

☑ **Additional Digit Required — Refer to the Tabular List for Digit Selection**   ▽ **Subterms under main terms may continue to next column or page**

56 — Volume 3   ▶◀ Revised Text   ● New Line   ▲ Revised Code   2015 ICD-9-CM

Resection — *see also* Excision, by site — *continued*

abdominoperineal (rectum), NOS 48.50
  pull-through (Altemeier) (Swenson) NEC 48.49
    Duhamel type 48.65
    laparoscopic 48.42
    not otherwise specified 48.40
    open 48.43
alveolar process and palate (en bloc) 27.32
aneurysm — *see* Aneurysmectomy
aortic valve (for subvalvular stenosis) 35.11
artery — *see* Arteriectomy
bile duct NEC 51.69
  common duct NEC 51.63
bladder (partial) (segmental) (transvesical) (wedge) 57.6
  complete or total 57.79
  lesion NEC 57.59
    transurethral approach 57.49
  neck 57.59
    transurethral approach 57.49
blood vessel — *see* Angiectomy
brain 01.59
  by
    stereotactic radiosurgery 92.30
      cobalt 60 92.32
      linear accelerator (LINAC) 92.31
      multi-source 92.32
      particle beam 92.33
      particulate 92.33
      radiosurgery NEC 92.39
      single source photon 92.31
  hemisphere 01.52
  lobe 01.53
breast (*see also* Mastectomy)
  quadrant 85.22
  segmental 85.23
broad ligament 69.19
bronchus (sleeve) (wide sleeve) 32.1
  block (en bloc) (with radical dissection of brachial plexus, bronchus, lobe of lung, ribs, and sympathetic nerves) 32.6
bursa 83.5
  hand 82.31
cecum (and terminal ileum)
  laparoscopic 17.32
  open and other 45.72
cerebral meninges 01.51
chest wall 34.4
clavicle 77.81
clitoris 71.4
colon (partial) (segmental)
  ascending (cecum and terminal ileum)
    laparoscopic 17.32
    open and other 45.72
  cecum (and terminal ileum)
    laparoscopic 17.32
    open and other 45.72
  complete
    laparoscopic 45.81
    open 45.82
    other 45.83
    unspecified 45.83
  descending (sigmoid)
    laparoscopic 17.36
    open and other 45.76
  for interposition 45.52
  Hartmann
    laparoscopic 17.35
    open and other 45.75
  hepatic flexure
    laparoscopic 17.33
    open and other 45.73
  laparoscopic 17.39
  left radical (hemicolon)
    laparoscopic 17.35
    open and other 45.75
  multiple segmental
    laparoscopic 17.31
    open and other 45.71
  open and other 45.79
  right radical (hemicolon) (ileocolectomy)
    laparoscopic 17.33
    open and other 45.73

Resection — *see also* Excision, by site — *continued*

colon — *continued*
  segmental NEC
    laparoscopic 17.39
    multiple
      laparoscopic 17.31
      open and other 45.71
    open and other 45.79
  sigmoid
    laparascopic 17.36
    open and other 45.76
  splenic flexure
    laparoscopic 17.35
    open and other 45.75
  total
    laparoscopic 45.81
    open 45.82
    other 45.83
    unspecified 45.83
  transverse
    laparoscopic 17.34
    open and other 45.74
conjunctiva, for pterygium 11.39
corneal graft 11.32
cornual (fallopian tube) (unilateral) 66.69
  bilateral 66.63
diaphragm 34.81
endaural 20.79
endorectal (pull-through) (Soave) 48.41
  combined abdominal, NOS 48.50
    laparoscopic 48.51
    open 48.52
    other 48.59
esophagus (partial) (subtotal) (*see also* Esophagectomy) 42.41
  total 42.42
exteriorized intestine — *see* Resection, intestine, exteriorized
fascia 83.44
  for graft 83.43
    hand 82.34
  hand 82.35
    for graft 82.34
gallbladder (total) 51.22
gastric (partial) (sleeve) (subtotal) NEC (*see also* Gastrectomy) 43.89
  with anastomosis NEC 43.89
    esophagogastric 43.5
    gastroduodenal 43.6
    gastrogastric 43.89
    gastrojejunal 43.7
  complete or total NEC 43.99
    with intestinal interposition 43.91
  laparoscopic 43.82
  radical NEC 43.99
    with intestinal interposition 43.91
  wedge 43.42
  endoscopic 43.41
hallux valgus (joint) (*see also* Bunionectomy)
  with prosthetic implant 77.59
hepatic
  duct 51.69
  flexure (colon)
    laparoscopic 17.33
    open and other 45.73
infundibula, heart (right) 35.34
intestine (partial) NEC
  cecum (with terminal ileum)
    laparoscopic 17.32
    open and other 45.72
  exteriorized (large intestine) 46.04
    small intestine 46.02
  for interposition 45.50
    large intestine 45.52
    small intestine 45.51
  hepatic flexure
    laparoscopic 17.33
    open and other 45.73
  ileum 45.62
    with cecum
      laparoscopic 17.32
      open and other 45.72
    laparoscopic 17.39
  large (partial) (segmental) NEC
    for interposition 45.52

Resection — *see also* Excision, by site — *continued*

intestine — *continued*
  large — *continued*
    laparoscopic 17.39
    multiple segmental
      laparoscopic 17.31
      open and other 45.71
    other 45.79
    total
      laparoscopic 45.81
      open 45.82
      other 45.83
      unspecified 45.83
    unspecified 45.79
    left hemicolon
      laparoscopic 17.35
      open and other 45.75
    multiple segmental (large intestine)
      laparoscopic 17.31
      open and other 45.71
      small intestine 45.61
    open and other 45.79
    right hemicolon
      laparoscopic 17.33
      open and other 45.73
    segmental (large intestine)
      laparoscopic 17.39
      multiple
        laparoscopic 17.31
        open and other 45.71
      open and other 45.79
      small intestine 45.62
        multiple 45.61
    sigmoid
      laparoscopic 17.36
      open and other 45.76
    small (partial) (segmental) NEC 45.62
      for interposition 45.51
      multiple segmental 45.61
      total 45.63
    total
      large intestine
        laparoscopic 45.81
        open 45.82
        other 45.83
        unspecified 45.83
      small intestine 45.63
joint structure NEC (*see also* Arthrectomy) 80.90
kidney (segmental) (wedge) 55.4
larynx (*see also* Laryngectomy)
  submucous 30.29
lesion — *see* Excision, lesion, by site
levator palpebrae muscle 08.33
ligament (*see also* Arthrectomy) 80.90
  broad 69.19
  round 69.19
  uterine 69.19
lip (wedge) 27.43
liver (partial) (wedge) 50.22
  lobe (total) 50.3
  total 50.4
lung (wedge) NEC 32.29
  endoscopic 32.28
  segmental (any part) 32.39
    thoracoscopic 32.30
  thoracoscopic 32.20
  volume reduction 32.22
    biologic lung volume reduction (BLVR) — *see* category 33.7 ☑
meninges (cerebral) 01.51
  spinal 03.4
mesentery 54.4
muscle 83.45
  extraocular 15.13
    with
      advancement or recession of other eye muscle 15.3
      suture of original insertion 15.13
  levator palpebrae 08.33
  Müller's, for blepharoptosis 08.35
  orbicularis oculi 08.20
  tarsal, for blepharoptosis 08.35
  for graft 83.43

Resection — *see also* Excision, by site — *continued*

muscle — *continued*
  for graft — *continued*
    hand 82.34
  hand 82.36
    for graft 82.34
  ocular — *see* Resection, muscle, extraocular
myocardium 37.33
nasal septum (submucous) 21.5
nerve (cranial) (peripheral) NEC 04.07
  phrenic 04.03
    for collapse of lung 33.31
  sympathetic 05.29
  vagus — *see* Vagotomy
nose (complete) (extended) (partial) (radical) 21.4
omentum 54.4
orbitomaxillary, radical 16.51
ovary (*see also* Oophorectomy, wedge) 65.22
  laparoscopic 65.24
palate (bony) (local) 27.31
  by wide excision 27.32
  soft 27.49
pancreas (total) (with synchronous duodenectomy) 52.6
  partial NEC 52.59
    distal (tail) (with part of body) 52.52
    proximal (head) (with part of body) (with synchronous duodenectomy) 52.51
    radical subtotal 52.53
  radical (one-stage) (two-stage) 52.7
  subtotal 52.53
pancreaticoduodenal (*see also* Pancreatectomy) 52.6
pelvic viscera (en masse) (female) 68.8
  male 57.71
penis 64.3
pericardium (partial) (for)
  chronic constrictive pericarditis 37.31
  drainage 37.12
  removal of adhesions 37.31
peritoneum 54.4
pharynx (partial) 29.33
phrenic nerve 04.03
  for collapse of lung 33.31
prostate (*see also* Prostatectomy)
  transurethral (punch) 60.29
pterygium 11.39
radial head 77.83
rectosigmoid (*see also* Resection, rectum) 48.69
rectum (partial) NEC 48.69
  with
    pelvic exenteration 68.8
    transsacral sigmoidectomy 48.61
  abdominoendorectal (combined), NOS 48.50
    laparoscopic 48.51
    open 48.52
    other 48.59
  abdominoperineal, NOS 48.50
    laparoscopic 48.51
    open 48.52
    other 48.59
    pull-through NEC 48.49
      Duhamel type 48.65
      laparoscopic 48.42
      not otherwise specified 48.40
      open 48.43
  anterior 48.63
    with colostomy (synchronous) 48.62
  Duhamel 48.65
  endorectal 48.41
    combined abdominal, NOS 48.50
      laparoscopic 48.51
      open 48.52
      other 48.59
  posterior 48.64
  pull-through NEC 48.49
    endorectal 48.41
    laparoscopic 48.42
    not otherwise specified 48.40
    open 48.43

☑ Additional Digit Required — Refer to the Tabular List for Digit Selection   ▽ Subterms under main terms may continue to next column or page

2015 ICD-9-CM   ▶◀ Revised Text   ● New Line   ▲ Revised Code   Volume 3 — 57

Resection — *see also* Excision, by site — *continued*
- rectum — *continued*
  - STARR procedure 48.74
  - submucosal (Soave) 48.41
    - combined abdominal, NOS 48.50
      - laparoscopic 48.51
      - open 48.52
      - other 48.59
- rib (transaxillary) 77.91
  - as operative approach — *omit code*
  - incidental to thoracic operation — *omit code*
- right ventricle (heart), for infundibular stenosis 35.34
- root (tooth) (apex) 23.73
  - with root canal therapy 23.72
  - residual or retained 23.11
- round ligament 69.19
- sclera 12.65
  - with scleral buckling (*see also* Buckling, scleral) 14.49
  - lamellar (for retinal reattachment) 14.49
    - with implant 14.41
- scrotum 61.3
- soft tissue NEC 83.49
  - hand 82.39
- sphincter of Oddi 51.89
- spinal cord (meninges) 03.4
- splanchnic 05.29
- splenic flexure (colon) 45.75
- sternum 77.81
- stomach (partial) (sleeve) (subtotal) NEC (*see also* Gastrectomy) 43.89
  - with anastomosis NEC 43.89
    - esophagogastric 43.5
    - gastroduodenal 43.6
    - gastrogastric 43.89
    - gastrojejunal 43.7
  - complete or total NEC 43.99
    - with intestinal interposition 43.91
  - fundus 43.89
  - laparoscopic 43.82
  - radical NEC 43.99
    - with intestinal interposition 43.91
  - wedge 43.42
    - endoscopic 43.41
- submucous
  - larynx 30.29
  - nasal septum 21.5
  - vocal cords 30.22
- synovial membrane (complete) (partial) (*see also* Synovectomy) 80.70
- tarsolevator 08.33
- tendon 83.42
  - hand 82.33
- thoracic structures (block) (en bloc) (radical) (brachial plexus, bronchus, lobes of lung, ribs, and sympathetic nerves) 32.6
- thorax 34.4
- tongue 25.2
  - wedge 25.1
- tooth root 23.73
  - with root canal therapy 23.72
  - apex (abscess) 23.73
    - with root canal therapy 23.72
  - residual or retained 23.11
- trachea 31.5
- transurethral
  - bladder NEC 57.49
  - prostate 60.29
- transverse colon
  - laparoscopic 17.34
  - open and other 45.74
- turbinates — *see* Turbinectomy
- ureter (partial) 56.41
  - total 56.42
- uterus — *see* Hysterectomy
- vein — *see* Phlebectomy
- ventricle (heart) 37.35
  - infundibula 35.34
- vesical neck 57.59
  - transurethral 57.49
- vocal cords (punch) 30.22

Respirator, volume-controlled (Bennett) (Byrd) — *see* Ventilation

Restoration
- cardioesophageal angle 44.66
  - laparoscopic 44.67
- dental NEC 23.49
  - by
    - application of crown (artificial) 23.41
    - insertion of bridge (fixed) 23.42
      - removable 23.43
- extremity — *see* Reattachment, extremity
- eyebrow 08.70
  - with graft 08.63
- eye socket 16.64
  - with graft 16.63
- tooth NEC 23.2
  - by
    - crown (artificial) 23.41
    - filling (amalgam) (plastic) (silicate) 23.2
    - inlay 23.3

Restrictive
- gastric band, laparoscopic 44.95

Resurfacing, hip 00.86
- acetabulum 00.87
  - with femoral head 00.85
- femoral head 00.86
  - with acetabulum 00.85
- partial NOS 00.85
  - acetabulum 00.87
  - femoral head 00.86
- total (acetabulum and femoral head) 00.85

Resuscitation
- artificial respiration 93.93
- cardiac 99.60
  - cardioversion 99.62
    - atrial 99.61
  - defibrillation 99.62
  - external massage 99.63
    - open chest 37.91
  - intracardiac injection 37.92
- cardiopulmonary 99.60
- endotracheal intubation 96.04
- manual 93.93
- mouth-to-mouth 93.93
- pulmonary 93.93

Resuture
- abdominal wall 54.61
- cardiac septum prosthesis 35.95
- chest wall 34.71
- heart valve prosthesis (poppet) 35.95
- wound (skin and subcutaneous tissue) (without graft) NEC 86.59

Retavase, infusion 99.10
Reteplase, infusion 99.10
Retightening (noninvasive)
- external fixator device — *omit code*
Retinaculotomy NEC — *see also* Division, ligament 80.40
- carpal tunnel (flexor) 04.43
Retraining
- cardiac 93.36
- vocational 93.85
Retrogasserian neurotomy 04.02
Revascularization
- cardiac (heart muscle) (myocardium) (direct) 36.10
  - with
    - bypass anastomosis
      - abdominal artery to coronary artery 36.17
      - aortocoronary (catheter stent) (homograft) (prosthesis) (saphenous vein graft) 36.10
        - one coronary vessel 36.11
        - two coronary vessels 36.12
        - three coronary vessels 36.13
        - four coronary vessels 36.14
      - gastroepiploic artery to coronary artery 36.17
      - internal mammary-coronary artery (single vessel) 36.15
        - double vessel 36.16
      - specified type NEC 36.19

Revascularization — *continued*
- cardiac — *continued*
  - with — *continued*
    - bypass anastomosis — *continued*
      - thoracic artery-coronary artery (single vessel) 36.15
        - double vessel 36.16
      - implantation of artery into heart (muscle) (myocardium) (ventricle) 36.2
    - indirect 36.2
    - specified type NEC 36.39
    - transmyocardial
      - endoscopic 36.33
      - endovascular 36.34
      - open chest 36.31
      - percutaneous 36.34
      - specified type NEC 36.32
      - thoracoscopic 36.33
Reversal, intestinal segment 45.50
- large 45.52
- small 45.51
Revision
- amputation stump 84.3
  - current traumatic — *see* Amputation
- anastomosis
  - biliary tract 51.94
  - blood vessel 39.49
  - gastric, gastrointestinal (with jejunal interposition) 44.5
  - intestine (large) 46.94
    - small 46.93
  - pleurothecal 03.97
  - pyelointestinal 56.72
  - salpingothecal 03.97
  - subarachnoid-peritoneal 03.97
  - subarachnoid-ureteral 03.97
  - ureterointestinal 56.72
- ankle replacement (prosthesis) 81.59
- anterior segment (eye) wound (operative) NEC 12.83
- arteriovenous shunt (cannula) (for dialysis) 39.42
- arthroplasty — *see* Arthroplasty
- bone flap, skull 02.06
- breast implant 85.93
- bronchostomy 33.42
- bypass graft (vascular) 39.49
  - abdominal-coronary artery 36.17
  - aortocoronary (catheter stent) (with prosthesis) (with saphenous vein graft) (with vein graft) 36.10
    - one coronary vessel 36.11
    - three coronary vessels 36.13
    - four coronary vessels 36.14
    - two coronary vessels 36.12
  - CABG — *see* Revision, aortocoronary bypass graft
  - chest tube — *see* intercostal catheter
  - coronary artery bypass graft (CABG) — *see* Revision, aortocoronary bypass graft, abdominal-coronary artery bypass, and internal mammary-coronary artery bypass
  - intercostal catheter (with lysis of adhesions) 34.04
    - thoracoscopic 34.06
  - internal mammary-coronary artery (single) 36.15
    - double vessel 36.16
- cannula, vessel-to-vessel (arteriovenous) 39.94
- canthus, lateral 08.59
- cardiac pacemaker
  - device (permanent) 37.89
  - electrode(s) (atrial) (transvenous) (ventricular) 37.75
  - pocket 37.79
- cardiac resynchronization defibrillator (CRT-D)
  - device 37.79
  - electrode(s) 37.75
  - pocket 37.79
- cardiac resynchronization pacemaker (CRT-P)
  - device (permanent) 37.89

Revision — *continued*
- cardiac resynchronization pacemaker — *continued*
  - electrode(s) (atria) (transvenous) (ventricular) 37.75
  - pocket 37.79
- cardioverter/defibrillator (automatic) pocket 37.79
- cholecystostomy 51.99
- cleft palate repair 27.63
- colostomy 46.43
- conduit, urinary 56.52
- cystostomy (stoma) 57.22
- disc — *see* Revision, intervertebral disc
- elbow replacement (prosthesis) 81.97
- enterostomy (stoma) 46.40
  - large intestine 46.43
  - small intestine 46.41
- enucleation socket 16.64
  - with graft 16.63
- esophagostomy 42.83
- exenteration cavity 16.66
  - with secondary graft 16.65
- extraocular muscle surgery 15.6
- fenestration, inner ear 20.62
- filtering bleb 12.66
- fixation device (broken) (displaced) (*see also* Fixation, bone, internal) 78.50
- flap or pedicle graft (skin) 86.75
- foot replacement (prosthesis) 81.59
- gastric anastomosis (with jejunal interposition) 44.5
- gastric band, laparoscopic 44.96
- gastric port device
  - laparoscopic 44.96
- gastroduodenostomy (with jejunal interposition) 44.5
- gastrointestinal anastomosis (with jejunal interposition) 44.5
- gastrojejunostomy 44.5
- gastrostomy 44.69
  - laparoscopic 44.68
- hand replacement (prosthesis) 81.97
- heart procedure NEC 35.95
- hip replacement NOS 81.53
  - acetabular and femoral components (total) 00.70
  - acetabular component only 00.71
  - acetabular liner and/or femoral head only 00.73
  - femoral component only 00.72
  - femoral head only and/or acetabular liner 00.73
  - partial
    - acetabular component only 00.71
    - acetabular liner and/or femoral head only 00.73
    - femoral component only 00.72
    - femoral head only and/or acetabular liner 00.73
  - total (acetabular and femoral components) 00.70
- Holter (-Spitz) valve 02.42
- ileal conduit 56.52
- ileostomy 46.41
- intervertebral disc, artificial (partial) (total) NOS 84.69
  - cervical 84.66
  - lumbar, lumbosacral 84.68
  - thoracic 84.67
- jejunoileal bypass 46.93
- jejunostomy 46.41
- joint replacement
  - acetabular and femoral components (total) 00.70
  - acetabular component only 00.71
  - acetabular liner and/or femoral head only 00.73
  - ankle 81.59
  - elbow 81.97
  - femoral component only 00.72
  - femoral head only and/or acetabular liner 00.73
  - foot 81.59
  - hand 81.97
  - hip 81.53

☑ Additional Digit Required — Refer to the Tabular List for Digit Selection · ▽ Subterms under main terms may continue to next column or page

58 — Volume 3 · ▶◀ Revised Text · ● New Line · ▲ Revised Code · 2015 ICD-9-CM

☑ Additional Digit Required — Refer to the Tabular List for Digit Selection   ▽ Subterms under main terms may continue to next column or page

60 — Volume 3   ▶◀ Revised Text   ● New Line   ▲ Revised Code   2015 ICD-9-CM

☑ **Additional Digit Required — Refer to the Tabular List for Digit Selection**   ▽ **Subterms under main terms may continue to next column or page**

Swinney operation (urethral reconstruction) 58.46

Switch, switching
  coronary arteries 35.84
  great arteries, total 35.84

Syme operation
  ankle amputation through malleoli of tibia and fibula 84.14
  urethrotomy, external 58.0

Sympathectomy NEC 05.29
  cervical 05.22
  cervicothoracic 05.22
  lumbar 05.23
  periarterial 05.25
  presacral 05.24
  renal 05.29
  thoracolumbar 05.23
  tympanum 20.91

Sympatheticotripsy 05.0

Symphysiotomy 77.39
  assisting delivery (obstetrical) 73.94
  kidney (horseshoe) 55.85

Symphysis, pleural 34.6

Synchondrotomy — see also Division, cartilage 80.40

Syndactylization 86.89

Syndesmotomy — see also Division, ligament 80.40

Synechiotomy
  endometrium 68.21
  iris (posterior) 12.33
    anterior 12.32

Synovectomy (joint) (complete) (partial) 80.70
  ankle 80.77
  elbow 80.72
  foot and toe 80.78
  hand and finger 80.74
  hip 80.75
  knee 80.76
  shoulder 80.71
  specified site NEC 80.79
  spine 80.79
  tendon sheath 83.42
    hand 82.33
  wrist 80.73

Syringing
  lacrimal duct or sac 09.43
  nasolacrimal duct 09.43
    with
      dilation 09.43
      insertion of tube or stent 09.44

T

Taarnhoj operation (trigeminal nerve root decompression) 04.41

Tack operation (sacculotomy) 20.79

Tactile Guidance System™ [TGS] — see category 17.4 ☑

Take-down
  anastomosis
    arterial 39.49
    blood vessel 39.49
    gastric, gastrointestinal 44.5
    intestine 46.93
    stomach 44.5
    vascular 39.49
    ventricular 02.43
  arterial bypass 39.49
  arteriovenous shunt 39.43
    with creation of new shunt 39.42
  cecostomy 46.52
  colostomy 46.52
  duodenostomy 46.51
  enterostomy 46.50
  esophagostomy 42.83
  gastroduodenostomy 44.5
  gastrojejunostomy 44.5
  ileostomy 46.51
  intestinal stoma 46.50
    large 46.52
    small 46.51
  jejunoileal bypass 46.93
  jejunostomy 46.51
  laryngostomy 31.62
  sigmoidostomy 46.52

Take-down — continued
  stoma
    bile duct 51.79
    bladder 57.82
    bronchus 33.42
    common duct 51.72
    esophagus 42.83
    gall bladder 51.92
    hepatic duct 51.79
    intestine 46.50
      large 46.52
      small 46.51
    kidney 55.82
    larynx 31.62
    rectum 48.72
    stomach 44.62
    thorax 34.72
    trachea 31.72
    ureter 56.83
    urethra 58.42
  systemic-pulmonary artery anastomosis 39.49
    in total repair of tetralogy of Fallot 35.81
  tracheostomy 31.72
  vascular anastomosis or bypass 39.49
  ventricular shunt (cerebral) 02.43

Talectomy 77.98

Talma-Morison operation (omentopexy) 54.74

Tamponade
  esophageal 96.06
  intrauterine (nonobstetric) 69.91
    after delivery or abortion 75.8
    antepartum 73.1
  vagina 96.14
    after delivery or abortion 75.8
    antepartum 73.1

Tanner operation (devascularization of stomach) 44.99

Tap
  abdomen 54.91
  chest 34.91
  cisternal 01.01
  cranial 01.09
  joint 81.91
  lumbar (diagnostic) (removal of dye) 03.31
  perilymphatic 20.79
  spinal (diagnostic) 03.31
  subdural (through fontanel) 01.09
  thorax 34.91

Tarsectomy 08.20
  de Grandmont 08.35

Tarsoplasty — see also Reconstruction, eyelid 08.70

Tarsorrhaphy (lateral) 08.52
  division or severing 08.02

Tattooing
  cornea 11.91
  skin 86.02

Tautening, eyelid for entropion 08.42

TAVI (transcatheter aortic valve implantation) 35.05

TAVR (transcatheter aortic valve replacement) 35.05

Telemetry (cardiac) 89.54

Teleradiotherapy
  beta particles 92.25
    intra-operative 92.41
  Betatron 92.24
  cobalt-60 92.23
  electrons 92.25
    intra-operative 92.41
  iodine-125 92.23
  linear accelerator 92.24
  neutrons 92.26
  particulate radiation NEC 92.26
  photons 92.24
  protons 92.26
  radioactive cesium 92.23
  radioisotopes NEC 92.23

Temperament assessment 94.02

Temperature gradient study — see also Thermography 88.89

Tendinoplasty — see Repair, tendon

Tendinosuture (immediate) (primary) — see also Suture, tendon 83.64

Tendinosuture — see also Suture, tendon — continued
  hand (see also Suture, tendon, hand) 82.45

Tendolysis 83.91
  hand 82.91

Tendoplasty — see Repair, tendon

Tenectomy 83.39
  eye 15.13
    levator palpebrae 08.33
    multiple (two or more tendons) 15.3
  hand 82.29
    levator palpebrae 08.33
  tendon sheath 83.31
    hand 82.21

Tenodesis (tendon fixation to skeletal attachment) 83.88
  Fowler 82.85
  hand 82.85

Tenolysis 83.91
  hand 82.91

Tenomyoplasty — see also Repair, tendon 83.88
  hand (see also Repair, tendon, hand) 82.86

Tenomyotomy — see Tenonectomy

Tenonectomy 83.42
  for graft 83.41
  hand 82.32
    hand 82.33
    for graft 82.32

Tenontomyoplasty — see Repair, tendon

Tenontoplasty — see Repair, tendon

Tenoplasty — see also Repair, tendon 83.88
  hand (see also Repair, tendon, hand) 82.86

Tenorrhaphy — see also Suture, tendon 83.64
  hand (see also Suture, tendon, hand) 82.45
  to skeletal attachment 83.88
    hand 82.85

Tenosuspension 83.88
  hand 82.86

Tenosuture — see also Suture, tendon 83.64
  hand (see also Suture, tendon, hand) 82.45
  to skeletal attachment 83.88
    hand 82.85

Tenosynovectomy 83.42
  hand 82.33

Tenotomy 83.13
  Achilles tendon 83.11
  adductor (hip) (subcutaneous) 83.12
  eye 15.12
    levator palpebrae 08.38
    multiple (two or more tendons) 15.4
  hand 82.11
  levator palpebrae 08.38
  pectoralis minor tendon (decompression thoracic outlet) 83.13
  stapedius 19.0
  tensor tympani 19.0

Tenovaginotomy — see Tenotomy

Tensing, orbicularis oculi 08.59

Termination of pregnancy
  by
    aspiration curettage 69.51
    dilation and curettage 69.01
    hysterectomy — see Hysterectomy
    hysterotomy 74.91
    intra-amniotic injection (saline) 75.0

Test, testing (for)
  14 C-Urea breath 89.39
  auditory function
    NEC 95.46
  Bender Visual-Motor Gestalt 94.02
  Benton Visual Retention 94.02
  cardiac (vascular)
    function NEC 89.59
    stress 89.44
      bicycle ergometer 89.43
      Masters' two-step 89.42
      treadmill 89.41
  Denver developmental (screening) 94.02
  fetus, fetal
    nonstress (fetal activity acceleration determinations) 75.34
    oxytocin challenge (contraction stress) 75.35

Test, testing — continued
  fetus, fetal — continued
    sensitivity (to oxytocin) — omit code
  function
    cardiac NEC 89.59
    hearing NEC 95.46
    muscle (by)
      electromyography 93.08
      manual 93.04
    neurologic NEC 89.15
    vestibular 95.46
      clinical 95.44
  glaucoma NEC 95.26
  hearing 95.47
    clinical NEC 95.42
  intelligence 94.01
  internal jugular-subclavian venous reflux 89.62
  intracarotid amobarbital (Wada) 89.10
  Masters' two-step stress (cardiac) 89.42
  muscle function (by)
    electromyography 93.08
    manual 93.04
  neurologic function NEC 89.15
  neurophysiologic monitoring intra-operative 00.94
  nocturnal penile tumescence 89.29
  provocative, for glaucoma 95.26
  psychologic NEC 94.08
  psychometric 94.01
  radio-cobalt B_{12} Schilling 92.04
  range of motion 93.05
  rotation (Bárány chair) (hearing) 95.45
  sleep disorder function — see categories 89.17-89.18
  Stanford-Binet 94.01
  Thallium stress (transesophageal pacing) 89.44
  tuning fork (hearing) 95.42
  Urea breath, (14 C) 89.39
  vestibular function NEC 95.46
    thermal 95.44
  Wada (hemispheric function) 89.10
  whispered speech (hearing) 95.42

TEVAP (transurethral electrovaporization of prostate) 60.29

Thalamectomy 01.41

Thalamotomy 01.41
  by stereotactic radiosurgery 92.32
    cobalt 60 92.32
    linear accelerator (LINAC) 92.31
    multi-source 92.32
    particle beam 92.33
    particulate 92.33
    radiosurgery NEC 92.39
    single source photon 92.31

Thal operation (repair of esophageal stricture) 42.85

Theleplasty 85.87

Therapy
  Antabuse 94.25
  aqueous oxygen (AO) 00.49
  art 93.89
  aversion 94.33
  behavior 94.33
  Bennett respirator — see category 96.7 ☑
  blind rehabilitation NEC 93.78
  Byrd respirator — see category 96.7 ☑
  carbon dioxide 94.25
  cobalt-60 92.23
  conditioning, psychiatric 94.33
  continuous positive airway pressure (CPAP) 93.90
    delivered by
      endotracheal tube — see category 96.7 ☑
      tracheostomy — see category 96.7 ☑
  croupette, croup tent 93.94
  daily living activities 93.83
    for the blind 93.78
  dance 93.89
  desensitization 94.33
  detoxification 94.25
  diversional 93.81
  domestic tasks 93.83

☑ Additional Digit Required — Refer to the Tabular List for Digit Selection   ▽ Subterms under main terms may continue to next column or page

2015 ICD-9-CM   ▶◀ Revised Text   ● New Line   ▲ Revised Code   Volume 3 — 63

Therapy — *continued*
  domestic tasks — *continued*
    for the blind 93.78
  Downstream® system 00.49
  educational (bed-bound children) (handi-
      capped) 93.82
  electroconvulsive (ECT) 94.27
  electroshock (EST) 94.27
    subconvulsive 94.26
  electrotonic (ETT) 94.27
  encounter group 94.44
  extinction 94.33
  family 94.42
  fog (inhalation) 93.94
  gamma ray 92.23
  group NEC 94.44
    for psychosexual dysfunctions 94.41
  hearing NEC 95.49
  heat NEC 93.35
    for cancer treatment 99.85
  helium 93.98
  hot pack(s) 93.35
  hyperbaric oxygen 93.95
    wound 93.59
  hyperthermia NEC 93.35
    for cancer treatment 99.85
  individual, psychiatric NEC 94.39
    for psychosexual dysfunction 94.34
  industrial 93.89
  infrared irradiation 93.35
  inhalation NEC 93.96
    nitric oxide 00.12
  insulin shock 94.24
  intermittent positive pressure breathing
      (IPPB) 93.91
  IPPB (intermittent positive pressure
      breathing) 93.91
  leech 99.99
  lithium 94.22
  LITT (laser interstitial thermal therapy) under
      guidance
    lesion
      brain 17.61
      breast 17.69
      head and neck 17.62
      liver 17.63
      lung 17.69
      prostate 17.69
      thyroid 17.62
  maggot 86.28
  manipulative, osteopathic (*see also* Manipu-
      lation, osteopathic) 93.67
  manual arts 93.81
  methadone 94.25
  mist (inhalation) 93.94
  music 93.84
  nebulizer 93.94
  neuroleptic 94.23
  nitric oxide 00.12
  occupational 93.83
  oxygen 93.96
    aqueous 00.49
    catalytic 93.96
    hyperbaric 93.95
      wound 93.59
    SuperSaturated 00.49
    wound (hyperbaric) 93.59
  paraffin bath 93.35
  physical NEC 93.39
    combined (without mention of compo-
        nents) 93.38
    diagnostic NEC 93.09
  play 93.81
    psychotherapeutic 94.36
  positive end expiratory pressure — *see* cat-
      egory 96.7 ☑
  psychiatric NEC 94.39
    drug NEC 94.25
      lithium 94.22
  radiation 92.29
    contact (150 KVP or less) 92.21
    deep (200-300 KVP) 92.22
    electron, intra-operative 92.41
    high voltage (200-300 KVP) 92.22
    low voltage (150 KVP or less) 92.21
    megavoltage 92.24

Therapy — *continued*
  radiation — *continued*
    orthovoltage 92.22
    particle source NEC 92.26
    photon 92.24
    radioisotope (teleradiotherapy) 92.23
    retinal lesion 14.26
    superficial (150 KVP or less) 92.21
    supervoltage 92.24
  radioisotope, radioisotopic NEC 92.29
    implantation or insertion 92.27
    injection or instillation 92.28
    teleradiotherapy 92.23
  radium (radon) 92.23
  recreational 93.81
  rehabilitation NEC 93.89
  respiratory NEC 93.99
    bi-level positive airway pressure [BiPAP]
        93.90
      delivered by
        endotracheal tube — *see* catego-
            ry 96.7 ☑
        tracheostomy — *see* category
            96.7 ☑
    continuous positive airway pressure
        [CPAP] 93.90
      delivered by
        endotracheal tube — *see* catego-
            ry 96.7 ☑
        tracheostomy — *see* category
            96.7 ☑
    endotracheal respiratory assistance —
        see category 96.7 ☑
    intermittent positive pressure breathing
        [IPPB] 93.91
    negative pressure (continuous) [CNP]
        93.99
    nitric oxide 00.12
    non-invasive positive pressure (NIPPV)
        93.90
    other continuous invasive (unspecified
        duration) 96.70
      for 96 consecutive hours or more
          96.72
      for less than 96 consecutive hours
          96.71
    positive end expiratory pressure [PEEP]
      invasive — *see* category 96.7 ☑
      non-invasive [NIPPV] 93.90
  root canal 23.70
    with
      apicoectomy 23.72
      irrigation 23.71
  shock
    chemical 94.24
    electric 94.27
      subconvulsive 94.26
    insulin 94.24
  speech 93.75
    for correction of defect 93.74
  SuperOxygenation (SSO₂) 00.49
  SuperSaturated oxygen 00.49
  ultrasound
    heat therapy 93.35
    hyperthermia for cancer treatment 99.85
    physical therapy 93.35
    therapeutic — *see* Ultrasound
  ultraviolet light 99.82
Thermocautery — *see* Cauterization
Thermography 88.89
  blood vessel 88.86
  bone 88.83
  breast 88.85
  cerebral 88.81
  eye 88.82
  lymph gland 88.89
  muscle 88.84
  ocular 88.82
  osteoarticular 88.83
  specified site NEC 88.89
  vein, deep 88.86
Thermokeratoplasty 11.74
Thermoplasty
  bronchoscopic, bronchial (lung) 32.27
Thermosclerectomy 12.62

Thermotherapy (hot packs) (paraffin bath)
    NEC 93.35
  prostate
    by
      microwave 60.96
      radiofrequency 60.97
    transurethral microwave thermotherapy
        (TUMT) 60.96
    transurethral needle ablation (TUNA)
        60.97
    TUMT (transurethral microwave ther-
        motherapy) 60.96
    TUNA (transurethral needle ablation)
        60.97
Thiersch operation
  anus 49.79
  skin graft 86.69
    hand 86.62
Thompson operation
  cleft lip repair 27.54
  correction of lymphedema 40.9
  quadricepsplasty 83.86
  thumb apposition with bone graft 82.69
Thoracectomy 34.09
  for lung collapse 33.34
Thoracentesis 34.91
Thoracocentesis 34.91
Thoracolysis (for collapse of lung) 33.39
Thoracoplasty (anterior) (extrapleural) (par-
    avertebral) (posterolateral) (complete)
    (partial) 33.34
Thoracoscopy, transpleural (for exploration)
    34.21
Thoracostomy 34.09
  for lung collapse 33.32
Thoracotomy (with drainage) 34.09
  as operative approach — *omit code*
  exploratory 34.02
**Thoratec® implantable ventricular assist
    device** (IVAD™) 37.66
**Thoratec® ventricular assist device (VAD)
    system** 37.66
Three-snip operation, punctum 09.51
Thrombectomy 38.00
  with endarterectomy — *see* Endarterectomy
  abdominal
    artery 38.06
    vein 38.07
  aorta (arch) (ascending) (descending) 38.04
  arteriovenous shunt or cannula 39.49
  bovine graft 39.49
  coronary artery 36.09
  head and neck vessel NEC 38.02
  intracranial vessel NEC 38.01
  lower limb
    artery 38.08
    vein 38.09
  mechanical
    endovascular
      head and neck 39.74
  pulmonary vessel 38.05
  thoracic vessel NEC 38.05
  upper limb (artery) (vein) 38.03
Thromboendarterectomy 38.10
  abdominal 38.16
  aorta (arch) (ascending) (descending) 38.14
  coronary artery 36.09
    open chest approach 36.03
  head and neck NEC 38.12
  intracranial NEC 38.11
  lower limb 38.18
  thoracic NEC 38.15
  upper limb 38.13
Thymectomy 07.80
  partial (open) (other) 07.81
    thoracoscopic 07.83
  total (open) (other) 07.82
    thoracoscopic 07.84
  transcervical 07.99
Thyrochondrotomy 31.3
Thyrocricoidectomy 30.29
Thyrocricotomy (for assistance in breathing)
    31.1
Thyroidectomy NEC 06.39
  by mediastinotomy (*see also* Thyroidectomy,
      substernal) 06.50

Thyroidectomy — *continued*
  with laryngectomy — *see* Laryngectomy
  complete or total 06.4
    substernal (by mediastinotomy)
        (transsternal route) 06.52
    transoral route (lingual) 06.6
  lingual (complete) (partial) (subtotal) (total)
      06.6
  partial or subtotal NEC 06.39
    with complete removal of remaining
        lobe 06.2
    submental route (lingual) 06.6
    substernal (by mediastinotomy)
        (transsternal route) 06.51
  remaining tissue 06.4
  submental route (lingual) 06.6
  substernal (by mediastinotomy) (transster-
      nal route) 06.50
    complete or total 06.52
    partial or subtotal 06.51
  transoral route (lingual) 06.6
  transsternal route (*see also* Thyroidectomy,
      substernal) 06.50
  unilateral (with removal of isthmus) (with
      removal of portion of other lobe)
      06.2
Thyroidorrhaphy 06.93
Thyroidotomy (field) (gland) NEC 06.09
  postoperative 06.02
Thyrotomy 31.3
  with tantalum plate 31.69
Tirofiban (HCl), infusion 99.20
Toilette
  skin — *see* Debridement, skin or subcuta-
      neous tissue
  tracheostomy 96.55
Token economy (behavior therapy) 94.33
Tomkins operation (metroplasty) 69.49
Tomography — *see also* Radiography
  abdomen NEC 88.02
  cardiac 87.42
  computerized axial NEC 88.38
    abdomen 88.01
    bone 88.38
      quantitative 88.98
    brain 87.03
    cardiac 87.41
    coronary 87.41
    head 87.03
    kidney 87.71
    skeletal 88.38
      quantitative 88.98
    thorax 87.41
  head NEC 87.04
  kidney NEC 87.72
  lung 87.42
  optical coherence (intravascular imaging)
    coronary vessel(s) 38.24
    non-coronary vessel(s) 38.25
  thorax NEC 87.42
Tongue tie operation 25.91
Tonography 95.26
Tonometry 89.11
Tonsillectomy 28.2
  with adenoidectomy 28.3
Tonsillotomy 28.0
Topectomy 01.32
Torek (-Bevan) operation (orchidopexy) (first
    stage) (second stage) 62.5
Torkildsen operation (ventriculocisternal
    shunt) 02.2 ☑
Torpin operation (cul-de-sac resection) 70.92
Toti operation (dacryocystorhinostomy) 09.81
Touchas operation 86.83
Touroff operation (ligation of subclavian
    artery) 38.85
Toxicology — *see* Examination, microscopic
TPN (total parenteral nutrition) 99.15
Trabeculectomy ab externo 12.64
Trabeculodialysis 12.59
Trabeculotomy ab externo 12.54
Trachelectomy 67.4
Trachelopexy 69.22
Tracheloplasty 67.69
Trachelorrhaphy (Emmet) (suture) 67.61
  obstetrical 75.51

☑ Additional Digit Required — Refer to the Tabular List for Digit Selection   ▽ Subterms under main terms may continue to next column or page

64 — Volume 3   ▶◀ Revised Text   ● New Line   ▲ Revised Code   2015 ICD-9-CM

☑ **Additional Digit Required** — Refer to the Tabular List for Digit Selection

▽ **Subterms under main terms may continue to next column or page**

Transplant, transplantation — *continued*
  toe (replacing absent thumb) (with amputation) 82.69 *[84.11]*
    to finger, except thumb 82.81 *[84.11]*
  tooth 23.5
  ureter to
    bladder 56.74
    ileum (external diversion) 56.51
      internal diversion only 56.71
    intestine 56.71
    skin 56.61
  vein (peripheral) 39.59
    renal, aberrant 39.55
  vitreous 14.72
    anterior approach 14.71
Transposition
  extraocular muscles 15.5
  eyelash flaps 08.63
    eye muscle (oblique) (rectus) 15.5
  finger (replacing absent thumb) (same hand) 82.61
    to
      finger, except thumb 82.81
      opposite hand (with ampu-tation) 82.69 *[84.01]*
  interatrial venous return 35.91
  jejunal (Henley) 43.81
  joint capsule (*see also* Arthroplasty) 81.96
  muscle NEC 83.79
    extraocular 15.5
    hand 82.59
  nerve (cranial) (peripheral) (radial anterior) (ulnar) 04.6
  nipple 85.86
  pterygium 11.31
  tendon NEC 83.76
    hand 82.57
  vocal cords 31.69
Transureteroureterostomy 56.75
Transversostomy — *see also* Colostomy 46.10
Trapping, aneurysm (cerebral) 39.52
Trauner operation (lingual sulcus extension) 24.91
Trephination, trephining
  accessory sinus — *see* Sinusotomy
  corneoscleral 12.89
  cranium 01.24
  nasal sinus — *see* Sinusotomy
  sclera (with iridectomy) 12.61
Trial (failed) forceps 73.3
Trigonectomy 57.6
Trimming, amputation stump 84.3
Triple arthrodesis 81.12
Trochanterplasty 81.40
Tsuge operation (macrodactyly repair) 82.83
Tuck, tucking — *see also* Plication
  eye muscle 15.22
    multiple (two or more muscles) 15.4
  levator palpebrae, for blepharoptosis 08.34
Tudor "rabbit ear" operation (anterior urethropexy) 59.79
Tuffier operation
  apicolysis of lung 33.39
  vaginal hysterectomy 68.59
    laparoscopically assisted (LAVH) 68.51
TULIP (transurethral ultrasound guided laser induced prostatectomy) 60.21
TUMT (transurethral microwave thermotherapy) **of prostate** 60.96
TUNA (transurethral needle ablation) of prostate 60.97
Tunnel, subcutaneous (antethoracic) 42.86
  with esophageal anastomosis 42.68
  esophageal 42.86
    with anastomosis — *see* Anastomosis, esophagus, antesternal
  pulse generator lead wire 86.99
    with initial procedure — *omit code*
Turbinectomy (complete) (partial) NEC 21.69
  by
    cryosurgery 21.61
    diathermy 21.61
  with sinusectomy — *see* Sinusectomy
Turco operation (release of joint capsules in clubfoot) 80.48
TURP (transurethral resection of prostate) 60.29

Tylectomy (breast) (partial) 85.21
Tympanectomy 20.59
  with tympanoplasty — *see* Tympanoplasty
Tympanogram 95.41
Tympanomastoidectomy 20.42
Tympanoplasty (type I) (with graft) 19.4
  with
    air pocket over round window 19.54
    fenestra in semicircular canal 19.55
    graft against
      incus or malleus 19.52
      mobile and intact stapes 19.53
    incudostapediopexy 19.52
  epitympanic, type I 19.4
  revision 19.6
  type
    II (graft against incus or malleus) 19.52
    III (graft against mobile and intact stapes) 19.53
    IV (air pocket over round window) 19.54
    V (fenestra in semicircular canal) 19.55
Tympanosympathectomy 20.91
Tympanotomy 20.09
  with intubation 20.01

U

UAE (uterine artery embolization), NOS 68.25
  with
    coils 68.24
    particulate agent (gelatin sponge) (gelfoam) (microspheres) (polyvinyl alcohol) (PVA) (spherical embolics) 68.25
Uchida operation (tubal ligation with or without fimbriectomy) 66.32
UFR (uroflowmetry) 89.24
Ultrafiltration 99.78
  hemodiafiltration 39.95
  hemodialysis (kidney) 39.95
  removal, plasma water 99.78
  therapeutic plasmapheresis 99.71
Ultrasonography
  abdomen 88.76
  aortic arch 88.73
  biliary tract 88.74
  breast 88.73
  deep vein thrombosis 88.77
  digestive system 88.74
  eye 95.13
  head and neck 88.71
  heart 88.72
  intestine 88.74
  intravascular — *see* Ultrasound, intravascular (IVUS)
  lung 88.73
  midline shift, brain 88.71
  multiple sites 88.79
  peripheral vascular system 88.77
  retroperitoneum 88.76
  therapeutic — *see* Ultrasound
  thorax NEC 88.73
  total body 88.79
  urinary system 88.75
  uterus 88.79
    gravid 88.78
Ultrasound
  diagnostic — *see* Ultrasonography
  fragmentation (of)
    cataract (with aspiration) 13.41
    urinary calculus, stones (Kock pouch) 59.95
  heart (intravascular) 88.72
    intracardiac (heart chambers) (ICE) 37.28
    intravascular (coronary vessels) (IVUS) 00.24
    non-invasive 88.72
  inner ear 20.79
  intravascular (IVUS) (VH™-IVUS) 00.29
    aorta 00.22
    aortic arch 00.22
    cerebral vessel, extracranial 00.21
    coronary vessel 00.24
    intrathoracic vessel 00.22
    other specified vessel 00.28
    peripheral vessel 00.23
    renal vessel 00.25

Ultrasound — *continued*
  intravascular — *continued*
    vena cava (inferior) (superior) 00.22
  therapeutic
    head 00.01
    heart 00.02
    neck 00.01
    other therapeutic ultrasound 00.09
    peripheral vascular vessels 00.03
    vessels of head and neck 00.01
  therapy 93.35
  VH™-IVUS — *see* Ultrasound, intravascular, by site
  virtual histology intravascular ultrasound — *see* Ultrasound, intravascular, by site
Umbilectomy 54.3
Unbridling
  blood vessel, peripheral 39.91
  celiac artery axis 39.91
Uncovering — *see* Incision, by site
Undercutting
  hair follicle 86.09
  perianal tissue 49.02
Unroofing — *see also* Incision, by site
  external
    auditory canal 18.02
    ear NEC 18.09
  kidney cyst 55.39
UPP (urethral pressure profile) 89.25
Upper GI series (x-ray) 87.62
UPPP (uvulopalatopharyngoplasty) 27.69 *[29.4]*
Uranoplasty (for cleft palate repair) 27.62
Uranorrhaphy (for cleft palate repair) 27.62
Uranostaphylorrhaphy 27.62
Urban operation (mastectomy) (unilateral) 85.47
  bilateral 85.48
Ureterectomy 56.40
  with nephrectomy 55.51
  partial 56.41
  total 56.42
Ureterocecostomy 56.71
Ureterocelectomy 56.41
Ureterocolostomy 56.71
Ureterocystostomy 56.74
Ureteroenterostomy 56.71
Ureteroileostomy (internal diversion) 56.71
  external diversion 56.51
Ureterolithotomy 56.2
Ureterolysis 59.02
  with freeing or repositioning of ureter 59.02
  laparoscopic 59.03
Ureteroneocystostomy 56.74
Ureteropexy 56.85
Ureteroplasty 56.89
Ureteroplication 56.89
Ureteroproctostomy 56.71
Ureteropyelography (intravenous) (diuretic infusion) 87.73
  percutaneous 87.75
  retrograde 87.74
Ureteropyeloplasty 55.87
Ureteropyelostomy 55.86
Ureterorrhaphy 56.82
Ureteroscopy 56.31
  with biopsy 56.33
Ureterosigmoidostomy 56.71
Ureterostomy (cutaneous) (external) (tube) 56.61
  closure 56.83
  ileal 56.51
Ureterotomy 56.2
Ureteroureterostomy (crossed) 56.75
  lumbar 56.41
  resection with end-to-end anastomosis 56.41
  spatulated 56.41
Urethral catheterization, indwelling 57.94
Urethral pressure profile (UPP) 89.25
Urethrectomy (complete) (partial) (radical) 58.39
  with
    complete cystectomy 57.79
    pelvic exenteration 68.8
    radical cystectomy 57.71

Urethrocystography (retrograde) (voiding) 87.76
Urethrocystopexy (by) 59.79
  levator muscle sling 59.71
  retropubic suspension 59.5
  suprapubic suspension 59.4
Urethrolithotomy 58.0
Urethrolysis 58.5
Urethropexy 58.49
  anterior 59.79
Urethroplasty 58.49
  augmentation 59.79
  collagen implant 59.72
  fat implant 59.72
  injection (endoscopic) of implant into urethra 59.72
  polytef implant 59.72
Urethrorrhaphy 58.41
Urethroscopy 58.22
  for control of hemorrhage of prostate 60.94
  perineal 58.21
Urethrostomy (perineal) 58.0
Urethrotomy (external) 58.0
  internal (endoscopic) 58.5
Uroflowmetry (UFR) 89.24
Urography (antegrade) (excretory) (intravenous) 87.73
  retrograde 87.74
Uteropexy (abdominal approach) (vaginal approach) 69.22
UVP (uvulopalatopharyngoplasty) 27.69 *[29.4]*
Uvulectomy 27.72
Uvulopalatopharyngoplasty (UPPP) 27.69 *[29.4]*
Uvulotomy 27.71

V

Vaccination (prophylactic) (against) 99.59
  anthrax 99.55
  brucellosis 99.55
  cholera 99.31
  common cold 99.51
  disease NEC 99.55
    arthropod-borne viral NEC 99.54
  encephalitis, arthropod-borne viral 99.53
  German measles 99.47
  hydrophobia 99.44
  infectious parotitis 99.46
  influenza 99.52
  measles 99.45
  mumps 99.46
  paratyphoid fever 99.32
  pertussis 99.37
  plague 99.34
  poliomyelitis 99.41
  rabies 99.44
  Rocky Mountain spotted fever 99.55
  rubella 99.47
  rubeola 99.45
  smallpox 99.42
  Staphylococcus 99.55
  Streptococcus 99.55
  tuberculosis 99.33
  tularemia 99.35
  tumor 99.28
  typhoid 99.32
  typhus 99.55
  undulant fever 99.55
  yellow fever 99.43
Vacuum extraction, fetal head 72.79
  with episiotomy 72.71
VAD
  vascular access device — *see* Vascular access device, totally implantable
  ventricular assist device — *see* Implant, heart assist system
Vagectomy (subdiaphragmatic) — *see also* Vagotomy 44.00
Vaginal douche 96.44
Vaginectomy 70.4
Vaginofixation 70.77
  with graft or prosthesis 70.78
Vaginoperineotomy 70.14
Vaginoplasty 70.79
Vaginorrhaphy 70.71
  obstetrical 75.69

☑ **Additional Digit Required — Refer to the Tabular List for Digit Selection**   ▽ **Subterms under main terms may continue to next column or page**

Vaginoscopy 70.21
Vaginotomy 70.14
  for
    culdocentesis 70.0
    pelvic abscess 70.12
Vagotomy (gastric) 44.00
  parietal cell 44.02
  selective NEC 44.03
    highly 44.02
    Holle's 44.02
    proximal 44.02
  truncal 44.01
Valvotomy — see Valvulotomy
Valvulectomy, heart — see Valvuloplasty, heart
Valvuloplasty
  heart, unspecified (without valve replacement) 35.10
    with prosthesis or tissue graft — see Replacement, heart, valve, by site
  aortic valve 35.11
    percutaneous (balloon) 35.96
  balloon, percutaneous 35.96
  combined with repair of atrial and ventricular septal defects — see Repair, endocardial cushion defect
  mitral valve
    balloon, percutaneous repair 35.96
    endovascular repair with implant 35.97
    open, without replacement 35.12
    percutaneous repair
      with implant (leaflet clip) 35.97
    transcatheter repair with implant 35.97
  open heart technique 35.10
  percutaneous (balloon) 35.96
  pulmonary valve 35.13
    in total repair of tetralogy of Fallot 35.81
    percutaneous (balloon) 35.96
  tricuspid valve 35.14
Valvulotomy
  heart (closed heart technique) (transatrial) (transventricular) 35.00
  aortic valve 35.01
  mitral valve 35.02
  open heart technique — see Valvuloplasty, heart
  pulmonary valve 35.03
    in total repair of tetralogy of Fallot 35.81
  tricuspid valve 35.04
Varicocelectomy, spermatic cord 63.1
Varicotomy, peripheral vessels (lower limb) 38.59
  upper limb 38.53
Vascular access device, totally implantable 86.07
Vascular closure, percutaneous puncture — omit code
Vascularization — see Revascularization
Vasectomy (complete) (partial) 63.73
Vasogram 87.94
Vasoligation 63.71
  gastric 38.86
Vasorrhaphy 63.81
Vasostomy 63.6
Vasotomy 63.6
Vasotripsy 63.71
Vasovasostomy 63.82
Vectorcardiogram (VCG) (with ECG) 89.53
Vectra® vascular access graft 86.07
Venectomy — see Phlebectomy
Venipuncture NEC 38.99
  for injection of contrast material — see Phlebography
Venography — see Phlebography
Venorrhaphy 39.32
Venotomy 38.00
  abdominal 38.07
  head and neck NEC 38.02
  intracranial NEC 38.01
  lower limb 38.09
  thoracic NEC 38.05
  upper limb 38.03

Venotripsy 39.98
Venovenostomy 39.29
Ventilation
  bi-level positive airway pressure [BiPAP] 93.90
    delivered by
      endotracheal tube — see category 96.7 ☑
      tracheostomy — see category 96.7 ☑
  continuous positive airway pressure [CPAP] 93.90
    delivered by
      endotracheal tube — see category 96.7 ☑
      tracheostomy — see category 96.7 ☑
  endotracheal respiratory assistance — see category 96.7 ☑
  intermittent positive pressure breathing [IPPB] 93.91
  mechanical, NOS 93.90
    by endotracheal tube — see category 96.7 ☑
    by tracheostomy — see category 96.7 ☑
    endotracheal respiratory assistance — see category 96.7 ☑
    invasive — see category 96.7 ☑
    non-invasive [NIPPV] 93.90
    other continuous invasive (unspecified duration) 96.70
      for 96 consecutive hours or more 96.72
      for less than 96 consecutive hours 96.71
    positive end expiratory pressure [PEEP]
      invasive — see category 96.7 ☑
      non-invasive [NIPPV] 93.90
  negative pressure (continuous) [CNP] 93.99
  non-invasive positive pressure (NIPPV) 93.90
Ventriculectomy, heart
  partial 37.35
Ventriculocholecystostomy 02.34
Ventriculocisternostomy 02.22
Ventriculocordectomy 30.29
Ventriculogram, ventriculography (cerebral) 87.02
  cardiac
    left ventricle (outflow tract) 88.53
      combined with right heart 88.54
    right ventricle (outflow tract) 88.52
      combined with left heart 88.54
    radionuclide cardiac 92.05
Ventriculomyocardiotomy 37.11
Ventriculoperitoneostomy 02.34
Ventriculopuncture 01.09
  through previously implanted catheter or reservoir (Ommaya) (Rickham) 01.02
Ventriculoseptopexy — see also Repair, ventricular septal defect 35.72
Ventriculoseptoplasty — see also Repair, ventricular septal defect 35.72
Ventriculostomy
  for
    external ventricular drainage (EVD) 02.21
    placement of ventricular catheter 02.21
    third (endoscopic) 02.22
Ventriculotomy
  cerebral 02.22
  heart 37.11
Ventriculoureterostomy 02.35
Ventriculovenostomy 02.32
Ventrofixation, uterus 69.22
Ventrohysteropexy 69.22
Ventrosuspension, uterus 69.22
VEP (visual evoked potential) 95.23
Version, obstetrical (bimanual) (cephalic) (combined) (internal) (podalic) 73.21
  with extraction 73.22
  Braxton Hicks 73.21
    with extraction 73.22
  external (bipolar) 73.91
  Potter's (podalic) 73.21
    with extraction 73.22
  Wigand's (external) 73.91

Version, obstetrical — continued
  Wright's (cephalic) 73.21
    with extraction 73.22
Vertebroplasty, percutaneous 81.65
Vesicolithotomy (suprapubic) 57.19
Vesicostomy 57.21
Vesicourethroplasty 57.85
Vesiculectomy 60.73
  with radical prostatectomy 60.5
Vesiculogram, seminal 87.92
  contrast 87.91
Vesiculotomy 60.72
Vestibuloplasty (buccolabial) (lingual) 24.91
Vestibulotomy 20.79
VH™-IVUS — see Ultrasound, intravascular, by site
Vicq D'azyr operation (larynx) 31.1
Vidal operation (varicocele ligation) 63.1
Vidianectomy 05.21
Villusectomy — see also Synovectomy 80.70
Vision check 95.09
Visual evoked potential (VEP) 95.23
Vitrectomy (mechanical) (posterior approach) 14.74
  with scleral buckling 14.49
  anterior approach 14.73
Vocational
  assessment 93.85
  retraining 93.85
  schooling 93.82
Voice training (postlaryngectomy) 93.73
von Kraske operation (proctectomy) 48.64
Voss operation (hanging hip operation) 83.19
Vulpius (-Compere) operation (lengthening of gastrocnemius muscle) 83.85
Vulvectomy (bilateral) (simple) 71.62
  partial (unilateral) 71.61
  radical (complete) 71.5
  unilateral 71.61
V-Y operation (repair)
  bladder 57.89
    neck 57.85
  ectropion 08.44
  lip 27.59
  skin (without graft) 86.89
  subcutaneous tissue (without skin graft) 86.89
  tongue 25.59

W

Wada test (hemispheric function) 89.10
Wang needle aspiration biopsy
  bronchus 33.24
  lung 33.27
Wardill operation 27.62
Ward-Mayo operation (vaginal hysterectomy) 68.59
  laparoscopically assisted (LAVH) 68.51
Washing — see Lavage and Irrigation
Waterston operation (aorta-right pulmonary artery anastomosis) 39.0
Watkins (-Wertheim) operation (uterus interposition) 69.21
Watson-Jones operation
  hip arthrodesis 81.21
  reconstruction of lateral ligaments, ankle 81.49
  shoulder arthrodesis (extra-articular) 81.23
  tenoplasty 83.88
Webbing (syndactylization) 86.89
Weir operation
  appendicostomy 47.91
  correction of nostrils 21.86
Wertheim operation (radical hysterectomy) 68.69
  laparoscopic 68.61
West operation (dacryocystorhinostomy) 09.81
Wheeler operation
  entropion repair 08.44
  halving procedure (eyelid) 08.24
Whipple operation (radical pancreaticoduodenectomy) 52.7
  Child modification (radical subtotal pancreatectomy) 52.53

Whipple operation — continued
  Rodney Smith modification (radical subtotal pancreatectomy) 52.53
Whitehead operation
  glossectomy, radical 25.4
  hemorrhoidectomy 49.46
White operation (lengthening of tendo calcaneus by incomplete tenotomy) 83.11
Whitman operation
  foot stabilization (talectomy) 77.98
  hip reconstruction 81.40
  repair of serratus anterior muscle 83.87
  talectomy 77.98
  trochanter wedge osteotomy 77.25
Wier operation (entropion repair) 08.44
Williams-Richardson operation (vaginal construction) 70.61
  with graft or prosthesis 70.63
Wilms operation (thoracoplasty) 33.34
Wilson operation (angulation osteotomy for hallux valgus) 77.51
Window operation
  antrum (nasal sinus) — see Antrotomy, maxillary
  aorticopulmonary 39.59
  bone cortex (see also Incision, bone) 77.10
    facial 76.09
  nasoantral — see Antrotomy, maxillary
  pericardium 37.12
  pleura 34.09
Winiwarter operation (cholecystoenterostomy) 51.32
Wiring
  aneurysm 39.52
  dental (for immobilization) 93.55
    with fracture-reduction — see Reduction, fracture
  orthodontic 24.7
Wirsungojejunostomy 52.96
Witzel operation (temporary gastrostomy) 43.19
Woodward operation (release of high riding scapula) 81.83
Wrapping, aneurysm (gauze) (methyl methacrylate) (plastic) 39.52

X

Xenograft 86.65
Xerography, breast 87.36
Xeromammography 87.36
Xiphoidectomy 77.81
X-ray
  chest (routine) 87.44
    wall NEC 87.39
  contrast — see Radiography, contrast
  diagnostic — see Radiography
  injection of radio-opaque substance — see Radiography, contrast
  skeletal series, whole or complete 88.31
  therapeutic — see Therapy, radiation

Y

Young operation
  epispadias repair 58.45
  tendon transfer (anterior tibialis) (repair of flat foot) 83.75
Yount operation (division of iliotibial band) 83.14

Z

Zancolli operation
  capsuloplasty 81.72
  tendon transfer (biceps) 82.56
Zeus® Robotic Surgical System — see category 17.4 ☑
Ziegler operation (iridectomy) 12.14
Zonulolysis (with lens extraction) — see also Extraction, cataract, intracapsular 13.19
Z-plasty
  epicanthus 08.59
  eyelid (see also Reconstruction, eyelid) 08.70
  hypopharynx 29.4
  skin (scar) (web contracture) 86.84
    with excision of lesion 86.3

☑ **Additional Digit Required** — Refer to the Tabular List for Digit Selection   ◹ Subterms under main terms may continue to next column or page

0. Procedures and Interventions, Not Elsewhere Classified (00)

✓3rd 00   Procedures and interventions, not elsewhere classified

✓4th 00.0   Therapeutic ultrasound

EXCLUDES   *diagnostic ultrasound (non-invasive) (88.71-88.79)*
intracardiac echocardiography [ICE] (heart chamber(s)) (37.28)
intravascular imaging (adjunctive) (00.21-00.29)

DEF: Interventional treatment modality using lower frequency and higher intensity levels of ultrasound energy than used in diagnostic ultrasound modality for the purpose of limiting intimal hyperplasia, or restenosis, associated with atherosclerotic vascular disease.

AHA: 4Q, '02, 90

00.01   Therapeutic ultrasound of vessels of head and neck
Anti-restenotic ultrasound
Intravascular non-ablative ultrasound

EXCLUDES   *diagnostic ultrasound of:*
eye (95.13)
head and neck (88.71)
that of inner ear (20.79)
ultrasonic:
angioplasty of non-coronary vessel (39.50)
embolectomy (38.01, 38.02)
endarterectomy (38.11, 38.12)
thrombectomy (38.01, 38.02)

00.02   Therapeutic ultrasound of heart
Anti-restenotic ultrasound
Intravascular non-ablative ultrasound

EXCLUDES   *diagnostic ultrasound of heart (88.72)*
ultrasonic ablation of heart lesion (37.34)
ultrasonic angioplasty of coronary vessels (00.66, 36.09)

00.03   Therapeutic ultrasound of peripheral vascular vessels
Anti-restenotic ultrasound
Intravascular non-ablative ultrasound

EXCLUDES   *diagnostic ultrasound of peripheral vascular system (88.77)*
ultrasonic angioplasty of:
non-coronary vessel (39.50)

00.09   Other therapeutic ultrasound

EXCLUDES   *ultrasonic:*
fragmentation of urinary stones (59.95)
percutaneous nephrostomy with fragmentation (55.04)
physical therapy (93.35)
transurethral guided laser induced prostatectomy (TULIP) (60.21)

✓4th 00.1   Pharmaceuticals

00.10   Implantation of chemotherapeutic agent
Brain wafer chemotherapy
Interstitial/intracavitary

EXCLUDES   *injection or infusion of cancer chemotherapeutic substance (99.25)*

DEF: Brain wafer chemotherapy: Placement of wafers containing antineoplastic agent against the wall of the resection cavity subsequent to the surgeon completing a tumor excision to deliver chemotherapy directly to the tumor site; used to treat glioblastoma multiforme (GBM).

AHA: 4Q, '02, 93

00.11   Infusion of drotrecogin alfa (activated)
Infusion of recombinant protein

AHA: 4Q, '02, 93
TIP: A recombinant version of naturally occurring activated protein C (APC), required to ensure the control of inflammation and clotting in blood vessels; used for patients with severe sepsis.

00.12   Administration of inhaled nitric oxide
Nitric oxide therapy

AHA: 4Q, '02, 94

00.13   Injection or infusion of nesiritide
Human B-type natriuretic peptide (hBNP)

AHA: 4Q, '02, 94
TIP: Used for the treatment of acutely decompensated congestive heart failure with dyspnea at rest or with minimal activity; is administered intravenously by infusion or bolus.

00.14   Injection or infusion of oxazolidinone class of antibiotics
Linezolid injection

AHA: 4Q, '02, 95

00.15   High-dose infusion interleukin-2 [IL-2]
Infusion (IV bolus, CIV) interleukin
Injection of aldesleukin

EXCLUDES   *low-dose infusion interleukin-2 (99.28)*

DEF: A high-dose anti-neoplastic therapy using a biological response modifier (BRM); the body naturally produces substances called interleukins, which are multi-function cytokines in the generation of an immune response.

AHA: 4Q, '03, 92

00.16   Pressurized treatment of venous bypass graft [conduit] with pharmaceutical substance
Ex-vivo treatment of vessel
Hyperbaric pressurized graft [conduit]

DEF: Ex-vivo process of delivering small nucleic acid molecules that block protein transcription factors essential for the expression of genes controlling cell proliferation into graft tissue under nondistending pressure; reduces intimal hyperplasia and vein graft failure.

00.17   Infusion of vasopressor agent

00.18   Infusion of immunosuppressive antibody therapy
Monoclonal antibody therapy
Polyclonal antibody therapy

INCLUDES   *during induction phase of solid organ transplantation*

AHA: 4Q, '05, 101

00.19   Disruption of blood brain barrier via infusion [BBBD]
Infusion of substance to disrupt blood brain barrier

Code also chemotherapy (99.25)
EXCLUDES   *other perfusion (39.97)*

DEF: Infusion of chemotherapy drug that temporarily allows the transport of materials into the brain through the blood brain barrier (BBB), which is the protective mechanism that limits transport of toxins while allowing necessary nutrients to pass from the blood vessels into the brain tissue; used in the treatment of brain cancers.

AHA: 4Q, '07, 103-104

✓4th 00.2   Intravascular imaging of blood vessels

NOTE   Real-time imaging of lumen of blood vessel(s) using sound waves
Endovascular ultrasonography
Intravascular [ultrasound] imaging of blood vessels
Intravascular ultrasound (IVUS)
Virtual histology intravascular ultrasound [VH-IVUS]

Code also any synchronous diagnostic or therapeutic procedures
EXCLUDES   *adjunct vascular system procedures, number of vessels treated (00.40-00.43)*
diagnostic procedures on blood vessels (38.21-38.29)
diagnostic ultrasound of peripheral vascular system (88.77)
intravascular imaging of vessel(s) by OCT (38.24-38.25)
magnetic resonance imaging (MRI) (88.91-88.97)
therapeutic ultrasound (00.01-00.09)

00.21   Intravascular imaging of extracranial cerebral vessels
Common carotid vessels and branches
Intravascular ultrasound (IVUS), extracranial cerebral vessels

EXCLUDES   *diagnostic ultrasound (non-invasive) of head and neck (88.71)*

✓3rd
✓4th   Additional Digit Required

00.22 Intravascular imaging of intrathoracic vessels
Aorta and aortic arch
Intravascular ultrasound (IVUS), intrathoracic vessels
Vena cava (superior) (inferior)
EXCLUDES *diagnostic ultrasound (non-invasive) of other sites of thorax (88.73)*

00.23 Intravascular imaging of peripheral vessels
Imaging of:
vessels of arm(s)
vessels of leg(s)
Intravascular ultrasound (IVUS), peripheral vessels
EXCLUDES *diagnostic ultrasound (non-invasive) of peripheral vascular system (88.77)*

00.24 Intravascular imaging of coronary vessels
Intravascular ultrasound (IVUS), coronary vessels
EXCLUDES *diagnostic ultrasound (non-invasive) of heart (88.72)*
intracardiac echocardiography [ICE] (ultrasound of heart chamber(s)) (37.28)

AHA: 3Q, '06, 8

00.25 Intravascular imaging of renal vessels
Intravascular ultrasound (IVUS), renal vessels
Renal artery
EXCLUDES *diagnostic ultrasound (non-invasive) of urinary system (88.75)*

00.28 Intravascular imaging, other specified vessel(s)

00.29 Intravascular imaging, unspecified vessel(s)

✓4ᵗʰ **00.3 Computer assisted surgery [CAS]**
CT-free navigation
Image guided navigation (IGN)
Image guided surgery (IGS)
Imageless navigation
That without the use of robotic(s) technology
Code also diagnostic or therapeutic procedure
EXCLUDES *robotic assisted procedures (17.41-17.49)*
stereotactic frame application only (93.59)
TIP: CAS includes three key activities: surgical planning, registration, and navigation; typically used in brain; cranial; ear, nose and throat (ENT); spinal; and orthopaedic surgeries.

00.31 Computer assisted surgery with CT/CTA
AHA: ▶4Q, '13, 88;◀ 4Q, '04, 113

00.32 Computer assisted surgery with MR/MRA
AHA: 4Q, '04, 113

00.33 Computer assisted surgery with fluoroscopy

00.34 Imageless computer assisted surgery

00.35 Computer assisted surgery with multiple datasets

00.39 Other computer assisted surgery
Computer assisted surgery NOS
AHA: ▶4Q, '13, 89◀

✓4ᵗʰ **00.4 Adjunct vascular system procedures**
NOTE These codes can apply to both coronary and peripheral vessels. These codes are to be used in conjunction with other therapeutic procedure codes to provide additional information on the number of vessels upon which a procedure was performed and/or the number of stents inserted. As appropriate, code both the number of vessels operated on (00.40-00.43), and the number of stents inserted (00.45-00.48).

Code also any:
angioplasty (00.61-00.62, 00.66, 39.50)
atherectomy (17.53-17.56)
endarterectomy (38.10-38.18)
insertion of vascular stent(s) (00.55, 00.63-00.65, 36.06-36.07, 39.90)
other removal of coronary artery obstruction (36.09)
AHA: 4Q, '05, 101

Stenting Techniques on Vessel Bifurcation

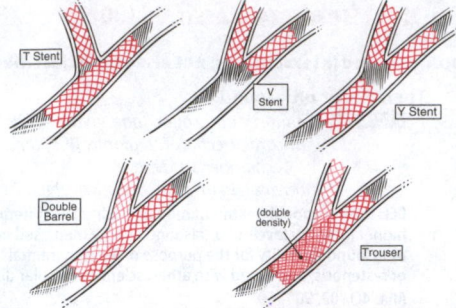

00.40 Procedure on single vessel
Number of vessels, unspecified
EXCLUDES *(aorto)coronary bypass (36.10-36.19)*
intravascular imaging of blood vessels (00.21-00.29)
AHA: ▶4Q, '13, 91;◀ 2Q, '12, 15; 4Q, '11, 166-167; 4Q, '10, 113; 2Q, '10, 8-9; 3Q, '09, 13; 2Q, '09, 12; 1Q, '07, 17; 3Q, '06, 8; 4Q, '05, 71, 106

00.41 Procedure on two vessels
EXCLUDES *(aorto)coronary bypass (36.10-36.19)*
intravascular imaging of blood vessels (00.21-00.29)
AHA: 3Q, '12, 5; 4Q, '06, 119; 4Q, '05, 105

00.42 Procedure on three vessels
EXCLUDES *(aorto)coronary bypass (36.10-36.19)*
intravascular imaging of blood vessels (00.21-00.29)

00.43 Procedure on four or more vessels
EXCLUDES *(aorto)coronary bypass (36.10-36.19)*
intravascular imaging of blood vessels (00.21-00.29)

00.44 Procedure on vessel bifurcation
NOTE This code is to be used to identify the presence of a vessel bifurcation; it does not describe a specific bifurcation stent. Use this code only once per operative episode, irrespective of the number of bifurcations in vessels.
AHA: ▶1Q, '13, 6;◀ 4Q, '06, 119

00.45 Insertion of one vascular stent
Number of stents, unspecified
AHA: 4Q, '11, 167; 4Q, '10, 113; 3Q, '09, 13; 4Q, '05, 71

00.46 Insertion of two vascular stents
AHA: ▶4Q, '13, 91;◀ 3Q, '12, 5; 2Q, '09, 12; 4Q, '05, 105-106

00.47 Insertion of three vascular stents
AHA: ▶4Q, '13, 91;◀ 4Q, '06, 119

00.48 Insertion of four or more vascular stents

00.49 SuperSaturated oxygen therapy
Aqueous oxygen (AO) therapy
SSO$_2$
SuperOxygenation infusion therapy

Code also any:
injection or infusion of thrombolytic agent (99.10)
insertion of coronary artery stent(s) (36.06-36.07)
intracoronary artery thrombolytic infusion (36.04)
number of vascular stents inserted (00.45-00.48)
number of vessels treated (00.40-00.43)
open chest coronary artery angioplasty (36.03)
other removal of coronary obstruction (36.09)
percutaneous transluminal coronary angioplasty [PTCA] (00.66)
procedure on vessel bifurcation (00.44)
transluminal coronary atherectomy (17.55)
EXCLUDES *other oxygen enrichment (93.96)*
other perfusion (39.97)
DEF: Method of reducing myocardial tissue damage via infusion of super-oxygenated blood directly to oxygen-deprived myocardial tissue in MI patients; typically performed as an adjunct procedure during PTCA or stent insertion.
AHA: 4Q, '08, 162

BI Bilateral Procedure   **NC** Non-covered Procedure   **LC** Limited Coverage Procedure   ▶◀ Revised Text   ● New Code   ▲ Revised Code Title

✓4ᵗʰ **00.5 Other cardiovascular procedures**
AHA: 4Q, '02, 95

00.50 Implantation of cardiac resynchronization pacemaker without mention of defibrillation, total system [CRT-P]

> **NOTE** Device testing during procedure — *omit code*

Biventricular pacemaker
Biventricular pacing without internal cardiac defibrillator
BiV pacemaker
Implantation of cardiac resynchronization (biventricular) pulse generator pacing device, formation of pocket, transvenous leads including placement of lead into left ventricular coronary venous system, and intraoperative procedures for evaluation of lead signals
That with CRT-P generator and one or more leads

> **EXCLUDES** *implantation of cardiac resynchronization defibrillator, total system [CRT-D] (00.51)*
> *insertion or replacement of any type pacemaker device (37.80-37.87)*
> *replacement of cardiac resynchronization: defibrillator, pulse generator only [CRT-D] (00.54)*
> *pacemaker, pulse generator only [CRT-P] (00.53)*

> **DEF:** Cardiac resynchronization pacemaker: CRT-P, or bi-ventricular pacing, adds a third lead to traditional pacemaker designs that connects to the left ventricle. The device provides electrical stimulation and coordinates ventricular contractions to improve cardiac output.
> AHA: 3Q, '05, 3-9; 4Q, '02, 100

00.51 Implantation of cardiac resynchronization defibrillator, total system [CRT-D]

> **NOTE** Device testing during procedure — *omit code*

BiV defibrillator
Biventricular defibrillator
Biventricular pacing with internal cardiac defibrillator
BiV ICD
BiV pacemaker with defibrillator
BiV pacing with defibrillator
Implantation of cardiac resynchronization (biventricular) pulse generator with defibrillator [AICD], formation of pocket, transvenous leads, including placement of lead into left ventricular coronary venous system, intraoperative procedures for evaluation of lead signals, and obtaining defibrillator threshold measurements
That with CRT-D generator and one or more leads

> **EXCLUDES** *implantation of cardiac resynchronization pacemaker, total system [CRT-P] (00.50)*
> *implantation or replacement of automatic cardioverter/ defibrillator, total system [AICD] (37.94)*
> *replacement of cardiac resynchronization defibrillator, pulse generator only [CRT-D] (00.54)*

> AHA: 2Q, '12, 14; 3Q, '08, 18; 1Q, '07, 16, 17; 3Q, '05, 3-9; 4Q, '02, 99, 100
> **TIP:** If an angiogram or a venogram is performed in conjunction with CRT-D placement, it should be coded separately; refer to subcategories 88.5 and 88.6.

00.52 Implantation or replacement of transvenous lead [electrode] into left ventricular coronary venous system

> **EXCLUDES** *implantation of cardiac resynchronization: defibrillator, total system [CRT-D] (00.51) pacemaker, total system [CRT-P] (00.50)*
> *initial insertion of transvenous lead [electrode] (37.70-37.72)*
> *replacement of transvenous atrial and/or ventricular lead(s) [electrodes] (37.76)*

00.53 Implantation or replacement of cardiac resynchronization pacemaker, pulse generator only [CRT-P]

> **NOTE** Device testing during procedure — *omit code*

Implantation of CRT-P device with removal of any existing CRT-P or other pacemaker device

> **EXCLUDES** *implantation of cardiac resynchronization pacemaker, total system [CRT-P] (00.50)*
> *implantation or replacement of cardiac resynchronization defibrillator, pulse generator only [CRT-D] (00.54)*
> *insertion or replacement of any type pacemaker device (37.80-37.87)*

> AHA: 3Q, '05, 3-9

00.54 Implantation or replacement of cardiac resynchronization defibrillator, pulse generator device only [CRT-D]

> **NOTE** Device testing during procedure — *omit code*

Implantation of CRT-D device with removal of any existing CRT-D, CRT-P, pacemaker, or defibrillator device

> **EXCLUDES** *implantation of automatic cardioverter/defibrillator pulse generator only (37.96)*
> *implantation of cardiac resynchronization defibrillator, total system [CRT-D] (00.51)*
> *implantation or replacement of cardiac resynchronization pacemaker, pulse generator only [CRT-P] (00.53)*

> AHA: 2Q, '12, 13,14; 3Q, '05, 3-9; 4Q, '02, 100

00.55 Insertion of drug-eluting stent(s) of other peripheral vessel(s)

Endograft(s)
Endovascular graft(s)
Stent graft(s)
Code also any:
   angioplasty of other non-coronary vessel(s) (39.50)
   atherectomy of other non-coronary vessel(s) (17.56)
   number of vascular stents inserted (00.45-00.48)
   number of vessels treated (00.40-00.43)
   procedure on vessel bifurcation (00.44)

> **EXCLUDES** *drug-coated peripheral stents, e.g., heparin coated (39.90)*
> *insertion of cerebrovascular stent(s) (00.63-00.65)*
> *insertion of drug-eluting coronary artery stent (36.07)*
> *insertion of drug-eluting stent(s) of superficial femoral artery (00.60)*
> *insertion of non-drug-eluting stent(s): coronary artery (36.06) peripheral vessel (39.90)*
> *that for other endovascular procedure (39.71-39.79)*

> AHA: 3Q, '12, 13; 4Q, '02, 101
> **TIP:** Drug-eluting stents gradually release a drug, such as Sirolimus, Taxol, or Paclitaxel into the vessel wall tissue over a period of 30 to 45 days to prevent the build-up of scar tissue that can narrow the reopened artery.

✓3ʳᵈ
✓4ᵗʰ Additional Digit Required   Valid OR Procedure   Non-OR Procedure   Adjunct Code
2015 ICD-9-CM   Volume 3 – 71

Procedures and Interventions, Not Elsewhere Classified

00.56–00.63

00.56 **Insertion or replacement of implantable pressure sensor with lead for intracardiac or great vessel hemodynamic monitoring**

> **NOTE** The sensor is physically connected by a lead to a separately implanted monitor

> Code also any associated implantation or replacement of subcutaneous monitor (00.57)

>> **EXCLUDES** circulatory monitoring (blood gas, arterial or venous pressure, cardiac output and coronary blood flow) (89.60-89.69)
>> insertion of implantable pressure sensor without lead for intracardiac or great vessel hemodynamic monitoring (38.26)

> **DEF:** Insertion of an implantable device consisting of a data storage system, a single lead with a pressure sensor tip and a wireless antenna that continuously collects data on heart rate, pressures, physical activity and temperature.
> **AHA:** 4Q, '06, 119

00.57 **Implantation or replacement of subcutaneous device for intracardiac or great vessel hemodynamic monitoring**

> Implantation of monitoring device with formation of subcutaneous pocket and connection to intracardiac pressure sensor via lead

> Code also any associated insertion or replacement of implanted pressure sensor with lead (00.56)

> **AHA:** 4Q, '06, 119

00.58 **Insertion of intra-aneurysm sac pressure monitoring device (intraoperative)**

> Insertion of pressure sensor during endovascular repair of abdominal or thoracic aortic aneurysm(s)

> **DEF:** Placement of a device in an aortic aneurysm sac during aneurysm repair to evaluate sac pressure before and after stent graft placement; helps detect endoleaks and prevents serious aneurysm complications.
> **AHA:** 4Q, '08, 163-165

00.59 **Intravascular pressure measurement of coronary arteries**

>> **INCLUDES** fractional flow reserve (FFR)

> Code also any synchronous diagnostic or therapeutic procedures

>> **EXCLUDES** intravascular pressure meas- urement of intrathoracic arteries (00.67)

> **AHA:** 4Q, '08, 163

√4ᵗʰ **00.6** **Procedures on blood vessels**

00.60 **Insertion of drug-eluting stent(s) of superficial femoral artery**

> Code also any:
> angioplasty of other non-coronary vessel(s) (39.50)
> atherectomy of other non-coronary vessel(s) (17.56)
> non-drug-eluting peripheral stents (39.90)
> number of vascular stents inserted (00.45-00.48)
> number of vessels treated (00.40-00.43)
> procedure on vessel bifurcation (00.44)

>> **EXCLUDES** insertion of drug-eluting stent(s) of other peripheral vessel (00.55)
>> that for other endovascular procedure (39.71-39.79)

> **DEF:** A self-expanding device made of nitinol, a thin, specialized durable metal coated with pharmacological agents that targets delivery of a drug directly to the arterial lesion to restore blood flow and reduce restenosis.
> **AHA:** 4Q, '10, 112-113

00.61 **Percutaneous angioplasty of extracranial vessel(s)**

> Carotid   Vertebral

> Code also any:
> injection or infusion of thrombolytic agent (99.10)
> number of vascular stents inserted (00.45-00.48)
> number of vessels treated (00.40-00.43)
> percutaneous atherectomy of extracranial vessel(s) (17.53)
> percutaneous insertion of carotid artery stent(s) (00.63)
> percutaneous insertion of other extracranial artery stent(s) (00.64)
> procedure on vessel bifurcation (00.44)

>> **EXCLUDES** angioplasty of other non-coronary vessel(s) (39.50)
>> atherectomy of other non-coronary vessel(s) (17.56)
>> removal of cerebrovascular obstruction of vessel(s) by open approach (38.01-38.02, 38.11-38.12, 38.31-38.32, 38.41-38.42)

> **AHA:** 3Q, '10, 17,18

⁷ 00.62 **Percutaneous angioplasty of intracranial vessel(s)** **NC**

> Basilar artery
> Intracranial portion of vertebral artery

> Code also any:
> injection or infusion of thrombolytic agent (99.10)
> number of vascular stents inserted (00.45-00.48)
> number of vessels treated (00.40-00.43)
> percutaneous atherectomy of intracranial vessel(s) (17.54)
> percutaneous insertion of intracranial stent(s) (00.65)
> procedure on vessel bifurcation (00.44)

>> **EXCLUDES** angioplasty of other non-coronary vessel(s) (39.50)
>> atherectomy of other non-coronary vessel(s) (17.56)
>> removal of cerebrovascular obstruction of vessel(s) by open approach (38.01-38.02, 38.11-38.12, 38.31-38.32, 38.41-38.42)

> **AHA:** 4Q, '11, 166

00.63 **Percutaneous insertion of carotid artery stent(s)**

> Includes the use of any embolic protection device, distal protection device, filter device, or stent delivery system
> Non-drug-eluting stent

> Code also any:
> number of vascular stents inserted (00.45-00.48)
> number of vessels treated (00.40-00.43)
> percutaneous angioplasty of extracranial vessel(s) (00.61)
> percutaneous atherectomy of extracranial vessel(s) (17.53)
> procedure on vessel bifurcation (00.44)

>> **EXCLUDES** angioplasty of other non-coronary vessel(s) (39.50)
>> atherectomy of other non-coronary vessel(s) (17.56)
>> insertion of coil-retention or embolization stent (39.72)
>> insertion of drug-eluting peripheral vessel stent(s) (00.55)

> **AHA:** 3Q, '10, 18

---

⁷ Noncovered except when reported with code 00.65.

BI Bilateral Procedure   **NC** Non-covered Procedure   **LC** Limited Coverage Procedure   ▶◀ Revised Text   ● New Code   ▲ Revised Code Title

72 – Volume 3   **2015 ICD-9-CM**

00.64 Percutaneous insertion of other extracranial artery stent(s)

Includes the use of any embolic protection device, distal protection device, filter device, or stent delivery system

Vertebral stent

Code also any:
number of vascular stents inserted (00.45-00.48)
number of vessels treated (00.40-00.43)
percutaneous angioplasty of extracranial vessel(s) (00.61)
percutaneous atherectomy of extracranial vessel(s) (17.53)
procedure on vessel bifurcation (00.44)

EXCLUDES *angioplasty of other non-coronary vessel(s) (39.50)*
atherectomy of other non-coronary vessel(s) (17.56)
insertion of coil-retention or embolization stent (39.72)
insertion of drug-eluting peripheral vessel stent(s) (00.55)

00.65 Percutaneous insertion of intracranial vascular stent(s)

Includes the use of any embolic protection device, distal protection device, filter device, or stent delivery system

Basilar stent

Code also any:
number of vascular stents inserted (00.45-00.48)
number of vessels treated (00.40-00.43)
percutaneous angioplasty of intracranial vessel(s) (00.62)
percutaneous atherectomy of intracranial vessel(s) (17.54)
procedure on vessel bifurcation (00.44)

EXCLUDES *angioplasty of other non-coronary vessel(s) (39.50)*
atherectomy of other non-coronary vessel(s) (17.56)
insertion of coil-retention or embolization stent (39.72)
insertion of drug-eluting peripheral vessel stent(s) (00.55)

00.66 Percutaneous transluminal coronary angioplasty [PTCA]

Balloon angioplasty of coronary artery
Percutaneous coronary angioplasty NOS
PTCA NOS

Code also any:
injection or infusion of thrombolytic agent (99.10)
insertion of coronary artery stent(s) (36.06-36.07)
intracoronary artery thrombolytic infusion (36.04)
number of vascular stents inserted (00.45-00.48)
number of vessels treated (00.40-00.43)
procedure on vessel bifurcation (00.44)
SuperSaturated oxygen therapy (00.49)
transluminal coronary atherectomy (17.55)

DEF: Balloon angioplasty: Insertion of catheter with inflation of balloon to flatten plaque and widen vessels.
AHA: ▶4Q, '13, 91;◀ 4Q, '12, 83, 85; 3Q, '12, 5; 4Q, '11, 167; 2Q, '10, 8-9; 2Q, '09, 12; 1Q, '07, 17; 3Q, '06, 8; 4Q, '05, 71, 101; The following references pertain to deleted PTCA codes (36.01, 36.02, 36.05): 1Q, '04, 10; 3Q, '03, 9; 4Q, '02, 114; 3Q, '02, 19; 1Q, '01, 9; 2Q, '01, 24; 1Q, '00, 11; 1Q, '99, 17; 4Q, '98, 74, 85; 1Q, '97, 3; 1Q, '94, 3; 3Q, '91, 24

PTCA (Balloon Angioplasty)

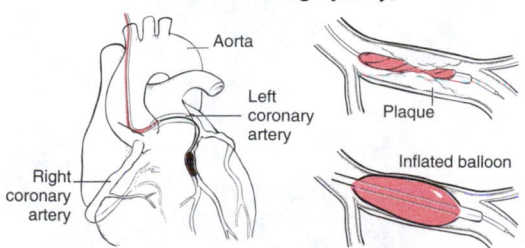

00.67 Intravascular pressure measurement of intrathoracic arteries

Assessment of:
aorta and aortic arch
carotid

Code also any synchronous diagnostic or therapeutic procedures
AHA: 4Q, '08, 163-164

00.68 Intravascular pressure measurement of peripheral arteries

Assessment of:
other peripheral vessels
vessels of arm(s)
vessels of leg(s)

Code also any synchronous diagnostic or therapeutic procedures
AHA: 4Q, '08, 163-164

00.69 Intravascular pressure measurement, other specified and unspecified vessels

Assessment of:
iliac vessels
intra-abdominal vessels
mesenteric vessels
renal vessels

Code also any synchronous diagnostic or therapeutic procedures

EXCLUDES *intravascular pressure measurement of:*
coronary arteries (00.59)
intrathoracic arteries (00.67)
peripheral arteries (00.68)

AHA: 4Q, '08, 163-164

✓4ᵗʰ **00.7 Other hip procedures**
AHA: 4Q, '05, 106

00.70 Revision of hip replacement, both acetabular and femoral components BI

Total hip revision

Code also any:
removal of (cement) (joint) spacer (84.57)
type of bearing surface, if known (00.74-00.77)

EXCLUDES *revision of hip replacement, acetabular component only (00.71)*
revision of hip replacement, fem- oral component only (00.72)
revision of hip replacement, not otherwise specified (81.53)
revision with replacement of acetabular liner and/or femoral head only (00.73)

AHA: 2Q, '08, 3, 4; 1Q, '08, 6; 4Q, '05, 113
TIP: Assign for a conversion from a previously placed hip hemiarthroplasty to a total hip joint replacement procedure.

00.71 Revision of hip replacement, acetabular component

Partial, acetabular component only
That with:
exchange of acetabular cup and liner
exchange of femoral head

Code also any type of bearing surface, if known (00.74-00.77)

EXCLUDES *revision of hip replacement, both acetabular and femoral components (00.70)*
revision of hip replacement, femoral component (00.72)
revision of hip replacement, not otherwise specified (81.53)
revision with replacement of acetabular liner and/or femoral head only (00.73)

AHA: 4Q, '05, 112

00.72   **Revision of hip replacement, femoral component**

Partial, femoral component only
That with:
    exchange of acetabular liner
    exchange of femoral stem and head

Code also any type of bearing surface, if known (00.74-00.77)

EXCLUDES   revision of hip replacement, acetabular component (00.71)
     revision of hip replacement, both acetabular and femoral components (00.70)
     revision of hip replacement, not otherwise specified (81.53)
     revision with replacement of acetabular liner and/or femoral head only (00.73)

00.73   **Revision of hip replacement, acetabular liner and/or femoral head only**

Code also any type of bearing surface, if known (00.74-00.77)

00.74   **Hip bearing surface, metal-on- polyethylene**

00.75   **Hip bearing surface, metal-on-metal**

AHA: 4Q, '06, 121

00.76   **Hip bearing surface, ceramic-on-ceramic**

AHA: 4Q, '05, 112

00.77   **Hip bearing surface, ceramic-on- polyethylene**

Hip bearing surface, oxidized zirconium-on-polyethylene

AHA: 4Q, '06, 120

√4th   **00.8**   **Other knee and hip procedures**

NOTE   Report up to two components using 00.81-00.83 to describe revision of knee replacements. If all three components are revised, report 00.80.

AHA: 4Q, '05, 113

00.80   **Revision of knee replacement, total (all components)**   BI

Replacement of femoral, tibial, and patellar components (all components)

Code also any removal of (cement) (joint) spacer (84.57)

EXCLUDES   revision of only one or two components (tibial, femoral or patellar component) (00.81-00.84)

AHA: 1Q, '08, 6
TIP: Assign for the revision of a unicompartment knee replacement to total knee arthroplasty; the procedure is still considered a revision, even though part of the component is being replaced for the first time.

00.81   **Revision of knee replacement, tibial component**

Replacement of tibial baseplate and tibial insert (liner)

EXCLUDES   revision of knee replacement, total (all components) (00.80)

AHA: 4Q, '05, 117

00.82   **Revision of knee replacement, femoral component**

That with replacement of tibial insert (liner)

EXCLUDES   revision of knee replacement, total (all components) (00.80)

AHA: 3Q, '06, 9; 4Q, '05, 117

00.83   **Revision of knee replacement, patellar component**

EXCLUDES   revision of knee replacement, total (all components) (00.80)

00.84   **Revision of total knee replacement, tibial insert (liner)**

Replacement of tibial insert (liner)

EXCLUDES   that with replacement of tibial component (tibial base plate and liner) (00.81)

00.85   **Resurfacing hip, total, acetabulum and femoral head**   BI

Hip resurfacing arthroplasty, total

AHA: 4Q, '06, 121

00.86   **Resurfacing hip, partial, femoral head**   BI

Hip resurfacing arthroplasty, NOS
Hip resurfacing arthroplasty, partial, femoral head

EXCLUDES   that with resurfacing of acetabulum (00.85)

AHA: 4Q, '06, 121

00.87   **Resurfacing hip, partial, acetabulum**   BI

Hip resurfacing arthroplasty, partial, acetabulum

EXCLUDES   that with resurfacing of femoral head (00.85)

AHA: 4Q, '06, 121

√4th   **00.9**   **Other procedures and interventions**

00.91   **Transplant from live related donor**

Code also organ transplant procedure

00.92   **Transplant from live non-related donor**

Code also organ transplant procedure

AHA: 1Q, '12, 13; 2Q, '08, 8; 4Q, '04, 117
TIP: Assign for a transplant from a patient who is designated as brain dead but is kept alive for organ harvesting.

00.93   **Transplant from cadaver**

Code also organ transplant procedure

AHA: 2Q, '11, 6

00.94   **Intra-operative neurophysiologic monitoring**

INCLUDES   cranial nerve, peripheral nerve and spinal cord testing performed intra-operatively

Intra-operative neurophysiologic testing
IOM
Nerve monitoring
Neuromonitoring
That by:
    brainstem auditory evoked potentials [BAEP]
    electroencephalogram [EEG]
    electromyogram [EMG]
    motor evoked potentials [MEP]
    nerve conduction study
    somatosensory evoked potentials [SSEP]
    transcranial Doppler

EXCLUDES   brain temperature monitoring (01.17)
     intracranial oxygen monitoring (01.16)
     intracranial pressure monitoring (01.10)
     plethysmogram (89.58)

DEF: Real-time testing techniques used in brain, spinal cord, and nerve procedures to assist in lesion excision and provide ongoing neurological functioning information and/or warning of impending neural structure injury.

AHA: ▶2Q, '13, 8;◄ 1Q, '11, 7; 2Q, '09, 4; 4Q, '07, 104

00.95   **Injection or infusion of glucarpidase**

AHA: 4Q, '12, 87

00.96   **Infusion of 4-Factor Prothrombin Complex Concentrate**

Infusion of 4F-PCC

EXCLUDES   transfusion of coagulation factors (99.06)
     transfusion of Factor IX complex (99.06)

AHA: ▶4Q, '13, 82, 83◄

BI   Bilateral Procedure   NC   Non-covered Procedure   LC   Limited Coverage Procedure   ▶◄ Revised Text   ● New Code   ▲ Revised Code Title

74 – Volume 3 · October 2014   **2015 ICD-9-CM**

1. Operations on the Nervous System (01-05)

✓3rd 01   **Incision and excision of skull, brain, and cerebral meninges**

✓4th 01.0   **Cranial puncture**

01.01   **Cisternal puncture**
Cisternal aspiration
Cisternal tap
EXCLUDES *pneumocisternogram (87.02)*
DEF: Needle insertion through subarachnoid space to withdraw cerebrospinal fluid.

01.02   **Ventriculopuncture through previously implanted catheter**
Puncture of ventricular shunt tubing
DEF: Piercing of artificial, fluid-diverting tubing in the brain for withdrawal of cerebrospinal fluid.

01.09   **Other cranial puncture**
Aspiration of:
    subarachnoid space
    subdural space
Cranial aspiration NOS
Puncture of anterior fontanel
Subdural tap (through fontanel)
AHA: 3Q, '09, 15-16; 4Q, '07, 107
TIP: Assign for aspiration of a subdural hematoma.

✓4th 01.1   **Diagnostic procedures on skull, brain, and cerebral meninges**

01.10   **Intracranial pressure monitoring**
INCLUDES insertion of catheter or probe for monitoring
AHA: ▶3Q, '13, 10;◀3Q, '09, 15-16; 4Q, '07, 105, 107
TIP: Several different devices are available that are connected to a catheter inserted via ventriculostomy, subarachnoid bolt, or screw; used to monitor intracranial pressure in patients with traumatic brain injury (TBI) or other serious brain disorders.

01.11   **Closed [percutaneous] [needle] biopsy of cerebral meninges**
Burr hole approach
DEF: Needle excision of tissue sample through skin into cerebral membranes; no other procedure performed.

01.12   **Open biopsy of cerebral meninges**
DEF: Open surgical excision of tissue sample from cerebral membrane.

01.13   **Closed [percutaneous] [needle] biopsy of brain**
Burr hole approach
Stereotactic method
DEF: Removal by needle of brain tissue sample through skin.
AHA: M-A, '87, 9

01.14   **Open biopsy of brain**
DEF: Open surgical excision of brain tissue sample.
AHA: 4Q, '12, 81

01.15   **Biopsy of skull**

01.16   **Intracranial oxygen monitoring**
Partial pressure of brain oxygen ($PbtO_2$)
INCLUDES insertion of catheter or probe for monitoring
AHA: ▶3Q, '13, 10;◀4Q, '07, 105, 107

01.17   **Brain temperature monitoring**
INCLUDES insertion of catheter or probe for monitoring
AHA: ▶3Q, '13, 10;◀4Q, '07, 105

01.18   **Other diagnostic procedures on brain and cerebral meninges**
EXCLUDES *brain temperature monitoring (01.17)*
cerebral:
    arteriography (88.41)
    thermography (88.81)
contrast radiogram of brain (87.01-87.02)
echoencephalogram (88.71)
electroencephalogram (89.14)
intracranial oxygen monitoring (01.16)
intracranial pressure monitoring (01.10)
microscopic examination of specimen from nervous system and of spinal fluid (90.01-90.09)
neurologic examination (89.13)
phlebography of head and neck (88.61)
pneumoencephalogram (87.01)
radioisotope scan:
    cerebral (92.11)
    head NEC (92.12)
tomography of head:
    C.A.T. scan (87.03)
    other (87.04)
AHA: ▶3Q, '13, 10;◀3Q, '98, 12

01.19   **Other diagnostic procedures on skull**
EXCLUDES *transillumination of skull (89.16)*
x-ray of skull (87.17)

✓4th 01.2   **Craniotomy and craniectomy**
EXCLUDES *decompression of skull fracture (02.02)*
exploration of orbit (16.01-16.09)
that as operative approach — omit code
DEF: Craniotomy: Incision into skull.
DEF: Craniectomy: Excision of part of skull.
AHA: 1Q, '91, 1

01.20   **Cranial implantation or replacement of neurostimulator pulse generator**
Code also any associated lead implantation (02.93)
EXCLUDES *implantation or replacement of subcutaneous neurostimulator pulse generator (86.94-86.98)*
DEF: Implantation or replacement of a small neurostimulator pulse generator in the cranium designed to treat medically intractable epilepsy, detect new-onset seizures, and apply stimulation at a seizure focus to suppress the seizure.
AHA: 4Q, '10, 113-114

01.21   **Incision and drainage of cranial sinus**
DEF: Incision for drainage, including drainage of air cavities in skull bones.

01.22   **Removal of intracranial neurostimulator lead(s)**
Code also any removal of neurostimulator pulse generator (86.05)
EXCLUDES *removal with synchronous replacement (02.93)*

01.23   **Reopening of craniotomy site**
DEF: Reopening of skull incision.

01.24   **Other craniotomy**
Cranial:
    decompression
    exploration
    trephination
Craniotomy NOS
Craniotomy with removal of:
    epidural abscess
    extradural hematoma
    foreign body of skull
EXCLUDES *removal of foreign body with incision into brain (01.39)*
AHA: 4Q, '10, 93; 2Q, '91, 14

01.25   **Other craniectomy**
Debridement of skull NOS
Sequestrectomy of skull
EXCLUDES *debridement of compound fracture of skull (02.02)*
strip craniectomy (02.01)
AHA: ▶2Q, '13, 18;◀1Q, '06, 6

✓3rd ✓4th Additional Digit Required   Valid OR Procedure   Non-OR Procedure   Adjunct Code

Operations on the Nervous System

01.26–02.14

01.26 Insertion of catheter(s) into cranial cavity or tissue
Code also any concomitant procedure (e.g. resection (01.59))
EXCLUDES *placement of intracerebral catheter(s) via burr hole(s) (01.28)*
AHA: 3Q, '09, 16; 4Q, '05, 117-118
TIP: Assign for balloon catheter placement in brain for infusion of liquid brachytherapy radioisotope for malignancy treatment; see also code 92.20 for infusion procedure.

01.27 Removal of catheter(s) from cranial cavity or tissue
AHA: 4Q, '05, 117-118

01.28 Placement of intracerebral catheter(s) via burr hole(s)
Convection enhanced delivery
Stereotactic placement of intracerebral catheter(s)
Code also infusion of medication
EXCLUDES *insertion of catheter(s) into cranial cavity or tissue(s) (01.26)*
DEF: The strategic neurosurgical placement of catheters via burr holes into targeted brain tissue, through which therapeutic agents such as antineoplastics are microinfused.
AHA: ▶3Q, '13, 10;◀ 3Q, '09, 16; 4Q, '06, 122

01.29 Removal of cranial neurostimulator pulse generator
AHA: 4Q, '10, 113-114

✓4th 01.3 Incision of brain and cerebral meninges

01.31 Incision of cerebral meninges
Drainage of:
intracranial hygroma
subarachnoid abscess (cerebral)
subdural empyema

01.32 Lobotomy and tractotomy
Division of:
brain tissue
cerebral tracts
Percutaneous (radiofrequency) cingulotomy
DEF: Lobotomy: Incision of nerve fibers of brain lobe, usually frontal.
DEF: Tractotomy: Severing of a nerve fiber group to relieve pain.

01.39 Other incision of brain
Amygdalohippocampotomy
Drainage of intracerebral hematoma
Incision of brain NOS
EXCLUDES *division of cortical adhesions (02.91)*
AHA: 4Q, '09, 83

✓4th 01.4 Operations on thalamus and globus pallidus

01.41 Operations on thalamus
Chemothalamectomy
Thalamotomy
EXCLUDES *that by stereotactic radiosurgery (92.30-92.39)*

01.42 Operations on globus pallidus
Pallidoansectomy
Pallidotomy
EXCLUDES *that by stereotactic radiosurgery (92.30-92.39)*

✓4th 01.5 Other excision or destruction of brain and meninges
AHA: 4Q, '93, 33

01.51 Excision of lesion or tissue of cerebral meninges
Decortication
Resection   } of (cerebral) meninges
Stripping of subdural membrane
EXCLUDES *biopsy of cerebral meninges (01.11-01.12)*

01.52 Hemispherectomy
DEF: Removal of one half of the brain. Most often performed for malignant brain tumors or intractable epilepsy.

01.53 Lobectomy of brain
DEF: Excision of a brain lobe.

01.59 Other excision or destruction of lesion or tissue of brain
Amygdalohippocampectomy
Curettage of brain
Debridement of brain
Marsupialization of brain cyst
Transtemporal (mastoid) excision of brain tumor
EXCLUDES *biopsy of brain (01.13-01.14)*
laser interstitial thermal therapy [LITT] of lesion or tissue of brain under guidance (17.61)
that by stereotactic radiosurgery (92.30-92.39)
AHA: 4Q, '05, 118; 3Q, '99, 7; 1Q, '99, 9; 3Q, '98, 12; 1Q, '98, 6

01.6 Excision of lesion of skull
Removal of granulation tissue of cranium
EXCLUDES *biopsy of skull (01.15)*
sequestrectomy (01.25)

✓3rd 02 Other operations on skull, brain, and cerebral meninges

✓4th 02.0 Cranioplasty
EXCLUDES *that with synchronous repair of encephalocele (02.12)*

02.01 Opening of cranial suture
Linear craniectomy
Strip craniectomy
DEF: Opening of the lines of junction between the bones of the skull for removal of strips of skull bone.

02.02 Elevation of skull fracture fragments
Debridement of compound fracture of skull
Decompression of skull fracture
Reduction of skull fracture
Code also any synchronous debridement of brain (01.59)
EXCLUDES *debridement of skull NOS (01.25)*
removal of granulation tissue of cranium (01.6)

02.03 Formation of cranial bone flap
Repair of skull with flap

02.04 Bone graft to skull
Pericranial graft (autogenous) (heterogenous)
AHA: ▶2Q, '13, 8;◀ 1Q, '11, 7

02.05 Insertion of skull plate
Replacement of skull plate
AHA: ▶2Q, '13, 8◀

02.06 Other cranial osteoplasty
Repair of skull NOS
Revision of bone flap of skull
DEF: Plastic surgery repair of skull bones.
AHA: 1Q, '06, 6; 1Q, '05, 11; 3Q, '98, 9

02.07 Removal of skull plate
EXCLUDES *removal with synchronous replacement (02.05)*

✓4th 02.1 Repair of cerebral meninges
EXCLUDES *marsupialization of cerebral lesion (01.59)*

02.11 Simple suture of dura mater of brain

02.12 Other repair of cerebral meninges
Closure of fistula of cerebrospinal fluid
Dural graft
Repair of encephalocele including synchronous cranioplasty
Repair of meninges NOS
Subdural patch
AHA: ▶2Q, '13, 8, 18◀

02.13 Ligation of meningeal vessel
Ligation of:
longitudinal sinus
middle meningeal artery

02.14 Choroid plexectomy
Cauterization of choroid plexus
DEF: Excision or destruction of the ependymal cells that form the membrane lining in the third, fourth, and lateral ventricles of the brain and secrete cerebrospinal fluid.

BI Bilateral Procedure   NC Non-covered Procedure   LC Limited Coverage Procedure   ▶◀ Revised Text   ● New Code   ▲ Revised Code Title

External Ventricular Drain (EVD)

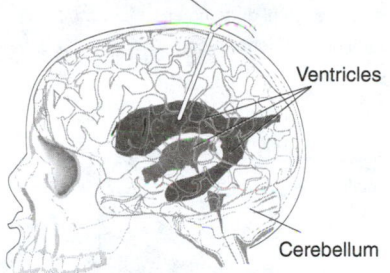

Shunt tubing to reservoir

Ventricles

Cerebellum

✓4ᵗʰ **02.2 Ventriculostomy**

AHA: 4Q, '11, 159-161

02.21 Insertion or replacement of external ventricular drain [EVD]

External ventricular drainage [EVD] setup
Replacement of external ventricular drain
Ventricular catheter placement for:
    drainage of cerebrospinal fluid [CSF]
    injection of medication or other substance
    sampling of cerebrospinal fluid [CSF]

EXCLUDES extracranial ventricular shunt (02.31-02.35, 02.39)
    intracranial ventricular shunt (02.22)
    other cranial puncture (01.09)
    ventricular shunt replacement (02.41-02.43)

DEF: Placement of a catheter into the ventricles for external drainage of cerebrospinal fluid into a container outside the body.

AHA: 4Q, '11, 161-162

02.22 Intracranial ventricular shunt or anastomosis

Anastomosis of ventricle to:
    cervical subarachnoid space
    cistern magna
Insertion of Holter valve into intracranial system
Shunt between two intracranial ventricles
That by endoscopy
Third ventriculostomy
Ventriculocisternostomy

DEF: Surgical creation of an opening of ventricle; often performed to drain cerebrospinal fluid in treating hydrocephalus.

✓4ᵗʰ **02.3 Extracranial ventricular shunt**

INCLUDES that with insertion of valve

DEF: Placement of shunt or creation of artificial passage leading from skull cavities to site outside skull to relieve excess cerebrospinal fluid created in the chorioid plexuses of the third and fourth ventricles of the brain.

02.31 Ventricular shunt to structure in head and neck

Ventricle to nasopharynx shunt
Ventriculomastoid anastomosis

02.32 Ventricular shunt to circulatory system

Ventriculoatrial anastomosis
Ventriculocaval shunt

02.33 Ventricular shunt to thoracic cavity

Ventriculopleural anastomosis

Extracranial Ventricular Shunt

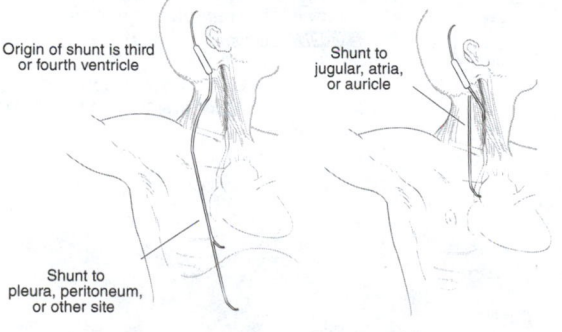

Origin of shunt is third or fourth ventricle

Shunt to jugular, atria, or auricle

Shunt to pleura, peritoneum, or other site

02.34 Ventricular shunt to abdominal cavity and organs

Ventriculocholecystostomy
Ventriculoperitoneostomy

02.35 Ventricular shunt to urinary system

Ventricle to ureter shunt

02.39 Ventricular shunt to extracranial site NEC

Ventricle to bone marrow shunt

✓4ᵗʰ **02.4 Revision, removal, and irrigation of ventricular shunt**

EXCLUDES revision of distal catheter of ventricular shunt (54.95)

02.41 Irrigation and exploration of ventricular shunt

Exploration of ventriculoperitoneal shunt at ventricular site
Re-programming of ventriculoperitoneal shunt

02.42 Replacement of ventricular shunt

Reinsertion of Holter valve
Revision of ventriculoperitoneal shunt at ventricular site

AHA: N-D, '86, 8

TIP: If a ventriculoperitoneal shunt is explored or revised at the peritoneal site, assign instead code 54.95.

02.43 Removal of ventricular shunt

AHA: N-D, '86, 8

✓4ᵗʰ **02.9 Other operations on skull, brain, and cerebral meninges**

EXCLUDES operations on:
    pineal gland (07.17, 07.51-07.59)
    pituitary gland [hypophysis] (07.13-07.15, 07.61-07.79)

02.91 Lysis of cortical adhesions

DEF: Breaking up of fibrous structures in brain outer layer.

02.92 Repair of brain

02.93 Implantation or replacement of intracranial neurostimulator lead(s)

Implantation, insertion, placement, or replacement of intracranial:
    brain pacemaker [neuropacemaker]
    depth electrodes
    epidural pegs
    electroencephalographic receiver
    foramen ovale electrodes
    intracranial electrostimulator
    subdural grids
    subdural strips

Code also any:
    insertion of cranial implantation or replacement of neurostimulator pulse generator (01.20)
    insertion of subcutaneous neurostimulator pulse generator (86.94-86.98)

AHA: 4Q, '97, 57; 4Q, '92, 28

02.94 Insertion or replacement of skull tongs or halo traction device

DEF: Halo traction device: Metal or plastic band encircles the head or neck secured to the skull with four pins and attached to a metal chest plate by rods; provides support and stability for the head and neck.

DEF: Skull tongs: Device inserted into each side of the skull used to apply parallel traction to the long axis of the cervical spine.

AHA: 3Q, '01, 8; 3Q, '96, 14

02.95 Removal of skull tongs or halo traction device

Operations on the Nervous System

02.96–03.53

Laminotomy with Decompression

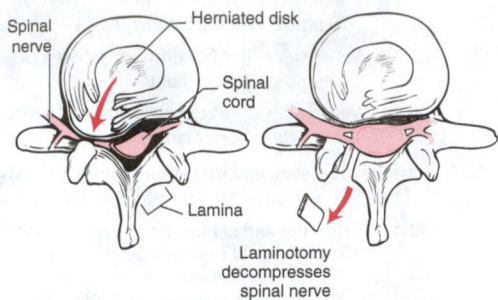

Spinal nerve — Herniated disk — Spinal cord — Lamina — Laminotomy decompresses spinal nerve

Lumbar Spinal Puncture

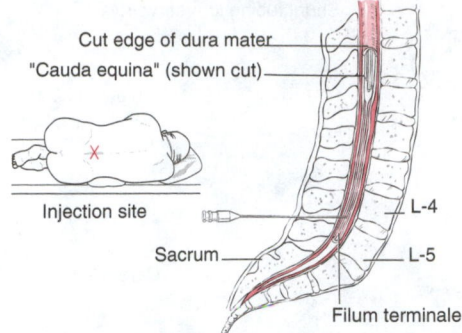

Cut edge of dura mater — "Cauda equina" (shown cut) — Injection site — Sacrum — Filum terminale — L-4 — L-5

02.96 Insertion of sphenoidal electrodes
AHA: 4Q, '92, 28

02.99 Other
EXCLUDES *chemical shock therapy (94.24)*
electroshock therapy:
subconvulsive (94.26)
other (94.27)

✓3rd 03 Operations on spinal cord and spinal canal structures
Code also any application or administration of an adhesion barrier substance (99.77)

✓4th 03.0 Exploration and decompression of spinal canal structures

03.01 Removal of foreign body from spinal canal

03.02 Reopening of laminectomy site

03.09 Other exploration and decompression of spinal canal
Decompression:
  laminectomy
  laminotomy
Expansile laminoplasty
Exploration of spinal nerve root
Foraminotomy
Code also any synchronous insertion, replacement and revision of posterior spinal motion preservation device(s), if performed (84.80-84.85)
EXCLUDES *drainage of spinal fluid by anastomosis*
(03.71-03.79)
laminectomy with excision of intervertebral
disc (80.51)
spinal tap (03.31)
that as operative approach — omit code
DEF: Decompression of spinal canal: Excision of bone pieces, hematoma or other lesion to relieve spinal cord pressure.
DEF: Expansile laminoplasty: Lamina is incised at the level of the pedicle to relieve pressure; no tissue is excised.
DEF: Foraminotomy: Removal of root opening between vertebrae to relieve nerve root pressure.
AHA: ▶2Q, '13, 18; 1Q, '13, 7;◀ 2Q, '11, 10; 4Q, '08, 109; 2Q, '08, 12; 4Q, '07, 117, 120; 1Q, '07, 10; 3Q, '04, 6; 4Q, '02, 109; 2Q, '02, 15; 4Q, '99, 14; 2Q, '97, 6; 2Q, '95, 9; 2Q, '95, 10; 2Q, '90, 22; S-Q, '86, 12

03.1 Division of intraspinal nerve root
Rhizotomy
DEF: Rhizotomy: Surgical severing of spinal nerve roots within spinal canal for pain relief.

✓4th 03.2 Chordotomy
DEF: Chordotomy: Surgical cutting of lateral spinothalamic tract of spinal cord to relieve pain.

03.21 Percutaneous chordotomy
Stereotactic chordotomy
DEF: Percutaneous chordotomy: Insertion of hollow needle through skin to interrupt spinal nerve root.
DEF: Stereotactic chordotomy: Use of three-dimensional imaging to locate spinal nerve root for surgical interruption.

03.29 Other chordotomy
Chordotomy NOS
Tractotomy (one-stage) (two-stage) of spinal cord
Transection of spinal cord tracts
DEF: Tractotomy (one stage) (two stages) of the spinal cord: Surgical incision or severing of a nerve tract of spinal cord.
DEF: Transection of spinal cord tracts: Use of transverse incision to divide spinal nerve root.

✓4th 03.3 Diagnostic procedures on spinal cord and spinal canal structures

03.31 Spinal tap
Lumbar puncture for removal of dye
EXCLUDES *lumbar puncture for injection of dye*
[myelogram] (87.21)
DEF: Puncture into lumbar subarachnoid space to tap cerebrospinal fluid.
AHA: ▶3Q, '13, 13;◀ 2Q, '90, 22

03.32 Biopsy of spinal cord or spinal meninges

03.39 Other diagnostic procedures on spinal cord and spinal canal structures
EXCLUDES *microscopic examination of specimen from*
nervous system or of spinal fluid
(90.01-90.09)
x-ray of spine (87.21-87.29)

03.4 Excision or destruction of lesion of spinal cord or spinal meninges
Curettage ⎫
Debridement ⎬ of spinal cord or spinal
Marsupialization of cyst ⎪ meninges
Resection ⎭
EXCLUDES *biopsy of spinal cord or meninges (03.32)*
AHA: ▶3Q, '13, 3;◀ 2Q, '08, 10; 3Q, '95, 5
TIP: A laminectomy is inherent to the excision of a spinal cord tumor; do not assign 03.09 separately.

✓4th 03.5 Plastic operations on spinal cord structures

03.51 Repair of spinal meningocele
Repair of meningocele NOS
DEF: Restoration of hernial protrusion of spinal meninges through defect in vertebral column.

03.52 Repair of spinal myelomeningocele
DEF: Restoration of hernial protrusion of spinal cord and meninges through defect in vertebral column.

03.53 Repair of vertebral fracture
Elevation of spinal bone fragments
Reduction of fracture of vertebrae
Removal of bony spicules from spinal canal
EXCLUDES *percutaneous vertebral augmentation*
(81.66)
percutaneous vertebroplasty (81.65)
AHA: 1Q, '07, 20; 4Q, '04, 126; 2Q, '02, 14; 4Q, '99, 11, 12, 13; 3Q, '96, 14

BI Bilateral Procedure   **NC** Non-covered Procedure   **LC** Limited Coverage Procedure   ▶◀ Revised Text   ● New Code   ▲ Revised Code Title

78 – Volume 3 • October 2014   **2015 ICD-9-CM**

03.59 Other repair and plastic operations on spinal cord structures

Repair of:	Repair of:
diastematomyelia	spinal meninges NOS
spina bifida NOS	vertebral arch defect
spinal cord NOS	

AHA: 4Q, '08, 109

TIP: Assign for repair of dural tears occurring during spinal surgery.

03.6 Lysis of adhesions of spinal cord and nerve roots

AHA: 2Q, '98, 18

√4th 03.7 Shunt of spinal theca

INCLUDES that with valve

DEF: Surgical passage created from spinal cord dura mater to another channel.

03.71 Spinal subarachnoid-peritoneal shunt

03.72 Spinal subarachnoid-ureteral shunt

03.79 Other shunt of spinal theca

Lumbar-subarachnoid shunt NOS
Pleurothecal anastomosis
Salpingothecal anastomosis

AHA: 1Q, '97, 7

03.8 Injection of destructive agent into spinal canal

√4th 03.9 Other operations on spinal cord and spinal canal structures

03.90 Insertion of catheter into spinal canal for infusion of therapeutic or palliative substances

Insertion of catheter into epidural, subarachnoid, or subdural space of spine with intermittent or continuous infusion of drug (with creation of any reservoir)

Code also any implantation of infusion pump (86.06)

03.91 Injection of anesthetic into spinal canal for analgesia

EXCLUDES that for operative anesthesia — omit code

AHA: 3Q, '00, 15; 1Q, '99, 8; 2Q, '98, 18

03.92 Injection of other agent into spinal canal

Intrathecal injection of steroid
Subarachnoid perfusion of refrigerated saline

EXCLUDES injection of:
    contrast material for myelogram (87.21)
    destructive agent into spinal canal (03.8)

AHA: 2Q, '03, 6; 3Q, '00, 15; 2Q, '98, 18

TIP: Assign, along with code 99.23 for a steroid injection into the spinal canal; if both steroid and other anesthetic agent are injected, assign 03.91, 03.92, and 99.23.

03.93 Implantation or replacement of spinal neurostimulator lead(s)

Code also any insertion of neurostimulator pulse generator (86.94-86.98)

AHA: 1Q, '00, 19

03.94 Removal of spinal neurostimulator lead(s)

Code also any removal of neurostimulator pulse generator (86.05)

03.95 Spinal blood patch

DEF: Injection of blood into epidural space to patch hole in outer spinal membrane made by previous spinal puncture; blood clots and fills hole.

03.96 Percutaneous denervation of facet

03.97 Revision of spinal thecal shunt

AHA: 2Q, '99, 4

03.98 Removal of spinal thecal shunt

03.99 Other

√3rd 04 Operations on cranial and peripheral nerves

√4th 04.0 Incision, division, and excision of cranial and peripheral nerves

EXCLUDES opticociliary neurectomy (12.79)
    sympathetic ganglionectomy (05.21-05.29)

04.01 Excision of acoustic neuroma

That by craniotomy

EXCLUDES that by stereotactic radiosurgery (92.3)

AHA: 2Q, '98, 20; 2Q, '95, 8; 4Q, '92, 26

04.02 Division of trigeminal nerve

Retrogasserian neurotomy

DEF: Transection of sensory root fibers of trigeminal nerve for relief of trigeminal neuralgia.

04.03 Division or crushing of other cranial and peripheral nerves

EXCLUDES that of:
    glossopharyngeal nerve (29.92)
    laryngeal nerve (31.91)
    nerves to adrenal glands (07.42)
    phrenic nerve for collapse of lung (33.31)
    vagus nerve (44.00-44.03)

AHA: 2Q, '98, 20

04.04 Other incision of cranial and peripheral nerves

04.05 Gasserian ganglionectomy

04.06 Other cranial or peripheral ganglionectomy

EXCLUDES sympathetic ganglionectomy (05.21-05.29)

04.07 Other excision or avulsion of cranial and peripheral nerves

Curettage
Debridement   } of peripheral nerve
Resection

Excision of peripheral neuroma [Morton's]

EXCLUDES biopsy of cranial or peripheral nerve (04.11-04.12)

AHA: 2Q, '95, 8; 4Q, '92, 26

√4th 04.1 Diagnostic procedures on peripheral nervous system

04.11 Closed [percutaneous] [needle] biopsy of cranial or peripheral nerve or ganglion

04.12 Open biopsy of cranial or peripheral nerve or ganglion

04.19 Other diagnostic procedures on cranial and peripheral nerves and ganglia

EXCLUDES microscopic examination of specimen from nervous system (90.01-90.09)
    neurologic examination (89.13)

04.2 Destruction of cranial and peripheral nerves

Destruction of cranial or peripheral nerves by:
  cryoanalgesia
  injection of neurolytic agent
  radiofrequency
Radiofrequency ablation

DEF: Radiofrequency ablation: High frequency radio waves are applied to injure the nerve resulting in interruption of the pain signal.

AHA: ▶1Q, '14, 8;◀ 3Q, '02, 10, 11; 4Q, '95, 74

04.3 Suture of cranial and peripheral nerves

√4th 04.4 Lysis of adhesions and decompression of cranial and peripheral nerves

04.41 Decompression of trigeminal nerve root

04.42 Other cranial nerve decompression

AHA: 3Q, '02, 13

04.43 Release of carpal tunnel

04.44 Release of tarsal tunnel

04.49 Other peripheral nerve or ganglion decompression or lysis of adhesions

Peripheral nerve neurolysis NOS

04.5 Cranial or peripheral nerve graft

04.6 Transposition of cranial and peripheral nerves

Nerve transplantation

DEF: Relocation of cranial or peripheral nerves without detaching or severing them.

√4th 04.7 Other cranial or peripheral neuroplasty

04.71 Hypoglossal-facial anastomosis

DEF: Surgical connection of hypoglossal nerve to facial nerve.

Release of Carpal Tunnel

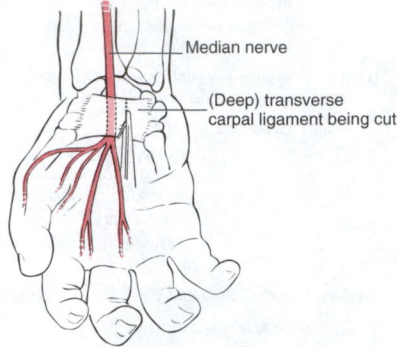

Median nerve

(Deep) transverse carpal ligament being cut

04.72 Accessory-facial anastomosis

DEF: Surgical connection of accessory nerve to facial nerve.

04.73 Accessory-hypoglossal anastomosis

DEF: Surgical connection of accessory nerve to hypoglossal nerve.

04.74 Other anastomosis of cranial or peripheral nerve

04.75 Revision of previous repair of cranial and peripheral nerves

04.76 Repair of old traumatic injury of cranial and peripheral nerves

04.79 Other neuroplasty

AHA: 1Q, '06, 11
TIP: Assign for application of a NeuraWrap nerve protector, an absorbable collagen implant that provides a nonconstricting encasement for injured peripheral nerves.

√4ᵗʰ **04.8 Injection into peripheral nerve**

EXCLUDES destruction of nerve (by injection of neurolytic agent) (04.2)

04.80 Peripheral nerve injection, not otherwise specified

04.81 Injection of anesthetic into peripheral nerve for analgesia

EXCLUDES that for operative anesthesia — omit code
AHA: 1Q, '00, 7

04.89 Injection of other agent, except neurolytic

EXCLUDES injection of neurolytic agent (04.2)

√4ᵗʰ **04.9 Other operations on cranial and peripheral nerves**

04.91 Neurectasis

DEF: Surgical stretching of peripheral or cranial nerve.

04.92 Implantation or replacement of peripheral neurostimulator lead(s)

Code also any insertion of neurostimulator pulse generator (86.94-86.98)
EXCLUDES implantation or replacement of carotid sinus stimulation lead(s) (39.82)
DEF: Placement of or removal and replacement of neurostimulator lead(s) during the same episode.
AHA: 2Q, '07, 8; 2Q, '06, 5; 2Q, '04, 7; 3Q, '01, 16; 2Q, '00, 22; 3Q, '96, 12

04.93 Removal of peripheral neurostimulator lead(s)

Code also any removal of neurostimulator pulse generator (86.05)
AHA: 3Q, '01, 16

04.99 Other

√3ʳᵈ **05 Operations on sympathetic nerves or ganglia**

EXCLUDES paracervical uterine denervation (69.3)

05.0 Division of sympathetic nerve or ganglion

EXCLUDES that of nerves to adrenal glands (07.42)

√4ᵗʰ **05.1 Diagnostic procedures on sympathetic nerves or ganglia**

05.11 Biopsy of sympathetic nerve or ganglion

05.19 Other diagnostic procedures on sympathetic nerves or ganglia

√4ᵗʰ **05.2 Sympathectomy**

DEF: Sympathectomy: Division of nerve pathway at a specific site of a sympathetic nerve.

05.21 Sphenopalatine ganglionectomy

05.22 Cervical sympathectomy

05.23 Lumbar sympathectomy

DEF: Excision, resection of lumber chain nerve group to relieve causalgia, Raynaud's disease, or lower extremity thromboangiitis.

05.24 Presacral sympathectomy

DEF: Excision or resection of hypogastric nerve network.

05.25 Periarterial sympathectomy

DEF: Removal of arterial sheath containing sympathetic nerve fibers.

05.29 Other sympathectomy and ganglionectomy

Excision or avulsion of sympathetic nerve NOS
Sympathetic ganglionectomy NOS
EXCLUDES biopsy of sympathetic nerve or ganglion (05.11)
optociliary neurectomy (12.79)
periarterial sympathectomy (05.25)
tympanosympathectomy (20.91)

√4ᵗʰ **05.3 Injection into sympathetic nerve or ganglion**

EXCLUDES injection of ciliary sympathetic ganglion (12.79)

05.31 Injection of anesthetic into sympathetic nerve for analgesia

05.32 Injection of neurolytic agent into sympathetic nerve

05.39 Other injection into sympathetic nerve or ganglion

√4ᵗʰ **05.8 Other operations on sympathetic nerves or ganglia**

05.81 Repair of sympathetic nerve or ganglion

05.89 Other

05.9 Other operations on nervous system

BI Bilateral Procedure   NC Non-covered Procedure   LC Limited Coverage Procedure   ▶◀ Revised Text   ● New Code   ▲ Revised Code Title

2. Operations on the Endocrine System (06-07)

✓3rd 06 Operations on thyroid and parathyroid glands
    INCLUDES incidental resection of hyoid bone

✓4th 06.0 Incision of thyroid field
    EXCLUDES *division of isthmus (06.91)*

    06.01 Aspiration of thyroid field
      Percutaneous or needle drainage of thyroid field
      EXCLUDES *aspiration biopsy of thyroid (06.11)*
           drainage by incision (06.09)
           postoperative aspiration of field (06.02)

    06.02 Reopening of wound of thyroid field
      Reopening of wound of thyroid field for:
        control of (postoperative) hemorrhage
        examination
        exploration
        removal of hematoma

    06.09 Other incision of thyroid field
      Drainage of hematoma
      Drainage of thyroglossal tract
      Exploration
        neck   } by incision
        thyroid (field)
      Removal of foreign body
      Thyroidotomy NOS
      EXCLUDES *postoperative exploration (06.02)*
           removal of hematoma by aspiration (06.01)

✓4th 06.1 Diagnostic procedures on thyroid and parathyroid glands

    06.11 Closed [percutaneous] [needle] biopsy of thyroid gland
      Aspiration biopsy of thyroid
      DEF: Insertion of needle-type device for removal of thyroid tissue sample.

    06.12 Open biopsy of thyroid gland

    06.13 Biopsy of parathyroid gland

    06.19 Other diagnostic procedures on thyroid and parathyroid glands
      EXCLUDES *radioisotope scan of:*
           parathyroid (92.13)
           thyroid (92.01)
           soft tissue x-ray of thyroid field (87.09)

06.2 Unilateral thyroid lobectomy
    Complete removal of one lobe of thyroid (with removal of isthmus or portion of other lobe)
    Hemithyroidectomy
    EXCLUDES *partial substernal thyroidectomy (06.51)*
    DEF: Excision of thyroid lobe.

✓4th 06.3 Other partial thyroidectomy

    06.31 Excision of lesion of thyroid
      EXCLUDES *biopsy of thyroid (06.11-06.12)*
           laser interstitial thermal therapy [LITT] of lesion or tissue of neck under guidance (17.62)
      DEF: Removal of growth on thyroid.

Thyroidectomy

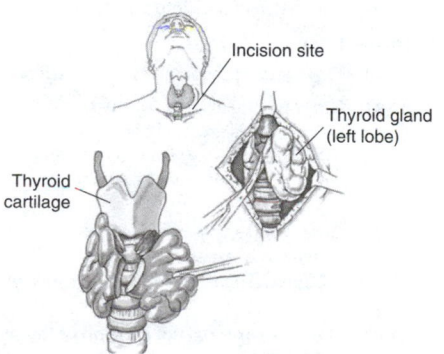

Incision site

Thyroid gland (left lobe)

Thyroid cartilage

06.39 Other
    Isthmectomy
    Partial thyroidectomy NOS
    EXCLUDES *partial substernal thyroidectomy (06.51)*

06.4 Complete thyroidectomy
    EXCLUDES *complete substernal thyroidectomy (06.52)*
           that with laryngectomy (30.3-30.4)

✓4th 06.5 Substernal thyroidectomy
    DEF: Removal of thyroid tissue below breastbone.

    06.50 Substernal thyroidectomy, not otherwise specified

    06.51 Partial substernal thyroidectomy

    06.52 Complete substernal thyroidectomy

06.6 Excision of lingual thyroid
    Excision of thyroid by: Excision of thyroid by:
      submental route   transoral route
    DEF: Excision of thyroid tissue at base of tongue.

06.7 Excision of thyroglossal duct or tract

✓4th 06.8 Parathyroidectomy
    DEF: Removal of parathyroid glands.

    06.81 Complete parathyroidectomy

    06.89 Other parathyroidectomy
      Parathyroidectomy NOS
      Partial parathyroidectomy
      EXCLUDES *biopsy of parathyroid (06.13)*

✓4th 06.9 Other operations on thyroid (region) and parathyroid

    06.91 Division of thyroid isthmus
      Transection of thyroid isthmus
      DEF: Cutting or division of tissue at narrowest point of thyroid.

    06.92 Ligation of thyroid vessels

    06.93 Suture of thyroid gland

    06.94 Thyroid tissue reimplantation
      Autotransplantation of thyroid tissue
      DEF: Placement of thyroid tissue graft into functional site.
      DEF: Autotransplantation of thyroid tissue: Tissue graft from patient's own thyroid tissue to another site on thyroid.

    06.95 Parathyroid tissue reimplantation
      Autotransplantation of parathyroid tissue
      DEF: Placement of parathyroid tissue graft into functional site.
      DEF: Autotransplantation of parathyroid tissue: Use of patient's own parathyroid tissue for graft.

    06.98 Other operations on thyroid glands

    06.99 Other operations on parathyroid glands

✓4th 07 Operations on other endocrine glands
    INCLUDES operations on:
        adrenal glands
        pineal gland
        pituitary gland
        thymus
    EXCLUDES *operations on:*
        aortic and carotid bodies (39.81-39.89)
        ovaries (65.0-65.99)
        pancreas (52.01-52.99)
        testes (62.0-62.99)

✓4th 07.0 Exploration of adrenal field
    EXCLUDES *incision of adrenal (gland) (07.41)*

    07.00 Exploration of adrenal field, not otherwise specified

    07.01 Unilateral exploration of adrenal field
      DEF: Investigation of one adrenal gland for diagnostic reasons.

    07.02 Bilateral exploration of adrenal field
      DEF: Investigation of both adrenal glands for diagnostic reasons.

Operations on the Endocrine System

07.1–07.83

✓4ᵗʰ **07.1 Diagnostic procedures on adrenal glands, pituitary gland, pineal gland, and thymus**

07.11 Closed [percutaneous] [needle] biopsy of adrenal gland

07.12 Open biopsy of adrenal gland

07.13 Biopsy of pituitary gland, transfrontal approach
DEF: Excision of pituitary gland tissue for exam through frontal bone.

07.14 Biopsy of pituitary gland, transsphenoidal approach
DEF: Excision of pituitary gland tissue for exam through sphenoid bone.

07.15 Biopsy of pituitary gland, unspecified approach

07.16 Biopsy of thymus

07.17 Biopsy of pineal gland

07.19 Other diagnostic procedures on adrenal glands, pituitary gland, pineal gland, and thymus
EXCLUDES microscopic examination of specimen from endocrine gland (90.11-90.19)
radioisotope scan of pituitary gland (92.11)

✓4ᵗʰ **07.2 Partial adrenalectomy**

07.21 Excision of lesion of adrenal gland
EXCLUDES biopsy of adrenal gland (07.11-07.12)

07.22 Unilateral adrenalectomy
Adrenalectomy NOS
EXCLUDES excision of remaining adrenal gland (07.3)
DEF: Excision of one adrenal gland.

07.29 Other partial adrenalectomy
Partial adrenalectomy NOS
AHA: 2Q, '05, 4
TIP: Assign in addition to a code from subcategory 55.5 if the documentation specifies radical nephrectomy, which includes adrenal gland resection.

07.3 Bilateral adrenalectomy
Excision of remaining adrenal gland
EXCLUDES bilateral partial adrenalectomy (07.29)

✓4ᵗʰ **07.4 Other operations on adrenal glands, nerves, and vessels**

07.41 Incision of adrenal gland
Adrenalotomy (with drainage)

07.42 Division of nerves to adrenal glands

07.43 Ligation of adrenal vessels

07.44 Repair of adrenal gland

07.45 Reimplantation of adrenal tissue
Autotransplantation of adrenal tissue
DEF: Autotransplantation of adrenal tissue: Use of tissue graft from the patient's own body.

07.49 Other

✓4ᵗʰ **07.5 Operations on pineal gland**

07.51 Exploration of pineal field
EXCLUDES that with incision of pineal gland (07.52)

07.52 Incision of pineal gland

07.53 Partial excision of pineal gland
EXCLUDES biopsy of pineal gland (07.17)

07.54 Total excision of pineal gland
Pinealectomy (complete) (total)

07.59 Other operations on pineal gland

✓4ᵗʰ **07.6 Hypophysectomy**
DEF: Excision, destruction of pituitary gland.

07.61 Partial excision of pituitary gland, transfrontal approach
Cryohypophysectomy, partial
Division of hypophyseal stalk
Excision of lesion of pituitary [hypophysis] | transfrontal approach
Hypophysectomy subtotal
Infundibulectomy, hypophyseal
EXCLUDES biopsy of pituitary gland, transfrontal approach (07.13)
DEF: Removal of partial pituitary gland through frontal bone.

07.62 Partial excision of pituitary gland, transsphenoidal approach
EXCLUDES biopsy of pituitary gland, transsphenoidal approach (07.14)
AHA: ▶1Q, '13, 7◀
DEF: Removal of partial pituitary gland through sphenoid bone.

07.63 Partial excision of pituitary gland, unspecified approach
EXCLUDES biopsy of pituitary gland NOS (07.15)

07.64 Total excision of pituitary gland, transfrontal approach
Ablation of pituitary by implantation (strontium-yttrium)(Y) | transfrontal approach
Cryohypophysectomy, complete
DEF: Removal of total pituitary gland through frontal bone.

07.65 Total excision of pituitary gland, transsphenoidal approach
DEF: Removal of total pituitary gland through sphenoid bone.

07.68 Total excision of pituitary gland, other specified approach
DEF: Destroy or remove pituitary gland by a specified approach, other than those listed.

07.69 Total excision of pituitary gland, unspecified approach
Hypophysectomy NOS
Pituitectomy NOS

✓4ᵗʰ **07.7 Other operations on hypophysis**

07.71 Exploration of pituitary fossa
EXCLUDES exploration with incision of pituitary gland (07.72)
DEF: Exploration of region of pituitary gland.

07.72 Incision of pituitary gland
Aspiration of:
craniobuccal pouch
craniopharyngioma
hypophysis
pituitary gland
Rathke's pouch

07.79 Other
Insertion of pack into sella turcica

✓4ᵗʰ **07.8 Thymectomy**

07.80 Thymectomy, not otherwise specified

07.81 Other partial excision of thymus
Open partial excision of thymus
EXCLUDES biopsy of thymus (07.16)
thoracoscopic partial excision of thymus (07.83)

07.82 Other total excision of thymus
Open total excision of thymus
EXCLUDES thoracoscopic total excision of thymus (07.84)

07.83 Thoracoscopic partial excision of thymus
EXCLUDES other partial excision of thymus (07.81)
AHA: 4Q, '07, 108

BI Bilateral Procedure   NC Non-covered Procedure   LC Limited Coverage Procedure   ▶◀ Revised Text   ● New Code   ▲ Revised Code Title

07.84   **Thoracoscopic total excision of**
    EXCLUDES *other total excision of thymus (07.82)*
    AHA: 4Q, '07, 108, 109

☑4ᵗʰ   07.9   **Other operations on thymus**

07.91   **Exploration of thymus field**
    EXCLUDES *exploration with incision of thymus (07.92)*

07.92   **Other incision of thymus**
    Open incision of thymus
    EXCLUDES *thoracoscopic incision of thymus (07.95)*

07.93   **Repair of thymus**

07.94   **Transplantation of thymus**
    DEF: Placement of thymus tissue grafts into functional area of gland.

07.95   **Thoracoscopic incision of thymus**
    EXCLUDES *other incision of thymus (07.92)*
    AHA: 4Q, '07, 108

07.98   **Other and unspecified thoracoscopic operations on thymus**
    AHA: 4Q, '07, 108

07.99   **Other and unspecified operations on thymus**
    Transcervical thymectomy
    EXCLUDES *other thoracoscopic operations on thymus (07.98)*

Operations on the Eye

08–08.84

3. Operations on the Eye (08-16)

✓3rd **08** **Operations on eyelids**
     INCLUDES operations on the eyebrow

✓4th **08.0** **Incision of eyelid**

     08.01 **Incision of lid margin**
         DEF: Cutting into eyelid edge.

     08.02 **Severing of blepharorrhaphy**
         DEF: Freeing of eyelids previously sutured shut.

     08.09 **Other incision of eyelid**

✓4th **08.1** **Diagnostic procedures on eyelid**

     08.11 **Biopsy of eyelid**

     08.19 **Other diagnostic procedures on eyelid**

✓4th **08.2** **Excision or destruction of lesion or tissue of eyelid**
     Code also any synchronous reconstruction (08.61-08.74)
     EXCLUDES biopsy of eyelid (08.11)

     08.20 **Removal of lesion of eyelid, not otherwise specified**
         Removal of meibomian gland NOS

     08.21 **Excision of chalazion**

     08.22 **Excision of other minor lesion of eyelid**
         Excision of:
           verruca
           wart

     08.23 **Excision of major lesion of eyelid, partial-thickness**
         Excision involving one-fourth or more of lid margin, partial-thickness
         DEF: Excision of lesion not in all eyelid layers.

     08.24 **Excision of major lesion of eyelid, full-thickness**
         Excision involving one-fourth or more of lid margin, full-thickness
         Wedge resection of eyelid
         DEF: Excision of growth in all eyelid layers, full thickness.
         AHA: 4Q, '11, 135

     08.25 **Destruction of lesion of eyelid**

✓4th **08.3** **Repair of blepharoptosis and lid retraction**

     08.31 **Repair of blepharoptosis by frontalis muscle technique with suture**
         DEF: Correction of drooping upper eyelid with suture of frontalis muscle.

     08.32 **Repair of blepharoptosis by frontalis muscle technique with fascial sling**
         DEF: Correction of drooping upper eyelid with fascial tissue sling of frontalis muscle.

     08.33 **Repair of blepharoptosis by resection or advancement of levator muscle or aponeurosis**
         DEF: Correction of drooping upper eyelid with levator muscle, extended, cut, or by expanded tendon.

     08.34 **Repair of blepharoptosis by other levator muscle techniques**

     08.35 **Repair of blepharoptosis by tarsal technique**
         DEF: Correction of drooping upper eyelid with tarsal muscle.

     08.36 **Repair of blepharoptosis by other techniques**
         Correction of eyelid ptosis NOS
         Orbicularis oculi muscle sling for correction of blepharoptosis

     08.37 **Reduction of overcorrection of ptosis**
         DEF: Correction, release of previous plastic repair of drooping eyelid.

     08.38 **Correction of lid retraction**
         DEF: Fixing of withdrawn eyelid into normal position.

✓4th **08.4** **Repair of entropion or ectropion**

     08.41 **Repair of entropion or ectropion by thermocauterization**
         DEF: Restoration of eyelid margin to normal position with heat cautery.

     08.42 **Repair of entropion or ectropion by suture technique**
         DEF: Restoration of eyelid margin to normal position by suture.

     08.43 **Repair of entropion or ectropion with wedge resection**
         DEF: Restoration of eyelid margin to normal position by removing tissue.

     08.44 **Repair of entropion or ectropion with lid reconstruction**
         DEF: Reconstruction of eyelid margin.

     08.49 **Other repair of entropion or ectropion**

✓4th **08.5** **Other adjustment of lid position**

     08.51 **Canthotomy**
         DEF: Incision into outer canthus of eye.

     08.52 **Blepharorrhaphy**
         Canthorrhaphy   Tarsorrhaphy
         DEF: Eyelids are partially sutured together; done to shorten palpebral fissure or protect cornea.

     08.59 **Other**
         Canthoplasty NOS
         Repair of epicanthal fold

✓4th **08.6** **Reconstruction of eyelid with flaps or grafts**
     EXCLUDES that associated with repair of entropion and ectropion (08.44)

     08.61 **Reconstruction of eyelid with skin flap or graft**
         DEF: Rebuild of eyelid by graft or flap method.
         AHA: 4Q, '11, 135

     08.62 **Reconstruction of eyelid with mucous membrane flap or graft**
         DEF: Rebuild of eyelid with mucous membrane graft or flap method.

     08.63 **Reconstruction of eyelid with hair follicle graft**
         DEF: Rebuild of eyelid with hair follicle graft.

     08.64 **Reconstruction of eyelid with tarsoconjunctival flap**
         Transfer of tarsoconjunctival flap from opposing lid
         DEF: Recreation of eyelid with tarsoconjunctival tissue.

     08.69 **Other reconstruction of eyelid with flaps or grafts**

✓4th **08.7** **Other reconstruction of eyelid**
     EXCLUDES that associated with repair of entropion and ectropion (08.44)
     TIP: Assign these codes twice for bilateral blepharoplasty procedures; medical necessity may require documentation of visual field loss.

     08.70 **Reconstruction of eyelid, not otherwise specified**
         AHA: 2Q, '96, 11

     08.71 **Reconstruction of eyelid involving lid margin, partial-thickness**
         DEF: Repair of eyelid margin not using all lid layers.

     08.72 **Other reconstruction of eyelid, partial-thickness**
         DEF: Reshape of eyelid not using all lid layers.

     08.73 **Reconstruction of eyelid involving lid margin, full-thickness**
         DEF: Repair of eyelid and margin using all tissue layers.

     08.74 **Other reconstruction of eyelid, full-thickness**
         DEF: Other repair of eyelid using all tissue layers.

✓4th **08.8** **Other repair of eyelid**

     08.81 **Linear repair of laceration of eyelid or eyebrow**

     08.82 **Repair of laceration involving lid margin, partial-thickness**
         DEF: Repair of laceration not involving all layers of eyelid margin.

     08.83 **Other repair of laceration of eyelid, partial thickness**
         DEF: Repair of eyelid tear not involving all eyelid layers.

     08.84 **Repair of laceration involving lid margin, full-thickness**
         DEF: Repair of eyelid margin tear involving all margin layers.

BI Bilateral Procedure   NC Non-covered Procedure   LC Limited Coverage Procedure   ▶◀ Revised Text   ● New Code   ▲ Revised Code Title

84 – Volume 3   2015 ICD-9-CM

Operations on the Eye

08.85   Other repair of laceration of eyelid, full-thickness
DEF: Repair of eyelid tear involving all layers.

08.86   Lower eyelid rhytidectomy
DEF: Removal of wrinkles from lower eyelid.

08.87   Upper eyelid rhytidectomy
DEF: Removal of wrinkles from upper eyelid.
AHA: 2Q, '96, 11

08.89   Other eyelid repair
AHA: 1Q, '00, 22

✓4th **08.9   Other operations on eyelids**

08.91   Electrosurgical epilation of eyelid
DEF: Electrical removal of eyelid hair roots.

08.92   Cryosurgical epilation of eyelid
DEF: Removal of eyelid hair roots by freezing.

08.93   Other epilation of eyelid

08.99   Other

✓3rd **09   Operations on lacrimal system**

09.0   Incision of lacrimal gland
Incision of lacrimal cyst (with drainage)

✓4th **09.1   Diagnostic procedures on lacrimal system**

09.11   Biopsy of lacrimal gland

09.12   Biopsy of lacrimal sac

09.19   Other diagnostic procedures on lacrimal system
EXCLUDES contrast dacryocystogram (87.05)
soft tissue x-ray of nasolacrimal duct (87.09)

✓4th **09.2   Excision of lesion or tissue of lacrimal gland**

09.20   Excision of lacrimal gland, not otherwise specified

09.21   Excision of lesion of lacrimal gland
EXCLUDES biopsy of lacrimal gland (09.11)

09.22   Other partial dacryoadenectomy
EXCLUDES biopsy of lacrimal gland (09.11)
DEF: Partial excision of tear gland.

09.23   Total dacryoadenectomy
DEF: Total excision of tear gland.

09.3   Other operations on lacrimal gland

✓4th **09.4   Manipulation of lacrimal passage**
INCLUDES removal of calculus
that with dilation
EXCLUDES contrast dacryocystogram (87.05)

09.41   Probing of lacrimal punctum
DEF: Exploration of tear duct entrance with flexible rod.

09.42   Probing of lacrimal canaliculi
DEF: Exploration of tear duct with flexible rod.

09.43   Probing of nasolacrimal duct
EXCLUDES that with insertion of tube or stent (09.44)
DEF: Exploration of passage between tear sac and nose with flexible rod.

09.44   Intubation of nasolacrimal duct
Insertion of stent into nasolacrimal duct
AHA: 2Q, '94, 11

09.49   Other manipulation of lacrimal passage

✓4th **09.5   Incision of lacrimal sac and passages**

09.51   Incision of lacrimal punctum

09.52   Incision of lacrimal canaliculi

09.53   Incision of lacrimal sac
DEF: Cutting into lacrimal pouch of tear gland.

09.59   Other incision of lacrimal passages
Incision (and drainage) of nasolacrimal duct NOS

09.6   Excision of lacrimal sac and passage
EXCLUDES biopsy of lacrimal sac (09.12)
DEF: Removal of pouch and passage of tear gland.

✓4th **09.7   Repair of canaliculus and punctum**
EXCLUDES repair of eyelid (08.81-08.89)

09.71   Correction of everted punctum
DEF: Repair of an outwardly turned tear duct entrance.

09.72   Other repair of punctum

09.73   Repair of canaliculus

✓4th **09.8   Fistulization of lacrimal tract to nasal cavity**

09.81   Dacryocystorhinostomy [DCR]
DEF: Creation of entrance between tear gland and nasal passage for tear flow.

09.82   Conjunctivocystorhinostomy
Conjunctivodacryocystorhinostomy [CDCR]
EXCLUDES that with insertion of tube or stent (09.83)
DEF: Creation of tear drainage path from lacrimal sac to nasal cavity through conjunctiva.

09.83   Conjunctivorhinostomy with insertion of tube or stent
DEF: Creation of passage between eye sac membrane and nasal cavity with tube or stent.

✓4th **09.9   Other operations on lacrimal system**

09.91   Obliteration of lacrimal punctum
DEF: Total destruction of tear gland opening in eyelid.

09.99   Other
AHA: 2Q, '94, 11
TIP: Assign for removal of nasolacrimal stent.

✓3rd **10   Operations on conjunctiva**

10.0   Removal of embedded foreign body from conjunctiva by incision
EXCLUDES removal of:
embedded foreign body without incision (98.22)
superficial foreign body (98.21)

10.1   Other incision of conjunctiva

✓4th **10.2   Diagnostic procedures on conjunctiva**

10.21   Biopsy of conjunctiva

10.29   Other diagnostic procedures on conjunctiva

✓4th **10.3   Excision or destruction of lesion or tissue of conjunctiva**

10.31   Excision of lesion or tissue of conjunctiva
Excision of ring of conjunctiva around cornea
EXCLUDES biopsy of conjunctiva (10.21)
DEF: Removal of growth or tissue from eye membrane.
AHA: 4Q, '00, 41; 3Q, '96, 7
TIP: Assign for excision of conjunctivochalasis.

10.32   Destruction of lesion of conjunctiva
EXCLUDES excision of lesion (10.31)
thermocauterization for entropion (08.41)
DEF: Destruction of eye membrane growth; not done by excision.

10.33   Other destructive procedures on conjunctiva
Removal of trachoma follicles

✓4th **10.4   Conjunctivoplasty**
DEF: Correction of conjunctiva by plastic surgery.

10.41   Repair of symblepharon with free graft
AHA: 3Q, '96, 7

10.42   Reconstruction of conjunctival cul-de-sac with free graft
EXCLUDES revision of enucleation socket with graft (16.63)
DEF: Rebuilding of eye membrane fold with graft of unattached tissue.

10.43   Other reconstruction of conjunctival cul-de-sac
EXCLUDES revision of enucleation socket (16.64)

10.44   Other free graft to conjunctiva

10.49   Other conjunctivoplasty
EXCLUDES repair of cornea with conjunctival flap (11.53)

10.5   Lysis of adhesions of conjunctiva and eyelid
Division of symblepharon (with insertion of conformer)

Operations on the Eye

08.85–10.5

Operations on the Eye

10.6–12.29

10.6 Repair of laceration of conjunctiva
> EXCLUDES that with repair of sclera (12.81)

✓4th **10.9 Other operations on conjunctiva**

10.91 Subconjunctival injection
> AHA: 3Q, '96, 7

10.99 Other

✓3rd **11 Operations on cornea**

11.0 Magnetic removal of embedded foreign body from cornea
> EXCLUDES that with incision (11.1)

11.1 Incision of cornea
> Incision of cornea for removal of foreign body

✓4th **11.2 Diagnostic procedures on cornea**

11.21 Scraping of cornea for smear or culture

11.22 Biopsy of cornea

11.29 Other diagnostic procedures on cornea

✓4th **11.3 Excision of pterygium**

11.31 Transposition of pterygium
> DEF: Cutting into membranous structure extending from eye membrane to cornea and suturing it in a downward position.

11.32 Excision of pterygium with corneal graft
> DEF: Surgical removal and repair of membranous structure extending from eye membrane to cornea using corneal tissue graft.

11.39 Other excision of pterygium

✓4th **11.4 Excision or destruction of tissue or other lesion of cornea**

11.41 Mechanical removal of corneal epithelium
> That by chemocauterization
> EXCLUDES that for smear or culture (11.21)
> DEF: Removal of outer layer of cornea by mechanical means.
> AHA: 3Q, '02, 20

11.42 Thermocauterization of corneal lesion
> DEF: Destruction of corneal lesion by electrical cautery.

11.43 Cryotherapy of corneal lesion
> DEF: Destruction of corneal lesion by freezing.

11.49 Other removal or destruction of corneal lesion
> Excision of cornea NOS
> EXCLUDES biopsy of cornea (11.22)

✓4th **11.5 Repair of cornea**

11.51 Suture of corneal laceration
> AHA: 3Q, '96, 7

11.52 Repair of postoperative wound dehiscence of cornea
> DEF: Repair of ruptured postoperative corneal wound.

11.53 Repair of corneal laceration or wound with conjunctival flap
> DEF: Correction corneal wound or tear with conjunctival tissue.

11.59 Other repair of cornea

✓4th **11.6 Corneal transplant**
> EXCLUDES excision of pterygium with corneal graft (11.32)

11.60 Corneal transplant, not otherwise specified
> NOTE To report donor sources — see codes 00.91-00.93
> Keratoplasty NOS

11.61 Lamellar keratoplasty with autograft
> DEF: Restoration of sight using patient's own corneal tissue, partial thickness.

11.62 Other lamellar keratoplasty
> DEF: Restoration of sight using donor corneal tissue, partial thickness.
> AHA: S-O, '85, 6

11.63 Penetrating keratoplasty with autograft
> Perforating keratoplasty with autograft
> TIP: Penetrating keratoplasty infers a full-thickness corneal transplant grafting procedure.

11.64 Other penetrating keratoplasty
> Perforating keratoplasty (with homograft)

11.69 Other corneal transplant

✓4th **11.7 Other reconstructive and refractive surgery on cornea**

11.71 Keratomileusis NC
> DEF: Restoration of corneal shape by removing portion of cornea, freezing, reshaping curve and reattaching it.

11.72 Keratophakia NC
> DEF: Correction of eye lens loss by dissecting the central zone of the cornea and replacing it with a thickened graft of the cornea.

11.73 Keratoprosthesis
> DEF: Placement of corneal artificial implant.

11.74 Thermokeratoplasty
> DEF: Reshaping and reforming cornea by heat application.

11.75 Radial keratotomy NC
> DEF: Incisions around cornea radius to correct nearsightedness.

11.76 Epikeratophakia NC
> DEF: Repair lens loss by cornea graft sutured to central corneal zone.

11.79 Other

✓4th **11.9 Other operations on cornea**

11.91 Tattooing of cornea

11.92 Removal of artificial implant from cornea

11.99 Other
> AHA: 3Q, '02, 20
> TIP: Assign for keratolimbal stem cell transplant, typically performed for aniridia and decreasing vision with deep vascular pannus of the eye.

✓3rd **12 Operations on iris, ciliary body, sclera, and anterior chamber**
> EXCLUDES operations on cornea (11.0-11.99)

✓4th **12.0 Removal of intraocular foreign body from anterior segment of eye**

12.00 Removal of intraocular foreign body from anterior segment of eye, not otherwise specified

12.01 Removal of intraocular foreign body from anterior segment of eye with use of magnet

12.02 Removal of intraocular foreign body from anterior segment of eye without use of magnet

✓4th **12.1 Iridotomy and simple iridectomy**
> EXCLUDES iridectomy associated with:
> cataract extraction (13.11-13.69)
> removal of lesion (12.41-12.42)
> scleral fistulization (12.61-12.69)

12.11 Iridotomy with transfixion

12.12 Other iridotomy
> Corectomy
> Discission of iris
> Iridotomy NOS
> DEF: Corectomy: Incision into iris (also called iridectomy).

12.13 Excision of prolapsed iris
> DEF: Removal of downwardly placed portion of iris.

12.14 Other iridectomy
> Iridectomy (basal) (peripheral) (total)
> DEF: Partial or total removal of iris.

✓4th **12.2 Diagnostic procedures on iris, ciliary body, sclera, and anterior chamber**

12.21 Diagnostic aspiration of anterior chamber of eye
> DEF: Suction withdrawal of fluid from anterior eye chamber for diagnostic reasons.

12.22 Biopsy of iris

12.29 Other diagnostic procedures on iris, ciliary body, sclera, and anterior chamber

---

BI Bilateral Procedure   NC Non-covered Procedure   LC Limited Coverage Procedure   ▶◀ Revised Text   ● New Code   ▲ Revised Code Title

√4th **12.3 Iridoplasty and coreoplasty**

DEF: Correction of abnormal iris or pupil by plastic surgery.

12.31 Lysis of goniosynechiae

Lysis of goniosynechiae by injection of air or liquid

DEF: Freeing of fibrous structures between cornea and iris by injecting air or liquid.

12.32 Lysis of other anterior synechiae

Lysis of anterior synechiae:
  NOS
  by injection of air or liquid

12.33 Lysis of posterior synechiae

Lysis of iris adhesions NOS

12.34 Lysis of corneovitreal adhesions

DEF: Release of adhesions of cornea and vitreous body.

12.35 Coreoplasty

Needling of pupillary membrane

DEF: Correction of an iris defect.

12.39 Other iridoplasty

√4th **12.4 Excision or destruction of lesion of iris and ciliary body**

12.40 Removal of lesion of anterior segment of eye, not otherwise specified

12.41 Destruction of lesion of iris, nonexcisional

Destruction of lesion of iris by:
  cauterization
  cryotherapy
  photocoagulation

12.42 Excision of lesion of iris

EXCLUDES biopsy of iris (12.22)

12.43 Destruction of lesion of ciliary body, nonexcisional

12.44 Excision of lesion of ciliary body

√4th **12.5 Facilitation of intraocular circulation**

12.51 Goniopuncture without goniotomy

DEF: Stab incision into anterior chamber of eye to relieve optic pressure.

12.52 Goniotomy without goniopuncture

DEF: Incision into Schlemm's canal to drain aqueous and relieve pressure.

12.53 Goniotomy with goniopuncture

12.54 Trabeculotomy ab externo

DEF: Incision into supporting connective tissue strands of eye capsule, via exterior approach.

12.55 Cyclodialysis

DEF: Creation of passage between anterior chamber and suprachoroidal space.

12.59 Other facilitation of intraocular circulation

√4th **12.6 Scleral fistulization**

EXCLUDES exploratory sclerotomy (12.89)

12.61 Trephination of sclera with iridectomy

DEF: Cut around sclerocornea to remove part of the iris.

12.62 Thermocauterization of sclera with iridectomy

DEF: Destruction of outer eyeball layer with partial excision of iris using heat.

Trabeculectomy Ab Externo

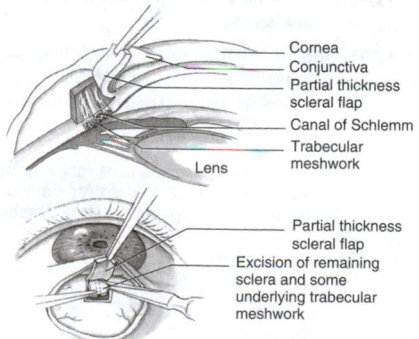

Cornea
Conjunctiva
Partial thickness scleral flap
Canal of Schlemm
Trabecular meshwork
Lens

Partial thickness scleral flap
Excision of remaining sclera and some underlying trabecular meshwork

12.63 Iridencleisis and iridotasis

DEF: Creation of permanent drain in iris by transposing or stretching iris tissue.

12.64 Trabeculectomy ab externo

DEF: Excision of supporting connective tissue strands of eye capsule, via exterior approach.

12.65 Other scleral fistulization with iridectomy

Holth's sclerectomy

DEF: Creation of outer eyeball layer passage with partial excision of iris.

12.66 Postoperative revision of scleral fistulization procedure

Revision of filtering bleb

EXCLUDES repair of fistula (12.82)

AHA: 2Q, '01, 16

12.67 Insertion of aqueous drainage device

Anterior chamber drainage device
Aqueous drainage shunt or stent
Eye valve implant
Filtration canal shunt or device

DEF: Placement of glaucoma drainage devices, shunts or valves that shunt aqueous fluid from the anterior chamber of the eye for absorption into the lymph and blood vessels around the eye.

AHA: 4Q, '11, 162

TIP: This procedure is typically for patients who have failed medical therapy and trabeculectomy.

12.69 Other fistulizing procedure

√4th **12.7 Other procedures for relief of elevated intraocular pressure**

12.71 Cyclodiathermy

DEF: Destruction of ciliary body tissue with heat.

12.72 Cyclocryotherapy

DEF: Destruction of ciliary body tissue by freezing.

12.73 Cyclophotocoagulation

DEF: Destruction of ciliary body tissue by high energy light source.

12.74 Diminution of ciliary body, not otherwise specified

12.79 Other glaucoma procedures

AHA: 2Q, '98, 16

TIP: Assign for suture lysis performed for elevated intraocular pressure status post trabeculectomy.

√4th **12.8 Operations on sclera**

EXCLUDES those associated with:
  retinal reattachment (14.41-14.59)
  scleral fistulization (12.61-12.69)

12.81 Suture of laceration of sclera

Suture of sclera with synchronous repair of conjunctiva

12.82 Repair of scleral fistula

EXCLUDES postoperative revision of scleral fistulization procedure (12.66)

12.83 Revision of operative wound of anterior segment, not elsewhere classified

EXCLUDES postoperative revision of scleral fistulization procedure (12.66)

12.84 Excision or destruction of lesion of sclera

12.85 Repair of scleral staphyloma with graft

DEF: Repair of protruding outer eyeball layer with a graft.

12.86 Other repair of scleral staphyloma

12.87 Scleral reinforcement with graft

DEF: Restoration of outer eyeball shape with tissue graft.

12.88 Other scleral reinforcement

12.89 Other operations on sclera

Exploratory sclerotomy

√4th **12.9 Other operations on iris, ciliary body, and anterior chamber**

12.91 Therapeutic evacuation of anterior chamber

Paracentesis of anterior chamber

EXCLUDES diagnostic aspiration (12.21)

Operations on the Eye

12.92–13.91

12.92 Injection into anterior chamber

Injection of:
air
liquid } into anterior chamber
medication

AHA: J-A, '84, 1

12.93 Removal or destruction of epithelial downgrowth from anterior chamber

EXCLUDES that with iridectomy (12.41-12.42)

DEF: Excision or destruction of epithelial overgrowth in anterior eye chamber.

12.97 Other operations on iris

12.98 Other operations on ciliary body

12.99 Other operations on anterior chamber

✓3rd **13 Operations on lens**

✓4th **13.0 Removal of foreign body from lens**

EXCLUDES removal of pseudophakos (13.8)

13.00 Removal of foreign body from lens, not otherwise specified

13.01 Removal of foreign body from lens with use of magnet

13.02 Removal of foreign body from lens without use of magnet

✓4th **13.1 Intracapsular extraction of lens**

Code also any synchronous insertion of pseudophakos (13.71)

AHA: S-O, '85, 6

13.11 Intracapsular extraction of lens by temporal inferior route

DEF: Extraction of lens and capsule via anterior approach through outer side of eyeball.

13.19 Other intracapsular extraction of lens

Cataract extraction NOS
Cryoextraction of lens
Erysiphake extraction of cataract
Extraction of lens NOS

13.2 Extracapsular extraction of lens by linear extraction technique

Code also any synchronous insertion of pseudophakos (13.71)

DEF: Excision of lens without the posterior capsule at junction between the cornea and outer eyeball layer by means of a linear incision.

AHA: S-O, '85, 6

13.3 Extracapsular extraction of lens by simple aspiration (and irrigation) technique

Irrigation of traumatic cataract

Code also any synchronous insertion of pseudophakos (13.71)

DEF: Removal of lens without the posterior capsule by suctioning and flushing out the area.

AHA: S-O, '85, 6

✓4th **13.4 Extracapsular extraction of lens by fragmentation and aspiration technique**

Code also any synchronous insertion of pseudophakos (13.71)

DEF: Removal of lens after division into smaller pieces with posterior capsule left intact.

AHA: S-O, '85, 6

TIP: Assign an additional code from subcategory 14.7 if a vitrectomy procedure is also performed with cataract extraction procedures.

13.41 Phacoemulsification and aspiration of cataract

AHA: 3Q, '96, 4; 1Q, '94, 16

13.42 Mechanical phacofragmentation and aspiration of cataract by posterior route

Code also any synchronous vitrectomy (14.74)

13.43 Mechanical phacofragmentation and other aspiration of cataract

Extraction of Lens (with insertion of intraocular lens prosthesis)

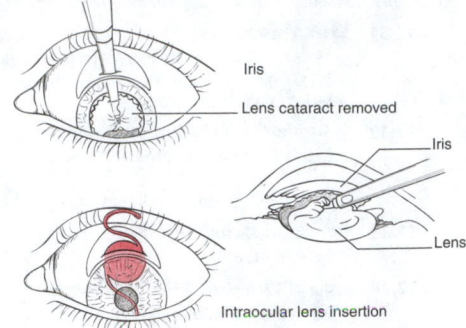

Iris
Lens cataract removed
Iris
Lens
Intraocular lens insertion

✓4th **13.5 Other extracapsular extraction of lens**

Code also any synchronous insertion of pseudophakos (13.71)

AHA: S-O, '85, 6

13.51 Extracapsular extraction of lens by temporal inferior route

DEF: Removal of lens through outer eyeball with posterior capsule left intact.

13.59 Other extracapsular extraction of lens

✓4th **13.6 Other cataract extraction**

Code also any synchronous insertion of pseudophakos (13.71)

AHA: S-O, '85, 6

13.64 Discission of secondary membrane [after cataract]

DEF: Breaking up of fibrotic lens capsule developed after previous lens extraction.

13.65 Excision of secondary membrane [after cataract]

Capsulectomy

DEF: Capsulectomy: Excision of lens capsule membrane after previous lens extraction.

13.66 Mechanical fragmentation of secondary membrane [after cataract]

DEF: Breaking up and removal of fibrotic lens capsule developed after previous lens extraction.

13.69 Other cataract extraction

✓4th **13.7 Insertion of prosthetic lens [pseudophakos]**

EXCLUDES implantation of intraocular telescope prosthesis (13.91)

DEF: Insertion of ocular implant, following lens extraction.

AHA: J-A, '84, 1

13.70 Insertion of pseudophakos, not otherwise specified

13.71 Insertion of intraocular lens prosthesis at time of cataract extraction, one-stage

Code also synchronous extraction of cataract (13.11-13.69)

AHA: 3Q, '96, 4

13.72 Secondary insertion of intraocular lens prosthesis

13.8 Removal of implanted lens

Removal of pseudophakos

✓4th **13.9 Other operations on lens**

AHA: 1Q, '00, 9

13.90 Operation on lens, not elsewhere classified

AHA: 4Q, '06, 123

13.91 Implantation of intraocular telescope prosthesis

Implantable miniature telescope

INCLUDES removal of lens, any method

EXCLUDES secondary insertion of ocular implant (16.61)

AHA: 4Q, '06, 123

TIP: This device is implanted in one eye, providing central vision; the nonimplanted eye can continue to provide peripheral vision for orientation and mobility.

BI Bilateral Procedure   NC Non-covered Procedure   LC Limited Coverage Procedure   ▶◀ Revised Text   ● New Code   ▲ Revised Code Title

88 – Volume 3   2015 ICD-9-CM

Laser Surgery (YAG)

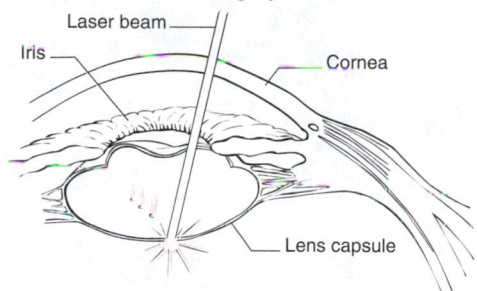

Laser beam
Iris
Cornea
Laser beam
Lens capsule

Scleral Buckling with Implant

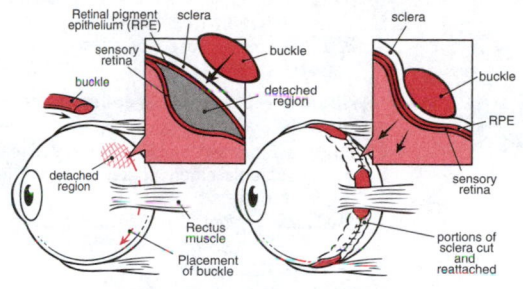

Retinal pigment epithelium (RPE)
sclera
buckle
sensory retina
detached region
buckle
detached region
sclera
buckle
RPE
sensory retina
Rectus muscle
Placement of buckle
portions of sclera cut and reattached

√3rd **14   Operations on retina, choroid, vitreous, and posterior chamber**

√4th **14.0   Removal of foreign body from posterior segment of eye**
EXCLUDES *removal of surgically implanted material (14.6)*

14.00 Removal of foreign body from posterior segment of eye, not otherwise specified

14.01 Removal of foreign body from posterior segment of eye with use of magnet

14.02 Removal of foreign body from posterior segment of eye without use of magnet

√4th **14.1   Diagnostic procedures on retina, choroid, vitreous, and posterior chamber**

14.11 Diagnostic aspiration of vitreous

14.19 Other diagnostic procedures on retina, choroid, vitreous, and posterior chamber

√4th **14.2   Destruction of lesion of retina and choroid**
INCLUDES destruction of chorioretinopathy or isolated chorioretinal lesion
EXCLUDES *that for repair of retina (14.31-14.59)*
DEF: Destruction of damaged retina and choroid tissue.

14.21 Destruction of chorioretinal lesion by diathermy

14.22 Destruction of chorioretinal lesion by cryotherapy

14.23 Destruction of chorioretinal lesion by xenon arc photocoagulation

14.24 Destruction of chorioretinal lesion by laser photocoagulation

14.25 Destruction of chorioretinal lesion by photocoagulation of unspecified type

14.26 Destruction of chorioretinal lesion by radiation therapy

14.27 Destruction of chorioretinal lesion by implantation of radiation source

14.29 Other destruction of chorioretinal lesion
Destruction of lesion of retina and choroid NOS

√4th **14.3   Repair of retinal tear**
INCLUDES repair of retinal defect
EXCLUDES *repair of retinal detachment (14.41-14.59)*

14.31 Repair of retinal tear by diathermy

14.32 Repair of retinal tear by cryotherapy

14.33 Repair of retinal tear by xenon arc photocoagulation

14.34 Repair of retinal tear by laser photocoagulation
AHA: 1Q, '94, 17

14.35 Repair of retinal tear by photocoagulation of unspecified type

14.39 Other repair of retinal tear

√4th **14.4   Repair of retinal detachment with scleral buckling and implant**
DEF: Placement of material around eye to indent sclera and close a hole or tear or to reduce vitreous traction.

14.41 Scleral buckling with implant
AHA: 3Q, '96, 6

14.49 Other scleral buckling
Scleral buckling with:
air tamponade
resection of sclera
vitrectomy
AHA: 1Q, '94, 16

√4th **14.5   Other repair of retinal detachment**
INCLUDES that with drainage

14.51 Repair of retinal detachment with diathermy

14.52 Repair of retinal detachment with cryotherapy

14.53 Repair of retinal detachment with xenon arc photocoagulation

14.54 Repair of retinal detachment with laser photocoagulation
AHA: N-D, '87, 10

14.55 Repair of retinal detachment with photocoagulation of unspecified type

14.59 Other

14.6   Removal of surgically implanted material from posterior segment of eye

√4th **14.7   Operations on vitreous**

14.71 Removal of vitreous, anterior approach
Open sky technique
Removal of vitreous, anterior approach (with replacement)
DEF: Removal of all or part of the eyeball fluid via the anterior segment of the eyeball.

14.72 Other removal of vitreous
Aspiration of vitreous by posterior sclerotomy

14.73 Mechanical vitrectomy by anterior approach
DEF: Removal of abnormal tissue in eyeball fluid to control fibrotic overgrowth in severe intraocular injury.
AHA: 3Q, '96, 4, 5

14.74 Other mechanical vitrectomy
Posterior approach
AHA: 4Q, '11, 106; 2Q, '10, 4-5; 3Q, '96, 4, 5

14.75 Injection of vitreous substitute
EXCLUDES *that associated with removal (14.71-14.72)*
AHA: 1Q, '98, 6; 3Q, '96, 4, 5; 1Q, '94, 17

14.79 Other operations on vitreous
AHA: 3Q, '99, 12; 1Q, '99, 11; 1Q, '98, 6
TIP: Assign for an endoscopic vitreous washout and reinjection of silicone oil.

√4th **14.8 Implantation of epiretinal visual prosthesis**

14.81 Implantation of epiretinal visual prosthesis
NOTE Includes lens removal, if present, scleral buckling, vitrectomy, epiretinal membrane peeling and pericardial grafting
EXCLUDES *implantation of intraocular telescope prosthesis (13.91)*
other operations on retina, choroid, and posterior chamber (14.9)
replacement of epiretinal visual prosthesis (14.83)
AHA: ▶4Q, '13, 83-85◀

Operations on the Eye

14.82–16.42

14.82 Removal of epiretinal visual prosthesis

> **NOTE** Includes 360-degree limbal peritomy and vitrectomy, if performed, and device extraction
>
> **EXCLUDES** *removal of eye prosthesis (97.31)*
>
> AHA: ▶4Q, '13, 83-85◀

14.83 Revision or replacement of epiretinal visual prosthesis

> **NOTE** Includes tack replacement, device relocation, and replacement of pericardial grafting, if needed
>
> **EXCLUDES** *implantation of epiretinal visual prosthesis (14.81)*
>
> AHA: ▶4Q, '13, 83-85◀

14.9 Other operations on retina, choroid, and posterior chamber

> AHA: 3Q, '96, 5
>
> TIP: Assign for epiretinal membrane peeling, which is typically performed with vitrectomy but is not an inherent component.

✓3rd **15 Operations on extraocular muscles**

> TIP: If a procedure is performed on the same muscle in both eyes, assign the appropriate code twice from subcategory 15.1 or 15.2.

✓4th **15.0 Diagnostic procedures on extraocular muscles or tendons**

15.01 Biopsy of extraocular muscle or tendon

15.09 Other diagnostic procedures on extraocular muscles and tendons

✓4th **15.1 Operations on one extraocular muscle involving temporary detachment from globe**

15.11 Recession of one extraocular muscle

> DEF: Detachment of exterior eye muscle with posterior reattachment to correct strabismus.
>
> AHA: 3Q, '96, 3

15.12 Advancement of one extraocular muscle

> DEF: Detachment of exterior eye muscle with forward reattachment to correct strabismus.

15.13 Resection of one extraocular muscle

15.19 Other operations on one extraocular muscle involving temporary detachment from globe

> **EXCLUDES** *transposition of muscle (15.5)*

✓4th **15.2 Other operations on one extraocular muscle**

15.21 Lengthening procedure on one extraocular muscle

> DEF: Extension of exterior eye muscle length.

15.22 Shortening procedure on one extraocular muscle

> DEF: Shortening of exterior eye muscle.

15.29 Other

15.3 Operations on two or more extraocular muscles involving temporary detachment from globe, one or both eyes

> AHA: 3Q, '96, 3

15.4 Other operations on two or more extraocular muscles, one or both eyes

15.5 Transposition of extraocular muscles

> **EXCLUDES** *that for correction of ptosis (08.31-08.36)*
>
> DEF: Relocation of exterior eye muscle to a more functional site.

15.6 Revision of extraocular muscle surgery

> DEF: Repair of previous exterior eye muscle surgery.

15.7 Repair of injury of extraocular muscle

> Freeing of entrapped extraocular muscle
> Lysis of adhesions of extraocular muscle
> Repair of laceration of extraocular muscle, tendon, or Tenon's capsule

15.9 Other operations on extraocular muscles and tendons

Lengthening Procedure on One Extraocular Muscle

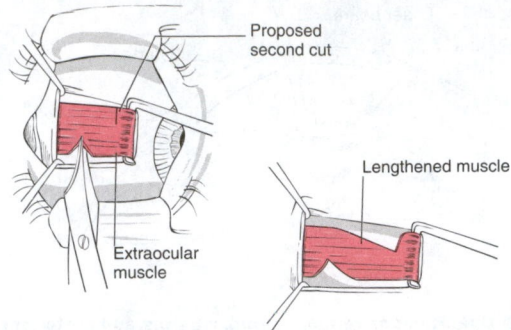

Proposed second cut

Lengthened muscle

Extraocular muscle

Shortening Procedure on One Extraocular Muscle

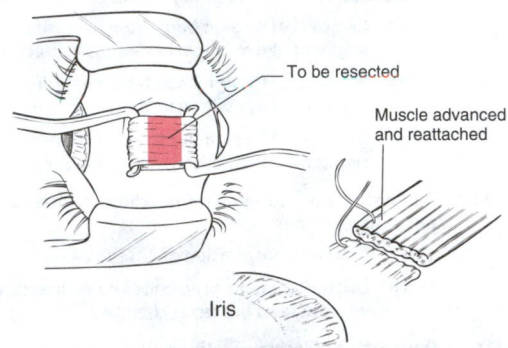

To be resected

Muscle advanced and reattached

Iris

16.02 Orbitotomy with insertion of orbital implant

> **EXCLUDES** *that with bone flap (16.01)*

16.09 Other orbitotomy

16.1 Removal of penetrating foreign body from eye, not otherwise specified

> **EXCLUDES** *removal of nonpenetrating foreign body (98.21)*
>
> DEF: Removal of foreign body from an unspecified site in eye.

✓4th **16.2 Diagnostic procedures on orbit and eyeball**

16.21 Ophthalmoscopy

16.22 Diagnostic aspiration of orbit

16.23 Biopsy of eyeball and orbit

16.29 Other diagnostic procedures on orbit and eyeball

> **EXCLUDES** *examination of form and structure of eye (95.11-95.16)*
> *general and subjective eye examination (95.01-95.09)*
> *microscopic examination of specimen from eye (90.21-90.29)*
> *objective functional tests of eye (95.21-95.26)*
> *ocular thermography (88.82)*
> *tonometry (89.11)*
> *x-ray of orbit (87.14, 87.16)*

✓4th **16.3 Evisceration of eyeball**

> DEF: Removal of eyeball, leaving sclera and occasionally cornea.

16.31 Removal of ocular contents with synchronous implant into scleral shell

> DEF: Removal of eyeball leaving outer eyeball layer with ocular implant into shell.

16.39 Other evisceration of eyeball

✓4th **16.4 Enucleation of eyeball**

> DEF: Removal of entire eyeball after severing eye muscles and optic nerves.

16.41 Enucleation of eyeball with synchronous implant into Tenon's capsule with attachment of muscles

> Integrated implant of eyeball
>
> DEF: Removal of eyeball with insertion of ocular implant and muscle attachment.

16.42 Enucleation of eyeball with other synchronous implant

| BI Bilateral Procedure | NC Non-covered Procedure | LC Limited Coverage Procedure | ▶◀ Revised Text | ● New Code | ▲ Revised Code Title |

16.49　Other enucleation of eyeball
Removal of eyeball NOS

√4th **16.5　Exenteration of orbital contents**

16.51　Exenteration of orbit with removal of adjacent structures
Radical orbitomaxillectomy
DEF: Removal of contents of bony cavity of eye as well as related tissues and structures.
DEF: Radical orbitomaxillectomy: Removal of contents of bony cavity of eye, related tissues and structures, and a portion of maxillary bone.

16.52　Exenteration of orbit with therapeutic removal of orbital bone

16.59　Other exenteration of orbit
Evisceration of orbit NOS
Exenteration of orbit with temporalis muscle transplant

√4th **16.6　Secondary procedures after removal of eyeball**
EXCLUDES　that with synchronous:
enucleation of eyeball (16.41-16.42)
evisceration of eyeball (16.31)

16.61　Secondary insertion of ocular implant
DEF: Insertion of ocular implant after previous eye removal.

16.62　Revision and reinsertion of ocular implant
DEF: Reimplant or correction of ocular implant.

16.63　Revision of enucleation socket with graft
DEF: Implant of tissue to correct socket after eye removal.

16.64　Other revision of enucleation socket

16.65　Secondary graft to exenteration cavity
DEF: Implant of tissue in place of eye after removal.

16.66　Other revision of exenteration cavity

16.69　Other secondary procedures after removal of eyeball

√4th **16.7　Removal of ocular or orbital implant**

16.71　Removal of ocular implant

16.72　Removal of orbital implant

√4th **16.8　Repair of injury of eyeball and orbit**

16.81　Repair of wound of orbit
EXCLUDES　reduction of orbital fracture (76.78-76.79)
repair of extraocular muscles (15.7)

16.82　Repair of rupture of eyeball
Repair of multiple structures of eye
EXCLUDES　repair of laceration of:
cornea (11.51-11.59)
sclera (12.81)

16.89　Other repair of injury of eyeball or orbit

√4th **16.9　Other operations on orbit and eyeball**
EXCLUDES　irrigation of eye (96.51)
prescription and fitting of low vision aids
(95.31-95.33)
removal of:
eye prosthesis NEC (97.31)
nonpenetrating foreign body from eye without
incision (98.21)

16.91　Retrobulbar injection of therapeutic agent
EXCLUDES　injection of radiographic contrast material
(87.14)
opticociliary injection (12.79)

16.92　Excision of lesion of orbit
EXCLUDES　biopsy of orbit (16.23)

16.93　Excision of lesion of eye, unspecified structure
EXCLUDES　biopsy of eye NOS (16.23)

16.98　Other operations on orbit

16.99　Other operations on eyeball

Operations on the Eye

16.49–16.99

Other Miscellaneous Diagnostic and Therapeutic Procedures

17–17.53

3A. Other Miscellaneous Diagnostic and Therapeutic Procedures (17)

√3ʳᵈ **17   Other miscellaneous procedures**

√4ᵗʰ **17.1   Laparoscopic unilateral repair of inguinal hernia**
> EXCLUDES *other and open unilateral repair of hernia (53.00-53.05)*
>
> AHA: 4Q, '08, 165-166

17.11   Laparoscopic repair of direct inguinal hernia with graft or prosthesis
> Laparoscopic repair of direct and indirect inguinal hernia with graft or prosthesis

17.12   Laparoscopic repair of indirect inguinal hernia with graft or prosthesis

17.13   Laparoscopic repair of inguinal hernia with graft or prosthesis, not otherwise specified

√4ᵗʰ **17.2   Laparoscopic bilateral repair of inguinal hernia**
> EXCLUDES *other and open bilateral repair of hernia (53.10-53.17)*
>
> AHA: 4Q, '08, 165-166

17.21   Laparoscopic bilateral repair of direct inguinal hernia with graft or prosthesis

17.22   Laparoscopic bilateral repair of indirect inguinal hernia with graft or prosthesis

17.23   Laparoscopic bilateral repair of inguinal hernia, one direct and one indirect, with graft or prosthesis

17.24   Laparoscopic bilateral repair of inguinal hernia with graft or prosthesis, not otherwise specified

17.3   Laparoscopic partial excision of large intestine
> EXCLUDES *other and open partial excision of large intestine (45.71-45.79)*
>
> AHA: 4Q, '08, 169-170

17.31   Laparoscopic multiple segmental resection of large intestine

17.32   Laparoscopic cecectomy

17.33   Laparoscopic right hemicolectomy

17.34   Laparoscopic resection of transverse colon

17.35   Laparoscopic left hemicolectomy

17.36   Laparoscopic sigmoidectomy

17.39   Other laparoscopic partial excision of large intestine

√4ᵗʰ **17.4   Robotic assisted procedures**
> NOTE This category includes use of a computer console with (3-D) imaging, software, camera(s), visualization and instrumentation *combined* with the use of robotic arms, device(s), or system(s) at the time of the procedure.
>
> Computer assisted robotic surgery
> Computer-enhanced robotic surgery
> Robotic procedure with computer assistance
> Surgeon-controlled robotic surgery
>
> Code first primary procedure
> EXCLUDES *computer assisted surgery (00.31-00.35, 00.39)*
> AHA: 4Q, '08, 172-174

17.41   Open robotic assisted procedure
> Robotic assistance in open procedure

17.42   Laparoscopic robotic assisted procedure
> Robotic assistance in laparoscopic procedure
> AHA: 3Q, '09, 5; 4Q, '08, 174

17.43   Percutaneous robotic assisted procedure
> Robotic assistance in percutaneous procedure

17.44   Endoscopic robotic assisted procedure
> Robotic assistance in endoscopic procedure

17.45   Thoracoscopic robotic assisted procedure
> Robotic assistance in thoracoscopic procedure

17.49   Other and unspecified robotic assisted procedure
> Robotic assistance in other and unspecified procedure
> EXCLUDES *endoscopic robotic assisted procedure (17.44)*
> *laparoscopic robotic assisted procedure (17.42)*
> *open robotic assisted procedure (17.41)*
> *percutaneous robotic assisted procedure (17.43)*
> *thoracoscopic robotic assisted procedure (17.45)*
>
> AHA: ►4Q, '13, 89◄

√4ᵗʰ **17.5   Additional cardiovascular procedures**
> AHA: 3Q, '12, 13; 4Q, '09, 139-140

17.51   Implantation of rechargeable cardiac contractility modulation [CCM], total system
> NOTE Device testing during procedure — *omit code*
>
> Implantation of CCM system includes formation of pocket, transvenous leads, including placement of leads, placement of catheter into left ventricle, intraoperative procedures for evaluation of lead signals, obtaining sensing threshold measurements, obtaining defibrillator threshold measurements.
>
> Includes implantation of device with removal of existing device
>
> Code also any concomitant:
> coronary bypass (36.10-36.19)
> extracorporeal circulation (39.61)
> insertion or replacement of automatic cardioverter/defibrillator, total system [AICD] 37.94
> EXCLUDES *implantation of CCM pulse generator only (17.52)*
>
> AHA: 4Q, '09, 141
> DEF: Device that delivers nonexcitatory impulses to the right ventricular septum during the absolute refractory period and signals that enhance myocardial strength and performance.

17.52   Implantation or replacement of cardiac contractility modulation [CCM] rechargeable pulse generator only
> NOTE Device testing during procedure — *omit code*
>
> Implantation of CCM device with removal of any existing CCM device
>
> Code also any concomitant:
> revision of device pocket (37.79)
> revision of lead [electrode] (37.75)

17.53   Percutaneous atherectomy of extracranial vessel(s)
> Directional atherectomy
> Excimer laser atherectomy
> Rotational atherectomy
> That by laser
> That by transluminal extraction
>
> Code also any:
> injection or infusion of thrombolytic agent (99.10)
> number of vascular stents inserted (00.45-00.48)
> number of vessels treated (00.40-00.43)
> percutaneous insertion of carotid artery stent(s) (00.63)
> percutaneous insertion of other extracranial artery stent(s) (00.64)
> procedure on vessel bifurcation (00.44)
> EXCLUDES *angioplasty of other non-coronary vessel(s) (39.50)*
> *atherectomy of intracranial vessel(s) (17.54)*
> *atherectomy of other non-coronary vessel(s) (17.56)*
> *removal of cerebrovascular obstruction of vessel(s) by open approach (38.01-38.02, 38.11-38.12, 38.31-38.32, 38.41-38.42)*
>
> AHA: 4Q, '11, 163-167
> TIP: This procedure may be performed instead of or in addition to angioplasty. If angioplasty is also performed, report it separately.

BI Bilateral Procedure   NC Non-covered Procedure   LC Limited Coverage Procedure   ►◄ Revised Text   ● New Code   ▲ Revised Code Title

17.54 Percutaneous atherectomy of intracranial vessel(s)

Directional atherectomy	That by laser
Excimer laser atherectomy	That by transluminal
Rotational atherectomy	extraction

Code also any:
    injection or infusion of thrombolytic agent (99.10)
    number of vascular stents inserted (00.45-00.48)
    number of vessels treated (00.40-00.43)
    percutaneous insertion of intracranial vascular
        stent(s) (00.65)
    procedure on vessel bifurcation (00.44)
    EXCLUDES angioplasty of other non-coronary vessel(s) (39.50)
        atherectomy of extracranial vessel(s) (17.53)
        atherectomy of other non-coronary vessel(s) (17.56)
        removal of cerebrovascular obstruction of
            vessel(s) by open approach
            (38.01-38.02, 38.11-38.12,
            38.31-38.32, 38.41-38.42)

AHA: 4Q, '11, 163-167
TIP: See tip under code 17.53

17.55 Transluminal coronary atherectomy

Directional atherectomy	That by percutaneous
Excimer laser atherectomy	approach
Rotational atherectomy	That by transluminal
That by laser	extraction

Code also any:
    injection or infusion of thrombolytic agent (99.10)
    insertion of coronary artery stent (36.06-36.07)
    intracoronary artery thrombolytic infusion (36.04)
    number of vascular stents inserted (00.45-00.48)
    number of vessels treated (00.40-00.43)
    procedure on vessel bifurcation (00.44)
    SuperSaturated oxygen therapy (00.49)
    transluminal coronary angioplasty (00.66)

AHA: 4Q, '11, 163-167
TIP: See tip under code 17.53

17.56 Atherectomy of other non-coronary vessel(s)

INCLUDES directional atherectomy
        excimer laser atherectomy
        rotational atherectomy
        that by laser
        that by transluminal extraction
Percutaneous transluminal angioplasty of:
    lower extremity vessels
    mesenteric artery
    renal artery
    upper extremity vessels

Code also any:
    injection or infusion of thrombolytic agent (99.10)
    insertion of drug-eluting peripheral vessel stent
        (00.55)
    insertion of non-drug-eluting peripheral vessel
        stent(s) or stent graft(s) (39.90)
    number of vascular stents inserted (00.45-00.48)
    number of vessels treated (00.40-00.43)
    procedure on vessel bifurcation (00.44)
    EXCLUDES percutaneous angioplasty of extracranial or
            intracranial vessel(s) (00.61-00.62)
        percutaneous angioplasty of other
            non-coronary vessel(s) (39.50)
        percutaneous atherectomy of extracranial
            vessel(s) (17.53)
        percutaneous atherectomy of intracranial
            vessel(s) (17.54)

AHA: 4Q, '11, 163-167
TIP: See tip under code 17.53

Laser Interstitial Thermal Therapy

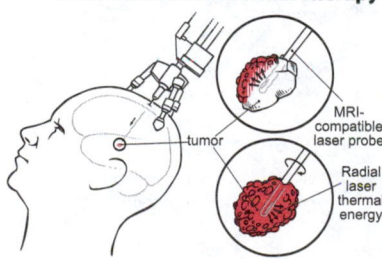

✓4th **17.6 Laser interstitial thermal therapy [LITT] under guidance**
        Focused laser interstitial thermal therapy [f-LITT] under MRI
            guidance
        MRI-guided LITT
        AHA: 4Q, '09, 141-143
        DEF: Selective, real-time thermal ablation of tumors using a laser
        probe placed directly into the tumor.

**17.61 Laser interstitial thermal therapy [LITT] of
lesion or tissue of brain under guidance**
        Focused laser interstitial thermal therapy [f-LITT]
            under MRI guidance
        MRI-guided LITT of lesion or tissue of brain
        EXCLUDES laser interstitial thermal therapy [LITT] of
                lesion or tissue of head under guidance
                (17.62)
        AHA: 4Q, '09, 143

**17.62 Laser interstitial thermal therapy [LITT] of lesion
or tissue of head and neck under guidance**
        Focused laser interstitial thermal therapy [f-LITT]
            under MRI guidance
        MRI-guided LITT of lesion or tissue of head and neck
        EXCLUDES laser interstitial thermal therapy [LITT] of
                lesion or tissue of brain under
                guidance (17.61)

**17.63 Laser interstitial thermal therapy [LITT] of
lesion or tissue of liver under guidance**
        Focused laser interstitial thermal therapy [f-LITT]
            under MRI guidance
        MRI-guided LITT of lesion or tissue of liver

**17.69 Laser interstitial thermal therapy [LITT] of lesion
or tissue of other and unspecified site under
guidance**
        Focused laser interstitial thermal therapy [f-LITT]
            under MRI guidance
        MRI-guided LITT of lesion or tissue of breast
        MRI-guided LITT of lesion or tissue of lung
        MRI-guided LITT of lesion or tissue of prostate
        EXCLUDES laser interstitial thermal therapy [LITT] of
                lesion or tissue of brain under
                guidance (17.61)
            laser interstitial thermal therapy [LITT] of
                lesion or tissue of head and neck under
                guidance (17.62)
            laser interstitial thermal therapy [LITT] of
                lesion or tissue of liver under guidance
                (17.63)

✓4th **17.7 Other diagnostic and therapeutic procedures**

17.70 Intravenous infusion of clofarabine
        EXCLUDES injection or infusion of cancer
                chemotherapeutic substance (99.25)
        AHA: 4Q, '09, 144

**17.71 Non-coronary intra-operative fluorescence vascular
angiography [IFVA]**
        Intraoperative laser arteriogram
        SPY arteriogram
        SPY arteriography
        EXCLUDES intra-operative coronary fluorescence
                vascular angiography (88.59)
        AHA: 4Q, '10,114-115

✓4th **17.8 Other adjunct procedures**
        NOTE These codes are to be used in conjunction with other
            therapeutic procedure codes to provide additional
            information on devices used as part of a procedure.

17.81 Insertion of antimicrobial envelope
        Use of anti-microbial (mesh) (prophylactic antibiotics
            embedded) envelope with the insertion of
            cardiovascular implantable electronic devices
            [CIED]

        Code first primary procedure:
            insertion of cardiovascular implantable electronic
                device(s) [CIED] (00.51, 00.53, 00.54, 37.94,
                37.96, 37.98)
        AHA: 4Q, '11, 167-168
        TIP: The envelope holds the device and releases
        antimicrobial agents to reduce postoperative infections.

Other Miscellaneous Diagnostic and Therapeutic Procedures

17.54–17.81

Operations on the Ear

18–19.3

4. Operations on the Ear (18-20)

√3rd **18   Operations on external ear**

INCLUDES   operations on:
    external auditory canal
    skin and cartilage of:
      auricle
      meatus

√4th **18.0   Incision of external ear**

EXCLUDES   removal of intraluminal foreign body (98.11)

18.01   Piercing of ear lobe
    Piercing of pinna

18.02   Incision of external auditory canal

18.09   Other incision of external ear

√4th **18.1   Diagnostic procedures on external ear**

18.11   Otoscopy
    DEF: Exam of the ear with instrument designed for visualization.

18.12   Biopsy of external ear

18.19   Other diagnostic procedures on external ear
    EXCLUDES   microscopic examination of specimen from ear (90.31-90.39)

√4th **18.2   Excision or destruction of lesion of external ear**

18.21   Excision of preauricular sinus
    Radical excision of preauricular sinus or cyst
    EXCLUDES   excision of preauricular remnant [appendage] (18.29)
    DEF: Excision of preauricular sinus or cyst with adjacent tissues.

18.29   Excision or destruction of other lesion of external ear
    Cauterization
    Coagulation
    Cryosurgery   } of external ear
    Curettage
    Electrocoagulation
    Enucleation
    Excision of:
      exostosis of external auditory canal
      preauricular remnant [appendage]
    Partial excision of ear
    EXCLUDES   biopsy of external ear (18.12)
      radical excision of lesion (18.31)
      removal of cerumen (96.52)

√4th **18.3   Other excision of external ear**
    EXCLUDES   biopsy of external ear (18.12)

18.31   Radical excision of lesion of external ear
    EXCLUDES   radical excision of preauricular sinus (18.21)
    DEF: Removal of damaged, diseased ear and adjacent tissue.

18.39   Other
    Amputation of external ear
    EXCLUDES   excision of lesion (18.21-18.29, 18.31)

18.4   Suture of laceration of external ear

18.5   Surgical correction of prominent ear
    Ear: Ear:
      pinning   setback
    DEF: Reformation of protruding outer ear.

18.6   Reconstruction of external auditory canal
    Canaloplasty of external auditory meatus
    Construction [reconstruction] of external meatus of ear:
      osseous portion
      skin-lined portion (with skin graft)
    DEF: Repair of outer ear canal.

√4th **18.7   Other plastic repair of external ear**

18.71   Construction of auricle of ear
    Prosthetic appliance for absent ear
    Reconstruction:
      auricle
      ear
    DEF: Reformation or repair of external ear flap.

18.72   Reattachment of amputated ear

18.79   Other plastic repair of external ear
    Otoplasty NOS
    Postauricular skin graft
    Repair of lop ear
    DEF: Postauricular skin graft: Graft repair behind ear.
    DEF: Repair of lop ear: Reconstruction of ear that is at right angle to head.
    AHA: 3Q, '03, 12

18.9   Other operations on external ear
    EXCLUDES   irrigation of ear (96.52)
      packing of external auditory canal (96.11)
      removal of:
        cerumen (96.52)
        foreign body (without incision) (98.11)

√3rd **19   Reconstructive operations on middle ear**

19.0   Stapes mobilization
    Division, otosclerotic: Remobilization of stapes
      material   Stapediolysis
      process   Transcrural stapes mobilization
    EXCLUDES   that with synchronous stapedectomy (19.11-19.19)
    DEF: Repair of innermost bone of middle ear to enable movement and response to sound.

√4th **19.1   Stapedectomy**
    EXCLUDES   revision of previous stapedectomy (19.21-19.29)
      stapes mobilization only (19.0)
    DEF: Removal of innermost bone of middle ear.

19.11   Stapedectomy with incus replacement
    Stapedectomy with incus:
      homograft
      prosthesis
    DEF: Removal of innermost bone of middle ear with autograft or prosthesis replacement.

19.19   Other stapedectomy

√4th **19.2   Revision of stapedectomy**

19.21   Revision of stapedectomy with incus replacement

19.29   Other revision of stapedectomy

19.3   Other operations on ossicular chain
    Incudectomy NOS
    Ossiculectomy NOS
    Reconstruction of ossicles, second stage
    DEF: Incudectomy: Excision of middle bone of middle ear, not otherwise specified.
    DEF: Ossiculectomy: Excision of middle ear bones, not otherwise specified.
    DEF: Reconstruction of ossicles, second stage: Repair of middle ear bones following previous surgery.

Stapedectomy with Incus Replacement

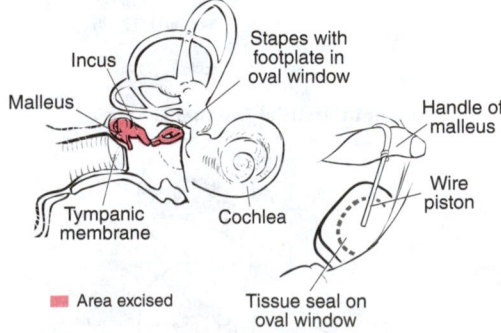

BI Bilateral Procedure   NC Non-covered Procedure   LC Limited Coverage Procedure   ▶◀ Revised Text   ● New Code   ▲ Revised Code Title

94 – Volume 3   **2015 ICD-9-CM**

Operations on the Ear

19.4–20.79

19.4 Myringoplasty

Epitympanic, type I
Myringoplasty by:
    cauterization
    graft
Tympanoplasty (type I)

DEF: Epitympanic, type I: Repair over or upon eardrum.
DEF: Myringoplasty by cauterization: Plastic repair of tympanic membrane of eardrum by heat.
DEF: Graft: Plastic repair using implanted tissue.
DEF: Tympanoplasty (type I): Reconstruction of eardrum to restore hearing.

√4th **19.5 Other tympanoplasty**

19.52 Type II tympanoplasty

Closure of perforation with graft against incus or malleus

19.53 Type III tympanoplasty

Graft placed in contact with mobile and intact stapes

AHA: M-A, '85, 15
TIP: Assign for a total ossicular replacement prosthesis (TORP) procedure.

19.54 Type IV tympanoplasty

Mobile footplate left exposed with air pocket between round window and graft

19.55 Type V tympanoplasty

Fenestra in horizontal semicircular canal covered by graft

19.6 Revision of tympanoplasty

DEF: Repair or correction of previous plastic surgery on eardrum.

19.9 Other repair of middle ear

Closure of mastoid fistula
Mastoid myoplasty
Obliteration of tympanomastoid cavity

DEF: Closure of mastoid fistula: Closing of abnormal channel in mastoid.
DEF: Mastoid myoplasty: Restoration or repair of mastoid muscle.
DEF: Obliteration of tympanomastoid cavity: Removal, total, of functional elements of middle ear.

√3rd **20 Other operations on middle and inner ear**

√4th **20.0 Myringotomy**

DEF: Myringotomy: Puncture of tympanic membrane or eardrum, also called tympanocentesis

20.01 Myringotomy with insertion of tube

Myringostomy

20.09 Other myringotomy

Aspiration of middle ear NOS

20.1 Removal of tympanostomy tube

√4th **20.2 Incision of mastoid and middle ear**

20.21 Incision of mastoid

20.22 Incision of petrous pyramid air cells

20.23 Incision of middle ear

Atticotomy
Division of tympanum
Lysis of adhesions of middle ear

EXCLUDES division of otosclerotic process (19.0)
    stapediolysis (19.0)
    that with stapedectomy (19.11-19.19)

√4th **20.3 Diagnostic procedures on middle and inner ear**

20.31 Electrocochleography

DEF: Measure of electric potential of eighth cranial nerve by electrode applied sound.

20.32 Biopsy of middle and inner ear

20.39 Other diagnostic procedures on middle and inner ear

EXCLUDES auditory and vestibular function tests (89.13, 95.41-95.49)
    microscopic examination of specimen from ear (90.31-90.39)

√4th **20.4 Mastoidectomy**

Code also any:
    skin graft (18.79)
    tympanoplasty (19.4-19.55)

EXCLUDES that with implantation of cochlear prosthetic device (20.96-20.98)

DEF: Mastoidectomy: Excision of bony protrusion behind ear.

20.41 Simple mastoidectomy

20.42 Radical mastoidectomy

20.49 Other mastoidectomy

Atticoantrostomy
Mastoidectomy:
    NOS
    modified radical

DEF: Atticoantrotomy: Opening of cavity of mastoid bone and middle ear.

√4th **20.5 Other excision of middle ear**

EXCLUDES that with synchronous mastoidectomy (20.41-20.49)

20.51 Excision of lesion of middle ear

EXCLUDES biopsy of middle ear (20.32)

20.59 Other

Apicectomy of petrous pyramid
Tympanectomy

√4th **20.6 Fenestration of inner ear**

20.61 Fenestration of inner ear (initial)

Fenestration of:
    labyrinth
    semicircular canals } with graft (skin)
    vestibule   (vein)

EXCLUDES that with tympanoplasty, type V (19.55)

DEF: Creation of inner ear opening.

20.62 Revision of fenestration of inner ear

√4th **20.7 Incision, excision, and destruction of inner ear**

20.71 Endolymphatic shunt

DEF: Insertion of tube to drain fluid in inner ear cavities.

20.72 Injection into inner ear

Destruction by injection (alcohol):
    inner ear
    semicircular canals
    vestibule

20.79 Other incision, excision, and destruction of inner ear

Decompression of labyrinth
Drainage of inner ear
Fistulization:
    endolymphatic sac
    labyrinth
Incision of endolymphatic sac
Labyrinthectomy (transtympanic)
Opening of bony labyrinth
Perilymphatic tap

EXCLUDES biopsy of inner ear (20.32)

DEF: Decompression of labyrinth: Controlled relief of pressure in cavities of inner ear.
DEF: Drainage of inner ear: Removal of fluid from inner ear.
DEF: Fistulization of endolymphatic sac: Creation of passage to fluid sac in inner ear cavities.
DEF: Fistulization of labyrinth: Creation of passage to inner ear cavities.
DEF: Incision of endolymphatic sac: Cutting into fluid sac in inner ear cavities.
DEF: Labyrinthectomy (transtympanic): Excision of cavities across eardrum.
DEF: Opening of bony labyrinth: Cutting into inner ear bony cavities.
DEF: Perilymphatic tap: Puncture or incision into fluid sac of inner ear cavities.

√3rd ✓4th Additional Digit Required   Valid OR Procedure   Non-OR Procedure   Adjunct Code

Operations on the Ear

20.8 Operations on Eustachian tube

Catheterization
Inflation
Injection (Teflon paste)   } of Eustachian tube
Insufflation (boric
     acid-salicylic acid)
Intubation
Politzerization

DEF: Catheterization: Passing catheter into passage between pharynx and middle ear.
DEF: Inflation: Blowing air, gas or liquid into passage between pharynx and middle ear to inflate.
DEF: Injection (Teflon paste): Forcing fluid (Teflon paste) into passage between pharynx and middle ear.
DEF: Insufflation (boric acid-salicylic acid): Blowing gas or liquid into passage between pharynx and middle ear.
DEF: Intubation: Placing tube into passage between pharynx and middle ear.
DEF: Politzerization: Inflating passage between pharynx and middle ear with Politzer bag.

✓4ᵗʰ **20.9 Other operations on inner and middle ear**

20.91 Tympanosympathectomy

DEF: Excision or chemical suppression of impulses of middle ear nerves.

20.92 Revision of mastoidectomy

AHA: 2Q, '98, 20
DEF: Correction of previous removal of mastoid cells from temporal or mastoid bone.

20.93 Repair of oval and round windows

Closure of fistula:
     oval window
     perilymph
     round window
DEF: Restoration of middle ear openings.

20.94 Injection of tympanum

20.95 Implantation of electromagnetic hearing device

Bone conduction hearing device
EXCLUDES cochlear prosthetic device (20.96-20.98)
AHA: 3Q, '07, 4; 4Q, '89, 5

20.96 Implantation or replacement of cochlear prosthetic device, not otherwise specified

Implantation of receiver (within skull) and insertion of electrode(s) in the cochlea
INCLUDES mastoidectomy
EXCLUDES electromagnetic hearing device (20.95)
AHA: 4Q, '89, 5

20.97 Implantation or replacement of cochlear prosthetic device, single channel

Implantation of receiver (within skull) and insertion of electrode in the cochlea
INCLUDES mastoidectomy
EXCLUDES electromagnetic hearing device (20.95)
AHA: 4Q, '89, 5

20.98 Implantation or replacement of cochlear prosthetic device, multiple channel

Implantation of receiver (within skull) and insertion of electrodes in the cochlea
INCLUDES mastoidectomy
EXCLUDES electromagnetic hearing device (20.95)
AHA: 4Q, '89, 5

20.99 Other operations on middle and inner ear

Attachment of percutaneous abutment (screw) for prosthetic device
Repair or removal of cochlear prosthetic device (receiver) (electrode)
EXCLUDES adjustment (external components) of cochlear prosthetic device (95.49)
     fitting of hearing aid (95.48)
AHA: 3Q, '07, 4; 4Q, '89, 7

BI Bilateral Procedure   **NC** Non-covered Procedure   **LC** Limited Coverage Procedure   ▶◀ Revised Text   ● New Code   ▲ Revised Code Title

96 – Volume 3   **2015 ICD-9-CM**

5. Operations on the Nose, Mouth, and Pharynx (21-29)

✓3rd 21 Operations on nose

INCLUDES operations on:
bone
skin } of nose

AHA: 1Q, '94, 5

✓4th 21.0 Control of epistaxis

21.00 Control of epistaxis, not otherwise specified

21.01 Control of epistaxis by anterior nasal packing

21.02 Control of epistaxis by posterior (and anterior) packing

21.03 Control of epistaxis by cauterization (and packing)

21.04 Control of epistaxis by ligation of ethmoidal arteries

21.05 Control of epistaxis by (transantral) ligation of the maxillary artery

21.06 Control of epistaxis by ligation of the external carotid artery

21.07 Control of epistaxis by excision of nasal mucosa and skin grafting of septum and lateral nasal wall

21.09 Control of epistaxis by other means

21.1 Incision of nose
Chondrotomy
Incision of skin of nose
Nasal septotomy
DEF: Chondrotomy: Incision or division of nasal cartilage.
DEF: Nasal septotomy: Incision into bone dividing nose into two chambers.

✓4th 21.2 Diagnostic procedures on nose

21.21 Rhinoscopy
DEF: Visualization of nasal passage with nasal speculum.

21.22 Biopsy of nose

21.29 Other diagnostic procedures on nose
EXCLUDES microscopic examination of specimen from nose (90.31-90.39)
nasal:
function study (89.12)
x-ray (87.16)
rhinomanometry (89.12)

✓4th 21.3 Local excision or destruction of lesion of nose
EXCLUDES biopsy of nose (21.22)
nasal fistulectomy (21.82)

21.30 Excision or destruction of lesion of nose, not otherwise specified

21.31 Local excision or destruction of intranasal lesion
Nasal polypectomy

21.32 Local excision or destruction of other lesion of nose
AHA: 2Q, '89, 16

21.4 Resection of nose
Amputation of nose

21.5 Submucous resection of nasal septum
DEF: Partial resection of nasal septum with mucosa reimplanted after excision.

✓4th 21.6 Turbinectomy
DEF: Partial or total removal of turbinate bones; inferior turbinate is most often excised.

21.61 Turbinectomy by diathermy or cryosurgery
DEF: Destruction of turbinate bone by heat or freezing.

21.62 Fracture of the turbinates
DEF: Surgical breaking of turbinate bones.

21.69 Other turbinectomy
EXCLUDES turbinectomy associated with sinusectomy (22.31-22.39, 22.42, 22.60-22.64)

Excision of Turbinate

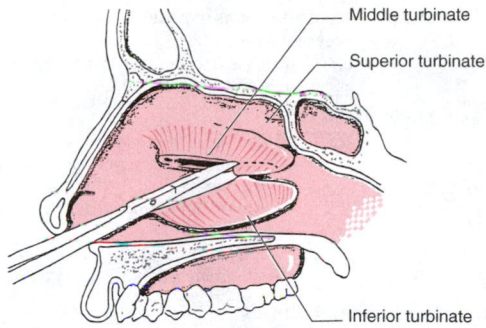

Middle turbinate
Superior turbinate
Inferior turbinate

✓4th 21.7 Reduction of nasal fracture

21.71 Closed reduction of nasal fracture

21.72 Open reduction of nasal fracture

✓4th 21.8 Repair and plastic operations on the nose

21.81 Suture of laceration of nose

21.82 Closure of nasal fistula
Nasolabial
Nasopharyngeal } fistulectomy
Oronasal
DEF: Sealing off crack or hole between nose and lip, nose and pharynx, or nose and mouth.

21.83 Total nasal reconstruction
Reconstruction of nose with:
arm flap
forehead flap
DEF: Plastic reformation of nasal structure with tissue flap from arm or forehead.

21.84 Revision rhinoplasty
Rhinoseptoplasty
Twisted nose rhinoplasty
DEF: Rhinoseptoplasty: Repair of nose and the bone dividing the nose into two chambers.
DEF: Twisted nose rhinoplasty: Repair of nose alignment following reconstructive surgery.

21.85 Augmentation rhinoplasty
Augmentation rhinoplasty with:
graft
synthetic implant
DEF: Implant of tissue or synthetic graft to enlarge nose.

21.86 Limited rhinoplasty
Plastic repair of nasolabial flaps
Tip rhinoplasty
DEF: Plastic repair of nasolabial flaps: Reconstruction of nasal area above lips.
DEF: Tip rhinoplasty: Reconstruction or restoration of nasal tip.

21.87 Other rhinoplasty
Rhinoplasty NOS

21.88 Other septoplasty
Crushing of nasal septum
Repair of septal perforation
EXCLUDES septoplasty associated with submucous resection of septum (21.5)
DEF: Crushing of nasal septum: Division and reconstruction of defects in bone dividing nasal chambers.
DEF: Repair of septal perforation: Repair of hole in bone dividing nasal chambers with adjacent tissue.

21.89 Other repair and plastic operations on nose
Reattachment of amputated nose

Operations on the Nose, Mouth, and Pharynx

21.9–24.2

√4ᵗʰ **21.9 Other operations on nose**

21.91 Lysis of adhesions of nose
Posterior nasal scrub
DEF: Posterior nasal scrub: Clearing out of abnormal adhesions in posterior nasal area.

21.99 Other
EXCLUDES dilation of frontonasal duct (96.21)
irrigation of nasal passages (96.53)
removal of:
intraluminal foreign body without incision (98.12)
nasal packing (97.32)
replacement of nasal packing (97.21)

√3ʳᵈ **22 Operations on nasal sinuses**

√4ᵗʰ **22.0 Aspiration and lavage of nasal sinus**

22.00 Aspiration and lavage of nasal sinus, not otherwise specified

22.01 Puncture of nasal sinus for aspiration or lavage

22.02 Aspiration or lavage of nasal sinus through natural ostium
DEF: Withdrawal of fluid and washing of nasal cavity through natural opening.

√4ᵗʰ **22.1 Diagnostic procedures on nasal sinus**

22.11 Closed [endoscopic] [needle] biopsy of nasal sinus

22.12 Open biopsy of nasal sinus

22.19 Other diagnostic procedures on nasal sinuses
Endoscopy without biopsy
EXCLUDES transillumination of sinus (89.35)
x-ray of sinus (87.15-87.16)

22.2 Intranasal antrotomy
EXCLUDES antrotomy with external approach (22.31-22.39)
DEF: Incision of intranasal sinus.

√4ᵗʰ **22.3 External maxillary antrotomy**

22.31 Radical maxillary antrotomy
Removal of lining membrane of maxillary sinus using Caldwell-Luc approach
DEF: Caldwell-Luc approach: Removal of membrane lining the maxillary cavity through incision above canine teeth.

22.39 Other external maxillary antrotomy
Exploration of maxillary antrum with Caldwell-Luc approach

√4ᵗʰ **22.4 Frontal sinusotomy and sinusectomy**

22.41 Frontal sinusotomy

22.42 Frontal sinusectomy
Excision of lesion of frontal sinus
Obliteration of frontal sinus (with fat)
EXCLUDES biopsy of nasal sinus (22.11-22.12)

√4ᵗʰ **22.5 Other nasal sinusotomy**

22.50 Sinusotomy, not otherwise specified

22.51 Ethmoidotomy

22.52 Sphenoidotomy

22.53 Incision of multiple nasal sinuses

√4ᵗʰ **22.6 Other nasal sinusectomy**
INCLUDES that with incidental turbinectomy
EXCLUDES biopsy of nasal sinus (22.11-22.12)

22.60 Sinusectomy, not otherwise specified

22.61 Excision of lesion of maxillary sinus with Caldwell-Luc approach

22.62 Excision of lesion of maxillary sinus with other approach

22.63 Ethmoidectomy
DEF: Removal of ethmoid cells and bone; includes excising partial or total mucosal lining.

22.64 Sphenoidectomy
DEF: Removal of wedge shaped sphenoid bone at base of brain.

√4ᵗʰ **22.7 Repair of nasal sinus**

22.71 Closure of nasal sinus fistula
Repair of oro-antral fistula

22.79 Other repair of nasal sinus
Reconstruction of frontonasal duct
Repair of bone of accessory sinus

22.9 Other operations on nasal sinuses
Exteriorization of maxillary sinus
Fistulization of sinus
EXCLUDES dilation of frontonasal duct (96.21)
DEF: Exteriorization of maxillary sinus: Creation of external maxillary cavity opening.
DEF: Fistulization of sinus: Creation of fistula canal in nasal cavity.

√3ʳᵈ **23 Removal and restoration of teeth**

√4ᵗʰ **23.0 Forceps extraction of tooth**

23.01 Extraction of deciduous tooth

23.09 Extraction of other tooth
Extraction of tooth NOS

√4ᵗʰ **23.1 Surgical removal of tooth**

23.11 Removal of residual root

23.19 Other surgical extraction of tooth
Odontectomy NOS
Removal of impacted tooth
Tooth extraction with elevation of mucoperiosteal flap

23.2 Restoration of tooth by filling

23.3 Restoration of tooth by inlay
DEF: Restoration of tooth by cementing in a molded filling.

√4ᵗʰ **23.4 Other dental restoration**

23.41 Application of crown

23.42 Insertion of fixed bridge

23.43 Insertion of removable bridge

23.49 Other

23.5 Implantation of tooth
DEF: Insertion of a sound tooth to replace extracted tooth.

23.6 Prosthetic dental implant
Endosseous dental implant
DEF: Implant of artificial denture within bone covering tooth socket.

√4ᵗʰ **23.7 Apicoectomy and root canal therapy**

23.70 Root canal, not otherwise specified

23.71 Root canal therapy with irrigation

23.72 Root canal therapy with apicoectomy
DEF: Removal of tooth root to treat damaged root canal tissue.

23.73 Apicoectomy

√3ʳᵈ **24 Other operations on teeth, gums, and alveoli**

24.0 Incision of gum or alveolar bone
Apical alveolotomy

√4ᵗʰ **24.1 Diagnostic procedures on teeth, gums, and alveoli**

24.11 Biopsy of gum

24.12 Biopsy of alveolus

24.19 Other diagnostic procedures on teeth, gums, and alveoli
EXCLUDES dental:
examination (89.31)
x-ray:
full-mouth (87.11)
other (87.12)
microscopic examination of dental specimen (90.81-90.89)

24.2 Gingivoplasty
Gingivoplasty with bone or soft tissue graft
DEF: Repair of gum tissue.

BI Bilateral Procedure   NC Non-covered Procedure   LC Limited Coverage Procedure   ▶◀ Revised Text   ● New Code   ▲ Revised Code Title

✓4th **24.3**   **Other operations on gum**

     24.31   **Excision of lesion or tissue of gum**
           EXCLUDES   *biopsy of gum (24.11)*
                    excision of odontogenic lesion (24.4)

     24.32   **Suture of laceration of gum**

     24.39   **Other**

24.4   **Excision of dental lesion of jaw**
     Excision of odontogenic lesion

24.5   **Alveoloplasty**
     Alveolectomy (interradicular) (intraseptal) (radical) (simple)
     (with graft or implant)
      EXCLUDES   *biopsy of alveolus (24.12)*
              en bloc resection of alveolar process and palate
              (27.32)
     DEF: Repair or correction of bony tooth socket.

24.6   **Exposure of tooth**

24.7   **Application of orthodontic appliance**
     Application, insertion, or fitting of:
       arch bars
       orthodontic obturator
       orthodontic wiring
       periodontal splint
      EXCLUDES   *nonorthodontic dental wiring (93.55)*

24.8   **Other orthodontic operation**
     Closure of diastema (alveolar) (dental)
     Occlusal adjustment
     Removal of arch bars
     Repair of dental arch
      EXCLUDES   *removal of nonorthodontic wiring (97.33)*

✓4th **24.9**   **Other dental operations**

     24.91   **Extension or deepening of buccolabial or lingual sulcus**

     24.99   **Other**
           EXCLUDES   *dental:*
                    debridement (96.54)
                    examination (89.31)
                    prophylaxis (96.54)
                    scaling and polishing (96.54)
                    wiring (93.55)
              fitting of dental appliance [denture] (99.97)
              microscopic examination of dental specimen
                    (90.81-90.89)
              removal of dental:
                    packing (97.34)
                    prosthesis (97.35)
                    wiring (97.33)
              replacement of dental packing (97.22)

✓3rd **25**   **Operations on tongue**

 ✓4th **25.0**   **Diagnostic procedures on tongue**

     25.01   **Closed [needle] biopsy of tongue**

     25.02   **Open biopsy of tongue**
           Wedge biopsy

     25.09   **Other diagnostic procedures on tongue**

25.1   **Excision or destruction of lesion or tissue of tongue**
      EXCLUDES   *biopsy of tongue (25.01-25.02)*
              frenumectomy:
                  labial (27.41)
                  lingual (25.92)
     AHA: 2Q, '02, 5
     TIP: Assign for tongue-based somnoplasty procedure, a temperature-controlled radiofrequency-based technology, used for treatment of obstructive sleep apnea.

25.2   **Partial glossectomy**

25.3   **Complete glossectomy**
     Glossectomy NOS
     Code also any neck dissection (40.40-40.42)

25.4   **Radical glossectomy**
     Code also any:
       neck dissection (40.40-40.42)
       tracheostomy (31.1-31.29)

✓4th **25.5**   **Repair of tongue and glossoplasty**

     25.51   **Suture of laceration of tongue**

     25.59   **Other repair and plastic operations on tongue**
           Fascial sling of tongue
           Fusion of tongue (to lip)
           Graft of mucosa or skin to tongue
        EXCLUDES   *lysis of adhesions of tongue (25.93)*
       AHA: 1Q, '97, 5
       TIP: Assign for genioglossus advancement, which may be performed in association with uvulopalatopharyngoplasty (UPPP).

✓4th **25.9**   **Other operations on tongue**

     25.91   **Lingual frenotomy**
           EXCLUDES   *labial frenotomy (27.91)*
       DEF: Extension of groove between cheek and lips or cheek and tongue.

     25.92   **Lingual frenectomy**
           EXCLUDES   *labial frenectomy (27.41)*
       DEF: Frenectomy: Removal of vertical membrane attaching tongue to floor of mouth.

     25.93   **Lysis of adhesions of tongue**

     25.94   **Other glossotomy**

     25.99   **Other**

✓3rd **26**   **Operations on salivary glands and ducts**
     INCLUDES   operations on:
           lesser salivary   ⎫
           parotid   ⎬ gland and duct
           sublingual   ⎪
           submaxillry   ⎭
     Code also any neck dissection (40.40-40.42)

     26.0   **Incision of salivary gland or duct**

 ✓4th **26.1**   **Diagnostic procedures on salivary glands and ducts**

     26.11   **Closed [needle] biopsy of salivary gland or duct**

     26.12   **Open biopsy of salivary gland or duct**

     26.19   **Other diagnostic procedures on salivary glands and ducts**
           EXCLUDES   *x-ray of salivary gland (87.09)*

 ✓4th **26.2**   **Excision of lesion of salivary gland**

     26.21   **Marsupialization of salivary gland cyst**
       DEF: Creation of pouch of salivary gland cyst to drain and promote healing.

     26.29   **Other excision of salivary gland lesion**
           EXCLUDES   *biopsy of salivary gland (26.11-26.12)*
              salivary fistulectomy (26.42)

 ✓4th **26.3**   **Sialoadenectomy**
     DEF: Removal of salivary gland.

     26.30   **Sialoadenectomy, not otherwise specified**

     26.31   **Partial sialoadenectomy**

     26.32   **Complete sialoadenectomy**
           En bloc excision of salivary gland lesion
           Radical sialoadenectomy

 ✓4th **26.4**   **Repair of salivary gland or duct**

     26.41   **Suture of laceration of salivary gland**

     26.42   **Closure of salivary fistula**
       DEF: Closing of abnormal opening in salivary gland.

     26.49   **Other repair and plastic operations on salivary gland or duct**
           Fistulization of salivary gland
           Plastic repair of salivary gland or duct NOS
           Transplantation of salivary duct opening

 ✓4th **26.9**   **Other operations on salivary gland or duct**

     26.91   **Probing of salivary duct**

     26.99   **Other**

✓3rd
✓4th Additional Digit Required   Valid OR Procedure   Non-OR Procedure   Adjunct Code
2015 ICD-9-CM   **Volume 3 – 99**

Operations on the Nose, Mouth, and Pharynx

27–28.0

√3rd **27 Other operations on mouth and face**

INCLUDES operations on:
- lips
- palate
- soft tissue of face and mouth, except tongue and gingiva

EXCLUDES operations on:
- gingiva (24.0-24.99)
- tongue (25.01-25.99)

27.0 Drainage of face and floor of mouth

Drainage of:
- facial region (abscess)
- fascial compartment of face
- Ludwig's angina

EXCLUDES drainage of thyroglossal tract (06.09)

27.1 Incision of palate

√4th **27.2 Diagnostic procedures on oral cavity**

27.21 Biopsy of bony palate

27.22 Biopsy of uvula and soft palate

27.23 Biopsy of lip

27.24 Biopsy of mouth, unspecified structure

27.29 Other diagnostic procedures on oral cavity

EXCLUDES soft tissue x-ray (87.09)

√4th **27.3 Excision of lesion or tissue of bony palate**

27.31 Local excision or destruction of lesion or tissue of bony palate

Local excision or destruction of palate by:
- cautery
- chemotherapy
- cryotherapy

EXCLUDES biopsy of bony palate (27.21)

27.32 Wide excision or destruction of lesion or tissue of bony palate

En bloc resection of alveolar process and palate

√4th **27.4 Excision of other parts of mouth**

27.41 Labial frenectomy

EXCLUDES division of labial frenum (27.91)

DEF: Removal of mucous membrane fold of lip.

27.42 Wide excision of lesion of lip

27.43 Other excision of lesion or tissue of lip

27.49 Other excision of mouth

EXCLUDES biopsy of mouth NOS (27.24)
- excision of lesion of:
  - palate (27.31-27.32)
  - tongue (25.1)
  - uvula (27.72)
- fistulectomy of mouth (27.53)
- frenectomy of:
  - lip (27.41)
  - tongue (25.92)

AHA: 2Q, '05, 8

TIP: Assign for "composite resection," which includes the mandible and floor of the mouth, performed for mandibular carcinoma. Codes for bone and lymph node resection should also be assigned.

√4th **27.5 Plastic repair of lip and mouth**

EXCLUDES palatoplasty (27.61-27.69)

27.51 Suture of laceration of lip

27.52 Suture of laceration of other part of mouth

27.53 Closure of fistula of mouth

EXCLUDES fistulectomy:
- nasolabial (21.82)
- oro-antral (22.71)
- oronasal (21.82)

27.54 Repair of cleft lip

27.55 Full-thickness skin graft to lip and mouth

27.56 Other skin graft to lip and mouth

27.57 Attachment of pedicle or flap graft to lip and mouth

AHA: 1Q, '96, 14

DEF: Repair of lip or mouth with tissue pedicle or flap still connected to original vascular base.

27.59 Other plastic repair of mouth

√4th **27.6 Palatoplasty**

27.61 Suture of laceration of palate

27.62 Correction of cleft palate

Correction of cleft palate by push-back operation

EXCLUDES revision of cleft palate repair (27.63)

27.63 Revision of cleft palate repair

Secondary:
- attachment of pharyngeal flap
- lengthening of palate

AHA: 1Q, '96, 14

27.64 Insertion of palatal implant

DEF: Nonabsorbable polyester implants placed into the soft palate at the back of the roof of the mouth; one implant placed at the soft palate midline and two are positioned on either side; used to support and stiffen the palate, reducing vibration (snoring).

27.69 Other plastic repair of palate

Code also any insertion of palatal implant (27.64)

EXCLUDES fistulectomy of mouth (27.53)

AHA: 3Q, '99, 22; 1Q, '97, 14; 3Q, '92, 18

TIP: Assign for uvulopalatopharyngoplasty (UPPP), along with code 29.4 Plastic operation on pharynx, along with additional codes for hyoid suspension and genioglossus advancement, if performed.

√4th **27.7 Operations on uvula**

27.71 Incision of uvula

27.72 Excision of uvula

EXCLUDES biopsy of uvula (27.22)

27.73 Repair of uvula

EXCLUDES that with synchronous cleft palate repair (27.62)
- uranostaphylorrhaphy (27.62)

27.79 Other operations on uvula

AHA: 3Q, '92, 18

√4th **27.9 Other operations on mouth and face**

27.91 Labial frenotomy

Division of labial frenum

EXCLUDES lingual frenotomy (25.91)

DEF: Division of labial frenum: Cutting and separating mucous membrane fold of lip.

27.92 Incision of mouth, unspecified structure

EXCLUDES incision of:
- gum (24.0)
- palate (27.1)
- salivary gland or duct (26.0)
- tongue (25.94)
- uvula (27.71)

27.99 Other operations on oral cavity

Graft of buccal sulcus

EXCLUDES removal of:
- intraluminal foreign body (98.01)
- penetrating foreign body from mouth without incision (98.22)

DEF: Graft of buccal sulcus: Implant of tissue into groove of interior cheek lining.

√3rd **28 Operations on tonsils and adenoids**

28.0 Incision and drainage of tonsil and peritonsillar structures

Drainage (oral) (transcervical) of:
- parapharyngeal ⎫
- peritonsillar   ⎬ abscess
- retropharyngeal ⎪
- tonsillar ⎭

BI Bilateral Procedure   NC Non-covered Procedure   LC Limited Coverage Procedure   ►◄ Revised Text   ● New Code   ▲ Revised Code Title

✓4th **28.1** **Diagnostic procedures on tonsils and adenoids**

28.11 **Biopsy of tonsils and adenoids**

28.19 **Other diagnostic procedures on tonsils and adenoids**

EXCLUDES *soft tissue x-ray (87.09)*

28.2 **Tonsillectomy without adenoidectomy**

AHA: 1Q, '97, 5; 2Q, '90, 23

28.3 **Tonsillectomy with adenoidectomy**

AHA: 2Q, '05, 16

28.4 **Excision of tonsil tag**

28.5 **Excision of lingual tonsil**

28.6 **Adenoidectomy without tonsillectomy**

Excision of adenoid tag

28.7 **Control of hemorrhage after tonsillectomy and adenoidectomy**

AHA: 2Q, '05, 16

✓4th **28.9** **Other operations on tonsils and adenoids**

28.91 **Removal of foreign body from tonsil and adenoid by incision**

EXCLUDES *that without incision (98.13)*

28.92 **Excision of lesion of tonsil and adenoid**

EXCLUDES *biopsy of tonsil and adenoid (28.11)*

28.99 **Other**

✓3rd **29** **Operations on pharynx**

INCLUDES operations on:
hypopharynx
nasopharynx
oropharynx
pharyngeal pouch
pyriform sinus

29.0 **Pharyngotomy**

Drainage of pharyngeal bursa

EXCLUDES *incision and drainage of retropharyngeal abscess (28.0)*
removal of foreign body (without incision) (98.13)

✓4th **29.1** **Diagnostic procedures on pharynx**

29.11 **Pharyngoscopy**

29.12 **Pharyngeal biopsy**

Biopsy of supraglottic mass

29.19 **Other diagnostic procedures on pharynx**

EXCLUDES *x-ray of nasopharynx:*
contrast (87.06)
other (87.09)

29.2 **Excision of branchial cleft cyst or vestige**

EXCLUDES *branchial cleft fistulectomy (29.52)*

✓4th **29.3** **Excision or destruction of lesion or tissue of pharynx**

AHA: 2Q, '89, 18

29.31 **Cricopharyngeal myotomy**

EXCLUDES *that with pharyngeal diverticulectomy (29.32)*

DEF: Removal of outward pouching of throat.

29.32 **Pharyngeal diverticulectomy**

29.33 **Pharyngectomy (partial)**

EXCLUDES *laryngopharyngectomy (30.3)*

29.39 **Other excision or destruction of lesion or tissue of pharynx**

29.4 **Plastic operation on pharynx**

Correction of nasopharyngeal atresia

EXCLUDES *pharyngoplasty associated with cleft palate repair (27.62-27.63)*

AHA: 3Q, '99, 22; 1Q, '97, 5; 3Q, '92, 18

DEF: Correction of nasopharyngeal atresia: Construction of normal opening for throat stricture behind nose.

TIP: Assign for uvulopalatopharyngoplasty (UPPP), secondary to code 27.69 Other plastic repair of the palate. Report additional codes for hyoid suspension and genioglossus advancement, if performed.

✓4th **29.5** **Other repair of pharynx**

29.51 **Suture of laceration of pharynx**

29.52 **Closure of branchial cleft fistula**

DEF: Sealing off an abnormal opening of the branchial fissure in throat.

29.53 **Closure of other fistula of pharynx**

Pharyngoesophageal fistulectomy

29.54 **Lysis of pharyngeal adhesions**

29.59 **Other**

AHA: 2Q, '89, 18

✓4th **29.9** **Other operations on pharynx**

29.91 **Dilation of pharynx**

Dilation of nasopharynx

29.92 **Division of glossopharyngeal nerve**

29.99 **Other**

EXCLUDES *insertion of radium into pharynx and nasopharynx (92.27)*
removal of intraluminal foreign body (98.13)

Operations on the Respiratory System

30–31.79

6. Operations on the Respiratory System (30-34)

√3rd **30 Excision of larynx**

√4th **30.0 Excision or destruction of lesion or tissue of larynx**

30.01 Marsupialization of laryngeal cyst
DEF: Incision of cyst of larynx with the edges sutured open to create pouch.

30.09 Other excision or destruction of lesion or lesion or tissue of larynx
Stripping of vocal cords
EXCLUDES biopsy of larynx (31.43)
laryngeal fistulectomy (31.62)
laryngotracheal fistulectomy (31.62)

30.1 Hemilaryngectomy
DEF: Excision of one side (half) of larynx.

√4th **30.2 Other partial laryngectomy**

30.21 Epiglottidectomy

30.22 Vocal cordectomy
Excision of vocal cords

30.29 Other partial laryngectomy
Excision of laryngeal cartilage

30.3 Complete laryngectomy
Block dissection of larynx (with thyroidectomy) (with synchronous tracheostomy)
Laryngopharyngectomy
EXCLUDES that with radical neck dissection (30.4)
AHA: 1Q, '12, 9

30.4 Radical laryngectomy
Complete [total] laryngectomy with radical neck dissection (with thyroidectomy) (with synchronous tracheostomy)

√3rd **31 Other operations on larynx and trachea**

31.0 Injection of larynx
Injection of inert material into larynx or vocal cords

31.1 Temporary tracheostomy
Temporary percutaneous dilatational tracheostomy [PDT]
Tracheotomy for assistance in breathing
Code also any synchronous bronchoscopy, if performed (33.21-33.24, 33.27)
AHA: ▶1Q, '13, 19;◀ 1Q, '97, 6
TIP: Assign for a procedure described as a mini-tracheostomy.

√4th **31.2 Permanent tracheostomy**

31.21 Mediastinal tracheostomy
DEF: Placement of artificial breathing tube in windpipe through mediastinum, for long-term use.

31.29 Other permanent tracheostomy
Permanent percutaneous dilatational tracheostomy [PDT]
Code also any synchronous bronchoscopy, if performed (33.21-33.24, 33.27)
EXCLUDES that with laryngectomy (30.3-30.4)
AHA: ▶1Q, '13, 19;◀ 4Q, '12, 84; 2Q, '05, 8; 2Q, '02, 6

31.3 Other incision of larynx or trachea
EXCLUDES that for assistance in breathing (31.1-31.29)

√4th **31.4 Diagnostic procedures on larynx and trachea**

31.41 Tracheoscopy through artificial stoma
EXCLUDES that with biopsy (31.43-31.44)
DEF: Exam of trachea by scope through an artificial opening.

Temporary Tracheostomy

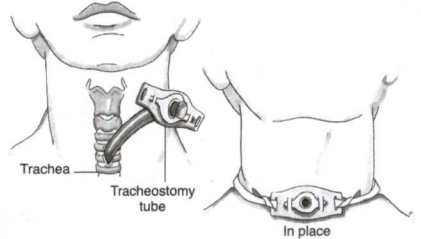

Closed Endoscopic Biopsy of Larynx

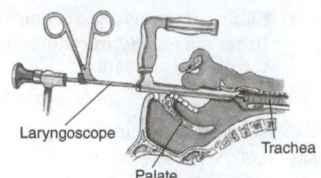

Laryngoscope   Trachea
Palate
Growth on vocal cord

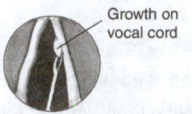

31.42 Laryngoscopy and other tracheoscopy
EXCLUDES that with biopsy (31.43-31.44)

31.43 Closed [endoscopic] biopsy of larynx

31.44 Closed [endoscopic] biopsy of trachea

31.45 Open biopsy of larynx or trachea

31.48 Other diagnostic procedures on larynx
EXCLUDES contrast laryngogram (87.07)
microscopic examination of specimen from larynx (90.31-90.39)
soft tissue x-ray of larynx NEC (87.09)

31.49 Other diagnostic procedures on trachea
EXCLUDES microscopic examination of specimen from trachea (90.41-90.49)
x-ray of trachea (87.49)

31.5 Local excision or destruction of lesion or tissue of trachea
EXCLUDES biopsy of trachea (31.44-31.45)
laryngotracheal fistulectomy (31.62)
tracheoesophageal fistulectomy (31.73)

√4th **31.6 Repair of larynx**

31.61 Suture of laceration of larynx

31.62 Closure of fistula of larynx
Laryngotracheal fistulectomy
Take-down of laryngostomy
DEF: Laryngotracheal fistulectomy: Excision and closing of passage between voice box and trachea.
DEF: Take-down of laryngostomy: Removal of laryngostomy tube and restoration of voice box.

31.63 Revision of laryngostomy

31.64 Repair of laryngeal fracture
DEF: Alignment and positioning of harder structures of larynx such as hyoid bone, following fracture.

31.69 Other repair of larynx
Arytenoidopexy   Graft of larynx
Cordopexy   Transposition of vocal cords
EXCLUDES construction of artificial larynx (31.75)
DEF: Arytenoidopexy: Fixation of pitcher-shaped cartilage in voice box.
DEF: Graft of larynx: Implant of graft tissue into voice box.
DEF: Transposition of the vocal cords: Placement of vocal cords into more functional positions.

√4th **31.7 Repair and plastic operations on trachea**

31.71 Suture of laceration of trachea

31.72 Closure of external fistula of trachea
Closure of tracheotomy

31.73 Closure of other fistula of trachea
Tracheoesophageal fistulectomy
EXCLUDES laryngotracheal fistulectomy (31.62)
DEF: Tracheoesophageal fistulectomy: Excision and closure of abnormal opening between windpipe and esophagus.

31.74 Revision of tracheostomy

31.75 Reconstruction of trachea and construction of artificial larynx
Tracheoplasty with artificial larynx

31.79 Other repair and plastic operations on trachea

BI Bilateral Procedure   NC Non-covered Procedure   LC Limited Coverage Procedure   ▶◀ Revised Text   ● New Code   ▲ Revised Code Title

102 – Volume 3 · October 2014   2015 ICD-9-CM

✓4ᵗʰ **31.9** **Other operations on larynx and trachea**

31.91 **Division of laryngeal nerve**

31.92 **Lysis of adhesions of trachea or larynx**

31.93 **Replacement of laryngeal or tracheal stent**
DEF: Removal and substitution of tubed molding into larynx or trachea.

31.94 **Injection of locally-acting therapeutic substance into trachea**

31.95 **Tracheoesophageal fistulization**
DEF: Creation of passage between trachea and esophagus.

31.98 **Other operations on larynx**
Dilation
Division of congenital web } of larynx
Removal of keel or stent
EXCLUDES removal of intraluminal foreign body from larynx without incision (98.14)
DEF: Dilation: Increasing larynx size by stretching.
DEF: Division of congenital web: Cutting and separating congenital membranes around larynx.
DEF: Removal of keel or stent: Removal of prosthetic device from larynx.

31.99 **Other operations on trachea**
EXCLUDES removal of:
intraluminal foreign body from trachea without incision (98.15)
tracheostomy tube (97.37)
replacement of tracheostomy tube (97.23)
tracheostomy toilette (96.55)
AHA: 3Q, '10, 6; 1Q, '97, 14
TIP: Assign for tracheal dilation associated with insertion of tracheobronchial endoprosthesis performed for treating benign tracheobronchial strictures or strictures produced by malignant neoplasms.

✓3ʳᵈ **32** **Excision of lung and bronchus**
INCLUDES rib section
sternotomy } as operative
sternum-splitting incision } approach
thoracotomy
Code also any synchronous bronchoplasty (33.48)
DEF: Rib resection: Cutting of ribs to access operative field.
DEF: Sternotomy: Cut through breastbone as an operative approach.
DEF: Sternum-splitting incision: Breaking through breastbone to access operative field.

✓4ᵗʰ **32.0** **Local excision or destruction of lesion or tissue of bronchus**
EXCLUDES biopsy of bronchus (33.24-33.25)
bronchial fistulectomy (33.42)
AHA: 4Q, '88, 11

32.01 **Endoscopic excision or destruction of lesion or tissue of bronchus**

32.09 **Other local excision or destruction of lesion or tissue of bronchus**
EXCLUDES that by endoscopic approach (32.01)

32.1 **Other excision of bronchus**
Resection (wide sleeve) of bronchus
EXCLUDES radical dissection [excision] of bronchus (32.6)
DEF: Resection (wide sleeve) of bronchus: Excision and partial, lengthwise removal of a lung branch.

✓4ᵗʰ **32.2** **Local excision or destruction of lesion or tissue of lung**

32.20 **Thoracoscopic excision of lesion or tissue of lung**
Thoracoscopic wedge resection
AHA: 4Q, '07, 109, 110

32.21 **Plication of emphysematous bleb**
DEF: Stitching of a swollen vesicle into folds or tuck.

32.22 **Lung volume reduction surgery** LC
DEF: Excision of portion of lung(s) to reduce respiratory effort in moderate to severe emphysema.
AHA: 1Q, '97, 6; 3Q, '96, 20; 4Q, '95, 64

32.23 **Open ablation of lung lesion or tissue**
AHA: 4Q, '06, 124

32.24 **Percutaneous ablation of lung lesion or tissue**
AHA: 4Q, '06, 124

Lung Volume Reduction

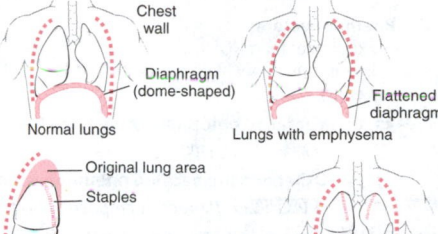

Chest wall
Diaphragm (dome-shaped)
Normal lungs
Flattened diaphragm
Lungs with emphysema
Original lung area
Staples
Diaphragm resumes a more domed shape
Lungs after surgery

32.25 **Thoracoscopic ablation of lung lesion or tissue**
EXCLUDES thoracoscopic excision of lesion or tissue of lung (32.20)
AHA: 4Q, '06, 124

32.26 **Other and unspecified ablation of lung lesion or tissue**
EXCLUDES bronchoscopic bronchial thermoplasty, ablation of smooth airway muscle (32.27)
AHA: 4Q, '06, 124

32.27 **Bronchoscopic bronchial thermoplasty, ablation of airway smooth muscle**
DEF: A transcatheter radiofrequency (RF)-based technology for severe asthma in which therapeutic heat is applied to the smooth muscle of the tracheobronchial tree and lungs to reduce bronchoconstriction.
AHA: 4Q, '10, 115-116

32.28 **Endoscopic excision or destruction of lesion or tissue of lung**
EXCLUDES ablation of lung lesion or tissue:
open (32.23)
other (32.26)
percutaneous (32.24)
thoracoscopic (32.25)
biopsy of lung (33.26-33.27)

32.29 **Other local excision or destruction of lesion or tissue of lung**
Resection of lung: Resection of lung:
NOS   wedge
EXCLUDES ablation of lung lesion or tissue:
open (32.23)
other (32.26)
percutaneous (32.24)
thoracoscopic (32.25)
biopsy of lung (33.26-33.27)
laser interstitial thermal therapy [LITT] of lesion or tissue of lung under guidance (17.69)
that by endoscopic approach (32.28)
thoracoscopic excision of lesion or tissue of lung (32.20)
wide excision of lesion of lung (32.3)
AHA: 3Q, '99, 3

✓4ᵗʰ **32.3** **Segmental resection of lung**
Partial lobectomy
AHA: 4Q, '07, 109

32.30 **Thoracoscopic segmental resection of lung**
AHA: 4Q, '07, 110

32.39 **Other and unspecified segmental resection of lung**
EXCLUDES thoracoscopic segmental resection of lung (32.30)

✓4ᵗʰ **32.4** **Lobectomy of lung**
Lobectomy with segmental resection of adjacent lobes of lung
EXCLUDES that with radical dissection [excision] of thoracic structures (32.6)
AHA: 4Q, '07, 109

32.41 **Thoracoscopic lobectomy of lung**
AHA: 4Q, '07, 110

32.49   **Other lobectomy of lung**
> EXCLUDES   *thoracoscopic lobectomy of lung (32.41)*

☑4th   **32.5**   **Pneumonectomy**
> Excision of lung NOS
> Pneumonectomy (with mediastinal dissection)
> AHA: 1Q, '99, 6

32.50   **Thoracoscopic pneumonectomy**
> AHA: 4Q, '07, 110

32.59   **Other and unspecified pneumonectomy**
> EXCLUDES   *thoracoscopic pneumonectomy (32.50)*

32.6   **Radical dissection of thoracic structures**
> Block [en bloc] dissection of bronchus, lobe of lung, brachial plexus, intercostal structure, ribs (transverse process), and sympathetic nerves

32.9   **Other excision of lung**
> EXCLUDES   *biopsy of lung and bronchus (33.24-33.27)*
> *pulmonary decortication (34.51)*

☑3rd   **33**   **Other operations on lung and bronchus**
> INCLUDES   rib section
> sternotomy
> sternum-splitting incision   }   as operative approach
> thoracotomy

33.0   **Incision of bronchus**

33.1   **Incision of lung**
> EXCLUDES   *puncture of lung (33.93)*

☑4th   **33.2**   **Diagnostic procedures on lung and bronchus**

33.20   **Thoracoscopic lung biopsy**
> EXCLUDES   *closed endoscopic biopsy of lung (33.27)*
> *closed [percutaneous] [needle] biopsy of lung (33.26)*
> *open biopsy of lung (33.28)*
> AHA: 4Q, '07, 110

33.21   **Bronchoscopy through artificial stoma**
> EXCLUDES   *that with biopsy (33.24, 33.27)*
> DEF: Visual exam of lung and its branches via tube through artificial opening.

33.22   **Fiber-optic bronchoscopy**
> EXCLUDES   *that with biopsy (33.24, 33.27)*
> DEF: Exam of lung and bronchus via flexible optical instrument for visualization.
> AHA: 1Q, '04, 4

33.23   **Other bronchoscopy**
> EXCLUDES   *that for:*
> *aspiration (96.05)*
> *biopsy (33.24, 33.27)*
> AHA: 3Q, '02, 18; 1Q, '99, 6

33.24   **Closed [endoscopic] biopsy of bronchus**
> Bronchoscopy (fiberoptic) (rigid) with:
> brush biopsy of "lung"
> brushing or washing for specimen collection
> excision (bite) biopsy
> Diagnostic bronchoalveolar lavage [BAL]
> Mini-bronchoalveolar lavage [mini-BAL]
> Transbronchoscopic needle aspiration [TBNA] of bronchus
> EXCLUDES   *closed biopsy of lung, other than brush biopsy of "lung" (33.26, 33.27)*
> *whole lung lavage (33.99)*
> DEF: Bronchoalveolar lavage (BAL): Saline is introduced into the subsegment of a lobe and retrieved using gentle suction; also called 'liquid biopsy'.
> DEF: Brush biopsy: Obtaining cell or tissue samples via bristled instrument without incision.
> AHA: 2Q, '09, 9, 16; 2Q, '06, 20; 3Q, '04, 9; 3Q, '02, 16; 4Q, '92, 27; 3Q, '91, 15

33.25   **Open biopsy of bronchus**
> EXCLUDES   *open biopsy of lung (33.28)*

Bronchoscopy with Bite Biopsy

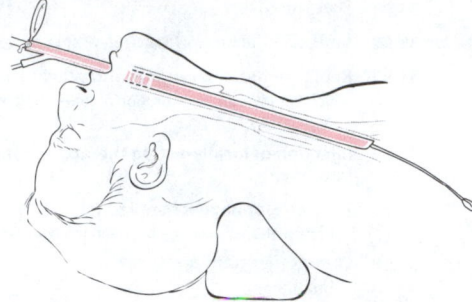

33.26   **Closed [percutaneous] [needle] biopsy of lung**
> Fine needle aspiration [FNA] of lung
> Transthoracic needle biopsy of lung [TTNB]
> EXCLUDES   *endoscopic biopsy of lung (33.27)*
> *thoracoscopic lung biopsy (33.20)*
> AHA: 3Q, '92, 12

33.27   **Closed endoscopic biopsy of lung**
> Fiber-optic (flexible) bronchoscopy with fluoroscopic guidance with biopsy
> Transbronchial lung biopsy
> Transbronchoscopic needle aspiration [TBNA] of lung
> EXCLUDES   *brush biopsy of "lung" (33.24)*
> *percutaneous biopsy of lung (33.26)*
> *thoracoscopic lung biopsy (33.20)*
> AHA: 1Q, '11, 18; 2Q, '09, 9, 16; 3Q, '04, 9; 3Q, '02, 16; 4Q, '92, 27; 3Q, '91, 15; S-O, '86, 11
> TIP: Transbronchial lung biopsy involves a biopsy taken endoscopically through the bronchus into the lung alveoli; if separate biopsies are taken of the bronchial and/or tracheal tissue, assign also 33.24.

33.28   **Open biopsy of lung**
> AHA: 3Q, '99, 3; 3Q, '92, 12

33.29   **Other diagnostic procedures on lung and bronchus**
> EXCLUDES   *bronchoalveolar lavage [BAL] (33.24)*
> *contrast bronchogram:*
> *endotracheal (87.31)*
> *other (87.32)*
> *endoscopic pulmonary airway flow measurement (33.72)*
> *lung scan (92.15)*
> *magnetic resonance imaging (88.92)*
> *microscopic examination of specimen from bronchus or lung (90.41-90.49)*
> *routine chest x-ray (87.44)*
> *ultrasonography of lung (88.73)*
> *vital capacity determination (89.37)*
> *x-ray of bronchus or lung NOS (87.49)*

☑4th   **33.3**   **Surgical collapse of lung**

33.31   **Destruction of phrenic nerve for collapse of lung**
> DEF: Therapeutic deadening or destruction of diaphragmatic nerve to collapse the lung.

33.32   **Artificial pneumothorax for collapse of lung**
> Thoracotomy for collapse of lung
> DEF: Forcing air or gas into diaphragmatic space to achieve therapeutic collapse of lung.
> DEF: Thoracotomy for collapse of lung: Incision into chest for therapeutic collapse of lung.

33.33   **Pneumoperitoneum for collapse of lung**
> DEF: Forcing air or gas into abdominal serous membrane to achieve therapeutic collapse of lung.

33.34   **Thoracoplasty**
> DEF: Removal of ribs for therapeutic collapse of lungs.

33.39   **Other surgical collapse of lung**
> Collapse of lung NOS

☑4th   **33.4**   **Repair and plastic operation on lung and bronchus**

33.41   **Suture of laceration of bronchus**

BI Bilateral Procedure   **NC** Non-covered Procedure   **LC** Limited Coverage Procedure   ▶◀ Revised Text   ● New Code   ▲ Revised Code Title

104 – Volume 3   2015 ICD-9-CM

33.42 **Closure of bronchial fistula**
Closure of bronchostomy   Fistulectomy:
Fistulectomy: bronchoesophageal
  bronchocutaneous   bronchovisceral
EXCLUDES *closure of fistula:*
bronchomediastinal (34.73)
bronchopleural (34.73)
bronchopleuromediastinal (34.73)
DEF: Closure of bronchostomy: Removal of bronchostomy tube and repair of surgical wound.
DEF: Fistulectomy: Closure of abnormal passage. Bronchocutaneous: Between skin and lung branch. Bronchoesophagus: Between esophagus and lung branch. Bronchovisceral: Between an internal organ and lung branch.

33.43 **Closure of laceration of lung**

33.48 **Other repair and plastic operations on bronchus**

33.49 **Other repair and plastic operations on lung**
EXCLUDES *closure of pleural fistula (34.73)*

√4ᵗʰ **33.5** **Lung transplant**
NOTE To report donor source — *see* codes 00.91-00.93
Code also cardiopulmonary bypass [extracorporeal circulation] [heart-lung machine] [39.61]
EXCLUDES *combined heart-lung transplantation (33.6)*
AHA: 4Q, '95, 75

33.50 **Lung transplantation, not otherwise specified** `LC`

33.51 **Unilateral lung transplantation** `LC`

33.52 **Bilateral lung transplantation** `LC`
Double-lung transplantation
En bloc transplantation
DEF: Sequential excision and implant of both lungs.

33.6 **Combined heart-lung transplantation** `LC`
NOTE To report donor source — *see* codes 00.91-00.93
Code also cardiopulmonary bypass [extracorporeal circulation] [heart-lung machine] (39.61)

√4ᵗʰ **33.7** **Other endoscopic procedures in bronchus or lung**
EXCLUDES *insertion of tracheobronchial stent (96.05)*

33.71 **Endoscopic insertion or replacement of bronchial valve(s), single lobe**
Endobronchial airflow redirection valve
Intrabronchial airflow redirection valve
EXCLUDES *endoscopic insertion or replacement of bronchial valve(s), multiple lobes (33.73)*
AHA: 4Q, '09, 144, 145; 4Q, '08, 175; 4Q, '06, 126
TIP: Bronchial valve placement is a less invasive treatment than lung volume reduction surgery (LVRS) or lung transplant in a patient with severe or end-stage emphysema or COPD.

33.72 **Endoscopic pulmonary airway flow measurement**
Assessment of pulmonary airway flow
Code also any diagnostic or therapeutic procedure, if performed
AHA: 4Q, '08, 174-175

33.73 **Endoscopic insertion or replacement of bronchial valve(s), multiple lobes**
Endobronchial airflow redirection valve
Intrabronchial airflow redirection valve
EXCLUDES *endoscopic insertion or replacement of bronchial valve(s), single lobe (33.71)*
AHA: 4Q, '09, 144,145
DEF: Minimally invasive treatment of air leaks resulting from disease, injury, or surgical intervention by the endoscopic placement of more than one bronchial valve.

33.78 **Endoscopic removal of bronchial device(s) or substances**
AHA: 4Q, '06, 126

33.79 **Endoscopic insertion of other bronchial device or substances**
Biologic lung volume reduction NOS (BLVR)
AHA: 4Q, '06, 126

√4ᵗʰ **33.9** **Other operations on lung and bronchus**

33.91 **Bronchial dilation**
AHA: 1Q, '97, 14

33.92 **Ligation of bronchus**
DEF: Tying off of a lung branch.

33.93 **Puncture of lung**
EXCLUDES *needle biopsy (33.26)*
AHA: ▶4Q, '13, 88◀
DEF: Piercing of lung with surgical instrument.

33.98 **Other operations on bronchus**
EXCLUDES *bronchial lavage (96.56)*
removal of intraluminal foreign body from bronchus without incision (98.15)

33.99 **Other operations on lung**
Whole lung lavage
EXCLUDES *other continuous mechanical ventilation (96.70-96.72)*
respiratory therapy (93.90-93.99)
AHA: 3Q, '02, 17

√3ʳᵈ **34** **Operations on chest wall, pleura, mediastinum, and diaphragm**
EXCLUDES *operations on breast (85.0-85.99)*

√4ᵗʰ **34.0** **Incision of chest wall and pleura**
EXCLUDES *that as operative approach — omit code*

34.01 **Incision of chest wall**
Extrapleural drainage
EXCLUDES *incision of pleura (34.09)*
DEF: Extrapleural drainage: Incision to drain fluid from external pleura.
AHA: 3Q, '00, 12; 1Q, '92, 13
TIP: Assign for removal of a broken sternal wire (S/P CABG procedure) when no replacement is implanted.

34.02 **Exploratory thoracotomy**

34.03 **Reopening of recent thoracotomy site**

34.04 **Insertion of intercostal catheter for drainage**
Chest tube
Closed chest drainage
Revision of intercostal catheter (chest tube) (with lysis of adhesions)
EXCLUDES *thoracoscopic drainage of pleural cavity (34.06)*
DEF: Insertion of catheter between ribs for drainage.
AHA: 2Q, '03, 7; 1Q, '99, 10; 2Q, '99, 12; 1Q, '95, 5; 1Q, '92, 12

34.05 **Creation of pleuroperitoneal shunt**
AHA: 4Q, '94, 50

34.06 **Thoracoscopic drainage of pleural cavity**
Evacuation of empyema
AHA: 4Q, '07, 110, 112

34.09 **Other incision of pleura**
Creation of pleural window for drainage
Intercostal stab
Open chest drainage
EXCLUDES *thoracoscopy (34.21)*
thoracotomy for collapse of lung (33.32)
DEF: Creation of pleural window: Creation of circumscribed drainage hole in serous membrane of chest.
DEF: Intercostal stab: Creation of penetrating stab wound between ribs.
DEF: Open chest drainage: Insertion of tube through ribs and serous membrane of chest for drainage.
AHA: 1Q, '07,14; 3Q, '02, 22; 1Q, '94, 7; 4Q, '94, 50

34.1 **Incision of mediastinum**
Code also any biopsy, if performed
EXCLUDES *mediastinoscopy (34.22)*
mediastinotomy associated with pneumonectomy (32.5)

√4ᵗʰ **34.2** **Diagnostic procedures on chest wall, pleura, mediastinum, and diaphragm**

34.20 **Thoracoscopic pleural biopsy**
AHA: 4Q, '07, 110

34.21 **Transpleural thoracoscopy**
DEF: Exam of chest through serous membrane using scope.
AHA: 3Q, '02, 27

Operations on the Respiratory System

34.22–34.99

34.22   **Mediastinoscopy**
> Code also any biopsy, if performed
> DEF: Exam of lung cavity and heart using scope.

34.23   **Biopsy of chest wall**

34.24   **Other pleural biopsy**
> EXCLUDES   *thoracoscopic pleural biopsy (34.20)*
> AHA: 3Q, '02, 22, 27; 1Q, '92, 14

34.25   **Closed [percutaneous] [needle] biopsy of mediastinum**

34.26   **Open biopsy of mediastinum**

34.27   **Biopsy of diaphragm**

34.28   **Other diagnostic procedures on chest wall, pleura, and diaphragm**
> EXCLUDES   *angiocardiography (88.50-88.58)*
>   *aortography (88.42)*
>   *arteriography of:*
>   *intrathoracic vessels NEC (88.44)*
>   *pulmonary arteries (88.43)*
>   *microscopic examination of specimen from chest wall, pleura, and diaphragm (90.41-90.49)*
>   *phlebography of:*
>   *intrathoracic vessels NEC (88.63)*
>   *pulmonary veins (88.62)*
>   *radiological examinations of thorax:*
>   *C.A.T. scan (87.41)*
>   *diaphragmatic x-ray (87.49)*
>   *intrathoracic lymphangiogram (87.34)*
>   *routine chest x-ray (87.44)*
>   *sinogram of chest wall (87.38)*
>   *soft tissue x-ray of chest wall NEC (87.39)*
>   *tomogram of thorax NEC (87.42)*
>   *ultrasonography of thorax (88.73)*

34.29   **Other diagnostic procedures on mediastinum**
> EXCLUDES   *mediastinal:*
>   *pneumogram (87.33)*
>   *x-ray NEC (87.49)*

34.3   **Excision or destruction of lesion or tissue of mediastinum**
> EXCLUDES   *biopsy of mediastinum (34.25-34.26)*
>   *mediastinal fistulectomy (34.73)*
> AHA: 2Q, '11, 12

34.4   **Excision or destruction of lesion of chest wall**
> Excision of lesion of chest wall NOS (with excision of ribs)
> EXCLUDES   *biopsy of chest wall (34.23)*
>   *costectomy not incidental to thoracic procedure (77.91)*
>   *excision of lesion of:*
>   *breast (85.20-85.25)*
>   *cartilage (80.89)*
>   *skin (86.2-86.3)*
>   *fistulectomy (34.73)*

✓4ᵗʰ 34.5   **Pleurectomy**

34.51   **Decortication of lung**
> EXCLUDES   *thoracoscopic decortication of lung (34.52)*
> DEF: Removal of thickened serous membrane for lung expansion.

34.52   **Thoracoscopic decortication of lung**
> AHA: 4Q, '07, 111, 113

34.59   **Other excision of pleura**
> Excision of pleural lesion
> EXCLUDES   *biopsy of pleura (34.24)*
>   *pleural fistulectomy (34.73)*

34.6   **Scarification of pleura**
> Pleurosclerosis
> EXCLUDES   *injection of sclerosing agent (34.92)*
> DEF: Destruction of fluid-secreting serous membrane cells of chest.
> AHA: 1Q, '92, 12

✓4ᵗʰ 34.7   **Repair of chest wall**

34.71   **Suture of laceration of chest wall**
> EXCLUDES   *suture of skin and subcutaneous tissue alone (86.59)*

34.72   **Closure of thoracostomy**

34.73   **Closure of other fistula of thorax**
> Closure of:
>   bronchopleural
>   bronchopleurocutaneous } fistula
>   bronchopleuromediastinal

34.74   **Repair of pectus deformity**
> Repair of:
>   pectus carinatum } (with implant)
>   pectus excavatum
> DEF: Pectus carinatum repair: Restoration of prominent chest bone defect with implant.
> DEF: Pectus excavatum: Restoration of depressed chest bone defect with implant.
> AHA: 2Q, '04, 6

34.79   **Other repair of chest wall**
> Repair of chest wall NOS
> AHA: 2Q, '04, 6; J-F, '87, 13
> TIP: Assign for removal and replacement of broken sternal wires (S/P CABG procedure), along with code 77.61 if sternal bone debridement was also performed.

✓4ᵗʰ 34.8   **Operations on diaphragm**

34.81   **Excision of lesion or tissue of diaphragm**
> EXCLUDES   *biopsy of diaphragm (34.27)*

34.82   **Suture of laceration of diaphragm**

34.83   **Closure of fistula of diaphragm**
> Thoracicoabdominal
> Thoracicogastric } fistulectomy
> Thoracicointestinal
> DEF: Fistulectomy: Closure of abnormal passage.

34.84   **Other repair of diaphragm**
> EXCLUDES   *repair of diaphragmatic hernia (53.7-53.82)*

34.85   **Implantation of diaphragmatic pacemaker**

34.89   **Other operations on diaphragm**

✓4ᵗʰ 34.9   **Other operations on thorax**

34.91   **Thoracentesis**
> DEF: Puncture of pleural cavity for fluid aspiration, also called pleurocentesis.
> AHA: 4Q, '12, 83; S-O, '85, 6

34.92   **Injection into thoracic cavity**
> Chemical pleurodesis
> Injection of cytotoxic agent or tetracycline
> Instillation into thoracic cavity
> Requires additional code for any cancer chemotherapeutic substance (99.25)
> EXCLUDES   *that for collapse of lung (33.32)*
> DEF: Chemical pleurodesis: Tetracycline hydrochloride injections to create adhesions between parietal and visceral pleura for treatment of pleural effusion.
> AHA: 3Q, '12, 24; 4Q, '07, 112; 1Q, '07, 14; 1Q, '92, 12; 2Q, '89, 17
> TIP: Assign for installation of biological glue and/or talc into the pleural cavity.

34.93   **Repair of pleura**

34.99   **Other**
> EXCLUDES   *removal of:*
>   *mediastinal drain (97.42)*
>   *sutures (97.43)*
>   *thoracotomy tube (97.41)*
> DEF: Pleural tent: Extrapleural mobilization of parietal pleura that allows draping of membrane over visceral pleura to eliminate intrapleural dead space and seal visceral pleura.
> AHA: 1Q, '00, 17; 1Q, '88, 9
> TIP: Assign for formation of a pleural tent, which involves extrapleural mobilization of the parietal pleura in the apex of the chest cavity.

BI Bilateral Procedure   **NC** Non-covered Procedure   **LC** Limited Coverage Procedure   ▶◀ Revised Text   ● New Code   ▲ Revised Code Title

106 – Volume 3   2015 ICD-9-CM

7. Operations on the Cardiovascular System (35-39)

√3ʳᵈ **35 Operations on valves and septa of heart**

INCLUDES sternotomy (median)
(tranverse) } as operative approach
thoracotomy

Code also any cardiopulmonary bypass [extracorporeal circulation] [heart-lung machine] (39.61)

√4ᵗʰ **35.0 Closed heart valvotomy or transcatheter replacement of heart valve**

> EXCLUDES percutaneous (balloon) valvuloplasty (35.96)
> DEF: Incision into valve to restore function.

35.00 Closed heart valvotomy, unspecified valve

35.01 Closed heart valvotomy, aortic valve

35.02 Closed heart valvotomy, mitral valve

35.03 Closed heart valvotomy, pulmonary valve

35.04 Closed heart valvotomy, tricuspid valve

35.05 Endovascular replacement of aortic valve

> NOTE Includes that with any balloon valvuloplasty; do not code separately

Implantation of transcatheter aortic valve
Replacement of aortic valve with tissue graft
(autograft) (bioprosthetic) (heterograft)
(homograft):
transarterial approach
transfemoral approach
TAVI (transcatheter aortic valve implantation)
TAVR (transcatheter aortic valve replacement)
> EXCLUDES open and other replacement of heart valve (35.20-35.28)

AHA: 4Q, '11, 169-175

35.06 Transapical replacement of aortic valve

> NOTE Includes that with any balloon valvuloplasty; do not code separately

Implantation of transcatheter aortic valve
Replacement of aortic valve with tissue graft
(autograft) (bioprosthetic) (heterograft)
(homograft):
intercostal approach
transventricular approach
That via transthoracic exposure, i.e. thoracotomy, sternotomy, or subxiphoid approach
> EXCLUDES open and other replacement of heart valve (35.20-35.28)

AHA: 4Q, '11, 169-175

35.07 Endovascular replacement of pulmonary valve

> NOTE Includes that with any balloon valvuloplasty; do not code separately

Implantation of transcatheter pulmonary valve
PPVI (percutaneous pulmonary valve implantation)
Replacement of pulmonary valve:
transfemoral approach
transvenous approach
That within previously created right ventricle to pulmonary artery conduit
TPVI (transcatheter pulmonary valve implantation)
> EXCLUDES open and other replacement of heart valve (35.20-35.28)

AHA: 4Q, '11, 169-175

35.08 Transapical replacement of pulmonary valve

> NOTE Includes that with any balloon valvuloplasty; do not code separately

Implantation of transcatheter pulmonary valve
Replacement of pulmonary valve:
intercostal approach
transventricular approach
That via transthoracic exposure, i.e. thoracotomy, sternotomy, or subxiphoid approach
> EXCLUDES open and other replacement of heart valve (35.20-35.28)

AHA: 4Q, '11, 169-175

35.09 Endovascular replacement of unspecified heart valve

> NOTE Includes that with any balloon valvuloplasty; do not code separately

Replacement of valve via:
intercostal approach
transventricular approach
> EXCLUDES open and other replacement of heart valve (35.20-35.28)

AHA: 4Q, '11, 169-175

√4ᵗʰ **35.1 Open heart valvuloplasty without replacement**

INCLUDES open heart valvotomy

Code also cardiopulmonary bypass, if performed [extracorporeal circulation] [heart-lung machine] (39.61)
> EXCLUDES that associated with repair of:
> endocardial cushion defect (35.54,35.63,35.73)
> percutaneous (balloon) valvuloplasty (35.96)
> valvular defect associated with atrial and ventricular septal defects (35.54, 35.63, 35.73)

> DEF: Incision into heart for plastic valve repair without replacing valve.

35.10 Open heart valvuloplasty without replacement, unspecified valve

35.11 Open heart valvuloplasty of aortic valve without replacement

> AHA: 2Q, '08, 13
> TIP: Assign for resuspension of aortic valve, in which 4-0 Prolene sutures are used to lift the valve into correct anatomical position, and a double layer of felt is placed on the inside and outside of the valve.

35.12 Open heart valvuloplasty of mitral valve without replacement

> AHA: 3Q, '10, 6; 1Q, '10, 14; 1Q, '97, 13

35.13 Open heart valvuloplasty of pulmonary valve without replacement

35.14 Open heart valvuloplasty of tricuspid valve without replacement

√4ᵗʰ **35.2 Open and other replacement of heart valve**

INCLUDES excision of heart valve with replacement

Code also cardiopulmonary bypass [extracorporeal circulation] [heart-lung machine] (39.61)
> EXCLUDES that associated with repair of:
> endocardial cushion defect (35.54,35.63, 35.73)
> valvular defect associated with atrial and ventricular septal defects (35.54, 35.63, 35.73)
> transapical replacement of heart valve (35.06, 35.08)
> transcatheter replacement of heart valve (35.05, 35.07)

> DEF: Removal and replacement of valve with tissue from patient, animal, other human, or prosthetic (synthetic) valve.

35.20 Open and other replacement of unspecified heart valve

That with tissue graft or prosthetic implant
> EXCLUDES endovascular replacement of unspecified heart valve (35.09)

35.21 Open and other replacement of aortic valve with tissue graft

Includes that by: Includes that by:
autograft   homograft
heterograft
> EXCLUDES endovascular replacement of aortic valve (35.05)
> transapical replacement of aortic valve (35.06)

AHA: 2Q, '97, 8

35.22 Open and other replacement of aortic valve

Replacement of aortic valve, NOS
That with prosthetic (partial) (synthetic) (total)
> EXCLUDES endovascular replacement of aortic valve (35.05)
> transapical replacement of aortic valve (35.06)

AHA: ▶4Q, '13, 102;◀ 4Q, '11, 152; 4Q, '08, 179; 1Q, '96, 11

Operations on the Cardiovascular System

35.23–35.55

35.23   **Open and other replacement of mitral valve with tissue graft**
Includes that by:
autograft
heterograft
homograft

35.24   **Open and other replacement of mitral valve**
Replacement of mitral valve, NOS
That with prosthetic (partial) (synthetic) (total)
EXCLUDES *percutaneous repair with implant or leaflet clip (35.97)*
AHA: 4Q, '97, 55

35.25   **Open and other replacement of pulmonary valve with tissue graft**
Includes that by:
autograft
heterograft
homograft
EXCLUDES *endovascular replacement of pulmonary valve (35.07)*
transapical replacement of pulmonary valve (35.08)
AHA: 1Q, '11, 24; 1Q, '07, 14; 1Q, '04, 16; 2Q, '97, 8
TIP: Assign for a Ross procedure, in which a patient's aortic valve is replaced by utilizing the pulmonary valve and the pulmonary valve is replaced with a homograft. Also assign code 35.21 for the aortic valve replacement.

35.26   **Open and other replacement of pulmonary valve**
Replacement of pulmonary valve, NOS
That with prosthetic (partial) (synthetic) (total)
EXCLUDES *endovascular replacement of pulmonary valve (35.07)*
transapical replacement of pulmonary valve (35.08)

35.27   **Open and other replacement of tricuspid valve with tissue graft**
Includes that by:
autograft
heterograft
homograft

35.28   **Open and other replacement of tricuspid valve**
Replacement of tricuspid valve, NOS
That with prosthetic (partial) (synthetic) (total)

√4ᵗʰ **35.3**   **Operations on structures adjacent to heart valves**
Code also cardiopulmonary bypass [extracorporeal circulation] [heart-lung machine] (39.61)

35.31   **Operations on papillary muscle**
Division
Reattachment } of papillary muscle
Repair

35.32   **Operations on chordae tendineae**
Division } chordae tendineae
Repair

35.33   **Annuloplasty**
Plication of annulus
DEF: Plication of annulus: Tuck stitched in valvular ring for tightening.
AHA: 1Q, '97, 13; 1Q, '88, 10
TIP: Do not assign unless the annuloplasty is the only procedure performed; if it included an operation on the leaflet as well, refer to valvuloplasty codes, which include the annuloplasty.

35.34   **Infundibulectomy**
Right ventricular infundibulectomy
DEF: Infundibulectomy: Excision of funnel-shaped heart passage.
DEF: Right ventricular infundibulectomy: Excision of funnel-shaped passage in right upper heart chamber.

35.35   **Operations on trabeculae carneae cordis**
Division } of trabeculae carneae cordis
Excision
Excision of aortic subvalvular ring

35.39   **Operations on other structures adjacent to valves of heart**
Repair of sinus of Valsalva (aneurysm)

√4ᵗʰ **35.4**   **Production of septal defect in heart**

35.41   **Enlargement of existing atrial septal defect**
Rashkind procedure
Septostomy (atrial) (balloon)
DEF: Enlargement of partition wall defect in lower heart chamber to improve function.
DEF: Rashkind procedure: Enlargement of partition wall defect between the two lower heart chambers by balloon catheter.

35.42   **Creation of septal defect in heart**
Blalock-Hanlon operation
DEF: Blalock-Hanlon operation: Removal of partition wall defect in lower heart chamber.

√4ᵗʰ **35.5**   **Repair of atrial and ventricular septa with prosthesis**
INCLUDES repair of septa with synthetic implant or patch
Code also cardiopulmonary bypass [extracorporeal circulation] [heart-lung machine] (39.61)

35.50   **Repair of unspecified septal defect of heart with prosthesis**
EXCLUDES *that associated with repair of:*
endocardial cushion defect (35.54)
septal defect associated with valvular defect (35.54)

35.51   **Repair of atrial septal defect with prosthesis, open technique**
Atrioseptoplasty
Correction of atrial septal defect
Repair: } with prosthesis
foramen ovale (patent)
ostium secundum defect
EXCLUDES *that associated with repair of:*
atrial septal defect associated with valvular and ventricular septal defects (35.54)
endocardial cushion defect (35.54)
DEF: Repair of opening or weakening in septum separating the atria; prosthesis implanted through heart incision.

35.52   **Repair of atrial septal defect with prosthesis, closed technique**
Insertion of atrial septal umbrella [King-Mills]
DEF: Correction of partition wall defect in lower heart chamber with artificial material, without incision into heart.
DEF: Insertion of atrial septal umbrella (King-Mills): Correction of partition wall defect in lower heart chamber with atrial septal umbrella.
AHA: 2Q, '05, 17; 3Q, '98, 11
TIP: Assign for Amplatzer balloon occlusion, used to repair cardiac anomalies; is implanted at the site of the defect via a catheter; typically performed in the cardiac catheterization lab.

35.53   **Repair of ventricular septal defect with prosthesis, open technique**
Correction of ventricular
septal defect } with prosthesis
Repair of supracristal defect
EXCLUDES *that associated with repair of:*
endocardial cushion defect (35.54)
ventricular defect associated with valvular and atrial septal defects (35.54)
AHA: 1Q, '07, 14

35.54   **Repair of endocardial cushion defect with prosthesis**
Repair:
atrioventricular canal
ostium primum defect } with prosthesis
valvular defect associated with (grafted to
atrial and ventricular septa)
septal defects
EXCLUDES *repair of isolated:*
atrial septal defect (35.51-35.52)
valvular defect (35.20, 35.22, 35.24, 35.26, 35.28)
ventricular septal defect (35.53)

35.55   **Repair of ventricular septal defect with prosthesis, closed technique**

BI Bilateral Procedure   **NC** Non-covered Procedure   **LC** Limited Coverage Procedure   ▶◀ Revised Text   ● New Code   ▲ Revised Code Title

108 – Volume 3   **2015 ICD-9-CM**

✓4ᵗʰ **35.6   Repair of atrial and ventricular septa with tissue graft**
Code also cardiopulmonary bypass [extracorporeal circulation] [heart-lung machine] (39.61)

35.60   Repair of unspecified septal defect of heart with tissue graft
EXCLUDES *that associated with repair of:*
endocardial cushion defect (35.63)
septal defect associated with valvular defect (35.63)

35.61   Repair of atrial septal defect with tissue graft
Atrioseptoplasty
Correction of atrial septal defect
Repair: ⎫
foramen ovale (patent) ⎬ with tissue graft
ostium secundum defect ⎭
EXCLUDES *that associated with repair of:*
atrial septal defect associated with valvular and ventricular septal defects (35.63)
endocardial cushion defect (35.63)

35.62   Repair of ventricular septal defect with tissue graft
Correction of ventricular ⎫
septal defect ⎬ with tissue
Repair of supracristal defect ⎭ graft
EXCLUDES *that associated with repair of:*
endocardial cushion defect (35.63)
ventricular defect associated with valvular and atrial septal defects (35.63)

35.63   Repair of endocardial cushion defect with tissue graft
Repair of:
artrioventricular canal ⎫
ostium primum defect ⎬
valvular defect associated with ⎬ with tissue
atrial and ventricular ⎬ graft
septal defects ⎭
EXCLUDES *repair of isolated:*
atrial septal defect (35.61)
valvular defect (35.20-35.21, 35.23, 35.25, 35.27)
ventricular septal defect (35.62)

✓4ᵗʰ **35.7   Other and unspecified repair of atrial and ventricular septa**
Code also cardiopulmonary bypass [extracorporeal circulation] [heart-lung machine] (39.61)

35.70   Other and unspecified repair of unspecified septal defect of heart
Repair of septal defect NOS
EXCLUDES *that associated with repair of:*
endocardial cushion defect (35.73)
septal defect associated with valvular defect (35.73)

35.71   Other and unspecified repair of atrial septal defect
Repair NOS: Repair NOS:
atrial septum   ostium secundum defect
foramen ovale (patent)
EXCLUDES *that associated with repair of:*
atrial septal defect associated with valvular and ventricular septal defects (35.73)
endocardial cushion defect (35.73)

35.72   Other and unspecified repair of ventricular septal defect
Repair NOS: Repair NOS:
supracristal defect   ventricular septum
EXCLUDES *that associated with repair of:*
endocardial cushion defect (35.73)
ventricular septal defect associated with valvular and atrial septal defects (35.73)

35.73   Other and unspecified repair of endocardial cushion defect
Repair NOS:
atrioventricular canal
ostium primum defect
valvular defect associated with atrial and ventricular septal defects
EXCLUDES *repair of isolated:*
atrial septal defect (35.71)
valvular defect (35.20, 35.22, 35.24, 35.26, 35.28)
ventricular septal defect (35.72)

✓4ᵗʰ **35.8   Total repair of certain congenital cardiac anomalies**
NOTE For partial repair of defect [e.g. repair of atrial septal defect in tetralogy of Fallot] — code to specific procedure

35.81   Total repair of tetralogy of Fallot
One-stage total correction of tetralogy of Fallot with or without:
commissurotomy of pulmonary valve
infundibulectomy
outflow tract prosthesis
patch graft of outflow tract
prosthetic tube for pulmonary artery
repair of ventricular septal defect (with prosthesis)
take-down of previous systemic-pulmonary artery anastomosis

35.82   Total repair of total anomalous pulmonary venous connection
One-stage total correction of total anomalous pulmonary venous connection with or without:
anastomosis between (horizontal) common pulmonary trunk and posterior wall of left atrium (side-to-side)
enlargement of foramen ovale
incision [excision] of common wall between posterior left atrium and coronary sinus and roofing of resultant defect with patch graft (synthetic)
ligation of venous connection (descending anomalous vein) (to left innominate vein) (to superior vena cava)
repair of atrial septal defect (with prosthesis)

35.83   Total repair of truncus arteriosus
One-stage total correction of truncus arteriosus with or without:
construction (with aortic homograft) (with prosthesis) of a pulmonary artery placed from right ventricle to arteries supplying the lung
ligation of connections between aorta and pulmonary artery
repair of ventricular septal defect (with prosthesis)

35.84   Total correction of transposition of great vessels, not elsewhere classified
Arterial switch operation [Jatene]
Total correction of transposition of great arteries at the arterial level by switching the great arteries, including the left or both coronary arteries, implanted in the wall of the pulmonary artery
EXCLUDES *baffle operation [Mustard] [Senning] (35.91)*
creation of shunt between right ventricle and pulmonary artery [Rastelli] (35.92)

Operations on the Cardiovascular System   **35.6–35.84**

Operations on the Cardiovascular System

35.9–36.06

☑⁴ᵗʰ **35.9 Other operations on valves and septa of heart**
Code also cardiopulmonary bypass, if performed [extracorporeal circulation] [heart-lung machine] (39.61)

35.91 Interatrial transposition of venous return
Baffle:
atrial
interatrial
Mustard's operation
Resection of atrial septum and insertion of patch to direct systemic venous return to tricuspid valve and pulmonary venous return to mitral valve
DEF: Atrial baffle: Correction of venous flow of abnormal or deviated lower heart chamber.
DEF: Interatrial baffle: Correction of venous flow between abnormal lower heart chambers.
DEF: Mustard's operation: Creates intra-atrial baffle using pericardial tissue to correct transposition of the great vessels.

35.92 Creation of conduit between right ventricle and pulmonary artery
Creation of shunt between right ventricle and (distal) pulmonary artery
EXCLUDES that associated with total repair of truncus arteriosus (35.83)
AHA: 1Q, '07, 14

35.93 Creation of conduit between left ventricle and aorta
Creation of apicoaortic shunt
Shunt between apex of left ventricle and aorta
AHA: 2Q, '09, 8

35.94 Creation of conduit between atrium and pulmonary artery
Fontan procedure
AHA: ▶1Q, '14, 9, 15◀

35.95 Revision of corrective procedure on heart
Replacement of prosthetic heart valve poppet
Resuture of prosthesis of:
septum
valve
EXCLUDES complete revision — code to specific procedure
replacement of prosthesis or graft of:
septum (35.50-35.63)
valve (35.20-35.28)
DEF: Replacement of prosthetic heart valve poppet: Removal and replacement of valve-supporting prosthesis.
DEF: Resuture of prosthesis of septum: Restitching of prosthesis in partition wall.
DEF: Resuture of prosthesis of valve: Restitching of prosthetic valve.

35.96 Percutaneous balloon valvuloplasty
Balloon dilation of valve
EXCLUDES endovascular replacement of heart valve (35.05, 35.07)
mitral valve repair with implant (35.97)
transapical replacement of heart valve (35.06, 35.08)
DEF: Percutaneous balloon valvuloplasty: Repair of valve with inflatable catheter.
AHA: 1Q, '11, 24; 3Q, '10, 16; 3Q, '09, 19; 3Q, '04, 10; M-J, '86, 6; N-D, '85, 10

35.97 Percutaneous mitral valve repair with implant
Endovascular mitral valve repair
Implantation of mitral valve leaflet clip
Transcatheter mitral valve repair
Code also any transesophageal echocardiography [TEE] (88.72)
EXCLUDES percutaneous balloon valvuloplasty (35.96)
AHA: 4Q, '10, 116-117
TIP: Assign for mitral valve reconstruction by use of the Evalve® Cardiovascular Valve Repair System or MitraClip® implant.

35.98 Other operations on septa of heart
AHA: 1Q, '07, 11

35.99 Other operations on valves of heart

☑³ʳᵈ **36 Operations on vessels of heart**
INCLUDES sternotomy (median)
(transverse) } as operative approach
thoracotomy
Code also any:
injection or infusion of platelet inhibitor (99.20)
injection or infusion of thrombolytic agent (99.10)
Code also cardiopulmonary bypass, if performed [extra- corporeal circulation] [heart-lung machine] (39.61)

☑⁴ᵗʰ **36.0 Removal of coronary artery obstruction and insertion of stent(s)**
AHA: 4Q, '95, 66; 2Q, '94, 13; 1Q, '94, 3; 2Q, '90, 23; N-D, '86, 8

36.03 Open chest coronary artery angioplasty
Coronary (artery):
endarterectomy (with patch graft)
thromboendarterectomy (with patch graft)
Open surgery for direct relief of coronary artery obstruction
Code also any:
insertion of drug-eluting coronary stent(s) (36.07)
insertion of non-drug-eluting coronary stent(s) (36.06)
number of vascular stents inserted (00.45-00.48)
number of vessels treated (00.40-00.43)
procedure on vessel bifurcation (00.44)
EXCLUDES that with coronary artery bypass graft (36.10-36.19)
DEF: Endarterectomy (with patch graft): Excision of thickened material within coronary artery; repair with patch graft.
DEF: Thromboendarterectomy (with patch graft): Excision of blood clot and thickened material within coronary artery; repair with patch graft.
DEF: Open surgery for direct relief of coronary artery obstruction: Removal of coronary artery obstruction through opening in chest.
AHA: 2Q, '01, 24; 3Q, '93, 7
TIP: Do not assign if the procedure was performed percutaneously; see instead code 00.66.

36.04 Intracoronary artery thrombolytic infusion
Enzyme infusion
Platelet inhibitor
That by direct coronary artery injection, infusion, or catheterization
EXCLUDES infusion of platelet inhibitor (99.20)
infusion of thrombolytic agent (99.10)
that associated with any procedure in 36.03
DEF: Infusion of clot breaking solution into intracoronary artery.
AHA: 4Q, '05, 102; 4Q, '02, 114; 3Q, '02, 20; 2Q, '01, 24; 4Q, '98, 85; 1Q, '97, 3; 4Q, '95, 67
TIP: If tPA infusion was performed in another facility within the previous 24 hours prior to arrival in the current facility, assign also diagnosis code V45.88.

36.06 Insertion of non-drug-eluting coronary artery stent(s)
Bare stent(s)   Endograft(s)
Bonded stent(s)   Endovascular graft(s)
Drug-coated stent(s),e.g.,   Stent graft(s)
heparin coated
Code also any:
number of vascular stents inserted (00.45-00.48)
number of vessels treated (00.40-00.43)
open chest coronary artery angioplasty (36.03)
percutaneous transluminal coronary angioplasty [PTCA] (00.66)
procedure on vessel bifurcation (00.44)
transluminal coronary atherectomy (17.55)
EXCLUDES insertion of drug-eluting coronary artery stent(s) (36.07)
DEF: Percutaneous implant of metal stent via catheter, to enlarge, maintain lumen size of coronary artery.
AHA: 4Q, '11, 167; 2Q, '09, 12; 4Q, '05, 71; 2Q, '04, 3; 4Q, '02, 101; 1Q,'01, 9; 2Q, '01, 24; 1Q, '00, 11; 1Q, '99, 17

BI Bilateral Procedure   NC Non-covered Procedure   LC Limited Coverage Procedure   ▶◀ Revised Text   ● New Code   ▲ Revised Code Title

36.07 **Insertion of drug-eluting coronary artery stent(s)**

Endograft(s)   Stent graft(s)
Endovascular graft(s)

Code also any:
number of vascular stents inserted (00.45-00.48)
number of vessels treated (00.40-00.43)
open chest coronary artery angioplasty (36.03)
percutaneous transluminal coronary angioplasty [PTCA] (00.66)
procedure on vessel bifurcation (00.44)
transluminal coronary atherectomy (17.55)

EXCLUDES *drug-coated stents, e.g., heparin coated (36.06)*
insertion of non-drug-eluting coronary artery stent(s) (36.06)

DEF: Drug-eluting stent technology developed to prevent the accumulation of scar tissue that can narrow reopened coronary arteries. A special polymer is used to coat the drug onto the stent, which slowly releases into the coronary artery wall tissue.

AHA: ▶4Q, '13, 91;◀ 3Q, '12, 5; 4Q, '05, 105-106; 4Q, '02, 101

36.09 **Other removal of coronary artery obstruction**

Coronary angioplasty NOS

Code also any:
number of vascular stents inserted (00.45-00.48)
number of vessels treated (00.40-00.43)
procedure on vessel bifurcation (00.44)

EXCLUDES *that by open angioplasty (36.03)*
that by percutaneous transluminal coronary angioplasty [PTCA] (00.66)
transluminal coronary atherectomy (17.55)

√4ᵗʰ **36.1** **Bypass anastomosis for heart revascularization**

NOTE Do not assign codes from series 00.40-00.43 with codes from series 36.10-36.19

Code also:
cardiopulmonary bypass [extracorporeal circulation] [heart-lung machine] (39.61)
pressurized treatment of venous bypass graft [conduit] with pharmaceutical substance, if performed (00.16)

DEF: Insertion of alternate vessel to bypass blocked coronary artery, correct coronary blood flow.

AHA: 4Q, '07, 121; 2Q, '96, 7; 3Q, '95, 7; 3Q, '93, 8; 1Q, '91, 7; 2Q, '90, 24; 4Q, '89, 3

TIP: The determining factor for coding an aortocoronary artery bypass graft operation is the number of coronary arteries involved rather than the number of grafts; the use of the sequential technique does not affect the code assignment.

36.10 **Aortocoronary bypass for heart revascularization, not otherwise specified**

Direct revascularization:
cardiac
coronary } with catheter stent,
hear muscle } prosthesis, or vein
myocardial } graft

Heart revascularization NOS

AHA: 2Q, '96, 7

36.11 **(Aorto)coronary bypass of one coronary artery**

AHA: 3Q, '02, 4, 9; 4Q, '89, 3

36.12 **(Aorto)coronary bypass of two coronary arteries**

AHA: 3Q, '02, 8; 4Q, '99, 15; 2Q, '96, 7; 3Q, '97, 14; 4Q, '89, 3

Coronary Bypass

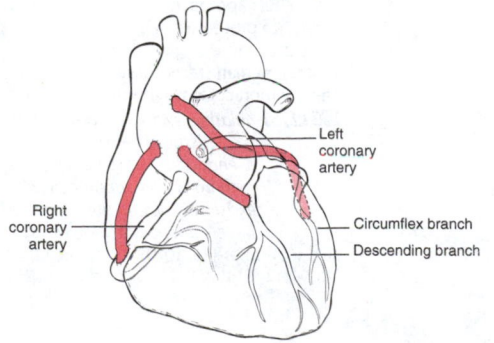

Left coronary artery

Right coronary artery

Circumflex branch

Descending branch

36.13 **(Aorto)coronary bypass of three coronary arteries**

AHA: 3Q, '02, 6, 7, 9; 2Q, '96, 7; 4Q, '89, 3

36.14 **(Aorto)coronary bypass of four or more coronary arteries**

AHA: 3Q, '02, 5; 2Q, '96, 7; 4Q, '89, 3

36.15 **Single internal mammary-coronary artery bypass**

Anastomosis (single):
mammary artery to coronary artery
thoracic artery to coronary artery

AHA: 3Q, '02, 4-9; 4Q, '99, 15; 3Q, '97, 14; 2Q, '96, 7

36.16 **Double internal mammary-coronary artery bypass**

Anastomosis, double:
mammary artery to coronary artery
thoracic artery to coronary artery

AHA: 3Q, '02, 6, 8, 9; 2Q, '96, 7

36.17 **Abdominal-coronary artery bypass**

Anastomosis:
gastroepiploic artery to coronary artery

AHA: 3Q, '97, 14; 4Q, '96, 64

36.19 **Other bypass anastomosis for heart revascularization**

AHA: 2Q, '96, 7

36.2 **Heart revascularization by arterial implant**

Implantation of:
aortic branches [ascending aortic branches] into heart muscle
blood vessels into myocardium
internal mammary artery [internal thoracic artery] into:
heart muscle
myocardium
ventricle
ventricular wall
Indirect heart revascularization NOS

√4ᵗʰ **36.3** **Other heart revascularization**

36.31 **Open chest transmyocardial revascularization**

DEF: Transmyocardial revascularization (TMR): Laser creation of channels through myocardium allows oxygenated blood flow from sinusoids to myocardial tissue.

36.32 **Other transmyocardial revascularization**

AHA: 4Q, '98, 74

36.33 **Endoscopic transmyocardial revascularization**

Thoracoscopic transmyocardial revascularization

AHA: 4Q, '06, 127

36.34 **Percutaneous transmyocardial revascularization**

Endovascular transmyocardial revascularization

AHA: 4Q, '06, 127

36.39 **Other heart revascularization**

Abrasion of epicardium   Myocardial graft:
Cardio-omentopexy   mediastinal fat
Intrapericardial poudrage   omentum
                           pectoral muscles

DEF: Cardio-omentopexy: Suture of omentum segment to heart after drawing segment through incision in diaphragm to improve blood supply.

DEF: Intrapericardial poudrage: Application of powder to heart lining to promote fusion.

√4ᵗʰ **36.9** **Other operations on vessels of heart**

Code also cardiopulmonary bypass [extracorporeal circulation] [heart-lung machine] (39.61)

36.91 **Repair of aneurysm of coronary vessel**

36.99 **Other operations on vessels of heart**

Exploration }
Incision } of coronary artery
Ligation }

Repair of arteriovenous fistula

AHA: 3Q, '03, 18; 1Q, '94, 3

√3ʳᵈ
√4ᵗʰ Additional Digit Required   Valid OR Procedure   Non-OR Procedure   Adjunct Code
2015 ICD-9-CM   October 2014 • Volume 3 – 111

Operations on the Cardiovascular System

37–37.33

√3ʳᵈ **37 Other operations on heart and pericardium**
Code also any injection or infusion of platelet inhibitor (99.20)

37.0 Pericardiocentesis
DEF: Puncture of the heart lining to withdraw fluid.
AHA: 1Q, '07, 11

√4ᵗʰ **37.1 Cardiotomy and pericardiotomy**
Code also cardiopulmonary bypass [extracorporeal circulation] [heart-lung machine] (39.61)

37.10 Incision of heart, not otherwise specified
Cardiolysis NOS

37.11 Cardiotomy

Incision of:	Incision of:
atrium	myocardium
endocardium	ventricle

37.12 Pericardiotomy
Pericardial window operation
Pericardiolysis
Pericardiotomy
DEF: Pericardial window operation: Incision into heart lining for drainage.
DEF: Pericardiolysis: Destruction of heart tissue lining.

√4ᵗʰ **37.2 Diagnostic procedures on heart and pericardium**

37.20 Non-invasive programmed electrical stimulation [NIPS]
EXCLUDES *catheter based invasive electro- physiologic testing (37.26)*
device interrogation only without arrhythmia induction (bedside check) (89.45-89.49)
that as part of intraoperative testing — omit code
DEF: Non-invasive testing of a previously implanted cardioverter-defibrillator to ensure proper lead placement and system function.
AHA: 4Q, '06, 128

37.21 Right heart cardiac catheterization
Cardiac catheterization NOS
EXCLUDES *that with catheterization of left heart (37.23)*
AHA: 3Q, '04, 10; 3Q, '03, 9; 2Q, '90, 23; M-J, '87, 11

37.22 Left heart cardiac catheterization
EXCLUDES *that with catheterization of right heart (37.23)*
AHA: 2Q, '10, 8-9; 4Q, '05, 71; 3Q, '05, 14; 3Q, '04, 10; 2Q, '04, 3; 1Q, '00, 21; 2Q, '90, 23; 4Q, '88, 4; M-J, '87, 11

37.23 Combined right and left heart cardiac catheterization
AHA: 1Q, '07, 11; 2Q, '05, 17; 3Q, '04, 10; 2Q, '01, 8; 1Q, '00, 20; 3Q, '98, 11; 2Q, '90, 23; M-J, '87, 11

37.24 Biopsy of pericardium

37.25 Biopsy of heart
AHA: 3Q, '03, 16; 3Q, '94, 8

37.26 Catheter based invasive electrophysiologic testing
Electrophysiologic studies [EPS]
Code also any concomitant procedure
EXCLUDES *device interrogation only without arrhythmia induction (bedside check) (89.45-89.49)*
His bundle recording (37.29)
non-invasive programmed electrical stimulation (NIPS) (37.20)
that as part of intraoperative testing — omit code
DEF: Diagnostic mapping and measurement of intracardiac electrical activity; requires inserting three to six catheters into heart blood vessels and positioning catheters under fluoroscopic guidance to determine site of the tachycardia or abnormal impulse pathway; may also be used to terminate arrhythmias.
AHA: 2Q, '11, 13; 3Q, '03, 23; 2Q, '03, 19; 1Q, '02, 8, 9; 1Q, '99, 3; 2Q, '97, 10; 3Q, '90, 11

Intracardiac Echocardiography

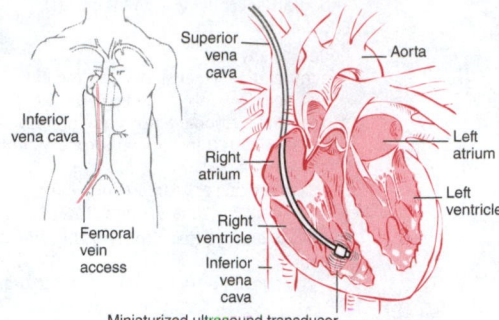

Miniaturized ultrasound transducer

37.27 Cardiac mapping
Code also any concomitant procedure
EXCLUDES *electrocardiogram (89.52)*
His bundle recording (37.29)
AHA: 2Q, '11, 13

37.28 Intracardiac echocardiography
Echocardiography of heart chambers
ICE
Code also any synchronous Doppler flow mapping (88.72)
EXCLUDES *intravascular imaging of coronary vessels (intravascular ultra-sound) (IVUS) (00.24)*
DEF: Creation of a two-dimensional graphic of heart using endoscopic echocardiographic equipment.
AHA: 4Q, '01, 62

37.29 Other diagnostic procedures on heart and pericardium
EXCLUDES *angiocardiography (88.50-88.58)*
cardiac function tests (89.41-89.69)
cardiovascular radioisotopic scan and function study (92.05)
coronary arteriography (88.55-88.57)
diagnostic pericardiocentesis (37.0)
diagnostic ultrasound of heart (88.72)
x-ray of heart (87.49)
AHA: S-O, '87, 3

√4ᵗʰ **37.3 Pericardiectomy and excision of lesion of heart**
Code also cardiopulmonary bypass [extracorporeal circulation] [heart-lung machine], if performed (39.61)

37.31 Pericardiectomy
Excision of:
adhesions of pericardium
constricting scar of:
epicardium
pericardium
DEF: Excision of a portion of heart lining.

37.32 Excision of aneurysm of heart
Repair of aneurysm of heart

37.33 Excision or destruction of other lesion or tissue of heart, open approach
Ablation or incision of heart tissue (cryoablation) (electrocurrent) (laser) (microwave) (radiofrequency) (resection) (ultrasound), open chest approach
Cox-maze procedure
Maze procedure
That by median sternotomy
That by thoracotomy without use of thoracoscope
EXCLUDES *ablation, excision or destruction of lesion or tissue of heart:*
endovascular approach (37.34)
thoracoscopic approach (37.37)
excision or destruction of left atrial appendage (LAA) (37.36)
AHA: 4Q, '10,118-119; 3Q, '10, 6; 3Q, '06, 13; 4Q, '03, 93-94; 2Q, '94, 12

BI Bilateral Procedure   NC Non-covered Procedure   LC Limited Coverage Procedure   ►◄ Revised Text   ● New Code   ▲ Revised Code Title

112 – Volume 3   **2015 ICD-9-CM**

37.34 Excision or destruction of other lesion or tissue of heart, endovascular approach

Ablation of heart tissue (cryoablation) (electrocurrent) (laser) (microwave) (radiofrequency) (ultrasound), via peripherally inserted catheter

Modified maze procedure, percutaneous approach

EXCLUDES *ablation, excision or destruction of lesion of tissue of heart:*
open approach (37.33)
thoracoscopic approach (37.37)

DEF: Destruction of heart tissue or lesion by freezing or electric current.

AHA: ▶3Q, '13, 10;◀ 2Q, '11, 13; 4Q, '10,118-119; 4Q, '03, 93-95; 1Q, '00, 20

TIP: If the ablation is performed via a right and left cardiac catheterization, report also code 37.23 and any associated procedures (e.g., angiography).

37.35 Partial ventriculectomy   NC

Ventricular reduction surgery
Ventricular remodeling

Code also any synchronous:
mitral valve repair (35.02, 35.12)
mitral valve replacement (35.23-35.24)

DEF: Removal of elliptical slice of ventricle between anterior and posterior papillary muscle; also called Batiste operation.

AHA: 4Q, '97, 54, 55

37.36 Excision, destruction, or exclusion of left atrial appendage [LAA]

INCLUDES thoracoscopic approach, minithoracotomy approach, percutaneous approach, endovascular approach, or subxiphoid approach

Clipping of left atrial appendage
Oversewing of left atrial appendage
Stapling of left atrial appendage
That by fastener or suture

Code also any:
concomitant (open) procedure performed
fluoroscopy (87.49)
transesophageal echocardiography (TEE) (88.72)

EXCLUDES *ablation, excision or destruction of lesion or tissue of heart, endovascular approach (37.34)*
excision or destruction of other lesion or tissue of heart, thoracoscopic approach (37.37)
insertion of left atrial appendage device (37.90)

DEF: Closure of LAA tissue via use of stapler, clip, or suture; performed for patients with atrial fibrillation for whom traditional anticoagulant therapies are contraindicated; prevents strokes and other embolic events.

AHA: 4Q, '08, 176

37.37 Excision or destruction of other lesion or tissue of heart, thoracoscopic approach

Ablation or incision of heart tissue (cryoablation) (electrocautery) (laser) (microwave) (radiofrequency) (resection) (ultrasound), via thoracoscope

Modified maze procedure, thoracoscopic approach

That via thoracoscopically-assisted approach (without thoracotomy) (with port access) (with subxiphoid incision)

EXCLUDES *ablation, excision or destruction of lesion or tissue of heart:*
endovascular approach (37.34)
open approach (37.33)
thoracoscopic excision or destruction of left atrial appendage [LAA] (37.36)

AHA: 1Q, '12, 14; 4Q, '10, 118-120

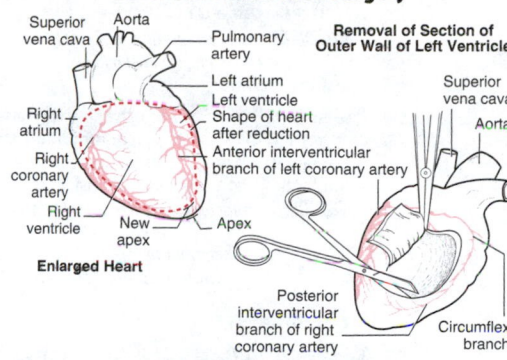

Ventricular Reduction Surgery

✓4th 37.4 Repair of heart and pericardium
AHA: 2Q, '90, 24

37.41 Implantation of prosthetic cardiac support device around the heart

Cardiac support device [CSD]
Epicardial support device
Fabric (textile) (mesh) device
Ventricular support device on surface of heart

Code also any:
cardiopulmonary bypass [extracorporeal circulation] [heart-lung machine] if performed (39.61)
mitral valve repair (35.02, 35.12)
mitral valve replacement (35.23-35.24)
transesophageal echocardiography (88.72)

EXCLUDES *circulatory assist systems (37.61-37.68)*

DEF: Cardiac support device: any device implanted around the ventricles of the heart for cardiac support.

DEF: Fabric (textile) (mesh) device: textile mesh net sutured around the heart for support.

AHA: 4Q, '05, 119-120

37.49 Other repair of heart and pericardium

AHA: 3Q, '08, 9

TIP: Assign for surgical ventricular restoration (SVR), performed to remodel or restore the left ventricle to a more normal size and shape in patients with akinetic parts of the heart.

✓4th 37.5 Heart replacement procedures
AHA: 4Q, '03, 96

37.51 Heart transplantation   LC

EXCLUDES *combined heart-lung transplantation (33.6)*

AHA: 4Q, '08, 182; 2Q, '05, 14

12 37.52 Implantation of total internal biventricular heart replacement system   LC

NOTE This procedure includes substantial removal of part or all of the biological heart. Both ventricles are resected, and the native heart is no longer intact. Ventriculectomy is included in this procedure; do not code separately.

Artificial heart

EXCLUDES *implantation of heart assist system [VAD] (37.62, 37.65, 37.66, 37.68)*

AHA: 4Q, '08, 181

Total Internal Biventricular Heart Replacement System

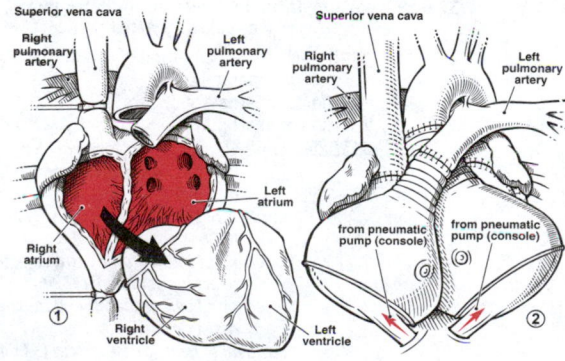

---

12 Limited coverage only when reported in combination with diagnosis code V70.7.

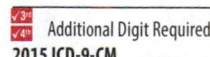

Additional Digit Required   Valid OR Procedure   Non-OR Procedure   Adjunct Code

2015 ICD-9-CM   **October 2014 • Volume 3 – 113**

37.53 Replacement or repair of thoracic unit of (total) replacement heart system NC

EXCLUDES replacement and repair of heart assist system [VAD] (37.63)

AHA: 4Q, '08, 181

37.54 Replacement or repair of other implantable component of (total) replacement heart system NC

Implantable battery   Transcutaneous energy
Implantable controller   transfer [TET] device

EXCLUDES replacement and repair of heart assist system [VAD] (37.63)
replacement or repair of thoracic unit of (total) replacement heart system (37.53)

AHA: 4Q, '08, 181

37.55 Removal of internal biventricular heart replacement system

Explantation of artificial heart

Code also any concomitant procedure, such as:
combined heart-lung transplantation (33.6)
heart transplantation (37.51)
implantation of internal biventricular heart replacement system (37.52)

EXCLUDES explantation [removal] of external heart assist system (37.64)
explantation [removal] of percutaneous external heart assist device (97.44)
nonoperative removal of heart assist system (97.44)
that with replacement or repair of heart replacement system (37.53, 37.54)

AHA: 4Q, '08, 180-182

√4th **37.6 Implantation of heart and circulatory assist system(s)**

EXCLUDES implantation of prosthetic cardiac support system (37.41)

DEF: Implant of device for assisting heart in circulating blood.
AHA: 4Q, '08, 177-179; 4Q, '95, 68

37.60 Implantation or insertion of biventricular external heart assist system

NOTE Device (outside the body but connected to heart) with external circulation pump. Ventriculotomy is included; do not code separately.

INCLUDES open chest (sternotomy) procedure for cannulae attachments

Temporary cardiac support for both left and right ventricles, inserted in the same operative episode

EXCLUDES implantation of internal biventricular heart replacement system (artificial heart) (37.52)
implant of pulsation balloon (37.61)
insertion of percutaneous external heart assist device (37.68)
insertion of temporary non-implantable extracorporeal circulatory assist device (37.62)

AHA: 4Q, '08, 179

37.61 Implant of pulsation balloon

AHA: 3Q, '05, 14

37.62 Insertion of temporary non-implantable extracorporeal circulatory assist device

NOTE Includes explantation of this device; do not code separately.
Insertion of heart assist system, NOS
Insertion of heart pump

EXCLUDES implantation of total internal biventricular heart replacement system [artificial heart] (37.52)
implant of external heart assist system (37.65)
insertion of implantable extracorporeal heart assist system (37.66)
insertion of percutaneous external heart assist device (37.68)
removal of heart assist system (37.64)

AHA: 4Q, '03, 116; 2Q, '90, 25

37.63 Repair of heart assist system

Replacement of parts of an existing ventricular assist device (VAD)

EXCLUDES replacement or repair of other implantable component of (total) replacement heart system [artificial heart] (37.54)
replacement or repair of thoracic unit of (total) replacement heart system [artificial heart] (37.53)

37.64 Removal of external heart assist system(s) or device(s)

Explantation of external device(s) providing left and right ventricular support
Explantation of single external device and cannulae

EXCLUDES explantation [removal] of percutaneous external heart assist device (97.44)
nonoperative removal of heart assist system (97.44)
temporary non-implantable extracorporeal circulatory assist device (37.62)
that with replacement of implant (37.63)

AHA: 4Q, '08, 177-178, 180

37.65 Implant of single ventricular (extracorporeal) external heart assist system

NOTE Device (outside the body but connected to heart) with external circulation and pump

NOTE Insertion or implantation of one external VAD for left or right heart support

INCLUDES open chest (sternotomy) procedure for cannulae attachments

Insertion of one device into one ventricle

EXCLUDES implantation of total internal biventricular heart replace- ment system (37.52)
implant of pulsation balloon (37.61)
insertion of implantable heart assist system (37.66)
insertion or implantation of two external VADs for simultaneous right and left heart support (37.60)
insertion of percutaneous external heart assist device (37.68)
that without sternotomy (37.62)

DEF: Insertion of short-term circulatory support device with pump outside body.

37.66 Insertion of implantable heart assist system LC

NOTE Device directly connected to the heart and implanted in the upper left quadrant of peritoneal cavity.This device can be used for either destination therapy (DT) or bridge-to-transplant (BTT).

Axial flow heart assist system
Diagonal pump heart assist system
Left ventricular assist device (LVAD)
Pulsatile heart assist system
Right ventricular assist device (RVAD)
Rotary pump heart assist system
Transportable, implantable heart assist system
Ventricular assist device (VAD) not otherwise specified

EXCLUDES implantation of total internal biventricular heart replacement system [artificial heart] (37.52)
implant of pulsation balloon (37.61)
insertion of percutaneous external heart assist device (37.68)

DEF: Insertion of long-term circulatory support device with pump in body.
AHA: 4Q, '03, 116; 1Q, '98, 8

37.67 Implantation of cardiomyostimulation system

NOTE Two-step open procedure consisting of tranfer of one end of the latissimus dorsi muscle; wrapping it around the heart; rib resection; implantation of epicardial cardiac pacing leads into the right ventricle; tunneling and pocket creation for the cardiomyostimulator.

AHA: 4Q, '98, 75; 1Q, '98, 8

BI Bilateral Procedure   NC Non-covered Procedure   LC Limited Coverage Procedure   ▶◀ Revised Text   ● New Code   ▲ Revised Code Title

114 – Volume 3   2015 ICD-9-CM

Ventricular Assist Devices

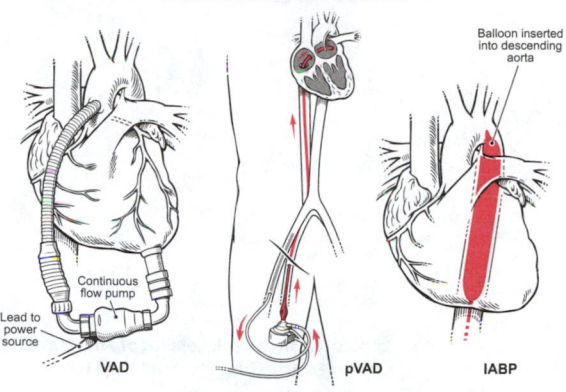

Balloon inserted into descending aorta

Continuous flow pump

Lead to power source

VAD   pVAD   IABP

37.68   Insertion of percutaneous external heart assist device

INCLUDES   percutaneous [femoral] insertion of cannulae attachments

Circulatory assist device
Extrinsic heart assist device
pVAD
Percutaneous heart assist device

AHA: 3Q, '09, 12; 2Q, '08, 12

TIP: Assign for placement of the Orqis device, an extracorporeal, minimally invasive cardiac system designed to increase blood velocity down the thoracic aorta; used for patients with CHF who respond poorly to medical treatment.

✓4ᵗʰ **37.7   Insertion, revision, replacement, and removal of leads; insertion of temporary pacemaker system; or revision of cardiac device pocket**

Code also any insertion and replacement of pacemaker device (37.80-37.87)

EXCLUDES   implantation or replacement of transvenous lead [electrode] into left ventricular cardiac venous system (00.52)

AHA: 1Q, '94, 16; 3Q, '92, 3; M-J, '87, 1

¹ **37.70   Initial insertion of lead [electrode], not otherwise specified**

EXCLUDES   insertion of temporary transvenous pacemaker system (37.78)
replacement of atrial and/or ventricular lead(s) (37.76)

¹ **37.71   Initial insertion of transvenous lead [electrode] into ventricle**

EXCLUDES   insertion of temporary transvenous pacemaker system (37.78)
replacement of atrial and/or ventricular lead(s) (37.76)

² **37.72   Initial insertion of transvenous leads [electrodes] into atrium and ventricle**

EXCLUDES   insertion of temporary transvenous pacemaker system (37.78)
replacement of atrial and/or ventricular lead(s) (37.76)

AHA: 4Q, '11, 168; 4Q, '08, 102; 2Q, '97, 4

¹ **37.73   Initial insertion of transvenous lead [electrode] into atrium**

EXCLUDES   insertion of temporary transvenous pacemaker system (37.78)
replacement of atrial and/or ventricular lead(s) (37.76)

⁴ **37.74   Insertion or replacement of epicardial lead [electrode] into epicardium**

Insertion or replacement of epicardial lead by:
sternotomy
thoracotomy

EXCLUDES   replacement of atrial and/or ventricular lead(s) (37.76)

AHA: 1Q, '07, 20; 3Q, '05, 3-9

37.75   Revision of lead [electrode]

Repair of electrode [removal with re-insertion]
Repositioning of lead(s) (AICD) (cardiac device) (CRT-D) (CRT-P) (defibrillator) (pacemaker) (pacing) (sensing) [electrode]
Revision of lead NOS

EXCLUDES   repositioning of temporary transvenous pacemaker system — omit code

AHA: 4Q, '12, 82, 88; 2Q, '12, 14; 3Q, '05, 8; 2Q, '99, 11

³ **37.76   Replacement of transvenous atrial and/or ventricular lead(s) [electrode]**

Removal or abandonment of existing transvenous or epicardial lead(s) with transvenous lead(s) replacement

EXCLUDES   replacement of epicardial lead [electrode] (37.74)

AHA: 3Q, '05, 3-9

37.77   Removal of lead(s) [electrode] without replacement

Removal:
epicardial lead (transthoracic approach)
transvenous lead(s)

EXCLUDES   removal of temporary transvenous pacemaker system — omit code
that with replacement of:
atrial and/or ventricular lead(s) [electrode] (37.76)
epicardial lead [electrode] (37.74)

37.78   Insertion of temporary transvenous pacemaker system

EXCLUDES   intraoperative cardiac pacemaker (39.64)

AHA: 3Q, '05, 7; 3Q, '93, 12; 1Q, '89, 2

37.79   Revision or relocation of cardiac device pocket

Debridement and reforming pocket (skin and subcutaneous tissue)
Insertion of loop recorder
Relocation of pocket [creation of new pocket] pacemaker or CRT-P
Removal of cardiac device/pulse generator without replacement
Removal of the implantable hemodynamic pressure sensor [lead] and monitor device
Removal without replacement of cardiac resynchronization defibrillator device
Repositioning of implantable hemodynamic pressure sensor [lead] and monitor device
Repositioning of pulse generator
Revision of cardioverter/defibrillator (automatic) pocket
Revision of pocket for intracardiac hemodynamic monitoring
Revision or relocation of CRT-D pocket
Revision or relocation of pacemaker, defibrillator, or other implanted cardiac device pocket

EXCLUDES   removal of loop recorder (86.05)

AHA: ▶2Q, '13, 18, 19;◀ 4Q, '12, 88; 3Q, '05, 3-9

✓4ᵗʰ **37.8   Insertion, replacement, removal, and revision of pacemaker device**

NOTE   Device testing during procedure — omit code

Code also any lead insertion, lead replacement, lead removal and/or lead revision (37.70-37.77)

EXCLUDES   implantation of cardiac resynchronization pacemaker, total system [CRT-P] (00.50)
implantation or replacement of cardiac resynchronization pacemaker pulse generator only [CRT-P] (00.53)

AHA: M-J, '87, 1

37.80   Insertion of permanent pacemaker, initial or replacement, type of device not specified

⁵ **37.81   Initial insertion of single-chamber device, not specified as rate responsive**

EXCLUDES   replacement of existing pacemaker device (37.85-37.87)

---

1 Valid OR procedure code if accompanied by one of the following codes: 37.80, 37.81, 37.82, 37.85, 37.86, 37.87
2 Valid OR procedure code if accompanied by one of the following codes: 37.80, 37.83
3 Valid OR procedure code if accompanied by one of the following codes: 37.80, 37.85, 37.86, 37.87
4 Valid OR procedure code if accompanied by one of the following codes: 37.80, 37.81, 37.82, 37.83, 37.85, 37.86, 37.87
5 Valid OR procedure code if accompanied by one of the following codes: 37.70, 37.71, 37.73, 37.74

✓3ʳᵈ
✓4ᵗʰ   Additional Digit Required   Valid OR Procedure   Non-OR Procedure   Adjunct Code

Insertion of Pacemaker

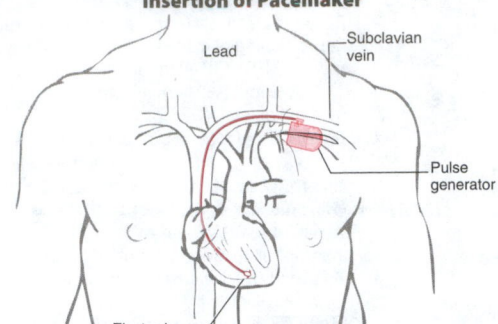

Lead
Subclavian vein
Pulse generator
Electrode

⁵ **37.82 Initial insertion of single-chamber device, rate responsive**

Rate responsive to physiologic stimuli other than atrial rate

EXCLUDES replacement of existing pacemaker device (37.85-37.87)

⁶ **37.83 Initial insertion of dual-chamber device**

Atrial ventricular sequential device

EXCLUDES replacement of existing pacemaker device (37.85-37.87)

AHA: 4Q, '11, 168; 4Q, '08, 102; 2Q, '97, 4

37.85 Replacement of any type pacemaker device with single-chamber device, not specified as rate responsive

37.86 Replacement of any type pacemaker device with single-chamber device, rate responsive

Rate responsive to physiologic stimuli other than atrial rate

37.87 Replacement of any type pacemaker device with dual-chamber device

Atrial ventricular sequential device

37.89 Revision or removal of pacemaker device

Removal without replacement of cardiac re-synchronization pacemaker device [CRT-P]
Repair of pacemaker device

EXCLUDES removal of temporary transvenous pacemaker system — omit code
replacement of existing pacemaker device (37.85-37.87)
replacement of existing pacemaker device with CRT-P pacemaker device (00.53)

AHA: N-D, '86, 1

✓4ᵗʰ **37.9 Other operations on heart and pericardium**

AHA: 3Q, '90, 11

37.90 Insertion of left atrial appendage device

Left atrial filter
Left atrial occluder
Transseptal catheter technique

DEF: Implantation of a filtering device within the left atrial appendage (LAA) to block emboli from exiting the LAA causing stroke or systemic thromboembolism.
AHA: 4Q, '04, 121

37.91 Open chest cardiac massage

EXCLUDES closed chest cardiac massage (99.63)
DEF: Massage of heart through opening in chest wall to reinstate or maintain circulation.
AHA: 4Q, '88, 12

37.92 Injection of therapeutic substance into heart

37.93 Injection of therapeutic substance into pericardium

Left Atrial Appendage Device Insertion

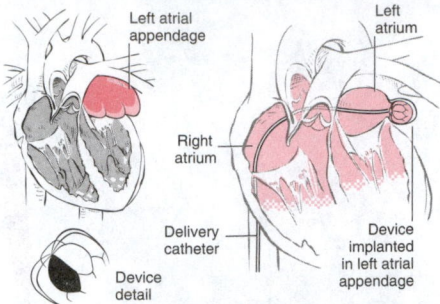

Left atrial appendage
Left atrium
Right atrium
Delivery catheter
Device implanted in left atrial appendage
Device detail

37.94 Implantation or replacement of automatic cardioverter/defibrillator, total system [AICD]

NOTE Device testing during procedure — omit code

Implantation of defibrillator with leads (epicardial patches), formation of pocket (abdominal fascia) (subcutaneous), any transvenous leads, intra-operative procedures for evaluation of lead signals, and obtaining defibrillator threshold measurements

Techniques:
lateral thoracotomy
medial sternotomy
subxiphoid procedure

Code also extracorporeal circulation, if performed (39.61)

Code also any concomitant procedure [e.g., coronary bypass (36.10-36.19) or CCM, total system (17.51)]

EXCLUDES implantation of cardiac resynchronization defibrillator, total system [CRT-D] (00.51)

DEF: Direct insertion of defibrillator/cardioverter system to deliver shock and restore heart rhythm.
AHA: ▶1Q, '13, 10;◀ 4Q, '12, 88; 4Q, '09, 141; 2Q, '03, 19; 3Q, '01, 5-7; 3Q, '99, 12; 1Q, '99, 3; 3Q, '90, 11; S-O, '87, 5
TIP: Assign for AICD placement, regardless of approach, whether by thoracotomy or by cephalic vein cutdown.

37.95 Implantation of automatic cardioverter/defibrillator lead(s) only

AHA: 4Q, '12, 88; 3Q, '90, 11

37.96 Implantation of automatic cardioverter/defibrillator pulse generator only

NOTE Device testing during procedure — omit code
EXCLUDES implantation or replacement of cardiac resynchronization defibrillator, pulse generator device only [CRT-D] (00.54)

AHA: 4Q, '12, 88; 3Q, '90, 11

37.97 Replacement of automatic cardioverter/defibrillator lead(s) only

EXCLUDES replacement of epicardial lead [electrode] into epicardium (37.74)
replacement of transvenous lead [electrode] into left ventricular coronary venous system (00.52)

AHA: 4Q, '12, 88; 3Q, '05, 3-9; 3Q, '90, 11

Automatic Implantable Cardioverter/Defibrillator

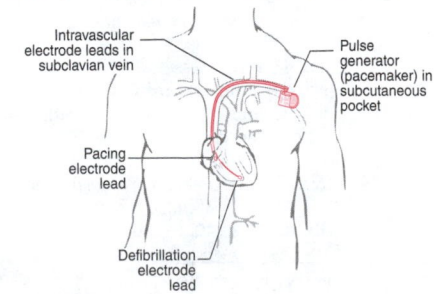

Intravascular electrode leads in subclavian vein
Pulse generator (pacemaker) in subcutaneous pocket
Pacing electrode lead
Defibrillation electrode lead

---

⁵ Valid OR procedure code if accompanied by one of the following codes: 37.70, 37.71, 37.73, 37.74
⁶ Valid OR procedure code if accompanied by one of the following codes: 37.72, 37.74

BI Bilateral Procedure   **NC** Non-covered Procedure   **LC** Limited Coverage Procedure   ▶◀ Revised Text   ● New Code   ▲ Revised Code Title

37.98 Replacement of automatic cardioverter defibrillator pulse generator only

> **NOTE** Device testing during procedure — *omit code*
> **EXCLUDES** *replacement of cardiac resynchronization defibrillator, pulse generator device only [CRT-D] (00.54)*
> **AHA:** 4Q, '12, 88; 1Q, '99, 3; 3Q, '90, 11

37.99 Other

> **EXCLUDES** *cardiac retraining (93.36)*
> *conversion of cardiac rhythm (99.60-99.69)*
> *implantation of prosthetic cardiac support device (37.41)*
> *insertion of left atrial appendage device (37.90)*
> *maze procedure (Cox-maze), open (37.33)*
> *maze procedure, endovascular approach (37.34)*
> *repositioning of pulse generator (37.79)*
> *revision of lead(s) (37.75)*
> *revision or relocation of pacemaker, defibrillator or other implanted cardiac device pocket (37.79)*
> **AHA:** 3Q, '05, 5; 2Q, '05, 14; 1Q, '97, 12; 1Q, '94, 19; 3Q, '90, 11; 1Q, '89, 11

√3ʳᵈ 38 Incision, excision, and occlusion of vessels

Code also any application or administration of an adhesion barrier substance (99.77)
Code also cardiopulmonary bypass [extracorporeal circulation] [heart-lung machine] (39.61)

> **EXCLUDES** *that of coronary vessels (00.66, 36.03, 36.04, 36.09, 36.10-36.99)*

The following fourth-digit subclassification is for use with appropriate categories in section 38.0, 38.1, 38.3, 38.5, 38.6, and 38.8 according to site. Valid fourth-digits are in [brackets] under each code.
  0 unspecified
  1 intracranial vessels
     Cerebral (anterior) (middle)
     Circle of Willis
     Posterior communicating artery
  2 other vessels of head and neck
     Carotid artery (common) (external) (internal)
     Jugular vein (external) (internal)
  3 upper limb vessels
     Axillary   Radial
     Brachial   Ulnar
  4 aorta
  5 other thoracic vessels
     Innominate   Subclavian
     Pulmonary (artery) (vein)   Vena cava, superior
  6 abdominal arteries
     Celiac   Mesenteric
     Gastric   Renal
     Hepatic   Splenic
     Iliac   Umbilical
       EXCLUDES *abdominal aorta (4)*
  7 abdominal veins
     Iliac   Splenic
     Portal   Vena cava (inferior)
     Renal
  8 lower limb arteries
     Femoral (common)   Popliteal
       (superficial)   Tibial
  9 lower limb veins
     Femoral   Saphenous
     Popliteal   Tibial

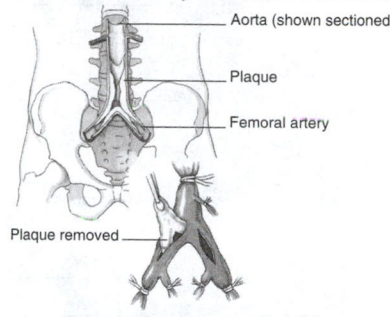

Endarterectomy of Aortic Bifurcation

Aorta (shown sectioned)
Plaque
Femoral artery
Plaque removed

§ √4ᵗʰ 38.0 Incision of vessel
[0-9]   Embolectomy   Thrombectomy
> **EXCLUDES** *endovascular removal of obstruction from head and neck vessel(s) (39.74)*
> *puncture or catheterization of any:*
>   *artery (38.91, 38.98)*
>   *vein (38.92-38.95, 38.99)*
> **AHA:** 2Q, '98, 23; **For code 38.04:** 4Q, '11, 108; **For code 38.08 and 38.09:** 1Q, '03, 17

§ √4ᵗʰ 38.1 Endarterectomy
[0-6,8]   Endarterectomy with:
             embolectomy
             patch graft
             temporary bypass during procedure
             thrombectomy
Code also any:
   number of vascular stents inserted (00.45-00.48)
   number of vessels treated (00.40-00.43)
   procedure on vessel bifurcation (00.44)
> **DEF:** Excision of tunica intima of artery to relieve arterial walls thickened by plaque or chronic inflammation.
> **AHA:** 1Q, '00, 16; 2Q, '99, 5; 2Q, '95, 16; **For code 38.12:** 3Q, '06, 20; 1Q, '02, 10

√4ᵗʰ 38.2 Diagnostic procedures on blood vessels
> **EXCLUDES** *adjunct vascular system procedures (00.40-00.43)*

38.21 Biopsy of blood vessel

38.22 Percutaneous angioscopy
> **EXCLUDES** *angioscopy of eye (95.12)*
> **DEF:** Exam with fiberoptic catheter inserted through peripheral artery to visualize inner lining of blood vessels.

38.23 Intravascular spectroscopy
> **INCLUDES** spectroscopy of both coronary and peripheral vessels
> Intravascular chemography
> Near infrared (NIR) spectroscopy
> **EXCLUDES** *intravascular imaging of:*
>   *coronary vessels (00.24, 38.24)*
>   *peripheral vessels (00.23, 38.25)*
> **DEF:** Method of identifying the chemical composition of coronary plaques by shining a near infrared (NIR) light at the plaque and measuring the amount of light reflected at different wavelengths.
> **AHA:** 4Q, '08, 182-183

38.24 Intravascular imaging of coronary vessel(s) by optical coherence tomography [OCT]
> **DEF:** Use of fiberoptic catheter probes that employ near-infrared electromagnetic radiation light to produce cross-sectional and enhanced resolution images of vessel plaque and intraluminal thrombus.
> **AHA:** 1Q, '10, 16-17

38.25 Intravascular imaging of non-coronary vessel(s) by optical coherence tomography [OCT]
> **EXCLUDES** *intravascular imaging of coronary vessel(s) by OCT (38.24)*
> **DEF:** Use of fiberoptic catheter probes that employ near-infrared electromagnetic radiation light to produce cross-sectional and enhanced resolution images of vessel plaque and intraluminal thrombus.
> **AHA:** 1Q, '10, 16-17

§ Requires fourth digit. Valid digits are in [brackets] under each code. See category 38 for definitions.

√3ʳᵈ
√4ᵗʰ Additional Digit Required   Valid OR Procedure   Non-OR Procedure   Adjunct Code
2015 ICD-9-CM   **Volume 3 – 117**

Operations on the Cardiovascular System

38.26–38.6

Methods of Vessel Anastomoses

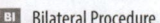

End-to-end

Side-to-side

Oblique cut

Fish mouth

Funnelization

End-to-side

38.26 Insertion of implantable pressure sensor without lead for intracardiac or great vessel hemodynamic monitoring

> **NOTE** The sensor is a standalone device and is not physically connected to a separately implanted monitor.

Leadless pressure sensor not physically connected to a separately implanted monitor

Single device combination leadless pressure sensor with integral monitor for intracardiac or great vessel (or branch thereof) hemodynamic monitoring

With or without internal batteries

Without leads

> **EXCLUDES** circulatory monitoring (blood gas, arterial or venous pressure, cardiac output and coronary blood flow (89.60-89.69)
> hemodynamic monitoring system with sensor and separately implanted monitor (00.56-00.57)
> insertion or replacement of implantable pressure sensor with lead for intracardiac or great vessel hemodynamic monitoring (00.56)

AHA: 4Q, '11, 175-176

38.29 Other diagnostic procedures on blood vessels

> **EXCLUDES** blood vessel thermography (88.86)
> circulatory monitoring (89.61-89.69)
> contrast:
>   angiocardiography (88.50-88.58)
>   arteriography (88.40-88.49)
>   phlebography (88.60-88.67)
> impedance phlebography (88.68)
> peripheral vascular ultrasonography (88.77)
> plethysmogram (89.58)

AHA: 3Q, '00, 16; 1Q, '99, 7

TIP: Assign for an artery test occlusion, performed to determine the feasibility of coil occlusion of an aneurysm.

§§ ✓4ᵗʰ **38.3 Resection of vessel with anastomosis**

[0-9]   Angiectomy

Excision of:
aneurysm (arteriovenous)
blood vessel (lesion) } with anastomosis

DEF: Reconstruction and reconnection of vessel after partial excision.

§ ✓4ᵗʰ **38.4 Resection of vessel with replacement**

[0-9]   Angiectomy

Excision of:
aneurysm (arteriovenous) or
blood vessel (lesion) } with replacement

Partial resection with replacement

> **EXCLUDES** endovascular repair of aneurysm (39.71-39.79)

Subcategory 38.4 requires the use of one of the following fourth-digit subclassifications to identify site:

0 unspecified

1 intracranial vessels
Cerebral (anterior) (middle)
Circle of Willis
Posterior communicating artery

2 other vessels of head and neck
Carotid artery (common) (external) (internal)
Jugular vein (external) (internal)

3 upper limb vessels
Axillary   Radial
Brachial   Ulnar

4 aorta, abdominal
Code also any thoracic vessel involvement (thoracoabdominal procedure) (38.45)

5 other thoracic vessels
Aorta (thoracic)   Subclavian
Innominate   Vena cava, superior
Pulmonary (artery) (vein)
Code also any abdominal aorta involvement (thoracoabdominal procedure) (38.44)

6 abdominal arteries
Celiac   Mesenteric
Gastric   Renal
Hepatic   Splenic
Iliac   Umbilical
> **EXCLUDES** abdominal aorta (4)

7 abdominal veins
Iliac   Splenic
Portal   Vena cava (inferior)
Renal

8 lower limb arteries
Femoral (common)(superficial)
Tibial

9 lower limb veins
Femoral   Saphenous
Popliteal   Tibial

DEF: Excision of aneurysm (arteriovenous): Excision and replacement of segment of stretched or bulging blood vessel.
DEF: Excision of blood vessel (lesion): Excision and replacement of segment of vessel containing lesion.
AHA: 2Q, '99, 5, 6; For code 38.44: 3Q, '06, 15; For code 38.45: ▶4Q, '13, 102;◀ 2Q, '08, 13; For code 38.48: 2Q, '08, 13

§§ ✓4ᵗʰ **38.5 Ligation and stripping of varicose veins**

[0-3,5,7,9] **EXCLUDES** ligation of varices:
   esophageal (42.91)
   gastric (44.91)

DEF: Ligation of varicose veins: Typing off vein with thread or wire to eliminate blood flow; stripping involves excising length of vein.
AHA: For code 38.59: 2Q, '97, 7
TIP: Do not assign a separate code for subfascial endoscopic perforator vein interruption, which is an integral part of the procedure.

§§ ✓4ᵗʰ **38.6 Other excision of vessels**

[0-9]   Excision of blood vessel (lesion) NOS
> **EXCLUDES** excision of vessel for aortocoronary bypass (36.10-36.14)
> excision with:
>   anastomosis (38.30-38.39)
>   graft replacement (38.40-38.49)
>   implant (38.40-38.49)

AHA: 3Q, '90, 17

§   Requires fourth digit. Valid digits are in [brackets] under each code. See subcategory 38.4 for definitions.
§§   Requires fourth digit. Valid digits are in [brackets] under each code. See category 38 for definitions.

BI Bilateral Procedure   **NC** Non-covered Procedure   **LC** Limited Coverage Procedure   ▶◀ Revised Text   ● New Code   ▲ Revised Code Title

118 – Volume 3 • October 2014   **2015 ICD-9-CM**

38.7   Interruption of the vena cava
　　Insertion of implant or sieve in vena cava
　　Ligation of vena cava (inferior) (superior)
　　Plication of vena cava
　　　DEF: Interruption of the blood flow through the venous heart vessels
　　　to prevent clots from reaching the chambers of the heart by means
　　　of implanting a sieve or implant, separating off a portion or by
　　　narrowing the venous blood vessels.
　　　AHA: 2Q, '07, 4; 2Q, '94, 9; S-O, '85, 5
　　　TIP: Assign this code for placement of a vena cava sieve, umbrella, or
　　　filter, regardless of the approach (open or percutaneous).

§§ √4th **38.8   Other surgical occlusion of vessels**
[0-9]
　　Clamping ⎫
　　Division ⎬ of blood vessel
　　Ligation ⎪
　　Occlusion ⎭
　　　EXCLUDES adrenal vessels (07.43)
　　　　esophageal varices (42.91)
　　　　gastric or duodenal vessel for ulcer (44.40-44.49)
　　　　gastric varices (44.91)
　　　　meningeal vessel (02.13)
　　　　percutaneous transcatheter infusion
　　　　　embolization (99.29)
　　　　spermatic vein for varicocele (63.1)
　　　　surgical occlusion of vena cava (38.7)
　　　　that for chemoembolization (99.25)
　　　　that for control of (postoperative) hemorrhage:
　　　　　anus (49.95)
　　　　　bladder (57.93)
　　　　　following vascular procedure (39.41)
　　　　　nose (21.00-21.09)
　　　　　prostate (60.94)
　　　　　tonsil (28.7)
　　　　　thyroid vessel (06.92)
　　　　transcatheter (infusion) 99.29
　　　AHA: 2Q, '90, 23; M-A, '87, 9; **For code 38.85:** 1Q, '03, 15; **For code 38.86:**
　　　1Q, '05, 14; N-D, '87, 4; **For code 38.89:** ▶1Q, '14, 6◀

√4th **38.9   Puncture of vessel**
　　　EXCLUDES that for circulatory monitoring (89.60-89.69)

　　38.91   Arterial catheterization
　　　AHA: ▶1Q, '13, 4;◀ 1Q, '05, 14; 1Q, '97, 3; 1Q, '95, 3; 2Q, '91,
　　　15; 2Q, '90, 23

　　38.92   Umbilical vein catheterization

　　38.93   Venous catheterization, not elsewhere classified
　　　EXCLUDES that for cardiac catheterization
　　　　　(37.21-37.23)
　　　　that for renal dialysis (38.95)
　　　　that with guidance (electrocardiogram)
　　　　　(fluoroscopy) (ultrasound) (38.97)
　　　AHA: 3Q, '10, 14; 3Q, '00, 9; 2Q, '98, 24; 1Q, '96, 3; 2Q, '96, 15;
　　　3Q, '91, 13; 4Q, '90, 14; 2Q, '90, 24; 3Q, '88, 13

　　38.94   Venous cutdown
　　　DEF: Incision of vein to place needle or catheter.

　　38.95   Venous catheterization for renal dialysis
　　　EXCLUDES insertion of totally implantable vascular
　　　　　access device [VAD] (86.07)
　　　AHA: 3Q, '12, 6; 4Q, '08, 193; 3Q, '98, 13; 2Q, '94, 11
　　　TIP: Do not assign for intravascular vessel-to-vessel cannula
　　　to create an external shunt; see instead code 39.93.
　　　TIP: Assign a separate subcategory 88.7 code for guidance
　　　by ultrasound.

　　38.97   Central venous catheter placement with guidance
　　　INCLUDES guidance by:
　　　　　electrocardiogram
　　　　　fluoroscopy
　　　　　ultrasound

　　38.98   Other puncture of artery
　　　EXCLUDES that for:
　　　　　arteriography (88.40-88.49)
　　　　　coronary arteriography (88.55-88.57)

Typical Venous Cutdown

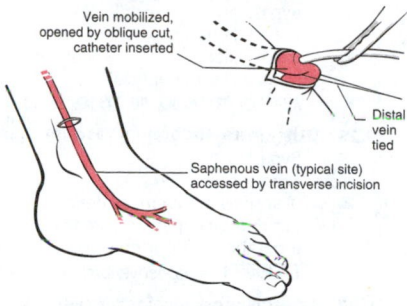

Vein mobilized, opened by oblique cut, catheter inserted
Distal vein tied
Saphenous vein (typical site) accessed by transverse incision

　　38.99   Other puncture of vein
　　　Phlebotomy
　　　EXCLUDES that for:
　　　　　angiography of veins (88.60-88.68)
　　　　　extracorporeal circulation (39.61, 50.92)
　　　　　injection or infusion of:
　　　　　sclerosing solution (39.92)
　　　　　therapeutic or prophylactic substance
　　　　　　(99.11-99.29)
　　　　　perfusion (39.96, 39.97)
　　　　　phlebography 88.60-88.68)
　　　　　transfusion (99.01-99.09)
　　　AHA: 4Q, '94, 50; 1Q, '88, 11

√3rd **39   Other operations on vessels**
　　　EXCLUDES those on coronary vessels (36.03-36.99)

　　39.0   Systemic to pulmonary artery shunt
　　　Descending aorta-pulmonary artery ⎫
　　　Left to right ⎬ anastomosis (graft)
　　　Subclavian-pulmonary ⎭
　　　Code also cardiopulmonary bypass [extracorporeal
　　　　circulation] [heart-lung machine] (39.61)
　　　DEF: Descending aorta-pulmonary artery anastomosis (graft):
　　　Connection of descending main heart artery to pulmonary artery.
　　　DEF: Left to right anastomosis (graft): Connection of systemic arterial
　　　blood vessel to venous pulmonary system.
　　　DEF: Subclavian-pulmonary anastomosis (graft): Connection of
　　　subclavian artery to pulmonary artery

　　39.1   Intra-abdominal venous shunt
　　　Anastomosis:
　　　　mesocaval
　　　　portacaval
　　　　portal vein to inferior vena cava
　　　　splenic and renal veins
　　　　transjugular intrahepatic portosystemic shunt [TIPS]
　　　EXCLUDES peritoneovenous shunt (54.94)
　　　DEF: Connection of two venous blood vessels within abdominal
　　　cavity.
　　　AHA: 2Q, '02, 4; 4Q, '94, 50; 4Q, '93, 31; 2Q, '93, 8

√4th **39.2   Other shunt or vascular bypass**
　　　Code also pressurized treatment of venous bypass graft
　　　　[conduit] with pharmaceutical substance,
　　　　if performed (00.16)
　　　DEF: Creation of supplemental blood flow to area with inadequate
　　　blood supply due to disease or injury of vessels.
　　　TIP: Assign separate codes for any concomitant procedures per-
　　　formed, such as arterial or venous thrombectomy or arteriography.

　　39.21   Caval-pulmonary artery anastomosis
　　　Code also cardiopulmonary bypass (39.61)

　　39.22   Aorta-subclavian-carotid bypass
　　　Bypass (arterial):
　　　　aorta to carotid and brachial
　　　　aorta to subclavian and carotid
　　　　carotid to subclavian

　　39.23   Other intrathoracic vascular shunt or bypass
　　　Intrathoracic (arterial) bypass graft NOS
　　　EXCLUDES coronary artery bypass (36.10-36.19)

　　39.24   Aorta-renal bypass

---

§§ Requires fourth digit. Valid digits are in [brackets] under each code. See category 38 for definitions.

√3rd
√4th
Additional Digit Required   Valid OR Procedure   Non-OR Procedure   Adjunct Code

Operations on the Cardiovascular System

39.25–39.52

39.25 Aorta-iliac-femoral bypass

Bypass: Bypass:
aortofemoral   aortopopliteal
aortoiliac   iliofemoral [iliac-femoral]
aortoiliac to popliteal
AHA: 1Q, '03, 16; 4Q, '90, 27; 1Q, '88, 10

39.26 Other intra-abdominal vascular shunt or bypass

Bypass:
aortoceliac
aortic-superior mesenteric
common hepatic-common iliac-renal
Intra-abdominal arterial bypass graft NOS
EXCLUDES   *peritoneovenous shunt (54.94)*

39.27 Arteriovenostomy for renal dialysis

Anastomosis for renal dialysis
Formation of (peripheral) arteriovenous fistula for renal [kidney] dialysis

Code also any renal dialysis (39.95)
AHA: 1Q, '07, 18; 1Q, '06, 10
TIP: Assign for creation of an internal shunt by arteriovenostomy for renal dialysis; includes transposition of the basilic vein.

39.28 Extracranial-intracranial (EC-IC) vascular bypass

AHA: 2Q, '92, 7; 4Q, '91, 22

39.29 Other (peripheral) vascular shunt or bypass

Bypass (graft):
axillary-brachial
axillary-femoral [axillofemoral] (superficial)
brachial
femoral-femoral
femoroperoneal
femoropopliteal (arteries)
femorotibial (anterior) (posterior)
popliteal
vascular NOS
EXCLUDES   *peritoneovenous shunt (54.94)*
AHA: 1Q, '03, 17; 2Q, '02, 8; 1Q, '02, 13; S-O, '85, 13

✓4th 39.3 Suture of vessel

Repair of laceration of blood vessel
EXCLUDES   *any other vascular puncture closure device — omit code*
suture of aneurysm (39.52)
that for control of hemorrhage (postoperative):
anus (49.95)
bladder (57.93)
following vascular procedure (39.41)
nose (21.00-21.09)
prostate (60.94)
tonsil (28.7)

39.30 Suture of unspecified blood vessel

39.31 Suture of artery

AHA: 4Q, '12, 81; 3Q, '06, 9

39.32 Suture of vein

✓4th 39.4 Revision of vascular procedure

39.41 Control of hemorrhage following vascular surgery

EXCLUDES   *that for control of hemorrhage (postoperative):*
anus (49.95)
bladder (57.93)
nose (21.00-21.09)
prostate (60.94)
tonsil (28.7)

39.42 Revision of arteriovenous shunt for renal dialysis

Conversion of renal dialysis:
end-to-end anastomosis to end-to-side
end-to-side anastomosis to end-to-end
vessel-to-vessel cannula to arteriovenous shunt
Removal of old arteriovenous shunt and creation of new shunt
EXCLUDES   *replacement of vessel-to-vessel cannula (39.94)*
AHA: 2Q, '94, 15; 4Q, '93, 33

39.43 Removal of arteriovenous shunt for renal dialysis

EXCLUDES   *that with replacement [revision] of shunt (39.42)*

39.49 Other revision of vascular procedure

Declotting (graft)
Revision of:
anastomosis of blood vessel
vascular procedure (previous)
DEF: Declotting (graft): Removal of clot from graft.
AHA: 2Q, '98, 17; 1Q, '97, 3; 2Q, '94, 15
TIP: Do not assign if a declotting procedure of an AV dialysis graft is performed as a component of a revision procedure; see instead code 39.42.

✓4th 39.5 Other repair of vessels

39.50 Angioplasty of other non-coronary vessel(s)

Percutaneous transluminal angioplasty (PTA) of non-coronary vessels:
lower extremity vessels
mesenteric artery
renal artery
upper extremity vessels

Code also any:
atherectomy of other non-coronary vessels(s) (17.56)
injection or infusion of thrombolytic agent (99.10)
insertion of drug-eluting peripheral vessel stent (00.55)
insertion of non-drug-eluting peripheral vessel stent(s) or stent grafts(s) (39.90)
number of vascular stents inserted (00.45-00.48)
number of vessels treated (00.40-00.43)
procedure on vessel bifurcation (00.44)
EXCLUDES   *percutaneous angioplasty of extracranial or intracranial vessel(s) (00.61-00.62)*
percutaneous atherectomy of extracranial or intracranial vessel(s) (17.53-17.54)
AHA: 3Q, '12, 13; 2Q, '12, 15; 3Q, '09, 13; 4Q, '06, 119; 3Q, '03, 10; 1Q, '02, 13; 2Q, '01, 23; 2Q, '00, 10; 1Q, '00, 12; 2Q, '98, 17; 1Q, '97, 3; 4Q, '96, 63; 4Q, '95, 66

39.51 Clipping of aneurysm

EXCLUDES   *clipping of arteriovenous fistula (39.53)*

39.52 Other repair of aneurysm

Repair of aneurysm by: Repair of aneurysm by:
coagulation   suture
electrocoagulation   wiring
filipuncture   wrapping
methyl methacrylate
EXCLUDES   *endovascular repair of aneurysm (39.71-39.79)*
re-entry operation (aorta) (39.54)
that with:
graft replacement (38.40-38.49)
resection (38.30-38.49, 38.60-38.69)
DEF: Application of device to repair abnormally stretched blood vessel and prevent a hemorrhage from vessel.
DEF: Repair of aneurysm by: Coagulation: Clotting or solidifying. Electrocoagulation: Electrically produced clotting. Filipuncture: Insertion of wire or thread. Methyl methacrylate: Injection or insertion of plastic material. Suture: Stitching. Wiring: Insertion of wire. Wrapping: Compression.
AHA: 3Q, '06, 15-16; 3Q, '02, 25, 26; 1Q, '99, 15, 16, 17; 1Q, '88, 10
TIP: Do not assign if any type of grafting material was used in the aneurysm repair; see instead subcategory 38.4 or endovascular repair subcategory 39.7.

BI Bilateral Procedure   NC Non-covered Procedure   LC Limited Coverage Procedure   ►◄ Revised Text   ● New Code   ▲ Revised Code Title

120 – Volume 3   **2015 ICD-9-CM**

39.53 **Repair of arteriovenous fistula**
Embolization of carotid cavernous fistula
Repair of arteriovenous fistula by:
  clipping
  coagulation
  ligation and division
  EXCLUDES *repair of:*
    arteriovenous shunt for renal dialysis
      (39.42)
    head and neck vessels, endovascular
      approach (39.72)
    that with:
      graft replacement (38.40-38.49)
      resection (38.30-38.49, 38.60-38.69)
DEF: Correction of arteriovenous fistula by application of clamps, causing coagulation or by tying off and dividing the connection.
AHA: 1Q, '00, 8
TIP: Do not assign for an embolization procedure performed by interventional radiologists via radiological guidance; it is not considered a surgical procedure; see instead code 99.29.

39.54 **Re-entry operation (aorta)**
Fenestration of dissecting aneurysm of thoracic aorta
Code also cardiopulmonary bypass [extracorporeal circulation] [heart-lung machine] (39.61)
DEF: Re-entry operation: Creation of passage between stretched wall of the vessel and major arterial channel to heart.
DEF: Fenestration of dissecting aneurysm of thoracic aorta: Creation of passage between stretched arterial heart vessel and functional part of vessel.

39.55 **Reimplantation of aberrant renal vessel**
DEF: Reimplant of renal vessel into normal position.

39.56 **Repair of blood vessel with tissue patch graft**
EXCLUDES *that with resection (38.40-38.49)*
AHA: ▶1Q, '14, 15;◄ 1Q, '04, 16

39.57 **Repair of blood vessel with synthetic patch graft**
EXCLUDES *that with resection (38.40-38.49)*

39.58 **Repair of blood vessel with unspecified type of patch graft**
EXCLUDES *that with resection (38.40-38.49)*

39.59 **Other repair of vessel**
Aorticopulmonary window operation
Arterioplasty NOS
Construction of venous valves (peripheral)
Plication of vein (peripheral)
Reimplantation of artery
Code also cardiopulmonary bypass [extracorporeal circulation] [heart-lung machine] (39.61)
EXCLUDES *interruption of the vena cava (38.7)*
    reimplantation of renal artery (39.55)
    that with:
      graft (39.56-39.58)
      resection (38.30-38.49, 38.60-38.69)
DEF: Aorticopulmonary window operation: Repair of abnormal opening between major heart arterial vessel above valves and pulmonary artery.
DEF: Construction of venous valves (peripheral): Reconstruction of valves within peripheral veins.
DEF: Plication of vein (peripheral): Shortening of peripheral vein.
DEF: Reimplantation of artery: Reinsertion of artery into its normal position.
AHA: 4Q, '93, 31; 2Q, '89, 17; N-D, '86, 8; S-O, '85, 5; M-A, '85, 15

39.6 **Extracorporeal circulation and procedures auxiliary to heart surgery**
AHA: 1Q, '95, 5

39.61 **Extracorporeal circulation auxiliary to open heart surgery**
Artificial heart and lung   Pump oxygenator
Cardiopulmonary bypass
EXCLUDES *extracorporeal hepatic assistance (50.92)*
    extracorporeal membrane oxygenation
      [ECMO] (39.65)
    hemodialysis (39.95)
    percutaneous cardiopulmonary bypass
      (39.66)
AHA: ▶4Q, '13, 102;◄ 3Q, '10, 6; 1Q, '10, 14; 2Q, '09, 8; 3Q, '08, 9; 2Q, '08, 13; 1Q, '04, 16; 3Q, '02, 5; 4Q, '97, 55; 3Q, '97, 14; 2Q, '97, 8; 2Q, '90, 24

39.62 **Hypothermia (systemic) incidental to open heart surgery**

39.63 **Cardioplegia**
Arrest:
  anoxic
  circulatory
DEF: Purposely inducing electromechanical cardiac arrest.

39.64 **Intraoperative cardiac pacemaker**
Temporary pacemaker used during and immediately following cardiac surgery
AHA: 1Q, '89, 2; M-J, '87, 3

39.65 **Extracorporeal membrane oxygenation [ECMO]**
EXCLUDES *extracorporeal circulation auxiliary to open*
      heart surgery (39.61)
    percutaneous cardiopulmonary bypass
      (39.66)
DEF: Creation of closed-chest, heart-lung bypass or Bard cardiopulmonary assist system with tube insertion.
AHA: 4Q, '11, 152; 2Q, '90, 23; 2Q, '89, 17; 4Q, '88, 5

39.66 **Percutaneous cardiopulmonary bypass**
Closed chest
EXCLUDES *extracorporeal circulation auxiliary to open*
      heart surgery (39.61)
    extracorporeal hepatic assistance (50.92)
    extracorporeal membrane oxygenation
      [ECMO] (39.65)
    hemodialysis (39.95)
DEF: Use of mechanical pump system to oxygenate and pump blood throughout the body via catheter in the femoral artery and vein.
AHA: 3Q, '96, 11

39.7 **Endovascular procedures on vessel(s)**
Embolization   Occlusion
Endoluminal repair   Removal
Implantation   Repair
EXCLUDES *angioplasty of other non-coronary vessel(s) (39.50)*
    atherectomy of other non-coronary vessel(s) (17.56)
    insertion of non-drug-eluting peripheral vessel
      stent(s) (39.90)
    other repair of aneurysm (39.52)
    percutaneous insertion of carotid artery stent(s)
      (00.63)
    percutaneous insertion of intracranial stent(s)
      (00.65)
    percutaneous insertion of other precerebral artery
      stent(s) (00.64)
    resection of abdominal aorta with replacement
      (38.44)
    resection of lower limb arteries with replacement
      (38.48)
    resection of thoracic aorta with replacement (38.45)
    resection of upper limb vessels with replacement
      (38.43)
    temporary therapeutic partial occlusion of vessel
      (39.77)

2015 ICD-9-CM
Additional Digit Required
Valid OR Procedure
Non-OR Procedure
Adjunct Code
October 2014 • Volume 3 – 121

Endovascular Repair of Abdominal Aortic Aneurysm

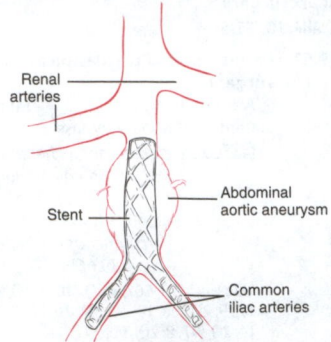

Renal arteries

Abdominal aortic aneurysm

Stent

Common iliac arteries

39.71 Endovascular implantation of other graft in abdominal aorta

Endovascular repair of abdominal aortic aneurysm with graft

Stent graft(s)

Code also intra-aneurysm sac pressure monitoring (intraoperative) (00.58)

EXCLUDES endovascular implantation of branching or fenestrated graft in aorta (39.78)

DEF: Replacement of a section of abdominal aorta with mesh graft via catheters inserted through femoral arteries.

AHA: ▶1Q, '13, 6;◄ 1Q, '02, 13; 4Q, '00, 63, 64

39.72 Endovascular (total) embolization or occlusion of head and neck vessels

Coil-retention stent

Embolization stent

Endograft(s)

Endovascular graft(s)

Liquid tissue adhesive (glue) embolization or occlusion

Other implant or substance for repair, embolization or occlusion

That for repair of aneurysm, arteriovenous malformation [AVM] or fistula

EXCLUDES embolization of head or neck vessels using bare coils (39.75)

embolization of head or neck vessels using bioactive coils (39.76)

mechanical thrombectomy of precerebral and cerebral vessels (39.74)

DEF: Coil embolization or occlusion: Utilizing x-ray guidance a neuro-microcatheter is guided from entry in the femoral artery in the groin to the site of the aneurysm of the head and neck vessels for delivery of micro-coils that stop blood flow to the arteriovenous malfomation (AVM).

AHA: ▶1Q, '13, 8;◄ 4Q, '02, 103

39.73 Endovascular implantation of graft in thoracic aorta

Endograft(s)

Endovascular graft(s)

Endovascular repair of defect of thoracic aorta with graft(s) or device(s)

Stent graft(s) or device(s)

That for repair of aneurysm, dissection, or injury

Code also intra-aneurysm sac pressure monitoring (intraoperative) (00.58)

EXCLUDES fenestration of dissecting aneurysm of thoracic aorta (39.54)

DEF: Intravascular transcatheter deployment of an expanding stent-graft for repair of thoracic aortic aneurysm, performed without opening the chest.

AHA: 4Q, '05, 120

39.74 Endovascular removal of obstruction from head and neck vessel(s)

Endovascular embolectomy

Endovascular thrombectomy of pre-cerebral and cerebral vessels

Mechanical embolectomy or thrombectomy

Code also:

any injection or infusion of thrombolytic agent (99.10)

number of vessels treated (00.40-00.43)

procedure on vessel bifurcation (00.44)

EXCLUDES endarterectomy of intracranial vessels and other vessels of head and neck (38.11-38.12)

occlusive endovascular embolization of head or neck vessels using bare coils (39.75)

occlusive endovascular embolization of head or neck vessel(s) using bioactive coils (39.76)

open embolectomy or thrombectomy (38.01-38.02)

AHA: 4Q, '06, 129

TIP: Mechanical thrombectomy represented by this code may also be documented as mechanical embolus removal in cerebral ischemia (MERCI®) extraction.

39.75 Endovascular embolization or occlusion of vessel(s) of head or neck using bare coils

Bare metal coils

Bare platinum coils [BPC]

That for treatment of aneurysm, arteriovenous malformation [AVM] or fistula

AHA: 4Q, '09, 145-146

39.76 Endovascular embolization or occlusion of vessel(s) of head or neck using bioactive coils

Biodegradable inner luminal polymer coils

Coil embolization or occlusion utilizing bioactive coils

Coils containing polyglycolic acid [PGA]

That for treatment of aneurysm, arteriovenous malformation [AVM] or fistula

AHA: 4Q, '09, 145-146

DEF: Enhanced aneurysm treatment by deployment of coils packed with novel polyglycol acid (PGA) or other bioactive substance to improve healing response.

39.77 Temporary (partial) therapeutic endovascular occlusion of vessel

Includes that of aorta

That by balloon catheter

Code also any: diagnostic arteriogram (88.40-88.49)

EXCLUDES any endovascular head or neck vessel procedure (39.72, 39.74-39.76)

diagnostic procedures on blood vessels (38.21-38.29)

permanent endovascular procedure (39.79)

AHA: 4Q, '11, 176-178

39.78 Endovascular implantation of branching or fenestrated graft(s) in aorta

AHA: 4Q, '11, 176-178

DEF: A tubular, fabric graft with specialized reinforced openings allowing physicians to custom fit and position the stent into vessel branches or bifurcations at complex anatomic sites.

TIP: These grafts provide an option for patients who are not anatomical candidates for traditional AAA grafts.

BI Bilateral Procedure   NC Non-covered Procedure   LC Limited Coverage Procedure   ▶◄ Revised Text   ● New Code   ▲ Revised Code Title

122 – Volume 3 · October 2014   2015 ICD-9-CM

39.79   **Other endovascular procedures on other vessels**
Endograft(s)
Endovascular graft(s)
Liquid tissue adhesive (glue) embolization or occlusion
Other coil embolization or occlusion
Other implant or substance for repair, embolization or occlusion
Repair of aneurysm
> **EXCLUDES**   *abdominal aortic aneurysm resection [AAA] (38.44)*
> *endovascular implantation of graft in abdominal aorta (39.71)*
> *endovascular implantation of graft in thoracic aorta (39.73)*
> *endovascular embolization or occlusion of head and neck vessels, bare metal coils (39.75)*
> *endovascular embolization or occlusion of head and neck vessels, bioactive coils (39.76)*
> *insertion of drug-eluting peripheral vessel stent(s) (00.55)*
> *insertion of non-drug-eluting peripheral vessel stent(s) (for other than aneurysm repair) (39.90)*
> *non-endovascular repair of arteriovenous fistula (39.53)*
> *other surgical occlusion of vessels — see category 38.8*
> *percutaneous transcatheter infusion (99.29)*
> *thoracic aortic aneurysm resection (38.45)*
> *transcatheter embolization for gastric or duodenal bleeding (44.44)*
> *uterine artery embolization with coils (68.24)*

AHA: ▶2Q, '13, 7;◀ 2Q, '12, 15; 4Q, '11, 138; 2Q, '10, 8-9; 1Q, '10, 21; 2Q, '09, 7-8; 2Q, '06, 22, 23; 4Q, '02, 103; 3Q, '01, 17,18; 4Q, '00, 64

☑️4ᵗʰ **39.8**   **Operations on carotid body, carotid sinus and other vascular bodies**
     AHA: 4Q, '10,121-124; 2Q, '07, 8

39.81   **Implantation or replacement of carotid sinus stimulation device, total system**
> **INCLUDES**   carotid explorations
Carotid sinus baroreflex activation device
Implantation of carotid sinus stimulator and lead(s)
> **EXCLUDES**   *implantation or replacement of carotid sinus stimulation lead(s) only (39.82)*
> *implantation or replacement of carotid sinus stimulation pulse generator only (39.83)*

DEF: A surgically implantable medical device that electrically activates the baroreflex; the system that helps regulate cardiovascular function to treat primary hypertension and hypertensive heart failure recalcitrant to medical therapy.
TIP: Assign for insertion of the Rheos Baroreflex Hypertension Therapy System.

39.82   **Implantation or replacement of carotid sinus stimulation lead(s) only**
> **EXCLUDES**   *implantation or replacement of carotid sinus stimulation device, total system (39.81)*

39.83   **Implantation or replacement of carotid sinus stimulation pulse generator only**
> **EXCLUDES**   *implantation or replacement of carotid sinus stimulation device, total system (39.81)*

     AHA: 4Q, '10, 125

39.84   **Revision of carotid sinus stimulation lead(s) only**
Repair of electrode [removal with re-insertion]
Repositioning of lead(s) [electrode]
     AHA: 4Q, '10, 121-124

39.85   **Revision of carotid sinus stimulation pulse generator**
Debridement and reforming pocket (skin and subcutaneous tissue)
Relocation of pocket [creation of new pocket]
Repositioning of pulse generator
Revision of carotid sinus stimulation pulse generator pocket

39.86   **Removal of carotid sinus stimulation device, total system**

39.87   **Removal of carotid sinus stimulation lead(s) only**

39.88   **Removal of carotid sinus stimulation pulse generator only**

39.89   **Other operations on carotid body, carotid sinus and other vascular bodies**
Chemodectomy
Denervation of:
   aortic body
   carotid body
Glomectomy, carotid
> **EXCLUDES**   *excision of glomus jugulare (20.51)*

DEF: Chemodectomy: Removal of a chemoreceptor vascular body.
DEF: Denervation of aortic body: Destruction of nerves attending the major heart blood vessels.
DEF: Denervation of carotid body: Destruction of nerves of carotid artery.
DEF: Glomectomy, carotid: Removal of the carotid artery framework.

☑️4ᵗʰ **39.9**   **Other operations on vessels**

39.90   **Insertion of non-drug-eluting peripheral (non-coronary) vessel stent(s)**
Bare stent(s)
Bonded stent(s)
Drug-coated stent(s), i.e., heparin coated
Endograft(s)
Endovascular graft(s)
Endovascular recanalization techniques
Stent graft(s)
Code also any:
   non-coronary angioplasty or atherectomy (39.50)
   number of vascular stents inserted (00.45-00.48)
   number of vessels treated (00.40-00.43)
   procedure on vessel bifurcation (00.44)
> **EXCLUDES**   *insertion of drug-eluting, peripheral vessel stent(s) (00.55)*
> *percutaneous insertion of carotid artery stent(s) (00.63)*
> *percutaneous insertion of intracranial stent(s) (00.65)*
> *percutaneous insertion of other precerebral artery stent(s) (00.64)*
> *that for aneurysm repair (39.71-39.79)*

AHA: 3Q, '12, 13; 3Q, '09, 13; 4Q, '06, 119; 4Q, '02, 101; 1Q, '00, 12; 4Q, '96, 63

39.91   **Freeing of vessel**
Dissection and freeing of adherent tissue:
   artery-vein-nerve bundle
   vascular bundle
     AHA: 3Q, '02, 12

39.92   **Injection of sclerosing agent into vein**
> **EXCLUDES**   *injection:*
> *esophageal varices (42.33)*
> *hemorrhoids (49.42)*

     AHA: 2Q, '92, 17

☑️3ʳᵈ
☑️4ᵗʰ   Additional Digit Required   Valid OR Procedure   Non-OR Procedure   Adjunct Code
2015 ICD-9-CM   **October 2014 • Volume 3 – 123**

External Arteriovenous Shunt

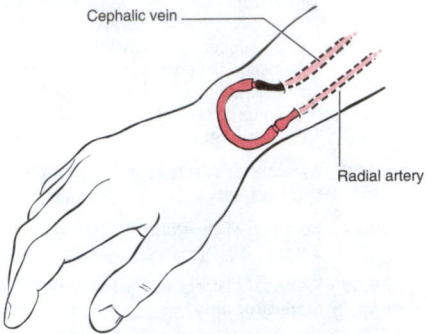

Cephalic vein

Radial artery

39.93   Insertion of vessel-to-vessel cannula

Formation of:

arteriovenous:
fistula }
shunt   } by external cannula

Code also any renal dialysis (39.95)

AHA: 3Q, '88, 13; S-O, '85, 5, 12

TIP: If the AV fistula or shunt catheter or device is considered totally implantable, assign instead 86.07.

39.94   Replacement of vessel-to-vessel cannula

Revision of vessel-to-vessel cannula

39.95   Hemodialysis

Artificial kidney   Hemofiltration
Hemodiafiltration   Renal dialysis

EXCLUDES peritoneal dialysis (54.98)

DEF: Filtration process to treat acute and chronic renal failure by eliminating toxic end products of nitrogen metabolism from blood.

AHA: 2Q, '11, 6; 4Q, '08, 193; 3Q, '07, 9; 1Q, '04, 22; 4Q, '03, 111; 2Q, '01, 2-14; 4Q, '00, 40; 2Q, '98, 20; S-O, '86, 11

39.96   Total body perfusion

Code also substance perfused (99.21-99.29)

39.97   Other perfusion

Perfusion NOS

Perfusion, local [regional] of:
carotid artery
coronary artery
head
lower limb
neck
upper limb

Code also substance perfused (99.21-99.29)

EXCLUDES perfusion of:
kidney (55.95)
large intestine (46.96)
liver (50.93)
small intestine (46.95)
SuperSaturated oxygen
therapy (00.49)

AHA: ▶3Q, '13, 10; ◀3Q, '96, 11

39.98   Control of hemorrhage, not otherwise specified

Angiotripsy
Control of postoperative hemorrhage NOS
Venotripsy

EXCLUDES control of hemorrhage (postoperative):
anus (49.95)
bladder (57.93)
following vascular procedure (39.41)
nose (21.00-21.09)
prostate (60.94)
tonsil (28.7)
that by:
ligation (38.80-38.89)
suture (39.30-39.32)

DEF: Angiotripsy: Clamping of tissue to stop arterial blood flow.

DEF: Venotripsy: Clamping of tissue to stop venous blood flow.

AHA: 2Q, '12, 10

39.99   Other operations on vessels

EXCLUDES injection or infusion of therapeutic or prophylactic substance (99.11-99.29)
transfusion of blood and blood components (99.01-99.09)

AHA: 1Q, '89, 11

TIP: Assign for removal of a vena cava filter via percutaneous transluminal approach via the jugular vein.

BI Bilateral Procedure   NC Non-covered Procedure   LC Limited Coverage Procedure   ▶◀ Revised Text   ● New Code   ▲ Revised Code Title

124 – Volume 3 • October 2014   2015 ICD-9-CM

8. Operations on the Hemic and Lymphatic Systems (40-41)

✓3rd **40   Operations on lymphatic system**

40.0   Incision of lymphatic structures

✓4th **40.1   Diagnostic procedures on lymphatic structures**

40.11   Biopsy of lymphatic structure
Transbronchoscopic needle aspiration [TBNA] of lymph node
AHA: 3Q, '10, 9; 4Q, '09, 74; 4Q, '08, 91

40.19   Other diagnostic procedures on lymphatic structures
EXCLUDES   lymphangiogram:
abdominal (88.04)
cervical (87.08)
intrathoracic (87.34)
lower limb (88.36)
upper limb (88.34)
microscopic examination of specimen (90.71-90.79)
radioisotope scan (92.16)
thermography (88.89)

✓4th **40.2   Simple excision of lymphatic structure**
EXCLUDES   biopsy of lymphatic structure (40.11)
DEF: Removal of lymphatic structure only.

40.21   Excision of deep cervical lymph node
AHA: 4Q, '99, 16

40.22   Excision of internal mammary lymph node

40.23   Excision of axillary lymph node
AHA: 2Q, '12, 4; 2Q, '02, 7

40.24   Excision of inguinal lymph node

40.29   Simple excision of other lymphatic structure
Excision of:
cystic hygroma
lymphangioma
Simple lymphadenectomy
DEF: Lymphangioma: Removal of benign congenital lymphatic malformation.
DEF: Simple lymphadenectomy: Removal of lymph node.
AHA: 1Q, '99, 6

40.3   Regional lymph node excision
Extended regional lymph node excision
Regional lymph node excision with excision of lymphatic drainage area including skin, subcutaneous tissue, and fat
DEF: Extended regional lymph node excision: Removal of lymph node group, including area around nodes.
AHA:1Q, '12, 9; 2Q, '92, 7
TIP: Assign for "selective neck dissection."

✓4th **40.4   Radical excision of cervical lymph nodes**
Resection of cervical lymph nodes down to muscle and deep fascia
EXCLUDES   that associated with radical laryngectomy (30.4)
TIP: Assign a code from this subcategory for procedures described as modified radical neck dissection.

40.40   Radical neck dissection, not otherwise specified

40.41   Radical neck dissection, unilateral
AHA: 2Q, '05, 8; 2Q, '99, 6
DEF: Total dissection of cervical lymph nodes on one side of neck.

40.42   Radical neck dissection, bilateral
DEF: Total dissection of cervical lymph nodes on both sides of neck.

✓4th **40.5   Radical excision of other lymph nodes**
EXCLUDES   that associated with radical mastectomy (85.45-85.48)

40.50   Radical excision of lymph nodes, not otherwise specified
Radical (lymph) node dissection NOS

40.51   Radical excision of axillary lymph nodes

40.52   Radical excision of periaortic lymph nodes

40.53   Radical excision of iliac lymph nodes

40.54   Radical groin dissection

40.59   Radical excision of other lymph nodes
EXCLUDES   radical neck dissection (40.40-40.42)

✓4th **40.6   Operations on thoracic duct**

40.61   Cannulation of thoracic duct
DEF: Placement of cannula in main lymphatic duct of chest.

40.62   Fistulization of thoracic duct
DEF: Creation of passage in main lymphatic duct of chest.

40.63   Closure of fistula of thoracic duct
DEF: Closure of fistula in main lymphatic duct of chest.

40.64   Ligation of thoracic duct
DEF: Tying off main lymphatic duct of chest.

40.69   Other operations on thoracic duct

40.9   Other operations on lymphatic structures
Anastomosis
Dilation
Ligation
Obliteration   } of peripheral lymphatics
Reconstruction
Repair
Transplantation
Correction of lymphedema of limb, NOS
EXCLUDES   reduction of elephantiasis of scrotum (61.3)

✓3rd **41   Operations on bone marrow and spleen**

✓4th **41.0   Bone marrow or hematopoietic stem cell transplant**
NOTE   To report donor source — see codes 00.91-00.93
EXCLUDES   aspiration of bone marrow from donor (41.91)
AHA: 4Q, '00, 64; 1Q, '91, 3; 4Q, '91, 26

41.00   Bone marrow transplant, not otherwise specified

8 **41.01   Autologous bone marrow transplant without purging**   NC
EXCLUDES   that with purging (41.09)
DEF: Transplant of patient's own bone marrow.

9 **41.02   Allogeneic bone marrow transplant with purging**   NC
Allograft of bone marrow with in vitro removal (purging) of T-cells
DEF: Transplant of bone marrow from donor to patient after donor marrow purged of undesirable cells.

9 **41.03   Allogeneic bone marrow transplant without purging**   NC
Allograft of bone marrow NOS

8 **41.04   Autologous hematopoietic stem cell transplant without purging**   NC
EXCLUDES   that with purging (41.07)
AHA: 4Q, '94, 52

9 **41.05   Allogeneic hematopoietic stem cell transplant without purging**   NC
EXCLUDES   that with purging (41.08)
AHA: 1Q, '11, 24; 1Q, '09, 9; 4Q, '97, 55

41.06   Cord blood stem cell transplant
AHA: 4Q, '97, 56

8 **41.07   Autologous hematopoietic stem cell transplant with purging**   NC
Cell depletion
AHA: 2Q, '06, 20-22
TIP: Assign for autologous peripheral blood stem cell boost reinfusion.

9 **41.08   Allogeneic hematopoietic stem cell transplant with purging**   NC
Cell depletion

8 **41.09   Autologous bone marrow transplant with purging**   NC
With extracorporeal purging of malignant cells from marrow
Cell depletion

---

8   Noncovered procedure only when the following diagnoses are present as either principal or secondary diagnosis: 204.00, 205.00, 205.10, 205.11, 206.00, 207.00, 208.00
9   Noncovered procedure only when the following diagnoses are present as either principal or secondary diagnosis: 203.00, 203.01

✓3rd   Additional Digit Required   Valid OR Procedure   Non-OR Procedure   Adjunct Code
✓4th
2015 ICD-9-CM

Partial Splenectomy

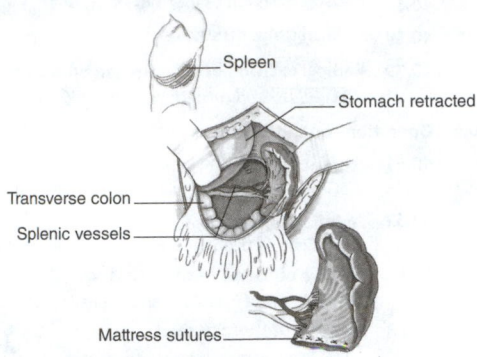

- Spleen
- Stomach retracted
- Transverse colon
- Splenic vessels
- Mattress sutures

Total Splenectomy

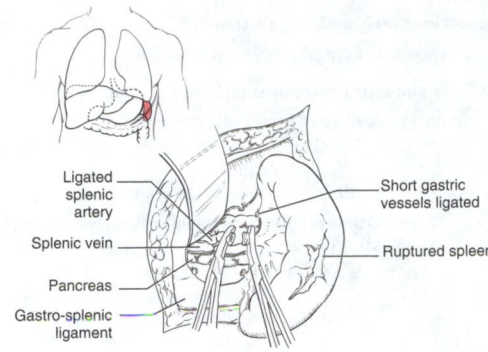

- Ligated splenic artery
- Splenic vein
- Pancreas
- Gastro-splenic ligament
- Short gastric vessels ligated
- Ruptured spleen

41.1	**Puncture of spleen**
   EXCLUDES *aspiration biopsy of spleen (41.32)*

41.2	**Splenotomy**

✓4ᵗʰ **41.3**	**Diagnostic procedures on bone marrow and spleen**

   41.31	**Biopsy of bone marrow**

   41.32	**Closed [aspiration] [percutaneous] biopsy of spleen**
      Needle biopsy of spleen

   41.33	**Open biopsy of spleen**

   41.38	**Other diagnostic procedures on bone marrow**
      EXCLUDES *microscopic examination of specimen from bone marrow (90.61-90.69)*
      radioisotope scan (92.05)

   41.39	**Other diagnostic procedures on spleen**
      EXCLUDES *microscopic examination of specimen from spleen (90.61-90.69)*
      radioisotope scan (92.05)

✓4ᵗʰ **41.4**	**Excision or destruction of lesion or tissue of spleen**
   Code also any application or administration of an adhesion barrier substance (99.77)
   EXCLUDES *excision of accessory spleen (41.93)*

   41.41	**Marsupialization of splenic cyst**
      DEF: Incision of cyst of spleen with edges sutured open to create pouch.

   41.42	**Excision of lesion or tissue of spleen**
      EXCLUDES *biopsy of spleen (41.32-41.33)*

   41.43	**Partial splenectomy**
      DEF: Partial removal of spleen.

41.5	**Total splenectomy**
   Splenectomy NOS
   Code also any application or administration of an adhesion barrier substance (99.77)
   AHA: ▶3Q, '13, 12◀

✓4ᵗʰ **41.9**	**Other operations on spleen and bone marrow**
   Code also any application or administration of an adhesion barrier substance (99.77)

   41.91	**Aspiration of bone marrow from donor for transplant**
      EXCLUDES *biopsy of bone marrow (41.31)*
      AHA: 1Q, '91, 3

   41.92	**Injection into bone marrow**
      EXCLUDES *bone marrow transplant (41.00-41.03)*
      AHA: 3Q, '96, 17
      TIP: Assign for intraosseous IV access, performed emergently for a dehydrated infant whose peripheral vein cannot be accessed.

   41.93	**Excision of accessory spleen**

   41.94	**Transplantation of spleen**

   41.95	**Repair and plastic operations on spleen**

   41.98	**Other operations on bone marrow**
      AHA: 2Q, '11, 10; 3Q, '08, 19

   41.99	**Other operations on spleen**

BI Bilateral Procedure   NC Non-covered Procedure   LC Limited Coverage Procedure   ▶◀ Revised Text   ● New Code   ▲ Revised Code Title

126 – Volume 3 • October 2014	2015 ICD-9-CM

9. Operations on the Digestive System (42-54)

☑3rd **42**   **Operations on esophagus**

☑4th **42.0**   **Esophagotomy**

42.01   **Incision of esophageal web**
> **DEF:** Cutting into congenital esophageal membrane.

42.09   **Other incision of esophagus**
> Esophagotomy NOS
> **EXCLUDES**   *esophagomyotomy (42.7)*
> *esophagostomy (42.10-42.19)*

☑4th **42.1**   **Esophagostomy**

42.10   **Esophagostomy, not otherwise specified**

42.11   **Cervical esophagostomy**
> **DEF:** Creation of opening into upper region of esophagus.

42.12   **Exteriorization of esophageal pouch**
> **DEF:** Transfer of section of esophageal pouch to exterior of the body.

42.19   **Other external fistulization of esophagus**
> Thoracic esophagostomy
> Code also any resection (42.40-42.42)

☑4th **42.2**   **Diagnostic procedures on esophagus**

42.21   **Operative esophagoscopy by incision**
> **DEF:** Esophageal examination with an endoscope through incision.

42.22   **Esophagoscopy through artificial stoma**
> **EXCLUDES**   *that with biopsy (42.24)*

42.23   **Other esophagoscopy**
> **EXCLUDES**   *that with biopsy (42.24)*
> **AHA:** 1Q, '00, 20; 3Q, '98, 11
> **TIP:** Two codes may be assigned to report transesophageal echocardiography (TEE): 88.72 for the diagnostic radiology portion of the procedure and 42.23 for the endoscopic approach.

42.24   **Closed [endoscopic] biopsy of esophagus**
> Brushing or washing for specimen collection
> Esophagoscopy with biopsy
> Suction biopsy of the esophagus
> **EXCLUDES**   *esophagogastroduodenoscopy [EGD] with closed biopsy (45.16)*
> **DEF:** Scope passed through mouth and throat to obtain biopsy specimen, usually by brushing and swabbing.

42.25   **Open biopsy of esophagus**

42.29   **Other diagnostic procedures on esophagus**
> **EXCLUDES**   *barium swallow (87.61)*
> *esophageal manometry (89.32)*
> *microscopic examination of specimen from esophagus (90.81-90.89)*
> **AHA:** 3Q, '96, 12

☑4th **42.3**   **Local excision or destruction of lesion or tissue of esophagus**

42.31   **Local excision of esophageal diverticulum**

42.32   **Local excision of other lesion or tissue of esophagus**
> **EXCLUDES**   *biopsy of esophagus (42.24-42.25)*
> *esophageal fistulectomy (42.84)*

42.33   **Endoscopic excision or destruction of lesion or tissue of esophagus**
> Ablation of esophageal neoplasm
> Control of esophageal bleeding
> Esophageal polypectomy } by endoscopic approach
> Espohageal varices
> Injection of esophageal varies
> **EXCLUDES**   *biopsy of esophagus (42.24-42.25)*
> *fistulectomy (42.84)*
> *open ligation of esophageal varices (42.91)*
> **AHA:** 4Q, '12, 85
> **TIP:** Assign for endoscopic sclerotherapy for bleeding esophageal varices.

42.39   **Other destruction of lesion or tissue of esophagus**
> **EXCLUDES**   *that by endoscopic approach (42.33)*

☑4th **42.4**   **Excision of esophagus**
> **EXCLUDES**   *esophagogastrectomy NOS 43.99)*

42.40   **Esophagectomy, not otherwise specified**

42.41   **Partial esophagectomy**
> Code also any synchronous:
> anastomosis other than end-to-end (42.51-42.69)
> esophagostomy (42.10-42.19)
> gastrostomy (43.11-43.19)
> **DEF:** Surgical removal of any part of esophagus.

42.42   **Total esophagectomy**
> Code also any synchronous:
> gastrostomy (43.11-43.19)
> interposition or anastomosis other than end-to-end (42.51-42.69)
> **EXCLUDES**   *esophagogastrectomy (43.99)*
> **AHA:** 4Q, '88, 11
> **DEF:** Surgical removal of entire esophagus.

☑4th **42.5**   **Intrathoracic anastomosis of esophagus**
> Code also any synchronous:
> esophagectomy (42.40-42.42)
> gastrostomy (43.1)
> **DEF:** Connection of esophagus to conduit within chest.

42.51   **Intrathoracic esophagoesophagostomy**
> **DEF:** Connection of both ends of esophagus within chest cavity.

42.52   **Intrathoracic esophagogastrostomy**
> **DEF:** Connection of esophagus to stomach within chest; follows esophagogastrectomy.

42.53   **Intrathoracic esophageal anastomosis with interposition of small bowel**

42.54   **Other intrathoracic esophagoenterostomy**
> Anastomosis of esophagus to intestinal segment NOS

42.55   **Intrathoracic esophageal anastomosis with interposition of colon**

42.56   **Other intrathoracic esophagocolostomy**
> Esophagocolostomy NOS

42.58   **Intrathoracic esophageal anastomosis with other interposition**
> Construction of artificial esophagus
> Retrosternal formation of reversed gastric tube
> **DEF:** Retrosternal anastomosis of reversed gastric tube: Formation of gastric tube behind breastbone.

42.59   **Other intrathoracic anastomosis of esophagus**
> **AHA:** 4Q, '88, 11

☑4th **42.6**   **Antesternal anastomosis of esophagus**
> Code also any synchronous:
> esophagectomy (42.40-42.42)
> gastrostomy (43.1)

42.61   **Antesternal esophagoesophagostomy**

42.62   **Antesternal esophagogastrostomy**

42.63   **Antesternal esophageal anastomosis with interposition of small bowel**

42.64   **Other antesternal esophagoenterostomy**
> Antethoracic:
> esophagoenterostomy
> esophagoileostomy
> esophagojejunostomy

42.65   **Antesternal esophageal anastomosis with interposition of colon**
> **DEF:** Connection of esophagus with colon segment.

42.66   **Other antesternal esophagocolostomy**
> Antethoracic esophagocolostomy

42.68   **Other antesternal esophageal anastomosis with interposition**

42.69   **Other antesternal anastomosis of esophagus**

42.7   **Esophagomyotomy**
> **DEF:** Division of esophageal muscle, usually distal.

☑3rd ☑4th **Additional Digit Required**   Valid OR Procedure   Non-OR Procedure   Adjunct Code

Operations on the Digestive System

42.8–43.99

√4ᵗʰ **42.8   Other repair of esophagus**

42.81   Insertion of permanent tube into esophagus
AHA: 1Q, '97, 15

42.82   Suture of laceration of esophagus

42.83   Closure of esophagostomy

42.84   Repair of esophageal fistula, not elsewhere classified
EXCLUDES repair of fistula:
bronchoesophageal (33.42)
esophagopleurocutaneous (34.73)
pharyngoesophageal (29.53)
tracheoesophageal (31.73)

42.85   Repair of esophageal stricture
AHA: ▶4Q, '13, 100◀

42.86   Production of subcutaneous tunnel without esophageal anastomosis
DEF: Surgical formation of esophageal passage, without cutting, and reconnection.

42.87   Other graft of esophagus
EXCLUDES antesternal esophageal anastomosis with interposition of:
colon (42.65)
small bowel (42.63)
antesternal esophageal anastomosis with other interposition (42.68)
intrathoracic esophageal anastomosis with interposition of:
colon (42.55)
small bowel (42.53)
intrathoracic esophageal anastomosis with other interposition (42.58)

42.89   Other repair of esophagus

√4ᵗʰ **42.9   Other operations on esophagus**

42.91   Ligation of esophageal varices
EXCLUDES that by endoscopic approach (42.33)
DEF: Destruction of dilated veins by suture strangulation.

42.92   Dilation of esophagus
Dilation of cardiac sphincter
EXCLUDES intubation of esophagus (96.03, 96.06-96.08)
DEF: Passing of balloon or hydrostatic dilators through esophagus to enlarge esophagus and relieve obstruction.

42.99   Other
EXCLUDES insertion of Sengstaken tube (96.06)
intubation of esophagus (96.03, 96.06-96.08)
removal of intraluminal foreign body from esophagus without incision (98.02)
tamponade of esophagus (96.06)

√3ʳᵈ **43   Incision and excision of stomach**
Code also any application or administration of an adhesion barrier substance (99.77)

43.0   Gastrotomy
EXCLUDES gastrostomy (43.11-43.19)
that for control of hemorrhage (44.49)
AHA: 3Q, '89, 14

√4ᵗʰ **43.1   Gastrostomy**
AHA: S-O, '85, 5

43.11   Percutaneous [endoscopic] gastrostomy [PEG]
Percutaneous transabdominal gastrostomy
DEF: Endoscopic positioning of tube through abdominal wall into stomach.

43.19   Other gastrostomy
EXCLUDES percutaneous [endoscopic] gastrostomy [PEG] (43.11)
AHA: 2Q, '12, 6; 1Q, '92, 14; 3Q, '89, 14
TIP: Do not report gastropexy suture of the stomach to the fascia separately when performed as an inherent part of gastrostomy to prevent leakage.

43.3   Pyloromyotomy
DEF: Cutting into longitudinal and circular muscular membrane between stomach and small intestine.

Partial Gastrectomy with Anastomosis to Duodenum

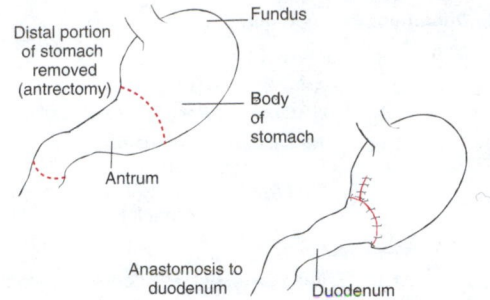

√4ᵗʰ **43.4   Local excision or destruction of lesion or tissue of stomach**

43.41   Endoscopic excision or destruction of lesion or tissue of stomach
Gastric polypectomy by endoscopic approach
Gastric varices by endoscopic approach
EXCLUDES biopsy of stomach (44.14-44.15)
control of hemorrhage (44.43)
open ligation of gastric varices (44.91)
AHA: 3Q, '96, 10

43.42   Local excision of other lesion or tissue of stomach
EXCLUDES biopsy of stomach (44.14-44.15)
gastric fistulectomy (44.62-44.63)
partial gastrectomy (43.5-43.89)

43.49   Other destruction of lesion or tissue of stomach
EXCLUDES that by endoscopic approach (43.41)
AHA: N-D, '87, 5; S-O, '85, 6

43.5   Partial gastrectomy with anastomosis to esophagus
Proximal gastrectomy

43.6   Partial gastrectomy with anastomosis to duodenum
Billroth I operation   Gastropylorectomy
Distal gastrectomy

43.7   Partial gastrectomy with anastomosis to jejunum
Billroth II operation
AHA: 3Q, '03, 7

√4ᵗʰ **43.8   Other partial gastrectomy**

43.81   Partial gastrectomy with jejunal transposition
Henley jejunal transposition operation
Code also any synchronous intestinal resection (45.51)

43.82   Laparoscopic vertical (sleeve) gastrectomy
EXCLUDES laparoscopic banding (44.95)
laparoscopic gastric restrictive procedure (44.95)
DEF: Removal of the majority of the stomach, the greater curvature, resulting in a long vertical shape with preservation of the pyloric valve and nerves of the stomach.
AHA: 4Q, '11, 178-179
TIP: This procedure requires no intestinal bypass or artificial device (such as the lap band), thereby reducing risk of dumping syndrome, intestinal obstruction, or other complications.

43.89   Open and other partial gastrectomy
Partial gastrectomy with bypass gastrogastrostomy
Sleeve resection of stomach
EXCLUDES laparoscopic sleeve gastrectomy (43.82)
AHA: 3Q, '03, 6-8

√4ᵗʰ **43.9   Total gastrectomy**

43.91   Total gastrectomy with intestinal interposition

43.99   Other total gastrectomy
Complete gastroduodenectomy
Esophagoduodenostomy with complete gastrectomy
Esophagogastrectomy NOS
Esophagojejunostomy with complete gastrectomy
Radical gastrectomy

Biliopancreatic Diversion Without Duodenal Switch

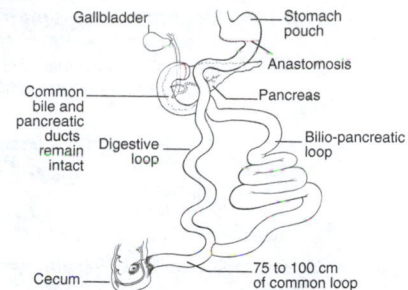

Biliopancreatic Diversion with Duodenal Switch

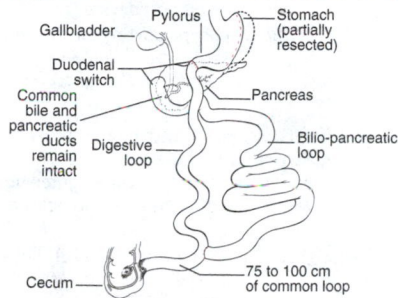

Types of Vagotomy Procedures

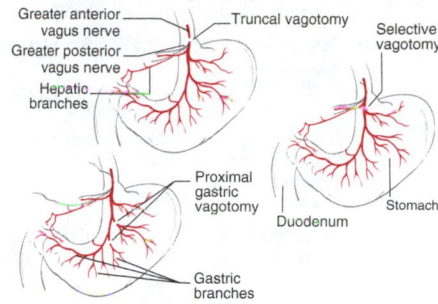

Roux-en-Y Operation (Gastrojejunostomy without gastrectomy)

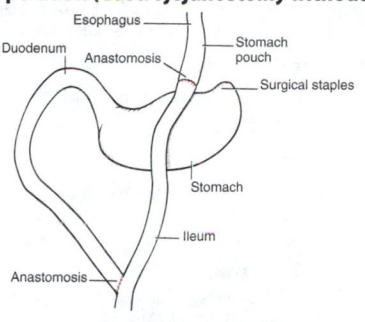

√3rd **44　Other operations on stomach**

Code also any application or administration of an adhesion barrier substance (99.77)

√4th **44.0　Vagotomy**

44.00　Vagotomy, not otherwise specified
Division of vagus nerve NOS
DEF: Cutting of vagus nerve to reduce acid production.

44.01　Truncal vagotomy
DEF: Surgical removal of vagus nerve segment near stomach branches.

44.02　Highly selective vagotomy
Parietal cell vagotomy
Selective proximal vagotomy
DEF: Cutting select gastric branches of vagus nerve to reduce acid production and preserve other nerve functions.

44.03　Other selective vagotomy

√4th **44.1　Diagnostic procedures on stomach**

44.11　Transabdominal gastroscopy
Intraoperative gastroscopy
EXCLUDES *that with biopsy (44.14)*

44.12　Gastroscopy through artificial stoma
EXCLUDES *that with biopsy (44.14)*

44.13　Other gastroscopy
EXCLUDES *that with biopsy (44.14)*
AHA: 1Q, '88, 15; N-D, '87, 5

44.14　Closed [endoscopic] biopsy of stomach
Brushing or washing for specimen collection
EXCLUDES *esophagogastroduodenoscopy [EGD] with closed biopsy (45.16)*
AHA: 1Q, '88, 15; N-D, '87, 5

44.15　Open biopsy of stomach

44.19　Other diagnostic procedures on stomach
EXCLUDES *gastric lavage (96.33)*
microscopic examination of specimen from stomach (90.81-90.89)
upper GI series (87.62)

√4th **44.2　Pyloroplasty**

44.21　Dilation of pylorus by incision
DEF: Cutting and suturing pylorus to relieve obstruction.

44.22　Endoscopic dilation of pylorus
Dilation with balloon endoscope
Endoscopic dilation of gastrojejunostomy site
AHA: 2Q, '01, 17
TIP: Assign for stent placement across an extrinsic obstruction of a gastrojejunostomy.

44.29　Other pyloroplasty
Pyloroplasty NOS　　　　Revision of pylorus
AHA: 3Q, '99, 3

√4th **44.3　Gastroenterostomy without gastrectomy**

44.31　High gastric bypass
Printen and Mason gastric bypass
DEF: Connection of middle part of small intestine to upper stomach to divert food passage from upper intestine.
AHA: M-J, '85, 17

44.32　Percutaneous (endoscopic) gastrojejunostomy
Bypass:　　　　　　　PEGJJ
　gastroduodenostomy
EXCLUDES *percutaneous (endoscopic) feeding jejunostomy (46.32)*
DEF: Percutaneous insertion of an endoscopically guided gastrostomy tube that provides an artificial opening into the gastric lumen and portion of the jejunum via the exterior abdominal wall.

44.38　Laparoscopic gastroenterostomy
Bypass:
　gastroduodenostomy
　gastroenterostomy
　gastrogastrostomy
Laparoscopic gastrojejunostomy without gastrectomy NEC
EXCLUDES *gastroenterostomy, open approach (44.39)*

44.39　Other gastroenterostomy
Bypass:　　　　　　　Bypass:
　gastroduodenostomy　　gastrogastrostomy
　gastroenterostomy
Gastrojejunostomy without gastrectomy NOS
AHA: 3Q, '03, 6; 1Q, '01, 16, 17

√4th **44.4　Control of hemorrhage and suture of ulcer of stomach or duodenum**

44.40　Suture of peptic ulcer, not otherwise specified

44.41　Suture of gastric ulcer site
EXCLUDES *ligation of gastric varices (44.91)*

44.42　Suture of duodenal ulcer site
AHA: J-F, '87, 11

44.43 **Endoscopic control of gastric or duodenal bleeding**
AHA: 2Q, '04, 12; 2Q, '92, 17; N-D, '87, 4

44.44 **Transcatheter embolization for gastric or duodenal bleeding**
EXCLUDES *surgical occlusion of abdominal vessels (38.86-38.87)*
DEF: Therapeutic blocking of stomach or upper small intestine blood vessel to stop hemorrhaging; accomplished by introducing various substances using a catheter.
AHA: 2Q, '11, 11; 1Q, '88, 15; N-D, '87, 4

44.49 **Other control of hemorrhage of stomach or duodenum**
That with gastrotomy

44.5 **Revision of gastric anastomosis**
Closure of:
  gastric anastomosis
  gastroduodenostomy
Closure of:
  gastrojejunostomy
  Pantaloon operation

√4ᵗʰ **44.6** **Other repair of stomach**

44.61 **Suture of laceration of stomach**
EXCLUDES *that of ulcer site (44.41)*

44.62 **Closure of gastrostomy**

44.63 **Closure of other gastric fistula**
Closure of:
  gastrocolic fistula
Closure of:
  gastrojejunocolic fistula

44.64 **Gastropexy**
DEF: Suturing of stomach into position.
AHA: M-J, '85, 17

44.65 **Esophagogastroplasty**
Belsey operation
Esophagus and stomach cardioplasty
AHA: M-J, '85, 17

44.66 **Other procedures for creation of esophagogastric sphincteric competence**
Fundoplication
Gastric cardioplasty
Nissen's fundoplication
Restoration of cardio-esophageal angle
EXCLUDES *that by laparoscopy (44.67)*
AHA: 3Q, '12, 6; 2Q, '03, 12; 2Q, '01, 3, 5, 6; 3Q, '98, 10; M-J, '85, 17
TIP: Do not assign a separate endoscopy code if performed by endoscopic approach.

44.67 **Laparoscopic procedures for creation of esophagogastric sphincteric competence**
Fundoplication
Gastric cardioplasty
Nissen's fundoplication
Restoration of cardio-esophageal angle
AHA: ▶1Q, '14, 7◀

44.68 **Laparoscopic gastroplasty**
Banding
Silastic vertical banding
Vertical banded gastroplasty (VBG)
Code also any synchronous laparoscopic gastroenterostomy (44.38)
EXCLUDES *insertion, laparoscopic adjustable gastric band (restrictive procedure) (44.95)*
other repair of stomach, open approach (44.61-44.65, 44.69)
AHA: ▶4Q, '13, 93◀

44.69 **Other**
Inversion of gastric diverticulum
Repair of stomach NOS
DEF: Inversion of gastric diverticulum: Turning stomach inward to repair outpouch of wall.
AHA: 3Q, '03, 8; 2Q, '01, 3; 3Q, '99, 3; M-J, '85, 17; N-D, '84, 13

√4ᵗʰ **44.9** **Other operations on stomach**

44.91 **Ligation of gastric varices**
EXCLUDES *that by endoscopic approach (43.41)*
DEF: Destruction of dilated veins by suture or strangulation.

44.92 **Intraoperative manipulation of stomach**
Reduction of gastric volvulus

44.93 **Insertion of gastric bubble (balloon)** NC

44.94 **Removal of gastric bubble (balloon)**

44.95 **Laparoscopic gastric restrictive procedure**
Adjustable gastric band and port insertion
EXCLUDES *laparoscopic gastroplasty (44.68)*
other repair of stomach (44.69)
AHA: ▶4Q, '13, 93◀

44.96 **Laparoscopic revision of gastric restrictive procedure**
Revision or replacement of:
  adjustable gastric band
  subcutaneous gastric port device

44.97 **Laparoscopic removal of gastric restrictive device(s)**
Removal of either or both:
  adjustable gastric band
  subcutaneous port device
EXCLUDES *nonoperative removal of gastric restrictive device(s) (97.86)*
open removal of gastric restrictive device(s) (44.99)

44.98 **(Laparoscopic) adjustment of size of adjustable gastric restrictive device**
Infusion of saline for device tightening
Withdrawal of saline for device loosening
Code also any:
  abdominal ultrasound (88.76)
  abdominal wall fluoroscopy (88.09)
  barium swallow (87.61)

44.99 **Other**
EXCLUDES *change of gastrostomy tube (97.02)*
dilation of cardiac sphincter (42.92)
gastric:
  cooling (96.31)
  freezing (96.32)
  gavage (96.35)
  hypothermia (96.31)
  lavage (96.33)
insertion of nasogastric tube (96.07)
irrigation of gastrostomy (96.36)
irrigation of nasogastric tube (96.34)
removal of:
  gastrostomy tube (97.51)
  intraluminal foreign body from stomach without incision (98.03)
replacement of:
  gastrostomy tube (97.02)
  (naso-)gastric tube (97.01)
AHA: 3Q, '04, 5

√3ʳᵈ **45** **Incision, excision, and anastomosis of intestine**
Code also any application or administration of an adhesion barrier substance (99.77)

√4ᵗʰ **45.0** **Enterotomy**
EXCLUDES *duodenocholedochotomy (51.41-51.42, 51.51)*
that for destruction of lesion (45.30-45.34)
that of exteriorized intestine (46.14, 46.24, 46.31)

45.00 **Incision of intestine, not otherwise specified**

45.01 **Incision of duodenum**

45.02 **Other incision of small intestine**

45.03 **Incision of large intestine**
EXCLUDES *proctotomy (48.0)*

√4ᵗʰ **45.1** **Diagnostic procedures on small intestine**
Code also any laparotomy (54.11-54.19)

45.11 **Transabdominal endoscopy of small intestine**
Intraoperative endoscopy of small intestine
EXCLUDES *that with biopsy (45.14)*
DEF: Endoscopic exam of small intestine through abdominal wall.
DEF: Intraoperative endoscope of small intestine: Endoscopic exam of small intestine during surgery.

45.12 **Endoscopy of small intestine through artificial stoma**
EXCLUDES *that with biopsy (45.14)*
AHA: M-J, '85, 17

BI Bilateral Procedure   NC Non-covered Procedure   LC Limited Coverage Procedure   ▶◀ Revised Text   ● New Code   ▲ Revised Code Title

Esophagogastroduodenoscopy

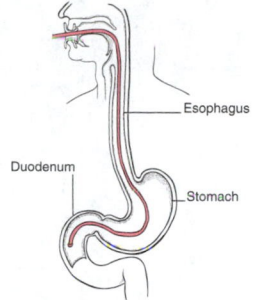

45.13   Other endoscopy of small intestine
Esophagogastroduodenoscopy [EGD]
EXCLUDES *that with biopsy (45.14, 45.16)*
AHA: 4Q, '12, 83, 85; 3Q, '04, 5; N-D, '87, 5

45.14   Closed [endoscopic] biopsy of small intestine
Brushing or washing for specimen collection
EXCLUDES *esophagogastroduodenoscopy [EGD] with closed biopsy (45.16)*

45.15   Open biopsy of small intestine
AHA: 2Q, '05, 12

45.16   Esophagogastroduodenoscopy [EGD] with closed biopsy
Biopsy of one or more sites involving esophagus, stomach, and/or duodenum
AHA: 3Q, '05, 17; 2Q, '01, 9

45.19   Other diagnostic procedures on small intestine
EXCLUDES *microscopic examination of specimen from small intestine (90.91-90.99)*
radioisotope scan (92.04)
ultrasonography (88.74)
x-ray (87.61-87.69)

√4ᵗʰ **45.2   Diagnostic procedures on large intestine**
Code also any laparotomy (54.11-54.19)

45.21   Transabdominal endoscopy of large intestine
Intraoperative endoscopy of large intestine
EXCLUDES *that with biopsy (45.25)*
DEF: Endoscopic exam of large intestine through abdominal wall.
DEF: Intraoperative endoscopy of large intestine: Endoscopic exam of large intestine during surgery.

45.22   Endoscopy of large intestine through artificial stoma
EXCLUDES *that with biopsy (45.25)*
DEF: Endoscopic exam of large intestine lining from rectum to cecum via colostomy stoma.

45.23   Colonoscopy
Flexible fiberoptic colonoscopy
EXCLUDES *endoscopy of large intestine through artificial stoma (45.22)*
flexible sigmoidoscopy (45.24)
rigid proctosigmoidoscopy (48.23)
transabdominal endoscopy of large intestine (45.21)
DEF: Endoscopic exam of descending colon, splenic flexure, transverse colon, hepatic flexure and cecum.
AHA: 3Q, '12, 23; 3Q, '05, 17; S-O, '85, 5

45.24   Flexible sigmoidoscopy
Endoscopy of descending colon
EXCLUDES *rigid proctosigmoidoscopy (48.23)*
DEF: Endoscopic exam of anus, rectum and sigmoid colon.

45.25   Closed [endoscopic] biopsy of large intestine
Biopsy, closed, of unspecified intestinal site
Brushing or washing for specimen collection
Colonoscopy with biopsy
EXCLUDES *proctosigmoidoscopy with biopsy (48.24)*
AHA: 1Q, '03, 10

45.26   Open biopsy of large intestine

45.27   Intestinal biopsy, site unspecified

45.28   Other diagnostic procedures on large intestine

45.29   Other diagnostic procedures on intestine, site unspecified
EXCLUDES *microscopic examination of specimen (90.91-90.99)*
scan and radioisotope function study (92.04)
ultrasonography (88.74)
x-ray (87.61-87.69)

√4ᵗʰ **45.3   Local excision or destruction of lesion or tissue of small intestine**

45.30   Endoscopic excision or destruction of lesion of duodenum
EXCLUDES *biopsy of duodenum (45.14-45.15)*
control of hemorrhage (44.43)
fistulectomy (46.72)
AHA: 2Q, '11, 7

45.31   Other local excision of lesion of duodenum
EXCLUDES *biopsy of duodenum (45.14-45.15)*
fistulectomy (46.72)
multiple segmental resection (45.61)
that by endoscopic approach (45.30)

45.32   Other destruction of lesion of duodenum
EXCLUDES *that by endoscopic approach (45.30)*
AHA: N-D, '87, 5; S-O, '85, 6

45.33   Local excision of lesion or tissue of small intestine, except duodenum
Excision of redundant mucosa of ileostomy
EXCLUDES *biopsy of small intestine (45.14-45.15)*
fistulectomy (46.74)
multiple segmental resection (45.61)

45.34   Other destruction of lesion of small intestine, except duodenum
AHA: 3Q, '12, 12; 2Q, '11, 7
TIP: Assign for endoscopic ablation of lesion of jejunum.

√4ᵗʰ **45.4   Local excision or destruction of lesion or tissue of large intestine**
AHA: N-D, '87, 11

45.41   Excision of lesion or tissue of large intestine
Excision of redundant mucosa of colostomy
EXCLUDES *biopsy of large intestine (45.25-45.27)*
endoscopic polypectomy of large intestine (45.42)
fistulectomy (46.76)
multiple segmental resection (17.31, 45.71)
that by endoscopic approach (45.42-45.43)

45.42   Endoscopic polypectomy of large intestine
EXCLUDES *that by open approach (45.41)*
DEF: Endoscopic removal of polyp from large intestine.
AHA: 2Q, '05, 16; 2Q, '90, 25

45.43   Endoscopic destruction of other lesion or tissue of large intestine
Endoscopic ablation of tumor of large intestine
Endoscopic control of colonic bleeding
EXCLUDES *endoscopic polypectomy of large intestine (45.42)*
AHA: 4Q, '02, 61
TIP: Assign for endoscopic treatment of a Dieulafoy lesion of the large intestine, regardless of technique.

45.49   Other destruction of lesion of large intestine
EXCLUDES *that by endoscopic approach (45.43)*

√4ᵗʰ **45.5   Isolation of intestinal segment**
Code also any synchronous:
anastomosis other than end-to-end (45.90-45.94)
enterostomy (46.10-46.39)

45.50   Isolation of intestinal segment, not otherwise specified
Isolation of intestinal pedicle flap
Reversal of intestinal segment
DEF: Isolation of small intestinal pedicle flap: Separation of intestinal pedicle flap.
DEF: Reversal of intestinal segment: Separation of intestinal segment.

Operations on the Digestive System

45.51–46.04

45.51   **Isolation of segment of small intestine**
Isolation of ileal loop
Resection of small intestine for interposition
AHA: 2Q, '05, 12; 3Q, '03, 6-8; 2Q, '03, 11; 3Q, '00, 7

45.52   **Isolation of segment of large intestine**
Resection of colon for interposition

√4th **45.6**   **Other excision of small intestine**
Code also any synchronous:
   anastomosis other than end-to-end (45.90-45.93, 45.95)
   colostomy (46.10-46.13)
   enterostomy (46.10-46.39)
EXCLUDES   *cecectomy (17.32, 45.72)*
          enterocolectomy (17.39, 45.79)
          gastroduodenectomy (43.6-43.99)
          ileocolectomy (17.33, 45.73)
          pancreatoduodenectomy (52.51-52.7)

45.61   **Multiple segmental resection of small intestine**
Segmental resection for multiple traumatic lesions of small intestine

45.62   **Other partial resection of small intestine**
Duodenectomy   Jejunectomy
Ileectomy
EXCLUDES   *duodenectomy with synchronous*
          pancreatectomy (52.51-52.7)
          resection of cecum and terminal ileum
          (17.32, 45.72)
AHA: 1Q, '10, 11; 1Q, '04, 10; 1Q, '03, 18

45.63   **Total removal of small intestine**

√4th **45.7**   **Open and other partial excision of large intestine**
Code also any synchronous:
   anastomosis other than end-to-end (45.92-45.94)
   enterostomy (46.10-46.39)
EXCLUDES   *laparoscopic partial excision of large intestine*
          (17.31-17.39)
AHA: 4Q, '92, 27

45.71   **Open and other multiple segmental resection of large intestine**
Segmental resection for multiple traumatic lesions of large intestine

45.72   **Open and other cecectomy**
Resection of cecum and terminal ileum

45.73   **Open and other right hemicolectomy**
Ileocolectomy   Right radical colectomy
AHA: 1Q, '11, 14; 3Q, '99, 10

45.74   **Open and other resection of transverse colon**

45.75   **Open and other left hemicolectomy**
EXCLUDES   *proctosigmoidectomy (48.41-48.69)*
          second stage Mikulicz operation (46.04)
DEF: Excision of left descending large intestine.
TIP: Assign for Hartmann procedure, typically involving resection of the sigmoid colon with the proximal end terminated as a colostomy and the distal end (rectum) oversewn. A true Hartmann procedure is done on the left side only.

45.76   **Open and other sigmoidectomy**
AHA: 3Q, '10, 12; 1Q, '96, 9; 3Q, '89, 15

45.79   **Other and unspecified partial excision of large intestine**
Enterocolectomy NEC
AHA: 1Q, '09, 5;1Q, '03, 18; 3Q, '97, 9; 2Q, '91, 16

√4th **45.8**   **Total intra-abdominal colectomy**
Excision of cecum, colon, and sigmoid
EXCLUDES   *coloproctectomy (48.41-48.69)*
AHA: 4Q, '08, 169-170

45.81   **Laparoscopic total intra-abdominal colectomy**
AHA: ▶2Q, '13, 20◀

45.82   **Open total intra-abdominal colectomy**

45.83   **Other and unspecified total intra-abdominal colectomy**
AHA: ▶2Q, '13, 20◀

Colectomy

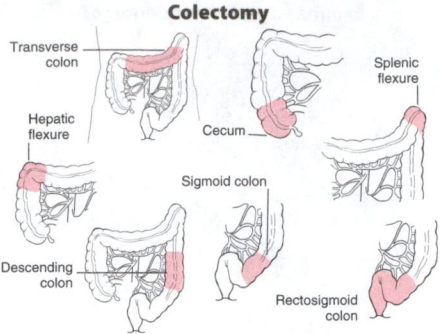

Transverse colon | Splenic flexure
Hepatic flexure | Cecum
Descending colon | Sigmoid colon | Rectosigmoid colon

Intestinal Anastomosis

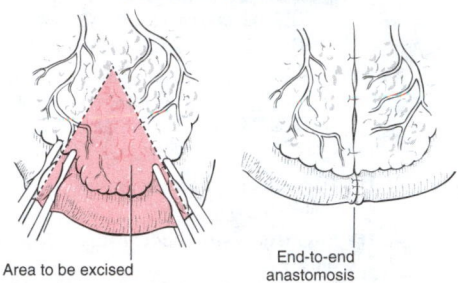

Area to be excised   End-to-end anastomosis

√4th **45.9**   **Intestinal anastomosis**
Code also any synchronous resection (45.31-45.8, 48.41-48.69)
EXCLUDES   *end-to-end anastomosis — omit code*

45.90   **Intestinal anastomosis, not otherwise specified**

45.91   **Small-to-small intestinal anastomosis**
AHA: 1Q, '10, 11; 3Q, '03, 6-8; M-J, '85, 17

45.92   **Anastomosis of small intestine to rectal stump**
Hampton procedure

45.93   **Other small-to-large intestinal anastomosis**
AHA: 1Q, '03, 18; N-D, '86, 11

45.94   **Large-to-large intestinal anastomosis**
EXCLUDES   *rectorectostomy (48.74)*
AHA: 1Q, '09, 5; 3Q, '89, 15

45.95   **Anastomosis to anus**
Formation of endorectal ileal pouch (J-pouch) (H-pouch) (S-pouch) with anastomosis of small intestine to anus
AHA: ▶2Q, '13, 20; ◀2Q, '05, 13

√3rd **46**   **Other operations on intestine**
Code also any application or administration of an adhesion barrier substance (99.77)

√4th **46.0**   **Exteriorization of intestine**
INCLUDES   loop enterostomy
          multiple stage resection of intestine
DEF: Bringing intestinal segment to body surface.

46.01   **Exteriorization of small intestine**
Loop ileostomy
AHA: ▶2Q, '13, 20◀

46.02   **Resection of exteriorized segment of small intestine**

46.03   **Exteriorization of large intestine**
Exteriorization of intestine NOS
First stage Mikulicz exteriorization of intestine
Loop colostomy

46.04   **Resection of exteriorized segment of large intestine**
Resection of exteriorized segment of intestine NOS
Second stage Mikulicz operation

BI Bilateral Procedure   NC Non-covered Procedure   LC Limited Coverage Procedure   ▶◀ Revised Text   ● New Code   ▲ Revised Code Title

132 – Volume 3 · October 2014   **2015 ICD-9-CM**

√4ᵗʰ 46.1 Colostomy
Code also any synchronous resection (45.49, 45.71-45.79, 45.8)
EXCLUDES loop colostomy (46.03)
that with abdominoperineal resection of rectum (48.5)
that with synchronous anterior rectal resection (48.62)
DEF: Creation of opening from large intestine through abdominal wall to body surface.

46.10 Colostomy, not otherwise specified

46.11 Temporary colostomy

46.13 Permanent colostomy

46.14 Delayed opening of colostomy

√4ᵗʰ 46.2 Ileostomy
Code also any synchronous resection (45.34, 45.61-45.63)
EXCLUDES loop ileostomy (46.01)
DEF: Creation of artificial anus by bringing ileum through abdominal wall to body surface.

46.20 Ileostomy, not otherwise specified

46.21 Temporary ileostomy

46.22 Continent ileostomy
DEF: Creation of opening from third part of small intestine through abdominal wall, with pouch outside abdomen.
AHA: M-J, '85, 17

46.23 Other permanent ileostomy

46.24 Delayed opening of ileostomy

√4ᵗʰ 46.3 Other enterostomy
Code also any synchronous resection (45.61-45.8)

46.31 Delayed opening of other enterostomy

46.32 Percutaneous (endoscopic) jejunostomy [PEJ]
Endoscopic conversion of gastrostomy to jejunostomy
Percutaneous (endoscopic) feeding enterostomy
EXCLUDES percutaneous [endoscopic] gastrojejunostomy (bypass) (44.32)
DEF: Percutaneous feeding enterostomy: Surgical placement of a (feeding) tube through the midsection of the small intestine through the abdominal wall.
DEF: Conversion of gastrostomy to jejunostomy: Endoscopic advancement of a jejunostomy tube through an existing gastrostomy tube into the proximal jejunum.
AHA: ▶3Q, '13, 15, 16;◄ 3Q, '10, 13

46.39 Other
Duodenostomy   Feeding enterostomy
AHA: 3Q, '89, 15

√4ᵗʰ 46.4 Revision of intestinal stoma
DEF: Revision of opening surgically created from intestine through abdominal wall, to skin surface.

46.40 Revision of intestinal stoma, not otherwise specified
Plastic enlargement of intestinal stoma
Reconstruction of stoma of intestine
Release of scar tissue of intestinal stoma
EXCLUDES excision of redundant mucosa (45.41)

46.41 Revision of stoma of small intestine
EXCLUDES excision of redundant mucosa (45.33)
AHA: 2Q, '05, 11

46.42 Repair of pericolostomy hernia

46.43 Other revision of stoma of large intestine
EXCLUDES excision of redundant mucosa (45.41)
AHA: 2Q, '02, 9
TIP: Assign for a relocation of a stoma.

√4ᵗʰ 46.5 Closure of intestinal stoma
Code also any synchronous resection (45.34, 45.49, 45.61-45.8)

46.50 Closure of intestinal stoma, not otherwise specified

46.51 Closure of stoma of small intestine

46.52 Closure of stoma of large intestine
Closure or take-down of cecostomy
Closure or take-down of colostomy
Closure or take-down of sigmoidostomy
AHA: 1Q, '09, 5; 2Q, '05, 4; 3Q, '97, 9; 2Q, '91, 16; N-D, '87, 8

√4ᵗʰ 46.6 Fixation of intestine

46.60 Fixation of intestine, not otherwise specified
Fixation of intestine to abdominal wall

46.61 Fixation of small intestine to abdominal wall
Ileopexy

46.62 Other fixation of small intestine
Noble plication of small intestine
Plication of jejunum
DEF: Noble plication of small intestine: Fixing small intestine into place with tuck in small intestine.
DEF: Plication of jejunum: Fixing small intestine into place with tuck in midsection.

46.63 Fixation of large intestine to abdominal wall
Cecocoloplicopexy   Sigmoidopexy (Moschowitz)

46.64 Other fixation of large intestine
Cecofixation   Colofixation

√4ᵗʰ 46.7 Other repair of intestine
EXCLUDES closure of:
ulcer of duodenum (44.42)
vesicoenteric fistula (57.83)

46.71 Suture of laceration of duodenum

46.72 Closure of fistula of duodenum

46.73 Suture of laceration of small intestine, except duodenum
AHA: 1Q, '10, 11

46.74 Closure of fistula of small intestine, except duodenum
EXCLUDES closure of:
artificial stoma (46.51)
vaginal fistula (70.74)
repair of gastrojejunocolic fistula (44.63)

46.75 Suture of laceration of large intestine

46.76 Closure of fistula of large intestine
EXCLUDES closure of:
gastrocolic fistula (44.63)
rectal fistula (48.73)
sigmoidovesical fistula (57.83)
stoma (46.52)
vaginal fistula (70.72-70.73)
vesicocolic fistula (57.83)
vesicosigmoidovaginal fistula (57.83)
AHA: 3Q, '99, 8

46.79 Other repair of intestine
Duodenoplasty
AHA: 3Q, '02, 11
TIP: Assign for duodenoplasty, typically performed for infants with congenital duodenal webs and stenosis.

√4ᵗʰ 46.8 Dilation and manipulation of intestine
AHA: 1Q, '03, 14

46.80 Intra-abdominal manipulation of intestine, not otherwise specified
Correction of intestinal   Reduction of:
malrotation   intestinal volvulus
Reduction of: intussusception
intestinal torsion
EXCLUDES reduction of intussusception with:
fluoroscopy (96.29)
ionizing radiation enema (96.29)
ultrasonography guidance (96.29)
DEF: Correction of intestinal malrotation: Repair of abnormal rotation.
DEF: Reduction of: Intestinal torsion: Repair of twisted segment. Intestinal volvulus: Repair of a knotted segment. Intussusception: Repair of prolapsed segment.
AHA: 4Q, '98, 82
TIP: Do not assign if the documentation indicates only "running or milking the bowel." This is an integral component of other procedures.

Operations on the Digestive System

46.81–48.33

46.81 Intra-abdominal manipulation of small intestine
AHA: ▶2Q, '13, 4◀

46.82 Intra-abdominal manipulation of large intestine
AHA: ▶2Q, '13, 4◀

46.85 Dilation of intestine
Dilation (balloon) of duodenum
Dilation (balloon) of jejunum
Endoscopic dilation (balloon) of large intestine
That through rectum or colostomy
EXCLUDES *with insertion of colonic stent (46.86-46.87)*
AHA: 3Q, '07, 5; 3Q, '89, 15

46.86 Endoscopic insertion of colonic stent(s)
Colonoscopy (flexible) (through stoma) with
transendoscopic stent placement
Combined with fluoroscopic-guided insertion
Stent endoprosthesis of colon
Through the scope [TTS] technique
EXCLUDES *other non-endoscopic insertion of colonic stent (46.87)*
AHA: 4Q, '09, 147

46.87 Other insertion of colonic stent(s)
INCLUDES that by:
fluoroscopic guidance only
rectal guiding tube
Non-endoscopic insertion
Code also any synchronous diagnostic procedure(s)
EXCLUDES *endoscopic insertion of colonic stent (46.86)*

✓4th **46.9 Other operations on intestines**

46.91 Myotomy of sigmoid colon

46.92 Myotomy of other parts of colon

46.93 Revision of anastomosis of small intestine

46.94 Revision of anastomosis of large intestine

46.95 Local perfusion of small intestine
Code also substance perfused (99.21-99.29)

46.96 Local perfusion of large intestine
Code also substance perfused (99.21-99.29)

46.97 Transplant of intestine   LC
NOTE To report donor source — see codes
00.91-00.93
AHA: 4Q, '00, 66

46.99 Other
Ileoentectropy
EXCLUDES *diagnostic procedures on intestine (45.11-45.29)*
dilation of enterostomy stoma (96.24)
intestinal intubation (96.08)
removal of:
intraluminal foreign body from large intestine without incision (98.04)
intraluminal foreign body from small intestine without incision (98.03)
tube from large intestine (97.53)
tube from small intestine (97.52)
replacement of:
large intestine tube or enterostomy device (97.04)
small intestine tube or enterostomy device (97.03)
AHA: 3Q, '99, 11; 1Q, '89, 11

✓3rd **47 Operations on appendix**
INCLUDES appendiceal stump
Code also any application or administration of an adhesion barrier
substance (99.77)

✓4th **47.0 Appendectomy**
EXCLUDES *incidental appendectomy, so described*
laparoscopic (47.11)
other (47.19)
AHA: 4Q, '96, 64; 3Q, '92, 12

47.01 Laparoscopic appendectomy
AHA: 1Q, '01, 15; 4Q, '96, 64

47.09 Other appendectomy
AHA: 4Q, '97, 52

✓4th **47.1 Incidental appendectomy**
DEF: Removal of appendix during abdominal surgery as prophylactic
measure, without significant appendiceal pathology.

47.11 Laparoscopic incidental appendectomy

47.19 Other incidental appendectomy
AHA: ▶2Q, '13, 4;◀ 4Q, '96, 65

47.2 Drainage of appendiceal abscess
EXCLUDES *that with appendectomy (47.0)*

✓4th **47.9 Other operations on appendix**

47.91 Appendicostomy
AHA: ▶1Q, '14, 15◀

47.92 Closure of appendiceal fistula

47.99 Other
Anastomosis of appendix
EXCLUDES *diagnostic procedures on appendix (45.21-45.29)*
AHA: ▶1Q, '14, 15;◀ 3Q, '01, 16
TIP: Assign for a Malone antegrade continence enema
procedure, in which the appendix is sutured to the
abdominal wall, creating an orifice through which the
patient can administer enemas via a small catheter through
the appendix and into the cecum.

✓3rd **48 Operations on rectum, rectosigmoid, and perirectal tissue**
Code also any application or administration of an adhesion barrier
substance (99.77)

48.0 Proctotomy
Decompression of imperforate anus
Panas' operation [linear proctotomy]
EXCLUDES *incision of perirectal tissue (48.81)*
DEF: Incision into rectal portion of large intestine.
DEF: Decompression of imperforate anus: opening a closed anus by
means of an incision.
DEF: Panas' operation (linear proctotomy): Linear incision into rectal
portion of large intestine.
AHA: 3Q, '99, 8

48.1 Proctostomy

✓4th **48.2 Diagnostic procedures on rectum, rectosigmoid, and
perirectal tissue**

48.21 Transabdominal proctosigmoidoscopy
Intraoperative proctosigmoidoscopy
EXCLUDES *that with biopsy (48.24)*

48.22 Proctosigmoidoscopy through artificial stoma
EXCLUDES *that with biopsy (48.24)*

48.23 Rigid proctosigmoidoscopy
EXCLUDES *flexible sigmoidoscopy (45.24)*
DEF: Endoscopic exam of anus, rectum and lower sigmoid
colon.
AHA: 1Q, '01, 8

48.24 Closed [endoscopic] biopsy of rectum
Brushing or washing for specimen collection
Proctosigmoidoscopy with biopsy
AHA: 1Q, '03, 14

48.25 Open biopsy of rectum

48.26 Biopsy of perirectal tissue

**48.29 Other diagnostic procedures on rectum,
rectosigmoid, and perirectal tissue**
EXCLUDES *digital examination of rectum (89.34)*
lower GI series (87.64)
microscopic examination of specimen from rectum (90.91-90.99)

✓4th **48.3 Local excision or destruction of lesion or tissue of rectum**

48.31 Radical electrocoagulation of rectal lesion or tissue
DEF: Destruction of lesion or tissue of rectal part of large
intestine.

48.32 Other electrocoagulation of rectal lesion or tissue
AHA: 2Q, '98, 18

48.33 Destruction of rectal lesion or tissue by laser

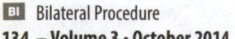

BI Bilateral Procedure   NC Non-covered Procedure   LC Limited Coverage Procedure   ▶◀ Revised Text   ● New Code   ▲ Revised Code Title

48.34 Destruction of rectal lesion or tissue by cryosurgery

48.35 Local excision of rectal lesion or tissue
> EXCLUDES biopsy of rectum (48.24-48.25)
> [endoscopic] polypectomy of rectum (48.36)
> excision of perirectal tissue (48.82)
> hemorrhoidectomy (49.46)
> rectal fistulectomy (48.73)

48.36 [Endoscopic] polypectomy of rectum
> AHA: 4Q, '95, 65

48.4 Pull-through resection of rectum
> Code also any synchronous anastomosis other than end-to-end (45.90, 45.92-45.95)
> AHA: 4Q, '08, 169-171

48.40 Pull-through resection of rectum, not otherwise specified
> Pull-through resection NOS
> EXCLUDES abdominoperineal pull-through NOS (48.50)

48.41 Soave submucosal resection of rectum
> Endorectal pull-through operation
> DEF: Soave submucosal resection: Resection of submucosal rectal part of large intestine by pull-through technique.
> DEF: Endorectal pull-through operation: Resection of interior large intestine by pull-through technique.

48.42 Laparoscopic pull-through resection of rectum

48.43 Open pull-through resection of rectum

48.49 Other pull-through resection of rectum
> Abdominoperineal pull-through
> Altemeier operation
> Swenson proctectomy
> EXCLUDES Duhamel abdominoperineal pull-through (48.65)
> laparoscopic pull-through resection of rectum (48.42)
> open pull-through resection of rectum (48.43)
> pull-through resection of rectum, not otherwise specified (48.40)
> DEF: Abdominoperineal pull-through: Resection of large intestine, latter part, by pull-through of abdomen, scrotum or vulva and anus.
> DEF: Swenson proctectomy: Excision of large intestine, rectal by pull-through and preserving muscles that close the anus.
> AHA: 2Q, '11, 13; 3Q, '01, 8; 2Q, '99, 13

48.5 Abdominoperineal resection of rectum
> INCLUDES with synchronous colostomy
> Combined abdominoendorectal resection
> Complete proctectomy
> Code also any synchronous anastomosis other than end-to-end (45.90, 45.92-45.95)
> EXCLUDES Duhamel abdominoperineal pull-through (48.65)
> that as part of pelvic exenteration (68.8)
> DEF: Rectal excision through cavities formed by abdomen, anus, vulva or scrotum.
> AHA: 4Q, '08, 169-172; 2Q, '97, 5

48.50 Abdominoperineal resection of the rectum, not otherwise specified

48.51 Laparoscopic abdominoperineal resection of the rectum
> AHA: ▶2Q, '13, 20◀

48.52 Open abdominoperineal resection of the rectum

48.59 Other abdominoperineal resection of the rectum
> EXCLUDES abdominoperineal resection of the rectum, NOS (48.50)
> laparoscopic abdominoperineal resection of the rectum (48.51)
> open abdominoperineal resection of the rectum (48.52)
> AHA: ▶2Q, '13, 20◀

48.6 Other resection of rectum
> Code also any synchronous anastomosis other than end-to-end (45.90, 45.92-45.95)

48.61 Transsacral rectosigmoidectomy
> DEF: Excision through sacral bone area of sigmoid and last parts of large intestine.

48.62 Anterior resection of rectum with synchronous colostomy
> DEF: Resection of front terminal end of large intestine and creation of colostomy.

48.63 Other anterior resection of rectum
> EXCLUDES that with synchronous colostomy (48.62)
> AHA: 1Q, '96, 9

48.64 Posterior resection of rectum

48.65 Duhamel resection of rectum
> Duhamel abdominoperineal pull-through

48.69 Other
> Partial proctectomy   Rectal resection NOS
> AHA: 2Q, '05, 13; J-F, '87, 11; N-D, '86, 11

48.7 Repair of rectum
> EXCLUDES repair of:
> current obstetric laceration (75.62)
> vaginal rectocele (70.50, 70.52, 70.53, 70.55)

48.71 Suture of laceration of rectum

48.72 Closure of proctostomy

48.73 Closure of other rectal fistula
> EXCLUDES fistulectomy:
> perirectal (48.93)
> rectourethral (58.43)
> rectovaginal (70.73)
> rectovesical (57.83)
> rectovesicovaginal (57.83)

48.74 Rectorectostomy
> Rectal anastomosis NOS
> Stapled transanal rectal resection (STARR)
> DEF: Rectal anastomosis: Connection of two cut portions of large intestine, rectal end.

48.75 Abdominal proctopexy
> Frickman procedure
> Ripstein repair of rectal prolapse
> DEF: Fixation of rectum to adjacent abdominal structures.

48.76 Other proctopexy
> Delorme repair of prolapsed rectum
> Proctosigmoidopexy
> Puborectalis sling operation
> EXCLUDES manual reduction of rectal prolapse (96.26)
> DEF: Delorme repair of prolapsed rectum: Fixation of rectal part of collapsed large intestine.
> DEF: Proctosigmoidopexy: Suturing rectal part of twisted large intestine.
> DEF: Puborectalis sling operation: Fixation of rectal part of large intestine by forming puborectalis muscle into sling.

48.79 Other repair of rectum
> Repair of old obstetric laceration of rectum
> EXCLUDES anastomosis to:
> large intestine (45.94)
> small intestine (45.92-45.93)
> repair of:
> current obstetrical laceration (75.62)
> vaginal rectocele (70.50, 70.52)

48.8 Incision or excision of perirectal tissue or lesion
> INCLUDES pelvirectal tissue
> rectovaginal septum

48.81 Incision of perirectal tissue
> Incision of rectovaginal septum

48.82 Excision of perirectal tissue
> EXCLUDES perirectal biopsy (48.26)
> perirectofistulectomy (48.93)
> rectal fistulectomy (48.73)

48.9 Other operations on rectum and perirectal tissue

48.91 Incision of rectal stricture

48.92 Anorectal myectomy
DEF: Excision of anorectal muscle.

48.93 Repair of perirectal fistula
EXCLUDES that opening into rectum (48.73)
DEF: Closure of abdominal passage in tissue around rectal part of large intestine.
AHA: 1Q, '07, 13
TIP: Assign for Seton placement, which is a cord or stitch that is passed through the path of the fistula; it generates a fibrous reaction, allowing for tissue ingrowth over a period of time.

48.99 Other
EXCLUDES digital examination of rectum (89.34)
dilation of rectum (96.22)
insertion of rectal tube (96.09)
irrigation of rectum (96.38-96.39)
manual reduction of rectal prolapse (96.26)
proctoclysis (96.37)
rectal massage (99.93)
rectal packing (96.19)
removal of:
impacted feces (96.38)
intraluminal foreign body from rectum without incision (98.05)
rectal packing (97.59)
transanal enema (96.39)

✓3rd **49 Operations on anus**
Code also any application or administration of an adhesion barrier substance (99.77)

✓4th **49.0 Incision or excision of perianal tissue**

49.01 Incision of perianal abscess
AHA: 2Q, '05, 10

49.02 Other incision of perianal tissue
Undercutting of perianal tissue
EXCLUDES anal fistulotomy (49.11)

49.03 Excision of perianal skin tags

49.04 Other excision of perianal tissue
EXCLUDES anal fistulectomy (49.12)
biopsy of perianal tissue (49.22)
AHA: 1Q, '01, 8

✓4th **49.1 Incision or excision of anal fistula**
EXCLUDES closure of anal fistula (49.73)

49.11 Anal fistulotomy

49.12 Anal fistulectomy

✓4th **49.2 Diagnostic procedures on anus and perianal tissue**

49.21 Anoscopy

49.22 Biopsy of perianal tissue

49.23 Biopsy of anus

49.29 Other diagnostic procedures on anus and perianal tissue
EXCLUDES microscopic examination of specimen from anus (90.91-90.99)

✓4th **49.3 Local excision or destruction of other lesion or tissue of anus**
Anal cryptotomy
Cauterization of lesion of anus
EXCLUDES biopsy of anus (49.23)
control of (postoperative) hemorrhage of anus (49.95)
hemorrhoidectomy (49.46)

49.31 Endoscopic excision or destruction of lesion or tissue of anus

49.39 Other local excision or destruction of lesion or tissue of anus
EXCLUDES that by endoscopic approach (49.31)
AHA: 1Q, '01, 8

Dynamic Gracioplasty

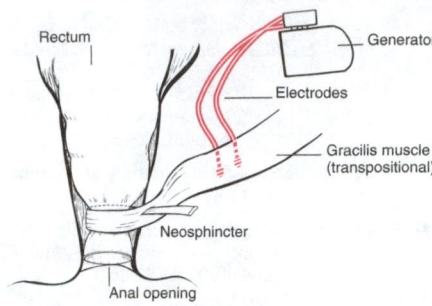

✓4th **49.4 Procedures on hemorrhoids**

49.41 Reduction of hemorrhoids
DEF: Manual manipulation to reduce hemorrhoids.

49.42 Injection of hemorrhoids

49.43 Cauterization of hemorrhoids
Clamp and cautery of hemorrhoids

49.44 Destruction of hemorrhoids by cryotherapy

49.45 Ligation of hemorrhoids
AHA: 4Q, '12, 81, 82

49.46 Excision of hemorrhoids
Hemorrhoidectomy NOS
AHA: 1Q, '07, 13

49.47 Evacuation of thrombosed hemorrhoids
DEF: Removal of clotted material from hemorrhoid.

49.49 Other procedures on hemorrhoids
Lord procedure

✓4th **49.5 Division of anal sphincter**

49.51 Left lateral anal sphincterotomy

49.52 Posterior anal sphincterotomy

49.59 Other anal sphincterotomy
Division of sphincter NOS

49.6 Excision of anus

✓4th **49.7 Repair of anus**
EXCLUDES repair of current obstetric laceration (75.62)

49.71 Suture of laceration of anus

49.72 Anal cerclage
DEF: Encircling anus with ring or sutures.

49.73 Closure of anal fistula
EXCLUDES excision of anal fistula (49.12)

49.74 Gracilis muscle transplant for anal incontinence
DEF: Moving pubic attachment of gracilis muscle to restore anal control.

49.75 Implantation or revision of artificial anal sphincter
Removal with subsequent replacement
Replacement during same or subsequent operative episode
AHA: 4Q, '02, 105

49.76 Removal of artificial anal sphincter
Explantation or removal without replacement
EXCLUDES revision with implantation during same operative episode (49.75)
AHA: 4Q, '02, 105

49.79 Other repair of anal sphincter
Repair of old obstetric laceration of anus
EXCLUDES anoplasty with synchronous hemorrhoidectomy (49.46)
repair of current obstetric laceration (75.62)
AHA: 2Q, '98, 16; 1Q, '97, 9

✓4th **49.9 Other operations on anus**
EXCLUDES dilation of anus (sphincter) (96.23)

49.91 Incision of anal septum

49.92 Insertion of subcutaneous electrical anal stimulator

BI Bilateral Procedure   NC Non-covered Procedure   LC Limited Coverage Procedure   ►◄ Revised Text   ● New Code   ▲ Revised Code Title

136 – Volume 3   2015 ICD-9-CM

49.93 **Other incision of anus**
Removal of:
   foreign body from anus with incision
   seton from anus
   EXCLUDES *anal fistulotomy (49.11)*
   removal of intraluminal foreign body
   without incision (98.05)

49.94 **Reduction of anal prolapse**
   EXCLUDES *manual reduction of rectal prolapse (96.26)*
   DEF: Manipulation of displaced anal tissue to normal position.

49.95 **Control of (postoperative) hemorrhage of anus**

49.99 **Other**

✓3rd **50** **Operations on liver**
Code also any application or administration of an adhesion barrier substance (99.77)

50.0 **Hepatotomy**
Incision of abscess of liver
Removal of gallstones from liver
Stromeyer-Little operation

✓4th **50.1** **Diagnostic procedures on liver**

50.11 **Closed (percutaneous) (needle) biopsy of liver**
Diagnostic aspiration of liver
AHA: 3Q, '05, 24; 4Q, '88, 12
TIP: When a laparotomy or other open procedure is performed and a needle biopsy of the liver is also performed, assign a separate code for the open procedure and code 50.11 for the needle biopsy.

50.12 **Open biopsy of liver**
Wedge biopsy
AHA: 3Q, '05, 24; 2Q, '05, 13

50.13 **Transjugular liver biopsy**
Transvenous liver biopsy
   EXCLUDES *closed (percutaneous) [needle] biopsy of liver (50.11)*
   laparoscopic liver biopsy (50.14)
AHA: 4Q, '07, 113

50.14 **Laparoscopic liver biopsy**
   EXCLUDES *closed (percutaneous) [needle] biopsy of liver (50.11)*
   open biopsy of liver (50.12)
   transjugular liver biopsy (50.13)
AHA: 4Q, '07, 113

50.19 **Other diagnostic procedures on liver**
   EXCLUDES *laparoscopic liver biopsy (50.14)*
   liver scan and radioisotope function study (92.02)
   microscopic examination of specimen from liver (91.01-91.09)
   transjugular liver biopsy (50.13)

✓4th **50.2** **Local excision or destruction of liver tissue or lesion**

50.21 **Marsupialization of lesion of liver**
   DEF: Exteriorizing lesion by incision and suturing cut edges to skin to create opening.

50.22 **Partial hepatectomy**
Wedge resection of liver
   EXCLUDES *biopsy of liver (50.11-50.12)*
   hepatic lobectomy (50.3)

50.23 **Open ablation of liver lesion or tissue**
AHA: 4Q, '06, 124

50.24 **Percutaneous ablation of liver lesion or tissue**
AHA: 4Q, '06, 124

50.25 **Laparoscopic ablation of liver lesion or tissue**
AHA: 4Q, '06, 124

50.26 **Other and unspecified ablation of liver lesion or tissue**
AHA: 4Q, '06, 124

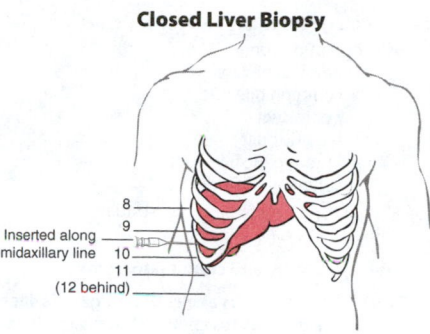

Closed Liver Biopsy

Inserted along midaxillary line
8
9
10
11
(12 behind)

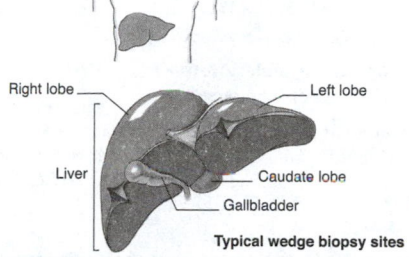

Liver Biopsy (Open, Wedge)

Right lobe
Left lobe
Liver
Caudate lobe
Gallbladder
Typical wedge biopsy sites

50.29 **Other destruction of lesion of liver**
Cauterization ⎫
Enucleation ⎬ of hepatic lesion
Evacuation ⎭
   EXCLUDES *ablation of liver lesion or tissue:*
   laparoscopic (50.25)
   open (50.23)
   other (50.26)
   percutaneous (50.24)
   laser interstitial thermal therapy [LITT] of lesion or tissue of liver under guidance (17.63)
   percutaneous aspiration of lesion (50.91)
AHA: ▶2Q, '13, 12;◄ 2Q, '03, 9

50.3 **Lobectomy of liver**
Total hepatic lobectomy with partial excision of other lobe

50.4 **Total hepatectomy**
AHA: 2Q, '08, 8

✓4th **50.5** **Liver transplant**
NOTE To report donor source — see codes 00.91-00.93

50.51 **Auxiliary liver transplant**   NC
Auxiliary hepatic transplantation leaving patient's own liver in situ

50.59 **Other transplant of liver**   LC
AHA: 4Q, '08, 120; 2Q, '08, 8

✓4th **50.6** **Repair of liver**

50.61 **Closure of laceration of liver**

50.69 **Other repair of liver**
Hepatopexy

✓4th **50.9** **Other operations on liver**
   EXCLUDES *lysis of adhesions (54.5)*

50.91 **Percutaneous aspiration of liver**
   EXCLUDES *percutaneous biopsy (50.11)*
   DEF: Incision into liver through body wall to withdraw fluid.

50.92 **Extracorporeal hepatic assistance**
Liver dialysis
   DEF: Devices used outside body to assist liver function.
AHA: 2Q, '01, 21

50.93 **Localized perfusion of liver**

50.94 **Other injection of therapeutic substance into liver**

50.99 **Other**
AHA: ▶2Q, '13, 12◄

✓3rd
✓4th Additional Digit Required   Valid OR Procedure   Non-OR Procedure   Adjunct Code
2015 ICD-9-CM   October 2014 • Volume 3 – 137

Operations on the Digestive System

51–51.59

✓3ʳᵈ **51** **Operations on gallbladder and biliary tract**

     INCLUDES operations on:
         ampulla of Vater
         common bile duct
         cystic duct
         hepatic duct
         intrahepatic bile duct
         sphincter of Oddi

     Code also any application or administration of an adhesion barrier substance (99.77)

✓4ᵗʰ **51.0** **Cholecystotomy and cholecystostomy**

     51.01 **Percutaneous aspiration of gallbladder**
         Percutaneous cholecystotomy for drainage
         That by: needle or catheter
         EXCLUDES *needle biopsy (51.12)*

     51.02 **Trocar cholecystostomy**
         DEF: Creating opening in gallbladder with catheter.
         AHA: 3Q, '89, 18

     51.03 **Other cholecystostomy**

     51.04 **Other cholecystotomy**
         Cholelithotomy NOS

✓4ᵗʰ **51.1** **Diagnostic procedures on biliary tract**
         EXCLUDES *that for endoscopic procedures classifiable to 51.64, 51.84-51.88, 52.14, 52.21, 52.93 -52.94, 52.97-52.98*

         AHA: 2Q, '97, 7

     51.10 **Endoscopic retrograde cholangiopancreatography [ERCP]**
         EXCLUDES *endoscopic retrograde:*
            cholangiography [ERC] (51.11)
            pancreatography [ERP] (52.13)
         DEF: Endoscopic and radioscopic exam of pancreatic and common bile ducts with contrast material injected through catheter in opposite direction of normal flow.
         AHA: 4Q, '03, 118; 3Q, '03, 17; 1Q, '01, 8; 2Q, '99, 13
         TIP: Do not assign separately if the ERCP was performed in conjunction with endoscopic sphincterotomy/papillotomy or other therapeutic biliary procedure.

     51.11 **Endoscopic retrograde cholangiography [ERC]**
         Laparoscopic exploration of common bile duct
         EXCLUDES *endoscopic retrograde:*
            cholangiopancreatography [ERCP] (51.10)
            pancreatography [ERP] (52.13)
         DEF: Endoscopic and radioscopic exam of common bile ducts with contrast material injected through catheter in opposite direction of normal flow.
         AHA: 1Q, '96, 12; 3Q, '89, 18; 4Q, '88, 7

     51.12 **Percutaneous biopsy of gallbladder or bile ducts**
         Needle biopsy of gallbladder

     51.13 **Open biopsy of gallbladder or bile ducts**

     51.14 **Other closed [endoscopic] biopsy of biliary duct or sphincter of Oddi**
         Brushing or washing for specimen collection
         Closed biopsy of biliary duct or sphincter of Oddi by procedures classifiable to 51.10-51.11, 52.13
         DEF: Endoscopic biopsy of muscle tissue around pancreatic and common bile ducts.

Laparoscopic Cholecystectomy by Laser

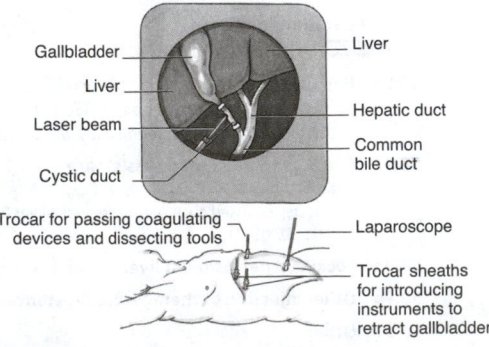

Gallbladder — Liver
Liver — Hepatic duct
Laser beam — Common bile duct
Cystic duct

Trocar for passing coagulating devices and dissecting tools — Laparoscope

Trocar sheaths for introducing instruments to retract gallbladder

---

     51.15 **Pressure measurement of sphincter of Oddi**
         Pressure measurement of sphincter by procedures classifiable to 51.10-51.11, 52.13
         DEF: Pressure measurement tests of muscle tissue surrounding pancreatic and common bile ducts.

     51.19 **Other diagnostic procedures on biliary tract**
         EXCLUDES *biliary tract x-ray (87.51-87.59)*
            microscopic examination of specimen from biliary tract (91.01-91.09)

✓4ᵗʰ **51.2** **Cholecystectomy**
         AHA: 1Q, '93, 17; 4Q, '91, 26; 3Q, '89, 18

     51.21 **Other partial cholecystectomy**
         Revision of prior cholecystectomy
         EXCLUDES *that by laparoscope (51.24)*
         AHA: 4Q, '96, 69

     51.22 **Cholecystectomy**
         EXCLUDES *laparoscopic cholecystectomy (51.23)*
         AHA: 4Q, '97, 52; 2Q, '91, 16

     51.23 **Laparoscopic cholecystectomy**
         That by laser
         DEF: Endoscopic removal of gallbladder.
         AHA: 4Q, '08, 174; 3Q, '98, 10; 4Q, '97, 52; 1Q, '96, 12; 2Q, '95, 11; 4Q, '91, 26

     51.24 **Laparoscopic partial cholecystectomy**
         AHA: 4Q, '96, 69

✓4ᵗʰ **51.3** **Anastomosis of gallbladder or bile duct**
         EXCLUDES *resection with end-to-end anastomosis (51.61-51.69)*

     51.31 **Anastomosis of gallbladder to hepatic ducts**

     51.32 **Anastomosis of gallbladder to intestine**

     51.33 **Anastomosis of gallbladder to pancreas**

     51.34 **Anastomosis of gallbladder to stomach**

     51.35 **Other gallbladder anastomosis**
         Gallbladder anastomosis NOS

     51.36 **Choledochoenterostomy**
         DEF: Connection of common bile duct to intestine.

     51.37 **Anastomosis of hepatic duct to gastrointestinal tract**
         Kasai portoenterostomy
         DEF: Kaisi portoenterostomy: A duct to drain bile from the liver is formed by anastomosing the porta hepatis to a loop of bowel.
         AHA: 2Q, '02, 12

     51.39 **Other bile duct anastomosis**
         Anastomosis of bile duct NOS
         Anastomosis of unspecified bile duct to:
            intestine
            liver
            pancreas
            stomach

✓4ᵗʰ **51.4** **Incision of bile duct for relief of obstruction**

     51.41 **Common duct exploration for removal of calculus**
         EXCLUDES *percutaneous extraction (51.96)*
         AHA: 1Q, '96, 12; 3Q, '89, 18; 4Q, '88, 7

     51.42 **Common duct exploration for relief of other obstruction**
         AHA: 3Q, '89, 18

     51.43 **Insertion of choledochohepatic tube for decompression**
         Hepatocholedochostomy
         AHA: 3Q, '89, 18; 4Q, '88, 7

     51.49 **Incision of other bile ducts for relief of obstruction**
         AHA: 3Q, '89, 18

✓4ᵗʰ **51.5** **Other incision of bile duct**
         EXCLUDES *that for relief of obstruction (51.41-51.49)*

     51.51 **Exploration of common duct**
         Incision of common bile duct
         AHA: 2Q, '97, 16; 1Q, '96, 12

     51.59 **Incision of other bile duct**
         AHA: 2Q, '97, 16; 3Q, '89, 18

BI Bilateral Procedure   **NC** Non-covered Procedure   **LC** Limited Coverage Procedure   ▶◀ Revised Text   ● New Code   ▲ Revised Code Title

Operations on the Digestive System

51.6–52.19

✓4ᵗʰ **51.6 Local excision or destruction of lesion or tissue of biliary ducts and sphincter of Oddi**
Code also anastomosis other than end-to-end (51.31, 51.36-51.39)
EXCLUDES biopsy of bile duct (51.12-51.13)

51.61 Excision of cystic duct remnant
AHA: 3Q, '89, 18

51.62 Excision of ampulla of Vater (with reimplantation of common duct)

51.63 Other excision of common duct
Choledochectomy
EXCLUDES fistulectomy (51.72)

51.64 Endoscopic excision or destruction of lesion of biliary ducts or sphincter of Oddi
Excision or destruction of lesion of biliary duct by procedures classifiable to 51.10-51.11, 52.13

51.69 Excision of other bile duct
Excision of lesion of bile duct NOS
EXCLUDES fistulectomy (51.79)

✓4ᵗʰ **51.7 Repair of bile ducts**

51.71 Simple suture of common bile duct

51.72 Choledochoplasty
Repair of fistula of common bile duct

51.79 Repair of other bile ducts
Closure of artificial opening of bile duct NOS
Suture of bile duct NOS
EXCLUDES operative removal of prosthetic device (51.95)

✓4ᵗʰ **51.8 Other operations on biliary ducts and sphincter of Oddi**

51.81 Dilation of sphincter of Oddi
Dilation of ampulla of Vater
EXCLUDES that by endoscopic approach (51.84)
DEF: Dilation of muscle around common bile and pancreatic ducts; to mitigate constriction obstructing bile flow.

51.82 Pancreatic sphincterotomy
Incision of pancreatic sphincter
Transduodenal ampullary sphincterotomy
EXCLUDES that by endoscopic approach (51.85)
DEF: Pancreatic sphincterotomy: Division of muscle around common bile and pancreatic ducts.
DEF: Transduodenal ampullary sphincterotomy: Incision into muscle around common bile and pancreatic ducts, closing approach through first section of small intestine.

51.83 Pancreatic sphincteroplasty

51.84 Endoscopic dilation of ampulla and biliary duct
Dilation of ampulla and biliary duct by procedures classifiable to 51.10-51.11, 52.13

51.85 Endoscopic sphincterotomy and papillotomy
Sphincterotomy and papillotomy by procedures classifiable to 51.10-51.11, 52.13
DEF: Incision of muscle around common bile and pancreatic ducts and closing the duodenal papilla.
AHA: 4Q, '03, 118; 3Q, '03, 17; 2Q, '97, 7

51.86 Endoscopic insertion of nasobiliary drainage tube
Insertion of nasobiliary tube by procedures classifiable to 51.10-51.11, 52.13

51.87 Endoscopic insertion of stent (tube) into bile duct
Endoprosthesis of bile duct
Insertion of stent into bile duct by procedures classifiable to 51.10-51.11, 52.13
EXCLUDES nasobiliary drainage tube (51.86)
replacement of stent (tube) (97.05)
AHA: 3Q, '03, 17

51.88 Endoscopic removal of stone(s) from biliary tract
Laparoscopic removal of stone(s) from biliary tract
Removal of biliary tract stone(s) by procedures classifiable to 51.10-51.11, 52.13
EXCLUDES percutaneous extraction of common duct stones (51.96)
AHA: 2Q, '00, 11; 2Q, '97, 7

51.89 Other operations on sphincter of Oddi

✓4ᵗʰ **51.9 Other operations on biliary tract**

51.91 Repair of laceration of gallbladder

51.92 Closure of cholecystostomy

51.93 Closure of other biliary fistula
Cholecystogastroenteric fistulectomy

51.94 Revision of anastomosis of biliary tract

51.95 Removal of prosthetic device from bile duct
EXCLUDES nonoperative removal (97.55)

51.96 Percutaneous extraction of common duct stones
AHA: 4Q, '88, 7

51.98 Other percutaneous procedures on biliary tract
Percutaneous biliary endoscopy via existing T-tube or other tract for:
dilation of biliary duct stricture
exploration (postoperative)
removal of stone(s) except common duct stone
Percutaneous transhepatic biliary drainage
EXCLUDES percutaneous aspiration of gallbladder (51.01)
percutaneous biopsy and/or collection of specimen by brushing or washing (51.12)
percutaneous removal of common duct stone(s) (51.96)
AHA: 1Q, '97, 14; 3Q, '89, 18; N-D, '87, 1

51.99 Other
Insertion or replacement of biliary tract prosthesis
EXCLUDES biopsy of gallbladder (51.12-51.13)
irrigation of cholecystostomy and other biliary tube (96.41)
lysis of peritoneal adhesions (54.5)
nonoperative removal of:
cholecystostomy tube (97.54)
tube from biliary tract or liver (97.55)

✓3ʳᵈ **52 Operations on pancreas**
INCLUDES operations on pancreatic duct
Code also any application or administration of an adhesion barrier substance (99.77)

✓4ᵗʰ **52.0 Pancreatotomy**

52.01 Drainage of pancreatic cyst by catheter

52.09 Other pancreatotomy
Pancreatolithotomy
EXCLUDES drainage by anastomosis (52.4, 52.96)
incision of pancreatic sphincter (51.82)
marsupialization of cyst (52.3)
DEF: Pancreatolithotomy: Incision into pancreas to remove stones.

✓4ᵗʰ **52.1 Diagnostic procedures on pancreas**

52.11 Closed [aspiration] [needle] [percutaneous] biopsy of pancreas

52.12 Open biopsy of pancreas

52.13 Endoscopic retrograde pancreatography [ERP]
EXCLUDES endoscopic retrograde:
cholangiography [ERC] (51.11)
cholangiopancreatography [ERCP] (51.10)
that for procedures classifiable to 51.14-51.15, 51.64, 51.84-51.88, 52.14, 52.21, 52.92-52.94, 52.97-52.98

52.14 Closed [endoscopic] biopsy of pancreatic duct
Closed biopsy of pancreatic duct by procedures classifiable to 51.10-51.11, 52.13

52.19 Other diagnostic procedures on pancreas
EXCLUDES contrast pancreatogram (87.66)
endoscopic retrograde pancreatography [ERP] (52.13)
microscopic examination of specimen from pancreas (91.01-91.09)

☑4ᵗʰ **52.2 Local excision or destruction of pancreas and pancreatic duct**

EXCLUDES   biopsy of pancreas (52.11-52.12, 52.14)
pancreatic fistulectomy (52.95)

52.21 Endoscopic excision or destruction of lesion or tissue of pancreatic duct

Excision or destruction of lesion or tissue of pancreatic duct by procedures classifiable to 51.10-51.11, 52.13

52.22 Other excision or destruction of lesion or tissue of pancreas or pancreatic duct

52.3 Marsupialization of pancreatic cyst

EXCLUDES   drainage of cyst by catheter (52.01)

DEF: Incision into pancreas and suturing edges to form pocket; promotes drainage and healing.

52.4 Internal drainage of pancreatic cyst

Pancreaticocystoduodenostomy
Pancreaticocystogastrostomy
Pancreaticocystojejunostomy

DEF: Withdrawing fluid from pancreatic cyst by draining it through a created passage to another organ.

DEF: Pancreaticocystoduodenostomy: Creation of passage from pancreatic cyst to first portion of small intestine.

DEF: Pancreaticocystogastrostomy: Creation of passage from pancreatic cyst to stomach.

DEF: Pancreaticocystojejunostomy: Creation of passage from pancreatic cyst to midsection of small intestine.

☑4ᵗʰ **52.5 Partial pancreatectomy**

EXCLUDES   pancreatic fistulectomy (52.95)

52.51 Proximal pancreatectomy

Excision of head of pancreas (with part of body)
Proximal pancreatectomy with synchronous duodenectomy

52.52 Distal pancreatectomy

Excision of tail of pancreas (with part of body)

52.53 Radical subtotal pancreatectomy

52.59 Other partial pancreatectomy

AHA: ▶3Q, '13, 12◀

52.6 Total pancreatectomy

Pancreatectomy with synchronous duodenectomy
AHA: 4Q, '96, 71

52.7 Radical pancreaticoduodenectomy

One-stage pancreaticoduodenal resection with choledochojejunal anastomosis, pancreaticojejunal anastomosis, and gastrojejunostomy
Two-stage pancreaticoduodenal resection (first stage) (second stage)
Radical resection of the pancreas
Whipple procedure

EXCLUDES   radical subtotal pancreatectomy (52.53)

DEF: Whipple procedure: pancreaticoduodenectomy involving the removal of the head of the pancreas and part of the small intestines; pancreaticojejunostomy, choledochojejunal anastomosis, and gastrojejunostomy included in the procedure.

AHA: 1Q, '01, 13

☑4ᵗʰ **52.8 Transplant of pancreas**

NOTE   To report donor source — see codes 00.91-00.93

[10] **52.80 Pancreatic transplant, not otherwise specified**   NC LC

52.81 Reimplantation of pancreatic tissue

[10] **52.82 Homotransplant of pancreas**   NC LC

52.83 Heterotransplant of pancreas   NC

52.84 Autotransplantation of cells of islets of Langerhans

Homotransplantation of islet cells of pancreas

DEF: Transplantation of Islet cells from pancreas to another location of same patient.

AHA: 4Q, '96, 70, 71

52.85 Allotransplantation of cells of islets of Langerhans

Heterotransplantation of islet cells of pancreas

DEF: Transplantation of Islet cells from one individual to another.

AHA: 4Q, '96, 70, 71

TIP: Assign also code 55.69 Other kidney transplantation, if a renal transplant is performed simultaneously.

52.86 Transplantation of cells of islets of Langerhans, not otherwise specified

AHA: 4Q, '96, 70

☑4ᵗʰ **52.9 Other operations on pancreas**

52.92 Cannulation of pancreatic duct

EXCLUDES   that by endoscopic approach (52.93)

DEF: Placement of tube into pancreatic duct, without an endoscope.

52.93 Endoscopic insertion of stent (tube) into pancreatic duct

Insertion of cannula or stent into pancreatic duct by procedures classifiable to 51.10-51.11, 52.13

EXCLUDES   endoscopic insertion of nasopancreatic drainage tube (52.97)
replacement of stent (tube) (97.05)

AHA: 2Q, '97, 7

52.94 Endoscopic removal of stone(s) from pancreatic duct

Removal of stone(s) from pancreatic duct by procedures classifiable to 51.10-51.11, 52.13

52.95 Other repair of pancreas

Fistulectomy } of pancreas
Simple suture

52.96 Anastomosis of pancreas

Anastomosis of pancreas (duct) to:
  intestine
  jejunum
  stomach

EXCLUDES   anastomosis to:
    bile duct (51.39)
    gallbladder (51.33)

52.97 Endoscopic insertion of nasopancreatic drainage tube

Insertion of nasopancreatic drainage tube by procedures classifiable to 51.10-51.11, 52.13

EXCLUDES   drainage of pancreatic cyst by catheter (52.01)
replacement of stent (tube) (97.05)

52.98 Endoscopic dilation of pancreatic duct

Dilation of Wirsung's duct by procedures classifiable to 51.10-51.11, 52.13

52.99 Other

Dilation of pancreatic [Wirsung's] duct } by open approach
Repair of pancreatic [Wirsung's] duct

EXCLUDES   irrigation of pancreatic tube (96.42)
removal of pancreatic tube (97.56)

Indirect Repair of Hernia

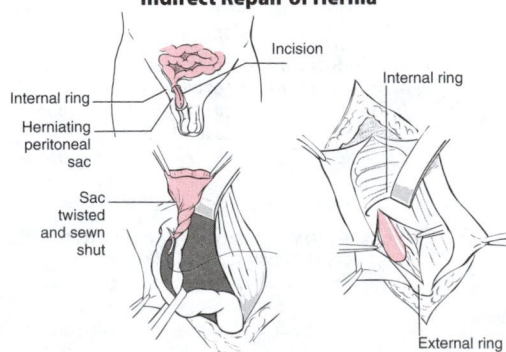

Incision
Internal ring
Internal ring
Internal ring
Herniating peritoneal sac
Sac twisted and sewn shut
External ring

---

[10] Noncovered procedure unless reported with code 55.69 or a diagnosis code from 250.x1 or 250.x3, or 251.3.

BI Bilateral Procedure   NC Non-covered Procedure   LC Limited Coverage Procedure   ▶◀ Revised Text   ● New Code   ▲ Revised Code Title

140 – Volume 3 · October 2014   **2015 ICD-9-CM**

Operations on the Digestive System

53–53.72

Indirect Inguinal Hernia

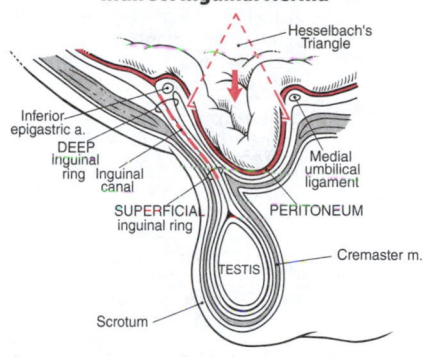

Direct Inguinal Hernia

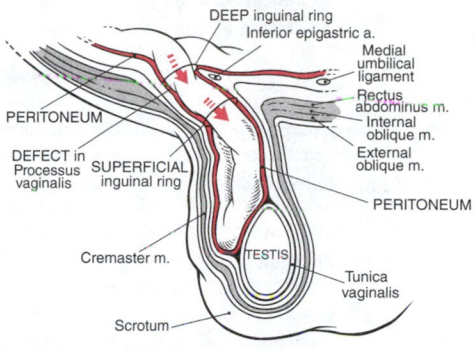

√3rd **53 Repair of hernia**

INCLUDES hernioplasty
herniorrhaphy

Code also any application or administration of an adhesion barrier substance (99.77)

EXCLUDES manual reduction of hernia (96.27)

DEF: Repair of hernia: Restoration of abnormally protruding organ or tissue.
DEF: Herniorrhaphy: Repair of hernia.
DEF: Herniotomy: Division of constricted, strangulated, irreducible hernia.
AHA: 3Q, '94, 8

√4th **53.0 Other unilateral repair of inguinal hernia**

EXCLUDES laparoscopic unilateral repair of inguinal hernia (17.11-17.13)

AHA: 4Q, '08, 165-167

53.00 Unilateral repair of inguinal hernia, not otherwise specified
Inguinal herniorrhaphy NOS
AHA: 3Q, '03, 10

53.01 Other and open repair of direct inguinal hernia
Direct and indirect inguinal hernia
AHA: 4Q, '96, 66

53.02 Other and open repair of indirect inguinal hernia

53.03 Other and open repair of direct inguinal hernia with graft or prosthesis

53.04 Other and open repair of indirect inguinal hernia with graft or prosthesis

53.05 Repair of inguinal hernia with graft or prosthesis, not otherwise specified

√4th **53.1 Other bilateral repair of inguinal hernia**

EXCLUDES laparoscopic bilateral repair of inguinal hernia (17.21-17.24)

AHA: 4Q, '08, 165-167

53.10 Bilateral repair of inguinal hernia, not otherwise specified

53.11 Other and open bilateral repair of direct inguinal hernia

53.12 Other and open bilateral repair of indirect inguinal hernia

53.13 Other and open bilateral repair of inguinal hernia, one direct and one indirect

53.14 Other and open bilateral repair of direct inguinal hernia with graft or prosthesis

53.15 Other and open bilateral repair of indirect inguinal hernia with graft or prosthesis

53.16 Other and open bilateral repair of inguinal hernia, one direct and one indirect, with graft or prosthesis

53.17 Bilateral inguinal hernia repair with graft or prosthesis, not otherwise specified

√4th **53.2 Unilateral repair of femoral hernia**

53.21 Unilateral repair of femoral hernia with graft or prosthesis

53.29 Other unilateral femoral herniorrhaphy

√4th **53.3 Bilateral repair of femoral hernia**

53.31 Bilateral repair of femoral hernia with graft or prosthesis

53.39 Other bilateral femoral herniorrhaphy

√4th **53.4 Repair of umbilical hernia**

EXCLUDES repair of gastroschisis (54.71)

AHA: 4Q, '08, 165-168

53.41 Other and open repair of umbilical hernia with graft or prosthesis

53.42 Laparoscopic repair of umbilical hernia with graft or prosthesis

53.43 Other laparoscopic umbilical herniorrhaphy

53.49 Other open umbilical herniorrhaphy

EXCLUDES other laparoscopic umbilical herniorrhaphy (53.43)
repair of umbilical hernia with graft or prosthesis (53.41, 53.42)

√4th **53.5 Repair of other hernia of anterior abdominal wall (without graft or prosthesis)**

53.51 Incisional hernia repair
AHA: 3Q, '03, 6

53.59 Repair of other hernia of anterior abdominal wall
Repair of hernia:
epigastric
hypogastric
spigelian
ventral
That by laparoscopic approach
AHA: 2Q, '06, 10; 3Q, '03, 6; 3Q, '96, 15

√4th **53.6 Repair of other hernia of anterior abdominal wall with graft or prosthesis**

AHA: 4Q, '08, 165-168

53.61 Other open incisional hernia repair with graft or prosthesis

EXCLUDES laparoscopic incisional hernia repair with graft or prosthesis (53.62)

AHA: 3Q, '03, 11

53.62 Laparoscopic incisional hernia repair with graft or prosthesis

53.63 Other laparoscopic repair of other hernia of anterior abdominal wall with graft or prosthesis
AHA: 2Q, '11, 18

53.69 Other and open repair of other hernia of anterior abdominal wall with graft or prosthesis

EXCLUDES other laparoscopic repair of other hernia of anterior abdominal wall with graft or prosthesis (53.63)

AHA: ▶4Q, '13, 95◀

√4th **53.7 Repair of diaphragmatic hernia, abdominal approach**

AHA: 4Q, '08, 165-168

53.71 Laparoscopic repair of diaphragmatic hernia, abdominal approach

53.72 Other and open repair of diaphragmatic hernia, abdominal approach

Operations on the Digestive System

53.75–54.3

53.75 Repair of diaphragmatic hernia, abdominal approach, not otherwise specified

EXCLUDES *laparoscopic repair of diaphragmatic hernia (53.71)*

other and open repair of diaphragmatic hernia (53.72)

√4ᵗʰ **53.8 Repair of diaphragmatic hernia, thoracic approach**

DEF: Repair of diaphragmatic hernia though abdomen and thorax.

53.80 Repair of diaphragmatic hernia with thoracic approach, not otherwise specified

Thoracoabdominal repair of diaphragmatic hernia

53.81 Plication of the diaphragm

DEF: Tuck repair of diaphragmatic hernia.

53.82 Repair of parasternal hernia

DEF: Repair of hernia protruding into breastbone area.

53.83 Laparoscopic repair of diaphragmatic hernia, with thoracic approach

AHA: 4Q, '08, 165-169

53.84 Other and open repair of diaphragmatic hernia, with thoracic approach

EXCLUDES *repair of diaphragmatic hernia with thoracic approach, NOS, (53.80)*

AHA: 4Q, '08, 165-169

53.9 Other hernia repair

Repair of hernia:　　Repair of hernia:
ischiatic　　　　　　omental
ischiorectal　　　　　retroperitoneal
lumbar　　　　　　　sciatic
obturator

EXCLUDES *relief of strangulated hernia with exteriorization of intestine (46.01, 46.03)*

repair of pericolostomy hernia (46.42)

repair of vaginal enterocele (70.92)

√3ʳᵈ **54 Other operations on abdominal region**

INCLUDES operations on:
epigastric region
flank
groin region
hypochondrium
inguinal region
loin region
mesentery
omentum
pelvic cavity
peritoneum
retroperitoneal tissue space

Code also any application or administration of an adhesion barrier substance (99.77)

EXCLUDES *hernia repair (53.00-53.9)*

obliteration of cul-de-sac (70.92)

retroperitoneal tissue dissection (59.00-59.09)

skin and subcutaneous tissue of abdominal wall (86.01-86.99)

54.0 Incision of abdominal wall

Drainage of:　　　　　Drainage of:
abdominal wall　　　　retroperitoneal abscess
extraperitoneal abscess

EXCLUDES *incision of peritoneum (54.95)*

laparotomy (54.11-54.19)

AHA: 2Q, '06, 23; 4Q, '05, 77; 1Q, '97, 11; N-D, '87, 12

TIP: Assign for incision and drainage (I&D) with debridement of abdominal wall surgical wound postoperative infection. Do not assign a separate debridement code; it's an integral component.

√4ᵗʰ **54.1 Laparotomy**

DEF: Incision into abdomen.

AHA: 1Q, '92, 13

54.11 Exploratory laparotomy

EXCLUDES *exploration incidental to intra-abdominal surgery — omit code*

DEF: Exam of peritoneal cavity through incision into abdomen.

AHA: 3Q, '89, 14; 4Q, '88, 12; J-F, '87, 11

TIP: An exploratory procedure followed by definitive surgery is coded only to the definitive surgery, except for procedures involving biopsy and/or incidental appendectomy.

54.12 Reopening of recent laparotomy site

Reopening of recent laparotomy site for:
control of hemorrhage
exploration
incision of hematoma

54.19 Other laparotomy

Drainage of intraperitoneal abscess or hematoma

EXCLUDES *culdocentesis (70.0)*

drainage of appendiceal abscess (47.2)

exploration incidental to intra-abdominal surgery — omit code

Ladd operation (54.95)

percutaneous drainage of abdomen (54.91)

removal of foreign body (54.92)

AHA: 3Q, '03, 17

√4ᵗʰ **54.2 Diagnostic procedures of abdominal region**

54.21 Laparoscopy

Peritoneoscopy

EXCLUDES *laparoscopic cholecystectomy (51.23)*

that incidental to destruction of fallopian tubes (66.21-66.29)

DEF: Endoscopic exam of peritoneal cavity through abdominal portal.

54.22 Biopsy of abdominal wall or umbilicus

54.23 Biopsy of peritoneum

Biopsy of:　　　　　Biopsy of:
mesentery　　　　　peritoneal implant
omentum

EXCLUDES *closed biopsy of:*

omentum (54.24)

peritoneum (54.24)

54.24 Closed [percutaneous] [needle] biopsy of intra-abdominal mass

Closed biopsy of:　　　Closed biopsy of:
omentum　　　　　　peritoneum
peritoneal implant

EXCLUDES *that of:*

fallopian tube (66.11)

ovary (65.11)

uterine ligaments (68.15)

uterus (68.16)

AHA: 4Q, '97, 57

54.25 Peritoneal lavage

Diagnostic peritoneal lavage

EXCLUDES *peritoneal dialysis (54.98)*

DEF: Irrigation of peritoneal cavity with siphoning of liquid contents for analysis.

AHA: 2Q, '98, 19; 4Q, '93, 28

54.29 Other diagnostic procedures on abdominal region

EXCLUDES *abdominal lymphangiogram (88.04)*

abdominal x-ray NEC (88.19)

angiocardiography of venae cavae (88.51)

C.A.T. scan of abdomen (88.01)

contrast x-ray of abdominal cavity (88.11-88.15)

intra-abdominal arteriography NEC (88.47)

microscopic examination of peritoneal and retroperitoneal specimen (91.11-91.19)

phlebography of:

intra-abdominal vessels NEC (88.65)

portal venous system (88.64)

sinogram of abdominal wall (88.03)

soft tissue x-ray of abdominal wall NEC (88.09)

tomography of abdomen NEC (88.02)

ultrasonography of abdomen and retroperitoneum (88.76)

54.3 Excision or destruction of lesion or tissue of abdominal wall or umbilicus

Debridement of abdominal wall

Omphalectomy

EXCLUDES *biopsy of abdominal wall or umbilicus (54.22)*

size reduction operation (86.83)

that of skin of abdominal wall (86.22, 86.26, 86.3)

AHA: 1Q, '89, 11

BI Bilateral Procedure　　NC Non-covered Procedure　　LC Limited Coverage Procedure　　▶◀ Revised Text　　● New Code　　▲ Revised Code Title

54.4 **Excision or destruction of peritoneal tissue**
Excision of:
appendices epiploicae
falciform ligament
gastrocolic ligament
lesion of:
mesentery
omentum
peritoneum
presacral lesion NOS
retroperitoneal lesion NOS
EXCLUDES *biopsy of peritoneum (54.23)*
endometrectomy of cul-de-sac (70.32)

✓4th **54.5** **Lysis of peritoneal adhesions**
Freeing of adhesions of: Freeing of adhesions of:
biliary tract peritoneum
intestines spleen
liver uterus
pelvic peritoneum
EXCLUDES *lysis of adhesions of:*
bladder (59.11)
fallopian tube and ovary (65.81, 65.89)
kidney (59.02)
ureter (59.02-59.03)
AHA: 3Q, '94, 8; 4Q, '90, 18
TIP: Code separately only if the documentation specifies that the adhesions were significant, caused symptoms, and/or increased the difficulty of the procedure being performed.

54.51 **Laparoscopic lysis of peritoneal adhesions**
AHA: 2Q, '11, 18; 4Q, '06, 134; 3Q, '03, 6-7; 4Q, '96, 65

54.59 **Other lysis of peritoneal adhesions**
AHA: ▶2Q, '13, 4;◀ 1Q, '10, 11; 3Q, '06, 15; 3Q, '03, 11; 1Q, '03, 14; 4Q, '96, 66

✓4th **54.6** **Suture of abdominal wall and peritoneum**

54.61 **Reclosure of postoperative disruption of abdominal wall**

54.62 **Delayed closure of granulating abdominal wound**
Tertiary subcutaneous wound closure
DEF: Closure of outer layers of abdominal wound; follows procedure to close initial layers of wound.

54.63 **Other suture of abdominal wall**
Suture of laceration of abdominal wall
EXCLUDES *closure of operative wound — omit code*

54.64 **Suture of peritoneum**
Secondary suture of peritoneum
EXCLUDES *closure of operative wound — omit code*

✓4th **54.7** **Other repair of abdominal wall and peritoneum**

54.71 **Repair of gastroschisis**
DEF: Repair of congenital fistula of abdominal wall.
AHA: 2Q, '02, 9

54.72 **Other repair of abdominal wall**
AHA: ▶4Q, '13, 95◀

54.73 **Other repair of peritoneum**
Suture of gastrocolic ligament

54.74 **Other repair of omentum**
Epiplorrhaphy
Graft of omentum
Omentopexy
Reduction of torsion of omentum
EXCLUDES *cardio-omentopexy (36.39)*
DEF: Epiplorrhaphy: Suture of abdominal serous membrane.
DEF: Graft of omentum: Implantation of tissue into abdominal serous membrane.
DEF: Omentopexy: Anchoring of abdominal serous membrane.
DEF: Reduction of torsion of omentum: Reduction of twisted abdominal serous membrane.
AHA: J-F, '87, 11

54.75 **Other repair of mesentery**
Mesenteric plication
Mesenteropexy
DEF: Creation of folds in mesentery for shortening.
DEF: Mesenteriopexy: Fixation of torn, incised mesentery.

✓4th **54.9** **Other operations of abdominal region**
EXCLUDES *removal of ectopic pregnancy (74.3)*

54.91 **Percutaneous abdominal drainage**
Paracentesis
EXCLUDES *creation of cutaneoperitoneal fistula (54.93)*
DEF: Puncture for removal of fluid.
AHA: 4Q, '07, 96; 3Q, '99, 9; 2Q, '99, 14; 3Q, '98, 12; 1Q, '92, 14; 2Q, '90, 25

54.92 **Removal of foreign body from peritoneal cavity**
AHA: 1Q, '89, 11

54.93 **Creation of cutaneoperitoneal fistula**
DEF: Creation of opening between skin and peritoneal cavity.
AHA: 2Q, '95, 10; N-D, '84, 6

54.94 **Creation of peritoneovascular shunt**
Peritoneovenous shunt
DEF: Peritoneal vascular shunt: Construction of shunt to connect peritoneal cavity with vascular system.
DEF: Peritoneovenous shunt: Construction of shunt to connect peritoneal cavity with vein.
AHA: 1Q, '94, 7; 1Q, '88, 9; S-O, '85, 6
TIP: Assign for insertion of a Denver shunt if it is described as a peritoneovascular shunt; if it is a Denver pleuroperitoneal shunt, assign instead 34.09.

54.95 **Incision of peritoneum**
Exploration of ventriculoperitoneal shunt at peritoneal site
Ladd operation
Revision of distal catheter of ventricular shunt
Revision of ventriculoperitoneal shunt at peritoneal site
EXCLUDES *that incidental to laparotomy (54.11-54.19)*
DEF: Ladd operation: Peritoneal attachment of incompletely rotated cecum, obstructing duodenum.
AHA: ▶ 2Q, '13, 4;◀ 4Q, '95, 65
TIP: If a ventriculoperitoneal shunt is explored or revised at the ventricular site, assign instead code 02.41 or 02.42.

54.96 **Injection of air into peritoneal cavity**
Pneumoperitoneum
EXCLUDES *that for:*
collapse of lung (33.33)
radiography (88.12-88.13, 88.15)

54.97 **Injection of locally-acting therapeutic substance into peritoneal cavity**
EXCLUDES *peritoneal dialysis (54.98)*

54.98 **Peritoneal dialysis**
EXCLUDES *peritoneal lavage (diagnostic) (54.25)*
DEF: Separation of blood elements by diffusion through membrane.
AHA: 4Q, '93, 28; N-D, '84, 6

54.99 **Other**
EXCLUDES *removal of:*
abdominal wall sutures (97.83)
peritoneal drainage device (97.82)
retroperitoneal drainage device (97.81)
AHA: 1Q, '99, 4

Operations on the Urinary System

55–55.54

10. Operations on the Urinary System (55-59)

✓3rd **55   Operations on kidney**
     INCLUDES   operations on renal pelvis
     Code also any application or administration of an adhesion barrier substance (99.77)
     EXCLUDES   perirenal tissue (59.00-59.09, 59.21-59.29, 59.91-59.92)

✓4th **55.0   Nephrotomy and nephrostomy**
     EXCLUDES   drainage by:
           anastomosis (55.86)
           aspiration (55.92)

55.01   Nephrotomy
     Evacuation of renal cyst
     Exploration of kidney
     Nephrolithotomy
     DEF: Nephrotomy: Incision into kidney.
     DEF: Evacuation of renal cyst: Draining contents of cyst.
     DEF: Exploration of kidney: Exploration through incision.
     DEF: Nephrolithotomy: Removal of kidney stone through incision.

55.02   Nephrostomy
     AHA: 2Q, '97, 4

55.03   Percutaneous nephrostomy without fragmentation
     Nephrostolithotomy, percutaneous (nephroscopic)
     Percutaneous removal of kidney stone(s) by:
         forceps extraction (nephroscopic)
         basket extraction
     Pyelostolithotomy, percutaneous (nephroscopic)
     With placement of catheter down ureter
     EXCLUDES   percutaneous removal by fragmentation (55.04)
           repeat nephroscopic removal during current episode (55.92)
     DEF: Insertion of tube through abdominal wall without breaking up stones.
     DEF: Nephrostolithotomy: Insertion of tube through the abdominal wall to remove stones.
     DEF: Basket extraction: Percutaneous removal of stone with grasping forceps.
     DEF: Pyelostolithotomy: Percutaneous removal of stones from funnel-shaped portion of kidney.
     AHA: 2Q, '96, 5

55.04   Percutaneous nephrostomy with fragmentation
     Percutaneous nephrostomy with disruption of kidney stone by ultrasonic energy and extraction (suction) through endoscope
     With placement of catheter down ureter
     With fluoroscopic guidance
     EXCLUDES   repeat fragmentation during current episode (59.95)
     DEF: Insertion of tube through abdominal wall into kidney to break up stones.
     AHA: 1Q, '89, 1; S-O, '86, 11

✓4th **55.1   Pyelotomy and pyelostomy**
     EXCLUDES   drainage by anastomosis (55.86)
           percutaneous pyelostolithotomy (55.03)
           removal of calculus without incision (56.0)

55.11   Pyelotomy
     Exploration of renal pelvis
     Pyelolithotomy

55.12   Pyelostomy
     Insertion of drainage tube into renal pelvis

✓4th **55.2   Diagnostic procedures on kidney**

55.21   Nephroscopy
     DEF: Endoscopic exam of renal pelvis; retrograde through ureter, percutaneous or open exposure.

55.22   Pyeloscopy
     DEF: Fluoroscopic exam of kidney pelvis, calyces and ureters; follows IV or retrograde injection of contrast.

55.23   Closed [percutaneous] [needle] biopsy of kidney
     Endoscopic biopsy via existing nephrostomy, nephrotomy, pyelostomy, or pyelotomy

55.24   Open biopsy of kidney

55.29   Other diagnostic procedures on kidney
     EXCLUDES   microscopic examination of specimen from kidney (91.21-91.29)
           pyelogram:
              intravenous (87.73)
              percutaneous (87.75)
              retrograde (87.74)
           radioisotope scan (92.03)
           renal arteriography (88.45)
           tomography:
              C.A.T scan (87.71)
              other (87.72)

✓4th **55.3   Local excision or destruction of lesion or tissue of kidney**

55.31   Marsupialization of kidney lesion
     DEF: Exteriorization of lesion by incising anterior wall and suturing cut edges to create open pouch.

55.32   Open ablation of renal lesion or tissue
     AHA: 4Q, '06, 124

55.33   Percutaneous ablation of renal lesion or tissue
     AHA: 4Q, '06, 124

55.34   Laparoscopic ablation of renal lesion or tissue
     AHA: 4Q, '06, 124

55.35   Other and unspecified ablation of renal lesion or tissue
     AHA: 4Q, '06, 124

55.39   Other local destruction or excision of renal lesion or tissue
     Obliteration of calyceal diverticulum
     EXCLUDES   ablation of renal lesion or tissue:
           laparoscopic (55.34)
           open (55.32)
           other (55.35)
           percutaneous (55.33)
           biopsy of kidney (55.23-55.24)
           partial nephrectomy (55.4)
           percutaneous aspiration of kidney (55.92)
           wedge resection of kidney (55.4)

55.4   Partial nephrectomy
     Calycectomy
     Wedge resection of kidney
     Code also any synchronous resection of ureter (56.40-56.42)
     DEF: Surgical removal of a part of the kidney.
     DEF: Calycectomy: Removal of indentations in kidney.

✓4th **55.5   Complete nephrectomy**
     Code also any synchronous excision of:
         adrenal gland (07.21-07.3)
         bladder segment (57.6)
         lymph nodes (40.3, 40.52-40.59)

55.51   Nephroureterectomy
     Nephroureterectomy with bladder cuff
     Total nephrectomy (unilateral)
     EXCLUDES   removal of transplanted kidney (55.53)
     DEF: Complete removal of the kidney and all or portion of the ureter.
     DEF: Nephroureterectomy with bladder cuff: Removal of kidney, ureter, and portion of bladder attached to ureter.
     DEF: Total nephrectomy (unilateral): Complete excision of one kidney.
     AHA: 2Q, '05, 4

55.52   Nephrectomy of remaining kidney
     Removal of solitary kidney
     EXCLUDES   removal of transplanted kidney (55.53)

55.53   Removal of transplanted or rejected kidney
     AHA: 4Q, 08, 83

55.54   Bilateral nephrectomy
     EXCLUDES   complete nephrectomy NOS (55.51)
     DEF: Removal of both kidneys same operative session.

BI Bilateral Procedure   NC Non-covered Procedure   LC Limited Coverage Procedure   ▶◀ Revised Text   ● New Code   ▲ Revised Code Title

Symphysiostomy for Horseshoe Kidney

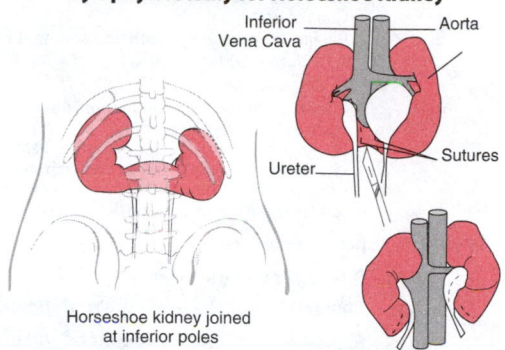

Horseshoe kidney joined at inferior poles

(Labels: Inferior Vena Cava, Aorta, Ureter, Sutures)

✓4th 55.6 Transplant of kidney

> **NOTE** To report donor source — see codes 00.91-00.93

55.61 Renal autotransplantation

55.69 Other kidney transplantation   **LC**

> AHA: 3Q, '12, 16; 2Q, '11, 6; 4Q, '04, 117; 4Q, '96, 71

55.7 Nephropexy

> Fixation or suspension of movable [floating] kidney

✓4th 55.8 Other repair of kidney

55.81 Suture of laceration of kidney

55.82 Closure of nephrostomy and pyelostomy

> **DEF:** Removal of tube from kidney and closure of site of tube insertion.

55.83 Closure of other fistula of kidney

55.84 Reduction of torsion of renal pedicle

> **DEF:** Restoration of twisted renal pedicle into normal position.

55.85 Symphysiotomy for horseshoe kidney

> **DEF:** Division of congenitally malformed kidney into two parts.

55.86 Anastomosis of kidney

> Nephropyeloureterostomy
> Pyeloureterovesical anastomosis
> Ureterocalyceal anastomosis
> **EXCLUDES** *nephrocystanastomosis NOS (56.73)*
> **DEF:** Nephropyeloureterostomy: Creation of passage between kidney and ureter.
> **DEF:** Pyeloureterovesical anastomosis: Creation of passage between kidney and bladder.
> **DEF:** Ureterocalyceal anastomosis: Creation of passage between ureter and kidney indentations.

55.87 Correction of ureteropelvic junction

55.89 Other

✓4th 55.9 Other operations on kidney

> **EXCLUDES** *lysis of perirenal adhesions (59.02)*

55.91 Decapsulation of kidney

> Capsulectomy ⎫
> Decortication ⎬ of kidney

55.92 Percutaneous aspiration of kidney (pelvis)

> Aspiration of renal cyst
> Renipuncture
> **EXCLUDES** *percutaneous biopsy of kidney (55.23)*
> **DEF:** Insertion of needle into kidney to withdraw fluid.
> AHA: N-D, '84, 20

55.93 Replacement of nephrostomy tube

55.94 Replacement of pyelostomy tube

55.95 Local perfusion of kidney

> **DEF:** Fluid passage through kidney.

55.96 Other injection of therapeutic substance into kidney

> Injection into renal cyst

55.97 Implantation or replacement of mechanical kidney

55.98 Removal of mechanical kidney

55.99 Other

> **EXCLUDES** *removal of pyelostomy or nephrostomy tube (97.61)*

✓3rd 56 Operations on ureter

Code also any application or administration of an adhesion barrier substance (99.77)

56.0 Transurethral removal of obstruction from ureter and renal pelvis

> Removal of:
> blood clot ⎫
> calculus ⎬ from ureter or renal pelvis without incision
> foreign body ⎭
> **EXCLUDES** *manipulation without removal of obstruction (59.8)*
> *that by incision (55.11,56.2)*
> *transurethral insertion of ureteral stent for passage of calculus (59.8)*
> **DEF:** Removal of obstruction by tube inserted through urethra to ureter.
> AHA: 1Q, '89, 1; S-O, '86, 12
> **TIP:** Assign for laser lithotripsy of the kidney or ureter, unless the documentation specifies extracorporeal shockwave lithotripsy (ESWL), see instead code 98.51.

56.1 Ureteral meatotomy

> **DEF:** Incision into ureteral meatus to enlarge passage.

56.2 Ureterotomy

> Incision of ureter for:
> drainage
> exploration
> removal of calculus
> **EXCLUDES** *cutting of ureterovesical orifice (56.1)*
> *removal of calculus without incision (56.0)*
> *transurethral insertion of ureteral stent for passage of calculus (59.8)*
> *urinary diversion (56.51-56.79)*
> AHA: S-O, '86, 10

✓4th 56.3 Diagnostic procedures on ureter

56.31 Ureteroscopy

56.32 Closed percutaneous biopsy of ureter

> **EXCLUDES** *endoscopic biopsy of ureter (56.33)*

56.33 Closed endoscopic biopsy of ureter

> Cystourethroscopy with ureteral biopsy
> Transurethral biopsy of ureter
> Ureteral endoscopy with biopsy through ureterotomy
> Ureteroscopy with biopsy
> **EXCLUDES** *percutaneous biopsy of ureter (56.32)*

56.34 Open biopsy of ureter

56.35 Endoscopy (cystoscopy) (looposcopy) of ileal conduit

> **DEF:** Endoscopic exam of created opening between ureters and one end of small intestine; other end used to form artificial opening.

56.39 Other diagnostic procedures on ureter

> **EXCLUDES** *microscopic examination of specimen from ureter (91.21-91.29)*

✓4th 56.4 Ureterectomy

Code also anastomosis other than end-to-end (56.51-56.79)
> **EXCLUDES** *fistulectomy (56.84)*
> *nephroureterectomy (55.51-55.54)*

56.40 Ureterectomy, not otherwise specified

56.41 Partial ureterotomy

> Excision of lesion of ureter
> Shortening of ureter with reimplantation
> **EXCLUDES** *biopsy of ureter (56.32-56.34)*

56.42 Total ureterectomy

✓4th **56.5**   **Cutaneous uretero-ileostomy**

56.51   **Formation of cutaneous uretero-ileostomy**
Construction of ileal conduit
External ureteral ileostomy
Formation of open ileal bladder
Ileal loop operation
Ileoureterostomy (Bricker's) (ileal bladder)
Transplantation of ureter into ileum with external diversion

> EXCLUDES   closed ileal bladder (57.87)
> replacement of ureteral defect by ileal segment (56.89)

DEF: Creation of urinary passage by connecting the terminal end of small intestine to ureter, then connecting to opening through abdominal wall.
DEF: Construction of ileal conduit: Formation of conduit from terminal end of small intestine.

56.52   **Revision of cutaneous uretero-ileostomy**
AHA: 3Q, '96, 15; 4Q, '88, 7

✓4th **56.6**   **Other external urinary diversion**

56.61   **Formation of other cutaneous ureterostomy**
Anastomosis of ureter to skin
Ureterostomy NOS

56.62   **Revision of other cutaneous ureterostomy**
Revision of ureterostomy stoma

> EXCLUDES   nonoperative removal of ureterostomy tube (97.62)

✓4th **56.7**   **Other anastomosis or bypass of ureter**

> EXCLUDES   ureteropyelostomy (55.86)

56.71   **Urinary diversion to intestine**
Anastomosis of ureter to intestine
Internal urinary diversion NOS

Code also any synchronous colostomy (46.10-46.13)

> EXCLUDES   external ureteral ileostomy (56.51)

56.72   **Revision of ureterointestinal anastomosis**

> EXCLUDES   revision of external ureteral ileostomy (56.52)

56.73   **Nephrocystanastomosis, not otherwise specified**

DEF: Connection of kidney to bladder.

56.74   **Ureteroneocystostomy**
Replacement of ureter with bladder flap
Ureterovesical anastomosis

DEF: Transfer of ureter to another site in bladder.
DEF: Ureterovesical anastomosis: Implantation of ureter into bladder.

56.75   **Transureteroureterostomy**

> EXCLUDES   ureteroureterostomy associated with partial resection (56.41)

DEF: Separating one ureter and joining the ends to the opposite ureter.

56.79   **Other**

✓4th **56.8**   **Repair of ureter**

56.81   **Lysis of intraluminal adhesions of ureter**

> EXCLUDES   lysis of periureteral adhesions (59.02-59.03)
> ureterolysis (59.02-59.03)

DEF: Destruction of adhesions within ureteral cavity.

56.82   **Suture of laceration of ureter**

56.83   **Closure of ureterostomy**

56.84   **Closure of other fistula of ureter**

56.85   **Ureteropexy**

56.86   **Removal of ligature from ureter**

56.89   **Other repair of ureter**
Graft of ureter
Replacement of ureter with ileal segment implanted into bladder
Ureteroplication

DEF: Graft of ureter: Tissue from another site for graft replacement or repair of ureter.
DEF: Replacement of ureter with ileal segment implanted into bladder and ureter replacement with terminal end of small intestine.
DEF: Ureteroplication: Creation of tucks in ureter.

✓4th **56.9**   **Other operations on ureter**

56.91   **Dilation of ureteral meatus**

56.92   **Implantation of electronic ureteral stimulator**

56.93   **Replacement of electronic ureteral stimulator**

56.94   **Removal of electronic ureteral stimulator**

> EXCLUDES   that with synchronous replacement (56.93)

56.95   **Ligation of ureter**

56.99   **Other**

> EXCLUDES   removal of ureterostomy tube and ureteral catheter (97.62)
> ureteral catheterization (59.8)

✓3rd **57**   **Operations on urinary bladder**
Code also any application or administration of an adhesion barrier substance (99.77)

> EXCLUDES   perivesical tissue (59.11-59.29, 59.91-59.92)
> ureterovesical orifice (56.0-56.99)

57.0   **Transurethral clearance of bladder**
Drainage of bladder without incision
Removal of:
blood clot
calculus   } from bladder without incision
foreign body

> EXCLUDES   that by incision (57.19)

AHA: S-O, '86, 11
DEF: Insertion of device through urethra to cleanse bladder.

✓4th **57.1**   **Cystotomy and cystostomy**

> EXCLUDES   cystotomy and cystostomy as operative approach — omit code

DEF: Cystotomy: Incision of bladder.
DEF: Cystostomy: Creation of opening into bladder.

57.11   **Percutaneous aspiration of bladder**

57.12   **Lysis of intraluminal adhesions with incision into bladder**

> EXCLUDES   transurethral lysis of intraluminal adhesions (57.41)

DEF: Incision into bladder to destroy lesions.

57.17   **Percutaneous cystostomy**
Closed cystostomy
Percutaneous suprapubic cystostomy

> EXCLUDES   removal of cystostomy tube (97.63)
> replacement of cystostomy tube (59.94)

DEF: Incision through body wall into bladder to insert tube.
DEF: Percutaneous (closed) suprapubic cystostomy: Incision above pubic arch, through body wall, into the bladder to insert tube.

57.18   **Other suprapubic cystostomy**

> EXCLUDES   percutaneous cystostomy (57.17)
> removal of cystostomy tube (97.63)
> replacement of cystostomy tube (59.94)

57.19   **Other cystotomy**
Cystolithotomy

> EXCLUDES   percutaneous cystostomy (57.17)
> suprapubic cystostomy (57.18)

AHA: 4Q, '95, 73; S-O, '86, 11

BI Bilateral Procedure   NC Non-covered Procedure   LC Limited Coverage Procedure   ▶◀ Revised Text   ● New Code   ▲ Revised Code Title

Operations on the Urinary System

Transurethral Cystourethroscopy

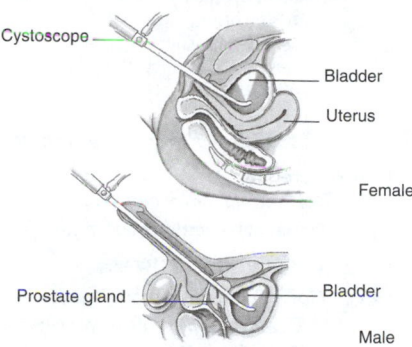

Cystoscope — Bladder — Uterus — Female

Prostate gland — Bladder — Male

✓4ᵗʰ **57.2 Vesicostomy**
     EXCLUDES   *percutaneous cystostomy (57.17)*
         suprapubic cystostomy (57.18)

     57.21 Vesicostomy
         Creation of permanent opening from bladder to skin using a bladder flap
         DEF: Creation of permanent opening from the bladder to the skin.

     57.22 Revision or closure of vesicostomy
         EXCLUDES   *closure of cystostomy (57.82)*

✓4ᵗʰ **57.3 Diagnostic procedures on bladder**

     57.31 Cystoscopy through artificial stoma

     57.32 Other cystoscopy
         Transurethral cystoscopy
         EXCLUDES   *cystourethroscopy with ureteral biopsy (56.33)*
                 retrograde pyelogram (87.74)
                 that for control of hemorrhage (postoperative):
                       bladder (57.93)
                       prostate (60.94)
         AHA: 1Q, '11, 25;1Q, '01, 14

     57.33 Closed [transurethral] biopsy of bladder

     57.34 Open biopsy of bladder
         AHA: 2Q, '05, 12

     57.39 Other diagnostic procedures on bladder
         EXCLUDES   *cystogram NEC (87.77)*
                 microscopic examination of specimen from bladder (91.31-91.39)
                 retrograde cystourethrogram (87.76)
                 therapeutic distention of bladder (96.25)

✓4ᵗʰ **57.4 Transurethral excision or destruction of bladder tissue**
     DEF: Destruction of bladder tissue with instrument inserted into urethra.

     57.41 Transurethral lysis of intraluminal adhesions

     57.49 Other transurethral excision or destruction of lesion or tissue of bladder
         Endoscopic resection of bladder lesion
         EXCLUDES   *transurethral biopsy of bladder (57.33)*
                 transurethral fistulectomy (57.83-57.84)

✓4ᵗʰ **57.5 Other excision or destruction of bladder tissue**
     EXCLUDES   *that with transurethral approach (57.41-57.49)*

     57.51 Excision of urachus
         Excision of urachal sinus of bladder
         EXCLUDES   *excision of urachal cyst of abdominal wall (54.3)*

     57.59 Open excision or destruction of other lesion or tissue of bladder
         Endometrectomy of bladder
         Suprapubic excision of bladder lesion
         EXCLUDES   *biopsy of bladder (57.33-57.34)*
                 fistulectomy of bladder (57.83-57.84)
         DEF: Endometrectomy of bladder: Removal of inner lining.
         DEF: Suprapubic excision of bladder lesion: Removal of lesion by excision above suprapubic bone arch.

57.6 Partial cystectomy
     Excision of bladder domeWedge resection of bladder
     Trigonectomy

✓4ᵗʰ **57.7 Total cystectomy**
     INCLUDES   total cystectomy with urethrectomy

     57.71 Radical cystectomy
         Pelvic exenteration in male
         Removal of bladder, prostate, seminal vesicles and fat
         Removal of bladder, urethra, and fat in a female
         Code also any:
             lymph node dissection (40.3, 40.5)
             urinary diversion (56.51-56.79)
         EXCLUDES   *that as part of pelvic exenteration in female (68.8)*
         DEF: Radical cystectomy: Removal of bladder and surrounding tissue.
         DEF: Pelvic exenteration in male: Excision of bladder, prostate, seminal vessels and fat.

     57.79 Other total cystectomy

✓4ᵗʰ **57.8 Other repair of urinary bladder**
     EXCLUDES   *repair of:*
             current obstetric laceration (75.61)
             cystocele (70.50-70.51)
         that for stress incontinence (59.3-59.79)

     57.81 Suture of laceration of bladder

     57.82 Closure of cystostomy

     57.83 Repair of fistula involving bladder and intestine
         Rectovesicovaginal   } fistulectomy
         Vesicosigmoidovaginal

     57.84 Repair of other fistula of bladder
         Cervicovesical
         Urethroperineovesical   } fistulectomy
         Uterovesical
         Vaginovesical
         EXCLUDES   *vesicoureterovaginal fistulectomy (56.84)*

     57.85 Cystourethroplasty and plastic repair of bladder neck
         Plication of sphincter of urinary bladder
         V-Y plasty of bladder neck
         DEF: Cystourethroplasty: Reconstruction of narrowed portion of bladder.
         DEF: Plication of sphincter or urinary bladder: Creation of tuck in bladder sphincter.
         DEF: V-Y plasty of bladder neck: Surgical reconstruction of the narrowed portion of bladder by V-Y technique.

     57.86 Repair of bladder exstrophy
         DEF: Surgical correction of a congenital bladder wall defect.

     57.87 Reconstruction of urinary bladder
         Anastomosis of bladder with isolated segment of ileum
         Augmentation of bladder
         Replacement of bladder with ileum or sigmoid [closed ileal bladder]
         Code also resection of intestine (45.50-45.52)
         DEF: Anastomosis of bladder with isolated segment of ileum: Creation of connection between bladder and separated terminal end of small intestine.
         AHA: 2Q, '05, 12; 2Q, '03, 11; 3Q, '00, 7
         TIP: Assign for closed continent ileovesicostomy, along with code 45.51 Isolation of segment of small intestine, for the continent ileovesicostomy; the ileum and bladder anastomoses are included.

     57.88 Other anastomosis of bladder
         Anastomosis of bladder to intestine NOS
         Cystocolic anastomosis
         EXCLUDES   *formation of closed ileal bladder (57.87)*

     57.89 Other repair of bladder
         Bladder suspension, not elsewhere classified
         Cystopexy NOS
         Repair of old obstetric laceration of bladder
         EXCLUDES   *repair of current obstetric laceration (75.61)*

57.2–57.89

Operations on the Urinary System

57.9–58.99

√4th **57.9   Other operations on bladder**

57.91   Sphincterotomy of bladder
Division of bladder neck
AHA: 2Q, '90, 26

57.92   Dilation of bladder neck

57.93   Control of (postoperative) hemorrhage of bladder

57.94   Insertion of indwelling urinary catheter

57.95   Replacement of indwelling urinary catheter

57.96   Implantation of electronic bladder stimulator   NC

57.97   Replacement of electronic bladder stimulator   NC

57.98   Removal of electronic bladder stimulator
EXCLUDES   *that with synchronous replacement (57.97)*

57.99   Other
EXCLUDES   *irrigation of:*
cystostomy (96.47)
other indwelling urinary catheter (96.48)
lysis of external adhesions (59.11)
removal of:
cystostomy tube (97.63)
other urinary drainage device (97.64)
therapeutic distention of bladder (96.25)

√3rd **58   Operations on urethra**
INCLUDES   operations on:
bulbourethral gland [Cowper's gland]
periurethral tissue

Code also any application or administration of an adhesion barrier substance (99.77)

58.0   Urethrotomy
Excision of urethral septum
Formation of urethrovaginal fistula
Perineal urethrostomy
Removal of calculus from urethra by incision
EXCLUDES   *drainage of bulbourethral gland or periurethral tissue (58.91)*
internal urethral meatotomy (58.5)
removal of urethral calculus without incision (58.6)

58.1   Urethral meatotomy
EXCLUDES   *internal urethral meatotomy (58.5)*
DEF: Incision of urethra to enlarge passage.

√4th **58.2   Diagnostic procedures on urethra**

58.21   Perineal urethroscopy

58.22   Other urethroscopy

58.23   Biopsy of urethra

58.24   Biopsy of periurethral tissue
DEF: Removal of tissue around urethra for biopsy.

58.29   Other diagnostic procedures on urethra and periurethral tissue
EXCLUDES   *microscopic examination of specimen from urethra (91.31-91.39)*
retrograde cystourethrogram (87.76)
urethral pressure profile (89.25)
urethral sphincter electromyogram (89.23)

√4th **58.3   Excision or destruction of lesion or tissue of urethra**
EXCLUDES   *biopsy of urethra (58.23)*
excision of bulbourethral gland (58.92)
fistulectomy (58.43)
urethrectomy as part of:
complete cystectomy (57.79)
pelvic evisceration (68.8)
radical cystectomy (57.71)

58.31   Endoscopic excision or destruction of lesion or tissue of urethra
Fulguration of urethral lesion

58.39   Other local excision or destruction of lesion or tissue of urethra
Excision of:
congenital valve }
lesion   } of urethra
stricture }
Urethrectomy
EXCLUDES   *that by endoscopic appoach (58.31)*

√4th **58.4   Repair of urethra**
EXCLUDES   *repair of current obstetric laceration (75.61)*

58.41   Suture of laceration of urethra

58.42   Closure of urethrostomy

58.43   Closure of other fistula of urethra
EXCLUDES   *repair of urethroperineovesical fistula (57.84)*

58.44   Reanastomosis of urethra
Anastomosis of urethra
DEF: Repair of severed urethra.

58.45   Repair of hypospadias or epispadias
AHA: 3Q, '97, 6; 4Q, '96, 35
DEF: Repair of abnormal urethral opening.

58.46   Other reconstruction of urethra
Urethral construction

58.47   Urethral meatoplasty
DEF: Reconstruction of urethral opening.

58.49   Other repair of urethra
Benenenti rotation of bulbous urethra
Repair of old obstetric laceration of urethra
Urethral plication
EXCLUDES   *repair of:*
current obstetric laceration (75.61)
urethrocele (70.50-70.51)
AHA: 1Q, '09, 15

58.5   Release of urethral stricture
Cutting of urethral sphincter
Internal urethral meatotomy
Urethrolysis
AHA: 1Q, '97, 13

58.6   Dilation of urethra
Dilation of urethrovesical junction
Passage of sounds through urethra
Removal of calculus from urethra without incision
EXCLUDES   *urethral calibration (89.29)*
AHA: ▶4Q, '13, 99;◀ 1Q, '11, 25; 1Q, '01, 14; 1Q, '97, 13

√4th **58.9   Other operations on urethra and periurethral tissue**

58.91   Incision of periurethral tissue
Drainage of bulbourethral gland
DEF: Incision of tissue around urethra.

58.92   Excision of periurethral tissue
EXCLUDES   *biopsy of periurethral tissue (58.24)*
lysis of periurethral adhesions (59.11-59.12)

58.93   Implantation of artificial urinary sphincter [AUS]
Placement of inflatable:
urethral sphincter
bladder sphincter
Removal with replacement of sphincter device [AUS]
With pump and/or reservoir

58.99   Other
Repair of inflatable sphincter pump and/or reservoir
Surgical correction of hydraulic pressure of inflatable sphincter device
Removal of inflatable urinary sphincter without replacement
EXCLUDES   *removal of:*
intraluminal foreign body from urethra without incision (98.19)
urethral stent (97.65)
AHA: 1Q, '09, 15

BI Bilateral Procedure   NC Non-covered Procedure   LC Limited Coverage Procedure   ▶◀ Revised Text   ● New Code   ▲ Revised Code Title

☑3ʳᵈ 59 Other operations on urinary tract

Code also any application or administration of an adhesion barrier substance (99.77)

☑4ᵗʰ 59.0 Dissection of retroperitoneal tissue

59.00 Retroperitoneal dissection, not otherwise specified

59.02 Other lysis of perirenal or periureteral adhesions

EXCLUDES *that by laparoscope (59.03)*

59.03 Laparoscopic lysis of perirenal or periureteral adhesions

AHA: 4Q, '06, 134

59.09 Other incision of perirenal or periureteral tissue

Exploration of perinephric area
Incision of perirenal abscess

DEF: Exploration of the perinephric area: Exam of tissue around the kidney by incision.

DEF: Incision of perirenal abscess: Incising abscess in tissue around kidney.

☑4ᵗʰ 59.1 Incision of perivesical tissue

DEF: Incising tissue around bladder.

59.11 Other lysis of perivesical adhesions

59.12 Laparoscopic lysis of perivesical adhesions

59.19 Other incision of perivesical tissue

Exploration of perivesical tissue
Incision of hematoma of space of Retzius
Retropubic exploration

☑4ᵗʰ 59.2 Diagnostic procedures on perirenal and perivesical tissue

59.21 Biopsy of perirenal or perivesical tissue

59.29 Other diagnostic procedures on perirenal tissue, perivesical tissue, and retroperitoneum

EXCLUDES *microscopic examination of specimen from:*
perirenal tissue (91.21-91.29)
perivesical tissue (91.31-91.39)
retroperitoneum NEC (91.11-91.19)
retroperitoneal x-ray (88.14-88.16)

59.3 Plication of urethrovesical junction

Kelly-Kennedy operation on urethra
Kelly-Stoeckel urethral plication

DEF: Suturing a tuck in tissues around urethra at junction with bladder; changes angle of junction and provides support.

59.4 Suprapubic sling operation

Goebel-Frangenheim-Stoeckel urethrovesical suspension
Millin-Read urethrovesical suspension
Oxford operation for urinary incontinence
Urethrocystopexy by suprapubic suspension

DEF: Suspension of urethra from suprapubic periosteum to restore support to bladder and urethra.

59.5 Retropubic urethral suspension

Burch procedure
Marshall-Marchetti-Krantz operation
Suture of periurethral tissue to symphysis pubis
Urethral suspension NOS

DEF: Suspension of urethra from pubic bone with suture placed from symphysis pubis to paraurethral tissues; elevates urethrovesical angle, restores urinary continence.

AHA: 1Q, '97, 11

59.6 Paraurethral suspension

Pereyra paraurethral suspension
Periurethral suspension

DEF: Suspension of bladder neck from fibrous membranes of anterior abdominal wall; upward traction applied; changes angle of urethra, improves urinary control.

☑4ᵗʰ 59.7 Other repair of urinary stress incontinence

59.71 Levator muscle operation for urethrovesical suspension

Cystourethropexy with levator muscle sling
Gracilis muscle transplant for urethrovesical suspension
Pubococcygeal sling

59.72 Injection of implant into urethra and/or bladder neck

Collagen implant
Endoscopic injection of implant
Fat implant
Polytef implant

DEF: Injection of collagen into submucosal tissues to increase tissue bulk and improve urinary control.

AHA: 4Q, '95, 72, 73

59.79 Other

Anterior urethropexy
Repair of stress incontinence NOS
Tudor "rabbit ear" urethropexy

DEF: Pubovaginal sling for treatment of stress incontinence: A strip of fascia is harvested and the vaginal epithelium is mobilized and then sutured to the midline at the urethral level to the rectus muscle to create a sling supporting the bladder.

DEF: Vaginal wall sling with bone anchors for treatment of stress incontinence: A sling for the bladder is formed by a suture attachment of vaginal wall to the abdominal wall. In addition, a suture is run from the vagina to a bone anchor placed in the pubic bone.

DEF: Transvaginal endoscopic bladder neck suspension for treatment of stress incontinence: Endoscopic surgical suturing of the vaginal epithelium and the pubocervical fascia at the bladder neck level on both sides of the urethra. Two supporting sutures are run from the vagina to an anchor placed in the pubic bone on each side.

AHA: 2Q, '01, 20; 1Q, '00, 14, 15, 19

59.8 Ureteral catheterization

Drainage of kidney by catheter
Insertion of ureteral stent
Ureterovesical orifice dilation

Code also any ureterotomy (56.2)

EXCLUDES *that for:*
retrograde pyelogram (87.74)
transurethral removal of calculus or clot from ureter and renal pelvis (56.0)

AHA: 2Q, '05, 12; 2Q, '03, 11; 3Q, '00, 7; 1Q, '89, 1; S-O, '86, 10
TIP: Assign code twice if ureteral stents were placed bilaterally.

☑4ᵗʰ 59.9 Other operations on urinary system

EXCLUDES *nonoperative removal of therapeutic device (97.61-97.69)*

59.91 Excision of perirenal or perivesical tissue

EXCLUDES *biopsy of perirenal or perivesical tissue (59.21)*

59.92 Other operations on perirenal or perivesical tissue

59.93 Replacement of ureterostomy tube

Change of ureterostomy tube
Reinsertion of ureterostomy tube

EXCLUDES *nonoperative removal of ureterostomy tube (97.62)*

59.94 Replacement of cystostomy tube

EXCLUDES *nonoperative removal of cystostomy tube (97.63)*

59.95 Ultrasonic fragmentation of urinary stones

Shattered urinary stones

EXCLUDES *percutaneous nephrostomy with fragmentation (55.04)*
shockwave disintegration (98.51)

AHA: 1Q, '89, 1; S-O, '86, 11

59.99 Other

EXCLUDES *instillation of medication into urinary tract (96.49)*
irrigation of urinary tract (96.45-96.48)

AHA: 2Q, '08, 14
TIP: Assign for removal of an infected pubovaginal sling.

☑3ʳᵈ
☑4ᵗʰ Additional Digit Required

2015 ICD-9-CM

Valid OR Procedure   Non-OR Procedure   Adjunct Code

Operations on the Urinary System

59–59.99

Operations on the Male Genital Organs

60–60.95

11. Operations on the Male Genital Organs (60-64)

☑3ʳᵈ **60** **Operations on prostate and seminal vesicles**
     INCLUDES operations on periprostatic tissue
     Code also any application or administration of an adhesion barrier substance (99.77)
     EXCLUDES that associated with radical cystectomy (57.71)

     60.0 **Incision of prostate** ♂
         Drainage of prostatic abscess
         Prostatolithotomy
         EXCLUDES drainage of periprostatic tissue only (60.81)

☑4ᵗʰ **60.1** **Diagnostic procedures on prostate and seminal vesicles**

       60.11 **Closed [percutaneous] [needle] biopsy of prostate** ♂
           Approach:
             transrectal
             transurethral
           Punch biopsy
           DEF: Excision of prostate tissue by closed technique for biopsy.

       60.12 **Open biopsy of prostate** ♂

       60.13 **Closed [percutaneous] biopsy of seminal vesicles** ♂
           Needle biopsy of seminal vesicles

       60.14 **Open biopsy of seminal vesicles** ♂

       60.15 **Biopsy of periprostatic tissue** ♂

       60.18 **Other diagnostic procedures on prostate and periprostatic tissue** ♂
           EXCLUDES microscopic examination of specimen from prostate (91.31-91.39)
                 x-ray of prostate (87.92)

       60.19 **Other diagnostic procedures on seminal vesicles** ♂
           EXCLUDES microscopic examination of specimen from seminal vesicles (91.31-91.39)
                 x-ray:
                   contrast seminal vesiculogram (87.91)
                   other (87.92)

☑4ᵗʰ **60.2** **Transurethral prostatectomy**
       EXCLUDES local excision of lesion of prostate (60.61)
       AHA: 2Q, '94, 9; 3Q, '92, 13

       60.21 **Transurethral (ultrasound) guided laser induced prostatectomy [TULIP]** ♂
           Ablation (contact) (noncontact) by laser
           AHA: 4Q, '95, 7

       60.29 **Other transurethral prostatectomy** ♂
           Excision of median bar by transurethral approach
           Transurethral electrovaporization of prostate (TEVAP)
           Transurethral enucleative procedure
           Transurethral prostatectomy NOS
           Transurethral resection of prostate (TURP)
           DEF: Excision of median bar by transurethral approach: Removal of fibrous structure of prostate.
           DEF: Transurethral enucleative procedure: Transurethral prostatectomy.
           AHA: 3Q, '97, 3

Transurethral Prostatectomy

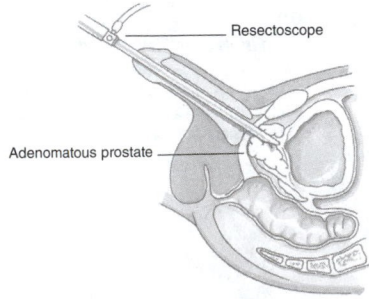

Resectoscope
Adenomatous prostate

60.3 **Suprapubic prostatectomy** ♂
         Transvesical prostatectomy
         EXCLUDES local excision of lesion of prostate (60.61)
                   radical prostatectomy (60.5)
         DEF: Resection of prostate through incision in abdomen above pubic arch.

60.4 **Retropubic prostatectomy** ♂
         EXCLUDES local excision of lesion of prostate (60.61)
                   radical prostatectomy (60.5)
         DEF: Removal of the prostate using an abdominal approach with direct cutting into prostatic capsule.

60.5 **Radical prostatectomy** ♂
         Prostatovesiculectomy
         Radical prostatectomy by any approach
         EXCLUDES cystoprostatectomy (57.71)
         DEF: Removal of prostate, epididymis and vas ampullae.
         DEF: Prostatovesiculectomy: Removal of prostate and epididymis.
         AHA: 3Q, '93, 12

☑4ᵗʰ **60.6** **Other prostatectomy**

       60.61 **Local excision of lesion of prostate** ♂
           EXCLUDES biopsy of prostate (60.11-60.12)
                 laser interstitial thermal therapy [LITT] of lesion or tissue of prostate under guidance (17.69)

       60.62 **Perineal prostatectomy** ♂
           Cryoablation of prostate
           Cryoprostatectomy
           Cryosurgery of prostate
           Radical cryosurcial ablation of prostate (RCSA)
           EXCLUDES local excision of lesion of prostate (60.61)
           DEF: Excision of prostate tissue through incision between scrotum and anus.
           AHA: 4Q, '95, 71

       60.69 **Other** ♂

☑4ᵗʰ **60.7** **Operations on seminal vesicles**

       60.71 **Percutaneous aspiration of seminal vesicle** ♂
           EXCLUDES needle biopsy of seminal vesicle (60.13)

       60.72 **Incision of seminal vesicle** ♂

       60.73 **Excision of seminal vesicle** ♂
           Excision of Müllerian duct cyst
           Spermatocystectomy
           EXCLUDES biopsy of seminal vesicle (60.13-60.14)
                 prostatovesiculectomy (60.5)

       60.79 **Other operations on seminal vesicles** ♂

☑4ᵗʰ **60.8** **Incision or excision of periprostatic tissue**

       60.81 **Incision of periprostatic tissue** ♂
           Drainage of periprostatic abscess

       60.82 **Excision of periprostatic tissue** ♂
           Excision of lesion of periprostatic tissue
           EXCLUDES biopsy of periprostatic tissue (60.15)

☑4ᵗʰ **60.9** **Other operations on prostate**

       60.91 **Percutaneous aspiration of prostate** ♂
           EXCLUDES needle biopsy of prostate (60.11)

       60.92 **Injection into prostate** ♂

       60.93 **Repair of prostate** ♂

       60.94 **Control of (postoperative) hemorrhage of prostate** ♂
           Coagulation of prostatic bed
           Cystoscopy for control of prostatic hemorrhage

       60.95 **Transurethral balloon dilation of the prostatic urethra** ♂
           DEF: Insertion and inflation of balloon to stretch the portion of the urethra that passes through the prostate.
           AHA: 4Q, '91, 23

BI Bilateral Procedure   NC Non-covered Procedure   LC Limited Coverage Procedure   ►◄ Revised Text   ● New Code   ▲ Revised Code Title

150 – Volume 3   2015 ICD-9-CM

60.96 Transurethral destruction of prostate tissue by microwave thermotherapy ♂

Transurethral microwave thermotherapy [TUMT] of prostate

EXCLUDES Prostatectomy:
other (60.61-60.69)
radical (60.5)
retropubic (60.4)
suprapubic (60.3)
transurethral (60.21-60.29)

AHA: 4Q, '00, 67

60.97 Other transurethral destruction of prostate tissue by other thermotherapy ♂

Radiofrequency thermotherapy
Transurethral needle ablation [TUNA] of prostate

EXCLUDES Prostatectomy:
other (60.61-60.69)
radical (60.5)
retropubic (60.4)
suprapubic (60.3)
transurethral (60.21-60.29)

AHA: 4Q, '00, 67

60.99 Other ♂

EXCLUDES prostatic massage (99.94)

AHA: 3Q, '90, 12

✓3rd **61 Operations on scrotum and tunica vaginalis**

61.0 Incision and drainage of scrotum and tunica vaginalis ♂

EXCLUDES percutaneous aspiration of hydrocele (61.91)

✓4th **61.1 Diagnostic procedures on scrotum and tunica vaginalis**

61.11 Biopsy of scrotum or tunica vaginalis ♂

61.19 Other diagnostic procedures on scrotum and tunica vaginalis ♂

61.2 Excision of hydrocele (of tunica vaginalis) ♂

Bottle repair of hydrocele of tunica vaginalis
EXCLUDES percutaneous aspiration of hydrocele (61.91)
DEF: Removal of fluid collected in serous membrane of testes.

61.3 Excision or destruction of lesion or tissue of scrotum ♂

Fulguration of lesion
Reduction of elephantiasis   } of scrotum
Partial scrotectomy

EXCLUDES biopsy of scrotum (61.11)
scrotal fistulectomy (61.42)

✓4th **61.4 Repair of scrotum and tunica vaginalis**

61.41 Suture of laceration of scrotum and tunica vaginalis ♂

61.42 Repair of scrotal fistula ♂

61.49 Other repair of scrotum and tunica vaginalis ♂
Reconstruction with rotational or pedicle flaps

✓4th **61.9 Other operations on scrotum and tunica vaginalis**

61.91 Percutaneous aspiration of tunica vaginalis ♂
Aspiration of hydrocele of tunica vaginalis

Hydrocelectomy

Scrotal skin incised
Sac opened
Fluid-filled sac mobilized
Excess tissue trimmed
Testis
Remaining sacular tissue folded back and sewn to itself to preclude recurrence ("bottle" procedure)

Orchiopexy with Detorsion of Testes

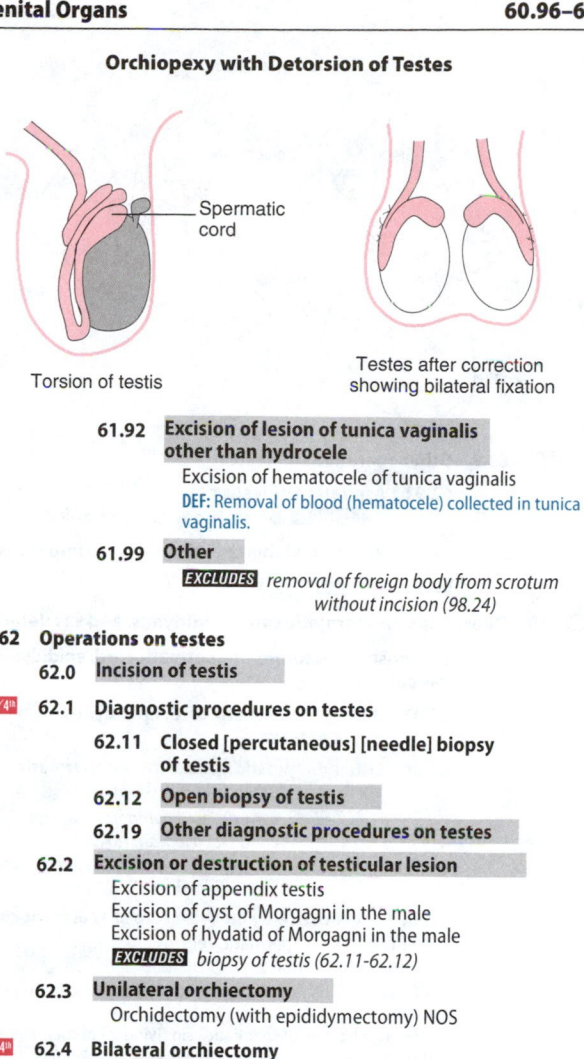

Torsion of testis

Spermatic cord

Testes after correction showing bilateral fixation

61.92 Excision of lesion of tunica vaginalis other than hydrocele ♂

Excision of hematocele of tunica vaginalis
DEF: Removal of blood (hematocele) collected in tunica vaginalis.

61.99 Other ♂

EXCLUDES removal of foreign body from scrotum without incision (98.24)

✓3rd **62 Operations on testes**

62.0 Incision of testis ♂

✓4th **62.1 Diagnostic procedures on testes**

62.11 Closed [percutaneous] [needle] biopsy of testis ♂

62.12 Open biopsy of testis ♂

62.19 Other diagnostic procedures on testes ♂

62.2 Excision or destruction of testicular lesion ♂

Excision of appendix testis
Excision of cyst of Morgagni in the male
Excision of hydatid of Morgagni in the male
EXCLUDES biopsy of testis (62.11-62.12)

62.3 Unilateral orchiectomy ♂
Orchidectomy (with epididymectomy) NOS

✓4th **62.4 Bilateral orchiectomy** ♂

Male castration
Radical bilateral orchiectomy (with epididymectomy)
Code also any synchronous lymph node dissection (40.3, 40.5)
DEF: Removal of both testes.
DEF: Radical bilateral orchiectomy (with epididymectomy): Excision of both testes and structures that store sperm.

62.41 Removal of both testes at same operative episode ♂
Bilateral orchidectomy NOS

62.42 Removal of remaining testis ♂
Removal of solitary testis

62.5 Orchiopexy ♂

Mobilization and replacement of testis in scrotum
Orchiopexy with detorsion of testis
Torek (-Bevan) operation (orchidopexy) (first stage) (second stage)
Transplantation to and fixation of testis in scrotum
DEF: Fixation of testis in scrotum.
DEF: Orchiopexy with detorsion of testis: Fixation and placement of testis in scrotum after correcting angle.
DEF: Torek operation (first stage) (second stage): Transfer of congenitally undescended testis from inguinal canal to scrotum.
DEF: Transplantation to and fixation of testis in scrotum: Transfer of displaced testis to scrotum.

✓4th **62.6 Repair of testes**

EXCLUDES reduction of torsion (63.52)

62.61 Suture of laceration of testis ♂

62.69 Other repair of testis ♂
Testicular graft

62.7 Insertion of testicular prosthesis ♂

✓3rd ✓4th Additional Digit Required   Valid OR Procedure   Non-OR Procedure   Adjunct Code

Operations on the Male Genital Organs

62.9–64.94

Varicocelectomy

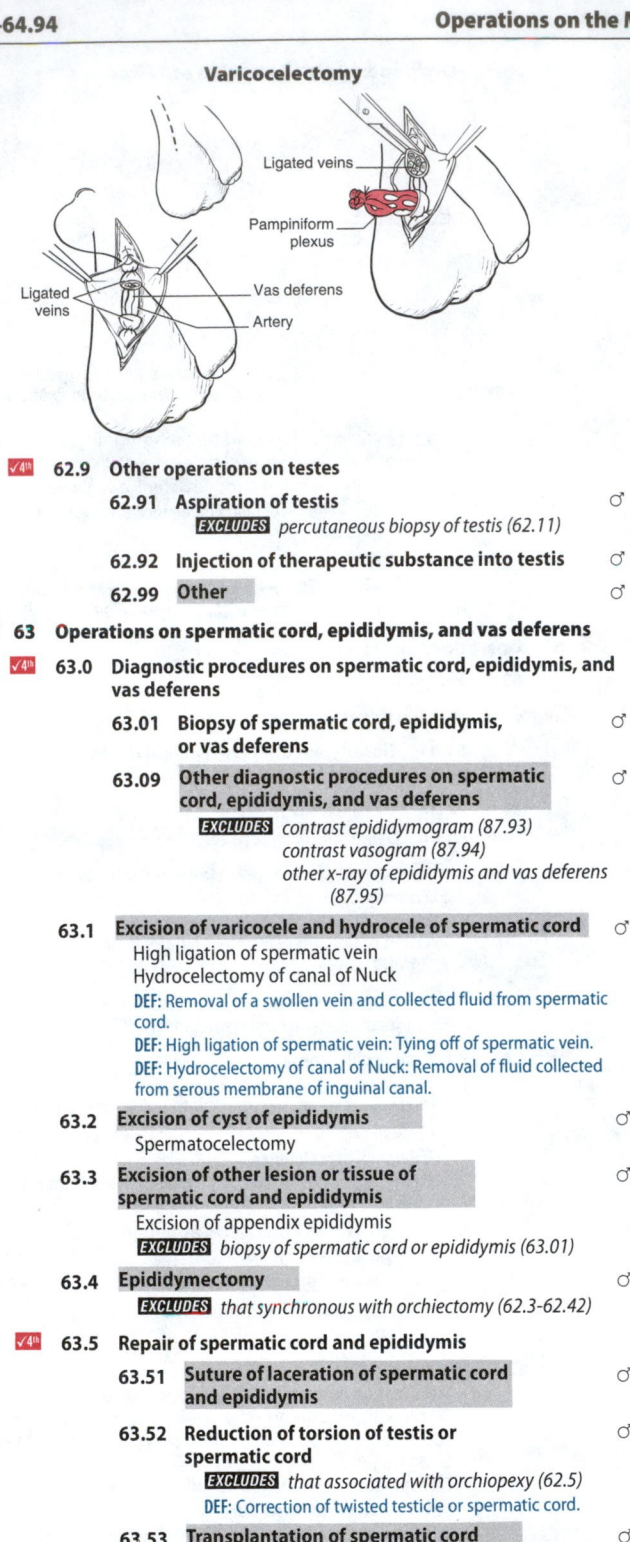

Ligated veins
Pampiniform plexus
Vas deferens
Ligated veins
Artery

✓4th 62.9 Other operations on testes

62.91 Aspiration of testis ♂
     EXCLUDES *percutaneous biopsy of testis (62.11)*

62.92 Injection of therapeutic substance into testis ♂

62.99 Other ♂

✓3rd 63 Operations on spermatic cord, epididymis, and vas deferens

✓4th 63.0 Diagnostic procedures on spermatic cord, epididymis, and vas deferens

63.01 Biopsy of spermatic cord, epididymis, or vas deferens ♂

63.09 Other diagnostic procedures on spermatic cord, epididymis, and vas deferens ♂
     EXCLUDES *contrast epididymogram (87.93)*
          contrast vasogram (87.94)
          other x-ray of epididymis and vas deferens (87.95)

63.1 Excision of varicocele and hydrocele of spermatic cord ♂
High ligation of spermatic vein
Hydrocelectomy of canal of Nuck
    DEF: Removal of a swollen vein and collected fluid from spermatic cord.
    DEF: High ligation of spermatic vein: Tying off of spermatic vein.
    DEF: Hydrocelectomy of canal of Nuck: Removal of fluid collected from serous membrane of inguinal canal.

63.2 Excision of cyst of epididymis ♂
Spermatocelectomy

63.3 Excision of other lesion or tissue of spermatic cord and epididymis ♂
Excision of appendix epididymis
     EXCLUDES *biopsy of spermatic cord or epididymis (63.01)*

63.4 Epididymectomy ♂
     EXCLUDES *that synchronous with orchiectomy (62.3–62.42)*

✓4th 63.5 Repair of spermatic cord and epididymis

63.51 Suture of laceration of spermatic cord and epididymis ♂

63.52 Reduction of torsion of testis or spermatic cord ♂
     EXCLUDES *that associated with orchiopexy (62.5)*
    DEF: Correction of twisted testicle or spermatic cord.

63.53 Transplantation of spermatic cord ♂

63.59 Other repair of spermatic cord and epididymis ♂

63.6 Vasotomy ♂
Vasostomy
    DEF: Vasotomy: Incision of ducts carrying sperm from testicles.
    DEF: Vasostomy: Creation of an opening into duct.

✓4th 63.7 Vasectomy and ligation of vas deferens

63.70 Male sterilization procedure, not otherwise specified NC ♂

63.71 Ligation of vas deferens NC ♂
Crushing of vas deferens
Division of vas deferens

63.72 Ligation of spermatic cord NC ♂

63.73 Vasectomy NC ♂
    AHA: 2Q, '98, 13

✓4th 63.8 Repair of vas deferens and epididymis

63.81 Suture of laceration of vas deferens and epididymis ♂

63.82 Reconstruction of surgically divided vas deferens ♂

63.83 Epididymovasostomy ♂
    DEF: Creation of new connection between vas deferens and epididymis.

63.84 Removal of ligature from vas deferens ♂

63.85 Removal of valve from vas deferens ♂

63.89 Other repair of vas deferens and epididymis ♂

✓4th 63.9 Other operations on spermatic cord, epididymis, and vas deferens

63.91 Aspiration of spermatocele ♂
    DEF: Puncture of cystic distention of epididymis.

63.92 Epididymotomy ♂
    DEF: Incision of epididymis.

63.93 Incision of spermatic cord ♂
    DEF: Incision into sperm storage structure.

63.94 Lysis of adhesions of spermatic cord ♂

63.95 Insertion of valve in vas deferens ♂

63.99 Other ♂

✓3rd 64 Operations on penis
    INCLUDES operations on:
       corpora cavernosa
       glans penis
       prepuce

64.0 Circumcision ♂
    DEF: Removal of penis foreskin.

✓4th 64.1 Diagnostic procedures on the penis

64.11 Biopsy of penis ♂

64.19 Other diagnostic procedures on penis ♂

64.2 Local excision or destruction of lesion of penis ♂
     EXCLUDES *biopsy of penis (64.11)*

64.3 Amputation of penis ♂

✓4th 64.4 Repair and plastic operation on penis

64.41 Suture of laceration of penis ♂

64.42 Release of chordee ♂
    DEF: Correction of downward displacement of penis.
    AHA: 4Q, '96, 34

64.43 Construction of penis ♂

64.44 Reconstruction of penis ♂

64.45 Replantation of penis ♂
Reattachment of amputated penis

64.49 Other repair of penis ♂
     EXCLUDES *repair of epispadias and hypospadias (58.45)*

64.5 Operations for sex transformation, not elsewhere classified NC ♂

✓4th 64.9 Other operations on male genital organs

64.91 Dorsal or lateral slit of prepuce ♂

64.92 Incision of penis ♂

64.93 Division of penile adhesions ♂

64.94 Fitting of external prosthesis of penis ♂
Penile prosthesis NOS

BI Bilateral Procedure   NC Non-covered Procedure   LC Limited Coverage Procedure   ►◄ Revised Text   ● New Code   ▲ Revised Code Title

64.95 Insertion or replacement of non-inflatable penile prosthesis ♂

Insertion of semi-rigid rod prosthesis into shaft of penis

EXCLUDES external penile prosthesis (64.94)
inflatable penile prosthesis (64.97)
plastic repair, penis (64.43-64.49)
that associated with:
construction (64.43)
reconstruction (64.44)

64.96 Removal of internal prosthesis of penis ♂

Removal without replacement of non-inflatable or inflatable penile prosthesis

64.97 Insertion or replacement of inflatable penile prosthesis ♂

Insertion of cylinders into shaft of penis and placement of pump and reservoir

EXCLUDES external penile prosthesis (64.94)
non-inflatable penile prosthesis (64.95)
plastic repair, penis (64.43-64.49)

64.98 Other operations on penis ♂

Corpora cavernosa-corpus spongiosum shunt
Corpora-saphenous shunt
Irrigation of corpus cavernosum

EXCLUDES removal of foreign body:
intraluminal (98.19)
without incision (98.24)
stretching of foreskin (99.95)

DEF: Corpora cavernosa-corpus spongiosum shunt: Insertion of shunt between erectile tissues of penis.

DEF: Corpora-saphenous shunt: Insertion of shunt between erectile tissue and vein of penis.

DEF: Irrigation of corpus cavernosum: Washing of erectile tissue forming dorsum and side of penis.

AHA: 3Q, '92, 9

TIP: Assign for arterialization of deep dorsal vein of penis, which involves anastomosis of the common femoral artery via a saphenous vein graft to the deep dorsal penile vein.

64.99 Other ♂

EXCLUDES collection of sperm for artificial insemination (99.96)

✓3rd ✓4th Additional Digit Required   Valid OR Procedure   Non-OR Procedure   Adjunct Code

Operations on the Female Genital Organs

65–66.02

12. Operations on the Female Genital Organs (65-71)

✓3rd **65** **Operations on ovary**
Code also any application or administration of an adhesion barrier substance (99.77)

✓4th **65.0** **Oophorotomy**
Salpingo-oophorotomy
DEF: Incision into ovary.
DEF: Salpingo-oophorotomy: Incision into ovary and the fallopian tube.

65.01 Laparoscopic oophorotomy ♀

65.09 Other oophorotomy ♀

✓4th **65.1** **Diagnostic procedures on ovaries**

65.11 Aspiration biopsy of ovary ♀

65.12 Other biopsy of ovary ♀

65.13 Laparoscopic biopsy of ovary ♀
AHA: 4Q, '96, 67

65.14 Other laparoscopic diagnostic procedures on ovaries ♀

65.19 Other diagnostic procedures on ovaries ♀
EXCLUDES microscopic examination of specimen from ovary (91.41-91.49)

✓4th **65.2** **Local excision or destruction of ovarian lesion or tissue**

65.21 Marsupialization of ovarian cyst ♀
EXCLUDES that by laparoscope (65.23)
DEF: Exteriorized cyst to outside by incising anterior wall and suturing cut edges to create open pouch.

65.22 Wedge resection of ovary ♀
EXCLUDES that by laparoscope (65.24)

65.23 Laparoscopic marsupialization of ovarian cyst ♀

65.24 Laparoscopic wedge resection of ovary ♀

65.25 Other laparoscopic local excision or destruction of ovary ♀

65.29 Other local excision or destruction of ovary ♀
Bisection ⎫
Cauterization ⎬ of ovary
Parial excision ⎭
EXCLUDES biopsy of ovary (65.11-65.13)
that by laparoscope (65.25)

✓4th **65.3** **Unilateral oophorectomy**

65.31 Laparoscopic unilateral oophorectomy ♀

65.39 Other unilateral oophorectomy ♀
EXCLUDES that by laparoscope (65.31)
AHA: 4Q, '96, 66

✓4th **65.4** **Unilateral salpingo-oophorectomy**

65.41 Laparoscopic unilateral salpingo-oophorectomy ♀
AHA: 4Q, '96, 67

65.49 Other unilateral salpingo-oophorectomy ♀

✓4th **65.5** **Bilateral oophorectomy**

65.51 Other removal of both ovaries at same operative episode ♀
Female castration
EXCLUDES that by laparoscope (65.53)

Oophorectomy

Fallopian tube
Fimbria
Ovary
Ovarian cyst

65.52 Other removal of remaining ovary ♀
Removal of solitary ovary
EXCLUDES that by laparoscope (65.54)

65.53 Laparoscopic removal of both ovaries at same operative episode ♀

65.54 Laparoscopic removal of remaining ovary ♀

✓4th **65.6** **Bilateral salpingo-oophorectomy**

65.61 Other removal of both ovaries and tubes at same operative episode ♀
EXCLUDES that by laparoscope (65.53)
AHA: 4Q, '12, 82; 4Q, '96, 65

65.62 Other removal of remaining ovary and tube ♀
Removal of solitary ovary and tube
EXCLUDES that by laparoscope (65.54)

65.63 Laparoscopic removal of both ovaries and tubes at the same operative episode ♀
AHA: 3Q, '09, 5; 4Q, '06, 133, 134; 4Q, '96, 68

65.64 Laparoscopic removal of remaining ovary and tube ♀

✓4th **65.7** **Repair of ovary**
EXCLUDES salpingo-oophorostomy (66.72)

65.71 Other simple suture of ovary ♀
EXCLUDES that by laparoscope (65.74)

65.72 Other reimplantation of ovary ♀
EXCLUDES that by laparoscope (65.75)
DEF: Grafting and repositioning of ovary at same site.

65.73 Other salpingo-oophoroplasty ♀
EXCLUDES that by laparoscope (65.76)

65.74 Laparoscopic simple suture of ovary ♀

65.75 Laparoscopic reimplantation of ovary ♀

65.76 Laparoscopic salpingo-oophoroplasty ♀

65.79 Other repair of ovary ♀
Oophoropexy

✓4th **65.8** **Lysis of adhesions of ovary and fallopian tube**

65.81 Laparoscopic lysis of adhesions of ovary and fallopian tube ♀
AHA: 4Q, '96, 67

65.89 Other lysis of adhesions of ovary and fallopian tube ♀
EXCLUDES that by laparoscope (65.81)

✓4th **65.9** **Other operations on ovary**

65.91 Aspiration of ovary ♀
EXCLUDES aspiration biopsy of ovary (65.11)

65.92 Transplantation of ovary ♀
EXCLUDES reimplantation of ovary (65.72, 65.75)

65.93 Manual rupture of ovarian cyst ♀
DEF: Breaking up an ovarian cyst using manual technique or blunt instruments.

65.94 Ovarian denervation ♀
DEF: Destruction of nerve tracts to ovary.

65.95 Release of torsion of ovary ♀

65.99 Other ♀
Ovarian drilling
AHA: N-D, '86, 9

✓3rd **66** **Operations on fallopian tubes**
Code also any application or administration of an adhesion barrier substance (99.77)

✓4th **66.0** **Salpingotomy and salpingostomy**

66.01 Salpingotomy ♀

66.02 Salpingostomy ♀

BI Bilateral Procedure   **NC** Non-covered Procedure   **LC** Limited Coverage Procedure   ▶◀ Revised Text   ● New Code   ▲ Revised Code Title

154 – Volume 3   2015 ICD-9-CM

✓4th 66.1 Diagnostic procedures on fallopian tubes

66.11 Biopsy of fallopian tube ♀

66.19 Other diagnostic procedures on fallopian tubes ♀

EXCLUDES *microscopic examination of specimen from fallopian tubes (91.41-91.49)*
radiography of fallopian tubes (87.82-87.83, 87.85)
Rubin's test (66.8)

✓4th 66.2 Bilateral endoscopic destruction or occlusion of fallopian tubes

INCLUDES bilateral endoscopic destruction or occlusion of fallopian tubes by:
culdoscopy
endoscopy
hysteroscopy
laparoscopy
peritoneoscopy
endoscopic destruction of solitary fallopian tube

DEF: Endoscopic blockage or destruction of both fallopian tubes.

DEF: Bilateral endoscopic destruction or occlusion of fallopian tubes by:

Culdoscopy: Endoscopic insertion through posterior structure of vagina.
Hysteroscopy: Endoscopic insertion through uterus.
Laparoscopy: Endoscopic insertion through abdomen.
Peritoneoscopy: Endoscopic insertion through abdominal serous membrane cavity.
Endoscopic destruction of solitary fallopian tube: Endoscopic destruction of one fallopian tube.

66.21 Bilateral endoscopic ligation and crushing of fallopian tubes NC ♀

66.22 Bilateral endoscopic ligation and division of fallopian tubes NC ♀

66.29 Other bilateral endoscopic destruction or occlusion of fallopian tubes NC ♀

✓4th 66.3 Other bilateral destruction or occlusion of fallopian tubes

INCLUDES destruction of solitary fallopian tube
EXCLUDES *endoscopic destruction or occlusion of fallopian tubes (66.21-66.29)*

66.31 Other bilateral ligation and crushing of fallopian tubes NC ♀

66.32 Other bilateral ligation and division of fallopian tubes NC ♀
Pomeroy operation

66.39 Other bilateral destruction or occlusion of fallopian tubes NC ♀
Female sterilization operation NOS

66.4 Total unilateral salpingectomy ♀

✓4th 66.5 Total bilateral salpingectomy

EXCLUDES *bilateral partial salpingectomy for sterilization (66.39)*
that with oophorectomy (65.61-65.64)

66.51 Removal of both fallopian tubes at same operative episode ♀

Endoscopic Ligation of Fallopian Tubes

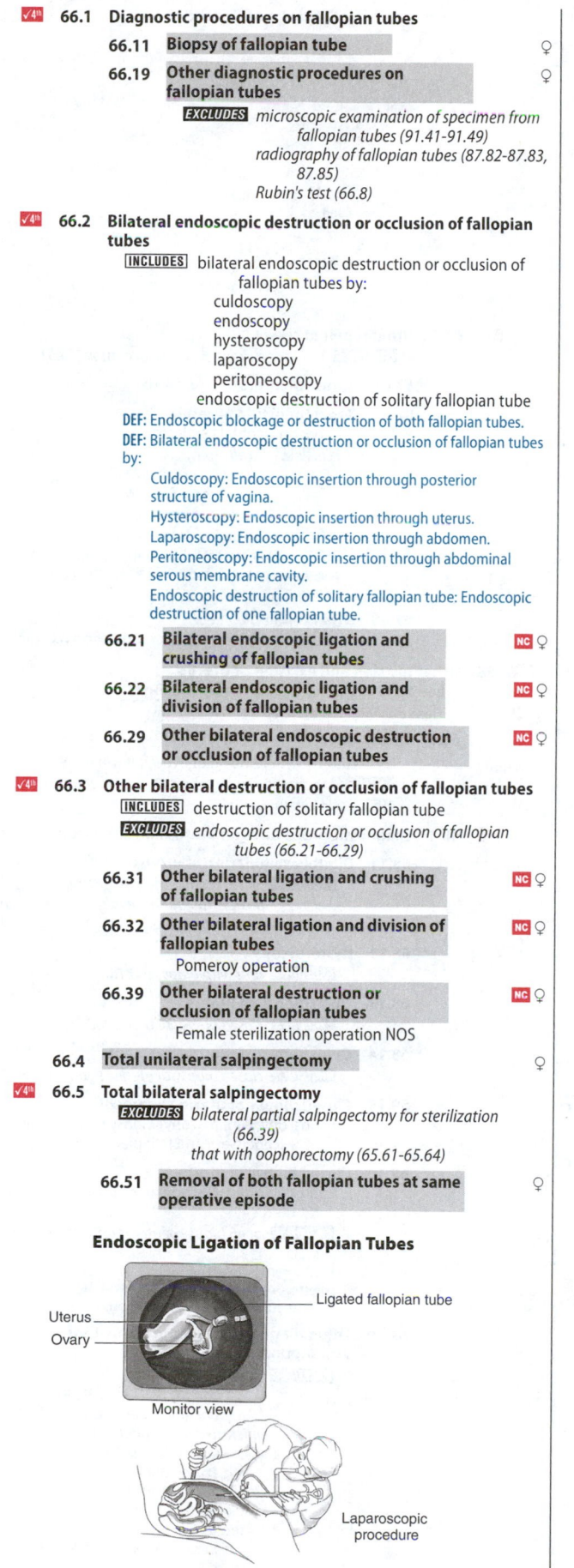

Uterus
Ovary
Ligated fallopian tube
Monitor view
Laparoscopic procedure

66.52 Removal of remaining fallopian tube ♀
Removal of solitary fallopian tube

✓4th 66.6 Other salpingectomy

INCLUDES salpingectomy by:
cauterization
coagulation
electrocoagulation
excision
EXCLUDES *fistulectomy (66.73)*

66.61 Excision or destruction of lesion of fallopian tube ♀
EXCLUDES *biopsy of fallopian tube (66.11)*

66.62 Salpingectomy with removal of tubal pregnancy ♀
Code also any synchronous oophorectomy (65.31, 65.39)
AHA: 3Q, '95, 15; S-O, '85, 14
TIP: If salpingectomy is not performed with removal of ectopic pregnancy, assign instead code 74.3 Removal of extratubal ectopic pregnancy.

66.63 Bilateral partial salpingectomy, not otherwise specified

66.69 Other partial salpingectomy ♀

✓4th 66.7 Repair of fallopian tube

66.71 Simple suture of fallopian tube ♀

66.72 Salpingo-oophorostomy ♀

66.73 Salpingo-salpingostomy ♀

66.74 Salpingo-uterostomy ♀

66.79 Other repair of fallopian tube ♀
Graft of fallopian tube
Reopening of divided fallopian tube
Salpingoplasty

DEF: Graft of fallopian: Repair of fallopian tube with implanted graft.
DEF: Reopening of divided fallopian tube: Reconnection of severed fallopian tube to restore patency.
DEF: Salpingoplasty: Plastic reconstruction of fallopian tube defect.
AHA: 2Q, '95, 10
TIP: When a patient is admitted for tubal ligation reversal, assign this code, along with diagnosis code V26.0 Tuboplasty or vasoplasty after previous sterilization, as the principal diagnosis.

66.8 Insufflation of fallopian tube ♀
Insufflation of fallopian tube with:
air
dye
gas
saline
Rubin's test
EXCLUDES *insufflation of therapeutic agent (66.95)*
that for hysterosalpingography (87.82-87.83)

DEF: Forceful blowing of gas or liquid into fallopian tubes to test patency.
DEF: Rubin's test: Introduction of carbon dioxide gas into fallopian tubes to test patency.

✓4th 66.9 Other operations on fallopian tubes

66.91 Aspiration of fallopian tube ♀

66.92 Unilateral destruction or occlusion of fallopian tube ♀
EXCLUDES *that of solitary tube (66.21-66.39)*

66.93 Implantation or replacement of prosthesis of fallopian tube ♀

66.94 Removal of prosthesis of fallopian tube ♀

66.95 Insufflation of therapeutic agent into fallopian tubes ♀

66.96 Dilation of fallopian tube ♀

66.97 Burying of fimbriae in uterine wall ♀
DEF: Implantation of fringed edges of fallopian tube into uterine wall.

✓3rd ✓4th Additional Digit Required
2015 ICD-9-CM
Valid OR Procedure
Non-OR Procedure
Adjunct Code
Volume 3 – 155

66.99   **Other**   ♀

> **EXCLUDES** *lysis of adhesions of ovary and tube (65.81, 65.89)*

AHA: 2Q, '94, 11

✓3rd **67**   **Operations on cervix**

Code also any application or administration of an adhesion barrier substance (99.77)

67.0   **Dilation of cervical canal**   ♀

> **EXCLUDES** *dilation and curettage (69.01-69.09)*
> *that for induction of labor (73.1)*

✓4th **67.1**   **Diagnostic procedures on cervix**

67.11   **Endocervical biopsy**   ♀

> **EXCLUDES** *conization of cervix (67.2)*

67.12   **Other cervical biopsy**   ♀

Punch biopsy of cervix NOS

> **EXCLUDES** *conization of cervix (67.2)*

67.19   **Other diagnostic procedures on cervix**   ♀

> **EXCLUDES** *microscopic examination of specimen from cervix (91.41-91.49)*

67.2   **Conization of cervix**   ♀

> **EXCLUDES** *that by:*
> *cryosurgery (67.33)*
> *electrosurgery (67.32)*

DEF: Removal of cone-shaped section from distal cervix; cervical function preserved.

✓4th **67.3**   **Other excision or destruction of lesion or tissue of cervix**

67.31   **Marsupialization of cervical cyst**   ♀

DEF: Incision and then suturing open of a cyst in the neck of the uterus.

67.32   **Destruction of lesion of cervix by cauterization**   ♀

Electroconization of cervix
LEEP (loop electrosurgical excision procedure)
LLETZ (large loop excision of the transformation zone)

DEF: Destruction of lesion of uterine neck by applying intense heat.
DEF: Electroconization of cervix: Electrocautery excision of multilayer cone-shaped section from uterine neck.

AHA: 1Q, '98, 3

67.33   **Destruction of lesion of cervix by cryosurgery**   ♀

Cryoconization of cervix

DEF: Destruction of lesion of uterine neck by freezing.
DEF: Cryoconization of cervix: Excision by freezing of multilayer cone-shaped section of abnormal tissue in uterine neck.

67.39   **Other excision or destruction of lesion or tissue of cervix**   ♀

> **EXCLUDES** *biopsy of cervix (67.11-67.12)*
> *cervical fistulectomy (67.62)*
> *conization of cervix (67.2)*

67.4   **Amputation of cervix**   ♀

Cervicectomy with synchronous colporrhaphy

DEF: Excision of lower uterine neck.
DEF: Cervicectomy with synchronous colporrhaphy: Excision of lower uterine neck with suture of vaginal stump.

✓4th **67.5**   **Repair of internal cervical os**

DEF: Repair of cervical opening defect.
AHA: 4Q, '01, 63; 3Q, '00, 11

67.51   **Transabdominal cerclage of cervix**   ♀

67.59   **Other repair of internal cervical os**   ♀

Cerclage of isthmus uteri   Shirodkar operation
McDonald operation   Transvaginal cerclage

> **EXCLUDES** *laparoscopically assisted supracervical hysterectomy [LASH] (68.31)*
> *transabdominal cerclage of cervix (67.51)*

DEF: Cerclage of isthmus uteri: Placement of encircling suture between neck and body of uterus.
DEF: Shirodkar operation: Placement of purse-string suture in internal cervical opening.

AHA: 4Q, '08, 125

Cerclage of Cervix

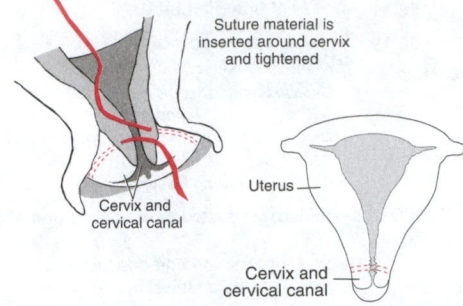

Suture material is inserted around cervix and tightened

Cervix and cervical canal

Uterus

Cervix and cervical canal

✓4th **67.6**   **Other repair of cervix**

> **EXCLUDES** *repair of current obstetric laceration (75.51)*

67.61   **Suture of laceration of cervix**   ♀

67.62   **Repair of fistula of cervix**   ♀

Cervicosigmoidal fistulectomy

> **EXCLUDES** *fistulectomy:*
> *cervicovesical (57.84)*
> *ureterocervical (56.84)*
> *vesicocervicovaginal (57.84)*

DEF: Closure of fistula in lower uterus.
DEF: Cervicosigmoidal fistulectomy: Excision of abnormal passage between uterine neck and torsion of large intestine.

67.69   **Other repair of cervix**   ♀

Repair of old obstetric laceration of cervix

✓3rd **68**   **Other incision and excision of uterus**

Code also any application or administration of an adhesion barrier substance (99.77)

68.0   **Hysterotomy**   ♀

Hysterotomy with removal of hydatidiform mole

> **EXCLUDES** *hysterotomy for termination of pregnancy (74.91)*

DEF: Incision into the uterus.

✓4th **68.1**   **Diagnostic procedures on uterus and supporting structures**

68.11   **Digital examination of uterus**   ♀

> **EXCLUDES** *pelvic examination, so described (89.26)*
> *postpartal manual exploration of uterine cavity (75.7)*

68.12   **Hysteroscopy**   ♀

> **EXCLUDES** *that with biopsy (68.16)*

68.13   **Open biopsy of uterus**   ♀

> **EXCLUDES** *closed biopsy of uterus (68.16)*

68.14   **Open biopsy of uterine ligaments**   ♀

> **EXCLUDES** *closed biopsy of uterine ligaments (68.15)*

68.15   **Closed biopsy of uterine ligaments**   ♀

Endoscopic (laparoscopy) biopsy of uterine adnexa, except ovary and fallopian tube

68.16   **Closed biopsy of uterus**   ♀

Endoscopic (laparoscopy) (hysteroscopy) biopsy of uterus

> **EXCLUDES** *open biopsy of uterus (68.13)*

AHA: 2Q, '12, 18
TIP: Assign for closed endometrial biopsy via Pipelle suction curette. Code assignment is based on the procedure performed, not the instrumentation.

68.19   **Other diagnostic procedures on uterus and supporting structures**   ♀

> **EXCLUDES** *diagnostic:*
> *aspiration curettage (69.59)*
> *dilation and curettage (69.09)*
> *microscopic examination of specimen from uterus (91.41-91.49)*
> *pelvic examination (89.26)*
> *radioisotope scan of:*
> *placenta (92.17)*
> *uterus (92.19)*
> *ultrasonography of uterus (88.78-88.79)*
> *x-ray of uterus (87.81-87.89)*

BI Bilateral Procedure   **NC** Non-covered Procedure   **LC** Limited Coverage Procedure   ▶◀ Revised Text   ● New Code   ▲ Revised Code Title

156 – Volume 3      **2015 ICD-9-CM**

☑4ᵗʰ **68.2 Excision or destruction of lesion or tissue of uterus**

68.21 Division of endometrial synechiae ♀

Lysis of intraluminal uterine adhesions

DEF: Separation of uterine adhesions.

DEF: Lysis of intraluminal uterine adhesion: Surgical destruction of adhesive, fibrous structures inside uterine cavity.

68.22 Incision or excision of congenital septum of uterus ♀

68.23 Endometrial ablation ♀

Dilation and curettage

Hysteroscopic endometrial ablation

DEF: Removal or destruction of uterine lining; usually by electrocautery or loop electrosurgical excision procedure (LEEP).

AHA: 4Q, '96, 68

TIP: The endometrium is ablated by a laser, radiofrequency electromagnetic energy, or electrocoagulation, via a roller ball or a U-shaped wire on the end of the hysteroscope.

68.24 Uterine artery embolization [UAE] with coils ♀

EXCLUDES *that without coils (68.25)*

AHA: 4Q, '11, 179-180

TIP: UAE may be performed for two purposes: to stop severe pelvic bleeding and to obstruct blood flow to uterine fibroids.

68.25 Uterine artery embolization [UAE] without coils ♀

Includes that by:
gelatin sponge
gelfoam
microspheres
particulate agent NOS
polyvinyl alcohol [PVA]
spherical embolics

EXCLUDES *that with coils (68.24)*

AHA: 4Q, '11, 179-180

TIP: UAE may be performed for two purposes: to stop severe pelvic bleeding and to obstruct blood flow to uterine fibroids.

68.29 Other excision or destruction of lesion of uterus ♀

Uterine myomectomy

EXCLUDES *biopsy of uterus (68.13)*
uterine fistulectomy (69.42)

AHA: 3Q, '06, 18; 1Q, '96, 14

☑4ᵗʰ **68.3 Subtotal abdominal hysterectomy**

68.31 Laparoscopic supracervical hysterectomy [LSH] ♀

Classic infrafascial SEMM hysterectomy [CISH]
Laparoscopically assisted supracervical hysterectomy [LASH]

DEF: A hysterectomy that spares the cervix and maintains the integrity of the pelvic floor; SEMM version of the supracervical hysterectomy, also called the classic infrafascial SEMM hysterectomy [CISH]; the cardinal ligaments, or lateral cervical ligaments that merge with the pelvic diaphragm remain intact.

AHA: 4Q, '03, 98-99

68.39 Other and unspecified subtotal abdominal hysterectomy ♀

Supracervical hysterectomy

EXCLUDES *classic infrafascial SEMM hysterectomy [CISH] (68.31)*
laparoscopic supracervical hysterectomy [LSH] (68.31)

AHA: 4Q, '03, 98

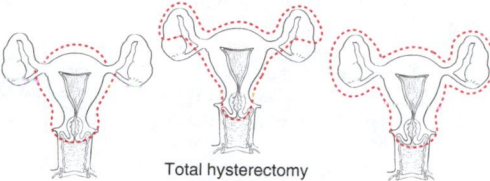

Vaginal Hysterectomy

Total hysterectomy (uterus only removed)

Total hysterectomy with bilateral salpingectomy (uterus and tubes removed)

Total hysterectomy with bilateral salpingo-oophorectomy (uterus, tubes, and ovaries removed)

☑4ᵗʰ **68.4 Total abdominal hysterectomy**

Code also any synchronous removal of tubes and ovaries (65.31-65.64)

EXCLUDES *radical abdominal hysterectomy, any approach (68.61-68.69)*

DEF: Complete excision of uterus and uterine neck through abdominal approach.

AHA: 4Q, '96, 65

68.41 Laparoscopic total abdominal hysterectomy ♀

Total laparoscopic hysterectomy [TLH]

AHA: 3Q, '09, 5; 4Q, '06, 130, 133

68.49 Other and unspecified total abdominal hysterectomy ♀

Hysterectomy:
extended

EXCLUDES *laparoscopic total abdominal hysterectomy (68.41)*

AHA: 4Q, '12, 82; 1Q, '12, 3-4; 4Q, '06, 130

☑4ᵗʰ **68.5 Vaginal hysterectomy**

Code also any synchronous:
removal of tubes and ovaries (65.31-65.64)
repair of cystocele or rectocele (70.50-70.52)
repair of pelvic floor (70.79)

DEF: Complete excision of the uterus by a vaginal approach.

68.51 Laparoscopically assisted vaginal hysterectomy [LAVH] ♀

AHA: 1Q, '12, 3-5; 4Q, '96, 68

68.59 Other and unspecified vaginal hysterectomy ♀

EXCLUDES *laparoscopically assisted vaginal hysterectomy (68.51)*
radical vaginal hysterectomy (68.71-68.79)

☑4ᵗʰ **68.6 Radical abdominal hysterectomy**

Code also any synchronous:
lymph gland dissection (40.3, 40.5)
removal of tubes and ovaries (65.31-65.64)

EXCLUDES *pelvic evisceration (68.8)*

DEF: Excision of uterus, loose connective tissue and smooth muscle around uterus and vagina via abdominal approach.

68.61 Laparoscopic radical abdominal hysterectomy ♀

Laparoscopic modified radical hysterectomy
Total laparoscopic radical hysterectomy [TLRH]

AHA: 4Q, '06, 130, 134

68.69 Other and unspecified radical abdominal hysterectomy ♀

Modified radical hysterectomy
Wertheim's operation

EXCLUDES *laparoscopic radical abdominal hysterectomy (68.61)*
laparoscopic total abdominal hysterectomy (68.41)

AHA: 4Q, '06, 130

Operations on the Female Genital Organs

68.7–69.99

√4th **68.7 Radical vaginal hysterectomy**
Code also any synchronous:
  lymph gland dissection (40.3, 40.5)
  removal of tubes and ovaries (65.31-65.64)
EXCLUDES abdominal hysterectomy, any approach
  (68.31-68.39, 68.41-68.49, 68.61-68.69, 68.9)
DEF: Excision of uterus, loose connective tissue and smooth muscle around uterus and vagina via vaginal approach.

68.71 Laparoscopic radical vaginal hysterectomy [LRVH] ♀
AHA: 4Q, '06, 130

68.79 Other and unspecified radical vaginal hysterectomy ♀
Hysterocolpectomy
Schauta operation
AHA: 4Q, '06, 130

68.8 Pelvic evisceration ♀
Removal of ovaries, tubes, uterus, vagina, bladder, and urethra (with removal of sigmoid colon and rectum)
Code also any synchronous:
  colostomy (46.10-46.13)
  lymph gland dissection (40.3, 40.5)
  urinary diversion (56.51-56.79)

68.9 Other and unspecified hysterectomy ♀
Hysterectomy NOS
EXCLUDES abdominal hysterectomy, any approach
  (68.31-68.39, 68.41-68.49, 68.61-68.69)
  vaginal hysterectomy, any approach (68.51-68.59,
  68.71-68.79)

√3rd **69 Other operations on uterus and supporting structures**
Code also any application or administration of an adhesion barrier substance (99.77)

√4th **69.0 Dilation and curettage of uterus**
EXCLUDES aspiration curettage of uterus (69.51-69.59)
DEF: Stretching of uterine neck to scrape tissue from walls.
TIP: If the documentation indicates dilation with both curettage and suction, assign instead code 69.59.

69.01 Dilation and curettage for termination of pregnancy ♀
AHA: 1Q, '98, 4

69.02 Dilation and curettage following delivery or abortion ♀
AHA: 3Q, '93, 6

69.09 Other dilation and curettage ♀
Diagnostic D and C
AHA: 1Q, '98, 4
TIP: Assign for D&C of a blighted ovum, which is not considered a viable pregnancy.

√4th **69.1 Excision or destruction of lesion or tissue of uterus and supporting structures**

69.19 Other excision or destruction of uterus and supporting structures ♀
EXCLUDES biopsy of uterine ligament (68.14)

√4th **69.2 Repair of uterine supporting structures**

69.21 Interposition operation ♀
Watkins procedure

69.22 Other uterine suspension ♀
Hysteropexy
Manchester operation
Plication of uterine ligament
DEF: Hysteropexy: Fixation or anchoring of uterus.
DEF: Manchester operation: Fixation or anchoring of uterus with supportive banding tissue of uterine neck and vagina.
DEF: Plication of uterine ligament: Creation of tucks in suppurative uterine banding tissue.
DEF: Repositioning or realignment of bladder and uterus.

69.23 Vaginal repair of chronic inversion of uterus ♀
DEF: Repositioning of inverted uterus via vaginal approach.

69.29 Other repair of uterus and supporting structures ♀

69.3 Paracervical uterine denervation ♀

Dilation and Curettage

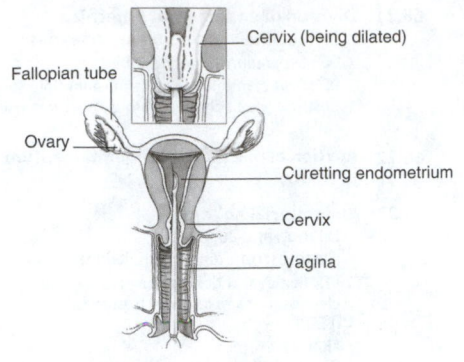

Cervix (being dilated)
Fallopian tube
Ovary
Curetting endometrium
Cervix
Vagina

√4th **69.4 Uterine repair**
EXCLUDES repair of current obstetric laceration (75.50-75.52)

69.41 Suture of laceration of uterus ♀

69.42 Closure of fistula of uterus ♀
EXCLUDES uterovesical fistulectomy (57.84)

69.49 Other repair of uterus ♀
Repair of old obstetric laceration of uterus

√4th **69.5 Aspiration curettage of uterus**
EXCLUDES menstrual extraction (69.6)

69.51 Aspiration curettage of uterus for termination of pregnancy ♀
Therapeutic abortion NOS

69.52 Aspiration curettage following delivery or abortion ♀

69.59 Other aspiration curettage of uterus ♀
AHA: 1Q, '98, 7

69.6 Menstrual extraction or regulation ♀
DEF: Induction of menstruation by low pressure suction.

69.7 Insertion of intrauterine contraceptive device ♀

√4th **69.9 Other operations on uterus, cervix, and supporting structures**
EXCLUDES obstetric dilation or incision of cervix (73.1, 73.93)

69.91 Insertion of therapeutic device into uterus ♀
EXCLUDES insertion of:
  intrauterine contraceptive device (69.7)
  laminaria (69.93)
  obstetric insertion of bag, bougie, or pack
  (73.1)

69.92 Artificial insemination ♀

69.93 Insertion of laminaria ♀
AHA: 2Q, '10, 6-7
DEF: Placement of laminaria, a sea kelp, in cervical os to induce labor; applied for six to 12 hours.

69.94 Manual replacement of inverted uterus ♀
EXCLUDES that in immediate postpartal period (75.94)

69.95 Incision of cervix ♀
EXCLUDES that to assist delivery (73.93)

69.96 Removal of cerclage material from cervix ♀
DEF: Removal of ring inserted to restore uterine neck competency.

69.97 Removal of other penetrating foreign body from cervix ♀
EXCLUDES removal of intraluminal foreign body from cervix (98.16)

69.98 Other operations on supporting structures of uterus ♀
EXCLUDES biopsy of uterine ligament (68.14)

69.99 Other operations on cervix and uterus ♀
EXCLUDES removal of:
  foreign body (98.16)
  intrauterine contraceptive device (97.71)
  obstetric bag, bougie, or pack (97.72)
  packing (97.72)

BI Bilateral Procedure   **NC** Non-covered Procedure   **LC** Limited Coverage Procedure   ►◄ Revised Text   ● New Code   ▲ Revised Code Title

✓3rd **70** **Operations on vagina and cul-de-sac**

Code also any application or administration of an adhesion barrier substance (99.77)

70.0 **Culdocentesis**　♀

DEF: Insertion of needle into upper vaginal vault encircling cervix to withdraw fluid.

AHA: 2Q, '90, 26

TIP: Assign for aspiration for sperm antibodies, which involves aspirating fluid from the female peritoneum or cul-de-sac area to check for the presence of sperm antibodies; assign separate codes for any tubal insufflation (66.8), and/or hysteroscopy (68.12).

✓4th **70.1** **Incision of vagina and cul-de-sac**

70.11 **Hymenotomy**　♀

70.12 **Culdotomy**　♀

DEF: Incision into pocket between terminal end of large intestine and posterior uterus.

70.13 **Lysis of intraluminal adhesions of vagina**　♀

70.14 **Other vaginotomy**　♀

Division of vaginal septum

Drainage of hematoma of vaginal cuff

DEF: Division of vaginal septum: Incision into partition of vaginal walls.

DEF: Drainage of hematoma of vaginal cuff: Incision into vaginal tissue to drain collected blood.

✓4th **70.2** **Diagnostic procedures on vagina and cul-de-sac**

70.21 **Vaginoscopy**　♀

70.22 **Culdoscopy**　♀

DEF: Endoscopic exam of pelvic viscera through incision in posterior vaginal wall.

70.23 **Biopsy of cul-de-sac**　♀

70.24 **Vaginal biopsy**　♀

70.29 **Other diagnostic procedures on vagina and cul-de-sac**　♀

✓4th **70.3** **Local excision or destruction of vagina and cul-de-sac**

70.31 **Hymenectomy**　♀

70.32 **Excision or destruction of lesion of cul-de-sac**　♀

Endometrectomy of cul-de-sac

EXCLUDES biopsy of cul-de-sac (70.23)

70.33 **Excision or destruction of lesion of vagina**　♀

EXCLUDES biopsy of vagina (70.24)
vaginal fistulectomy (70.72-70.75)

70.4 **Obliteration and total excision of vagina**　♀

Vaginectomy

EXCLUDES obliteration of vaginal vault (70.8)

DEF: Vaginectomy: Removal of vagina.

✓4th **70.5** **Repair of cystocele and rectocele**

70.50 **Repair of cystocele and rectocele**　♀

EXCLUDES repair of cystocele and rectocele with graft or prosthesis (70.53)

DEF: Repair of anterior and posterior vaginal wall bulges.

70.51 **Repair of cystocele**　♀

Anterior colporrhaphy (with urethrocele repair)

EXCLUDES repair of cystocele and rectocele with graft or prosthesis (70.53)
repair of cystocele with graft or prosthesis (70.54)

AHA: N-D, '84, 20

70.52 **Repair of rectocele**　♀

Posterior colporrhaphy

EXCLUDES repair of cystocele and rectocele with graft or prosthesis (70.53)
repair of rectocele with graft or prosthesis (70.55)
STARR procedure (48.74)

AHA: 2Q, '11, 10; 1Q, '06, 12

70.53 **Repair of cystocele and rectocele with graft or prosthesis**　♀

Use additional code for biological substance (70.94) or synthetic substance (70.95), if known

AHA: 4Q, '07, 114-115

70.54 **Repair of cystocele with graft or prosthesis**　♀

Anterior colporrhaphy (with urethrocele repair)

Use additional code for biological substance (70.94) or synthetic substance (70.95), if known

AHA: 2Q, '11, 10; 4Q, '07, 114-115

70.55 **Repair of rectocele with graft or prosthesis**　♀

Posterior colporrhaphy

Use additional code for biological substance (70.94) or synthetic substance (70.95), if known

AHA: 4Q, '07, 114-115

✓4th **70.6** **Vaginal construction and reconstruction**

70.61 **Vaginal construction**　♀

AHA: 3Q, '06, 18

70.62 **Vaginal reconstruction**　♀

AHA: N-D, '84, 20

70.63 **Vaginal construction with graft or prosthesis**

Use additional code for biological substance (70.94) or synthetic substance (70.95), if known

EXCLUDES vaginal construction (70.61)

AHA: 4Q, '07, 114-115

70.64 **Vaginal reconstruction with graft or prosthesis**

Use additional code for biological substance (70.94) or synthetic substance (70.95), if known

EXCLUDES vaginal reconstruction (70.62)

AHA: 4Q, '07, 114-115

✓4th **70.7** **Other repair of vagina**

EXCLUDES lysis of intraluminal adhesions (70.13)
repair of current obstetric laceration (75.69)
that associated with cervical amputation (67.4)

70.71 **Suture of laceration of vagina**　♀

AHA: N-D, '84, 20

70.72 **Repair of colovaginal fistula**　♀

DEF: Correction of abnormal opening between midsection of large intestine and vagina.

70.73 **Repair of rectovaginal fistula**　♀

DEF: Correction of abnormal opening between last section of large intestine and vagina.

70.74 **Repair of other vaginoenteric fistula**　♀

DEF: Correction of abnormal opening between vagina and intestine other than mid or last sections.

70.75 **Repair of other fistula of vagina**　♀

EXCLUDES repair of fistula:
rectovesicovaginal (57.83)
ureterovaginal (56.84)
urethrovaginal (58.43)
uterovaginal (69.42)
vesicocervicovaginal (57.84)
vesicosigmoidovaginal (57.83)
vesicoureterovaginal (56.84)
vesicovaginal (57.84)

70.76 **Hymenorrhaphy**　♀

DEF: Closure of vagina with suture of hymenal ring or hymenal remnant flaps.

70.77 **Vaginal suspension and fixation**　♀

DEF: Repair of vaginal protrusion, sinking or laxity by suturing vagina into position.

70.78 **Vaginal suspension and fixation with graft or prosthesis**　♀

Use additional code for biological substance (70.94) or synthetic substance (70.95), if known

AHA: 4Q, '07, 114-115

70.79 **Other repair of vagina**　♀

Colpoperineoplasty

Repair of old obstetric laceration of vagina

Operations on the Female Genital Organs

70.8–71.9

70.8 Obliteration of vaginal vault ♀
LeFort operation
DEF: LeFort operation: Uniting or sewing together vaginal walls.

✓4th **70.9 Other operations on vagina and cul-de-sac**

70.91 Other operations on vagina ♀
EXCLUDES *insertion of:*
diaphragm (96.17)
mold (96.15)
pack (96.14)
pessary (96.18)
suppository (96.49)
removal of:
diaphragm (97.73)
foreign body (98.17)
pack (97.75)
pessary (97.74)
replacement of:
diaphragm (97.24)
pack (97.26)
pessary (97.25)
vaginal dilation (96.16)
vaginal douche (96.44)

70.92 Other operations on cul-de-sac ♀
Obliteration of cul-de-sac
Repair of vaginal enterocele
AHA: 4Q, '94, 54
DEF: Repair of vaginal enterocele: Elimination of herniated cavity within pouch between last part of large intestine and posterior uterus.

70.93 Other operations on cul-de-sac with graft or prosthesis ♀
Repair of vaginal enterocele with graft or prosthesis
Use additional code for biological substance (70.94) or synthetic substance (70.95), if known
AHA: 4Q, '07, 114-115

70.94 Insertion of biological graft ♀
Allogenic material or substance
Allograft
Autograft
Autologous material or substance
Heterograft
Xenogenic material or substance
Code first these procedures when done with graft or prosthesis:
Other operations on cul-de-sac (70.93)
Repair of cystocele (70.54)
Repair of cystocele and rectocele (70.53)
Repair of rectocele (70.55)
Vaginal construction (70.63)
Vaginal reconstruction (70.64)
Vaginal suspension and fixation (70.78)
AHA: 4Q, '07, 116

70.95 Insertion of synthetic graft or prosthesis ♀
Artificial tissue
Code first these procedures when done with graft or prosthesis:
Other operations on cul-de-sac (70.93)
Repair of cystocele (70.54)
Repair of cystocele and rectocele (70.53)
Repair of rectocele (70.55)
Vaginal construction (70.63)
Vaginal reconstruction (70.64)
Vaginal suspension and fixation (70.78)
AHA: 4Q, '07, 116

✓3rd **71 Operations on vulva and perineum**
Code also any application or administration of an adhesion barrier substance (99.77)

✓4th **71.0 Incision of vulva and perineum**

71.01 Lysis of vulvar adhesions ♀

71.09 Other incision of vulva and perineum ♀
Enlargement of introitus NOS
EXCLUDES *removal of foreign body without incision (98.23)*

Marsupialization

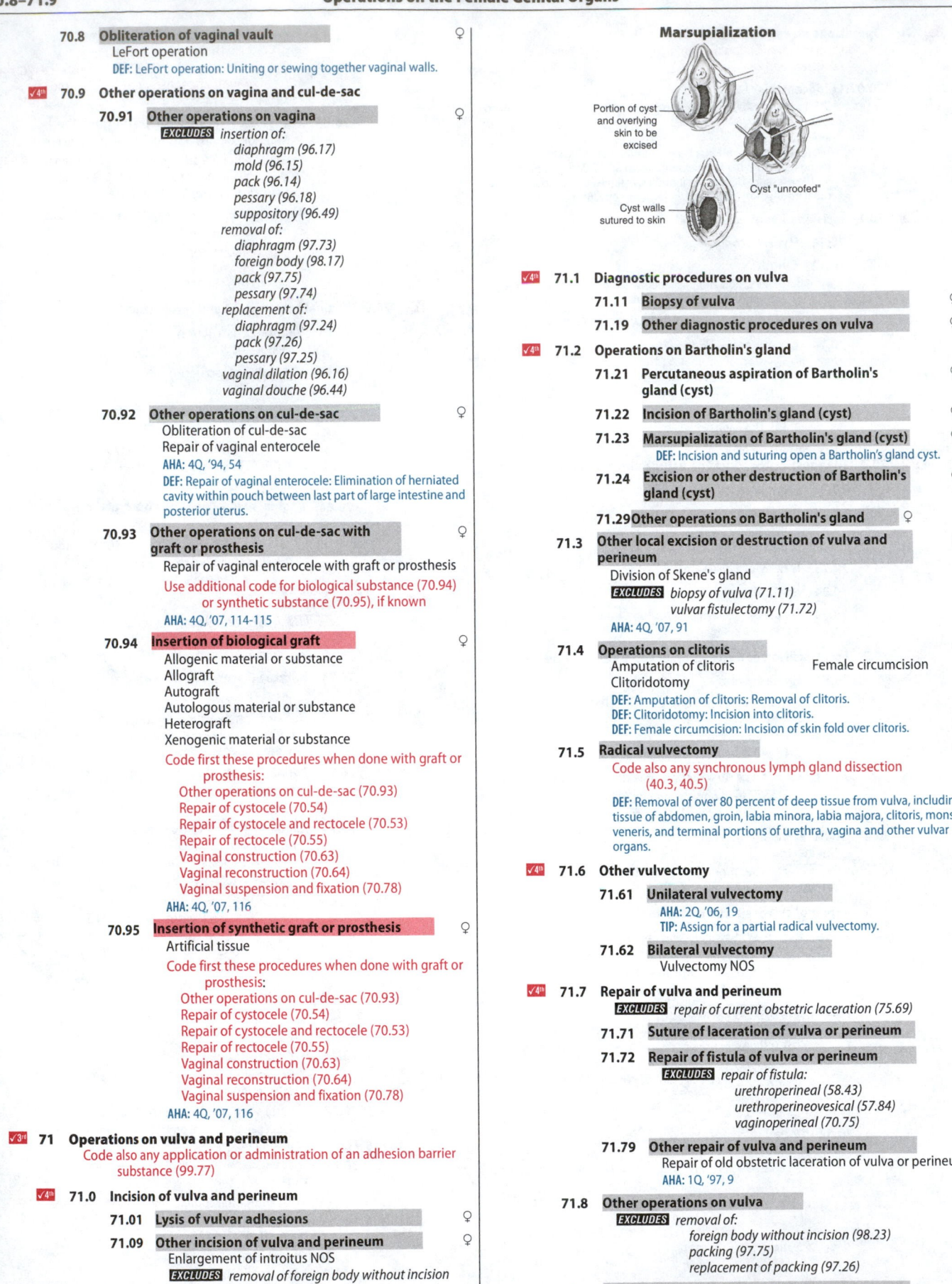

Portion of cyst and overlying skin to be excised

Cyst "unroofed"

Cyst walls sutured to skin

✓4th **71.1 Diagnostic procedures on vulva**

71.11 Biopsy of vulva ♀

71.19 Other diagnostic procedures on vulva ♀

✓4th **71.2 Operations on Bartholin's gland**

71.21 Percutaneous aspiration of Bartholin's gland (cyst) ♀

71.22 Incision of Bartholin's gland (cyst) ♀

71.23 Marsupialization of Bartholin's gland (cyst) ♀
DEF: Incision and suturing open a Bartholin's gland cyst.

71.24 Excision or other destruction of Bartholin's gland (cyst) ♀

71.29 Other operations on Bartholin's gland ♀

71.3 Other local excision or destruction of vulva and perineum ♀
Division of Skene's gland
EXCLUDES *biopsy of vulva (71.11)*
vulvar fistulectomy (71.72)
AHA: 4Q, '07, 91

71.4 Operations on clitoris ♀
Amputation of clitoris   Female circumcision
Clitoridotomy
DEF: Amputation of clitoris: Removal of clitoris.
DEF: Clitoridotomy: Incision into clitoris.
DEF: Female circumcision: Incision of skin fold over clitoris.

71.5 Radical vulvectomy ♀
Code also any synchronous lymph gland dissection (40.3, 40.5)
DEF: Removal of over 80 percent of deep tissue from vulva, including tissue of abdomen, groin, labia minora, labia majora, clitoris, mons veneris, and terminal portions of urethra, vagina and other vulvar organs.

✓4th **71.6 Other vulvectomy**

71.61 Unilateral vulvectomy ♀
AHA: 2Q, '06, 19
TIP: Assign for a partial radical vulvectomy.

71.62 Bilateral vulvectomy ♀
Vulvectomy NOS

✓4th **71.7 Repair of vulva and perineum**
EXCLUDES *repair of current obstetric laceration (75.69)*

71.71 Suture of laceration of vulva or perineum ♀

71.72 Repair of fistula of vulva or perineum ♀
EXCLUDES *repair of fistula:*
urethroperineal (58.43)
urethroperineovesical (57.84)
vaginoperineal (70.75)

71.79 Other repair of vulva and perineum ♀
Repair of old obstetric laceration of vulva or perineum
AHA: 1Q, '97, 9

71.8 Other operations on vulva ♀
EXCLUDES *removal of:*
foreign body without incision (98.23)
packing (97.75)
replacement of packing (97.26)

71.9 Other operations on female genital organs ♀
AHA: 4Q, '04, 90; 1Q, '03, 13
TIP: Assign for reversal of the type III female circumcision.

| BI Bilateral Procedure | NC Non-covered Procedure | LC Limited Coverage Procedure | ►◄ Revised Text | ● New Code | ▲ Revised Code Title |

13. Obstetrical Procedures (72-75)

✓3rd **72 Forceps, vacuum, and breech delivery**

72.0 Low forceps operation ♀
Outlet forceps operation

72.1 Low forceps operation with episiotomy ♀
Outlet forceps operation with episiotomy

✓4th **72.2 Mid forceps operation**

72.21 Mid forceps operation with episiotomy ♀

72.29 Other mid forceps operation ♀

✓4th **72.3 High forceps operation**

72.31 High forceps operation with episiotomy ♀

72.39 Other high forceps operation ♀

72.4 Forceps rotation of fetal head ♀
DeLee maneuver   Kielland rotation
Key-in-lock rotation   Scanzoni's maneuver
Code also any associated forceps extraction (72.0-72.39)

✓4th **72.5 Breech extraction**

72.51 Partial breech extraction with forceps to aftercoming head ♀

72.52 Other partial breech extraction ♀

72.53 Total breech extraction with forceps to aftercoming head ♀

72.54 Other total breech extraction ♀

72.6 Forceps application to aftercoming head ♀
Piper forceps operation
EXCLUDES *partial breech extraction with forceps to aftercoming head (72.51)*
total breech extraction with forceps to aftercoming head (72.53)

✓4th **72.7 Vacuum extraction**
INCLUDES Malström's extraction

72.71 Vacuum extraction with episiotomy ♀

72.79 Other vacuum extraction ♀
AHA: 2Q, '06, 5
TIP: This code may be assigned with the appropriate code from category 74 Cesarean section and removal of fetus, when a vacuum is applied during cesarean surgery.

72.8 Other specified instrumental delivery ♀

72.9 Unspecified instrumental delivery ♀

✓3rd **73 Other procedures inducing or assisting delivery**

✓4th **73.0 Artificial rupture of membranes**

73.01 Induction of labor by artificial rupture of membranes ♀
Surgical induction NOS
EXCLUDES *artificial rupture of membranes after onset of labor (73.09)*
AHA: 3Q, '00, 5

73.09 Other artificial rupture of membranes ♀
Artificial rupture of membranes at time of delivery

Breech Extraction

Breech presentation

Delivery of legs

Baby rotated for delivery of arms

Umbilicus

73.1 Other surgical induction of labor ♀
Induction by cervical dilation
EXCLUDES *injection for abortion (75.0)*
insertion of suppository for abortion (96.49)

✓4th **73.2 Internal and combined version and extraction**

73.21 Internal and combined version without extraction ♀
Version NOS

73.22 Internal and combined version with extraction ♀

73.3 Failed forceps ♀
Application of forceps without delivery   Trial forceps

73.4 Medical induction of labor ♀
EXCLUDES *medication to augment active labor — omit code*
AHA: 2Q, '10, 6-7

✓4th **73.5 Manually assisted delivery**

73.51 Manual rotation of fetal head ♀

73.59 Other manually assisted delivery ♀
Assisted spontaneous delivery   Credé maneuver
AHA: 4Q, '98, 76

73.6 Episiotomy ♀
Episioproctotomy
Episiotomy with subsequent episiorrhaphy
EXCLUDES *that with:*
high forceps (72.31)
low forceps (72.1)
mid forceps (72.21)
outlet forceps (72.1)
vacuum extraction (72.71)
AHA: 4Q, '08, 192; 1Q, '92, 10

73.8 Operations on fetus to facilitate delivery ♀
Clavicotomy on fetus
Destruction of fetus
Needling of hydrocephalic head

✓4th **73.9 Other operations assisting delivery**

73.91 External version ♀

73.92 Replacement of prolapsed umbilical cord ♀

73.93 Incision of cervix to assist delivery ♀
Dührssen's incisions

73.94 Pubiotomy to assist delivery ♀
Obstetrical symphysiotomy

73.99 Other ♀
EXCLUDES *dilation of cervix, obstetrical, to induce labor (73.1)*
insertion of bag or bougie to induce labor (73.1)
removal of cerclage material (69.96)

✓3rd **74 Cesarean section and removal of fetus**
Code also any synchronous:
hysterectomy (68.3-68.4, 68.6, 68.8)
myomectomy (68.29)
sterilization (66.31-66.39, 66.63)
AHA: 2Q, '06, 5

74.0 Classical cesarean section ♀
Transperitoneal classical cesarean section
AHA: 4Q, '11, 133

74.1 Low cervical cesarean section ♀
Lower uterine segment cesarean section
AHA: 1Q, '01, 11

74.2 Extraperitoneal cesarean section ♀
Supravesical cesarean section

74.3 Removal of extratubal ectopic pregnancy ♀
Removal of:
ectopic abdominal pregnancy
fetus from peritoneal or extraperitoneal cavity following uterine or tubal rupture
EXCLUDES *that by salpingostomy (66.02)*
that by salpingotomy (66.01)
that with synchronous salpingectomy (66.62)
AHA: 4Q, '92, 25; 2Q, '90, 25; 2Q, '90, 27; 1Q, '89, 11

Obstetrical Procedures

74.4–75.99

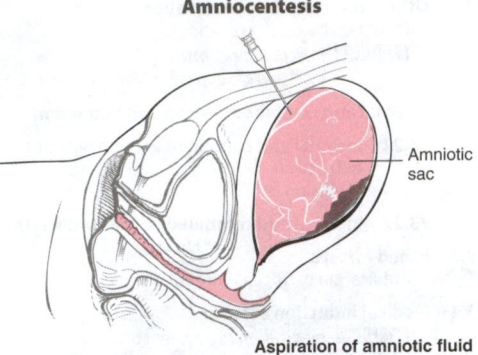

Amniocentesis

Amniotic sac

Aspiration of amniotic fluid

74.4   Cesarean section of other specified type   ♀

Peritoneal exclusion cesareansection
Transperitoneal cesarean section NOS
Vaginal cesarean section

✓4th **74.9   Cesarean section of unspecified type**

74.91   Hysterotomy to terminate pregnancy   ♀
Therapeutic abortion by hysterotomy

74.99   Other cesarean section of unspecified type   ♀
Cesarean section NOS
Obstetrical abdominouterotomy
Obstetrical hysterotomy

✓3rd **75   Other obstetric operations**

75.0   Intra-amniotic injection for abortion   ♀
Injection of:

prostaglandin ⎫
saline ⎭ for induction of abortion

Termination of pregnancy by intrauterine injection
EXCLUDES *insertion of prostaglandin suppository for abortion (96.49)*

75.1   Diagnostic amniocentesis   ♀

75.2   Intrauterine transfusion   ♀
Exchange transfusion in utero
Insertion of catheter into abdomen of fetus for transfusion
Code also any hysterotomy approach (68.0)

✓4th **75.3   Other intrauterine operations on fetus and amnion**
Code also any hysterotomy approach (68.0)

75.31   Amnioscopy   ♀
Fetoscopy
Laparoamnioscopy
AHA: 3Q, '06, 16-17

75.32   Fetal EKG (scalp)   ♀

75.33   Fetal blood sampling and biopsy   ♀

75.34   Other fetal monitoring   ♀
Antepartum fetal nonstress test
Fetal monitoring, not otherwise specified
EXCLUDES *fetal pulse oximetry (75.38)*

75.35   Other diagnostic procedures on fetus and amnion   ♀
Intrauterine pressure determination
EXCLUDES *amniocentesis (75.1)*
diagnostic procedures on gravid uterus and placenta (87.81, 88.46, 88.78, 92.17)
AHA: 3Q, '06, 16-17

75.36   Correction of fetal defect   ♀

75.37   Amnioinfusion   ♀
Code also injection of antibiotic (99.21)
AHA: 4Q, '98, 76
TIP: This procedure involves the controlled instillation of sterile normal saline or lactated Ringers solution into the uterine cavity to replace the amniotic fluid.

75.38   Fetal pulse oximetry   ♀
Transcervical fetal oxygen saturation monitoring
Transcervical fetal SpO$_2$ monitoring
DEF: Single-use sensor inserted through the birth canal and positioned to rest against the fetal cheek, forehead, or temple; infrared beam of light aimed at the fetal skin is reflected back through the sensor for analysis.
AHA: 4Q, '01, 64

75.4   Manual removal of retained placenta   ♀
EXCLUDES *aspiration curettage (69.52)*
dilation and curettage (69.02)
AHA: 3Q, '06, 11

✓4th **75.5   Repair of current obstetric laceration of uterus**

75.50   Repair of current obstetric laceration of uterus, not otherwise specified   ♀

75.51   Repair of current obstetric laceration of cervix   ♀

75.52   Repair of current obstetric laceration of corpus uteri   ♀
AHA: 2Q, '08, 8
TIP: Assign for B-Lynch procedure performed to control intraoperative hemorrhage during a cesarean section.

✓4th **75.6   Repair of other current obstetric laceration**
Code also episiotomy, if performed (73.6)
AHA: 1Q, '92, 11

75.61   Repair of current obstetric laceration of bladder and urethra   ♀

75.62   Repair of current obstetric laceration of rectum and sphincter ani   ♀

75.69   Repair of other current obstetric laceration   ♀
Episioperineorrhaphy   Repair of:
Repair of: vagina
   pelvic floor   vulva
   perineum   Secondary repair of
             episiotomy
AHA: 4Q, '08, 192; 4Q, '07, 12

75.7   Manual exploration of uterine cavity, postpartum   ♀

75.8   Obstetric tamponade of uterus or vagina   ♀
EXCLUDES *antepartum tamponade (73.1)*

✓4th **75.9   Other obstetric operations**

75.91   Evacuation of obstetrical incisional hematoma of perineum   ♀
Evacuation of hematoma of:
   episiotomy
   perineorrhaphy

75.92   Evacuation of other hematoma of vulva or vagina   ♀

75.93   Surgical correction of inverted uterus   ♀
Spintelli operation
EXCLUDES *vaginal repair of chronic inversion of uterus (69.23)*

75.94   Manual replacement of inverted uterus   ♀

75.99   Other   ♀
AHA: 3Q, '06, 16-17

BI Bilateral Procedure   **NC** Non-covered Procedure   **LC** Limited Coverage Procedure   ►◄ Revised Text   ● New Code   ▲ Revised Code Title

162 – Volume 3   2015 ICD-9-CM

14. Operations on the Musculoskeletal System (76-84)

✓3rd 76 Operations on facial bones and joints

> **EXCLUDES** accessory sinuses (22.00-22.9)
> nasal bones (21.00-21.99)
> skull (01.01-02.99)

✓4th 76.0 Incision of facial bone without division

76.01 Sequestrectomy of facial bone
Removal of necrotic bone chip from facial bone

76.09 Other incision of facial bone
Reopening of osteotomy site of facial bone
> **EXCLUDES** osteotomy associated with orthognathic surgery (76.61-76.69)
> removal of internal fixation device (76.97)

✓4th 76.1 Diagnostic procedures on facial bones and joints

76.11 Biopsy of facial bone

76.19 Other diagnostic procedures on facial bones and joints
> **EXCLUDES** contrast arthrogram of temporomandibular joint (87.13)
> other x-ray (87.11-87.12, 87.14-87.16)

AHA: N-D, '87, 12

76.2 Local excision or destruction of lesion of facial bone
> **EXCLUDES** biopsy of facial bone (76.11)
> excision of odontogenic lesion (24.4)

✓4th 76.3 Partial ostectomy of facial bone

76.31 Partial mandibulectomy
Hemimandibulectomy
> **EXCLUDES** that associated with temporomandibular arthroplasty (76.5)

DEF: Partial excision of lower jawbone.
DEF: Hemimandibulectomy: Excision of one-half of lower jawbone.
AHA: 2Q, '05, 8
TIP: Assign for "composite resection," which includes the mandible and floor of the mouth, along with code 27.49 Other excision of mouth.

76.39 Partial ostectomy of other facial bone
Hemimaxillectomy (with bone graft or prosthesis)
DEF: Partial excision of facial bone other than lower jawbone.
DEF: Hemimaxillectomy (with bone graft or prosthesis): Excision of one side of upper jawbone and restoration with bone graft or prosthesis.
AHA: J-F, '87, 14

✓4th 76.4 Excision and reconstruction of facial bones

76.41 Total mandibulectomy with synchronous reconstruction

76.42 Other total mandibulectomy

76.43 Other reconstruction of mandible
> **EXCLUDES** genioplasty (76.67-76.68)
> that with synchronous total mandibulectomy (76.41)

AHA: 2Q, '03, 13

76.44 Total ostectomy of other facial bone with synchronous reconstruction
DEF: Total facial bone excision with reconstruction during same operative session.
AHA: 3Q, '93, 6

76.45 Other total ostectomy of other facial bone

76.46 Other reconstruction of other facial bone
> **EXCLUDES** that with synchronous total ostectomy (76.44)

76.5 Temporomandibular arthroplasty
AHA: 4Q, '99, 20

✓4th 76.6 Other facial bone repair and orthognathic surgery

Code also any synchronous:
bone graft (76.91)
synthetic implant (76.92)
> **EXCLUDES** reconstruction of facial bones (76.41-76.46)

76.61 Closed osteoplasty [osteotomy] of mandibular ramus
Gigli saw osteotomy
DEF: Reshaping and restoration of lower jawbone projection; closed surgical field, which is a limited "key hole" incision.
DEF: Gigli saw osteotomy: Plastic repair using a flexible wire with saw teeth.

76.62 Open osteoplasty [osteotomy] of mandibular ramus

76.63 Osteoplasty [osteotomy] of body of mandible

76.64 Other orthognathic surgery on mandible
Mandibular osteoplasty NOS
Segmental or subapical osteotomy
AHA: 2Q, '04, 9, 10

76.65 Segmental osteoplasty [osteotomy] of maxilla
Maxillary osteoplasty NOS

76.66 Total osteoplasty [osteotomy] of maxilla

76.67 Reduction genioplasty
Reduction mentoplasty
DEF: Reduction of protruding chin or lower jawbone.

76.68 Augmentation genioplasty
Mentoplasty:
NOS
with graft or implant
DEF: Extension of the lower jawbone to a functional position by means of plastic surgery.

76.69 Other facial bone repair
Osteoplasty of facial bone NOS

✓4th 76.7 Reduction of facial fracture
> **INCLUDES** internal fixation

Code also any synchronous:
bone graft (76.91)
synthetic implant (76.92)
> **EXCLUDES** that of nasal bones (21.71-21.72)

76.70 Reduction of facial fracture, not otherwise specified

76.71 Closed reduction of malar and zygomatic fracture

76.72 Open reduction of malar and zygomatic fracture

76.73 Closed reduction of maxillary fracture

76.74 Open reduction of maxillary fracture

76.75 Closed reduction of mandibular fracture

76.76 Open reduction of mandibular fracture

76.77 Open reduction of alveolar fracture
Reduction of alveolar fracture with stabilization of teeth

76.78 Other closed reduction of facial fracture
Closed reduction of orbital fracture
> **EXCLUDES** nasal bone (21.71)

76.79 Other open reduction of facial fracture
Open reduction of orbit rim or wall
> **EXCLUDES** nasal bone (21.72)

✓4th 76.9 Other operations on facial bones and joints

76.91 Bone graft to facial bone
Autogenous
Bone bank } graft to facial bone
Heterogenous

76.92 Insertion of synthetic implant in facial bone
Alloplastic implant to facial bone

76.93 Closed reduction of temporomandibular dislocation

76.94 Open reduction of temporomandibular dislocation

✓3rd ✓4th Additional Digit Required   Valid OR Procedure   Non-OR Procedure   Adjunct Code

76.95 Other manipulation of temporomandibular joint

76.96 Injection of therapeutic substance into temporomandibular joint

76.97 Removal of internal fixation device from facial bone

> EXCLUDES removal of:
> dental wiring (97.33)
> external mandibular fixation device NEC (97.36)

76.99 Other

✓3ʳᵈ **77 Incision, excision, and division of other bones**

> EXCLUDES laminectomy for decompression (03.09)
> operations on:
> accessory sinuses (22.00-22.9)
> ear ossicles (19.0-19.55)
> facial bones (76.01-76.99)
> joint structures (80.00-81.99)
> mastoid (19.9-20.99)
> nasal bones (21.00-21.99)
> skull (01.01-02.99)

The following fourth-digit subclassification is for use with appropriate categories in section 77 to identify the site. Valid fourth-digit categories are in [brackets] under each code.
   0 unspecified site
   1 scapula, clavicle, and thorax [ribs and sternum]
   2 humerus
   3 radius and ulna
   4 carpals and metacarpals
   5 femur
   6 patella
   7 tibia and fibula
   8 tarsals and metatarsals
   9 other
      Pelvic bones
      Phalanges (of foot) (of hand)
      Vertebrae

§ ✓4ᵗʰ **77.0 Sequestrectomy**
[0-9]
> DEF: Excision and removal of dead bone.

§ ✓4ᵗʰ **77.1 Other incision of bone without division**
[0-9]
> Reopening of osteotomy site
> EXCLUDES aspiration of bone marrow, (41.31, 41.91)
> removal of internal fixation device (78.60-78.69)
> AHA: For code 77.17: 1Q, '02, 3
> DEF: Incision into bone without division of site.

§ ✓4ᵗʰ **77.2 Wedge osteotomy**
[0-9]
> EXCLUDES that for hallux valgus (77.51)
> DEF: Removal of wedge-shaped piece of bone.

§ ✓4ᵗʰ **77.3 Other division of bone**
[0-9]
> Osteoarthrotomy
> EXCLUDES clavicotomy of fetus (73.8)
> laminotomy or incision of vertebra (03.01-03.09)
> pubiotomy to assist delivery (73.94)
> sternotomy incidental to thoracic operation — omit code

§ ✓4ᵗʰ **77.4 Biopsy of bone**
[0-9]
> AHA: For code 77.45: 2Q, '98, 12; For code 77.49: 3Q, '06, 13

✓4ᵗʰ **77.5 Excision and repair of bunion and other toe deformities**

77.51 **Bunionectomy with soft tissue correction and osteotomy of the first metatarsal**
> DEF: Incision and removal of big toe bony prominence and reconstruction with soft tissue.

77.52 **Bunionectomy with soft tissue correction and arthrodesis**
> DEF: Removal of big toe bony prominence and reconstruction with soft tissue and joint fixation.

77.53 **Other bunionectomy with soft tissue correction**

77.54 **Excision or correction of bunionette**
> That with osteotomy
> DEF: Resection of fifth metatarsal head via exposure of joint; includes imbrication of capsule.

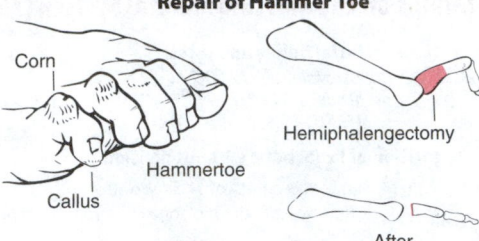

Repair of Hammer Toe

Corn

Hemiphalengectomy

Hammertoe

Callus

After

77.56 **Repair of hammer toe**
> Filleting ⎫
> Fusion ⎬ of hammer toe
> Phalangectomy (partial) ⎭
> DEF: Repair of clawlike toe defect by joint fusion, or partial removal of toe via traction technique.

77.57 **Repair of claw toe**
> Capsulotomy ⎫
> Fusion ⎬
> Phalangectomy (partial) ⎬ of claw toe
> Tendon lengthening ⎭
> DEF: Repair of clawlike toe defect by joint fusion, partial removal of toe, joint capsule incision or lengthening of fibrous muscle attachment.

77.58 **Other excision, fusion, and repair of toes**
> Cockup toe repair
> Overlapping toe repair
> That with use of prosthetic materials

77.59 **Other bunionectomy**
> Resection of hallux valgus joint with insertion of prosthesis
> DEF: Resection of hallux valgus joint with insertion of prosthesis: Cutting away part of big toe with prosthesis insertion to correct bony prominence.

§ ✓4ᵗʰ **77.6 Local excision of lesion or tissue of bone**
[0-9]
> EXCLUDES biopsy of bone (77.40-77.49)
> debridement of compound fracture (79.60-79.69)
> AHA: For code 77.61: 4Q, '10, 131; 3Q, '01, 9; For code 77.65: ▶3Q, '13, 5;◀ 4Q, '04, 128; S-O, '85, 4; For code 77.67: ▶3Q, '13, 5;◀ 1Q, '02, 3; 1Q, '99, 8; For code 77.68: 4Q, '12, 83; For code 77.69: 1Q, '08, 4; 2Q, '00, 18
> TIP: Assign for debridement procedures that extend to bone.

§ ✓4ᵗʰ **77.7 Excision of bone for graft**
[0-9]
> AHA: 2Q, '07, 5; 4Q, '99, 11, 13; For code 77.71: 3Q, '03, 19; For code 77.79: ▶2Q, '13, 8;◀ 1Q, '08, 5; 2Q, '03, 13; 4Q, '02, 107, 109-110; 2Q, '02, 16; 2Q, '00 12, 13; 4Q, '99, 11, 13

§ ✓4ᵗʰ **77.8 Other partial ostectomy**
[0-9]
> Condylectomy
> EXCLUDES amputation (84.00-84.19, 84.91)
> arthrectomy (80.90-80.99)
> excision of bone ends associated with:
>   arthrodesis (81.00-81.39, 81.62-81.66)
>   arthroplasty (81.40-81.59, 81.71-81.85)
> excision of cartilage (80.5-80.6, 80.80-80.99)
> excision of head of femur with synchronous replacement (00.70-00.73, 81.51-81.53)
> hemilaminectomy (03.01-03.09)
> laminectomy (03.01-03.09)
> ostectomy for hallux valgus (77.51-77.59)
> partial amputation:
>   finger (84.01)
>   thumb (84.02)
>   toe (84.11)
> resection of ribs incidental to thoracic operation — omit code
> that incidental to other operation — omit code
> AHA: For code 77.89: 2Q, '02, 8

§ ✓4ᵗʰ **77.9 Total ostectomy**
[0-9]
> EXCLUDES amputation of limb (84.00-84.19, 84.91)
> that incidental to other operation — omit code
> AHA: For code 77.95: ▶1Q, '14, 12◀

---

§   Requires fourth digit. Valid digits are in [brackets] under each code. See category 77 for codes and definitions.

BI Bilateral Procedure   NC Non-covered Procedure   LC Limited Coverage Procedure   ▶◀ Revised Text   ● New Code   ▲ Revised Code Title

164 – Volume 3 · October 2014

2015 ICD-9-CM

✓3rd **78   Other operations on bones, except facial bones**

EXCLUDES operations on:
> accessory sinuses (22.00-22.9)
> facial bones (76.01-76.99)
> joint structures (80.00-81.99)
> nasal bones (21.00-21.99)
> skull (01.01-02.99)

The following fourth-digit subclassification is for use with appropriate categories in section 78 to identify the site. Valid fourth-digit categories are in [brackets] under each code.

0 unspecified site
1 scapula, clavicle, and thorax [ribs and sternum]
2 humerus
3 radius and ulna
4 carpals and metacarpals
5 femur
6 patella
7 tibia and fibula
8 tarsals and metatarsals
9 other
> Pelvic bones
> Phalanges (of foot) (of hand)
> Vertebrae

§ ✓4th **78.0   Bone graft**
[0-9]
Bone:
> bank graft
> graft (autogenous) (heterogenous)
That with debridement of bone graft site (removal of sclerosed, fibrous, or necrotic bone or tissue)
Transplantation of bone

Code also any excision of bone for graft (77.70-77.79)

EXCLUDES that for bone lengthening (78.30-78.39)

AHA: 2Q, '02, 11; 2Q, '98, 12; 3Q, '94, 10; 1Q, '91, 3;
For code 78.06: 3Q, '12, 11
TIP: Assign a code from this subcategory whether the documentation indicates bone or bone marrow as the grafting material.

§ ✓4th **78.1   Application of external fixator device**
[0-9]
Fixator with insertion of pins/wires/screws into bone

Code also any type of fixator device, if known (84.71-84.73)

EXCLUDES other immobilization, pressure, and attention to wound (93.51-93.59)

AHA: 2Q, '94, 4; For code 78.12: 4Q, '05, 129

§ ✓4th **78.2   Limb shortening procedures**
[0,2-5,7-9] Epiphyseal stapling
Open epiphysiodesis
Percutaneous epiphysiodesis
Resection/osteotomy

§ ✓4th **78.3   Limb lengthening procedures**
[0,2-5,7-9] Bone graft with or without internal fixation devices or osteotomy
Distraction technique with or without corticotomy/osteotomy

Code also any application of an external fixation device (78.10-78.19)

§ ✓4th **78.4   Other repair or plastic operations on bone**
[0-9]
Other operation on bone NEC
Repair of malunion or nonunion fracture NEC

EXCLUDES application of external fixation device (78.10-78.19)
> limb lengthening procedures (78.30-78.39)
> limb shortening procedures (78.20-78.29)
> osteotomy (77.3)
> reconstruction of thumb (82.61-82.69)
> repair of pectus deformity (34.74)
> repair with bone graft (78.00-78.09)

AHA: 3Q, '91, 20; 4Q, '88, 11; For code 78.41: ▶1Q, '13, 5;◄ 2Q, '02, 16;
For code 78.47: 3Q, '91, 20; For code 78.49: 3Q, '04, 9; 2Q, '03, 22; 3Q, '02, 12; 2Q, '02, 14, 15; 4Q, '99, 22; 1Q, '97, 5

§ ✓4th **78.5   Internal fixation of bone without fracture reduction**
[0-9]
Internal fixation of bone (prophylactic)
Reinsertion of internal fixation device
Revision of displaced or broken fixation device

EXCLUDES arthroplasty and arthrodesis (81.00-81.85)
> bone graft (78.00-78.09)
> insertion of sternal fixation device with rigid plates (84.94)
> limb shortening procedures (78.20-78.29)
> that for fracture reduction (79.10-79.19, 79.30-79.59)

AHA: 2Q, '99, 11; 2Q, '94, 4; For code 78.52: 2Q, '10, 6; For code 78.55: 2Q, '10, 6; For code 78.59: 3Q, '04, 6; 2Q, '03, 15; 4Q, '99, 13

§ ✓4th **78.6   Removal of implanted devices from bone**
[0-9]
External fixator device (invasive)
Internal fixation device
Removal of bone growth stimulator (invasive)
Removal of internal limb lengthening device
Removal of pedicle screw(s) used in spinal fusion

EXCLUDES removal of cast, splint, and traction device (Kirschner wire) (Steinmann pin) (97.88)
> removal of posterior spinal motion preservation (facet replacement, pedicle-based dynamic stabilization, interspinous process) device(s) (80.09)
> removal of skull tongs or halo traction device (02.95)

AHA: 1Q, '00, 15; For code 78.67: 2Q, '03, 14; For code 78.69: 4Q, '02, 110; 2Q, '00, 18

§ ✓4th **78.7   Osteoclasis**
[0-9]
DEF: Surgical breaking or rebreaking of bone.

§ ✓4th **78.8   Diagnostic procedures on bone, not elsewhere classified**
[0-9]
EXCLUDES biopsy of bone (77.40-77.49)
> magnetic resonance imaging (88.94)
> microscopic examination of specimen from bone (91.51-91.59)
> radioisotope scan (92.14)
> skeletal x-ray (87.21-87.29, 87.43, 88.21-88.33)
> thermography (88.83)

§ ✓4th **78.9   Insertion of bone growth stimulator**
[0-9]
Insertion of:
> bone stimulator (electrical) to aid bone healing
> osteogenic electrodes for bone growth stimulation
> totally implanted device (invasive)
EXCLUDES non-invasive (transcutaneous) (surface) stimulator (99.86)

✓3rd **79   Reduction of fracture and dislocation**

INCLUDES application of cast or splint
> reduction with insertion of traction device (Kirschner wire) (Steinmann pin)

Code also any:
> application of external fixator device (78.10-78.19)
> type of fixator device, if known (84.71-84.73)
EXCLUDES external fixation alone for immobilization of fracture (93.51-93.56, 93.59)
> internal fixation without reduction of fracture (78.50-78.59)
> operations on:
>> facial bones(76.70-76.79)
>> nasal bones (21.71-21.72)
>> orbit (76.78-76.79)
>> skull (02.02)
>> vertebrae (03.53)
> removal of cast or splint (97.88)
> replacement of cast or splint (97.11-97.14)
> traction alone for reduction of fracture (93.41-93.46)

The following fourth-digit subclassification is for use with appropriate categories in section 79 to identify the site. Valid fourth-digit categories are in [brackets] under each code.

0 unspecified site
1 humerus
2 radius and ulna
> Arm NOS
3 carpals and metacarpals
> Hand NOS
4 phalanges of hand
5 femur
6 tibia and fibula
> Leg NOS
7 tarsals and metatarsals
> Foot NOS
8 phalanges of foot
9 other specified bone

§ ✓4th **79.0   Closed reduction of fracture without internal fixation**
[0-9]
EXCLUDES that for separation of epiphysis (79.40-79.49)
DEF: Manipulative realignment of fracture; without incision or internal fixation.
AHA: 2Q, '94, 3; 3Q, '89, 17; 4Q, '88, 11; For code 79.01: 4Q, '05, 129; For code 79.05: 3Q, '89, 16

§ ✓4th **79.1   Closed reduction of fracture with internal fixation**
[0-9]
EXCLUDES that for separation of epiphysis (79.40-79.49)
DEF: Manipulative realignment of fracture; with internal fixation but without incision.
AHA: 2Q, '94, 4; 4Q, '93, 35; 1Q, '93, 27

§ Requires fourth digit. Valid digits are in [brackets] under each code. See appropriate category for codes and definitions.

§ ✓4ᵗʰ **79.2** **Open reduction of fracture without internal fixation**
[0-9]
> **EXCLUDES** *that for separation of epiphysis (79.50-79.59)*
> AHA: 2Q, '94, 3

§ ✓4ᵗʰ **79.3** **Open reduction of fracture with internal fixation**
[0-9]
> **EXCLUDES** *that for separation of epiphysis (79.50-79.59)*
> **DEF:** Realignment of fracture with incision and internal fixation.
> AHA: 2Q, '98, 12; 3Q, '94, 10; 2Q, '94, 3; 4Q, '93, 35; **For code 79.32:** 1Q, '07, 7; **For code 79.35:** 1Q, '07, 4; **For code 79.36:** 2Q, '12,11-12
> **TIP:** When arthroscopy assists with visualization of the surgical site, do not report the arthroscopy separately.

§ ✓4ᵗʰ **79.4** **Closed reduction of separated epiphysis**
[0-2,5,6,9] Reduction with or without internal fixation
> **DEF:** Manipulative reduction of expanded joint end of long bone to normal position without incision.

§ ✓4ᵗʰ **79.5** **Open reduction of separated epiphysis**
[0-2,5,6,9] Reduction with or without internal fixation
> **DEF:** Reduction of expanded joint end of long bone with incision.

§ ✓4ᵗʰ **79.6** **Debridement of open fracture site**
[0-9] Debridement of compound fracture
> **DEF:** Removal of damaged tissue at fracture site.
> AHA: 3Q, '95, 12; 3Q, '89, 16
> **TIP:** Do not assign a skin/soft tissue debridement procedure code (e.g., 86.22) in addition to the open fracture debridement code; all debridement is included.

✓4ᵗʰ **79.7** **Closed reduction of dislocation**
> **INCLUDES** closed reduction (with external traction device)
> **EXCLUDES** *closed reduction of dislocation of temporomandibular joint (76.93)*
> **DEF:** Manipulative reduction of displaced joint without incision; with or without external traction.

79.70 **Closed reduction of dislocation of unspecified site**

79.71 **Closed reduction of dislocation of shoulder**

79.72 **Closed reduction of dislocation of elbow**

79.73 **Closed reduction of dislocation of wrist**

79.74 **Closed reduction of dislocation of hand and finger**

79.75 **Closed reduction of dislocation of hip**

79.76 **Closed reduction of dislocation of knee**
> AHA: N-D, '86, 7

79.77 **Closed reduction of dislocation of ankle**

79.78 **Closed reduction of dislocation of foot and toe**

79.79 **Closed reduction of dislocation of other specified sites**

✓4ᵗʰ **79.8** **Open reduction of dislocation**
> **INCLUDES** open reduction (with internal and external fixation devices)
> **EXCLUDES** *open reduction of dislocation of temporomandibular joint (76.94)*
> **DEF:** Reduction of displaced joint via incision; with or without internal and external fixation.

79.80 **Open reduction of dislocation of unspecified site**

79.81 **Open reduction of dislocation of shoulder**

79.82 **Open reduction of dislocation of elbow**

79.83 **Open reduction of dislocation of wrist**

79.84 **Open reduction of dislocation of hand and finger**

79.85 **Open reduction of dislocation of hip**

79.86 **Open reduction of dislocation of knee**

79.87 **Open reduction of dislocation of ankle**

79.88 **Open reduction of dislocation of foot and toe**

79.89 **Open reduction of dislocation of other specified sites**

§ ✓4ᵗʰ **79.9** **Unspecified operation on bone injury**
[0-9]

✓3ʳᵈ **80** **Incision and excision of joint structures**
> **INCLUDES** operations on:
> capsule of joint
> cartilage
> condyle
> ligament
> meniscus
> synovial membrane
> **EXCLUDES** *cartilage of:*
> *ear (18.01-18.9)*
> *nose (21.00-21.99)*
> *temporomandibular joint (76.01-76.99)*

> The following fourth-digit subclassification is for use with appropriate categories in section 80 to identify the site:
>
> | | |
> |---|---|
> | 0 unspecified site | 6 knee |
> | 1 shoulder | 7 ankle |
> | 2 elbow | 8 foot and toe |
> | 3 wrist | 9 other specified sites |
> | 4 hand and finger | Spine |
> | 5 hip | |

§ ✓4ᵗʰ **80.0** **Arthrotomy for removal of prosthesis,**
[0-9] **without replacement**
> **INCLUDES** removal of posterior spinal motion preservation (dynamic stabilization, facet replacement, interspinous process) device(s)
>
> Code also any:
> insertion of (cement) (joint) (methylmethacrylate) spacer (84.56)
> removal of (cement) (joint) (methylmethacrylate) spacer (84.57)
> **EXCLUDES** *removal of pedicle screws used in spinal fusion (78.69)*
> **DEF:** Incision into joint to remove prosthesis.
> AHA: 4Q, '09, 148-149; **For code 80.05:** 3Q, '12, 14; 2Q, '08, 4, 5; **For code 80.06:** 3Q, '12, 15; 2Q, '97, 10
> **TIP:** Assign 80.05 for a Girdlestone procedure, in which an infected hip prosthesis is removed without replacement, until the surgical site heals.

§ ✓4ᵗʰ **80.1** **Other arthrotomy**
[0-9] Arthrostomy
> **EXCLUDES** *that for:*
> *arthrography (88.32)*
> *arthroscopy (80.20-80.29)*
> *injection of drug (81.92)*
> *operative approach — omit code*
> **DEF:** Incision into joint; other than to remove prosthesis.
> **DEF:** Arthrostomy: Creation of opening into joint.
> AHA: **For code 80.15:** 3Q, '06, 22-23; **For code 80.16:** 3Q, '06, 23

§ ✓4ᵗʰ **80.2** **Arthroscopy**
[0-9]
> AHA: 3Q, '93, 5; 1Q, '93, 23

§ ✓4ᵗʰ **80.3** **Biopsy of joint structure**
[0-9] Aspiration biopsy
> AHA: **For code 80.39:** 3Q, '05, 13-14

§ ✓4ᵗʰ **80.4** **Division of joint capsule, ligament, or cartilage**
[0-9] Goldner clubfoot release
> Heyman-Herndon(-Strong) correction of metatarsus varus
> Release of:
> adherent or constrictive joint capsule
> joint
> ligament
> **EXCLUDES** *symphysiotomy to assist delivery (73.94)*
> *that for:*
> *carpal tunnel syndrome (04.43)*
> *tarsal tunnel syndrome (04.44)*
> **DEF:** Incision and separation of joint tissues, including capsule, fibrous bone attachment or cartilage.
> AHA: **For code 80.49:** 2Q, '02, 16

✓4ᵗʰ **80.5** **Excision, destruction and other repair of intervertebral disc**

80.50 **Excision, destruction and other repair of intervertebral disc, unspecified**
> Unspecified as to excision or destruction

---

§ Requires fourth digit. Valid digits are in [brackets] under each code. See appropriate category for codes and definitions.

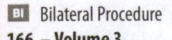 Bilateral Procedure   **NC** Non-covered Procedure   **LC** Limited Coverage Procedure   ►◄ Revised Text   ● New Code   ▲ Revised Code Title

166 – Volume 3   2015 ICD-9-CM

80.51   Excision of intervertebral disc

NOTE   Requires additional code for any concomitant decompression of spinal nerve root at different level from excision site

Diskectomy

Level:
  cervical
  thoracic
  lumbar (lumbosacral)

Removal of herniated nucleus pulposus

That by laminotomy or hemilaminectomy

That with decompression of spinal nerve root at same level

Code also any:
  concurrent spinal fusion (81.00-81.08)
  repair of the anulus fibrosus (80.53-80.54)

EXCLUDES   intervertebral chemonucleolysis (80.52)
  laminectomy for exploration of intraspinal canal (03.09)
  laminotomy for decompression of spinal nerve root only (03.09)
  that for insertion of (non-fusion) spinal disc replacement device (84.60-84.69)
  that with corpectomy, (vertebral) (80.99)

DEF: Discectomy: Removal of intervertebral disc.

DEF: Removal of a herniated nucleus pulposus: Removal of displaced intervertebral disc, central part.

AHA: 2Q, '09, 4-5; 4Q, '08, 184; 2Q, '08, 14; 1Q, '08, 5; 1Q, '07, 9; 1Q, '06, 12; 4Q, '04, 133; 3Q, '03, 12; 1Q, '96, 7; 2Q, '95, 9; 2Q, '90, 27; S-O, '86, 12

80.52   Intervertebral chemonucleolysis

With aspiration of disc fragments

With diskography

Injection of proteolytic enzyme into intervertebral space (chymopapain)

EXCLUDES   injection of anesthetic substance (03.91)
  injection of other substances (03.92)

DEF: Destruction of intervertebral disc via injection of enzyme.

80.53   Repair of the anulus fibrosus with graft or prosthesis

INCLUDES   microsurgical suture repair with fascial autograft
  soft tissue re-approximation repair with tension bands
  surgical mesh repair

Anular disc repair

Closure (sealing) of the anulus fibrosus defect

Code also any:
  application or administration of adhesion barrier substance, if performed (99.77)
  intervertebral discectomy, if performed (80.51)
  locally harvested fascia for graft (83.43)

DEF: Adjunct procedure involving closure of defect in annulus fibrosis (ring of cartilage and fibrous tissue surrounding nucleus pulposus of IV disc) following discectomy surgery; prevents later disc herniation.

AHA: 4Q, '08, 183-184

80.54   Other and unspecified repair of the anulus fibrosus

Anular disc repair

Closure (sealing) of the anulus fibrosus defect

Microsurgical suture repair without fascial autograft

Percutaneous repair of the anulus fibrosus

Code also any:
  application or administration of adhesion barrier substance, if performed (99.77)
  intervertebral discectomy, if performed (80.51)

DEF: Adjunct procedure involving closure of defect in annulus fibrosis (ring of cartilage and fibrous tissue surrounding nucleus pulposus of IV disc) following discectomy surgery; prevents later disc herniation.

AHA: 4Q, '08, 183-184

80.59   Other destruction of intervertebral disc

Destruction NEC   That by laser

AHA: 3Q, '02, 10

TIP: Assign for intradiscal electrothermal therapy (IDET), whereby thermal energy (heat) is directed into the outer disc wall (annulus) and inner disc contents (nucleus) via a heating coil, decreasing the pressure inside the disc.

80.6   Excision of semilunar cartilage of knee

Excision of meniscus of knee

AHA: 2Q, '03, 18; 3Q, '00, 4; 2Q, '96, 3; 1Q, '93, 23

§ √4th **80.7   Synovectomy**
[0-9]
Complete or partial resection of synovial membrane

EXCLUDES   excision of Baker's cyst (83.39)

DEF: Excision of inner membrane of joint capsule.

§ √4th **80.8   Other local excision or destruction of lesion of joint**
[0-9]
AHA: For code 80.86: 1Q, '08, 7

§ √4th **80.9   Other excision of joint**
[0-9]
EXCLUDES   cheilectomy of joint (77.80-77.89)
  excision of bone ends (77.80-77.89)

AHA: For code 80.99: 1Q, '07, 20

√3rd **81   Repair and plastic operations on joint structures**

√4th **81.0   Spinal fusion**

NOTE   Spinal fusion is classified by the anatomic portion (column) fused and the technique (approach) used to perform the fusion.

For the anterior column, the body (corpus) of adjacent vertebrae are fused (interbody fusion). The anterior column can be fused using an anterior, lateral, or posterior technique.

For the posterior column, posterior structures of adjacent vertebrae are fused (pedicle, lamina, facet, transverse process, or "gutter" fusion). A posterior column fusion can be performed using a posterior, posterolateral, or lateral transverse technique.

INCLUDES   arthrodesis of spine with:
  bone graft
  internal fixation

Code also any:
  insertion of interbody spinal fusion device (84.51)
  insertion of recombinant bone morphogenetic protein (84.52)
  synchronous excision of (locally) harvested bone for graft (77.70-77.79)
  the total number of vertebrae fused (81.62-81.64)

EXCLUDES   corrections of pseudarthrosis of spine (81.30-81.39)
  refusion of spine (81.30-81.39)

DEF: Spinal fusion: Immobilization of spinal column.

DEF: Anterior interbody fusion: Arthrodesis by excising disc and cartilage end plates with bone graft insertion between two vertebrae.

DEF: Lateral fusion: Arthrodesis by decorticating and bone grafting lateral surface of zygapophysial joint, pars interarticularis and transverse process.

DEF: Posterior fusion: Arthrodesis by decorticating and bone grafting of neural arches between right and left zygapophysial joints.

DEF: Posterolateral fusion: Arthrodesis by decorticating and bone grafting zygapophysial joint, pars interarticularis and transverse processes.

AHA: 4Q, '10,125-127; 4Q, '03, 99

TIP: Assign also code 03.53 if the fusion was performed for treatment of acute traumatic spinal fracture.

81.00   Spinal fusion, not otherwise specified

81.01   Atlas-axis spinal fusion

Craniocervical fusion ⎫ by anterior transoral
C1–C2 fusion   ⎬ or posterior
Occiput C2 fusion   ⎭ technique

81.02   Other cervical fusion of the anterior column, anterior technique

Arthrodesis of C2 level or below:
  anterior interbody fusion
  anterolateral technique

AHA: ▶2Q, '13, 26;◀ 4Q, '03, 101; 1Q, '01, 6; 1Q, '96, 7

§   Requires fourth digit. Valid digits are in [brackets] under each code. See category 80 for codes and definitions.

√3rd
√4th Additional Digit Required

2015 ICD-9-CM

Valid OR Procedure   Non-OR Procedure   Adjunct Code

Operations on the Musculoskeletal System

81.03–81.32

Types of Grafts for Anterior Arthrodesis

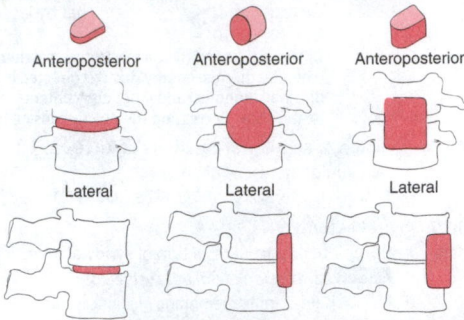

Subtalar Joint Arthroereisis

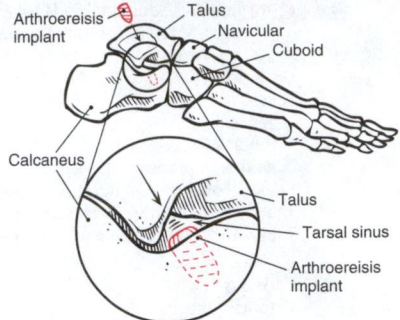

81.03   **Other cervical fusion of the posterior column, posterior technique**

Arthrodesis of C2 level or below, posterolateral technique

AHA: ▶2Q, '13, 26◀

81.04   **Dorsal and dorsolumbar fusion of the anterior column, anterior technique**

Arthrodesis of thoracic or thoracolumbar region:
    anterior interbody fusion
    anterolateral technique
Extracavitary technique

AHA: 3Q, '03, 19

81.05   **Dorsal and dorsolumbar fusion of the posterior column, posterior technique**

Arthrodesis of thoracic or thoracolumbar region, posterolateral technique

AHA: 2Q, '02, 16; 4Q, '99, 11

81.06   **Lumbar and lumbosacral fusion of the anterior column, anterior technique**

Anterior lumbar interbody fusion [ALIF]
Arthrodesis of lumbar or lumbosacral region:
    anterior interbody fusion
    anterolateral technique
    retroperitoneal
    transperitoneal
Direct lateral interbody fusion [DLIF]
Extreme lateral interbody fusion [XLIF]

AHA: 2Q, '08, 14; 1Q, '07, 20; 4Q, '05, 122; 4Q, '02, 107; 4Q, '99, 11

81.07   **Lumbar and lumbosacral fusion of the posterior column, posterior technique**

Facet fusion
Posterolateral technique
Transverse process technique

AHA: 2Q, '11, 10; 2Q, '09, 4; 4Q, '02, 108

81.08   **Lumbar and lumbosacral fusion of the anterior column, posterior technique**

Arthrodesis of lumbar or lumbosacral region, posterior interbody fusion
Axial lumbar interbody fusion [AxiaLIF]
Posterior lumbar interbody fusion [PLIF]
Transforaminal lumbar interbody fusion [TLIF]

AHA: 2Q, '09, 4-5; 1Q, '08, 5; 1Q, '06, 12, 13; 4Q, '05, 122-123; 4Q, '02, 107, 109; 2Q, '00, 12, 13; 4Q, '99, 13; 2Q, '95, 9

✓4ᵗʰ   **81.1**   **Arthrodesis and arthroereisis of foot and ankle**

INCLUDES   arthrodesis of foot and ankle with:
    bone graft
    external fixation device

DEF: Fixation of foot or ankle joints.

81.11   **Ankle fusion**

Tibiotalar fusion

81.12   **Triple arthrodesis**

Talus to calcaneus and calcaneus to cuboid and navicular

81.13   **Subtalar fusion**

EXCLUDES   arthroereisis (81.18)

81.14   **Midtarsal fusion**

81.15   **Tarsometatarsal fusion**

81.16   **Metatarsophalangeal fusion**

81.17   **Other fusion of foot**

81.18   **Subtalar joint arthroereisis**

DEF: Insertion of an endoprosthesis to limit excessive valgus motion of the subtalar joint; nonfusion procedure to prevent pronation.

AHA: 4Q, '05, 124

✓4ᵗʰ   **81.2**   **Arthrodesis of other joint**

INCLUDES   arthrodesis with:
    bone graft
    external fixation device
    excision of bone ends and compression

81.20   **Arthrodesis of unspecified joint**

81.21   **Arthrodesis of hip**

81.22   **Arthrodesis of knee**

81.23   **Arthrodesis of shoulder**

81.24   **Arthrodesis of elbow**

81.25   **Carporadial fusion**

81.26   **Metacarpocarpal fusion**

81.27   **Metacarpophalangeal fusion**

81.28   **Interphalangeal fusion**

81.29   **Arthrodesis of other specified joints**

✓4ᵗʰ   **81.3**   **Refusion of spine**

NOTE   Spine fusion is classified by the anatomic portion (column) fused and the technique (approach) used to perform the fusion.

For the anterior column, the body (corpus) of adjacent vertebrae are fused (interbody fusion). The anterior column can be fused using an anterior, lateral, or posterior technique.

For the posterior column, posterior structures of adjacent vertebrae are fused (pedicle, lamina, facet, transverse process, or "gutter" fusion). A posterior column fusion can be performed using a posterior, posterolateral, or lateral transverse technique.

INCLUDES   arthrodesis of spine with:
    bone graft
    internal fixation
    correction of pseudarthrosis of spine

Code also any:
    insertion of interbody spinal fusion device (84.51)
    insertion of recombinant bone morphogenetic protein (84.52)
    synchronous excision of (locally) harvested bone for graft (77.70-77.79)
    the total number of vertebrae fused (81.62-81.64)

AHA: 4Q, '10,125-127; 4Q, '03, 99; 4Q, '01, 64

81.30   **Refusion of spine, not otherwise specified**

81.31   **Refusion of atlas-axis spine**

Craniocervical fusion   ⎫ by anterior transoral
C1-C2 fusion   ⎬ or posterior
Occiput C2 fusion   ⎭ technique

81.32   **Refusion of other cervical spine, anterior column, anterior technique**

Arthrodesis of C2 level or below:
    anterior interbody fusion
    anterolateral technique

BI Bilateral Procedure   NC Non-covered Procedure   LC Limited Coverage Procedure   ▶◀ Revised Text   ● New Code   ▲ Revised Code Title

168 – Volume 3 · October 2014   **2015 ICD-9-CM**

81.33 **Refusion of other cervical spine, posterior column, posterior technique**

Arthrodesis of C2 level or below, posterolateral technique

81.34 **Refusion of dorsal and dorsolumbar spine, anterior column, anterior technique**

Arthrodesis of thoracic or thoracolumbar region:
anterior interbody fusion
anterolateral technique
Extracavitary technique

81.35 **Refusion of dorsal and dorsolumbar spine, posterior column, posterior technique**

Arthrodesis of thoracic or thoracolumbar region, posterolateral technique

81.36 **Refusion of lumbar and lumbosacral spine, anterior column, anterior technique**

Anterior lumbar interbody fusion [ALIF]
Arthrodesis of lumbar or lumbosacral region:
anterior interbody fusion
anterolateral technique
retroperitoneal
transperitoneal
Direct lateral interbody fusion [DLIF]
Extreme lateral interbody fusion [XLIF]
AHA: 4Q, '05, 122-123

81.37 **Refusion of lumbar and lumbosacral spine, posterior column, posterior technique**

Facet fusion
Posterolateral technique
Transverse process technique

81.38 **Refusion of lumbar and lumbosacral spine, anterior column, posterior technique**

Arthrodesis of lumbar or lumbosacral region, posterior interbody fusion
Axial lumbar interbody fusion [AxiaLIF]
Posterior lumbar interbody fusion [PLIF]
Transforaminal lumbar interbody fusion [TLIF]
AHA: 4Q, '05, 122-123; 4Q, '02, 110

81.39 **Refusion of spine, not elsewhere classified**

√4th 81.4 Other repair of joint of lower extremity

INCLUDES arthroplasty of lower extremity with:
external traction or fixation
graft of bone (chips) or cartilage
internal fixation device
AHA: S-O, '85, 4

81.40 **Repair of hip, not elsewhere classified**

81.42 **Five-in-one repair of knee**

Medial meniscectomy, medial collateral ligament repair, vastus medialis advancement, semitendinosus advancement, and pes anserinus transfer

81.43 **Triad knee repair**

Medial meniscectomy with repair of the anterior cruciate ligament and the medial collateral ligament
O'Donoghue procedure

81.44 **Patellar stabilization**

Roux-Goldthwait operation for recurrent dislocation of patella

DEF: Roux-Goldthwait operation: Stabilization of patella via lateral ligament transposed at insertion beneath undisturbed medial insertion; excision of capsule ellipse and medial patella retinaculum; capsule reefed for lateral patella hold.

81.45 **Other repair of the cruciate ligaments**

AHA: M-A, '87, 12

81.46 **Other repair of the collateral ligaments**

81.47 **Other repair of knee**

AHA: 2Q, '06, 13; 2Q, '03, 18; 1Q, '00, 12, 13; 1Q, '96, 3; 3Q, '93, 5
TIP: Assign for Unispacer™ arthroplasty for degenerative arthritis of the knee; the device fits between the natural structures of the knee and helps to stabilize knee alignment.

81.49 **Other repair of ankle**

AHA: 2Q, '01, 15; 3Q, '00, 4

√4th 81.5 Joint replacement of lower extremity

NOTE Removal of prior prothesis — *omit code*
INCLUDES arthroplasty of lower extremity with:
external traction or fixation
graft of bone (chips) or cartilage
internal fixation device or prosthesis
AHA: 4Q, '09, 149; S-O, '85, 4

81.51 **Total hip replacement**   BI

Replacement of both femoral head and acetabulum by prosthesis
Total reconstruction of hip
Code also any type of bearing surface, if known (00.74-00.77)
DEF: Repair of both surfaces of hip joint with prosthesis.
AHA: 2Q, '09, 11; 4Q, '04, 113; 2Q, '91, 18

81.52 **Partial hip replacement**   BI

Bipolar endoprosthesis
Code also any type of bearing surface, if known (00.74-00.77)
DEF: Repair of single surface of hip joint with prosthesis.
AHA: 2Q, '91, 18

81.53 **Revision of hip replacement, not otherwise specified**

Revision of hip replacement, not specified as to component(s) replaced, (acetabular, femoral or both)
Code also any:
removal of (cement) (joint) spacer (84.57)
type of bearing surface, if known (00.74-00.77)
EXCLUDES revision of hip replacement, components specified (00.70-00.73)
AHA: 4Q, '05, 125; 3Q, '97, 12

81.54 **Total knee replacement**   BI

Bicompartmental
Partial knee replacement
Tricompartmental
Unicompartmental (hemijoint)
AHA: ▶1Q, '14, 12; 4Q, '13, 100; 3Q, '13, 11; 2Q, '13, 17◀
DEF: Repair of a knee joint with prosthetic implant in one, two, or three compartments.

Total Hip Replacement

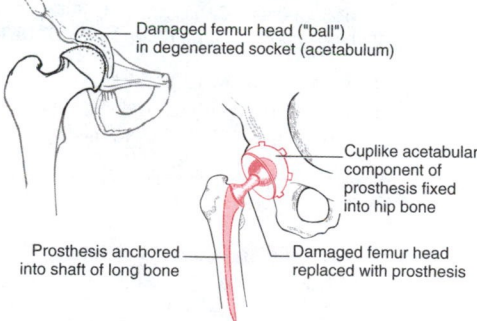

Damaged femur head ("ball") in degenerated socket (acetabulum)

Cuplike acetabular component of prosthesis fixed into hip bone

Prosthesis anchored into shaft of long bone

Damaged femur head replaced with prosthesis

Partial Hip Replacement

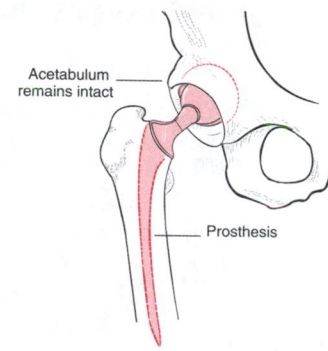

Acetabulum remains intact

Prosthesis

Total Knee Replacement

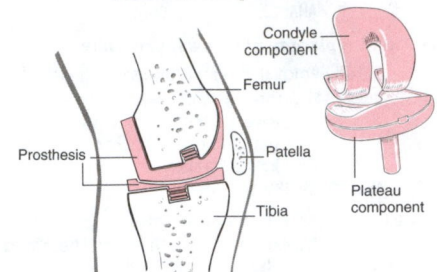

Vertebroplasty

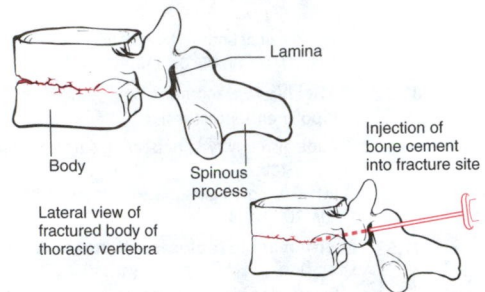

81.55 **Revision of knee replacement, not otherwise specified**

Code also any removal of (cement) (joint) spacer (84.57)

EXCLUDES arthrodesis of knee (81.22)
revision of knee replacement, components specified (00.80-00.84)

AHA: 4Q, '05, 113; 2Q, '97, 10

81.56 **Total ankle replacement** [BI]

81.57 **Replacement of joint of foot and toe**

81.59 **Revision of joint replacement of lower extremity, not elsewhere classified**

✓4ᵗʰ **81.6** **Other procedures on spine**

NOTE **Number of vertebrae**

The vertebral spine consists of 25 vertebrae in the following order and number:
cervical: C1 (atlas), C2 (axis), C3, C4, C5, C6, C7
thoracic or dorsal: T1, T2, T3, T4, T5, T6, T7, T8, T9, T10, T11, T12
lumbar and sacral: L1, L2, L3, L4, L5, S1

Coders should report only one code from the series 81.62-81.64 to show the total number of vertebrae fused on the patient.
Code also the level and approach of the fusion or refusion (81.00-81.08, 81.30-81.39)

AHA: 4Q, '03, 99

81.62 **Fusion or refusion of 2-3 vertebrae**

AHA: 2Q, '11, 10; 1Q, '10, 23; 2Q, '09, 4-5; 2Q, '08, 14; 1Q, '08, 5; 1Q, '07, 20; 1Q, '06, 12, 13; 4Q, '05, 123; 4Q, '03, 99

81.63 **Fusion or refusion of 4-8 vertebrae**

AHA: 1Q, '10, 23; 4Q, '03, 99-101

81.64 **Fusion or refusion of 9 or more vertebrae**

AHA: 4Q, '03, 99

81.65 **Percutaneous vertebroplasty**

Injection of bone void filler (cement) (polymethylmethacrylate) (PMMA) into the diseased or fractured vertebral body

EXCLUDES kyphoplasty (81.66)
percutaneous vertebral augmentation (81.66)

AHA: 4Q, '12, 84; 2Q, '08, 15

Percutaneous Vertebral Augmentation

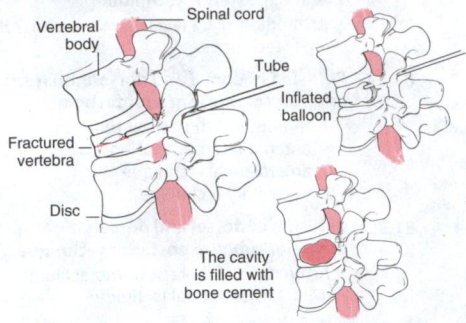

The cavity is filled with bone cement

81.66 **Percutaneous vertebral augmentation**

Arcuplasty
Insertion of inflatable balloon, bone tamp, or other device displacing (removing) (compacting) bone to create a space (cavity) (void) prior to the injection of bone void filler (cement) (polymethylmethacrylate) (PMMA) or other substance
Kyphoplasty
SKyphoplasty
Spineoplasty

EXCLUDES percutaneous vertebroplasty (81.65)

AHA: 1Q, '07, 5, 7; 3Q, '06, 13; 4Q, '04, 126

TIP: A vertebral bone biopsy is not integral to this procedure. If performed, report also code 77.49.

✓4ᵗʰ **81.7** **Arthroplasty and repair of hand, fingers, and wrist**

INCLUDES arthroplasty of hand and finger with:
external traction or fixation
graft of bone (chips) or cartilage
internal fixation device or prosthesis

EXCLUDES operations on muscle, tendon, and fascia of hand (82.01-82.99)

DEF: Plastic surgery of hand, fingers and wrist joints.

81.71 **Arthroplasty of metacarpophalangeal and interphalangeal joint with implant**

81.72 **Arthroplasty of metacarpophalangeal and interphalangeal joint without implant**

AHA: 1Q, '93, 28

81.73 **Total wrist replacement**

81.74 **Arthroplasty of carpocarpal or carpometacarpal joint with implant**

81.75 **Arthroplasty of carpocarpal or carpometacarpal joint without implant**

AHA: 3Q, '93, 8

81.79 **Other repair of hand, fingers, and wrist**

✓4ᵗʰ **81.8** **Arthroplasty and repair of shoulder and elbow**

INCLUDES arthroplasty of upper limb NEC with:
external traction or fixation
graft of bone (chips) or cartilage
internal fixation device or prosthesis

81.80 **Other total shoulder replacement**

EXCLUDES reverse total shoulder replacement (81.88)

AHA: 2Q, '08, 5

81.81 **Partial shoulder replacement**

81.82 **Repair of recurrent dislocation of shoulder**

AHA: 3Q, '95, 15

81.83 **Other repair of shoulder**

AHA: 1Q, '02, 9; 4Q, '01, 51; 2Q, '00, 14; 3Q, '93, 5
TIP: Assign for SLAP (superior labral anterior posterior—glenoid labrum lesion) repair.

81.84 **Total elbow replacement**

Partial elbow replacement

81.85 **Other repair of elbow**

[BI] Bilateral Procedure   [NC] Non-covered Procedure   [LC] Limited Coverage Procedure   ▶◀ Revised Text   ● New Code   ▲ Revised Code Title

170 – Volume 3   **2015 ICD-9-CM**

Arthrocentesis

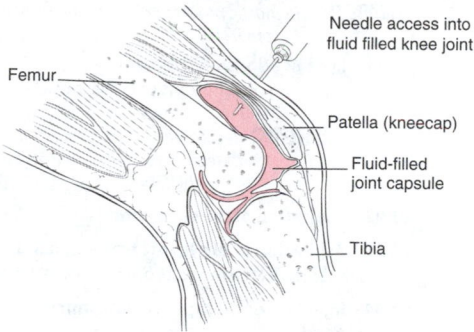

Needle access into
fluid filled knee joint

Femur

Patella (kneecap)

Fluid-filled
joint capsule

Tibia

81.88 **Reverse total shoulder replacement**
Reverse ball-and-socket of the shoulder
EXCLUDES conversion of prior (failed) total shoulder
replacement (arthroplasty) to reverse
total shoulder replacement (81.97)
AHA: 4Q, '10, 129-130

√4th **81.9** **Other operations on joint structures**

81.91 **Arthrocentesis**
Joint aspiration
EXCLUDES that for:
arthrography (88.32)
biopsy of joint structure (80.30-80.39)
injection of drug (81.92)
DEF: Insertion of needle to withdraw fluid from joint.

81.92 **Injection of therapeutic substance into joint or
ligament**
AHA: 3Q, '10, 14; 2Q, '00, 14; 3Q, '89, 16

81.93 **Suture of capsule or ligament of upper
extremity**
EXCLUDES that associated with arthroplasty
(81.71-81.75, 81.80-81.81, 81.84)

81.94 **Suture of capsule or ligament of ankle and foot**
EXCLUDES that associated with arthroplasty
(81.56-81.59)

81.95 **Suture of capsule or ligament of other lower
extremity**
EXCLUDES that associated with arthroplasty
(81.51-81.55, 81.59)

81.96 **Other repair of joint**

81.97 **Revision of joint replacement of upper extremity**
Partial
Removal of cement spacer
Revision of arthroplasty of shoulder
Total
AHA: 1Q, '04, 12

81.98 **Other diagnostic procedures on joint
structures**
EXCLUDES arthroscopy (80.20-80.29)
biopsy of joint structure (80.30-80.39)
microscopic examination of specimen from
joint (91.51-91.59)
thermography (88.83)
x-ray (87.21-87.29, 88.21-88.33)

81.99 **Other**
AHA: 4Q, '05, 124

√3rd **82** **Operations on muscle, tendon, and fascia of hand**
INCLUDES operations on:
aponeurosis
synovial membrane (tendon sheath)
tendon sheath

√4th **82.0** **Incision of muscle, tendon, fascia, and bursa of hand**

82.01 **Exploration of tendon sheath of hand**
Incision of   } tendon sheath of
Removal of rice bodies in } hand
EXCLUDES division of tendon (82.11)
DEF: Incision into and exploration of the hand's muscle and
its accompanying supportive, connective tissue, bands, and
sacs.

82.02 **Myotomy of hand**
EXCLUDES myotomy for division (82.19)
DEF: Incision into hand muscle.

82.03 **Bursotomy of hand**

82.04 **Incision and drainage of palmar or thenar space**

82.09 **Other incision of soft tissue of hand**
EXCLUDES incision of skin and subcutaneous tissue
alone (86.01-86.09)
AHA: N-D, '87, 10

√4th **82.1** **Division of muscle, tendon, and fascia of hand**

82.11 **Tenotomy of hand**
Division of tendon of hand

82.12 **Fasciotomy of hand**
Division of fascia of hand

82.19 **Other division of soft tissue of hand**
Division of muscle of hand

√4th **82.2** **Excision of lesion of muscle, tendon, and fascia of hand**

82.21 **Excision or lesion of tendon sheath of hand**
Ganglionectomy of tendon sheath (wrist)

82.22 **Excision of lesion of muscle of hand**

82.29 **Excision of other lesion of soft tissue of hand**
EXCLUDES excision of lesion of skin and subcutaneous
tissue (86.21-86.3)

√4th **82.3** **Other excision of soft tissue of hand**
Code also any skin graft (86.61-86.62, 86.73)
EXCLUDES excision of skin and subcutaneous tissue (86.21-86.3)

82.31 **Bursectomy of hand**

82.32 **Excision of tendon of hand for graft**
DEF: Resection and excision of fibrous tissue connecting
bone to hand muscle for grafting.

82.33 **Other tenonectomy of hand**
Tenosynovectomy of hand
EXCLUDES excision of lesion of:
tendon (82.29)
sheath (82.21)
DEF: Removal of fibrous bands connecting muscle to bone
of hand.
DEF: Tenosynovectomy of hand: Excision of fibrous band
connecting muscle and bone of hand and removal of
coverings.

82.34 **Excision of muscle or fascia of hand for graft**

82.35 **Other fasciectomy of hand**
Release of Dupuytren's contracture
EXCLUDES excision of lesion of fascia (82.29)
DEF: Excision of fibrous connective tissue; other than for
grafting or removing lesion.
DEF: Release of Dupuytren's contracture: Excision of fibrous
connective tissue to correct flexion of fingers.

82.36 **Other myectomy of hand**
EXCLUDES excision of lesion of muscle (82.22)

82.39 **Other excision of soft tissue of hand**
EXCLUDES excision of skin (86.21-86.3)
excision of soft tissue lesion (82.29)

√4th **82.4** **Suture of muscle, tendon, and fascia of hand**

82.41 **Suture of tendon sheath of hand**

82.42 **Delayed suture of flexor tendon of hand**
DEF: Suture of fibrous band between flexor muscle and
bone; following initial repair.

82.43 **Delayed suture of other tendon of hand**

82.44 **Other suture of flexor tendon of hand**
EXCLUDES delayed suture of flexor tendon of hand
(82.42)

82.45 **Other suture of other tendon of hand**
EXCLUDES delayed suture of other tendon of hand
(82.43)

82.46 **Suture of muscle or fascia of hand**

✓4th **82.5 Transplantation of muscle and tendon of hand**
AHA: 1Q, '93, 28

82.51 Advancement of tendon of hand
DEF: Detachment of fibrous connective muscle band and bone with reattachment at advanced point of hand.

82.52 Recession of tendon of hand
DEF: Detachment of fibrous band of muscle and bone with reattachment at drawn-back point of hand.

82.53 Reattachment of tendon of hand

82.54 Reattachment of muscle of hand

82.55 Other change in hand muscle or tendon length

82.56 Other hand tendon transfer or transplantation
EXCLUDES pollicization of thumb (82.61)
transfer of finger, except thumb (82.81)
AHA: 2Q, '99, 10; 4Q, '98, 40

82.57 Other hand tendon transposition
AHA: 1Q, '93, 28; 3Q, '93, 8

82.58 Other hand muscle transfer or transplantation

82.59 Other hand muscle transposition

✓4th **82.6 Reconstruction of thumb**
INCLUDES digital transfer to act as thumb
Code also any amputation for digital transfer (84.01, 84.11)

82.61 Pollicization operation carrying over nerves and blood supply
DEF: Creation or reconstruction of a thumb with another digit, commonly the index finger.

82.69 Other reconstruction of thumb
"Cocked-hat" procedure [skin flap and bone]
Grafts:
bone   } to thumb
skin (pedicle)

✓4th **82.7 Plastic operation on hand with graft or implant**

82.71 Tendon pulley reconstruction
Reconstruction for opponensplasty
DEF: Reconstruction of fibrous band between muscle and bone of hand.

82.72 Plastic operation on hand with graft of muscle or fascia

82.79 Plastic operation on hand with other graft or implant
Tendon graft to hand
AHA: J-F, '87, 6

✓4th **82.8 Other plastic operations on hand**

82.81 Transfer of finger, except thumb
EXCLUDES pollicization of thumb (82.61)
AHA: 2Q, '05, 7
TIP: Assign this code, along with code 84.11 Amputation of toe, for a procedure in which a toe is transferred to the site of previous traumatic finger amputation.

82.82 Repair of cleft hand
DEF: Correction of fissure defect of hand.

82.83 Repair of macrodactyly
DEF: Reduction in size of abnormally large fingers.

82.84 Repair of mallet finger
DEF: Repair of flexed little finger.

82.85 Other tenodesis of hand
Tendon fixation of hand NOS
DEF: Fixation of fibrous connective band between muscle and bone of hand.

82.86 Other tenoplasty of hand
Myotenoplasty of hand
DEF: Myotenoplasty of hand: Plastic repair of muscle and fibrous band connecting muscle to bone.

82.89 Other plastic operations on hand
Plication of fascia
Repair of fascial hernia
EXCLUDES that with graft or implant (82.71-82.79)

✓4th **82.9 Other operations on muscle, tendon, and fascia of hand**
EXCLUDES diagnostic procedures on soft tissue of hand (83.21-83.29)

82.91 Lysis of adhesions of hand
Freeing of adhesions of fascia, muscle, and tendon of hand
EXCLUDES decompression of carpal tunnel (04.43)
that by stretching or manipulation only (93.26)

82.92 Aspiration of bursa of hand

82.93 Aspiration of other soft tissue of hand
EXCLUDES skin and subcutaneous tissue (86.01)

82.94 Injection of therapeutic substance into bursa of hand

82.95 Injection of therapeutic substance into tendon of hand

82.96 Other injection of locally-acting therapeutic substance into soft tissue of hand
EXCLUDES subcutaneous or intramuscular injection (99.11-99.29)

82.99 Other operations on muscle, tendon, and fascia of hand

✓3rd **83 Operations on muscle, tendon, fascia, and bursa, except hand**
INCLUDES operations on:
aponeurosis
synovial membrane of bursa and tendon sheaths
tendon sheaths
EXCLUDES diaphragm (34.81-34.89)
hand (82.01-82.99)
muscles of eye (15.01-15.9)

✓4th **83.0 Incision of muscle, tendon, fascia, and bursa**

83.01 Exploration of tendon sheath
Incision of tendon sheath
Removal of rice bodies from tendon sheath
DEF: Incision of external covering of fibrous cord for exam.
DEF: Removal of rice bodies from tendon sheath: Incision and removal of small bodies resembling grains of rice.

83.02 Myotomy
EXCLUDES cricopharyngeal myotomy (29.31)
AHA: 4Q, '08, 135; 2Q, '89, 18

83.03 Bursotomy
Removal of calcareous deposit of bursa
EXCLUDES aspiration of bursa (percutaneous) (83.94)

83.09 Other incision of soft tissue
Incision of fascia
EXCLUDES incision of skin and subcutaneous tissue alone (86.01-86.09)
AHA: 1Q, '09, 10

✓4th **83.1 Division of muscle, tendon, and fascia**

83.11 Achillotenotomy

83.12 Adductor tenotomy of hip
DEF: Incision into fibrous attachment between adductor muscle and hip bone.

83.13 Other tenotomy
Aponeurotomy   Tendon transection
Division of tendon   Tenotomy for thoracic
Tendon release   outlet decompression
DEF: Aponeurotomy: Incision and separation of fibrous cords attaching a muscle to bone to aid movement.
DEF: Division of tendon: Separation of fibrous band connecting muscle to bone.
DEF: Tendon release: Surgical detachment of fibrous band from muscle and/or bone.
DEF: Tendon transection: Incision across width of fibrous bands between muscle and bone.
DEF: Tenotomy for thoracic outlet decompression: Incision of fibrous muscle with separation from bone to relieve compressed thoracic outlet.

BI Bilateral Procedure   NC Non-covered Procedure   LC Limited Coverage Procedure   ▶◀ Revised Text   ● New Code   ▲ Revised Code Title

172 – Volume 3   2015 ICD-9-CM

83.14 Fasciotomy

Division of fascia
Division of iliotibial band
Fascia stripping
Release of Volkmann's contracture by fasciotomy
DEF: Division of fascia: Incision to separate fibrous connective tissue.
DEF: Division of iliotibial band: Incision to separate fibrous band connecting tibial bone to muscle in flank.
DEF: Fascia stripping: Incision and lengthwise separation of fibrous connective tissue.
DEF: Release of Volkmann's contracture by fasciotomy: Divisional incision of connective tissue to correct defect in flexion of finger(s).
AHA: 4Q, '06, 102; 3Q, '98, 8
TIP: Assign for all fasciotomy procedures, regardless of whether the approach is open or endoscopic. For fasciotomy of hand, see code 82.12.

83.19 Other division of soft tissue

Division of muscle
Muscle release
Myotomy for thoracic outlet decompression
Myotomy with division
Scalenotomy
Transection of muscle

83.2 Diagnostic procedures on muscle, tendon, fascia, and bursa, including that of hand

83.21 Open biopsy of soft tissue

EXCLUDES biopsy of chest wall (34.23)
closed biopsy of skin and subcutaneous tissue (86.11)

83.29 Other diagnostic procedures on muscle, tendon, fascia, and bursa, including that of hand

EXCLUDES microscopic examination of specimen (91.51-91.-59)
soft tissue x-ray (87.09, 87.38-87.39, 88.09, 88.35, 88.37)
thermography of muscle (88.84)

83.3 Excision of lesion of muscle, tendon, fascia, and bursa

EXCLUDES biopsy of soft tissue (83.21)

83.31 Excision of lesion of tendon sheath

Excision of ganglion of tendon sheath, except of hand

83.32 Excision of lesion of muscle

Excision of:
heterotopic bone
muscle scar for release of Volkmann's contracture
myositis ossificans
DEF: Heterotopic bone: Bone lesion in muscle.
DEF: Muscle scar for release of Volkmann's contracture: Scarred muscle tissue interfering with finger flexion.
DEF: Myositis ossificans: Bony deposits in muscle.

83.39 Excision of lesion of other soft tissue

Excision of Baker's cyst
EXCLUDES bursectomy (83.5)
excision of lesion of skin and subcutaneous tissue (86.3)
synovectomy (80.70-80.79)
AHA: 3Q, '10, 11; 2Q, '05, 3; 2Q, '97, 6

83.4 Other excision of muscle, tendon, and fascia

83.41 Excision of tendon for graft

83.42 Other tenonectomy

Excision of:
aponeurosis
tendon sheath
Tenosynovectomy

83.43 Excision of muscle or fascia for graft

AHA: ▶2Q, '13, 8;◀ 1Q, '11, 7

83.44 Other fasciectomy

DEF: Excision of fascia; other than for graft.
AHA: ▶4Q, '13, 96◀

83.45 Other myectomy

Debridement of muscle NOS
Scalenectomy
DEF: Scalenectomy: Removal of thoracic scaleni muscle tissue.
AHA: 1Q, '99, 8
TIP: Do not assign a skin/soft tissue debridement procedure code (e.g., 86.22) in addition to the muscle debridement (83.45) code; all more superficial debridement is included when multilayer debridement is performed at the same site.

83.49 Other excision of soft tissue

83.5 Bursectomy

AHA: 2Q, '06, 15; 2Q, '99, 11

83.6 Suture of muscle, tendon, and fascia

83.61 Suture of tendon sheath

83.62 Delayed suture of tendon

83.63 Rotator cuff repair

DEF: Repair of musculomembranous structure around shoulder joint capsule.
AHA: 4Q, '11, 136; 1Q, '06, 6; 2Q, '93, 8

83.64 Other suture of tendon

Achillorrhaphy
Aponeurorrhaphy
EXCLUDES delayed suture of tendon (83.62)
DEF: Achillorrhaphy: Suture of fibrous band connecting Achilles tendon to heel bone.
DEF: Aponeurorrhaphy: Suture of fibrous cords connecting muscle to bone.

83.65 Other suture of muscle or fascia

Repair of diastasis recti

83.7 Reconstruction of muscle and tendon

EXCLUDES reconstruction of muscle and tendon associated with arthroplasty

83.71 Advancement of tendon

DEF: Detaching fibrous cord between muscle and bone with reattachment at advanced point.

83.72 Recession of tendon

DEF: Detaching fibrous cord between muscle and bone with reattachment at drawn-back point.

83.73 Reattachment of tendon

83.74 Reattachment of muscle

83.75 Tendon transfer or transplantation

83.76 Other tendon transposition

83.77 Muscle transfer or transplantation

Release of Volkmann's contracture by muscle transplantation

83.79 Other muscle transposition

83.8 Other plastic operations on muscle, tendon, and fascia

EXCLUDES plastic operations on muscle, tendon, and fascia associated with arthroplasty

83.81 Tendon graft

AHA: 3Q, '12, 11

83.82 Graft of muscle or fascia

AHA: ▶2Q, '13, 8;◀ 1Q, '10, 7; 3Q, '01, 9

83.83 Tendon pulley reconstruction

DEF: Reconstruction of fibrous cord between muscle and bone at any site other than hand.

83.84 Release of clubfoot, not elsewhere classified

Evans operation on clubfoot

83.85 Other change in muscle or tendon length

Hamstring lengthening
Heel cord shortening
Plastic achillotenotomy
Tendon plication
DEF: Plastic achillotenotomy: Increase in heel cord length.
DEF: Tendon plication: Surgical tuck of tendon.

83.86 Quadricepsplasty

DEF: Correction of quadriceps femoris muscle.

Operations on the Musculoskeletal System

83.87–84.18

83.87   **Other plastic operations on muscle**
Musculoplasty
Myoplasty
AHA: 1Q, '97, 9

83.88   **Other plastic operations on tendon**
Myotenoplasty   Tenodesis
Tendon fixation   Tenoplasty
AHA: ▶2Q, '13, 23◀

83.89   **Other plastic operations on fascia**
Fascia lengthening   Plication of fascia
Fascioplasty

✓4th **83.9**   **Other operations on muscle, tendon, fascia, and bursa**
EXCLUDES   nonoperative:
    manipulation (93.25-93.29)
    stretching (93.27-93.29)

83.91   **Lysis of adhesions of muscle, tendon, fascia, and bursa**
EXCLUDES   that for tarsal tunnel syndrome (04.44)
DEF: Separation of created fibrous structures from muscle, connective tissues, bands and sacs.

83.92   **Insertion or replacement of skeletal muscle stimulator**
Implantation, insertion, placement, or replacement of skeletal muscle:
    electrodes
    stimulator
AHA: 2Q, '99, 10

83.93   **Removal of skeletal muscle stimulator**

83.94   **Aspiration of bursa**

83.95   **Aspiration of other soft tissue**
EXCLUDES   that of skin and subcutaneous tissue (86.01)

83.96   **Injection of therapeutic substance into bursa**

83.97   **Injection of therapeutic substance into tendon**

83.98   **Injection of locally-acting therapeutic substance into other soft tissue**
EXCLUDES   subcutaneous or intramuscular injection (99.11-99.29)
AHA: 2Q, '06, 11

83.99   **Other operations on muscle, tendon, fascia, and bursa**
Suture of bursa

✓3rd **84**   **Other procedures on musculoskeletal system**

✓4th **84.0**   **Amputation of upper limb**
EXCLUDES   revision of amputation stump (84.3)

84.00   **Upper limb amputation, not otherwise specified**
Closed flap amputation
Kineplastic amputation
Open or guillotine amputation } of upper limb NOS
Revision of current traumatic amputation
DEF: Closed flap amputation: Sewing a created skin flap over stump end of upper limb.
DEF: Kineplastic amputation: Amputation and preparation of stump of upper limb to permit movement.
DEF: Open or guillotine amputation: Straight incision across upper limb; used when primary closure is contraindicated.
DEF: Revision of current traumatic amputation: Reconstruction of traumatic amputation of upper limb to enable closure.

84.01   **Amputation and disarticulation of finger**
EXCLUDES   ligation of supernumerary finger (86.26)

84.02   **Amputation and disarticulation of thumb**

84.03   **Amputation through hand**
Amputation through carpals

84.04   **Disarticulation of wrist**

84.05   **Amputation through forearm**
Forearm amputation

84.06   **Disarticulation of elbow**
DEF: Amputation of forearm through elbow joint.

84.07   **Amputation through humerus**
Upper arm amputation

84.08   **Disarticulation of shoulder**
DEF: Amputation of arm through shoulder joint.

84.09   **Interthoracoscapular amputation**
Forequarter amputation
DEF: Removal of upper arm, shoulder bone and collarbone.

✓4th **84.1**   **Amputation of lower limb**
EXCLUDES   revision of amputation stump (84.3)

84.10   **Lower limb amputation, not otherwise specified**
Closed flap amputation
Kineplastic amputation } of lower limb
Open or guillotine amputation   NOS
Revision of current traumatic amputation
DEF: Closed flap amputation: Sewing a created skin flap over stump of lower limb.
DEF: Kineplastic amputation: Amputation and preparation of stump of lower limb to permit movement.
DEF: Open or guillotine amputation: Straight incision across lower limb; used when primary closure is contraindicated.
DEF: Revision of current traumatic amputation: Reconstruction of traumatic amputation of lower limb to enable closure.

84.11   **Amputation of toe**
Amputation through metatarsophalangeal joint
Disarticulation of toe
Metatarsal head amputation
Ray amputation of foot (disarticulation of the metatarsal head of the toe extending across the forefoot, just proximal to the metatarsophalangeal crease)
EXCLUDES   ligation of supernumerary toe (86.26)
AHA: 2Q, '05, 7; 4Q, '99, 19

84.12   **Amputation through foot**
Amputation of forefoot
Amputation through middle of foot
Chopart's amputation
Midtarsal amputation
Transmetatarsal amputation (amputation of the forefoot, including the toes)
EXCLUDES   Ray amputation of foot (84.11)
DEF: Amputation of forefoot: Removal of foot in front of joint between toes and body of foot.
DEF: Chopart's amputation: Removal of foot with retention of heel, ankle and other associated ankle bones.
DEF: Midtarsal amputation: Amputation of foot through tarsals.
DEF: Transmetatarsal amputation: Amputation of foot through metatarsals.
AHA: 4Q, '99, 19

84.13   **Disarticulation of ankle**
DEF: Removal of foot through ankle bone.

84.14   **Amputation of ankle through malleoli of tibia and fibula**

84.15   **Other amputation below knee**
Amputation of leg through tibia and fibula NOS

84.16   **Disarticulation of knee**
Batch, Spitler, and McFaddin amputation
Mazet amputation
S.P. Roger's amputation
DEF: Removal of lower leg through knee joint.

84.17   **Amputation above knee**
Amputation of leg through femur
Amputation of thigh
Conversion of below-knee amputation into above-knee amputation
Supracondylar above-knee amputation
AHA: 1Q, '05, 16; 1Q, '05, 16; 3Q, '03, 14

84.18   **Disarticulation of hip**
DEF: Removal of leg through hip joint.

BI Bilateral Procedure   NC Non-covered Procedure   LC Limited Coverage Procedure   ▶◀ Revised Text   ● New Code   ▲ Revised Code Title

84.19 **Abdominopelvic amputation**
Hemipelvectomy
Hindquarter amputation
DEF: Removal of leg and portion of pelvic bone.
DEF: Hemipelvectomy: Removal of leg and lateral pelvis.

✓4ᵗʰ **84.2** **Reattachment of extremity**
AHA: 1Q, '95, 8

84.21 **Thumb reattachment**

84.22 **Finger reattachment**

84.23 **Forearm, wrist, or hand reattachment**

84.24 **Upper arm reattachment**
Reattachment of arm NOS

84.25 **Toe reattachment**

84.26 **Foot reattachment**

84.27 **Lower leg or ankle reattachment**
Reattachment of leg NOS

84.28 **Thigh reattachment**

84.29 **Other reattachment**

84.3 **Revision of amputation stump**
Reamputation
Secondary closure ⎫ of stump
Trimming ⎭
EXCLUDES *revision of current traumatic amputation [revision by
further amputation of current injury]
(84.00-84.19, 84.91)*

AHA: 4Q, '99, 15; 2Q, '98, 15; 4Q, '88, 12
TIP: Only assign if the documentation indicates that the amputation
stump revision involves transecting the entire circumference of the
bone.

✓4ᵗʰ **84.4** **Implantation or fitting of prosthetic limb device**

84.40 **Implantation or fitting of prosthetic limb
device, not otherwise specified**

84.41 **Fitting of prosthesis of upper arm and shoulder**

84.42 **Fitting of prosthesis of lower arm and hand**

84.43 **Fitting of prosthesis of arm, not otherwise specified**

84.44 **Implantation of prosthetic device of arm**

84.45 **Fitting of prosthesis above knee**

84.46 **Fitting of prosthesis below knee**

84.47 **Fitting of prosthesis of leg, not otherwise specified**

84.48 **Implantation of prosthetic device of leg**
AHA: ▶1Q, '14, 12◀

✓4ᵗʰ **84.5** **Implantation of other musculoskeletal devices and
substances**
EXCLUDES *insertion of (non-fusion) spinal disc replacement
device (84.60-84.69)*

84.51 **Insertion of interbody spinal fusion device**
Insertion of:
cages (carbn, ceramic, metal, plastic or titanium)
interbody fusion cage
synthetic cages or spacers
threaded bone dowels
Code also refusion of spine (81.30-81.39)
Code also spinal fusion (81.00-81.08)
AHA: 2Q, '09, 5; 2Q, '08, 14; 1Q, '07, 20; 4Q, '05, 123; 1Q, '04,
21; 4Q, '02, 108-110

84.52 **Insertion of recombinant bone
morphogenetic protein**
rhBMP
That via collagen sponge, coral, ceramic and other
carriers
Code also primary procedure performed:
fracture repair (79.00-79.99)
spinal fusion (81.00-81.08)
spinal refusion (81.30-81.39)
DEF: Surgical implantation of bone morphogenetic proteins
(BMP) and recombinant BMP (rhBMP) to induce new bone
growth formation; clinical applications include delayed
unions and nonunions, fractures, and spinal fusions.
AHA: 2Q, '09, 4-5; 4Q, '02, 110

Spinal Fusion with Metal Cage

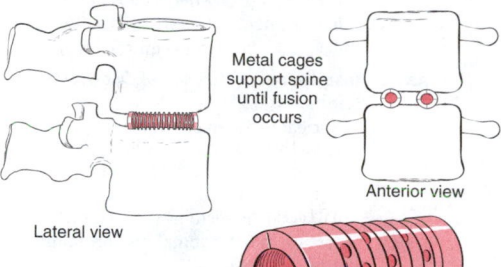

Metal cages
support spine
until fusion
occurs

Lateral view

Anterior view

Spinal fusion
with metal cages

Detail

84.53 **Implantation of internal limb lengthening device
with kinetic distraction**
Code also limb lengthening procedure (78.30-78.39)

84.54 **Implantation of other internal limb lengthening
device**
Implantation of internal limb lengthening device, not
otherwise specified (NOS)
Code also limb lengthening procedure (78.30-78.39)

84.55 **Insertion of bone void filler**
Insertion of:
acrylic cement (PMMA)
bone void cement
calcium based bone void filler
polymethylmethacrylate (PMMA)
EXCLUDES *that with percutaneous vertebral
augmentation (81.66)
that with percutaneous vertebroplasty
(81.65)*
AHA: 4Q, '04, 128

84.56 **Insertion or replacement of (cement) spacer**
Insertion or replacement of joint
(methylmethacrylate) spacer
AHA: ▶3Q, '13, 5;◀3Q, '12, 14, 15; 2Q, '08, 4; 4Q, '05, 124

84.57 **Removal of (cement) spacer**
Removal of joint (methylmethacrylate) spacer
AHA: 2Q, '08, 4, 5; 4Q, '05, 113, 124-125

84.59 **Insertion of other spinal devices**
EXCLUDES *initial insertion of pedicle screws with spinal
fusion — omit code
insertion of facet replacement device(s)
(84.84)
insertion of interspinous process device(s)
(84.80)
insertion of pedicle-based dynamic
stabilization device(s) (84.82)*
AHA: 1Q, '07, 9, 10

✓4ᵗʰ **84.6** **Replacement of spinal disc**
INCLUDES non-fusion arthroplasty of the spine with insertion
of artificial disc prosthesis

84.60 **Insertion of spinal disc prosthesis, not
otherwise specified**
Replacement of spinal disc, NOS
INCLUDES diskectomy (discectomy)

84.61 **Insertion of partial spinal disc prosthesis,
cervical**
Nuclear replacement device, cervical
Partial artificial disc prosthesis (flexible), cervical
Replacement of nuclear disc (nucleus pulposus),
cervical
INCLUDES diskectomy (discectomy)

84.62 **Insertion of total spinal disc prosthesis,
cervical**
Replacement of cervical spinal disc, NOS
Replacement of total spinal disc, cervical
Total artificial disc prosthesis (flexible), cervical
INCLUDES diskectomy (discectomy)

Operations on the Musculoskeletal System

84.19–84.62

Operations on the Musculoskeletal System

84.63–84.81

84.63   **Insertion of spinal disc prosthesis, thoracic**

Artificial disc prosthesis (flexible), thoracic
Replacement of thoracic spinal disc, partial or total
[INCLUDES] diskectomy (discectomy)

84.64   **Insertion of partial spinal disc prosthesis, lumbosacral**

Nuclear replacement device, lumbar
Partial artificial disc prosthesis (flexible), lumbar
Replacement of nuclear disc (nucleus pulposus), lumbar
[INCLUDES] diskectomy (discectomy)

[11] **84.65**   **Insertion of total spinal disc prosthesis, lumbosacral**   `NC`

Replacement of lumbar spinal disc, NOS
Replacement of total spinal disc, lumbar
Total artificial disc prosthesis (flexible), lumbar
[INCLUDES] diskectomy (discectomy)
AHA: 4Q, '04, 133

84.66   **Revision or replacement of artificial spinal disc prosthesis, cervical**

Removal of (partial) (total) spinal disc prosthesis with synchronous insertion of new (partial) (total) spinal disc prosthesis, cervical
Repair of previously inserted spinal disc prosthesis, cervical

84.67   **Revision or replacement of artificial spinal disc prosthesis, thoracic**

Removal of (partial) (total) spinal disc prosthesis with synchronous insertion of new (partial) (total) spinal disc prosthesis, thoracic
Repair of previously inserted spinal disc prosthesis, thoracic

84.68   **Revision or replacement of artificial spinal disc prosthesis, lumbosacral**

Removal of (partial) (total) spinal disc prosthesis with synchronous insertion of new (partial) (total) spinal disc prosthesis, lumbosacral
Repair of previously inserted spinal disc prosthesis, lumbosacral

84.69   **Revision or replacement of artificial spinal disc prosthesis, not otherwise specified**

Removal of (partial) (total) spinal disc prosthesis with synchronous insertion of new (partial) (total) spinal disc prosthesis
Repair of previously inserted spinal disc prosthesis

✓4th **84.7**   **Adjunct codes for external fixator devices**

Code also any primary procedure performed:
application of external fixator device (78.10, 78.12-78.13, 78.15, 78.17-78.19)
reduction of fracture and dislocation (79.00-79.89)
AHA: 4Q, '05, 127-129

84.71   **Application of external fixator device, monoplanar system**

[EXCLUDES] other hybrid device or system (84.73)
ring device or system (84.72)
DEF: Instrumentation that provides percutaneous neutralization, compression, and /or distraction of bone in a single plane by applying force within that plane.
AHA: 4Q, '05, 129

84.72   **Application of external fixator device, ring system**

Ilizarov type
Sheffield type
[EXCLUDES] monoplanar device or system (84.71)
other hybrid device or system (84.73)
DEF: Instrumentation that provides percutaneous neutralization, compression, and/or distraction of bone through 360 degrees of force application.

External Fixator Devices

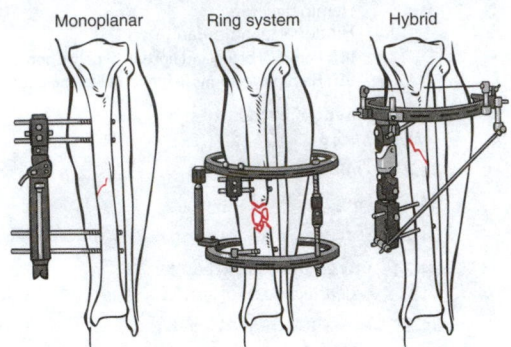

Monoplanar   Ring system   Hybrid

84.73   **Application of hybrid external fixator device**

Computer (assisted) (dependent) external fixator device
Hybrid system using both ring and monoplanar devices
[EXCLUDES] monoplanar device or system, when used alone (84.71)
ring device or system, when used alone (84.72)
DEF: Instrumentation that provides percutaneous neutralization, compression, and /or distraction of bone by applying multiple external forces using monoplanar and ring device combinations.

✓4th **84.8**   **Insertion, replacement and revision of posterior spinal motion preservation device(s)**

Dynamic spinal stabilization device(s)
[INCLUDES] any synchronous facetectomy (partial, total) performed at the same level
Code also any synchronous surgical decompression (foraminotomy, laminectomy, laminotomy), if performed (03.09)
[EXCLUDES] fusion of spine (81.00-81.08, 81.30-81.39)
insertion of artificial disc prosthesis (84.60-84.69)
insertion of interbody spinal fusion device (84.51)
AHA: 4Q, '07, 116-120

84.80   **Insertion or replacement of interspinous process device(s)**

Interspinous process decompression device(s)
Interspinous process distraction device(s)
[EXCLUDES] insertion or replacement of facet replacement device (84.84)
insertion or replacement of pedicle-based dynamic stabilization device (84.82)

84.81   **Revision of interspinous process device(s)**

Repair of previously inserted interspinous process device(s)
[EXCLUDES] revision of facet replacement device(s) (84.85)
revision of pedicle-based dynamic stabilization device (84.83)

Posterior Spinal Motion Preservation Devices

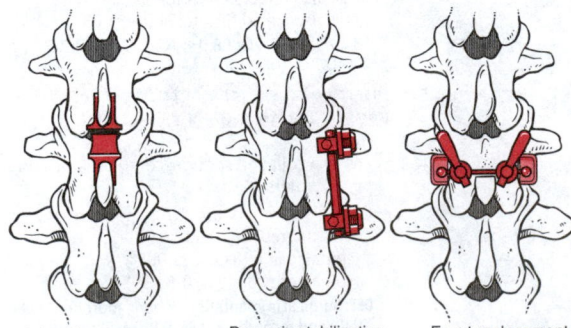

Interspinous devices   Dynamic stabilization   Facet replacement

---

[11] Noncovered except when patient is 60 years or less.

BI Bilateral Procedure   **NC** Non-covered Procedure   **LC** Limited Coverage Procedure   ▶◀ Revised Text   ● New Code   ▲ Revised Code Title

176 – Volume 3   **2015 ICD-9-CM**

84.82 **Insertion or replacement of pedicle-based dynamic stabilization device(s)**

EXCLUDES   initial insertion of pedicle screws with spinal
    fusion — omit code
    insertion or replacement of facet
     replacement device(s) (84.84)
    insertion or replacement of interspinous
     process device(s) (84.80)
    replacement of pedicle screws used in spinal
     fusion (78.59)

AHA: 2Q, '11, 10

84.83 **Revision of pedicle-based dynamic stabilization device(s)**

Repair of previously inserted pedicle-based dynamic
   stabilization device(s)

EXCLUDES   removal of pedicle screws used in spinal
    fusion (78.69)
    replacement of pedicle screws used in spinal
     fusion (78.59)
    revision of facet replacement device(s)
     (84.85)
    revision of interspinous process device(s)
     (84.81)

84.84 **Insertion or replacement of facet replacement device(s)**

Facet arthroplasty

EXCLUDES   initial insertion of pedicle screws with spinal
    fusion — omit code
    insertion or replacement of interspinous
     process device(s) (84.80)
    insertion or replacement of pedicle-based
     dynamic stabilization device(s) (84.82)
    replacement of pedicle screws used in spinal
     fusion (78.59)

AHA: 4Q, '07, 120

84.85 **Revision of facet replacement device(s)**

Repair of previously inserted facet replacement
   device(s)

EXCLUDES   removal of pedicle screws used in spinal
    fusion (78.69)
    replacement of pedicle screws used in spinal
     fusion (78.59)
    revision of interspinous process device(s)
     (84.81)
    revision of pedicle-based dynamic
     stabilization device(s) (84.83)

√4ᵗʰ **84.9** **Other operations on musculoskeletal system**

EXCLUDES   nonoperative manipulation (93.25-93.29)

84.91 **Amputation, not otherwise specified**

84.92 **Separation of equal conjoined twins**

84.93 **Separation of unequal conjoined twins**

Separation of conjoined twins NOS

84.94 **Insertion of sternal fixation device with rigid plates**

EXCLUDES   insertion of sternal fixation device for
    internal fixation of fracture (79.39)
    internal fixation of bone without fracture
     reduction (78.59)

AHA: 4Q, '10, 130-131

84.99 **Other**

Operations on the Integumentary System

15. Operations on the Integumentary System (85-86)

√3ʳᵈ **85**   **Operations on the breast**

INCLUDES   operations on the skin and subcutaneous tissue of:
- breast } female or male
- previous mastectomy site
- revision of previous mastectomy site

85.0   **Mastotomy**

Incision of breast (skin) Mammotomy

EXCLUDES   aspiration of breast (85.91)
removal of implant (85.94)

AHA: 1Q, '04, 3; 2Q, '90, 27

√4ᵗʰ **85.1**   **Diagnostic procedures on breast**

85.11   **Closed [percutaneous] [needle] biopsy of breast**

DEF: Mammatome biopsy: Excision of breast tissue using a needle inserted through a small incision, followed by a full cut circle of tissue surrounding the core biopsy to obtain multiple contiguous directional sampling for definitive diagnosis and staging of cancer.

AHA: 2Q, '00, 10; 3Q, '89, 17

85.12   **Open biopsy of breast**

DEF: Excision of breast tissue for examination.

AHA: 3Q, '89, 17; M-A, '86, 11

TIP: If an entire breast lesion is excised, assign instead code 85.21 Local excision of lesion of breast.

85.19   **Other diagnostic procedures on breast**

EXCLUDES   mammary ductogram (87.35)
mammography NEC (87.37)
manual examination (89.36)
microscopic examination of specimen (91.61-91.69)
thermography (88.85)
ultrasonography (88.73)
xerography (87.36)

√4ᵗʰ **85.2**   **Excision or destruction of breast tissue**

EXCLUDES   mastectomy (85.41-85.48)
reduction mammoplasty (85.31-85.32)

85.20   **Excision or destruction of breast tissue, not otherwise specified**

EXCLUDES   laser interstitial thermal therapy [LITT] of lesion or tissue of breast under guidance (17.69)

85.21   **Local excision of lesion of breast**

Lumpectomy
Removal of area of fibrosis from breast

EXCLUDES   biopsy of breast (85.11-85.12)

AHA: 3Q, '12, 3; 2Q, '90, 27; 3Q, '89, 17; M-A, '86, 11

85.22   **Resection of quadrant of breast**

85.23   **Subtotal mastectomy**

EXCLUDES   quadrant resection (85.22)

DEF: Excision of a large portion of breast tissue.

AHA: 2Q, '92, 7

85.24   **Excision of ectopic breast tissue**

Excision of accessory nipple

DEF: Excision of breast tissue outside normal breast region.

85.25   **Excision of nipple**

EXCLUDES   excision of accessory nipple (85.24)

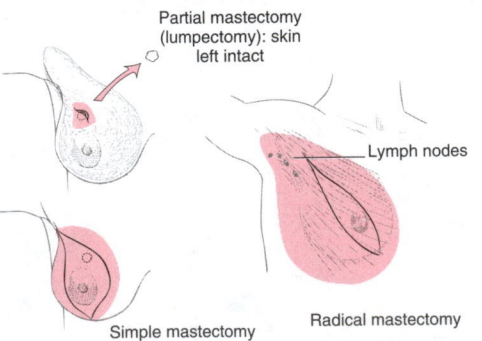

Mastectomy

Partial mastectomy (lumpectomy): skin left intact

Lymph nodes

Simple mastectomy

Radical mastectomy

√4ᵗʰ **85.3**   **Reduction mammoplasty and subcutaneous mammectomy**

AHA: 4Q, '95, 79, 80

85.31   **Unilateral reduction mammoplasty**

Unilateral:
amputative mammoplasty
size reduction mammoplasty

85.32   **Bilateral reduction mammoplasty**

Amputative mammoplasty
Biesenberger operation
Reduction mammoplasty (for gynecomastia)

85.33   **Unilateral subcutaneous mammectomy with synchronous implant**

EXCLUDES   that without synchronous implant (85.34)

DEF: Removal of mammary tissue, leaving skin and nipple intact with implant of prosthesis.

85.34   **Other unilateral subcutaneous mammectomy**

Removal of breast tissue with preservation of skin and nipple
Subcutaneous mammectomy NOS

DEF: Excision of mammary tissue, leaving skin and nipple intact.

85.35   **Bilateral subcutaneous mammectomy with synchronous implant**

EXCLUDES   that without synchronous implant (85.36)

DEF: Excision of mammary tissue, both breasts, leaving skin and nipples intact; with prostheses.

85.36   **Other bilateral subcutaneous mammectomy**

√4ᵗʰ **85.4**   **Mastectomy**

85.41   **Unilateral simple mastectomy**

Mastectomy:
NOS
complete

DEF: Removal of one breast.

85.42   **Bilateral simple mastectomy**

Bilateral complete mastectomy

DEF: Removal of both breasts.

AHA: 2Q, '11, 12

85.43   **Unilateral extended simple mastectomy**

Extended simple mastectomy NOS
Modified radical mastectomy
Simple mastectomy with excision of regional lymph nodes

DEF: Removal of one breast and lymph nodes under arm.

AHA: 2Q, '12, 4; 2Q, '92, 7; 3Q, '91, 24; 2Q, '91, 21

TIP: Modified radical mastectomy includes sentinel node biopsy, a regional axillary lymph resection for staging. Do not report separately.

85.44   **Bilateral extended simple mastectomy**

AHA: 2Q, '92, 7; 3Q, '91, 24; 2Q, '91, 21

85.45   **Unilateral radical mastectomy**

Excision of breast, pectoral muscles, and regional lymph nodes [axillary, clavicular, supraclavicular]
Radical mastectomy NOS

DEF: Removal of one breast and regional lymph nodes, pectoral muscle and adjacent tissue.

AHA: 2Q, '91, 21

TIP: Do not assign a separate code for lymph node excision (subcategory 40.3 or 40.5); the service is included in the radical mastectomy code.

85.46   **Bilateral radical mastectomy**

AHA: 2Q, '91, 21

85.47   **Unilateral extended radical mastectomy**

Excision of breast, muscles, and lymph nodes [axillary, clavicular, supraclavicular, internal mammary, and mediastinal]
Extended radical mastectomy NOS

DEF: Removal of one breast, regional and middle chest lymph nodes, chest muscle and adjacent tissue.

85.48   **Bilateral extended radical mastectomy**

DEF: Removal of both breasts, regional and middle chest lymph nodes, chest muscle and adjacent tissue.

Operations on the Integumentary System

85–85.48

✓4ᵗʰ 85.5 Augmentation mammoplasty
EXCLUDES *that associated with subcutaneous mammectomy (85.33, 85.35)*
DEF: Plastic surgery to increase breast size.
AHA: 3Q, '97, 12; 4Q, '95, 76, 80

85.50 Augmentation mammoplasty, not otherwise specified

85.51 Unilateral injection into breast for augmentation
EXCLUDES *injection of fat graft of breast (85.55)*

85.52 Bilateral injection into breast for augmentation
Injection into breast for augmentation NOS
EXCLUDES *injection of fat graft of breast (85.55)*

85.53 Unilateral breast implant
AHA: 2Q, '00 18; 2Q, '98, 14

85.54 Bilateral breast implant
Breast implant NOS

85.55 Fat graft to breast
INCLUDES extraction of fat for autologous graft
Autologous fat transplantation or transfer
Fat graft to breast NOS
Fat graft to breast with or without use of enriched graft
Micro-fat grafting
EXCLUDES *that with reconstruction of breast (85.70-85.79)*
AHA: 4Q, '10, 132-134

85.6 Mastopexy
DEF: Anchoring of pendulous breast.

✓4ᵗʰ 85.7 Total reconstruction of breast
AHA: 4Q, '08, 185-187; 4Q, '95, 77; 1Q, '93, 27
TIP: When a patient is admitted for breast reconstruction following mastectomy, assign diagnosis code V51.0 as the principal or first-listed diagnosis.

85.70 Total reconstruction of breast, not otherwise specified
Perforator flap, free

85.71 Latissimus dorsi myocutaneous flap
AHA: 2Q, '11, 12

85.72 Transverse rectus abdominis myocutaneous [TRAM] flap, pedicled
EXCLUDES *transverse rectus abdominis myocutaneous (TRAM) flap, free (85.73)*

85.73 Transverse rectus abdominis myocutaneous [TRAM] flap, free
EXCLUDES *transverse rectus abdominis myocutaneous (TRAM) flap, pedicled (85.72)*
AHA: 4Q, '10, 115

85.74 Deep inferior epigastric artery perforator [DIEP] flap, free

85.75 Superficial inferior epigastric artery [SIEA] flap, free

85.76 Gluteal artery perforator [GAP] flap, free

85.79 Other total reconstruction of breast
EXCLUDES *deep inferior epigastric artery perforator [DIEP] flap, free (85.74)*
gluteal artery perforator [GAP] flap, free (85.76)
latissimus dorsi myocutaneous flap (85.71)
perforator flap, free (85.70)
superficial inferior epigastric artery [SIEA] flap, free (85.75)
total reconstruction of breast, not otherwise specified (85.70)
transverse rectus abdominis myocutaneous [TRAM] flap, free (85.73)
transverse rectus abdominis myocutaneous [TRAM] flap, pedicled (85.72)

✓4ᵗʰ 85.8 Other repair and plastic operations on breast
EXCLUDES *that for:*
augmentation (85.50-85.54)
reconstruction (85.70-85.76, 85.79)
reduction (85.31-85.32)
AHA: 4Q, '95, 77

85.81 Suture of laceration of breast

85.82 Split-thickness graft to breast

85.83 Full-thickness graft to breast
AHA: 4Q, '95, 77

85.84 Pedicle graft to breast
DEF: Implantation of transferred muscle tissue still connected to vascular source.
AHA: 4Q, '95, 77

85.85 Muscle flap graft to breast
AHA: 4Q, '95, 77

85.86 Transposition of nipple
DEF: Relocation of nipple.
AHA: 4Q, '95, 78

85.87 Other repair or reconstruction of nipple
AHA: 4Q, '95, 78

85.89 Other mammoplasty

✓4ᵗʰ 85.9 Other operations on the breast

85.91 Aspiration of breast
EXCLUDES *percutaneous biopsy of breast (85.11)*

85.92 Injection of therapeutic agent into breast
EXCLUDES *that for augmentation of breast (85.51-85.52, 85.55)*

85.93 Revision of implant of breast
AHA: 2Q, '98, 14; 4Q, '95, 76

85.94 Removal of implant of breast
AHA: 2Q, '98, 14; 3Q, '92, 4

85.95 Insertion of breast tissue expander
Insertion (soft tissue) of tissue expander (one or more) under muscle or platysma to develop skin flaps for donor use
AHA: ▶4Q, '13, 96;◄ 2Q, '11, 12

85.96 Removal of breast tissue expander(s)
AHA: 2Q, '00, 18; 4Q, '95, 77

85.99 Other
AHA: 2Q, '12, 8

✓3ʳᵈ 86 Operations on skin and subcutaneous tissue
INCLUDES operations on:
hair follicles
male perineum
nails
sebaceous glands
subcutaneous fat pads
sudoriferous glands
superficial fossae
EXCLUDES *those on skin of:*
anus (49.01-49.99)
breast (mastectomy site) (85.0-85.99)
ear (18.01-18.9)
eyebrow (08.01-08.99)
eyelid (08.01-08.99)
female perineum (71.01-71.9)
lips (27.0-27.99)
nose (21.00-21.99)
penis (64.0-64.99)
scrotum (61.0-61.99)
vulva (71.01-71.9)

✓4ᵗʰ 86.0 Incision of skin and subcutaneous tissue

86.01 Aspiration of skin and subcutaneous tissue
Aspiration of:
abscess
hematoma   } of nail, skin, or subcutaneous tissue
seroma
AHA: 3Q, '89, 16

✓3ʳᵈ
✓4ᵗʰ Additional Digit Required   Valid OR Procedure   Non-OR Procedure   Adjunct Code

86.02 Injection or tattooing of skin lesion or defect

Insertion
Injection } of filling material
Pigmenting of skin
DEF: Pigmenting of skin: Adding color to skin.

86.03 Incision of pilonidal sinus or cyst

EXCLUDES marsupialization (86.21)

86.04 Other incision with drainage of skin and subcutaneous tissue

EXCLUDES drainage of:
fascial compartments of face and mouth (27.0)
palmar or thenar space (82.04)
pilonidal sinus or cyst (86.03)
AHA: ▶3Q, '13, 15;◄ 1Q, '09, 11; 4Q, '04, 76
TIP: If extensive debridement is performed along with the I&D procedure, assign instead code 86.22.

86.05 Incision with removal of foreign body or device from skin and subcutaneous tissue

Removal of carotid sinus baroreflex activation device
Removal of loop recorder
Removal of neurostimulator pulse generator (single array, dual array)
Removal of tissue expander(s) from skin or soft tissue other than breast tissue
EXCLUDES removal of foreign body without incision (98.20-98.29)
AHA: 2Q, '96, 15; N-D, '87, 10; N-D, '86, 9

86.06 Insertion of totally implantable infusion pump

Code also any associated catheterization
EXCLUDES insertion of totally implantable vascular access device (86.07)
AHA: 2Q, '99, 4; 4Q, '90, 14

86.07 Insertion of totally implantable vascular access device [VAD]

Totally implanted port
EXCLUDES insertion of totally implantable infusion pump (86.06)
DEF: Placement of vascular access infusion catheter system under skin to allow for frequent manual infusions into blood vessel.
AHA: 1Q, '01, 13; 1Q, '96, 3; 2Q, '94, 11; 3Q, '91, 13; 4Q, '90, 15

86.09 Other incision of skin and subcutaneous tissue

Creation of thalamic stimulator pulse generator pocket, new site
Escharotomy
Exploration:
sinus tract, skin
superficial fossa
Relocation of subcutaneous device pocket NEC
Reopening subcutaneous pocket for device revision without replacement
Undercutting of hair follicle
EXCLUDES creation of loop recorder pocket, new site and insertion/relocation of device (37.79)
creation of pocket for implantable, patient-activated cardiac event recorder and insertion/relocation of device (37.79)
removal of catheter from cranial cavity (01.27)
that for drainage (86.04)
that of:
cardiac pacemaker pocket, new site (37.79)
fascial compartments of face and mouth (27.0)
AHA: ▶4Q, '13, 86;◄ 1Q, '05, 17; 2Q, '04, 7, 8; 4Q, '00, 68; 4Q, '99, 21; 4Q, '97, 57; 3Q, '89, 17; N-D, '86, 1; N-D, '84, 6

✓4ᵗʰ 86.1 Diagnostic procedures on skin and subcutaneous tissue

86.11 Closed biopsy of skin and subcutaneous tissue

AHA: 4Q, '08, 99

86.19 Other diagnostic procedures on skin and subcutaneous tissue

EXCLUDES microscopic examination of specimen from skin and subcutaneous tissue (91.61-91.79)

✓4ᵗʰ 86.2 Excision or destruction of lesion or tissue of skin and subcutaneous tissue

86.21 Excision of pilonidal cyst or sinus

Marsupialization of cyst
EXCLUDES incision of pilonidal cyst or sinus (86.03)
DEF: Marsupialization of cyst: Incision of cyst and suturing edges to skin to open site.

86.22 Excisional debridement of wound, infection, or burn

Removal by excision of:
devitalized tissue
necrosis
slough
EXCLUDES debridement of:
abdominal wall (wound) (54.3)
bone (77.60-77.69)
muscle (83.45)
of hand (82.36)
nail (bed) (fold) (86.27)
nonexcisional debridement of wound, infection, or burn (86.28)
open fracture site (79.60-79.69)
pedicle or flap graft (86.75)
AHA: 3Q, '12, 3; 2Q, '11, 11; 3Q, '08, 8; 1Q, '08, 3-4; 3Q, '06, 19; 2Q, '06, 11; 1Q, '05, 14; 4Q, '04, 138; 3Q, '02, 23; 2Q, '00, 9; 1Q, '99, 8; 2Q, '92, 17; 3Q, '91, 18; 3Q, '89, 16; 4Q, '88, 5; N-D, '86, 1
TIP: Assign only if the debridement involves skin and subcutaneous tissues; any deeper structures (e.g., muscle, bone) are coded elsewhere.

86.23 Removal of nail, nail bed, or nail fold

86.24 Chemosurgery of skin

Chemical peel of skin
DEF: Chemicals applied to destroy skin tissue.
DEF: Chemical peel of skin: Chemicals used to peel skin layers.

86.25 Dermabrasion

That with laser
EXCLUDES dermabrasion of wound to remove embedded debris (86.28)
DEF: Removal of wrinkled or scarred skin with fine sandpaper, wire, brushes or laser.

86.26 Ligation of dermal appendage

EXCLUDES excision of preauricular appendage (18.29)
DEF: Tying off extra skin.

86.27 Debridement of nail, nail bed, or nail fold

Removal of:
necrosis
slough
EXCLUDES removal of nail, nail bed, or nail fold (86.23)

86.28 Nonexcisional debridement of wound, infection, or burn

Debridement NOS
Maggot therapy
Removal of devitalized tissue, necrosis, and slough by such methods as:
brushing
irrigation (under pressure)
scrubbing
washing
Ultrasonic debridement
Water scalpel (jet)
DEF: Removal of damaged skin by methods other than excision.
AHA: ▶1Q, '13, 15;◄ 4Q, '11, 182; 2Q, '10, 11; 3Q, '09, 13; 1Q, '07, 10, 11; 1Q, '05, 14; 2Q, '04, 5, 6; 4Q, '03, 110; 2Q, '03, 15; 3Q, '02, 23; 2Q, '01, 18; 3Q, '91, 18; 4Q, '88, 5
TIP: Assign for VersaJet debridement, regardless of depth of tissue debrided.

BI Bilateral Procedure   **NC** Non-covered Procedure   **LC** Limited Coverage Procedure   ▶◄ Revised Text   ● New Code   ▲ Revised Code Title

86.3 **Other local excision or destruction of lesion or tissue of skin and subcutaneous tissue**

Destruction of skin by:
cauterization
cryosurgery
fulguration
laser beam
That with Z-plasty
EXCLUDES *adipectomy (86.83)*
biopsy of skin (86.11)
wide or radical excision of skin (86.4)
Z-plasty without excision (86.84)
AHA: 1Q, '96, 15; 2Q, '90, 27; 1Q, '89, 12; 3Q, '89, 18; 4Q, '88, 7

86.4 **Radical excision of skin lesion**

Wide excision of skin lesion involving underlying or adjacent structure
Code also any lymph node dissection (40.3-40.5)
AHA: 4Q, '09, 74

✓4th **86.5** **Suture or other closure of skin and subcutaneous tissue**

86.51 **Replantation of scalp**

86.59 **Closure of skin and subcutaneous tissue of other sites**
Adhesives (surgical)(tissue)
Staples
Sutures
EXCLUDES *application of adhesive strips (butterfly) — omit code*
AHA: 4Q, '99, 23

✓4th **86.6** **Free skin graft**
INCLUDES excision of skin for autogenous graft
EXCLUDES *construction or reconstruction of:*
penis (64.43-64.44)
trachea (31.75)
vagina (70.61-70.64)
DEF: Transplantation of skin to another site.

86.60 **Free skin graft, not otherwise specified**

86.61 **Full-thickness skin graft to hand**
EXCLUDES *heterograft (86.65)*
homograft (86.66)

86.62 **Other skin graft to hand**
EXCLUDES *heterograft (86.65)*
homograft (86.66)

86.63 **Full-thickness skin graft to other sites**
EXCLUDES *heterograft (86.65)*
homograft (86.66)

86.64 **Hair transplant**
EXCLUDES *hair follicle transplant to eyebrow or eyelash (08.63)*

86.65 **Heterograft to skin**
Pigskin graft
Porcine graft
EXCLUDES *application of dressing only (93.57)*
DEF: Implantation of nonhuman tissue.
AHA: 3Q,'02, 23

86.66 **Homograft to skin**
Graft to skin of:
amnionic membrane } from donor
skin
DEF: Implantation of tissue from human donor.

86.67 **Dermal regenerative graft**
Artificial skin, NOS
Creation of "neodermis"
Decellularized allodermis
Integumentary matrix implants
Prosthetic implant of dermal layer of skin
Regenerate dermal layer of skin
EXCLUDES *heterograft to skin (86.65)*
homograft to skin (86.66)
DEF: Replacement of dermis and epidermal layer of skin by cultured or regenerated autologous tissue; used to treat full-thickness or deep partial-thickness burns; also called cultured epidermal autograft (CEA).
AHA: 3Q, '10, 7-8; 3Q, '06, 19; 4Q, '98, 76, 79

86.69 **Other skin graft to other sites**
EXCLUDES *heterograft (86.65)*
homograft (86.66)
AHA: 1Q, '10, 7; 4Q, '99, 15

✓4th **86.7** **Pedicle grafts or flaps**
EXCLUDES *construction or reconstruction of:*
penis (64.43-64.44)
trachea (31.75)
vagina (70.61-70.64)
DEF: Full thickness skin and subcutaneous tissue partially attached to the body by a narrow strip of tissue so that it retains its blood supply. The unattached portion is sutured to the defect.

86.70 **Pedicle or flap graft, not otherwise specified**

86.71 **Cutting and preparation of pedicle grafts or flaps**
Elevation of pedicle from its bed
Flap design and raising
Partial cutting of pedicle or tube
Pedicle delay
EXCLUDES *pollicization or digital transfer (82.61,82.81)*
revision of pedicle (86.75)
DEF: Elevation of pedicle from its bed: Separation of tissue implanted from its bed.
DEF: Flap design and raising: Planing and elevation of tissue to be implanted.
DEF: Pedicle delay: Elevation and preparation of tissue still attached to vascular bed; delayed implant.
AHA: 4Q, '01, 66

86.72 **Advancement of pedicle graft**
AHA: 3Q, '99, 9, 10

86.73 **Attachment of pedicle or flap graft to hand**
EXCLUDES *pollicization or digital transfer (82.61, 82.81)*

86.74 **Attachment of pedicle or flap graft to other sites**
Attachment by:
advanced flap
double pedicled flap
pedicle graft
rotating flap
sliding flap
tube graft
DEF: Advanced flap: Sliding tissue implant into new position.
DEF: Double pedicle flap: Implant connected to two vascular beds.
DEF: Pedicle graft: Implant connected to vascular bed.
DEF: Rotating flap: Implant rotated along curved incision.
DEF: Sliding flap: Sliding implant to site.
DEF: Tube graft: Double tissue implant to form tube with base connected to original site.
AHA: 3Q, '99, 9; 1Q, '96, 15

86.75 **Revision of pedicle or flap graft**
Debridement } of pedicle or flap graft
Defatting
DEF: Connection of implant still attached to its vascular tissue.

✓4th **86.8** **Other repair and reconstruction of skin and subcutaneous tissue**

86.81 **Repair for facial weakness**

86.82 **Facial rhytidectomy**
Face lift
EXCLUDES *rhytidectomy of eyelid (08.86-08.87)*
DEF: Revision and tightening of excess, wrinkled facial skin.

Operations on the Integumentary System

86.83–86.99

86.83 Size reduction plastic operation

Liposuction

Reduction of adipose tissue of:

    abdominal wall (pendulous)

    arms (batwing)

    buttock

    thighs (trochanteric lipomatosis)

EXCLUDES   *breast (85.31-85.32)*

         liposuction to harvest fat graft (86.90)

DEF: Excision and plastic repair of excess skin and underlying tissue.

AHA: 2Q, '06, 10

TIP: Assign for abdominoplasty or panniculectomy performed after a morbid obesity surgical procedure and significant weight loss.

86.84 Relaxation of scar or web contracture of skin

Z-plasty of skin

EXCLUDES   *Z-plasty with excision of lesion (86.3)*

86.85 Correction of syndactyly

DEF: Plastic repair of webbed fingers or toes.

86.86 Onychoplasty

DEF: Plastic repair of nail or nail bed.

86.87 Fat graft of skin and subcutaneous tissue

INCLUDES   extraction of fat for autologous graft

Autologous fat transplantation or transfer

Fat graft NOS

Fat graft of skin and subcutaneous tissue with or without use of enriched graft

Micro-fat grafting

EXCLUDES   *fat graft to breast (85.55)*

AHA: ▶1Q, '13, 7◀

86.89 Other repair and reconstruction of skin and subcutaneous tissue

EXCLUDES   *mentoplasty (76.67-76.68)*

AHA: 4Q, '02, 107; 1Q, '00, 26; 2Q, '98, 20; 2Q, '93, 11; 2Q, '92, 17

✓4ᵗʰ 86.9 Other operations on skin and subcutaneous tissue

86.90 Extraction of fat for graft or banking

Harvest of fat for extraction of cells for future use

Liposuction to harvest fat graft

EXCLUDES   *that with graft at same operative episode (85.55, 86.87)*

86.91 Excision of skin for graft

Excision of skin with closure of donor site

EXCLUDES   *that with graft at same operative episode (86.60-86.69)*

86.92 Electrolysis and other epilation of skin

EXCLUDES   *epilation of eyelid (08.91-08.93)*

86.93 Insertion of tissue expander

Insertion (subcutaneous) (soft tissue) of expander (one or more) in scalp (subgaleal space), face, neck, trunk except breast, and upper and lower extremities for development of skin flaps for donor use

EXCLUDES   *flap graft preparation (86.71)*

         tissue expander, breast (85.95)

86.94 Insertion or replacement of single array neurostimulator pulse generator, not specified as rechargeable

Pulse generator (single array, single channel, single port) for intracranial, spinal, and peripheral neurostimulator

Code also any associated lead implantation (02.93, 03.93, 04.92)

EXCLUDES   *cranial implantation or replacement of neurostimulator pulse generator (01.20)*

         insertion or replacement of single array rechargeable neurostimulator pulse generator (86.97)

AHA: 4Q, '04, 135

86.95 Insertion or replacement of multiple array neurostimulator pulse generator, not specified as rechargeable

Pulse generator (multiple array, multiple channel, multiple port) for intracranial, spinal, and peripheral neurostimulator

Code also any associated lead implantation (02.93, 03.93, 04.92)

EXCLUDES   *cranial implantation or replacement of neurostimulator pulse generator (01.20)*

         insertion or replacement of (multiple array) rechargeable neurostimulator pulse generator (86.98)

86.96 Insertion or replacement of other neurostimulator pulse generator

Code also any associated lead implantation (02.93, 03.93, 04.92)

EXCLUDES   *cranial implantation or replacement of neurostimulator pulse generator (01.20)*

         insertion of multiple array neurostimulator pulse generator (86.95, 86.98)

         insertion of single array neurostimulator pulse generator (86.94, 86.97)

AHA: 2Q, '07, 8; 2Q, '06, 5-6

86.97 Insertion or replacement of single array rechargeable neurostimulator pulse generator

Rechargeable pulse generator (single array, single channel, single port) for intracranial, spinal, and peripheral neurostimulator

Code also any associated lead implantation (02.93, 03.93, 04.92)

EXCLUDES   *cranial implantation or replacement of neurostimulator pulse generator (01.20)*

AHA: 4Q, '05, 130

86.98 Insertion or replacement of multiple array (two or more) rechargeable neurostimulator pulse generator

Rechargeable pulse generator (multiple array, multiple channel, multiple port) for intracranial, spinal, and peripheral neurostimulator

Code also any associated lead implantation (02.93, 03.93, 04.92)

EXCLUDES   *cranial implantation or replacement of neurostimulator pulse generator (01.20)*

AHA: 4Q, '05, 130

86.99 Other

EXCLUDES   *removal of sutures from:*

         abdomen (97.83)

         head and neck (97.38)

         thorax (97.43)

         trunk NEC (97.84)

    wound catheter:

         irrigation (96.58)

         replacement (97.15)

AHA: 4Q, '97, 57; N-D, '86, 1

BI Bilateral Procedure   **NC** Non-covered Procedure   **LC** Limited Coverage Procedure   ▶◀ Revised Text   ● New Code   ▲ Revised Code Title

182 – Volume 3 · October 2014   **2015 ICD-9-CM**

16. Miscellaneous Diagnostic and Therapeutic Procedures (87-99)

✓3ʳᵈ 87   Diagnostic radiology

✓4ᵗʰ 87.0   Soft tissue x-ray of face, head, and neck
EXCLUDES angiography (88.40-88.68)

87.01   Pneumoencephalogram
DEF: Radiographic exam of cerebral ventricles and subarachnoid spaces with injection of air or gas for contrast.

87.02   Other contrast radiogram of brain and skull
Pneumocisternogram
Pneumoventriculogram
Posterior fossa myelogram
DEF: Pneumocisternogram: radiographic exam of subarachnoid spaces after injection of gas or contrast.
DEF: Pneumoventriculography: radiographic exam of cerebral ventricles after injection of gas or contrast.
DEF: Posterior fossa myelogram: radiographic exam of posterior channel of spinal cord after injection of gas or contrast.

87.03   Computerized axial tomography of head
C.A.T. scan of head
AHA: 3Q, '05, 12; 3Q, '99, 7

87.04   Other tomography of head

87.05   Contrast dacryocystogram
DEF: Radiographic exam of tear sac after injection of contrast.

87.06   Contrast radiogram of nasopharynx

87.07   Contrast laryngogram

87.08   Cervical lymphangiogram
DEF: Radiographic exam of lymph vessels of neck with or without contrast.

87.09   Other soft tissue x-ray of face, head, and neck
Noncontrast x-ray of:
  adenoid
  larynx
  nasolacrimal duct
  nasopharynx
  salivary gland
  thyroid region
  uvula
EXCLUDES x-ray study of eye (95.14)

✓4ᵗʰ 87.1   Other x-ray of face, head, and neck
EXCLUDES angiography (88.40-88.68)

87.11   Full-mouth x-ray of teeth

87.12   Other dental x-ray
Orthodontic cephalogram or cephalometrics
Panorex examination of mandible
Root canal x-ray

87.13   Temporomandibular contrast arthrogram

87.14   Contrast radiogram of orbit

87.15   Contrast radiogram of sinus

87.16   Other x-ray of facial bones
X-ray of:
  frontal area
  mandible
  maxilla
  nasal sinuses
  nose
  orbit
  supraorbital area
  symphysis menti
  zygomaticomaxillary complex

87.17   Other x-ray of skull
Lateral projection ⎫
Sagittal projection ⎬ of skull
Tangential projection ⎭
DEF: Lateral projection: Side to side view of head.
DEF: Sagittal projection: View of body in plane running midline from front to back.
DEF: Tangential projection: Views from adjacent skull surfaces.

✓4ᵗʰ 87.2   X-ray of spine

87.21   Contrast myelogram
DEF: Radiographic exam of space between middle and outer spinal cord coverings after injection of contrast.

87.22   Other x-ray of cervical spine

87.23   Other x-ray of thoracic spine

87.24   Other x-ray of lumbosacral spine
Sacrococcygeal x-ray

87.29   Other x-ray of spine
Spinal x-ray NOS

✓4ᵗʰ 87.3   Soft tissue x-ray of thorax
EXCLUDES angiocardiography (88.50-88.58)
          angiography (88.40-88.68)

87.31   Endotracheal bronchogram
DEF: Radiographic exam of main branch of lung with contrast introduced through windpipe.

87.32   Other contrast bronchogram
Transcricoid bronchogram
DEF: Transcricoid bronchogram: Radiographic exam of main branch of lung with contrast introduced through cartilage of neck.

87.33   Mediastinal pneumogram
DEF: Radiographic exam of cavity containing heart, esophagus and adjacent structures.

87.34   Intrathoracic lymphangiogram
DEF: Radiographic exam of lymphatic vessels within chest; with or without contrast.

87.35   Contrast radiogram of mammary ducts
DEF: Radiographic exam of mammary ducts; with contrast.

87.36   Xerography of breast
DEF: Radiographic exam of breast via selenium-coated plates.

87.37   Other mammography
AHA: 3Q, '89, 17; 2Q, '90, 28; N-D, '87, 1
TIP: Assign as an additional code when mammographic localization is performed immediately prior to breast lesion biopsy or excision. Wire localization is included.

87.38   Sinogram of chest wall
Fistulogram of chest wall
DEF: Fistulogram of chest wall: Radiographic exam of abnormal opening in chest.

87.39   Other soft tissue x-ray of chest wall

✓4ᵗʰ 87.4   Other x-ray of thorax
EXCLUDES angiocardiography (88.50-88.58)
          angiography (88.40-88.68)

87.41   Computerized axial tomography of thorax
C.A.T. scan of heart
C.A.T. scan ⎫
Crystal linea scan of x-ray beam ⎪
Electronic subtraction ⎬ of thorax
Photoelectric response ⎪
Tomography with use of computer, x-rays, and camera ⎭

87.42   Other tomography of thorax
Cardiac tomogram
EXCLUDES C.A.T. scan of heart (87.41)
DEF: Radiographic exam of chest plane.

87.43   X-ray of ribs, sternum, and clavicle
Examination for:
cervical rib
fracture

87.44   Routine chest x-ray, so described
X-ray of chest NOS

87.49   Other chest x-ray
X-ray of:
bronchus NOS
diaphragm NOS
heart NOS
lung NOS
mediastinum NOS
trachea NOS

✓4th   **87.5   Biliary tract x-ray**

87.51   Percutaneous hepatic cholangiogram
DEF: Radiographic exam of bile tract of gallbladder; with
needle injection of contrast into bile duct of liver.
AHA: 2Q, '90, 28; N-D, '87, 1

87.52   Intravenous cholangiogram
DEF: Radiographic exam of bile ducts; with intravenous
contrast injection.

87.53   Intraoperative cholangiogram
DEF: Radiographic exam of bile ducts with contrast;
following gallbladder removal.
AHA: 1Q, '96, 12; 2Q, '90, 28; 3Q, '89, 18; 4Q, '88, 7

87.54   Other cholangiogram

87.59   Other biliary tract x-ray
Cholecystogram

✓4th   **87.6   Other x-ray of digestive system**

87.61   Barium swallow

87.62   Upper GI series

87.63   Small bowel series

87.64   Lower GI series

87.65   Other x-ray of intestine

87.66   Contrast pancreatogram

87.69   Other digestive tract x-ray

✓4th   **87.7   X-ray of urinary system**
EXCLUDES   angiography of renal vessels (88.45, 88.65)

87.71   Computerized axial tomography of kidney
C.A.T. scan of kidney

87.72   Other nephrotomogram
DEF: Radiographic exam of kidney plane.

87.73   Intravenous pyelogram
Diuretic infusion pyelogram
DEF: Radiographic exam of lower kidney, with intravenous
contrast injection.
DEF: Diuretic infusion pyelogram: Radiographic exam of
lower kidney with diuretic contrast.

87.74   Retrograde pyelogram
TIP: The diagnostic cystoscopy service is included in the
retrograde pyelogram code; do not assign 57.32 separately.

87.75   Percutaneous pyelogram

87.76   Retrograde cystourethrogram
DEF: Radiographic exam of bladder and urethra with
contrast injected through catheter into bladder.

87.77   Other cystogram

87.78   Ileal conduitogram
DEF: Radiographic exam of passage created between ureter
and artificial opening into abdomen.
AHA: M-J, '87, 11

87.79   Other x-ray of the urinary system
KUB x-ray

Ureteropyelography

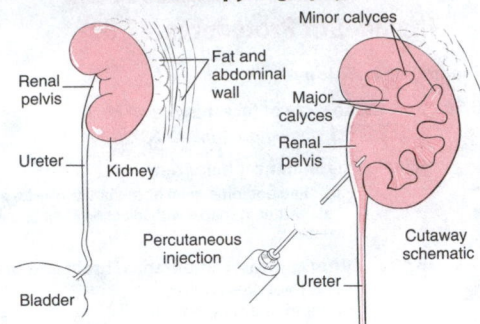

Minor calyces
Renal pelvis
Fat and abdominal wall
Major calyces
Renal pelvis
Ureter
Kidney
Percutaneous injection
Cutaway schematic
Ureter
Bladder

✓4th   **87.8   X-ray of female genital organs**

87.81   X-ray of gravid uterus   ♀
Intrauterine cephalometry by x-ray

87.82   Gas contrast hysterosalpingogram   ♀
DEF: Radiographic exam of uterus and fallopian tubes with
gas contrast.

87.83   Opaque dye contrast hysterosalpingogram   ♀

87.84   Percutaneous hysterogram   ♀
DEF: Radiographic exam of uterus with contrast
injected through body wall.

87.85   Other x-ray of fallopian tubes and uterus ♀

87.89   Other x-ray of female genital organs   ♀

✓4th   **87.9   X-ray of male genital organs**

87.91   Contrast seminal vesiculogram   ♂

87.92   Other x-ray of prostate and seminal vesicles ♂

87.93   Contrast epididymogram   ♂

87.94   Contrast vasogram   ♂

87.95   Other x-ray of epididymis and vas deferens ♂

87.99   Other x-ray of male genital organs   ♂

✓3rd   **88   Other diagnostic radiology and related techniques**

✓4th   **88.0   Soft tissue x-ray of abdomen**
EXCLUDES   angiography (88.40-88.68)

88.01   Computerized axial tomography of abdomen
C.A.T. scan of abdomen
EXCLUDES   C.A.T. scan of kidney (87.71)
AHA: 2Q, '98, 13

88.02   Other abdomen tomography
EXCLUDES   nephrotomogram (87.72)

88.03   Sinogram of abdominal wall
Fistulogram of abdominal wall
DEF: Radiographic exam of abnormal abdominal passage.

88.04   Abdominal lymphangiogram
DEF: Radiographic exam of abdominal lymphatic vessels
with contrast.

88.09   Other soft tissue x-ray of abdominal wall

✓4th   **88.1   Other x-ray of abdomen**

88.11   Pelvic opaque dye contrast radiography

88.12   Pelvic gas contrast radiography
Pelvic pneumoperitoneum

88.13   Other peritoneal pneumogram

88.14   Retroperitoneal fistulogram

88.15   **Retroperitoneal pneumogram**

88.16   **Other retroperitoneal x-ray**

88.19   **Other x-ray of abdomen**
Flat plate of abdomen
AHA: 3Q, '99, 9

✓4ᵗʰ 88.2   **Skeletal x-ray of extremities and pelvis**
EXCLUDES   contrast radiogram of joint (88.32)

88.21   **Skeletal x-ray of shoulder and upper arm**

88.22   **Skeletal x-ray of elbow and forearm**

88.23   **Skeletal x-ray of wrist and hand**

88.24   **Skeletal x-ray of upper limb, not otherwise specified**

88.25   **Pelvimetry**
DEF: Imaging of pelvic bones to measure pelvic capacity.

88.26   **Other skeletal x-ray of pelvis and hip**

88.27   **Skeletal x-ray of thigh, knee, and lower leg**

88.28   **Skeletal x-ray of ankle and foot**

88.29   **Skeletal x-ray of lower limb, not otherwise specified**

✓4ᵗʰ 88.3   **Other x-ray**

88.31   **Skeletal series**
X-ray of whole skeleton

88.32   **Contrast arthrogram**
EXCLUDES   that of temporomandibular joint (87.13)

88.33   **Other skeletal x-ray**
EXCLUDES   skeletal x-ray of:
extremities and pelvis (88.21-88.29)
face, head, and neck (87.11-87.17)
spine (87.21-87.29)
thorax (87.43)

88.34   **Lymphangiogram of upper limb**

88.35   **Other soft tissue x-ray of upper limb**

88.36   **Lymphangiogram of lower limb**

88.37   **Other soft tissue x-ray of lower limb**
EXCLUDES   femoral angiography (88.48, 88.66)

88.38   **Other computerized axial tomography**
C.A.T. scan NOS
EXCLUDES   C.A.T. scan of:
abdomen (88.01)
head (87.03)
heart (87.41)
kidney (87.71)
thorax (87.41)
AHA: 3Q, '05, 13-14

88.39   **X-ray, other and unspecified**

✓4ᵗʰ 88.4   **Arteriography using contrast material**
NOTE   The fourth-digit subclassification identifies the site to be viewed, not the site of injection.
INCLUDES   angiography of arteries
arterial puncture for injection of contrast material
radiography of arteries (by fluoroscopy)
retrograde arteriography
EXCLUDES   arteriography using:
radioisotopes or radionuclides (92.01-92.19)
ultrasound (88.71-88.79)
fluorescein angiography of eye (95.12)
DEF: Electromagnetic wave photography of arteries with contrast.
AHA: N-D, '85, 14

88.40   **Arteriography using contrast material, unspecified site**

88.41   **Arteriography of cerebral arteries**
Angiography of:
basilar artery
carotid (internal)
vertebral artery
posterior cerebral circulation
AHA: 1Q, '00, 16; 1Q, '99, 7; 1Q, '97, 3

88.42   **Aortography**
Arteriography of aorta and aortic arch
AHA: 2Q, '10, 8-9; 1Q, '99, 17

88.43   **Arteriography of pulmonary arteries**

88.44   **Arteriography of other intrathoracic vessels**
EXCLUDES   angiocardiography (88.50-88.58)
arteriography of coronary arteries (88.55-88.57)

88.45   **Arteriography of renal arteries**

88.46   **Arteriography of placenta**   ♀
Placentogram using contrast material

88.47   **Arteriography of other intra-abdominal arteries**
AHA: 2Q, '09, 7; 1Q, '00, 18; N-D, '87, 4

88.48   **Arteriography of femoral and other lower extremity arteries**
AHA: 2Q, '06, 23; 3Q, '03, 10; 1Q, '03, 17; 2Q, '96, 6; 2Q, '89, 17

88.49   **Arteriography of other specified sites**
AHA: 2Q, '10, 8-9

✓4ᵗʰ 88.5   **Angiocardiography using contrast material**
INCLUDES   arterial puncture and insertion of arterial catheter for injection of contrast material
cineangiocardiography
selective angiocardiography

Code also synchronous cardiac catheterization (37.21-37.23)
EXCLUDES   angiography of pulmonary vessels (88.43, 88.62)
DEF: Electromagnetic wave photography of heart and great vessels with contrast.
AHA: 3Q, '08, 18; 3Q, '92, 10; M-J, '87, 11

88.50   **Angiocardiography, not otherwise specified**

88.51   **Angiocardiography of venae cavae**
Inferior vena cavography
Phlebography of vena cava (inferior) (superior)

88.52   **Angiocardiography of right heart structures**
Angiocardiography of:
pulmonary valve
right atrium
right ventricle (outflow tract)
EXCLUDES   intra-operative fluorescence vascular angiography (88.59)
that combined with left heart angiocardiography (88.54)
AHA: 1Q, '07, 16

88.53   **Angiocardiography of left heart structures**
Angiocardiography of:
aortic valve
left atrium
left ventricle (outflow tract)
EXCLUDES   intra-operative fluorescence vascular angiography (88.59)
that combined with right heart angiocardiography (88.54)
AHA: 1Q, '07, 11, 17; 4Q, '05, 71; 3Q, '05, 14; 1Q, '00, 20; 4Q, '88, 4

88.54   **Combined right and left heart angiocardiography**
EXCLUDES   intra-operative fluorescence vascular angiography (88.59)

88.55   **Coronary arteriography using a single catheter**
Coronary arteriography by Sones technique
Direct selective coronary arteriography using a single catheter
EXCLUDES   intra-operative fluorescence vascular angiography (88.59)
AHA: 2Q, '06, 25-26; 3Q, '02, 20

88.56   **Coronary arteriography using two catheters**
Coronary arteriography by:
Judkins technique
Ricketts and Abrams technique
Direct selective coronary arteriography using two catheters
EXCLUDES   intra-operative fluorescence vascular angiography (88.59)
AHA: 3Q, '06, 8; 1Q, '00, 20; 4Q, '88, 4

88.57 Other and unspecified coronary arteriography

Coronary arteriography NOS

EXCLUDES *intra-operative fluorescence vascular angiography (88.59)*

AHA: 1Q, '07, 15; 2Q, '06, 25; 4Q, '05, 71; 3Q, '05, 14; 2Q, '05, 17; 1Q, '00, 21

88.58 Negative-contrast cardiac roentgenography

Cardiac roentgenography with injection of carbon dioxide

88.59 Intra-operative coronary fluorescence vascular angiography

Intraoperative laser arteriogram (SPY)

SPY arteriogram

SPY arteriography

DEF: Coronary artery bypass grafting (CABG) procedure imaging technology; utilizes dye with high-speed digital infrared photography. Sequence is performed for each graft; provides information on graft patency, vessel size, blood flow velocities.

AHA: 4Q, '10, 114-115; 4Q, '07, 121

✓4ᵗʰ **88.6 Phlebography**

NOTE The fourth-digit subclassification (88.60-88.67) identifies the site to be viewed, not the site of injection.

INCLUDES angiography of veins

radiography of veins (by fluoroscopy)

retrograde phlebography

venipuncture for injection of contrast material

venography using contrast material

EXCLUDES *angiography using:*

radioisotopes or radionuclides (92.01-92.19)

ultrasound (88.71-88.79)

fluorescein angiography of eye (95.12)

DEF: Electromagnetic wave photography of veins with contrast.

88.60 Phlebography using contrast material, unspecified site

88.61 Phlebography of veins of head and neck using contrast material

88.62 Phlebography of pulmonary veins using contrast material

88.63 Phlebography of other intrathoracic veins using contrast material

AHA: 3Q, '08, 18

88.64 Phlebography of the portal venous system using contrast material

Splenoportogram (by splenic arteriography)

88.65 Phlebography of other intra-abdominal veins using contrast material

88.66 Phlebography of femoral and other lower extremity veins using contrast material

AHA: 2Q, '06, 23

88.67 Phlebography of other specified sites using contrast material

88.68 Impedance phlebography

✓4ᵗʰ **88.7 Diagnostic ultrasound**

INCLUDES echography

non-invasive ultrasound

ultrasonic angiography

ultrasonography

EXCLUDES *intravascular imaging (adjunctive) (IVUS) (00.21-00.29)*

that for intraoperative monitoring (00.94)

therapeutic ultrasound (00.01-00.09)

DEF: Graphic recording of anatomical structures via high frequency, sound-wave imaging and computer graphics.

AHA: 3Q, '12, 6

88.71 Diagnostic ultrasound of head and neck

Determination of midline shift of brain

Echoencephalography

EXCLUDES *eye (95.13)*

AHA: 1Q, '02, 10; 1Q, '92, 11

88.72 Diagnostic ultrasound of heart

Echocardiography

Transesophageal echocardiography

EXCLUDES *echocardiography of heart chambers (37.28)*

intracardiac echocardiography (ICE) (37.28)

intravascular (IVUS) imaging of coronary vessels (00.24)

AHA: 1Q, '07, 11; 3Q, '05, 14; 2Q, '05, 17; 4Q, '04, 121; 1Q, '04, 16; 1Q, '00, 20, 21; 1Q, '99, 6; 3Q, '98, 11

TIP: Assign also code 42.23 Esophagoscopy, NEC, when a transesophageal echocardiogram is performed.

88.73 Diagnostic ultrasound of other sites of thorax

Aortic arch ⎫

Breast ⎬ ultrasonography

Lung ⎭

88.74 Diagnostic ultrasound of digestive system

88.75 Diagnostic ultrasound of urinary system

88.76 Diagnostic ultrasound of abdomen and retroperitoneum

AHA: 2Q, '99, 14

88.77 Diagnostic ultrasound of peripheral vascular system

Deep vein thrombosis ultrasonic scanning

EXCLUDES *adjunct vascular system procedures (00.40-00.43)*

AHA: 4Q, '99, 17; 1Q, '99, 12; 1Q, '92, 11

88.78 Diagnostic ultrasound of gravid uterus ♀

Intrauterine cephalometry:

echo

ultrasonic

Placental localization by ultrasound

AHA: 2Q, '10, 6-7; 4Q, '08, 125

88.79 Other diagnostic ultrasound

Ultrasonography of:

multiple sites

nongravid uterus

total body

✓4ᵗʰ **88.8 Thermography**

DEF: Infrared photography to determine various body temperatures.

88.81 Cerebral thermography

88.82 Ocular thermography

88.83 Bone thermography

Osteoarticular thermography

88.84 Muscle thermography

88.85 Breast thermography

88.86 Blood vessel thermography

Deep vein thermography

88.89 Thermographay of other sites

Lymph gland thermography

Thermography NOS

✓4ᵗʰ **88.9 Other diagnostic imaging**

88.90 Diagnostic imaging, not elsewhere classified

AHA: 2Q, '06, 25-26

88.91 Magnetic resonance imaging of brain and brain stem

EXCLUDES *intraoperative magnetic resonance imaging (88.96)*

laser interstitial thermal therapy [LITT] of lesion or tissue of brain under guidance (17.61)

real-time magnetic resonance imaging (88.96)

AHA: ▶3Q, '13, 10◀

BI Bilateral Procedure   NC Non-covered Procedure   LC Limited Coverage Procedure   ▶◀ Revised Text   ● New Code   ▲ Revised Code Title

88.92 Magnetic resonance imaging of chest and myocardium
For evaluation of hilar and mediastinal lymphadenopathy
EXCLUDES *laser interstitial thermal therapy [LITT] of lesion or tissue of breast under guidance (17.69)*
laser interstitial thermal therapy [LITT] of lesion or tissue of lung under guidance (17.69)
AHA: 2Q, '10, 13

88.93 Magnetic resonance imaging of spinal canal
Spinal cord levels:
cervical
thoracic
lumbar (lumbosacral)
Spinal cord
Spine

88.94 Magnetic resonance imaging of musculoskeletal
Bone marrow blood supply
Extremities (upper) (lower)

88.95 Magnetic resonance imaging of pelvis, prostate, and bladder
EXCLUDES *laser interstitial thermal therapy (LITT) of lesion or tissue of prostate under guidance (17.69)*

88.96 Other intraoperative magnetic resonance imaging
iMRI
Real-time magnetic resonance imaging
AHA: 4Q, '02, 111

88.97 Magnetic resonance imaging of other and unspecified sites
Abdomen
Eye orbit
Face
Neck
EXCLUDES *laser interstitial thermal therapy (LITT) of lesion or tissue of other and unspecified site under guidance (17.69)*

88.98 Bone mineral density studies
Dual photon absorptiometry
Quantitative computed tomography (CT) studies
Radiographic densitometry
Single photon absorptiometry
DEF: Dual photon absorptiometry: Measurement of bone mineral density by comparing dissipation of emission from two separate photoelectric energy peaks.
DEF: Quantitative computed tomography (CT) studies: Computer assisted analysis of x-ray absorption through bone to determine density.
DEF: Radiographic densiometry: Measurement of bone mineral density by degree of bone radiopacity.
DEF: Single photon absorptiometry: Measurement of bone mineral density by degree of dissipation of emission from one photoelectric energy peak emitted by gadolinium 153.

√3rd 89 Interview, evaluation, consultation, and examination

√4th 89.0 Diagnostic interview, consultation, and evaluation
EXCLUDES *psychiatric diagnostic interview (94.11-94.19)*

89.01 Interview and evaluation, described as brief
Abbreviated history and evaluation

89.02 Interview and evaluation, described as limited
Interval history and evaluation

89.03 Interview and evaluation, described as comprehensive
History and evaluation of new problem

89.04 Other interview and evaluation

89.05 Diagnostic interview and evaluation, not otherwise specified

89.06 Consultation, described as limited
Consultation on a single organ system

89.07 Consultation, described as comprehensive

89.08 Other consultation

89.09 Consulation, not otherwise specified

√4th 89.1 Anatomic and physiologic measurements and manual examinations — nervous system and sense organs
EXCLUDES *ear examination (95.41-95.49)*
eye examination (95.01-95.26)
the listed procedures when done as part of a general physical examination (89.7)

89.10 Intracarotid amobarbital test
Wada test
DEF: Amobarbital injections into internal carotid artery to induce hemiparalysis to determine the hemisphere that controls speech and language.

89.11 Tonometry
DEF: Pressure measurements inside eye.

89.12 Nasal function study
Rhinomanometry
DEF: Rhinomanometry: Measure of degree of nasal cavity obstruction.

89.13 Neurologic examination

89.14 Electroencephalogram
EXCLUDES *that with polysomnogram (89.17)*
DEF: Recording of electrical currents in brain via electrodes to detect epilepsy, lesions and other encephalopathies.
AHA: ▶3Q, '13, 10;◀ 3Q, '05, 12

89.15 Other nonoperative neurologic function tests
AHA: 3Q, '95, 5; 2Q, '91, 14; J-F, '87, 16; N-D, '84, 6

89.16 Transillumination of newborn skull
DEF: Light passed through newborn skull for diagnostic purposes.

89.17 Polysomnogram
Sleep recording
DEF: Graphic studies of sleep patterns.

89.18 Other sleep disorder function tests
Multiple sleep latency test [MSLT]

89.19 Video and radio-telemetered electroencephalographic monitoring
Radiographic } EEG Monitoring
Video
EXCLUDES *intraoperative monitoring (00.94)*
AHA: 1Q, '92, 17; 2Q, '90, 27

√4th 89.2 Anatomic and physiologic measurements and manual examinations — genitourinary system
EXCLUDES *the listed procedures when done as part of a general physical examination (89.7)*
AHA: 1Q, '90, 27

89.21 Urinary manometry
Manometry through:
indwelling ureteral catheter
nephrostomy
pyelostomy
ureterostomy
DEF: Measurement of urinary pressure by:
Indwelling urinary catheter: Semipermanent urinary catheter.
Nephrostomy: Opening into pelvis of kidney.
Pyelostomy: Opening in lower kidney.
Ureterostomy: Opening into ureter.

89.22 Cystometrogram
DEF: Pressure recordings at various stages of bladder filling.

89.23 Urethral sphincter electromyogram

89.24 Uroflowmetry [UFR]
DEF: Continuous recording of urine flow.

89.25 Urethral pressure profile [UPP]

89.26 Gynecological examination ♀
Pelvic examination

89.29 Other nonoperative genitourinary system measurements
Bioassay of urine
Renal clearance
Urine chemistry
AHA: N-D, '84, 6

√4ᵗʰ 89.3 Other anatomic and physiologic measurements and manual examinations

> EXCLUDES *the listed procedures when done as part of a general physical examination (89.7)*

89.31 Dental examination
Oral mucosal survey
Periodontal survey

89.32 Esophageal manometry
DEF: Measurement of esophageal fluid and gas pressures.
AHA: 3Q, '96, 13

89.33 Digital examination of enterostomy stoma
Digital examination of colostomy stoma

89.34 Digital examination of rectum

89.35 Transillumination of nasal sinuses

89.36 Manual examination of breast

89.37 Vital capacity determination
> EXCLUDES *endoscopic pulmonary airway flow measurement (33.72)*

DEF: Measurement of expelled gas volume after full inhalation.

89.38 Other nonoperative respiratory measurements
Plethysmography for measurement of respiratory function
Thoracic impedance plethysmography
> EXCLUDES *endoscopic pulmonary airway flow measurement (33.72)*

DEF: Plethysmography for measurement of respiratory function: Registering changes in respiratory function as noted in blood circulation.
AHA: S-O, '87, 6

89.39 Other nonoperative measurements and examinations
^{14}C-Urea breath test
Basal metabolic rate [BMR]
Gastric:
   analysis
   function NEC
> EXCLUDES *body measurement (93.07)*
> *cardiac tests (89.41-89.69)*
> *fundus photography (95.11)*
> *limb length measurement (93.06)*

AHA: 2Q, '01, 9; 3Q, '00, 9; 3Q, '96, 12; 1Q, '94, 18; N-D, '84, 6
TIP: Assign for Kinevac stimulation of the gallbladder, performed for analysis of function and examination of bile.

√4ᵗʰ 89.4 Cardiac stress tests, pacemaker and defibrillator checks

89.41 Cardiovascular stress test using treadmill
AHA: 1Q, '88, 11

89.42 Masters' two-step stress test
AHA: 1Q, '88, 11

89.43 Cardiovascular stress test using bicycle ergometer
DEF: Electrocardiogram during exercise on bicycle with device capable of measuring muscular, metabolic and respiratory effects of exercise.
AHA: 1Q, '88, 11

89.44 Other cardiovascular stress test
Thallium stress test with or without transesophageal pacing

89.45 Artificial pacemaker rate check
Artificial pacemaker function check NOS
Bedside device check of pacemaker or cardiac resynchronization pacemaker [CRT-P]
Interrogation only without arrhythmia induction
> EXCLUDES *catheter based invasive electrophysiologic testing (37.26)*
> *non-invasive programmed electrical stimulation [NIPS] (arrhythmia induction) (37.20)*

AHA: 3Q, '10, 9; 1Q, '02, 3

89.46 Artificial pacemaker artifact wave form check

89.47 Artificial pacemaker electrode impedance check

89.48 Artificial pacemaker voltage or amperage threshold check

89.49 Automatic implantable cardioverter/ defibrillator (AICD) check
Bedside check of an AICD or cardiac resynchronization defibrillator [CRT-D]
Checking pacing thresholds of device
Interrogation only without arrhythmia induction
> EXCLUDES *catheter based invasive electrophysiologic testing (37.26)*
> *non-invasive programmed electrical stimulation [NIPS] (arrhythmia induction) (37.20)*

AHA: 4Q, '04, 136

√4ᵗʰ 89.5 Other nonoperative cardiac and vascular diagnostic procedures
> EXCLUDES *fetal EKG (75.32)*

89.50 Ambulatory cardiac monitoring
Analog devices [Holter-type]
AHA: 4Q, '99, 21; 4Q, '91, 23

89.51 Rhythm electrocardiogram
Rhythm EKG (with one to three leads)

89.52 Electrocardiogram
ECG NOS
EKG (with 12 or more leads)
AHA: 1Q, '88, 11; S-O, '87, 6

89.53 Vectorcardiogram (with ECG)

89.54 Electrographic monitoring
Telemetry
> EXCLUDES *ambulatory cardiac monitoring (89.50)*
> *electrographic monitoring during surgery — omit code*

DEF: Evaluation of heart electrical activity by continuous screen monitoring.
DEF: Telemetry: Evaluation of heart electrical activity; with radio signals at distance from patient.
AHA: 4Q, '91, 23; 1Q, '88, 11

89.55 Phonocardiogram with ECG lead

89.56 Carotid pulse tracing with ECG lead
> EXCLUDES *oculoplethysmography (89.58)*

89.57 Apexcardiogram (with ECG lead)
AHA: J-F, '87, 16

89.58 Plethysmogram
Penile plethysmography with nerve stimulation
> EXCLUDES *plethysmography (for):*
> *measurement of respiratory function (89.38)*
> *thoracic impedance (89.38)*

DEF: Determination and recording of blood pressure variations present or passing through an organ.
AHA: S-O, '87, 7

89.59 Other nonoperative cardiac and vascular measurements
AHA: 2Q, '10, 11; 3Q, '05, 21; 3Q, '03, 23; 2Q, '92, 12

√4ᵗʰ 89.6 Circulatory monitoring
> EXCLUDES *electrocardiographic monitoring during surgery — omit code*
> *implantation or replacement of subcutaneous device for intracardiac hemodynamic monitoring (00.57)*
> *insertion or replacement of implantable pressure sensor (lead) for intracardiac hemodynamic monitoring (00.56)*

AHA: M-J, '87, 11

89.60 Continuous intra-arterial blood gas monitoring
Insertion of blood gas monitoring system and continuous monitoring of blood gases through an intra-arterial sensor
AHA: 4Q, '02, 111

BI Bilateral Procedure   NC Non-covered Procedure   LC Limited Coverage Procedure   ►◄ Revised Text   ● New Code   ▲ Revised Code Title

188 – Volume 3   2015 ICD-9-CM

Central Venous Pressure Monitoring

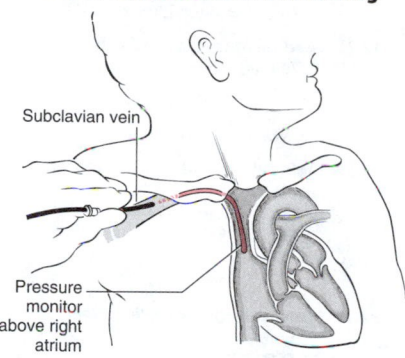

Subclavian vein

Pressure monitor above right atrium

89.61 Systemic arterial pressure monitoring
> **EXCLUDES** *intra-aneurysm sac pressure monitoring (intraoperative) (00.58)*
> *intravascular pressure measurement of intrathoracic arteries (00.67)*
> *intravascular pressure measurement of peripheral arteries (00.68)*

89.62 Central venous pressure monitoring
> **EXCLUDES** *intravascular pressure measurement, other specified and unspecified vessels (00.69)*

89.63 Pulmonary artery pressure monitoring
> **EXCLUDES** *pulmonary artery wedge monitoring (89.64)*

89.64 Pulmonary artery wedge monitoring
> Pulmonary capillary wedge [PCW] monitoring
> Swan-Ganz catheterization
> **DEF:** Monitoring pulmonary artery pressure via catheter inserted through right lower and upper heart chambers into pulmonary artery and advancing the balloon-tip to wedge it in the distal pulmonary artery branch.

89.65 Measurement of systemic arterial blood gases
> **EXCLUDES** *continuous intra-arterial blood gas monitoring (89.60)*

89.66 Measurement of mixed venous blood gases

89.67 Monitoring of cardiac output by oxygen consumption technique
> Fick method
> **DEF:** Fick method: Indirect measure of cardiac output through blood volume flow over pulmonary capillaries; determines oxygen absorption by measurement of arterial oxygen content versus venous oxygen content.

89.68 Monitoring of cardiac output by other technique
> Cardiac output monitor by thermodilution indicator
> **DEF:** Cardiac output monitor by thermodilution indicator: Injection of ice cold dextrose solution into right lower heart chamber; temperature sensitive catheter monitors disappearance from beat to beat to measure expelled blood volume.

89.69 Monitoring of coronary blood flow
> Coronary blood flow monitoring by coincidence counting technique
> **EXCLUDES** *intravascular pressure measurement of coronary arteries (00.59)*

89.7 General physical examination

89.8 Autopsy

√3rd **90 Microscopic examination - I**

The following fourth-digit subclassification is for use with categories in section 90 to identify type of examination:
1 bacterial smear
2 culture
3 culture and sensitivity
4 parasitology
5 toxicology
6 cell block and Papanicolaou smear
9 other microscopic examination

§ √4th **90.0** Microscopic examination of specimen from nervous
[1-6,9] system and of spinal fluid

§ √4th **90.1** Microscopic examination of specimen from endocrine
[1-6,9] gland, not elsewhere classified

§ √4th **90.2** Microscopic examination of specimen from eye
[1-6,9]

§ √4th **90.3** Microscopic examination of specimen from ear, nose,
[1-6,9] throat, and larynx

§ √4th **90.4** Microscopic examination of specimen from trachea,
[1-6,9] bronchus, pleura, lung, and other thoracic specimen, and of sputum

§ √4th **90.5** Microscopic examination of blood
[1-6,9]

§ √4th **90.6** Microscopic examination of specimen from spleen and of
[1-6,9] bone marrow

§ √4th **90.7** Microscopic examination of specimen from lymph node
[1-6,9] and of lymph

§ √4th **90.8** Microscopic examination of specimen from upper
[1-6,9] gastrointestinal tract and of vomitus

§ √4th **90.9** Microscopic examination of specimen from lower
[1-6,9] gastrointestinal tract and of stool

√3rd **91 Microscopic examination - II**

The following fourth-digit subclassification is for use with categories in section 91 to identify type of examination:
1 bacterial smear
2 culture
3 culture and sensitivity
4 parasitology
5 toxicology
6 cell block and Papanicolaou smear
9 other microscopic examination

§ √4th **91.0** Microscopic examination of specimen from liver, biliary
[1-6,9] tract, and pancreas

§ √4th **91.1** Microscopic examination of peritoneal and retroperitoneal
[1-6,9] specimen

§ √4th **91.2** Microscopic examination of specimen from kidney,
[1-6,9] ureter, perirenal and periureteral tissue

§ √4th **91.3** Microscopic examination of specimen from bladder,
[1-6,9] urethra, prostate, seminal vesicle, perivesical tissue, and of urine and semen

§ √4th **91.4** Microscopic examination of specimen from female ♀
[1-6,9] genital tract
> Amnionic sac
> Fetus

§ √4th **91.5** Microscopic examination of specimen from
[1-6,9] musculoskeletal system and of joint fluid
> Microscopic examination of:
> bone
> bursa
> cartilage
> fascia
> ligament
> muscle
> synovial membrane
> tendon

---

§   Requires fourth digit. Valid digits are in [brackets] under each code. See appropriate category for codes and definitions.

√3rd √4th **Additional Digit Required**   Valid OR Procedure   Non-OR Procedure   Adjunct Code

§ ✓4th **91.6 Microscopic examination of specimen from skin and**
[1-6,9] **other integument**
Microscopic examination of:
hair
nails
skin
EXCLUDES *mucous membrane — code to organ site*
that of operative wound (91.71-91.79)

§ ✓4th **91.7 Microscopic examination of specimen from operative**
[1-6,9] **wound**

§ ✓4th **91.8 Microscopic examination of specimen from other site**
[1-6,9]

§ ✓4th **91.9 Microscopic examination of specimen from unspecified**
[1-6,9] **site**

✓3rd **92 Nuclear medicine**

✓4th **92.0 Radioisotope scan and function study**

92.01 Thyroid scan and radioisotope function studies
Iodine-131 uptake
Protein-bound iodine
Radio-iodine uptake

92.02 Liver scan and radioisotope function study

92.03 Renal scan and radioisotope function study
Renal clearance study

92.04 Gastrointestinal scan and radioisotope function
study
Radio-cobalt B$_{12}$ Schilling test
Radio-iodinated triolein study

92.05 Cardiovascular and hematopoietic scan and
radioisotope function study
Bone marrow
Cardiac output
Circulation time   } scan or function
Radionuclide cardiac   study
    ventriculogram
Spleen
AHA: 2Q, '92, 7; 1Q, '88, 11

92.09 Other radioisotope function studies

✓4th **92.1 Other radioisotope scan**

92.11 Cerebral scan
Pituitary

92.12 Scan of other sites of head
EXCLUDES *eye (95.16)*

92.13 Parathyroid scan

92.14 Bone scan

92.15 Pulmonary scan

92.16 Scan of lymphatic system

92.17 Placental scan   ♀

92.18 Total body scan

92.19 Scan of other sites

✓4th **92.2 Therapeutic radiology and nuclear medicine**
EXCLUDES *that for:*
ablation of pituitary gland (07.64-07.69)
destruction of chorioretinal lesion (14.26-14.27)
DEF: Radiation and nuclear isotope treatment of diseased tissue.
AHA: 3Q, '92, 5

92.20 Infusion of liquid brachytherapy radioisotope
I-125 radioisotope
Intracavitary brachytherapy
EXCLUDES *removal of radioisotope*
AHA: 4Q, '05, 117-118
TIP: Refer to codes 01.26 and 01.27 for placement or
removal of balloon catheter used for liquid brachytherapy
radioisotope infusion.

92.21 Superficial radiation
Contact radiation [up to 150 KVP]

92.22 Orthovoltage radiation
Deep radiation [200-300 KVP]

92.23 Radioisotopic teleradiotherapy
Teleradiotherapy using:
cobalt-60
iodine-125
radioactive cesium

92.24 Teleradiotherapy using photons
Megavoltage NOS
Supervoltage NOS
Use of:
Betatron
linear accelerator

92.25 Teleradiotherapy using electrons
Beta particles
EXCLUDES *intra-operative electron radiation therapy*
(92.41)

92.26 Teleradiotherapy of other particulate radiation
Neutrons
Protons NOS

92.27 Implantation or insertion of radioactive elements
Intravascular brachytherapy
Code also incision of site
EXCLUDES *infusion of liquid brachytherapy radioisotope*
(92.20)
AHA: 1Q, '04, 3-4; 1Q, '00, 11, 12; 3Q, '94, 11; 1Q, '88, 4

92.28 Injection or instillation of radioisotopes
Injection or infusion of radioimmunoconjugate
Intracavitary injection or instillation
Intravenous injection or instillation
Iodine-131 [I-131] tositumomab
Radioimmunotherapy
Ytrium-90 [Y-90] ibritumomab tiuxetan
EXCLUDES *infusion of liquid brachytherapy radioisotope*
(92.20)

92.29 Other radiotherapeutic procedure
AHA: ▶1Q, '13, 8;◀ 3Q, '06, 14-15

✓4th **92.3 Stereotactic radiosurgery**
Code also stereotactic head frame application (93.59)
EXCLUDES *stereotactic biopsy*
DEF: Ablation of deep intracranial lesions; single procedure;
placement of head frame for 3-D analysis of lesion, followed by
radiation treatment from helmet attached to frame.
AHA: 4Q, '98, 79; 4Q, '95, 70
TIP: Do not assign when stereotactic technique is used to obtain the
coordinates for the exact location of a brain tumor, after which open
craniotomy is performed. See instead subcategory 01.5.

92.30 Stereotactic radiosurgery, not otherwise
specified

92.31 Single source photon radiosurgery
High energy x-rays
Linear accelerator (LINAC)
AHA: ▶4Q, '13, 89◀

92.32 Multi-source photon radiosurgery
Cobalt 60 radiation
Gamma irradiation
AHA: 4Q, '04, 113

92.33 Particulate radiosurgery
Particle beam radiation (cyclotron)
Proton accelerator

92.39 Stereotactic radiosurgery, not elsewhere
classified

✓4th **92.4 Intra-operative radiation procedures**

92.41 Intra-operative electron radiation therapy
IOERT
That using a mobile linear accelerator
DEF: Use of a mobile linear accelerator unit that delivers
precision electron radiation beam radiation to highly
focused anatomic sites, protecting the normal surrounding
tissues from exposure.
AHA: 4Q, '07, 122

---

§ Requires fourth digit. Valid digits are in [brackets] under each code. See category 91 for codes and definitions.

BI Bilateral Procedure   NC Non-covered Procedure   LC Limited Coverage Procedure   ▶◀ Revised Text   ● New Code   ▲ Revised Code Title

✓3rd **93   Physical therapy, respiratory therapy, rehabilitation, and related procedures**

✓4th   **93.0   Diagnostic physical therapy**
AHA: N-D, '86, 7

93.01   Functional evaluation

93.02   Orthotic evaluation

93.03   Prosthetic evaluation

93.04   Manual testing of muscle function
AHA: J-F, '87, 16

93.05   Range of motion testing
AHA: J-F, '87, 16

93.06   Measurement of limb length

93.07   Body measurement
Girth measurement
Measurement of skull circumference

93.08   Electromyography
EXCLUDES   eye EMG (95.25)
that for intraoperative monitoring (00.94)
that with polysomnogram (89.17)
urethral sphincter EMG (89.23)
DEF: Graphic recording of electrical activity of muscle.
AHA: J-F, '87, 16

93.09   Other diagnostic physical therapy procedure

✓4th   **93.1   Physical therapy exercises**
AHA: J-F, '87, 16; N-D, '86, 7

93.11   Assisting exercise
EXCLUDES   assisted exercise in pool (93.31)

93.12   Other active musculoskeletal exercise

93.13   Resistive exercise

93.14   Training in joint movements

93.15   Mobilization of spine

93.16   Mobilization of other joints
EXCLUDES   manipulation of temporomandibular joint (76.95)

93.17   Other passive musculoskeletal exercise

93.18   Breathing exercise

93.19   Exercise, not elsewhere classified

✓4th   **93.2   Other physical therapy musculoskeletal manipulation**
AHA: N-D, '86, 7

93.21   Manual and mechanical traction
EXCLUDES   skeletal traction (93.43-93.44)
skin traction (93.45-93.46)
spinal traction (93.41-93.42)

93.22   Ambulation and gait training

93.23   Fitting of orthotic device

93.24   Training in use of prosthetic or orthotic device
Training in crutch walking

93.25   Forced extension of limb

93.26   Manual rupture of joint adhesions
DEF: Therapeutic application of force to rupture adhesions restricting movement.

93.27   Stretching of muscle or tendon

93.28   Stretching of fascia

93.29   Other forcible correction of deformity
AHA: N-D, '85, 11

✓4th   **93.3   Other physical therapy therapeutic procedures**

93.31   Assisted exercise in pool

93.32   Whirlpool treatment

93.33   Other hydrotherapy

93.34   Diathermy

93.35   Other heat therapy
Acupuncture with smouldering moxa
Hot packs
Hyperthermia NEC
Infrared irradiation
Moxibustion
Paraffin bath
EXCLUDES   hyperthermia for treatment of cancer (99.85)
DEF: Moxibustion: Igniting moxa, a Chinese plant, for counterirritation of skin.
DEF: Paraffin bath: Hot wax treatment.

93.36   Cardiac retraining
DEF: Cardiac rehabilitation regimen following myocardial infarction or coronary bypass graft procedure.

93.37   Prenatal training
Training for natural childbirth

93.38   Combined physical therapy without mention of the components

93.39   Other physical therapy
AHA: 2Q, '05, 6; 4Q, '03, 105 -106, 108-110; 3Q, '97, 12; 3Q, '91, 15

✓4th   **93.4   Skeletal traction and other traction**

93.41   Spinal traction using skull device
Traction using:
caliper tongs
Crutchfield tongs
halo device
Vinke tongs
EXCLUDES   insertion of tongs or halo traction device (02.94)
DEF: Applying device to head to exert pulling force on spine.
AHA: 3Q, '01, 8; 3Q, '96, 14; 2Q, '94, 3

93.42   Other spinal traction
Cotrel's traction
EXCLUDES   cervical collar (93.52)
DEF: Pulling force exerted on spine without skull device.

93.43   Intermittent skeletal traction

93.44   Other skeletal traction
Bryant's
Dunlop's   } traction
Lyman Smith
Russell's

93.45   Thomas' splint traction
DEF: Thomas splint: Placement of ring around thigh, attached to rods running length of leg for therapeutic purposes.

93.46   Other skin traction of limbs
Adhesive tape traction
Boot traction
Buck's traction
Gallows traction

✓4th   **93.5   Other immobilization, pressure, and attention to wound**
EXCLUDES   external fixator device (84.71-84.73)
wound cleansing (96.58-96.59)

93.51   Application of plaster jacket
EXCLUDES   Minerva jacket (93.52)

93.52   Application of neck support
Application of:
cervical collar
Minerva jacket
molded neck support

93.53   Application of other cast

93.54   Application of splint
Plaster splint
Tray splint
EXCLUDES   periodontal splint (24.7)

93.55   Dental wiring
EXCLUDES   that for orthodontia (24.7)

Miscellaneous Diagnostic and Therapeutic Procedures

93.56–93.98

93.56   Application of pressure dressing
Application of:
Gibney bandage
Robert Jones' bandage
Shanz dressing

93.57   Application of other wound dressing
Porcine wound dressing
AHA: ►4Q, '13, 97;◄ 3Q, '12, 15; 3Q, '02, 23
TIP: Assign for MatriStem (extracellular matrix wound powder) when applied to damaged or amputated skin to facilitate tissue regeneration and promote wound healing.

93.58   Application of pressure trousers
Application of:
anti-shock trousers
MAST trousers
vasopneumatic device
AHA: 3Q, '96, 13

93.59   Other immobilization, pressure, and attention to wound
Elastic stockings
Electronic gaiter
Intermittent pressure device
Oxygenation of wound (hyperbaric)
Stereotactic head frame application
Strapping (non-traction)
Velpeau dressing
AHA: 3Q, '99, 7; 1Q, '99, 12, 13; 1Q, '91, 11; 1Q, '89, 12

✓4th 93.6   Osteopathic manipulative treatment

93.61   Osteopathic manipulative treatment for general mobilization
General articulatory treatment

93.62   Osteopathic manipulative treatment using high-velocity, low-amplitude forces
Thrusting forces

93.63   Osteopathic manipulative treatment using low-velocity, high-amplitude forces
Springing forces

93.64   Osteopathic manipulative treatment using isotonic, isometric forces

93.65   Osteopathic manipulative treatment using indirect forces

93.66   Osteopathic manipulative treatment to move tissue fluids
Lymphatic pump

93.67   Other specified osteopathic manipulative treatment

✓4th 93.7   Speech and reading rehabilitation and rehabilitation of the blind

93.71   Dyslexia training

93.72   Dysphasia training
DEF: Speech training to coordinate and arrange words in proper sequence.

93.73   Esophageal speech training
DEF: Speech training after voice box removal; sound is produced by vibration of air column in esophagus against the cricopharangeal sphincter.

93.74   Speech defect training

93.75   Other speech training and therapy
AHA: 4Q, '03, 105, 109; 4Q, '97, 36; 3Q, '97, 12

93.76   Training in use of lead dog for the blind

93.77   Training in braille or Moon

93.78   Other rehabilitation for the blind

✓4th 93.8   Other rehabilitation therapy

93.81   Recreational therapy
Diversional therapy
Play therapy
EXCLUDES   play psychotherapy (94.36)

93.82   Educational therapy
Education of bed-bound children
Special schooling for the handicapped

93.83   Occupational therapy
Daily living activities therapy
EXCLUDES   training in activities of daily living for the blind (93.78)
AHA: 2Q, '05, 6; 4Q, '03, 105-106, 108, 110; 3Q, '97, 12

93.84   Music therapy

93.85   Vocational rehabilitation
Sheltered employment
Vocational:
assessment
retraining
training

93.89   Rehabilitation, not elsewhere classified
AHA: 2Q, '05, 6

✓4th 93.9   Respiratory therapy
EXCLUDES   insertion of airway (96.01-96.05)
other continuous invasive (through endotracheal tube or tracheostomy) mechanical ventilation (96.70-96.72)

93.90   Non-invasive mechanical ventilation
NOTE   Patients admitted on *non-invasive* mechanical ventilation that subsequently require *invasive* mechanical ventilation; code both types of mechanical ventilation
Bi-level airway pressure
BiPAP without (delivery through) endotracheal tube or tracheostomy
CPAP without (delivery through) endotracheal tube or tracheostomy
Mechanical ventilation NOS
Non-invasive positive pressure (NIPPV)
Non-invasive PPV
NPPV
That delivered by non-invasive interface:
face mask
nasal mask
nasal pillow
oral mouthpiece
oronasal mask
EXCLUDES   invasive (through endotracheal tube or tracheostomy) continuous mechanical ventilation (96.70-96.72)
DEF: Noninvasive ventilation support system that augments the ability to breathe spontaneously without the insertion of an endotracheal tube or tracheostomy.
AHA: 4Q, '08, 187-189; 1Q, '08, 8-9; 3Q, '04, 3; 1Q, '02, 12, 13; 3Q, '98, 14; 4Q, '91, 21

93.91   Intermittent positive pressure breathing [IPPB]
AHA: 4Q, '91, 21

93.93   Nonmechanical methods of resuscitation
Artificial respiration
Manual resuscitation
Mouth-to-mouth resuscitition
AHA: 2Q, '03, 17

93.94   Respiratory medication administered by nebulizer
Mist therapy

93.95   Hyperbaric oxygenation
EXCLUDES   oxygenation of wound (93.59)

93.96   Other oxygen enrichment
Catalytic oxygen therapy
Cytoreductive effect
Oxygenators
Oxygen therapy
EXCLUDES   oxygenation of wound (93.59)
SuperSaturated oxygen therapy (00.49)

93.97   Decompression chamber

93.98   Other control of atmospheric pressure and composition
Antigen-free air conditioning
Helium therapy
EXCLUDES   inhaled nitric oxide therapy (INO) (00.12)
AHA: 1Q, '02, 14

93.99 **Other respiratory procedures**
Continuous negative pressure ventilation [CNP]
Postural drainage
AHA: 4Q, '03, 108; 3Q, '99, 11; 4Q, '91, 22

✓3ʳᵈ **94** **Procedures related to the psyche**

✓4ᵗʰ **94.0** **Psychologic evaluation and testing**

94.01 **Administration of intelligence test**
Administration of:
Stanford-Binet
Wechsler Adult Intelligence Scale
Wechsler Intelligence Scale for Children

94.02 **Administration of psychologic test**
Administration of:
Bender Visual-Motor Gestalt Test
Benton Visual Retention Test
Minnesota Multiphasic Personality Inventory
Wechsler Memory Scale

94.03 **Character analysis**

94.08 **Other psychologic evaluation and testing**

94.09 **Psychologic mental status determination, not otherwise specified**

✓4ᵗʰ **94.1** **Psychiatric interviews, consultations, and evaluations**

94.11 **Psychiatric mental status determination**
Clinical psychiatric mental status determination
Evaluation for criminal responsibility
Evaluation for testimentary capacity
Medicolegal mental status determination
Mental status determination NOS

94.12 **Routine psychiatric visit, not otherwise specified**

94.13 **Psychiatric commitment evaluation**
Pre-commitment interview

94.19 **Other psychiatric interview and evaluation**
Follow-up psychiatric interview NOS

✓4ᵗʰ **94.2** **Psychiatric somatotherapy**
DEF: Biological treatment of mental disorders.

94.21 **Narcoanalysis**
Narcosynthesis

94.22 **Lithium therapy**

94.23 **Neuroleptic therapy**

94.24 **Chemical shock therapy**

94.25 **Other psychiatric drug therapy**
AHA: S-O, '86, 4

94.26 **Subconvulsive electroshock therapy**

94.27 **Other electroshock therapy**
Electroconvulsive therapy (ECT)
EST

94.29 **Other psychiatric somatotherapy**

✓4ᵗʰ **94.3** **Individual psychotherapy**

94.31 **Psychoanalysis**

94.32 **Hypnotherapy**
Hypnodrome
Hypnosis

94.33 **Behavior therapy**
Aversion therapy
Behavior modification
Desensitization therapy
Extinction therapy
Relaxation training
Token economy

94.34 **Individual therapy for psychosexual dysfunction**
EXCLUDES that performed in group setting (94.41)

94.35 **Crisis intervention**

94.36 **Play psychotherapy**

94.37 **Exploratory verbal psychotherapy**

94.38 **Supportive verbal psychotherapy**

94.39 **Other individual psychotherapy**
Biofeedback

✓4ᵗʰ **94.4** **Other psychotherapy and counseling**

94.41 **Group therapy for psychosexual dysfunction**

94.42 **Family therapy**

94.43 **Psychodrama**

94.44 **Other group therapy**

94.45 **Drug addiction counseling**

94.46 **Alcoholism counseling**

94.49 **Other counseling**

✓4ᵗʰ **94.5** **Referral for psychologic rehabilitation**

94.51 **Referral for psychotherapy**

94.52 **Referral for psychiatric aftercare**
That in:
halfway house
outpatient (clinic) facility

94.53 **Referral for alcoholism rehabilitation**

94.54 **Referral for drug addiction rehabilitation**

94.55 **Referral for vocational rehabilitation**

94.59 **Referral for other psychologic rehabilitation**

✓4ᵗʰ **94.6** **Alcohol and drug rehabilitation and detoxification**
AHA: 2Q, '91, 12

94.61 **Alcohol rehabilitation**
DEF: Program designed to restore social and physical functioning, free of the dependence of alcohol.

94.62 **Alcohol detoxification**
DEF: Treatment of physical symptoms during withdrawal from alcohol dependence.

94.63 **Alcohol rehabilitation and detoxification**

94.64 **Drug rehabilitation**
DEF: Program designed to restore social and physical functioning, free of the dependence of drugs.

94.65 **Drug detoxification**
DEF: Treatment of physical symptoms during withdrawal from drug dependence.

94.66 **Drug rehabilitation and detoxification**

94.67 **Combined alcohol and drug rehabilitation**

94.68 **Combined alcohol and drug detoxification**

94.69 **Combined alcohol and drug rehabilitation and detoxification**

✓3ʳᵈ **95** **Ophthalmologic and otologic diagnosis and treatment**

✓4ᵗʰ **95.0** **General and subjective eye examination**

95.01 **Limited eye examination**
Eye examination with prescription of spectacles

95.02 **Comprehensive eye examination**
Eye examination covering all aspects of the visual system

95.03 **Extended ophthalmologic work-up**
Examination (for):
glaucoma
neuro-ophthalmology
retinal disease

95.04 **Eye examination under anesthesia**
Code also type of examination

95.05 **Visual field study**

95.06 **Color vision study**

95.07 **Dark adaptation study**
DEF: Exam of eye's adaption to dark.

95.09 **Eye examination, not otherwise specified**
Vision check NOS

✓3ʳᵈ ✓4ᵗʰ Additional Digit Required   Valid OR Procedure   Non-OR Procedure   Adjunct Code

Miscellaneous Diagnostic and Therapeutic Procedures

95.1–96.25

✓4th **95.1** **Examinations of form and structure of eye**

95.11 **Fundus photography**

95.12 **Fluorescein angiography or angioscopy of eye**

95.13 **Ultrasound study of eye**

95.14 **X-ray study of eye**

95.15 **Ocular motility study**

95.16 **P$_{32}$ and other tracer studies of eye**

✓4th **95.2** **Objective functional tests of eye**
> EXCLUDES *that with polysomnogram (89.17)*

95.21 **Electroretinogram [ERG]**

95.22 **Electro-oculogram [EOG]**

95.23 **Visual evoked potential [VEP]**
> DEF: Measuring and recording evoked visual responses of body and senses.

95.24 **Electronystagmogram [ENG]**
> DEF: Monitoring of brain waves to record induced and spontaneous eye movements.

95.25 **Electromyogram of eye [EMG]**

95.26 **Tonography, provocative tests, and other glaucoma testing**

✓4th **95.3** **Special vision services**

95.31 **Fitting and dispensing of spectacles**

95.32 **Prescription, fitting, and dispensing of contact lens**

95.33 **Dispensing of other low vision aids**

95.34 **Ocular prosthetics**

95.35 **Orthoptic training**

95.36 **Ophthalmologic counselling and instruction**
Counselling in:
adaptation to visual loss
use of low vision aids

✓4th **95.4** **Nonoperative procedures related to hearing**

95.41 **Audiometry**
Békésy 5-tone audiometry
Impedance audiometry
Stapedial reflex response
Tympanogram
Subjective audiometry

95.42 **Clinical test of hearing**
Tuning fork test
Whispered speech test

95.43 **Audiological evaluation**
Audiological evaluation by:
Bárány noise machine
blindfold test
delayed feedback
masking
Weber lateralization

95.44 **Clinical vestibular function tests**
Thermal test of vestibular function

95.45 **Rotation tests**
Bárány chair
> DEF: Irrigation of ear canal with warm or cold water to evaluate vestibular function.

95.46 **Other auditory and vestibular function tests**

95.47 **Hearing examination, not otherwise specified**

95.48 **Fitting of hearing aid**
> EXCLUDES *implantation of electromagnetic hearing device (20.95)*
>
> AHA: 4Q, '89, 5

95.49 **Other nonoperative procedures related to hearing**
Adjustment (external components) of cochlear prosthetic device

Endotracheal Intubation

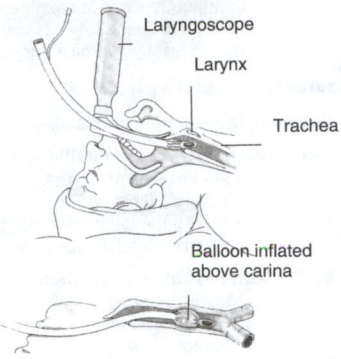

Laryngoscope

Larynx

Trachea

Balloon inflated above carina

✓3rd **96** **Nonoperative intubation and irrigation**

✓4th **96.0** **Nonoperative intubation of gastrointestinal and respiratory tracts**

96.01 **Insertion of nasopharyngeal airway**

96.02 **Insertion of oropharyngeal airway**

96.03 **Insertion of esophageal obturator airway**

96.04 **Insertion of endotracheal tube**
> AHA: ▶1Q, '13, 10;◀ 4Q, '10, 80; 2Q, '09, 11; 1Q, '07, 11; 2Q, '06, 8; 4Q, '05, 88; 3Q, '05, 10; 2Q, '05, 19

96.05 **Other intubation of respiratory tract**
> EXCLUDES *endoscopic insertion or replacement of bronchial device or substance (33.71, 33.79)*
>
> AHA: 1Q, '97, 14

96.06 **Insertion of Sengstaken tube**
Esophageal tamponade
> DEF: Insertion of Sengstaken tube: Nonsurgical emergency measure to stop esophageal bleeding using compression exerted by inflated balloons; additional tube ports to aspirate blood and clots.

96.07 **Insertion of other (naso-) gastric tube**
Intubation for decompression
> EXCLUDES *that for enteral infusion of nutritional substance (96.6)*
>
> AHA: 4Q, '08, 139

96.08 **Insertion of (naso-) intestinal tube**
Miller-Abbott tube (for decompression)
> AHA: 3Q, '12, 23

96.09 **Insertion of rectal tube**
Replacement of rectal tube

✓4th **96.1** **Other nonoperative insertion**
> EXCLUDES *nasolacrimal intubation (09.44)*

96.11 **Packing of external auditory canal**

96.14 **Vaginal packing** ♀

96.15 **Insertion of vaginal mold** ♀

96.16 **Other vaginal dilation** ♀

96.17 **Insertion of vaginal diaphragm** ♀

96.18 **Insertion of other vaginal pessary** ♀

96.19 **Rectal packing**

✓4th **96.2** **Nonoperative dilation and manipulation**

96.21 **Dilation of frontonasal duct**

96.22 **Dilation of rectum**

96.23 **Dilation of anal sphincter**

96.24 **Dilation and manipulation of enterostomy stoma**

96.25 **Therapeutic distention of bladder**
Intermittent distention of bladder

BI Bilateral Procedure   **NC** Non-covered Procedure   **LC** Limited Coverage Procedure   ▶◀ Revised Text   ● New Code   ▲ Revised Code Title

194 – Volume 3 • October 2014   2015 ICD-9-CM

96.26   **Manual reduction of rectal prolapse**

96.27   **Manual reduction of hernia**

96.28   **Manual reduction of enterostomy prolapse**
      AHA: N-D, '87, 11

96.29   **Reduction of intussusception of alimentary tract**
      With:
         fluoroscopy
         ionizing radiation enema
         ultrasonography guidance
      Hydrostatic reduction
      Pneumatic reduction
      EXCLUDES   *intra-abdominal manipulation of intestine,*
                   not otherwise specified (46.80)
      AHA: 4Q, '98, 82

√4ᵗʰ   **96.3**   **Nonoperative alimentary tract irrigation, cleaning, and local instillation**

96.31   **Gastric cooling**
      Gastric hypothermia
      DEF: Reduction of internal stomach temperature.

96.32   **Gastric freezing**

96.33   **Gastric lavage**

96.34   **Other irrigation of (naso-)gastric tube**

96.35   **Gastric gavage**
      DEF: Food forced into stomach.

96.36   **Irrigation of gastrostomy or enterostomy**

96.37   **Proctoclysis**
      DEF: Slow introduction of large amounts of fluids into lower large intestine.

96.38   **Removal of impacted feces**
      Removal of impaction:
         by flushing manually

96.39   **Other transanal enema**
      Rectal irrigation
      EXCLUDES   *reduction of intussusception of alimentary*
                   tract by ionizing radiation enema
                   (96.29)
      AHA: 3Q, '12, 23

√4ᵗʰ   **96.4**   **Nonoperative irrigation, cleaning, and local instillation of other digestive and genitourinary organs**

96.41   **Irrigation of cholecystostomy and other biliary tube**

96.42   **Irrigation of pancreatic tube**

96.43   **Digestive tract instillation, except gastric gavage**

96.44   **Vaginal douche**   ♀

96.45   **Irrigation of nephrostomy and pyelostomy**

96.46   **Irrigation of ureterostomy and ureteral catheter**

96.47   **Irrigation of cystostomy**

96.48   **Irrigation of other indwelling urinary catheter**

96.49   **Other genitourinary instillation**
      Insertion of prostaglandin suppository
      AHA: 1Q, '01, 5

√4ᵗʰ   **96.5**   **Other nonoperative irrigation and cleaning**

96.51   **Irrigation of eye**
      Irrigation of cornea
      EXCLUDES   *irrigation with removal of foreign body*
                   (98.21)

96.52   **Irrigation of ear**
      Irrigation with removal of cerumen

96.53   **Irrigation of nasal passages**

96.54   **Dental scaling, polishing, and debridement**
      Dental prophylaxis
      Plaque removal

96.55   **Tracheostomy toilette**

96.56   **Other lavage of bronchus and trachea**
      EXCLUDES   *diagnostic bronchoalveolar lavage (BAL)*
                   (33.24)
                   whole lung lavage (33.99)
      AHA: 3Q, '02, 18

96.57   **Irrigation of vascular catheter**
      AHA: 3Q, '93, 5

96.58   **Irrigation of wound catheter**

96.59   **Other irrigation of wound**
      Wound cleaning NOS
      EXCLUDES   *debridement (86.22, 86.27-86.28)*
      AHA: 3Q, '12, 3; S-O, '85, 7

96.6   **Enteral infusion of concentrated-nutritional substances**

√4ᵗʰ   **96.7**   **Other continuous invasive mechanical ventilation**
      BiPAP delivered through endotracheal tube or tracheostomy (invasive interface)
      CPAP delivered through endotracheal tube or tracheostomy (invasive interface)
      Endotracheal respiratory assistance
      Invasive positive pressure ventilation [IPPV]
      Mechanical ventilation through invasive interface
      That by tracheostomy
      Weaning of an intubated (endotracheal tube) patient
      Code also any associated:
         endotracheal tube insertion (96.04)
         tracheostomy (31.1-31.29)
      EXCLUDES   *continuous negative pressure ventilation [CNP] (iron*
                   lung) (cuirass) (93.99)
                   intermittent positive pressure breathing [IPPB] (93.91)
                   non-invasive bi-level positive airway pressure [BiPAP] (93.90)
                   non-invasive continuous positive airway pressure [CPAP] (93.90)
                   non-invasive positive pressure (NIPPV) (93.90)
                   that by face mask (93.90-93.99)
                   that by nasal cannula (93.90-93.99)
                   that by nasal catheter (93.90-93.99)

NOTE   **Endotracheal intubation**

To calculate the number of hours (duration) of continuous mechanical ventilation during a hospitalization, begin the count from the start of the (endotracheal) intubation. The duration ends with (endotracheal) extubation.

If a patient is intubated prior to admission, begin counting the duration from the time of the admission. If a patient is transferred (discharged) while intubated, the duration would end at the time of transfer (discharge).

For patients who begin on (endotracheal) intubation and subsequently have a tracheostomy performed for mechanical ventilation, the duration begins with the (endotracheal) intubation and ends when the mechanical ventilation is turned off (after the weaning period).

NOTE   **Tracheostomy**

To calculate the number of hours of continuous mechanical ventilation during a hospitalization, begin counting the duration when mechanical ventilation is started. The duration ends when the mechanical ventilator is turned off (after the weaning period).

If a patient has received a tracheostomy prior to admission and is on mechanical ventilation at the time of admission, begin counting the duration from the time of admission. If a patient is transferred (discharged) while still on mechanical ventilation via tracheostomy, the duration would end at the time of the transfer (discharge).

AHA: ▶2Q, '13, 25; 1Q, '13, 12-13;◀ 3Q, '10, 3-4; 4Q, '08, 187-190 3Q, '04, 3; 2Q, '92, 13; 4Q, '91, 16; 4Q, '91, 18; 4Q, '91, 21

TIP: Do not assign if the patient is not intubated or does not have a tracheostomy. Refer to subcategory 93.9 for noninvasive mechanical ventilation.

96.70   **Continuous invasive mechanical ventilation of unspecified duration**
Invasive mechanical ventilation NOS

96.71   **Continuous invasive mechanical ventilation for less than 96 consecutive hours**
AHA: ▶1Q, '13, 10;◀ 4Q, '10, 80; 2Q, '09, 11; 3Q, '07, 6; 2Q, '06, 8; 3Q, '05, 10; 3Q, '04, 11; 2Q, '02, 19; 1Q, '02, 12; 1Q, '01, 6

[13]96.72   **Continuous invasive mechanical ventilation for 96 consecutive hours or more**
AHA: ▶1Q, '13, 12;◀ 2Q, '05, 19; 1Q, '04, 23

✓3rd **97   Replacement and removal of therapeutic appliances**

✓4th **97.0   Nonoperative replacement of gastrointestinal appliance**

97.01   **Replacement of (naso-)gastric or esophagostomy tube**

97.02   **Replacement of gastrostomy tube**
AHA: 1Q, '97, 11

97.03   **Replacement of tube or enterostomy device of small intestine**
AHA: 1Q, '03, 10

97.04   **Replacement of tube or enterostomy device of large intestine**

97.05   **Replacement of stent (tube) in biliary or pancreatic duct**
AHA: 2Q, '99, 13

✓4th **97.1   Nonoperative replacement of musculoskeletal and integumentary system appliance**

97.11   **Replacement of cast on upper limb**

97.12   **Replacement of cast on lower limb**

97.13   **Replacement of other cast**

97.14   **Replacement of other device for musculoskeletal immobilization**
Splinting
Strapping

97.15   **Replacement of wound catheter**

97.16   **Replacement of wound packing or drain**
EXCLUDES repacking of:
dental wound (97.22)
vulvar wound (97.26)

✓4th **97.2   Other nonoperative replacement**

97.21   **Replacement of nasal packing**

97.22   **Replacement of dental packing**

97.23   **Replacement of tracheostomy tube**
AHA: N-D, '87, 11

97.24   **Replacement and refitting of vagina diaphragm**   ♀

97.25   **Replacement of other vaginal pessary**   ♀

97.26   **Replacement of vaginal or vulvar packing or drain**   ♀

97.29   **Other nonoperative replacements**
AHA: 3Q, '99, 9; 3Q, '98, 12

✓4th **97.3   Nonoperative removal of therapeutic device from head and neck**

97.31   **Removal of eye prosthesis**
EXCLUDES removal of ocular implant (16.71)
removal of orbital implant (16.72)

97.32   **Removal of nasal packing**

97.33   **Removal of dental wiring**

97.34   **Removal of dental packing**

97.35   **Removal of dental prosthesis**

97.36   **Removal of other external mandibular fixation device**

97.37   **Removal of tracheostomy tube**

97.38   **Removal of sutures from head and neck**

Intraaortic Balloon Pump

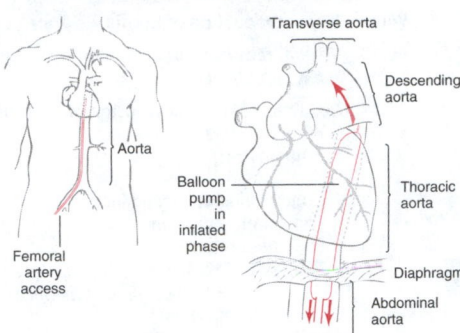

97.39   **Removal of other therapeutic device from head and neck**
EXCLUDES removal of skull tongs (02.94)

✓4th **97.4   Nonoperative removal of therapeutic device from thorax**

97.41   **Removal of thoracotomy tube or pleural cavity drain**
AHA: 1Q, '99, 10

97.42   **Removal of mediastinal drain**

97.43   **Removal of sutures from thorax**

97.44   **Nonoperative removal of heart assist system**
Explantation [removal] of circulatory assist device
Explantation [removal] of percutaneous external heart assist device
Removal of extrinsic heart assist device
Removal of pVAD
Removal of percutaneous heart assist device
DEF: Non-invasive removal of ventricular assist systems, or intraaortic balloon pump, which is a balloon catheter placed into the descending thoracic aorta and timed to inflate and deflate with the patient's own heart rhythm to aid in blood circulation.
AHA: 4Q, '01, 65

97.49   **Removal of other device from thorax**
EXCLUDES endoscopic removal of bronchial device(s) or substances (33.78)
AHA: N-D, '86, 9

✓4th **97.5   Nonoperative removal of therapeutic device from digestive system**

97.51   **Removal of gastrostomy tube**

97.52   **Removal of tube from small intestine**

97.53   **Removal of tube from large intestine or appendix**

97.54   **Removal of cholecystostomy tube**

97.55   **Removal of T-tube, other bile duct tube, or liver tube**
Removal of bile duct stent
AHA:1Q, '01, 8
TIP: Assign also code 51.10 if a biliary stent was removed via ERCP guidance.

97.56   **Removal of pancreatic tube or drain**

97.59   **Removal of other device from digestive system**
Removal of rectal packing

✓4th **97.6   Nonoperative removal of therapeutic device from urinary system**

97.61   **Removal of pyelostomy and nephrostomy tube**
DEF: Nonsurgical removal of tubes from lower part of kidney.

97.62   **Removal of ureterostomy tube and ureteral catheter**

97.63   **Removal of cystostomy tube**

97.64   **Removal of other urinary drainage device**
Removal of indwelling urinary catheter

97.65   **Removal of urethral stent**

---

[13] LOS must be => 4 days

BI Bilateral Procedure   **NC** Non-covered Procedure   **LC** Limited Coverage Procedure   ▶◀ Revised Text   ● New Code   ▲ Revised Code Title

196 – Volume 3 · October 2014   **2015 ICD-9-CM**

97.69   Removal of other device from urinary system

✓4th   **97.7**   Nonoperative removal of therapeutic device from genital system

     97.71   Removal of intrauterine contraceptive device   ♀

     97.72   Removal of intrauterine pack   ♀

     97.73   Removal of vaginal diaphragm   ♀

     97.74   Removal of other vaginal pessary   ♀

     97.75   Removal of vaginal or vulvar packing   ♀

     97.79   Removal of other device from genital tract
               Removal of sutures

✓4th   **97.8**   Other nonoperative removal of therapeutic device

     97.81   Removal of retroperitoneal drainage device

     97.82   Removal of peritoneal drainage device
               AHA: 2Q, '90, 28; S-O, '86, 12

     97.83   Removal of abdominal wall sutures

     97.84   Removal of sutures from trunk, not elsewhere classified

     97.85   Removal of packing from trunk, not elsewhere classified

     97.86   Removal of other device from abdomen

     97.87   Removal of other device from trunk

     97.88   Removal of external immobilization device
               Removal of:
                   brace
                   cast
                   splint

     97.89   Removal of other therapeutic device

✓3rd   **98**   **Nonoperative removal of foreign body or calculus**

✓4th   **98.0**   Removal of intraluminal foreign body from digestive system without incision
         EXCLUDES removal of therapeutic device (97.51-97.59)
         DEF: Retrieval of foreign body from digestive system lining without incision.

     98.01   Removal of intraluminal foreign body from mouth without incision

     98.02   Removal of intraluminal foreign body from esophagus without incision

     98.03   Removal of intraluminal foreign body from stomach and small intestine without incision

     98.04   Removal of intraluminal foreign body from large intestine without incision

     98.05   Removal of intraluminal foreign body from rectum and anus without incision

✓4th   **98.1**   Removal of intraluminal foreign body from other sites without incision
         EXCLUDES removal of therapeutic device (97.31-97.49, 97.61-97.89)

     98.11   Removal of intraluminal foreign body from ear without incision

     98.12   Removal of intraluminal foreign body from nose without incision

     98.13   Removal of intraluminal foreign body from pharynx without incision

     98.14   Removal of intraluminal foreign body from larynx without incision

     98.15   Removal of intraluminal foreign body from trachea and bronchus without incision
         EXCLUDES endoscopic removal of bronchial device(s) or substances (33.78)

     98.16   Removal of intraluminal foreign body from uterus without incision   ♀
         EXCLUDES removal of intrauterine contraceptive device (97.71)

     98.17   Removal of intraluminal foreign body from vagina without incision   ♀

     98.18   Removal of intraluminal foreign body from artificial stoma without incision

     98.19   Removal of intraluminal foreign body from urethra without incision

✓4th   **98.2**   Removal of other foreign body without incision
         EXCLUDES removal of intraluminal foreign body (98.01-98.19)

     98.20   Removal of foreign body, not otherwise specified

     98.21   Removal of superficial foreign body from eye without incision

     98.22   Removal of other foreign body without incision from head and neck
               Removal of embedded foreign body from eyelid or conjunctiva without incision

     98.23   Removal of foreign body from vulva without incision   ♀

     98.24   Removal of foreign body from scrotum or penis without incision   ♂

     98.25   Removal of other foreign body without incision from trunk except scrotum, penis, or vulva

     98.26   Removal of foreign body from hand without incision
               AHA: N-D, '87, 10

     98.27   Removal of foreign body without incision from upper limb, except hand

     98.28   Removal of foreign body from foot without incision

     98.29   Removal of foreign body without incision from lower limb, except foot

✓4th   **98.5**   Extracorporeal shockwave lithotripsy [ESWL]
         Lithotriptor tank procedure
         Disintegration of stones by extracorporeal induced shockwaves
         That with insertion of stent
         DEF: Breaking of stones with high voltage condenser device synchronized with patient R waves.

     98.51   Extracorporeal shockwave lithotripsy [ESWL] of the kidney, ureter and/or bladder
               AHA: 4Q, '95, 73; 1Q, '89, 2
               TIP: If the lithotripsy is documented with an endoscopic approach (e.g., cystoscopic), do not assign 98.51, assign instead 56.0 and 59.95; if by percutaneous nephrostomy, do not assign 98.51, assign instead 55.04.

     98.52   Extracorporeal shockwave lithotripsy [ESWL] of the gallbladder and/or bile duct   `NC`

     98.59   Extracorporeal shockwave lithotripsy of other sites   `NC`

Extracorporeal Shock Wave Lithotripsy

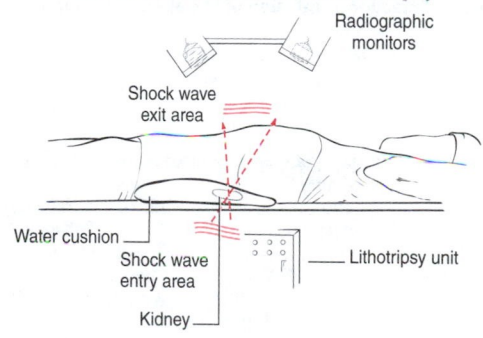

✓3rd ✓4th   Additional Digit Required   Valid OR Procedure   Non-OR Procedure   Adjunct Code

Miscellaneous Diagnostic and Therapeutic Procedures

99–99.24

√3ʳᵈ **99   Other nonoperative procedures**

√4ᵗʰ **99.0   Transfusion of blood and blood components**
Use additional code for that done via catheter or cutdown (38.92-38.94)

99.00   Perioperative autologous transfusion of whole blood or blood components
Intraoperative blood collection
Postoperative blood collection
Salvage
DEF: Salvaging patient blood with reinfusion during perioperative period.
AHA: 4Q, '95, 69

99.01   Exchange transfusion
Transfusion:
    exsanguination
    replacement
DEF: Repetitive withdrawal of blood, replaced by donor blood.
AHA: 2Q, '89, 15

99.02   Transfusion of previously collected autologous blood
Blood component
DEF: Transfusion with patient's own previously withdrawn and stored blood.
AHA: 4Q, '95, 69; 1Q, '90, 10; J-A, '85, 16

99.03   Other transfusion of whole blood
Transfusion:
    blood NOS
    hemodilution
    NOS

99.04   Transfusion of packed cells
AHA: 4Q, '11, 146; 4Q, '10, 80

99.05   Transfusion of platelets
Transfusion of thrombocytes

99.06   Transfusion of coagulation factors
Transfusion of antihemophilic factor
EXCLUDES   infusion of 4-Factor Prothrombin Complex Concentrate (00.96)

99.07   Transfusion of other serum
Transfusion of plasma
EXCLUDES   injection [transfusion] of:
    antivenin (99.16)
    gamma globulin (99.14)

99.08   Transfusion of blood expander
Transfusion of Dextran

99.09   Transfusion of other substance
Transfusion of:
    blood surrogate
    granulocytes
EXCLUDES   transplantation [transfusion] of bone marrow (41.00-41.09)
AHA: 1Q, '11, 24

√4ᵗʰ **99.1   Injection or infusion of therapeutic or prophylactic substance**
INCLUDES   injection or infusion given:
    hypodermically   ⎫
    intramuscularly   ⎬ acting locally or
    intravenously   ⎭   systemically

99.10   Injection or infusion of thrombolytic agent
Alteplase   Tenecteplase
Anistreplase   Tissue plasminogen activator
Reteplase   (TPA)
Streptokinase   Urokinase
EXCLUDES   aspirin — omit code
    GP IIb/IIIa platelet inhibitors (99.20)
    heparin (99.19)
    SuperSaturated oxygen therapy (00.49)
    warfarin — omit code
AHA: ▶4Q, '13, 99;◀ 4Q, '12, 85; 2Q, '12, 15; 2Q, '11, 4; 3Q, '10, 5; 2Q, '06, 22; 4Q, '05, 101-103; 2Q, '01, 7-9, 23; 4Q, '98, 83
TIP: If a tPA infusion is started in another facility within 24 hours of transferring to the current facility, assign diagnosis code V45.88, whether or not the infusion is continued in the current facility.

99.11   Injection of Rh immune globulin
Injection of:
    Anti-D (Rhesus) globulin
    RhoGAM

99.12   Immunization for allergy
Desensitization

99.13   Immunization for autoimmune disease

99.14   Injection or infusion of immunoglobulin
Injection of immune sera
Injection or infusion of gamma globulin

99.15   Parenteral infusion of concentrated nutritional substances
Hyperalimentation
Total parenteral nutrition [TPN]
Peripheral parenteral nutrition [PPN]
DEF: Administration of greater than necessary amount of nutrients via other than the alimentary canal (e.g., infusion).
AHA: 4Q, '03, 104

99.16   Injection of antidote
Injection of:
    antivenin
    heavy metal antagonist

99.17   Injection of insulin

99.18   Injection or infusion of electrolytes

99.19   Injection of anticoagulant
EXCLUDES   infusion of drotrecogin alfa (activated) (00.11)

√4ᵗʰ **99.2   Injection or infusion of other therapeutic or prophylactic substance**
INCLUDES   injection or infusion given:
    hypodermically   ⎫
    intramuscularly   ⎬ acting locally or
    intravenously   ⎭   systemically
Use additional code for:
    injection (into):
      breast (85.92)
      bursa (82.94, 83.96)
      intraperitoneal (cavity) (54.97)
      intrathecal (03.92)
      joint (76.96, 81.92)
      kidney (55.96)
      liver (50.94)
      orbit (16.91)
      other sites — see Alphabetic Index
    perfusion:
      NOS (39.97)
      intestine (46.95, 46.96)
      kidney (55.95)
      liver (50.93)
      total body (39.96)
EXCLUDES   SuperSaturated oxygen therapy (00.49)

99.20   Injection or infusion of platelet inhibitor
Glycoprotein IIb/IIIa inhibitor
GP IIb-IIIa inhibitor
GP IIb/IIIa inhibitor
EXCLUDES   infusion of heparin (99.19)
    injection or infusion of thrombolytic agent (99.10)
AHA: 3Q, '06, 8; 2Q, '04, 3; 4Q, '02, 114; 4Q, '98, 85

99.21   Injection of antibiotic
EXCLUDES   injection or infusion of oxazolidinone class of antibiotics (00.14)
AHA: 3Q, '10, 11; 4Q, '98, 76; 2Q, '90, 24; M-A, '87, 9

99.22   Injection of other anti-infective
EXCLUDES   injection or infusion of oxazolidinone class of antibiotics (00.14)

99.23   Injection of steroid
Injection of cortisone
Subdermal implantation of progesterone
AHA: 3Q, '00, 15; 1Q, '99, 8; 3Q, '96, 7; 3Q, '92, 9; S-O, '85, 7

99.24   Injection of other hormone
AHA: 1Q, '06, 9

BI   Bilateral Procedure   NC   Non-covered Procedure   LC   Limited Coverage Procedure   ▶◀ Revised Text   ● New Code   ▲ Revised Code Title

99.25 Injection or infusion of cancer chemotherapeutic substance
Chemoembolization
Injection or infusion of antineoplastic agent
Use additional code for disruption of blood brain barrier, if performed [BBBD] (00.19)
EXCLUDES immunotherapy, antineoplastic (00.15, 99.28)
implantation of chemotherapeutic agent (00.10)
injection of radioisotope (92.28)
injection or infusion of biological response modifier [BRM] as an antineoplastic agent (99.28)
intravenous infusion of clofarabine (17.70)
AHA: 1Q, '12, 13; 2Q, '11, 4; 4Q, '09, 79; 4Q, '08, 82; 4Q, '07, 104; 2Q, '03, 6, 16; 4Q, '02, 93; 1Q, '99, 4; 1Q, '98, 6; 3Q, '96, 11; 4Q, '95, 67; 2Q, '92, 7; 1Q, '92, 12; 1Q, '88, 8; N-D, '86, 11

99.26 Injection of tranquilizer

99.27 Iontophoresis
DEF: Iontophoresis: Introduction of soluble salts into tissues via electric current.

99.28 Injection or infusion of biological response modifier [BRM] as an antineoplastic agent
Immunotherapy, antineoplastic
Infusion of cintredekin besudotox
Interleukin therapy
Low-dose interleukin-2 [IL-2] therapy
Tumor vaccine
EXCLUDES high-dose infusion interleukin-2 [IL-2] (00.15)
AHA: 4Q, '06, 123; 4Q, '03, 92; 2Q, '99, 8; 2Q, '98, 10; 4Q, '94, 51

99.29 Injection or infusion of other therapeutic or prophylactic substance
EXCLUDES administration of neuroprotective agent (99.75)
immunization (99.31-99.59)
infusion of blood brain barrier disruption substance (00.19)
injection of sclerosing agent into:
esophageal varices (42.33)
hemorrhoids (49.42)
veins (39.92)
injection or infusion of:
human B-type natriuretic peptide (hBNP) (00.13)
nesiritide (00.13)
platelet inhibitor (99.20)
thrombolytic agent (99.10)
uterine artery embolization without coils (68.25)
AHA: 4Q, '11, 179-180; 2Q, '10, 4-5, 6-7, 14; 1Q, '10, 21; 1Q, '07, 11; 2Q, '03, 10; 3Q, '02, 19, 24; 1Q, '01, 15; 2Q, '00, 14; 1Q, '00, 8, 18, 23; 4Q, '99, 17; 3Q, '99, 21; 4Q, '98, 83; 2Q, '98, 17, 18, 23, 24; 1Q, '98, 6; 2Q, '97, 11; 1Q, '97, 3; 4Q, '95, 67; 2Q, '95, 12; 4Q, '90, 14; 2Q, '90, 23; 2Q, '89, 17; 1Q, '88, 9; N-D, '87, 4; S-O, '87, 11

√4ᵗʰ **99.3 Prophylactic vaccination and inoculation against certain bacterial diseases**
DEF: Administration of a killed bacteria suspension to produce immunity.

99.31 Vaccination against cholera

99.32 Vaccination against typhoid and paratyphoid fever
Administration of TAB vaccine

99.33 Vaccination against tuberculosis
Administration of BCG vaccine

99.34 Vaccination against plague

99.35 Vaccination against tularemia

99.36 Administration of diphtheria toxoid
EXCLUDES administration of:
diphtheria antitoxin (99.58)
diphtheria-tetanus-pertussis, combined (99.39)

99.37 Vaccination against pertussis
EXCLUDES administration of diphtheria-tetanus-pertussis, combined (99.39)

99.38 Administration of tetanus toxoid
EXCLUDES administration of:
diphtheria-tetanus-pertussis, combined (99.39)
tetanus antitoxin (99.56)

99.39 Administration of diphtheria-tetanus- pertussis, combined

√4ᵗʰ **99.4 Prophylactic vaccination and inoculation against certain viral diseases**
DEF: Administration of a killed virus suspension to produce immunity.

99.41 Administration of poliomyelitis vaccine

99.42 Vaccination against smallpox

99.43 Vaccination against yellow fever

99.44 Vaccination against rabies

99.45 Vaccination against measles
EXCLUDES administration of measles-mumps-rubella vaccine (99.48)

99.46 Vaccination against mumps
EXCLUDES administration of measles-mumps-rubella vaccine (99.48)

99.47 Vaccination against rubella
EXCLUDES administration of measles-mumps-rubella vaccine (99.48)

99.48 Administration of measles-mumps-rubella vaccine

√4ᵗʰ **99.5 Other vaccination and inoculation**

99.51 Prophylactic vaccination against the common cold

99.52 Prophylactic vaccination against influenza

99.53 Prophylactic vaccination against arthropod-borne viral encephalitis

99.54 Prophylactic vaccination against other arthropod-borne viral diseases

99.55 Prophylactic administration of vaccine against other diseases
Vaccination against:
anthrax
brucellosis
Rocky Mountain spotted fever
Staphylococcus
Streptococcus
typhus
AHA: 2Q, '00, 9; 1Q, '94, 10

99.56 Administration of tetanus antitoxin

99.57 Administration of botulism antitoxin

99.58 Administration of other antitoxins
Administration of:
diphtheria antitoxin
gas gangrene antitoxin
scarlet fever antitoxin

99.59 Other vaccination and inoculation
Vaccination NOS
EXCLUDES injection of:
gamma globulin (99.14)
Rh immune globulin (99.11)
immunization for:
allergy (99.12)
autoimmune disease (99.13)

√4ᵗʰ **99.6 Conversion of cardiac rhythm**
EXCLUDES open chest cardiac:
electric stimulation (37.91)
massage (37.91)
DEF: Correction of cardiac rhythm.

99.60 Cardiopulmonary resuscitation, not otherwise specified
AHA: 1Q, '94, 16

99.61 **Atrial cardioversion**
DEF: Application of electric shock to upper heart chamber to restore normal heart rhythm.

99.62 **Other electric countershock of heart**
Cardioversion:
  NOS
  external
Conversion to sinus rhythm
Defibrillation
  External electrode stimulation
AHA: ▶1Q, '13, 10;◀1Q, '07, 17

99.63 **Closed chest cardiac massage**
Cardiac massage NOS
Manual external cardiac massage
DEF: Application of alternating manual pressure over breastbone to restore normal heart rhythm.

99.64 **Carotid sinus stimulation**

99.69 **Other conversion of cardiac rhythm**
AHA: 4Q, '88, 11

✓4ᵗʰ **99.7** **Therapeutic apheresis or other injection, administration, or infusion of other therpeutic or prophylactic substance**

99.71 **Therapeutic plasmapheresis**
EXCLUDES *extracorporeal immunoadsorption [ECI] (99.76)*

99.72 **Therapeutic leukopheresis**
Therapeutic leukocytapheresis

99.73 **Therapeutic erythrocytapheresis**
Therapeutic erythropheresis
AHA: 1Q, '94, 20

99.74 **Therapeutic plateletpheresis**

99.75 **Administration of neuroprotective agent**
DEF: Direct application of neuroprotective agent (e.g., nimodipine) to miinimize ischemic injury by inhibiting toxic neurotransmitters, blocking free ions, removing free radicals, and causing vasodilation.
AHA: 4Q, '00, 68

99.76 **Extracorporeal immunoadsorption**
Removal of antibodies from plasma with protein A columns
AHA: 4Q, '02, 112

99.77 **Application or administration of adhesion barrier substance**
AHA: 1Q, '10, 11; 4Q, '02, 113

99.78 **Aquapheresis**
Plasma water removal
Ultrafiltration [for water removal]
EXCLUDES *hemodiafiltration (39.95)*
hemodialysis (39.95)
therapeutic plasmapheresis (99.71)

99.79 **Other**
Apheresis (harvest) of stem cells
AHA: 3Q, '08, 19; 1Q, '06, 12, 13; 1Q, '05, 16; 4Q, '97, 55

✓4ᵗʰ **99.8** **Miscellaneous physical procedures**

99.81 **Hypothermia (central) (local)**
EXCLUDES *gastric cooling (96.31)*
gastric freezing (96.32)
that incidental to open heart surgery (39.62)
AHA: 3Q, '10, 14

99.82 **Ultraviolet light therapy**
Actinotherapy

99.83 **Other phototherapy**
Phototherapy of the newborn
EXCLUDES *extracorporeal photochemotherapy (99.88)*
photocoagulation of retinal lesion (14.23-14.25, 14.33-14.35, 14.53-14.55)
DEF: Treating disease with light rays of various concentrations.
AHA: 2Q, '89, 15

99.84 **Isolation**
Isolation after contact with infectious disease
Protection of individual from his surroundings
Protection of surroundings from individual

99.85 **Hyperthermia for treatment of cancer**
Hyperthermia (adjunct therapy) induced by microwave, ultrasound, low energy radio frequency, probes (interstitial), or other means in the treatment of cancer
Code also any concurrent chemotherapy or radiation therapy
AHA: 3Q, '96, 11; 3Q, '89, 17

99.86 **Non-invasive placement of bone growth stimulator**
Transcutaneous (surface) placement of pads or patches for stimulation to aid bone healing
EXCLUDES *insertion of invasive or semi-invasive bone growth stimulators (device) (percutaneous electrodes) (78.90-78.99)*

99.88 **Therapeutic photopheresis**
Extracorporeal photochemotherapy
Extracorporeal photopheresis
EXCLUDES *other phototherapy (99.83)*
ultraviolet light therapy (99.82)
DEF: Extracorporeal photochemotherapy: Treating disease with drugs that react to ultraviolet radiation or sunlight.
AHA: 2Q, '99, 7

✓4ᵗʰ **99.9** **Other miscellaneous procedures**

99.91 **Acupuncture for anesthesia**

99.92 **Other acupuncture**
EXCLUDES *that with smouldering moxa (93.35)*

99.93 **Rectal massage (for levator spasm)**

99.94 **Prostatic massage** ♂

99.95 **Stretching of foreskin** ♂

99.96 **Collection of sperm for artificial insemination** ♂

99.97 **Fitting of denture**

99.98 **Extraction of milk from lactating breast** ♀

99.99 **Other**
Leech therapy

BI Bilateral Procedure | NC Non-covered Procedure | LC Limited Coverage Procedure | ▶◀ Revised Text | ● New Code | ▲ Revised Code Title

200 – Volume 3 • October 2014 | 2015 ICD-9-CM